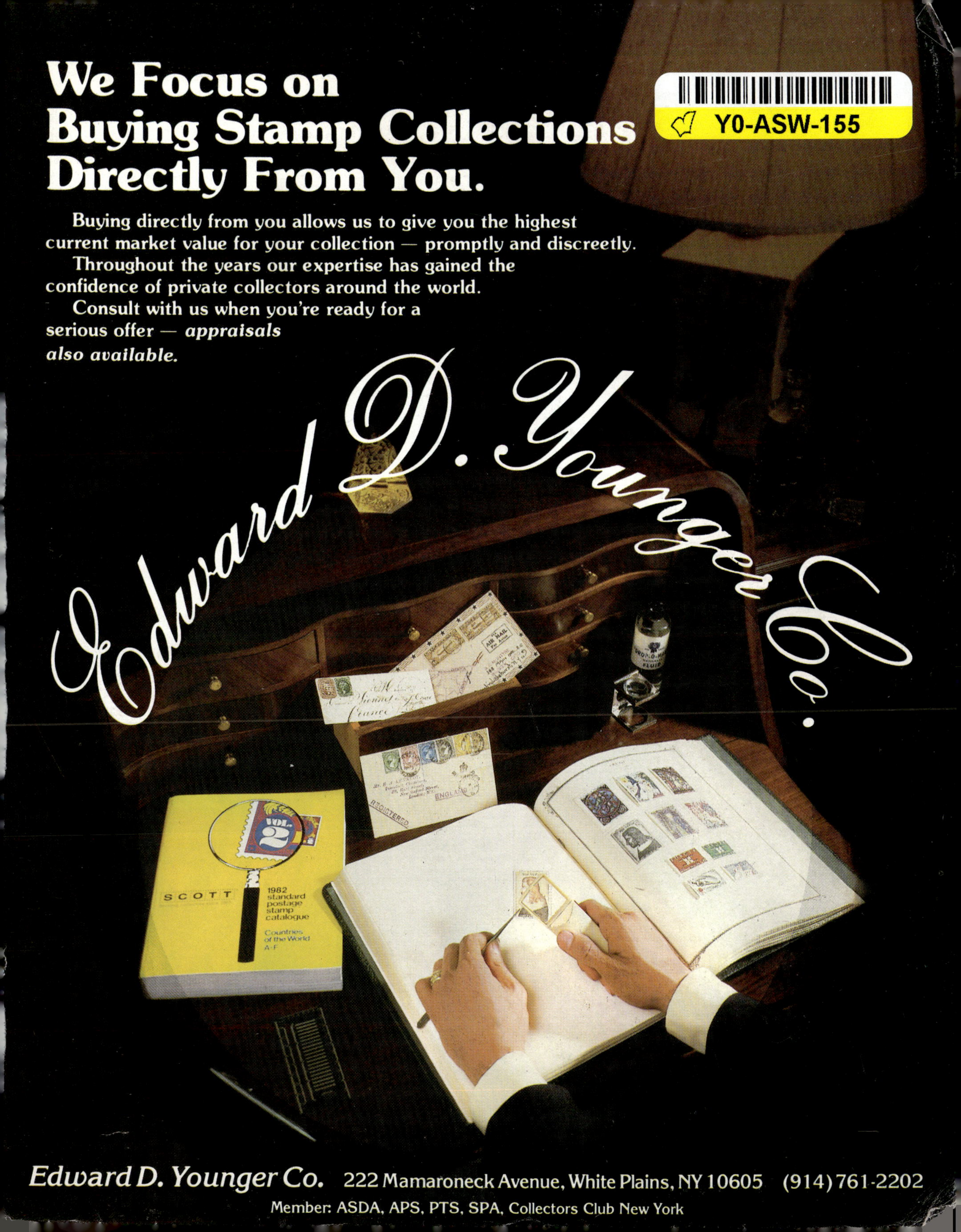

We Focus on
Buying Stamp Collections
Directly From You.
Buying directly from you allows us to give you the highest current market value for your collection — promptly and discreetly.
Throughout the years our expertise has gained the confidence of private collectors around the world.
Consult with us when you're ready for a serious offer — appraisals also available.
Edward D. Younger Co.
SCOTT
1982 standard postage stamp catalogue
Countries of the World A-F
AIR MAIL
REGISTERED
ENGLAND
Edward D. Younger Co. 222 Mamaroneck Avenue, White Plains, NY 10605 (914) 761-2202
Member: ASDA, APS, PTS, SPA, Collectors Club New York

U.S. Post Office breaks Olympic record.

The 1983-84 Olympic series, the largest ever issued by the U.S. Postal Service, makes an outstanding addition to your collection.

And what a way to start someone you love on a hobby that's filled with excitement and wonder.

24 spectacular stamps track Olympic events from high jumping to ice dancing. All designed by the award-winning sports illustrator Bob Peak.

Collect the whole set, now available at the Post Office. And make this Olympic experience your most complete. Ever.

© USPS 1984

STANDARD POSTAGE STAMP CATALOGUE

1985

One Hundred and Forty-first Edition
in Four Volumes

VOLUME IV

EUROPEAN COUNTRIES and COLONIES
INDEPENDENT NATIONS of
AFRICA, ASIA, LATION AMERICA
P—Z

Publisher—BERT TAUB
President—BENJAMIN FRANKLIN BAILAR
Vice-President—ESTELLE DENARO
Catalogue Editor Emeritus—JAMES B. HATCHER
Executive Editor—WILLIAM W. CUMMINGS
Editor—ELAINE MILANO
New Issues Editor—BARBARA A. WEINFIELD
Staff Editors—STEPHEN W. BRAHAM, MARTIN FRANKEVICZ
Associate Editors—IRVING KOSLOW, GEORGE A. McNAMARA,
WILLIAM N. SALOMON, BERT TAUB
Production Coordinator—GAIL D. ISRAEL
Vice-President, Sales-Marketing—BRIAN KOSLOW
Advertising Sales—ELEANOR KASMIR

Copyright © 1984 by

SCOTT PUBLISHING CO.

3 East 57th St., New York, N.Y. 10022

ACKNOWLEDGMENT

The Editor thanks all those many good friends of Scott who have helped this year or in previous years in the task of revising the Standard Catalogue. They have generously shared their stamp knowledge with others through this medium.

No list of aides can be complete, and several helpers prefer anonymity. The following men are chiefly those who have undertaken to assist on one or more specific countries:

Bruce W. Ball
John K. Bash
Brian M. Bleckwenn
Herbert J. Bloch
William G. Bogg
John R. Boker, Jr.
Paul Brenner
George W. Brett

Alex A. Cohen
Herbert E. Conway

Ellery Denison
Pandelis J. Drossos

Daniel S. Franklin

Frank P. Geiger
Henry Gitner
Brian M. Green
David Gronbeck-Jones

Mihran B. Hagopian
Calvet M. Hahn
J. Hannaney
Leo John Harris
Clifford O. Herrick
Juan J. Holler
Robert L. Huggins
J. R. Hughes

Lewis S. Kaufman
Ernest A. Kehr

Joseph E. Landry, Jr.
Andrew Levitt

David MacDonnell
Robert L. Markovits

Robert P. Odenweller

Souren Panirian
Frank E. Patterson III
Gilbert N. Plass
Henrik Pollak

Alex Rendon
Stanley J. Richmond
Milo D. Rowell

Otto G. Schaffling
Richard Schwartz
Alfredo M. Seiferheld
F. Burton Sellers
Michael Shamilzadeh
James W. Smith
Sherwood Springer
Willard F. Stanley

Carlos Vieiro

Richard A. Washburn
John M. Wilson
Paul B. Woodward
Edmund H. Wright

Among the organizations that have helped are:

AMERICAN AIR MAIL SOCIETY
102 Arbor Road, Cinnaminson, NJ 08077

AMERICAN PHILATELIC SOCIETY
P.O. Box 8000, State College, Pa. 16801

AMERICAN REVENUE ASSOCIATION
Bruce Miller, Sec'y, 701 S. First Ave., Suite 332, Arcadia, CA 91006

AMERICAN STAMP DEALERS' ASSOCIATION
5 Dakota Drive, Suite 102, Lake Success, NY 11042

ARABIAN PHILATELIC ASSOCIATION
Aramco, Box 1929, Dhahran, Saudi Arabia

BRAZIL PHILATELIC ASSOCIATION
Tony DeBellis, 30 W. 60th St., New York, NY 10023

BUREAU ISSUES ASSOCIATION
59 West Germantown Pike, Norristown, PA 19401

CANADIAN STAMP DEALERS' ASSOCIATION
John H. Talman, 35 Victoria St., Toronto, Canada M5C 2A1

CANAL ZONE STUDY GROUP
Alfred R. Bew, Sec'y., 29 S. South Carolina Ave., Atlantic City, N.J. 08401

CHINA STAMP SOCIETY
J. Lewis Blackburn, Pres., 21816 8th Place W., Bothell, WA 98011

CONFEDERATE STAMP ALLIANCE
Brian M. Green, c/o Philatelic Foundation, 270 Madison Ave., New York, NY 10016

COSTA RICA COLLECTORS, Society of
Rt. 4, Box 472, Marble Falls, TX 78654

CROATIAN PHILATELIC SOCIETY
1512 Lancelot Rd., Borger, TX 79007

CZECHOSLOVAK PHILATELY, Society for
87 Carmita Ave., Rutherford, N.J. 07070

EIRE PHILATELIC ASSOCIATION
Robert C. Jones, Sec'y., 8 Beach St., Brockton, MA 02402

ESTONIAN PHILATELIC SOCIETY
Rudolf Hamar, Pres., 243 E. 34th St., New York, N.Y. 10016

FRANCE & COLONIES PHILATELIC SOCIETY
Walter Parshall, Sec'y., 103 Spruce St., Bloomfield, N.J. 07003

GERMANY PHILATELIC SOCIETY
c/o Fred Behrendt, Sec'y., P.O. Box 2034, Westminster, Maryland 21157

GUATEMALA COLLECTORS, International Society of
Henry B. Madden, Pres., 4003 N. St. Charles St., Baltimore, MD 21218

HELLENIC PHILATELIC Society of America
Dr. Nicholas Asimakopulos, Sec'y, 541 Cedar Hill Ave., Wyckoff, N.J. 07481

JAPANESE PHILATELY, International Society for
Kenneth Kamholz Sec'y., P.O. Box 1283, Haddonfield, NJ 08033

KOREA STAMP SOCIETY, INC.
Forrest W. Calkins, Sec'y., P.O. Box 1057, Grand Junction, Colo. 81502

MEXICO-ELMHURST PHILATELIC SOCIETY INTERNATIONAL
Quintus Fernando, Sec'y., 2402 E. 8th St., Tucson, AZ 85719

OCEANIA PHILATELIC SOCIETY
William Hagan, Pres., 1523 East Meadowbrook Drive, Loveland, OH 45140

PHILATELIC FOUNDATION
270 Madison Ave., New York, N.Y. 10016

POLONUS PHILATELIC SOCIETY
864 N. Ashland Ave., Chicago, Ill. 60622

PORTUGUESE PHILATELY, International Society for
Nancy M. Gaylord, 1116 Marineway West, North Palm Beach, FL 33408

ROSSICA, Society of Russian Philately
Norman Epstein, Treas., 33 Crooke Ave., Brooklyn, N.Y. 11226

EL SALVADOR, Associated Collectors of
Robert Fisher, Box 306, Oaks, Pa. 19456

SCANDINAVIAN COLLECTORS CLUB
Robert B. Brandeberry, 58 W. Salisbury Dr., Wilmington, DE 19809

TURKEY & OTTOMAN PHILATELIC SOCIETY
William A. Sandrik, Box 6126, Washington, DC 20044

UNITED POSTAL STATIONERY SOCIETY
P.O. Box 48, Redlands, CA 92373

ISBN 0-89487-065-3
Library of Congress Card No. 2-3301

CONTENTS OF VOLUME IV

See Index at back of book for page numbers

Nations of Europe, Africa, Asia and their colonies, and Latin America appear alphabetically in Vols. II, III and IV.

Vol. II runs from A to F (Territory of the Afars and Issas through Funchal).

Vol. III covers G to O (Gabon through Oltre Giuba).

Vol. IV covers P to Z (Panama through Zambezia).

See Vol. I for United States and Affiliated Territories, United Nations, and British Commonwealth of Nations.

COPYRIGHT NOTICE

The contents of this book, are owned exclusively by Scott Publishing Co. and all rights thereto are reserved under the Pan American and Universal Copyright Conventions.

Copyright © 1984
by Scott Publishing Co., New York, N.Y. Printed in U.S.A.

COPYRIGHT NOTE
Permission is hereby given for the use of material in this book and covered by copyright if:
(a) The material is used in advertising matter, circulars or price lists for the purpose of offering stamps for sale or purchase at the prices listed therein; and
(b) Such use is incidental to the business of buying and selling stamps and is limited in scope and length, i.e., it does not cover a substantial protion of the total number of stamps issued by any country or of any special category of stamps of any country; and
(c) Such material is not used as part of any catalogue, stamp album or computerized or other system based upon the Scott catalogue numbers, or in any updated valuations of stamps not offered for sale or purchase; and
(d) Such use is not competitive with the business of the copyright owner.
Any use of the material in this book which does not satisfy all the foregoing conditions is forbidden in any form unless permission in each instance is given in writing by the copyright owner.

TRADEMARK NOTICE

The terms SCOTT, SCOTT'S, SCOTT CATALOGUE NUMBERING SYSTEM, SCOTT CATALOGUE NUMBER, SCOTT NUMBER and abbreviations thereof, are trademarks of Scott Publishing Co., used to identify its publications and its copyrighted system for identifying and classifying postage stamps for dealers and collectors. These trademarks are to be used only with the prior consent of Scott Publishing Co.

No part of this work may be reproduced in any form or by any means, electronic or mechanical, including photocopying, without permission in writing from Scott Publishing Co.

The Scott Standard Postage Catalogue accepts all advertisements in good faith, but does not endorse or assume any responsibility for the contents of advertisements.

SPECIAL NOTICES

This Catalogue lists adhesive postage stamps of the various countries, except for the United States where additional listings cover revenue stamps and postal stationery.

To facilitate identification, the following style of listing is used:

Canada

41	A24	3c bright vermilion	17.50	30
	a.	3c rose carmine	300.00	6.00

The number (41) in the first column is the index or identification number; the letter and number combination (A24) indicates the design and refers to the illustration having this (A24) designation; next comes the denomination (3c) followed by the color (bright vermilion); the prices are in two columns at the right, the first (17.50) being that of an unused stamp and the last (30) of a canceled one. This is known as a major listing or variety.

Variations from so-called "normal" stamps are listed in small type and designated by lowercase letters of the alphabet. These are called minor varieties. When they immediately follow the major listing in the catalogue the original index and design numbers are understood to be the same. In the preceding example, the minor variety, No. 41a, differs from the major variety, No. 41, only in shade; its design, perforation, etc., remain unchanged.

When year, perforation, watermark or printing method is mentioned, the description applies to all succeeding listings until a change is noted. The heading note "Without Gum" applies only to the set it precedes.

When a stamp is printed in black on colored paper, the color of the paper alone is given in italics.

With stamps printed in two or more colors, the color given first is that of the frame or outer parts of the design starting at upper left corner. The colors that follow are those of the vignette or inner parts of the design.

For some sets which include both vertical and horizontal format stamps, a single illustration is used, with the various designs and formats described beneath the illustration.

ABBREVIATIONS

The most frequently used abbreviations are:
Imperf. = Imperforate. Perf. = Perforated. Wmk. = Watermark. Unwmkd. = Unwatermarked. Litho. = Lithographed. Photo. = Photogravure. Engr. = Engraved. Typo. = Typographed.

When no color is given for an overprint or surcharge, it is understood to be in black. Abbreviations are sometimes used, as (B) or (Bk) Black, (Bl) Blue, (R) Red, (G) Green, etc.

NEW ISSUE LISTINGS

Scott's Chronicle of New Issues appears regularly in the Scott Stamp Monthly and reports new listings.

CONDITION

Condition is the all-important factor of price. Prices quoted are for stamps in fine condition. Extra fine copies often bring higher prices, while unused stamps without gum or with partial gum usually sell for less than copies with full original gum. Prices given in this Catalogue for unused stamps are for specimens which have the major part of the original gum on the back, except, of course, those varieties which were issued without gum. In certain countries, such as Brunswick, a note indicates that prices are for specimens without gum. **Slightly defective stamps which are off-center, heavily canceled, faded or stained are usually sold at large discounts. Damaged stamps which are torn or mutilated or have serious defects seldom bring more than a small fraction of the price of a fine specimen.**

Standards of condition vary greatly in the stamps of different countries. Early United States, Great Britain, Victoria and Japan stamps, for example, were poorly perforated and as a rule heavily canceled. They cannot be obtained in as fine condition as stamps from countries where more care was taken in perforating and lighter cancellations applied.

PRICING LIMITATIONS

Each price appearing in this Catalogue represents an estimate by the editors of the current value basis for a fine specimen offered by an informed stamp dealer to an informed customer (stamp collector). They are not intended to reflect prices in transactions between dealers or between collectors and dealers as such transactions may involve adjustments based on the dealers' profit margins.

Sales may be made at lower figures by reason of individual bargaining, the effect of dealer profit margins and mark-ups, poor condition of the stamp, changes in popularity, temporary over-supply, local custom, the "vest pocket dealer," or the many other reasons which can cause deviations in price. Sales also may occur at higher prices because of exceptionally fine condition, unusual postal markings, unexpected political changes, or newly discovered philatelic and other information.

The publishers and editors endeavor to obtain more than one judgment of the prices and to incorporate in their pricing the various price factors listed above, but there can be no assurance that all of the prices listed are accurate estimates of prices which would be paid in actual transactions. Some of the stamps listed have not traded recently, but the pricing is based on the editors estimates of the probable prices which the stamp would command if the were offered for sale to a collector. The users of this Catalogue should not enter into any transaction solely in reliance on the prices, valuations or stamp availability information set forth in the Catalogue. Persons wishing to further establish the value of a particular stamp or other material may wish to consult with recognized stamp experts and dealers and review current information or recent developments which could affect stamp prices.

The prices listed in this Catalogue may not reflect current markets due to the lapse of time between the preparation of text and the distribution and use of this Catalogue. The publisher assumes no obligation to revise the prices during the distribution period of this Catalogue or to advise users of other factors, such as stamp availability, political and economic conditions or collecting preferences, all of which may have an immediate positive or negative impact on prices. The editors endeavor to balance these factors with their general understanding of stamp pricing considerations to avoid unnecessary fluctuations in the prices included in this Catalogue.

It should be noted that the editors of this Catalogue may also deal in stamps and may maintain substantial personal stamp collections. They may buy, sell and deal in stamps for their own account and for the account of others and therefore may have both a direct and indirect interest in the price of the stamps. In some cases, the references to prices may reflect valuations of their personal holdings or stamps in which they deal for themselves and others.

Prices in italics indicate infrequent sales, lack of pricing information, or that the market value is fluctuating excessively. The condition of early issues of many countries varies greatly. In some instances very fine to superb copies are rarely obtainable. Many of these older issues are priced in italics because the actual value is determined by the condition of each individual stamp.

The absence of price does not necessarily indicate that the stamp is scarce or rare. In the United States listings, a dash in the price column means that the stamp is known in a stated form or variety, but that information is lacking or insufficient for pricing.

The minimum price of a stamp is fixed at 5¢ to cover the dealer's labor and service cost of sorting, cataloguing and filling orders individually, but the sum of these list prices does not properly represent the "value" of a packet of unsorted or unmounted stamps sold in bulk which generally consists of only the cheaper stamps.

Unused prices are for stamps that have been hinged, through mid-1953 in the British area and 1960 in the U.S., unhinged thereafter. Where used are considerably higher than unused, the price applies to a stamp showing a distinct contemporary postmark of origin.

Beginning around 1900, sometimes earlier, prices for sets are given for most issues of five or more stamps. Unless otherwise noted, the set price excludes minor varieties. The parenthetical number in the set-price line tells the number of stamps in the priced total. Set prices are the sum of the individual prices.

Many countries sell canceled-to-order stamps at a marked reduction of face value. (Exceptions include Australia, Netherlands, France and Switzerland, which sell or have sold CTO stamps at full face value.) It is almost impossible to identify such stamps, if the gum has been removed, as the official government canceling devices are used. Examples on cover and used in the proper period are worth more.

HOW TO ORDER FROM YOUR DEALER

It is not necessary to write the full description of a stamp as listed in this Catalogue. All that is needed is the name of the country, the index number and whether unused or used. For example, "Japan Scott No. 422 unused" is sufficient to identify the stamp of Japan listed as: "422 A206 5y brown."

ADDENDA and NUMBER CHANGES

Stamps received too late to be included in the body of the Catalogue are listed in the Addenda at the back of this volume.

A list of stamps whose catalogue numbers have been changed from those of the preceding edition appears at the back of this volume.

EXAMINATION

Scott Publishing Co. cannot undertake to pass upon genuineness or condition of stamps, due to the time and responsibility involved, but refers collectors to the several expert committees which undertake this work. Neither can Scott Publishing Co. undertake to appraise or identify. The Company cannot take responsibility for unsolicited stamps or covers.

The 1981 edition of the *Scott Standard Postage Stamp Catalogue* was the first to be produced by computer typesetting procedures. For each of the preceding one-hundred thirty-six editions, the *Scott Catalogue* was prepared by "hot-metal" technology. Hot-metal typesetting (using Linotype, Monotype and copper engravings for most of the illustrations) was the state of the art in the early 1900's when the *Catalogue* took its present form. Today, however, hot-metal is a dying art, and it is both slow and expensive.

In order to prepare the *Scott Catalogue* for computer typesetting, several years of systems design, data entry and proofreading were required. Due to the literally millions of characters that have been processed, there will undoubtedly be errors. The editors hope that readers will point out any corrections to the *Catalogue* text.

The advantages of the computer approach are severalfold: the timeliness of price changes in future editions will be improved; the quality of the illustrations will remain constant rather than deteriorating each year: and finally, all of the *Catalogue* information will eventually be incorporated into a "data base" of prices from which new publishing products can be derived for collectors and investors.

COLOR ABBREVIATIONS

amb	amber	chnt	chestnut	ind	indigo	redsh	reddish
anil	aniline	choc	chocolate	int	intense	res	reseda
ap	apple	chr	chrome	lav	lavender	ros	rosine
aqua	aquamarine	cit	citron	lem	lemon	ryl	royal
az	azure	cl	claret	lil	lilac	sal	salmon
bis	bister	cob	cobalt	lt	light	saph	sapphire
bl	blue	cop	copper	mag	magenta	scar	scarlet
bld	blood	crim	crimson	man	manila	sep	sepia
blk	black	cr	cream	mar	maroon	sien	sienna
bril	brilliant	dk	dark	mv	mauve	sil	silver
brn	brown	dl	dull	multi	multicolored	sl	slate
brnsh	brownish	dp	deep	mlky	milky	stl	steel
brnz	bronze	db	drab	myr	myrtle	turq	turquoise
brt	bright	emer	emerald	ol	olive	ultra	ultramarine
brnt	burnt	gldn	golden	olvn	olivine	ven	venetian
car	carmine	grysh	grayish	org	orange	ver	vermilion
cer	cerise	grn	green	pck	peacock	vio	violet
chlky	chalky	grnsh	greenish	pnksh	pinkish	yel	yellow
cham	chamois	hel	heliotrope	Prus	Prussian	yelsh	yellowish
		hn	henna	pur	purple		

INFORMATION FOR COLLECTORS

The anatomy of a stamp can be divided into the following parts: paper, watermark, separation, impression, design and gum.

PAPER

Paper is a material composed of a compacted web of cellulose fibers formed into sheets. The fibers most often used for the paper on which stamps are printed are mulberry bark, wood, straw and certain grasses, with linen or cotton rags added for greater strength. These fibers are ground, bleached and boiled until they are reduced to a slushy pulp known as "stuff." Sizing, or weak glue, and coloring matter may be added to the pulp. Thin coatings of pulp are poured on sieve-like frames which allow the water to run off while retaining the matted pulp. When it is almost dry, the appearance of the pulp is converted by mechanical processes. It may be passed through smooth or engraved rollers (dandy rolls) or placed between cloth in a press that flattens and dries the product under pressure, thus forming a sheet of paper.

Stamp paper falls broadly into two divisions—"wove" and "laid." The differences in appearance are caused by the surface of the frame onto which the pulp is first fed. If the surface is smooth and even, the paper will be of uniform texture throughout, showing no light and dark areas when held up to a light. This is called **Wove Paper.** Early paper making machines poured the pulp on to continuously circulating webs of felt, but modern machines feed the pulp on to a cloth-like screen made of closely interwoven fine wires. This paper, when held up to a light, will show little dots or points, very close together. Technically, it is called "wire wove," but because it is the most common form, it is generally known as "wove paper." Any United States or British stamp printed after 1880 will furnish an example of wire wove paper.

The frames utilized for **Laid Paper** are made of closely spaced parallel wires, with cross wires at wider intervals. Obviously a greater thickness of the pulp will settle between the wires, and the paper, when held up to a light, will show alternate light and dark lines. The spacing and the thickness of the lines may vary, but on any one sheet of paper, they are all alike. (Russia Nos. 31-38.)

If the lines are spaced quite far apart, like the ruling on a writing tablet, the paper is called **Batonné** from the French word meaning a staff. Batonné paper may be either wove or laid. If it is laid, fine laid lines can be seen between the batons. The laid lines, which are actually a form of watermark, may be geometrical figures such as squares, diamonds, rectangles, or wavy lines.

When the lines form little squares, the paper is called **Quadrille.** When they form rectangles instead of squares, the paper is called **Oblong Quadrille.** (Mexico—Guadalajara Nos. 38-41.)

Paper is also classified as thick or thin, hard or soft, and by color if dye was added during production, such as yellowish, greenish, bluish and reddish.

Pelure Paper is an extremely thin, hard and often brittle paper. It is sometimes bluish or grayish. (Serbia No. 170.)

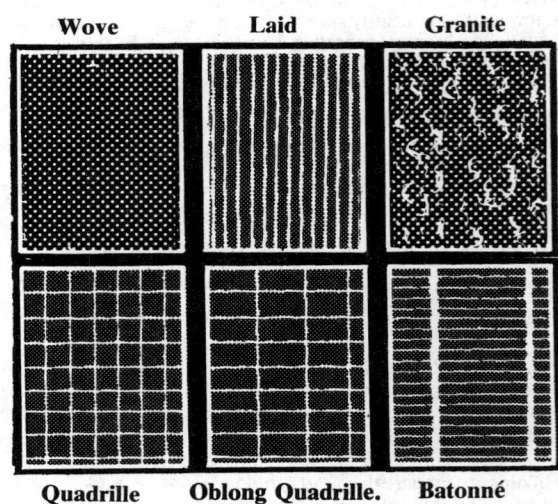

Wove   Laid   Granite

Quadrille   Oblong Quadrille.   Batonné

Native Paper is a term applied to the handmade papers on which some of the early stamps of the Indian States were printed. Japanese paper, originally made of mulberry fibers and rice flour, is part of this group. (Japan Nos. 1-18.)

Manila Paper, often used to make stamped envelopes and wrappers, is a coarse textured stock, usually smooth on one side and rough on the other. It is made in a variety of colors.

Silk Paper, introduced by the British in 1847 as a safeguard against counterfeiting, has scattered bits of colored silk thread in it. Silk-thread paper has continuous threads of colored silk arranged so that one or more threads run through the stamp or postal stationery. (Great Britain Nos. 5-8.)

Granite Paper, not to be confused with either of the silk papers, is filled with minute fibers of various colors and lengths in the paper substance. (Austria Nos. 172-175.)

Chalky Paper is coated with a chalk-like substance to discourage the cleaning and reuse of canceled stamps. As the design is imprinted on the water-soluble coating of the stamp, any attempts to remove a cancellation will destroy the stamp. **Collectors are warned not to soak these stamps in any fluid.** If one is to be removed from envelope paper, a good way is to wet the paper from underneath until the gum dissolves enough to slip the stamp off it. (St. Kitts-Nevis Nos. 89-90.)

India Paper, originally introduced from China about 1750, is sometimes referred to as China Paper. It is a thin, opaque paper often used for plate and die proofs by many countries.

Information for Collectors

Double Paper in philately has two distinct meanings. The first, used experimentally as a means to discourage re-use, is two-ply paper, usually of a thick and thin sheet, joined together during the process of manufacture. Any attempt to remove a cancellation would destroy the design which is printed on the thin paper. The second occurs on the rotary press when the printer glues the end of one paper roll onto the next roll to save time in feeding the paper through the press. Stamp designs are printed over the joined paper and if overlooked by inspectors, may get into post-office stocks.

Goldbeater's Skin, used for the 1886 issue of Prussia, was made of a tough translucent paper. The design was printed in reverse on the back of the stamp, and the gum applied on top of the printing. It is impossible to remove them from the paper to which they are affixed without destroying the design.

Ribbed Paper has an uneven, corrugated surface made by passing it through ridged rollers. (Exists on some copies of U.S. No. 163.)

Various other substances that have been used for stamp manufacture include aluminum, copper, silver and gold foil, plastic, silk and cotton fabrics. Most of these are considered novelties designed for sale to novice collectors.

Multiple Watermarks of Crown Agents and Burma

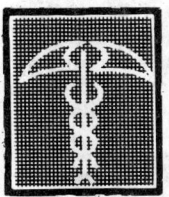  

Watermarks of Uruguay, Vatican and Jamaica

WATERMARKS

Watermarks are an integral part of the paper as they are formed in the process of manufacture. They consist of small designs such as crowns, stars, anchors, letters, etc. formed of wire or cut from metal that are soldered to the surface of the dandy roll or mold. These pieces of metal (referred to as "bits") impress a design into the paper which may be seen by holding the stamp up to the light. They are more easily seen in a watermark detector, a small black tray. The stamp is placed face down in the tray and dampened with carbon tetrachloride or lighter fluid, which brings up the watermark in dark lines against a lighter background.

WARNING. Some inks used in the photogravure process dissolve in watermark fluids. (See SOLUBLE PRINTING INKS.) There are also electric watermark detectors that come with plastic discs of various colors. When the light is turned on the watermark can be seen through the disc that neutralizes the color of the stamp.

Watermarks may be found reversed, inverted, sideways or diagonal, as seen from the back of the stamp, depending on the position of the printing plates or the manner in which paper was fed through the press. On machine-made paper they normally read from right to left. In a "multiple watermark" the design is repeated closely throughout the sheet. In a "sheet watermark" the design appears only once on the sheet, but extends over many stamps. Individual stamps may carry only a small fraction or none of the watermark.

"Marginal watermarks" occur in the margins of sheets or panes of stamps. Outside the border of some papers a large row of letters may spell the name of the country or of the manufacturer of the paper. Careless press feeding may cause parts of these letters to show on stamps of the outer rows. **For easier reference watermarks are numbered in the Scott Catalogue. See numerical index of Watermarks at back of this volume.**

SEPARATION

Separation is the general term used to describe methods of separating stamps. The earliest issues, such as the 1840 Penny Blacks, did not have any means provided for separating and were intended to be cut apart with scissors. These are called imperforate stamps. As many stamps that were first issued imperforate were later issued perforated, care must be observed in buying imperforate stamps to be sure they are really imperforate and not perforated copies that have been trimmed. Although sometimes priced as singles, it is recommended that imperforate varieties of normally perforated stamps be collected in pairs or larger pieces as indisputable evidence of their imperforate character.

Separation is effected by two general methods, rouletting and perforating. In rouletting the paper is cut partly or wholly through, but no paper is removed. In perforating a part of the paper is removed. Rouletting derives its name from the French roulette, a spur-like wheel. As the wheel is rolled over the paper, each point makes a small cut. The number of cuts made in two centimeters determines the gauge of the roulette. This is fully explained under "Perforation."

ROULETTING: The shape and arrangement of the teeth on the wheels varies. French names are usually used to describe the various roulettes:

Percé en lignes: rouletted in lines. The paper receives short, straight cuts in lines. (Mexico No. 500.)

Percé en points: pin-perforated. Round, equidistant holes are pricked through the paper, but no paper is removed, which distinguishes it from a small perforation. (Mexico Nos. 242-256.)

Information for Collectors

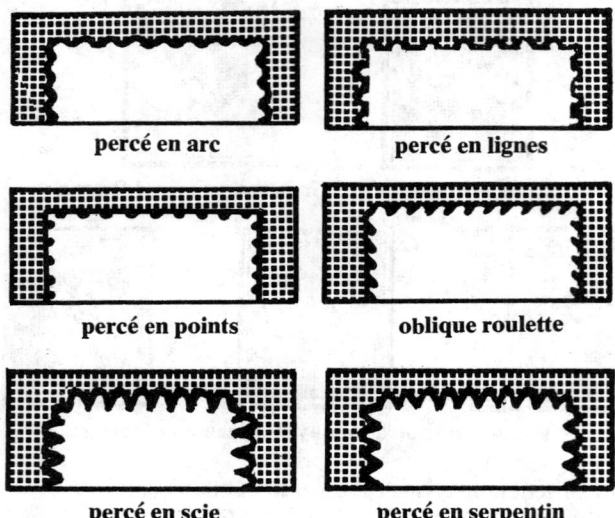

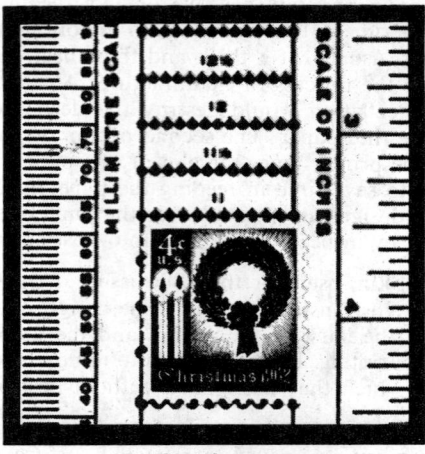

Perforation gauge

Percé en arc and percé en scie: pierced in an arc or sawtoothed rouletted, forming half circles or small triangles. (Hanover Nos. 25-29.)

Percé en serpentin: serpentine roulette. The cuts form a serpentine or wavy line. (Brunswick Nos. 13-22.)

PERFORATION: The second chief style of separation of stamps, and the one which is in universal use today, is called perforating. By this process the paper between the stamps is cut away in a line of holes, usually round, leaving little bridges of paper between the stamps to hold them together. These little bridges, which project from the stamp when it is torn from the sheet are called the teeth of the perforation. As the size of the perforation is sometimes the only way to differentiate between two otherwise identical stamps, it is necessary to be able to measure and describe them. This is done with a perforation gauge, a ruler-like device that has dots to show how many perforations can be counted in the space of 2 centimeters, the space universally adopted as the length in which perforations are measured. Run your stamp along the gauge until the dots on it fit exactly into the perforations. If the number alongside the dots into which it fits is 11, this means that 11 perforations fit between two centimeters and the stamp is described as "perf. 11." If the gauge of the perforations on the top and bottom of a stamp differs from that on the sides, it is called a "compound perforation." In measuring compound perforations the gauge at the top and bottom is always given first, then the sides. Thus a stamp that measures 10½ at top and bottom and 11 at the sides is described as "10½ x 11." (U.S. No. 1526.)

A perforation with small holes and teeth close together is called a "fine perforation." One with large holes and teeth far apart is a "coarse perforation." If the holes are jagged rather than clean cut, it is called "rough perforation." Blind perforations are the slight impressions left by the perforating pins if they fail to puncture the paper. Multiples showing blind perfs may command a slight premium over normally perforated stamps.

PRINTING PROCESSES

ENGRAVING (Intaglio): Master Die—The initial operation in the engraving process is the making of the master die. The die is a small flat block of soft steel on which the stamp design is recess engraved in reverse.

The original art is reduced photographically to the appropriate size, and serves as a tracing guide for the initial outline of the design. After the engraving is completed, the die is hardened to withstand the stress and pressures of subsequent transfer operations.

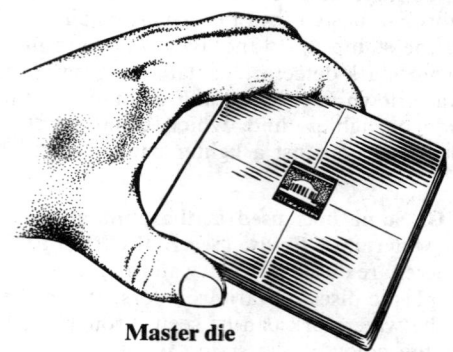

Master die

Transfer Roll—The next operation is the making of the transfer roll which, as the name implies, is the medium used to transfer the subject from the die to the plate. A blank roll of soft steel, mounted on a mandrel, is placed under the bearers of a transfer press, so as to allow it to roll freely on its axis. The hardened die is placed on the bed of the press and the face of the transfer roll is brought to bear on the die under pressure. The bed is then rocked back and forth under increasing pressure until the soft steel of the roll is forced into every engraved line of the die. The resulting impression on the roll is known as a "relief" or a "relief transfer." When the required number of reliefs are "rocked in," the soft steel transfer roll is also hardened.

Information for Collectors

A "relief" is the normal reproduction of the design on the die in reverse. A "defective relief" may occur during the "rocking in" process due to a minute piece of foreign material lodging on the die, or other causes. Imperfections in the steel of the transfer roll may result in a breaking away of parts of the design. If the damaged relief is continued in use, it will transfer a repeating defect to the plate. Sometimes reliefs are deliberately altered. "Broken relief" and "altered relief" are terms used to designate these changed conditions.

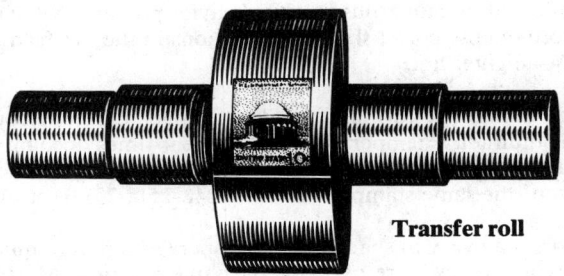
Transfer roll

Plate—The final step in the procedure is the making of the printing plate. A flat piece of soft steel replaces the die on the bed of the transfer press and one of the reliefs on the transfer roll is brought to bear on it. The position on the plate is determined by position dots, which have been lightly marked on the plate in advance. After the position of the relief is determined, pressure is brought to bear and, by following the same method used in making the transfer roll, a transfer is entered, This transfer reproduces in reverse and in detail the design of the relief. As many transfers are entered on the plate as there are to be subjects.

After the required transfers have been entered, the position dots, layout dots and lines, scratches, etc. are generally burnished out. Any required *guide lines, plate numbers* or other *marginal markings* are added. A proof impression is then taken and if "certified" (approved), the plate is machined for fitting to the press, hardened and sent to the plate vault ready for use.

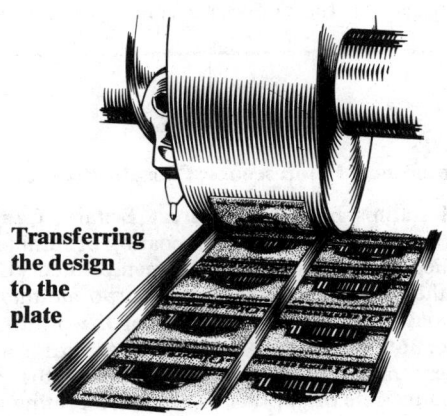
Transferring the design to the plate

On press, the plate is inked and the surface automatically wiped clean, leaving the ink only in the depressed lines. Damp paper under pressure is forced down into the engraved depressed lines, thereby receiving the ink. Consequently, the lines on engraved stamps are slightly raised; and, conversely, slight depressions occur on the back of the stamp.

The expressions *taille douce,* engraved, line engraved and steel plate all designate substantially the same processes for producing engraved stamps.

Rotary Press—Engraved stamps were printed only with flat plates until 1915, when rotary press printing was introduced. *Rotary press plates,* after being certified, require additional machining. They are curved to fit the press cylinder and "gripper slots" are cut into the back of each plate to receive the "grippers," which hold the plate securely on the press, after which the plate is hardened. Stamps printed from rotary press plates are usually longer or wider than the same stamps printed from flat press plates. The stretching of the plate during the curving process causes this enlargement.

Re-entry—In order to execute a re-entry the transfer roll is reapplied to the plate, usually at some time after it has been put to press. Thus worn-out designs can be resharpened by carefully re-entering the transfer roll. If the transfer roll is not precisely in line with the impression on the plate, the registration will not be true and a double transfer will result. After a plate has been curved for the rotary press, it is impossible to make a re-entry.

Double Transfer—A description of the condition of a transfer on a plate that shows evidence of a duplication of all, or a portion of the design. It is usually the result of the changing of the registration between the transfer roll and the plate during the rocking-in of the original entry.

It is sometimes necessary to remove the original transfer from a plate and repeat the process a second time. If the finished re-transfer shows indications of the original impression due to incomplete erasure, the result is also a double transfer.

Re-engraved—Either the die that has been used to make a plate or the plate itself may have its "temper" drawn (softened) and be re-cut. The resulting impressions from such a re-engraved die or plate may differ slightly from the original issue, and are known as "re-engraved."

Short Transfer—It sometimes happens that the transfer roll is not rocked its entire length in entering a transfer on a plate, with the result that the finished transfer fails to show the complete design. This is known as a "short transfer." (U.S. No. 8, type III of 1851-56 1c.)

TYPOGRAPHY (Letterpress, Surface Printing)—As related to the printing of postage stamps, typography is the reverse of engraving. It includes all printing wherein the design is raised above the surface area, whether it is wood, metal, or in some instances hard rubber.

The master die is made in much the same manner as the engraved die. However, in this instance the area not being utilized as a printing surface is cut away, leaving the surface area raised. The original die is then reproduced by stereotyping or electrotyping. The resulting electrotypes are assembled in the required number and format of the desired sheet of stamps. The plate used in printing the stamps is an electroplate of these assembled electrotypes.

Ink is applied to the raised surface and the pressure of the press transfers the ink impression to the paper. Again, as opposed to engraving, the fine lines of typography are impressed on the surface of the stamp. When viewed from the back (as on a typewritten page) the corresponding linework will be raised slightly above the surface.

PHOTOGRAVURE (Rotogravure, Heliogravure)—In this process the basic principles of photography are applied to a sensitized metal plate, as opposed to photographic paper. The design is photographically transferred to the plate through a halftone screen, breaking the reproduction into tiny dots. The plate is treated chemically and the dots form depressions of varying depths, depending on the degrees of shade in the design. The depressions in the plate hold the ink, which is lifted out when the paper is pressed against the plate, in a manner similar to that of engraved printing.

LITHOGRAPHY—This process is based on the principle that oil and water will not mix. The design is drawn by hand or transferred from an engraving to the surface of a lithographic stone or metal plate in a greasy (oily) ink. The stone (or plate) is wet with an acid fluid, causing it to repel the printing ink in all areas not covered by the greasy ink.

Transfers are made from the original stone or plate by means of transfer paper. A series of duplicate transfers are grouped and these in turn are transferred to the final printing plate.

Photolithography—The application of photographic processes to lithography. This process allows greater flexibility of design, relating to use of halftone screens combined with linework.

Offset—A development of the lithographic process. A rubber-covered blanket cylinder takes up the impression from the inked lithographic plate. From the "blanket" the impression is *offset* or transferred to the paper. Because of its greater flexibility and speed, offset printing has largely displaced lithography. Since the processes and results are almost identical, stamps printed by either method are designated as lithographed.

Sometimes two or even three printing methods are combined in producing stamps.

EMBOSSED (RELIEF) PRINTING—A method in which the design is sunk in the metal of the die and the printing is done against a yielding platen, such as leather or linoleum, which is forced up into the depression of the die, thus forming the design on the paper in relief.

Embossing may be done without color (Sardinia Nos. 4-6); with color printed around the embossed area (Great Britain No. 5 and most U.S. envelopes); and with color in exact registration with the embossed subject (Canada Nos. 656-657).

INK COLORS: Pigments or dyes, usually of mineral origin, are used in the manufacture of inks or colored papers on which stamps are printed. The tone of any given color may be affected by numerous factors: heavier pressure will cause a more intense color; slight interruptions in the ink feed will cause a lighter tint.

Hand-mixed ink formulas produced under different conditions (humidity, temperature) at different times account for notable color variations in early printings, mostly 19th century, of the same stamp (U.S. Nos. 248-250, 279B, etc.).

Colors may vary in shade because papers of different quality and consistency were used for the same printing. Most pelure papers, for example, show a richer color when compared to wove or laid papers. (Russia No. 181a.)

The very nature of the printing processes can cause a variety of differences in shades or hues of the same stamp. Some of these shades are scarcer than others, and are of particular interest to the advanced collector.

SOLUBLE PRINTING INKS. WARNING. Most stamp colors are permanent. That is, they are not seriously affected by light or water. Some colors may fade from excessive exposure to light. Other stamps are printed in inks which dissolve easily in water or in benzine, carbon tetrachloride or other fluids used to detect watermarks. These inks were often used intentionally to prevent the removal of cancellations.

Benzine affects most photogravure printings. Water affects all aniline prints, those on safety paper, and some photogravure printings. All the above are called *fugitive colors*.

TAGGED STAMPS

(Luminescence, Fluorescence, Phosphorescence)

Some tagged stamps have bars (Great Britain, Canada), frames (South Africa), or an overall coating of luminescent material applied after the stamps have been printed (United States). Another tagging method is to incorporate the luminescent material into some or all colors of the printing ink (Australia No. 366, Netherlands No. 478). A third is to mix the luminescent material with the pulp during the paper manufacturing process or apply it as a surface coating afterwards. These are called "fluorescent" papers. (Switzerland Nos. 510-514, Germany No. 848.)

Information for Collectors

The treated stamps show up in specific colors when exposed to ultraviolet light. The wave length of the luminescent material determines the colors and activates the triggering mechanism of the electronic machinery for sorting, facing or canceling letters.

Various fluorescent substances have been used as paper whiteners, but the resulting "hi-brite papers" show up differently under ultraviolet light and do not trigger the machines. They are not noted in the Catalogue.

Introduced in Great Britain in 1959 on an experimental basis, tagging in its various forms is now used by many countries to expedite the handling of mail. Following Great Britain were Germany ('61); Canada and Denmark ('62); United States, Australia, Netherlands and Switzerland ('63); Belgium and Japan ('66); Sweden and Norway ('67); Italy ('68); Russia ('69), and so forth.

Certain stamps were issued both with and without the luminescent factor. In these instances, the "tagged" variety is listed in the United States, Canada, Great Britain and Switzerland, and is noted in some of the other countries.

GUM

The gum on a stamp's back may be smooth, crinkly, dark, white, colored or tinted, and either obvious or virtually invisible as on Canada No. 453 or Rwanda Nos. 287-294. Most stamp gumming has been carried out with adhesives using gum arabic or dextrine as a base, but certain polymers such as polyvinyl alcohol (PVA) have been used extensively since World War II. The PVA gum which Harrison & Sons of Great Britain introduced in 1968 is dull, slightly yellowish and almost invisible.

Stamps having full **original gum** sell for more than those from which the gum has been removed. Reprints may have gum differing from the originals.

REPRINTS AND REISSUES

Reprints are impressions of stamps (usually obsolete) made from the original plates or stones. If valid for postage and from obsolete issues, they are called reissues. If they are from current issues, they are *second, third,* etc. *printings*. If designated for a particular purpose, they are called *special printings*.

When reprints are not valid for postage, but made from original dies and plates by authorized persons they are *official reprints*—to distinguish them from *private reprints* made from original plates and dies by private hands. *Official reproductions* or imitations are made from new dies and plates by government authorization.

For the 1876 Centennial, the U.S. government made official imitations of its first postage stamps, which are listed as Nos. 3-4; official reprints of the demonetized pre-1861 issues; reissued the 1869 stamps and made special printings of the current 1875 denominations. An example of the private reprint is that of the New Haven postmaster's provisional.

Most reprints differ slightly from the original stamp in some characteristic such as gum, paper, perforation, color, watermark (or lack thereof). Sometimes the details have been followed so meticulously that only a student of that stamp can tell the reprint from the original.

REMAINDERS AND CANCELED TO ORDER

Some countries sell their stock of old stamps when a new issue replaces them. The **remainders** are usually canceled with a punch hole, a heavy line or bar, or a more or less regular cancellation to avoid postal use. The most famous merchant of remainders was Nicholas F. Seebeck, who arranged printing contracts between the Hamilton Bank Note Co., of which he was a director, and several Central and Latin American countries in the 1880's and 1890's. The contracts provided that the plates and all remainders of the yearly issues became the property of Hamilton, and Seebeck saw to it that ample stock remained. The "Seebecks," both remainders and reprints, were standard packet fillers for decades.

Some countries also issue stamps **canceled to order** (CTO), either in sheets with original gum or stuck onto pieces of paper or envelopes and canceled. Such CTO items generally are worth less than postally used stamps. Most can be detected by the presence of gum. However, as the CTO practice goes back at least to 1885, the gum inevitably has been washed off some stamps so they could pass for postally used. The normally applied postmarks usually differ slightly and specialists can tell the difference. When applied individually to envelopes by philatelically minded persons, CTO material is known as *favor canceled* and generally sells at large discounts.

CINDERELLAS AND FACSIMILES

Cinderella is a catchall term used by collectors of phantoms, fantasies, bogus items, municipal issues, exhibition seals, local revenues, transportation stamps, labels, poster stamps, etc. Cinderellas are not issued by any national government for postal purposes. Some cinderella collectors include local postage issues, telegraph stamps, essays and proofs, forgeries and counterfeits.

A fantasy is an adhesive created for a nonexisting stamp issuing authority. Fantasy items range from imaginary countries (Kingdom of Sedang or Principality of Trinidad) to nonexisting locals (Winans City Post), or nonexisting transportation lines (McRobish & Co.'s Acapulco-San Francisco Line). On the other hand, if the entity exists and might have issued stamps or did issue other stamps, the items are *bogus* stamps. These would include the Mormon postage stamps of Utah, S. Allan Taylor's Guatemala and Paraguay inventions, the propaganda issues for the South Moluccas and the adhesives of the Page & Keyes local post of Boston.

Both fantasies and bogus issues are sometimes called *phantoms*.

Facsimiles are copies or imitations made to represent original stamps, but which do not pretend to be originals. A catalogue illustration is such a facsimile. Illustrations from the Moëns catalogue of the last century were occasionally colored and passed as stamps. Since the beginning of stamp collecting, facsimiles have been made for collectors as space fillers or for reference. They often carry the words "facsimile," "falsch" (German), "sanko" or "mozo" (Japanese), or "faux" (French) overprinted on the face or stamped on the back. Naturally, they have only curio value.

COUNTERFEITS OR FORGERIES

Postal counterfeits or **postal forgeries** are unauthorized imitations of stamps intended to deprive the post of revenue. They often command higher prices than the genuine stamps they imitate. Sales are illegal and governments can, and do, prosecute.

The first postal forgery was of Spain's 4-cuartos carmine of 1854, No. 25. The forgers lithographed it, though the original was typographed. Apparently they were not satisfied and soon made an engraved forgery which is fairly common, unlike the scarce lithographed counterfeit. Postal forgeries quickly followed in Spain, Austria, Naples, Sardinia and the Roman States.

An infamous counterfeit to defraud the government is the 1-shilling Great Britain "Stock Exchange" forgery of 1872 used on telegrams at the exchange that year. It escaped detection until a stamp dealer noticed it in 1898. Recent postal counterfeits include the U.S. 4c Lincoln and the 8c Eisenhower as well as Canada's 6c orange of 1968 (which was later faked in turn).

Because the governments concerned did not issue them, the *wartime propaganda* stamps of both World Wars may be classed as postal counterfeits. They were put out by other governments or resistance groups.

Philatelic forgeries or *counterfeits* are unauthorized imitations of stamps designed to deceive and defraud collectors. Such spurious items first appeared on the market around 1860 and most old-time collections contain one or more. Many are crude and easily spotted even by the non-specialist, but some can deceive the better-than-average collector.

An important supplier of these early philatelic forgeries was the Hamburg printer, Gebrüder Spiro. Many others indulged in this craft including S. Allan Taylor, George Hussey, James Chute, Georges Foure, Benjamin & Sarpy, Julius Goldner, E. Oneglia and L. H. Mercier. Among the noted 20th century forgers are Francois Fournier, Jean Sperati and the prolific Raoul DeThuin.

Most classic rarities, many medium priced stamps and, in this century, cheap stamps on a wholesale basis destined for beginners' packets, have been fraudulently produced. However, few new philatelic forgeries have appeared in recent decades and virtually no new frauds of valuable classics. Successful imitation of engraved work is virtually impossible.

It has proven far easier to produce a fake by altering a genuine stamp than to duplicate a stamp completely.

REPAIRS AND FAKES

Most collectors will not object to restoration of a stamp or cover, although they will not accept repairs on the same basis. *Restoration* in this sense includes cleaning with a soft eraser or soap and water. It may include the ironing out of a crease or removal of a cellophane tape stain. Removal of old hinges is acceptable. Some collectors believe that freshening of a stamp is valid restoration, whether done by the removal of oxides, "toning," or the effect of wax paper left on stamps shipped to the tropics between such sheets. Regumming may have been acceptable restoration half a century ago, but today it is considered faking. Restored stamps or covers do not normally sell at a discount, and may even change hands at a premium.

Repairs include filling in thin spots, mending tears by reweaving, adding a missing corner or perforation "tooth." Repaired stamps sell at substantial discounts.

Fakes are genuine stamps altered in some way to make them more desirable and sold without revealing the alterations. According to one major student, 30,000 varieties of fakes were known in the 1950's. The number has grown. The widespread existence of fakes makes it important for collectors to study their philatelic holdings and relevant literature. For the same reason they should buy from reputable dealers who will guarantee their stamps and make full prompt refund should a purchase be declared not genuine by some mutually agreed-upon authority. Because fakes always have some genuine characteristics, it is not always possible to obtain unanimity among expert students regarding specific items. These students may change their opinions as philatelic knowledge increases. More than 80 per cent of all fakes on the market today are regummed, reperforated or altered in regard to overprints, surcharges or cancellations.

Stamps can be chemically treated to alter or eliminate colors. For example a pale rose can be recolored into a blue of a higher value, or a "missing color" variety created. Designs may be changed by "painting," or a stroke or dot added or bleached out to turn an ordinary variety into a scarce stamp. Part of a stamp can be bleached and reprinted in a different version, achieving an inverted center or frame. Margins can be added or repairs done so deceptively that the stamp moves from the repaired to the fake category.

The fakers have not left the backs of stamps untouched. They may create false watermarks or add fake grills (or press out genuine ones). A thin India paper proof may be glued onto a thicker backing to "create" an issued stamp, or a cardboard proof may be shaved down. Silk threads have been impressed in and stamps have been split so that a rare paper variety, from a cheap stamp, can be applied as a back to falsely identify the stamp. However, the most common back treatment is regumming.

Information for Collectors

Some operators openly advertise "foolproof" application of "original gum" to stamps that lack it. This is faking, not counterfeiting. As few early stamps have survived without being hinged, the large number of never-hinged examples now offered for sale suggests the extent of regumming that has been and is being done. Regumming may be used to hide repairs and thin spots, but dipping in watermark fluid will often reveal these flaws.

The fakers also tamper with separations. Ingenious ways to add margins are known, and perforated wide-margin stamps may be falsely represented as imperforate when trimmed. Reperforating is commonly done to create scarce coil or perforation varieties and to eliminate the straight-edge stamps found in sheet margin positions of many earlier issues. Custom has made straight edges less desirable and the fakers have obliged by reperforating them so extensively that many are now uncommon if not rare.

Another main field of the faker is that of the overprint, surcharge and cancellation. The forging of rare surcharges or overprints began in the 1880's or 1890's. These forgeries are sometimes difficult to detect, but the better experts have probably identified almost all of them. Only occasionally are the overprints or cancellations removed to create unoverprinted stamps or unused items. The SPECIMEN overprints are sometimes removed—scraping and repainting is one way—to create unoverprinted varieties. Cheap revenues or pen-canceled stamps are used to generate "unused" stamps for further faking by adding other markings. The quartz lamp and a high-powered magnifying glass help in detecting cancellation removals.

The big problem, however, is the addition of overprints, surcharges or cancellations—many quite dangerous. Plating of the stamps or the overprint can be an important detecting method.

Fake postmarks can range from numerous spurious fancy cancellations, to the host of markings applied to transatlantic covers to create rare uses. With the advance of cover collecting and the wide interest in postal history, a fertile new field for fakers arose. Some have tried to create entire covers. Others specialize in adding stamps, tied by fake cancellations, to genuine stampless covers, or replacing cheaper or damaged stamps with more valuable ones. Detailed study of rates and postmarks (including the analysis of "breaks" in each handstamp over a period), ink analysis, etc. will usually unmask the fraud.

TERMINOLOGY

BOOKLETS: Many countries have issued stamps in small booklets for the convenience of users. They are usually sold by the post office at a small premium. Booklets have been issued in all sizes and forms, often with advertising on the covers, on the panes of stamps or on the interleaving. The panes may be printed from special plates or made from regular sheets. All panes from booklets issued by the United States and many from those of other countries are straight edged on the bottom and both sides, but perforated between the stamps. Any unit in the pane, either printed or blank, which is not a postage stamp, is called a *label* in the catalogue listings.

CANCELLATIONS: The marks or obliterations put on a stamp by the postal authorities to show that it has done service and is no longer valid for postage. If it is made with a pen, it is called a pen cancellation. When the location of the post office appears in the cancellation, it is called a town cancellation. When it calls attention to a cause or celebration, it is a slogan cancellation. Many other types and styles of cancellations exist, such as duplex, numerals, targets, etc.

COIL STAMPS—Stamps issued in rolls for use in affixing and vending machines. Those of the United States, Canada, etc., are perforated horizontally or vertically only, with the outer edges imperforate. Coil stamps of some countries (Great Britain) are perforated on all four sides.

COVERS: Envelopes, with or without adhesive postage stamps, which have passed through the mail and bear postal or other markings of philatelic interest. Before the introduction of envelopes (1840), people folded letters and wrote the address on the outside. Many people covered their letters with an extra sheet of paper on the outside for the address. Hence the word "cover." Used air letter sheets, stamped envelopes, and other items of postal stationery are also referred to as "covers."

ERRORS: Stamps having some unintentional deviation from the normal. Errors include, but are not limited to, mistakes in color, paper or watermark; inverted centers (or frames), surcharges or overprints, and double impressions. A factually wrong or misspelled inscription, if it appears on all examples of a stamp, is not classified as a philatelic error. (Panama No. J1).

OVERPRINTED AND SURCHARGED STAMPS: Overprinting is wording placed on stamps to alter the place of use ("Canal Zone" on U.S. issues); to adapt them for a special purpose ("Porto" on Denmark's 1913-20 regular issues for use as postage dues, Nos. J1-J7); or for a special occasion (Guatemala Nos. 374-378).

The term **surcharge** is used when the overprint changes or restates the value (1923 "Inflation Issues" of Germany; Australia No. 580).

Surcharges and overprints may be handstamped, typeset or, occasionally, lithographed or engraved.

PRECANCELS: Stamps canceled by the issuing government before they are sold at the post office. Precanceling is done to expedite the handling of large mailings.

In the United States precancellations generally identify the point of origin. That is, the city and state names (or initials) appear, usually centered by an arrangement of parallel lines.

In France the abbreviation **Affranchts** in a semicircle together with the word **Postes** is the general form. Belgian precancellations are usually a square box in which the name of the city appears. Netherlands' precancellations have the name of the city enclosed between a large and small circle, sometimes called a "life-saver."

Precancellations of other countries usually follow these patterns, but may be any arrangement of bars, boxes and city names.

PROOFS AND ESSAYS: Proofs are impressions taken from an approved die, plate or stone in which the design and color are the same as the stamp issued to the public. Trial color proofs are impressions taken from approved dies, plates or stones in varying colors. An essay is the impression of a design that differs in some way from the stamp as issued.

PROVISIONALS: Stamps issued on short notice and intended for temporary use pending the arrival of regular (definitive) issues. They are usually issued to meet contingencies: changes in government or currency; shortage of necessary postage values, or military occupation.

In the 1840's, postmasters in certain American cities issued stamps that were valid only at specific post offices. Postmasters of the Confederate States also issued stamps with limited validity. These are known as Postmasters' Provisionals.

SE-TENANT: Joined together, referring to an unsevered pair, strip or block of stamps differing in design, denomination or overprint (U.S. Nos. 1530-1537).

TETE BECHE: A pair of stamps in which one is upside down in relation to the other. Some of these are the result of intentional sheet arrangement (Morocco Nos. B10-B11). Others occurred when one or more electrotypes were accidentally placed upside down on the plate (Colombia No. 57a). Separation of course destroys the tête bêche variety.

SPECIMENS: One of the regulations of the Universal Postal Union requires member nations to send samples of all stamps they put into service to the International Bureau in Switzerland. These are then sent to all other member nations as samples of what stamps are valid for postage. Many are overprinted, handstamped or initial-perforated "Specimen," "Canceled" or "Muestra." Some are marked with bars across the denominations (China), punched holes (Czechoslovakia) or back inscriptions (Mongolia).

Stamps distributed to government officials or for publicity purposes, and stamps submitted by private security printers for official approval may also receive such defacements.

These markings prevent postal use, and all such items are generally known as "specimens."

CLASSIFICATION OF STAMPS

The various functions of stamps are classified by their names. Postage stamps; air post stamps; postage due stamps for unpaid postage, collected at time of delivery; late fee stamps, a special fee for forwarding a letter after regular mail delivery; registration stamps, fee for keeping special record of letter and ensuring its delivery; special delivery and express stamps, for delivery of letter in advance of regular delivery. With the exception of regular postage, all numbers in the catalogue include a prefix letter denoting the class to which the stamp belongs. (B=Semi-Postal; C=Air Post; E=Special Delivery; J=Postage Due; O=Official; CO=Air Post Official; etc.).

CATALOGUE TERMS TRANSLATED

English	French	German	Spanish	Italian
Air mail	Poste aérienne	Flugpost	Correo aéreo	Posta aerea
Back	Verso	Rückseitig	Dorso	Dorso
Background	Fond	Hintergrund	Fondo	Sfondo
Bar	Barre	Balken	Barra	Barra
Bisected stamp	Timbre coupé	Halbiert	Partido en dos	Frazionato
Block of four	Bloc de quatre	Viererblock	Bloque de cuatro	Blocco di quattro
Booklet	Carnet	Heftchen	Cuadernillo	Libretto
Bottom	Bas	Unten	Abajo	Basso
Bright	Vif	Lebhaft	Vivo	Vivo
Broken	Interrompu	Unterbrochen	Interrumpido	Interrotto
Cancellation	Oblitération	Entwertung	Matasello	Annullamento
Cancellation to order	Oblitération de complaisance	Gefälligkeitsabstempelung	Matasello de complacencia	Annullamento di compiacenza
Canceled	Annulé	Gestempelt	Cancelado	Annullato
Center	Centre du timbre	Mittelstück	Centro	Centro
Centering	Centrage	Zentrierung	Centrado	Centratura
Chalky paper	Papier couché	Kreidepapier	Papel estucado	Carta gessata
Circle	Cercle	Kreis	Circulo	Circolo
Coat of arms	Armoiries	Wappen	Escudo de armas	Arme
Coil	Rouleau de timbres	Markenrolle	Rollo de sellos	Rollo di francobolli
Color	Couleur	Farbe	Color	Colore
Comb perforation	Dentelure en peigne	Kammzähnung	Dentado de peine	Dentalletura e pettine
Commemorative	Commémoratif	Gedenkausgabe	Conmemorativo	Commemorativo
Corner	Angle	Ecke	Esquina	Angolo
Counterfeit	Faux	Fälschung	Falsificación	Falsificazione
Cover	Lettre	Brief	Carta	Lettera
Crescent	Croissant	Halbmond	Media luna	Luna crescente
Crown	Couronne	Krone	Corona	Corona
Cut square	Coupure	Ausschnitt	Recorte	Ritaglio
Dark	Foncé	Dunkel	Oscuro	Oscuro
Date	Date	Datum	Fecha	Data
Definitive	Définitif	Freimarken	Definitivo	Definitivo
Design	Dessin	Zeichnung	Diseño	Disegno
Die	Matrice	Urstempel	Cuño	Conio
District	District	Bezirk	Distrito	Distretto
Double	Double	Doppelt	Doble	Doppio
Dull	Terne	Trüb	Turbio	Smorto
Embossing	Impression en relief	Prägedruck	Impresión en relieve	Rilievo
Engraved	Gravé	Graviert	Grabado	Inciso
Error	Erreur	Fehler	Error	Errore
Essay	Essai	Probedruck	Ensayo	Saggio
Figure	Chiffre	Ziffer	Cifra	Cifra
Forerunner	Précurseur	Vorläufer	Precursor	Precursore
Forgery	Faux	Fälschung	Falsificación	Falsificazione
Frame	Cadre	Rahmen	Marco	Cornice
Genuine	Authentique	Echt	Auténtico	Autentico
Glossy paper	Papier glacé	Glanzpapier	Papel lustre	Carta patinata
Granite paper	Papier mélangé de fils de soie	Faserpapier	Papel con filamentos	Carta con fili di seta
Gum	Gomme	Gummi	Goma	Gomma
Gutter	Interpanneau	Zwischensteg	Espacio blanco entre dos grupos	Interspazio
Half	Moitié	Hälfte	Mitad	Metà
Handstamp	Cachet à la main	Handstempel	Matasello manual	Annullamento manuale

Catalogue Terms Translated

English	French	German	Spanish	Italian
Imperforate	Non-dentelé	Geschnitten	Sin dentar	Non dentellato
Inscription	Inscription	Inschrift	Inscripción	Dicitura
Inverted	Renversé	Kopfstehend	Invertido	Capovolto
Issue	Emission	Ausgabe	Emisión	Emissione
King	Roi	König	Rey	Re
Kingdom	Royaume	Königreich	Reino	Regno
Laid	Vergé	Gestrichen	Listado	Vergato
Large	Grand	Gross	Grande	Grosso
Late fee stamp	Timbre pour lettres en retard	Verspätungsmarke	Sello para cartas retardadas	Francobollo per le lettere in ritardo
Left	Gauche	Links	Izquierda	Sinistro
Light	Clair	Hell	Claro	Chiaro
Line perforation	Dentelure en lignes	Linienzähnung	Dentado en linea	Dentellatura lineare
Lithography	Lithographie	Steindruck	Litografia	Litografia
Lozenges	Losanges	Rauten	Rombos	Losanghe
Margin	Marge	Rand	Borde	Margine
Multiple	Multiple	Mehrfach	Multiple	Multiplo
Narrow	Étroit	Eng	Estrecho	Stretto
Network	Burelage	Netz	Burelage	Rete
Newspaper stamp	Timbre pour journaux	Zeitungsmarke	Sello para periódicos	Francobollo per giornali
Not issued	Non émis	Nicht verausgabt	No emitido	Non emesso
Numeral	Chiffre	Ziffer	Cifra	Numerale
Occupation	Occupation	Besetzung	Ocupación	Occupazione
Official stamp	Timbre de service	Dienstmarke	Sello de servicio	Francobollo servizio
Oval	Ovale	Eiförmig	Óvalo	Ovale
Overprint	Surcharge	Aufdruck	Sobrecarga	Soprastampa
Pair	Paire	Paar	Pareja	Coppia
Pale	Pâle	Blass	Pálido	Pallido
Pane	Panneau	Gruppe	Grupo	Gruppo
Paper	Papier	Papier	Papel	Carta
Parcel post stamp	Timbre pour colis postaux	Paketmarke	Sello para paquete postal	Francobollo per pacchi postali
Pen canceled	Oblitéré à plume	Federzugentwertung	Cancelado a pluma	Annullato a penna
Perforated	Dentelé	Gezähnt	Dentado	Dentellato
Perforation	Dentelure	Zähnung	Dentar	Dentellatura
Photogravure	Héliogravure	Rastertiefdruck	Fotograbado	Rotocalco
Piece	Fragment	Briefstück	Fragmento	Frammento
Pin perforation	Percé en points	In Punkten durchstochen	Horadado con alfileres	Perforato a punti
Plate	Planche	Platte	Plancha	Lastra
Postage due stamp	Timbre-taxe	Portomarke	Sello de tasa	Segnatasse
Postage stamp	Timbre-poste	Briefmarke	Sello de correos	Francobollo postale
Postal forgery	Faux pour servir	Postfälschung	Falso por correo	Falso per posta
Postal tax stamp	Timbre surtaxe obligatoire	Zwangszuschlagsmarke	Sello de sobretasa obligatorio	Francobollo per sopratassa obligatorio
Postmark	Oblitération postale	Poststempel	Matasello	Bollo
Price	Prix	Preis	Precio	Prezzo
Printing	Impression	Druck	Impresión	Stampa
Private	Privé	Privat	Privado	Privato
Proof	Epreuve	Druckprobe	Prueba de impresión	Prova
Quadrille	Quadrillé	Gegittert	Cuadriculado	Quadriglia
Quarter	Un quart	Viertel	Un cuarto	Quarto
Recess printing	Impression en taille douce	Tiefdruck	Grabado	Incisione
Reengraving	Regravure	Neugravierung	Regrabado	Rincisione

Catalogue Terms Translated

English	French	German	Spanish	Italian
Reentry	Double frappe	Nachgravierung	Regrabado	Doppia incisione
Registration stamp	Timbre pour lettre recommandée	Einschreibemarke	Sello de certificado	Francobollo per lettere raccomandate
Reprint	Réimpression	Nachdruck	Reimpresión	Ristampa
Revenue stamp	Timbre fiscal	Stempelmarke	Sello fiscal	Francobollo fiscale
Reversed	Retourné	Umgekehrt	Invertido	Rovesciato
Ribbed	Cannelé	Geriffelt	Acanalado	Scanalatura
Right	Droite	Rechts	A la derecha	Destro
Rotary printing	Impression par cylindre	Walzendruck	Impresión cilindrica	Stampa rotativa
Roulette	Perçage	Durchstich	Picadura	Foratura
Rouletted	Percé	Durchstochen	Picado	Forato
Semipostal stamp	Timbre de bienfaisance	Wohltätigkeitsmarke	Sello de beneficencia	Francobollo di beneficenza
Serpentine roulette	Percé en serpentin	Schlangenartiger Durchstich	Picado a serpentina	Perforazione a serpentina
Set	Série	Satz	Serie	Serie
Set price	Prix de la série	Satzpreis	Precio por serie	Prezzo per serie
Se-tenant	Se-tenant	Zusammendruck	Combinación	Combinazione
Shade	Nuance	Tönung	Tono	Gradazione di colore
Sheet	Feuille	Bogen	Hoja	Foglio
Side	Côté	Seite	Lado	Lato
Small	Petit	Klein	Pequeño	Piccolo
Souvenir sheet	Bloc commémoratif	Block, gedenkblock	Hojita-bloque conmemorativa	Foglietto commemorativo
Special delivery stamp	Timbre pour exprès	Eilmarke	Sello de urgencia	Francobollo per espressi
Specimen	Spécimen	Muster	Muestra	Saggio
Strip	Bande	Streifen	Tira	Striscia
Surcharge	Surcharge	Zuschlag	Sobrecarga	Soprastampa
Surtax	Surtaxe	Zuschlag	Sobretasa	Sopratassa
Tête bêche	Tête-bêche	Kehrdruck	Tête-bêche	Tête-bêche
Thick	Épais	Dick	Grueso	Spesso
Thin	Mince	Dünn	Delgado	Smilzo
Tinted paper	Papier teinté	Getöntes papier	Papel coloreado	Carta colorata
Top	Haut	Oben	Arriba	Alto
Typography	Typographie	Buchdruck	Tipografía	Tipografia
Unused	Neuf	Ungebraucht	Nuevo	Nuovo
Used	Oblitéré	Gebraucht	Usado	Usato
War tax stamp	Timbre d'impôt de guerre	Kriegssteuermarke	Sello de impuesto de guerra	Francobollo per tassa di guerra
Watermark	Filigrane	Wasserzeichen	Filigrana	Filigrana
Wide	Espacé	Weit	Ancho	Largo
With	Avec	Mit	Con	Con
Without	Sans	Ohne	Sin	Senza
Worn	Usé	Abgenutzt	Gastado	Usato
Wove paper	Papier ordinaire	Einfaches Papier	Papel avitelado	Carta unita

CATALOGUE COLORS TRANSLATED

English	French	German	Spanish	Italian
Apple green	Verte-pomme	Apfelgrün	Verde manzana	Verde mela
Bister	Bistre	Bister	Bistre	Bistro
Black	Noir	Schwarz	Negro	Nero
Blue	Bleu	Blau	Azul	Azzurro
Brick red	Rouge-brique	Ziegelrot	Rojo ladrillo	Rosso di mattone
Bronze	Bronze	Bronze	Bronce	Bronzo
Brown	Brun	Braun	Castaño, pardo	Bruno
Buff	Chamois	Sämisch	Anteado	Camoscio
Carmine	Carmin	Karmin	Carmin	Carminio
Cerise	Cerise	Kirschrot	Color de ceresa	Color ciliegia
Chalky blue	Bleu terne	Kreideblau	Azul turbio	Azzurro smorto
Chamois	Chamois	Sämisch	Anteado	Camoscio
Chestnut	Marron	Kastanienbraun	Castaño rojo	Marrone
Chocolate	Chocolat	Schokoladebraun	Chocolate	Cioccolato
Chrome yellow	Jaune-chrome	Chromgelb	Amarillo cromo	Giallo croma
Citron	Citron	Zitronengelb	Cidra	Cedro
Claret	Lie de vin	Weinrot	Rojo vinoso	Vinaccia
Cobalt	Cobalt	Kobaltblau	Cobalto	Cobalto
Copper red	Rouge-cuivre	Kupferrot	Rojo cobre	Rosso di rame
Cream	Crème	Rahmfarbe	Crema	Crema
Crimson	Cramoisi	Karmesin	Carmesi	Cremisi
Emerald	Vert-émeraude	Smaragdgrün	Esmeralda	Smeraldo
Flesh	Chair	Fleischfarben	Carne	Carnicino
Gray	Gris	Grau	Gris	Grigio
Green	Vert	Grün	Verde	Verde
Indigo	Indigo	Indigo	Azul indigo	Indaco
Lake	Lie de vin	Lackfarbe	Laca	Lacca
Lemon	Jaune-citron	Zitronengelb	Limón	Limone
Lilac	Lilas	Lila	Lila	Lilla
Magenta	Magenta	Magentarot	Magenta	Magenta
Mauve	Mauve	Malvenfarbe	Malva	Malva
Milky blue	Bleu laiteux	Milchblau	Azul lechoso	Azzurro di latte
Moss green	Vert mousse	Moosgrün	Verde musgo	Verde muscosa
Multicolored	Polychrome	Mehrfarbig	Multicolores	Policromo
Ocher	Ocre	Ocker	Ocre	Ocra
Olive	Olive	Oliv	Oliva	Oliva
Orange	Orange	Orange	Naranja	Arancio
Pink	Rose	Rosa	Rosa	Rosa
Plum	Prune	Pflaumenfarbe	Color de ciruela	Prugna
Prussian blue	Bleu de Prusse	Preussischblau	Azul de Prusia	Azzurro di Prussia
Purple	Pourpre	Purpur	Púrpura	Porpora
Red	Rouge	Rot	Rojo	Rosso
Rose	Rose	Rosa	Rosa	Rosa
Rosine	Rose vif	Lebhaftrosa	Rosa vivo	Rosa vivo
Royal blue	Bleu-roi	Königsblau	Azul real	Azzurro reale
Rust	Brun-rouille	Rostbraun	Castaño oxidado	Castagna
Sage green	Vert-sauge	Salbeigrün	Verde salvia	Verde salvia
Salmon	Saumon	Lachs	Salmón	Salmone
Scarlet	Écarlate	Scharlach	Escarlata	Scarlatto
Sea green	Vert de mer	Seegrün	Verde mar	Verde mare
Sepia	Sépia	Sepia	Sepia	Seppia
Sienna	Terre de Sienne	Siena	Siena	Siena
Sky blue	Bleu ciel	Himmelblau	Azul celeste	Azzurro cielo
Slate	Ardoise	Schiefer	Pizarra	Ardesia
Steel blue	Bleu acier	Stahlblau	Azul acero	Azzurro acciaio
Straw	Jaune-paille	Strohgelb	Amarillo pajizo	Giallo pallido
Turquoise blue	Bleu-turquoise	Türkisblau	Azul turquesa	Azzurro turchese
Ultramarine	Outremer	Ultramarin	Ultramar	Oltremare
Vermilion	Vermillon	Zinnober	Cinabrio	Vermiglione
Violet	Violet	Violett	Violeta	Violetto
Yellow	Jaune	Gelb	Amarillo	Giallo

List of Colonies, Former Colonies, Offices and Territories Controlled by Parent States

BELGIUM
Belgian Congo
Ruanda-Urundi

DENMARK
Danish West Indies
Faroe Islands
Greenland
Iceland

FRANCE
Colonies, Past and Present, and Controlled Territories

Afars and Issas, Terr. of
Alaouites
Alexandretta
Algeria
Alsace and Lorraine
Ajouan
Annam & Tonkin
Benin
Cambodia (Khmer)
Cameroun
Castellorizo
Chad
Cilicia
Cochin China
Comoro Islands
Dahomey
Diego Suarez
Djibouti (Somali Coast)
Fezzan
French Congo
French Equatorial Africa
French Guiana
French Guinea
French India
French Morocco
French Polynesia (Oceania)
French Southern & Antarctic Territories
French Sudan
French West Africa
Gabon
Germany
Ghadames
Grand Comoro
Guadeloupe
Indo-China
Inini
Ivory Coast
Laos
Latakia
Lebanon
Madagascar
Martinique
Mauritania
Mayotte
Memel
Middle Congo
Mohéli
New Caledonia
New Hebrides
Niger Territory
Nossi-Bé
Obock
Reunion
Rouad, Ile
Ste.-Marie de Madagascar
St. Pierre & Miquelon
Senegal
Senegambia & Niger
Somali Coast
Syria
Tahiti
Togo
Tunisia
Ubangi-Shari
Upper Senegal & Niger
Upper Volta
Viet Nam
Wallis & Futuna Islands

Post Offices in Foreign Countries
China
Crete
Egypt
Turkish Empire
Zanzibar

GERMANY
Early States
Baden
Bavaria
Bergedorf
Bremen
Brunswick
Hamburg
Hanover
Lubeck
Mecklenburg-Schwerin
Mecklenburg-Strelitz
Oldenburg
Prussia
Saxony
Schleswig-Holstein
Wurttemberg

Former Colonies
Cameroun (Kamerun)
Caroline Islands
German East Africa
German New Guinea
German South-West Africa
Kiauchau
Mariana Islands
Marshall Islands
Samoa
Togo

ITALY
Early States
Modena
Parma
Romagna
Roman States
Sardinia
Tuscany
Two Sicilies
Naples
Neapolitan Provinces
Sicily

Former Colonies, Controlled Territories, Occupation Areas
Aegean Islands
  Calimno (Calino)
  Caso
  Cos (Coo)
  Karki (Carchi)
  Leros (Lero)
  Lipso
  Nisiros (Nisiro)
  Patmos (Patmo)
  Piscopi
  Rodi (Rhodes)
  Scarpanto
  Simi
  Stampalia
Castellorizo
Corfu
Cyrenaica
Eritrea
Ethiopia (Abyssinia)
Fiume
Ionian Islands
  Cephalonia
  Ithaca
  Paxos
Italian East Africa
Libya
Oltre Giuba
Saseno
Somalia (Italian Somaliland)
Tripolitania

Post Offices in Foreign Countries
"Estero" *
Austria
China
  Peking
  Tientsin
Crete
Tripoli
Turkish Empire
  Constantinople
Turkish Empire (cont.)
  Durazzo
  Janina
  Jerusalem
  Salonika
  Scutari
  Smyrna
  Valona

* Stamps overprinted "ESTERO" were used in various parts of the world.

NETHERLANDS
Netherlands Antilles (Curacao)
Netherlands Indies
Netherlands New Guinea
Surinam (Dutch Guiana)

PORTUGAL
Colonies, Past and Present, and Controlled Territories
Angola
Angra
Azores
Cape Verde
Funchal
Horta
Inhambane
Kionga
Lourenço Marques
Macao
Madeira
Mozambique
Mozambique Co.
Nyassa
Ponta Delgada
Portuguese Africa
Portuguese Congo
Portuguese Guinea
Portuguese India
Quelimane
St. Thomas & Prince Isls.
Tete
Timor
Zambezia

RUSSIA
Allied Territories and Republics, Occupation Areas

Armenia
Aunus (Olonets)
Azerbaijan
Batum
Estonia
Far Eastern Republic
Georgia
Karelia
Latvia
Lithuania
North Ingermanland
Ostland
Russian Turkestan
Siberia
South Russia
Tannu Tuva
Transcaucasian
    Federated Republics
Ukraine
Wenden (Livonia)
Western Ukraine

SPAIN
Colonies, Past and Present, and Controlled Territories

Agüera, La
Cape Juby
Cuba
Elobey, Annobon & Corisco
Fernando Po
Ifni
Mariana Islands
Philippines
Puerto Rico
Rio de Oro
Rio Muni
Spanish Guinea
Spanish Morocco
Spanish Sahara
Spanish West Africa

Post Offices in Foreign Countries

Morocco
Tangier
Tetuan

COMMON DESIGN TYPES

Pictured in this section are issues where one illustration has been used for a number of countries in the Catalogue. Not included in this section are overprinted stamps or those issues which are illustrated in each country.

EUROPA

Europa Issue, 1956
The design symbolizing the cooperation among the six countries comprising the Coal and Steel Community is illustrated in each country.

Belgium	444–445
France	805–806
Germany	748–749
Italy	715–716
Luxembourg	318–320
Netherlands	368–369

Europa Issue, 1958

"E" and Dove
CD1

European Postal Union at the service of European integration.

1958, Sept. 13

Belgium	478–479
France	889–890
Germany	790–791
Italy	750–751
Luxembourg	341–343
Netherlands	375–376
Saar	317–318

Europa Issue, 1959

6-Link Endless Chain
CD2

1959, Sept. 19

Belgium	479–498
France	929–930
Germany	805–806
Italy	791–792
Luxembourg	354–355
Netherlands	379–380

Europa Issue, 1960

19-Spoke Wheel
CD3

First anniversary of the establishment of C.E.P.T. (Conférence Européenne des Administrations des Postes et des Télécommunications.) The spokes symbolize the 19 founding members of the Conference.

1960, Sept.

Belgium	518–519
Denmark	379
Finland	376–377
France	970–971
Germany	818–820
Great Britain	377–378
Greece	688
Iceland	327–328
Ireland	175–176
Italy	809–810
Luxembourg	374–375
Netherlands	385–386
Norway	387
Portugal	866–867
Spain	941–942
Sweden	562–563
Switzerland	400–401
Turkey	1493–1494

Europa Issue, 1961

19 Doves Flying as One
CD4

The 19 doves represent the 19 members of the Conference of European Postal and Telecommunications Administrations, C.E.P.T.

1961–62

Belgium	536–537
Cyprus	201–203
France	1005–1006
Germany	844–845
Great Britain	383–384
Greece	718–719
Iceland	340–341
Italy	845–846
Luxembourg	382–383
Netherlands	387–388
Spain	1010–1011
Switzerland	410–411
Turkey	1518–1520

Europa Issue 1962

Young Tree with 19 Leaves
CD5

The 19 leaves represent the 19 original members of C.E.P.T.

1962–63

Belgium	546–547
Cyprus	219–221
France	1045–1046
Germany	852–853
Greece	739–740
Iceland	348–349
Ireland	184–185
Italy	860–861
Luxembourg	386–387
Netherlands	394–395
Norway	414–415
Switzerland	416–417
Turkey	1553–1555

Europa Issue, 1963

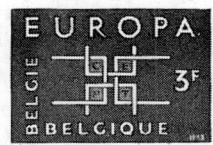

Stylized Links, Symbolizing Unity
CD6

1963, Sept.

Belgium	562–563
Cyprus	229–231
Finland	419
France	1074–1075
Germany	867–868
Greece	768–769
Iceland	357–358
Ireland	188–189
Italy	880–881
Luxembourg	403–404
Netherlands	416–417
Norway	441–442
Switzerland	429
Turkey	1602–1603

Europa Issue, 1964

Symbolic Daisy
CD7

5th anniversary of the establishment of C.E.P.T. The 22 petals of the flower symbolize the 22 members of the Conference.

1964, Sept.

Austria	738
Belgium	578–579
Cyprus	244–246
France	1109–1110
Germany	897–898
Greece	801–802
Iceland	367–368
Ireland	196–197
Italy	894–895
Luxembourg	411–412
Monaco	590–591
Netherlands	428–429
Norway	458
Portugal	931–933
Spain	1262–1263
Switzerland	438–439
Turkey	1628–1629

Europa Issue, 1965

Leaves and "Fruit"
CD8

1965

Belgium	600–601
Cyprus	262–264
Finland	437
France	1131–1132
Germany	934–935
Greece	833–834
Iceland	375–376
Ireland	204–205
Italy	915–916
Luxembourg	432–433
Monaco	616–617
Netherlands	438–439
Norway	475–476
Portugal	958–960
Switzerland	469
Turkey	1665–1666

Europa Issue, 1966

Symbolic Sailboat
CD9

1966, Sept.

Andorra, French	172
Belgium	622–628
Cyprus	275–277
France	1163–1164
Germany	963–964
Greece	862–863
Iceland	384–385
Ireland	216–217
Italy	942–943
Liechtenstein	415
Luxembourg	440–441
Monaco	639–640
Netherlands	441–442
Norway	496–497
Portugal	980–982
Switzerland	477–478
Turkey	1718–1719

Europa Issue, 1967

Cogwheels
CD10

xvii

COMMON DESIGN TYPES

1967

Andorra, French	174-175
Belgium	641-642
Cyprus	297-299
France	1178-1179
Greece	891-892
Germany	969-970
Iceland	389-390
Ireland	232-233
Italy	951-952
Liechtenstein	420
Luxembourg	449-450
Monaco	669-670
Netherlands	444-447
Norway	504-505
Portugal	994-996
Spain	1465-1466
Switzerland	482
Turkey	B120-B121

Europa Issue, 1968

Golden Key with C.E.P.T. Emblem
CD11

1968

Andorra, French	182-183
Belgium	664-665
Cyprus	314-316
France	1209-1210
Germany	983-984
Greece	916-917
Iceland	395-396
Ireland	242-243
Italy	979-980
Liechtenstein	442
Luxembourg	466-467
Monaco	689-691
Netherlands	452-453
Portugal	1019-1021
San Marino	687
Spain	1526
Turkey	1775-1776

Europa Issue, 1969

"EUROPA" and "CEPT"
CD12

Tenth anniversary of C.E.P.T.

1969

Andorra, French	188-189
Austria	837
Belgium	683-684
Cyprus	326-328
Denmark	458
Finland	483
France	1245-1246
Germany	996-997
Great Britain	585
Greece	947-948
Iceland	406-407
Ireland	270-271
Italy	1000-1001
Jugoslavia	1003-1004
Liechtenstein	453
Luxembourg	474-475
Monaco	722-724
Netherlands	475-476
Norway	533-534
Portugal	1038-1040
San Marino	701-702
Spain	1567
Sweden	814-816
Switzerland	500-501
Turkey	1799-1800
Vatican	470-472

Europa Issue, 1970

Interwoven Threads
CD13

1970

Andorra, French	196-197
Belgium	708-709
Cyprus	340-342
France	1271-1272
Germany	1018-1019
Greece	985, 987
Iceland	420-421
Ireland	279-281
Italy	1013-1014
Jugoslavia	1024-1025
Liechtenstein	470
Luxembourg	489-490
Monaco	768-770
Netherlands	483-484
Portugal	1060-1062
San Marino	729-730
Spain	1607
Switzerland	515-516
Turkey	1848-1849

Europa Issue, 1971

"Fraternity, Cooperation, Common Effort"—CD14

1971

Andorra, French	205-206
Belgium	742-743
Cyprus	365-367
Finland	504
France	1304
Germany	1064-1065
Greece	1029-1030
Iceland	429-430
Ireland	305-306
Italy	1038-1039
Jugoslavia	1052-1053
Liechtenstein	485
Luxembourg	500-501
Malta	425-427
Monaco	797-799
Netherlands	488-489
Portugal	1094-1096
San Marino	749-750
Spain	1675-1676
Switzerland	531-532
Turkey	1876-1877

Europa Issue, 1972

Sparkles, Symbolic of Communications
CD15

1972

Andorra, French	210-211
Andorra, Spanish	62
Belgium	768-769
Cyprus	380-382
Finland	512-513
France	1341
Germany	1089-1090
Greece	1049-1050
Iceland	439-440
Ireland	316-317
Italy	1065-1066
Jugoslavia	1100-1101
Liechtenstein	504
Luxembourg	512-513
Malta	450-453
Monaco	831-832
Netherlands	494-495
Portugal	1141-1143
San Marino	771-772
Spain	1718
Switzerland	544-545
Turkey	1907-1908

Europa Issue, 1973

Post Horn and Arrows
CD16

1973

Andorra, French	319-320
Andorra, Spanish	76
Belgium	782-783
Cyprus	396-398
Finland	526
France	1367
Germany	1114-1115
Greece	1090-1092
Iceland	447-448
Ireland	329-330
Italy	1108-1109
Jugoslavia	1138-1139
Liechtenstein	528-529
Luxembourg	523-524
Malta	469-471
Monaco	866-867
Netherlands	504-505
Norway	604-605
Portugal	1170-1172
San Marino	802-803
Spain	1753
Switzerland	580-581
Turkey	1935-1936

PORTUGAL & COLONIES

Vasco da Gama Issue

Fleet Departing—CD20

Fleet Arriving at Calicut
CD21

Embarking at Rastello—CD22

Muse of History
CD23

Flagship San Gabriel, da Gama and Camoens
CD24

Archangel Gabriel, the Patron Saint
CD25

Flagship San Gabriel
CD26

Vasco da Gama
CD27

Fourth centenary of Vasco da Gama's discovery of the route to India.

1898

Azores	93-100
Macao	67-74
Madeira	37-44
Portugal	147-154
Port. Africa	1-8
Port. India	189-196
Timor	45-52

Pombal Issue
POSTAL TAX

Marquis de Pombal
CD28

Planning Reconstruction of Lisbon, 1755
CD29

Pombal Monument, Lisbon
CD30

Sebastiao José de Carvalho e Mello, Marquis de Pombal (1699-1782), statesman, rebuilt Lisbon after earthquake of 1755. Tax was for the erection of Pombal monument. Obligatory on all mail on certain days throughout the year.

1925

Angola	RA1-RA3
Azores	RA9-RA11
Cape Verde	RA1-RA3
Macao	RA1-RA3
Madeira	RA1-RA3
Mozambique	RA1-RA3
Portugal	RA11-RA13
Port. Guinea	RA1-RA3
Port. India	RA1-RA3
St. Thomas & Prince Islands	RA1-RA3
Timor	RA1-RA3

COMMON DESIGN TYPES

Pombal Issue
POSTAL TAX DUES

Marquis de Pombal
CD31

Planning Reconstruction of Lisbon, 1755
CD32

Pombal Monument, Lisbon
CD33

1925

Angola	RAJ1-RAJ3
Azores	RAJ2-RAJ4
Cape Verde	RAJ1-RAJ3
Macao	RAJ1-RAJ3
Madeira	RAJ1-RAJ3
Mozambique	RAJ1-RAJ3
Portugal	RAJ2-RAJ4
Port. Guinea	RAJ1-RAJ3
Port. India	RAJ1-RAJ3
St. Thomas & Prince Islands	RAJ1-RAJ3
Timor	RAJ1-RAJ3

Vasco da Gama
CD34

Mousinho de Albuquerque   **Dam**
CD35   CD36

Prince Henry the Navigator
CD37

Affonso de Albuquerque
CD38

1938-39

Angola	274-291
Cape Verde	234-251
Macao	289-305
Mozambique	270-287
Port. Guinea	233-250
Port. India	439-453
St. Thomas & Prince Islands	302-319, 323-340
Timor	223-239

Plane over Globe
CD39

1938-39

Angola	C1-C9
Cape Verde	C1-C9
Macao	C7-C15
Mozambique	C1-C9
Port. Guinea	C1-C9
Port. India	C1-C8
St. Thomas & Prince Islands	C1-C18
Timor	C1-C9

Lady of Fatima Issue

Our Lady of the Rosary, Fatima, Portugal
CD40

1948-49

Angola	315-318
Cape Verde	266
Macao	336
Mozambique	325-328
Port. Guinea	271
Port. India	480
St. Thomas & Prince Islands	351
Timor	254

A souvenir sheet of 9 stamps was issued in 1951 to mark the extension of the 1950 Holy Year. The sheet contains: Angola No. 316, Cape Verde No. 266, Macao No. 336, Mozambique No. 325, Portuguese Guinea No. 271, Portuguese India Nos. 480, 485, St. Thomas & Prince Islands No. 351, Timor No. 254.
The sheet also contains a portrait of Pope Pius XII and is inscribed "Encerramento do Ano Santo, Fatima 1951." It was sold for 11 escudos.

Holy Year Issue

Church Bells and Dove   **Angel Holding Candelabra**
CD41   CD42

Holy Year, 1950.

1950-51

Angola	331-332
Cape Verde	268-269
Macao	339-340
Mozambique	330-331
Port. Guinea	273-274
Port. India	490-491, 496-503
St. Thomas & Prince Islands	353-354
Timor	258-259

A souvenir sheet of 8 stamps was issued in 1951 to mark the extension of the Holy Year. The sheet contains: Angola No. 331, Cape Verde No. 269, Macao No. 340, Mozambique No. 331, Portuguese Guinea No. 275, Portuguese India No. 490, St. Thomas & Prince Islands No. 354, Timor No. 258, some with colors changed. The sheet contains doves and is inscribed "Encerramento do Ano Santo, Fatima 1951." It was sold for 17 escudos.

Holy Year Conclusion Issue

Our Lady of Fatima
CD43

Conclusion of Holy Year. Sheets contain alternate vertical rows of stamps and labels bearing quotation from Pope Pius XII, different for each colony.

1951

Angola	357
Cape Verde	270
Macao	352
Mozambique	356
Port. Guinea	275
Port. India	506
St. Thomas & Prince Islands	355
Timor	270

Medical Congress Issue

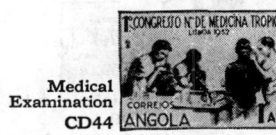

Medical Examination
CD44

First National Congress of Tropical Medicine, Lisbon, 1952.
Each stamp has a different design.

1952

Angola	358
Cape Verde	287
Macao	364
Mozambique	359
Port. Guinea	276
Port. India	516
St. Thomas & Prince Islands	356
Timor	271

POSTAGE DUE STAMPS

CD45

1952

Angola	J37-J42
Cape Verde	J31-J36
Macao	J53-J58
Mozambique	J51-J56
Port. Guinea	J40-J45
Port. India	J47-J52
St. Thomas & Prince Islands	J52-J57
Timor	J31-J36

Sao Paulo Issue

Father Manuel da Nobrega and View of Sao Paulo
CD46

400th anniversary of the founding of Sao Paulo, Brazil.

1954

Angola	385
Cape Verde	297
Macao	382
Mozambique	395
Port. Guinea	291
Port. India	530
St. Thomas & Prince Islands	369
Timor	279

Tropical Medicine Congress Issue

Securidaca Longipedunculata
CD47

Sixth International Congress for Tropical Medicine and Malaria, Lisbon, Sept. 1958.
Each stamp shows a different plant.

1958

Angola	409
Cape Verde	303
Macao	392
Mozambique	404
Port. Guinea	295
Port. India	569
St. Thomas & Prince Islands	371
Timor	289

Sports Issue

Flying
CD48

Each stamp shows a different sport.

COMMON DESIGN TYPES

1962

Angola	433–438
Cape Verde	320–325
Macao	394–399
Mozambique	424–429
Port. Guinea	299–304
St. Thomas & Prince Islands	374–379
Timor	313–318

Anti-Malaria Issue

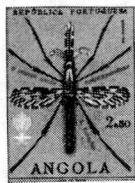

Anopheles Funestus and
Malaria Eradication Symbol
CD49

World Health Organization drive to eradicate malaria.

1962

Angola	439
Cape Verde	326
Macao	400
Mozambique	430
Port. Guinea	305
St. Thomas & Prince Islands	380
Timor	319

Airline Anniversary Issue

Map of Africa, Super Constellation
and Jet Liner
CD50

Tenth anniversary of Transportes Aéreos Portugueses (TAP).

1963

Angola	490
Cape Verde	327
Mozambique	434
Port. Guinea	318
St. Thomas & Prince Islands	381

National Overseas Bank Issue

Antonio Teixeira de Sousa
CD51

Centenary of the National Overseas Bank of Portugal.

1964, May 16

Angola	509
Cape Verde	328
Port. Guinea	319
St. Thomas & Prince Islands	382
Timor	320

ITU Issue

ITU Emblem and
St. Gabriel
CD52

Centenary of the International Communications Union.

1965, May 17

Angola	511
Cape Verde	329
Macao	402
Mozambique	464
Port. Guinea	320
St. Thomas & Prince Islands	383
Timor	321

National Revolution Issue

St. Pauls's Hospital, and Commercial
and Industrial School
CD53

40th anniversary of the National Revolution.
Different buildings on each stamp.

1966, May 28

Angola	525
Cape Verde	338
Macao	403
Mozambique	465
Port. Guinea	329
St. Thomas & Prince Islands	392
Timor	322

Navy Club Issue

Mendes Barata and Cruiser
Dom Carlos I
CD54

Centenary of Portugal's Navy Club.
Each stamp has a different design.

1967, Jan. 31

Angola	527–528
Cape Verde	339–340
Macao	412–413
Mozambique	478–479
Port. Guinea	330–331
St. Thomas & Prince Islands	393–394
Timor	323–324

Admiral Coutinho Issue

Admiral Gago Coutinho and his
First Ship
CD55

Centenary of the birth of Admiral Carlos Viegas Gago Coutinho (1869–1959), explorer and aviation pioneer.
Each stamp has a different design.

1969, Feb. 17

Angola	547
Cape Verde	355
Macao	417
Mozambique	484
Port. Guinea	335
St. Thomas & Prince Islands	397
Timor	335

Administration Reform Issue

Luiz Augusto
Rebello
da Silva
CD56

Centenary of the administration reforms of the overseas territories.

1969, Sept. 25

Angola	549
Cape Verde	357
Macao	419
Mozambique	491
Port. Guinea	337
St. Thomas & Prince Islands	399
Timor	338

Marshal Carmona Issue

Marshal A. O.
Carmona
CD57

Birth centenary of Marshal Antonio Oscar Carmona de Fragoso (1869–1951), President of Portugal.
Each stamp has a different design.

1970, Nov. 15

Angola	563
Cape Verde	359
Macao	422
Mozambique	493
Port. Guinea	340
St. Thomas & Prince Islands	403
Timor	341

Olympic Games Issue

Racing Yachts and Olympic Emblem
CD59

20th Olympic Games, Munich, Aug. 26–Sept. 11.
Each stamp shows a different sport.

1972, June 20

Angola	569
Cape Verde	361
Macao	426
Mozambique	504
Port. Guinea	342
St. Thomas & Prince Islands	408
Timor	343

Lisbon-Rio de Janeiro Flight Issue

"Santa Cruz" over
Fernando de Noronha
CD60

50th anniversary of the Lisbon to Rio de Janeiro flight by Arturo de Sacadura and Coutinho, March 30–June 5, 1922.
Each stamp shows a different stage of the flight.

1972, Sept. 20

Angola	570
Cape Verde	362
Macao	427
Mozambique	505
Port. Guinea	343
St. Thomas & Prince Islands	409
Timor	344

WMO Centenary Issue

WMO Emblem
CD61

Centenary of international meteorological cooperation.

1973, Dec. 15

Angola	571
Cape Verde	363
Macao	429
Mozambique	509
Port. Guinea	344
St. Thomas & Prince Islands	410
Timor	345

FRENCH COMMUNITY

Colonial Exposition Issue

People of French Empire
CD70

Women's Heads
CD71

France Showing Way to Civilization
CD72

"Colonial Commerce"
CD73

International Colonial Exposition, Paris 1931.

COMMON DESIGN TYPES

1931

Cameroun	213–216
Chad	60–63
Dahomey	97–100
Fr. Guiana	152–155
Fr. Guinea	116–119
Fr. India	100–103
Fr. Polynesia	76–79
Fr. Sudan	102–105
Gabon	120–123
Guadeloupe	138–141
Indo-China	140–142
Ivory Coast	92–95
Madagascar	169–172
Martinique	129–132
Mauritania	65–68
Middle Congo	61–64
New Caledonia	176–179
Niger	73–76
Reunion	122–125
St. Pierre & Miquelon	132–135
Senegal	138–141
Somali Coast	135–138
Togo	254–257
Ubangi-Shari	82–85
Upper Volta	66–69
Wallis & Futuna Isls.	85–88

Paris International Exposition Issue
Colonial Arts Exposition Issue

"Colonial Resources"
CD74   CD77

Overseas Commerce
CD75

Exposition Buildings and Women
CD76

"France and the Empire"
CD78

Cultural Treasures of the Colonies
CD79

Souvenir sheets contain one imperf. stamp.

1937

Cameroun	217–222A
Dahomey	101–107
Fr. Equatorial Africa	27–32, 73
Fr. Guiana	162–168
Fr. Guinea	120–126
Fr. India	104–110
Fr. Polynesia	117–123
Fr. Sudan	106–112
Guadeloupe	148–154
Indo-China	193–199
Inini	41
Ivory Coast	152–158
Kwangchowan	132
Madagascar	191–197
Martinique	179–185
Mauritania	69–75
New Caledonia	208–214
Niger	72–83
Reunion	167–173
St. Pierre & Miquelon	165–171
Senegal	172–178
Somali Coast	139–145
Togo	258–264
Wallis & Futuna Isls.	89

Curie Issue

Pierre and Marie Curie
CD80

40th anniversary of the discovery of radium. The surtax was for the benefit of the International Union for the Control of Cancer.

1938

Cameroun	B1
Dahomey	B2
France	B76
Fr. Equatorial Africa	B1
Fr. Guiana	B3
Fr. Guinea	B2
Fr. India	B6
Fr. Polynesia	B5
Fr. Sudan	B1
Guadeloupe	B3
Indo-China	B14
Ivory Coast	B2
Madagascar	B2
Martinique	B2
Mauritania	B3
New Caledonia	B4
Niger	B1
Reunion	B4
St. Pierre & Miquelon	B3
Senegal	B2
Somali Coast	B2
Togo	B1

Caillié Issue

René Caillié and Map of Northwestern Africa
CD81

Death centenary of René Caillié (1799–1838), French explorer.
All three denominations exist with colony name omitted.

1939

Dahomey	108–110
Fr. Guinea	161–163
Fr. Sudan	113–115
Ivory Coast	160–162
Mauritania	109–111
Niger	84–86
Senegal	188–190
Togo	265–267

New York World's Fair Issue

Natives and New York Skyline
CD82

1939

Cameroun	223–224
Dahomey	111–112
Fr. Equatorial Africa	78–79
Fr. Guiana	169–170
Fr. Guinea	164–165
Fr. India	111–112
Fr. Polynesia	124–125
Fr. Sudan	116–117
Guadeloupe	155–156
Indo-China	203–204
Inini	42–43
Ivory Coast	163–164
Kwangchowan	121–122
Madagascar	209–210
Martinique	186–187
Mauritania	112–113
New Caledonia	215–216
Niger	87–88
Reunion	174–175
St. Pierre & Miquelon	205–206
Senegal	191–192
Somali Coast	179–180
Togo	268–269
Wallis & Futuna Isls.	90–91

French Revolution Issue

Storming of the Bastille
CD83

150th anniversary of the French Revolution. The surtax was for the defense of the colonies.

1939

Cameroun	B2–B6
Dahomey	B3–B7
Fr. Equatorial Africa	B4–B8, CB1
Fr. Guiana	B4–B8, CB1
Fr. Guinea	B3–B7
Fr. India	B7–B11
Fr. Polynesia	B6–B10, CB1
Fr. Sudan	B2–B6
Guadeloupe	B4–B8
Indo-China	B15–B19, CB1
Inini	B1–B5
Ivory Coast	B3–B7
Kwangchowan	B1–B5
Madagascar	B3–B7, CB1
Martinique	B3–B7
Mauritania	B4–B8
New Caledonia	B5–B9, CB1
Niger	B2–B6
Reunion	B5–B9, CB1
St. Pierre & Miquelon	B4–B8
Senegal	B4–B8, CB1
Somali Coast	B3–B7
Togo	B2–B6
Wallis & Futuna Isls.	B1–B5

Plane over Coastal Area
CD85

All five denominations exist with colony name omitted.

1940

Dahomey	C1–C5

Fr. Guinea	C1–C5
Fr. Sudan	C1–C5
Ivory Coast	C1–C5
Mauritania	C1–C5
Niger	C1–C5
Senegal	C12–C16
Togo	C1–C5

Colonial Infantryman
CD86

1941

Cameroun	B13B
Dahomey	B13
Fr. Equatorial Africa	B8B
Fr. Guiana	B10
Fr. Guinea	B13
Fr. India	B13
Fr. Polynesia	B12
Fr. Sudan	B12
Guadeloupe	B10
Indo-China	B19B
Inini	B7
Ivory Coast	B13
Kwangchowan	B7
Madagascar	B9
Martinique	B9
Mauritania	B14
New Caledonia	B11
Niger	B12
Reunion	B11
St. Pierre & Miquelon	B8B
Senegal	B14
Somali Coast	B9
Togo	B10B
Wallis & Futuna Isls.	B7

Cross of Lorraine and Four-motor Plane
CD87

1941-5

Cameroun	C1–C7
Fr. Equatorial Africa	C17–C23
Fr. Guiana	C9–C10
Fr. India	C1–C6
Fr. Polynesia	C3–C9
Fr. West Africa	C1–C3
Guadeloupe	C1–C2
Madagascar	C37–C43
Martinique	C1–C2
New Caledonia	C7–C13
Reunion	C18–C24
St. Pierre & Miquelon	C1–C7
Somali Coast	C1–C7

Transport Plane
CD88

Caravan and Plane—CD89

COMMON DESIGN TYPES

1942

Dahomey	C6-C13
Fr. Guinea	C6-C13
Fr. Sudan	C6-C13
Ivory Coast	C6-C13
Mauritania	C6-C13
Niger	C6-C13
Senegal	C17-C25
Togo	C6-C13

Red Cross Issue

Marianne
CD90

The surtax was for the French Red Cross and national relief.

1944

Cameroun	B28
Fr. Equatorial Africa	B38
Fr. Guiana	B12
Fr. India	B14
Fr. Polynesia	B13
Fr. West Africa	B1
Guadeloupe	B12
Madagascar	B15
Martinique	B11
New Caledonia	B13
Reunion	B15
St. Pierre & Miquelon	B13
Somali Coast	B13
Wallis & Futuna Isls.	B9

Eboué Issue

Félix Eboué
CD91

Félix Eboué, first French colonial administrator to proclaim resistance to Germany after French surrender in World War II.

1945

Cameroun	296-297
Fr. Equatorial Africa	156-157
Fr. Guiana	171-172
Fr. India	210-211
Fr. Polynesia	150-151
Fr. West Africa	15-16
Guadeloupe	187-188
Madagascar	259-260
Martinique	196-197
New Caledonia	274-275
Reunion	238-239
St. Pierre & Miquelon	322-323
Somali Coast	238-239

Victory Issue

Victory
CD92

European victory of the Allied Nations in World War II.

1946, May 8

Cameroun	C8
Fr. Equatorial Africa	C24
Fr. Guiana	C11
Fr. India	C7
Fr. Polynesia	C10
Fr. West Africa	C4
Guadeloupe	C3
Indo-China	C19
Madagascar	C44
Martinique	C3
New Caledonia	C14
Reunion	C25
St. Pierre & Miquelon	C8
Somali Coast	C8
Wallis & Futuna Isls.	C1

Chad to Rhine Issue

Leclerc's Departure from Chad
CD93

Battle at Cufra Oasis
CD94

Tanks in Action, Mareth
CD95

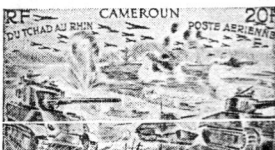

Normandy Invasion
CD96

Entering Paris
CD97

Liberation of Strasbourg
CD98

"Chad to the Rhine" march, 1942-44, by Gen. Jacques Leclerc's column, later French 2nd Armored Division.

1946, June 6

Cameroun	C9-C14
Fr. Equatorial Africa	C25-C30
Fr. Guiana	C12-C17
Fr. India	C8-C13
Fr. Polynesia	C11-C16
Fr. West Africa	C5-C10
Guadeloupe	C4-C9
Indo-China	C20-C25
Madagascar	C45-C50
Martinique	C4-C9
New Caledonia	C15-C20
Reunion	C26-C31
St. Pierre & Miquelon	C9-C14
Somali Coast	C9-C14
Wallis & Futuna Isls.	C2-C7

UPU Issue

French Colonials, Globe and Plane
CD99

75th anniversary of the Universal Postal Union.

1949, July 4

Cameroun	C29
Fr. Equatorial Africa	C34
Fr. India	C17
Fr. Polynesia	C20
Fr. West Africa	C15
Indo-China	C26
Madagascar	C55
New Caledonia	C24
St. Pierre & Miquelon	C18
Somali Coast	C18
Togo	C18
Wallis & Futuna Isls.	C10

Tropical Medicine Issue

Doctor Treating Infant
CD100

The surtax was for charitable work.

1950

Cameroun	B29
Fr. Equatorial Africa	B39
Fr. India	B15
Fr. Polynesia	B14
Fr. West Africa	B3
Madagascar	B17
New Caledonia	B14
St. Pierre & Miquelon	B14
Somali Coast	B14
Togo	B11

Military Medal Issue

Medal, Early Marine and Colonial Soldier
CD101

Centenary of the creation of the French Military Medal.

1952

Cameroun	332
Comoro Isls.	39
Fr. Equatorial Africa	186
Fr. India	233
Fr. Polynesia	179
Fr. West Africa	57
Madagascar	286
New Caledonia	295
St. Pierre & Miquelon	345
Somali Coast	267
Togo	327
Wallis & Futuna Isls.	149

Liberation Issue

Allied Landing, Victory Sign and Cross of Lorraine
CD102

10th anniversary of the liberation of France.

1954, June 6

Cameroun	C32
Comoro Isls.	C4
Fr. Equatorial Africa	C38
Fr. India	C18
Fr. Polynesia	C23
Fr. West Africa	C17
Madagascar	C57
New Caledonia	C25
St. Pierre & Miquelon	C19
Somali Coast	C19
Togo	C19
Wallis & Futuna Isls.	C11

FIDES Issue

Plowmen
CD103

Efforts of FIDES, the Economic and Social Development Fund for Overseas Possessions (Fonds d' Investissement pour le Developpement Economique et Social.)

Each stamp has a different design.

1956

Cameroun	326-329
Comoro Isls.	43
Fr. Polynesia	181
Madagascar	292-295
New Caledonia	303
Somali Coast	268
Togo	331

Flower Issue

Euadania
CD104

Each stamp shows a different flower.

1958-9

Cameroun	333
Comoro Isls.	45
Fr. Equatorial Africa	200-201
Fr. Polynesia	192
Fr. So. & Antarctic Terr.	11
Fr. West Africa	79-83
Madagascar	301-302
New Caledonia	304-305
St. Pierre & Miquelon	357

COMMON DESIGN TYPES

xxiii

Somali Coast	270
Togo	348-349
Wallis & Futuna Isls.	152

Human Rights Issue

Sun, Dove and U. N. Emblem
CD105

10th anniversary of the signing of the Universal Declaration of Human Rights.

1958

Comoro Isls.	44
Fr. Equatorial Africa	202
Fr. Polynesia	191
Fr. West Africa	85
Madagascar	300
New Caledonia	306
St. Pierre & Miquelon	356
Somali Coast	274
Wallis & Futuna Isls.	153

C.C.T.A. Issue

Map of Africa and Cogwheels
CD106

10th anniversary of the Commission for Technical Cooperation in Africa south of the Sahara.

1960

Cameroun	335
Cent. African Rep.	3
Chad	66
Congo, P.R.	90
Dahomey	138
Gabon	150
Ivory Coast	180
Madagascar	9
Mali	117
Mauritania	104
Niger	89
Upper Volta	89

Air Afrique Issue, 1961

Modern and Ancient Africa, Map and Planes
CD107

Founding of Air Afrique (African Airlines).

1961-62

Cameroun	C37
Cent. African Rep.	C5
Chad	C7
Congo, P.R.	C5
Dahomey	C17
Gabon	C5
Ivory Coast	C18
Mauritania	C17
Niger	C22
Senegal	C31
Upper Volta	C4

Anti-Malaria Issue

Malaria Eradication Emblem
CD108

World Health Organization drive to eradicate malaria.

1962, Apr. 7

Cameroun	B36
Cent. African Rep.	B1
Chad	B1
Comoro Isls.	B1
Congo, P.R.	B3
Dahomey	B15
Gabon	B4
Ivory Coast	B15
Madagascar	B19
Mali	B1
Mauritania	B16
Niger	B14
Senegal	B16
Somali Coast	B15
Upper Volta	B1

Abidjan Games Issue

Relay Race
CD109

Abidjan Games, Ivory Coast, Dec. 24-31, 1961. Each stamp shows a different sport.

1962

Chad	83-84
Cent. African Rep.	19-20
Congo, P.R.	103-104
Gabon	163-164
Niger	109-111
Upper Volta	103-105

African and Malagasy Union Issue

Flag of African and Malagasy Union
CD110

First anniversary of the Union.

1962, Sept. 8

Cameroun	373
Cent. African Rep.	21
Chad	85
Congo, P.R.	105
Dahomey	155
Gabon	165
Ivory Coast	198
Madagascar	332
Mauritania	170
Niger	112
Senegal	211
Upper Volta	106

Telstar Issue

Telstar and Globe Showing Andover and Pleumeur-Bodou
CD111

First television connection of the United States and Europe through the Telstar satellite, July 11-12, 1962.

1962-63

Andorra, French	154
Comoro Isls.	C7
Fr. Polynesia	C29
Fr. So. & Antarctic Terr.	C5
New Caledonia	C33
Somali Coast	C31
St. Pierre & Miquelon	C26
Wallis & Futuna Isls.	C17

Freedom From Hunger Issue

World Map and Wheat Emblem
CD112

United Nations Food and Agriculture Organization's "Freedom from Hunger" campaign.

1963, Mar. 21

Cameroun	B37-B38
Cent. African Rep.	B2
Chad	B2
Congo, P.R.	B4
Dahomey	B16
Gabon	B5
Ivory Coast	B16
Madagascar	B21
Mauritania	B17
Niger	B15
Senegal	B17
Upper Volta	B2

Red Cross Centenary Issue

Centenary Emblem
CD113

Centenary of the International Red Cross.

1963, Sept. 2

Comoro Isls.	55
Fr. Polynesia	205
New Caledonia	328
St. Pierre & Miquelon	367
Somali Coast	297
Wallis & Futuna Isls.	165

African Postal Union Issue

UAMPT Emblem, Radio Masts, Plane and Mail
CD114

Establishment of the African and Malagasy Posts and Telecommunications Union, UAMPT.

1963, Sept. 8

Cameroun	C47
Cent. African Rep.	C10
Chad	C9
Congo, P.R.	C13
Dahomey	C19
Gabon	C13
Ivory Coast	C25
Madagascar	C75
Mauritania	C22
Niger	C27
Rwanda	36
Senegal	C32
Upper Volta	C9

Air Afrique Issue, 1963

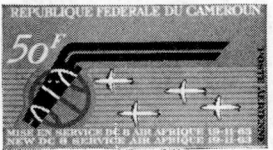

Symbols of Flight
CD115

First anniversary of Air Afrique and inauguration of DC-8 service.

1963, Nov. 19

Cameroun	C48
Chad	C10
Congo, P.R.	C14
Gabon	C18
Ivory Coast	C26
Mauritania	C26
Niger	C35
Senegal	C33

Europafrica Issue

Europe and Africa Linked Together
CD116

Signing of an economic agreement between the European Economic Community and the African and Malagasy Union, Yaoundé, Cameroun, July 20, 1963.

1963-64

Cameroun	402
Chad	C11
Cent. African Rep.	C12
Congo, P.R.	C16

COMMON DESIGN TYPES

Gabon	C19
Ivory Coast	217
Niger	C43
Upper Volta	C11

Human Rights Issue

Scales of Justice and Globe
CD117

15th anniversary of the Universal Declaration of Human Rights.

1963, Dec. 10

Comoro Isls.	58
Fr. Polynesia	206
New Caledonia	329
St. Pierre & Miquelon	368
Somali Coast	300
Wallis & Futuna Isls.	166

PHILATEC Issue

Stamp Album, Champs Elysées Palace and Horses of Marly
CD118

"PHILATEC," International Philatelic and Postal Techniques Exhibition, Paris, June 5–21, 1964.

1963–64

Comoro Isls.	60
France	1078
Fr. Polynesia	207
New Caledonia	341
St. Pierre & Miquelon	369
Somali Coast	301
Wallis & Futuna Isls.	167

Cooperation Issue

Maps of France and Africa and Clasped Hands
CD119

Cooperation between France and the French-speaking countries of Africa and Madagascar.

1964

Cameroun	409–410
Cent. African Rep.	39
Chad	103
Congo, P.R.	121
Dahomey	193
France	1111
Gabon	175
Ivory Coast	221
Madagascar	360
Mauritania	181
Niger	143
Senegal	236
Togo	495

ITU Issue

Telegraph, Syncom Satellite and ITU Emblem
CD120

Centenary of the International Telecommunication Union.

1965, May 17

Comoro Isls.	C14
Fr. Polynesia	C33
Fr. So. & Antarctic Terr.	C8
New Caledonia	C40
New Hebrides	124–125
St. Pierre & Miquelon	C29
Somali Coast	C36
Wallis & Futuna Isls.	C20

French Satellite A-1 Issue

Diamant Rocket and Launching Installations
CD121

Launching of France's first satellite, Nov. 26, 1965.

1965–66

Comoro Isls.	C15–C16
France	1137–1138
Fr. Polynesia	C40–C41
Fr. So. & Antarctic Terr.	C9–C10
New Caledonia	C44–C45
St. Pierre & Miquelon	C30–C31
Somali Coast	C39–C40
Wallis & Futuna Isls.	C22–C23

French Satellite D-1 Issue

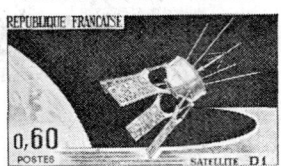

D-1 Satellite in Orbit
CD122

Launching of the D-1 satellite at Hammaguir, Algeria, Feb. 17, 1966.

1966

Comoro Isls.	C17
France	1148
Fr. Polynesia	C42
Fr. So. & Antarctic Terr.	C11
New Caledonia	C46
St. Pierre & Miquelon	C32
Somali Coast	C49
Wallis & Futuna Isls.	C24

Air Afrique Issue, 1966

Planes and Air Afrique Emblem
CD123

Introduction of DC-8F planes by Air Afrique.

1966

Cameroun	C79
Cent. African Rep.	C35
Chad	C26
Congo, P.R.	C42
Dahomey	C42
Gabon	C47
Ivory Coast	C32
Mauritania	C57
Niger	C63
Senegal	C47
Togo	C54
Upper Volta	C31

African Postal Union Issue, 1967

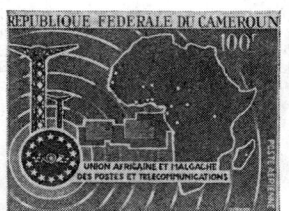

Telecommunications Symbols and Map of Africa
CD124

Fifth anniversary of the establishment of the African and Malagasy Union of Posts and Telecommunications, UAMPT.

1967

Cameroun	C90
Cent. African Rep.	C46
Chad	C37
Congo, P.R.	C57
Dahomey	C61
Gabon	C58
Ivory Coast	C34
Madagascar	C85
Mauritania	C65
Niger	C75
Rwanda	C1–C3
Senegal	C60
Togo	C81
Upper Volta	C50

Monetary Union Issue

Gold Token of the Ashantis, 17–18th Centuries
CD125

Fifth anniversary of the West African Monetary Union.

1967, Nov. 4

Dahomey	244
Ivory Coast	259
Mauritania	238
Niger	204
Senegal	294

Togo	623
Upper Volta	181

WHO Anniversary Issue

Sun, Flowers and WHO Emblem
CD126

20th anniversary of the World Health Organization.

1968, May 4

Afars & Issas	317
Comoro Isls.	73
Fr. Polynesia	241–242
Fr. So. & Antarctic Terr.	31
New Caledonia	367
St. Pierre & Miquelon	377
Wallis & Futuna Isls.	169

Human Rights Year Issue

Human Rights Flame
CD127

International Human Rights Year.

1968, Aug. 10

Afars & Issas	322–323
Comoro Isls.	76
Fr. Polynesia	243–244
Fr. So. & Antarctic Terr.	32
New Caledonia	369
St. Pierre & Miquelon	382
Wallis & Futuna Isls.	170

2nd PHILEXAFRIQUE Issue

Gabon No. 131 and Industrial Plant
CD128

Opening of PHILEXAFRIQUE, Abidjan, Feb. 14.
Each stamp shows a local scene and stamp.

1969, Feb. 14

Cameroun	C118
Cent. African Rep.	C65
Chad	C48
Congo, P.R.	C77
Dahomey	C94
Gabon	C82
Ivory Coast	C38–C40
Madagascar	C92
Mali	C65
Mauritania	C80
Niger	C104
Senegal	C68
Togo	C104
Upper Volta	C62

COMMON DESIGN TYPES

Concorde Issue

Concorde in Flight
CD129

First flight of the prototype Concorde super-sonic plane at Toulouse, Mar. 1, 1969.

1969
Afars & Issas	C56
Comoro Isls.	C29
France	C42
Fr. Polynesia	C50
Fr. So. & Antarctic Terr.	C18
New Caledonia	C63
St. Pierre & Miquelon	C40
Wallis & Futuna Isls.	C30

Development Bank Issue

Bank Emblem—CD130

Fifth anniversary of the African Development Bank.

1969
Cameroun	499
Chad	217
Congo, P.R.	181–182
Ivory Coast	281
Mali	127–128
Mauritania	267
Niger	220
Senegal	317–318
Upper Volta	201

ILO Issue

ILO Headquarters, Geneva, and Emblem
CD131

50th anniversary of the International Labor Organization.

1969–70
Afars & Issas	337
Comoro Isls.	83
Fr. Polynesia	251–252
Fr. So. & Antarctic Terr.	35
New Caledonia	379
St. Pierre & Miquelon	396
Wallis & Futuna Isls.	172

ASECNA Issue

Map of Africa, Plane and Airport
CD132

10th anniversary of the Agency for the Security of Aerial Navigation in Africa and Madagascar (ASECNA, Agence pour la Sécurité de la Navigation Aérienne en Afrique et à Madagascar).

1969–70
Cameroun	500
Cent. African Rep.	119
Chad	222
Congo, P.R.	197
Dahomey	269
Gabon	260
Ivory Coast	287
Mali	130
Niger	221
Senegal	321
Upper Volta	204

U.P.U. Headquarters Issue

U.P.U. Headquarters and Emblem
CD133

New Universal Postal Union headquarters, Bern, Switzerland.

1970
Afars & Issas	342
Algeria	443
Cameroun	503–504
Cent. African Rep.	125
Chad	225
Comoro Isls.	84
Congo, P.R.	216
Fr. Polynesia	261–262
Fr. So. & Antarctic Terr.	36
Gabon	258
Ivory Coast	295
Madagascar	444
Mali	134–135
Mauritania	283
New Caledonia	382
Niger	231–232
St. Pierre & Miquelon	397–398
Senegal	328–329
Tunisia	535
Wallis & Futuna Isls.	173

De Gaulle Issue

General de Gaulle, 1940
CD134

First anniversary of the death of Charles de Gaulle, (1890–1970), President of France.

1971–72
Afars & Issas	356–357
Comoro Isls.	104–105
France	1322–1325
Fr. Polynesia	270–271
Fr. So. & Antarctic Terr.	52–53
New Caledonia	393–394
Reunion	377, 380
St. Pierre & Miquelon	417–418
Wallis & Futuna Isls.	177–178

African Postal Union Issue, 1971

Carved Stool, UAMPT Building, Brazzaville, Congo
CD135

10th anniversary of the establishment of the African and Malagasy Posts and Telecommunications Union, UAMPT. Each stamp has a different native design.

1971, Nov. 13
Cameroun	C177
Cent. African Rep.	C89
Chad	C94
Congo, P.R.	C136
Dahomey	C146
Gabon	C120
Ivory Coast	C47
Mauritania	C113
Niger	C164
Rwanda	C8
Senegal	C105
Togo	C166
Upper Volta	C97

West African Monetary Union Issue

African Couple, City, Village and Commemorative Coin
CD136

10th anniversary of the West African Monetary Union.

1972, Nov. 2
Dahomey	300
Ivory Coast	331
Mauritania	299
Niger	258
Senegal	374
Togo	825
Upper Volta	280

African Postal Union Issue, 1973

Telecommunications Symbols and Map of Africa
CD137

11th anniversary of the African and Malagasy Posts and Telecommunications Union (UAMPT).

1973, Sept. 12
Cameroun	574
Cent. African Rep.	194
Chad	272
Congo, P.R.	289
Dahomey	311
Gabon	320
Ivory Coast	361
Madagascar	500
Mauritania	304
Niger	287
Rwanda	540
Senegal	393
Togo	849
Upper Volta	285

Philexafrique II—Essen Issue

Buffalo and Dahomey
No. C33
CD138

Wild Ducks and Baden
No. 1
CD139

Designs: Indigenous fauna, local and German stamps.
Types CD138–CD139 printed horizontally and vertically se-tenant in sheets of 10 (2x5). Label between horizontal pairs alternately commemorates Philexafrique II, Libreville, Gabon, June 1978, and 2nd International Stamp Fair, Essen, Germany, Nov. 1–5.

1978-1979
Benin	C285–C286
Central Africa	C200–C201
Chad	C238–C239
Congo Republic	C245–C246
Djibouti	C121–C122
Gabon	C215–C216
Ivory Coast	C64–C65
Mali	C356–C357
Mauritania	C185–C186
Niger	C291–C292
Rwanda	C12–C13
Senegal	C146–C147
Togo	C363–C364
Upper Volta	C253–C254

HISTORICAL FOOTNOTES

Scouting Year: 75th anniversary of scouting and 125th birth anniversary of its founder, Lord Baden-Powell (1857-1941).

Robert Koch: Centenary of tuberculosis bacillus discovery by Robert Koch (1843-1910), German physician. Awarded 1905 Nobel Prize for physiology and medicine; also discovered cholera bacillus, 1883.

George Washington: 250th birth anniversary of George Washington (1732-1799), first U.S. president.

Charles Darwin: Death centenary of Charles Darwin (1809-1882), British naturalist. Traveled through South America and Australasia, 1831-1836, aboard the Beagle developing his theory of evolution. Published findings in *On the Origin of Species,* 1859.

Norman Rockwell (1894-1978): American illustrator who is best known for his paintings of people in everyday situations. Many of his works have been on the covers of *The Saturday Evening Post, Boy's Life, American Boy* and *St. Nicholas.*

Lewis B. Carroll (1832-1898): English author of the childhood classics *Alice in Wonderland* and *Through the Looking Glass.* He also wrote many works on mathematics under his real name, Charles Lutwidge Dodgson.

World Cup Soccer: The 12th World Cup Soccer Championship was held in Spain from June 13th to July 11th. The series, held every 4 years, opened in Barcelona with Belgium over Argentina before a crowd of 95,000. The 52 games were held in 17 stadiums in 14 cities with 24 participating teams. The final game was played in Madrid with Italy defeating Germany by a score of 3 to 1.

19th Universal Postal Union Congress, Hamburg, Germany, June 18-July 27; attended by approx. 750 delegates from 166 member countries.

AUSIPEX '84 Intl. Stamp Exhibition, Melbourne, Australia, Sept. 21-30.

PHILATELIA '84 Intl. Stamp Exhibition, Stuttgart, Germany, Oct. 5-7.

FILACENTO '84 Intl. Stamp Exhibition, The Hague, Netherlands, Sept. 6-9.

14th Winter Olympic Games, Sarajevo, Jugoslavia, Feb. 8-19, 1984.

23rd Olympic Games, Los Angeles, July 28-Aug. 12, 1984.

SCOTT'S STANDARD POSTAGE STAMP CATALOGUE

PANAMA
(păn'ȧ·mä')

LOCATION — In Central America between Costa Rica and Colombia.
GOVT. — Republic.
AREA — 29,208 sq. mi.
POP. — 1,770,000 (est. 1977).
CAPITAL — Panama.

Formerly a department of the Republic of Colombia, Panama gained its independence in 1903. Dividing the country at its center is the Canal Zone, site of the Panama Canal, a strip of land ten miles wide, leased to the United States of America.

100 Centavos = 1 Peso
100 Centesimos = 1 Balboa (1906)

Issued under Colombian Dominion

Coat of Arms
A1   A2

Lithographed.
1878   Imperf.   Unwmkd.

Thin Wove Paper.

1	A1	5c gray grn	30.00	30.00
a.		5c yel grn	30.00	30.00
2	A1	10c blue	75.00	85.00
3	A1	20c rose red	40.00	45.00
4	A2	50c buff	1,750.	

All values of this issue are known rouletted unofficially.

Medium Thick Paper.

5	A1	5c bl grn	30.00	30.00
6	A1	10c blue	75.00	
7	A2	50c orange	15.00	

Nos. 5–7 were printed before Nos. 1–4, according to Panamanian archives.
Prices for used Nos. 1–5 are for handstamped postal cancellations.

These stamps have been reprinted in a number of shades, on thin to moderately thick, white or yellowish paper. They are without gum or with white, crackly gum. Some of the 50c stamps appear to have been reprinted from the original stone; they are all in a golden yellow shade, less brownish than the orange originals. All values have been reprinted from new stones made from retouched dies. The marks of retouching are plainly to be seen in the sea and clouds. On the original 10c the shield in the upper left corner has two blank sections; on the reprints the design of this shield is completed. The impression of these reprints is frequently blurred.

Map of Panama
A3   A4

1887-88   Perf. 13½.

8	A3	1c green	1.25	1.50
9	A3	2c pink ('88)	1.25	1.75
a.		2c sal	1.25	1.75
10	A3	5c blue	1.25	60
11	A3	10c yellow	1.25	70
a.		Imperf., pair		
12	A3	20c lilac	1.50	1.50
13	A3	50c brn ('88)	2.00	1.25
a.		Imperf.		
		Nos. 8-13 (6)	8.50	6.80

1892   Pelure Paper.

14	A3	50c brown	2.25	1.50

The stamps of this issue have been reprinted on papers of slightly different colors from those of the originals. These are: 1c yellow green, 2c deep rose, 5c bright blue, 10c straw, 20c violet. The 50c is printed from a very worn stone, in a lighter brown than the originals. The series includes a 10c on lilac paper. All these stamps are to be found perforated, imperforate, imperforate horizontally or imperforate vertically. At the same time that these were made, impressions were struck upon a variety of glazed and surface-colored papers.

Wove Paper

1892-96   Engraved.   Perf. 12.

15	A4	1c green	35	35
16	A4	2c rose	50	40
17	A4	5c blue	75	75
18	A4	10c orange	40	40
19	A4	20c vio ('95)	60	50
20	A4	50c bis brn ('96)	60	50
21	A4	1p lake ('96)	7.00	5.00
		Nos. 15-21 (7)	10.20	7.90

Preceding Issues Surcharged:

HABILITADO.   HABILITADO.
1894   1894
1   **1**
CENTAVO.   CENTAVO.
a   b

HABILITADO.   HABILITADO.
1894   1894
5   **5**
CENTAVOS.   CENTAVOS.
c   d

HABILITADO.   HABILITADO.
1894   1894
5   **10**
CENTAVOS.   CENTAVOS.
e   f

HABILITADO.
1894
10
CENTAVOS,
g

1894   Black Surcharge

22	(a)	1c on 2c rose	65	65
a.		Inverted surcharge	3.50	3.50
b.		Double surcharge		
23	(b)	1c on 2c rose	50	50
a.		"CCNTAVO"	3.50	3.50
b.		Inverted surcharge	3.50	3.50
c.		Double surcharge	7.00	7.00

Red Surcharge

24	(c)	5c on 20c lil	1.50	1.50
a.		Inverted surcharge	11.00	11.00
b.		Double surcharge		
c.		Without "HABILITADO"		
25	(d)	5c on 20c lil	2.50	2.50
a.		"CCNTAVOS"	9.00	9.00
b.		Inverted surcharge	11.00	11.00
c.		Double surcharge		
d.		Without "HABILITADO"		
26		5c on 20c lil	4.00	4.00
a.		Inverted surcharge	11.00	11.00
b.		Double surcharge		
27	(f)	10c on 50c brn	2.00	2.00
a.		"1894" omitted		
b.		Double surcharge		
c.		"CCNTAVOS"	15.00	
28	(g)	10c on 50c brn	11.00	11.00
a.		"CCNTAVOS"	35.00	
b.		Inverted surcharge		

Pelure Paper.

29	(f)	10c on 50c brn	2.50	2.35
a.		"1894" omitted	4.00	
b.		Inverted surcharge	11.00	11.00
30	(g)	10c on 50c brn	8.00	8.00
a.		"CCNTAVOS"		
b.		Without "HABILITADO"		
c.		Inverted surcharge	20.00	20.00
d.		Double surcharge		
		Nos. 22-30 (9)	32.65	32.50

There are several settings of these surcharges. Usually the surcharge is about 15½ mm. high, but in one setting it is only 13 mm. All the types are to be found with a comma after "CENTAVOS". Nos. 24, 25, 26, 29 and 30 exist with the surcharge printed sideways. Nos. 23, 24 and 29 may be found with an inverted "A" instead of "V" in "CENTAVOS". There are also varieties caused by dropped or broken letters.

Issues of the Republic.
Issued in the City of Panama.
Stamps of 1892-96 Overprinted:

Handstamped   REPUBLICA DE
                PANAMA
                a

1903, Nov. 16   Rose Handstamp.

51	A4	1c green	1.00	85
52	A4	2c rose	2.50	2.50
53	A4	5c blue	75	75
54	A4	10c yellow	1.25	1.25
55	A4	20c violet	2.00	2.00
56	A4	50c bis brn	5.00	5.00
57	A4	1p lake	35.00	35.00
		Nos. 51-57 (7)	47.50	47.35

Blue Black Handstamp.

58	A4	1c green	1.00	75
59	A4	2c rose	75	75
60	A4	5c blue	4.00	4.00
61	A4	10c yellow	2.50	2.50
62	A4	20c violet	6.00	6.00
63	A4	50c bis brn	6.00	6.00
64	A4	1p lake	35.00	35.00
		Nos. 58-64 (7)	55.25	55.00

The stamps of this issue are to be found with the handstamp placed horizontally, vertically or diagonally; inverted; double; double, one inverted; double, both inverted; in pairs, one without handstamp; etc.

This handstamp has been reprinted in brown rose on the 1, 5, 20 and 50c, in purple on the 1, 2, 50c and 1p, and in magenta on the 5, 10, 20 and 50c. Reprints were also made in rose and black when the handstamp was nearly worn out, so that the "R" of "REPUBLICA" appears to be shorter than usual, and the bottom part of "LI" has been broken off. The "P" of "PANAMA" leans to the left and the tops of "NA" are broken. Many of these varieties are found inverted, double, etc.

Overprinted PANAMA PANAMA

1903, Dec. 3   b

Bar in Similar Color to Stamp.
Black Overprint.

65	A4	2c rose	1.25	1.25
a.		"PANAMA" 15mm long	1.75	
b.		Violet bar	5.00	
66	A4	5c blue	100.00	
a.		"PANAMA" 15mm long	100.00	
67	A4	10c yellow	1.25	1.50
a.		"PANAMA" 15mm long	3.50	
b.		Horizontal ovpt.	15.00	

Gray Black Overprint.

68	A4	2c rose	1.00	1.00
a.		"PANAMA" 15mm long	1.25	

Carmine Overprint.

69	A4	5c blue	1.25	1.50
a.		"PANAMA" 15mm long		
b.		Bar only	25.00	22.50
c.		Double overprint		
70	A4	20c violet	4.00	4.00
a.		"PANAMA" 15mm long	5.00	
b.		Double overprint, one in blk	30.00	
		Nos. 65, 67-70 (5)	8.75	9.25

This overprint was set up to cover fifty stamps. "PANAMA" is normally 13mm. long and 1¾mm. high but, in two rows in each sheet, it measures 15 to 16mm. This word may be found with one or more of the letters taller than usual; with one, two or three inverted "V"s instead of "A"s; with an inverted "Y" instead of "A"; an inverted "N"; an "A" with accent; and a fancy "P". Owing to misplaced impressions, stamps exist with "PANAMA" once only, twice on one side, or three times.

Overprinted in Red PANAMA PANAMA

1903, Dec.   c

71	A4	1c green	50	50
a.		"PANAMA" 15mm long	75	
b.		"PANAMA" reading down	3.00	
c.		"PANAMA" reading up and down	3.00	
d.		Double overprint	7.00	
72	A4	2c rose	35	35
a.		"PANAMA" 15mm long	75	
b.		"PANAMA" reading down		
c.		"PANAMA" reading up and down	3.00	
d.		Double overprint	7.00	
73	A4	20c violet	1.25	1.25
a.		"PANAMA" 15mm long	2.00	
b.		"PANAMA" reading down		
c.		"PANAMA" reading up and down	7.00	7.00
d.		Double overprint	15.00	15.00
74	A4	50c bis brn	2.50	2.50
a.		"PANAMA" 15mm long	4.00	
b.		"PANAMA" reading up and down	11.00	11.00
c.		Double overprint	5.00	5.00

PANAMA

75	A4	1p lake	6.00	6.00
a.		"PANAMA" 15mm long	5.00	
b.		"PANAMA" reading up and down	16.00	16.00
c.		Double ovpt.	15.00	
d.		Inverted ovpt.		22.50
		Nos. 71-75 (5)	10.60	10.60

Setting "c" appears to be a re-arrangement (or two very similar re-arrangements) of setting "b". The overprint covers fifty stamps. "PANAMA" usually reads upward but sheets of the 1, 2 and 20c exist with the word reading upward on one half the sheet and downward on the other half. In one re-arrangement one stamp in fifty has the word reading in both directions. Nearly all the varieties of setting "b" are repeated in setting "c" excepting the inverted "V" and fancy "P". There are also additional varieties of large letters and "PANAMA" occasionally has an "A" missing or inverted. There are misplaced impressions, as of setting "b".

Overprinted in Red PANAMA PANAMA
d

1904-05

76	A4	1c green	35	35
a.		Both words reading up	1.50	
b.		Both words reading down	3.00	
c.		Double overprint		
d.		Pair, one without overprint	7.50	
e.		"PANAAM"	22.50	
f.		Inverted "M" in "PANAMA"	75	
77	A4	2c rose	35	35
a.		Both words reading up	2.50	
b.		Both words reading down	2.50	
c.		Double overprint	11.00	
d.		Double overprint, one inverted	15.00	
e.		Inverted "M" in "PANAMA"	75	
78	A4	5c blue	40	40
a.		Both words reading up	3.50	
b.		Both words reading down	4.00	
c.		Inverted overprint	12.50	
d.		"PANAAM"	27.50	
e.		"PAMAMA"	9.00	
f.		"PAMANA"	5.00	
g.		Inverted "M" in "PANAMA"	1.50	
h.		Double overprint	22.50	
79	A4	10c yellow	40	40
a.		Both words reading up	5.00	
b.		Both words reading down	5.00	
c.		Double overprint	15.00	
d.		Inverted overprint	7.50	
e.		"PANAAM"	11.00	
f.		Inverted "M" in "PANAMA"	2.50	
g.		Red brown overprint	8.00	5.00
80	A4	20c violet	2.00	1.50
a.		Both words reading up	5.00	
b.		Both words reading down	10.00	
81	A4	50c bis brn	3.50	3.00
a.		Both words reading up	11.00	
b.		Both words reading down	11.00	
c.		Double overprint		
82	A4	1p lake	5.00	5.00
a.		Both words reading up	12.50	
b.		Both words reading down	12.50	
c.		Double overprint		
d.		Double overprint, one inverted	22.50	
		Nos. 76-82 (7)	12.00	11.00

This overprint is also set up to cover fifty stamps. One stamp in each fifty has "PANAMA" reading upward at both sides. Another has the word reading downward at both sides, a third has an inverted "V" in place of the last "A" and a fourth has a small thick "N". In a resetting all these varieties are corrected except the inverted "V". There are misplaced overprints as before.

Later printings show other varieties and have the bar 2½ instead of 2mm. wide. The colors of the various printings of Nos. 76 to 82 range from carmine to almost pink.

Experts consider the black overprint on the 50c to be bogus.

The 20c violet and 50c bistre brown exist with bar 2½mm. wide, including the error "PAMANA", but are not known to have been issued. Some copies have been cancelled "to oblige".

Issued in Colon.
Handstamped in Magenta or Violet REPUBLICA DE PANAMA
e

On Stamps of 1892-96.

1903-04

101	A4	1c green	50	50
102	A4	2c rose	65	65
103	A4	5c blue	75	75
104	A4	10c yellow	2.00	2.00
105	A4	20c violet	4.00	4.00
106	A4	1p lake	100.00	100.00

On Stamps of 1887-92.
Ordinary Wove Paper.

107	A3	50c brown	20.00	20.00
		Nos. 101-107 (7)	127.90	127.90

Pelure Paper.

| 108 | A3 | 50c brown | | 85.00 |

Handstamped in Magenta, Violet or Red PANAMA
f

On Stamps of 1892-96.

109	A4	1c green	5.00	5.00
110	A4	2c rose	5.00	5.00
111	A4	5c blue	5.00	5.00
112	A4	10c yellow	8.00	8.00
113	A4	20c violet	12.50	12.50
114	A4	1p lake	85.00	85.00

On Stamps of 1887-92.
Ordinary Wove Paper.

115	A3	50c brown	35.00	35.00
		Nos. 109-115 (7)	155.50	155.50

Pelure Paper.

| 116 | A3 | 50c brown | 50.00 | 50.00 |

The first note after No. 64 applies also to Nos. 101-116.

The handstamps on Nos. 109-116 have been counterfeited.

REPUBLICA DE PANAMA
Stamps with this overprint were a private speculation. They exist on cover.

Overprinted República de Panamá.
g

On Stamps of 1892-96.
Carmine Overprint.

129	A4	1c green	50	50
a.		Inverted overprint	8.00	
b.		Double overprint	3.00	
c.		Double overprint, one inverted	8.00	
130	A4	5c blue	60	60

Brown Overprint.

131	A4	1c green	15.00	
a.		Double overprint, one inverted		

Black Overprint.

132	A4	1c green	40.00	40.00
a.		Vertical overprint	50.00	
b.		Inverted overprint	50.00	
c.		Double overprint, one inverted	50.00	
133	A4	2c rose	60	60
a.		Inverted overprint		
134	A4	10c yellow	60	60
a.		Inverted overprint	22.50	
b.		Double overprint	7.50	
135	A4	20c violet	60	60
a.		Inverted overprint	5.00	
b.		Double overprint	7.00	
136	A4	1p lake	17.50	17.50

On Stamps of 1887-88.
Blue Overprint.
Ordinary Wove Paper.

| 137 | A3 | 50c brown | 3.50 | 3.50 |

Pelure Paper.

138	A3	50c brown	3.50	3.50
a.		Double overprint	15.00	

This overprint is set up to cover fifty stamps. In each fifty there are four stamps without accent on the last "a" of "Panama", one with accent on the "a" of "Republica" and one with a thick, upright "l".

Overprinted in Carmine REPUBLICA DE PANAMA.

On Stamp of 1892-96.

139	A4	20c violet	75.00	75.00
a.		Double overprint		

Issued in Bocas del Toro.
Stamps of 1892-96 Overprinted.

Handstamped in Violet R DE PANAMA
k

1903-04

151	A4	1c green	22.50	17.50
152	A4	2c rose	22.50	17.50
153	A4	5c blue	27.50	22.50
154	A4	10c yellow	15.00	10.00
155	A4	20c violet	50.00	40.00
156	A4	50c bis brn	100.00	75.00
157	A4	1p lake	150.00	150.00
		Nos. 151-157 (7)	387.50	332.50

The handstamp is known double and inverted. Counterfeits exist.

Handstamped in Violet Panama
l

158	A4	1c green	75.00	
159	A4	2c rose	75.00	
160	A4	5c blue	90.00	
161	A4	10c yellow	110.00	
162	A4	1p lake	250.00	

Handstamp "l" was applied to these 5 stamps only by favor, experts state. Counterfeits are numerous.

General Issues

A5

1905, Feb. 4 Engraved Perf. 12

179	A5	1c green	75	60
180	A5	2c rose	1.00	75

Issued to commemorate Panama's Declaration of Independence from the Colombian Republic, November 3, 1903.

Surcharged in Vermilion on Stamps of 1892-96 Issue:

Panamá Panamá 1 ct.

1906

181	A4	1c on 20c vio	35	35
a.		"Panrma"	3.00	3.00
b.		"Pnnama"	3.00	3.00
c.		"Pauama"	3.00	3.00
d.		Inverted surcharge	5.00	5.00
e.		Double surcharge	4.00	4.00
f.		Double surcharge, one inverted		

PANAMÁ PANAMÁ 2 cts.

182	A4	2c on 50c bis brn	35	35
a.		3rd "A" of "PANAMA" inverted	3.00	3.00
b.		Both "PANAMA" reading down	5.00	5.00
c.		Double surcharge		
d.		Inverted surcharge	3.50	

The 2c on 20c violet was never issued to the public.

Carmine Surcharge.

183	A4	5c on 1p lake	75	60
a.		Both "PANAMA" reading down	8.00	8.00
b.		"5" omitted		
c.		Double surcharge		
d.		Inverted surcharge		
e.		3rd "A" of "PANAMA" inverted	7.00	7.00

On Stamp of 1903-04, No. 75.

184	A4	5c on 1p lake	75	60
a.		"PANAMA" 15mm long		
b.		"PANAMA" reading up and down		
c.		Both "PANAMA" reading down		
d.		Inverted surcharge		
e.		Double surcharge		
f.		3rd "A" of "PANAMA" inverted		

National Flag
A6

Vasco Núñez de Balboa
A7

Hernández de Córdoba
A8

Coat of Arms
A9

Justo Arosemena
A10

Manuel J. Hurtado
A11

José de Obaldía
A12

Tomás Herrera
A13

PANAMA

José de Fábrega
A14

1906-07   Engraved   Perf. 11½
185	A6	½c org & multi	60	50
186	A7	1c dk grn & blk	60	50
187	A8	2c scar & blk	75	50
188	A9	2½c red org	75	50
189	A10	5c bl & blk	1.00	50
a.		5c ultra & blk	1.25	75
190	A11	8c pur & blk	1.25	1.00
191	A12	10c vio & blk	1.25	75
192	A13	25c brn & blk	3.00	1.50
193	A14	50c black	7.00	5.00
		Nos. 185-193 (9)	16.20	10.75

Inverted centers exist of Nos. 185-187, 189, 189a, 190-193. Price, each $20. Nos. 185-193 exist imperf.

Map   Balboa
A17   A18

Córdoba   Arms
A19   A20

Arosemena   Obaldía
A21   A23

1909-15   Perf. 12
195	A17	½c org ('11)	75	60
a.		Booklet pane of 6		
196	A17	½c rose ('15)	90	70
197	A18	1c dk grn & blk	90	70
a.		Inverted center		
b.		Bkt. pane of 6	80.00	
198	A19	2c red & blk	90	40
a.		Bklt. pane of 6	80.00	
199	A20	2½c red org	1.25	40
200	A21	5c bl & blk	1.50	40
a.		Bklt. pane of 6	80.00	
201	A23	10c vio & blk	3.00	1.50
a.		Booklet pane of 6		
		Nos. 195-201 (7)	9.20	4.70

Balboa Sighting Pacific Ocean,
His Dog at His Feet—A24

1913, Sept.
202	A24	2½c dk grn & yel grn	1.25	1.00

Issued to commemorate the 400th anniversary of Balboa's discovery of the Pacific Ocean.

Panama Exposition Issue.

Chorrera Falls—A25

Map of Panama Canal
A26

Balboa Taking Possession
of the Pacific—A27

Ruins of Cathedral
of Old Panama—A28

Palace of Arts—A29

Gatun Locks—A30

Culebra Cut—A31

Santo Domingo Monastery's
Flat Arch—A32

1915-16   Perf. 12
204	A25	½c ol grn & blk	75	50
205	A26	1c dk grn & blk	90	50
206	A27	2c car & blk	1.00	50
a.		2c ver & blk ('16)	1.00	50
207				

Manuel J. Hurtado—A33

1916
213	A33	8c vio & blk	5.00	3.50

S. S. "Panama" in Culebra Cut
August 11, 1914
A34

S. S. "Panama" in Culebra Cut
August 11, 1914
A35

S. S. "Cristobal" in Gatun Lock
A36

1918
214	A34	12c pur & blk	20.00	7.50
215	A35	15c brt bl & blk	12.50	4.00
216	A36	24c yel brn & blk	20.00	4.00

208	A28	2½c scar & blk	1.00	60
209	A29	3c vio & blk	1.25	75
210	A30	5c bl & blk	1.75	60
a.		Center inverted	750.00	600.00
211	A31	10c org & blk	3.50	1.25
212	A32	20c brn & blk	15.00	6.00
a.		Center inverted	400.00	
		Nos. 204-212 (8)	25.15	10.70

No. 208 Surcharged in Dark Blue

1519   **1919**

2 CENTESIMOS 2

1919, Aug. 15
217	A28	2c on 2½c scar & blk	60	60
a.		Inverted surcharge	12.50	12.50
b.		Double surcharge	15.00	15.00

City of Panama, 400th anniversary.

Dry Dock at Balboa
A38

Ship in Pedro Miguel Lock
A39

1920   Engraved
218	A38	50c org & blk	22.50	12.50
219	A39	1b dk vio & blk	30.00	20.00

Centenary of Independence Issue.

Arms of
Panama City   José Vallarino
A40   A41

"Land Gate"   Simón Bolivar
A42   A43

Statue of   Bolívar's
Cervantes   Tribute
A44   A45

Carlos   Municipal Building
de Ycaza   in 1821 and 1921
A46   A47

Statue of Balboa   Spanish Church
A48   A49

Herrera   Fábrega
A50   A51

PANAMA

1921, Nov.

220	A40	½c orange	75	40
221	A41	1c green	75	30
222	A42	2c carmine	1.00	40
223	A43	2½c red	2.00	1.50
224	A44	3c dl vio	2.00	1.50
225	A45	5c blue	1.25	60
226	A46	8c ol grn	6.00	3.50
227	A47	10c violet	3.50	2.00
228	A48	15c lt bl	5.00	2.50
229	A49	20c ol brn	5.00	3.00
230	A50	24c blk brn	9.00	6.00
231	A51	50c black	17.50	9.00
		Nos. 220-231 (12)	57.75	32.70

Centenary of Independence.

Hurtado
A52

Arms
A53

1921, Nov. 28

232	A52	2c dk grn	75	50

Issued to commemorate the birth centenary of Manuel José Hurtado (1821-1887), president and folklore writer.

No. 208 Surcharged in Black
1923

2 CENTESIMOS 2

1923

233	A28	2c on 2½c scar & blk	50	50

Surcharge varieties include wrong or omitted date, double surcharge and pair, one without surcharge. Price $2.50 each. Two stamps in each sheet have a bar above "CENTESIMOS."

1924, May   Engraved

234	A53	½c orange	25	12
235	A53	1c dk grn	25	12
236	A53	2c carmine	35	12
237	A53	5c dk bl	60	20
238	A53	10c dk vio	75	30
239	A53	12c ol grn	1.00	60
240	A53	15c ultra	1.25	60
241	A53	24c yel brn	3.00	90
242	A53	50c orange	7.00	1.75
243	A53	1b black	10.00	4.00
		Nos. 234-243 (10)	24.45	8.71

Bolívar Congress Issue.

Bolívar
A54

Statue of Bolívar
A55

Bolívar Hall
A56

1926, June 10   Perf. 12½

244	A54	½c orange	50	20
245	A54	1c dk grn	50	20
246	A54	2c scarlet	60	35
247	A54	4c gray	60	35
248	A54	5c dk bl	90	60
249	A55	8c lilac	1.50	90
250	A55	10c dl vio	1.25	85
251	A55	12c ol grn	2.00	1.25
252	A55	15c ultra	2.50	1.50
253	A55	20c brown	5.00	2.25
254	A56	24c blk vio	7.00	1.75
255	A56	50c black	12.50	6.00
		Nos. 244-255 (12)	34.85	16.20

Lindbergh's Airplane,
"The Spirit of St. Louis"
A57

Lindbergh's Airplane and
Map of Panama
A58

1928, Jan. 9   Typo.   Rouletted 7

256	A57	2c dk red & blk, sal	75	50
257	A58	5c dk bl, grn	1.00	75

Commemorating the visit of Colonel Charles A. Lindbergh to Central America by airplane.

No. 232 Overprinted in Red

1903
NOV 3 BRE
1928

1928, Nov. 1   Perf. 12

258	A52	2c dk grn	40	25

25th anniversary of the Republic.

1830 - 1930

No. 247 Surcharged in Black

17 DE DICIEMBRE

UN CENTESIMO

1930, Dec. 17   Perf. 12½, 13

259	A54	1c on 4c gray	35	30

Issued in commemoration of the centenary of the death of Simón Bolívar, the Liberator.

Nos. 244-246 Overprinted

in Red or Blue.

1932   Perf. 12½

260	A54	½c org (R)	30	30
261	A54	1c dk grn (R)	35	25
a.		Double overprint	27.50	
262	A54	2c scar (Bl)	25	25

No. 252 Surcharged in Red

263	A55	10c on 15c ultra	1.00	50
a.		Double surcharge	85.00	

No. 220 Overprinted as in 1932 in Black.

1933   Perf. 12

Overprint 19mm. Long

264	A40	½c orange	50	30
a.		Overprint 17mm. Long		

Dr. Manuel
Amador Guerrero
A60

1933, July 3   Engr.   Perf. 12½

265	A60	2c dk red	60	30

Commemorative of the centenary of the birth of Dr. Manuel Amador Guerrero, founder of the Republic of Panama and its first President.

No. 251 Surcharged in Red
HABILITADA
10 c.

1933

266	A55	10c on 12c ol grn	1.50	1.00

No. 253 Overprinted in Red **HABILITADA**

267	A55	20c brown	2.00	1.50

José Domingo
de Obaldía
A61

Eusebio
A. Morales
A62

Quotation
from
Emerson
A63

National Institute—A64

Justo A. Facio
A65

Pablo Arosemena
A66

1934, July   Engraved   Perf. 14

268	A61	1c dk grn	1.25	75
269	A62	2c scarlet	1.25	75
270	A63	5c dk bl	2.00	1.25
271	A64	10c brown	4.00	2.00
272	A65	12c yel org	7.00	3.00
273	A66	15c Prus bl	10.00	3.50
		Nos. 268-273 (6)	25.50	11.25

Issued in commemoration of the 25th anniversary of the First National Institute.

Nos. 248, 227 Overprinted in Black or Red **HABILITADA**

1935-36   Perf. 12½, 12

274	A54	5c dk bl	60	40
275	A47	10c vio (R) ('36)	1.00	50

No. 225 Surcharged in Red **HABILITADA B. 0.01**

1936   Perf. 11½

276	A45	1c on 5c bl	60	50
a.		Lines of surcharge 1½mm between	10.00	

1836 1936

No. 241 Surcharged in Blue

2 CENTESIMOS

1936, Sept. 24   Perf. 12

277	A53	2c on 24c yel brn	60	60
a.		Double surch.	30.00	

Issued in commemoration of the centenary of the birth of Pablo Arosemena, president of Panama in 1910-12. See Nos. C19-C20.

Ruins of
Custom
House,
Portobelo
A67

Designs: 1c, Panama Tree. 2c, "La Pollera." 5c, Simon Bolívar. 10c, Cathedral Tower Ruins, Old Panama. 15c, Francisco García y Santos. 20c, Madden Dam, Panama Canal. 25c, Columbus. 50c, Gaillard Cut. 1b, Panama Cathedral.

1936   Engraved   Perf. 11½

278	A67	½c yel org	60	30
279	A67	1c bl grn	60	30
280	A67	2c car rose	60	30
281	A67	5c blue	1.00	40
282	A67	10c dk vio	1.50	60
283	A67	15c turq bl	1.50	85
284	A67	20c red	2.50	1.50
285	A67	25c blk brn	3.00	2.00
286	A67	50c orange	8.00	4.00
287	A67	1b black	20.00	12.50
		Nos. 278-287 (10)	39.30	22.75

Issued to commemorate the 4th Postal Congress of the Americas and Spain. See Nos. C21-C26.

Stamps of 1936 Overprinted in Red or Blue

1937

288	A67	½c yel org (R)	50	30
a.		Inverted overprint	27.50	
289	A67	1c bl grn (R)	60	30
290	A67	2c car rose (Bl)	60	30
291	A67	5c bl (R)	60	40
292	A67	10c dk vio (R)	1.50	60
293	A67	15c turq bl (R)	8.00	4.50

PANAMA

294	A67	20c red (Bl)	2.50	1.50
295	A67	25c blk brn (R)	4.00	2.00
296	A67	50c org (Bl)	10.00	6.00
297	A67	1b blk (R)	20.00	12.50
		Nos. 288-297 (10)	48.30	28.40

See also Nos. C27–C32.

Stamps of 1921-26 Overprinted in Red or Blue

1937, July   Perf. 12, 12½

298	A54	½c org (R)	1.25	1.00
a.		Inverted overprint	40.00	
299	A41	1c grn (R)	40	35
a.		Inverted overprint	40.00	
300	A54	1c dk grn (R)	40	35
301	A52	2c dk grn (R)	50	30
302	A54	2c scar (Bl)	50	40

Stamps of 1921-26 Surcharged in Red

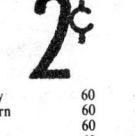

1937-38 2c

303	A54	2c on 4c gray	60	40
304	A46	2c on 8c ol grn	60	40
305	A55	2c on 8c lil	60	40
306	A55	2c on 10c dl vio	60	40
307	A55	2c on 12c ol grn	60	40
308	A48	2c on 15c lt bl	60	40
309	A50	2c on 24c blk brn	60	40
310	A51	2c on 50c blk	60	40
		Nos. 298-310 (13)	7.85	5.60

Ricardo Arango A77

Juan A. Guizado A78

Fire Fighting—A79

Modern Fire Fighting Equipment A80

Firemen's Monument A81

David H. Brandon A82

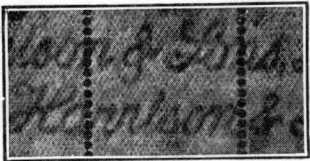

Wmk. 233

Perf. 14x14½, 14½x14
Wmkd. "Harrison & Sons, London" in Script Letters. (233)

1937, Nov. 25   Photogravure

311	A77	½c org red	60	30
312	A78	1c green	60	30
313	A79	2c red	60	40
314	A80	5c brt bl	90	40
315	A81	10c purple	1.50	90
316	A82	12c yel grn	2.50	90
		Nos. 311-316,C40-C42 (9)	10.20	5.65

50th anniversary of the Fire Department.

Cathedral Tower and Statue of Liberty, Flags of Panama and United States—A83

Engraved and Lithographed.

1938, Dec. 7   Perf. 12½ Unwmkd.
Center in Black; Flags in Red and Ultramarine.

317	A83	1c dp grn	60	30
318	A83	2c carmine	75	35
319	A83	5c blue	1.25	60
320	A83	12c olive	2.50	90
321	A83	15c brt ultra	3.00	1.50
		Nos. 317-321 (5)	8.10	3.65

Issued to commemorate the 150th anniversary of the Constitution of the United States of America. See also Nos. C49-C53.

No. 236 Overprinted in Black

1938, June 5   Perf. 12

| 321A | A53 | 2c carmine | 40 | 35 |
| b. | | Inverted overprint | 35.00 | |

Opening of the Normal School at Santiago, Veraguas Province, June 5, 1938. See Nos. C53A–C53B.

Gatun Lake A84

Designs: 1c, Pedro Miguel Locks. 2c, Allegory. 5c, Culebra Cut. 10c, Ferryboat. 12c, Aerial View of Canal. 15c, Gen. William C. Gorgas. 50c, Dr. Manuel A. Guerrero. 1b, Woodrow Wilson.

1939, Aug. 15 Engraved Perf. 12½

322	A84	½c yellow	50	10
323	A84	1c dp bl grn	60	15
324	A84	2c dl rose	75	20
325	A84	5c dl bl	1.25	25
326	A84	10c dk vio	1.50	60
327	A84	12c ol grn	1.50	75
328	A84	15c ultra	1.50	1.00
329	A84	50c orange	2.50	
330	A84	1b dk brn	7.50	5.00
		Nos. 322-330 (9)	19.10	8.05

Issued to commemorate the 25th anniversary of the opening of the Panama Canal. See Nos. C54-C61.

Stamps of 1924 Overprinted in Black or Red

CONSTITUCION 1941

1941, Jan. 2   Perf. 12

331	A53	½c orange	50	30
332	A53	1c dk grn (R)	50	35
333	A53	2c carmine	50	35
334	A53	5c dk bl (R)	60	30
335	A53	10c dk vio (R)	90	60
336	A53	15c ultra (R)	2.00	90
337	A53	50c dp org	10.00	5.00
338	A53	1b blk (R)	22.50	9.00
		Nos. 331-338 (8)	37.50	16.75

Issued to commemorate the new constitution of Panama which became effective Jan. 2, 1941. See Nos. C67–C71.

Liberty A93

Black Overprint

1942, Feb. 19   Engraved

| 339 | A93 | 10c purple | 1.25 | 1.00 |

Surcharged with New Value.

| 340 | A93 | 2c on 5c dk bl | 1.00 | 75 |

See also No. C72.

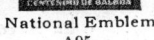

National Emblem A95

Farm Girl A96

Flags of Panama and Costa Rica A94

1942   Engr. & Litho.

| 341 | A94 | 2c rose red, dk bl & dp rose | 45 | 35 |

Issued to commemorate the first anniversary of the settlement of the Costa Rica-Panama border dispute. See No. C73.

Cart Laden with Sugar Cane (Inscribed "ACARRERO DE CAÑA") A97

Balboa Taking Possession of the Pacific—A98

Golden Altar of San José A99

San Blas Indian Woman and Child A101

Santo Tomas Hospital A100

Modern Highway—A102

Engraved; Flag on ½c Litho.

1942

342	A95	½c dl vio, bl & car	10	6
343	A96	1c dk grn	15	8
344	A97	2c vermilion	25	10
345	A98	5c dp bl & blk	30	12
346	A99	10c car rose & org	60	30
347	A100	15c lt bl & blk	1.00	75
348	A101	50c org red & ol blk	2.25	1.50
349	A102	1b black	3.50	1.00
		Nos. 342-349 (8)	8.15	3.91

See also Nos. 357, 365, 376, 377, 380, 395 and 409.

Flag of Panama A103

Arms of Panama A104

Engraved; Flag on 2c Litho.

1947, Apr.   Perf. 12½ Unwmkd.

| 350 | A103 | 2c car, bl & red | 20 | 15 |
| 351 | A104 | 5c dp bl | 25 | 25 |

Issued to commemorate the second anniversary of the National Constitutional Assembly of 1945.

No. 241 Surcharged in Black

Habilitada CORREOS B/. 0.50

1947   Perf. 12

| 352 | A53 | 50c on 24c yel brn | 1.50 | 1.50 |
| a. | | "Habilitada" | 3.00 | 3.00 |

Nos. C6C, C75, C74 and C87 Surcharged in Black or Carmine

HABILITADA CORREOS B/. 0.01½

353	AP5	½c on 8c gray blk	12	12
a.		"B/.0.01½ CORREOS" (transposed)	4.00	4.00
354	AP34	½c on 8c dk ol brn & blk (C)	12	12

PANAMA

355	AP34	1c on 7c rose car	18	18
356	AP42	2c on 8c vio	25	18
		Nos. 352-356 (5)	2.17	2.10

Flag Type of 1942.
1948   Engraved and Litho.

357	A95	½c car, org, bl & dp car	20	15

Monument to Firemen of Colon
A105

American-La France Fire Engine
A106

Designs: 20c, Firemen and hose cart. 25c, New Central Fire Station, Colon. 50c, Maximino Walker. 1b, J. J. A. Ducruet.

1948   Engraved
Center in Black.

358	A105	5c dp car	30	20
359	A106	10c orange	50	30
360	A106	20c gray bl	1.00	55
361	A106	25c chocolate	1.00	75
362	A105	50c purple	2.00	75
363	A105	1b dp grn	3.00	1.75
		Nos. 358-363 (6)	7.80	4.30

Issued to commemorate the 50th anniversary of the founding of the Colon Fire Department.

Cervantes
A107

1948   Perf. 12½   Unwmkd.

364	A107	2c car & blk	40	20

Issued to commemorate the 400th anniversary of the birth of Miguel de Cervantes Saavedra, novelist, playwright and poet. See Nos. C105-C106.

Oxcart Type of 1942 Redrawn.
Inscribed:
"ACARREO DE CAÑA".

1948   Perf. 12.

365	A97	2c vermilion	60	15

No. 365 Surcharged or Overprinted in Black

1949, May 23

366	A97	1c on 2c ver	25	15
367	A97	2c vermilion	25	15
a.		Inverted overprint	3.00	
		Nos. 366-367, C108-C111 (6)	6.15	5.95

Issued to commemorate the centenary of the incorporation of Chiriqui Province.

Stamps and Types of 1942-48 Issues Overprinted in Black or Red

1949, Sept.   Engraved

368	A96	1c dk grn	25	15
369	A97	2c ver (#365)	40	20
370	A98	5c bl (R)	60	35
		Nos. 368-370, C114-C118 (8)	8.00	6.05

Issued to commemorate the 75th anniversary of the formation of the Universal Postal Union.
Overprint on No. 368 is slightly different and smaller, 15½x12mm.

Francisco Javier de Luna   Dr. Carlos J. Finlay
A108   A109

1949, Dec. 7   Perf. 12½

371	A108	2c car & blk	35	20

Issued to commemorate the 200th anniversary of the founding of the University of San Javier. See No. C119.

1950, Jan. 12   Perf. 12   Unwmkd.

372	A109	2c car & gray blk	50	20

Issued to honor Dr. Carlos J. Finlay (1833-1915), Cuban physician and biologist who found that a mosquito transmitted yellow fever. See also No. C120.

Nos. 343, 357 and 345, Overprinted or Surcharged in Carmine or Black

CENTENARIO del Gral. José de San Martín 17 de Agosto de 1950

1950, Aug. 17

373	A96	1c dk grn	20	12
374	A95	2c on ½c car, org, bl & dp car (Bk)	25	15
375	A98	5c dp bl & blk	35	25
		Nos. 373-375, C121-C125 (8)	6.80	5.02

Issued to commemorate the centenary of the death of Gen. José de San Martin. The overprint is in four lines on No. 375.

Types of 1942.
1950   Engraved

376	A97	2c ver & blk	20	8
377	A98	5c blue	40	15

No. 376 is inscribed "ACARREO DE CAÑA".

Nos. 376 and 377 Overprinted in Green or Carmine

Tercer Centenario del Natalicio de San Juan Bautista de La Salle.
1651-1951

1951, Sept. 26

378	A97	2c ver & blk (G)	20	15
379	A98	5c bl (C)	35	20

Issued to commemorate the 500th anniversary of the birth of St. Jean-Baptiste de la Salle.
The overprint exists (a) inverted on both stamps, (b) with top line omitted and second line repeated in its place. Price, each $12.50.

Altar Type of 1942.
1952   Engraved   Perf. 12

380	A99	10c pur & org	50	25

No. 357 Surcharged "1952" and New Value in Black.

1952

381	A95	1c on ½c multi	20	8

Queen Isabella I and Arms
A110

1952, Oct. 20   Engraved   Perf. 12½
Center in Black

382	A110	1c green	12	10
383	A110	2c carmine	18	12
384	A110	5c dk bl	25	15
385	A110	10c purple	35	15
		Nos. 382-385, C131-C136 (10)	8.97	7.47

Issued to commemorate the 500th anniversary of the birth of Queen Isabella I of Spain.

No. 380 and Type of 1942 Surcharged "B/.0.01 1953" in Black or Carmine.

1953   Perf. 12.

387	A99	1c on 10c pur & org	10	8
388	A100	1c on 15c blk (C)	20	8

A similar surcharge on No. 346 was privately applied.

Baptism of the Flag
A111

Manuel Amador Guerrero and Senora de Amador
A112

Designs: 12c, Santos Jorge A. and Jeronimo de la Ossa. 20c, Revolutionary Junta. 50c, Old city hall. 1b, National coinage.

1953, Nov. 3   Engraved   Perf. 12

389	A111	2c purple	20	10
390	A112	5c red org	25	8
391	A112	12c dp red vio	50	20
392	A112	20c sl gray	75	35
393	A111	50c org yel	1.75	90
394	A112	1b blue	3.75	1.90
		Nos. 389-394 (6)	7.20	3.53

Issued to commemorate the 50th anniversary of the founding of the Republic of Panama. See Nos. C140-C145.

Farm Girl Type of 1942.
1954   Perf. 12.   Unwmkd.

395	A96	1c dp car rose	8	6

Surcharged with New Value in Black.

396	A96	3c on 1c dp car rose	12	8

Monument to Gen. Tomas Herrera
A113

1954   Lithographed.   Perf. 12½

397	A113	3c purple	25	10

Centenary of the death of Gen. Tomas Herrera. See Nos. C148-C149.

Tocumen International Airport
A114

1955

398	A114	½c org brn	6	5

Pres. J. A. Remon Cantera
A115

1955, June 1

399	A115	3c lil rose & blk	25	10

Issued in tribute to Pres. José Antonio Remon Cantera, 1908-1955. See No. C153.

Victor de la Guardia y Ayala and Miguel Chiari
A116

1955, Sept. 13

400	A116	5c violet	25	10

Centenary of province of Coclé.

Ferdinand de Lesseps—A117

First Excavation of Panama Canal—A118

PANAMA

Design: 50c, Theodore Roosevelt.
1955, Nov. 16
401	A117	3c rose brn, *rose*	45	12
402	A118	25c vio bl, *lt bl*	1.00	75
403	A117	50c vio, *lt vio*	2.25	1.50
	Nos. 401-403, C155-C156 (5)		6.95	4.97

Issued to commemorate the 150th anniversary of the birth of Ferdinand de Lesseps, French promoter connected with building of Panama Canal. Imperforates exist, but were not sold at any post office.

Arms of Panama City
A119

Carlos A. Mendoza
A120

Perf. 12½
1956, Aug. 17   Litho.   Unwmkd.
404	A119	3c green	18	8

Issued to commemorate the sixth Inter-American Congress of Municipalities, Panama City, Aug. 14-19, 1956.
For souvenir sheet see C182a.

Wmk. 311
Wmkd. Star and RP Multiple. (311)
1956, Sept. 13
405	A120	10c rose red & dp grn	30	18

Issued to commemorate the centenary of the birth of Pres. Carlos A. Mendoza.

National Archives
A121

Design: 25c, Pres. Belisario Porras.
1956, Nov. 27
406	A121	15c gray	60	30
407	A121	25c dk car rose & bluish blk	90	60

Issued to commemorate the centenary of the birth of Pres. Belisario Porras. See Nos. C183-C184.

Pan-American Highway, Panama—A122

1957, Aug. 1
408	A122	3c gray grn	20	8

Issued to publicize the 7th Pan-American Highway Congress. See Nos. C185-C187.

Hospital Type of 1942.
Engraved.
1957   Perf. 12   Unwmkd.
409	A100	15c black	50	25

Manuel Espinosa Batista
A123

Flags of 21 American Nations
A124

Perf. 12½
1957, Sept. 20   Litho.   Wmk. 311
410	A123	5c grn & ultra	20	10

Issued to commemorate the centenary of the birth of Manuel Espinosa B., independence leader.

No. 398 Surcharged "1957" and New Value in Violet or Black.
1957   Unwmkd.
411	A114	1c on ½c org brn (V)	8	5
412	A114	3c on ½c org brn	15	8

No. 391 Surcharged "1958," New Value and Dots.
1958   Engraved.   Perf. 12
413	A112	3c on 12c dp red vio	15	6

Perf. 12½
1958, July 10   Litho.   Unwmkd.
Center yellow & black; flags in national colors.
414	A124	1c lt gray	10	5
415	A124	2c brt yel grn	15	6
416	A124	3c red org	20	6
417	A124	7c vio bl	35	12
	Nos. 414-417, C203-C206 (8)		5.53	4.59

Issued to commemorate the 10th anniversary of the Organization of American States.

Brazilian Pavilion, Brussels Fair
A125

Pavilions: 3c, Argentina. 5c, Venezuela. 10c, Great Britain.
1958, Sept. 8   Wmk. 311
418	A125	1c org yel & emer	8	6
419	A125	3c lt bl & ol	15	6
420	A125	5c lt brn & sl	20	10
421	A125	10c aqua & redsh brn	30	25
	Nos. 418-421, C207-C209 (7)		4.98	4.67

World's Fair, Brussels, Apr. 17-Oct. 19. A souvenir sheet containing Nos. 418-421 and C207-C209 is listed as No. C209a.

Pope Pius XII as Young Man
A126

U. N. Headquarters Building
A127

Lithographed.
1959, Jan.   Perf. 12½   Wmk. 311
422	A126	3c org brn	20	10

Issued in memory of Pope Pius XII, 1876-1958. See Nos. C210-C212a.

Human Rights Issue
Design: 15c, Humanity looking into sun.
1959, Apr. 14   Wmk. 311
423	A127	3c mar & ol	10	8
424	A127	15c org & emer	50	35
	Nos. 423-424, C213-C217 (7)		5.35	4.90

Issued to commemorate the 10th anniversary (in 1958) of the signing of the Universal Declaration of Human Rights.

Nos. 423-424 Overprinted in Dark Blue

8A REUNION
C.E.P.A.L.
MAYO 1959

1959, May 16
425	A127	3c mar & ol	15	12
426	A127	15c org & emer	50	30
	Nos. 425-426, C218-C221 (6)		5.30	4.24

Issued to commemorate the 8th Reunion of the Economic Commission for Latin America.

Eusebio A. Morales
A128

National Institute
A129

Portrait: 13c, Abel Bravo.
Perf. 12½
1959, July 27   Litho.   Wmk. 311
427	A128	3c car rose	12	6
428	A128	13c brt grn	40	20
429	A129	21c lt bl	60	40
	Nos. 427-429, C222-C223 (5)		1.49	88

50th anniversary, National Institute.

Soccer
A130

Fencing
A131

Designs: 3c, Swimming. 20c, Hurdling.
1959, Oct. 26
430	A130	1c gray & emer	8	6
431	A130	3c brt bl & red brn	15	8
432	A130	20c emer & red brn	70	60
	Nos. 430-432, C224-C226 (6)		2.81	2.39

Issued to commemorate the 3rd Pan American Games, Chicago, Aug. 27-Sept. 7, 1959.

Attractive slip cases are available for most Scott Albums.

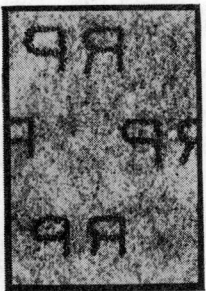

Wmk. 343
Wmkd. RP Multiple. (343)
1960, Sept. 22   Litho.   Perf. 12½
Design: 5c, Soccer.
433	A131	3c lt vio & mag	15	8
434	A131	5c bl grn & emer	25	10
	Nos. 433-434, C234-C237 (6)		2.82	2.13

Issued to commemorate the 17th Olympic Games, Rome, Aug. 25-Sept. 11.

Agricultural Products and Cattle
A132

1961, Mar. 3   Perf. 12½   Wmk. 311
435	A132	3c bl grn	15	6

Issued to publicize the second agricultural and livestock census, Apr. 16, 1961.

Children's Hospital
A133

1961, May 2
436	A133	3c grnsh bl	12	6

Issued to commemorate the 25th anniversary of the Lions Club of Panama.

Flags of Panama and Costa Rica
A134

1961, Oct. 2   Perf. 12½   Wmk. 343
437	A134	3c car & bl	18	10

Issued to commemorate the meeting of Presidents Mario Echandi of Costa Rica and Roberto F. Chiari of Panama at Paso Canoa, Apr. 21, 1961. See No. C251.

Arms of Colon
A135

Mercury and Cogwheel
A136

PANAMA

1962, Feb. 28   Litho.   Wmk. 311

| 438 | A135 | 3c car, yel & vio bl | 12 | 6 |

Issued to publicize the third Central American Municipal Assembly, Colon, May 13–17. See No. C255.

1962, March 16   Wmk. 343

| 439 | A136 | 3c red org | 10 | 6 |

First industrial and commercial census.

Social Security Hospital
A137

1962, June 1   Perf. 12½

| 440 | A137 | 3c ver & gray | 10 | 6 |

Opening of the Social Security Hospital.

Church of San Francisco de Veraguas
A138

Ruins of Cathedral of Panama
A139

Designs: 3c, David Cathedral. 5c, Natá Church. 10c, Don Bosco Church. 15c, Church of the Virgin of Carmen. 20c, Colon Cathedral. 25c, Greek Orthodox Temple. 50c, Cathedral of Panama. 1b, Protestant Church of Colon.

1962–64   Litho.   Wmk. 343
Buildings in Black

441	A138	1c red & bl	6	5
442	A139	2c red & yel	8	6
443	A138	3c vio & yel	10	6
444	A139	5c rose & lt grn	15	10
445	A139	10c grn & yel	30	8
445A	A139	10c red & bl ('64)	30	18
446	A139	15c ultra & lt grn	40	25
447	A139	20c red & pink	45	35
448	A138	25c grn & pink	60	40
449	A139	50c ultra & pink	1.25	80
450	A139	1b lil & yel	3.25	2.75
		Nos. 441-450 (11)	6.94	5.18

Issued to publicize freedom of religion in Panama. Issue dates: No. 445A, June 4, 1964; others, July 20, 1962. See Nos. C256-C265; souvenir sheet No. C264a.

Panama Canal Bridge during Construction
A140

1962, Oct. 12   Perf. 12½

| 451 | A140 | 3c car & gray | 12 | 6 |

Issued to commemorate the opening of the Panama Canal Bridge (Thatcher Ferry Bridge), Oct. 12, 1962. See No. C273.

Fire Brigade Exercises, Inauguration of Aqueduct, 1906
A141

Portraits of Fire Brigade Officials: 3c, Lt. Col. Luis Carlos Endara P., Col. Raul Arango N. and Major Ernesto Arosemena A. 5c, Guillermo Patterson Jr., David F. de Castro, Pres. T. Gabriel Duque, Telmo Rugliancich and Tomas Leblanc.

1963   Perf. 12½   Wmk. 311

452	A141	1c emer & blk	5	5
453	A141	3c vio bl & blk	10	6
454	A141	5c mag & blk	15	10
		Nos.452-454, C279-C281 (6)	1.55	1.31

Issued to commemorate the 75th anniversary (in 1962) of the Panamanian Fire Brigade.

Nos. 440, 443, 451, 453 and 407 Surcharged "VALE" and New Value in Black or Red.

1963   Perf. 12½   Wmk. 343

455	A137	4c on 3c ver & gray	20	8
456	A138	4c on 3c vio & yel	20	8
457	A140	4c on 3c car & gray	20	8

**   Wmk. 311**

458	A141	4c on 3c vio bl & blk	20	8
459	A121	10c on 25c dk car rose & bluish blk (R)	50	15
		Nos.455-459 (5)	1.30	47

Pres. Francisco J. Orlich, Costa Rica
A142

Vasco Nuñez de Balboa
A143

Flags and Presidents: 2c, Luis A. Somoza, Nicaragua. 3c, Dr. Ramon Villeda M., Honduras. 4c, Roberto F. Chiari, Panama.

**   Perf. 12½x12**

1963, Dec. 18   Litho.   Unwmkd.
Portrait in Slate Green

460	A142	1c lt grn, red & ultra	15	15
461	A142	2c lt bl, red & ultra	18	18
462	A142	3c pale pink, red & ultra	25	18
463	A142	4c rose, red & ultra	30	25

Issued to commemorate the meeting of Central American Presidents with Pres. John F. Kennedy, San José, March 18–20, 1963. See also Nos. C292-C294.

1964, Jan. 22   Photo.   Perf. 13

| 464 | A143 | 4c grn, pale rose | 15 | 15 |

Issued to commemorate the 450th anniversary of Balboa's discovery of the Pacific Ocean. See also No. C295.

No. C231 Surcharged in Red:
"Correos B/. 0.10"
Lithographed

1964   Perf. 12½   Wmk. 311

| 465 | AP74 | 10c on 21c lt bl | 25 | 20 |

Type of 1962 Overprinted in Red:
"HABILITADA"

1964   Wmk. 343

| 466 | A138 | 1b red, bl & blk | 2.50 | 2.25 |

Eleanor Roosevelt
A147

Keel-billed Toucan
A148

**   Perf. 12x12½**

1964, Oct. 9   Litho.   Unwmkd.

| 478 | A147 | 4c car & blk, grnsh | 18 | 12 |

Issued to honor Eleanor Roosevelt (1884–1962). See Nos. C345-C345a.

Canceled to Order

Canceled sets of new issues have been sold by the government. Postally used copies are worth more.

1965, Oct. 27   Perf. 14   Unwmkd.

Song Birds: 2c, Scarlet macaw. 3c, Red-crowned woodpecker. 4c, Blue-gray tanager (horiz.).

479	A148	1c brt pink & multi	5	5
480	A148	2c multi	5	5
481	A148	3c brt vio & multi	8	6
482	A148	4c org yel & multi	10	8
		Nos. 479-482, C346-C347 (6)	65	52

Snapper—A149
Design: 2c, Dolphin.

1965, Dec. 7   Lithographed

483	A149	1c multi	8	5
484	A149	2c multi	12	6
		Nos. 483-484, C348-C351 (6)	1.98	1.52

No. 448 Surcharged
1966, June 27 Perf. 12½ Wmk. 343

| 485 | A138 | 13c on 25c grn & pink | 45 | 25 |

The "25c" has not been obliterated.

Hen and Chicks
A150

Domestic Animals: 3c Rooster. 5c, Pig (horiz.). 8c, Cow (horiz.).

1967, Feb. 3   Perf. 14   Unwmkd.

486	A150	1c multi	6	5
487	A150	3c multi	8	5
488	A150	5c multi	13	8
489	A150	8c multi	21	12
		Nos. 486-489, C360-C363 (8)	3.15	2.42

New World Anhinga
A151

Birds: 1c, Quetzals. 3c, Turquoise-browed motmot. 4c, Double-collared aracari (horiz.). 5c, Macaw. 13c, Belted kingfisher.

1967, July 20

490	A151	½c lt bl & multi	5	5
491	A151	1c lt gray & multi	5	5
492	A151	3c pink & multi	10	5
493	A151	4c lt grn & multi	12	6
494	A151	5c buff & multi	15	8
495	A151	13c yel & multi	45	25
		Nos. 490-495 (6)	92	54

Red Deer, by Franz Marc
A152

Animal Paintings by Franz Marc: 3c, Tiger (vert.). 5c, Monkeys. 8c, Blue Fox.

1967, Sept. 1   Perf. 14

496	A152	1c multi	5	5
497	A152	3c multi	10	5
498	A152	5c multi	15	8
499	A152	8c multi	30	12
		Nos. 496-499, C364-C367 (8)	2.80	1.70

Map of Panama, People and Houses
A153

Design: 10c, Map of Americas and people (vert.).

Wmkd. MEX and Eagle in Circle, Multiple. (350)

1969, Aug.   Photogravure

| 500 | A153 | 5c vio bl | 15 | 10 |
| 501 | A153 | 10c brt rose lil | 30 | 20 |

Issued to publicize the 1970 census.

Cogwheel—A154

PANAMA

1969, Aug.

502 A154 13c yel & dk bl gray 30 25

Issued to commemorate the 50th anniversary of Rotary International of Panama.

Cornucopia and Map of Panama
A155
Perf. 14½x15

1969, Oct. 10 Litho. Unwmkd.

503 A155 10c lt bl & multi 25 15

Issued to commemorate the first anniversary of the October 11 Revolution.

Map of Panama and Ruins — Natá Church
A156 — A157

Designs: 5c, Farmer, wife and mule. 13c, Hotel Continental. 20c, Church of the Virgin of Carmen. 21c, Gold altar, San José Church. 25c, Del Rey bridge. 30c, Dr. Justo Arosemena monument. 34c, Cathedral of Panama. 38c, Municipal Palace. 40c, French Plaza. 50c, Thatcher Ferry Bridge (Bridge of the Americas). 59c, National Theater.

Perf. 14½x15, 15x14½

1969-70 Litho. Unwmkd.

504	A156	3c org & blk	10	6
505	A156	5c lt bl grn ('70)	15	6
506	A157	8c dl brn ('70)	25	20
507	A156	13c emer & blk	35	18
508	A156	20c vio brn ('70)	45	45
509	A157	21c yel ('70)	45	45
510	A156	25c lt bl grn ('70)	60	40
511	A157	30c blk ('70)	70	60
512	A156	34c org brn ('70)	80	60
513	A156	38c brt bl ('70)	85	60
514	A156	40c org yel ('70)	90	60
515	A156	50c brt rose lil & blk	1.20	90
516	A156	59c brt rose lil ('70)	1.35	80

Nos. 504-516 (13) 8.25 5.70

Stadium and Discus Thrower
A158

Flor del Espíritu Santo
A159

Wmk. 365
Wmkd. Argentine Arms, 'Casa de Moneda de la Nacion' & 'RA' Mult. (365)

1970, Jan. 6 Litho. Perf. 13½

517	A158	1c ultra & multi	5	5
518	A158	2c ultra & multi	5	5
519	A158	3c ultra & multi	8	7
520	A158	5c ultra & multi	13	8
521	A158	10c ultra & multi	27	15
522	A158	13c ultra & multi	35	20
523	A159	13c pink & multi	35	20
524	A158	25c ultra & multi	65	50
525	A158	30c ultra & multi	80	65

Nos. 517-525, C368-C369 (11) 3.98 2.85

Issued to publicize the 11th Central American and Caribbean Games, Feb. 28–Mar. 14.

Office of Comptroller General, 1970
A160

Designs: 3c, Alejandro Tapia and Martin Sosa, first Comptrollers, 1931–34 (horiz.). 8c, Comptroller's emblem. 13c, Office of Comptroller General, 1955–70 (horiz.).

1971, Feb. 25 Litho. Wmk. 365

526	A160	3c yel & multi	9	5
527	A160	5c brn, buff & gold	15	8
528	A160	8c gold & multi	25	12
529	A160	13c blk & multi	40	22

Comptroller General's Office, 40th anniversary.

Indian Alligator Design — Education Year Emblem, Map of Panama
A161 — A162

Perf. 13½

1971, Aug. 18 Wmk. 343

530 A161 8c multi 25 20

Fifth anniversary of SENAPI (Servicio Nacional de Artesanía y Pequeñas Industrias).

1971, Aug. 19 Lithographed

531 A162 1b multi 2.50 1.75

International Education Year, 1970.

Congress Emblem
A163

1972, Aug. 25

532 A163 25c multi 85 50

9th Inter-American Conference of Saving and Loan Associations, Panama City, Jan. 23–29, 1971.

UPU Headquarters, Bern
A164

Design: 30c, Universal Postal Union Monument, Bern (vert.).

1971, Dec. 14 Wmk. 343

| 533 | A164 | 8c multi | 25 | 12 |
| 534 | A164 | 30c multi | 85 | 50 |

Inauguration of Universal Postal Union Headquarters, Bern, Switzerland.

Cow, Pig and Produce
A165

1971, Dec. 15

535 A165 3c yel, brn & blk 9 5

3rd agricultural census.

Map of Panama and "4-S" Emblem
A166

1971, Dec. 16

536 A166 2c multi 6 5

Rural youth 4-S program.

UNICEF Emblem, Children
A167

Perf. 13½

1972, Sept. 12 Wmk. 365

537 A167 1c yel & multi 5 5

25th anniversary (in 1971) of the United Nations International Children's Fund (UNICEF). See Nos. C390-C392a.

Tropical Fruits
A168

1972, Sept. 13 Multicolored

538 A168 1c shown 5 5

| 539 | A168 | 2c Isla de Noche | 9 | 5 |
| 540 | A168 | 3c Carnival float, vert. | 9 | 7 |

Nos. 538-540, C393-C395 (6) 1.35 79

Tourist publicity.

Nos. 516, 531 and 511 Surcharged in Red

CONSEJO DE SEGURIDAD
15 · 21 Marzo 1973

Perf. 14½x15, 15x14½, 13½

1973, Mar. 16 Unwmkd. Wmk. 343

541	A156	8c on 59c brt rose lil	15	12
542	A162	10c on 1b multi	20	18
543	A157	13c on 30c blk	30	20

U.N. Security Council Meeting, Panama City, Mar. 15–21. Surcharges differ in size and are adjusted to fit shape of stamp. See No. C402.

José Daniel Crespo, Educator
A169

Perf. 13½

1973, June 20 Litho. Wmk. 365

544 A169 3c lt bl & multi 10 8

Nos. 544,C403-C413 (12) 7.80 3.38

Nos. 511-512 and 509 Surcharged in Red

VALE 13¢

Perf. 15x14½, 14½x15

1974, Nov. 11 Unwmkd.

545	A157	5c on 30c blk	10	7
546	A156	10c on 34c org brn	20	14
547	A157	13c on 21c yel	26	20

Nos. 545-547, C417-C421 (8) 1.27 93

Surcharge vertical on No. 546.

Bolivar, Thatcher Ferry Bridge, Men with Flags
A170

Perf. 12½

1976, Mar. 30 Litho. Unwmkd.

548 A170 6c multi 12 8

150th anniversary of Congress of Panama. See Nos. C426-C428.

Evibacus Princeps
A171

PANAMA

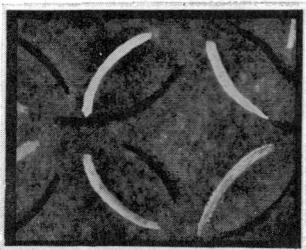

Wmk. 377
Wmkd. Interlocking Circles (377)
Designs: 3c, Ptitosarcus sinuosus (vert.). 4c, Acanthaster planci. 7c, Starfish. 1b, Mithrax spinossimus.

Perf. 12½x13, 13x12½

1976, May 6   Lithographed
549	A171	2c multi	5	5
550	A171	3c multi	6	5
551	A171	4c multi	8	6
552	A171	7c multi	14	10
	Nos. 549-552, C429-C430 (6)		1.21	.81

Souvenir Sheet
Imperf.
| 553 | A171 | 1b multi | | 4.50 |

Marine life. No. 553 contains one stamp, multicolored margin with black inscription. Size: 100x100mm.

Flag Bearer from Bolivar Monument
A172

Bolivar and Argentine Flag
A173

Designs: Stamps of type A172 show details of Bolivar Monument, Panama City; type A173 shows head of Bolivar and flags of Latin American countries.

Lithographed
1976, June 22 Perf. 13½ Unwmkd.
Yellow & Multicolored

554	A172	20c shown	40	30
555	A173	20c shown	40	30
556	A173	20c Bolivia	40	30
557	A173	20c Brazil	40	30
558	A173	20c Chile	40	30
559	A172	20c Battle scene	40	30
560	A173	20c Colombia	40	30
561	A173	20c Costa Rica	40	30
562	A173	20c Cuba	40	30
563	A173	20c Ecuador	40	30
564	A173	20c El Salvador	40	30
565	A173	20c Guatemala	40	30
566	A173	20c Guyana	40	30
567	A173	20c Haiti	40	30
568	A172	20c Assembly	40	30
569	A172	20c Liberated people	40	30
570	A173	20c Honduras	40	30
571	A173	20c Jamaica	40	30
572	A173	20c Mexico	40	30
573	A173	20c Nicaragua	40	30
574	A173	20c Panama	40	30
575	A173	20c Paraguay	40	30
576	A173	20c Peru	40	30
577	A173	20c Dominican Republic	40	30
578	A172	20c Bolivar and flag bearer	40	30
579	A173	20c Surinam	40	30
580	A173	20c Trinidad-Tobago	40	30
581	A173	20c Uruguay	40	30
582	A173	20c Venezuela	40	30

| 583 | A172 | 20c Indian delegation | 40 | 30 |
| | Nos. 554-583 (30) | | 12.00 | 9.00 |

Souvenir Sheet
584	A172	Sheet of 3		3.50
a.	30c, Bolivar and flag bearer			.75
b.	30c, Monument, top			.75
c.	40c, Inscription tablet			1.00

Amphictyonic Congress of Panama, sesquicentennial. Nos. 554-583 printed se-tenant in sheets of 30 (6x5) with black marginal inscription and control number. No. 584 perf. and imperf., has green marginal inscription. Size: 81x122mm.

Nicanor Villalaz, Designer of Coat of Arms
A174

National Lottery Building, Panama City
A175

1976, Nov. 12   Litho.   **Perf. 12½**
| 585 | A174 | 5c dk bl | 10 | 8 |
| 586 | A175 | 6c multi | 12 | 8 |

Contadora Island
A176

1976, Dec. 29   **Perf. 12½**
| 587 | A176 | 3c multi | 15 | 5 |

Presidents Carter and Omar Torrijos Signing Panama Canal Treaties
A177

1978, Jan.   Litho.   Perf. 12
Size: 90x40mm.
588	A177	Strip of 3	2.00	
a.	3c multi		6	
b.	40c multi		80	
c.	50c multi		1.00	

Perf. 14
Size: 36x26mm.
| 589 | A177 | 23c multi | 46 | 32 |

Signing of Panama Canal Treaties, Washington, D.C., Sept. 7, 1977.

Presidents Carter and Torrijos Signing Treaties—A178
Design: 3c, Treaty signing.

1978, Nov. 13   Litho.   **Perf. 12**
590	A178	Strip of 3	1.75	
a.	5c multi (30x40mm)		10	
b.	35c multi (30x40mm)		70	
c.	41c multi (45x40mm)		82	

Size: 36x26mm.
| 591 | A178 | 3c multi | 6 | 5 |

Signing of Panama Canal Treaties, Panama City, Panama, June 6, 1978.

World Trade Center, Colon
A179

1978   Litho.   Perf. 12
| 592 | A179 | 6c multi | 12 | 8 |

Free Zone of Colon, 30th anniversary.

Melvin Jones, Lions Emblem
A180

1978, Dec. 5
| 593 | A180 | 50c multi | 1.00 | 80 |

Birth centenary of Melvin Jones, founder of Lions International.

Soldier with Children, Ship, Flag
A181

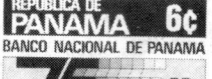

"75," Coat of Arms
A182

Rotary Emblem, "75"
A183

Pres. Torrijos and Carter, Flags, Ship
A184

UPU Emblem, Globe
A185

Boy and Girl Inside Heart
A186

1979, Oct. 1   Litho.   **Perf. 14**
594	A181	3c multi	6	5
595	A182	6c multi	12	8
596	A183	17c multi	35	25
597	A184	23c multi	45	30
598	A185	35c multi	70	45
599	A186	50c multi	1.00	65
	Nos. 594-599 (6)		2.68	1.77

Return of Canal Zone to Panama, October 1 (3c, 23c); National Bank, 75th anniversary; Rotary International, 75th anniversary; 18th Universal Postal Union Congress, Rio de Janeiro, Sept.—Oct., 1979; International Year of the Child.

Colon Station, St. Charles Hotel, Engraving—A187

Postal Headquarters, Balboa, Inauguration—A188

Return of Canal Zone to Panama, Oct. 1, 1979—A189

Census of the Americas—A190

Panamanian Tourist and Convention Center Opening—A191

PANAMA

Inter-American Development Bank,
25th Anniversary—A192

Canal Zone Centenary—A193

Olympic Stadium, Moscow '80
Emblem—A194

1980, June 17		Litho.		Perf. 12	
600	A187	1c rose vio		5	5
601	A188	3c multi		6	5
602	A189	6c multi		12	8
603	A190	17c multi		35	25
604	A191	23c multi		45	30
605	A192	35c multi		70	45
606	A193	41c pale rose & blk		82	55
607	A194	50c multi		1.00	65
		Nos. 600-607 (8)		3.55	2.38

Transpanamanian Railroad centenary (1c); 22nd Summer Olympic Games, Moscow, July 19-Aug. 3 (50c).

La Salle
Congregation,
75th Anniv.
(1979)
A195

Louis Braille
A196

1981, May 15		Litho.		Perf. 12	
608	A195	17c multi		35	25

1981, May 15					
609	A196	23c multi		45	30

Intl. Year of the Disabled.

Bull's Blood—A197

1981, June 26		Litho.		Perf. 12	
610	A197	3c shown		6	5
611	A197	6c Lory, vert.		12	8
612	A197	41c Hummingbird, vert.		82	55
613	A197	50c Toucan		1.00	65

Apparition of the
Virgin to St. Catherine
Laboure,
150th Anniv.—A198

1981, June 26		Litho.		Perf. 12	
614	A198	35c multi		70	50

Pres. Torrijos and Bayano Dam—A199
Wmk. 343

1982, Mar.		Litho.		Perf. 10½	
615	A199	17c multi		35	25

National Solidarity—A200
Wmk. 343

1981, Nov. 30		Litho.		Perf. 10½	
616	A200	3c multi		6	5

First Death Anniv. of Pres. Omar
Torrijos Herrera—A201
Wmk. 381: "Panama" and Design

1982, May 14		Litho.		Perf. 10½	
617	A201	5c Aerial view		10	6
618	A201	6c Army camp		12	8
619	A201	50c Felipillo Engineering Works		1.00	60
		Nos. 617-619, C433-C434 (5)		2.74	1.64

Ricardo J. Alfaro (1882-1977),
Statesman—A202

Designs: Photos by Luiz Gutierrez Cruz.

1982, Aug. 18			Wmk. 381		
620	A202	3c multi		6	5

See Nos. C436-C437.

1983 World Cup—A203
Wmk. 381 "Panama" and Design

1982			Litho.	Perf. 10½	
621	A203	50c Italian team		1.00	55

See Nos. C438-C440.

Chamber of Commerce Expo Comer '83,
Jan. 12-16—A204
Wmk. 381

1983		Litho.		Perf. 10½	
622	A204	17c multi		34	20

Visit of Pope
John Paul II
A205

Bank Emblem
A206

Various portraits of the Pope. 35c airmail.

Wmk. 382 (Stars)

1983, Mar. 1		Litho.		Perf. 12x11	
623	A205	6c multi		12	8
624	A205	17c multi		34	20
625	A205	35c multi		70	40

1983, Mar. 18					
626	A206	50c multi		1.00	60

24th Council Meeting of Inter-American Development Bank, Mar. 21-23.

Simon Bolivar
(1783-1830)—A207

1983,		Litho.		Perf. 12	
627	A207	50c multi		1.00	60

Souvenir Sheet
Imperf.

| 628 | A207 | 1b like 50c | 2.00 | 1.25 |

No. 628 has black control number. Size: 86x76mm.

World Communications Year—A208

1983, Oct. 9		Litho.		Perf. 14	
629	A208	30c UPAE emblem		60	35
630	A208	40c WCY emblem		80	48
631	A208	50c UPU emblem		1.00	60
632	A208	60c Dove in flight		1.20	75

Souvenir Sheet
Imperf.

| 633 | A208 | 1b multi | 2.00 | 1.25 |

No. 633 contains designs of Nos. 629-632 without denominations. Margin shows coat of arms; black marginal inscription. Size: 151x150mm.

Freedom of Worship—A209

1983, Oct. 21		Litho.		Perf. 11½	
634	A209	3c Panama Mosque		6	5
635	A209	5c Bahai Temple		10	6
636	A209	6c St. Francis Church		12	8
637	A209	17c Shevet Ahim Synagogue		34	20

Ricardo Miro
(1883-1940),
Poet
A210

The Prophet,
by Alfredo
Sinclair
A211

Famous Men: 3c, Richard Newman (1883-1946), educator. 5c, Cristobal Rodriguez (1883-1943), politician. 6c, Alcibiades Arosemena (1883-1958), industrialist and financier. 35c, Cirilo Martinez (1883-1924), linguist.

1983, Nov. 8		Litho.		Perf. 14	
638	A210	1c multi		5	5
639	A210	3c multi		6	5
640	A210	5c multi		10	6
641	A210	6c multi		12	8
642	A210	35c multi		70	42
		Nos 638-642 (5)		1.03	66

1983, Dec. 12				Perf. 12	

Paintings: No. 643, Village House, by Juan Manuel Cedeno. No. 644, Large Nude, by Manuel Chong Neto. 3c, On Another Occasion, by Spiros Vamvas. 6c, Punta Chame Landscape, by Guillermo Trujillo. 28c, Neon Light, by Alfredo Sinclair. 41c, Highland Girls, by Al Sprague. 1b, Bright Morning, by Ignacio Mallol Pibernat. Nos. 643-647, 650 horiz.

643	A211	1c multi		5	5
644	A211	1c multi		5	5
645	A211	3c multi		6	5
646	A211	6c multi		12	8
647	A211	28c multi		56	34
648	A211	35c multi		70	42
649	A211	41c multi		82	50
650	A211	1b multi		2.00	1.20
		Nos 643-650 (8)		4.36	2.69

PANAMA

AIR POST STAMPS.
Special Delivery Stamp No. E3
Surcharged in Dark Blue

VEINTICINCO CENTESIMOS

1929, Feb. 8 Perf. 12½ Unwmkd.
C1	SD1	25c on 10c org	1.50	1.25
a.		Inverted surcharge	35.00	35.00

Nos. E3–E4 Overprinted in Blue

CORREO AEREO

1929
C2	SD1	10c orange	75	75
a.		Inverted overprint	25.00	20.00
b.		Double overprint	25.00	20.00

Some specialists claim the red overprint is a proof impression.

With Additional Surcharge of New Value.
C3	SD1	15c on 10c org	75	75
C4	SD1	25c on 20c dk brn	1.75	1.50
a.		Double surcharge	20.00	20.00

No. E3 Surcharged in Blue

CORREO AEREO 5 CENTESIMOS

1930, Jan. 25
C5	SD1	5c on 10c org	75	75

No. 219 Overprinted in Red

CORREO AEREO

1930, Feb. 28 Perf. 12
C6	A39	1b dk vio & blk	25.00	17.50

Airplane over Map of Panama
AP5   AP6

1930–41 Engraved Perf. 12
C6A	AP5	5c bl ('41)	20	6
C6B	AP5	7c rose car ('41)	35	10
C6C	AP5	8c gray blk ('41)	35	10
C7	AP5	15c dp grn	45	6
C8	AP5	20c rose	50	8
C9	AP5	25c dp bl	1.00	1.00
		Nos. C6A–C9 (6)	2.85	1.40

See also No. C112.

1930, Aug. 4 Perf. 12½
C10	AP6	5c ultra	20	8
C11	AP6	10c orange	35	30
C12	AP6	30c dp vio	8.00	6.00
C13	AP6	50c dp red	2.00	75
C14	AP6	1b black	8.00	5.00
		Nos. C10–C14 (5)	18.55	12.13

Amphibian
AP7

1931, Nov. Typo. Without Gum
C15	AP7	5c dp bl	1.25	1.25
a.		5c gray bl	1.25	1.25
b.		Horizontal pair, imperf. between	75.00	

Issued Nov. 24 to commemorate the start of regular airmail service between Panama City and the western provinces, but valid only on Nov. 28–29 on mail carried by aquaplane "3 Noviembre."

Many sheets have a papermaker's watermark "DOLPHIN BOND" in double-lined capitals.

No. C9 Surcharged in Red 19 mm. long

HABILITADA 20 C.

1932, Dec. 14 Perf. 12
C16	AP5	20c on 25c dp bl	5.00	75

Surcharge 17 mm. long.
C16A	AP5	20c on 25c dp bl	300.00	4.00

Special Delivery Stamp No. E4
Overprinted in Red or Black

CORREO AEREO

1934 Perf. 12½
C17	SD1	20c dk brn	1.25	75
C17A	SD1	20c dk brn (Bk)	100.00	85.00

Surcharged In Black

CORREO AEREO 10 CENTESIMOS

1935, June
C18	SD1	10c on 20c dk brn	1.25	75

Same Surcharge with Small "10."
C18A	SD1	10c on 20c dk brn	75.00	7.50
b.		Horiz. pair, imperf. vert.	150.00	

Nos. 234 and 242 Surcharged in Blue

1836–1936 CORREO AEREO 5 CENTESIMOS

1936, Sept. 24
C19	A53	5c on ½c org	375.00	375.00
C20	A53	5c on 50c org	1.50	1.25
a.		Double surcharge	60.00	60.00

Issued in commemoration of the centenary of the birth of President Pablo Arosemena.

It is claimed that No. C19 was not regularly issued.

Urracá Monument
AP8

Human Genius Uniting the Oceans
AP9

Designs: 20c, Panama City. 30c, Balboa Monument. 50c, Pedro Miguel Locks. 1b, Palace of Justice.

1936, Dec. 1 Engraved. Perf. 12
C21	AP8	5c blue	1.00	50
C22	AP9	10c yel org	1.25	90
C23	AP9	20c red	3.00	2.00
C24	AP8	30c dk vio	5.00	4.00
C25	AP9	50c car rose	12.50	9.00
C26	AP9	1b black	15.00	10.00
		Nos. C21–C26 (6)	37.75	26.40

Issued to commemorate the 4th Postal Congress of the Americas and Spain.

Nos. C21–C26 Overprinted in Red or Blue

U P U

1937, Mar. 29
C27	AP8	5c bl (R)	60	60
a.		Invert. ovpt.	50.00	
C28	AP9	10c yel org (Bl)	1.00	75
C29	AP9	20c red (Bl)	2.50	2.00
a.		Double ovpt.	50.00	
C30	AP8	30c dk vio (R)	6.00	5.00
C31	AP9	50c car rose (Bl)	25.00	25.00
a.		Double ovpt.	175.00	
C32	AP9	1b blk (R)	30.00	25.00
		Nos. C27–C32 (6)	65.10	58.35

Regular Stamps of 1921–26 Surcharged in Red

CORREO AEREO 5¢

1937, June 30 Perf. 12, 12½
C33	A55	5c on 15c ultra	1.00	1.00
C34	A55	5c on 20c brn	1.00	1.00
C35	A47	5c on 10c vio	2.50	2.00

Regular Stamps of 1920–26 Surcharged in Red

CORREO AEREO 5¢

C36	A56	5c on 24c blk vio	1.00	1.00
C37	A39	5c on 1b dk vio & blk	75	75
C38	A56	10c on 50c blk	3.00	2.50
a.		Inverted surcharge	27.50	

No. 248 Overprinted in Red

CORREO AEREO

Perf. 12½
C39	A54	5c dk bl	1.00	1.00
a.		Double overprint	27.50	
		Nos. C33–C39 (7)	10.25	9.25

Fire Dept. Badge
AP14

Florencio Arosemena
AP15

José Gabriel Duque
AP16

Perf. 14x14½

1937, Nov. 25 Photo. Wmk. 233
C40	AP14	5c blue	75	50
C41	AP15	10c orange	1.00	60
C42	AP16	20c crimson	1.75	75

50th anniversary of the Fire Department.

Basketball
AP17

Baseball
AP18

Designs: 7c, Swimming. 8c, Boxing. 15c, Soccer.

Perf. 14x14½, 14½x14

1938, Feb. 2
C43	AP17	1c rose red	1.75	45
C44	AP17	2c green	1.75	20
C45	AP18	7c gray blk	2.50	50
C46	AP18	8c red brn	2.50	50
C47	AP17	15c ultra	6.00	2.50
a.		Souv. sheet of 5	20.00	20.00
b.		As "a", No. C43 omitted	4,000.	
		Nos. C43–C47 (5)	14.50	4.15

4th Central American Caribbean Games. No. C47a measures 140x140mm. and contains one each of Nos. C43–C47 plus arms and inscriptions.

Cathedral Tower and Statue of Liberty, Flags of Panama and U.S.—AP22

Engraved and Lithographed.

1938, Dec. 7 Perf. 12½ Unwmkd.

Center in Black, Flags in Red and Ultra.
C49	AP22	7c gray	55	45
C50	AP22	8c brt ultra	80	45
C51	AP22	15c red brn	1.00	1.00
C52	AP22	50c orange	12.50	12.50
C53	AP22	1b black	12.50	12.50
		Nos. C49–C53 (5)	27.35	26.90

Issued in commemoration of the 150th anniversary of the Constitution of the United States of America.

PANAMA

Nos. C12 and C7 Surcharged in Red

1938, June 5   Perf. 12½, 12

C53A	AP6	7c on 30c dp vio	60	60
c.	Double surch.		27.50	
d.	Invtd. surch.		35.00	
C53B	AP5	8c on 15c dp grn	60	60
e.	Invtd surch.		35.00	

Opening of the Normal School at Santiago, Veraguas Province, June 5, 1938. The 8c surcharge has no bars.

Belisario Porras AP23

Designs: 2c, William Howard Taft. 5c, Pedro J. Sosa. 10c, Lucien Bonaparte Wise. 15c, Armando Reclus. 20c, Gen. George W. Goethals. 50c, Ferdinand de Lesseps. 1b, Theodore Roosevelt.

1939, Aug. 15   Engraved.

C54	AP23	1c dl rose	50	15
C55	AP23	2c dp bl grn	50	18
C56	AP23	5c indigo	75	30
C57	AP23	10c dk vio	1.00	35
C58	AP23	15c ultra	2.00	50
C59	AP23	20c rose pink	5.00	2.50
C60	AP23	50c dk brn	6.00	1.25
C61	AP23	1b black	10.00	7.00
	Nos. C54-C61 (8)		25.75	12.23

Opening of Panama Canal, 25th anniversary.

Flags of the 21 American Republics—AP31

1940, Apr. 15   Unwmkd.

C62	AP31	15c blue	65	50

Pan American Union, 50th anniversary.

Stamps of 1939-40 Surcharged in Black:

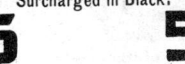

1940, Aug. 12

C63	AP23 (a)	5c on 15c lt ultra	35	35
a.	"7 AEREO 7" on 15c lt ultra (#C58)		60.00	60.00
C64	AP31 (b)	7c on 15c ultra	60	40
C65	AP23 (c)	7c on 20c rose pink	60	40
C66	AP31 (d)	8c on 15c bl	60	40

Stamps of 1924-30 Overprinted in Black or Red:

1941, Jan. 2   Perf. 12½, 12

C67	SD1 (e)	7c on 10c org	1.25	1.25
C68	A53 (f)	15c on 24c yel brn (R)	4.00	3.00
C69	AP5 (g)	20c rose	4.00	3.00
C70	AP6 (g)	50c dp red	9.00	6.00
C71	AP6 (g)	1b blk (R)	20.00	12.50
	Nos. C67-C71 (5)		38.25	25.75

Issued in commemoration of the new constitution of Panama which became effective January 2, 1941.

Liberty AP32 Black Overprint.

1942, Feb. 19   Engraved   Perf. 12

C72	AP32	20c chnt brn	3.00	2.50

Flags of Panama and Costa Rica AP33

Engraved and Lithographed.

1942, Apr. 25   Unwmkd.

C73	AP33	15c dp grn, dk bl & dp rose	85	20

Issued to commemorate the first anniversary of the settlement of the Costa Rica-Panama border dispute.

Swordfish—AP34

J. D. Arosemena Normal School AP35

Alejandro Meléndez G. AP40

Designs: 8c, Gate of Glory, Portobelo. 15c, Taboga Island, Balboa Harbor. 50c, Firehouse. 1b, Gold animal figure.

1942, June 4   Engr.   Perf. 12

C74	AP34	7c rose car	75	25
C75	AP34	8c dk ol brn & blk	25	10
C76	AP34	15c dk vio	40	10
C77	AP35	20c red brn	50	10
C78	AP34	50c ol grn	1.25	60
C79	AP34	1b blk & org yel	3.25	1.75
	Nos. C74-C79 (6)		6.40	2.90

See also Nos. C96-C99, C113 and C126.

1943, Dec. 16

Design: 5b, Ernesto T. Lefevre.

C80	AP40	3b dk ol gray	8.00	8.00
C81	AP40	5b dk bl	12.00	10.00

Nos. C6C and C7 Surcharged in Carmine

AEREO B/. 0.10 1947

1947, Mar. 8   Perf. 12

C82	AP5	5c on 8c gray blk	20	15
a.	Double overprint		40.00	
C83	AP5	10c on 15c dp grn	75	50

Nos. C74 to C76 Surcharged in Black or Carmine

AEREO B/. 0.10 1947

C84	AP34	5c on 7c rose car (Bk)	25	25
a.	Double surch.		500.00	
C85	AP34	5c on 8c dk ol brn & blk	25	25
C86	AP34	10c on 15c dk vio	40	35
a.	Double surch.		15.00	15.00

National Theater AP42

1947, Apr. 7   Engraved   Unwmkd.

C87	AP42	8c violet	60	40

Issued to commemorate the second anniversary of the National Constitutional Assembly of 1945.

Manuel Amador Guerrero AP43

Manuel Espinosa B. AP44

Designs: 5c, José Agustín Arango. 10c, Federico Boyd. 15c, Ricardo Arias. 50c, Carlos Constantino Arosemena. 1b, Nicanor de Obarrio. 2b, Tomas Arias.

Center in Black.

1948, Feb. 11   Perf. 12½

C88	AP43	3c blue	50	35
C89	AP43	5c brown	50	35
C90	AP43	10c orange	50	35
C91	AP43	15c dp cl	50	35
C92	AP44	20c dp car	1.00	75
C93	AP44	50c dk gray	2.00	1.00
C94	AP44	1b green	6.00	5.00
C95	AP44	2b yellow	13.50	10.00
	Nos. C88-C95 (8)		24.50	18.15

Issued to honor members of the Revolutionary Junta of 1903.

Types of 1942.

1948, June 14   Perf. 12

C96	AP34	2c carmine	1.50	15
C97	AP34	15c ol gray	50	20
C98	AP35	20c green	50	25
C99	AP34	50c rose car	8.50	5.00

Franklin D. Roosevelt and Juan D. Arosemena AP45

Four Freedoms AP46

Monument to F. D. Roosevelt AP47

Franklin D. Roosevelt AP49

Map showing Boyd-Roosevelt Trans-Isthmian Highway AP48

1948, Sept. 15   Perf. 12½

C100	AP45	5c dp car & blk	25	20
C101	AP46	10c yel org	45	40
C102	AP47	20c dl grn	50	50
C103	AP48	50c dp ultra & blk	1.25	1.10
C104	AP49	1b gray blk	2.50	2.00
	Nos. C100-C104 (5)		4.95	4.20

Issued in tribute to Franklin Delano Roosevelt (1882-1945).

Monument to Cervantes AP50

PANAMA

Design: 10c, Don Quixote attacking windmill.
1948, Nov. 15

C105	AP50	5c dk bl & blk	25	15
C106	AP50	10c pur & blk	50	40

Issued to commemorate the 400th anniversary of the birth of Miguel de Cervantes Saavedra, novelist, playwright and poet.

No. C106 Overprinted in Carmine
"CENTENARIO DE
JOSE GABRIEL DUQUE"

"18 de Enero de 1949"
1949, Jan.

C107	AP50	10c pur & blk	60	55
a.		Inverted ovpt.	12.00	

Issued to commemorate the centenary of the birth of José Gabriel Duque (1849-1918), newspaper publisher and philanthropist.

Nos. C96, C6A, C97 and C99
Overprinted in Black or Red

1949, May

C108	AP34(h)	2c carmine	25	25
a.		Double ovpt.	7.50	
C109	AP5(i)	5c bl (R)	40	40
C110	AP34(h)	15c ol gray (R)	1.00	1.00
C111	AP34(h)	50c rose car	4.00	4.00

Issued to commemorate the centenary of the incorporation of Chiriqui Province.

Types of 1930-42.
Design: 10c, Gate of Glory, Portobelo.
1949, Aug. 4   Perf. 12

C112	AP5	5c orange	25	12
C113	AP34	10c dk bl & blk	30	20

Stamps of 1943-49 Overprinted or
Surcharged in Black, Green or Red

1949, Sept. 9

C114	AP34	2c carmine	25	25
a.		Inverted ovpt.	20.00	
b.		Double ovpt.	20.00	
C115	AP5	5c org (G)	75	50
a.		Inverted ovpt.	12.00	
b.		Double ovpt.	30.00	
c.		Double ovpt., one inverted	30.00	
C116	AP34	10c dk bl & blk (R)	75	60
C117	AP40	25c on 3b dk ol gray (R)	1.00	1.00
C118	AP34	50c rose car	4.00	3.00
		Nos. C114-C118 (5)	6.75	5.35

Issued to commemorate the 75th anniversary of the formation of the Universal Postal Union.
No. C115 has small overprint, 15½x12mm., like No. 368. Overprint on Nos. C114, C116 and C118 as illustrated. Surcharge on No. C117 is arranged vertically, 29x18mm.

University of San Javier
AP51

1949, Dec. 7   Engraved.   Perf. 12½

C119	AP51	5c dk bl & blk	50	20

See note after No. 371.

Mosquito—AP52
1950, Jan. 12   Perf. 12

C120	AP52	5c dp ultra & gray blk	2.00	1.00

Issued to honor Dr. Carlos J. Finlay.
See note after No. 372.

Nos. C96, C112,
C113 and C9
Overprinted
in Black
or Carmine
(5 or 4 lines)

CENTENARIO
del Gral. José
de San Martín
17 de Agosto
de 1950

1950, Aug. 17   Unwmkd.

C121	AP34	2c carmine	50	40
C122	AP5	5c orange	50	50
C123	AP34	10c dk bl & blk (C)	75	60
C124	AP5	25c dp bl (C)	1.25	1.00

Same on No. 362, Overprinted "AEREO"

C125	A105	50c pur & blk (C)	3.00	2.00
		Nos. C121-C125 (5)	6.00	4.50

Issued to commemorate the centenary of the death of Gen. José de San Martín.

Firehouse Type of 1942.
1950, Oct. 30   Engraved

C126	AP34	50c dp bl	3.00	1.50

Nos. C113 and C81 Surcharged
in Carmine or Orange
AEREO
B/.0.02

X   1952   X
1952, Feb. 20

C127	AP34	2c on 10c dk bl & blk	25	15
a.		Pair, one without surcharge	400.00	
C128	AP34	5c on 10c dk bl & blk (O)	30	12
b.		Pair, one without surcharge	400.00	
C128A	AP40	1b on 5b dk bl	40.00	40.00

The surcharge on No. C128A is arranged to fit stamp, with four bars covering value panel at bottom, instead of crosses.

Nos. 376 and 380
Surcharged "AEREO 1952" and
New Value in Carmine or Black.
1952, Aug. 1

C129	A97	5c on 2c ver & blk (C)	20	12
a.		Inverted surcharge	35.00	
C130	A99	25c on 10c pur & org	1.00	90

Isabella Type of Regular Issue
Engraved
1952, Oct. 20 Perf. 12½ Unwmkd.
Center in Black

C131	A110	4c red org	12	10
C132	A110	5c ol grn	15	10
C133	A110	10c orange	50	45
C134	A110	25c gray bl	80	50
C135	A110	50c chocolate	1.50	90
C136	A110	1b black	5.00	4.75
		Nos. C131-C136 (6)	8.07	6.80

Issued to commemorate the 500th anniversary of the birth of Queen Isabella I of Spain.

No. C113 Surcharged "5 1953"
in Carmine.
1953, Apr. 22   Perf. 12

C137	AP34	5c on 10c dk bl & blk	50	15

Masthead of
La Estrella
AP54
1953, July

C138	AP54	5c rose car	25	20
C139	AP54	10c blue	35	30

Centenary of Panama's first newspaper, La Estrella.

Act of Independence
AP55

Senora de Remon and
Pres. José A. Remon Cantera
AP56

Designs: 7c, Pollera. 25c, National flower. 50c, Marcos A. Salazar, Esteban Huertas and Domingo Diaz A. 1b, Dancers.
1953, Nov.

C140	AP55	2c dp ultra	13	10
C141	AP56	5c dp grn	20	10
C142	AP56	7c gray	30	20
C143	AP56	25c black	2.50	1.00
C144	AP56	50c dk brn	1.50	1.00
C145	AP56	1b red org	4.50	2.00
		Nos. C140-C145 (6)	9.13	4.40

Founding of republic, 50th anniversary.

Nos. C138-C139 Surcharged with New
Value in Black or Red
1953-54

C146	AP54	1c on 5c rose car ('54)	10	6
C147	AP54	1c on 10c bl (R)	10	6

Gen. Herrera at Conference Table
AP57
Design: 1b, Gen. Herrera leading troops.
1954, Dec. 4   Litho.   Perf. 12½

C148	AP57	6c dp grn	20	10
C149	AP57	1b scar & blk	5.00	4.25

Issued to commemorate the centenary of the death of Gen. Tomas Herrera.

Rotary
Emblem
and Map
AP58
1955, Feb. 23

C150	AP58	6c rose vio	20	10
C151	AP58	21c red	75	50
C152	AP58	1b black	6.50	4.00
a.		1b vio blk	8.00	6.50

Issued to commemorate the 50th anniversary of the founding of Rotary International.

Pres. J. A. Remon
Cantera
AP59
1955, June 1

C153	AP59	6c rose vio & blk	25	10

Issued in tribute to Pres. José Antonio Remon Cantera, 1908–1955.

No. C151 Surcharged

B/.xxxxxxxx0.15

1955, Dec. 7

C154	AP58	15c on 21c red	60	50

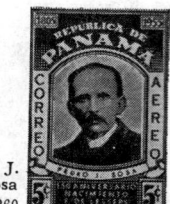

Pedro J.
Sosa
AP60

First Barge
Going
through
Canal and
de Lesseps
AP61

Lithographed.
1955, Nov. 22 Perf. 12½ Unwmkd.

C155	AP60	5c grn, lt grn	25	10
C156	AP61	1b red lil & blk	3.00	2.50

Issued to commemorate the 150th anniversary of the birth of Ferdinand de Lesseps. Imperforates exist.

Pres. Dwight
D. Eisenhower
AP62

Statue
of Bolivar
AP63

PANAMA

Bolivar Hall
AP64

Portraits—Presidents: C158, Pedro Aramburu, Argentina. C159, Dr. Victor Paz Estenssoro, Bolivia. C160, Dr. Juscelino Kubitschek O., Brazil. C161, Gen. Carlos Ibanez del Campo, Chile. C162, Gen. Gustavo Rojas Pinilla, Colombia. C163, Jose Figueres, Costa Rica. C164, Gen. Fulgencio Batista y Zaldivar, Cuba. C165, Gen. Hector B. Trujillo Molina, Dominican Rep. C166, José Maria Velasco Ibarra, Ecuador. C167, Col. Carlos Castillo Armas, Guatemala. C168, Gen. Paul E. Magloire, Haiti. C169, Julio Lozano Diaz, Honduras. C170, Adolfo Ruiz Cortines, Mexico. C171, Gen. Anastasio Somoza, Nicaragua. C172, Ricardo Arias Espinosa, Panama. C173, Gen. Alfredo Stroessner, Paraguay. C174, Gen. Manuel Odria, Peru. C175, Col. Oscar Osorio, El Salvador. C176, Dr. Alberto F. Zubiria, Uruguay. C177, Gen. Marcos Perez Jimenez, Venezuela. 1b, Simon Bolivar.

1956, July 18

C157	AP62	6c rose car & vio bl	1.00	50
C158	AP62	6c brt grnsh bl & blk	40	30
C159	AP62	6c bis & blk	40	30
C160	AP62	6c emer & blk	40	30
C161	AP62	6c lt grn & brn	40	30
C162	AP62	6c yel & grn	40	30
C163	AP62	6c brt vio & grn	40	30
C164	AP62	6c dl pur & vio bl	40	30
C165	AP62	6c red lil & sl grn	40	30
C166	AP62	6c cit & vio bl	40	30
C167	AP62	6c ap grn & brn	40	30
C168	AP62	6c brn & vio bl	40	30
C169	AP62	6c brt car & grn	40	30
C170	AP62	6c red & brn	40	30
C171	AP62	6c lt bl & grn	40	30
C172	AP62	6c blk & grn	40	30
C173	AP62	6c org & blk	40	30
C174	AP62	6c bluish gray & brn	40	30
C175	AP62	6c sal rose & blk	40	30
C176	AP62	6c dk grn & vio bl	40	30
C177	AP62	6c dk org brn & dk grn	40	30
C178	AP63	20c dk bluish gray	1.00	75
C179	AP64	50c green	1.50	1.50
C180	AP63	1b brown	4.00	2.50
		Nos. C157-C180 (24)	15.50	11.25

Issued to commemorate the Pan-American Conference, Panama City, July 21–22, 1956, and the 130th anniversary of the first Pan-American Conference. Imperforates exist.

Ruins of First Town Council Building
AP65

Design: 50c, City Hall, Panama City.

1956, Aug. 14

C181	AP65	25c red	75	50
C182	AP65	50c black	1.50	1.35
	a.	Souvenir sheet of 3	3.50	3.50

Issued to commemorate the sixth Inter-American Congress of Municipalities, Panama City, Aug. 14–19, 1956.
No. C182a contains one each of Nos. 404, C181–C182, imperf., with inscription in gold border. The sheet measures 125x76mm. and sold for 85c.

Monument
AP66

St. Thomas Hospital
AP67

1956, Nov. 27 Wmk. 311

C183	AP66	5c green	15	8
C184	AP67	15c dk car	40	30

Issued to commemorate the centenary of the birth of Pres. Belisario Porras.

Highway Construction
AP68

Designs: 20c, Road through jungle, Darien project. 1b, Map of Americas showing Pan-American Highway.

Lithographed.
1957, Aug. 1 *Perf. 12½* Wmk. 311

C185	AP68	10c black	30	18
C186	AP68	20c lt bl & blk	1.00	50
C187	AP68	1b green	4.25	3.75
	a.	AP65 Souvenir sheet of 3, unwmkd.	10.00	10.00

Nos. C185–C187a were issued to publicize the 7th Pan-American Highway Congress.
No. C187a is No. C182a overprinted in black: "VII° CONGRESSO INTERAMERICANO DE CARRETERAS 1957."

No. C153 Surcharged "1957" and New Value.

1957, Aug. 13 Unwmkd.

C188	AP59	10c on 6c rose vio & blk	30	25

Remon Polyclinic
AP69

Customs House, Portobelo
AP70

Buildings: C191, Portobelo Castle. C192, San Jeronimo Castle. C193, Remon Hippodrome. C194, Legislature. C195, Interior and Treasury Department. C196, El Panama Hotel. C197, San Lorenzo Castle.

Lithographed.
1957, Oct. *Perf. 12½* Wmk. 311

Design in Black.

C189	AP69	10c lt bl	35	18
C190	AP70	10c lilac	35	18
C191	AP70	10c gray	35	18
C192	AP70	10c lil rose	35	18
C193	AP70	10c ultra	35	18
C194	AP70	10c brn ol	35	18
C195	AP70	10c org yel	35	18
C196	AP70	10c yel grn	35	18
C197	AP70	1b red	3.75	2.75
		Nos. C189-C197 (9)	6.55	4.19

No. C148 Surcharged with New Value and "1958" in Red

1958, Feb. 11 Unwmkd.

C198	AP57	5c on 6c dp grn	30	10

United Nations Emblem
AP71

Flags of Panama and U.N.
AP72

1958, March 5 Litho. Wmk. 311

C199	AP71	10c brt grn	30	15
C200	AP71	21c lt ultra	60	50
C201	AP71	1b lt ultra	1.25	1.00
C202	AP72	1b gray, ultra & car	4.00	3.75
	a.	Souvenir sheet of 4	9.00	9.00

Issued to commemorate the tenth anniversary of the United Nations (in 1955).
No. C202a measures 127x102mm. and contains one each of Nos. C199–C202, imperf. Marginal inscription in carmine and ultramarine. The sheet also exists with the 10c and 50c omitted.

OAS Type of Regular Issue, 1958.
Designs: 10c, 1b, Flags of 21 American Nations. 50c, Headquarters in Washington.

1958, July 10 *Perf. 12½* Unwmkd.
Center yellow and black; flags in national colors.

C203	A124	5c lt bl	18	12
C204	A124	10c car rose	30	18
C205	A124	50c gray	1.00	1.00
C206	A124	1b black	3.25	3.00

Issued to commemorate the 10th anniversary of the Organization of American States.

Type of Regular Issue.
Pavilions: 15c, Vatican City. 50c, United States. 1b, Belgium.

1958, Sept. 8 *Perf. 12½* Wmk. 311

C207	A125	15c gray & lt vio	50	45
C208	A125	50c dk gray & org brn	1.25	1.25
C209	A125	1b brt vio & bluish grn	2.50	2.50
	a.	Souv. sheet of 7	6.00	6.00

World's Fair, Brussels, Apr. 17–Oct. 19.
No. C209a contains one each of Nos. 418–421 and C207–C209 with marginal inscription and fair emblem in slate and light brown. Size: 128½x102mm. Sold for 2b.

Pope Type of Regular Issue
Portraits of Pius XII: 5c, As cardinal. 30c, Wearing papal tiara. 50c, Enthroned.

1959, Jan. 21 Litho. Wmk. 311

C210	A126	5c violet	20	18
C211	A126	30c lil rose	90	75
C212	A126	50c bl gray	1.50	1.35
	a.	Souvenir sheet of 4	3.00	3.00

Issued in memory of Pope Pius XII, 1876–1958.
No. C212a measures 127x85½mm. and contains one each of Nos. C210–C212 and No. 422, imperf, and watermarked sideways. Marginal inscriptions and ornaments in colors of stamps. Sold for 1b. The sheet also exists with 30c omitted. No. C212a with C.E.P.A.L. overprint is listed as No. C221a.

Human Rights Issue
Type of Regular Issue, 1959.
Designs: 5c, Humanity looking into sun. 10c, 20c, Torch and U. N. emblem. 50c, U. N. Flag. 1b, U. N. Headquarters building.

1959, Apr. 14 *Perf. 12½*

C213	A127	5c emer & bl	15	12
C214	A127	10c gray & org brn	25	15
C215	A127	20c brn & gray	50	45
C216	A127	50c grn & ultra	1.35	1.25
C217	A127	1b red & bl	2.50	2.50
		Nos. C213-C217 (5)	4.75	4.47

Issued to commemorate the 10th anniversary (in 1958) of the signing of the Universal Declaration of Human Rights.

Nos. C213–C215, C212a Overprinted and C216 Surcharged in Red or Dark Blue

```
8a REUNION
C.E.P.A.L.
MAYO 1959
```

1959, May 16

C218	A127	5c emer & bl (R)	15	12
C219	A127	10c gray & org brn (Bl)	35	20
C220	A127	20c brn & gray (R)	65	50
C221	A127	1b on 50c grn & ultra (R)	3.50	3.00
	a.	Souvenir sheet of 4	7.00	7.00

Issued to commemorate the 8th Reunion of the Economic Commission for Latin America.
This overprint also exists on Nos. C216–C217. These have been disavowed by Panama's postmaster general.
No. C221a is No. C212a with two-line black overprint at top of sheet: "8a. REUNION DE LA C.E.P.A.L. MAYO 1959."

Type of Regular Issue, 1959.
Portraits: 5c, Justo A. Facio, Rector. 10c, Ernesto de la Guardia, Jr., Pres. of Panama.

Lithographed.
1959, July 27 *Perf. 12½* Wmk. 311

C222	A128	5c black	12	10
C223	A128	10c black	25	12

Issued to publicize the 50th anniversary of the National Institute.

Type of Regular Issue, 1959.
Designs: 5c, Boxing. 10c, Baseball. 50c, Basketball.

1959, Oct. 26 *Perf. 12½* Wmk. 311

C224	A130	5c blk & red brn	18	15
C225	A130	10c gray & red brn	35	25
C226	A130	50c lt ultra & org	1.35	1.25

Issued to commemorate the 3rd Pan American Games, Chicago, Aug. 27–Sept. 7, 1959.

Nos. C143–C145 Overprinted in Vermilion, Red or Black

```
NACIONES UNIDAS
AÑO MUNDIAL.
REFUGIADOS.
1959–1960
```

Engraved.
1960, Feb. 6 *Perf. 12* Unwmkd.

C227	AP56	5c blk (V)	50	50
C228	AP56	50c dk brn (R)	1.00	1.00
C229	AP56	1b red org	2.65	2.50

Issued to publicize World Refugee Year, July 1, 1959–June 30, 1960.
The revenues from the sale of Nos. C227–C229 went to the United Nations Refugee Fund.

PANAMA

Administration Building,
National University
AP74

Designs: 21c, Humanities building. 25c, Medical school. 30c, Dr. Octavio Mendez Pereria first rector of University.

Perf. 12½

1960, Mar. 23 Litho. Wmk. 311

C230	AP74	10c brt grn	20	15
C231	AP74	21c lt bl	45	30
C232	AP74	25c ultra	65	50
C233	AP74	30c black	75	55

Issued to commemorate the 25th anniversary of the founding of the National University.

Olympic Games Issue
Type of Regular Issue, 1960

Designs: 5c, Basketball. 10c, Bicycling (horiz.). 25c, Javelin thrower. 50c, Athlete with Olympic torch.

Wmkd. RP Multiple (343).

1960, Sept. 22 Perf. 12½

C234	A131	5c org & red	12	10
C235	A131	10c ocher & blk	30	20
C236	A131	25c lt bl & dk bl	65	55
C237	A131	50c brn & blk	1.35	1.10
a.		Souvenir sheet of 2	3.50	3.50

Issued to commemorate the 17th Olympic Games, Rome, Aug. 25–Sept. 11. No. C237a contains one each of Nos. C236–C237, imperf., blue margin with black inscription. Size: 126x76mm.

Citizens' Silhouettes
AP75

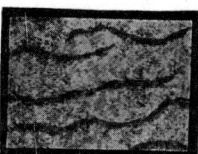

Wmkd. Wavy Lines (229)

Design: 10c, Heads and map of Central America.

1960 Lithographed

| C238 | AP75 | 5c black | 10 | 10 |
| C239 | AP75 | 10c brown | 25 | 20 |

Issued to publicize the 6th census of population and the 2nd census of dwellings (No. C238), Dec. 11, 1960, and the All America Census, 1960 (No. C239).

Boeing 707 Jet Liner
AP76

1960, Dec. 1 Perf. 12½ Wmk. 343

C240	AP76	5c lt grnsh bl	15	10
C241	AP76	10c emerald	25	20
C242	AP76	20c red brn	60	40

Souvenir Sheet

U.N. Emblem—AP77

Lithographed

1961, March 7 Imperf. Wmk. 311

| C243 | AP77 | 80c blk & car rose | 2.25 | 2.25 |

Issued to commemorate the 15th anniversary (in 1960) of the United Nations. No. C243 measures 63x76mm. with carmine rose marginal ornaments and black inscription and control number.

No. C243 Overprinted in Blue with Large Uprooted Oak Emblem and "Ano de los Refugiados."

1961, June 2

| C244 | AP77 | 80c blk & car rose | 5.00 | 5.00 |

Issued to commemorate World Refugee Year, July 1, 1959–June 30, 1960.

Lions International Issue
Type of Regular Issue, 1961.

Designs: 5c, Helen Keller School for the Blind. 10c, Children's summer camp. 21c, Arms of Panama and Lions emblem.

1961, May 2 Perf. 12½ Wmk. 311

C245	A133	5c black	12	10
C246	A133	10c emerald	30	12
C247	A133	21c ultra, yel & red	55	40

Issued to commemorate the 25th anniversary of the Lions Club of Panama.

HABILITADA
en
B/.0.01

Nos. C230 and C236 Surcharged in Black or Red

1961 Wmk. 311 (1c); Wmk. 343

C248	AP74	1c on 10c brt grn	15	10
C249	A131	1b on 25c lt bl & dk bl (Bk)	2.50	2.25
C250	A131	1b on 25c lt bl & dk bl (R)	2.50	2.25

Pres. Roberto F. Chiari
and Pres. Mario Echandi
AP78

Lithographed

1961, Oct. 2 Perf. 12½ Wmk. 343

| C251 | AP78 | 1b blk & gold | 2.25 | 2.25 |

Issued to commemorate the meeting of the Presidents of Panama and Costa Rica at Paso Canoa, Apr. 21, 1961.

Dag Hammarskjold
AP79

1961, Dec. 27 Perf. 12½

| C252 | AP79 | 10c black | 30 | 20 |

Issued in memory of Dag Hammarskjold, Secretary General of the United Nations, 1953–61.

No. C230 Surcharged

Vale B/. 0.15

1962, Feb. 21 Wmk. 311

| C253 | AP74 | 15c on 10c brt grn | 45 | 30 |

XX

No. C236 Surcharged

VALE B/. 1.00

Wmk. 343

| C254 | A131 | 1b on 25c lt bl & dk bl | 2.25 | 2.00 |

City Hall,
Colon
AP80

1962, Feb. 28 Litho. Wmk. 311

| C255 | AP80 | 5c vio bl & blk | 25 | 15 |

Issued to publicize the third Central American Municipal Assembly, Colon, May 13–17.

Church Type of Regular Issue, 1962.

Designs: 5c, Church of Christ the King. 7c, Church of San Miguel. 8c, Church of the Sanctuary. 10c, Saints Church. 15c, Church of St. Ann. 21c, Canal Zone Synagogue (Now used as USO Center). 25c, Panama Synagogue. 30c, Church of St. Francis. 50c, Protestant Church, Canal Zone. 1b, Catholic Church, Canal Zone.

Lithographed

1962–64 Perf. 12½ Wmk. 343

Buildings in Black

C256	A138	5c pur & buff	10	10
C257	A138	7c lil rose & brt pink	18	15
C258	A139	8c pur & bl	20	15
C259	A139	10c lil & sal	25	15
C259A	A139	10c grn & dl red brn ('64)	30	30
C260	A139	15c red & buff	35	30
C261	A138	21c brn & bl	50	45
C262	A138	25c bl & pink	60	50
C263	A139	30c lil rose & bl	70	65
C264	A138	50c lil & lt grn	1.10	1.00
a.		Souvenir sheet of 4	3.00	3.00
C265	A139	1b bl & sal	2.25	2.00
		Nos. C256–C265 (11)	6.53	5.75

Issued to publicize freedom of religion in Panama. Issue dates: No. C259A, June 4, 1964; others, July 20, 1962. No. C264a contains one each of Nos. 448–449 and C262 and C264 imperf. with black marginal inscription. Size: 133x107 mm.

Nos. C234 and C236 Overprinted and Surcharged "IX JUEGOS C.A. Y DEL CARIBE KINGSTON-1962" and Games Emblem in Black, Green, Orange or Red.

1962 Perf. 12½ Wmk. 343

C266	A131	5c org & red	20	18
C267	A131	10c on 25c lt bl & dk bl (G)	35	30
C268	A131	15c on 25c lt bl & dk bl (O)	55	50
C269	A131	20c on 25c lt bl & dk bl (R)	65	60
C270	A131	25c lt bl & dk bl	80	70
		Nos. C266–C270 (5)	2.55	2.28

Issued to commemorate the Ninth Central American and Caribbean Games, Kingston, Jamaica, Aug. 11–25.

VALE

Nos. CB1–CB2
Surcharged

.20 ¢

XX

1962, May 3 Wmk. 311

| C271 | SPAP1 | 10c on 5c + 5c car rose | 1.75 | 1.25 |
| C272 | SPAP1 | 20c on 10c + 10c vio bl | 2.75 | 1.25 |

Type of Regular Issue, 1962.

Design: 10c, Canal bridge completed.

Lithographed

1962, Oct. 12 Perf. 12½ Wmk. 343

| C273 | A140 | 10c bl & blk | 25 | 20 |

See note after No. 451.

John H. Glenn,
"Friendship 7"
Capsule
AP81

UPAE
Emblem
AP82

Designs: 10c, "Friendship 7" capsule and globe (horiz.). 31c, Capsule in space (horiz.). 50c, Glenn with space helmet.

1962, Oct. 19 Perf. 12½ Wmk. 311

C274	AP81	5c rose red	15	15
C275	AP81	10c yellow	30	25
C276	AP81	31c blue	1.25	90
C277	AP81	50c emerald	1.50	1.25
a.		Souvenir sheet of 4	3.50	3.50

Issued to commemorate the first orbital flight of U.S. astronaut Lt. Col. John H. Glenn, Jr., Feb. 20, 1962. No. C277a contains one each of Nos. C274–C277, imperf. Green background with rose red inscription and black control number. Sold for 1b. Size: 76x100mm.

1963, Jan. 8 Litho. Wmk. 343

| C278 | AP82 | 10c multi | 25 | 15 |

Issued to commemorate the 50th anniversary of the founding of the Postal Union of the Americas and Spain, UPAE.

Type of Regular Issue

Designs: 10c, Fire Engine "China", Plaza de Santa Ana. 15c, 14th Street team. 21c, Fire Brigade emblem.

1963, Jan. 22 Perf. 12½ Wmk. 311

C279	A141	10c org & blk	25	20
C280	A141	15c lil & blk	30	25
C281	A141	21c gold, red & ultra	70	65

See note after No. 454.

PANAMA

"FAO" and Wheat Emblem
AP83

1963, Mar. 21 Lithographed
C282 AP83 10c grn & red 30 25
C283 AP83 15c ultra & red 40 35
Issued for the "Freedom from Hunger" campaign of the U.N. Food and Agriculture Organization.

No. C245 Overprinted in Yellow, Orange or Green:
"XXII Convención/Leonística/Centroamericana/Panamá, 18–21/Abril 1963"
1963, Apr. 18 Perf. 12½ Wmk. 311
C284 A133 5c blk (Y) 15 12
C285 A133 5c blk (O) 15 12
C286 A133 5c blk (G) 15 12
Issued to commemorate the 22nd Central American Lions Congress, Panama, April 18–21.

HABILITADO
No. C230 Surcharged:
Vale B/.0.04
1963, June 11
C287 AP74 4c on 10c brt grn 12 6

Nos. 445 and 432 Overprinted "AEREO" Vertically
1963 Perf. 12½ Wmk. 343
C288 A139 10c grn, yel & blk 25 20

Wmk. 311
C289 A130 20c emer & red brn 45 35

No. C234 Overprinted: "LIBERTAD DE PRENSA 20-VIII-63"
1963, Aug. 20 Wmk. 343
C290 A131 5c org & red 15 12
Freedom of Press Day, Aug. 20, 1963.

No. C232 Surcharged in Red: "VALE 10¢"
1963, Oct. 9 Perf. 12½ Wmk. 311
C291 AP74 10c on 25c ultra 25 20

Type of Regular Issue, 1963
Flags and Presidents: 5c, Julio A. Rivera, El Salvador. 10c, Miguel Ydígoras, Guatemala. 21c, John F. Kennedy, USA.
Perf. 12½x12
1963, Dec. 18 Litho. Unwmkd.
Portrait in Slate Green.
C292 A142 5c yel, red & ultra 45 45
C293 A142 10c bl, red & ultra 75 60
C294 A142 21c org yel, red & ultra 2.25 2.00

See note after No. 463.

Balboa Type of Regular Issue, 1964
1964, Jan. 22 Photo. Perf. 13
C295 A143 10c dk vio, pale pink 30 25

See note after No. 464.

No. C261 Surcharged in Red: "VALE B/.0.50"
Lithographed
1964 Perf. 12½ Wmk. 343
C296 A138 50c on 21c brn, bl & blk 1.50 1.10

Type of 1962 Overprinted: "HABILITADA"
C297 A139 1b emer, yel & blk 2.75 2.50

Nos. 434 and 444 Surcharged: "Aéreo B/.0.10"
1964 Perf. 12½ Wmk. 343
C298 A131 10c on 5c bl grn & emer 30 20
C299 A139 10c on 5c rose, lt grn & blk 30 20

St. Patrick's Cathedral, New York
AP84

Cathedrals: 21c, St. Stephen's, Vienna. No. C302, St. Sofia's, Sofia. C303, Notre Dame, Paris. No. C304, Cologne. C305, St. Paul's. No. C306, Metropolitan, Athens. C307, St. Elizabeth's, Kosice, Czechoslovakia (inscr. Kassa, Hungary). No. C308, New Delhi. C309, Milan. C310, Guadalupe Basilica. C311, New Church, Delft, Netherlands. C312, Lima. C313, St. John's, Prague. C314, Lisbon. C315, St. Basil's, Moscow. C316, Toledo. C317, Stockholm. C318, Basel. C319, St. George's Patriarchal Church, Istanbul. 1b, Panama City. 2b, St. Peter's Basilica, Rome.

Engraved
1964, Feb. 17 Perf. 12 Unwmkd.
Center in Black
C300 AP84 21c olive 75 50
C301 AP84 21c chocolate 75 50
C302 AP84 21c aqua 75 50
C303 AP84 21c red brn 75 50
C304 AP84 21c magenta 75 50
C305 AP84 21c red 75 50
C306 AP84 21c org red 75 50
C307 AP84 21c blue 75 50
C308 AP84 21c brown 75 50
C309 AP84 21c green 75 50
C310 AP84 21c vio bl 75 50
C311 AP84 21c dk sl grn 75 50
C312 AP84 21c violet 75 50
C313 AP84 21c black 75 50
C314 AP84 21c emerald 75 50
C315 AP84 21c dp vio 75 50
C316 AP84 21c ol grn 75 50
C317 AP84 21c car rose 75 50
C318 AP84 21c Prus grn 75 50
C319 AP84 21c dk brn 75 50
C320 AP84 1b dk bl 3.00 1.50
C321 AP84 2b yel grn 6.00 3.00
  a. Souv. sheet of 6 12.50 12.50
Nos. C300-C321 (22) 24.00 14.50

Issued to commemorate Vatican II, the 21st Ecumenical Council of the Roman Catholic Church.
No. C321a contains 6 imperf. stamps similar to Nos. C300, C303, C305, C315, C320 and C321. Black marginal inscription and red control number. Size: 198x138mm. Sold for 3.85b.
Six stamps of this set (Nos. C300, C305, C309, C319, C321a) were overprinted "1964." The overprint is olive bister on the stamps, yellow on the souvenir sheet. The overprint is reported to exist also in yellow gold on the same six stamps and in olive bister on the souvenir sheet.

Roosevelt Type of Regular Issue
Perf. 12x12½
1964, Oct. 9 Litho. Unwmkd.
C345 A147 20c grn & blk, buff 70 60
  a. Souv. sheet of 1 imperf. 1.10 1.10
Issued to honor Eleanor Roosevelt (1884–1962). No. C345a contains two imperf. stamps similar to Nos. 478 and C345. Lilac margin with white inscription and red control number. Size: 87x76mm.

Bird Type of Regular Issue, 1965.
Song Birds: 5c, Common troupial (horiz.). 10c, Crimson-backed tanager (horiz.).
1965, Oct. 27 Perf. 14 Unwmkd.
C346 A148 5c dp org & multi 12 10
C347 A148 10c brt bl & multi 25 18

Fish Type of Regular Issue
Designs: 8c, Shrimp. 12c, Hammerhead. 13c, Atlantic sailfish. 25c, Seahorse (vert.).
1965, Dec. 7 Lithographed
C348 A149 8c multi 25 18
C349 A149 12c multi 38 30
C350 A149 13c multi 40 33
C351 A149 25c multi 75 60

English Daisy and Emblem
AP85

Designs (Junior Chamber of Commerce Emblem and): No. C353, Hibiscus. No. C354, Orchid. No. C355, Water lily. No. C356, Gladiolus. No. C357, Flor del Espíritu Santo.

1966, Mar. 16
C352 AP85 30c brt pink & multi 75 60
C353 AP85 30c sal & multi 75 60
C354 AP85 30c pale yel & multi 75 60
C355 AP85 40c lt grn & multi 1.25 75
C356 AP85 40c bl & multi 1.25 75
C357 AP85 40c pink & multi 1.25 75
Nos. C352-C357 (6) 6.00 4.05

Issued to commemorate the 50th anniversary of the Junior Chamber of Commerce.

Nos. C224 and C236 Surcharged
1966, June 27 Perf. 12½ Wmk. 311
C358 A130 3c on 5c blk & red brn 12 10

Wmk. 343
C359 A131 13c on 25c lt & dk bl 45 35

The old denominations are not obliterated on Nos. C358–C359.

Animal Type of Regular Issue, 1967
Domestic Animals: 10c, Pekingese dog. 13c, Zebu (horiz.). 30c, Cat. 40c, Horse (horiz.).
1967, Feb. 3 Perf. 14 Unwmkd.
C360 A150 10c multi 32 25
C361 A150 13c multi 40 32
C362 A150 30c multi 85 70
C363 A150 40c multi 1.10 85

Young Hare, by Dürer
AP86

Designs: 10c, St. Jerome and the Lion, by Albrecht Dürer. 20c, Lady with the Ermine, by Leonardo Da Vinci. 30c, The Hunt, by Delacroix (horiz.).
1967, Sept. 1
C364 AP86 10c blk, buff & car 30 20
C365 AP86 13c lt yel & multi 40 25

C366 AP86 20c multi 60 35
C367 AP86 30c multi 90 60

Games Type of Regular Issue and

San Blas Indian Girl
AP87

Design: 13c, Thatcher Ferry bridge.
1970, Jan. 6 Litho. Perf. 13½
C368 A158 13c multi 40 25
C369 AP87 30c multi 85 65

See notes after No. 525.

Juan D. Arosemena and Arosemena Stadium
AP88

Designs: 2c, 3c, 5c, like 1c. No. C374, Basketball. No. C375, New Panama Gymnasium. No. C376, Revolution Stadium. No. C377, Panamanian man and woman in Stadium. 30c, Stadium, eternal flame, arms of Mexico, Puerto Rico and Cuba.

Wmkd. Argentine Arms & 'RA' (365)
1970, Oct. 5 Perf. 13½
C370 AP88 1c pink & multi 5 5
C371 AP88 2c pink & multi 5 5
C372 AP88 3c pink & multi 6 5
C373 AP88 5c pink & multi 10 7
C374 AP88 13c lt bl & multi 26 20
C375 AP88 13c lil & multi 26 20
C376 AP88 13c yel & multi 26 20
C377 AP88 13c grn & multi 26 20
C378 AP88 30c yel & multi 60 45
  a. Souvenir sheet 75 75
Nos. C370-C378 (9) 1.90 1.47
Issued to commemorate the 11th Central American and Caribbean Games, Feb. 28–Mar. 14. No. C378a contains one imperf. stamp similar to No. C378. Bright pink margin with black commemorative inscription and control number. Size: 85x75mm.

Astronaut on Moon
AP89

EXPO '70 Emblem and Pavilion
AP90

Design: No. C380, U.S. astronauts Charles Conrad, Jr., Richard F. Gordon, Jr. and Alan L. Bean.
1971 Perf. 13½ Wmk. 343
C379 AP89 13c gold & multi 50 30
C380 AP89 13c grn & multi 50 30

Man's first landing on the moon, Apollo 11, July 20, 1969 (No. C379) and Apollo 12 moon mission, Nov. 14–24, 1969.
Issue date: No. C379, Aug. 20; No. C380, Aug. 23.

1971, Aug. 24 Lithographed
C381 AP90 10c pink & multi 20 20
EXPO '70 International Exposition, Osaka, Japan, Mar. 15–Sept. 13.

PANAMA

Flag of Panama
AP91

Design: 13c, Map of Panama superimposed on Western Hemisphere, and tourist year emblem.

1971, Dec. 11   Wmk. 343

| C382 | AP91 | 5c multi | 15 | 10 |
| C383 | AP91 | 13c multi | 40 | 25 |

Proclamation of 1972 as Tourist Year of the Americas.

Mahatma Gandhi
AP92

1971, Dec. 17

| C384 | AP92 | 10c blk & multi | 30 | 20 |

Centenary of the birth of Mohandas K. Gandhi (1869–1948), leader in India's fight for independence.

Central American Independence Issue

Flags of Central American States
AP92a

1971, Dec. 20

| C385 | AP92a | 13c multi | 40 | 25 |

Panama No. 4
AP93

1971, Dec. 21

| C386 | AP93 | 8c red, dk bl & blk | 25 | 12 |

2nd National Philatelic and Numismatic Exposition, 1970.

Natá Church
AP94

1972, Sept. 7   Wmk. 365

| C387 | AP94 | 40c lt bl & multi | 1.10 | 60 |

450th anniversary of the founding of Natá.

Telecommunications Emblem
AP95

1972, Sept. 8

| C388 | AP95 | 13c lt bl, dp bl & blk | 26 | 20 |

3rd World Telecommunications Day (in 1971).

Apollo 14
AP96

1972, Sept. 11

| C389 | AP96 | 13c tan & multi | 85 | 35 |

Apollo 14 U.S. moon mission, Jan. 1–Feb. 9, 1971.

Shoeshine Boy Counting Coins
AP97

1972, Sept. 12

Multicolored

C390	AP97	5c shown	10	7
C391	AP97	8c Mother & Child	16	10
C392	AP97	50c UNICEF emblem	1.00	60
a.		Souvenir sheet	1.75	1.75

25th anniversary (in 1971) of the United Nations International Children's Fund (UNICEF). No. C392a contains one imperf. stamp similar to No. C392. Black marginal inscription and control number. Size: 85x75mm.

San Blas Cloth, Cuna Indians
AP98

1972, Sept. 13

Multicolored

C393	AP98	5c shown	15	10
C394	AP98	8c Beaded necklace, Guaymi Indians	25	12
C395	AP98	25c View of Portobelo	75	40
a.		Souv. sheet of 2	1.25	1.25

Tourist publicity. No. C395a contains 2 imperf. stamps similar to Nos. C393 and C395. Black marginal inscription and control number. Size: 96x128mm.

Baseball and Games' Emblem
AP99

Designs (Games' Emblem and): 10c, Basketball (vert.). 13c, Torch (vert.). 25c, Boxing. 50c, Map and flag of Panama, Bolivar. 1b, Medals.

Perf. 12½

1973, Feb. 9   Litho.   Unwmkd.

C396	AP99	8c rose red & yel	20	12
C397	AP99	10c blk & ultra	25	15
C398	AP99	13c bl & multi	40	25
C399	AP99	25c blk, yel grn & red	75	38
C400	AP99	50c grn & multi	1.75	75
C401	AP99	1b multi	3.50	1.50
		Nos. C396-401 (6)	6.85	3.15

7th Bolivar Games, Panama City, Feb. 17–March 3.

No. C387 Surcharged in Red Similar to No. 542.

1973, Mar. 16   Perf. 13½   Wmk. 365

| C402 | AP94 | 13c on 40c multi | 35 | 20 |

U.N. Security Council Meeting, Panama City, Mar. 15–21.

Portrait Type of Regular Issue 1973

Designs: 5c, Isabel Herrera Obaldia, educator. 8c, Nicolas Victoria Jaén, educator. 10c, Forest Scene, by Roberto Lewis. No. C406, Portrait of a Lady, by Manuel E. Amador. No. C407, Ricardo Miró, poet. 20c, Portrait, by Isaac Benitez. 21c, Manuel Amador Guerrero, statesman. 25c, Belisario Porras, statesman. 30c, Juan Demostenes Arosemena, statesman. 34c, Octavio Mendez Pereira, writer. 38c, Ricardo J. Alfaro, writer.

1973, June 20   Litho.   *Perf. 13½*

C403	A169	5c pink & multi	15	10
C404	A169	8c pink & multi	25	15
C405	A169	10c gray & multi	30	20
C406	A169	13c pink & multi	50	25
C407	A169	13c pink & multi	50	25
C408	A169	20c bl & multi	75	30
C409	A169	21c yel & multi	75	35
C410	A169	25c pink & multi	75	40
C411	A169	30c gray & multi	1.00	50
C412	A169	34c lt bl & multi	1.25	60
C413	A169	38c lt bl & multi	1.50	70
		Nos. C403-C413 (11)	7.70	3.80

Famous Panamanians.

Nos. C403, C410, and C412 Overprinted in Black or Red

1923
1973

Bodas de Oro
Escuela Profesional
Isabel Herrera Obaldía

1973, Sept. 14   Litho.   *Perf. 13½*

C414	A169	5c pink & multi	20	10
C415	A169	25c pink & multi	75	40
C416	A169	34c bl & multi (R)	1.25	75

50th anniversary of the Isabel Herrera Obaldia Professional School.

Nos. C395, C408, C413, C412 and C409 Surcharged in Red

VALE 8¢

1974, Nov. 11   Litho.   *Perf. 13½*

C417	AP98	1c on 25c multi	5	5
C418	A169	3c on 20c multi	6	5
C419	A169	8c on 38c multi	16	10
C420	A169	10c on 34c multi	20	15
C421	A169	13c on 21c multi	26	20
		Nos. C417-C421 (5)	73	55

Women's Hands, Panama Map, UN and IWY Emblems
AP100

Victoria Sugar Plant, Sugar Cane, Map of Veraguas Province
AP101

Unwmkd.

1975, May 6   Litho.   *Perf. 12½*

| C422 | AP100 | 17c bl & multi | 60 | 25 |
| a. | | Souvenir sheet | 1.00 | 1.00 |

International Women's Year 1975. No. C422a contains one typographed imperf. stamp similar to No. C422; black marginal inscription with IWY emblem. Without gum. Size: 88x76mm.

1975, Oct. 9   Litho.   *Perf. 12½*

Designs: 17c, Bayano electrification project and map of Panama (horiz.). 33c, Tocumen International Airport and map (horiz.).

C423	AP101	17c bl, buff & blk	50	20
C424	AP101	27c ultra & yel grn	75	35
C425	AP101	33c bl & multi	1.00	40

7th anniversary of the Oct. 11, 1968, Revolution.

Bolivar Statue and Flags
AP102

Bolivar Hall, Panama City
AP103

Design: 41c, Bolivar with flag of Panama, ruins of Old Panama City.

1976, Mar.

C426	AP102	23c multi	46	30
C427	AP103	35c multi	70	42
C428	AP102	41c multi	82	55

150th anniversary of Congress of Panama.
Issue dates: 23c, Mar. 15; others Mar. 30.

Marine Life Type of 1976

Designs: 17c, Diodon hystrix (vert.). 27c, Pocillopora damicornis.

Perf. 13x12½, 12½x13

1976, May 6   Litho.   Wmk. 377

| C429 | A171 | 17c multi | 34 | 20 |
| C430 | A171 | 27c multi | 54 | 35 |

Marine life.

PANAMA

Cerro Colorado AP104
1976, Nov. 12 Litho. *Perf. 12½*
C431 AP104 23c multi   46 30
Cerro Colorado copper mines, Chiriqui Province.

Genl. Omar Torrijos Herrera (1929-1981)—AP105

1982, Feb. Litho. *Perf. 10½*
C432 AP105 23c multi   50 32

Herrera Type of 1982
Wmk. 311
1982, May 14 Litho. *Perf. 10½*
C433 A201 35c Security Council reunion, 1973   70 42
C434 A201 41c Torrijos Airport   82 48

Souvenir Sheet
Imperf.
C435 A201 23c like #C432   2.00 1.50

No. C435 has blue margin; black control number. Size: 86x75mm. Sold for 1b.

Alfaro Type of 1982
Photos by Luiz Gutierrez Cruz.
1982, Aug. 18 Wmk. 381
C436 A202 17c multi   34 20
C437 A202 23c multi   45 28

World Cup Type of 1982
Wmk. 381 "Panama" and Design
1982 Litho. *Perf. 10½*
C438 A203 23c Map   45 28
C439 A203 35c Pele, vert.   70 42
C440 A203 41c Cup, vert.   82 48

1b imperf. souvenir sheet exists in design of 23c; black control number. Size; 85x75mm.

Nicolas A. Solano (1882-1943), Tuberculosis Researcher—AP106

1983, Feb. 8 Wmk. 382 (Stars) Litho. *Perf. 10½*
C441 AP106 23c brown   50 30

AIR POST SEMI-POSTAL STAMPS

"The World Against Malaria" SPAP1

Lithographed
1961, Dec. 20 *Perf. 12½* Wmk. 311
CB1 SPAP1 5c + 5c car rose   1.25 85
CB2 SPAP1 10c + 10c vio bl   1.25 85
CB3 SPAP1 15c + 15c dk grn   1.25 85

Issued to support the World Health Organization's drive to eradicate malaria.

SPECIAL DELIVERY STAMPS.

Nos. 211-212 Overprinted in Red **EXPRESO**

1926 *Perf. 12* Unwmkd.
E1 A31 10c org & blk   7.00 3.00
    a. "EXPRESO"   40.00
E2 A32 20c brn & blk   9.00 3.00
    a. "EXPESO"   40.00
    b. Double overprint   35.00 35.00

Bicycle Messenger SD1
1929 Engraved *Perf. 12½*
E3 SD1 10c orange   1.50 1.00
E4 SD1 20c dk brn   3.00 1.50

REGISTRATION STAMPS.
Issued under Colombian Dominion.

R1

Engraved
1888 *Perf. 13½* Unwmkd.
F1 R1 10c gray   12.50 8.00

Imperforate and part-perforate copies without gum and those on surface-colored paper are reprints.

R2
Magenta, Violet or Blue Black Handstamped Overprint
1898 *Perf. 12*
F2 R2 10c yellow   9.00 8.00
The handstamp on No. F2 was also used as a postmark.

R3

1900 Lithographed. *Perf. 11.*
F3 R3 10c lt bl   5.00 4.50
1901
F4 R3 10c brn red   40.00 37.50

R4

1902 Blue Black Surcharge.
F5 R4 20c on 10c brn red   30.00 27.50

Issues of the Republic.
Issued in the City of Panama.
Registration Stamps of Colombia Handstamped:

R9

Handstamped in Blue **REPUBLICA DE PANAMA**
Black or Rose
a
1903-04 *Imperf.*
F6 R9 20c red brn, bl   50.00 50.00
F7 R9 20c bl, bl (R)   50.00 50.00

Reprints exist of Nos. F6 and F7; see note after No. 64.

With Additional Surcharge in Rose **10.**
F8 R9 10c on 20c red brn, bl   70.00 70.00
    b. "10" in bl blk   70.00 70.00
F9 R9 10c on 20c bl, bl   70.00 70.00

Handstamped in Rose **Panamá**

.10
F10 R9 10c on 20c red brn, bl   70.00 70.00
F11 R9 10c on 20c bl, bl   50.00 50.00

Issued in Colon.
Regular Issues Handstamped "R/COLON" in Circle (as on F2) Together with Other Overprints and Surcharges.

Handstamped **REPUBLICA DE PANAMA**

1903-04 *Perf. 12*
F12 A4 10c yellow   3.00 3.00

Handstamped **PANAMA**
F13 A4 10c yellow   25.00

Overprinted in Red **PANAMA** **PANAMA**
                      c   *d*
F14 A4 10c yellow   3.00 3.00

Overprinted in Black **República de Panamá.**
                          g
F15 A4 10c yellow   7.00 7.00

The handstamps on Nos. F12 to F15 are in magenta, violet or red; various combinations of these colors are to be found. They are struck in various positions, including double, inverted, one handstamp omitted, etc.

Colombia No. F13 Handstamped Type "e" In Violet
Imperf.
F16 R9 20c red brn, bl   70.00 70.00

Overprinted Type "g" in Black
F17 R9 20c red brn, bl   7.00 7.00

No. F17 Surcharged in Manuscript
F18 R9 10c on 20c red brn, bl   70.00 70.00

No. F17 Surcharged in Purple **10**
F19 R9 10c on 20c red brn, bl   100.00 100.00

No. F17 Surcharged in Violet **10**
F20 R9 10c on 20c red brn, bl   100.00 100.00

The varieties of the overprint type "g" which are described after No. 138 are also to be found on the Registration and Acknowledgment of Receipt stamps. It is probable that Nos. F17 to F20 inclusive owe their existence more to speculation than to postal necessity.

Issued in Bocas del Toro.
Colombia Nos. F17 and F13 Handstamped in Violet
R DE PANAMA
k
1903-04
F21 R9 20c bl, bl   150.00 150.00
F22 R9 20c red brn, bl   150.00 150.00

No. F21 Surcharged in Manuscript in Violet or Red
F23 R9 10c on 20c bl, bl   175.00 175.00

Colombia Nos. 13, 17 Handstamped in Violet **Panama**
l

Surcharged in Manuscript (a) "10"
(b) "10cs" in Red
F25 R9 10 on 20c red brn, bl   80.00 80.00
F26 R9 10cs on 20c bl, bl   60.00 60.00

No. F25 without surcharge is bogus, according to leading experts.

General Issue.

R5

1904 Engraved *Perf. 12*
F27 R5 10c green   1.00 75

Nos. 190 and 213 Surcharged in Red **R 5 cts.**

1916-17
F29 A11 5c on 8c pur & blk   3.00 3.00
    a. "5" inverted   75.00
    b. Large, round "5"   10.00
    c. Inverted surcharge   15.00 15.00
    d. Tête bêche surcharge

PANAMA

F30 A33 5c on 8c vio & blk
('17) 3.50 1.25
a. Inverted surcharge 11.00 11.00
b. Tête bêche surcharge
c. Double surcharge 50.00
Stamps similar to No. F30, overprinted in green were unauthorized.

INSURED LETTER STAMPS.
Stamps of 1939 Surcharged in Black

0 05   0 05

SEGURO POSTAL

HABILITADO

1942	Perf. 12½		Unwmkd.
G1	AP23	5c on 1b blk	60 50
G2	A84	10c on 1b dk brn	1.00 75
G3	AP23	25c on 50c dk brn	2.50 1.25

ACKNOWLEDGMENT OF RECEIPT STAMPS.
Issued under Colombian Dominion.

Experts consider this handstamp—"A.R. / COLON / COLOMBIA"—to be a cancellation or a marking intended for a letter to receive special handling. It was applied at Colon to various stamps in 1897–1904 in different colored inks for philatelic sale. It exists on cover, usually with the bottom line removed by masking the handstamp.

Nos. 17–18 Handstamped in Rose

1902
H4 A4 5c blue 7.50 7.50
H5 A4 10c yellow 15.00 15.00
This handstamp was also used as a postmark.

Issues of the Republic.
Issued in the City of Panama.
Colombia No. H3 Handstamped.

Handstamped in Rose   REPUBLICA DE PANAMA
                           a

1903–04 *Imperf.* Unwmkd.
H9 AR2 10c bl, *bl* 11.00 11.00
Reprints exist of No. H9, see note after No. 64.

No. H9 Surcharged with New Value.

H10 AR2 5c on 10c bl, *bl* 4.00 4.00

Colombia No. H3 Handstamped in Rose   Panamá
                                          n

H11 AR2 10c bl, *bl* 20.00 20.00

Issued in Colon.
Handstamped in Magenta or Violet   REPUBLICA DE PANAMA
Imperf.
H17 AR2 10c bl, *bl* 15.00 15.00

Handstamped   PANAMA
H18 AR2 10c bl, *bl* 100.00 100.00

Overprinted in Black   *República de Panamá.*
H19 AR2 10c bl, *bl* 11.00 11.00

No. H19 Surcharged in Manuscript
H20 AR2 10c on 5c on 10c bl, *bl* 125.00 125.00

Issued in Bocas del Toro.
Colombia No. H3 Handstamped in Violet   Panama
                                           l
and Surcharged in Manuscript in Red

1904
H21 AR2 5c on 10c bl, *bl*
No. H21 without surcharge is bogus.

General Issue

AR3

1904 *Engraved.* *Perf. 12.*
H22 AR3 5c blue 1.25 1.25

No. 199 Overprinted in Violet   A. R.

1916
H23 A20 2½c red org 1.25 1.25
a. "R.A." for "A.R." 65.00
b. Double ovpt. 11.00
c. Inverted ovpt. 11.00

LATE FEE STAMPS.
Issues of the Republic.
Issued in the City of Panama.
Colombia No. I4 Handstamped in Rose or Blue Black

LF3   REPUBLICA DE PANAMA
         a

1903–04 *Imperf.* Unwmkd.
I1 LF3 5c pur, *rose* 11.00 11.00
I2 LF3 5c pur, *rose* (Bl Blk) 15.00 15.00
Reprints exist of Nos. I1 and I2; see note after No. 64.

General Issue.

LF4

1904 *Engraved.* *Perf. 12.*
I3 LF4 2½c lake 1.00 1.00

No. 199 Overprinted with Typewriter   Retardo

1910, Aug. 12
I4 A20 2½c red org 150.00 150.00
Used only on Aug. 12–13.

Handstamped

1910
I5 A20 2½c red org 75.00 75.00

No. 195 Surcharged in Green   RETARDO
                                UN CENTÉSIMO

1917
I6 A17 1c on ½c org 1.00 1.00
a. "UN CENTESIMO" inverted 65.00
b. Double surcharge 15.00
c. Inverted surcharge 9.00 9.00

Same Surcharge on No. 196.
1921
I7 A17 1c on ½c rose 30.00 30.00

POSTAGE DUE STAMPS.

San Geronimo Castle Gate, Portobelo
D1

Statue of Columbus   Pedro J. Sosa
D2   D4

Design: 4c, Capitol, Panama City.

Engraved
1915 *Perf. 12* Unwmkd.
J1 D1 1c ol brn 2.25 40
J2 D2 2c ol brn 3.00 35
J3 D1 4c ol brn 4.00 75
J4 D4 10c ol brn 3.00 1.00
Type D1 was intended to show a gate of San Lorenzo Castle, Chagres, and is so inscribed.

Numeral of Value
D5

1930 *Perf. 12½*
J5 D5 1c emerald 1.00 35
J6 D5 2c dk red 1.00 30
J7 D5 4c dk bl 1.50 40
J8 D5 10c violet 1.50 60

PANAMA

POSTAL TAX STAMPS.

Pierre and Marie Curie
PT1
Engraved.

1939		Perf. 12.		Unwmkd.	
RA1	PT1	1c rose car		75	20
RA2	PT1	1c green		75	20
RA3	PT1	1c orange		75	20
RA4	PT1	1c blue		75	20

See also Nos. RA6–RA18, RA24–RA27, RA30.

Stamp of 1924
Overprinted in Black

1940				
RA5	A53	1c dk grn	2.00	1.50

1941		Inscribed 1940.		
RA6	PT1	1c rose car	60	15
RA7	PT1	1c green	60	15
RA8	PT1	1c orange	60	15
RA9	PT1	1c blue	60	15

1942		Inscribed 1942.		
RA10	PT1	1c violet	60	20

1943		Inscribed 1943.		
RA11	PT1	1c rose car	60	20
RA12	PT1	1c green	60	20
RA13	PT1	1c orange	60	20
RA14	PT1	1c blue	60	20

1945		Inscribed: 1945.		
RA15	PT1	1c rose car	60	25
RA16	PT1	1c green	60	25
RA17	PT1	1c orange	60	25
RA18	PT1	1c blue	60	25

Nos. 234 and 235
Surcharged
in Black or Red

CANCER
B/. 0.01
1947

1946		Perf. 12		Unwmkd.	
RA19	A53	1c on ½c org		75	20
RA20	A53	1c on 1c dk grn (R)		75	20

Same Surcharged in Black
on Nos. 239 and 241.

1947				
RA21	A53	1c on 12c ol grn	60	20
RA22	A53	1c on 24c yel brn	60	20

Surcharged in Red on No. 342.

RA23	A95	1c on ½c dl vio, bl & car	60	15

Type of 1939.
Inscribed: 1947.

1947				
RA24	PT1	1c rose car	60	10
RA25	PT1	1c green	60	10
RA26	PT1	1c orange	60	10
RA27	PT1	1c blue	60	10

Nos. C100 and C101 Surcharged in Black

a

b

1949		Perf. 12½		Unwmkd.	
RA28	AP45	(a) 1c on 5c dp car & blk		50	12
a.		Inverted surcharge		15.00	
RA29	AP46	(b) 1c on 10c yel org		50	12

Type of 1939 Inscribed "1949"

1949		Perf. 12		
RA30	PT1	1c brown		60	10

The tax from the sale of Nos. RA1–RA30 was used for the control of cancer.

Stadium—PT2

Torch Emblem   Discobolus
PT3   PT4

Design: No. RA33, Stadium, different view.
Engraved.

1951		Perf. 12½		Unwmkd.	
RA31	PT2	1c car & blk		1.00	25
RA32	PT3	1c dk bl & blk		1.00	25
RA33	PT2	1c grn & blk		1.00	25

1952
Design: No. RA34, Turners' emblem.

RA34	PT3	1c org & blk	1.00	25
RA35	PT4	1c pur & blk	2.50	25

The tax from the sale of Nos. RA31–RA35 was used to promote physical education.

Boys Doing Farm Work—PT5
Lithographed.

1958		Perf. 12½		Wmk. 311	
		Size: 35x24mm.			
RA36	PT5	1c rose red & gray		20	8

Type of 1958 Inscribed "1959"
1959		Size: 35x24mm.		
RA37	PT5	1c gray & emer	12	8
RA38	PT5	1c vio bl & gray	12	8

Type of 1958 Inscribed "1960"

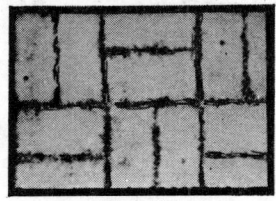

Wmk. 334

1960		Wmkd. Rectangles (334)	Perf. 13½	
		Size: 32x23mm.		
RA39	PT5	1c car & gray	12	10

Nos. C235
and C241
Surcharged
in Black
or Red

1 ¢

"Rehabilitación
de Menores"

1961		Perf. 12½	Wmk. 343	
RA40	A131	1c on 10c ocher & blk	15	10
RA41	AP76	1c on 10c emer (R)	15	10
a.		Invtd. surch.		

Girl at
Sewing
Machine
PT6

Wmkd. RP Multiple (343).

1961, Nov. 24		Litho.	Perf. 12½	
RA42	PT6	1c brt vio	10	7
RA43	PT6	1c rose lil	10	7
RA44	PT6	1c yellow	10	7
RA45	PT6	1c blue	10	7
RA46	PT6	1c emerald	10	7
		Nos. RA42–RA46 (5)	50	35

1961, Dec. 1
Design: Boy with hand saw.

RA47	PT6	1c red lil	10	7
RA48	PT6	1c rose	10	7
RA49	PT6	1c orange	10	7
RA50	PT6	1c blue	10	7
RA51	PT6	1c gray	10	7
		Nos. RA47–RA51 (5)	50	35

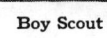

Boy Scout   Map of
PT7   Panama, Flags
                 PT8

Designs: Nos. RA57–RA61, Girl Scout.
Perf. 12½

1964, Feb. 7		Litho.	Wmk. 343	
RA52	PT7	1c olive	10	5
RA53	PT7	1c gray	10	5
RA54	PT7	1c lilac	10	5
RA55	PT7	1c car rose	10	5
RA56	PT7	1c blue	10	5
RA57	PT7	1c bluish grn	10	5
RA58	PT7	1c violet	10	5
RA59	PT7	1c orange	10	5

RA60	PT7	1c yellow	10	5
RA61	PT7	1c brn org	10	5
		Nos. RA52–RA61 (10)	1.00	50

The tax from Nos. RA36–RA61 was for youth rehabilitation.

Perf. 12½
1973, Jan. 22		Litho.	Unwmkd.	
RA62	PT8	1c black	5	5

7th Bolivar Sports Games, Feb. 17–Mar. 3, 1973. The tax was for a new post office in Panama City.

Farm Cooperative
PT9

Designs: No. RA64, 5b silver coin. No. RA65, Victoriano Lorenzo. No. RA66, RA69, Cacique Urraca. No. RA67–RA68, RA70, Post Office.

1973–75				
RA63	PT9	1c brt yel grn & ver	10	6
RA64	PT9	1c gray & red	10	6
RA65	PT9	1c ocher & red	10	6
RA66	PT9	1c org & red	10	6
RA67	PT9	1c bl & red	10	6
RA68	PT9	1c blk ('74)	10	6
RA69	PT9	1c org ('74)	10	6
RA70	PT9	1c ver ('75)	15	6
		Nos. RA63–RA70 (8)	85	48

The tax was for a new post office in Panama City.

Stamps of 1969–1973
Surcharged in Violet,
Blue, Yellow, Black
or Carmine

VALE 1¢
PRO EDIFICIO

Perf. 14½x15, 15x14½, 13½
Lithographed

1975		Unwmkd., Wmk. 343, 365		
		Multicolored		
RA75	A168	1c on 1c (#538; VB)	10	8
RA76	A168	1c on 2c (#539; Y)	10	8
RA77	A164	1c on 30c (#534; B)	10	8
RA78	A157	1c on 30c (#511; B)	10	8
RA79	A156	1c on 40c (#514; B)	10	8
RA80	A156	1c on 50c (#515; B)	10	8
RA81	A169	1c on 20c (#C408; C)	5	5
RA82	A169	1c on 25c (#C410; B)	10	8
RA83	AP98	1c on 25c (#C395; B)	10	8
RA84	A169	1c on 30c (#C411; B)	10	8
RA85	AP94	1c on 40c (#C387; C)	10	88
		Nos. RA75–RA85 (11)	1.10	

The tax was for a new post office in Panama City. Surcharge vertical, reading down on No. RA75 and up on Nos. RA76, RA78 and RA83. Nos. RA75–RA85 were obligatory on all mail.

PT10   PT11

1980, Dec. 3		Litho.	Perf. 12	
RA86	PT10	2c Boys	5	5
RA87	PT10	2c Boy and chicks	5	5
RA88	PT10	2c Working in fields	5	5
RA89	PT10	2c Boys feeding piglet	5	5
a.		Souvenir sheet of 4	2.00	

Tax was for Children's Village (Christmas 1980). Nos. RA86–RA89 se-tenant and were obligatory on all mail. No. RA89a contains Nos. RA86–RA89; black marginal inscription and control number. Size: 155x170mm. Sold for 1b.

1981, Nov. 1		Litho.	Perf. 12	
RA90	PT11	2c Boy, pony	5	5
RA91	PT11	2c Nativity	5	5
RA92	PT11	2c Tree	5	5
RA93	PT11	2c Church	5	5

Souvenir Sheet
RA94		Sheet of 4	10.00	
a–d.		PT11 2c, Children's drawings		

Tax was for Children's Village. Nos. RA90–RA93 se-tenant and were obligatory on all mail. No. RA94 has black marginal inscription and control number. Size: 131x140mm. Sold for 5b.

PT12

1982, Nov. 1   Litho.   *Perf. 13½x12½*
RA95	PT12	2c Carpentry	5	5
RA96	PT12	2c Beekeeping	5	5
RA97	PT12	2c Pig farming, vert.	5	5
RA98	PT12	2c Gardening, vert.	5	5

Tax was for Children's Village (Christmas 1982). Nos. RA95-RA96 and RA97-RA98 se-tenant and were obligatory on all mail.

Children's Drawings—PT13

1983, Nov. 1   Litho.   *Perf. 14½*
RA99	PT13	2c Annunciation	5	5
RA100	PT13	2c Bethlehem and Star	5	5
RA101	PT13	2c Church and Houses	5	5
RA102	PT13	2c Flight into Egypt	5	5

2 undenominated souvenir sheets exist showing designs of Nos. RA99, RA101 and Nos. RA100, RA102 respectively.

PARAGUAY

(păr'à·gwä ; pä'rä·gwī')

LOCATION — In South America, bounded by Bolivia, Brazil and Argentina.
GOVT. — Republic.
AREA. — 157,042 sq. mi.
POP. — 2,800,000 (1977).
CAPITAL — Asunción.

10 Reales = 100 Centavos = 1 Peso
100 Céntimos = 1 Guarani (1944)

Prices of early Paraguay stamps vary according to condition. Quotations for Nos. 1-9 are for fine copies. Very fine to superb specimens sell at much higher prices, and inferior or poor copies sell at reduced prices, depending on the condition of the individual specimen.

Vigilant Lion Supporting Liberty Cap
A1   A2

A3
Lithographed.

1870, Aug. 1		Imperf.	Unwmkd.	
1	A1	1r rose	6.00	6.00
2	A2	2r blue	70.00	70.00
3	A3	3r black	120.00	120.00

Unofficial reprints of 2r in blue and other colors are on thicker paper than originals. They show a colored dot in upper part of "S" of "DOS" in upper right corner.

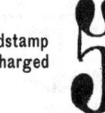

Handstamp Surcharged

1878		Black Surcharge.		
4	A1	5c on 1r rose	60.00	60.00
5	A2	5c on 2r bl	200.00	175.00
5E	A3	5c on 3r blk	350.00	300.00
		Blue Surcharge.		
5F	A1	5c on 1r rose	60.00	60.00
5H	A2	5c on 2r bl	700.00	700.00
6	A3	5c on 3r blk	200.00	200.00

The surcharge may be found inverted, double, sideways and omitted.

The originals are surcharged in dull black or dull blue. The reprints are in intense black and bright blue. The reprint surcharges are over-inked and show numerous breaks in the handstamp.

Handstamp Surcharged

		Black Surcharge.		
7	A2	5c on 2r bl	350.00	250.00
8	A3	5c on 3r blk	275.00	225.00
		Blue Surcharge.		
9	A3	5c on 3r blk	150.00	150.00
a.	Double surcharge, large and small "5"		800.00	800.00

The surcharge on Nos. 7, 8 and 9 is usually placed sideways. It may be found double or inverted on Nos. 8 and 9.
Nos. 4 to 9 have been extensively counterfeited.

A4   A4a

1879		Lithographed.	Perf. 12½.	
		Thin Paper		
10	A4	5r orange	75	
11	A4	10r red brn	90	
a.	Imperf.			
b.	Imperf. vert., pair		20.00	

Nos. 10 and 11 were never placed in use.

1879-81		**Thin Paper**		
12	A4a	5c org brn	1.75	1.75
13	A4a	10c bl grn ('81)	2.50	2.50

Reprints of Nos. 10-13 are imperf., perf. 11½, 12, 12½ or 14. They have yellowish gum and the 10c is deep green.

A5

A6   A7
Lithographed

1881, Aug.			Perf. 11½-13½	
14	A5	1c blue	90	75
a.	Imperf., pair		3.50	3.50
15	A6	2c rose red	90	75
a.	2c dl org red		90	75
b.	Imperf., pair		3.50	3.50
c.	Horiz. or vert. pair, imperf. between		3.00	3.00
16	A7	4c brown	90	75
a.	Imperf., pair		3.50	3.50
b.	Horiz. or vert. pair, imperf. between		3.00	3.00

A8   A9
Handstamped in Black or Gray.

1881, July			Perf. 12½	
17	A8	1c on 10c bl grn	10.00	10.00
18	A9	2c on 10c bl grn	10.00	10.00

A10
Handstamped.

1884, May 8			Imperf.	
19	A10	1c on 1r rose	4.00	3.50

The surcharges on Nos. 17-19 exist double, inverted and in pairs with one omitted. Counterfeits exist.

Seal of the Treasury
A11   A12

1884, Aug. 3 Litho.			Perf. 11½, 12½	
20	A11	1c green	50	35
a.	Imperf., pair		2.00	
21	A11	2c rose red	50	35
a.	Imperf., pair		3.50	
22	A11	5c blue	50	35
a.	Imperf., pair		7.50	

Shades exist.

Perf. 11½, 11½x12, 12½x11½.
1887		**Typographed.**		
23	A12	1c green	25	12
24	A12	2c rose	25	15
25	A12	5c blue	40	25
26	A12	7c brown	85	60
27	A12	10c lilac	60	35
28	A12	15c orange	60	35
29	A12	20c pink	60	35
	Nos. 23-29 (7)		3.55	2.17

See also Nos. 42-45.

Symbols of Liberty from Coat of Arms   Pres. Cándido Bareiro
A13   A14

1889, Feb.		Litho.	Perf. 11½	
30	A13	15c red vio	2.50	2.50
a.	Imperf., pair		10.00	10.00

Oval Overprint Handstamped in Violet.

1892, Oct. 12			Perf. 12x12½	
31	A14	10c vio bl	9.00	4.00

Discovery of America by Columbus, 400th anniversary. Overprint reads: "1492 / 12 DE OCTUBRE / 1892." Sold only on day of issue.

Cirilo A. Rivarola   Salvador Jovellanos
A15   A16

Juan B. Gil   Higinio Uriarte
A17   A18

Cándido Bareiro   Gen. Bernardino Caballero
A19   A20

Gen. Patricio Escobar   Juan G. González
A21   A22

1892-96		Litho.	Perf. 12x12½	
32	A15	1c gray (centavos)	20	10
33	A15	1c gray (centavo) ('96)	20	12
34	A16	2c green	20	10
a.	Chalky paper ('96)		20	12
35	A17	4c carmine	20	10
a.	Chalky paper ('96)		25	15
36	A18	5c vio ('93)	25	10
a.	Chalky paper ('96)		20	15
37	A19	10c vio bl (punched) ('93)	35	30
	Unpunched ('96)		7.00	2.00
38	A19	10c dl bl ('96)	30	25
39	A20	14c yel brn	85	75
40	A21	20c red ('93)	1.25	75
41	A22	30c lt grn	1.75	1.25
	Nos. 32-41 (10)		5.55	3.82

The 10c violet blue (No. 37) was, until 1896, issued punched with a circular hole in order to prevent it being fraudulently overprinted as No. 31.
Nos. 33 and 38 are on chalky paper.

Seal Type of 1887.
1892		**Typographed.**		
42	A12	40c sl bl	3.50	1.75
43	A12	60c yellow	1.50	75
44	A12	80c lt bl	1.25	75
45	A12	1p ol grn	1.25	75

A23   A24

1895, Aug. 1			Perf. 11½x12	
46	A23	5c on 7c brn	50	30

Telegraph Stamps Surcharged
1896, Apr.		Engraved	Perf. 11½	
		Denomination in Black		
47	A24	5c on 2c brn & gray	75	50
a.	Inverted surcharge		20.00	20.00
48	A24	5c on 4c yel & gray	75	50
a.	Inverted surcharge		15.00	15.00

Provisorio
Nos. 28, 42   **10**
Surcharged   **Centavos**

1898-99			**Typographed**	
49	A12	10c on 15c org ('99)	90	70
a.	Inverted surcharge		27.50	27.50
b.	Double surcharge		17.50	17.50
50	A12	10c on 40c sl bl	40	30

Surcharge on No. 49 has small "c."

Telegraph Stamps Surcharged
1900, May 14		Engr.	Perf. 11½	
50A	A24	5c on 30c grn, gray & blk	2.50	1.75
50B	A24	10c on 50c dl vio, gray & blk	6.00	4.00

The basic telegraph stamps are like those used for Nos. 47-48, but the surcharges on Nos. 50A-50B consist of "5 5" and "10 10" above a blackout rectangle covering the engraved denominations.
A 40c red, bluish gray and black telegraph stamp (basic type of A24) was used provisionally in August, 1900, for postage. Price, postally used, $10.

PARAGUAY

Seal of the Treasury
A25
Perf. 11½, 12

1900, Sept.   Engraved
51	A25	2c gray	20	15
52	A25	3c org brn	25	18
53	A25	5c dk grn	25	18
54	A25	8c dk brn	30	20
55	A25	10c car rose	30	20
56	A25	24c dp bl	60	30
	Nos. 51-56 (6)		1.90	1.21

Small Figures.
1901, Apr.   Litho.   *Perf. 11½*
57	A25	2c rose	30	18
58	A25	5c vio brn	30	20
59	A25	40c blue	1.25	45

1901-02   Larger Figures.
60	A25	1c gray grn ('02)	20	12
61	A25	2c gray	20	15
a.	Half used as 1c on cover			75
62	A25	4c pale bl	20	15
63	A25	5c violet	30	18
64	A25	8c gray brn ('02)	25	20
65	A25	10c rose red ('02)	35	20
66	A25	28c org ('02)	60	35
67	A25	40c blue	60	30
	Nos. 60-67 (8)		2.70	1.65

J. B. Egusquiza
A26   A27

Chalky Paper
1901. Sept. 24   Typo.   *Perf. 12x12½*
| 68 | A26 | 1p slate | 60 | 40 |

1902, Aug.   Red Surcharge.
| 69 | A27 | 20c on 24c dp bl | 50 | 30 |
| a. | Inverted surcharge | | 12.50 | |

A27a   A28

Black Surcharge.
1902, Dec. 22   *Perf. 12x12½*
70	A27a	1c on 14c yel brn	35	20
a.	No period after "cent"		1.75	1.50
b.	Comma after "cent"		1.25	1.00
c.	Accent over "Un"		1.25	1.00

1903   *Perf. 11½*
| 71 | A28 | 5c on 60c yel | 50 | 30 |
| 72 | A28 | 5c on 80c lt bl | 35 | 20 |

A29

A30   A31

1902-03   *Perf. 12*
| 73 | A29 | 1c on 1p sl ('03) | 25 | 18 |
| a. | No period after "cent" | | 3.25 | 3.00 |

Perf. 11½.
74	A30	5c on 8c gray brn	50	30
a.	No period after "cent"		1.75	1.50
b.	Double surcharge		7.00	6.00
76	A31	5c on 28c org	50	35
a.	No period after "cent"		1.75	1.50
b.	Comma after "cent"		75	60

The surcharge on Nos. 73 and 74 is found reading both upward and downward.

Sentinel Lion with Right Paw Ready to Strike for "Peace and Justice"
A32   A33

Perf. 11½
1903, Feb. 28   Litho.   Unwmkd.
77	A32	1c gray	30	20
78	A32	2c bl grn	35	25
79	A32	5c blue	50	20
80	A32	10c org brn	60	25
81	A32	20c carmine	60	30
82	A32	30c dp bl	75	30
83	A32	60c purple	2.00	1.25
	Nos. 77-83 (7)		5.10	2.75

1903, Sept.
84	A33	1c yel grn	25	15
85	A33	2c red org	25	15
86	A33	5c dk bl	30	20
87	A33	10c purple	40	25
88	A33	20c dk grn	1.25	60
89	A33	30c ultra	1.50	40
90	A33	60c ocher	1.50	1.00
	Nos. 84-90 (7)		5.45	2.75

Nos. 84–90 exist imperf. Price for pairs, $6 each for 1c-20c, $8 for 30c, $10 for 60c.
The three-line overprint "Gobierno provisorio Ago. 1904" is fraudulent.

Sentinel Lion at Rest
A35   A36
Perf. 11½, 12, 11½x12.

1905-10   Dated "1904"   Engr.
91	A35	1c orange	25	10
92	A35	1c ver ('07)	25	10
93	A35	1c grnsh bl ('06)	25	15
94	A35	2c ver ('06)	25	15
95	A35	2c ol grn ('07)	50.00	
96	A35	2c car rose ('08)	25	15
97	A35	5c dk bl	25	15
98	A35	5c sl bl ('06)	25	15
99	A35	5c yel ('06)	25	15
100	A35	10c bis ('06)	25	15
101	A35	10c emer ('07)	25	15
102	A35	10c dp ultra ('08)	25	15
103	A35	20c vio ('06)	60	40
104	A35	20c bis ('07)	60	40
105	A35	20c ap grn ('07)	60	25
106	A35	30c turq bl ('06)	60	25
107	A35	30c bl gray ('07)	60	25
108	A35	30c dl lil ('08)	75	35
109	A35	60c choc ('07)	50	30
110	A35	60c org brn ('07)	6.00	2.50
111	A35	60c sal pink ('10)	6.00	2.50
	Nos. 91-94, 96-111 (20)		18.90	8.70

All but Nos. 92 and 104 exist imperf. Price for pair, $6 each, except No. 95 at $35 and Nos. 109–111 at $15 each pair.

1904, Aug.   Litho.   *Perf. 11½*
| 112 | A36 | 10c blue | 50 | 30 |
| a. | Imperf., pair | | 6.00 | |

No. 112 Surcharged in Black

1904, Dec.
| 113 | A36 | 30c on 10c bl | 75 | 50 |

Issued to celebrate peace between a successful revolutionary party and the government previously in power.

Governmental Palace, Asunción
A37
Dated "1904"

1906-10   Engr.   *Perf. 11½, 12*
Center in Black
114	A37	1p brt rose	2.50	1.50
115	A37	1p brn org ('07)	1.00	50
116	A37	1p ol gray ('07)	1.00	50
117	A37	2p turq ('07)	50	35
118	A37	2p lake ('09)	50	40
119	A37	2p brn org ('10)	60	40
120	A37	5p red ('07)	1.50	1.00
121	A37	5p ol grn ('10)	1.50	1.00
122	A37	5p dl bl ('10)	1.50	1.00
123	A37	10p brn org ('07)	1.40	1.00
124	A37	10p dp bl ('10)	1.40	1.00
125	A37	10p choc ('10)	1.50	1.00
126	A37	20p org ('07)	3.50	3.25
127	A37	20p vio ('10)	3.50	3.25
128	A37	20p yel ('10)	3.50	3.25
	Nos. 114-128 (15)		25.40	19.40

Habilitado en 5 CENTAVOS
Nos. 94 and 95 Surcharged

1907
129	A35	5c on 2c ver	40	30
a.	"5" omitted		2.00	2.00
b.	Inverted surcharge		2.50	2.50
c.	Double surcharge			
d.	Double surcharge, one inverted		2.00	2.00
e.	Double surcharge, both inverted		12.00	12.00
130	A35	5c on 2c ol grn	50	30
a.	"5" omitted		2.00	2.00
b.	Inverted surcharge		2.00	2.00
c.	Double surcharge		4.00	4.00
d.	Bar omitted		4.00	4.00

Habilitado en 5 CENTAVOS
Official Stamps of 1906-08 Surcharged

1908
131	O17	5c on 10c bis	35	25
a.	Double surcharge		6.00	6.00
132	O17	5c on 10c vio	35	25
a.	Inverted surcharge		3.00	3.00
133	O17	5c on 20c emer	35	25
134	O17	5c on 20c vio	35	25
a.	Inverted surcharge		3.00	3.00
135	O17	5c on 30c sl bl	1.00	1.00
136	O17	5c on 30c turq bl	1.00	1.00
a.	Inverted surcharge			
b.	Double surcharge		6.00	6.00
137	O17	5c on 60c choc	25	20
a.	Double surcharge		12.00	12.00
138	O17	5c on 60c red brn	40	25
a.	Inverted surcharge		75	75
	Nos. 131-138 (8)		4.05	3.45

Same Surcharge on Official Stamps of 1903.
139	A32	5c on 30c dp bl	2.50	2.25
140	A32	5c on 60c pur	1.00	60
a.	Double surcharge		5.00	5.00

Habilitado
Official Stamps of 1906-08 Overprinted
141	O17	5c dp bl	40	25
a.	Inverted overprint		3.00	3.00
b.	Bar omitted		9.00	9.00
c.	Double overprint		4.00	4.00
142	O17	5c sl bl	50	40
a.	Inverted overprint		2.50	2.50
b.	Double overprint		3.50	3.50
c.	Bar omitted		9.00	9.00
143	O17	5c grnsh bl	30	20
a.	Inverted overprint		2.50	2.50
b.	Bar omitted		7.50	7.50
144	O18	1p brn org & blk	50	45
a.	Double overprint		2.00	2.00
b.	Double overprint, one inverted		2.50	2.50
c.	Triple overprint, two inverted		4.25	4.25
145	O17	1p brt rose & blk	85	70
a.	Bar omitted			
	Nos. 141-145 (5)		2.55	2.00

Habilitado en 5 CENTAVOS
Regular Issues of 1906-08 Surcharged

1908
146	A35	5c on 1c grnsh bl	15	15
a.	Inverted surcharge		1.00	1.00
b.	Double surcharge		1.50	1.50
c.	"5" omitted		3.00	3.00
147	A35	5c on 2c car rose	15	10
a.	Inverted surcharge		1.00	1.00
b.	"5" omitted		2.50	2.50
c.	Double surcharge		1.50	1.50
d.	Double surcharge, one inverted			
148	A35	5c on 60c org brn	25	15
a.	Inverted surcharge		1.50	1.50
b.	"5" omitted		2.00	2.00
149	A35	5c on 60c sal pink	25	20
a.	Double surcharge		1.00	1.00
b.	Double surcharge, one inverted		7.00	7.00
150	A35	5c on 60c choc	20	15
a.	Inverted surcharge		2.50	2.50
151	A35	20c on 1c grnsh bl	25	20
a.	Inverted surcharge			
152	A35	20c on 2c ver	10.00	10.00
153	A35	20c on 2c car rose	6.00	6.00
a.	Inverted surch.		25.00	
154	A35	20c on 30c dl lil	40	35
a.	Inverted surcharge			
b.	Double surcharge			
155	A35	20c on 30c turq bl	3.00	3.00
	Nos. 146-155 (10)		20.65	20.30

Same Surcharge on Regular Issue of 1901-02.
156	A25	5c on 28c org	2.50	2.25
157	A25	5c on 40c dk bl	75	60
a.	Inverted surcharge		3.00	3.00

Same Surcharge on Official Stamps of 1908
158	O17	5c on 10c emer	35	25
a.	Double surcharge			
159	O17	5c on 10c red lil	35	25
a.	Double surcharge		4.00	4.00
b.	"5" omitted		3.00	3.00
160	O17	5c on 20c bis	75	60
a.	Double surcharge		2.50	2.50
161	O17	5c on 20c sal pink	75	60
a.	"5" omitted		3.50	3.50
162	O17	5c on 30c bl gray	25	20
163	O17	5c on 30c yel	15	10
a.	"5" omitted		3.00	3.00
b.	Inverted surcharge		2.50	2.50
164	O17	5c on 60c org brn	40	25
a.	Double surcharge		10.00	10.00
165	O17	5c on 60c dp ultra	25	15
a.	Inverted surcharge		5.00	5.00
b.	"5" omitted		3.00	
	Nos. 158-165 (8)		3.25	2.45

PARAGUAY

		Same Surcharge on No. O52		
166	A32	20c on 5c bl	2.50	2.00
a.		Inverted surcharge	6.00	7.50

Habilitado en
20
Surcharged
CENTAVOS

1908 On Stamp of 1887.

167	A12	20c on 2c car	5.00	4.00
a.		Inverted surcharge	15.00	

On Official Stamps of 1892.

168	A12	5c on 15c org	5.00	3.50
169	A12	5c on 20c pink	75.00	65.00
170	A12	5c on 50c gray	30.00	25.00
170A	A12	20c on 5c bl	3.00	2.50
b.		Inverted surcharge	17.50	17.50

Nos. 151, 152, 153, 155, 167, 170A, while duly authorized, all appear to have been sold to a single individual, and although they paid postage, it is doubtful whether they can be considered as ever having been placed on sale to the public.

Habilitado 1908
Surcharged
(Date in Red)
UN CENTAVO

1908–09

171	O18	1c on 1p brt rose & blk	40	30
172	O18	1c on 1p lake & blk	35	25
173	O18	1c on 1p brn org & blk ('09)	1.75	1.25

Varieties of surcharge on Nos. 171–173 include: "CETTAVO"; date omitted, double or inverted; third line double or omitted.

Types of 1905–1910 Overprinted 1908

1908, Mar. 5 — Perf. 11½

174	A35	1c emerald	15	10
175	A35	5c yellow	15	12
176	A35	10c lil brn	20	15
177	A35	20c yel org	15	10
178	A35	30c red	50	40
179	A35	60c magenta	40	35
180	A37	1p lt bl	25	20
		Nos. 174-180 (7)	1.80	1.42

Overprinted 1909

1909, Sept.

181	A35	1c bl gray	15	10
182	A35	1c scarlet	15	12
183	A35	5c dk grn	15	12
184	A35	5c bp org	15	12
185	A35	10c rose	25	20
186	A35	10c bis brn	25	20
187	A35	20c yellow	15	12
188	A35	20c violet	20	15
189	A35	30c org brn	60	40
190	A35	30c dl bl	60	40
		Nos. 181-190 (10)	2.65	1.93

Coat of Arms above Numeral of Value
A38

"The Republic"
A39

1910–21 Lithographed. Perf. 11½

191	A38	1c gray blk	12	8
192	A38	5c brt vio	15	8
a.		Pair, imperf. between	2.00	2.00
193	A38	5c bl grn ('19)	15	8
194	A38	5c lt bl ('21)	15	8
195	A38	10c yel grn	15	8
196	A38	10c dp vio ('19)	20	8
197	A38	10c red ('21)	15	8
198	A38	20c red	15	8
199	A38	50c car rose	60	30
200	A38	75c dp bl	25	20
a.		Diag. half perforated ('11)	25	20
		Nos. 191-200 (10)	2.07	1.04

Nos. 191–200 exist imperforate.
No. 200a was authorized for use as 20c.

1911 Engraved.

201	A39	1c ol grn & blk	15	8
202	A39	2c dk bl & blk	20	15
203	A39	5c car & ind	30	20
204	A39	10c dp bl & brn	35	20
205	A39	20c ol grn & ind	35	20
206	A39	50c lil & ind	60	30
207	A39	75c ol grn & red lil	60	30
		Nos. 201-207 (7)	2.55	1.43

Centenary of National Independence.
The 1c, 2c, 10c and 50c exist imperf.
Price for pairs, $3 each.

Habilitada
No. 199 Surcharged
en
VEINTE

1912

208	A38	20c on 50c car rose	20	10
a.		Inverted surcharge	2.00	2.00
b.		Double surcharge	2.00	2.00
c.		Bar omitted	3.50	3.50

National Coat of Arms
A40

1913 Engraved. Perf. 11½

209	A40	1c gray	5	5
210	A40	2c orange	5	5
211	A40	5c lilac	5	5
212	A40	10c green	5	5
213	A40	20c dl red	5	5
214	A40	40c rose	10	5
215	A40	75c dp bl	15	5
216	A40	80c yellow	15	10
217	A40	1p lt bl	15	10
218	A40	1.25p pale bl	30	20
219	A40	3p grnsh bl	35	15
		Nos. 209-219 (11)	1.45	90

Nos. J7-J10 Overprinted
HABILITADO
1918

HABILITADO EN 0.05
Nos. J10 and 214 Surcharged
1918

220	D2	5c yel brn	10	8
221	D2	10c yel brn	10	8
222	D2	20c yel brn	15	15
223	D2	40c yel brn	20	15

224	D2	5c on 40c yel brn	15	15
225	A40	30c on 40c rose	15	10
		Nos. 220-225 (6)	85	71

Nos. 220–225 exist with surcharge inverted, double and double with one inverted.
The surcharge "Habilitado—1918—5 cents 5" on the 1c gray official stamps of 1914, is bogus.

HABILITADO
No. J11 Overprinted
1920

229	D2	1p yel brn	20	10
a.		Inverted overprint	1.25	1.25
b.		Double overprint		
c.		Double overprint, one inverted		
d.		Double overprint inverted		
e.		"AABILITADO"	1.50	1.50
f.		"1929" for "1920"	1.50	1.50
g.		Ovpt. lines 8mm apart	40	

HABILITADO
Nos. 216 and 219 Surcharged en 0.50
1920

230	A40	50c on 80c yel	25	12
231	A40	1.75p on 3p grnsh bl	1.50	1.25

Same Surcharge on No. J12

232	D2	1p on 1.50p yel brn	45	18

Nos. 230–232 exist with various surcharge errors, including inverted, double, double inverted and double with one inverted.

Parliament Building A41

1920 Lithographed. Perf. 11½

233	A41	50c red & blk	45	25
a.		"CORRLOS"	3.00	3.00
234	A41	1p lt bl & blk	1.25	60
235	A41	1.75p dk bl & blk	25	20
236	A41	3p org & blk	2.00	30

Issued to commemorate the fiftieth anniversary of the Constitution.
All values exist imperforate and Nos. 233, 235 and 236 with center inverted. It is doubtful that any of these varieties were regularly issued.

No. 215 Surcharged 50
1920

237	A40	50c on 75c dp bl	60	15

Nos. 200, 215 Surcharged 50
1921

241	A38	50c on 75c dp bl	20	10
242	A40	50c on 75c dp bl	30	10

A42

1922, Feb. 8 Litho. Perf. 11½

243	A42	50c car & dk bl	20	15
a.		Imperf. pair	1.00	
b.		Center inverted	17.50	17.50
244	A42	1p dk bl & blk	20	15
a.		Imperf. pair	1.00	
b.		Center inverted	22.50	22.50

"C" overprints, listed under Nos. L1–L37, were applied to Nos. 243–244 and various stamps of types A40, A44–A52, A54, A57–A60 and D2.

Rendezvous of Conspirators A43

1922-23

245	A43	1p dp bl	20	15
246	A43	1p scar & dk bl ('23)	25	15
247	A43	1p red vio & gray ('23)	25	15
248	A43	1p org & gray ('23)	30	15
249	A43	5p dk vio	75	35
250	A43	5p dk bl & org brn ('23)	75	35
251	A43	5p dl red & lt bl ('23)	75	35
252	A43	5p emer & blk ('23)	75	35
		Nos. 245-252 (8)	4.00	2.00

Issued to commemorate National Independence.

No. 218 Surcharged "Habilitado en $1¡—1924" in Red.
1924

253	A40	1p on 1.25p pale vio	15	15

This stamp was for use in Asunción. Nos. L3 to L5 were for use in the interior, as is indicated by the "C" in the surcharge.

Map of Paraguay A44

1924 Lithographed Perf. 11½

254	A44	1p dk bl	15	7
255	A44	2p car rose	25	12
256	A44	4p lt bl	35	18
a.		Perf. 12	75	18

Nos. 254–256 exist imperf. Price $6 each pair.

Gen. José E. Díaz A45

Columbus A46

1925-26 Perf. 11½, 12

257	A45	50c red	15	10
258	A45	1p dk bl	20	15
259	A45	1p emer ('26)	15	10

Nos. 257–258 exist imperf. Price $2 each pair.

1925 Perf. 11½

260	A46	1p blue	40	20
a.		Imperf. pair	4.00	

Nos. 194, 214-215, J12 Surcharged
Habilitado en
1 centavo
in Black or Red

1926

261	A38	1c on 5c lt bl	10	5
262	A40	7c on 40c rose	20	12
263	A40	15c on 75c dp bl (R)	10	8
264	D2	1.50p on 1.50p yel brn	25	15

25

PARAGUAY

Nos. 194, 179 and 256 Surcharged
"Habilitado" and New Values.

1927

265	A38	2c on 5c lt bl	5	5
266	A35	50c on 60c mag	20	20
a.		Invtd. surcharge	4.00	
267	A44	1.50p on 4p lt bl	15	8

Official Stamp of 1914 Surcharged
"Habilitado" and New Value.

| 268 | O19 | 50c on 75c dp bl | 10 | 8 |

National Emblem
A47

Pedro Juan Caballero
A48

Map of Paraguay
A49

Fulgencio Yegros
A50

Ignacio Iturbe
A51

Oratory of the Virgin, Asunción
A52

Perf. 12, 11, 11½, 11x12

1927-38   Typographed

269	A47	1c lt red ('31)	10	10
270	A47	2c org red ('30)	10	10
271	A47	7c lilac	10	10
272	A47	7c emer ('29)	10	10
273	A47	10c gray grn ('28)	10	10
a.		10c lt grn ('31)	10	10
274	A47	10c lil rose ('30)	10	10
275	A47	10c lt bl ('35)	10	10
276	A47	20c dl bl ('28)	10	10
277	A47	20c lil brn ('30)	10	10
278	A47	20c lt vio ('31)	10	10
279	A47	20c rose ('35)	10	10
280	A47	50c ultra	10	10
281	A47	50c dl red ('28)	10	10
282	A47	50c org ('30)	15	15
283	A47	50c gray ('31)	10	10
284	A47	50c brn vio ('34)	10	10
285	A47	50c rose ('36)	10	10
286	A47	70c ultra ('28)	15	15
287	A48	1p emerald	10	10
288	A48	1p org red ('30)	10	10
289	A48	1p brn org ('34)	10	10
290	A49	1.50p brown	15	10
291	A49	1.50p lil ('28)	30	10
292	A49	1.50p rose red ('32)	15	10
293	A50	2.50p bister	10	10
294		3p gray	40	30
295	A51	3p rose red ('36)	15	10
296	A51	3p brt vio ('36)	10	10
297	A52	5p chocolate	40	35
298	A52	5p vio ('36)	20	10
299	A52	5p pale org ('38)	15	10
300	A49	20p red ('29)	2.75	2.25
301	A49	20p emer ('29)	2.75	2.25
302	A49	20p vio brn ('29)	2.75	2.25
		Nos. 269-302 (34)	12.55	10.40

No. 281 is also known perf. 10½x11½.
Papermaker's watermarks are sometimes found on No. 271 ("GLORIA BOND" in double-lined circle) and No. 280 ("Extra Vencedor Bond").

Arms of Juan de Salazar de Espinosa
A53

Columbus
A54

1928, Aug. 15   Perf. 12

| 303 | A53 | 10p vio brn | 2.00 | 1.50 |

Issued in commemoration of Juan de Salazar de Espinosa, founder of Asunción.
A papermaker's watermark ("INDIAN BOND EXTRA STRONG S.&C") is sometimes found on Nos. 303, 305-307.

1928   Lithographed.

304	A54	10p ultra	1.00	50
305	A54	10p vermilion	1.00	50
306	A54	10p dp red	1.00	50

President Rutherford B. Hayes of U.S.A. and Villa Occidental
A55

1928, Nov. 20   Perf. 12

| 307 | A55 | 10p gray brn | 7.50 | 3.75 |
| 308 | A55 | 10p red brn | 7.50 | 3.75 |

Issued to commemorate the 50th anniversary of the Hayes' Chaco decision.

Portraits of Archbishop Bogarin
A56

1930, Aug. 15

309	A56	1.50p lake	2.00	1.50
310	A56	1.50p turq bl	2.00	1.50
311	A56	1.50p dl vio	2.00	1.50

Issued to honor Archbishop Juan Sinforiano Bogarin, first archbishop of Paraguay.

Habilitado
No. 272
Surcharged
en
CINCO

1930

| 312 | A47 | 5c on 7c emer | 10 | 10 |

A57

1930-39   Typo.   Perf. 11½, 12

313	A57	10p brown	1.00	40
314	A57	10p brn red, bl ('31)	1.00	40
315	A57	10p dk bl, pink ('32)	1.00	40
316	A57	10p gray brn ('36)	75	35
317	A57	10p gray ('37)	75	35
318	A57	10p bl ('39)	30	25
		Nos. 313-318 (6)	4.80	2.15

60th anniversary of the first Paraguayan postage stamp.

Gunboat "Humaitá"—A58

1931   Perf. 12

| 319 | A58 | 1.50p purple | 75 | 45 |

Issued to commemorate the 60th anniversary of the Constitution. See Nos. C39-C53.

View of San Bernardino—A59

1931, Aug.

| 320 | A59 | 1p lt grn | 50 | 30 |

Issued in commemoration of the 50th anniversary of the founding of San Bernardino.

Nos. 309-310 Overprinted in Blue or Red

**FELIZ
AÑO NUEVO
1932**

1931, Dec. 31

| 321 | A56 | 1.50p lake (Bl) | 1.50 | 1.50 |
| 322 | A56 | 1.50p turq bl (R) | 1.50 | 1.50 |

Map of the Gran Chaco
A60

1932-35   Typographed.   Perf. 12

| 323 | A60 | 1.50p dp vio | 30 | 20 |
| 324 | A60 | 1.50p rose ('35) | 20 | 15 |

Nos. C74-C78 Surcharged

**CORREOS
1 PESO
FELIZ AÑO NUEVO
1933**

1933   Litho.

325	AP18	50c on 4p ultra	50	40
326	AP18	1p on 8p red	1.00	75
327	AP18	1.50p on 12p bl grn	1.00	75
328	AP18	2p on 16p dk vio	1.00	75
329	AP18	5p on 20p org brn	2.50	2.00
		Nos. 325-329 (5)	6.00	4.65

Flag of the Race Issue

Flag with Three Crosses: Caravels of Columbus
A61

1933, Oct. 10   Litho.   Perf. 11

330	A61	10c red brn, ol grn & vio	15	12
331	A61	20c dl red, pale bl & vio	15	12
332	A61	50c bl grn, ver & vio	20	12
333	A61	1p sl gray, yel brn & vio	20	18
334	A61	1.50p dk bl, yel grn & vio	20	18
335	A61	2p blk brn, bl grn & vio	50	50
336	A61	5p ol grn, org brn & vio	1.00	1.00
337	A61	10p pale bl, blk brn & vio	1.00	1.00
		Nos. 330-337 (8)	3.40	3.22

Commemorating the 441st anniversary of the sailing of Christopher Columbus from the port of Palos, August 3rd, 1492, on his first voyage to the New World.

Monstrance
A62

Arms of Asunción
A63

1937, Aug.   Perf. 11½   Unwmkd.

338	A62	1p dk bl, yel & red	10	8
339	A62	3p dk bl, yel & red	12	10
340	A62	10p dk bl, yel & red	25	20

Issued in commemoration of the first National Eucharistic Congress at Asuncion.

1937, Aug.

341	A63	50c vio & buff	5	5
342	A63	1p bis & lt grn	6	6
343	A63	3p red & lt bl	10	8
344	A63	10p car rose & buff	25	18
345	A63	20p bl & db	30	30
		Nos. 341-345 (5)	76	64

Issued in commemoration of the 400th anniversary of the founding of Asuncion.

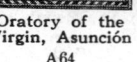
Oratory of the Virgin, Asunción
A64

Carlos Antonio Lopez
A65

PARAGUAY

José Eduvigis Diaz
A66

1938-39 Typographed. Perf. 11, 12.
346	A64	5p ol grn	35	15
347	A64	5p pale rose ('39)	50	20
348	A64	11p vio brn	35	20

Issued in commemoration of the 400th anniversary of the founding of Asunción.

1939   **Perf. 12.**
349	A65	2p lt ultra & pale brn	35	25
350	A66	2p lt ultra & brn	40	30

Reburial of ashes of Pres. Carlos Antonio Lopez (1790–1862) and Gen. José Eduvigis Diaz in the National Pantheon, Asunción.

Pres. Patricio Escobar
and Ramon Zubizarreta
A67

Pres. Bernardino Caballero and
Senator José S. Decoud
A68

1939-40 Lithographed Perf. 11½
Heads in Black.
351	A67	50c dl org ('40)	12	10
352	A67	1p lt vio ('40)	25	15
353	A67	2p red brn ('40)	35	20
354	A68	5p lt ultra	50	30
		Nos. 351-354, C122-C123 (6)	17.72	15.25

Issued in commemoration of the 50th anniversary of the founding of the University of Asunción.
Varieties of this issue include inverted heads (50c, 1p, 2p); doubled heads; Caballero and Decoud heads in 50c frame: imperforates and part-perforates. Copies with inverted heads were not officially issued.

Coats of Arms—A69

Pres. Baldomir of Uruguay,
Flags of Paraguay, Uruguay
A70

Designs: 2p, Pres. Benavides, Peru. 3p, U.S Eagle and Shield. 5p, Pres. Alessandri, Chile. 6p, Pres. Vargas, Brazil. 10p, Pres. Ortiz, Argentina.

Engraved; Flags Lithographed
1939   **Perf. 12**
Flags in National Colors
355	A69	50c vio bl	25	20
356	A70	1p olive	20	12
357	A70	2p bl grn	25	18
358	A70	3p sepia	50	35
359	A70	5p orange	40	30
360	A70	6p dl vio	1.00	80
361	A70	10p bis brn	75	50
		Nos. 355-361 (7)	3.35	2.45

First Buenos Aires Peace Conference. See also Nos. C113–121.

Coats of Arms of New York
and Asunción—A76

1939, Nov. 30
362	A76	5p scarlet	30	25
363	A76	10p dp bl	60	45
364	A76	11p dk bl grn	80	70
365	A76	22p ol blk	1.00	85

New York World's Fair. See also Nos. C124–C126.

Paraguayan   Paraguayan
Soldier   Woman
A77   A78

Cowboys   Plowing
A79   A80

View of Paraguay River
A81

Oxcart—A82

Pasture—A83

Piraretá Falls—A84

1940, Jan. 1 Photo. Perf. 12½
366	A77	50c dp org	20	15
367	A78	1p brt red vio	25	20
368	A79	3p brt grn	35	25
369	A80	5p chestnut	50	25
370	A81	10p magenta	50	30
371	A82	20p violet	1.00	75
372	A83	50p cob bl	2.50	1.00
373	A84	100p black	5.00	3.00
		Nos. 366-373 (8)	10.30	5.90

Second Buenos Aires Peace Conference.

Map of the Americas
A85

1940, May Engraved Perf. 12
374	A85	50c red org	12	8
375	A85	1p green	20	12
376	A85	5p dk bl	35	20
377	A85	10p brown	1.00	80
		Nos. 374-377, C127-C130 (8)	10.42	7.10

Pan American Union, 50th anniversary.

Reproduction of   Sir Rowland
Type A1   Hill
A86   A87

Reproductions of Types A2 and A3
A88   A89

1940, Aug. 15 Photo. Perf. 13½
378	A86	1p aqua & brt red vio	1.20	50
379	A87	5p dp yel grn & red brn	1.50	65
380	A88	6p org brn & ultra	3.50	1.25
381	A89	10p ver & blk	3.50	2.00

Postage stamp centenary.

Dr. José Francia
A90   A91

1940, Sept. 20 Engr. Perf. 12
382	A90	50c car rose	25	20
383	A91	50c plum	25	20
384	A90	1p brt grn	25	20
385	A91	5p dp bl	25	20

Centenary of the death of Dr. José Francia (1766–1840), dictator of Paraguay, 1814–1840.

No. 366
Surcharged
in Black

1940, Sept. 7 Perf. 12½
| 386 | A77 | 5p on 50c dp org | 40 | 40 |

Issued in honor of President José F. Estigarribia who died in a plane crash Sept. 7, 1940.

No. 360 Overprinted in Black
Visita al Paraguay
Agosto de 1941
1941, Aug. Perf. 12
| 387 | A70 | 6p multi | 40 | 40 |

Issued in commemoration of the visit of President Vargas of Brazil to Paraguay.

Nos. C113-C115
Overprinted "HABILITADO"
and Bars in Blue or Red.
1942, Jan. 17 Perf. 12½
388	AP25	1p multi (Bl)	25	20
389	AP26	3p multi (R)	30	20
390	AP27	5p multi (R)	35	20

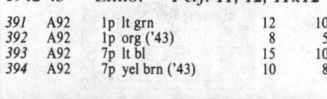

Coat of Arms
A92

1942-43 Litho. Perf. 11, 12, 11x12
391	A92	1p lt grn	12	10
392	A92	1p org ('43)	8	5
393	A92	7p lt bl	15	10
394	A92	7p yel brn ('43)	10	8

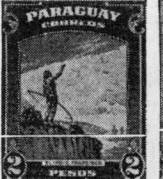 

The Indian   Arms of
Francisco   Irala
A93   A95

PARAGUAY

Domingo Martinez de Irala
and His Vision—A94

Engraved
1942, Aug. 15   Perf. 12   Unwmkd.
395	A93	2p green	1.50	60
396	A94	5p rose	1.50	60
397	A95	7p sapphire	1.50	50
	Nos. 395-397, C131-C133 (6)	22.25	17.20

400th anniversary of Asunción.

President Higinio   Christopher
Morinigo and   Columbus
Scenes of Industry   A97
and Agriculture
A96

1943, Aug. 15
| 398 | A96 | 7p blue | 18 | 15 |

1943, Aug. 15
399	A97	50c violet	40	30
400	A97	1p gray brn	30	20
401	A97	5p dk grn	1.00	25
402	A97	7p brt ultra	50	20

Issued to commemorate the 450th anniversary of the discovery of America.

No. 296   Habilitado
Surcharged in Black   **en**
                                      un céntimo
1944   Perf. 12, 11, 11½, 11x12
| 403 | A51 | 1c on 3p brt vio | 10 | 8 |

Nos. 398 and 402 Surcharged
"1944 / 5 Centimos 5" in Red.
1944   Perf. 12.
| 404 | A96 | 5c on 7p bl | 24 | 12 |
| 405 | A97 | 5c on 7p brt ultra | 24 | 12 |

Imperforates
Starting with No. 406, many Paraguayan stamps exist imperforate.

Primitive Postal Service
among Indians
A98

Ruins of Humaitá Church
A99

 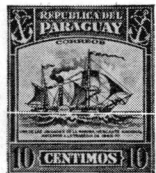

Locomotive of   Early
early Paraguayan   Merchant
Railroad   Ship
A100   A102

Marshal
Francisco
S. Lopez
A101

Port   Birthplace of
Asunción   Paraguay's
A103   Liberation
                            A104

Monument to
Heroes of Itororó
A105

Engraved.
1944-45   Perf. 12½   Unwmkd.
406	A98	1c black	15	10
407	A99	2c cop brn ('45)	25	20
408	A100	5c lt ol	60	30
409	A101	7c lt bl ('45)	25	15
410	A102	10c grn ('45)	60	40
411	A103	15c dk bl ('45)	60	40
412	A104	50c blk brn	1.00	90
413	A105	1g dk rose car ('45)	2.00	1.00
	Nos. 406-413 (8)	5.45	3.45

See also Nos. 435, 437, 439, 441, C134-C146, C158-C162.

No. 409 Surcharged in Red
5   5

1945
| 414 | A101 | 5c on 7c lt bl | 18 | 15 |

Handshake, Map and Flags
of Paraguay and Panama
A106

Designs: 3c, Venezuela Flag. 5c, Colombia Flag. 2g, Peru Flag.

Engraved; Flags Lithographed in National Colors.
1945, Aug. 15   Perf. 12½   Unwmkd.
415	A106	1c dk grn	10	10
416	A106	3c lake	15	12
417	A106	5c bl blk	20	12
418	A106	2g brown	2.50	1.75

Issued to commemorate the goodwill visits of President Higinio Morinigo during 1943. See also Nos. C147-C153.

Nos. B6 to B9 Surcharged "1945"
and New Value in Black.
1945   Engraved   Perf. 12
419	SP4	2c on 7p+3p red brn	15	12
420	SP4	2c on 7p+3p pur	15	15
421	SP4	2c on 7p+3p car rose	15	12
422	SP4	5c on 7p+3p saph	20	15
423	SP4	5c on 7p+3p red brn	30	15
424	SP4	5c on 7p+3p pur	30	15
425	SP4	5c on 7p+3p car rose	30	15
426	SP4	5c on 7p+3p saph	30	15
	Nos. 419-426 (8)	1.90	1.14

Similar Surcharge in Red
on Nos. 409, 398 and 402.
Perf. 12½, 12.
427	A101	5c on 7c lt bl	25	18
428	A96	5c on 7p bl	30	20
429	A97	5c on 7p brt ultra	35	25

Nos. 427-429 exist with black surcharge.

Coat of Arms
("U.P.U." at bottom)
A110

1946   Litho.   Perf. 11, 12, 11x12
| 430 | A110 | 5c gray | 8 | 6 |

See also Nos. 459-463, 478-480, 498-506, 525-536, 633-646.

Nos. B6 to B9 Surcharged "1946"
and New Value in Black.
1946   Perf. 12
431	SP4	5c on 7p+3p red brn	75	50
432	SP4	5c on 7p+3p pur	75	50
433	SP4	5c on 7p+3p car rose	75	50
434	SP4	5c on 7p+3p saph	75	50

First Telegraph
in South America
A111

Monument to   Colonial Jesuit
Antequera   Altar
A112   A113

Engraved.
1946, Sept. 21   Perf. 12½   Unwmkd.
435	A102	1c rose car	8	6
436	A111	2c purple	10	9
437	A98	5c ultra	15	10
438	A112	10c org yel	20	18
439	A105	15c brn ol	25	25
440	A113	50c dp grn	75	45
441	A104	1g brt ultra	1.50	85
	Nos. 435-441 (7)	3.03	1.98

See also Nos. C135-C138, C143.

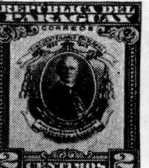

Marshal Francisco Solano Lopez
A114

1947, May 15   Perf. 12
442	A114	1c purple	6	6
443	A114	2c org red	8	6
444	A114	5c green	12	6
445	A114	15c ultra	15	15
446	A114	50c dk grn	60	60
	Nos. 442-446 (5)	1.01	99

See also Nos. C163-C167.

 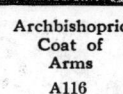

Juan Sinforiano   Archbishopric
Bogarin,   Coat of
Archbishop of   Arms
Asunción   A116
A115

Projected   Vision
Monument of the   of Projected
Sacred Heart   Monument
of Jesus   A118
A117

1948, Jan. 6   Engr.   Perf. 12½
447	A115	2c dk bl	12	12
448	A116	5c dp car	10	8
449	A117	10c gray blk	20	15
450	A118	15c green	40	25

Issued to commemorate the 50th anniversary of the establishment of the Archbishopric of Asunción.
See also Nos. C168-C175.

"Political Enlightenment"
A119

Engraved and Lithographed
1948, Sept. 11
| 451 | A119 | 5c car red & bl | 10 | 10 |
| 452 | A119 | 15c red org, red & bl | 20 | 18 |

Issued to honor the Barefeet, a political group. See Nos. C176-C177.

PARAGUAY

C. A. Lopez, J. N. Gonzalez
and Freighter Paraguari
A120

1949   Lithographed
Centers in Carmine, Black,
Ultramarine and Blue.

453	A120	2c orange	6	6
454	A120	5c bl vio	10	6
455	A120	10c black	12	10
456	A120	15c violet	20	12
457	A120	50c bl grn	30	18
458	A120	1g dl vio brn	50	30
	Nos. 453-458 (6)		1.28	82

Paraguay's merchant fleet centenary.

Type of 1946.

1950   Perf. 10½.   Unwmkd.

459	A110	5c red	5	5
460	A110	10c blue	6	5
461	A110	50c rose lil	7	5
462	A110	1g pale vio	18	12

1951   Coarse Impression.

| 463 | A110 | 30c green | 8 | 6 |

Blocks of Four of
Nos. 459, 460
and 463
Overprinted
in Various Colors

(Illustration Reduced
One-Half)

1951, Apr. 18

464	A110	5c red (Bk), block	30	25
465	A110	10c bl (R), block	50	35
466	A110	30c grn (V), block	75	60

Issued to commemorate the First Economic Congress of Paraguay, Apr. 18, 1951.

Columbus Lighthouse—A121

1952, Feb. 11   Perf. 10

467	A121	2c org brn	5	5
468	A121	5c lt ultra	5	5
469	A121	10c rose	6	6
470	A121	15c lt bl	6	6
471	A121	20c lilac	8	8
472	A121	50c orange	20	20
473	A121	1g bluish grn	35	35
	Nos. 467-473 (7)		85	85

Silvio Pettirossi
A122

1954, Mar. Lithographed   Perf. 10

474	A122	5c blue	5	5
475	A122	20c rose pink	5	5
476	A122	50c vio brn	8	8
477	A122	60c lt vio	20	15
	Nos. 474-477, C201-C204 (8)		1.15	1.10

Issued to honor Silvio Pettirossi, aviator.

Arms Type of 1946

1954   Perf. 11

| 478 | A110 | 10c vermilion | 5 | 5 |

Perf. 10

478A	A110	10c ver, redrawn	5	5
479	A110	10g orange	50	40
480	A110	50g vio brn	2.50	2.00

No. 478A measures 20½x24mm., has 5 frame lines at left and 6 at right. No. 478 measures 20x24½mm., has 6 frame lines at left and 5 at right.

Three National Heroes—A123

1954, Aug. 15   Litho.   Perf. 10

481	A123	5c lt vio	5	5
482	A123	20c lt blue	5	5
483	A123	50c rose pink	6	6
484	A123	1g org brn	10	10
485	A123	2g bl grn	20	20
	Nos. 481-485 (5)		46	46

Issued to honor Marshal Francisco S. Lopez, Pres. Carlos A. Lopez and Gen. Bernardino Caballero.
See also Nos. C216-C220.

Pres. Alfredo Stroessner
and Pres. Juan D. Peron
A124

Photogravure and Lithographed

1955, Apr.   Perf. 13x13½   Wmk. 90
Frames and Flags
in Blue and Carmine

486	A124	5c brn, yel brn & sal pink	5	5
487	A124	10c lil rose, dp cl & cr	5	5
488	A124	50c gray, blk & cr	6	6
489	A124	1.30g rose lil, rose vio & cr	12	10
490	A124	2.20g ultra, dk bl & cr	25	18
	Nos. 486-490, C221-C224 (9)		1.34	1.10

Visit of Pres. Juan D. Peron of Argentina.

Jesuit Ruins, Trinidad Belfry—A125

Santa Maria
Cornice
A126

Jesuit Ruins: 20c, Corridor at Trinidad. 2.50g, Tower of Santa Rosa. 5g, San Cosme gate. 15g, Church of Jesus. 25g, Niche at Trinidad.

Perf. 12½x12, 12x12½

1955, June 19   Engr.   Unwmkd.

491	A125	5c org yel	5	5
492	A125	20c ol bis	6	5
493	A126	50c lt red brn	8	5
494	A126	2.50g olive	8	5
495	A125	5g yel brn	12	8
496	A125	15g bl grn	45	30
497	A126	25g dp grn	90	50
	Nos. 491-497 (7)		1.74	1.08

Issued to commemorate the 25th anniversary of the priesthood of Monsignor Rodriguez. See also Nos. C225-C232.

Arms Type of 1946.
Perf. 10, 11 (No. 500)

1956-58   Lithographed   Unwmkd.

498	A110	5c brn ('57)	5	5
499	A110	30c red brn ('57)	5	5
500	A110	45c gray ol	5	5
500A	A110	90c lt vio bl	5	5
501	A110	2c ocher	8	8
502	A110	2.20g lil rose	10	10
503	A110	3g ol bis ('58)	6	6
503A	A110	4.20g emer ('57)	10	8
504	A110	5g ver ('57)	15	10
505	A110	10g lt grn ('57)	30	20
506	A110	20g bl ('57)	60	45
	Nos. 498-506 (11)		1.59	1.27

No. 500A exists with four-line, carmine overprint: "DIA N. UNIDAS 24 Octubre 1945-1956". It was not regularly issued and no decree authorizing it is known.

Soldiers, Angel and Asuncion
Cathedral—A127

Design: Nos. 513-519, Soldier and nurse in medallion and flags.

Perf. 13½

1957, June 12   Photo.   Unwmkd.
Granite Paper.
Flags in Red and Blue

508	A127	5c bl grn	5	5
509	A127	10c carmine	5	5
510	A127	15c ultra	5	5
511	A127	20c dp cl	5	5
512	A127	25c gray blk	5	5
513	A127	30c lt bl	5	5
514	A127	40c gray blk	5	5
515	A127	50c dk car	5	5
516	A127	1g bluish grn	5	5
517	A127	1.30g ultra	8	5
518	A127	1.50g dp cl	8	5
519	A127	2g brt grn	15	8
	Nos. 508-519 (12)		76	63

Issued to honor the heroes of the Chaco war. See Nos. C233-C245.

Statue of St. Ignatius
(Guarani Carving)
A128

Blessed Roque Gonzales
and St. Ignatius—A129

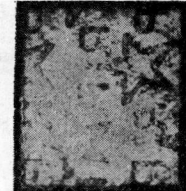

Wmk. 319
Design: 1.50g, St. Ignatius and San Ignacio Monastery.

Wmkd. Stars and R P Multiple (319)
1958, Mar. 15   Litho.   Perf. 11

520	A128	50c dk red brn	5	5
521	A129	50c lt bl grn	5	5
522	AP91	1.50g brt vio	6	5
523	A128	3g lt bl	15	8
524	A129	6.25g rose car	25	18
	Nos. 520-524 (5)		56	41

Issued to commemorate the 4th centenary of the death of St. Ignatius of Loyola (1491-1556).
See also Nos. 704-707.

Arms Type of 1946.

1958-64 Lithographed   Perf. 10, 11

525	A110	45c gray ol	5	5
526	A110	50c rose vio	5	5
527	A110	70c lt brn ('59)	5	5
527A	A110	90c vio bl	5	5
528	A110	1g violet	5	5
529	A110	1.50g lil ('59)	5	5
529A	A110	2g bis ('64)	5	6
530	A110	3g ol bis ('59)	8	6
531	A110	4.50g lt ultra ('59)	10	10
531A	A110	5g rose red ('59)	12	10
531B	A110	10g bl grn ('59)	30	20
532	A110	12.45g yel grn	25	20
533	A110	15g dl org	30	25
534	A110	30g citron	55	40
535	A110	50g brn red	85	60
536	A110	100g gray vio	1.70	1.25
	Nos. 525-536 (16)		4.60	3.51

Pres. Alfredo Stroessner
A130

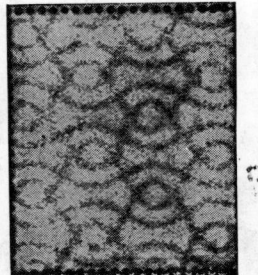

Wmk. 320

Wmkd. Interlacing Lines (320)
1958, Aug. 15   Litho.   Perf. 13½
Center in Slate.

537	A130	10c sal pink	5	5
538	A130	15c violet	5	5
539	A130	25c yel grn	5	5
540	A130	30c lt fawn	5	5
541	A130	50c rose car	12	8
542	A130	75c lt ultra	12	8

PARAGUAY

543	A130	5g lt bl grn	20	15
544	A130	10g brown	20	15
	Nos. 537-544 (8)		84	66

Issued to commemorate the re-election of President General Alfredo Stroessner. See also Nos. C246-C251.

Nos. 491-497 Surcharged in Red

Perf. 12½x12, 12x12½
1959, May 14 Engraved Unwmkd.

545	A125	1.50g on 5c org yel	5	5
546	A125	1.50g on 20c ol bis	5	5
547	A126	1.50g on 50c lt red brn	5	5
548	A126	3g on 2.50g ol	10	10
549	A125	6.25g on 5g yel brn	15	15
550	A126	20g on 15g bl grn	50	50
551	A126	30g on 25g dp grn	75	75
	Nos. 545-551 (7)		1.65	1.65

The surcharge is made to fit the stamps. See also Nos. C252-C259. Counterfeits of surcharge exist.

Goalkeeper Catching Soccer Ball
A131

World Refugee Year Emblem
A132

1960, Mar. 18 Photo. Perf. 12½

556	A131	30c brt red & bl grn	5	5
557	A131	50c plum & dk bl	5	5
558	A131	75c ol grn & org	5	5
559	A131	1.50g dk vio & bl grn	10	10
	Nos. 556-559, C262-C264 (7)		2.15	2.15

Olympic Games of 1960.

1960, Apr. 7 Litho. Perf. 11

560	A132	25c sal & yel grn	15	10
561	A132	50c lt yel grn & red org	20	15
562	A132	70c lt brn & lil rose	60	40
563	A132	1.50g lt bl & ultra	60	50
564	A132	3g gray & bis brn	1.25	1.00
	Nos. 560-564, C265-C268 (9)		18.05	8.65

Issued to publicize World Refugee Year, July 1, 1959-June 30, 1960 (1st issue).

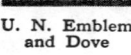

U. N. Emblem and Dove
A133

Flags of U.N. and Paraguay and U.N. Emblem
A134

Designs: 3g, Hand holding scales. 6g, Hands breaking chains. 20g, Flame.

1960, Apr. 21 Perf. 12½x13

565	A133	1g dk car & bl	5	5
566	A133	3g bl & org	6	6
567	A133	6g gray grn & sal	8	8
568	A133	20g ver & yel	25	25
	Nos. 565-568, C269-C271 (7)		3.84	3.84

Issued to commemorate the United Nations' Declaration of Human Rights. Miniature sheets exist, perf. and imperf., containing one each of Nos. 565-568, all printed in purple and orange. Size: 139x94mm.

Perf. 13x13½
1960, Oct. 24 Photo. Unwmkd.

569	A134	30c lt bl, red & bl	5	5
570	A134	75c yel, red & bl	5	5
571	A134	90c pale lil, red & bl	6	6
	Nos. 569-571, C272-C273 (5)		38	38

15th anniversary of the United Nations.

International Bridge, Arms of Brazil, Paraguay
A135

Truck Carrying Logs
A136

1961, Jan. 26 Litho. Perf. 14

572	A135	15c green	5	5
573	A135	30c dl bl	5	5
574	A135	50c orange	5	5
575	A135	75c vio bl	5	5
576	A135	1g violet	7	7
	Nos. 572-576, C274-C277 (9)		1.92	1.74

Issued to commemorate the inauguration of the International Bridge between Paraguay and Brazil.

Photogravure

1961, Apr. 10 Perf. 13 Unwmkd.

Designs: 90c, 2g, Logs on river barge. 1g, 5g, Radio tower.

577	A136	25c yel grn & rose car	10	5
578	A136	90c bl & yel	10	5
579	A136	1g car rose & org	10	5
580	A136	2g ol grn & sal	15	10
581	A136	5g lil & emer	20	15
	Nos. 577-581, C278-C281 (9)		3.30	2.65

Issued to publicize Paraguay's progress, "Paraguay en Marcha."

P. J. Caballero, José G. R. Francia, F. Yegros, Revolutionary Leaders
A137

1961, May 16 Litho. Perf. 14½

582	A137	30c green	5	5
583	A137	50c lil rose	5	5
584	A137	90c violet	5	5
585	A137	1.50g Prus bl	5	5
586	A137	3g ol bis	6	6
587	A137	4g ultra	10	8
588	A137	5g brown	12	10
	Nos. 582-588 (7)		48	44

Issued to commemorate the 150th anniversary of Independence (1st issue). See also Nos. C282-C287.

"Chaco Peace"
A138

Puma
A139

1961, June 12 Perf. 14x14½

589	A138	25c vermilion	5	5
590	A138	30c green	5	5
591	A138	50c red brn	5	5
592	A138	1g brt vio	5	5
593	A138	2g dk bl gray	8	8
	Nos. 589-593, C288-C290 (8)		2.63	2.48

Issued to commemorate the Chaco Peace and the 150th anniversary of Independence (2nd issue).

1961, Aug. 16 Perf. 14 Unwmkd.

594	A139	75c dl vio	6	6
595	A139	1.50g brown	8	8
596	A139	4.50g green	12	12
597	A139	10g Prus bl	25	25
	Nos. 594-597, C291-C293 (7)		6.51	6.01

Issued to commemorate the 150th anniversary of Independence (3rd issue).

University Seal
A140

Hotel Guarani
A141

1961, Sept. 18 Perf. 14x14½

598	A140	15c ultra	5	5
599	A140	25c dk red	5	5
600	A140	75c bl grn	5	5
601	A140	1g orange	6	6
	Nos. 598-601, C294-C296 (7)		1.56	1.56

Issued to commemorate the founding of the Catholic University in Asuncion and the 150th anniversary of Independence (4th issue).

1961, Oct. 14 Litho. Perf. 15

602	A141	50c sl bl	5	5
603	A141	1g green	5	5
604	A141	4.50g lilac	20	20
	Nos. 602-604, C297-C300 (7)		1.70	1.60

Issued to commemorate the opening of the Hotel Guarani and the 150th anniversary of Independence (5th issue).

Tennis Racket and Balls in Flag Colors—A142

1961, Oct. 16 Litho. Perf. 11

605	A142	35c multi	5	5
606	A142	75c multi	5	5
607	A142	1.50g multi	6	6
608	A142	2.25g multi	8	8

609	A142	4g multi	15	39
	Nos. 605-609 (5)		39	

Issued to commemorate the 28th South American Tennis Championships, Asuncion, Oct. 15-23 (1st issue). Some specialists question the status of this issue. See Nos. C301-C303.
Imperforates exist in changed colors as well as two imperf. souvenir sheets with stamps in changed colors.

Uprooted Oak Emblem
A145

Tennis Player
A146

Lithographed

1961, Dec. 30 Perf. 11 Unwmkd.

619	A145	10c ultra & lt bl	5	
620	A145	25c mar & org	5	
621	A145	50c car rose & pink	5	
622	A145	75c dk bl & yel grn	5	

Issued for World Refugee Year, 1959-60 (2nd issue). Imperforates in changed colors and souvenir sheets exist. Some specialists question the status of this issue. See Nos. C307-C309.

1962, Jan. 5 Perf. 15x14½

623	A146	35c Prus bl	5	5
624	A146	75c dk vio	5	5
625	A146	1.50g red brn	6	5
626	A146	2.25g emerald	8	6
	Nos. 623-626, C310-C313 (8)		2.69	2.66

Issued to commemorate the 28th South American Tennis Championships, 1961 (second issue) and the 150th anniversary of Independence (6th issue).

Scout Bugler
A147

1962, Feb. 6 Perf. 11
Olive Green Center

627	A147	10c dp mag	5	
628	A147	20c red org	5	
629	A147	25c dk brn	5	
630	A147	30c emerald	5	
631	A147	50c indigo	5	
	Nos. 627-631 (5)		25	

Issued to honor the Boy Scouts. Imperfs. in changed colors exist. Some specialists question the status of this issue. See Nos. C314-C316.

Arms Type of 1946

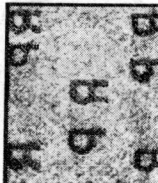

Wmk. 347

PARAGUAY

Wmkd. RP Multiple (347)
1962–68   Lithographed   Perf. 11

634	A110	50c stl bl ('63)	5	5
635	A110	70c dl lil ('63)	5	5
636	A110	1.50g vio ('63)	5	5
637	A110	3g dp bl ('68)	5	5
638	A110	4.50g redsh brn ('67)	6	5
639	A110	5g lil ('64)	7	5
640	A110	10g car rose ('63)	14	10
641	A110	12.45g ultra	17	15
642	A110	15.45g ver	23	18
643	A110	18.15g lilac	27	20
644	A110	20g lt brn ('63)	28	22
645	A110	50g dl red brn ('67)	70	35
646	A110	100g bl gray ('63)	1.40	85
		Nos. 634-646 (13)	3.52	2.35

Map and Laurel Branch
A148

U.N. Emblem
A149

Perf. 14x14½
1962, Apr. 14   Unwmkd.

647	A148	50c ocher	5	5
648	A148	75c vio bl	5	5
649	A148	1g purple	5	5
650	A148	1.50g brt grn	5	5
651	A148	4.50g vermilion	10	10
		Nos. 647-651, C320-C321 (7)	1.40	1.40

Issued for the Day of the Americas and to commemorate the 150th anniversary of Independence (7th issue).

1962, Apr. 23   Perf. 15

652	A149	50c bis brn	5	5
653	A149	75c dp cl	5	5
654	A149	1g Prus bl	5	5
655	A149	2g org brn	6	6
		Nos. 652-655, C322-C325 (8)	3.71	3.71

Issued to honor the United Nations and to commemorate the 150th anniversary of Independence (8th issue).

Malaria Eradication Emblem and Mosquito
A150

Design: 75c, 1g, 1.50g, Microscope, anopheles mosquito and eggs.

Perf. 14x13½
1962, May 23   Wmk. 346

656	A150	30c pink, ultra & blk	5	5
657	A150	50c bis, grn & blk	5	5
658	A150	75c rose red, blk & bis	5	5
659	A150	1g brt grn, blk & bis	6	6
660	A150	1.50g dl red brn, blk & bis	5	5
		Nos. 656-660 (5)	25	

Issued for the World Health Organization drive to eradicate malaria. Imperforates exist in changed colors. Some specialists question the status of this issue. See Nos. C326–C330.

Stadium
A151

Perf. 13½x14
1962, July 28   Litho.   Wmk. 346

661	A151	15c yel & dk brn	5	5
662	A151	25c brt grn & dk brn	5	5
663	A151	30c lt vio & dk brn	5	5
664	A151	40c dl org & dk brn	5	5
665	A151	50c brt yel grn & dk brn	5	5
		Nos. 661-665 (5)	20	

World Soccer Championships, Chile, May 30–June 17. Some specialists question the status of this issue. Imperfs. exist. See Nos. C331–C333.

Freighter
A152

Designs: Various merchantmen.

Perf. 14½x15
1962, July 31   Unwmkd.

666	A152	30c bis brn	5	5
667	A152	90c sl bl	5	5
668	A152	1.50g brn red	6	6
669	A152	2g green	8	8
670	A152	4.20g vio bl	16	16
		Nos. 666-670, C334-C335 (7)	1.37	1.22

Issued to honor the merchant marine.

Friendship 7" Capsule over South America
A153

Perf. 13½x14
1962, Sept. 4   Litho.   Wmk. 346

671	A153	15c dk bl & bis	5	5
672	A153	25c vio brn & bis	5	5
673	A153	30c dk sl grn & bis	5	5
674	A153	40c dk gray & bis	5	5
675	A153	50c dk vio & bis	5	5
		Nos. 671-675 (5)	25	

Issued to publicize U.S. manned space flights. Imperfs. in changed colors exist. Some specialists question the status of this issue. See Nos. C336–C338.

Discus Thrower
A154

Lithographed
1962, Oct 1

676	A154	15c blk & yel	5	5
677	A154	25c blk & lt grn	5	5
678	A154	30c blk & pink	5	5
679	A154	40c blk & pale vio	5	5
680	A154	50c blk & lt bl	5	5
		Nos. 676-680 (5)	25	

Issued to publicize the Olympic Games from Amsterdam 1928 to Tokyo 1964. Each stamp is inscribed with date and place of various Olympic Games. Imperfs. in changed colors exist. Some specialists question the status of this issue. See Nos. C339–C341.

Peace Dove and Cross
A155

Perf. 14½
1962, Oct. 11   Litho.   Unwmkd.

681	A155	50c olive	5	5
682	A155	70c dk bl	5	5
683	A155	1.50g bister	5	5
684	A155	2g violet	5	5
685	A155	3g brick red	8	8
		Nos. 681-685, C342-C347 (11)	3.04	2.34

Vatican II, the 21st Ecumenical Council of the Roman Catholic Church, which opened Oct. 11, 1962.

Pres. Alfredo Stroessner
A156

1963. Aug. 6   Perf. 11   Wmk. 347

686	A156	50c ol gray & sep	5	5
687	A156	75c buff & sep	6	6
688	A156	1.50g lt lil & sep	12	12
689	A156	3g emer & sep	25	12
		Nos. 686-689, C348-C350 (7)	2.83	2.10

Third presidential term of Alfredo Stroessner.

Popes Paul VI, John XXIII and St. Peter's, Rome
A157

1964, May 23

690	A157	1.50g cl & org	5	5
691	A157	3g cl & dk grn	6	5
692	A157	4g cl & bis	8	6
		Nos. 690-692, C351-C353 (6)	3.04	2.51

National holiday of St. Maria Auxiliadora (Our Lady of Perpetual Help).

Coats of Arms of Paraguay and France
A158

Design: 3g, Presidents Stroessner and de Gaulle.

1964, Oct. 6

693	A158	1.50g brown	5	5
694	A158	3g ultra	6	5
695	A158	4g gray	8	6
		Nos. 693-695, C354-C356 (6)	3.04	3.51

Visit of Pres. Charles de Gaulle of France.

Map of Americas
A159

Overprint: "Centenario de la Epopeya Nacional 1.864–1.870"

1965, Apr. 26   Perf. 11   Wmk. 347

696	A159	1.50g dl grn	5	5
697	A159	3g car red	8	8
698	A159	4g dk bl	10	10
		Nos. 696-698, C357-C358 (5)	1.51	1.15

Centenary of National Epic. Not issued without overprint.

Cattleya Warscewiczii
A160

1965, June 28   Perf. 14½   Unwmkd.

699	A160	20c purple	5	5
700	A160	30c blue	5	5
701	A160	90c brt mag	5	5
702	A160	1.50g green	12	12
703	A160	4.50g orange	8	8
		Nos. 699-703, C359-C361 (8)	2.15	1.46

150th anniversary of Independence (1811–1961).

St. Ignatius Type of 1958
1966, Apr. 20   Perf. 11   Wmk. 347

704	A129	15c ultra	6	6
705	A129	25c ultra	6	6
706	A129	75c ultra	8	8
707	A129	90c ultra	8	8
		Nos. 704-707, C362-C365 (8)	1.32	1.06

Issued to commemorate the 350th anniversary of the founding of San Ignacio Guazu Monastery.

Rubén Darío
A161

Globe and Lions Emblem—A162

1966, July 16

708	A161	50c ultra	5	5
709	A161	70c bis brn	5	5
710	A161	1.50g rose car	5	5
711	A161	3g violet	8	8
712	A161	4g grnsh bl	5	5
713	A161	5g black	5	5
		Nos. 708-713, C366-C370 (11)	2.78	1.58

Issued to commemorate the 50th anniversary of the death of Rubén Darío (pen name of Felix Rubén Garcia Sarmiento, 1867–1916), Nicaraguan poet, newspaper correspondent and diplomat.

1967, May 9   Lithographed

Designs: 1.50g, 3g, Melvin Jones. 4g, 5g, Lions' Headquarters, Chicago.

714	A162	50c lt vio	5	5
715	A162	70c blue	5	5
716	A162	1.50g ultra	5	5
717	A162	3g brown	5	5
718	A162	4g Prus grn	6	6
719	A162	5g ol gray	8	8
		Nos. 714-719, C371-C375 (11)	2.22	1.59

50th anniversary of Lions International.

PARAGUAY

WHO Emblem
A163

1968, Aug. 12   Perf. 11   Wmk. 347

720	A163	3g bluish grn	5	5
721	A163	4g brt pink	5	5
722	A163	5g bis brn	5	5
723	A163	10g violet	10	8
		Nos. 720-723, C376-C378 (7)	3.05	1.95

Issued to commemorate the 20th anniversary of the World Health Organization and the centenary of the national epic.

"World United in Peace"
A164

1969, June 28   Perf. 11   Wmk. 347

724	A164	50c rose	5	5
725	A164	70c ultra	5	5
726	A164	1.50g lt brn	5	5
727	A164	3g lil rose	8	8
728	A164	4g emerald	10	10
729	A164	5g violet	14	14
730	A164	10g brt lil	26	26
		Nos. 724-730 (7)	73	73

Peace Week.

Francisco Solano Lopez—A165   **Paraguay No. 2 A166**

1970, March 1   Perf. 11   Wmk. 347

731	A165	1g bis brn	5	5
732	A165	2g violet	5	5
733	A165	3g brt pink	5	5
734	A165	4g rose cl	5	5
735	A165	5g blue	7	6
736	A165	10g brt grn	14	10
		Nos. 731-736, C382-C385 (10)	1.88	1.41

Centenary of the death of Marshal Francisco Solano Lopez (1827-1870), President of Paraguay.

1970, Aug. 15   Lithographed

Designs (First Issue of Paraguay): 2g, 10g, No. 1. 3g, No. 3. 5g, No. 2.

737	A166	1g car rose	5	5
738	A166	2g ultra	5	5
739	A166	4g org brn	8	5
740	A166	5g violet	12	10
741	A166	10g lilac	24	18
		Nos. 737-741, C386-C388 (8)	2.89	2.35

Centenary of stamps of Paraguay.

UNESCO and Paraguay Emblems, Globe, Teacher and Pupil
A167

1971, May 18

742	A167	3g ultra	5	5
743	A167	5g lilac	7	6
744	A167	10g emerald	14	10
		Nos. 742-744, C389-C392 (7)	1.99	1.46

International Education Year.

UNICEF Emblem
A168

1972, Jan. 24   Granite Paper

745	A168	1g red brn	5	5
746	A168	2g ultra	5	5
747	A168	3g lil rose	5	5
748	A168	4g violet	6	5
749	A168	5g emerald	7	5
750	A168	10g claret	14	10
		Nos. 745-750, C393-C395 (9)	1.45	1.11

25th anniversary (in 1971) of the United Nations International Children's Fund (UNICEF).

Acaray Dam
A169

Designs: 2g, Francisco Solano Lopez monument. 3g, Friendship Bridge. 5g, Tebicuary River Bridge. 10g, Hotel Guarani.

1972, Nov. 16   Perf. 13½x13
Granite Paper

751	A169	1g sepia	5	5
752	A169	2g brown	5	5
753	A169	3g brt ultra	5	5
754	A169	5g brt pink	7	6
755	A169	10g dl grn	14	10
		Nos. 751-755, C396-C399 (9)	3.09	2.26

Tourism Year of the Americas.

OAS Emblem   **Hand Holding Letter**
A170   **A171**

1973   Lithographed   Perf. 13x13½
Granite Paper

756	A170	1g multi	5	5
757	A170	2g multi	5	5
758	A170	3g multi	5	5
759	A170	4g multi	6	5
760	A170	5g multi	12	6
761	A170	10g multi	14	10
		Nos. 756-761, C400-C403 (10)	3.15	2.31

25th anniversary of the Organization of American States.

Perf. 11

1973, July 10   Litho.   Wmk. 347

| 762 | A171 | 2g lil rose & blk | 5 | 5 |

No. 762 was issued originally as a non-obligatory stamp to benefit mailmen, but its status was changed to regular postage.

Exhibition Emblem
A172

1973, Aug. 11   Perf. 13x13½
Granite Paper

763	A172	1g org brn	5	5
764	A172	2g vermilion	5	5
765	A172	3g blue	5	5
766	A172	4g emerald	6	5
767	A172	5g lilac	7	6
		Nos. 763-767, C404-C405 (7)	93	73

EXPOPAR 73, Paraguayan Industrial Exhibition.

"U.P.U.," Pantheon, Carrier Pigeon, Globe
A173
Perf. 13½x13

1975, Feb.   Wmk. 347

768	A173	1g blk & lil	5	5
769	A173	2g blk & rose red	5	5
770	A173	3g blk & ultra	5	5
771	A173	5g blk & bl	7	6
772	A173	10g blk & lil rose	14	12
		Nos. 768-772, C406-C407 (7)	99	88

Centenary of Universal Postal Union.

Institute of Higher Education
A174
Perf. 13½x13

1976, Mar. 16   Litho.   Wmk. 347

| 773 | A174 | 5g vio, blk & red | 7 | 5 |
| 774 | A174 | 10g ultra, blk & red | 14 | 12 |

Inauguration of Institute of Higher Education, Sept. 23, 1974. See No. C408.

Rotary Emblem
A175

1976, Mar. 16   Perf. 13x13½

| 775 | A175 | 3g blk, bl & cit | 5 | 5 |
| 776 | A175 | 4g car, bl & cit | 5 | 5 |

Rotary International, 70th anniversary. See No. C409.

IWY Emblem, Woman's Head
A176

1976, Mar. 16

| 777 | A176 | 1g ultra & brn | 5 | 5 |
| 778 | A176 | 2g car & brn | 5 | 5 |

International Women's Year 1975. See No. C410.

Mburucuya Flowers
A177

Weaver with Ostrich Feather Panel
A178

Designs: 1g, Ostrich feather panel. 2g, Black palms.

Perf. 13x13½

1977   Litho.   Wmk. 347

779	A178	1g multi	5	5
780	A177	2g multi	5	5
781	A177	3g multi	5	5
782	A178	5g multi	15	10
		Nos. 779-782, C411-C412 (6)	1.40	1.00

Issue dates: 2g, 3g, Apr. 25; 1g, 5g, June 27.

Francisco Solano Lopez
A179
Wmk. 347

1977, July 24   Litho.   Perf. 13x13½

| 783 | A179 | 10g brown | 25 | 15 |

Marshal Francisco Solano Lopez (1827-1870), President of Paraguay, sesquicentennial of birth. See Nos. C413-C414.

National College
A180

PARAGUAY

		Wmk. 347			
1978		Litho.	Perf. 13½x13		
784	A180	3g claret		5	5
785	A180	4g vio bl		7	5
786	A180	5g lilac		8	6
	Nos. 784-786, C415-C417 (6)		1.42	1.06

Centenary of National College in Asuncion.

José Estigarribia, Bugler, Flag of Paraguay—A181

1978		Photo.	Perf. 13x13½		
787	A181	3g multi		5	5
788	A181	5g multi		8	6
789	A181	10g multi		16	12
	Nos. 787-789, C418-C420 (6)		1.49	1.13

Induction of José Felix Estigarribia (1888-1940), general and president of Paraguay, into Salon de Bronce (National Heroes' Hall of Fame).

Congress Emblem
A182
Lithographed

1979, Aug.	Perf. 13x13½	Wmk. 347		
790	A182	10g red, bl & blk	16	12

22nd Latin-American Tourism Congress, Asuncion. See No. C418.

Pilar City Bicentennial—A183

		Wmk. 347			
1980, July 17		Litho.	Perf. 13½x13		
791	A183	5g multi		8	6

See No. C422.

Paraguay Airlines Boeing 707 Service Inauguration—A183a

		Wmk. 347			
1980, Sept. 17		Litho.	Perf. 13½x13		
791A	A183a	20g multi		32	24

See No. C422A.

UPU Membership Centenary—A184

1981, Aug. 18		Litho.	Perf. 13½x13		
792	A184	5g rose lake & blk		8	6
793	A184	10g lil & blk		16	12
	Nos. 792-793, C427-C429 (5)		1.76	1.32

25th Anniv. of Stroessner City—A185
Design: Itaipua Dam, Pres. Stroessner.

		Wmk. 347			
1983, Jan. 22		Litho.	Perf. 13½x13		
794	A185	3g multi		5	5
795	A185	5g multi		8	6
796	A185	10g multi		16	12
797	A185	20g multi		32	24
798	A185	25g multi		40	30
799	A185	50g multi		80	60

Nos. 797-799 airmail.

See "Special Notices" at the front of this volume for data on the listing methods of this Catalogue, abbreviations, condition, prices and examination.

Unused Prices

Catalogue prices for unused stamps through 1960 are for hinged copies in fine condition.
Never-hinged unused stamps issued before 1961 often sell above Catalogue prices. Current never-hinged prices for various countries will be found in the Scott Stamp Market Update.

Recent issues are recorded in the Scott Chronicle of New issues beginning with Vol. 1, No. 2.
Previous issues are recorded in For the Record at the back of this volume.

PARAGUAY

SEMI-POSTAL STAMPS

Red Cross Nurse—SP1
Typographed.

1930, July 22   *Perf. 12*   Unwmkd.
B1	SP1	1.50p + 50c gray vio	2.00	1.25
B2	SP1	1.50p + 50c dp rose	2.00	1.25
B3	SP1	1.50p + 50c dk bl	2.00	1.25

The surtax was for the benefit of the Red Cross Society of Paraguay.

College of Agriculture—SP2

1930
B4	SP2	1.50p + 50c bl, *pink*	50	50

The surtax was for the benefit of the Agricultural Institute.
The sheet of No. B4 has a papermaker's watermark: "Vencedor Bond".
A 1.50p + 50c red on yellow was prepared but not regularly issued. Price 40 cents.

Red Cross Headquarters SP3   Our Lady of Asunción SP4

1932
B5	SP3	50c + 50c rose	50	40

1941   Engraved
B6	SP4	7p + 3p red brn	60	50
B7	SP4	7p + 3p pur	60	50
B8	SP4	7p + 3p car rose	60	50
B9	SP4	7p + 3p saph	60	50

No. 361 Surcharged in Black

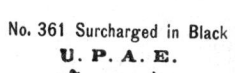

1944
B10	A70	10c on 10p multi	70	50

The surtax was for the victims of the San Juan earthquake in Argentina.

No. C169 Surcharged in Carmine
"AYUDA AL ECUADOR 5 + 5"

1949   *Perf. 12½*   Unwmkd.
B11	AP62	5c + 5c on 30c dk bl	15	15

The surtax was for the victims of the Ecuador earthquake.

AIR POST STAMPS

Official Stamps of 1913 Surcharged   **Correo Aéreo Habilitado en $ 2:85**

1929, Jan. 1   *Perf. 11½*   Unwmkd.
C1	O19	2.85c on 5c lil	1.75	1.25
C2	O19	5.65c on 10c grn	1.00	75
C3	O19	11.30c on 50c rose	1.50	1.00

Counterfeits of surcharge exist.

Regular Issues of 1924-27 Surcharged as in 1929

1929, Feb. 26   *Perf. 12*
C4	A51	3.40p on 3p gray	3.50	2.25
a.		Surcharged "Correo—en $3.40—Habilitado—Aereo."	17.50	
b.		Double surcharge	17.50	
c.		"A'ero" instead of "A'ereo"		
C5	A44	6.80p on 4p lt bl	3.50	2.25
a.		Surcharged "Correo—Aereo—en $6.80—Habilitado."	17.50	
C6	A52	17p on 5p choc	3.50	2.25
a.		Surcharged "Correo—Habilitado—Habilitado—en 17p"	9.00	
b.		Double surcharge	17.50	

Wings—AP1

Pigeon with Letter—AP2

Airplanes—AP3

1929-31   Typographed.   *Perf. 12*
C7	AP1	2.85p gray grn	1.25	90
a.		Imperf. (pair)	75.00	
C8	AP1	2.85p turq grn ('31)	60	40
C9	AP2	5.65p brown	1.75	50
C10	AP2	5.65p scar ('31)	75	50
C11	AP3	11.30p chocolate	1.25	80
a.		Imperf. (pair)	75.00	
C12	AP3	11.30p dp bl ('31)	60	50
		Nos. C7-C12 (6)	6.20	3.90

Sheets of these stamps sometimes show portions of a papermaker's watermark "Indian Bond C. Extra Strong."
Excellent counterfeits are plentiful.

Regular Issues of 1924-28 Surcharged in Black or Red   **Correo Aéreo Habilitado en $ 3.40**

1929   *Perf. 11½, 12*
C13	A47	95c on 7c lil	40	30
C14	A47	1.90p on 20c dl bl	40	30
C15	A44	3.40p on 4p lt bl (R)	50	40
a.		Double surcharge	4.00	
C16	A44	4.75p on 4p lt bl (R)	90	75
a.		Double surcharge	4.00	
C17	A51	6.80p on 3p gray	1.25	1.00
a.		Double surcharge	6.00	
C18	A52	17p on 5p choc	3.50	3.00
a.		Horiz. pair, imperf. between	50.00	
		Nos. C13-C18 (6)	6.95	5.75

Six stamps in the sheet of No. C17 have the "$" and numerals thinner and narrower than the normal type.

Airplane and Arms AP4   Cathedral of Asunción AP5

Airplane and Globe AP6

1930   *Perf. 12*
C19	AP4	95c dp red, *pink*	60	50
C20	AP4	95c dk bl, *bl*	60	50
C21	AP5	1.90p lt red, *pink*	60	50
C22	AP5	1.90p vio, *vio*	60	50
C23	AP6	6.80p blk, *lt bl*	60	50
C24	AP6	6.80p pin, *pink*	60	60
		Nos. C19-C24 (6)	3.60	3.10

Sheets of Nos. C19-C24 have a papermaker's watermark: "Extra Vencedor Bond."
Counterfeits exist.

Stamps and Types of 1927-28 Overprinted in Red   **CORREO AEREO**

1930
C25	A47	10c ol grn	20	15
a.		Double overprint	5.00	
C26	A47	20c dl bl	25	15
a.		"CORREO CORREO" instead of "CORREO AEREO"	5.00	
b.		"AEREO AEREO" instead of "CORREO AEREO"	5.00	
C27	A48	1p emerald	1.25	1.00
C28	A51	3p gray	1.25	1.00

AP7   AP8

AP9   AP10

1930   Red or Black Surcharge
C29	AP7	5c on 10c gray grn (R)	10	10
a.		"AEREO" omitted	30.00	
C30	AP7	5c on 70c ultra (R)	10	10
a.		Vert. pair, imperf. between	40.00	
C31	AP10	20c on 1p org red	35	35
a.		"CORREO" double	6.00	6.00
b.		"AEREO" double	6.00	6.00
C32	AP7	40c on 50c org (R)	25	20
a.		"AEREO" omitted	9.00	9.00
b.		"CORREO" double	6.00	6.00
c.		"AEREO" double	6.00	6.00
C33	AP8	6p on 10p red	2.00	1.50
C34	AP9	10p on 20p red	9.00	7.50
C35	AP9	10p on 20p vio brn	9.00	7.50
		Nos. C29-C35 (7)	20.80	17.25

Declaration of Independence AP11

1930, May 14   Typographed
C36	AP11	2.85p dk bl	60	50
C37	AP11	3.40p dk grn	60	40
C38	AP11	4.75p dp lake	60	40

Issued in commemoration of the National Independence Day, May 14, 1811.

Gunboat "Paraguay"—AP12

1931-39   *Perf. 11½, 12.*
C39	AP12	1p claret	25	25
C40	AP12	1p dk bl ('36)	25	25
C41	AP12	2p orange	30	30
C42	AP12	2p dk brn ('36)	30	30
C43	AP12	3p turq grn	60	55
C44	AP12	3p lt ultra ('36)	60	60
C45	AP12	3p brt rose ('39)	50	50
C46	AP12	6p dk grn	75	75
C47	AP12	6p vio ('36)	90	80
C48	AP12	6p dl bl ('39)	70	70
C49	AP12	10p vermilion	1.75	1.65
C50	AP12	10p bluish grn ('35)	2.50	2.50
C51	AP12	10p yel brn ('36)	2.00	2.00
C52	AP12	10p dk bl ('36)	1.25	1.25
C53	AP12	10p lt pink ('39)	1.75	1.75
		Nos. C39-C53 (15)	14.40	14.15

Issued in commemoration of the first constitution of Paraguay as a Republic and the arrival of the "Paraguay" and "Humaita."
Counterfeits of Nos. C39 to C53 are plentiful.

Regular Issue of 1924 Surcharged   **3 3 Correo Aéreo**

"Graf Zeppelin"

1931, Aug. 22
C54	A44	3p on 4p lt bl	13.00	10.00

Correo Aéreo Overprinted

"Graf Zeppelin"

C55	A44	4p lt bl	13.00	10.00

On Nos. C54-C55 the Zeppelin is handstamped. The rest of the surcharge or overprint is typographed.

PARAGUAY

War Memorial
AP13

Orange Tree
and Yerba Mate
AP14

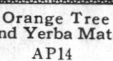

Yerba Mate
AP15

Palms
AP16

Eagle
AP17

1931-36 Lithographed.

C56	AP13	5c lt bl	15	10
a.	Horizontal pair, imperf. between		12.50	
C57	AP13	5c dp grn ('33)	12	12
C58	AP13	5c lt red ('33)	25	12
C59	AP13	5c vio ('35)	10	10
C60	AP14	10c dp vio	15	15
C61	AP14	10c brn lake ('33)	15	15
C62	AP14	10c yel brn ('33)	15	10
C63	AP14	10c ultra ('35)	10	10
a.	Imperf., pair		11.00	
C64	AP15	20c red	15	12
C65	AP15	20c dl bl ('33)	25	25
C66	AP15	20c emer ('33)	20	15
C67	AP15	20c yel brn ('35)	10	10
a.	Imperf., pair		7.50	
C68	AP16	40c dp grn	20	18
C69	AP16	40c sl bl ('35)	15	10
C70	AP16	40c red ('36)	25	20
C71	AP17	80c dl bl	20	18
C72	AP17	80c dl grn ('33)	30	25
C73	AP17	80c scar ('33)	25	18
	Nos. C56-C73 (18)		3.22	2.60

Airship "Graf Zeppelin"—AP18

1932, April Lithographed

C74	AP18	4p ultra	2.25	2.00
a.	Imperf., pair		10.00	
C75	AP18	8p red	3.50	2.50
C76	AP18	12p bl grn	2.75	2.25
C77	AP18	16p dk vio	6.00	4.00
C78	AP18	20p org brn	6.00	5.50
	Nos. C74-C78 (5)		20.50	16.25

"Graf Zeppelin"
over Brazilian Terrain
AP19

"Graf Zeppelin" over Atlantic
AP20

1933, May 5

C79	AP19	4.50p dp bl	2.50	2.00
C80	AP19	9p dp rose	5.00	4.00
a.	Horizontal pair, imperf. between		250.00	
C81	AP19	13.50p bl grn	5.00	4.00
C82	AP20	22.50p bis brn	12.50	10.00
C83	AP20	45p dl vio	17.50	17.50
	Nos. C79-C83 (5)		42.50	37.50

Excellent counterfeits are plentiful.

Posts and Telegraph Building,
Asunción—AP21

1934-37 Perf. 11½.

C84	AP21	33.75p ultra	3.00	2.50
C85	AP21	33.75p car ('35)	3.00	2.50
	33.75p rose ('37)		2.50	2.50
C86	AP21	33.75p emer ('36)	4.00	3.00
C87	AP21	33.75p bis brn ('36)	1.00	1.00

Nos. C79-C83
Overprinted in Black **1934**

1934, May 26

C88	AP19	4.50p dp bl	3.00	2.50
C89	AP19	9p dp rose	3.50	3.00
C90	AP19	13.50p bl grn	10.00	9.00
C91	AP20	22.50p bis brn	8.00	7.00
C92	AP20	45p dl vio	17.50	16.00
	Nos. C88-C92 (5)		42.00	37.50

Types of 1933 Issue
Overprinted in Black **1935**

1935

C93	AP19	4.50p rose red	4.00	3.00
C94	AP19	9p lt grn	5.00	4.00
C95	AP19	13.50p brown	15.00	12.00
C96	AP20	22.50p violet	12.50	11.00
C97	AP20	45p blue	35.00	30.00
	Nos. C93-C97 (5)		71.50	60.00

Tobacco Plant—AP22

1935-39 Typographed.

C98	AP22	17p lt brn	4.00	4.00
C99	AP22	17p carmine	7.50	7.50
C100	AP22	17p dk bl	5.00	5.00
C101	AP22	17p pale yel grn ('39)	3.00	3.00

Excellent counterfeits are plentiful.

Church of
Incarnation
AP23

1935-38

C102	AP23	102p carmine	7.50	6.00
C103	AP23	102p blue	7.50	6.00
C103A	AP23	102p ind ('36)	5.00	5.00
C104	AP23	102p yel brn	5.50	5.50
a.	Imperf. (pair)		30.00	
C105	AP23	102p vio ('37)	2.50	2.50
C106	AP23	102p brn org ('38)	2.25	2.25
	Nos. C102-C106 (6)		30.25	27.25

Excellent counterfeits are plentiful.

Habilitado
Types of 1934-35
Surcharged in Red

en $ 24.—

1937, Aug. 1

C107	AP21	24p on 33.75p sl bl	1.00	75
C108	AP23	65p on 102p ol bis	2.50	1.75
C109	AP23	84p on 102p bl grn	2.50	1.50

Plane over Asunción
AP24

Typographed

1939, Aug. 3 Perf. 10½, 11½.

C110	AP24	3.40p yel grn	1.00	1.00
C111	AP24	3.40p org brn	60	50
C112	AP24	3.40p indigo	60	50

Buenos Aires Peace Conference Issue.

Flags of Paraguay and Bolivia
AP25

Coats of Arms
AP26

President Ortiz of Argentina,
Flags of Paraguay, Argentina
AP27

Map of Paraguay with New
Chaco Boundary—AP28

Designs: 10p, Pres. Vargas, Brazil. 30p, Pres. Alessandri, Chile. 50p, U. S. Eagle and Shield. 100p, Pres. Benavides, Peru. 200p, Pres. Baldomir, Uruguay.

Engraved; Flags Lithographed

1939, Nov. Perf. 12½

Flags in National Colors

C113	AP25	1p red brn	15	12
C114	AP26	3p dk bl	20	15
C115	AP27	5p ol blk	20	18
C116	AP27	10p violet	25	20
C117	AP27	30p orange	40	25
C118	AP27	50p blk brn	60	40
C119	AP27	100p brt grn	90	80
C120	AP27	200p green	6.00	3.50
C121	AP28	500p black	15.00	12.50
	Nos. C113-C121 (9)		23.70	18.10

Pres. Bernardino Caballero and
Senator José S. Decoud—AP34

1939, Sept. Litho. Perf. 12

C122	AP34	28p rose & blk	7.50	6.50
C123	AP34	90p yel grn & blk	9.00	8.00

Issued in commemoration of the 50th anniversary of the founding of the University of Asunción.

Map with Asunción-New
York Air Route
AP35

1939, Nov. 30 Engraved.

C124	AP35	30p brown	5.50	4.00
C125	AP35	80p orange	7.00	6.00
C126	AP35	90p purple	11.50	11.00

New York World's Fair.

Map of the
Americas
AP36

1940, May Perf. 12

C127	AP36	20p rose car	50	35
C128	AP36	70p vio bl	1.25	45
C129	AP36	100p Prus grn	1.50	1.10
C130	AP36	500p dk vio	5.50	4.00

Issued in commemoration of the 50th anniversary of the founding of the Pan American Union.

The Indian
Francisco
AP37

Arms of
Irala
AP39

PARAGUAY

Domingo Martinez de Irala and His Vision—AP38

1942, Aug. 15				
C131	AP37	20p dp plum	1.50	1.25
C132	AP38	70p fawn	4.25	3.25
C133	AP39	500p ol gray	12.00	11.00

400th anniversary of Asunción.

Imperforates
Starting with No. C134, many Paraguayan air mail stamps exist imperforate.

Port of Asunción
AP40

First Telegraph in South America
AP41

Early Merchant Ship
AP42

Birthplace of Paraguay's Liberation
AP43

Monument to Antequera
AP44

Locomotive of First Paraguayan Railroad
AP45

Monument to Heroes of Itororó
AP46

Primitive Postal Service among Indians
AP48

Government House
AP47

Colonial Jesuit Altar
AP49

Ruins of Humaitá Church
AP50

Oratory of the Virgin
AP51

Marshal Francisco S. Lopez
AP52

1944-45		Perf. 12½	Unwmkd.	
C134	AP40	1c blue	10	8
C135	AP41	2c green	15	12
C136	AP42	3c brn vio	25	18
C137	AP43	5c brt bl grn	20	15
C138	AP44	10c dk vio	30	25
C139	AP45	20c dk brn	60	30
C140	AP46	30c lt bl	40	40
C141	AP47	40c olive	65	60
C142	AP48	70c brn red	85	80
C143	AP49	1g org yel	2.00	1.35
C144	AP50	2g cop brn	2.50	2.00
C145	AP51	5g blk brn	6.75	6.00
C146	AP52	10g indigo	15.00	13.50
	Nos. C134-C146 (13)		29.75	25.73

See also Nos. C158-C162.

Handshake, Map and Flags of Paraguay and Ecuador
AP53

Designs: (Flags.) 40c, Bolivia. 70c, Mexico. 1g, Chile. 2g, Brazil. 5g, Argentina. 10g, U.S.

Engraved; Flags Lithographed in National Colors.

1945, Aug. 15				
C147	AP53	20c orange	50	45
C148	AP53	40c olive	50	40
C149	AP53	70c lake	55	50
C150	AP53	1g sl bl	90	90
C151	AP53	2g bl vio	1.50	1.50
C152	AP53	5g green	2.00	2.00
C153	AP53	10g brown	9.00	9.00
	Nos. C147-C153 (7)		14.95	14.75

Issued to commemorate the goodwill visits of President Higinio Morinigo during 1943.
Sizes: Nos. C147-C151, 30x26mm.; 5g, 32x28mm.; 10g, 33x30mm.

Nos. C139-C142 Surcharged "1946" and New Value in Black.

1946		Engraved.	Perf. 12½	
C154	AP45	5c on 20c dk brn	1.00	1.00
C155	AP46	5c on 30c lt bl	1.00	1.00
C156	AP47	5c on 40c ol	1.00	1.00
C157	AP48	5c on 70c brn red	1.00	1.00

Types of 1944-45
1946, Sept. 21		Engraved.		
C158	AP50	10c dp car	10	10
C159	AP40	20c emerald	15	15
C160	AP47	1g brn org	75	75
C161	AP52	5g purple	2.25	2.25
C162	AP51	10g rose car	7.50	7.50
	Nos. C158-C162 (5)		10.75	10.75

Marshal Francisco Solano Lopez
AP60

1947, May 15			Perf. 12	
C163	AP60	32c car lake	20	20
C164	AP60	64c org brn	40	40
C165	AP60	1g Prus grn	60	60
C166	AP60	5g Prus grn & brn vio	2.00	2.00
C167	AP60	10g dk car rose & dk yel grn	3.00	3.00
	Nos. C163-C167 (5)		6.20	6.20

Archbishopric Coat of Arms
AP61

Projected Monument of the Sacred Heart of Jesus
AP62

Vision of Projected Monument
AP63

Juan Sinforiano Bogarin, Archbishop of Asunción
AP64

1948, Jan. 6		Perf. 12½	Unwmkd.	
Size: 25½x31mm.

C168	AP61	20c gray blk	12	10
C169	AP62	30c dk bl	15	15
C170	AP63	40c lilac	25	18
C171	AP64	70c org red	35	35
C172	AP62	1g brn red	45	45
C173	AP63	2g red	1.50	1.50

Size: 25½x34mm.

C174	AP64	5g brt car & dk bl	2.25	2.25
C175	AP61	10g dk grn & brn	3.25	3.25
	Nos. C168-C175 (8)		8.32	8.23

Issued to commemorate the 50th anniversary of the establishment of the Archbishopric of Asunción.

Type of Regular Issue of 1948 Inscribed "AEREO."
1948, Sept. 11		Engr. & Litho.		
C176	A119	69c dk grn, red & bl	1.00	1.00
C177	A119	5g dk bl, red & bl	4.50	3.50

The Barefeet, a political group.

No. C171 Surcharged in Black

1949, June 29				
C178	AP64	5c on 70c org red	25	25

Issued in tribute to Archbishop Juan Sinforiano Bogarin, 1863-1949.

Symbols of U.P.U.
AP65

Franklin D. Roosevelt
AP66

1950, Sept. 4	Engr.	Perf. 13½x13		
C179	AP65	20c grn & vio	30	30
C180	AP65	30c rose vio & brn	35	35
C181	AP65	50c gray & grn	40	40
C182	AP65	1g bl & brn	45	45
C183	AP65	5g rose & blk	1.00	1.00
	Nos. C179-C183 (5)		2.50	2.50

Issued to commemorate the 75th anniversary (in 1949) of the formation of the Universal Postal Union.

Engraved; Flags Lithographed
1950, Oct. 2		Perf. 12½		

Flags in Carmine & Violet Blue.

C184	AP66	20c red	15	15
C185	AP66	30c black	15	15
C186	AP66	50c claret	25	18
C187	AP66	1g dk gray grn	35	40
C188	AP66	5g dp bl	90	85
	Nos. C184-C188 (5)		1.80	1.73

Issued in tribute to Franklin D. Roosevelt, 1882-1945.

Urn Containing Remains of Columbus
AP67

1952, Feb. 11		Litho.	Perf. 10	
C189	AP67	10c ultra	6	6
C190	AP67	20c green	6	6
C191	AP67	30c lilac	8	8
C192	AP67	40c rose	10	10

PARAGUAY

C193	AP67	50c bis brn	12	12
C194	AP67	1g blue	15	15
C195	AP67	2g orange	30	30
C196	AP67	5g red brn	60	60
	Nos. C189-C196 (8)		1.47	1.47

Queen Isabella I
AP68

1952, Oct. 12

C197	AP68	1g vio bl	15	15
C198	AP68	2g chocolate	25	25
C199	AP68	5g dl gry	50	50
C200	AP68	10g lil rose	1.10	1.10

Issued to commemorate the 500th anniversary of the birth of Queen Isabella I of Spain (1951).

Silvio Pettirossi
AP69

1954, March

C201	AP69	40c brown	8	8
C202	AP69	55c green	12	12
C203	AP69	80c ultra	12	12
C204	AP69	1.30g gray bl	45	45

Issued to honor Silvio Pettirossi, aviator.

Church of San Roque—AP70

1954, June 20 Engraved Perf. 12x13

C205	AP70	20c carmine	10	8
C206	AP70	30c brn vio	10	8
C207	AP70	50c ultra	10	8
C208	AP70	1g red brn & bl grn	15	15
C209	AP70	1g red brn & lil rose	15	15
C210	AP70	1g red brn & blk	15	15
C211	AP70	1g red brn & org	15	15
a.		Miniature sheet of 4	60	60
C212	AP70	5g dk red brn & vio	25	25
C213	AP70	5g dk red brn & ol grn	25	25
C214	AP70	5g dk red brn & org yel	25	25
C215	AP70	5g dk red brn & yel org	25	25
a.		Miniature sheet of 4	1.25	1.25
	Nos. C205-C215 (11)		1.90	1.84

Centenary (in 1953) of the establishment of the Church of San Roque, Asuncion. Nos. C211a and C215a contain typographed reproductions respectively of Nos. C208-C211 and C212-C215. They are perforated 12x12½. Issued without gum. Size: 124x108mm.

Three National Heroes—AP71

Lithographed.

1954, Aug. 15 Perf. 10 Unwmkd.

C216	AP71	5g violet	30	30
C217	AP71	10g ol grn	55	55
C218	AP71	20g gray brn	1.00	85
C219	AP71	50g vermilion	2.25	2.25
C220	AP71	100g blue	7.50	7.50
	Nos. C216-C220 (5)		11.60	11.45

Issued to honor Marshal Francisco S. Lopez, Pres. Carlos A. Lopez and Gen. Bernardino Caballero.

Pres. Alfredo Stroessner
and Pres. Juan D. Peron
AP72

Photogravure and Lithographed

1955, Apr. Perf. 13x13½ Wmk. 90

Frames & Flags in Blue & Carmine

C221	AP72	60c ol grn & cr	6	6
C222	AP72	2g bl grn & cr	15	15
C223	AP72	3g brn org & cr	25	20
C224	AP72	4.10g brt rose pink & cr	35	30

Visit of Pres. Juan D. Peron of Argentina.

Jesuit Ruins, Trinidad Belfry
AP73

Santa Maria Cornice
AP74

Jesuit Ruins: 3g, Corridor at Trinidad. 6g, Tower of Santa Rosa. 10g, San Cosme gate. 20g, Church of Jesus. 30g, Niche at Trinidad. 50g, Sacristy at Trinidad.

Perf. 12½x12, 12x12½

1955, June 19 Engraved Unwmkd.

C225	AP73	2g aqua	8	8
C226	AP73	3g ol grn	8	8
C227	AP73	4g lt bl grn	8	8
C228	AP74	6g brown	8	8
C229	AP73	10g rose	12	12
C230	AP73	20g brn ol	20	20
C231	AP74	30g dk grn	80	60
C232	AP74	50g dp aqua	80	80
	Nos. C225-C232 (8)		2.24	2.04

Issued to commemorate the 25th anniversary of the priesthood of Monsignor Rodriguez.

Soldier and Flags
AP75

"Republic" and Soldier
AP76

Photogravure

1957, June 12 Perf. 13½ Unwmkd.

Granite Paper
Flags in Red and Blue

C233	AP75	10c ultra	5	5
C234	AP75	15c dp cl	5	5
C235	AP75	20c red	5	5
C236	AP75	25c lt bl	5	5
C237	AP75	50c bluish grn	5	5
C238	AP75	1g rose car	5	5
C239	AP76	1.30g dp cl	10	6
C240	AP76	1.50p lt bl	10	6
C241	AP76	2g emerald	10	6
C242	AP76	4.10g red	10	6
C243	AP76	5g gray blk	15	10
C244	AP76	10g bluish grn	20	15
C245	AP76	25g ultra	25	15
	Nos. C233-C245 (13)		1.55	1.19

Issued to honor the heroes of the Chaco war.

Type of Stroessner Regular Issue, 1958.

1958, Aug. 16 Litho. Wmk. 320

Center in Slate.

C246	A130	12g rose lil	50	50
C247	A130	18g orange	60	60
C248	A130	23g org brn	1.00	1.00
C249	A130	36g emerald	1.00	1.00
C250	A130	50g citron	1.25	1.25
C251	A130	65g gray	2.00	2.00
	Nos. C246-C251 (6)		6.35	6.35

Issued to commemorate the re-election of President General Alfredo Stroessner.

Nos. C225-C232 Surcharged in Red

Perf. 12½x12, 12x12½

1959, May 26 Engr. Unwmkd.

C252	AP73	4g on 2g aqua	20	15
C253	AP73	12.45g on 3g ol grn	35	30
C254	AP74	18.15g on 6g brn ol	50	45
C255	AP73	23.40g on 10g rose	70	55
C256	AP73	34.80g on 20g brn ol	1.00	75
C257	AP74	36g on 4g lt bl grn	1.10	80
C258	AP74	43.95g on 30g dk grn	1.30	90
C259	AP74	100g on 50g dp aqua	3.00	2.00
	Nos. C252-C259 (8)		8.15	5.90

The surcharge is made to fit the stamps. Counterfeits of surcharge exist.

U.N. Emblem
AP77

Typographed.

1959, Aug. 27 Perf. 11 Unwmkd.

C260	AP77	5g ocher & ultra	1.00	80

Issued to commemorate the visit of Dag Hammarskjold, Secretary General of the United Nations, Aug. 27–29.

Map and U. N. Emblem
AP78

Uprooted Oak Emblem
AP79

1959, Oct. 24 Litho. Perf. 10

C261	AP78	12.45g bl & sal	40	30

United Nations Day, Oct. 24, 1959.

Type of Regular Issue
(Olympic Games)

Design: Basketball.

1960, Mar. 18 Photo. Perf. 12½

C262	A131	12.45g red & dk bl	40	40
C263	A131	18.15g lil & gray ol	50	50
C264	A131	36g bl grn & rose car	1.00	1.00

Issued to publicize the 1960 Olympic Games. The Paraguayan Philatelic Agency reported as spurious the imperf. souvenir sheet reproducing one of No. C264.

1960, Apr. 7 Litho. Perf. 11

C265	AP79	4g grn & pink	1.25	75
C266	AP79	12.45g bl & yel grn	3.00	1.25
C267	AP79	18.15g car & ocher	5.00	1.50
C268	AP79	23.40g red org & bl	6.00	3.00

Issued to publicize World Refugee Year, July 1, 1959–June 30, 1960 (1st issue).

Type of Regular Issue, 1960.
(Human Rights)

Designs: 40g, U.N. Emblem. 60g, Hands holding scales. 100g, Flame.

1960, Apr. 21 Perf. 12½x13

C269	A133	40g dk ultra & red	75	75
C270	A133	60g grnsh bl & org	90	90
C271	A133	100g dk ultra & red	1.75	1.75

Issued to commemorate the United Nations' Declaration of Human Rights. An imperf. miniature sheet exists, containing one each of Nos. C269-C271, all printed in green and vermilion. Size: 139x94mm.

Type of Regular Issue
(United Nations)

Perf. 13x13½

1960, Oct. 24 Photo. Unwmkd.

C272	A134	3g org, red & bl	10	10
C273	A134	4g pale grn, red & bl	12	12

15th anniversary of the United Nations.

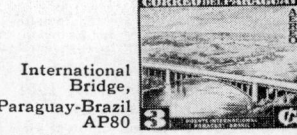

International Bridge, Paraguay-Brazil
AP80

1961, Jan. 26 Litho. Perf. 14

C274	AP80	3g carmine	15	12
C275	AP80	12.45g brn lake	35	30
C276	AP80	18.15g Prus grn	40	35
C277	AP80	36g dk bl	75	70
a.		Souvenir sheet of 4	1.50	1.50

Issued to commemorate the inauguration of the International Bridge between Paraguay and Brazil. No. C277a contains one each of Nos. C274-C277, imperf. Marginal inscription in dark blue and Prussian green. Size: 123x180mm.

"Paraguay en Marcha"
Type of 1961.

Designs: 12.45g, Truck carrying logs. 18.15g, Logs on river barge. 22g, Radio tower. 36g, Jet plane.

1961, Apr. 10 Perf. 13

C278	A136	12.45g yel & vio bl	50	40
C279	A136	18.15g pur & ocher	60	50

PARAGUAY

C280	A136	22g ultra & ocher	75	60
C281	A136	36g brt grn & yel	80	75

Issued to publicize Paraguay's progress.

Declaration
of Independence—AP81
1961, May 16   Litho.   Perf. 14½

C282	AP81	12.45g dl red brn	25	25
C283	AP81	18.15g dk bl	40	35
C284	AP81	23.40g green	50	45
C285	AP81	30g lilac	60	55
C286	AP81	36g rose	80	75
C287	AP81	44g olive	1.00	.90
		Nos. C282-C287 (6)	3.55	3.25

Issued to commemorate the 150th anniversary of Independence (1st issue).

"Paraguay" and   South American
Clasped Hands   Tapir
AP82   AP83
1961, June 12   Perf. 14x14½

C288	AP82	3g vio bl	30	30
C289	AP82	4g rose cl	30	30
C290	AP82	100g gray grn	1.75	1.60

Issued to commemorate the Chaco Peace and the 150th anniversary of Independence (2nd issue).

1961, Aug 16   Perf. 14   Unwmkd.

C291	AP83	12.45g claret	1.50	1.00
C292	AP83	18.15g ultra	1.50	1.50
C293	AP83	34.80g red brn	3.00	3.00

Issued to commemorate the 150th anniversary of Independence (3rd issue).

Type of Regular Issue, 1961
(Catholic University)
1961, Sept. 18   Perf. 14x14½

C294	A140	3g bis brn	15	15
C295	A140	12.45g lil rose	40	40
C296	A140	36g blue	80	80

Issued to commemorate the founding of the Catholic University in Asuncion and the 150th anniversary of Independence (4th issue).

Type of Regular Issue, 1961
(Hotel Guarani)
Design: Hotel Guarani, different view.
1961, Oct. 14   Litho.   Perf. 15

C297	A141	3g dl red brn	10	10
C298	A141	4g ultra	12	12
C299	A141	18.15g orange	50	45
C300	A141	36g rose car	80	75

Issued to commemorate the opening of the Hotel Guarani and the 150th anniversary of Independence (5th issue).

Type of Regular Issue, 1961
(Tennis Championships)
1961, Oct. 16 Perf. 11   Unwmkd.

C301	A142	12.45g multi		50
C302	A142	20g multi		90
C303	A142	50g multi		2.00

Issued to commemorate the 28th South American Tennis Championships, Asuncion, Oct. 15–23 (1st issue). Some specialists question the status of this issue. Two imperf. souvenir sheets exist containing four 12.45s stamps each in a different color with simulated perforations and black marginal inscription. Size: 104x158mm.

Type of Regular Issue, 1961.
(World Refugee Year)
Design: Oak emblem rooted in ground, wavy-lined frame.
1961, Dec. 30

C307	A145	18.15g brn & red		75
C308	A145	36g car & emer		1.50
C309	A145	50g emer & org		2.00

Issued for World Refugee Year, 1959–60 (2nd issue). Imperforates in changed colors and souvenir sheets exist. Some specialists question the status of this issue.

Type of Regular Issue, 1962
(Tennis Championships)
Design: Map of South America and tennis player using backhand stroke.
1962, Jan. 5   Perf. 15x14½

C310	A146	4g carmine	15	15
C311	A146	12.45g red lil	40	40
C312	A146	20g bl grn	80	80
C313	A146	50g org brn	1.10	1.10

Issued to commemorate the 28th South American Tennis Championships, 1961 (second issue) and the 150th anniversary of Independence (6th issue).

Lord Baden-Powell
AP84
1962, Feb. 6   Perf. 11

C314	AP84	12.45g car rose & bl		60
C315	AP84	36g car rose & emer		1.75
C316	AP84	50g car rose & org yel		2.50

Issued to honor the Boy Scouts. Imperfs. in changed colors and perf. and imperf. souvenir sheets exist. Some specialists question the status of this issue.

Pres. Alfredo Stroessner
and Prince Philip
AP85
1962, Mar. 9   Lithographed
Portraits in Ultramarine

C317	AP85	12.45g grn & buff	25	25
C318	AP85	18.15g red & pink	35	35
C319	AP85	36g brn & yel	65	65

Visit of Prince Philip, Duke of Edinburgh. Perf. and imperf. souvenir sheets exist.

Type of Regular Issue, 1962
(Day of the Americas)
Design: 20g, 50g, Hands holding globe.
Perf. 14x14½
1962, Apr. 14   Unwmkd.

C320	A148	20g lil rose	35	35
C321	A148	50g orange	75	75

See note after No. 651.

Type of Regular Issue, 1962
(United Nations)
Design: U.N. Headquarters, New York.
1962, Apr. 23   Perf. 15

C322	A149	12.45g dl vio	50	50
C323	A149	18.15g ol grn	75	75

C324	A149	23.40g brn red	1.00	1.00
C325	A149	30g carmine	1.25	1.25

See note after No. 655.

Type of Regular Issue, 1962
(Malaria Eradication)
Designs: 3g, 4g, Malaria eradication emblem. 12.45g, 18.15g, 36g, Mosquito, U.N. emblem and microscope.
Perf. 14x13½
1962, May 23   Wmk. 346

C326	A150	3g bl, red & blk		8
C327	A150	4g grn, red & blk		10
C328	A150	12.45g ol bis, grn & blk		35
C329	A150	18.15g rose lil, red & blk		75
C330	A150	36g rose red, vio bl & blk		2.00

Issued for the World Health Organization drive to eradicate malaria. Imperforates exist in changed colors. Two souvenir sheets exist, one containing one copy of No. C330, the other an imperf. 36g in blue, red & black. Gray margins; size 105x70mm. Some specialists question the status of this anti-malaria issue.

Soccer Players and Globe
AP86
1962, July 28   Lithographed

C331	AP86	12.45g brt rose, blk & vio		75
C332	AP86	18.15g lt red brn, blk & vio		1.10
C333	AP86	36g gray grn, blk & brn		2.25

Issued to commemorate the World Soccer Championships, Chile, May 30–June 17, 1962. A souvenir sheet contains one copy of No. C333 with dull orange marginal inscription and emblem. Size: 105x70mm. Some specialists question the status of this issue.

Ship's Wheel   Lt. Col. John H.
                            Glenn, Jr. and
                          Lt. Cmdr. Scott
                                 Carpenter
AP87   AP88
Design: 44g, Like 12.45g with diagonal colorless band in background.
Perf. 15x14½
1962, July 31   Unwmkd.

C334	AP87	12.45g dk red	25	20
C335	AP87	44g blue	75	65

Issued to honor the Merchant Marine.

Perf. 13½x14
1962, Sept. 4   Litho.   Wmk. 346

C336	AP88	12.45g car lake & gray		25
C337	AP88	18.15g red lil & gray		40
C338	AP88	36g dl cl & gray		80

Issued to publicize U.S. manned space flights. Imperfs. in changed colors and two souvenir sheets exist. Some specialists question the status of this issue.

Olympic Games Type of Regular Issue, 1962
Design (Olympic flame and): 12.45g, Melbourne, 1956. 18.15g, Rome, 1960. 36g, Tokyo, 1964.
1962, Oct. 1

C339	A154	12.45g brt grn, lt grn & choc		25
C340	A154	18.15g ol brn, yel & choc		40
C341	A154	36g rose red, pink & choc		80

Issued to publicize the Olympic Games. Imperfs. in changed colors and two souvenir sheets exist. Some specialists question the status of this issue.

Dove Symbolizing Holy Ghost
AP89
Perf. 14½
1962, Oct. 11   Litho.   Unwmkd.

C342	AP89	5g vio bl	14	12
C343	AP89	10g brt grn	26	20
C344	AP89	12.45g lake	28	22
C345	AP89	18.15g orange	50	40
C346	AP89	23.40g violet	58	42
C347	AP89	36g rose red	1.00	70
		Nos. C342-C347 (6)	2.76	2.06

Vatican II. See note after No. 685.

Stroessner Type of 1963
1963, Aug. 6   Litho.   Wmk. 347

C348	A156	12.45g pink & cl	35	30
C349	A156	18.15g pink & grn	50	45
C350	A156	36g pink & vio	1.50	1.00

Third presidential term of Alfredo Stroessner. A 36g imperf. souvenir sheet exists.

National Holiday Type of 1964
Design: Asuncion Cathedral, Popes Paul VI and John XXIII.
1964, May 23

C351	A157	12.45g sl grn & lem	35	30
C352	A157	18.15g pur & lem	50	45
C353	A157	36g vio bl & lem	2.00	1.60

National holiday of St. Maria Auxilliadora (Our Lady of Perpetual Help).

De Gaulle Visit Type of 1964
Designs: 12.45g, 36g, Presidents Stroessner and de Gaulle. 18.15g, Coats of Arms of Paraguay and France.
1964, Oct. 6

C354	A158	12.45g lilac	35	30
C355	A158	18.15g bl grn	50	45
C356	A158	36g magenta	2.00	1.60

Visit of Pres. Charles de Gaulle of France.

National Epic Type of 1965
1965, Apr. 26 Perf. 11 Wmk. 347

C357	A159	12.45g brn & blk	28	22
C358	A159	36g brt lil & blk	1.00	70

Centenary of National Epic. Not issued without overprint.

Ceibo
Tree
AP90

PARAGUAY

1965, June 28 *Perf. 14½* **Unwmkd.**

C359	AP90	3g brn red	8	6
C360	AP90	4g green	10	8
C361	AP90	66g brn org	1.65	1.00

150th anniversary of Independence (1811-1961).

St. Ignatius and San Ignacio Monastery
AP91

1966, Apr. 20 *Perf. 11* **Wmk. 347**

C362	AP91	3g brown	6	5
C363	AP91	12.45g sepia	20	15
C364	AP91	18.15g sepia	30	20
C365	AP91	23.40g sepia	50	40

Issued to commemorate the 350th anniversary of the founding of San Ignacio Guazu Monastery.

"Paraguay de Fuego" by Dario — AP92
Medical Laboratory "Health" — AP93

1966, July 16 Lithographed

C366	AP92	12.45g blue	15	12
C367	AP92	18.15g red lil	20	18
C368	AP92	23.40g org brn	50	20
C369	AP92	36g brt grn	75	35
C370	AP92	50g rose car	85	40
		Nos. C366-C370 (5)	2.45	1.25

See note after No. 713.

1967, May 9 **Wmk. 347**

Designs: 12.45g, 18.15g, Library "Education."

C371	AP93	12.45g dk brn	15	12
C372	AP93	18.15g violet	20	18
C373	AP93	23.40g rose cl	25	20
C374	AP93	36g Prus bl	60	35
C375	AP93	50g rose car	70	40
		Nos. C371-C375 (5)	1.90	1.25

50th anniversary of Lions International.

WHO Emblem — AP94
Torch, Book, Houses — AP95

1968, Aug. 12 Litho. *Perf. 11*

C376	AP94	36g blk brn	60	35
C377	AP94	50g rose cl	70	45
C378	AP94	100g brt bl	1.50	90

Issued to commemorate the 20th anniversary of the World Health Organization, and the centenary of the national epic.

1969, June 28 *Perf. 11* **Wmk. 347**

C379	AP95	36g blue	1.00	
C380	AP95	50g bis brn	1.25	
C381	AP95	100g rose car	2.50	

National drive for teachers' homes.

Solano Lopez Type of Regular Issue
1970, March 1 *Perf. 11* **Wmk. 347**

C382	A165	15g lt Prus bl	21	15
C383	A165	20g org brn	28	20
C384	A165	30g gray grn	42	30
C385	A165	40g gray brn	56	40

See note after No. 736.

Centenary Type of Regular Issue
1970, Aug. 15 Lithographed

Designs (First Issue of Paraguay): 15g, No. 3. 30g, No. 2. 36g, No. 1.

C386	A166	15g vio brn	45	36
C387	A166	30g dp grn	90	72
C388	A166	36g brt pink	1.00	84

Centenary of stamps of Paraguay.

UNESCO Type of Regular Issue
Perf. 11

1971, May 18 Litho. **Wmk. 347**

C389	A167	20g claret	28	20
C390	A167	25g brt pink	35	25
C391	A167	30g brown	40	30
C392	A167	50g gray ol	70	50

International Education Year.

UNICEF Type of Regular Issue
1972, Jan. 24 Granite Paper

C393	A168	20g brt bl	28	20
C394	A168	25g lt ol	35	25
C395	A168	30g dk brn	40	30

See note after No. 750.

Tourism Year Type of Regular Issue
Designs: 20g, Bus and car on highway. 25g, Hospital of Institute for Social Service. 50g, "Presidente Stroessner" of state merchant marine. 100g, "Electra C" of Paraguayan airlines.

1972, Nov. 16 *Perf. 13½x13*
Granite Paper

C396	A169	20g rose car	28	20
C397	A169	25g gray	35	25
C398	A169	50g violet	70	50
C399	A169	100g brt lil	1.40	1.00

Tourism Year of the Americas.

OAS Type of Regular Issue
1973 Lithographed *Perf. 13x13½*
Granite Paper

C400	A170	20g multi	28	20
C401	A170	25g multi	35	25
C402	A170	50g multi	70	50
C403	A170	100g multi	1.40	1.00

25th anniversary of the Organization of American States.

Exhibition Type of Regular Issue
1973, Aug. 11 Litho. *Perf. 13x13½*
Granite Paper

| C404 | A172 | 20g lil rose | 28 | 20 |
| C405 | A172 | 25g rose cl | 35 | 25 |

EXPOPAR 73, Paraguayan Industrial Exhibition.

UPU Type of 1974
Perf. 13½x13

1975, Feb. **Wmk. 347**

| C406 | A173 | 20g blk & brn | 28 | 25 |
| C407 | A173 | 25g blk & emer | 35 | 30 |

Centenary of Universal Postal Union.

Institute Type of 1976
Perf. 13½x13

1976, Mar. 16 Litho. **Wmk. 347**

| C408 | A174 | 30g brn, blk & red | 42 | 35 |

Inauguration of Institute of Higher Education.

Rotary Type of 1976
1976, Mar. 16 *Perf. 13½x13*

| C409 | A175 | 25g emer, bl & lem | 35 | 25 |

Rotary International, 70th anniversary.

IWY Type of 1976
1976, Mar. 16 **Wmk. 347**

| C410 | A176 | 20g grn & brn | 28 | 20 |

International Women's Year 1975.

Types of 1977
Designs: 20g, Rose tabebuia. 25g, Woman holding ceramic pot.

1977 Litho. *Perf. 13x13½*

| C411 | A177 | 20g multi | 50 | 35 |
| C412 | A178 | 25g multi | 60 | 40 |

Issue dates: 20g, Apr. 25; 25g, June 27.

Marshal Type of 1977
1977, July 24 Litho. **Wmk. 347**

| C413 | A179 | 50g dk vio | 1.00 | 75 |
| C414 | A179 | 100g green | 2.00 | 1.50 |

Marshal Francisco Solano Lopez, sesquicentennial of birth.

National College Type 1978
Wmk. 347

1978 Litho. *Perf. 13½x13*

C415	A180	20g brown	32	25
C416	A180	25g vio blk	40	30
C417	A180	30g brt grn	50	35

Centenary of National College in Asuncion.

Estigarribia Type of 1978
1978 Photo. *Perf. 13½x13*

C418	A181	20g multi	32	24
C419	A181	25g multi	40	30
C420	A181	30g multi	48	36

Induction of José Felix Estigarribia (1888-1940), general and president of Paraguay, into Salon de Bronce (National Heroes' Hall of Fame).

Tourism Type of 1979
Lithographed

1979, Aug. *Perf. 13½x13* **Wmk. 347**

| C421 | A182 | 50g red, bl & blk | 80 | 60 |

22nd Latin-American Tourism Congress, Asuncion.

Pilar Type of 1980
Wmk. 347

1980, July 17 Litho. *Perf. 13½x13*

| C422 | A183 | 25g multi | 40 | 30 |

Jet Type of 1980
Wmk. 347

1980, Sept. 17 Litho. *Perf. 13½x13*

| C422A | A183a | 100g multi | 1.60 | 1.25 |

Metropolitan Seminary Centenary—AP96
Wmk. 347

1981, Mar. 26 Litho. *Perf. 13½x13*

C423	AP96	5g ultra	8	6
C424	AP96	10g red brn	16	12
C425	AP96	25g green	40	30
C426	AP96	50g gray	80	60

UPU Issue
Wmk. 347

1981, Aug. 18 Litho. *Perf. 13½x13*

C427	A184	20g grn & blk	32	24
C428	A184	25g lt red brn & blk	40	30
C429	A184	50g bl & blk	80	60

Mother Maria Mazzarello (1837-1881), Co-Founder of Daughters of Mary
AP97

1981, Dec. 30 Litho. *Perf. 13x13½*

C430	AP97	20g blk & grn	32	24
C431	AP97	25g blk & red brn	40	30
C432	AP97	50g blk & gray vio	80	60

PARAGUAY

D1   D2

POSTAGE DUE STAMPS.

Lithographed

1904 Perf. 11½ Unwmkd.

J1	D1	2c green	40	35
J2	D1	4c green	40	35
J3	D1	10c green	40	35
J4	D1	20c green	40	35

1913 **Engraved**

J5	D2	1c yel brn	10	5
J6	D2	2c yel brn	10	8
J7	D2	5c yel brn	10	8
J8	D2	10c yel brn	15	10
J9	D2	20c yel brn	15	10
J10	D2	40c yel brn	15	10
J11	D2	1p yel brn	15	10
J12	D2	1.50p yel brn	20	15
		Nos. J5-J12 (8)	1.10	76

INTERIOR OFFICE ISSUES.

The "C" signifies "Campaña" (rural). These stamps were sold by Postal Agents in country districts, who received a commission on their sales. These stamps were available for postage in the interior but not in Asunción or abroad.

Nos. 243-244 Overprinted in Red

1922

L1	A42	50c car & dk bl	20	10
L2	A41	1p dk bl & brn	25	15

The overprint on Nos. L1-L2 exists double or inverted. Counterfeits exist.

Nos. 215, 218, J12 Surcharged

C
Habilitado
en
$ 1:—
1924

1924

L3	A40	50c on 75c dp bl	15	5
L4	A40	1p on 1.25p pale bl	15	5
L5	D2	1p on 1.50p yel brn	15	12

Nos. L3-L4 exist imperf.

Nos. 254, 257-260 Overprinted

C in Black or Red.

1924-26

L6	A45	50c red ('25)	10	5
L7	A44	1p dk bl (R)	10	8
L8	A45	1p dk bl (R) ('25)	10	5
L9	A46	1p bl (R) ('25)	12	6
L10	A45	1p emer ('26)	10	5
		Nos. L6-L10 (5)	52	29

Nos. L6, L8-L9 exist imperf. Price $5 each pair.

Same Overprint on Stamps and Type of 1927-36 in Red or Black.

1927-39

L11	A47	50c ultra (R)	10	10
L12	A47	50c dl red ('28)	10	10
L13	A47	50c org ('29)	10	10
L14	A47	50c lt bl ('30)	10	10
L15	A47	50c gray (R) ('31)	10	10
L16	A47	50c bluish grn (R) ('33)	10	10
L17	A47	50c vio (R) ('34)	10	10
L18	A48	1p emerald	10	10
L19	A48	1p org red ('29)	10	10
L20	A48	1p lil brn ('31)	10	10
L21	A48	1p dk bl (R) ('33)	10	10
L22	A48	1p brt vio (R) ('35)	10	10
L23	A49	1.50p brown	10	10
a.		Double overprint	3.00	
L24	A49	1.50p lil ('28)	10	10
L25	A49	1.50p dl bl (R)	10	10
L26	A50	2.50p bis ('28)	30	12
L27	A50	2.50p vio (R) ('36)	10	10
L28	A51	3p gray (R)	15	10
L29	A51	3p rose red ('39)	18	10
L30	A52	5p vio (R) ('36)	12	10
L31	A57	10p gray brn (R) ('36)	60	50
		Nos. L11-L31 (21)	2.95	2.52

Types of 1931-35 and No. 305 Overprinted in Black or Red

1931-36

L32	A59	1p lt red	10	10
L33	A58	1.50p dp bl (R)	10	10
L34	A60	1.50p bis brn ('32)	12	10
L35	A60	1.50p grn (R) ('34)	12	10
L36	A60	1.50p bl (R) ('35)	12	10
L37	A54	10p vermilion	2.50	2.50
		Nos. L32-L37 (6)	3.06	3.00

OFFICIAL STAMPS.

O1

O2   O3

O4   O5

O6   O7

Lithographed

1886, Aug. 20 Imperf. Unwmkd.

O1	O1	1c orange	5.00	5.00
O2	O2	2c violet	5.00	5.00
O3	O3	5c red	5.00	5.00
O4	O4	7c green	5.00	5.00
O5	O5	10c brown	5.00	5.00
O6	O6	15c sl bl	5.00	5.00
a.		Wavy lines on face of stamp		
b.		"OFICIAL" omitted	2.00	
O7	O7	20c claret	5.00	5.00
		Nos. O1-O7 (7)	35.00	35.00

Nos. O1 to O7 have the date and various control marks and letters printed on the back of each stamp in blue and black.
The overprints exist inverted on all values.

Nos. O1 to O7 have been reprinted from new stones made from slightly retouched dies.

O8

O9   O10

O11   O12

O13   O14

1886 Perf. 11½

O8	O8	1c dk grn	1.00	1.00
O9	O9	2c scarlet	1.00	1.00
O10	O10	5c dl bl	1.00	1.00
O11	O11	7c orange	1.00	1.00
O12	O12	10c lake	1.00	1.00
O13	O13	15c brown	1.00	1.00
O14	O14	20c blue	1.00	1.00
		Nos. O8-O14 (7)	7.00	7.00

The overprint exists inverted on all values. Price $3.

No. 20 Overprinted

1886, Sept. 1

| O15 | A11 | 1c dk grn | 3.00 | 3.00 |

O15

Handstamped Surcharge in Black

1889 Imperf.

O16	O15	3c on 15c vio	3.00	2.00
O17	O15	5c on 15c red brn	3.00	2.00

Perf. 11½

O18	O15	1c on 15c mar	3.00	2.00
O19	O15	2c on 15c mar	3.00	2.00

Counterfeits of Nos. O16-O19 abound.

Regular Issue of 1887 Handstamp Overprinted in Violet

Typographed

1890 Perf. 11½-12½ & Compounds

O20	A12	1c green	25	20
O21	A12	2c rose red	25	20
O22	A12	5c blue	25	20
O23	A12	7c brown	7.50	5.00
O24	A12	10c lilac	25	20
O25	A12	15c orange	95	50
O26	A12	20c pink	75	60
		Nos. O20-O26 (7)	10.25	6.95

Nos. O20-O26 exist with double overprint and all but the 20c with inverted overprint.
Nos. O20-O22, O24-O26 exist with blue overprint. The status is questioned. Price, set $30.

Stamps and Type of 1887 Regular Issue Overprinted in Black

1892

O33	A12	1c green	18	12
O34	A12	2c rose red	18	12
O35	A12	5c blue	18	12
O36	A12	7c brown	3.50	2.00
O37	A12	10c lilac	1.25	45
O38	A12	15c orange	35	18
O39	A12	20c pink	45	20
O40	A12	50c gray	25	25
		Nos. O33-O40 (8)	6.34	3.44

No. 26 Overprinted

1893

| O41 | A12 | 7c brown | 20.00 | 10.00 |

Counterfeits of No. O41 exist.

O16

1901, Feb. Engr. Perf. 11½, 12½

O42	O16	1c dl bl	40	40
O43	O16	2c rose red	15	12
O44	O16	4c dk brn	15	12
O45	O16	5c dk grn	15	12
O46	O16	8c org brn	15	15
O47	O16	10c car rose	20	20
O48	O16	20c dp bl	30	25
		Nos. O42-O48 (7)	1.50	1.36

A 12c deep green, type O16, was prepared but not issued.

No. 45 Overprinted Oficial

1902 Perf. 12 x 12½

| O49 | A12 | 1p ol grn | 18 | 18 |
| a. | | Inverted overprint | 20.00 | |

Counterfeits of No. O49a exist.

Regular Issue of 1903 Overprinted

1903 Perf. 11½.

O50	A32	1c gray	15	10
O51	A32	2c bl grn	15	10
O52	A32	5c blue	18	12
O53	A32	10c org brn	15	10
O54	A32	20c carmine	15	10
O55	A32	30c dp bl	15	10
O56	A32	60c purple	25	20
		Nos. O50-O56 (7)	1.18	82

O17   O18

1905-08 Engraved Perf. 11½, 12

O57	O17	1c gray grn	30	15
O58	O17	1c ol grn ('05)	40	15
O59	O17	1c brn org ('06)	90	20
O60	O17	1c ver ('08)	50	25
O61	O17	2c brn org	30	15
O62	O17	2c gray grn ('05)	30	15
O63	O17	2c red ('06)	1.50	50
O64	O17	2c gray ('08)	75	40
O65	O17	5c dp bl ('06)	40	25
O66	O17	5c gray bl ('08)	3.00	2.00
O67	O17	5c grnsh bl ('08)	1.50	1.25
O68	O17	10c vio ('06)	25	15
O69	O17	20c vio ('08)	1.25	75
		Nos. O57-O69 (13)	11.35	6.35

1908

O70	O17	10c bister	7.00	
O71	O17	10c emerald	7.00	
O72	O17	10c red lil	9.00	
O73	O17	20c bister	6.00	

PARAGUAY—PERU

O74	O17	20c sal pink	7.00
O75	O17	20c green	7.00
O76	O17	30c turq bl	7.00
O77	O17	30c bl gray	7.00
O78	O17	30c yellow	3.00
O79	O17	60c chocolate	7.00
O80	O17	60c org brn	8.00
O81	O17	60c dp ultra	6.00
O82	O18	1p brt rose & blk	50.00
O83	O18	1p lake & blk	50.00
O84	O18	1p brn org & blk	50.00
		Nos. O70-O84 (15)	231.00

Nos. O70-O84 were not issued, but were surcharged or overprinted for use as regular postage stamps. See Nos. 131, 133, 135-138, 144-145, 158-165, 171-173.

O19

1913   **Perf. 11½**

O85	O19	1c gray	10	5
O86	O19	2c orange	10	6
O87	O19	5c lilac	10	5
O88	O19	10c green	10	6
O89	O19	20c dl red	10	8
O90	O19	50c rose	10	8
O91	O19	75c dp bl	10	8
O92	O19	1p dl bl	10	10
O93	O19	2p yellow	25	25
		Nos. O85-O93 (9)	1.05	81

Type of Regular Issue of 1927-38
Overprinted in Red **OFICIAL**

1935

O94	A47	10c lt ultra	10	5
O95	A47	50c violet	10	6
O96	A48	1p orange	10	5
O97	A60	1.50p green	15	10
O98	A50	2.50p violet	15	12
		Nos. O94-O98 (5)	60	38

Overprint is diagonal on 1.50p.

President Escobar and Ramon Zubizarreta
O20

1940   **Lithographed.**   **Perf. 12.**

O99	O20	50c red brn & blk	10	6
O100	O20	1p rose pink & blk	10	7
O101	O20	2p lt bl grn & blk	10	7
O102	O20	5p ultra & blk	10	8
O103	O20	10p lt vio & blk	15	10
O104	O20	50p dp org & blk	60	50
		Nos. O99-O104 (6)	1.15	88

Issued in commemoration of the 50th anniversary of the founding of the University of Asunción.

PARMA
See Italian States group preceding Italy in Vol. III.

PERSIA
See Iran, Vol. III.

PERU
(pĕ·rōō′)
LOCATION—West coast of South America.
GOVT.—Republic.
AREA—496,093 sq. mi.
POP.—16,580,000 (est. 1977).
CAPITAL—Lima.

8 Reales = 1 Peso
100 Centavos = 10 Dineros = 5 Pesetas = 1 Peso
100 Centavos = 1 Sol (1874)

Prices of early Peru stamps vary according to condition. Quotations for Nos. 1-15 are for fine copies. Very fine to superb specimens sell at much higher prices, and inferior or poor copies sell at reduced prices, depending on the condition of the individual specimen.

Sail and Steamship
A1
Design: 2r, Ship sails eastward.
Engraved.

1857, Dec. 1   **Imperf.**   **Unwmkd.**

1	A1	1r bl, bl	2,250.	2,500.
2	A1	2r brn red, bl	2,750.	3,750.

The Pacific Steam Navigation Co. gave a quantity of these stamps to the Peruvian government so that a trial of prepayment of postage by stamps might be made.
Stamps of 1 and 2 reales, printed in various colors on white paper, laid and wove, were prepared for the Pacific Steam Navigation Co. but never put in use. Price $50 each on wove paper, $400 each on laid paper.

Coat of Arms
A2   **A3**

A4

Wavy Lines in Spandrels.
1858, Mar. 1   **Lithographed**

3	A2	1d dp bl	250.00	40.00
4	A3	1p rose red	1,100.	175.00
5	A4	½peso rose red	4,750.	4,500.
6	A4	½peso buff	2,250.	800.00
a.		½peso org yel	2,250.	800.00

A5   **A6**
Large Letters.
1858, Dec.   **Double-lined Frame**

7	A5	1d sl bl	325.00	40.00
8	A6	1p red	325.00	70.00

A7   **A8**

1860-61   Zigzag Lines in Spandrels

9	A7	1d blue	125.00	11.00
a.		Prus bl	125.00	20.00
b.		Cornucopia on white ground	300.00	65.00
c.		Zigzag lines broken at angles	200.00	25.00
10	A8	1p rose	325.00	30.00
a.		1p brick red	325.00	30.00
b.		Cornucopia on white ground	325.00	30.00

Retouched,
10 lines instead of 9 in left label.

11	A8	1p rose	165.00	35.00
a.		Pelure paper	275.00	35.00

A9   **A10**

1862-63   **Embossed.**

12	A9	1d red	20.00	4.00
a.		Arms embossed sideways	600.00	125.00
b.		Thick paper	40.00	12.50
c.		Diagonal half used on cover		200.00
13	A10	1p brn ('63)	125.00	40.00
a.		Diagonal half used on cover		1,500.

Counterfeits of Nos. 13 and 15 exist.

A11

1868-72

14	A11	1d green	15.00	3.00
a.		Arms embossed inverted	2,250.	800.00
b.		Diagonal half used on cover		500.00
15	A10	1p org ('72)	125.00	40.00
a.		Diagonal half used on cover		40.00

Nos. 12-15, 19 and 20 were printed in horizontal strips. Stamps may be found printed on two strips of paper where the strips were joined by overlapping.

Llamas
A12

A13   **A14**

1866-67   **Engraved**   **Perf. 12**

16	A12	5c green	7.00	1.00
17	A13	10c vermilion	7.00	2.00
18	A14	20c brown	30.00	5.00
a.		Diagonal half used on cover		550.00

See also Nos. 109, 111, 113.

Locomotive and Arms
A15

1871, Apr.   **Embossed**   **Imperf.**

19	A15	5c scarlet	100.00	35.00
a.		5c pale red	100.00	35.00

Issued to commemorate the 20th anniversary of the first railway in South America, linking Lima and Callao.
The so-called varieties "ALLAO" and "CALLA" are due to over-inking.

Llama
A16

1873, Mar.   **Rouletted Horiz.**

20	A16	2c dk ultra	50.00	500.00

Counterfeits are plentiful.

Sun God of the Incas
A17

Coat of Arms
A18   **A19**

A20   **A21**

A22   **A23**

Embossed with Grill.
1874-84   **Engraved**   **Perf. 12**

21	A17	1c org ('79)	75	60
22	A18	2c dk vio	1.00	75
23	A19	5c bl ('77)	1.25	40
24	A19	5c ultra ('79)	12.00	2.00
25	A20	10c grn ('76)	40	35
a.		Imperf., pair	40.00	
26	A20	10c sl ('84)	3.00	35
a.		Diagonal half used as 5c on cover		
27	A21	20c brn red	2.00	1.00

28	A22	50c green	12.00	3.00
29	A23	1s rose	2.00	1.75
		Nos. 21-29 (9)	34.40	10.20

No. 25a lacks the grill.

No. 26 with overprint "DE OFICIO" is said to have been used to frank mail of Gen. A. A. Caceres during the civil war against Gen. Miguel Iglesias, provisional president. Experts question its status.

1880

30	A17	1c green	2.00	
31	A18	2c rose	2.00	

Nos. 30 and 31 were prepared for use but not issued without overprint.

See also Nos. 104–108, 110, 112, 114–115.

Stamps of 1874-80 Overprinted in Red, Blue or Black

Reduced illustration

1880, Jan. 5

32	A17	1c grn (R)	75	60
a.		Inverted overprint	15.00	15.00
b.		Double overprint	20.00	20.00
33	A18	2c rose (Bl)	1.25	1.00
a.		Inverted overprint	15.00	15.00
b.		Double overprint	20.00	17.50
34	A18	2c rose (Bk)	60.00	45.00
a.		Inverted overprint		
b.		Double overprint		
35	A19	5c ultra (R)	2.00	1.50
a.		Inverted overprint	15.00	15.00
b.		Double overprint	20.00	20.00
36	A22	50c grn (R)	35.00	22.50
a.		Inverted overprint	60.00	60.00
b.		Double overprint	70.00	70.00
37	A23	1s rose (Bl)	90.00	60.00
a.		Inverted overprint	150.00	150.00
b.		Double overprint	150.00	150.00

Stamps of 1874-80 Overprinted in Red or Blue

Reduced illustration

1881, Jan. 28

38	A17	1c grn (R)	1.00	75
a.		Inverted overprint	12.50	12.50
b.		Double overprint	20.00	20.00
39	A18	2c rose (Bl)	17.50	12.50
a.		Inverted overprint	25.00	20.00
b.		Double overprint	35.00	30.00
40	A19	5c ultra (R)	1.50	1.00
a.		Inverted overprint	20.00	20.00
b.		Double overprint	30.00	30.00
41	A22	50c grn (R)	600.00	350.00
a.		Invtd. overprint	750.00	
42	A23	1s rose (Bl)	110.00	90.00
a.		Inverted ovpt.	200.00	

Reprints of Nos. 38 to 42 were made in 1884. In the overprint the word "PLATA" is 3 mm. high instead of 2½ mm. The cross bars of the letters "A" of that word are set higher than on the original stamps. The 5c is printed in blue instead of ultramarine.

For stamps of 1874–80 overprinted with Chilean arms or small UPU "horseshoe," see Nos. N11–N23.

Stamps of 1874–79 Handstamped in Black or Blue

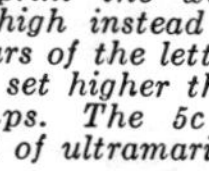

1883

65	A17	1c org (Bk)	1.25	1.00
66	A17	1c org (Bl)	60.00	
68	A19	5c ultra (Bk)	9.00	6.00
69	A20	10c grn (Bk)	85	75
70	A20	10c grn (Bl)	6.00	5.00
71	A22	50c grn (Bk)	8.00	4.00
73	A23	1s rose (Bk)	13.50	7.50

This overprint is found in 11 types.

The 1c green, 2c dark violet and 20c brown red, overprinted with triangle, are fancy varieties made for sale to collectors and never placed in regular use.

Overprinted Triangle and "Union Postal Universal Peru" in Oval.

1883

77	A22	50c grn (R & Bk)	150.00	85.00
78	A23	1s rose (Bl & Bk)	175.00	125.00

The 1c green, 2c rose and 5c ultramarine, overprinted with triangle and "U. P. U. Peru" oval, were never placed in regular use.

Overprinted Triangle and "Union Postal Universal Lima" in Oval.

1883

79	A17	1c grn (R & Bl)	65.00	50.00
80	A17	1c grn (R & Bk)	6.00	5.00
a.		Oval overprint inverted		
b.		Double overprint of oval		
81	A18	2c rose (Bl & Bk)	6.00	5.00
82	A19	5c ultra (R & Bk)	10.00	7.50
83	A19	5c ultra (R & Bl)	10.00	7.50
84	A22	50c grn (R & Bk)	175.00	125.00
85	A23	1s rose (Bl & Bk)	250.00	175.00

Some authorities question the status of No. 79.

Nos. 80, 81, 84 and 85 were reprinted in 1884. They have the second type of oval overprint with "PLATA" 3mm. high.

Overprinted Triangle and

86	A17	1c grn (Bk & Bk)	90	75
a.		Horseshoe inverted	15.00	
87	A17	1c grn (Bl & Bk)	5.00	4.00
88	A18	2c ver (Bk & Bk)	1.00	75
89	A19	5c bl (Bk & Bk)	1.25	1.00
90	A19	5c bl (Bl & Bk)	10.00	9.00
91	A19	5c bl (R & Bk)	*2,000.*	*1,500.*

Overprinted Horseshoe Alone

1883, Oct. 23

95	A17	1c green	1.75	1.25
96	A18	2c vermilion	1.75	*6.00*
a.		Double overprint		
97	A19	5c blue	2.50	2.25
98	A19	5c ultra	27.50	20.00
99	A22	50c rose	90.00	90.00
100	A23	1s ultra	40.00	30.00

The 2c violet overprinted with the above design in red and triangle in black also the 1c green overprinted with the same combination plus the horseshoe in black, are fancy varieties made for sale to collectors.

No. 23 Overprinted in Black

1884, April 28

103	A19	5c blue	1.00	60
a.		Double overprint	7.50	7.50

Stamps of 1c and 2c with the above overprint, also with the above and "U. P. U. LIMA" oval in blue or "CORREOS LIMA" in a double-lined circle in red, were made to sell to collectors and were never placed in use.

Without Overprint or Grill

1886-95

104	A17	1c dl vio	50	25
105	A17	1c ver ('95)	60	35
106	A18	2c green	75	25
107	A18	2c dp ultra ('95)	50	35
108	A19	5c orange	75	30
109	A12	5c cl ('95)	1.50	75
110	A20	10c slate	40	20
111	A13	10c org ('95)	1.25	50
112	A21	20c blue	6.00	1.00
113	A14	20c dp ultra ('95)	10.00	2.00
114	A22	50c red	2.00	1.00
115	A23	1s brown	1.75	75
		Nos. 104-115 (12)	26.00	7.70

Overprinted Horseshoe in Black and Triangle in Rose Red.

1889

116	A17	1c green	75	65
a.		Horseshoe inverted	7.50	

Nos. 30 and 25 Overprinted "Union Postal Universal Lima" in Oval in Red.

1889, Sept. 1

117	A17	1c green	1.25	1.00
117A	A20	10c green	2.25	1.50

The overprint on Nos. 117 and 117A is of the second type with "PLATA" 3 mm. high.

Stamps of 1874-80 Overprinted in Black

Pres. Remigio Morales Bermúdez

1894, Oct. 23

118	A17	1c orange	75	65
a.		Inverted overprint	11.00	11.00
b.		Double overprint	11.00	11.00
119	A17	1c green	60	50
a.		Inverted overprint	5.00	5.00
b.		Double inverted overprint	7.50	7.50
120	A18	2c violet	60	50
a.		Diagonal half used as 1c		
b.		Inverted overprint	11.00	11.00
c.		Double overprint	11.00	
121	A18	2c rose	60	50
a.		Double overprint	11.00	11.00
b.		Inverted overprint	11.00	11.00
122	A19	5c blue	3.00	2.00
122A	A19	5c ultra	5.00	2.00
b.		Inverted overprint	15.00	15.00
123	A20	10c green	60	50
a.		Inverted overprint	11.00	11.00
124	A22	50c green	2.00	1.75
a.		Inverted overprint	15.00	15.00
		Nos. 118-124 (8)	13.15	8.40

Same, with Additional Overprint of Horseshoe.

125	A18	2c vermilion	50	40
a.		Head inverted	4.00	4.00
b.		Head double	7.50	7.50
126	A19	5c blue	1.25	75
a.		Head inverted	11.00	11.00
127	A22	50c rose	60.00	40.00
a.		Head double	70.00	60.00
b.		Head inverted		
128	A23	1s ultra	135.00	125.00
a.		Both overprints inverted	165.00	150.00
b.		Head double	165.00	150.00

A23a

Vermilion Surcharge.

1895 ***Perf. 11½***

129	A23a	5c on 5c grn	10.00	7.50
130	A23a	10c on 10c ver	8.00	6.00
131	A23a	20c on 20c brn	9.00	7.00
132	A23a	50c on 50c ultra	10.00	7.50
133	A23a	1s on 1s red brn	15.00	10.00
		Nos. 129-133 (5)	52.00	38.00

Nos 129–133 were used only in Tumbes. The basic stamps were prepared by revolutionaries in northern Peru.

"Liberty"

A23b A23c

1895, Sept. 8 **Engraved**

134	A23b	1c gray vio	2.25	1.25
135	A23b	2c green	2.25	1.25
136	A23b	5c yellow	2.25	1.25
137	A23b	10c ultra	2.25	1.25
138	A23c	20c orange	2.25	1.75
139	A23c	50c dk bl	12.00	7.50
140	A23c	1s car lake	60.00	40.00
		Nos. 134-140 (7)	83.25	54.25

Commemorative of the success of the revolution against the government of General Caceres and of the election of President Pierola.

Manco Capac, Founder of Inca Dynasty

A24

Francisco Pizarro Conqueror of the Inca Empire

A25

General José de La Mar

A26

1896–1900

141	A24	1c ultra	50	20
a.		1c bl (error)	60.00	50.00
142	A24	1c yel grn ('98)	50	10
143	A24	2c blue	50	20
144	A24	2c scar ('99)	50	12
145	A25	5c indigo	75	25
146	A25	5c grn ('97)	75	10
147	A25	5c grnsh bl ('99)	50	8
148	A25	10c yellow	1.25	35
149	A25	10c gray blk ('00)	1.25	15
150	A25	20c orange	2.50	35
151	A26	50c car rose	5.00	1.25
152	A26	1s org red	7.50	1.50
153	A26	2s claret	3.00	1.25
		Nos. 141-153 (13)	24.50	5.90

The 5c in black is a chemical changeling.

Paucartambo Bridge

A27

PERU

Post and Telegraph Building, Lima
A28

Pres. Nicolás de Piérola
A29

1897, Dec. 31

154	A27	1c dp ultra	1.00	50
155	A28	2c brown	1.00	35
156	A29	5c brt rose	1.50	40

Opening of new P.O. in Lima.

A30   A31

1897, Nov. 8

157	A30	1c bister	60	50
a.		Inverted overprint	4.00	4.00
b.		Dbl. overprint	15.00	15.00

1899

| 158 | A31 | 5s org red | 2.50 | 2.00 |
| 159 | A31 | 10s bl grn | 600.00 | 550.00 |

Pres. Eduardo de Romaña
A32

Admiral Miguel L. Grau
A33

Col. Francisco Bolognesi
A33a

Pres. Romaña
A33b

Frame Litho., Center Engr.

1900

| 160 | A32 | 22c yel grn & blk | 12.00 | 1.25 |

1901, Jan.

161	A33	1c grn & blk	1.00	35
162	A33a	2c red & blk	1.00	35
163	A33b	5c dl vio & blk	1.50	35

Advent of 20th century.

Municipal Hygiene Institute
Lima
A34   A35

1902   Engraved.

| 164 | A34 | 22c green | 50 | 30 |

1905

| 165 | A35 | 12c dp bl & blk | 1.00 | 35 |

Same Surcharged in Red or Violet

1907

166	A35	1c on 12c dp bl & blk (R)	40	30
a.		Inverted surch.	12.00	12.00
b.		Double surch.	12.00	12.00
167	A35	2c on 12c dp bl & blk (V)	75	50
a.		Double surcharge	12.00	12.00
b.		Inverted surch.	12.00	12.00

Monument of Bolognesi
A36

Admiral Grau
A37

Llama
A38

Statue of Bolívar
A39

Columbus Monument
A44

City Hall, Lima, formerly an Exhibition Building
A40

School of Medicine, Lima
A41

Post and Telegraph Building, Lima—A42

Grandstand at Santa Beatrix Race Track—A43

1907

168	A36	1c yel grn & blk	35	20
169	A37	2c red & vio	35	20
170	A38	4c ol grn	6.00	90
171	A39	5c bl & blk	60	15
172	A40	10c red brn & blk	1.50	35
173	A41	20c dk grn & blk	27.50	75
174	A42	50c black	27.50	1.00
175	A43	1s pur & grn	160.00	2.50
176	A44	2s dp bl & blk	150.00	150.00
		Nos. 168-176 (9)	373.80	156.05

Manco Capac
A45

Columbus
A46

Pizarro
A47

San Martín
A48

Bolívar—A49

La Mar—A50

Ramón Castilla
A51

Grau
A52

Bolognesi
A53

1909

177	A45	1c gray	20	10
178	A46	2c green	20	10
179	A47	4c vermilion	35	15
180	A48	5c violet	20	10
181	A49	10c dp bl	50	15
182	A50	12c pale bl	1.25	20
183	A51	20c brn red	1.50	35
184	A52	50c yellow	5.00	50
185	A53	1s brn red & blk	12.00	50
		Nos. 177-185 (9)	21.20	2.15

No. 165 Surcharged in Red

1913, Jan.

| 186 | A35 | 8c on 12c dp bl & blk | 1.00 | 35 |

Stamps of 1899-1908 Surcharged in Magenta:

a   *b*

c

1915

On Issues of 1898—1900.

187	A24 (a)	1c on 1c yel grn	22.50	17.50
a.		Inverted surcharge	32.50	27.50
188	A25 (a)	1c on 10c gray blk	1.25	85

On Issue of 1905.

| 189 | A35 (c) | 2c on 12c dp bl & blk | 35 | 25 |
| a. | | Inverted surcharge | | |

On Issue of 1907.

190	A36 (a)	1c on 1c yel grn & blk	1.00	75
191	A37 (a)	1c on 2c red & vio	1.50	1.25
192	A38 (b)	1c on 4c ol grn	2.50	2.00
a.		Inverted surcharge	6.00	6.00
193	A40 (b)	1c on 10c red brn & blk	50	30
a.		Inverted surcharge	3.75	3.75
193C	A40 (c)	2c on 10c red brn & blk	125.00	125.00
194	A41 (c)	2c on 20c dk grn & blk	17.50	17.50
195	A42 (c)	2c on 50c blk	2.50	2.50

Stamps of 1909 Surcharged in Red, Green or Violet

d

e   *f*

1916

196	A50 (d)	1c on 12c pale bl (R)	25	20
a.		Double surcharge	3.00	3.00
b.		Green surcharge	7.00	7.00
197	A51 (d)	1c on 20c brn red (G)	25	20
198	A52 (d)	1c on 50c yel (G)	25	20
a.		Inverted surcharge	3.00	3.00

PERU

199	A47 (e)	2c on 4c ver (V)	25	20
200	A53 (f)	10c on 1s red & blk (G)	60	40
a.		"VALF"	5.00	5.00
		Nos. 196-200 (5)	1.60	1.20

Official Stamps of 1909–14
Overprinted or Surcharged in Green or Red:

g h

1916

201	O1	1c red (G)	20	20
202	O1	2c on 50c ol grn (R)	25	25
203	O1	10c bis brn (G)	30	20

Postage Due Stamps of 1909
Surcharged in Violet-Black.

204	D7	2c on 1c brn	60	60
205	D7	2c on 5c brn	20	20
206	D7	2c on 10c brn	20	20
207	D7	2c on 50c brn	20	20
		Nos. 201-207 (7)	1.95	1.85

Many copies of Nos. 187 to 207 have a number of pin holes. It is stated that these holes were made at the time the surcharges were printed. The varieties which we list of the 1915 and 1916 issues were sold to the public at post offices. Many other varieties which were previously listed are now known to have been delivered to one speculator or to have been privately printed by him from the surcharging plates which he had acquired.

No. 179 Surcharged in Black

Un Centavo

1917

208	A47	1c on 4c ver	35	25
a.		Double surcharge	6.00	6.00
b.		Inverted surcharge	6.00	6.00

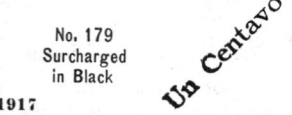

San Martín
A54

Columbus at Salamanca
A62

Funeral of Atahualpa
A63

Battle of Arica,
"Arica, the Last Cartridge"
A64

Designs: 2c, Bolívar. 4c, José Gálvez. 5c, Manuel Pardo. 8c, Grau. 10c, Bolognesi. 12c, Castilla. 20c, General Cáceres.

1918 Engraved
Centers in Black.

209	A54	1c orange	15	10
210	A54	2c green	20	10
211	A54	4c lake	35	10
212	A54	5c dp ultra	25	5
213	A54	8c red brn	90	40
214	A54	10c grnsh bl	50	10
215	A54	12c dl vio	1.25	25
216	A54	20c ol grn	1.50	25
217	A62	50c vio brn	7.00	50
218	A63	1s grnsh bl	15.00	75
219	A64	2s dp ultra	27.50	1.00
		Nos. 209-219 (11)	54.60	3.60

Augusto B. Leguía
A65

1919, Dec. Lithographed

220	A65	5c bl & blk	25	25
a.		Imperf.	50	50
b.		Center inverted	15.00	15.00
221	A65	5c brn & blk	25	25
a.		Imperf.	50	50
b.		Center inverted	15.00	15.00

Commemorative of the Constitution of 1919.

San Martín
A66

Thomas Cochrane
A70

Oath of Independence—A69

Designs: 2c, Field Marshal Arenales. 4c, Field Marshal Las Heras. 10c, Martin Jean Guisse. 12c, Vidal. 20c, Leguia. 50c, San Martin monument. 1s, San Martin and Leguia.

1921, July 28 Engr.; 7c Litho.

222	A66	1c ol brn & red brn	50	20
a.		Center inverted	550.00	550.00
223	A66	2c green	50	25
224	A66	4c car rose	1.50	75
225	A69	5c ol brn	60	20
226	A70	7c violet	1.25	50
227	A66	10c ultra	1.25	50
228	A66	12c blk & sl	4.00	60
229	A66	20c car & gray blk	4.00	1.00
230	A66	50c vio brn & dl vio	12.50	3.00
231	A69	1s car rose & yel grn	17.50	6.00
		Nos. 222-231 (10)	43.60	13.00

Centenary of Independence.

A76 A77

1923

232	A76	5c on 8c red brn & blk	60	30

Red Brown Surcharge.

1924

233	A77	4c on 5c ultra & blk	40	25
a.		Inverted surcharge	5.00	5.00
b.		Double surcharge, one inverted	7.00	7.00

Simón Bolívar
A78 A79 A80

Perf. 14, 14 x 14½, 14½, 13½.

1924 Engr.; Photo. (4c, 5c)

234	A78	2c ol grn	50	10
235	A79	4c yel grn	75	15
236	A79	5c black	1.50	15
237	A80	10c carmine	75	10
238	A78	20c ultra	1.50	20
239	A78	50c dl vio	5.00	1.00
240	A78	1s yel brn	12.00	3.00
241	A78	2s dl bl	35.00	15.00
		Nos. 234-241 (8)	57.00	19.70

Centenary of the Battle of Ayacucho which ended Spanish power in South America.
No. 237 exists imperf.

José Tejada Rivadeneyra
A81

Mariano Melgar
A82

Iturregui
A83

Leguía
A84

José de La Mar
A85

Monument of José Olaya
A86

Statue of María Bellido
A87

De Saco
A88

José Leguía
A89

1924-29 Engraved Perf. 12
Size: 18½x23mm.

242	A81	2c ol gray	15	5
243	A82	4c dk gray	15	10
244	A83	8c black	2.50	1.25
245	A84	10c org red	25	10
245A	A85	15c dp bl ('28)	75	25
246	A86	20c blue	1.00	20
247	A85	20c yel ('29)	1.50	25
248	A87	50c violet	7.00	50
249	A88	1s bis brn	10.00	1.25
250	A89	2s ultra	27.50	5.00
		Nos. 242-250 (10)	50.80	8.95

See also Nos. 258, 260, 276-282.

No. 246 Surcharged in Red:

DOS Centavos DOS Centavos
1925   1925
a   b

1925

251	A86(a)	2c on 20c bl	450.00	
252	A86(b)	2c on 20c bl	1.25	75
a.		Inverted surcharge	50.00	50.00
b.		Double surch., one inverted	75.00	75.00

No. 245 Overprinted **Plebiscito**

1925

253	A84	10c org red	1.00	1.00
a.		Invtd. ovpt.	20.00	20.00

This stamp was for exclusive use on letters from the plebiscite provinces of Tacna and Arica, and posted on the Peruvian transport "Ucayali" anchored in the port of Arica.

No. 213 Surcharged:

Habilitada   Habilitada
2 Cts.   2 centavos
1929   1929
a   b

1929

255	A54(a)	2c on 8c red brn & blk	75	75
256	A54(b)	2c on 8c red brn & blk	1.00	1.00

No. 247 Surcharged

**Habilitada
15 cts.
1929**

257	A86	15c on 20c yel	1.00	1.00
a.		Inverted surcharge	10.00	10.00

Coil Stamps.
Stamps of 1924 Issue.

1929 Perf. 14 Horizontally

258	A81	2c ol gray	50.00	25.00
260	A84	10c org red	60.00	20.00

Postal Tax Stamp of 1928 Overprinted

**Habilitada
Franqueo**
Perf. 12.

1930

261	PT6	2c dk vio	50	50
a.		Inverted ovpt.	4.00	4.00

No. 247 Surcharged

**Habilitada
2 Cts.
1930**

262	A86	2c on 20c yel	35	35

PERU

Air Post Stamp
of 1928
Surcharged

Habilitada Franqueo 2 Cts. 1930

263	AP1	2c on 50c dk grn	30	20
a.		"Habitada"	1.50	1.50

Coat of Arms — A91   Lima Cathedral — A92

Designs: 10c, Children's Hospital. 50c, Madonna and Child.

Perf. 12 x 11½, 11½ x 12.

1930, July 5 Lithographed

264	A91	2c green	1.25	85
265	A92	5c scarlet	3.00	1.75
266	A92	10c dk bl	2.00	1.25
267	A91	50c bis brn	27.50	15.00

Issued in connection with the Sixth Pan American Congress for Child Welfare. By error the stamps are inscribed "Seventh Congress."

Type of 1924
Overprinted
in Black, Green
or Blue

1930, Dec. 22 Photo. *Perf. 15x14*
Size: 18¼x22mm.

268	A84	10c org red (Bk)	25	6
a.		Inverted overprint	15.00	15.00
b.		Without ovpt.	10.00	10.00
c.		Double surch.	7.50	7.50

Same with Additional Surcharge of Numerals in Each Corner.

269	A84	2c on 10c org red (G)	10	8
a.		Inverted surcharge	17.50	
270	A84	4c on 10c org red (G)	20	
a.		Double surch.	12.50	12.50

Engraved.
Perf. 12.
Size: 19x23½mm.

271	A84	15c on 10c org red (Bl)	30	20
a.		Inverted surcharge	15.00	15.00
b.		Double surch.	15.00	15.00

Bolívar — A95

1930, Dec. 16 Lithographed

272	A95	2c buff	50	30
273	A95	4c red	1.00	45
274	A95	10c bl grn	50	35
275	A95	15c sl gray	1.00	75

Issued in commemoration of the centenary of the death of General Simón Bolívar.

Types of 1924-29 Issues.
Size: 18x22mm.

1931 Photogravure. *Perf. 15 x14.*

276	A81	2c ol grn	25	10
277	A82	4c dk grn	25	10
279	A85	15c dp bl	75	15
280	A86	20c yellow	1.50	30

281	A87	50c violet	1.50	40
282	A88	1s ol brn	2.50	50
		Nos. 276-282 (6)	6.75	1.55

Pizarro — A96

Old Stone Bridge, Lima — A97

1931, July 28 Litho. *Perf. 11*

283	A96	2c sl bl	3.00	2.00
284	A96	4c dp brn	3.00	2.00
285	A96	15c dk grn	3.00	2.00
286	A97	10c rose red	3.00	2.00
287	A97	10c mag & lt grn	3.00	2.00
288	A97	15c yel & bl gray	3.00	2.00
289	A97	15c dk sl & red	3.00	2.00
		Nos. 283-289 (7)	21.00	14.00

First Peruvian Philatelic Exhibition, Lima, July, 1931.

Manco Capac — A99   Sugar Cane Field — A102   Picking Cotton — A103

Oil Refinery — A100   Guano Deposits — A104

Mining — A105   Llamas — A106

1931-32 *Perf. 11, 11x11½*

292	A99	2c ol blk	35	10
293	A100	4c dk grn	75	25
295	A102	10c red org	1.25	12
a.		Vertical pair, imperf. between	40.00	
296	A103	15c turq bl	2.00	25
297	A104	20c yellow	5.00	40
298	A105	50c gray lil	6.00	40
299	A106	1s brn ol	15.00	1.00
		Nos. 292-299 (7)	30.35	2.52

Arms of Piura — A107

1932, July 28 *Perf. 11½x12*

300	A107	10c dk bl	8.50	7.50
301	A107	15c dp vio	8.50	7.50

Issued to commemorate the 400th anniversary of the founding of the city of Piura. On sale one day. Counterfeits exist. See also No. C3.

Parakas — A108   Chimu — A109

Inca — A110

Perf. 11½, 12, 11½x12

1932, Oct. 15

302	A108	10c dk vio	25	6
303	A109	15c brn red	50	15
304	A110	50c dk bl	75	25

Issued in commemoration of the fourth centenary of the Spanish conquest of Peru.

Arequipa and El Misti — A111   President Luis M. Sánchez Cerro — A112

Monument to Simón Bolívar at Lima — A115   Statue of Liberty — A116

1932-34 Photogravure *Perf. 13½*

305	A111	2c black	25	8
306	A111	2c bl blk	25	8
307	A111	2c grn ('34)	25	8
308	A111	4c dk brn	25	8
309	A111	4c org ('34)	25	8
310	A112	10c vermilion	20.00	9.00
311	A115	15c ultra	50	8
312	A115	15c mag ('34)	50	12
313	A115	20c red brn	75	15
314	A115	20c vio ('34)	75	20
315	A115	50c dk grn ('33)	1.00	18
316	A115	1s dp org	7.00	35
317	A115	1s org brn	9.00	50
		Nos. 305-317 (13)	40.75	10.98

1934

| 318 | A116 | 10c rose | 75 | 5 |

Pizarro — A117

Coronation of Huascar — A118

The Inca — A119

1934-35 *Perf. 13.*

319	A117	10c crimson	25	6
320	A117	15c ultra	75	8
321	A118	20c dp bl ('35)	1.50	10
322	A118	50c dp red brn	1.50	20
323	A119	1s dk vio	3.50	50
		Nos. 319-323 (5)	7.50	94

Pizarro and the Thirteen — A120

Belle of Lima — A122   Francisco Pizarro — A123

Designs: 4c, Lima Cathedral. 1s, Veiled woman of Lima.

1935, Jan 18 *Perf. 13½*

324	A120	2c brown	50	30
325	A120	4c violet	75	55
326	A122	10c rose red	75	30
327	A123	15c ultra	1.25	60
328	A120	20c sl gray	2.00	75
329	A120	50c ol grn	3.00	1.50
330	A122	1s Prus bl	7.00	3.50
331	A123	2s org brn	16.00	12.50
		Nos. 324-331 (8)	31.25	20.00

Issued to commemorate the fourth centenary of the founding of Lima. See Nos. C6–C12.

View of Ica — A125

Lake Huacachina, Health Resort — A126

PERU

Grapes
A127

Cotton Boll
A128

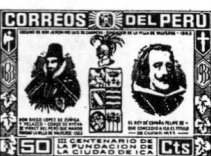

Zuniga y Velazco and
Philip IV—A129

Supreme God
of the Nazcas
A130

Engraved; Photogravure (10c).   **Perf. 12½**

332	A125	4c gray bl	1.50	1.50
333	A126	5c dk car	50	1.50
334	A127	10c magenta	6.00	2.50
335	A126	20c green	2.50	1.75
336	A128	35c dk car	12.00	6.00
337	A129	50c org & brn	8.00	6.00
338	A130	1s pur & red	22.50	15.00
		Nos. 332-338 (7)	53.00	34.25

Issued in commemoration of the tercentenary of the founding of the City of Ica.

Pizarro and the Thirteen—A131

1935–36   **Photogravure**   **Perf. 13½**

339	A131	2c dp vio	15	10
340	A131	4c bl grn ('36)	20	12

"San Cristóbal,"
First Peruvian Warship
A132

Naval College at Punta—A133

Independence Square, Callao
A134

Aerial View of Callao
A135

Plan of Walls of Callao in 1746
A137

Grand Marshal José de La Mar
A138

Packetboat "Sacramento"
A139

Viceroy José Antonio
Manso de Velasco
A140

Fort Maipú
A141

Plan of Fort Real Felipe
A142

Design: 15c, Docks and Custom House.

1936, Aug. 27   **Photo.**   **Perf. 12½**

341	A132	2c black	1.00	30
342	A133	4c bl grn	1.00	25
343	A134	5c yel brn	1.00	20
344	A135	10c bl gray	1.00	30
345	A135	15c green	1.00	35
346	A137	20c dk brn	1.00	35
347	A138	50c purple	2.00	70
348	A139	1s ol grn	17.50	2.50

Engraved.

349	A140	2s violet	22.50	10.00
350	A141	5s carmine	32.50	20.00
351	A142	10s red org & brn	80.00	60.00
		Nos. 341-351 (11)	160.50	94.95

Issued to commemorate the centenary of the founding of the Province of Callao. See No. C13.

Nos. 340, 321
and 323
Surcharged in Black

Habilitado S. 0.10 Cts.

1936   **Perf. 13½, 13.**

353	A131	2c on 4c bl grn	10	8
a.		"0.20" for "0.02"	5.00	5.00
354	A118	10c on 20c dp bl	20	20
a.		Double surch.	5.00	
b.		Inverted surch.	5.00	
355	A119	10c on 1s dk vio	30	30

Many varieties of the surcharge are found on these stamps: no period after "S", no period after "Cts", period after "2", "S" omitted, various broken letters, etc. The surcharge on No. 355 is horizontal.

Peruvian Cormorants
(Guano Deposits)
A143

Oil Well
at Talara
A144

"El Chasqui"
(Inca Courier)
A145

Avenue of the Republic, Lima
A146

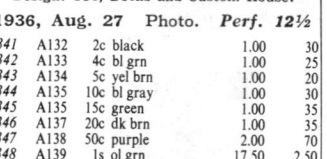

Municipal Palace and
Museum of Natural History
A147

San Marcos University at Lima
A148

Post Office,
Lima
A149

Viceroy Manuel de
Amat y Junyent
A150

Joseph A.
de Pando y Riva
A151

Dr. José Dávila
Condemarin
A152

1936–37   **Photogravure**   **Perf. 12½**

356	A143	2c lt brn	75	20
357	A143	2c grn ('37)	1.00	15
358	A144	4c blk brn	75	35
359	A144	4c int blk ('37)	40	20
360	A145	10c crimson	50	10
361	A145	10c ver ('37)	15	8
362	A146	15c ultra	1.00	20
363	A146	15c brt bl ('37)	30	10
364	A147	20c black	1.00	25
365	A147	20c blk brn ('37)	35	15
366	A148	50c org yel	4.00	75
367	A148	50c dk gray vio ('37)	1.00	25
368	A149	1s brn vio	7.50	1.00
369	A149	1s ultra ('37)	2.00	30

Engraved

370	A150	2s ultra	16.50	3.00
371	A150	2s dk vio ('37)	5.00	50
372	A151	5s sl bl	16.50	3.00
373	A152	10s dk vio & brn	85.00	35.00
		Nos. 356-373 (18)	143.70	45.58

A particular stamp may be scarce, but if few want it, its market potential may remain relatively low.

PERU

No. 370 Surcharged in Black *Habilit. Un Sol*

1937
374	A150	1s on 2s ultra	4.00	3.50

Children's Holiday Center, Ancón
A153

Chavin Pottery
A154

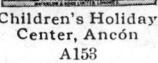
Highway Map of Peru
A155

Archaeological Museum, Lima
A156

Industrial Bank of Peru
A157

Worker's Houses, Lima
A158

Toribio de Luzuriaga
A159

Historic Fig Tree
A160

Idol from Temple of Chavin
A161

Mt. Huascarán
A162

Imprint: "Waterlow & Sons Limited, Londres".

1938, July 1 Photo. *Perf. 12½, 13*
375	A153	2c emerald	10	5
376	A154	4c org brn	15	5
377	A155	10c scarlet	30	5
378	A156	15c ultra	40	5
379	A157	20c magenta	20	5
380	A158	50c grnsh bl	60	5
381	A159	1s dp cl	1.50	10
382	A160	2s green	5.00	30

Engraved.
383	A161	5s dl vio & brn	12.50	75
384	A162	10s blk & ultra	20.00	1.00
		Nos. 375-384 (10)	40.75	2.45

See also Nos. 410-418, 426-433, 438-441.

Palace Square—A163

Lima Coat of Arms—A164

Government Palace—A165

1938, Dec. 9 Photo. *Perf. 12½*
385	A163	10c sl grn	75	30

Engraved and Lithographed.
386	A164	15c blk, gold, red & bl	1.25	40

Photogravure
387	A165	1s olive	3.00	1.25

Issued in commemoration of the 8th Pan-American Conference at Lima, December, 1938. See also Nos. C62-C64.

No. 377 Surcharged in Black *Habilitada 5 cts.*

1940 *Perf. 13*
388	A155	5c on 10c scar	15	8
a.		Inverted surcharge		

National Radio Station
A166

Overprint: "FRANQUEO POSTAL"

1941 Lithographed *Perf. 12*
389	A166	50c dl yel	3.00	25
390	A166	1s violet	3.00	30
391	A166	2s dl gray grn	7.50	75
392	A166	5s fawn	40.00	12.50
393	A166	10s rose vio	65.00	10.00
		Nos. 389-393 (5)	118.50	23.80

Gonzalo Pizarro and Orellana
A167

Francisco de Orellana
A168

Francisco Pizarro
A169

Map of South America with Amazon as Spaniards Knew It in 1542
A170

Gonzalo Pizarro
A171

Discovery of the Amazon River
A172

1943, Feb. *Perf. 12½*
394	A167	2c crimson	15	10
395	A168	4c slate	20	10
396	A169	10c yel brn	30	15
397	A170	15c vio bl	75	30
398	A171	20c yel ol	30	20
399	A172	25c dl org	3.00	50
400	A168	30c dp mag	50	30
401	A170	50c bl grn	1.00	60
402	A167	70c violet	4.00	1.00
403	A171	80c lt bl	4.00	1.00
404	A172	1s cocoa brn	6.00	1.00
405	A169	5s int blk	11.00	6.00
		Nos. 394-405 (12)	31.20	11.25

Issued to commemorate the 400th anniversary of the discovery of the Amazon River by Francisco de Orellana in 1542.

No. 377 Surcharged in Black *10 Ctvs.*

1943 *Perf. 13*
406	A155	10c on 10c scar	15	6

Samuel Finley Breese Morse
A173

1944 *Perf. 12½*
407	A173	15c lt bl	25	18
408	A173	30c ol gray	75	25

Centenary of invention of the telegraph.

Types of 1938.
Imprint: "Columbian Bank Note Co."
1945-47 Lithographed. *Perf. 12½*
410	A153	2c green	6	5
411	A154	4c org brn ('46)	8	5
412	A156	15c ultra	12	5
413	A157	20c magenta	2.50	8
414	A158	50c grnsh bl	25	6
415	A159	1s vio brn	40	10
416	A160	2s dl grn	1.00	12
417	A161	5s dl vio & brn	6.00	50
418	A162	10s blk & ultra ('47)	7.50	75
		Nos. 410-418 (9)	17.91	1.76

No. 415 Surcharged in Black *Habilitada S|o. 0.20*

1946
419	A159	20c on 1s vio brn	35	12
a.		Surch. reading down	12.50	12.50

A174

A175

A176

A177

PERU

A178

Overprint: "Habilitada I Congreso Nac. de Turismo Lima-1947"

Perf. 12½

1947, Apr. 15		Litho.	Unwmkd.	
420	A174	15c blk & car	40	20
421	A175	1s ol brn	55	30
422	A176	1.35s yel grn	55	40
423	A177	3s Prus bl	1.25	75
424	A178	5s dl grn	2.75	1.35
		Nos. 420-424 (5)	5.50	3.00

1st National Tourism Congress, Lima. The basic stamps were prepared, but not issued, for the 5th Pan American Highway Congress of 1944.

Types of 1938
Photogravure.
Imprint: "Waterlow & Sons Limited, Londres."

1949-51		Perf. 13x13½, 13½x13.		
426	A154	4c chocolate	6	5
427	A156	15c aqua	8	5
428	A157	20c bl vio	12	5
429	A158	50c red brn	25	5
430	A159	1s blk brn	45	8
431	A160	2s ultra	1.00	15

Engraved.
Perf. 12½.

432	A161	5s ultra & red brn ('50)		
433	A162	10s dk bl grn & blk ('51)	1.25	50
			3.00	1.00
		Nos. 426-433 (8)	6.21	1.93

Monument to Admiral Miguel L. Grau
A179

1949, June 6			Perf. 12½	
434	A179	10c ultra & bl grn	15	5

Types of 1938.
Imprint: "Inst. de Grav. Paris."

1951		Perf. 12½x12, 12x12½.		
438	A156	15c pck grn	8	5
439	A157	20c violet	10	5
440	A158	50c org brn	15	5
441	A159	1s dk brn	30	10

Nos. 375 and 438 Surcharged in Black

HABILITADA
S/. 0.01

1951-52		Perf. 12½, 12½x12		
445	A153	1c on 2c emer	6	5
446	A156	10c on 15c pck grn	8	5
446A	A156	10c on 15c pck grn (small surch.) ('52)	8	5

On No. 446A "S/. 0.10" is in smaller type measuring 11½mm. See also No. 456.
Nos. 445-446A exist with surcharge double.

Water Promenade	Post Boy
A180	A181

Designs: 4c, 50c, 1s and 2s, Various buildings, Lima. 20c, Post Office Street, Lima. 5s, Lake Llanganuco, Ancachs. 10s, Ruins of Machu-Picchu.

Overprint: "V Congreso Panamericano de Carreteras 1951"

1951, Oct. 13		Perf. 12	Unwmkd.	
		Black Overprint.		
447	A180	2c dk grn	6	5
448	A180	4c brt red	8	5
449	A181	15c gray	12	6
450	A181	20c ol brn	15	6
451	A180	50c dp plum	18	8
452	A180	1s blue	30	10
453	A180	2s dp bl	45	15
454	A180	5s brn lake	1.50	1.50
455	A181	10s chocolate	2.50	1.25
		Nos. 447-455 (9)	5.34	3.30

Issued to commemorate the 5th Pan-American Congress of Highways, 1951.

No. 438 Surcharged in Black

HABILITADA
S/. 0.05

1952		Perf. 12½x12	Unwmkd.	
456	A156	5c on 15c pck grn	10	6

Tourist Hotel, Tacna	Vicuña
A182	A183

Contour Farming, Cuzco	Gen. Marcos Perez Jimenez
A184	A185

Designs: 5c, Fishing boat and principal fish. 10c, Matarani. 15c, Locomotive No. 80 and coaches. 25c, Engineering school. 30c, Ministry of Public Health and Social Assistance. 1s, Paramonga fortress. 2s, Monument to Native Farmer.

Imprint: "Thomas De La Rue & Co. Ltd."
Perf. 13, 12 (A184)

1952-53		Lithographed	Unwmkd.	
457	A182	2c red lil ('53)	8	5
458	A182	5c green	8	5
459	A182	10c yel grn ('53)	18	5
460	A182	15c gray ('53)	8	5
461	A182	20c red brn ('53)	50	15
462	A182	25c rose red	18	5
463	A182	30c ind ('53)	13	5
464	A184	50c grn ('53)	60	10
465	A184	1s brown	40	8
466	A184	2s Prus grn ('53)	45	12
		Nos. 457-466 (10)	2.67	75

See also Nos. 468-478, 483-488, 497-501, C184-C185, C209.

1956, July 25		Engr.	Perf. 13½x13	
467	A185	25c brown	8	5

Issued to commemorate the visit of Gen. Marcos Perez Jimenez, President of Venezuela, June 1955.

Types of 1952-53
Designs as before.
Imprint: "Thomas De La Rue & Co. Ltd."

1957-59		Lithographed	Perf. 13, 12	
468	A182	15c brn ('59)	35	5
469	A182	25c grn ('59)	35	5
470	A182	30c rose red	18	8
471	A184	50c dl pur	30	8
472	A184	1s lt vio bl	40	10
473	A184	2s gray ('58)	55	15
		Nos. 468-473 (6)	2.13	51

Types of 1952-53
Designs as Before
Imprint:
"Joh. Enschedé en Zonen-Holland"
Perf. 12½x13½, 13½x12½, 13x14.

1960		Lithographed.	Unwmkd.	
474	A183	20c lt red brn	25	6
475	A182	30c lil rose	15	5
476	A184	50c rose vio	18	6
477	A184	1s lt vio bl	27	8
478	A184	2s gray	55	12
		Nos. 474-478 (5)	1.40	37

No. 475 measures 33x22mm. No. 470 measures 32x22½ mm.

Symbols of the Eucharist	Trumpeting Angels
A186	A187

Design: 50c, Cross and "JHS".

1960, Aug. 10		Photo.	Perf. 11½	
479	A186	50c ultra, blk & dk red	20	12
480	A186	1s multi	40	20

Nos. 479-480 were intended for voluntary use to help finance the 6th National Eucharistic Congress at Piura, Aug. 25-28, 1960. Authorized for payment of postage on day of issue only, Aug. 10, but through misunderstanding within the Peruvian postal service they were accepted for payment of postage by some post offices until late in December. Re-authorized for postal use, they were again sold and used, starting in July, 1962. See Nos. RA37-RA38.

1961, Dec. 20		Litho.	Perf. 10½	
481	A187	20c brt bl	45	12

Christmas 1961.
Valid for postage for one day, Dec. 20. Used thereafter as a voluntary seal to benefit a fund for postal employees.

Centenary Cedar, Main Square, Pomabamba—A188
Engraved

1962, Sept. 7		Perf. 13	Unwmkd.	
482	A188	1s red & grn	60	20

Issued to commemorate the centenary (in 1961) of Pomabamba province.

Types of 1952-53
Designs: 20c, Vicuña. 30c, Port of Matarani. 40c, Gunboat. 50c, Contour farming. 60c, Tourist hotel, Tacna. 1s, Paramonga, Inca fortress.

Imprint: "Thomas De La Rue & Co. Ltd."
Perf. 13x13½, 13½x13, 12 (A184)

1962, Nov. 19		Litho.	Wmk. 346	
483	A183	20c rose cl	20	10
484	A182	30c dk bl	15	5
485	AP49	40c orange	20	5
486	A184	50c lt bluish grn	20	5
487	A182	60c grnsh blk	25	10
488	A184	1s rose	35	15
		Nos. 483-488 (6)	1.35	50

Wheat Emblem and Symbol of Agriculture, Industry
A189

1963, July 23		Perf. 12½	Unwmkd.	
489	A189	1s red org & ocher		

Issued for the "Freedom from Hunger" campaign of the U.N. Food and Agriculture Organization. See also No. C190.

Alliance for Progress Emblem	Pacific Fair Emblem
A190	A191

1964, June 22		Litho.	Perf. 12x12½	
490	A190	40c multi	6	5

Issued to honor the Alliance for Progress. See note after U.S. No. 1234. See Nos. C192-C193.

1965, Oct. 30		Litho.	Perf. 12x12½	
491	A191	1.50s multi	20	10
492	A191	2.50s multi	40	18
493	A191	3.50s multi	50	30

4th International Pacific Fair, Lima, Oct. 30-Nov. 14.

Santa Claus and Letter
A192

1965, Nov. 2			Perf. 11	
494	A192	20c red & blk	18	6
495	A192	50c grn & blk	30	6
496	A192	1s bl & blk	60	12

Christmas 1965.
Valid for postage for one day, Nov. 2. Used Nov. 3, 1965-Jan. 31, 1966, as voluntary seals for the benefit of a fund for postal employees. See Nos. 522-524.

Types of 1952-62
Designs: 20c, Vicuña. 30c, Port of Matarani. 40c, Gunboat. 50c, Contour farming. 1s, Paramonga, Inca fortress.

Imprint: "I.N.A."
Perf. 12, 13½x14 (A184)

1966, Aug. 8		Litho.	Unwmkd.	
497	A183	20c brn red	8	5
498	A182	30c dk bl	7	5
499	AP49	40c orange	8	5
500	A184	50c gray grn	10	5
501	A184	1s rose	15	8
		Nos. 497-501 (5)	48	28

PERU

Postal Tax Stamps Nos. RA40, RA43 Surcharged

X Habilitado X   XX Habilitado

S. 0.10   **S/. 0.10**
a   *b*
Perf. 14x14½, 12½x12

1966, May 9   Lithographed
501A	PT11 (a)	10c on 2c lt brn		5	5
501B	PT14 (b)	10c on 3c lt car		5	5

Map of Peru, Cordillera Central and Pelton Wheel
A193

1966, Nov. 24   Photo.   Perf. 13½x14
502	A193	70c bl, blk & vio bl		12	10

Issued to commemorate the opening of the Huinco Hydroelectric Center. See No. C205.

Inca Wind Vane and Sun
A194

Perf. 13½x14
1967, Apr. 18   Photo.   Unwmkd.
503	A194	90c dp lil rose, blk & gold		12	8

Issued to publicize the 6-year building program. See No. C212.

Pacific Fair Emblem
A195

1967, Oct. 9   Photo.   Perf. 12
504	A195	1s gold, dk grn & blk		12	8

Issued to publicize the 5th International Pacific Fair, Lima, Oct. 27-Nov. 12. See No. C216.

Gold Alligator, Mochica Culture
A196

Designs (gold sculptures of the pre-Inca Yunca tribes): 2.60s, Bird (vert.). 3.60s, Lizard. 4.60s, Bird (vert.). 5.60s, Jaguar.

1968, Aug. 16   Photo.   Perf. 12
Sculptures in Gold Yellow and Brown
505	A196	1.90s dp mag		20	12
506	A196	2.60s black		25	15
507	A196	3.60s dp mag		40	20
508	A196	4.60s black		45	20
509	A196	5.60s dp mag		50	25
		Nos. 505-509 (5)		1.80	92

See also Nos. B1-B5.

Indian and Wheat
A197

1969, Mar. 3   Perf. 11
Black Surcharge
510	A197	2.50s on 90c brn & yel		20	15
511	A197	3s on 90c lil & brn		25	20
512	A197	4s on 90c rose & grn		35	25
		Nos. 510-512, C232-C233 (5)		1.70	1.15

Agrarian Reform Law.
Nos. 510-512 were not issued without surcharge.

Flag, Worker Holding Oil Rig and Map—**A198**

1969, Apr. 9   Litho.   Perf. 12
513	A198	2.50s multi		20	15
514	A198	3s gray & multi		25	20
515	A198	4s lil & multi		30	25
516	A198	5.50s lt bl & multi		40	30

Issued to commemorate the nationalization of the Brea Parinas oilfields, Oct. 9, 1968.

Kon Tiki Raft, Globe and Jet
A199

1969, June 17   Litho.   Perf. 11
517	A199	2.50s dp bl & multi		20	10
		Nos. 517, C238-C241 (5)		1.14	82

Issued to publicize the 1st Peruvian Airlines (APSA) flight to Europe.

Capt. José A. Quiñones Gonzales
A200

1969, July 23   Litho.   Perf. 11
518	A200	20s red & multi		1.75	90

Issued in memory of Capt. José A. Quiñones Gonzales (1914-1941), military aviator. See No. C243.

Freed Andean Farmer
A201

1969, Aug. 28   Litho.   Perf. 11
519	A201	2.50s dk bl, lt bl & red		20	12

Issued to commemorate the enactment of the Agrarian Reform Law of June 24, 1969. See Nos. C246-C247.

Adm. Miguel Grau
A202

1969, Oct. 8   Litho.   Perf. 11
520	A202	50s dk bl & multi		3.50	2.50

Issued for Navy Day.

Flags and "6"
A203

1969, Nov. 14
521	A203	2.50s gray & multi		18	12

Issued to publicize the Sixth International Pacific Trade Fair, Lima, Nov. 14-30. See Nos. C251-C252.

Santa Claus Type of 1965
Design: Santa Claus and letter inscribed "FELIZ NAVIDAD Y PROSPERO AÑO NUEVO."

1969, Dec. 1   Litho.   Perf. 11
522	A192	20c red & blk		8	8
523	A192	20c org & blk		8	8
524	A192	20c brn & blk		8	8

Christmas 1969.
Valid for postage for one day, Dec. 1, 1969. Used after that date as postal tax stamps.

Gen. Francisco Bolognesi and Soldier **A204**   Puma-shaped Jug, Vicus Culture **A205**

1969, Dec. 9
525	A204	1.20s lt ultra, blk & gold		15	5

Army Day, Dec. 9. See No. C253.

1970, Feb. 23   Litho.   Perf. 11
526	A205	2.50s buff, blk & brn		20	12
		Nos. 526, C281-C284 (5)		1.80	1.32

The indexes in each volume of the Scott Catalogue contain many listings which help to identify stamps.

Ministry of Transport and Communications
A206

1970, Apr. 1   Lithographed   Perf. 11
527	A206	40c org & gray		5	5
528	A206	40c gray & blk		5	5
529	A206	40c brick red & gray		5	5
530	A206	40c brt pink & gray		5	5
531	A206	40c org brn & gray		5	5
		Nos. 527-531 (5)			

Issued to commemorate the first anniversary of the Ministry of Transport and Communications.

Anchovy
A207

Fish: No. 533, Pacific hake.

1970, Apr. 30   Litho.   Perf. 11
532	A207	2.50s vio bl & multi		20	10
533	A207	2.50s vio bl & multi		20	10
		Nos. 532-533, C285-C287 (5)		1.25	58

Nos. 532-533 are printed se-tenant in sheet with Nos. C285-C287, arranged in horizontal strips of five.

Composite Head: Soldier and Farmer
A208

1970, June 24   Litho.   Perf. 11
534	A208	2.50s gold & multi		25	10

Issued to publicize a "United people and army building a new Peru." See Nos. C290-C291.

Cadets, Chorrillos College, and Arms
A209

Designs (Coat of Arms and): No. 536, Cadets of La Punta Naval College. No. 537, Cadets of Las Palmas Air Force College.

1970, July 27   Litho.   Perf. 11
535	A209	2.50s blk & multi		65	25
536	A209	2.50s blk & multi		65	25
537	A209	2.50s blk & multi		65	25

Issued to publicize Peru's military colleges. Nos. 535-537 printed se-tenant.

PERU

Courtyard, Puruchuco Fortress, Lima
A210

1970, Aug. 6

538	A210 2.50s multi	20	10
	Nos. 538, C294-C297 (5)	1.89	85

Issued for tourist publicity.

Nativity, Cuzco School
A211

Paintings: 1.50s, Adoration of the Kings, Cuzco School. 1.80s, Adoration of the Shepherds, Peruvian School.

1970, Dec. 23   Litho.   Perf. 11

539	A211 1.20s multi	8	5
540	A211 1.50s multi	10	6
541	A211 1.80s multi	15	8

Christmas 1970.

St. Rosa of Lima
A212

1971, Apr. 12   Litho.   Perf. 11

| 542 | A212 2.50s multi | 20 | 10 |

300th anniversary of the canonization of St. Rosa of Lima (1586–1617), first native-born American Saint.

Tiahuanacoide Cloth—A213
Design: 2.50s, Chancay cloth.

1971, Apr. 19

543	A213 1.20s bl & multi	15	5
544	A213 2.50s yel & multi	30	10
	Nos. 543-544, C306-C308 (5)	1.98	60

Nazca Sculpture, 5th Century, and Seriolella
A214

1971, June 7   Litho.   Perf. 11

545	A214 1.50s multi	20	6
	Nos. 545, C309-C312 (5)	3.10	83

Publicity for 200-mile zone of sovereignty of the high seas.

Mateo Garcia Pumacahua
A215

Portraits: No. 547, Mariano Melgar. No. 548, Micaela Bastidas. No. 549, Jose Faustino Sanchez Carrion. No. 550, Francisco Antonia de Zela. No. 551, Jose Baquijano y Carrillo. No. 552, Martin Jorge Guise.

1971

546	A215 1.20s ver & blk	10	5
547	A215 1.20s gray & multi	10	5
548	A215 1.50s dk bl & multi	12	6
549	A215 2s dk bl & multi	15	8
550	A215 2.50s ultra & multi	20	10
551	A215 2.50s gray & multi	20	10
552	A215 2.50s dk bl & multi	20	10
	Nos. 546-552 (7)	1.07	54

150th anniversary of independence, and to honor the heroes of the struggle for independence.

Issue dates: Nos. 546, 550, May 10; Nos. 547, 551, July 5; Nos. 548-549, 552, July 27.

See Nos. C313-C325.

Gongora Portentosa
A216

Designs: Various Peruvian orchids.

1971, Sept. 27   Perf. 13½x13

553	A216 1.50s pink & multi	18	6
554	A216 2s pink & multi	25	8
555	A216 2.50s pink & multi	27	10
556	A216 3s pink & multi	33	12
557	A216 3.50s pink & multi	50	12
	Nos. 553-557 (5)	1.53	48

"Progress of Liberation," by Teodoro Nuñez Ureta
A217

Design: 3.50s, Detail from painting by Teodoro Nuñez Ureta.

1971, Nov. 4   Perf. 13x13½

558	A217 1.20s multi	10	5
559	A217 3.50s multi	30	15

2nd Ministerial meeting of the "Group of 77." See No. C331.

Plaza de Armas, Lima, 1843
A218

Design: 3.50s, Plaza de Armas, Lima, 1971.

1971, Nov. 6

560	A218 3s pale grn & blk	40	12
561	A218 3.50s lt brick red & blk	50	15

3rd Annual International Stamp Exhibition, EXFILIMA '71, Lima, Nov. 6–14.

Army Coat of Arms
A219

1971, Dec. 9   Litho.   Perf. 13½x13

| 562 | A219 8.50s multi | 85 | 30 |

Sesquicentennial of Peruvian Army.

Flight into Egypt
A220

Old Stone Sculptures of Huamanga: 2.50s, Three Kings. 3s, Nativity.

1971, Dec. 18   Perf. 13x13½

563	A220 1.80s multi	27	8
564	A220 2.50s multi	38	10
565	A220 3s gray & multi	50	12

Christmas 1971. See Nos. 597–599.

Fisherman, by J. M. Ugarte Elespuru
A221

Gold Statuette, Chimu, c. 1500
A222

Paintings by Peruvian Workers: 4s, Threshing Grain in Cajamarca, by Camilo Blas. 6s, Huanca Highlanders, by José Sabogal.

1971, Dec. 30   Perf. 13½x13

566	A221 3.50s blk & multi	50	15
567	A221 4s blk & multi	65	15
568	A221 6s blk & multi	90	20

To publicize the revolution and change of order.

1972, Jan. 31   Litho.   Perf. 13½x13

Ancient Jewelry: 4s, Gold drummer, Chimu. 4.50s, Quartz figurine, Lambayeque culture, 5th century. 5.40s, Gold necklace and pendant, Mochiqua, 4th century. 6s, Gold insect, Lambayeque culture, 14th century.

569	A222 3.90s red, blk & ocher	45	15
570	A222 4s red, blk & ocher	45	15
571	A222 4.50s brt bl, blk & ocher	55	16
572	A222 5.40s red, blk & ocher	65	18
573	A222 6s red, blk & ocher	75	20
	Nos. 569-573 (5)	2.85	84

Popeye Catalufa
A223

Fish: 1.50s, Guadara. 2.50s, Jack mackerel.

1972, Mar. 20   Perf. 13x13½

574	A223 1.20s lt bl & multi	12	5
575	A223 1.50s lt bl & multi	15	6
576	A223 2.50s lt bl & multi	25	10
	Nos. 574-576, C333-C334 (5)	1.32	53

Seated Warrior, Mochica
A224

"Bringing in the Harvest" (July)
A225

Designs (painted pottery jugs of Mochica culture, 5th century): 1.50s, Helmeted head. 2s, Kneeling deer. 2.50s, Helmeted head. 3s, Kneeling warrior.

1972, May 8   Perf. 13½x13

Background Emerald

577	A224 1.20s multi	18	5
578	A224 1.50s multi	22	6
579	A224 2s multi	33	8
580	A224 2.50s multi	42	10
581	A224 3s multi	55	10
	Nos. 577-581 (5)	1.70	39

1972-73   Litho.   Perf. 13½x13

Designs: Monthly woodcuts from Calendario Incaico.

Black Vignette & Inscriptions

582	A225 2.50s red brn, July	50	10
583	A225 3s grn, Aug.	90	10
584	A225 2.50s rose, Sept.	50	10
585	A225 3s lt bl, Oct.	75	10
586	A225 2.50s org, Nov.	75	10
587	A225 3s lil, Dec.	75	10
588	A225 2.50s brn, Jan. ('73)	50	10
589	A225 3s pale grn, Feb. ('73)	75	10
590	A225 2.50s bl, Mar. ('73)	50	10
591	A225 3s org, Apr. ('73)	75	10
592	A225 2.50s lil rose, May ('73)	50	10
593	A225 3s yel & blk June ('73)	75	10
	Nos. 582-593 (12)	7.90	1.20

400th anniversary of publication of the Calendario Incaico by Felipe Guaman Poma de Ayala.

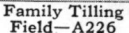

Family Tilling Field—A226

Oil Derricks
A228

Sovereignty of the Sea (Inca Frieze)
A227

PERU

51

```
            Perf. 13½x13, 13x13½
1972, Oct. 31              Lithographed
594  A226   2s multi            15     6
595  A227   2.50s multi         20    10
596  A228   3s gray & multi     25    10
```
4th anniversaries of land reforms and the nationalization of the oil industry and 15th anniversary of the claim to a 200-mile zone of sovereignty of the sea.

Christmas Type of 1971

Designs (Sculptures): 1.50s, Holy Family, wood (vert.). 2s, Holy Family with lambs, stone. 2.50s, Holy Family in stable, stone (vert.).

```
1972, Nov. 30
597  A220  1.50s buff & multi   15     5
598  A220   2s buff & multi     20     6
599  A220  2.50s buff & multi   25    10
```
Christmas 1972; 17th–18th centuries sculptures from Huamanga.

Morning Glory
A228

Mayor on Horseback, by Fierro
A229

```
1972, Dec. 29   Litho.   Perf. 13
              Multicolored
600  A228  1.50s  shown         15     5
601  A228  2.50s  Amaryllis     25    10
602  A228   3s   Liabum excelsum 30    10
603  A228  3.50s Bletia (orchid) 33   12
604  A228   5s   Cantua buxifolia 42  20
       Nos. 600-604 (5)       1.45   57
```

```
1973, Aug. 13   Litho.   Perf. 13
```
Paintings by Fierro: 2s, Man and Woman, 1830. 2.50s, Padre Abregu Riding Mule. 3.50s, Dancing Couple. 4.50s, Bullfighter Estevan Arredondo on Horseback.

```
605  A229  1.50s sal & multi    15     5
606  A229   2s sal & multi      20     8
607  A229  2.50s sal & multi    25    13
608  A229  3.50s sal & multi    35    15
609  A229  4.50s sal & multi    60    25
       Nos. 605-609 (5)       1.55    66
```
170th anniversary of the birth of Francisco Pancho Fierro (1803–1879), painter.

Presentation in the Temple
A230

Paintings of the Cuzqueña School: 2s, Holy Family (vert.). 2.50s, Adoration of the Kings.

```
1973, Nov. 30  Litho.   Perf. 13x13½
610  A230  1.50s multi         12     5
611  A230   2s multi           15     6
612  A230  2.50s multi         20    10
           Christmas 1973.
```

Peru No. 20
A231

```
1974, Mar. 1  Lithographed  Perf. 13
613  A231   6s gray & dk bl     60    25
```
25th anniversary of the Peruvian Philatelic Association.

Non-ferrous Smelting Plant, La Oroya
A232

Colombia Bridge, San Martin
A233

Designs: 8s, 10s, Different views, Santiago Antunez Dam, Tayacaja.

```
1974           Litho.   Perf. 13x13½
614  A232  1.50s blue            8     5
615  A233   2s multi            10     6
616  A232   3s rose cl          18    10
617  A232  4.50s green          25    18
618  A233   8s multi            45    24
619  A233  10s multi            55    30
       Nos. 614-619 (6)       1.61    93
```
"Peru Determines its Destiny."
Issue Dates: 2s, 8s, 10s, July 1. 1.50s, 3s, 4.50s, Dec. 6.

Battle of Junin, by Felix Yañez
A234

Design: 2s, 3s, Battle of Ayacucho, by Felix Yañez.

```
1974           Litho.   Perf. 13x13½
620  A234  1.50s multi          15     5
621  A234   2s multi            15     5
622  A234  2.50s multi          20    15
623  A234   3s multi            25    15
```
Sesquicentennial of the Battles of Junin and Ayacucho.
Issue dates: 1.50s, 2.50s, Aug. 6. 2s, 3s, Oct. 9.
See Nos. C400-C404.

Indian Madonna
A235

```
1974, Dec. 20  Litho.   Perf. 13½x13
624  A235  1.50s multi          12     5
         Christmas 1974.  See No. C417.
```

Maria Parado de Bellido
A236

International Women's Year Emblem
A237

Designs (IWY Emblem, Peruvian Colors and): 2s, Micaela Bastidas. 2.50s, Juana Alarco de Dammert.

```
          Perf. 13x13½, 13½x13
1975, Sept. 8            Lithographed
625  A236  1.50s bl grn, red & blk  20    5
626  A237   2s blk & red             25    6
627  A236  2.50s pink, blk & red     30    8
628  A237   3s red, blk & ultra      50    8
```
International Women's Year 1975.

St. Juan Macias
A238

```
1975, Nov. 14         Perf. 13½x13
629  A238   5s blk & multi       40    16
```
Canonization of Juan Macias in 1975.

Louis Braille
A239

```
          Perf. 13x13½
1976, Mar. 2          Lithographed
630  A239  4.50s gray, red & blk  50    15
```
Sesquicentennial of the invention of Braille system of writing for the blind by Louis Braille (1809–1852).

Peruvian Flag
A240

```
1976, Aug. 29  Litho.  Perf. 13½x13
631  A240   5s gray, blk & red    24    16
```
Revolutionary Government, Phase II, 1st anniversary.

St. Francis, by El Greco
A241

Indian Mother
A242

```
1976, Dec. 9   Litho.   Perf. 13½x13
632  A241   5s gold, buff & brn   50    16
```
St. Francis of Assisi, 750th death anniversary.

```
1976, Dec. 23
633  A242   4s multi              50    12
         Christmas 1976.
```

Chasqui Messenger
A243

"X" over Flags
A244

```
1977    Lithographed   Perf. 13½x13
634  A243   6s grnsh bl & blk    60    20
635  A243   8s red & blk         60    20
636  A243  10s ultra & blk       75    40
637  A243  12s lt grn & blk      75    50
```
See Nos. C465–C467.

```
1977, Nov. 25  Litho.  Perf. 13½x13
638  A244  10s multi             30    15
```
10th International Pacific Fair, Lima, Nov. 16–27.

Republican Guard Badge
A245

Indian Nativity
A246

```
1977, Dec. 1
639  A245  12s multi             35    20
```
58th anniversary of Republican Guard.

```
1977, Dec. 23
640  A246   8s multi             16    10
         Christmas 1977. See No. C483.
```

Nos. 495, 494, 496 Surcharged with New Value and Bar in Red, Dark Blue or Black:
"FRANQUEO / 10.00 / RD-0161-77"

```
1977, Dec.                Perf. 11
641  A192  10s on 50c grn & blk (R)   20   15
642  A192  20s on 20c red & blk (DB)  40   30
643  A192  30s on 1s bl & blk (B)     60   50
```

Inca Head
A247

```
1978    Lithographed   Perf. 13½x13
644  A247   6s brt grn           12     8
645  A247  10s red               20    15
646  A247  16s red brn           32    32
       Nos. 644-646, C486-C489 (7)  4.92  3.75
```

PERU

Flags of Germany, Argentina, Austria, Brazil—A248

Argentina '78 Emblem and Flags of Participants: No. 648, 652, Hungary, Iran, Italy, Mexico. No. 649, 653, Scotland, Spain, France, Netherlands. No. 650, 654, Peru, Poland, Sweden and Tunisia. No. 651, like No. 647.

1978		Litho.		Perf. 13x13½	
647	A248	10s bl & multi		20	15
648	A248	10s bl & multi		20	15
649	A248	10s bl & multi		20	15
650	A248	10s bl & multi		20	15
651	A248	16s bl & multi		16	10
652	A248	16s bl & multi		16	10
653	A248	16s bl & multi		16	10
654	A248	16s bl & multi		16	10
	Nos. 647-654 (8)			1.44	1.00

11th World Soccer Cup Championship, Argentina, June 1–25. Nos. 647–650 and 651–654 printed se-tenant in blocks of 4. Issue dates: Nos. 647–650, June 28. Nos. 651–654, Dec. 4.

Thomas Faucett, Planes of 1928, 1978 A249

1978, Oct. 19   Litho.   Perf. 13

655	A249	40s multi	60	40

Faucett Aviation, 50th anniversary.

Nazca Bowl, Huaco A250

1978–79   Litho.   Perf. 13x13½

656	A250	16s vio bl ('79)	20	10
657	A250	20s grn ('79)	25	15
658	A250	25s lt grn ('79)	30	20
659	A250	35s rose red ('79)	50	25
660	A250	45s dk brn	60	35
661	A250	50s black	75	38
662	A250	55s car rose ('79)	75	40
663	A250	70s lil rose ('79)	90	55
664	A250	75s blue	1.00	58
665	A250	80s sal ('79)	1.00	60
667	A250	200s brt vio ('79)	2.50	1.50
	Nos. 656-667 (11)		8.75	5.06

Peruvian Nativity A252

Ministry of Education, Lima A253

1978, Dec. 28 Litho. Perf. 13½x13

672	A252	16s multi	20	10

1979, Jan. 4

| 673 | A253 | 16s multi | 20 | 10 |

National Education Program.

Nos. RA40, B1–B5 and 509 Surcharged in Various Colors. No. RA40 Overprinted also:

Habilitado Dif.-Porte S/. 2.00 *a*

SOBRE TASA OFICIAL S/. 3.00 *b*

Habilitado R.D. N° 0118 S/. 35.00 *c*

Perf. 14x14½, 12, 12x12½, 12½x12

1978, July–Aug.   Litho., Photo.
Light Brown; Multicolored

674	PT11(a)	2s on 2c (O)	5	5
675	PT11(b)	3s on 2c (Bk)	5	5
676	PT11(b)	4s on 2c (G)	5	5
677	PT11(b)	5s on 2c (V)	5	5
678	PT11(b)	6s on 2c (DBl)	6	5
679	SP1	20s on 1.90s + 90c (G)	20	15
680	SP1	30s on 2.60s + 1.30s (Bl)	30	25
681	PT11(c)	35s on 2c (C)	35	30
682	PT11(c)	50s on 2c (LtBl)	50	40
683	SP1	55s on 3.60s + 1.80s (VBl)	55	45
684	SP1	65s on 4.60s + 2.30s (Go)	65	50
685	A196	80s on 5.60s (VBl)	80	65
686	SP1	85s on 20s + 10s (Bk)	85	60
	Nos. 674-686 (13)		4.46	3.70

Surcharge on Nos. 679–680, 683–684, 686 includes heavy bar over old denomination.

Battle of Iquique A254

Heroes' Crypt A255

Col. Francisco Bolognesi A256

War of the Pacific: #688, Col. Jose J. Inclan. #689, Corvette Union running Arica blockade. #690, Battle of Angamos, Aguirre, Miguel Grau (1838•1879), Perre. #690A, Lt. Col. Pedro Ruiz Gallo. 85s, Marshal Andres A. Caceres. #692, Naval Battle of Angamos. #697, Col. Bolognesi's Reply, by Angeles de la Cruz. #698, Col. Alfonso Ugarte on horseback.

Lithographed

1979–80   Perf. 13½x13, 13x13½

687	A254	14s multi	12	8
688	A256	25s multi	25	18
689	A254	25s multi	25	18
690	A254	25s multi	25	18
690A	A256	25s multi ('80)	25	18
691	A256	85s multi	85	60
692	A254	100s multi	1.00	65
693	A256	100s multi	1.00	65
694	A256	115s multi	1.10	68
695	A254	200s multi	1.80	1.20
696	A256	200s multi	1.80	1.20
697	A254	200s multi	1.80	1.20
698	A254	200s multi	1.80	1.20

Red Cross A257

1979, May 4   Perf. 13x13½

699	A257	16s multi	15	15

Centenary of Peruvian Red Cross.

Billiard Balls A258

Arms of Cuzco A259

1979, June 4   Perf. 13½x13

| 700 | A258 | 34s multi | 40 | 20 |

1979, June 24

| 701 | A259 | 50s multi | 50 | 30 |

Inca Sun Festival, Cuzco.

Peru Colors, Tacna Monument—A260

1979, Aug. 28   Litho.   Perf. 13½x13

| 702 | A260 | 16s multi | 20 | 10 |

Return of Tacna Province to Peru, 50th anniversary.

Telecom 79—A261

1979, Sept. 20

| 703 | A261 | 15s multi | 15 | 10 |

3rd World Telecommunications Exhibition, Geneva, Sept. 20-26.

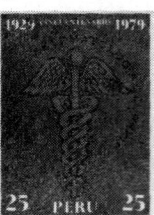

Caduceus—A262

World Map, "11," Fair Emblem—A263

1979, Nov. 13

| 704 | A262 | 25s multi | 30 | 18 |

Stomatology Academy of Peru, 50th anniversary; 4th International Congress.

1979, Nov. 24

| 705 | A263 | 55s multi | 55 | 40 |

11th Pacific International Trade Fair, Lima, Nov. 14-25.

Gold Jewelry—A264

1979, Dec. 19   Perf. 13½x13

| 706 | A264 | 85s multi | 85 | 60 |

Larco Herrera Archaeological Museum.

Christmas 1979—A265

1979, Dec. 27   Litho.   Perf. 13x13½

| 707 | A265 | 25s multi | 30 | 18 |

Unused Prices

Catalogue prices for unused stamps through 1960 are for hinged copies in fine condition. Never-hinged unused stamps issued before 1961 often sell above Catalogue prices. Current never-hinged prices for various countries will be found in the Scott StampMarket Update.

See "Special Notices" at the front of this volume for data on the listing methods of this Catalogue, abbreviations, condition, prices and examination.

PERU

Queen Sofia and King Juan Carlos I, Visit to Peru—A266

1979		Litho.		Perf. 13×13½	
708	A266	75s multi		80	22

No. RA40 Surcharged in Black, Green or Blue

1979, Oct. 8
709	PT11	7s on 2c brn	8	5
710	PT11	9s on 2c brn (G)	10	5
711	PT11	15s on 2c brn (B)	16	10

Nos. 702, 687, 700, 663 Surcharged

1980, Apr. 14 Litho. Perf. 13½x13, 13x13½
712	A260	20s on 16s multi	20	15
713	A254	25s on 14s multi	25	18
714	A258	65s on 34s multi	65	50
715	A250	80s on 70s lil rose	80	58
		Nos. 712-715, C501-C502 (6)	2.70	1.93

Liberty Holding Arms of Peru—A267

Civic duties: 15s, respect the Constitution. 20s, honor country. 25s, vote. 30s, military service. 35s, pay taxes. 45s, contribute to national progress. 50s, respect rights.

1980 **Litho.**
716	A267	15s grnsh bl	15	10
717	A267	20s sal pink	20	15
718	A267	25s ultra	25	18
719	A267	30s lil rose	30	22
720	A267	35s black	35	25
721	A267	45s lt bl grn	45	35
722	A267	50s brown	50	35
		Nos. 716-722 (7)	2.20	1.60

Chimu Cult Cup—A268

1980, July 9 Litho.
| 723 | A268 | 35s multi | 35 | 25 |

Map of Peru and Liberty—A269

Return to Civilian Government—A270

1980, Sept. 9 Litho. Perf. 13½x13, 13x13½
724	A269	25s multi	25	18
725	A270	35s multi	35	25

Machu Picchu—A271

1980, Nov. 10 Litho. Perf. 13x13½
| 726 | A271 | 25s multi | 25 | 18 |

World Tourism Conference, Manila, Sept. 27.

Tupac Amaru Rebellion Bicentennial—A272

1980, Dec.22 Litho. Perf. 13½x13
| 727 | A272 | 25s multi | 25 | 18 |

Christmas 1980—A273

1980, Dec. 31 Litho. Perf. 13
| 728 | A273 | 15s multi | 15 | 10 |

Death Sesquicentennial (1980) of Simon Bolivar—A274

1981, Jan. 28 Litho. Perf. 13½x13
| 729 | A274 | 40s multi | 40 | 30 |

Nos. 725, 667, 694 Surcharged

1981 **Litho. Perf. 13x13½**
730	A270	25s on 35s multi	25	16
731	A250	85s on 200s brt vio	85	65
732	A256	100s on 115s multi	1.00	75

Return to Constitutional Government, July 28, 1980—A275

1981, Mar. 26 Litho. Perf. 13½x13
| 733 | A275 | 25s multi | 25 | 18 |

Tupac Amaru and Micaela Bastidas, Bronze Sculptures, by Miguel Baca-Rossi—A276

1981, May 18 Litho. Perf. 13½x13
| 734 | A276 | 60s multi | 60 | 45 |

Rebellion of Tupac Amaru and Micaela Bastidas bicentenary.

Carved Stone Head, Huamachuco Tribe—A277

Designs: Nos. 739, 742, 749 Pottery vase, Inca (vert.). No. 740, Head (diff. vert.). Nos. 743, 749A-749B, Huaco idol (fish), Nazca. 100s, Pallasca (vert.). 140s, Puma:

1981 **Litho. Perf. 13½x13, 13x13½**
738	A277	30s dp rose lil	30	20
739	A277	40s org ('82)	40	25
740	A277	40s ultra	40	25
742	A277	80s brn ('82)	80	50
743	A277	80s red ('82)	80	50
745	A277	100s lil rose	1.00	65
748	A277	140s lt bl grn	1.40	90
749	A277	180s grn ('82)	1.80	1.15
749A	A277	240s grnsh bl ('82)	2.40	1.50
749B	A277	280s vio ('82)	2.80	1.75
		Nos. 738-749B (10)	12.10	7.65

Postal and Philatelic Museum, 50th. Anniv. A278

1981, May 31 Litho. Perf. 13½x13
| 750 | A278 | 130s multi | 1.30 | 90 |

1979 Constitution Assembly President Victor Raul Haya de la Torre—A279

1981, Oct. 7 Litho. Perf. 13½x13
| 751 | A279 | 30s pur & gray | 30 | 20 |

Inca Messenger, by Guaman Poma (1526-1613)—A280

1981 **Litho. Perf. 12**
752	A280	30s lil & blk	30	20
753	A280	40s ver & blk	40	25
754	A280	130s brt yel grn & blk	1.30	80
755	A280	140s brt bl & blk	1.40	90
756	A280	200s yel brn & blk	2.00	1.25
		Nos. 752-756 (5)	5.40	3.40

Christmas 1981. Issue dates: 30s, 40s, 200s, Dec. 21; others, Dec. 31.

Intl. Year of the Disabled—A280a

1981 **Litho. Perf. 13½x13**
| 756A | A280a | 100s multi | 1.00 | 65 |

Nos. 377, C130, C143, J56, O33, RA36, RA39, RA40, RA42, RA43 Surcharged in Brown, Black, Orange, Red, Green or Blue

1982
757	PT11	10s on 2c (#RA40, Br)	5	5
758	A155	10s on 10c (#377, Bk)	5	5
759	D7	80s on 10c (#J56, Bk)	20	12
760	O1	80s on 10c (#O33, Bk)	20	12
761	PT14	80s on 3c (#RA43, O)	20	12
762	PT17	100s on 10c (#RA42, R)	24	16
763	AP57	100s on 2.20s (#C130, R)	24	16
764	PT14	150s on 3c (#RA39, G)	36	24
765	PT14	180s on 3c (#RA43, R)	45	30
766	PT14	200s on 3c (#RA43, Bl)	50	32
767	AP60	240s on 1.25s (#C143, R)	60	40
768	PT15	280s on 5c (#RA36, Bk)	70	45
		Nos. 757-768 (12)	3.79	2.49

Nos. 763, 767 airmail.

PERU

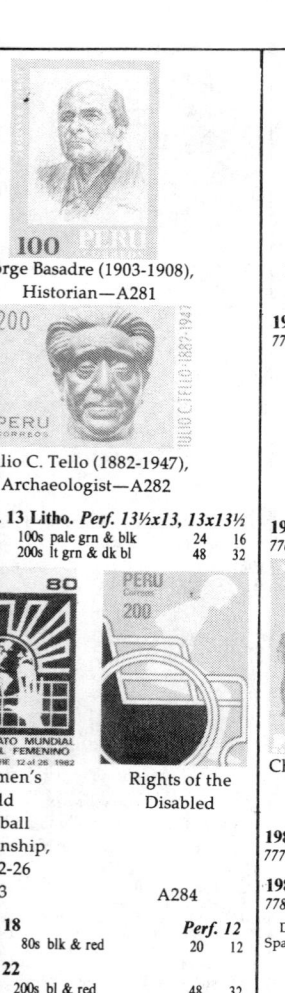

Jorge Basadre (1903-1908), Historian—A281

Julio C. Tello (1882-1947), Archaeologist—A282

1982, Oct. 13 Litho. Perf. 13½x13, 13½x13½
| 769 | A281 | 100s pale grn & blk | 24 | 16 |
| 770 | A282 | 200s lt grn & dk bl | 48 | 32 |

9th Women's World Volleyball Championship, Sept. 12-26 A283

Rights of the Disabled A284

1982, Oct. 18 Perf. 12
| 771 | A283 | 80s blk & red | 20 | 12 |

1982, Oct. 22
| 772 | A284 | 200s bl & red | 48 | 32 |

Brena Campaign Centenary—A285

1982, Oct. 26 Perf. 13x13½
| 773 | A285 | 70s Andres Caceres medallion | 16 | 10 |

1982 World Cup—A286

1982, Nov. 2 Perf. 12
| 774 | A286 | 80s multi | 20 | 12 |

16th Intl. Congress of Latin Notaries, Lima, June—A287

1982, Nov. 6
| 775 | A287 | 500s Emblem | 1.20 | 80 |

Handicrafts Year—A288

1982, Nov. 24 Perf. 13x13½
| 776 | A288 | 200s Clay bull figurine | 48 | 32 |

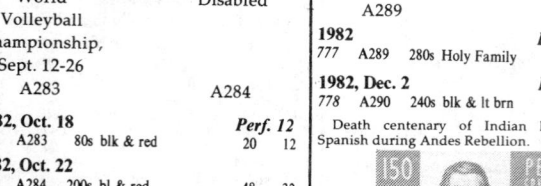

Christmas 1982   Pedro Vilcapaza
A289   A290

1982
| 777 | A289 | 280s Holy Family | 68 | 45 |

1982, Dec. 2 Perf. 13½x13
| 778 | A290 | 240s blk & lt brn | 60 | 40 |

Death centenary of Indian leader against Spanish during Andes Rebellion.

Jose Davila Condemarin (1799-1882), Minister of Posts (1849-76)—A291

1982, Dec. 10 Perf. 13x13½
| 779 | A291 | 150s bl & blk | 36 | 24 |

10th Anniv. of Intl. Potato Study Center, Lima—A292

1982, Dec. 27 Perf. 13x13½
| 780 | A292 | 240s multi | 60 | 40 |

450th Anniv. of City of San Miguel de Piura—A293

1982, Dec. 31 Perf. 13x13½
| 781 | A293 | 280s Arms | 68 | 45 |

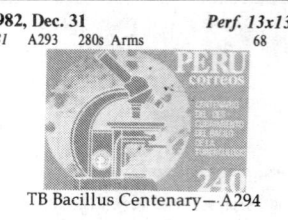

TB Bacillus Centenary—A294

1983, Jan. 18 Perf. 12
| 782 | A294 | 240s Microscope, slide | 60 | 40 |

St. Teresa of Jesus of Avila (1515-1582), by Jose Espinoza de los Monteros, 1682—A295

1983, Mar. 1
| 783 | A295 | 100s multi | 24 | 16 |

10th Anniv. of State Security Service—A296

1983, Mar. 8
| 784 | A296 | 100s bl & org | 24 | 16 |

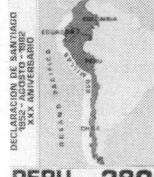

Horseman's Ornamental Silver Shoe, 19th Cent.—A297

1983, Mar. 18
| 785 | A297 | 250s multi | 62 | 42 |

30th Anniv. of Santiago Declaration—A298

1983, Mar. 25
| 786 | A298 | 280s Map | 68 | 45 |

25th Anniv. of Lima-Bogota Airmail Service—A299

1983, Apr. 8
| 787 | A299 | 150s Jet | 36 | 24 |

75th Anniv. of Lima and Callao State Lotteries—A300

1983, Apr. 26
| 788 | A300 | 100s multi | 24 | 16 |

Nos. 739, 773, 771, 778, 780, 782, 781, 786, 777, 749, 774 Surcharged in Black or Green.

1983 Litho.
789	A277	100s on 40s org	24	16
790	A285	100s on 70s multi	24	16
791	A283	100s on 80s blk & red	24	16
792	A290	100s on 240s multi	24	16
793	A292	100s on 240s multi	24	16
794	A294	100s on 240s ol grn	24	16
795	A293	150s on 280s multi (G)	36	24
796	A298	150s on 280s multi	36	24
797	A289	200s on 280s multi	50	32
798	A277	300s on 180s grn	75	50
799	A277	400s on 180s grn	1.00	65
800	A286	500s on 80s multi	1.25	80

Military Ships—A301

1983 Perf. 12
| 801 | A301 | 150s Cruiser Almirante Grau, 1907 | 36 | 24 |
| 802 | A301 | 350s Submarine Ferre, 1913 | 85 | 55 |

Simon Bolivar Birth Bicentenary
A302

Christmas 1983
A303

1983, Dec. 13 Litho. Perf. 14
| 803 | A302 | 100s blk & lt bl | 24 | 16 |

1983, Dec. 16
| 804 | A303 | 100s Virgin and Child | 24 | 16 |

PERU

SEMI-POSTAL STAMPS

Gold Funerary Mask
SP1

Designs: 2.60s+1.30s, Ceremonial knife (vert.). 3.60s+1.80s, Ceremonial vessel. 4.60s+2.30s, Goblet with precious stones (vert.). 20s+10s, Earplug.

Perf. 12x12½, 12½x12

1966, Aug. 16   Photo.   Unwmk.

B1	SP1	1.90s + 90c multi	50	50
B2	SP1	2.60s + 1.30s multi	60	60
B3	SP1	3.60s + 1.80s multi	90	90
B4	SP1	4.60s + 2.30s multi	1.25	1.25
B5	SP1	20s + 10s multi	5.00	5.00
		Nos. B1-B5 (5)	8.25	8.25

The designs show gold objects of the 12th–13th centuries Chimu culture. The surtax was for tourist publicity.

AIR POST STAMPS.

No. 248 Overprinted in Black

Servicio Aéreo

1927, Dec. 10   Perf. 12   Unwmkd.

C1	A87	50c violet	55.00	37.50

Two types of overprint. Counterfeits exist.

President Augusto Bernardino Leguía
AP1

Coat of Arms of Piura
AP2

1928, Jan. 12   Engraved

C2	AP1	50c dk grn	1.00	50

1932, July 28   Lithographed

C3	AP2	50c scarlet	30.00	27.50

Issued to commemorate the 400th anniversary of the city of Piura. On sale one day. Counterfeits exist.

Airplane in Flight
AP3

1934, Feb.   Engraved   Perf. 12½

C4	AP3	2s blue	5.00	50
C5	AP3	5s brown	12.00	1.00

Funeral of Atahualpa
AP4

Palace of Torre-Tagle
AP7

Designs: 35c, Mt. San Cristobal. 50c, Avenue of Barefoot Friars. 10s, Pizarro and the Thirteen.

1935, Jan. 18   Photo.   Perf. 13½

C6	AP4	5c emerald	50	25
C7	AP4	35c brown	75	50
C8	AP4	50c org yel	1.25	1.00
C9	AP4	1s plum	2.50	1.50
C10	AP7	2s red org	4.00	3.00
C11	AP4	5s dp cl	16.50	9.00
C12	AP4	10s dk bl	65.00	50.00
		Nos. C6-C12 (7)	90.50	65.25

4th centenary of founding of Lima.
Nos. C6–C12 overprinted "Radio Nacional" are revenue stamps.

"La Callao,"
First Locomotive in South America
AP9

1936, Aug. 27   Perf. 12½

C13	AP9	35c gray blk	4.00	2.00

Issued in commemoration of the centenary of the founding of the Province of Callao.

Nos. C4–C5 Surcharged "Habilitado" and New Value, like Nos. 353–355

1936, Nov. 4

C14	AP3	5c on 2s bl	50	10
C15	AP3	25c on 5s brn	1.00	40
	a.	Double surch.	20.00	20.00
	b.	No period between "O" and "25 Cts"	2.00	2.00
	c.	Inverted surch.	25.00	

There are many broken letters in this setting.

La Mar Park, Lima—AP10

Jorge Chávez—AP14

Aerial View of Peruvian Coast
AP16

View of the "Sierra"
AP17

St. Rosa of Lima
AP22

Designs: 15c, Mail Steamer "Inca" on Lake Titicaca. 20c, Native Queña (flute) Player and Llama. 30c, Ram at Model Farm, Puno. 50c, Mines of Peru. 1s, Train in Mountains. 1.50s, Jorge Chavez Aviation School. 2s, Transport Plane. 5s, Aerial View of Virgin Forests.

1936-37   Photogravure.   Perf. 12½

C16	AP10	5c brt grn	30	10
C17	AP10	5c emer ('37)	35	15
C18	AP10	15c lt ultra	75	15
C19	AP10	15c bl ('37)	50	20
C20	AP10	20c gray blk	2.00	20
C21	AP10	20c pale ol grn ('37)	1.25	25
C22	AP14	25c mag ('37)	60	15
C23	AP10	30c hn brn	6.00	1.25
C24	AP10	30c dk ol brn ('37)	1.75	25
C25	AP14	35c brown	4.00	3.50
C26	AP10	50c yellow	60	50
C27	AP10	50c brn vio ('37)	90	25
C28	AP16	70c Prus grn	8.00	6.00
C29	AP16	70c pck grn ('37)	1.25	75
C30	AP17	80c brn blk	9.00	7.00
C31	AP17	80c ol blk ('37)	1.75	75
C32	AP10	1s ultra	6.00	60
C33	AP10	1s red brn ('37)	3.50	35
C34	AP14	1.50s red brn	10.00	8.00
C35	AP14	1.50s org yel ('37)	6.00	60

Engraved.

C36	AP10	2s dp bl	20.00	10.00
C37	AP10	2s yel grn ('37)	12.50	1.00
C38	AP16	5s green	25.00	5.00
C39	AP22	10s car & brn	225.00	165.00
		Nos. C16-C39 (24)	347.00	212.00

Air Post Stamps of 1936 Surcharged in Black or Red

Habilit.
Un Sol

1936, June 26

C40	AP10	15c on 30c hn brn	1.00	55
C41	AP14	15c on 35c brn	1.00	35
C42	AP16	15c on 70c Prus grn	6.00	4.00
C43	AP17	25c on 80c brn blk (R)	6.00	4.00
C44	AP10	1s on 2s dp bl	10.00	5.00
		Nos. C40-C44 (5)	24.00	13.90

Surcharge on No. C43 is vertical, reading down.

First Flight in Peru, 1911
AP23

Jorge Chávez
AP24

Airport of Limatambo at Lima
AP25

Map of Aviation Lines from Peru
AP26

Designs: 10c, Juan Bielovucic (1889–?) flying over Lima race course, Jan. 14, 1911. 15c, Jorge Chavez-Dartnell (1887–1910), French-born Peruvian aviator who flew from Brixen to Domodossola in the Alps and died of plane-crash injuries.

1937, Sept. 15   Engraved.   Perf. 12

C45	AP23	10c violet	50	15
C46	AP24	15c dk grn	75	15
C47	AP25	25c gray brn	50	15
C48	AP26	1s black	2.50	1.75

Issued in commemoration of the Inter-American Technical Conference of Aviation, September, 1937.

Government Restaurant at Callao
AP27

Monument on the Plains of Junin
AP28

Rear Admiral Manuel Villar
AP29

View of Tarma
AP30

Dam, Ica River
AP31

View of Iquitos
AP32

Highway and Railroad Passing
AP33

Mountain Road
AP34

Plaza San Martín, Lima
AP35

PERU

National Radio of Peru
AP36

Stele from Chavin Temple
AP37

Ministry of Public Works, Lima
AP38

Crypt of the Heroes, Lima
AP39

Imprint: "Waterlow & Sons Limited, Londres."
1938, July 1 Photo. Perf. 12½, 13

C49	AP27	5c vio brn	12	6
C50	AP28	15c dk brn	12	5
C51	AP29	20c dp mag	60	20
C52	AP30	25c dp grn	20	5
C53	AP31	30c orange	18	5
C54	AP32	50c green	50	45
C55	AP33	70c sl bl	1.00	8
C56	AP34	80c olive	1.50	15
C57	AP35	1s sl grn	12.50	6.00
C58	AP36	1.50s purple	3.00	12

Engraved.

C59	AP37	2s ind & org brn	4.00	75
C60	AP38	5s brown	25.00	1.00
C61	AP39	10s ol grn & ind	100.00	50.00
		Nos. C49-C61 (13)	148.72	58.96

See also Nos. C73-C75, C89-C93, C103.

Torre-Tagle Palace
AP40

National Congress Building
AP41

Manuel Ferreyros, José Gregorio Paz Soldán and Antonio Arenas—AP42
1938, Dec. 9 Photo. Perf. 12½

C62	AP40	25c brt ultra	1.25	75
C63	AP41	1.50s brn vio	3.50	2.50
C64	AP42	2s black	2.25	1.50

8th Pan-American Conference at Lima.

Habilit.
Surcharged in Black
0.15
1942 Perf. 13.

C65	AP30	15c on 25c dp grn	2.00	15

Types of 1938.
Lithographed.
Imprint: "Columbian Bank Note Co."
1945-46 Perf. 12½. Unwmkd.

C73	AP27	5c vio brn	20	5
C74	AP31	30c orange	40	8
C75	AP36	1.50s pur ('46)	65	50

Nos. C73 and C54
Overprinted in Black

PRIMER VUELO
PIA
LIMA - NUEVA YORK

1947, Sept. 25 Perf. 12½, 13

C76	AP27	5c vio brn	10	10
C77	AP32	50c green	20	15

Issued to commemorate the first Peru International Airways flight from Lima to New York City, September 27-28, 1947.

Peru-Great Britain Air Route — AP43
Basketball Players — AP44

Designs: 5s, Discus thrower. 10s, Rifleman.
1948, July 29 Photo. Perf. 12½

C78	AP43	1s blue	4.50	4.50

Carmine Overprint, "AEREO".

C79	AP44	2s red brn	6.50	6.00
C80	AP44	5s yel grn	11.00	10.00
C81	AP44	10s yellow	12.50	12.50
a.		Souvenir sheet, perf. 13	42.50	42.50

Issued to publicize Peru's participation in the 1948 Olympic Games held at Wembley, England, during July and August. Postally valid for four days, July 29-Aug. 1, 1948. Proceeds went to the Olympic Committee.
No. C81a measures 116x151mm, and contains one each of Nos. C78 to C81, and blue inscriptions in upper and lower margins. A surtax of 2 soles was for the Children's Hospital.
Remainders of Nos. C78-C81 and C81a were overprinted "Melbourne 1956" and placed on sale Nov. 19, 1956, at all post offices as "voluntary stamps" with no postal validity. Clerks were permitted to postmark them to please collectors, and proceeds were to help pay the cost of sending Peruvian athletes to Australia. On April 14, 1957, postal authorities declared these stamps valid for one day, April 15, 1957. The overprint was applied to 10,000 sets and 21,000 souvenir sheets. Price, set, $10; sheet, $10.

No. C55
Surcharged in Red

Habilitada.
S/. 0.10

1948, Dec. Perf. 13

C82	AP33	10c on 70c sl bl	15	6
C83	AP33	20c on 70c sl bl	15	6
C84	AP33	55c on 70c sl bl	25	8

Nos. C52, C55 and C56
Surcharged in Black

Habilitada
S/. 0.10

1949, Mar. 25

C85	AP30	5c on 25c dp grn	15	8
C86	AP30	10c on 25c dp grn	15	6
C87	AP33	15c on 70c sl bl	20	8
C88	AP34	30c on 80c ol	1.25	20

The surcharge is vertical, reading up, on No. C87.

Types of 1938.
Photogravure.
Imprint: "Waterlow & Sons Limited, Londres."
1949-50 Perf. 13x13½, 13½x13

C89	AP27	5c ol bis	10	5
C90	AP31	30c red	15	5
C91	AP33	70c blue	25	5
C92	AP34	80c cerise	60	20
C93	AP36	1.50s vio brn ('50)	50	30
		Nos. C89-C93 (5)	1.60	65

Air View, Reserva Park, Lima—AP45

Flags of the Americas and Spain—AP46

Designs: 30c, National flag. 55c, Huancayo Hotel. 95c, Blanca-Ancash Cordillera. 1.50s, Arequipa Hotel. 2s, Coal chute and dock, Chimbote. 5s, Town hall, Miraflores. 10s, Hall of National Congress, Lima.

Overprinted "U. P. U. 1874-1949"
in Red or Black.
1951, Apr. 2 Engraved. Perf. 12

C94	AP45	5c bl grn	10	10
C95	AP45	30c blk & car	20	15
a.		Inverted ovpt.		
C96	AP45	55c yel grn (Bk)	20	15
C97	AP45	95c dk grn	30	25
C98	AP45	1.50s dp car (Bk)	40	35
C99	AP45	2s dp bl	50	45
C100	AP45	5s rose car (Bk)	6.00	6.00
C101	AP45	10s purple	8.00	9.00
C102	AP46	20s dk brn & ultra	14.00	14.00
		Nos. C94-C102 (9)	29.70	30.45

Issued to commemorate the 75th anniversary (in 1949) of the formation of the Universal Postal Union.
Nos. C94-C102 exist without overprint, but were not regularly issued. Price, set, $200.

Type of 1938.
Imprint: "Inst. de Grav. Paris."
1951, May Engr. Perf. 12½x12

C103	AP27	5c ol bis	12	5

Type of 1938
Surcharged in Black

HABILITADA
S|o. 0.25

1951

C108	AP31	25c on 30c rose red	20	8

Thomas de San Martin y Contreras and Jerónimo de Aliaga y Ramirez
AP47

San Marcos University—AP48

Designs: 50c, Church and convent of Santo Domingo. 1.20s, P. de Peralta Barnuevo, T. de San Martin y Contreras and J. Baquijano y Carrillo de Cordova. 2s, T. Rodriguez de Mendoza, J. Hipolito Unanue y Pavon and J. Cayetano Heredia y Garcia. 5s, Arms of the University, 1571 and 1735.

Lithographed.
1951, Dec. 10 Perf. 11½x12½

C109	AP47	30c gray	15	8
C110	AP48	40c ultra	15	8
C111	AP48	50c car rose	20	15
C112	AP47	1.20s emerald	30	25
C113	AP47	2s slate	50	20
C114	AP47	5s multi	2.25	30
		Nos. C109-C114 (6)	3.55	1.06

Issued to commemorate the 400th anniversary of the founding of San Marcos University.

River Gunboat Marañon
AP49

Peruvian Cormorants
AP50

Tobacco Plant
AP52

National Airport, Lima
AP51

PERU

Garcilaso de la Vega
AP53

Manco Capac Monument
AP54

Designs: 1.50s, Housing Unit No. 3. 2.20s, Inca Solar Observatory.
Imprint: "Thomas De La Rue & Co. Ltd."

1953-60   Perf. 13, 12.   Unwmkd.

C115	AP49	40c yel grn	10	8
a.		40c bl grn ('57)	12	8
C116	AP50	75c dk brn	1.00	20
C116A	AP50	80c pale brn red ('60)	40	8
C117	AP51	1.25s blue	20	10
C118	AP49	1.50s cerise	25	15
C119	AP51	2.20s dk bl	1.50	25
C120	AP52	3s brown	1.25	35
C121	AP53	5s bister	1.00	20
C122	AP54	10s dl vio brn	2.50	50
		Nos. C115-C122 (9)	8.20	1.91

See also Nos. C158-C162, C182-C183, C186-C189, C210-C211.

Queen Isabella I
AP55

Fleet of Columbus—AP56
Perf. 12½x11½, 11½x12½.

1953, June 18   Engr.   Unwmkd.

C123	AP55	40c dp car	25	15
C124	AP56	1.25s emerald	40	25
C125	AP56	2.15s dp plum	80	45
C126	AP56	2.20s black	1.25	45

Issued to commemorate the 500th anniversary (in 1951) of the birth of Queen Isabella I of Spain.

Arms of Lima and Bordeaux
AP57

Designs: 50c, Eiffel Tower and Cathedral of Lima. 1.25s, Admiral Dupetit-Thouars and frigate "La Victorieuse." 2.20s, Presidents Coty and Prado and exposition hall.

1957, Sept. 16   Perf. 13

C127	AP57	40c cl, grn & ultra	15	12
C128	AP57	50c grn, blk & hn brn	15	8
C129	AP57	1.25s bl, ind & dk grn	30	20
C130	AP57	2.20s bluish blk, bl & red brn	60	40

Issued to publicize the French Exposition, Lima, Sept. 15-Oct. 1.

Pre-Stamp Postal Markings
AP58

Designs: 10c, 1r Stamp of 1857. 15c, 2r Stamp of 1857. 25c, 1d Stamp of 1860. 30c, 1p Stamp of 1858. 40c, 4p Stamp of 1858. 1.25s, José Davila Condemarin. 2.20s, Ramon Castilla. 5s, Pres. Manuel Prado. 10s, Shield of Lima containing stamps.

1957, Dec. 1   Engraved   Unwmkd.
Perf. 12½x13

C131	AP58	5c sil & blk	8	6
C132	AP58	10c lil rose & bl	8	6
C133	AP58	15c grn & red brn	8	6
C134	AP58	25c org yel & bl	8	6
C135	AP58	30c vio brn & org brn	8	6
C136	AP58	40c blk & bis	15	8
C137	AP58	1.25s dk bl & dk brn	45	35
C138	AP58	2.20s red & sl bl	75	60
C139	AP58	5s lil rose & mar	1.75	1.50
C140	AP58	10s ol grn & lil	3.00	2.25
		Nos. C131-C140 (10)	6.50	5.08

Issued to commemorate the centenary of Peruvian postage stamps. No. C140 issued to publicize the Peruvian Centenary Philatelic Exhibition (PEREX).

Carlos Paz Soldan
AP59

Port of Callao and Pres. Manuel Prado
AP60

Perf. 14 x 13½, 13½ x 14

1958, Apr. 7   Litho.   Wmk. 116

C141	AP59	40c brn & pale rose	15	8
C142	AP59	1s grn & lt grn	22	12
C143	AP60	1.25s dl pur & ind	35	20

Issued to commemorate the centenary of the telegraph connection between Lima and Callao and the centenary of the political province of Callao.

Flags of France and Peru
AP61

Cathedral of Lima and Lady
AP62

Designs: 1.50s, Horseback rider and mall in Lima. 2.50s, Map of Peru showing national products.

1958, May 20   Engraved   Unwmkd.
Perf. 12½x13, 13x12½

C144	AP61	50c dl vio, bl & car	15	8
C145	AP62	65c multi	20	10
C146	AP62	1.50s bl, brn vio & ol	40	18
C147	AP61	2.50s sl grn, grnsh bl & cl	50	25

Issued to publicize the Peruvian Exhibition in Paris, May 20-July 10.

Bro. Martin de Porres Velasquez
AP63

First Royal School of Medicine
(Now Ministry of Government and Police)
AP64

Designs: 1.20s, Daniel Alcides Carrion Garcia. 1.50s, Jose Hipolito Unanue Pavon.

Perf. 13x13½, 13½x13

1958, July 24   Litho.   Unwmkd.

C148	AP63	60c multi	15	8
C149	AP63	1.20s multi	20	12
C150	AP63	1.50s multi	25	15
C151	AP64	2.20s black	35	30

Issued to commemorate the centenary of the birth of Daniel A. Carrion (1857-1885), medical martyr.

Gen. Ignacio Alvarez Thomas
AP65

1958, Nov. 13   Perf. 13x12½

C152	AP65	1.10s brn lake, bis & ver	30	20
C153	AP65	1.20s blk, bis & ver	35	25

Issued to commemorate the centenary of the death of General Ignacio Alvarez Thomas (1787-1857), fighter for South American independence.

"Justice" and Emblem
AP66

1958, Nov. 13
Star in Blue and Olive Bistre.

C154	AP66	80c emerald	12	10
C155	AP66	1.10s red org	15	18
C156	AP66	1.20s ultra	25	18
C157	AP66	1.50s lil rose	30	18

Issued to commemorate the 150th anniversary of the Lima Bar Association.

Types of 1953-57
Designs: 80c, Peruvian cormorants. 3.80s, Inca Solar Observatory.
Imprint: "Joh. Enschedé en Zonen-Holland"
Perf. 12½x14, 14x13, 13x14

1959, Dec. 9   Unwmkd.

C158	AP50	80c brn red	20	8
C159	AP52	3s lt grn	1.00	40
C160	AP51	3.80s orange	1.75	50
C161	AP53	5s brown	1.00	50
C162	AP54	10s org ver	2.00	80
		Nos. C158-C162 (5)	5.95	2.28

WRY Emblem, Dove, Rainbow and Farmer
AP67

Peruvian Cormorant Over Ocean
AP68

1960, Apr. 7   Litho.   Perf. 14x13

C163	AP67	80c multi	50	45
C164	AP67	4.30s multi	1.00	75
a.		Souvenir sheet of 2	15.00	15.00

Issued to publicize World Refugee Year, July 1, 1959-June 30, 1960.
No. C164a contains one each of Nos. C163-C164, imperf., with marginal inscriptions in black. Size: 150x100mm. Sold for 15 sol.

1960, May 30   Perf. 14x13½

C165	AP68	1s multi	60	15

International Pacific Fair, Lima, 1959.

PERU

Lima Coin of 1659
AP69

1961, Jan. 19 Perf. *13x14* Unwmkd.

| C166 | AP69 | 1s org brn & gray | 20 | 12 |
| C167 | AP69 | 2s Prus bl & gray | 35 | 25 |

Issued to commemorate the first National Numismatic Exposition, Lima, 1959, and the 300th anniversary of the first dated coin (1659) minted at Lima.

The Earth—AP70

1961, Mar. 8 Litho. Perf. *13½x14*

| C168 | AP70 | 1s multi | 85 | 20 |

International Geophysical Year, 1957–58.

Frigate Amazonas
AP71

1961, Mar. 8 Engraved Perf. *13½*

C169	AP71	50c brn & grn	12	10
C170	AP71	80c dl vio & red org	15	12
C171	AP71	1s grn & sep	40	18

Issued to commemorate the centenary (in 1958) of the trip around the world by the Peruvian frigate Amazonas.

Machu Picchu Sheet

A souvenir sheet was issued Sept. 11, 1961, to commemorate the 50th anniversary of the discovery of the ruins of Machu Picchu, ancient Inca city in the Andes, by Hiram Bingham. It contains two bi-colored imperf. airmail stamps, 5s and 10s, lithographed in a single design picturing the mountaintop ruins. The sheet was valid for one day and was sold in a restricted manner. Price $7.50.

Olympic Torch,   Fair Emblem
Laurel and Globe   and Llama
AP72   AP73

1961, Dec. 13 Perf. *13* Unwmkd.

C172	AP72	5s gray & ultra	75	50
C173	AP72	10s gray & car	1.50	90
a.	Souv. sheet		4.00	4.00

Issued to commemorate the 17th Olympic Games, Rome, Aug. 25–Sept. 11, 1960.
No. C173a contains one each of Nos. C172–C173, imperf., with black marginal inscription. Size: 99x79mm.

1962, Jan. Litho. Perf. *10½x11*

| C174 | AP73 | 1s multi | 30 | 20 |

2nd International Pacific Fair, Lima, 1961.

Map Showing Disputed Border,
Peru-Ecuador—AP74

1962, May 25 Perf. *10½*
Gray Background

C175	AP74	1.30s blk, red & car rose	30	25
C176	AP74	1.50s blk, red & emer	35	30
C177	AP74	2.50s blk, red & dk bl	45	40

Issued to commemorate the 20th anniversary of the settlement of the border dispute with Ecuador by the Protocol of Rio de Janeiro.

Cahuide and Cuauhtémoc
AP75

1962, May 25 Engraved Perf. *13*

C178	AP75	1s dk car rose, red & brt grn	20	12
C179	AP75	2s grn, red & brt grn	35	20
C180	AP75	3s brn, red & brt grn	50	25

Issued to commemorate the exhibition of Peruvian art treasures in Mexico.

Agriculture, Industry
and Archaeology
AP76
Lithographed

1962, Sept. 7 Litho. Perf. *14x13½*

| C181 | AP76 | 1s blk & gray | 12 | 10 |

Issued to commemorate the centenary (in 1961) of Pallasca Ancash province.

Types of 1953–60

Designs: 1.30s, Guanayes. 1.50s, Housing Unit No. 3. 1.80s, Locomotive No. 80 (like No. 480). 2s, Monument to Native Farmer. 3s, Tobacco plant. 4.30s, Inca Solar Observatory. 5s, Garcilaso de la Vega. 10s, Inca Monument.

Imprint: "Thomas De La Rue
& Co. Ltd."
Lithographed

1962–63 Perf. *13* Wmk. 346

C182	AP50	1.30s pale yel	30	20
C183	AP49	1.50s claret	35	15
C184	A182	1.80s dk bl	40	15

Perf. *12*

C185	A184	2s emer ('63)	42	20
C186	AP52	3s lil rose	60	25
C187	AP51	4.30s orange	1.10	45
C188	AP53	5s citron	1.10	50

Perf. *13½x14*

| C189 | AP54 | 10s vio bl ('63) | 2.00 | 1.00 |
| | Nos. C182-C189 (8) | | 6.27 | 2.90 |

Freedom from Hunger Issue
Type of Regular Issue

1963, July 23 Perf. *12½* Unwmkd.

| C190 | A189 | 4.30s lt grn & ocher | 75 | 60 |

Issued for the "Freedom from Hunger" campaign of the U.N. Food and Agriculture Organization.

Jorge Chávez   Fair
and Wing   Poster
AP77   AP78
Engraved

1964, Feb. 20 Perf. *13* Unwmkd.

| C191 | AP77 | 5s org brn, dk brn & bl | 1.00 | 50 |

Issued to commemorate the 50th anniversary of the first crossing of the Alps by air (Sept. 23, 1910) by the Peruvian aviator Jorge Chávez.

Alliance for Progress
Type of Regular Issue

Design: 1.30s, Same, horizontal.

Perf. *12½x12*, *12x12½*

1964, June 22   Lithographed

| C192 | A190 | 1.30s multi | 20 | 18 |
| C193 | A190 | 3s multi | 40 | 35 |

Issued to honor the Alliance for Progress.

1965, Jan. 15 Perf. *14½* Unwmkd.

| C194 | AP78 | 1s multi | 15 | 12 |

3rd International Pacific Fair, Lima 1963.

Basket, Globe,   St. Martin de Porres
Pennant   AP80
AP79

1965, Apr. 19   Perf. *12x12½*

| C195 | AP79 | 1.30s vio & red | 35 | 18 |
| C196 | AP79 | 4.30s bis brn & red | 85 | 45 |

4th Women's International Basketball Championship.

1965, Oct. 29 Litho. Perf. *11*

Designs: 1.80s, St. Martin's miracle: dog, cat and mouse feeding from same dish. 4.30s, St. Martin with cherubim in Heaven.

C197	AP80	1.30s gray & multi	25	12
C198	AP80	1.80s gray & multi	35	15
C199	AP80	4.30s gray & multi	75	40

Issued to commemorate the canonization of St. Martin de Porres Velasquez (1579–1639), on May 6, 1962.

Victory
Monument, Lima,
and Battle Scene
AP81

Designs: 3.60s, Monument and Callao Fortress. 4.60s, Monument and José Galvez.

Perf. *14x13½*

1966, May 2   Photo.   Unwmkd.

C200	AP81	1.90s multi	40	30
C201	AP81	3.60s brn, yel & bis	60	40
C202	AP81	4.60s multi	90	60

Issued to commemorate the centenary of Peru's naval victory over the Spanish Armada at Callao, May, 1866.

Civil Guard
Emblem
AP82

Design: 1.90s, Emblem and various activities of Civil Guard.

1966, Aug. 30 Photo. Perf. *13½x14*

| C203 | AP82 | 90c multi | 12 | 12 |
| C204 | AP82 | 1.90s dp lil rose, gold & blk | 25 | 20 |

Centenary of the Civil Guard.

Type of Regular Issue

1966, Nov. 24 Photo. Perf. *13½x14*

| C205 | A193 | 1.90s lil, blk & vio bl | 25 | 20 |

Opening of Huinco Hydroelectric Center.

Sun Symbol, Ancient Carving
AP83

Designs: 3.60s, Map of Peru and spiral (horiz.). 4.60s, Globe with map of Peru.

Perf. *14x13½*, *13½x14*

1967, Feb. 16   Lithographed

C206	AP83	2.60s red org & blk	35	25
C207	AP83	3.60s dp bl & blk	50	35
C208	AP83	4.60s tan & multi	60	45

Issued to commemorate the photography exhibition "Peru Before the World" which opened simultaneously in Lima, Madrid, Santiago de Chile and Washington, Sept. 27, 1966.

Types of 1953–60

Designs: 2.60s, Monument to Native Farmer. 3.60s, Tobacco plant. 4.60s, Inca Solar Observatory.

Imprint: "I.N.A."

1967, Jan. Perf. *13½x14*, *14x13½*

C209	A184	2.60s brt grn	35	25
C210	AP52	3.60s lil rose	50	30
C211	AP51	4.60s orange	60	40

PERU

Wind Vane and Sun Type of Regular Issue
Perf. 13½x14
1967, Apr. 18 Photo. Unwmkd.
C212 A194 1.90s yel brn, blk & gold 25 20
Six-year building program.

St. Rosa of Lima
by Angelino
Medoro
AP84

Lions Emblem
AP85

St. Rosa Painted by: 2.60s. Carlo Maratta. 3.60s, Cuzquena School, 17th century.

1967, Aug. 30 Photo. *Perf. 13½*
C213 AP84 1.90s blk, gold & multi 50 20
C214 AP84 2.60s blk, gold & multi 75 25
C215 AP84 3.60s blk, gold & multi 1.00 35

Issued to commemorate the 350th anniversary of the death of St. Rosa of Lima.

Fair Type of Regular Issue
1967, Oct. 27 Photo. *Perf. 12*
C216 A195 1s gold, brt red lil & blk 15 10
Issued to publicize the 5th International Pacific Fair, Lima, Oct. 27–Nov. 12.

1967, Dec. 29 Litho. *Perf. 14x13½*
C217 AP85 1.60s brt bl & vio bl, grysh 20 15
50th anniversary of Lions International.

Decorated Jug,
Nazca Culture
AP86

Antarqui, Inca
Messenger
AP87

Designs (painted pottery jugs of pre-Inca Nazca culture): 2.60s, Falcon. 3.60s, Round jug decorated with grain-eating bird. 4.60s, Two-headed snake. 5.60s, Marine bird.

1968, June 4 Photo. *Perf. 12*
C218 AP86 1.90s multi 20 18
C219 AP86 2.60s multi 25 20
C220 AP86 3.60s blk & multi 35 30
C221 AP86 4.60s brn & multi 45 40
C222 AP86 5.60s gray & multi 55 50
Nos. C218-C222 (5) 1.80 1.58

1968, Sept. 2 Litho. *Perf. 12*
Design: 5.60s, Alpaca and jet liner.
C223 AP87 3.60s multi 45 18
C224 AP87 5.60s red, blk & brn 65 25

Issued to commemorate the 12th anniversary of Peruvian Airlines (APSA).

Human Rights Flame
AP88

1968, Sept. 5 Photo. *Perf. 14x13½*
C225 AP88 6.50s brn, red & grn 35 30
International Human Rights Year 1968.

Discobolus and Mexico
Olympics Emblem
AP89

1968, Oct. 19 Photo. *Perf. 13½*
C226 AP89 2.30s yel, brn & dk bl 20 12
C227 AP89 3.50s yel grn, sl bl & red 28 18
C228 AP89 5s brt pink, blk & ultra 40 25
C229 AP89 6.50s lt bl, mag & brn 55 35
C230 AP89 8s lil, ultra & car 60 40
C231 AP89 9s org, vio & grn 65 45
Nos. C226-C231 (6) 2.68 1.75

Issued to commemorate the 19th Olympic Games, Mexico City, Oct. 12–27.

Hand, Corn and Field
AP90

1969, Mar. 3 Litho. *Perf. 11*
C232 AP90 5.50s on 1.90s grn & yel 40 25
C233 AP90 6.50s on 1.90s bl, grn & yel 50 30

Agrarian Reform Law. Nos. C232–C233 were not issued without surcharge.

Peruvian Silver 8-reales Coin, 1568
AP91

1969, Mar. 17 Litho. *Perf. 12*
C234 AP91 5s yel, gray & blk 30 20
C235 AP91 5s bl grn, gray & blk 30 20

Issued to commemorate the 400th anniversary of the first Peruvian coinage.

Ramon
Castilla
Monument
AP92

Design: 10s, Pres. Ramon Castilla.
1969, May 30 Photo. *Perf. 13½*
Size: 27x40mm.
C236 AP92 5s emer & ind 45 20

Perf. 12
Size: 21x37mm.
C237 AP92 10s plum & brn 1.00 45

Issued to commemorate the centenary of the death of Ramon Castilla (1797–1867), president of Peru (1845–1851 and 1855–1862), on the occasion of the unveiling of the monument in Lima.

Airline Type of Regular Issue
1969, June 17 Litho. *Perf. 11*
C238 A199 3s org & multi 15 12
C239 A199 4s multi 20 15
C240 A199 5.50s ver & multi 27 20
C241 A199 6.50s vio & multi 32 25

First Peruvian Airlines (APSA) flight to Europe.

Radar Antenna, Satellite and Earth
AP93

1969, July 14 Litho. *Perf. 11*
C242 AP93 20s multi 1.50 85
  a. Souv. sheet 1.75 1.75

Issued to commemorate the opening of the Lurin satellite earth station near Lima. No. C242a contains one imperf. stamp with simulated perforations similar to No. C242. Light blue margin with black commemorative inscription and control number. Size: 109x80mm.

Gonzales Type of Regular Issue
1969, July 23 Litho. *Perf. 11*
C243 A200 20s red & multi 1.75 80
Issued in memory of Capt. José A. Quiñones Gonzales (1914–1941), military aviator.

WHO Emblem
AP94

1969, Aug. 14 Photo. *Perf. 12*
C244 AP94 5s gray, red brn, gold & blk 25 20
C245 AP94 6.50s dl org, gray bl, gold & blk 32 25

Issued to commemorate the 20th anniversary (in 1968) of the World Health Organization.

Agrarian Reform Type of Regular Issue
1969, Aug. 28 Litho. *Perf. 11*
C246 A201 3s lil & blk 15 12
C247 A201 4s brn & buff 20 18
Issued to commemorate the enactment of the Agrarian Reform Law of June 24, 1969.

Garcilaso
de la Vega
AP95

Designs: 2.40s, De la Vega's coat of arms. 3.50s, Title page of "Commentarios Reales que tratan del origen de los Yncas," Lisbon, 1609.

1969, Sept. 18 Litho. *Perf. 12x12½*
C248 AP95 2.40s emer, sil & blk 15 10
C249 AP95 3.50s ultra, buff & blk 20 15
C250 AP95 5s sil, yel, blk & brn 30 20
  a. Souv. sheet of 3 1.35 1.35

Issued to commemorate the 351st anniversary of the death of Garcilaso de la Vega, called "Inca" (1539–1616), historian of Peru.

No. C250a contains 3 imperf. stamps similar to Nos. C248–C250. Pink margin with black commemorative inscription. Size: 127½x88½mm.

Fair Type of Regular Issue, 1969
1969, Nov. 14 Litho. *Perf. 11*
C251 A203 3s bis & multi 15 12
C252 A203 4s multi 20 15
Issued to publicize the Sixth International Pacific Trade Fair, Lima, Nov. 14–30.

Bolognesi Type of Regular Issue
1969, Dec. 9 Litho. *Perf. 11*
C253 A204 50s lt brn, blk & gold 4.50 2.00

Issued for Army Day, 1970.

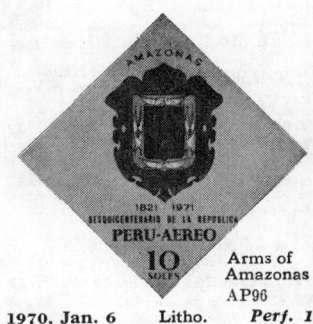
Arms of
Amazonas
AP96

1970, Jan. 6 Litho. *Perf. 11*
C254 AP96 10s multi 50 45

ILO
Emblem
AP97

1970, Jan. 16
C278 AP97 3s dk vio bl & lt ultra 25 12

Issued to commemorate the 50th anniversary of the International Labor Organization.

PERU

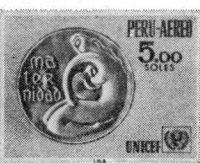

Motherhood and UNICEF Emblem
AP98

1970, Jan. 16   Photo.   Perf. 13½x14
C279	AP98	5s yel, gray & blk	35	20
C280	AP98	6.50s brt pink, gray & blk	50	30

Issued to honor UNICEF (United Nations International Children's Fund).

Vicus Culture Type of Regular Issue, 1970
Ceramics of Vicus Culture, 6th–8th Centuries: 3s, Squatting warrior. 4s, Jug. 5.50s, Twin jugs. 6.50s, Woman and jug.

1970, Feb. 23   Litho.   Perf. 11
C281	A205	3s buff, blk & brn	25	20
C282	A205	4s buff, blk & brn	30	25
C283	A205	5.50s buff, blk & brn	45	35
C284	A205	6.50s buff, blk & brn	60	40

Fish Type of Regular Issue
Fish: No. C285, Swordfish. No. C286, Yellowfin tuna. 5.50s, Wolf fish.

1970, Apr. 30   Litho.   Perf. 11
C285	A207	3s vio bl & multi	20	8
C286	A207	4s vio bl & multi	23	10
C287	A207	5.50s vio bl & multi	40	15

Nos. C285–C287 are printed se-tenant in sheet with Nos. 532–533, arranged in horizontal strips of five.

Telephone   U.N. Headquarters, N.Y.
AP99   AP100

1970, June 12   Litho.   Perf. 11
C288	AP99	5s multi	40	15
C289	AP99	10s multi	80	35

Issued to commemorate the nationalization of the Peruvian telephone system, Mar. 25, 1970.

Soldier-Farmer Type of Regular Issue

1970, June 24   Litho.   Perf. 11
C290	A208	3s gold & multi	30	10
C291	A208	5.50s gold & multi	45	20

Issued to publicize a "United people and army building a new Peru."

1970, June 26
C292	AP100	3s vio bl & lt bl	15	10

25th anniversary of United Nations.

Rotary Club Emblem—AP101

1970, July 18
C293	AP101	10s blk, red & gold	1.10	30

Rotary Club of Lima, 50th anniversary.

Tourist Type of Regular Issue
Designs: 3s, Ruins of Sun Fortress, Trujillo. 4s, Sacsayhuaman Arch, Cuzco (vert.). 5.50s, Arch and Lake Titicaca, Puno (vert.). 10s, Machu Picchu, Cuzco (vert.).

1970, Aug. 6   Litho.   Perf. 11
C294	A210	3s multi	22	10
C295	A210	4s multi	30	10
C296	A210	5.50s multi	42	20
C297	A210	10s multi	75	30
a.		Souvenir sheet of 5	2.50	2.50

No. C297a contains 5 imperf. stamps similar to Nos. 538, C294–C297 with simulated perforations. Pale bister margin with black inscription and control number. Size: 125x93½mm.

Procession, Lord of Miracles
AP102

Designs: 4s, Cockfight, by T. Nuñez Ureta. 5.50s, Altar of Church of the Nazarene (vert.). 6.50s, Procession, by J. Vinatea Reinoso. 8s, Procession, by José Sabogal (vert.).

1970, Nov. 30   Litho.   Perf. 11
C298	AP102	3s blk & multi	22	10
C299	AP102	4s blk & multi	30	15
C300	AP102	5.50s blk & multi	40	20
C301	AP102	6.50s blk & multi	50	25
C302	AP102	8s blk & multi	60	30
		Nos. C298–C302 (5)	2.02	1.00

October Festival in Lima.

"Tight Embrace" (from ancient monolith)
AP103

1971, Feb. 8   Litho.   Perf. 11
C303	AP103	4s ol gray, yel & red	35	15
C304	AP103	5.50s dk bl, pink & red	45	20
C305	AP103	6.50s sl, buff & red	50	25

Issued to express Peru's gratitude to the world for aid after the Ancash earthquake, May 31, 1970.

Textile Type of Regular Issue
Designs: 3s, Chancay tapestry (vert.). 4s, Chancay lace. 5.50s, Paracas cloth (vert.).

1971, Apr. 19   Litho.   Perf. 11
C306	A213	3s multi	38	10
C307	A213	4s grn & multi	50	15
C308	A213	6.50s multi	65	20

Fish Type of Regular Issue
Fish Sculptures and Fish: 3.50s, Chimu Inca culture, 14th century and Chilean sardine. 4s, Mochica culture, 5th century, and engraulis ringens. 5.50s, Chimu culture, 13th century, and merluccius peruanos. 8.50s, Nazca culture, 3rd century, and brevoortis maculatachicaes.

1971, June 7   Litho.   Perf. 11
C309	A214	3.50s multi	45	15
C310	A214	4s multi	55	15
C311	A214	5.50s multi	75	20
C312	A214	8.50s multi	1.15	30

Publicity for the 200-mile zone of sovereignty of the high seas.

Independence Type of 1971
Designs (Paintings): No. C313, Toribio Rodriguez de Mendoza. No. C314, José de la Riva Aguero. No. C315, Francisco Vidal. 3.50s, José de San Martin. No. C317, Juan P. Viscardo y Guzman. No. C318, Hipolito Unanue. 4.50s, Liberation Monument, Paracas. No. C320, José G. Condorcanqui-Tupac Amaru. No. C321, Francisco J. de Luna Pizarro. 6s, March of the Numancia Battalion (horiz.). 7.50s, Peace Tower, monument for Alvarez de Arenales (horiz.). 9s, Liberators' Monument, Lima (horiz.). 10s, Independence Proclamation in Lima (horiz.).

1971   Lithographed   Perf. 11
C313	A215	3s brt mag & blk	18	10
C314	A215	3s gray & multi	18	10
C315	A215	3s dk bl & multi	18	10
C316	A215	3.50s dk bl & multi	22	13
C317	A215	4s emer & blk	25	15
C318	A215	4s gray & multi	25	15
C319	A215	4.50s dk bl & multi	27	17
C320	A215	5.50s brn & blk	33	20
C321	A215	5.50s gray & multi	33	20
C322	A215	6s dk bl & multi	35	22
C323	A215	7.50s dk bl & multi	45	27
C324	A215	9s dk bl & multi	55	30
C325	A215	10s dk bl & multi	60	30
		Nos. C313–C325 (13)	4.14	2.39

150th anniversary of independence, and to honor the heroes of the struggle for independence. Sizes: 6s, 10s, 45x35mm. 7.50s, 9s, 41x39mm. Others 31x49mm. Issue dates: Nos. C313, C317, C320, May 10; Nos. C314, C318, C321, July 5; others July 27.

Ricardo Palma   Weight Lifter
AP104   AP105

1971, Aug. 27   Perf. 13
C326	AP104	7.50s ol bis & blk	90	27

Sesquicentennial of National Library. Ricardo Palma (1884–1912) was a writer and director of the library.

1971, Sept. 15
C327	AP105	7.50s brt bl & blk	75	27

25th World Weight Lifting Championships, Lima.

Flag, Family, Soldier's Head
AP106

1971, Oct. 4
C328	AP106	7.50s blk, lt bl & red	75	27
a.		Souvenir sheet	1.50	1.50

3rd anniversary of the revolution of the armed forces. No. C328a contains one imperf. stamp similar to No. C328. Black marginal inscription and control number. Size: 109x81mm.

"Sacramento"
AP107

1971, Oct. 8
C329	AP107	7.50s lt bl & dk bl	55	27

Sesquicentennial of Peruvian Navy.

Peruvian Order of the Sun
AP108

1971, Oct. 8
C330	AP108	7.50s multi	55	30

Sesquicentennial of the Peruvian Order of the Sun.

Liberation Type of Regular Issue
Design: 50s, Detail from painting "Progress of Liberation," by Teodoro Nuñez Ureta.

1971, Nov. 4   Litho.   Perf. 13x13½
C331	A217	50s multi	4.50	1.50

2nd Ministerial meeting of the "Group of 77."

Fair Emblem
AP109

1971, Nov. 12   Perf. 13
C332	AP109	4.50s multi	30	20

7th Pacific International Trade Fair.

Fish Type of Regular Issue
Fish: 3s, Pontinus furcirhinus dubius. 5.50s, Hogfish.

1972, Mar. 20   Litho.   Perf. 13x13½
C333	A223	3s lt bl & multi	30	12
C334	A223	5.50s lt bl & multi	50	20

Teacher and Children, by Teodoro Nuñez Ureta
AP110

1972, Apr. 10   Litho.   Perf. 13x13½
C335	AP110	6.50s multi	50	25

Enactment of Education Reform Law.

White-tailed Trogon
AP111

1972, June 19   Litho.   Perf. 13½x13
Multicolored
C336	AP111	2s shown	22	8
C337	AP111	2.50s *Amazonian umbrellabird*	28	10
C338	AP111	3s *Peruvian cock-of-the-rock*	35	12
C339	AP111	6.50s *Cuvier's toucan*	70	23
C340	AP111	8.50s *Blue-crowned motmot*	1.00	35
		Nos. C336–C340 (5)	2.55	88

PERU

Quipu and Map of Americas
AP112

Inca Runner, Olympic Rings
AP113

1972, Aug. 21

C341   AP112   5s blk & multi   35   20

4th Interamerican Philatelic Exhibition, EXFILBRA, Rio de Janeiro, Aug. 26–Sept. 2.

1972, Aug. 28

C342   AP113   8s buff & multi   85   23

20th Olympic Games, Munich, Aug. 26–Sept. 11.

Woman of Catacaos, Piura
AP114

Funerary Tower, Sillustani, Puno
AP115

Regional Costumes: 2s, Tupe (Yauyos) woman of Lima. 4s, Indian with bow and arrow, from Conibo, Loreto. 4.50s, Man with calabash, Cajamarca. 5s, Moche woman, Trujillo. 6.50s, Man and woman of Ocongate, Cuzco. 8s, Chucupana woman, Ayacucho. 8.50s, Cotuncha woman, Junin. 10s, Woman of Puno dancing "Pandilla."

1972–73

C343	AP114	2s blk & multi	15	6
C344	AP114	3.50s blk & multi	30	15
C345	AP114	4s blk & multi	35	15
C346	AP114	4.50s blk & multi	40	15
C346A	AP114	5s blk & multi	38	15
C347	AP114	6.50s blk & multi	55	22
C347A	AP114	8s blk & multi	60	28
C347B	AP114	8.50s blk & multi	65	30
C348	AP114	10s blk & multi	80	30
	Nos. C343-C348 (9)		4.18	1.76

Issue dates: 3.50s, 4s and 6.50s, Sept. 29, 1972. 2s, 4.50s and 10s, Apr. 30, 1973. 5s, 8s and 8.50s, Oct. 15, 1973.

Perf. 13½x13, 13x13½

1972, Oct. 16   Lithographed

Archaeological Monuments: 1.50s, Stone of the 12 angles, Cuzco. 3.50s, Ruins of Chavin, Ancash (horiz.). 5s, Wall and gate, Chavin, Ancash (horiz.). 8s, Ruins of Machu Picchu (horiz.).

C349	AP115	1.50s multi	20	5
C350	AP115	3.50s multi	35	12
C351	AP115	4s multi	40	12
C352	AP115	5s multi	50	15
C353	AP115	8s multi	1.00	30
	Nos. C349-C353 (5)		2.45	74

Inca Poncho
AP116

Designs: Inca ponchos, various textile designs.

1973, Jan. 29   Litho.   Perf. 13½x13

C354	AP116	2s multi	15	6
C355	AP116	3.50s multi	30	10
C356	AP116	4s multi	30	10
C357	AP116	5s multi	40	15
C358	AP116	8s multi	75	24
	Nos. C354-C358 (5)		1.90	67

Goblets and Ring, Mochica, 10th Century
AP117

Antique Jewelry: 2.50s, Golden hands and arms, Lambayeque, 12th century. 4s, Gold male statuette, Mochica, 8th century. 5s, Two gold brooches, Nazca, 8th century. 8s, Flayed puma, Mochica, 8th century.

1973, Mar. 19   Litho.   Perf. 13½x13

C359	AP117	1.50s multi	15	5
C360	AP117	2.50s multi	20	8
C361	AP117	4s multi	30	12
C362	AP117	5s multi	40	15
C363	AP117	8s multi	75	24
	Nos. C359-C363 (5)		1.80	64

Andean Condor
AP118

Indian Guide, by José Sabogal
AP119

Protected Animals: 5s, Vicuña. 8s, Spectacled bear.

1973, Apr. 16   Litho.   Perf. 13½x13

C364	AP118	4s blk & multi	30	12
C365	AP118	5s blk & multi	40	15
C366	AP118	8s blk & multi	65	24

See Nos. C372–C376, C408–C409.

1973, May 7   Litho.   Perf. 13½x13

Peruvian Paintings: 8.50s, Portrait of a Lady, by Daniel Hernandez. 20s, Man Holding Figurine, by Francisco Laso.

C367	AP119	1.50s multi	10	5
C368	AP119	8.50s multi	55	25
C369	AP119	20s multi	1.35	60

Basket and World Map
AP120

1973, May 26   Perf. 13x13½

| C370 | AP120 | 5s green | 40 | 15 |
| C371 | AP120 | 20s lil rose | 1.60 | 60 |

1st International Basketball Festival.

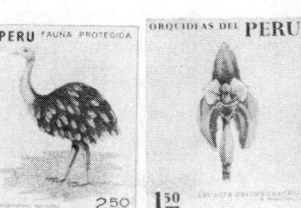

Darwin's Rhea
AP121

Orchid
AP122

1973, Sept. 3   Litho.   Perf. 13½x13
Multicolored

C372	AP121	2.50s *shown*	20	8
C373	AP121	3.50s *Giant otter*	27	10
C374	AP121	6s *Greater flamingo*	45	18
C375	AP121	8.50s *Bush dog* (horiz.)	65	25
C376	AP121	10s *Chinchilla* (horiz.)	75	30
	Nos. C372-C376 (5)		2.32	91

Protected animals.

1973, Sept. 27

Designs: Various orchids.

C377	AP122	1.50s blk & multi	15	5
C378	AP122	2.50s blk & multi	25	8
C379	AP122	3s blk & multi	30	10
C380	AP122	3.50s blk & multi	35	10
C381	AP122	8s blk & multi	85	24
	Nos. C377-C381 (5)		1.90	57

Pacific Fair Emblem
AP123

1973, Nov. 14   Litho.   Perf. 13½x13

C382   AP123   8s blk, red & gray   75   30

8th International Pacific Fair, Lima.

Cargo Ship ILO
AP124

Designs: 2.50s, Boats of Pescaperu fishing organization. 8s, Jet and seagull.

1973, Dec. 14   Litho.   Perf. 13

C383	AP124	1.50s multi	12	5
C384	AP124	2.50s multi	20	8
C385	AP124	8s multi	65	24

Issued to promote government enterprises.

Lima Monument
AP125

1973, Nov. 27   Perf. 13

C386   AP125   8.50s red & multi   65   25

50th anniversary of Air Force Academy. Monument honors Jorge Chavez, Peruvian aviator.

Bridge at Yananacu, by Enrique Camino Brant
AP126

Paintings: 10s, Peruvian Birds, by Teodoro Nuñez Ureta (vert.). 50s, Boats of Totora, by Jorge Vinatea Reinoso.

Perf. 13x13½, 13½x13

1973, Dec. 28

C387	AP126	8s multi	60	24
C388	AP126	10s multi	75	28
C389	AP126	50s multi	3.50	1.50

Moral House, Arequipa
AP127

Landscapes: 2.50s, El Misti Mountain, Arequipa. 5s, Puya Raymondi (cacti), (vert.). 6s, Huascaran Mountain. 8s, Lake Querococha. Views on 5s, 6s, 8s are views in White Cordilleras Range, Ancash Province.

1974, Feb. 11

C390	AP127	1.50s multi	15	5
C391	AP127	2.50s multi	20	8
C392	AP127	5s multi	35	15
C393	AP127	6s multi	45	20
C394	AP127	8s multi	75	24
	Nos. C390-C394 (5)		1.90	72

San Jeronimo's, Cuzco
AP128

Churches of Peru: 3.50s, Cajamarca Cathedral. 5s, San Pedro's, Zepita-Puno (horiz.). 6s, Cuzco Cathedral. 8.50s, Santo Domingo, Cuzco.

1974, May 6

C395	AP128	1.50s multi	10	5
C396	AP128	3.50s multi	25	10
C397	AP128	5s multi	33	12
C398	AP128	6s multi	40	18
C399	AP128	8.50s multi	75	24
	Nos. C395-C399 (5)		1.83	69

Surrender at Ayacucho, by Daniel Hernandez
AP129

Designs: 6s, Battle of Junin, by Felix Yañex. 7.50s, Battle of Ayachucho, by Felix Yañez.

1974   Litho.   Perf. 13x13½

C400	AP129	3.50s multi	25	12
C401	AP129	6s multi	50	18
C402	AP129	7.50s multi	60	20
C403	AP129	8.50s multi	75	27
C404	AP129	10s multi	1.00	10
	Nos. C400-C404 (5)		3.10	1.07

Sesquicentennial of the Battles of Junin and Ayacucho and of the surrender at Ayacucho.

Issue dates: 7.50s, Aug. 6. 6s, Oct. 9. Others, Dec. 9.

PERU

Chavin Stone, Ancash
AP130

Machu Picchu, Cuzco
AP131

Designs: Nos. C407, C409, Different bas-reliefs from Chavin Stone. No. C408, Baths of Tampumacchay, Cuzco. No. C410, Ruins of Kencco, Cuzco.

Perf. 13½x13, 13x13½

1974, Mar. 25

C405	AP130	3s multi	20	10
C406	AP131	3s multi	20	10
C407	AP130	5s multi	30	12
C408	AP131	5s multi	30	12
C409	AP130	10s multi	60	30
C410	AP131	10s multi	60	30
	Nos. C405-C410 (6)		2.20	1.04

Cacajao Rubicundus
AP132

1974, Oct. 21 *Perf.13½x13*

C411	AP132	8s multi	60	25
C412	AP132	20s multi	1.50	60

Protected animals.

Inca Gold Mask
AP133

1974, Nov. 8 *Perf. 13x13½*

C413	AP133	8s yel & multi	60	25

8th World Mining Congress, Lima.

Chalan, Horseman's Cloak
AP134

1974, Nov. 11 Litho. *Perf. 13½x13*

C414	AP134	5s multi	40	15
C415	AP134	8.50s multi	75	25

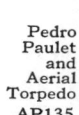 

Pedro Paulet and Aerial Torpedo
AP135

1974, Nov. 28 Litho. *Perf. 13x13½*

C416	AP135	8s bl & vio	60	25

Centenary of Universal Postal Union. Pedro Paulet, inventor of the mail-carrying aerial torpedo.

Christmas Type of 1974
Design: 6.50s, Indian Nativity scene.

1974, Dec. 20 *Perf. 13½x13*

C417	A235	6.50s multi	40	20

Christmas 1974.

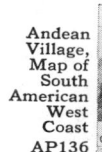 

Andean Village, Map of South American West Coast
AP136

1974, Dec. 30

C418	AP136	6.50s multi	50	20

Meeting of Communications Ministers of Andean Pact countries.

Map of Peru, Modern Buildings, UN Emblem
AP137

1975, Mar. 12 Litho. *Perf. 13x13*

C419	AP137	6s blk, gray & red	50	20

2nd United Nations Industrial Development Organization Conference, Lima.

Nos. C187, C211 and C160 Surcharged with New Value and Heavy Bar in Dark Blue

Lithographed

1975, April *Perf. 12* **Wmk. 346**
Perf. 13½x14, 13x14 **Unwmkd.**

C420	AP51	2s on 4.30s org	20	6
C421	AP51	2.50s on 4.60s org	35	12
C422	AP51	5s on 3.80s org	50	15

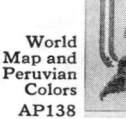 

World Map and Peruvian Colors
AP138

1975, Aug. 25 Litho. *Perf. 13x13½*

C423	AP138	6.50s lt bl, vio bl & red	75	25

Conference of Foreign Ministers of Non-aligned Countries.

Map of Peru and Flight Route
AP139

1975, Oct. 23 Litho. *Perf. 13x13½*

C424	AP139	8s red, pink & blk	1.00	25

AeroPeru's first flights: Lima–Rio de Janeiro, Lima–Los Angeles.

Fair Poster
AP140

Col. Francisco Bolognesi
AP141

1975, Nov. 21 Litho. *Perf. 13½x13*

C425	AP140	6s blk, bis & red	75	20

9th International Pacific Fair, Lima, 1975.

1975, Dec. 23 Litho. *Perf. 13½x13*

C426	AP141	20s multi	2.50	50

160th birth anniversary of Col. Francisco Bolognesi.

Indian Mother and Child
AP142

Inca Messenger, UPAE Emblem
AP143

1976, Feb. 23 Litho. *Perf. 13½x13*

C427	AP142	6s gray & multi	75	20

Christmas 1975.

1976, Mar. 19 Litho. *Perf. 13½x13*

C428	AP143	5s red, blk & tan	75	15

11th Congress of the Postal Union of the Americas and Spain, UPAE.

Nos. C187, C211, C160, C209, C210 Surcharged in Dark Blue or Violet Blue (No Bar)

Perf. 12, 13x14, 13½x14, 14x13½

1976 **Wmk. 346, Unwmkd.**

C429	AP51	2s on 4.30s org	15	6
C430	AP51	3.50s on 4.60s org	25	10
C431	AP51	4.50s on 3.80s org	30	14
C432	AP51	5s on 4.30s org	40	15
C433	AP51	6s on 4.60s org	50	18
C434	A184	10s on 2.60s brt grn	75	30
C435	AP52	50s on 3.60s lil rose (VB)	3.00	2.00
	Nos. C429-C435 (7)		5.35	2.93

Stamps of 1962-67 Surcharged with New Value and Heavy Bar in Black, Red, Green, Dark Blue or Orange

Perf. 14x13½, 11, 13½x14, 12

1976-77 **Unwmkd., Wmk. 346**

C436	AP52	1.50s on 3.60s (Bk) #C210	15	5
C437	A184	2s on 2.60s (R) #C209 ('77)	25	6
C438	AP52	2s on 3.60s (G) #C210	25	6
C439	AP80	2s on 4.30s (Bk) #C199	25	8
C440	A184	3s on 2.60s (Bk) #C209 ('77)	25	9
C441	A184	4s on 2.60s (DBl) #C209	25	12
C442	AP52	4s on 3.60s (DBl) #C210 ('77)	25	12
C443	AP51	5s on 4.30s (R) #C187	35	15
C444	AP83	6s on 4.60s (Bk) #C208 ('77)	50	18
C445	AP51	6s on 4.60s (DBl) #C211 ('77)	50	18
C446	AP51	7s on 4.30s (Bk) #C187 ('77)	60	20
C447	AP52	7.50s on 3.60s (DBl) #C210	60	22
C448	AP52	8s on 3.60s (O) #C210	75	24
C449	AP51	10s on 4.30s (Bk) #C187 ('77)	75	30
C450	AP52	10s on 4.60s (DBl) #C211	75	30
C451	AP86	24s on 3.60s (Bk) #C220 ('77)	2.00	70
C452	AP86	28s on 4.60s (Bk) #C221 ('77)	2.50	80
C453	AP86	32s on 5.60s (Bk) #C222 ('77)	2.50	95
C454	A184	50s on 2.60s (O) #C209 ('77)	4.00	1.50
C455	AP52	50s on 3.60s (G) #C210	4.00	1.50
	Nos. C436-C455 (20)		21.45	7.78

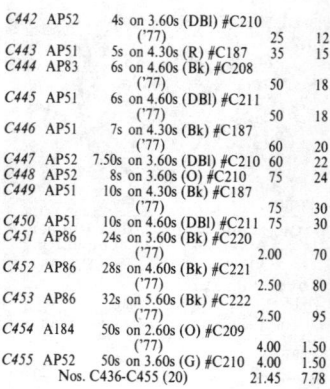

Map of Tacna and Tarata Provinces
AP144

1976, Aug. 28 Litho. *Perf. 13½x13*

C456	AP144	10s multi	1.00	20

Re-incorporation of Tacna Province into Peru, 47th anniversary.

Investigative Police Badge
AP145

"Declaration of Bogota"
AP146

1976, Sept. 15 Litho. *Perf. 13½x13*

C457	AP145	20s multi	2.00	60

Investigative Police of Peru, 54th anniversary.

1976, Sept. 22

C458	AP146	10s multi	1.00	30

Declaration of Bogota for cooperation and world peace, 10th anniversary.

Pal Losonczi and Map of Hungary
AP147

PERU

1976, Nov. 2   Litho.   *Perf. 13½x13*
C459   AP147   7s ultra & blk   75   20
Visit of Pres. Pal Losonczi of Hungary, Oct. 1976.

Map of Amazon Basin, Colors of Peru and Brazil
AP148

1976, Dec. 16   Litho.   *Perf. 13*
C460   AP148   10s bl & multi   1.00   30
Visit of Gen. Ernesto Geisel, president of Brazil, Nov. 5, 1976.

Liberation Monument, Lima
AP149

1977, Mar. 9   Litho.   *Perf. 13x13½*
C461   AP149   20s red buff & blk   1.25   60
Army Day.

Map of Peru and Venezuela, South America
AP150

1977, Mar. 14
C462   AP150   12s buff & multi   75   35
Meeting of Pres. Francisco Morales Bermudez Cerrutti of Peru and Pres. Carlos Andres Perez of Venezuela, Dec. 1976.

Electronic Tree   Map of Peru, Refinery, Tanker
AP151   AP152

1977, May 30   Litho.   *Perf. 13½x13*
C463   AP151   20s gray, red & blk   2.00   60
World Telecommunications Day.

1977, July 13   Litho.   *Perf. 13½x13*
C464   AP152   14s multi   1.25   35
Development of Bayovar oil complex.

Messenger Type of 1977

1977   Litho.   *Perf. 13½x13*
C465   A243   24s mag & blk   1.75   75
C466   A243   28s bl & blk   2.00   75
C467   A243   32s rose brn & blk   2.50   1.00

Arms of Arequipa   Gen. Jorge Rafael Videla
AP153   AP154

1977, Sept. 3   Litho.   *Perf. 13½x13*
C468   AP153   10s multi   30   15
Gold of Peru Exhibition, Arequipa 1977.

1977, Oct. 8   Litho.   *Perf. 13½x13*
C469   AP154   36s multi   1.00   40
Visit of Jorge Rafael Videla, president of Argentina.

Stamps of 1953-67 Surcharged with New Value and Heavy Bar in Black, Dark Blue or Green

Perf. 13½x14, 14x13½, 12, 12½x11½, 13½, 13x14

1977   Unwmkd., Wmk. 346
C470   AP83   2s on 3.60s (Bk) #C207   10   5
C471   AP51   2s on 4.60s (DB) #C211   10   5
C472   AP51   4s on 4.60s (DB) #C211   10   5
C473   AP51   5s on 4.30s (Bk) #C187   15   5
C474   AP52   5s on 3.60s (Bk) #C210   15   5
C475   AP55   10s on 2.15s (Bk) #C215   25   10
C476   AP52   10s on 3.60s (DB) #C210   25   10
C477   AP84   10s on 3.60s (Bk) #C215   25   10
C478   AP52   20s on 3.60s (DB) #C210   50   20
C479   AP51   100s on 3.80s (G) #C160   6.00   4.00
Nos. C470-C479 (10)   7.85   4.75

Nos. C223-C224 Surcharged with New Value, Heavy Bars and: "FRANQUEO"

1977   Lithographed   *Perf. 12*
C480   AP87   6s on 3.60s multi   30   20
C481   AP87   8s on 3.60s multi   40   25
C482   AP87   10s on 5.60s multi   75   35

Adm. Miguel Grau
AP155

1977, Dec. 15   Litho.   *Perf. 13½x13*
C483   AP155   28s multi   55   40
Navy Day. Miguel Grau (1838-1879), Peruvian naval commander.

Christmas Type of 1977
Design: 20s, Indian Nativity.

1977, Dec. 23
C484   A246   20s multi   75   30
Christmas 1977.

Andrés Bello, Flag and Map of Participants
AP156

1978, Jan. 12   Lithographed   *Perf. 13*
C485   AP156   30s multi   60   40
8th Meeting of Education Ministers honoring Andrés Bello, Lima.

Inca Type of 1978

1978   Litho.   *Perf. 13½x13*
C486   A247   24s dp rose lil   48   35
C487   A247   30s salmon   60   45
C488   A247   65s brt bl   1.30   1.00
C489   A247   95s dk bl   1.90   1.50

Antenna, ITU Emblem
AP157

1978, July 3   Litho.   *Perf. 13x13½*
C490   AP157   50s gray & multi   1.00   70
10th World Telecommunications Day.

San Martin, Flag Colors of Peru and Argentina
AP158

1978, Sept. 4   Litho.   *Perf. 13½x13*
C491   AP158   30s multi   60   45
Gen. José de San Martin (1778-1850), soldier and statesman, protector of Peru.

Stamps of 1965-67 Surcharged "Habilitado / R.D. No. 0118" and New Value in Red, Green, Violet Blue or Black

1978   Lithographed
C492   AP83   34s on 4.60s multi (R) #C208   35   25
C493   AP79   40s on 4.30s multi (G) #C196   40   30
C494   A184   70s on 2.60s brt grn (VB) #C209   70   60
C495   AP52   110s on 3.60s lil rose (Bk) #C210   1.10   1.00
C496   AP80   265s on 4.30s gray & multi (Bk) #C199   2.65   2.25
Nos. C492-C496 (5)   5.20   4.40

Stamps and Type of 1968-78 Surcharged in Violet Blue, Black or Red

1978   Lithographed
C497   AP86   25s on 4.60s brn & multi (VB) #C221   25   20
C498   A247   45s on 28s dk grn (Bk)   45   35
C499   A247   75s on 28s dk grn (R)   75   60
C500   AP86   105s on 5.60s gray & multi (R) #C222   1.10   1.00

Nos. C498-C499 not issued without surcharge.

Nos. C486, C467 Surcharged

1980, Apr. 14   Litho.   *Perf. 13½x13*
C501   A247   35s on 24s dp rose lil   35   22
C502   A243   45s on 32s rose brn & blk   45   30

No. C130 Surcharged in Black.

1981, Nov.   Engr.   *Perf. 13*
C503   AP57   30s on 2.20s multi   30   20
C504   AP57   40s on 2.20s multi   40   25

No. C130 Surcharged and Overprinted in Green:
"12 Feria / Internacional / del / Pacifico 1981"

1981, Nov. 30
C505   AP57   140s on 2.20s multi   1.40   1.00
12th Intl. Pacific Fair.

A well-informed dealer has services to offer that would be helpful toward building your collection.

Use the **Yellow Pages** to fulfill your philatelic requirements.

PERU

AIR POST SEMI-POSTAL STAMPS

Chavin Griffin
SPAP1

Designs: 1.50s+1s, Bird. 3s+2.50s, Cat. 4.30s+3s, Mythological figure (vert.). 6s+4s, Chavin god (vert.).

Perf. 12½x12, 12x12½

1963, Apr. 18 Litho. Wmk. 346
Design in Gray and Brown

CB1	SPAP1	1s + 50c sal pink	25	25
CB2	SPAP1	1.50s + 1s bl	25	25
CB3	SPAP1	3s + 2.50s lt grn	75	75
CB4	SPAP1	4.30s + 3s grn	1.00	1.00
CB5	SPAP1	6s + 4s cit	1.25	1.25
	Nos. CB1-CB5 (5)		3.50	3.50

The designs are from ceramics found by archaeological excavations of the 14th century Chavin culture. The surtax was for the excavations fund.

Henri Dunant
and Centenary
Emblem
SPAP2

Perf. 12½x12

1964, Jan. 29 Unwmkd.
Emblem in Gray & Red

CB6	SPAP2	1.30s + 70c pale rose & sl grn	25	25
CB7	SPAP2	4.30s + 1.70s lt bl & sl grn	65	65

Centenary of International Red Cross.

SPECIAL DELIVERY STAMPS.

Regular Issue of 1900 Overprinted in Black

1908 Perf. 12. Unwmkd.

E1	A25	10c gray blk	27.50	20.00

Regular Issue of 1907 Overprinted in Violet

1909

E2	A40	10c red brn & blk	37.50	22.50

Regular Issue of 1909 Handstamped in Violet

1910

E3	A49	10c dp bl	25.00	20.00

Two handstamps were used to make No. E2. Impressions from them measure 22½x6½mm. and 24x6½mm.
Counterfeits exist of Nos. E1-3.

POSTAGE DUE STAMPS.

Coat of Arms
D1

Steamship and Llama
D2   D3

D4   D5

Engraved.
With Grill.

1874–86 Perf. 12 Unwmkd.

J1	D1	1c bis ('79)	25	20
a.		Without grill ('86)	15	
J2	D2	5c vermilion	35	25
a.		Without grill ('86)	20	
J3	D3	10c orange	50	40
a.		Without grill ('86)	30	
J4	D4	20c blue	75	50
a.		Without grill ('86)	50	
J5	D5	50c brown	12.50	4.00
a.		Without grill ('86)		

A 2c green exists, but was not regularly issued.

Overprinted in
Blue or Red

1881 "PLATA" 2½mm. High.

J6	D1	1c bis (Bl)	5.00	4.00
J7	D2	5c ver (Bl)	10.00	9.00
a.		Double overprint	25.00	25.00
b.		Inverted ovpt.		
J8	D3	10c org (Bl)	10.00	9.00
a.		Inverted overprint	25.00	25.00
J9	D4	20c bl (R)	35.00	30.00
J10	D5	50c brn (Bl)	80.00	75.00

In the reprints of this overprint "PLATA" is 3 mm. high instead of 2½ mm. Besides being struck in the regular colors it was also applied to the 1, 5, 10 and 50c in red and the 20c in blue.

Overprinted
in Red

1881

J11	D1	1c bister	7.50	7.50
J12	D2	5c vermilion	10.00	9.00
J13	D3	10c orange	12.00	10.00
J14	D4	20c blue	35.00	27.50
J15	D5	50c brown	110.00	90.00

Originals of Nos. J11 to J15 are overprinted in brick-red, oily ink; reprints in thicker, bright red ink. The 5c exists with reprinted overprint in blue.

Overprinted
"Union Postal Universal Lima Plata", in Oval in first named color and Triangle in second named color.

1883

J16	D1	1c bis (Bl & Bk)	6.00	4.00
J17	D1	1c bis (Bk & Bl)	10.00	9.00
J18	D2	5c ver (Bl & Bk)	10.00	9.00
J19	D3	10c org (Bl & Bk)		7.50
J20	D4	20c bl (R & Bk)	650.00	650.00
J21	D5	50c brn (Bl & Bk)	80.00	75.00

Reprints of Nos. J16 to J21 have the oval overprint with "PLATA" 3mm. high. The 1c also exists with the oval overprint in red.

Overprinted in
Black

1884

J22	D1	1c bister	50	50
J23	D2	5c vermilion	60	60
J24	D3	10c orange	75	60
J25	D4	20c blue	1.25	75
J26	D5	50c brown	4.00	1.50
	Nos. J22-J26 (5)		7.10	3.95

The triangular overprint is found in 11 types.

Overprinted "Lima Correos" in Circle in Red and Triangle in Black.

1884

J27	D1	1c bister	17.50	15.00

Reprints of No. J27 have the overprint in bright red. At the time they were made the overprint was also printed on the 5, 10, 20 and 50c Postage Due stamps.

Postage due stamps overprinted with Sun and "CORREOS LIMA" (as shown above No. 103), alone or in combination with the "U. P. U. LIMA" oval or "LIMA CORREOS" in double-lined circle, are fancy varieties made to sell to collectors and never placed in use.

Overprinted

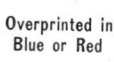 

1896-97

J28	D1	1c bister	40	35
a.		Double overprint		
J29	D2	5c vermilion	40	35
a.		Double overprint		
b.		Inverted ovpt.		
J30	D3	10c orange	50	50
a.		Inverted overprint		
J31	D4	20c blue	75	60
J32	A22	50c red ('97)	85	75
J33	A23	1s brn ('97)	1.25	1.00
a.		Double overprint		
b.		Inverted ovpt.		
	Nos. J28-J33 (6)		4.15	3.55

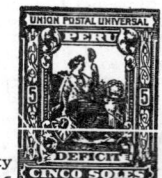

Liberty
D6

1899 Engraved

J34	D6	5s yel grn	1.50	7.50
J35	D6	10s dl vio	1,100.	1,250.

No. 159 Surcharged in Black

1902

DEFICIT
CINCO CENTAVOS

J36	A31	5c on 10s bl grn	1.50	1.25
a.		Double surcharge	17.50	17.50

No. J4 Surcharged in Black

DÉFICIT
UN CENTAVO

J37	D4	1c on 20c bl	75	60
a.		"DEFICIT" omitted	10.00	3.00
b.		"DEFICIT" double	10.00	3.00
c.		"UN CENTAVO" double	10.00	3.00
d.		"UN CENTAVO" omitted	12.50	9.00

Surcharged Vertically like No. J36.

J38	D4	5c on 20c bl	1.50	1.50

Similar Surcharge on No. J35.

J39	D6	1c on 10s dl vio	75	75

D7

1909 Engraved. Perf. 12.

J40	D7	1c red brn	50	20
J41	D7	5c red brn	50	20
J42	D7	10c red brn	60	25
J43	D7	50c red brn	90	30

1921

Size: 18¼x22mm.

J44	D7	1c vio brn	25	25
J45	D7	2c vio brn	25	25
J46	D7	5c vio brn	40	30
J47	D7	10c vio brn	60	25
J48	D7	50c vio brn	2.00	75
J49	D7	1s vio brn	9.00	3.00
J50	D7	2s vio brn	12.00	3.50
	Nos. J44-J50 (7)		24.50	8.30

Nos. J49 and J50 have the circle at the center replaced by a shield containing "S/.", in addition to the numeral.
In 1929 during a shortage of regular postage stamps, some of the Postage Due stamps of 1921 were used instead.

Type of 1909-22.
Size: 18¾x23mm.

J50A	D7	2c vio brn	60	25
J50B	D7	10c vio brn	1.00	25

Type of 1909-22 Issues.

1932 Photogravure Perf. 14½x14

J51	D7	2c vio brn	60	25
J52	D7	10c vio brn	1.00	25

Regular Stamps
of 1934-35
Overprinted in Black

"Deficit"

1935 Perf. 13.

J53	A131	2c dp cl	60	25
J54	A117	10c crimson	75	60

Type of 1909-32.
Size: 19x23mm.
Imprint: "Waterlow & Sons, Limited, Londres."

1936 Engraved. Perf. 12½.

J55	D7	2c lt brn	25	20
J56	D7	10c gray grn	60	25

PERU

OFFICIAL STAMPS.

Regular Issue
of 1886
Overprinted in Red

a

1890, Feb. 2

O2	A17	1c dl vio	2.00	2.00
a.		Double overprint	12.50	12.50
O3	A18	2c green	2.00	2.00
a.		Double overprint	12.50	12.50
b.		Inverted ovpt.	12.50	12.50
O4	A19	5c orange	2.50	2.50
a.		Inverted ovpt.	12.50	12.50
b.		Double overprint	12.50	12.50
O5	A20	10c slate	1.25	1.00
a.		Double overprint	12.50	12.50
b.		Inverted overprint	12.50	12.50
O6	A21	20c blue	4.00	3.00
a.		Double overprint	12.50	12.50
b.		Inverted overprint	12.50	12.50
O7	A22	50c red	6.00	3.00
a.		Inverted ovpt.	17.50	
b.		Double overprint		
O8	A23	1s brown	7.50	5.00
a.		Double overprint	25.00	25.00
b.		Inverted overprint	25.00	25.00

Nos. 118–124 (Bermudez Ovpt.)
Overprinted Type "a" in Red.

1894, Oct.

O9	A17	1c green	2.00	1.75
a.		"Gobierno" and head inverted	10.00	8.00
b.		Double overprint of "Gobierno"		
O10	A17	1c orange	35.00	30.00
O11	A18	2c rose	2.00	1.75
a.		Overprinted head inverted	15.00	15.00
b.		Both overprints inverted		
O12	A18	2c violet	2.00	1.75
a.		"Gobierno" double		
O13	A19	5c ultra	35.00	30.00
a.		Both overprints inverted		
O14	A19	5c blue	15.00	13.50
O15	A20	10c green	5.00	4.00
O16	A22	50c red	7.50	7.00

Nos. 125–126 ("Horseshoe" Ovpt.)
Overprinted Type "a" in Red.

O17	A18	2c vermilion	2.50	2.25
O18	A19	5c blue	2.50	2.25

Nos. 105, 107, 109, 113 Overprinted
Type "a" in Red.

1895, May

O19	A17	1c vermilion	12.50	12.50
O20	A18	2c dp ultra	12.50	12.50
O21	A12	5c claret	10.00	9.00
O22	A14	20c dp ultra	10.00	9.00

Nos. O2–O22 have been extensively counterfeited.

Nos. 141, 148, 149,
151 Overprinted in
Black

1896-1901

O23	A24	1c ultra	20	15
O24	A25	10c yellow	1.50	75
a.		Double overprint		
O25	A25	10c gray blk ('01)	20	15
O26	A26	50c brt rose	60	40

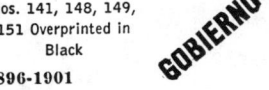

1909–14 Engraved *Perf. 12*
Size: 18½ x 22mm.

O27	O1	1c red	15	10
O28	O1	1c brn red	15	10
a.		1c org ('14)	35	25
O29	O1	10c bis brn ('14)	20	10
a.		10c vio brn		
O30	O1	50c ol grn ('14)	1.00	50
a.		50c bl grn	1.50	50

Size: 18¾ x 23½mm.

O30B	O1	10c vio brn	50	25
		Nos. O27–O30B (5)	2.20	1.20

1933 Photogravure. *Perf. 15x14*

O31	O1	10c vio brn	50	20

No. 319
Overprinted
in Black

"Servicio
Oficial"

1935 *Perf. 13.* Unwmkd.

O32	A117	10c crimson	15	10

Type of 1909-33.
Imprint: "Waterlow & Sons,
Limited, Londres."

1936 Engraved *Perf. 12½*
Size: 19x23 mm.

O33	O1	10c lt brn	15	10
O34	O1	50c gray grn	50	30

PARCEL POST STAMPS.

PP1

PP2

PP3

Typeset.

1897 *Perf. 12* Unwmkd.

Q1	PP1	1c dl lil	3.50	2.75
Q2	PP2	2c bister	4.00	3.50
a.		2c ol	4.00	3.50
b.		2c yel	4.00	3.50
c.		Laid paper	100.00	100.00
Q3	PP2	5c dk bl	15.00	10.00
		Tête bêche pair	500.00	
Q4	PP3	10c vio brn	20.00	15.00
Q5	PP3	20c rose red	25.00	20.00
Q6	PP3	50c bl grn	65.00	50.00
		Nos. Q1-Q6 (6)	132.50	101.25

Surcharged
in Black

UN
CENTAVO

1903–04

Q7	PP3	1c on 20c rose red	17.00	15.00
Q8	PP3	1c on 50c bl grn	17.00	15.00
Q9	PP3	5c on 10c vio brn	110.00	90.00
a.		Inverted surch.	165.00	150.00
b.		Double surch.		

POSTAL TAX STAMPS.
Plebiscite Issues.

These stamps were not used in Tacna and Arica (which were under Chilean occupation) but were used in Peru to pay a supplementary tax on letters, etc.
It was intended that the money derived from the sale of these stamps should be used to help defray the expenses of the plebiscite.

Morro
Arica
PT1

Adm. Grau and Col. Bolognesi
Reviewing Troops—PT2

Bolognesi
Monument
PT3

Lithographed

1925-26 *Perf. 12* Unwmkd.

RA1	PT1	5c dp bl	1.75	50
RA2	PT1	5c rose red	1.25	35
RA3	PT1	5c yel grn	1.00	35
RA4	PT2	10c brown	3.50	1.25
RA5	PT3	50c bl grn	25.00	12.50
		Nos. RA1-RA5 (5)	32.50	14.95

PT4

1926

RA6	PT4	2c orange	35	20

PT5

1927–28

RA7	PT5	2c dp org	75	15
RA8	PT5	2c red brn	75	20
RA9	PT5	2c dk bl	75	20
RA10	PT5	2c gray vio	50	15
RA11	PT5	2c bl grn ('28)	50	15
RA12	PT5	20c red	3.00	1.25
		Nos. RA7-RA12 (6)	6.25	2.10

PT6

1928 Engraved

RA13	PT6	2c dk vio	30	15

The use of the Plebiscite stamps was discontinued July 26, 1929, after the settlement of the Tacna-Arica controversy with Chile.

Unemployment Fund Issues.

These stamps were required in addition to the ordinary postage, on every letter or piece of postal matter. The money obtained by their sale was to assist the unemployed.

Habilitada
Pro
Desocupados
2 Cts.

Nos. 273–275
Surcharged

1931

RA14	A95	2c on 4c red	1.00	50
a.		Invtd. surch.	5.00	5.00
RA15	A95	2c on 10c bl grn	75	50
a.		Invtd. surch.	5.00	5.00
RA16	A95	2c on 15c sl gray	75	50
a.		Invtd. surch.	5.00	5.00

"Labor"
PT7

Blacksmith
PT8

Two types of Nos. RA17–RA18:
I. Imprint 15mm.
II. Imprint 13¾mm.
Perf. 12 x 11½, 11½ x 12.

1931-32 Lithographed.

RA17	PT7	2c emer (I)	10	10
a.		Type II	10	
RA18	PT7	2c rose car (I) ('32)	10	10
a.		Type II	10	

1932-34

RA19	PT8	2c dp gray	10	10
RA20	PT8	2c pur ('34)	10	10

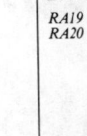

Monument of
2nd of May
PT9

Perf. 13, 13½, 13x13½

1933-35 Photogravure

RA21	PT9	1c bl vio	20	10
RA22	PT9	1c org ('34)	20	10
RA23	PT9	1c brn vio ('35)	20	8

No. 307
Overprinted in Black

Pro-Desocupados
a
Perf. 13½.

1934

RA24	A111	2c green	15	8
a.		Inverted ovpt.	2.00	1.75

No. 339
Overprinted in Black

Pro
Desocupados

1935

RA25	A131	2c dp cl	10	8

No. 339 Overprinted Type "a" in Black.

1936 *Perf. 13½.* Unwmkd.

RA26	A131	2c dp cl	10	8

PERU

**No. RA23
Overprinted in Black** *"Ley 8310"*

1936 *Perf. 13x13½*
RA27	PT9	2c brn vio	15	10
a.		Double ovpt.	2.00	
b.		Overprint reading down	2.00	
c.		Overprint double, reading down	2.00	

St. Rosa of Lima — PT10
"Protection" by John Q. A. Ward — PT11

1937 Engraved. *Perf. 12.*
RA28	PT10	2c car rose	20	5

Nos. RA27 and RA28 represented a tax to help erect a church.

Imprint: "American Bank Note Company"
1938 Lithographed
RA29	PT11	2c brown	20	8

The tax was to help the unemployed.

**Type of 1938 Redrawn.
Imprint: "Columbian Bank Note Company."**
1943 *Perf. 12½*
RA30	PT11	2c dl cl brn	15	8

See note above No. RA14. See also Nos. RA34, RA40.

PT12 — PT13

1949 *Perf. 12½, 12*
Black Surcharge.
RA31	PT12	3c on 4c vio bl	75	8
RA32	PT13	3c on 10c bl	75	8

The tax was for an education fund.

Symbolical of Education — PT14
Emblem of Congress — PT15

1950 Typographed *Perf. 14*
Size: 16½x21mm.
RA33	PT14	3c dp car	20	8

See also Nos. RA35, RA39, RA43.

**Type of 1938.
Imprint:
"Thomas De La Rue & Co. Ltd."**
1951 Lithographed
RA34	PT11	2c lt redsh brn	20	8

**Type of 1950.
Imprint: "Thomas De La Rue & Company, Limited."**
1952 *Perf. 14, 13* Unwmkd.
Size: 16½x21½mm.
RA35	PT14	3c brn car	20	8

1954 Rouletted 13.
RA36	PT15	5c bl & red	30	8

The tax was to help finance the National Marian Eucharistic Congress.

Piura Arms and Congress Emblem
PT16

1960 Lithographed. *Perf. 10½*
RA37	PT16	10c ultra, red, grn & yel	25	8
a.		Green ribbon inverted		
RA38	PT16	10c ultra & red	25	12

Nos. RA37-RA38 were used to help finance the 6th National Eucharistic Congress, Piura, Aug. 25-28. Obligatory on all domestic mail until Dec. 31, 1960. Both stamps exist imperf.

**Type of 1950.
Imprint: "Bundesdruckerei Berlin"**
1961 *Perf. 14*
Size: 17½x22½mm.
RA39	PT14	3c dp car	12	10

**Type of 1938
Imprint:
"Harrison and Sons Ltd"**
1962, Apr. Litho. *Perf. 14x14½*
RA40	PT11	2c lt brn	15	8

Symbol of Eucharist
PT17

1962, May 8 Rouletted 11
RA41	PT17	10c bl & org	12	10

Issued to raise funds for the Seventh National Eucharistic Congress, Huancayo, 1964. Obligatory on all domestic mail.

1962 Imprint: "Iberia"
RA42	PT17	10c bl & org	12	10

Type of 1950
1965, Apr. Litho. *Perf. 12½x12*
Imprint: "Thomas De La Rue"
Size: 18x22mm.
RA43	PT14	3c lt car	25	15

Type of 1962 Overprinted in Red with three "X," Bars and:
"Periodista / Peruano / LEY / 16078"
1966, July 2 Litho. Pin Perf.
Imprint "Iberia"
RA44	PT17	10c vio & org	12	10

Certain countries cancel stamps in full sheets and sell them (usually with gum) for less than face value. Dealers generally sell "CTO" (canceled to order) stamps for much less than postally used copies.

**No. RA43
Surcharged
in Green
or Black**

HABILITADO
"Fondo del
Periodista
Peruano"
Ley 16078
S/o. 0.10
b

HABILITADO

Habilitado
«Fondo del
Periodista
Peruano»
Ley 16078
S/. 0.10
c

"Fondo del
Periodista
Peruano"
Ley 16078
S/o. 0.10
d

1966-67 *Perf. 12x12½*
RA45	PT14 (b)	10c on 3c lt car (G)	1.25	15
RA46	PT14 (c)	10c on 3c lt car (Bk)	1.00	10
RA47	PT14 (c)	10c on 3c lt car (G)	20	12
RA48	PT14 (d)	10c on 3c lt car (G)	35	15

The surtax of Nos. RA44-RA48 was for the Peruvian Journalists' Fund.

Pen Made of Newspaper — PT18
Temple at Chan-Chan — PT19

1967, Dec. Litho. *Perf. 11*
RA49	PT18	10c dk red & blk	10	10

The surtax was for the Peruvian Journalists' fund.

1967, Dec. 27
Designs: No. RA51, Side view of temple. Nos. RA52-RA55, Various stone bas-reliefs from Chan-Chan.
RA50	PT19	20c bl & grn	10	5
RA51	PT19	20c multi	10	5
RA52	PT19	20c brt bl & blk	10	5
RA53	PT19	20c emer & blk	10	5
RA54	PT19	20c sep & blk	10	5
RA55	PT19	20c lil rose & blk	10	5
		Nos. RA50-RA55 (6)	60	30

The surtax was for the excavations at Chan-Chan, northern coast of Peru. (Mochica-Chimu pre-Inca period).

Type of 1967 Surcharged in Red:
"VEINTE / CENTAVOS / R.S. 16-8-68"

Designs: No. RA56, Handshake. No. RA57, Globe and pen.

1968, Oct. Litho. *Perf. 11*
RA56	PT18	20c on 50c multi	15	15
RA57	PT18	20c on 1s multi	10	10

Nos. RA56-RA57 without surcharge were not obligatory tax stamps.
No. C199 surcharged "PRO NAVIDAD/ Veinte Centavos/R.S. 5-11-68" was not a compulsory postal tax stamp.

No. RA43 Surcharged Similar to Type "c."
1968, Oct. *Perf. 12½x12*
RA58	PT14	20c on 3c lt car	10	10

Surcharge lacks quotation marks and 4th line reads: Ley 17050.

PERU—Ancachs to Chiclayo

OCCUPATION STAMPS.
Issued under Chilean Occupation.
Stamps formerly listed as Nos. N1–N10 are regular issues of Chile canceled in Peru.

Stamps of Peru, 1874-80,
Overprinted in Red,
Blue or Black

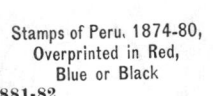

1881-82			Perf. 12.	
N11	A17	1c org (Bl)	75	1.50
a.	Inverted overprint			
N12	A18	2c dk vio (Bk)	75	6.00
a.	Inverted overprint		25.00	
b.	Double overprint		35.00	
N13		2c rose (Bk)	2.50	35.00
a.	Inverted overprint			
N14	A19	5c bl (R)	85.00	125.00
a.	Inverted overprint			
N15	A19	5c ultra (R)	135.00	150.00
N16	A20	10c grn (R)	75	2.50
a.	Inverted overprint		10.00	10.00
b.	Double overprint		17.50	17.50
N17	A21	20c brn red (Bl)	150.00	175.00

Reprints of No. N17 have the overprint in bright blue; on the originals it is in dull ultramarine. Nos. N11 and N12 exist with reprinted overprint in red or yellow. There are numerous counterfeits with the overprint in both correct and fancy colors.

Same, with Additional
Overprint in Black

1882				
N19	A17	1c grn (R)	1.00	1.50
a.	Arms inverted		12.50	15.00
b.	Arms double		8.00	10.00
c.	Horseshoe inverted		17.50	20.00
N20	A19	5c bl (R)	1.50	1.50
a.	Arms inverted		20.00	22.50
b.	Arms double		20.00	22.50
N21	A22	50c rose (Bk)	3.00	4.00
a.	Arms inverted		15.00	
N22	A22	50c rose (Bl)	3.00	5.00
N23	A23	1s ultra (R)	6.00	8.00
a.	Arms inverted		20.00	
b.	Horseshoe inverted		25.00	
c.	Arms and horseshoe inverted		30.00	
d.	Arms double		20.00	
	Nos. N19-N23 (5)		14.50	20.00

PROVISIONAL ISSUES.
Stamps Issued in Various Cities of Peru during the Chilean Occupation of Lima and Callao.
During the Chilean-Peruvian War which took place in 1879 to 1882, the Chilean forces occupied Lima and Callao, the two largest cities in Peru. As these cities were the source of supply of postage stamps, Peruvians in other sections of the country were left without stamps and were forced to the expedient of making provisional issues from whatever material was at hand. Many of these were former cancelling devices made over for this purpose.
Counterfeits exist of many of the overprinted stamps.

ANCACHS
(än'kächs')
(See Note under "Provisional Issues")

Regular Issue of Peru,
Overprinted in Manuscript in Black

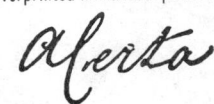

1884		Perf. 12	Unwmkd.	
1N1	A19	5c blue	80.00	75.00

Regular Issues of Peru,
Overprinted in Black

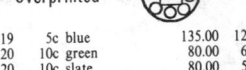

| 1N2 | A19 | 5c blue | 27.50 | 25.00 |

Overprinted

1N3	A19	5c blue	135.00	125.00
1N4	A20	10c green	80.00	60.00
1N5	A20	10c slate	80.00	50.00

Same, with Additional Overprint "FRANCA"

| 1N6 | A20 | 10c green | 120.00 | 60.00 |

Overprinted

| 1N7 | A19 | 5c blue | 45.00 | 40.00 |
| 1N8 | A20 | 10c green | 45.00 | 40.00 |

Same, with Additional Overprint "FRANCA"

| 1N9 | A20 | 10c green | | |

A1
Revenue Stamp of Peru, 1878-79,
Overprinted in Black
"CORREO Y FISCAL" and "FRANCA".

| 1N10 | A1 | 10c yellow | 55.00 | 50.00 |

APURIMAC
(ä'pōō·rē'mäk)
(See Note under "Provisional Issues").

Provisional Issue of Arequipa
Overprinted in Black

ADMON. PRAL. DE
CORREOS DEL DEPto DE
APURIMAC
ABANCAY

Overprint Covers Two Stamps.

1885		Imperf.	Unwmkd.	
2N1	A6	10c gray	135.00	125.00

Some experts question the status of No. 2N1.

AREQUIPA
(ä'rȧ·kē'pȧ)
(See Note under "Provisional Issues")

A1   A2
Coat of Arms
Overprint ("PROVISIONAL 1881–1882") in Black

1881, Jan.		Imperf.	Unwmkd.	
3N1	A1	10c blue	4.00	5.00
a.	10c ultra		4.00	4.00
b.	Double overprint		17.50	20.00
c.	Overprinted on back of stamp		12.50	15.00
3N2	A2	25c rose	4.00	9.00
a.	"2" in upper left corner inverted		12.50	
b.	"Cevtavos"		12.50	15.00
c.	Double overprint		17.50	20.00

The overprint also exists on 5s yellow. The overprints "1883" in large figures or "Habilitado 1883" are fraudulent.

With Additional
Overprint
Handstamped
in Red

1881, Feb.

| 3N3 | A1 | 10c blue | 5.00 | 5.00 |
| a. | 10c ultra | | 20.00 | 12.50 |

A4
1883   Lithographed.

| 3N7 | A4 | 10c dl rose | 5.00 | 7.50 |
| a. | 10c ver | | 5.00 | 7.50 |

Overprinted in Blue like No. 3N3.

| 3N9 | A4 | 10c vermilion | 7.50 | 7.50 |
| a. | 10c dl rose | | 7.50 | 6.00 |

Reprints of No. 3N9 are in different colors from the originals, orange, bright red, etc. They are printed in sheets of 20 instead of 25.

Redrawn.

| 3N10 | A4 | 10c brick red (Bl) | | 250.00 |

The redrawn stamp has small triangles without arabesques in the lower spandrels. The palm branch at left of the shield and other parts of the design have been redrawn.

Same Overprint in Black, Violet or Magenta
On Regular Issues of Peru.

Embossed with Grill.

1884		Perf. 12.		
3N11	A17	1c org (Bk, V or M)	10.00	10.00
3N12	A18	2c dk vio (Bk)	10.00	10.00
3N13	A19	5c bl (Bk, V or M)	3.00	2.00
a.	5c ultra (Bk or M)		12.50	12.00
3N15	A20	10c sl (Bk)	5.00	4.00
3N16	A21	20c brn red (Bk or M)	40.00	40.00
3N18	A22	50c grn (Bk or V)	40.00	40.00
3N20	A23	1s rose (Bk or V)	50.00	50.00

A5   A6

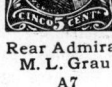

Rear Admiral   Col. Francisco
M. L. Grau   Bolognesi
A7   A8

Same Overprint as on Previous Issues.

1885		Imperf.		
3N22	A5	5c ol (Bk)	10.00	10.00
a.	Without overprint		10.00	10.00
3N23	A6	10c gray (Bk)	10.00	9.00
a.	Without overprint		8.00	6.00
3N25	A7	5c bl (Bk)	10.00	9.00
a.	Without overprint		8.00	6.00
3N26	A8	10c ol (Bk)	10.00	6.00
a.	Without overprint		8.00	6.00

These stamps have been reprinted without overprint; they exist however with forged overprint. Originals are on thicker paper with distinct mesh, reprints on paper without mesh.

AYACUCHO
(ī'yä·kōō'chō)
(See Note under "Provisional Issues")

Provisional Issue
of Arequipa
Overprinted
in Black

1881		Imperf.	Unwmkd.	
4N1	A1	10c blue	110.00	100.00
a.	10c ultra		110.00	100.00

CHACHAPOYAS
(chä·chä·pō'yäs)
(See Note under "Provisional Issues")

Regular Issue of Peru
Overprinted
in Black

1884		Perf. 12.	Unwmkd.	
5N1	A19	5c ultra	135.00	125.00

CHALA
(chä'lä)
(See Note under "Provisional Issues")

Regular Issues
of Peru
Overprinted
in Black

1884		Perf. 12	Unwmkd.	
6N1	A19	5c blue	12.50	10.00
6N2	A20	10c slate	15.00	12.50

CHICLAYO
(chĕ·klä'yō)
(See Note under "Provisional Issues")

Regular Issue
of Peru
Overprinted
in Black

FRANCA

1884		Perf. 12	Unwmkd.	
7N1	A19	5c blue	25.00	15.00

Same, Overprinted FRANCA

| 7N2 | A19 | 5c blue | 50.00 | 35.00 |

CUZCO
(kōōs'kō)
(See Note under "Provisional Issues")

Provisional Issues of Arequipa Overprinted in Black

		1881-85	Imperf.	Unwmkd.
8N1	A1	10c blue	70.00	60.00
8N2	A4	10c red	70.00	60.00

Overprinted "CUZCO" in an oval of dots.

| 8N5 | A5 | 5c olive | 110.00 | 100.00 |
| 8N6 | A6 | 10c gray | 80.00 | 75.00 |

Regular Issue of Peru Overprinted in Black "CUZCO" in a Circle.
Perf. 12.

| 8N7 | A19 | 5c blue | 25.00 | 25.00 |

Provisional Issues of Arequipa Overprinted in Black

		1883		Imperf.
8N9	A4	10c red	15.00	15.00

Same Overprint in Black on Regular Issues of Peru.
1884   *Perf. 12.*

| 8N10 | A19 | 5c blue | 25.00 | 25.00 |
| 8N11 | A20 | 10c slate | 25.00 | 15.00 |

Same Overprint in Black on Provisional Issues of Arequipa.
Imperf.

| 8N12 | A5 | 5c olive | 50.00 | 50.00 |
| 8N13 | A6 | 10c gray | 15.00 | 15.00 |

Postage Due Stamps of Peru Surcharged in Black

Perf. 12.

| 8N14 | D1 | 10c on 1c bis | 165.00 | 150.00 |
| 8N15 | D3 | 10c on 10c org | 165.00 | 150.00 |

HUACHO
(wä'chō)
(See Note under "Provisional Issues")

Regular Issues of Peru Overprinted in Black

1884   *Perf. 12.*   Unwmkd.

9N1	A19	5c blue	15.00	15.00
9N2	A20	10c green	9.00	9.00
9N3	A20	10c slate	25.00	25.00

MOQUEGUA
(mō·kā'gwä)
(See Note under "Provisional Issues")

Provisional Issues of Arequipa Overprinted in Violet

Overprint 27mm. wide (illustration reduced).

		1881-83	Imperf.	Unwmkd.
10N1	A1	10c blue	65.00	60.00
10N2	A4	10c red ('83)	65.00	60.00

Same Overprint on Regular Issues of Peru in Violet.

		1884	Perf. 12.	
10N3	A17	1c orange	65.00	60.00
10N4	A19	5c blue	55.00	45.00

Red Overprint.

| 10N5 | A19 | 5c blue | 45.00 | 40.00 |

Same Overprint in Violet on Provisional Issues of Peru of 1880.
Perf. 12.

10N6	A17	1c grn (R)	12.50	10.00
10N7	A18	2c rose (Bl)	15.00	15.00
10N8	A19	5c bl (R)	30.00	30.00

Same Overprint in Violet on Provisional Issue of Arequipa.
1885   *Imperf.*

| 10N9 | A6 | 10c gray | 85.00 | 75.00 |

Regular Issues of Peru Overprinted in Violet

Perf. 12.

| 10N10 | A19 | 5c blue | 165.00 | 100.00 |
| 10N11 | A20 | 10c slate | 70.00 | 40.00 |

Same Overprint in Violet on Provisional Issue of Arequipa.
Imperf.

| 10N12 | A6 | 10c gray | 110.00 | 100.00 |

PAITA
(pī'tä)
(See Note under "Provisional Issues")

Regular Issues of Peru Overprinted

Black Overprint.

		1884	Perf. 12	Unwmkd.
11N1	A19	5c blue	35.00	35.00
11N2	A20	10c green	22.50	22.50
11N3	A20	10c slate	35.00	35.00

Red Overprint.

| 11N4 | A19 | 5c blue | 35.00 | 35.00 |

Overprint lacks ornaments on Nos. 11N4-11N5.

Violet Overprint.
Letters 5½ mm. High.

| 11N5 | A19 | 5c ultra | 35.00 | 35.00 |
| a. | | 5c bl | | |

PASCO
(päs'kō)
(See Note under "Provisional Issues")

Regular Issues of Peru Overprinted in Magenta or Black

		1884	Perf. 12	Unwmkd.
12N1	A19	5c bl (M)	25.00	20.00
a.		5c ultra (M)	35.00	35.00
12N2	A20	10c grn (Bk)	50.00	45.00
12N3	A20	10c sl (Bk)	100.00	85.00

PISCO
(pēs'kō)
(See Note under "Provisional Issues")

Regular Issue of Peru Overprinted in Black

		1884	Perf. 12.	Unwmkd.
13N1	A19	5c blue	275.00	250.00

PIURA
(pyōō'rä)
(See Note under "Provisional Issues")

Regular Issues of Peru Overprinted in Black

		1884	Perf. 12.	Unwmkd.
14N1	A19	5c blue	30.00	15.00
a.		5c ultra	40.00	40.00
14N2	A21	20c brn red	125.00	125.00
14N3	A22	50c green	300.00	300.00

Same Overprint in Black on Provisional Issues of Peru of 1881.

14N4	A17	1c grn (R)	35.00	35.00
14N5	A18	2c rose (Bl)	60.00	60.00
14N6	A19	5c ultra (R)	75.00	75.00

Regular Issues of Peru Overprinted in Violet, Black or Blue

14N7	A19	5c bl (V)	25.00	15.00
a.		5c ultra (V)	25.00	15.00
b.		5c ultra (Bk)	25.00	15.00
14N8	A21	20c brn red (Bk)	125.00	125.00
14N9	A21	20c brn red (Bl)	125.00	125.00

Same Overprint in Black on Provisional Issues of Peru of 1881.

14N10	A17	1c grn (R)	30.00	30.00
14N11	A19	5c bl (R)	35.00	35.00
a.		5c ultra (R)	60.00	60.00

Regular Issues of Peru Overprinted in Black

| 14N13 | A19 | 5c blue | 6.00 | 5.00 |
| 14N14 | A21 | 20c brn red | 125.00 | 125.00 |

Regular Issues of Peru Overprinted in Black

| 14N15 | A19 | 5c ultra | 110.00 | 100.00 |
| 14N16 | A21 | 20c brn red | 200.00 | 175.00 |

Same Overprint on Postage Due Stamp of Peru.

| 14N18 | D3 | 10c orange | 150.00 | 125.00 |

PUNO
(pōō'nō)
(See Note under "Provisional Issues")

Provisional Issue of Arequipa Overprinted in Violet or Blue

Diameter of outer circle 20½mm., PUNO 11½mm. wide, M 3½mm. wide. Other types of this overprint are fraudulent.

		1882-83	Imperf.	Unwmkd.
15N1	A1	10c bl (V)	25.00	25.00
a.		10c ultra (V)	30.00	30.00
15N3	A2	25c red (V)	40.00	30.00
15N4	A4	10c dl rose (Bl)	40.00	40.00
		10c ver (Bl)	40.00	40.00

The overprint also exists on 5s yellow of Arequipa.

Same Overprint in Magenta on Regular Issues of Peru.

		1884	Perf. 12.	
15N5	A17	1c orange	17.50	17.50
15N6	A18	2c violet	65.00	65.00
15N7	A19	5c blue	12.50	12.50

Violet Overprint.

| 15N8 | A19 | 5c blue | 12.50 | 12.50 |
| a. | | 5c ultra | 17.50 | 17.50 |

Same Overprint in Black on Provisional Issues of Arequipa.
1885   *Imperf.*

15N10	A5	5c olive	25.00	20.00
15N11	A6	10c gray	8.00	8.00
15N12	A8	10c olive	15.00	15.00

Regular Issues of Peru Overprinted in Magenta

		1884	Perf. 12.	
15N13	A17	1c orange	15.00	12.50
15N14	A18	2c violet	20.00	17.50
15N15	A19	5c blue	8.00	8.00
a.		5c ultra	16.00	16.00
15N16	A20	10c green		
15N17	A21	20c brn red	125.00	125.00
15N18	A22	50c green		

YCA
(ē'kä)
(See Note under "Provisional Issues")

Regular Issues of Peru Overprinted in Violet

		1884	Perf. 12	Unwmkd.
16N1	A17	1c orange	60.00	60.00
16N3	A19	5c blue	17.50	12.50

Black Overprint.

| 16N5 | A19 | 5c blue | 15.00 | 10.00 |

Magenta Overprint.

| 16N6 | A19 | 5c blue | 15.00 | 10.00 |
| 16N7 | A20 | 10c slate | 45.00 | 45.00 |

Regular Issues of Peru Overprinted in Black

| 16N12 | A19 | 5c blue | 225.00 | 200.00 |
| 16N13 | A21 | 20c brown | 275.00 | 250.00 |

PERU—Yca—PHILIPPINES 69

Regular Issues of Peru Overprinted in Carmine

16N14	A19	5c blue	200.00	175.00
16N15	A20	10c slate	250.00	225.00

Same, with Additional Overprint

16N21	A19	5c blue	225.00	200.00
16N22	A21	20c brn red	350.00	300.00

Various other stamps exist with the overprints "YCA" and "YCA VAPOR" but they are not known to have been issued. Some of them were made to fill a dealer's order and others are reprints or merely cancellations.

PHILIPPINES
(fĭl'ĭ-pēnz; -pĭnz)

LOCATION—A group of 7,100 islands and islets in the Malay Archipelago, north of Borneo, in the North Pacific Ocean.
GOVT.—Republic.
AREA—115,748 sq. mi.
POP.—45,030,000 (1977).
CAPITAL—Quezon City.

The islands were ceded to the United States by Spain in 1898. On November 15, 1935, they were given their independence, subject to a transition period which ended July 4, 1946. On that date the Commonwealth became the "Republic of the Philippines."

8 Cuartos = 1 Real
100 Centavos de Peso = 1 Peso (1864)
100 Centimos de Escudo = 1 Escudo (1871)
100 Centimos de Peseta = 1 Peseta (1872)
1000 Milesimas de Peso = 100 Centimos or Centavos = 1 Peso (1878)
100 Cents = 1 Dollar (1899)
100 Centavos = 1 Peso (1906)
100 Centavos (Sentimos) = 1 Peso (Piso) (1946)

Prices of early Philippine stamps vary according to condition. Quotations for Nos. 1–32 are for fine copies. Very fine to superb specimens sell at much higher prices, and inferior or poor copies sell at reduced prices, depending on the condition of the individual specimen.

Issued under Spanish Dominion.

The stamps of Philippine Islands punched with a round hole had been withdrawn from use and punched to indicate that they were no longer available for postage. In this condition they sell for only a trifle, as compared to postally used copies.

Queen Isabella II
A1   A2

Engraved.
1854   *Imperf.*   *Unwmkd.*
1	A1	5c orange	1,850.	375.00
a.		5c brn org	2,100.	450.00
2	A1	10c carmine	575.00	225.00
a.		10c pale rose	900.00	350.00

4	A2	1r sl bl	600.00	225.00
a.		1r bl	800.00	350.00
b.		1r ultra	800.00	350.00
c.		"CORROS"	4,000.	1,500.
5	A2	2r green	900.00	210.00
a.		2r yel grn	900.00	275.00

Forty varieties of each value.

A3

1855   **Lithographed**
| 6 | A3 | 5c pale ver | 1,850. | 575.00 |

Four varieties.

Redrawn
| 7 | A3 | 5c vermilion | 9,000. | 1,200. |

In the redrawn stamp the inner circle is smaller and is not broken by the labels at top and bottom. Only one variety.

Queen Isabella II
A4   A5

Wmk. 104
Typographed
Wmkd. Loops. (104)
1856
| 8 | A4 | 1r grn, bl | | 120.00 |
| 9 | A4 | 2r car, bl | | 165.00 |

Nos. 8 and 9 can be distinguished from the Cuban stamps of 1855 only by the cancellations.

1859, Jan. 1   Litho.   Unwmkd.
10	A5	5c vermilion	18.00	8.00
a.		5c scar	22.50	12.50
b.		5c org	37.50	18.00
11	A5	10c rose	18.00	11.50

Four varieties of each value.

Dot after CORREOS
A6   A7

1861–62
| 12 | A6 | 5c vermilion | 26.50 | 12.50 |
| 13 | A7 | 5c dl red ('62) | 32.50 | 14.00 |

Colon after CORREOS
A8   A8a

A9   A10

1863
14	A8	5c vermilion	18.00	9.00
15	A8	10c carmine	42.50	22.50
16	A8	1r violet	675.00	300.00
17	A8	2r blue	600.00	275.00
18	A8	1r gray grn	250.00	100.00
19	A8a	1r green	120.00	52.50
20	A9	1r emer		45.00

No. 18 has "CORREOS" 10½mm. long, the point of the bust is rounded and is about 1mm. from the circle which contains 94 pearls.
No. 20 has "CORREOS" 11mm. long, and the bust ends in a sharp point which nearly touches the circle of 76 pearls.

1864   Typographed.
21	A10	3⅛c buff	3.75	1.85
22	A10	6²⁄₈c grn, rose	3.75	1.10
23	A10	12½c bl, sal	6.75	1.10
24	A10	25c red, buff	9.00	3.75

Preceding Issues Handstamped **HABILITADO POR LA NACION**

1868–74
25	A2	1r sl bl ('74)	2,650.	1,200.
25A	A2	2r grn ('74)	5,250.	1,150.
26	A4	1r grn, bl ('73)	180.00	90.00
27	A4	2r car, bl ('73)	225.00	90.00
28	A5	10c rose ('74)	90.00	52.50
29	A7	5c red ('73)	90.00	45.00
30	A8	5c ver ('72)	67.50	37.50
31	A8	1r vio ('72)	675.00	450.00
32	A8	2r bl ('72)	600.00	375.00
33	A8a	1r gray grn ('71)	240.00	60.00
34	A9	1r emer ('71)	62.50	27.50
35	A10	3⅛c buff	13.50	6.00
36	A10	6²⁄₈c grn, rose	13.50	6.00
37	A10	12½c bl, sal	45.00	22.50
38	A10	25c ver, buff	20.00	13.00

"Spain"   King Amadeo
A11   A12

1870   Typographed   Perf. 14
39	A11	5c blue	38.50	3.75
40	A11	10c dp grn	8.25	3.25
41	A11	20c brown	45.00	18.50
42	A11	40c rose	60.00	11.50

1872
43	A12	12c rose	10.00	3.50
a.		Imperf.	60.00	
44	A12	16c blue	85.00	18.50
a.		16c ultra	120.00	60.00
45	A12	25c gray lil	10.00	3.50
		25c lil	16.50	11.00
46	A12	62c violet	22.50	5.25
47	A12	1p25c yel brn	47.50	15.00

 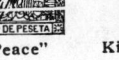

"Peace"   King Alfonso XII
A13   A14

1874
48	A13	12c gray lil	11.50	3.00
49	A13	25c ultra	3.75	1.50
50	A13	62c rose	30.00	3.00
51	A13	1p25c brown	150.00	30.00
a.		Imperf.	300.00	

1875–77
52	A14	2c rose	2.25	60
53	A14	2c dk bl ('77)	140.00	60.00
54	A14	6c org ('77)	9.00	2.25
55	A14	10c bl ('77)	3.50	75
56	A14	12c lilac	3.75	75
57	A14	20c vio brn	12.00	3.00
58	A14	25c dp grn	9.00	75

Imperforates of type A14 probably are from proof or trial sheets.

Nos. 52, 63 Handstamp Surcharged in Black or Blue

HABILITADO 12 CS P.TA

1877–79
59	A14	12c on 2c rose (Bk)	45.00	13.50
60	A16	12c on 25m blk (Bk) ('79)	45.00	13.50
61	A16	12c on 25m blk (Bl) ('79)	150.00	110.00

Surcharge exists inverted on Nos. 59–60, double on No. 59.

A16

1878–79   Typographed
62	A16	0.0625 (62½m) gray	37.50	10.00
62A	A16	0.0625 (62½m) lil	37.50	10.00
63	A16	25m black	2.65	40
64	A16	25m brn ('79)	45.00	18.00
65	A16	50m dl lil	22.50	7.50
66	A16	100m carmine	67.50	22.50
67	A16	100m yel grn ('79)	7.00	1.85
68	A16	125m blue	3.75	50
69	A16	200m rose ('79)	22.50	4.50
70	A16	200m vio rose ('79)	165.00	90.00
71	A16	250m bis ('79)	7.50	1.85

Imperforates of type A16 probably are from proof or trial sheets.

Stamps of 1878-79 Surcharged:

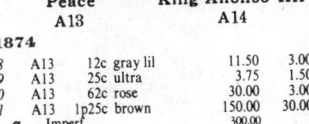

1879
72	A16(a)	2c on 25c grn	40.00	9.00
a.		Double surcharge		
73	A16(a)	8c on 100m car	32.50	9.00
a.		"COREROS"	90.00	45.00
74	A16(b)	2c on 25m grn	62.50	22.50
75	A16(b)	8c on 100m car	57.50	27.50

Canceled-to-order stamps are often from remainders. Most collectors of canceled stamps prefer postally used specimens.

A well informed dealer can help the collector build his collection. He is the one to turn to when philatelic property must be sold.

PHILIPPINES

A19

Original state: The medallion is surrounded by a heavy line of color of nearly even thickness, touching the line below "Filipinas"; the opening in the hair above the temple is narrow and pointed.

1st retouch: The line around the medallion is thin, except at the upper right, and does not touch the horizontal line above it; the opening in the hair is slightly wider and rounded; the lock of hair above the forehead is shaped like a broad "V" and ends in a point; there is a faint white line below it, which is not found on the original. The shape of the hair and the width of the white line vary.

2nd retouch: The lock of hair is less pointed; the white line is much broader.

1880-86 Typographed

76	A19	2c rose	45	30
77	A19	2½c brown	3.00	30
78	A19	2⁴⁄₈c ultra ('82)	65	30
79	A19	2⁴⁄₈c ultra, 1st retouch ('83)	45	30
80	A19	2⁴⁄₈c ultra, 2nd retouch ('86)	7.50	75
81	A19	5c gray ('82)	45	30
a.		5c gray bl	75	40
82	A19	6²⁄₈c dp grn ('82)	2.65	1.50
83	A19	8c yel brn	8.25	2.25
84	A19	10c green	300.00	140.00
85	A19	10c brn lil ('82)	1.50	30
a.		10c brn vio	2.50	1.25
86	A19	12½c brt rose ('82)	90	30
87	A19	20c bis brn ('82)	1.50	30
88	A19	25c dk brn ('82)	1.85	30

See also Nos. 137-139.

Stamps and Type of 1880-86 Handstamp Surcharged in Black, Green or Red:

c

d

e   f

1881-88   Black Surcharge.

89	A19 (c)	2c on 2½c brn	3.75	1.50
90	A19 (f)	10c on 2⁴⁄₈c ultra (#79) ('87)	40.00	10.00
91	A19 (f)	10c on 2⁴⁄₈c ultra (#80) ('87)	6.00	1.50
92	A19 (d)	20c on 8c brn ('83)	9.00	2.75
93	A19 (d)	1r on 2c car ('83)	45.00	25.00
94	A19 (d)	2r on 2⁴⁄₈c ultra ('83)	6.00	1.50

Green Surcharge.

95	A19 (e)	8c on 2c car ('83)	6.00	1.85
96	A19 (d)	10c on 2c car ('83)	4.00	1.85
97	A19 (d)	1r on 2c car ('83)	90.00	37.50
98	A19 (d)	1r on 5c gray bl ('83)	6.00	2.75
99	A19 (d)	1r on 8c brn ('83)	9.00	2.75

Red Surcharge.

100	A19 (f)	1c on 2⁴⁄₈c ultra (#79) ('87)	90	60
101	A19 (f)	1c on 2⁴⁄₈c ultra (#80) ('87)	2.50	1.25
102	A19 (d)	16c on 2⁴⁄₈c ultra ('83)	9.00	2.75
103	A19 (d)	1r on 2c car ('83)	6.00	2.75
104	A19 (d)	1r on 5c bl gray ('83)	14.00	4.75

Surcharges exist double or inverted on many of Nos. 89-104.

Handstamp Surcharged in Magenta

g

h

1887

105	A19 (g)	8c on 2⁴⁄₈c ultra (#79)	90	45
106	A19 (g)	8c on 2⁴⁄₈c ultra (#80)	1.00	1.00

1888

107	A19 (h)	2⁴⁄₈c on 1c gray grn	1.20	80
108	A19 (h)	2⁴⁄₈c on 5c bl gray	1.50	60
109	N1 (h)	2⁴⁄₈c on ⅛c grn	50	22
110	A19 (h)	2⁴⁄₈c on 50m bis	2.10	1.00
111	A19 (h)	2⁴⁄₈c on 10c grn	1.50	60

No. 109 is surcharged on a newspaper stamp of 1886-89 and has the inscriptions shown on cut N1.

On Revenue Stamps.

R1

R2

R3

Handstamp Surcharged in Black, Yellow, Green, Red or Magenta:

j

k

HABILITADO PARA CORREOS

m

1881-88   Black Surcharge.

112	R1 (c)	2c on 10c bis	24.00	13.00
113	R1 (j)	2c on 10c bis	2.50	90
114	R1 (j)	2⁴⁄₈c on 2r bl	210.00	90.00
115	R1 (j)	8c on 10c bis	210.00	100.00
116	R1 (j)	8c on 2r bl	8.25	2.50
118	R1 (d)	1r on 12⁴⁄₈c gray bl ('83)	7.00	3.75
119	R1 (d)	1r on 10c bis ('82)	10.00	3.75

Yellow Surcharge.

120	R2 (e)	2c on 200m grn ('82)	5.50	2.50
121	R1 (d)	16c on 2r bl ('83)	4.75	2.85

Green Surcharge.

122	R1 (d)	1r on 10c bis ('83)	12.00	3.75

Red Surcharge.

123	R1 (d+j)	2r on 8c on 2r bl ('82)	40.00	15.00
124	R1 (d)	1r on 12⁴⁄₈c gray bl ('83)	5.00	3.00
125	R1 (k)	6²⁄₈c on 12⁴⁄₈c gray bl ('85)	5.75	2.50
126	R3 (d)	1r on 10p bis ('83)	45.00	27.50
127	R1 (m)	1r green	100.00	75.00
127A	R1 (m)	2r blue	210.00	120.00
128	R2 (d)	1r on 1p grn ('83)	32.50	18.00
129	R2 (d)	1r on 200m grn ('83)	80.00	45.00

Magenta Surcharge.

130	R2 (h)	2⁴⁄₈c on 200m grn ('88)	3.75	1.50
131	R2 (h)	2⁴⁄₈c on 20c brn ('88)	12.00	5.75

On Telegraph Stamps.

T1

T2

Surcharged in Red, Black or Magenta

1883-88

132	T1 (d)	2r on 250m ultra (R)	10.00	3.75
133	T1 (d)	20c on 250m ultra (Bk)	50.00	30.00
134	T1 (d)	2r on 250m ultra (Bk)	12.00	5.50
135	T1 (d)	1r on 20c on 250m ultra (R & Bk)	7.50	4.50

Magenta Surcharge.

136	T2 (h)	2⁴⁄₈c on 1c bis (M) ('88)	90	60

Type of 1880-86 Redrawn.

1887-88

137	A19	50m bister	75	40
138	A19	1c yel brn ('88)	75	30
139	A19	6c yel brn ('88)	12.00	2.25

King Alfonso XIII
A36

1890-97   Typographed

140	A36	1c vio ('92)	75	30
141	A36	1c rose ('94)	4.50	1.85
142	A36	1c bl grn ('96)	2.25	60
143	A36	1c cl ('97)	9.50	3.75
144	A36	2c claret	22	15
145	A36	2c vio ('92)	30	22
146	A36	2c dk brn ('94)	22	10
147	A36	2c ultra ('96)	38	38
148	A36	2c gray brn ('96)	10	10
149	A36	2½c dl bl	45	15
150	A36	2½c ol gray ('92)	30	22
151	A36	5c dk bl	45	15
152	A36	5c dk ol gray	90	30
153	A36	5c grn ('92)	38	30
154	A36	5c lil ('92)	300.00	125.00
155	A36	5c vio brn ('96)	7.50	2.75
156	A36	5c bl grn ('96)	4.50	1.50
157	A36	6c brn vio ('92)	30	22
158	A36	6c red org ('94)	75	22
159	A36	6c car rose ('96)	4.50	2.25
160	A36	8c yel grn	22	8
161	A36	8c ultra ('92)	75	30
162	A36	8c red brn ('94)	38	10
163	A36	10c bl grn	1.50	8
164	A36	10c pale cl ('91)	90	22
165	A36	10c cl ('92)	38	8
166	A36	10c yel brn ('96)	38	8

167	A36	12⅘c yel grn	30	15
168	A36	12⅘c org ('94)	90	22
169	A36	15c red brn ('92)	90	30
170	A36	15c rose ('94)	90	38
171	A36	15c bl grn ('96)	2.25	1.50
172	A36	20c rose	35.00	13.00
173	A36	20c sal ('91)	10.00	3.75
174	A36	20c gray brn ('92)	2.25	38
175	A36	20c dk vio ('94)	4.50	1.85
176	A36	20c org ('96)	3.75	1.50
177	A36	25c brown	5.50	1.50
178	A36	25c dl bl ('91)	2.25	30
179	A36	40c dk vio ('97)	12.50	3.75
180	A36	80c cl ('97)	24.00	7.50

Many of Nos. 140–180 exist imperf.

Stamps of Previous Issues Handstamp Surcharged in Blue, Red, Black or Violet

1897 **Blue Surcharge.**

181	A36	5c on 5c grn	2.25	1.25
182	A36	15c on 15c red brn	2.50	1.20
183	A36	20c on 20c gray brn	6.75	4.25

Red Surcharge.

184	A19	5c on 5c bl gray	3.50	1.85
185	A36	5c on 5c grn	2.50	1.35

Black Surcharge.

186	A19	5c on 5c bl gray	4.00	3.00
187	A36	5c on 5c grn	22.50	12.50
188	A36	15c on 15c rose	3.00	1.75
189	A36	20c on 20c dk vio	21.00	11.00
190	A36	20c on 25c brn	13.50	8.50

Violet Surcharge.

191	A36	15c on 15c rose	5.00	3.00

Inverted, double and other variations of this surcharge exist.

The surcharge on No. 186 is in a mixture of black and red inks.

Impressions in violet black are believed to be reprints. The following varieties are known: 5c on 5c blue green, 15c on 15c rose, 15c on 15c red brown, 20c on 20c gray brown, 20c on 20c dark violet, 20c on 25c brown. These surcharges are to be found double, inverted, etc.

King Alfonso XIII
A39

1898 **Typographed**

192	A39	1m org brn	10	10
193	A39	2m org brn	10	10
194	A39	3m org brn	15	10
195	A39	4m org brn	3.25	90
196	A39	5m org brn	10	10
197	A39	1c blk vio	10	10
198	A39	2c dk bl grn	10	10
199	A39	3c dk brn	10	10
200	A39	4c orange	7.00	3.75
201	A39	5c car rose	15	10
202	A39	6c dk bl	75	45
203	A39	8c gray brn	38	22
204	A39	10c vermilion	1.15	70
205	A39	15c dl ol grn	1.15	60
206	A39	20c maroon	1.15	75
207	A39	40c violet	75	60
208	A39	60c black	3.25	1.50
209	A39	80c red brn	3.25	1.50
210	A39	1p yel grn	7.50	4.75
211	A39	2p sl bl	15.00	5.25

Nos. 192–211 exist imperf. Price $1,000.

Issued under U.S. Administration

Regular Issues of the United States Overprinted in Black

On No. 260.

1899–1900 ***Perf. 12*** **Unwmkd.**

212	A96	50c orange	400.00	225.00

On Nos. 279a, 279d, 267, 268, 281a, 282C, 283, 284, 275 and 275a.

Wmkd. Double-lined USPS. (191)

213	A87	1c yel grn	3.75	90
214	A88	2c org red, type III	1.75	60
a.		2c car, type III	2.25	1.00
b.		Booklet pane of 6 ('00)	325.00	175.00
215	A89	3c purple	6.00	1.75
216	A91	5c blue	6.00	1.50
a.		Inverted overprint		2,000.
217	A94	10c brn, type I	20.00	5.00
217A	A94	10c org brn, type II	250.00	50.00
218	A95	15c ol grn	30.00	7.50
a.		15c lt ol grn	35.00	12.50
219	A96	50c orange	110.00	35.00
a.		50c red org		
		Nos. 213-219 (8)	427.50	102.25

On Nos. 280b, 282 and 272.

1901

220	A90	4c org brn	20.00	5.00
221	A92	6c lake	25.00	8.00
222	A93	8c vio brn	27.50	8.00

On Nos. 276, 276A, 277a and 278.

Red Overprint.

223	A97	$1 blk, type I	450.00	250.00
223A	A97	$1 blk, type II	2,500.	1,250.
224	A98	$2 dk bl	700.00	350.00
225	A99	$5 dk grn	1,500.	1,000.

On Nos. 300–313 and shades.

1903-04 **Black Overprint.**

226	A115	1c bl grn	3.50	40
227	A116	2c carmine	7.50	1.50
228	A117	3c brt vio	75.00	15.00
229	A118	4c brn ('04)	80.00	25.00
a.		4c org brn	80.00	20.00
230	A119	5c blue	12.00	1.25
231	A120	6c brnsh lake ('04)	85.00	20.00
232	A121	8c vio blk ('04)	40.00	15.00
233	A122	10c pale red brn ('04)	22.50	3.50
a.		10c red brn	25.00	5.00
b.		Pair, one without overprint		1,250.
234	A123	13c pur blk	35.00	17.50
a.		13c brn vio	35.00	17.50
235	A124	15c ol grn	50.00	12.00
236	A125	50c orange	160.00	50.00
		Nos. 226-236 (11)	570.50	161.15

Red Overprint.

237	A126	$1 black	625.00	275.00
238	A127	$2 dk bl ('04)	1,750.	800.00
239	A128	$5 dk grn ('04)	2,100.	1,200.

On No. 319 in Black.

1904

240	A129	2c carmine	5.50	2.50
a.		Bklt. pane of 6	1,200.	

José Rizal
A40

Arms of Manila
A41

Wmk. 191

Designs: 4c, Pres. William McKinley. 6c, Fernando Magellan. 8c, Miguel Lopez de Legaspi. 10c, Gen. Henry W. Lawton. 12c, Lincoln. 16c, Adm. William T. Sampson. 20c, Washington. 26c, Francisco Carriedo. 30c, Benjamin Franklin.

Each Inscribed "Philippine Islands / United States of America".

Wmkd. Double-lined PIPS. (191PI)

1906, Sept. 8 **Engraved** ***Perf. 12***

241	A40	2c dp grn	30	6
a.		2c yel grn ('10)	50	6
b.		Booklet pane of 6	200.00	
242	A40	4c carmine	40	6
a.		4c car lake ('10)	75	6
b.		Booklet pane of 6	200.00	
243	A40	6c violet	1.25	15
244	A40	8c brown	2.25	75
245	A40	10c blue	1.65	10
246	A40	12c brn lake	5.00	2.25
247	A40	16c vio blk	3.25	25
248	A40	20c org brn	3.75	40
249	A40	26c vio brn	6.00	2.50
250	A40	30c ol grn	4.50	1.60
251	A41	1p orange	20.00	11.00
252	A41	2p black	35.00	1.50
253	A41	4p dk bl	100.00	17.50
254	A41	10p dk grn	200.00	85.00
		Nos. 241-254 (14)	383.35	123.12

Change of Colors

1909-13 ***Perf. 12.***

255	A40	12c red org	8.00	3.00
256	A40	16c ol grn	2.00	50
257	A40	20c yellow	7.50	1.50
258	A40	26c bl grn	1.50	80
259	A40	30c ultra	10.00	4.00
260	A41	1p pale vio	27.50	6.00
260A	A41	2p vio brn ('13)	75.00	3.00
		Nos. 255-260A (7)	131.50	18.80

Wmk. 190

Wmkd. Single-lined PIPS. (190PI)

1911 ***Perf. 12***

261	A40	2c green	60	10
a.		Booklet pane of 6	175.00	
262	A40	4c car lake	3.00	12
a.		4c car		
b.		Booklet pane of 6	175.00	
263	A40	6c dp vio	1.75	10
264	A40	8c brown	8.00	50
265	A40	10c blue	3.00	10
266	A40	12c orange	2.00	50
267	A40	16c ol grn	2.25	20
268	A40	20c yellow	2.00	15
a.		20c org	2.00	15
269	A40	26c bl grn	2.75	30
270	A40	30c ultra	2.75	50
271	A41	1p pale vio	20.00	50
272	A41	2p vio brn	25.00	1.00
273	A41	4p dp bl	650.00	60.00
274	A41	10p dp grn	200.00	20.00
		Nos. 261-274 (14)	923.10	84.07

1914

275	A40	30c gray	10.00	65

1914-23 ***Perf. 10.***

276	A40	2c green	1.25	12
a.		Booklet pane of 6	185.00	
277	A40	4c carmine	1.25	15
a.		Booklet pane of 6	185.00	
278	A40	6c lt vio	25.00	12.50
a.		6c dp vio	27.50	7.00
279	A40	8c brown	25.00	9.00
280	A40	10c dk bl	17.50	25
281	A40	16c ol grn	60.00	4.50
282	A40	20c orange	15.00	1.00
283	A40	30c gray	40.00	3.50
284	A41	1p pale vio	95.00	4.00
		Nos. 276-284 (9)	280.00	35.02

1918–26 ***Perf. 11***

285	A40	2c green	16.50	4.00
a.		Bklt. pane of 6	550.00	
286	A40	4c carmine	25.00	2.50
a.		Bklt. pane of 6	550.00	
287	A40	6c dp vio	30.00	1.75
287A	A40	8c lt brn	200.00	40.00
288	A40	10c dk bl	40.00	1.75
289	A40	16c ol grn	85.00	6.50
289A	A40	20c orange	45.00	9.00
289C	A40	30c gray	40.00	15.00
289D	A41	1p pale vio	50.00	15.00
		Nos. 285-289D (9)	531.50	95.50

1917–25 ***Perf. 11*** **Unwmkd.**

290	A40	2c yel grn	10	5
a.		2c dk grn	12	5
b.		Vert. pair, imperf. horiz.		
c.		Horiz. pair, imperf. btwn.	750.00	
d.		Vertical pair, imperf. between	1,750.	
e.		Booklet pane of 6	20.00	
291	A40	4c carmine	10	5
a.		4c lt rose	25	5
b.		Booklet pane of 6	17.50	
292	A40	6c dp vio	30	8
a.		6c lil	40	8
b.		6c red vio	40	10
c.		Booklet pane of 6	200.00	
293	A40	8c yel brn	20	12
a.		8c org brn	20	12
294	A40	10c dp bl	20	8
295	A40	12c red org	40	15
296	A40	16c lt ol grn	50.00	25
a.		16c ol bis	50.00	50
297	A40	20c org yel	35	10
298	A40	26c green	55	65
a.		26c bl grn	70	40
299	A40	30c gray	50	10
300	A41	1p pale vio	27.50	1.25
a.		1p red lil	27.50	1.25
b.		1p pale rose lil	27.50	1.50
301	A41	2p vio brn	25.00	75
302	A41	4p blue	18.50	50
a.		4p dk bl	18.50	50
		Nos. 290-302 (13)	123.70	4.13

1923–26

Design: 16c, Adm. George Dewey.

303	A40	16c ol bis	75	15
a.		16c ol grn	1.35	15
304	A41	10p dp grn ('26)	60.00	8.00

Legislative Palace
A42

1926, Dec. 20 ***Perf. 12*** **Unwmkd.**

319	A42	2c grn & blk	50	30
a.		Horiz. pair, imperf. between	250.00	
b.		Vert. pair, imperf. between	400.00	
320	A42	4c car & blk	50	40
a.		Horiz. pair, imperf. between	250.00	
b.		Vert. pair, imperf. between	325.00	
321	A42	16c ol grn & blk	1.00	85
a.		Horiz. pair, imperf. between	300.00	
b.		Vert. pair, imperf. between	400.00	
c.		Double impression of center	500.00	
322	A42	18c lt brn & blk	1.25	75
a.		Double impression of center	500.00	
b.		Vert. pair, imperf. between	400.00	
323	A42	20c org & blk	1.75	1.25
a.		20c org & brn	300.00	
b.		Imperf., pair	400.00	400.00
c.		As "a", imperf., pair	350.00	
d.		Vert. pair, imperf. between	400.00	
324	A42	24c gray & blk	1.50	1.00
a.		Vert. pair, imperf. between	400.00	
325	A42	1p rose lil & blk	60.00	35.00
a.		Vert. pair, imperf. between	450.00	
		Nos. 319-325 (7)	66.50	39.55

Opening of the Legislative Palace.

PHILIPPINES

Coil Stamp
Rizal Type of 1906
1928   **Perf. 11 Vertically**

| 326 | A40 | 2c green | 7.50 | 7.50 |

Types of 1906-23
1925   **Imperf.**   **Unwmkd.**

340	A40	2c yel grn ('31)	12	12
341	A40	4c car rose ('31)	20	20
342	A40	6c vio ('31)	2.00	2.00
343	A40	8c brn ('31)	1.75	1.75
344	A40	10c bl ('31)	2.00	2.00
345	A40	12c dp org ('31)	3.00	3.00
346	A40	16c ol grn (*Dewey*) ('31)	2.25	2.25
347	A40	20c org yel ('31)	2.25	2.25
348	A40	26c grn ('31)	2.25	2.25
349	A40	30c lt gray ('31)	2.50	2.50
350	A41	1p lt vio ('31)	8.00	8.00
351	A41	2p brn vio ('31)	20.00	20.00
352	A41	4p bl ('31)	60.00	60.00
353	A41	10p grn ('31)	175.00	175.00
		Nos. 340-353 (14)	281.32	281.32

Two imperforate issues were made, in 1925 and 1931. They differ in shade.

Mount Mayon, Luzon
A43

Post Office, Manila
A44

Pier No. 7, Manila Bay
A45

Vernal Falls, Yosemite Park, California (See footnote)
A46

Rice Planting
A47

Rice Terraces
A48

Baguio Zigzag
A49

1932, May 3   **Perf. 11**

354	A43	2c yel grn	75	35
355	A44	4c rose car	50	35
356	A45	12c orange	75	75
357	A46	18c red org	25.00	12.50
358	A47	20c yellow	1.00	80
359	A48	24c dp vio	1.50	1.00
360	A49	32c ol brn	1.50	1.15
		Nos. 354-360 (7)	31.00	16.90

The 18c vignette was intended to show Pagsanjan Falls in Laguna, central Luzon, and is so labeled. Through error the stamp pictures Vernal Falls in Yosemite National Park, California.

Nos. 302, 302a Surcharged in Orange or Red

1932

368	A41	1p on 4p bl (O)	2.50	50
a.		1p on 4p dk bl (O)	3.50	1.50
369	A41	2p on 4p dk bl (R)	4.50	1.00
a.		2p on 4p bl (R)	4.50	1.00

Baseball Players
A50

Tennis Player
A51

Basketball Players
A52

Typographed.

1934, Apr. 14   **Perf. 11½**

380	A50	2c yel brn	20	20
381	A51	6c ultra	40	35
a.		Vert. pair, imperf. btwn.	400.00	
382	A52	16c vio brn	75	75
a.		Imperf. horizontally (pair)	400.00	

Tenth Far Eastern Championship Games.

José Rizal
A53

Woman and Carabao
A54

La Filipina
A55

Pearl Fishing
A56

Fort Santiago
A57

Salt Spring
A58

Magellan's Landing, 1521
A59

"Juan de la Cruz"
A60

Rice Terraces
A61

"Blood Compact," 1565
A62

Barasoain Church, Malolos
A63

Battle of Manila Bay, 1898
A64

Montalban Gorge
A65

George Washington
A66

1935, Feb. 15   **Engraved.**   **Perf. 11**

383	A53	2c rose	5	5
384	A54	4c yel grn	5	5
385	A55	6c dk brn	9	6
386	A56	8c violet	12	12
387	A57	10c rose car	25	20
388	A58	12c black	18	15
389	A59	16c dk bl	18	12
390	A60	20c lt ol grn	25	6
391	A61	26c indigo	35	35
392	A62	30c org red	35	35
393	A63	1p red org & blk	2.50	1.85
394	A64	2p bis brn & blk	5.00	1.75
395	A65	4p bl & blk	5.00	3.75
396	A66	5p grn & blk	10.00	2.25
		Nos. 383-396 (14)	24.37	11.11

Commonwealth Issues

The Temples of Human Progress
A67

1935, Nov. 15

397	A67	2c car rose	15	10
398	A67	6c dp vio	20	15
399	A67	16c blue	30	20
400	A67	36c yel grn	50	45
401	A67	50c brown	80	80
		Nos. 397-401 (5)	1.95	1.70

Issued in commemoration of the inauguration of the Philippine Commonwealth on Nov. 15th, 1935.

José Rizal
A68

President Manuel L. Quezon
A69

PHILIPPINES

1936, June 19			Perf. 12	
402	A68	2c yel brn	10	10
403	A68	6c sl bl	15	10
a.		Imperf. vertically, pair	600.00	
404	A68	36c red brn	60	60

Issued to commemorate the 75th anniversary of the birth of José Rizal.

1936, Nov. 15			Perf. 11	
408	A69	2c org brn	6	6
409	A69	6c yel grn	12	10
410	A69	12c ultra	18	15

Issued in commemoration of the first anniversary of the Commonwealth.

Stamps of 1935 Overprinted in Black

COMMON-WEALTH *a*   COMMONWEALTH *b*

1936-37			Perf. 11.	
411	A53 (a)	2c rose	6	6
a.		Booklet pane of 6	3.25	1.00
412	A54 (b)	4c yel grn ('37)	75	40
413	A55 (b)	6c dk brn	25	10
414	A56 (b)	8c vio ('37)	35	30
415	A57 (b)	10c rose car	20	6
a.		"Commonwealth"		
416	A58 (b)	12c blk ('37)	20	8
417	A59 (b)	16c dk bl	25	20
418	A60 (a)	20c lt ol grn ('37)	75	50
419	A61 (b)	26c ind ('37)	65	45
420	A62 (b)	30c org red	30	15
421	A63 (b)	1p red org & blk	1.00	30
422	A64 (b)	2p bis brn & blk ('37)	7.00	3.00
423	A65 (b)	4p bl & blk ('37)	25.00	4.00
424	A66 (b)	5p grn & blk ('37)	2.50	1.65
		Nos. 411-424 (14)	39.28	11.24

Map of Philippines A70   Arms of Manila A71

1937, Feb. 3				
425	A70	2c yel grn	10	6
426	A70	6c lt brn	18	10
427	A70	12c sapphire	20	10
428	A70	20c dp org	35	15
429	A70	36c dp vio	60	50
430	A70	50c carmine	70	35
		Nos. 425-430 (6)	2.13	1.26

33rd Eucharistic Congress.

1937, Aug. 27			Perf. 11	
431	A71	10p gray	6.50	3.00
432	A71	20p hn brn	3.50	2.00

Stamps of 1935 Overprinted in Black

COMMON-WEALTH *a*   COMMONWEALTH *b*

1938-40			Perf. 11.	
433	A53 (a)	2c rose ('39)	8	5
a.		Booklet pane of 6	3.75	1.00
b.		"WEALTH COMMON-"	2,500.	
c.		Hyphen omitted		
434	A54 (a)	4c yel grn ('40)	60	50
435	A55 (a)	6c dk brn ('39)	8	8
a.		6c gldn brn	10	8
436	A56 (b)	8c vio ('39)	10	10
a.		"Commonwealth"	60.00	
437	A57 (b)	10c rose car ('39)	10	6
438	A58 (b)	12c blk ('40)	10	9
439	A59 (b)	16c dk bl	18	10
440	A60 (b)	20c lt ol grn ('39)	20	10
441	A61 (b)	26c ind ('40)	30	30
442	A62 (b)	30c org red ('39)	1.60	85
443	A63 (b)	1p red org & blk	60	25
444	A64 (b)	2p bis brn & blk	4.00	1.00
445	A65 (b)	4p bl & blk ('40)	65.00	65.00
446	A66 (b)	5p grn & blk ('40)	7.00	4.00
		Nos. 433-446 (14)	79.94	72.48

Overprint "b" measures 18½x13¾mm. No. 433b occurs in booklet pane, No. 433a, position 5; all copies are straight-edged, left and bottom.

Stamps of 1917-37 Surcharged in Red, Violet or Black

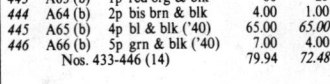

Foreign Trade Week.

1939, July 5				
449	A54	2c on 4c yel grn (R)	10	8
450	A40	6c on 26c bl grn (V)	20	20
a.		6c on 26c grn	1.00	45
451	A71	50c on 20p hn brn (Bk)	1.25	1.25

President Quezon Taking Oath of Office A74   José Rizal A75

1940, Feb. 8				
458	A74	2c dk org	10	8
459	A74	6c dk grn	15	12
460	A74	12c purple	30	15

4th anniversary of Commonwealth.

Rotary Press Printing.
Size: 19 x 22½ mm.

1941, Apr. 14			Perf. 11x10½	
461	A75	2c ap grn	5	5

Triumphal Arch A72   Malacañan Palace A73

1939, Nov. 15			Perf. 11	
452	A72	2c yel grn	10	8
453	A72	6c carmine	15	10
454	A72	12c brt bl	25	10

1939, Nov. 15				
455	A73	2c green	10	6
456	A73	6c orange	15	10
457	A73	12c carmine	25	8

Nos. 452-457 commemorate the 4th anniversary of the Commonwealth.

Flat Plate Printing.
Size: 18¾ x 22 mm.

1941-43			Perf. 11	
462	A75	2c ap grn ('43)	12	6
a.		2c pale ap grn	25	6
b.		Booklet pane of 6 (ap grn) ('43)	1.50	1.50
c.		Booklet pane of 6 (pale ap grn)	4.00	3.50

No. 462 was issued only in booklet panes and all copies have straight edges. Further printings were made in 1942 and 1943 in different shades from the first supply of stamps sent to the islands.

Philippine Stamps of 1935-41, Handstamped in Violet   VICTORY

1944			Perf. 11, 11x10½.	
463	A53	2c rose (On 411)	225.00	125.00
a.		Booklet pane of 6	1,850.	
463B	A53	2c rose (On 433)	1,450.	1,450.
464	A75	2c ap grn (On 461)	2.00	2.00
465	A54	4c yel grn (On 384)	25.00	25.00
466	A55	6c dk brn (On 385)	1,250.	750.00
467	A69	6c yel grn (On 409)	100.00	85.00
468	A55	6c dk brn (On 413)	500.00	300.00
469	A72	6c car (On 453)	125.00	100.00
470	A73	6c org (On 456)	450.00	300.00
471	A74	6c dk grn (On 459)	150.00	90.00
472	A56	8c vio (On 436)	12.50	15.00
473	A57	10c rose car (On 415)	100.00	60.00
474	A57	10c rose car (On 437)	125.00	75.00
475	A69	12c ultra (On 410)	250.00	110.00
476	A72	12c brt bl (On 454)	3,000.	1,400.
477	A74	12c pur (On 460)	150.00	100.00
478	A58	16c dk bl (On 389)	600.00	
479	A59	16c dk bl (On 417)	300.00	120.00
480	A59	16c dk bl (On 439)	120.00	100.00
481	A60	20c lt ol grn (On 440)	27.50	27.50
482	A62	30c org red (On 420)	175.00	125.00
483	A62	30c org red (On 442)	250.00	135.00
484	A63	1p red org & blk (On 443)	7,000.	4,500.

Types of 1935-37 Overprinted

VICTORY   VICTORY

COMMON-WEALTH *a*   COMMONWEALTH *b*

1945			Perf. 11.	
485	A53 (a)	2c rose	10	6
486	A54 (b)	4c yel grn	12	8
487	A55 (b)	6c gldn brn	15	10
488	A56 (b)	8c violet	20	18
489	A57 (b)	10c rose car	20	15
490	A58 (b)	12c black	30	18
491	A59 (b)	16c dk bl	40	15
492	A60 (b)	20c lt ol grn	45	12
493	A62 (b)	30c org red	60	50
494	A63 (b)	1p red org & blk	1.75	40
		Nos. 485-494 (10)	4.27	1.92

Nos. 431-432 Overprinted in Black   VICTORY

1945				
495	A71	10p gray	50.00	15.00
496	A71	20p hn brn	40.00	17.50

José Rizal A76

Rotary Press Printing.

1946, May 28			Perf. 11x10½	
497	A76	2c sepia	10	6

Republic

Philippine Girl Holding Flag of the Republic A77

Engraved.

1946, July 4			Perf. 11 Unwmkd.	
500	A77	2c carmine	30	30
501	A77	6c green	50	30
502	A77	12c blue	75	50

Issued to commemorate the independence of the Philippines, July 4, 1946.

No. 497 Overprinted in Brown

PHILIPPINES 50TH ANNIVERSARY MARTYRDOM OF RIZAL 1896~1946

1946, Dec. 30			Perf 11x10½	
503	A76	2c sepia	30	25

Issued to commemorate the 50th anniversary of the execution of José Rizal.

Rizal Monument A78   Bonifacio Monument A79

Jones Bridge A80   Santa Lucia Gate A81

Mayon Volcano A82   Avenue of Palms A83

1947			Engraved Perf. 12	
504	A78	4c blk brn	20	5
505	A79	10c red org	25	8

PHILIPPINES

506	A80	12c dp bl	35	12
507	A81	16c sl gray	2.00	1.25
508	A82	20c red brn	60	15
509	A83	50c dl grn	1.50	1.00
510	A83	1p violet	3.00	75
		Nos. 504-510 (7)	7.90	3.40

Manuel L. Quezon—A84

1947, May 1   Typographed.

| 511 | A84 | 1c green | 18 | 12 |

Pres. Manuel A. Roxas
Taking Oath of Office
A85

1947, July 4   **Perf. 12½**   **Unwmkd.**

512	A85	4c car rose	30	25
513	A85	6c dk grn	70	70
514	A85	16c purple	1.50	1.00

First anniversary of republic.

Souvenir Sheet.

A86

1947, Nov. 28   *Imperf.*

| 515 | A86 | Sheet of four | 1.00 | 1.00 |
| a. | | 1c brt grn | 20 | 20 |

Marginal inscription in carmine. Size: 63½x84½mm.

United Nations Emblem
A87

1947, Nov. 24   **Perf. 12½**

516	A87	4c dk car & pink	2.00	1.75
a.		Imperf.	3.00	3.00
517	A87	6c pur & pale vio	3.00	3.00
a.		Imperf.	3.00	3.00
518	A87	12c dp bl & pale bl	3.50	3.50
a.		Imperf.	3.00	3.00

Issued to honor the conference of the Economic Commission in Asia and the Far East, held at Baguio.

Gen. Douglas MacArthur—A88

1948, Feb. 3   Engraved.   *Perf. 12*

519	A88	4c purple	50	25
520	A88	6c rose car	1.00	75
521	A88	16c brt ultra	1.75	75

Threshing Rice
A89

1948, Feb. 23   Typo.   *Perf. 12½*

522	A89	2c grn & pale yel grn	1.50	1.00
523	A89	6c brn & cr	1.75	1.25
524	A89	18c dp bl & pale bl	5.00	4.00

Issued to honor the conference of the United Nations Food and Agriculture Organization, held at Baguio. No. 524 exists imperf. See No. C67.

Manuel A. Roxas   José Rizal
A90   A91

1948, July 15   Engraved   *Perf. 12*

| 525 | A90 | 2c black | 30 | 20 |
| 526 | A90 | 4c black | 40 | 30 |

Issued in tribute to President Manuel A. Roxas who died April 15, 1948.

1948, June 19   Unwmkd.

| 527 | A91 | 2c brt grn | 6 | 5 |
| a. | | Booklet pane of 6 | 2.00 | |

Scout   Sampaguita,
Saluting   National Flower
A92   A93

1948, Oct. 31   Typo.   *Imperf.*

528	A92	2c choc & grn	50	25
a.		Perf. 11½	1.50	75
529	A92	4c choc & pink	60	40
a.		Perf. 11½	1.75	1.10

Issued to commemorate the 25th anniversary of the foundation of the Boy Scouts of the Philippines.
No. 528 exists part perforate.

1948, Dec. 8   *Perf. 12½*

| 530 | A93 | 3c blk, pale bl & grn | 50 | 40 |

U.P.U. Monument, Bern
A94

Engraved.

1949, Oct. 9   *Perf. 12*   Unwmkd.

531	A94	4c green	20	10
532	A94	6c dl vio	28	10
533	A94	18c bl gray	95	30

Souvenir Sheet.
Imperf.

534	A94	Sheet of three	85	70
a.		4c grn	20	15
b.		6c dl vio	25	20
c.		18c bl	30	30

Issued in sheets measuring 106x91½ mm. Marginal inscriptions at top and bottom in blue. In 1960 an unofficial, 3-line overprint ("President D. D. Eisenhower/Visit to the Philippines/June 14-16, 1960") was privately applied to No. 534. Nos. 531 to 534 were issued to commemorate the 75th anniversary of the formation of the Universal Postal Union. See also No. 901.

Gen. Gregorio del Pilar
at Tirad Pass
A95

1949, Dec. 2   *Perf. 12*

| 535 | A95 | 2c red brn | 20 | 15 |
| 536 | A95 | 4c green | 40 | 35 |

Issued to mark the 50th anniversary of the death of Gen. Gregorio P. del Pilar and fifty-two of his men at Tirad Pass.

Globe   Red Lauan
A96   Tree
           A97

1950, Mar. 1

537	A96	2c purple	25	10
538	A96	6c dk grn	35	10
539	A96	18c dp bl	75	25
		Nos. 537-539, C68-C69 (5)	3.35	1.05

Issued to publicize the 5th World Congress of the Junior Chamber of Commerce, Manila, March 1-8, 1950.

1950, Apr. 14

| 540 | A97 | 2c green | 20 | 10 |
| 541 | A97 | 4c purple | 55 | 30 |

Issued on the occasion of the 50th anniversary of the Bureau of Forestry.

F. D. Roosevelt   Lions Club
with his Stamps   Emblem
A98   A99

1950, May 22

542	A98	4c dk brn	30	25
543	A98	6c car rose	50	45
544	A98	18c blue	1.25	90

Issued to honor Franklin D. Roosevelt and to commemorate the 25th anniversary of the formation of the Philatelic Association of the Philippines. See also No. C70.

1950, June 4   Engraved.

| 545 | A99 | 2c orange | 65 | 65 |
| 546 | A99 | 4c violet | 85 | 85 |

Issued to commemorate the convention of the Lions Club, Manila, June 1950. See also Nos. C71-C72.

Pres. Elpidio Quirino Taking Oath
A100

1950, July 4   *Perf. 12*   Unwmkd.

547	A100	2c car rose	10	15
548	A100	4c magenta	20	15
549	A100	6c bl grn	30	25

Issued on the occasion of the 4th anniversary of the Republic of the Philippines.

No. 527 Surcharged in Black.

1950, Sept. 20

| 550 | A91 | 1c on 2c brt grn | 8 | 5 |

Dove over Globe—A101

1950, Oct. 23

551	A101	5c green	40	30
552	A101	6c rose car	40	30
553	A101	18c ultra	85	65

Baguio Conference of 1950.

Headman of Barangay
Inspecting Harvest
A102

Lithographed.

1951, Mar. 31   *Perf. 12½*

554	A102	5c dl grn	25	10
a.		Imperf.	25	25
555	A102	6c red brn	40	40
a.		Imperf.	40	40
556	A102	18c vio bl	1.00	1.00
a.		Imperf.	1.00	1.00

The government's Peace Fund campaign.

Arms of Manila   Arms of Cebu
A103   A104

Arms of   Arms of
Zamboanga   Iloilo
A105   A106

1951   Engraved.   *Perf. 12*
Various Frames.

557	A103	5c purple	60	50
558	A103	6c gray	40	32
559	A103	18c brt ultra	60	50

Various Frames.

560	A104	5c crim rose	60	50
561	A104	6c bis brn	40	32
562	A104	18c violet	60	50

PHILIPPINES

		Various Frames.		
563	A105	5c bl grn	70	55
564	A105	6c red brn	45	35
565	A105	18c lt bl	70	55
		Various Frames.		
566	A106	5c brt grn	80	65
567	A106	6c violet	55	40
568	A106	18c dp bl	80	65
		Nos. 557-568 (12)	7.20	5.79

Issue dates: A103, Feb. 3. A104, Apr. 27. A105, June 19. A106, Aug. 26.

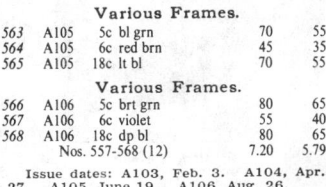

U. N. Emblem and Girl Holding Flag
A107

Liberty Holding Declaration of Human Rights
A108

1951, Oct. 24   Perf. 11½ Unwmkd.

569	A107	5c red	75	35
570	A107	6c bl grn	60	35
571	A107	18c vio bl	1.50	90

United Nations Day, Oct. 24, 1951.

1951, Dec. 10   Perf. 12

572	A108	5c green	60	35
573	A108	6c red org	80	60
574	A108	18c ultra	1.50	90

Universal Declaration of Human Rights.

Students and Department Seal
A109

1952, Jan. 31

| 575 | A109 | 5c org red | 60 | 50 |

Issued to commemorate the 50th anniversary (in 1951) of the Philippine Educational System.

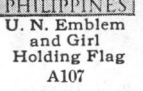

Milkfish and Map—A111

1952, Oct. 27   Perf. 12½

| 578 | A111 | 5c org brn | 1.35 | 85 |
| 579 | A111 | 6c dp bl | 85 | 65 |

Issued to publicize the 4th Indo-Pacific Fisheries Council Meeting, Quezon City, Oct. 23–Nov. 7, 1952.

Maria Clara
A112

1952, Nov. 16

| 580 | A112 | 5c dp bl | 60 | 12 |
| 581 | A112 | 6c brown | 60 | 20 |

Issued to publicize the first Pan-Asian Philatelic Exhibition, PANAPEX, Manila, Nov. 16–22, 1952. See also No. C73.

Wright Park, Baguio City
A113

Francisco Baltazar, Poet
A114

1952, Dec. 15   Perf. 12

| 582 | A113 | 5c red org | 80 | 80 |
| 583 | A113 | 6c dp bl grn | 1.20 | 1.00 |

Issued to publicize the third Lions District Convention, Baguio City.

1953, Mar. 27

| 584 | A114 | 5c citron | 55 | 45 |

National Language Week.

"Gateway to the East"
A115

Presidents Quirino and Sukarno
A116

1953, Apr. 30

| 585 | A115 | 5c turq grn | 40 | 12 |
| 586 | A115 | 6c vermilion | 50 | 20 |

Philippines International Fair.

1953, Oct. 5   Engr. & Litho.

| 587 | A116 | 5c multi | 25 | 15 |
| 588 | A116 | 6c multi | 30 | 30 |

Second anniversary of the visit of Indonesia's President Sukarno.

Marcelo H. del Pilar
A117

Portraits: 1c, Manuel L. Quezon. 2c, José Abad Santos (different frame). 3c, Apolinario Mabini (different frame). 10c, Father José Burgos. 20c, Lapu-Lapu. 25c, Gen. Antonio Luna. 50c, Cayetano Arellano. 60c, Andres Bonifacio. 2p, Graciano L. Jaena.

Perf. 12, 12½, 13, 14x13½

1952-60   Engraved.

589	A117	1c red brn ('53)	5	5
590	A117	2c gray ('60)	5	5
591	A117	3c brick red ('59)	7	5
592	A117	5c crim rose	10	5
595	A117	10c ultra ('55)	20	5
597	A117	20c car lake ('55)	40	5
598	A117	25c yel grn ('58)	50	25
599	A117	50c org ver ('59)	1.00	35
600	A117	60c car rose ('58)	1.25	50
601	A117	2p violet	4.00	1.25
		Nos. 589-601 (10)	7.62	2.65

Doctor Examining Boy
A118

1953, Dec. 16

| 603 | A118 | 5c lil rose | 40 | 35 |
| 604 | A118 | 6c ultra | 50 | 45 |

Issued to commemorate the 50th anniversary of the founding of the Philippine Medical Association.

First Philippine Stamp, Magellan's Landing and Manila Scene—A119

1954, Apr. 25   Perf. 13

Stamp of 1854 in Orange.

605	A119	5c purple	75	50
606	A119	18c dp bl	1.50	1.25
607	A119	30c green	3.50	3.00
		Nos. 605-607, C74-C76 (6)	14.75	12.50

Centenary of Philippine postage stamps.

Nos. 592 and 509 Overprinted or Surcharged in Black

1954, Apr. 23   Perf. 12

| 608 | A117 | 5c crim rose | 1.50 | 1.25 |
| 609 | A83 | 18c on 50c dl grn | 2.75 | 2.00 |

Issued to publicize the first National Boy Scout Jamboree, Quezon City, April 23-30, 1954. The surcharge on No. 609 is reduced to fit the size of the stamp.

Discus Thrower and Games Emblem
A120

Designs: 18c, Swimmer. 30c, Boxers.

1954, May 31   Perf. 13

610	A120	5c dk bl, bl	1.10	75
611	A120	18c dk grn, grn	1.75	1.25
612	A120	30c dp cl, rose	2.75	2.25

2nd Asian Games, Manila, May 1-9.

Nos. 505 and 508 Surcharged in Blue

1954, Sept. 6   Perf. 12

| 613 | A79 | 5c on 10c red org | 25 | 15 |
| 614 | A82 | 18c on 20c red brn | 85 | 80 |

Issued to publicize the Manila Conference, 1954. The surcharge is arranged to obliterate the original denomination.

Allegory of Independence
A121

"Immaculate Conception," by Murillo
A122

1954, Nov. 30   Perf. 13

| 615 | A121 | 5c dk car | 35 | 25 |
| 616 | A121 | 18c dp bl | 1.00 | 60 |

Issued to commemorate the 56th anniversary of the declaration of the first Philippine Independence.

1954, Dec. 30   Perf. 12

| 617 | A122 | 5c blue | 55 | 40 |

Issued to mark the end of the Marian Year.

Mayon Volcano, Moro Vinta and Rotary Emblem
A123

1955, Feb. 23 Engraved.   Perf. 13

| 618 | A123 | 5c dl bl | 30 | 15 |
| 619 | A123 | 18c dk car rose | 1.00 | 75 |

Rotary International, 50th anniversary. See also No. C77.

Allegory of Labor
A124

Pres. Ramon Magsaysay
A125

1955, May 26   Perf. 13x12½

| 620 | A124 | 5c brown | 50 | 40 |

Issued in connection with the Labor-Management Congress, Manila, May 26-28, 1955.

1955, July 4   Perf. 12½

621	A125	5c blue	25	20
622	A125	20c red	75	75
623	A125	30c green	1.25	1.25

9th anniversary of the Republic.

Village Well—A126

1956, Mar. 16   Perf. 12½x13½

| 624 | A126 | 5c violet | 40 | 40 |
| 625 | A126 | 20c dl grn | 90 | 85 |

Issued to publicize the drive for improved health conditions in rural areas.

PHILIPPINES

No. 592 Overprinted — WCOTP CONFERENCE MANILA

1956, Aug. 1   *Perf. 12*   Unwmkd.
626   A117   5c crim rose   50   45

Issued to commemorate the fifth Annual Conference of the World Confederation of Organizations of the Teaching Profession, Manila, Aug. 1-8, 1956.

Nurse and Disaster Victims
A127

Engr.; Cross Litho. in Red
1956, Aug. 30
627   A127   5c violet   65   60
628   A127   20c gray brn   85   70

Issued to commemorate 50 years of Red Cross Service in the Philippines.

Monument to U. S. Landing, Leyte—A128
1956-57   Lithographed   *Perf. 12½*
629   A128   5c car rose   15   15
a.   Imperf. ('57)   65   65

Issued to commemorate the landing of the U.S. forces under Gen. Douglas MacArthur on Leyte, Oct. 20, 1944.

Santo Tomas University
A129
1956, Nov. 13   Photo.   *Perf. 11½*
630   A129   5c brn car & choc   50   35
631   A129   60c lil & red brn   2.00   1.75

Issued in honor of the University of Santo Tomas.

Statue of Christ by Rizal
A130
1956, Nov. 28   Engraved   *Perf. 12*
632   A130   5c gray ol   40   30
633   A130   20c rose car   85   80

Issued in connection with the Second National Eucharistic Congress, Manila, Nov. 28-Dec. 2, and to commemorate the centenary of the Feast of the Sacred Heart.

Nos. 561, 564 and 567 Surcharged with New Value in Blue or Black.
1956   *Perf. 12*   Unwmkd.
634   A104   5c on 6c bis brn (Bl)   20   20
635   A105   5c on 6c red brn (Bl)   20   20
636   A106   5c on 6c vio (Bk)   20   20

Girl Scout, Emblem and Tents
A131
1957, Jan. 19   Litho.   *Perf. 12½*
637   A131   5c dk bl   50   50
a.   Imperf.   65   65

Issued to commemorate the centenary of the Scout movement and for the Girl Scout World Jamboree, Quezon City, Jan. 19-Feb. 2, 1957.

Copies of Nos. 637 and 637a (No. 48 in sheet) exist with heavy black rectangular handstamps obliterating erroneous date at left, denomination and cloverleaf emblem.

Pres. Ramon Magsaysay
A132
1957, Aug. 31   Engraved.   *Perf. 12*
638   A132   5c black   15   10

Issued to commemorate Pres. Ramon Magsaysay, (1907-1957).

"Spoliarium" by Juan Luna
A133
1957, Oct. 23   *Perf. 14x14½*
639   A133   5c rose car   18   12

Issued to commemorate the centenary of the birth of Juan Luna, painter.

Sergio Osmena and First National Assembly
A134
1957, Oct. 16   *Perf. 12½x13½*
640   A134   5c bl grn   18   15

Issued to commemorate the 50th anniversary of the First Philippine Assembly and to honor Sergio Osmeña, Speaker of the Assembly.

Nos. 595 and 597 Surcharged in Carmine or Black

1957, Dec. 30   *Perf. 14x13½*
641   A117   5c on 10c ultra (C)   25   25
642   A117   10c on 20c car lake   35   35

Issued to commemorate the inauguration of Carlos P. Garcia as president and Diosdado Macapagal as vice-president, Dec. 30.

University of the Philippines
A135
1958   Engraved   *Perf. 13½x13*
643   A135   5c dk car rose   45   20

Issued to commemorate the 50th anniversary of the founding of the University of the Philippines.

Pres. Carlos P. Garcia
A136

Granite Paper
1958   Photogravure   *Perf. 11½*
644   A136   5c multi   15   12
645   A136   20c multi   60   45

12th anniversary of Philippine Republic.

Manila Cathedral—A137
Engraved
1958, Dec. 8   *Perf. 13x13½, 12*
646   A137   5c multi   30   20

Issued to commemorate the inauguration of the rebuilt Manila Cathedral, Dec. 8, 1958.

No. 592 Surcharged **OneCentavo**
1959   *Perf. 12*
647   A117   1c on 5c crim rose   20   5

Nos. B4-B5 Surcharged with New Values and Bars
1959   *Perf. 13*
648   SP4   1c on 2c + 2c red   8   8
649   SP5   6c on 4c + 4c vio   12   12

Issued on Feb. 3, 1959, the 14th anniversary of the liberation of Manila from the Japanese forces.

Philippine Flag
A138
1959, Feb. 8   *Perf. 13*   Unwmkd.
650   A138   6c dp ultra, yel & dp car   10   10
651   A138   20c dp car, yel & dp ultra   25   25

Seal of Bulacan Province
A139
1959   Engraved   *Perf. 13*
652   A139   6c lt yel grn   10   8
653   A139   20c rose red   35   25

Issued in conjunction with the 60th anniversary of the Malolos constitution.

1959
Design: 6c, 25c, Seal of Capiz Province and portrait of Pres. Roxas.
654   A139   6c lt brn   10   10
655   A139   25c purple   35   30

Issued on the 11th anniversary of the death of Pres. Manuel A. Roxas.

Seal of Bacolod City—A140
1959
656   A140   6c bl grn   15   10
657   A140   10c rose lil   25   15

Nos. 658-803 were reserved for the rest of a projected series showing seals and coats of arms of provinces and cities.

Mines View Park, Baguio
A141
Perf. 13½ (6c, 25c), 12 (6c)
1959, Sept. 1
804   A141   6c brt grn   20   15
805   A141   25c rose red   40   30

Issued to commemorate the 50th anniversary of the city of Baguio.

No. 533 Surcharged in Red

1959, Oct. 24   *Perf. 12*
806   A94   6c on 18c bl   15   10

Issued for United Nations Day, Oct. 24.

PHILIPPINES

Maria Cristina Falls
A142

Photogravure.

1959, Nov. 18		Perf. 13½, 12		
807	A142	6c vio & dp yel grn	18	10
808	A142	30c grn & brn	55	40

No. 504
Surcharged with New Value and Bars

1959		Engraved	Perf. 12	
809	A78	1c on 4c blk brn	12	5

Manila Atheneum Emblem
A143

1959, Dec. 10			Perf. 13½, 12	
810	A143	6c ultra	10	10
811	A143	30c rose red	55	40

Issued to commemorate the centenary of the Manila Atheneum (Ateneo de Manila), a school, and to mark a century of progress in education.

Manuel Quezon   José Rizal
A144   A145

1959-60		Engraved	Perf. 13	
812	A144	1c ol gray ('60)	10	5
		Perf. 14x12		
813	A145	6c gray bl	15	5

A146

Photogravure.

1960		Perf. 12½x13½	Unwmkd.	
814	A146	6c brn & gold	20	15

Issued to commemorate the 25th anniversary of the Philippine Constitution. See No. C82.

Site of Manila Pact
A147

1960		Engraved	Perf. 12½	
815	A147	6c emerald	10	10
816	A147	25c orange	45	35

Issued to commemorate the 5th anniversary (in 1959) of the Congress of the Philippines establishing the South-East Asia Treaty Organization (SEATO).

Sunset at Manila Bay and Uprooted Oak Emblem
A148

1960, Apr. 7		Photo.	Perf. 13½	
817	A148	6c multi	10	10
818	A148	25c multi	45	35

Issued to publicize World Refugee Year, July 1, 1959–June 30, 1960.

A149

1960, July 29			Perf. 13½	
819	A149	5c lt grn, red & gold	15	8
820	A149	6c bl, red & gold	20	12

Issued to commemorate the 50th anniversary of the founding of the Philippine Tuberculosis Society.

Basketball—A150
Design: 10c, Runner.

1960, Nov. 30			Perf. 13x13½	
821	A150	6c lt grn & brn	18	10
822	A150	10c rose lil & brn	25	15

Issued to commemorate the 17th Olympic Games, Rome, Aug. 25–Sept. 11. See also Nos. C85–C86.

Presidents Eisenhower and Garcia and Presidential Seals
A151

1960, Dec. 30			Perf. 13½	
823	A151	6c multi	25	20
824	A151	20c ultra, red & yel	60	30

Issued to commemorate the visit of Pres. Dwight D. Eisenhower to the Philippines, June 14, 1960.

Nos. 539, 616, 619, 553, 606 and 598 Surcharged with New Values and Bars in Red or Black.

1960-61		Engr.	Perf. 12, 13, 12½	
825	A96	1c on 18c dp bl (R)	5	5
826	A121	5c on 18c dp bl (R)	15	10
827	A123	5c on 18c dp car rose	30	25
828	A101	10c on 18c ultra (R)	25	20
829	A119	10c on 18c dp bl & org (R)	30	25
830	A117	20c on 25c yel grn ('61)	30	20
		Nos. 825-830 (6)	1.35	1.05

On No. 830, no bars are overprinted, the surcharge "20 20" serving to cancel the old denomination.

Mercury and Globe—A152

1961, Jan. 23		Photo.	Perf. 13½	
831	A152	6c red brn, bl, blk & gold	12	10

Issued to commemorate the Manila Postal Conference, Jan. 10–23. See also No. C87.

Nos. B10, B11 and B11a Surcharged "2nd National Boy Scout Jamboree Pasonanca Park" and New Value in Black or Red

1961, May 2		Engraved	Perf. 13	
		Yellow Paper		
832	SP8	10c on 6c+4c car	15	15
833	SP8	30c on 25c+5c bl (R)	50	50
a.		Tete beche, wht (10c on 6c+4c & I 30c on 25c+5c) (Bk)	75	75

Issued to publicize the Second National Boy Scout Jamboree, Pasonanca Park, Zamboanga City.

De la Salle College, Manila
A153

1961, June 16		Photo.	Perf. 11½	
834	A153	6c multi	10	8
835	A153	10c multi	25	12

Issued to commemorate the 50th anniversary of the founding of De la Salle College, Manila.

José Rizal as Student—A154
Designs: 6c, Rizal and birthplace at Calamba, Laguna. 10c, Rizal and parents. 20c, Rizal with Juan Luna and F. R. Hidalgo in Madrid. 30c, Rizal's execution.

1961		Perf. 13½	Unwmkd.	
836	A154	5c multi	10	7
837	A154	6c multi	10	8
838	A154	10c grn & red brn	25	20
839	A154	20c brn red & grnsh bl	35	30
840	A154	30c vio, lil & org brn	50	40
		Nos. 836-840 (5)	1.30	1.05

Centenary of the birth of José Rizal.

Nos. 815–816 Overprinted

IKA
15 KAARAWAN
Republika ng Pilipinas
Hulyo 4, 1961

1961, July 4		Engraved	Perf. 12½	
841	A147	6c emerald	30	30
842	A147	25c orange	50	50

15th anniversary of the Republic.

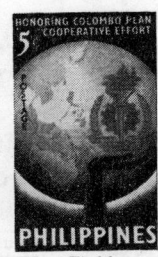

Colombo Plan Emblem and Globe Showing Member Countries
A155

1961, Oct. 8		Photo.	Perf. 13x11½	
843	A155	5c multi	10	10
844	A155	12c multi	12	10

Issued to commemorate the 7th anniversary of the admission of the Philippines to the Colombo Plan.

Government Clerk—A156

1961, Dec. 9		Perf. 12½	Unwmkd.	
845	A156	6c vio, bl & red	20	10
846	A156	10c gray bl & red	45	25

Issued to honor the Philippine government employees.

No. C83 Surcharged

6¢ PAAF GOLDEN JUBILEE 1911 1961

1961, Nov. 30		Engr.	Perf. 14x14½	
847	AP11	6c on 10c car	20	20

Issued to commemorate the 50th anniversary of the Philippine Amateur Athletic Federation.

PHILIPPINES

No. 655 Surcharged with
New Value and:
"MACAPAGAL-PELAEZ INAUGURATION
DEC. 30, 1961"

1961, Dec. 30   Perf. 12½
848 A139   6c on 25c pur   22   10

Issued to commemorate the inauguration of President Diosdado Macapagal and Vice-President Emanuel Pelaez.

No. B8 Surcharged

1962, Jan. 23 Photo. Perf. 13½x13
849 SP7   6c on 5c grn & red   15   8

Vanda Orchids   Apolinario Mabini
A157   A158

Orchids: 6c, White mariposa. 10c, Sander's dendrobe. 20c, Sanggumay.

1962, Mar. 9 Photo. Perf. 13½x14
Dark Blue Background
850 A157   5c rose, grn & yel   12   12
851 A157   6c grn & yel   18   18
852 A157   10c grn, car & brn   20   20
853 A157   20c lil, brn & grn   32   32
   a. Se-tenant block of 4, #850-853   85   85
   b. As "a," imperf.   1.25   1.25

Printed in sheets of 40, containing 10 blocks of Nos. 850-853 se-tenant.

Perf. 13½; 14 (1s); 13x12
(#857, 10s).
1962-69 Engraved   Unwmkd.

Portraits: 1s, Manuel L. Quezon. 3s, Marcelo H. del Pilar. 6s, José Rizal. No. 857A Rizal (wearing shirt). 10s, Father José Burgos. 20s, Lapu-Lapu. 30s, Rajah Soliman. 50s, Cayetano Arellano. 70s, Sergio Osmena. 1p (No. 863), Emilio Jacinto. 1p (No. 864), José M. Panganiban.

854 A158   1s org brn ('63)   5   5
855 A158   3s rose red   5   5
856 A158   5s car rose ('63)   5   5
857 A158   6s dk red brn   5   5
857A A158   6s pck bl ('64)   10   5
858 A158   10s brt pur ('63)   12   5
859 A158   20s Prus bl ('63)   20   5
860 A158   30s vermilion   38   10
861 A158   50s vio ('63)   60   12
862 A158   70s brt bl ('63)   75   35
863 A158   1p grn ('63)   1.50   30
864 A158   1p dp org ('69)   90   40
Nos. 854-864 (12)   4.80   1.62

Pres. Macapagal Taking Oath of Office—A159

1962 Photogravure Perf. 13½
Vignette Multicolored
865 A159   6s blue   10   5
866 A159   10s green   15   10
867 A159   30s violet   45   15

Issued to commemorate the swearing in of President Diosdado Macapagal, Dec. 30, 1961.

Volcano in Lake Taal and
Malaria Eradication Emblem
A160

1962, Oct. 24 Perf. 11½ Unwmkd.
Granite Paper
868 A160   6s multi   10   10
869 A160   10s multi   15   10
870 A160   70s multi   1.10   75

Issued on United Nations Day for the World Health Organization drive to eradicate malaria.

No. 598 Surcharged in Red
1762   1962
BICENTENNIAL
Diego Silang
Revolt
20

1962, Nov. 15 Engraved Perf. 12
871 A117   20s on 25c yel grn   30   25

Issued to commemorate the bicentennial of the Diego Silang revolt in Ilocos Province.

No. B6 Overprinted with Sideways Chevron Obliterating Surtax.

1962, Dec. 23   Perf. 12
872 SP6   5c on 5c+1c dp bl   15   12

Nos. 855, 857 Surcharged with New Value and Old Value Obliterated.

1963   Perf. 13½
873 A158   1s on 3s rose red   6   5
Perf. 13x12
874 A158   5s on 6s dk red brn   10   5

No. 601 Surcharged

1963, June 12   Perf. 12
875 A117   6s on 2p vio   15   10
876 A117   20s on 2p vio   35   35
877 A117   70s on 2p vio   1.00   85

Issued to publicize the Diego Silang Bicentennial Art and Philatelic Exhibition, ARPHEX, Manila, May 28-June 30.

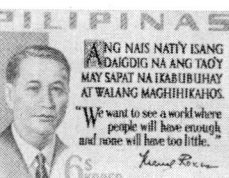

Pres. Manuel Roxas
A161

1963-73 Engraved Perf. 13½
878 A161   6s brt bl & blk, bluish   10   5
879 A161   30s brn & blk   55   15

Portrait: Pres. Ramon Magsaysay.
880 A161   6s lil & blk   10   5
881 A161   30s yel grn & blk   45   12

Portrait: Pres. Elpidio Quirino.
882 A161   6s brn & blk ('65)   10   5
883 A161   30s rose lil & blk ('65)   45   12

Portrait: Gen. (Pres.) Emilio Aguinaldo.
883A A161   6s dp cl & blk ('66)   10   5
883B A161   30s bl & blk ('66)   45   12

Portrait: Pres. José P. Laurel.
883C A161   6s lt red brn & blk ('66)   10   5
883D A161   30s bl & blk ('66)   45   10

Portrait: Pres. Manuel L. Quezon.
883E A161   10s bl gray & blk ('67)   10   5
883F A161   30s lt vio & blk ('67)   45   12

Portrait: Pres. Sergio Osmeña.
883G A161   10s rose lil & blk ('70)   10   5
883H A161   40s grn & blk ('70)   45   10

Portrait: Pres. Carlos P. Garcia.
883I A161   10s multi ('73)   10   5
883J A161   30s multi ('73)   45   12
Nos. 878-883J (16)   4.50   1.35

Nos. 878-883J honor former presidents.

Globe, Flags of   Red Cross
Thailand, Korea,   Centenary
China, Philippines   Emblem
A162   A163

1963, Aug. 26 Photo. Perf. 13½x13
884 A162   6s dk grn & multi   8   6
885 A162   20s dk grn & multi   28   15

Issued to commemorate the first anniversary of the Asian-Oceanic Postal Union.

1963, Sept. 1   Perf. 11½
886 A163   5s lt vio, gray & red   10   5
887 A163   6s ultra, gray & red   10   5
888 A163   20s grn, gray & red   30   20

Centenary of the International Red Cross.

Bamboo Dance
A164

Folk Dances: 6s, Dance with oil lamps. 10s, Duck dance. 20s, Princess Gandingan's rock dance.

1963, Sept. 15 Perf. 14 Unwmkd.
889 A164   5s multi   10   10
890 A164   6s multi   12   12
891 A164   10s multi   20   20
892 A164   20s multi   35   35

Printed in sheets of 40, containing 10 blocks of Nos. 889-892 se-tenant.

Pres. Macapagal and Filipino Family
A165

1963, Sept. 28   Perf. 14
893 A165   5s bl & multi   8   5
894 A165   6s yel & multi   10   6
895 A165   20s lil & multi   25   18

Issued to publicize Pres. Macapagal's 5-year Socioeconomic Program.

Presidents Lopez Mateos and Macapagal—A166

1963, Sept. 28 Photo. Perf. 13½
896 A166   6s multi   10   8
897 A166   30s multi   30   20

Issued to commemorate the visit of Pres. Adolfo Lopez Mateos of Mexico to the Philippines.

Andres Bonifacio—A167

1963, Nov. 30 Perf. 12 Unwmkd.
898 A167   5s gold, brn, gray & red   6   5
899 A167   6s sil, brn, gray & red   8   5
900 A167   25s brnz, brn, gray & red   38   35

Issued to commemorate the centenary of the birth of Andres Bonifacio, national hero and poet.

Souvenir Sheet
No. 534 Overprinted:
"UN ADOPTION/DECLARATION OF HUMAN RIGHTS/15TH ANNIVERSARY DEC. 10, 1963"

1963, Dec. 10 Engraved Imperf.
901 A94   Sheet of three   85   85

Issued to commemorate the 15th anniversary of the Universal Declaration of Human Rights.

Woman holding Sheaf of Rice
A168

1963, Dec. 20 Photo. Perf. 13½x13
902 A168   6s brn & multi   10   5

Issued for the "Freedom from Hunger" campaign of the U.N. Food and Agriculture Organization. See also Nos. C88-C89.

PHILIPPINES

Bamboo Organ Apolinario Mabini
A169 A170

1964, May 4 Perf. 13½

903	A169	5s multi	10	5
904	A169	6s multi	10	5
905	A169	20s multi	30	20

The bamboo organ in the Church of Las Piñas, Rizal, was built by Father Diego Cera, 1816–1822.

Wmkd. "Harrison & Sons, London." in Script. (233)

1964, July 23 Photo. Perf. 14½

906	A170	6s pur & gold	10	5
907	A170	10s red brn & gold	15	10
908	A170	30s brt grn & gold	35	25

Issued to commemorate the centenary of the birth of Apolinario Mabini (1864–1903), national hero and a leader of the 1898 revolution.

Flags Surrounding Pres. Macapagal Signing
SEATO Emblem Agricultural Land
A171 Reform Code
  A172

Perf. 13

1964, Sept. 8 Photo. Unwmkd.
Flags and Emblem Multicolored

909	A171	6s dk bl & yel	8	5
910	A171	10s dp grn & yel	15	10
911	A171	25s dk brn & yel	32	25

Issued to commemorate the 10th anniversary of the South-East Asia Treaty Organization (SEATO).

1964, Dec. 21 Perf. 14½ Wmk. 233

| 912 | A172 | 3s multi | 7 | 5 |
| 913 | A172 | 8s multi | 8 | 5 |

Issued to commemorate the signing of the Agricultural Land Reform Code. See also No. C90.

Basketball
A173

1964, Dec. 28 Perf. 14½x14
Sport: 10s, Women's relay race. 20s, Hurdling. 30s, Soccer.

915	A173	6s lt bl, dk brn & gold	10	8
	a.	Imperf.	15	15
916	A173	10s gold, pink & dk brn	20	10
	a.	Imperf.	25	
	b.	Gold omitted		
917	A173	20s gold, dk brn & yel	35	20
	a.	Imperf.	50	50
918	A173	30s emer, dk brn & gold	45	35
	a.	Imperf.	60	60

18th Olympic Games, Tokyo, Oct. 10–25.

Presidents Lubke and Macapagal and Coats of Arms—A174

1965, Apr. 19 Perf. 13½ Unwmkd.

919	A174	6s ol grn & multi	8	5
920	A174	10s multi	15	5
921	A174	25s dp bl & multi	28	25

Issued to commemorate the visit of Pres. Heinrich Lubke of Germany, Nov. 18–23, 1964.

Emblems of Manila Observatory and Weather Bureau—A175

1965, May 22 Photo. Perf. 13½

922	A175	6s lt ultra & multi	8	5
923	A175	20s lt vio & multi	18	8
924	A175	50s bl grn & multi	60	40

Issued to commemorate the centenary of the Meteorological Service in the Philippines.

Pres. John F. Kennedy
A176

Perf. 14½x14

1965, May 29 Wmk. 233
Center Multicolored

925	A176	6s gray	15	5
926	A176	10s brt vio	20	10
927	A176	25s ultra	50	30

Issued in memory of President John F. Kennedy (1917–63).
Nos. 925–927 exist with ultramarine of tie omitted.
The 6s and 30s exist imperf. Price, each $30.

King and Queen of Thailand, Pres. and Mrs. Macapagal
A177

Perf. 12½x13

1965, June 12 Unwmkd.

928	A177	2s brt bl & multi	5	5
929	A177	6s bis & multi	10	5
930	A177	30s red & multi	35	20

Issued to commemorate the visit of King Phumiphon Aduldet and Queen Sirikit of Thailand, July 1963.

Princess Beatrix and Evangelina Macapagal—A178

Perf. 13x12½

1965, July 4 Photo. Unwmkd.

931	A178	2s bl & multi	5	5
932	A178	6s blk & multi	10	5
933	A178	10s multi	15	10

Issued to commemorate the visit of Princess Beatrix of the Netherlands, Nov. 21–23, 1962.

Cross and Rosary Held Before Map of Philippines
A179

Design: 6s, Map of Philippines, cross and Legaspi-Urdaneta monument.

1965, Oct. 4 Perf. 13 Unwmkd.

| 934 | A179 | 3s multi | 10 | 5 |
| 935 | A179 | 6s multi | 15 | 5 |

Issued to commemorate the 400th anniversary of the Christianization of the Philippines. See also Nos. C91–C92 and souvenir sheet No. C92a.

Presidents Sukarno and Macapagal and Prime Minister Tunku Abdul Rahman
A180

1965, Nov. 25 Perf. 13
Flags of Indonesia, Philippines and Malaysia in Red, Yellow and Dark Blue

936	A180	6s dk bl	10	5
937	A180	10s chocolate	10	10
938	A180	25s green	30	20

Signing of the Manila Accord (Mapilindo) by Malaya, Philippines and Indonesia.

Bicyclists and Globe
A181

Perf. 13½

939	A181	6s multi	5	5
940	A181	10s multi	15	10
941	A181	25s multi	30	20

Issued to commemorate the Second Asian Cycling Championship, Philippines, Nov. 28–Dec. 5.

Nos. B21–B22 Surcharged

10s

MARCOS-LOPEZ INAUGURATION DEC. 30, 1965

1965, Dec. 30 Engraved Perf. 13

| 942 | SP12 | 10s on 6s + 4s grn & rose lil | 15 | 15 |
| 943 | SP12 | 30s on 30s + 5s brt bl & cl | 38 | 38 |

Issued to commemorate the inauguration of President Ferdinand Marcos and Vice-President Fernando Lopez.

Antonio Regidor
A182

1966, Jan. 21 Perf. 12x11

| 944 | A182 | 6s blue | 10 | 5 |
| 945 | A182 | 30s brown | 35 | 30 |

Issued to honor Dr. Antonio Regidor, Secretary of the High Court of Manila and President of Public Instruction.

No. 857A Overprinted in Red:
"HELP ME STOP / SMUGGLING / Pres. MARCOS"

1966, May 1 Engraved Perf. 13½

| 946 | A158 | 6s pck bl | 15 | 6 |

Issued to publicize the anti-smuggling drive of the government.
No. 946 exists with overprint inverted, double, double with one inverted, and double with both inverted.

Girl Scout Giving Scout Sign
A183

1966, May 26 Litho. Perf. 13x12½

947	A183	3s ultra & multi	5	5
948	A183	6s emer & multi	8	5
949	A183	20s brn & multi	20	12

Philippine Girl Scouts, 25th anniversary.

Pres. Marcos Taking Oath of Office
A184

PHILIPPINES

1966, June 12   **Perf. 12½**
950	A184	6s bl & multi	10	5
951	A184	20s emer & multi	15	10
952	A184	30s yel & multi	35	30

Issued to commemorate the inauguration of President Ferdinand E. Marcos, Dec. 30, 1965.

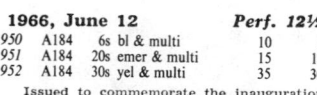

Seal of Manila and Historical Scenes
A185

1966, June 24
| 953 | A185 | 6s multi | 10 | 10 |
| 954 | A185 | 30s multi | 30 | 25 |

Adoption of the new seal of Manila.

Old and New Philippine National Bank Buildings
A186

Designs: 6s, Entrance to old bank building and 1p silver coin.

1966, July 22   **Photo.**   **Perf. 14x13½**
| 955 | A186 | 6s gold, ultra, sil & blk | 12 | 5 |
| 956 | A186 | 10s multi | 25 | 10 |

Issued to commemorate the 50th anniversary of the Philippine National Bank. See also No. C93.

Post Office, Annex Three
A187

1966, Oct. 1   **Perf. 14½**   **Wmk. 233**
957	A187	6s lt vio, yel & grn	8	5
958	A187	10s rose cl, yel & grn	12	10
959	A187	20s ultra, yel & grn	30	15

60th anniversary of Postal Savings Bank.

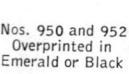 

Nos. 950 and 952 Overprinted in Emerald or Black

Unwmkd.
1966, Oct. 24   **Litho.**   **Perf. 12½**
| 960 | A184 | 6s multi (E) | 10 | 10 |
| 961 | A184 | 30s multi | 40 | 35 |

Manila Summit Conference, Oct. 23–27.

Nos. 915a–918a Overprinted

50th ANNIVERSARY LIONS INTERNATIONAL 1967

Photogravure
1967, Jan. 14   **Imperf.**   **Wmk. 233**
962	A173	6s lt bl, dk brn & gold	8	6
963	A173	10s gold, dk brn & pink	15	12
964	A173	20s gold, dk brn & yel	30	30
965	A173	30s emer, dk brn & gold	45	45

Issued to commemorate the 50th anniversary of Lions International. The Lions emblem is in the lower left corner on the 6s, in the upper left corner on the 10s and in the upper right corner on the 30s.

"Succor" by Fernando Amorsolo
A188

Lithographed
1967, May 15   **Perf. 14**   **Unwmkd.**
966	A188	5s sep & multi	10	5
967	A188	20s bl & multi	20	10
968	A188	2p grn & multi	1.75	1.00

25th anniversary of the Battle of Bataan.

Nos. 857A and 913 Surcharged

1967, Aug.   **Engraved**   **Perf. 13½**
| 969 | A158 | 4s on 6s pck bl | 8 | 5 |

Perf. 14½   **Photo.**   **Wmk. 233**
| 970 | A172 | 5s on 6s multi | 8 | 5 |

Issue dates: 4s, Aug. 10; 5s, Aug. 7.

Gen. Douglas MacArthur and Paratroopers Landing on Corregidor—A189

Lithographed
1967, Aug. 31   **Perf. 14**   **Unwmkd.**
| 971 | A189 | 6s multi | 15 | 15 |
| 972 | A189 | 5p multi | 4.00 | 3.50 |

25th anniversary, Battle of Corregidor.

Bureau of Posts, Manila, Jones Bridge over Pasig River
A190

1967, Sept. 15 Litho.   **Perf. 14x13½**
973	A190	4s multi & blk	20	5
974	A190	20s multi & red	20	10
975	A190	50s multi & vio	50	40

65th anniversary of the Bureau of Posts.

Philippine Nativity Scene
A191

1967, Dec. 1   **Photo.**   **Perf. 13½**
| 976 | A191 | 10s multi | 15 | 15 |
| 977 | A191 | 40s multi | 45 | 35 |

Christmas 1967.

Chinese Garden, Rizal Park, Presidents Marcos and Chiang Kai-shek—A192

Designs (Presidents' heads and scenes in Chinese Garden, Rizal Park, Manila): 10s, Gate. 20s, Landing pier.

1967–68   **Photo.**   **Perf. 13½**
978	A192	5s multi	5	5
979	A192	10s multi ('68)	12	8
980	A192	20s multi	20	12

Sino-Philippine Friendship Year 1966–67.

Makati Center Post Office, Mrs. Marcos and Rotary Emblem
A193

1968, Jan. 9   **Litho.**   **Perf. 14**
981	A193	10s bl & multi	12	12
982	A193	20s grn & multi	25	25
983	A193	40s multi	45	45

Issued to commemorate the first anniversary of the Makati Center Post Office.

Nos. 882, 883C and B27 Surcharged with New Value and Two Bars.

1968
984	A161	5s on 6s grn & blk	7	5
985	A161	5s on 6s lt red brn & blk	7	5
986	SP14	10s on 6s+5s ultra & red	10	

Felipe G. Calderon, Barasoain Church and Malolos Constitution
A194

1968, Apr. 4   **Litho.**   **Perf. 14**
987	A194	10s lt ultra & multi	8	6
988	A194	40s grn & multi	35	35
989	A194	75s multi	65	60

Issued to commemorate the centenary of the birth of Felipe G. Calderon (1868–1909), lawyer and author of the Malolos Constitution.

Earth and Transmission from Philippine Station to Satellite
A195

1968, Oct. 21   **Photo.**   **Perf. 13½**
990	A195	10s blk & multi	15	12
991	A195	40s multi	45	35
992	A195	75s multi	75	60

Issued to commemorate the inauguration of the Philcomsat Station in Tany, Luzon, May 2, 1968.

Tobacco Industry and Tobacco Board's Emblem—A196

1968, Nov. 15   **Photo.**   **Perf. 13½**
993	A.96	10s blk & multi	10	8
994	A.96	40s bl & multi	35	30
995	A.96	70s crim & multi	60	50

Philippine tobacco industry.

Kudyapi
A197

Philippine Musical Instruments: 20s, Ludag (drum). 30s, Kulintangan. 50s, Subing (bamboo flute).

1968, Nov. 22   **Photo.**   **Perf. 13½**
996	A197	10s multi	8	6
997	A197	15s multi	15	12
998	A197	30s multi	28	25
999	A197	50s multi	45	40

Concordia College
A198

1968, Dec. 8   **Perf. 13x13½**
1000	A198	10s multi	12	8
1001	A198	20s multi	20	18
1002	A198	70s multi	60	50

Issued to commemorate the centenary of the Colegio de la Concordia, Manila, a Catholic women's school. Issued Dec. 8 (Sunday), but entered the mail Dec. 9.

Singing Children
A199

PHILIPPINES

1968, Dec. 16   *Perf. 13½*

1003	A199	10s multi	10	8
1004	A199	40s multi	40	35
1005	A199	75s multi	75	60

Christmas 1968.

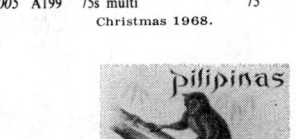

Tarsier
A200

Animals: 10s, Tamarau. 20s, Carabao. 75s, Mouse deer.

1969, Jan. 8   Photo.   *Perf. 13½*

1006	A200	2s blk & multi	5	5
1007	A200	10s multi	10	5
1008	A200	20s org & multi	15	12
1009	A200	75s grn & multi	75	60

Opening of the hunting season.

Emilio Aguinaldo and Historical Building, Cavite—A201

1969, Jan. 23   Litho.   *Perf. 14*

1010	A201	10s yel & multi	15	10
1011	A201	40s bl & multi	45	28
1012	A201	70s multi	75	60

Issued to commemorate the centenary of the birth of Emilio Aguinaldo (1869–1964), commander of Filipino forces in rebellion against Spain.

Guard Turret, San Andres Bastion, Manila, and Rotary Emblem
A202

1969, Jan. 29   Photo.   *Perf. 12½*

| 1013 | A202 | 10s ultra & multi | 12 | 8 |

Issued to commemorate the 50th anniversary of the Manila Rotary Club. See Nos. C96–C97.

Claro M. Recto
A203

1969, Feb. 10   Engraved   *Perf. 13*

| 1014 | A203 | 10s brt rose lil | 8 | 5 |

Issued to honor Senator Claro M. Recto (1890–1960), lawyer and Supreme Court judge.

PHILATELIC WEEK
NOV. 24–30, 1968

No. 973 Overprinted

1969, Feb. 14   Litho.   *Perf. 14x13½*

| 1015 | A190 | 4s multi & blk | 15 | 6 |

Issued to commemorate Philatelic Week, Nov. 24–30, 1968.

José Rizal College, Mandaluyong
A204

1969, Feb. 19   Photo.   *Perf. 13*

1016	A204	10s multi	10	8
1017	A204	40s multi	35	25
1018	A204	50s multi	45	38

Issued to commemorate the 50th anniversary of the founding of Rizal College.

No. 948 Surcharged in Red with New Value, 2 Bars and: "4th NATIONAL BOY / SCOUT JAMBOREE / PALAYAN CITY—MAY, 1969"

1969, May 12   Litho.   *Perf. 13x12½*

| 1019 | A183 | 5s on 6s multi | 12 | 8 |

Map of Philippines, Red Crescent, Cross, Lion and Sun Emblems
A205

1969, May 26   Photo.   *Perf. 12½*

1020	A205	10s gray, ultra & red	10	6
1021	A205	40s lt ultra, dk bl & red	40	25
1022	A205	75s bis, brn & red	60	55

Issued to commemorate the 50th anniversary of the League of Red Cross Societies.

Pres. and Mrs. Marcos Harvesting Miracle Rice
A206

1969, June 13   Photo.   *Perf. 14*

1023	A206	10s multi	10	6
1024	A206	40s multi	40	30
1025	A206	75s multi	60	55

Issued to publicize the introduction of IR8 (miracle) rice, produced by the International Rice Research Institute.

Holy Child of Leyte and Map of Leyte—A207

1969, June 30   *Perf. 13½*

| 1026 | A207 | 5s emer & multi | 6 | 5 |
| 1027 | A207 | 10s crim & multi | 10 | 8 |

Issued to commemorate the 80th anniversary of the return of the image of the Holy Child of Leyte to Tacloban. See No. C98.

Philippine Development Bank
A208

1969, Sept. 12   Photo.   *Perf. 13½*

1028	A208	10s dk bl, blk & grn	10	7
1029	A208	40s rose car, blk & grn	50	25
1030	A208	75s brn, blk & grn	75	55

Issued to commemorate the inauguration of the new building of the Philippine Development Bank in Makati, Rizal.

Common Birdwing
A209

Butterflies: 20s, Tailed jay. 30s, Red Helen. 40s, Birdwing.

1969, Sept. 15   Photo.   *Perf. 13½*

1031	A209	10s multi	10	6
1032	A209	20s multi	17	10
1033	A209	30s multi	30	20
1034	A209	40s multi	45	28

World's Children and UNICEF Emblem
A210

1969, Oct. 6

1035	A210	10s bl & multi	8	5
1036	A210	20s multi	15	12
1037	A210	30s multi	25	20

Issued for the 15th anniversary of Universal Children's Day.

Monument and Leyte Landing
A211

1969, Oct. 20   *Perf. 13½x14*

1038	A211	5s lt grn & multi	8	5
1039	A211	10s yel & multi	15	8
1040	A211	40s pink & multi	45	28

Issued to commemorate the 25th anniversary of the landing of the U.S. forces under Gen. Douglas MacArthur on Leyte, Oct. 20, 1944.

Philippine Cultural Center, Manila—A212

1969, Nov. 4   Photo.   *Perf. 13½*

| 1041 | A212 | 10s ultra | 10 | 8 |
| 1042 | A212 | 30s brt rose lil | 30 | 25 |

Issued to publicize the Cultural Center of the Philippines, containing theaters, a museum and libraries.

Nos. 889–892 Surcharged or Overprinted: "1969 PHILATELIC WEEK"

1969, Nov. 24   Photo.   *Perf. 14*

1043	A164	5s multi	5	5
1044	A164	5s on 6s multi	5	5
1045	A164	10s multi	12	10
1046	A164	10s on 20s multi	12	10

Philatelic Week, Nov. 23–29.

Melchora Aquino
A213

1969, Nov. 30   *Perf. 12½*

1047	A213	10s multi	8	6
1048	A213	20s multi	15	10
1049	A213	30s dk bl & multi	25	15

Issued to commemorate the 50th anniversary of the death of Melchora Aquino (Tandang Sora; 1812–1919), the Grand Old Woman of the Revolution.

No. 950 Surcharged with New Value, 2 Bars and:

"PASINAYA, IKA -2 PANUNUNGKU-LAN / PANGULONG FERDINAND E. MARCOS / DISYEMBRE 30, 1969"

1969, Dec. 30   Litho.   *Perf. 12½*

| 1050 | A184 | 5s on 6s multi | 20 | 6 |

Issued to commemorate the inauguration of Pres. Ferdinand E. Marcos and Vice Pres. Fernando Lopez for a second term, Dec. 30.

Pouring Ladle and Iligan Steel Mills—A214

1970, Jan. 20   Photo.   *Perf. 13½*

1051	A214	10s ver & multi	8	6
1052	A214	20s multi	15	12
1053	A214	30s ultra & multi	25	18

Issued to publicize the Iligan Integrated Steel Mills, Northern Mindanao, the first Philippine steel mills.

Nos. 857A, 904 and 906 Surcharged with New Value and Two Bars

Engraved

1970, Apr. 30   *Perf. 13½ Unwmkd.*

| 1054 | A158 | 4s on 6s pck bl | 5 | 5 |

Photogravure

| 1055 | A169 | 5s on 6s multi | 5 | 5 |

PHILIPPINES

Perf. 14½ Wmk. 233
1056 A170 5s on 6s pur & gold 5 5

New U.P.U. Headquarters and Monument, Bern—A215
Photogravure
1970, May 20 *Perf. 13½* Unwmkd.
1057 A215 10s bl, dk bl & yel 10 6
1058 A215 30s lt grn, dk bl & yel 32 18

Issued to commemorate the inauguration of the new Universal Postal Union Headquarters in Bern.

Emblem, Mayon Volcano and Filipina—A216
1970, Sept. 6 Photo. *Perf. 13½x14*
1059 A216 10s brt bl & multi 8 10
1060 A216 20s multi 18 12
1061 A216 30s multi 30 15

Issued to publicize the 15th International Conference on Social Welfare, Manila, Sept. 6–12.

Crab, by Alexander Calder, and Map of Philippines—A217
1970, Oct. 5 *Perf. 13½x13½*
1062 A217 10s emer & multi 12 10
1063 A217 40s multi 35 20
1064 A217 50s ultra & multi 50 30

Campaign against cancer.

Scaled Tridacna A218

Sea Shells: 10s, Royal spiny oyster. 20s, Venus comb. 40s, Glory of the sea.
1970, Oct. 19 Photo. *Perf. 13½*
1065 A218 5s blk & multi 5 5
1066 A218 10s dk grn & multi 12 6
1067 A218 20s multi 25 12
1068 A218 40s dk bl & multi 50 30

Nos. 922, 953 and 955 Surcharged **4ˢ FOUR**
Photogravure; Lithographed
1970, Oct. 26 *Perf. 13½, 12½*
1069 A175 4s on 6s multi 5 5
1070 A185 4s on 6s multi 5 5
1071 A186 4s on 6s multi 5 5

One line surcharge on No. 1071.

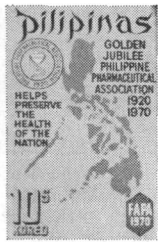

Map of Philippines and FAPA Emblem A219
1970, Nov. 16 Photo. *Perf. 13½*
1072 A219 10s dp org & multi 12 6
1073 A219 50s lt vio & multi 60 30

Issued to commemorate the opening of the 4th General Assembly of the Federation of Asian Pharmaceutical Associations (FAPA) and the 3rd Asian Congress of Pharmaceutical Sciences.

Hundred Islands of Pangasinan, Peddler's Cart—A220

Designs: 20s, Tree house in Pasonanca Park, Zamboanga City. 30s, Sugar industry, Negros Island, Mt. Kanlaon, Woman and Carabao statue, symbolizing agriculture. 2p, Miagao Church, Iloilo, and horse-drawn calesa.
1970, Nov. 12 *Perf. 12½x13½*
1074 A220 10s multi 8 8
1075 A220 20s multi 18 15
1076 A220 30s multi 27 25
1077 A220 2p multi 1.60 1.00

Tourist publicity. See Nos. 1086–1097.

No. 884 Surcharged: "UPU-AOPU / Regional Seminar / Nov. 23–Dec. 5, 1970 / TEN 10s"
1970, Nov. 22 Photo. *Perf. 13½x13*
1078 A162 10s on 6s multi 15 15

Universal Postal Union and Asian-Oceanic Postal Union Regional Seminar, Nov. 23–Dec. 5.

No. 915 Surcharged Vertically: "1970 PHILATELIC WEEK"
Perf. 14½x14
1970, Nov. 22 Wmk. 233
1079 A173 10s on 6s multi 15 5
Philatelic Week, Nov. 22–28.

Pope Paul VI, Map of Far East and Australia—A221
Unwmkd.
1970, Nov. 27 Photo. *Perf. 13½x14*
1080 A221 10s ultra & multi 12 10
1081 A221 30s multi 27 20

Visit of Pope Paul VI, Nov. 27–29, 1970. See No. C99.

Mariano Ponce A222

1970, Dec. 30 Engraved *Perf. 14½*
1082 A222 10s rose car 12 5

Mariano Ponce (1863–1918), editor and legislator. See also Nos. 1136–1137.

PATA Emblem A223

1971, Jan. 21 Photo. *Perf. 14½*
1083 A223 5s brt grn & multi 7 5
1084 A223 10s bl & multi 15 8
1085 A223 70s brn & multi 45 35

Pacific Travel Association (PATA), 20th annual conference, Manila, Jan. 21–29.

Tourist Type of 1970

Designs: 10s, Filipina and Ang Nayong (7 village replicas around man-made lagoon). 20s, Woman and fisherman, Estancia. 30s, Pagsanjan Falls. 5p, Watch Tower, Punta Cruz, Boho.
Perf. 12½x13½
1971, Feb. 15 Photogravure
1086 A220 10s multi 6 6
1087 A220 20s multi 12 10
1088 A220 30s multi 25 25
1089 A220 5p multi 2.00 2.00

1971, Apr. 19
Designs: 10s, Cultured pearl farm, Davao. 20s, Coral divers, Davao, Mindanao. 40s, Moslem Mosque, Zamboanga. 1p, Rice terraces, Banaue.
1090 A220 10s multi 8 6
1091 A220 20s multi 15 12
1092 A220 40s multi 25 18
1093 A220 1p multi 55 45

1971, May 3
Designs: 10s, Spanish cannon, Zamboanga. 30s, Magellan's cross, Cebu City. 50s, Big Jar monument in Calamba, Laguna. 70s, Mayon Volcano, Legaspi.
1094 A220 10s multi 8 6
1095 A220 30s multi 15 12
1096 A220 50s multi 25 25
1097 A220 70s multi 50 30

Family and Emblem A224
1971, March 21 Photo. *Perf. 13½*
1098 A224 20s lt grn & multi 12 10
1099 A224 40s pink & multi 25 20

Regional Conference of the International Planned Parenthood Federation for Southeast Asia and Oceania, Baguio City, March 21–27.

No. 955 Surcharged **FIVE 5ˢ**
1971, June 10 Photo. *Perf. 14x13½*
1100 A186 5s on 6s multi 15 5

Allegory of Law—A225
1971, June 15 Photo. *Perf. 13*
1101 A225 15s org & multi 12 8
60th anniversary of the University of the Philippines Law College. See No. C100.

Manila Anniversary Emblem A226
1971, June 24
1102 A226 10s multi 10 8
400th anniversary of the founding of Manila. See No. C101.

Santo Tomas University, Arms of Schools of Medicine and Pharmacology—A227
1971, July 8 Photo. *Perf. 13½*
1103 A227 5s yel & multi 8 8
Centenary of the founding of the Schools of Medicine and Surgery, and Pharmacology at the University of Santo Tomas, Manila. See No. C102.

No. 957 Surcharged

1971, July 11 *Perf. 14½* Wmk. 233
1104 A187 5s on 6s multi 7 7
World Congress of University Presidents, Manila.

Our Lady of Guia Appearing to Filipinos and Spanish Soldiers—A228
1971, July 8 Photo. *Perf. 13½*
1105 A228 10s multi 10 8
1106 A228 75s multi 50 45

4th centenary of appearance of the statue of Our Lady of Guia, Ermita, Manila.

PHILIPPINES

Bank Building, Plane, Car and Workers—A229

1971, Sept. 14   Perf. 12½

1107	A229	10s bl & multi	8	6
1108	A229	30s lt grn & multi	27	25
1109	A229	1p multi	60	50

70th anniversary of the First National City Bank in the Philippines.

No. 944 Surcharged

Perf. 12x11

1971, Nov. 24   Engr.   Unwmkd.

| 1110 | A182 | 4s on 6s bl | 10 | 5 |
| 1111 | A182 | 5s on 6s bl | 12 | 5 |

No. 957 Surcharged

1971—PHILATELIC WEEK

Photogravure

1971, Nov. 24   Perf. 14½   Wmk. 233

| 1112 | A187 | 5s on 6s multi | 8 | 6 |

Philatelic Week, 1971.

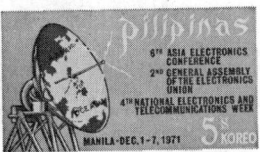
Radar with Map of Far East and Oceania—A230

1972, Feb. 29   Photo.   Perf. 14x14½

| 1113 | A230 | 5s org yel & multi | 8 | 5 |
| 1114 | A230 | 40s red org & multi | 50 | 30 |

Electronics Conferences, Manila, Dec. 1–7, 1971.

Fathers Gomez, Burgos and Zamora
A231

1972, Apr. 3   Perf. 13x12½

| 1115 | A231 | 5s gold & multi | 5 | 5 |
| 1116 | A231 | 60s gold & multi | 40 | 40 |

Centenary of the deaths of Fathers Mariano Gomez, José Burgos and Jacinto Zamora, martyrs for Philippine independence from Spain.

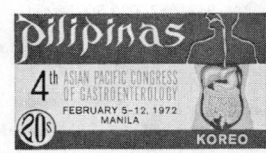
Digestive Tract—A232

1972, Apr. 11   Photo.   Perf. 12½x13

| 1117 | A232 | 20s ultra & multi | 18 | 12 |

4th Asian Pacific Congress of Gastroenterology, Manila, Feb. 5–12. See No. C103.

No. 953 Surcharged

1972, Apr. 20   Perf. 12½

| 1118 | A185 | 5s on 6s multi | 5 | 5 |

No. 069 with Two Bars over "G." and "O."

1972, May 16   Engraved   Perf. 13½

| 1119 | A158 | 50s violet | 40 | 25 |

Nos. 883A, 909 and 929 Surcharged with New Value and 2 Bars

1972, May 29   Engraved   Perf. 13½

| 1120 | A161 | 10s on 6s dp cl & blk | 10 | 5 |

Photo. Perf. 13

| 1121 | A171 | 10s on 6s multi | 10 | 5 |

Perf. 12½x13

| 1122 | A177 | 10s on 6s multi | 10 | 5 |

Independence Monument, Manila—A233

1972, May 31   Photo.   Perf. 13x12½

1123	A233	5s brt bl & multi	15	5
1124	A233	50s red & multi	75	20
1125	A233	60s emer & multi	1.00	30

Visit ASEAN countries (Association of South East Asian Nations).

"K", Skull and Crossbones
A234 EVOLUTION OF THE PHILIPPINE FLAG

Development of Philippine Flag: No. 1126, 3 "K's" in a row ("K" stands for Katipunan). No. 1127, 3 "K's" as triangle. No. 1128, One "K." No. 1130, 3 "K's," sun over mountain on white triangle. No. 1131, Sun over 3 "K's." No. 1132, Tagalog "K" in sun. No. 1133, Sun with human face. No. 1134, Tricolor flag, forerunner of present flag. No. 1135, Present flag. Nos. 1126, 1128, 1130–1131, 1133, 1135 inscribed in Tagalog.

1972, June 12   Photo.

1126	A234	5s ultra & red	28	22
1127	A234	30s ultra & red	28	22
1128	A234	30s ultra & red	28	22
1129	A234	30s ultra & blk	28	22
1130	A234	30s ultra & red	28	22
1131	A234	30s ultra & red	28	22
1132	A234	30s ultra & red	28	22
1133	A234	30s ultra & red	28	22
1134	A234	30s ultra, red & blk	28	22
1135	A234	30s ultra, yel & red	28	22
		Block of 10	2.75	2.50

Nos. 1126–1135 printed se-tenant in sheets of 50 (5x10).

Portrait Type of 1970

Portraits: 40s, Gen. Miguel Malvar. 1p, Julian Felipe.

1972   Engraved   Perf. 14

| 1136 | A222 | 40s rose red | 30 | 5 |
| 1137 | A222 | 1p dp bl | 85 | 30 |

Honoring Gen. Miguel Malvar (1865–1911), revolutionary leader, and Julian Felipe (1861–1944), composer of Philippine national anthem.

Issue dates: 40s, July 10; 1p, June 26.

Parrotfish
A235

1972, Aug. 14   Photo.   Perf. 13
Multicolored

1138	A235	5s shown	5	5
1139	A235	10s Sunburst butterflyfish	12	6
1140	A235	20s Moorish idol	25	12

Tropical fish. See No. C104.

Development Bank of the Philippines
A236

1972, Sept. 12

1141	A236	10s gray bl & multi	8	6
1142	A236	20s lil & multi	15	10
1143	A236	60s tan & multi	50	30

25th anniversary of the Development Bank of the Philippines.

Pope Paul VI—A237

1972, Sept. 26   Perf. 14   Unwmkd.

| 1144 | A237 | 10s lt grn & multi | 6 | 6 |
| 1145 | A237 | 50s lt vio & multi | 40 | 30 |

First anniversary (in 1971) of the visit of Pope Paul VI to the Philippines, and for his 75th birthday. See No. C105.

Nos. 880, 899 and 925 Surcharged with New Value and 2 Bars

1972, Sept. 29   Engr.   Perf. 13½

| 1146 | A161 | 10s on 6s lil & blk | 8 | 5 |

Photo. Perf. 12

| 1147 | A167 | 10s on 6s multi | 8 | 5 |

Perf. 14½x14   Wmk. 233

| 1148 | A176 | 10s on 6s multi | 8 | 5 |

Charon's Bark, by Resurrección Hidalgo
A238

Paintings: 10s, Rice Workers' Meal, by F. Amorsolo. 30s, "Spain and the Philippines," by Juan Luna (vert.). 70s, Song of Maria Clara, by F. Amorsolo.

Photogravure

1972, Oct. 16   Perf. 14x13   Unwmkd.

Size: 38x40mm.

| 1149 | A238 | 5s sil & multi | 5 | 5 |
| 1150 | A238 | 10s sil & multi | 10 | 6 |

Size: 24x56mm.

| 1151 | A238 | 30s sil & multi | 25 | 25 |

Size: 38x40mm.

| 1152 | A238 | 70s sil & multi | 50 | 50 |

25th anniversary of the organization of the Stamp and Philatelic Division.

Lamp, Nurse, Emblem—A239

1972, Oct. 22   Perf. 12½x13½

1153	A239	5s vio & multi	5	5
1154	A239	10s bl & multi	6	5
1155	A239	70s org & multi	40	35

50th anniversary of the Philippine Nursing Association.

Heart, Map of Philippines
A240

1972, Oct. 24   Perf. 13

1156	A240	5s pur, emer & red	5	5
1157	A240	10s bl, emer & red	10	6
1158	A240	30s emer, bl & red	25	20

"Your heart is your health," World Health Month.

First Mass on Limasawa, by Carlos V. Francisco—A241

84 PHILIPPINES

1972, Oct. 31 **Perf. 14**
1159 A241 10s brn & multi 10 8
450th anniversary of the first mass in the Philippines, celebrated by Father Valderama on Limasawa, Mar. 31, 1521. See No. C106.

Nos. 878, 882, 899 Surcharged: "ASIA PACIFIC SCOUT CONFERENCE NOV. 1972"

1972, Nov. 13 **Engr.** **Perf. 13½**
1160 A161 10s on 6s bl & blk 10 8
1161 A161 10s on 6s grn & blk 10 8
Photogravure **Perf. 12**
1162 A167 10s on 6s multi 10 8
Asia Pacific Scout Conference, Nov. 1972.

Torch, Olympic Emblems—A242
Photogravure
1972, Nov. 15 **Perf. 12½x13½**
1163 A242 5s bl & multi 5 5
1164 A242 10s multi 10 6
1165 A242 70s org & multi 50 40
20th Olympic Games, Munich, Aug. 26–Sept. 11.

Nos. 896 and 919 Surcharged with New Value, Two Bars and: "1972 PHILATELIC WEEK"

1972, Nov. 23 **Photo.** **Perf. 13½**
1166 A166 10s on 6s multi 10 10
1167 A174 10s on 6s multi 10 10
Philatelic Week 1972.

Manunggul Burial Jar, 890–710 B.C. A243
Designs: No. 1169, Ngipet Duldug Cave ritual earthenware vessel, 155 B.C. No. 1170, Metal age chalice, 200-600 A.D. No. 1171, Earthenware vessel, 15th century.

1972, Nov. 29
1168 A243 10s grn & multi 8 5
1169 A243 10s lil & multi 8 5
1170 A243 10s bl & multi 8 5
1171 A243 10s yel & multi 8 5

College of Pharmacy and Univ. of the Philippines Emblems—A244
1972, Dec. 11 **Perf. 12½x13½**
1172 A244 5s lt vio & multi 7 5
1173 A244 10s yel & multi 8 5
1174 A244 30s ultra & multi 30 20
60th anniversary of the College of Pharmacy of the University of the Philippines.

Christmas Lantern Makers, by Jorgé Pineda A245

1972, Dec. 14 **Photo.** **Perf. 12½**
1175 A245 10s dk bl & multi 10 5
1176 A245 30s brn & multi 25 15
1177 A245 50s grn & multi 40 35
Christmas 1972.

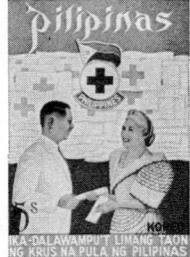

Red Cross Flags, Pres. Roxas and Mrs. Aurora Quezon A246

1972, Dec. 21
1178 A246 5s ultra & multi 5 5
1179 A246 20s multi 15 12
1180 A246 30s brn & multi 25 20
25th anniversary of the Philippine Red Cross.

Nos. 894 and 936 Surcharged with New Value and 2 Bars
1973, Jan. 22 **Photo.** **Perf. 14, 13**
1181 A246 10s on 6s multi 8 5
1182 A180 10s on 6s multi 8 5

San Luis University, Luzon—A247
1973, Mar. 1 **Photo.** **Perf. 13½x14**
1183 A247 5s multi 5 5
1184 A247 10s yel & multi 6 5
1185 A247 75s multi 45 40
60th anniversary of San Luis University, Baguio City, Luzon.

Jesus Villamor and Fighter Planes A248
1973, Apr. 9 **Photo.** **Perf. 13½x14**
1186 A248 10s multi 8 5
1187 A248 2p multi 1.10 1.10
Col. Jesus Villamor (1914–1971), World War II aviator who fought for liberation of the Philippines.

Nos. 932, 957, 070 Surcharged with New Values and 2 Bars
1973, Apr. 23 **Photo.** **Perf. 13x13½**
1188 A178 5s on 6s multi 7 5
Perf. 14½ **Wmk. 233**
1189 A187 5s on 6s multi 7 5
Engraved **Unwmkd.**
1190 A222 15s on 10s rose car 10 5
Two additional bars through "G.O." on No. 1190.

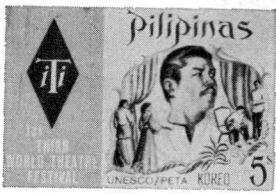

ITI Emblem, Performance and Actor Vic Silayan—A249
1973, May 15 **Photo.** **Perf. 13x12½**
1191 A249 5s bl & multi 5 5
1192 A249 10s yel grn & multi 10 6
1193 A249 50s org & multi 30 20
1194 A249 70s rose & multi 45 28
1st Third World Theater Festival, sponsored by the UNESCO affiliated International Theater Institute, Manila, Nov. 19–30, 1971.

Josefa Llanes Escoda A250

Designs: No. 1196, Gabriela Silang. No. 1197, Rafael Palma. 30s, José Rizal. 60s, Marcela Agoncillo. 90s, Teodoro R. Yangco. 1.10p, Dr. Pio Valenzuela. 1.20p, Gregoria de Jesus. No. 1204, Pedro A. Paterna. No. 1205, Teodora Alonso. 1.80p, Edilberto Evangelista. 5p, Fernando M. Guerrero.

1973–78 **Engraved** **Perf. 14½**
1195 A250 15s sepia 8 5
Lithographed **Perf. 12½**
1196 A250 15s vio ('74) 8 5
1197 A273 15s emer ('74) 8 5
1198 A250 30s vio bl ('78) 10 5
1199 A250 60s dl red brn 35 35
1200 A273 90s brt bl ('74) 45 22
1201 A273 1.10p brt bl ('74) 55 25
1202 A250 1.20p dl red ('78) 40 20
1203 A250 1.50p lil rose 75 65
1204 A273 1.50p brn ('74) 75 30
1205 A250 1.80p green 90 80
1206 A250 5p blue 2.50 2.50
Nos. 1195-1208 (12) 6.99 5.47

1973–74 **Imperf.**
1196a A250 15s vio ('74) 10 10
1197a A273 15s emer ('74) 10 10
1199a A250 60s dl red brn 36 36
1200a A273 90s brt bl ('74) 55 50
1202a A273 1.10p brt bl ('74) 65 65
1204a A273 1.50p lil rose 65 65
1205a A273 1.50p brn ('74) 90 90
1206a A250 1.80p green 90 90
1208a A250 5p blue 2.50 2.50
Nos. 1196a-1208a (9) 6.81 6.66

Honoring: Josefa Llanes Escoda (1898–1942), leader of Girl Scouts and Federation of Women's Clubs (No. 1195). Gabriela Silang (1731–1763), "the Ilocana Joan of Arc" (No. 1196). Rafael Palma (1874–1939), journalist, statesman, educator (No. 1197). Marcela Agoncillo (1859–1946), designer of first Philippine flag, 1898 (60s). Teodoro R. Yangco (1861–1939), patriot and philanthropist (90s). Dr. Pio Valenzuela (1869–1956), physician and newspaperman (1.10p). Pedro A. Paterno (1857–1911), lawyer, writer, patriot (No. 1204). Teodora Alonso (1827–1911), mother of José Rizal (No. 1205). Edilberto Evangelista (1862–1897), army engineer, patriot (1.80p). Fernando Maria Guerrero (1873–1929), journalist, political leader (5p). José Rizal (1861–1896), national hero. Gregoria de Jesus, independence leader.

No. 857A surcharged with New Value and 2 Bars in Black and Overprinted in Red: "HELP ME STOP / SMUGGLING / Pres. MARCOS"
1973, June 4 **Engraved** **Perf. 13½**
1209 A158 5s on 6s pck bl 5 5
Anti-smuggling campaign.

No. 925 Surcharged
1973, June 4 **Wmk. 233**
1210 A176 5s on 6s multi 5 5
10th anniversary of death of John F. Kennedy (1917–1963).

Pres. Marcos, Farm Family, Unfurling of Philippine Flag—A251
Perf. 12½x13½
1973, Sept. 24 **Photo.** **Unwmkd.**
1211 A251 15s ultra & multi 10 10
1212 A251 45s red & multi 25 25
1213 A251 90s multi 50 50
75th anniversary of Philippine independence and 1st anniversary of proclamation of martial law.

Imelda Romualdez Marcos A252
1973, Oct. 31 **Photo.** **Perf. 13**
1214 A252 15s dl bl & multi 10 10
1215 A252 50s multi 28 28
1216 A252 60s lil & multi 35 35
Imelda Romualdez Marcos, First Lady of the Philippines.

Presidential Palace, Manila, Pres. and Mrs. Marcos—A253
1973, Nov. 15 **Litho.** **Perf. 14**
1217 A253 15s rose & multi 10 10
1218 A253 50s ultra & multi 25 25
See No. C107.

INTERPOL Emblem A254

PHILIPPINES

1973, Dec. 18   Photo.   *Perf. 13*
| 1219 | A254 | 15s ultra & multi | 15 | 10 |
| 1220 | A254 | 65s lt grn & multi | 45 | 25 |

50th anniversary of International Criminal Police Organization.

Cub and Boy Scouts — A255

Design: 15s, Various Scout activities; inscribed in Tagalog.

1973–74   Lithographed   *Perf. 12½*
1221	A255	15s bis & emer	12	10
a.		Imperf. ('74)	15	15
1222	A255	65s bis & brt bl	42	35
a.		Imperf. ('74)	60	60

50th anniversary of Philippine Boy Scouts.

Issue dates: Nos. 1221–1222, Dec. 28, 1973. Nos. 1221a–1222a, Feb. 4, 1974, although first day covers are dated Dec. 28, 1973.

Manila, Bank Emblem and Farmers — A256

Designs: 60s, Old bank building. 1.50p, Modern bank building.

1974, Jan. 3   Photo.   *Perf. 12½x13½*
1223	A256	15s sil & multi	8	6
1224	A256	60s sil & multi	30	18
1225	A256	1.50p sil & multi	75	45

25th anniversary of the Central Bank of the Philippines.

UPU Emblem, Maria Clara Costume — A257

Filipino Costumes: 60s, Balintawak and UPU emblem. 80s, Malong costume and UPU emblem.

1974, Jan. 15   *Perf. 12½*
1226	A257	15s multi	8	6
1227	A257	60s multi	32	20
1228	A257	80s multi	45	28

Centenary of Universal Postal Union.

No. 1192 Surcharged in Red with New Value, 2 Bars and: "1973 / PHILATELIC WEEK"

1974, Feb. 4   Photo.   *Perf. 13x12½*
| 1229 | A249 | 15s on 10s multi | 12 | 6 |

Philatelic Week, 1973. First day covers exist dated Nov. 26, 1973.

Nos. 1186 and 1136 Overprinted and Surcharged

1974, Mar. 25   Photo.   *Perf. 13½x14*
| 1230 | A248 | 15s on 10s multi | 8 | 6 |

Engraved   *Perf. 14*
| 1231 | A222 | 45s on 40s rose red | 22 | 18 |

25th anniversary of Lions International of the Philippines. The overprint on No. 1230 arranged to fit shape of stamp.

Pediatrics Congress Emblem and Map of Participating Countries — A258

1974, Apr. 30   Litho.   *Perf. 12½*
1232	A258	30s brt bl & red	15	9
a.		Imperf.	20	12
1233	A258	1p dl grn & red	50	30
a.		Imperf.	65	50

Asian Congress of Pediatrics, Manila, Apr. 30–May 4.

Nos. 912, 954–955 Surcharged with New Value and Two Bars   *Perf. 14½*
| 1234 | A172 | 5s on 3s multi | 5 | 5 |

Litho.   *Perf. 12½   Unwmkd.*
| 1235 | A185 | 5s on 6s multi | 5 | 5 |

Photo.   *Perf. 14x13½*
| 1236 | A186 | 5s on 6s multi | 5 | 5 |

WPY Emblem — A259

1974, Aug. 15   Litho.   *Perf. 12½*
1237	A259	5s org & blk blk	5	5
a.		Imperf.	5	5
1238	A259	2p lt grn & dk bl	90	50
a.		Imperf.	1.00	75

World Population Year, 1974.

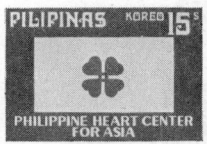

Red Feather Community Chest Emblem — A260

Wmk. 372
Wmkd. "K" and "P" Multiple (372)

1974, Sept. 5   Litho.   *Perf. 12½*
1239	A260	15s brt bl & red	10	5
a.		Imperf.	15	15
1240	A260	40s emer & red	25	15
a.		Imperf.	30	30
1241	A260	45s red brn & red	30	15
a.		Imperf.	30	30

25th anniversary of the Philippine Community Chest.

Sultan Kudarat, Flag, Order and Map of Philippines — A261

Perf. 13½x14

1975, Jan. 13   Photo.   *Unwmkd.*
| 1242 | A261 | 15s multi | 12 | 5 |

Sultan Mohammad Dipatuan Kudarat, 16th–17th century ruler.

Mental Health Association Emblem — A262

Lithographed

1975, Jan. 20   *Perf. 12½   Wmk. 372*
1243	A262	45s emer & org	20	15
a.		Imperf.	30	30
1244	A262	1p emer & pur	40	30
a.		Imperf.	50	50

Philippine Mental Health Association, 25th anniversary.

4-Leaf Clover — A263

1975, Feb. 14
1245	A263	15s vio bl & red	8	5
a.		Imperf.	14	14
1246	A263	50s emer & red	20	20
a.		Imperf.	28	28

Philippine Heart Center for Asia, inauguration.

Military Academy, Cadet and Emblem — A264

Perf. 13½x14

1975, Feb. 17   Unwmkd.
| 1247 | A264 | 15s grn & multi | 15 | 10 |
| 1248 | A264 | 45s plum & multi | 38 | 25 |

Philippine Military Academy, 70th anniversary.

Helping the Disabled — A265

Perf. 12½, Imperf.

1975, Mar. 17   Wmk. 372
| 1249 | A265 | Block of 10 | 2.40 | 2.00 |
| a. | | Imperf. (any perf) | 18 | 12 |

25th anniversary (in 1974) of Philippine Orthopedic Association.

Nos. B43, B50–B51 Surcharged with New Value and Two Bars

Litho., *Perf. 12½*; Photo., *Perf. 13½*

1975, Apr. 15   Unwmkd.
1250	SP18	5s on 15s+5s	5	5
1251	SP16	60s on 70s+5s	35	30
1252	SP18	1p on 1.10p+5s	40	35

"Grow and Preserve Forests"
A266   A267

1975, May 19   Litho.   *Perf. 14½*
| 1253 | A266 | 45s blk, brn & grn | 22 | 15 |
| 1254 | A267 | 45s blk, brn & grn | 22 | 15 |

Forest conservation. Nos. 1253–1254 printed se-tenant in sheets of 100.

Jade Vine — A268

1975, June 9   Photo.   *Perf. 14½*
| 1255 | A268 | 15s multi | 15 | 5 |

Imelda R. Marcos, IWY Emblem — A269

Civil Service Emblem — A270

PHILIPPINES

Wmk. 372
1975, July 2   Litho.   *Perf. 12½*

1256	A269	15s bl & blk	12	12
a.		Imperf.	15	15
1257	A269	80s pink, bl & grn	50	40
a.		Imperf.	50	50

International Women's Year 1975.

1975, Sept. 19   Litho.   *Perf. 12½*

1258	A270	15s multi	10	8
a.		Imperf.	12	12
1259	A270	50s multi	20	15
a.		Imperf.	32	32

Dam and Emblem A271

1975, Sept. 30

1260	A271	40s org & vio bl	15	15
a.		Imperf.	25	25
1261	A271	1.50p brt rose & vio bl	65	50
a.		Imperf.	80	80

Manila Harbor, 1875 A272

Perf. 13x13½

1975, Nov. 4   Unwmkd.

| 1262 | A272 | 1.50p red & multi | 70 | 40 |

Hong Kong and Shanghai Banking Corporation, centenary of Phillipines service.

Norberto Romualdez (1875–1941), Scholar and Legislator A273

Jose Rizal Monument, Luneta Park A273a

Noted Filipinos: No. 1264, Rafael Palma (1874–1939), journalist, statesman, educator. No. 1265, Rajah Kalantiaw, chief of Panay, author of ethical-penal code (1443). 65s, Emilio Jacinto (1875–1899), patriot. No. 1269, Gen. Gregorio del Pilar (1875–1899), military hero. No. 1270, Lope K. Santos (1879–1963), grammarian, writer. 1.60p, Felipe Agoncillo (1859–1941), lawyer, cabinet member.

Lithographed
1975-81   *Perf. 12½*   Wmk. 372

1264	A273	30s brn ('77)	8	5
1265	A273	30s dp rose ('78)	8	5
1266	A273a	40s yel & blk ('81)	22	10
1267	A273	60s violet	22	10
			35	35
1268	A273	65s lil rose	25	10
a.		Imperf.	38	38
1269	A273	90s lil rose	33	12
a.		Imperf.	50	50
1270	A273	90s grn ('78)	24	10
1272	A273	1.60p blk ('76)	75	25
		Nos. 1264-1272 (8)	2.17	87

See Nos. 1195-1208.

A274

1975, Nov. 22   Litho.   *Perf. 12½*

1275	A274	60s multi	25	20
1276	A274	1.50p multi	60	50

40th anniversary of 1st landing of the Pan American World Airways China Clipper in the Philippines.

Nos. 1199 and 1205 Overprinted

AIRMAIL EXHIBITION NOV 22-DEC 9

1975, Nov. 22   Unwmkd.

1277	A250	60s dl red brn	25	25
1278	A273	1.50p brown	50	50

Airmail Exhibition, Nov. 22–Dec. 9.

APO Emblem A275

1975, Nov. 24   Wmk. 372

1279	A275	5s ultra & multi	8	5
a.		Imperf.	10	10
1280	A275	1p bl & multi	55	40
a.		Imperf.	60	60

Amateur Philatelists' Organization, 25th anniversary.

San Agustin Church A276

Philippine Churches: 30s, Morong Church (horiz.). 45s, Basilica of Taal (horiz.). 60s, San Sebastian Church.

1975, Dec. 23   Litho.   *Perf. 12½*

1281	A276	20s bluish grn	12	12
a.		Imperf.	20	20
1282	A276	30s yel org & blk	18	12
a.		Imperf.	25	25
1283	A276	45s rose, brn & blk	25	18
a.		Imperf.	30	30
1284	A276	60s yel, bis & blk	30	25
a.		Imperf.	50	50

Holy Year 1975.

Conductor's Hands A277

1976, Jan. 27

1285	A277	5s org & multi	5	5
1286	A277	50s multi	30	25

Manila Symphony Orchestra, 50th anniversary.

PAL Planes of 1946 and 1976 A278

1976, Feb. 14

1287	A278	60s bl & multi	25	15
1288	A278	1.50p red & multi	65	50

Philippine Airlines, 30th anniversary.

National University A279

1976, Mar. 30

1289	A279	45s bl, vio bl & yel	20	15
1290	A279	60s lt bl, vio bl & pink	30	20

National University, 75th anniversary.

Eye Examination A280

1976, Apr. 7   Litho.   *Perf. 12½*

| 1291 | A280 | 15s multi | 12 | 5 |

World Health Day: "Foresight prevents blindness."

Book and Emblem A281

1976, May 24   Unwmkd.

| 1292 | A281 | 1.50p grn & multi | 70 | 60 |

National Archives, 75th anniversary.

Santo Tomas University, Emblems A282

1976, June 7   Wmk. 372

1293	A282	15s yel & multi	10	5
1294	A282	50s multi	25	20

Colleges of Education and Science, Santo Tomas University, 50th anniversary.

Maryknoll College—A283

Wmk. 372

1976, July 26   Litho.   *Perf. 12½*

1295	A283	15s lt bl & multi	10	5
1296	A283	1.50p bis & multi	65	50

Maryknoll College, Quezon City, 50th anniversary.

No. 1164 Surcharged in Dark Violet

15s = Montreal 1976 21st OLYMPICS CANADA

1976, July 30   Photo.   *Perf. 12½x13½*

| 1297 | A242 | 15s on 10s multi | 15 | 10 |

21st Olympic Games, Montreal, Canada, July 17–Aug. 1.

Police College, Manila—A284

1976, Aug. 8   Litho.   *Perf. 12½*

1298	A284	15s multi	10	8
a.		Imperf.	15	15
1299	A284	60s multi	30	20
a.		Imperf.	50	50

Philippine Constabulary, 75th anniversary.

Surveyors—A285

1976, Sept. 2   Wmk. 372

| 1300 | A285 | 80s multi | 35 | 30 |

Bureau of Lands, 75th anniversary.

Monetary Fund and World Bank Emblems A286

Virgin of Antipollo A287

1976, Oct. 4   Litho.   *Perf. 12½*

1301	A286	60s multi	25	20
1302	A286	1.50p multi	65	50

Joint Annual Meeting of the Board of Governors of the International Monetary Fund and the World Bank, Manila, Oct. 4–8.

PHILIPPINES

1976, Nov. 26   *Perf. 12½*
1303   A287   30s multi   12   8
1304   A287   90s multi   32   22

Virgin of Antipolo, Our Lady of Peace and Good Voyage, 350th anniversary of arrival of statue in the Philippines and 50th anniversary of the canonical coronation.

No. 1184 Surcharged with New Value and 2 Bars and Overprinted:
"1976 PHILATELIC WEEK"
Unwmkd.
1976, Nov. 26 Photo.   *Perf. 13½x14*
1305   A247   30s on 10s multi   12   8

Philatelic Week 1976.

People Going to Church
A288

Wmk. 372
1976, Dec. 1   Litho.   *Perf. 12½*
1306   A288   15s bl & multi   5   5
1307   A288   30s bl & multi   18   10

Christmas 1976.

Symbolic Diamond and Book
A289

Galicano Apacible
A290

1976, Dec. 13
1308   A289   30s grn & multi   15   10
1309   A289   75s grn & multi   35   25

Philippine Educational System, 75th anniversary.

No. 1202 and 1208 Surcharged with New Value and 2 Bars
1977, Jan. 17   **Unwmkd.**
1310   A273   1.20p on 1.10p bl   50   40
1311   A250   3p on 5p bl   1.00   90

Wmk. 372
1977   Lithographed   *Perf. 12½*
Design: 30s, José Rizal.
1313   A290   30s multi   12   5
1318   A290   2.30p multi   80   55

Dr. José Rizal (1861-1896) physician, poet and national hero (30s). Dr. Galicano Apacible (1864-1949), physician, statesman (2.30p).
Issue dates: 30s, Feb. 16; 2.30p, Jan. 24.

Emblem, Flags, Map of AOPU
A291

1977, Apr. 1   **Wmk. 372**
1322   A291   50s multi   15   10
1323   A291   1.50p multi   50   40

Asian-Oceanic Postal Union (AOPU), 15th anniversary.

Cogwheels and Worker
A292

1977, Apr. 21   *Perf. 12½*
1324   A292   90s blk & multi   40   35
1325   A292   2.30p blk & multi   75   65

Asian Development Bank, 10th anniversary.

Farmer at Work and Receiving Money
A293

1977, May 14   Litho.   **Wmk. 372**
1326   A293   30s org red & multi   12   5

National Commission on Countryside Credit and Collection, campaign to strengthen the rural credit system.

Solicitor General's Emblem
A294

1977, June 30   Litho.   *Perf. 12½*
1327   A294   1.65p multi   50   30

Office of the Solicitor General, 75th anniversary.

Conference Emblem
A295

1977, July 29   Litho.   *Perf. 12½*
1328   A295   2.20p bl & multi   70   40

8th World Conference of the World Peace through Law Center, Manila, Aug. 21-26.

ASEAN Emblem
A296

1977, Aug. 8
1329   A296   1.50p grn & multi   55   30

Association of South East Asian Nations (ASEAN), 10th anniversary.

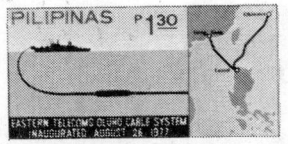

Cable-laying Ship, Map Showing Cable Route—A297
1977, Aug. 26   Litho.   *Perf. 12½*
1330   A297   1.30p multi   45   30

Inauguration of underwater telephone cable linking Okinawa, Luzon and Hong Kong.

President Marcos
A298

1977, Sept. 11   **Wmk. 372**
1331   A298   30s multi   12   5
1332   A298   2.30p multi   85   55

Ferdinand E. Marcos, president of the Philippines, 60th birthday.

People Raising Flag
A299

1977, Sept. 21   Litho.   *Perf. 12½*
1333   A299   30s multi   12   5
1334   A299   2.30p multi   85   55

5th anniversary of "New Society."

Bishop Gregorio Aglipay
A300

1977, Oct. 1   Litho.   *Perf. 12½*
1335   A300   30s multi   10   5
1336   A300   90s multi   35   20

Philippine Independent Aglipayan Church, 75th anniversary.

Fairchild FC-2 over World Map—A301
1977, Oct. 28   **Wmk. 372**
1337   A301   2.30p multi   80   50

First scheduled Pan American airmail service, Key West to Havana, 50th anniversary.

No. 1280 Surcharged with New Value, 2 Bars and Overprinted in Red:
"1977 / PHILATELIC / WEEK"
1977, Nov. 22   Litho.   *Perf. 12½*
1338   A275   90s on 1p multi   30   20

Philatelic Week.

Children Celebrating and Star from Lantern
A302

1977, Dec. 1   **Unwmkd.**
1339   A302   30s multi   12   5
1340   A302   45s multi   22   8

Christmas 1977.

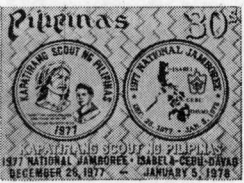

Scouts and Map showing Jamboree Locations—A303
1977, Dec. 27
1341   A303   30s multi   12   5

National Boy Scout Jamboree, Tumauini, Isabela; Capitol Hills, Cebu City; Mariano Marcos, Davao, Dec. 27, 1977–Jan. 5, 1978.

Far Eastern University Arms
A304

1978, Jan. 26   Litho.   **Wmk. 372**
1342   A304   30s gold & multi   12   5

Far Eastern University, 50th anniversary.

Sipa
A305

Designs: Various positions of Sipa ballgame.
1978, Feb. 28   *Perf. 12½*
1343   A305   5s bl & multi   5   5
1344   A305   10s bl & multi   5   5
1345   A305   40s bl & multi   18   10
1346   A305   75s bl & multi   38   5

Nos. 1343-1346 printed se-tenant with continuous design.

87

PHILIPPINES

Arms of Meycauayan—A306
1978, Apr. 21   Litho.   Perf. 12½
1347 A306 1.05p multi   35   18
400th anniversary of Meycauayan, founded 1578–1579.

Moro Vinta and UPU Emblem A307
Designs (UPU Emblem and): 2.50p, No. 1350b, Horse-drawn mail cart. No. 1350a, like 5p. No. 1350c, Steam locomotive. No. 1350d, Three-master.
1978, June 9   Litho.   Perf. 13½
1348 A307 2.50p multi   90   60
1349 A307 5p multi   1.80 1.20
Souvenir Sheet   Perf. 12½x13
1350   Sheet of 4   15.00
 a. A307 7.50p multi   3.25 3.25
 b. A307 7.50p multi   3.25 3.25
 c. A307 7.50p multi   3.25 3.25
 d. A307 7.50p multi   3.25 3.25
CAPEX International Philatelic Exhibition, Toronto, Ont., June 9–18. No. 1350 has red marginal inscription. Size of stamps: 36½x25mm; sheet: 90x73mm. No. 1350 exists imperf. in changed colors.

Andres Bonifacio Monument, by Guillermo Tolentino—A308
Wmk. 372
1978, July 10   Litho.   Perf. 12½
1351 A308 30s multi   12   5

Rook, Knight and Globe A309
1978, July 17
1352 A309 30s vio bl & red   10   5
1353 A309 2p vio bl & red   65   45
World Chess Championship, Anatoly Karpov and Viktor Korchnoi, Baguio City, 1978.

Miners A310
1978, Aug. 12   Litho.   Perf. 12½
1354 A310 2.30p multi   70   40
75th anniversary of Benguet gold mining industry.

Manuel Quezon and Quezon Memorial A311
1978, Aug. 19
1355 A311 30s multi   8   5
1356 A311 1p multi   35   15
Manuel Quezon (1878–1944), first president of Commonwealth of the Philippines.

Law Association Emblem, Philippine Flag—A312
1978, Aug. 27   Litho.   Perf. 12½
1357 A312 2.30p multi   70   50
58th International Law Conference, Manila, Aug. 27–Sept. 2.

Sergio Osmeña A313
1978, Sept. 8
1358 A313 30s multi   8   5
1359 A313 1p multi   35   15
Pres. Sergio Osmeña (1878–1961).

Map Showing Cable Route, Cable-laying Ship—A314
1978, Sept. 30
1360 A314 1.40p multi   45   28
ASEAN Submarine Cable Network, Philippines-Singapore cable system, inauguration.

Basketball, Games' Emblem A315
1978, Oct. 1
1361 A315 30s multi   8   5
1362 A315 2.30p multi   70   50
8th Men's World Basketball Championship, Manila, Oct. 1–15.

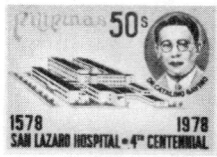
San Lazaro Hospital and Dr. Catalino Gavino—A316
1978, Oct. 13   Litho.   Perf. 12½
1363 A316 50s multi   18   6
1364 A316 90s multi   30   15
San Lazaro Hospital, 400th anniversary.

Nurse Vaccinating Child A317
1978, Oct. 24
1365 A317 30s multi   10   5
1366 A317 1.50p multi   55   30
Eradication of smallpox.

No. 1268 Surcharged

1978, Nov. 23
1367 A273 60s on 65s lil rose 22   10
Philatelic Week.

"The Telephone Across Country and World"
A318   A319
Wmk. 372
1978, Nov. 28   Litho.   Perf. 12½
1368 A318 30s multi   10   5
1369 A319 2p multi   65   45
Philippine Long Distance Telephone Company, 50th anniversary. Nos. 1368–1369 printed se-tenant in sheets of 30.

A little time given to study of the arrangement of the Scott Catalogue can make it easier to use effectively.

Traveling Family—A320
1978, Nov. 28
1370 A320 30s multi   10   5
1371 A320 1.35p multi   50   20
Decade of Philippine children.

Church and Arms of Agoo A321
1978, Dec. 7   Litho.   Perf. 12½
1372 A321 30s multi   12   5
1373 A321 45s multi   18   8
400th anniversary of the founding of Agoo.

Church and Arms of Balayan A322
1978, Dec. 8
1374 A322 30s multi   10   5
1375 A322 90s multi   32   15
400th anniversary of the founding of Balayan.

Dr. Honoria Acosta Sison A323
1978, Dec. 15
1376 A323 30s multi   12   5
Dr. Honoria Acosta Sison (1888–1970), first Philippine woman physician.

Family, Houses, U.N. Emblem—A324
1978, Dec.   Litho.   Perf. 12½
1377 A324 30s multi   10   5
1378 A324 3p multi   1.00   60
30th anniversary of Universal Declaration of Human Rights.

Chaetodon Trifasciatus A325
Fish: 1.20p, Balistoides niger. 2.20p, Rhinecanthus aculeatus. 2.30p, Chelmon rostratus. No. 1383, Chaetodon mertensi. No. 1384, Euxiphipops xanthometapon.

PHILIPPINES

1978, Dec. 29			Perf. 14	
1379	A325	30s multi	10	5
1380	A325	1.20p multi	40	15
1381	A325	2.20p multi	65	35
1382	A325	2.30p multi	70	40
1383	A325	5p multi	1.60	85
1384	A325	5p multi	1.60	85
	Nos. 1379-1384 (6)		5.05	2.65

Carlos P. Romulo,
U.N. Emblem—A326

1979, Jan. 14		Litho.	Perf. 12½	
1385	A326	30s multi	10	5
1386	A326	2p multi	75	40

Carlos P. Romulo (b. 1899–), president of U.N. General Assembly and Security Council.

Rotary Emblem and "60" A327

Rosa Sevilla de Alvero A328

1979, Jan. 26			Wmk. 372	
1387	A327	30s multi	12	5
1388	A327	2.30p multi	85	35

Rotary Club of Manila, 60th anniversary.

1979, Mar. 4		Litho.	Perf. 12½	
1389	A328	30s rose	10	5

Rosa Sevilla de Alvero, educator and writer, birth centenary.

Oil Well and Map of Palawan A329

Wmk. 372

1979, Mar. 21		Litho.	Perf. 12½	
1390	A329	30s multi	12	5
1391	A329	45s multi	18	8

First Philippine oil production, Nido Oil Reef Complex, Palawan.

Merrill's Fruit Doves—A330

Birds: 1.20p, Brown tit babbler. 2.20p, Mindoro imperial pigeons. 2.30p, Steere's pittas. No. 1396, Koch's red-breasted pittas. No. 1397, Philippine eared nightjar.

Perf. 14x13½

1979, Apr. 16			Unwmkd.	
1392	A330	30s multi	10	5
1393	A330	1.20p multi	40	15
1394	A330	2.20p multi	65	35
1395	A330	2.30p multi	70	40
1396	A330	5p multi	1.60	85
1397	A330	5p multi	1.60	85
	Nos. 1392-1397 (6)		5.05	2.65

Association Emblem and Reader A331

Wmk. 372

1979, Apr. 3		Litho.	Perf. 12½	
1398	A331	30s multi	10	5
1399	A331	75s multi	25	10
1400	A331	1p multi	35	12

Association of Special Libraries of the Philippines, 25th anniversary.

UNCTAD Emblem A332

Wmk. 372

1979, May 3		Litho.	Perf. 12½	
1401	A332	1.20p multi	35	15
1402	A332	2.30p multi	75	30

5th Session of United Nations Conference on Trade and Development, Manila, May 3–June 1.

Civet Cat A333

1979, May 14			Perf. 14	
1403	A333	30s multi	10	5
1404	A333	1.20p multi	40	20
1405	A333	2.20p multi	65	35
1406	A333	2.30p multi	70	40
1407	A333	5p multi	1.60	85
1408	A333	5p multi	1.60	85
	Nos. 1403-1408 (6)		5.05	2.70

Philippine Animals: 1.20p, Macaque. 2.20p, Wild boar. 2.30p, Dwarf leopard. No. 1407, Asiatic dwarf otter. No. 1408, Anteater.

Dish Antenna A334

Design: 1.30p, World map.

1979, May 17		Litho.	Perf. 12½	
1409	A334	90s multi	28	10
1410	A334	1.30p multi	42	15

11th World Telecommunications Day, May 17.

Mussaenda Donna Evangelina A335

Philippine Mussaendas: 1.20p, Dona Esperanza. 2.20p, Dona Hilaria. 2.30p, Dona Aurora. No. 1415, Gining Imelda. No. 1416, Dona Trining.

1979, June 11		Litho.	Perf. 14	
1411	A335	30s multi	10	5
1412	A335	1.20p multi	40	5
1413	A335	2.20p multi	65	35
1414	A335	2.30p multi	70	40
1415	A335	5p multi	1.60	85
1416	A335	5p multi	1.60	85
	Nos. 1411-1416 (6)		3.15	1.70

Manila Cathedral, Coat of Arms A336

1979, June 25		Litho.	Perf. 12½	
1417	A336	30s multi	10	5
1418	A336	75s multi	25	10
1419	A336	90s multi	30	15

Archdiocese of Manila, 400th anniversary.

Patrol Boat, Naval Arms A337

1979, June 26				
1420	A337	30s multi	8	5
1421	A337	45s multi	12	8

Philippine Navy Day.

Man Breaking Chains, Broken Syringe A338

1979, July 23		Litho.	Perf. 12½	
1422	A338	30s multi	10	5
1423	A338	90s multi	30	15
1424	A338	1.05p multi	38	18

Fight drug abuse.

Afghan Hound—A339

Designs: 90s, Striped tabbies. 1.20p, Dobermann pinscher. 2.20p, Siamese cats. 2.30p, German shepherd. 5p, Chinchilla cats.

1979, Aug. 6			Perf. 14	
1425	A339	30s multi	10	5
1426	A339	90s multi	30	15
1427	A339	1.20p multi	42	20
1428	A339	2.20p multi	70	25
1429	A339	2.30p multi	75	65
1430	A339	5p multi	1.60	75
	Nos. 1425-1430 (6)		3.87	2.05

Children Playing, IYC Emblem A340

Designs: Children playing and IYC emblem (diff.).

1979, Aug. 31		Litho.	Perf. 12½	
1431	1340	15s multi	5	5
1432	1340	20s multi	8	5
1433	1340	25s multi	10	5
1434	A340	1.20p multi	30	15

International Year of the Child.

Hands Holding Emblem A341

1979, Sept. 27		Litho.	Perf. 12½	
1435	A341	30s multi	8	5
1436	A341	1.35p multi	42	15

Methodism in the Philippines, 80th anniversary.

Emblem and Coins—A342

Wmk. 372

1979, Nov. 15		Litho.	Perf. 12½	
1437	A342	30s multi	8	5

Philippine Numismatic and Antiquarian Society, 50th anniversary.

Concorde over Manila and Paris—A343

Design: 2.20p, Concorde over Manila.

1979, Nov. 22				
1438	A343	1.05p multi	32	25
1439	A343	2.20p multi	70	50

Air France service to Manila, 25th anniversary.

No. 1272 Surcharged in Red

1979, Nov. 23				
1440	A273	90s on 1.60p blk	30	15

Philatelic Week. Surcharge similar to No. 1367.

Transport Association Emblem—A344

1979, Nov. 27				
1441	A344	75s multi	25	12
1442	A344	2.30p multi	70	50

International Air Transport Association, 35th annual general meeting, Manila.

Unused Prices

Catalogue prices for unused stamps through 1960 are for hinged copies in fine condition.

Local Government Year—A345

1979, Dec. 14   Litho.   *Perf. 12½*
| 1443 | A345 | 30s multi | 12 | 8 |
| 1444 | A345 | 45s multi | 18 | 12 |

Mother and Children, Ornament—A346

Christmas 1979: 90s, Stars.

1979, Dec. 17
| 1445 | A346 | 30s multi | 12 | 8 |
| 1446 | A346 | 90s multi | 35 | 22 |

Rheumatic Pain Spots and Congress Emblem A347

Wmk. 372

1980, Jan. 20   Litho.   *Perf. 12½*
| 1447 | A347 | 30s multi | 16 | 8 |
| 1448 | A347 | 90s multi | 48 | 22 |

Southeast Asia and Pacific Area League Against Rheumatism, 4th Congress, Manila, Jan. 19-24.

Gen. Douglas MacArthur—A348

Designs: 30s, MacArthur's birthplace (Little Rock, Ark) and burial place (Norfolk, Va.). 2.30p, MacArthur's cap, sunglasses and pipe. 5p, MacArthur and troops wading ashore at Leyte, Oct. 20, 1944.

1980, Jan. 26   Wmk. 372   *Perf. 12½*
1449	A348	30s multi	16	8
1450	A348	75s multi	35	18
1451	A348	2.30p multi	1.15	75

Souvenir Sheet
| 1452 | A348 | 5p multi | 2.75 | 1.50 |

Gen. Douglas MacArthur (1880-1964). Margin of No. 1452 contains signature and quote. Size: 76×76mm.

COLORS
Please refer to page v for a complete list of color abbreviations used in this book.

Knights of Columbus of Philippines, 75th Anniversary—A349

1980, Feb. 14
| 1453 | A349 | 30s multi | 16 | 8 |
| 1454 | A349 | 1.35p multi | 68 | 40 |

Philippine Military Academy, 75th Anniversary—A350

Wmk. 372

1980, Feb. 17   Litho.   *Perf. 12½*
| 1455 | A350 | 30s multi | 16 | 8 |
| 1456 | A350 | 1.20p multi | 60 | 30 |

Philippines Women's University, 75th Anniversary—A351

1980, Feb. 21
| 1457 | A351 | 30s multi | 16 | 8 |
| 1458 | A351 | 1.05p multi | 55 | 25 |

Disaster Relief—A352

Rotary International, 75th Anniversary (Paintings by Carlos Botong Francisco): Nos. 1459 and 1460 each in continuous design.

1980, Feb. 23   *Perf. 12½*
1459		Strip of 5, dp yel & multi	80	40
a.		30s, single stamp	16	8
1460		Strip of 5, yel grn & multi	5.75	2.75
a.		2.30p, single stamp	1.15	75

6th Centenary of Islam in Philippines—A353

Wmk. 372

1980, Mar. 28   Litho.   *Perf. 12½*
| 1461 | A353 | 30s multi | 16 | 8 |
| 1462 | A353 | 1.30p multi | 65 | 30 |

Hand Crushing Cigarette, WHO Emblem—A354

1980, Apr. 14
| 1463 | A354 | 30s multi | 16 | 8 |
| 1464 | A354 | 75s multi | 35 | 20 |

World Health Day (Apr. 7); anti-smoking campaign.

Philippine Girl Scouts, 40th Anniversary—A355

Wmk. 372

1980, May 26   Litho.   *Perf. 12½*
| 1465 | A355 | 30s multi | 16 | 8 |
| 1466 | A355 | 2p multi | 55 | 28 |

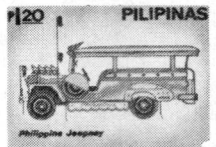
Jeepney (Public Jeep)—A356

1980, June 24   Litho.   *Perf. 12½*
| 1467 | A356 | 30s *Jeepney* (diff.) | 16 | 8 |
| 1468 | A356 | 1.20p *shown* | 60 | 30 |

Nos. 1272, 1206 Surcharged in Red

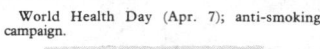

Wmk. 372 (1.35p)

1980, Aug. 1   Litho.   *Perf. 12½*
| 1469 | A273 | 1.35p on 1.60p blk | 68 | 34 |
| 1470 | A250 | 1.50p on 1.80p grn | 80 | 40 |

Independence, 82nd Anniversary.

Association Emblem—A357

1980, Aug. 1   Wmk. 372
| 1471 | A357 | 30s multi | 16 | 8 |
| 1472 | A357 | 2.30p multi | 1.15 | 75 |

International Association of Universities, 7th General Conference, Manila, Aug. 25-30.

Congress Emblem, Map of Philippines—A358

Wmk. 372

1980, Aug. 18   Litho.   *Perf. 12½*
1473	A358	30s lt grn & blk	16	8
1474	A358	75s lt bl & blk	35	20
1475	A358	2.30p sal & blk	1.15	60

International Federation of Library Associations and Institutions, 46th Congress, Manila, Aug. 18-23.

Kabataang Barangay (New Society), 5th Anniversary—A359

1980, Sept. 19   Litho.   *Perf. 12½*
1476	A359	30s multi	16	8
1477	A359	40s multi	22	10
1478	A359	1p multi	55	28

Nos. 1389, 1422, 1443, 1445, 1327 Surcharged in Blue, Black or Red

Wmk. 372

1980, Sept. 26   Litho.   *Perf. 12½*
1479	A328	40s on 30s rose (Bl)	22	10
1480	A338	40s on 30s multi	22	10
1481	A345	40s on 30s multi	22	10
1482	A346	40s on 30s multi (R)	22	10
1483	A294	2p on 1.65p multi (R)	1.10	55
		Nos. 1479-1483 (5)	1.98	95

Catamaran, Conference Emblem—A360

1980, Sept. 27
| 1484 | A360 | 30s multi | 16 | 8 |
| 1485 | A360 | 2.30p multi | 1.25 | 75 |

World Tourism Conference, Manila, Sept. 27.

Stamp Day
A361

U.N. Headquarters and Emblem, Flag of Philippines
A362

1980, Oct. 9
1486	A361	40s multi	22	10
1487	A361	1p multi	55	28
1488	A361	2p multi	1.10	55

PHILIPPINES

1980, Oct. 20
| 1489 | A362 | 40s shown | 22 | 10 |
| 1490 | A362 | 3.20p U.N. and Philippine flags, U.N. headquarters | 1.75 | 1.25 |

United Nations, 35th anniversary.

Murex Alabaster—A363

1980, Nov. 2
1491	A363	40s shown	22	10
1492	A363	60s Bursa bubo	32	16
1493	A363	1.20p Homalocantha zamboi	60	30
1494	A363	2p Xenophora pallidula	1.10	55

INTERPOL Emblem on Globe—A364
Wmk. 372
1980, Nov. 5 **Litho.**
1495	A364	40s multi	22	10
1496	A364	1p multi	55	26
1497	A364	3.20p multi	1.75	1.25

49th General Assembly Session of INTERPOL (International Police Organization), Manila, Nov. 13-21.

Central Philippine University, 75th Anniversary—A365
Unwmkd.
1980, Nov. 17
| 1498 | A365 | 40s multi | 22 | 10 |
| 1499 | A365 | 3.20p multi | 1.75 | 1.25 |

No. 1257 Surcharged
Wmk. 372
1980, Nov. 21 **Litho.** **Perf. 12½**
| 1500 | A269 | 1.20p on 80s multi | 60 | 30 |

Philatelic Week 1980. Surcharge similar to No. 1367.

No. 1358 Surcharged

1980, Nov. 30
| 1501 | A313 | 40s on 30s multi | 22 | 10 |

APO Philatelic Society, 30th anniversary.

Christmas Tree, Present and Candy Cane—A366

1980, Dec. 15 **Unwmkd.** **Litho.** **Perf. 12½**
| 1502 | A366 | 40s multi | 22 | 10 |

Christmas 1980.

No. 1467 Surcharged

1981, Jan. 2
| 1503 | A356 | 40c on 30s multi | 22 | 10 |

Nos. 1370, 1257 Surcharged in Red or Black

1981
| 1504 | A320 | 10s on 30s (R) multi | 5 | 5 |
| 1505 | A269 | 85s on 80s multi | 48 | 22 |

Issue dates: 10s, Jan. 12; 85s, Jan. 2.

Heinrich Von Stephan, UPU Emblem—A367
1981, Jan. 30
| 1506 | A367 | 3.20p multi | 1.75 | 90 |

Heinrich von Stephan (1831-1897), founder of Universal Postal Union, birth sesquicentennial.

Pope John Paul II Greeting Crowd—A368

Designs: 90s, Pope, signature (vert.). 1.20p Pope, cardinals (vert.). 3p, Pope giving blessing, Vatican arms, Manila Cathedral. 7.50p, Pope, light on map of Philippines (vert.).

1981, Feb. 17 **Unwmkd.** **Perf. 13½x14**
1507	A368	90s multi	50	24
1508	A368	1.20p multi	65	32
1509	A368	2.30p multi	1.30	60
1510	A368	3p multi	1.65	78

Souvenir Sheet
| 1511 | A368 | 7.50p multi | 4.25 | 2.00 |

Visit of Pope John Paul, Feb. 17-22. No. 1511 has multicolored margin showing Vatican arms. Size: 76x92mm.

Nos. 1364, 1423, 1268, 1446, 1261, 1206, 1327 Surcharged

Wmk. 372, Unwmked.
1981 **Litho.** **Perf. 12½**
1512	A316	40s on 90s multi	22	10
1513	A338	40s on 90s multi	22	10
1514	A270	40s on 65s lil rose	22	10
1515	A346	40s on 90s multi	22	10
1517	A271	1p on 1.50p brt rose & vio bl	62	25
1518	A250	1.20p on 1.80p grn	65	32
1519	A294	1.20p on 1.65p multi	65	32
1520	A271	2p on 1.50p brt rose & vio bl	1.25	50

Nos. 1512-1520 (8) 4.05 1.79

Inter-Parliamentary Session—A369
1981, Apr. 20 **Wmk. 372**
| 1521 | A369 | 2p multi | 1.10 | 55 |
| 1522 | A369 | 3.20p multi | 1.75 | 90 |

68th Spring Meeting of the Inter-Parliamentary Union, Manila, Apr. 20-25.

Unless otherwise stated, all issues on granite paper.

Bubble Coral A370
Wmk. 372
1981, May 22 **Litho.** **Perf. 12½**
1523	A370	40s shown	22	10
1524	A370	40s Branching coral	22	10
1525	A370	40s Brain coral	22	10
1526	A370	40s Table coral	22	10

Nos. 1523-1526 se-tenant.

Philippine Motor Assoc., 50th Anniv.—A371

Designs: Vintage cars. Nos. 1527-1530 se-tenant.

1981, May 25
1527	A371	40s Presidents car	22	10
1528	A371	40s 1930	22	10
1529	A371	40s 1937	22	10
1530	A371	40s shown	22	10

Re-inauguration of Pres. Ferdinand E. Marcos—A372

1981, June 30
| 1531 | A372 | 40s multi | 22 | 10 |

Souvenir Sheet
Imperf.
| 1532 | A372 | 5p multi | 2.75 | 1.25 |

No. 1531 exists imperf. Size of No. 1532: 79x78mm.

St. Ignatius Loyola, Founder of Jesuit Order—A373

400th Anniv. of Jesuits in Philippines: No. 1534, Jose, Rizal, Ateneo University. No. 1535, Father Federico Faura, Manila Observatory. No. 1536, Father Saturnino Urios, map of Philippines. Nos. 1533-1536 se-tenant.

1981, July 31
1533	A373	40s multi	22	10
1534	A373	40s multi	22	10
1535	A373	40s multi	22	10
1536	A373	40s multi	22	10

Souvenir Sheet
Imperf.
| 1537 | A373 | 2p multi | 1.25 | 50 |

No. 1537 contains vignettes of Nos. 1533-1536. Size: 89x88mm.

Gen. Gregorio del Pilar (1875-1899)—A374

Design: 40s, Isabelo de los Reyes (1867-1938), labor union founder. No. 1540, Magsaysay. No. 1541, Francisco Dagohoy. No. 1543, Ambrosia R. Bautista, signer of Declaration of Independence, 1898, No. 1544, Juan Sumulong (1875-1942), statesman. 2.30p, Nicanor Abelardo (1893-1934), composer. 3.20p, Gen. Vicente Lim (1888-1945), first Philippine graduate of West Point.

Wmk. 372
1981-82 **Litho.** **Perf. 12½**
1538	A374	40s grnsh bl	22	10
1539	A374	1p blk & red brn	62	25
1540	A374	1.20p blk & lt red brn	65	32
1541	A374	1.20p brn	65	32
1543	A374	2p blk & red brn	1.25	50
1544	A374	2p	1.25	50
1545	A374	2.30p lt red brn	1.30	55
1546	A374	3.20p gray bl	1.75	90

Chief Justice Fred Ruiz Castro 67th Birth Anniv. A375

Intl. Year of the Disabled A376

1981, Sept. 2
| 1551 | A375 | 40s multi | 22 | 10 |

Wmk. 372
1981, Oct. 24 **Litho.** **Perf. 12½**
Granite Paper
| 1552 | A376 | 40s multi | 22 | 10 |
| 1553 | A376 | 3.20p multi | 1.75 | 90 |

PHILIPPINES

24th Intl. Red Cross
Conference,
Manila, Nov. 7-14
A376a

1981, Nov. 7
1554	A376a	40s multi	22	10
1555	A376a	2p multi	1.25	50
1556	A376a	3.20p multi	1.75	90

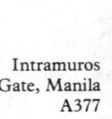

Intramuros
Gate, Manila
A377

1981, Nov. 13
| 1557 | A377 | 40s black | 22 | 10 |

Manila Park Zoo Concert Series, Nov.
20-30—A378

1981, Nov. 20
| 1558 | A378 | 40s multi | 22 | 10 |

No. 1329 Overprinted "1981 Philatelic
Week" and Surcharged.

Wmk. 372

1981, Nov. 23 *Litho.* *Perf. 12½*
| 1559 | A296 | 1.20p on 1.50p multi | 65 | 32 |

Nos. 1205, 1347, 1371 Surcharged.

1981, Nov. 25 *Litho.* *Perf. 12½*
1560	A306	40s on 1.05p multi	22	10
1561	A320	40s on 1.35p multi	22	10
1562	A273	1.20p on 1.50p brn	65	32

11th Southeast Asian Games, Manila,
Dec. 6-15—A379

1981, Dec. 3
1563	A379	40s Running	22	10
1564	A379	1p Bicycling	62	25
1565	A379	2p Pres. Marcos, Intl. Olympic Pres. Samaranch	1.25	50
1566	A379	2.30p Soccer	1.30	60
1567	A379	2.80p Shooting	1.60	72
1568	A379	3.20p Bowling	1.75	90
	Nos 1563-1568 (6)		6.74	3.07

Manila Intl. Film Festival, Jan.
18-29—A380

Wmk. 372
1982, Jan. 18 *Litho.* *Perf. 12½*
1569	A380	40s Film Center	22	10
1570	A380	2p Golden trophy, vert.	1.25	50
1571	A380	3.20p Trophy, diff., vert.	1.75	90

Manila Metropolitan Waterworks and
Sewerage System Centenary—A381

1982, Jan. 22
| 1572 | A381 | 40s blue | 22 | 10 |
| 1573 | A381 | 1.20p brown | 65 | 32 |

Nos. 1268, 1302, 1328 Surcharged in
Black.

1982, Jan. 28
1574	A273	1p on 65s lil rose	62	30
1575	A286	1p on 1.50p multi	62	30
1576	A295	3.20p on 2.20p multi	1.75	90

Scouting Year—A382

1982, Feb. 22
| 1577 | A382 | 40s Portrait | 22 | 10 |
| 1578 | A382 | 2p Scout giving salute | 1.25 | 50 |

25th Anniv. of Children's Museum and
Library Foundation—A383

1982, Feb. 25
| 1579 | A383 | 40s Mural | 22 | 10 |
| 1580 | A383 | 1.20p Children playing | 65 | 32 |

77th Anniv. of Philippine Military
Academy—A384

Wmk. 372
1982, Mar. 25 *Litho.* *Perf. 12½*
| 1581 | A384 | 40s multi | 22 | 10 |
| 1582 | A384 | 1p multi | 62 | 30 |

40th Bataan Day—A385

1982, Apr. 9
| 1583 | A385 | 40s Soldier | 22 | 10 |
| 1584 | A385 | 2p "Reunion for Peace" | 1.25 | 50 |

Souvenir Sheet
| 1585 | A385 | 3.20p Cannon, flag | 1.75 | 1.00 |

No. 1585 contains one stamp (38x28mm., imperf.); multicolored margin shows emblem. Size: 76x76mm.

No. B27 Surcharged.

1982 *Photo.* *Perf. 13½*
| 1586 | SP9 | 10s on 6 + 5s multi | 6 | 5 |

Aurora Aragon Quezon (1888-1949),
Former First Lady—A386

1982, Apr. 28 *Litho.* *Perf. 12½*
| 1587 | A386 | 1p rose pink | 62 | 30 |

7th Towers Awards—A387

1982, May 1
| 1588 | A387 | 40s Man holding award | 22 | 10 |
| 1589 | A387 | 1.20p Award | 65 | 32 |

United Nations Conference on Human
Environment, 10th Anniv.—A388

1982, June 5
| 1590 | A388 | 40s Turtle | 22 | 10 |
| 1591 | A388 | 3.20p Philippine eagle | 1.75 | 90 |

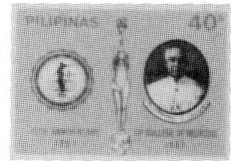

75th Anniv. of Univ. of Philippines
College of Medicine—A389

1982, June 10
| 1592 | A389 | 40s multi | 22 | 10 |
| 1593 | A389 | 3.20p multi | 1.75 | 90 |

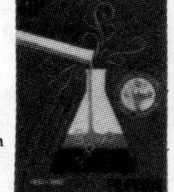

Natl.
Livelihood
Movement
A390

Adamson
Univ., 50th
Anniv.
A391

1982, June 12
| 1594 | A390 | 40s multi | 22 | 10 |

1982, June 21
| 1595 | A391 | 40s bl & multi | 22 | 10 |
| 1596 | A391 | 1.20p lt vio & multi | 65 | 32 |

Social Security,   Pres. Marcos,
25th Anniv.   65th Birthday
A392   A393

1982, Sept. 1 *Perf. 13½x13*
| 1597 | A392 | 40s multi | 22 | 10 |
| 1598 | A392 | 1.20p multi | 65 | 32 |

1982, Sept. 11 *Perf. 13½x13*
1599	A393	40s sil & multi	22	10
1600	A393	3.20p sil & multi	1.75	90
a.		Souvenir sheet of 2	2.00	1.00

No. 1600a contains Nos. 1599-1600 (imperf.); multicolored margin shows arms, black inscription. Size: 76x76mm.

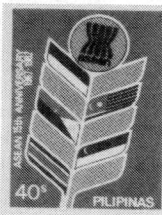

15th Anniv. of Assoc. of Southeast
Asian Nations (ASEAN)—A394

1982, Sept. 22 *Litho.* *Perf. 12½*
| 1601 | A394 | 40s Flags | 22 | 10 |

St. Teresa of Avila (1515-1582)—A395

PHILIPPINES

1982, Oct. 15   *Perf. 13x13½*
1602	A395	40s Text	22	10
1603	A395	1.20p Map	65	32
1604	A395	2p Map	1.25	50

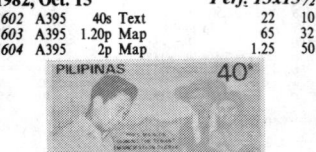

10th Anniv. of Tenant Farmers' Emancipation Decree—A396

      Wmk. 372
1982, Oct. 21   Litho.   *Perf. 13x13½*
| 1605 | A396 | 40s Pres. Marcos signing law | 22 | 10 |

350th Anniv. of St. Isabel College—A397

1982, Oct. 22
| 1606 | A397 | 40s multi | 22 | 10 |
| 1607 | A397 | 1p multi | 62 | 25 |

Reading Campaign—A398

1982, Nov. 4
| 1608 | A398 | 40s yel & multi | 22 | 10 |
| 1609 | A398 | 2.30p grn & multi | 1.30 | 55 |

42nd Skal Club World Congress, Manilla, Nov. 7-12—A399

1982, Nov. 7
| 1610 | A399 | 40s Heads | 22 | 10 |
| 1611 | A399 | 2p Chief | 1.25 | 50 |

25th Anniv. of Bayanihan Folk Arts Center—A400

Designs: Various folk dances.

1982, Nov. 10   Litho.   *Perf. 13x13½*
| 1612 | A400 | 40s multi | 22 | 10 |
| 1613 | A400 | 2.80p multi | 1.60 | 72 |

TB Bacillus Centenary—A401

1982, Dec. 7   Wmk. 372
| 1614 | A401 | 40s multi | 22 | 10 |
| 1615 | A401 | 2.80p multi | 1.60 | 72 |

Christmas 1982—A402

1982, Dec. 10
| 1616 | A402 | 40s multi | 22 | 10 |
| 1617 | A402 | 1p multi | 62 | 25 |

Philatelic Week, Nov. 22-28—A403

      Wmk. 372
1982, Nov. 28   Litho.   *Perf. 13x13½*
| 1618 | A403 | 40s yel & multi | 22 | 10 |
| 1619 | A403 | 1p sil & multi | 62 | 25 |

Visit of Pres. Marcos to the US, Sept.—A404

1982, Dec. 18
1620	A404	40s multi	22	10
1621	A404	3.20p multi	1.90	85
a.		Souvenir sheet of 2	2.25	1.00

No. 1621a contains Nos. 1620-1621. Size: 76x77mm.

| UN World Assembly on Aging, July 26-Aug. 6 A405 | Senate Pres. Eulogio Rodreiguez, Sr. (1883-1964) A406 |

1982, Dec. 24
| 1622 | A405 | 1.20p Woman | 65 | 32 |
| 1623 | A405 | 2p Man | 1.25 | 50 |

1983, Jan. 21
| 1624 | A406 | 40s grn & multi | 22 | 10 |
| 1625 | A406 | 1.20p org & multi | 65 | 32 |

1983 Manila Intl. Film Festival, Jan. 24-Feb. 4—A407

1983, Jan. 24
| 1626 | A407 | 40s blk & multi | 22 | 10 |
| 1627 | A407 | 3.20p PINK & multi | 1.90 | 85 |

Beatification of Lorenzo Ruiz (1981)—A408

      Wmk. 372
1983, Feb. 18   Litho.   *Perf. 13x13½*
| 1628 | A408 | 40s multi | 22 | 10 |
| 1629 | A408 | 1.20p multi | 65 | 32 |

400th Anniv. of Local Printing Press—A409

1983, Mar. 14
| 1630 | A409 | 40s blk & grn | 22 | 10 |

Safety at Sea—A410

1983, Mar. 17   *Perf. 13½x13*
| 1631 | A410 | 40s multi | 22 | 10 |

25th anniv. of Inter-Governmental Maritime Consultation Org. Convention.

Intl. Org. of Supreme Audit Institutions, 11th Congress, Manila, Apr. 19-27—A411

      Wmk. 372
1983, Apr. 8   Litho.   *Perf. 13x13½*
1632	A411	40s Symbols	22	10
1633	A411	2.80p Emblem	1.60	72
a.		Souvenir sheet of 2	2.00	1.00

No. 1633a contains Nos. 1632-1633, imperf. Size: 76x76mm.

Type of 1982 Overprinted in Red:
"7th BSP NATIONAL JAMBOREE 1983"

1983, Apr. 13   *Perf. 12½*
| 1634 | A390 | 40s multi | 22 | 10 |

Boy Scouts of Philippines jamboree.

No. 1249 Surcharged.

1983, Apr. 15
| 1635 | | Block of 10 | 2.25 | 1.00 |
| a. | A265 | 40s on 45s, any single grn | 22 | 10 |

75th Anniv. of Dental Assoc.—A412

      Wmk. 372
1983, May 9   Litho.   *Perf. 13½x13*
| 1636 | A412 | 40s multi | 22 | 10 |

75th Anniv. of University of the Philippines—A413

      Wmk. 372
1983, June 17   Litho.   *Perf. 13½x13*
| 1637 | A413 | 40s Statue | 22 | 10 |
| 1638 | A413 | 1.20p Statue, diff., diamond | 65 | 32 |

Visit of Japanese Prime Minister Yasuhiro Nakasone, May 6-8—A414

      Wmk. 372
1983, June 20   Litho.   *Perf. 13x13½*
| 1639 | A414 | 40s multi | 22 | 10 |

25th Anniv. of Natl. Science and Technology Authority—A415

1983, July 11
1640	A415	40s Animals, produce	22	10
1641	A415	40s Heart, food, pill	22	10
1642	A415	40s Factories, windmill, car	22	10
1643	A415	40s Chemicals, house, book	22	10

Science Week. Nos. 1640-1643 se-tenant.

PHILIPPINES

World Communications Year—A416

		Wmk. 372	Litho.	Perf. 12½
1983, Oct. 24
1644 A416 3.20p multi 1.90 85

Philippine Postal System Bicentennial A417

1983, Oct. 31
1645 A417 40s multi 22 10

Christmas 1983—A418
Star of the East and Festival Scene in continuous design.

1983, Nov. 15 Litho. Perf. 12½
1646 Strip of 5 1.10 50
a. A418 40s single stamp 22 10
b. Souvenir sheet 1.10

Xavier University, 50th Anniv.—A419

1983, Dec. 1 Litho. Perf. 14
1647 A419 40s multi 22 10
1648 A419 60s multi 34 15

Ministry of Labor and Employment, Golden Jubilee—A420

1983, Dec. 8 Litho. Perf. 12½
1649 A420 40s brt ultra & multi 22 10
1650 A420 60s gold & multi 34 15

50th Anniv. of Women's Suffrage Movement—A421

1983, Dec. 7
1651 A421 40s multi 22 10
1652 A421 60s multi 34 15

Philatelic Week—A422
Stamp Collecting: a. Cutting. b. Sorting. c. Soaking. d. Affixing hinges. e. Mounting stamp.

1983, Dec. 20
1653 Strip of 5 1.40 60
a.-e. A422 50s multi 28 12

Emancipation Type of 1982

1983 Litho. Perf. 13
Size: 32x22mm.
1654 A396 40s multi 5 5

Philippine Cockatoo A423

Princess Tarhata Kiram A424

1984, Jan. 9 Perf. 14
1655 A423 40s shown 5 5
1656 A423 2.30p Guaiabero 34 15
1657 A423 2.80p Crimson-spotted racket-tailed parrots 40 16
1658 A423 3.20p Large-billed parrot 45 18
1659 A423 3.60p Tanygnathus sumatranus 50 20
1660 A423 5p Hanging parakeets 70 28
 Nos. 1655-1660 (6) 2.44 1.02

1984, Jan. 16 Perf. 13
1661 A424 3p grn & red 42 16

1984, Jan. 23 Perf. 13½x13
1662 A425 40s blk & multi 5 5
1663 A425 60s red & multi 5 5

1984, Feb. 9 Perf. 13
1664 A426 60s blk & bl grn 5 5
1665 A426 3.60p red & bl grn 50 20

Nos. 1549, 1599, 1618 Surcharged.

1984, Feb. 20
1666 A393 50s on 40s multi 8 5
1667 A403 60s on 40s multi 8 5
1668 A374 3.60p on 3.20p gray bl 50 20

Portrait Type of 1981

Designs: No. 1672, Gen. Artemio Ricarte. No. 1673, Teodoro M. Kalaw. No. 1674, Pres. Carlos P. Garcia.

1984 Litho. Perf. 12½x13
1672 A374 60s blk & lt brn 8 5
1673 A374 60s blk & pur 8 5
1674 A374 60s black 8 5

Issue dates: No. 1672, Mar. 22; No. 1673, Mar. 31; No. 1674, June 14.

Types of 1982

1984
1681 A390 60s #1594 8 5
1682 A374 1.80p #1549 25 10
1683 A374 2.40p #1548 35 15
1684 A386 3.60p Quezon 50 20
1685 A374 4.20p #1547 58 25

Issue dates: No. 1685, Mar. 26; others May 5.

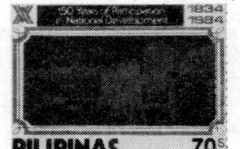
Ayala Corp. Sesquicentenary—A427
Night Views of Manila.

1984, Apr. 25 Litho. Perf. 13x13½
1686 A427 70s multi 12 5
1687 A427 3.60p multi 50 20

ESPAÑA '84—A428

1984, Apr. 27 Perf. 14
1688 A428 2.50p multi 40 18
1689 A428 5p multi 80 35
1690 Sheet of 4 5.00 2.25
a. A428 7.50p like #1689 1.20 55
b. A428 7.50p multi 1.20 55
c. A428 7.50p multi 1.20 55
d. A428 7.50p like #1688 1.20 55

Size of No. 1690: 100x73mm.

Maria Pax Mendoza Guazon—A429

1984, May 26 Perf. 13
1691 A429 60s brt bl & red 8 5
1692 A429 65s brt bl, red & blk 10 5

Designs: 2.50p, Our Lady of the Most Holy Rosary with St. Dominic, by C. Francisco. 5p, Spoliarium, by Juan Luna. No. 1690b, Blessed Virgin of Manila as Patroness of Voyages, Galleon showing map of Panama-Manila. No. 1609c, Illustrations from The Monkey and the Turtle, by Rizal (first children's book published in Philippines, 1885.)

PHILIPPINES

SEMI-POSTAL STAMPS.
Republic.

Epifanio de los Santos, Trinidad H. Pardo and Teodoro M. Kalaw
SP1

Doctrina Christiana, Cover Page
SP2

"Noli Me Tangere," Cover Page
SP3

Engraved
1949, Apr. 1   Perf. 12   Unwmkd.

B1	SP1	4c +2c sep	1.00	75
B2	SP2	6c +4c vio	3.00	2.00
B3	SP3	18c +7c bl	4.00	3.50

The surtax was for restoration of war-damaged public libraries.

War Widow and Children
SP4

Disabled Veteran
SP5

1950, Nov. 30

| B4 | SP4 | 2c +2c red | 10 | 12 |
| B5 | SP5 | 4c +4c vio | 40 | 40 |

The surtax was for war widows and children and disabled veterans of World War II.

Mrs. Manuel L. Quezon
SP6

1952, Aug. 19   Perf. 12

| B6 | SP6 | 5c +1c dp bl | 15 | 15 |
| B7 | SP6 | 6c +2c car rose | 40 | 40 |

The surtax was used to encourage planting and care of fruit trees among Philippine children. See also No. 872.

Quezon Institute
SP7

Photogravure
1958, Aug. 19   Perf. 13½, 12

Cross in Red

| B8 | SP7 | 5c +5c grn | 15 | 15 |
| B9 | SP7 | 10c +5c dp vio | 45 | 45 |

These stamps were obligatory on all mail from Aug. 19–Sept. 30.

The surtax on all semi-postals from Nos. B8–B9 onward was for the Philippine Tuberculosis Society unless otherwise stated.

Scout Cooking
SP8

Design: 25c+5c, Archery.

1959   Engraved   Perf. 13
Yellow Paper.

B10	SP8	6c +4c car	18	18
B11	SP8	25c +5c bl	60	60
a.		Nos. B10-B11 tête bêche, white	1.20	1.20
		Nos. B10-B11, CB1-CB3 (5)	4.48	4.48

Issued to publicize the 10th Boy Scout World Jamboree, Makiling National Park, July 17–26. The surtax was to finance the Jamboree.
For souvenir sheet see No. CB3a.

Nos. B8-B9 Surcharged in Red
HELP
FIGHT
3+5
TB

1959 Photogravure Perf. 13½, 12
Cross in Red.

B12	SP7	3c +5c on 5c +5c grn	15	15
a.		"3+5" and bars omitted		
B13	SP7	6c +5c on 10c +5c dp vio	20	20

Bohol Sanatorium—SP9

1959, Aug. 19 Engraved Perf. 12
Cross in Red.

| B14 | SP9 | 6c +5c yel grn | 15 | 15 |
| B15 | SP9 | 25c +5c vio bl | 50 | 40 |

No. B8 Surcharged "Help Prevent TB" and New Value.
Photogravure

1960, Aug. 19   Perf. 13½, 12

| B16 | SP7 | 6c +5c on 5c +5c grn & red | 25 | 20 |

Roxas Memorial T.B. Pavilion
SP10

Photogravure
1961, Aug. 19 Perf. 11½ Unwmkd.

| B17 | SP10 | 6c +5c brn & red | 25 | 20 |

Emiliano J. Valdes T.B. Pavilion
SP11

1962, Aug. 19
Cross in Red

B18	SP11	6s +5s dk vio	20	15
B19	SP11	30s +5s ultra	50	40
B20	SP11	70s +5s brt bl	1.25	1.00

José Rizal Playing Chess
SP12

Design: 30s+5s, Rizal fencing.

1962, Dec. 30 Engraved Perf. 13

| B21 | SP12 | 6s +4s grn & rose lil | 30 | 30 |
| B22 | SP12 | 30s +5s brt bl & cl | 60 | 60 |

Surtax for Rizal Foundation.

Map of Philippines and Cross
SP13

1963, Aug. 19 Perf. 13 Unwmkd.

B23	SP13	6s +5s vio & red	12	6
B24	SP13	10s +5s grn & red	20	15
B25	SP13	50s +5s brn & red	75	50

Negros Oriental T.B. Pavilion
SP14

1964, Aug. 19 Photo. Perf. 13½
Cross in Red

B26	SP14	5s +5s brt pur	10	5
B27	SP14	5s +5s ultra	15	5
B28	SP14	30s +5s brn	50	40
B29	SP14	70s +5s grn	1.00	90

No. B27 Surcharged in Red with New Value and Two Bars

1965, Aug. 19
Cross in Red

| B30 | SP14 | 1s +5s on 6s +5s ultra | 12 | 5 |
| B31 | SP14 | 3s +5s on 6s +5s ultra | 18 | 10 |

Stork-billed Kingfisher
SP15

Birds: 5s+5s, Rufous hornbill. 10s+5s, Monkey-eating eagle. 30s+5s, Great-billed parrot.

1967, Aug. 19 Photo. Perf. 13½
Cross in Red

B32	SP15	1s +5s multi	10	10
B33	SP15	5s +5s multi	10	10
B34	SP15	10s +5s multi	15	15
B35	SP15	30s +5s multi	50	50

1969, Aug. 15 Litho. Perf. 13½

Birds: 1s+5s, Three-toed woodpecker. 5s+5s, Philippine trogon. 10s+5s, Mt. Apo lorikeet. 40s+5s, Scarlet minivet.
Cross in Red

B36	SP15	1s +5s multi	10	10
B37	SP15	5s +5s multi	15	15
B38	SP15	10s +5s multi	25	20
B39	SP15	40s +5s multi	50	50

Julia V. de Ortigas and Tuberculosis Society Building
SP16

1970, Aug. 3 Photo. Perf. 13½
Cross in Red

B40	SP16	1s +5s multi	10	5
B41	SP16	5s +5s multi	15	15
B42	SP16	30s +5s multi	50	50
B43	SP16	70s +5s multi	65	65

Mrs. Julia V. de Ortigas was president of the Philippine Tuberculosis Society, 1932–1969.

Mabolo, Santol, Chico, Papaya
SP17

Philippine Fruits: 10s+5s, Balimbing, atis, mangosteen, macupa, bananas. 40s+5s, Susong-kalabao, avocado, duhat, watermelon, guava, mango. 1p+5s, Lanzones, oranges, sirhuelas, pineapple.

1972, Aug. 1 Litho. Perf. 13
Cross in Red

B44	SP17	1s +5s multi	5	5
B45	SP17	10s +5s multi	10	10
B46	SP17	40s +5s multi	35	35
B47	SP17	1p +5s multi	70	70

Nos. B45–B46 Surcharged with New Value and 2 Bars

1973, June 15

| B48 | SP17 | 15s +5s on 10s +5s multi | 15 | 15 |
| B49 | SP17 | 60s +5s on 40s +5s multi | 45 | 45 |

PHILIPPINES

Dr. Basilio J. Valdes and Veterans Memorial Hospital—SP18

1974, July 8   Litho.   Perf. 12½
Cross in Red

B50	SP18	15s +5s bl grn	10	10
	a.	Imperf.	15	15
B51	SP18	1.10p +5s vio bl	55	50
	a.	Imperf.	70	70

Dr. Valdes (1892-1970) was president of Philippine Tuberculosis Society.

AIR POST STAMPS.
Madrid-Manila Flight Issue.

Regular Issue of 1917-26 Overprinted in Red or Violet

1926, May 13   Perf. 11.   Unwmkd.

C1	A40	2c grn (R)	4.00	3.25
C2	A40	4c car (V)	5.00	3.75
	a.	Inverted overprint	1,100.	
C3	A40	6c lil (R)	27.50	10.00
C4	A40	8c org brn (V)	27.50	11.00
C5	A40	10c dp bl (V)	27.50	11.00
C6	A40	12c red org (V)	32.50	16.50
C7	A40	16c lt ol grn (Sampson) (V)	1,350.	1,000.
C8	A40	16c ol bis (Sampson) (R)	1,850.	1,500.
C9	A40	16c ol grn (Dewey) (V)	32.50	16.50
C10	A40	20c org yel (V)	32.50	16.50
C11	A40	26c bl grn (V)	32.50	16.50
C12	A40	30c gray (V)	32.50	16.50
C13	A41	2p vio brn (R)	350.00	250.00
C14	A41	4p dk bl (R)	600.00	350.00
C15	A41	10p dp grn (V)	900.00	600.00

Same Overprint on No. 269.
Wmkd. Single-lined PIPS. (190PI)
Perf. 12

C16	A40	26c bl grn (V)	1,850.	

Same Overprint on No. 284.
Perf. 10

C17	A41	1p pale vio (V)	110.00	75.00

Issued to commemorate the flight of Spanish aviators Gallarza and Loriga from Madrid to Manila.

London-Orient Flight Issue.

Regular Issue of 1917-25 Overprinted in Red

1928, Nov. 9   Perf. 11   Unwmkd.

C18	A40	2c green	60	40
C19	A40	4c carmine	60	50
C20	A40	6c violet	2.25	1.75
C21	A40	8c org brn	2.50	2.25
C22	A40	10c dp bl	2.50	2.25
C23	A40	12c red org	3.50	3.00
C24	A40	16c ol grn (Dewey)	2.75	2.25
C25	A40	20c org yel	3.50	3.00
C26	A40	26c bl grn	10.00	7.50
C27	A40	30c gray	10.00	7.50

Same Overprint on No. 271.
Wmkd. Single-lined PIPS. (190PI)
Perf. 12.

C28	A41	1p pale vio	35.00	35.00
		Nos. C18-C28 (11)	73.20	65.40

Commemorating an airplane flight from London to Manila.

Nos. 354-360 Overprinted

1932, Sept. 27   Perf. 11   Unwmkd.

C29	A43	2c yel grn	45	45
C30	A44	4c rose car	50	50
C31	A45	12c orange	80	80
C32	A46	18c red org	4.00	4.00
C33	A47	20c yellow	2.25	2.25
C34	A48	24c dp vio	2.25	2.25
C35	A49	32c ol brn	2.25	2.25
		Nos. C29-C35 (7)	12.50	12.50

Issued to commemorate the visit of Capt. Wolfgang von Gronan on his round-the-world flight.

Regular Issue of 1917-25 Overprinted

1933, Apr. 11

C36	A40	2c green	45	45
C37	A40	4c carmine	50	50
C38	A40	6c dp vio	80	80
C39	A40	8c org brn	1.75	1.65
C40	A40	10c dk bl	1.50	1.25
C41	A40	12c orange	1.25	1.25
C42	A40	16c ol grn (Dewey)	1.25	1.25
C43	A40	20c yellow	1.25	1.25
C44	A40	26c green	1.50	1.50
	a.	26c bl grn	2.50	2.50
C45	A40	30c gray	2.00	1.85
		Nos. C36-C45 (10)	12.25	11.75

Commemorating the flight from Madrid to Manila of aviator Fernando Rein y Loring.

No. 290b Overprinted

1933, May 26   Perf. 11.   Unwmkd.

C46	A40	2c green	65	50

Regular Issue of 1932 Overprinted

C47	A44	4c rose car	10	8
C48	A45	12c orange	50	18
C49	A47	20c yellow	50	30
C50	A48	24c dp vio	50	35
C51	A49	32c ol brn	75	45
		Nos. C46-C51 (6)	3.00	1.86

Nos. 387 and 392 Overprinted in Gold

P.I.-U.S. INITIAL FLIGHT December-1935

1935, Dec. 2

C52	A57	10c rose car	25	25
C53	A62	30c org red	50	50

Issued to commemorate the China Clipper flight from Manila to San Francisco, December 2-5, 1935.

Regular Issue of 1917-25 Surcharged in Various Colors

MANILA-MADRID ARNAIZ-CALVO FLIGHT-1936 2 CENTAVOS 2

1936, Sept. 6   Perf. 11.

C54	A40	2c on 4c car (Bl)	8	6
C55	A40	6c on 12c red org (V)	15	12
C56	A40	16c on 26c bl grn (Bk)	30	30
	a.	16c on 26c grn	1.50	1.00

Issued to commemorate the Manila-Madrid flight by aviators Antonio Arnaiz and Juan Calvo.

Regular Issue of 1917-37 Surcharged in Black or Red

1939, Feb. 17

C57	A40	8c on 26c bl grn (Bk)	1.00	55
	a.	8c on 26c grn (Bk)	2.00	2
C58	A71	1p on 10p gray (R)	3.00	2.50

Issued to commemorate the first Air Mail Exhibition, held Feb. 17-19, 1939.

Moro Vinta and Clipper AP1

1941, June 30

C59	AP1	8c carmine	1.10	70
C60	AP1	20c ultra	1.40	55
C61	AP1	60c bl grn	2.00	1.00
C62	AP1	1p sepia	1.00	65

No. C47 Handstamped in Violet   VICTORY

1944, Dec. 3   Perf. 11.   Unwmkd.

C63	A44	4c rose car	1,650.	1,000.

Republic.

Manuel L. Quezon and Franklin D. Roosevelt AP2

Engraved.

1947, Aug. 19   Perf. 12   Unwmkd.

C64	AP2	6c dk grn	75	75
C65	AP2	40c red org	1.50	1.50
C66	AP2	80c dp bl	4.00	4.00

Threshing Rice AP3

1948, Feb. 23   Typo.   Perf. 12½

C67	AP3	40c dk car & pink	20.00	12.50

Issued to honor the conference of the United Nations' Food and Agriculture Organization, held at Baguio.

Globe AP4

1950, Mar. 1   Engraved.   Perf. 12.

C68	AP4	30c dp org	75	30
C69	AP4	50c car rose	1.25	30

Issued to publicize the 5th World Congress of the Junior Chamber of Commerce, Manila, March 1-8, 1950.

Scott's International Album provides spaces for an extensive representative collection of the world's postage stamps.

PHILIPPINES

Souvenir Sheet.

Franklin D. Roosevelt
and Stamp Collection
AP5

May 22, 1950 *Imperf.*
C70 AP5 80c dp grn 1.75 1.75
Issued in sheets measuring 60½ x 50½ mm., to honor Franklin D. Roosevelt and to commemorate the 25th anniversary of the formation of the Philatelic Association of the Philippines.

Lions Club Emblem — AP6   Maria Clara in 19th Century Costume — AP7

1950, June 2 *Perf. 12*
C71 AP6 30c emerald 90 70
C72 AP6 50c ultra 1.15 90
a. Souvenir sheet 2.00 2.00
Issued to commemorate the convention of the Lions Club, Manila, June 1950.
No. C72a measures 91 x 88 mm., and contains one each of Nos. C71 and C72. Inscriptions in top and bottom margins in orange.

1952, Nov. 16 *Perf. 12½*
C73 AP7 30c rose car 1.20 1.00
Issued to publicize the first Pan-Asian Philatelic Exhibition, PANAPEX, Manila, Nov. 16-22, 1952.

First Philippine Stamp,
Magellan's Landing and
Manila Scene
AP8

1954, April 25 *Perf. 13*
1854 Stamp in Orange.
C74 AP8 10c dk brn 1.50 1.25
C75 AP8 20c dk grn 2.50 2.00
C76 AP8 50c carmine 5.00 4.50
Centenary of Philippine postage stamps.

Mayon Volcano, Moro Vinta
and Rotary Emblem — AP9

1955, Feb. 23
C77 AP9 50c bl grn 1.90 1.25
Issued to commemorate the 50th anniversary of the founding of Rotary International.

Lt. José Gozar
AP10

Portraits: 20c, 50c, Lt. Gozar. 30c, 70c, Lt. Basa.
1955 Engraved. *Perf. 13*
C78 AP10 20c dp vio 65 20
C79 AP10 30c red 75 20
C80 AP10 50c bluish grn 1.00 30
C81 AP10 70c blue 1.65 1.25
Issued in honor of Lt. José Gozar and Lt. Cesar Fernando Basa, Filipino aviators in World War II.

Constitution Type of Regular Issue.
1960, Feb. 8 Photo. *Perf. 12½x13½*
C82 A146 30c brt bl & sil 45 35
Issued to commemorate the 25th anniversary of the Philippine Constitution.

Air Force Plane of 1935 and Saber Jet
AP11

1960, May 2 Engr. *Perf. 14x14½*
C83 AP11 10c carmine 25 15
C84 AP11 20c ultra 50 35
25th anniversary of Philippine Air Force.

Olympic Type of Regular Issue
Designs: 30c, Sharpshooter. 70c, Woman swimmer.
1960, Nov. 30 Photo. *Perf. 13x13½*
C85 A150 30c org & brn 60 50
C86 A150 70c grnsh bl & vio brn 1.20 1.00
Issued to commemorate the 17th Olympic Games, Rome, Aug. 25-Sept. 11.

Postal Conference
Type of Regular Issue, 1961
1961, Feb. 23 *Perf. 13½x13*
C87 A152 30c multi 40 32
Manila Postal Conference, Jan. 10-23.

Freedom from Hunger
Type of Regular Issue
1963, Dec. 20 Photogravure
C88 A168 30s lt grn & multi 40 30
C89 A168 50s multi 65 50
Issued for the "Freedom from Hunger" campaign of the U.N. Food and Agriculture Organization.

Land Reform
Type of Regular Issue
1964, Dec. 21 *Perf. 14½ Wmk. 233*
C90 A172 30s multi 35 30
Issued to commemorate the signing of the Agricultural Land Reform Code.

Mass Baptism by
Father Andres de Urdaneta, Cebu
AP12

Design: 70s, World map showing route of the Cross from Spain to Mexico to Cebu, and two galleons.

Perf. 13
1965, Oct. 4 Photo. *Unwmkd.*
C91 AP12 30s multi 35 20
C92 AP12 70s multi 80 45
a. Souvenir sheet of 4 2.00 2.00
Issued to commemorate the 400th anniversary of the Christianization of the Philippines. No. C92a contains four imperf. stamps similar to Nos. 934-935 and C91-C92 with simulated perforation. Brown marginal inscription. Size: 169x 106mm.

Souvenir Sheet

Family and Progress Symbols
AP13

1966, July 22 Photo. *Imperf.*
C93 AP13 70s multi 90 90
Issued to commemorate the 50th anniversary of the Philippine National Bank. No. C93 contains one stamp with simulated perforation superimposed on a facsimile of a 50p banknote of 1916. Size of stamp: 55x27mm.; sheet, 156x69mm.

Eruption of Taal Volcano
and Refugees — AP14

1967, Oct. 1 Photo. *Perf. 13½x13*
C94 AP14 70s multi 75 65
Eruption of Taal Volcano, Sept. 28, 1965.

Eruption of
Taal Volcano
AP15

1968, Oct. 1 Litho. *Perf. 13½*
C95 AP15 70s multi 75 75
Eruption of Taal Volcano, Sept. 28, 1965.

Rotary Type of 1969
1969, Jan. 29 Photo. *Perf. 12½*
C96 A202 40s grn & multi 35 25
C97 A202 75s red & multi 75 60
50th anniversary of Manila Rotary Club.

Holy Child Type of Regular Issue
1969, June 30 Photo. *Perf. 13½*
C98 A207 40s ultra & multi 40 28
See note after No. 1027.

Pope Type of Regular Issue
1970, Nov. 27 Photo. *Perf. 13½x14*
C99 A221 40s vio & multi 40 27
Visit of Pope Paul VI, Nov. 27-29, 1970.

Law College Type of Regular Issue
1971, June 15 *Perf. 13*
C100 A225 1p grn & multi 65 60

Manila Type of Regular Issue
1971, June 24
C101 A226 1p multi & bl 65

Santo Tomas Type of Regular Issue
1971, July 8 Photo. *Perf. 13½*
C102 A227 2p lt bl & multi 1.30 1.10
See note after No. 1103.

Congress Type of Regular Issue
1972, Apr. 11 Photo. *Perf. 13½x13*
C103 A232 40s grn & multi 35 30
4th Asian Pacific Congress of Gastroenterology, Manila, Feb. 5-12.

Tropical Fish Type of Regular Issue
1972, Aug. 14 Photo. *Perf. 13*
Multicolored
C104 A235 50s Dusky angelfish 60 30

Pope Paul VI Type of Regular Issue
1972, Sept. 26 Photo. *Perf. 14*
C105 A237 60s lt bl & multi 45 45
See note after No. 1145.

First Mass Type of Regular Issue
1972, Oct. 31 Photo. *Perf. 14*
C106 A241 60s multi 40 35
See note after No. 1159.

Presidential Palace Type of Regular Issue
1973, Nov. 15 Litho. *Perf. 14*
C107 A253 60s multi 30 30

No. C92a Surcharged and Overprinted
with U.S. Bicentennial Emblems and:
"U.S.A. BICENTENNIAL / 1776-1976"
in Black
Unwmkd.
1976, Sept. 23 Photo. *Imperf.*
C108 Sheet of 4 65 65
a. A179 5s on 3s multi 5 5
b. A179 5s on 6s multi 5 5
c. AP12 15s on 30s multi 12 12
d. AP12 50s on 70s multi 37 35
American Bicentennial. Nos. C108a-C108d are overprinted with Bicentennial emblem and 2 bars over old denomination. Inscription and 2 Bicentennial emblems overprinted in margin. Overprint and surcharges exist in red.

Souvenir Sheet

Netherlands No. 1 and Philippines
No. 1 and Windmill — AP16

1977, May 26 Litho. *Perf. 14½*
C109 Sheet of 3 10.00 10.00
a. 7.50p multi, single stamp 2.75 2.75
AMPHILEX '77, International Stamp Exhibition, Amsterdam, May 26-June 5. No. C109 contains 3 No. C109a, multicolored margin. Size: 72x90mm. Exists imperf. Price $17.50.

Souvenir Sheet

Philippines and Spain Nos. 1,
Bull and Matador — AP17

1977, Oct. 7 Litho. *Perf. 12½x13*
C110 AP17 Sheet of 3 12.00 12.00
a. 7.50p multi, single stamp 3.00 3.00
ESPAMER '77 (Exposicion Filatelica de America y Europa), Barcelona, Spain, Oct. 7-13. No. C110 contains 3 No. C110a, multicolored margin with ESPAMER emblems. Size: 75x90mm.
Exists imperf. Price $17.50.

Nos. B10 and
CB3a Surcharged

50$

JULY 4-14, 1979
QUEZON CITY

			Perf. 13	
1979, July 5	Engr.			
C111	SP8	90s on 6c + 4c car, yel	25	25

Souvenir Sheet
White Paper

C112		Sheet of 5	1.00	1.00
a.	SP8	50s on 6c + 4c car		15
b.	SP8	50s on 25c + 5c bl		15
c.	SP8	50s on 30c + 10c grn		15
d.	SP8	50s on 70c + 20c red brn		15
e.	SP8	50s on 80c + 20c vio		15

First Scout Philatelic Exhibition, Quezon City, July 4–14, commemorating 25th anniversary of First National Jamboree. Surcharge on No. C111 includes "AIRMAIL." Violet marginal inscriptions on No. C112 overprinted with heavy bars; new commemorative inscriptions and Scout emblem added. Size: 171x89mm.

See "Special Notices" at the front of this volume for data on the listing methods of this Catalogue, abbreviations, condition, prices and examination.

Unused Prices
Catalogue prices for unused stamps through 1960 are for hinged copies in fine condition.
Never-hinged unused stamps issued before 1961 often sell above Catalogue prices. Current never-hinged prices for various countries will be found in the Scott StampMarket Update.

WE STOCK OVER 267 COUNTRIES!

If you need stamps issued before 1960 to complete your collection

SEND US YOUR WANTLIST OR CALL TODAY!

(References Please)

EST. 1937

**Stampazine Inc.
3 E. 57th St.
N.Y., N.Y. 10022
(212) PL2-5905**

PHILIPPINES

AIR POST SEMI-POSTAL STAMPS
Type of Semi-Postal Issue, 1959.
Designs: 30c+10c, Bicycling. 70c+20c, Scout with plane model. 80c+20c, Pres. Carlos P. Garcia and scout shaking hands.

Engraved.
1959, July 17   Perf. 13.   Unwmkd.

CB1	SP8	30c + 10c grn	60	60
CB2	SP8	70c + 20c red brn	1.25	1.25
CB3	SP8	80c + 20c vio	1.85	1.85
a.		Souvenir sheet of five	3.00	3.00

Issued to publicize the 10th Boy Scout World Jamboree, Makiling National Park, July 17–26. The surtax was to finance the Jamboree.

No. CB3a measures 171x89mm. and contains one each of Nos. CB1–CB3 and types of Nos. B10–B11 on white paper. Marginal inscription in violet. Sold for 4p.

SPECIAL DELIVERY STAMPS.
United States No. E5 Overprinted in Red **PHILIPPINES**

Wmkd. Double-lined USPS. (191)
1901, Oct. 15   Perf. 12

E1	SD3	10c dk bl	110.00	125.00

Special Delivery Messenger SD2

Wmkd. Double-lined PIPS. (191PI)
1906   Engraved.

E2	SD2	20c ultra	22.50	7.00
a.		20c pale ultra	22.50	9.00

Special Printing.
Overprinted in Red as No. E1 on United States No. E6.
1907

E2A	SD4	10c ultra	1,400.	

Wmkd. Single-lined PIPS. (190PI)
1911

E3	SD2	20c dp ultra	17.50	9.00

1916   Perf. 10

E4	SD2	20c dp ultra	140.00	40.00

1919   Perf. 11.   Unwmkd.

E5	SD2	20c ultra	45	25
a.		20c pale ultra	75	25
b.		20c dl vio	45	25

Type of 1906 Issue.
1925-31   Imperf.

E6	SD2	20c dl vio ('31)	15.00	17.50

Type of 1919 Overprinted in Black   COMMONWEALTH
1939   Perf. 11.

E7	SD2	20c bl vio	30	30

Nos. E5b and E7, Handstamped in Violet   VICTORY
1944   Perf. 11

E8	SD2	20c dl vio (On E5b)	300.00	225.00
E9	SD2	20c bl vio (On E7)	225.00	165.00

Type SD2 Overprinted "VICTORY" As No. 486
1945

E10	SD2	20c bl vio	85	85
a.		"IC" close together	3.50	3.50

Republic

Manila Post Office and Messenger SD3

Engraved.
1947, Dec. 22   Perf. 12   Unwmkd.

E11	SD3	20c rose lil	75	55

Post Office Building, Manila, and Hands with Letter—SD4

1962, Jan. 23   Perf. 13½x13

E12	SD4	20c lil rose	38	30

SPECIAL DELIVERY OFFICIAL STAMP.
Type of 1906 Issue Overprinted **O.B.**
1931   Perf. 11.   Unwmkd.

EO1	SD2	20c dl vio	85	65
a.		No period after "B"	20.00	15.00
b.		Double ovpt.		

POSTAGE DUE STAMPS.
Postage Due Stamps of the United States Nos. J38 to J44 Overprinted in Black   **PHILIPPINES**

Wmkd. Double-lined USPS. (191)
1899, Aug. 16   Perf. 12

J1	D2	1c dp cl	4.00	1.75
J2	D2	2c dp cl	5.00	1.75
J3	D2	5c dp cl	10.00	3.75
J4	D2	10c dp cl	12.50	6.00
J5	D2	50c dp cl	150.00	90.00
		Nos. J1-J5 (5)	181.50	103.25

No. J1 was used to pay regular postage September 5–19, 1902.

1901, Aug. 31

J6	D2	3c dp cl	15.00	10.00
J7	D2	30c dp cl	175.00	100.00

Post Office Clerk D3

Engraved.
1928, Aug. 21   Perf. 11   Unwmkd.

J8	D3	4c brn red	15	15
J9	D3	6c brn red	15	15
J10	D3	8c brn red	15	15
J11	D3	10c brn red	20	20
J12	D3	12c brn red	20	20
J13	D3	16c brn red	25	20
J14	D3	20c brn red	20	20
		Nos. J8-J14 (7)	1.30	1.30

No. J8 Surcharged in Blue   3 CVOS. 3
1937

J15	D3	3c on 4c brn red	25	15

Nos. J8 to J14 Handstamped in Violet   VICTORY
1944

J16	D3	4c brn red	120.00	
J17	D3	6c brn red	85.00	
J18	D3	8c brn red	90.00	
J19	D3	10c brn red	85.00	
J20	D3	12c brn red	85.00	
J21	D3	16c brn red	90.00	
J22	D3	20c brn red	90.00	

Republic

D4

Engraved.
1947, Oct. 20   Perf. 12   Unwmkd.

J23	D4	3c rose car	25	25
J24	D4	4c brt vio bl	60	50
J25	D4	6c ol grn	75	75
J26	D4	10c orange	1.00	1.00

OFFICIAL STAMPS
Official Handstamped Overprints.

"Officers purchasing stamps for government business may, if they so desire, overprint them with the letters 'O.B.' either in writing with black ink or by rubber stamps but in such a manner as not to obliterate the stamp that postmasters will be unable to determine if the stamps have been previously used". C. M. Cotterman, Director of Posts, December 26, 1905.

Beginning with January 1, 1906, all branches of the Insular Government used postage stamps to prepay postage instead of franking them as before. Some officials used manuscript, some utilized the typewriting machines, some made press-printed overprints, but by far the larger number provided themselves with rubber stamps. The majority of these read "O.B." but other forms were: "OFFICIAL BUSINESS" or "OFFICIAL MAIL" in two lines, with variations on many of these.

These "O.B." overprints are known on U. S. 1899-1901 stamps; on 1903-06 stamps in red and blue; on 1906 stamps in red, blue, black, yellow and green.

"O.B." overprints were also made on the centavo and peso stamps of the Philippines, per order of May 25, 1907.

Beginning in 1926 the stamps were overprinted and issued by the Government, but some post offices continued to handstamp "O.B."

Regular Issue of 1926 Overprinted in Red   OFFICIAL
1926, Dec. 20   Perf. 12   Unwmkd.

O1	A42	2c grn & blk	2.50	1.75
O2	A42	4c car & blk	2.50	1.60
a.		Vertical pair, imperf. between	325.00	
O3	A42	18c lt brn & blk	7.00	6.00
O4	A42	20c org & blk	6.00	2.00

Issued to commemorate the opening of the Legislative Palace.

Regular Issue of 1917-26 Overprinted   O.B.
1931   Perf. 11.

O5	A40	2c green	6	5
a.		No period after "B"	8.50	4.00
b.		No period after "O"		
O6	A40	4c carmine	8	5
a.		No period after "B"	8.50	4.00
O7	A40	6c dp vio	10	8
O8	A40	8c yel brn	10	8
O9	A40	10c dp bl	40	12
O10	A40	12c red org	25	15
O11	A40	16c lt ol grn (Dewey)	25	10
a.		No period after "B"	22.50	
		16c ol bis	1.50	30
O12	A40	20c org yel	30	10
a.		No period after "B"	12.50	12.50
O13	A40	26c green	45	45
		26c bl grn	1.25	1.00
O14	A40	30c gray	40	35
		Nos. O5-O14 (10)	2.39	1.53

Same Overprint on Regular Issue of 1935.
1935

O15	A53	2c rose	6	5
a.		No period after "B"	8.50	4.00
O16	A54	4c yel grn	6	5
a.		No period after "B"	8.50	6.00
O17	A55	6c dk brn	10	6
a.		No period after "B"	13.50	13.50
O18	A56	8c violet	12	12
O19	A57	10c rose car	15	6
O20	A58	12c black	20	15
O21	A59	16c dk bl	20	15
O22	A60	20c lt ol grn	20	15
O23	A61	26c indigo	40	35
O24	A62	30c org red	45	40
		Nos. O15-O24 (10)	1.94	1.54

Same Overprint on Overprinted Issue of 1936-37.
1937-38   Perf. 11

O25	A53	2c rose	8	5
a.		No period after "B"	5.00	2.50
O26	A60	20c lt ol grn ('38)	1.00	75

Regular Issue of 1935, Overprinted in Black: O. B.   O. B.   COMMONWEALTH   COMMONWEALTH
a   b
1938-40   Perf. 11

O27	A53(a)	2c rose	8	5
a.		Hyphen omitted	12.00	7.50
b.		No period after "B"	15.00	10.00
O28	A54(b)	4c yel grn	10	8
O29	A55(a)	6c dk brn	15	6
O30	A56(b)	8c violet	15	10
O31	A57(b)	10c rose car	17	10
a.		No period after "O"	20.00	20.00
O32	A58(b)	12c black	18	18
O33	A59(b)	16c dk bl	25	12
O34	A60(a)	20c lt ol grn ('40)	35	35
O35	A61(b)	26c indigo	45	45
O36	A62(b)	30c org red	40	40
		Nos. O27-O36 (10)	2.28	1.89

No. 461 Overprinted in Black   O. B.
c
1941, Apr. 14   Perf. 11x10½   Unwmkd.

O37	A75	2c ap grn	5	5

Official Stamps Handstamped in Violet   VICTORY
1944   Perf. 11, 11x10½.

O38	A53	2c rose (On O27)	130.00	85.00
O39	A75	2c ap grn (On O37)	5.00	3.00
O40	A54	4c yel grn (On O16)	25.00	20.00
O40A	A55	6c dk brn (On O29)	3,000.	
O41	A57	10c rose car (On O31)	100.00	
O42	A60	20c lt ol grn (On O22)	3,500.	
O43	A60	20c lt ol grn (On O26)	1,400.	

No. 497 Overprinted Type "c" in Black
Perf. 11x10½
1946, June 19   Unwmkd.

O44	A76	2c sepia	6	5

Republic

Nos. 504, 505 and 507

Overprinted in Black **O. B.**

d

1948 *Perf. 12.* **Unwmkd.**

O50	A78	4c blk brn	15	5
a.		Invtd. ovpt.	35.00	
b.		Dbl. ovpt.	35.00	
O51	A79	10c red org	30	5
O52	A81	16c sl gray	1.90	75

The overprint on No. O51 comes in two sizes: 13mm., applied in Manila, and 12½mm., applied in New York.

Nos. 527, 508 and 509

Overprinted in Black **O. B.**

e

Overprint Measures 14mm.

O53	A91	2c brt grn	55	5

1949

O54	A82	20c red brn	75	15

Overprint Measures 12mm.

O55	A83	50c dl grn	1.25	75

No. 550 Overprinted Type "e" in Black.

Overprint Measures 14mm.

1950

O56	A91	1c on 2c brt grn	10	5

Nos. 589, 592, 595 and 597 Overprinted in Black **O. B.**

f

Overprint Measures 15mm.

1952-55

O57	A117	1c red brn ('53)	8	5
O58	A117	5c crim rose	15	5
O59	A117	10c ultra ('55)	25	5
O60	A117	20c car lake ('55)	60	8

No. 647 Overprinted **O B**

g

1959 Engraved *Perf. 12*

O61	A117	1c on 5c crim rose	8	5

No. 813 Overprinted Type "f".

Overprint measures 16½mm.

1959

O62	A145	6c gray bl	20	8

Nos. 856-861 Overprinted

G. O. h **G. O.** j

G. O. k G.O. l

1962-64 *Perf. 13½*

O63	A158(j)	5s car rose ('63)	5	5

Perf. 13x12

O64	A158(h)	6s dk red brn	7	5

Perf. 13½

O65	A158(k)	6s pck bl ('64)	8	5
O66	A158(j)	10s brt pur ('63)	12	5
O67	A158(j)	20s Prus bl ('63)	20	5
O68	A158(j)	30s vermilion	40	15
O69	A158(k)	50s vio ('63)	60	15
		Nos. O63-O69 (7)	1.52	55

"G.O." stands for "Gawaing Opisyal," Tagalog for "Official Business."

On 6s overprint "k" is 10mm. wide.

No. 1082 Overprinted Type "l".

1970, Dec. 30 **Engraved** *Perf. 14*

O70	A222	10s rose car	10	5

NEWSPAPER STAMPS

N1

Typographed.

1886-89 *Perf. 14.* **Unwmkd.**

P1	N1	⅛c yel grn	38	15
P2	N1	1m rose	38	15
P3	N1	2m blue	38	15
P4	N1	5m dk brn	38	15

N2

1890-96

P5	N2	⅛c dk vio	15	15
P6	N2	⅛c grn ('92)	1.50	38
P7	N2	⅛c org brn ('94)	22	8
P8	N2	⅛c dl bl ('96)	1.10	60
P9	N2	1m dk vio	15	15
P10	N2	1m grn ('92)	3.00	75
P11	N2	1m ol gray ('94)	22	8
P12	N2	1m ultra ('96)	38	8
P13	N2	2m dk vio	15	15
P14	N2	2m grn ('92)	3.00	75
P15	N2	2m ol gray ('94)	22	8
P16	N2	2m brn ('96)	38	8
P17	N2	5m dk vio	15	15
P18	N2	5m grn ('92)	120.00	30.00
P19	N2	5m ol gray ('94)	22	8
P20	N2	5m dp bl grn ('96)	2.75	1.10

Imperfs. exist of Nos. P8, P9, P11, P12, P16, P17 and P20.

OCCUPATION STAMPS

Issued under Japanese Occupation.

Nos. 461, 438 and 439

Overprinted with Bars in Black.

Perf. 11x10½, 11.

1942-43 **Unwmkd.**

N1	A75	2c ap grn	6	6
a.		Pair, one without overprint		
N2	A58	12c blk ('43)	15	15
N3	A59	16c dk bl	4.50	3.50

Nos. 435, 442, 443 and 423

Surcharged in Black

5 a

b 16 16

50 CENTAVOS 50 c

1 1

ONE PESO d

Perf. 11.

N4	A55(a)	5(c) on 6c gldn brn	10	10
a.		Top bar shorter, thinner	10	10
b.		5(c) on 6c dk brn	10	10
c.		As "b", top bar shorter and thinner	10	10
N5	A62(b)	16(c) on 30c org red ('43)	20	20
N6	A63(c)	50c on 1p red org & blk ('43)	60	60
a.		Dbl. surch.		200.00
N7	A65(d)	1p on 4p bl & blk ('43)	67.50	52.50

On Nos. N4 and N4b, the top bar measures 1½x22½ mm. On Nos. N4a and N4c, the top bar measures 1x21 mm. and the "5" is smaller and thinner.

No. 384 Surcharged in Black

CONGRATULATIONS
FALL OF
BATAAN AND
CORREGIDOR
1942
2

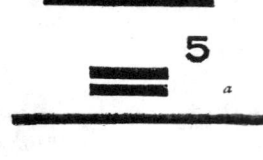

1942, May 18

N8	A54	2c on 4c yel grn	2.50	2.00

Issued to commemorate Japan's capture of Bataan and Corregidor. The American-Filipino forces finally surrendered May 7, 1942.

No. 384 Surcharged in Black

ダイトーアセンソー
イツシユーネンキネン
12-8-1942 5

1942, Dec. 8

N9	A54	5c on 4c yel grn	45	30

Issued to commemorate the first anniversary of the "Greater East Asia War".

Nos. C59 and C62 Surcharged in Black

ヒトー ギヨーセイフ
イツシユーネン キネン
1-23-43
2

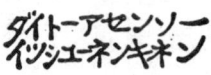

1943, Jan. 23

N10	AP1	2c on 8c car	20	20
N11	AP1	5c on 1p sep	40	40

Issued to commemorate the first anniversary of the Philippine Executive Commission.

Nipa Hut
OS1

Rice Planting
OS2

Mt. Mayon and Mt. Fuji
OS3

Moro Vinta
OS4

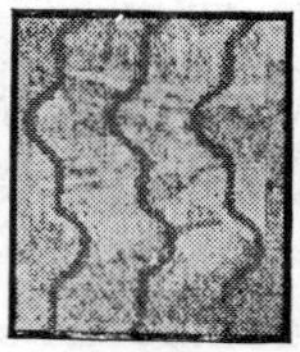

Wmk. 257

Engraved,

Typographed (2c, 6c, 25c)

Wmkd. Curved Wavy Lines. (257)

1943-44 ***Perf. 13***

N12	OS1	1c dp org	5	5
N13	OS2	2c brt grn	5	5
N14	OS1	4c sl grn	5	5
N15	OS3	5c org brn	5	5
N16	OS2	6c red	8	8
N17	OS3	10c bl grn	6	6
N18	OS4	12c stl bl	75	75
N19	OS4	16c dk brn	6	6
N20	OS1	20c rose vio	85	85
N21	OS3	21c violet	15	15
N22	OS2	25c pale brn	6	5
N23	OS3	1p dp car	18	15
N24	OS4	2p dl vio	1.75	1.50
N25	OS4	5p dk ol	6.00	5.00
		Nos. N12-N25 (14)	10.14	8.85

Map of Manila Bay Showing Bataan and Corregidor
OS5

1943, May 7 **Photo.** **Unwmkd.**

N26	OS5	2c car red	12	12
N27	OS5	5c brt grn	18	18

Issued to commemorate the first anniversary of the fall of Bataan and Corregidor.

No. 440 Surcharged in Black

Limbagan
1593 - 1943
12 12

1943, June 20 **Engr.** ***Perf. 11***

N28	A60	12c on 20c lt ol grn	25	20
a.		Double surcharge		

Issued to commemorate the 350th anniversary of the printing press in the Philippines. "Limbagan" is Tagalog for "printing press."

Rizal Monument, Filipina and Philippine Flag
OS6

PHILIPPINES—POLAND

PHILIPPINES (continued)

1943, Oct. 14   Photo.   Perf. 12

N29	OS6	5c lt bl	10	10
N30	OS6	12c orange	14	14
a.		Imperf.	16	16
N31	OS6	17c rose pink	16	16
a.		Imperf.	22	22

Issued to commemorate the "Independence of the Philippines." Japan granted "independence" Oct. 14, 1943, when the puppet republic was founded.
The imperforate stamps were issued without gum.

José Rizal   Rev. José Burgos
OS7   OS8

Apolinario Mabini—OS9

1944, Feb. 17   Litho.   Perf. 12

N32	OS7	5c blue	22	22
a.		Imperf.	22	22
N33	OS8	12c carmine	12	12
a.		Imperf.	12	12
N34	OS9	17c dp org	16	16
a.		Imperf.	16	16

Nos. C60 and C61 Surcharged in Black

1944, May 7   Perf. 11

N35	AP1	5c on 20c ultra	50	50
N36	AP1	12c on 60c bl grn	1.00	1.00

Issued to commemorate the second anniversary of the fall of Bataan and Corregidor.

José P. Laurel—OS10
Without Gum.

1945, Jan. 12   Litho.   Imperf.

N37	OS10	5c dl vio brn	7	6
N38	OS10	7c bl grn	10	8
N39	OS10	20c chlky bl	15	12

Issued belatedly on Jan. 12, 1945, to commemorate the first anniversary of the puppet Philippine Republic, Oct. 14, 1944. "S" stands for "sentimos".

OCCUPATION SEMI-POSTAL STAMPS.

Woman, Farming and Cannery
OSP1

1942, Nov. 12   Perf. 12   Unwmkd.

NB1	OSP1	2c + 1c pale vio	15	15
NB2	OSP1	5c + 1c brt grn	10	10
NB3	OSP1	16c + 2c org	12.00	10.00

Issued to promote the campaign to produce and conserve food. The surtax aided the Red Cross.

Souvenir Sheet.

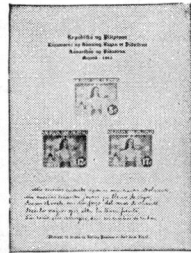

OSP2
Without Gum.

1943, Oct. 14   Imperf.

NB4	OSP2	Sheet of three	27.50	2.00

Issued to commemorate the "Independence of the Philippines."
No. NB4 contains one each of Nos. N29a-N31a. Lower inscription from Rizal's "Last Farewell." Size: 127x177mm. Sold for 2.50p.

Nos. N18, N20 and N21 Surcharged in Black

BAHÂ
1943
+21

1943, Dec. 8   Perf. 13   Wmk. 257

NB5	OS4	12c +21c stl bl	15	15
NB6	OS1	20c +36c rose vio	12	12
NB7	OS3	21c +40c vio	15	15

The surtax was for the benefit of victims of a Luzon flood. "Baha" is Tagalog for "flood."

Souvenir Sheet.

OSP3
Lithographed
Without Gum.

1944, Feb. 9   Imperf.   Unwmkd.

NB8	OSP3	Sheet of three	2.00	2.50

No. NB8 contains one each of Nos. N32a–N34a.
Sheet sold for 1p, surtax going to a fund for the care of heroes' monuments. Size: 101x143mm.

OCCUPATION POSTAGE DUE STAMP.

No. J15 Overprinted with Bar in Blue.

1942, Oct. 14   Perf. 11   Unwmkd.

NJ1	D3	3c on 4c brn red	20.00	10.00

On copies of No. J15, two lines were drawn in India ink with a ruling pen across "United States of America" by employees of the Short Paid Section of the Manila Post Office to make a provisional 3c postage due stamp which was used from Sept. 1, 1942, (when the letter rate was raised from 2c to 5c) until Oct. 14 when No. NJ1 went on sale.

OCCUPATION OFFICIAL STAMPS.

Nos. 461, 413, 435, 435a and 442 Overprinted or Surcharged in Black with Bars and Perf. 11x10½, 11.

公用
(K. P.)

1943-44   Unwmkd.

NO1	A75	2c ap grn	8	8
a.		Double ovpt.		
NO2	A55	5(c) on 6c dk brn (On No. 413) ('44)	17.50	17.50
NO3	A55	5(c) on 6c gldn brn (On No. 435a)	15	15
a.		Narrower spacing between bars	20	20
b.		5(c) on 6c dk brn (On No. 435)	15	12
c.		As "b", narrower spacing between bars	20	20
NO4	A62	16c on 30c org red	45	45
a.		Wider spacing between bars	45	45

On Nos. NO3 and NO3b, the bar deleting "United States of America" is 9¾ to 10mm. above the bar deleting "Common.". On Nos. NO3a and NO3c, the spacing is 8 to 8½ mm.
On No. NO4 the center bar is 19 mm. long, 3¼ mm. below the top bar and 6 mm. above the Japanese characters. On No. NO4a, the center bar is 20½ mm. long, 9 mm. below the top bar and 1 mm. above the Japanese characters.
"K. P." stands for Kagamitang Pampamahalaan, "Official Business" in Tagalog.

Nos. 435 and 435a Surcharged in Black

5
REPUBLIKA NG
PILIPINAS
(K. P.)

1944   Perf. 11.

NO5	A55	5c on 6c gldn brn	10	10
a.		5c on 6c dk brn	10	10

Nos. O34 and C62 Overprinted in Black

Pilipinas
REPUBLIKA
—
K.P.
a
REPUBLIKA NG PILIPINAS
(K. P.)
—
b

NO6	A60(a)	20c lt ol grn	35	35
NO7	AP1(b)	1p sepia	1.00	1.00

Since 1867 American stamp collectors have been using the Scott Catalogue to identify their stamps and Scott Albums to house their collections.

POLAND
(pō′lănd)

LOCATION—In Europe between Russia and Germany.
GOVT.—Republic.
AREA—120,664 sq. mi.
POP.—34,700,000 (est. 1977).
CAPITAL—Warsaw.

100 Kopecks = 1 Ruble
100 Fenigi = 1 Marka (1918)
100 Halerzy = 1 Korona (1918)
100 Groszy = 1 Zloty (1924)

Prices for No. 1 are for fine copies. Very fine to superb specimens sell at much higher prices, and inferior or poor copies sell at reduced prices, depending on the condition of the individual specimen.

Issued under Russian Dominion.

Coat of Arms
A1
Perf. 11½ to 12½.

1860   Typographed.   Unwmkd.

1	A1	10k bl & rose	650.00	275.00
a.		10k bl & car	800.00	350.00
b.		10k dk bl & rose	800.00	350.00
c.		Added bl frame for inner oval	1,200.	600.00
d.		Imperf.		

Used for letters within the Polish territory and to Russia. Postage on all foreign letters was paid in cash.
These stamps were superseded by those of Russia in 1865.

Issues of the Republic.

Local issues were made in various Polish cities during the German occupation. In the early months of the Republic many issues were made by overprinting the German occupation stamps with the words "Poczta Polska" and an eagle or bars often with the name of the city. These issues were not authorized by the Government but were made by the local authorities and restricted to local use. In 1916 a series of stamps was issued for the Polish Legion and in 1917-18 the Polish Expeditionary Force used surcharged Russian stamps. The regularity of these issues is questioned.

Warsaw Issues.

Statue of   Coat of Arms
Sigismund III   of Warsaw
A2   A3

Polish Eagle   Sobieski Monument
A4   A5

POLAND

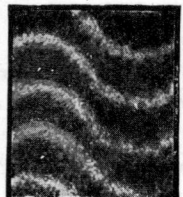
Wmk. 145

Stamps of the Warsaw Local Post Surcharged.
Wmkd. Wavy Lines. (145)

1918, Nov. 17 — Perf. 11½

11	A2	5f on 2gr brn & buff	1.00	85
a.		Inverted surcharge	40.00	40.00
12	A3	10f on 6gr grn & buff	85	75
a.		Inverted surcharge	6.00	6.00
13	A4	25f on 10gr rose & buff	2.00	1.75
a.		Inverted surcharge	12.00	12.00
14	A5	50f on 20gr lt bl & buff	5.25	5.00
a.		Inverted surcharge	150.00	150.00

Nos. 11-14 exist imperforate.

Occupation Stamps Nos. N6 to N16 Overprinted or Surcharged:

a   b

Wmkd. Lozenges. (125)

1918-19 — Perf. 14, 14½

15	A16	3(pf) brn ('19)	19.00	12.50
16	A22	5(pf) on 2½pf gray	35	35
17	A16	5(pf) on 3pf brn	4.00	2.50
18	A16	5(pf) green	75	60
19	A16	10(pf) carmine	15	15
20	A22	15(pf) dk vio	15	15
21	A16	20(pf) blue	25	25
a.		20pf ultra	500.00	500.00
23	A22	25(pf) on 7½pf org	35	20
24	A16	30(pf) org & blk, buff	15	15
25	A16	40(pf) lake & blk	50	50
26	A16	60(pf) magenta	75	75
		Nos. 15-26 (11)	26.40	18.10

There are two settings of this overprint. The first printing, issued Dec. 5, 1918, has space of 3½mm. between the middle two bars. The second printing, issued Jan. 15, 1919, has space of 4½mm. No. 15 comes only in the second setting; all others in both.

Varieties of this overprint and surcharge are numerous: double; inverted; misspellings (Pocata, Poczto, Pelska); letters omitted, inverted or wrong font; 3 bars instead of 4, etc.

Lublin Issue.

A6   A7

Austrian Military Semi-Postal Stamps of 1918 Overprinted.
Perf. 12½x13

1918, Dec. 5 — Unwmkd.

27	A6	10h gray grn	9.00	7.50
a.		Inverted ovpt.	25.00	25.00
28	A7	20h magenta	9.00	7.50
a.		Inverted ovpt.	25.00	25.00
29	A6	45h blue	9.00	7.50
a.		Inverted ovpt.	25.00	25.00

Austrian Military Stamps of 1917 Surcharged

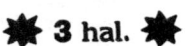

1918-19 — Perf. 12½

30	M3	3hal on 3h ol gray	30.00	25.00
a.		Invtd. surch.	200.00	200.00
b.		Perf. 11½	27.50	22.50
c.		Perf. 11½x12½	40.00	40.00
31	M3	3hal on 15h brt rose	3.75	3.00
a.		Inverted surch.	20.00	20.00

Surcharged in Black

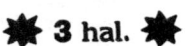

32	M3	10hal on 30h sl grn	3.75	2.50
a.		Inverted surch.	20.00	20.00
b.		Brown surcharge (error)	60.00	50.00
34	M3	25hal on 40h ol bis	6.00	4.00
a.		Inverted surch.	30.00	30.00
b.		Perf. 11½	15.00	6.00
35	M3	45hal on 60h rose	4.00	3.50
a.		Inverted surch.	20.00	20.00
36	M3	45hal on 80h dl bl	7.00	7.00
a.		Inverted surch.	30.00	30.00
37	M3	50hal on 60h rose	4.00	3.50
a.		Inverted surch.	20.00	20.00

Similar surcharge with bars instead of stars over original value

38	M3	45hal on 80h dl bl	7.50	7.00
a.		Inverted surch.	20.00	20.00

Overprinted

39	M3	50h dp grn	32.50	25.00
a.		Inverted overprint	80.00	80.00
40	M3	90h dk vio	5.00	4.00
a.		Inverted ovpt.	20.00	20.00
		Nos. 30-40 (10)	103.50	84.50

Cracow Issues.
Austrian Stamps of 1916-18 Overprinted

POCZTA POLSKA

1919, Jan. 17 — Typographed

41	A37	3h brt vio	200.00	185.00
42	A37	5h lt grn	225.00	185.00
43	A37	6h dp org	22.50	17.50
a.		Inverted ovpt.	400.00	
44	A37	10h magenta	210.00	185.00
45	A37	12h lt bl	22.50	16.00
46	A39	40h ol grn	17.50	15.00
a.		Inverted ovpt.	100.00	100.00
b.		Double ovpt.	300.00	
47	A39	50h bl grn	7.50	6.00
a.		Inverted ovpt.		1,250.
48	A39	60h dp bl	5.00	4.00
a.		Inverted ovpt.	100.00	75.00
49	A39	80h org brn	4.00	3.50
b.		Double ovpt.	75.00	75.00
			100.00	100.00
50	A39	90h red vio	650.00	550.00
51	A39	1k car, yel	8.00	6.00

Engraved.

52	A40	2k blue	5.00	4.00
53	A40	3k car rose	55.00	45.00
54	A40	4k yel grn	80.00	75.00
55	A40	10k dp vio	3,750.	4,000.

The 3k is on granite paper.
The overprint on Nos. 52 to 55 is slightly larger than illustration and different ornament between lines of type.

Same Overprint on Nos. 168-171.

1919 — Typographed

56	A42	15h dl red	7.50	7.00
57	A42	20h dk grn	75.00	80.00
58	A42	25h blue	750.00	650.00
59	A42	30h dl vio	150.00	125.00

POLSKA POCZTA

Austria No. 157 Surcharged

25

1919, Jan. 24

60	A39	25h on 80h org brn	3.00	3.00
a.		Inverted surcharge	60.00	60.00

Excellent counterfeits of Nos. 27 to 60 exist.

Polish Eagle
A9
Without gum

1919, Feb. 25 — Litho. — Imperf.
Yellowish Paper

61	A9	2h gray	40	40
62	A9	3h dl vio	40	40
63	A9	5h green	10	10
64	A9	6h orange	10.00	10.00
65	A9	10h lake	10	10
66	A9	15h brown	10	10
67	A9	20h ol grn	40	40

Bluish Paper.

68	A9	25h car	10	10
69	A9	50h indigo	10	10
70	A9	70h dp bl	40	40
71	A9	1k ol gray & car	75	60
		Nos. 61-71 (11)	12.85	12.70

Nos. 61-71 exist with privately applied perforations.

Posen (Poznan) Issue.

A9a   A9b

German Stamps of 1906-20 Overprinted in Black.
Perf. 14, 14½

1919, Aug. 5 — Wmk. 125

72	A9a	5pf on 2pf gray	25.00	17.50
73	A9a	5pf on 7½pf org	2.50	1.50
a.		Inverted surch.	125.00	
74	A9a	5pf on 20pf bl vio	2.00	1.25
75	A9b	10pf on 25pf org & blk, yel	5.00	3.25
76	A9b	10pf on 40pf lake & blk	2.75	1.50
		Nos. 72-76 (5)	37.25	25.00

Germany Nos. 96 and 98 Surcharged in Red or Green:

a   b

1919, Sept. 15

77	A22	5pf on 2pf gray (R)	225.00	175.00
a.		Inverted surcharge		3,000.
78	A22	10pf on 7½pf org (G)	175.00	125.00

Nos. 77-78 are a provisional issue for use in Gniezno.
Counterfeit surcharges abound.

For Northern Poland.

Eagle and Fasces, Symbolical of United Poland
A10   A11

"Agriculture"   "Peace"
A12   A13

Polish Cavalryman—A14
Wove or Ribbed Paper.

1919, Jan. 27 — Imperf.

81	A10	3f bis brn	15	10
82	A10	5f green	15	8
83	A10	10f red vio	15	8
84	A10	15f dp rose	15	10
85	A11	20f dp bl	15	10
86	A11	25f ol grn	15	10
87	A11	50f bl grn	15	10
88	A12	1m violet	1.50	1.00
89	A12	1.50m dp grn	2.75	1.75
90	A12	2m dk brn	3.25	2.00
91	A13	2.50m org brn	8.50	5.00
92	A14	5m red vio	10.00	5.25
		Nos. 81-92 (12)	27.05	15.66

POLAND

Perf. 10, 11, 11½, 10x11½, 11½x10.

1919-20				
93	A10	3f bis brn	8	6
94	A10	5f green	8	6
95	A10	10f red vio	8	6
96	A10	10f brn ('20)	8	6
97	A10	15f dp rose	8	6
98	A10	15f ver ('20)	8	6
99	A11	20f dp bl	8	6
100	A11	25f ol grn	8	6
101	A11	40f brt vio ('20)	8	6
102	A11	50f bl grn	8	6
103	A12	1m violet	50	50
105	A12	1.50m dp grn	1.00	50
106	A12	2m dk brn	1.00	50
107	A13	2.50m org brn	1.50	1.25
108	A14	5m red vio	2.50	1.25
	Nos. 93-108 (15)		7.30	4.35

Several denominations among Nos. 81-132 are found with double impression or in pairs imperf. between.
See also Nos. 140-152C, 170-175.

For Southern Poland.

A15   A16

A17

A18   A19

1919, Jan. 27			Imperf.	
109	A15	3h red brn	10	10
110	A15	5h emerald	10	10
111	A15	10h orange	10	10
112	A15	15h vermilion	10	10
113	A16	20h gray brn	10	10
114	A16	25h lt bl	10	10
115	A16	50h org brn	15	10
116	A17	1k dk grn	25	15
117	A17	1.50k red brn	3.00	2.50
118	A17	2k dk bl	1.75	1.50
119	A18	2.50k dk vio	7.00	4.00
120	A19	5k sl bl	8.00	5.00
	Nos. 109-120 (12)		20.75	13.85

Perf. 10, 11½, 10x11½, 11½x10.

121	A15	3h red brn	5	5
122	A15	5h emerald	5	5
123	A15	10h orange	5	5
124	A15	15h vermilion	5	5
125	A16	20h gray brn	5	5
126	A16	25h lt bl	5	5
127	A16	50h org brn	5	5
128	A17	1k dk grn	20	10
129	A17	1.50k red brn	50	10
130	A17	2k dk bl	50	10
131	A18	2.50k dk vio	60	20
132	A19	5k sl bl	1.00	40
	Nos. 121-132 (12)		3.15	1.25

National Assembly Issue.

A20   Adalbert Trampczynski A22

Ignace Jan Paderewski A21

Eagle Watching Ship A24

Designs: 25f, Gen. Josef Pilsudski. 1m, Griffin.

Wove or Ribbed Paper.

1919-20			Perf. 11½	
133	A20	10f red vio	20	10
134	A20	15f brn red	50	25
a.	Imperf., pair		25.00	
135	A22	20f dp brn (21x25mm)	40	30
136	A22	20f dp brn (17x20mm)('20)	75	95
137	A21	25f ol grn	25	18
138	A24	50f Prus bl	30	20
139	A24	1m purple	40	30
	Nos. 133-139 (7)		2.80	2.28

First National Assembly of Poland.

General Issue.
Perf. 9 to 14½ and Compound.

1919		Thin Laid Paper		
140	A11	25f ol grn	8	5
141	A11	50f bl grn	8	5
142	A12	1m dk gray	35	10
143	A12	2m bis brn	1.00	15
144	A13	3m red brn	50	15
a.	Pair, imperf. vert.		7.50	7.50
145	A14	5m red vio	25	15
146	A14	6m dp rose	25	15
a.	Pair, imperf. vert.		10.00	10.00
147	A14	10m brn red	35	20
	Horizontal pair, imperf.		10.00	10.00
148	A14	20m gray grn	60	35
	Nos. 140-148 (9)		3.46	1.35

Type of 1919 Redrawn.
Perf. 9 to 14½ and Compound.

1920-22		Thin Laid or Wove Paper.		
149	A10	1m red	10	6
150	A10	2m gray grn	15	6
151	A10	3m lt bl	15	6
152	A10	4m rose red	15	6
152A	A10	5m dk vio	15	6
a.	Pair, imperf. vert.		7.50	7.50
152C	A10	8m gray brn ('22)	30	20
	Nos. 149-152C (6)		1.00	10

The word "POCZTA" is in smaller letters and the numerals have been enlarged.
The color of No. 152A varies from dark violet to red brown.

No. 101 Surcharged

Perf. 10, 11½, 10x11½, 11½x10.

1921, Jan. 25		Thick Wove Paper		
153	A10	3m on 40f brt vio	25	15
a.	Double surcharge		15.00	15.00
b.	Inverted surcharge		20.00	20.00

Sower and Rainbow of Hope A27

Perf. 9 to 14½ and Compound.

1921		Lithographed		
		Thin Laid or Wove Paper.		
		Size: 28x22mm.		
154	A27	10m sl bl	20	10
155	A27	15m lt brn	25	10
155A	A27	20m red	20	15

Signing of peace treaty with Russia.
See also No. 191.

Sun (Peace) Breaking into Darkness (Despair) A28

"Peace" and "Agriculture" A29

"Peace" A30
Perf. 11, 11½, 12, 12½, 13 and Compound.

1921, May 2				
156	A28	2m green	1.50	60
157	A28	3m blue	1.50	60
158	A28	4m red	1.00	60
	4m car rose (error)		175.00	
159	A29	6m car rose	1.25	60
160	A29	10m sl bl		75
161	A30	25m dk vio	2.50	1.50
162	A30	50m sl bl & buff	1.50	1.00
	Nos. 156-162 (7)		10.25	5.65

Issued to commemorate the Constitution.

Polish Eagle A31

Perf. 9 to 14½ and Compound.

1921-23				
163	A31	25m vio & buff	10	10
164	A31	50m car & buff	10	10
a.	Imperf. horizontally			
165	A31	100m blk brn & org	10	10
166	A31	200m blk & rose ('23)	25	15
167	A31	300m ol grn ('23)	25	15
168	A31	400m brn ('23)	25	15
169	A31	500m brn ('23)	25	15
169A	A31	1000m org ('23)	25	10
169B	A31	2000m dl bl ('23)	25	10
	Nos. 163-169B (9)		1.80	1.15

Types of 1919 and

Miner A32

Perf. 9 to 14½ and Compound.

1922-23				
170	A10	5f blue	10	15
171	A10	10f lt vio	10	15
172	A11	20f pale red	10	15
173	A11	40f vio brn	10	15
174	A11	50f orange	10	15
175	A11	75f bl grn	10	15
176	A32	1m black	15	20
177	A32	1.25m dk grn	15	25
178	A32	2m dp rose	15	25
179	A32	3m emerald	15	25
180	A32	4m dp ultra	15	25
181	A32	5m yel brn	15	25
182	A32	6m red org	20	25
183	A32	10m lil brn	20	25
184	A32	20m dp vio	20	30
185	A32	50m ol grn	25	35
187	A32	80m ver ('23)	50	1.00
188	A32	100m vio ('23)	50	1.00
189	A32	200m org ('23)	1.50	3.00
190	A32	300m pale bl ('23)	4.50	5.00
	Nos. 170-190 (20)		9.35	13.50

This issue was to commemorate the union of Upper Silesia with Poland.
There were two printings of Nos. 176 to 190, the first being from flat plates, the second from rotary press on thin paper with perforations 12½.
Nos. 173 and 175 are printed from new plates showing larger value numerals and a single "f".

Sower Type Redrawn.
Size: 25x21mm.

1922	Thick or Thin Wove Paper			
191	A27	20m carmine	40	40

In this stamp the design has been strengthened and made more distinct, especially the ground and the numerals in the upper corners.

Nicolaus Copernicus A33   Father Stanislaus Konarski A34

1923		*Perf. 10 to 12½.*		
192	A33	1000m indigo	90	40
193	A34	3000m brown	50	40
a.	"Konapski"		10.00	7.50
194	A33	5000m rose	90	40

Nos. 192 and 194 commemorate the 450th anniversary of the birth of Nicolaus Copernicus (1473-1543), the astronomer. No. 193 commemorates the death of Stanislaus Konarski (1700-1773), educator, and the creation by the Polish Parliament of the Commission of Public Instruction.

No. 163 Surcharged

Perf. 9 to 14½ and Compound.

1923				
195	A31	10000m on 25m vio & buff	20	10
a.	Double surcharge		5.00	
b.	Inverted surcharge		7.50	

Stamps of 1921 Surcharged **MK 25,000 MK**

196	A27	25000m on 20m red	40	15
a.	Double surcharge		5.00	5.00
b.	Inverted surcharge		10.00	
197	A27	50000m on 10m grnsh bl	20	12
a.	Double surcharge		5.00	5.00
b.	Inverted surcharge		7.50	7.50

No. 191 Surcharged **MK 25,000 MK**

198	A27	25000m on 20m car	30	12
a.	Double surcharge		5.00	5.00
b.	Inverted surcharge		7.50	

No. 150 Surcharged with New Value.

1924				
199	A10	20000m on 2m gray grn	50	20
a.	Inverted surcharge		7.50	7.50
b.	Double surcharge		5.00	5.00

Type of 1919 Issue Surcharged with New Value.

200	A10	100000m on 5m red brn	20	10
a.	Double surcharge		5.00	5.00
b.	Inverted surcharge		7.50	

POLAND

Arms of Poland
A35

Perf. 10 to 14½ and Compound.
1924   Lithographed
Thin Paper.

205	A35	10,000m lil brn	40	30
206	A35	20,000m ol grn	40	20
207	A35	30,000m scarlet	1.25	40
208	A35	50,000m ap grn	2.75	40
209	A35	100,000m brn org	80	35
210	A35	200,000m lt bl	40	15
211	A35	300,000m red vio	80	80
212	A35	500,000m brn	80	80
213	A35	1,000,000m pale rose	80	3.50
214	A35	2,000,000m dk grn	1.25	8.00
		Nos. 205-214 (10)	9.65	14.50

Arms of Poland   President Stanislaus Wojciechowski
A36   A37

Perf. 10 to 13½ and Compound.
1924

215	A36	1g org brn	40	10
216	A36	2g dk brn	40	10
217	A36	3g orange	50	10
218	A36	5g ol grn	1.00	10
219	A36	10g bl grn	1.25	8
220	A36	15g red	1.25	8
221	A36	20g blue	2.50	20
222	A36	25g red brn	3.50	40
a.		25g ind	2,500.	
223	A36	30g dp vio	15.00	30
a.		30g gray bl	250.00	
224	A36	40g indigo	4.00	40
225	A36	50g magenta	3.50	35

Perf. 11½, 12.

226	A37	1z scarlet	17.50	1.25
		Nos. 215-226 (12)	50.80	3.46

Holy Gate of Wilno (Vilnius)   Poznan Town Hall
A38   A39

Sigismund Monument, Warsaw   Wawel Castle at Cracow
A40   A41

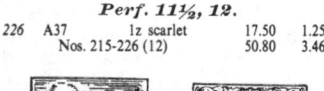

Sobieski Statue at Lwow
A42

Ship of State
A43

Perf. 10 to 13.
1925-27

227	A38	1g bis brn	50	20
228	A42	2g brn ol	60	35
229	A40	3g blue	2.25	25
230	A39	5g yel grn	2.25	10
231	A40	10g violet	2.25	10
232	A41	15g rose red	2.00	10
233	A43	20g dl red	2.50	15
234	A38	24g gray bl	9.00	1.50
235	A42	30g dk bl	3.50	15
236	A41	40g lt bl ('27)	4.00	15
237	A43	45g dk vio	9.00	25
		Nos. 227-237 (11)	37.85	3.30

1926-27   Redrawn.

238	A40	3g blue	3.00	35
239	A39	5g yel grn	3.50	15
240	A40	10g violet	5.00	15
241	A41	15g rose red	5.00	15

On Nos. 229 to 232 inclusive the lines representing clouds touch the numerals. On the redrawn stamps the numerals have white outlines, separating them from the cloud lines.

Marshal Pilsudski   Frederic Chopin
A44   A45

1927 Typographed   Perf. 12½, 11½

242	A44	20g red brn	3.00	15
243	A45	40g dp ultra	20.00	1.25

See also No. 250.

President Ignacy Moscicki—A46

1927, May 4   Perf. 11½

245	A46	20g red	4.00	50

Dr. Karol Kaczkowski   Julius Slowacki
A47   A48

1927, May 27   Perf. 11½, 12½

246	A47	10g gray grn	3.00	2.00
247	A47	25g carmine	6.00	3.00
248	A47	40g dk bl	9.25	3.00

Issued to commemorate the fourth International Congress of Military Medicine and Pharmacy, Warsaw, May 30-June 4, 1927.

1927, June 28   Perf. 12½

249	A48	20g rose	4.00	40

Commemorating the transfer from Paris to Cracow of the remains of Julius Slowacki, poet.

Pilsudski Type of 1927.
1928   Design Redrawn
Perf. 11½, 12x11½, 12½x13.

250	A44	25g yel brn	3.00	20

Souvenir Sheet.

A49

1928, May 3   Engr.   Perf. 12½

251	A49	Sheet of two	375.00	400.00
a.		50g blk brn	100.00	100.00
b.		1z blk brn	100.00	100.00

Issued to commemorate the First National Philatelic Exhibition at Warsaw, May 3 to 13, 1928. Sold to each purchaser of a ticket to the Warsaw Philatelic Exhibition, which cost 1.50 zloty. Sheets measure 117x88mm.

Marshal Pilsudski   Pres. Moscicki
A49a   A50

Perf. 10½ to 14 and Compound.
1928-31   Wove Paper.

253	A49a	50g bluish sl	4.00	10
254	A49a	50g bl grn ('31)	15.00	25

See also No. 315.

Perf. 12x12½, 11½ to 13½ and Compound.
1928   Laid Paper.

255	A50	1z blk, cr	10.00	25
a.		Horizontally laid paper ('30)	80.00	3.00

See also Nos. 305, 316.

General Josef Bem   Henryk Sienkiewicz
A51   A52

Wove Paper.
1928, May   Typo.   Perf. 12½

256	A51	25g rose red	3.50	35

Issued in commemoration of the return from Syria to Poland of the ashes of General Josef Bem.

1928, Oct.

257	A52	15g ultra	3.00	10

Eagle Arms   "Swiatowid," Ancient Slav God
A53   A54

1928-29   Perf. 12x12½

258	A53	5g dk vio	50	5
259	A53	10g green	1.50	15
260	A53	25g red brn	85	10

1928, Dec. 15   Perf. 12½x12

261	A54	25g brown	3.00	20

Issued in connection with the Poznan Agricultural Exhibition.

King John III Sobieski   Stylized Soldiers
A55   A56

1930, July   Perf. 12x12½

262	A55	75g claret	6.00	25

1930, Nov. 1   Perf. 12½

263	A56	5g vio brn	50	10
264	A56	15g dk bl	2.00	35
265	A56	25g red brn	1.75	10
266	A56	30g dl red	7.00	3.50

Centenary of insurrection of 1830.

Kosciuszko, Washington, Pulaski
A57

Laid Paper.
1932, May 3   Perf. 11½

267	A57	30g brown	2.50	40

Commemorative of the 200th anniversary of the birth of George Washington.

 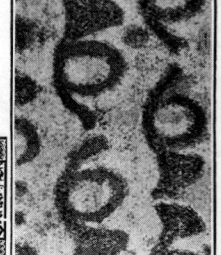

Coat of Arms
A58   Wmk. 234

Wmkd. Multiple Post Horns. (234)
1932-33   Typo.   Perf. 12x12½

268	A58	5g dl vio ('33)	50	5
269	A58	10g green	50	5
270	A58	15g red brn ('33)	50	5
271	A58	20g gray	1.00	6
272	A58	25g buff	1.25	6
273	A58	30g dp rose	4.00	6
274	A58	60g blue	30.00	25
		Nos. 268-274 (7)	37.75	58

City Hall of Torun
A59

POLAND

1933, Jan. 2   Engr.   *Perf. 11½*
275   A59   60g dk bl   30.00   1.00

Commemorative of the 700th anniversary of the founding of the City of Torun by the Grand Master of the Knights of the Teutonic Order.
See also No. B28.

Altar Panel of
St. Mary's Church, Cracow
A60

Perf. 11½-12½ & Compound
Laid Paper.

1933, July 10   Unwmkd.
277   A60   80g red brn   17.50   1.75

Issued to commemorate the 400th anniversary of the death of Veit Stoss, sculptor and woodcarver.

John III Sobieski and Allies before Vienna, painted by Jan Matejko
A61

1933, Sept. 12   Laid Paper
278   A61   1.20z indigo   30.00   5.00

Issued in commemoration of the 250th anniversary of the deliverance of Vienna by the Polish and allied forces under command of John III Sobieski, King of Poland, when besieged by the Turks in 1683.

Cross of Independence   Josef Pilsudski
A62   **A63**

Perf. 12½

1933, Nov. 11   Typo.   Wmk. 234
279   A62   30g scarlet   10.00   45

15th anniversary of independence.

Type of 1932
Overprinted
in Red or Black

**Wyst. Filat.
1934
Katowice**

1934, May 5   Perf. 12
280   A58   20g gray (R)   30.00   22.50
281   A58   30g dp rose   30.00   22.50

Katowice Philatelic Exhibition.

*Perf. 11½ to 12½
and Compound.*

1934, Aug. 6   Engr.   Unwmkd.
282   A63   25g gray bl   1.25   35
283   A63   30g blk brn   3.00   50

Polish Legion, 20th anniversary.

Nos. 274, 277-278
Surcharged in Black or Red

1934   *Perf. 12 x 12½.*   Wmk. 234
284   A58   55g on 60g bl   7.50   50

Unwmkd.
Perf. 11½-12½ & Compound
285   A60   25g on 80g red brn   6.00   50
286   A61   1z on 1.20z ind (R)   20.00   3.00
  a.   Figure "1" in surcharge 5mm
     high instead of 4½mm   20.00   3.00

Surcharge of No. 286 includes bars.

Pilsudski Mourning Issue.

Marshal Pilsudski—**A64**
Perf. 11 to 13 and Compound.

1935
287   A64   5g black   1.00   20
288   A64   15g black   1.00   30
289   A64   25g black   2.00   25
290   A64   45g black   5.00   1.75
291   A64   1z black   9.50   5.75
    Nos. 287-291 (5)   18.50   8.25

Nos. 287 and 288 are typographed, Nos. 290 and 291 lithographed. No. 289 exists both typographed and lithographed.
See No. B35b.

Nos. 270, 282
Overprinted
in Blue or Red

**Kopiee
Marszalka
Piłsudskiego**

1935   *Perf. 12 x 12½.*   Wmk. 234
292   A58   15g red brn   1.25   75

Perf. 11½, 11½ x 12½.   Unwmkd.
293   A63   25g gray bl (R)   4.00   2.25

Issued in connection with the proposed memorial to Marshal Pilsudski, the stamps were sold at Cracow exclusively.

"The Dog Cliff"   President Ignacy Moscicki
A65   **A75**

Designs: 10g, "Eye of the Sea." 15g, M. S. "Pilsudski." 20g, View of Pieniny. 25g, Belvedere Palace. 30g, Castle in Mira. 45g, Castle at Podhorce. 50g, Cloth Hall, Cracow. 60g, Raczynski Library, Poznan. 1z, Cathedral, Wilno.

1935-36 Typographed *Perf. 12½x13*
294   A65   5g vio bl   1.00   8
295   A65   10g yel grn   1.00   8
296   A65   15g Prus grn   3.00   8
297   A65   20g vio blk   1.50   10
    Engraved.
298   A65   25g myr grn   1.25   8
299   A65   30g rose red   3.50   25
300   A65   45g plum ('36)   1.75   25
301   A65   50g blk ('36)   1.75   25
302   A65   55g bl ('36)   15.00   50
303   A65   1z brn ('36)   6.00   1.25
304   A75   3z blk brn   4.00   4.00
    Nos. 294-304 (11)   39.75   6.92

See also Nos. 308-311.

Type of 1928 inscribed
"1926 . 3 . VI . 1936"
on Bottom Margin.

1936, June 3
305   A50   1z ultra   7.50   5.00

Issued in commemoration of the tenth anniversary of the Presidency of Ignacy Moscicki.

Nos. 299, 302 Overprinted in Blue or Red
**GORDON-BENNETT 30.VIII.
1936**

1936, Aug. 15
306   A65   30g rose red   15.00   7.50
307   A65   55g bl (R)   15.00   7.50

Issued to commemorate the Gordon-Bennett International Balloon Race.

Scenic Type of 1935-36.

Designs: 5g, Church at Czestochowa. 10g, Maritime Terminal, Gdynia. 15g, University, Lwow. 20g, Municipal Building, Katowice.

1937   Engraved.   *Perf. 12½.*
308   A65   5g vio brn   25   8
309   A65   10g green   75   8
310   A65   15g red brn   50   8
311   A65   20g org brn   75   25

Marshal Smigly-Rydz   President Moscicki
A80   **A81**

1937   *Perf. 12½ x13.*
312   A80   25g sl grn   30   10
313   A80   55g blue   75   15

Souvenir Sheets.

1937   Types of 1928-37
314   A80   25g dk brn, sheet of
     four   27.50   35.00
  a.   Single stamp   2.00   3.00
315   A49a   50g dp bl, sheet of
     four   27.50   35.00
  a.   Single stamp   2.00   3.00
316   A50   1z gray blk, sheet of
     four   27.50   35.00
  a.   Single stamp   2.00   3.00

Each of the above stamps is printed in a block of four on a sheet of paper measuring 111x125 mm. Inscribed in red at top; "26VI—I.VII—1937" with the Romanian coat of arms at the left and the Polish at the right.
Issued in commemoration of the visit of King Carol of Romania to Poland, June 26th to July 1st, 1937.
See No. B35c.

1938, Feb. 1   *Perf. 12½*
317   A81   15g sl grn   25   10
318   A81   30g rose vio   1.00   25

71st birthday of President Moscicki.

Kosciuszko, Paine and Washington and View of New York City
A82

1938, Mar. 17   *Perf. 12x12½*
319   A82   1z gray bl   2.00   3.00

Issued in commemoration of the 150th anniversary of the Constitution of the United States of America.

Boleslaus I
and Emperor
Otto III
at Gnesen   Marshal Pilsudski
A83   **A95**

Designs: 10g, King Casimir III. 15g, King Ladislas II Jagello and Queen Hedwig. 20g, King Casimir IV. 25g, Treaty of Lublin. 30g, King Stephen Bathory commending Wielock, the peasant. 45g, Stanislas Zolkiewski and Jan Chodkiewicz. 50g, John III Sobieski entering Vienna. 55g, Union of nobles, commoners and peasants. 75g, Dabrowski, Kosciuszko and Poniatowski. 1z, Polish soldiers. 2z, Romuald Traugutt.

1938, Nov. 11   Engr.   *Perf. 12½*
320   A83   5g red org   10   10
321   A83   10g green   10   10
322   A83   15g fawn   30   20
323   A83   20g pck bl   50   25
324   A83   25g dl bl   15   15
325   A83   30g rose red   75   20
326   A83   45g black   50   25
327   A83   50g brt red vio   3.00   20
328   A83   55g ultra   1.00   15
329   A83   75g dl grn   2.50   1.75
330   A83   1z orange   2.00   1.50
331   A83   2z car rose   10.00   10.00
332   A95   3z gray blk   10.00   15.00
   Nos. 320-332 (13)   30.90   29.85

Issued in commemoration of the 20th anniversary of Poland's independence. See also No. 339.

Souvenir Sheet.

Marshal Pilsudski
Gabriel Narutowicz
President Moscicki
Marshal Smigly-Rydz
A96

1938, Nov. 11   *Perf. 12½*
333   A96   Sheet of four   17.50   22.50
  a.   25g dl vio (Pilsudski)   1.00   1.25
  b.   25g dl vio (Narutowicz)   1.00   1.25
  c.   25g dl vio (President Moscicki)   1.00   1.25
  d.   25g dl vio (Marshal
     Smigly-Rydz)   1.00   1.25

Issued to commemorate the 20th anniversary of Poland's independence. Sheets measure 101½x125mm.

Poland Welcoming
Teschen People   Skier
A97   **A98**

1938, Nov. 11
334   A97   25g dl vio   2.00   50

Issued to commemorate the restoration of the Teschen territory ceded by Czechoslovakia.

1939, Feb. 6
335   A98   15g org brn   1.25   1.75
336   A98   25g dl vio   1.75   75
337   A98   30g rose red   2.50   1.75
338   A98   55g brt ultra   7.00   6.00

International Ski Meet, Zakopane, Feb. 11–19.

POLAND

Type of 1938.
Design: 15g, King Ladislas II Jagello and Queen Hedwig.
Re-engraved

1939, Mar. 2   Perf. 12½
| 339 | A83 | 15g redsh brn | 45 | 15 |

No. 322 with crossed swords and helmet at lower left. No. 339, swords and helmet have been removed.

Marshal Pilsudski Reviewing Troops
A99

1939, Aug. 1   Engraved
| 340 | A99 | 25g dl rose vio | 75 | 95 |

Polish Legion, 25th anniversary.
See No. B35a.

Polish Peoples Republic

Romuald Traugutt   Tadeusz Kosciuszko
A100   A101
Design: 1z, Jan Henryk Dabrowski.

Perf. 11½

1944, Sept. 7   Litho.   Unwmkd.
Without Gum
341	A100	25g crim rose	45.00	50.00
342	A101	50g dp grn	55.00	65.00
343	A101	1z dp ultra	50.00	65.00

Counterfeits exist.

Polish Eagle
A103

Grunwald Monument, Cracow
A104

1944, Sept. 13   Photo.   Perf. 12½
344	A103	25g dp red	75	60
a.		25g dl red, typo.		95
345	A104	50g dk sl grn	60	25

No. 344a was not put on sale without surcharge. See Nos. 346, 349a, C20.

No. 344 Surcharged in Black
— 1 zł —
31.XII.1943
K. R. N.
31.XII.1944
a
— 2 zł —
P. K. W. N.
31.XII.1944
b
— 3 zł —
31.XII.1944
R. T. R. P.
c

1944-45
345A	A103	1z on 25g	2.25	2.75
345B	A103	2z on 25g ('45)	2.25	2.75
345C	A103	3z on 25g ('45)	2.25	2.75

Issued to honor Polish government agencies.
K. R. N.—Krajowa Rada Narodowa (Polish National Council), P. K. W. N.—Polski Komitet Wyzwolenia Narodu (Polish National Liberation Committee) and R. T. R. P.— Rzad Tymczasowy Rzeczypospolitej Polskiej (Temporary Administration of the Polish Republic).

No. 344a Surcharged in Brown

1'50 ZŁ

1945, Sept. 1
| 346 | A103 | 1.50z on 25g dl red | 60 | 25 |
| a. | | 1.50z on 25g dp red, #344 | 350.00 | 250.00 |

— 3 zł —
No. 344 Surcharged in Blue
Kielce
15. I. 1945

1945, Feb. 12
347	A103	3z on 25g red	5.00	6.00
348	A103	3z on 25g red (Radom, 16. I. 1945)	3.50	4.25
349	A103	3z on 25g red (Warszawa, 17. I. 1945)	7.50	8.00
a.		3z on 25g dl red, #344a	100.00	125.00
350	A103	3z on 25g red (Czestochowa, 17. I. 1945)	3.50	4.25
351	A103	3z on 25g red (Krakow, 19. I. 1945)	3.50	4.25
352	A103	3z on 25g red (Lodz, 19. I. 1945)	3.50	4.25
353	A103	3z on 25g red (Gniezno, 22. I. 1945)	3.50	4.25
354	A103	3z on 25g red (Bydgoszcz, 23. I. 1945)	3.50	4.25

355	A103	3z on 25g red (Kalisz, 24. I. 1945)	3.50	4.25
356	A103	3z on 25g red (Zakopane, 29. I. 1945)	3.50	4.25
		Nos. 347-356 (10)	40.50	48.00

Dates overprinted are those of liberation for each city.

Grunwald Monument, Cracow   Kosciuszko Statue, Cracow
A105   A106

Cloth Hall, Cracow   Copernicus Memorial
A107   A108

Wawel Castle—A109

1945, Apr. 10   Photo.   Perf. 10½, 11
357	A107	50g dk vio brn	25	15
a.		50g dk brn	75	50
358	A106	1z hn brn	50	35
359	A107	2z sapphire	75	50
360	A108	3z dp red vio	2.00	75
361	A109	5z bl grn	5.00	5.50
		Nos. 357-361 (5)	8.50	7.25

Liberation of Cracow Jan. 19, 1945.
Nos. 357 to 361 exist imperforate.
No. 357a is a coarser printing from a new plate showing designer's name (J. Wilczyk) in lower left margin. No. 357 does not show his name.

Nos. 341 and 342 Surcharged in Black or Red:
5 zł

22.I.1863.
d
5 zł. =

24. III. 1794

1945   Perf. 11½
| 362 | A100(d) | 5z on 25g crim rose | 32.50 | 37.50 |
| 363 | A101(e) | 5z on 50g dp grn (R) | 8.00 | 10.00 |

No. 362 was issued without gum.

No. 345 Surcharged in Brown

1 ZŁ

1945, Sept. 10   Perf. 12½
| 364 | A104 | 1z on 50g dk sl grn | 50 | 25 |

Lodz Skyline   Kosciuszko Monument, Lodz
A110   A111

Flag Bearer Carrying Wounded Comrade
A112

1945   Litho.   Perf. 11; 9 (3z)
365	A110	1z dp ultra	75	25
366	A111	3z dl red vio	85	50
367	A112	5z dp car	3.00	3.00

Nos. 365 and 367 commemorate the liberation of Lodz and Warsaw.

Grunwald Battle Scene   Eagle Breaking Fetters and Manifesto of Freedom
A113   A114

1945, July 16
| 368 | A113 | 5z dp bl | 8.00 | 9.00 |

Battle of Grunwald (Tannenberg), July 15, 1410.

1945, July 22
| 369 | A114 | 3z rose car | 12.50 | 15.00 |

Issued to commemorate the 1st anniversary of the liberation of Poland.

Krantor, Danzig   Stock Tower, Danzig
A115   A116

Ancient High Gate, Danzig
A117

POLAND

1945, Sept. 15   Photo.   **Unwmkd.**

370	A115	1z olive	15	10
371	A116	2z sapphire	25	10
372	A117	3c dk vio	75	25

Recovery of Poland's access to the sea at Danzig. Exist imperf. Price, set $15.

Civilian and Soldiers in Rebellion
A118

1945, Nov. 29

| 373 | A118 | 10z black | 8.00 | 9.00 |

Issued to commemorate the 115th anniversary of the "November Uprising" against the Russians, November 29th, 1830.

Warsaw Castle, 1939 and 1945
A119

Designs—Views of Warsaw, 1939 and 1945: 3z, Cathedral of St. John. 3.50z, City Hall. 6z, Post Office. 8z, Army General Staff Headquarters. 10z, Holy Cross Church.

1945–46   *Imperf.*   **Unwmkd.**

374	A119	1.50z crimson	25	10
375	A119	3z dk bl	40	10
376	A119	3.50z lt bl grn	1.00	50
377	A119	6z gray blk ('46)	40	25
378	A119	8z brn ('46)	2.00	50
379	A119	10z dk vio ('46)	90	25
	Nos. 374-379 (6)		4.95	1.70

Nos. 374 to 379 Overprinted in Black

WARSZAWA WOLNA
17 Styczeń
1945—1946

1946, Jan. 17

383	A119	1.50z crimson	1.25	2.00
384	A119	3z dk bl	1.25	2.00
385	A119	3.50z lt bl grn	1.25	2.00
386	A119	6z gray blk	1.25	2.00
387	A119	8z brown	1.25	2.00
388	A119	10z dk vio	1.25	2.00
	Nos. 383-388 (6)		7.50	12.00

Issued to commemorate the first anniversary of the liberation of Warsaw, January 17, 1945.

Polish Revolutionist
A125

Infantry Advancing
A126

1946, Jan. 22   **Perf. 11**

| 389 | A125 | 6z sl bl | 6.00 | 7.00 |

Revolt of Jan. 22, 1863.

1946, May 9

| 390 | A126 | 3z brown | 35 | 15 |

Polish freedom, first anniversary.

Premier Edward Osubka-Morawski
Pres. Boleslaw Bierut and
Marshal Michael Rola-Zymierski
A127

Perf. 11x10½

1946, July 22   **Unwmkd.**

| 391 | A127 | 3z purple | 3.00 | 3.75 |

Bedzin Castle
A128

Duke Henry IV of Silesia, from Tomb at Wroclaw
A129

Lanckrona Castle
A130

1946, Sept. 1   Photogravure   *Imperf.*

392	A128	5z ol gray	25	10
393	A128	5z brown	25	10

Perf. 10½.

| 394 | A129 | 6z gray blk | 50 | 25 |

Imperf.

| 395 | A130 | 10z dp bl | 1.25 | 35 |

Perforated copies of Nos. 392, 393 and 395 are said to have been privately made.

Jan Matejko, Jacek Malczewski, Josef Chelmonski
A131

1947

Adam Chmielowski (Brother Albert)
A132

Designs: 3z, Chopin. 5z, Wojciech Boguslawski, Helena Modjeska and Stefan Jaracz. 6z, Alexander Swietochowski, Stephen Zeromski and Boleslaw Prus. 10z, Marie Sklodowska Curie. 15z, Stanislaw Wyspianski, Juliusz Slowacki and Jan Kasprowicz. 20z, Adam Mickiewicz.

Perf. 11, Imperf.

396	A131	1z blue	30	15
397	A132	2z brown	50	25
398	A132	3z Prus grn	75	25
399	A131	5z ol grn	1.00	25
400	A131	6z gray grn	2.00	95
401	A132	10z gray brn	1.25	25
402	A131	15z sepia	2.25	75
403	A132	20z gray blk	2.25	1.00
	Nos. 396-403 (8)		10.55	3.85

No. 394 Surcharged in Red

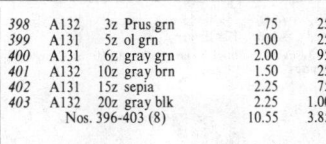

1947, Feb. 25   **Perf. 10½**

| 404 | A129 | 5z on 6z gray blk | 50 | 30 |

Types of 1947.

1947   Photogravure   *Perf. 11, Imperf.*

405	A131	1z sl gray	25	20
406	A132	2z orange	25	15
407	A132	3z ol grn	1.75	50
408	A131	5z ol brn	50	15
409	A131	6z car rose	75	30
410	A132	10z blue	1.25	25
411	A131	15z chnt brn	1.00	50
412	A132	20z dk vio	75	75
a.	Souvenir sheet of 8		200.00	250.00
	Nos. 405-412 (8)		6.50	2.80

No. 412a measures 210x128mm. and contains one each of Nos. 405 to 412, perf. 11½. Marginal decorations and inscriptions, including "Kultura Polska," in olive green and carmine. The sheet has a face value of 62z and a surtax of 438z.

Laborer   Farmer
A139   A140

Fisherman   Miner
A141   A142

1947, Aug. 20   Engr.   **Perf. 13**

413	A139	5z rose brn	1.25	25
414	A140	10z brt bl grn	25	10
415	A141	15z dk bl	1.50	25
416	A142	20z brn blk	1.00	15

Allegory of the Revolution
A143

Insurgents
A144

1948, Mar. 15   Photo.   **Perf. 11**

| 417 | A143 | 15z brown | 40 | 20 |

Centenary of the Revolution of 1848. See Nos. 430–432.

1948, Apr. 19

| 418 | A144 | 15z gray blk | 1.00 | 2.00 |

Issued to commemorate the 5th anniversary of the ghetto uprising, Warsaw, April 19, 1943.

Decorated Bicycle Wheel
A145

1948, May 1

| 419 | A145 | 15z brt rose & bl | 2.50 | 1.50 |

Issued to commemorate the 1st International Bicycle Peace Race, Warsaw-Prague-Warsaw.

Launching Ship   Loading Freighter
A146   A147

Design: 35z, Racing yacht "Gen. Mariusz Zaruski."

1948, June 22

420	A146	6z violet	1.50	1.75
421	A147	15z brn car	1.75	1.75
422	A147	35z sl gray	3.00	3.00

Issued to honor the Polish Merchant Marine.

Cyclists
A148   A149

1948, June 22

423	A148	3z gray	1.75	75
424	A148	6z brown	1.75	1.25
425	A148	15z green	1.75	1.75

Issued to publicize the 7th Circuit of Poland Bicycle Race, June 22 to July 4, 1948.

1948, July 15

426	A149	6z blue	50	50
427	A149	15z red	1.25	50
428	A149	18z rose brn	1.00	25
429	A149	35z dk brn	1.00	50

Issued to publicize an exhibition to commemorate the recovery of Polish territories, Wroclaw, 1948.

Gen. Henryk Dembinski and Gen. Josef Bem
A150

Symbolical of United Youth
A151

Designs: 35z, S. Worcell, P. Sciegienny and E. Dembowski. 60z, Friedrich Engels and Karl Marx.

1948, July 15

430	A150	30z dk brn	75	50
431	A150	35z ol grn	3.50	50
432	A150	60z brt rose	1.00	75

Issued to commemorate the centenary of the Revolution of 1848. See also No. 417.

POLAND

1948, Aug. 8
433 A151 15z blue 75 35
Issued to publicize the International Congress of Democratic Youth, Warsaw, August 1948.

Stagecoach Leaving Torun Gate
A152

1948, Sept. 4
434 A152 15z brown 75 50
Philatelic Exhibition, Torun, September, 1948.

Clock Dial and Locomotive — A153
Pres. Boleslaw Bierut — A154

1948, Oct. 6 Perf. 11½
435 A153 18z blue 6.00 6.00
Issued to publicize the European Railroad Schedule Conference, Cracow.

1948–49 Perf. 11, 11½ Unwmkd.
436 A154 2z org ('49) 5 5
437 A154 3z bl grn ('49) 10 10
438 A154 5z brown 5 5
439 A154 6z slate 50 25
440 A154 10z vio ('49) 15 5
441 A154 15z dp car 25 8
442 A154 18z gray grn 60 35
443 A154 30z blue 95 25
444 A154 35z vio brn 3.00 50
Nos. 436–444 (9) 5.65 1.68

Workers Carrying Flag
A155

Designs: 15z, Marx, Engels, Lenin and Stalin. 25z, Ludwig Warynski.
Inscribed: "Kongres Jednosci Klasy Robotniczej 8. XII. 1948."

1948, Dec. 8 Perf. 11
445 A155 5z crimson 85 25
446 A155 15z dl vio 85 75
447 A155 25z brown 1.75 60

Redrawn. Dated: "XII. 1948."
Designs as before.

1948, Dec. 15 Perf. 11½
448 A155 5z brn car 2.50 1.50
449 A155 15z brt bl 2.50 1.50
450 A155 25z dk grn 3.50 3.00
Issued to publicize the Congress of the Union of the Working Class, Warsaw, December, 1948.

"Socialism"
A156

Designs: 5z, "Labor." 15z, "Peace."

Photogravure.
1949, May 31 Perf. 11½ Unwmkd.
451 A156 3z car rose 1.25 1.00

452 A156 5z dp bl 1.25 1.00
453 A156 15z dp grn 1.75 1.75
Issued to publicize the 8th Trade Union Congress, June 5, 1949.

Warsaw Scene
A157

Pres. Boleslaw Bierut — A158
Radio Station — A159

1949, July 22 Perf. 13x12½, 12½x13. Lithographed
454 A157 10z gray blk 3.25 1.50
455 A158 15z lil rose 2.00 1.75
456 A159 35z gray bl 2.00 1.50
Issued to commemorate the fifth anniversary of "People's Poland."

Stagecoach and World Map
A160

Designs: 30z, Ship and map. 80z, Plane and map.

Perf. 13x12½

1949, Oct. 10 Engraved
457 A160 6z gray pur 1.00 1.75
458 A160 30z blue 2.50 1.75
459 A160 80z dl grn 6.00 4.00
Issued to commemorate the 75th anniversary of the formation of the Universal Postal Union.

Symbolical of United Poland
A161

1949 Perf. 13½x13
460 A161 5z brn red 1.25 30
461 A161 10z rose red 30 10
462 A161 15z green 30 10
463 A161 35z dk brn 1.00 60
Issued to publicize the Congress of the People's Movement for Unity.

Adam Mickiewicz — A162
Frederic Chopin — A163

Design: 35z, Juliusz Slowacki.

1949, Dec. 5 Perf. 12½
464 A162 10z brn vio 3.50 2.00
465 A163 15z brn rose 5.00 3.00
466 A162 35z dp bl 3.50 2.00

Mail Delivery — A164
Adam Mickiewicz and Pushkin — A165

1950, Jan. 21
467 A164 15z red vio 3.00 1.75
Issued to publicize the 3rd Congress of P. T. T. Trade Unions, January 21-23, 1950.

1949, Dec. 15
468 A165 15z lilac 3.50 1.75
Polish-Soviet friendship.

Pres. Boleslaw Bierut — A166
Julian Marchlewski — A167

1950, Feb. 25 Engr. Perf. 12x12½
469 A166 15z red 50 25
See also Nos. 478–484, 490–496.

1950, Mar. 23 Photo. Perf. 11x10½
470 A167 15z gray blk 1.00 60
Issued to commemorate the 25th anniversary of the death of Julian Marchlewski, author and political leader.

Reconstruction, Warsaw — A168
Perf. 11, 12 and Compounds of 13

1950, Apr. 15
471 A168 5z dk brn 20 8
See also No. 497.

Worker Holding Hammer, Flag and Olive Branch — A169
Workers of Three Races with Flag — A170

1950, Apr. 26 Perf. 11½
472 A169 10z dp lil rose 1.50 35
473 A170 15z brn ol 1.50 20
60th anniversary of Labor Day.

 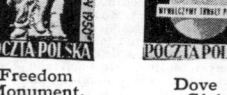

Freedom Monument, Poznan — A171
Dove on Globe — A172

1950, Apr. 27
474 A171 15z chocolate 35 18
Poznan Fair, Apr. 29–May 14, 1950.

1950, May 15 Unwmkd.
475 A172 10z dk grn 1.00 25
476 A172 15z dk brn 50 10
Issued to commemorate the Day of International Action for World Peace.

Polish Workers — A173
Hibner, Kniewski and Rutkowski — A174

1950, July 20 Perf. 12½x13
477 A173 15z vio bl 25 10
Issued to publicize Poland's 6-year plan. See also Nos. 507A – 510, 539.

Bierut Type of 1950, No Frame

1950 Engraved Perf. 12x12½
478 A166 5z dl grn 5 5
479 A166 10z dl red 8 5
480 A166 15z dp bl 1.00 25
481 A166 20z vio brn 25 10
482 A166 25z yel brn 45 10
482A A166 30z rose brn 50 25
483 A166 40z brown 40 10
484 A166 50z olive 1.50 50
Nos. 478–484 (8) 4.23 1.40

1950, Aug. 18 Photo. Perf. 11
485 A174 15z gray blk 2.50 95
Issued to commemorate the 25th anniversary of the execution of three Polish revolutionists, Ladislaus Hibner, Ladislaus Kniewski and Heinrich Rutkowski.

Worker and Dove — A175
Dove by Picasso — A176

1950, Aug. 31 Engr. Perf. 12½
486 A175 15z gray grn 50 15
Polish Peace Congress, Warsaw, 1950.

"GROSZY"

To provide denominations needed as a result of the currency revaluation of Oct. 28, 1950, each post office was authorized to surcharge stamps of its current stock with the word "Groszy." Many types and sizes of this surcharge exist. The surcharge was applied to most of Poland's 1946–1950 issues. All stamps of that period could receive the surcharge upon request of anyone.

1950, Nov. 13
487 A176 40g blue 1.50 50
488 A176 45g brn red 50 15
2nd World Peace Congress.

Josef Bem and Battle Scene — A177

POLAND

109

1950, Dec. 10
| 489 | A177 | 45g blue | 2.50 | 1.75 |

Issued to commemorate the centenary of the death of Gen. Josef Bem.

Type of 1950 with Frame Omitted.
Perf. 12x12½

1950, Dec. 16		Engr.	Unwmkd.	
490	A166	5g brn vio	10	8
491	A166	10g bluish grn	15	8
492	A166	15g dp yel grn	10	6
493	A166	25g dk red	10	6
493A	A166	30g red	20	8
494	A166	40g vermilion	15	8
495	A166	45g dp bl	1.00	30
496	A166	75g brown	75	25
	Nos. 490-496 (8)		2.55	99

Reconstruction Type of 1950.
Photogravure.

1950		*Perf. 11, 11x11½, 13x11.*		
497	A168	15g green	20	8

Woman and Doves
A178

1951, Mar. 2 Engr. *Perf. 12½*
| 498 | A178 | 45g dk red | 45 | 25 |

Issued to publicize the Congress of Women, March 3-4, 1951.

Gen. Jaroslaw Dabrowski
A179

1951, Mar. 24 *Perf. 12x12½*
| 499 | A179 | 45g dk grn | 35 | 20 |

Issued to commemorate the 80th anniversary of the Insurrection of Paris and the death of Gen. Jaroslaw Dabrowski.

Dove Type of 1950 Surcharged.
Perf. 12½
| 500 | A176 | 45g on 15z brn red | 65 | 25 |

Worker and Flag	Steel Mill, Nowa Hute
A180	A181

1951, Apr. 25 Photo. *Perf. 14x11*
| 501 | A181 | 45g scarlet | 35 | 15 |

Issued to publicize Labor Day, May 1, 1951.

1951 Engraved. *Perf. 12½*
502	A181	40g dk bl	10	5
503	A181	45g black	15	5
504	A181	60g brown	30	8
505	A181	90g dk car	55	15

Pioneer Saluting	Boy and Girl Pioneers
A182	A183

1951, Apr. 1 Photogravure
| 506 | A182 | 30g ol brn | 1.00 | 75 |
| 507 | A183 | 45g brt grnsh bl | 7.50 | 1.00 |

Issued to publicize Children's Day, June 1, 1951.

Workers Type of 1950.
Engraved.

1951		*Perf. 12½x13.*	Unwmkd.	
507A	A173	45g vio bl	15	10
508	A173	75g blk brn	25	10
509	A173	1.15z dk grn	60	30
510	A173	1.20z dk red	40	30

Issued to publicize Poland's 6-year plan.

Stanislaw Staszyk	Congress Emblem
A184	A186

Z. F. von Wroblewski and Karol S. Olszewski—A185

Portraits: 40g, Marie Sklodowska Curie. 60g, Marceli Nencki. 1.15z, Nicolaus Copernicus.

Photogravure.

1951, Apr. 25 *Perf. 12½, 14x11*
511	A184	25g car rose	2.25	2.00
512	A184	40g ultra	25	25
513	A185	45g purple	7.00	1.75
514	A184	60g green	75	25
515	A184	1.15z claret	2.00	1.00
516	A186	1.20z gray	1.25	75
	Nos. 511-516 (6)		13.50	6.00

Issued to publicize the first Congress of Polish Science.

Feliks E. Dzerzhinski
A187

1951, July 5 Engr. *Perf. 12x12½*
| 517 | A187 | 45g chnt brn | 35 | 10 |

Issued to commemorate the 25th anniversary of the death of Feliks E. Dzerzhinski, Polish revolutionary, organizer of Russian secret police.

Pres. Boleslaw Bierut—A188

1951, July 22 *Perf. 12½*
518	A188	45g dk car	50	25
519	A188	60g dp grn	15.00	7.50
520	A188	90g dp bl	1.00	50

Issued to commemorate the 7th anniversary of the formation of the Polish People's Republic.

Flag and Sports Emblem
A189

Perf. 12½, 14x11

1951, Sept. 8 Photogravure
| 521 | A189 | 45g green | 1.50 | 75 |

Issued to publicize the National Sports Festival, 1951.

Type of 1950 with Frame Omitted Surcharged with New Value in Black.

1951, Sept. 1 Engr. *Perf. 12½x11½*
| 522 | A166 | 45g on 35z org red | 35 | 15 |

Youths Encircling Globe—A190

1951, Aug. 5 Photo. *Perf. 12½x11*
| 523 | A190 | 40g dp ultra | 60 | 30 |

Issued to publicize the third World Youth Festival, Berlin, Aug. 5-19, 1951.

Joseph V. Stalin	Frederic Chopin and Stanislaw Moniuszko
A191	A192

1951, Oct. 30 Engr. *Perf. 12½*
| 524 | A191 | 45g lake | 25 | 10 |
| 525 | A191 | 90g gray blk | 50 | 25 |

Issued to publicize the month of Polish-Soviet friendship, Nov. 1951.

1951, Nov. 15 Unwmkd.
| 526 | A192 | 45g gray | 35 | 10 |
| 527 | A192 | 90g brnsh red | 75 | 35 |

Festival of Polish Music, 1951.

Apartment House Construction	Coal Mining
A193	A194

Design: Nos. 529-530, Electrical installation.

1951-52
Inscribed: "Plan 6," etc.
528	A193	30g dl grn	10	6
529	A193	30g gray blk ('52)	10	8
530	A193	45g red ('52)	25	15
531	A194	90g chocolate	45	15
532	A193	1.15z vio brn ('52)	40	15
533	A194	1.20z dp bl ('52)	50	20
	Nos. 528-533, B68-B69A (9)		3.65	1.59

Poland's 6-year plan.

Pawel Finder
A195

Portrait: 1.15z, Malgorzata Fornalska.

1952, Jan. 18
| 534 | A195 | 90g chocolate | 35 | 15 |
| 535 | A195 | 1.15z red org | 45 | 30 |

Issued to commemorate the 10th anniversary the founding of the Polish Workers Party.

Flag, Workman, Mother and Child
A196

1952, Mar. 8 *Perf. 12½x12*
| 536 | A196 | 1.20z dp car | 50 | 25 |

Issued to publicize International Women's Day, Mar. 8, 1952. See also No. B64.

Gen. Karol Swierczewski-Walter	Pres. Boleslaw Bierut
A197	A198

1952, Mar. 28 *Perf. 12½*
| 537 | A197 | 90g bl gray | 50 | 15 |

Issued to commemorate the fifth anniversary of the death of Gen. Karol Swierczewski-Walter (1896-1947). See No. B65.

1952, Apr. 18
| 538 | A198 | 90g dl grn | 1.00 | 75 |

Issued to commemorate the 60th anniversary of the birth of Pres. Boleslaw Bierut. See also Nos. B66-B67.

Souvenir Sheet

A199

1951, Nov. 15
539	A199	Sheet of four	17.50	15.00
a.	45g red brn (A173)		2.00	1.50
b.	75g red brn (A173)		2.00	1.50
c.	1.15z red brn (A173)		2.00	1.50
d.	1.20z red brn (A173)		2.00	1.50

Issued in sheets measuring 90x119mm., to publicize the Polish Philatelic Association Congress, Warsaw, 1951. Sold for 5 zloty.

Workers with Flag—A200

POLAND

1952, May 1   *Perf. 12½*   Unwmkd.
540   A200   75g dp grn   40   25
Labor Day, May 1, 1952. See No. B70.

J. I. Kraszewski
A201

Portraits: 1z, Hugo Kollontaj. 1.15z, Marja Konopnicka.

1952, May   Various Frames.
541   A201   25g brn vio   40   25
542   A201   1z yel grn   40   15
543   A201   1.15z red brn   75   60
Nos. 541-543, B71-B72 (5)   2.30   1.40

Nikolai Gogol   Gymnast
A202   A203

1952, June 5
544   A202   25g dp grn   1.25   65
Issued to commemorate the 100th anniversary of the death of Nikolai V. Gogol, writer.

1952, June 21   Photo.   *Perf. 13*
545   A203   1.15z grn (*Runners*)   1.75   1.25
546   A203   1.20z dl red   75   75

See also Nos. B75-B76.

Racing Cyclists   Shipyard Worker and Collier
A204   A205

1952, Apr. 25   *Perf. 13½*
547   A204   40g blue   1.50   75
Issued to commemorate the 5th International Peace Bicycle Race, Warsaw-Berlin-Prague.

1952, June 28   Engr.   *Perf. 12½*
548   A205   90g vio brn   1.00   50
Issued to publicize Shipbuilders' Day, 1952. See also Nos. B77-B78.

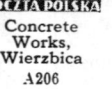

Concrete Works, Wierzbica   Bugler
A206   A207

1952, June 17
549   A206   3z gray   1.25   50
550   A206   10z brn red   2.00   35

1952, July 17   *Perf. 12½x12*
551   A207   90g brown   50   25
Youth Festival, 1952. See Nos. B79-B80.

Celebrating New Constitution   Power Plant, Jaworzno
A208   A209

1952, July 22   Photo.   *Perf. 12½*
552   A208   3z vio & dk brn   50   35
Issued to commemorate the proclamation of a new constitution. See also No. B81.

1952, Aug. 7   Engraved
553   A209   1z black   75   40
554   A209   1.50z dp grn   75   25
See also No. B82.

Grywald   Parachute Descent
A210   A211

1952, Aug. 18
Design: 1z, Niedzica.
555   A210   60g dk grn   75   75
556   A210   1z red ("Niedzica")   1.25   15
   a.   1z red ("Niedziga")   3.00   75

See also No. B85.

1952, Aug. 23
557   A211   90g dp bl   95   75
Issued to publicize Aviation Day, Aug. 23, 1952. See also Nos. B86-B87.

Avicenna   Shipbuilding
A212   A213

Portrait: 90g, Victor Hugo.

1952, Sept. 1
558   A212   75g red brn   50   25
559   A212   90g sepia   40   15
Issued to commemorate the anniversaries of the births of Avicenna (1000th) and Victor Hugo (150th).

1952, Sept. 10
560   A213   5g dp grn   15   5
561   A213   15g red brn   25   15
Reconstruction of Danzig shipyards.

Assault on the Winter Palace, 1917
A214

1952, Nov. 7   *Perf. 12x12½*
562   A214   60g dk brn   75   50
35th Anniv. of the Russian Revolution. See #B92. Exists imperf. Price $20.

Auto Assembly Plant, Zeran   Dove
A215   A216

1952, Dec. 12   *Perf. 12½*
563   A215   1.15z brown   60   25
See also No. B99.

1952, Dec. 12   Photogravure
564   A216   30g green   75   30
565   A216   60g ultra   1.50   75
Issued to publicize the Congress of Nations for Peace, Vienna, Dec. 12-19, 1952.

Soldier with Flag   Karl Marx
A217   A218

1953, Feb. 2   *Perf. 11*   Unwmkd.
Flag in Carmine.
566   A217   60g ol gray   4.00   1.00
567   A217   80g bl gray   90   75
Issued to commemorate the 10th anniversary of the Battle of Stalingrad.

1953, Mar. 14   *Perf. 12½*
568   A218   60g dk bl   22.50   12.50
569   A218   80g dk brn   1.00   50
Issued to commemorate the 70th anniversary of the death of Karl Marx.

Cyclists and Arms of Warsaw   Flag and Globe
A219   A220

Arms: No. 571, Berlin. No. 572, Prague.

1953, Apr. 30
570   A219   80g dk brn   1.00   50
571   A219   80g dk grn   1.00   50
572   A219   80g red   15.00   11.00
Issued to commemorate the 6th International Peace Bicycle Race, Warsaw-Berlin-Prague.

1953, Apr. 28
573   A220   60g vermilion   1.50   75
574   A220   80g carmine   65   15
Issued to publicize Labor Day, May 1, 1953.

Boxer
A221

Design: 95g, Boxing match.

1953, May 17
575   A221   40g red brn   1.00   50
576   A221   80g orange   15.00   5.50
577   A221   95g vio brn   2.50   1.50
Issued to publicize the European Championship Boxing Matches, Warsaw, May 17-24, 1953.

Copernicus Watching Heavens, by Jan Matejko—A222

Nicolaus Copernicus
A223

Perf. 12x12½, 12½x12.

1953, May 22   Engraved
578   A222   20g brown   1.50   50
579   A223   80g dp bl   12.50   6.50
Issued to commemorate the 480th anniversary of the birth of Nicolaus Copernicus, astronomer.

Fishing Boat   Old Part of Warsaw
A224   A225

Design: 1.35z, Freighter "Czech."

1953, July 15   *Perf. 12½*
580   A224   80g dk grn   1.95   50
581   A224   1.35z dp bl   3.00   1.25
Issued for Merchant Marine Day.

1953, July 15   Photogravure
582   A225   20g red brn   20   10
583   A225   2.35z blue   2.00   1.25
Issued to commemorate the 36th anniversary of the proclamation of "People's Poland."

Students of Two Races   Schoolgirl and Dove
A226   A227

Design: 1.35z, Congress badge (similar to A7?).

1953, Aug. 24
584   A226   40g dk brn   25   15
585   A227   1.35z green   75   10
586   A227   1.50z blue   1.75   1.25
Nos. 584-586, C32-C33 (5)   5.25   2.70
Issued to publicize the third World Congress of Students, Warsaw, 1953.

POLAND

Nurse Feeding Baby
A228

Design: 1.75z, Nurse instructing mother.

1953, Nov. 21
| 587 | A228 | 80g rose car | 9.00 | 5.00 |
| 588 | A228 | 1.75z dp grn | 50 | 25 |

Issued to publicize Poland's Social Health Service.

Mieczyslaw Kalinowski — A229
Battle Scene, Polish and Soviet Flags — A230

Portrait: 1.75z, Roman Pazinski.

1953, Oct. 10
589	A229	45g brown	3.00	2.50
590	A230	80g brn lake	50	10
591	A229	1.75z ol gray	50	20

Issued to commemorate the 10th anniversary of Poland's People's Army.

Jan Kochanowski — A231
Courtyard, Wawel Castle — A232

Portrait: 1.35z, Mikolaj Rej.

1953, Nov. 10 Engraved
592	A231	20g red brn	20	10
593	A232	80g dp plum	50	10
594	A231	1.35z gray blk	1.75	75

Issued for the "Renaissance Year."

Palace of Culture, Warsaw
A233

Designs: 1.75z, Constitution Square. 2z, Old Section, Warsaw.

1953, Nov. 30 Perf. 12x12½
595	A233	80g vermilion	10.00	1.50
596	A233	1.75z dp bl	75	50
597	A233	2z vio brn	6.00	3.00

Issued for the reconstruction of Warsaw.

Ice Dancer — A236
Skier — A237

Design: 2.85z, Ice hockey player.

1953, Dec. 31 Litho. Perf. 12½
602	A236	80g blue	1.50	50
603	A237	95g bl grn	2.00	75
604	A236	2.85z dk red	5.00	3.00

Canceled to Order
The government stamp agency began late in 1951 to sell canceled sets of new issues. Prices in the second ("used") column are for these canceled-to-order stamps. Postally used copies are worth more.

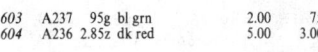

Children at Play
A238

Designs: 80g, Girls on the way to school. 1.50z, Two students in class.

1953, Dec. 31 Photogravure
605	A238	10g violet	25	10
606	A238	80g red brn	1.00	45
607	A238	1.50z dk grn	5.00	2.75

Krynica Spa — A239
Dunajec Canyon, Pieniny Mountains — A240

Designs: 80g, Lake Morskie-Oko, Tatra Mts. 2z, Windmill and framework, Ciechocinek.

1953, Dec. 16
608	A239	20g bl & rose brn	25	15
609	A240	80g bl grn & dk vio	1.50	1.25
610	A240	1.75z ol bis & dk grn	1.00	15
611	A239	2z brick red & blk	1.50	25

Electric Passenger Train — A241
Spinning Mill, Worker — A242

1954, Jan. 26 Engraved

Design: 80g, Electric locomotive and cars.

| 612 | A241 | 60g dp bl | 9.00 | 5.50 |
| 613 | A241 | 80g red brn | 75 | 25 |

1954, Mar. 24 Photogravure
Designs: 40g, Woman letter carrier. 80g, Woman tractor driver.

614	A242	20g dp brn	1.00	50
615	A242	40g dp bl	75	20
616	A242	80g dk brn	1.00	25

Flags and May Flowers — A243
"Peace" Uniting Three Capitals — A244

1954, Apr. 28
617	A243	40g chocolate	75	50
618	A243	60g dp bl	75	20
619	A243	80g car rose	75	30

Issued to publicize Labor Day, May 1, 1954.

1954, Apr. 29 Perf. 12½x12
Design: No. 621, Dove, olive branch and wheel.
| 620 | A244 | 80g red brn | 70 | 25 |
| 621 | A244 | 80g dp bl | 75 | 25 |

Issued to publicize the 7th International Bicycle Tour, May 2-17, 1954.

Glider and Framed Clouds
A245 — A246

1954, Apr. 30 Engraved Perf. 11½
| 622 | A245 | 25g gray | 85 | 30 |
| 623 | A245 | 80g brn car | 30 | 10 |

Issued to publicize the third Trade Union Congress, Warsaw 1954.

1954, May 31 Photo. Perf. 12½

Designs: 60g, Glider and flags. 1.35z, Glider and large cloud.

624	A246	45g dk grn	75	12
625	A246	60g purple	3.00	1.50
626	A246	60g brown	1.50	25
627	A246	1.35z blue	2.00	50

International Glider Championships, Leszno.

Fencing — A247
Handstand on Horizontal Bars — A248

Design: 1z, Relay racers.

1954, July 17
628	A247	25g vio brn	1.50	50
629	A248	60g Prus bl	2.50	25
630	A247	1z vio red	1.50	75

Javelin Throwers — A249
Studzianki Battle Scene — A250

1954, July 17 Perf. 12
| 631 | A249 | 60g rose brn & dk red brn | 2.50 | 40 |
| 632 | A249 | 1.55z gray & blk | 1.00 | 60 |

Nos. 628-632 were issued to publicize the second Summer Spartacist Games, 1954.

1954, Aug. 24 Perf. 12½
Design: 1z, Soldier and flag bearer.
| 633 | A250 | 60g dk grn | 2.00 | 75 |
| 634 | A250 | 1z vio brn | 7.50 | 2.50 |

10th anniversary, Battle of Studzianki.

Railway Signal — A251
Farmer Picking Fruit — A252

Design: 60g, Modern train.

1954, Sept. 9
| 635 | A251 | 40g dl bl | 1.50 | 50 |
| 636 | A251 | 60g black | 5.00 | 1.25 |

Issued to publicize Railwaymen's Day.

1954, Sept. 15
| 637 | A252 | 40g violet | 1.75 | 95 |
| 638 | A252 | 60g black | 75 | 25 |

Month of Polish-Soviet friendship.

View of Elblag — A253
Chopin and Piano — A254

Cities: 45g, Danzig. 60g, Torun. 1.40z, Malbork. 1.55z, Olsztyn.

1954, Oct. 16 Engr. Perf. 12x12½
639	A253	20g dk car, bl	2.75	1.25
640	A253	45g brn, yel	25	10
641	A253	60g dk grn, cit	30	10
642	A253	1.40z dk bl, pink	65	10
643	A253	1.55z dk brn, cr	1.00	25
		Nos. 639-643 (5)	4.95	1.80

Issued to commemorate the 500th anniversary of Pomerania's return to Poland.

1954, Nov. 8 Photo. Perf. 12½
644	A254	45g dk brn	35	8
645	A254	60g dk grn	65	15
646	A254	1z dk bl	1.50	70

Issued to publicize the fifth International Competition of Chopin's Music.

Coal Mine — A255

Designs: 20g, Soldier, flag and map. 25g, Steel mill. 40g, Relaxing worker in deck chair. 45g, Building construction. 60g, Tractor in field. 1.15z, Lublin Castle. 1.40z, Books and publications. 1.55z, Loading ship. 2.10z, Attacking tank.

Photogravure; Center Engraved

1954-55 Perf. 12½x12
647	A255	10g red brn & choc	1.25	15
648	A255	20g rose & grnsh blk	75	45
649	A255	25g bis & ch ('55)	1.75	25
650	A255	40g yel org & choc	50	25
651	A255	45g cl & vio brn	1.00	
652	A255	60g emer & red brn ('55)	1.00	35
653	A255	1.15z brt bl grn & sep	1.00	75
654	A255	1.40z org & choc	10.00	3.50
655	A255	1.55z bl & ind	2.00	1.00
656	A255	2.10z ultra & ind	3.50	2.00
		Nos. 647-656 (10)	22.75	8.95

10th anniversary of "People's Poland." Issue dates: 25g, 60g, 1955. Others, Dec. 23, 1954.

POLAND

Photogravure; Center Lithographed
(Designs same as above.)

1954, Oct. 30
| 656A | A255 | 25g bis & blk | 2.75 | 1.50 |
| 656B | A255 | 60g emer & red brn | 1.50 | 1.00 |

Insurgents Attacking Russians
A256

Designs: 60g, Gen. Tadeusz Kosciuszko and insurgents. 1.40z, Kosciuszko leading attack in Cracow.

1954, Nov. 30   Engr.   Perf. 12½
657	A256	40g grnsh blk	50	20
658	A256	60g vio brn	75	25
659	A256	1.40z dk gray	1.75	1.00

Issued to commemorate the 160th anniversary of the Insurrection of 1794.

Bison
A257

Animals: 60g, European elk. 1.90z, Chamois. 3z, Beaver.

Engr.; Background Photo.

1954, Dec. 22
660	A257	45g yel grn & blk brn	50	25
661	A257	60g emer & dk brn	50	25
662	A257	1.90z bl & blk brn	75	25
663	A257	3z bl grn & dk brn	2.25	75

Exist imperf. Price, set $6.

Liberators Entering Warsaw **Frederic Chopin**
A258   A259

Design: 60g, Allegory of freedom.

1955, Jan. 17   Photogravure
| 664 | A258 | 40g red brn | 75 | 50 |
| 665 | A258 | 60g dl bl | 2.00 | 95 |

Liberation of Warsaw, 10th anniversary.

1955, Feb. 22   Engraved
| 666 | A259 | 40g dk brn | 40 | 10 |
| 667 | A259 | 60g indigo | 75 | 30 |

Issued to publicize the fifth International Competition of Chopin's Music, Feb. 22 – Mar. 21, 1955.

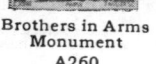

Brothers in Arms Monument   **Sigismund III**
A260   A261

Warsaw monuments: 5g, Mermaid. 10g, Feliks E. Dzerzhinski. 40g, Nicolaus Copernicus. 45g, Marie Sklodowska Curie. 60g, Adam Mickiewicz. 1.55z, Jan Kilinski.

1955, May 3   Perf. 12½   Unwmkd.
668	A260	5g dk grn, *grnsh*	5	5
669	A260	10g vio brn, *yel*	5	5
670	A261	15g blk brn, *bluish*	5	5
671	A260	20g dk bl, *pink*	5	5
672	A260	40g vio, *vio*	50	15
673	A261	45g vio brn, *cr*	75	35
674	A260	60g dk bl, *gray*	50	15
675	A261	1.55z sl bl, *grysh*	1.35	50
	Nos. 668-675 (8)		3.30	1.35

See also Nos. 737 - 739.

Palace of Culture and Flags of Poland and USSR
A262

Design: 60g, Monument.

Perf. 12½x12, 11

1955, Apr. 21   Photogravure
676	A262	40g rose red	25	10
677	A262	40g lt brn	75	45
678	A262	60g Prus bl	30	10
679	A262	60g dk ol brn	30	10

Issued to commemorate the 10th anniversary of the Polish-USSR treaty of friendship.

Arms and Bicycle Wheels   **Poznan Town Hall and Fair Emblem**
A263   A264

Design: 60g, Three doves above road.

1955, Apr. 25   Perf. 12
| 680 | A263 | 40g chocolate | 55 | 25 |
| 681 | A263 | 60g ultra | 35 | 10 |

Issued to commemorate the 8th International Peace Bicycle Race, Prague-Berlin-Warsaw.

1955, June 10   Photo.   Perf. 12½
| 682 | A264 | 40g brt ultra | 50 | 25 |
| 683 | A264 | 60g dl red | 25 | 10 |

Issued to commemorate the 24th International Fair at Poznan, July 3-24, 1955.

"Laikonik" Carnival Costume
A265

A265a

1955, June 16   Typo.   Perf. 12
Multicolored Centers
684	A265	20g emer & hn	50	35
685	A265a	40g brt org & lil	75	10
686	A265	60g bl & car	2.25	45

Issued to commemorate Cracow Celebration Days.

Pansies
A266

Designs: 40g, 60g, (No. 690), Dove and Tower of Palace of Science and Culture. 45g, Pansies. 60g, (No. 691), 1z, "Peace" (POKOJ) and Warsaw Mermaid.

1955, July 13   Litho.   Perf. 12
687	A266	25g vio brn, org & car	25	10
688	A266	40g gray bl & gray blk	25	10
689	A266	45g brn lake, yel & car	50	15
690	A266	60g sep & org	40	25
691	A266	60g ultra & lt bl	40	25
692	A266	1z pur & lt bl	1.25	75
	Nos. 687-692 (6)		3.05	1.60

Exist imperf. Price, set $5.

Issued to commemorate the fifth World Festival of Youth in Warsaw, July 31–August 14, 1955. Exist imperf. Price, set $4.

Motorcyclists   **Stalin Palace of Culture and Science, Warsaw**
A267   A268

1955, July 20   Photo.   Perf. 12½
| 693 | A267 | 40g chocolate | 45 | 30 |
| 694 | A267 | 60g dk grn | 35 | 10 |

Issued to commemorate the 13th International Motorcycle Race in the Tatra Mountains, August 7–9, 1955.

1955, July 21
695	A268	60g ultra	25	10
696	A268	60g gray	25	10
697	A268	75g bl grn	50	25
698	A268	75g brown	50	25

Issued to commemorate Polish National Day, July 22, 1955. Sheets contain alternating copies of the 60g values or the 75g values respectively.

Athletes   **Stadium**
A269   A270

Designs: 40g, Hammer throwing. 1z, Basketball. 1.35z, Sculling. 1.55z, Swimming.

1955, July 27   Perf. 12½   Unwmkd.
699	A269	20g chocolate	10	5
700	A269	40g plum	20	10
701	A270	60g dl bl	40	10
702	A269	1z org ver	75	20
703	A269	1.35z dl vio	1.00	20
704	A269	1.55z pck grn	1.50	75
	Nos. 699-704 (6)		3.95	1.40

2nd International Youth Games, 1955. Exist imperf. Price, set $4.50.

Town Hall, Szczecin (Stettin)   **Revolutionaries with Flag**
A271   A272

Designs: 40g, Cathedral, Wroclaw (Breslau). 60g, Town Hall, Zielona Gora (Grunberg). 95g, Town Hall, Opole (Oppeln).

1955, Sept. 22   Engr.   Perf. 11½
705	A271	25g dl grn	15	15
706	A271	40g red brn	20	8
707	A271	60g vio bl	50	10
708	A271	95g dk gray	75	35

Issued to commemorate the tenth anniversary of the acquisition of Western Polish Territories.

Perf. 12x12½

1955, Sept. 30   Photogravure
| 709 | A272 | 40g dk brn | 40 | 30 |
| 710 | A272 | 60g dk car rose | 35 | 15 |

Revolution of 1905, 50th anniversary.

Adam Mickiewicz
A273

Mickiewicz Monument, Paris
A274

Designs: 60g, Death mask. 95g, Statue, Warsaw.

1955, Oct. 10   Perf. 12x12½, 12½
711	A273	20g dk brn	20	8
712	A274	40g brn org & dk brn	25	10
713	A274	60g grn & brn	25	10
714	A274	95g brn red & blk	1.00	65

Issued to commemorate the centenary of the death of Adam Mickiewicz, poet, and to publicize the celebration of Mickiewicz year.

Teacher and Child   **Rook and Hands**
A275   A276

Design: 60g, Flame and open book.

Perf. 12½x13

1955, Oct. 21   Unwmkd.
| 715 | A275 | 40g brown | 2.00 | 50 |
| 716 | A275 | 60g ultra | 3.50 | 1.50 |

Issued in honor of the 50th anniversary of the Polish Teachers' Trade Union.

POLAND

1956, Feb. 9 — Perf. 12½
Design: 60g, Chess Knight and hands.
717	A276	40g dk red	2.25	1.50
718	A276	60g blue	2.25	30

First World Chess Championship of the Deaf and Dumb, Feb. 9–23.

Captain and S. S. Kilinski—A277

Designs: 10g, Sailor and barges. 20g, Dock worker and S.S. Pokoj. 45g, Shipyard and worker. 60g, Fisherman, S. S. Chopin and trawlers.

1956, Mar. 16 — Perf. 12x12½ Engraved
719	A277	5g green	5	5
720	A277	10g car lake	5	5
721	A277	20g dp ultra	10	5
722	A277	45g rose brn	75	35
723	A277	60g vio brn	50	5
	Nos. 719-723 (5)	1.45	55

Snowflake and Ice Skates A278
Cyclist A279

Designs: 40g, Snowflake and Ice Hockey sticks. 60g, Snowflake and Skis.

1956, Mar. 7 — Photo. Perf. 12½
724	A278	20g brt ultra & blk	5.00	1.75
725	A278	40g brt grn & vio bl	75	10
726	A278	60g lil & lake	75	15

Issued to commemorate the XI World Students Winter Sport Championship, March 7-13, 1956.

1956, Apr. 25
727	A279	40g dk bl	1.25	75
728	A279	60g dk grn	25	15

9th International Peace Bicycle Race, Warsaw-Berlin-Prague, May 1–15.

Zakopane Mountains and Shelter A280

Designs: 40g, Map, compass and knapsack. 60g, Map of Poland and canoe. 1.15z, Skis and mountains.

1956, May 25
729	A280	30g dk grn	25	10
730	A280	40g lt red brn	25	10
731	A280	60g blue	1.00	75
732	A280	1.15z dl pur	50	20

Issued to publicize the Polish Tourist industry.

No. 593 Surcharged with New Values.

1956, July 6 — Engr. Perf. 12½
733	A232	10g on 80g dp plum	35	15
734	A232	40g on 80g dk brn	25	8
735	A232	60g on 80g dk grn	50	10
736	A232	1.35z on 80g dp plum	1.00	60

The size and type of surcharge and obliteration of old value differ for each denomination.

1956, July 10 — Type of 1955
Warsaw Monuments: 30g, Ghetto Monument. 40g, John III Sobieski. 1.55z, Prince Joseph Poniatowski.

737	A260	30g black	25	5
738	A260	40g red brn, *grnsh*	50	35
739	A260	1.55z vio brn, *pnksh*	75	25

No. 737 measures 22½x28mm., instead of 21x27mm.

Polish and Russian Dancers—A281
Design: 60g, Open book and cogwheels.

1956, Sept. 14 — Litho. Perf. 12
740	A281	40g brn red & brn	60	35
741	A281	60g bis & red	35	15

Polish-Soviet Friendship month.

Ludwiga Warzynska and Children A282
Bee on Clover and Beehive A283

1956, Sept. 17 — Photo. Perf. 12½
742	A282	40g dl red brn	50	35
743	A282	60g blue	35	10

Issued in honor of a heroic school teacher who saved three children from a burning house.

1956, Oct. 30 — Litho. Unwmkd.
Design: 60g, Father Jana Dzierzona.
744	A283	40g org yel & brn	1.00	50
745	A283	60g yel & brn	30	10

Issued to commemorate the 50th anniversary of the death of Father Jana Dzierzona, the inventor of the modernized beehive.

"Lady with the Ermine" by Leonardo da Vinci A284

Designs: 40g, Niobe. 60g, Madonna by Veit Stoss.

1956 — Engraved Perf. 11½x11
746	A284	40g dk grn	3.00	1.25
747	A284	60g dk vio	1.00	40
748	A284	1.55z chocolate	2.00	40

Issued to publicize International Museum Week (UNESCO), Oct. 8–14.

Fencer—A285

Designs: 20g, Boxer. 25g, Sculling. 40g, Steeplechase racer. 60g, Javelin thrower. No. 755, Woman gymnast. No. 756, Woman broad jumper.

1956 — Engraved Perf. 11½
750	A285	10g sl & chnt	20	10
751	A285	20g lt brn & dl vio	35	10
752	A285	25g lt bl & blk	50	25
753	A285	40g brt bl grn & redsh brn	40	10
754	A285	60g rose car & ol brn	50	20
755	A285	1.55z lt vio & sep	2.00	1.50
756	A285	1.55z org & chnt	1.25	35
	Nos. 750-756 (7)	5.20	2.60

Issued to commemorate the 16th Olympic Games in Melbourne, Nov. 22–Dec. 8.

15th Century Mailman A286

Lithographed and Engraved.
1956, Nov. 30 — Perf. 12½ Unwmkd.
757	A286	60g lt bl & blk	1.25	90

Issued on the occasion of the reopening of the Postal Museum in Wroclaw (Breslau).

Skier and Snowflake A287
Ski Jumper and Snowflake A288

Design: 1z, Skier in right corner.

1957, Jan. 18 — Photo. Perf. 12½
758	A287	40g blue	40	10
759	A288	60g dk grn	40	15
760	A287	1z purple	75	45

Issued to publicize 50 years of skiing in Poland.

Globe and Tree A289

United Nations Emblem A290
United Nations Headquarters A291

1957, Feb. 26 — Photo. Perf. 12
761	A289	5g mag & brt grnsh bl	40	30
762	A290	15g bl & gray	50	30
763	A291	40g brt bl grn & gray	1.00	75

Issued in honor of the United Nations. Exist imperf. Price, set $6.

An imperf. souvenir sheet exists, containing a 1.50z stamp in a redrawn design similar to A291. The stamp is blue and bright bluish green, marginal decorations are gray and yellow. Sheet size: 57–59mmx70mm. Price, $12, unused or canceled.

Skier A292
Sword, Foil and Saber on World Map A293

1957, Mar. 22 — Perf. 12½
764	A292	60g blue	75	35
765	A292	60g brown	1.00	50

Issued to commemorate the 12th anniversary of the death of the skiers Bronislaw Czech and Hanna Marusarzowna.

1957, Apr. 20 — Perf. 12½ Unwmkd.
Designs: No. 767, Fencer facing right. No. 768, Fencer facing left.
766	A293	40g dp plum	75	50
767	A293	60g carmine	50	10
768	A293	60g ultra	50	15
a.		Nos. 767-768 se-tenant	1.25	50

Issued to commemorate the World Youth Fencing Championships, Warsaw.

Nos. 767–768 are printed se-tenant in the sheet, the fencers facing each other with swords crossed on No. 768.

Dr. Sebastian Petrycy A294
Bicycle Wheel and Carnation A295

Doctors' Portraits: 20g, Wojciech Oczko. 40g, Jedrzei Sniadecki. 60g, Tytus Chalubinski. 1z, Wladyslaw Bieganski. 1.35z, Jozef Dietl. 2.50z, Benedykt Dybowski. 3z, Henryk Jordan.

Portraits Engraved, Inscriptions Typographed

1957 — Perf. 11½
769	A294	10g sep & ultra	5	5
770	A294	20g emer & cl	5	5
771	A294	40g gray & org red	10	5
772	A294	60g bl & pale brn	50	35
773	A294	1z org & dk bl	25	10
774	A294	1.35z gray brn & grn	30	10
775	A294	2.50z dl vio & lil rose	60	10
776	A294	3z vio & ol brn	75	15
	Nos. 769-776 (8)	2.60	95

Issued in honor of famous Polish Physicians of the past.

1957, May 4 — Photo. Perf. 12½
Design: 1.50z, Cyclist.
777	A295	60g ultra	75	35
778	A295	1.50z brt car rose	25	20

Issued to commemorate the 10th International Peace Bicycle Race, Warsaw-Berlin-Prague.

POLAND

Poznan Fair Emblem A296   Turk's Cap A297

1957, June 8 Litho. Unwmkd.
779 A296 60g ultra   30   15
780 A296 2.50z lt bl grn   40   15

Issued to publicize the 26th Fair at Poznan.

1957, Aug. 12 Photo. Perf. 12
Flowers: No. 782, Carline Thistle. No. 783, Sea Holly. No. 784, Edelweiss. No. 785, Lady's-slipper.

781 A297 60g bl grn & cl   30   10
782 A297 60g gray, grn & yel   30   10
783 A297 60g lt bl & grn   30   10
784 A297 60g gray & yel grn   30   10
785 A297 60g lt grn, mar & yel   1.25 50
      Nos. 781-785 (5)   2.45 90

Fire Fighter A298   Town Hall, Leipzig and Congress Emblem A299

Designs: 60g, Child and flames. 2.50z, Grain and flames.

1957, Sept. 11 Perf. 12
786 A298 40g blk & red   10   5
787 A298 60g dk grn & org red   10   5
788 A298 2.50z vio & red   60   30

Issued to publicize the International Fire Brigade Conference, Warsaw.

1957, Sept. 25 Photo. Perf. 12½
789 A299 60g violet   18   10

Issued to publicize the fourth International Trade Union Congress, Leipzig, Oct. 4-15.

"Girl Writing Letter" by Fragonard A300   Karol Libelt A301

1957, Oct. 9 Perf. 12
790 A300 2.50z dk bl grn   75   15

Issued for Stamp Day, Oct. 9.

1957, Nov. 15 Photo. Perf. 12½
791 A301 60g car lake   25   10

Issued to commemorate the centenary of the Poznan Scientific Society and to honor Karol Libelt, politician and philosopher.

Broken Chain and Revolutionary Flag A302   Jan A. Komensky (Comenius) A303

Design: 2.50z, Lenin Statue, Poronin.

1957, Nov. 7
792 A302 60g brt bl & red   10   8
793 A302 2.50z blk & red brn   40   20

Issued to commemorate the 40th anniversary of the Russian Revolution.

1957, Dec. 11 Perf. 12
794 A303 2.50z brt car   35   10

Issued to commemorate the 300th anniversary of the publication of "Didactica Opera Omnia."

Henri Wieniawski A304   Andrzej Strug A305

1957, Dec. 2 Perf. 12½
795 A304 2.50z blue   35   10

Issued to publicize the third Wieniawski Violin Competition in Poznan.

1957, Dec. 16 Perf. 12½ Unwmkd.
796 A305 2.50z brown   30   12

Issued to commemorate the 20th anniversary of the death of Andrzej Strug, novelist.

Joseph Conrad and "Torrens" A306

1957, Dec. 30 Engr. Perf. 12x12½
797 A306 60g brn, grnsh   20   10
798 A306 2.50z dk bl, pink   60   25

Issued to commemorate the centenary of the birth of Joseph Conrad, Polish-born English writer.

Postilion and Stylized Plane A307   Town Hall at Biecz A308

1958 Lithographed Perf. 12½
Designs: 40g, Tomb of Prosper Prowano, globe with plane and satellite. 60g, St. Mary's Church, Cracow, mail coach and plane. 95g, Mail coach and postal bus. 2.10z, Medieval postman and train. 3.40z, Medieval galleon and modern ships.

799 A307 40g lt bl & vio brn   5   5
800 A307 60g pale vio & blk   10   5
801 A307 95g lem & vio   10   5
802 A307 2.10z gray & ultra   80   40
803 A307 2.50z brt bl & blk   60   20
804 A307 3.40z aqua & mar   60   20
      Nos. 799-804 (6)   2.25 95

Issued to commemorate the 400th anniversary of the Polish posts. Imperfs. exist of all but No. 803.

1958, Mar. 29 Engr. Perf. 12½
Town Halls: 40g, Wroclaw. 60g, Tarnow (horiz.). 2.10z, Danzig. 2.50z, Zamosc.

805 A308 20g green   5   5
806 A308 40g brown   10   5
807 A308 60g dk bl   10   5
808 A308 2.10z rose lake   40   10
809 A308 2.50z violet   60   30
      Nos. 805-809 (5)   1.25 55

Giant Pike Perch A309

Fishes: 60g, Salmon (vert.). 2.10z, Pike (vert.). 2.50z, Trout (vert.). 6.40z, Grayling (horiz.).

1958, Apr. 22 Photo. Perf. 12
810 A309 40g bl, blk, grn & yel   15   10
811 A309 60g yel grn, dk grn & bl 15   10
812 A309 2.10z dk bl, grn & yel   45   20
813 A309 2.50z pur, blk & yel grn 2.00 40
814 A309 6.40z bl grn, brn & red 1.25   50
      Nos. 810-814 (5)   4.00 1.30

Casimir Palace, Warsaw University A310   Stylized Glider and Cloud A311

1958, May 14 Perf. 12½ Unwmkd.
815 A310 2.50z vio bl   30   12

Issued to commemorate the 140th anniversary of the University of Warsaw.

1958, June 14 Lithographed
Design: 2.50z, Design reversed.

816 A311 60g gray bl & blk   20   10
817 A311 2.50z gray & blk   50   25

Issued to publicize the 7th International Glider Competitions.

Fair Emblem A312   Armed Postman and Mail Box A313

1958, June 9
818 A312 2.50z blk & rose   30   15

Issued to publicize the 27th Fair at Poznan.

1958, Sept. 1 Engraved Perf. 11
819 A313 60g dk bl   25   10

Issued to commemorate the 19th anniversary of the defense of the Polish post office at Danzig. Inscribed: "You were the first."

Letter, Quill and Postmark A314   Polar Bear A315

1958, Oct. 9 Lithographed
820 A314 60g blk, bl grn & ver   75   45

Issued for Stamp Day. Exists imperf.

Perf. 12½x12
1958, Sept. 30 Photogravure
Design: 2.50z, Rocket and Sputnik.

821 A315 60g black   30   10
822 A315 2.50z dk bl   90   25

Issued to commemorate the International Geophysical Year, 1957-58.

Partisan's Cross A316

Designs: 60g, Virtuti Militari Cross. 2.50z, Grunwald Cross.

1958, Oct. 10 Perf. 11
823 A316 40g blk, grn & ocher   25   10
824 A316 60g blk, bl & yel   25   10
825 A316 2.50z multi   1.00 35

Issued to commemorate the 15th anniversary of the Polish People's Army.

17th Century Ship A317   UNESCO Building Paris A318

Design: 2.50z, Polish immigrants.

1958, Oct. 29 Perf. 11
826 A317 60g dk sl grn   15   10
827 A317 2.50z dk car rose   50   20

Issued to commemorate the 350th anniversary of the arrival of the first Polish immigrants in America.

1958, Nov. 3 Unwmkd.
828 A318 2.50z yel grn & blk   60   20

Issued to commemorate the opening of UNESCO (U. N. Educational, Scientific and Cultural Organization) Headquarters in Paris, Nov. 3.

Stagecoach—A319

Wmk. 326

Wmkd. Post Horn Multiple (326)

1958, Oct. 26 Engr. *Perf. 12½*

829	A319	2.50z sl, *buff*	1.25	75
a.		Souvenir sheet of 6	10.00	10.00

Issued to commemorate the philatelic exhibition in honor of the 400th anniversary of the Polish post, Warsaw, Oct. 25-Nov. 10.
No. 829a measures 131½x139mm. with marginal inscription in slate.

Souvenir Sheet.

1958, Dec. 12 *Imperf.* Unwmkd.

Printed on Silk

830	A319	50z dk bl	12.50	12.50

400th anniversary of the Polish posts.
No. 830 measures 87½x75mm. with marginal inscription in dark blue.

Stanislaw Wyspianski
A320

Kneeling Figure
A321

Portrait: 2.50z, Stanislaw Moniuszko.

1958, Nov. 25 Engr. *Perf. 12½*

831	A320	60g dk vio	15	10
832	A320	2.50z dk sl grn	55	25

Issued to honor Stanislaw Wyspianski, painter and poet, and Stanislaw Moniuszko, composer.

1958, Dec. 10 Lithographed

833	A321	2.50z lt brn & red brn	45	20

Issued to commemorate the tenth anniversary of the signing of the Universal Declaration of Human Rights.

Red Flag
A322

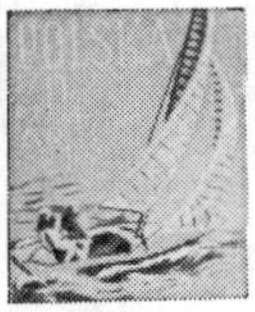

Sailing
A323

1958, Dec. 16 Photogravure

834	A322	60g plum & red	15	8

Issued to commemorate the 40th anniversary of the Communist Party of Poland.

1959, Jan. 3

Sports: 60g, Girl archer. 95g, Soccer. 2z, Horsemanship.

835	A323	40g lt bl & vio bl	35	20
836	A323	60g sal & brn vio	30	15
837	A323	95g grn & brn vio	50	35
838	A323	2z dp bl & lt grn	45	35

Hand at Wheel
A324

Wheat, Hammer and Flag
A325

Design: 1.55z, Factory.

Perf. 12½

1959, Mar. 10 Wmk. 326

839	A324	40gr red, bis & blk	10	5
840	A325	60gr multi	10	7
841	A324	1.55z gray, ver & blk	60	25

Issued to publicize the 3rd Workers Congress.

Amanita Phalloides—A326

Designs: Various mushrooms.

1959, May 8 Photo. *Perf. 11½*

842	A326	20g yel, grn & brn	1.75	75
843	A326	30g multi	25	10
844	A326	40g multi	75	10
845	A326	60g yel grn, brn & ocher	75	10
846	A326	1z multi	50	15
847	A326	2.50z bl, grn & brn	1.00	25
848	A326	3.40z multi	1.25	50
849	A326	5.60z dl yel, brn & grn	3.75	2.00
		Nos. 842-849 (8)	10.00	3.95

"Storks," by Jozef Chelmonski
A327

Paintings: 60g, Mother and Child, Stanislaw Wyspianski (vert.). 1z, Mme. de Romanet, Henryk Rodakowski (vert.). 1.50z, Old Man and Death, Jacek Malczewski (vert.). 6.40z, River Scene, Aleksander Gierymski.

1959 Engraved. *Perf. 12, 12½x12*

850	A327	40g gray grn	25	15
851	A327	60g dl pur	30	15
852	A327	1z int blk	50	15
853	A327	1.50z brown	75	40
854	A327	6.40z blue	3.00	1.00
		Nos. 850-854 (5)	4.80	1.85

Issued in honor of Polish painters. Nos. 850 and 854 measure 36x28mm.; Nos. 851 and 853, 28x36mm.; No. 852, 28x37mm.

Miner and Globe
A328

Map of Poland and Symbol of Agriculture
A329

1959, July 1 Lithographed

855	A328	2.50z multi	45	15

Issued to commemorate the 3rd Miners' Conference, Katowice, July 1959.

Perf. 12x12½

1959, July 21 Wmk. 326

Map of Poland and: 60g, Symbol of industry. 1.50z, Symbol of art and science.

856	A329	40g blk, bl & grn	10	5
857	A329	60g blk & ver	14	5
858	A329	1.50z blk & bl	25	15

Issued to commemorate 15 years of the Peoples' Republic of Poland.

Lazarus Ludwig Zamenhof
A330

Map of Austria and Flower
A331

Design: 1.50z, Star, globe and flag.

1959, July 24 *Perf. 12½*

859	A330	60g blk & grn, *ol*	15	10
860	A330	1.50z ultra, grn & red, *gray*	75	25

Issued to commemorate the centenary of the birth of Lazarus Ludwig Zamenhof, author of Esperanto, and in conjunction with the Esperanto Congress in Warsaw.

1959, July 27 Lithographed

861	A331	60g sep, red & grn, *yel*	10	10
862	A331	2.50z bl, red, & grn, *gray*	75	30

Issued to publicize the 7th World Youth Festival, Vienna, July 26-Aug. 14.

Symbolic Plane
A332

Perf. 12½

1959, Aug. 24 Wmk. 326

863	A332	60g vio bl, grnsh bl & blk	25	8

Issued to commemorate the 30th anniversary of LOT, the Polish airline.

Sejm (Parliament) Building
A333

Perf. 12x12½

1959, Aug. 27 Photogravure

864	A333	60g lt grn, blk & red	10	7
865	A333	2.50z vio gray, blk & red	60	35

Issued for the 48th Interparliamentary Conference in Warsaw.

No. 640 Overprinted in Blue:
"BALPEX I—GDANSK 1959"

1959, Aug. 30 Engr. Unwmkd.

866	A253	45g brn, *yel*	80	60

Issued to publicize the International Philatelic Exhibition of Baltic States at Danzig.

Stylized Dove and Globe
A334

Perf. 12½

1959, Sept. 1 Photo. Wmk. 326

867	A334	60g bl & gray	15	7

Issued to commemorate the tenth anniversary of the World Peace Movement.

Red Cross Nurse
A335

Designs: 60g, Nurse. 2.50z, Henri Dunant.

1959, Sept. 21 Litho. *Perf. 12½*

Size: 21 x 26 mm.

868	A335	40g red, lt grn & blk	15	8
869	A335	60g bis brn, brn & red	15	10

Perf. 11

Size: 23 x 23 mm.

870	A335	2.50z red, pink & blk	75	50

Issued to commemorate the 40th anniversary of the Polish Red Cross and the centenary of the Red Cross.

Polish-Chinese Friendship Society Emblem
A336

Flower Made of Stamps
A337

Lithographed.

1959, Sept. 28 *Perf. 11* Wmk. 326

871	A336	60g multi	50	25
872	A336	2.50z multi	35	20

Issued to publicize Polish-Chinese friendship.

1959, Oct. 9 *Perf. 12½*

873	A337	60g lt grnsh bl, grn & red	15	8
874	A337	2.50z red, grn & vio	50	30

Issued for Stamp Day, 1959.

Sputnik 3—A338

Designs: 60g, Rocket. 2.50z, Earth, moon and Sputnik 2.

1959, Nov. 7 Photo. Wmk. 326

875	A338	40g Prus bl & gray	40	20
876	A338	60g mar & blk	60	40
877	A338	2.50z grn & dk bl	1.75	1.00

Issued on the 42nd anniversary of the Russian Revolution to commemorate the landing of the Soviet moon rocket.
Exist imperf. Price, set $4.75.

Child Doing Homework
A339

Charles Darwin
A340

POLAND

Design: 60g, Three children leaving school.

Lithographed & Engraved
1959, Nov. 14 Perf. 11½
| 878 | A339 | 40g grn & dk brn | 15 | 8 |
| 879 | A339 | 60g bl & red | 25 | 10 |

Issued to publicize the "1,000 Schools" campaign for the 1,000th anniversary of Poland.

1959, Dec. 10 Engr. Perf. 11
Portraits: 40g, Dmitri I. Mendeleev. 60g, Albert Einstein. 1.50z, Louis Pasteur. 1.55z, Isaac Newton. 2.50z, Nicolaus Copernicus.
880	A340	20g dk bl	10	5
881	A340	40g ol gray	15	5
882	A340	60g claret	15	5
883	A340	1.50g dk vio brn	25	10
884	A340	1.55z dk grn	75	25
885	A340	2.50z violet	1.75	1.00
		Nos. 880-885 (6)	3.15	1.50

Issued to honor famous scientists.

Man from Rzeszow A341 — Woman from Rzeszow A342

Regional Costumes: 40g, Cracow. 60g, Kurpiow. 1z, Silesia. 2z, Lowicz. 2.50z, Mountain people. 3.10z, Kujawy. 3.40z, Lublin. 5.60z, Szamotull. 6.50z, Lubuski.

Engraved & Photogravure
Perf. 12, Imperf.
1959-60 Wmk. 326
886	A341	20g sl grn & blk	10	10
887	A342	20g sl grn & blk	10	10
888	A341	40g lt bl & rose car ('60)	10	10
889	A342	40g rose car & bl ('60)	10	10
890	A341	60g blk & pink	10	10
891	A342	60g blk & pink	10	10
892	A341	1z grnsh red & dk red	15	10
893	A342	1z grnsh bl & dk red	15	10
894	A341	2z yel & ultra ('60)	25	15
895	A342	2z yel & ultra ('60)	25	15
896	A341	2.50z grn & rose lil	50	20
897	A342	2.50z grn & rose lil	50	20
898	A341	3.10z yel grn & sl grn ('60)	60	20
899	A342	3.10z yel grn & sl grn ('60)	60	20
900	A341	3.40z gray grn & brn ('60)	75	25
901	A342	3.40z gray grn & brn ('60)	75	25
902	A341	5.60z yel grn & gray bl	2.00	75
903	A342	5.60z yel grn & gray bl	2.00	75
904	A341	6.50z vio & gray grn ('60)	1.75	60
905	A342	6.50z vio & gray grn ('60)	1.75	60
		Nos. 886-905 (20)	12.60	5.10

Piano A343 — Frederic Chopin A344

Design: 1.50z, Musical note and manuscript.

1960, Feb. 22 Litho. Perf. 12
| 906 | A343 | 60g brt vio & blk | 25 | 30 |
| 907 | A343 | 1.50z blk, gray & red | 75 | 25 |

Engraved.
Perf. 12½x12
| 908 | A344 | 2.50z black | 1.75 | 95 |

Nos. 906-908 issued to commemorate the 150th anniversary of the birth of Frederic Chopin and to publicize the Chopin music competition.

Stamp of 1860 A345

Designs: 60g, Ski meet stamp of 1939. 1.35z, Design from 1860 issue. 1.55z, 1945 liberation stamp. 2.50z, 1957 stamp day stamp.

Perf. 11½x11
Litho. (40g, 1.35z); Litho. & Photo.
1960, Mar. 21 Wmk. 326
909	A345	40g multi	25	10
910	A345	60g vio, ultra & blk	50	25
911	A345	1.35z gray, red & bl	1.25	60
912	A345	1.55z grn, car & blk	1.25	35
913	A345	2.50z ap grn, dk grn & blk	1.50	60
		Nos. 909-913 (5)	4.75	1.90

Centenary of Polish stamps. Nos. 909-913 were also issued in sheets of four. Price, $500.

Discus Thrower, Amsterdam 1928 A346

Polish Olympic Victories: No. 915, Runner. No. 916, Bicyclist. No. 917, Steeplechase. No. 918, Trumpeters. No. 919, Boxers. No. 920, Olympic flame. No. 921 Woman jumper.

Perf. 12x12½
Lithographed and Embossed
1960, June 15 Unwmkd.
914	A346	60g bl & blk	25	15
915	A346	60g car rose & blk	25	15
916	A346	60g vio & blk	25	15
917	A346	60g bl grn & blk	25	15
918	A346	2.50z ultra & blk	75	30
919	A346	2.50z chnt & blk	75	30
920	A346	2.50z red & blk	75	30
921	A346	2.50z emer & blk	75	30
		Nos. 914-921 (8)	4.00	1.80

Issued to commemorate the 17th Olympic Games, Rome, Aug. 25–Sept. 11.
Nos. 914-917 and Nos. 918-921 are printed se-tenant in the sheets. The oval lines of each set of 4 stamps form the stadium oval.
Nos. 914-921 exist imperf. Price, set $6.

Tomb of King Ladislas II Jagello A347

Battle of Grunwald by Jan Matejko—A348

Design: 90g, Detail from Grunwald monument.

Engraved
1960 Perf. 11x11½ Wmk. 326
| 922 | A347 | 60g vio brn | 50 | 20 |
| 923 | A347 | 90g ol gray | 1.00 | 50 |

Size: 78x37mm.
| 924 | A348 | 2.50z dk gray | 3.00 | 1.50 |

550th anniversary, Battle of Grunwald.

The Annunciation A349

Designs (Carvings by Veit Stoss, St. Mary's Church, Cracow): 30g, Nativity. 40g, Adoration of the Kings. 60g, The Resurrection. 2.50z, The Ascension. 5.60z, Descent of the Holy Ghost. 10z, The Assumption of the Virgin (vert.).

Engraved
1960 Perf. 12 Wmk. 326
925	A349	20g Prus bl	30	10
926	A349	30g lt red brn	15	10
927	A349	40g violet	40	15
928	A349	60g dl grn	40	15
929	A349	2.50z rose lake	1.25	40
930	A349	5.60z dk brn	7.50	4.50
		Nos. 925-930 (6)	10.00	5.40

Miniature Sheet
Imperf.
| 931 | A349 | 10z black | 8.00 | 6.50 |

No. 931 contains one vertical stamp which measures 72x95mm. Sheet size: 84x105mm.

Ignacy Jan Paderewski A350

1960, Sept. 26 Perf. 12½
| 932 | A350 | 2.50z black | 45 | 15 |

Issued to commemorate the centenary of the birth of Ignacy Jan Paderewski, statesman and musician.

Lukasiewicz and Kerosene Lamp A351

Engraved and Photogravure
1960, Sept. 14 Perf. 11
| 933 | A351 | 60g cit & blk | 20 | 8 |

Issued to commemorate the 5th Pharmaceutical Congress, and to honor Ignacy Lukasiewicz, chemist-pharmacist.

No. 909 Overprinted:
"DZIEN ZNACZKA 1960"
1960 Lithographed Perf. 11½x11
| 934 | A345 | 40g multi | 1.25 | 1.00 |

Issued for Stamp Day, 1960.

Great Bustard—A352

Birds: 20g, Raven. 30g, Great cormorant. 40g, Black stork. 50g, Eagle owl. 60g, White-tailed sea eagle. 75g, Golden eagle. 90g, Short-toed eagle. 2.50z, Rock thrush. 4z, European kingfisher. 5.60z, Wall creeper. 6.50z, European roller.

Photogravure
1960 Perf. 11½ Unwmkd.
Birds in Natural Colors.
935	A352	10g gray & blk	15	10
936	A352	20g pale grn & blk	20	15
937	A352	30g pale grn & blk	20	15
938	A352	40g pale grn & blk	25	20
939	A352	50g pale grn & blk	25	15
940	A352	60g pale grn & blk	25	15
941	A352	75g pale grn & blk	50	15
942	A352	90g pale grn & blk	50	25
943	A352	2.50z pale ol gray & blk	3.50	2.50
944	A352	4z pale ol gray & blk	1.75	90
945	A352	5.60z pale ol gray & blk	3.00	1.00
946	A352	6.50z pale ol gray & blk	6.00	2.00
		Nos. 935-946 (12)	16.55	8.70

Gniezno A353 — Front Page of "Merkuriusz" A354

The male and female costume stamps of each denomination were printed se-tenant in sheets of 56.

POLAND

Historic Towns: 10g, Cracow. 20g, Warsaw. 40g, Poznan. 50g, Plock. 60g, Kalisz. No. 952A, Tczew. 80g, Frombork. 90g, Torun. 95g, Puck (ships). 1z, Slupsk. 1.15z, Gdansk (Danzig). 1.35z, Wroclaw. 1.50z, Szczecin. 1.55z, Opole. 2z, Kolobrzeg. 2.10z, Legnica. 2.50z, Katowice. 3.10z, Lodz. 5.60z, Walbrzych.

Engraved
1960-61 Perf. 11½, 13x12½

947	A353	5g red brn	8	5
948	A353	10g green	8	5
949	A353	20g dk brn	8	5
950	A353	40g vermilion	8	5
951	A353	50g violet	8	5
952	A353	60g rose cl	8	5
952A	A353	60g lt ultra ('61)	25	8
953	A353	80g blue	15	5
954	A353	90g brn ('61)	25	10
955	A353	95g ol gray	15	5

Engraved and Lithographed

956	A353	1z org & gray	15	5
957	A353	1.15z sl grn & sal	15	10
958	A353	1.35z lil rose & lt grn	15	10
959	A353	1.50z sep & palm	15	10
960	A353	1.55z car lake & buff	15	10
961	A353	2z dk bl & pink	25	10
962	A353	2.10z sep & yel	20	10
963	A353	2.50z dl vio & pale grn	30	15
964	A353	3.10z ver & gray	40	15
965	A353	5.60z sl grn & lt grn	1.00	20
		Nos. 947-965 (20)	4.18	1.73

Lithographed and Embossed
1961 Perf. 12 Wmk. 326

Newspapers: 60g, "Proletaryat," first issue, Sept. 15, 1883. 2.50z, "Rzeczpospolita," first issue, July 23, 1944.

966	A354	40g blk, ultra & emer	75	35
967	A354	60g blk, org brn & yel	75	35
968	A354	2.50z blk, vio & bl	4.50	4.00

Issued to commemorate the 300th anniversary of the Polish newspaper Merkuriusz.

Ice Hockey
A355

Part of Cogwheel
A356

Sports: 60g, Ski jump. 1z, Soldiers on skis. 1.50z, Slalom.

1961, Feb. 1 Litho. Wmk. 326

969	A355	40g lt vio, blk & yel	50	25
970	A355	60g lt ultra, blk & car	1.50	75
971	A355	1z lt bl, ol & red	7.50	3.00
972	A355	1.50z grnsh bl, blk & yel	1.25	50

Issued to commemorate the First Winter Spartacist Games of Friendly Armies.

1961, Feb. 11 Perf. 12½

973	A356	60g red & blk	25	8

Fourth Congress of Polish Engineers.

Maj. Yuri A. Gagarin
A357

Design: 60g, Globe and path of rocket.

1961, Apr. 27 Photo. Perf. 12

974	A357	40g dk red & blk	1.25	50
975	A357	60g ultra, blk & car	75	30

Issued to commemorate the first man in space, Yuri Gagarin, Apr. 12, 1961.

Emblem of Poznan Fair
A358

1961, May 25 Litho. Perf. 12½x12

977	A358	40g brt bl, blk & red org	15	7
978	A358	1.50z red org, blk & brt bl	35	12
a.		Souv. sheet of 2	3.50	2.50

Issued to publicize the 30th International Fair at Poznan.
No. 978a contains two of No. 978 with simulated perforation and blue marginal inscriptions. Sold for 4.50z. Size: 122x 51mm. Issued July 29, 1961.

Tadeusz Kosciuszko
A359

Famous Poles: No. 979, Mieszko I. No. 980, Casimir Wielki. No. 981, Casimir Jagello. No. 982, Nicolaus Copernicus. No. 983, Andrzej Frycz Modrzewski.

Photogravure and Engraved
1961, June 15 Perf. 11x11½
Black Inscriptions and Designs

979	A359	60g chlky bl	15	6
980	A359	60g dp rose	15	6
981	A359	60g slate	15	10
982	A359	60g dl vio	95	35
983	A359	60g lt brn	20	12
984	A359	60g ol gray	20	12
		Nos. 979-984 (6)	1.80	81

See also Nos. 1059-1064, 1152-1155.

Trawler—A360

Designs: Various Polish Cargo Ships.

Lithographed
1961, June 24 Perf. 11 Unwmkd.

985	A360	60g multi	50	15
986	A360	1.55z multi	60	15
987	A360	2.50z multi	1.00	45
988	A360	3.40z multi	1.20	75
989	A360	4z multi	2.00	1.50
990	A360	5.60z multi	4.50	2.75
		Nos. 985-990 (6)	9.80	5.75

Issued to honor the Polish ship industry. Sizes (width): 60g, 2.50z, 54mm.; 1.55z, 3.40z, 4z, 80mm.; 5.60z, 108mm.

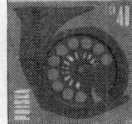
Post Horn and Telephone Dial
A361

Designs (Post horn and): 60g, Radar screen. 2.50z, Conference emblem, globe.

1961, June 26

991	A361	40g sl, gray & red org	15	8
992	A361	60g gray, yel & vio	15	8
993	A361	2.50z ol bis, brt bl & vio bl	50	25
a.		Souv. sheet of 3	3.50	2.50

Issued to commemorate the Conference of Communications Ministers of Communist Countries, Warsaw.
No. 993a contains one each of Nos. 991-993. Marginal inscription in violet. Size: 108x66mm. Sold for 5z.

Seal of Opole, 13th Century
A362

Cement Works, Opole
A363

Designs: No. 996, Tombstone of Henry IV and seal, Wroclaw. No. 997, Apartment houses, Wroclaw. No. 998, Seal of Conrad II and Silesian eagle. No. 999, Steel works, Gorzow. No. 1000, Seal of Prince Barnim I. No. 1001, Seaport, Szczecin. No. 1002, Seal of Princess Elizabeth. No. 1003, Factory, Szczecinek. No. 1004, Seal of Unislaw. No. 1005, Shipyard, Gdansk. No. 1005A, Tower, Frombork Cathedral. No. 1005B, Chemical Laboratory, Kortowo, Olsztyn.

Engraved
1961-62 Perf. 11 Wmk. 326
Western Territories

994	A362	40g brn, grysh	10	5
995	A363	40g brn, grysh	10	5
996	A362	60g vio, pink	15	10
997	A363	60g vio, pink	15	10
998	A362	95g grn, bluish ('62)	25	15
999	A363	95g grn, bluish ('62)	25	15
1000	A362	2.50z ol grn, grnsh	50	25
1001	A363	2.50z ol grn, grnsh	50	25

Northern Territories

1002	A362	60g vio bl, bluish ('62)	15	10
1003	A363	60g vio bl, bluish ('62)	15	10
1004	A362	1.55z brn, buff ('62)	25	10
1005	A363	1.55z brn, buff ('62)	25	10
1005A	A362	2.50z sl bl, grysh ('62)	50	25
1005B	A363	2.50z sl bl, grysh ('62)	50	25
		Nos. 994-1005B (14)	3.80	2.00

Sheets of 56 with alternating rows of horizontal and vertical stamps. The horizontal stamps also alternate with a label with commemorative inscription. Each sheet contains 28 se-tenant pairs of types A362-A363 with label.

Kayak Race Start and "E"
A364

Designs: 60g, Four-man canoes and "E". 2.50z, Paddle, Polish flag and "E" (vert.).

Lithographed
1961, Aug. 18 Perf. 12½ Wmk. 326

1006	A364	40g bl grn, yel & red	25	10
1007	A364	60g multi	25	10
1008	A364	2.50z multi	1.50	70

6th European Canoe Championships, Poznan, Aug. 18-20.

Exist imperf. Price, set $3.

Maj. Gherman Titov, Star, Globe, Orbit—A365

Dove and Earth—A366
Perf. 12x12½

1961, Aug. 24 Photo. Unwmkd.

1009	A365	40g pink, blk & red	45	15
1010	A366	60g bl & blk	45	15

Issued to commemorate the manned space flight of Vostok 2, Aug. 6-7, in which Russian Maj. Gherman Titov orbited the earth 17 times.

Insurgents' Monument, St. Ann's Mountain
A367

Design: 1.55z, Cross of Silesian Insurgents.

Lithographed
1961, Sept. 15 Perf. 12 Wmk. 326

1011	A367	60g gray & emer	15	8
1012	A367	1.55z gray & bl	35	20

Issued to commemorate the 40th anniversary of the third Silesian uprising.

"PKO," Initials of Polish Savings Bank
A368

Designs (Initials and): No. 1014, Bee and clover. No. 1015, Ant. No. 1016, Squirrel. 2.50z, Savings bankbook.

POLAND

1961, Oct. 2   Perf. 12   Wmk. 326

1013	A368	40g ver, blk & org	30	15
1014	A368	60g bl, blk & brt pink	30	15
1015	A368	60g bis brn, blk & ocher	30	10
1016	A368	60g brt grn, blk & dl red	30	10
1017	A368	2.50z car rose, gray & blk	3.00	2.00
		Nos. 1013-1017 (5)	4.20	2.50

Issued to publicize Savings Month.

Mail Cart, by Jan Chelminski
A369

1961, Oct. 9   Engraved   Perf. 12x12½

1018	A369	60g dp grn	45	15
1019	A369	60g vio brn	45	15

Issued to commemorate the 40th anniversary of the Polish Postal Museum and for Stamp Day.

Congress Emblem
A370

1961, Nov. 20   Perf. 12   Wmk. 326

1020	A370	60g black	15	8

Issued to publicize the Fifth World Congress of Trade Unions, Moscow, Dec. 4-16.

Seal of Kopasyni Family, 1284   **Child and Syringe**
A371   **A372**

Designs: 60g, Seal of Bytom, 14th century. 2.50z, Emblem of International Miners Congress, 1958.

1961, Dec. 4   Litho.   Perf. 11x11½

1021	A371	40g multi	25	10
1022	A371	60g bl, gray bl & vio bl	25	10
1023	A371	2.50z yel grn, grn & blk	75	25

Issued to commemorate 1,000 years of the Polish mining industry.

Perf. 12½x12, 12x12½
1961, Dec. 11

Designs: 60g, Children of three races (horiz.). 2.50z, Mother, child and milk bottle.

1024	A372	40g lt bl & blk	20	10
1025	A372	60g org & blk	20	10
1026	A372	2.50z brt bl grn & blk	75	35

Issued to commemorate the 15th anniversary of UNICEF (U.N. International Children's Emergency Fund).

Emblem
A373

Design: 60g, Map with oil pipe line from Siberia to Central Europe.

1961, Dec. 12   Perf. 12   Wmk. 326

1027	A373	40g dk red, yel & vio bl	30	10
1028	A373	60g vio bl, bl & red	25	8

Issued to commemorate the 15th session of the Council of Mutual Economic Assistance of the Communist States.

Ground Beetle
A374

Black Apollo Butterfly
A375

Insects: 30g, Violet runner. 40g, Alpine longicorn beetle. 50g, Great oak capricorn beetle. 60g, Gold runner. 80g, Stag-horned beetle. 1.35z, Death's-head moth. 1.50z, Tiger-striped swallowtail butterfly. 1.55z, Apollo butterfly. 2.50z, Red ant. 5.60z, Bumble bee.

1961, Dec. 30   Photo.   Unwmkd.
Insects in Natural Colors

1029	A374	20g bis brn	25	15
1030	A374	30g pale gray grn	25	10
1031	A374	40g pale yel grn	25	10
1032	A374	50g bl grn	25	8
1033	A374	60g dl rose lil	25	15
1034	A374	80g pale grn	35	15

Perf. 11½

1035	A375	1.15z ultra	45	20
1036	A375	1.35z sapphire	45	20
1037	A375	1.50z bluish grn	75	25
1038	A375	1.55z brt pur	65	25
1039	A375	2.50z brt grn	2.50	60
1040	A375	5.60z org brn	9.50	5.00
		Nos. 1029-1040 (12)	15.90	7.25

Worker with Gun   **Women Skiers**
A376   **A377**

Designs: No. 1042, Worker with trowel and gun. No. 1043, Worker with hammer. No. 1044, Worker at helm. No. 1045, Worker with dove and banner.

Perf. 12½x12
1962, Jan. 5   Litho.   Unwmkd.

1041	A376	60g red, blk & grn	15	8
1042	A376	60g red, blk & sl	15	8
1043	A376	60g blk & vio bl, red	15	8
1044	A376	60g blk & bis, red	25	8
1045	A376	60g blk & gray, red	25	15
		Nos. 1041-1045 (5)	95	47

Polish Workers' Party, 20th anniversary.

Lithographed and Embossed
1962, Feb. 14   Perf. 12

Designs: 60g, Long distance skier. 1.50z, Ski jump (vert.). 10z, FIS emblem (vert.).

1046	A377	40g gray, red & gray bl	15	10
a.		40g sep, red & dl bl	70	20
1047	A377	60g gray, red & gray bl	30	15
a.		60g sep, red & dl bl	90	50
1048	A377	1.50z gray, red & gray bl	45	30
a.		1.50z gray, lil & red	2.50	1.50

Souvenir Sheet
Imperf.

1049	A377	10z gray, red & gray bl	4.50	3.50

Issued to commemorate the World Ski Championships at Zakopane (FIS). No. 1049 contains one stamp with simulated perforation and gray blue inscription. The sheet sold for 15z. Size: 67x80mm.
Each of Nos. 1046-1048 exists in a souvenir sheet of four, with top marginal inscription in gray. Size of the three sheets: 110x92½mm. Price, set of 3, $75.

Broken Flower and Prison Cloth (Auschwitz)—A378

Maidenek Concentration Camp
A379

Design: 1.50z, Proposed memorial, Treblinka concentration camp.

Engraved
1962, Apr. 3   Perf. 11½   Wmk. 326

1050	A378	40g sl bl	25	10
1051	A379	60g dk gray	35	15
1052	A378	1.50z dk vio	75	35

Issued during International Resistance Movement Month to commemorate the millions who died in concentration camps, 1940-45.

Bicyclist—A380

Designs: 2.50z, Cyclists in race. 3.40z, Wheel and arms of Berlin, Prague and Warsaw.

Lithographed
1962, Apr. 27   Perf. 12   Unwmkd.

1053	A380	60g bl & blk	20	10
1054	A380	2.50z yel & blk	60	20
1055	A380	3.40z lil & blk	90	30

Issued to commemorate the 15th International Peace Bicycle Race, Warsaw-Berlin-Prague.
Size of Nos. 1053 and 1055: 36x22mm. No. 1054: 74x22mm.

Lenin in Bialy Dunajec   **Karol Swierczewski-Walter**
A381   **A382**

Designs: 60g, Lenin. 2.50z, Lenin and Cracow fortifications.

Engraved and Photogravure
Perf. 11x11½
1962, May 25   Wmk. 326

1056	A381	40g pale grn & Prus grn	75	25
1057	A381	60g pink & dp cl	25	15
1058	A381	2.50z yel & dk brn	50	25

Issued to commemorate the 50th anniversary of Lenin's arrival in Poland.

Famous Poles Type of 1961.

Famous Poles: No. 1059, Adam Mickiewicz. No. 1080, Juliusz Slowacki. No. 1061, Frederic Chopin. No. 1062, Romuald Traugutt. No. 1063, Jaroslaw Dabrowski. No. 1064, Marja Konopnicka.

1962, June 20   Engr. & Photo.
Black Inscriptions and Designs

1059	A359	60g dl grn	35	20
1060	A359	60g brn org	20	10

Lithographed
Perf. 12x12½

1061	A359	60g dl bl	20	10
1062	A359	60g brn ol	20	10
1063	A359	60g rose lil	20	10
1064	A359	60g bl grn	20	8
		Nos. 1059-1064 (6)	1.35	68

Perf. 11x11½
1962, July 14   Engr.   Unwmkd.

1065	A382	60g black	15	8

Issued to commemorate the 15th anniversary of the death of General Karol Swierczewski-Walter, organizer of the new Polish army.

Crocus   **The Poisoned Well by Jacek Malczewski**
A383   **A384**

Flowers: No. 1067, Orchid. No. 1068, Monkshood. No. 1069, Gas plant. No. 1070, Water lily. No. 1071, Gentian. No. 1072, Daphne mezereum. No. 1073, Cowbell. No. 1074, Anemone. No. 1075, Globeflower. No. 1076, Snowdrop. No. 1077, Adonis vernalis.

POLAND

1962, Aug. 8 Perf. 12 Unwmkd.
Flowers in Natural Colors
1066	A383	60g dl yel & red	25	20
1067	A383	60g redsh brn & vio	95	50
1068	A383	60g pink & lil	15	10
1069	A383	90g ol & grn	25	10
1070	A383	90g yel grn & red	25	15
1071	A383	1t ol grn & red	25	15
1072	A383	1.50z gray bl & bl	40	20
1073	A383	1.50z yel grn & dk grn	75	25
1074	A383	1.50z Prus grn & dk bl	40	20
1075	A383	2.50z gray grn & dk bl	1.00	70
1076	A383	2.50z dk bl grn & dk bl	1.00	70
1077	A383	2.50z gray bl & grn	1.50	75
	Nos. 1066-1077 (12)	7.15	4.00

1962, Aug. 15 Engraved Wmk. 326
|1078|A384|60g buff|35|15|

Issued in sheets of 40 with alternating label for FIP Day (Federation Internationale de Philatelie), Sept. 1. Also issued in miniature sheet of four. Price, $25.

Pole Vault—A385

Designs: 60g, Relay race. 90g, Javelin. 1z, Hurdles. 1.50z, High jump. 1.55z, Discus. 2.50z, 100m. dash. 3.40z, Hammer throw.

Lithographed
1962, Sept. 12 Perf. 11 Unwmkd.
1079	A385	40g multi	10	5
1080	A385	60g multi	10	5
1081	A385	90g multi	15	10
1082	A385	1z multi	20	10
1083	A385	1.50z multi	25	15
1084	A385	1.55z multi	30	15
1085	A385	2.50z multi	50	25
1086	A385	3.40z multi	1.25	50
	Nos. 1079-1086 (8)	2.85	1.35

7th European Athletic Championships, Belgrade, Sept. 12-16. Exist imperf. Price, set $5.

Anopheles Mosquito — A386
Pavel R. Popovich and Andrian G. Nikolayev — A387

Designs: 1.50z, Malaria blood cells. 2.50z, Cinchona flowers. 3z, Anopheles mosquito.

1962, Oct. 1 Perf. 13x12 Wmk. 326
1087	A386	60g ol blk, dk brn & bl grn	15	5
1088	A386	1.50z red, gray & brt vio	30	10
1089	A386	2.50z multi	65	25

Miniature Sheet
Imperf.
|1090|A386|3z multi|1.50|1.00|

Issued for the World Health Organization drive to eradicate malaria. No. 1090 contains one stamp; green and violet blue margin. Size: 60x78mm.

1962, Oct. 6 Perf. 12½x12
Design: 2.50z, Two stars in orbit around earth. 10z, Two stars in orbit.
|1091|A387|60g vio, blk & cit|20|5|
|1092|A387|2.50z Prus bl, blk & red|40|25|

Souvenir Sheet
Perf. 12x11
|1093|A387|10z sl bl, blk & red|3.00|2.50|

Issued to commemorate the first Russian group space flight, Vostoks III and IV, Aug. 11-15, 1962. No. 1093 contains one stamp with design of stamp extending into slate blue and black sheet margin. Size: 68x93½mm.

Woman Mailing Letter A388
Mazovian Princes' Mansion, Warsaw A389

1962, Oct. 9 Engr. Perf. 12½x12
|1094|A388|60g black|15|8|
|1095|A388|2.50z red brn|60|20|

Issued for Stamp Day, 1962. The design is from the painting "A Moment of Decision," by Anthony Kamienski.

1962, Oct. 13 Lithographed
|1096|A389|60g red & blk|25|8|

Issued to commemorate the 25th anniversary of the founding of the Polish Democratic Party.

Cruiser "Aurora"—A390

Photogravure and Engraved
1962, Nov. 3 Perf. 11
|1097|A390|60g red & dk bl|25|8|

Issued to commemorate the 45th anniversary of the Russian October revolution.

Janusz Korczak by K. Dunikowski A391
King on Horseback A392

Designs: (Illustrations from King Matthew books): 90g, King giving fruit to Island girl. 1z, King handcuffed and soldier with sword. 2.50z, King with dead bird. 5.60z, King ice skating in moonlight.

Lithographed
1962, Nov. 12 Perf. 13x12 Unwmkd.
1098	A391	40g brn, bis & sep	20	10
1099	A392	60g multi	20	10
1100	A392	90g multi	40	10
1101	A392	1z multi	40	10
1102	A392	2.50z brn, yel & brt grn	75	20
1103	A392	5.60z brn, dk bl & grn	2.75	1.25
	Nos. 1098-1103 (6)	4.70	2.20

Issued to commemorate the 20th anniversary of the death of Dr. Janusz Korczak (Henryk Goldszmit), physician, pedagogue and writer, in the Treblinka concentration camp, Aug. 5, 1942.

View of Old Warsaw—A393

1962, Nov. 26 Perf. 11 Wmk. 326
|1104|A393|3.40z multi|60|35|
|a.|Sheet of 4|5.00|4.00|

Issued to commemorate the 5th Trade Union Congress, Warsaw, Nov. 26-Dec. 1. No. 1104a contains 4 stamps and has black marginal inscription. Size: 135x82mm.

Orphan Mary and the Dwarf A394

Various Scenes from "Orphan Mary and the Dwarfs" by Marja Konopnicka.

Lithographed
1962, Dec. 31 Perf. 13x12 Unwmkd.
1105	A394	40g multi	50	20
1106	A394	60g multi	3.00	1.50
1107	A394	1.50z multi	75	15
1108	A394	1.55z multi	75	20
1109	A394	2.50z multi	95	50
1110	A394	3.40z multi	3.00	2.00
	Nos. 1105-1110 (6)	8.95	4.55

Issued to commemorate the 120th anniversary of the birth of Marja Konopnicka, poet and fairy tale writer.

Romuald Traugutt—A395

Perf. 11½x11
1963, Jan. 31 Wmk. 326
|1111|A395|60g aqua, blk & pale pink|25|8|

Issued to commemorate the centenary of the 1863 insurrection and to honor its leader, Romuald Traugutt.

Tractor and Wheat—A396

Designs: 60g, Man reaping and millet. 2.50z, Combine and rice.

Perf. 12x12½
1963, Feb. 25 Litho. Wmk. 326
1112	A396	40g gray, bl, blk & ocher	30	5
1113	A396	60g brn red, blk, brn & grn	1.00	35
1114	A396	2.50z yel, buff, blk & grn	80	25

Issued for the "Freedom from Hunger" campaign of the U.N. Food and Agriculture Organization.

Cocker Spaniel—A397

Dogs: 30g, Polish sheep dog. 40g, Boxer. 50g, Airedale terrier (vert.). 60g, French bulldog (vert.). 1z, Poodle (vert.). 2.50z, Hunting dog. 3.40z, Sheep dog (vert.). 6.50z, Great Dane.

1963, Mar. 25 Perf. 12½ Unwmkd.
1115	A397	20g lil, blk & org brn	20	10
1116	A397	30g rose car & blk	25	10
1117	A397	40g lil, blk & yel brn	30	10
1118	A397	50g multi	40	10
1119	A397	60g lt bl & blk	50	25
1120	A397	1z yel grn & blk	90	75
1121	A397	2.50z org, blk & brn	1.75	70
1122	A397	3.40z red org & blk	3.50	1.50
1123	A397	6.50z brt yel & blk	6.50	4.50
	Nos. 1115-1123 (9)	14.30	8.00

Egyptian Ship A398
Fighter and Ruins of Warsaw Ghetto A399

Ancient Ships: 10g, Phoenician merchant ship. 20g, Greek trireme. 30g, 3rd century merchantman. 40g, Scandinavian "Gokstad." 60g, Frisian "Kogge." 1z, 14th century "Holk." 1.15z, 15th century "Caraca."

Photo. (Background) & Engr.
1963, Apr. 5 Perf. 11½
1124	A398	5g brn, tan	5	5
1125	A398	10g grn, gray grn	5	5
1126	A398	20g ultra, gray	5	5
1127	A398	30g blk, gray ol	10	5
1128	A398	40g lt bl, bluish	10	5
1129	A398	60g cl, gray	15	8
1130	A398	1z blk, bl	25	10
1131	A398	1.15z grn, pale rose	75	25
	Nos. 1124-1131 (8)	1.50	68

See also Nos. 1206-1213, 1299-1306.

Perf. 11½x11
1963, Apr. 19 Wmk. 326
|1132|A399|2.50z gray brn & gray|50|20|

Issued to commemorate the 20th anniversary of the Warsaw Ghetto Uprising.

POLAND

Centenary Emblem
A400

Perf. 12½x12

1963, May 8   Litho.   Unwmkd.

| 1133 | A400 | 2.50z bl, yel & red | 75 | 25 |

Issued to commemorate the centenary of the founding of the International Red Cross. Every other stamp in sheet inverted.

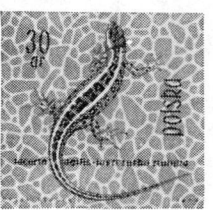

Sand Lizard
A401

Designs: 40g, Smooth snake. 50g, European pond turtle. 60g, Grass snake. 90g, Slow worm. 1.15z, European tree frog. 1.35z, Alpine newt. 1.50z, Crested newt. 1.55z, Green toad. 2.50z, Fire-bellied toad. 3z, Fire salamander. 3.40z, Natterjack.

Photogravure
1963, June 1   Perf. 11½   Unwmkd.
Reptiles and Amphibians in Natural Colors

1134	A401	30g grnsh gray & blk	15	5
1135	A401	40g gray ol & blk	15	5
1136	A401	50g bis brn & blk	25	10
1137	A401	60g tan & blk	25	10
1138	A401	90g gray grn & blk	25	10
1139	A401	1.15z gray & blk	25	10
1140	A401	1.35z gray bl & dk bl	45	25
1141	A401	1.50z bluish grn & blk	75	35
1142	A401	1.55z bluish gray & blk	45	25
1143	A401	2.50z gray vio & blk	45	25
1144	A401	3z gray grn & blk	1.25	.65
1145	A401	3.40z gray & blk	3.50	2.50
		Nos. 1134-1145 (12)	8.15	4.55

Foil, Saber, Sword and Helmet
A402

Designs: 40g, Fencers and knights in armor. 60g, Fencers and dragoons. 1.15z, Contemporary and 18th cent. fencers. 1.55z, Fencers and old houses, Danzig. 6.50z, Arms of Danzig (vert.).

Perf. 12x12½, 12½x12

1963, June 29   Litho.   Unwmkd.

1146	A402	20g brn & org	10	5
1147	A402	40g dk bl & bl	10	8
1148	A402	60g red & dp org	15	8
1149	A402	1.15z grn & emer	30	12
1150	A402	1.55z vio & lil	60	25
1151	A402	6.50z yel brn, mar & yel	2.25	75
		Nos. 1146-1151 (6)	3.55	1.33

Issued to commemorate the 28th World Fencing Championships, Danzig, July 15-28. A souvenir sheet exists containing one each of Nos. 1147-1150. Blue marginal inscription, gray control number. Size: 111x95mm.   Price $30.

Famous Poles Type of 1961
Famous Poles: No. 1152, Ludwik Warynski. No. 1153, Ludwik Krzywicki. No. 1154, Marie Sklodowska Curie. No. 1155, Karol Swierczewski-Walter.

Perf. 12x12½

1963, July 20   Wmk. 326
Black Inscriptions and Designs

1152	A359	60g red brn	10	8
1153	A359	60g gray brn	10	8
1154	A359	60g blue	30	15
1155	A359	60g green	15	8

Valeri Bykovski—A403

Designs: 60g, Valentina Tereshkova. 6.50z, Rockets "Falcon" and "Mew" and globe.

Lithographed
1963, Aug. 26   Perf. 11   Unwmkd.

1156	A403	40g ultra, emer & blk	20	5
1157	A403	60g grn, ultra & blk	20	8
1158	A403	6.50z multi	1.50	50

Issued to commemorate the space flights of Valeri Bykovski June 14-19, and Valentina Tereshkova, first woman cosmonaut, June 16-19, 1963.

Basketball—A404

Designs: Various positions of ball, hands and players. 10z, Town Hall, People's Hall and Arms of Wroclaw.

1963, Sept. 16   Perf. 11½   Unwmkd.

1159	A404	40g multi	5	5
1160	A404	50g fawn, grn & blk	10	6
1161	A404	60g red, lt grn & blk	10	8
1162	A404	90g multi	15	10
1163	A404	2.50z multi	30	20
1164	A404	5.60z multi	1.75	70
		Nos. 1159-1164 (6)	2.45	1.19

Souvenir Sheet
Imperf.

| 1165 | A404 | 10z multi | 2.75 | 2.00 |

Issued to commemorate the 13th European Men's Basketball Championship, Wroclaw, Oct. 4-13. No. 1165 contains one stamp; white inscription on fawn margin also commemorates the simultaneous European Sports Stamp Exhibition. Sheet sold for 15z. Size: 75x86mm.

Eagle and Ground-to-Air Missile
A405

Designs (Eagle and): 40g, Destroyer. 60g, Jet fighter plane. 1.35z, Tank. 1.55z, Self-propelled rocket launcher. 2.50z, Amphibious troop carrier. 3z, Swords and medieval and modern soldiers.

1963, Oct. 1   Perf. 12x12½

1166	A405	20g multi	10	5
1167	A405	40g vio, grn & red	10	5
1168	A405	60g multi	15	5
1169	A405	1.15z multi	20	10
1170	A405	1.35z multi	25	10
1171	A405	1.55z multi	25	15
1172	A405	2.50z multi	35	15
1173	A405	3z multi	75	35
		Nos. 1166-1173 (8)	2.15	1.00

Polish People's Army, 20th anniversary.

"Love Letter" by Wladyslaw Czachórski—A406

Engraved
1963, Oct. 9   Perf. 11½   Unwmkd.

| 1174 | A406 | 60g dk red brn | 30 | 15 |

Issued for Stamp Day.

Nos. 1156-1158 Overprinted: "23-28 X. 1963" and name of astronaut.

1963   Lithographed   Perf. 11

1175	A403	40g ultra, emer & blk	45	15
1176	A403	60g grn, ultra & blk	55	20
1177	A403	6.50z multi	2.50	1.25

Issued to commemorate the visit of Valentina Tereshkova and Valeri Bykovski to Poland, Oct. 23-28. The overprints are: 40g, W. F. Bykowski w Polsce; 60g, W. W. Tierieszkowa/w Polsce; 6.50z, W. F. BYKOWSKI I W. W. TIERIESZKOWA W POLSCE.

Konstantin E. Tsiolkovsky's Rocket and Rocket Speed Formula
A407

American and Russian Space Crafts: 40g, Sputnik 1. 50g, Explorer 1. 60g, Lunik 2. 1z, Lunik 3. 1.50z, Vostok 1. 1.55z, Friendship 7. 2.50z, Vostoks 3 & 4. 5.60z, Mariner 2. 6.50z, Mars 1.

Perf. 12½x12

1963, Nov. 11   Litho.   Unwmkd.
Black Inscriptions

1178	A407	30g dl bl grn & gray	5	5
1179	A407	40g lt ol grn & gray	5	5
1180	A407	50g vio bl & gray	10	5
1181	A407	60g brn org & gray	10	5
1182	A407	1z brt grn & gray	10	8
1183	A407	1.50z org red & gray	20	8
1184	A407	1.55z bl & gray	20	10
1185	A407	2.50z lil & gray	40	15
1186	A407	5.60z brt yel grn & gray	1.00	40
1187	A407	6.50z grnsh bl & gray	1.50	50
		Nos. 1178-1187 (10)	3.70	1.48

Conquest of space. A souvenir sheet contains 2 each of #1186-1187.

Price $55.

Arab Stallion "Comet"—A408

Horses from Mazury Region
A409

Horses: 30g, Tarpans (wild horses). 40g, Horse from Sokolka. 50g, Arab mares and foals (horiz.). 90g, Steeplechasers (horiz.). 1.55z, Arab stallion "Witez II." 2.50z, Head of Arab horse, facing right. 4z, Mixed breeds (horiz.). 6.50z, Head of Arab horse, facing left.

Perf. 11½x11 (A408); 12½x12, 12
1963, Dec. 30   Photogravure

1188	A408	20g blk, yel & car	10	10
1189	A408	30g multi	20	10
1190	A408	40g multi	20	10

Sizes: 75x26mm. (50g, 90g, 4z); 28x38mm. (60g, 1.55z, 2.50z, 6.50z).

1191	A409	50g multi	25	15
1192	A409	60g yel, dp rose & blk	25	15
1193	A409	90g multi	35	15
1194	A409	1.55z multi	60	25
1195	A409	2.50z multi	90	25
1196	A409	4z multi	2.00	75
1197	A409	6.50z yel, dl bl & blk	3.50	2.50
		Nos. 1188-1197 (10)	8.35	4.50

Issued to publicize Polish horse breeding.

Ice Hockey—A410

Sports: 30g, Slalom. 40g, Skiing. 60g, Speed skating. 1z, Ski jump. 2.50z, Tobogganing. 5.60z, Cross-country skiing. 6.50z, Figure skating pair.

1964, Jan. 25   Litho.   Perf. 12x12½

1198	A410	20g multi	5	5
1199	A410	30g multi	8	5
1200	A410	40g multi	8	5
1201	A410	60g multi	10	5
1202	A410	1z multi	30	10
1203	A410	2.50z multi	60	20
1204	A410	5.60z multi	1.00	50
1205	A410	6.50z multi	1.75	95
		Nos. 1198-1205 (8)	3.96	1.95

9th Winter Olympic Games, Innsbruck, Jan. 29-Feb. 9. A souvenir sheet contains 2 each of #1203, 1205.

Price $25.

Ship Type of 1963
Sailing Ships: 1.35z, Caravel of Columbus (vert.). 1.50z, Galleon. 1.55z, Polish warship, 1627 (vert.). 2z, Dutch merchant ship (vert.). 2.10z, Line ship. 2.50z, Frigate. 3z, 19th century merchantman. 3.40z, "Dar Pomorza," 20th century school ship (vert.).

1964, Mar. 19   Engraved   Perf. 12½

1206	A398	1.35z ultra	15	8
1207	A398	1.50z claret	15	8
1208	A398	1.55z black	20	8

POLAND

1209	A398	2z violet	20	8
1210	A398	2.10z green	25	8
1211	A398	2.50z car rose	30	15
1212	A398	3z ol grn	50	15
1213	A398	3.40z brown	75	25
	Nos. 1206-1213 (8)		2.50	95

European Cat
A411

King Casimir III, the Great
A412

Designs: 40g, 60g, 1.55z, 2.50z, 6.50z, Various European cats. 50g, Siamese cat. 90g, 1.35z, 3.40z, Various Persian cats. 60g, 90g, 1.35z, 1.55z horizontal.

1964, Apr. 30   Litho.   Perf. 12½
Cats in Natural Colors;
Black Inscriptions.

1216	A411	30g yellow	25	15
1217	A411	40g orange	25	15
1218	A411	50g yellow	25	15
1219	A411	60g brt grn	50	15
1220	A411	90g lt brn	25	15
1221	A411	1.35z emerald	25	15
1222	A411	1.55z vio bl	75	30
1223	A411	2.50z lilac	2.25	90
1224	A411	3.40z rose	2.50	1.50
1225	A411	6.50z violet	5.00	2.50
	Nos. 1216-1225 (10)		12.25	6.10

Engraved
1964, May 5   Perf. 11x11½
Designs: No. 1227, Hugo Kollataj. No. 1228, Jan Dlugosz. No. 1229, Nicolaus Copernicus. 2.50z, King Ladislas II, Jagello and Queen Jadwiga.
Size: 22x35mm.

1226	A412	40g dl cl	15	5
1227	A412	40g green	15	5
1228	A412	60g violet	25	5
1229	A412	60g dk brn	30	5

Size: 35½x37mm.

1230	A412	2.50z gray brn	70	25
	Nos. 1226-1230 (5)		1.55	45

Issued to commemorate the 600th anniversary of the founding of the Jagellonian University in Cracow.

Lapwing
A413

Waterfowl: 40g, White-spotted bluethroat. 50g, Black-tailed godwit. 60g, Osprey. 90g, Gray heron. 1.35z, Little gull. 1.55z, Shoveler. 5.60z, Arctic loon. 6.50z, Great crested grebe.

Photogravure
1964, June 5 Perf. 11½ Unwmkd.
Birds in Natural Colors;
Black Inscriptions
Size: 34x34mm.

1231	A413	30g chlky bl	10	5
1232	A413	40g bister	10	5
1233	A413	50g brt yel grn	12	5

Perf. 11½x11
Size: 34x48mm.

1234	A413	60g blue	12	5
1235	A413	90g lemon	20	10
1236	A413	1.35z green	50	10

Perf. 11½.
Size: 34x34mm.

1237	A413	1.55z olive	50	25
1238	A413	5.60z bl grn	1.25	60
1239	A413	6.50z brt grn	2.00	95
	Nos. 1231-1239 (9)		4.89	2.20

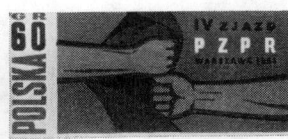
Hands Holding Red Flag—A414

Designs: No. 1241, Red and white ribbon around hammer. No. 1242, Hammer and rye. No. 1243, Brick wall under construction and red flag.

1964, June 15   Litho.   Perf. 11

1240	A414	60g ol bis, red, blk & pink	15	8
1241	A414	60g red, gray & blk	15	8
1242	A414	60g mag, blk & yel	15	8
1243	A414	60g gray, red, sal & blk	15	8

Issued to commemorate the fourth congress of the Polish United Workers Party.

Symbols of Peasant-Worker Alliance
A415

Atom Symbol and Book
A416

Shipyard, Danzig—A417

Designs: No. 1245, Stylized oak. No. 1247, Factory and cogwheel. No. 1248, Tractor and grain. No. 1249, Pen, brush, mask and ornament. No. 1251, Lenin Metal Works, Nowa Huta. No. 1252, Cement factory, Chelm. No. 1253, Power Station, Turoszow. No. 1254, Oil refinery, Plock. No. 1255, Sulphur mine, Tarnobrzeg.

1964   Lithographed   Perf. 12x12½

1244	A415	60g red, org & blk	15	8
1245	A415	60g grn, red, ocher, bl & blk	15	8

Perf. 11
Photogravure

1246	A416	60g gray & dp vio bl	15	6
1247	A416	60g brt bl & blk	15	6
1248	A416	60g emer & blk	15	6
1249	A416	60g org & red	15	6

Photogravure and Engraved

1250	A417	60g dl bl grn & ultra	15	6
1251	A417	60g brt pink & pur	15	6
1252	A417	60g gray & gray brn	15	6
1253	A417	60g grn & sl grn	15	6
1254	A417	60g sal & cl	15	6
1255	A417	60g cit & sep	15	6
	Nos. 1244-1255 (12)		1.80	76

Issued to commemorate the 20th anniversary of the Polish People's Republic.

Warsaw Fighters, 1944
A418

1964, Aug. 1   Litho.   Perf. 12½x12

| 1256 | A418 | 60g multi | 25 | 10 |

Issued to commemorate the 20th anniversary of the Warsaw insurrection against German occupation.

Running—A419

Women's High Jump—A420

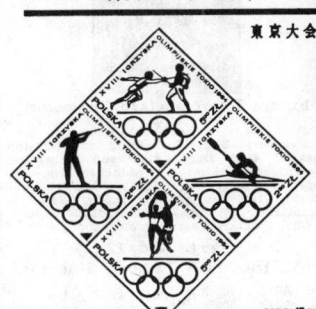
Olympic Sports—A421

Sport: 40g, Rowing (single). 60g, Weight lifting. 90g, Relay race (square). 1z, Boxing (square). 2.50z, Soccer (square). 6.50z, Diving.

Lithographed
1964, Aug. 17   Perf. 11   Unwmkd.

1257	A419	20g multi	10	5
1258	A419	40g grnsh bl, bl & yel	12	5
1259	A419	60g vio bl, red & rose lil	15	10
1260	A419	90g dk brn, red & yel	25	10
1261	A419	1z dk vio, lil & gray	25	10
1262	A419	2.50z multi	60	25
1263	A420	5.60z multi	1.50	75
1264	A420	6.50z multi	2.50	1.25
	Nos. 1257-1264 (8)		5.47	2.60

Souvenir Sheet
Imperf.

1265	A421	Sheet of 4, multi	4.50	3.00
a.		2.50z Sharpshooting	50	35
b.		2.50z Canoeing	50	35
c.		5z Fencing	50	35
d.		5z Basketball	50	35

Issued to commemorate the 18th Olympic Games, Tokyo, Oct. 10-25. Size of sheet No. 1265: 80x104mm.; size of stamps in sheet: 24x24mm. A souvenir sheet containing 2 each of Nos. 1263-1264 with black marginal inscription exists. Size: 84x112mm. Price $30.

Warsaw Mermaid and Stars
A422

Stefan Zeromski by Monika Zeromska
A423

1964, Sept. 7   Perf. 12½x12½

| 1266 | A422 | 2.50z vio & blk | 45 | 15 |

Issued to commemorate the 15th Astronautical Congress, Warsaw, Sept. 7-12.

1964, Sept. 21   Photo.   Perf. 12½

| 1267 | A423 | 60g ol gray | 25 | 8 |

Issued to commemorate the centenary of the birth of Stefan Zeromski (1864-1925), writer.

Gun and Hand Holding Hammer
A424

Globe and Red Flag
A425

1964, Sept. 21   Litho.   Perf. 11

| 1268 | A424 | 60g brt grn, blk & red | 25 | 8 |

Issued to commemorate the Third Miners' Militia Congress, Warsaw, Sept. 24-26.

1964, Sept. 28   Photo.   Perf. 12½

| 1269 | A425 | 60g blk & red org | 25 | 8 |

First Socialist International, centenary.

POLAND

Stagecoach by Jozef Brodowski
A426

1964, Oct. 9 Engraved Perf. 11½

| 1270 | A426 | 60g green | 25 | 8 |
| 1271 | A426 | 60g lt brn | 25 | 8 |

Issued for Stamp Day.

Eleanor Roosevelt
A427

1964, Oct. 10   Perf. 12½

| 1272 | A427 | 2.50z black | 30 | 15 |

Issued to honor Eleanor Roosevelt (1884–1962).

Proposed Monument for Defenders of Westerplatte, 1939
A428

Polish Soldiers Crossing Oder River, 1945
A429

Designs: No. 1274, Virtuti Military Cross. No. 1275, Nike, proposed monument for the martyrs of Bydgoszcz (woman with sword and torch). No. 1277, Battle of Studzianki, 1944.

Perf. 12x11, 11x12

1964, Nov. 16 Engraved Unwmkd.

1273	A428	40g bl vio	15	8
1274	A428	40g slate	15	8
1275	A428	60g dk bl	15	8
1276	A429	60g dk bl grn	15	8
1277	A429	60g grnsh blk	15	8
		Nos. 1273-1277 (5)	75	40

Issued to commemorate the struggle and martyrdom of the Polish people, 1939–45. The vertical stamps are printed in sheets of 56 stamps (8x7) with 7 labels in each outside vertical row. The horizontal stamps are printed in sheets of 50 stamps (5x10) with 10 labels in each outside vertical row. See Nos. 1366-1368.

Attractive slip cases are available for most Scott Albums.

Souvenir Sheet

Col. Vladimir M. Komarov, Boris B. Yegorov and Dr. Konstantin Feoktistov
A430

1964, Nov. 21 Litho. Perf. 11½x11

1278	A430	Souv. sheet of 3	1.50	1.00
	a.	60g red & blk (Komarov)	30	12
	b.	60g brt grn & blk (Feoktistov)	30	12
	c.	60g ultra & blk (Yegorov)	30	12

Issued to commemorate the Russian three-manned space flight in space ship Voskhod, Oct. 12–13, 1964. No. 1278 has bright green marginal inscription. Size of stamps: 27x36mm.; size of sheet: 113½x64mm.

Cyclamen
A431

Garden Flowers: 30g, Freesia. 40g, Monique rose. 50g, Peony. 60g, Royal lily. 90g, Oriental poppy. 1.35z, Tulip. 1.50z, Narcissus. 1.55z, Begonia. 2.50z, Carnation. 3.40z, Iris. 5.60z, Camellia.

1964, Nov. 30 Photogravure Perf. 11

Size: 35½x35½mm.

Flowers in Natural Colors

1279	A431	20g violet	10	5
1280	A431	30g dp lil	10	5
1281	A431	40g blue	10	5
1282	A431	50g vio bl	10	5
1283	A431	60g lilac	12	5
1284	A431	90g dp grn	15	8

Size: 26x37½mm.

1285	A431	1.35z dk bl	25	12
1286	A431	1.50z dp car	75	50
1287	A431	1.55z green	25	10
1288	A431	2.50z ultra	65	20
1289	A431	3.40z redsh brn	1.25	50
1290	A431	5.60z ol gray	2.25	1.25
		Nos. 1279-1290 (12)	6.07	3.00

Future Interplanetary Spacecraft
A432

Designs: 30g, Launching of Russian rocket. 40g, Dog Laika and launching tower. 60g, Lunik 3 photographing far side of the Moon. 1.55z, Satellite exploring the ionosphere. 2.50z, Satellite "Elektron 2" exploring radiation belt. 5.60z, "Mars 1" between Mars and Earth.

Perf. 12½x12

1964, Dec. 30 Litho. Unwmkd.

1291	A432	20g multi	8	5
1292	A432	30g multi	8	5
1293	A432	40g ol grn, blk & bl	10	5
1294	A432	60g dk bl, blk & dk red	15	8
1295	A432	1.55z gray & multi	50	10
1296	A432	2.50z multi	1.00	25
1297	A432	5.60z multi	1.65	60
		Nos. 1291-1297, B108 (8)	5.81	1.90

Issued to publicize space research.

Warsaw Mermaid, Ruins and New Buildings—A433

1965, Jan. 15 Engr. Perf. 11x11½

| 1298 | A433 | 60g sl grn | 15 | 8 |

Liberation of Warsaw, 20th anniversary.

Ship Type of 1963

Designs as before.

1965, Jan. 25 Engraved Perf. 12½

1299	A398	5g dk brn	5	5
1300	A398	10g sl grn	5	5
1301	A398	20g sl bl	5	5
1302	A398	30g gray ol	5	5
1303	A398	40g dk bl	5	5
1304	A398	60g claret	10	8
1305	A398	1z red brn	20	10
1306	A398	1.15z dk red brn	25	10
		Nos. 1299-1306 (8)	80	53

Edaphosaurus—A434

Dinosaurs: 30g, Cryptocleidus (vert.). 40g, Brontosaurus. 60g, Mesosaurus (vert.). 90g, Stegosaurus. 1.15z, Brachiosaurus (vert.). 1.35z, Styracosaurus. 3.40z, Corythosaurus (vert.). 5.60z, Rhamphorhynchus (vert.). 6.50z, Tyrannosaurus.

1965, Mar. 5 Litho. Perf. 12½

1307	A434	20g multi	10	8
1308	A434	30g multi	10	8
1309	A434	40g multi	15	8
1310	A434	60g multi	15	8
1311	A434	90g multi	50	15
1312	A434	1.15z multi	25	15
1313	A434	1.35z multi	30	15
1314	A434	3.40z multi	75	25
1315	A434	5.60z multi	1.50	50
1316	A434	6.50z multi	2.50	1.25
		Nos. 1307-1316 (10)	6.30	2.77

See also Nos. 1395-1403.

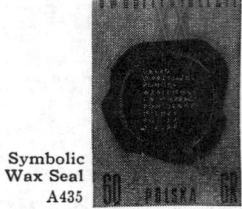
Symbolic Wax Seal
A435

Russian and Polish Flags, Oil Refinery-Chemical Plant, Plock
A436

1965, Apr. 21 Perf. 12½x12, 12½

| 1317 | A435 | 60g multi | 15 | 8 |
| 1318 | A436 | 60g multi | 15 | 8 |

Issued to commemorate the 20th anniversary of the signing of the Polish-Soviet treaty of friendship, mutual assistance and postwar cooperation.

Polish Eagle and Town Coats of Arms
A437

1965, May 8 Engraved Perf. 11½

| 1319 | A437 | 60g car rose | 25 | 8 |

Issued to commemorate the 20th anniversary of regaining the Western and Northern Territories.

Dove—A438

1965, May 8 Litho. Perf. 12x12½

| 1320 | A438 | 60g red & blk | 25 | 8 |

Victory over Fascism, 20th anniversary.

ITU Emblem
A439

"The People's Friend" and Clover
A440

Factory and Rye—A441

Perf. 12½x12

1965, May 17 Litho. Unwmkd.

| 1321 | A439 | 2.50z brt bl, lil, yel & blk | 50 | 15 |

Issued to commemorate the centenary of the International Telecommunication Union.

1965, June 5 Perf. 11

| 1322 | A440 | 40g multi | 15 | 5 |
| 1323 | A441 | 60g multi | 15 | 8 |

Issued to commemorate the 70th anniversary of the "Popular Movement" in Poland.

Finn Class Yachts—A442

POLAND

Yachts: 30g, Dragon class. 40g, 5.5-m. class. 50g, Group of Finn class. 60g, V-class. 1.35z, Group of Cadet class. 4z, Group of Star class. 5.60z, Two Flying Dutchmen. 6.50z, Two Amethyst class. 15z, Finn class race. (30g, 60g, 5.60z vertical)

Lithographed
1965, June 14 Perf. 12½ Unwmkd.

1324	A442	30g multi	15	8
1325	A442	40g multi	15	8
1326	A442	50g multi	20	8
1327	A442	60g multi	20	8
1328	A442	1.35z multi	25	15
1329	A442	4z multi	85	40
1330	A442	5.60z multi	1.50	75
1331	A442	6.50z multi	2.25	1.25
		Nos. 1324-1331 (8)	5.55	2.87

Miniature Sheet
Perf. 11

1332	A442	15z multi	3.00	2.00

Issued to publicize the World Championships of Finn Class Yachts, Gdynia, July 22–29. No. 1332 contains one stamp (size: 48x22mm.), gray margin. Size of sheet: 79x59mm.

Marx and Lenin
A443

Photogravure and Engraved
1965, June 14 Perf. 11½x11

1333	A443	60g vermilion	15	8

Issued to commemorate the 6th Conference of Ministers of Post of Communist Countries, Peking, June 21–July 15.

Warsaw's Coat of Arms, 17th Century—A444

Old Town Hall, 18th Century
A445

Designs: 10g, Artifacts, 13th century. 20g, Tombstone of last Duke of Mazovia. 60g, Barbican, Gothic-Renaissance castle. 1.50z, Arsenal, 19th century. 1.55z, National Theater. 2.50z, Staszic Palace. 3.40z, Woman with sword from Heroes' Memorial and Warsaw Mermaid seal.

Perf. 11x11½, 11½x11, 12x12½, 12½x12

1965, July 21 Engraved Unwmkd.

1334	A444	5g car rose	5	5
1335	A444	10g green	5	5
1336	A445	20g vio bl	5	5
1337	A445	40g brown	5	5
1338	A445	60g orange	8	5
1339	A445	1.50z black	8	5
1340	A445	1.55z gray bl	25	10
1341	A445	2.50z lilac	40	15

Photogravure and Engraved
Perf. 11½

1342	A444	3.40z cit & blk	1.25	75
		Nos. 1334-1342 (9)	2.33	1.33

700th anniversary of Warsaw. No. 1342 measures 50x62mm. It is perforated all around, with lower right quarter perforated to form a 21x26mm. stamp within a stamp. It was issued in sheets of 25 (5x5).

IQSY Emblem
A446

Designs: 2.50z, Radar screen, Torun. 3.40z, Solar system.

1965, Aug. 9 Lithographed

1343	A446	60g vio, ver, brt grn & blk	15	5
a.		60g ultra, org, yel, bl & blk	15	5
1344	A446	2.50z red, yel, pur & blk	50	15
a.		2.50z red brn, yel, gray & blk	50	15
1345	A446	3.40z org & multi	65	25
a.		3.40z ol gray & multi	65	25

International Quiet Sun Year, 1964–65.

Odontoglossum Grande A447   **Weight Lifting** A448

Orchids: 30g, Cypripedium hibridum. 40g, Lycaste skinneri. 50g, Cattleya. 60g, Vanda sanderiana. 1.35z, Cypripedium hibridum. 4z, Sobralia. 5.60z, Disa grandiflora. 6.50z, Cattleya labiata.

1965, Sept. 6 Photo. Perf. 12½x12

1346	A447	20g multi	10	8
1347	A447	30g multi	10	8
1348	A447	40g multi	10	8
1349	A447	50g multi	20	8
1350	A447	60g multi	20	8
1351	A447	1.35z multi	35	15
1352	A447	4z multi	75	50
1353	A447	5.60z multi	1.50	75
1354	A447	6.50z multi	2.50	1.25
		Nos. 1346-1354 (9)	5.80	3.05

1965, Oct. 8 Photo. Unwmkd.

Sport: 40g, Boxing. 50g, Relay race, men. 60g, Fencing. 90g, Women's 80-meter hurdles. 3.40z, Relay race, women. 6.50z, Hop, step and jump. 7.10z, Volleyball, women.

1355	A448	30g gold & multi	15	10
1356	A448	40g gold & multi	15	10
1357	A448	50g sil & multi	15	10
1358	A448	60g gold & multi	15	10
1359	A448	90g sil & multi	25	10
1360	A448	3.40z gold & multi	75	25
1361	A448	6.50z gold & multi	1.25	75
1362	A448	7.10z brnz & multi	1.50	1.00
		Nos. 1355-1362 (8)	4.35	2.50

Issued to commemorate the victories won by the Polish team in 1964 Olympic Games. Each denomination printed in sheets of eight stamps and two center labels showing medals. Margin inscribed in Polish and Japanese Olympic rings in border. Size: 184x106mm.

Mail Coach, by Piotr Michalowski
A449

Design: 2.50z, Departure of Coach, by Piotr Michalowski.

1965, Oct. 9 Engr. Perf. 11x11½

1363	A449	60g brown	25	10
1364	A449	2.50z sl grn	40	15

Issued for Stamp Day, 1965. Sheets of 50 with labels se-tenant inscribed "Dzien Znaczka 1965 R."

U.N. Emblem A450   **Memorial, Plaszow** A451

1965, Oct. 24 Litho. Perf. 12½x12

1365	A450	2.50z ultra	40	15

20th anniversary of United Nations.

Engraved
1965, Nov. 29 Perf. 12x11, 11x12

Designs: 1367, Kielce Memorial. No. 1368, Chelm Memorial. (horiz.).

1366	A451	60g grnsh gray	25	10
1367	A451	60g chocolate	25	10
1368	A451	60g black	25	10

Note after No. 1277 applies also to Nos. 1366-1368.

Wolf
A452

Animals: 30g, Lynx. 40g, Red fox. 50g, Badger. 60g, Brown bear. 1.50z, Wild boar. 2.50z, Red deer. 5.60z, European bison. 7.10z, Moose.

1965, Nov. 30 Photo. Perf. 11½

1369	A452	20g multi	10	8
1370	A452	30g multi	10	8
1371	A452	40g multi	10	8
1372	A452	50g multi	10	8
1373	A452	60g multi	15	8
1374	A452	1.50z multi	75	25
1375	A452	2.50z multi	75	25
1376	A452	5.60z multi	1.75	95
1377	A452	7.10z multi	2.50	1.75
		Nos. 1369-1377 (9)	6.30	3.60

Gig
A452

Horse-drawn carriages, Lancut Museum: 40g, Coupé. 50g, Lady's basket. 60g, Vis-a-vis. 90g, Cab. 1.15z, Berlinka. 2.50z, Hunting break. 6.50z, Caleche à la Daumont. 7.10z, English break.

1965, Dec. 30 Litho. Perf. 11

Size: 50x23mm.

1378	A453	20g multi	15	5
1379	A453	40g lil & multi	15	5
1380	A453	50g org & multi	15	10
1381	A453	60g fawn & multi	15	10
1382	A453	90g yel & multi	15	10

Size: 76x23mm.

1383	A453	1.15z multi	25	15
1384	A453	2.50z ol & multi	65	35
1385	A453	6.50z multi	1.50	75

Size: 103x23mm.

1386	A453	7.10z bl & multi	2.75	1.50
		Nos. 1378-1386 (9)	6.00	3.15

Cargo Ship (No. 1389)—A454

Designs: No. 1387, Supervising Technical Organization (NOT) emblem, symbols of industry. No. 1388, Pit head and miners' badge (vert.). No. 1390, Chemical plant, Plock. No. 1391, Combine. No. 1392, Railroad train. No. 1393, Building crane (vert.). No. 1394, Pavilion and emblem of 35th International Poznan Fair.

1966 Lithographed Perf. 11

1387	A454	60g multi	15	8
1388	A454	60g multi	15	8
1389	A454	60g multi	15	8
1390	A454	60g multi	15	8
1391	A454	60g multi	15	8
1392	A454	60g multi	15	8
1393	A454	60g multi	15	8
1394	A454	60g multi	15	8
		Nos. 1387-1394 (8)	1.20	64

Issued to commemorate the 20th anniversary of the nationalization of Polish industry. No. 1394 also commemorates the 35th International Poznan Fair. Nos. 1387-1388 issued in connection with the 5th Congress of Polish Technicians, Katowice. Printed in sheets of 20 stamps and 20 labels with commemorative inscription within cogwheel on each label. Dates of issue: Nos. 1387-1388, Feb. 10; others, May 21.

Dinosaur Type of 1965.
1966, March 5 Litho. Perf. 12½

Prehistoric Vertebrates: 20g, Dinichthys. 30g, Eusthenopteron. 40g, Ichthyostega. 50g, Mastodonsaurus. 60g, Cynognathus. 2.50z, Archaeopteryx (vert.). 3.40z, Brontotherium. 6.50z, Machairodus. 7.10z, Mammoth.

1395	A434	20g multi	10	5
1396	A434	30g multi	10	5
1397	A434	40g multi	10	5
1398	A434	50g multi	10	5
1399	A434	60g multi	30	10
1400	A434	2.50z multi	50	25
1401	A434	3.40z multi	75	35
1402	A434	6.50z multi	1.50	75
1403	A434	7.10z multi	2.75	1.50
		Nos. 1395-1403 (9)	6.20	3.15

Henryk Sienkiewicz
A455

Photogravure and Engraved
1966, March 30 Perf. 11½

1404	A455	60g dl yel	30	10

Issued to commemorate the 120th anniversary of the birth and the 50th anniversary of the death of Henryk Sienkiewicz (1846–1916), author and winner of 1905 Nobel Prize.

 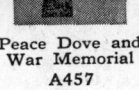

Soccer Game A456   **Peace Dove and War Memorial** A457

POLAND

Designs: Various phases of soccer. Each stamp inscribed with the place and the result of final game in various preceding soccer championships.

1966, May 6   Perf. 13x12

1405	A456	20g multi	5	5
1406	A456	40g multi	5	5
1407	A456	60g multi	15	8
1408	A456	90g multi	25	10
1409	A456	1.50z multi	50	20
1410	A456	3.40z multi	75	25
1411	A456	6.50z multi	1.50	60
1412	A456	7.10z multi	2.25	1.00
	Nos. 1405-1412 (8)		5.50	2.33

Issued to publicize the World Cup Soccer Championship, Wembley, England, July 11-30. Each denomination printed in sheets of 10 (5x2), with ornamental border and commemorative inscription. See also No. B109.

Typographed and Engraved
1966, May 9   Perf. 11½

| 1413 | A457 | 60g sil & multi | 15 | 8 |

21st anniversary of victory over Fascism.

Women's Relay Race
A458

Designs: 20g, Start of men's short distance race (vert.). 60g, Javelin (vert.). 90g, Women's 80-meter hurdles. 1.35z, Discus (vert.). 3.40z, Finish of men's medium distance race. 6.50z, Hammer throw (vert.). 7.10z, High jump.

    Perf. 11½x11, 11x11½
1966, June 18   Lithographed

1414	A458	20g multi	5	5
1415	A458	40g multi	5	5
1416	A458	60g multi	10	8
1417	A458	90g multi	15	8
1418	A458	1.35z multi	25	10
1419	A458	3.40z multi	75	25
1420	A458	6.50z multi	1.00	50
1421	A458	7.10z multi	1.25	75
	Nos. 1414-1421 (8)		3.60	1.86

Souvenir Sheet
Design: 5z, Long distance race.
    Imperf.

| 1422 | A458 | 5z multi | 1.75 | 1.00 |

Issued to publicize the European Athletic Championships, Budapest, August, 1966. Nos. 1422 contains one horizonal stamp (size: 57x27mm.); gray margin shows track and violet blue inscription. Size: 109x64 mm.

Polish Eagle
A459

Flowers and Farm Produce
A460

Designs: Nos. 1424, 1426, Flag of Poland. Nos. 1425, Polish Eagle.

Photogravure and Embossed
    Perf. 12½x12
1966, July 21   Unwmkd.

1423	A459	60g gold, red & blk	15	10
1424	A459	60g gold, red & blk	15	10
1425	A459	2.50z gold, red & blk	45	25
1426	A459	2.50z gold, red & blk	45	25

Issued to commemorate the 1000th anniversary of Poland. Nos. 1423-1424 and 1425-1426 printed in 2 sheets of 10 (5x2); top row in each sheet in eagle design, bottom row in flag design.

1966, Aug. 15   Photo.   Perf. 11

Designs: 60g, Woman holding loaf of bread. 3.40z, Farm girls holding harvest wreath.

    Size: 22x50mm.

| 1427 | A460 | 40g gold & multi | 35 | 12 |
| 1428 | A460 | 60g gold & multi | 35 | 12 |

    Size: 48x50mm.

| 1429 | A460 | 3.40z vio bl & multi | 1.00 | 65 |

Issued to publicize the harvest festival.

Chrysanthemum
A461

Flowers: 20g, Poinsettia. 30g, Centaury. 40g, Rose. 60g, Zinnias. 90g, Nasturtium. 1.35z, Dahlia. 6.50z, Sunflower. 7.10z, Magnolia.

1966, Sept. 1   Perf. 11½
Flowers in Natural Colors

1430	A461	10g gold & blk	10	5
1431	A461	20g gold & blk	10	5
1432	A461	30g gold & blk	10	5
1433	A461	40g gold & blk	10	5
1434	A461	60g gold & blk	15	10
1435	A461	90g gold & blk	1.25	50
1436	A461	5.60z gold & blk	1.50	50
1437	A461	6.50z gold & blk	2.25	1.00
1438	A461	7.10z gold & blk	1.75	1.25
	Nos. 1430-1438 (9)		7.30	3.55

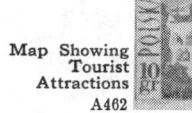

Map Showing Tourist Attractions
A462

Designs: 20g, Lighthouse, Hel. 40g, Amethyst yacht on Masurian Lake. No. 1442, Poniatowski Bridge, Warsaw, and sailboat. No. 1443, Mining Academy, Kielce. 1.15z, Dunajec Gorge. 1.35z, Old oaks, Rogalin. 1.55z, Planetarium, Katowice. 2z, M.S. Batory and globe.

    Perf. 12½x12, 11½x12
1966, Sept. 15   Engraved

1439	A462	10g car rose	5	5
1440	A462	20g ol gray	5	5
1441	A462	40g grysh bl	5	5
1442	A462	60g redsh brn	10	5
1443	A462	60g black	10	5
1444	A462	1.15z green	18	10
1445	A462	1.35z vermilion	20	10
1446	A462	1.55z violet	25	10
1447	A462	2z dk gray	30	15
	Nos. 1439-1447 (9)		1.28	70

Stableman with Percherons, by Piotr Michalowski
A463

Design: 2.50z, "Horses and Dogs" by Michalowski.

1966, Sept. 8   Perf. 11x11½

| 1448 | A463 | 60g gray brn | 15 | 8 |
| 1449 | A463 | 2.50z green | 30 | 15 |

Issued for Stamp Day, 1966.

Capital of Romanesque Column from Tyniec and Polish Flag
A464

Engraved and Photogravure
1966, Oct. 7   Perf. 11½

| 1450 | A464 | 60g dk brn & rose | 15 | 8 |

Polish Cultural Congress.

Soldier
A465

1966, Oct. 20   Litho.   Perf. 11x11½

| 1451 | A465 | 60g blk, ol grn, & dl red | 25 | 8 |

Issued to commemorate the participation of the Polish Jaroslaw Dabrowski Brigade in the Spanish Civil War.

Green Woodpecker
A466

Forest Birds: 10g, The eight birds of the set combined. 30g, Eurasian jay. 40g, European golden oriole. 60g, Hoopoe. 2.50z, European redstart. 4z, Siskin (finch). 6.50z, Chaffinch. 7.10z, Great tit.

1966, Nov. 17   Photo.   Perf. 11½
Birds in Natural Colors; Black Inscription.

1452	A466	10g lt grn	15	8
1453	A466	20g dl vio bl	15	8
1454	A466	30g dl grn	15	8
1455	A466	40g gray	15	8
1456	A466	60g gray grn	15	8
1457	A466	2.50z lt ol grn	50	30
1458	A466	4z dl vio	1.75	60
1459	A466	6.50z green	1.25	75
1460	A466	7.10z gray bl	2.50	1.25
	Nos. 1452-1460 (9)		6.75	3.30

Ceramic Ram, c. 4000 B.C.
A467

Designs: No. 1462, Bronze weapons and ornaments, c. 3500 B.C. (horiz.). No. 1463, Biskupin, settlement plan, 2500 B.C.

1966, Dec. 10   Engr.   Perf. 11x11½

1461	A467	60g dl vio brn	20	10
1462	A467	60g brown	20	10
1463	A467	60g green	20	10

Polish Eagle, Hammer and Grain—A468

Designs: 60g, Eagle and map of Poland.

1966, Dec. 20   Litho.   Perf. 11

| 1464 | A468 | 40g brn, red & bluish lil | 10 | 5 |
| 1465 | A468 | 60g brn, red & ol grn | 15 | 8 |

Millenium of Poland.

Gemini, American Spacecraft
A469

Spacecraft: 20g, Vostok (USSR). 60g, Ariel 2 (Great Britain). 1.35z, Proton 1 (USSR). 1.50z, FR 1 (France). 3.40z, Alouette (Canada). 6.50z, San Marco 1 (Italy). 7.10z, Luna 9 (USSR).

1966, Dec. 20   Perf. 11½x11

1466	A469	20g tan & multi	5	5
1467	A469	40g brn & multi	5	5
1468	A469	60g gray & multi	8	5
1469	A469	1.35z multi	25	10
1470	A469	1.50z multi	25	10
1471	A469	3.40z multi	60	25
1472	A469	6.50z multi	1.20	45
1473	A469	7.10z multi	1.45	75
	Nos. 1466-1473 (8)		3.93	1.80

Dressage—A470

Horses: 20g, Horse race. 40g, Jump. 60g, Steeplechase. 90g, Trotting. 5.90z, Polo. 6.60z, Stallion "Ofir." 7z, Stallion "Skowronek."

1967, Feb. 25   Photo.   Perf. 12½

1474	A470	10g ultra & multi	10	5
1475	A470	20g org & multi	10	5
1476	A470	40g ver & multi	15	6
1477	A470	60g multi	20	8
1478	A470	90g grn & multi	35	10
1479	A470	5.90z multi	1.25	35
1480	A470	6.60z multi	1.50	75
1481	A470	7z vio & multi	3.25	1.75
	Nos. 1474-1481 (8)		6.90	3.19

Issued to commemorate the 150th anniversary of the Janov Podlaski stud farm.

Memorial at Auschwitz (Oswiecim)
A471

POLAND

Emblem of
Memorials
Administration
A472

Designs (Memorials at): No. 1484, Oswiecim-Monowice. No. 1485, Westerplatte. No. 1486, Lodz-Radugoszcz. No. 1487, Stutthof. No. 1488, Lambinowice-Jencom. No. 1489, Zagan.

1967   Engraved   *Perf. 11½x11, 11x11½*

1482	A471	40g brn ol	10	5
1483	A472	40g dl vio	10	5
1484	A472	40g black	10	5
1485	A472	40g green	10	5
1486	A472	40g black	10	5
1487	A471	40g ultra	10	5
1488	A471	40g brown	10	5
1489	A472	40g dp plum	10	5
	Nos. 1482-1489 (8)		80	40

Issued to commemorate the martyrdom and fight of the Polish people, 1939-45. Issue dates: Nos. 1482-1484, Apr. 10. Nos. 1485-1487, Oct. 9. Nos. 1488-1489, Dec. 28.
See also Nos. 1620-1624.

Striped
Butterfly-
fish
A473

Tropical fish: 10g, Imperial angelfish. 40g, Barred butterflyfish. 60g, Spotted triggerfish. 90g, Undulate triggerfish. 1.50z, Striped triggerfish. 4.50z, Blackeye butterflyfish. 6.60z, Blue angelfish. 7z, Saddleback butterflyfish.

1967, Apr. 1   Litho.   *Perf. 11x11½*

1492	A473	5g multi	10	5
1493	A473	10g multi	10	5
1494	A473	40g multi	15	8
1495	A473	60g multi	20	10
1496	A473	90g multi	20	10
1497	A473	1.50z multi	25	15
1498	A473	4.50z multi	95	50
1499	A473	6.60z multi	1.20	75
1500	A473	7z multi	2.00	1.25
	Nos. 1492-1500 (9)		5.15	3.03

Bicyclists—A474

1967, May 5   Litho.   *Perf. 11*

1501	A474	60g multi	25	10

Issued to commemorate the 20th Warsaw-Berlin-Prague Bicycle Race.

Men's
100-meter
Race
A475

Sports and Olympic Rings: 40g, Steeplechase. 60g, Women's relay race. 90g, Weight lifter. 1.35z, Hurdler. 3.40z, Gymnast on vaulting horse. 6.60z, High jump. 7z, Boxing.

1967, May 24   Litho.   *Perf. 11*

1502	A475	20g multi	10	5
1503	A475	40g multi	10	5
1504	A475	60g multi	10	5
1505	A475	90g multi	15	8
1506	A475	1.35z multi	25	10
1507	A475	3.40z multi	60	20
1508	A475	6.60z multi	1.00	35
1509	A475	7z multi	1.25	75
	Nos. 1502-1509 (8)		3.55	1.63

Issued to publicize the 19th Olympic Games, Mexico City, 1968. Nos. 1502-1509 printed in sheets of 8, (2x4) with label showing emblem of Polish Olympic Committee between each two horizontal stamps; black marginal inscription. See also No. B110.

Badge of
Socialist
Working
Brigade
A476

1967, June 2

1510	A476	60g multi	15	8

Issued to publicize the 6th Congress of Polish Trade Unions. Printed in sheets of 20 stamps and 20 labels and in miniature sheets of 4 stamps and 4 labels.

Mountain
Arnica
A477

Medicinal Plants: 60g, Columbine. 3.40z, Gentian. 4.50z, Ground pine. 5z, Iris sibirica. 10z, Azalea pontica.

1967, June 14   *Perf. 11½x11*
Flowers in Natural Colors

1511	A477	40g blk & brn org	5	5
1512	A477	60g blk & lt bl	5	8
1513	A477	3.40z blk & dp org	60	20
1514	A477	4.50z blk & lt vio	65	25
1515	A477	5z blk & mar	70	25
1516	A477	10z blk & bis	1.50	75
	Nos. 1511-1516 (6)		3.55	1.58

Monument
for Silesian
Insurgents
A478

1967, July 21   Litho.   *Perf. 11½*

1517	A478	60g multi	15	8

Issued to commemorate the unveiling of the monument for the Silesian Insurgents of 1919-21 at Katowice, July, 1967.

Marie
Curie
A479

Designs: No. 1519, Curie statue, Warsaw. No. 1520, Nobel Prize diploma.

1967, Aug. 1   Engr.   *Perf. 11½x11*

1518	A479	60g dk car rose	30	15
1519	A479	60g violet	20	10
1520	A479	60g sepia	30	15

Issued to commemorate the centenary of the birth of Marie Sklodowska Curie (1867-1934), discoverer of radium and polonium.

Sign Language
and Emblem
A480

1967, Aug. 1   Litho.   *Perf. 11x11½*

1521	A480	60g brt bl & blk	15	8

Issued to publicize the 5th Congress of the World Federation of the Deaf, Warsaw, Aug. 10-17.

Flowers of the Meadows
A481

Flowers: 40g, Poppy. 60g, Morning glory. 90g, Pansy. 1.15z, Common pansy. 2.50z, Corn cockle. 3.40z, Wild aster. 4.50z, Common pimpernel. 7.90z, Chicory.

1967, Sept. 5   Photo.   *Perf. 11½*

1522	A481	20g multi	8	5
1523	A481	40g multi	8	5
1524	A481	60g multi	8	8
1525	A481	90g multi	15	10
1526	A481	1.15z multi	20	10
1527	A481	2.50z multi	45	25
1528	A481	3.40z multi	60	25
1529	A481	4.50z multi	1.25	75
1530	A481	7.90z multi	1.50	75
	Nos. 1522-1530 (9)		4.39	2.38

Wilanow Palace, by
Wincenty Kasprzycki
A482

Engraved and Photogravure

1967, Oct. 9   *Perf. 11½*

1531	A482	60g ol blk & lt bl	15	8

Issued for Stamp Day, 1967.

Cruiser Aurora—A483

Designs: No. 1533, Lenin and library. No. 1534, Luna 10, earth and moon.

1967, Oct. 9   Litho.   *Perf. 11*

1532	A483	60g gray, red & blk	20	10
1533	A483	60g gray, dl blk & blk	20	10
1534	A483	60g gray, red & blk	25	15

Issued to commemorate the 50th anniversary of the Russian Revolution.

Tadeusz Kosciusko
A485

Engraved and Photogravure

1967, Oct. 14   *Perf. 12x11*

1540	A485	60g choc & ocher	15	8
1541	A485	2.50z sl grn & rose car	30	20

Issued to commemorate the 150th anniversary of the death of Tadeusz Kosciusko (1746-1817), Polish patriot and general in the American Revolution.

Vanessa
Butterfly
A486

Designs: Various Butterflies.

1967, Oct. 14   Litho.   *Perf. 11½*
Butterflies in Natural Colors

1542	A486	10g green	10	10
1543	A486	20g lt vio bl	10	10
1544	A486	40g yel grn	10	10
1545	A486	60g gray	15	10
1546	A486	2z lemon	25	15
1547	A486	2.50z Prus grn	30	15
1548	A486	3.40z blue	55	25
1549	A486	4.50z rose lil	1.75	75
1550	A486	7.90z bister	3.00	1.75
	Nos. 1542-1550 (9)		6.30	3.45

Polish
Woman,
by
Antoine
Watteau
A487

Paintings from Polish Museums: 20g, Lady with the Ermine, by Leonardo da Vinci. 60g, Dog Fighting Heron, by Abraham Hondius. 2z, Guitarist after the Hunt, by J. Baptiste Greuze. 2.50z, Tax Collectors, by Marinus van Reymerswaele. 3.40z, Portrait of Daria Flodorowna, by Fiodor St. Rokotov. 4.50z, Still Life with Lobster, by Jean de Heem (horiz.). 6.60z, Landscape (from the Good Samaritan), by Rembrandt (horiz.).

Perf. 11½x11, 11x11½

1967, Nov. 15   Photogravure

1551	A487	20g gold & multi	20	10
1552	A487	40g gold & multi	15	8
1553	A487	60g gold & multi	15	8
1554	A487	2z gold & multi	35	20
1555	A487	2.50z gold & multi	50	25
1556	A487	3.40z gold & multi	75	25
1557	A487	4.50z gold & multi	1.75	75
1558	A487	6.60z gold & multi	2.00	1.25
	Nos. 1551-1558 (8)		5.85	2.96

POLAND

Ossolinski Medal, Book and Flags
A488

1967, Dec. 12   Litho.   Perf. 11

| 1559 | A488 | 60g lt bl, red & lt brn | 25 | 8 |

Issued to commemorate the 150th anniversary of the founding of the Ossolineum, a center for scientific and cultural activities, by Count Josef Maximilian Ossolinski.

Wladyslaw S. Reymont
A489

1967, Dec. 12

| 1560 | A489 | 60g dk brn, ocher & red | 25 | 8 |

Issued to commemorate the centenary of the birth of Wladyslaw Stanislaw Reymont (1867–1924), writer, Nobel Prize winner.

Ice Hockey
A490

Designs: 60g, Skiing. 90g, Slalom. 1.35z, Speed skating. 1.55z, Long-distance skiing. 2z, Sledding. 7z, Biathlon. 7.90z, Ski jump.

1968, Jan. 10

1561	A490	40g multi	8	5
1562	A490	60g multi	10	8
1563	A490	90g multi	15	8
1564	A490	1.35z multi	25	10
1565	A490	1.55z multi	25	10
1566	A490	2z multi	30	15
1567	A490	7z multi	1.00	50
1568	A490	7.90z multi	1.50	75
		Nos. 1561-1568 (8)	3.63	1.81

Issued to publicize the 10th Winter Olympic Games, Grenoble, France, Feb. 6-18, 1968.

Puss in Boots
A491

Fairy Tales: 40g, The Fox and the Raven. 60g. Mr. Twardowski (man flying on a cock). 2z, The Fisherman and the Fish. 2.50z, Little Red Riding Hood. 3.40z, Cinderella. 5.50z, Thumbelina. 7z, Snow White.

1968, Mar. 15   Litho.   Perf. 12½

1569	A491	20g multi	5	5
1570	A491	40g lt vio & multi	5	5
1571	A491	60g multi	15	8
1572	A491	2z ol & multi	30	20
1573	A491	2.50z ver & multi	40	30
1574	A491	3.40z multi	70	45
1575	A491	5.50z multi	95	60
1576	A491	7z multi	1.75	1.00
		Nos. 1569-1576 (8)	4.30	2.40

Bird-of-Paradise Flower
A492

Exotic Flowers: 10g, Clianthus dampieri. 20g, Passiflora quadrangularis. 40g, Coryphanta vivipara. 60g, Odontonia. 90g, Protea cynaroides.

1968, May 15   Litho.   Perf. 11½

1577	A492	10g sep & multi	10	6
1578	A492	20g multi	10	6
1579	A492	30g brn & multi	10	6
1580	A492	40g ultra & multi	10	6
1581	A492	60g multi	15	8
1582	A492	90g multi	25	10
		Nos. 1577-1582, B111-B112 (8)	3.75	1.87

"Peace" by Henryk Tomaszewski
A493

Design: 2.50z, Poster for Gounod's Faust, by Jan Lenica.

1968, May 29   Litho.   Perf. 11½x11

| 1583 | A493 | 60g gray & multi | 15 | 8 |
| 1584 | A493 | 2.50z gray & multi | 30 | 15 |

Issued to publicize the 2nd International Poster Biennial Exhibition, Warsaw.

Zephyr Glider
A494

Polish Gliders: 90g, Storks. 1.50z, Swallow. 3.40z, Flies. 4z, Seal. 5.50z, Pirate.

1968, May 29   Perf. 12½

1585	A494	60g multi	8	5
1586	A494	90g multi	15	8
1587	A494	1.50z multi	25	10
1588	A494	3.40z multi	75	25
1589	A494	4z multi	1.00	50
1590	A494	5.50z multi	1.25	75
		Nos. 1585-1590 (6)	3.48	1.73

11th International Glider Championships, Leszno.

Child Holding Symbolic Stamp
A495

Sosnowiec Memorial
A496

Design: No. 1592, Balloon over Poznan Town Hall.

1968, July 2   Litho.   Perf. 11½x11

| 1591 | A495 | 60g multi | 20 | 10 |
| 1592 | A495 | 60g multi | 20 | 10 |

Issued to commemorate 75 years of Polish philately and to publicize the "Tematica 1968" stamp exhibition in Poznan. Printed in sheets of 12 (4x3) se-tenant, arranged checkerwise, with light blue marginal inscription.

Photogravure and Engraved

1968, July 20   Perf. 11x11½

| 1593 | A496 | 60g brt rose lil & blk | 20 | 8 |

The monument by Helena and Roman Husarski and Witold Ceckiewicz was unveiled Sept. 16, 1967, to honor the revolutionary deeds of Silesian workers and miners.

Relay Race and Sculptured Head
A497

Sports and Sculptures: 40g, Boxing. 60g. Basketball. 90g, Long jump. 2.50z, Women's javelin. 3.40z, Athlete on parallel bars. 4z, Bicycling. 7.90z, Fencing.

1968, Sept. 2   Litho.   Perf. 11x11½
Size: 35x26mm.

1594	A497	30g sep & multi	5	5
1595	A497	40g brn org, brn & blk	5	5
1596	A497	60g gray & multi	8	5
1597	A497	90g vio & multi	12	8
1598	A497	2.50z multi	30	10
1599	A497	3.40z brt grn, blk & lt ultra	55	15
1600	A497	4z multi	60	25
1601	A497	7.90z multi	1.15	50
		Nos. 1594-1601, B113 (9)	5.65	2.73

Issued to publicize the 19th Olympic Games, Mexico City, Oct. 12-27.

Jewish Woman with Lemons, by Aleksander Gierymski
A498

Polish Paintings: 40g, Knight on Bay Horse, by Piotr Michalowski. 60g, Fisherman, by Leon Wyczolkowski. 1.35z, Eliza Parenska, by Stanislaw Wyspianski. 1.50z, "Manifest," by Wojciech Weiss. 4.50z, Stancyk (Jester), by Jan Matejko (horiz.). 5z, Children's Band, by Tadeusz Makowski (horiz.). 7z, Feast II, by Zygmunt Waliszewski (horiz.).

Perf. 11½x11, 11x11½

1968, Oct. 10   Lithographed

1602	A498	40g gray & multi	10	5
1603	A498	60g gray & multi	10	5
1604	A498	1.15z gray & multi	15	10
1605	A498	1.35z gray & multi	25	10
1606	A498	1.50z gray & multi	50	25
1607	A498	4.50z gray & multi	75	35
1608	A498	5z gray & multi	1.25	45
1609	A498	7z gray & multi	1.50	75
		Nos. 1602-1609 (8)	4.60	2.10

Issued in sheets of 4 stamps and 2 labels inscribed with painter's name.

"September, 1939" by M. Bylina
A499

Paintings: No. 1611, Partisans, by L. Maciag. No. 1612, Tank in Battle, by M. Bylina. No. 1613, Monte Cassino, by A. Boratynski. No. 1614, Tanks Approaching Warsaw, by S. Garwatowski. No. 1615, Battle on the Neisse, by M. Bylina. No. 1616, On the Oder, by K. Mackiewicz. No. 1617, "In Berlin," by M. Bylina. No. 1618, Warship "Blyskawica" by M. Mokwa. No. 1619, "Pursuit" (fighter planes), by T. Kulisiewicz.

Litho., Typo. and Engraved

1968, Oct. 12   Perf. 11½

1610	A499	40g pale yel, ol & vio	10	5
1611	A499	40g lil, red lil & ind	10	5
1612	A499	40g gray, dk bl & ol	10	5
1613	A499	40g pale sal, org brn & blk	10	5
1614	A499	60g pale grn, dk grn & plum	10	5
1615	A499	60g gray, vio bl & blk	20	10
1616	A499	60g pale grn, ol grn & vio brn	20	10
1617	A499	60g pink, car & grnsh blk	20	10
1618	A499	60g pink, brn & grn	20	10
1619	A499	60g lt bl, grnsh bl & blk	20	10
		Nos. 1610-1619 (10)	1.50	75

Polish People's Army, 25th anniversary.

Memorial Types of 1967

Designs: No. 1620, Tomb of the Unknown Soldier, Warsaw. No. 1621, Nazi War Crimes Memorial, Zamosc. No. 1622, Guerrilla Memorial, Plichno. No. 1623, Guerrilla Memorial, Kartuzy. No. 1624, Polish Insurgents' Memorial, Poznan.

Perf. 11½x11, 11x11½

1968, Nov. 15   Engraved

1620	A471	40g slate	10	5
1621	A472	40g dl red	10	5
1622	A472	40g dk bl	10	5
1623	A471	40g sepia	10	5
1624	A472	40g sepia	10	5
		Nos. 1620-1624 (5)	50	25

Issued to commemorate the martyrdom and fight of the Polish people, 1939–45.

Strikers, S. Lentz
A500

Paintings: No. 1626, "Manifesto," by Wojciech Weiss. No. 1627, Party members, by F. Kowarski (horiz.).

Perf. 11½x11, 11x11½

1968, Nov. 11   Lithographed

1625	A500	60g dk red & multi	15	8
1626	A500	60g dk red & multi	15	8
1627	A500	60g dk red & multi	15	8

Issued to publicize the 5th Congress of the Polish United Workers' Party.

POLAND

Departure for the Hunt, by
Wojciech Kossak—A501

Hunt Paintings: 40g, Hunting with Falcon, by Juliusz Kossak. 60g, Wolves' Raid, by A. Wierusz-Kowalski. 1.50z, Bear Hunt, by Julian Falat. 2.50z, Fox Hunt, by T. Sutherland. 3.40z, Boar Hunt, by Frans Snyders. 4.50z, Hunters' Rest, by W. G. Pierow. 8.50z, Lion Hunt in Morocco, by Delacroix.

1968, Nov. 20   Perf. 11

1628	A501	20g multi	8	5
1629	A501	40g multi	8	5
1630	A501	60g multi	10	5
1631	A501	1.50z multi	35	10
1632	A501	2.50z multi	30	15
1633	A501	3.40z multi	60	20
1634	A501	4.50z multi	1.25	60
1635	A501	8.50z multi	2.25	1.25
		Nos. 1628-1635 (8)	5.01	2.45

Afghan Greyhound
A502

Dogs: 20g, Maltese. 40g, Rough-haired fox terrier (vert.). 1.50z, Schnauzer. 2.50z, English setter. 3.40z, Pekinese. 4.50z, German shepherd. 8.50z, Pointer.

1969, Feb. 2 Perf. 11x11½, 11½x11
Dogs in Natural Colors

1636	A502	20g gray & brt grn	25	15
1637	A502	40g gray & org	40	20
1638	A502	60g gray & lil	40	20
1639	A502	1.50z gray & blk	40	25
1640	A502	2.50z gray & brt pink	65	35
1641	A502	3.40z gray & dk grn	1.25	50
1642	A502	4.50z gray & ver	2.25	1.00
1643	A502	8.50z gray & vio	5.00	2.25
		Nos. 1636-1643 (8)	10.60	4.90

Issued to publicize the General Assembly of the International Kennel Federation, Warsaw, May 1969.

Eagle-on-Shield House Sign
A503

1969, Feb. 23 Litho. Perf. 11½x11

| 1644 | A503 | 60g gray, red & blk | 15 | 8 |

9th Congress of Democratic Movement.

Sheaf of Wheat
A504

1969, Mar. 29 Litho. Perf. 11½x11

| 1645 | A504 | 60g multi | 15 | 8 |

Issued to publicize the 5th Congress of the United Peasant Party, Warsaw, March 29-31.

Runner—A505

Designs (Olympic Rings and): 20g, Woman gymnast. 40g, Weight lifting. 60g, Women's javelin.

1969, Apr. 25 Litho. Perf. 11½x11

1646	A505	10g org & multi	5	5
1647	A505	20g ultra & multi	5	5
1648	A505	40g yel & multi	8	5
1649	A505	60g red & multi	15	8
		Nos. 1646-1649, B114-B117 (8)	3.78	1.61

Issued to commemorate the 50th anniversary of the Polish Olympic Committee, and the 75th anniversary of the International Olympic Committee.

Sailboat and Lighthouse,
Kolobrzeg Harbor—A506

Designs: 40g, Tourist map of Swietokrzyski National Park. 60g, Ruins of 16th century castle, Niedzica (vert.). 1.50z, Castle of the Dukes of Pomerania and ship, Szczecin. 2.50z, View of Torun and Vistula. 3.40z, View of Klodzko (vert.). 4z, View of Sulejow. 4.50z, Market Place, Kazimierz Dolny (vert.).

1969, May 20 Lithographed Perf. 11

1650	A506	40g multi	5	5
1651	A506	60g multi	8	5
1652	A506	1.35z multi	10	6
1653	A506	1.50z multi	15	10
1654	A506	2.50z multi	20	12
1655	A506	3.40z multi	35	18
1656	A506	4z multi	50	25
1657	A506	4.50z multi	75	35
		Nos. 1650-1657 (8)	2.18	1.16

Issued for tourist publicity. Printed in sheets of 15 stamps and 15 labels. Domestic plants on labels of 40g, 60g and 1.35z, coats of arms on others. See also Nos. 1731-1735.

World Map and
Sailboat Opty
A507

1969, June 21 Litho. Perf. 11x11½

| 1658 | A507 | 60g multi | 30 | 10 |

Issued to commemorate Leonid Teliga's one-man voyage around the world, Casablanca, Jan. 21, 1967, to Las Palmas, Apr. 16, 1969.

Nicolaus Copernicus,
Woodcut by Tobias Stimer
A508

Designs: 60g, Copernicus, by Jeremias Falck, 15th century globe and map of constellations. 2.50z, Copernicus, painting by Jan Matejko and map of heliocentric system.

Photo., Engr. and Litho.
1969, June 26   Perf. 11½

1659	A508	40g dl yel, sep & dp car	25	10
1660	A508	60g grnsh gray, blk & dp car	25	10
1661	A508	2.50z lt vio brn, ol & dp car	75	35

Issued to commemorate the 500th anniversary of the birth of Nicolaus Copernicus (1473-1543), astronomer.

"Memory" Pathfinders' Cross and Protectors' Badge
A509

Frontier Guard and Embossed Arms of Poland
A510

Coal Miner—A511

Designs: No. 1663, "Defense," military eagle and Pathfinders' cross. No. 1664, "Labor," map of Poland and Pathfinders' cross.

Photo., Engr. and Typo.
1969, July 19   Perf. 11x11½

1662	A509	60g ultra, blk & red	20	10
1663	A509	60g grn, blk & red	20	10
1664	A509	60g car, blk & grn	20	10

5th National Alert of Polish Pathfinders' Union.

1969, July 21   Litho. & Embossed

Designs: No. 1666, Oil refinery-chemical plant, Plock. No. 1667, Combine harvester. No. 1668, Rebuilt Grand Theater, Warsaw. No. 1669, Marie Curie-Sklodowska University and Monument, Lublin. No. 1671, Chemical industry (sulphur) worker. No. 1672, Steelworker. No. 1673, Ship builder and ship.

1665	A510	60g red & multi	10	5
1666	A510	60g red & multi	10	5
1667	A510	60g red & multi	10	5
1668	A510	60g red & multi	10	5
1669	A510	60g red & multi	10	5

Lithographed
Perf. 11½x11

1670	A511	60g gray & multi	10	5
1671	A511	60g gray & multi	10	5
1672	A511	60g gray & multi	10	5
1673	A511	60g gray & multi	10	5
		Nos. 1665-1673 (9)	90	45

Issued to commemorate the 25th anniversary of the Polish People's Republic. Nos. 1665-1669 are printed se-tenant in sheets of 20 (5x4); Nos. 1670-1673 are se-tenant in sheets of 20 (4x5).

Landing Module on Moon, and Earth
A512

1969, Aug. 21 Litho. Perf. 12x12½

| 1674 | A512 | 2.50z multi | 1.50 | 75 |

Issued to commemorate man's first landing on the moon, July 20, 1969. U.S. astronauts Neil A. Armstrong and Col. Edwin E. Aldrin, Jr., with Lieut. Col. Michael Collins piloting Apollo 11. Issued in sheets of 8 stamps and 2 tabs with decorative border. One tab shows Apollo 11 with lunar landing module, the other shows module's take-off from moon. Price, sheet. $30, used $15.

Motherhood, by
Stanislaw Wyspianski—A513

Polish Paintings: 40g, "Hamlet," by Jacek Malczewski. 60g, Indian Summer (sleeping woman), by Jozef Chelmonski. 2z, Two Girls, by Olga Boznanska (vert.). 2.50z, "The Sun of May" (Breakfast on the Terrace), by Jozef Mehoffer (vert.). 3.40z, Woman Combing her Hair, by Wladyslaw Slewinski. 5.50z, Still Life, by Jozef Pankiewicz. 7z, The Abduction of the King's Daughter, by Witold Wojtkiewicz.

Perf. 11x11½, 11½x11
1969, Sept. 4   Photogravure

1675	A513	20g gold & multi	5	5
1676	A513	40g gold & multi	5	5
1677	A513	60g gold & multi	15	10
1678	A513	2z gold & multi	30	20
1679	A513	2.50z gold & multi	30	20
1680	A513	3.40z gold & multi	50	30
1681	A513	5.50z gold & multi	1.25	60
1682	A513	7z gold & multi	2.00	1.00
		Nos. 1675-1682 (8)	4.60	2.50

Issued in sheets of 4 stamps and 2 labels inscribed with painter's name.

Nike
A514

1969, Sept. 19 Litho. Perf. 11½x11

| 1683 | A514 | 60g gray, red & bis | 15 | 8 |

Issued to publicize the 4th Congress of the Union of Fighters for Freedom and Democracy.

POLAND

Details from Memorial,
Maidanek Concentration Camp
A515

1969, Sept. 20   Perf. 11
1684 A515 40g brt lil, gray & blk   25   10

Issued to commemorate the unveiling of a monument to the victims of the Maidanek concentration camp. The monument was designed by the sculptor Wiktor Tolkin.

Costumes from
Krczonow, Lublin
A516

Regional Costumes: 60g, Lowicz. 1.15z, Rozbark, Katowice. 1.35z, Lower Silesia, Wroclaw. 1.50z, Opoczno, Lodz. 4.50z, Sacz, Cracow. 5z, Highlanders, Cracow. 7z, Kurpiow, Warsaw.

1969, Sept. 30 Litho. Perf. 11½x11
1685 A516 40g multi   5   5
1686 A516 60g multi   8   5
1687 A516 1.15z multi   16   8
1688 A516 1.35z multi   20   10
1689 A516 1.50z multi   24   14
1690 A516 4.50z multi   80   45
1691 A516 5z multi   1.25   75
1692 A516 7z multi   1.00   55
     Nos. 1685-1692 (8)   3.78 2.17

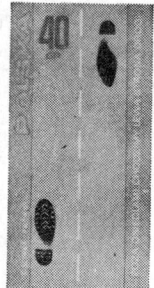

"Walk at Left"
A517

Designs: 60g, "Drive Carefully" (horses on road). 2.50z, "Lower your Lights" (automobiles on road).

1969, Oct. 4   Perf. 11
1693 A517 40g multi   5   5
1694 A517 60g multi   10   8
1695 A517 2.50z multi   35   15

Issued to publicize traffic safety.

ILO Emblem
and Welder's
Mask
A518

1969, Oct. 20   Perf. 11x11½
1696 A518 2.50z vio bl & ol 25   10

Issued to commemorate the 50th anniversary of the International Labor Organization.

Bell
Foundry
A519

Miniatures from Behem's Code, completed 1505: 60g, Painter's studio. 1.35z, Wood carvers. 1.55z, Shoemaker. 2.50z, Cooper. 3.40z, Bakery. 4.50z, Tailor. 7z, Bowyer's shop.

1969, Nov. 12 Litho. Perf. 12½
1697 A519 40g gray & multi   5   5
1698 A519 60g gray & multi   10   5
1699 A519 1.35z gray & multi   20   10
1700 A519 1.55z gray & multi   24   14
1701 A519 2.50z gray & multi   35   20
1702 A519 3.40z gray & multi   50   30
1703 A519 4.50z gray & multi   75   40
1704 A519 7z gray & multi   1.50   75
     Nos. 1697-1704 (8)   3.69 1.99

Angel
A520

Folk Art (Sculptures): 40g, Sorrowful Christ (head). 60g, Sorrowful Christ (seated figure). 2z, Crying woman. 2.50z, Adam and Eve. 3.40z, Woman with birds.

1969, Dec. 19 Litho. Perf. 12½
Size: 21x36mm.
1705 A520 20g lt bl & multi   6   5
1706 A520 40g lil & multi   8   5
1707 A520 60g multi   12   8
1708 A520 2z multi   30   15
1709 A520 2.50z multi   36   20
1710 A520 3.40z multi   50   30
     Nos. 1705-1710, B118-B119 (8) 3.77 1.86

Leopold
Staff
(1878-
1957)
A521

Portraits: 60g, Wladyslaw Broniewski (1897-1962). 1.35z, Leon Kruczkowski (1900-1962). 1.50z, Julian Tuwim (1894-1953). 1.55z, Konstanty Ildefons Galczynski (1905-1953). 2.50z, Maria Dabrowska (1889-1965). 3.40z, Zofia Nalkowska (1885-1954).

Litho., Typo. and Engraved
1969, Dec. 30   Perf. 11x11½
1711 A521 40g ol grn & blk, grnsh   6   5
1712 A521 60g dp car & blk, pink   8   5
1713 A521 1.35z vio bl & blk, grysh 20   10
1714 A521 1.50z pur & blk, pink   25   10
1715 A521 1.55z dp grn & blk, grnsh 25   12
1716 A521 2.50z ultra & blk, gray   35   15
1717 A521 3.40z red brn & blk, pink 50   25
     Nos. 1711-1717 (7)   1.69   82

Issued to honor Polish writers.

Statue
of Nike
and
Polish
Colors
A522

1970, Jan. 17 Photo. Perf. 11½
1718 A522 60g sil, gold, red & blk 30   12

Warsaw liberation, 25th anniversary.

Medieval Print
Shop and
Modern Color
Proofs
A523

1970, Jan. 20 Litho. Perf. 11½x11
1719 A523 60g multi   15   8

Centenary of Polish printers' trade union.

Ring-
necked
Pheasant
A524

Game Birds: 40g, Mallard drake. 1.15z, Woodcock. 1.35z, Ruffs (males). 1.50z, Wood pigeon. 3.40z, Black grouse. 7z, Gray partridges (cock and hen). 8.50z, Capercaillie cock giving mating call.

1970, Feb. 28 Litho. Perf. 11½
1720 A524 40g multi   15   10
1721 A524 60g multi   1.50   25
1722 A524 1.15z multi   15   10
1723 A524 1.35z multi   20   10
1724 A524 1.50z multi   50   25
1725 A524 3.40z multi   50   25
1726 A524 7z multi   2.25 1.25
1727 A524 8.50z multi   1.50 1.50
     Nos. 1720-1727 (8)   7.75 3.80

Lenin in his Kremlin Study, Oct.
1918, and Polish Lenin Steel Mill
A525

Designs: 60g, Lenin addressing 3rd International Congress in Leningrad, 1920, and Luna 13. 2.50z, Lenin with delegates to 10th Russian Communist Party Congress, Moscow, 1921, dove and globe.

Engraved and Typographed
1970, Apr. 22   Perf. 11
1728 A525 40g grnsh blk & dl red   8   5
1729 A525 60g sep & dp lil rose   15   8
  a.   Souvenir sheet of 4   1.50   75
1730 A525 2.50z bluish blk & ver   35   20

Birth centenary of Lenin (1870-1924), Russian communist leader.
No. 1729a commemorates the Cracow International Philatelic Exhibition. It contains 4 of No. 1729 with vermilion marginal inscription. Size: 133x81mm.

Tourist Type of 1969

Designs: No. 1731, Townhall, Wroclaw (vert.). No. 1732, Cathedral, Piast Castle tower and church towers, Opole. No. 1733, Castle, Legnica. No. 1734, Castle Tower, Bolkow. No. 1735, Town Hall, Brzeg.

1970, May 9 Litho. Perf. 11
Multicolored
1731 A506 60g Wroclaw   25   10
1732 A506 60g Opole   25   10
1733 A506 60g Legnica   25   10
1734 A506 60g Bolkow   25   10
1735 A506 60g Brzeg   25   10
     Nos. 1731-1735 (5)   1.25   50

Issued for tourist publicity. Printed in sheets of 15 stamps and 15 labels, showing coats of arms.

Polish
and
Russian
Soldiers
before
Branden-
burg Gate
A526

Flower, Eagle
and Arms of
7 Cities
A527

Lithographed and Engraved
1970, May 9   Perf. 11
1736 A526 60g tan & multi   15   8
                      Perf. 11½
1737 A527 60g sil, red & sl grn   15   8

Issued to commemorate the 25th anniversary of victory over Germany and of Polish administration of the Oder-Neisse border area.

Peasant
Movement
Flag
A528

1970, May 15 Litho. Perf. 11½
1738 A528 60g ol & multi   25   8

Issued to commemorate the 75th anniversary of the Polish peasant movement.

U.P.U. Head-
quarters
A529

POLAND

1970, May 20

| 1739 | A529 | 2.50z bl & vio bl | 25 | 12 |

Issued to commemorate the inauguration of the new Universal Postal Union Headquarters in Bern.

Soccer
A530

1970, May 30   *Perf. 11½x11*

| 1740 | A530 | 60g multi | 35 | 20 |

Issued to commemorate the European Soccer Cup Finals. Printed in sheets of 15 stamps and 15 se-tenant labels inscribed with the scores of the games.

Lamp of Learning
A531

1970, June 3   *Perf. 11½*

| 1741 | A531 | 60g blk, bis & red | 15 | 8 |

Plock Scientific Society, 150th anniversary.

Cross-country Race
A532

Designs: No. 1743, Runners from ancient Greek vase. No. 1744, Archer, drawing by W. Skoczylas.

1970, June 16 Photo. *Perf. 11x11½*

1742	A532	60g yel & multi	25	12
1743	A532	60g blk & multi	25	12
1744	A532	60g dk bl & multi	25	12

Issued in connection with the 10th session of the International Olympic Academy. See No. B120.

Copernicus, by Bacciarelli and
View of Bologna
A533

Designs: 60g, Copernicus, by W. Lesseur and view of Padua. 2.50z, Copernicus, by Zinck Nora and view of Ferrara.

Photo., Engr. and Typo.

1970, June 26   *Perf. 11½*

1745	A533	40g org & multi	15	8
1746	A533	60g ol & multi	15	8
1747	A533	2.50z multi	60	30

Issued to commemorate the 500th anniversary of the birth of Nicolaus Copernicus (1473–1543), Polish astronomer.

Aleksander Orlowski (1777–1832),
Self-portrait—A534

Miniatures: 40g, Jan Matejko (1838–1893), self-portrait. 60g, King Stefan Batory (1533–1586), anonymous painter. 2z, Maria Leszczynska (1703–1768), anonymous French painter. 2.50z, Maria Walewska (1789–1817), by Jacquotot Marie-Victoire. 3.40z, Tadeusz Kosciuszko (1746–1817), by Jan Rustem. 5.50z, Samuel Bogumil Linde (1771–1847), by G. Landolfi. 7z, Michal Oginski (1728–1800), by Windisch Nanette.

Lithographed and Photogravure

1970, Aug. 27   *Perf. 11½*

1748	A534	20g gold & multi	15	8
1749	A534	40g gold & multi	15	8
1750	A534	60g gold & multi	15	8
1751	A534	2z gold & multi	25	15
1752	A534	2.50z gold & multi	50	25
1753	A534	3.40z gold & multi	75	40
1754	A534	5.50z gold & multi	1.25	65
1755	A534	7z gold & multi	2.00	1.00
		Nos. 1748-1755 (8)	5.20	2.69

Nos. 1748–1755 printed in sheets of 4 stamps and 2 labels. The miniatures show famous Poles and are from collections in the National Museums in Warsaw and Cracow.

Poster for
Chopin
Competition
A535

Photogravure and Engraved

1970, Sept. 8   *Perf. 11x11½*

| 1756 | A535 | 2.50z blk & vio | 30 | 15 |

The 8th International Chopin Piano Competition, Warsaw, Oct. 7-25.

U.N.
Emblem
A536

1970, Sept. 8 Photo. *Perf. 11½*

| 1757 | A536 | 2.50z multi | 30 | 15 |

United Nations, 25th anniversary.

Poles
A537

Design: 60g, Family, home and Polish flag.

1970, Sept. 15 Litho. *Perf. 11½x11*

| 1758 | A537 | 40g gray & multi | 20 | 10 |
| 1759 | A537 | 60g multi | 25 | 12 |

National Census, Dec. 8, 1970.

Grunwald Cross and Warship
Piorun (Thunderbolt)—A538

Designs (Grunwald Cross and Warship): 60g, Orzel (Eagle). 2.50z, Garland.

1970, Sept. 25 Engr. *Perf. 11½x11*

1760	A538	40g sepia	20	10
1761	A538	60g black	25	10
1762	A538	2.50z dp brn	75	25

Issued to honor the Polish Navy during World War II.

Cellist,
by Jerzy
Nowosielski
A539

Paintings: 40g, View of Lodz, by Benon Liberski. 60g, Studio Concert, by Waclaw Taranczewski. 1.50z, Still Life, by Zbigniew Pronaszko. 2z, Woman Hanging up Laundry, by Andrzej Wroblewski. 3.40z, "Expressions," by Maria Jarema (horiz.). 4z, Canal in the Forest, by Piotr Potworowski (horiz.). 8.50z, "The Sun," by Wladyslaw Strzeminski (horiz.).

1970, Oct. 9   Photo.   *Perf. 11½*

1763	A539	20g multi	5	5
1764	A539	40g multi	5	5
1765	A539	60g multi	10	5
1766	A539	1.50z multi	25	15
1767	A539	2z multi	30	20
1768	A539	3.40z multi	45	20
1769	A539	4z multi	75	35
1770	A539	8.50z multi	1.50	75
		Nos. 1763-1770 (8)	3.45	1.80

Issued for Stamp Day.

Luna 16 Landing
on Moon—A540

Stag
A541

1970, Nov. 20 Litho. *Perf. 11½x11*

| 1771 | A540 | 2.50z multi | 50 | 20 |

Luna 16 Russian unmanned, automatic moon mission, Sept. 12–24. Issued in sheets of 8 stamps and 2 tabs with bluish black commemorative inscription. One tab shows rocket launching; the other, parachute landing of capsule. Price, sheet $12.50, used $7.50.

1970, Dec. 23 Photo. *Perf. 11½x12*

Designs from 16th Century Tapestries in Wawel Castle: 1.15z, Stork. 1.35z, Leopard fighting dragon. 2z, Man's head. 2.50z, Child holding bird. 4z, God, Adam and Eve. 4.50z, Panel with monogram of King Sigismund Augustus. 5.50z, Poland's coat of arms.

1772	A541	60g multi	10	5
1773	A541	1.15z pur & multi	20	10
1774	A541	1.35z multi	22	12
1775	A541	2z sep & multi	35	18
1776	A541	2.50z dk bl & multi	45	20
1777	A541	4z grn & multi	1.00	45
1778	A541	4.50z multi	1.25	65
		Nos. 1772-1778 (7)	3.57	1.75

See No. B121.

Souvenir Sheet
Imperf.

| 1779 | A541 | 5.50z blk & multi | 1.50 | 75 |

No. 1779 contains one stamp (size: 48x57mm.), gray margin and black inscription. Size: 62x89mm.

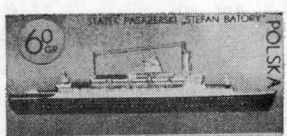

Transatlantic Liner Stefan Batory
A542

Polish Ships: 40g, School sailing ship Dar Pomorza. 1.15z, Ice breaker Perkun. 1.35z, Rescue ship R-1. 1.50z, Freighter Ziemia Szczecinska. 2.50z, Tanker Beskidy. 5z, Express freighter Hel. 8.50z, Ferry Gryf.

1971, Jan. 30 Photo. *Perf. 11*

1780	A542	40g ver & multi	5	5
1781	A542	60g multi	10	5
1782	A542	1.15z bl & multi	18	10
1783	A542	1.35z yel & multi	20	12
1784	A542	1.50z multi	25	12
1785	A542	2.50z vio & multi	45	20
1786	A542	5z multi	95	45
1787	A542	8.50z bl & multi	1.50	75
		Nos. 1780-1787 (8)	3.68	1.84

Checiny
Castle
A543

Polish Castles: 40g, Wisnicz. 60g, Bedzin. 2z, Ogrodzieniec. 2.50z, Niedzica. 3.40z, Kwidzyn. 4z, Pieskowa Skala. 8.50z, Lidzbark Warminski.

1971, March 5 Litho. *Perf. 11*

1788	A543	20g multi	5	5
1789	A543	40g multi	5	5
1790	A543	60g multi	10	8
1791	A543	2z multi	28	10
1792	A543	2.50z multi	30	15
1793	A543	3.40z multi	48	25
1794	A543	4z multi	55	35
1795	A543	8.50z multi	1.25	75
		Nos. 1788-1795 (8)	3.06	1.78

Fighting in Pouilly Castle, Jaroslaw
Dabrowski and Walery Wroblewski
A544

POLAND

1971, March 3   Perf. 12½x12½
1796   A544   60g vio bl, brn & red   15   8

Centenary of the Paris Commune.

Seedlings   Bishop Marianos
A545   A546

Designs: 60g, Forest.   1.50z, Clearing.

1971, Mar. 30 Photo.   Perf. 11½x11
Sizes: 26x34mm. (40g, 1.50z); 26x47mm. (60g)

1797	A545	40g grn & multi	15	5
1798	A545	60g grn & multi	25	8
1799	A545	1.50z grn & multi	50	20

Proper forest management.

1971, Apr. 20
Frescoes from Faras Cathedral, Nubia, 8th–12th centuries: 60g, St. Anne. 1.15z, 1.50z, 7z, Archangel Michael (diff. frescoes). 1.35z, Hermit Anamon of Tuna el Gabel. 4.50z, Cross with symbols of four Evangelists. 5z, Christ protecting Nubian dignitary.

1800	A546	40g gold & multi	5	5
1801	A546	60g gold & multi	10	8
1802	A546	1.15z gold & multi	18	10
1803	A546	1.35z gold & multi	25	12
1804	A546	1.50z gold & multi	30	15
1805	A546	4.50z gold & multi	90	35
1806	A546	5z gold & multi	95	40
1807	A546	7z gold & multi	1.20	60
		Nos. 1800-1807 (8)	3.93	1.85

Polish archaeological excavations in Nubia.

Silesian Insurrectionists—A547

1971, May 3   Photo.   Perf. 11
1808   A547   60g dk red brn & gold   20   8
  a.   Souv. sheet of 3   1.50   75

50th anniversary of the 3rd Silesian uprising. Printed in sheets of 15 stamps and 15 labels showing Silesian Insurrectionists monument in Katowice. No. 1808a contains 3 No. 1808 with 3 labels. Dark red brown marginal inscription. Size: 107½x 107½mm.

Peacock on the Lawn, by Dorota, 4 years old
A548

Children's Drawings and UNICEF Emblem: 40g, Our Army (horiz.). 60g, Spring. 2z, Cat with Ball (horiz.). 2.50z, Flowers in Vase. 3.40z, Friendship (horiz.). 5.50z, Clown. 7z, The Unknown Planet (horiz.).

1971, May 20 Perf. 11½x11, 11x11½

1809	A548	20g multi	5	5
1810	A548	40g multi	5	5
1811	A548	60g multi	10	6
1812	A548	2z multi	25	14
1813	A548	2.50z multi	30	16
1814	A548	3.40z multi	50	24
1815	A548	5.50z multi	75	40
1816	A548	7z multi	1.25	60
		Nos. 1809-1816 (8)	3.25	1.70

25th anniversary of UNICEF (United Nations Children's Fund).

Fair Emblem
A549

1971, June 1 Photo.   Perf. 11½x11
1817   A549   60g ultra, blk & dk car   15   8

40th International Poznan Fair, June 13–22.

Collegium Maius, Cracow—A550

Designs: 40g, Copernicus House, Torun (vert.). 2.50z, Olsztyn Castle. 4z, Frombork Cathedral (vert.).

1971, June   Litho.   Perf. 11

1818	A550	40g multi	15	8
1819	A550	60g blk, red brn & sep	20	10
1820	A550	2.50z multi	45	20
1821	A550	4z multi	75	35

Nicolaus Copernicus (1473–1543), astronomer. Printed in sheets of 15 with labels showing portrait of Copernicus, page from "Euclid's Geometry," astrolabe or drawing of heliocentric system, respectively.

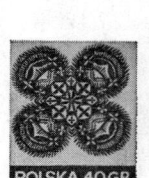 

Paper Cut-out   Worker, by Xawery Dunikowski
A551   A552

Designs: Various paper cut-outs (folk art).
Photo., Engr. and Typo.

1971, July 12   Perf. 12x11½

1822	A551	20g blk & brt grn, bluish	5	5
1823	A551	40g sl grn & dk ol, lt gray	5	5
1824	A551	60g brn & bl, gray	10	8
1825	A551	1.15z plum & brn, buff	15	10
1826	A551	1.35z dk grn & ver, yel grn	25	12
		Nos. 1822-1826 (5)	60	40

1971, July 21 Photo.   Perf. 11½x12
Sculptures: No. 1828, Founder, by Xawery Dunikowski. No. 1829, Miners, by Magdalena Wiecek. No. 1830, Woman harvester, by Stanislaw Horno-Poplawski.

1827	A552	40g sil & multi	10	6
1828	A552	40g sil & multi	10	6
1829	A552	60g sil & multi	25	15
1830	A552	60g sil & multi	25	15
	a.	Souvenir sheet of 4	1.50	75

No. 1830a contains one each of Nos. 1827–1830. Black marginal inscription commemorating 11th Philatelic Exhibition in Szczecin. Size: 157x85mm.

Punched Tape and Cogwheel
A553

1971, Sept. 2 Litho.   Perf. 11x11½
1831   A553   60g pur & red   15   8

6th Congress of Polish Technicians, held at Poznan, February, 1971.

Angel, by Jozef   Water Lilies, by
Mehoffer, 1901   Wyspianski
A554   A555

Stained Glass Windows: 60g, Detail from "The Elements" by Stanislaw Wyspianski, 1904. 1.35z, Apollo, by Wyspianski. 1.55z, Two Kings, 14th century. 3.40z, Flight into Egypt, 14th century. 5.50z, St. Jacob the Elder, 14th century.

1971, Sept. 15 Photo.   Perf. 11½x11

1832	A554	20g gold & multi	5	5
1833	A555	40g gold & multi	5	5
1834	A555	60g gold & multi	10	8
1835	A555	1.35z gold & multi	25	10
1836	A554	1.55z gold & multi	30	12
1837	A554	3.40z gold & multi	50	20
1838	A554	5.50z gold & multi	75	35
		Nos. 1832-1838, B122 (8)	3.26	1.77

Mrs. Fedorowicz, by Witold Pruszkowski (1846–1896)
A556

Paintings of Women: 50g, Woman with Book, by Tytus Czyzewski (1885–1945). 60g, Girl with Chrysanthemums, by Olga Boznanska (1865–1940). 2.50z, Girl in Red Dress, by Jozef Pankiewicz (1866–1940; horiz.). 3.40z, Nude, by Leon Chwistek (1884–1944; horiz.). 4.50z, Strange Garden (woman), by Jozef Mehoffer (1869–1946). 5z, Artist's Wife with White Hat, by Zbigniew Pronaszko (1885–1958).

Perf. 11½x11, 11x11½

1971, Oct. 9   Lithographed

1839	A556	40g gray & multi	5	5
1840	A556	50g gray & multi	5	5
1841	A556	60g gray & multi	10	8
1842	A556	2.50z gray & multi	35	15
1843	A556	3.40z gray & multi	50	20
1844	A556	4.50z gray & multi	75	35
1845	A556	5z gray & multi	1.00	50
		Nos. 1839-1845, B123 (8)	4.05	1.93

Stamp Day, 1971. Printed in sheets of 4 stamps and 2 labels inscribed "Women in Polish Paintings."

Krolewski Castle, Warsaw

1971, Oct. 14 Photo. Perf. 11x11½
1846   A557   60g gold, blk & brt red   15   8

P-11C Dive Bombers
A558

Planes and Polish Air Force Emblem: 1.50z, PZL 23-A Karas fighters. 3.40z, PZL Los bomber.

1971, Oct. 14

1847	A558	90g multi	20	10
1848	A558	1.50z bl, red & blk	25	10
1849	A558	3.40z multi	55	25

Martyrs of the Polish Air Force, 1939.

Lunar Rover and Astronauts
A559

Design: No. 1851, Lunokhod 1 on moon (vert.).

Perf. 11x11½, 11½x11

1971, Nov. 17

| 1850 | A559 | 2.50z multi | 35 | 15 |
| 1851 | A559 | 2.50z multi | 35 | 15 |

Apollo 15 U.S. moon exploration mission, July 26–Aug. 7 (No. 1850); Luna 17 unmanned automated U.S.S.R. moon mission, Nov. 10–17 (No. 1851). Printed in sheets of 6 stamps and 2 labels, with marginal inscriptions.

Worker at Helm
A560

Shipbuilding
A561

Designs: No. 1853, Worker. No. 1855, Apartment houses under construction. No. 1856, "Bison" combine harvester. No. 1857, Polish Fiat 125. No. 1858, Mining tower. No. 1859, Chemical plant.

1971, Dec. 8   Perf. 11½x11

1852	A560	60g gray, ultra & red	15	8
1853	A560	60g red & gray	15	8
		Strip of 2 + label	30	16

POLAND

Perf. 11x11½

1854	A561	60g red, gold & blk	15	8
1855	A561	60g red, gold & blk	15	8
1856	A561	60g red, gold & blk	15	8
1857	A561	60g red, gold & blk	15	8
1858	A561	60g red, gold & blk	15	8
1859	A561	60g red, gold & blk	15	8
		Block of 6	90	50
a.		Souvenir sheet of 6	1.00	60
		Nos. 1852-1859 (8)	1.20	64

6th Congress of the Polish United Worker's Party. Nos. 1852–1853 printed se-tenant in sheets of 30 with 15 labels showing congress emblem. Nos. 1854–1859 printed se-tenant in sheets of 36 with outline of map of Poland extending over block of 6 stamps. No. 1859a contains one each of Nos. 1854–1859. Black marginal inscription. Size: 100x115mm.

Cherry Blossoms—A562

Blossoms: 20g, Niedzwiecki's apple. 40g, Pear. 60g, Peach. 1.15z, Japanese magnolia. 1.35z, Red hawthorne. 2.50z, Apple. 3.40z, Red chestnut. 5z, Acacia robinia. 8.50z, Cherry.

1971, Dec. 28 Litho. Perf. 12½
Blossoms in Natural Colors

1860	A562	10g dl bl & blk	8	5
1861	A562	20g grnsh bl & blk	8	5
1862	A562	40g lt vio & blk	10	5
1863	A562	60g grn & blk	15	10
1864	A562	1.15z Prus bl & blk	25	15
1865	A562	1.35z ocher & blk	30	20
1866	A562	2.50z grn & blk	75	40
1867	A562	3.40z ocher & blk	75	40
1868	A562	5z tan & blk	1.00	50
1869	A562	8.50z bis & blk	2.00	1.00
		Nos. 1860-1869 (10)	5.11	2.75

Fighting Worker, by J. Jarnuszkiewicz
A563

Photogravure and Engraved
1972, Jan. 5 Perf. 11½

1870	A563	60g red & blk	15	8

Polish Workers' Party, 30th anniversary.

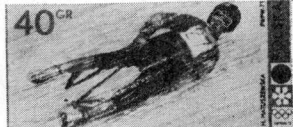

Luge and Sapporo '72 Emblem—A564

Designs (Sapporo '72 Emblem and): 60g, Women's slalom (vert.). 1.65z, Biathlon (vert.). 2.50z, Ski jump.

1972, Jan. 12 Photo. Perf. 11

1871	A564	40g sil & multi	15	8
1872	A564	60g sil & multi	18	10
1873	A564	1.65z sil & multi	40	25
1874	A564	2.50z sil & multi	75	40

11th Winter Olympic Games, Sapporo, Japan, Feb. 3–13. See No. B124.

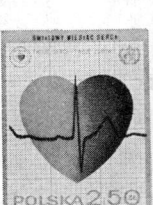

Heart and Electrocardiogram A565   **Bicyclists Racing** A566

1972, Mar. 28 Photo. Perf. 11½x11

1875	A565	2.50z bl, red & blk	30	15

"Your heart is your health," World Health Day.

1972, May 2 Perf. 11

1876	A566	60g sil & multi	15	8

25th Warsaw-Berlin-Prague Bicycle Race.

Berlin Monument A567   **Olympic Runner** A568

1972, May 9 Engr. Perf. 11½x11

1877	A567	60g grnsh blk	15	8

Unveiling of monument for Polish soldiers and German anti-Fascists in Berlin, May 14, 1972.

1972, May 20 Perf. 11½x11

Designs (Olympic Rings and "Motion" Symbol and): 30g, Archery. 40g, Boxing. 60g, Fencing. 2.50z, Wrestling. 3.40z, Weight lifting. 5z, Bicycling. 8.50z, Sharpshooting.

1878	A568	20g multi	10	5
1879	A568	30g multi	10	5
1880	A568	40g multi	10	5
1881	A568	60g gray & multi	15	10
1882	A568	2.50z multi	40	25
1883	A568	3.40z multi	75	35
1884	A568	5z bl & multi	1.00	45
1885	A568	8.50z multi	1.75	85
		Nos. 1878-1885 (8)	4.35	2.05

20th Olympic Games, Munich, Aug. 26–Sept. 10. See No. B125.

Vistula and Cracow A569

1972, May 28 Photo. Perf. 11½x11

1886	A569	60g red, grn & ocher	15	8

50th anniversary of Polish Immigrants Society in Germany (Rodlo).

Knight of King Mieszko I A570

1972, June 12

1887	A570	60g gold, red brn, yel & blk	15	8

Millennium of the Battle of Cedynia (Cidyny).

Cheetah—A571

1972, Aug. 20 Litho. Perf. 12½
Buff & Multicolored

1888	A571	20g shown	20	10
1889	A571	40g Giraffe (vert.)	20	10
1890	A571	60g Toco toucan	20	10
1891	A571	1.35z Chimpanzee	30	15
1892	A571	1.65z Gibbon	40	25
1893	A571	3.40z Crocodile	50	30
1894	A571	4z Kangaroo	1.50	75
1895	A571	4.50z Tiger (vert.)	3.25	1.75
1896	A571	7z Zebra	3.75	2.00
		Nos. 1888-1896 (9)	10.30	5.50

Zoo animals.

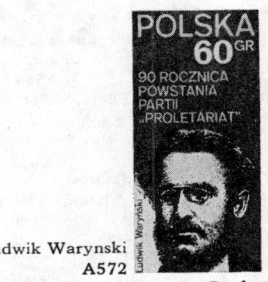

Ludwik Warynski A572

1972, Sept. 1 Photo. Perf. 11

1897	A572	60g multi	15	8

90th anniversary of Proletariat Party, founded by Ludwik Warynski. Printed in sheets of 25 stamps each se-tenant with label showing masthead of party newspaper "Proletariat."

Feliks Dzerzhinski A573

1972, Sept. 11 Litho. Perf. 11x11½

1898	A573	60g red & blk	15	8

95th anniversary of the birth of Feliks Dzerzhinski (1877–1926), Russian politician of Polish descent.

Congress Emblem A574

1972, Sept. 15 Photo. Perf. 11½x11

1899	A574	60g multi	15	8

25th Congress of the International Cooperative Union, Warsaw, Sept. 1972.

"In the Barracks," by Moniuszko A575

Scenes from Operas or Ballets by Moniuszko: 20g, The Countess. 40g, The Frightful Castle. 60g, Halka. 1.15z, A New Don Quixote. 1.35z, Verbum Nobile. 1.55z, Ideal. 2.50z, Paria.

Photogravure and Engraved
1972, Sept. 15 Perf. 11½

1900	A575	10g gold & vio	5	5
1901	A575	20g gold & dk brn	5	5
1902	A575	40g gold & sl grn	5	5
1903	A575	60g gold & ind	8	5
1904	A575	1.15z gold & dk bl	20	10
1905	A575	1.35z gold & dk bl	30	15
1906	A575	1.55z gold & grnsh blk	30	15
1907	A575	2.50z gold & dk brn	60	35
		Nos. 1900-1907 (8)	1.63	95

Centenary of the death of Stanislaw Moniuszko (1819–1872), composer.

"Amazon," by Piotr Michalowski A576

Paintings: 40g, Ostañ Daszkiewicz, by Jan Matejko. 60g, "Summer Rain" (dancing woman), by Wojciech Gerson. 2z, Woman from Naples, by Aleksander Kotsis. 2.50z, Girl Taking Bath, by Pantaleon Szyndler. 3.40z, Count of Thun (child), by Artur Grottger. 4z, Rhapsody (old man), by Stanislaw Wyspianski. 60g and 2.50z inscribed "DZIEN ZNACZKA 1972."

1972, Sept. 28 Photo. Perf. 10½x11

1908	A576	30g gold & multi	15	5
1909	A576	40g gold & multi	15	5
1910	A576	60g gold & multi	15	8
1911	A576	2z gold & multi	30	15
1912	A576	2.50z gold & multi	30	20
1913	A576	3.40z gold & multi	55	25
1914	A576	4z gold & multi	1.25	60
		Nos. 1908-1914, B126 (8)	4.85	2.38

Stamp Day 1972.

Copernicus, by Jacob van Meurs, 1654, Heliocentric System—A577

POLAND

Portraits of Copernicus: 60g, 16th century etching and Prussian coin, 1530. 2.50z, by Jeremiah Falck, 1645, and coat of arms of King of Prussia, 1520. 3.40z, Copernicus with lily of the valley, and page from Theophilactus Simocatta's "Letters on Customs."

1972, Sept. 28   Litho.   Perf. 11x11½

1915	A577	40g brt bl & blk	5	5
1916	A577	60g ocher & blk	10	5
1917	A577	2.50z red & blk	30	15
1918	A577	3.40z yel grn & blk	60	35

500th anniversary of the birth of Nicolaus Copernicus (1473–1543), astronomer. See No. B127.

Nos. 1337–1338 Surcharged in Red or Black

50 GR X = 1 50 ZŁ
a   b

1972   Engr.   Perf. 11½x11

1919	A445(a)	50g on 40g brn (R)	5	5
1920	A445(a)	90g on 40g brn (R)	9	5
1921	A445(a)	1z on 40g brn (R)	10	5
1922	A445(b)	1.50z on 60g org	15	5
1923	A445(b)	2.70z on 60g org (R)	30	15
1924	A445(b)	4z on 60g org	40	20
1925	A445(b)	4.50z on 60g org	45	25
1926	A445(b)	4.90z on 60g org	55	30
Nos. 1919-1926 (8)			2.09	1.10

Issue dates: Nos. 1919–1920, Nov. 17; others Oct. 2.

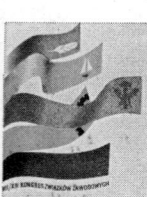

The Little Soldier, by E. Piwowarski
A578

1972, Oct. 16   Litho.   Perf. 11½

1927	A578	60g rose & blk	15	8

Children's hospital "Centrum Zdrowia Dzieka," to be built as memorial to children killed during Nazi regime.

Warsaw Royal Castle, 1656, by Erik J. Dahlbergh
A579

1972, Oct. 16   Photo.   Perf. 11x11½

1928	A579	60g vio, bl & blk	15	8

Rebuilding of Warsaw Castle, destroyed during World War II.

Ribbons with Symbols of Trade Union Activities
A580

Mountain Lodge, Chocholowska Valley
A581

1972, Nov. 13   Perf. 11½x11

1929	A580	60g multi	15	8

7th and 13th Polish Trade Union congresses, Nov. 13–15.

1972, Nov. 13   Perf. 11

Mountain Lodges in Tatra National Park: 60g, Hala Ornak, West Tatra (horiz.). 1.55z, Hala Gasienicowa. 2.50z, Morskie Oro, Rybiego Potoku Valley

1930	A581	40g multi	8	5
1931	A581	60g multi	15	8
1932	A581	1.55z multi	25	10
1933	A581	1.65z multi	25	15
1934	A581	2.50z multi	50	25
Nos. 1930-1934 (5)			1.23	63

Japanese Azalea—A582

Flowering Shrubs: 50g, Alpine rose. 60g, Pomeranian honeysuckle. 1.65z, Chinese quince. 2.50z, Viburnum. 3.40z, Rhododendron. 4z, Mock orange. 8.50z, Lilac.

1972, Dec. 15   Litho.   Perf. 12½

1935	A582	40g gray & multi	5	5
1936	A582	50g bl & multi	8	5
1937	A582	60g multi	15	5
1938	A582	1.65z ultra & multi	30	15
1939	A582	2.50z ocher & multi	45	20
1940	A582	3.40z multi	55	30
1941	A582	4z multi	1.00	35
1942	A582	8.50z multi	2.00	95
Nos. 1935-1942 (8)			4.58	2.10

Emblem   Copernicus
A583   A584

1972, Dec. 15   Photo.   Perf. 11½

1943	A583	60g red & multi	15	8

5th Congress of Socialist Youth Union.

Coil Stamps

1972, Dec. 28   Photo.   Perf. 14

1944	A584	1z dp cl	20	10
1945	A584	1.50z yel brn	35	15

500th anniversary of the birth of Nicolaus Copernicus (1473–1543), astronomer. Black control number on back of every 5th stamp.

Piast Knight, 10th Century
A585

Polish Cavalry: 40g, Knight, 13th century. 60g, Knight of Ladislas Jagello, 15th century (horiz.). 1.35z, Hussar, 17th century. 4z, National Guard Uhlan, 18th century. 4.50z, Congress Kingdom Period, 1831. 5z, Light cavalry, 1939 (horiz.). 7z, Light cavalry, People's Army, 1945.

1972, Dec. 28   Perf. 11

1946	A585	20g vio & multi	5	5
1947	A585	40g multi	10	5
1948	A585	60g org & multi	15	8
1949	A585	1.35z org & multi	25	10
1950	A585	4z org & multi	60	25
1951	A585	4.50z org & multi	75	35
1952	A585	5z brn & multi	1.25	50
1953	A585	7z multi	1.75	75
Nos. 1946-1953 (8)			4.90	2.13

Man and Woman, Sculpture by Viera Muchina
A586

Design: 60g, Globe with Red Star.

1972, Dec. 30

1954	A586	40g gray & multi	10	5
1955	A586	60g blk, red & vio bl	15	10

50th anniversary of the Soviet Union.

Copernicus, by M. Bacciarelli
A587

Portraits of Copernicus: 1.50z, painted in Torun, 16th century. 2.70z, by Zinck Nor. 4z, from Strasbourg clock. 4.90z, Copernicus in his Observatory, by Jan Matejko (horiz.).

Perf. 11½x11, 11x11½

1973, Feb. 18   Photogravure

1956	A587	1z brn & multi	15	8
1957	A587	1.50z multi	20	10
1958	A587	2.70z multi	35	15
1959	A587	4z multi	75	35
1960	A587	4.90z multi	1.00	50
Nos. 1956-1960 (5)			2.45	1.23

500th anniversary of the birth of Nicolaus Copernicus (1473–1543), astronomer.

Piast Coronation Sword, 12th Century
A588

Lenin Monument, Nowa Huta
A589

Polish Art: No. 1962, Kruzlowa Madonna, c. 1410. No. 1963, Hussar's armor, 17th century. No. 1964, Wawel head, wood, 16th century. No. 1965, Cock, sign of Rifle Fraternity, 16th century. 2.70z, Cover of Queen Anna Jagiellonka's prayer book (eagle), 1582. 4.90z, Skarbimierz Madonna, wood, c. 1340. 8.50z, The Nobleman Tenczynski, portrait by unknown artist, 17th century.

1973, Mar. 28   Photo.   Perf. 11½x11

1961	A588	50g vio & multi	5	5
1962	A588	1z lt bl & multi	15	6
1963	A588	1z ultra & multi	15	6
1964	A588	1.50z bl & multi	20	10
1965	A588	1.50z grn & multi	20	10
1966	A588	2.70z multi	35	18
1967	A588	4.90z multi	65	30
1968	A588	8.50z blk & multi	1.75	75
Nos. 1961-1968 (8)			3.50	1.60

1973, Apr. 28   Litho.   Perf. 11x11½

1969	A589	1z multi	15	8

Unveiling of Lenin Monument at Nowa Huta.

Envelope Showing Postal Code
A590

1973, May 5   Perf. 11x11½

1970	A590	1.50z multi	20	10

Introduction of postal code system in Poland.

Wolf—A591

1973, May 21   Photo.   Perf. 11
Multicolored

1971	A591	50g shown	10	5
1972	A591	1z Mouflon	15	10
1973	A591	1.50z Moose	20	10
1974	A591	2.70z Capercaillie	40	16
1975	A591	3z Deer	45	20
1976	A591	4.50z Lynx	75	35
1977	A591	4.90z European hart	1.95	75
1978	A591	5z Wild boar	1.25	
Nos. 1971-1978 (8)			6.50	2.96

International Hunting Committee Congress and 50th anniversary of Polish Hunting Association.

US Satellite "Copernicus" over Earth
A592

Design: No. 1980, USSR satellite Salut over earth.

1973, June 20

1979	A592	4.90z multi	75	50
1980	A592	4.90z multi	75	50

American and Russian astronomical observatories in space. No. 1979 issued in sheets of 6 stamps and 2 labels showing constellations and Nicolaus Copernicus. Dark blue margin with white and red inscription. No. 1980 issued in sheets of 6 stamps and 2 labels showing astronauts and Sojuz 11. White margin with blue and red inscription.

Flame Rising from Book
A593

1973, June 26   Lithographed

1981	A593	1.50z bl & multi	20	10

2nd Polish Science Congress, Warsaw, June 26–29.

POLAND

Arms of Poznan on 14th Century Seal
A594

Marcel Nowotko
A595

Perf. 11½x11, 11x11½

1973, June 30

Designs (Polska '73 Emblem and): 1.50z, Tombstone of Nicolas Tomicki, 1524. 2.70z, Kalisz paten, 12th century. 4z, Lion knocker from bronze gate, Gniezno, 12th century (horiz.).

1982	A594	1z pink & multi	15	8
1983	A594	1.50z org & multi	20	10
1984	A594	2.70z buff & multi	35	18
1985	A594	4z yel & multi	60	25

POLSKA 73 International Philatelic Exhibition, Poznan, Aug. 19–Sept. 2. See No. B128.

1973, Aug. 8 Litho. Perf. 11½x11

| 1986 | A595 | 1.50z red & blk | 20 | 10 |

80th anniversary of the birth of Marcel Nowotko (1893–1942), labor leader, member of Central Committee of Communist Party of Poland.

Emblem and Orchard—A596

Designs (Human Environment Emblem and): 90g, Grazing cows. 1z, Stork's nest. 1.50z, Pond with fish and water lilies. 2.70z, Flowers on meadow. 4.90z, Underwater fauna and flora. 5z, Forest scene. 6.50z, Still life.

1973, Aug. 30 Photo. Perf. 11

1987	A596	50g blk & multi	6	5
1988	A596	90g blk & multi	10	5
1989	A596	1z blk & multi	10	5
1990	A596	1.50z blk & multi	20	10
1991	A596	2.70z blk & multi	30	18
1992	A596	4.90z blk & multi	85	35
1993	A596	5z blk & multi	1.25	45
1994	A596	6.50z blk & multi	2.00	70
		Nos. 1987-1994 (8)	4.86	1.93

Protection of the environment.

Motorcyclist—A597

Perf. 11½

| 1995 | A597 | 1.50z sil & multi | 20 | 10 |

Finals in individual world championship motorcycle race on cinder track, Chorzów, Sept. 2.

Scott's editorial staff cannot undertake to identify, authenticate or appraise stamps and postal markings.

Tank
A598

1973, Oct. 12 Litho. Perf. 12½

Multicolored

1996	A598	1z shown	15	8
1997	A598	1z Fighter plane	15	8
1998	A598	1.50z Missile	35	15
1999	A598	1.50z Warship	35	15

Polish People's Army, 30th anniversary.

Grzegorz Piramowicz—A599

Design: 1.50z, J. Sniadecki, Hugo Kollataj and Julian Ursyn Niemcewicz.

Perf. 11½x11

1973, Oct. 13 Photo. & Engr.

| 2000 | A599 | 1z buff & dk brn | 15 | 8 |
| 2001 | A599 | 1.50z gray & sl grn | 20 | 10 |

Bicentenary of the National Education Commission.

Henryk Arctowski, and Penguins
A600

Polish Scientists: No. 2003, Pawel Edmund Strzelecki and Kangaroo. No. 2004, Benedykt Tadeusz Dybowski and Lake Baikal. No. 2005, Stefan Szolc-Rogozinski, sailing ship "Lucja-Margaret." 2z, Bronislaw Malinowski, Trobriand Island drummers. 2.70z, Stefan Drzewiecki and submarine. 3z, Edward Adolf Strasburger and plants. 8z, Ignacy Domeyko, geological strata.

1973, Nov. 30 Photo. Perf. 10½x11

2002	A600	1z gold & multi	10	5
2003	A600	1z gold & multi	10	5
2004	A600	1.50z gold & multi	15	8
2005	A600	1.50z gold & multi	15	8
2006	A600	2z gold & multi	25	12
2007	A600	2.70z gold & multi	35	16
2008	A600	3z gold & multi	50	25
2009	A600	8z gold & multi	1.50	75
		Nos. 2002-2009 (8)	3.10	1.54

Polish Flag
A601

1973, Dec. 15 Photo. Perf. 11½x11

| 2010 | A601 | 1.50z dp ultra, red & gold | 20 | 10 |

25th anniversary of Polish United Workers' Party.

Jelcz-Berliet Bus
A602

Designs: Polish automotives.

1973, Dec. 28 Photo. Perf. 11x11½

Multicolored

2011	A602	50g shown	5	5
2012	A602	90g Jelcz 316	12	5
2013	A602	1z Polski Fiat 126p	15	8
2014	A602	1.50z Polski Fiat 125p	20	10
2015	A602	4z Nysa M-521 bus	60	35
2016	A602	4.50z Star 660 truck	75	45
		Nos. 2011-2016 (6)	1.87	1.08

Iris
A603

Flowers: 1z, Dandelion. 1.50z, Rose. 3z, Thistle. 4z, Cornflowers. 4.50z, Clover. (Paintings by Stanislaw Wyspianski.)

1974, Jan. 22 Engr. Perf. 12x11½

2017	A603	50g lilac	6	5
2018	A603	1z green	12	5
2019	A603	1.50z red org	20	8
2020	A603	3z dp vio	50	20
2021	A603	4z vio bl	75	25
2022	A603	4.50z emerald	90	35
		Nos. 2017-2022 (6)	2.53	98

Cottage, Kurpie
A604

Designs: 1.50z, Church, Sekowa. 4z, Town Hall, Sulmierzyce. 4.50z, Church, Lachowice. 4.90z, Windmill, Sobienie-Jeziory. 5z, Orthodox Church, Ulucz.

1974, Mar. 5 Photo. Perf. 11x11½

2023	A604	1z multi	15	6
2024	A604	1.50z yel & multi	20	9
2025	A604	4z pink & multi	50	24
2026	A604	4.50z lt bl & multi	55	28
2027	A604	4.90z multi	60	28
2028	A604	5z pink & multi	75	30
		Nos. 2023-2028 (6)	2.75	1.25

Mail Coach and UPU Emblem
A605

Embroidery from Cracow
A606

1974, Mar. 30 Perf. 11½x12

| 2029 | A605 | 1.50z multi | 25 | 15 |

Centenary of Universal Postal Union.

1974, May 7 Photo. Perf. 11½x11

Designs (Embroideries from): 1.50z, Lowicz. 4z, Slask.

2030	A606	50g multi	6	5
2031	A606	1.50z multi	20	8
2032	A606	4z multi	60	30
a.		Souv. sheet of 3, imperf.	2.00	1.50
b.		Souv. sheet of 3, perf. 11½x11	6.00	4.50

SOCPHILEX IV International Philatelic Exhibition, Katowice, May 18–June 2.

No. 2032a contains 3 imperf. stamps similar to No. 2032. Violet margin with silver inscription and white lace pattern from Koniakow. Size: 68x170mm. Sold for 17z.

No. 2032b is similar to No. 2032a, with white margin, blue inscription, silver lace and perf. 11½x11. Sold for 17z plus 15z for 4 envelopes.

Association Emblem
A607

Soldier and Dove
A608

1974, May 8 Litho. Perf. 12x11½

| 2033 | A607 | 1.50z gray & red | 18 | 8 |

5th Congress of the Association of Combatants for Liberty and Democracy, Warsaw, May 8–9.

1974, May 9 Perf. 11½x11

| 2034 | A608 | 1.50z org, lt bl & blk | 18 | 8 |

29th anniversary of victory over Fascism.

Comecon Building, Moscow
A609

1974, May 15 Perf. 11x11½

| 2035 | A609 | 1.50z gray bl, bis & red | 18 | 8 |

25th anniversary of the Council of Mutual Economic Assistance.

Soccer Ball and Games' Emblem
A610

Design: No. 2037, Soccer players, Olympic rings and 1972 medal.

1974, June 15 Photo. Perf. 11x11½

2036	A610	4.90z ol & multi	75	35
a.		Souvenir sheet of 4 + 2 labels	4.00	2.00
2037	A610	4.90z ol & multi	75	35
a.		Souvenir sheet of 4	20.00	10.00

World Cup Soccer Championship, Munich, June 13–July 7.

No. 2036a issued to commemorate Poland's silver medal in 1974 Championship. It contains 4 No. 2036 and 2 labels showing medal and names of team members. Silver marginal inscription. Size: 106x 120mm.

No. 2037a contains 2 each of Nos. 2036-2037. Black marginal inscription. Size: 116x83mm.

POLAND

Sailing Ship, 16th Century
A611

Chess, by Jan Kochanowski
A612

Polish Sailing Ships: 1.50z, "Dal," 1934. 2.70z, "Opty," sailed around the world, 1969. 4z, "Dar Pomorza," winner "Operation Sail," 1972. 4.90z, "Polonez," sailed around the world, 1973.

1974, June 29 Litho. Perf. 11½x11

2038	A611	1z multi	10	6
2039	A611	1.50z multi	15	10
2040	A611	2.70z multi	30	18
2041	A611	4z grn & multi	75	40
2042	A611	4.90z dp bl & multi	1.00	50
		Nos. 2038-2042 (5)	2.30	1.24

1974, July 15 Litho. Perf. 11½x11

Design: 1.50z, "Education," etching by Daniel Chodowiecki.

2043	A612	1z multi	15	8
2044	A612	1.50z multi	35	20

10th International Chess Festival, Lublin.

Man and Map of Poland
A613

Polish Eagle
A614

1974, July 21 Photo. Perf. 11½x11

2045	A613	1.50z blk, gold & red	20	10
2046	A614	1.50z sil & multi	20	8
2047	A614	1.50z red & multi	20	10

30th anniversary of the People's Republic of Poland.

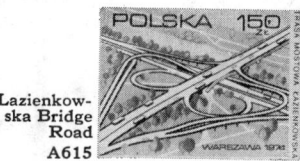

Lazienkowska Bridge Road
A615

1974, July 21 Perf. 11x11½

| 2048 | A615 | 1.50z multi | 20 | 10 |

Opening of Lazienkowska Bridge over Vistula south of Warsaw.

Strawberries and Congress Emblem
A616

1974, Sept. 10 Photo. Perf. 11½
Multicolored

2049	A616	50g shown	5	5
2050	A616	90g Black currants	12	5
2051	A616	1z Apples	15	6
2052	A616	1.50z Cucumbers	20	10
2053	A616	2.70z Tomatoes	30	20
2054	A616	4.50z Peas	50	32
2055	A616	4.90z Pansies	75	40
2056	A616	5z Nasturtiums	1.50	75
		Nos. 2049-2056 (8)	3.57	1.93

19th International Horticultural Congress, Warsaw, Sept. 1974.

Civic Militia and Security Service Badge
A617

Polish Child, by Lukasz Orlowski
A618

1974, Oct. 3 Photo. Perf. 11½x11

| 2057 | A617 | 1.50g multi | 18 | 8 |

30th anniversary of the Civic Militia and the Security Service.

1974, Oct. 9

Polish paintings of Children: 90g, Girl with Pigeon, Anonymous artist, 19th century. 1z, Girl, by Stanislaw Wyspianski. 1.50z, The Orphan from Poronin, by Wladyslaw Slewinski. 3z, Peasant Boy, by Kazimierz Sichulski. 4.50z, Florentine Page, by Aleksander Gierymski. 4.90z, The Artist's Son Tadeusz, by Piotr Michalowski. 6.50z, Boy with Doe, by Aleksander Kotsis.

2058	A618	50g multi	5	5
2059	A618	90g multi	12	5
2060	A618	1z multi	15	6
2061	A618	1.50z multi	20	10
2062	A618	3z multi	45	20
2063	A618	4.50z multi	60	30
2064	A618	4.90z multi	75	40
2065	A618	6.50z multi	1.00	50
		Nos. 2058-2065 (8)	3.32	1.66

Children's Day. The 1z and 1.50z are inscribed "Dzien Znaczka (Stamp Day) 1974."

Cracow Manger—A619

King Sigismund Vasa—A620

Designs: 1.50z, Flight into Egypt, 1465. 4z, King Jan Olbracht.

1974, Dec. 2 Litho. Perf. 11½x11

2066	A619	1z multi	15	8
2067	A619	1.50z multi	20	10
2068	A620	2z multi	30	15
2069	A620	4z multi	75	50

Masterpieces of Polish art.

Angler
A621

Designs: 1.50z, Hunter with bow and arrow. 4z, Boy snaring geese. 4.50z, Beekeeper. Designs from 16th century woodcuts.

1974–77 Engr. Perf. 11½x11

2070	A621	1z black	10	5
2071	A621	1.50z indigo	15	6
2071A	A621	4z sl grn	40	20
2071B	A621	4.50z dk brn	45	25

Issue dates: 1z, 1.50z, Dec. 30, 1974. 4z, 4.50z, Dec. 12, 1977.

Pablo Neruda, by Osvaldo Guayasamin
A622

1974, Dec. 31 Litho. Perf. 11½x11

| 2072 | A622 | 1.50z multi | 18 | 8 |

Pablo Neruda (1904–1973), Chilean poet.

Nike Monument and Opera House, Warsaw—A623

1975, Jan. 17 Photogravure Perf. 11

| 2073 | A623 | 1.50z multi | 18 | 8 |

30th anniversary of the liberation of Warsaw.

Hobby Falcon
A624

"Auschwitz"
A625

1975, Jan. 23 Perf. 11½x12
Multicolored

2074	A624	1z Lesser kestrel, male	15	8
2075	A624	1z same, female	15	8
2076	A624	1.50z Red-footed falcon, male	25	10
2077	A624	1.50z same, female	25	10
2078	A624	2z shown	40	20
2079	A624	4z Kestrel	75	35
2080	A624	4z Merlin	1.50	75
2081	A624	8z Peregrine	3.00	1.30
		Nos. 2074-2081 (8)	6.45	2.91

Falcons. Stamps of same denominations printed se-tenant in sheets of 50.

Photogravure and Engraved
1975, Jan. 27 Perf. 11½x11

| 2082 | A625 | 1.50z red & blk | 20 | 10 |

30th anniversary of the liberation of Auschwitz (Oswiecim) concentration camp.

Women's Hurdle Race
A626

Designs: 1.50z, Pole vault. 4z, Hop, step and jump. 4.90z, Sprinting.

1975, Mar. 8 Litho. Perf. 11x11½

2083	A626	1z multi	15	6
2084	A626	1.50z ol & multi	20	8
2085	A626	4z multi	60	20
2086	A626	4.90z grn & multi	75	35

6th European Indoor Athletic Championships, Katowice, March 1975.

St. Anne, by Veit Stoss, Arphila Emblem
A627

1975, Apr. 15 Photo. Perf. 11x11½

| 2087 | A627 | 1.50z multi | 20 | 10 |

ARPHILA 75, International Philatelic Exhibition, Paris, June 6–10.

Amateur Radio Union Emblem, Globe
A628

1975, Apr. 15 Litho. Perf. 11x11½

| 2088 | A628 | 1.50z multi | 18 | 8 |

International Amateur Radio Union Conference, Warsaw, Apr. 1975.

Mountain Guides' Badge and Sudetic Mountains—A629

Designs: No. 2089, Pine, badge and Tatra Mountains (vert.). No. 2090, Gentian and Tatra Mountains (vert.). No. 2092, Yew branch with berries, and Sudetic Mountains. No. 2093, River, Beskids Mountains and badge (vert.). No. 2094, Arnica and Beskids Mountains (vert.).

1975, Apr. 30 Photo. Perf. 11

2089	A629	1z multi	10	6
2090	A629	1z multi	10	6
2091	A629	1.50z multi	15	8
2092	A629	1.50z multi	15	8
2093	A629	4z multi	75	35
2094	A629	4z multi	75	35
		Nos. 2089-2094 (6)	2.00	98

Centenary of Polish Mountain Guides Organizations. Stamps of same denomination printed se-tenant in sheets of 50, showing continuous design.

Hands Holding Tulips and Rifle
A630

Warsaw Treaty Members' Flags
A631

1975, May 9 Perf. 11½x11

| 2095 | A630 | 1.50z bl & multi | 18 | 8 |

30th anniversary of the end of World War II and victory over Fascism.

POLAND 135

1975, May 14

| 2096 | A631 | 1.50z bl & multi | 18 | 8 |

20th anniversary of the signing of the Warsaw Treaty (Bulgaria, Czechoslovakia, German Democratic Rep., Hungary, Poland, Romania, USSR).

Cock and Hen, Congress Emblem
A632

1975, June 23 Photo. Perf. 12x11½
Multicolored

2097	A632	50g shown	10	5
2098	A632	1z Geese	15	8
2099	A632	1.50z Cattle	25	10
2100	A632	2z Cow	40	15
2101	A632	3z Arabian stallion	60	20
2102	A632	4z Wielkopolska horses	75	25
2103	A632	4.50z Pigs	1.25	60
2104	A632	5z Sheep	2.50	95
		Nos. 2097-2104 (8)	6.00	2.38

20th Congress of the European Zootechnical Federation, Warsaw.

Apollo and Soyuz Linked in Space
A633

Designs: No. 2106, Apollo. No. 2107, Soyuz.

1975, July 15 Perf. 11x11½

2105	A633	1.50z dp ultra & multi	20	10
2106	A633	4.90z dp ultra & multi	75	35
2107	A633	4.90z dp ultra & multi	75	35
a.		Souvenir sheet of 6 + 2 labels	12.00	6.00

Apollo Soyuz space test project (Russo-American cooperation), launching July 15; link-up, July 17. Nos. 2106-2107 printed se-tenant. No. 2107a contains 2 each of Nos. 2105-2107, 2 labels and black and red marginal inscription. Size: 119x155 mm.

Health Fund Emblem
A634

1975, July 12 Perf. 11½x11

| 2108 | A634 | 1.50z sil, blk & bl | 18 | 8 |

National Fund for Health Protection.

"E" and Polish Flag
A635

1975, July 30 Litho. Perf. 11x11½

| 2109 | A635 | 4z lt bl, red & blk | 55 | 20 |

European Security and Cooperation Conference, Helsinki, July 30–Aug. 1.

U.N. Emblem and Sunburst
A636

1975, July 25

| 2110 | A636 | 4z bl & multi | 55 | 20 |

30th anniversary of the United Nations.

Bolek and Lolek
A637

Cartoon Characters and Children's Health Center Emblem: 1z, Jacek and Agatka. 1.50z, Reksio, the dog. 4z, Telesfor, the dragon.

1975, Aug. 30 Photo. Perf. 11x11½

2111	A637	50g vio bl & multi	5	5
2112	A637	1z multi	15	8
2113	A637	1.50z multi	20	10
2114	A637	4z multi	75	35

Children's television programs.

Circular Bar Graph and Institute's Emblem
A638

IWY Emblem, White, Yellow and Brown Women
A639

1975, Sept. 1 Litho. Perf. 11½x11

| 2115 | A638 | 1.50z multi | 18 | 8 |

International Institute of Statistics, 40th session, Warsaw, Sept. 1975.

1975, Sept. 8 Photogravure

| 2116 | A639 | 1.50z multi | 18 | 8 |

International Women's Year 1975.

First Poles Arriving on "Mary and Margaret" 1608—A640

George Washington
A641

Designs: 1.50z, Polish glass blower and glass works, Jamestown, 1608. 2.70z, Helena Modrzejewska (1840-1909), Polish actress, came to US in 1877. 4z, Casimir Pulaski (1747-1779), and 6.40z, Tadeusz Kosciusko (1748-1817), heroes of American War of Independence.

1975, Sept. 24 Litho. Perf. 11x11½

2117	A640	1z blk & multi	15	6
2118	A640	1.50z blk & multi	20	8
2119	A640	2.70z blk & multi	35	15
2120	A640	4z blk & multi	50	25
2121	A640	6.40z blk & multi	75	40
		Nos. 2117-2121 (5)	1.95	94

Souvenir Sheet
Perf. 12

2122	A641	Sheet of 3	2.25	1.25
a.		4.90z shown	60	20
b.		4.90z Kosciusko	60	20
c.		4.90z Pulaski	60	20

American Revolution, bicentenary. No. 2122 contains 3 stamps and 3 labels showing respectively: American flag and Polish inscription; Polish flag and English inscription; raising the flag at Yorktown. Size: 115x100mm.

Albatross Biplane, 1918–1925
A642

Design: 4.90z, IL 62 jet, 1975.

1975, Sept. 25 Perf. 11x11½

| 2123 | A642 | 2.40z buff & multi | 25 | 10 |
| 2124 | A642 | 4.90z gray & multi | 75 | 30 |

50th anniversary of Polish air post stamps.

Frederic Chopin
A643

1975, Oct. 7 Photogravure

| 2125 | A643 | 1.50z gold, lt vio & blk | 18 | 8 |

9th International Chopin Piano Competition, Warsaw, Oct. 7–28. Printed in sheets of 50 stamps with alternating labels with commemorative inscription.

Dunikowski, Self-portrait
A644

1975, Oct. 9 Perf. 11½x11

Sculptures: 1z, "Breath." 1.50z, "Maternity."

2126	A644	50g sil & multi	5	5
2127	A644	1z sil & multi	15	10
2128	A644	1.50z sil & multi	20	10

Stamp Day 1975, and for the birth centenary of Xawery Dunikowski (1875-1964), sculptor. See No. B131.

Town Hall, Zamosc
A645

Lodz, by Wladyslaw Strzeminski
A646

Design: 1z, Arcades, Kazimierz Dolny (horiz.).

1975, Nov. 11 Photo. Perf. 14
Coil Stamps

| 2129 | A645 | 1z ol grn | 15 | 5 |
| 2130 | A645 | 1.50z rose brn | 20 | 8 |

European Architectural Heritage Year 1975. Black control number on back of every fifth stamp of Nos. 2129–2130.

1975, Nov. 22 Litho. Perf. 12½

| 2131 | A646 | 4.50z multi | 75 | 30 |
| a. | | Souvenir sheet | 1.50 | 90 |

Lodz 75, 12th Polish Philatelic Exhibition, commemorating 25th anniversary of Polish Philatelists Union. No. 2131a contains one stamp; gray and violet blue margin. Size: 79x102mm.

Piast Family Eagle
A647

Designs: 1.50z, Seal of Prince Boleslaw of Legnica. 4z, Coin of Prince Jerzy Wilhelm (1660–1675).

1975, Nov. 29 Engr. Perf. 11x11½

2132	A647	1z green	15	8
2133	A647	1.50z brown	20	10
2134	A647	4z dl vio	50	25

Piast dynasty's influence on the development of Silesia.

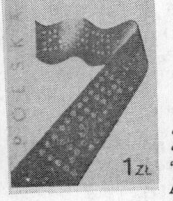

"7" Inscribed "ZJAZD" and "PZPR"
A648

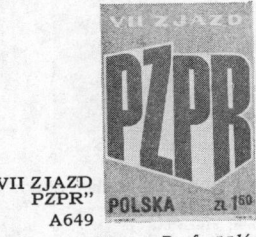

"VII ZJAZD PZPR"
A649

1975, Dec. 8 Photo. Perf. 11½x11

| 2135 | A649 | 1z lt bl & multi | 12 | 5 |
| 2136 | A649 | 1.50z sil, red & ultra | 18 | 8 |

7th Congress of Polish United Workers' Party.

Ski Jump
A650

Designs (Winter Olympic Games Emblem and): 1z, Ice hockey. 1.50z, Slalom. 2z, Speed skating. 4z, Luge. 6.40z, Biathlon.

1976, Jan. 10 Perf. 11x11½

2137	A650	50g sil & multi	5	5
2138	A650	1z sil & multi	15	8
2139	A650	1.50z sil & multi	20	10
2140	A650	2z sil & multi	30	12
2141	A650	4z sil & multi	60	25
2142	A650	6.40z sil & multi	1.10	50
		Nos. 2137-2142 (6)	2.40	1.10

12th Winter Olympic Games, Innsbruck, Austria, Feb. 4–15.

POLAND

Engine by Richard Trevithick, 1803—A651

Locomotives by: 1z, M. Murray and J. Blenkinsop, 1810. No. 2145, George Stephenson's Rocket, 1829. No. 2146, Polish electric locomotive, 1969. 2.70z, Stephenson, 1837. 3z, Joseph Harrison, 1840. 4.50z, Thomas Rogers, 1855. 4.90z, Chrzanow (Polish), 1922.

1976, Feb. 13 Photo. Perf. 11½x12

2143	A651	50g multi	5	5
2144	A651	1z multi	15	8
2145	A651	1.50z multi	20	10
2146	A651	1.50z multi	20	10
2147	A651	2.70z multi	40	20
2148	A651	3z multi	40	20
2149	A651	4.50z multi	1.50	75
2150	A651	4.90z multi	1.75	85
Nos. 2143-2150 (8)			4.65	2.33

History of the locomotive.

Telephone, Radar and Satellites, ITU Emblem—A652

1976, Mar. 10 Perf. 11

2151 A652 1.50z multi 20 8

Centenary of first telephone call by Alexander Graham Bell, Mar. 10, 1876.

Atom Symbol and Flags of Communist Countries A653

1976, Mar. 10 Litho. Perf. 11½

2152 A653 1.50z multi 20 8

Joint Institute of Nuclear Research, Dubna, USSR, 20th anniversary.

Ice Hockey A654

Design: 1.50z, Like 1z, reversed.

1976, Apr. 8 Photo. Perf. 11½x11

| 2153 | A654 | 1z multi | 12 | 8 |
| 2154 | A654 | 1.50z multi | 25 | 12 |

Ice Hockey World Championship 1976, Katowice.

Soldier and Map of Sinai A655

1976, Apr. 30 Photo. Perf. 11x11½

2155 A655 1.50z multi 18 8

Polish specialist troops serving with U.N. Forces in Sinai Peninsula.

No. 2155 printed se-tenant with label with commemorative inscription.

Sappers' Monument, by Stanislaw Kulow, Warsaw A656

Interphil 76, Philadelphia A657

Design: No. 2157, First Polish Army Monument, by Bronislaw Koniuszy, Warsaw.

1976, May 8 Perf. 11½

| 2156 | A656 | 1z gold & multi | 12 | 6 |
| 2157 | A656 | 1z sil & multi | 12 | 6 |

Memorials unveiled on 30th anniversary of World War II victory.

1976, May 20 Litho. Perf. 11½x11

2158 A657 8.40z gray & multi 95 55

Interphil 76, International Philatelic Exhibition, Philadelphia, Pa., May 29–June 6.

Wielkopolski Park and Owl—A658

National Parks: 1z, Wolinski Park and eagle. 1.50z, Slowinski Park and sea gull. 4.50z, Bieszczadzki Park and lynx. 5z, Ojcowski Park and bat. 6z, Kampinoski Park and elk.

1976, May 22 Photo. Perf. 12x11½

2159	A658	90g multi	10	6
2160	A658	1z multi	10	6
2161	A658	1.50z multi	15	10
2162	A658	4.50z multi	55	30
2163	A658	5z multi	60	35
2164	A658	6z multi	75	42
Nos. 2159-2164 (6)			2.25	1.29

U.N. Headquarters, Dove-shaped Globe—A659

1976, June 29 Litho. Perf. 11x11½

2165 A659 8.40z multi 95 55

U.N. postage stamps, 25th anniversary.

Fencing and Olympic Rings A660

1976, June 30 Photogravure
Multicolored

2166	A660	50g shown	6	5
2167	A660	1z Bicycling	12	6
2168	A660	1.50z Soccer	18	10
2169	A660	4.20z Boxing	50	28
2170	A660	6.90z Weight lifting	80	48
2171	A660	8.40z Running	95	60
Nos. 2166-2171 (6)			2.61	1.57

21st Olympic Games, Montreal, Canada, July 17–Aug. 1. See No. B132.

Polish Theater, Poznan A662

1976, July 12 Litho. Perf. 11x11½

2173 A662 1.50z gray ol & org 18 8

Polish Theater in Poznan, centenary.

Czekanowski, Lake Baikal A663

1976, Sept. 3 Photo. Perf. 11x11½

2174 A663 1.50z sil & multi 18 8

Aleksander Czekanowski (1833–1876), geologist, death centenary.

Siren A664

Designs: 1z, Sphinx (vert.). 2z, Lion. 4.20z, Bull. 4.50z, Goat. Designs from Corinthian vases, 7th century B.C.

Perf. 11x11½, 11½x11

1976, Oct. 30 Photogravure

2175	A664	1z gold & multi	10	6
2176	A664	1.50z gold & multi	15	8
2177	A664	2z gold & multi	25	15
2178	A664	4.20z gold & multi	50	30
2179	A664	4.50z gold & multi	55	32
Nos. 2175-2179, B133 (6)			3.55	1.86

Stamp Day 1976.

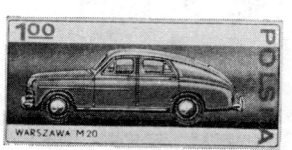

Warszawa M20—A665

Designs (Automobiles): 1.50z, Warszawa 223. 2z, Syrena 104. 4.90z, Polski Fiat 125.

1976, Nov. 6 Photo. Perf. 11

2180	A665	1z multi	12	6
2181	A665	1.50z multi	18	8
2182	A665	2z multi	25	15
2183	A665	4.90z multi	60	32
a.	Souvenir sheet of 4		1.75	90

Zeran Automobile Factory, Warsaw, 25th anniversary. No. 2183a contains one each of Nos. 2180–2183 and 2 decorative labels; silver marginal inscription. Size: 135x 107mm.

Pouring Ladle A666

Virgin and Child, Epitaph, 1425 A667

1976, Nov. 26 Litho. Perf. 11

2184 A666 1.50z multi 18 8

First steel production at Katowice Foundry.

Design: 6z, The Beautiful Madonna, sculpture, c. 1410.

1976, Dec. 15

| 2185 | A667 | 1z multi | 12 | 6 |
| 2186 | A667 | 6z multi | 75 | 40 |

Polish Trade Union Emblem A668

1976, Dec. 29

2187 A668 1.50z multi 18 8

8th Polish Trade Union Congress.

Tanker Zawrat Unloading, Gdansk—A669

Designs: No. 2189, Ferry Gryf and cars at pier, Gdansk. No. 2190, Loading containers, Gdynia. No. 2191, "Stefan Batory" and "People of the Sea" monument, Gdynia. 2z, Barge and cargoship "Ziemia Szczecinska", Szczecin. 4.20z, Coal loading installations, Swinoujscie. 6.90z, Liner, hydrofoil and lighthouse, Kolobrzeg. 8.40z, Map of Polish Coast with ports, ships and emblem of Union of Polish Ports.

1976, Dec. 29 Photo. Perf. 11

2188	A669	1z multi	12	6
2189	A669	1z multi	12	6
2190	A669	1.50z multi	18	8
2191	A669	1.50z multi	18	8
2192	A669	2z multi	12	25
2193	A669	4.20z multi	50	24
2194	A669	6.90z multi	85	42
2195	A669	8.40z multi	95	50
Nos. 2188-2195 (8)			3.02	1.69

Polish ports.

Nurse Helping Old Woman A670

Civilian Defense Medal A671

POLAND 137

1977, Jan. 24 Litho. Perf. 11½x11
2196 A670 1.50z multi 18 8
Polish Red Cross.

1977, Feb. 26 Litho. Perf. 11
2197 A671 1.50z multi 18 8
Civilian Defense.

Ball on the Road—A672

1977, Mar. 12 Photogravure
2198 A672 1.50z ol & multi 18 8
Social Action Committee (founded 1966), "Stop, Child on the Road!"

Dewberry A673
Designs: Forest fruits.

1977, Mar. 17 Multicolored Perf. 11½x11
2199 A673 50g shown 5 5
2200 A673 90g Cranberry 10 5
2201 A673 1z Wild strawberry 12 6
2202 A673 1.50z Bilberry 18 8
2203 A673 2z Raspberry 25 12
2204 A673 4.50z Blueberry 55 32
2205 A673 6z Dog rose 70 42
2206 A673 6.90z Hazelnut 85 48
Nos. 2199-2206 (8) 2.80 1.58

Flags of USSR and Poland as Computer Tape A674
Emblem and Graph A675

1977, Apr. 4 Litho. Perf. 11½x11
2207 A674 1.50z red & multi 18 8
Scientific and technical cooperation between Poland and USSR, 30th anniversary.

1977, Apr. 22
2208 A675 1.50z red & multi 18 8
7th Congress of Polish Engineers.

Venus, by Rubens A676

Rubens Paintings: 1.50z, Bathsheba. 5z, Helene Fourment. 6z, Self-portrait.

1977, Apr. 30 Frame in Gray Brown Perf. 11½
2209 A676 1z multi 12 6
2210 A676 1.50z multi 18 8
2211 A676 5z multi 60 35
2212 A676 6z multi 70 42
Peter Paul Rubens (1577–1640), Flemish painter, 400th birth anniversary. See No. B134.

Peace Dove A677

1977, May 6 Perf. 11½x11½
2213 A677 1.50z blk, ultra & yel 18 8
Congress of World Council of Peace, Warsaw, May 6–11.

Bicyclist A678

1977, May 6 Photogravure
2214 A678 1.50z gray & multi 18 8
30th International Peace Bicycling Race, Warsaw-Berlin-Prague.

Wolf A679
Violinist, by Jacob Toorenvliet A680

Designs (Wildlife Fund Emblem): No. 2216, Great bustard. No. 2217, Kestrel. 6z, Otter.

1977, May 12 Photo. Perf. 11½x11
2215 A679 1z sil & multi 12 6
2216 A679 1.50z sil & multi 18 8
2217 A679 1.50z sil & multi 18 8
2218 A679 6z sil & multi 70 42
Wildlife protection.

1977, May 16
2219 A680 6z gold & multi 75 42
AMPHILEX '77 International Philatelic Exhibition, Amsterdam, May 26–June 5. No. 2219 issued in sheets of 6.

Midsummer Bonfire A681

Folk Customs: 1z, Easter cock. 1.50z, Dousing the women on Easter Monday. 3z, Harvest festival. 6z, Christmas procession with crèche. 8.40z, Wedding dance. 1z, 1.50z, 3z, 6z vertical.

Perf. 11x11½, 11½x11
1977, June 13 Photogravure
2220 A681 90g multi 10 5
2221 A681 1z multi 12 5
2222 A681 1.50z multi 18 8
2223 A681 3z multi 35 15
2224 A681 6z multi 70 35
2225 A681 8.40z multi 95 45
Nos. 2220-2225 (6) 2.40 1.13

Henryk Wieniawski and Musical Symbol A682

1977, June 30 Litho. Perf. 11½x11
2226 A682 1.50z gold, blk & red 18 8
Wieniawski Music Festivals, Poznan: 5th International Lute Competition, June 30–July 10, and 7th International Violin Competition, Nov. 13–27.

Parnassius Apollo—A683

Butterflies: No. 2228, Nymphalis polychloros. No. 2229, Papilio machaon. No. 2230, Nymphalis antiopa. 5z, Fabriciana adippe. 6.90z, Argynnis paphia.

1977, Aug. 22 Photo. Perf. 11
2227 A683 1z multi 12 5
2228 A683 1z multi 12 5
2229 A683 1.50z multi 18 8
2230 A683 1.50z multi 18 8
2231 A683 5z multi 95 30
2232 A683 6.90z multi 1.50 75
Nos. 2227-2232 (6) 3.05 1.31

Arms of Slupsk, Keyboard A684
Feliks Dzerzhinski A685

1977, Sept. 3 Perf. 11½
2233 A684 1.50z multi 18 8
Slupsk Piano Festival.

1977, Sept. 10 Litho. Perf. 11½x11
2234 A685 1.50z ol bis & sep 18 8
Feliks E. Dzerzhinski (1877–1926), organizer and head of Russian Secret Police (Cheka), birth centenary.

Earth and Sputnik A686

1977, Oct. 1 Litho. Perf. 11x11½
2235 A686 1.50z ultra & car 20 10
a. Souvenir sheet of 3 90 60
60th anniversary of the Russian Revolution and 20th anniversary of Sputnik space flight. Printed in sheets of 15 stamps and 15 carmine labels showing Winter Palace, Leningrad. No. 2235a contains 3 No. 2235 and 3 labels, arranged checkerwise; carmine and ultramarine marginal inscription. Size: 100x125mm.

Boleslaw Chobry's Denarius, 11th Century A687

Silver Coins: 1z, King Kazimierz Wielki's Cracow groszy, 14th century. 1.50z, Legniza-Brzeg-Wolow thaler, 17th century. 4.20z, King Augustus III guilder, Gdansk, 18th century. 4.50z, 5z (ship), 1936. 6z, 100z, Poland's millenium, 1966.

1977, Oct. 9 Photo. Perf. 11½x11
2236 A687 50g sil & multi 5 5
2237 A687 1z sil & multi 12 5
2238 A687 1.50z sil & multi 18 8
2239 A687 4.20z sil & multi 60 25
2240 A687 4.50z sil & multi 75 35
2241 A687 6z sil & multi 1.25 50
Nos. 2236-2241 (6) 2.95 1.29
Stamp Day.

Monastery, Przasnysz A688

Designs: No. 2242, Wolin Gate (vert.). No. 2243, Church, Debno (vert.). No. 2245, Cathedral, Plock. 6z, Castle, Kornik. 6.90z, Palace and Garden, Wilanow.

Perf. 11½x11, 11x11½
1977, Nov. 21 Photogravure
2242 A688 1z multi 12 6
2243 A688 1z multi 12 6
2244 A688 1.50z multi 18 8
2245 A688 1.50z multi 18 8
2246 A688 6z multi 70 30
2247 A688 6.90z multi 85 40
Nos. 2242-2247 (6) 2.15 98
Architectural landmarks.

Vostok (USSR) and Mercury (USA) A689

1977, Dec. 28 Photo. Perf. 11x11½
2248 A689 6.90z ultra & multi 85 50
a. Souvenir sheet of 6 6.00 3.00
20 years of space conquest. No. 2248a contains 6 No. 2248 (2 tete-beche pairs) and 2 labels, one showing Sputnik 1 "4.X.1957," the other Explorer 1 and "31.1.1958." Designs of various spacecraft in margin. Size: 119x157mm.

DN Class Iceboats—A690
Design: No. 2250, One iceboat.

POLAND

1978, Feb. 6 Litho. Perf. 11
| 2249 | A690 | 1.5z lt ultra & blk | 20 | 8 |
| 2250 | A690 | 1.5z lt ultra & blk | 20 | 8 |

6th World Iceboating Championships, Feb. 6–11. Nos. 2249–2250 printed se-tenant with label in between, sheets of 16 stamps and 8 labels showing Championship emblem.

Electric Locomotive, Katowice Station, 1957—A691

Locomotives in Poland: No. 2252, Narrow-gauge engine and Gothic Tower, Znin. No. 2253, Pm36 and Cegielski factory, Poznan, 1936. No. 2254, Electric train and Otwock Station, 1936. No. 2255, Marki Train and Warsaw Stalow Station, 1907. 4.50z, Ty51 coal train and Gdynia Station, 1933. 5z, Tr21 and Chrzanow factory, 1920. 6z, "Cockerill" and Vienna Station, 1848.

1978, Feb. 28 Photo. Perf. 12x11½
2251	A691	50g multi	5	5
2252	A691	1z multi	12	5
2253	A691	1z multi	12	5
2254	A691	1.50z multi	18	10
2255	A691	1.50z multi	18	10
2256	A691	4.50z multi	55	25
2257	A691	5z multi	60	30
2258	A691	6z multi	75	40
		Nos. 2251-2258 (8)	2.55	1.30

Pierwsze Wzloty, 1896, and Czeslaw Tanski—A692

Polish Sport Planes: 1z, Zwyciezcy-Challenge, 1932, F. Zwirko and S. Wigura (vert.). 1.50z, RWD-5 bis over South Atlantic, 1933, and S. Skarzynski (vert.). 4.20z, MI-2 helicopter over mountains, Pezetel emblem (vert.). 6.90z, PZL-104 Wilga 35, Pezetel emblem. 8.40z, Motoszybowiec SZD-45 Ogar.

Perf. 11x11½, 11½x11
2259	A692	50g multi	5	5
2260	A692	1z multi	12	6
2261	A692	1.50z multi	18	8
2262	A692	4.20z multi	50	20
2263	A692	6.90z multi	85	40
2264	A692	8.40z multi	1.00	45
		Nos. 2259-2264 (6)	2.70	1.24

Soccer A693 **Poster A694**
Design: 6.90z, Soccer ball (horiz.).

Perf. 11½x11, 11x11½
1978, May 12 Litho.
| 2265 | A693 | 1.50z multi | 18 | 10 |
| 2266 | A693 | 6.90z multi | 85 | 50 |

11th World Cup Soccer Championships, Argentina, June 1–25.

1978, June 1 Perf. 12x11½
| 2267 | A694 | 1.50z multi | 18 | 8 |

7th International Poster Biennale, Warsaw.

Fair Emblem A695

1978, June 10 Perf. 11
| 2268 | A695 | 1.50z multi | 18 | 8 |

50th International Poznan Fair.

Polonez Passenger Car—A696

1978, June 10 Photo. Perf. 11
| 2269 | A696 | 1.50z multi | 18 | 8 |

Maj. Miroslaw Hermaszewski A697

Design: 6.90z, Hermaszewski, globe and trajectory (horiz.).

Perf. 11½x11, 11x11½
1978, June 27 Photogravure
| 2270 | A697 | 1.50z multi | 20 | 10 |
| 2271 | A697 | 6.90z multi | 85 | 40 |

First Polish cosmonaut on Russian space mission. Printed in sheets of 6 stamps and 2 labels.

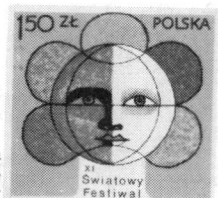

Youth Festival Emblem A698

1978, July 12 Litho. Perf. 11½
| 2272 | A698 | 1.50z multi | 18 | 8 |

11th Youth Festival, Havana, July 28–Aug. 5.

Souvenir Sheet

Flowers—A699

1978, July 20 Perf. 11½x11
| 2273 | A699 | 1.50z gold & multi | 30 | 15 |

30th anniversary of Polish Youth Movement. No. 2273 has multicolored margin showing emblems of various youth organizations. Size: 69x79mm.

Anopheles Mosquito and Blood Cells A700

Design: 6z, Tsetse fly and blood cells.

1978, Aug. 19 Litho. Perf. 11½x11
| 2274 | A700 | 1.50z multi | 18 | 8 |
| 2275 | A700 | 6z multi | 75 | 35 |

4th International Parasitological Congress.

Norway Maple, Environment Emblem A701 **Jan Zizka, Battle of Grunwald, by Jan Matejko A702**

Designs (Human Environment Emblem and): 1z, English oak. 1.50z, White poplar. 4.20z, Scotch pine. 4.50z, White willow. 6z, Birch.

1978, Sept. 6 Photo. Perf. 14
2276	A701	50g gold & multi	5	5
2277	A701	1z gold & multi	12	5
2278	A701	1.50z gold & multi	18	6
2279	A701	4.20z gold & multi	50	16
2280	A701	4.50z gold & multi	55	25
2281	A701	6z gold & multi	75	30
		Nos. 2276-2281 (6)	2.15	87

Protection of the environment.

Souvenir Sheet

1978, Sept. 8 Perf. 11½x11
| 2282 | A702 | 6z gold & multi | 85 | 60 |

PRAGA '78 International Philatelic Exhibition, Prague, Sept. 8–17. No. 2282 has gold margin with red inscription and PRAGA '78 emblem. Size: 68x78mm.

Letter, Telephone and Satellite A703

1978, Sept. 20 Litho. Perf. 11
| 2283 | A703 | 1.50z multi | 18 | 8 |

20th anniversary of the Organization of Ministers of Posts and Telecommunications of Warsaw Pact countries.

Peace, by Andre le Brun A704

1978-79 Litho. Perf. 11½ (1z), 12½
2284	A704	1z violet	12	5
2285	A704	1.50z steel bl ('79)	18	8
2286	A704	2z brn ('79)	20	10
2287	A704	2.50z ultra ('79)	25	12

Polish Unit, U.N. Middle East Emergency Force—A706

Designs: No. 2289, Color Guard, Kosziusko Division (4 soldiers). No. 2290, Color Guard, field training (3 soldiers).

1978, Oct. 6 Photo. Perf. 12x11½
2289	A706	1.50z multi	18	8
2290	A706	1.50z multi	18	8
2291	A706	1.50z multi	18	8

35th anniversary of People's Army.

Young Man, by Raphael A707

1978, Oct. 9 Perf. 11
| 2292 | A707 | 6z multi | 75 | 30 |

Stamp Day 1978.

Dr. Korczak and Children A708

1978, Oct. 11 Litho. Perf. 11½x11
| 2293 | A708 | 1.50z multi | 18 | 8 |

Dr. Janusz Korczak, physician, educator, writer, birth centenary.

Wojciech Boguslawski (1757–1829) A709

Portraits: 1z, Aleksander Fredro (1795–1878). 1.50z, Juliusz Slowacki (1809–1849). 2z, Adam Mickiewicz (1798–1855). 4.50z, Stanislaw Wyspianski (1869–1907). 6z, Gabriela Zapolska (1857–1921).

1978, Nov. 11 Litho. Perf. 11½
2294	A709	50g multi	5	5
2295	A709	1z multi	12	5
2296	A709	1.50z multi	18	8
2297	A709	2z multi	25	10
2298	A709	4.50z multi	55	20
2299	A709	6z multi	75	35
		Nos. 2294-2299 (6)	1.90	83

Polish dramatists.

POLAND

Polish Combatants Monument, and Eiffel Tower, Paris—A710

1978, Nov. 2 Photo. *Perf. 11x11½*
2300 A710 1.50z brn, red & bl   18   8

Przewalski Mare and Colt A711

Animals: 1z, Polar bears. 1.50z, Indian elephants. 2z, Jaguars. 4.20z, Gray seals. 4.50z, Hartebeests. 6z, Mandrills.

1978, Nov. 10
2301 A711   50g multi   5   5
2302 A711   1z multi   12   5
2303 A711 1.50z multi   18   8
2304 A711   2z multi   25   10
2305 A711 4.20z multi   50   16
2306 A711 4.50z multi   55   20
2307 A711   6z multi   75   30
     Nos. 2301-2307 (7)   2.40   94

Warsaw Zoological Gardens, 50th anniversary.

Adolf Warski (1868-1937) A712

Party Emblem A713

Portraits: No. 2309, Julian Lenski (1889-1937). No. 2310, Aleksander Zawadzki (1899-1964). No. 2311, Stanislaw Dubois (1901-1942).

Perf. 11½x11, 11x11½   Photogravure

2308 A712 1.50z red & brn   18   8
2309 A712 1.50z red & blk   18   8
2310 A712 1.50z red & dk vio   18   8
2311 A712 1.50z red & dk bl   18   8
2312 A713 1.50z blk, red & gold   18   8
     Nos. 2308-2312 (5)   90   40

Polish United Workers' Party, 30th anniversary.

LOT Planes, 1929 and 1979 A714

1979, Jan. 2 Photo. *Perf. 11x11½*
2313 A714 6.90z gold & multi   70   30
LOT, Polish airline, 50th anniversary.

Train and IYC Emblem—A715

Designs (Children's Paintings): 1z, Children with toys. 1.50z, Children in meadow. 6z, Family.

1979, Jan. 13   *Perf. 11*
2314 A715   50g multi   5   5
2315 A715   1z multi   12   5
2316 A715 1.50z multi   18   10
2317 A715   6z multi   75   35

International Year of the Child.

Artist's Wife, by Karol Mondral A716

Modern Polish Graphic Arts: 50g, "Lightning," by Edmund Bartlomiejcyk (horiz.). 1.50z, Musicians, by Tadeusz Kulisiewicz. 4.50z, Portrait of a Brave Man, by Wladyslaw Skoczylas.

Perf. 11½x12, 12x11½   Engraved

1979, Mar. 5
2318 A716   50g brt vio   5   5
2319 A716   1z sl grn   12   5
2320 A716 1.50z bl gray   18   8
2321 A716 4.50z vio bl   55   25

Andrzej Frycz-Modrzewski, Stefan Batory, Jan Zamoyski—A717
Photogravure and Engraved

1979, Mar. 12   *Perf. 12x11½*
2322 A717 1.50z cr & sep   15   8

Royal Tribunal in Piotrkow Trybunalski, 400th anniversary.

Pole Vault and Olympic Emblem A718

Designs (Olympic Emblem and): 1.50z, High jump. 6z, Cross-country skiing. 8.40z, Equestrian.

1979, Mar. 26 Photo. *Perf. 12x11½*
2323 A718   1z multi   10   5
2324 A718 1.50z multi   15   8
2325 A718   6z multi   60   25
2326 A718 8.40z multi   85   35

1980 Olympic Games.

Flounder—A720

Fish and Environmental Protection Emblem: 90g, Perch. 1z, Grayling. 1.50z, Salmon. 2z, Trout. 4.50z, Pike. 5z, Carp. 6z, Catfish and frog.

1979, Apr. 26 Photo. *Perf. 11½x11*
2327 A720   50g multi   5   5
2328 A720   90g multi   12   5
2329 A720   1z multi   12   5
2330 A720 1.50z multi   18   8
2331 A720   2z multi   25   10
2332 A720 4.50z multi   55   25
2333 A720   5z multi   60   25
2334 A720   6z multi   75   35
     Nos. 2327-2334 (8)   2.62 1.18

Polish angling, centenary, and protection of the environment.

A721

1979, Apr. 30 Litho. *Perf. 11x11½*
2335 A721 1.50z multi   18   8

Council for Mutual Economic Aid of Socialist Countries, 30th anniversary.

Faces and Emblem A722

1979, May 7   *Perf. 11*
2336 A722 1.50z red & blk   18   8

6th Congress of Association of Fighters for Liberty and Democracy, Warsaw, May 7-8.

St. George's Church, Sofia A723

1979, May 15 Photo. *Perf. 11x11½*
2337 A723 1.50z multi   18   8

Philaserdica '79 Philatelic Exhibition, Sofia, Bulgaria, May 18-27.

Pope John Paul II, Cracow Cathedral A723

Designs: 8.40z, Pope John Paul II, Auschwitz-Birkenau Memorial. 50z, Pope John Paul II.

1979, June 2 Photo. *Perf. 11x11½*
2338 A723 1.50z multi   25   10
2339 A723 8.40z multi   1.00   50

Souvenir Sheet
Perf. 11½x11
2340 A723   50z multi   5.50 5.00

Visit of Pope John Paul II to Poland, June 2-11. No. 2340 contains one stamp (26x35mm.); gray and gold margin shows church facade. Size: 63x79mm.
A variety of No. 2340 with silver margin exists.

Paddle Steamer Prince Ksawery and Old Warsaw—A724

Designs: 1.50z, Steamer Gen. Swierczewski and Gdansk, 1914. 4.50z, Tug Aurochs and Plock, 1960. 6z, Motor ship Mermaid and modern Warsaw, 1959.

1979, June 15 Litho. *Perf. 11*
2341 A724   1z multi   12   6
2342 A724 1.50z multi   18   8
2343 A724 4.50z multi   55   25
2344 A724   6z multi   75   35

Vistula River navigation, 150th anniversary.

Kosciuszko Monument, Detroit A725

1979, July 1 Photo. *Perf. 11½*
2345 A725 8.40z multi   85   45

Gen. Tadeusz Kosziuszko (1746-1807), Polish soldier and statesman who served in American Revolution.

Mining Machinery   Eagle and People
A726   A727

Design: 1.50z, Salt crystals.

1979, July 14 Photo. *Perf. 14*
2346 A726 1z lt brn & blk   10   5
2347 A726 1.50z bl grn & blk   18   8

Wieliczka ancient rock-salt mines.

1979, July 21   *Perf. 11½x11*
Design: No. 2349, Man with raised hand and flag.

2348 A727 1.50z red, bl & gray   18   8
2349 A727 1.50z sil, red & blk   18   8

35 years of Polish People's Republic.

POLAND

Souvenir Sheet
1979, Sept. 2 Photo. Perf. 11½x11
2350 A727 Sheet of 2, multi 75 50

13th National Philatelic Exhibition. No. 2350 contains Nos. 2348–2349 and label with exhibition emblem. Silver and white margin; black marginal inscription. Size: 120x85mm.

Poland No. 1, Rowland Hill—A728

1979, Aug. 16 Litho. Perf. 11½x11
2351 A728 6z multi 75 35

Rowland Hill (1795–1879), originator of penny postage.

Souvenir Sheet

The Rape of Europa, by Bernardo Strozzi—A729

1979, Aug. 20 Photo. Perf. 11x11½
2352 A729 10z multi 1.25 75

Europhil '79, International Philatelic Exhibition. No. 2352 has blue and gold margin showing emblems of various philatelic exhibitions. Size: 81x70mm.

Wojciech Jastrzebowski—A730

1979, Aug. 27 Perf. 11½x11
2353 A730 1.50z multi 18 8

Economic Congress.

Postal Workers' Monument—A731

1979, Sept. 1 Perf. 11x11½
2354 A731 1.50z multi 18 8

40th anniversary of Polish postal workers' resistance to Nazi invaders. See No. B137.

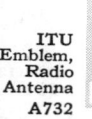

ITU Emblem, Radio Antenna—A732

1979, Sept. 24 Perf. 11x11½
2355 A732 1.50z multi 18 8

International Radio Consultative Committee (CCIR) of the International Telecommunications Union, 50th anniversary.

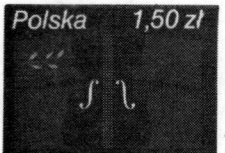

Violin—A733

1979, Sept. 25 Lithographed
2356 A733 1.50z dk bl, org, grn 18 8

Henryk Wieniawski Young Violinists' Competition, Lublin.

Pulaski Monument, Buffalo—A734   Gen. Franciszek Jozwiak—A735

1979, Oct. 1 Photo. Perf. 11½x12
2357 A734 8.40z multi 85 35

Gen. Casimir Pulaski (1748–1779), Polish nobleman who served in American Revolutionary War, death bicentenary.

1979, Oct. 3 Perf. 11½x11
2358 A735 1.50z bl, gold 18 8

35th anniversary of Civil and Military Security Service, founded by Gen. Franciszek Jozwiak (1895–1966).

Drive-in Post Office—A736

Designs: 1.50z, Parcel sorting. 4.50z, Loading mail train. 6z, Mobile post office.

1979, Oct. 9 Perf. 11½
2359 A736 1z multi 12 6
2360 A736 1.50z multi 18 8
2361 A736 4.50z multi 55 25
2362 A736 6z multi 75 35

Stamp Day.

Holy Family—A737

Design: 6.90z, Nativity (horiz.).

Perf. 11½×11, 11×11½
1979, Dec. 4 Photo.
2363 A737 2z multi 25 10
2364 A737 6.90z multi 75 35

Soyuz 30 and Salyut 6—A738

Space Achievements: 1.50z, Kopernik 500 and Copernicus satellite. 2z, Lunik 2 and Ranger 7. 4.50z, Yuri Gagarin and Vostok. 6.90z, Neil Armstrong and Apollo 11.

1979, Dec. 28 Photo. Perf. 11½×11
2365 A738 1z multi 12 5
2366 A738 1.50z multi 18 10
2367 A738 2z multi 25 12
2368 A738 4.50z multi 55 25
2369 A738 6.90z multi 75 35
  a. Souvenir sheet of 5 2.25 1.75
     Nos. 2365-2369 (5) 1.85 87

No. 2369a contains Nos. 2365–2369, tete beche plus label; dark blue marginal inscription and stars. Size: 120×102½mm.

Trotters—A739

Designs: Horse Paintings.
1980, Jan. 31 Photo. Perf. 11½x12
2370 A739 1z Stagecoach 10 5
2371 A739 2z Horse, trainer 20 10
2372 A739 2.50z shown 25 12
2373 A739 3z Fox hunt 30 15
2374 A739 4z Sled 40 20
2375 A739 6z Hay cart 60 30
2376 A739 6.50z Pairs 65 32
2377 A739 6.90z Hurdles 70 35
  Nos. 2370-2377 (8) 3.20 1.59

Sierakov horse stud farm, 150th anniversary.

Party Slogan on Map of Poland—A740   Janusza Stannego—A741

1980, Feb. 11 Photo. Perf. 11½x11
2378 A740 2.50z multi 30 15
2379 A741 2.50z multi 30 15

Polish United Workers' Party, 8th Congress.

Equestrian, Olympic Rings—A742

1980, Mar. 31 Perf. 12x11½
2380 A742 2z shown 25 10
2381 A742 2.50z Archery 30 15
2382 A742 6.50z Biathlon 75 35
2383 A742 8.40z Volleyball 85 42

13th Winter Olympic Games, Lake Placid, N.Y., Feb. 12-24 (6.50z); 22nd Summer Olympic Games, Moscow, July 19-Aug. 3. See No. B138.

Map and Old Town Hall, 1591, Zamosc—A743

1980, Apr. 3 Litho. Perf. 11½
2384 A743 2.50z multi 30 15

Zamosc, 400th anniversary.

Arms of Poland and Russia—A744

1980, Apr. 21 Litho. Perf. 11½
2385 A744 2.50z multi 30 15

Treaty of Friendship, Cooperation and Mutual Assistance between Poland and USSR, 35th anniversary.

Lenin, 110th Birth Anniversary—A745

1980, Apr. 22 Photo. Perf. 11
2386 A745 2.50z multi 30 15

See "Special Notices" at the front of this volume for data on the listing methods of this Catalogue, abbreviations, condition, prices and examination.

POLAND

Workers Marching — A746

Dove Over Liberation Date — A747

1980, May 1   Perf. 11½x11
2387   A746   2.50z multi   30   15
Revolution of 1905, 75th anniversary.

1980, May 9   Perf. 11½x12
2388   A747   2.50z multi   30   15
Victory over fascism, 35th anniversary.

Arms of Treaty-signing Countries — A748

1980, May 14   Litho.   Perf. 11½x11
2389   A748   2z red & blk   25   10
Signing of Warsaw Pact (Bulgaria, Czechoslovakia, German Democratic Rep., Hungary, Poland, Romania, USSR), 25th anniversary.

Caverns, (1961 Expedition) Map of Cuba — A749

1980, May 22   Photo.   Perf. 14
2390   A749   2z shown   25   10
2391   A749   2z Seals, Antarctica, 1959   25   10
2392   A749   2.50z Ethnology, Mongolia, 1963   30   15
2393   A749   2.50z Archaeology, Syria, 1959   30   15
2394   A749   6.50z Mountain climbing, Nepal, 1978   75   35
2395   A749   8.40z Paleontology, Mongolia, 1963   85   42
    Nos. 2390-2395 (6)   2.70   1.27

Unused Prices

Catalogue prices for unused stamps through 1960 are for hinged copies in fine condition. Never-hinged unused stamps issued before 1961 often sell above Catalogue prices. Current never-hinged prices for various countries will be found in the Scott StampMarket Update.

Malachowski Lyceum, Arms of Polish Order of Labor — A750

1980, June 7   Photo.   Perf. 11x12
2396   A750   2z blk & dl grn   25   10
Malachowski Lyceum (oldest school in Plock), 800th anniversary.

1980, June 30   Perf. 11½x11
2397   A751   2z shown   25   10
2398   A751   2z Clathrus ruber   25   10
2399   A751   2.50z Phallus hadriani   30   15
2400   A751   2.50z Strobilomyces floccopus   30   15
2401   A751   8z Sparassis crispa   80   40
2402   A751   10.50z Langermannia gigantea   1.05   52
    Nos. 2397-2402 (6)   2.95   1.42

Xerocomus Parasiticus — A751

Sandomierz Millenium — A752

1980, July 12   Photo.   Perf. 11x11½
2403   A752   2.50z dk brn   25   12

"Lwow," T. Ziolkowski — A753

Ships and Teachers: 2.50z, Antoni Garnuszewski, A. Garnuszewski. 6z, Zenit, A. Ledochowski. 6.50z, Jan Turlejski, K. Porebski. 6.90z, Horyzon, G. Kanski. 8.40z, Dar Pomorza, K. Maciejewicz.

1980, July 21   Litho.   Perf. 11
2404   A753   2z multi   25   10
2405   A753   2.50z multi   30   15
2406   A753   6z multi   70   30
2407   A753   6.50z multi   75   32
2408   A753   6.90z multi   75   35
2409   A753   8.40z multi   85   42
    Nos. 2404-2409 (6)   3.90   1.79
Marize Maritime High School.

Atropa Belladonna — A754

Designs: Medicinal plants.

1980, Aug. 15   Litho.   Perf. 11½x11
2410   A754   2z shown   25   10
2411   A754   2.50z Datura innoxia   30   15
2412   A754   3.40z Valeriana   35   18
2413   A754   5z Mentha piperita   60   25
2414   A754   6.50z Calendula   75   35
2415   A754   8z Salvia officinalis   80   40
    Nos. 2410-2415 (6)   3.05   1.43

Jan Kochanowski (1530-1584), Poet — A755

1980, Aug. 20   Perf. 11
2416   A755   2.50z multi   30   15

United Nations, 35th Anniversary — A756

1980, Sept. 19   Photo.   Perf. 11x11½
2417   A756   8.40z multi   85   42

Chopin Piano Competition — A757

1980, Oct. 2   Litho.   Perf. 11½
2418   A757   6.90z blk & tan   75   35

Mail Pick-up — A758

1980, Oct. 9   Photo.   Perf. 12x11½
2419   A758   2z shown   25   10
2420   A758   2.50z Letter sorting   30   12
2421   A758   6z Loading mail plane   75   30
2422   A758   6.50z Mail boxes   75   32
   a. Souvenir sheet of 4   6.00   4.00
Stamp Day. No. 2422a contains Nos. 2419-2422; black marginal inscription. Size: 123x94mm.

Girl Embracing Dove, U.N. Emblem — A759

1980, Nov. 21   Litho.   Perf. 11x11½
2423   A759   8.40z multi   85   42
U.N. Declaration on the Preparation of Societies for Life in Peace.

Battle of Olzynska Grochowska, by W. Kossak — A760

1980, Nov. 29   Photo.   Perf. 11
2424   A760   2.50z multi   30   15
Battle of Olzynska Grochowska, 1830.

Horse-drawn Fire Engine — A761

Designs: Horse-drawn vehicles.

1980, Dec. 16
2425   A761   2z shown   25   10
2426   A761   2.50z Passenger coach   30   15
2427   A761   3z Beer wagon   35   15
2428   A761   5z Sled   60   25
2429   A761   6z Bus   70   35
2430   A761   6.50z Two-seater   75   35
    Nos. 2425-2430 (6)   2.95   1.35

Honor to the Silesian Rebels, by Jan Borowczak — A762

Pablo Picasso — A763

1981, Jan. 22   Engr.   Perf. 11½
2431   A762   2.50z gray grn   30   15
Silesian uprising, 60th anniversary.

1981, Mar. 10   Photo.   Perf. 11½x11
2432   A763   8.40z multi   85   45
   a. Miniature sheet of 2 + 2 labels   2.25   1.25
Pablo Picasso (1881-1973), artist, birth centenary. No. 2432 se-tenant with label showing A Crying Woman. No. 2432a has black marginal inscription. Size: 94½x129mm. Sold for 20.80z.

POLAND

Balloon Flown by Pilatre de Rozier, 1783—A764

Gordon Bennett Cup (Balloons): No. 2434, J. Blanchard, J. Jeffries, 1875. 2.50z, F. Godard, 1850. 3z, F. Hynek, Z. Burzynski, 1933. 6z, Z. Burzynski, N. Wysocki, 1935. 6.50z, B. Abruzzo, M. Anderson, P. Newman, 1978. 10.50z, Winners' names, 1933-1935, 1938.

1981, Mar. 25   Photo.   Perf. 11½x12

2433	A764	2z multi	25	10
2434	A764	2z multi	25	10
2435	A764	2.50z multi	30	15
2436	A764	5z multi	35	15
2437	A764	6z multi	70	35
2438	A764	6.50z multi	75	35
	Nos. 2433-2438 (6)		2.60	1.20

Souvenir Sheet Imperf.

2439 A76410.50z multi   1.75 1.00

No. 2439 has gold decorative margin. Size: 58½x98mm.

Iphegenia, by Franz Anton Maulbertsch (1724-1796), WIPA '81 Emblem —A765

1981, May 11   Litho.   Perf. 11½

2440 A765 10.50z multi   1.25 35

WIPA '81 International Philatelic Exhibition, Vienna, May 22-31.

Wroclaw, 1493
A766

Gen. Wladyslaw Sikorski (1881-1943)
A767

1981, May 15   Photo.   Perf. 14

2441 A766 6.50z brown   75 35

See Nos. 2456-2459.

1981, May 20   Perf. 11½x11

2442 A767 6.50z multi   75 35

Kwan Vase, 18th Cent.
A768

1981, June 15

2443	A768	1z shown	10	5
2444	A768	2z Cup, saucer, 1820	25	10
2445	A768	2.50z Jug, 1820	30	15
2446	A768	5z Portrait plate, 1880	60	25
2447	A768	6.50z Vase, 1900	75	35
2448	A768	8.40z Basket, 1840	85	40
	Nos. 2443-2448 (6)		2.85	1.32

Intl. Architects Union, 14th Congress, Warsaw
A769

1981, July 15   Litho.

2449 A769 2.50z multi   30 15

Moose, Rifle and Pouch—A770

1981, July 30

2450	A770	2z shown	20	10
2451	A770	2z Boar	20	10
2452	A770	2.50z Fox	25	12
2453	A770	2.50z Elk	25	12
2454	A770	6.50z Greylag goose	65	32
2455	A770	6.50z Fen duck, horiz.	65	32
	Nos. 2450-2455 (6)		2.20	1.08

City Type of 1981

1981, July 28   Photo.   Perf. 11x11½

2456	A766	4z Gdansk, 1652, vert.	40	20
2457	A766	5z Krakow, 1493, vert.	50	25
2458	A766	6z Legnica, 1744	60	30
2459	A766	8z Warsaw, 1618	80	40

A770a

1982, Nov. 2   Photo.   Perf. 11½

2461	12z Vistula River	30	15
2463	17z Kasimierz Dolny	42	20
2466	25z Danzig	62	30

Wild Bison
A771

1981, Aug. 27   Perf. 11½x11

2471 Strip of 5   3.75 2.25
a.-e. 6.50z, any single   75 45

60th Anniv. of Polish Tennis Federation
A772

1981, Sept. 17   Photo.   Perf. 11x11½

2472 A772 6.50z multi   75 35

Model Airplane—A773

1981, Sept. 24   Perf. 14

2473	A773	1z shown	10	5
2474	A773	2z Boats	25	10
2475	A773	2.50z Racing cars	30	15
2476	A773	4.20z Gliders	50	25
2477	A773	6.50z Radio-controlled racing cars	75	35
2478	A773	8z Yachts	80	40
	Nos. 2473-2478 (6)		2.70	1.30

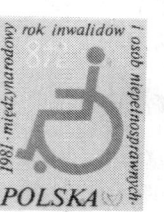

Intl. Year of the Disabled
A774

Stamp Day
A775

1981, Sept. 25   Litho.   Perf. 11½x11

2479 A774 8.40z multi   85 42

1981, Oct. 9   Photo.   Perf. 14

| 2480 | A775 | 2.50z Pistol, 18th cent., horiz. | 30 | 15 |
| 2481 | A775 | 8.40z Sword, 18th cent. | 85 | 42 |

Henri Wieniawski (1835-1880), Violinist and Composer
A776

Bronislaw Wesolowski (1870-1919)
A777

1981, Oct. 10   Perf. 11½x12

2482 A776 2.50z multi   30 15

1981, Oct. 15   Litho.

Working Movement Leaders: 2z, Malgorzata Fornalska (1902-1944). 2.50z, Maria Koszutska (1876-1939). 6.50z, Marcin Kasprzak (1860-1905).

2483	A777	50g grn & blk		5	5
2484	A777	2z bl & blk	25	10
2485	A777	2.50z brn & blk	30	15
2486	A777	6.50z lil rose & blk	75	35

World Food Day
A778

1981, Oct. 16   Perf. 11½x11

2487 A778 6.90z multi   75 35

Old Theater, Cracow, 200th Anniv.—A779

Theater Emblem and: 2z, Helena Modrzejewska (1840-1909), actress. 2.50z, Stanislaw Kozmian (1836-1922), theater director, 1865-1885, founder of Cracow School. 6.50z, Konrad Swinarski (1929-1975), stage manager.

1981, Oct. 17   Photo. & Engr.   Perf. 12x11½

2488	A779	2z multi	25	10
2489	A779	2.50z multi	30	15
2490	A779	6.50z multi	65	35
2491	A779	8z multi	80	40

Souvenir Sheet

Vistula River Project—A780

1981, Dec. 20   Litho.   Perf. 11½x12

2492 A780 10.50z multi   1.25 75

No. 2492 has gray and gold margin. Size: 63x51mm.

Flowering Succulent Plants—A781

1981, Dec. 22   Photo.   Perf. 13

2493	A781	90g Epiphyllopsis gaertneri	8	5
2494	A781	1z Cereus tonduzii	12	5
2495	A781	2z Cylindropuntia leptocaulis	25	10
2496	A781	2.50z Cylindroppuntia fulgida	30	15
2497	A781	2.50z Caralluma lugardi	30	15
2498	A781	6.50z Nopalea cochenillifera	65	32
2499	A781	6.50z Lithops helmutii	65	32
2500	A78110.50z Cylindropuntia spinosior	1.25	55
	Nos. 2493-2500 (8)	3.60	1.69

Polish Workers' Party, 40th Anniv.
A782

Stoneware Plate, 1890
A783

POLAND

1982, Jan. 5   Photo.   *Perf. 11½x11*
2501   A782   2.50z multi   25   12

1982, Jan. 20
Porcelain or Stoneware: 2z, Plate, mug, 1790. 2.50z, Soup tureen, gravy dish, 1830. 6z, Salt and pepper dish, 1844. 8z, Stoneware jug, 1840. 10.50z, Stoneware figurine, 1740.

2502	A783	1z multi	10	5
2503	A783	2z multi	20	10
2504	A783	2.50z multi	25	12
2505	A783	6z multi	60	30
2506	A783	8z multi	80	40
2507	A783	10.50z multi	1.05	52
	Nos. 2502-2507 (6)		3.00	1.49

Ignacy Lukasiewicz (1822-1882), Oil Lamp Inventor — A784

Karol Szymanowski (1882-1937), Composer — A785

Designs: Various oil lamps.

1982, Mar. 22   Photo.   *Perf. 11½x11*

2508	A784	1z multi	10	5
2509	A784	2z multi	20	10
2510	A784	2.50z multi	25	12
2511	A784	3.50z multi	35	18
2512	A784	9z multi	90	45
2513	A784	10z multi	1.00	50
	Nos. 2508-2513 (6)		2.80	1.40

1982, Apr. 8
2514   A785   2.50z dk brn & gold   25   12

Victory in Challenge Trophy Flights — A786

1982, May 5   Photo.   *Perf. 11x11½*
2515   A786   27z RWD-6 monoplane   2.75   1.40
2516   A786   31z RWD-9   3.10   1.55
   a. Souvenir sheet of 2   6.00   3.00

No. 2516a contains Nos. 2515-2516; multicolored margin shows map of flights. Size: 90x103mm.

Henryk Szienkewicz (1846-1916), Writer — A787

1982 World Cup — A788

Polish Nobel Prize Winners: 15z, Wladyslaw Reymont (1867-1925), writer, 1924. 25z, Marie Curie (1867-1934), physicist 1903, 1911. 31z, Czeslaw Milosz (b. 1911), poet, 1980.

1982, May 10   Litho.   *Perf. 11½x11*

2517	A787	3z blk & dk grn	30	15
2518	A787	15z blk & brn	1.50	75
2519	A787	25z black	2.50	1.25
2520	A787	31z blk & gray	3.10	1.55

Perf. 11½x11, 11x11½
1982, May 28   Photo.

2521	A788	25z Ball	2.50	1.25
2522	A788	27z Bull, ball, horiz.	2.75	1.40

Souvenir Sheet

Maria Kaziera Sobieska — A789

1982, June 11   Photo.   *Perf. 11½x11*
2523   A789   65z multi   6.50   3.00

PHILEXFRANCE '82 Intl. Stamp Exhibition, Paris, June 11-21. No. 2523 has pale blue and gold margin. Size: 69x87mm.

Assoc. Presidents Stanislaw Sierakowski and Boleslaw Domanski — A790

1982, July 20   Litho.
2524   A790   4.50z multi   45   22

Assoc. of Poles in Germany, 60th anniv.

2nd UN Conference on Peaceful Uses of Outer Space, Vienna, Aug. 9-21 — A791

1982, Aug. 9   Photo.
2525   A791   31z Globe   3.00   1.50

No. 2441 Surcharged

1982, Aug. 20
2526   A766   10z on 6.50z brn   1.00   50

Black Madonna of Jasna Gora, 600th Anniv. — A792

Workers' Movement — A793

Designs: 2.50z, Father Augustin Kordecki (1603-1673). 25z, Siege of Jasna Gora by Swedes, 1655 (horiz.).

1982, Aug. 26   *Perf. 11*
2527   A792   2.50z multi   25   12
2528   A792   25z multi   2.50   1.25
2529   A792   65z multi   6.50   3.00

A souvenir sheet of 2 No. 2529 exists.

1982, Sept. 3   *Perf. 11½x11*
2530   A793   6z multi   60   30

Norbert Barlicki (1880-1941) — A794

Carved Head, Wawel Castle — A795

Workers' Activists: 6z, Pawel Finder (1904-1944). 15z, Marian Buczek (1896-1939). 20z, Cezaryna Wojnarowska (1861-1911). 29z, Ignacy Daszynski (1866-1936).

1982, Sept. 10   *Perf. 12x11½*

2531	A794	5z multi	50	25
2532	A794	6z multi	60	30
2533	A794	15z multi	1.50	75
2534	A794	20z multi	2.00	1.00
2535	A794	29z multi	2.90	1.45
	Nos. 2531-2535 (5)		7.50	3.75

1982, Sept. 25
2536   A795   60z Woman's head   4.50   2.00
2537   A795   100z Man's head   7.50   3.00

TB Bacillus Centenary — A796

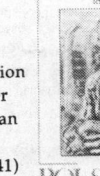

Sanctification of Father Maximilian Kolbe (1894-1941) — A797

1982, Sept. 22   *Perf. 11½x11*
2538   A796   10z Koch   40   20
2539   25z Oko Bujwid
              (1857-1942),
              bacteriologist   1.00   50

1982, Oct.
2540   A797   27z multi   1.00   50

50th Anniv. of Polar Research — A798

1982, Oct. 25   Litho.   *Perf. 11½*
2541   A798   27z multi   1.00   50

Stanislaw Zaremba (1863-1942), Mathematician — A799

Mathematicians: 6z, Waclaw Sierpinski (1882-1969). 12z, Zygmunt Janiszewski (1888-1920). 15z, Stefan Banach (1892-1945).

1982, Nov. 23   Photo.   *Perf. 11x11½*
2542   A799   5z multi   20   10
2543   A799   6z multi   25   12
2544   A799   12z multi   45   22
2545   A799   15z multi   60   30

First Anniv. of Military Rule — A800

1982, Dec. 13   *Perf. 12x11½*
2546   A800   2.50z Commemorative medal,
              obverse and reverse   10   5

Cracow Monuments Restoration — A801

POLAND

1982, Dec. 20 Litho. *Perf. 11½x11*
2547 A801 15z Deanery portal 60 30
2548 A801 25z Law College portal 1.00 50

Souvenir Sheet
Litho. & Engr. *Imperf.*
2549 A801 65z City map 2.50 1.50

No. 2549 contains one stamp (22x27mm.); margin shows old buildings. Size: 77x95mm.

Map of Poland, by Bernard Wapowski, 1526—A802

Maps: 6z, Warsaw, Polish Kingdom Quartermaster, 1839. 8z, Poland, Romer's Atlas, 1908. 25z, Krakow, by A. Buchowiecki, 1703, astrolabe, 17th cent.

1982, Dec. 28 Litho. *Perf. 11½*
2550 A802 5z multi 20 10
2551 A802 6z multi 25 12
2552 A802 8z multi 35 18
2553 A802 25z multi 1.00 50

120th Anniv. of 1863 Uprising—A803

1983, Jan. 22 Photo. *Perf. 12x11½*
2554 A803 6z The Battle, by Arthur Grottger (1837-1867) 25 12

Warsaw Theater Sesquicentennial—A804

1983, Feb. 24 Photo. *Perf. 11*
2555 A804 6z multi 25 12

10th Anniv. of UN Conference on Human Environment, Stockholm—A805

1983, Mar. 24 Litho. *Perf. 11½*
2556 A805 5z Wild flowers 20 10
2557 A805 6z Swan, carp, eel 25 12
2558 A805 17z Hoopoe 65 32
2559 A805 30z Fish 1.20 60
2560 A805 31z Deer, fawn, buffalo 1.25 62
2561 A805 38z Fruit 1.50 75

Karol Kurpinski (1785-1857), Composer—A806

Famous People: 6z, Maria Jasnorzewska Pawlikowska (1891-1945), poet. 17z, Stanislaw Szober (1879-1938), linguist. 25z, Tadeusz Banachiewicz (1882-1954), astronomer. 27z, Jaroslaw Iwaszkiewicz (1894-1980), writer. 31z, Wladyslaw Tatarkiewicz (1886-1980), Philosopher, art historian.

1983, Mar. 25 Photo. *Perf. 11½x11*
2562 A806 5z tan & brn 20 10
2563 A806 6z pink & vio 25 12
2564 A806 17z dk grn & lt grn 65 32
2565 A806 25z bis & brn 1.00 50
2566 A806 27z lt bl & dk bl 1.10 55
2567 A806 31z vio & pur 1.25 62

Polish Medalists in 22nd Olympic Games, 1980—A807

1983, Apr. 5 *Perf. 11x11½*
2568 A807 5z Steeple chase 20 10
2569 A807 6z Equestrian 25 12
2570 A807 15z Soccer, 1982 World Cup 60 30
2571 A807 27 + 5z Pole vault 1.25 65

Warsaw Ghetto Uprising, 40th Anniv. A808

Customs Cooperation Council, 30th Anniv. A809

1983, Apr. 19 Photo. *Perf. 11½x11*
2572 A808 6z Heroes' Monument, by Natan Rappaport 25 12

Se-tenant with label showing anniversary medal.

1983, Apr. 28
2573 A809 5z multi 20 10

Second Visit of Pope John Paul II—A810

Portraits of Pope. 31z vert.

1983, June 16 Photo. *Perf. 11*
2574 A810 31z multi 1.25 60
2575 A810 65z multi 2.50 1.25
 a. Souvenir sheet 2.60 1.50

No. 2575a contains No. 2575. Size: 108x82mm.

Army of King John III Sobieski—A811

1983, July 5 *Perf. 11½x11*
2576 A811 5z Dragoons 20 10
2577 A811 5z Knight in armor 20 10
2578 A811 6z Non-commissioned infantry officers 25 12
2579 A811 15z Light cavalryman 60 30
2580 A811 27z Hussars 1.10 55

750th Anniv. of Torun Municipality—A812

1983, Photo. *Perf. 11*
2581 A812 6z multi 25 12
 a. Souv. sheet of 4 1.00 75

60th Anniv. of Polish Boxing Union—A813

1983, Nov. 4 Litho. *Perf. 11½x11*
2582 A813 6z multi 25 12

Enigma Decoding Machine, 50th Anniv. A813a

Girl Near House A813b

1983, Aug. 16 Litho. *Perf. 11½x11*
2582A A813a 5z multi 20 10
1983 Photo. *Perf. 11½x12*
2582B A813b 6z multi 25 12

Portrait of King John III Sobieski—A814

300th Anniv. of Victory over the Turks in Vienna (King's Portraits by): No. 2584, Unkown court painter. No. 2585, Sobieski on Horseback, by Francesco Trevisani (1656-1746). 25z, Jerzy Eleuter Szymonowicz-Siemiginowski (1660-1711). 65z+10z, Sobieski at Vienna, by Jan Matejko (1838-1893). Size of No. 2587: 99x75mm.

1983, Sept. 12 *Perf. 11*
2583 A814 5z multi 20 10
2584 A814 6z multi 25 12
2585 A814 6z multi 25 12
2586 A814 25z multi 1.00 50

Souvenir Sheet
Imperf.
2587 A814 65 + 10z multi 3.00 2.00

Polish Peoples' Army, 40th Anniv.—A815

Designs: No. 2588, General Bronislaw Zygmunt Berling (1896-1980). No. 2589, Wanda Wasilewska (1905-1964). No. 2591, Troop formation.

1983, Oct. 12 Photo. *Perf. 11*
2588 A815 5z multi, vert. 20 10
2589 A815 5z multi, vert. 20 10
2590 A815 6z multi, vert. 25 12
2591 A815 6z multi 25 12

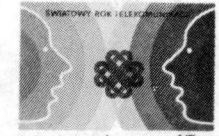

World Communications Year—A816

1983, Oct. 18 Photo. *Perf. 11*
2592 A816 15z multi 60 30

Cracow Monuments Restoration—A817

POLAND

1983, Nov. 25   Litho.   *Perf. 11*

2593	A817	5z Cloth Hall	24	12
2594	A817	6z Town Hall Tower vert.	30	16

Traditional Hats
A793

Natl. People's Council, 40th Anniv.
A794

1983, Dec. 16   Photo.   *Perf. 11½x11*

2595	A793	5z Biskupianski	24	12
2596	A793	5z Rozbarski	24	12
2597	A793	6z Warminsko-Mazurski	30	16
2598	A793	6z Cieszynski	30	16
2599	A793	25z Kurpiowski	1.20	60
2600	A793	38z Lubuski	1.85	90
		Nos. 2595-2600 (6)	4.13	2.06

1983, Dec. 31

2601	A794	6z Hand holding sword (poster)	30	16

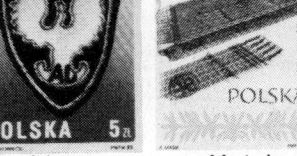

People's Army, 40th Anniv.
A795

Musical Instruments
A796

1984, Jan. 1   Litho.   *Perf. 11½x11*

2602	A795	5z Gen. Bem Brigade badge	24	12

1984, Feb. 10   Photo.

2603	A796	5z Dulcimer	24	12
2604	A796	6z Drum, tambourine	30	15
2605	A796	10z Accordion	50	25
2606	A796	15z Double bass	75	38
2607	A796	17z Bagpipes	85	42
2608	A796	29z Figurines by Tadeusz Zak	1.45	72
		Nos. 2603-2608 (6)	4.09	2.04

Wincenty Witos (1874-1945), Prime Minister—A797

1984, Mar. 2   Litho.   *Perf. 11½x11*

2609	A797	6z grn & sep	30	15

Local Flowers (Clematis Varieties)—A798

1984, Mar. 26   Photo.   *Perf. 11x11½*

2610	A798	5z Lanuginosa	25	12
2611	A798	6z Tangutica	30	15
2612	A798	10z Texensis	50	25
2613	A798	17z Alpina	85	42
2614	A798	25z Vitalba	1.25	62
2615	A798	27z Montana	1.35	68
		Nos. 2610-2615 (6)	4.50	2.24

The Ecstasy of St. Francis, by El Greco—A799

1984, Apr. 21   *Perf. 11*

2616	A799	27z multi	1.35	68

1984 Summer Olympics—A800

1984, Apr. 25   Litho.   *Perf. 11x11½*

2617	A800	5z Handball	25	12
2618	A800	6z Fencing	30	15
2619	A800	15z Bicycling	75	38
2620	A800	16z Running	80	40
2621	A800	17z Running, diff.	85	42
	a.	Souvenir sheet of 2	2.25	
2622	A800	31z Skiing (winter games)	1.55	80
		Nos. 2617-2622 (6)	4.50	2.27

No. 2621a contains Nos. 2620-2621; margin shows Olympic medals. Size: 129x79mm. Sold for 43z.

Battle of Monte Casino, 40th Anniv.—A801

1984, May 18   Photo.   *Perf. 11½x11*

2623	A801	15z Memorial Cross	75	38

POLAND
Rarities to New Issues

MINT • USED • YEAR SETS

Comprehensive 29 page pricelist, only $1.

Wasserman Philatelics

P.O. Box 3932, Stn 'B'
Winnipeg, Manitoba
R2W 5H9
Canada

POLAND

Yearly Units - New Issues

Mint — Used — Covers
FDCs — Locals
Dependable, Cordial &
Complete Service
Most Complete Stock
1860-1983
(Dealers' inquiries invited)

Price list on request

Roman J. Burkiewicz

Polish Philatelic Hdqrs.
P.O. Box 160
Frisco, CO 80443

POLAND

SEMI-POSTAL STAMPS.
Regular Issue of 1919 Surcharged in Violet:

1919, May 3		Imperf.	Unwmkd.
B1	A10(a) 5f + 5f grn	20	30
B2	A10(a) 10f + 5f red vio	1.50	80
B3	A10(a) 15f + 5f dp red	40	35
B4	A11(b) 25f + 5f ol grn	40	35
B5	A11(b) 50f + 5f bl grn	60	40

Perf. 11½.

B6	A10(a) 5f + 5f grn	20	20
B7	A10(a) 10f + 5f red vio	35	30
B8	A10(a) 15f + 5f dp red	20	20
B9	A11(b) 25f + 5f ol grn	25	20
B10	A11(b) 50f + 5f bl grn	50	35
Nos. B1-B10 (10)		4.60	3.45

Commemorative of the First Polish Philatelic Exhibition. The surtax benefited the Polish White Cross Society.

Regular Issue of 1920 Surcharged in Carmine

Thin Laid Paper

1921, Mar. 5		Perf. 9	
B11	A14 5m + 30m red vio	6.50	10.00
B12	A14 6m + 30m dp rose	6.00	10.00
B13	A14 10m + 30m lt red	15.00	15.00
B14	A14 20m + 30m gray grn	45.00	45.00

Counterfeits, differently perforated, exist of Nos. B11–14.

Light of Knowledge
SP1 SP2

1925, Jan. 1	Typo.	Perf. 12½.	
B15	SP1 1g org brn	15.00	20.00
B16	SP1 2g dk brn	15.00	20.00
B17	SP1 3g orange	15.00	20.00
B18	SP1 5g ol grn	15.00	20.00
B19	SP1 10g bl grn	15.00	20.00
B20	SP1 15g red	15.00	20.00
B21	SP1 20g blue	15.00	20.00
B22	SP1 25g red brn	15.00	20.00
B23	SP1 30g dp vio	15.00	20.00
B24	SP1 40g indigo	45.00	20.00
B25	SP1 50g magenta	15.00	20.00
Nos. B15-B25 (11)		195.00	220.00

"Na Skarb" means "National Funds". These stamps were sold at a premium of 50 groszy each, for charity.

1927, May 3		Perf. 11½.	
B26	SP2 10g + 5g choc & grn	8.00	4.00
B27	SP2 20g + 5g dk bl & buff	8.00	4.00

"NA OSWIATE" means "For Public Instruction". The surtax aided an Association of Educational Societies.

Torun Type of 1933

1933, May 21		Engraved	
B28	A59 60g (+40g) red brn, buff	22.50	17.50

Issued in connection with the Philatelic Exhibition at Torun, May 21 to 28, 1933, and sold at a premium of 40g to aid the exhibition funds.

Souvenir Sheet.

Stagecoach and Wayside Inn
SP3
Engraved

1938, May 3	Perf. 12, Imperf.		
B29	SP3 Sheet of four	125.00	100.00
a.	45g grn	7.50	7.50
b.	55g bl	7.50	7.50

Issued to commemorate the 5th Philatelic Exhibition at Warsaw, May 3–8. The sheet contains two 45g and two 55g stamps. Size: 133½x102mm. Sold for 3z, a surtax of 1z.

Souvenir Sheet.

Stratosphere Balloon over Mountains
SP4

1938, Sept. 15		Perf. 12½	
B31	SP4 75g dp vio, sheet	90.00	65.00

Issued in advance of a proposed Polish stratosphere flight. Sheets measure 76½x125mm. Sold for 2z, a surtax of 1.25z.

Winterhelp Issue.

SP5

1938-39			
B32	SP5 5g + 5g red org	75	1.25
B33	SP5 25g + 10g dk vio ('39)	1.00	2.00
B34	SP5 55g + 15g brt ultra ('39)	2.25	3.25

Souvenir Sheet.

SP6

1939, Aug. 1			
B35	SP6 Sheet of three	22.50	22.50
a.	25g dk bl gray (Marshal Pilsudski Reviewing Troops)	2.00	1.75
b.	25g dk bl gray (Marshal Pilsudski)	2.00	1.75
c.	25g dk bl gray (Marshal Smigly-Rydz)	2.00	1.75

Issued in sheets measuring 102x124½ mm, in commemoration of the 25th anniversary of the founding of the Polish Legion. The sheets sold for 1.75z, the 1z surtax going to the National Defense fund.

Polish People's Republic.

Polish Warship
SP7

Sailing Vessel SP8   Polish Naval Ensign and Merchant Flag SP9

Crane and Krantor, Danzig
SP10
Typographed.

1945, Apr. 24	Perf. 11	Unwmkd.	
B36	SP7 50g + 2z red	3.50	4.50
B37	SP8 1z + 3z dp bl	3.50	4.50
B38	SP9 2z + 4z dk car	3.50	4.50
B39	SP10 3z + 5z ol grn	3.50	4.50

Issued to commemorate the 25th anniversary of the founding of the Polish Maritime League.

City Hall, Poznan—SP11

1945, June 16		Photogravure	
B40	SP11 1z + 5z grn	17.50	20.00

Postal Workers' Convention, Poznan, June 16, 1945. Exists imperf.

Last Stand at Westerplatte
SP12

1945, Sept. 1			
B41	SP12 1z + 9z stl bl	15.00	17.50

Polish army's last stand at Westerplatte, Sept. 1, 1939. Exists imperf.

"United Industry"—SP13

1945, Nov. 18 Perf. 11. Unwmkd.
B42 SP13 1.50z + 8.50z sl blk 6.00 6.50

Trade Unions Congress, Warsaw, Nov. 18, 1945.

Polish Volunteers in Spain
SP14

1946, Mar. 10			
B43	SP14 3z + 5z red	3.00	3.50

Issued to commemorate the participation of the Jaroslaw Dabrowski Brigade in the Spanish Civil War.

14th Century Piast Eagle and Soldiers SP15   "Death" Spreading Poison Gas over Majdenek Prison Camp SP16

1946, May 2			
B44	SP15 3z + 7z brn	95	75

Silesian uprisings of 1919-21, 1939-45.

1946, Apr. 29			
B45	SP16 3z + 5z Prus grn	2.50	3.50

Issued to recall Maidenek, a concentration camp of World War II near Lublin.

Bydgoszcz (Bromberg) Canal SP17   Map of Polish Coast and Baltic Sea SP18

1946, Apr. 19	Perf. 11.	Unwmkd.	
B46	SP17 3z + 2z ol blk	17.50	20.00

Issued to commemorate the 600th anniversary of Bydgoszcz (Bromberg).

1946, July 21			
B47	SP18 3z + 7z dp bl	75	95

Issued to commemorate the Maritime Holiday of 1946. The surtax was for the Polish Maritime League.

Salute to P. T. T. Casualty and Views of Danzig—SP19

POLAND

1946, Sept. 14

| B48 | SP19 | 3z +12z sl | 1.00 | 1.50 |

Issued in honor of Polish postal employees killed in the German attack on Danzig, September, 1939.

School Children
SP20

Designs: 6z+24z, Courtyard of Jagellon University, Cracow. 11z+19z, Gregor Piramowicz (1735-1801), founder of Education Commission.

1946, Oct. 10 Perf. 11½ Unwmkd.

B49	SP20	3z +22z dk red	35.00	42.50
B49A	SP20	6z +24z dk bl	35.00	42.50
B49B	SP20	11z +19z dk grn	35.00	42.50
c.		Souvenir sheet of 3	425.00	450.00

Polish educational work. Surtax was for International Bureau of Education.
No. B49c contains one each of Nos. B49-B49B with blue marginal inscriptions and control number. Sold for 100z. Size: 128-129x80mm.

Stanislaw Stojalowski, Jakob Bojko. Jan Stapinski and Wincenty Witos
SP21

1946, Dec. 1

B50	SP21	5z +10z bl grn	1.50	1.50
B51	SP21	5z +10z dl bl	1.50	1.50
B52	SP21	5z +10z dk ol	1.50	1.50

Issued to commemorate the 50th anniversary of the Peasant Movement. The surtax was for education and cultural improvement among the Polish peasantry.

No. 391 Surcharged in Red

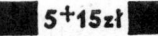

1947, Feb. 4 Perf. 11x10½

| B53 | A127 | 3z +7z pur | 7.00 | 8.00 |

Issued to commemorate the opening of the Polish Parliament, January 19, 1947.

No. 344 Surcharged in Blue

1947, Feb. 21 Perf. 12½

| B54 | A103 | 5z +15z on 25g dp red | 2.50 | 3.00 |

Ski Championship Meet, Zakopane.

Emil Zegadlowicz
SP22

1947, Mar. 1 Photo. Perf. 11

| B55 | SP22 | 5z +15z dl gray grn | 1.00 | 1.00 |

Nurse and War Victims
SP23

Adam Chmielowski
SP24

1947, June 1 Perf. 10½

| B56 | SP23 | 5z +5z ol blk & red | 1.50 | 2.00 |

The surtax was for the Red Cross.

1947, Dec. 21 Perf. 11

| B57 | SP24 | 2z +18z dk vio | 75 | 95 |

Zamkowy Square and Proposed Highway
SP25

1948, Nov. 1

| B58 | SP25 | 15z +5z grn | 35 | 30 |

The surtax was to aid in the reconstruction of Warsaw.

Infant and TB Crosses
SP26

Marceli Nowotko
SP27

1948, Dec. 16 Perf. 11½

Various Portraits of Children

B59	SP26	3z +2z dl grn	2.50	1.75
B60	SP26	5z +5z brn	2.50	1.75
B61	SP26	6z +4z vio	2.00	1.75
B62	SP26	15z +10z car lake	2.00	1.75

Alternate vertical rows of stamps and ten different labels. The surtax was for anti-tuberculosis work among children.

Perf. 12½

1952, Jan. 18 Unwmkd.

| B63 | SP27 | 45g +15g dk car | 35 | 25 |

Issued to commemorate the 10th anniversary of the founding of the Polish Workers Party.

Types of Regular Issues of 1952.

1952, Mar. 8 Perf. 12½x12.

| B64 | A196 | 45g +15g choc | 40 | 15 |

Issued to publicize International Women's Day March 8, 1952.

1952, Mar. 28 Perf. 12½

| B65 | A197 | 45g +15g choc | 45 | 15 |

Issued to commemorate the fifth anniversary of the death of Gen. Karol Swierczewski-Walter.

1952, Apr. 18

| B66 | A198 | 45g +15g red | 75 | 35 |
| B67 | A198 | 1.20z +15g ultra | 75 | 30 |

Issued to commemorate the 60th anniversary of the birth of Pres. Boleslaw Bierut.

Type of Regular Issue of 1951-52
Inscribed "Plan 6," etc.

Design: 45g+15g, Electrical installation.

1952

B68	A193	30g +15g brn red	50	20
B69	A193	45g +15g choc	1.00	35
B69A	A194	1.20z +15g red org	35	25

Issued to publicize Poland's 6-year plan.

Type of Regular Issue of 1952.

1952, May 1

| B70 | A200 | 45g +15g car rose | 20 | 10 |

Issued to publicize Labor Day, May 1, 1952.

Similar to Regular Issue of 1952.
Portraits: 30g+15g, Marja Konopnicka. 45g+15g, Hugo Kollatai.

1952, May Different Frames

| B71 | A201 | 30g +15g bl grn | 50 | 20 |
| B72 | A201 | 45g +15g bl grn | 35 | 20 |

Issue dates: No. B71, May 10. No. B72, May 20.

Leonardo da Vinci
SP28

1952, June 1

| B73 | SP28 | 30g +15g ultra | 1.25 | 75 |

Issued to commemorate the 500th anniversary of the birth of Leonardo da Vinci.

Pres. Bierut and Children—SP29

Photogravure

1952, June 1 Perf. 13½x14

| B74 | SP29 | 45g +15g bl | 1.50 | 75 |

Issued to publicize International Children's Day June 1, 1952.

Swimmers
SP30

Design: 45g+15g, Soccer players and trophy.

1952, June 21 Perf. 13

| B75 | SP30 | 30g +15g bl | 4.50 | 2.00 |
| B76 | SP30 | 45g +15g pur | 2.00 | 50 |

Yachts
SP31

"Dar Pomorza"
SP32

1952, June 28 Engr. Perf. 12½

| B77 | SP31 | 30g +15g dp bl grn | 3.00 | 95 |
| B78 | SP32 | 45g +15g dp ultra | 75 | 35 |

Shipbuilders' Day, 1952.

Workers on Holiday
SP33

Students
SP34

Perf. 12½x12, 12x12½

1952, July 17

| B79 | SP33 | 30g +15g dp grn | 35 | 30 |
| B80 | SP34 | 45g +15g red | 75 | 25 |

Issued to publicize the Youth Festival, 1952.

Constitution Type of Regular Issue.

1952, July 22 Photo. Perf. 11.

| B81 | A208 | 45g +15g lt bl grn & dk brn | 1.25 | 35 |

Proclamation of a new constitution.

Power Plant Type of Regular Issue.

1952, Aug. 7 Engr. Perf. 12½.

| B82 | A209 | 45g +15g red | 75 | 10 |

Ludwik Warynski
SP36

Church of Frydman
SP37

1952, July 31

| B83 | SP36 | 30g +15g dk red | 50 | 20 |
| B84 | SP36 | 45g +15g blk brn | 45 | 35 |

70th anniversary of the birth of Ludwik Warynski, political organizer.

1952, Aug. 18

| B85 | SP37 | 45g +15g vio brn | 1.50 | 50 |

Aviator Watching Glider
SP38

Henryk Sienkiewicz
SP39

Design: 45g+15g, Pilot entering plane.

1952, Aug. 23

| B86 | SP38 | 30g +15g grn | 75 | 50 |
| B87 | SP38 | 45g +15g brn red | 3.00 | 1.50 |

Issued to publicize Aviation Day, Aug. 23, 1952.

1952, Oct. 25

| B88 | SP39 | 45g +15g vio brn | 45 | 30 |

Issued to honor Henryk Sienkiewicz (1846-1916), author of "Quo Vadis" and other novels, Nobel prizewinner (literature, 1905).

POLAND

Revolution Type of Regular Issue.
1952, Nov. 7   Perf. 12x12½
B92	A214	45g +15g red brn	1.00	25

Issued to commemorate the 35th anniversary of the Russian Revolution. Exists imperforate.

Lenin   Miner
SP42   SP43

1952, Nov. 7   Perf. 12½
B93	SP42	30g +15g vio brn	30	20
B94	SP42	45g +15g brn	85	50
a.	"LENIN" omitted		30.00	

Issued to publicize the month of Polish-Soviet friendship, November 1952.

1952, Dec. 4
B95	SP43	45g +15g blk brn	25	15
B96	SP43	1.20z +15g brn	60	30

Miners' Day, December 4, 1952.

Henryk   Truck Factory,
Wieniawski   Lublin
and Violin   SP45
SP44

1952, Dec. 5   Photogravure
B97	SP44	30g +15g dk grn	75	50
B98	SP44	45g +15g pur	3.50	1.00

Issued to honor Henryk Wieniawski and to publicize the second International Violin Competition.

Type of Regular Issue of 1952.
1952, Dec. 12   Engraved
B99	A215	45g +15g dp grn	35	15

1953, Feb. 20
B100	SP45	30g +15g dp bl	25	25
B101	SP45	60g +20g vio brn	50	10

Souvenir Sheets

Town Hall in Poznan
SP46

Photogravure and Lithographed
1955, July 7   Imperf.
B102	SP46	2z pck grn & ol grn	4.00	2.50
B103	SP46	3z car rose & ol blk	22.50	15.00

Issued to commemorate the 6th Polish Philatelic Exhibition in Poznan. Sheets measure 50x69mm. They sold for 3z and 4.50z respectively.

"Peace" (POKOJ) and
Warsaw Mermaid
SP47

Design: 1z, Pansies (A266) and inscription on map of Europe, Africa and Asia.

1955, Aug. 3
B104	SP47	1z bis, rose vio & yel	3.00	2.00
B105	SP47	2z ol gray, ultra & lt bl	15.00	10.00

Issued to commemorate the International Philatelic Exhibition in Warsaw, August 1-14, 1955. Sheets measure 61x83mm. They sold for 2z and 3z respectively.

Souvenir Sheet.

Chopin and Liszt
SP48
Photogravure

1956, Oct. 25   Imperf.
B106	SP48	4z dk bl grn	30.00	20.00

No. B106 measures 55x76mm. with marginal inscription in dark blue green and violet brown. Issued for the Day of the Stamp and to emphasize Polish-Hungarian friendship. The sheet sold for 6z.

Souvenir Sheet

Stamp of 1860
SP49
Lithographed

1960, Sept. 4   Perf. 11   Wmk. 326
B107	SP49	Sheet of four	50.00	45.00
a.	10z +10z bl, red & blk		10.00	10.00

Issued to commemorate the International Philatelic Exhibition "POLSKA 60" Warsaw, Sept. 3–11. No. B107 contains four stamps with black marginal inscription. Size: 78½x106mm. Sold only with 5z ticket to exhibition.

Type of Space Issue, 1964.
Design: 6.50z+2z, Yuri A. Gagarin in space capsule.

Perf. 12½x12
1964, Dec. 30   Unwmkd.
B108	A432	6.50z +2z Prus grn & multi	2.25	95

Issued to publicize space research.

Miniature Sheet

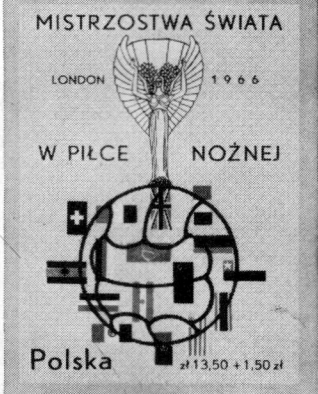

Jules Rimet Cup and Flags of
Participating Countries
SP50

1966, May 9   Litho.   Imperf.
B109	SP50	13.50z +1.50z gray & multi	3.50	2.00

Issued to publicize the World Cup Soccer Championship, Wembley, England, July 11–30. Size: 61x81mm.

Helpful notes abound in the "Information for Collectors" section at the front of this volume.

Souvenir Sheet

J. Kusocinski, Olympic Winner
10,000-Meter Race, 1932
SP51

1967, May 24   Litho.   Imperf.
B110	SP51	10z +5z multi	3.00	1.50

Issued to publicize the 19th Olympic Games, Mexico City, 1968. Simulated perforations. Size: 64x85mm.

Flower Type of Regular Issue
Flowers: 4z+2z, Abutilon. 8z+4z, Rosa polyantha hybr.

1968, May 15   Litho.   Perf. 11½
B111	A492	4z +2z vio & multi	1.00	50
B112	A492	8z +4z lt vio & multi	2.00	95

Olympic Type of Regular Issue, 1968
Design: 10z+5z, Runner with Olympic torch and Chin cultic carved stone disc showing Mayan ball player and game's scoreboard.

1968, Sept. 2   Litho.   Perf. 11½
Size: 56x45mm.
B113	A497	10z +5z multi	2.75	1.50

Issued to publicize the 19th Olympic Games, Mexico City, Oct. 12–27. The surtax was for the Polish Olympic Committee.

Olympic Type of Regular Issue, 1969
Designs (Olympic Rings and): 2.50z+50g, Women's discus. 3.40z+1z, Running. 4z+1.50z, Boxing. 7z+2z, Fencing.

1969, Apr. 25   Litho.   Perf. 11½x11
B114	A505	2.50z +50g multi	50	15
B115	A505	3.40z +1z multi	60	25
B116	A505	4z +1.50z multi	90	35
B117	A505	7z +2z multi	1.45	65

See note after No. 1649.

Folk Art Type of Regular Issue
Designs: 5.50z+1.50z, Choir. 7z+1.50z, Organ grinder.

1969, Dec. 19   Litho.   Perf. 11½x11
Size: 24x36mm.
B118	A520	5.50z +1.50z multi	1.00	45
B119	A520	7z +1.50z multi	1.35	60

Souvenir Sheet
Sports Type of Regular Issue
Design: 10z+5z, "Horse of Glory," by Z. Kaminski.

1970, June 16   Photo.   Imperf.
B120	A532	10z +5z multi	2.75	1.50

The surtax was for the Polish Olympic Committee. No. B120 contains one imperf. stamp with simulated perforations and the Olympic Laurel badge of the Polish Olympic Committee in green bordered margin. Size: 70x101mm.

POLAND

Souvenir Sheet
Tapestry Type of Regular Issue
Design: 7z+3z, Satyrs holding monogram of King Sigismund Augustus.
1970, Dec. 23   Photo.   Imperf.
B121 A541 7z + 3c multi   1.75   1.00
B121 contains one stamp, gray margin and black inscription. Size: 62x89mm.

Type of Regular Issue
Design: 8.50z+4z, Virgin Mary, 15th century stained glass window.
1971, Sept. 15   Perf. 11½x11
B122 A555 8.50z + 4z multi   1.50   85

Painting Type of Regular Issue
Design: 7z+1z, Nude, by Wojciech Weiss (1875–1950).
1971, Oct. 9   Lithographed
B123 A556 7z + 1z multi   1.25   55
Stamp Day 1971.

Souvenir Sheet
Olympic Type of Regular Issue
Design: 10z+5z, Slalom and Sapporo '72 emblem (vert.).
1972, Jan. 12   Photo.   Imperf.
B124 A564 10z + 5z multi   2.50   1.50
11th Winter Olympic Games, Sapporo, Japan, Feb. 3–13. No. B124 contains one stamp with simulated perforations (27x52mm.). Mountain design in margin with silver inscription and border. Size of sheet: 84x68½mm.

Souvenir Sheet
Olympic Type of Regular Issue
Design: 10z+5z, Archery (like 30g).
1972, May 20   Photo.   Perf. 11½x11
B125 A568 10z + 5z multi   2.50   1.50
20th Olympic Games, Munich, Aug. 26–Sept. 10. No. B125 contains one stamp. Black inscription, multicolored Olympic rings and "Motion" symbol in margin. Size: 67x79mm.

Painting Type of Regular Issue, 1972.
Design: 8.50z+4z, Portrait of a Young Lady, by Jacek Malczewski (horiz.).
1972, Sept. 28   Photo.   Perf. 11x10½
B126 A576 8.50z + 4z multi   2.50   1.00
Stamp Day 1972.

Souvenir Sheet

Copernicus
SP52
Engraved and Photogravure
1972, Sept. 28   Perf. 11½
B127 SP52 10z + 5z vio bl, gray & car   2.75   1.50
500th anniversary of the birth of Nicolaus Copernicus (1473–1543), astronomer. No. B127 shows the Ptolemaic and Copernican concepts of solar system by L'Harmonica Microcosmica, by Cellarius, 1660. Marginal inscription "EXPOSITION PHILATELIQUE MONDIALE POLSKA 73 Poznan." Size: 62x100mm.

Souvenir Sheet

Poznan, 1740, by F. B. Werner
SP53
1973, Aug. 19   Imperf.
B128 SP53 10z + 5z ol & dk brn   3.00   1.75
a.   10z + 5z pale lil & dk brn   9.00   8.00

POLSKA 73 International Philatelic Exhibition, Poznan, Aug. 19–Sept. 2. No. B128 contains one stamp with simulated perforations. Brown marginal inscription and POLSKA 73 emblem with Copernicus portrait in margin. Size: 90x66mm.
No. B128a was sold only in combination with an entrance ticket.

Copernicus, by Marcello Baciarelli
SP54
1973, Sept. 27   Photo.   Perf. 11x11½
B129 SP54 4z + 2z multi   90   50
Stamp Day. The surtax was for the reconstruction of the Royal Castle in Warsaw.

Souvenir Sheet

Montreal Olympic Games Emblem—SP55
Photogravure and Engraved
1975, Mar. 8   Perf. 12
B130 SP55 10z + 5z sil & grn   2.50   1.75
21st Olympic Games, Montreal, July 17–Aug. 8, 1976. Size of No. B130: 75x60mm.

Dunikowski Type of 1975
Design: 8z+4z, Mother and Child, from Silesian Insurrectionist Monument, by Dunikowski.
1975, Oct. 9   Photo.   Perf. 11½x11
B131 A644 8z + 4z multi   2.00   95
Stamp Day 1975, and for the birth centenary of Xawery Dunikowski (1875–1964), sculptor.

Souvenir Sheet

Volleyball—SP56
Engraved and Photogravure
1976, June 30   Perf. 11½
B132 SP56 10z + 5z blk & car   2.00   1.25
21st Olympic Games, Montreal, Canada, July 17–Aug. 1. No. B132 contains one perf. 11½ stamp and is perf. 11½ all around. Black marginal design. Size: 75x93mm.

Corinthian Art Type 1976
Design: 8z+4z, Winged Sphinx (vert.).
1976, Oct. 30   Photo.   Perf. 11½x11
B133 A664 8z + 4z multi   2.00   95
Stamp Day 1976.

Souvenir Sheet

Stoning of St. Stephen, by Rubens—SP57
1977, Apr. 30   Engr.   Perf. 12x11½
B134 SP57 8z + 4z sep   1.75   1.25
Peter Paul Rubens (1577–1640), Flemish painter, 400th birth anniversary. No. B134 is arranged similar to type SP55 but with sheet margins perforated all around and stamp on top; orange and sepia commemorative inscription and Rubens' signature. Overall size: 75x60mm.

Souvenir Sheet

Kazimierz Gzowski
SP58
1978, June 6   Photo.   Perf. 11½x11
B135 SP58 8.40z + 4z multi   1.50   1.00
CAPEX, '78 Canadian International Philatelic Exhibition, Toronto, Ont., June 9–18. No. B135 has multicolored margin showing Niagara Falls. Size: 69x78mm.
K. S. Gzowski (1813–1898), Polish engineer and lawyer living in Canada, built International Bridge over Niagara River.

Souvenir Sheet

Olympic Rings—SP59
1979, May 19   Engr.   Imperf.
B136 SP59 10z + 5z blk   2.00   1.25
1980 Olympic Games. No. B136 has black and dark red margin. Size: 103x63 mm.

Monument Type of 1979
Souvenir Sheet
1979, Sept. 1   Photo.   Imperf.
B137 A731 10z + 5z multi   2.00   1.25
40th anniversary of Polish postal workers' resistance to Nazi invaders. No. B137 has multicolored margin showing military medal. Size: 79x70mm. Surtax was for monument.

Olympic Type of 1980
Souvenir Sheet
1980, Mar. 31   Photo.   Perf. 11x11½
B138 A74210.50z + 5z Kayak   2.00   1.25
22nd Summer Olympic Games, Moscow, July 19–Aug. 3. No. B138 contains one stamp (42x30mm.); multicolored margin shows kayak race and Olympic emblems. Size: 87x69½mm.

Intercosmos Cooperative Space Program—SP60
1980, Apr. 12   Perf. 11½x11
B139 SP60 6.90z + 3z multi   2.00   1.00
No. B139 has multicolored margin showing cosmonauts and Intercosmos emblem. Size: 64x79mm.

1970 Uprising Memorial—SP61
Designs: 2.50z + 1z, Triple Crucifix, Gdansk (27x46mm.). 6.50z + 1z, Monument, Gdynia.
1981, Dec. 16   Photo.   Perf. 11½x12
B140 SP61 2.50 + 1z blk & red   1.25   75
B141 SP61 6.50 + 1z blk & lil   2.50   1.50

POLAND

AIR POST STAMPS.

Biplane
AP1

Perf. 12½

		1925, Sept. 10 Typo.	Unwmkd.	
C1	AP1	1g lt bl	75	1.25
C2	AP1	2g orange	75	1.25
C3	AP1	3g yel brn	75	1.25
C4	AP1	5g dk brn	75	1.25
C5	AP1	10g dk grn	2.00	85
C6	AP1	15g red vio	3.00	1.50
C7	AP1	20g ol grn	10.00	3.50
C8	AP1	30g dl rose	7.00	3.50
C9	AP1	45g dk vio	10.00	5.00
		Nos. C1-C9 (9)	35.00	19.35

Capt. Franciszek Zwirko
and Stanislaus Wigura
AP2

Perf. 11½ to 12½ and Compound.

		1933, Apr. 15 Engraved Wmk. 234		
C10	AP2	30g gray grn	15.00	1.25

Issued in commemoration of the winning of the circuit of Europe flight by two Polish aviators in 1932. The stamp was available for both air mail and ordinary postage.

Nos. C7 and C10 Overprinted in Red

		1934, Aug. 28 Perf. 12½ Unwmkd.		
C11	AP1	20g ol grn	18.00	9.00

Perf. 11½ Wmk. 234

| C12 | AP2 | 30g gray grn | 8.00 | 2.75 |

Polish People's Republic

Douglas Plane over Ruins
of Warsaw
AP3

Photogravure.

		1946, Mar. 5 Perf. 11 Unwmkd.		
C13	AP3	5z grnsh blk	50	15
a.		Without control no.	5.00	50
C14	AP3	10z dk vio	50	15
C15	AP3	15z blue	1.50	35
C16	AP3	20z rose brn	1.00	15
C17	AP3	25z dk bl grn	2.00	50
C18	AP3	30z red	3.00	75
		Nos. C13-C18 (6)	8.50	2.05

The 10z, 20z and 30z were issued only with control number in lower right stamp margin. The 15z and 25z exist only without number. The 5z comes both ways. Nos. C13–C18 exist imperforate.

Nos. 345, 344 and 344a Surcharged in Red or Black:

ZŁ 40 ZŁ
LOTNICZA
a
LOTNICZA
ZŁ 50 ZŁ
b

		1947, Sept. 10 Perf. 12½		
C19	A104(a)	40z on 50g dk sl grn (R)	2.50	1.25
C20	A103(b)	50z on 25g dl red	3.00	2.50
a.		50z on 25g dp red	4.00	2.50

Centaur
AP4

1948 Perf. 11.

C21	AP4	15z dk vio	2.50	30
C22	AP4	25z dp bl	1.25	20
C23	AP4	30z brown	95	35
C24	AP4	50z dk grn	95	30
C25	AP4	75z gray blk	1.75	60
C26	AP4	100z red org	1.50	40
		Nos. C21-C26 (6)	8.90	2.15

Pres. F. D. Roosevelt
AP5

Airplane Mechanic and Propeller
AP5a

Designs: 100z, Casimir Pulaski. 120z, Tadeusz Kosciusko.

Granite Paper

		1948, Dec. 30 Photo. Perf. 11½		
C26A	AP5	80z bl blk	20.00	35.00
C26B	AP5	100z purple	22.50	25.00
C26C	AP5	120z dp bl	22.50	25.00
d.		Souvenir sheet of 3	250.00	275.00

No. C26d contains stamps similar to Nos. C26A–C26C with colors changed: 80z ultramarine, 100z carmine rose, 120z dark green. Border and marginal inscription in dark green and carmine rose. Control number in pale green. Sold for 500z. Size: 159x94mm.

		1950, Feb. 6 Engr. Perf. 12½		
C27	AP5a	500z rose lake	5.00	4.00

Seaport
AP6

Designs: 90g, Mechanized farm. 1.40z. Warsaw. 5z, Steel mill.

1952, Apr. 10 Perf. 12x12½

C28	AP6	55g int bl	20	10
C29	AP6	90g dl grn	35	10
C30	AP6	1.40z vio brn	50	15
C31	AP6	5z gray blk	1.50	50

Nos. C28–C31 exist imperf. Price $8.

Congress Badge
AP7

1953, Aug. 23 Photo. Imperf.

| C32 | AP7 | 55g brn lil | 1.50 | 30 |
| C33 | AP7 | 75g brn org | 1.00 | 90 |

Issued to publicize the third World Congress of Students, Warsaw 1953.

Souvenir Sheet

AP8

1954, May 23 Engr. Perf. 12x12½

| C34 | AP8 | 5z gray grn, sheet | 35.00 | 32.50 |

Issued in sheets measuring 57x76mm. on the occasion of the third congress of the Polish Philatelic Association, Warsaw, 1954. Sold for 7.50 zlotys. A similar sheet, imperf. and in dark blue, was issued but had no postal validity.

Paczkow Castle, Luban
AP9

Plane over "Peace" Steelworks
AP10

Designs: 80g, Kazimierz, Dolny. 1.15z, Wawel castle, Cracow. 1.50z, City Hall, Wroclaw. 1.55z, Laziersky Square, Warsaw. 1.95z, Cracow gate, Lublin.

1954, July 9 Perf. 12½

C35	AP9	60g dk gray grn	25	15
C36	AP9	80g red	20	10
C37	AP9	1.15z black	1.50	50
C38	AP9	1.50z rose lake	60	25
C39	AP9	1.55z dp gray bl	60	15
C40	AP9	1.95z chocolate	1.25	40
		Nos. C35-C40 (6)	4.40	1.55

Unwmkd.; Wmk. 326 ('58 Values)
1957-58 Engr. & Photo. Perf. 12½

Plane over: 1.50z, Castle Square, Warsaw. 3.40z, Old Market, Cracow. 3.90z, King Boleslaw Chrobry Wall, Szczecin. 4z, Karkonosze mountains. 5z, Danzig. 10z, Ruins of Liwa Castle. 15z, Old City, Lublin. 20z, Kasprowy Wierch Peak and cable car. 30z, Porabka dam. 50z. M. S. Batory and Gdynia harbor.

C41	AP10	90g blk & pink	15	8
C42	AP10	1.50z brn & sal	20	6
C43	AP10	3.40z sep & buff	40	10
C44	AP10	3.90z dk brn & cit	75	20
C45	AP10	4z ind & lt grn	35	8
C46	AP10	5z mar & gray ('58)	60	15
C47	AP10	10z sep & grn ('58)	1.25	25
C48	AP10	15z vio bl & pale bl	1.50	50
C49	AP10	20z vio blk & lem ('58)	3.00	70
C50	AP10	30z ol gray & bis ('58)	4.00	1.50
C51	AP10	50z dk bl & gray ('58)	7.25	3.00
		Nos. C41-C51 (11)	19.45	6.92

1959, May 23 Litho. Wmk. 326

| C52 | AP10 | 10z sepia | 2.00 | 1.50 |
| a. | | With 5z label | 2.75 | 2.50 |

65th anniv. of the Polish Philatelic Society. Sheet of 6 stamps and 2 each of 3 different labels. Each label carries an added charge of 5z for a fund to build a Society clubhouse in Warsaw.

Jantar Glider
AP11

Designs: 10z, Mi6 transport helicopter. 20z, PZL-106 Kruk, crop spraying plane. 50z, Plane over Warsaw Castle.

Engraved
1976-78 Perf. 11½ Unwmkd.

C53	AP11	5z bl grn	50	30
C54	AP11	10z dk brn	1.00	60
C55	AP11	20z grnsh blk	2.00	1.20
C56	AP11	50z claret	5.00	3.00

Contemporary aviation.
Issue dates: 5z, Mar. 27, 1976. 20z, Feb. 15, 1977. 50z, Feb. 2, 1978.

AIR POST SEMI-POSTAL STAMP
Polish People's Republic

Wing of Jet Plane and Letter
SPAP1

Photogravure.
1957, Mar. 28 Perf. 11½ Unwmkd.

| CB1 | SPAP1 | 4z + 2z bl | 4.00 | 4.00 |
| | | Souv. sheet | 7.50 | 4.00 |

7th Polish National Philatelic Exhibition, Warsaw. Sheet of 12 with 4 diagonally arranged gray labels.

No. CB1a contains one 4z+2z ultramarine, type SPAP1, imperf., with marginal inscriptions in bright pink. Size: 56x75mm.

POSTAGE DUE STAMPS.
Cracow Issues.

Postage Due Stamps of Austria, 1916, Overprinted in Black or Red

POCZTA ◇ POLSKA

1919, Jan. 10 Perf. 12½ Unwmkd.

J1	D4	5h rose red	10.00	9.00
J2	D4	10h rose red	2,750.	3,250.
J3	D4	15h rose red	5.00	4.00
a.		Invtd. ovpt.		200.00
J4	D4	20h rose red	675.00	675.00
J5	D4	25h rose red	25.00	20.00
J6	D4	30h rose red	1,000.	925.00
J7	D4	40h rose red	350.00	300.00
J8	D5	1k ultra (R)	3,500.	3,500.

POLAND

J9	D5	5k ultra (R)	3,500.	3,500.
J10	D5	10k ultra (R)	10,000.	10,000.
a.		Blk. ovpt.	15,000.	15,000.

The overprint on Nos. J8 to J10 is slightly larger than illustration and has different ornament between lines of type.

D6
Type of Austria, 1916-18,
Surcharged in Black.
1919, Jan. 10

J11	D6	15h on 36h vio	400.00	300.00
J12	D6	50h on 42h choc	40.00	40.00
a.		Double surch.	400.00	400.00

Counterfeits exist of Nos. J1 to J12.

Regular Issues.

Numerals of Value
D7   D8
1919   Typographed.   Perf. 11½.

J13	D7	2(f) red org	15	10
J14	D7	4(f) red org	10	10
J15	D7	5(f) red org	10	10
J16	D7	10(f) red org	10	10
J17	D7	20(f) red org	10	10
J18	D7	30(f) red org	10	10
J19	D7	50(f) red org	10	10
J20	D7	100(f) red org	50	50
J21	D7	500(f) red org	1.75	1.50
J22	D7	2(h) dk bl	15	10
J23	D7	4(h) dk bl	15	15
J24	D7	5(h) dk bl	15	15
J25	D7	10(h) dk bl	15	15
J26	D7	20(h) dk bl	15	10
J27	D7	30(h) dk bl	15	10
J28	D7	50(h) dk bl	15	10
J29	D7	100(h) dk bl	35	25
J30	D7	500(h) dk bl	1.25	1.00
		Nos. J13-J30 (18)	5.65	4.65

Thin Laid Paper.
1920   Perf. 9, 10, 11½

J31	D7	20(f) dk bl	50	50
J32	D7	100(f) dk bl	25	25
J33	D7	200(f) dk bl	40	50
J34	D7	500(f) dk bl	25	25

6 Mk.
Regular Issue
of 1919
Surcharged

dopłata

1921, Jan. 25   Wove Paper   Imperf.

J35	A9	6m on 15h brn	50	50
J36	A9	6m on 25h car	50	50
J37	A9	20m on 10h lake	1.25	1.25
J38	A9	20m on 50h ind	1.50	1.50
J39	A9	35m on 70h dp bl	13.50	13.50
		Nos. J35-J39 (5)	17.25	17.25

Perf. 9 to 14½ and Compound
1921-22
Typographed
Thin Laid or Wove Paper.
Size: 17 x 22 mm.

J40	D8	1m indigo	20	15
J41	D8	2m indigo	20	15
J42	D8	4m indigo	20	15
J43	D8	6m indigo	20	15
J44	D8	8m indigo	20	15
J45	D8	20m indigo	20	15
J46	D8	50m indigo	20	15
J47	D8	100m indigo	35	25
		Nos. J40-J47 (8)	1.75	1.30

Nos. J44-J45, J41 Surcharged
Perf. 9 to 14½ and Compound.
1923, Nov.

J48	D8	10,000(m) on 8m ind	25	10
J49	D8	20,000(m) on 20m ind	25	20
J50	D8	50,000(m) on 2m ind	1.50	1.00

Type of 1921-22 Issue.
1923   Typographed.   Perf. 12½.
Size: 19x24mm.

J51	D8	50m indigo	15	10
J52	D8	100m indigo	15	10
J53	D8	200m indigo	15	10
J54	D8	500m indigo	15	10
J55	D8	1000m indigo	15	10
J56	D8	2000m indigo	15	10
J57	D8	10,000m indigo	10	10
J58	D8	20,000m indigo	10	10
J59	D8	30,000m indigo	10	10
J60	D8	50,000m indigo	20	15
J61	D8	100,000m indigo	25	15
J62	D8	200,000m indigo	30	10
J63	D8	300,000m indigo	50	25
J64	D8	500,000m indigo	50	15
J65	D8	1,000,000m indigo	1.00	50
J66	D8	2,000,000m indigo	1.50	50
J67	D8	3,000,000m indigo	3.00	75
		Nos. J51-J67 (17)	8.45	3.40

D9   D10
Perf. 10 to 13½ and Compound.
1924   Size: 20x25½mm.

J68	D9	1g brown	35	20
J69	D9	2g brown	35	20
J70	D9	4g brown	35	20
J71	D9	6g brown	75	20
J72	D9	10g brown	4.00	30
J73	D9	15g brown	3.25	35
J74	D9	20g brown	8.00	35
J75	D9	25g brown	6.50	35
J76	D9	30g brown	1.50	35
J77	D9	40g brown	1.50	35
J78	D9	50g brown	1.50	35
J79	D9	1z brown	1.25	50
J80	D9	2z brown	1.25	50
J81	D9	3z brown	2.50	2.00
J82	D9	5z brown	2.50	2.00
		Nos. J68-J82 (15)	35.55	6.85

Nos. J68-J69 and J72-J75 exist measuring 19½x24½mm.

1930, July   Perf. 12½.

J83	D10	5g ol brn	1.00	35

Postage Due
Stamps of 1924
Surcharged

50 groszy

Perf. 10 to 13½ and Compound.
1934-38

J84	D9	10g on 2z brn ('38)	50	30
J85	D9	15g on 2z brn	50	30
J86	D9	20g on 1z brn	50	30
J87	D9	20g on 5z brn	2.50	60
J88	D9	25g on 40g brn	1.50	60
J89	D9	30g on 40g brn	1.00	60
J90	D9	50g on 40g brn	1.00	75
J91	D9	50g on 3z brn ('35)	2.00	1.00
		Nos. J84-J91 (8)	9.50	4.45

No. 255a
Surcharged
in Red
or Indigo

1934-36   Laid Paper

J92	A50	10g on 1z blk, cr (R) ('36)	1.00	25
a.		Vertically laid paper (No. 255)	35.00	25.00
J93	A50	20g on 1z blk, cr (R) ('36)	3.00	95
J94	A50	25g on 1z blk, cr (I)	1.00	35
a.		Vertically laid paper (No. 255)	32.50	25.00

D11
Typographed
1939, Nov. 25   Perf. 12½x12

J95	D11	5g dk bl grn	15	10
J96	D11	10g dk bl grn	15	10
J97	D11	15g dk bl grn	15	10
J98	D11	20g dk bl grn	75	25
J99	D11	25g dk bl grn	25	20
J100	D11	30g dk bl grn	50	25
J101	D11	50g dk bl grn	1.00	1.50
J102	D11	1z dk bl grn	3.00	2.00
		Nos. J95-J102 (8)	5.95	4.50

Polish People's Republic.

Post Horn with   Polish
Thunderbolts   Eagle
D12   D13
Perf. 11x10½
1945, May 20   Litho.   Unwmkd.
Size: 25½x19mm.

J103	D12	1z org brn	15	10
J104	D12	2z org brn	20	15
J105	D12	3z org brn	25	20
J106	D12	5z org brn	35	30

Type of 1945
Perf. 11, 11½ (P) or Imperf. (I)
1946-49   Photogravure
Size: 29x21½mm.

J106A	D12	1z org brn (P) ('49)	20	15
J107	D12	2z org brn (P,I)	20	15
J108	D12	3z org brn (P,I)	20	15
J109	D12	5z org brn (I)	20	15
J110	D12	6z org brn (I)	20	15
J111	D12	10z org brn (I)	25	20
J112	D12	15z org brn (P,I)	35	30
J113	D12	25z org brn (P,I)	50	45
J114	D12	100z brn (P) ('49)	1.00	50
J115	D12	150z brn (P) ('49)	1.75	50
		Nos. J106A-J115 (10)	4.85	2.70

1950   Engraved.   Perf. 12x12½.

J116	D13	5z red brn	10	8
J117	D13	10z red brn	10	8
J118	D13	15z red brn	15	10
J119	D13	20z red brn	25	10
J120	D13	25z red brn	25	15
J121	D13	50z red brn	75	20
J122	D13	100z red brn	1.25	75
		Nos. J116-J122 (7)	2.90	1.86

1951-52

J123	D13	5g red brn	10	5
J124	D13	10g red brn	10	5
J125	D13	15g red brn	10	5
J126	D13	20g red brn	15	10
J127	D13	25g red brn	20	10
J128	D13	30g red brn	25	15
J129	D13	50g red brn	30	20
J130	D13	60g red brn	35	20
J131	D13	90g red brn	45	25
J132	D13	1z red brn	70	45
J133	D13	2z red brn	1.25	75
J134	D13	5z brn vio	3.00	1.75
		Nos. J123-J134 (12)	6.95	4.10

1953, Apr.   Photogravure
Without imprint

J135	D13	5g red brn	15	8
J136	D13	10g red brn	15	8
J137	D13	15g red brn	15	8
J138	D13	20g red brn	15	8
J139	D13	25g red brn	20	10
J140	D13	30g red brn	30	15
J141	D13	50g red brn	50	25
J142	D13	60g red brn	60	30
J143	D13	90g red brn	75	40
J144	D13	1z red brn	95	45
J145	D13	2z red brn	1.75	95
		Nos. J135-J145 (11)	5.65	2.92

OFFICIAL STAMPS.

O1
Perf. 10, 11½, 10x11½, 11½x10.
1920, Feb. 1   Litho.   Unwmkd.

O1	O1	3(f) vermilion	10	15
O2	O1	5(f) vermilion	20	25
O3	O1	10(f) vermilion	20	25
O4	O1	15(f) vermilion	20	25
O5	O1	25(f) vermilion	20	25
O6	O1	50(f) vermilion	20	25
O7	O1	100(f) vermilion	30	35
O8	O1	150(f) vermilion	40	50
O9	O1	200(f) vermilion	40	50
O10	O1	300(f) vermilion	40	50
O11	O1	600(f) vermilion	75	50
		Nos. O1-O11 (11)	3.35	3.75

Numerals Larger.
Stars inclined outward.
Thin Laid Paper.
1920, Nov. 20   Perf. 11½.

O12	O1	5(f) red	10	20
O13	O1	10(f) red	40	50
O14	O1	15(f) red	25	35
O15	O1	25(f) red	75	1.00
O16	O1	50(f) red	50	75
		Nos. O12-O16 (5)	2.00	2.80

               Polish Eagle
O3   O4
Wmkd. Multiple Post Horns. (234)
1933, Aug. 1 Typo. Perf. 12x12½.

O17	O3	(30g) vio (Zwyczajna)	1.25	15
O18	O3	(80g) red (Polecona)	3.00	35

1935, Apr. 1

O19	O4	(25g) bl vio (Zwyczajna)	15	10
O20	O4	(55g) car (Polecona)	30	15

Stamps inscribed "Zwyczajna" or "Zwykła" were for ordinary official mail. Those with "Polecona" were for registered official mail.

Polish People's Republic

Polish Eagle
O5

POLAND

Perf. 11, 14
1945, July 1 Photo. Unwmkd.
O21	O5	(5z) bl vio (*Zwykla*)		50	10
a.		Imperf.		1.50	1.50
O22	O5	(10z) red (*Polecona*)		1.00	25
a.		Imperf.		2.50	2.00

Control number at bottom right: M-01705 on No. O21; M-01706 on No. O22.

Type of 1945 Redrawn
1946, July 31
O23	O5	(5z) dl bl vio (*Zwykla*)	30	10
O24	O5	(10z) dl rose red (*Polecona*)	50	15

The redrawn stamps appear blurred and the eagle contains fewer lines of shading. Control number at bottom right: M-01709 on Nos. O23–O26.

Redrawn Type of 1946.
1946, July 31 Imperf.
O25	O5	(60g) dl bl vio (*Zwykla*)	50	15
O26	O5	(1.55z) dl rose red (*Polecona*)	50	25

Type of 1945, 2nd Redrawing
No Control Number at Lower Right
Perf. 11, 11½, 11x12½
1952 Unwmkd.
O27	O5	(60g) bl (*Zwykla*)	30	15
O28	O5	(1.55z) red (*Polecona*)	50	25

Redrawn Type of 1952.
1954 Perf. 13x11, 11½, 14
O29	O5	(60g) sl gray (*Zwykla*)	1.75	75

O6

Perf. 11x11½, 12x12½
1954, Aug. 15 Engraved
O30	O6	(60g) dk bl (*Zwykla*)	35	15
O31	O6	(1.55z) red (*Polecona*)	60	30

Polish People's Republic, 10th anniversary.

NEWSPAPER STAMPS.
Austrian Newspaper Stamps of 1916 Overprinted **POCZTA POLSKA**

1919, Jan. 10 Imperf. Unwmkd.
P1	N9	2h brown	12.00	10.00
P2	N9	4h green	3.50	2.50
P3	N9	6h dk bl	3.50	2.50
P4	N9	10h orange	40.00	37.50
P5	N9	30h claret	7.00	6.00
		Nos. P1-P5 (5)	66.00	58.50

OCCUPATION STAMPS.
Issued under German Occupation.
German Stamps of 1905 Overprinted

Perf. 14, 14½
1915, May 12 Wmk. 125
N1	A16	3pf brown	75	50
N2	A16	5pf green	2.00	50
N3	A16	10pf carmine	2.00	50
N4	A16	20pf ultra	3.00	75
N5	A16	40pf lake & blk	12.00	6.00
		Nos. N1-N5 (5)	19.75	8.25

German Stamps of 1905–17 Overprinted **Gen.-Gouv. Warschau**

1916–17
N6	A22	2½pf gray	50	35
N7	A16	3pf brown	1.00	75
N8	A16	5pf green	1.00	50
N9	A22	7½pf orange	75	50
N10	A16	10pf carmine	1.00	35
N11	A22	15pf yel brn	6.00	3.00
N12	A22	15pf dk vio ('17)	50	50
N13	A16	20pf ultra	6.00	3.00
N14	A16	30pf org & blk, *buff*	7.50	3.75
N15	A16	40pf lake & blk	2.50	35
N16	A16	60pf magenta	3.00	35
		Nos. N6-N16 (11)	25.75	11.15

6 Groschen 6

German Stamps of 1934 Surcharged in Black

Deutsche Post OSTEN

1939, Dec. 1 Perf. 14 Wmk. 237
N17	A64	6g on 3(pf) bis	50	50
N18	A64	8g on 4(pf) dl bl	50	60
N19	A64	12g on 6(pf) dk grn	50	50
N20	A64	16g on 8(pf) ver	1.25	1.50
N21	A64	20g on 10(pf) choc	50	50
N22	A64	24g on 12(pf) dp car	50	40
N23	A64	30g on 15(pf) mar	1.00	1.25
N24	A64	40g on 20(pf) brt bl	85	65
N25	A64	50g on 25(pf) ultra	85	1.00
N26	A64	60g on 30(pf) ol grn	85	65
N27	A64	80g on 40(pf) red vio	1.25	1.10
N28	A64	1z on 50(pf) dk grn & blk	3.00	2.00
N29	A64	2z on 100(pf) org & blk	6.00	4.50
		Nos. N17-N29 (13)	17.55	15.15

Stamps of Poland 1937, Surcharged in Black or Brown

1940 Perf. 12½, 12½x13 Unwmkd.
N30	A80	24g on 25g sl grn	2.50	2.50
N31	A81	40g on 30g rose vio	85	85
N32	A80	50g on 55g bl	75	75

Similar Surcharge on Stamps of 1938-39.
N33	A83	2g on 5g red org	40	55
N34	A83	4(g) on 5g red org	40	55
N35	A83	6(g) on 10g grn	40	55
N36	A83	8(g) on 10g grn (Br)	50	55
N37	A83	10(g) on 10g grn	40	55
N38	A83	12(g) on 15g redsh brn (On No. 339)	50	55
N39	A83	16(g) on 15g redsh brn (On No. 339)	50	55
N40	A83	24g on 25g dl vio	40	55
N41	A83	30(g) on 30g rose red	75	75
N42	A83	50(g) on 50g brt red vio	75	75
N43	A83	60(g) on 55g ultra	12.50	12.50
N44	A83	80(g) on 75g dl grn	12.50	12.50
N45	A83	1z on 1z org	12.50	12.50
N46	A83	2z on 2z car rose	7.00	7.50
N47	A95	3z on 3z gray blk	7.00	7.50

Similar Surcharge on Semi-Postal Stamps of 1939.
N48	SP5	30g on 5g + 5g red org	75	85
N49	SP5	40g on 25g + 10g dk vio	75	85

N50	SP5	1z on 55g + 15g brt ultra	10.00	10.00

Similar Surcharge on Postage Due Stamps of 1939.
Perf. 12½ x 12.
N51	D11	50(g) on 20g dk bl grn	1.50	1.75
N52	D11	50(g) on 25g dk bl grn	15.00	12.50
a.		Invtd. surch.		
N53	D11	50(g) on 30g dk bl grn	35.00	35.00
N54	D11	50(g) on 50g dk bl grn	1.50	1.25
N55	D11	50(g) on 1z dk bl grn	2.50	1.50
		Nos. N30-N55 (26)	127.60	126.20

The surcharge on Nos. N30 to N55 is arranged to fit the shape of the stamp and obliterate the original denomination. On some values, "General Gouvernement" appears at the bottom.

St. Florian's Gate, Cracow — OS1   Palace, Warsaw — OS13

Designs: 8g, Watch Tower, Cracow. 10g, Cracow Gate, Lublin. 12g, Courtyard and statue of Copernicus. 20g, Dominican Church, Cracow. 24g, Wawel Castle, Cracow. 30g, Church Lublin. 40g, Arcade, Cloth Hall, Cracow. 48g, City Hall, Sandomierz. 50g, Court House, Cracow. 60g, Courtyard, Cracow. 80g, St. Mary's Church, Cracow.

Photogravure.
1940–41 Perf. 14 Unwmkd.
N56	OS1	6(g) brown	40	65
N57	OS1	8(g) brn org	75	65
N58	OS1	8(g) bl blk ('41)	40	50
N59	OS1	10(g) emerald	30	28
N60	OS1	12(g) dk grn	2.50	35
N61	OS1	12(g) dp vio ('41)	40	50
N62	OS1	20(g) dk ol brn	75	1.00
N63	OS1	24(g) hn brn	20	10
N64	OS1	30(g) purple	25	25
N65	OS1	30(g) vio brn ('41)	25	50
N66	OS1	40(g) sl blk	30	20
N67	OS1	48(g) chnt brn ('41)	75	85
N68	OS1	50(g) brt bl	25	20
N69	OS1	60(g) sl grn	30	30
N70	OS1	80(g) dl pur	50	40
N71	OS13	1z rose lake	2.50	1.25
N72	OS13	1z Prus grn ('41)	75	50
		Nos. N56-N72 (17)	11.55	8.48

Cracow Castle and City, 15th Century — OS14

1941, Apr. 20 Engr. Perf. 14½
N73	OS14	10z red & ol blk	2.00	3.00

Printed in sheets of 8.

Rondel and Florian's Gate, Cracow—OS15

Design: 4z, Tyniec Monastery, Vistula River.
1941 Perf. 13½x14
N74	OS15	2z dk ultra	50	50
N75	OS15	4z sl grn	75	85

Adolf Hitler — OS17

Photogravure.
1941–43 Perf. 14. Unwmkd.
N76	OS17	2(g) gray blk	15	15
N77	OS17	6(g) gldn brn	15	15
N78	OS17	8(g) sl bl	15	15
N79	OS17	10(g) green	15	15
N80	OS17	12(g) purple	15	15
N81	OS17	16(g) org red	50	75
N82	OS17	20(g) blk brn	15	15
N83	OS17	24(g) henna	15	15
N84	OS17	30(g) rose vio	35	25
N85	OS17	32(g) dk bl grn	60	75
N86	OS17	40(g) brt bl	20	15
N87	OS17	48(g) chestnut	75	60
N88	OS17	50(g) vio bl ('43)	25	25
N89	OS17	60(g) dk ol ('43)	25	25
N90	OS17	80(g) dk vio ('43)	25	25
		Nos. N76-N90 (15)	4.55	4.50

A 20g black brown exists with head of Hans Frank substituted for that of Hitler. It was printed and used by Resistance movements.
Nos. N76-N80, N82-N90 exist imperf.

1942–44 Engraved Perf. 12½.
N91	OS17	50(g) vio bl	50	50
N92	OS17	60(g) dk ol	50	50
N93	OS17	80(g) dk red vio	50	50
N94	OS17	1(z) sl grn	75	75
a.		Perf. 14 ('44)	1.50	1.50
N95	OS17	1.20(z) dk brn	75	85
a.		Perf. 14 ('44)	1.50	1.75
N96	OS17	1.60(z) bl vio	1.00	1.00
a.		Perf. 14 ('44)	2.00	2.50
		Nos. N91-N96 (6)	4.00	4.10

Exist imperf.

Rondel and Florian's Gate, Cracow — OS18

Designs: 4z, Tyniec Monastery, Vistula River. 6z, View of Lwow. 10z, Cracow Castle and City, 15th Century.

1943–44 Perf. 13½x14.
N100	OS18	2z sl grn	25	25
N101	OS18	4z dk gray vio	40	50
N102	OS18	6z sep ('44)	60	75
N103	OS18	10z org brn & gray blk	75	1.00

OCCUPATION SEMI-POSTAL STAMPS.
Issued under German Occupation.
Types of 1940 Occupation Postage Stamps Surcharged in Red

Photogravure.
1940, Aug. 17 Perf. 14. Unwmkd.
NB1	OS1	12(g) + 8(g) ol gray	3.00	3.50
NB2	OS1	24(g) + 16(g) ol gray	3.00	3.50
NB3	OS1	50(g) + 50(g) ol gray	4.00	4.00
NB4	OS1	80(g) + 80(g) ol gray	4.00	4.00

POLAND—Offices in Danzig

German Peasant Girl in Poland
OSP1

Designs: 24g+26g, Woman wearing scarf. 30g+20g, Similar to type OSP4.

1940, Oct. 26   Engr.   Perf. 14½
Thick Paper.

NB5	OSP1	12(g) + 38(g) dk sl grn	3.00	3.50
NB6	OSP1	24(g) + 26(g) cop red	3.00	3.50
NB7	OSP1	30(g) + 20(g) dk pur	3.50	4.00

Issued to commemorate the first anniversary of the General Government.

German Peasant
OSP4

1940, Dec. 1   Perf. 12.

NB8	OSP4	12(g) + 8(g) dk grn	1.25	2.00
NB9	OSP4	24(g) + 16(g) rose red	1.50	2.50
NB10	OSP4	30(g) + 30(g) vio brn	2.00	3.00
NB11	OSP4	50(g) + 50(g) ultra	2.50	3.50

The surtax was for war relief.

Adolf Hitler—OSP5
Thick Cream Paper
Engraved.

1942, Apr. 20   Perf. 11   Unwmkd.

NB12	OSP5	30(g) + 1z brn car	50	75
NB13	OSP5	50(g) + 1z dk ultra	50	75
NB14	OSP5	1.20(z) + 1z brn	50	75

To commemorate Hitler's 53rd birthday. Printed in sheets of 25, with marginal inscription: 20. April 1942.

Ancient Lublin—OSP6

Designs: 24g+6g, 1z+1z, Modern Lublin.

1942, Aug. 15   Photo.   Perf. 12½

NB15	OSP6	12(g) + 8(g) rose vio	15	25
NB16	OSP6	24(g) + 6(g) hn	15	25
NB17	OSP6	50(g) + 50(g) dp bl	25	50
NB18	OSP6	1z + 1z dp grn	35	75

600th anniversary of Lublin.

Veit Stoss   **Adolf Hitler**
OSP8   OSP13

Designs: 24g+26g, Hans Durer. 30g+30g, Johann Schuch. 50g+50g, Joseph Elsner. 1z+1z, Nicolaus Copernicus.

1942, Nov. 20   Engr.   Perf. 13½x14

NB19	OSP8	12(g) + 18g dl pur	15	25
NB20	OSP8	24(g) + 26g dl hn	15	25
NB21	OSP8	30(g) + 30g dl rose vio	15	25
NB22	OSP8	50(g) + 50g dl bl vio	25	40
NB23	OSP8	1(z) + 1z dl myr grn	50	75
	Nos. NB19-NB23 (5)		1.20	1.90

1943, Apr. 20

NB24	OSP13	12(g) + 1z pur	15	25
NB25	OSP13	24(g) + 1z rose car	25	40
NB26	OSP13	84(g) + 1z myr grn	50	75

To commemorate Hitler's 54th birthday.

Type of 1942 Overprinted in Black

24. MAI 1543   24. MAI 1943

1943, May 24

NB27	OSP8	1(z) + 1z rose lake	75	95

To commemorate the 400th anniversary of the death of the astronomer, Nicolaus Copernicus (1473-1543). Printed in sheets of 10, with marginal inscription in rose lake.

Cracow Gate,   **Adolf**
Lublin   **Hitler**
OSP14   OSP19

Designs: 24g+76g, Cloth Hall, Cracow. 30g+70g, New Government Building, Radom. 50g+1z, Bruhl Palace, Warsaw. 1z+2z, Town Hall, Lwow. The center of the designs is embossed with the emblem of the National Socialist Party.

1943   Photo., Embossed

NB28	OSP14	12(g) + 38(g) dk grn	15	25
NB29	OSP14	24(g) + 76(g) red	15	25
NB30	OSP14	30(g) + 70(g) rose vio	15	25
NB31	OSP14	50(g) + 1z brt bl	15	25
NB32	OSP14	1z + 2z bl blk	35	75
	Nos. NB28-NB32 (5)		95	1.75

3rd anniversary of the National Socialist Party in Poland.

1944, Apr. 20   Photo.   Perf. 14x13½.

NB33	OSP19	12(g) + 1z grn	15	25
NB34	OSP19	24(g) + 1z rose car	15	25
NB35	OSP19	84(g) + 1z dk vio	20	40

To commemorate Hitler's 55th birthday. Printed in sheets of 25 with decorative border.

Conrad Celtis
OSP20

Designs: 24g+26g, Andreas Schluter. 30g+30g, Hans Boner. 50g+50g, Augustus II. 1z+1z, Georg Gottlieb Pusch.

1944, July 15   Engr.   Perf. 13½x14

NB36	OSP20	12(g) + 18g dk grn	15	25
NB37	OSP20	24(g) + 26g dk red	15	25
NB38	OSP20	30(g) + 30g rose vio	15	25
NB39	OSP20	50(g) + 50g ultra	20	35
NB40	OSP20	1(z) + 1z dl red brn	25	50
	Nos. NB36-NB40 (5)		90	1.60

Cracow Castle—OSP25

1944, Oct. 26   Perf. 14½

NB41	OSP25	10z + 10z red & blk	12.50	17.50
a.		Imperf.	12.50	
b.		10z + 10z car & grnsh blk	20.00	25.00

To commemorate the fifth anniversary of the General Government, October 26, 1944. Printed in sheets of 8, with marginal inscription in black.

OCCUPATION RURAL DELIVERY STAMPS.
Issued under German Occupation.

OSD1
Perf. 13½

1940, Dec. 1   Photo.   Unwmkd.

NL1	OSD1	10g red org	1.00	1.25
NL2	OSD1	20g red org	1.00	1.50
NL3	OSD1	30g red org	1.00	1.50
NL4	OSD1	50g red org	3.00	3.50

OCCUPATION OFFICIAL STAMPS.
Issued under German Occupation.

Eagle and Swastika
OOS1
Perf. 12, 13½x14

1940, Apr.   Photo.   Unwmkd.
Size: 31x23 mm.

NO1	OOS1	6g lt brn	1.75	2.00
NO2	OOS1	8g gray	1.75	2.00
NO3	OOS1	10g green	1.75	2.00
NO4	OOS1	12g dk grn	2.50	2.25
NO5	OOS1	20g dk brn	2.50	4.00
NO6	OOS1	24g hn brn	30.00	1.00
NO7	OOS1	30g rose lake	3.50	4.00
NO8	OOS1	40g dl vio	3.50	5.50
NO9	OOS1	48g dl ol	10.00	6.00
NO10	OOS1	50g ryl bl	2.50	3.50
NO11	OOS1	60g dk ol grn	2.00	2.50
NO12	OOS1	80g rose vio	2.00	2.50

Size: 35x26 mm.

NO13	OOS1	1z gray blk & brn vio	5.00	6.00
NO14	OOS1	3z gray blk & chnt	5.00	6.00
NO15	OOS1	5z gray blk & org brn	6.00	7.50
	Nos. NO1-NO15 (15)		79.75	56.75

1940   Perf. 12
Size: 21¼x16¼ mm.

NO16	OOS1	6g brown	75	85
NO17	OOS1	8g slate	1.00	1.25
NO18	OOS1	10g dp green	1.75	1.50
NO19	OOS1	12g sl grn	1.95	1.50
NO20	OOS1	20g blk brn	7.50	7.50
NO21	OOS1	24g cop brn	75	85
NO22	OOS1	30g rose lake	1.00	1.20
NO23	OOS1	40g dl pur	1.75	1.50
NO24	OOS1	50g ryl bl	2.00	1.75
	Nos. NO16-NO24 (9)		18.45	17.90

Nazi Emblem and Cracow Castle
OOS2

1943   Photogravure   Perf. 14

NO25	OOS2	6(g) brown	15	25
NO26	OOS2	8(g) sl bl	15	25
NO27	OOS2	10(g) green	15	25
NO28	OOS2	12(g) dk vio	75	25
NO29	OOS2	16(g) red org	15	50
NO30	OOS2	20(g) dk brn	25	25
NO31	OOS2	24(g) dk red	75	25
NO32	OOS2	30(g) rose vio	25	25
NO33	OOS2	40(g) blue	25	25
NO34	OOS2	60(g) ol grn	25	25
NO35	OOS2	80(g) dl cl	50	25
NO36	OOS2	100(g) sl blk	75	1.00
	Nos. NO25-NO36 (12)		4.35	4.00

POLISH OFFICES ABROAD.
OFFICES IN DANZIG.

Poland
Nos. 215-225
Overprinted

PORT GDAŃSK

Perf. 11½x12

1925, Jan. 5   Unwmkd.

1K1	A36	1g org brn	50	1.50
1K2	A36	2g gk brn	75	3.00
1K3	A36	3g orange	75	1.50
1K4	A36	5g ol grn	20.00	7.50
1K5	A36	10g bl grn	9.00	2.50
1K6	A36	15g red	45.00	5.00
1K7	A36	20g blue	2.50	1.50
1K8	A36	25g red brn	2.50	1.50
1K9	A36	30g dp vio	2.50	1.50
1K10	A36	40g indigo	2.50	1.50
1K11	A36	50g magenta	6.00	2.00
	Nos. 1K1-1K11 (11)		92.00	29.00

Same Overprint on Poland Nos. 230-231

1926   Perf. 11½, 12

1K11A	A39	5g yel grn	60.00	50.00
1K12	A40	10g violet	14.00	17.50

No. 232 Overprinted

PORT GDAŃSK

1926-27

1K13	A41	15g rose red	65.00	40.00

Same Overprint on Redrawn Stamps of 1926-27. Perf. 13.

1K14	A39	5g yel grn	2.00	1.75

POLAND—Offices in Danzig—Offices in Turkish Empire—Exile Government

1K15	A40	10g violet	6.00	2.00
1K16	A41	15g rose red	4.00	4.00
1K17	A43	20g dl red	3.00	1.75
	Nos. 1K13-1K17 (5)		80.00	49.50

Same Overprint on Poland Nos. 250, 255
1928-30   *Perf. 12½*

1K18	A44	25g yel brn	5.00	2.50

Laid Paper.
Perf. 11½ x12, 12½ x11½.

1K19	A50	1z blk, cr ('30)	40.00	30.00

Poland Nos. 258-260 Overprinted **PORT GDAŃSK**
1929-30   *Perf. 12x12½*

1K20	A53	5g dk vio	2.25	1.50
1K21	A53	10g grn ('30)	2.25	1.50
1K22	A53	25g red brn	3.50	1.50

Same Overprint on Poland No. 257.
1931, Jan. 5   *Perf. 12½*

1K23	A52	15g ultra	4.00	4.00

Poland No. 255 Overprinted in Dark Blue **PORT GDAŃSK**
1933, July 1   *Laid Paper*   *Perf. 11½*

1K24	A50	1z blk, cr	100.00	125.00

Counterfeits exist of No. 1K24.

Poland Nos. 268-270 Overprinted in Black **PORT GDAŃSK**
Wmkd. Multiple Post Horns. (234)
1934-36   *Perf. 12 x12½*

1K25	A58	5g dl vio	4.00	3.00
1K26	A58	10g grn ('36)	40.00	80.00
1K27	A58	15g brn grn	4.00	3.00

Poland Nos. 294, 296, 298 Overprinted in Black in one or two lines **PORT GDAŃSK**
1935-36   *Perf. 12½x13.*   *Unwmkd.*

1K28	A65	5g vio bl	4.00	3.00
1K29	A65	15g Prus grn	7.50	8.00
1K30	A65	25g myr grn	4.00	2.00

Same Overprint in Black on Poland Nos. 308, 310
1937, June 5

1K31	A65	5g vio bl	1.00	1.50
1K32	A65	15g red brn	1.00	1.50

Counterfeit overprints are known on Nos. 1K1-1K32.

Polish Merchants Selling Wheat in Danzig, 16th Century
A2

1938, Nov. 11   *Engr.*   *Perf. 12½*

1K33	A2	5g red org	1.00	1.25
1K34	A2	15g red brn	1.00	1.25
1K35	A2	25g dl vio	1.00	1.25
1K36	A2	55g brt ultra	4.00	4.00

OFFICES IN THE TURKISH EMPIRE.
Stamps of Poland 1919, Overprinted in Carmine **LEVANT**
1919, May   *Perf. 11½.*   *Unwmkd.*
Wove Paper.

2K1	A10	3f bis brn	35.00	40.00
2K2	A10	5f green	35.00	40.00
2K3	A10	10f red vio	35.00	40.00
2K4	A10	15f red	35.00	40.00
2K5	A11	20f dp bl	35.00	40.00
2K6	A11	25f ol grn	35.00	40.00
2K7	A11	50f bl grn	35.00	40.00

Overprinted L E V A N T

2K8	A12	1m violet	35.00	40.00
2K9	A12	1.50m dp grn	35.00	40.00
2K10	A12	2m dk grn	35.00	40.00
2K11	A13	2.50m org brn	35.00	40.00
2K12	A14	5m red vio	35.00	40.00
	Nos. 2K1-2K12 (12)		420.00	480.00

Counterfeit cancellations are plentiful.
Reprints are lighter, shiny red.
Price, set $25.
Polish stamps with "P.P.C." overprint (Poste Polonaise Constantinople) were used on consular mail for a time.

Stamps of 1919-20 Overprinted in Red:

a   *b*

1921, May 25   Thin Laid Paper

2K13	A10 (a)	1m red		1.25
2K14	A10 (a)	2m gray grn		1.75
2K15	A10 (a)	3m lt bl		1.50
2K16	A10 (a)	4m rose red		2.00
2K17	A14 (b)	6m dp rose		2.50
2K18	A14 (b)	10m brn red		5.00
2K19	A14 (b)	20m gray grn		7.50
	Nos. 2K13-2K19 (7)			21.50

Nos. 2K13-2K19 were not issued.
Counterfeits exist of Nos. 2K1-2K19.

EXILE GOVERNMENT IN GREAT BRITAIN
These stamps were issued by the Polish government in exile for letters posted from Polish merchant ships and warships.

United States Embassy Ruins, Warsaw
A1

Polish Ministry of Finance Ruins, Warsaw
A2

Destruction of Mickiewicz Monument, Cracow
A3

Polish Submarine "Orzel"
A8

Ruins of Warsaw
A4

Polish Machine Gunners
A5

Armored Tank
A6

Polish Planes in Great Britain
A7

Perf. 12½, 11½x12.

1941, Dec. 15   *Engr.*   *Unwmkd.*

3K1	A1	5g rose vio	.50	.75
3K2	A2	10g dk bl grn	1.00	1.00
3K3	A3	25g black	1.50	1.75
3K4	A4	55g dk bl	2.00	2.25
3K5	A5	75g ol grn	5.00	5.50
3K6	A6	80g dk car rose	5.00	5.50
3K7	A7	1z sl bl	5.00	5.50
3K8	A8	1.50z cop brn	5.00	6.00
	Nos. 3K1-3K8 (8)		25.00	28.25

These stamps were used for correspondence carried on Polish ships and, on certain days, in Polish Military camps in Great Britain.

Polish Air Force in Battle of the Atlantic
A9

Polish Army in France, 1939-40
A11

Polish Merchant Navy
A10

Polish Army in Narvik, Norway, 1940
A12

The Homeland Fights On
A15

Polish Army in Libya, 1941-42
A13

General Sikorsky and Polish Soldiers in the Middle East, 1943
A14

The Secret Press in Poland
A16

1943, Nov. 1

3K9	A9	5g rose lake	.50	1.00
3K10	A10	10g dk bl grn	1.00	1.50
3K11	A11	25g dk vio	1.00	1.50
3K12	A12	55g sapphire	1.50	2.50
3K13	A13	75g brn car	2.50	3.50
3K14	A14	80g rose car	3.50	4.50
3K15	A15	1z ol blk	3.50	4.50
3K16	A16	1.50z black	4.00	5.00
	Nos. 3K9-3K16 (8)		17.50	24.00

Nos. 3K5 to 3K8 Surcharged in Blue

MONTE CASSINO
18. V. 1944

Perf. 12½, 11½x12.
1944, June 27   *Unwmkd.*

3K17	A5	45g on 75g ol grn	8.00	9.00
3K18	A6	55g on 80g dk car rose	8.00	9.00
3K19	A7	80g on 1z sl bl	8.00	9.00
3K20	A8	1.20z on 1.50z cop brn	8.00	9.00

Issued to commemorate the capture of Monte Cassino by the Poles, May 18, 1944.

POLAND—Exile Government—PONTA DELGADA—PORTUGAL

SEMI-POSTAL STAMP.

Heroic Defenders of Warsaw
SP1
Engraved.
1945, Feb. 3 Perf. 11½. Unwmkd.
3KB1 SP1   1z +2z sl grn   5.00   6.50

Issued to commemorate the Warsaw uprising of August 1 to October 3, 1944.

PONTA DELGADA
(pŏn'tȧ děl·gä'thȧ)

LOCATION — An administrative district of the Azores comprising the islands of São Miguel and Santa Maria.
GOVT.—A district of Portugal.
AREA—342 sq. mi.
POP.—124,000 (approx.).
CAPITAL—Ponta Delgada.

1000 Reis = 1 Milreis

King Carlos
A1   A2
Perf. 11½, 12½, 13½.
1892-93   Typographed.   Unwmkd.
1   A1   5r yellow   60   60
 a.   Diagonal half used as 2½r on piece   2.50
 b.   Perf. 11½   5.25   4.00
2   A1   10r redsh vio   1.75   1.00
3   A1   15r chocolate   2.25   1.50
4   A1   20r lavender   2.75   1.40
 a.   Perf. 13½   4.50   2.75
5   A1   25r dp grn   1.75   60
6   A1   50r ultra   4.00   1.50
7   A1   75r carmine   7.50   5.25
8   A1   80r yel grn   10.00   8.00
9   A1   100r brn, yel   7.50   5.25
10 A1   150r car, rose   35.00 30.00
11 A1   200r dk bl, bl   30.00 25.00
12 A1   300r dk bl, sal   40.00 30.00

The reprints are on paper slightly thinner that that of the originals, and unsurfaced. They have white gum and clean-cut perf. 13½ or 11½. Lowest priced, $1.50 each.

1897-1905   Perf. 11½
Name and Value in Black
except Nos. 25 and 34.

13   A2   2½r gray   30   20
14   A2   5r orange   30   20
15   A2   10r lt grn   30   20
16   A2   15r brown   6.00   4.00
17   A2   15r gray grn ('99)   1.00   75
18   A2   20r dl vio   1.25   80
19   A2   25r sea grn   2.00   75
20   A2   25r rose red ('99)   30
21   A2   50r blue   1.75   1.25
22   A2   50r ultra ('05)   12.00   9.00
23   A2   65r sl bl ('98)   60   55
 a.   Imperf.
24   A2   75r rose   4.00   2.75
25   A2   75r brn & car, yel
              ('05)   10.00   7.50
26   A2   80r violet   2.00   1.00
27   A2   100r dk bl, bl   2.00   1.50
28   A2   115r org brn, rose ('98) 1.75   1.25
29   A2   120r gray brn, buff ('98) 1.75   1.25
30   A2   150r lt brn, buff   1.75   1.40
31   A2   180r sl, pnksh ('98) 1.75   1.25
32   A2   200r red vio, pnksh 6.00   3.75
33   A2   300r bl, rose   6.00   3.75
 a.   Perf. 12½   35.00 27.50
34   A2   500r blk & red, bl 12.00   8.50
 a.   Perf. 12½   16.50 10.00
         Nos. 13-34 (22)   75.25 51.90

The stamps of Ponta Delgada were superseded by those of the Azores, which in 1931 were replaced by those of Portugal.

PORTO RICO
(See Puerto Rico.)

PORTUGAL
(pŏr'tu̇·gȧl)

LOCATION — In southern Europe, lying on the western coast of the Iberian Peninsula.
GOVT.—Republic.
AREA—35,510 sq. mi.
POP.—9,730,000 (est. 1976).
CAPITAL—Lisbon.

Figures for area and population include the Azores and Madeira, which are integral parts of the Republic. The Republic was established in 1910. See Azores, Funchal, Madeira.

1000 Reis = 1 Milreis
10 Reis = 1 Centimo
100 Centavos = 1 Escudo (1912)

Prices of early Portugal stamps vary according to condition. Quotations for Nos. 1-51 are for fine copies. Very fine to superb specimens sell at much higher prices, and inferior or poor copies sell at reduced prices, depending on the condition of the individual specimen.

Queen Maria II
A1   A2

A3   A4
Typographed; Embossed
1853   Imperf.   Unwmkd.
1   A1   5r org brn   1,900.   700.00
2   A2   25r blue   875.00   15.00
3   A3   50r dp yel grn 2,500.   700.00
 a.   50r bl grn   3,250.   900.00
4   A4   100r lilac   9,000. 1,600.

The stamps of the 1853 issue were reprinted in 1864, 1885, 1905 and 1953. Many stamps of subsequent issues were reprinted in 1885 and 1905. The reprints of 1864 are on thin white paper with white gum. The originals have brownish gum which often stains the paper. The reprints of 1885 are on a stout, very white paper. They are usually ungummed, but occasionally have a white gum with yellowish spots. The reprints of 1905 are on creamy white paper of ordinary quality with shiny white gum. When perforated the reprints of 1885 have a rather rough perforation 13½ with small holes; those of 1905 have a clean-cut perforation 13½ with large holes making sharp pointed teeth.

The colors of the reprints usually differ from those of the originals, but actual comparison is necessary.

The reprints are often from new dies which differ slightly from those used for the originals.

5 reis: There is a defect in the neck which makes the Adam's apple appear very large in the first reprint. The later ones can be distinguished by the paper and the shades and by the absence of the pendant curl.

25 reis: The burelage of the ground work in the original is sharp and clear, while in the 1864 reprints it is blurred in several places; the upper and lower right hand corners are very thick and blurred. The central oval is less than ½ mm. from the frame at the sides of the originals and fully ¾ mm. in the 1885 and 1905 reprints.

50 reis: In the reprints of 1864 and 1885 there is a small break in the upper right hand diagonal line of the frame, and the initials of the engraver (F. B. F.) which in the originals are plainly discernible in the lower part of the bust, do not show. The reprints of 1905 have not the break in the frame and the initials are distinct.

100 reis: The small vertical lines at top and bottom at each side of the frame are heavier in the reprints of 1864 than in the originals. The reprints of 1885 and 1905 can be distinguished only by the paper, gum and shades.

Reprints of 1953 have thick paper, no gum and dates "1853/1953" on back.

Prices of lowest-cost reprints (1885) of Nos. 1-3, $50 each; of No. 4, $100.

King Pedro V
A5   A6

A7   A8

1855   With Straight Hair
TWENTY-FIVE REIS:
 Type I. Pearls mostly touch each other and oval outer line.
 Type II. Pearls are separate from each other and oval outer line.

5   A5   5r red brn   2,500.   800.00
6   A6   25r bl, type II   700.00   27.50
 a.   25r bl, type I   900.00   30.00
7   A7   50r green   350.00   70.00
8   A8   100r lilac   700.00   75.00

Several types of No. 5 exist, differing in number of pearls encircling head (74 to 89) and other details.

All values were reprinted in 1885 and 1905. Price for lowest-cost, $15 each.

1856   With Curled Hair.
TWENTY-FIVE REIS:
 Type I. The network is fine (single lines).
 Type II. The network is coarse (double lines).

9   A5   5r brn (shades)   350.00   35.00
10 A5   5r bl, type II   300.00   14.00
 a.   25r bl, type I   2,500.   40.00

1858
11 A6   25r rose, type II 225.00   4.00

The 5r dark brown, formerly listed and sold at about $1.00, is now believed by the best authorities to be a reprint made before 1866. It is printed on thin yellowish white paper with yellowish white gum and is known only unused. The same remarks will apply to a 25r blue which is common unused but not known used. It is printed from a die which was not used for the issued stamps but the differences are slight and can only be told by expert comparison.

Nos. 9 and 10, also 10a in rose, were reprinted in 1885 and Nos. 9, 10, 10a and 11 in 1905. Price of lowest-cost reprints, $15 each.

King Luiz
A9   A10

A11   A12

A13

1862-64
FIVE REIS.
 Type I.   The distance between "5" and "reis" is 3 mm.
 Type II. The distance between "5" and "reis" is 2 mm.

12 A9   5r brn, type I   70.00   7.00
 a.   5r brn, type II   125.00 20.00
13 A10 10r orange   90.00 35.00
14 A11 25r rose   90.00   4.00
15 A12 50r yel grn   450.00 70.00
16 A13 100r lil ('64)   600.00 75.00

All values were reprinted in 1885 and all except the 25r in 1905. Price of lowest-cost reprints, $15 each.

King Luiz
A14   A15

1866-67   Imperf.
17 A14 5r black   100.00   8.00
18 A14 10r yellow   175.00 80.00
19 A14 20r bister   130.00 50.00
20 A14 25r rose ('67)   175.00   4.00
21 A14 50r green   250.00 55.00
22 A14 80r orange   225.00 60.00
23 A14 100r dk lil ('67) 250.00 70.00
24 A14 120r blue   275.00 55.00

Some values with unofficial percé en croix (diamond) perforation were used in Madeira.

All values were reprinted in 1885 and 1905. Price $12.50 each.

PORTUGAL

1867-70   Typographed; Embossed   Perf. 12½

25	A14	5r black	125.00	30.00
26	A14	10r yellow	225.00	80.00
27	A14	20r bis ('69)	250.00	80.00
28	A14	25r rose	60.00	5.00
29	A14	50r grn ('68)	250.00	80.00
30	A14	80r org ('69)	325.00	90.00
31	A14	100r lil ('69)	250.00	90.00
32	A14	120r blue	200.00	55.00
33	A14	240r pale vio ('70)	750.00	350.00

Two types each of 5r and 100r differ in the position of the "5" at upper right and the "100" at lower right in relation to the end of the label.

Nos. 25-33 were reprinted in 1885 and 1905. Some of the 1885 reprints were perforated 12½ as well as 13½. Price of the lowest-cost reprints, $12.50 each.

1870-84   Perf. 12½, 13½

34	A15	5r black	40.00	4.00
a.		Imperf.	875.00	
b.		Perf. 11		450.00
c.		Perf. 14	150.00	50.00
35	A15	10r yel ('71)	60.00	15.00
a.		Imperf.	875.00	
b.		Perf. 11		450.00
c.		Perf. 14	275.00	175.00
36	A15	10r bl grn ('79)	200.00	100.00
37	A15	10r yel grn ('80)	90.00	15.00
38	A15	15r lil brn ('75)	70.00	15.00
39	A15	20r bister	55.00	9.00
a.		Imperf.	875.00	
b.		Perf. 11		350.00
40	A15	20r rose ('84)	200.00	25.00
41	A15	25r rose	20.00	1.75
a.		Imperf.	875.00	
b.		Perf. 11		350.00
c.		Perf. 14	275.00	12.50
42	A15	50r pale grn	100.00	10.00
b.		Perf. 11		450.00
43	A15	50r bl ('79)	200.00	25.00
44	A15	80r orange	80.00	5.00
a.		Perf. 14	400.00	275.00
b.		Perf. 11		450.00
45	A15	100r pale lil ('71)	45.00	4.50
a.		Perf. 11	500.00	275.00
46	A15	120r bl, perf. 12½ ('71)	225.00	60.00
a.		Perf. 13½		
47	A15	150r pale bl ('76)	275.00	100.00
a.		Imperf.		
48	A15	150r yel ('80)	110.00	7.00
49	A15	240r pale vio ('73)	1,200.	700.00
b.		Perf. 11		
50	A15	300r dl vio ('76)	110.00	20.00
51	A15	1000r blk ('84)	200.00	45.00

Two types each of 15r, 20r and 80r differ in the distance between the figures of value.

All values of the issues of 1870-84 were reprinted in 1885 and 1905. Price of the lowest-cost reprints, $12.50 each.

King Luiz
A16   A17

A18   A19

1880-81   Typo.   Perf. 12½, 13½

52	A16	5r black	17.50	2.50
53	A17	25r bluish gray	185.00	12.50
54	A18	25r gray	17.50	2.00
55	A18	25r brn vio ('81)	17.50	2.00
56	A19	50r bl ('81)	210.00	10.00

All values were reprinted in 1885 and 1905. Price of the lowest-cost reprints, $5 each.

A20   A21

King Luiz
A22   A23

A24   A24a

1882-87   Perf. 11½, 12½, 13½

57	A20	2r blk ('84)	9.00	7.50
58	A21	5r blk ('83)	9.00	1.25
59	A22	10r grn ('84)	22.50	2.25
60	A23	25r brown	15.00	1.50
61	A24	50r blue	25.00	1.50
62	A24a	500r blk ('84)	375.00	225.00
63	A24a	500r vio p. 12½ ('87)	175.00	30.00
a.		Perf. 13½	350.00	250.00

The stamps of the 1882-87 issues were reprinted in 1885, 1893 and 1905. Price of the lowest-cost reprints, $6 each.

A25   A26

1887

64	A25	20r rose	30.00	11.00
65	A26	25r violet	17.50	1.25
66	A26	25r lil rose	17.50	1.25

Nos. 64-66 were reprinted in 1905. Price $5 each.

King Carlos
A27

1892-93   Perf. 11½, 12½, 13½

67	A27	5r orange	7.50	1.50
68	A27	10r redsh vio	12.00	1.50
69	A27	15r chocolate	9.00	3.00
70	A27	20r lavender	15.00	5.25
71	A27	25r dk grn	17.50	1.50
72	A27	50r blue	22.50	4.50
73	A27	75r car ('93)	45.00	5.25
a.		Perf. 11½	150.00	7.50
74	A27	80r yel grn	52.50	27.50
75	A27	100r brn, *buff* ('93)	40.00	3.00
a.		Invtd. ovpt.	175.00	7.50
76	A27	150r car, *rose* ('93)	90.00	25.00
77	A27	200r dk bl, *bl* ('93)	90.00	27.50
78	A27	300r dk bl, *sal* ('93)	105.00	30.00

Nos. 76-78 were reprinted in 1900 (perf. 11½), and all values in 1905 (perf. 13½). Prices of the lowest-cost reprints of Nos. 67-75, $6 each; of Nos. 76-78, $12 each.

Stamps and Types of Previous Issues Overprinted in Black or Red:

PROVISORIO   PROVISORIO
a   *b*

PROVISORIO
c

1892

79	A21 (a)	5r gray blk	11.00	5.25
a.		Double ovpt.	300.00	165.00
80	A22 (b)	10r green	11.00	5.25
a.		Invtd. ovpt.		
b.		Double ovpt.	300.00	200.00

1892-93

81	A21 (c)	5r gray blk (R)	7.50	4.50
82	A22 (c)	10r grn (R)	9.00	5.25
a.		Inverted overprint	75.00	75.00
83	A25 (c)	20r rose	15.00	10.00
84	A26 (c)	25r rose lil	7.50	3.75
85	A24 (c)	50r bl (R) ('93)	52.50	42.50

1893

86	A15 (c)	15r bis brn (R)	9.00	6.00
87	A15 (c)	80r yellow	75.00	60.00

Nos. 86-87 are found in two types each. See note below No. 51.

Some of Nos. 79-87 were reprinted in 1900 and all values in 1905. Price of lowest-cost reprint, $10.

Stamps and Types of Previous Issues Overprinted or Surcharged in Black or Red:

1893
PROVISORIO
d

1893
PROVISORIO
20 rs.
e

1893   Perf. 11½, 12½

88	A21 (d)	5r gray blk (R)	13.00	9.00
89	A22 (d)	10r grn (R)	16.00	12.00
a.		"1938"	175.00	150.00
b.		"1863"	175.00	150.00
90	A25 (d)	20r rose	30.00	25.00
a.		Invtd. ovpt.		
91	A26 (e)	20r on 25r lil rose	30.00	22.50
92	A26 (e)	25r lil rose	75.00	60.00
a.		Invtd. ovpt.	150.00	150.00
93	A24 (d)	50r bl (R)	67.50	52.50

Perf. 12½

94	A15 (e)	50r on 80r yel	90.00	75.00
95	A15 (e)	75r on 80r yel	60.00	52.50
96	A15 (d)	80r yellow	67.50	60.00

Nos. 94-96 are found in two types each. See note below No. 51.

Some of Nos. 88-96 were reprinted in 1900 and all values in 1905. Price of lowest-cost reprint, $10 each.

Prince Henry the Navigator Issue.

Prince Henry on his Ship
A46

Prince Henry
Directing Fleet Maneuvers
A47

Symbolic of Prince Henry's Studies
A48

1894   Lithographed.   Perf. 14

97	A46	5r orange	3.00	90
98	A46	10r magenta	3.75	90
99	A46	15r red brn	6.00	2.25
100	A46	20r dl vio	7.50	3.00
101	A47	25r gray grn	6.00	1.25
102	A47	50r blue	12.00	3.00
103	A47	75r car rose	24.00	7.50
104	A47	80r yel grn	27.50	11.00
105	A47	100r lt brn, *pale buff*	20.00	7.50

Engraved.

106	A48	150r lt car, *pale rose*	57.50	12.50
107	A48	300r dk bl, *sal buff*	67.50	17.50
108	A48	500r dp vio, *pale lil*	150.00	45.00
109	A48	1000r gray blk, *grysh*	185.00	60.00
		Nos. 97-109 (13)	569.75	172.30

Commemorating the fifth centenary of the birth of Prince Henry the Navigator.

King Carlos
A49

Value in Black or Red (※ 122, 131, 131a)

1895-1905   Typographed   Perf. 11½

110	A49	2½r gray	30	8
a.		Imperf.		
111	A49	5r orange	25	8
		Booklet pane of 6		
112	A49	10r lt grn	35	8
		Booklet pane of 6		
113	A49	15r brown	60.00	3.00
114	A49	15r gray grn ('99)	30.00	2.25
115	A49	20r gray vio	45	15
		Booklet pane of 6		
116	A49	25r sea grn	45.00	15
117	A49	25r car rose ('99)	30	5
		Booklet pane of 6		
118	A49	50r blue	60.00	45
		Booklet pane of 6		
119	A49	50r ultra ('05)	35	20
		Booklet pane of 6		
120	A49	65r sl bl ('98)	40	20
121	A49	75r rose	70.00	3.00
122	A49	75r brn, *yel* ('05)	90	60

PORTUGAL

123	A49	80r violet	1.25	90
124	A49	100r dk bl, *bl*	60	30
125	A49	115r org brn, *pink*('98)	3.00	2.25
126	A49	130r gray brn, *straw*('98)	2.25	1.25
127	A49	150r lt brn, *straw*	72.50	14.00
128	A49	180r sl, *pnksh*('98)	9.00	7.50
129	A49	200r red lil, *pnksh*	2.25	90
130	A49	300r bl, *rose*	2.50	1.50
131	A49	500r blk, *bl* ('96)	5.25	3.75
a.		Perf. 12½	100.00	25.00
		Nos. 110-131 (22)	366.90	42.64

Several values of the above type exist without figures of value, also with figures inverted or otherwise misplaced but they were not regularly issued.

St. Anthony and his Vision
A50

St. Anthony Preaching to Fishes
A51

St. Anthony Ascends to Heaven
A52

St. Anthony, from Portrait
A53

1895   Typographed
Perf. 11½, 12½ and Compound.

132	A50	2½r black	3.00	1.75

Lithographed.

133	A51	5r brn org	3.50	1.75
134	A51	10r red lil	6.50	4.00
135	A51	15r chocolate	8.00	6.00
136	A51	20r gray vio	8.00	6.00
137	A51	25r grn & vio	5.00	1.50
138	A52	50r bl & brn	25.00	12.50
139	A52	75r rose & brn	30.00	20.00
140	A52	80r lt grn & brn	50.00	37.50
141	A52	100r choc & blk	37.50	17.50
142	A53	150r car & bis	115.00	75.00
143	A53	200r bl & bis	115.00	75.00
144	A53	300r sl & bis	150.00	90.00
145	A53	500r vio brn & grn	300.00	210.00
146	A53	1000r vio & grn	500.00	325.00
		Nos. 132-146 (15)	1,356.50	883.50

Commemorating the seventh centenary of the birth of Saint Anthony of Padua. Stamps have eulogy in Latin printed on the back.

Vasco da Gama Issue
Common Design Types
1898   Engraved.   *Perf. 12½ to 16.*

147	CD20	2½r bl grn	90	40
148	CD21	5r red	90	40
149	CD22	10r red vio	6.00	1.75
150	CD23	25r yel grn	4.25	45
151	CD24	50r dk bl	7.00	3.00
152	CD25	75r vio brn	27.50	9.00
153	CD26	100r bis brn	22.50	7.50
154	CD27	150r bister	45.00	22.50
		Nos. 147-154 (8)	114.05	45.00

Commemorating the fourth centenary of Vasco da Gama's discovery of the route to India.

King Manuel II
A62   A63

1910   Typographed.   *Perf. 14½x15.*

156	A62	2½r violet	25	10
157	A62	5r black	25	10
a.		Booklet pane of 6		
158	A62	10r gray grn	30	25
159	A62	15r lil brn	1.75	1.40
160	A62	20r carmine	90	75
a.		Booklet pane of 6		
161	A62	25r vio brn	60	10
a.		Booklet pane of 6		
162	A62	50r dk bl	1.10	60
a.		Booklet pane of 6		
163	A62	75r bis brn	7.00	4.00
164	A62	80r slate	2.25	1.75
165	A62	100r brn, *lt grn*	9.00	3.00
166	A62	200r dk grn, *sal*	4.50	3.00
167	A62	300r azure	6.00	4.50
168	A63	500r ol grn & vio brn	12.50	11.00
169	A63	1000r dk bl & blk	25.00	22.50
		Nos. 156-169 (14)	71.40	53.05

Preceding Issue Overprinted in Carmine or Green

1910

170	A62	2½r violet	30	15
171	A62	5r black	30	15
a.		Booklet pane of 6		
172	A62	10r gray grn	2.50	90
a.		Booklet pane of 6		
173	A62	15r lil brn	75	60
174	A62	20r car (G)	3.00	2.25
a.		Booklet pane of 6		
175	A62	25r vio brn	75	25
a.		Booklet pane of 6		
176	A62	50r dk bl	5.25	2.25
a.		Booklet pane of 6		
177	A62	75r bis brn	8.00	4.50
178	A62	80r slate	2.50	1.75
179	A62	100r brn, *lt grn*	1.50	75
180	A62	200r dk grn, *sal*	2.25	1.50
181	A62	300r azure	3.25	3.00
182	A63	500r ol grn & vio brn	8.00	7.50
183	A63	1000r dk bl & blk	17.50	15.00
		Nos. 170-183 (14)	55.85	40.55

The numerous inverted and double overprints on this issue were unofficially and fraudulently made. The 50r with blue overprint is a fraud.

Common Design Types
pictured in section at front of book.

Vasco da Gama Issue Overprinted or Surcharged:

REPUBLICA
a

REPUBLICA   **REPUBLICA**

REIS 15 REIS   **1$000**
b   *c*

1911   *Perf. 12½ to 16*

185	CD20(a)	2½r bl grn	30	25
a.		Inverted overprint	12.50	12.50
186	CD21(b)	15r on 5r red	45	40
a.		Inverted surcharge	12.50	12.50
187	CD23(a)	25r yel grn	45	30
188	CD24(a)	50r dk bl	2.25	1.10
a.		Inverted overprint	12.50	12.50
189	CD25(a)	75r vio brn	30.00	25.00
190	CD26(b)	80r on 150r bis	3.75	3.00
191	CD26(a)	100r bis brn	3.75	1.75
a.		Inverted overprint	15.00	15.00
192	CD22(c)	1000r on 10r red vio	30.00	25.00
		Nos. 185-192 (8)	70.95	56.80

Postage Due Stamps of 1898 Overprinted or Surcharged for Regular Postage:

REPUBLICA

REPUBLICA   **R$ 300 R$**
d   *e*

1911   *Perf. 12*

193	D1(d)	5r black	45	30
a.		Double overprint, one inverted	10.00	10.00
194	D1(d)	10r magenta	60	45
195	D1(d)	20r orange	3.00	2.25
196	D1(d)	200r brn, *buff*	37.50	30.00
197	D1(e)	300r on 50r sl	25.00	20.00
198	D1(e)	500r on 100r car, *pink*	15.00	7.50
a.		Invtd. surch.	50.00	50.00
		Nos. 193-198 (6)	81.55	60.50

Vasco da Gama Issue of Madeira Overprinted or Surcharged Types "a", "b" and "c".

1911   *Perf. 12½ to 16*

199	CD20(a)	2½r bl grn	2.00	1.50
200	CD21(b)	15r on 5r red	1.75	1.50
a.		Inverted surcharge	7.00	7.00
201	CD23(a)	25r yel grn	4.50	3.75
202	CD24(a)	50r dk bl	7.50	7.00
a.		Inverted overprint	17.50	17.50
203	CD25(a)	75r vio brn	6.00	4.50
a.		Inverted overprint	17.50	17.50
204	CD27(b)	80r on 150r bis	4.75	4.50
a.		Inverted surcharge	25.00	25.00
205	CD26(a)	100r bis brn	16.00	6.00
a.		Inverted overprint	35.00	35.00
206	CD22(c)	1000r on 10r red vio	20.00	16.00
		Nos. 199-206 (8)	65.25	44.75

Ceres
A64

With Imprint.
Typographed.

1912-31   *Perf. 15x14, 12x11½.*

207	A64	¼c dk ol	15	5
208	A64	½c black	15	5
209	A64	1c dp grn	1.00	10
210	A64	1c choc ('18)	10	5
211	A64	1½c chocolate	5.00	1.25
212	A64	1½c dp grn ('18)	15	6
213	A64	2c carmine	5.00	45
214	A64	2c org ('18)	25	5
215	A64	2c yel ('24)	30	15
216	A64	2c choc ('26)	60	35
217	A64	2½c violet	20	5
218	A64	3c car rose ('17)	15	5
219	A64	3c ultra ('21)	15	5
220	A64	3½c lt grn ('18)	15	5
221	A64	4c lt grn ('19)	25	5
222	A64	4c org ('26)	35	25
223	A64	5c dp bl	5.00	20
224	A64	5c yel brn ('18)	60	15
225	A64	5c ol brn ('21)	25	5
226	A64	5c blk brn ('31)	50	25
227	A64	6c pale rose ('20)	35	6
228	A64	6c brn ('24)	40	15
229	A64	6c red brn ('30)	15	10
230	A64	7½c yel brn	5.00	1.00
231	A64	7½c dp bl ('18)	25	8
232	A64	8c slate	30	8
233	A64	8c bl grn ('22)	30	25
234	A64	8c org ('24)	25	25
235	A64	10c org brn	50	10
236	A64	10c red ('31)	35	5
237	A64	12c bl gray ('20)	1.50	45
238	A64	12c dp grn ('21)	30	20
239	A64	13½c chlky bl ('20)	75	50
240	A64	14c dk bl, *yel* ('20)	2.00	2.00
241	A64	14c brt vio ('21)	30	25
242	A64	15c plum	1.50	60
243	A64	15c blk ('23)	25	10
244	A64	16c brt ultra ('24)	75	75
245	A64	20c vio brn, *grn*	11.00	1.50
246	A64	20c brn, *buff* ('20)	15.00	2.00
247	A64	20c dk brn ('21)	50	50
248	A64	20c dp grn ('23)	1.00	50
249	A64	20c gray ('24)	25	15
250	A64	24c grnsh bl ('21)	35	20
251	A64	25c sal pink ('23)	25	8
252	A64	25c lt gray ('26)	75	50
253	A64	25c bl grn ('30)	1.00	25
254	A64	30c brn, *pink*	85.00	7.50
255	A64	30c lt brn, *yel* ('17)	3.50	75
256	A64	30c gray brn ('21)	35	20
257	A64	30c dk brn ('24)	2.50	1.25
258	A64	32c dp grn ('24)	75	50
259	A64	36c red ('21)	50	15
260	A64	40c dk bl ('23)	1.00	75
261	A64	40c choc ('24)	50	15
262	A64	40c grn ('26)	65	35
263	A64	48c rose ('24)	3.50	85
264	A64	50c org, *sal*	9.00	1.50
265	A64	50c yel ('21)	45	15
266	A64	50c bis ('30)	1.50	1.00
267	A64	50c red brn ('30)	1.50	60
268	A64	60c bl ('21)	75	30
269	A64	64c pale ultra ('24)	2.00	1.75
270	A64	75c dl rose ('23)	6.25	3.00
271	A64	75c car rose ('30)	1.50	60
272	A64	80c brn rose ('21)	7.50	2.00
273	A64	80c vio ('24)	1.00	20
274	A64	80c dk grn ('30)	1.75	50
275	A64	90c chlky bl ('21)	1.25	50
276	A64	96c dp rose ('26)	17.50	13.50
277	A64	1e dp grn, *bl*	11.00	1.50
278	A64	1e vio ('21)	2.00	75
a.		Perf. 15x14	90.00	30.00
279	A64	1e dk bl ('23)	3.75	1.65
280	A64	1e gray vio ('24)	2.00	30
281	A64	1e brn lake ('30)	5.00	75
282	A64	1.10e yel brn ('21)	2.50	75
283	A64	1.20e yel brn ('21)	1.75	75
284	A64	1.20e buff ('24)	30.00	20.00
285	A64	1.20e pur brn ('31)	3.00	75
286	A64	1.25e dk bl ('31)	2.25	90
287	A64	1.50e blk vio ('23)	7.50	2.25

157

PORTUGAL

288	A64	1.50e lil ('24)	10.00	3.00
289	A64	1.60e dp bl ('24)	7.50	1.50
290	A64	2e sl grn ('21)	27.50	2.50
291	A64	2e red vio ('31)	17.00	6.50
292	A64	2.40e ap grn ('26)	125.00	90.00
293	A64	3e pink ('26)	110.00	85.00
294	A64	3.20e gray grn ('24)	17.50	9.00
295	A64	4.50e org ('31)	45.00	32.50
296	A64	5e emer ('24)	15.00	5.00
297	A64	10e pink ('24)	75.00	25.00
298	A64	20e pale turq ('24)	185.00	125.00
		Nos. 207-298 (92)	921.05	469.56

Presidents of Portugal
and Brazil and Aviators
Cabral and Coutinho—A65

1923   Lithographed.   Perf. 14.

299	A65	1c brown	10	10
300	A65	2c orange	10	10
301	A65	3c ultra	10	10
302	A65	4c yel grn	10	10
303	A65	5c bis brn	10	10
304	A65	10c brn org	10	10
305	A65	15c black	10	10
306	A65	20c bl grn	10	10
307	A65	25c rose	10	10
308	A65	30c ol brn	75	75
309	A65	40c chocolate	10	10
310	A65	50c yellow	15	15
311	A65	75c violet	30	30
312	A65	1e dp bl	45	45
313	A65	1.50e ol grn	75	75
314	A65	2e myr grn	1.40	1.40
		Nos. 299-314 (16)	4.80	4.80

Issued to commemorate the flight of Sacadura Cabral and Gago Coutinho from Portugal to Brazil.

Camoëns at Ceuta
A66

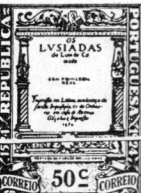

Camoëns Saving
the Lusiads
A67

Luis de
Camoëns
A68

First Edition
of the Lusiads
A69

Monument
to Camoëns
A72

Camoëns Dying
A70

Tomb of Camoëns
A71

Engr.; Values Typo. in Black

1924, Nov. 11   Perf. 14, 14½.

315	A66	2c lt bl	24	20
316	A66	3c orange	24	20
317	A66	4c dk gray	24	20
318	A66	5c yel grn	24	20
319	A66	6c lake	24	20
320	A67	8c org brn	24	20
321	A67	10c gray vio	24	20
322	A67	15c ol grn	24	20
323	A67	16c vio brn	24	20
324	A67	20c dp org	24	20
325	A68	25c lilac	24	20
326	A68	30c dk brn	24	20
327	A68	32c dk grn	50	50
328	A68	40c ultra	24	20
329	A68	48c red brn	1.25	1.25
330	A69	50c red org	1.25	1.25
331	A69	64c green	1.25	1.25
332	A69	75c dk vio	1.25	1.25
333	A69	80c bister	1.25	1.25
334	A69	96c lake	1.25	1.25
335	A70	1e slate	1.00	1.00
336	A70	1.20e lt brn	2.25	2.25
337	A70	1.50e red	1.25	1.25
338	A70	1.60e dk bl	1.25	1.25
339	A70	2e ap grn	2.25	2.25
340	A71	2.40e grn, grn	3.75	3.75
341	A71	3e dk bl, bl	1.40	1.40
a.		Value double	90.00	
b.		Value omitted		
342	A71	3.20e green	1.40	1.40
343	A71	4.50e orange	3.75	3.00
344	A71	10e dk brn, pnksh	6.75	5.50
345	A72	20e dk vio, lil	9.00	6.00
		Nos. 315-345 (31)	45.17	39.65

Issued to commemorate the 400th anniversary of the birth of Luis de Camoens, poet.

Castello-Branco's House
at Sao Miguel de Seide
A73

Castello-Branco's Study
A74

Camillo
Castello-Branco
A75

Teresa
de Albuquerque
A76

Mariana and
João de Cruz
A77

Simão
de Botelho
A78

1925, Mar. 26   Perf. 12½.

346	A73	2c orange	20	15
347	A73	3c green	20	15
348	A73	4c ultra	20	15
349	A73	5c scarlet	20	15
350	A73	6c brn vio	20	15
a.		"6" and "C" omitted		
351	A74	8c blk brn	20	15
352	A74	10c pale bl	20	15
353	A75	15c ol grn	25	20
354	A74	16c red org	30	15
355	A74	20c dk vio	30	15
356	A74	25c car rose	30	15
357	A74	30c bis brn	30	15
358	A74	32c green	1.00	1.00
359	A75	40c grn & blk	30	20
360	A74	48c red brn	2.00	1.75
361	A76	50c bl grn	75	50
362	A76	64c org brn	3.00	3.00
363	A76	75c gray blk	1.00	1.00
364	A75	80c brown	1.00	1.00
365	A76	96c car rose	1.50	1.50
366	A76	1e gray vio	1.00	75
367	A76	1.20e yel grn	1.50	1.40
368	A77	1.50e dk bl, bl	12.50	11.00
369	A75	1.60e indigo	3.75	2.25
370	A77	2e dk grn, grn	5.25	2.25
371	A77	2.40e red, org	35.00	27.50
372	A77	3e lake, bl	50.00	37.50
373	A77	3.20e green	25.00	25.00
374	A75	4.50e red & blk	11.00	3.00
375	A77	10e brn, yel	11.00	3.00
376	A78	20e orange	12.50	2.00
		Nos. 346-376 (32)	181.90	127.45

Issued to commemorate the centenary of the birth of Camillo Castello-Branco, novelist.

First Independence Issue.

Alfonso the
Conqueror, First
King of Portugal
A79

Filipa de Vilhena
Arming
her Sons
A82

Batalha Monastery
and King John I
A80

Battle of Aljubarrota
A81

King John IV
(The Duke
of Braganza)
A83

Independence
Monument,
Lisbon
A84

1926, Aug. 13   Perf. 14, 14½.

Center in Black.

377	A79	2c orange	20	15
378	A80	3c ultra	20	15
379	A80	4c yel grn	20	15
380	A80	5c blk brn	20	15
381	A79	6c ocher	20	15
382	A80	15c dk grn	20	15
383	A79	16c dp bl	50	50
384	A81	20c dl vio	60	50
385	A82	25c scarlet	60	50
386	A82	32c dp grn	75	75
387	A82	40c yel brn	25	25
388	A80	46c carmine	2.25	2.25
389	A82	50c ol bis	2.25	2.25
390	A83	64c bl grn	3.25	3.25
391	A82	75c red brn	3.25	3.25
392	A84	96c dl red	4.50	4.50
393	A83	1e blk vio	6.00	6.00
394	A81	1.60e myr grn	7.50	7.50
395	A84	3e plum	25.00	25.00
396	A84	4.50e ol grn	27.50	27.50
397	A81	10e carmine	45.00	45.00
		Nos. 377-397 (21)	130.40	129.90

The use of these stamps instead of the regular issue was obligatory on Aug. 13th and 14th, Nov. 30th and Dec. 1st, 1926.

Surcharged

and bars.

1926   Center in Black.

397A	A80	2c on 5c blk brn	85	85
397B	A80	2c on 46c car	85	85
397C	A83	2c on 64c bl grn	85	85
397D	A82	3c on 75c red brn	85	85
397E	A84	3c on 96c dl red	85	85
397F	A83	3c on 1e blk vio	85	85
397G	A81	4c on 1.60e myr grn	5.00	5.00
397H	A84	4c on 3e plum	2.75	2.75
397J	A84	6c on 4.50e ol grn	2.75	2.75
397K	A81	6c on 10e car	2.75	2.75
		Nos. 397A-397K (10)	18.35	18.35

There are two styles of the ornaments in these surcharges.

PORTUGAL

Ceres
A85

Without Imprint

1926, Dec. 2   Typo.   Perf. 13½x14

398	A85	2c chocolate	5	5
399	A85	3c brt bl	5	5
400	A85	4c dp org	5	5
401	A85	5c dp brn	5	5
402	A85	6c org brn	6	5
403	A85	10c org red	5	5
404	A85	15c black	5	5
405	A85	16c ultra	15	8
406	A85	25c gray	15	5
407	A85	32c dp grn	40	25
408	A85	40c bl grn	20	5
409	A85	48c rose	1.00	1.00
410	A85	50c ocher	70	35
411	A85	64c dp bl	1.10	1.00
412	A85	80c violet	3.00	30
413	A85	96c car rose	1.50	1.25
414	A85	1e red brn	8.25	60
415	A85	1.20e yel brn	9.00	90
416	A85	1.60e dk bl	1.10	30
417	A85	2e green	13.00	60
418	A85	3.20e ol grn	4.25	30
419	A85	4.50e yellow	4.00	1.00
420	A85	5e brn ol	75.00	1.40
421	A85	10e red	5.50	1.10
		Nos. 398-421 (24)	128.66	11.58

Second Independence Issue.

Gonçalo Mendes
da Maia
A86

Dr. João
das Regras
A88

Guimarães
Castle
A87

Battle of Montijo
A89

Brites
de Almeida
A90

João Pinto
Ribeiro
A91

1927, Nov. 29   Engr.   Perf. 14
Center in Black

422	A86	2c brown	20	20
423	A87	3c ultra	20	20
424	A88	4c orange	20	20
425	A88	5c ol brn	20	20
426	A89	6c org brn	20	20
427	A87	15c blk brn	30	30
428	A88	16c dp bl	75	75
429	A86	25c gray	75	75
430	A89	32c bl grn	1.75	1.75
431	A90	40c yel grn	60	60
432	A86	48c brn red	8.50	8.50
433	A87	80c dk vio	7.00	6.50
434	A90	96c dl red	11.00	9.00
435	A88	1.60c myr grn	12.00	11.00
436	A91	4.50e bister	18.00	16.00
		Nos. 422-436 (15)	61.65	56.15

The use of these stamps instead of the regular issue was compulsory on Nov. 29th, 30th, Dec. 1st, 2nd, 1927. The money derived from their sale was used for the purchase of a palace for a war museum, the organization of an international exposition in Lisbon, in 1940, and for fêtes to be held in that year in commemoration of the eighth centenary of the founding of Portugal and the third centenary of its restoration.

Third Independence Issue.

Gualdim
Paes
A93

The Siege of
Santarem
A94

Battle of Rolica—A95

Battle of Atoleiros
A96

Joana
de Gouveia
A97

Matias
de Albuquerque
A98

Center in Black
1928, Nov. 27

437	A93	2c lt bl	20	20
438	A94	3c lt grn	20	20
439	A95	4c lake	20	20
440	A96	5c ol grn	20	20
441	A97	6c org brn	20	20
442	A94	15c slate	55	55
443	A95	16c dk vio	55	55
444	A93	25c ultra	60	60
445	A97	32c dp grn	2.50	2.50
446	A96	40c ol brn	40	40
447	A95	50c red org	7.50	7.50
448	A94	80c lt gray	7.50	7.50
449	A97	96c carmine	15.00	15.00
450	A96	1e claret	22.50	20.00
451	A93	1.60e dk bl	9.00	9.00
452	A98	4.50e yellow	9.00	9.00
		Nos. 437-452 (16)	76.10	73.60

Obligatory Nov. 27-30. See note after No. 436.

Surcharged in Black.
A99

1928-29   Perf. 12x11½, 15x14.

453	A99	4c on 8c org	30	20
454	A99	4c on 30c dk brn	30	20
455	A99	10c on ¼c dk ol	40	25
a.		Inverted surch.	2.50	
456	A99	10c on ½c blk (R)	55	25
a.		Perf. 15x14	75	60
457	A99	10c on 1c choc	55	25
a.		Perf. 15x14	52.50	45.00
458	A99	10c on 4c grn	30	20
a.		Perf. 15x14	70.00	52.50
459	A99	10c on 4c org	30	30
460	A99	10c on 5c ol brn	30	25
461	A99	15c on 16c bl	40	30
462	A99	15c on 16c ultra	1.50	90
463	A99	15c on 20c brn	22.50	22.50
464	A99	15c on 20c gray	40	30
465	A99	15c on 24c grnsh bl	1.75	40
466	A99	15c on 25c gray	40	40
467	A99	15c on 25c sal pink	40	25
468	A99	16c on 32c dp grn	75	75
469	A99	40c on 2c org	30	20
470	A99	40c on 2c yel	4.00	3.00
471	A99	40c on 2c choc	30	25
472	A99	40c on 3c ultra	30	30
473	A99	40c on 50c vio	30	25
474	A99	40c on 60c dl bl	75	45
a.		Perf. 15x14	6.00	6.00
475	A99	40c on 64c pale ultra	75	60
476	A99	40c on 75c dl rose	75	60
477	A99	40c on 80c vio	60	45
478	A99	40c on 90c chlky bl	4.00	1.50
a.		Perf. 15x14	7.50	7.00
479	A99	40c on 1e gray vio	60	40
480	A99	40c on 1.10e yel brn	60	50
481	A99	80c on 6c pale rose	60	40
482	A99	80c on 6c choc	60	35
483	A99	80c on 48c rose	90	80
484	A99	80c on 1.50e lil	1.50	80
485	A99	96c on 1.20e yel grn	2.50	2.25
486	A99	96c on 1.20e buff	2.50	2.25
487	A99	1.60e on 2e sl grn	17.50	16.00
488	A99	1.60e on 3.20e gray grn	7.00	6.00
489	A99	1.60e on 20e pale turq	7.00	6.00
		Nos. 453-489 (37)	84.45	70.85

Stamps of 1912-26
Overprinted
in Black or Red   **Revalidado**

1929   Perf. 12x11½

490	A64	10c org brn	30	20
a.		Perf. 15x14	55.00	55.00
491	A64	15c blk (R)	30	20
492	A64	40c lt grn	30	20
493	A64	40c chocolate	30	20
494	A64	96c dp rose	4.50	2.75
495	A64	1.60e brt bl	9.00	8.25
a.		Double ovpt.		
		Nos. 490-495 (6)	14.70	11.80

Liberty
A100

"Portugal"
Holding Volume
of "Lusiads"
A101

1929, May   Perf. 12x11½

496	A100	1.60e on 5c red brn	7.50	6.00

1931-38   Typographed.   Perf. 14.

497	A101	4c bis brn	15	5
498	A101	5c ol gray	15	5
499	A101	6c lt gray	15	5
500	A101	10c dk vio	15	5
501	A101	15c gray blk	15	5
502	A101	16c brt bl	1.10	45
503	A101	25c dp grn	3.00	20
a.		Imperf.		
504	A101	25c brt bl ('33)	3.00	25
505	A101	30c dk grn ('33)	1.25	25
506	A101	40c org red	7.50	5
507	A101	48c fawn	90	35
508	A101	50c lt brn	15	5
509	A101	75c car rose	4.50	1.25
510	A101	80c emerald	25	5
511	A101	95c car rose ('33)	12.00	5.25
512	A101	1e claret	35.00	5
513	A101	1.20e ol grn	2.25	80
514	A101	1.25e dk bl	1.25	5
515	A101	1.60e dk bl ('33)	25.00	3.50
516	A101	1.75e dk bl ('38)	35	5
517	A101	2e dl vio	55	5
518	A101	4.50e orange	1.50	6
519	A101	5e yel grn	1.50	6
		Nos. 497-519 (23)	101.80	13.02

Birthplace of St. Anthony
A102

Font where
St. Anthony
was Baptized
A103

Lisbon
Cathedral
A104

St. Anthony with
Infant Jesus
A105

Santa Cruz
Cathedral
A106

St. Anthony's Tomb at Padua
A107

1931, June   Typo.   Perf. 12

528	A102	15c plum	40	20
		Lithographed.		
529	A103	25c gray & pale grn	75	40
530	A104	40c gray brn & buff	45	30

PORTUGAL

531	A105	75c dl rose & pale rose	18.00	11.00	
532	A106	1.25e gray & pale bl	37.50	25.00	
533	A107	4.50e gray vio & lil	18.00	3.00	
		Nos. 528-533 (6)	75.10	39.90	

Commemorating the seventh centenary of the death of St. Anthony of Padua and Lisbon.

Nuno Alvares Pereira
A108

1931, Nov. 1   Typo.   Perf. 12x11½

534	A108	15c black	1.00	75
535	A108	25c gray grn & blk	1.00	60
536	A108	40c orange	2.50	60
a.		Value omitted	25.00	25.00
537	A108	75c car rose	17.00	12.50
538	A108	1.25e dk bl & pale bl	25.00	18.00
539	A108	4.50e choc & lt grn	110.00	50.00
a.		Value omitted	175.00	175.00
		Nos. 534-539 (6)	156.50	82.45

Issued in commemoration of the fifth centenary of the death of Nuno Alvares Pereira (1360-1431), Portuguese warrior and statesman.

Nos. 528-533 Surcharged   40 C.

1933   Perf. 12.

543	A104	15c on 40c gray brn & buff 55		30
544	A102	40c on 15c plum	1.00	45
545	A103	40c on 25c gray & pale grn	1.00	40
546	A105	40c on 75c dl rose & pale rose	5.50	3.50
547	A106	40c on 1.25e gray & pale bl	5.50	3.50
548	A107	40c on 4.50e gray vio & lil	5.50	3.50
		Nos. 543-548 (6)	19.05	11.65

Nos. 534-539 Surcharged   15 C.

1933   Perf. 12x11½

549	A108	15c on 40c org	45	30
550	A108	40c on 15c blk	2.25	1.75
551	A108	40c on 25c gray grn	60	40
552	A108	40c on 75c car rose	5.50	3.50
553	A108	40c on 1.25e dk bl	5.50	3.50
554	A108	40c on 4.50e choc & lt grn	5.50	3.50
		Nos. 549-554 (6)	19.80	12.95

President Carmona
A109

Head of a Colonial
A110

1934, May 28   Typo.   Perf. 11½.

556	A109	40c brt vio	15.00	10

1934, July   Perf. 11½x12.

558	A110	25c dk brn	1.75	50
559	A110	40c scarlet	10.00	20
560	A110	1.60e dk bl	25.00	13.00

Colonial Exposition.

Roman Temple, Evora
A111

Prince Henry the Navigator
A112

"All for the Nation"
A113

Coimbra Cathedral
A114

1935-41   Perf. 11½x12

561	A111	4c black	20	5
562	A111	5c blue	20	5
563	A111	6c choc ('36)	20	5

Perf. 11½, 12x11½ (1.75e)

564	A112	10c turq grn	5.00	15
565	A112	15c red brn	20	5
a.		Booklet pane of 4		
566	A113	25c dp bl	3.50	20
567	A113	40c brown	30	5
a.		Booklet pane of 4		
568	A113	1e rose red	2.00	30
568A	A114	1.75e blue	60.00	1.00
568B	A113	10c gray blk ('41)	12.50	1.25
569	A113	20e turq grn ('41)	15.00	1.00
		Nos. 561-569 (11)	99.10	4.15

Queen Maria
A115

Rod and Bowl of Aesculapius
A116

Typographed, Head Embossed.

1935, June 1   Perf. 11½

570	A115	40c scarlet	1.00	15

First Portuguese Philatelic Exhibition.

1937, July 24   Typo.   Perf. 11½x12

571	A116	25c blue	7.50	75

Issued in commemoration of the centenary of the establishment of the School of Medicine in Lisbon and Oporto.

Gil Vicente
A117

Grapes
A118

1937

572	A117	40c dk brn	15.00	10
573	A117	1e rose red	1.75	10

Issued to commemorate the 400th anniversary of the death of Gil Vicente (1465-1536), Portuguese playwright. Design shows him in cowherd role in his play, "Auto do Vaqueiro."

1938   Perf. 11½

575	A118	15c brt pur	1.00	50
576	A118	25c brown	1.35	90
577	A118	40c dp red lil	8.00	25
578	A118	1.75e dp bl	22.50	14.00

Issued in connection with the International Vineyard and Wine Congress.

Emblem of Portuguese Legion
A119

1940, Jan. 27   Perf. 11½   Unwmkd.

579	A119	5c dl yel	25	15
580	A119	10c violet	30	15
581	A119	15c brt bl	35	15
582	A119	25c brown	13.00	50
583	A119	40c dk grn	20.00	15
584	A119	80c yel grn	1.00	25
585	A119	1e brt red	17.50	1.50
586	A119	1.75e dk bl	5.00	2.25
a.		Souvenir sheet of 8	200.00	200.00
		Nos. 579-586 (8)	57.40	5.10

Issued in honor of the Portuguese Legion. No. 586a measures 157 x 171mm. and contains one each of Nos. 579-586 with marginal date "1939." The sheet sold for 5.50e, the proceeds going to various charities.

Portuguese World Exhibition
A120

King John IV
A121

Discoveries Monument, Belém
A122

King Alfonso I
A123

Perf. 12x11½, 11½x12

1940-41   Engraved

587	A120	10c brn vio	20	15
588	A121	15c dk grnsh bl	20	8
589	A122	25c dk sl grn	90	30
590	A121	35c yel grn	50	25
591	A123	40c ol bis	1.25	7
592	A120	80c dk vio	4.00	20
593	A122	1e dk red	7.00	50
594	A123	1.75e ultra	4.00	1.50
a.		Souvenir sheet of 8 ('41)	40.00	40.00
		Nos. 587-594 (8)	18.05	3.05

The 10c and 80c commemorate the Portuguese International Exhibition, Lisbon; 15c and 35c, 300th anniversary of the restoration of the monarchy; 40c and 1.75e, 800th anniversary of Portuguese independence. No. 594a contains one each of Nos. 587-594; ornamental border. Sold for 10e. Size: 159x223mm.

Sir Rowland Hill
A124

1940-41   Typo.   Perf. 11½x12

595	A124	15c dk vio brn	40	18
596	A124	25c dp org brn	40	20
597	A124	35c green	40	25
598	A124	40c brn vio	40	10
599	A124	50c turq grn	10.00	3.00
600	A124	80c lt bl	1.25	60
601	A124	1e crimson	9.00	1.50
602	A124	1.75e dk bl	4.00	2.75
a.		Souvenir sheet of 8 ('41)	32.50	32.50
		Nos. 595-602 (8)	25.85	8.58

Postage stamp centenary. No. 602a contains one each of Nos. 595-602 and marginal date "1940." Sold for 10e. Size: 161x153mm.

Fisherwoman of Nazare
A126

Native of Coimbra
A127

Native of Saloio
A128

Fisherwoman of Lisbon
A129

Native of Olhão
A130

Native of Aveiro
A131

Native of Madeira
A132

Native of Viana do Castelo
A133

Rancher of Ribatejo — A134

Peasant of Alentejo — A135

1941, Apr. 4 Typo. *Perf. 11½.*

605	A126	4c sage grn	15	10
606	A127	5c org brn	20	10
607	A128	10c red vio	1.50	15
608	A129	15c lt yel grn	20	15
609	A130	25c rose vio	1.25	15
610	A131	40c yel grn	20	10
611	A132	80c lt bl	1.50	60
612	A133	1e rose red	5.00	70
613	A134	1.75e dl bl	5.00	2.50
614	A135	2e red org	25.00	17.50
a.		Sheet of ten	60.00	60.00
		Nos. 605-614 (10)	40.00	22.05

No. 614a measures 163x146mm. and contains one each of Nos. 605–614, with monogram and "1941" in margins. The sheet sold for 10e.

Ancient Sailing Vessel — A136

1943 *Perf. 14.*

615	A136	5c black	5	5
616	A136	10c fawn	5	5
617	A136	15c lil gray	10	5
618	A136	20c dl vio	5	5
619	A136	30c brn vio	5	5
620	A136	35c dk bl grn	7	5
621	A136	50c plum	20	5
622	A136	1e dp rose	1.75	5
623	A136	1.75e indigo	10.00	25
624	A136	2e dl cl	75	5
625	A136	2.50e crim rose	1.25	5
626	A136	3.50e grnsh bl	6.00	35
627	A136	5e dp org	50	5
628	A136	10e bl gray	80	5
629	A136	15e bl grn	11.00	35
630	A136	20e ol gray	32.50	25
631	A136	50e salmon	125.00	40
		Nos. 615-631 (17)	190.12	2.20

See also Nos. 702 - 710.

Farmer — A137

Postrider — A138

1943, Oct. *Perf. 11½.*

632	A137	10c dl bl	40	12
633	A137	50c red	40	12

Congress of Agricultural Science.

1944, May Unwmkd.

634	A138	10c dk vio brn	20	15
635	A138	50c purple	30	15
636	A138	1e cerise	1.50	25
637	A138	1.75e brt bl	1.40	1.25
a.		Sheet of four	17.50	17.50

3rd Philatelic Exhibition, Lisbon.
No. 637a contains one each of Nos. 634–637; marginal decorations. Sold for 7.50e. Size: 82x122mm.

Portrait of Avellar Brotero — A139

Statue of Brotero — A140

1944–45 Typo. *Perf. 11½x12*

638	A139	10c chocolate	20	12
639	A140	50c dl grn	1.00	16
640	A140	1e carmine	3.25	50
641	A139	1.75e dk bl	2.50	1.25
a.		Sheet of four ('45)	25.00	25.00

Issued to commemorate the 200th anniversary of the birth of Avellar Brotero, botanist.
No. 641a measures 145x195mm. and contains one each of Nos. 638-641 and marginal decorations. The sheet sold for 7.50e.

Gil Eannes — A141

Designs: 30c, Joao Goncalves Zarco. 35c, Bartolomeu Dias. 50c, Vasco da Gama. 1e, Pedro Alvares Cabral. 1.75e, Fernando Magellan. 2e, Goncalo Velho. 3.50e, Diogo Cao.

1945, July 29 Engr. *Perf. 13½.*

642	A141	10c vio brn	10	10
643	A141	30c yel brn	20	10
644	A141	35c bl grn	30	20
645	A141	50c dk ol grn	40	10
646	A141	1e vermilion	2.00	30
647	A141	1.75e sl bl	2.25	1.25
648	A141	2e black	2.50	75
649	A141	3.50e car rose	6.50	3.00
a.		Sheet of eight	20.00	20.00
		Nos. 642-649 (8)	14.25	5.80

Portuguese navigators of 15th and 16th centuries.
No. 649a contains one each of Nos. 642–649; marginal decorations. Sold for 15e. Size: 167x172mm.

Pres. Antonio Oscar de Fragoso Carmona — A149

Astrolabe — A150

Perf. 11½

1945, Nov. 12 Photo. Unwmkd.

650	A149	10c brt vio	10	8
651	A149	30c cop brn	10	8
652	A149	35c dk grn	10	8
653	A149	50c dk ol	50	16
654	A149	1e dk red	4.00	40
655	A149	1.75e dk bl	5.00	2.00
656	A149	2e dp cl	20.00	2.50
657	A149	3.50e sl blk	12.50	3.25
a.		Sheet of eight	100.00	100.00
		Nos. 650-657 (8)	42.30	8.55

No. 657a measures 135½x98mm. and contains one each of Nos. 650–657 and decorative border. The sheet sold for 15e.

1945–46 Lithographed

658	A150	10c lt brn	10	8
659	A150	50c gray grn	30	10
660	A150	1e brn red	2.00	45
661	A150	1.75e dl chlky bl	2.50	2.00
a.		Sheet of four ('46)	20.00	20.00

Issued to commemorate the centenary of the Portuguese Naval School.
No. 661a measures 114½x135mm. and contains one each of Nos. 658 - 661, marginal decorations and "1945." The sheet sold for 7.50e.

Silves Castle—A151

Almourol Castle—A152

Designs—Castles: 30c, Leiria. 35c, Feira. 50c, Guimaraes. 1.75e, Lisbon. 2e, Braganca. 3.50e, Ourem.

1946, June 1 Engraved

662	A151	10c brn vio	10	8
663	A151	30c brn red	20	14
664	A151	35c ol grn	20	18
665	A151	50c gray blk	40	14
666	A152	1e brt car	10.00	65
667	A152	1.75e dk bl	9.00	2.00
a.		Sheet of four	75.00	75.00
668	A152	2e dk gray grn	25.00	1.75
669	A152	3.50e org brn	11.00	4.00
		Nos. 662-669 (8)	55.90	8.94

No. 667a is printed on buff granite paper. The sheet measures 135 x 102 mm., and sold for 12.50e.

Figure with Tablet and Arms — A153

Madonna and Child — A154

1946, Nov. 19 *Perf. 12x11½*

670	A153	50c dk bl	30	15
a.		Sheet of four	50.00	50.00

Issued to commemorate the centenary of the establishment of the Bank of Portugal.
No. 670a measures 155x143½mm. and has a border and marginal inscriptions. The sheet sold for 7.50e.

1946, Dec. 8 *Perf. 13½* Unwmkd.

671	A154	30c gray blk	40	12
672	A154	50c dp grn	40	12
673	A154	1e rose car	2.00	60
674	A154	1.75e brt bl	3.00	1.50
a.		Sheet of four ('47)	20.00	20.00

Issued to commemorate the 300th anniversary of the proclamation making the Virgin Mary patroness of Portugal.
No. 674a measures 108½x159mm. and contains one each of Nos. 671-674, and marginal decorations and inscriptions. The sheet sold for 7.50e.

Shepherdess, Caramullo — A155

Surrender of the Moors, 1147 — A163

Designs: 30c, Timbrel player, Malpique. 35c, Flute player, Monsanto. 50c, Woman of Avintes. 1e, Field laborer, Maia. 1.75e, Woman of Algarve. 2e, Bastonet player, Miranda. 3.50e, Woman of the Azores.

1947, Mar. 1 Photo. *Perf. 11½*

675	A155	10c rose vio	10	8
676	A155	30c dk red	10	8
677	A155	35c dk ol grn	20	12
678	A155	50c dk brn	40	7
679	A155	1e red	4.00	40
680	A155	1.75e sl bl	4.00	2.75
681	A155	2e pck bl	20.00	1.75
682	A155	3.50e sl blk	12.50	3.50
a.		Sheet of eight	110.00	110.00
		Nos. 675-682 (8)	41.30	8.75

No. 682a measures 135x98mm. and contains one each of Nos. 675-682, and decorative border. The sheet sold for 15e.

1947, Oct. 13 Engraved *Perf. 12½*

683	A163	5c bl grn	10	10
684	A163	20c dk car	30	20
685	A163	50c violet	50	20
686	A163	1.75e dk bl	4.00	3.00
687	A163	2.50e chocolate	6.00	5.00
688	A163	3.50e sl blk	10.00	9.00
		Nos. 683-688 (6)	20.90	17.50

Issued to commemorate the 800th anniversary of the conquest of Lisbon from the Moors.

St. John de Britto — A164, A165

1948, May 28 *Perf. 11½x12*

689	A164	30c green	20	15
690	A165	50c dk brn	20	15
691	A164	1e rose car	5.00	1.10
692	A165	1.75e blue	6.50	1.75

Issued to commemorate the 300th anniversary of the birth of St. John de Britto.

Architecture and Engineering — A166

King John I — A167

1948, May 28 *Perf. 13x12½*

693	A166	50c vio brn	20	8

Issued to publicize the Exposition of public Works and the National Congress of Engineering and Architecture, 1948.

Photogravure.

1949, May 6 *Perf. 11½* Unwmkd.

Designs: 30c, Philippa of Lancaster. 35c, Prince Ferdinand. 50c, Prince Henry the Navigator. 1e, Nuno Alvarez Pereira. 1.75e, John das Regras. 2e, Fernao Lopes. 3.50e, Affonso Domingues.

694	A167	10c brn vio & cr	20	10
695	A167	30c dk bl grn & cr	20	12
696	A167	35c dk ol grn & cr	20	15
697	A167	50c dp bl & cr	90	25
698	A167	1e dk red & cr	90	25
699	A167	1.75e dk gray & cr	8.00	7.00
700	A167	2e dk gray bl & cr	4.00	75
701	A167	3.50e dk brn & gray	14.00	13.00
a.		Sheet of 8	32.50	32.50
		Nos. 694-701 (8)	28.40	21.62

No. 701a contains one each of Nos. 694–701 and ornamental border. Sold for 15e.

Ship Type of 1942.

1948–49 Typographed *Perf. 14*

702	A136	80c dp grn	2.50	20
703	A136	1e dp cl ('48)	1.25	5

PORTUGAL

704	A136	1.20e dp car	2.50	18
705	A136	1.50e olive	20.00	15
706	A136	1.80e yel org	20.00	1.50
707	A136	2e dp bl	2.50	6
708	A136	4e orange	22.50	1.25
709	A136	6e yel grn	45.00	1.50
710	A136	7.50e grnsh gray	14.00	1.25
Nos. 702-710 (9)			130.25	6.14

Angel, Coimbra Museum A168 — Symbols of the U.P.U. A169

1949, Dec. 20 Engr. Perf. 13x14

| 711 | A168 | 1e red brn | 7.00 | 8 |
| 712 | A168 | 5e ol brn | 75 | 20 |

Issued to publicize the 16th International Congress of History and Art.

1949, Dec. 29

713	A169	1e brn vio	30	10
714	A169	2e dp bl	70	20
715	A169	2.50e dp grn	3.00	60
716	A169	4e brn red	8.00	3.00

Issued to commemorate the 75th anniversary of the formation of the Universal Postal Union.

Madonna of Fatima A170 — St. John of God Helping Ill Man A171

1950, May 13 Perf. 11½x12

717	A170	50c dk grn	60	12
718	A170	1e dk brn	2.25	15
719	A170	2e blue	4.00	1.00
720	A170	5e lilac	52.50	18.50

Issued to commemorate the Holy Year, 1950, and to honor "Our Lady of the Rosary" at Fatima.

1950, Oct. 30 Engraved Unwmkd.

721	A171	20c gray vio	20	17
722	A171	50c cerise	40	18
723	A171	1e ol grn	80	20
724	A171	1.50e dp org	7.50	2.00
725	A171	2e blue	5.50	90
726	A171	4e chocolate	20.00	4.50
Nos. 721-726 (6)			34.40	7.95

Issued to commemorate the 400th anniversary of the death of St. John of God.

Guerra Junqueiro A172 — Fisherman and Catch A173

1951, Mar. 2 Litho. Perf. 13½

| 727 | A172 | 50c dk brn | 2.50 | 30 |
| 728 | A172 | 1e dk sl gray | 60 | 15 |

Birth centenary of Guerra Junqueiro, poet.

1951, Mar. 9

| 729 | A173 | 50c gray grn, *buff* | 2.50 | 50 |
| 730 | A173 | 1e rose lake, *buff* | 80 | 12 |

3rd National Congress of Fisheries.

Dove A174

Pope Pius XII A175

1951, Oct. 11

731	A174	20c dk brn & buff	20	10
732	A174	90c dk ol grn & cr	2.00	80
733	A175	1e dp cl & pink	2.00	8
734	A175	2.30e dk bl grn & bl	5.00	1.00

End of the Holy Year.

15th Century Colonists, Terceira A176

1951, Oct. 24 Perf. 13x13½

| 735 | A176 | 50c dk bl, *sal* | 1.25 | 60 |
| 736 | A176 | 1e dk brn, *cr* | 80 | 60 |

Issued to commemorate the 500th anniversary (in 1950) of the colonizing of the island of Terceira.

Student, Soldiers and Workers A177

1951, Nov. 22 Perf. 13½x13

| 737 | A177 | 1e vio brn | 1.35 | 15 |
| 738 | A177 | 2.30e dk bl | 1.25 | 50 |

Issued to commemorate the 25th anniversary of the national revolution.

16th Century Coach A178
Designs: Various coaches.

Perf. 13x13½

1952, Jan. 8 Engraved Unwmkd.

739	A178	10c purple	10	6
740	A178	20c ol gray	15	10
741	A178	50c stl bl	40	12
742	A178	90c green	75	60
743	A178	1e red org	85	15
744	A178	1.40e rose pink	3.00	2.50
745	A178	1.50e rose brn	3.50	1.50
746	A178	2.30e dp ultra	1.10	65
Nos. 739-746 (8)			9.85	5.68

Issued to honor the National Museum of Coaches.

Symbolical of NATO A179

1952, Apr. 4 Litho. Perf. 12½

| 747 | A179 | 1e grn & blk | 8.00 | 30 |
| 748 | A179 | 3.50e gray & vio bl | 125.00 | 20.00 |

Issued to commemorate the third anniversary of the signing of the North Atlantic Treaty.

Hockey Players on Roller Skates A180

1952, June 28 Perf. 13x13½

| 749 | A180 | 1e dk bl & gray | 3.00 | 20 |
| 750 | A180 | 3.50e dk red brn | 5.00 | 2.00 |

Issued to publicize the 8th World Championship Hockey-on-Skates matches.

Francisco Gomes Teixeira A181 — St. Francis and Two Boys A182

1952, Nov. 25 Perf. 14x14½

| 751 | A181 | 1e cerise | 60 | 12 |
| 752 | A181 | 2.30e dp bl | 3.75 | 3.25 |

Issued to commemorate the centenary of the birth of Francisco Gomes Teixeira (1851–1932), mathematician.

1952, Dec. 23 Perf. 13½

753	A182	1e dk grn	70	18
754	A182	2e dp cl	1.25	50
755	A182	3.50e chlky bl	14.00	8.50
756	A182	5e dk pur	20.00	2.50

Issued to commemorate the 400th anniversary of the death of St. Francis Xavier.

Marshal Carmona Bridge—A183
Designs: 1.40e, "28th of May" Stadium. 2e, University City, Coimbra. 3.50e, Salazar Dam.

1952, Dec. 10 Perf. 12½ Unwmkd.
Buff Paper.

757	A183	1e red brn	40	10
758	A183	1.40e dl pur	6.50	3.75
759	A183	2e dk grn	4.00	1.40
760	A183	3.50e dk bl	7.00	2.50

Issued to commemorate the centenary of the foundation of the Ministry of Public Works.

Equestrian Seal of King Diniz A184

1953–56 Lithographed

761	A184	5c grn, *cit*	5	5
762	A184	10c ind, *sal*	5	5
763	A184	20c org red, *cit*	5	5
763A	A184	30c rose lil, *cr* ('56)	8	5
764	A184	50c gray	5	5
765	A184	90c dk grn, *bl*	4.50	20
766	A184	1e vio brn, *rose*	10	5
767	A184	1.40e rose red	4.50	50
768	A184	1.50e red, *cr*	20	5
769	A184	2e gray	20	5
770	A184	2.30e blue	5.00	40
771	A184	2.50e gray blk, *sal*	25	5
772	A184	5e rose vio, *cr*	65	5
773	A184	10e bl, *cit*	1.25	5
774	A184	20e bis brn, *cit*	2.50	10
775	A184	50e rose vio	6.25	20
Nos. 761-775 (16)			25.68	2.00

St. Martin of Braga A185 — Guilherme Gomes Fernandes A186

Perf. 13x13½

1953, Feb. 26 Unwmkd.

| 776 | A185 | 1e gray blk & gray | 1.25 | 15 |
| 777 | A185 | 3.50e dk brn & yel | 8.50 | 5.50 |

Issued to commemorate the 14th centenary of the arrival of St. Martin of Dume on the Iberian peninsula.

1953, Mar. 28 Perf. 13

| 778 | A186 | 1e red vio | 1.00 | 15 |
| 779 | A186 | 2.30e dp bl | 6.50 | 5.50 |

Issued to commemorate the birth of Guilherme Gomes Fernandes, General Inspector of the Firemen of Porto.

Emblems of Automobile Club A187

1953, Apr. 15 Perf. 12½

| 780 | A187 | 1e dk grn & yel grn | 1.00 | 20 |
| 781 | A187 | 3.50e dk brn & buff | 8.00 | 5.50 |

Issued to commemorate the 50th anniversary of the Portuguese Automobile Club.

Princess St. Joanna A188 — Queen Maria II A189

1953, May 14 Litho. Perf. 14½x14 Unwmkd.

| 782 | A188 | 1e blk & gray grn | 1.50 | 20 |
| 783 | A188 | 3.50e dk bl & bl | 10.00 | 6.50 |

Issued to commemorate the 500th anniversary of the birth of Princess St. Joanna.

PORTUGAL

1953, Oct. 3   Photo.   *Perf. 13½*
Background of Lower Panel in Gold.

784	A189	50c red brn	20	10
785	A189	1e cl brn	20	10
786	A189	1.40e dk vio	1.50	1.00
787	A189	2.30e dp bl	2.50	1.75
788	A189	3.50e vio bl	2.50	2.00
789	A189	4.50e dk brn	2.00	1.00
790	A189	5e dk ol grn	4.25	70
791	A189	20e red vio	35.00	3.50
	Nos. 784-791 (8)		48.15	10.15

Issued to commemorate the centenary of Portugal's first postage stamp.

Allegory
A190

1954, Sept. 22   *Perf. 13*

792	A190	1e bl & dk grnsh bl	60	10
793	A190	1.50e buff & dk brn	1.00	30

Issued to commemorate the 150th anniversary of the founding of the State Secretariat for Financial Affairs.

Open Textbook
A191

Cadet and College Arms
A192

1954, Oct. 15   Lithographed

794	A191	50c blue	15	6
795	A191	1e red	20	5
796	A191	2e dk grn	11.00	50
797	A191	2.50e org brn	12.50	1.10

National literacy campaign.

1954, Nov. 17

798	A192	1e choc & lt grn	1.25	15
799	A192	3.50e dk bl & gray grn	3.00	1.75

150th anniversary of the Military College.

Manuel da Nobrega and Crucifix
A193

King Alfonso I
A194

1954, Dec. 17   Engr.   *Perf. 14x13*

800	A193	1e brown	60	10
801	A193	2.30e dp bl	16.00	14.00
802	A193	3.50e gray grn	8.00	1.25
803	A193	5e green	16.00	1.75

Issued to commemorate the 400th anniversary of the founding of Sao Paulo, Brazil.

1955, Mar. 17   *Perf. 13½x13*

Kings: 20c, Sancho I. 50c, Alfonso II. 90c, Sancho II. 1e, Alfonso III. 1.40e, Diniz. 1.50e, Alfonso IV. 2e, Pedro I. 2.30e, Ferdinand I.

804	A194	10c rose vio	10	10
805	A194	20c dk ol grn	10	10
806	A194	50c dk bl grn	30	15
807	A194	90c green	90	60
808	A194	1e red brn	60	10
809	A194	1.40e car rose	3.00	2.00
810	A194	1.50e ol brn	1.50	75
811	A194	2e dp org	4.25	2.00
812	A194	2.30e vio bl	4.25	2.50
	Nos. 804-812 (9)		15.00	8.30

Telegraph Pole
A195

A. J. Ferreira da Silva
A196

1955, Sept. 16   Litho.   *Perf. 13½*

813	A195	1e ocher & hn brn	40	15
814	A195	2.30e gray grn & Prus bl	5.50	2.00
815	A195	3.50e lem & dp grn	5.50	1.50

Issued to commemorate the centenary of the telegraph system in Portugal.

1956, May 8   Photo.   Unwmkd.

816	A196	1e bl & dk bl	40	10
817	A196	2.30e grn & dk grn	4.25	3.25

Issued to commemorate the centenary of the birth of Prof. Antonio Joaquim Ferreira da Silva, chemist.

Steam Locomotive, 1856
A197

Madonna, 15th Century
A198

Design: 1.50e, 2e, Electric train, 1956.

1956, Oct. 28   Litho.   *Perf. 13*

818	A197	1e lt & dk ol grn	40	10
819	A197	1.50e Prus bl & lt grnsh bl	1.50	35
820	A197	2e dk org brn & bis	10.00	1.25
821	A197	2.50e choc & brn	12.50	1.75

Centenary of the Portuguese railways.

1956, Dec. 8   Photogravure

822	A198	1e dp grn & lt ol grn	40	10
823	A198	1.50e dk red brn & ol bis	75	20

Mothers' Day, Dec. 8.

J. B. Almeida Garrett
A199

1957, Mar. 7   Engr.   *Perf. 13½x14*

824	A199	1e sepia	45	12
825	A199	2.30e lt pur	10.50	8.00
826	A199	3.50e dl grn	13	45
827	A199	5e rose car	16.00	6.50

Issued in honor of Joao Baptista da Silva Leitao de Almeida Garrett, poet.

Cesario Verde
A200

Exhibition Emblems
A201

1957, Dec. 12   Litho.   *Perf. 13½*

828	A200	1e cit & brn	70	6
829	A200	3.30e gray grn, yel grn & dk ol	1.50	1.00

Issued in honor of Jose Joaquim de Cesario Verde (1855-1886), poet.

1958, Apr. 7

830	A201	1e multi	65	12
831	A201	3.30e multi	1.50	1.25

Issued for the Universal and International Exposition at Brussels.

Queen St. Isabel
A202

Institute for Tropical Medicine
A203

Design: 2e, 5e, St. Teotonio.

Perf. 14½x14

1958, July 10   Photo.   Unwmkd.

832	A202	1e rose brn & buff	30	8
833	A202	2e dk grn & buff	50	20
834	A202	2.50e pur & buff	1.75	20
835	A202	5e brn & buff	2.50	40

1958, Sept. 4   Litho.   *Perf. 13*

836	A203	1e dk grn & lt gray	80	10
837	A203	2.50e bl & pale bl	2.50	50

Issued to publicize the 6th International Congress for Tropical Medicine and Malaria, Lisbon, Sept. 1958, and the opening of the new Tropical Medicine Institute.

Cargo Ship and Loading Crane—A204

1958, Nov. 27   *Perf. 13*   Unwmkd.

838	A204	1e brn & dk brn	1.00	10
839	A204	4.50e vio bl & dk bl	1.50	70

Issued to commemorate the 2nd National Congress of the Merchant Marine, Porto.

Queen Leonor
A205

1958, Dec. 17

840	A205	1e multi	30	12
841	A205	1.50e bis, blk, bl & dk bis brn	2.00	20

a. Dark bis brn omitted

842	A205	2.30e multi	1.75	60
843	A205	4.10e multi	1.25	80

Issued to commemorate the 500th anniversary of the birth of Queen Leonor.

Arms of Aveiro
A206

Symbols of Hope and Peace
A207

1959, Aug. 30   Litho.   *Perf. 13*

844	A206	1e ol bis, brn, gold & sil	50	10
845	A206	5e grnsh gray, gold & sil	3.00	45

Millennium of Aveiro.

1960, Mar. 2   *Perf. 12½*

846	A207	1e lt vio & blk	85	15
847	A207	3.50e gray & dk grn	3.50	2.00

Issued to commemorate the 10th anniversary (in 1959) of the North Atlantic Treaty Organization.

Open Door to "Peace" and WRY Emblem
A208

Glider
A209

1960, Apr. 7   *Perf. 13*   Unwmkd.

848	A208	20c multi	8	5
849	A208	1e multi	75	5
850	A208	1.80e yel grn, org & blk	50	40

Issued to publicize World Refugee Year, July 1, 1959–June 30, 1960.

1960, May 2

Designs: 1.50e, Plane. 2e, Plane and parachutes. 2.50e, Model plane.

851	A209	1e yel, gray & bl	20	5
852	A209	1.50e multi	80	20
853	A209	2e bl grn, yel & blk	1.10	50
854	A209	2.50e grnsh bl, ocher & red	1.75	60

Issued to commemorate the 50th anniversary (in 1959) of the Aero Club of Portugal.

Father Cruz
A210

University of Evora Seal
A211

1960, July 18   *Perf. 13*   Unwmkd.

855	A210	1e dp brn	40	10
856	A210	4.30e Prus bl & blk	4.25	4.00

Issued to honor Father Cruz, "father of the poor."

PORTUGAL

1960, July 18   **Lithographed**
857	A211	50c vio bl	10	6
858	A211	1e red brn & yel	30	10
859	A211	1.40e rose cl & rose	1.00	80

Issued to commemorate the 400th anniversary of the founding of the University of Evora.

Arms of Prince Henry
A212

Arms of Lisbon and Symbolic Ship
A213

Designs: 2.50e, Caravel. 3.50e, Prince Henry. 5e, Prince Henry's motto. 8e, Prince Henry's sloop. 10e, Old chart of Sagres region of Portugal.

1960, Aug. 4   **Photo.**   *Perf. 12x12½*
860	A212	1e gold & multi	20	5
861	A212	2.50e gold & multi	1.75	40
862	A212	3.50e gold & multi	2.50	1.25
863	A212	5e gold & multi	3.75	50
864	A212	8e gold & multi	60	50
865	A212	10e gold & multi	6.00	1.60
		Nos. 860-865 (6)	14.80	4.30

Issued to commemorate the 500th anniversary of the death of Prince Henry the Navigator.

Europa Issue, 1960
Common Design Type
1960, Sept. 16   **Litho.**   *Perf. 13*
Size: 31x21mm.
| 866 | CD3 | 1e ultra & gray bl | 40 | 6 |
| 867 | CD3 | 3.50e brn red & rose red | 2.75 | 1.50 |

1960, Nov. 17   *Perf. 13*
| 868 | A213 | 1e gray ol, blk & vio bl | 70 | 10 |
| 869 | A213 | 3.30e bl, blk & ultra | 6.00 | 4.50 |

Issued to commemorate the Fifth National Philatelic Exhibition, Lisbon, part of the Prince Henry the Navigator festivities. (The ship in the design is in honor of Prince Henry.)

Flag and Laurel
A214

1960, Dec. 20   **Litho.**   *Perf. 13*
| 870 | A214 | 1e multi | 20 | 10 |

50th anniversary of the Republic.

King Pedro V
A215

1961, Aug. 3   **Engraved**   *Perf. 13*
| 871 | A215 | 1e gray brn & dk grn | 50 | 5 |
| 872 | A215 | 6.50e dk bl & blk | 1.50 | 50 |

Issued to commemorate the centenary of the founding of the Faculty of Letters, Lisbon University.

Setubal Sea Gate and Ships
A216

1961, Aug. 24   **Litho.**   *Perf. 12x11½*
| 873 | A216 | 1e gold & multi | 40 | 6 |
| 874 | A216 | 4.30e gold & multi | 5.00 | 5.00 |

Centenary of the city of Setubal.

Clasped Hands and CEPT Emblem
A217

Tomar Castle and River Nabao
A218

Europa Issue, 1961
1961, Sept. 18   *Perf. 13½x13*
875	A217	1e bl & lt bl	20	6
876	A217	1.50e grn & brt grn	1.10	1.10
877	A217	3.50e brn, pink & red	1.75	1.75

1962, Jan. 26   *Perf. 11½x12*
| 878 | A218 | 1e gold & multi | 30 | 5 |
| 879 | A218 | 3.50e gold & multi | 1.50 | 1.40 |

800th anniversary of the city of Tomar.

National Guardsman
A219

Archangel Gabriel
A220

1962, Feb. 20   *Perf. 13½*   **Unwmkd.**
880	A219	1e multi	20	7
881	A219	2e multi	1.75	35
882	A219	2.50e multi	1.50	35

Issued to commemorate the 50th anniversary of the Republican National Guard.

1962, Mar. 24   **Litho.**   *Perf. 13*
| 883 | A220 | 1e ol, pink & red brn | 70 | 6 |
| 884 | A220 | 3.50e ol, pink & dk grn | 45 | 25 |

Issued for St. Gabriel's Day. St. Gabriel is patron of telecommunications.

Tents and Scout Emblem
A221

1962, June 11   *Perf. 13*   **Unwmkd.**
885	A221	20c gray, bis, yel & blk	5	5
a.		Double impression of gray frame lettering		
886	A221	50c multi	10	8
887	A221	1e multi	70	9
888	A221	2.50e multi	2.50	30
889	A221	3.50e multi	1.00	40
890	A221	6.50e multi	90	50
		Nos. 885-890 (6)	5.25	1.42

Issued to commemorate the 50th anniversary of the Portuguese Boy Scouts and the 18th Boy Scout World Conference, Sept. 19-24, 1961.

Children Reading
A222

Designs: 1e, Vaccination. 2.80e, Children playing ball. 3.50e, Guarding sleeping infant.

1962, Sept. 10   **Litho.**   *Perf. 13½*
891	A222	50c bluish grn, yel & blk	10	5
892	A222	1e pale bl, yel & blk	70	6
893	A222	2.80e dp org yel & blk	1.00	1.00
894	A222	3.50e dl rose, yel & blk	1.50	1.00

Issued to commemorate the Tenth International Congress of Pediatrics, Lisbon, Sept. 9-15.

Europa Issue, 1962

19-Cell Honeycomb
A223

1962, Sept. 17
895	A223	1e bl, dk bl & gold	30	5
896	A223	1.50e lt & dk grn & gold	1.25	50
897	A223	3.50e dp rose, mar & gold	1.00	80

The 19 cells represent the 19 original members of the Conference of European Postal and Telecommunications Administrations, C.E.P.T.

St. Zenon, the Courier
A224

European Soccer Cup and Emblem
A225

1962, Dec. 1   *Perf. 13½*   **Unwmkd.**
898	A224	1e multi	30	6
899	A224	2e multi	1.10	60
900	A224	2.80e multi	1.50	1.50

Issued for Stamp Day.

1963, Feb. 5   *Perf. 13½*
| 901 | A225 | 1e multi | 90 | 6 |
| 902 | A225 | 4.30e multi | 1.25 | 1.00 |

Issued to commemorate the victories of the Benfica Club of Lisbon in the 1961 and 1962 European Soccer Championships.

Wheat Emblem
A226

1963, Mar. 21   **Lithographed**
903	A226	1e multi	30	6
904	A226	3.30e multi	1.25	1.00
905	A226	3.50e multi	1.75	70

Issued for the "Freedom from Hunger" campaign of the U.N. Food and Agriculture Organization.

Stagecoach—A227

1963, May 7   *Perf. 12x11½*
906	A227	1e gray, lt & dk bl	30	5
907	A227	1.50e bis, dk brn & lil rose	1.25	35
908	A227	5e org brn, dk brn & rose lil	40	10

Issued to commemorate the centenary of the first International Postal Conference, Paris, 1863.

St. Vincent de Paul by Monsaraz
A228

1963, July 10   **Photo.**   *Perf. 13½x14*
Gold Inscription
909	A228	20c lt bl & ultra	10	5
a.		Gold inscription omitted	70.00	
910	A228	1e gray & sl	40	5
911	A228	2.80e grn & sl	1.00	90
a.		Gold inscription omitted	80.00	
912	A228	5e dp rose car & sl	1.75	50

Issued to commemorate the tercentenary of the death of St. Vincent de Paul.

Emblem of Order and Knight
A229

1963, Aug. 13   **Litho.**   *Perf. 11½*
913	A229	1e multi	30	5
914	A229	1.50e multi	40	14
915	A229	2.50e multi	1.75	50

Issued to commemorate the 800th anniversary of the Military Order of Avis.

Europa Issue, 1963

Stylized Bird—A230

1963, Sept. 16   *Perf. 13½*
916	A230	1e lt bl, gray & blk	30	10
917	A230	1.50e grn, gray & blk	1.50	30
918	A230	3.50e red, gray & blk	1.75	1.00

PORTUGAL

	Jet Plane A231		Apothecary Jar A232	

1963, Dec. 1   Perf. 13½   Unwmkd.

919	A231	1e dk bl & lt bl	30	8
920	A231	2.50e dk grn & yel grn	1.25	40
921	A231	3.50e org brn & org	1.50	80

Issued to commemorate the 10th anniversary of Transportes Aéreos Portugueses, TAP.

1964, Apr. 9   Lithographed

922	A232	50c brn ol, dk brn & blk	20	8
923	A232	1e rose brn, dp cl & blk	30	6
924	A232	4.30e dk gray, sl & blk	5.00	5.00

Issued to commemorate the 4th centenary of the publication (in Goa, Apr. 10, 1563) of "Coloquios Dos Simples e Drogas" (Herbs and Drugs in India) by Garcia D'Orta.

Emblem of National Overseas Bank A233	Mt. Sameiro Church A234

1964, May 19   Perf. 13½   Unwmkd.

925	A233	1e bis, yel & dk bl	20	6
926	A233	2.50e ocher, yel & grn	1.75	50
927	A233	3.50e bis, yel & brn	1.25	65

Centenary of National Overseas Bank.

1964, June 5   Lithographed

928	A234	1e red brn, bis & dl brn	20	6
929	A234	2e brn, bis & dl brn	1.40	50
930	A234	5e dk vio bl, bis & gray	1.75	65

Issued to commemorate the centenary of the Shrine of Our Lady of Mt. Sameiro, Braga.

Europa Issue, 1964
Common Design Type
1964, Sept. 14   Perf. 13½   Unwmkd.
Size: 19x32mm.

931	CD7	1e bl, lt bl & dk bl	30	6
932	CD7	3.50e rose brn, buff & dk brn	1.40	60
933	CD7	4.30e grn, yel grn & dk grn	2.25	2.00

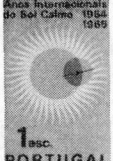 

Partial Eclipse of Sun A235	Olympic Rings, Emblems of Portugal and Japan A236

1964

| 934 | A235 | 1e multi | 35 | 10 |
| 935 | A235 | 8e multi | 1.40 | 60 |

International Quiet Sun Year, 1964-65.

1964, Dec. 1   Perf. 13½   Unwmkd.
Black Inscriptions; Olympic Rings in Pale Yellow

936	A236	20c tan, red & vio bl	10	5
937	A236	1e ultra, red & vio bl	30	6
938	A236	1.50e yel grn, red & vio bl	1.25	50
939	A236	6.50e rose lil, red & vio bl	1.75	1.50

18th Olympic Games, Tokyo, Oct. 10-25.

Eduardo Coelho A237	Traffic Signs and Signals A238

1964, Dec. 28   Litho.   Perf. 13½

| 940 | A237 | 1e multi | 30 | 6 |
| 941 | A237 | 5e multi | 1.75 | 60 |

Issued to commemorate the centenary of the founding of Portugal's first newspaper, "Diario de Noticias," and to honor the founder, Eduardo Coelho, journalist.

1965, Feb. 15   Lithographed

942	A238	1e yel, red & emer	40	5
943	A238	3.30e multi	4.00	4.00
944	A238	3.50e red, yel & emer	1.75	80

Issued to publicize the First National Traffic Congress, Lisbon, Feb. 15-19.

Ferdinand I, Duke of Braganza A239	Coimbra Gate, Angel with Censer and Sword A240

1965, Mar. 16   Perf. 13½   Unwmkd.

| 945 | A239 | 1e rose brn & blk | 20 | 6 |
| 946 | A239 | 10e Prus grn & blk | 2.00 | 70 |

Issued to commemorate the 500th anniversary of the city of Braganza (in 1964).

1965, Apr. 27   Perf. 11½x12

947	A240	1e bl & multi	20	10
948	A240	2.50e multi	1.75	60
949	A240	5e multi	1.75	1.00

Issued to commemorate the 9th centenary (in 1964) of the capture of the city of Coimbra from the Moors.

ITU Emblem A241

1965, May 17   Perf. 13½

950	A241	1e bis brn, ol grn & ol	20	5
951	A241	3.50e ol, rose cl & dp cl	1.40	60
952	A241	6.50e yel grn, dl bl & sl bl	1.00	90

Issued to commemorate the centenary of the International Telecommunication Union.

Calouste Gulbenkian A242

1965, July 20   Litho.   Perf. 13½

| 953 | A242 | 1e multi | 70 | 10 |
| 954 | A242 | 8e multi | 80 | 50 |

Issued to honor Calouste Gulbenkian (1869-1955), oil industry pioneer and sponsor of the Gulbenkian Foundation.

Red Cross A243

1965, Aug. 17   Perf. 13½   Unwmkd.

955	A243	1e grn, red & blk	20	5
956	A243	4e ol, red & blk	2.00	60
957	A243	4.30e lt rose brn, red & blk	10.00	10.00

Centenary of the Portuguese Red Cross.

Europa Issue, 1965
Common Design Type
1965, Sept. 27   Litho.   Perf. 13
Size: 31x24mm.

958	CD8	1e saph, grnsh bl & dk bl	20	10
959	CD8	3.50e rose brn, sal & brn	1.75	60
960	CD8	4.30e yel grn, sal & dk grn	4.00	3.50

Military Plane A244

1965, Oct. 20   Perf. 13½

961	A244	1e ol grn, red & dk grn	20	5
962	A244	2e sep, red & dk grn	1.00	30
963	A244	5e chlky bl, red & dk grn	1.75	80

Issued to commemorate the 50th anniversary of the founding of the Portuguese Air Force.

Woman A245	Chrismon with Alpha and Omega A246

Designs: Characters from Gil Vicente Plays.

1965, Dec. 1   Litho.   Perf. 13½

964	A245	20c ol, pale yel & blk	10	5
965	A245	1e brn, pale yel & blk	30	6
966	A245	2.50e dk red, buff & blk	2.50	30
967	A245	6.50e bl, gray & blk	70	60

Issued to commemorate the 500th anniversary of the birth of Gil Vicente (1465?-1536?).

1966, March 28   Litho.   Perf. 13½

968	A246	1e ol bis, gold & blk	50	10
969	A246	3.30e gray, gold & blk	3.25	3.25
970	A246	5e rose cl, gold & blk	2.50	90

Issued to commemorate the Congress of the International Committee for the Defense of Christian Civilization, Lisbon.

Symbols of Peace and Labor A247

1966, May 28   Litho.   Perf. 13½

971	A247	1e dk bl, sl bl & lt sl bl	20	5
972	A247	3.50e ol, ol brn, & lt ol	1.50	70
973	A247	4e dk brn, brn car & dl rose	1.25	60

40th anniversary of National Revolution.

Knight Giraldo on Horseback A248

1966, June 8

| 974 | A248 | 1e multi | 70 | 10 |
| 975 | A248 | 8e multi | 1.00 | 45 |

Issued to commemorate the 800th anniversary of the conquest of Evora from the Moors.

Salazar Bridge A249

Designs: 2.80e, 4.30e, View of bridge (vert.).

1966, Aug. 6   Litho.   Perf. 13½

976	A249	1e gold & red	15	5
977	A249	2.50e gold & ultra	1.75	50
978	A249	2.80e sil & dp ultra	1.75	1.25
979	A249	4.30e sil & dk grn	1.75	1.25

Issued to commemorate the opening of the Salazar Bridge over the Tejo River, Lisbon.

Europa Issue, 1966
Common Design Type
1966, Sept. 26   Litho.   Perf. 11½x12
Size: 26x32mm.

980	CD9	1e bl & blk	15	5
981	CD9	3.50e red brn & blk	2.00	1.00
982	CD9	4.30e yel grn & blk	2.25	1.75

Pestana — A250	Bocage — A251

PORTUGAL

Portraits: 20c, Câmara Pestana (1863–1899), bacteriologist. 50c, Egas Moniz (1874–1955), neurologist. 1e, Antonio Pereira Coutinho (1851–1939), botanist. 1.50e, José Corrêa da Serra (1750–1823), botanist. 2e, Ricardo Jórge (1858–1938), hygienist and anthropologist. 2.50e, J. Liete de Vasconcelos (1858–1941), ethnologist. 2.80e, Maximiano Lemos (1860–1923), medical historian. 4.30e, José Antonio Serrano, anatomist.

1966 Dec. 1   Litho.   Perf. 13½
Portrait and Inscription in Dark Brown and Bister

983	A250	20c gray grn	5	5
984	A250	50c orange	10	5
985	A250	1e lemon	20	5
986	A250	1.50e bis brn	30	15
987	A250	2e brn org	1.75	15
988	A250	2.50e pale grn	2.00	30
989	A250	2.80e salmon	2.00	2.00
990	A250	4.30e Prus bl	2.50	2.50
		Nos. 983-990 (8)	8.90	5.25

Issued to honor Portuguese scientists.

1966, Dec. 28 Litho. Perf. 11½x12

991	A251	1e bis, grnsh gray & blk	18	5
992	A251	2e brn org, grnsh gray & blk	60	25
993	A251	6e gray, grnsh gray & blk	1.10	60

Issued to commemorate the 200th anniversary of the birth of Manuel Maria Barbosa du Bocage (1765–1805), poet.

Europa Issue, 1967
Common Design Type
1967, May 2 Lithographed Perf. 13
Size: 21½x31mm.

994	CD10	1e lt bl, Prus bl & blk	20	10
995	CD10	3.50e sal, brn red & blk	1.75	50
996	CD10	4.30e yel grn, ol grn & blk	2.50	1.75

Apparition of Our Lady of Fatima
A252

Statues of Roman Senators
A253

Designs: 2.80e, Church and Golden Rose. 3.50e, Statue of the Pilgrim Virgin, with lilies and doves. 4e, Doves holding crown over Chapel of the Apparition.

1967, May 13   Perf. 11½x12

997	A252	1e multi	15	10
998	A252	2.80e multi	1.25	1.25
999	A252	3.50e multi	60	25
1000	A252	4e multi	70	30

Issued to commemorate the 50th anniversary of the apparition of the Virgin Mary to 3 shepherd children at Fatima.

1967, June 1   Litho.   Perf. 13

1001	A253	1e gold & rose cl	15	5
1002	A253	2.50e gold & dl bl	1.75	30
1003	A253	4.30e gold & gray grn	70	60

Introduction of a new civil law code.

Shipyard, Margueira, Lisbon
A254

Design: 2.80e, 4.30e, Ship's hull and map showing location of harbor.

1967, June 23

1004	A254	1e aqua & multi	15	5
1005	A254	2.80e multi	75	60
1006	A254	3.50e multi	80	40
1007	A254	4.30e multi	1.00	80

Issued to commemorate the inauguration of the Lisnave Shipyard at Margueira, Lisbon.

Symbols of Healing
A255

Flags of EFTA Nations
A256

1967, Oct. 8   Litho.   Perf. 13½

1008	A255	1e multi	20	8
1009	A255	2e multi	1.00	30
1010	A255	5e multi	1.75	75

Issued to publicize the 6th European Congress of Rheumatology, Lisbon, Oct. 8–13.

1967, Oct. 24   Litho.   Perf. 13½

1011	A256	1e bis & multi	15	5
1012	A256	3.50e buff & multi	1.00	70
1013	A256	4.30e gray & multi	3.00	3.00

Issued to publicize the European Free Trade Association. See note after Norway No. 501.

Tables of the Law
A257

1967, Dec. 27   Litho.   Perf. 13½

1014	A257	1e olive	15	5
1015	A257	2e red brn	1.00	30
1016	A257	5e green	1.50	80

Centenary of abolition of death penalty.

Bento de Goes
A258

1968, Feb. 14 Engr. Perf. 12x11½

| 1017 | A258 | 1e ol, ind & dk brn | 60 | 8 |
| 1018 | A258 | 8e org brn, dl pur & ol | 90 | 50 |

Issued to commemorate the 360th anniversary (in 1967) of the death of Bento de Goes (1562–1607), Jesuit explorer of the route to China.

Europa Issue, 1968
Common Design Type
1968, Apr. 29   Litho.   Perf. 13
Size: 31x21mm.

1019	CD11	1e multi	20	5
1020	CD11	3.50e multi	1.50	1.00
1021	CD11	4.30e multi	3.00	3.00

Mother's and Child's Hands
A259

1968, May 26   Litho.   Perf. 13½

1022	A259	1e lt gray, blk & red	20	5
1023	A259	2e sal, blk & red	1.00	40
1024	A259	5e lt bl, blk & red	1.50	65

Issued to commemorate the 30th anniversary of the Mothers' Organization for National Education.

"Victory over Disease" and WHO Emblem
A260

1968, July 10   Litho.   Perf. 12½

1025	A260	1e multi	20	5
1026	A260	3.50e multi	1.10	40
1027	A260	4.30e tan & multi	8.00	8.00

Issued for the 20th anniversary of the World Health Organization.

Madeira Grapes and Wine
A261

João Fernandes Vieira
A262

Designs: 1e, Fireworks on New Year's Eve. 1.50e, Mountains and valley. 3.50e, Woman doing Madeira embroidery. 4.30e, João Gonçalves Zarco. 20e, Muschia aurea (flower).

Perf. 12x11½, 11½x12
1968, Aug. 17   Lithographed

1028	A261	50c multi	10	5
1029	A261	1e multi	15	5
1030	A261	1.50e multi	45	10
1031	A261	2.80e multi	2.00	2.00
1032	A262	3.50e multi	1.75	40
1033	A262	4.30e multi	8.00	8.00
1034	A262	20e multi	4.50	1.50
		Nos. 1028-1034 (7)	16.95	12.10

Issued to publicize Madeira and the Lubrapex 1968 stamp exhibition. Design descriptions in Portuguese, French and English printed on back of stamps.

Pedro Alvares Cabral
A263

Cabral's Fleet
A264

Design: 3.50e, Cabral's coat of arms (vert.).

Perf. 12x12½, 12½x12
1969, Jan. 30   Engraved

| 1035 | A263 | 1e vio bl, bl & gray bl | 40 | 10 |
| 1036 | A263 | 3.50e dp cl | 3.50 | 1.40 |

Lithographed

| 1037 | A264 | 6.50e grn & multi | 2.50 | 1.50 |

Issued to commemorate the 5th centenary of the birth of Pedro Alvarez Cabral (1468–1520), navigator, discoverer of Brazil. Nos. 1035–1037 have description of the designs printed on the back in Portuguese, French and English.

Europa Issue, 1969
Common Design Type
1969, Apr. 28   Litho.   Perf. 13
Size: 31x22½mm.

1038	CD12	1e dp bl & multi	15	10
1039	CD12	3.50e multi	1.75	60
1040	CD12	4.30e grn & multi	2.75	2.50

King José I and Arms of National Press
A265

1969, May 14 Litho. Perf. 11½x12

1041	A265	1e multi	20	10
1042	A265	2e multi	1.25	30
1043	A265	8e multi	1.75	30

Bicentenary of the National Press.

ILO Emblem
A266

1969, May 28   Perf. 13

1044	A266	1e bluish grn, blk & sil	15	10
1045	A266	3.50e red, blk & sil	1.25	60
1046	A266	4.30e brt bl, blk & sil	2.00	2.00

Issued to commemorate the 50th anniversary of the International Labor Organization.

Juan Cabrillo Rodriguez
A267

Vianna da Motta, by Columbano Bordalo Pinheiro
A268

PORTUGAL

1969, July 16   Litho.   Perf. 11½x12

1047	A267	1e multi	15	10
1048	A267	2.50e multi	1.40	30
1049	A267	6.50e multi	1.00	60

Bicentenary of San Diego, Calif., and honoring Juan Cabrillo Rodriguez, explorer of California coast.
Backs inscribed. See note below No. 1034.

1969, Sept. 24   Litho.   Perf. 12

| 1050 | A268 | 1e multi | 55 | 10 |
| 1051 | A268 | 9e gray & multi | 90 | 50 |

Issued to commemorate the centenary of the birth of Vianna da Motta (1868–1948), pianist and composer.

Gago Coutinho and 1922 Seaplane
A269

Design: 2.80e, 4.30e, Adm. Coutinho and Coutinho sextant.

1969, Oct. 22

1052	A269	1e grnsh gray, dk & lt brn	15	10
1053	A269	2.80e yel bis, dk & lt brn	1.40	1.25
1054	A269	3.30e gray bl, dk & lt brn	1.75	1.60
1055	A269	4.30e lt rose brn, dk & lt brn	1.75	1.60

Issued to commemorate the centenary of the birth of Admiral Carlos Viegas Gago Coutinho (1869–1959), explorer and aviation pioneer.

Vasco da Gama
A270

Designs: 2.80e, Da Gama's coat of arms. 3.50e, Map showing route to India and compass rose (horiz.). 4e, Da Gama's fleet (horiz.).

Perf. 12x11½, 11½x12

1969, Dec. 30   Lithographed

1056	A270	1e multi	40	10
1057	A270	2.80e multi	2.75	2.50
1058	A270	3.50e multi	3.00	80
1059	A270	4e multi	3.00	80

500th anniversary of the birth of Vasco da Gama (1469–1525), navigator who found sea route to India.
Design descriptions in Portuguese, French and English printed on back of stamps.

Europa Issue, 1970
Common Design Type

1970, May 4   Litho.   Perf. 13½
Size: 31x22mm.

1060	CD13	1e dk bl & pale yel	40	10
1061	CD13	3.50e red brn & pale yel	1.75	90
1062	CD13	4.30e ol & pale yel	2.50	2.00

Distillation Plant
A271

Design: 2.80e, 6e, Catalytic cracking tower.

1970, June 5   Litho.   Perf. 13

1063	A271	1e dk bl & dl bl	15	6
1064	A271	2.80e sl grn & pale grn	1.25	1.25
1065	A271	3.30e dk ol grn & ol	1.25	1.25
1066	A271	6e dk brn & dl ocher	1.25	80

Opening of the Oporto Oil Refinery.

Marshal Carmona and Oak Leaves
A272

Designs: 2.50e, Carmona, Portuguese coat of arms and laurel. 7e, Carmona and ferns.

Lithographed, Engraved
1970, July 1   Perf. 12x12½

1067	A272	1e ol grn & blk	15	6
1068	A272	2.50e red, ultra & blk	1.40	40
1069	A272	7e sl bl & blk	1.25	90

Issued to commemorate the centenary of the birth of Marshal Antonio Oscar de Fragoso Carmona (1869–1951), President of Portugal, 1926–1951.

Emblem of Plant Research Station
A273

1970, July 29   Lithographed

1070	A273	1e multi	15	5
1071	A273	2.50e multi	1.25	30
1072	A273	5e multi	1.40	70

Issued to commemorate the 25th anniversary of the Plant Research Station at Elvas.

Compass Rose and EXPO Emblem
A274

Designs: 5e, Monogram of Christ (IHS) and EXPO emblem. 6.50e, "Portugal and Japan" as written in old manuscripts, and EXPO emblem.

1970, Sept. 16   Litho.   Perf. 13

1073	A274	1e gold & multi	20	5
1074	A274	5e sil & multi	1.00	40
1075	A274	6.50e multi	1.75	1.75

Issued to commemorate EXPO '70 International Exhibition, Osaka, Japan, March 15–Sept. 13. See No. C11.

Castle (from Arms of Santarem)
A275

Designs: No. 1077, Star and wheel, from Covilha coat of arms. 2.80e, Ram and Covilha coat of arms. 4e, Knights on horseback and Santarem coat of arms.

1970, Oct. 7   Litho.   Perf. 12x11½

1076	A275	1e multi	30	8
1077	A275	1e ultra & multi	30	8
1078	A275	2.80e red & multi	2.25	2.25
1079	A275	4e gray & multi	1.10	90

Nos. 1076 and 1079 commemorate the centenary of the City of Santarem; Nos. 1077–1078 commemorate the centenary of the City of Covilha.

Paddle-steamer Great Eastern Laying Cable
A276

Designs: 2.80e, 4e, Cross section of cable.

1970, Nov. 21   Litho.   Perf. 14

1080	A276	1e multi	15	8
1081	A276	2.50e multi	1.50	45
1082	A276	2.80e multi	1.75	1.75
1083	A276	4e multi	1.60	1.00

Centenary of the Portugal-Great Britain submarine telegraph cable.

Grapes and Woman Filling Baskets
A277

Designs: 1e, Worker carrying basket of grapes, and jug. 3.50e, Glass of wine, and barge with barrels on River Douro. 7e, Wine bottle and barrels.

1970, Dec. 20   Litho.   Perf. 12x11½

1084	A277	50c multi	8	5
1085	A277	1e multi	25	5
1086	A277	3.50e multi	1.25	25
1087	A277	7e multi	90	70

Publicity for port wine export.

Mountain Windmill, Bussaco Hills   Francisco Franco (1885–1955)
A278   A279

Windmills: 50c, Beira Litoral Province. 1e, Estremadura Province. 2e, St. Miguel, Azores. 3.30e, Porto Santo, Madeira. 5e, Pico, Azores.

1971, Feb. 24   Litho.   Perf. 13

1088	A278	20c multi	15	5
1089	A278	50c lt bl & multi	10	5
1090	A278	1e gray & multi	40	10
1091	A278	2e multi	95	15
1092	A278	3.30e ocher & multi	2.00	2.00
1093	A278	5e multi	2.25	80
		Nos. 1088–1093 (6)	5.75	3.15

Backs inscribed. See note below No. 1034.

Europa Issue, 1971
Common Design Type

1971, May 3   Photo.   Perf. 14
Size: 32x22mm.

1094	CD14	1e dk bl, lt grn & blk	40	20
1095	CD14	3.50e red brn, yel & blk	1.50	40
1096	CD14	7.50e ol, yel & blk	2.25	1.50

Perf. 11½x12½; 13½
(2.50e, 4e)

1971, July 7   Engraved

Designs: 1e, Antonio Teixeira Lopes (1866–1942). 1.50e, Antonio Augusto da Costa Mota (1862–1930). 2.50e, Rui Roque Gameiro (1906–1935). 3.50e, José Simoes de Almeida (nephew; 1880–1950). 4e, Francisco dos Santos (1878–1930).

1097	A279	20c black	8	5
a.		Perf. 13½	1.25	20
1098	A279	1e claret	15	5
1099	A279	1.50e sepia	40	20
1100	A279	2.50e dk bl	1.00	20
1101	A279	3.50e car rose	1.00	25
1102	A279	4e gray grn	2.25	25
		Nos. 1097–1102 (6)	4.88	3.00

Portuguese sculptors.

Pres. Antonio Salazar
A280

1971, July 27   Engraved   Perf. 13½

1103	A280	1e multi	15	5
a.		Perf. 12½x12	30.00	2.25
1104	A280	5e multi	1.00	25
1105	A280	10e multi	1.50	60
a.		Perf. 12½x12	8.00	1.00

Wolframite Crystals
A281

Minerals: 2.50e, Arsenopyrite (gold). 3.50e, Beryllium. 6.50e, Chalcopyrite (copper).

1971, Sept. 24   Litho.   Perf. 12

1106	A281	1e multi	15	5
1107	A281	2.50e car & multi	1.75	50
1108	A281	3.50e grn & multi	60	20
1109	A281	6.50e bl & multi	90	60

Spanish-Portuguese-American Economic Geology Congress.

Town Gate, Castelo Branco   Weather Recording Station and Barograph Charts
A282   A283

Designs: 3e, Memorial column. 12.50e, Arms of Castelo Branco (horiz.).

1971, Oct. 7   Perf. 14

1110	A282	1e multi	20	5
1111	A282	3e multi	1.40	40
1112	A282	12.50e multi	1.00	55

Bicentenary of Castelo Branco as a town.

1971, Oct. 29   Perf. 13½

Designs: 4e, Stratospheric weather balloon and weather map of southwest Europe and North Africa. 6.50e, Satellite and aerial map of Atlantic Ocean off Portugal.

1113	A283	1e buff & multi	15	5
1114	A283	4e multi	1.75	70
1115	A283	6.50e blk, dl red brn & org	90	45

25 years of Portuguese meteorological service.

PORTUGAL

Missionaries and Ship
A284

1971, Nov. 24

1116	A284	1e gray, ultra & blk	15	5
1117	A284	3.30e dp bis, lil & blk	1.40	1.40
1118	A284	4.80e ol, grn & blk	1.50	1.40

400th anniversary of the martyrdom of a group of Portuguese missionaries on the way to Brazil.

"Man"
A285

Designs: 3.30e, "Earth" (animal, vegetable, mineral). 3.50e, "Air" (birds). 4.50e, "Water" (fish).

1971, Dec. 22   Litho.   *Perf. 12*

1119	A285	1e brn & multi	8	5
1120	A285	3.30e lt bl, yel & grn	55	40
1121	A285	3.50e lt bl, rose & vio	60	10
1122	A285	4.50e lt bl, grn & ultra	2.25	1.00

Nature conservation.

City Hall, Sintra
A286

Designs: 5c, Aqueduct, Lisbon. 50c, University, Coimbra. 1e, Torre dos Clerigos, Porto. 1.50e, Belem Tower, Lisbon. 2.50e, Castle, Vila da Feira. 3e, Misericordia House, Viana do Castelo. 3.50e, Window, Tomar Convent. 8e, Ducal Palace, Guimaraes. 10e, Cape Girao, Madeira. 20e, Episcopal Garden, Castelo Branco. 100e, Lakes of Seven Cities, Azores.

1972–73   Litho.   *Perf. 12½*
Size: 22x17½mm.

1123	A286	5c gray, grn & blk	15	10
1124	A286	50c gray bl, blk & org	8	5
1125	A286	1e grn, blk & brn	8	5
1126	A286	1.50e bl, bis & blk	10	5
1127	A286	2.50e brn, dk brn & gray	15	5
1128	A286	3e yel, blk & brn	25	6
1129	A286	3.50e dp org, sl & brn	15	6
1130	A286	8e blk, ol & grn	1.50	10

Perf. 13½
Size: 31x22mm.

1131	A286	10e gray, blk & multi	45	10
1132	A286	20e grn & multi	3.00	25
1133	A286	50e gray bl, ocher & blk	1.50	45
1134	A286	100e grn & multi	3.00	1.20
		Nos. 1123-1134 (12)	10.41	2.57

"CTT" and year date printed in minute gray multiple rows on back of stamps. Issue dates: 1e, 1.50e, 50e, 100e, Mar. 1; 50c, 3e, 10e, 20e, Dec. 6, 1972; 5c, 2.50e, 3.50e, 8e, Sept. 5, 1973.
See Nos. 1207–1214.

Tagging

Starting in 1975, phosphor (bar or L-shape) was applied to the face of most definitives and commemoratives.
Stamps issued both with and without tagging include Nos. 1124–1125, 1128, 1130–1131, 1209, 1213–1214, 1250, 1253, 1257, 1260, 1263.

Window, Pinhel Church   **Heart and Pendulum**
A287   **A288**

Designs: 1e, Arms of Pinhel (horiz.). 7.50e, Stone lantern.

1972, Mar. 29   *Perf. 13½*

1135	A287	1e bl & multi	15	5
	a.	Perf. 11½x12½	30.00	
1136	A287	2.50e multi	1.40	20
1137	A287	7.50e bl & multi	1.00	60

Bicentenary of Pinhel as a town.

1972, Apr. 24

Designs: 4e, Heart and spiral pattern. 9e, Heart and continuing coil pattern.

1138	A288	1e vio & red	15	5
1139	A288	4e grn & red	2.00	60
1140	A288	9e brn & red	90	55

"Your heart is your health," World Health Day.

Europa Issue 1972
Common Design Type

1972, May 1   *Perf. 13½*
Size: 21x31mm.

1141	CD15	1e gray & multi	15	5
1142	CD15	3.50e sal & multi	75	40
1143	CD15	6e grn & multi	1.50	45

Trucks
A289

1972, May 17   Litho.   *Perf. 13½*
Multicolored

1144	A289	1e shown	15	5
1145	A289	4.50e Taxi	1.50	70
1146	A289	8e Autobus	1.40	80

13th Congress of International Union of Road Transport (I.R.U.), Estoril, May 15–18.

Soccer, Olympic Rings
A290

1972, July 26   Litho.   *Perf. 14*
Multicolored

1147	A290	50c shown	6	5
1148	A290	1e Running	10	5
1149	A290	1.50e Equestrian	25	10
1150	A290	3.50e Swimming, women's	60	30
1151	A290	4.50e Yachting	90	75
1152	A290	5e Gymnastics, women's	1.40	50
		Nos. 1147-1152 (6)	3.31	1.75

20th Olympic Games, Munich, Aug. 26–Sept. 11.

Marquis of Pombal   **Tomé de Sousa**
A291   **A292**

1972, Aug. 28   *Perf. 13½*
Multicolored

1153	A291	1e shown	15	5
1154	A291	2.50e Scientific apparatus	1.40	35
1155	A291	8e Seal of Univ. of Coimbra	1.25	80

Bicentenary of the Pombaline reforms of University of Coimbra.

1972, Oct. 5   Litho.   *Perf. 13½*

Designs: 2.50e, José Bonifacio. 3.50e, Dom Pedro IV. 6e, Allegory of Portuguese-Brazilian Community.

1156	A292	1e gray & multi	15	5
1157	A292	2.50e grn & multi	70	20
1158	A292	3.50e multi	70	15
1159	A292	6e bl & multi	1.25	60

150th anniversary of Brazilian independence.

Sacadura Cabral, Gago Coutinho and Plane
A293

Designs: 2.50e, 3.80e, Map of flight from Lisbon to Rio de Janeiro. 2.80e, Like 1e.

1972, Nov. 15   *Perf. 11½x12½*

1160	A293	1e bl & multi	15	6
	a.	Perf. 13½	15.00	60
1161	A293	2.50e multi	75	20
1162	A293	2.80e multi	90	80
1163	A293	3.80e multi	1.25	1.00
	a.	Perf. 13½	37.50	1.50

50th anniversary of the Lisbon to Rio de Janeiro flight by Commander Arturo de Sacadura Cabral and Adm. Carlos Viegas Gago Coutinho, Mar. 30–June 5, 1922.

Luiz Camoëns
A294

Designs: 3e, Hand saving manuscript from sea. 10e, Symbolic of man's questioning and discovering the unknown.

1972, Dec. 27   Litho.   *Perf. 13*

1164	A294	1e org brn, buff & blk	15	5
1165	A294	3e dl bl, lt grn & blk	1.00	30
1166	A294	10e red brn, buff & yel	1.60	60

4th centenary of the publication of The Lusiads by Luiz Camoëns (1524–1580).

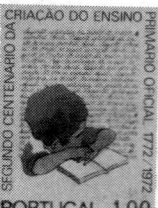

Graphs and Sequence Count
A295

Designs: 4e, Odometer. 9e, Graphs.

1973, Apr. 11   Litho.   *Perf. 14½*

1167	A295	1e gray & multi	15	5
1168	A295	4e gray & multi	1.25	35
1169	A295	9e gray & multi	1.00	45

Productivity Conference '72, Jan. 17–22, 1972.

Europa Issue 1973
Common Design Type

1973, Apr. 30   *Perf. 13*
Size: 31x29mm.

1170	CD16	1e multi	15	5
1171	CD16	4e brn red & multi	2.00	40
1172	CD16	6e grn & multi	2.50	50

Gen. Medici, Arms of Brazil and Portugal
A296

Designs: 2.80e, 4.80e, Gen. Medici, and world map.

Lithographed and Engraved

1973, May 16   *Perf. 12x11½*

1173	A296	1e dk grn, blk & sep	15	5
1174	A296	2.80e ol & multi	80	60
1175	A296	3.50e dk bl, blk & buff	80	60
1176	A296	4.80e multi	60	55

Visit of Gen. Emilio Garrastazu Medici, President of Brazil, to Portugal.

Child and Birds
A297

Designs: 4e, Child and flowers. 7.50e, Child.

1973, May 28   Litho.   *Perf. 13*

1177	A297	1e ultra & multi	15	5
1178	A297	4e multi	1.25	25
1179	A297	7.50e bis & multi	1.40	70

To pay renewed attention to children.

Transportation, Weather Map
A298

Designs: 3.80e, Communications: telegraph, telephone, radio, satellite. 6e, Postal service: mailbox, truck, mail distribution diagram.

1973, June 25

1180	A298	1e multi	10	5
1181	A298	3.80e multi	40	20
1182	A298	6e multi	90	70

Ministry of Communications, 25th anniversary.

Pupil and Writing Exercise
A299

PORTUGAL

169

Designs: 4.50e, Illustrations from 18th century primer. 5.30e, School and children, by 9-year-old Marie de Luz (horiz.). 8e, Symbolic chart of teacher-pupil link (horiz.).

1973, Oct. 24 Litho. Perf. 13

1183	A299	1e bl & multi	15	5
1184	A299	4.50e brn & multi	1.00	25
1185	A299	5.30e lt bl & multi	90	70
1186	A299	8e grn & multi	1.60	70

Bicentenary of primary state school education.

Oporto Streetcar, 1910
A300

Designs: 1e, Horse-drawn streetcar, 1872. 3.50e, Double-decker Leyland bus, 1972.

1973, Nov. 7 Size: 31½x34mm.

| 1187 | A300 | 1e brn, yel & blk | 15 | 10 |
| 1188 | A300 | 3.50e choc & multi | 1.75 | 1.10 |

Size: 37½x27mm. Perf. 12½

| 1189 | A300 | 7.50e buff & multi | 1.40 | 80 |

Centenary of public transportation in Oporto.

Servicemen's League Emblem
A301

Death of Nuño Gonzalves
A302

Designs: 2.50e, Sailor, soldier and aviator. 11e, Military medals.

1973, Nov. 28 Litho. Perf. 13

1190	A301	1e multi	15	5
1191	A301	2.50e multi	1.50	25
1192	A301	11e dk bl & multi	1.10	45

50th anniversary of the Servicemen's League.

1973, Dec. 19

| 1193 | A302 | 1e sl bl & org | 10 | 5 |
| 1194 | A302 | 10e vio brn & org | 90 | 10 |

600th anniversary of the heroism of Nuño Gonzalves, alcaide of Faria Castle.

Damião de Gois, by Dürer (?)
A303

"The Exile," by Soares dos Reis
A304

Designs: 4.50e, Title page of Cronica de Principe D. Joao. 7.50e, Lute and score of Dodecachordon.

1974, Apr. 5 Lithographed Perf. 12

1195	A303	1e multi	15	5
1196	A303	4.50e multi	75	30
1197	A303	7.50e multi	1.00	40

400th anniversary of the death of Damião de Gois (1502–1574), humanist, writer, composer.

Europa Issue 1974

1974, Apr. 29 Litho. Perf. 13

1198	A304	1e multi	15	5
1199	A304	4e dk red & multi	3.00	45
1200	A304	6e dk grn & multi	3.50	60

Pattern of Light Emission
A305

Designs: 4.50e, Spiral wave radiation pattern. 5.30e, Satellite and earth.

1974, June 26 Litho. Perf. 14

1201	A305	1.50e gray ol	15	8
1202	A305	4.50e dk bl	2.00	70
1203	A305	5.30e brt rose lil	60	45

Establishment of satellite communications network via Intelsat among Portugal, Angola and Mozambique.

Diffusion of Hertzian Waves
A306

Designs (Symbolic): 3.30e, Messages through space. 10e, Navigation help.

1974, Sept. 4 Litho. Perf. 12

1204	A306	1.50e multi	15	8
1205	A306	3.30e multi	1.00	50
1206	A306	10e multi	2.00	60

Centenary of the birth of Guglielmo Marconi (1874–1937), Italian electrical engineer and inventor.

Buildings Type of 1972–73

Designs: 10c, Ponte do Lima (Roman bridge). 30c, Alcobaça Monastery, interior. 2e, City Hall, Bragança. 4e, New Gate, Braga. 4.50e, Dolmen of Carrazeda. 5e, Roman Temple, Evora. 6e, Leca do Balio Monastery. 7.50e, Almourol Castle.

1974, Sept. 18 Litho. Perf. 12½
Size: 22x17½mm.

1207	A286	10c multi	15	10
1208	A286	30c multi	15	5
1209	A286	2e multi	16	5
1210	A286	4e multi	60	8
1211	A286	4.50e multi	1.10	8
1212	A286	5e multi	9.00	8
1213	A286	6e multi	3.00	20
1214	A286	7.50e multi	1.50	15
		Nos. 1207-1214 (8)	15.66	79

"CTT" and year date printed in minute gray multiple rows on back of stamps.

Postilion, Truck and Letter
A307

Designs: 2e, Hand holding letter. 3.30e, Packet and steamship. 4.50e, Pigeon and letters. 5.30e, Hand holding sealed letter. 20e, Old and new locomotives.

1974, Oct. 9 Lithographed Perf. 13

1220	A307	1.50e brn & multi	15	10
1221	A307	2e multi	90	10
1222	A307	3.30e ol & multi	25	18
1223	A307	4.50e multi	1.00	70
1224	A307	5.30e multi	75	60
1225	A307	20e multi	2.75	1.75
a.		Souvenir sheet of 6	7.50	7.50
		Nos. 1220-1225 (5)		3.43

Centenary of Universal Postal Union. No. 1225a contains one each of Nos. 1220-1225, arranged to show a continuous design with a globe in center. Blue and indigo marginal design and inscription. Size: 106x146mm. Sold for 50c.

Luisa Todi, Singer (1753–1833)
A308

Marcos Portugal, Composer (1762–1838)
A309

Portuguese Musicians: 2e, João Domingos Bomtempo (1775–1842). 2.50e, Carlos Seixas (1704–1742). 3e, Duarte Lobo (1565–1646). 5.30e, João de Sousa Carvalho (1745–1798).

1974, Oct. 30 Litho. Perf. 12

1226	A308	1.50e brt pink	15	8
1227	A308	2e vermilion	1.50	30
1228	A308	2.50e brown	1.10	12
1229	A308	3e bluish blk	75	30
1230	A308	5.30e sl grn	1.00	85
1231	A309	11e rose lake	1.00	75
		Nos. 1226-1231 (6)	5.50	2.40

Coat of Arms of Beja
A310

Designs: 3.50e, Men of Beja in costumes from Roman times to date. 7e, Moorish Arches and view across plains.

1974, Nov. 13

1232	A310	1.50e multi	15	8
1233	A310	3.50e multi	1.50	60
1234	A310	7e multi	2.50	70

2,000th anniversary of Beja.

Annunciation
A311

Rainbow and Dove
A312

Designs: 4.50e, Adoration of the Shepherds. 10e, Flight into Egypt. Designs show Portuguese costumes from Nazare township.

1974, Dec. 4 Lithographed Perf. 13

1235	A311	1.50e red & multi	15	8
1236	A311	4.50e multi	3.50	50
1237	A311	10e bl & multi	2.50	50

Christmas 1974.

1974, Dec. 18 Perf. 12

1238	A312	1.50e multi	15	8
1239	A312	3.50e multi	3.50	70
1240	A312	5e multi	2.50	50

Armed Forces Movement of Apr. 25, 1974.

Egas Moniz
A313

Designs: 3.30e, Lobotomy probe and Nobel Prize medal, 1949. 10e, Cerebral angiograph, 1927.

1974, Dec. 27 Engr. Perf. 11½x12

1241	A313	1.50e yel & multi	15	8
1242	A313	3.30e brn & ocher	45	40
1243	A313	10e gray & ultra	2.00	40

Egas Moniz (1874–1955), brain surgeon, birth centenary.

Soldier as Farmer, Farmer as Soldier
A314

1975, Mar. 21 Litho. Perf. 12

1244	A314	1.50e grn & multi	20	8
1245	A314	3e gray & multi	2.50	35
1246	A314	4.50e multi	3.00	60

Cultural progress and citizens' guidance campaign.

Hands and Dove
A315

Designs: 4.50e, Brown hands reaching for dove. 10e, Dove with olive branch and arms of Portugal.

1975, Apr. 23 Litho. Perf. 13½

1247	A315	1.50e red & multi	15	8
1248	A315	4.50e brn & multi	2.50	40
1249	A315	10e grn & multi	3.00	50

Movement of April 25th, first anniversary. Slogans in Portuguese, French and English printed on back of stamps.

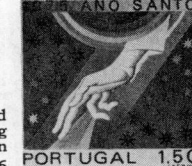

God's Hand Reaching Down
A316

Designs: 4.50e, Jesus' hand holding up cross. 10e, Dove (Holy Spirit) descending.

1975, May 13 Litho. Perf. 13½

1250	A316	1.50e multi	15	8
1251	A316	4.50e plum & multi	3.00	60
1252	A316	10e bl & multi	3.75	1.00

Holy Year 1975.

Europa Issue 1975

Horseman of the Apocalypse, 12th Century
A317

Design: 10e, The Poet Fernando Pessoa, by Almada Negreiros (1893–1970).

1975, May 26

| 1253 | A317 | 1.50e multi | 30 | 8 |
| 1254 | A317 | 10e multi | 5.50 | 50 |

PORTUGAL

Assembly Building
A318

1975, June 2   Litho.   Perf. 13½

| 1255 | A318 | 2e red, blk & yel | 20 | 6 |
| 1256 | A318 | 20e emer, blk & yel | 4.00 | 1.50 |

Opening of Constituent Assembly.

Hikers
A319

Designs: 4.50e, Campsite on lake. 5.30e, Mobile homes on the road.

1975, Aug. 4   Litho.   Perf. 13½

1257	A319	2e multi	90	6
1258	A319	4.50e multi	1.50	40
1259	A319	5.30e multi	60	40

36th Rally of the International Federation of Camping and Caravanning, Santo Andre Lake.

People and Sapling
A320

Designs: (UN Emblem and): 4.50e, People and dove. 20e, People and grain.

1975, Sept. 17   Litho.   Perf. 13½

1260	A320	2e grn & multi	40	6
1261	A320	4.50e vio & multi	1.50	40
1262	A320	20e multi	3.75	1.00

United Nations, 30th anniversary.

Icarus and Rocket
A321

Designs: 4.50e, Apollo and Soyuz in space. 5.30e, Robert H. Goddard, Robert Esnault-Pelterie, Hermann Oberth and Konstantin Tsiolkovski. 10e, Sputnik, man in space, moon landing module.

1975, Sept. 26   Litho.   Perf. 13½
Size: 30½x26½mm.

1263	A321	2e grn & multi	40	6
1264	A321	4.50e brn & multi	1.75	50
1265	A321	5.30e lil & multi	60	40

Size: 65x28mm.

| 1266 | A321 | 10e bl & multi | 4.00 | 70 |

26th Congress of International Astronautical Federation, Lisbon, Sept. 1975.

Land Survey
A322

Designs: 8e, Ocean survey. 10e, People of many races and globe.

1975, Nov. 19   Litho.   Perf. 12x12½

1267	A322	2e ocher & multi	30	6
1268	A322	8e bl & multi	1.50	50
1269	A322	10e dk vio & multi	3.00	50

Centenary of Lisbon Geographical Society.

Arch and Trees
A323

Designs: 8e, Plan, pencil and ruler. 10e, Hand, old building and brick tower.

1975, Nov. 28   Perf. 13½

1270	A323	2e dk bl & gray	30	6
1271	A323	8e dk car & gray	2.50	50
1272	A323	10e ocher & multi	2.75	50

European Architectural Heritage Year 1975.

Nurse and Hospital Ward
A324

Designs (IWY Emblem and): 2e, Farm workers. 3.50e, Secretary. 8e, Factory worker.

1975, Dec. 30   Litho.   Perf. 13½

1273	A324	50c multi	10	5
1274	A324	2e multi	1.25	10
1275	A324	3.50e multi	1.25	30
1276	A324	8e multi	1.50	60
a.		Souvenir sheet of 4	4.50	4.50

International Women's Year 1975. No. 1276a contains 4 stamps similar to Nos. 1273–1276 in slightly changed colors; blue and gray marginal inscription and IWY emblem. Size: 102x115mm. Sold for 25e.

Pen Nib as Plowshare
A325

1976, Feb. 6   Litho.   Perf. 12

| 1277 | A325 | 3e dk bl & red org | 40 | 10 |
| 1278 | A325 | 20e org, ultra & red | 3.75 | 1.50 |

Portuguese Society of Writers, 50th anniversary.

Telephones, 1876, 1976
A326

Design: 10.50e, Alexander Graham Bell and telephone.

1976, Mar. 10   Litho.   Perf. 12x12½

| 1279 | A326 | 3e yel grn, grn & blk | 1.00 | 10 |
| 1280 | A326 | 10.50e rose, red & blk | 3.00 | 45 |

Centenary of first telephone call by Alexander Graham Bell, March 10, 1876.

Industry and Shipping
A327

Design: 1e, Garment, food and wine industries.

1976, Apr. 7   Litho.   Perf. 12½

| 1281 | A327 | 50c red brn | 40 | 5 |
| 1282 | A327 | 1e slate | 55 | 5 |

Support of national production.

Europa Issue 1976

Carved Spoons, Olive Wood
A328

Designs: 20e, Gold filigree pendant, silver box and CEPT emblem.

1976, May 3   Litho.   Perf. 12x12½
Tagged

| 1283 | A328 | 3e ol & multi | 40 | 8 |
| 1284 | A328 | 20e tan & multi | 7.50 | 2.75 |

Stamp Collectors
A329

Designs: 7.50e, Stamp exhibition and hand canceler. 10e, Printing and designing stamps.

1976, May 29   Litho.   Perf. 14½

1285	A329	3e multi	15	8
1286	A329	7.50e multi	1.00	25
1287	A329	10e multi	2.00	40

Interphil 76, International Philatelic Exhibition, Philadelphia, Pa., May 29–June 6.

King Ferdinand I
A330

Designs: 5e, Plowshare, farmers chasing off hunters. 10e, Harvest.

1976, July 2   Litho.   Perf. 12

1288	A330	3e lt bl & multi	30	8
1289	A330	5e yel grn & multi	2.00	25
1290	A330	10e multi	2.50	50
a.		Souvenir sheet of 3	5.00	5.00

Agricultural reform law (compulsory cultivation of uncultivated lands), 600th anniversary. No. 1290a contains one each of Nos. 1288–1290, black marginal inscription with text of law of May 28, 1375. Size: 230x148mm. Sold for 30e.

Torch Bearer
A331

Designs (Montreal Games' Emblem, Maple Leaf and): 7e, Women's relay race. 10.50e, Olympic flame.

1976, July 16   Perf. 13½

1291	A331	3e red & multi	30	8
1292	A331	7e red & multi	2.00	60
1293	A331	10.50e red & multi	3.00	60

21st Olympic Games, Montreal, Canada, July 17–Aug. 1.

Farm
A332

1976, Sept. 15   Litho.   Perf. 13½
Tagged
Multicolored

1294	A332	3e shown	90	8
1295	A332	3e Ship	90	8
1296	A332	3e City	90	8
1297	A332	3e Factory	90	8
a.		Souvenir sheet of 4	10.50	10.50

Fight against illiteracy. No. 1297a contains one each of Nos. 1294–1297, perf. 12; light gray marginal inscription. Size: 147x104mm. Sold for 25e.

Azure-winged Magpie
A333

Designs: 5e, Lynx. 7e, Portuguese laurel cherry. 10.50e, Little wild carnations.

1976, Sept. 30   Litho.   Perf. 12

1298	A333	3e multi	40	8
1299	A333	5e multi	1.50	8
1300	A333	7e multi	1.50	40
1301	A333	10.50e multi	2.00	60

Portucale 77, 2nd International Thematic Exhibition, Oporto, Oct. 29–Nov. 6, 1977.

Exhibition Hall
A334

Design: 20e, Symbolic stamp and emblem.

1976, Oct. 9   Litho.   Perf. 13½

1302	A334	3e bl & multi	30	8
1303	A334	20e ocher & multi	3.50	1.40
a.		Souvenir sheet of 2	4.00	4.00

6th Luso-Brazilian Philatelic Exhibition, LUBRAPEX 76, Oporto, Oct. 9. No. 1303a contains one each of Nos. 1302–1303, gray margin shows view of Oporto. Size: 180x 142mm. Sold for 30e.

Bank Emblem and Family
A335

Designs: 7e, Emblem and grain. 15e, Emblem and cog wheels.

1976, Oct. 29   Perf. 12

1304	A335	3e org & multi	15	8
1305	A335	7e grn & multi	1.75	50
1306	A335	15e bl & multi	2.50	70

Trust Fund Bank centenary.

Sheep Grazing on Marsh
A336

Designs: 3e, Drainage ditches. 5e, Fish in water. 10e, Ducks flying over marsh.

1976, Nov. 24   Litho.   Perf. 14

1307	A336	1e multi	30	10
1308	A336	3e multi	75	12
1309	A336	5e multi	1.50	20
1310	A336	10e multi	2.00	40

Protection of wetlands.

PORTUGAL

171

"Liberty"
A337

1976, Nov. 30   Litho.   Perf. 13½

| 1311 | A337 | 3e gray, grn & ver | 90 | 8 |

Constitution of 1976.

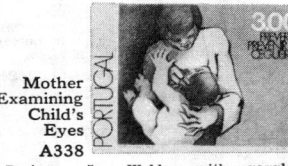
Mother Examining Child's Eyes
A338

Designs: 5e, Welder with goggles. 10.50e, Blind woman reading Braille.

1976, Dec. 13

1312	A338	3e multi	30	8
1313	A338	5e multi	1.50	35
1314	A338	10.50e multi	2.00	90

World Health Day and campaign against blindness.

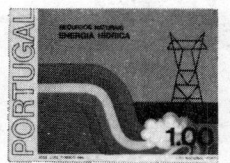
Hydro-electric Energy
A339

Abstract Designs: 4e, Fossil fuels. 5e, Geothermal energy. 10e, Wind power. 15e, Solar energy.

1976, Dec. 30

1315	A339	1e multi	20	10
1316	A339	4e multi	60	15
1317	A339	5e multi	75	15
1318	A339	10e multi	1.40	40
1319	A339	15e multi	2.50	60
		Nos. 1315-1319 (5)	5.45	1.40

Sources of energy.

Map of Council of Europe Members
A340

1977, Jan. 28   Litho.   Perf. 12

| 1320 | A340 | 8.50e multi | 75 | 60 |
| 1321 | A340 | 10e multi | 75 | 60 |

Portugal's joining Council of Europe.

Alcoholic and Bottle
A341

Designs (Bottle and): 5e, Symbolic figure of broken life. 15e, Bars blotting out the sun.

1977, Feb. 4   Perf. 13

1322	A341	3e multi	15	8
1323	A341	5e ocher & multi	60	15
1324	A341	15e org & multi	1.40	50

Anti-alcoholism Day and 10th anniversary of Portuguese Anti-alcoholism Society.

Trees Tapped for Resin
A342

Designs: 4e, Trees stripped for cork. 7e, Trees and logs. 15e, Trees at seashore as windbreakers.

1977, Mar. 21   Litho.   Perf. 13½

1325	A342	1e multi	15	5
1326	A342	4e multi	40	15
1327	A342	7e multi	1.40	30
1328	A342	15e multi	1.50	60

Forests, a natural resource.

"Suffering"
A343

Designs: 6e, Man exercising. 10e, Group exercising. All designs include emblems of World Health Organization and Portuguese Institute for Rheumatology.

1977, Apr. 13   Litho.   Perf. 12x12½

1329	A343	4e blk, brn & ocher	25	8
1330	A343	6e blk, bl & vio	1.00	60
1331	A343	10e blk, pur & red	90	40

International Rheumatism Year.

Europa 1977

Southern Plains Landscape
A344

Design: 8.50e, Northern mountain valley.

1977, May 2

1332	A344	4e multi	25	8
1333	A344	8.50e multi	1.25	60
	a.	Miniature sheet of 6	30.00	30.00

No. 1333a contains 3 each of Nos. 1332-1333; ocher marginal inscription. Size: 147x96mm.

Pope John XXI Enthroned
A345

Petrus Hispanus, the Physician
A346

1977, May 20   Litho.   Perf. 13½

| 1334 | A345 | 4e multi | 25 | 10 |
| 1335 | A346 | 15e multi | 60 | 40 |

Pope John XXI (Petrus Hispanus), only Pope of Portuguese descent, 7th death centenary.

Compass Rose, Camoens Quotation
A347

1977, June 8   Perf. 12

| 1336 | A347 | 4e multi | 25 | 10 |
| 1337 | A347 | 8.50e multi | 70 | 45 |

Camoens Day and to honor Portuguese overseas communities.

Student, Computer and Book
A348

Designs (Book and): No. 1339, Folk dancers, flutist and boat. No. 1340, Tractor drivers. No. 1341, Atom and people.

1977, July 20   Litho.   Perf. 12x12½

1338	A348	4e multi	40	10
1339	A348	4e multi	40	10
1340	A348	4e multi	40	10
1341	A348	4e multi	40	10
	a.	Souvenir sheet of 4	4.50	4.50

Continual education. No. 1341a contains one each of Nos. 1338-1341; brown and ultramarine inscription and emblem in margin. Size: 148x96mm. Sold for 20e.

Pyrites, Copper, Chemical Industry
A349

Designs: 5e, Marble, statue, public buildings. 10e, Iron ore, girders, crane. 20e, Uranium ore, atomic diagram.

1977, Oct. 4   Litho.   Perf. 12x11½

1342	A349	4e multi	25	10
1343	A349	5e multi	70	20
1344	A349	10e multi	75	30
1345	A349	20e multi	2.25	80

Natural resources from the subsoil.

Alexandre Herculano
A350

1977, Oct. 19   Engr.   Perf. 12x11½

| 1346 | A350 | 4e multi | 25 | 10 |
| 1347 | A350 | 15e multi | 1.00 | 30 |

Alexandre Herculano de Carvalho Araujo (1810-1877), historian, novelist, death centenary.

Maria Pia Bridge
A351

Design: 4e, Arrival of first train, ceramic panel by Jorge Colaco, St. Bento railroad station.

1977, Nov. 4   Litho.   Perf. 12x11½

| 1348 | A351 | 4e multi | 25 | 10 |
| 1349 | A351 | 10e multi | 1.25 | 1.00 |

Centenary of extension of railroad across Douro River.

Poveiro Bark
A352

Coastal Fishing Boats: 3e, Do Mar bark. 4e, Nazaré bark. 7e, Algarve skiff. 10e, Xavega bark. 15e, Bateira de Buarcos.

1977, Nov. 19   Perf. 12

1350	A352	2e multi	60	8
1351	A352	3e multi	30	8
1352	A352	4e multi	30	15
1353	A352	7e multi	45	15
1354	A352	10e multi	90	60
1355	A352	15e multi	1.75	60
	a.	Souvenir sheet of 6	4.50	4.50
		Nos. 1350-1355 (6)	4.30	1.66

PORTUCALE 77, 2nd International Topical Exhibition. Oporto, Nov. 19-20. No. 1355a contains one each of Nos. 1350-1355; gray margin with black inscription. Size: 148x105mm. Sold for 60e.

Nativity
A353

Children's Drawings: 7e, Nativity. 10e, Holy Family (vert.). 20e, Star and Christ Child (vert.).

Perf. 12x11½, 11½x12

1977, Dec. 12   Lithographed

1356	A353	4e multi	25	10
1357	A353	7e multi	1.10	28
1358	A353	10e multi	1.10	40
1359	A353	20e multi	3.00	80

Christmas 1977.

Old Desk and Computer
A354

Designs: Work tools, old and new.

1978-83   Litho.   Perf. 12½

Size: 22x17mm.

1360	A354	50c Medical	5	5
1361	A354	1e Household	5	5
1362	A354	2e Communications	8	5
1363	A354	3e Garment making	10	5
1364	A354	4e Office	12	5
1365	A354	5e Fishing craft	15	5
1366	A354	5.50e Weaving	18	5
1367	A354	6e Plows	20	5
1368	A354	6.50e Aviation	20	5
1369	A354	7e Printing	25	5
1370	A354	8e Carpentry	25	5
1371	A354	8.50e Potter's wheel	25	5
1372	A354	9e Photography	30	8
1373	A354	10e Saws	30	8
1373A	A354	12.50e Compasses ('83)	25	5
1373B	A354	16e Mail processing ('83)	32	16

Perf. 13½

Size: 31x22mm.

1374	A354	20e Construction	60	15
1375	A354	30e Steel industry	90	18
1376	A354	40e Transportation	1.25	30
1377	A354	50e Chemistry	1.50	25
1378	A354	100e Shipbuilding	3.00	50
1379	A354	250e Telescopes	5.00	50

Red Mediterranean Soil
A355

Designs: 5e, Stone formation. 10e, Alluvial soil. 20e, Black soil.

1978, Mar. 6   Litho.   Perf. 12

1380	A355	4e multi	25	10
1381	A355	5e multi	30	10
1382	A355	10e multi	55	40
1383	A355	20e multi	2.00	55

Soil, a natural resource.

PORTUGAL

Street Crossing
A356

Designs: 2e, Motorcyclist. 2.50e, Children in back seat of car. 5e, Hands holding steering wheel. 9e, Driving on country road. 12.50e, "Avoid drinking and driving."

1978, Apr. 19   Litho.   Perf. 12

1384	A356	1e multi	8	5
1385	A356	2e multi	15	5
1386	A356	2.50e multi	45	5
1387	A356	5e multi	70	10
1388	A356	9e multi	1.10	45
1389	A356	12.50e multi	1.50	70

Road safety campaign.

Europa Issue 1978

Roman Tower, Belmonte
A357

Design: 40e, Belém Monastery of Hieronymite monks (inside).

1978, May 2

1390	A357	10e multi	45	15
1391	A357	40e multi	2.00	1.00
a.	Souvenir sheet of 4		17.00	17.00

No. 1391a contains 2 each of Nos. 1390–1391, imperf.; gray marginal inscription. Size: 111x95mm. Sold for 120e.

Trajan's Bridge
A358

Roman Tablet from Bridge
A359

1978, June 14   Litho.   Perf. 13½

| 1392 | A358 | 10e multi | 30 | 10 |
| 1393 | A359 | 20e multi | 1.50 | 50 |

1900th anniversary of Chaves (Aquae Flaviae).

Running
A360

Designs: 10e, Bicycling. 12.50e, Watersport. 15e, Soccer.

1978, July 24   Litho.   Perf. 12

1394	A360	5e multi	25	10
1395	A360	10e multi	35	20
1396	A360	12.50e multi	75	50
1397	A360	15e multi	75	30

Sport for all the people.

Pedro Nuñes
A361

Design: 20e, "Nonio" navigational instrument and diagram from "Tratado da Rumaçao do Globo."

1978, Aug. 9   Litho.   Perf. 12x11½

| 1398 | A361 | 5e multi | 30 | 10 |
| 1399 | A361 | 20e multi | 1.50 | 40 |

Pedro Nuñes (1502–1578), navigator and cosmographer.

Trawler, Frozen Fish Processing, Can of Sardines—A362

Fishing Industry: 9e, Deep-sea trawler, loading and unloading at dock. 12.50e, Trawler with radar and instruction in use of radar. 15e, Trawler with echo-sounding equipment, microscope and test tubes.

1978, Sept. 16   Litho.   Perf. 12x11½

1400	A362	5e multi	25	10
1401	A362	9e multi	30	15
1402	A362	12.50e multi	75	30
1403	A362	15e multi	1.00	30

Natural resources.

Postrider
A363

Designs: No. 1405, Carrier pigeon. No. 1406, Envelopes. No. 1407, Pen.

1978, Oct. 30   Litho.   Perf. 12

1404	A363	5e yel & multi	40	10
1405	A363	5e bl gray & multi	40	10
1406	A363	5e grn & multi	40	10
1407	A363	5e red & multi	40	10

Introduction of Postal Code.

Human Figure, Flame Emblem
A364

Design: 40e, Human figure pointing the way and flame emblem.

1978, Dec. 7   Litho.   Perf. 12

1408	A364	14e multi	45	10
1409	A364	40e multi	2.00	1.00
a.	Souvenir sheet of 4		5.00	5.00

Universal Declaration of Human Rights, 30th anniversary and 25th anniversary of European Declaration. No. 1409a contains 2 each Nos. 1408–1409; gray marginal inscription. Size: 120x100mm.

Sebastiao Magalhaes Lima—A365

1978, Dec. 7

| 1410 | A365 | 5e multi | 30 | 10 |

Sebastiao Magalhaes Lima (1850–1928), lawyer, journalist, statesman.

Mail Boxes and Scale
A366

Designs: 5e, Telegraph and condenser lens. 10e, Portugal Nos. 2–3 and postal card printing press, 1879. 14e, Book and bookcases, 1879, 1979.

1978, Dec. 20

1411	A366	4e multi	25	10
1412	A366	5e multi	30	10
1413	A366	10e multi	55	20
1414	A366	14e multi	1.25	60
a.	Souvenir sheet of 4		3.00	3.00

Centenary of Postal Museum and Postal Library; 125th anniversary of Portuguese stamps (10e). No. 1414a contains Nos. 1411–1414; gray marginal inscription. Size: 120x99mm. Sold for 40e.

Emigrant at Railroad Station—A367

Designs: 14e, Farewell at airport. 17e, Emigrant greeting child at railroad station.

1979, Feb. 21   Litho.   Perf. 12

1415	A367	5e multi	15	10
1416	A367	14e multi	45	30
1417	A367	17e multi	1.25	65

Portuguese emigration.

Automobile Traffic
A368

Designs: 5e, Pneumatic drill. 14e, Man with bull horn.

1979, Mar. 14   Perf. 13½

1418	A368	4e multi	8	5
1419	A368	5e multi	10	5
1420	A368	14e multi	28	14

Combat noise pollution.

NATO Emblem
A369

1979, Apr. 4   Litho.   Perf. 12

1421	A369	5e multi	20	10
1422	A369	50e multi	2.00	1.00
a.	Souvenir sheet of 4		6.00	6.00

North Atlantic Treaty Organization, 30th anniversary. No. 1422a contains 2 each of Nos. 1421–1422. Ultramarine marginal inscription. Size: 120x100mm.

Europa Issue 1979

Mail Delivery, 16th Century
A370

Design: 40e, Mail delivery, 19th century.

1979, Apr. 30   Litho.   Perf. 12

1423	A370	14e multi	28	15
1424	A370	40e multi	80	40
a.	Souvenir sheet of 4		10.00	10.00

No. 1424a contains 2 each of Nos. 1423–1424; gray marginal inscription. Size: 120x113mm.

Mother, Infant, Dove
A371

Designs (IYC Emblem and): 5.50e, Children playing ball. 10e, Child in nursery school. 14e, Black and white boys.

1979, June 1   Litho.   Perf. 12x12½

1425	A371	5.50e multi	12	5
1426	A371	6.50e multi	14	8
1427	A371	10e multi	20	10
1428	A371	14e multi	28	15
a.	Souvenir sheet of 4		3.00	3.00

International Year of the Child. No. 1428a contains Nos. 1425–1428. Gray marginal inscription. Size: 111x104mm. Sold for 40e.

Salute to the Flag
A372

1979, June 8

| 1429 | A372 | 6.50e multi | 14 | 8 |
| a. | Souvenir sheet of 9 | | 3.50 | 3.50 |

Portuguese Day. No. 1429a has gray marginal inscription. Size: 148x125mm.

Pregnant Woman
A373

Designs: 17e, Boy sitting in a cage. 20e, Face, and hands using hammer.

1979, June 6   Litho.   Perf. 12x12½

1430	A373	6.50e multi	14	8
1431	A373	17e multi	35	18
1432	A373	20e multi	40	20

Help for the mentally retarded.

Children Reading Book, UNESCO Emblem
A374

Design: 17e, Teaching deaf child, and UNESCO emblem.

1979, June 25

| 1433 | A374 | 6.50e multi | 14 | 8 |
| 1434 | A374 | 17e multi | 35 | 18 |

International Bureau of Education, 50th anniversary.

See "Special Notices" at the front of this volume for data on the listing methods of this Catalogue, abbreviations, condition, prices and examination.

PORTUGAL

Water Cart, Brasiliana '79 Emblem
A375

Brasiliana '79 Philatelic Exhibition: 5.50e, Wine sledge. 6.50e, Wine cart. 16e, Covered cart. 19e, Mogadouro cart. 20e, Sand cart.

1979, Sept. 15   Litho.   *Perf. 12*

1435	A375	2.50e multi	5	5
1436	A375	5.50e multi	12	5
1437	A375	6.50e multi	14	8
1438	A375	16e multi	32	16
1439	A375	19e multi	38	20
1440	A375	20e multi	40	20
	1435-1440 (6)		2.79	1.38

Antonio José de Almeida (1866-1929)
A376

Republican Leaders: 6.50e, Afonso Costa (1871-1937). 10e, Teofilo Braga (1843-1924). 16e, Bernardino Machado (1851-1944). 19.50e, Joao Chagas (1863-1925). 20e, Elias Garcia (1830-1891).

1979, Oct. 4   *Perf. 12½×12*

1441	A376	5.50e multi	12	5
1442	A376	6.50e multi	14	8
1443	A376	10e multi	20	10
1444	A376	16e multi	32	16
1445	A376	19.50e multi	40	20
1446	A376	20e multi	40	20
	Nos. 1441-1446 (6)		3.12	1.53

See Nos. 1454-1459.

Red Cross and Family—A377

Red Cross and: 20e, Doctor examining elderly man.

1979, Oct. 26   *Perf. 12×12½*

| 1447 | A377 | 6.50e multi | 14 | 8 |
| 1448 | A377 | 20e multi | 40 | 20 |

National Health Service Campaign.

Holy Family, 17th Century Mosaic
A378

Mosaics, Lisbon Tile Museum: 6.50e, Nativity, 16th century. 16e, Flight into Egypt, 18th century.

1979, Dec. 5   Litho.   *Perf. 12×12½*

1449	A378	5.50e multi	12	5
1450	A378	6.50e multi	14	8
1451	A378	16e multi	32	16

Christmas 1979.

Rotary International, 75th Anniversary—A379

1980, Feb. 22   *Perf. 12x11½*

| 1452 | A379 | 16e shown | 32 | 16 |
| 1453 | A379 | 50e Emblem, torch | 1.00 | 50 |

Portrait Type of 1979

Leaders of the Republican Movement: 3.50e, Alvaro de Castro (1878-1928). 5.50e, Antonio Sergio (1883-1969). 6.50e, Norton de Matos (1867-1955). 11e, Jaime Cortesao (1884-1960). 16e, Teixeira Gomes (1860-1941). 20e, Jose Domingues dos Santos (1885-1958). Nos. 1454-1459 horizontal.

1980, Mar. 19

1454	A376	3.50e multi	8	5
1455	A376	5.50e multi	12	5
1456	A376	6.50e multi	14	8
1457	A376	11e multi	22	12
1458	A376	16e multi	32	16
1459	A376	20e multi	40	20
	Nos. 1454-1459 (6)		1.28	66

Europa Issue 1980

Serpa Pinto (1864-1900), Explorer of Africa—A380

1980, Apr. 14

1460	A380	16e shown	32	16
1461	A380	60e Vasco da Gama (1468-1524)	1.20	60
a.	Souvenir sheet of 4		5.00	5.00

No. 1461a contains 2 each Nos. 1460-1461. Silver margin shows Europa emblem. Size: 108x110mm.

Barn Owl—A381

1980, May 6   Litho.   *Perf. 12x11½*

1462	A381	6.50e shown	14	8
1463	A381	16e Red fox	32	16
1464	A381	19.50e Timber wolf	40	20
1465	A381	20e Golden eagle	40	20
a.	Souvenir sheet of 4		3.00	3.00

European Campaign for the Protection of Species and their Habitat (Lisbon Zoo animals); London 1980 International Stamp Exhibition, May 6-14. No. 1465a contains Nos. 1462-1465; blue margin shows London 1980 emblem. Size: 110½x108mm.

Luiz Camoëns—A382

1980, June 9   Litho. & Engr.   *Perf. 11½x12*

| 1466 | A382 | 6.50e multi | 14 | 8 |
| 1467 | A382 | 20e multi | 40 | 20 |

Luiz Camoëns (1524-1580), 400th death anniversary. Nos. 1466-1467 each se-tenant with label showing poetry text.

Mendes Pinto and Chinese Men—A383

1980, June 30   Litho.   *Perf. 12x11½*

| 1468 | A383 | 6.50e shown | 14 | 8 |
| 1469 | A383 | 10e Battle at sea | 20 | 10 |

A Peregrinacao (The Peregrination,) by Fernao Mendes Pinto (1509-1583), written in 1580, published in 1614.

St. Vincent and Old Lisbon—A384

Designs: 8e, Lantern Tower, Evora Cathedral. 11e, Jesus with top hat, Miranda do Douro Cathedral, and mountain. 16e, Our Lady of the Milk, Braga Cathedral, and Canicada Dam. 19.50e, Pulpit, Santa Cruz Monastery, Coimbra, and Aveiro River. 20e, Algarve chimney, and Rocha Beach.

1980, Sept. 17   Litho.   *Perf. 12x12½*

1470	A384	6.50e multi	14	6
1471	A384	8e multi	16	8
1472	A384	11e multi	22	12
1473	A384	16e multi	32	16
1474	A384	19.50e multi	40	20
1475	A384	20e multi	40	20
	Nos. 1470-1475 (6)		1.64	82

World Tourism Conference, Manila, Sept. 27.

Caravel, Lubrapex '80 Emblem—A385

1980, Oct. 18   Litho.   *Perf. 12x11½*

1476	A385	6.50e shown	14	6
1477	A385	8e Three-master Nau	16	8
1478	A385	16e Galleon	32	16
1479	A385	19.50e Paddle steamer	40	20
a.	Souvenir sheet of 4		2.50	2.50

Lubrapex '80 Stamp Exhibition, Lisbon, Oct. 18-26. No. 1479a contains Nos. 1476-1479; light green marginal inscription. Size: 132x88mm.

Car Emitting Gas Fumes—A386

1980, Oct. 31

| 1480 | A386 | 6.50e Light bulbs | 14 | 8 |
| 1481 | A386 | 16e shown | 32 | 16 |

Energy conservation.

Student, School and Sextant—A387

1980, Dec. 19   Litho.   *Perf. 12x11½*

| 1482 | A387 | 6.50e Founder, book, emblem | 14 | 8 |
| 1483 | A387 | 19.50e shown | 40 | 20 |

Lisbon Academy of Science bicentennial.

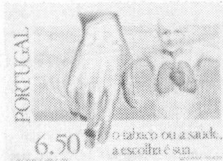

Man with Diseased Heart and Lungs, Hand Holding Cigarette—A388

1980, Dec. 19   *Perf. 13½*

| 1484 | A388 | 6.50e shown | 14 | 8 |
| 1485 | A388 | 19.50e Healthy man rejecting cigarette | 40 | 20 |

Anti-smoking campaign.

Census Form and Houses—A389

1981, Jan. 1   Litho.   *Perf. 13½*

| 1486 | A389 | 6.50e Form, head | 14 | 8 |
| 1487 | A389 | 16e shown | 32 | 16 |

Fragata on Tejo River—A390

1981, Feb. 23   Litho.   *Perf. 12x12½*

1488	A390	8e shown	16	8
1489	A390	8.50e Rabelo, Douro River	18	8
1490	A390	10e Moliceiro, Aveiro River	20	10
1491	A390	16e Barco, Lima River	32	16
1492	A390	19.50e Carocho, Minho River	40	20
1493	A390	20e Varino, Tejo River	40	20
	Nos. 1488-1493 (6)		1.66	82

PORTUGAL

Rajola Tile, Valencia, 15th Century—A391

1981, Mar. 16		Litho.		*Perf. 11½x12*	
1494	A391	8.50e multi		18	10
a.		Miniature sheet of 6		1.25	1.00

No. 1494a has red and black marginal inscriptions. Size: 102x146mm.

1981, June 13		Litho.		*Perf. 11½x12*	
Design: Moresque tile, Coimbra 16th cent.
1495	A391	8.50e multi		18	10
a.		Miniature sheet of 6		1.25	1.00

No. 1495a has red and black marginal inscription. Size: 102x146mm.

1981, Aug. 28		Litho.		*Perf. 11½x12*	
Design: No. 1496, Arms of Duke of Braganza, 1510.
1496	A391	8.50e multi		18	10
a.		Miniature sheet of 6		1.25	1.00

No. 1496a has red brown and black marginal inscription. Size: 147x102mm.

1981, Dec. 16		Litho.		*Perf. 11½x12*	
Design: No. 1497, Pisanos design, 1595.
1497	A391	8.50e multi		18	10
a.		Miniature sheet of 6		1.25	1.00
b.		Souvenir sheet of 4		1.00	50

No. 1497b contains Nos. 1494-1497, red brown and tan margin. Size: 102x120mm.

Perdigueiro—A392

1981, Mar. 16			*Perf. 12*	
1498	A392	7e Cao de agua	14	8
1499	A392	8.50e Serra de aires	18	8
1500	A392	15e shown	30	15
1501	A392	22e Podengo	44	22
1502	A392	25.50e Castro laboreiro	55	25
1503	A392	35.50e Serra da estrela	75	35
		Nos. 1498-1503 (6)	2.36	1.13

Portuguese Kennel Club, 50th anniversary.

Workers and Rainbow—A393

1981, Apr. 30		Litho.		*Perf. 12x12½*	
1504	A393	8.50e shown		18	8
1505	A393	25.50e Rainbow, demonstration		55	25

International Workers' Day.

Dancer in National Costume—A394

Europa Issue 1981

1981, May 11			*Perf. 13½*	
1506	A394	22e shown	44	22
1507	A394	48e Painted boat, horiz.	1.00	50
a.		Souvenir sheet of 4	4.00	2.50

No. 1507a contains 2 each Nos. 1506-1507, blue green marginal inscription. Size: 108x110mm.

St. Anthony Writing—A395

St. Anthony of Lisbon, 750th Anniversary of Death: 70e, Blessing people.

1981, June 13		Litho.		*Perf. 12x11½*	
1508	A395	8.50e multi		18	8
1509	A395	70e multi		1.40	70

500th Anniv. of King Joao II Accession—A396

1981, Aug. 28		Litho.		*Perf. 12x11½*	
1510	A396	8.50e shown		18	8
1511	A396	27e Joao II leading army		55	30

125th Anniv. of Portuguese Railroads—A397

Designs: Locomotives.

1981, Oct. 28		Litho.		*Perf. 12x11½*	
1512	A397	8.50e Dom Luis, 1862		18	8
1513	A397	19e Pacific 500, 1925		38	20
1514	A397	27e ALCO 1500, 1948		55	30
1515	A397	33.50e BB 2600 ALSTHOM, 1974		70	35

Christmas 1981
A399

Designs: Clay creches.

1981, Dec. 16			*Perf. 12½x12*	
1520	A399	7e multi	14	8
1521	A399	8.50e multi	18	8
1522	A399	27e multi	55	30

800th Birth Anniv. of St. Francis of Assisi—A400

1982, Jan. 20		Litho.		*Perf. 12½x12*	
1523	A400	8.50e With animals		18	8
1524	A400	27e Building church		55	30

Centenary of Figueira da Foz—A401

1982, Feb. 24		Litho.		*Perf. 13½*	
1525	A401	10e St. Catherine Fort		20	10
1526	A401	19e Tagus Bridge, ships		38	20

25th Anniv. of European Economic Community—A402

1982, Feb. 24			*Perf. 12x11½*	
1527	A402	27e multi	55	28
a.		Souvenir sheet of 4	2.25	1.15

No. 1527a has black and yellow margin. Size: 155x89mm.

Tile Type of 1981

Design: Italo-Flemish pattern, 17th cent.

1982, Mar. 24		Litho.		*Perf. 11½x12*	
1528	A391	10e multi		20	10
a.		Miniature sheet of 6		1.25	60

No. 1528a has red and black marginal inscription. Size: 147x102mm.

1982, June 11		Litho.		*Perf. 12x11½*	

Design: 10e, Oriental fabric pattern altar frontal, 17th cent.

| 1529 | A391 | 10e multi | | 20 | 10 |
| a. | | Miniature sheet of 6 | | 1.25 | 60 |

No. 1529a has red and black marginal inscription. Size: 146x102mm.

1982, Sept. 22		Litho.		*Perf. 12*	
Design: No. 1530, Greek cross, 1630-1640.
1530	A391	10e multi		20	10
a.		Miniature sheet of 6		1.25	60

No. 1530a has red and black marginal inscription. Size: 147x101mm.

1982, Dec. 15		Litho.		*Perf. 11½x12*	
Design: No. 1531, Blue and white design, Mother of God Convent, Lisbon, 1670.
1531	A391	10e red & bl		20	10
a.		Miniature sheet of 6		1.25	60
b.		Souvenir sheet of 4		80	40

No. 1531b contains Nos. 1528-1531; red marginal inscription. Size: 102x120mm.

Major Sporting Events of 1982—A403

Designs: 27e, Lisbon Sail. 33.50e, 25th Roller-hockey Championships, Lisbon and Barcelos, May 1-16. 50e, Intl. 470 Class World Championships, Cascais Bay. 75e, Espana '82 World Cup Soccer.

1982, Mar. 24			*Perf. 12x12½*	
1532	A403	27e multi	55	28
1533	A403	33.50e multi	68	34
1534	A403	50e multi	1.00	50
1535	A403	75e multi	1.50	75

Telephone Centenary—A404

1982, Apr. 14		Litho.		*Perf. 11½x12*	
1536	A404	10e Phone, 1882		20	10
1537	A404	27e 1887		55	30

Europa 1982—A405

Design: Embassy of King Manuel to Pope Leo X, 1514.

1982, May 3			*Perf. 12x11½*	
1538	A405	33.50e multi	65	35
a.		Miniature sheet of 4	2.75	1.50

No. 1538a has gray and black marginal inscription. Size: 141x101mm.

Visit of Pope John Paul II—A406

Designs: Pope John Paul and cathedrals.

1982, May 13			*Perf. 14*	
1539	A406	10e Fatima	20	10
1540	A406	27e Sameiro	55	30
1541	A406	33.50e Lisbon	70	35
a.		Miniature sheet of 6	3.00	1.50

No. 1541a contains 2 each Nos. 1539-1541; dark blue marginal inscription. Size: 139x80mm.

PORTUGAL

Tejo Estuary Nature Reserve Birds—A407

1982, June 11   *Perf. 11½x12*
1542	A407	10e Dunlin	20	10
1543	A407	19e Red-crested pochard	40	20
1544	A407	27e Greater flamingo	55	30
1545	A40733.50e Black-winged stilt		70	35

PHILEXFRANCE '82 Stamp Exhibition, Paris, June 11-21.

TB Bacillus Centenary—A408

1982, July 27   *Perf. 12x11½*
| 1546 | A408 | 27e Koch | 55 | 30 |
| 1547 | A40833.50e Virus, lungs | | 70 | 35 |

Don't Drink and Drive!—A409

1982, Sept. 22   *Perf. 12*
| 1548 | A409 | 10e multi | 20 | 10 |

Boeing 747—A410

Lubrapex '82 Stamp Exhibition (Historic Flights): 10e, South Atlantic crossing, 1922. 19e, South Atlantic night crossing, 1927. 33.50e, Lisbon-Rio de Janeiro discount fare flights, 1960-1967. 50e, Portugal-Brazil service, 10th anniv.

1982, Oct. 15   *Perf. 12x11½*
1549	A410	10e Fairey III D MK2	20	10
1550	A410	19e Dornier DO	40	20
1551	A41033.50e DC-7C		70	35
1552	A410	50e shown	1.00	50
a.	Souvenir sheet of 4		2.50	1.25

No. 1552a contains Nos. 1549-1552; blue margin shows balloonist. Size: 156x98mm.

Marques de Pombal, Statesman, 200th Anniv. of Death—A411

1982, Nov. 24   *Litho.*   *Perf. 12x11½*
| 1553 | A411 | 10e multi | 20 | 10 |

75th Anniv. of Port Authority of Lisbon—A412

1983, Jan. 5   *Perf. 12½*
| 1554 | A412 | 10e Ships | 20 | 10 |

1983, Jan. 5   *Perf. 12x11½*
| 1555 | A413 | 27e multi | 55 | 30 |

French Alliance Centenary—A413

Export Effort—A414

1983, Jan. 28
| 1556 | A414 | 10e multi | 20 | 10 |

World Communications Year—A415

1982, Feb. 23   *Litho.*   *Perf. 11½x12*
| 1557 | A415 | 10e bl & multi | 20 | 10 |
| 1558 | A41533.50e lt brn & multi | | 70 | 35 |

Naval Uniforms and Ships—A416

1983, Feb. 23   *Perf. 13½*
1559	A416	12.50e Midshipman, 1782, Vasco da Gama	25	12
1560	A416	25e Sailor, 1845, Estefania	50	25
1561	A416	30e Sargent, 1900, Adamastor	60	30
1562	A416	37.50e Midshipman, 1892, Comandante Joao Belo	75	40
a. Bklt. pane, #1559-1562		4.25	

Tile Type of 1981

Design: No. 1563, Hunting scene, 1680.

1983, Mar. 16   *Perf. 12x11½*
| 1563 | A39112.50e multi | | 25 | 12 |
| a. | Miniature sheet of 6 | | 1.50 | |

Design: No. 1564, Birds, 18th cent.

1983, June 16   *Litho.*
| 1564 | A391 | 12.50e multi | 25 | 12 |
| a. | Miniature sheet of 6 | | 1.50 | |

1983, Oct. 19   *Litho.*

Design: No. 1565, Flowers and Birds, 18th cent.
| 1565 | A391 | 12.50e multi | 25 | 12 |
| a. | Miniature sheet of 6 | | 1.50 | |

1983, Nov. 23   *Litho.*   *Perf. 12x11½*

Design: 12.50e, Figurative tile, 18th cent.
1566	A391	12.50e multi	25	12
a.	Miniature sheet of 6		1.50	
b.	Souvenir sheet of 4		1.00	

No. 1566b contains Nos. 1563-1566. Size: 102x120mm.

17th European Arts and Sciences Exhibition, Lisbon—A417

Portuguese Discoveries and Renaissance Euroe: 11e, Helmet, 16th cent. 12.50e, Astrolabe. 25e, Ships, Flemish tapestry. 30e, Column capital, 12th cent. 37.50e, Hour glass. 40e, Chinese panel painting.

1983, Apr. 6
1567	A417	11e multi	22	10
1568	A41712.50e multi		25	12
1569	A417	25e multi	50	25
1570	A417	30e multi	60	30
1571	A41737.50e multi		75	38
1572	A417	40e multi	80	40
a.	Souvenir sheet of 6		3.25	1.75

No. 1572a contains Nos. 1567-1572. Size: 115x118mm.

Europa Issue 1983

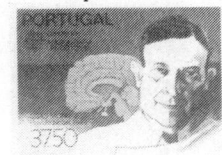

Egas Moniz (1874-1955), Cerebral Angiography and Pre-frontal Leucotomy Pioneer—A418

1983, May 5   *Perf. 12½*
| 1573 | A418 | 37.50e multi | 75 | 38 |
| a. | Souvenir sheet of 4 | | 3.00 | 1.50 |

Margin shows portrait. Size: 140x115mm.

European Conference of Ministers of Transport—A419

1983, May 16
| 1574 | A419 | 30e multi | 60 | 30 |

Endangered Sea Mammals—A420

1983, July 29   *Litho.*   *Perf. 12x11½*
1575	A420	12.50e Sea wolf	25	12
1576	A420	30e Dolphin	60	30
1577	A420	37.50e Killer whale	75	38
1578	A420	80e Humpback whale	1.60	80
a.	Souvenir sheet of 4		3.25	1.75

BRASILIANA '83 Intl. Stamp Exhibition, Rio de Janeiro, July 29-Aug. 7. No. 1578a contains Nos. 1575-1578. Size: 134x82mm.

600th Anniv. of Revolution of 1383—A421

1983, Sept. 14   *Perf. 13½*
| 1579 | A421 | 12.50e Death of Joao Fernandes Andeiro | 25 | 12 |
| 1580 | A421 | 30e Rebellion | 60 | 30 |

First Manned Balloon Flight—A422

Designs: 16e, Bartolomeu Lourenco de Gusmao, Passarola flying machine. 51e, Montgolfier Balloon, first flight.

1983, Nov. 9   *Litho.*   *Perf. 12x11½*
| 1581 | A422 | 16e multi | 32 | 16 |
| 1582 | A422 | 51e multi | 1.00 | 50 |

Christmas 1983—A423

Stained Glass Windows, Monastery at Batalha: 12.50e, Adoration of the Magi. 30e, Flight to Egypt.

1983, Nov. 23   *Perf. 12½*
| 1583 | A423 | 12.50e multi | 25 | 12 |
| 1584 | A423 | 30e multi | 60 | 30 |

Lisbon Zoo Centenary—A424

1984, Jan. 18   *Litho.*   *Perf. 12x11½*
1585	A424	16e Siberian tigers	32	16
1586	A424	16e White rhinoceros	32	16
1587	A424	16e Damalisco Albifronte	32	16
1588	A424	16e Cheetahs	32	16

Nos. 1585-1588 se-tenant.

Military Type of 1983

Air Force Dress Uniforms and Planes: 16e, 1954; Hawker Hurricane II, 1943. 35e, 1960; Republic F-84G Thunderjet. 40e, Paratrooper, 1966; 2502 Nord Noratlas, 1960. 51e, 1966; Corsair II, 1982.

1984, Feb. 15   Litho.   Perf. 13½
1589	A416	16e multi	32	16
1590	A416	35e multi	70	35
1591	A416	40e multi	80	40
1592	A416	51e multi	1.05	52
a.		Bklt. pane of 4 (#1589-1592)	2.90	

Tile Type of 1981

Design: 16e, Royal arms, 19th cent.

1984, Mar. 8   Litho.   Perf. 12x11½
1593	A391	16e multi	24	12
a.		Miniature sheet of 6	1.50	

1984, July 18   Litho.   Perf. 12x11½

Design: 16e, Pombal Palace wall tile, 19th cent.

1594	A391	16e multi	24	12
a.		Miniature sheet of 6	1.50	

Size: 146x102mm.

25th Lisbon Intl. Fair, May 9-13—A425

Events: 40e, World Food Day. 51e, 15th Rehabilitation Intl. World Congress, Lisbon, June 4-8 (vert.).

1984, Apr. 3
1597	A425	35e multi	52	26
1598	A425	40e multi	60	30
1599	A425	51e multi	75	38

April 25th Revolution, 10th Anniv.—A426

1984, Apr. 25   Perf. 13½
1600	A426	16e multi	24	12

Europa (1959-84)—A427

1984, May 2   Perf. 12x11½
1601	A427	51e multi	75	38
a.		Souvenir sheet of 4	3.00	1.50

Size of No. 1601a: 141x115mm.

LUBRAPEX '84 and Natl. Early Art Museum Centenary—A428

Paintings: 16e, Nun, 15th cent. 40e, St. John, by Master of the Retable of Santiago, 16th cent. 51e, View of Lisbon, 17th cent. 66e, Cabeca de Jovem, by Domingos Sesqueira, 19th cent.

1984, May 9   Litho.   Perf. 12x11½
1602	A428	16e multi	24	12
1603	A428	40e multi	60	30
1604	A428	51e multi	75	38
1605	A428	66e multi	1.00	50
a.		Souvenir sheet of 4	2.75	1.50

No. 1605a contains Nos. 1602-1605; tan and black margin. Size: 110x110mm.

1984 Summer Olympics—A429

1984, June 5
1606	A429	35e Fencing	52	26
1607	A429	40e Gymnastics	60	30
1608	A429	51e Running	75	38
1609	A429	80e Pole vault	1.20	60

Souvenir Sheet
1610	A429	100e Hurdles	1.50	75

No. 1610 has multicolored margin showing runners. Size: 90x93mm.

PORTUGAL

For the advanced collector.
We buy and sell
specialized material.

George Alevizos
2716 Ocean Park Blvd. Ste. 1020
Santa Monica, CA 90405
Telephone: 213/450-2543

PORTUGAL — Azores

AIR POST STAMPS.

Symbol of Aviation AP1

Typographed.

1936-41   *Perf. 12x11½.*   Unwmkd.

C1	AP1	1.50e dk bl		45	30
C2	AP1	1.75e red org		75	30
C3	AP1	2.50e rose red		1.10	30
C4	AP1	3e brt bl ('41)		11.50	9.00
C5	AP1	4e dp yel grn ('41)		18.00	13.00
C6	AP1	5e car lake		1.10	25
C7	AP1	10e brn lake		2.75	25
C8	AP1	15e org ('41)		11.50	6.00
C9	AP1	20e blk brn		6.00	1.25
C10	AP1	50e brn vio ('41)		150.00	55.00

Nos. C1–C10 exist imperf.

EXPO Type of Regular Issue
1970, Sept. 16   Litho.   *Perf. 13*

C11	A274	3.50e sil & multi		55	30

Issued to commemorate EXPO '70 International Exhibition, Osaka, Japan, March 15–Sept. 13.

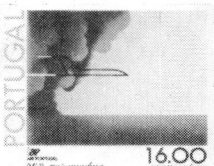

TAP-Airline of Portugal 35th Anniversary—AP2

Design: 19e, Jet flying past sun.

1979, Sept. 21   Litho.   *Perf. 12×11½*

C12	AP2	16e multi		32	16
C13	AP2	19e multi		40	20

See "Special Notices" at the front of this volume for data on the listing methods of this Catalogue, abbreviations, condition, prices and examination.

Regional Issues

Starting in 1980, stamps inscribed Azores and Madeira were valid and sold in Portugal.

Azores

Azores No. 2—A33

Design: 19.50e, Azores No. 6.

1980, Jan. 2   Litho.   *Perf. 12*

314	A33	6.50e multi	15	8
315	A33	19.50e multi	40	20
a.		Souvenir sheet of 2	60	30

No. 315a contains Nos. 314-315; multicolored margin shows view of Islands, after print by Pedrozo, 1868. Size: 140×115½mm.

Map of Azores—A34

1980, Sept. 17   Litho.   *Perf. 12x11½*

316	A34	50c shown	5	5
317	A34	1e Cathedral	5	5
318	A34	5e Windmill	10	5
319	A34	6.50e Local women	14	8
320	A34	8e Coastline	16	8
321	A34	30e Ponta Delgada	60	30

World Tourism Conference, Manila, Sept. 27.

Europa Issue 1981

St. Peter's Cavalcade, St. Miguel Island—A35

1981, May 11   Litho.   *Perf. 12*

322	A35	22e multi	45	20
a.		Souvenir sheet of 2	90	50

No. 322a has multicolored margin showing mounted procession. Size: 140x116mm.

Bulls Attacking Spanish Soldiers A36

Battle of Salga Valley, 400th Anniv.: 33.50e, Friar Don Pedro leading citizens.

1981, July 24   Litho.   *Perf. 12x11½*

323	A36	8.50e multi	20	10
324	A36	33.50e multi	65	30

Tolpis Azorica A37

Designs: Local flora.

1981, Sept. 21   Litho.   *Perf. 12½x12*

325	A37	7e shown	14	6
326	A37	8.50e Ranunculus azoricus	18	8
327	A37	20e Platanthera micranta	40	20
328	A37	50e Laurus azorica	1.00	50
a.		Bklt. pane of 4 (#325-328)	1.75	

1982, Jan. 29   Litho.   *Perf. 12½x12*

329	A37	4e Myosotis azorica	8	5
330	A37	10e Lactuca watsoniana	20	10
331	A37	27e Vicia dennesiana	55	30
332	A37	33.50e Azorina vidalii	70	35
a.		Bklt. pane of 4	1.60	

See Nos. 338-341.

Europa 1982—A38

1982, May 3   Litho.   *Perf. 12x11½*

333	A38	33.50e Heroes of Mindelo embarkation, 1832	70	35
a.		Souvenir sheet of 3	2.10	1.05

No. 333a has multicolored margin. Size: 140x114mm.

Chapel of the Holy Ghost—A39

Designs: Various Chapels of the Holy Ghost.

1982, Nov. 24   Litho.   *Perf. 12½x12*

334	A39	27e multi	55	30
335	A39	33.50e multi	70	35

Europa 1983—A40

1983, May 5   Litho.   *Perf. 12½*

336	A40	37.50e Geothermal energy	75	38
a.		Souvenir sheet of 3	2.25	1.25

Margin shows energy plant. Size: 114x139mm.

Flag of the Autonomous Region—A41

1983, May 23   Litho.   *Perf 12x11½*

337	A41	12.50e multi	25	12

Flower Type of 1981

1983, June 16   *Perf. 12½x12*

338	A37	12.50e St. John's wort	25	12
339	A37	30e Prickless bramble	60	30
340	A37	37.50e Romania bush	75	38
341	A37	100e Common juniper	2.00	1.00
a.		Bklt. pane of 4 (#338-341)	3.60	

Women Wearing Terceira Cloaks—A42

1984, Mar. 8   Litho.   *Perf. 13½*

342	A42	16e Jesters costumes, 18th cent.	24	12
343	A42	51e shown	75	38

Europa (1959-84)—A43

1984, May 2   *Perf. 12½x11½*

344	A43	51e multi	75	38
a.		Souvenir sheet of 3	2.25	1.25

Size of No. 344a: 115x140mm.

Madeira
Type of Azores, 1980

Designs: 6.50e, Madeira No. 2. 19.50e, Madeira No. 5.

1980, Jan. 2 Litho. *Perf. 12*

66	A33	6.50e multi	15	8
67	A33	19.50e multi	40	20
a.		Souvenir sheet of 2	60	30

No. 67a contains Nos. 66-67. Multicolored margin shows Ilehu Fortress after print by Pedrozo, 1864. Size: 140×115½mm.

Grapes and Wine—A7

1980, Sept. 17 Litho. *Perf. 12x11½*

68	A7	50c Bullock cart	5	5
69	A7	1e shown	5	5
70	A7	5e Produce map of Madeira	10	5
71	A7	6.50e Basket and lace	15	8
72	A7	8 Orchid	16	8
73	A7	30e Madeira boat	60	30
		Nos. 68-73 (6)	1.11	61

World Tourism Conference, Manila, Sept. 27.

Europa Issue 1981

O Bailinho Folk Dance—A8

1981, May 11 Litho. *Perf. 12*

| 74 | A8 | 22e multi | 45 | 30 |
| a. | | Souvenir sheet of 2 | 90 | 50 |

No. 74a has multicolored margin showing folk dancers. Size: 140x115mm.

Explorer Ship—A9

1981, July 1 Litho. *Perf. 12x11½*

| 75 | A9 | 8.50e shown | 18 | 8 |
| 76 | A9 | 33.50e Map | 70 | 35 |

Discovery of Madeira anniv.

Dactylorhiza Foliosa—A10

Designs: Local flora.

1981, Oct. 6 Litho. *Perf. 12½x12*

77	A10	7e shown	14	6
78	A10	8.50e Echium candicans	18	8
79	A10	20e Geranium maderense	40	20
80	A10	50e Isoplexis sceptrum	1.00	50
a.		Bklt. pane of 4 (#77-80)	1.75	

Europa 1982—A11

1982, May 3 Litho. *Perf. 12x11½*

| 81 | A11 | 33.50e Sugar mills, 15th cent. | 70 | 35 |
| a. | | Souvenir sheet of 3 | 2.25 | 1.10 |

No. 81a has multicolored margin. Size: 140x115mm.

Flower Type of 1981

1982, Aug. 31 Litho. *Perf. 12½x12*

82	A10	9e Goodyera macrophylla	18	9
83	A10	10e Armeria maderensis	20	10
84	A10	27e Viola paradoxa	55	30
85	A10	33.50e Scilla maderensis	70	35
a.		Bklt. pane of 4 (#82-85)	1.75	

Brinco Dancing Dolls—A12

1982, Dec. 15 Litho. *Perf. 13½*

| 86 | A12 | 27e shown | 55 | 30 |
| 87 | A12 | 33.50e Dancers | 70 | 35 |

Europa 1983—A13

1983, May 5 Litho. *Perf. 12½*

| 88 | A13 | 37.50e Levadas irrigation system | 75 | 38 |
| a. | | Souvenir sheet of 3 | 2.25 | 1.25 |

Margin shows canal. Size: 114x140mm.

Flag of the Autonomous Region—A14

1983, July 1 Litho. *Perf. 12x11½*

| 89 | A14 | 12.50e multi | 25 | 12 |

Flower Type of 1981

1983, Oct. 19 Litho. *Perf. 12½x12*

90	A10	12.50e Matthiola maderensis	25	12
91	A10	30e Erica maderensis	60	30
92	A10	37.50e Cirsium latifolium	75	38
93	A10	100e Clethra arborea	2.00	1.00
a.		Bklt. pane of 4 (#90-93)	3.60	

Europa (1959-84)—A15

1984, May 2 Litho. *Perf. 12x11½*

| 94 | A15 | 51e multi | 75 | 38 |
| a. | | Souvenir sheet of 3 | 2.25 | 1.25 |

Size of No. 94a: 115x140mm.

PORTUGAL

J19	D2	50r car (G)	2.50	1.25
J20	D2	100r dl bl	2.50	1.50
		Nos. J14-J20 (7)	6.70	3.75
		See note after No. 183.		

1915, Mar. 18 — Typographed

J21	D3	½c brown	15	15
J22	D3	1c orange	15	15
J23	D3	2c claret	15	15
J24	D3	3c green	15	15
J25	D3	4c gray vio	15	15
J26	D3	5c carmine	15	15
J27	D3	10c dk bl	20	15
		Nos. J21-J27 (7)	1.10	1.05

1921-27

J28	D3	½c gray grn ('22)	10	10
J29	D3	4c gray grn ('27)	10	10
J30	D3	8c gray grn ('23)	12	10
J31	D3	10c gray grn ('22)	20	12
J32	D3	12c gray grn	15	12
J33	D3	16c gray grn ('23)	18	15
J34	D3	20c gray grn	18	15
J35	D3	24c gray grn	15	12
J36	D3	32c gray grn ('23)	30	20
J37	D3	36c gray grn	30	20
J38	D3	40c gray grn ('23)	30	25
J39	D3	48c gray grn ('23)	35	20
J40	D3	50c gray grn	35	20
J41	D3	60c gray grn	35	20
J42	D3	72c gray grn	50	20
J43	D3	80c gray grn ('23)	3.25	90
J44	D3	1.20e gray grn	1.75	80
		Nos. J28-J44 (17)	8.63	4.11

POSTAGE DUE STAMPS.
Vasco da Gama Issue.

The Zamorin of Calicut Receiving Vasco da Gama
D1

Typographed.

1898, May 1   Perf. 12   Unwmkd.
Denomination in Black.

J1	D1	5r black	2.75	1.50
a.		Value and "Continente" omitted		
J2	D1	10r lil & blk	3.50	2.00
J3	D1	20r org & blk	6.50	3.50
J4	D1	50r sl & blk	17.50	6.50
J5	D1	100r car & blk, *pink*	65.00	30.00
J6	D1	200r brn & blk, *buff*	75.00	40.00

D2   D3

1904   Perf. 11½ x 12

J7	D2	5r brown	35	20
J8	D2	10r orange	1.75	75
a.		Imperf.		
J9	D2	20r lilac	6.50	2.75
J10	D2	30r gray grn	2.00	1.75
J11	D2	40r gray vio	2.25	1.75
J12	D2	50r carmine	45.00	4.50
a.		Imperf.		
J13	D2	100r dl bl	3.00	1.75
a.		Imperf.		
		Nos. J7-J13 (7)	60.85	13.45

Preceding Issue Overprinted in Carmine or Green

1910

J14	D2	5r brown	30	20
J15	D2	10r orange	35	20
J16	D2	20r lilac	35	20
J17	D2	30r gray grn	35	20
J18	D2	40r gray vio	35	20

J72	D6	1e vio bl, dk bl & lt bl	5	5
J73	D6	2e grn, dk grn & lt grn	5	5
J74	D6	3e lt grn, grn & yel ('75)	10	5
J75	D6	4e bl grn, dk grn & yel ('75)	10	5
J76	D6	5e cl, dp cl & pink	10	5
J77	D6	9e vio, dk vio & pink ('75)	20	10
J78	D6	10e lil, pur & pale vio ('75)	20	10
J79	D6	20e red, brn & pale vio ('75)	40	20
		Nos. J65-J79 (15)	1.55	1.00

D4   D5

1932-33

J45	D4	5c buff	25	25
J46	D4	10c lt bl	25	25
J47	D4	20c pink	60	30
J48	D4	30c bl grn	60	30
J49	D4	40c lt grn	60	30
J50	D4	50c gray	60	30
J51	D4	60c rose	1.00	70
J52	D4	80c vio brn	5.00	1.50
J53	D4	1.20e gray ol ('33)	7.00	4.00
		Nos. J45-J53 (9)	15.90	7.90

1940, Feb. 1   Perf. 12½   Unwmkd.

J54	D5	5c bis, perf. 14	15	10
J55	D5	10c rose lil	15	10
J56	D5	20c dk car rose	15	10
J57	D5	30c purple	15	10
J58	D5	40c cerise	15	10
J59	D5	50c brt bl	15	10
J60	D5	60c yel grn	15	10
J61	D5	80c scarlet	20	10
J62	D5	1e brown	25	10
J63	D5	2e dk rose vio	50	20
J64	D5	5e org yel, perf. 14	1.50	1.00
a.		Perf. 12½		
		Nos. J54-J64 (11)	3.50	2.10

Nos. J54-J64 were first issued perf. 14. In 1955 all but the 5c were reissued in perf. 12½.

D6

1967-75   Litho.   Perf. 11½

J65	D6	10c dp org, red brn & yel	5	5
J66	D6	20c bis, dk brn & yel	5	5
J67	D6	30c org, red brn & yel	5	5
J68	D6	40c ol bis, dk brn & yel	5	5
J69	D6	50c ultra, dk bl & bl	5	5
J70	D6	60c grnsh bl, dk grn & lt bl	5	5
J71	D6	80c bl, dk bl & lt bl	5	5

OFFICIAL STAMPS.

No. 567 Overprinted in Black

1938   Perf. 11½   Unwmkd.

O1	A113	40c brown	25	6

O1

1952, Sept.   Litho.   Perf. 12½

O2	O1	blk & cr	10	5

1975, June

O3	O1	blk & yel	70	30

Lettering on No. O3 is black on yellow panel.

NEWSPAPER STAMPS.

N1

Perf. 11½, 12½, 13½.

1876   Typographed   Unwmkd.

P1	N1	2½r bister	6.00	75
a.		2½r ol grn	6.00	75

Various shades.

PARCEL POST STAMPS.

Mercury and Commerce
PP1

Typographed.

1920-22   Perf. 12   Unwmkd.

Q1	PP1	1c lil brn	18	10
Q2	PP1	2c orange	18	10
Q3	PP1	5c lt brn	18	10
Q4	PP1	10c red brn	20	15
Q5	PP1	20c gray bl	25	15
Q6	PP1	40c car rose	30	15
Q7	PP1	50c black	40	20
Q8	PP1	60c dk bl ('21)	40	20
Q9	PP1	70c gray brn ('21)	2.50	1.00
Q10	PP1	80c ultra ('21)	2.50	1.00
Q11	PP1	90c lt vio ('21)	2.50	1.00
Q12	PP1	1e lt grn	2.50	60
Q13	PP1	2e pale lil ('22)	6.00	1.00
Q14	PP1	3e ol ('22)	8.00	2.00
Q15	PP1	4e ultra ('22)	12.50	3.00
Q16	PP1	5e gray ('22)	20.00	2.50
Q17	PP1	10e choc ('22)	55.00	4.50
		Nos. Q1-Q17 (17)	113.59	17.75

Parcel Post Package
PP2

1936   Perf. 11½

Q18	PP2	50c ol brn	25	10
Q19	PP2	1e bis brn	25	10
Q20	PP2	1.50e purple	30	10
Q21	PP2	2e car lake	1.25	12
Q22	PP2	2.50e ol grn	1.25	12
Q23	PP2	4.50e brn lake	2.50	25
Q24	PP2	5e violet	4.50	25
Q25	PP2	10e orange	9.00	80
		Nos. Q18-Q25 (8)	19.30	1.84

PORTUGAL

POSTAL TAX STAMPS.

These stamps represent a special fee for the delivery of postal matter on certain days in each year. The money derived from their sale is applied to works of public charity.

Regular Issues Overprinted in Carmine ASSISTENCIA

Perf. 14½x15

1911, Oct. 4 Unwmkd.

| RA1 | A62 | 10r gray grn | 2.50 | 1.00 |

The 20r carmine of this type was for use on telegrams.

1912, Oct. 4 *Perf. 15x14½*

| RA2 | A64 | 1c dp grn | 2.25 | 1.00 |

The 2c carmine of this type was for use on telegrams.

"Lisbon" PT1   "Charity" PT2

1913, June 8 Litho. *Perf. 12x11½*

| RA3 | PT1 | 1c dk grn | 50 | 35 |

The 2c dark brown of this type was for use on telegrams.

1915, Oct. 4 Typographed

| RA4 | PT2 | 1c carmine | 25 | 20 |

The 2c plum of this type was for use on telegrams.

No. RA4 Surcharged 15 ctvs.

1924, Oct. 4

| RA5 | PT2 | 15c on 1c dl red | 60 | 35 |

The 30c on 2c claret of this type was for use on telegrams.

Charity Type of 1915 Issue.

1925, Oct. 4 *Perf. 12½*

| RA6 | PT2 | 15c carmine | 30 | 25 |

The 30c brown violet of this type was for use on telegrams.

Comrades of the Great War Issue.

Muse of History with Tablet PT3

1925, Apr. 8 Litho. *Perf. 11.*

RA7	PT3	10c brown	50	40
RA8	PT3	10c green	50	40
RA9	PT3	10c rose	50	40
RA10	PT3	10c ultra	50	40

The use of these stamps, in addition to the regular postage, was obligatory on certain days of the year. If the tax represented by these stamps was not prepaid, it was collected by means of Postal Tax Due Stamp No. RAJ1.

Pombal Issue Common Design Types
Engraved; Value and "Continente" Typographed in Black.

1925, May 8 *Perf. 12½*

RA11	CD28	15c ultra	15	8
RA12	CD29	15c ultra	60	50
RA13	CD30	15c ultra	60	50

Olympic Games Issue.

Hurdler PT7

1928 Lithographed *Perf. 12*

| RA14 | PT7 | 15c dl red & blk | 5.00 | 4.00 |

The use of this stamp, in addition to the regular postage, was obligatory on May 22nd, 23rd and 24th, 1928. Ten per cent. of the money thus obtained was retained by the Postal Administration; the balance was given to a Committee in charge of Portuguese participation in the Olympic games at Amsterdam.

POSTAL TAX DUE STAMPS.

PTD1   PTD2

Comrades of the Great War Issue.
Typographed.

1925 *Perf. 11x11½.* Unwmkd.

| RAJ1 | PTD1 | 20c brn org | 1.00 | 1.00 |

See Note after No. RA10.

Pombal Issue. Common Design Types

1925 *Perf. 12½.*

RAJ2	CD31	30c ultra	75	75
RAJ3	CD32	30c ultra	75	75
RAJ4	CD33	30c ultra	75	75

When the compulsory tax was not paid by the use of stamps Nos. RA11 to RA13, double the amount was collected by means of Nos. RAJ2 to RAJ4.

Olympic Games Issue.

1928 Lithographed. *Perf. 11½*

| RAJ5 | PTD2 | 30c lt red & blk | 5.00 | 5.00 |

FRANCHISE STAMPS.

These stamps are supplied by the Government to various charitable, scientific and military organizations for franking their correspondence. This franking privilege was withdrawn in 1938.

FOR THE RED CROSS SOCIETY.

F1

Typographed

1889–1915 *Perf. 11½* Unwmkd.

1S1	F1	rose & blk ('15)	20	10
a.		ver & blk ('08)	1.00	75
b.		red & blk, perf. 12½	15.00	2.00

No. 1S1 Overprinted in Green

1917

| 1S3 | F1 | rose & blk | 50.00 | 45.00 |
| a. | | Inverted overprint | 75.00 | 65.00 |

Olympic Games Issue.

"Charity" Extending Hope to Invalid. F1a

1926 Lithographed. *Perf. 14.*
Inscribed "LISBOA".

| 1S4 | F1a | blk & red | 5.00 | 5.00 |

Inscribed "DELEGACOES".

| 1S5 | F1a | blk & red | 5.00 | 5.00 |

No. 1S4 was for use in Lisbon. No. 1S5 was for the Red Cross chapters outside Lisbon.

Camoëns Issue of 1924 Overprinted in Black or Red

1927

1S6	A68	40c ultra	75
1S7	A68	48c red brn	75
1S8	A69	64c green	75
1S9	A69	75c dk vio	75
1S10	A71	4.50e org (R)	75
1S11	A71	10e dk brn, pnksh	75
		Nos. 1S6–1S11 (6)	4.50

CRUZ VERMELHA Porte franco 1927

Camoëns Issue of 1924 Overprinted in Red

Porte franco 1928

1928

1S12	A67	15c ol grn	75
1S13	A67	16c vio brn	75
1S14	A68	25c lilac	75
1S15	A68	40c ultra	75
1S16	A70	1.20e lt brn	75
1S17	A70	2e ap grn	75
		Nos. 1S12-1S17 (6)	4.50

Camoëns Issue of 1924 Overprinted in Red

Porte franco 1929

1929

1S18	A68	30c dk brn	75
1S19	A68	40c ultra	75
1S20	A69	80c bister	75
1S21	A70	1.50e red	75
1S22	A70	1.60e dk bl	75
1S23	A70	2.40e grn, grn	75
		Nos. 1S18-1S23 (6)	4.50

Same Overprint Dated "1930"

1930

1S24	A68	40c ultra	75
1S25	A69	50c red org	75
1S26	A69	96c lake	75
1S27	A70	1.60e dk bl	75
1S28	A71	3e dk bl, bl	75
1S29	A72	20e dk vio, lil	75
		Nos. 1S24-1S29 (6)	4.50

Camoëns Issue of 1924 Overprinted in Red

Porte franco 1931

1931

1S30	A68	25c lilac	75
1S31	A68	32c dk grn	75
1S32	A68	40c ultra	75
1S33	A69	96c lake	75

1S34	A70	1.60e dk bl	75
1S35	A71	3.20e green	75
		Nos. 1S30-1S35 (6)	4.50

Same Overprint Dated "1932"

1931

1S36	A67	20c dp org	1.00
1S37	A68	40c ultra	1.00
1S38	A68	48c red brn	1.00
1S39	A69	64c green	1.00
1S40	A70	1.60e dk bl	1.00
1S41	A71	10e dk brn, pnksh	1.00
		Nos. 1S36-1S41 (6)	6.00

Nos. 1S6–1S11 Overprinted in Red
1933
f

1932

1S42	A68	40c ultra	1.25
1S43	A68	48c red brn	1.25
1S44	A69	64c green	1.25
1S45	A69	75c dk vio	1.25
1S46	A71	4.50e orange	1.25
1S47	A71	10e dk brn, pnksh	1.25
		Nos. 1S42-1S47 (6)	7.50

Nos. 1S6-1S11 Overprinted type "f" Dated "1934"

1933

1S48	A68	40c ultra	1.25
1S49	A68	48c red brn	1.25
1S50	A69	64c green	1.25
1S51	A69	75c dk vio	1.25
1S52	A71	4.50e orange	1.25
1S53	A71	10e dk brn, pnksh	1.25
		Nos. 1S48-1S53 (6)	7.50

Nos. 1S6-1S11 Overprinted type "f" Dated "1935"

1935

1S54	A68	40c ultra	1.50
1S55	A68	48c red brn	1.50
1S56	A69	64c green	1.50
1S57	A69	75c dk vio	1.50
1S58	A71	4.50e orange	1.50
1S59	A71	10e dk brn, pnksh	1.50
		Nos. 1S54-1S59 (6)	9.00

Camoëns Issue of 1924 Overprinted in Black or Red

Cruz Vermelha Porte Franco 1935

1935

1S60	A68	25c lilac	75
1S61	A68	40c ultra (R)	75
1S62	A69	50c red org	75
1S63	A70	1e slate	75
1S64	A70	2e ap grn	75
1S65	A72	20e dk vio, lil	75
		Nos. 1S60-1S65 (6)	4.50

Camoëns Issue of 1924 Overprinted in Red

1936

1S66	A68	30c dk brn	75
1S67	A68	32c dk grn	75
1S68	A69	80c bister	75
1S69	A70	1.20e lt brn	75
1S70	A71	3e dk bl, bl	75

PORTUGAL—PORTUGUESE AFRICA—PORTUGUESE CONGO

1S71	A71	4.50e blk, *yel*	75	
	Nos. 1S66-1S71 (6)		4.50	

After the government withdrew the franking privilege in 1938, the Portuguese Red Cross Society distributed charity labels which lacked postal validity.

No. 1S4 Overprinted "1935".

1936		*Perf. 14.*	Unwmkd.	
1S72	F1a	blk & red	3.75	3.75

Same Stamp with Additional Overprint "Delegacoes".

| 1S73 | F1a | blk & red | 3.75 | 3.75 |

FOR CIVILIAN RIFLE CLUBS.

Rifle Club Emblem
F2
Perf. 11½ x 12.

1899-1910		Typographed.	Unwmkd.	
2S1	F2	bl grn & car ('99)	20.00	20.00
2S2	F2	brn & yel grn ('00)	20.00	20.00
2S3	F2	car & buff ('01)	2.50	2.50
2S4	F2	bl & org ('02)	2.50	2.50
2S5	F2	grn & org ('03)	2.50	2.50
2S6	F2	lt brn & car ('04)	2.50	2.50
2S7	F2	mar & ultra ('05)	2.50	2.50
2S8	F2	ultra & buff ('06)	2.50	2.50
2S9	F2	choc & yel ('07)	2.50	2.50
2S10	F2	car & ultra ('08)	2.50	2.50
2S11	F2	bl & yel grn ('09)	2.50	2.50
2S12	F2	bl grn & brn, *pink* ('10)	2.50	2.50
	Nos. 2S1-2S12 (12)		65.00	65.00

FOR THE GEOGRAPHICAL SOCIETY OF LISBON.

Coat of Arms
F3   F4
Lithographed.

1903-34		*Perf. 11½.*	Unwmkd.	
3S1	F3	blk, rose, bl & red	9.00	2.50
3S2	F3	bl, yel, red & grn ('09)	11.00	4.00
3S3	F4	blk, org, bl & red ('11)	1.50	1.00
3S4	F4	blk & brn org ('22)	3.00	3.00
3S5	F4	blk & bl ('24)	12.50	5.00
3S6	F4	blk & rose ('26)	4.00	2.50
3S7	F4	blk & grn ('27)	4.00	2.50
3S8	F4	bl, yel & red ('29)	2.50	1.50
3S9	F4	bl, red & vio ('30)	2.50	1.50
3S10	F4	dp bl, lil & red ('31)	2.50	1.50
3S11	F4	bis brn & red ('32)	2.50	1.50
3S12	F4	lt grn & red ('33)	2.50	1.50
3S13	F4	bl & red ('34)	2.50	1.50
	Nos. 3S1-3S13 (13)		62.00	29.50

No. 3S12 with three-line overprint, "C.I.C.I. Portugal 1933," was not valid for postage and was sold only to collectors. No. 3S2 was reprinted in 1933. Green vertical lines behind "Porte Franco" omitted. Price $7.50.

F5

1934		Lithographed.	*Perf. 11½.*	
3S15	F5	bl & red	1.75	1.50

1935-38			*Perf. 11.*	
3S16	F5	blue	6.00	6.00
3S17	F5	dk bl & red ('36)	2.50	2.50
3S18	F5	lil & red ('37)	1.75	1.25
3S19	F5	blk, grn & car ('38)	1.75	1.25

The inscription in the inner circle is omitted on No. 3S16.

FOR THE NATIONAL AID SOCIETY FOR CONSUMPTIVES.

F10
Perf. 11½ x 12

1904, July		Typo.	Unwmkd.	
4S1	F10	brn & grn	3.50	3.50
4S2	F10	car & yel	3.50	3.50

PORTUGUESE AFRICA

(pŏr'tû·gēz; -gēs ăf'rĭ·kà)

For use in any of the Portuguese possessions in Africa.

1000 Reis = 1 Milreis
100 Centavos = 1 Escudo

Vasco da Gama Issue.
Common Design Types
Perf. 13½ to 15½

1898, Apr. 1		Engr.	Unwmkd.	
1	CD20	2½r bl grn	1.25	1.25
2	CD21	5r red	1.25	1.25
3	CD22	10r red vio	1.25	1.25
4	CD23	25r yel grn	1.25	1.25
5	CD24	50r dk bl	1.50	1.50
6	CD25	75r vio brn	6.75	6.75
7	CD26	100r bis brn	5.75	5.75
8	CD27	150r bister	8.50	8.50
	Nos. 1-8 (8)		27.50	27.50

Commemorating Vasco da Gama's voyage to India.

POSTAGE DUE STAMPS.

D1
Typographed.

1945		*Perf. 11½ x 12*	Unwmkd.	

Denomination in Black.

J1	D1	10c claret	25	35
J2	D1	20c purple	25	35
J3	D1	30c dp bl	25	35
J4	D1	40c chocolate	25	35
J5	D1	50c red vio	40	55
J6	D1	1e org brn	1.10	1.25
J7	D1	2e yel grn	2.00	2.50
J8	D1	3e brt car	3.50	4.00
J9	D1	5e org yel	7.50	8.00
	Nos. J1-J9 (9)		15.50	17.70

WAR TAX STAMPS.

Liberty—WT1
Perf. 12 x 11½, 15 x 14.

1919		Typographed.	Unwmkd.	

Overprinted in Black, Orange or Carmine.

MR1	WT1	1c grn (Bk)	60	60
MR2	WT1	4c grn (O)	60	60
MR3	WT1	5c grn (C)	60	60

Some authorities consider No. MR2 a revenue stamp.

PORTUGUESE CONGO

(pŏr'tû·gēz ; -gēs kŏng'ō)

LOCATION — The northernmost district of the Portuguese Angola Colony on the southwest coast of Africa.

CAPITAL—Cabinda.

Stamps of Angola replaced those of Portuguese Congo.

1000 Reis = 1 Milreis
100 Centavos = 1 Escudo (1913)

King Carlos
A1   A2
Perf. 11½, 12½, 13½.

1894, Aug. 5		Typo.	Unwmkd.	
1	A1	5r yellow	80	60
a.		Perf. 13½	14.00	11.50
2	A1	10r redsh vio	1.50	80
a.		Perf. 13½	17.50	13.50
3	A1	15r chocolate	2.75	2.00
4	A1	20r lavender	2.00	1.50
5	A1	25r green	1.40	75
6	A1	50r lt bl	3.00	2.00
7	A1	75r rose	4.50	3.00
a.		Perf. 12½	15.00	13.50
8	A1	80r yel grn	7.50	5.50
a.		Perf. 12½	15.00	10.00
9	A1	100r brn, *yel*	5.50	3.25
a.		Perf. 13½	22.50	15.00
10	A1	150r car, *rose*	10.00	9.00
11	A1	200r dk bl, *bl*	10.00	9.00
12	A1	300r dk bl, *sal*	12.50	10.00
	Nos. 1-12 (12)		61.45	47.40

1898-1903			*Perf. 11½*	

Name & Value in Black except 500r

13	A2	2½r gray	30	25
14	A2	5r orange	30	25
15	A2	10r lt grn	45	30
16	A2	15r brown	1.25	1.00
17	A2	15r gray grn ('03)	75	50
18	A2	20r gray vio	80	60
19	A2	25r sea grn	1.25	75
20	A2	25r car rose ('03)	90	65
21	A2	50r dp bl	1.50	1.25
22	A2	50r brn ('03)	2.50	1.50
23	A2	65r dl bl ('03)	7.50	6.50
24	A2	75r rose	3.00	3.00
25	A2	75r red lil ('03)	3.00	2.50
26	A2	80r violet	3.00	3.00
27	A2	100r dk bl, *bl*	2.50	2.00
28	A2	115r org brn, *pink* ('03)	6.50	6.00
29	A2	130r brn, *straw* ('03)	9.50	9.00
30	A2	150r brn, *buff*	3.50	3.00
31	A2	200r red lil, *pnksh*	4.50	3.00
32	A2	300r dk bl, *rose*	3.50	3.00
33	A2	400r dl bl, *straw* ('03)	9.00	8.50
34	A2	500r blk & red, *bl* ('01)	15.00	9.00
35	A2	700r vio, *yelsh* ('01)	27.50	15.00
	Nos. 13-35 (23)		108.00	80.35

Surcharged in Black

1902		*Perf. 11½, 12½, 13½*		

On Issue of 1894.

36	A1	65r on 15r choc	3.75	2.75
a.		Perf. 11½	12.50	7.50
37	A1	65r on 20r lav	3.75	2.75
38	A1	65r on 25r grn	3.75	2.75
a.		Perf. 11½	14.00	7.50
39	A1	65r on 300r bl, *sal*	5.00	5.00
40	A1	115r on 10r red vio	3.75	3.00
41	A1	115r on 50r lt bl	3.00	2.50
42	A1	130r on 5r yel	3.75	2.75
a.		Inverted surch.	10.00	10.00
43	A1	130r on 75r rose	3.50	2.75
a.		Perf. 12½	6.75	5.50
44	A1	130r on 100r brn, *yel*	3.75	2.75
a.		Inverted surch.	17.50	15.00
b.		Perf. 11½	16.50	12.50
45	A1	400r on 80r yel grn	1.75	1.35
46	A1	400r on 150r car, *rose*	1.35	1.10
47	A1	400r on 200r bl, *bl*	1.35	1.10

On Newspaper Stamp of 1894.

48	N1	115r on 2½r brn	3.75	2.75
a.		Inverted surch.	10.00	10.00
	Nos. 36-48 (13)		42.20	33.30

Nos. 16, 19, 21 and 24 Overprinted In Black

PROVISORIO

1902			*Perf. 11½*	
49	A2	15r brown	1.75	1.25
50	A2	25r sea grn	1.75	1.25
51	A2	50r blue	1.75	1.25
52	A2	75r rose	4.00	2.75

No. 23 Surcharged

50 RÉIS

1905				
53	A2	50r on 65r dl bl	3.75	2.25

Angola Stamps of 1898-1903
(Port. Congo type A2)
Overprinted or Surcharged:

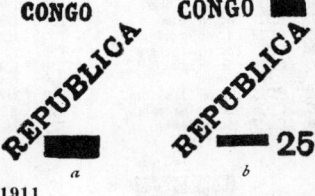

1911				
54	(a)	2½r gray	1.00	80
55	(a)	5r orange	1.50	1.25
56	(a)	10r lt grn	1.50	1.25
57		"REPUBLICA" inverted	10.00	10.00
	(a)	15r gray grn	1.50	1.25
a.		"REPUBLICA" inverted	10.00	10.00

PORTUGUESE CONGO—PORTUGUESE GUINEA

58	(b)	25r on 200r red vio, *pnksh*	2.50	2.00
a.		"REPUBLICA" inverted	10.00	10.00
b.		"CONGO" double	10.00	10.00

Thin Bar and "CONGO"
as Type "b".

59	(a)	2½r gray	1.00	80
		Nos. 54-59 (6)	9.00	7.35

Issue of 1898-1903
Overprinted in
Carmine or Green

REPUBLICA

1911

60	A2	2½r gray	20	20
a.		Inverted overprint		
61	A2	5r orange	25	20
62	A2	10r lt grn	25	20
63	A2	15r gray grn	30	25
64	A2	20r gray vio	30	25
65	A2	25r car rose (G)	30	25
a.		Inverted overprint	5.00	5.00
66	A2	70r brown	30	30
67	A2	75r red lil	75	50
68	A2	100r dk bl, *bl*	75	60
69	A2	115r org brn, *pink*	1.50	1.00
70	A2	130r brn, *straw*	1.50	1.00
71	A2	200r red vio, *pnksh*	2.25	1.75
72	A2	400r dl bl, *straw*	2.25	1.75
73	A2	500r blk & red, *bl*	3.00	2.00
74	A2	700r vio, *yelsh*	3.00	2.00
		Nos. 60-74 (15)	16.90	12.25

Vasco da Gama Issue of Various
Portuguese Colonies Surcharged
REPUBLICA
CONGO
¼ C.

1913
On Stamps of Macao.

75	CD20	¼c on ½a bl grn	1.50	1.50
76	CD21	½c on 1a red	1.50	1.50
77	CD22	1c on 2a red vio	1.50	1.50
78	CD23	2½c on 4a yel grn	1.50	1.50
79	CD24	5c on 8a dk bl	1.50	1.50
80	CD25	7½c on 12a vio brn	3.00	3.00
81	CD26	10c on 16a bis brn	2.25	2.25
82	CD27	15c on 24a bis	2.25	2.25
		Nos. 75-82 (8)	15.00	15.00

On Stamps of Portuguese Africa.

83	CD20	¼c on 2½r bl grn	1.00	1.00
84	CD21	½c on 5r red	1.00	1.00
85	CD22	1c on 10r red vio	1.00	1.00
86	CD23	2½c on 25r yel grn	1.00	1.00
87	CD24	5c on 50r dk bl	1.50	1.50
88	CD25	7½c on 75r vio brn	2.75	2.75
89	CD26	10c on 100r bis brn	1.50	1.50
a.		Inverted surch.	15.00	15.00
90	CD27	15c on 150r bis	1.75	1.75
		Nos. 83-90 (8)	11.50	11.50

On Stamps of Timor.

91	CD20	¼c on ½a bl grn	1.50	1.50
92	CD21	½c on 1a red	1.50	1.50
93	CD22	1c on 2a red vio	1.50	1.50
94	CD23	2½c on 4a yel grn	1.50	1.50
95	CD24	5c on 8a dk bl	1.50	1.50
a.		Double surch.	15.00	15.00
96	CD25	7½c on 12a vio brn	3.00	3.00
97	CD26	10c on 16a bis brn	2.25	2.25
98	CD27	15c on 24a bis	2.25	2.25
		Nos. 91-98 (8)	15.00	15.00

Ceres
A3

1914 Typographed. *Perf. 15x14.*
Name and Value in Black.

99	A3	¼c ol brn	45	35
a.		Inscriptions inverted		
100	A3	½c black	65	40
101	A3	1c bl grn	2.75	1.75
102	A3	1½c lil brn	1.25	75
103	A3	2c carmine	1.25	75
104	A3	2½c lt vio	35	25
105	A3	5c dp bl	75	60
106	A3	7½c yel brn	1.00	75
107	A3	8c slate	1.50	1.00
108	A3	10c org brn	1.50	1.00
109	A3	15c plum	1.75	1.00
110	A3	20c yel grn	2.00	1.50
111	A3	30c brn, *grn*	2.50	1.75
112	A3	40c brn, *pink*	3.50	2.50
113	A3	50c org, *sal*	3.50	2.50
114	A3	1e grn, *bl*	4.50	2.50
		Nos. 99-114 (16)	29.20	19.35

Issue of 1898-1903 Overprinted
Locally in Green or Red

1914-18 *Perf. 11½*

117	A2	50r brn (G)	75	60
118	A2	75r rose (G)	75.00	75.00
119	A2	75r red lil (G)	90	75
120	A2	100r bl, *bl* (R)	75	60
121	A2	200r red vio, *pink* (G)	1.25	1.00
122	A2	400r dl bl, *straw* (R) ('18)	50.00	35.00
123	A2	500r blk & red, *bl* (R)	35.00	27.50

No. 118 was not regularly issued.
Same on Nos. 51-52

124	A2	50r bl (R)	90	50
125	A2	75r rose (G)	1.50	90

Same on No. 53

126	A2	50r on 65r dl bl (R)	1.00	70
		Nos. 117, 119-126 (9)	92.05	67.55

Provisional Issue of 1902
Overprinted Type "c" in Red

1915 *Perf. 11½, 13½*

127	A1	115r on 10r red vio	30	25
a.		Perf. 13½	15.00	12.00
128	A1	115r on 50r lt bl	30	25
a.		Perf. 11½	1.75	60
129	A1	130r on 5r yel	35	30
130	A1	130r on 75r rose	1.50	60
131	A1	130r on 100r brn, *buff*	50	35
135	N1	115r on 2½r brn	50	25

Nos. 49, 51 Overprinted Type "c"

136	A2	15r brown	50	30
137	A2	50r blue	50	30

No. 53 Overprinted Type "c"

138	A2	50r on 65r dl bl	50	30
		Nos. 127-138 (9)	4.95	2.90

NEWSPAPER STAMP

N1
Perf. 12½, 13½
1894, Aug. 5 Typo. Unwmkd.
| P1 | N1 | 2½r brown | 80 | 60 |

Common Design Types
pictured in section at front of book.

PORTUGUESE GUINEA

(pŏr′tû·gēz gĭn′ĭ)

LOCATION—On the west coast of Africa between Senegal and Guinea.
GOVT.—Former Portuguese Overseas Territory.
AREA—13,944 sq. mi.
POP.—560,000 (est. 1970).
CAPITAL—Bissau.

The territory, including the Bissagos Islands, became an independent republic on Sept. 10, 1974. See Guinea-Bissau in Vol. III.

1000 Reis = 1 Milreis
100 Centavos = 1 Escudo (1913)

Prices of early Portuguese Guinea stamps vary according to condition. Quotations for Nos. 1-7 are for fine copies. Very fine to superb specimens sell at much higher prices, and inferior or poor copies sell at reduced prices, depending on the condition of the individual specimen.

Stamps of Cape Verde,
1877-85 **GUINÉ**
Overprinted in Black

Without Gum (Nos. 1-7)

1881 *Perf. 12½.* Unwmkd.

1	A1	5r black	1,100.	1,000.
1A	A1	10r yel	1,250.	1,000.
2	A1	20r bister	500.00	300.00
3	A1	25r rose	1,250.	950.00
4	A1	40r blue	1,100.	1,000.
a.		Cliché of Mozambique in Cape Verde plate	6,250.	6,000.
4B	A1	50r green	1,250.	1,000.
5	A1	100r lilac	300.00	250.00
6	A1	200r orange	700.00	600.00
7	A1	300r brown	700.00	600.00

Overprinted
in Red or Black **GUINÉ**

1881-85 *Perf. 12½, 13½*

8	A1	5r blk (R)	2.75	2.75
9	A1	10r yellow	150.00	125.00
10	A1	10r grn ('85)	6.50	4.75
11	A1	20r bister	2.00	1.75
12	A1	20r rose ('85)	6.50	4.75
a.		Double overprint		
13	A1	25r carmine	1.75	1.25
a.		Perf. 13½	62.50	30.00
14	A1	25r vio ('85)	2.50	1.50
a.		Double overprint		
15	A1	40r blue	150.00	100.00
a.		Cliché of Mozambique in Cape Verde plate	1,000.	800.00
16	A1	40r grn ('85)	1.50	1.25
a.		Cliché of Mozambique in Cape Verde plate	30.00	27.50
b.		Imperf.		
c.		As "a," imperf.		
d.		Double ovpt.		
17	A1	50r green	175.00	100.00
18	A1	50r bl ('85)	4.50	2.25
a.		Imperf.		
b.		Double overprint		
19	A1	100r lilac	6.00	3.75
a.		Inverted overprint		
20	A1	200r orange	8.50	6.50

21	A1	300r yel brn	12.00	9.50
a.		300r lake brn	12.00	9.50

Varieties of this overprint may be found without accent on "E" of "GUINE", or with grave instead of acute accent.

Stamps of the 1879-85 issues were reprinted on a smooth white chalky paper, ungummed, and on thin white paper with shiny white gum and clean-cut perforation 13½. Price of lowest selling reprints, $1 each.

King Luiz
A3

1886 Typo. *Perf. 12½, 13½*

22	A3	5r gray blk	3.75	2.25
a.		Imperf.		
23	A3	10r green	5.50	2.75
b.		Perf. 13½	5.50	4.50
24	A3	20r carmine	7.00	3.75
25	A3	25r red lil	6.75	4.25
a.		Imperf.		
26	A3	40r chocolate	6.00	5.00
a.		Perf. 12½	75.00	45.00
27	A3	50r blue	11.00	4.50
a.		Imperf.		
28	A3	80r gray	11.00	11.00
a.		Perf. 12½	75.00	50.00
29	A3	100r brown	11.00	11.00
a.		Perf. 12½	30.00	15.00
30	A3	200r gray lil	30.00	15.00
31	A3	300r orange	35.00	22.50
a.		Perf. 13½	185.00	150.00

Reprinted in 1905 on thin white paper with shiny white gum and clean-cut perforation 13½. Nos. 22, 27-29, price $2 each. Nos. 23, 25-26, 30-31, price $20 each.

King Carlos
A4   A5

1893-94 *Perf. 11½*

32	A4	5r yellow	1.40	90
a.		Perf. 12½	2.00	1.25
33	A4	10r red vio	1.40	90
34	A4	15r chocolate	1.50	1.25
35	A4	20r lavender	1.50	1.25
36	A4	25r bl grn	1.50	1.25
37	A4	50r lt bl	2.75	1.75
a.		Perf. 12½	7.50	4.50
38	A4	75r rose	9.00	6.50
39	A4	80r lt grn	9.00	6.50
40	A4	100r brn, *buff*	9.00	6.50
41	A4	150r car, *rose*	9.00	7.50
42	A4	200r dk bl, *bl*	10.00	7.50
43	A4	300r dk bl, *sal*	13.00	10.00
		Nos. 32-43 (12)	69.05	51.80

Almost all of Nos. 32-43 were issued without gum.

1898-1903 *Perf. 11½*
Name & Value in Black except 500r

44	A5	2½r gray	35	30
45	A5	5r orange	35	30
46	A5	10r lt grn	35	30
47	A5	15r brown	3.00	1.75
48	A5	15r gray grn ('03)	1.40	1.10
49	A5	20r gray vio	1.25	90
50	A5	25r sea grn	1.75	90
51	A5	25r car ('03)	80	60
52	A5	50r dk bl	2.50	1.25
53	A5	50r brn ('03)	1.85	1.40
54	A5	65r dl bl ('03)	7.50	6.00
55	A5	75r rose	13.50	7.00
56	A5	75r lil ('03)	1.75	1.75
57	A5	80r brt vio	3.00	2.00
58	A5	100r dk bl, *bl*	1.75	1.75
a.		Perf. 12½	45.00	20.00

PORTUGUESE GUINEA

59	A5	115r org brn, *pink* ('03)	7.50	5.50
60	A5	130r brn, *straw* ('03)	7.50	5.50
61	A5	150r lt brn, *buff*	7.50	3.00
62	A5	200r red lil, *pnksh*	7.50	3.50
63	A5	300r bl, *rose*	6.50	3.50
64	A5	400r dl bl, *straw* ('03)	7.50	5.50
65	A5	500r blk & red, *bl* ('01)	9.00	6.00
66	A5	700r vio, *yelsh* ('01)	15.00	9.00
		Nos. 44-66 (23)	111.10	68.80

Stamps issued in 1903 were without gum.

Issue of 1886
Surcharged in Black or Red

65 RÉIS

1902, Oct. 20 Perf. 12½, 13½

67	A3	65r on 10r grn	5.00	5.00
68	A3	65r on 20r car	5.00	5.00
69	A3	65r on 25r red lil	5.00	5.00
70	A3	115r on 40r choc	4.50	4.50
a.		Perf. 13½	9.00	9.00
71	A3	115r on 50r bl	4.50	4.50
72	A3	115r on 300r org	6.25	6.25
73	A3	130r on 80r gray	6.25	6.25
74	A3	130r on 100r brn	6.25	6.25
a.		Perf. 13½	12.50	12.50
75	A3	400r on 200r gray lil	10.00	10.00
76	A3	400r on 5r gray blk (R)	20.00	20.00
		Nos. 67-76 (10)	72.75	72.75

Reprints of No. 76 are in black and have clean-cut perforation 13½. Price $2 each.

Same Surcharge on Issue of 1893-94.
Perf. 11½, 12½, 13½

77	A4	65r on 10r red vio	4.00	4.00
78	A4	65r on 15r choc	4.00	4.00
79	A4	65r on 20r lav	4.00	4.00
80	A4	65r on 50r lt bl	2.75	2.75
81	A4	115r on 5r yel	4.00	4.00
a.		Inverted surcharge	25.00	25.00
b.		Perf. 12½	25.00	25.00
82	A4	115r on 25r bl grn	4.00	4.00
83	A4	130r on 150r car, *rose*	5.50	5.50
84	A4	130r on 200r dk bl, *bl*	5.50	5.50
85	A4	130r on 300r dk bl, *sal*	5.00	5.00
86	A4	400r on 75r rose	2.00	2.00
87	A4	400r on 80r lt grn	2.00	2.00
88	A4	400r on 100r brn, *buff*	2.00	2.00

Same Surcharge on No. P1

89	N1	115r on 2½r brn	4.50	4.50
		Nos. 77-89 (13)	49.25	49.25

Issue of 1898
Overprinted in Black

PROVISORIO

1902, Oct. 20 Perf. 11½

90	A5	15r brown	1.75	1.10
91	A5	25r sea grn	1.75	1.10
92	A5	50r dk bl	2.25	1.50
93	A5	75r rose	4.50	3.75

No. 54 Surcharged in Black

50 RÉIS

1905

94	A5	50r on 65r dl bl	4.50	2.50

Issue of 1898-1903
Overprinted in Carmine or Green

REPUBLICA

1911 Perf. 11½

95	A5	2½r gray	40	30
a.		Inverted overprint	3.00	3.00

96	A5	5r orange	40	30
97	A5	10r lt grn	75	45
98	A5	15r gray grn	75	45
99	A5	20r gray vio	75	45
100	A5	25r car (G)	75	45
a.		Double overprint	7.50	7.50
101	A5	50r brown	50	40
102	A5	75r lilac	50	40
103	A5	100r dk bl, *bl*	1.50	70
104	A5	115r org brn, *pink*	1.50	70
105	A5	130r brn, *straw*	1.50	70
106	A5	200r red lil, *pink*	5.50	3.00
107	A5	400r dl bl, *straw*	2.50	1.35
108	A5	500r blk & red, *bl*	2.50	1.35
109	A5	700r vio, *yelsh*	3.75	2.00
		Nos. 95-109 (15)	23.55	13.00

Issued without gum: Nos. 101-102, 104-105, 107.

Issue of 1898-1903
Overprinted in Red

Without Gum (Nos. 110-115)

1913 Perf. 11½

110	A5	15r gray grn	7.50	5.50
111	A5	75r lilac	7.50	5.50
a.		Inverted ovpt.		
112	A5	100r bl, *bl*	4.75	3.50
a.		Inverted ovpt.		
113	A5	200r red lil, *pnksh*	20.00	20.00
a.		Inverted ovpt.		

Same Overprint on Nos. 90 and 93 in Red.

114	A5	15r brown	7.50	6.00
a.		"REPUBLICA" double		
b.		"REPUBLICA" inverted		
115	A5	75r rose	7.50	6.00
a.		"REPUBLICA" inverted		
		Nos. 110-115 (6)	54.75	46.50

Vasco da Gama Issue of Various Portuguese Colonies Surcharged

REPUBLICA GUINE ¼ C.

1913 On Stamps of Macao.

116	CD20	¼c on ½a bl grn	2.00	2.00
117	CD21	½c on 1a red	2.00	2.00
118	CD22	1c on 2a red vio	2.00	2.00
119	CD23	2½c on 4a yel grn	2.00	2.00
120	CD24	5c on,8a dk bl	2.00	2.00
121	CD25	7½c on 12a vio brn	3.50	3.50
122	CD26	10c on 16a bis brn	2.00	2.00
a.		Invtd. surch.	20.00	20.00
123	CD27	15c on 24a bis	3.00	3.00
		Nos. 116-123 (8)	18.50	18.50

On Stamps of Portuguese Africa.

124	CD20	¼c on 2½c bl grn	1.50	1.50
125	CD21	½c on 5r red	1.50	1.50
126	CD22	1c on 10r red vio	1.50	1.50
127	CD23	2½c on 25r yel grn	1.50	1.50
128	CD24	5c on 50r dk bl	1.50	1.50
129	CD25	7½c on 75r vio brn	4.00	4.00
130	CD26	10c on 100r bis brn	1.50	1.50
131	CD27	15c on 150r bis	4.50	4.50
		Nos. 124-131 (8)	17.50	17.50

On Stamps of Timor.

132	CD20	¼c on ½a bl grn	1.75	1.75
133	CD21	½c on 1a red	1.75	1.75
134	CD22	1c on 2a red viv	1.75	1.75
135	CD23	2½c on 4a yel grn	1.75	1.75
136	CD24	5c on 8a dk bl	1.75	1.75
137	CD25	7½c on 12a vio brn	3.50	3.50
138	CD26	10c on 16a bis brn	1.75	1.75
139	CD27	15c on 24a bis	3.50	3.50
		Nos. 132-139 (8)	17.75	17.75

Ceres A6

1914-26 Perf. 15x14, 12x11½
Name and Value in Black.

140	A6	¼c ol brn	10	7
141	A6	½c black	10	8
142	A6	1c bl grn	1.50	1.50
143	A6	1c yel grn ('22)	10	8
144	A6	1½c lil brn	15	8
145	A6	2c carmine	10	8
146	A6	2c gray ('25)	20	1.00
147	A6	2½c lt vio	15	6
148	A6	3c org ('22)	15	1.00
149	A6	4c dp red ('22)	20	1.00
150	A6	4½c gray ('22)	20	1.00
151	A6	5c dp bl	75	50
152	A6	5c brt bl ('22)	20	10
153	A6	6c lil ('22)	20	1.00
154	A6	7c ultra ('22)	30	1.00
155	A6	7½c yel brn	20	10
156	A6	8c slate	20	8
157	A6	10c org brn	15	8
158	A6	12c bl grn ('22)	75	35
159	A6	15c plum	9.00	6.00
160	A6	15c brn rose ('22)	60	35
161	A6	20c yel grn	20	10
162	A6	24c ultra ('25)	2.25	2.25
163	A6	25c brn ('25)	2.75	2.75
164	A6	30c brn, *grn*	6.50	6.00
165	A6	30c gray grn ('22)	80	25
166	A6	40c brn, *pink*	3.50	3.50
167	A6	40c turq bl ('22)	80	40
168	A6	50c org, *sal*	3.50	3.50
169	A6	50c vio ('25)	1.60	70
170	A6	60c dk bl ('22)	1.75	70
171	A6	60c dp rose ('26)	2.50	2.50
172	A6	80c brt rose ('22)	1.60	90
173	A6	1e grn, *bl*	4.50	4.50
174	A6	1e pale rose ('22)	2.50	1.25
175	A6	1e ind ('26)	2.75	2.75
176	A6	2e dk vio ('22)	2.75	1.60
177	A6	5e buff ('25)	10.00	6.00
178	A6	10e ('25)	20.00	12.50
179	A6	20e pale turq ('25)	50.00	22.50
		Nos. 140-179 (40)	135.55	90.18

Provisional Issue of 1902
Overprinted in Carmine

1915 Perf. 11½, 12½, 13½

180	A3	115r on 40r choc	80	70
a.		Perf. 13½	9.00	6.50
181	A3	115r on 50r bl	80	70
182	A3	130r on 80r gray	3.00	2.00
a.		Perf. 12½	25.00	20.00
183	A3	130r on 100r brn	2.75	2.00
a.		Perf. 13½	12.00	9.50
184	A4	115r on 5r yel	90	75
a.		Perf. 11½		
185	A4	115r on 25r bl grn	90	70
186	A4	130r on 150r car, *rose*	1.25	90
187	A4	130r on 200r bl, *bl*	90	75
188	A4	130r on 300r dk bl, *sal*	90	75
189	N1	115r on 2½r brn	1.25	90
a.		Perf. 13½	13.50	12.50
b.		Inverted ovpt.	12.50	12.50

On Nos. 90, 92, 94
Perf. 11½

190	A5	15r brown	90	75
191	A5	50r dk bl	90	75
192	A5	50r on 65r dl bl	90	75
		Nos. 180-192 (13)	16.15	12.40

Nos. 64, 66 Overprinted

REPUBLICA

1919 Without Gum Perf. 11½

193	A5	400r dl bl, *straw*	13.50	11.00
194	A5	700r vio, *yelsh*	6.75	4.50

Nos. 140, 141 and 59 Surcharged:

$04 centavos **$12 CENTAVOS**
  a   b
Without Gum

1920, Sept. Perf. 15x14, 11½

195	A6(a)	4c on ¼c ol brn	4.00	2.50
196	A6(a)	6c on ½c blk	3.75	2.50
197	A5(b)	12c on 115r org brn, *pink*	5.00	4.00

República

Nos. 86-88 Surcharged

40 C.

1925 Perf. 11½

203	A4	40c on 400r on 75r	1.00	80
204	A4	40c on 400r on 80r	80	70
205	A4	40c on 400r on 100r	80	70

Nos. 171-172, 176 Surcharged

70 C.

1931 Perf. 12x11½

211	A6	50c on 60c dp rose	1.60	1.25
212	A6	70c on 80c pink	1.75	1.60
213	A6	1.40e on 2e dk vio	4.00	3.00

Ceres A7

Wmkd. Maltese Cross. (232)

1933 Perf. 12 x 11½

214	A7	1c bister	8	7
215	A7	5c ol brn	10	8
216	A7	10c violet	10	10
217	A7	15c black	15	10
218	A7	20c gray	15	10
219	A7	30c dk grn	15	12
220	A7	40c dk org	30	20
221	A7	45c lt bl	60	45
222	A7	50c lt brn	60	45
223	A7	60c ol grn	60	45
224	A7	70c org brn	75	60
225	A7	80c emerald	90	75
226	A7	85c dp rose	2.00	1.25
227	A7	1e red brn	1.00	75
228	A7	1.40e dk bl	3.00	1.75
229	A7	2e red vio	2.50	2.00
230	A7	5e ap grn	6.50	4.50
231	A7	10e ol vio	12.50	6.50
232	A7	20e orange	45.00	19.00
		Nos. 214-232 (19)	76.98	39.22

Common Design Types
Engraved
Name and Value Typographed in Black.

1938 Perf. 13½ x 13. Unwmkd.

233	CD34	1c gray grn	9	9
234	CD34	5c org brn	12	12
235	CD34	10c dk car	12	10
236	CD34	15c dk vio brn	20	15
237	CD34	20c slate	45	30
238	CD35	30c rose vio	45	30
239	CD35	35c brt grn	50	35
240	CD35	40c brown	50	35
241	CD35	50c brt red vio	50	35
242	CD36	60c gray blk	50	35
243	CD36	70c brn vio	50	35
244	CD36	80c orange	1.00	75
245	CD36	1e red	1.00	75
246	CD37	1.75e blue	1.50	90
247	CD37	2e brn car	4.00	1.50
248	CD37	5e ol grn	5.00	2.00
249	CD38	10e ol vio	6.00	2.75
250	CD38	20e red brn	25.00	5.00
		Nos. 233-250 (18)	47.43	16.14

Common Design Types
pictured in section at front of book.

PORTUGUESE GUINEA

Fort of Cacheu—A8

Nuno Tristam
A9

Ulysses S. Grant
A10

Designs: 3.50e, Teixeira Pinto. 5e, Honorio Barreto. 20e, Bissau Church.

Lithographed.
1946-47   Perf. 11   Unwmkd.

251	A8	30c gray & lt gray	85	60
252	A9	50c blk & pink	50	40
253	A9	50c gray grn & lt grn	50	40
254	A10	1.75e bl & lt bl	3.00	1.50
255	A10	3.50e red & pink	4.50	2.00
256	A10	5e lt brn & buff	10.00	5.00
257	A8	20e vio & lt vio	15.00	7.00
a.		Sheet of seven ('47)	70.00	70.00
		Nos. 251-257 (7)	34.35	16.90

Discovery of Guinea, 500th anniversary. No. 257a contains one each of Nos. 251–257. Size: 175½x221mm. Sold for 40 escudos.
Issue date: Nos. 251-257, Jan. 12, 1946.

Guinea Village
A11

U.P.U. Symbols
A12

Designs: 10c, Crowned crane. 20c, 3.50e, Tribesman 35c, 5e, Woman in ceremonial dress. 50c, Musician. 70c, Man. 80c, 20e, Girl. 1e, 2e, Drummer. 1.75e, Antelope.

1948, Apr.   Photo.   Perf. 11½.

258	A11	5c chocolate	20	20
259	A11	10c lt vio	1.50	1.10
260	A11	20c dl rose	50	40
261	A11	35c green	50	40
262	A11	50c dp org	30	30
263	A11	70c dp gray bl	50	50
264	A11	80c dl grn	60	50
265	A11	1e rose red	1.00	60
266	A11	1.75e ultra	5.50	2.00
267	A11	2e blue	15.00	5.00
268	A11	3.50e org brn	2.00	1.10
269	A11	5e slate	3.00	1.50
270	A11	20e violet	9.00	4.00
a.		Sheet of 13	75.00	75.00
		Nos. 258-270 (13)	39.60	13.75

No. 270a measures 176 x 158 mm., and contains one each of Nos. 258 to 270 plus two labels. Marginal inscriptions and border in gray and black. Sheet sold for 40 escudos.

Lady of Fatima Issue.
Common Design Type
1948, Oct.   Litho.   Perf. 14½.

271 CD40 50c dp grn   3.50 3.00
Visit of the statue of Our Lady of Fatima.

1949, Oct.   Perf. 14.
272 A12 2e dp org & cr   3.50 2.50
Universal Postal Union, 75th anniversary.

Holy Year Issue.
Common Design Types
1950, May   Perf. 13x13½.

273 CD41 1e brn lake   2.00 1.25
274 CD42 3e bl grn   3.00 2.00
Issued to commemorate the Holy Year, 1950.

Holy Year Extension Issue.
Common Design Type
1951, Oct.   Perf. 14.

275 CD43 1e choc & pale brn   80 60

Medical Congress Issue.
Common Design Type
Design: Physical examination.
1952   Perf. 13½

276 CD44 50c pur & choc   40 30
National Congress of Tropical Medicine, Lisbon.

Exhibition Entrance
A13

Stamp of Portugal and Arms of Colonies
A14

1953, Jan.   Litho.   Perf. 13

277	A13	10c brn lake & ol	15	12
278	A13	50c dk bl & bis	80	40
279	A13	3e blk, dk brn & sal	2.00	1.00

Issued to commemorate the Exhibition of Sacred Missionary Art held at Lisbon in 1951.

1953   Photogravure   Unwmkd.
Stamp and Arms Multicolored.

280 A14 50c lem & gray bl   90 70
Centenary of Portugal's first postage stamps.

Analeptes Trifasciata
A15

1953   Perf. 11½.
Various Beetles in Natural Colors.

281	A15	5c yellow	10	10
282	A15	10c blue	10	10
283	A15	30c org ver	10	10
284	A15	50c yel grn	20	20
285	A15	70c gray brn	40	30
286	A15	1e orange	40	30
287	A15	2e pale ol grn	1.00	30
288	A15	3e lil rose	1.50	75
289	A15	5e lt bl grn	2.50	80
290	A15	10e lilac	3.50	1.10
		Nos. 281-290 (10)	9.80	4.05

Sao Paulo Issue
Common Design Type
1954   Lithographed.   Perf. 13½

291 CD46 1e lil rose, bl gray & blk   30 20
Sao Paulo, 400th anniversary.

Belem Tower, Lisbon, and Colonial Arms
A16

1955, Apr. 14

292	A16	1e bl & multi	30	20
293	A16	2.50e gray & multi	60	40

Issued to publicize the visit of Pres. Francisco H. C. Lopes.

Fair Emblem, Globe and Arms
A17

1958   Perf. 12x11½   Unwmkd.
294 A17 2.50e multi   70 50
World's Fair at Brussels.

Tropical Medicine Congress Issue
Common Design Type
Design: Maytenus senegalensis.
1958   Perf. 13½

295 CD47 5e multi   2.50 1.25
6th International Congress of Tropical Medicine and Malaria, Lisbon, Sept. 1958.

Honorio Barreto
A18

Nautical Astrolabe
A19

1959, Apr. 29   Litho.   Perf. 13½
296 A18 2.50e multi   30 20
Issued to commemorate the centenary of the death of Honorio Barreto, governor of Portuguese Guinea.

1960, June 25   Perf. 13½
297 A19 2.50e multi   30 20
Issued to commemorate the 500th anniversary of the death of Prince Henry the Navigator.

Traveling Medical Unit
A20

1960   Perf. 14½   Unwmkd.
298 A20 1.50e multi   30 20
Issued to commemorate the 10th anniversary of the Commission for Technical Co-operation in Africa South of the Sahara (C.C.T.A.).

Sports Issue
Common Design Type
Sports: 50c, Automobile race. 1e, Tennis. 1.50e, Shot put. 2.50e, Wrestling. 3.50e, Trapshooting. 15e, Volleyball.
1962, Jan. 18   Litho.   Perf. 13½
Multicolored Designs

299	CD48	50c lt brn	10	10
300	CD48	1e lt lil	80	30
301	CD48	1.50e gray ol	30	20
302	CD48	2.50e yellow	50	20
303	CD48	3.50e salmon	50	25
304	CD48	15e pale lil	1.70	1.00
		Nos. 299-304 (6)	3.90	2.05

Anti-Malaria Issue
Common Design Type
Design: Anopheles gambiae.
1962   Perf. 13½   Unwmkd.

305 CD49 2.50e multi   60 40
Issued for the World Health Organization drive to eradicate malaria.

African Spitting Cobra
A21

Snakes: 35c, African rock python. 70c, Boomslang. 80c, West African mamba. 1.50e, Smythe's water snake. 2e, Common night adder (horiz.). 2.50e, Green swamp snake. 3.50e, Brown house snake. 4e, Spotted wolf snake. 5e, Common puff adder. 15e, Striped beauty snake. 20e, African egg-eating snake (horiz.).

1963, Jan. 17   Litho.   Perf. 13½

306	A21	20c multi	20	12
307	A21	35c multi	20	12
308	A21	70c multi	40	30
309	A21	80c multi	40	30
310	A21	1.50e multi	60	30
311	A21	2e multi	40	20
312	A21	2.50e multi	1.25	30
313	A21	3.50e multi	30	20
314	A21	4e multi	40	30
315	A21	5e multi	40	30
316	A21	15e multi	90	60
317	A21	20e multi	1.25	80
		Nos. 306-317 (12)	6.70	3.84

Airline Anniversary Issue
Common Design Type
1963   Lithographed   Perf. 14½

318 CD50 2.50e lt brn & multi   70 30
Issued to commemorate the 10th anniversary of Transportes Aéreos Portugueses.

National Overseas Bank Issue
Common Design Type
Design: 2.50e, João de Andrade Córvo.
1964, May 16   Perf. 13½

319 CD51 2.50e multi   60 35
Issued to commemorate the centenary of the National Overseas Bank of Portugal.

ITU Issue
Common Design Type
1965, May 17   Perf. 14½   Unwmkd.

320 CD52 2.50e lt bl & multi   1.75 80

PORTUGUESE GUINEA

Soldier, 1548
A22

Designs: 40c, Rifleman, 1578. 60c, Rifleman, 1640. 1e, Grenadier, 1721. 2.50e, Fusiliers captain, 1740. 4.50e, Infantryman, 1740. 7.50e, Sergeant major, 1762. 10e, Engineers' officer, 1806.

1966, Jan. 8   Litho.   *Perf. 13½*

321	A22	25c multi	18	12
322	A22	40c multi	20	12
323	A22	60c multi	25	15
324	A22	1e multi	35	17
325	A22	2.50e multi	1.00	35
326	A22	4.50e multi	1.75	1.00
327	A22	7.50e multi	1.75	1.25
328	A22	10e multi	2.25	1.50
		Nos. 321-328 (8)	7.73	4.66

National Revolution Issue
Common Design Type

Design: 2.50e, Berta Craveiro Lopes School and Central Pavilion of Bissau Hospital.

1966, May 28   Litho.   *Perf. 11½*

329   CD53   2.50e multi   50   30
National Revolution, 40th anniversary.

Navy Club Issue
Common Design Type

Designs: 50c, Capt. Oliveira Muzanty and cruiser Republica. 1e, Capt. Afonso de Cerqueira and torpedo boat Guadiana.

1967, Jan. 31   Litho.   *Perf. 13*

330	CD54	50c multi	25	10
331	CD54	1e multi	75	50

Centenary of Portugal's Navy Club.

Sacred Heart of Jesus Monument and Chapel of the Apparition
A23

Pres. Rodrigues Thomas—A24

1967, May 13   *Perf. 12½x13*

332   A23   50c multi   20   15

Issued to commemorate the 50th anniversary of the appearance of the Virgin Mary to three shepherd children at Fatima.

1968, Feb. 2   Litho.   *Perf. 13½*

333   A24   1e multi   30   20

Issued to commemorate the 1968 visit of Pres. Americo de Deus Rodrigues Thomaz.

Cabral's Coat of Arms
A25

1968, Apr. 22   Litho.   *Perf. 14*

334   A25   2.50e multi   50   20

500th anniversary, birth of Pedro Alvares Cabral, navigator who took possession of Brazil for Portugal.

Admiral Coutinho Issue
Common Design Type

Design: 1e, Adm. Coutinho and astrolabe.

1969, Feb. 17   Litho.   *Perf. 14*

335   CD55   1e multi   30   20

Da Gama Coat of Arms
A26

Arms of King Manuel I
A27

Vasco da Gama Issue

1969, Aug. 29   Litho.   *Perf. 14*

336   A26   2.50e multi   30   20

Issued to commemorate the 500th anniversary of the birth of Vasco da Gama (1469–1524), navigator.

Administration Reform Issue
Common Design Type

1969, Sept. 25   Litho.   *Perf. 14*

337   CD56   50c multi   20   10

King Manuel I Issue

1969, Dec. 1   Litho.   *Perf. 14*

338   A27   2e multi   30   20

Issued to commemorate the 500th anniversary of the birth of King Manuel I.

Pres. Ulysses S. Grant and View of Bolama
A28

1970, Oct. 25   Litho.   *Perf. 13½*

339   A28   2.50e multi   40   20

Centenary of Pres. Grant's arbitration in 1868 of Portuguese-English dispute concerning Bolama.

Marshal Carmona Issue
Common Design Type

Design: 1.50e, Antonio Oscar Carmona in general's uniform.

1970, Nov. 15   Litho.   *Perf. 14*

340   CD57   1.50e multi   30   20

Luiz Camoëns
A29

1972, May 25   Litho.   *Perf. 13*

341   A29   50c brn org & multi   20   15

4th centenary of publication of The Lusiads by Luiz Camoëns (1524–1580).

Olympic Games Issue
Common Design Type

Design: 2.50e, Weight lifting, hammer throw and Olympic emblem.

1972, June 20   *Perf. 14x13½*

342   CD59   2.50e multi   40   20

20th Olympic Games, Munich, Aug. 26–Sept. 11.

Lisbon-Rio de Janeiro Flight Issue
Common Design Type

Design: 1e, "Lusitania" taking off from Lisbon.

1972, Sept. 20   Litho.   *Perf. 13½*

343   CD60   1e multi   30   15

WMO Centenary Issue
Common Design Type

1973, Dec. 15   Litho.   *Perf. 13*

344   CD61   2e lt brn & multi   30   20

Centenary of international meteorological cooperation.

AIR POST STAMPS.
Common Design Type
Name and Value in Black.
Perf. 13½x13

1938, Sept. 19   Engr.   Unwmkd.

C1	CD39	10c scarlet	65	50
C2	CD39	20c purple	65	50
C3	CD39	50c orange	70	50
C4	CD39	1e ultra	90	60
C5	CD39	2e lil brn	6.25	4.50
C6	CD39	3e dk grn	2.00	1.25
C7	CD39	5e red brn	5.00	1.50
C8	CD39	9e rose car	5.50	3.25
C9	CD39	10e magenta	13.00	4.00
		Nos. C1-C9 (9)	34.65	16.60

No. C7 exists with overprint "Exposicao Internacional de Nova York, 1939–1940" and Trylon and Perisphere.

POSTAGE DUE STAMPS.

D1   D2

Without Gum (Nos. J1–J29)
Typographed

1904   *Perf. 12*   Unwmkd.

J1	D1	5r yel grn	50	40
J2	D1	10r slate	50	40
J3	D1	20r yel brn	50	40
J4	D1	30r red org	1.50	1.25
J5	D1	50r gray brn	1.50	1.25
J6	D1	60r red brn	3.00	2.00
J7	D1	100r lilac	3.00	2.00
J8	D1	130r dl bl	3.00	2.00
J9	D1	200r carmine	4.00	3.50
J10	D1	500r violet	10.00	4.50
		Nos. J1-J10 (10)	27.50	17.70

Same Overprinted in Carmine or Green

REPUBLICA

1911

J11	D1	5r yel grn	25	20
J12	D1	10r slate	25	20
J13	D1	20r yel brn	45	30
J14	D1	30r red org	45	30
J15	D1	50r gray brn	45	30
J16	D1	60r red brn	1.00	75
J17	D1	100r lilac	2.00	1.00
J18	D1	130r dl bl	2.00	1.00
J19	D1	200r car (G)	2.00	1.50
J20	D1	500r violet	1.25	1.00
		Nos. J10-J20 (10)	10.10	6.55

Nos. J2–J10 Overprinted

REPUBLICA

1919

J21	D1	10r slate	5.50	5.50
J22	D1	20r yel brn	6.00	6.00
J23	D1	30r red org	3.50	3.50
J24	D1	50r gray brn	1.50	1.50
J25	D1	60r red brn	135.00	135.00
J26	D1	100r lilac	1.50	1.50
J27	D1	130r dl bl	20.00	20.00
J28	D1	200r carmine	2.00	2.00
J29	D1	500r violet	16.50	16.50
		Nos. J21-J24, J26-J29 (8)	56.50	56.50

No. J25 was not regularly issued but exists on genuine covers.

1921

J30	D2	½c yel grn	15	10
J31	D2	1c slate	15	10
J32	D2	2c org brn	15	10
J33	D2	3c orange	15	10
J34	D2	5c gray brn	15	10
J35	D2	6c lt brn	15	10
J36	D2	10c red vio	30	30
J37	D2	13c dl bl	30	30
J38	D2	20c carmine	30	30
J39	D2	50c gray	30	30
		Nos. J30-J39 (10)	2.10	1.80

Common Design Type
Photogravure and Typographed.

1952   *Perf. 14*   Unwmkd.
Numeral in Red, Frame Multicolored.

J40	CD45	10c ol grn	6	6
J41	CD45	30c purple	5	10
J42	CD45	50c dk grn	5	5
J43	CD45	1e vio bl	20	20
J44	CD45	2e ol bl	30	30
J45	CD45	5e brn red	65	65
		Nos. J40-J45 (6)	1.31	1.36

WAR TAX STAMPS.

WT1

Perf. 11½x12

1919, May 20   Typo.   Unwmkd.

MR1	WT1	10r brn, buff & blk	25.00	15.00
MR2	WT1	40r brn, buff & blk	25.00	15.00
MR3	WT1	50r brn, buff & blk	25.00	15.00

The 40r is not overprinted "REPUBLICA".
Some authorities consider Nos. MR2–MR3 to be revenue stamps.

NEWSPAPER STAMP.

N1

Perf. 12½, 13½

1893   Typographed   Unwmkd.

P1   N1   2½r brown   90   60

POSTAL TAX STAMPS.
Pombal Issue
Common Design Types
Engraved.

1925   *Perf. 12½*   Unwmkd.

RA1	CD28	15c red & blk	75	75
RA2	CD29	15c red & blk	75	75
RA3	CD30	15c red & blk	75	75

PORTUGUESE GUINEA—PORTUGUESE INDIA

Coat of Arms—PT7
Without Gum (Nos. RA4–RA16)

1934, Apr. 1		Typo.	Perf. 11½	
RA4	PT7	50c red brn & grn	10.00	4.50

Coat of Arms
PT8   PT9

1938-40

| RA5 | PT8 | 50c ol bis & cit | 7.50 | 6.00 |
| RA6 | PT8 | 50c lt grn & ol brn ('40) | 7.50 | 6.00 |

1942 Perf. 11
| RA7 | PT9 | 50c blk & yel | 2.00 | 1.00 |

1959, July Unwmkd.
| RA8 | PT9 | 30c dk ocher & blk | 20 | 20 |

See also Nos. RA24–RA26.

Lusignian Cross
PT10   PT11

1967 Typo. Perf. 11x11½
RA9	PT10	50c pink, red & blk	2.00	2.00
RA10	PT10	1e grn, red & blk	2.00	2.00
RA11	PT10	5e gray, red & blk	3.25	3.25
RA12	PT10	10e lt bl, red & blk	6.00	6.00

The tax was for national defense.
A 50e was used for revenue only.

1967, Aug. Typographed Perf. 11
RA13	PT11	50c pink, blk & red	1.25	1.25
RA14	PT11	1e pale grn, blk & red	1.25	1.25
RA15	PT11	5e gray, blk & red	2.50	2.50
RA16	PT11	10e lt bl, blk & red	3.50	3.50

The tax was for national defense.

Carved Figurine
PT12

Art from Bissau Museum: 1e, Tree of Life, with 2 birds (horiz.). No. RA19, Man wearing horned headgear ("Vaca Bruto"). No. RA20, As RA19, inscribed "Tocador de Bombolon." 2.50e, The Magistrate. 5e, Man bearing burden on head. 10e, Stylized pelican.

1968 Lithographed Perf. 13½
RA17	PT12	50c gray & multi	10	8
a.	Yellow paper		1.00	
RA18	PT12	1e multi	15	12
RA19	PT12	2e lt bl & multi (Vaca Bruto)	15	
RA20	PT12	2e (Tocador de Bombolon)	15.00	
RA21	PT12	2.50e multi	40	30
RA22	PT12	5e multi	60	50
RA23	PT12	10e multi	1.25	1.00
		Nos. RA17-RA19, RA21-RA23 (6)	2.80	2.25

Obligatory on all inland mail Mar. 15–Apr. 15 and Dec. 15–Jan. 15, and all year on parcels.
A souvenir sheet embracing Nos. RA17–RA19 and RA21–RA23 exists. The stamps have simulated perforations. Price $3.50.

Arms Type of 1942
1968 Typographed Perf. 11
Without Gum
RA24	PT9	2.50e lt bl & blk	40	40
RA25	PT9	5e grn & blk	75	75
RA26	PT9	10e dp bl & blk	1.50	1.50

No. RA20 Surcharged
$50

1968 Lithographed Perf. 13½
| RA27 | PT12 | 50c on 2e multi | 50 | 50 |
| RA28 | PT12 | 1e on 2e multi | 50 | 50 |

Black and White Hands Holding Sword   Mother and Children
PT13   PT14

1968 Lithographed Perf. 13½
RA29	PT13	50c pink & multi	5	5
RA30	PT13	1e multi	10	10
RA31	PT13	2e yel & multi	25	25
RA32	PT13	2.50e buff & multi	35	35
RA33	PT13	3e multi	40	40
RA34	PT13	4e gray & multi	45	45
RA35	PT13	5e multi	65	65
RA36	PT13	10e multi	1.50	1.50
		Nos. RA29-RA36 (8)	3.75	3.75

The surtax was for national defense. Other denominations exist: 8e, 9e, 15e.

1971, June Litho. Perf. 13½
RA37	PT14	50c multi	15	15
RA38	PT14	1e multi	15	15
RA39	PT14	2e multi	20	20
RA40	PT14	40r blue (sic 3e)	30	30
RA41	PT14	4e multi	35	35
RA42	PT14	5e multi	60	60
RA43	PT14	10e multi	1.10	1.10
		Nos. RA37-RA43 (7)	2.85	2.85

A 20e exists.

POSTAL TAX DUE STAMPS.
Pombal Issue
Common Design Types
1925 Perf. 12½ Unwmkd.
RAJ1	CD31	30c red & blk	75	75
RAJ2	CD32	30c red & blk	75	75
RAJ3	CD33	30c red & blk	75	75

PORTUGUESE INDIA
(pŏr'tů·gĕz; -gĕs ĭn'dĭ·å)

LOCATION — West coast of the Indian peninsula.
GOVT.—Former Portuguese colony.
AREA—1,537 sq. mi.
POP.—649,000 (1958).
CAPITAL—Panjim (Nova-Goa).

The colony was seized by India on Dec. 18, 1961, and annexed by that republic.

1000 Reis = 1 Milreis
12 Reis = 1 Tanga (1881-82)
(Real = singular of Reis)
16 Tangas = 1 Rupia
100 Centavos = 1 Escudo (1959)

Prices of early Portuguese India stamps vary according to condition. Quotations for Nos. 1–55 are for fine copies. Very fine to superb specimens sell at much higher prices, and inferior or poor copies sell at reduced prices, depending on the condition of the individual specimen.

Numeral of Value
A1   A2

A1: Large figures of value. "REIS" in Roman capitals. "S" and "R" of "SERVICO" smaller and "E" larger than the other letters. 33 lines in background. Side ornaments of four dashes.
A2: Large figures of value. "REIS" in block capitals. "S," "E" and "R" same size as other letters of "SERVICO". 44 lines in background. Side ornaments of five dots.

Handstamped from a Single Die.
Perf. 13 to 18 & Compound
1871, Oct. 1 Unwmkd.
Thin Transparent Brittle Paper.
1	A1	10r black	450.00	350.00
2	A1	20r dk car	1,200.	300.00
3	A1	40r Prus bl	400.00	300.00
4	A1	100r yel grn	450.00	350.00
5	A1	200r ocher yel	550.00	375.00

1872
Thick Soft Wove Paper.
5A	A1	10r black	1,250.	300.00
6	A1	20r dk car	1,250.	275.00
7	A1	20r org ver	1,250.	275.00
8	A1	200r ocher yel	1,250.	700.00
9	A1	300r dp red vio		1,500.

The 600r and 900r of type A1 are bogus.

Perf. 12½ to 14½ & Compound
1872
10	A2	10r black	200.00	80.00
11	A2	20r vermilion	225.00	70.00
a.	"20" omitted			1,000.
12	A2	40r blue	75.00	55.00
a.	Tête bêche pr.		4,500.	
13	A2	100r dp grn	87.50	62.50
14	A2	200r yellow	300.00	250.00
15	A2	300r red vio	275.00	175.00
a.	Imperf.			
16	A2	600r red vio	185.00	150.00
a.	"600" double		500.00	
17	A2	900r red vio	210.00	175.00

An unused 100r blue green exists with watermark of lozenges and gray burelage on back. Experts believe it to be a proof.

White Laid Paper.
18	A2	10r black	40.00	35.00
a.	Tête bêche pair		6,000.	
19	A2	20r vermilion	37.50	30.00

20	A2	40r blue	62.50	55.00
a.	"40" double		300.00	
b.	Tête bêche pair		1,500.	1,500.
21	A2	100r green	75.00	62.50
a.	"100" double		350.00	
22	A2	200r yellow	185.00	165.00

1873 Re-issues.
Thin Bluish Toned Paper
23	A2	20r vermilion	185.00	150.00
24	A1	10r black	12.50	10.00
a.	"1" inverted		185.00	125.00
b.	"10" double		400.00	
25	A1	20r vermilion	10.00	9.00
a.	"20" double		400.00	
b.	"20" inverted			
26	A1	300r dp vio	100.00	87.50
a.	"300" double		400.00	
27	A1	600r dp vio	125.00	110.00
a.	"600" double		400.00	
b.	"600" inverted		625.00	
28	A1	900r dp vio	125.00	110.00
a.	"900" double		400.00	
b.	"900" triple		1,000.	

Nos. 23 to 26 are re-issues of Nos. 11, 5A, 7, and 9. The paper is thinner and harder than that of the 1871-72 stamps and slightly transparent. It was originally bluish white but is frequently stained yellow by the gum.

A3   A4
A3: Same as A1 with small figures.
A4: Same as A2 with small figures.

1874
Thin Bluish Toned Paper
29	A3	10r black	37.50	30.00
30	A3	20r vermilion	450.00	300.00
a.	"20" double			700.00

1875
31	A4	10r black	30.00	22.50
32	A4	15r rose	12.50	10.00
a.	"15" inverted		400.00	
b.	"15" double			
33	A4	20r vermilion	87.50	40.00
a.	"O" missing		625.00	
b.	"20" sideways		625.00	
c.	"20" double			

A5   A6
A5: Re-cutting of A1. Small figures. "REIS" in Roman capitals. Letters larger. "V" of "SERVICO" barred. 33 lines in background. Side ornaments of five dots.
A6: First re-cutting of A2. Small figures. "REIS" in block capitals. Letters re-cut. "V" of "SERVICO" barred. 41 lines above and 43 below "REIS". Side ornaments of five dots.

Perf. 12½ to 13½ & Compound
1876
34	A5	10r black	21.00	16.50
35	A5	20r vermilion	18.50	14.00
a.	"20" double			
36	A6	10r black	6.25	4.00
a.	Double impression			
b.	"10" double		400.00	
37	A6	15r rose	400.00	300.00
a.	"15" omitted		1,000.	
38	A6	20r vermilion	25.00	18.50
39	A6	40r blue	125.00	100.00
40	A6	100r green	185.00	150.00
a.	Imperf.			
41	A6	200r yellow	750.00	625.00
42	A6	300r violet	500.00	400.00
a.	"300" omitted			
43	A6	600r violet	750.00	700.00
44	A6	900r violet	875.00	750.00

A7

A8

A9

A7: Same as A5 with addition of a star above and a bar below the value.

A8: Second re-cutting of A2. Same as A6 but 41 lines both above and below "REIS". Star above and bar below value.

A9: Third re-cutting of A2. 41 lines above and 38 below "REIS". Star above and bar below value. White line around central oval.

1877

45	A7	10r black	30.00	20.00
46	A8	10r black	45.00	30.00
47	A9	10r black	30.00	22.50
a.		"10" omitted		
48	A9	15r rose	30.00	25.00
49	A9	20r vermilion	10.00	8.00
50	A9	40r blue	20.00	18.50
a.		"40" omitted		
51	A9	100r green	87.50	62.50
a.		"100" omitted		
52	A9	200r yellow	90.00	80.00
53	A9	300r violet	125.00	110.00
54	A9	600r violet	125.00	110.00
55	A9	900r violet	125.00	110.00

No. 47, 20r, 40r and 200r exist imperf.

Portuguese Crown—A10

Typographed.

1877, July 15 ***Perf. 12½, 13½***

56	A10	5r black	4.50	3.00
57	A10	10r yellow	9.00	6.25
a.		Imperf.		
58	A10	20r bister	7.50	5.75
59	A10	25r rose	12.50	8.75
60	A10	40r blue	18.50	14.00
a.		Perf. 12½	200.00	125.00
61	A10	50r yel grn	25.00	18.50
62	A10	100r lilac	15.00	12.50
63	A10	200r orange	25.00	18.00
64	A10	300r yel brn	30.00	25.00

1880-81

65	A10	10r green	10.00	8.00
66	A10	25r slate	40.00	27.50
a.		Perf. 12½	80.00	50.00
67	A10	25r violet	25.00	17.50
68	A10	40r yellow	30.00	25.00
69	A10	50r dk bl	20.00	17.50

The stamps of the 1877-81 issues were reprinted in 1885, on stout very white paper, ungummed and with rough perforation 13½. They were again reprinted in 1905 on thin white paper with shiny white gum and clean-cut perforation 13½ with large holes. Price of the lowest-cost reprint, $1 each.

Stamps of 1871-77
Surcharged with New Values.
Black Surcharge.

1881

70	A1	1½r on 20r dk car (#2)		*400.00*
71	A1	1½r on 20r org ver (#7)		*325.00*
72	A2	1½r on 20r ver (#11)		*300.00*
73	A1	1½r on 20r ver (#25)	200.00	175.00
74	A4	1½r on 20r ver (#33)	110.00	100.00
a.		Inverted surcharge		
75	A5	1½r on 20r ver (#35)	100.00	80.00
76	A6	1½r on 20r ver (#38)	110.00	100.00
77	A9	1½r on 20r ver (#49)	185.00	125.00
78	A4	5r on 15r rose (#32)	2.50	2.50
a.		Double surcharge		
b.		Inverted surcharge		
78C	A6	5r on 15r rose (#37)	150.00	150.00
79	A5	5r on 20r ver (#35)	3.00	3.00
a.		Double surcharge		
b.		Inverted surcharge		
80	A6	5r on 20r ver (#38)	2.00	2.00
a.		Double surcharge		
b.		Inverted surcharge		
81	A9	5r on 20r ver (#49)	5.00	4.00
a.		Double surcharge		
b.		Invtd. surcharge		

Red Surcharge.

82	A2	5r on 10r blk (#18)	*225.00*	*225.00*
83	A1	5r on 10r blk (#24)	*300.00*	*250.00*
84	A3	5r on 10r blk (#29)	*1,200.*	
85	A4	5r on 10r blk (#31)	*100.00*	*100.00*
86	A5	5r on 10r blk (#34)	6.00	6.00
a.		Double surcharge		
87	A6	5r on 10r blk (#36)	7.50	6.25
a.		Inverted surcharge		
88	A7	5r on 10r blk (#45)	75.00	40.00
a.		Inverted surcharge		
89	A8	5r on 10r blk (#46)	62.50	45.00
90	A9	5r on 10r blk (#47)	37.50	30.00
a.		Inverted surcharge		
b.		Double surcharge		

Similar Surcharge, Handstamped.
Black Surcharge.

1883

91	A5	1½r on 10r blk (#34)		*400.00*
92	A6	1½r on 10r blk (#36)		*350.00*
93	A9	1½r on 10r blk (#47)	*350.00*	*300.00*
94	A1	4½r on 40r bl (#3)		*375.00*
95	A2	4½r on 40r bl (#12)	30.00	30.00
96	A2	4½r on 40r bl (#20)	30.00	30.00
98	A6	4½r on 40r bl (#39)	30.00	30.00
99	A1	4½r on 100r yel grn (#4)		*375.00*
100	A2	4½r on 100r grn (#13)	35.00	35.00
101	A2	4½r on 100r grn (#21)	35.00	35.00
102	A6	4½r on 100 grn (#40)	35.00	35.00
104	A1	6r on 100r yel grn (#4)		*625.00*
105	A2	6r on 100r grn (#13)		*225.00*
106	A2	6r on 100r grn (#21)	*175.00*	*135.00*
107	A6	6r on 100r grn (#40)	*250.00*	*175.00*
108	A1	6r on 200r ocher yel (#5)	*400.00*	*300.00*
109	A2	6r on 200r yel (#14)		*180.00*
110	A2	6r on 200r yel (#22)	*175.00*	*175.00*
111	A6	6r on 200r yel (#41)		*375.00*
112	A9	6r on 200r yel (#52)	*350.00*	*350.00*

Stamps of 1877-81
Surcharged in Black **1½**

1881-82

113	A10	1½r on 5r blk	1.30	90
a.		With additional surcharge "4½" in bl	45.00	37.50
114	A10	1½r on 10r grn	1.30	1.10
a.		With additional surcharge "6"	62.50	55.00
115	A10	1½r on 20r bis	11.00	7.50
a.		Inverted surcharge		
b.		Double surcharge		
c.		Pair, one without surcharge		
116	A10	1½r on 25r sl	35.00	27.50
117	A10	1½r on 100r lil	55.00	40.00
118	A10	4½r on 10r grn	175.00	150.00
119	A10	4½r on 20r bis	3.50	2.25
a.		Inverted surcharge		
120	A10	4½r on 25r vio	9.00	7.50
121	A10	4½r on 100r lil	100.00	80.00
122	A10	6r on 10r yel	35.00	27.50
123	A10	6r on 10r grn	10.00	6.50
124	A10	6r on 20r bis	17.50	11.00
125	A10	6r on 25r sl	30.00	20.00
126	A10	6r on 25r vio	2.50	2.00
127	A10	6r on 40r bl	87.50	75.00
128	A10	6r on 40r yel	40.00	30.00
129	A10	6r on 50r grn	40.00	30.00
130	A10	6r on 50r bl	62.50	50.00

Surcharged in Black **1 T**

131	A10	1t on 10r grn	125.00	110.00
a.		With additional surcharge "6"		
132	A10	1t on 20r bis	40.00	37.50
133	A10	1t on 25r sl	37.50	27.50
134	A10	1t on 25r vio	12.50	8.75
135	A10	1t on 40r bl	16.50	11.00
136	A10	1t on 50r grn	50.00	35.00
137	A10	1t on 50r bl	25.00	17.50
138	A10	1t on 100r lil	20.00	11.00
139	A10	1t on 200r org	40.00	35.00
140	A10	2t on 25r sl	30.00	25.00
a.		Small "T"	50.00	30.00
141	A10	2t on 25r vio	13.00	11.00
142	A10	2t on 40r bl	40.00	30.00
143	A10	2t on 40r yel	50.00	40.00
144	A10	2t on 50r grn	15.00	12.50
a.		Inverted surcharge		
145	A10	2t on 50r bl	95.00	80.00
146	A10	2t on 100r lil	11.00	9.00
147	A10	2t on 200r org	35.00	30.00
148	A10	2t on 300r brn	30.00	25.00
149	A10	4t on 10r grn	14.00	11.00
a.		Inverted surcharge		
150	A10	4t on 50r grn	12.50	10.00
a.		With additional surcharge "2"	100.00	80.00
151	A10	4t on 200r org	37.50	30.00
152	A10	8t on 20r bis	30.00	25.00
153	A10	8t on 25r rose	175.00	150.00
154	A10	8t on 40r bl	45.00	37.50
155	A10	8t on 100r lil	35.00	30.00
156	A10	8t on 200r org	30.00	25.00
157	A10	8t on 300r brn	45.00	37.50

1882 Blue Surcharge.

158	A10	4½r on 5r blk	8.00	7.00

Similar Surcharge, Handstamped.

1883

159	A10	1½r on 5r blk	12.50	8.75
160	A10	1½r on 10r grn	12.50	6.25
161	A10	4½r on 100r lil	*175.00*	*150.00*

The "2" in "½" is 3mm. high, instead of 2mm. as on Nos. 113, 114 and 121.

The handstamp is known double on Nos. 159–161.

A12

1882-83 Typographed.

With or Without Accent on "E" of "REIS".

162	A12	1½r black	60	50
a.		"½" for "1½"		
163	A12	4½r ol bis	60	50
164	A12	6r green	80	50
165	A12	1t rose	80	50
166	A12	2t blue	80	50
167	A12	4t lilac	3.00	2.50
168	A12	8t orange	3.00	3.00

There were three printings of the 1882-83 issue. The first had "REIS" in thick letters with acute accent on the "E." The second had "REIS" in thin letters with accent on the "E." The third had the "E" without accent. In the first printing the "E" sometimes had a grave or circumflex accent.

The third printing may be divided into two sets, with or without a small circle in the cross of the crown.

Stamps doubly printed or with value omitted, double, inverted or misplaced are printer's waste.

Nos. 162–168 were reprinted on thin white paper, with shiny white gum and clean-cut perforation 13½. Price of lowest-cost reprint, $1 each.

"REIS" no serifs.
A13

"REIS" with serifs.
A14

1883 Lithographed. ***Imperf.***

169	A13	1½r black	1.40	1.00
a.		Tête bêche pair		
b.		"1½" double	300.00	275.00
170	A13	4½r ol grn	15.00	10.00
a.		"4½" omitted	300.00	275.00
171	A13	6r green	15.00	10.00
a.		Tête bêche pair	1,000.	
b.		"6" omitted	300.00	275.00
172	A14	1½r black	60.00	15.00
a.		"1½" omitted	300.00	275.00
173	A14	6r green	52.50	35.00
a.		"6" omitted	300.00	275.00

Nos. 169–171 exist with unofficial perf. 12.

King Luiz
A15

King Carlos
A16

Perf. 12½, 13½

1886, Apr. 29 **Embossed**

174	A15	1½r black	2.00	1.00
a.		Perf. 13½	150.00	90.00
175	A15	4½r bister	2.50	1.25
a.		Perf. 13½	30.00	15.00
176	A15	6r dp grn	2.75	1.50
a.		Perf. 13½	30.00	15.00
177	A15	1t brt rose	4.00	2.25
178	A15	2t dp bl	7.50	4.00
179	A15	4t gray vio	7.50	4.00
180	A15	8t orange	7.50	4.00
		Nos. 174-180 (7)	33.75	18.00

Nos. 178–179 were reprinted. Originals have yellow gum. Reprints have white gum and clean-cut perforation 13½. Price, $1 each.

Typographed.

1895-96 ***Perf. 11½, 12½, 13½.***

181	A16	1½r black	1.00	45
182	A16	4½r pale org	1.00	45
a.		Perf. 13½	6.50	1.50
183	A16	6r green	1.00	50
a.		Perf. 12½	3.00	1.25
184	A16	9r gray lil	4.00	3.00
185	A16	1t lt bl	1.25	60
a.		Perf. 12½	4.50	2.00
186	A16	2t rose	1.00	60
a.		Perf. 12½	3.75	2.00
187	A16	4t dk bl	1.50	75
a.		Perf. 12½	3.75	2.00

188	A16	8t brt vio	3.50	2.50
		Nos. 181-188 (8)	14.25	8.85

No. 184 was reprinted. Reprints have white gum, and clean-cut perforation 13½. Price $10.

Vasco da Gama Issue.

Common Design Types

1898, May 1 Engr. *Perf. 14 to 15*

189	CD20	1½r bl grn	1.00	1.00
190	CD21	4½r red	1.00	1.00
191	CD22	6r red vio	1.00	1.00
192	CD23	9r yel grn	1.10	1.10
193	CD24	1t dk bl	1.75	1.75
194	CD25	2t vio brn	2.00	2.00
195	CD26	4t bis brn	2.25	2.25
196	CD27	8t bister	4.50	4.50
		Nos. 189-196 (8)	14.60	14.60

Vasco da Gama's voyage to India, 1497–99.

King Carlos
A17

1898–1903 Typographed. *Perf. 11½*

Name and Value in Black except No. 219.

197	A17	1r gray ('02)	30	20
198	A17	1½r orange	25	15
199	A17	1½r sl ('02)	30	20
200	A17	2r org ('02)	30	25
201	A17	2½r yel brn ('02)	40	30
202	A17	3r dp bl ('02)	30	20
203	A17	4½r lt grn	75	45
204	A17	6r brown	75	45
205	A17	6r gray grn ('02)	30	20
206	A17	9r dl vio	75	45
a.		9r gray lil	2.00	2.00
208	A17	1t sea grn	75	45
209	A17	1t car rose ('02)	50	20
210	A17	2t blue	1.00	45
a.		Perf. 13½	25.00	7.00
211	A17	2t brn ('02)	2.00	1.25
212	A17	2½t dl bl ('02)	7.50	6.00
213	A17	4t bl, *bl*	2.50	1.00
214	A17	5t brn, *straw* ('02)	2.50	1.50
215	A17	8t red lil, *pnksh*	2.00	1.50
216	A17	8t red vio, *pink* ('02)	5.50	2.50
217	A17	12t bl, *pink*	3.50	2.00
218	A17	12t grn, *pink* ('02)	5.50	2.75
219	A17	1rp blk & red, *bl*	7.50	4.50
220	A17	1rp dl bl, *straw* ('02)	10.50	6.00
221	A17	2rp vio, *yelsh*	11.00	6.50
222	A17	2rp gray blk, *straw* ('03)	17.50	12.00
		Nos. 197-222 (25)	84.15	51.45

Several stamps of this issue exist without value or with value inverted but they are not known to have been issued in this condition. The 1r and 6r in carmine rose are believed to be color trials.

No. 210 Surcharged in Black — **1½ Reis**

1900

223	A17	1½r on 2t bl	3.00	75
a.		Inverted surcharge		
b.		Perf. 13½	25.00	20.00

Stamps of 1885-96 Surcharged in Black or Red — **1 REAL**

On Stamps of 1886.

1902 *Perf. 12½, 13½*

224	A15	1r on 2t bl	1.00	50
225	A15	2r on 4½r bis	40	25
a.		Inverted surcharge		
b.		Double surcharge		
226	A15	2½r on 6r grn	40	25
227	A15	3r on 1t rose	40	25
228	A15	2½t on 1½r blk (R)	1.75	1.25
229	A15	2½t on 4t gray vio	3.00	1.50
230	A15	5t on 8t org	75	50
a.		Perf. 12½	30.00	17.50

On Stamps of 1895-96.

Perf. 11½, 12½, 13½

231	A16	1r on 6r grn	40	25
232	A16	2r on 8t brt vio	40	25
233	A16	2½r on 9r gray vio	40	25
234	A16	3r on 4½r yel	1.50	90
a.		Inverted surcharge	10.00	10.00
235	A16	3r on 1t lt bl	1.25	80
236	A16	2½t on 1½r blk (R)	2.00	75
237	A16	5t on 2t rose	2.00	75
a.		Perf. 12½	37.50	17.50
238	A16	5t on 4t dk bl	2.00	75
a.		Perf. 12½	37.50	17.50
		Nos. 224-238 (15)	17.65	9.20

Nos. 224, 229, 231, 233, 234, 235 and 238 were reprinted in 1905. They have whiter gum than the originals and very clean-cut perf. 13½. Price 75 cents each.

Nos. 204, 208, 210 Overprinted — **PROVISORIO**

1902 *Perf. 11½*

239	A17	6r brown	1.75	90
a.		Inverted overprint		
240	A17	1t sea grn	1.75	90
241	A17	2t blue	1.75	90
a.		Perf. 13½	150.00	100.00

No. 212 Surcharged in Black — **2 TANGAS**

1905

243	A17	2t on 2½t dl bl	1.75	1.60

Stamps of 1898-1903 Overprinted in Lisbon in Carmine or Green — **REPUBLICA**

1911

244	A17	1r gray	15	10
a.		Inverted overprint	2.00	2.00
245	A17	1½r slate	20	12
a.		Double overprint	2.00	2.00
246	A17	2r orange	25	20
a.		Double overprint		
b.		Inverted overprint	3.00	3.00
247	A17	2½r yel brn	30	15
248	A17	3r dp bl	25	12
249	A17	4½r lt grn	35	25
250	A17	6r gray grn	20	10
251	A17	9r gray lil	25	20
252	A17	1t car rose (G)	35	20
253	A17	2t brown	35	20
254	A17	4t bl, *bl*	1.35	1.10
255	A17	5t brn, *straw*	1.50	1.10
256	A17	8t vio, *pink*	4.50	2.50
257	A17	12t grn, *pink*	4.50	2.50
258	A17	1rp dl bl, *straw*	6.25	4.50
259	A17	2rp gray blk, *straw*	8.00	6.50
		Nos. 244-259 (16)	28.75	19.84

A18

Prices are for pairs, both halves.

1911 Perforated Diagonally.

260	A18	1r on 2r org	75	65
a.		Without diagonal perf.	2.00	1.50
b.		Cut diagonally instead of perf.	2.50	2.00

Common Design Types pictured in section at front of book.

Stamps of Preceding Issues Perforated Vertically through the Middle and Each Half Surcharged with New Value:

3 REIS — 3 REIS (a) — 6 REIS — 6 REIS (b)

1912–13

Prices are for pairs, both halves of the stamp

On Issue of 1898-1903.

260C	A17(a)	1r on 2r org	25	20
261	A17(a)	1r on 1t car	25	20
262	A17(a)	1r on 5t brn, *straw*	30.00	15.00
263	A17(b)	1r on 5t brn, *straw*	3.75	3.00
264	A17(a)	1½r on 2½r yel brn	70	60
264C	A17(a)	1½r on 4½r lt grn	15.00	7.50
265	A17(a)	1½r on 9r gray lil	50	40
266	A17(a)	1½r on 4t bl, *bl*	50	40
267	A17(a)	2r on 2½r yel brn	75	40
268	A17(a)	2r on 4t bl, *bl*	1.00	65
269	A17(a)	3r on 2½r yel brn	75	45
270	A17(a)	3r on 2t brn	1.00	50
271	A17(a)	6r on 4½r lt grn	1.00	65
272	A17(a)	6r on 9r gray lil	80	50
273	A17(b)	6r on 9r dl vio	4.50	3.75
274	A17(b)	6r on 8t red vio, *pink*	1.50	90

On Provisional Issue of 1902.

275	A16(b)	1r on 5t on 2t rose	10.00	7.50
276	A16(b)	1r on 5t on 4t bl	7.50	6.25
277	A15(b)	1r on 5t on 8t org	2.50	1.75
278	A15(a)	2r on 2½r on 6r grn	2.50	2.00
279	A16(a)	2r on 2½r on 9r gray vio	18.50	16.50
280	A16(b)	3r on 5t on 2t rose	7.50	6.25
281	A16(b)	3r on 5t on 4t bl	7.50	6.25
282	A15(b)	3r on 5t on 8t org	2.50	1.75

On Issue of 1911.

283	A17(a)	1r on 1r gray	25	20
283B	A17(a)	1r on 2r org	25	20
284	A17(a)	1r on 1t car	35	20
285	A17(a)	1r on 5t brn, *straw*	40	30
285A	A17(b)	1r on 5t brn, *straw*		
285B	A17(a)	1½r on 4½r lt grn	50	30
286	A17(a)	3r on 2t brn	10.00	7.50
289	A17(a)	6r on 9r gray lil	65	50

There are several settings of these surcharges and many minor varieties of the letters and figures, notably a small "6". Nos. 260–289 were issued mostly without gum.

More than half of Nos. 260C–289 exist with inverted or double surcharge, or with bisecting perforation omitted. The legitimacy of these varieties is questioned. Price of inverted surcharges, $3–$15; double surcharges, $1–$4; perf. omitted, $1.50–$15.

Similar surcharges made without official authorization on stamps of type A17 are: 2r on 2½r, 3r on 2½r, 3r on 5t, and 6r on 4½r.

Vasco da Gama Issue Overprinted — **REPUBLICA**

1913

290	CD20	1½r bl grn	35	30
291	CD21	4½r red	35	30
a.		Double overprint		
292	CD22	6r red vio	45	35
a.		Double overprint		
293	CD23	9r yel grn	50	35
294	CD24	1t dk bl	1.00	65
295	CD25	2t vio brn	2.00	1.25
296	CD26	4t org brn	1.25	1.00
297	CD27	8t bister	2.25	1.50
		Nos. 290-297 (8)	8.15	5.70

Issues of 1898-1913 Overprinted Locally in Red — **REPÚBLICA**

1913-15

On Issues of 1898-1903.

300	A17	2r orange	4.00	3.50
301	A17	2½r yel brn	60	45
302	A17	3r dp bl	4.50	3.75
303	A17	4½r lt grn	1.60	1.25
304	A17	6r gray grn	11.00	10.00
305	A17	9r gray lil	1.40	1.00
306	A17	1t sea grn	11.00	9.00
307	A17	2t blue	20.00	11.00
309	A17	4t bl, *bl*	10.00	8.00
310	A17	5t brn, *straw*	17.50	11.00
311	A17	8t red vio, *pink*	20.00	15.00
312	A17	12t grn, *pink*	3.00	2.00
313	A17	1rp blk & red, *bl*	17.50	13.00
314	A17	1rp dl bl, *straw*	6.00	5.00
315	A17	2rp gray blk, *straw*	10.00	8.00
316	A17	2rp vio, *yelsh*	8.00	6.00
		Nos. 300-316 (16)	146.10	107.95

Inverted or double overprints exist on 2½r, 4½r, 9r, 1rp and 2rp.

Nos. 300–316 were issued without gum except 4½r and 9r.

Nos. 302, 304, 306, 307, 310, 311 and 313 were not regularly issued. Nor were the 1½r, 2t brown and 12t blue on pink with preceding overprint.

Same Overprint in Red or Green.

On Provisional Issue of 1902.

317	A15	1r on 2t bl	5.50	4.50
a.		"REPUBLICA" inverted		
318	A15	2r on 4½r bis	5.50	4.50
a.		"REPUBLICA" inverted		
319	A15	2½r on 6r grn	75	50
a.		"REPUBLICA" inverted	4.50	4.50
320	A15	2½r on 4t gray vio	15.00	10.00
321	A15	3r on 1t rose (R)	4.00	3.50
323	A15	5t on 8t org (G)	3.75	3.75
a.		Red overprint	3.75	3.75
324	A16	1r on 6r grn	5.50	4.50
325	A16	2r on 8t vio	5.50	4.50
a.		Inverted surcharge		
327	A16	3r on 4½r yel	15.00	10.00
328	A16	3r on 1t lt bl	15.00	10.00
329	A16	5t on 2t rose (G)	3.00	2.50
330	A16	5t on 4t bl (G)	3.00	2.75
331	A16	5t on 4t bl (R)	3.00	2.75
a.		"REPUBLICA" inverted		
b.		"REPUBLICA" double		
		Nos. 317-331 (13)	84.50	63.75

The 2½r on 1½r of types A15 and A16, the 3r on 1t (A15) and 2½r on 9r (A16) were clandestinely printed.

Some authorities question the status of No. 317-318, 320-321, 324, 327-328.

Same Overprint on Nos. 240–241

1913-15

334	A17	1t sea grn	6.00	4.50
335	A17	2t blue	5.50	5.00

This overprint was applied to No. 239 without official authorization.

On Issue of 1912-13

Perforated through the Middle.

Prices are for pairs, both halves of the stamp.

336	A17(a)	1r on 2r org	3.50	3.00
340	A17(a)	1½r on 4½r lt grn	3.50	3.00
341	A17(a)	1½r on 9r gray lil	2.75	2.50
342	A17(a)	1½r on 4t bl, *bl*	4.50	4.00
343	A17(a)	2r on 2½r yel brn	2.50	2.25

PORTUGUESE INDIA

344	A17(a)	2r on 4t bl, *bl*	4.50	3.50
345	A17(a)	3r on 2½r yel brn	2.75	2.50
346	A17(a)	3r on 2t brn	3.00	3.00
347	A17(a)	6r on 4½r lt grn	1.00	1.00
348	A17(a)	6r on 9r gray lil	1.75	1.75
350	A17(b)	6r on 8t red vio, *pink*	1.75	1.75
352	A16(b)	1r on 5t on 4t bl	20.00	17.50
354	A15(a)	2r on 2½r on 6r grn	2.75	2.50
		Nos. 334-354 (15)	65.75	57.75

The 1r on 5t (A15), 1r on 1t (A17), 1½r on 2½r (A17), 3r on 5t on 8t (A15), and 6r on 9r (A17) were clandestinely printed.
Nos. 336, 347 exist with inverted surcharge.
Some authorities question the status of Nos. 341-345, 352 and 354.

Ceres
A21

Typographed
1913-21 *Perf.* 12x11½, 15x14.
Name and Value in Black.

357	A21	1r ol brn	30	30
358	A21	1½r yel grn	30	30
a.		Imperf.		
359	A21	2r black	50	40
360	A21	2½r ol grn	35	30
361	A21	3r lilac	35	20
362	A21	4½r org brn	35	20
363	A21	5r bl grn	75	50
364	A21	6r lil brn	35	20
365	A21	9r ultra	70	30
366	A21	10r carmine	75	40
367	A21	1t lt vio	35	30
368	A21	2t dp bl	75	35
369	A21	3t yel brn	50	40
370	A21	4t slate	2.00	1.00
371	A21	8t plum	5.00	3.50
372	A21	12t grn, *grn*	4.00	2.75
373	A21	1rp brn, *pink*	22.50	12.50
374	A21	2rp org, *sal*	15.00	10.00
375	A21	3rp grn, *bl*	17.50	11.00
		Nos. 357-375 (19)	72.30	44.90

The 1, 2, 2½, 3, 4½r, 1, 2, and 4t exist with the black inscriptions inverted and the 2½r with them double, one inverted, but it is not known that any of these were regularly issued.
See also Nos. 401-410.

Nos. 249, 251-253, 256-259
Surcharged in Black **1½ REIS**

1914

376	A17	1½r on 4½r grn	35	30
377	A17	1½r on 9r gray lil	45	30
378	A17	1½r on 12t grn, *pink*	60	45
379	A17	3r on 1t car rose	50	30
380	A17	3r on 2t brn	3.50	2.50
381	A17	3r on 8t red vio, *pink*	2.75	2.75
382	A17	3r on 1rp dl bl, *straw*	55	40
383	A17	3r on 2rp gray blk, *straw*	75	60

There are three varieties of the "2" in "1½r".
Nos. 376-377 exist with inverted surcharge.

The only foreign revenue stamps listed in this Catalogue are those authorized for prepayment of postage.

Vasco da Gama Issue
Surcharged in Black **REPUBLICA 1½ REIS**

384	CD21	1½r on 4½r red	45	30
385	CD23	1½r on 9r yel grn	60	35
386	CD24	3r on 1t dk bl	45	30
387	CD25	3r on 2t vio brn	80	50
388	CD26	3r on 4t org brn	35	30
389	CD27	3r on 8t bis	2.00	1.50
		Nos. 376-389 (14)	14.10	10.90

Double, inverted and other surcharge varieties exist on Nos. 384-386, 389.

Stamps of 1898-1903
Surcharged in Red **REPÚBLICA 1½ REIS**

1915

390	A17	1½r on 4½r grn	25.00	17.50
a.		"REPUBLICA" omitted		
b.		"REPUBLICA" inverted		
391	A17	1½r on 9r gray lil	10.00	7.50
a.		"REPUBLICA" omitted		
392	A17	1½r on 12t grn, *pink*	75	50
394	A17	3r on 2t brn	4.00	3.00
395	A17	3r on 1rp dl bl, *straw*	15.00	
396	A17	3r on 2rp gray blk, *straw*	5.00	4.00

Nos. 390, 390a, 390b, 391, 391a and 395 were not regularly issued. The 3r on 2½r (A17) was surcharged without official authorization.

Preceding Issues
Overprinted in Carmine **REPUBLICA**

1915
On No. 230

397	A15	5t on 8t org	1.50	1.10

On Nos. 241, 243

398	A17	2t blue	80	80
399	A17	2t on 2½t dl bl	1.35	1.00

No. 359
Surcharged in Carmine **1½ REAL**

1922

400	A21	1½r on 2r blk	50	45

Ceres Type of 1913-21.
1922-25 Typographed *Perf.* 12x11½
Name and Value in Black.

401	A21	4r blue	1.40	1.00
402	A21	1½t gray grn	1.10	70
403	A21	2½t turq bl	1.25	1.00
404	A21	3t4r yel brn	4.50	3.00
405	A21	4t gray ('25)	1.50	60
406	A21	8t dl rose	7.50	5.00
407	A21	1rp gray brn	17.00	13.00
408	A21	2rp yellow	17.00	14.00
409	A21	3rp bluish grn	25.00	20.00
410	A21	5rp car rose	30.00	22.50
		Nos. 401-410 (10)	106.25	80.80

Vasco da Gama and Flagship
A22

1925, Jan. 30 Litho. Without Gum

411	A22	6r brown	3.75	2.50
412	A22	1t red vio	5.00	3.00

Issued to commemorate the 400th anniversary of the death of Vasco da Gama (1469?-1524), Portuguese navigator.

Monument to
St. Francis
A23

Image of
St. Francis
A25

Autograph of St. Francis
A24

Image of
St. Francis
A26

Tomb of
St. Francis
A28

Church of Bom Jesus at Goa
A27

1931, Dec. 3 *Perf.* 14

414	A23	1r gray grn	80	70
415	A24	2r brown	80	70
416	A25	6r red vio	1.25	80
417	A26	1½t yel brn	5.00	3.00
418	A27	2t dp bl	7.25	4.50
419	A28	2½t lt red	11.00	5.50
		Nos. 414-419 (6)	26.10	15.20

Issued in commemoration of the Exposition of St. Francis Xavier at Goa, in December, 1931.

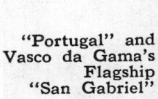

Nos. 371 and 404
Surcharged **2½ T.**

1931-32 *Perf.* 15x14, 12x11½

420	A21	1½r on 8t plum ('32)	1.25	80
423	A21	2½t on 3t4r yel brn	16.50	13.00

"Portugal" and
Vasco da Gama's
Flagship
"San Gabriel"
A29

Wmkd. Maltese Cross. (232)
1933 Typographed *Perf.* 11½x12

424	A29	1r bister	12	5
425	A29	2r ol brn	15	6
426	A29	4r violet	15	6
427	A29	6r dk grn	15	6
428	A29	8r black	18	5
429	A29	1t gray	20	12
430	A29	1½t dp rose	25	12
431	A29	2t brown	30	12
432	A29	2½t dk bl	1.25	30
433	A29	3t brt bl	1.25	30
434	A29	5t red org	1.25	30
435	A29	1rp ol grn	6.00	2.50
436	A29	2rp maroon	11.00	5.00
437	A29	3rp orange	12.50	6.00
438	A29	5rp ap grn	30.00	25.00
		Nos. 424-438 (15)	64.75	40.04

Common Design Types
Perf. 13½x13
1938, Sept. 1 Engr. Unwmkd.
Name and Value in Black.

439	CD34	1r gray grn	8	7
440	CD34	2r org brn	10	10
441	CD34	3r dk vio brn	10	12
442	CD34	6r brt grn	12	10
443	CD35	10r dk car	40	30
444	CD35	1t brt red vio	40	30
445	CD35	1½t red	45	30
446	CD37	2t orange	45	30
447	CD37	2½t blue	45	30
448	CD37	3t slate	90	30
449	CD36	5t rose vio	1.50	90
450	CD36	1rp brn car	5.00	90
451	CD36	2rp ol grn	6.00	3.00
452	CD38	3rp bl vio	12.50	6.50
453	CD38	5rp red brn	27.50	15.00
		Nos. 439-453 (15)	55.95	15.59

Stamps of 1933
Surcharged in Black **1 tanga**

Perf. 11½x12
1941, June Wmk. 232

454	A29	1t on 1½t dp rose	2.25	1.75
455	A29	1t on 1rp ol grn	2.25	1.75
456	A29	1t on 2rp mar	2.25	1.75
457	A29	1t on 5rp ap grn	2.25	1.75

Nos. 430-431
Surcharged **3 RÉIS**

1943

458	A29	3r on 1½t dp rose	1.00	75
459	A29	1t on 2t brn	2.25	2.00

PORTUGUESE INDIA

Nos. 434, 428, 437 and 432
Surcharged in Dark Blue or Carmine

1 REAL

a

6 Réis

b

			Perf. 11½x12	**Wmk. 232**	
1945-46					
460	A29 (a)	1r on 5t red org (Dk Bl)		90	60
461	A29 (b)	2r on 8r blk (C)		70	50
462	A29 (b)	3r on 3rp org (Bl) ('46)		2.00	1.75
463	A29 (b)	6r on 2½t dk bl (C)		2.25	1.75

St. Francis Xavier
A30

Luis de Camoens
A31

Garcia de Orta
A32

St. John de Britto
A33

Arch of the Viceroy
A34

Affonso de Albuquerque
A35

Vasco da Gama
A36

Francisco de Almeida
A37

Perf. 11½

1946, May 28			Litho.	Unwmkd.	
464	A30	1r blk & gray blk		30	30
465	A31	2r rose brn & pale rose brn		30	30
466	A32	6r ocher & dl yel		30	30
467	A33	7r vio & pale vio		1.50	60
468	A34	9r sep & buff		1.50	60
469	A35	1t dk sl grn & sl grn		1.50	60
470	A36	3½t ultra & pale ultra		1.75	1.25
471	A37	1rp choc & bis brn		4.00	1.50
a.		Min. sheet of 8		15.00	15.00
		Nos. 464-471 (8)		11.15	5.45

No. 471a measures 166x229mm. and contains one each of Nos. 464-471, and decorative border. The sheet sold for 1½ rupias.

No. 428, 431 and 433
Surcharged
in Carmine
or Black

1 Real

c

1946		**Perf. 11½x12**	**Wmk. 232**	
472	A29 (c)	1r on 8r blk (C)	75	50
473	A29 (b)	3r on 2t brn	75	60
474	A29 (b)	6r on 3t brt bl	2.25	2.00

Type of 1946 and

Joao de Castro
A38

José Vaz
A39

Luis de Ataide
A40

Duarte Pacheco Pereira
A41

Lithographed

1948		**Perf. 11½**	Unwmkd.	
475	A38	3r brt ultra & lt bl	90	50
476	A30	1t dk grn & yel grn	1.25	75
477	A39	1½t dk pur & dl vio	2.00	1.25
478	A40	2½t brt ver	2.50	1.75
479	A41	7½t dk brn & org brn	4.00	2.50
a.		Min. sheet of 5	15.00	15.00
		Nos. 475-479 (5)	10.65	6.75

No. 476 measures 21x31mm.
No. 479a measures 106x146mm. and contains one each of Nos. 475-479. Marginal inscriptions in gray. The sheet sold for 1 rupia.

Lady of Fatima Issue
Common Design Type

1948			**Perf. 14½**	
480	CD40	1t dk bl grn	3.50	3.00

Visit of statue of Our Lady of Fatima.

Our Lady of Fatima
A42

1949		Lithographed	**Perf. 14**	
481	A42	1r blue	80	60
482	A42	3r org yel	80	60
483	A42	9r dk car rose	1.50	1.00
484	A42	2t green	3.75	1.50
485	A42	9t org red	4.00	1.75
486	A42	2rp dk vio brn	7.50	3.75
487	A42	5rp ol grn	16.50	7.00
488	A42	8rp vio bl	35.00	12.50
		Nos. 481-488 (8)	69.85	28.70

Issued to honor Our Lady of the Rosary at Fatima, Portugal.

U. P. U. Issue.

U.P.U. Symbols
A42a

1949, Oct.				
489	A42a	2½t scar & pink	2.00	1.50

U.P.U., 75th anniversary.

Holy Year Issue.
Common Design Types

1950, May			**Perf. 13x13½**	
490	CD41	1r ol bis	1.00	50
491	CD42	2t dk gray grn	1.25	75

See also Nos. 496-503.

1 Real

No. 443
Surcharged
in Black

1950			**Perf. 13½x13**	
492	CD35	1r on 10r dk car	25	25
493	CD35	2r on 10r dk car	25	25

Similar Surcharge on No. 447
in Black or Red.

| 494 | CD37 | 1r on 2½t bl | 25 | 25 |
| 495 | CD37 | 3r on 2½t bl (R) | 40 | 30 |

Letters with serifs, small (lower case) "r" in "real" and "réis".

Holy Year Issue
Common Design Types

1951	Lithographed.		**Perf. 13½.**	
496	CD41	1r dp car rose	30	30
497	CD41	2r emerald	35	30
498	CD42	3r red brn	40	30
499	CD41	6r gray	40	40
500	CD41	9r brt pink	1.00	65
501	CD41	1t bl vio	1.00	65
502	CD42	2t yellow	1.00	65
503	CD41	4t vio brn	1.00	65
		Nos. 496-503 (8)	5.45	3.90

Issued to commemorate the Holy Year (1950).

No. 447 with Surcharge Similar to
Nos. 492-493 in Red.

1951			**Perf. 13½x13**	
504	CD37	6r on 2½t bl (R)	40	30
505	CD37	1t on 2½t bl (R)	25	25

Letters with serifs, small (lower case) "r" in "réis".

Holy Year Extension Issue
Common Design Type

1951	Lithographed	**Perf. 14**	
506	CD43	1rp bl vio & pale vio	1.50	1.00

Extension of the Holy Year into 1951.

José Vaz
A43

Ruins of
Sancoale Church
A44

Design: 12t, Altar.

1951	Lithographed	**Perf. 14½**	
	Dated: "1651-1951."		
507	A43	1r Prus bl & pale bl	10	10
508	A43	2r ver & red brn	10	10
509	A43	3r gray blk & gray	50	25
510	A43	1t vio bl & ind	10	5
511	A43	2t dp cl & cl	25	20
512	A43	3t ol grn & blk	50	20
513	A43	9t ind & ultra	65	40
514	A44	10t lil & vio	1.00	50
515	A44	12t blk brn & brn	1.50	75
		Nos. 507-515 (9)	4.70	2.55

Issued to commemorate the 300th anniversary of the birth of José Vaz.

Medical Congress Issue.
Common Design Type
Design: Medical School, Goa.

1952		**Perf. 13½.**	Unwmkd.	
516	CD44	4½t blk & lt bl	4.00	2.00

National Congress of Tropical Medicine, Lisbon.

St. Francis Xavier Issue

Statue of Saint Francis Xavier
A44a

1952, Oct. 25		Litho.	**Perf. 14**	
517	A44a	6r aqua & multi	30	25
518	A44a	2t cr & multi	2.00	65
519	A44a	5t pink & sil	4.00	1.25

Souvenir Sheets

A45

PORTUGUESE INDIA

St. Francis Xavier and
his Tomb, Goa—A46
Perf. 13.

520	A45	9t brn & dk brn	10.00	10.00
a.		Single stamp	6.00	6.00

Issued in sheets measuring 90x100mm., with central design and background in gray, frame and inscriptions in black.

521	A46	Sheet of two	10.00	10.00
a.		4t org buff & blk	3.00	3.00
b.		8t sl & blk	3.00	3.00

Issued in sheets measuring 79x65mm., with border in light blue and inscriptions in black.
Nos. 517 to 521 were issued to commemorate the 400th anniversary of the death of St. Francis Xavier.

Numeral St. Francis Xavier
A47 A48

1952, Dec. 4 Litho. *Perf. 13½*

522	A47	3t black	6.00	6.00
523	A48	5t dk vio & blk	6.00	6.00
a.		Strip of 2 + label	25.00	25.00

Issued to publicize Portuguese India's first stamp exhibition, Goa, 1952.
No. 523a consists of a tête bêche pair of Nos. 522-523 separated by a label publicizing the exhibition.

Statue of Stamp of Portugal
Virgin Mary and Arms of
A49 Colonies
  A49a

1953, Jan.

524	A49	6r dk & lt bl	20	20
525	A49	1t brn & buff	75	60
526	A49	3t dk pur & pale ol	2.50	1.25

Exhibition of Sacred Missionary Art held at Lisbon in 1951.

Stamp Centenary Issue.
1953 Typographed
Stamp and Arms Multicolored.

| 527 | A49a | 1t pale grn & bl grn | 80 | 60 |

Centenary of Portugal's first postage stamps.

C. A. da Gama
Pinto
A50

1954, Apr. 10 Litho. *Perf. 11½*

| 528 | A50 | 3r gray & ol grn | 15 | 10 |
| 529 | A50 | 2t blk & gray blk | 25 | 25 |

Issued to commemorate the centenary of the birth of C. A. da Gama Pinto, ophthalmologist and author.

Sao Paulo Issue
Common Design Type
1954, Oct. 2 Perf. 13½ Unwmkd.

| 530 | CD46 | 2t dk Prus bl, bl & blk | 30 | 30 |

Sao Paulo, 400th anniversary.

Affonso Msgr. Sebastiao
de Albuquerque Rodolfo
School Dalgado
A51 A52

1955, Feb. 26

| 531 | A51 | 9t multi | 1.00 | 60 |

Issued to commemorate the centenary (in 1954) of the founding of the Affonso de Albuquerque National School.

1955, Nov. 15 Perf. 13½ Unwmkd.

| 532 | A52 | 1r multi | 20 | 20 |
| 533 | A52 | 1t multi | 50 | 25 |

Issued to commemorate the centenary of the birth of Msgr. Sebastiao Rodolfo Dalgado.

Francisco Manuel Antonio
de Almeida de Susa
A53 A54

Map of Bassein
by Pedro Barreto
de Resendo, 1635
A55

Portraits: 9r, Affonso de Albuquerque. 1t, Vasco da Gama. 1½t, Filipe Nery Xavier. 3t, Nuno da Cunha. 4t, Agostinho Vicente Lourenco. 8t, Jose Vaz. 9t, Manuel Godinho de Heredia. 10t, Joao de Castro. 2rp, Antonio Caetano Pacheco. 3rp, Constantino de Bragancas.
Maps of ancient forts, drawn in 1635: 2½t, Mombaim (Bombay). 3½t, Damao (Daman). 5t, Diu. 12t, Cochin. 1rp, Goa.
Inscribed:
"450 Aniversario da Fundacao do Estado da India 1505-1955."
Perf. 11½x12 (A53),
Perf. 14½ (A54),
Perf. 12½ (A55).

1956, Mar. 24 Unwmkd.

534	A53	3r multi	20	20
535	A54	6r multi	20	20
536	A53	9r multi	40	20
537	A53	1t multi	40	30
538	A54	1½t multi	20	20
539	A53	2t multi	2.75	1.50
540	A55	2½t multi	1.50	75
541	A53	3t multi	40	20
542	A55	3½t multi	1.50	75
543	A54	4t multi	20	20
544	A55	5t multi	75	35
545	A54	8t multi	60	40
546	A54	9t multi	60	40
547	A53	10t multi	50	30
548	A55	12t multi	1.25	75
549	A55	1rp multi	2.00	1.50
550	A54	2rp multi	1.50	80
551	A53	3rp multi	2.00	1.25
Nos. 534-551 (18)			16.95	10.35

Issued to commemorate the 450th anniversary of the Portuguese settlements in India.

Map of Damao Arms of Vasco
and Nagar Aveli da Gama
A56 A57

1957 Lithographed. *Perf. 11½*
Map and Inscriptions in Black,
Red, Ochre and Blue

552	A56	3r gray & buff	10	10
553	A56	6r bl grn & pale lem	10	10
554	A56	3t pink & lt gray	15	10
555	A56	6t blue	25	25
556	A56	1t ol bis & lt vio gray	60	50
557	A56	1t vio & pale gray	1.75	1.00
558	A56	3rp cit & pink	2.00	1.25
559	A56	5rp mag & pink	3.00	2.50
Nos. 552-559 (8)			7.95	5.80

Perf. 13x13½
1958, Apr. 3 Unwmkd.

Arms of: 6r, Lopo Soares de Albergaria. 9r, Francisco de Almeida. 1t, Garcia de Noronha. 3t, Alfonso de Albuquerque. 5t, Joao de Castro. 11t, Luis de Ataide. 1r, Nuno da Cunha.

Arms in Original Colors.
Inscriptions in Black and Red.

560	A57	2r buff & ocher	10	10
561	A57	6r gray & ocher	10	10
562	A57	9r pale bl & emer	10	10
563	A57	1t pale cit & brn	20	10
564	A57	4t pale bl grn & lil	25	15
565	A57	5t buff & bl	30	20
566	A57	11t pink & lt brn	50	40
567	A57	1rp pale grn & mar	80	60
Nos. 560-567 (8)			2.35	1.75

Brussels Fair Issue

Exhibition Emblem
and View
A58

1958, Dec. 15 Litho. *Perf. 14½*

| 568 | A58 | 1rp multi | 60 | 40 |

World's Fair, Brussels, Apr. 17-Oct. 19.

Tropical Medicine Congress Issue
Common Design Type
Design: Holarrhena antidysenterica.

1958, Dec. 15 *Perf. 13½*

| 569 | CD47 | 5t gray, brn, grn & red | 1.00 | 40 |

6th International Congress of Tropical Medicine and Malaria, Lisbon, Sept. 1958.

Stamps of 1955-58 Surcharged
with New Values and Bars.
1959, Jan. 1 Litho. Unwmkd.
Multicolored

570	A57	5c on 2r (No. 560)	15	10
571	A56	10c on 3r (No. 552)	10	10
572	A57	15c on 6r (No. 561)	10	10
573	A57	20c on 9r (No. 562)	10	10
574	A57	30c on 1t (No. 563)	12	10
575	A55	40c on 1t (No. 539)	20	15
576	A55	40c on 2½t (No. 540)	40	30
577	A55	40c on 3½t (No. 542)	20	10
578	A55	50c on 3t (No. 554)	15	10
579	A53	80c on 3t (No. 541)	15	10
580	A53	80c on 10t (No. 547)	75	65
581	A53	80c on 3rp (No.551)	90	80
582	A57	1e on 4t (No. 564)	15	10
583	A57	1.50e on 5t (No. 565)	20	20
584	A56	2e on 6t (No. 555)	30	30
585	A56	2.50e on 1t (No. 556)	35	35
586	A57	4e on 1t (No. 566)	50	50
587	A56	4.50e on 1rp (No. 567)	55	50
588	A56	5e on 2rp (No.557)	55	50
589	A56	10c on 3rp (No. 558)	1.75	1.25
590	A56	30c on 5rp (No. 559)	4.00	1.50
Nos. 570-590 (21)			11.67	7.90

Types of 1946-1958 Surcharged with
New Values: Old Values Obliterated.
1959 Lithographed. Unwmkd.

591	A39	40c on 1½t dl pur	25	10
592	A54	40c on 1½t multi	25	12
593	CD46	40c on 2t bl & gray	80	60
594	A49	80c on 3t blk & pale cit	25	10
595	A36	80c on 3½t dk bl	40	15
596	CD47	80c on 5t gray, brn, grn & red	40	30
597	A58	80c on 1rp multi	80	40
Nos. 591-597 (7)			3.15	1.77

Coin, Manuel I Arms of
A59 Prince Henry
  A60

Various Coins from the Reign of Manuel I (1495-1521) to the Republic.

Perf. 13½x13
1959, Dec. 1 Litho. Unwmkd
Inscriptions in Black and Red.

598	A59	5c lt bl & gold	6	6
599	A59	10c pale brn & gold	6	6
600	A59	15c pale grn & gray	5	5
601	A59	30c sal & gray	5	5
602	A59	40c pale yel & gray	6	5
603	A59	50c lil & gray	6	5
604	A59	60c pale yel grn & gray	8	5
605	A59	80c lt bl & gray	8	8
606	A59	1e ocher & gray	10	8
607	A59	1.50e bl & gray	15	10
608	A59	2e pale bl & gold	20	15
609	A59	2.50e pale gray & gold	25	15
610	A59	3e cit & gray	30	18
611	A59	4e pink & gray	40	20
612	A59	4.40e pale bl & vio brn	50	40
613	A59	5e pale dl vio & gray	60	40
614	A59	10e brt yel & gray	1.25	75
615	A59	20e beige & gray	2.25	1.50
616	A59	30e brt yel grn & lt cop brn	3.50	2.25
617	A59	50c lt gray & gray	6.00	4.00
Nos. 598-617 (20)			16.00	10.58

PORTUGUESE INDIA — PUERTO RICO

1960, June 25 — *Perf. 13½*
618 A60 3c multi 50 40

Issued to commemorate the 500th anniversary of the death of Prince Henry the Navigator.
Portugal continued to print special-issue stamps for its lost colony after its annexation by India Dec. 18, 1961. Stamps of India were first used on Dec. 29. Stamps of Portuguese India remained valid until Jan. 5, 1962.

AIR POST STAMPS.
Common Design Type
Perf. 13½x13
1938, Sept. 1 Engr. Unwmkd.
Name and Value in Black.

C1	CD39	1t scarlet	60	35
C2	CD39	2½t purple	80	35
C3	CD39	3½t orange	80	40
C4	CD39	4½t ultra	1.75	60
C5	CD39	7t lil brn	2.00	80
C6	CD39	7½t dk grn	3.00	1.00
C7	CD39	9t red brn	5.00	1.50
C8	CD39	11t magenta	6.00	1.50
		Nos. C1-C8 (8)	19.95	6.50

No. C4 exists with overprint "Exposicao Internacional de Nova York, 1939-1940" and Trylon and Perisphere.

POSTAGE DUE STAMPS.

D1
Typographed.
Perf. 11½ Unwmkd.
1904
Name and Value in Black

J1	D1	2r gray grn	20	20
J2	D1	3r yel grn	20	20
J3	D1	4r orange	20	20
J4	D1	5r slate	20	20
J5	D1	6r gray	20	20
J6	D1	9r yel brn	30	30
J7	D1	1t red org	60	50
J8	D1	2t gray brn	1.25	1.00
J9	D1	5t dl bl	2.75	2.50
J10	D1	10t carmine	2.75	2.50
J11	D1	1rp dl vio	8.00	4.50
		Nos. J1-J11 (11)	16.65	12.30

Nos. J1-J11 Overprinted in Carmine or Green

1911

J12	D1	2r gray grn	10	10
J13	D1	3r yel grn	10	10
J14	D1	4r orange	15	10
J15	D1	5r slate	15	10
J16	D1	6r gray	20	20
J17	D1	9r yel brn	30	20
J18	D1	1t red org	35	30
J19	D1	2t gray brn	60	50
J20	D1	5t dl bl	1.25	1.10
J21	D1	10t car (G)	2.00	1.50
J22	D1	1rp dl vio	3.00	2.00
		Nos. J12-J22 (11)	8.20	6.20

Nos. J1-J11 Overprinted

1914

J23	D1	2r gray grn	25	25
J24	D1	3r yel grn	25	25
J25	D1	4r orange	25	25
J26	D1	5r slate	25	25
J27	D1	6r gray	50	40
J28	D1	9r yel brn	50	50
J29	D1	1t red org	75	50
J30	D1	2t gray brn	2.75	1.50
J31	D1	5t dl bl	2.50	2.00
J32	D1	10t carmine	3.75	2.50
J33	D1	1rp dl vio	6.25	4.25
		Nos. J23-J33 (11)	18.00	12.65

Nos. 432, 433 and 434 Surcharged in Red or Black "3 RÉIS"

1943 — *Perf. 11½x12.* Wmk. 232

J34	A29	3r on 2½t dk bl (R)	60	40
J35	A29	6r on 3t brt bl (R)	80	80
J36	A29	1t on 5t red org (Bk)	1.75	1.50

D2
1945 Typographed. Unwmkd.
Country Name and Denomination in Black.

J37	D2	2r brt car	75	75
J38	D2	3r blue	75	75
J39	D2	4r org yel	75	75
J40	D2	6r yel grn	75	75
J41	D2	1t bis brn	75	75
J42	D2	2t chocolate	75	75
		Nos. J37-J42 (6)	4.50	4.50

Nos. 467 and 471 Surcharged in Carmine or Black "Porteado 2 Réis"

1951, Jan. 1 *Perf. 11½*

J43	A33	2r on 7r vio & pale vio (C)	60	50
J44	A33	3r on 7r vio & pale vio (C)	60	60
J45	A37	1t on 1rp choc & bis brn	60	60
J46	A37	2t on 1rp choc & bis brn	60	50

Common Design Type
1952 Photo. & Typo. *Perf. 14*
Numeral in Red; Frame Multicolored.

J47	CD45	2r olive	20	15
J48	CD45	3r black	20	15
J49	CD45	6r dk bl	20	15
J50	CD45	1t dk car	30	20
J51	CD45	2t orange	50	50
J52	CD45	10t vio bl	2.00	2.00
		Nos. J47-J52 (6)	3.40	3.15

Nos. J47-J49 and J51-52 Surcharged with New Value and Bars.
1959, Jan.
Numeral in Red; Frame Multicolored.

J53	CD45	5c on 2r ol	20	15
J54	CD45	10c on 3r blk	20	15
J55	CD45	15c on 6r dk bl	25	20
J56	CD45	60c on 2t org	80	80
J57	CD45	60c on 10t vio bl	1.75	1.50
		Nos. J53-J57 (5)	3.20	2.80

WAR TAX STAMPS.

WT1
Perf. 15x14
1919, Apr. 15 Typo. Unwmkd.
Overprinted in Black or Carmine.
Denomination in Black.

MR1	WT1	0:00:05,48rp grn (Bk)	1.50	1.25
MR2	WT1	0:01:09,94rp grn (Bk)	3.75	2.00
MR3	WT1	0:02:03,43rp grn (C)	3.75	2.00

Some authorities consider No. MR2 a revenue stamp.

POSTAL TAX STAMPS.
Pombal Issue.
Common Design Types
1925 *Perf. 12½.* Unwmkd.

RA1	CD28	6r rose & blk	60	60
RA2	CD29	6r rose & blk	60	60
RA3	CD30	6r rose & blk	60	60

Mother and Child
PT1
1948 Lithographed. *Perf. 11.*

RA4	PT1	6r yel grn	3.00	3.00
RA5	PT1	1t carmine	3.00	3.00

Type of 1948 Surcharged with New Value and Bar in Black.
1951

RA6	PT1	1t on 6r car	3.00	2.25

1952 Type of 1948.

RA7	PT1	1t gray	2.50	2.00

1953

RA7A	PT1	1t red org	2.50	1.75

No. RA5 Overprinted in Black «Revalidado P. A. P.»
1953

RA8	PT1	1t carmine	6.50	6.50

Type of 1948 Typographed.
1954

RA9	PT1	6r pale bis	4.00	4.00

Mother and Child
PT2   PT3

1956 Surcharged in Black. Typographed *Perf. 11*

RA10	PT2	1t on 4t bl	12.50	12.50

Lithographed. *Perf. 13*

RA11	PT3	1t blk, pale grn & red	1.25	75

Type of 1948 Redrawn.
1956 *Perf. 11*
Without Gum.

RA12	PT1	1t bluish grn	3.75	3.75

Denomination in white oval at left.

No. RA11 Surcharged with New Value and Bars in Red
1957 *Perf. 13½*

RA13	PT3	6r on 1t blk, pale grn & red	1.00	75

Type of 1956.
1958 *Perf. 13* Unwmkd.

RA14	PT3	1t dk bl, sal & grn	1.00	75

No. RA14 Surcharged with New Values and Four Bars.
1959, Jan. Litho. *Perf. 13*

RA15	PT3	20c on 1t	60	60
RA16	PT3	40c on 1t	60	60

Arms and People Seeking Help
PT4

1960 *Perf. 13½*

RA17	PT4	20c brn & red	30	30

POSTAL TAX DUE STAMPS.
Pombal Issue.
Common Design Types
1925 *Perf. 12½.* Unwmkd.

RAJ1	CD31	1t rose & blk	60	60
RAJ2	CD32	1t rose & blk	60	60
RAJ3	CD33	1t rose & blk	60	60

See note after Portugal No. RAJ4.

PRUSSIA

See German States group preceding Germany in Vol. III.

PUERTO RICO
(Porto Rico)
(pwĕr'tü rē'kō)

LOCATION—A large island in the West Indies, east of Hispaniola.
GOVT.—Former Spanish Colony.
AREA—3,435 sq. mi.
POP.—953,243 (1899).
CAPITAL—San Juan.
The island was ceded to the United States by the Treaty of 1898.

100 Centimes = 1 Peseta
1000 Milesimas = 100 Centavos = 1 Peso (1881)
100 Cents = 1 Dollar (1898)

Issued under Spanish Dominion.

Puerto Rican stamps of 1855-73, a part of the Spanish colonial period, were also used in Cuba. They are listed as Cuba Nos. 1-4, 9-14, 18-21, 32-34, 35A-37, 39-41, 43-45, 47-49, 51-53, 55-57.

Stamps of Cuba Overprinted in Black:

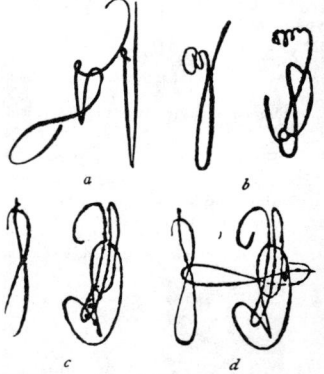

a   b
c   d

1873 *Perf. 14.* Unwmkd.
1 A10 (a) 25c gray 37.50 2.25

PUERTO RICO

2	A10 (a)	50c brown	90.00	8.50
3	A10 (a)	1p red brn	165.00	22.50

1874

4	A11 (b)	25c ultra	24.00	3.00

1875

5	A12 (b)	25c ultra	22.50	3.50
6	A12 (b)	50c green	30.00	4.00
a.		Invtd. ovpt.	200.00	100.00
7	A12 (b)	1p brown	110.00	16.50

1876

8	A13 (c)	25c bl gray	4.75	2.25
9	A13 (c)	50c ultra	12.00	3.75
10	A13 (c)	1p brown	35.00	10.00
11	A13 (d)	25c bl gray	15.00	1.50
12	A13 (d)	1p black	45.00	10.00

Varieties of overprint on Nos. 8–11 include: inverted, double, partly omitted.

King Alfonso XII
A5   A6

1877   Typographed

13	A5	5c yel brn	5.00	2.25
a.		5c car (error)	225.00	175.00
14	A5	10c carmine	15.00	3.00
a.		10c brn (error)	225.00	175.00
15	A5	15c dp grn	21.00	10.00
16	A5	25c ultra	9.00	1.90
17	A5	50c bister	15.00	4.50

Same, Dated "1878".

1878

18	A5	5c ol bis	17.00	18.00
19	A5	10c red brn	165.00	90.00
20	A5	25c dp grn	3.00	1.50
21	A5	50c ultra	8.50	2.25
22	A5	1p bister	15.00	5.25

Same, Dated "1879".

1879

23	A5	5c lake	11.50	4.50
24	A5	10c dk brn	11.50	4.50
25	A5	15c dk ol grn	11.50	4.50
26	A5	25c blue	3.75	1.85
27	A5	50c dk grn	11.50	4.00
28	A5	1p gray	35.00	15.00

Imperforates of type A5 are from proof or trial sheets.

1880

29	A6	¼c dp grn	32.50	13.00
30	A6	½c brt rose	7.50	2.25
31	A6	1c brn lil	12.50	8.00
32	A6	2c gray lil	7.50	4.00
33	A6	3c buff	7.50	4.00
34	A6	4c black	7.50	4.00
35	A6	5c gray grn	3.75	1.85
36	A6	10c rose	4.50	2.25
37	A6	15c yel brn	7.50	3.00
38	A6	25c gray bl	3.75	1.50
39	A6	40c gray	12.50	1.50
40	A6	50c dk brn	18.00	8.00
41	A6	1p ol bis	42.50	10.00

Same, Dated "1881".

1881

42	A6	½m lake	38	15
43	A6	1m violet	38	22
44	A6	2m pale rose	65	38
45	A6	4m brt grn	1.10	30
46	A6	6m brn lil	1.10	55
47	A6	8m ultra	2.65	1.10
48	A6	1c gray grn	4.00	1.10
49	A6	2c lake	4.75	2.65
50	A6	3c dk brn	10.00	4.50
51	A6	5c gray bl	3.75	38
52	A6	8c brown	6.75	1.10
53	A6	10c slate	24.00	7.50
54	A6	20c ol bis	30.00	9.00

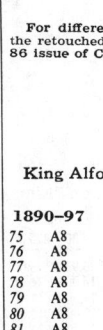

King Alfonso XII
A7

1882–86

55	A7	½m rose	38	15
a.		½m sal rose	45	35
56	A7	½m lake ('84)	75	60
57	A7	1m pale lake	75	60
58	A7	1m brt rose ('84)	38	15
59	A7	2m violet	38	15
60	A7	4m brn lil	38	15
61	A7	6m brown	60	15
62	A7	8m yel grn	60	15
63	A7	1c gray grn	38	15
64	A7	2c rose	1.50	15
65	A7	3c yellow	4.50	1.85
a.		Cliché of 8c in plate of 3c	160.00	
66	A7	3c yel brn ('84)	4.50	75
a.		Cliché of 3c in plate of 3c	32.50	
67	A7	5c gray bl	15.00	90
68	A7	5c gray bl, 1st retouch ('84)	15.00	3.50
69	A7	5c gray bl, 2nd retouch ('86)	140.00	7.50
70	A7	8c gray brn	4.00	15
71	A7	10c dk grn	4.00	38
72	A7	20c gray lil	5.75	38
a.		20c ol grn (error)	75.00	
73	A7	40c blue	37.50	12.00
74	A7	80c ol bis	47.50	13.00

For differences between the original and the retouched stamps see note on the 1883–86 issue of Cuba.

King Alfonso XIII
A8

1890–97

75	A8	½m black	38	10
76	A8	½m ol gray ('92)	10	10
77	A8	½m red brn ('94)	10	10
78	A8	½m dl vio ('96)	10	10
79	A8	1m emerald	45	10
80	A8	1m dk vio ('92)	10	10
81	A8	1m ultra ('94)	10	10
82	A8	1m dp brn ('96)	10	10
83	A8	2m lil rose	38	10
84	A8	2m vio brn ('92)	10	10
85	A8	2m red org ('94)	10	10
86	A8	2m yel grn ('96)	10	10
87	A8	4m dk ol grn	15.00	7.50
88	A8	4m ultra ('92)	10	10
89	A8	4m yel brn ('94)	10	10
90	A8	4m bl grn ('96)	75	38
91	A8	6m dk brn	45.00	15.00
92	A8	6m pale rose ('92)	18	10
93	A8	8m ol bis	45.00	30.00
94	A8	8m yel grn ('92)	18	10
95	A8	1c yel brn	38	10
96	A8	1c bl grn ('91)	75	15
97	A8	1c vio brn ('94)	4.50	22
98	A8	1c cl ('96)	45	10
99	A8	2c dk vio	1.50	1.10
100	A8	2c red brn ('92)	1.10	15
101	A8	2c lil ('94)	1.85	22
102	A8	2c org brn ('96)	45	10
103	A8	3c sl bl	10.00	1.10
104	A8	3c org ('92)	1.10	15
105	A8	3c ol gray ('94)	4.50	22
106	A8	3c bl ('96)	13.50	38
107	A8	3c cl brn ('97)	30	10
108	A8	4c sl bl ('94)	1.10	22
109	A8	4c gray brn ('96)	60	10
110	A8	5c brn vio	15.00	60
111	A8	5c yel grn ('94)	3.75	45
112	A8	5c bl grn ('92)	90	10
113	A8	5c bl ('96)	30	10
114	A8	6c org ('94)	45	10
115	A8	6c vio ('96)	30	10
116	A8	8c ultra	20.00	2.25
117	A8	8c gray brn ('92)	22	10
118	A8	8c dl vio ('94)	8.50	1.50
119	A8	8c car rose ('96)	1.85	1.10
120	A8	10c rose	6.00	1.10
a.		10c sal rose	13.50	3.50
121	A8	10c lil rose ('92)	1.10	22
122	A8	20c red org	6.75	4.75
123	A8	20c lil ('92)	1.85	38
124	A8	20c car rose ('94)	1.10	22
125	A8	20c ol gray ('96)	4.50	1.10
126	A8	40c orange	110.00	40.00
127	A8	40c sl bl ('92)	4.50	2.25
128	A8	40c cl ('94)	5.25	3.50
129	A8	40c sal ('96)	4.50	2.25
130	A8	80c yel grn	300.00	150.00
131	A8	80c org ('92)	11.50	6.00
132	A8	80c blk ('97)	30.00	12.00

Imperforates of type A8 were not issued and are variously considered to be proofs or printer's waste.

Landing of Columbus on Puerto Rico
A9

King Alfonso XIII
A10

1893   Lithographed   Perf. 12

133	A9	3c dk grn	175.00	42.50

400th anniversary, landing of Columbus on Puerto Rico. Counterfeits exist.

1898   Typographed.

135	A10	1m org brn	10	10
136	A10	2m org brn	10	10
137	A10	3m org brn	10	10
138	A10	4m org brn	1.50	55
139	A10	1c blk vio	10	10
140	A10	1c blk vio	10	10
a.		Tête bêche pair	1,350.	
141	A10	2c dk bl grn	10	10
142	A10	3c dk brn	10	10
143	A10	4c orange	1.50	80
144	A10	5c brt rose	10	10
145	A10	6c dk bl	22	10
146	A10	8c gray brn	22	10
147	A10	10c vermilion	10	10
148	A10	15c dl vio	22	10
149	A10	20c maroon	1.85	55
150	A10	40c violet	1.35	1.20
151	A10	60c black	1.35	1.20
152	A10	80c red brn	4.50	4.00
153	A10	1p yel grn	9.00	7.50
154	A10	2p sl bl	21.00	6.50
		Nos. 135-154 (20)	43.73	25.50

Nos. 135-154 exist imperf. Price, set $1,200.

Stamps of 1890-97 Handstamped in Rose or Purple (8c)

Habilitado PARA 1898 y 99.

1898

154A	A8	½m dl vio	12.00	6.00
155	A8	1m dp brn	2.00	2.00
156	A8	2m yel grn	40	40
157	A8	4m bl grn	40	40
158	A8	1c claret	75	1.00
159	A8	2c org brn	75	1.00
160	A8	3c blue	21.00	10.00
161	A8	3c cl brn	50	50
162	A8	4c gray brn	50	50
163	A8	4c sl bl	12.50	8.50
164	A8	5c yel grn	7.50	7.50
165	A8	5c blue	45	45
166	A8	6c violet	45	40
167	A8	8c car rose (P)	75	45
a.		Rose overprint	7.00	7.00
168	A8	20c ol gray	1.50	1.50
169	A8	40c salmon	3.50	3.50
170	A8	80c black	21.00	15.00

As usual with handstamps there are many inverted, double and similar varieties. Counterfeits of Nos. 154A–170 abound.

Issued under U.S. Administration

Ponce Issue.

A11

1898		Imperf.		Unwmkd.
200	A11	5c vio, yelsh		4,500.

Counterfeits exist of Nos. 200–201.

Coamo Issue.

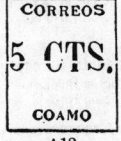

A12

1898		Imperf.		Unwmkd.
201	A12	5c black	400.00	400.00

There are ten varieties in the setting. The stamps bear the control mark "F. Santiago" in violet.

United States
Nos. 279a, 267, 281a, 272 and 282C
Overprinted in Black at 36° angle

PORTO RICO

Wmkd. Double-lined USPS. (191)
1899   Perf. 12

210	A87	1c yel grn	6.50	1.75
a.		Overprint at 25° angle	9.00	2.50
211	A88	2c car, type III	6.00	1.50
a.		Overprint at 25° angle	7.50	1.50
212	A91	5c blue	9.00	2.25
213	A93	8c vio brn	30.00	17.50
a.		Overprint at 25° angle	35.00	19.00
c.		"PORTO RIC"	90.00	90.00
214	A94	10c brn, type I	21.00	6.00
		Nos. 210-214 (5)	72.50	29.00

Misspellings of the overprint, actually broken letters (PORTO RICU, PORTU RICO, FORTO RICO), are found on 1c, 2c, 8c and 10c.

United States
Nos. 279a and 267
Overprinted Diagonally In Black

PUERTO RICO

1900

215	A87	1c yel grn	5.50	1.75
216	A88	2c carmine	5.00	1.25
a.		2c red	5.50	1.25
b.		Inverted ovpt.		3,000.

POSTAGE DUE STAMPS.

United States
Nos. J38, J39 and J42
Overprinted in Black at 36° angle

PORTO RICO

Wmkd. Double-lined USPS. (191)
1899   Perf. 12

J1	D2	1c dp cl	22.00	8.00
a.		Overprint at 25° angle	27.50	
J2	D2	2c dp cl	15.00	7.50
a.		Overprint at 25° angle	20.00	8.50
J3	D2	10c dp cl	150.00	55.00
a.		Overprint at 25° angle	175.00	65.00

Stamps of Puerto Rico were replaced by those of the United States.

PUERTO RICO—QUELIMANE—REUNION

WAR TAX STAMPS.

Stamps of 1890-94 Overprinted or Surcharged by Handstamp

IMPUESTO DE GUERRA

1898   Perf. 14   Unwmkd.

Purple Overprint or Surcharge.

MR1	A8	1c yel brn	8.00	6.00
MR2	A8	2c on 2m org	3.75	3.00
MR3	A8	2c on 5c bl grn	4.50	3.75
MR4	A8	2c dk vio	45	30
MR5	A8	2c lilac	90	90
MR6	A8	2c red brn	45	30
MR7	A8	5c bl grn	45	30
MR8	A8	5c on 5c bl grn	5.25	3.75

Rose Surcharge.

MR9	A8	2c on 2m org	1.85	1.85
MR10	A8	5c on 1m dk vio	30	30
MR11	A8	5c on 1m dl bl	45	45

Magenta Surcharge.

MR12	A8	5c on 1m dk vio	30	30
MR13	A8	5c on 1m dl bl	2.50	2.50

Nos. MR2 to MR13 were issued as War Tax Stamps (2c on letters or sealed mail; 5c on telegrams) but, during the early days of the American occupation, they were accepted for ordinary postage.
Double, inverted and similar varieties of overprints are numerous in this issue.

QUELIMANE
(kĕl'ĕ·mä'nĕ)

LOCATION — A district of the Mozambique Province in Portuguese East Africa.
GOVT. — Part of the Portuguese East Africa Colony.
AREA — 39,800 sq. mi.
POP. — 877,000 (approx.).
CAPITAL — Quelimane.

This district was formerly a part of Zambezia. Quelimane stamps were replaced by those of Mozambique.

100 Centavos = 1 Escudo

Vasco da Gama Issue of Various Portuguese Colonies Surcharged as

REPUBLICA
QUELIMANE
¼ C.

1913   Perf. 12½ to 16.   Unwmkd.

On Stamps of Macao.

1	CD20	¼c on ½a bl grn	2.00	2.00
2	CD21	½c on 1a red	2.00	2.00
3	CD22	1c on 2a red vio	2.00	2.00
4	CD23	2½c on 4a yel grn	2.00	2.00
5	CD24	5c on 8a dk bl	2.00	2.00
6	CD25	7½c on 12a vio brn	3.00	3.00
7	CD26	10c on 16a bis brn	2.00	2.00
a.		Inverted surcharge	10.00	
8	CD27	15c on 24a bis	2.00	2.00
		Nos. 1-8 (8)	17.00	17.00

On Stamps of Portuguese Africa.

9	CD20	¼c on 2½r bl grn	2.00	2.00
10	CD21	½c on 5r red	2.00	2.00
11	CD22	1c on 10r red vio	2.00	2.00
12	CD23	2½c on 25r yel grn	2.00	2.00
13	CD24	5c on 50r dk bl	2.00	2.00
14	CD25	7½c on 75r vio brn	3.00	3.00
15	CD26	10c on 100r bis	2.00	2.00
16	CD27	15c on 150r bis	2.00	2.00
		Nos. 9-16 (8)	17.00	17.00

Common Design Types
pictured in section at front of book.

On Stamps of Timor.

17	CD20	¼c on ½a bl grn	2.00	2.00
18	CD21	½c on 1a red	2.00	2.00
19	CD22	1c on 2a red vio	2.00	2.00
20	CD23	2½c on 4a yel grn	2.00	2.00
21	CD24	5c on 8a dk bl	2.00	2.00
22	CD25	7½c on 12a vio brn	3.00	3.00
23	CD26	10c on 16a bis brn	2.00	2.00
24	CD27	15c on 24a bis	2.00	2.00
		Nos. 17-24 (8)	17.00	17.00

Ceres
A1

1914   Typographed.   Perf. 15 x 14.

Name and Value in Black.

25	A1	¼c ol brn	1.00	1.25
26	A1	½c black	1.50	1.25
27	A1	1c bl grn	1.35	1.00
a.		Imperf.		
28	A1	1½c lil brn	1.75	1.40
29	A1	2c carmine	1.75	1.40
30	A1	2½c lt vio	60	45
31	A1	5c dp bl	1.50	1.25
32	A1	7½c yel brn	1.25	1.00
33	A1	8c slate	1.75	1.25
34	A1	10c org brn	1.25	1.00
35	A1	15c plum	2.75	2.25
36	A1	20c yel grn	1.25	1.00
37	A1	30c brn, grn	3.50	2.50
38	A1	40c brn, pink	3.50	2.50
39	A1	50c org, sal	3.50	2.50
40	A1	1e grn, bl	5.00	4.00
		Nos. 25-40 (16)	33.20	26.00

REUNION
(rĕ·ün'yŭn)

LOCATION — An island in the Indian Ocean about 400 miles east of Madagascar.
GOVT. — Former French colony.
AREA — 970 sq. mi.
POP. — 490,000 (est. 1974).
CAPITAL — St. Denis.

The colony of Réunion became an integral part of the Republic, acquiring the same status as the departments in metropolitan France, under a law effective Jan. 1, 1947.
On Jan. 1, 1975, stamps of France replaced those inscribed or overprinted "CFA."

100 Centimes = 1 Franc

Prices of early Reunion stamps vary according to condition. Quotations for Nos. 1-2 are for fine copies. Very fine to superb specimens sell at much higher prices, and inferior or poor copies sell at reduced prices, depending on the condition of the individual specimen.

A1    **A2**

Typographed

1852   Imperf.   Unwmkd.

1	A1	15c blue	17,500.	10,000.
2	A2	30c blue	17,500.	10,000.

Four varieties of each value.
The reprints are printed on a more bluish paper than the originals. They have a frame of a thick and a thin line, instead of one thick and two thin lines. Price $12 each.

Stamps of French Colonies Surcharged or Overprinted in Black:

1885

3	A1(a)	5c on 40c org, yelsh	190.00	190.00
a.		Inverted surcharge	550.00	550.00
4	A1 (a)	25c on 40c org, yelsh	25.00	22.50
a.		Inverted surcharge	175.00	175.00
b.		Double surcharge	175.00	175.00
5	A5(a)	5c on 30c brn, yelsh	25.00	22.50
a.		"5" invtd	675.00	675.00
b.		Double surcharge	175.00	175.00
6	A4(a)	5c on 40c org, yelsh(I)	21.00	17.50
a.		5c on 40c org, yelsh(II)	800.00	800.00
b.		Inverted surcharge	175.00	175.00
c.		Double surcharge	175.00	175.00
7	A8(a)	5c on 30c brn, yelsh	3.25	3.25
8	A8(a)	5c on 40c ver, straw	45.00	37.50
a.		Inverted surcharge	175.00	175.00
b.		Double surcharge	175.00	175.00
9	A8(a)	10c on 40c ver, straw	4.75	4.00
10	A8(a)	20c on 30c brn yelsh	32.50	25.00

Overprint Type "b"
With or Without Accent on "E"

1891

11	A4	40c org, yelsh (I)	275.00	225.00
a.		40c org, yelsh (II)	1,750.	1,750.
12	A7	80c car, pnksh	30.00	25.00
13	A8	30c brn, yelsh	16.00	16.00
14	A8	40c ver, straw	11.50	11.50
15	A8	75c car, rose	210.00	210.00
16	A8	1fr brnz grn, straw	22.50	21.00

Perf. 14 x 13½.

17	A9	1c lil bl	1.75	1.25
a.		Inverted overprint	8.00	8.00
b.		Double ovpt.	15.00	15.00
18	A9	2c brn, buff	2.25	1.75
a.		Inverted overprint	8.00	8.00
19	A9	4c cl, lav	3.75	3.25
a.		Inverted overprint	25.00	25.00
20	A9	5c grn, grnsh	3.75	2.50
a.		Inverted overprint	12.00	12.00
b.		Double ovpt.	18.00	17.50
21	A9	10c lavender	15.00	2.50
a.		Inverted overprint	22.50	22.50
b.		Double ovpt.	25.00	22.50
22	A9	15c blue	22.00	3.00
a.		Inverted overprint	37.50	37.50
23	A9	20c red, grn	16.00	10.00
a.		Inverted overprint	45.00	45.00
b.		Double surch.	40.00	37.50
24	A9	25c rose	16.00	3.25
a.		Invt. ovpt.	45.00	45.00
25	A9	35c dp vio, yel	13.00	10.00
a.		Inverted overprint	52.50	52.50
26	A9	40c red, straw	32.50	26.50
a.		Inverted overprint	75.00	75.00

27	A9	75c car, rose	325.00	300.00
a.		Inverted overprint	525.00	525.00
28	A9	1fr brnz grn, straw	275.00	250.00
a.		Inverted overprint	525.00	525.00

The varieties "RUNION", "RUENION", "REUNIONR", "REUNIOU" and "REUNOIN" are found on most stamps of this group. There are also many broken letters.

No. 23 with Additional Surcharge in Black:

02c   2

c   d

2   2

e   f

1891

29	A9(c)	02c on 20c red, grn	3.75	3.75
30	A9(c)	15c on 20c red, grn	6.00	6.00
31	A9(d)	2c on 20c red, grn	1.20	1.20
32	A9(e)	2c on 20c red, grn	90	65
33	A9(f)	2c on 20c red, grn	1.75	1.75

Navigation and Commerce
A14

1892-1905   Typographed.
Name of Colony in Blue or Carmine.

34	A14	1c bl	45	45
35	A14	2c brn, buff	45	45
36	A14	4c cl, lav	80	80
37	A14	5c grn, grnsh	2.75	1.00
38	A14	5c yel grn ('00)	60	55
39	A14	10c lavender	3.00	1.00
40	A14	10c red ('00)	75	65
41	A14	15c bl, quadrille paper	10.00	1.25
42	A14	15c gray ('00)	2.35	50
43	A14	20c red, grn	7.50	4.75
44	A14	25c rose	7.50	1.00
a.		"Reunion" double	110.00	95.00
45	A14	25c bl ('00)	9.00	8.50
46	A14	30c brn, bis	8.00	4.75
47	A14	40c red, straw	10.00	8.00
48	A14	50c car, rose	30.00	17.50
a.		"Reunion" in red and bl	110.00	110.00
49	A14	50c brn, az ("Reunion" in car) ('00)	21.00	16.00
50	A14	50c brn, az ("Reunion" in bl) ('05)	26.00	19.00
51	A14	75c dp vio, org	26.00	16.00
a.		"Reunion" double	110.00	100.00
52	A14	1fr brnz grn, straw	20.00	12.50
a.		"Reunion" double	115.00	100.00
		Nos. 34-52 (19)	186.15	118.65

French Colonies No. 52
Surcharged in Black:

2c   2c   2c

g   h   j

1893

53	A9(g)	2c on 20c red, grn	80	80
54	A9(h)	2c on 20c red, grn	1.60	1.60
55	A9(j)	2c on 20c red, grn	7.50	7.50

REUNION

Reunion
Nos. 47–48, 51–52
Surcharged
in Black

5 c.
k

1901

56	A14(k)	5c on 40c red, *straw*	1.50	1.50
a.		Inverted surcharge	14.00	12.00
b.		No bar	55.00	55.00
c.		Thin "5"		
d.		"5" inverted	150.00	150.00
57	A14(k)	5c on 50c car, *rose*	2.00	2.00
a.		Inverted surcharge	14.00	12.00
b.		No bar	55.00	55.00
c.		Thin "5"		
58	A14(k)	15c on 75c vio, *org*	6.50	6.50
a.		Inverted surcharge	14.00	12.00
b.		No bar	55.00	55.00
c.		Thin "5" and small "1"		
d.		As "c," invtd.	12.00	11.00
59	A14(k)	15c on 1fr brnz grn, *straw*	6.50	6.50
a.		Inverted surcharge	14.00	12.00
b.		No bar	55.00	55.00
c.		Thin "5" and small "1"		
d.		As "c," invtd.	12.00	11.00

Map of Réunion
A19

Coat of Arms and
View of St. Denis
A20

View of St. Pierre—A21

1907-30   Typographed

60	A19	1c vio & car rose	6	6
61	A19	2c brn & ultra	6	6
a.		Imperf. (pair)	45.00	
62	A19	4c ol grn & red	10	10
63	A19	5c grn & red	8	6
64	A19	5c ol y & vio ('22)	5	5
65	A19	10c car & grn	75	10
66	A19	10c grn ('22)	8	8
67	A19	10c brn red & org red, bluish ('26)	10	10
68	A19	15c blk & ultra	5	
69	A19	15c gray grn & bl grn ('26)	15	15
70	A19	15c bl & lt red ('28)	15	15
71	A20	20c gray grn & bl grn	10	6
72	A20	25c dp bl & vio brn	1.00	75
73	A20	25c lt brn & bl ('22)	13	13
74	A20	30c yel brn & grn	22	18
75	A20	30c rose & pale rose ('22)	15	15
76	A20	30c gray & car rose ('26)	12	12
77	A20	30c dp grn & yel grn ('28)	45	45
78	A20	35c ol grn & bl	45	18
79	A20	40c gray grn & brn ('25)	10	10
80	A20	45c vio & car rose	45	18
81	A20	45c red brn & ver ('26)	22	22
82	A20	45c vio & red org ('28)	1.00	1.00
83	A20	50c red brn & ultra	1.00	38
84	A20	50c bl & ultra ('22)	10	10
85	A20	50c yel & vio ('26)	10	10
86	A20	60c dk bl & yel brn ('26)	10	10
87	A20	65c vio & lt bl ('28)	45	38
88	A20	75c red & car rose	22	15
89	A20	75c ol brn & red vio ('28)	90	75
90	A20	90c brn red & brt red ('30)	3.25	3.00
91	A21	1fr ol grn & bl	30	30
92	A21	1fr bl ('26)	28	28
93	A21	1fr yel brn & lav ('28)	38	22
94	A21	1.10fr org brn & rose lil ('28)	50	38
95	A21	1.50fr dk bl & ultra ('30)	4.50	3.00
96	A21	2fr red & grn	1.75	1.25
97	A21	3fr red vio ('30)	4.75	3.25
98	A21	5fr car & vio brn	3.75	2.00
		Nos. 60-98 (39)	28.35	20.12

Stamps of
1892-1900
Surcharged in
Black or Carmine

05   **10**
m   *n*

1912

99	A14(m)	5c on 2c brn, *buff*	38	38
100	A14(m)	5c on 15c gray (C)	38	38
a.		Inverted surcharge	67.50	67.50
101	A14(m)	5c on 20c red, *grn*	50	50
102	A14(m)	5c on 25c *rose* (C)	38	38
103	A14(m)	5c on 30c brn, *bis* (C)	38	38
104	A14(n)	10c on 40c red, *straw*	38	38
105	A14(n)	10c on 50c brn, *az* (C)	1.40	1.40
106	A14(n)	10c on 75c dp vio, *org*	4.00	4.00
		Nos. 99-106 (8)	7.80	7.80

Two spacings between the surcharged numerals
are found on Nos. 99 to 106.

No. 62
Surcharged

0,01

1917

107	A19	1c on 4c ol grn & red	60	60
a.		Inverted surcharge	20.00	20.00
b.		Double surch.	32.50	32.50

Stamps and Types
of 1907-30
Surcharged
in Black or Red

40
≡

1922-33

108	A20	40c on 20c grn & yel ('22)	30	30
109	A20	50c on 45c red brn & ver ('33)	45	38
109A	A20	50c on 45c vio & red org ('33)	140.00	140.00
b.		Double surch.	675.00	
110	A20	50c on 65c vio & lt bl ('22)	45	38
111	A20	60c on 75c red & rose ('22)	22	22
112	A19	65c on 15c blk & ultra (R) ('25)	50	50
113	A19	85c on 15c blk & ultra (R) ('25)	50	50
114	A20	85c on 75c red & cer ('25)	50	50
115	A20	90c on 75c brn red & rose red ('27)	65	65
		Nos.108-109,110-115 (8)	3.57	3.43

Stamps and Type of 1907-30
Surcharged with New Value and Bars
in Black or Red.

1924-27

116	A21	25c on 5fr car & brn	30	30
a.		Double surcharge	40.00	
117	A21	1.25fr on 1fr bl (R) ('26)	22	22
a.		Double surch.	40.00	40.00
118	A21	1.50fr on 1fr ind & ultra, *bluish* ('27)	30	30
a.		Double surcharge	52.50	52.50
119	A21	3fr on 5fr dl red & lt bl ('27)	90	90
120	A21	10fr on 5fr bl grn & brn red ('27)	6.50	5.75
121	A21	20fr on 5fr blk brn & rose ('27)	9.00	7.50
		Nos. 116-121 (6)	17.22	14.97

Colonial Exposition Issue.
Common Design Types
1931   Engraved   *Perf. 12½.*
Name of Country
Typographed in Black.

122	CD70	40c dp grn	1.25	1.25
123	CD71	50c violet	1.60	1.60
124	CD72	90c red org	1.60	1.60
125	CD73	1.50fr dl bl	1.60	1.60

Cascade of
Salazie
A22

Waterfowl Lake and Anchain Peak
A23

Léon Dierx Museum, St. Denis
A24

Perf. 12, 12½ and Compound.
1933-40   Engraved

126	A22	1c violet	5	5
127	A22	2c dk brn	5	5
128	A22	3c rose vio ('40)	5	5
129	A22	4c ol grn	5	5
130	A22	5c red org	8	5
131	A22	10c ultra	5	5
132	A22	15c black	5	5
133	A22	20c indigo	8	5
134	A22	25c red brn	10	10
135	A22	30c dk grn	12	12
136	A23	35c grn ('38)	22	22
137	A23	40c ultra	12	10
138	A23	40c brn blk ('40)	15	15
139	A23	45c red vio	38	30
140	A23	45c grn ('40)	15	15
141	A23	50c red	6	6
142	A23	55c brn org ('38)	22	18
143	A23	60c dl bl ('40)	15	15
144	A23	65c ol grn	60	38
145	A23	70c ol grn ('40)	15	15
146	A23	75c dk brn	1.75	1.50
147	A23	80c blk ('38)	22	22
148	A23	90c carmine	80	65
149	A23	90c dl rose vio ('39)	22	22
150	A23	1fr green	75	15
151	A23	1fr dk car ('38)	50	22
152	A23	1fr blk ('40)	8	8
153	A24	1.25fr org brn	22	18
154	A24	1.25fr brt car rose ('39)	38	38
155	A24	1.40fr pck bl ('40)	22	22
156	A24	1.50fr ultra	5	5
157	A22	1.60fr dk car rose ('40)	38	38
158	A24	1.75fr ol grn	28	22
159	A22	1.75fr dk bl ('38)	28	22
160	A24	2fr vermilion	15	15
161	A22	2.25fr brt ultra ('39)	65	65
162	A22	2.50fr chnt ('40)	38	38
163	A24	3fr purple	15	15
164	A24	5fr magenta	30	22
165	A24	10fr dk bl	38	25
166	A24	20fr red brn	65	50
		Nos. 126-166 (41)	11.67	9.46

Paris International
Exposition Issue.
Common Design Types
1937   *Perf. 13*

167	CD74	20c dp vio	75	75
168	CD75	30c dk grn	75	75
169	CD76	40c car rose	75	75
170	CD77	50c dk brn & blk	75	75
171	CD78	90c red	75	75
172	CD79	1.50fr ultra	75	75
		Nos. 167-172 (6)	4.50	4.50

Colonial Arts Exhibition Issue.
Souvenir Sheet.
Common Design Type
1937   *Imperf.*

173	CD74	3fr ultra	2.50	2.50

Issued in sheets measuring 118x99mm.
containing one stamp.

New York World's Fair Issue.
Common Design Type
1939   Engraved   *Perf. 12½x12*

174	CD82	1.25fr car lake	45	45
175	CD82	2.25fr ultra	45	45

St. Denis Roadstead and
Marshal Pétain
A25

1941   *Perf. 11½x12*   *Unwmkd.*

176	A25	1fr brown	22	
177	A25	2.50fr blue	22	

Nos. 176–177 were issued by the Vichy
goverment, and were not placed on sale in
Réunion.

No. 144
Surcharged
in Carmine

≡ **1f**

1943

177A	A23	1fr on 65c ol grn	45	5

REUNION

V1

Stamps of the above design and stamps of type A26, without "RF", were issued in 1943 and 1944 by the Vichy Government, but were not placed on sale in Réunion.

Stamps of 1907 Overprinted in Blue Violet

France Libre
q

1943   *Perf. 14 x 13½.*   Unwmkd.

178	A19(q)	4c ol gray & pale red	1.40	1.40
179	A20(q)	75c red & lil rose	38	38
180	A21(q)	5fr car & vio brn	22.50	22.50

Stamps of 1933-40 Overprinted in Carmine, Black or Blue Violet

France Libre
r

Perf. 12½.

181	A22(r)	1c rose vio (C)	22	22
182	A22(r)	2c blk brn (C)	22	22
183	A22(r)	3c rose vio (C)	22	22
184	A22(r)	4c ol yel (C)	22	22
185	A22(r)	5c red org	22	22
186	A22(r)	10c ultra (C)	22	22
187	A22(r)	15c blk (C)	22	22
188	A22(r)	20c ind (C)	22	22
189	A22(r)	25c red brn (BlV)	22	22
190	A22(r)	30c dk grn (C)	22	22
191	A23(q)	35c green	22	22
192	A23(q)	40c dl ultra (C)	22	22
193	A23(q)	40c brn blk (C)	22	22
194	A23(q)	45c red vio	22	22
195	A23(q)	45c green	22	22
196	A23(q)	50c org red	22	22
197	A23(q)	55c brn org	22	22
198	A23(q)	60c dl bl (C)	1.25	1.25
199	A23(q)	65c ol grn (C)	22	22
200	A23(q)	70c ol grn (C)	75	75
201	A23(q)	75c dk brn (C)	1.40	1.40
202	A23(q)	80c blk (C)	22	22
203	A23(q)	90c dl rose vio	22	22
204	A23(q)	1fr green	22	22
205	A23(q)	1fr dk car	22	22
206	A23(q)	1fr blk (C)	90	90
207	A24(q)	1.25fr org brn (BlV)	22	22
208	A24(q)	1.25fr brt car rose	75	75
209	A22(r)	1.40fr pck bl (C)	60	60
210	A24(q)	1.50fr ultra (C)	22	22
211	A22(r)	1.60fr dk car rose	75	75
212	A24(q)	1.75fr ol grn (C)	32	32
213	A22(r)	1.75fr dk bl (C)	1.50	1.50
214	A24(q)	2fr vermilion	22	22
215	A22(r)	2.25fr brt ultra (C)	75	75
216	A22(r)	2.50fr chnt (BlV)	2.25	2.25
217	A24(q)	3fr pur (C)	22	22
218	A24(q)	5fr brn lake (BlV)	75	75
219	A24(q)	10fr dk bl (C)	2.50	2.50
220	A24(q)	20fr red brn (BlV)	4.25	4.25

New York World's Fair Issue Overprinted in Black or Carmine.

221	CD82(q)	1.25 fr car lake	90	90
222	CD82(q)	2.25 fr ultra (C)	90	90
		Nos. 178-222 (45)	50.52	50.52

No. 177A Overprinted Type "q".

1943   *Perf. 12½.*   Unwmkd.

223	A23	1fr on 65c ol grn	22	22

Produce of Réunion—A26

1943   Photo.   *Perf. 14½x14*

224	A26	5c dl brn	6	6
225	A26	10c dk bl	6	6
226	A26	25c emerald	6	6
227	A26	30c dp org	6	6
228	A26	40c dk sl grn	15	15
229	A26	80c rose vio	22	22
230	A26	1fr red brn	18	18
231	A26	1.50fr crimson	22	22
232	A26	2fr black	22	22
233	A26	2.50fr ultra	22	22
234	A26	4fr dk vio	22	22
235	A26	5fr bister	22	22
236	A26	10fr dk brn	45	45
237	A26	20fr dk grn	60	60
		Nos. 224-237 (14)	3.16	3.16

Eboue Issue. Common Design Type

1945   Engraved   *Perf. 13*

238	CD91	2fr black	30	30
239	CD91	25fr Prus grn	45	45

Nos. 224, 226 and 233 Surcharged with New Values and Bars in Carmine or Black.

1945   *Perf. 14½x14*

240	A26	50c on 5c dl brn (C)	5	5
241	A26	60c on 5c dl brn (C)	5	5
242	A26	70c on 5c dl brn (C)	6	6
243	A26	1.20fr on 5c dl brn (C)	15	15
244	A26	2.40fr on 25c emer	15	15
245	A26	3fr on 25c emer	28	28
246	A26	4.50fr on 25c emer	30	30
247	A26	15fr on 2.50fr ultra (C)	40	40
		Nos. 240-247 (8)	1.44	1.44

Cliff
A27

Cutting Sugar Cane
A28

Common Design Types
pictured in section at front of book.

Cascade   Banana Tree
A29   A30

Mountain Scene
A31

Ship Approaching Réunion
A32
Photogravure.

1947   *Perf. 13½*   Unwmkd.

249	A27	10c org & grnsh blk	5	5
250	A27	30c org & brt bl	6	6
251	A27	40c org & vio	8	8
252	A28	50c bl grn & brn	12	12
253	A28	60c dk bl & brn	12	12
254	A28	80c brn & ol brn	22	22
255	A29	1fr dl bl & vio brn	12	12
256	A29	1.20fr bl grn & gray	22	22
257	A29	1.50fr org & vio brn	22	22
258	A30	2fr bl & bl grn	22	22
259	A30	3fr vio brn & bl grn	22	22
260	A30	3.60fr dl red & rose red	22	22
261	A30	4fr gray bl & buff	22	22
262	A31	5fr rose lil & brn	22	22
263	A31	6fr bl & brn	42	35
264	A31	10fr org & ultra	60	45
265	A32	15fr gray bl & vio brn	1.50	1.25
266	A32	20fr bl & org	2.00	1.60
267	A32	25fr rose lil & brn	2.40	2.00
		Nos. 249-267 (19)	9.23	7.96

Stamps of France, 1945–49, Surcharged in Black or Carmine:

1949   *Perf. 14x13½, 13.*   Unwmkd.

268	A154(a)	10c on 30c blk, red org & yel	28	12
269	A155(a)	30c on 50c brn, yel & red	25	18
270	A146(a)	50c on 1fr rose red	35	20
271	A146(a)	60c on 2fr lt bl grn	5.50	60
272	A147(b)	1fr on 3fr dp rose	55	30
273	A147(b)	2fr on 4fr lt bl grn	2.25	40
274	A147(b)	2.50fr on 5fr bl	12.00	7.25
275	A147(b)	3fr on 6fr crim rose	1.20	40
276	A147(b)	4fr on 10fr brt vio	1.20	35
277	A162(a)	5fr on 20fr sl gray (C)	2.25	55
278	A146(b)	6fr on 12fr ultra	3.50	70
279	A160(a)	7fr on 12fr rose car	3.25	1.25
280	A165(a)	8fr on 25fr dk bl (C)	16.00	2.75
281	A165(a)	10fr on 25fr blk brn (C)	90	45
282	A174(a)	11fr on 18fr dk bl (C)	4.50	1.65
		Nos. 268-282 (15)	53.98	17.15

The letters "C. F. A." are the initials of "Colonies Francaises d'Afrique," referring to the currency which is expressed in French Africa francs. The surcharge on Nos. 277, 279, 282 includes two bars.

1950   *Perf. 14 x 13½.*

283	A182(a)	10c on 50c bl, red & yel	20	12
284	A182(a)	1fr on 2fr grn, yel & red (#619)	5.75	3.25
285	A147(b)	2fr on 5fr lt grn	6.25	2.75

Surcharged Type "a" and Bars.

1950-51   *Perf. 13.*

286	A188	5fr on 20fr dk red	4.50	75
287	A185	8fr on 25fr dp ultra ('51)	2.75	45

Stamps of France, 1951-52, Surcharged in Black or Red.

1951-52   *Perf. 14x13½, 13.*

288	A182(a)	50c on 1fr bl, red & yel	32	18
289	A182(a)	1fr on 2fr vio bl, red & yel (#662)	55	30
290	A147(b)	2fr on 5fr dl vio	80	70
291	A147(b)	3fr on 6fr grn	3.50	1.25
292	A220(a)	5fr on 20fr dk pur ('52)	90	50
293	A147(b)	6fr on 12fr red org ('52)	3.50	60
294	A215(a)	8fr on 20fr vio ('52)	3.25	55
295	A147(b)	9fr on 18fr cer	5.50	2.75
296	A208(a)	15fr on 30fr ind (C)	2.25	50
		Nos. 288-296 (9)	20.57	7.33

The surcharge on Nos. 292, 294 and 296 include two bars.

France, No. 697 Surcharged Type "a" in Black.

1953   *Perf. 14x13½*

297	A182	50c on 1fr blk, red & yel	32	18

France, No. 688 Surcharged in Black

3F CFA
c

Perf. 13.

298	A230	3fr on 6fr dp plum & car	60	35

France Nos. 703 and 705 Surcharged Type "a" in Red or Blue.

1954

299	A235	8fr on 40fr choc & ind (R)	13.00	3.75
300	A235	20fr on 75fr org & cl	50.00	22.50

REUNION

France Nos. 698, 721, 713, and 715 Surcharged Type "a" in Black.
Perf. 14x13½, 13.

301	A182	1fr on 2fr brn, bl & yel	50	30
302	A241	4fr on 10fr aqua & org brn	1.30	60
303	A238	8fr on 40fr dk brn, vio brn & org brn	3.50	35
304	A238	20fr on 75fr dp car & mag	4.00	70

The surcharge on Nos. 303 and 304 includes two bars.

France Nos. 737, 719 and 722-724 Surcharged in Black or Red.

305	A182(a)	1fr on 2fr blk, red & yel	45	15
306	A241(a)	2fr on 6fr ultra, ind & dk grn (R)	40	30
307	A242(a)	6fr on 12fr rose vio & dk vio	2.00	60
308	A241(a)	9fr on 18fr bl, dk grn & ind	5.75	3.75
309	A241(a)	10fr on 20fr blk brn, bl grn & red brn	2.50	55
	Nos. 299-309 (11)		83.40	33.55

The surcharge on Nos. 306-308 includes two bars; on No. 309 three bars.

France No. 720 Surcharged Type "c" in Red, Bars at Lower Left.
1955 *Perf. 13*

310	A241	3fr on 8fr brt bl & dk grn	80	40

France Nos. 785, 774-779 Surcharged Type "a" in Black or Red.
Typographed, Engraved.
1955-56 *Perf. 14x13½, 13*

311	A182	50c on 1fr bl, red & yel	15	12
312	A265	2fr on 6fr car lake ('56)	75	40
313	A265	3fr on 8fr ind	55	30
314	A265	4fr on 10fr dp ultra	55	0
315	A265	5fr on 12fr vio & brn (R)	1.00	30
316	A265	6fr on 18fr bluish grn & ind (R)	65	25
317	A265	10fr on 25fr org brn & red brn	1.10	35
	Nos. 311-317 (7)		4.75	1.92

The surcharge on Nos. 312-317 includes two bars.

France Nos. 801-804 Surcharged Type "a" or "b" in Black or Red.
1956 *Engraved.* *Perf. 13*

318	A280(a)	8fr on 30fr gray vio & blk (R)	1.75	28
319	A280(b)	9fr on 40fr brn & vio brn	2.75	1.10
320	A280(a)	15fr on 50fr rose vio & vio	2.25	90
321	A280(a)	20fr on 75fr ind, grn & bl (R)	3.00	1.10

The surcharge on Nos. 318, 319 and 321 includes two bars.

France Nos. 837 and 839 Surcharged Type "a" in Red.
1957 *Perf. 13*

322	A294	7fr on 15fr dk bl grn & sep	1.00	30
323	A265	17fr on 70fr blk & dl grn	3.50	1.60

The surcharge on Nos. 322-323 includes two bars.
No. 322 has three types of "7" in the sheet of 50. There are 34 of the "normal" 7; 10 of a slightly thinner 7, and six of a slightly thicker 7.

France Nos. 755-756, 833-834, 851-855, 908, 949 Surcharged in Black or Red Type "a", "b" or

50ᶠCFA

d
Typographed, Engraved
1957-60 *Perf. 14x13½, 13*

324	A236(b)	2fr on 6fr org	32	12
325	A302(b)	3fr on 10fr dk ol bis & vio brn ('58)	32	20
326	A236(b)	4fr on 12fr red lil	2.00	55
327	A236(b)	5fr on 10fr brt grn	1.25	40
328	A303(b)	6fr on 18fr ind & dk brn	55	30
329	A302(b)	9fr on 25fr bl gray & vio brn (R) ('58)	80	40
330	A252(a)	10fr on 20fr ultra (R)	80	25
331	A252(a)	12fr on 25fr rose red	3.25	45
332	A303(b)	17fr on 35fr car rose & lake	2.50	80
333	A302(a)	20fr on 50fr ol grn & ol bis	1.25	65
334	A302(a)	25fr on 85fr dp cl	2.25	1.00
335	A339(a)	50fr on 1fr vio bl, bl & grn ('60)	1.75	65
	Nos. 324-335 (12)		17.04	5.77

e *f*

The surcharge includes two bars on Nos. 324, 326-327, 329-331, 333 and 335.

France Nos. 973, 939 and 968 Surcharged

2ᶠ CFA   12ᶠCFA

1961-63 Typographed Perf. 14x13½

336	A318(e)	2fr on 5c multi	12	12
337	A336(e)	5fr on 10c brt grn	17	18
338	A336(b)	5fr on 10c brt grn ('63)	1.00	35
339	A349(f)	12fr on 25c lake & gray	32	8

The surcharge on No. 337 includes three bars. No. 338 has "b" surcharge and two bars.

France Nos. 943, 941 and 946 Surcharged "CFA" and New Value in Two Lines in Black or Red.
Engraved, Typographed.
1961 *Perf. 13, 14x13½ Unwmkd.*

340	A338	7fr on 15c bl & ind	90	35
341	A337	10fr on 20c grnsh bl & car rose	20	15
342	A339	20fr on 20c sl grn & lt cl (R)	11.00	3.00

Surcharge on No. 342 includes 3 bars.

France Nos. 1047-1048 Surcharged with New Value, "CFA" and Two Bars
1963, Jan. 2 Engraved Perf. 13

343	A394	12fr on 25c gray, yel & grn	50	35
344	A395	25fr on 50c dk bl, grn & ultra	60	45

Issued to commemorate the first television connection of the United States and Europe through the Telstar satellite, July 11-12, 1962.

France Nos. 1040-1041, 1007 and 1009 Surcharged Similarly to Type "e".
Typographed, Engraved
1963 *Perf. 14x13½, 13*

345	A318	2fr on 5c ver, ultra & yel	8	6
346	A318	5fr on 10c red, ultra & yel	10	6
347	A372	7fr on 15c bl & pur	30	20
348	A372	20fr on 45c vio bl, red brn & grn	90	40

Two-line surcharge on No. 345; No. 347 has currency expressed in capital "F" and two heavy bars through old value; two thin bars on No. 348.

France No. 1078 Surcharged Type "e" in Two Lines in Dark Blue.
1964, Feb. 8 Engraved Perf. 13

349	CD118	12fr on 25c dk gray, sl grn & dk car	70	50

Issued to publicize "PHILATEC," International Philatelic and Postal Techniques Exhibition, Paris, June 5-21, 1964.

France Nos. 1092, 1094 and 1102 Surcharged with New Value and "CFA"
Typographed, Engraved
1964 *Perf. 14x13½, 13*

350	A318	1fr on 2c emer, vio bl & yel	5	5
351	A318	6fr on 18c multi	28	28
352	A420	35fr on 70c sl, grn & car	80	60

Surcharge on No. 352 includes two bars.

France Nos. 1096, 1126 and 1070 Surcharged with New Value and "CFA"
1965

353	A318	15fr on 30c vio bl & red	35	10
354	A440	25fr on 50c multi	60	45
355	A408	30fr on 60c ultra, dk grn & hn brn	80	60

Two bars obliterate old denomination on Nos. 354-355.

Etienne Regnault, "Le Taureau" and Coast of Reunion
A33

1965, Oct. 3 Engraved Perf. 13

356	A33	15fr bluish blk & dk car	40	22

Tercentenary of settlement of Reunion.

France No. 985 Surcharged with New Value, Two Bars and "CFA".
1966, Feb. 13 Engraved Perf. 13

357	A360	10fr on 20c bl & car	20	18

French Satellite A-1 Issue
France Nos. 1137-1138 Surcharged with New Value, Two Bars and "CFA" in Red
1966, March 27 Engraved Perf. 13

358	CD121	15fr on 30c Prus bl, brt bl & blk	55	45
359	CD121	30fr on 60c blk, Prus bl & brt bl	70	65
a.	Strip of 2 + label		1.30	

France Nos. 1142, 1143, 1101 and 1127 Surcharged with New Value, "CFA" and Two Bars
1967-69 *Typo.* *Perf. 14x13*

360	A446	2fr on 5c bl & red	20	15

Photogravure

360A	A446	10fr on 20c multi ('69)	22	15

Engraved

361	A421	20fr on 40c multi	45	40
362	A439	30fr on 60c red & red brn	60	40

EXPO '67 Issue
France No. 1177 Surcharged with New Value, "CFA" and Two Bars
1967, June 12 Engraved Perf. 13

363	A473	30fr on 60c dl bl & bl grn	55	40

Issued to commemorate the International Exhibition EXPO '67, Montreal, Apr. 28-Oct. 27.

Lions Issue
France No. 1196 Surcharged in Violet Blue with New Value, "CFA" and Two Bars
1967, Oct. 29 Engraved Perf. 13

364	A485	20fr on 40c dk car & vio bl	60	40

50th anniversary of Lions International.

France No. 1130 Surcharged in Violet Blue with New Value, "CFA" and Two Bars
1968, Feb. 26 Engraved Perf. 13

365	A440	50fr on 1fr gray, grn & brn	90	45

France No. 1224 Surcharged with New Value, "CFA" and Two Bars
1968, Oct. 21 Engraved Perf. 13

366	A508	20fr on 40c multi	50	40

20 years of French Polar expeditions.

France Nos. 1230-1231 Surcharged with New Value, "CFA" and Two Bars.
1969, Apr. 13 Engraved Perf. 13

367	A486	15fr on 30c grn	30	20
368	A486	20fr on 40c dp car	35	15

France No. 1255 Surcharged with New Value, "CFA" and Two Bars
1969, Aug. 18 Engraved Perf. 13

370	A526	35fr on 70c multi	90	40

Issued to commemorate the 200th anniversary of Napoleon Bonaparte (1769-1821).

France No. 1294 Surcharged with New Value and "CFA"
1971, Jan. 16 Engraved Perf. 13

371	A555	25fr on 50c rose car	40	20

France No. 1301 Surcharged with New Value and "CFA"
1971, Apr. 13 Engraved Perf. 13

372	A562	40fr on 80c multi	80	45

France No. 1309 Surcharged with New Value, "CFA" and 2 Bars
1971, June 5 Engraved Perf. 13

373	A569	15fr on 40c multi	30	25

Aid for rural families.

France No. 1312 Surcharged with New Value and "CFA"
1971, Aug. 30 Engraved Perf. 13

374	A571	45fr on 90c multi	60	40

France No. 1320 Surcharged with New Value and "CFA"
1971, Oct. 18

375	A573	45fr on 90c multi	75	50

40th anniversary of the first assembly of presidents of artisans' guilds.

Réunion Chameleon
A34

1971, Nov. 8 Photo. Perf. 13

376	A34	25fr multi	50	25

Nature protection.

REUNION

Common Design Type and

De Gaulle in
Brazzaville, 1944
A35

Designs: No. 377, Gen. de Gaulle, 1940.
No. 379, de Gaulle entering Paris, 1944.
No. 380, Pres. de Gaulle, 1970.

1971, Nov. 9   Engraved

377	CD134	25fr black	60	45
378	A35	25fr ultra	60	45
379	A35	25fr rose red	60	45
380	CD134	25fr black	60	45
a.		Strip of 4 + label	2.75	2.00

First anniversary of the death of Charles de Gaulle (1890-1970), president of France. Nos. 377-380 printed se-tenant in sheets of 20 containing 5 strips of 4 plus labels with Cross of Lorraine and inscription.

France No. 1313 Surcharged with New Value and "CFA"

1972, Jan. 17   Engr.   Perf. 13

| 381 | A570 | 50fr on 1.10fr multi | 80 | 60 |

Map of South
Indian Ocean,
Penguin and
Ships
A36

1972, Jan. 31   Engraved   Perf. 13

| 382 | A36 | 45fr blk, bl & ocher | 80 | 65 |

Bicentenary of the discovery of the Crozet and Kerguelen Islands.

France No. 1342 Surcharged with New Value, "CFA" and 2 Bars in Red

1972, May. 8   Engr.   Perf. 13

| 383 | A590 | 15fr on 40c red | 32 | 25 |

20th anniversary of Blood Donors' Association of Post and Telecommunications Employees.

France Nos. 1345-1346 Surcharged with New Value, "CFA" and 2 Bars

1972, June 5   Typo.   Perf. 14x13

| 384 | A593 | 15fr on 30c multi | 32 | 20 |
| 385 | A593 | 25fr on 50c multi | 40 | 30 |

Introduction of postal code system.

France No. 1377 Surcharged with New Value, "CFA" and 2 Bars in Ultramarine

1973, June 12   Engraved   Perf. 13

| 386 | A620 | 45fr on 90c multi | 70 | 55 |

France Nos. 1374, 1336 Surcharged with New Value, "CFA" in Ultramarine or Red

1973   Engraved   Perf. 13

| 387 | A617 | 50fr on 1fr multi (U) | 60 | 55 |
| 388 | A586 | 100fr on 2fr multi (R) | 1.60 | 80 |

Issue dates: 50fr, June 24; 100fr, Oct. 13.
On No. 388, two bars cover "2.00".

France No. 1231C Surcharged with New Value, "CFA" and 2 Bars

1973, Nov.   Typo.   Perf. 14x13

| 389 | A486 | 15fr on 30c bl grn | 32 | 28 |

France No. 1390 Surcharged with New Value, "CFA" and 2 Bars in Red.

1974, Jan. 20   Engraved   Perf. 13

| 390 | A633 | 25fr on 50c multi | 55 | 35 |

ARPHILA 75 Philatelic Exhibition, Paris, June 1975.

France Nos. 1394-1397 Surcharged "100 FCFA" in Black, Ultramarine or Brown

Engr. (※391, 393),
Photo. (※392, 394).

1974   Perf. 12x13, 13x12
Multicolored

391	A637	100fr on 2fr (Bk)	1.40	90
392	A638	100fr on 2fr (U)	1.25	90
393	A639	100fr on 2fr (Br)	1.25	90
394	A640	100fr on 2fr (U)	1.25	90

Nos. 391-394 printed in sheets of 25 with alternating labels publicizing "ARPHILA 75," Paris June 6-16, 1975. Two bars obliterate original denomination on Nos. 391-393.

France No. 1401 Surcharged "45 FCFA" and 2 Bars in Red

1974, Apr. 29   Engraved   Perf. 13

| 395 | A644 | 45fr on 90c multi | 70 | 50 |

Reorganized sea rescue organization.

France No. 1415 Surcharged with New Value, 2 Bars and "FCFA" in Ultramarine.

1974, Oct. 6   Engraved   Perf. 13

| 396 | A657 | 60fr on 1.20fr multi | 90 | 70 |

Centenary of Universal Postal Union.

France Nos. 1292A and 1294B Surcharged with New Value and "FCFA" in Ultramarine

1974, Oct. 19   Typo.   Perf. 14x13

| 397 | A555 | 30fr on 60c grn | 1.25 | 90 |

Engraved   Perf. 13

| 398 | A555 | 40fr on 80c car rose | 1.40 | 1.10 |

SEMI-POSTAL STAMPS.

Regular Issue of 1907
Surcharged in
Black or Red

1915   Perf. 14x13½.   Unwmkd.

B1	A19	10c +5c car & grn (Bk)	40.00	37.50
a.		Inverted surcharge	100.00	95.00
B2	A19	10c +5c car & grn (R)	50	50
a.		Inverted surcharge	30.00	30.00

1916

Regular Issue of 1907
Surcharged in Red

| B3 | A19 | 10c +5c car & grn | 45 | 45 |

Curie Issue
Common Design Type

1938   Perf. 13

| B4 | CD80 | 1.75fr + 50c brt ultra | 6.25 | 6.25 |

French Revolution Issue.
Common Design Type

1939   Photogravure   Unwmkd.
Name and Value Typo. in Black.

B5	CD83	45(c) +25(c) grn	4.00	4.00
B6	CD83	70(c) +30(c) brn	4.00	4.00
B7	CD83	90(c) +35(c) red org	4.00	4.00
B8	CD83	1fr +1fr rose pink	4.00	4.00
B9	CD83	2.25fr +2fr bl	4.00	4.00
		Nos. B5-B9 (5)	20.00	20.00

Common Design Type and

Artillery
Colonel
SP1

Colonial Infantry
SP2

1941   Perf. 13½   Unwmkd.

B10	SP1	1fr +1fr red		55
B11	CD86	1.50fr +3fr cl		55
B12	SP2	2.50fr +1fr bl		55

Nos. B10-B12 were issued by the Vichy government and were not placed on sale in Reunion.
In 1944 the Vichy government surcharged Nos. 176-177 with "OEUVRES COLONIALES" and surtax, changing the denomination of the 2.50fr to 50c. These were not placed on sale in Reunion.

Red Cross Issue
Common Design Type

1944   Perf. 14½ x 14.

| B15 | CD90 | 5fr +20fr blk | 45 | 45 |

The surtax was for the French Red Cross and national relief.

France Nos. B365-B366 Surcharged with New Value, "CFA" and Two Bars.

1962, Dec. 10   Engraved   Perf. 13
Cross in Red

| B16 | SP219 | 10fr +5fr on 20c+10c redsh brn | 1.75 | 1.75 |
| B17 | SP219 | 12fr +5fr on 25c+10c dl grn | 1.75 | 1.75 |

The surtax was for the Red Cross.

France Nos. B374-B375 Surcharged with New Value, "CFA" and Two Bars in Red

1963, Dec. 9
Cross in Red

| B18 | SP223 | 10fr +5fr on 20c+10c blk | 2.75 | 2.75 |
| B19 | SP223 | 12fr +5fr on 25c+10c sl grn | 2.75 | 2.75 |

Issued to commemorate the centenary of the International Red Cross. The surtax was for the Red Cross.

France Nos. B385-B386 Surcharged with New Value, "CFA" and Two Bars in Dark Blue

1964, Dec. 13   Perf. 13   Unwmkd.
Cross in Carmine

| B20 | SP230 | 10fr +5fr on 20c+10c blk | 1.00 | 1.00 |
| B21 | SP230 | 12fr +5fr on 25c+10c blk | 1.00 | 1.00 |

Issued to honor Jean Nicolas Corvisart (1755-1821) and Dominique Larrey (1766-1842), physicians. The surtax was for the Red Cross.

France Nos. B392-B393 Surcharged with New Value, "CFA" and Two Bars

1965, Dec. 12   Engraved   Perf. 13
Cross in Carmine

| B22 | SP233 | 12fr +5fr on 25c+10c sl | 1.00 | 1.00 |
| B23 | SP233 | 15fr +5fr on 30c+10c dl red brn | 1.00 | 1.00 |

The surtax was for the Red Cross.

France Nos. B402-B403 Surcharged with New Value, "CFA" and Two Bars

1966, Dec. 11   Engraved   Perf. 13
Cross in Carmine

| B24 | SP237 | 12fr +5fr on 25c+10c grn | 1.10 | 1.00 |
| B25 | SP237 | 15fr +5fr on 30c+10c sl | 1.10 | 1.00 |

The surtax was for the Red Cross.

France Nos. B409-B410 Surcharged with New Value, "CFA" and Two Bars

1967, Dec. 17   Engraved   Perf. 13
Cross in Carmine

| B26 | SP240 | 12fr +5fr on 25c+10c dl vio & lt brn | 2.00 | 2.00 |
| B27 | SP240 | 15fr +5fr on 30c+10c grn & lt brn | 2.00 | 2.00 |

The surtax was for the Red Cross.

France Nos. B421-B424 Surcharged with New Value, "CFA" and Two Bars

1968-69   Engraved   Perf. 13
Cross in Carmine

B28	SP244	12fr +5fr on 25c+10c pur & sl bl	1.25	1.00
B29	SP244	15fr +5fr on 30c+10c brn		1.00
B30	SP244	20fr +7fr on 40c+15c dk brn & bl ('69)	90	90
B31	SP244	20fr +7fr on 40c+15c pur & Prus bl ('69)	90	90

The surtax was for the Red Cross.

France No. B425 Surcharged with New Value, "CFA" and Two Bars

1969, Mar. 17   Engraved   Perf. 13

| B32 | SP245 | 15fr +5fr on 30c+10c multi | 75 | 75 |

Issued for Stamp Day.

France No. B440 Surcharged with New Value, "CFA" and Two Bars.

1970, Mar. 16   Engraved   Perf. 13

| B33 | SP249 | 20fr +5fr on 40c+10c multi | 75 | 60 |

Issued for stamp day.

France Nos. B443-B444 Surcharged with New Value "CFA" and Two Bars

1970, Dec. 14   Engraved   Perf. 13
Cross in Carmine

| B34 | SP252 | 20fr +7fr on 40c+15c grn | 2.00 | 1.75 |
| B35 | SP252 | 20fr +7fr on 40c+15c cop red | 2.00 | 1.75 |

The surtax was for the Red Cross.

France No. B451 Surcharged wth New Value, "CFA" and Two Bars

1971, Mar. 29   Engraved   Perf. 13

| B36 | SP254 | 25fr +5fr on 50c+10c multi | 60 | 50 |

Stamp Day, 1971.

France Nos. B452-B453 Surcharged with New Value, "CFA" and Two Bars

1971, Dec. 13
Cross in Carmine

| B37 | SP255 | 15fr +5fr on 30c+10c vio bl | 90 | 90 |
| B38 | SP255 | 25fr +5fr on 50c+10c dp car | 90 | 90 |

The surtax was for the Red Cross.

France No. B460 Surcharged with New Value and "CFA"

1972, Mar. 20   Engr.   Perf. 13

| B39 | SP257 | 25fr +5fr on 50c+10c multi | 60 | 60 |

Stamp Day 1972.

REUNION

France Nos. B461–B462 Surcharged with
New Value, "CFA" and Two Bars in
Red or Green.

1972, Dec. 16 Engraved Perf. 13

| B40 | SP258 | 15fr +5fr on 30c+10c sl grn & red (R) | 75 | 75 |
| B41 | SP258 | 25fr +5fr on 50c+10c red (G) | 90 | 90 |

Surtax was for the Red Cross.

France No. B470 Surcharged with New
Value, "CFA" and Two Bars in Red

1973, Mar. 26 Engraved Perf. 13

| B42 | SP260 | 25fr +5fr on 50c+10c grnsh bl | 1.10 | 90 |

Stamp Day, 1973.

France Nos. B471–B472 Surcharged with
New Value, "CFA" and Two Bars
in Red

1973, Dec. 3 Engraved Perf. 13

| B43 | SP261 | 15 +5fr on 30c+10c sl grn & red | 80 | 80 |
| B44 | SP261 | 25 +5fr on 50c+10c | 1.00 | 1.00 |

Surtax was for the Red Cross.

France No. B477 Surcharged
"25 + 5 FCFA"

1974, Mar. 11 Engraved Perf. 13

| B45 | SP263 | 25fr +5fr on 50c+10c multi | 40 | 40 |

Stamp Day 1974.

France Nos. B479–B480 Surcharged with
New Value, "FCFA" and Two Bars in
Green or Red

1974, Nov. 30 Engraved Perf. 13
Multicolored

| B46 | SP265 | 30fr +7fr on 60c+15c (G) | 80 | 80 |
| B47 | SP266 | 40fr +7fr on 80c+15c (R) | 1.00 | 1.00 |

Surtax was for the Red Cross.

AIR POST STAMPS.

No. 141 Overprinted in Blue
RÉUNION - FRANCE
par avion
« ROLAND GARROS »

1937, Jan. 23 Perf. 12½ Unwmkd.

C1	A23	50c red	165.00	150.00
	a.	Pair, one without ovpt.	750.00	750.00
	b.	Inverted ovpt.		1,850.

Issued for the flight of the "Roland Garros" from Reunion to France by aviators Laurent, Lenier and Touge in Jan.–Feb., 1937.

Airplane and
Landscape
AP2

1938, Mar. 1 Engraved. Perf. 12½

C2	AP2	3.65(fr) sl bl & car	35	35
C3	AP2	6.65(fr) brn & org red	35	35
C4	AP2	9.65(fr) car & ultra	35	35
C5	AP2	12.65(fr) brn & grn	70	70

Plane and
Bridge over
East River
AP3

Plane and
Landscape
AP4

1942, Oct. 19 Perf. 12x12½

C6	AP3	50c ol & pur	20	
C7	AP3	1fr dk bl & scar	20	
C8	AP3	2fr brn & blk	22	
C9	AP3	3fr rose lil & grn	35	
C10	AP3	5fr red org & red brn	35	

Frame Engraved,
Center Photogravure.

C11	AP4	10fr dk grn, red org & vio	32	
C12	AP4	20fr dk bl, brn vio & red	45	
C13	AP4	50fr brn car, Prus grn & bl	50	
		Nos. C6–C13 (8)	2.59	

There is doubt whether Nos. C6–C13 were officially placed in use.

V2

Stamps of the above design were issued in 1943 by the Vichy Government, but were not placed on sale in Réunion.

Nos. C2–C5
Overprinted in
Black or Carmine

**France
Libre**

1943 Perf. 12½ Unwmkd.

C14	AP2	3.65fr sl bl & car	1.50	1.50
C15	AP2	6.65fr brn & org red	1.50	1.50
C16	AP2	9.65fr car & ultra (C)	1.50	1.50
C17	AP2	12.65fr brn & grn	1.50	1.50

Common Design Type
1944 Photogravure. Perf. 14½x14.

C18	CD87	1fr dk org	18	18
C19	CD87	1.50fr red red	18	18
C20	CD87	5fr brn red	22	22
C21	CD87	10fr black	30	30
C22	CD87	25fr ultra	30	30
C23	CD87	50fr dk grn	60	60
C24	CD87	100fr plum	60	60
		Nos. C18–C24 (7)	2.08	2.08

Victory Issue
Common Design Type
1946, May 8 Engraved. Perf. 12½

| C25 | CD92 | 8fr ol gray | 45 | 45 |

Issued to commemorate the European victory of the Allied Nations in World War II.

Chad to Rhine Issue
Common Design Types
1946, June 6

C26	CD93	5fr orange	50	50
C27	CD94	10fr sepia	50	50
C28	CD95	15fr grnsh blk	50	50
C29	CD96	20fr lil rose	60	60

C30	CD97	25fr grnsh bl	65	65
C31	CD98	50fr green	65	65
		Nos. C26–C31 (6)	3.40	3.40

Shadow of Plane—AP5

Plane over
Réunion
AP6

Air View of Réunion and
Shadow of Plane—AP7
Perf. 13x12½

1947, Mar. 24 Photo. Unwmkd.

C32	AP5	50fr ol grn & bl gray	4.50	3.75
C33	AP6	100fr dk brn & org	6.75	6.00
C34	AP7	200fr dk bl & org	7.50	7.50

France,
Nos. C18 to C21
Surcharged

**20F
CFA**
c

and Bars, in Carmine or Black

1949 Perf. 13 Unwmkd.

C35	AP7	20fr on 40fr dk grn (C)	1.40	50
C36	AP8	25fr on 50fr rose pink	1.65	60
C37	AP9	50fr on 100fr dk bl (C)	4.50	2.00
C38	AP10	100fr on 200fr red	22.50	13.00

France Nos. C24, C26 and C27 Surcharged
Type "c" and Bars in Black.

1949–51

C39	AP12	100fr on 200fr dk bl grn ('51)	62.50	21.00
C40	AP12	200fr on 500fr brt red	26.50	16.50
C41	AP13	500fr on 1000fr sep, bl ('51)	175.00	140.00

France Nos. C29–C32 Surcharged "CFA,"
New Value and Bars in Blue or Red.

1954, Feb. 10

C42	AP15(c)	50fr on 100fr red brn & bl	1.50	40
C43	AP15	100fr on 200fr blk brn & vio bl (R)	3.75	80
C44	AP15(c)	200fr on 500fr car & org	16.50	12.50
C45	AP15	500fr on 1000fr vio brn, bl grn & ind	18.00	10.00

France Nos. C35–C36 Surcharged "CFA,"
New Values and Bars in Red or Black.

1957–58 Engraved Perf. 13

| C46 | AP17 | 200fr on 500fr dp ultra & blk (R) | 13.50 | 5.25 |
| C47 | AP17 | 500fr on 1000fr lil, ol blk & blk ('58) | 20.00 | 10.00 |

France Nos. C37, C39–C40 Surcharged
"CFA," New Value and Bars
in Red or Black

1961–64

C48	AP15	100fr on 2fr vio bl & ultra	3.00	1.10
C49	AP17	200fr on 5fr dp ultra & blk	4.50	1.75
C50	AP17	500fr on 10fr lil, ol & blk (B) ('64)	12.50	5.25

France No. C41 Surcharged "CFA,"
New Value and Two Bars in Red

1967, Jan. 27 Engraved Perf. 13

| C51 | AP17 | 100fr on 2fr sl bl & ind | 1.50 | 60 |

France No. C45 Surcharged in Red with
"CFA," New Value and Two Bars
in Red

1972, May 14 Engraved Perf. 13

| C52 | AP21 | 200fr on 5fr multi | 3.50 | 1.50 |

AIR POST
SEMI-POSTAL STAMPS.

French Revolution Issue
Common Design Type

1939 Perf. 13 Unwmkd.
Name and Value Typographed
in Orange.

| CB1 | CD83 | 3.65fr +4fr brn blk | 9.50 | 9.50 |

V3

Stamps of the above design and type of Cameroun V10 inscribed "Réunion" were issued in 1942 by the Vichy Government, but were not placed on sale in Réunion.

POSTAGE DUE STAMPS.

D1   D2

Type-set.
1889–92 Imperf. Unwmkd.
Yellowish or Bluish White Paper.

J1	D1	5c black	9.50	4.50
J2	D1	10c black	12.00	4.50
J3	D1	15c blk ('92)	26.50	12.00
J4	D1	20c black	22.50	11.00
J5	D1	30c black	18.50	9.50

Ten varieties of each value.
Nos. J1–J5 exist with double impression.
Prices $12.50–$25.

REUNION—RIO DE ORO

REUNION

1907 Typo. Perf. 14x13½

J6	D2	5c car, yel	22	22
J7	D2	10c bl, bl	22	22
J8	D2	15c bluish	25	25
J9	D2	20c carmine	25	25
J10	D2	30c grn, grnsh	45	45
J11	D2	50c red, grn	50	50
J12	D2	60c car, bl	50	50
J13	D2	1fr violet	85	85
		Nos. J6-J13 (8)	3.24	3.24

Type of 1907 Issue Surcharged = 2F. =

1927

J14	D2	2fr on 1fr org red	3.75	3.75
J15	D2	3fr on 1fr org brn	3.75	3.75

Arms of Réunion D3 — Numeral D4

1933 Engraved. Perf. 13 x 13½

J16	D3	5c dp vio	6	6
J17	D3	10c dk grn	6	6
J18	D3	15c org brn	6	6
J19	D3	20c lt red	8	8
J20	D3	30c ol grn	15	15
J21	D3	50c ultra	22	22
J22	D3	60c blk brn	22	22
J23	D3	1fr lt vio	18	18
J24	D3	2fr dp bl	18	18
J25	D3	3fr carmine	25	25
		Nos. J16-J25 (10)	1.46	1.46

1947 Photogravure. Perf. 13. Unwmkd.

J26	D4	10c dk vio	5	5
J27	D4	30c brown	6	6
J28	D4	50c bl grn	10	10
J29	D4	1fr orange	15	15
J30	D4	2fr red vio	18	18
J31	D4	3fr red brn	20	20
J32	D4	4fr blue	45	45
J33	D4	5fr hn brn	45	45
J34	D4	10fr sl grn	45	45
J35	D4	20fr vio bl	55	55
		Nos. J26-J35 (10)	2.64	2.64

France, Nos. J83 to J92 Surcharged in Black — **50c CFA**

1949-53

J36	D5	10c on 1fr brt ultra	8	8
J37	D5	50c on 2fr turq bl	12	12
J38	D5	1fr on 3fr brn org	18	18
J39	D5	2fr on 4fr dp vio	45	45
J40	D5	3fr on 5fr brt pink	3.00	2.25
J41	D5	5fr on 10fr red org	90	75
J42	D5	10fr on 20fr ol bis	2.25	2.00
J43	D5	20fr on 50fr dk grn ('50)	6.50	3.25
J44	D5	50fr on 100fr dp grn ('53)	16.00	9.00
		Nos. J36-J44 (9)	29.48	18.08

Same Surcharge on France Nos. J93, J95-J96.

1962-63 Typo. Perf. 14x13½

J46	D6	1fr on 5c brt pink ('63)	1.00	1.00
J47	D6	10fr on 20c ol bis ('63)	1.75	1.75
J48	D6	20fr on 50c dk grn	14.00	9.50

France Nos. J98-J103 Surcharged New Value and "CFA"

1964-71 Perf. 14x13½ Unwmkd.

J49	D7	1fr on 5c car rose, red & grn	8	8
J50	D7	5fr on 10c car rose, brt bl & grn	12	12
J51	D7	7fr on 15c brn, brn & red	22	18
J52	D7	10fr on 20c multi ('71)	75	60
J53	D7	15fr on 30c brn, ultra & grn	22	18

J54	D7	20fr on 50c vio bl, car & grn	35	28
J55	D7	50fr on 1fr vio bl, lil & grn	1.00	80
		Nos. J49-J55 (7)	2.74	2.24

PARCEL POST STAMP.

No. 40 Overprinted Colis Postaux

1906 Perf. 14x13½ Unwmkd.

Q1	A14	10c red	5.25	5.25

RIO DE ORO

(rē′ō dā ō′rō)

LOCATION — On the northwest coast of Africa, bordering on the Atlantic Ocean.
GOVT. — Spanish Colony.
AREA — 71,600 sq. mi.
POP. — 24,000.
CAPITAL — Villa Cisneros.

Rio de Oro became part of Spanish Sahara.

100 Centimos = 1 Peseta

King Alfonso XIII
A1 — A2

Typographed.
Control Numbers on Back in Blue

1905 Perf. 14 Unwmkd.

1	A1	1c bl grn	3.50	1.75
2	A1	2c claret	3.50	1.75
3	A1	3c brnz grn	3.50	1.75
4	A1	4c dk brn	3.50	1.75
5	A1	5c org red	3.50	1.75
6	A1	10c dk gray brn	3.50	1.75
7	A1	15c red brn	3.50	1.75
8	A1	25c dk bl	62.50	17.50
9	A1	50c dk grn	32.50	8.00
10	A1	75c dk vio	32.50	11.50
11	A1	1p org brn	24.00	5.00
12	A1	2p buff	67.50	26.50
13	A1	3p dl vio	47.50	11.50
14	A1	4p bl grn	47.50	11.50
15	A1	5p dl bl	65.00	21.00
16	A1	10p pale red	150.00	52.50
		Nos. 1-16 (16)	553.50	177.25

No. 8 Handstamp Surcharged in Rose

1907

17	A1	15c on 25c dk bl	185.00	50.00

The surcharge exists inverted, double and in violet, normally positioned.

Control Numbers on Back in Blue

1907 Typographed.

18	A2	1c claret	3.25	2.25
19	A2	2c black	3.25	2.25
20	A2	3c dk brn	3.25	2.25
21	A2	4c red	3.25	2.25
22	A2	5c blk brn	3.25	2.25
23	A2	10c chocolate	3.25	2.25
24	A2	15c dk bl	3.25	2.25
25	A2	25c dp grn	8.00	2.25
26	A2	50c blk vio	8.00	2.25
27	A2	75c org brn	8.00	2.25
28	A2	1p orange	13.00	2.25
29	A2	2p dl vio	5.00	2.25
30	A2	3p bl grn	5.00	2.25
	a.	Cliché of 4p in plate of 3p	250.00	150.00

31	A2	4p dk bl	10.00	3.75
32	A2	5p red	10.00	3.75
33	A2	10p dp grn	10.00	7.50
		Nos. 18-33 (16)	99.75	44.25

1907 Nos. 9-10 Handstamp Surcharged in Red — **10 Cens**

1907

34	A1	10c on 50c dk grn	52.50	14.00
	a.	"10" omitted	135.00	75.00
35	A1	10c on 75c dk vio	52.50	14.00

No. 12 Handstamp Surcharged in Violet — **1908 2 Cens**

1908

36	A1	2c on 2p buff	45.00	14.00

No. 36 is found with "1908" measuring 11 mm. and 12 mm.

Same Surcharge in Red on No. 26

38	A2	10c on 50c blk vio	30.00	5.50

A 5c on 10c (No. 23) was not officially issued.

Nos. 25, 27-28 Handstamp Surcharged Type "a" in Red, Violet or Green.

1908

39	A2	15c on 25c dp grn (R)	32.50	6.00
40	A2	15c on 75c org brn (V)	42.50	8.00
	a.	Green surcharge	52.50	20.00
41	A2	15c on 1p org (V)	42.50	8.00
42	A2	15c on 1p org (R)	42.50	15.00
43	A2	15c on 1p org (G)	42.50	15.00
		Nos. 39-43 (5)	202.50	52.00

As this surcharge is handstamped, it exists in several varieties: double, inverted, in pairs with one surcharge omitted, etc.

A3

1908 Imperf.

44	A3	5c on 50c grn (C)	115.00	47.50
45	A3	5c on 50c grn (V)	165.00	80.00

The surcharge, which is handstamped, exists in many variations. Nos. 44-45 are found with and without control numbers on back.

King Alfonso XIII
A4

Control Numbers on Back in Blue

1909 Typographed. Perf. 14½

46	A4	1c red	60	40
47	A4	2c orange	60	40
48	A4	5c dk grn	60	40
49	A4	10c org red	60	40
50	A4	15c bl grn	60	40
51	A4	20c dk vio	1.50	60
52	A4	25c dp bl	1.50	60
53	A4	30c claret	1.50	60
54	A4	40c chocolate	1.50	60
55	A4	50c red vio	2.50	60

56	A4	1p dk brn	3.75	2.50
57	A4	4p car rose	4.25	3.50
58	A4	10p claret	9.00	5.00
		Nos. 46-58 (13)	28.50	16.00

Stamps of 1905 Handstamped in Black — **1910 10 Céntimos**

1910

60	A1	10c on 5p bl	12.50	11.00
a.		Red surcharge	70.00	42.50
62	A1	10c on 10p pale red	12.50	11.00
a.		Violet surcharge	110.00	55.00
b.		Green surcharge	110.00	55.00
65	A1	15c on 3p dl vio	12.50	11.00
a.		Imperf.	110.00	
66	A1	15c on 4p bl grn	12.50	11.00
a.		10c on 4p bl grn	550.00	150.00

See note after No. 43.

Nos. 31 and 33 Surcharged in Red or Violet — **2**

1911-13 — **Cents**

67	A2	2c on 4p bl grn (R)	10.00	3.50
68	A2	5c on 10p dp grn (V)	25.00	3.50

Nos. 29-30 Surcharged in Black — **10 Céntimos**

69	A2	10c on 2p dl vio	13.50	3.50
69A	A2	10c on 3p bl grn ('13)	135.00	15.00

Nos. 30, 32 Handstamped Type "a"

69B	A2	15c on 3p bl grn ('13)	100.00	8.00
70	A2	15c on 5p red	10.00	3.75
		Nos. 67-70 (6)	293.50	37.25

King Alfonso XIII
A5 — A6

Control Numbers on Back in Blue

1912 Typographed. Perf. 13½

71	A5	1c car rose	30	15
72	A5	2c lilac	30	15
73	A5	5c dp grn	30	15
74	A5	10c red	30	15
75	A5	15c brn org	30	15
76	A5	20c brown	30	15
77	A5	25c dl bl	30	15
78	A5	30c dk vio	30	15
79	A5	40c bl grn	30	15
80	A5	50c lake	30	15
81	A5	1p red	2.25	60
82	A5	4p claret	5.00	2.50
83	A5	10p dk brn	7.00	3.00
		Nos. 71-83 (13)	17.25	7.60

Control Numbers on Back in Blue

1914 Perf. 13.

84	A6	1c ol blk	30	15
85	A6	2c maroon	30	15
86	A6	5c dp grn	30	15
87	A6	10c org red	30	15
88	A6	15c org red	30	15
89	A6	20c dp cl	30	15
90	A6	25c dk bl	30	15
91	A6	30c bl grn	30	15
92	A6	40c brn org	30	15
93	A6	50c dk brn	30	15
94	A6	1p dl lil	2.25	2.00
95	A6	4p car rose	5.50	2.00
96	A6	10p dl vio	7.00	4.75
		Nos. 84-96 (13)	17.75	10.25

RIO DE ORO—RIO MUNI

1917
Nos. 71–83 Overprinted in Black

1917			Perf. 13½	
97	A5	1c car rose	8.00	75
98	A5	2c lilac	8.00	75
99	A5	5c dp grn	2.50	75
100	A5	10c red	2.50	75
101	A5	15c org brn	2.50	75
102	A5	20c brown	2.50	75
103	A5	25c dl bl	2.50	75
104	A5	30c dk vio	2.50	75
105	A5	40c bl grn	2.50	75
106	A5	50c lake	2.50	75
107	A5	1p red	11.00	3.00
108	A5	4p claret	15.00	3.75
109	A5	10p dk brn	25.00	5.75
	Nos. 97-109 (13)		87.00	20.00

Nos. 97–109 exist with overprint inverted or double (price 50 percent over normal) and in dark blue (price twice normal).

King Alfonso XIII
A7
Control Numbers on Back in Blue

1919	Typo.		Perf. 13	
114	A7	1c brown	80	50
115	A7	2c claret	80	50
116	A7	5c lt grn	80	50
117	A7	10c carmine	80	50
118	A7	15c orange	80	50
119	A7	20c orange	80	50
120	A7	25c blue	80	50
121	A7	30c green	80	50
122	A7	40c vermilion	80	50
123	A7	50c brown	80	50
124	A7	1p lilac	5.25	3.00
125	A7	4p rose	8.50	5.00
126	A7	10p violet	13.00	7.25
	Nos. 114-126 (13)		34.75	20.25

A8 **A9**
Control Numbers on Back in Blue

1920			Perf. 13	
127	A8	1c gray lil	80	50
128	A8	2c rose	80	50
129	A8	5c lt red	80	50
130	A8	10c lilac	80	50
131	A8	15c lt brn	80	50
132	A8	20c grnsh bl	80	50
133	A8	25c yellow	80	50
134	A8	30c dl bl	4.50	3.25
135	A8	40c orange	2.75	1.25
136	A8	50c dl rose	2.75	1.25
137	A8	1p gray grn	2.75	1.25
138	A8	4p lil rose	5.25	3.00
139	A8	10p brown	12.00	7.00
	Nos. 127-139 (13)		35.60	20.50

Control Numbers on Back in Blue

1922				
140	A9	1c yellow	80	50
141	A9	2c red brn	80	50
142	A9	5c bl grn	80	50
143	A9	10c pale red	80	50
144	A9	15c myr grn	80	50
145	A9	20c turq bl	80	50
146	A9	25c dp bl	80	50
147	A9	30c dp rose	1.50	1.25
148	A9	40c violet	1.50	1.25
149	A9	50c orange	1.50	1.25
150	A9	1p red	4.50	2.00
151	A9	4p claret	8.00	4.25
152	A9	10p dk brn	12.50	7.50
	Nos. 140-152 (13)		35.10	21.00

For subsequent issues see Spanish Sahara.

RIO MUNI

LOCATION—West Africa, bordering on Cameroun and Gabon Republics.
GOVT.—Province of Spain
AREA—9,500 sq. mi.
POP.—183,377 (1960).
CAPITAL—Bata.

Rio Muni and the island of Fernando Po are the two provinces that constitute Spanish Guinea. Separate stamp issues for the two provinces were decreed in 1960. Spanish Guinea Nos. 1–84 were used only in the territory now called Rio Muni.

Rio Muni united with Fernando Po on Oct. 12, 1968, to form the Republic of Equatorial Guinea.

100 Centimos = 1 Peseta

Boy Reading and Missionary **Quina Plant**
A1 **A2**
Photogravure

1960	Perf. 13x12½		Unwmkd.	
1	A1	25c dl vio bl	6	6
2	A1	50c ol brn	6	6
3	A1	75c dl grysh pur	6	6
4	A1	1p org ver	6	6
5	A1	1.50p brt bl grn	6	6
6	A1	2p red lil	20	6
7	A1	3p sapphire	45	6
8	A1	5p red brn	1.25	8
9	A1	10p lt ol grn	2.25	25
	Nos. 1-9 (9)		4.45	75

1960 Perf. 13x12½
Design: 80c, Croton plant.

| 10 | A2 | 35c sl grn | 5 | 5 |
| 11 | A2 | 80c Prus grn | 10 | 5 |

See Nos. B1-B2.

Map of Rio Muni—A3
Designs: 50c, 1p, Gen. Franco. 70c, Government Palace.

1961, Oct. 1 Perf. 12½x13

12	A3	25c gray vio	6	5
13	A3	50c ol brn	6	5
14	A3	70c brt grn	6	5
15	A3	1p red org	15	5

25th anniversary of the nomination of Gen. Francisco Franco as Chief of State.

Rio Muni Headdress
A4

Design: 50c, Rio Muni idol.
1962, July 10 Perf. 13x12½

16	A4	25c violet	6	5
17	A4	50c green	8	5
18	A4	1p org brn	15	5

Issued for child welfare.

Cape Buffalo—A5
Design: 35c, Gorilla (vert.).
Perf. 13x12½, 12½x13

1962, Nov. 23 Photo. Unwmkd.

19	A5	15c dk ol grn	6	5
20	A5	35c magenta	6	5
21	A5	1p brn org	20	5

Issued for Stamp Day.

Mother and Child **Father Joaquin Juanola**
A6 **A7**

1963, Jan. 29 Perf. 13x12½

| 22 | A6 | 50c green | 10 | 5 |
| 23 | A6 | 1p brn org | 10 | 5 |

Issued to help the victims of the Seville flood.

1963, July 6 Perf. 13x12½
Design: 50c, Blessing hand, cross and palms.

24	A7	25c dl vio	5	5
25	A7	50c brn ol	5	5
26	A7	1p org red	15	5

Issued for child welfare.

Praying Child and Arms **Branch of Copal Tree**
A8 **A9**

1963, July 12

| 27 | A8 | 50c dl grn | 10 | 5 |
| 28 | A8 | 1p redsh brn | 10 | 5 |

Issued for Barcelona flood relief.

Perf. 13x12½, 12½x13
1964, Mar. 6 Photogravure
Design: 50c, Flowering quina (horiz.).

29	A9	25c brt vio	5	5
30	A9	50c bl grn	5	5
31	A9	1p dk car rose	15	5

Issued for Stamp Day 1963.

Tree Pangolin—A10

Design: 50c, Chameleon.
1964, June 1 Perf. 13x12½

32	A10	25c vio blk	5	5
33	A10	50c ol gray	6	5
34	A10	1p fawn	15	5

Issued for child welfare.

Dwarf Crocodile—A11
1964, July 1
Designs: 15c, 70c, 3p, Dwarf crocodile. 25c, 1p, 5p, Leopard. 50c, 1.50p, 10p, Black rhinoceros.

35	A11	15c lt brn	5	5
36	A11	25c violet	5	5
37	A11	50c olive	5	5
38	A11	70c green	10	5
39	A11	1p brn car	50	5
40	A11	1.50p bl grn	50	5
41	A11	3p dk bl	75	6
42	A11	5p brown	2.25	60
43	A11	10p green	6.50	1.25
	Nos. 35-43 (9)		10.75	2.21

Greshoff's Tree Frog—A12
Design: 1p, Helmet guinea fowl (vert.).
Perf. 13x12½, 12½x13
1964, Nov. 23 Photo. Unwmkd.

44	A12	50c green	5	5
45	A12	1p dp cl	6	5
46	A12	1.50p bl grn	15	6

Issued for Stamp Day, 1964.

Woman's Head **Woman Chemist**
A13 **A14**
Design: 1.50p, Logger.

1964 Photogravure Perf. 13x12½

47	A13	50c dp grn	6	5
48	A14	1p red org	6	5
49	A14	1.50p bl grn	15	6

Issued to commemorate 25 years of peace.

Goliath Beetle—A15
Beetle: 1p, Acridoxena hewaniana.
1965, June 1 Photo. Perf. 12½x13

50	A15	50c Prus grn	5	5
51	A15	1p sepia	6	5
52	A15	1.50p black	15	6

Issued for child welfare.

RIO MUNI—ROMANIA

Ring-necked Pheasant
A16

Leopard and Arms of Rio Muni
A17

Perf. 13x12½, 12½x13

		1965, Nov. 23	Photogravure		
53	A16	50c grnsh gray		6	5
54	A17	1p sepia		45	6
55	A16	2.50p lilac		2.00	50

Issued for Stamp Day, 1965.

Elephant and Parrot
A18

Design: 1.50p, Lion and boy.

Perf. 12½x13

		1966, June 1	Photo.	Unwmkd.	
56	A18	50c olive		6	5
57	A18	1p dk pur		6	5
58	A18	1.50p brt Prus bl		15	6

Issued for child welfare.

Water Chevrotain
A19

Designs: 40c, 4p, Tree pangolin (vert.).

		1966, Nov. 23	Photo.	Perf. 13	
59	A19	10c brn & yel brn		5	5
60	A19	40c brn & yel		5	5
61	A19	1.50p bl & rose lil		6	6
62	A19	4p dk bl & emer		25	15

Issued for Stamp Day, 1966.

A20

Designs: 40c, 4p, Vine creeper.

		1967, June 1	Photo.	Perf. 13	
63	A20	10c grn & yel		5	5
64	A20	40c blk, rose car & grn		5	5
65	A20	1.50p bl & org		6	6
66	A20	4p blk & grn		25	15

Issued for child welfare.

Potto
A21

Designs: 1p, River hog (horiz.). 3.50p, African golden cat (horiz.).

		1967, Nov. 23	Photo.	Perf. 13	
67	A21	1p blk & red brn		6	6
68	A21	1.50p brn & grn		6	6
69	A21	3.50p org brn & grn		30	20

Issued for Stamp Day 1967.

Zodiac Issue

Cancer
A22

Signs of the Zodiac: 1.50p, Taurus. 2.50p, Gemini.

		1968, Apr. 25	Photo.	Perf. 13	
70	A22	1p brt mag, lt yel		6	6
71	A22	1.50p brn, pink		6	6
72	A22	2.50p dk vio, yel		25	15

Issued for child welfare.

SEMI-POSTAL STAMPS
Type of Regular Issue, 1960

Designs: 10c+5c, Croton plant. 15c+5c, Flower and leaves of croton.

Photogravure

		1960	Perf. 13x12½	Unwmkd.	
B1	A2	10c +5c mar		6	6
B2	A2	15c +5c bis brn		6	6

The surtax was for child welfare.

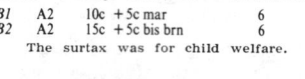
Bishop Juan de Ribera
SP1

Design: 20c+5c, The clown Pablo de Valladolid by Velazquez. 30c+10c, Juan de Ribera statue.

		1961	Perf. 13x12½		
B3	SP1	10c +5c rose brn		6	6
B4	SP1	20c +5c dk sl grn		6	6
B5	SP1	30c +10c ol brn		6	6
B6	SP1	50c +20c brn		12	6

Issued for Stamp Day, 1960.

Mandrill—SP2

Design: 25c+10c, Elephant (vert.).

		Perf. 12½x13, 13x12½			
		1961, June 21		Unwmkd.	
B7	SP2	10c + 5c rose brn		6	6
B8	SP2	25c +10c gray vio		6	6
B9	SP2	80c +20c dk grn		15	6

The surtax was for child welfare.

Statuette
SP3

Design: 25c+10c, 1p+10c, Male figure.

		1961, Nov. 23		Perf. 13x12½	
B10	SP3	10c + 5c rose brn		6	6
B11	SP3	25c +10c dk pur		6	6
B12	SP3	30c +10c ol blk		6	6
B13	SP3	1p +10c red org		12	6

Issued for Stamp Day 1961.

ROMAGNA

See Italian States group preceding Italy in Vol. III.

ROMANIA

(rū-ˈmā-nē-ə, rō-ˈma-nyə)

Rumania, Roumania

LOCATION—In southeastern Europe bordering on the Black Sea.
GOVT.—Republic.
AREA—91,584 sq. mi.
POP.—21,530,000 (1977).
CAPITAL—Bucharest.

Romania was formed in 1859 from a union of the principalities of Moldavia and Walachia. It became a kingdom in 1881. Following World War I the original territory was considerably enlarged by the addition of Bessarabia, Bukovina, Transylvania, Crisana, Maramures and Banat. The republic was established in 1948.

40 Parale = 1 Piastre
100 Bani = 1 Leu (plural "Lei") (1868)

Prices of early Romanian stamps vary according to condition. Quotations for Nos. 1–14 are for fine copies. Very fine to superb specimens sell at much higher prices, and inferior or poor copies sell at reduced prices, depending on the condition of the individual specimen.

Moldavia.

Coat of Arms
A1   A2

Handstamped.

		1858, July	Imperf.	Unwmkd.	
		Laid Paper.			
1	A1	27pa rose		25,000.	6,500.
a.		Tête bêche pair			
2	A1	54pa bl, grn		5,500.	2,600.
3	A1	108pa bl, rose		18,500.	6,000.
		Wove Paper.			
4	A1	81pa bl, bl		27,500.	27,500.

Cut to shape or octagonally, Nos. 1–4 sell for one-fourth to one-third of these prices.

		1858	**Bluish Wove Paper.**		
5	A2	5pa black		15,000.	5,500.
6	A2	40pa blue		175.00	125.00
a.		Tête bêche pair		850.00	2,250.
7	A2	80pa red		9,000.	650.00
a.		Tête bêche pair			

		1859	**White Wove Paper.**		
8	A2	5pa black		10,500.	5,500.
a.		Tête bêche pair			
b.		Frame broken at bottom		110.00	
c.		As "b", tête bêche pair		450.00	
9	A2	40pa blue		110.00	80.00
a.		Tête bêche pair		450.00	1,350.
10	A2	80pa red		375.00	160.00
b.		Tête bêche pair		1,300.	4,000.

No. 8b has a break in the frame at bottom below "A". It was never placed in use.

Moldavia-Walachia.

Coat of Arms
A3

Printed by Hand from Single Dies

		1862	**White Laid Paper**		
11	A3	3pa orange		275.00	3,000.
a.		3pa yel		275.00	3,000.
b.		Tête bêche pair			
12	A3	6pa carmine		275.00	300.00
		Tête bêche pair			
13	A3	6pa red		275.00	300.00
14	A3	30pa blue		75.00	100.00
a.		Tête bêche pair		200.00	

		White Wove Paper.			
15	A3	3pa org yel		50.00	225.00
a.		3pa lem		100.00	225.00
b.		Tête bêche pair		200.00	1,500.
16	A3	6pa carmine		40.00	150.00
		Tête bêche pair		160.00	
17	A3	6pa vermilion		30.00	90.00
		Tête bêche pair		120.00	
18	A3	30pa blue		45.00	27.50
a.		Tête bêche pair		175.00	

Nos. 11 to 18 inclusive were printed with a hand press, one at a time, from single dies. The impressions were very irregularly placed and occasionally overlapped. Sheets contained thirty-two stamps in four rows of eight. The third and fourth rows were printed inverted, thus making the second and third rows tête bêche, foot to foot. All values come in distinct shades, frequently even on the same sheet. The paper of this and the following issues through No. 52 often shows a bluish, grayish or yellowish tint.

Typographed from Plates.

		1864	**White Wove Paper.**		
19	A3	3pa yellow		35.00	1,750.
a.		Tête bêche pair		160.00	
b.		Pair, one sideways		100.00	
20	A3	6pa dp rose		4.00	
a.		Tête bêche pair		22.50	
b.		Pair, one sideways		11.00	
21	A3	30pa dp bl		5.00	50.00
a.		Tête bêche pair		25.00	
b.		Pair, one sideways		12.50	
c.		Bluish wove paper		125.00	

Stamps of 1862 and 1864 issues can usually be distinguished by colors. In the 1862 issue the 3pa and 6pa are often blurred and appear greasy; the 30pa is usually clearly printed. The 30pa of 1864 usually has a large dot at left of eagle's crown.

Plates for the 1864 issue contained 40 clichés in 5 rows of 8. The first and second rows were inverted. Clichés in the third row were placed sideways, 4 with head to right and 4 with head to left, making one tête bêche pair. The fourth and fifth rows were normally placed.

No. 20 was never placed in use. All values exist in shades, light to dark.

Counterfeit cancellations exist on Nos. 11–21.

ROMANIA

Three stamps in this design—2pa, 5pa, 20pa—were printed on white wove paper in 1864, but never placed in use. Price, set $10.

Romania.

Prince Alexandru Ioan Cuza
A4

TWENTY PARALES.
Type I. The central oval does not touch the inner frame. The "I" of "DECI" extends above and below the other letters.
Type II. The central oval touches the frame at the bottom. The "I" of the "DECI" is the same height as the other letters.

Lithographed.
1865, Jan.   Imperf.   Unwmkd.

22	A4	2pa orange	25.00	125.00
a.		2pa yel	35.00	150.00
b.		2pa ocher	125.00	275.00
23	A4	5pa blue	15.00	150.00
24	A4	20pa red, type I	6.00	9.00
a.		Bluish paper	200.00	
25	A4	20pa red, type II	6.00	9.00
a.		Bluish paper	200.00	

The 20pa types are found se-tenant.

White Laid Paper.

26	A4	2pa orange	30.00	100.00
a.		2pa ocher	75.00	
27	A4	5pa blue	60.00	375.00

Prince Carol—A5

Type I   Type II
A6   A7

TWENTY PARALES.
Type I. A6. The Greek border at the upper right goes from right to left.
Type II. A7. The Greek border at the upper right goes from left to right.

1866-67   Thin Wove Paper.

29	A5	2pa yellow	6.00	35.00
a.		Thick paper	40.00	275.00
30	A5	5pa dk bl	25.00	275.00
a.		5pa ind	100.00	750.00
b.		Thick paper	35.00	350.00
31	A6	20pa rose, type I	6.00	7.50
a.		Dot in Greek border, thin paper	525.00	175.00
b.		Thick paper	110.00	65.00
c.		Dot in Greek border, thick paper	150.00	100.00
32	A7	20pa rose, type II	6.00	7.50
a.		Thick paper	110.00	65.00

The 20pa types are found se-tenant.
Faked cancellations are known on Nos. 22-27, 29-32.
The white dot of Nos. 31a and 31c occurs in extreme upper right border.
Thick paper was used in 1866, thin in 1867.

Prince Carol
A8   A9

1868-70

33	A8	2b orange	17.50	12.00
a.		2b yel	35.00	50.00
34	A8	3b vio ('70)	20.00	20.00
35	A8	4b dk bl	55.00	27.50
36	A8	18b scarlet	225.00	9.00
a.		18b rose	225.00	9.00

1869

37	A9	5b org yel	50.00	25.00
a.		5b dp org	60.00	25.00
38	A9	10b blue	20.00	12.00
a.		10b ultra	60.00	25.00
b.		10b ind	75.00	35.00
40	A9	15b vermilion	50.00	17.50
41	A9	25b org & bl	32.50	15.00
42	A9	50b bl & red	190.00	20.00
a.		50b ind & red	210.00	22.50

No. 40 on laid paper was not issued. All copies have a pale blue circular cancellation. Price $1,750.

Prince Carol
A10   A11

1871-72   Imperf.

43	A10	5b rose	32.50	12.00
a.		5b ver	35.00	15.00
44	A10	10b org yel	50.00	20.00
a.		Laid paper	400.00	400.00
45	A10	10b blue	140.00	35.00
46	A10	15b red	150.00	100.00
47	A10	50b ol brn	27.50	25.00

1872

48	A10	10b ultra	20.00	27.50
a.		Laid paper	100.00	150.00
b.		10b grnsh bl	140.00	175.00
49	A10	50b ind & red	210.00	300.00

No. 48 is a provisional issue printed from a new plate in which the head is placed further right.
Faked cancellations are found on No. 49.

1872   Wove Paper.   Perf. 12½.

50	A10	5b rose	37.50	20.00
a.		5b ver	1,300.	700.00
51	A10	10b blue	50.00	17.50
a.		10b ultra	65.00	22.50
52	A10	25b dk brn	20.00	20.00

No. 43a with faked perforation is frequently offered as No. 50a.

Tinted Paper.
Paris Print, Fine Impression.
1872   Typo.   Perf. 14x13½

53	A11	1½b brnz grn, bluish	4.00	50
54	A11	3b grn, bluish	12.50	1.00
55	A11	5b bis, pale buff	7.50	75
56	A11	10b blue	8.00	75
57	A11	15b red brn, pale buff	80.00	5.00
58	A11	25b org, pale buff	80.00	6.50
59	A11	50b rose, pale rose	100.00	10.00

Nos. 53-59 exist imperf.

Bucharest Print, Rough Impression
Perf. 11, 11½, 13½, and Compound.
1876-79

60	A11	1½b brnz grn, bluish	6.00	50
61	A11	5b bis, yelsh	17.50	60
b.		Printed on both sides		125.00
62	A11	10b bl, yelsh ('77)	17.50	75
a.		10b pale bl, yelsh	17.50	75
b.		10b dk bl, yelsh	25.00	
d.		Cliché of 5b in plate of 10b ('79)	275.00	125.00
63	A11	10b ultra ('77)	30.00	1.00
64	A11	15b red brn, yelsh	45.00	1.25
65	A11	30b org red, yelsh ('78)	150.00	9.00
a.		Printed on both sides		350.00

No. 62d has been reprinted in dark blue. The originals are in dull blue. Price of reprint, $30.

Perf. 11, 11½, 13½ and Compound.
1879

66	A11	1½b blk, yelsh	2.50	20
b.		Imperf.	20.00	
67	A11	3b ol grn, bluish	8.50	85
c.		Diagonal half used as 1½b on cover		
68	A11	5b grn, bluish	3.00	25
69	A11	10b rose, yelsh	10.00	30
b.		Cliché of 5b in plate of 10b	150.00	900.00
70	A11	15b rose red, yelsh	45.00	5.00
71	A11	25b bl, yelsh	35.00	4.00
72	A11	50b bis, yelsh	70.00	4.00

There are two varieties of the numerals on the 15b and 50b.

No. 69b has been reprinted in dark rose. Originals are in pale rose. Price of reprint, $30.

King Carol I
A12   A13

1880   White Paper.

73	A12	15b brown	10.00	50
74	A12	25b blue	17.50	75
a.		Imperf., pair	100.00	

1885-89   Perf. 13½, 11½ & Compound.

75	A13	1½b black	1.75	35
a.		Printed on both sides		
76	A13	3b violet	5.00	50
c.		Half used as 1½b on cover		
77	A13	5b green	45.00	5.00
78	A13	15b red brn	10.00	75
79	A13	25b blue	10.00	75

Tinted Paper.

80	A13	1½b blk, bluish	3.50	60
81	A13	3b vio, bluish	4.00	90
82	A13	3b ol grn, bluish	3.50	50
83	A13	5b bl grn, bluish	4.00	50
84	A13	10b rose, pale buff	5.00	50
85	A13	15b red brn, pale buff	17.50	50
86	A13	25b bl, pale buff	17.50	1.25
87	A13	50b bis, pale buff	60.00	5.00

Wmk. 163
This is not a true watermark, having been impressed after the paper was manufactured.

Thin Pale Yellowish Paper.
1889   Wmkd. Coat of Arms. (163)

88	A13	1½b black	25.00	2.00
89	A13	3b violet	20.00	2.00
90	A13	5b green	20.00	2.25
91	A13	10b rose	20.00	2.00
92	A13	15b red brn	60.00	4.00
93	A13	25b dk bl	35.00	3.50

King Carol I
A14   A15

Perf. 13½, 11½ & Compound
1890

94	A14	1½b maroon	3.50	50
95	A14	3b violet	25.00	1.00
96	A14	5b emerald	7.50	75
97	A14	10b red	8.00	1.25
a.		10b rose	17.50	3.00
98	A14	15b dk brn	20.00	1.50
99	A14	25b gray bl	15.00	1.50
100	A14	50b orange	65.00	12.50

1891   Unwmkd.

101	A14	1½b lil rose	1.25	25
b.		Printed on both sides		60.00
102	A14	3b lilac	1.50	25
a.		3b vio	2.00	35
b.		Printed on both sides		
c.		Impressions of 5b on back	100.00	100.00
103	A14	5b emerald	2.00	40
104	A14	5b pale red	8.50	50
		Printed on both sides	125.00	110.00
105	A14	15b gray brn	9.50	30
106	A14	25b gray bl	6.00	50
107	A14	50b orange	65.00	4.00

Nos. 101-107 exist imperf.

1891

108	A15	1½b claret	1.25	80
109	A15	3b lilac	1.50	80
110	A15	5b emerald	3.50	3.00
111	A15	10b red	4.00	3.00
112	A15	15b gray brn	1.25	1.00

Stamps of type A15 were issued in commemoration of the 25th year of the reign of King Carol I.

Wmk. 164

1894   Wmkd. P R (164)

113	A14	3b lilac	8.50	1.50
114	A14	5b pale grn	6.50	1.50
115	A14	25b gray bl	10.00	3.00
116	A14	50b orange	20.00	8.00

King Carol I
A17   A18

A19   A20

ROMANIA

A21   A23

Wmk. 200

1893-98 Wmkd. P R (164 & 200)

117	A17	1b pale brn	75	8
118	A17	1½b black	60	10
119	A18	3b chocolate	75	6
120	A19	5b blue	90	6
a.		Cliché of the 25b in the plate of 5b	70.00	100.00
121	A19	5b yel grn ('98)	3.50	8
a.		5b emer	4.25	25
122	A20	10b emerald	2.50	6
123	A20	10b rose ('98)	4.25	25
124	A21	15b rose	2.25	6
125	A21	15b blk ('98)	4.50	35
126	A19	25b violet	2.50	8
127	A19	25b ind ('98)	7.00	35
128	A19	40b gray grn	12.50	30
129	A19	50b orange	11.00	35
130	A23	1 l bis & rose	12.50	75
131	A23	2 l org & brn	20.00	1.50
		Nos. 117-131 (15)	85.50	4.43

This watermark may be found in two sizes, 12 and 15mm. high. (Wmks. 164 and 200). The paper also varies in thickness.

A 3b orange of type A18; 10b brown, type A20; 15b rose, type A21, and 25b bright green with similar but different border, all watermarked "P R", were prepared but never issued.

Price, each $7.50.
See #132-157, 224-229.

King Carol I
A24

Thin Paper, Tinted Rose on Back.
Perf. 11½, 13½ and Compound
1900-03 Unwmkd.

132	A17	1b pale brn	50	10
133	A24	1b brn ('01)	75	10
134	A24	1b blk ('03)	75	10
135	A18	3b red brn	60	6
136	A19	5b emerald	90	6
137	A20	10b rose	90	6
a.		10b org (error)	40.00	40.00
138	A21	15b black	1.25	8
139	A21	15b lil gray ('01)	1.50	8
140	A21	15b dk vio ('03)	2.50	8
141	A19	25b blue	2.50	10
142	A19	40b gray grn	8.00	15
143	A19	50b orange	10.00	20
144	A23	1 l bis & rose ('01)	22.50	25
145	A23	1 l grn & blk ('03)	17.50	60
146	A23	2 l org & brn ('01)	22.50	1.25
147	A23	2 l red brn & blk ('03)	20.00	1.25
		Nos. 132-147 (16)	112.65	4.52

No. 132 inscribed BANI; Nos. 133-134 BAN.

Wmk. 167
(Reduced illustration.)
Wmkd. Coat of Arms Covering 25 Stamps. (167)

1900, July

148	A17	1b pale brn	3.50	2.00
149	A18	3b red brn	4.50	2.00
150	A19	5b emerald	8.00	2.25
151	A20	10b rose	7.00	2.00
152	A21	15b black	9.50	2.00
153	A19	25b blue	12.50	3.00
154	A19	40b gray grn	20.00	3.50
155	A19	50b orange	20.00	4.00
156	A23	1 l bis & rose	25.00	6.00
157	A23	2 l org & brn	25.00	6.00
		Nos. 148-157 (10)	135.00	32.75

Mail Coach Leaving P.O.—A25
Thin Paper, Tinted Rose on Face.
1903 Perf. 14 x 13½. Unwmkd.

158	A25	1b gray brn	1.50	75
159	A25	3b brn vio	2.75	1.00
160	A25	5b pale grn	4.00	1.75
161	A25	10b rose	3.00	1.75
162	A25	15b black	3.00	1.50
163	A25	25b blue	12.50	7.00
164	A25	40b dl grn	15.00	8.00
165	A25	50b orange	20.00	10.00
		Nos. 158-165 (8)	61.75	31.75

Counterfeits are plentiful.
See note after No. 172.
See also No. 428.

King Carol I and Façade of New Post Office
A26

Thick Toned Paper.
1903 Engraved Perf. 13½x14

166	A26	15b black	3.00	2.50
167	A26	25b blue	7.50	3.75
168	A26	40b gray grn	8.00	5.00
169	A26	50b orange	8.00	5.00
170	A26	1 l dk brn	9.00	5.00
171	A26	2 l dl red	52.50	20.00
a.		2 l org (error)	75.00	32.50
172	A26	5 l dl vio	75.00	40.00
		Nos. 166-172 (7)	163.00	81.25

Nos. 158 to 172 were issued to commemorate the opening of the new Post Office in Bucharest.
Counterfeits exist.

Prince Carol Taking Oath of Allegiance, 1866
A27

Prince in Royal Carriage
A28

Prince Carol at Calafat in 1877
A29

Prince Carol Shaking Hands with His Captive, Osman Pasha
A30

Carol I as Prince in 1866 and King in 1906
A31

Romanian Army Crossing Danube—A32

Romanian Troops Return to Bucharest in 1878
A33

Prince Carol at Head of His Command in 1877
A34

King Carol I at the Cathedral in 1896
A35

King Carol I at Shrine of St. Nicholas, 1904
A36

1906 Engraved. Perf. 12.

176	A27	1b bis & blk	25	20
177	A28	3b red brn & blk	35	25
178	A29	5b dp grn & blk	75	25
179	A30	10b car & blk	30	20
180	A31	15b dl vio & blk	25	20
181	A32	25b ultra & blk	3.00	1.00
a.		25b ol grn & blk	3.00	1.00
182	A33	40b dk brn & blk	75	50
183	A34	50b bis brn & blk	90	50
184	A35	1 l ver & blk	1.00	75
185	A36	2 l org & blk	1.00	90
		Nos. 176-185 (10)	8.55	4.75

Commemorating the 40 years' rule of Carol I as Prince and King.
No. 181a was never placed in use. Cancellations were by favor.

King Carol I
A37

1906

186	A37	1b bis & blk	25	15
187	A37	3b red brn & blk	80	30
188	A37	5b dp grn & blk	30	15
189	A37	10b car & blk	30	15
190	A37	15b dl vio & blk	65	25
191	A37	25b ultra & blk	7.50	3.75
a.		Head inverted		
192	A37	40b dk brn & blk	85	40
193	A37	50b bis brn & blk	85	40
194	A37	1 l red & blk	1.00	40
195	A37	2 l org & blk	1.00	40
		Nos. 186-195 (10)	13.50	6.35

25th anniversary of the Kingdom.

Plowman and Angel
A38

Exposition Building
A39

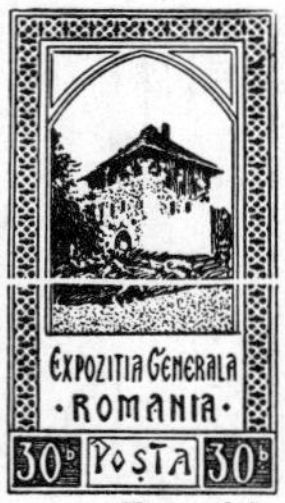
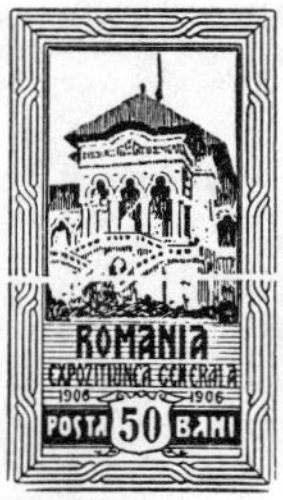

Exposition Buildings
A40 A41

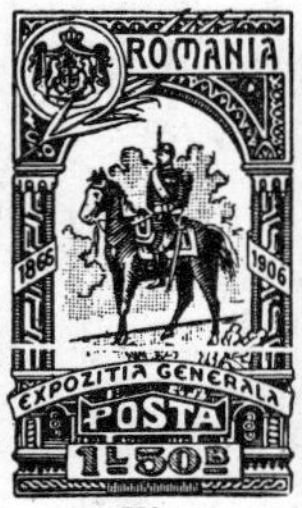
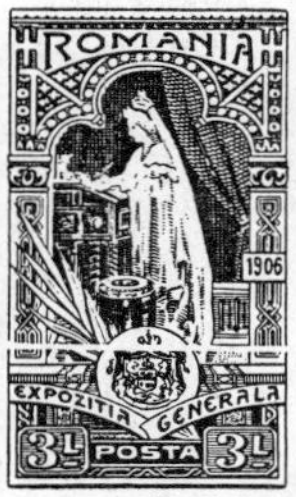

King Carol I — A42
Queen Elizabeth (Carmen Sylva) — A43

1906 Typo. *Perf. 11½, 13½*

196	A38	5b yel grn & blk	2.50	60
197	A38	10b car & blk	2.50	60
198	A39	15b vio & blk	3.50	1.00
199	A39	25b bl & blk	3.50	1.00
200	A40	30b red & blk brn	4.25	1.00
201	A40	40b grn & blk brn	4.25	1.25
202	A41	50b org & blk	4.25	1.75
203	A41	75b lt brn & dk brn	4.25	2.00
204	A42	1.50 l red lil & blk brn	20.00	11.00
a.		Center inverted		
205	A42	2.50 l yel & brn	20.00	11.00
a.		Center inverted		
206	A43	3 l brn org & brn	20.00	11.00
		Nos. 196-206 (11)	89.00	42.20

Nos. 196 to 206 were issued to publicize the General Exposition. They were sold at post offices July 29-31, 1906, and were valid only for those three days. Those sold at the exposition are overprinted "S E" in black. Remainders were sold privately, both unused and cancelled to order, by the Exposition promoters.

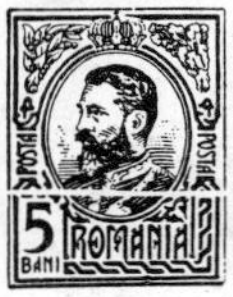
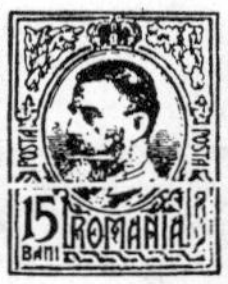
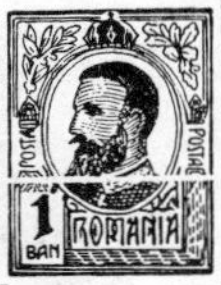

King Carol I
A44 A45 A46

Perf. 11½, 13½ & Compound

1908-18 Engraved.

207	A44	5b pale yel grn	1.50	30
208	A44	10b carmine	1.25	10
209	A45	15b purple	12.50	1.75
210	A44	25b dp bl	1.25	10
211	A44	40b brt grn	75	10
212	A44	40b dk brn ('18)	3.00	1.00
213	A44	50b orange	60	10
214	A44	50b lt red ('18)	1.25	50
215	A44	1 l brown	1.25	25
216	A44	2 l red	5.50	2.00
		Nos. 207-216 (10)	28.85	6.20

Perf. 13½x14, 11½, 13½ & Compound

1909-18 Typographed

217	A46	1b black	12	5
218	A46	3b red brn	20	5
219	A46	5b yel grn	12	5
220	A46	10b rose	20	5
221	A46	15b dl vio	15.00	9.00
222	A46	15b ol grn	25	10
223	A46	15b red brn ('18)	45	30
		Nos. 217-223 (7)	16.34	9.60

Nos. 217–219, 222 exist imperf.
No. 219 in black is a chemical changeling.

Types of 1893–99.

1911–19 White Paper. Unwmkd.

224	A17	1½b straw	75	50
225	A19	25b dp bl ('18)	50	10
226	A19	40b gray brn ('19)	1.00	50
227	A19	50b dl red ('19)	60	30
228	A23	1 l gray grn ('18)	1.25	35
229	A23	2 l org ('18)	1.50	35
		Nos. 224-229 (6)	5.60	2.10

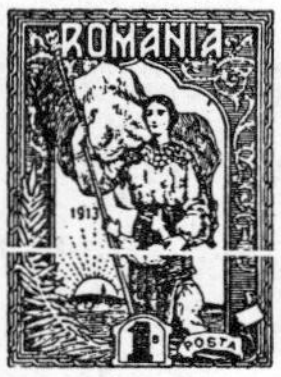
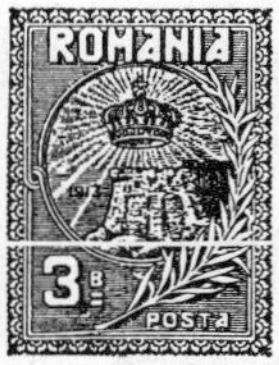

Romania Holding Flag — A47
Romanian Crown and Old Fort on Danube — A48

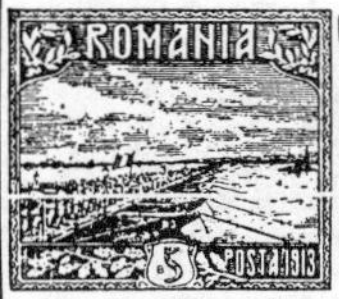
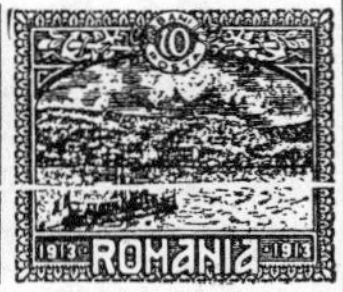

Troops Crossing Danube — A49
View of Turtucaia — A50

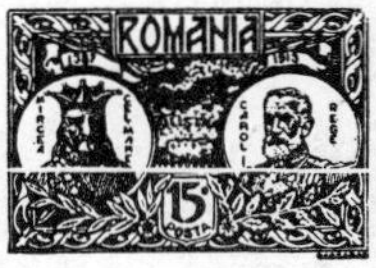

Mircea the Great and Carol I — A51

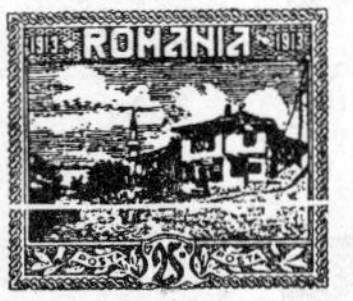

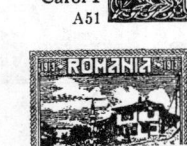

View of Silistra — A52

Perf. 11½x13½, 13½x11½

1913, Dec. 25

230	A47	1b black	30	25
231	A48	3b ol gray & choc	75	50
232	A49	5b yel grn & blk brn	40	25
233	A50	10b org & gray	40	25
234	A51	15b bis & vio	65	30
235	A52	25b bl & choc	1.10	65
236	A49	40b bis & red vio	2.00	1.25
237	A48	50b yel & bl	4.00	2.25
238	A48	1 l bl & ol bis	12.50	6.00
239	A48	2 l org red & rose	15.00	10.00
		Nos. 230-239 (10)	37.10	21.70

Romania's annexation of Silistra.

No. 217 Handstamped in Red

25
BANI

Perf. 13½x14, 11½, 13½ & Compound

1918, May 1

240	A46	25b on 1b blk	40	25

This handstamp is found inverted.

No. 219 and 220 Overprinted in Black

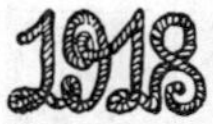

1918

241	A46	5b yel grn	50	25
a.		Invtd. overprint	7.50	4.00
b.		Double overprint	7.50	
242	A46	10b rose	50	25
a.		Invtd. overprint	7.50	4.00
b.		Double overprint	7.50	

Nos. 217, 219 and 220 Overprinted in Red or Black

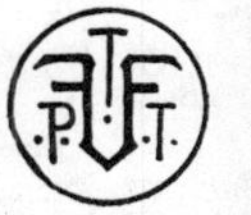

1919, Nov. 8

245	A46	1b blk (R)	25	15
a.		Inverted overprint	2.50	
b.		Double overprint	5.00	3.00
246	A46	5b yel grn (Bk)	25	15
a.		Double overprint	5.00	4.00
b.		Inverted overprint	2.50	2.50
247	A46	10b rose (Bk)	25	15
a.		Inverted overprint	2.50	2.50
b.		Double overprint	5.00	3.50

Commemorating the recovery of Transylvania and the return of the King to Bucharest.

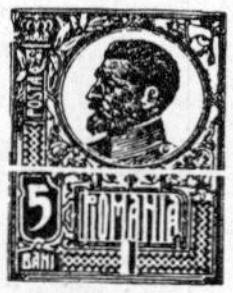

King Ferdinand — A53

1920–22 Typographed

248	A53	1b black	20	10
249	A53	5b yel grn	20	6
250	A53	10b rose	20	6
251	A53	15b red brn	60	15
252	A53	25b dp bl	1.25	18
253	A53	25b brown	60	10
254	A53	40b gray brn	1.00	15
255	A53	50b salmon	25	6
256	A53	1 l gray grn	1.00	8
257	A53	1 l rose	60	25
258	A53	2 l orange	1.00	25
259	A53	2 l dp bl	1.00	25
260	A53	2 l rose ('22)	2.50	1.50
		Nos. 248-260 (13)	10.40	3.19

Nos. 248–260 are printed on two papers: coarse, grayish paper with bits of colored fiber, and thinner white paper of better quality.
Nos. 248–251, 253 exist imperf.

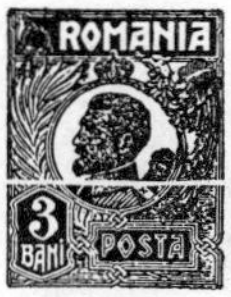

King Ferdinand — A54

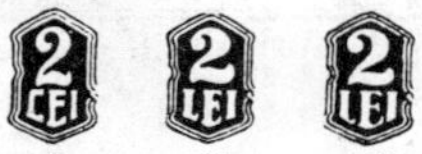

I II III

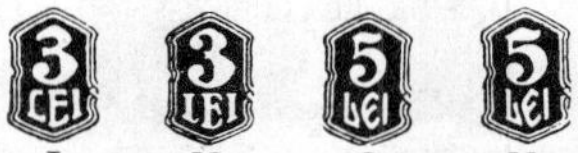

I II I II

TWO LEI.
Type I. The "2" is thin, with tail 2½mm. wide. Top of "2" forms a hook.
Type II. The "2" is thick, with tail 3mm. wide. Top of "2" forms a ball.
Type III. The "2" is similar to type II. The "E" of "LEI" is larger and about 2mm. wide.

THREE LEI.
Type I. Top of "3" begins in a point. Top and middle bars of "E" of "LEI" are without serifs.
Type II. Top of "3" begins in a ball. Top and middle bars of "E" of "LEI" have serifs.

FIVE LEI.
Type I. The "5" is 2½mm. wide. The end of the final stroke of the "L" of "LEI" almost touches the vertical stroke.
Type II. The "5" is 3mm. wide and the lines are broader than in type I. The end of the final stroke of the "L" of "LEI" is separated from the vertical by a narrow space.

Perf. 13½x14, 11½, 13½ & Compound

1920-26

261	A54	3b black	20	10
262	A54	5b black	10	5
263	A54	10b yel grn ('25)	10	5
a.		10b ol grn ('25)	45	
264	A54	25b bis brn	20	10
265	A54	25b salmon	20	10
266	A54	30b violet	25	10
267	A54	50b orange	15	5
268	A54	60b gray grn	75	40
269	A54	1 l violet	25	5
270	A54	2 l rose (I)	1.00	25
a.		2 l cl (I)	17.50	
271	A54	2 l lt grn (II)	65	10
a.		2 l lt grn (I)	1.00	15
b.		2 l lt grn (III)	80	10
272	A54	3 l bl (I)	2.00	35
273	A54	3 l buff (II)	75	25
a.		3 l buff (I)	4.00	60
274	A54	3 l sal (II)	30	5
a.		3 l sal (I)	1.50	1.00
275	A54	3 l car rose (II)	60	8
276	A54	5 l emer (I)	1.50	25
277	A54	5 l lt brn (II)	60	8
a.		5 l lt brn (I)	1.50	30
278	A54	6 l blue	2.25	75
279	A54	6 l carmine	3.50	1.25
280	A54	6 l ol grn ('26)	2.25	50
281	A54	7½ l pale bl	1.75	30
282	A54	10 l dp bl	1.75	25
		Nos. 261-282 (22)	21.10	5.46

Nos. 273 and 273a, also 274 and 274a, are found se-tenant. The 50b exists in three types.

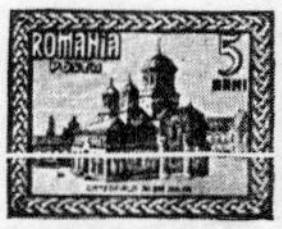
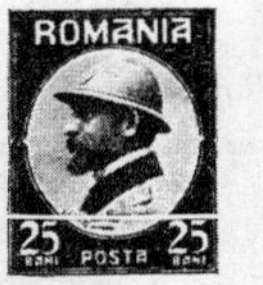

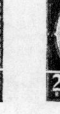

Alba Iulia Cathedral — A55
King Ferdinand — A56

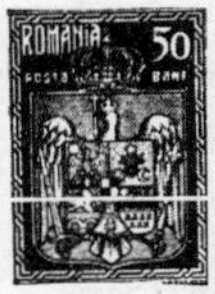
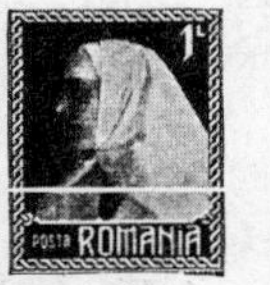

Coat of Arms — A57
Queen Marie as Nurse — A58

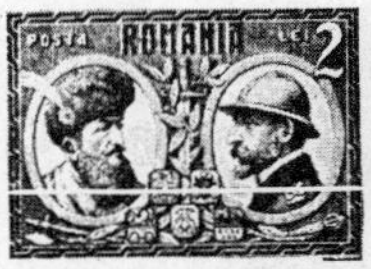
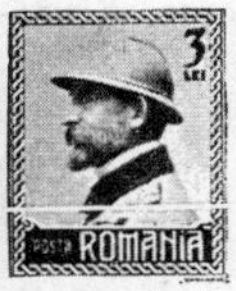

Michael the Brave and King Ferdinand — A59
King Ferdinand — A60

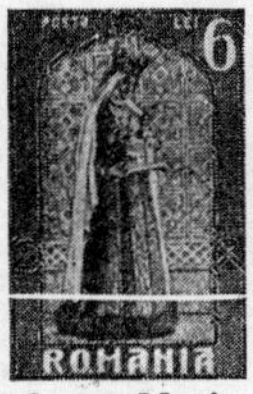
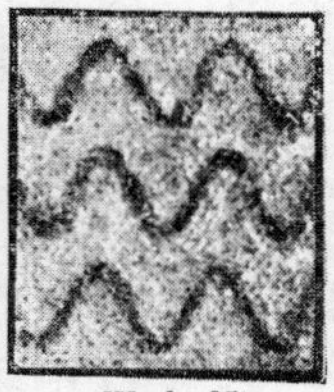

Queen Marie — A61
Wmk. 95

Perf. 13½x14, 13½, 11½ & Compound

Wmkd. Wavy Lines. (95)

1922, Oct. 15 Photogravure

283	A55	5b black	10	10
a.		Engraver's name omitted	3.50	2.00

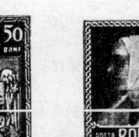

206 ROMANIA

284	A56	25b chocolate	25	20
285	A57	50b dp grn	20	10
286	A58	1 l ol grn	25	20
287	A59	2 l carmine	25	20
288	A60	3 l blue	1.75	75
289	A61	6 l violet	7.50	3.50
		Nos. 283-289 (7)	10.30	5.05

Issued in connection with the coronation of King Ferdinand I and Queen Marie on Oct. 15, 1922, at Alba Iulia. All values exist imperforate.

King Ferdinand
A62   A63

1926, July 1   Perf. 11   Unwmkd.

291	A62	10b yel grn	25	25
292	A62	25b orange	25	25
293	A62	50b org brn	25	25
294	A63	1 l dk vio	25	25
295	A63	2 l dk grn	25	25
296	A63	3 l brn car	25	25
297	A63	5 l blk brn	25	25
298	A63	6 l ol	25	25
a.		6 l brt bl (error)	100.00	100.00
300	A63	9 l slate	25	25
301	A63	10 l brt bl	25	25
b.		10 l brn car (error)	100.00	100.00
		Nos. 291-301 (10)	2.50	2.50

60th birthday of King Ferdinand. Exist imperf. Imperf. examples with watermark 95 are proofs.

King Carol I and King Ferdinand
A69

King Ferdinand—A70

A71

1927, Aug. 1   Perf. 13½

308	A69	25b brn vio	30	30
309	A70	30b gray blk	30	30
310	A71	50b dk grn	30	30
311	A69	1 l bluish sl	30	30
312	A70	2 l dp grn	35	35
313	A70	3 l violet	50	50
314	A71	4 l dk brn	60	60
315	A70	4.50 l hn brn	2.00	2.00
316	A70	5 l red brn	60	60
317	A71	6 l carmine	1.25	1.25
318	A69	7.50 l grnsh bl	90	90
319	A69	10 l brt bl	1.25	1.25
		Nos. 308-319 (12)	8.65	8.65

50th anniversary of Romania's independence from Turkish suzerainty. Some values exist imperf. All exist imperf. and with value numerals omitted.

King Michael
A72   A73

Perf. 13½x14 (25b, 50b); 13½

1928-29   Typo.   Unwmkd.

Size: 19 x 25mm.

320	A72	25b black	20	8
321	A72	30b fawn ('29)	35	8
322	A72	50b ol grn	20	8

Photogravure.

Size: 18½ x 24½ mm.

323	A73	1 l violet	25	8
324	A73	2 l dp grn	40	8
325	A73	3 l brt rose	75	8
326	A73	5 l red brn	1.00	8
327	A73	7.50 l ultra	5.50	40
328	A73	10 l blue	4.50	15
		Nos. 320-328 (9)	13.15	1.11

See also Nos. 343-345, 353-357.

Parliament House, Bessarabia
A74

Designs: 1 l, 2 l, Parliament House, Bessarabia. 3 l, 5 l, 20 l, Hotin Fortress. 7.50 l, 10 l, Fortress Cetatea Alba.

1928, Apr. 29   Perf. 13½   Wmk. 95

329	A74	1 l dp grn	75	35
330	A74	2 l dp brn	75	35
331	A74	3 l blk brn	75	35
332	A74	5 l car lake	95	50
333	A74	7.50 l ultra	1.00	75
334	A74	10 l Prus bl	2.50	1.50
335	A74	20 l blk vio	3.00	2.00
		Nos. 329-335 (7)	9.70	5.80

Issued in celebration of the tenth anniversary of the reunion of Bessarabia with Romania.

King Carol I and King Michael
A77

View of Constanta Harbor
A78

Trajan's Monument at Adam Clisi
A79

Cernavoda Bridge—A80

1928, Oct. 25

336	A77	1 l bl grn	80	40
337	A78	2 l red brn	80	40
338	A77	3 l gray blk	1.00	40
339	A79	5 l dl lil	1.25	60
340	A79	7.50 l ultra	1.50	60
341	A80	10 l blue	2.00	1.00
342	A80	20 l car rose	3.00	1.25
		Nos. 336-342 (7)	10.35	4.65

Issued in commemoration of the fiftieth anniversary of the union of Dobruja with Romania.

Michael Types of 1928-29

Perf. 13½x14

1928, Sept. 1   Typo.   Wmk. 95

| 343 | A72 | 25b black | 35 | 15 |

Photogravure.

| 344 | A73 | 7.50 l ultra | 1.75 | 75 |
| 345 | A73 | 10 l blue | 3.50 | 50 |

Ferdinand I; Stephen the Great; Michael the Brave; Corvin and Constantine Brancoveanu
A81

Union with Transylvania   Avram Jancu
A82   A83

Prince Michael   Castle
the Brave   Bran
A84   A85

King Ferdinand I
A86

1929, May 10   Photo.   Wmk. 95

347	A81	1 l dk vio	1.00	50
348	A82	2 l ol grn	1.00	50
349	A83	3 l vio brn	1.25	60
350	A84	4 l cerise	1.35	60
351	A85	5 l orange	2.25	1.10

| 352 | A86 | 10 l brt bl | 2.75 | 1.50 |
| | | Nos. 347-352 (6) | 9.60 | 4.80 |

Union of Transylvania and Romania.

Michael Type of 1928.

1930   Perf. 14½x14   Unwmkd.

Size: 18x23 mm.

353	A73	1 l dp vio	50	10
354	A73	2 l dp grn	75	10
355	A73	3 l car rose	1.50	10
356	A73	7.50 l ultra	3.00	65
357	A73	10 l dp bl	7.50	5.00
		Nos. 353-357 (5)	13.25	5.95

Stamps of 1928-30   8 IUNIE 1930
Overprinted

On Nos. 320-322, 326, 328

1930, June 8   Typographed
Perf. 13½ x14, 13½.

359	A72	25b black	20	10
360	A72	30b fawn	20	10
361	A72	50b ol grn	15	10

Photogravure.

Size: 18½x24½mm.

| 362 | A73 | 5 l red brn | 55 | 10 |
| 362A | A73 | 10 l brt bl | 4.00 | 1.00 |

On Nos. 353-357

Perf. 14½x14

Size: 18x23 mm

363	A73	1 l dp vio	15	10
364	A73	2 l dp grn	20	10
365	A73	3 l car rose	25	10
366	A73	7.50 l ultra	1.75	75
367	A73	10 l dp bl	1.75	25

On Nos. 343-344

Typo.   Wmk. 95
Perf. 13½x14, 13½

| 368 | A72 | 25b black | 60 | 20 |

Photogravure.

Size: 18½x24½ mm.

| 368A | A73 | 7.50 l ultra | 2.50 | 75 |
| | | Nos. 359-368A (12) | 12.30 | 3.65 |

Accession to the throne by King Carol II. This overprint exists on No. 345.

King Carol II
A87   A88   A89

Wmk. 225

Wmkd.
Crown over PTT, Multiple. (225)

1930   Perf. 13½, 14, 14x13½

369	A87	25b black	25	6
370	A87	50b chocolate	45	20
371	A87	1 l dk vio	30	5
372	A87	2 l gray grn	40	5
373	A88	3 l car rose	75	5
374	A88	4 l org red	1.00	5
375	A88	6 l car brn	1.25	5
376	A88	7.50 l ultra	1.50	15
377	A89	10 l dp bl	1.75	10
378	A89	16 l pck grn	7.00	15
379	A89	20 l orange	7.00	40
		Nos. 369-379 (11)	21.65	1.31

Exist imperf. See Nos. 405-414.

ROMANIA

A90   A91

1930, Dec. 24   *Perf. 13½*   *Unwmkd.*

380	A90	1 l dl vio	1.00	30
381	A91	2 l green	1.00	30
382	A91	4 l vermilion	1.50	30
383	A91	6 l brn car	3.50	30

First census in Romania.

King Carol II—A92

King Carol I   King Ferdinand
A93   A96

King Carol II—A94

King Carol II, King Ferdinand and King Carol I—A95

1931, May 10   *Photo.*   *Wmk. 225*

384	A92	1 l gray vio	3.50	1.25
385	A93	2 l green	4.50	1.25
386	A94	6 l red brn	6.50	2.25
387	A95	10 l blue	11.00	4.50
388	A96	20 l orange	12.50	7.00
		Nos. 384-388 (5)	38.00	16.25

50th anniversary of Romanian Kingdom.

Using Bayonet
A97

Romanian Infantryman 1870   Romanian Infantry 1830
A98   A99

King Carol I   Infantry Advance
A100   A101

King Ferdinand   King Carol II
A102   A103

1931, May 10

389	A97	25 b gray blk	1.25	80
390	A98	50 b dk red brn	1.75	90
391	A99	1 l gray vio	2.00	1.00
392	A100	2 l dp grn	3.50	1.50
393	A101	3 l car rose	7.50	4.50
394	A102	7.50 l ultra	10.00	6.00
395	A103	16 l bl grn	12.50	8.00
		Nos. 389-395 (7)	38.50	22.70

Centenary of the Romanian Army.

Naval Cadet Ship "Mircea"   King Carol II
A104   A108

Designs: 10 l, Ironclad. 16 l, Light cruiser. 20 l, Destroyer.

1931, May 10

396	A104	6 l red brn	5.50	2.50
397	A104	10 l blue	5.50	2.50
398	A104	16 l bl grn	20.00	4.50
399	A104	20 l orange	11.00	6.00

50th anniversary of the Romanian Navy.

Engraved.

1931   *Perf. 12*   *Unwmkd.*

400	A108	30 l ol bis & bl bl	75	35
401	A108	50 l red & dk bl	2.75	75
402	A108	100 l dk grn & bl bl	3.50	1.00

Exist imperf.

Carol II, Ferdinand, Carol I
A109

Wmk. 230

Wmkd. Crowns and Monograms. (230)

1931, Nov. 1   *Photo.*   *Perf. 13½*

403	A109	16 l Prus grn	10.00	50

Exists imperf.

Carol II Types of 1930-31
Perf. 13½, 14, 14½ and Compound.

1932   *Wmk. 230*

405	A87	25 b black	50	10
406	A87	50 b dk brn	70	15
407	A87	1 l dk vio	1.25	10
408	A87	2 l gray grn	1.25	10
409	A88	3 l car rose	2.00	10
410	A88	4 l org red	3.50	10
411	A88	6 l car brn	6.50	15
412	A88	7.50 l ultra	10.00	50
413	A89	10 l dp bl	100.00	75
414	A89	20 l orange	100.00	7.50
		Nos. 405-414 (10)	225.70	9.55

Alexander the Good   King Carol II
A110   A111

1932, May   *Perf. 13½*

415	A110	6 l car brn	10.00	7.50

500th anniversary of the death of Alexander the Good, Prince of Moldavia, 1400-1432.

1932, June

416	A111	10 l brt bl	10.00	60

Exists imperf.

Cantacuzino and Gregory Ghika, Founders of Coltea and Pantelimon Hospitals
A112

Session of the Congress
A113

Aesculapius and Hygeia
A114

1932, Sept.   *Perf. 13½*

417	A112	1 l car rose	7.00	5.00
418	A113	6 l dp org	17.50	8.00
419	A114	10 l brt bl	27.50	15.00

Ninth International History of Medicine Congress, Bucharest.

Bull's Head and Post Horn   Coat of Arms
A116   A120

Lion Rampant and Bridge   Dolphins   Eagle and Castles
A117   A118   A119

Eagle and Post Horn   Bull's Head and Post Horn
A121   A122

1932, Nov. 20   *Typo.*   *Imperf.*

421	A116	25 b black	1.25	25
422	A117	1 l violet	1.75	50
423	A118	2 l green	2.25	60
424	A119	3 l car rose	2.75	75
425	A120	6 l red brn	3.50	90
426	A121	7.50 l lt bl	5.00	1.50
427	A122	10 l dk bl	7.00	4.00
		Nos. 421-427 (7)	23.50	8.50

Issued to commemorate the 75th anniversary of the first Moldavian stamps.

Mail Coach Type of 1903.

1932, Nov. 20   *Perf. 13½*

428	A25	16 l bl grn	10.00	5.00

Commemorating the 30th anniversary of the opening of the new Post Office, Bucharest, in 1903.

Arms of City of Turnu-Severin, Ruins of Tower of Emperor Severus
A123

Inauguration of Trajan's Bridge
A124

ROMANIA

Prince Carol
Landing at Turnu-Severin
A125

Bridge over the Danube
A126

Photogravure.

1933, June 2   Perf. 14½x14

429	A123	25b gray grn	50	30
430	A124	50b dl bl	1.00	40
431	A125	1 l blk brn	1.00	45
432	A126	2 l ol blk	2.50	70

Centenary of the incorporation in Walachia of the old Roman City of Turnu-Severin.
Exist imperf.

Queen Elizabeth and King Carol I
A127

Profiles of Kings Carol I,
Ferdinand and Carol II
A128

Castle Peles, Sinaia
A129

1933, Aug.

433	A127	1 l dk vio	2.50	1.75
434	A128	3 l ol brn	2.50	1.75
435	A129	6 l vermilion	3.00	2.50

50th anniversary of the erection of Castle Peles, the royal summer residence at Sinaia.
Exist imperf.

King Carol II
A130   A131

King Carol II
A132

1934, Aug.   Perf. 13½

436	A130	50b brown	75	40
437	A131	2 l gray grn	1.25	50
438	A131	4 l red	2.00	60
439	A132	6 l dp cl	6.00	40

Nos. 436, 439 exist imperf.

Child and   Woman and
Grapes—A133   Fruit—A134

1934, Sept. 14

| 440 | A133 | 1 l dl grn | 2.75 | 2.00 |
| 441 | A134 | 2 l vio brn | 2.75 | 2.00 |

National Fruit Week, Sept. 14–21.
Exist imperf.

Crisan, Horia and Closca—A135

Designs: 2 l, Crisan. 6 l, Closca. 10 l, Horia.

1935, Feb. 28

442	A135	1 l purple	75	50
443	A135	2 l green	1.00	75
444	A135	6 l brown	2.00	1.00
445	A135	10 l blue	4.00	2.00

150th anniversary of the death of three Romanian martyrs. Exist imperf.

King Carol II
A139   A140

A141   A142

A143

Wmkd.
Crowns and Monograms. (230)
1935-40 Photogravure.   Perf. 13½.

446	A139	25b blk brn	8	5
447	A142	50b brown	10	6
448	A140	1 l purple	20	5
449	A141	2 l green	25	5
449A	A141	2 l dk bl grn ('40)	60	60
450	A142	3 l dp rose	25	10
450A	A142	3 l grnsh bl ('40)	75	75
451	A141	4 l vermilion	1.00	8
452	A140	5 l rose car ('40)	1.00	1.00
453	A143	6 l maroon	80	5
454	A140	7.50 l ultra	1.50	35
454A	A142	8 l mag ('40)	1.50	1.50
455	A141	9 l brt ultra ('40)	2.25	2.25
456	A141	10 l brt bl	75	30
456A	A143	12 l sl bl ('40)	1.25	1.25
457	A139	15 l dk brn ('40)	1.25	1.25
458	A143	16 l Prus bl	1.50	20
459	A143	20 l orange	1.00	40
460	A143	24 l dk car ('40)	2.00	2.00

Nos. 446-460 (19)   18.03   12.29

Exist imperf.

Nos. 454, 456
Overprinted
in Red   CEHOSLOVACIA   YUGOSLAVIA
          1920-1936

1936, Dec. 5

| 461 | A140 | 7.50 l ultra | 5.00 | 3.50 |
| 462 | A142 | 10 l brt bl | 5.00 | 3.50 |

16th anniversary of the Little Entente.
Overprints in silver or gold are fraudulent.

Birthplace of Ion Creanga
A144

Ion Creanga—A145

1937, May 15

463	A144	2 l green	1.00	70
464	A145	3 l car rose	1.00	70
465	A144	4 l dp vio	1.50	1.00
466	A145	6 l red brn	1.50	1.25

Birth centenary of Ion Creanga (1837–1889), writer. Exist imperf.

Cathedral at
Curtea de Arges
A146

1937, July 1

| 467 | A146 | 7.50 l ultra | 2.00 | 80 |
| 468 | A146 | 10 l blue | 3.50 | 70 |

The Little Entente (Romania, Czechoslovakia, Jugoslavia). Exist imperf.

Souvenir Sheet.

A146a

Surcharged in Black with New Values.
1937, Oct. 25   Perf. 13½   Unwmkd.

469	A146a	Sheet of four	5.00	5.00
a.		2 l on 20 l org	50	50
b.		6 l on 10 l brt bl	50	50
c.		10 l on 6 l mar	50	50
d.		20 l on 2 l grn	50	50

Promotion of the Crown Prince Michael to the rank of Lieutenant on his 17th birthday. Size: 123x151mm.

Arms of Romania, Greece,
Turkey and Jugoslavia
A147

Perf. 13x13½

1938, Feb. 10   Wmk. 230

| 470 | A147 | 7.50 l ultra | 1.50 | 1.00 |
| 471 | A147 | 10 l blue | 2.50 | 1.00 |

The Balkan Entente.

A148

King Carol II
A149   A150

1938, May 10   Perf. 13½

472	A148	3 l dk car	50	30
473	A149	6 l vio brn	50	30
474	A150	10 l blue	75	40

New Constitution of Feb. 27, 1938.

Prince Carol at Calatorie, 1866
A151

ROMANIA

At Calafat—A152

Examining Plans for a Monastery
A153

Sigmaringen and Peles Castles
A154

Prince Carol and Carmen Sylva (Queen Elizabeth)
A155

Prince Carol, Age 6
A156

1866
A157

1877
A158

Equestrian Statue
A159

Battle of Plevna
A160

On Horseback
A161

1914
A162

King Carol I and Queen Elizabeth
A163

Cathedral of Curtea de Arges
A164
Perf. 14, 14x13½, 13½
Wmkd.
Crowns and Monograms. (230)
1939, Apr. 10

475	A151	25b ol blk	10	7
476	A152	50b vio brn	10	10
477	A153	1 l dk pur	25	12
478	A154	1.50 l green	12	7
a.		Booklet pane of 4		
479	A155	2 l myr grn	15	8
480	A156	3 l red org	15	8
a.		Booklet pane of 8		
481	A157	4 l rose lake	20	9
a.		Booklet pane of 8		
482	A158	5 l black	12	6
a.		Booklet pane of 8		
483	A159	7 l ol blk	15	6
a.		Booklet pane of 6		
b.		Booklet pane of 6		
484	A160	8 l dk bl	30	15
485	A161	10 l dp mag	35	20
486	A162	12 l dl bl	50	25
a.		Booklet pane of 6		
487	A163	15 l ultra	60	30
488	A164	16 l Prus grn	1.50	75
		Nos. 475-488 (14)	4.59	2.38

Centenary of the birth of King Carol I.

Souvenir Sheets

A164a
1939-40   *Perf. 14x13½*

488A A164a Sheet of 3   3.00 3.00
  d. Imperf. ('40)   4.50 4.50
No. 488A contains one each of Nos. 475, 476 and 478. Size: 140½x117½mm. Sold for 20 l, the surtax for national defense.

A164b
488B A164b Sheet of 4   3.00 3.00
  e. Imperf. ('40)   4.50 4.50

488C A164b Sheet of 4   3.00 3.00
  f. Imperf. ('40)   4.50 4.50

No. 488B contains one each of Nos. 480–482 and 486, perf. 14x15½. Size: 127x146½mm.
No. 488C contains one each of Nos. 479, 483, 484 and 485, perf. 14x15½. Size: 125x146mm. Nos. 488B–488C sold for 50 l, the surtax for national defense.
Nos. 488A–488C and 488d–488f were overprinted "PRO-PATRIA 1940" to aid the armament fund. Price, set of 6, $100.
Nos. 488A–488C exist with overprint of "ROMA BERLIN 1940" and bars, but these are not recognized as having been officially issued.

Romanian Pavilion
A165

Romanian Pavilion
A166

1939, May 8   *Perf. 14x13½, 13½*

489	A165	6 l brn car	50	50
490	A166	12 l brt bl	50	50

New York World's Fair.

Mihail Eminescu
A167   A168

1939, May 22   *Perf. 13½*

491	A167	5 l ol gray	60	60
492	A168	7 l brn car	60	60

50th anniversary of the death of Mihail Eminescu, poet.

Three Types of Locomotives—A169

Modern Train—A170

Wood-burning Locomotive
A171

Streamlined Locomotive
A172

Railroad Terminal
A173

1939, June 10   *Typo.*   *Perf. 14*

493	A169	1 l red vio	70	50
494	A170	4 l dp rose	90	50
495	A171	5 l gray lil	1.00	50
496	A171	7 l claret	1.25	60
497	A172	12 l blue	1.50	1.50
498	A173	15 l green	3.25	2.00
		Nos. 493-498 (6)	8.60	5.60

Romanian Railways, 70th anniversary.

Arms of Romania, Greece Turkey and Jugoslavia
A174
Perf. 13½

1940, May 27   *Photo.*   *Wmk. 230*

504	A174	12 l lt ultra	50	50
505	A174	16 l dl bl	50	50

The Balkan Entente.

King Michael
A175

Prince Duca
A176

1940-42   *Perf. 14*   *Wmk. 230*

506	A175	25b Prus grn	6	5
506A	A175	50b dk grn ('42)	6	5
507	A175	1 l purple	8	5
508	A175	2 l red org	10	5
508A	A175	4 l sl ('42)	6	5
509	A175	5 l rose pink	10	5
509A	A175	7 l dp bl ('42)	6	6
510	A175	10 l dp mag	30	5
511	A175	12 l dl bl	6	5
511A	A175	13 l dk vio ('42)	6	10
512	A175	16 l Prus bl	30	5
513	A175	20 l brown	1.50	5
514	A175	30 l yel grn	20	6
515	A175	50 l ol brn	25	10
516	A175	100 l rose brn	35	15
		Nos. 506-516 (15)	3.54	97

See also Nos. 535A-553.

1941, Oct. 6   *Perf. 13½*

517	A176	6 l lt brn	20	20
518	A176	12 l dk vio	25	25
519	A176	24 l brt bl	30	30

Issued to commemorate the crossing of the Dniester River by Romanian forces invading Russia.
Each of Nos. 517–519 exists in an imperf., ungummed souvenir sheet of four with marginal inscriptions including "1943." These were prepared by the civil government of Trans-Dniestria to be sold for 300 lei apiece to aid the Red Cross, but were not recognized by the national government at Bucharest. The sheets reached philatelic channels in 1946.

See also Nos. 554-557.

ROMANIA

Hotin Chapel, Bessarabia
A177

Sucevita Monastery, Bucovina
A179

Inscribed "Basarabia" or "Bucovina" at bottom.

Designs: 50b, 9.50 l, Hotin Fortress, Bessarabia. 1.50 l, Soroca Fortress, Bessarabia. 2 l, 5.50 l, Tighina Fortress, Bessarabia. 3 l, Dragomirna Monastery, Bucovina. 6.50 l, Cetatea Alba Fortress, Bessarabia. 10 l, 130 l, Putna Monastery, Bucovina. 13 l, Milisauti Monastery, Bucovina. 26 l, St. Nicholas Monastery, Suceava, Bucovina. 39 l, Rughi Monastery, Bessarabia.

1941, Dec. 1 — Perf. 13½

520	A177	25b rose car	5	5
521	A179	50b red brn	5	5
522	A179	1 l dp vio	6	6
523	A179	1.50 l green	6	5
524	A179	2 l brn org	6	8
525	A179	3 l dk ol grn	20	10
526	A177	5 l ol blk	25	10
527	A179	5.50 l brown	25	15
528	A179	6.50 l magenta	55	35
529	A179	9.50 l gray blk	55	35
530	A179	10 l dk vio brn	35	10
531	A177	13 l sl bl	45	20
532	A179	17 l brn car	55	15
533	A179	26 l gray grn	65	40
534	A179	39 l bl grn	1.00	60
535	A179	130 l yel org	3.75	2.50
	Nos. 520-535 (16)		8.83	5.29

See also Nos. B179–B187.

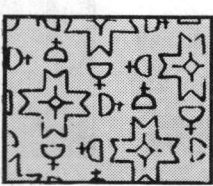

Wmk. 276
Type of 1940-42.

Wmkd. Cross and Crown Multiple. (276)

1943-45 — Perf. 14

535A	A175	25b Prus grn ('44)	5	5
536	A175	50b dk grn ('44)	5	5
537	A175	1 l dk vio ('43)	5	5
538	A175	2 l red org ('43)	5	5
539	A175	3 l red brn ('44)	5	5
540	A175	3.50 l brn ('43)	5	5
541	A175	4 l slate	5	5
542	A175	4.50 l dk brn ('43)	5	5
543	A175	5 l rose car	5	5
544	A175	6.50 l dl vio	5	5
545	A175	7 l dp bl	5	5
546	A175	10 l dp mag	5	5
547	A175	11 l brt ultra	6	5
548	A175	12 l dk bl	5	5
549	A175	15 l ryl bl	7	5
550	A175	16 l dp bl	5	5
551	A175	20 l brn ('43)	5	5
551A	A175	29 l ultra ('45)	80	50
552	A175	30 l yel grn	25	7
553	A175	50 l ol blk	35	20
	Nos. 535A-553 (20)		2.28	1.62

Prince Duca Type of 1941.

1943 — Perf. 13½

554	A176	3 l red org	10	10
555	A176	6 l dl brn	20	20
556	A176	12 l dl vio	25	25
557	A176	24 l brt bl	35	35

Andrei Saguna
A188

Andrei Muresanu
A189

Designs: 4.50 l, Samuel Micu. 11 l, Gheorghe Sincai. 15 l, Michael the Brave. 31 l, Gheorghe Lazar. 35 l, Avram Jancu. 41 l, Simeon Barnutiu. 55 l, Three Heroes. 61 l, Petru Maior.

1945 Inscribed "1944." Perf. 14.

558	A188	25b rose red	35	35
559	A189	50b orange	25	25
560	A189	4.50 l brown	25	25
561	A188	11 l lt ultra	25	25
562	A188	15 l Prus grn	25	25
563	A189	31 l dl vio	25	25
564	A188	35 l bl blk	25	25
565	A188	41 l ol gray	25	25
566	A189	55 l red brn	25	25
567	A189	61 l dp mag	25	25
	Nos. 558-567, B251 (11)		3.35	3.10

Romania's liberation. The men pictured are Transylvanians.

King Michael
A198   A199

King Michael
A200   A201

1945 Photogravure

568	A198	50b gray bl	5	5
569	A199	1 l dl brn	5	5
570	A198	2 l violet	5	5
571	A198	2 l sepia	5	5
572	A199	4 l yel grn	5	5
573	A200	5 l dp mag	5	5
574	A198	10 l blue	5	5
575	A198	15 l magenta	5	5
576	A198	20 l dl bl	5	5
577	A200	25 l red org	5	5
578	A200	35 l brown	5	5
579	A199	40 l car rose	5	5
580	A199	50 l pale ultra	5	5
581	A200	55 l red	5	5
582	A200	75 l Prus grn	5	5
583	A201	80 l orange	8	5
584	A201	100 l dp red brn	5	5
585	A201	160 l yel grn	5	5
586	A201	200 l dk ol grn	35	5
587	A201	400 l dl vio	6	5
	Nos. 568-587 (20)		1.34	1.00

Nos. 571, 573, 580, 581, 585 and 587 are printed on toned paper, Nos. 576, 577, 583, 584 and 586 on both toned and white papers, others on white paper only.

See also Nos. 610-624, 651-660.

Mail Carrier—A202

Telegraph Operator
A203

Lineman—A204

Post Office, Bucharest
A205

1945, July 20 Perf. 13 Wmk. 276

588	A202	100 l dk brn	1.00	1.00
589	A202	100 l gray ol	1.00	1.00
590	A203	150 l brown	1.50	1.50
591	A203	150 l brt rose	1.50	1.50
592	A204	250 l lt gray ol	1.75	1.75
593	A204	250 l blue	1.75	1.75
594	A205	500 l dp mag	15.00	15.00
	Nos. 588-594 (7)		23.50	23.50

Issued in sheets of 4.

I. Ionescu, G. Titeica
A. O. Idachimescu
and V. Cristescu
A207

Allegory of Learning
A208

1945, Sept. 5 — Perf. 13½

596	A207	2 l sepia	15	15
597	A208	80 l bl blk	25	25

50th anniversary of "Gazeta Matematica," mathematics journal.

Cernavoda Bridge
A209

1945, Sept. 26 — Perf. 14

| 598 | A209 | 80 l bl blk | 25 | 15 |

50th anniversary of Cernavoda Bridge.

Blacksmith and Plowman
A210

1946, Mar. 6

| 599 | A210 | 80 l blue | 25 | 20 |

Agrarian reform law of Mar. 23, 1945.

Atheneum, Bucharest
A211

Numeral in Wreath
A212

Georges Enescu
A213

Perf. 13½

1946, Apr. 26 Photo. Wmk. 276

600	A211	10 l dk bl	15	10
601	A212	20 l red brn	15	10
602	A212	55 l pck bl	15	10
603	A213	80 l purple	30	25
a.		Tête bêche pair	60	65
604	A212	160 l red org	15	15
	Nos. 600-604, B330-B331 (7)		2.35	2.20

Issued to commemorate the 25th anniversary of the Philharmonic Society.

Mechanic
A214

Designs: No. 606, Laborer. No. 607, Sower. No. 608, Reaper. 200 l, Students.

1946, May 1 — Perf. 13½x13

605	A214	10 l Prus grn	60	60
606	A214	10 l dk car rose	5	5
607	A214	20 l dl bl	60	60
608	A214	20 l dk red brn	5	5
609	A214	200 l brt red	15	15
	Nos. 605-609 (5)		1.45	1.45

Issued to publicize Labor Day, May, 1, 1946.

ROMANIA

Michael Types of 1945.
Photogravure.
1946   *Perf. 14*   *Wmk. 276*
Toned Paper

610	A198	10 l brt red brn	6	5
611	A198	20 l vio brn	6	5
612	A201	80 l blue	6	5
613	A198	137 l yel grn	6	5
614	A201	160 l chlky bl	6	5
615	A201	200 l red org	6	5
616	A201	300 l sapphire	6	5
617	A201	360 l sepia	6	5
618	A199	400 l red org	6	5
619	A201	480 l brn red	6	5
620	A201	600 l dk ol grn	6	5
621	A201	1000 l Prus grn	6	5
622	A198	1500 l Prus grn	6	5
623	A201	2400 l magenta	10	8
624	A201	3700 l dl bl	10	5
		Nos. 610-624 (15)	98	76

Demetrius Cantemir — A219   Soccer — A222

Designs: 100 l, "Cultural Ties." 300 l, "Economic Ties."

1946, Oct. 20   *Perf. 13½*

625	A219	80 l dk brn	15	15
626	A219	100 l dp bl	15	15
627	A219	300 l bl blk	15	15

Issued to publicize Romania-Soviet friendship. See Nos. B338-B339.

1946, Sept. 1   *Perf. 11½, Imperf.*

Designs: 20 l, Diving. 50 l, Running. 80 l, Mountain climbing.

628	A222	10 l dp bl	50	50
629	A222	20 l brt red	50	50
630	A222	50 l dp vio	50	50
631	A222	80 l chocolate	50	50
		Nos. 628-631, B340, C26, CB6 (7)	4.60	4.60

Issued in sheets of 16.

Weaving — A226   Child Receiving Bread — A227

Transporting Relief Supplies — A228   CGM Congress Emblem — A229

Photogravure.
1946, Nov. 20   *Perf. 14*   *Wmk. 276*

636	A226	80 l dk ol brn	10	10
		Nos. 636, B342-B345 (5)	70	68

Issued for the Democratic Women's Organization of Romania. See No. CB7.

Perf. 13½x14, 14x13½
1947, Jan. 15

637	A227	300 l dk ol brn	25	20
638	A228	600 l magenta	25	20

Issued to publicize the social relief fund. See also Nos. B346-B348.

1947, Feb. 10   *Perf. 13½*

639	A229	200 l blue	25	15
640	A229	300 l orange	25	15
a.		Se-tenant with No. 639	50	50
b.		Se-tenant with No. 641	50	50
641	A229	600 l crimson	25	15

Issued to commemorate the Congress of the United Labor Unions ("CGM"). Printed in sheets of 18 comprising 3 pairs of each denomination. Sheet yields 3 each of Nos. 640a and 640b.

Peace in Chariot — A230

Peace — A231   Dove of Peace — A233

Flags of United States, Russia, Great Britain and Romania — A232

Perf. 14x13½, 13½x14
1947, Feb. 25

642	A230	300 l dl vio	15	15
643	A231	600 l dk org brn	15	15
644	A232	3000 l blue	15	15
645	A233	7200 l sage grn	15	15

Issued to commemorate the signing of the peace treaty of February 10, 1947.

King Michael — A234

1947   *Perf. 13½*
Size: 25x30 mm.

646	A234	3000 l blue	20	15
647	A234	7200 l dl vio	20	15
648	A234	15,000 l brt bl	30	15
649	A234	21,000 l magenta	30	20
650	A234	36,000 l violet	50	30
		Nos. 646-650 (5)	1.50	95

See also Nos. 661-664.

Michael Types of 1945.
Photogravure.
1947   *Perf. 14*   *Wmk. 276*

651	A199	10 l red brn	6	5
652	A200	20 l magenta	6	5
653	A198	80 l blue	6	5
654	A199	200 l brt red	6	5
655	A198	500 l magenta	6	5
656	A200	860 l vio brn	8	5
657	A199	2500 l ultra	6	5
658	A198	5000 l sl gray	15	8
659	A198	8000 l Prus grn	25	15
660	A201	10,000 l dk brn	15	15

Type of 1947.
Size: 18x21½mm.

661	A234	1000 l gray bl	5	5
662	A234	5500 l yel grn	8	5
663	A234	20,000 l brn	10	6
664	A234	50,000 l red org	25	15
		Nos. 651-664 (14)	1.47	1.04

Harvesting Wheat — A235

Designs: 1 l, Log raft. 2 l, River steamer. 3 l, Resita. 5 l, Cathedral of Curtea de Arges. 10 l, View of Bucharest. 12 l, 36 l, Cernavoda Bridge. 15 l, 32 l, Port of Constantsa. 20 l, Petroleum field.

1947, Aug. 15   *Perf. 14½x14*

666	A235	50b red org	10	5
667	A235	1 l red brn	10	5
668	A235	2 l bl gray	10	5
669	A235	3 l rose crim	25	8
670	A235	5 l brt ultra	30	10
671	A235	10 l brt bl	35	10
672	A235	12 l violet	50	15
673	A235	15 l dp ultra	75	20
674	A235	20 l dk brn	1.50	50
675	A235	32 l vio brn	3.00	1.00
676	A235	36 l dk car rose	3.00	50
		Nos. 666-676 (11)	9.95	2.88

Beehive, Savings Emblem — A236

1947, Oct. 31   *Perf. 13½*

677	A236	12 l dk car rose	35	25

World Savings Day, Oct. 31, 1947.

People's Republic

Map, Workers and Children — A237

1948, Jan. 25   *Perf. 14½x14*

678	A237	12 l brt ultra	50	20

Issued to publicize the census of 1948.

Government Printing Plant and Press — A238

1948   *Perf. 14½x14*

679	A238	6 l magenta	1.75	1.00
680	A238	7.50 l dk Prus grn	1.00	25
b.		Tête bêche pair	2.50	1.75

75th anniversary of Stamp Division of Romanian State Printing Works. Issue dates: No. 680, Feb. 12. No. 679, May 20.

Romanian and Bulgarian Peasants Shaking Hands — A239

1948, Mar. 25   *Wmk. 276*

680A	A239	32 l red brn	70	35

Romanian-Bulgarian friendship.

Allegory of the People's Republic — A240

1948, Apr. 8   *Photo.*   *Perf. 14x14½*

681	A240	1 l car rose	65	25
682	A240	2 l dl org	65	35
683	A240	12 l dp bl	1.00	60

New constitution.

Nos. 666 to 676 Overprinted in Black

1948, Mar.   *Perf. 14½x14*

684	A235	50b red org	40	20
685	A235	1 l red brn	40	12
686	A235	2 l bl gray	1.00	20
687	A235	3 l rose crim	1.00	20
688	A235	5 l brt ultra	1.50	20
689	A235	10 l brt bl	2.00	25
690	A235	12 l violet	2.25	30
691	A235	15 l dp ultra	2.25	35
692	A235	20 l dk brn	3.00	60
693	A235	32 l vio brn	8.00	2.00
694	A235	36 l dk car rose	8.00	2.00
		Nos. 684-694 (11)	29.80	6.42

Romanian Newspapers — A241

1948, Sept. 12

695	A241	10 l red brn	35	15

Issued to publicize the Week of the Democratic Press, Sept. 12-19. See Nos. B396-B398.

No. 680A Surcharged with New Value in Black.

1948, Aug. 17

696	A239	31 l on 32 l red brn	1.00	35

Monument to Soviet Soldier — A242   Proclamation of Islaz — A243

ROMANIA

1948, Oct. 29 Photo. Perf. 14x14½
697 A242 10 l dk red 75 60
Sheets of 50 stamps and 50 labels. See Nos. B399–B400, CB16.

1948, June 1 Perf. 14½x14
698 A243 11 l car rose 60 30
Nos. 698, B409-B412 (5) 5.55 5.20
Centenary of Revolution of 1848.

Arms of
Romanian People's Republic
A243a

1948, July 8 Wmk. 276
698A A243a 50 b red ("Lei 0.50") 55 55
698B A243a 1 l red brn 35 5
698C A243a 2 l dk grn 35 5
698D A243a 3 l grnsh blk 50 8
698E A243a 4 l chocolate 50 8
698F A243a 5 l ultra 50 10
698G A243a 10 l dp bl 1.50 8

"Bani" instead of "Lei"
698H A243a 50 b red ("Bani 0.50") 65 30
Nos. 698A-698H (8) 4.90 1.29

See also Nos. 712-717.

Nicolae Balcescu—A244

Wmk. 289
Wmkd. RPR Multiple. (289)

1948, Dec. 20
699 A244 20 l scarlet 60 20
Issued to honor Nicolae Balcescu (1819–1852), writer.

Release from Bondage—A245

1948, Dec. 30 Perf. 13½
700 A245 5 l brt rose 45 25
First anniversary of the Republic.

Lenin   Folk Dance
A246   A247

1949, Jan. 21
701 A246 20 l black 50 25
Issued to commemorate the 25th anniversary of the death of Lenin (Vladimir Ilyich Ulianov). No. 701 exists imperf.

1949, Jan. 24 Perf. 13½
702 A247 10 l dp bl 50 25
Issued to commemorate the 90th anniversary of the union of the Danubian Principalities.

Ion C. Frimu
and Revolutionary Scene
A248

1949, Mar. 22 Perf. 14½x14
703 A248 20 l red 50 25
No. 703 exists imperf.

Aleksander S. Pushkin
A249

1949, May 20 Perf. 14x14½
704 A249 11 l car rose 75 30
705 A249 30 l Prus grn 1.10 45
Issued to commemorate the 150th anniversary of the birth of Aleksander S. Pushkin.

Globe and Post Horn
A250

Evolution of Mail
Transportation
A251

Perf. 13½, 14½x14
1949, June 30 Photo. Wmk. 289
706 A250 20 l org brn 2.50 1.75
707 A251 30 l brt bl 1.75 1.25
Issued to commemorate the 75th anniversary of the formation of the Universal Postal Union.

Russian Army Entering
Bucharest, August, 1944
A252

Perf. 14½x14, Imperf.
1949, Aug. 23
708 A252 50 l choc, bl grn 1.00 50
Issued to commemorate the fifth anniversary of the liberation of Romania by the Soviet army in August, 1944.

"Long Live Romanian-Soviet Amity"
A253

1949, Nov. 1 Perf. 13½x14½
709 A253 20 l dp red 50 40
Issued to publicize a national week of Romanian Soviet friendship celebration, Nov. 1–7, 1949. Exists imperf.

Symbols of   Joseph V.
Transportation   Stalin
A254   A256

1949, Dec. 10 Perf. 13½
710 A254 11 l blue 75 30
711 A254 20 l crimson 75 30
Issued to publicize an International Conference of Transportation Unions, December 10, 1949.
Alternate vertical rows of stamps and labels in sheet. Exist imperf.

Arms Type of 1948.
1949–50 Perf. 14x13½ Wmk. 289
712 A243a 50 b red ("Lei 0.50") 50 30
713 A243a 1 l red brn 50 10
714 A243a 2 l dk grn 50 10
714A A243a 3 l grnsh blk 95 20
715 A243a 5 l ultra 75 20
716 A243a 5 l rose vio ('50) 1.00 10
717 A243a 10 l dp bl 1.25 25
Nos. 712-717 (7) 5.45 1.25

1949, Dec. 21 Perf. 13½
718 A256 31 l ol blk 60 25
Stalin's 70th birthday. Exists imperf.

Mihail   Poem: "Life"
Eminescu
A257   A258
Designs: No. 721, "Third Letter." No. 722, "Angel and Demon." No. 723, "Emperor and Proletariat."
Inscribed:
"Mihail Eminescu 1850–1950."

1950, Jan. 15 Photo. Wmk. 289
719 A257 11 l blue 75 30
720 A258 11 l purple 1.25 35
721 A258 11 l dk grn 75 75
722 A258 11 l red brn 75 30
723 A258 11 l rose pink 75 30
Nos. 719-723 (5) 4.25 2.00
Issued to commemorate the centenary of the birth of Mihail Eminescu, poet.

Fair at Dragaica—A259

Ion Andreescu
(Self-portrait)
A260

Village Well—A261
Perf. 14½x14, 14x14½
1950, Mar. 25
724 A259 5 l dk gray grn 75 35
725 A260 11 l ultra 1.25 35
726 A261 20 l brown 1.40 75
Issued to commemorate the centenary of the birth of Ion Andreescu, painter. No. 725 also exists imperf.

Graph
and
Factories
A262
Design: 31 l, Tractor and Oil Derricks.
Inscribed: "Planul de Stat 1950."
Perf. 14½x14
1950, Apr. 23 Wmk. 289
727 A262 11 l red 90 35
728 A262 31 l violet 1.25 60
Issued to publicize the 1950 plan for increased industrial production. No. 727 also exists imperf.

 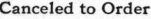
Young Man   Arms of
Holding Flag   Republic
A263   A264

1950, May 1 Perf. 14x14½
729 A263 31 l org red 60 30
Labor Day, May 1. Exists imperf.

Canceled to Order
Canceled sets of new issues have long been sold by the government. Prices in the second ("used") column are for these canceled-to-order stamps. Postally used copies are worth more.

ROMANIA

1950		Photogravure.	Perf. 12½	
730	A264	50 b black	25	10
731	A264	1 l red	10	5
732	A264	2 l ol gray	8	5
733	A264	3 l violet	15	5
734	A264	4 l rose lil	10	5
735	A264	5 l red brn	15	5
736	A264	6 l dp grn	15	7
737	A264	7 l vio brn	25	6
738	A264	7.50 l blue	35	15
739	A264	10 l dk brn	80	5
740	A264	11 l rose car	80	5
741	A264	15 l dp bl	45	5
742	A264	20 l Prus grn	50	15
743	A264	31 l dl grn	75	10
744	A264	36 l dk org brn	1.25	45
		Nos. 730-744 (15)	6.13	1.48

See also Nos. 947-961 which have similar design with white denomination figures.

Bugler and Drummer
A265

Designs: 11 l, Three school children. 31 l, Drummer, flag-bearer and bugler.

1950, May 25			Perf. 14½x14	
745	A265	8 l blue	75	50
746	A265	11 l rose vio	1.25	75
747	A265	31 l org ver	2.50	1.50

Issued to commemorate the first anniversary of the formation of the Young Pioneers organization.

Factory Worker
A266

Aurel Vlaicu and his First Plane
A267

1950, July 20		Photo.	Perf. 14x14½	
748	A266	11 l red brn	50	30
749	A266	11 l red	50	30
750	A266	11 l blue	50	30
751	A266	11 l blk brn	50	30

Issued to commemorate the second anniversary of the nationalization of industry.

1950, July 22	Perf. 12½	Wmk. 289		
752	A267	3 l dk grn	50	20
753	A267	6 l dk bl	60	20
754	A267	8 l ultra	60	20

Issued to honor Aurel Vlaicu (1882-1913), pioneer of Romanian aviation.

Mother and Child
A268

Lathe and Operator
A269

1950, Sept. 9			Perf. 13½	
755	A268	11 l rose red	45	30
756	A268	20 l dk ol brn	45	30

Issued to publicize the Congress of the Committees for the Struggle for Peace.

Statue of Soviet Soldier
A270

1950, Oct. 6			Perf. 14x14½	
757	A270	30 l red brn	75	35

Issued to publicize the celebration of Romanian-Soviet friendship, Oct. 7-Nov. 7, 1950.

No. 741 Overprinted in Carmine

TRĂIASCĂ PRIETENIA ROMÂNO-MAGHIARĂ

1950, Oct. 6			Perf. 12½	
758	A264	15 l dp bl	65	25

Romanian-Hungarian friendship.

"Agriculture," "Manufacturing" and Sports Badge—A271

Designs: 5 l, Student workers and Sports badge. 11 l, Track team and badge. 31 l, Calisthenics and badge.

1950, Oct. 30			Perf. 14½x14	
759	A271	3 l rose car	1.00	75
760	A271	5 l red brn	75	50
761	A271	5 l brt bl	75	50
762	A271	11 l green	75	50
763	A271	31 l brn ol	1.75	1.25
		Nos. 759-763 (5)	5.00	3.50

"Industry"
A273

A272

"Agriculture"—A274

1950, Nov. 2			Perf. 13½	
764	A272	11 l blue	45	30
765	A272	11 l red org	45	30

3rd Soviet-Romanian Friendship Congress.

Perf. 14x14½, 14½x14				
1951, Feb. 9		Photo.	Wmk. 289	
766	A273	11 l red brn	20	15
767	A274	31 l dp bl	60	30

Issued to commemorate the Industry and Agriculture Exposition. Exist imperf.

Ski Jump—A275

Ski Descent—A276

Designs: 5 l, Skating. 20 l, Hockey. 31 l, Bobsledding.

1951, Jan. 28			Perf. 13½	
768	A275	4 l blk brn	50	15
769	A275	5 l vermilion	75	30
770	A276	11 l dp bl	1.40	45
771	A275	20 l org brn	1.50	1.00
772	A275	31 l dk gray grn	3.00	1.75
		Nos. 768-772 (5)	7.15	3.65

9th World University Winter Games.

Medal for Work
A277

Orders: 4 l, Star of the Republic, Classes III, IV & V. 11 l, Work. 35 l, Star of the Republic, Classes I & II.

1951, May 1			Perf. 13½	
773	A277	2 l ol gray	45	30
774	A277	4 l blue	45	30
775	A277	11 l crimson	45	30
776	A277	35 l org brn	50	30

Labor Day. Exist imperf.

Camp of Young Pioneers
A278

Pioneers Greeting Stalin
A279

Admitting New Pioneers
A280

Perf. 14x14½, 14½x14.

1951, May 8				
777	A278	1 l gray grn	1.50	1.00
778	A279	11 l blue	1.50	35
779	A280	35 l red	1.25	45

Romanian Young Pioneers Organization.

Woman Orator and Flags
A281

Ion Negulici
A282

1951, Mar. 8			Perf. 14x14½	
780	A281	11 l org brn	50	15

Woman's Day, Mar. 8. Exists imperf.

1951, June 20			Perf. 14x14½	
781	A282	35 l rose red	1.25	90

Issued to commemorate the centenary of the death of Ion Negulici, painter.

Bicyclists
A283

1951, July 9			Perf. 14½x14	
782	A283	11 l chnt brn	2.00	1.00
a.		Tête bêche pair	5.50	5.00

The 1951 Bicycle Tour of Romania.

Festival Badge
A284

Boy and Girl with Flag
A285

Youths Encircling Globe
A286

1951, Aug. 1			Perf. 13½	
783	A284	1 l scarlet	75	35
784	A285	5 l dp bl	75	35
785	A286	11 l dp plum	1.10	75

3rd World Youth Festival, Berlin.

Filimon Sarbu
A287

"Romania Raising the Masses"
A288

214 ROMANIA

"Revolutionary Romania"—A289

1951, July 23   Perf. 14x14½
786 A287   11 l dk brn   45   15

Issued to commemorate the 10th anniversary of the death of Filimon Sarbu, patriot.

Perf. 14x14½, 14½x14
1951, July 23
787 A288   11 l yel brn   1.25   50
788 A288   11 l rose vio   1.25   50
789 A289   11 l dk grn   1.25   50
790 A289   11 l org red   1.25   50

Issued to commemorate the centenary of the death of C. D. Rosenthal, painter.

Scanteia Building
A290

1951, Aug. 16   Perf. 14½x14
791 A290   11 l blue   60   15

Issued to commemorate the 20th anniversary of the founding of the newspaper Scanteia.

Miner in Dress Uniform   Order for National Defense
A291   A293

Design: 11 l, Miner in work clothes.

1951, Aug. 12   Perf. 14x14½
792 A291   5 l blue   35   25
793 A291   11 l plum   35   15

Issued to publicize Miner's Day.

1951, Aug. 12   Perf. 14x14½
794 A293   10 l crimson   50   20

Choir   Music Week Emblem
A294   A295

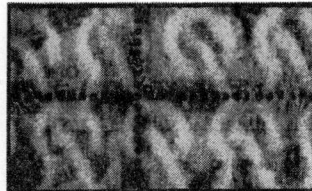

Wmk. 358

Wmkd. RPR Multiple in Endless Rows (358)
Design: No. 796, Orchestra and dancers.

1951, Sept. 22 Photo. Perf. 13½
795 A294   11 l blue   50   30
796 A294   11 l red brn   75   60
797 A295   11 l purple   50   30

Issued to publicize Music Week, Sept. 22–30, 1951.

Soldier   Oil Field
A296   A297

1951, Oct. 2
798 A296   11 l blue   50   20

Issued to publicize Army Day, Oct. 2, 1951.

1951-52
Designs: 2 l, Coal mining. 3 l, Romanian soldier. 4 l, Smelting ore. 5 l, Agricultural machinery. 6 l, Canal construction. 7 l, Agriculture. 8 l, Self-education. 11 l, Hydroelectric production. 35 l, Manufacturing.

799 A297   1 l blk brn   15   6
800 A297   2 l chocolate   15   6
801 A297   3 l scarlet   35   13
802 A297   4 l yel brn ('52) 20   15
803 A297   5 l green   35   10
804 A297   6 l brt bl ('52)   1.25   40
805 A297   7 l emerald   50   40
806 A297   8 l brn ('52)   50   40
807 A297   11 l blue   35   10
808 A297   35 l purple   1.35   80
    Nos. 799-808, C35-C36 (12) 10.40 7.10

Issued to publicize the 1951-55 Five Year Plan.

Arms of Soviet Union and Romania
A298

1951, Oct. 7   Wmk. 358
809 A298   4 l chnt brn, cr   35   15
810 A298   35 l org red   90   45

Issued to publicize the month of Romanian-Soviet friendship, Oct. 7–Nov. 7, 1951.

Pavel   Railroad
Tcacenco   Conductor
A299   A300

1951, Dec. 15   Perf. 14x14½
811 A299   10 l ol brn & dk brn 50 25

Issued to commemorate the 26th anniversary of the death of Pavel Tcacenco, revolutionary.

1952, Mar. 24   Perf. 13½
812 A300   55b dk brn   2.00   60
Railroad Workers' Day, Feb. 16.

Ion L. Caragiale
A301

Announcing Caragiale Celebration
A302

Designs: No. 814, Book and painting "1907." No. 815, Bust and wreath.

1952, Apr. 1 Perf. 13½, 14½x14
Inscribed: ".... I. L. Caragiale."
813 A301 55b chlky bl   95   25
814 A302 55b scarlet   95   25
815 A302 55b dp grn   95   25
816 A302 1 l brown   2.75 1.00

Issued to commemorate the centenary of the birth of Ion L. Caragiale, dramatist.

Types of 1952 Surcharged with New Value in Black or Carmine.
1952-53
817 A302 20b on 11 l scar (As No. 814) 1.00 75
818 A302 55b on 11 l dp grn (As No. 815) (C) 1.25 95
819 A301 75b on 11 l chlky bl (C) 2.00 1.25

Various Issues Surcharged with New Values in Carmine or Black.
On No. 678, Census.
Perf. 14x13½.
819A A237 55b on 12 l ultra 6.00 3.25
On No. 683, New Constitution.
Perf. 14.
820   A240 50b on 12 l dp bl 3.50 2.25
On No. 698, Revolution.
820A A243 1.75 l on 11 l car rose (Bk) 20.00 10.00

On Nos. 704–705, Pushkin.
1952   Wmk. 358
821   A249 10b on 11 l car rose (Bk) 3.50 1.75
822   A249 10b on 30 l Prus grn 3.50 1.75

On Nos. 719–723, Eminescu.
Perf. 13½x13, 13x13½.
823   A257 10b on 11 l bl   1.75 1.75
824   A258 10b on 11 l pur   1.75 1.75
825   A258 10b on 11 l dk grn 1.75 1.75
826   A258 10b on 11 l red brn (Bk) 1.75 1.75
827   A258 10b on 11 l rose pink (Bk) 1.75 1.75

On Nos. 724–725, Andreescu.
Perf. 14.
827A A259 55b on 5 l dk gray grn 6.50 3.50
827B A260 55b on 11 l ultra 6.50 3.50

On Nos. 727–728, Production Plan.
Perf. 14½x14.
827C A262 20b on 11 l red (Bk)   2.25 1.00
827D A262 20b on 31 l vio   2.25 1.00

On No. 729, Labor Day.
Perf. 14.
827E A263 55b on 31 l org red (Bk) 3.50 3.50

On Nos. 730–739 and 741–744, National Arms.
Perf. 12½.
828 A264 3b on 1 l red (Bk)   90   60
829 A264 3b on 2 l ol gray (Bk)   1.50   75
830 A264 3b on 4 l rose lil (Bk)   90   60
831 A264 3b on 5 l red brn (Bk)   1.50   75
832 A264 3b on 7.50 l bl (Bk)   4.25 1.75
833 A264 3b on 10 l dk brn (Bk)   1.50   75
834 A264 55b on 50b blk brn   4.25   90
835 A264 55b on 3 l vio   4.25   90
836 A264 55b on 6 l dp grn   4.25   90
837 A264 55b on 7 l vio brn   4.25   90
838 A264 55b on 15 l dp bl   6.50   90
839 A264 55b on 20 l Prus grn   4.25   90
840 A264 55b on 31 l dl grn   4.25   90
841 A264 55b on 36 l dk org brn   6.50   90

On Nos. 745–747, Young Pioneers.
Perf. 14.
841A A265 55b on 8 l bl   10.00 7.00
841B A265 55b on 11 l rose vio   10.00 7.00
841C A265 55b on 31 l org ver (Bk) 10.00 7.00

On Nos. 752–754, Vlaicu.
Perf. 12½.
842 A267 10b on 3 l dk grn 1.75   90
843 A267 10b on 6 l dk bl   1.75   90
844 A267 10b on 8 l ultra   1.75   90
Original denomination cancelled with an "✕."

On No. 756, Peace Congress.
Perf. 13½.
844A A269 20b on 20 l dk ol brn 2.25 1.75

On No. 759, Sports.
Perf. 14½x14.
845 A271 55b on 3 l rose car (Bk) 17.50 15.00

On No. 767, Exposition.
846 A274 55b on 31 l dp bl   7.50 6.00

On Nos. 771–772, Winter Games.
Perf. 13½.
847 A275 55b on 21 l org brn (Bk) 25.00 10.00
848 A275 55b on 31 l dk gray grn 25.00 10.00

On Nos. 773–776, Labor Medals.
849 A277 20b on 2 l ol gray   5.00 2.75
850 A277 20b on 4 l bl   5.00 2.75
851 A277 20b on 11 l crim (Bk) 5.00 2.75
852 A277 20b on 35 l org brn (Bk) 5.00 2.75

On No. 779, Young Pioneers.
Perf. 14x14½.
853 A280 55b on 35 l red (Bk) 15.00 11.00
On No. 792, Miners' Day.
854 A291 55b on 5 l bl   10.00 7.00
On No. 794, Defense Order.
855 A293 55b on 10 l crim (Bk) 6.00 4.00

On Nos. B409–B412, 1848 Revolution.
1952   Perf. 13x13½.   Wmk. 276
856 SP2801.75 l on 21+21 car lake (Bk) 10.00 3.50
857 SP2811.75 l on 51+51 dk vio 10.00 3.50
858 SP2821.75 l on 101+101 dk ol brn 10.00 3.50
859 SP2801.75 l on 361+181 dp bl 10.00 3.50

On Nos. 799–808, 5-Year Plan.
Perf. 13½.
Wmk. 358
860 A297 35b on 1 l blk brn   2.50 1.25
861 A297 35b on 2 l choc   10.00 1.50

ROMANIA

862	A297	35b on 3 l scar (Bk)	5.00	2.50
863	A297	35b on 4 l yel brn (Bk)	6.00	3.00
a.		Red surcharge	25.00	20.00
864	A297	35b on 5 l grn	5.00	5.00
865	A297	1 l on 6 l brt bl	7.50	7.50
866	A297	1 l on 7 l emer	6.00	3.00
867	A297	1 l on 8 l brn	6.00	6.00
868	A297	1 l on 11 l bl	7.50	3.75
869	A297	1 l on 35 l pur	7.50	3.00

On Nos. 809–810, Romanian-Soviet Friendship.

| 870 | A298 | 10b on 4 l chnt brn, cr (Bk) | 2.00 | 1.25 |
| 871 | A298 | 10b on 35 l org red (Bk) | 2.00 | 1.25 |

On No. 811, Tcacenco. *Perf. 13½x14.*

| 872 | A299 | 10b on 10 l ol brn & dk brn | 2.00 | 1.25 |

Ivan P. Pavlov
A302a
Wmk. 358

1952, Apr. 14 Photo. *Perf. 13½x13*

| 873 | A302a | 1 l red brn | 2.50 | 75 |

Issued to commemorate the meeting of Romanian-Soviet doctors in Bucharest.

Hammer and Sickle Medal
A303

1952, May 1

| 874 | A303 | 55b org brn & chnt brn | 1.00 | 20 |

Issued for Labor Day.

Medal for Motherhood — A304
Leonardo da Vinci — A305

Medals: 55b, Maternal glory. 1.75 l, Mother-Heroine.

1952, Apr. 7 *Perf. 13½x13*

875	A304	20b plum & sl gray	45	15
876	A304	55b hn brn	1.00	25
877	A304	1.75 l rose red & brn buff	2.50	60

International Women's Day.

1952, July 3

| 878 | A305 | 55b purple | 2.50 | 75 |

Issued to commemorate the 500th anniversary of the birth of Leonardo da Vinci.

Gogol and Scene from Taras Bulba
A306

Nikolai V. Gogol
A307

1952, Apr. 1 *Perf. 13½x14, 14x13½*

| 879 | A306 | 55b dp bl | 1.25 | 30 |
| 880 | A307 | 1.75 l ol gray | 1.75 | 75 |

Issued to commemorate the centenary of the death of Nikolai V. Gogol, Russian writer.

Pioneers Saluting—A308

Labor Day Paraders Returning
A309

Design: 55b, Pioneers studying nature.

1952, May 21 *Perf. 14*

881	A308	20b brown	1.00	15
882	A308	55b dp grn	2.50	25
883	A309	1.75 l blue	4.50	50

Third anniversary of Romanian Pioneers.

Infantry Attack, Painting by Grigorescu
A310

Miner
A311

Design: 1.10 l, Romanian and Russian soldiers.

1952, June 7 *Perf. 13x13½*

| 884 | A310 | 50b rose brn | 75 | 10 |
| 885 | A310 | 1.10 l blue | 1.25 | 40 |

Issued to commemorate the 75th anniversary of the Independence Proclamation of 1877.

1952, Aug. 11 Wmk. 358

| 902 | A311 | 20b rose red | 1.25 | 25 |
| 903 | A311 | 55b purple | 1.25 | 15 |

Issued to publicize the Day of the Miner.

Book and Globe
A312

Students in Native Dress
A314

Chemistry Student
A313

Design: 55b, Students playing soccer.

Perf. 13½x13, 13½x14, 13x13½.

1952, Sept. 5

904	A312	10b dp bl	15	5
905	A313	20b orange	70	40
906	A312	55b dp grn	1.00	20
907	A314	1.75 l rose red	1.60	60

Issued to publicize the International Student Union Congress, Bucharest, September 1952.

Soldier, Sailor and Aviator
A316

1952, Oct. 2 *Perf. 14*

| 909 | A316 | 55b blue | 80 | 15 |

Armed Forces Day, Oct. 2, 1952.

"Russia" Leading Peace Crusade
A317

Allegory: Romanian-Soviet Friendship
A318

Perf. 13½x13, 13x13½.

1952, Oct. 7

| 910 | A317 | 55b vermilion | 1.10 | 25 |
| 911 | A318 | 1.75 l blk brn | 2.75 | 65 |

Issued to publicize the month of Romanian-Soviet friendship, October 1952.

Rowing on Lake Snagov
A319

Nicolae Balcescu
A320

Design: 1.75 l, Athletes marching with flags.

1952, Oct. 20

| 912 | A319 | 20b dp bl | 4.00 | 40 |
| 913 | A319 | 1.75 l rose red | 7.00 | 1.00 |

1952, Nov. 29

| 914 | A320 | 55b gray | 2.50 | 45 |
| 915 | A320 | 1.75 l lem bis | 6.00 | 90 |

Issued to commemorate the centenary of the death of Nicolae Balcescu, poet.

Arms of Republic
A321

1952, Dec. 6 Wmk. 358

| 916 | A321 | 55b dl grn | 1.25 | 30 |

5th anniversary of socialist constitution.

Arms and Industrial Symbols
A322

1953, Jan. 8 *Perf. 12½x13½*

| 917 | A322 | 55b bl, yel & red | 1.50 | 50 |

Issued to commemorate the fifth anniversary of the proclamation of the People's Republic.

Matei Millo, Costache Caragiale and Aristita Romanescu
A323

1953, Feb. Photo. *Perf. 13x13½*

| 918 | A323 | 55b brt ultra | 2.50 | 50 |

Issued to commemorate the centenary of the founding of the National Theater of I. L. Caragiale.

Iron Foundry Worker
A324

Worker
A325

Design: No. 921, Driving Tractor.

1953, Feb. *Perf. 13½x13, 13x13½*

919	A324	55b sl grn	50	20
920	A325	55b blk brn	50	20
921	A325	55b orange	1.00	50

Issued to commemorate the third Congress of the Syndicate of the Romanian People's Republic.

"Strike at Grivita," Painted by G. Miclossy
A326

Arms of Romanian People's Republic
A327

215

ROMANIA

1953, Feb. 16			Perf. 13x13½	
922	A326	55b chestnut	1.25	20

Issued to commemorate the 20th anniversary of the strike of Feb. 16, 1933 in the oil industry.

1953			Perf. 12½	
923	A327	5b crimson	25	8
924	A327	55b purple	90	15

Flags of Romania and Russia, Farm Machinery
A328

1953, Mar. 24			Perf. 14	
925	A328	55b dk brn, bl	1.25	45

Issued to commemorate the 5th anniversary of the signing of a treaty of friendship and mutual assistance between Russia and Romania.

Map and Medal A329   Rug A330

Folk Dance
A330a

1953, Mar. 24

| 926 | A329 | 55b dk gray grn | 3.00 | 75 |
| 927 | A329 | 55b chestnut | 4.00 | 75 |

Issued to publicize the 20th World Championship Table Tennis Matches held in Budapest, 1953.

1953

Designs: 10b, Ceramics. 20b, Costume of Campulung (Muscel). 55b, Apuseni Mts. costume.

Inscribed: "Arta Populara Romaneasca."

928	A330	10b dp grn	75	6
929	A330	20b red brn	1.50	15
929A	A330a	35b purple	2.25	20
930	A330	55b vio bl	3.50	6
931	A330	1 l brt red vio	5.00	50
	Nos. 928-931 (5)		13.00	1.16

Romanian Folk Arts.

Karl Marx A331   Children Planting Tree A332

Physics Class—A333

1953, May 21			Perf. 13½x13	
932	A331	1.55 l ol brn	1.75	90

Issued to commemorate the 70th anniversary of the death of Karl Marx.

1953, May 21			Perf. 14	

Design: 55b, Flying model planes.

933	A332	35b dp grn	1.00	25
934	A332	55b dl bl	1.75	35
935	A333	1.75 l brown	4.00	90

Women and Flags A334   Discus Thrower A335

Students Offering Teacher Flowers
A336

1953, June 18			Perf. 13½x13	
936	A334	55b red brn	1.25	25

Issued to publicize the third World Congress of Women, Copenhagen, 1953.

1953, Aug. 2		Perf. 14	Wmk. 358	

Designs: 55b, Students reaching toward dove. 1.75 l, Dance in local costumes.

937	A335	20b orange	1.00	15
938	A335	55b dp bl	1.75	25
939	A336	65b scarlet	2.25	75
940	A336	1.75 l red vio	6.50	1.00

Issued to publicize the fourth World Youth Festival, Bucharest, Aug. 2-16, 1953.

Waterfall A337   Wheat Field A338

Design: 55b, Forester holding seedling.

1953, July 29			Photogravure	
941	A337	20b vio bl	1.00	25
942	A338	38b dl grn	2.50	1.00
943	A337	55b lt brn	2.75	45

Issued to publicize the Month of the Forest.

Vladimir V. Mayakovsky
A339

1953, Aug. 22				
944	A339	55b brown	1.25	25

Issued to commemorate the 60th anniversary of the birth of V. V. Mayakovsky, poet.

Miner Using Drill
A340

1953, Sept. 19				
945	A340	1.55 l sl blk	2.25	50

Issued to publicize Miners' Day.

Arms of Republic
A342

1952-53			Perf. 12½	
		Size: 20x24mm.		
947	A342	3b dp org	60	25
948	A342	5b crimson	80	5
949	A342	7b dk bl grn	80	25
950	A342	10b chocolate	1.00	5
951	A342	20b dp bl	1.25	5
952	A342	35b blk brn	2.50	10
953	A342	50b dk gray grn	3.25	5
954	A342	55b purple	8.25	8
		Size: 24x29mm.		
955	A342	1.10 l dk brn	6.25	35
956	A342	1.75 l violet	25.00	50
957	A342	2 l ol blk	6.50	60
958	A342	2.35 l org brn	8.00	40
959	A342	2.55 l dp org	10.00	50
960	A342	3 l dk gray grn	10.00	40
961	A342	5 l dp crim	12.50	75
	Nos. 947-961 (15)		96.70	4.38

Stamps of similar design with value figures in color are Nos. 730-744.

Postal Administration Building and Telephone Employees
A343

Designs: 55b, Postal Adm. Bldg. and Letter carrier. 1 l, Map and communications symbols. 1.55 l, Postal Adm. Bldg. and Telegraph employees.

1953, Oct. 20	Perf. 14	Wmk. 358		
964	A343	20b dk red brn	30	15
965	A343	55b ol grn	50	20
966	A343	1 l brt bl	1.25	30
967	A343	1.55 l rose brn	1.75	75

Issued to commemorate the 50th anniversary of the construction of the Postal Administration Building.

Liberation Medal A344   Soldier and Flag A345

1953, Oct. 20			Perf. 14x13½	
968	A344	55b dk brn	75	15

Issued to commemorate the 9th anniversary of the liberation of Romania.

1953, Oct. 2			Perf. 13½	
969	A345	55b ol grn	1.00	50

Issued to publicize Army Day, October 2, 1953.

Girl with Model Plane
A346

Designs: 20b, Parachute landing. 55b, Glider and pilot. 1.75 l, Plane in flight.

1953, Oct. 20			Perf. 14	
970	A346	10b org & dk gray grn	3.00	45
971	A346	20b org brn & dk ol grn	6.00	25
972	A346	55b dk scar & rose lil	10.00	75
973	A346	1.75 l dk rose vio & brn	14.00	1.00

Issued to popularize civil aviation.

Workers and Flags
A347

Design: 1.55 l, Spasskii Tower and lock on Volga-Don Canal.

1953, Nov. 25			Perf. 13x13½	
974	A347	55b brown	75	20
975	A347	1.55 l rose brn	1.10	50

Issued to publicize the month of Romanian-Soviet friendship, Oct. 7–Nov. 7, 1953.

Hemispheres and Clasped Hands
A348

Workers, Flags and Globe
A349

1953, Nov. 25			Perf. 14	
976	A348	55b dk ol	60	25
977	A349	1.25 l crimson	1.50	60

World Congress of Trade Unions, 1953.

Ciprian Porumbescu A350   Harvesting Machine A351

ROMANIA

1953, Dec. 16
978 A350 55b purple 5.00 50
Issued to commemorate the centenary of the birth of Ciprian Porumbescu (1853–1883), composer.

Perf. 13x13½
1953, Dec. 16 **Wmk. 358**
Designs: 35b, Tractor in field. 2.55 l, Cattle.
979 A351 10b sepia 35 8
980 A351 35b dk brn 50 25
981 A351 2.55 l org brn 4.00 1.00

Aurel Vlaicu A352
Lenin A353

1953, Dec. 26 **Perf. 14**
982 A352 50b vio bl 1.25 35
Issued to commemorate the 40th anniversary of the death of Aurel Vlaicu, aviation pioneer.

1954, Jan. 21 **Perf. 13½**
983 A353 55b dk red brn, *buff* 1.25 35
30th anniversary of the death of Lenin.

Red Deer A354

Designs: 55b, Children planting trees. 1.75 l, Mountain scene.

1954, Apr. 1
Yellow Surface-colored Paper
984 A354 20b dk brn 2.25 30
985 A354 55b violet 2.50 30
986 A354 1.75 l dk bl 5.00 90
To publicize the Month of the Forest, April, 1954.

Calimanesti Rest Home A355

Workers' Rest Homes: 1.55 l, Sinaia. 2 l, Predeal. 2.35 l, Tusnad. 2.55 l, Govora.

1954, Apr. 15 **Perf. 14**
987 A355 5b blk brn, *cr* 35 15
988 A355 1.55 l dk vio brn, *bl* 1.50 30
989 A355 2 l dk grn, *pink* 2.50 35
990 A355 2.35 l ol blk, *grnsh* 2.50 1.00
991 A355 2.55 l dk red brn, *cit* 3.50 1.25
  Nos. 987-991 (5) 10.35 3.05

Octav Bancila A356
Globe, Child, Dove and Flowers A357

1954, May 26 **Perf. 13½**
992 A356 55b red brn & dk grn 4.00 2.00
Issued to commemorate the 10th anniversary of the death of Octav Bancila, painter.

1954, June 1 **Perf. 13½**
993 A357 55b brown 1.50 50
Issued to publicize Children's Day, June 1, 1954.

Girl Feeding Calf A358

Designs: 55b, Girl holding sheaf of grain. 1.75 l, Young students.

1954, July 5 **Perf. 14**
994 A358 20b grnsh blk 35 25
995 A358 55b blue 75 35
996 A358 1.75 l car rose 2.00 65

Stephen the Great A359
Loading Coal on Conveyor Belt A360

1954, July 10
997 A359 55b vio brn 2.25 65
Issued to commemorate the 450th anniversary of the death of Stephen of Moldavia (1433?–1504).

1954, Aug. 8 **Perf. 13x13½**
998 A360 1.75 l black 2.00 75
Issued to publicize Miners' Day, 1954.

Victor Babes A361
Applicant Requesting Loan A362

1954, Aug. 15 **Perf. 14**
999 A361 55b rose red 2.00 25
Issued to commemorate the centenary of the birth of Victor Babes, serologist.

1954, Aug. 20
Design: 55b, Mutual aid declaration.
1000 A362 20b dp vio 40 15
1001 A362 55b dk redsh brn 65 35
Issued to commemorate the fifth anniversary of the founding of the Mutual Aid Organization.

Sailor and Naval Scene A363
Monument to Soviet Soldier A364

1954, Aug. 19 **Perf. 13x13½**
1002 A363 55b dp bl 1.25 35
Issued to publicize Navy Day.

1954, Aug. 23 **Perf. 13½x13**
1003 A364 55b scar & pur 1.25 35
Issued to commemorate the 10th anniversary of Romania's liberation.

House of Culture A365

Academy of Music, Bucharest A366
Aviator A367

Designs: 55b, Scanteia building. 1.55 l, Radio station.

1954, Sept. 6 **Perf. 14, 13½x13**
1004 A365 20b vio bl 30 10
1005 A366 38b violet 65 35
1006 A365 55b vio brn 65 20
1007 A366 1.55 l red brn 1.25 40
Issued to publicize Romania's cultural progress during the decade following liberation.

Perf. 13½x13
1954, Sept. 13 **Wmk. 358**
1008 A367 55b blue 1.50 35
Issued to publicize Aviation Day.

Chemical Plant and Oil Derricks A368
Dragon Pillar, Peking A369

1954, Sept. 21 **Perf. 13x13½**
1009 A368 55b gray 2.25 50
Issued to publicize the International Conference of chemical and petroleum workers, Bucharest, September 1954.

1954, Oct. 7 **Perf. 14**
1010 A369 55b dk ol grn, *cr* 2.25 50
Week of Chinese Culture.

D. T. Neculuta A370
ARLUS Emblem A371

1954, Oct. 17 **Perf. 13½x13**
1011 A370 55b purple 1.75 35
Issued to commemorate the 50th anniversary of the death of Dumitru Th. Neculuta, poet.

1954, Oct. 22 **Perf. 14**
Design:
65b, Romanian and Russian women embracing.
1012 A371 55b rose car 75 25
1013 A371 65b dk pur 85 35
Month of Romanian-Soviet Friendship.

Gheorghe Tattarescu A372
Barbu Iscovescu A373

1954, Oct. 24 **Perf. 13½x13**
1014 A372 55b cerise 2.25 35
Issued to commemorate the 60th anniversary of the death of Gheorghe Tattarescu (1820–1894), painter.

1954, Nov. 3 **Perf. 14**
1015 A373 1.75 l red brn 3.50 75
Issued to commemorate the centenary of the death of Barbu Iscovescu, painter.

Wild Boar A374
Globe and Clasped Hands A375

Designs: 65b, Couple planting tree. 1.20 l, Logging.

Perf. 13½x13
1955, Mar. 15 **Wmk. 358**
1016 A374 35b brown 1.00 30
1017 A374 65b turq bl 1.75 35
1018 A374 1.20 l dk red 3.50 1.00
Month of the Forest, 1955.

1955, Apr. 5 **Photogravure**
1019 A375 25b car rose 60 30
Issued to publicize the International Conference of Universal Trade Unions (Federation Syndicale Mondiale), Vienna, April 1955.

Teletype A376
Lenin A377

1955, Dec. 20 **Perf. 13½x13**
1020 A376 50b lilac 1.25 25
Issued to commemorate the centenary of the Romanian telegraph system.

1955, Apr. 22 **Perf. 13½x14**
Various Portraits of Lenin.
1021 A377 20b ol bis & brn 35 25

ROMANIA

| 1022 | A377 | 55b cop brn | 65 | 35 |
| 1023 | A377 | 1 l vermilion | 1.00 | 45 |

85th anniversary of the birth of Lenin.

Chemist
A378

Volleyball
A379

Designs: 5b, Steelworker. 10b, Aviator. 20b, Miner. 30b, Tractor driver. 35b, Pioneer. 40b, Girl student. 55b, Mason. 1 l, Sailor. 1.55 l, Spinner. 2.35 l, Soldier. 2.55 l, Electrician.

1955–56 Perf. 14 Wmk. 358

1024	A378	3b blue	20	8
1025	A378	5b violet	10	5
1026	A378	10b chocolate	20	5
1027	A378	20b lil rose	30	5
1027A	A378	30b vio bl ('56)	75	15
1028	A378	35b grnsh bl	50	10
1028A	A378	40b slate	1.25	20
1029	A378	55b ol gray	75	5
1030	A378	1 l purple	1.50	5
1031	A378	1.55 l brn lake	2.50	5
1032	A378	2.35 l bis brn	4.00	45
1033	A378	2.55 l slate	4.25	45
		Nos. 1024-1033 (12)	16.30	1.73

1955, June 17

Design: 1.75 l, Woman volleyball player.

| 1034 | A379 | 55b red vio, *pink* | 3.00 | 1.00 |
| 1035 | A379 | 1.75 l lil rose, *cr* | 7.00 | 1.00 |

European Volleyball Championships, Bucharest.

Globe, Flag and Dove
A379a

Girls with Dove and Flag
A380

1955, May 7 Photo. Perf. 13½

| 1035A | A379a | 55b ultra | 1.00 | 35 |

Peace Congress, Helsinki.

1955, June 1 Perf. 13½x14

| 1036 | A380 | 55b dk red brn | 1.00 | 35 |

International Children's Day, June 1.

Russian War Memorial, Berlin
A381

Theodor Aman Museum
A382

1955, May 9

| 1037 | A381 | 55b dp bl | 1.00 | 35 |

Victory over Germany, 10th anniversary.

1955, June 28 Perf. 13½, 14

Bucharest Museums: 55b, Lenin and Stalin Museum. 1.20 l, Popular Arts Museum. 1.75 l, Arts Museum. 2.55 l, Simu Museum.

1038	A382	20b rose lil	30	20
1039	A382	55b brown	65	20
1040	A382	1.20 l gray blk	95	65
1041	A382	1.75 l sl grn	1.75	65
1042	A382	2.55 l rose vio	3.25	75
		Nos. 1038-1042 (5)	6.90	2.45

Nos. 1038, 1040 and 1042 measure 29x24½mm. Nos. 1039 and 1041 measure 32½x23mm.

Sharpshooter
A383

1955, Sept. 11 Perf. 13½

| 1043 | A383 | 1 l pale brn & sep | 6.00 | 90 |

Issued to commemorate the European Sharpshooting Championship meeting in Bucharest, September 11–18, 1955.

Fire Truck, Farm and Factory—A384

1955, Sept. 13 Wmk. 358

| 1044 | A384 | 55b carmine | 90 | 30 |

Firemen's Day, Sept. 13.

Bishop Dosoftei
A385

Mother and Child
A386

Portraits: No. 1046, Stolnicul Constantin Cantacuzino. No. 1047, Dimitrie Cantemir. No. 1048, Enachita Vacarescu. No. 1049, Anton Pann.

1955, Sept. 9 Photogravure

1045	A385	55b bluish gray	90	45
1046	A385	55b dp vio	90	45
1047	A385	55b ultra	90	45
1048	A385	55b rose vio	90	45
1049	A385	55b ol gray	90	45
		Nos. 1045-1049 (5)	4.50	2.25

Issued to honor Romanian writers.

1955, July 7 Perf. 13½x14

| 1050 | A386 | 55b ultra | 1.25 | 35 |

World Congress of Mothers, Lausanne.

Pioneers and Train Set
A387

Rowing
A388

1955 Perf. 12½

Designs: 20b, Pioneers studying nature. 55b, Home of the Pioneers.

1051	A387	10b brt ultra	25	10
1052	A387	20b grnsh bl	75	15
1053	A387	55b dp plum	2.00	45

Fifth anniversary of the Pioneer headquarters, Bucharest.

1955, Aug. 22 Perf. 13x13½

Design: 1 l, Sculling.

| 1054 | A388 | 55b dk ol grn | 5.00 | 80 |

| 1055 | A388 | 1 l dp bl | 8.50 | 1.00 |

Issued to commemorate the European Women's Rowing Championship on Lake Snagov, August 4–7, 1955.

Insect Pest Control
A389

I. V. Michurin
A390

1955, Oct. 15 Perf. 14x13½

1056	A389	10b brt grn	40	10
1057	A389	20b lil rose	40	10
1058	A389	55b vio bl	1.00	15
1059	A389	1 l dp cl	1.75	65

Issued to publicize quality products of Romanian agriculture. See also Nos. 1068–1071.

1955, Oct. 25 Perf. 13½x14

| 1060 | A390 | 55b Prus bl | 1.25 | 35 |

Issued to commemorate the 100th anniversary of the birth of I. V. Michurin, Russian agricultural scientist.

Congress Emblem
A391

Globes and Olive Branches
A392

1955, Oct. 20 Perf. 13x13½

| 1061 | A391 | 20b cr & ultra | 45 | 15 |

Issued to publicize the fourth Soviet-Romanian Congress, Bucharest, Oct. 1955.

1955, Oct. 1 Perf. 13½x13

Design: 1 l, Three workers holding FSM banner.

| 1062 | A392 | 55b dk ol grn | 45 | 15 |
| 1063 | A392 | 1 l ultra | 75 | 15 |

International Trade Union Organization (Federation Syndicale Mondiale), 10th anniversary.

Sugar Beets
A393

Sheep and Shepherd
A394

Designs: 20b, Cotton. 55b, Flax. 1.55 l, Sun Flower.

1955, Nov. 10 Perf. 13½

1064	A393	10b plum	50	20
1065	A393	20b sl grn	65	25
1066	A393	55b brt ultra	1.75	50
1067	A393	1.55 l dk red brn	4.00	75

1955, Dec. 10 Perf. 14x13½

Stock Farming: 10b, Pigs. 35b, Cattle. 55b, Horses.

1068	A394	5b yel grn & brn	35	25
1069	A394	10b ol bis & dk vio	75	25
1070	A394	35b brick red & brn	1.50	35
1071	A394	55b dk ol bis & brn	3.25	75

Issued to publicize animal husbandry.

Hans Christian Andersen
A395

Portraits: 55b, Adam Mickiewicz. 1 l, Friedrich von Schiller. 1.55 l, Baron de Montesquieu. 1.75 l, Walt Whitman. 2 l, Miguel de Cervantes.

Perf. 13½x14

1956, Dec. 17 Engraved Unwmkd.

1072	A395	20b sl bl	45	20
1073	A395	55b dp ultra	1.00	20
1074	A395	1 l grnsh blk	1.25	25
1075	A395	1.55 l vio brn	3.50	75
1076	A395	1.75 l dl vio	4.00	1.25
1077	A395	2 l rose lake	4.00	1.25
		Nos. 1072-1077 (6)	14.20	3.90

Anniversaries of famous writers.

Bank Book and Savings Bank
A396

Perf. 14x13½

1956, Dec. 29 Photo. Wmk. 358

| 1078 | A396 | 55b dp vio | 1.50 | 1.00 |
| 1079 | A396 | 55b blue | 75 | 15 |

Issued to publicize the advantage of systematic saving in a bank.

Census Date—A397

Design: 1.75 l, Family group.

Inscribed:

"Recensamintul Populatiei"

1956, Feb. 3 Perf. 13½

1080	A397	55b dp org	45	15
1081	A397	1.75 l emer & red brn	1.25	50
a.		Center inverted	250.00	250.00

National Census, Feb. 21, 1956.

Ring-necked Pheasant
A398

Great Bustard
A399

Street Fighting, Paris, 1871
A400

ROMANIA

Animals: 20b, Hare (No. 1082). 20b, Bustard (No. 1083). 35b, Trout. 50b, Boar. 55b, Brown bear (No. 1087). 1 l, Lynx. 1.55 l, Red squirrel. 2 l, Chamois. 3.25 l, Pintail (duck). 4.25 l, Fallow deer.

1956		Perf. 14		Wmk. 358
1082	A398	20b grn & blk	1.00	75
1083	A399	20b cit & gray blk	1.00	75
1084	A399	35b brt bl & blk	1.00	75
1085	A398	50b dp ultra & brn blk	1.50	1.20
1086	A398	55b ol bis & ind	1.75	1.25
1087	A398	55b dk bl grn & dk red brn	1.75	1.25
1088	A398	1 l dk grn & red brn	2.50	2.00
1089	A399	1.55 l lt ultra & red brn	4.50	3.00
1090	A398	1.75 l sl grn & dk brn	5.00	4.00
1091	A398	2 l ultra & brn blk	13.50	10.00
1092	A399	3.25 l lt grn & blk brn	10.00	7.50
1093	A399	4.25 l brn org & dk brn	13.50	9.50
	Nos. 1082-1093 (12)		57.50	41.95

Exist imperf. in changed colors.
Price, set $35.

1956, May 29 — Perf. 13½
| 1094 | A400 | 55b vermilion | 1.10 | 35 |

85th anniversary of Commune of Paris.

Globe and Child — A400a   Oak Tree — A401

1956, June 1 — Photo. — Perf. 13½x14
| 1095 | A400a | 55b dp vio | 1.25 | 70 |

Issued for International Children's Day. The sheet of 100 contains 10 labels, each with "Peace" printed on it in one of 10 languages.

1956, June 11 — Litho. — Wmk. 358
Design: 55b, Logging train in timberland.
| 1096 | A401 | 20b dk bl grn, *pale grn* | 1.00 | 25 |
| 1097 | A401 | 55b brn blk, *pale grn* | 2.75 | 50 |

Month of the Forest, 1956.

Romanian Academy — A402

1956, June 19 — Photo. — Perf. 14
| 1098 | A402 | 55b dk grn & dl yel | 1.25 | 40 |

90th anniversary of Romanian Academy.

Red Cross Worker A403   Woman Speaker and Globe A404

1956, June 7
| 1099 | A403 | 55b ol & red | 2.00 | 50 |

Issued to publicize the Romanian Red Cross Congress, June 7–9, 1956.

1956, June 14
| 1100 | A404 | 55b dk bl grn | 1.10 | 35 |

Issued to publicize the International Conference of Working Women, Budapest, June 14-17, 1956.

Traian Vuia and Planes A405

1956, June 21 — Perf. 13x13½
| 1101 | A405 | 55b grnsh blk & brn | 1.10 | 35 |

50th anniversary of first flight by Traian Vuia, near Paris.

Ion Georgescu — A406

1956, June 25 — Perf. 14x13½
| 1102 | A406 | 55b dk red brn & dk grn | 1.75 | 35 |

Birth centenary of Ion Georgescu (1856-1898), sculptor.

White Cabbage Butterfly — A407

June Bug — A408

Design: 55b, Colorado potato beetle.

Perf. 14x13½, 13½x14

1956, July 30
1103	A407	10b dp vio, pale yel & blk	4.00	35
1104	A407	55b ol blk & yel	6.00	50
1105	A408	1.75 l lt ol & dp plum	8.00	7.50
1106	A408	1.75 l gray ol & dk vio brn	8.00	90

Campaign against insect pests.

Girl Holding Sheaf of Wheat A409   Dock Workers on Strike A410

1956 — Perf. 13½x14
| 1107 | A409 | 55b dl pur ("1949-1956") | 2.25 | 50 |
| a. | | "1951-1956" (error) | 5.00 | 3.50 |

7th anniversary of collective farming.

1956, Aug. 6
| 1108 | A410 | 55b dk red brn | 75 | 25 |

Issued to commemorate the 50th anniversary of the dock workers' strike at Galati.

Title Page and Printer A411   Maxim Gorki A412

1956, Aug. 13 — Perf. 13½
| 1109 | A411 | 55b ultra | 75 | 25 |

Issued to commemorate the 25th anniversary of the publication of "Scanteia" (The Spark).

1956, Aug. 29 — Perf. 13½x14
| 1110 | A412 | 55b brown | 75 | 25 |

Maxim Gorki (1868–1936), Russian writer.

Theodor Aman A413   Primrose and Snowdrops A414

1956, Sept. 24 — Engraved
| 1111 | A413 | 55b gray blk | 1.25 | 35 |

Issued to commemorate the 125th anniversary of the birth of Theodor Aman, painter.

1956, Sept. 26 — Photo. — Perf. 14x14½
Flowers: 55b, Daffodil and violets. 1.75 l, Snapdragon and bellflowers. 3 l, Poppies and lilies of the valley.

Flowers in Natural Colors.
1112	A414	5b bl, yel & red	75	25
1113	A414	55b blk, yel & red	1.75	50
1114	A414	1.75 l ind, pink & yel	4.50	50
1115	A414	3 l bl grn, dk brn & yel	6.50	1.25

Olympic Rings and Torch A415   Janos Hunyadi A416

Designs: 55b, Water polo. 1 l, Gymnastics. 1.55 l, Canoeing. 1.75 l, High jump.

1956, Oct. 25 — Perf. 13½x14
1116	A415	20b vermilion	35	20
1117	A415	55b ultra	75	20
1118	A415	1 l lil rose	1.10	30
1119	A415	1.55 l lt bl grn	1.75	30
1120	A415	1.75 l dp pur	2.25	75
	Nos. 1116-1120 (5)		6.20	1.75

Issued to commemorate the 16th Olympic Games, Melbourne, Nov. 22-Dec. 8.

1956, Oct. — Wmk. 358
| 1121 | A416 | 55b dp vio | 1.10 | 35 |

Issued to commemorate the 500th anniversary of the death of Janos Hunyadi (1387–1456), national hero of Hungary. No. 1121 is found se-tenant with label showing Hunyadi Castle.

Benjamin Franklin A417   Georges Enescu as a Boy A418

Portraits: 35b, Sesshu (Toyo Oda). 40b, G. B. Shaw. 50b, Ivan Franco. 55b, Pierre Curie. 1 l, Henrik Ibsen. 1.55 l, Fedor Dostoevski. 1.75 l, Heinrich Heine 2.55l, Mozart. 3.25 l, Rembrandt.

1956 — Unwmkd.
1122	A417	20b vio bl	35	10
1123	A417	35b rose lake	40	15
1124	A417	40b chocolate	45	20
1125	A417	50b brn blk	55	15
1126	A417	55b dk ol	65	15
1127	A417	1 l dk bl grn	1.00	25
1128	A417	1.55 l dp pur	1.50	20
1129	A417	1.75 l brt bl	2.00	45
1130	A417	2.55 l rose vio	2.75	75
1131	A417	3.25 l dk bl	3.00	1.75
	Nos. 1122-1131 (10)		12.65	4.15

Issued in honor of great personalities of the world.

1956, Dec. 29 — Engraved
Portrait: 1.75 l, Georges Enescu as an adult.
| 1132 | A418 | 55b ultra | 75 | 25 |
| 1133 | A418 | 1.75 l dp cl | 1.75 | 50 |

Issued to commemorate the 75th anniversary of the birth of Georges Enescu, musician and composer.

Fighting Peasants, by Octav Bancila A419

1957, Feb. 28 — Photo. — Wmk. 358
| 1134 | A419 | 55b dk bl gray | 1.10 | 25 |

50th anniversary of Peasant Uprising.

Stephen the Great A420

ROMANIA

1957, Apr. 24   *Perf. 13½x14*

| 1147 | A420 | 55b brown | 75 | 25 |
| 1148 | A420 | 55b ol blk | 1.10 | 25 |

Issued to commemorate the 500th anniversary of the enthronement of Stephen the Great, Prince of Moldavia.

Dr. George Marinescu, Marinescu Institute and Congress Emblem — A421

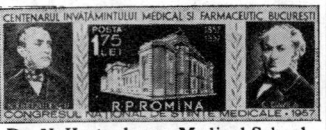

Dr. N. Kretzulescu, Medical School, Dr. C. Davila — A422

Designs: 35b, Dr. I. Cantacuzino and Cantacuzino Hospital. 55b, Dr. V. Babes and Babes Institute.

1957, May 5   *Perf. 14x13½*

1149	A421	20b dp grn	45	5
1150	A421	35b dp red brn	60	25
1151	A421	55b red lil	1.00	45
1152	A422	1.75 l brt ultra & dk red	3.00	1.00

Issued to publicize the National Congress of Medical Science, Bucharest May 5–6. No. 1152 also commemorates the centenary of medical and pharmaceutical teaching in Bucharest. It measures 66x23mm.

Dove and Handle Bars — A423

Design: 55b, Cyclist.

1957, May 29   *Perf. 13½x14*

| 1153 | A423 | 20b brt ultra | 30 | 15 |
| 1154 | A423 | 55b dk brn | 90 | 30 |

10th International Bicycle Peace Race.

Woman Watching Gymnast A424   Woman Gymnast on Bar A425

Designs: 55b, Vaulting horse. 1.75 l, Acrobat.

1957, May 21   *Perf. 13½*

1155	A424	20b emerald	30	15
1156	A425	35b brt red	55	25
1157	A425	55b brt bl	1.10	35
1158	A424	1.75 l red lil	3.00	75

Issued to publicize the European Women's Gymnastic meet, Bucharest.

The first price column gives the catalogue value of an unused stamp, the second that of a used stamp.

Sliderule, Caliper & Atomic Symbol A426   Rhododendron Hirsutum A427

1957, May 29   *Perf. 14*   *Wmk. 358*

Photogravure.

| 1159 | A426 | 55b blue | 1.00 | 25 |
| 1160 | A426 | 55b brn red | 1.75 | 45 |

Issued to publicize the 2nd Congress of the Society of Engineers and Technicians, Bucharest, May 29–31.

1957, June 22   Litho.   Unwmkd.

Carpathian Mountain Flowers: 10b, Daphne Blagayana. 20b, Lilium Bulbiferum L. 35b, Leontopodium Alpinum. 55b, Gentiana Acaulis L. 1 l, Dianthus Callizonus. 1.55 l, Primula Carpatica Griseb. 1.75 l, Anemone Montana Hoppe.

Light Gray Background.

1161	A427	5b brt rose	30	10
1162	A427	10b dk grn	45	15
1163	A427	20b red org	55	25
1164	A427	35b olive	80	20
1165	A427	55b ultra	1.00	25
1166	A427	1 l red	1.50	40
1167	A427	1.55 l yellow	2.75	45
1168	A427	1.75 l dk pur	5.00	35
		Nos. 1161-1168 (8)	12.35	2.05

Nos. 1161–1168 also come se-tenant with a decorative label.

"Oxcart" by Grigorescu A428   Nicolae Grigorescu A429

Painting: 1.75 l, Battle scene.

1957, June 29   Photo.   *Wmk. 358*

1169	A428	20b dk bl grn	75	15
1170	A429	55b dp brn	1.50	30
1171	A428	1.75 l chlky bl	4.00	1.25

Issued to commemorate the 50th anniversary of the death of Nicolae Grigorescu, painter.

Warship A430

1957, Aug. 3   *Perf. 13x13½*

| 1172 | A430 | 1.75 l Prus bl | 1.50 | 45 |

Issued for Navy Day, 1957.

Young Couple A431

Festival Emblem — A432

Folk Dance — A433

Design: 55b, Girl with flags on hoop.

Perf. 14x14½, 14x14x12½ (A432), 13½x12½ (A433)

1957, July 28

1173	A431	20b red lil	30	10
1174	A431	55b emerald	45	15
1175	A432	1 l red org	1.10	60
1176	A433	1.75 l ultra	2.00	90

Issued to commemorate the Moscow 1957 Youth Festival. No. 1173 measures 23x34mm. No. 1174 measures 22x38mm. No. 1175 was printed in sheets of 50, alternating with 40 labels inscribed "Peace and Friendship" in 20 languages.

Bugler A434   Girl Holding Dove A435

1957, Aug. 30   *Perf. 14*   *Wmk. 358*

| 1177 | A434 | 20b brt pur | 1.10 | 25 |

Issued to commemorate the 80th anniversary of the Russo-Turkish war.

1957, Sept. 3   *Perf. 13½*

| 1178 | A435 | 55b Prus grn & red | 1.10 | 25 |

Issued in honor of the Red Cross.

Battle Scene A436

1957, Aug. 31

| 1179 | A436 | 1.75 l brown | 1.25 | 45 |

Issued to commemorate the 40th anniversary of the battle of Marasesti.

Jumper and Dove A437

Designs: 55b, Javelin thrower and bison. 1.75 l, Runner and stag.

1957, Sept. 14   Photo.   *Perf. 13½*

1180	A437	20b brt bl & blk	45	15
1181	A437	55b yel & blk	1.00	35
1182	A437	1.75 l brick red & blk	3.50	90

International Athletic Meet, Bucharest.

Statue of Ovid, Constanta A438

1957, Sept. 20   Photo.   *Wmk. 358*

| 1183 | A438 | 1.75 l vio bl | 2.50 | 60 |

Issued to commemorate the 2000th anniversary of the birth of the Roman poet Publius Ovidius Naso.

Oil Field — A439

Design: 55b, Horse pulling drill, 1857.

1957, Oct. 5

1184	A439	20b dl red brn	30	10
1185	A439	20b indigo	30	10
1186	A439	55b vio blk	75	50

Centenary of Romanian oil industry.

Congress Emblem — A440

1957, Sept. 28

| 1187 | A440 | 55b ultra | 65 | 25 |

Issued to publicize the fourth International Trade Union Congress, Leipzig, Oct. 4–15.

Young Couple, Lenin Banner A441   Endre Ady A442

Designs: 35b, Lenin and Flags (horizontal). 55b, Lenin statue.

1957, Nov. 6   *Perf. 14x14½, 14½x14*

1188	A441	10b crimson	20	6
1189	A441	35b plum	35	12
1190	A441	55b brown	50	35

Russian Revolution, 40th anniversary.

1957, Dec. 5   *Perf. 14*

| 1191 | A442 | 55b ol brn | 90 | 25 |

Issued to commemorate the 80th anniversary of the birth of Endre Ady, Hungarian poet.

Oath of Bobilna — A443

ROMANIA

221

Bobilna Monument
A444

Black-winged Stilt
A445

1957, Nov. 30
| 1192 | A443 | 50b dp plum | 45 | 10 |
| 1193 | A444 | 55b sl bl | 60 | 25 |

Issued to commemorate the 520th anniversary of the insurrection of the peasants of Bobilna in 1437.

Perf. 13½x14, 14x13½
1957, Dec. 27   Photo.   Wmk. 358

Animals: 10b, Great white egret. 20b, White spoonbill. 50b, Sturgeon. 55b, Ermine (horiz.). 1.30 l, White pelican (horiz.).

1194	A445	5b red brn & gray	10	8
1195	A445	10b emer & ocher	20	8
1196	A445	20b brt red & ocher	25	10
1197	A445	50b bl grn & ocher	65	15
1198	A445	55b dp cl & gray	75	20
1199	A445	1.30 l pur & org	2.50	50
Nos. 1194-1199, C53-C54 (8)		14.45	3.61

Sputnik 2 and Laika—A446

1957, Dec. 20   Perf. 14x13½
| 1200 | A446 | 1.20 l bl & dk brn | 2.50 | 75 |
| 1201 | A446 | 1.20 l grnsh bl & choc | 2.50 | 75 |

Dog Laika, "first space traveler."

Romanian Arms, Flags—A447

Designs: 55b, Arms, "Industry and Agriculture." 1.20 l, Arms, "Art, Science and Sport" (soccer)."

1957, Dec. 30   Perf. 13½
1202	A447	25b ultra, red & ocher	30	10
1203	A447	55b dl yel	60	15
1204	A447	1.20 l crim rose	1.00	50

Issued to commemorate the 10th anniversary of the proclamation of the Peoples' Republic.

Flag and Wreath—A448

1958, Feb. 15   Perf. 13½   Unwmkd.
| 1205 | A448 | 1 l dk bl & red, buff | 75 | 30 |
| 1206 | A448 | 1 l brn & red, buff | 75 | 30 |

Grivita Strike, 25th anniversary.

Television, Radio Antennas
A449

Design: 1.75 l, Telegraph pole and wires.

1958, Mar. 21   Perf. 14x13½
| 1207 | A449 | 55b brt vio | 60 | 25 |
| 1208 | A449 | 1.75 l dp mag | 1.75 | 50 |

Issued to commemorate the Telecommunications Conference in Moscow, Dec. 3–17, 1957.

Nicolae Balcescu
A450

Fencer in Global Mask
A451

Romanian Writers: 10b, Ion Creanga. 35b, Alexandru Vlahuta. 55b, Mihail Eminescu. 1.75 l, Vasile Alecsandri. 2 l, Barbu S. Delavrancea.

1958   Perf. 14x14½   Wmk. 358
1209	A450	5b bluish blk	25	10
1210	A450	10b int blk	40	15
1211	A450	35b dk bl	45	15
1212	A450	55b dk red brn	75	25
1213	A450	1.75 l blk brn	1.50	35
1214	A450	2 l dk sl grn	2.50	45
Nos. 1209-1214 (6)		5.85	1.45

1958, Apr. 5   Perf. 14½x14
| 1215 | A451 | 1.75 l brt pink | 1.75 | 50 |

Issued to publicize the Youth Fencing World Championships at Bucharest.

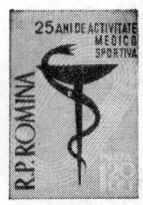 

Stadium and Health Symbol
A452

Globe and Dove
A453

1958, Apr. 16   Perf. 14x14½
| 1216 | A452 | 1.20 l lt grn & red | 1.75 | 30 |

25 years of sports medicine.

1958, May 15   Photogravure
| 1217 | A453 | 55b brt bl | 75 | 30 |

Issued to publicize the 4th Congress of the International Democratic Women's Federation, June, 1958.

Carl von Linné
A454

Lepiota Procera
A456

Portraits: 20b, Auguste Comte. 40b, William Blake. 55b, Mikhail I. Glinka. 1 l, Henry W. Longfellow. 1.75 l, Carlo Goldoni. 2 l, Jan A. Komensky.

Perf. 14x14½
1958, May 31   Unwmkd.
1218	A454	10b Prus grn	15	8
1219	A454	20b brown	30	10
1220	A454	40b dp lil	50	20
1221	A454	55b dp bl	75	15
1222	A454	1 l dp mag	1.10	20
1223	A454	1.75 l dp vio bl	1.75	45
1224	A454	2 l olive	3.00	60
Nos. 1218-1224 (7)		7.55	1.78

Issued to honor great personalities of the world.

1958, July   Litho.   Unwmkd.

Mushrooms: 10b, Clavaria aurea. 20b, Amanita caesarea. 30b, Lactarius deliciosus. 35b, Armillaria mellea. 55b, Coprinus comatus. 1 l, Morchella conica. 1.55 l, Psalliota campestris. 1.75 l, Boletus edulis. 2 l, Cantharellus cibarius.

1225	A456	5b gray bl & brn	10	5
1226	A456	10b ol, ocher & brn	10	5
1227	A456	20b gray, red & yel	25	5
1228	A456	30b grn & dp grn	35	10
1229	A456	35b lt bl & yel brn	40	10
1230	A456	55b pale grn, fawn & brn	65	15
1231	A456	1 l bl grn, ocher & brn	1.00	20
1232	A456	1.55 l gray, lt gray & pink	1.55	30
1233	A456	1.75 l emer & buff	2.00	30
1234	A456	2 l dl bl & org yel	3.50	50
Nos. 1225-1234 (10)		9.85	1.85

Antarctic Map and Emil Racovita
A457

Design: 1.20 l, Cave and Racovita.

1958, July 30   Photo.   Perf. 14½x14
| 1235 | A457 | 55b ind & lt bl | 1.10 | 25 |
| 1236 | A457 | 1.20 l oli bis & dk vio | 2.00 | 35 |

Issued to commemorate the 90th anniversary of the birth of Emil Racovita, explorer and naturalist.

Armed Forces Monument
A458

Designs: 75b, Soldier guarding industry. 1.75 l, Sailor raising flag and ship.

1958, Oct. 2   Perf. 13½x13
1237	A458	55b org brn	25	10
1238	A458	75b dp mag	45	15
1239	A458	1.75 l brt bl	1.10	35

Issued for the Day of the Armed Forces, Oct. 2. See also No. C55.

Scott's International Album provides spaces for an extensive representative collection of the world's postage stamps.

Woman from Oltenia
A459

Man from Oltenia
A460

Regional Costumes: 40b, Tara Oasului. 50b, Transylvania. 55b, Muntenia. 1 l, Banat. 1.75 l, Moldavia.

Lithographed
1958   Perf. 13½x14   Unwmkd.
| 1240 | A459 | 35b blk & red, dl yel | 30 | 15 |
| 1241 | A460 | 35b blk & red, dl yel | 30 | 15 |

Designs in Dark Brown and Deep Carmine.
1242	A459	40b pale brn	35	25
1243	A460	40b pale brn	35	25
1244	A459	50b lt lil	40	15
1245	A460	50b lt lil	40	15
1246	A459	55b gray	60	20
1247	A460	55b gray	60	20
1248	A459	1 l rose	1.25	30
1249	A460	1 l rose	1.25	30
1250	A459	1.75 l aqua	1.75	45
1251	A460	1.75 l aqua	1.75	45
Nos. 1240-1251 (12)		9.30	3.00

Same denoms. se-tenant with label between.

Exist imperf. Price, set $25.

Printer and Hand Press
A461

Moldavia Stamp of 1858
A462

Designs: 55b, Scissors cutting strips of 1858 stamps. 1.20 l, Postillion and mail coach. 1.30 l, Postillion blowing horn and courier on horseback. 1.75 l, 2 l, 3.30 l, Various denominations of 1858 issue.

1958, Nov. 15   Engr.   Perf. 14½x14
1252	A461	35b vio bl	30	7
1253	A461	55b dk red brn	60	10
1254	A461	1.20 l dl bl	1.25	18
1255	A461	1.30 l brn vio	1.50	30
1256	A462	1.55 l gray brn	1.75	45
1257	A462	1.75 l rose cl	2.00	65
1258	A462	2 l dl vio	2.50	1.25
1259	A462	3.30 l dl red brn	3.75	1.50
Nos. 1252-1259 (8)		13.65	4.50

Centenary of Romanian stamps. See #C57.

Exist imperf. Price, set $25.

Bugler
A463

Runner
A464

ROMANIA

1958, Dec. 10   Photo.   Perf. 13½x13

| 1260 | A463 | 55b crim rose | 75 | 25 |

Decade of teaching reforms.

Perf. 13½x14

1958, Dec. 9   Wmk. 358

| 1261 | A464 | 1 l dp brn | 1.50 | 45 |

Third Youth Spartacist Sports Meet.

Building and Flag
A465

Prince Alexandru Ioan Cuza
A466

1958, Dec. 16

| 1262 | A465 | 55b dk car rose | 50 | 15 |

Workers' Revolution, 40th anniversary.

Perf. 14x13½

1959, Jan. 27   Unwmkd.

| 1263 | A466 | 1.75 l dk bl | 1.25 | 45 |

Centenary of the Romanian Union.

Friedrich Handel
A467

Corn
A468

Sheep
A469

Portraits: No. 1265, Robert Burns. No. 1266, Charles Darwin. No. 1267, Alexander Popov. No. 1268, Shalom Aleichem.

1959, Apr. 25   Photo.   Perf. 13½x14

1264	A467	55b brown	60	15
1265	A467	55b indigo	60	25
1266	A467	55b slate	60	15
1267	A467	55b carmine	60	15
1268	A467	55b purple	60	15
		Nos. 1264-1268 (5)	3.00	85

Various cultural anniversaries in 1959.

Perf. 13½x14, 14x13½

1959, June 1   Photo.   Wmk. 358

Designs: No. 1270, Sunflower and bee. No. 1271, Sugar beet and refinery. No. 1273, Cattle. No. 1274, Rooster and hens. No. 1275, Tractor and grain. No. 1276, Loaded farm wagon. No. 1277, Farm couple and "10".

1269	A468	55b brt grn	45	10
1270	A468	55b red org	45	10
1271	A468	55b red lil	45	10
1272	A469	55b ol grn	45	10
1273	A469	55b red brn	45	10
1274	A469	55b yel brn	45	10
1275	A469	55b blue	45	10
1276	A469	55b brown	45	10

Unwmkd.

| 1277 | A469 | 5 l dp red lil | 4.00 | 1.25 |
| | | Nos. 1269-1277 (9) | 7.60 | 2.05 |

Issued to commemorate the 10th anniversary of collective farming. Nos. 1272–1276 measure 33x23mm.; No. 1277 measures 38x27mm.

Young Couple
A470

Steel Worker and Farm Woman
A471

Design: 1.60 l, Dancer in folk costume.

Perf. 13½x14

1959, July 15   Unwmkd.

| 1278 | A470 | 1 l brt bl | 75 | 20 |
| 1279 | A470 | 1.60 l car rose | 1.25 | 35 |

Issued to publicize the 7th World Youth Festival, Vienna, July 26–Aug. 14.

1959, Aug. 23   Litho.   Perf. 13½x14

| 1280 | A471 | 55b multi | 75 | 30 |
| a. | | Souv. sheet | 1.50 | 1.00 |

Issued to commemorate the 15th anniversary of Romania's liberation from the Germans.
No. 1280a is ungummed, imperf. and measures 50x73mm. The blue, yellow and red vignette shows large "XV" and Romanian flag. Brown 1.20 l denomination and inscription in margin.

Prince Vlad Tepes and Document
A472

Designs: 40b, Nicolae Balcescu Street. No. 1283, Atheneum. No. 1284, Printing Combine. 1.55b, Opera House. 1.75 l, Stadium.

1959, Sept. 20   Photogravure

Centers in Gray.

1281	A472	20b blue	75	25
1282	A472	40b brown	1.25	20
1283	A472	55b bis brn	1.75	35
1284	A472	55b rose lil	2.00	35
1285	A472	1.55 l pale vio	4.00	75
1286	A472	1.75 l bluish grn	5.00	1.00
		Nos. 1281-1286 (6)	14.75	2.90

Issued to commemorate the 500th anniversary of the founding of Bucharest. See No. C71.

No. 1261 Overprinted with Shield in Silver, inscribed:

"Jocurile Bucaresti Balcanice 1959"

1959, Sept. 12   Wmk. 358

| 1287 | A464 | 1 l dp brn | 7.50 | 7.50 |

Issued to commemorate the Balkan Games.

Soccer
A473

Motorcycle Race
A474

Sports: 40b, Ice hockey. 55b, Field ball. 1 l, Horse race. 1.50 l, Boxing. 1.55 l, Rugby. 1.60 l, Tennis.

Lithographed.

1959   Perf. 13½.   Unwmkd.

1288	A473	20b multi	25	5
1289	A474	35b multi	35	5
1290	A474	40b multi	40	5
1291	A473	55b multi	55	5
1292	A473	1 l multi	75	15
1293	A473	1.50 l multi	1.25	30
1294	A474	1.55 l multi	1.50	40
1295	A474	1.60 l multi	1.75	60
		Nos. 1288-1294, C72 (9)	9.25	2.40

Russian Icebreaker "Lenin"
A475

1959, Oct. 25   Photo.   Perf. 14½x13½

| 1296 | A475 | 1.75 l bl vio | 2.00 | 45 |

First atomic ice-breaker.

Stamp Album and Magnifying Glass
A476

Purple Foxglove
A477

1959, Nov. 15   Perf. 14   Wmk. 358

| 1297 | A476 | 1.60 l vio bl + 40b label | 1.75 | 75 |

Issued for Stamp Day.
Stamp and label were printed alternately in sheet. The 40b went to the Romanian Association of Philatelists.

1959, Dec. 15   Typo.   Unwmkd.

Medicinal Flowers in Natural Colors

1298	A477	20b shown	15	5
1299	A477	40b Peppermint	30	5
1300	A477	55b Cornflower	45	5
1301	A477	55b Daisies	55	5
1302	A477	1 l Autumn crocus	75	5
1303	A477	1.20 l Monkshood	85	6
1304	A477	1.55 l Poppies	1.25	40
1305	A477	1.60 l Linden	1.35	50
1306	A477	1.75 l Dog rose	1.50	50
1307	A477	3.20 l Buttercup	3.00	85
		Nos. 1298-1307 (10)	10.15	2.56

Cuza University, Jassy—A478

1960, Nov. 26   Photo.   Wmk. 358

| 1308 | A478 | 55b brown | 60 | 25 |

Centenary of Cuza University, Jassy.

Gheorghe Cosbuc
A479

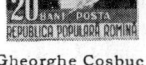
Huchen (Salmon)
A480

Portraits: 40b, Ion Luca Caragiale. 50b, Grigore Alexandrescu. 55b, Alexandru Donici. 1 l, Costache Negruzzi. 1.55 l, Dimitrie Bolintineanu.

1960, Jan. 20   Perf. 14

1309	A479	20b bluish blk	15	10
1310	A479	40b dp lil	35	25
1311	A479	50b brown	50	25
1312	A479	55b vio brn	55	25
1313	A479	1 l violet	1.00	30
1314	A479	1.55 l dk bl	1.75	45
		Nos. 1309-1314 (6)	4.30	1.60

Issued in honor of various Romanian writers.

1960, Feb. 1   Engr.   Unwmkd.

Designs: 55b, Greek tortoise. 1.20 l, Shelduck.

1315	A480	20b blue	30	10
1316	A480	55b brown	50	15
1317	A480	1.20 l dk pur	1.25	30
		Nos. 1315-1317, C76-C78 (6)	7.30	1.45

Woman, Dove and Globe
A481

Lenin
A482

1960, Mar. 1   Photo.   Perf. 14

| 1318 | A481 | 55b vio bl | 75 | 35 |

Issued to commemorate 50 years of International Women's Day, March 8.

1960, Apr. 22   Perf. 13½   Wmk. 358

Designs: 55b, Lenin statue, Bucharest. 1.55b, Head of Lenin.

| 1319 | A482 | 40b magenta | 45 | 15 |
| 1320 | A482 | 55b vio bl | 75 | 25 |

Souvenir Sheet

| 1321 | A482 | 1.55 l carmine | 2.25 | 1.50 |

Issued to commemorate the 90th anniversary of the birth of Lenin. No. 1321 measures 63x75mm. with carmine marginal inscription and ornaments.

Heroes Monument
A483

Design: 55b, Soviet war memorial.

1960, May 9   Perf. 14   Wmk. 358

1322	A483	40b vio bl	55	20
1323	A483	55b vio bl	55	15
a.		Strip of 2 (Nos. 1322-1323 and label)	2.50	1.00

15th anniversary of the liberation.
Nos. 1322–1323 exist imperf., printed in deep magenta. Price, set $3; label strip, $3.75.

Swimming—A484

Sports: 55b, Women's gymnastics. 1.20 l, High jump. 1.60 l, Boxing. 2.45 l, Canoeing.

ROMANIA

Typographed
1960, June   Perf. 14   Unwmkd.
Gray Background.

1326	A484	40b bl & yel	50	35
1327	A484	55b blk, yel & emer	60	35
1328	A484	1.20 l emer & brick red	1.35	75
1329	A484	1.60 l bl, yel & blk	2.50	1.00
1330	A484	2.45 l blk, emer & brick red	2.50	1.75
		Nos. 1326-1330 (5)	7.45	4.20

17th Olympic Games, Rome, Aug. 25–Sept. 11.
Nos. 1326–1330 were printed in one sheet, including se-tenant strips of two kinds in alternate rows: (a.) 40b, 55b and 1.20 l, (b.) 1.60 l, 2.45 l and two labels. When the two strips are placed together, the Olympic rings join. Gutters inscribed "Jocurile Olimpice—Roma—1960" separate the rows.

Exist imperf. (3.70 l replaced 2.45 l). Price, set $20.

Swimming
A485

1960		Photogravure	Wmk. 358	
1331	A485	20b chlky bl	20	10
1332	A485	40b dk brn red	40	10
1333	A485	55b blue	60	10
1334	A485	1 l rose red	75	15
1335	A485	1.60 l rose lil	1.25	35
1336	A485	2 l dl vio	1.75	65
		Nos. 1331-1336 (6)	4.95	1.45

Souvenir Sheets
Perf. 11½

| 1337 | A486 | 5 l ultra | 7.50 | 5.00 |

Imperf.

| 1338 | A486 | 6 l dl red | 12.50 | 7.50 |

Nos. 1326–1338 issued to commemorate the 17th Olympic Games, Rome, Aug. 25–Sept. 11.
Nos. 1337–1338 measure 90x69½mm.

Olympic Flame, Stadium—A486
Sports: 40b, Women's gymnastics. 55b, High jump. 1 l, Boxing. 1.60 l, Canoeing. 2 l, Soccer.

Badge, Worker and Factories
A487

Lithographed
1960, June 20   Perf. 13½   Unwmkd.

| 1339 | A487 | 55b red org & dk car | 60 | 25 |

Romanian Workers' Party, 3rd congress.

Leo Tolstoy
A488

Portraits: 20b, Mark Twain. 35b, Hokusai. 40b, Alfred de Musset. 55b, Daniel Defoe. 1 l, Janos Bolyai. 1.20 l, Anton Chekov. 1.55 l, Robert Koch. 1.75 l, Frederick Chopin.

Photogravure

1960		Perf. 14	Wmk. 358	
1340	A488	10b dl pur	10	6
1341	A488	20b olive	15	8
1342	A488	35b blue	20	8
1343	A488	40b sl grn	25	15
1344	A488	55b dl brn vio	55	15
1345	A488	1 l Prus grn	90	35
1346	A488	1.20 l dk car rose	1.25	15
1347	A488	1.55 l gray bl	1.50	25
1348	A488	1.75 l brown	1.75	40
		Nos. 1340-1348 (9)	6.65	1.67

Various cultural anniversaries.

Students   **Piano and Books**
A489   **A490**

Designs: 5b, Diesel locomotive. 10b, Dam. 20b, Miner with drill. 30b, Ambulance and doctor. 35b, Textile worker. 50b, Nursery. 55b, Timber industry. 60b, Harvester. 75b, Feeding cattle. 1 l, Atomic reactor. 1.20 l, Oil derricks. 1.50 l, Coal mine. 1.55 l, Loading ship. 1.60 l, Athlete. 1.75 l, Bricklayer. 2 l, Steam roller. 2.40 l, Chemist. 3 l, Radio and television.

Photogravure

1960		Perf. 14	Wmk. 358	
1349	A489	3b brt lil rose	10	5
1350	A489	5b ol bis	5	5
1351	A489	10b vio gray	8	5
1352	A489	20b bl vio	8	5
1353	A489	30b vermilion	12	5
1354	A489	35b crimson	12	5
1355	A490	40b ocher	15	5
1356	A490	50b bluish vio	20	5
1357	A490	55b blue	20	5
1358	A490	60b green	20	5
1359	A490	75b gray ol	35	5
1360	A490	1 l car rose	60	5
1361	A489	1.20 l black	45	5
1362	A489	1.50 l plum	60	5
1363	A490	1.55 l Prus grn	60	5
1364	A490	1.60 l dp bl	65	5
1365	A489	1.75 l red brn	75	5
1366	A489	2 l dk ol gray	90	10
1367	A490	2.40 l brt lil	1.00	15
1368	A489	3 l grysh bl	1.25	20
		Nos. 1349-1368, C86 (21)	10.20	1.55

Ovid Statue at Constanta
A491

Black Sea Resorts: 35b, Constanta harbor. 40b, Vasile Rosita beach and vase. 55b, Ionian column and Mangalia beach. 1 l, Eforie. 1.60 l, Eforie and sailboat.

1960, Aug. 2   Litho.   Unwmkd.

1369	A491	20b multi	14	5
1370	A491	35b multi	20	5
1371	A491	40b multi	24	5
1372	A491	55b multi	30	5
1373	A491	1 l multi	75	15
1374	A491	1.60 l multi	1.10	25
		Nos. 1369-1374, C87 (7)	4.23	1.05

Emblem   **Petrushka,**
A492   **Russian Puppet**
                 A493

Designs: Various Puppets.

1960, Aug. 20   Typographed

1375	A492	20b multi	10	5
1376	A493	40b multi	20	5
1377	A493	55b multi	30	5
1378	A493	1 l multi	60	10
1379	A493	1.20 l multi	65	20
1380	A493	1.75 l multi	1.00	35
		Nos. 1375-1380 (6)	2.85	81

International Puppet Theater Festival.

Children on Sled   **Globe and**
A494   **Peace Banner**
                        A495

Children's Sports: 35b, Boys playing ball (horiz.). 55b, Ice skating (horiz.). 1 l, Running. 1.75 l, Swimming (horiz.).

Lithographed
1960, Oct. 1   Perf. 14   Unwmkd.

1381	A494	20b multi	15	5
1382	A494	35b multi	25	10
1383	A494	55b multi	45	15
1384	A494	1 l multi	60	15
1385	A494	1.75 l multi	1.25	35
		Nos. 1381-1385 (5)	2.70	80

Perf. 13½x14

1960, Nov. 26   Photo.   Wmk. 358

| 1386 | A495 | 55b brt bl & yel | 45 | 15 |

Issued to commemorate the 15th anniversary of the International Youth Federation.

Worker and Flags
A496

Perf. 14x13

1960, Nov. 26   Litho.   Unwmkd.

| 1387 | A496 | 55b dk car & red org | 45 | 15 |

40th anniversary of the general strike.

Carp
A497

1960, Dec. 5   Typographed
Fish: 20b, Pikeperch. 40b, Black Sea turbot. 55b, Allis shad. 1 l, Wels (catfish.) 1.20 l, Sterlet. 1.60 l, Huchen (salmon).

1388	A497	10b multi	10	5
1389	A497	20b multi	10	5
1390	A497	40b multi	45	10
1391	A497	55b multi	55	15
1392	A497	1 l multi	1.25	15
1393	A497	1.20 l multi	1.25	25
1394	A497	1.60 l multi	1.75	30
		Nos. 1388-1394 (7)	5.45	1.00

Kneeling Woman   **Steelworker by**
and Grapes   **I. Irimescu**
A498   **A499**

Designs: 30b, Farmers drinking (horiz.). 40b, Loading grapes into basket (horiz.). 55b, Woman cutting grapes. 75b, Vintner with basket. 1 l, Woman filling basket with grapes. 1.20 l, Vintner with jug. 5 l, Antique wine jug.

1960, Dec. 20   Litho.   Perf. 14

1395	A498	20b brn & gray	15	6
1396	A498	30b red org & pale grn	25	6
1397	A498	40b dp ultra & gray el	45	8
1398	A498	55b emer & buff	60	18
1399	A498	75b dk car rose & pale grn	60	20
1400	A498	1 l Prus grn & gray el	75	35
1401	A498	1.20 l org brn & pale bl	1.25	55
		Nos. 1395-1401 (7)	4.05	1.48

Souvenir Sheet
Imperf.

| 1402 | A498 | 5 l dk car rose & bis | 4.50 | 2.25 |

Each stamp represents a different wine-growing region: Dragasani, Dealul Mare, Odobesti, Cotnari, Tirnave, Minis, Murfatlar and Pietroasa.
No. 1402 contains one imperf. stamp. Margin inscribed "Viticultura 1960" names of wine-growing regions and medals in deep ultramarine, pale green and gold. Size: 95x115mm.

Perf. 13½x14, 14x13½

1961, Feb. 16   Photo.   Unwmkd.
Modern Sculptures: 10b, G. Doja, I. Vlad. 20b, Meeting, B. Caragea. 40b, Georges Enescu, A. Angnel. 50b, Mihail Eminescu, C. Baraschi. 55b, Peasant Revolt, 1907, M. Constantinescu (horiz.). 1 l, "Peace," I. Jalea. 1.55 l, Building Socialism, C. Medrea. 1.75 l, Birth of an Idea, A. Szobotka.

1403	A499	5b car rose	10	5
1404	A499	10b violet	10	5
1405	A499	20b ol blk	15	10
1406	A499	40b ol bis	20	10
1407	A499	50b blk brn	25	15
1408	A499	55b org ver	30	15
1409	A499	1 l dp plum	60	20
1410	A499	1.55 l brt ultra	80	20
1411	A499	1.75 l green	1.50	30
		Nos. 1403-1411 (9)	4.00	1.30

ROMANIA

Peter Poni, and Chemical Apparatus
A500

Scientists: 20b, A. Saligny and Danube bridge, Cernavoda. 55b, C. Budeanu and electrical formula. 1.55 l, Gh. Titeica and geometrical symbol.

1961, Apr. 11 Litho. Perf. 13½x13
Portraits in Brown Black

1412	A500	10b pink & vio bl	10	5
1413	A500	20b cit & mar	15	6
1414	A500	55b bl & red	35	10
1415	A500	1.55 l ocher & lil	1.25	35

Issued to honor Romanian scientists.

Freighter "Galati"—A501

Ships: 40b, Passenger ship "Oltenita." 55b, Motorboat "Tomis." 1 l, Freighter "Arad." 1.55 l, Tugboat. 1.75 l, Freighter "Dobrogea."

1961, Apr. 25 Typo. Perf. 14x13

1416	A501	20b multi	10	5
1417	A501	40b multi	20	8
1418	A501	55b multi	30	10
1419	A501	1 l multi	45	15
1420	A501	1.55 l multi	1.00	25
1421	A501	1.75 l multi	1.25	35
	Nos. 1416-1421 (6)		3.30	98

Marx, Lenin and Engels on Red Flag—A502

Designs: 55b, Workers. 1 l, "Industry and Agriculture" and Workers Party Emblem.

1961, Apr. 29 Lithographed

| 1422 | A502 | 33b red, bl & ocher | 30 | 6 |
| 1423 | A502 | 55b mar, red & gray | 45 | 15 |

Souvenir Sheet
Imperf.

| 1424 | A502 | 1 l multi | 1.75 | 95 |

Issued to commemorate 40th anniversary of the Romanian Communist Party. No. 1424 has blue inscription, yellow and red ornaments in margin. Sheet measures: 114x79mm.; the stamp measures: 55x33 mm.

Roe Deer and Bronze Age Hunting Scene
A503

Lynx and Prehistoric Hunter
A504

Designs: 35b, Boar and Roman hunter. 40b, Brown bear and Roman tombstone. 55b, Red deer, 16th cent. hunter. 75b, Red fox and feudal hunter. 1 l, Black goat and modern hunter. 1.55 l, Rabbit and hunter with dog. 1.75 l, Badger and hunter. 2 l, Roebuck and hunter.

1961, July Perf. 13x14, 14x13

1425	A503	10b multi	5	5
1426	A504	20b multi	15	5
1427	A504	35b multi	30	5
1428	A504	40b multi	35	5
1429	A503	55b multi	35	5
1430	A504	75b multi	45	15
1431	A503	1 l multi	75	15
1432	A503	1.55 l multi	1.50	20
1433	A503	1.75 l multi	2.25	30
1434	A503	2 l multi	2.75	45
	Nos. 1425-1434 (10)		8.90	1.50

Georges Enescu
A505

1961, Sept. 7 Litho. Perf. 14x13

| 1435 | A505 | 3 l pale vio & vio brn | 2.00 | 45 |

Second International Georges Enescu Festival, Bucharest.

Peasant Playing Panpipe **Heraclitus**
A506 A507

Peasants playing musical instruments: 20b, Alpenhorn (horiz.). 40b, Flute. 55b, Guitar. 60b, Bagpipe. 1 l, Zither.

Typographed

1961 Perf. 13x14, 14x13 Unwmkd.
Tinted Paper

1436	A506	10b multi	5	6
1437	A506	20b multi	15	6
1438	A506	40b multi	30	8
1439	A506	55b multi	60	10
1440	A506	60b multi	60	20
1441	A506	1 l multi	85	30
	Nos. 1436-1441 (6)		2.55	80

Perf. 13½x13

1961, Oct. 25 Photo. Wmk. 358

Portraits: 20b, Francis Bacon. 40b, Rabindranath Tagore. 55b, Domingo F. Sarmiento. 1.35 l, Heinrich von Kleist. 1.75 l, Mikhail V. Lomonosov.

1442	A507	10b maroon	15	5
1443	A507	20b brown	15	5
1444	A507	40b Prus grn	20	6
1445	A507	55b cerise	30	6
1446	A507	1.35 l brt bl	1.00	15
1447	A507	1.75 l purple	1.35	20
	Nos. 1442-1447 (6)		3.15	57

Swimming
A508

Gold Medal, Boxing
A509

Designs: No. 1449, Olympic torch. No. 1450, Water polo, Melbourne. No. 1451, Women's high jump, Rome.

1961, Oct. 30 Photo. Unwmkd.

Perf. 14x14½

1448	A508	20b bl gray	25	15
1449	A508	20b vermilion	25	15
1450	A508	55b ultra	50	25
1451	A508	55b blue	50	25

Perf. 10½
Size: 33x33mm.

Gold Medals: 35b, Pistol shooting, Melbourne. 40b, Sharpshooting, Rome. 55b, Wrestling. 1.35 l, Woman's high jump. 1.75 l, Three medals for canoeing.

Medals in Ochre

1452	A509	10b Prus grn	17	10
1453	A509	35b brown	35	15
1454	A509	40b plum	40	15
1455	A509	55b org red	50	20
1456	A509	1.35 l dp ultra	1.10	15

Size: 46x32mm.

| 1457 | A509 | 1.75 l dp car rose | 1.50 | 45 |
| | Nos. 1452-1457 (6) | | 4.02 | 1.20 |

Romania's gold medals in 1956, 1960 Olympics.

#1452-1457 exist imperf. Price, set $10. A Souvenir sheet of one 4 l dark red & ocher was issued.
Price unused $9, canceled $6.

Congress Emblem **Primrose**
A510 A511

1961, Dec. Litho. Perf. 13½x14

| 1458 | A510 | 55b dk car rose | 75 | 45 |

Issued to publicize the Fifth World Congress of Trade Unions, Moscow, Dec. 4–16.

Perf. 14x13½, 13½x14

1961, Sept. 15

Designs: 20b, Sweet William. 25b, Peony. 35b, Prickly pear. 40b, Iris. 55b, Buttercup. 1 l, Hepatica. 1.20 l, Poppy. 1.55 l, Gentian. 1.75 l, Carol Davilla and Dimitrie Brindza. 20b, 25b, 40b, 55b, 1.20 l, 1.55 l, are vertical.

1459	A511	10b multi	8	5
1460	A511	20b multi	10	5
1461	A511	25b multi	15	5
1462	A511	35b multi	30	5
1463	A511	40b multi	35	5
1464	A511	55b multi	45	10
1465	A511	1 l multi	60	15
1466	A511	1.20 l multi	75	20
1467	A511	1.55 l multi	1.50	45
	Nos. 1459-1467 (9)		4.28	1.15

Souvenir Sheet
Imperf.

| 1468 | A511 | 1.75 l car, blk & grn | 4.50 | 2.25 |

Nos. 1459–1468 issued to commemorate the centenary of the Bucharest Botanical Garden. No. 1468 contains one stamp with ochre and gray green ornamental border. Size: 105x72mm.

#1459-1467 exist imperf. Price, set $8.

United Nations Emblem **Cock and Savings Book**
A512 A513

Designs: 20b, Map of Balkan peninsula and dove. 40b, Men of three races.

1961, Nov. 27 Perf. 13½x14

1469	A512	20b bl, yel & pink	35	10
1470	A512	40b multi	75	18
1471	A512	55b org, lil & yel	1.00	25

Issued to commemorate the 15th anniversary of the United Nations. Nos. 1470–1471 are each printed with alternating yellow labels.

Exist imperf. Price, set $5.

1962, Feb. 15 Typo. Perf. 13½

Designs: 55b, Honeycomb, bee and savings book.

| 1472 | A513 | 40b multi | 35 | 15 |
| 1473 | A513 | 55b multi | 35 | 25 |

Issued to publicize Savings Day.

Soccer Player and Map of Europe **Wheat, Map and Tractor**
A514 A515

Lithographed

1962, Apr. 20 Perf. 13x14 Unwmkd.

| 1474 | A514 | 55b emer & red brn | 75 | 35 |

Issued to commemorate the European Junior Soccer Championships, Bucharest.

1962, Apr. 27 Perf. 13½x14

Designs: 55b, Medal honoring agriculture. 1.55 l, Sheaf of wheat, hammer & sickle.

1475	A515	40b org & dk car	30	10
1476	A515	55b yel, car & brn	35	10
1477	A515	1.55 l multi	1.00	35

Collectivization of agriculture.

Canoe Race
A516

ROMANIA

Designs: 20b, Kayak. 40b, Eight-man shell. 55b, Two-man skiff. 1 l, Yachts. 1.20 l, Motorboats. 1.55 l, Sailboat. 3 l, Water slalom.

1962, May 15   Photo.   Perf. 14x13
Vignette in Bright Blue

1478	A516	10b lil rose	5	5
1479	A516	20b ol gray	15	5
1480	A516	40b red brn	20	5
1481	A516	55b ultra	35	5
1482	A516	1 l red	45	5
1483	A516	1.20 l dp plum	90	15
1484	A516	1.55 l orange	1.25	25
1485	A516	3 l violet	2.25	50
		Nos. 1478-1485 (8)	5.60	1.15

These stamps were also issued imperf. with color of denomination and inscription changed.
Price, set unused $10, canceled $4.50.

Ion Luca Caragiale
A517

Portraits: 40b, Jean Jacques Rousseau. 1.75 l, Aleksander I. Herzen. 3.30 l, Ion Luca Caragiale (as a young man).

1962, June 9   Perf. 13½x14

1486	A517	40b dk sl grn	30	15
1487	A517	55b magenta	35	15
1488	A517	1.75 l dp bl	1.25	30

Souvenir Sheet
Perf. 11½

| 1489 | A517 | 3.30 l brown | 4.25 | 2.25 |

No. 1486 commemorates the 250th anniversary of the birth of J. J. Rousseau, French philosopher, Nos. 1487 and 1489 commemorate the 50th anniversary of the death of I. L. Caragiale, Romanian author, and No. 1488 commemorates the 150th anniversary of the birth of A. I. Herzen, Russian writer. No. 1489 contains one stamp (32x55mm), marginal design shows titles of works by Caragiale. Size of sheet: 91x121mm.

Globes Surrounded with Flags
A518
Typographed

1962, July 6   Perf. 11   Unwmkd.

| 1490 | A518 | 55b multi | 60 | 20 |

Issued to publicize the 8th Youth Festival for Peace and Friendship, Helsinki, July 28–Aug. 6, 1962.

Traian Vuia   Fieldball Player and Globe
A519   A520

Perf. 13½x14
1962, July 20   Photo.   Wmk. 358
Portraits: 20b, Al. Davila. 35b, Vasile Pirvan. 40b, Ion Negulici. 55b, Grigore Cobilescu. 1 l, Dr. Gheorghe Marinescu. 1.20 l, Ion Cantacuzino. 1.35 l, Victor Babes. 1.55 l, C. Levaditi.

1491	A519	15b brown	15	10
1492	A519	20b dl red brn	15	10
1493	A519	35b brn mag	20	10
1494	A519	40b bl vio	20	10
1495	A519	55b brt bl	30	10
1496	A519	1 l dp ultra	35	10
1497	A519	1.20 l crimson	60	15
1498	A519	1.35 l Prus grn	75	20
1499	A519	1.55 l purple	1.50	20
		Nos. 1491-1499 (9)	4.20	1.30

Perf. 13x14
1962, May 12   Litho.   Unwmkd.

| 1500 | A520 | 55b yel & vio | 75 | 15 |

Issued to commemorate the 2nd International Women's Fieldball Championships, Bucharest.

Same Surcharged in Violet Blue:
"Campioana Mondială 5 lei"
1962, July 31

| 1501 | A520 | 5 l on 55b yel & vio | 6.00 | 3.50 |

Issued to commemorate the Romanian victory in the 2nd International Women's Fieldball Championships.

Rod Fishing
A521
Various Fishing Scenes

1962, July 25   Perf. 14x13

1502	A521	10b multi	15	5
1503	A521	25b multi	15	5
1504	A521	40b bl & brick red	20	10
1505	A521	55b multi	30	10
1506	A521	75b sl, gray & bl	45	15
1507	A521	1 l multi	70	25
1508	A521	1.75 l multi	1.10	25
1509	A521	3.25 l multi	2.00	45
		Nos. 1502-1509 (8)	5.05	1.40

No. 1474 Surcharged in Dark Blue:
"1962 Campioană Europeană 2 lei"
1962, July 31

| 1510 | A514 | 2 l on 55b emer & red brn | 3.00 | 2.00 |

Issued to commemorate Romania's victory in the European Junior Soccer Championships, Bucharest.

Child and Butterfly   Handicraft
A522   A523

Designs: 30b, Girl feeding bird. 40b, Boy and model sailboat. 55b, Children writing (horiz.). 1.20 l, Girl at piano, and boy playing violin. 1.55 l, Pioneers camping (horiz.).

Lithographed
1962, Aug. 25   Perf. 13x14, 14x13

1511	A522	20b lt bl, red & brn	15	8
1512	A522	30b org, bl & red brn	15	8
1513	A522	40b chlky bl, dp org & Prus bl	20	12
1514	A522	55b cit, bl & red	35	8
1515	A522	1.20 l car, brn & dk vio	60	25
1516	A522	1.55 l bis, red & vio	1.25	25
		Nos. 1511-1516 (6)	2.70	86

1962, Oct. 12   Perf. 13x14
Designs: 10b, Food and drink. 20b, Chemical industry. 40b, Chinaware. 55b, Leather industry. 75b, Textiles. 1 l, Furniture. 1.20 l, Electrical appliances. 1.55 l, Household goods (sewing machine and pots).

1517	A523	5b multi	15	8
1518	A523	10b multi	10	8
1519	A523	20b multi	10	8
1520	A523	40b multi	30	8
1521	A523	55b multi	30	8
1522	A523	75b multi	35	8
1523	A523	1 l multi	50	10
1524	A523	1.20 l multi	90	25
1525	A523	1.55 l multi	1.50	30
		Nos. 1517-1525, C126 (10)	5.70	1.48

4th Sample Fair, Bucharest.

Lenin   Bull
A524   A525

1962, Nov. 7   Perf. 10½

| 1526 | A524 | 55b vio bl, red & bis | 50 | 20 |

Issued to commemorate the 45th anniversary of the Russian October Revolution.

1962, Nov. 20   Perf. 14x13, 13x14
Designs: 20b, Sheep (horiz.). 40b, Merino ram (horiz.). 1 l, York pig. 1.35 l, Cow. 1.55 l, Heifer (horiz.). 1.75 l, Pigs (horiz.).

1527	A525	20b ultra & blk	15	10
1528	A525	40b bl, yel & sep	20	10
1529	A525	55b ocher, buff & sl grn	30	12
1530	A525	1 l gray, yel & brn	45	15
1531	A525	1.35 l dl grn, choc & blk	60	25
1532	A525	1.55 l org red, dk brn & blk	1.00	35
1533	A525	1.75 l dk vio bl, yel & org	1.25	65
		Nos. 1527-1533 (7)	3.95	1.72

Arms, Factory and Harvester
A526

Perf. 14½x13½
1962, Dec. 30   Litho.   Unwmkd.

| 1534 | A526 | 1.55 l multi | 1.50 | 30 |

Issued to commemorate the 15th anniversary of the Romanian People's Republic.

Strikers at Grivita, 1933
A527

1963, Feb. 16   Perf. 14x13½

| 1535 | A527 | 1.75 l red, vio & yel | 1.10 | 25 |

Issued to commemorate the 30th anniversary of the strike of railroad and oil industry workers at Grivita.

Tractor Driver and "FAO" Emblem   Tomatoes
A528   A529

Designs: 55b, Farm woman, cornfield and combine. 1.55 l, Child drinking milk and milking machine. 1.75 l, Woman with basket of grapes and vineyard.

1963, Mar. 21 Photo. Perf. 14½x13

1536	A528	40b vio bl	15	10
1537	A528	55b bis brn	25	10
1538	A528	1.55 l rose red	75	20
1539	A528	1.75 l green	1.25	30

Issued for the "Freedom from Hunger" campaign of the U.N. Food and Agriculture Organization.

Perf. 13½x14, 14x13½
1963, Apr. 25   Litho.   Unwmkd.
Designs: 40b, Hot peppers. 55b, Radishes. 75b, Eggplant. 1.20 l, Mild peppers. 3.25 l, Cucumbers (horiz.).

1540	A529	35b multi	15	10
1541	A529	40b multi	20	10
1542	A529	55b multi	25	10
1543	A529	75b multi	35	15
1544	A529	1.20 l multi	90	20
1545	A529	3.25 l multi	2.00	60
		Nos. 1540-1545 (6)	3.85	1.25

Woman Swimmer at Start   Chicks
A530   A531

Designs: 30b, Crawl (horiz.). 55b, Butterfly stroke (horiz.). 1 l, Backstroke (horiz.). 1.35 l, Breaststroke (horiz.). 1.55 l, Woman diver. 2 l, Water polo.

1963, June 15 Perf. 13x14, 14x13

1546	A530	25b yel brn, emer & gray	15	8
1547	A530	30b ol grn, gray & yel	20	8
1548	A530	55b bl, gray & red	30	10
1549	A530	1 l grn, gray & red	45	15
1550	A530	1.35 l ultra, car & gray	60	20
1551	A530	1.55 l pur, gray & org	1.10	25
1552	A530	2 l car rose, gray & org	1.25	75
		Nos. 1546-1552 (7)	4.05	1.61

ROMANIA

1963, May 23 *Perf. 10½*
Domestic poultry: 30b, Hen. 40b, Goose. 55b, White cock. 70b, Duck. 1 l, Hen. 1.35 l, Tom turkey. 3.20 l, Hen.

Fowl in Natural Colors; Inscription in Dark Blue

1553	A531	20b ultra	15	5
1554	A531	30b tan	15	8
1555	A531	40b org brn	18	8
1556	A531	55b brt grn	22	8
1557	A531	70b lilac	45	10
1558	A531	1 l blue	60	15
1559	A531	1.35 l ocher	90	20
1560	A531	3.20 l yel grn	1.75	75
Nos. 1553-1560 (8)			4.40	1.49

Women and Globe
A532

1963, June 15 *Photo.* *Perf. 14x13*

| 1561 | A532 | 55b dk bl | 45 | 15 |

Issued to commemorate the International Women's Congress, Moscow, June 24–29.

William M. Thackeray, Writer
A533

Portraits: 50b, Eugene Delacroix, painter. 55b, Gheorghe Marinescu, physician. 1.55 l, Giuseppe Verdi, composer. 1.75 l, Stanislavski, actor and producer.

1963, July *Perf. 14x13* *Unwmkd.*
Portrait in Black

1562	A533	40b pale vio	20	10
1563	A533	50b bis brn	30	15
1564	A533	55b olive	40	20
1565	A533	1.55 l rose brn	80	25
1566	A533	1.75 l pale vio bl	1.25	30
Nos. 1562-1566 (5)			2.95	1.00

Walnuts
A534

Designs: 20b, Plums. 40b, Peaches. 55b, Strawberries. 1 l, Grapes. 1.55 l, Apples. 1.60 l, Cherries. 1.75 l, Pears.

1963, Sept. 15 *Litho.* *Perf. 14x13½*
Fruits in Natural Colors

1567	A534	10b pale yel & brn ol	10	10
1568	A534	20b pale pink & red org	10	10
1569	A534	40b lt bl & bl	20	10
1570	A534	55b dl yel & rose car	25	10
1571	A534	1 l pale vio & vio	45	15
1572	A534	1.55 l yel grn & ultra	35	15
1573	A534	1.60 l yel & bis	1.25	20
1574	A534	1.75 l lt bl & grn	1.25	30
Nos. 1567-1574 (8)			4.35	1.20

Women Playing Volleyball and Map of Europe
A535

Designs: 40b, Three men players. 55b, Three women players. 1.75 l, Two men players. 3.20 l, Europa Cup.

1963, Oct. 22 *Perf. 13½x14*

1575	A535	5b gray & lil rose	15	8
1576	A535	40b gray & vio bl	30	10
1577	A535	55b gray & grnsh bl	50	15
1578	A535	1.75 l gray & org brn	90	30
1579	A535	3.20 l gray & vio	1.75	75
Nos. 1575-1579 (5)			3.60	1.38

Issued to commemorate the European Volleyball Championships, Oct. 22–Nov. 4.

Pine Tree, Branch and Cone
A536

Design: 1.75 l, Beech forest and branch.

Photogravure
1963, Dec. 5 *Perf. 13½* *Unwmkd.*

| 1580 | A536 | 55b dk grn | 25 | 15 |
| 1581 | A536 | 1.75 l dk bl | 75 | 30 |

Reforestation program.

Silkworm Moth   18th Century
A537   House, Ploesti
                  ### A538

Designs: 20b, Chrysalis, moth and worm. 40b, Silkworm on leaf. 55b, Bee over mountains (horiz.). 60b, 1.20 l, 1.35 l, 1.60 l, Bees pollinating various flowers (horiz.).

1963, Dec. 12 *Litho.* *Perf. 13x14*

1582	A537	10b multi	15	8
1583	A537	20b multi	20	10
1584	A537	40b multi	30	10
1585	A537	55b multi	45	15
1586	A537	60b multi	60	20
1587	A537	1.20 l multi	1.00	25
1588	A537	1.35 l multi	1.25	35
1589	A537	1.60 l multi	1.75	35
Nos. 1582-1589 (8)			5.65	1.58

1963, Dec. 25 Engraved Perf. 13

Peasant Houses from Village Museum, Bucharest: 40b, Oltenia, 1875 (horiz.). 55b, Hunedoara, 19th Cent. (horiz.). 75b, Oltenia, 19th Cent. 1 l, Brasov, 1847. 1.20 l, Bacau, 19th Cent. 1.75 l, Arges, 19th Cent.

1590	A538	20b claret	15	10
1591	A538	40b blue	20	10
1592	A538	55b dl vio	30	10
1593	A538	75b green	35	10
1594	A538	1 l brn & mar	60	10
1595	A538	1.20 l gray ol	75	15
1596	A538	1.75 l dk brn & ultra	1.35	25
Nos. 1590-1596 (7)			3.70	90

Ski Jump
A539

Sports: 20b, Speed skating. 40b, Ice hockey. 55b, Women's figure skating. 60b, Slalom. 75b, Biathlon. 1 l, Bob-sledding. 1.20 l, Cross-country skiing.

1963, Nov. 25 *Litho.* *Perf. 14*

1597	A539	10b red & dk bl	15	6
1598	A539	20b ultra & red brn	20	6
1599	A539	40b emer & red brn	30	6
1600	A539	55b vio & red brn	45	12
1601	A539	60b org & vio bl	60	30
1602	A539	75b lil rose & dk bl	75	30
1603	A539	1 l bis & vio bl	1.25	50
1604	A539	1.20 l grnsh bl & vio	1.35	70
Nos. 1597-1604 (8)			5.05	2.10

Issued to publicize the 9th Winter Olympic Games, Innsbruck, Jan. 29–Feb. 9, 1964.

Exist imperf. in changed colors. Price, set $10.

A souvenir sheet contains one imperf. stamp, a 1.50-lei ultramarine and red stamp showing the Olympic Ice Stadium at Innsbruck and the Winter Games emblem. Size: 124x79½mm.

Price $12.

Elena Teodorini   Munteanu
as Carmen   Murgoci and
A540   Congress Emblem
                    ### A541

Designs: 10b, George Stephanescu, founder of Romanian opera. 35b, Ion Bajenaru as Petru Rares. 40b, D. Popovici as Alberich. 55b, Hariclea Darclée as Tosca. 75b, George Folescu as Boris Godunov. 1 l, Jean Athanasiu as Rigoletto. 1.35 l, Traian Grosavescu as Duke in Rigoletto. 1.55 l, N. Leonard as Hoffmann.

1964, Jan. 20 *Photo.* *Perf. 13*
Portrait in Dark Brown

1605	A540	10b olive	6	5
1606	A540	20b ultra	8	5
1607	A540	35b green	15	5
1608	A540	40b grnsh bl	18	5
1609	A540	55b car rose	30	5
1610	A540	75b lilac	30	5
1611	A540	1 l blue	60	15
1612	A540	1.35 l brt vio	1.25	30
1613	A540	1.55 l red org	1.40	30
Nos. 1605-1613 (9)			4.62	1.05

1964, Feb. 5 *Perf. 13* *Unwmkd.*

| 1614 | A541 | 1.60 l brt bl, ind & bis | 1.10 | 20 |

Issued to commemorate the 8th International Soil Congress, Bucharest.

Asculphaid
A542

Insects: 10b, Thread-waisted wasp. 35b, Wasp. 40b, Rhyparioides metelkana moth. 55b, Tussock moth. 1.20 l, Kanetisa circe butterfly. 1.55 l, Beetle. 1.75 l, Horned beetle.

1964, Feb. 20 *Perf. 14x13*
Insects in Natural Colors

1615	A542	5b pale lil	10	10
1616	A542	10b lt bl & red	15	10
1617	A542	35b pale grn	20	8
1618	A542	40b ol grn	25	8
1619	A542	55b ultra	30	15
1620	A542	1.20 l pale grn & red	60	15
1621	A542	1.55 l yel & brn	90	15
1622	A542	1.75 l org & red	1.00	25
Nos. 1615-1622 (8)			3.50	1.06

Tobacco Plant   Jumping
A543   A544

Garden flowers: 20b, Geranium. 40b, Fuchsia. 55b, Chrysanthemum. 75b, Dahlia. 1 l, Lily. 1.25 l, Day lily. 1.55 l, Marigold.

1964, March 25 *Perf. 13x14*

1623	A543	10b dk bl, grn & bis	10	5
1624	A543	20b gray, grn & red	10	5
1625	A543	40b pale grn, grn & red	20	5
1626	A543	55b grn, lt grn & lil	30	5
1627	A543	75b cit, red & grn	35	5
1628	A543	1 l dp cl, rose cl, grn & org	50	10
1629	A543	1.25 l sal, vio bl & grn	80	20
1630	A543	1.55 l red brn, yel & grn	1.00	20
Nos. 1623-1630 (8)			3.35	85

Photogravure
1964, Apr. 25 *Perf. 13* *Unwmkd.*

Horse Show Events: 40b, Dressage (horiz.). 1.35 l, Jumping. 1.55 l, Galloping (horiz.).

1631	A544	40b lt bl, rose brn & blk	20	15
1632	A544	55b lil, red & brn	30	15
1633	A544	1.35 l brt grn, red & dk bl	90	30
1634	A544	1.55 l pale yel, bl & dp cl	1.35	30

Hogfish   Mihail
A545   Eminescu
                    ### A546

Fish (Constanta Aquarium): 10b, Peacock blenny. 20b, Mediterranean scad. 40b, Sturgeon. 50b, Sea horses. 55b, Yellow gurnard. 1 l, Beluga. 3.20 l, Stingray.

1964, May 10 Lithographed *Perf. 14*

1635	A545	5b multi	7	5
1636	A545	10b multi	8	5
1637	A545	20b multi	15	5
1638	A545	40b multi	20	5
1639	A545	50b multi	30	10
1640	A545	55b multi	30	10
1641	A545	1 l multi	75	15
1642	A545	3.20 l multi	1.80	35
Nos. 1635-1642 (8)			3.65	90

Photogravure
1964, June 20 *Perf. 13* *Unwmkd.*
Portraits in Dark Brown

Portraits: 20b, Ion Creanga. 35b, Emil Girleanu. 55b, Michelangelo. 1.20 l, Galileo Galilei. 1.75 l, William Shakespeare.

1643	A546	5b green	10	8
1644	A546	20b magenta	15	8
1645	A546	35b vermilion	35	10
1646	A546	55b bister	40	12

ROMANIA

1647	A546	1.20 l ultra	70	25
1648	A546	1.75 l violet	1.00	35
	Nos. 1643-1648 (6)		2.70	98

Issued to commemorate the 50th anniversary of the death of Emil Girleanu, writer; the 75th anniversary of the deaths of Ion Creanga and Mihail Eminescu, writers; the 400th anniversary of the death of Michelangelo and the births of Galileo and Shakespeare.

Road through Gorge — A547 **High Jump** — A548

Designs: 55b, Lake Bilea and cottage. 1 l, Ski lift, Polana Brasov. 1.35 l, Ceahlaul peak and Lake Bicaz (horiz.). 1.75 l, Hotel Alpin.

1964, June 29 — Engraved

1649	A547	40b rose brn	20	10
1650	A547	55b dk bl	30	10
1651	A547	1 l dl pur	50	10
1652	A547	1.35 l pale brn	75	15
1653	A547	1.75 l green	90	30
	Nos. 1649-1653 (5)		2.65	75

Issued for tourist publicity.

1964, July 28 — Photogravure

Designs: 40b, Javelin throw. 55b, Running. 1 l, Discus throw. 1.20 l, Hurdling. 1.55 l, Map and flags of Balkan countries.

Size: 23x37½mm.

1654	A548	30b ver, yel & yel grn	20	8
1655	A548	40b grn, yel, brn & vio	20	10
1656	A548	55b gldn brn, yel & bl grn	35	12
1657	A548	1 l brt bl, yel, brn & red	75	15
1658	A548	1.20 l pur, yel, brn & grn	85	20

Lithographed
Size: 23x45mm.

| 1659 | A548 | 1.55 l multi | 1.50 | 45 |
| | Nos. 1654-1659 (6) | | 3.85 | 1.20 |

The 1964 Balkan Games.

Factory — A549

Designs: 55b, Flag and Coat of Arms (vert.). 75b, Combine. 1.20 l, Apartment buildings. 2 l, Flag, coat of arms, industrial and agricultural scenes. 55b, 2 l, Inscribed "A XX A aniversare a eliberarii patriei!"

1964, Aug. 23 — Photo. Perf. 13

1660	A549	55b multi	20	15
1661	A549	60b multi	30	15
1662	A549	75b multi	30	25
1663	A549	1.20 l multi	60	25

Souvenir Sheet
Imperf.

| 1664 | A549 | 2 l multi | 1.75 | 1.10 |

Issued to commemorate the 20th anniversary of Romania's liberation. No. 1664 contains one stamp (110x70mm.). Size of sheet: 134x95mm.

High Jump — A550

Sport: 30b, Wrestling. 35b, Volleyball. 40b, Canoeing. 55b, Fencing. 1.20 l, Women's gymnastics. 1.35 l, Soccer. 1.55 l, Sharpshooting.

1964, Sept. 1 — Lithographed
Olympic Rings in Blue, Yellow, Black, Green and Red

1665	A550	20b yel & blk	30	5
1666	A550	30b lil & blk	30	5
1667	A550	35b grnsh bl & blk	30	5
1668	A550	40b pink & blk	35	5
1669	A550	55b lt yel grn & blk	50	5
1670	A550	1.20 l org & blk	1.00	30
1671	A550	1.35 l ocher & blk	1.25	45
1672	A550	1.55 l bl & blk	1.35	75
	Nos. 1665-1672 (8)		5.35	1.76

18th Olympic Games, Tokyo, Oct. 10–25. Nos. 1665–1669 exist imperf., in changed colors. Three other denominations exist, 1.60 l, 2 l and 2.40 l, imperf. Price, set of 8, unused $12, canceled $7.50.
An imperf. souvenir sheet contains a 3.25 l stamp showing a runner; Olympic torch and rings on yellow margin. Size: 80x110mm.
Price unused $12, canceled $7.50.

Georges Enescu, Piano Keys and Neck of Violin — A551

Designs: 55b, Enescu at piano. 1.60 l, Enescu Festival medal. 1.75 l, Enescu bust by G. Anghel.

1964, Sept. 5 — Engraved

1673	A551	10b bl grn	10	8
1674	A551	55b vio blk	30	15
1675	A551	1.60 l dk red brn	80	30
1676	A551	1.75 l dk bl	1.40	35

Third International Georges Enescu Festival, Bucharest, Sept., 1964.

Black Swans — A552

Designs: 5b, Indian python. 35b, Ostriches. 40b, Crowned cranes. 55b, Tigers. 1 l, Lions. 1.55 l, Grevy's zebras. 2 l, Bactrian camels.

Perf. 14x13
1964, Sept. 28 — Litho. Unwmkd.

1677	A552	5b multi	8	5
1678	A552	10b multi	12	5
1679	A552	35b multi	20	5
1680	A552	40b multi	30	5
1681	A552	55b multi	40	5
1682	A552	1 l multi	75	16
1683	A552	1.55 l multi	1.50	25
1684	A552	2 l multi	2.00	30
	Nos. 1677-1684 (8)		5.35	99

Issued to publicize the Bucharest Zoo.

C. Brincoveanu, Stolnicul Cantacuzino, Gheorghe Lazar and Academy — A553

Designs: 40b, Alexandru Ioan Cuza, medal and University. 55b, Masks, curtain, harp, keyboard and palette (vert.). 75b, Women students in laboratory and auditorium. 1 l, Savings Bank building.

Perf. 13x13½, 13½x13
1964, Oct. 14 — Photogravure

1685	A553	20b multi	15	8
1686	A553	40b multi	20	8
1687	A553	55b multi	30	15
1688	A553	75b multi	35	20
1689	A553	1 l dk brn, yel & org	60	40
	Nos. 1685-1689 (5)		1.60	93

No. 1685 commemorates the 250th anniversary of the Royal Academy; Nos. 1686 and 1688 commemorate the centenary of the University of Bucharest; No. 1687 commemorates the centenary of the Academy of Art and No. 1689 commemorates the centenary of the Savings Bank.

Soldier's Head and Laurel — A554

1964, Oct. 25 — Litho. Perf. 12x12½

| 1690 | A554 | 55b ultra & lt bl | 35 | 15 |

Issued for Army Day.

Canadian Kayak Singles Gold Medal, Melbourne, 1956 — A555
Strawberries — A556

Romanian Olympic Gold Medals: 30b, Boxing, Melbourne, 1956. 35b, Rapid Silhouette Pistol, Melbourne, 1956. 40b, Women's High Jump, Rome, 1960. 55b, Wrestling, Rome, 1960. 1.20 l, Clay Pigeon Shooting, Rome, 1960. 1.35 l, High Jump, Tokyo, 1964. 1.55 l, Javelin, Tokyo, 1964.

1964, Nov. 30 Photo. Perf. 13½
Medals in Gold and Brown

1691	A555	20b pink & ultra	20	5
1692	A555	30b yel & ultra	30	5
1693	A555	35b bluish grn & ultra	40	5
1694	A555	40b lil & ultra	60	5
1695	A555	55b org & ultra	70	5
1696	A555	1.20 l ol grn & ultra	1.00	15
1697	A555	1.35 l gldn brn & ultra	1.35	50
1698	A555	1.55 l rose lil & ultra	1.75	50
	Nos. 1691-1698 (8)		6.30	1.40

Issued to honor Romanian athletes, who won gold medals in three Olympic Games. Nos. 1691–1695 exist imperf., in changed colors. Three other denominations exist, 1.60 l, 2 l and 2.40 l, imperf. Price, set of 8, unused $9, canceled $3.
A 10 l souvenir sheet shows the 1964 Olympic gold medal and world map. Size: 140x110mm.
Price unused $10, canceled $5.

1964, Dec. 20 Litho. Perf. 13½x14
Designs: 35b, Blackberries. 40b, Raspberries. 55b, Rose hips. 1.20 l, Blueberries. 1.35 l, Cornelian cherries. 1.55 l, Hazelnuts. 2.55 l, Cherries.

1703	A556	5b gray, red & grn	5	5
1704	A556	35b ocher, grn & dk vio bl	15	5
1705	A556	40b pale vio, car & grn	20	5
1706	A556	55b yel grn, grn & red	25	6
1707	A556	1.20 l sal grn, grn, brn & ind	60	14
1708	A556	1 l lt bl, grn & red	70	14
1709	A556	1.55 l gldn brn, grn & ocher	1.25	25
1710	A556	2.55 l ultra, grn & red	2.00	45
	Nos. 1703-1710 (8)		5.20	1.19

Syncom 3 — A557 **U.N. Headquarters, N.Y.** — A558

Space Satellites: 40b, Syncom 3 over TV antennas. 55b, Ranger 7 reaching moon close-up (horiz.). 1 l, Ranger 7 and moon close-up (horiz.). 1.20 l, Voskhod. 5 l, Konstantin Feoktistov, Vladimir M. Komarov, Boris B. Yegorov and Voskhod.

Perf. 13x14, 14x13
1965, Jan. 5 Litho. Unwmkd.
Size: 22x38mm., 38x22mm.

1711	A557	30b multi	20	10
1712	A557	40b multi	30	10
1713	A557	55b multi	45	10
1714	A557	1 l multi	55	10
1715	A557	1.20 l multi, horiz.	90	20

Perf. 13½x13
Size: 52x30mm.

| 1716 | A557 | 5 l multi | 3.00 | 95 |
| | Nos. 1711-1716 (6) | | 5.40 | 1.55 |

1965, Jan. 25 Perf. 12x12½
Design: 1.60 l, Arms and flag of Romania, and U.N. emblem.

1717	A558	55b ultra, red & gold	40	18
1718	A558	1.60 l ultra, red, gold & yel	85	25

Issued to commemorate the 20th anniversary of the United Nations and the 10th anniversary of Romania's membership in the United Nations.

Greek Tortoise — A559

Reptiles: 10b, Bull lizard. 20b, Three-lined lizard. 55b, Slow worm. 60b, Sand viper. 1 l, Desert lizard. 1.20 l, Orsini's viper. 1.35 l, Caspian whipsnake. 3.25 l, Four-lined snake.

ROMANIA

1965, Feb. 25 Photo. Perf. 13½

1719	A559	5b multi	5	5
1720	A559	10b multi	10	5
1721	A559	20b multi	10	5
1722	A559	40b multi	15	5
1723	A559	55b multi	20	10
1724	A559	60b multi	30	10
1725	A559	1 l multi	40	15
1726	A559	1.20 l multi	75	15
1727	A559	1.35 l multi	85	25
1728	A559	3.25 l multi	1.75	35
		Nos. 1719-1728 (10)	4.65	1.30

White Persian Cats
A560

Designs: 1.35 l, Siamese cat. Others, Various European cats. (5b, 10b, 3.25 l horizontal.)

1965, Mar. 20 Lithographed
Size: 41x29mm., 29x41mm.
Cats in Natural Colors

1729	A560	5b brn org & blk	5	5
1730	A560	10b brt bl & blk	5	5
1731	A560	40b yel grn, yel & blk	20	12
1732	A560	55b rose red & blk	30	10
1733	A560	60b yel & blk	35	10
1734	A560	75b lt vio & blk	60	10
1735	A560	1.35 l red org & blk	90	15

Perf. 13x13½
Size: 62x29mm.

1736	A560	3.25 l blue	2.50	60
		Nos. 1729-1736 (8)	4.95	1.27

No. 1714 Surcharged in Violet

RANGER 9
24 - 3 - 1965

5 Lei

1965, Apr. 25 Perf. 14x13

1737	A557	5 l on 1 l multi	20.00	20.00

Issued to commemorate the flight of the U. S. rocket Ranger 9 to the moon, March 24, 1965.

Dante Alighieri
A561

Portraits: 40b, Ion Bianu, philologist and historian. 55b, Anton Bacalbasa, writer. 60b, Vasile Conta, philosopher. 1 l, Jean Sibelius, Finnish composer. 1.35 l, Horace, Roman poet.

1965, May 10 Photo. Perf. 13½
Portrait in Black.

1738	A561	40b chlky bl	15	8
1739	A561	55b bister	20	10
1740	A561	60b lt lil	20	15
1741	A561	1 l dl red brn	35	20
1742	A561	1.35 l olive	75	20
1743	A561	1.75 l org red	1.10	40
		Nos. 1738-1743 (6)	2.75	1.23

ITU Emblem, Old and New Communication Equipment
A562

1965, May 15 Engraved

| 1744 | A562 | 1.75 l ultra | 1.10 | 30 |

Issued to commemorate the centenary of the International Communication Union.

Iron Gate, Danube—A562a

Arms of Jugoslavia and Romania and Djerdap Dam—A562b

Design: 55b (50d), Iron Gate hydroelectric plant and dam.

Perf. 12½x12

1965, May 20 Litho. Unwmkd.

1745	A562a	30b (25d) lt bl & grn	5	5
1746	A562a	55b (50d) lt bl & dk red	60	8

Miniature Sheet
Perf. 13½x13

1747	A562b	Sheet of 4	3.75	3.75
a.		80b multi	25	15
b.		1.20 l multi	45	25

Issued simultaneously by Romania and Jugoslavia to commemorate the start of construction of the Iron Gate hydroelectric plant and dam. Valid for postage in both countries.
No. 1747 contains one each of Nos. 1747a, 1747b and Jugoslavia Nos. 771a and 771b. Only Nos. 1747a and 1747b were valid in Romania. Size: 104x80mm. Sold for 4 l. See Jugoslavia Nos. 769-771.

Small-bore Rifle Shooting, Kneeling
A563

Designs: 4b, Rifle shooting, prone. 55b, Rapid-fire pistol and map of Europe. 1 l, Free pistol and map of Europe. 1.60 l, Small-bore rifle, standing, and map of Europe. 2 l, 5 l, Marksmen in various shooting positions (all horizontal).

Perf. 12x12½, 12½x12
1965, May 30 Litho. Unwmkd.
Size: 23x43mm. 43x23mm.

1748	A563	20b multi	10	6
1749	A563	40b dl grn, pink & blk	15	6
1750	A563	55b multi	30	6
1751	A563	1 l pale grn, blk & ocher	60	15
1752	A563	1.60 l multi	75	20

Perf. 13½
Size: 51x28mm.

1753	A563	2 l multi	1.10	45
		Nos. 1748-1753 (6)	3.00	98

European Shooting Championships, Bucharest.
Nos. 1749–1752 were issued imperf. in changed colors. Two other denominations exist, 3.25 and 5 l, imperf. Price, set of 6, unused $7.50, canceled $3.

Fat-Frumos and the Giant
A564

Fairy Tales: 40b, Fat-Frumos on horseback and Ileana Cosinzeana. 55b, Harap Alb and the Bear. 1 l, "The Moralist Wolf." 2 l, "The Ox and the Calf." 3.20 l, Wolf and bear pulling sled.

1965, June 25 Photo. Perf. 13

1756	A564	20b multi	10	5
1757	A564	40b multi	20	5
1758	A564	55b multi	25	5
1759	A564	1 l multi	65	12
1760	A564	1.35 l multi	75	16
1761	A564	2 l multi	1.25	30
		Nos. 1756-1761 (6)	3.20	73

Bee and Blossoms
A565

Lt. Col. Gordon Cooper and Lt. Com. Charles Conrad, Gemini 3 and Globe
A566

Design: 1.60 l, Exhibition Hall (horiz.).

Perf. 12x12½, 12½x12
1965, July 28 Litho. Unwmkd.

1762	A565	55b org, bl & pink	40	10
1763	A565	1.60 l multi	75	30

Issued to publicize the 20th Congress of the International Federation of Beekeeping Associations (Apimondia), Bucharest, Aug. 26-31.

1965, Aug. 25 Litho. Perf. 12x12½

Designs: 1.75 l, Col. Pavel Belyayev, Lt. Col. Alexei Leonov and Voskhod 2. 2.40 l, Early Bird over globe.

1764	A566	1.75 l dk bl, bl & ver	1.10	20
1765	A566	2.40 l multi	1.50	35
1766	A566	3.20 l dk bl, lt bl & ver	2.75	45

Issued to honor achievements in space.

European Quail
A567

Birds: 10b, Eurasian woodcock. 20b, Eurasian snipe. 40b, Turtle dove. 55b, Mallard. 60b, White-fronted goose. 1 l, Eurasian crane. 1.20 l, Glossy Ibis. 1.35 l, Mute swan. 3.25 l, White pelican.

1965, Sept. 10 Photo. Perf. 13½
Size: 34x34mm.
Birds in Natural Colors

1767	A567	5b red brn & rose lil	15	5
1768	A567	10b red brn & yel grn	15	5
1769	A567	20b brn & bl grn	25	5
1770	A567	40b lil & grn	30	5
1771	A567	55b brt grn & lt brn	30	5
1772	A567	60b dl org & bl	40	5
1773	A567	1 l red & lil	55	15
1774	A567	1.20 l dk brn & grn	85	20
1775	A567	1.35 l org & ultra	1.00	20

Size: 32x73mm.

1776	A567	3.25 l ultra & sep	2.50	65
		Nos. 1767-1776 (10)	6.45	1.50

Marx and Lenin
A568

Vasile Alecsandri
A569

1965, Sept. 6 Photogravure

| 1777 | A568 | 55b red, blk & yel | 45 | 20 |

Issued to commemorate the Sixth Conference of Postal Ministers of Communist Countries, Peking, June 21–July 15.

1965, Oct. 9 Perf. 13½ Unwmkd.

| 1778 | A569 | 55b red brn, dk brn & gold | 45 | 20 |

75th anniversary of the death of Vasile Alecsandri (1821-1890), statesman and poet.

Bird-of-Paradise Flower
A570

Flowers from Cluj Botanical Gardens: 10b, Stanhope orchid. 20b, Paphiopedilum insigne. 30b, Zanzibar water lily (horiz.). 40b, Ferocactus (horiz.). 55b, Cotton blossom (horiz.). 1 l, Hibiscus (horiz.). 1.35 l, Gloxinia. 1.75 l, Victoria water lily (horiz.). 2.30 l, Hibiscus, bird-of-paradise flower and greenhouse.

ROMANIA

Perf. 12x12½, 12½x12
1965, Oct. 25   Lithographed
Size: 23x43, 43x23mm.
Flowers in Natural Colors

1779	A570	5b brown	5	5
1780	A570	10b green	5	5
1781	A570	20b dk bl	10	5
1782	A570	30b vio bl	15	5
1783	A570	40b red brn	15	5
1784	A570	55b dk red	20	5
1785	A570	1 l ol grn	45	5
1786	A570	1.35 l violet	75	15
1787	A570	1.75 l dk grn	1.25	20

Perf. 13½
Size: 52x30mm.

| 1788 | A570 | 2.30 l green | 1.75 | 75 |

Nos. 1779-1788 (10)   4.90   1.45

The orchid on No. 1780 is attached to the bottom of the limb.

Running   Pigeon and Post Horn
A571   A572

Sports: 1.55 l, Soccer. 1.75 l, Woman diver. 2 l, Mountaineering. 5 l, Canoeing (horiz.).

1965, Nov. 10   Photo.   Perf. 13½

1789	A571	55b multi	20	5
1790	A571	1.55 l multi	75	15
1791	A571	1.75 l multi	85	20
1792	A571	2 l multi	90	30
1793	A571	5 l multi	2.25	60

Nos. 1789-1793 (5)   4.95   1.30

Issued to publicize the Spartacist Games. No. 1793 commemorates the Romanian victory in the European Kayak Championships.

1965, Nov. 15   Engraved

Designs: 1 l, Pigeon on television antenna and post horn (horiz.). 1.75 l, Flying pigeon and post horn (horiz.).

1794	A572	55b car & vio bl + 45b label	60	15
1795	A572	1 l arm & brn	60	25
1796	A572	1.75 l ol grn & sep	1.10	35

Issued for Stamp Day. No. 1794 is printed with alternating label showing post rider and emblem of Romanian Philatelists' Association and 45b additional charge. Stamp and label are imperf. between.

Chamois and Hunting Trophy
A573

Designs (Hunting Trophy and): 1 l, Brown bear. 1.60 l, Red deer. 1.75 l, Wild boar. 3.20 l, Antlers of red deer.

1965, Dec. 10   Photo.   Perf. 13½
Size: 37x22mm.

1797	A573	55b rose lil, yel & brn	25	6
1798	A573	1 l brt grn, red & brn	50	8
1799	A573	1.60 l lt vio bl, org & brn	80	10
1800	A573	1.75 l rose, grn & blk	1.25	30

Size: 48x36½mm.

| 1801 | A573 | 3.20 l gray, gold, blk & org | 2.00 | 60 |

Nos. 1797-1801 (5)   4.80   1.14

Probe III Photographing Moon
A574

Designs: 5b, Proton I space station (vert.). 15b, Molniya I telecommunication satellite (vert.). 3.25 l, Mariner IV and Mars picture (vert.). 5 l, Gemini 5.

Perf. 12x12½, 12½x12
1965, Dec. 25   Lithographed

1802	A574	5b multi	15	5
1803	A574	10b vio bl, red & gray	20	5
1804	A574	15b pur, gray & org	20	5
1805	A574	3.25 l vio bl, blk & red	3.00	45
1806	A574	5 l dk bl, gray & red org	5.00	1.00

Nos. 1802-1806 (5)   8.55   1.60

Achievements in space research.

Cocker Spaniel
A575

Hunting Dogs: 5b, Dachshund (triangle). 40b, Retriever. 55b, Terrier. 60b, Red setter. 75b, White setter. 1.55 l, Pointers (rectangle). 3.25 l, Duck hunter with retriever (rectangle).

1965, Dec. 28   Photo.   Perf. 13½
Size: 30x42mm.

| 1807 | A575 | 5b multi | 10 | 5 |

Size: 33½x33½mm.

1808	A575	10b multi	15	5
1809	A575	40b multi	25	5
1810	A575	60b multi	30	5
1811	A575	60b multi	40	15
1812	A575	75b multi	70	15

Size: 43x28mm.

| 1813 | A575 | 1.55 l multi | 1.25 | 30 |
| 1814 | A575 | 3.25 l multi | 4.00 | 1.50 |

Nos. 1807-1814 (8)   7.15   2.30

Chessboard, Queen and Jester
A576

Designs (Chessboard and): 20b, 1.60 l, Pawn and emblem. 55b, 1 l, Rook and knight on horseback.

1966, Feb. 25   Litho.   Perf. 13

1815	A576	20b multi	15	5
1816	A576	40b multi	25	10
1817	A576	55b multi	40	10
1818	A576	1 l multi	85	15
1819	A576	1.60 l multi	1.50	20
1820	A576	3.25 l multi	3.50	1.00

Nos. 1815-1820 (6)   6.65   1.60

Chess Olympics in Cuba.

Tractor, Grain and Sun
A577

1966, March 5

| 1821 | A577 | 55b lt grn & ocher | 35 | 10 |

Issued to commemorate the founding congress of the National Union of Cooperative Farms.

Gheorghe Gheorghiu-Dej   Congress Emblem
A578   A579

1966, March   Photo.   Perf. 13½

| 1822 | A578 | 55b gold & blk | 35 | 10 |
| a. | | 5 l souv. sheet | 8.00 | 8.00 |

Issued to commemorate the first anniversary of the death of Pres. Gheorghe Gheorghiu-Dej (1901–65). No. 1822a contains design similar to No. 1822 with signature of Gheorghiu-Dej; marginal border, denomination and "Posta Romana" in red, dates and inscription in black, gold flags and gray control number. Size: 90x99½mm.

1966, March 21   Perf. 13x14½

| 1823 | A579 | 55b yel & red | 35 | 10 |

1966 Congress of Communist Youth.

Folk Dancers of Moldavia
A580

Folk Dances: 40b, Oltenia. 55b, Maramaros. 1 l, Muntenia. 1.60 l, Banat. 2 l, Transylvania.

1966, Apr. 4   Engraved   Perf. 13½
Center in Black

1824	A580	30b lilac	15	10
1825	A580	40b brick red	15	10
1826	A580	55b brt bl grn	30	10
1827	A580	1 l maroon	60	10
1828	A580	1.60 l dk bl	1.25	20
1829	A580	2 l yel grn	2.25	60

Nos. 1824-1829 (6)   4.70   1.20

Soccer Game
A581

Designs: 10b, 15b, 55b, 1.75 l, Scenes of soccer play. 4 l, Jules Rimet Cup.

1966, Apr. 25   Litho.   Unwmkd.

1830	A581	5b multi	10	10
1831	A581	10b multi	15	10
1832	A581	15b multi	20	10
1833	A581	55b multi	85	10
1834	A581	1.75 l multi	2.00	25
1835	A581	4 l gold & multi	4.50	1.25
a.		10 l souv. sheet	7.50	6.00

Nos. 1830-1835 (6)   7.80   1.90

Issued to publicize the World Cup Soccer Championship, Wembley, England, July 11–30.

No. 1835a contains one 10 l multicolored stamp in design of 4 l, but larger (32x46 mm.) and imperf. Gold marginal inscription and gray ornament; pale green control number. No gum. Sheet size: 85x100 mm. Issued June 20.

Symbols of Industry
A582

1966, May 14   Photogravure

| 1836 | A582 | 55b multi | 35 | 10 |

Romanian Trade Union Congress.

Red-breasted Flycatcher   Venus 3 (Russia)
A583   A584

Song Birds: 10b, Red crossbill. 15b, Great reed warbler. 20b, European redstart. 55b, European robin. 1.20 l, White-spotted bluethroat. 1.55 l, Yellow wagtail. 3.20 l, Common penduline tit.

1966, May 25   Photo.   Perf. 13½

1837	A583	5b gold & multi	5	5
1838	A583	10b sil & multi	5	5
1839	A583	15b gold & multi	15	5
1840	A583	20b sil & multi	25	7
1841	A583	55b sil & multi	40	10
1842	A583	1.20 l gold & multi	65	10
1843	A583	1.55 l sil & multi	3.25	75
1844	A583	3.20 l gold & multi	3.75	75

Nos. 1837-1844 (8)   8.55   1.92

1966, June 25

Designs: 20b, FR-1 (France). 1.60 l, Luna 9 (Russia). 5 l, Gemini 6 and 7 (U.S.A.).

1845	A584	10b dp vio, gray & red	15	10
1846	A584	20b ultra, blk & red	25	10
1847	A584	1.60 l bl, blk & red	1.00	20
1848	A584	5 l bl, blk, brn & red	2.75	1.25

International achievements in space.

ROMANIA

Urechia Nestor
A585

Portraits: 5b, George Cosbuc. 10b, Gheorghe Sincai. 40b, Aron Pumnul. 55b, Stefan Luchian. 1 l, Sun Yat-sen. 1.35 l, Gottfried Wilhelm Leibniz. 1.60 l, Romain Rolland. 1.75 l, Ion Ghica. 3.25 l, Constantin Cantacuzino.

1966, June 28

1849	A585	5b grn, blk & dk bl	10	5
1850	A585	10b rose car, grn & blk	10	5
1851	A585	20b grn, plum & blk	15	5
1852	A585	40b vio bl, brn & blk	15	5
1853	A585	55b brn org, bl grn & blk	30	5
1854	A585	1 l ocher, vio & blk	40	12
1855	A585	1.35 l bl & blk	50	14
1856	A585	1.60 l brt grn, dl vio & blk	80	20
1857	A585	1.75 l org, dl vio & blk	80	20
1858	A585	3.25 l bl, dk car & blk	1.50	45
	Nos. 1849-1858 (10)		4.80	1.36

Cultural anniversaries.

Country House,
by Gheorghe Petrascu—A586

Paintings: 10b, Peasant Woman, by Nicolae Grigorescu (vert.). 20b, Reapers at Rest, by Camil Ressu. 55b, Man with the Blue Cap, by Van Eyck (vert.). 1.55 l, Train Compartment, by Daumier. 3.25 l, Betrothal of the Virgin, by El Greco (vert.).

1966, July 25   Gold Frame   Unwmkd.

1859	A586	5b Prus grn & brn org	30	15
1860	A586	10b red brr. & crim	30	15
1861	A586	20b brn & brt grn	30	20
1862	A586	55b vio bl & lil	50	30
1863	A586	1.55 l dk sl grn & org	2.25	90
1864	A586	3.25 l vio & ultra	5.00	2.50
	Nos. 1859-1864 (6)		8.65	4.20

See also Nos. 1907–1912.

Hottonia Palustris
A587

Marine Flora: 10b, Ceratophyllum submersum. 20b, Aldrovanda vesiculosa. 40b, Callitriche verna. 55b, Vallisneria spiralis. 1 l, Elodea Canadensis rich. 1.55 l, Hippuris vulgaris. 3.25 l, Myriophyllum spicatum.

1966, Aug. 25   Litho.   Perf. 13½

Size: 28x40mm.

1865	A587	5b multi	5	5
1866	A587	10b multi	10	5
1867	A587	20b multi	10	5
1868	A587	40b multi	15	7
1869	A587	55b multi	25	8
1870	A587	1 l multi	75	10
1871	A587	1.55 l multi	1.10	35

Size: 28x50mm.

1872	A587	3.25 l multi	2.25	55
	Nos. 1865-1872 (8)		4.75	1.30

Derivation of
the Meter
A588

Design: 1 l, Metric system symbols.

1966, Sept. 10   Photo.   Perf. 13½

1873	A588	55b sal & ultra	40	10
1874	A588	1 l lt grn & vio	65	10

Introduction of metric system in Romania, centenary.

Statue of Ovid
and Medical
School Emblem
A589

Line Integral
Denoting Work
A590

I. H. Radulescu, M. Kogalniceanu
and T. Savulescu—A591

Design: 1 l, Academy centenary medal.

1966, Sept. 30

Size: 22x27mm.

1875	A589	40b lil gray, ultra, sep & gold	25	10
1876	A590	55b gray, brn, red & gold	25	10

Size: 22x34mm.

1877	A589	1 l ultra, brn & gold	55	10

Size: 66x28mm.

1878	A591	3 l org, dk brn & gold	1.50	60

Centenary of the Romanian Academy.

Crawfish
A592

Molluscs and Crustaceans: 10b, Nassa reticulata (vert.). 20b, Stone crab. 40b, Campylaea trizona. 55b, Helix lucorum. 1.35 l, Mytilus galloprovincialis. 1.75 l, Lymnaea stagnalis. 3.25 l, Anodonta cygnaea. (10b, 40b, 55b, 1.75 l, are snails; 1.35 l, 3.25 l, are bivalves).

1966, Oct. 15
Animals in Natural Colors

1879	A592	5b dp org	5	5
1880	A592	10b lt bl	5	5
1881	A592	20b pale lil	7	5
1882	A592	40b yel grn	20	10
1883	A592	55b car rose	30	5
1884	A592	1.35 l brt grn	75	20
1885	A592	1.75 l ultra	90	40
1886	A592	3.25 l brt org	2.25	75
	Nos. 1879-1886 (8)		4.57	1.75

Cave
Bear
A593

Prehistoric Animals: 10b, Mammoth. 15b, Bison. 55b, Cave elephant. 1.55 l, Stags. 4 l, Dinotherium.

1966, Nov. 25

Size: 36x22mm.

1887	A593	5b ultra, bl grn & red brn	5	5
1888	A593	10b vio, emer & brn	5	5
1889	A593	15b ol, grn & dk brn	5	5
1890	A593	55b lil, emer & brn	30	8
1891	A593	1.55 l ultra, grn & brn	1.00	25

Size: 43x27mm.

1892	A593	4 l rose car, grn & brn	2.25	1.00
	Nos. 1887-1892 (6)		3.70	1.48

Putna
Monastery
A594

1966   Photogravure   Perf. 13½

1893	A594	2 l multi	1.00	25

Putna Monastery, 500th anniversary.

Yuri A. Gagarin
and Vostok 1
A595

Russian Achievements in Space: 10b, Trajectory of Sputnik 1 around globe (horiz.). 25b, Valentina Tereshkova and globe with trajectory of Vostok 6. 40b, Andrian G. Nikolayev, Pavel R. Popovich and globe with trajectory of Vostok 8. 55b, Alexei Leonov walking in space.

1967, Feb. 15   Photo.   Perf. 13½

1894	A595	10b sil & multi	5	5
1895	A595	20b sil & multi	6	5
1896	A595	25b sil & multi	15	5
1897	A595	40b sil & multi	25	12
1898	A595	55b sil & multi	45	15
	Nos. 1894-1898, C163-C166 (9)	6.51	1.82

Ten years of space exploration.

Barn Owl
A596

Birds of Prey: 20b, Eagle owl. 40b, Saker falcon. 55b, Egyptian vulture. 75b, Osprey. 1 l, Griffon vulture. 1.20 l, Lammergeier. 1.75 l, Cinereous vulture.

1967, Mar. 20   Photo.   Unwmkd.
Birds in Natural Colors

1899	A596	10b vio & ol	5	5
1900	A596	20b bl & org	10	5
1901	A596	40b emer & org	15	6
1902	A596	55b yel grn & ocher	20	8
1903	A596	75b rose lil & grn	25	10
1904	A596	1 l yel org & blk	50	16
1905	A596	1.20 l cl & yel	1.25	18
1906	A596	1.75 l sal pink & gray	1.75	75
	Nos. 1899-1906 (8)		4.25	1.43

Painting Type of 1966

Paintings: 10b, Woman in Fancy Dress, by Ion Andreescu. 20b, Washwomen, by J. Al. Steriadi. 40b, Women weavers, by St. Dimitrescu (vert.). 1.55 l, Venus and Amor, by Lucas Cranach (vert.). 3.20 l, Hercules and the Lion of Numea, by Rubens. 5 l, Haman Asking Esther's Forgiveness, by Rembrandt (vert.).

1967, Mar. 30   Perf. 13½
Gold Frame

1907	A586	10b dp bl & rose red	10	5
1908	A586	20b dp grn & bis	15	5
1909	A586	40b car & bl	25	6
1910	A586	1.55 l dp plum & lt ultra	90	20
1911	A586	3.20 l brn & org	1.50	35
1912	A586	5 l ol grn & org	3.25	1.00
	Nos. 1907-1912 (6)		6.15	1.71

Mlle.
Pogany,
by
Brancusi
A597

Sculptures: 5b, Girl's head. 10b, The Sleeping Muse (horiz.). 20b, The Infinite Column. 40b, The Kiss (horiz.). 55b, Earth Wisdom (seated woman). 3.25 l, Gate of the Kiss.

Photogravure
1967, Apr. 27 Perf. 13½ Unwmkd.

1913	A597	5b dl yel, blk brn & ver	5	5
1914	A597	10b bl grn, blk & lil	5	5
1915	A597	20b lt bl, blk & rose red	15	5
1916	A597	40b pink, sep & brt grn	25	10
1917	A597	55b yel grn, blk & ultra	40	15
1918	A597	1.20 l bluish lil, ol blk & org	75	25
1919	A597	3.25 l emer, blk & cer	1.85	75
	Nos. 1913-1919 (7)		3.50	1.40

Issued to commemorate the 10th anniversary of the death of Constantin Brancusi (1876–1957), sculptor.

Coins
of
1867
A598

ROMANIA

Design: 1.20 l, Coins of 1966.
1967, May 4
| 1920 | A508 | 55b multi | 35 | 15 |
| 1921 | A508 | 1.20 l multi | 75 | 35 |

Centenary of Romanian monetary system.

Infantry Soldier, by
Nicolae Grigorescu
A599

1967, May 9
| 1922 | A599 | 55b multi | 90 | 20 |

Issued to commemorate the 90th anniversary of Romanian independence.

Peasants Marching, by
Stefan Luchian
A600

Painting: 40b, Fighting Peasants, by Octav Bancila (vert.).

1967, May 20 Perf. 13½ Unwmkd.
| 1923 | A600 | 40b multi | 50 | 10 |
| 1924 | A600 | 1.55 l multi | 2.00 | 1.00 |

60th anniversary of Peasant Uprising.

Centaury
A601

Carpathian Flora: 40b, Hedge mustard. 55b, Columbine. 1.20 l, Alpine violet. 1.75 l, Bell flower. 4 l, Dryas (horiz.).

1967, June 10 Photogravure
Flowers in Natural Colors
1925	A601	20b ocher	10	10
1926	A601	40b violet	15	10
1927	A601	55b bis & brn red	25	12
1928	A601	1.20 l yel & red brn	50	20
1929	A601	1.75 l bluish grn & car	75	30
1930	A601	4 l lt ultra	1.90	85
	Nos. 1925-1930 (6)	3.65	1.67

Fortifications,
Sibiu
A602

Map of Romania and
ITY Emblem—A603

Designs: 40b, Cris Castle. 55b, Wooden Church, Plopis. 1.60 l, Ruins of Nuamtulua Fortress. 1.75 l, Mogosoala Palace. 2.25 l, Voronet Church.

1967, June 29 Photo. Perf. 13½
Size: 33x33mm.
1931	A602	20b ultra & multi	10	5
1932	A602	40b vio & multi	15	10
1933	A602	55b multi	20	10
1934	A602	1.60 l multi	60	15
1935	A602	1.75 l multi	75	20

Size: 48x36mm.
| 1936 | A602 | 2.25 l bl & multi | 1.25 | 40 |
| | Nos. 1931-1936 (6) | 3.05 | 1.00 |

Souvenir Sheet
Imperf.
| 1937 | A603 | 5 l lt bl, ultra & blk | 4.00 | 2.00 |

Issued for International Tourist Year, 1967. No. 1937 has pale blue control number. Size: 101x90mm.

The Attack at Marasesti,
by E. Stoica—A604

1967, July 24 Perf. 13½ Unwmkd.
| 1938 | A604 | 55b gray, Prus bl & brn | 50 | 20 |

Issued to commemorate the 50th anniversary of the Battle of Marasesti and Oituz.

Dinu Lipatti,
Pianist
A605

Designs: 20b, Al. Orascu, architect. 40b, Gr. Antipa, zoologist. 55b, M. Kogalniceanu, statesman. 1.20 l, Jonathan Swift, writer. 1.75 l, Marie Curie, scientist.

1967, July 29 Photo. Perf. 13½
1939	A605	10b ultra, blk & pur	10	5
1940	A605	20b org brn, blk & ultra	10	5
1941	A605	40b bl grn, blk & org brn	15	10
1942	A605	55b dp rose, blk & dk ol grn	20	10
1943	A605	1.20 l ol, blk & brn	45	20
1944	A605	1.75 l dl bl, blk & bl grn	90	30
	Nos. 1939-1944 (6)	1.85	80

Cultural anniversaries.

Wrestlers   Congress Emblem
A606   A607

Designs: 20b, 55b, 1.20 l, 2 l, Various fight scenes and world map (20b, 2 l horizontal); on 2 l maps are large and wrestlers small).

1967, Aug. 28
1945	A606	10b ol & multi	10	8
1946	A606	20b cit & multi	15	10
1947	A606	55b bis & multi	20	10
1948	A606	1.20 l multi	50	25
1949	A606	2 l ultra, gold & dp car	1.25	60
	Nos. 1945-1949 (5)	2.20	1.13

Issued to commemorate the World Greco-Roman Wrestling Championships, Bucharest.

1967, Aug. 28
| 1950 | A607 | 1.60 l lt bl, ultra & dp car | 75 | 20 |

Issued to commemorate the International Linguists' Congress, Bucharest, Aug. 28–Sept. 2.

Ice Skating
A608

Designs: 40b, Biathlon. 55b, 5 l, Bobsledding. 1 l, Skiing. 1.55 l, Ice Hockey. 2 l, Emblem of 10th Winter Olympic Games. 2.30 l, Ski jump.

1967, Sept. 28 Photo. Perf. 13½x13
1951	A608	20b lt bl & multi	10	5
1952	A608	40b multi	15	10
1953	A608	55b bl & multi	20	10
1954	A608	1 l lil & multi	30	20
1955	A608	1.55 l multi	55	20
1956	A608	2 l gray & multi	90	25
1957	A608	2.30 l multi	1.50	50
	Nos. 1951-1957 (7)	3.70	1.40

Souvenir Sheet
Imperf.
| 1958 | A608 | 5 l lt bl & multi | 5.00 | 4.50 |

Issued to publicize the 10th Winter Olympic Games, Grenoble, France, Feb. 6-18, 1968.
Nos. 1951-1957 issued in sheets of 10 (5x2) and 5 labels.
No. 1958 contains one stamp; gray marginal inscription and emblem. Size: 78½x99½mm.

Curtea
de Arges
Monastery
A609

1967, Nov. 1 Perf. 13½ Unwmkd.
| 1959 | A609 | 55b multi | 45 | 10 |

Issued to commemorate the 450th anniversary of the Curtea de Arges Monastery.

Romanian Academy Library—A610

1967, Sept. 25 Lithographed
| 1960 | A610 | 55b ocher, gray & dk bl | 45 | 10 |

Issued to commemorate the centenary of the founding of the Romanian Academy Library, Bucharest.

Karl Marx
and Title Page   Lenin
A611   A612

1967, Nov. 4 Photogravure
| 1961 | A611 | 40b rose cl, blk & yel | 35 | 15 |

Issued to commemorate the centenary of the publication of "Das Kapital" by Karl Marx.

1967, Nov. 3
| 1962 | A612 | 1.20 l red, blk & gold | 60 | 15 |

Issued to commemorate the 50th anniversary of the Russian October Revolution.

Monorail
Leaving U.S.
EXPO
Pavilion
A613

Designs: 1 l, EXPO emblem and atom symbol. 1.60 l, Cup, world map and EXPO emblem. 2 l, EXPO emblem.

1967, Nov. 28 Photogravure
1963	A613	55b grnsh bl, vio & blk	20	12
1964	A613	1 l red, blk & gray	45	18
1965	A613	1.60 l multi	75	35
1966	A613	2 l multi	1.00	40

Issued to commemorate EXPO '67 International Exhibition, Montreal, Apr. 28–Oct. 27. No. 1965 also commemorates Romania's victory in the World Fencing Championships in Montreal.

Truck   Arms of the
A614   Republic
              A615

ROMANIA

Diesel Locomotive	Map Showing Telephone Network
A616	A617

Designs: 10b, Communications emblem (vert.). 20b, Train. 35b, Plane. 50b, Telephone (vert.). 60b, Small loading truck. 1.20 l, Autobus. 1.35 l, Helicopter. 1.50 l, Trolley bus. 1.55 l, Radio station and tower. 1.75 l, Highway. 2 l, Mail truck. 2.40 l, Television tower. 3.20 l, Jet plane. 3.25 l, Steamship. 4 l, Electric train. 5 l, World map and teletype.

Photo.; Engraved (type A615)
1967–68   Perf. 13½

1967	A614	5b lt ol grn ('68)	5	5
1968	A614	10b hn brn ('68)	5	5
1969	A614	20b gray ('68)	7	5
1970	A614	35b bl blk ('68)	13	5
1971	A615	40b vio bl	14	5
1972	A615	50b org ('68)	17	5
1973	A615	55b dl org	19	5
1974	A614	60b org brn ('68)	21	5

Size: 22½x28mm., 28x22½mm.

1975	A616	1 l emer ('68)	33	5
1976	A617	1.20 l red lil ('68)	40	5
1977	A617	1.35 l brt bl ('68)	45	5
1978	A616	1.50 l rose red ('68)	50	5
1979	A616	1.55 l dk brn ('68)	50	5
1980	A615	1.60 l rose red	55	5
1981	A617	1.75 l dp grn ('68)	60	5
1982	A617	2 l cit ('68)	90	5
1983	A617	2.40 l dk bl ('68)	1.10	5
1984	A617	3 l grnsh bl	1.10	5
1985	A617	3.20 l ocher ('68)	1.50	5
1986	A616	3.25 l ultra ('68)	1.50	5
1987	A617	4 l lil rose ('68)	1.65	5
1988	A617	5 l vio ('68)	1.90	5
		Nos. 1967-1988 (22)	13.99	1.10

No. 1984 was issued to commemorate the 40th anniversary of the first automatic telephone exchange and to commemorate the introduction of automatic telephone service. See also Nos. 2078–2079, 2269–2284.

Coat of Arms, Symbols of Agriculture and Industry
A618

Designs: 55b, Coat of arms. 1.60 l, Romanian flag. 1.75 l, Coat of arms and symbols of arts and education.

1967, Dec. 26 Photo. Perf. 13½
Size: 27x48mm.

| 1989 | A618 | 40b multi | 15 | 8 |
| 1990 | A618 | 55b multi | 20 | 12 |

Size: 33½x48mm.

| 1991 | A618 | 1.60 l multi | 50 | 25 |

Size: 27x48mm.

| 1992 | A618 | 1.75 l multi | 90 | 35 |

20th anniversary of the republic.

Souvenir Sheet

Anemones, by Stefan Luchian
A619

1968, Mar. 30   Litho.   Imperf.

| 1993 | A619 | 10 l multi | 7.50 | 7.50 |

Issued to commemorate the centenary of the birth of Stefan Luchian, Romanian painter. No. 1993 has gold and black marginal inscription and gray control number on back. Size: 90x100mm.

Portrait of a Lady, by Misu Popp
A620

Paintings: 10b, The Reveille of Romania, by Gheorghe Tattarescu. 20b, Composition, by Teodorescu Sionion (horiz.). 35b, The Judgment of Paris, by Hendrick van Balen (horiz.). 55b, Little Girl with Red Kerchief, by Nicolae Grigorescu. 60b, The Mystical Betrothal of St. Catherine, by Lamberto Sustris (horiz.). 1 l, Old Nicolas, the Zither Player, by Stefan Luchian. 1.60 l, Man with a Skull, by Dierick Bouts (?). 1.75 l, Madonna and Child with Fruit Basket, by Jan van Bylert. 2.40 l, Medor and Angelica, by Sebastiano Ricci (horiz.). 3 l, Summer, by Jacob Jordaens (horiz.). 3.20 l, 5 l, Ecce Homo, by Titian.

1968   Photogravure   Perf. 13½
Gold Frame
Size: 28x49mm.

| 1994 | A620 | 10b multi | 5 | 5 |

Size: 48½x36½, 36x48½mm.

1995	A620	20b multi	5	5
1996	A620	35b multi	14	8
1997	A620	40b multi	20	8
1998	A620	55b multi	20	8
1999	A620	60b multi	30	10
2000	A620	1 l multi	50	12
2001	A620	1.60 l multi	75	20
2002	A620	1.75 l multi	75	25
2003	A620	2.40 l multi	1.35	45
2004	A620	3 l multi	1.50	75
2005	A620	3.20 l multi	2.50	1.00
		Nos. 1994-2005 (12)	8.29	3.21

Miniature Sheet
Imperf.

| 2006 | A620 | 5 l multi | 6.50 | 6.50 |

No. 2006 contains one stamp with gold frame and ultramarine design in margin. Size: 74x90mm.
Issue dates: 40b, 55b, 1, 1.60, 2.40, 3.20 and 5 lei, Mar. 28. Others, Sept. 9.
See also Nos. 2088–2094, 2124–2130.

Human Rights Flame	WHO Emblem
A621	A622

1968, May 9   Perf. 13½   Unwmkd.

| 2007 | A621 | 1 l multi | 50 | 25 |

Issued for International Human Rights Year.

1968, May 14   Photogravure

| 2008 | A622 | 1.60 l multi | 75 | 35 |

Issued to commemorate the 20th anniversary of the World Health Organization.

"Prince Dragos Hunting Bison," by Nicolae Grigorescu—A623

1968, May 17

| 2009 | A623 | 1.60 l multi | 90 | 35 |

Issued to publicize the 15th Hunting Congress, Mamaia, May 23–29.

Pioneers and Liberation Monument
A624

1968, June 9   Photo.   Perf. 13½

Designs (Pioneers): 40b, receiving scarfs. 55b, building model planes and boat. 1 l, as radio amateurs. 1.60 l, folk dancing. 2.40 l, Girl Pioneers in camp.

2010	A624	5b multi	5	5
2011	A624	40b multi	14	8
2012	A624	55b multi	24	8
2013	A624	1 l multi	45	20
2014	A624	1.60 l multi	75	30
2015	A624	2.40 l multi	1.00	35
		Nos. 2010-2015 (6)	2.63	1.06

Ion Ionescu de la Brad
A625

1968, June 24
Size: 28x43mm.

Designs: 55b, Emil Racovita. 1.60 l, Prince Mircea of Walachia.

| 2016 | A625 | 40b multi | 30 | 5 |
| 2017 | A625 | 55b grn & multi | 30 | 6 |

Size: 28x48mm.

| 2018 | A625 | 1.60 l gold & multi | 75 | 25 |

Issued to commemorate: 40b, sesquicentennial of the birth of Ion Ionescu de la Brad (1818–91); 55b, centenary of the birth of Emil Racovita (1868–1947), explorer and naturalist; 1.60 l, 550th anniversary of the death of Prince Mircea (1386–1418). Dates of issue: 40b, 55b, June 24; 1.60 l, June 22.

Geranium
A626

Designs: Various geraniums.

1968, July 20   Photo.   Perf. 13½

2019	A626	10b multi	5	5
2020	A626	20b multi	7	5
2021	A626	40b multi	14	8
2022	A626	55b multi	19	10
2023	A626	60b multi	21	15
2024	A626	1.20 l multi	45	20
2025	A626	1.35 l multi	60	28
2026	A626	1.60 l multi	1.25	35
		Nos. 2019-2026 (8)	2.96	1.26

Avram Iancu, by B. Iscovescu and Demonstrating Students
A627

Designs (Demonstrating Students and): 55b, Nicolae Balcescu, by Gheorghe Tattarescu. 1.60 l, Vasile Alecsandri, by N. Livaditti.

1968, July 25

2027	A627	55b gold & multi	30	8
2028	A627	1.20 l gold & multi	75	15
2029	A627	1.60 l gold & multi	1.10	35

120th anniversary of 1848 revolution.

Boxing	Atheneum and Harp
A628	A629

Aztec Calendar Stone and: 10b, Javelin, Women's. 20b, Woman diver. 40b, Volleyball. 60b, Wrestling. 1.20 l, Fencing. 1.35 l, Canoeing. 1.60 l, Soccer. 5 l, Running.

1968, Aug. 28

2030	A628	10b multi	5	5
2031	A628	20b multi	8	5
2032	A628	40b multi	16	10
2033	A628	55b multi	19	10
2034	A628	60b multi	21	15
2035	A628	1.20 l multi	60	15

ROMANIA

2036	A628	1.35 l multi	75	35
2037	A628	1.60 l multi	1.10	40
	Nos. 2030-2037 (8)		3.14	1.45

Souvenir Sheet
Imperf.

2038	A628	5 l multi	3.75	2.50

Issued to publicize the 19th Olympic Games, Mexico City, Oct. 12-17. No. 2038 contains one stamp with inscription, Olympic rings and control number in margin. Size: 76x89mm.

1968, Aug. 20 Litho. *Perf. 12x12½*

2039	A629	55b multi	35	15

Centenary of the Philharmonic Orchestra.

Globe and Emblem
A630

1968, Oct. 4 Litho. *Perf. 13½*

2040	A630	1.60 l ultra & gold	75	20

Issued to commemorate the 20th anniversary of the International Federation of Photographic Art.

Moldovita Monastery Church
A631

Historic Monuments: 10b, "The Triumph of Trajan," Roman metope (vert.). 55b, Cozia monastery church. 1.20 l, Court of Tirgoviste Palace. 1.55 l, Palace of Culture, Jassy. 1.75 l, Corvinus Castle, Hunedoara.

1968, Nov. 25 Engraved *Perf. 13½*

2041	A631	10b dk bl, ol & brn	5	5
2042	A631	40b rose car, bl & brn	14	5
2043	A631	55b ultra, ol, brn & vio	20	6
2044	A631	1.20 l yel, mar & gray	45	12
2045	A631	1.55 l bl & lt grn	75	25
2046	A631	1.75 l org, blk & ol	1.00	40
	Nos. 2041-2046 (6)		2.59	93

Mute Swan
A632

Protected Birds and Animals: 20b, European stilts. 40b, Sheldrakes. 55b, Egret feeding young. 60b, Golden eagle. 1.20 l, Great bustards. 1.35 l, Chamois. 1.60 l, Bison.

1968, Dec. 20 Photo. *Perf. 13½*

2047	A632	10b pink & multi	5	5
2048	A632	20b multi	8	5
2049	A632	40b lil & multi	14	5
2050	A632	55b ol & multi	19	6
2051	A632	60b multi	30	7
2052	A632	1.20 l multi	65	15
2053	A632	1.35 l bl & multi	75	20
2054	A632	1.60 l multi	90	35
	Nos. 2047-2054 (8)		3.06	98

Michael the Brave's Entry into Alba Iulia, by D. Stoica—A633

Designs: 1 l, "The Round Dance of Union," by Theodor Aman. 1.75 l, Assembly of Alba Iulia.

1968, Dec. 1 Litho. *Perf. 13½*

2055	A633	55b gold & multi	30	10
2056	A633	1 l gold & multi	45	15
2057	A633	1.75 l gold & multi	1.00	35
a.	Souv. sheet of 3		2.25	2.25

Issued to commemorate the 50th anniversary of the union of Transylvania and Romania. No. 2057a contains 3 imperf. stamps similar to Nos. 2055-2057. Gold marginal inscription and ribbon in national colors. Size: 120x110mm. Sold for 4 l.

Woman from Neamt
A634

Regional Costumes: 40b, Man from Neamt. 55b, Woman from Hunedoara. 1 l, Man from Hunedoara. 1.60 l, Woman from Brasov. 2.40 l, Man from Brasov.

1968, Dec. 28 *Perf. 12x12½*

2058	A634	5b org & multi	5	5
2059	A634	40b bl & multi	14	5
2060	A634	55b multi	22	8
2061	A634	1 l brn & multi	40	15
2062	A634	1.60 l brn & multi	85	20
2063	A634	2.40 l multi	1.50	50
	Nos. 2058-2063 (6)		3.16	1.03

1969, Feb. 15

Regional Costumes: 5b, Woman from Dolj. 40b, Man from Dolj. 55b, Woman from Arges. 1 l, Man from Arges. 1.60 l, Woman from Timisoara. 2.40 l, Man from Timisoara.

2064	A634	5b multi	5	5
2065	A634	40b multi	14	8
2066	A634	55b lil & multi	22	10
2067	A634	1 l rose & multi	40	18
2068	A634	1.60 l multi	85	30
2069	A634	2.40 l brn & multi	1.50	50
	Nos. 2064-2069 (6)		3.16	1.21

Fencing
A635

Sports: 20b, Women's javelin. 40b, Canoeing. 1.20 l, Boxing. 1 l, Volleyball. 1.60 l, Swimming. 1.60 l, Wrestling. 2.40 l, Soccer.

1969, Mar. 10 Photo. *Perf. 13½*
Denominations Black, Athletes in Gray.

2070	A635	10b pale brn	5	5
2071	A635	20b violet	7	5
2072	A635	40b blue	14	8
2073	A635	55b red	15	10
2074	A635	1 l green	35	16
2075	A635	1.20 l brt bl	45	20
2076	A635	1.60 l cerise	65	25
2077	A635	2.40 l dp green	1.00	40
	Nos. 2070-2077 (8)		2.86	1.29

Type of Regular Issue
Designs: 40b, Power lines. 55b, Dam.

1969, Jan. 10 Photo. *Perf. 13½*

2078	A614	40b ultra	14	6
2079	A614	55b rose red	25	10

Painting Type of 1968

Paintings (Nudes): 10b, Woman Carrying Jug, by Gheorghe Tattarescu. 20b, Reclining Woman, by Theodor Pallady (horiz.). 35b, Seated Woman, by Nicolae Tonitza. 60b, Venus and Amor, 17th century Flemish School. 1.75b, 5 l, Diana and Endimion, by Marco Liberi. 3 l, The Three Graces, by Alessandro Varotari.

1969, Mar. 27 Photo. *Perf. 13½*
Gold Frame
Size: 37x49mm., 49x37mm.

2088	A620	10b multi	15	5
2089	A620	20b multi	20	6
2090	A620	35b multi	30	10
2091	A620	60b multi	50	15
2092	A620	1.75 l multi	1.00	50

Size: 27½x48½mm.

2093	A620	3 l multi	2.25	90
	Nos. 2088-2093 (6)		4.40	1.76

Miniature Sheet
Imperf.

2094	A620	5 l multi	5.00	5.00

No. 2094 contains one stamp (size: 36½x48½mm.) with simulated perforations and gold marginal ornaments. Size: 71x90½mm. Gray control number on back.
No. 2093 is incorrectly inscribed Hans von Aachen.

ILO Emblem Symbolic Head
A636 A637

1969, Apr. 9 Photo. *Perf. 13½*

2095	A636	55b multi	50	12

International Labor Organization, 50th anniversary.

1969, Apr. 28

2096	A637	55b ultra & multi	45	30
2097	A637	1.50 l red & multi	1.35	1.00

Issued to publicize Romania's cultural and economic cooperation with European countries.

Communications Symbol
A638

1969, May 12 Photo. *Perf. 13½*

2098	A638	55b vio bl & bluish gray	40	15

Issued to publicize the 7th Session of the Conference of Postal and Telecommunications Ministers, Bucharest.

Boxers, Referee and Map of Europe
A639

Map of Europe and: 40b, Two boxers. 55b, Sparring. 1.75 l, Referee declaring winner.

1969, May 24

2099	A639	35b multi	13	6
2100	A639	40b multi	14	10
2101	A639	55b multi	35	14
2102	A639	1.75 l bl & multi	90	35

European Boxing Championships, Bucharest, May 31-June 8.

Apatura Ilia
A640

Designs: Various butterflies and moths.

1969, June 25 Photo. *Perf. 13½*
Insects in Natural Colors

2103	A640	5b yel grn	5	5
2104	A640	10b rose mag	5	5
2105	A640	20b violet	7	5
2106	A640	40b bl grn	14	5
2107	A640	55b brt bl	19	5
2108	A640	1 l blue	45	20
2109	A640	1.20 l vio bl	60	30
2110	A640	2.40 l yel bis	1.20	40
	Nos. 2103-2110 (8)		2.75	1.15

Communist Party Flag
A641

1969, Aug. 6 Photo. *Perf. 13½*

2111	A641	55b multi	40	10

Issued to commemorate the 10th Romanian Communist Party Congress.

Torch, Atom Diagram and Book Broken Chain
A642 A643

Designs: 40b, Symbols of agriculture, science and industry. 1.75 l, Pylon, smokestack and cogwheel.

1969, Aug. 10

2112	A642	35b multi	15	6
2113	A642	40b grn & multi	20	8
2114	A642	1.75 l multi	75	25

Issued to publicize the exhibition showing the achievements of Romanian economy during the last 25 years.

ROMANIA

1969, Aug. 23

Designs: 55b, Construction work. 60b, Flags.

2115	A643	10b multi	5	5
2116	A643	55b yel & multi	25	12
2117	A643	60b multi	35	14

Issued to commemorate the 25th anniversary of Romania's liberation from fascist rule.

Juggler on Unicycle
A644

Branesti Mask
A645

Circus Performers: 20b, Clown. 35b, Trapeze artists. 60b, Dressage and woman trainer. 1.75 l, Woman in high wire act. 3 l, Performing tiger and trainer.

1969, Sept. 29   Photo.   *Perf. 13½*

2118	A644	10b lt bl & multi	5	5
2119	A644	20b lem & multi	7	5
2120	A644	35b lil & multi	13	5
2121	A644	60b multi	20	6
2122	A644	1.75 l multi	80	20
2123	A644	3 l ultra & multi	1.65	45
		Nos. 2118-2123 (6)	2.90	85

Painting Type of 1968

Paintings: 10b, Venetian Senator, Tintoretto School. 20b, Sofia Kretzulescu, by Gheorghe Tattarescu. 35b, Phillip IV, by Velazquez. 60b, Man Reading and Child, by Hans Memling. 1.75 l, Doamnei d'Aguesseau, by Madame Vigée-Lebrun. 3 l, Portrait of a Woman, by Rembrandt. 5 l, The Return of the Prodigal Son, by Bernardino Licinio (horiz.).

1969   *Gold Frame*
Size: 36½x49mm.

2124	A620	10b multi	5	5
2125	A620	20b multi	7	5
2126	A620	35b multi	13	5
2127	A620	60b multi	35	6
2128	A620	1.75 l multi	90	20
2129	A620	3 l multi	1.40	60
		Nos. 2124-2129 (6)	2.90	1.01

Miniature Sheet
Imperf.

2130	A620	5 l gold & multi	3.75	2.50

No. 2130 contains one stamp with simulated perforations and gray blue control number in margin. Size: 90x77mm.
Issue dates: 5 l, July 31. Others, Oct. 1.

1969, Nov. 24   Photo.   *Perf. 13½*

Masks from: 55b, Tudora. 1.55 l, Birsesti. 1.75 l, Rudaria.

2131	A645	40b org & multi	14	7
2132	A645	55b multi	20	8
2133	A645	1.55 l red & multi	75	30
2134	A645	1.75 l multi	90	35

Armed Forces Memorial
A646

1969, Oct. 25

2135	A646	55b red, blk & gold	25	10

25th anniversary of the People's Army.

Locomotives of 1869 and 1969
A647

1969, Oct. 31

2136	A647	55b sil & multi	35	20

Issued to commemorate the centenary of the Bucharest-Filaret-Giurgevo railroad.

Apollo 12 Landing Module
A648

1969, Nov. 24

2137	A648	1.50 l multi	95	75

Issued to commemorate the second landing on the moon, Nov. 19, 1969, astronauts Captains Alan Bean, Charles Conrad, Jr. and Richard Gordon.
Printed in sheets of 4 with 4 labels (one label with names of astronauts, one with Apollo 12 emblem and 2 silver labels with picture of landing module, Intrepid).

Mother Goose in Goat Disguise
A649

Designs: 55b, Children singing and decorated tree, Sorcova. 1.50 l, Drummer and singer, Buhaiul. 2.40 l, Singer and bell ringer, Plugusurol.

1969, Dec. 25   Photo.   *Perf. 13½*

2138	A649	40b bis & multi	14	10
2139	A649	55b lil & multi	20	12
2140	A649	1.50 l bl & multi	75	30
2141	A649	2.40 l multi	1.10	45

Issued for New Year 1970.

The Last Judgment (detail), Voronet Monastery—A650

North Moldavian Monastery Frescoes: 10b, Stephen the Great and family, Voronet. 20b, Three prophets, Sucevita. 60b, St. Nicholas (scene from his life), Sucevita (vert.). 1.75 l, Siege of Constantinople, 7th century, Moldovita. 3 l, Plowman, Voronet (vert.).

1969, Dec. 15

2142	A650	10b gold & multi	5	5
2143	A650	20b gold & multi	7	5
2144	A650	35b gold & multi	13	8
2145	A650	60b gold & multi	21	9
2146	A650	1.75 l gold & multi	60	30
2147	A650	3 l gold & multi	1.90	50
		Nos. 2142-2147 (6)	2.96	1.10

Ice Hockey
A651

Designs: 55b, Goalkeeper. 1.20 l, Two players with puck. 2.40 l, Player and goalkeeper.

1970, Jan. 20   Photo.   *Perf. 13½*

2148	A651	20b yel & multi	7	5
2149	A651	55b multi	25	15
2150	A651	1.20 l pink & multi	55	35
2151	A651	2.40 l lt bl & multi	1.10	55

Issued to publicize the World Ice Hockey Championships, Bucharest and Galati, Feb. 24–March 5.

Pasqueflower
A652

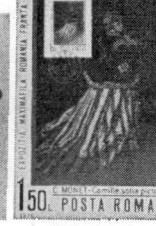
Camille, by Claude Monet (Maximum Card)—A654

Flowers: 10b, Adonis vernalis. 20b, Thistle. 40b, Almond tree blossoms. 55b, Iris. 1 l, Flax. 1.20 l, Sage. 2.40 l, Peony.

1970, Feb. 25   Photo.   *Perf. 13½*

2152	A652	5b yel & multi	5	5
2153	A652	10b grn & multi	5	5
2154	A652	20b lt bl & multi	8	5
2155	A652	40b vio & multi	16	7
2156	A652	55b ultra & multi	19	8
2157	A652	1 l multi	35	20
2158	A652	1.20 l red & multi	60	25
2159	A652	2.40 l multi	1.25	40
		Nos. 2152-2159 (8)	2.73	1.15

1970, Mar. 23

Design: 1 l, Pagoda and EXPO '70 emblem.
Size: 34x50mm.

Japanese Print and EXPO '70 Emblem
A653

Size: 29x92mm.

2161	A653	1 l gold & multi	45	30

Issued to publicize EXPO '70 International Exhibition, Osaka, Japan, Mar. 15–Sept. 13.

2160	A653	20b gold & multi	15	5

A souvenir sheet exists with perforated label in pagoda design of 1-lei. Yellow margin inscribed in Romanian, English and Japanese, with computer-dot outlines of young women in kimono and occidental dress. Size: 180x120mm. Issued Nov. 28, 1970. Price $3.

Alexandru I. Cuza, by C. Popp de Szathmary
A655

Lenin
A656

1970, Apr. 19   Photo.   *Perf. 13½*

2162	A654	1.50 l gold & multi	75	20

Issued to publicize the Franco-Romanian Maximafil Philatelic Exhibition.

1970, Apr. 20   Photo.   *Perf. 13½*

2163	A655	55b gold & multi	30	10

Issued to commemorate the 150th anniversary of the birth of Alexandru Ioan Cuza (1820–1866), prince of Romania.

1970, Apr. 21   Photo.   *Perf. 13½*

2164	A656	40b dk red & multi	20	10

Centenary of birth of Lenin (1870–1924).

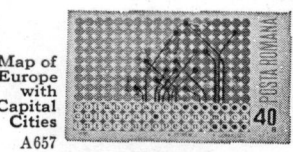
Map of Europe with Capital Cities
A657

1970, Apr. 28

2165	A657	40b grn, brn org & blk	75	50
2166	A657	1.50 l ultra, yel brn & blk	1.50	1.00

Issued to publicize Inter-European cultural and economic cooperation.

Victory Monument, Romanian and Russian Flags
A658

1970, May 9

2167	A658	55b red & multi	25	10

Issued to commemorate the 25th anniversary of victory over the Germans.

Greek Silver Drachm, 5th Century B.C.
A659

Coins: 20b, Getic-Dacian silver didrachm, 2nd–1st centuries B.C. 35b, Emperor Trajan's copper sestertius, 106 A.D. 60b, Mircea ducat, 1400. 1.75 l, Stephen the Great's silver groschen, 1460. 3 l, Brasov klippe-taler, 1601 (vert.).

1970, May 15

2168	A659	10b ultra, blk & sil	8	6
2169	A659	20b hn brn, blk & sil	12	8
2170	A659	35b grn, dk brn & gold	18	10
2171	A659	60b brn, blk & sil	24	15
2172	A659	1.75 l brt bl, blk & sil	72	35
2173	A659	3 l dk car, blk & sil	1.50	50
		Nos. 2168-2173 (6)	2.84	1.25

ROMANIA

Soccer Players and Ball
A660

1970, May 26   Perf. 13½
Designs: Soccer ball and various scenes from soccer game.
2174	A660	40b multi	16	12
2175	A660	55b multi	19	15
2176	A660	1.75 l bl & multi	75	35
2177	A660	3.30 l multi	1.40	60

Souvenir Sheet
2178	A660	Souv. sheet of 4	3.75	2.75
a.		1.20 l multi	42	20
b.		1.50 l multi	50	25
c.		1.55 l multi	54	30
d.		1.75 l multi	55	30

Issued to publicize the 9th World Soccer Championships for the Jules Rimet Cup, Mexico City, May 30–June 21. No. 2178 contains 4 stamps similar to Nos. 2174–2177, but with only one quarter of the soccer ball on each stamp, forming one large ball in the center of the block. Blue margin with commemorative inscription. Size: 108x108mm.

Moldovita Monastery
A661

Designs: Frescoes from North Moldavian Monasteries.

1970, June 29   Perf. 13½
Size: 36½x49mm.
2179	A661	10b gold & multi	8	6

Size: 27½x49mm.
2180	A661	20b gold & multi	12	8

Size: 36½x49, 48x37mm.
2181	A661	40b gold & multi	20	15
2182	A661	55b gold & multi	30	20
2183	A661	1.75 l gold & multi	65	40
2184	A661	3 l gold & multi	1.75	70
		Nos. 2179-2184 (6)	3.10	1.59

Miniature Sheet
2185	A661	5 l gold & multi	2.50	2.50

No. 2185 contains one stamp. Gray control number. Size: 90x77½mm.

Friedrich Engels
A662

1970, July 10   Photo.   Perf. 13½
2186	A662	1.50 l multi	75	25

Issued to commemorate the sesquicentennial of the birth of Friedrich Engels (1820–1895), German socialist.

Aerial View of Iron Gate Power Station
A663

1970, July 13
2187	A663	35b bl & multi	20	10

Issued to publicize the hydroelectric plant at the Iron Gate of the Danube.

Cargo Ship
A664

1970, July 17
2188	A664	55b bl & multi	25	10

Issued to commemorate the 75th anniversary of the Romanian merchant marine.

Exhibition Hall and Oil Derrick
A665

1970, July 20
2189	A665	1.50 l multi	75	20

International Bucharest Fair, Oct. 13–24.

U.P.U. Headquarters, Bern
A666

1970, Aug. 17   Photo.   Perf. 13½
2190	A666	1.50 l ultra & sl grn	75	20

Issued to commemorate the opening of the Universal Postal Union Headquarters in Bern.

Education Year Emblem
A667

Iceberg Rose
A668

1970, Aug. 17
2191	A667	55b blk, pur & red	25	10

Issued for International Education Year.

1970, Aug. 21
Roses: 35b, Wiener charme. 55b, Pink luster. 1 l, Piccadilly. 1.50 l, Orange Delbard. 2.40 l, Sibelius.
2192	A668	20b dk red, grn & yel	8	5
2193	A668	35b vio, yel & grn	13	10
2194	A668	55b bl, rose & grn	19	15
2195	A668	1 l grn, car rose & yel	45	20
2196	A668	1.50 l dk red & grn	65	35
2197	A668	2.40 l brt bl, dp red & grn	1.25	50
		Nos. 2192-2197 (6)	2.75	1.35

Spaniel and Pheasant, by Jean B. Oudry
A669

Paintings: 10b, The Hunt, by Domenico Brandi. 35b, The Hunt, by Jan Fyt. 60b, After the Chase, by Jacob Jordaens. 1.75 l, 5 l, Game Merchant, by Frans Snyders (horiz.). 3 l, The Hunt, by Adriaen de Gryeff. Sizes: 37x49mm. (10b, 35b); 35x33mm. (20b, 60b, 3 l); 49x37mm. (1.75 l, 3 l).

1970, Sept. 20   Photo.   Perf. 13½
2198	A669	10b gold & multi	6	5
2199	A669	20b gold & multi	12	8
2200	A669	35b gold & multi	15	10
2201	A669	60b gold & multi	30	18
2202	A669	1.75 l gold & multi	85	50
2203	A669	3 l gold & multi	1.75	85
		Nos. 2198-2203 (6)	3.23	1.76

Miniature Sheet
2204	A669	5 l gold & multi	3.00	3.00

No. 2204 contains one stamp and gray control number in margin. Size: 88x78 mm.

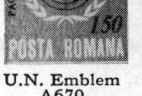

U.N. Emblem
A670

Mother and Child—A671

1970, Sept. 29
2205	A670	1.50 l lt bl, ultra & blk	75	20

25th anniversary of the United Nations.

1970, Sept. 25
Designs: 1.50 l, Red Cross relief trucks and tents. 1.75 l, Rebuilding houses.
2206	A671	55b bl gray, blk & ol	25	10
2207	A671	1.50 l ol, blk & car	65	15
		Strip of 3 (#2206-2207, C179)	1.95	1.00
2208	A671	1.75 l bl & multi	85	35

Issued to publicize the plight of the victims of the Danube flood. Nos. 2206–2207 and C179 are printed se-tenant.

Arabian Thoroughbred—A672

Horses: 35b, American trotter. 55b, Ghidran (Anglo-American). 1 l, Northern Moravian. 1.50 l, Trotter thoroughbred. 2.40 l, Lippizaner.

1970, Oct. 10   Photo.   Perf. 13½
2209	A672	20b blk & multi	8	5
2210	A672	35b blk & multi	13	10
2211	A672	55b blk & multi	19	15
2212	A672	1 l blk & multi	45	25
2213	A672	1.50 l blk & multi	75	25
2214	A672	2.40 l blk & multi	1.65	50
		Nos. 2209-2214 (6)	3.25	1.30

See also Nos. 2227–2232.

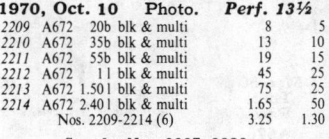

Ludwig van Beethoven
A673

1970, Nov. 2
2215	A673	55b multi	35	10

Bicentenary of the birth of Ludwig van Beethoven (1770–1827), composer.

Abstract, by Joan Miró—A674

1970, Dec. 10   Photo.   Perf. 13½
2216	A674	3 l ultra & multi	1.75	1.25

Souvenir Sheet
Imperf.
2217	A674	5 l ultra & multi	3.25	3.25

Plight of the Danube flood victims. No. 2216 issued in sheets of 5 stamps and label with signature of Miró and date of flood. No. 2217 contains one stamp with simulated perforation, marginal inscription and control number. Size: 78x95mm.

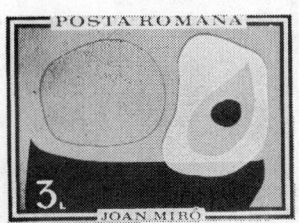

The Sense of Sight, by Gonzales Coques
A675

"The Senses," paintings by Gonzales Coques (1614–1684): 20b, Hearing. 35b, Smell. 60b, Taste. 1.75 l, Touch. 3 l, Bruckenthal Museum, Sibiu. 5 l, View of Sibiu, 1808 (horiz.).

1970, Dec. 15   Photo.   Perf. 13½
2218	A675	10b gold & multi	6	5
2219	A675	20b gold & multi	12	8
2220	A675	35b gold & multi	15	10
2221	A675	60b gold & multi	25	10
2222	A675	1.75 l gold & multi	85	50
2223	A675	3 l gold & multi	1.50	85
		Nos. 2218-2223 (6)	2.93	1.68

Miniature Sheet
Imperf.
2224	A675	5 l gold & multi	3.00	3.00

No. 2224 contains one stamp with blue ornamental frame and gray control number in front. Size: 89½x77½mm.

ROMANIA

Men of Three Races
A676

1971, Feb. 23 Photo. Perf. 13½
2225 A676 1.50 l multi 75 20
International year against racial discrimination.

Tudor Vladimirescu, by Theodor Aman
A677

1971, Feb. 20
2226 A677 1.50 l gold & multi 75 20
Sesquicentennial of the death of Tudor Vladimirescu, patriot.

German Shepherd
A677a

Dogs: 35b, Bulldog. 55b, Fox terrier. 1 l, Setter. 1.50 l, Cocker spaniel. 2.40 l, Poodle.

1971, Feb. 22
2227	A677a	20b blk & multi	12	8
2228	A677a	35b blk & multi	20	10
2229	A677a	55b blk & multi	35	15
2230	A677a	1 l blk & multi	50	25
2231	A677a	1.50 l blk & multi	75	45
2232	A677a	2.40 l blk & multi	1.50	80
		Nos. 2227-2232 (6)	3.42	1.83

Paris Commune Congress Emblem
A678 A679

1971, Mar. 15 Photo. Perf. 13½
2233 A678 40b multi 20 10
Centenary of the Paris Commune.

1971, March 23
2234 A679 55b multi 25 10
Romanian Trade Unions Congress.

Rock Formation
A680

Designs: 10b, Bicazului Gorge (vert.). 55b, Winter resort. 1 l, Danube Delta view. 1.50 l, Lakeside resort. 2.40 l, Venus, Jupiter, Neptune Hotels on Black Sea.

1971, Apr. 15
Size: 23x38, 38x23mm.
2235	A680	10b multi	6	5
2236	A680	40b multi	15	10
2237	A680	55b multi	25	15
2238	A680	1 l multi	45	28
2239	A680	1.50 l multi	75	40

Size: 76½x28mm.
| 2240 | A680 | 2.40 l multi | 1.25 | 65 |
| | | Nos. 2235-2240 (6) | 2.91 | 1.63 |

Tourist publicity.

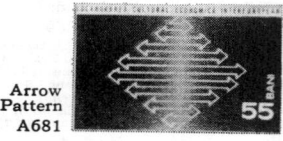

Arrow Pattern
A681

Design: 1.75 l, Wave pattern.

1971, Apr. 28 Photo. Perf. 13½
2241 A681 55b multi 1.00 85
2242 A681 1.75 l multi 2.00 1.50
Inter-European Cultural and Economic Collaboration. Sheets of 10.

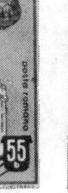

Historical Museum Demonstration, by A. Anastasiu
A682 A684

Communist Party Emblem
A683

1971, May 7 Photo. Perf. 13½
2243 A682 55b bl & multi 25 10
For Romania's Historical Museum.

1971, May 8
Design: 35b, Reading Proclamation, by Stefan Szonyi.
2244	A684	35b multi	15	5
2245	A683	40b multi	20	8
2246	A684	55b multi	25	10

50th anniversary of the Romanian Communist Party.

Souvenir Sheets

Dancing the Hora, by Theodor Aman—A686

1971, May 25 Photo. Perf. 13½
2247 A685 Sheet of 6, multi 5.50 5.00
a. 1.20 l shown
b. 1.20 l Maid by V. Dimitrov-Maystora 80 60
c. 1.20 l Rosa Botzaris, by Joseph Stieler 80 60
d. 1.20 l Woman in Costume, by Katarina Ivanovic 80 60
e. 1.20 l Argeseanca, by Carol Popp de Szathmary 80 60
f. 1.20 l Woman in Modern Dress, by Calli Ibrahim 80 60
2248 A686 5 l multi 3.00 3.00
Balkanphila III Stamp Exhibition, Bucharest, June 27—July 2.
No. 2247 contains 6 stamps in 3 rows and 6 labels showing exhibition emblem and "60b." Blue marginal inscription. Size: 175x211mm. No. 2248 contains one stamp and has silver marginal inscription. Size: 90x77½mm.

Pomegranate Flower
A687

Flowers: 35b, Slipperwort. 55b, Lily. 1 l, Mimulus. 1.50 l, Morning-glory. 2.40 l, Leaf cactus (horiz.).

1971, June 20
2249	A687	20b ultra & multi	12	8
2250	A687	35b red & multi	15	8
2251	A687	55b ultra & multi	20	10
2252	A687	1 l car & multi	50	20
2253	A687	1.50 l car & multi	85	25
2254	A687	2.40 l ultra & multi	1.40	50
		Nos. 2249-2254 (6)	3.22	1.21

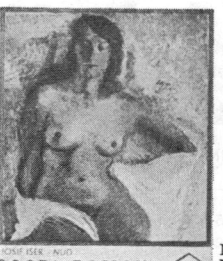

Nude, by Iosif Iser
A688

Paintings of Nudes: 20b, by Camil Ressu. 35b, by Nicolae Grigorescu. 60b, by Eugene Delacroix (odalisque). 1.75 l, by Auguste Renoir. 3 l, by Palma il Vecchio (Venus and Amor). 5 l, by Il Bronzino (Venus and Amor). 60b, 3 l, 5 l, horiz.

1971, July 25 Photo. Perf. 13½
Size: 38x50mm., 49x39mm., 29x50mm. (20b).
2255	A688	10b gold & multi	5	5
2256	A688	20b gold & multi	8	8
2257	A688	35b gold & multi	13	10
2258	A688	60b gold & multi	20	12
2259	A688	1.75 l gold & multi	65	35
2260	A688	3 l gold & multi	2.50	75
		Nos. 2255-2260 (6)	3.61	1.45

Miniature Sheet
Imperf.
2261 A688 5 l gold & multi 3.00 3.00
No. 2261 contains one stamp. Size: 89x77½mm.

Ships in Storm, by B. Peters—A689

Paintings of Ships by: 20b, Ludolf Backhuysen. 35b, Andries van Eertvelt. 60b, M. W. Arnold. 1.75 l, Ivan Konstantinovich Aivazovski. 3 l, Jean Steriadi. 5 l, N. Darascu (vert.).

1971, Sept. 15 Photo. Perf. 13½
2262	A689	10b gold & multi	5	5
2263	A689	20b gold & multi	8	5
2264	A689	35b gold & multi	13	8
2265	A689	60b gold & multi	20	12
2266	A689	1.75 l gold & multi	65	40
2267	A689	3 l gold & multi	1.50	72
		Nos. 2262-2267 (6)	2.61	1.42

Miniature Sheet
2268 A689 5 l gold & multi 2.50 2.50
No. 2268 contains one stamp. Size: 77x90mm.

Types of Regular Issue
Designs as Before and: 3.60 l, Mail collector. 4.80 l, Mailman. 6 l, Ministry of Posts.

1971 Photogravure Perf. 13½
Size: 16½x23mm., 23x16½mm.
2269	A616	1 l emerald	33	5
2270	A617	1.20 l red lil	40	5
2271	A617	1.35 l brt bl	45	5
2272	A616	1.50 l org red	50	5
2273	A616	1.55 l sepia	50	5
2274	A617	1.75 l dp grn	55	5
2275	A617	2 l citron	65	5
2276	A616	2.40 l dk bl	80	5
2277	A617	3 l grnsh bl	1.00	5
2278	A617	3.20 l ocher	1.00	5
2279	A616	3.25 l ultra	1.25	5
2280	A616	3.60 l blue	1.50	5
2281	A617	4 l lil rose	1.75	6
2282	A616	4.80 l grnsh bl	1.90	5
2283	A617	5 l violet	2.00	10
2284	A616	6 l dp mag	2.25	15
		Nos. 2269-2284 (16)	16.83	99

Prince Neagoe Basarab Theodor Pallady (Painter)
A690 A691

1971, Sept. 20 Perf. 13½
2288 A690 60b gold & multi 30 15
450th anniversary of the death of Prince Neagoe Basarab of Walachia.

ROMANIA

1971, Oct. 12 Photo. Perf. 13½
Portraits of: 55b, Benvenuto Cellini (1500–1571), sculptor. 1.50 l, Antoine Watteau (1684–1721), painter. 2.40 l, Albrecht Dürer (1471–1528), painter.

2289	A691	40b gold & multi	15	10
2290	A691	55b gold & multi	21	12
2291	A691	1.50 l gold & multi	45	25
2292	A691	2.40 l gold & multi	1.00	35

Anniversaries of famous artists.

Proclamation of Cyrus the Great
A692

Figure Skating
A693

1971, Oct. 12
| 2293 | A692 | 55b multi | 20 | 10 |

2500th anniversary of the founding of the Persian empire by Cyrus the Great.

1971, Oct. 25
Designs: 20b, Ice hockey. 40b, Biathlon (skier). 55b, Bobsledding. 1.75 l, Skiing. 3 l, Sapporo '72 emblem. 5 l, Olympic flame and emblem.

2294	A693	10b lt bl, blk & red	5	5
2295	A693	20b multi	8	5
2296	A693	40b multi	16	10
2297	A693	55b lt bl, blk & red	19	12
2298	A693	1.75 l lt bl, blk & red	80	35
2299	A693	3 l lt bl, blk & red	1.35	60
		Nos. 2294-2299 (6)	2.63	1.27

Miniature Sheet
Imperf.
| 2300 | A693 | 5 l multi | 3.00 | 3.00 |

11th Winter Olympic Games, Sapporo, Japan, Feb. 3–13, 1972. Nos. 2294–2296 printed se-tenant in sheets of 15 (5x3); Nos. 2297–2298 printed se-tenant in sheets of 10 (5x2). No. 2300 contains one stamp (37x50mm.). Size of sheet: 78x90mm.

St. George and the Dragon
A694

Frescoes from North Moldavian Monasteries: 10b, 20b, 40b, Moldovita. 55b, 1.75 l, 5 l, Voronet. 3 l, Arborea (horiz.).

1971, Nov. 30 Photo. Perf. 13½
2301	A694	10b gold & multi	5	5
2302	A694	20b gold & multi	9	5
2303	A694	40b gold & multi	18	10
2304	A694	55b gold & multi	21	12
2305	A694	1.75 l gold & multi	95	42
2306	A694	3 l gold & multi	1.50	90
		Nos. 2301-2306 (6)	2.98	1.64

Miniature Sheet
Imperf.
| 2307 | A694 | 5 l gold & multi | 2.50 | 1.50 |

No. 2307 contains one stamp (44x56 mm.). Size of sheet: 78x89mm.

Ferdinand Magellan
A695

Designs: 55b, Johannes Kepler and observation tower. 1 l, Yuri Gagarin and rocket orbiting earth. 1.50 l, Baron Ernest Rutherford, atom, nucleus and chemical apparatus.

1971, Dec. 20
2308	A695	40b grn, brt rose & dk bl	18	6
2309	A695	55b lil, blk & gray grn	21	8
2310	A695	1 l vio & multi	45	25
2311	A695	1.50 l red brn, grn & bl	65	36

450th anniversary of the death of Magellan (1480?–1521), navigator (40b); 400th anniversary of the birth of Kepler (1571–1630), astronomer (55b); Gagarin, first man in space, 10th anniversary (1 l); centenary of birth of Ernest R. Rutherford (1871–1937), British physicist (1.50 l).

Matei Millo
A696

Young Communists Union Emblem
A697

1971, Dec.
| 2312 | A696 | 55b bl & multi | 21 | 8 |
| 2313 | A696 | 1 l pur & multi | 40 | 20 |

75th anniversary of the death of Matei Millo (1814–1896), playwright (55b); centenary of the birth of Nicolae Iorga (1871–1940), historian and politician (1 l).

1972, Feb.
| 2314 | A697 | 55b dk bl, red & gold | 25 | 10 |

Young Communists Union, 50th anniversary.

Lynx Cubs—A698

Young Animals: 35b, Foxes. 55b, Roe fawns. 1 l, Wild pigs. 1.50 l, Wolves. 2.40 l, Bears.

1972, Mar. 10 Photo. Perf. 13½
2315	A698	20b multi	9	5
2316	A698	35b multi	14	8
2317	A698	55b bl & multi	21	12
2318	A698	1 l multi	45	30
2319	A698	1.50 l multi	60	40
2320	A698	2.40 l grn & multi	1.50	50
		Nos. 2315-2320 (6)	2.99	1.45

Wrestling
A699

Designs (Olympic Rings and): 20b, Canoeing. 55b, Soccer. 1.55 l, Women's high jump. 2.90 l, Boxing. 6.70 l, Field ball.

1972, Apr. 25 Photo. Perf. 13½
2321	A699	10b yel & multi	5	5
2322	A699	20b multi	9	5
2323	A699	55b gray & multi	21	12
2324	A699	1.55 l grn & multi	45	25
2325	A699	2.90 l multi	85	35
2326	A699	6.70 l lil & multi	2.00	75
		Nos. 2321-2326 (6)	3.65	1.57

20th Olympic Games, Munich, Aug. 26–Sept. 10. See No. C186–C187.

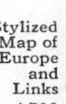
Stylized Map of Europe and Links
A700

Design: 2.90 l, Entwined arrows and links.

1972, Apr. 28
| 2327 | A700 | 1.75 l dp car, gold & blk | 1.40 | 1.10 |
| 2328 | A700 | 2.90 l grn, gold & blk | 1.75 | 1.50 |

Inter-European Cultural and Economic Collaboration. Nos. 2327–2328 printed se-tenant.

UIC Emblem and Trains
A701

1972, May 20 Photo. Perf. 13½
| 2329 | A701 | 55b dp car rose, blk & gold | 25 | 10 |

50th anniversary, International Railway Union (UIC).

Souvenir Sheet

"Summer," by Peter Brueghel the Younger—A702

1972, May 20 Perf. 13x13½
| 2330 | A702 | 6 l gold & multi | 3.00 | 3.00 |

Belgica 72, International Philatelic Exhibition, Brussels, June 24–July 9. No. 2330 contains one stamp; gold margin with white inscription and Belgica 72 emblem. Size: 89x77mm.

Peony
A703

Protected Flowers: 40b, Pink. 55b, Edelweiss. 60b, Nigritella rubra. 1.35 l, Narcissus. 2.90 l, Lady's slipper.

1972, June 5 Photo. Perf. 13
Flowers in Natural Colors
2331	A703	20b dk vio bl	9	5
2332	A703	40b chocolate	12	8
2333	A703	55b dp bl	20	10
2334	A703	60b dk grn	25	18
2335	A703	1.35 l violet	75	25
2336	A703	2.90 l dk Prus bl	1.35	60
		Nos. 2331-2336 (6)	2.76	1.26

Saligny Bridge, Cernavoda—A704

Danube Bridges: 1.75 l, Giurgeni Bridge, Vadul. 2.75 l, Friendship Bridge, Giurgiu-Ruse.

1972, June 25 Photo. Perf. 13½
2337	A704	1.35 l bl & multi	40	22
2338	A704	1.75 l bl & multi	50	28
2339	A704	2.75 l bl & multi	1.00	38

North Railroad Station, Bucharest
A705

1972, July 4
| 2340 | A705 | 55b ultra & multi | 25 | 10 |

Centenary of the North Railroad Station, Bucharest.

Water Polo and Olympic Rings
A706

Designs (Olympic Rings and): 20b, Pistol shoot. 55b, Discus. 1.55 l, Gymnastics, women's. 2.75 l, Canoeing. 6.40 l, Fencing.

1972, July 5 Photo. Perf. 13½
2341	A706	10b ol, gold & lil	5	5
2342	A706	20b red, gold & grn	7	5
2343	A706	55b grn, gold & brn	18	12
2344	A706	1.55 l vio, gold & ol	45	25
2345	A706	2.75 l bl, gold & gray	90	35
2346	A706	6.40 l pur, gold & gray	2.10	75
		Nos. 2341-2346 (6)	3.75	1.57

20th Olympic Games, Munich, Aug. 26–Sept. 11. See No. C187.

Stamp Printing Press
A707

ROMANIA

1972, July 25

| 2347 | A707 | 55b multi | 25 | 10 |

Centenary of the stamp printing office.

Stefan Popescu, Self-portrait
A708

1972, Aug. 10
Multicolored

2348	A708	55b shown	15	6
2349	A708	1.75 l Octav Bancila	40	28
2350	A708	2.90 l Gheorghe Petrascu	75	32
2351	A708	6.50 l Ion Andreescu	1.75	60

Self-portraits by Romanian painters.

Runner with Torch, Olympic Rings
A709

City Hall Tower, Sibiu
A710

1972, Aug. 13

| 2352 | A709 | 55b sil, bl & cl | 25 | 10 |

Olympic torch relay from Olympia, Greece, to Munich, Germany, passing through Romania.

1972, Photo. Perf. 13

Designs: 1.85 l, St. Michael's Cathedral, Cluj. 2.75 l, Sphinx Rock, Mt. Bucegi (horiz.). 3.35 l, Heroes' Monument, Bucharest. 3.45 l, Sinaia Castle (horiz.). 5.15 l, Hydroelectric Works, Arges (horiz.). 5.60 l, Church of the Epiphany, Iasi. 6.20 l, Bran Castle. 6.40 l, Hunedoara Castle (horiz.). 6.80 l, Polytechnic Institute, Bucharest (horiz.). 7.05 l, Black Church, Brasov. 8.45 l, Atheneum, Bucharest. 9.05 l, Excavated Coliseum, Sarmizegetusa (horiz.). 9.10 l, Hydroelectric Station, Iron Gate (horiz.). 9.85 l, Monument, Cetatea. 11.90 l, Republic Palace (horiz.). 12.75 l, Television Station. 13.30 l, Arch, Alba Iulia (horiz.). 16.20 l, Clock Tower, Sighisoara.

Size: 23x18mm., 17x24mm.

2353	A710	1.85 l brt pur	50	5
2354	A710	2.75 l gray	75	5
2355	A710	3.35 l magenta	90	5
2356	A710	3.45 l green	80	5
2357	A710	5.15 l brt bl	1.40	5
2358	A710	5.60 l blue	1.50	5
2359	A710	6.20 l cerise	1.60	5
2360	A710	6.40 l sepia	1.75	5
2361	A710	6.80 l rose red	1.75	5
2362	A710	7.05 l black	2.00	5
2363	A710	8.45 l rose red	2.25	5
2364	A710	9.05 l dl grn	2.50	5
2365	A710	9.10 l ultra	2.50	5
2366	A710	9.85 l green	2.75	5

Size: 19½x29, 29x21mm.

2367	A710	10 l dp brn		25
2368	A710	11.90 l bluish blk	3.25	25
2369	A710	12.75 l dk vio	3.50	25
2370	A710	13.30 l dl red	3.75	25
2371	A710	16.20 l ol grn	4.50	25
		Nos. 2353-2371, C193 (20)	44.70	2.20

View of Satu-Mare
A711

1972, Oct. 5

| 2372 | A711 | 55b multi | 30 | 10 |

Millennium of Satu-Mare.

Tennis Racket and Davis Cup
A712

1972, Oct. 10 Perf. 13½

| 2373 | A712 | 2.75 l multi | 1.25 | 35 |

Final tennis match for the Davis Cup between Romania and USA, Bucharest, Oct. 13-15.

Venice, by Gheorge Petrascu—A713

Paintings of Venice by: 20b, N. Darascu. 55b, Petrascu. 1.55 l, Marius Bunescu. 2.75 l, N. Darascu (vert.). 6 l, Petrascu. 6.40 l, Marius Bunescu.

1972, Oct. 20

2374	A713	10b gray & multi	5	5
2375	A713	20b gray & multi	8	6
2376	A713	55b gray & multi	15	10
2377	A713	1.55 l gray & multi	40	25
2378	A713	2.75 l gray & multi	80	35
2379	A713	6.40 l gray & multi	2.00	75
		Nos. 2374-2379 (6)	3.48	1.56

Souvenir Sheet

| 2380 | A713 | 6 l gray & multi | 2.50 | 2.50 |

No. 2380 contains one stamp and has decorative gray margin. Size: 89x79mm.

Fencing, Bronze Medal
A714

Apollo 1, 2 and 3
A715

Designs: 20b, Team handball, bronze medal. 35b, Boxing, silver medal. 1.45 l, Hurdles, women's, silver medal. 2.75 l, Pistol shoot, silver medal. 6.20 l, Wrestling, gold medal.

1972, Oct. 28

2381	A714	10b red org & multi	5	5
2382	A713	20b lt grn & multi	8	5
2383	A714	35b multi	12	6
2384	A714	1.45 l multi	40	25
2385	A714	2.75 l ocher & multi	80	35
2386	A714	6.20 l bl & multi	2.00	70
		Nos. 2381-2386 (6)	3.45	1.46

Romanian medalists at 20th Olympic Games. See No. C191.

1972, Dec. 27 Photo. Perf. 13½
Multicolored

2387	A715	10b shown	5	5
2388	A715	35b Grissom, Chaffee and White, 1967	10	5
2389	A715	40b Apollo 4, 5, 6	12	6
2390	A715	55b Apollo 7, 8	12	8
2391	A715	1 l Apollo 9, 10	25	15
2392	A715	1.20 l Apollo 11, 12	35	15
2393	A715	1.85 l Apollo 13, 14	50	20
2394	A715	2.75 l Apollo 15, 16	75	30
2395	A715	3.60 l Apollo 17	1.25	60
		Nos. 2387-2395 (9)	3.49	1.64

Highlights of U.S. Apollo space program. See No. C192.

"25" and Flags
A716

Designs: 1.20 l, "25" and national emblem. 1.75 l, "25" and factory.

1972, Dec. 25

2396	A716	55b bl & multi	18	6
2397	A716	1.20 l yel & multi	50	15
2398	A716	1.75 l ver & multi	60	25

25th anniversary of the Republic.

European Bee-eater
A717

Globeflowers
A718

Designs: No. 2400, Red-breasted goose. No. 2401, Penduline tit. No. 2403, Garden Turk's-cap. No. 2404, Gentian.

1973, Feb. 5 Photo. Perf. 13

2399	A717	1.40 l gray & multi	35	15
2400	A717	1.85 l multi	50	25
2401	A717	2.75 l bl & multi	1.00	30
		Strip of 3	2.00	90
2402	A718	1.40 l multi	35	15
2403	A718	1.85 l yel & multi	50	25
2404	A718	2.75 l multi	1.00	30
		Strip of 3	2.00	90

Nature protection. Nos. 2399-2401 and 2402-2404 printed se-tenant horizontally in 2 sheets of 15 (3x5).

Nicolaus Copernicus
A719

1973, Feb. 19 Photo. Perf. 13x13½

| 2405 | A719 | 2.75 l multi | 90 | 40 |

500th anniversary of the birth of Nicolaus Copernicus (1473-1543), Polish astronomer. Printed with alternating label publicizing International Philatelic Exhibition, Poznan, Aug. 19-Sept. 2.

Suceava Woman
A720

D. Paciurea (Sculptor)
A721

Regional Costumes: 40b, Suceava man. 55b, Harghita woman. 1.75 l, Harghita man. 2.75 l, Gorj woman. 6.40 l, Gorj man.

1973, Mar. 15

2406	A720	10b lt bl & multi	5	5
2407	A720	40b multi	12	10
2408	A720	55b bis & multi	15	10
2409	A720	1.75 l lil & multi	45	15
2410	A720	2.75 l multi	70	20
2411	A720	6.40 l multi	1.75	65
		Nos. 2406-2411 (6)	3.22	1.25

1973, Mar. 26

Portraits: 40b, I. Slavici (1848-1925), writer. 55b, G. Lazar (1779-1823), writer. 6.40 l, A. Flechtenmacher (1823-1898), composer.

2412	A721	10b multi	5	5
2413	A721	40b multi	12	5
2414	A721	55b multi	20	6
2415	A721	6.40 l multi	1.50	70

Anniversaries of famous artists.

Map of Europe
A722

Design: 3.60 l, Symbol of collaboration.

1973, Apr. 28 Photo. Perf. 13½

| 2416 | A722 | 3.35 l dp bl & gold | 1.40 | 1.00 |
| 2417 | A722 | 3.60 l brt mag & gold | 1.75 | 1.50 |

Inter-European cultural and economic cooperation. Nos. 2416-2417 printed se-tenant in sheets of 10 with blue marginal inscription.

Souvenir Sheet

The Rape of Proserpina, by Hans von Aachen—A723

1973, May 5

| 2418 | A723 | 12 l gold & multi | 4.00 | 3.50 |

IBRA Munchen 1973, International Stamp Exhibition, Munich, May 11-20. No. 2418 contains one stamp, gold marginal inscription and IBRA emblem. Size: 90x78mm.

ROMANIA 239

Prince Alexander I. Cuza — A724
Hand with Hammer and Sickle — A725

1973, May 5   Photo.   *Perf. 13½*
| 2419 | A724 | 1.75 l multi | 75 | 25 |

Centenary of the death of Alexander Ioan Cuza (1820-1873), prince of Romania, Moldavia and Walachia.

1973, May 5
| 2420 | A725 | 40b gold & multi | 25 | 10 |

Workers and Peasants Party, 25th anniversary.

Romanian Flag, Bayonets Stabbing Swastika — A726
WMO Emblem, Weather Satellite — A727

1973, May 5
| 2421 | A726 | 55b multi | 25 | 10 |

Anti-fascist Front, 40th anniversary.

1973, June 15
| 2422 | A727 | 2 l ultra & multi | 75 | 30 |

Centenary of international meteorological cooperation.

 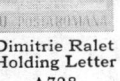

Dimitrie Ralet Holding Letter — A728
Dimitrie Cantemir — A729

1973, June 20
2423	A728	40b multi	12	6
2424	A728	60b multi	18	8
2425	A728	1.55 l multi	45	25

"The Letter on Romanian Portraits." Socfilex III Philatelic Exhibition, Bucharest, July 20-29. See Nos. B432-B433.

1973, June 25

Design: 6 l, Portrait of Cantemir in oval frame.
| 2426 | A729 | 1.75 l multi | 70 | 30 |

Souvenir Sheet
| 2427 | A729 | 6 l multi | 2.50 | 2.00 |

300th anniversary of the birth of Dimitrie Cantemir (1673-1723), Prince of Moldavia, writer. No. 2427 contains one stamp (size: 38x50mm.), date in margin. Size: 77x90mm.

Plate — A730

1973, July 25   Photo.   *Perf. 13½*

Designs: 10b, Fibulae (vert.). 55b, Jug (vert.). 1.55 l, Necklaces and fibula. 2.75 l, Plate (vert.). 6.80 l, Octagonal bowl with animal handles. 12 l, Breastplate (vert.).

2428	A730	10b vio bl & multi	5	5
2429	A730	20b grn & multi	6	5
2430	A730	55b red & multi	15	8
2431	A730	1.55 l multi	40	20
2432	A730	2.75 l plum & multi	75	30
2433	A730	6.80 l multi	1.75	70
		Nos. 2428-2433 (6)	3.16	1.38

Souvenir Sheet
| 2434 | A730 | 12 l multi | 4.00 | 3.50 |

Roman gold treasure of Pietroasa, 4th century. No. 2434 contains one stamp, gold margin with white inscription and greenish control number. Size: 77x90mm.

 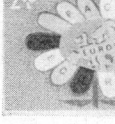

Symbolic Flower, Map of Europe — A731

1973, Oct. 2   Photo.   *Perf. 13½*

Design: 5 l, Map of Europe, symbolic tree.
2435	A731	2.75 l multi	1.25	1.00
2436	A731	5 l multi	2.00	1.50
		Sheet of 4 + 2 labels	7.50	7.50

Conference for European Security and Cooperation, Helsinki, Finland, July 1973. Nos. 2435-2436 printed in sheets containing 2 each of Nos. 2435-2436 and 2 labels showing Conference Hall, Helsinki, and U.N. Building, Geneva; red marginal inscription. Size: 152x80mm.

Jug and Cloth, Oboga — A732

Designs: 20b, Plate and Pitcher, Vama. 55b, Bowl, Marginea. 1.55 l, Pitcher and plate, Sibiu-Saschiz. 2.75 l, Bowl and jug, Pisc. 6.80 l, Figurine (fowl), Oboga.

1973, Oct. 15   *Perf. 13*
2437	A732	10b gold & multi	5	5
2438	A732	20b gold & multi	6	5
2439	A732	55b gold & multi	15	8
2440	A732	1.55 l sil & multi	40	20
2441	A732	2.75 l sil & multi	70	30
2442	A732	6.80 l sil & multi	1.75	70
		Nos. 2437-2442 (6)	3.11	1.38

Pottery and cloths from various regions of Romania.

Women Workers, by G. Saru — A733

Paintings of Workers: 20b, Construction Site, by M. Bunescu (horiz.). 55b, Shipyard Workers, by H. Catargi (horiz.). 1.55 l, Worker, by Catargi. 2.75 l, Miners, by A. Phoebus. 6.80 l, Spinner, by Nicolae Grigorescu. 12 l, Farmers at Rest, by Stefan Popescu (horiz.).

1973, Nov. 26   Photo.   *Perf. 13½*
2443	A733	10b gold & multi	5	5
2444	A733	20b gold & multi	6	5
2445	A733	55b gold & multi	15	6
2446	A733	1.55 l gold & multi	40	20
2447	A733	2.75 l gold & multi	70	30
2448	A733	6.80 l gold & multi	1.75	70
		Nos. 2443-2448 (6)	3.11	1.36

Miniature Sheet
| 2449 | A733 | 12 l gold & multi | 4.00 | 3.50 |

No. 2449 contains one stamp. Size: 90x77mm.

City Hall, Craiova — A734
Tugboat under Bridge — A735

Designs: 10b, Infinite Column, by Constantin Brancusi (vert.). 20b, Heroes' Mausoleum, Marasesti. 35b, Risnov Citadel. 40b, Densus Church (vert.). 50b, Blaj Church (vert.). 55b, Maldaresti Fortress. 60b, National Theater, Iasi. 1 l, Curtea-de-Arges Monastery (vert.). 1.20 l, Tirgu-Mures Citadel. 1.45 l, Cargoship Dimbovita. 1.50 l, Muntenia passenger ship. 1.55 l, Three-master Mircea. 1.75 l, Motorship Transilvania. 2.20 l, Ore carrier Oltul. 3.65 l, Trawler Mures. 4.70 l, Tanker Arges.

1973-74   Photogravure   *Perf. 13*
2450	A734	5b lake	5	5
2451	A734	10b brt bl	5	5
2452	A734	20b orange	6	5
2453	A734	35b green	11	5
2454	A734	40b dk vio	12	5
2455	A734	50b ultra	16	5
2456	A734	55b org brn	18	5
2457	A734	60b carmine	20	5
2458	A734	1 l dp ultra	33	5
2459	A734	1.20 l ol grn	40	8
2460	A735	1.35 l gray	45	5
2461	A735	1.45 l dl bl	48	5
2462	A735	1.50 l car rose	50	5
2463	A735	1.55 l vio bl	50	5
2464	A735	1.75 l sl grn	58	5
2465	A735	2.20 l brt bl	72	5
2466	A735	3.65 l dl lil	1.20	10
2467	A735	4.70 l vio brn	1.55	15
		Nos. 2450-2467 (18)	7.64	1.08

Issue dates: Nos. 2450-2459, Dec. 15, 1973. Nos. 2460-2467, Jan. 28, 1974.

Boats at Montfleur, by Claude Monet — A736

Paintings: 40b, Church of Moret, by Alfred Sisley (vert.). 55b, Orchard in Bloom, by Camille Pissarro. 1.75 l, Portrait of Jeanne, by Pissarro (vert.). 2.75 l, Landscape, by Auguste Renoir. 3.60 l, Portrait of a Girl, by Paul Cezanne (vert.). 10 l, Women Taking Bath, by Renoir (vert.).

1974, Mar. 15   Photo.   *Perf. 13½*
2468	A736	20b bl & multi	6	5
2469	A736	40b bl & multi	12	6
2470	A736	55b bl & multi	18	8
2471	A736	1.75 l bl & multi	40	15
2472	A736	2.75 l bl & multi	70	30
2473	A736	3.60 l bl & multi	1.20	50
		Nos. 2468-2473 (6)	2.66	1.16

Souvenir Sheet
| 2474 | A736 | 10 l bl & multi | 3.50 | 2.50 |

Impressionistic paintings. No. 2474 contains one stamp; gray margin designed to look like canvas. Size: 77x89mm.

Harness Racing — A737

Designs: Various horse races.

1974, Apr. 5   Photo.   *Perf. 13½*
2475	A737	40b ver & multi	12	8
2476	A737	55b bis & multi	15	8
2477	A737	60b multi	20	14
2478	A737	1.55 l multi	40	20
2479	A737	2.75 l multi	70	40
2480	A737	3.45 l multi	1.15	60
		Nos. 2475-2480 (6)	2.72	1.50

Centenary of horse racing in Romania.

Nicolae Titulescu — A738

1974, Apr. 16
| 2481 | A738 | 1.75 l multi | 50 | 20 |

Interparliamentary Session, Bucharest, Apr. 1974. Nicolae Titulescu (1883-1941) was the first Romanian delegate to the League of Nations.

Souvenir Sheet

Roman Memorial with First Reference to Napoca (Cluj) — A739

1974, Apr. 18 Photogravure *Perf. 13*
| 2482 | A739 | 10 l multi | 3.50 | 2.50 |

1850th anniversary of the elevation of the Roman settlement of Napoca (Cluj) to a municipality. No. 2482 contains one stamp, buff margin and black inscription. Size: 77x91mm.

Stylized Map of Europe — A740

Design: 3.45 l, Satellite over earth.

1974, Apr. 25   Photo.   *Perf. 13½x13*
| 2483 | A740 | 2.20 l multi | 1.25 | 1.00 |
| 2484 | A740 | 3.45 l multi | 1.75 | 1.50 |

Inter-European Cultural Economic Cooperation. Nos. 2483-2484 printed se-tenant in sheet of 10 with gold marginal inscription.

ROMANIA

Young Pioneers with Banners, by Pepene Cornelia—A741

1974, Apr. 25   Photo.   *Perf. 13½*

| 2485 | A741 | 55b multi | 30 | 10 |

25th anniversary of the Romanian Pioneers Organization.

Mail Motorboat, UPU Emblem
A742

Designs (UPU Emblem and): 40b, Mail train. 55b, Mailplane and truck. 1.75 l, Mail delivery by motorcycle. 2.75 l, Mailman delivering letter to little girl. 3.60 l, Young stamp collectors. 4 l, Mail collection. 6 l, Modern post office.

1974, May 11

2486	A742	20b gray & multi	6	5
2487	A742	40b multi	12	8
2488	A742	55b ultra & multi	15	8
2489	A742	1.75 l multi	40	30
2490	A742	2.75 l brn & multi	70	40
2491	A742	3.60 l org & multi	1.00	60
	Nos. 2486-2491 (6)		2.43	1.51

Souvenir Sheet

2492	A742	Sheet of 2	3.75	3.75
a.	4 l multi		1.25	
b.	6 l multi		2.00	

Centenary of Universal Postal Union. No. 2492 has red marginal inscription and black control number. Size: stamps, 28x24mm.; sheet, 90x78mm. An imperf. airmail UPU souvenir sheet of one (10 l) exists. The multicolored stamp is 49x38mm. The sheet, with violet blue inscription and marginal design, has black control number. Size: 106½x80mm. This sheet is not known to have been sold to the public at post offices.

No. 2382 Surcharged with New Value and Overprinted:

"ROMÂNIA / CAMPIOANA / MONDIALĂ / 1974"

1974, May 13

| 2493 | A714 | 1.75 l on 20b multi | 2.25 | 1.50 |

Romania's victory in World Handball Championship, 1974.

Soccer and Games Emblem
A743

"25"
A744

Designs: Games emblem and various scenes from soccer game.

1974, June 25   *Perf. 13½*

2494	A743	20b pur & multi	6	5
2495	A743	40b multi	12	8
2496	A743	55b ultra & multi	15	10
2497	A743	1.75 l brn & multi	45	30
2498	A743	2.75 l multi	70	40
2499	A743	3.60 l vio & multi	1.00	60
	Nos. 2494-2499 (6)		2.48	1.53

Souvenir Sheet

| 2500 | A743 | 10 l multi | 3.50 | 3.00 |

World Cup Soccer Championship, Munich, June 13–July 7. No. 2500 contains one horizontal stamp (50x38mm.), light blue margin and black control number. Size: 89x77mm. An imperf. 10 l airmail souvenir sheet exists showing a globe as soccer ball and satellite. Gray blue margin showing Soccer Cup, radio tower and stadium; black control number. Size: 106½x79mm.

1974, June 10

| 2501 | A744 | 55b bl & multi | 30 | 10 |

25th anniversary of the Council for Mutual Economic Assistance (COMECON).

UN Emblem and People
A745

Hand Drawing Peace Dove
A746

1974, June 25   Photo.   *Perf. 13½*

| 2502 | A745 | 2 l multi | 50 | 20 |

World Population Year.

1974, June 28

| 2503 | A746 | 2 l ultra & multi | 50 | 20 |

25 years of the National and International Movement to Uphold the Cause of Peace.

Ioan, Prince of Wallachia
A747

Hunedoara Iron and Steel Works
A749

Soldier, Industry and Agriculture
A748

Designs: 1.10 l, Avram Iancu (1824–1872). 1.30 l, Dr. C. I. Parhon (1874–1969). 1.40 l, Bishop Dosoftei (1624–1693).

1974   Photogravure   *Perf. 13*

2504	A747	20b blue	6	5
2505	A748	55b car rose	10	6
2506	A749	1 l sl grn	20	10
2507	A747	1.10 l dk gray ol	25	10
2508	A747	1.30 l dp mag	30	12
2509	A747	1.40 l dk vio	40	15
	Nos. 2504-2509 (6)		1.31	58

No. 2505 issued for Army Day, No. 2506 for 220th anniversary of Hunedoara Iron and Steel works; others for anniversaries of famous Romanians. Issue dates: 1 l, June 17; others June 25.

Romanians and Flags—A750

Design: 40b, Romanian and Communist flags forming "XXX" (vert.).

1974, Aug. 20

| 2510 | A750 | 40b gold, ultra & car | 12 | 5 |
| 2511 | A750 | 55b yel & multi | 18 | 8 |

30th anniversary of Romania's liberation from Fascist rule.

Souvenir Sheet

View, Stockholm—A751

1974, Sept. 10   Photo.   *Perf. 13*

| 2512 | A751 | 10 l multi | 3.50 | 2.75 |

Stockholmia 74 International Philatelic Exhibition, Stockholm, Sept. 21–29. No. 2512 contains one stamp, black marginal inscription. Size: 90x78mm.

Thistle
A752

Designs: 40b, Checkered lily. 55b, Yew. 1.75 l, Azalea. 2.75 l, Forget-me-not. 3.60 l, Pinks.

1974, Sept. 15

2513	A752	20b plum & multi	6	5
2514	A752	40b multi	12	8
2515	A752	55b multi	15	10
2516	A752	1.75 l multi	40	30
2517	A752	2.75 l brn & multi	70	40
2518	A752	3.60 l multi	1.00	60
	Nos. 2513-2518 (6)		2.43	1.53

Nature protection.

Isis, First Century A.D.
A753

Designs: 40b, Serpent, by Glycon. 55b, Emperor Trajan, bronze bust. 1.75 l, Roman woman, statue, 3rd century. 2.75 l, Mithraic bas-relief. 3.60 l, Roman man, statue, 3rd century.

1974, Oct. 20   Photo.   *Perf. 13*

2519	A753	20b multi	6	5
2520	A753	40b ultra & multi	12	5
2521	A753	55b multi	15	9
2522	A753	1.75 l multi	40	20
2523	A753	2.75 l brn & multi	70	30
2524	A753	3.60 l multi	1.00	40
	Nos. 2519-2524 (6)		2.43	1.06

Archaeological art works excavated in Romania.

Romanian Communist Party Emblem
A754

Design: 1 l, similar to 55b.

1974, Nov. 20

| 2525 | A754 | 55b blk, red & gold | 15 | 6 |
| 2526 | A754 | 1 l blk, red & gold | 25 | 12 |

9th Romanian Communist Party Congress.

Discobolus and Olympic Rings
A755

1974, Nov. 11

| 2527 | A755 | 2 l ultra & multi | 75 | 25 |

Romanian Olympic Committee, 60th anniversary.

Skylab
A756

1974, Dec. 14   Photo.   *Perf. 13*

| 2528 | A756 | 2.50 l multi | 90 | 50 |

Skylab, manned U.S. space laboratory. No. 2528 printed in sheets of 4 stamps and 4 labels, showing Skylab, globe and black inscriptions. Black control number. A 10 l imperf. souvenir sheet exists showing Skylab. Size: 80x107mm.

Field Ball and Games' Emblem
A757

ROMANIA

Designs: 1.75 l, 2.20 l, Various scenes from field ball; 1.75 l, vertical.

1975, Jan. 3
2529	A757	55b ultra & multi	15	6
2530	A757	1.75 l yel & multi	40	20
2531	A757	2.20 l multi	50	20

World University Field Ball Championship.

Rocks and Birches, by Andreescu
A758

Paintings: 40b, Farm Woman with Green Kerchief. 55b, Winter in the Woods. 1.75 l, Winter in Barbizon (horiz.). 2.75 l, Self-portrait. 3.60 l, Main Road (horiz.).

1975, Jan. 24
2532	A758	20 b gold & multi	6	5
2533	A758	40 b gold & multi	12	8
2534	A758	55 b gold & multi	15	10
2535	A758	1.75 l gold & multi	40	30
2536	A758	2.75 l gold & multi	70	40
2537	A758	3.60 l gold & multi	1.00	60
	Nos. 2532-2537 (6)		2.43	1.53

Ion Andreescu (1850–1882), painter.

Torch with Flame in Flag Colors and Coat of Arms
A759

1975, Feb. 1
| 2538 | A759 | 40b multi | 20 | 8 |

Romanian Socialist Republic, 10th anniversary.

Vaslui Battle, by O. Obedeanu
A760

1975, Feb. 8 Photo. Perf. 13½
| 2539 | A760 | 55b gold & multi | 25 | 8 |

500th anniversary of the battle at the High Bridge, Stephan the Great's victory over the Turks.

Woman Spinning, by Nicolae Grigorescu
A761

Michelangelo, Self-portrait
A762

1975, Mar. 1
| 2540 | A761 | 55b gold & multi | 25 | 8 |

International Women's Year 1975.

1975, Mar. 10
| 2541 | A762 | 5 l multi | 1.25 | 55 |

500th birth anniversary of Michelangelo Buonarroti (1475–1564), Italian sculptor, painter and architect.

Souvenir Sheet

Escorial Palace and España 75 Emblem—A763

1975, Mar. 15 Photo. Perf. 13
| 2542 | A763 | 10 l multi | 3.00 | 2.50 |

España 75 International Philatelic Exhibition, Madrid, Apr. 4–13.

Letter with Postal Code, Pigeon
A764

1975, Mar. 26 Photo. Perf. 13½
| 2543 | A764 | 55b bl & multi | 25 | 8 |

Introduction of postal code system.

Children's Science Pavilion—A765

1975, Apr. 10 Photo. Perf. 13
| 2544 | A765 | 4 l multi | 1.10 | 40 |

Oceanexpo 75, International Exhibition, Okinawa, July 20, 1975–Jan. 1976.

Peonies, by N. Tonitza
A766

Design: 3.45 l, Chrysanthemums, by St. Luchian.

1975, Apr. 28
| 2545 | A766 | 2.20 l gold & multi | 90 | 75 |
| 2546 | A766 | 3.45 l gold & multi | 1.50 | 1.40 |

Inter-European Cultural and Economic Cooperation. Nos. 2544–2545 printed checkerwise in sheets of 10 (2x5) with blue marginal inscription.

1875 Meter Convention Emblem
A767

1975, May 10 Photo. Perf. 13
| 2547 | A767 | 1.85 l bl, blk & gold | 50 | 20 |

Centenary of International Meter Convention, Paris, 1875.

Mihail Eminescu and his Home
A768

1975, June 5
| 2548 | A768 | 55b multi | 25 | 15 |

Mihail Eminescu (1850–1889), poet, 125th birth anniversary.

Marble Plaque and Dacian Coins 1st–2nd Centuries—A769

1975, May 26
| 2549 | A769 | 55b multi | 25 | 8 |

2000th anniversary of the founding of Alba Iulia (Apulum).

Souvenir Sheet

"On the Bank of the Seine," by Th. Pallady—A770

1975, May 26
| 2550 | A770 | 10 l multi | 3.50 | 2.75 |

ARPHILA 75, Paris, June 6–16. No. 2550 has gold marginal inscription and post horns. Size: 77x89mm.

Albert Schweitzer
A771

1974, Dec. 20 Photo. Perf. 13½
| 2551 | A771 | 40b blk brn | 15 | 5 |

Dr. Albert Schweitzer (1875–1965), medical missionary.

Ana Ipatescu
A772

1975, June 2 Photo. Perf. 13½
| 2552 | A772 | 55b lil rose | 25 | 8 |

Ana Ipatescu, fighter in 1848 revolution.

Policeman with Walkie-talkie
A773

1975, Sept. 1
| 2553 | A773 | 55b brt bl | 30 | 8 |

Publicity for traffic rules.

Monument and Projected Reconstruction, Adam Clissi—A777

Roman Monuments: 55b, Emperor Trajan, bas-relief (vert.). 1.20 l, Trajan's column, Rome (vert.). 1.55 l, Governor Decibalus, bas-relief (vert.). 2 l, Excavated Roman city, Turnu-Severin. 2.25 l, Trajan's Bridge, ruin and projected reconstruction. No. 2569, Roman fortifications (vert.).

1975, June 26 Photo. Perf. 13½
2563	A777	55b red brn & blk	18	10
2564	A777	1.20 l vio bl & blk	35	20
2565	A777	1.55 l grn & blk	35	22
2566	A777	1.75 l dl rose & multi	50	28
2567	A777	2 l dl yel & blk	60	40
2568	A777	2.25 l brt bl & blk	70	50
	Nos. 2563-2568 (6)		2.68	1.70

Souvenir Sheet

| 2569 | A777 | 10 l multi | 3.75 | 3.00 |

European Architectural Heritage Year. No. 2569 contains one stamp; blue and gold margin with black control number. Size: 78x90mm.

An imperf. 10 l gold and dark brown souvenir sheet exists showing the Roman wolf suckling Romulus and Remus. Gray and gold margin with red control number. Size: 80x160mm.

A similar souvenir sheet exists with the Roman wolf 10 l, blue and multicolored margins, black inscriptions including "ESSEN 1978", red control number, imperf. Size: 75x91mm. It appeared in 1978, honoring the International Stamp Fair, Essen, Germany.

Michael the Brave, by Sadeler
A778

ROMANIA

Michael the Brave Statue—A779

Designs: 1.20 l, Ottoman Messengers Offering Gifts to Michael the Brave, by Theodor Aman (horiz.). 2.75 l, Michael the Brave in Battle of Calugareni, by Aman.

1975, July 7

2571	A778	55b gold & blk	15	10
2572	A778	1.20 l gold & multi	30	20
2573	A778	2.75 l gold & multi	75	40

Souvenir Sheet
Imperf.

| 2574 | A779 | 10 l gold & multi | 20.00 | 20.00 |

First political union of Romanian states under Michael the Brave, 375th anniversary. No. 2574 has red control number. Size: 70x109mm.

No. 2574 issued Sept. 20.

Larkspur
A780

1975, Aug. 15   Photo.   Perf. 13½
Multicolored

2575	A780	20b shown	6	5
2576	A780	40b Field poppies	12	5
2577	A780	55b Xeranthemum annuum	15	10
2578	A780	1.75 l Rockrose	40	20
2579	A780	2.75 l Meadow sage	70	40
2580	A780	3.60 l Wild chicory	1.00	55
		Nos. 2575-2580 (6)	2.43	1.35

No. 2541 Overprinted in Red:

**Tîrg internaţional
de mărci poştale**

Riccione — Italia
23–25 august 1975

1975, Aug. 23

| 2581 | A762 | 5 l multi | 2.50 | 1.25 |

International Philatelic Exhibition, Riccione, Italy, Aug. 23–25.

Map Showing Location of
Craiova, 1750—A781

1975, Sept. 15   Photo.   Perf. 13½

2582	A781	Strip of 3	80	40
a.		20b ocher, yel, red & blk	10	8
b.		55b ocher, yel, red & blk	20	15
c.		1 l ocher, yel, red & blk	35	20

1750th anniversary of first documentation of Daco-Getian settlement of Pelendava and 500th anniversary of documentation of Craiova.
Size of Nos. 2582a, 2582c: 25x32mm.; of No. 2582b: 80x32mm.

Muntenian Rug—A782

Designs: Romanian Peasant Rugs: 40b, Banat. 55b, Oltenia. 1.75 l, Moldavia. 2.75 l, Oltenia. 3.60 l, Maramures.

1975, Oct. 5   Photo.   Perf. 13½

2583	A782	20b dk bl & multi	6	5
2584	A782	40b blk & multi	12	8
2585	A782	55b multi	15	10
2586	A782	1.75 l blk & multi	50	20
2587	A782	2.75 l multi	70	40
2588	A782	3.60 l blk & multi	1.00	50
		Nos. 2583-2588 (6)	2.53	1.33

Minibus
A783

1975, Nov. 5   Photo.   Perf. 13½
Multicolored

2589	A783	20b shown	6	5
2590	A783	40b Gasoline truck	12	5
2591	A783	55b Jeep	15	10
2592	A783	1.75 l Flat-bed truck	50	20
2593	A783	2.75 l Dacia automobile	70	40
2594	A783	3.60 l Dump truck	1.00	50
		Nos. 2589-2594 (6)	2.53	1.30

Souvenir Sheet

Winter, by Peter Brueghel,
the Younger—A784

1975, Nov. 25   Photo.   Perf. 13½

| 2595 | A784 | 10 l multi | 3.50 | 3.00 |

THEMABELGA International Topical Philatelic Exhibition, Brussels, Dec. 13–21. No. 2595 has gold margin with white inscription and claret emblem. Size: 89x77 mm.

Luge and Olympic Games'
Emblem—A785

Designs: (Innsbruck Olympic Games' Emblem and): 40b, Biathlon (vert.). 55b, Woman skier. 1.75 l, Ski jump. 2.75 l, Woman figure skater. 3.60 l, Ice hockey. 10 l, Two-man bobsled.

1976, Jan. 12   Photo.   Perf. 13½

2596	A785	20b bl & multi	8	5
2597	A785	40b multi	10	8
2598	A785	55b multi	25	12
2599	A785	1.75 l ol & multi	45	20
2600	A785	2.75 l multi	75	30
2601	A785	3.60 l multi	1.20	55
		Nos. 2596-2601 (6)	6.33	4.30

Souvenir Sheet

| 2602 | A785 | 10 l multi | 3.50 | 3.00 |

12th Winter Olympic Games, Innsbruck, Austria, Feb. 4–15. No. 2602 has yellow green and ultramarine marginal design, showing cross-country skiing. Size: 90x78mm. An imperf. 10 l souvenir sheet exists showing slalom; Romanian flag, Games' emblem and red control number in margin. Size: 107x79mm.

Washington at Valley Forge,
by W. T. Trego—A786

Paintings: 40b, Washington at Trenton, by John Trumbull (vert.). 55b, Washington Crossing the Delaware, by Emanuel Leutze. 1.75 l, The Capture of the Hessians, by Trumbull. 2.75 l, Jefferson, by Thomas Sully (vert.). 3.60 l, Surrender of Cornwallis at Yorktown, by Trumbull. 10 l, Signing of the Declaration of Independence, by Trumbull.

1976, Jan. 25   Photo.   Perf. 13½

2603	A786	20b gold & multi	6	5
2604	A786	40b gold & multi	12	5
2605	A786	55b gold & multi	15	10
2606	A786	1.75 l gold & multi	40	20
2607	A786	2.75 l gold & multi	75	40
2608	A786	3.60 l gold & multi	1.10	50
		Nos. 2603-2608 (6)	2.58	1.30

Souvenir Sheet

| 2609 | A786 | 10 l gold & multi | 3.50 | 2.75 |

American Bicentennial. No. 2609 also commemorates Interphil 76 International Philatelic Exhibition, Philadelphia, Pa., May 29–June 6. Printed in horizontal rows of 4 stamps with centered label showing Bicentennial emblem.
No. 2609 has red, blue and gold marginal inscription and Bicentennial emblem. Size: 90x78mm.

Prayer,
by
Brancusi
A787

Designs: 1.75 l, Architectural Assembly, by Brancusi. 3.60 l, Constantin Brancusi.

1976, Feb. 15   Photo.   Perf. 13½

2610	A787	55b pur & multi	18	6
2611	A787	1.75 l bl & multi	40	20
2612	A787	3.60 l multi	1.00	45

Constantin Brancusi (1876-1957), sculptor, birth centenary.

Anton
Davidoglu
A788

Archives
Museum
A789

Designs: 55b, Vlad Tepes. 1.20 l, Costache Negri.

1976, Feb. 25

2613	A788	40b grn & multi	12	5
2614	A788	55b grn & multi	18	15
2615	A788	1.20 l grn & multi	30	15
2616	A788	1.75 l grn & multi	40	20

Anniversaries: Anton Davidoglu (1876-1958), mathematician; Prince Vlad Tepes, commander in war against the Turks (d. 1476); Costache Negri (1812-1876), Moldavian freedom fighter; Romanian National Archives Museum, founded 1926.

Dr. Carol Davila
A790

Vase with King
Decebalus Portrait
A791

Designs: 1.75 l, Nurse with patient. 2.20 l, First aid.

1976, Apr. 20

2617	A790	55b multi	15	6
2618	A790	1.75 l multi	40	15
2619	A790	2.20 l yel & multi	50	20

Romanian Red Cross centenary. See No. C199.

1976, May 13

Design: 3.45 l, Vase with portrait of King Michael the Bold.

| 2620 | A791 | 2.20 l bl & multi | 1.00 | 75 |
| 2621 | A791 | 3.45 l multi | 2.00 | 1.75 |

Inter-European Cultural Economic Co-operation. Nos. 2620-2621 each printed in sheets of 4 with marginal inscriptions.

ROMANIA

Coat of Arms	Spiru Haret
A792	A793

1976, June 12

| 2622 | A792 | 1.75 l multi | 50 | 15 |

1976, June 25

| 2628 | A793 | 20b multi | 20 | 8 |

Spiru Haret (1851–1912), mathematician, 125th birth anniversary.

Woman Athlete
A794

Designs (Romanian Olympic Emblem and): 40b, Boxing. 55b, Team handball. 1.75 l, 2-man scull (horiz.). 2.75 l, Gymnast on rings (horiz.). 3.60 l, 2-man canoe (horiz.). 10 l, Woman gymnast (horiz.).

1976, June 25   Photo.   Perf. 13½

2629	A794	20b org & multi	6	5
2630	A794	40b multi	12	5
2631	A794	55b multi	18	6
2632	A794	1.75 l multi	50	15
2633	A794	2.75 l vio & multi	75	30
2634	A794	3.60 l bl & multi	1.00	45
		Nos. 2629-2634 (6)	2.61	1.06

Souvenir Sheet

| 2635 | A794 | 10 l rose & multi | 3.50 | 3.00 |

21st Olympic Games, Montreal, Canada, July 17–Aug. 1. No. 2635 contains one stamp (49x37mm.); blue and rose marginal inscription and ornaments, black control number. Size: 90x77mm.
An imperf. airmail 10 l souvenir sheet exists showing Olympia Stadium, Montreal; ultramarine margin with space design and red control number. Size: 107x80mm.

Inscribed Stone Tablets, Banat—A795

Designs: 40b, Hekate, Bacchus, bas-relief. 55b, Ceramic fragment, bowl, coins. 1.75 l, Bowl, urn and cup. 2.75 l, Sword, lance and tombstone. 3.60 l, Lances, urn. 10 l, Clay vessel and silver coins.

1976, July 25

2636	A795	20b multi	6	5
2637	A795	40b multi	12	5
2638	A795	55b org & multi	18	6
2639	A795	1.75 l multi	40	20
2640	A795	2.75 l fawn & multi	70	30
2641	A795	3.60 l multi	1.00	45
		Nos. 2636-2641 (6)	2.46	1.11

Souvenir Sheet

| 2642 | A795 | 10 l yel & multi | 3.50 | 3.00 |

Daco-Roman archaeological treasures. No. 2642, issued Mar. 25, has light yellow green margin and black inscription. Size: 77x90mm. An imperf. 10 l souvenir sheet exists showing a silver and gold vase and silver coins; red control number. Size: 79x107mm.

Wolf Statue, 4th Century Map
A796

1976, Aug. 25

| 2643 | A796 | 55b multi | 25 | 10 |

1600th anniversary of the founding of Buzau.

Red Deer and Hunting Horn A797

Game: 40b, Brown bear. 55b, Chamois. 1.75 l, Boar. 2.75 l, Red fox. 3.60 l, Lynx.

1976, Sept. 20

2644	A797	20b buff & multi	6	5
2645	A797	40b buff & multi	12	5
2646	A797	55b buff & multi	15	6
2647	A797	1.75 l buff & multi	40	20
2648	A797	2.75 l buff & multi	70	30
2649	A797	3.60 l buff & multi	1.00	45
		Nos. 2644-2649 (6)	2.43	1.11

Dan Grecu, Bronze Medal—A798

Nadia Comaneci
A799

Designs: 40b, Fencing, bronze medal. 55b Gheorge Megelea (Javelin), bronze medal. 1.75 l, Handball, silver medal. 2.75 l, Boxing, 1 bronze, 2 silver medals. 3.60 l, Wrestling, silver and bronze medals. 10 l, Vasile Daba (kayak), gold and silver medals (vert.).

1976, Oct. 20   Photo.   Perf. 13½

2650	A798	20b multi	6	5
2651	A798	40b car & multi	12	5
2652	A798	55b grn & multi	18	6
2653	A798	1.75 l red & multi	58	22
2654	A798	2.75 l bl & multi	90	40
2655	A798	3.60 l multi	1.20	60
2656	A799	5.70 l multi	1.70	70
		Nos. 2650-2656 (7)	4.74	2.08

Souvenir Sheet

| 2657 | A798 | 10 l multi | 3.50 | 3.00 |

Romanian Olympic medalists. No. 2657 contains one stamp, size: 37x50mm.; Prussian blue margin with gold Romanian Olympic emblem and black control number. Size: 89x78mm.

Milan Cathedral—A800

1976, Oct. 20   Photo.   Perf. 13½

| 2658 | A800 | 4.75 l multi | 1.25 | 60 |

ITALIA 76 International Philatelic Exhibition, Milan, Oct. 14–24.

Oranges and Carnations, by Luchian—A801

Paintings by Stefan Luchian (1868–1916): 40b, Flower arrangement. 55b, Vase with flowers. 1.75 l, Roses. 2.75 l, Cornflowers. 3.60 l, Carnations in vase.

1976, Nov. 5

2659	A801	20b multi	6	5
2660	A801	40b multi	12	5
2661	A801	55b multi	15	6
2662	A801	1.75 l multi	40	20
2663	A801	2.75 l multi	70	30
2664	A801	3.60 l multi	1.00	45
		Nos. 2659-2664 (6)	2.43	1.11

Arms of Alba
A802

Designs: Arms of Romanian counties.

1976–77   Photogravure   Perf. 13½
Multicolored

2665	A802	55b shown	14	5
2666	A802	55b Arad	14	5
2667	A802	55b Arges	14	5
2668	A802	55b Bacau	14	5
2669	A802	55b Bihor	14	5
2670	A802	55b Bistrita-Nasaud	14	5
2671	A802	55b Botosani	14	5
2672	A802	55b Brasov	14	5
2673	A802	55b Braila	14	5
2674	A802	55b Buzau	14	5
2675	A802	55b Caras-Severin	14	5
2676	A802	55b Cluj	14	5
2677	A802	55b Constanta	14	5
2678	A802	55b Covasna	14	5
2679	A802	55b Dimbovita	14	5
2680	A802	55b Dolj	14	5
2681	A802	55b Galati	14	5
2682	A802	55b Gorj	14	5
2683	A802	55b Harghita	14	5
2684	A802	55b Hunedoara	14	5
2685	A802	55b Ialomita	14	5
2686	A802	55b Iasi	14	5
2687	A802	55b Ilfov	14	5
2688	A802	55b Maramures	14	5
2689	A802	55b Mehedinti	14	5
2690	A802	55b Mures	14	5
2691	A802	55b Neamt	14	5
2692	A802	55b Olt	14	5
2693	A802	55b Prahova	14	5
2694	A802	55b Salaj	14	5
2695	A802	55b Satu-Mare	14	5
2696	A802	55b Sibiu	14	5
2697	A802	55b Suceava	14	5
2698	A802	55b Teleorman	14	5
2699	A802	55b Timis	14	5
2700	A802	55b Tulcea	14	5
2701	A802	55b Vaslui	14	5
2702	A802	55b Vilcea	14	5
2703	A802	55b Vrancea	14	5
2704	A802	55b Postal emblem	14	5
		Nos. 2665-2704 (40)	5.60	2.00

Sheets of 50 (10x5) contain 5 designs: Nos. 2665–2669; 2670–2674; 2675–2679; 2680–2684; 2685–2689; 2690–2694; 2695–2699; 2700–2704. Each row of 10 contains 5 pairs of each design.
Issue dates: Nos. 2665–2679, Dec. 20, 1976. Nos. 2680–2704, Sept. 5, 1977.

Oxcart, by Grigorescu—A803

Paintings by Nicolae Grigorescu: 1 l, Self-portrait (vert.). 1.50 l, Shepherdess. 2.15 l, Woman Spinning with Distaff. 3.40 l, Shepherd (vert.). 4.80 l, Rest at Well.

1977, Jan. 20   Photo.   Perf. 13½

2705	A803	55b gray & multi	10	5
2706	A803	1 l gray & multi	20	10
2707	A803	1.50 l gray & multi	30	15
2708	A803	2.15 l gray & multi	45	20
2709	A803	3.40 l gray & multi	75	25
2710	A803	4.80 l gray & multi	1.10	35
		Nos. 2705-2710 (6)	2.90	1.10

Nicolae Grigorescu (1838–1907), 70th death anniversary.

Cheia Telecommunications Station
A804

1977, Feb. 1

| 2711 | A804 | 55b multi | 15 | 8 |

Red Deer
A805

ROMANIA

Protected Birds and Animals: 1 l, Mute swan. 1.50 l, Egyptian vulture. 2.15 l, Bison. 3.40 l, White-headed ruddy duck. 4.80 l, Kingfisher.

1977, Mar. 20   Photo.   Perf. 13½

2712	A805	55b multi	14	5
2713	A805	1 l multi	20	10
2714	A805	1.50 l multi	30	15
2715	A805	2.15 l multi	50	20
2716	A805	3.40 l multi	75	25
2717	A805	4.80 l multi	1.10	35
	Nos. 2712-2717 (6)		2.99	1.10

Calafat Artillery Unit,
by Sava Hentia—A806

Paintings: 55b, Attacking Infantryman, by Oscar Obedeanu (vert.). 1.50 l, Infantry Attack in Winter, by Stefan Luchian (vert.). 2.15 l, Battle of Plevna (after etching). 3.40 l, Artillery, by Nicolae Ion Grigorescu. 10 l, Battle of Grivita, 1877.

1977

2718	A806	55b gold & multi	14	5
2719	A806	1 l gold & multi	20	10
2720	A806	1.50 l gold & multi	30	10
2721	A806	2.15 l gold & multi	45	15
2722	A806	3.40 l gold & multi	75	25
	Nos. 2718-2722, B442 (5)		3.44	1.28

Souvenir Sheet

| 2723 | A806 | 10 l gold & multi | 3.50 | 3.00 |

Centenary of Romania's independence. No. 2723 has multicolored margin showing independence leaders and black control number. Size: 89x78mm. A 10 l imperf. souvenir sheet exists showing victorious return of army, Dobruja, 1878.
Issue dates: Nos. 2718-2722, May 9; No. 2723, Apr. 25.

Sinaia,
Carpathian
Mountains
A807

Design: 2.40 l, Hotels, Aurora, Black Sea.

1977, May 17

| 2724 | A807 | 2 l gold & multi | 1.50 | 1.25 |
| 2725 | A807 | 2.40 l gold & multi | 2.00 | 1.75 |

Inter-European Cultural and Economic Cooperation. Nos. 2724-2725 printed in sheets of 4 with marginal inscriptions.

Petru Rares   Ion Luca Caragiale
A808   A809

1977, June 10   Photo.   Perf. 13½

| 2726 | A808 | 40b multi | 15 | 8 |

450th anniversary of the elevation of Petru Rares to Duke of Moldavia.

1977, June 10

| 2727 | A809 | 55b multi | 18 | 8 |

Ion Luca Caragiale (1852-1912), writer, 125th birth anniversary.

Red Cross Nurse, Children,
Emblems—A810

1977, June 10

| 2728 | A810 | 1.50 l multi | 40 | 15 |

23rd International Red Cross Conference, Bucharest.

Arch of Triumph, Bucharest
A811

1977, June 10

| 2729 | A811 | 2.15 l multi | 60 | 20 |

60th anniversary of the Battles of Marasesti and Oituz.

Peaks of San Marino, Exhibition
Emblem—A812

1977, Aug. 28   Photo.   Perf. 13½

| 2730 | A812 | 4 l brt bl & multi | 1.00 | 35 |

Centenary of San Marino stamps, and San Marino '77 Philatelic Exhibition, San Marino, Aug. 28-Sept. 4.

Vaulting—A813

Gymnasts: 40b, Woman dancer. 55b, Man on parallel bars. 1 l, Woman on balance beam. 2.15 l, Man on rings. 4.80 l, Woman on double bars.

1977, Sept. 25   Photo.   Perf. 13½

2731	A813	20b multi	6	5
2732	A813	40b multi	12	5
2733	A813	55b multi	14	6
2734	A813	1 l multi	28	10
2735	A813	2.15 l multi	50	20
2736	A813	4.80 l multi	1.25	45
	Nos. 2731-2736 (6)		2.35	91

"Carpati" near Cazane.
Iron Gate—A814

Designs: 1 l, "Mircesti" at Orsova. 1.50 l, "Oltenita" at Calafat. 2.15 l, Water bus at Giurgiu. 3 l, "Herculane" at Tulcea. 3.40 l, "Muntenia" in Nature preserve, Sulina. 4.80 l, Map of Danube Delta with Sulina Canal. 10 l, Danubius, god of Danube, from Trajan's Column, Rome (vert.).

1977, Dec. 28

2737	A814	55b multi	10	6
2738	A814	1 l multi	20	10
2739	A814	1.50 l multi	35	15
2740	A814	2.15 l multi	60	20
2741	A814	3 l multi	85	30
2742	A814	3.40 l multi	95	30
2743	A814	4.80 l multi	1.35	45
	Nos. 2737-2743 (7)		4.40	1.56

Souvenir Sheet

| 2744 | A814 | 10 l multi | 4.00 | 3.00 |

European Danube Commission. No. 2744 has gray margin with blue inscription and black control number; marginal design shows Roman legionaries crossing Danube on pontoon bridge, from Trajan's Column. Size: 81x70mm. A 10 l imperf. souvenir sheet exists showing map of Danube from Regensburg to the Black Sea.

Flag and
Arms of
Romania
A815

Designs: 1.20 l, Computer production in Romania. 1.75 l, National Theater, Craiova.

1977, Dec. 30

2745	A815	55b multi	14	6
2746	A815	1.20 l multi	25	12
2747	A815	1.75 l multi	40	20

Proclamation of Republic, 30th anniversary.

Dancers
A816

Designs: Romanian male folk dancers.

1977, Nov. 28   Photo.   Perf. 13½

2748	A816	20b multi	6	5
2749	A816	40b multi	12	5
2750	A816	55b multi	12	6
2751	A816	1 l multi	20	10
2752	A816	2.15 l multi	55	20
2753	A816	4.80 l multi	1.25	45
	Nos. 2748-2753 (6)		2.30	91

Souvenir Sheet

| 2754 | A816 | 10 l multi | 3.00 | 3.00 |

No. 2754 has lemon decorative margin. Size: 80x70mm.

Firiza
Dam
A817

Hydroelectric Stations and Dams: 40b, Negovanu. 55b, Piatra Neamt. 1 l, Izvorul Muntelui-Bicaz. 2.15 l, Vidraru. 4.80 l, Iron Gate.

1978, Mar. 10   Photo.   Perf. 13½

2755	A817	20b multi	6	5
2756	A817	40b multi	12	5
2757	A817	55b multi	14	6
2758	A817	1 l multi	20	10
2759	A817	2.15 l multi	50	20
2760	A817	4.80 l multi	1.00	45
	Nos. 2755-2760 (6)		2.02	91

Soccer and
Argentina '78
Emblem
A818

Designs: Various soccer scenes and Argentina '78 emblem.

1978, Apr. 15

2761	A818	55b bl & multi	10	6
2762	A818	1 l org & multi	20	10
2763	A818	1.50 l yel grn & multi	25	10
2764	A818	2.15 l ver & multi	45	15
2765	A818	3.40 l bl grn & multi	75	30
2766	A818	4.80 l lil rose & multi	1.00	40
	Nos. 2761-2766 (6)		2.75	1.11

11th World Cup Soccer Championship, Argentina '78, June 1-25. See No. C222.

King Decebalus of Dacia Statue, Deva
A819

Design: 3.40 l, King Mircea the Elder of Wallachia statue, Tulcea, and ship.

1978, May 22   Photo.   Perf. 13½

| 2767 | A819 | 1.30 l gold & multi | 1.00 | 80 |
| 2768 | A819 | 3.40 l gold & multi | 1.50 | 1.25 |

Inter-European Cultural and Economic Cooperation. Nos. 2767-2768 printed in sheets of 4 with marginal inscriptions and control number.

 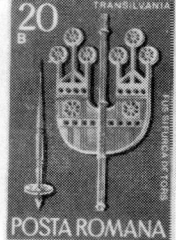

Worker, Factory,   Spindle and
Flag   Handle,
                                  Transylvania
A821   A822

ROMANIA

1978, June 11 Photo. *Perf. 13½*
2770 A821 55b multi   18   8
Nationalization of industry, 30th anniversary.

1978, June 20
Wood Carvings: 40b, Cheese molds, Muntenia. 55b, Spoons, Oltenia. 1 l, Barrel, Moldavia. 2.15 l, Ladle and mug, Transylvania. 4.80 l, Water bucket, Oltenia.
2771 A822 20b multi   6   5
2772 A822 40b multi   12   5
2773 A822 55b multi   12   6
2774 A822 1 l multi   20 10
2775 A822 2.15 l multi 45 20
2776 A822 4.80 l multi 1.00 40
   Nos. 2771-2776 (6) 1.95 86

Danube Delta—A823
Designs: 1 l, Bran Castle (vert.). 1.50 l, Monastery, Suceava, Moldavia. 2.15 l, Caves, Oltenia. 3.40 l, Ski lift, Brasov. 4.80 l, Mangalia, Black Sea. 10 l, Strehaia Fortress (vert.).

1978, July 20 Photo. *Perf. 13½*
2777 A823 55b multi   10   6
2778 A823 1 l multi   20 10
2779 A823 1.50 l multi 30 15
2780 A823 2.15 l multi 45 15
2781 A823 3.40 l multi 75 30
2782 A823 4.80 l multi 1.00 40
   Nos. 2777-2782 (6) 2.80 1.11

Miniature Sheet
2783 A823 10 l multi 3.50 3.00
Tourist publicity. No. 2783 contains one stamp (37x51mm). Black margin shows bridge and moat. Size: 80x70mm. Issued July 30.

Electronic Microscope
A824
Designs: 40b, Hydraulic excavator. 55b, Computer center. 1.50 l, Oil derricks. 3 l, Harvester combine (horiz.). 3.40 l, Petrochemical plant.

1978, Aug. 15 Photo. *Perf. 13½*
2784 A824 20b multi   6   5
2785 A824 40b multi   12   5
2786 A824 55b multi   12   6
2787 A824 1.50 l multi 30 10
2788 A824 3 l multi   60 10
2789 A824 3.40 l multi 80 35
   Nos. 2784-2789 (6) 2.00 81
Industrial development.

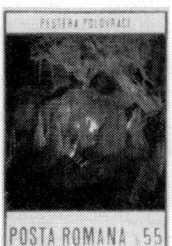 

Polovraci Cave,   "Racial Equality"
Carpathians   A826
   A825

Caves: 1 l, Topolnita. 1.50 l, Ponoare. 2.15 l, Ratei, Mt. Bucegi. 3.40 l, Closani, Mt. Motrului. 4.80 l, Epuran. 1 l, 1.50 l, 4.80 l, Mt. Mehedinti.

1978, Aug. 25 Photo. *Perf. 13½*
2790 A825 55b multi   10   6
2791 A825 1 l multi   20 10
2792 A825 1.50 l multi 30 10
2793 A825 2.15 l multi 45 20
2794 A825 3.40 l multi 75 25
2795 A825 4.80 l multi 1.00 40
   Nos. 2790-2795 (6) 2.80 1.11

1978, Sept. 28
2796 A826 3.40 l multi 75 30
Anti-Apartheid Year.

Gold Bas-relief
A827
Designs: 40b, Gold armband. 55b, Gold cameo ring. 1 l, Silver bowl. 2.15 l, Eagle from Roman standard (vert.). 4.80 l, Silver armband.

1978, Sept. 25
2797 A827 20b multi   6   5
2798 A827 40b multi   12   5
2799 A827 55b multi   12   6
2800 A827 1 l multi   20 10
2801 A827 2.15 l multi 45 20
2802 A827 4.80 l multi 1.00 40
   Nos. 2797-2802 (6) 1.95 86
Daco-Roman archaeological treasures. An imperf. 10 l souvenir sheet exists showing gold helmet (vert.); red control number. Size: 74x90mm.

Woman Gymnast, Games' Emblem
A828
Designs (Games' Emblem and): 1 l, Running. 1.50 l, Skiing. 2.15 l, Equestrian. 3.40 l, Soccer. 4.80 l, Handball.

1978, Sept. 15
2803 A828 55b multi   10   6
2804 A828 1 l multi   10 10
2805 A828 1.50 l multi 30 15
2806 A828 2.15 l multi 45 20
2807 A828 3.40 l multi 75 30
2808 A828 4.80 l multi 1.00 40
   Nos. 2803-2808 (6) 2.70 1.31

Ptolemaic Map of Dacia
A829
Designs: 55b, Meeting House of Romanian National Council, Arad. 1.75 l, Pottery vases, 8th-9th centuries, found near Arad. Nos. 2809-2811 printed se-tenant.

1978, Oct. 21 Photo. *Perf. 13½*
2809 A829 40b multi   10   5
2810 A829 55b multi   10   6
2811 A829 1.75 l multi 40 18
2,000th anniversary of founding of Arad.

Assembly at   Warrior,
Alba Julia, 1919   Bas-relief
   A830   A831
Design: 1 l, Open book and Romanian flag.

1978, Dec. 1
2812 A830 55b gold & multi 10   6
2813 A830 1 l gold & multi 20 10
60th anniversary of national unity.

1979 Photo. *Perf. 13½*
Design: 1.50 l, Warrior on horseback, bas-relief.
2814 A831 55b multi   14   6
2815 A831 1.50 l multi 30 12
2,050 years since establishment of first centralized and independent Dacian state.

"Heroes of Vaslui"   Ice Hockey,
     A832   Globe,
                          Emblem
                           A833
Children's Drawings: 1 l, Building houses. 1.50 l, Folk music of Tica. 2.15 l, Industrial landscape (horiz.). 3.40 l, winter customs (horiz.). 4.80 l, Pioneer festival (horiz.).

1979, Mar. 1
2816 A832 55b multi   10   6
2817 A832 1 l multi   20 10
2818 A832 1.50 l multi 30 10
2819 A832 2.15 l multi 45 15
2820 A832 3.40 l multi 75 25
2821 A832 4.80 l multi 1.00 40
   Nos. 2816-2821 (6) 2.80 1.06
International Year of the Child.

1979, Mar. 16 Photo. *Perf. 13½*
Design: 3.40 l, Ice hockey players, globe and emblem.
2822 A833 1.30 l multi 25 12
2823 A833 3.40 l multi 75 25
European Youth Ice Hockey Championship, Miercurea-Ciuc (1.30 l) and World Ice Hockey Championship, Galati (3.40 l). Printed se-tenant.

Dog's-tooth Violet
A834
Protected Flowers: 1 l, Alpine violet. 1.50 l, Linum borzaeanum. 2.15 l, Persian bindweed. 3.40 l, Primula auricula. 4.80 l, Transylvanian columbine.

1979, Apr. 25 Photo. *Perf. 13½*
2824 A834 55b multi   10   6
2825 A834 1 l multi   20 10
2826 A834 1.50 l multi 30 15
2827 A834 2.15 l multi 45 15
2828 A834 3.40 l multi 75 30
2829 A834 4.80 l multi 1.00 35
   Nos. 2824-2829 (6) 2.80 1.11

Mail Coach and Post Rider, 19th Century
A835

1979, May 3 Photo. *Perf. 13*
2830 A835 1.30 l multi 45 15
Inter-European Cultural and Economic Cooperation. Printed in sheets of 4 with marginal inscription and control number. See No. C231.

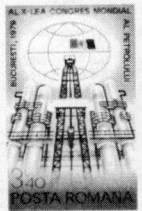 

Oil Rig   Girl
and Refinery   Pioneer
  A836   A837

1979, May 24 Photo. *Perf. 13*
2832 A836 3.40 l multi 75 25
10th World Petroleum Congress, Bucharest.

1979, June 20
2833 A837 55b multi   18   8
30th anniversary of Romanian Pioneers.

Children with Flowers, IYC Emblem
A838
Designs (IYC Emblem and): 1 l, Kindergarten. 2 l, Pioneers with rabbit. 4.60 l, Drummer, trumpeters, flags.

1979, July 18 Photo. *Perf. 13½*
2834 A838 40b multi   12   5
2835 A838 1 l multi   20 10
2836 A838 2 l multi   45 20
2837 A838 4.60 l multi 1.00 40
International Year of the Child.

Lady in a Garden,   Stefan
by Tattarescu   Gheorghiu
    A839   A840

Paintings by Gheorghe Tattarescu: 40b, Mountain woman. 55b, Mountain man. 1 l, Portrait of Gh. Magheru. 2.15 l, The artist's daughter. 4.80 l, Self-portrait.

ROMANIA

1979, June 16

2838	A839	20b multi	6	5
2839	A839	40b multi	10	5
2840	A839	55b multi	10	6
2841	A839	1 l multi	20	10
2842	A839	2.15 l multi	45	20
2843	A839	4.80 l multi	1.00	40
		Nos. 2838-2843 (6)	1.91	86

1979, Aug.

Designs: 55b, Gheorghe Lazar monument. 2.15 l, Lupeni monument. 4.60 l, Women in front of Memorial Arch.

2844	A840	40b multi	10	5
2845	A840	55b multi	10	6
2846	A840	2.15 l multi	45	15
2847	A840	4.60 l multi	1.00	35

State Theater, Tirgu-Mures—A841

Modern Architecture: 40b, University, Brasov. 55b, Political Administration Buildings, Baia Mare. 1 l, Stefan Gheorghiu Academy, Bucharest. 2.15 l, Political Administration Building, Botosani. 4.80 l, House of Culture, Tirgoviste.

1979, June 25

2848	A841	20b multi	6	5
2849	A841	40b multi	10	5
2850	A842	55b multi	10	6
2851	A841	1 l multi	20	10
2852	A841	2.15 l multi	45	20
2853	A841	4.80 l multi	1.00	40
		Nos. 2848-2853 (6)	1.91	86

Flags of Russia and Romania—A842

Design: 1 l, Workers' Militia, by L. Suhar (horiz.).

1979, Aug. 20   Photo.   Perf. 13½

2854	A842	55b multi	10	6
2855	A842	1 l multi	25	10

Liberation from Fascism, 35th anniversary.

Cargo Ship Galati—A843

Romanian Ships: 1 l, Cargo ship Bucuresti. 1.50 l, Ore carrier Resita. 2.15 l, Ore carrier Tomis. 3.40 l, Tanker Dacia. 4.80 l, Tanker Independenta.

1979, Aug. 27   Photo.   Perf. 13½

2856	A843	55b multi	10	6
2857	A843	1 l multi	20	10
2858	A843	1.50 l multi	30	15
2859	A843	2.15 l multi	45	15
2860	A843	3.40 l multi	75	25
2861	A843	4.80 l multi	1.00	40
		Nos. 2856-2861 (6)	2.80	1.11

Olympic Stadium, Melbourne, 1956, Moscow '80 Emblem—A844

Moscow '80 Emblem and Olympic Stadiums: 1 l, Rome, 1960. 1.50 l, Tokyo, 1964. 2.15 l, Mexico City, 1968. 3.40 l, Munich, 1972. 4.80 l, Montreal, 1976. 10 l, Moscow, 1980.

1979, Oct. 23   Photo.   Perf. 13½

2862	A844	55b multi	10	6
2863	A844	1 l multi	20	10
2864	A844	1.50 l multi	30	15
2865	A844	2.15 l multi	45	15
2866	A844	3.40 l multi	75	25
2867	A844	4.80 l multi	1.00	40
		Nos. 2862-2867 (6)	2.80	1.11

Souvenir Sheet

2868	A844	10 l multi	3.00	3.00

22nd Summer Olympic Games, Moscow, July 19-Aug. 3, 1980. No. 2868 contains one stamp (50×38mm). Yellow and brown margin shows satellite and stadium; black control number. Size: 79½× 69mm.

Arms of Alba Iulia—A845

Designs: Arms of Romanian cities.

1979, Oct. 25   Multicolored

2869	A845	1.20 l	shown	25	12
2870	A845	1.20 l	Arad	25	12
2871	A845	1.20 l	Bacau	25	12
2872	A845	1.20 l	Baia-Mare	25	12
2873	A845	1.20 l	Birlad	25	12
2874	A845	1.20 l	Botosani	25	12
2875	A845	1.20 l	Braila	25	12
2876	A845	1.20 l	Brasov	25	12
2877	A845	1.20 l	Buzau	25	12
2878	A845	1.20 l	Calarasi	25	12
2879	A845	1.20 l	Cluj	25	12
2880	A845	1.20 l	Constanta	25	12
2881	A845	1.20 l	Craiova	25	12
2882	A845	1.20 l	Dej	25	12
2883	A845	1.20 l	Deva	25	12
2884	A845	1.20 l	Turnu-Severin	25	12
2885	A845	1.20 l	Focsani	25	12
2886	A845	1.20 l	Galati	25	12
2887	A845	1.20 l	Gheorghe Gheorghiu-Dej	25	12
2888	A845	1.20 l	Giurgiu	25	12
2889	A845	1.20 l	Hunedoara	25	12
2890	A845	1.20 l	Iasi	25	12
2891	A845	1.20 l	Lugoj	25	12
2892	A845	1.20 l	Medias	25	12
2893	A845	1.20 l	Odorheiu Seguiesc	25	12

1980, Jan. 5

2894	A845	1.20 l	Oradea	25	12
2895	A845	1.20 l	Petrosani	25	12
2896	A845	1.20 l	Piatra-Neamt	25	12
2897	A845	1.20 l	Pitesti	25	12
2898	A845	1.20 l	Ploiesti	25	12
2899	A845	1.20 l	Resita	25	12
2900	A845	1.20 l	Rimnicu-Vilcea	25	12
2901	A845	1.20 l	Roman	25	12
2902	A845	1.20 l	Satu-Mare	25	12
2903	A845	1.20 l	Sibiu	25	12
2904	A845	1.20 l	Siget-Marmatiei	25	12
2905	A845	1.20 l	Sighisoara	25	12
2906	A845	1.20 l	Suceava	25	12
2907	A845	1.20 l	Tecuci	25	12
2908	A845	1.20 l	Timisoara	25	12
2909	A845	1.20 l	Tirgoviste	25	12
2910	A845	1.20 l	Tirgu-Jiu	25	12
2911	A845	1.20 l	Tirgu-Mures	25	12
2912	A845	1.20 l	Tulcea	25	12
2913	A845	1.20 l	Turda	25	12
2914	A845	1.20 l	Turnu Magurele	25	12
2915	A845	1.20 l	Bucharest	25	12
		Nos. 2869-2915 (47)		11.75	5.64

Maramures Woman—A846

Regional Costumes: 40b, Maramures man. 55b, Vrancea woman. 1.50 l, Vrancea man. 3 l, Padureni woman. 3.40 l, Padureni man.

1979, Oct. 27

2916	A846	20b multi	6	5
2917	A846	40b multi	10	5
2918	A846	55b multi	10	6
2919	A846	1.50 l multi	35	15
2920	A846	3 l multi	70	25
2921	A846	3.40 l multi	80	30
		Nos. 2916-2921 (6)	2.11	86

Snapdragons, by Stefan Luchian A847

Flower Paintings by Luchian: 60b, Triple chrysanthemums. 1.55 l, Potted flowers on stairs.

1979, July 27

2922	A847	40b multi	10	5
2923	A847	60b multi	18	8
2924	A847	1.55 l multi	35	16

Socfilex, International Philatelic Exhibition, Bucharest. See. Nos. B445-B446.

Romanian Communist Party, 12th Congress—A848

1979, Oct.

2925	A848	5 l multi	1.75	75

Blue and gray margin shows factory. Size: 70× 80mm.

Figure Skating, Lake Placid '80 Emblem, Olympic Rings—A849

1979, Dec. 27   Photo.   Perf. 13½

Multicolored

2926	A849	55b shown	10	6
2927	A849	1 l Downhill skiing	20	10
2928	A849	1.50 l Biathlon	30	15
2929	A849	2.15 l Two-man bobsledding	45	20
2930	A849	3.40 l Speed skating	75	25
2931	A849	4.80 l Ice hockey	1.00	35
		Nos. 2926-2931	2.80	1.11

Souvenir Sheet

2932	A849	10 l Ice hockey, diff.	3.00	1.25

13th Winter Olympic Games, Lake Placid, N.Y., Feb. 12-24, 1980. No. 2932 contains one stamp (38×50mm). Multicolored margin shows mountains and trees; black control number. Size: 71×78mm. An imperf. 10 l air post souvenir sheet exists showing four-man bobsledding; red control number. Size: 90×75½mm.

"Calugareni", Expo Emblem—A850

1979, Dec. 29

2933	A850	55b shown	10	6
2934	A850	1 l "Orleans"	20	10
2935	A850	1.50 l No. 1059, type fawn	30	15
2936	A850	2.15 l No. 15021, type 1E	45	15
2937	A850	3.40 l "Pacific"	75	30
2938	A850	4.80 l Electric engine 060-EA	1.00	35
		Nos. 2933-2938 (6)	2.80	1.11

Souvenir Sheet

2939	A850	10 l Diesel electric	3.00	3.00

International Transport Exposition, Hamburg, June 8-July 1. No. 2939 contains one stamp (50×40mm.); light blue margin, Expo emblem. Size: 81×71mm.

Dacian Warrior, Trajan's Column, Rome—A851

Design: 1.50 l, Two warriors.

1980, Feb. 9   Photo.   Perf. 13½

2940	A851	55b multi	10	6
2941	A851	1.50 l multi	30	12

2,050 years since establishment of first centralized and independent Dacian state.

Unused Prices

Catalogue prices for unused stamps through 1960 are for hinged copies in fine condition.

ROMANIA

Kingfisher—A852

1980, Mar. 25   Photo.   Perf. 13½
2942	A852	55b	shown	14	6
2943	A852	1 l	Great white heron, vert.	20	10
2944	A852	1.50 l	Red-breasted goose	30	15
2945	A852	2.15 l	Red deer, vert.	45	20
2946	A852	3.40 l	Roe deer	75	25
2947	A852	4.80 l	European bison, vert.	1.00	40
		Nos. 2942-2947 (6)		2.84	1.16

European Nature Protection Year. A 10 l imperf. souvenir sheet exists showing bears; red control number. See No. C232.

Souvenir Sheets

George Enescu Playing Violin—A853

1980, May 6
2948		Sheet of 4 multi	1.75	75
a.	A853 1.30 l	shown	38	14
b.	A853 1.30 l	Conducting	38	14
c.	A853 1.30 l	Playing piano	38	14
d.	A853 1.30 l	Composing	38	14
2949		Sheet of 4 multi	4.00	1.25
a.	A853 3.40 l	Beethoven in library	95	30
b.	A853 3.40 l	Portrait	95	30
c.	A853 3.40 l	At piano	95	30
d.	A853 3.40 l	Composing	95	30

Inter-European Cultural and Economic Cooperation. Nos. 2948-2949 have gold marginal inscription, black control number. Size: 107½x82mm.

Vallota	Tudor
Purpurea	Vladimirescu
A854	A855

1980, Apr. 10   Photo.   Perf. 13½
2950	A854	55b	shown	14	6
2951	A854	1 l	Eichhornia crasipes	20	10
2952	A854	1.50 l	Sprekelia Formosissima	30	15
2953	A854	2.15 l	Hypericum calycinum	45	20
2954	A854	3.40 l	Camellia japonica	75	25
2955	A854	4.80 l	Nelumbo nucifera	1.00	40
		Nos. 2950-2955 (6)		2.84	1.16

1980, Apr. 24

Designs: 55b, Mihail Sadoveanu. 1.50 l, Battle against Hungarians. 2.15 l, Tudor Arghezi. 3 l, Horea.

2956	A855	40b	multi	10	5
2957	A855	55b	multi	10	6
2958	A855	1.50 l	multi	30	15
2959	A855	2.15 l	multi	45	20
2960	A855	3 l	multi	60	25
		Nos. 2956-2960 (5)		1.55	71

Anniversaries: 40b, Tudor Vladimirescu (1780-1821), leader of 1821 revolution, 200th birth anniversary; 55b, Mihail Sadoveanu (1880-1961), author, birth centenary; 1.50 l, Victory of Posada; 2.15 l, Tudor Arghezi (1880-1967), poet, birth centenary; 3 l, Horea (1730-1785), leader of 1784 uprising, 250th birth anniversary.

Dacian Fruit Bowl and Cup
A856

1980, May 8
| 2961 | A856 | 1 l | multi | 20 | 10 |

Petrodava City, 2000th anniversary.

Javelin, Moscow '80 Emblem
A857

1980, June 20   Photo.   Perf. 13½
2962	A857	55b	shown	14	6
2963	A857	1 l	Fencing	20	10
2964	A857	1.50 l	Shooting	30	15
2965	A857	2.15 l	Kayak	45	20
2966	A857	3.40 l	Wrestling	75	25
2967	A857	4.80 l	Rowing	1.00	40
		Nos. 2962-2967 (6)		2.84	1.16

Souvenir Sheet

| 2968 | A857 | 10 l | Handball | 3.00 | 3.00 |

22nd Summer Olympic Games, Moscow, July 19-Aug. 3. No. 2968 contains one stamp (38x50mm.). Multicolored margin shows handball plays; black control number. Size: 91x78½mm. An imperf. 10 l air post souvenir sheet exists showing gymnast; red control number. Size: 116x79½mm.

Congress	Fireman
Emblem	Rescuing Child
A858	A859

1980, Aug. 10   Photo.   Perf. 13½
| 2969 | A858 | 55b | multi | 14 | 6 |

15th International Historical Sciences Congress, Bucharest.

1980, Aug. 25
| 2970 | A859 | 55b | multi | 14 | 6 |

Firemen's Day (Sept. 13).

Chinese and Romanian Young
Pioneers at Stamp Show—A860

1980, Sept. 18
| 2971 | A860 | 1 l | multi | 20 | 10 |

Romanian-Chinese Philatelic Exhibition, Bucharest.

Souvenir Sheet

Parliament Building, Bucharest—A861

1980, Sept. 30
| 2972 | A861 | 10 l | multi | 3.00 | 3.00 |

European Security Conference, Madrid. Multicolored margin shows flag of Romania; black control number. An imperf. 10 l air post souvenir sheet exists showing Plaza Mayor, Madrid; red control number. Size: 78½x91mm.

Knights and Chessboard—A862

1980, Oct. 1   Photo.   Perf. 13½
2973	A862	55b	shown	14	6
2974	A862	1 l	Rooks	20	10
2975	A862	2.15 l	Man	45	20
2976	A862	4.80 l	Woman	1.00	40

Chess Olympiad, Valletta, Malta, Nov. 20-Dec. 8.

Dacian Warrior—A863

1980, Oct. 15
2977	A863	20b	shown	6	5
2978	A863	40b	Moldavian soldier, 15th cent.	12	5
2979	A863	55b	Walachian horseman, 17th cent.	12	6
2980	A863	1 l	Flag bearer, 19th cent.	20	10
2981	A863	1.50 l	Infantryman, 19th cent.	30	15
2982	A863	2.15 l	Lancer, 19th cent.	45	20
2983	A863	4.80 l	Mounted Elite Corps Guard, 19th cent.	1.00	45
		Nos. 2977-2983 (7)		2.25	1.06

Burebista Sculpture—864

1980, Nov. 5   Photo.   Perf. 13½
| 2984 | A864 | 2 l | multi | 40 | 20 |

2050 years since establishment of first centralized and independent Dacian state.

George	
Oprescu	
(1881-1969), Art	National
Critic	Dog Show
A865	A866

Famous Men: 2.15 l, Marius Bunescu (1881-1971), painter. 3.40 l, Ion Georgescu (1856-1898), sculptor.

1981, Feb. 20   Photo.   Perf. 13½
2985	A865	1.50 l	multi	30	15
2986	A865	2.15 l	multi	45	20
2987	A865	3.40 l	multi	75	35

1981, Mar. 15

Designs: Dogs (40b, 1 l, 1.50 l, 3.40 l horiz.).

2988	A866	40b	Mountain sheepdog	12	5
2989	A866	55b	Saint Bernard	12	6
2990	A866	1 l	Fox terrier	20	10
2991	A866	1.50 l	German shepherd	30	15
2992	A866	2.15 l	Boxer	45	20
2993	A866	3.40 l	Dalmatian	75	35
2994	A866	4.80 l	Poodle	1.00	50
		Nos. 2988-2994 (7)		2.94	1.41

River Steamer Stefan cel Mare—A867

1981, Mar. 25
2995	A867	55b	shown	10	6
2996	A867	1 l	Vas de Supraveghere	20	10
2997	A867	1.50 l	Tudor Vladimirescu	35	15
2998	A867	2.15 l	Dredger Sulina	45	20
2999	A867	3.40 l	Republica Populara Romana	75	35
3000	A867	4.80 l	Sulina Canal	1.00	50
		Nos. 2995-3000 (6)		2.85	1.36

Souvenir Sheet

| 3001 | A867 | 10 l | Galati | 3.00 | 3.00 |

European Danube Commission, 125th anniversary. No. 3001 has multicolored margin showing river scene and Commission flag; black control number. Size: 90x78mm. An imperf. 10 l souvenir sheet exists showing map of Danube; red control number. Size: 106x80mm.

ROMANIA

Carrier Pigeon—A868

Designs: Various carrier pigeons and doves.

1981, Apr. 15		Photo.	Perf. 13½	
3002	A868	40b multi	10	5
3003	A868	55b multi	12	6
3004	A868	1 l multi	20	10
3005	A868	1.50 l multi	30	15
3006	A868	2.15 l multi	45	20
3007	A868	3.40 l multi	75	35
	Nos. 3002-3007 (6)		1.92	.91

Romanian Communist Party, 60th Anniv. A869

Singing Romania Festival A871

Folkdance, Moldavia A870

1981, Apr. 22 Photo. *Perf. 13½*
3008 A869 1 l multi   20   10

1981, May 4 Photo. *Perf. 13½*

Designs: Regional folkdances.

3009		Sheet of 4, multi	2.75	1.00
a.	A870 2.50 l shown		65	22
b.	A870 2.50 l Transylvania		65	22
c.	A870 2.50 l Banat		65	22
d.	A870 2.50 l Muntenia		65	22
3010		Sheet of 4, multi	2.75	1.00
a.	A870 2.50 l Maramures		65	22
b.	A870 2.50 l Dobruja		65	22
c.	A870 2.50 l Oltenia		65	22
d.	A870 2.50 l Crisana		65	22

Inter-European Cultural and Economic Cooperation. Nos. 3009-3010 have gold marginal inscription; black control number.

1981, July 15

3011	A871	55b Industry	15	6
3012	A871	1.50 l Electronics	35	15
3013	A871	2.15 l Agriculture	50	25
3014	A871	3.40 l Culture	75	45

University '81 Games, Bucharest A872

Theodor Aman, Artist, Birth Sesquicentennial A873

1981, July 17

3015	A872	1 l Book, flag	20	10
3016	A872	2.15 l Emblem	50	25
3017	A872	4.80 l Stadium, horiz.	1.00	50

1981, July 28

Aman Paintings: 40b, Self-portrait. 55b, Battle of Giurgiu. 1 l, The Family Picnic. 1.50 l, The Painter's Studio. 2.15 l, Woman in Interior. 3.40 l, Aman Museum, Bucharest. 55b, 1 l, 1.50 l, 3.40 l horiz.

3018	A873	40b multi	12	5
3019	A873	55b multi	15	6
3020	A873	1 l multi	20	10
3021	A873	1.50 l multi	40	15
3022	A873	2.15 l multi	50	25
3023	A873	3.40 l multi	85	35
	Nos. 3018-3023 (6)		2.22	.96

Thinker of Cernavoda, 3rd Cent. BC—A874

1981, July 30
3024 A874 3.40 l multi   75   35
16th Science History Congress.

Blood Donation Campaign—A875

1981, Aug. 15 Photo. *Perf. 13½*
3025 A875 55b multi   15   6

Bucharest Central Military Hospital Sesquicentennial—A876

1981, Sept. 1
3026 A876 55b multi   15   6

Romanian Musicians A877

1981, Sept. 20

3027	A877	40b George Enescu (1881-1955)	12	5
3028	A877	55b Paul Constantinescu (1909-1963)	15	6
3029	A877	1 l Dinu Lipatti (1917-1950)	20	10
3030	A877	1.50 l Ionel Periea (1900-1970)	40	20
3031	A877	2.15 l Ciprian Porumbescu (1853-1883)	50	25
3032	A877	3.40 l Mihail Jora (1891-1971)	75	35
	Nos. 3027-3032 (6)		2.12	1.01

Stamp Day—A879

1981, Nov. 5 Photo. *Perf. 13½*
3034 A879 2 l multi   50   20

Children's Games A880

Espana '82 World Cup Soccer A881

Illustrations by Eugen Palade (40b, 55b, 1 l) and Norman Rockwell.

1981, Nov. 25

3035	A880	40b Hopscotch	12	5
3036	A880	55b Soccer	15	6
3037	A880	1 l Riding stick horse	20	10
3038	A880	1.50 l Snagging the Big One	40	15
3039	A880	2.15 l A Patient Friend	50	25
3040	A880	3 l Doggone It	70	30
3041	A880	4 l Puppy Love	80	50
	Nos. 3035-3041, C243 (8)		3.75	1.76

1981, Dec. 28

Designs: Various soccer players.

3042	A881	55b multi	15	6
3043	A881	1 l multi	25	10
3044	A881	1.50 l multi	40	15
3045	A881	2.15 l multi	50	25
3046	A881	3.40 l multi	75	35
3047	A881	4.80 l multi	1.10	55

Souvenir Sheet

3048 A881 10 l multi   3.00   3.00

No. 3048 contains one stamp (38x50mm.); multicolored margin shows cup, emblem, black control number. Size: 90x78mm. An imperf. 10 l air post souvenir sheet exists showing game; red control number. Size: 106x80mm.

Prince Alexander the Good of Moldavia (ruled 1400-1432)—A882

Designs: 1.50 l, Bogdan Petriceicu Hasdeu (1838-1907), scholar. 2.15 l, Nicolae Titulescu (1882-1941), diplomat.

1982, Jan. 30 Photo. *Perf. 13½*

3049	A882	1 l multi	30	15
3050	A882	1.50 l multi	40	20
3051	A882	2.15 l multi	55	30

Bucharest Subway System—A883

1982, Feb. 25

3052	A883	60b Union Square station entrance	20	12
3053	A883	2.40 l Heroes' Station platform	60	35

60th Anniv. of Communist Youth Union—A884

1982

3054	A884	1 l multi	30	10
3055	A884	1.20 l Construction worker	30	10
3056	A884	1.50 l Farm workers	40	15
3057	A884	2 l Research	50	25
3058	A884	2.50 l Workers	75	35
3059	A884	3 l Musicians, dancers	85	40
	Nos. 3054-3059 (6)		3.10	1.35

Dog Sled—A885

1982, Mar. 28 Photo. *Perf. 13½*

3060	A885	55b Dog rescuing child	15	6
3061	A885	1 l Shepherd, dog, vert.	25	10
3062	A885	3 l Hunting dog, vert.	80	50
3063	A885	3.40 l shown	90	50
3064	A885	4 l Spitz, woman, vert.	1.00	60
3065	A885	4.80 l Guide dog, woman, vert.	1.20	65
3066	A885	5 l Dalmatian, girl, vert.	1.40	70
3067	A885	6 l Saint Bernard	1.50	60
	Nos. 3060-3067 (8)		7.20	3.71

Bran Castle, Brasov, 1377—A886

1982, May 6

3068		Sheet of 4, multi	2.75	1.00
a.	A886 2.50 l shown		65	22
b.	A886 2.50 l Hunedoara, Corvinilor, 1409		65	22
c.	A886 2.50 l Sinaia, 1873		65	22
d.	A886 2.50 l Iasi, 1905		65	22
3069		Sheet of 4, multi	2.75	1.00
a.	A886 2.50 l Neuschwanstein		65	22
b.	A886 2.50 l Stolzenfels		65	22
c.	A886 2.50 l Katz-Loreley		65	22
d.	A886 2.50 l Linderhof		65	22

Inter-European Cultural and Economic Cooperation. Nos. 3068-3069 have gold marginal inscription; black control number. Size: 109x83mm.

ROMANIA

Souvenir Sheet

Constantin Brancusi in Paris Studio—A887

1982, June 5
| 3070 | A887 | 10 l multi | 3.00 | 3.00 |

PHILEXFRANCE '82 Intl. Stamp Exhibition, Paris, June 11-21. Size: 70x81mm.

Gloria C-16 Combine Harvester—A888

1982, June 29
3071	A888	50b shown	12	5
3072	A888	1 l Dairy farm	25	12
3073	A888	1.50 l Apple orchard	42	15
3074	A888	2.50 l Vineyard	60	30
3075	A888	3 l Irrigation	75	38

Nos. 3071-3075, C250 (6)

Souvenir Sheet
| 3076 | A888 | 10 l Village | 3.00 | 3.00 |

Agricultural modernization. No. 3076 contains one stamp (50x38mm.); multicolored margin shows farm; black control number. Size: 70x81mm.

Souvenir Sheet

European Security and Cooperation Conference (10th Anniv.), Madrid—A889

1982, Sept. 25   *Imperf.*
| 3077 | A889 | 10 l multi | 3.00 | 3.00 |

Red control number. Size: 105x81mm. An imperf. 15 l souvenir sheet exists showing airmail stamps; red control number. Size: 106x80mm.

Resort Hotels and Beaches
A890

1 l, 2.50 l, 3 l, 5 l horiz.

1982, Aug. 30   Photo.   Perf. 13½
3078	A890	50b Baile Felix	12	5
3079	A890	1 l Predeal	30	12
3080	A890	1.50 l Baile Herculane	42	15
3081	A890	2.50 l Eforie Nord	60	30
3082	A890	3 l Olimp	85	35
3083	A890	5 l Neptun	1.40	60

Nos. 3078-3083 (6)   3.69   1.57

1982, Sept. 6
3084	A891	1 l Legend, horiz.	30	12
3085	A891	1.50 l Contrasts, horiz.	42	15
3086	A891	3.50 l Relay Runner, horiz.	90	40
3087	A891	4 l shown	1.10	60

Souvenir Sheet

Merry Peasant Girl, by Nicolae Grigorescu (d. 1907)—A892

1982, Sept. 30   Photo.   Perf. 13½
| 3088 | A892 | 10 l multi | 2.50 | 2.50 |

Black control number. Size: 70x80mm.

Bucharest Intl. Fair—A893

1982, Oct. 2
| 3089 | A893 | 2 l Exhibition Hall, flag | 50 | 25 |

Savings Week, Oct. 25-31
A894

Stamp Day
A895

1982, Oct. 25
| 3090 | A894 | 1 l Girl holding bank book | 25 | 12 |
| 3091 | A894 | 2 l Poster | 50 | 25 |

1982, Nov. 10
| 3092 | A895 | 1 l Woman letter carrier | 25 | 12 |
| 3093 | A895 | 2 l Mailman | 50 | 25 |

Scene from Ileana Sinziana, by Petre Ispirescu
A896

Arms, Colors, Book
A897

Fairytales: 50b, The Youngest Child and the Golden Apples, by Petre Ispirescu. 1 l, The Bear Hoaxed by the Fox, by Ion Creanga. 1.50 l, The Prince of Tear, by Mihai Eminescu. 2.50 l, The Little Bag with Two Coins Inside, by Ion Creanga. 5 l, Danila Prepeleac, by Ion Creanga.

1982, Nov. 30
3094	A896	50b multi	12	6
3095	A896	1 l multi	25	12
3096	A896	1.50 l multi	38	15
3097	A896	2.50 l multi	62	25
3098	A896	3 l multi	75	30
3099	A896	5 l multi	1.25	60

Nos. 3094-3099 (6)   3.37   1.48

1982, Dec. 16
| 3100 | A897 | 1 l Closed book | 25 | 12 |
| 3101 | A897 | 2 l Open book | 50 | 25 |

Natl. Communist Party Conference, Bucharest, Dec. 16-18.

Wooden Flask, Suceava—A898

1982, Dec. 22   Photo.   Perf. 13½
3102	A898	50b shown	12	6
3103	A898	1 l Ceramic plate, Radauti	25	12
3104	A898	1.50 l Wooden scoop, Valea Mare	38	18
3105	A898	2 l Plate, jug, Vama	50	25
3106	A898	3 l Butter churn, wooden bucket, Moldavia	75	38
3107	A898	3.50 l Ceramic plates, Lehceni	90	45
3108	A898	4 l Wooden spoon, platter, Cluj	1.00	50
3109	A898	5 l Bowl, plate, Marginea	1.25	62

Size: 23x29mm., 29x23mm.

3110	A898	6 l Jug, flask, Bihor	1.50	75
3111	A898	7 l Spindle, shuttle, Transylvania	1.75	90
3112	A898	7.50 l Water buckets, Suceava	1.90	95
3113	A898	8 l Jug, Oboga: plate, Horezu	2.00	1.00
3114	A898	10 l Water buckets, Hunedoara, Suceava	2.50	1.25
3115	A898	20 l Wooden flask, beakers, Horezu	5.00	2.50
3116	A898	30 l Wooden spoons, Alba	7.50	3.75
3117	A898	50 l Ceramic dishes, Horezu	12.50	6.25

Nos. 3102-3117 (16)   39.80   19.91

1.50 l, 3.50 l, 10 l, 30 l horiz.

35th Anniv. of Republic
A899

Grigore Manolescu (1857-92), as Hamlet
A900

1982, Dec. 27
| 3118 | A899 | 1 l Symbols of development | 25 | 12 |
| 3119 | A899 | 2 l Flag | 50 | 25 |

1983, Feb. 28

Actors or Actresses in Famous Roles: 50b, Matei Millo (1814-1896) in The Discontented. 1 l, Mihail Pascaly (1829-1882) in Director Milo. 1.50 l, Aristizza Romanescu (1854-1918), in The Dogs. 2 l, C. I. Nottara (1859-1935) in Snowstorm. 3 l, Agatha Birsescu (1857-1939) in Medea. 4 l, Ion Brezeanu (1869-1940) in The Lost Letter. 5 l, Aristide Demetriad (1872-1930) in The Despotic Prince.

3120	A900	50b multi	12	6
3121	A900	1 l multi	25	12
3122	A900	1.50 l multi	38	15
3123	A900	2 l multi	50	25
3124	A900	2.50 l multi	62	25
3125	A900	3 l multi	75	30
3126	A900	4 l multi	1.00	50
3127	A900	5 l multi	1.25	60

Nos. 3120-3127 (8)   4.87   2.23

Hugo Grotius (1583-1645), Dutch Jurist—A901

1983, Apr. 30
| 3128 | A901 | 2 l brown | 50 | 25 |

Romanian-Made Vehicles—A902

1983, May 3
3129	A902	50b ARO-10	12	6
3130	A902	1 l Dacia 1300 station wagon	25	12
3131	A902	1.50 l ARO-242 jeep	38	15
3132	A902	2.50 l ARO-244	62	25
3133	A902	4 l Dacia 1310	1.00	50
3134	A902	5 l OLTCIT club passenger car	1.25	60

Nos. 3129-3134 (6)

Johannes Kepler (1571-1630)—A903

ROMANIA

Famous Men: No. 3135: b. Alexander von Humboldt (1769-1859), explorer. c. Goethe (1749-1832). d. Richard Wagner (1813-1883), composer. No. 3136: a. Ioan Andreescu (1850-1882), painter. b. George Constantinescu (1881-1965), engineer. c. Tudor Arghezi (1880-1967), poet. d. C.I. Parhon (1874-1969), endocrinologist.

1983, May 16

3135		Sheet of 4, multi	3.00	1.25
a.-d.	A903 31		75	30
3136		Sheet of 4, multi	3.00	1.35
a.-d.	A903 31		75	30

Inter-European Cultural and Economic Cooperation. Nos. 3135-3136 have gold marginal inscription; black control numbers. Size: 110x81mm.

Workers' Struggle, 50th Anniv.—A904

1983, July 22   Photo.   Perf. 13½

3137	A904	2 l sil & multi	50	25

Birds—A905

1983, Oct. 28   Photo.   Perf. 13½

3138	A905	50b Luscinia svecica	12	6
3139	A905	1 l Sturnus roseus	25	12
3140	A905	1.50 l Coracias garrulus	38	18
3141	A905	2.50 l Merops apiaster	62	30
3142	A905	4 l Emberiza schoeniclus	1.00	50
3143	A905	5 l Lanius minor	1.25	62
		Nos. 3138-3143 (6)	3.62	1.78

Water Sports—A906

1983, Sept. 16   Photo.   Perf. 13½

3144	A906	50b Kayak	12	6
3145	A906	1 l Water polo	25	12
3146	A906	1.50 l Canadian one-man canoes	38	18
3147	A906	2.50 l Diving	62	30
3148	A906	4 l Singles rowing	1.00	50
3149	A906	5 l Swimming	1.25	62
		Nos. 3144-3149 (6)	3.62	1.78

Stamp Day—A907

1983, Oct. 24

3150	A907	1 l Mailman on bicycle	25	12
3151	A907	50 l Flag	90	45

Souvenir Sheet

3152	A907	10 l Unloading mail plane	2.50	2.50

No. 3152 is airmail, contains one stamp (38x51mm.). Size: 91x79mm.

Geum Reptans—A908

Flora (No. 3154): b. Papaver dubium. c. Carlina acaulis. d. Paeonia peregrina. e. Gentiana excisa. Fauna (No. 3155): a. Sciurus vulgaria. b. Grammia quenselii. c. Dendrocopos medius. d. Lynx. e. Tichodroma muraria.

1983, Oct. 28   Photo.   Perf. 13½

3154		Strip of 5	1.25	65
a.-e.	A908	1 l multi	25	12
3155		Strip of 5	1.25	65
a.-e.	A908	1 l multi	25	12

Issued in sheets of 15; black control numbers. Size: 153x163mm.

Lady with Feather, by Cornelius Baba A909

Pact with Romania, 65th Anniv. A910

1983, Nov. 3

3156	A909	1 l shown	25	12
3157	A909	2 l Citizens	50	25
3158	A909	3 l Farmers, horiz.	75	38
3159	A909	4 l Resting in the Field, horiz.	1.00	50

1983, Nov. 30

3160	A910	1 l Banner, emblem	25	12
3161	A910	2 l Congress building, flags	50	25

Flags of Participating Countries, Post Office, Mailman—A911

1983, Dec. 17

3162	A911	1 l shown	25	12
3163	A911	2 l Congress building, woman letter carrier	50	25

Souvenir Sheet

3164	A911	10 l Flags, Congress building	2.50	2.50

BALKANFILA '83 Stamp Exhibition, Bucharest. No. 3164 contains one stamp (38x50mm.). Size: 91x79mm.

Orient Express Centenary (Paris-Istanbul)—A912

1983, Dec. 30

3165	A912	10 l Leaving Gara de Nord, Bucharest, 1883	2.50	2.50

Black control number. Size: 91x79mm.

1984 Winter Olympics—A913

1984, Jan. 14

3166	A913	50b Cross-country skiing	12	6
3167	A913	1 l Biathlon	25	12
3168	A913	1.50 l Figure skating	38	18
3169	A913	2 l Speed skating	50	25
3170	A913	3 l Hockey	75	38
3171	A913	3.50 l Bobsledding	90	45
3172	A913	4 l Luge	1.00	50
3173	A913	5 l Skiing	1.25	62
		Nos. 3166-3173 (8)	5.15	2.56

A 10 l imperf souvenir sheet exists showing ski jumping; red control number. Size: 108x81mm.

Souvenir Sheet

Union of Moldavia and Walachia Provinces, 125th Anniv.—A914

Design: 10 l, Prince Alexandru Ioan Cuza, arms.

1984, Jan. 24   Photo.   Perf. 13½

3174	A914	10 l multi	1.75	1.75

Multicolored decorative margin with text. Size: 90x79mm.

Palace of Udriste Naturel (1596-1658), Chancery Official—A915

Famous Men: 1 l, Miron Costin (1633-91), poet. 1.50 l, Cisan (Marcu Giurgiu), (1733-85), peasant revolt leader. 2 l, Simion Barnutiu (1808-64), scientist. 3.50 l, Duiliu Zamfirescu (1858-1922), poet. 4 l, Nicolas Milescu (1636-1708), Court official.

1984, Feb. 8

3175	A915	50b multi	8	5
3176	A915	1 l multi	16	8
3177	A915	1.50 l multi	24	12
3178	A915	2 l multi	32	16
3179	A915	3.50 l multi	56	28
3180	A915	4 l multi	65	32
		Nos. 3175-3180 (6)	2.01	1.01

Orsova Bridge—A917

Bridges: No. 3182: b. Arges. c. Basarabi. d. Ohaba. No. 3183: a. Kohlbrand-Germany. b. Bosfor-Turcia. c. Europa-Austria. d. Turnului-Anglia.

1984, Apr. 24

3182		Sheet of 4	2.00	2.00
a.-d.	A917 31		50	50
3183		Sheet of 4	2.00	2.00
a.-d.	A917 31		50	50

Inter-European Cultural and Economic Cooperation. Nos. 3182-3183 have gold marginal inscription; black control number. Size: 109x82mm.

ROMANIA & EASTERN EUROPE

Albania
Bulgaria
Czechoslovakia
Finland
Hungary
East Germany (DDR)
Jugoslavia
Poland
Russia & Associated Territories

WANT LISTS INVITED
Personalized collection building service.
Lists available on request.

R.J.B. Mail Sales
R. J. Burkiewicz
P.O. Box 160
Frisco, CO 80443

ROMANIA

SEMI-POSTAL STAMPS.

Queen Elizabeth Spinning — SP1
The Queen Weaving — SP2

Perf. 11½, 11½x13½

1906, Jan. 14 Typo. Unwmkd.

B1	SP1	3b (+7b) brn	3.00	2.00
B2	SP1	5b (+10b) lt grn	3.00	2.00
B3	SP1	10b (+10b) rose red	10.00	4.75
B4	SP1	15b (+10b) vio	8.00	4.00

1906, Mar. 18

B5	SP2	3b (+7b) org brn	3.00	2.00
B6	SP2	5b (+10b) bl grn	3.00	2.00
B7	SP2	10b (+10b) car	10.00	4.75
B8	SP2	15b (+10b) red vio	8.00	4.00

Queen as War Nurse—SP3

1906, Mar. 23 Perf. 11½, 13½x11½

B9	SP3	3b (+7b) org brn	3.00	2.00
B10	SP3	5b (+10b) bl grn	3.00	2.00
B11	SP3	10b (+10b) car	10.00	4.75
B12	SP3	15b (+10b) red vio	8.00	4.00

Booklet panes of 4 exist of Nos. B1–B3, B5–B7, B9–B12.
Counterfeits of Nos. B1–B12 are plentiful.

SP4

1906, Aug. 4 Perf. 12

B13	SP4	3b (+7b) ol brn, buff & bl	1.50	1.00
B14	SP4	5b (+10b) grn, rose & buff	2.00	1.00
B15	SP4	10b (+10b) rose red, buff & bl	3.50	2.50
B16	SP4	15b (+10b) vio, buff & bl	9.00	3.75

Guardian Angel Bringing Poor to Crown Princess Marie — SP5

1907, Feb. Engr. Perf. 11 Center in Brown

B17	SP5	3b (+7b) org brn	4.00	1.50
B18	SP5	5b (+10b) dk grn	2.50	.60
B19	SP5	10b (+10b) dk car	2.50	.60
B20	SP5	15b (+10b) dl vio	2.00	.50

Nos. B1–B20 were sold for more than face value. The surtax, shown in parenthesis, was for charitable purposes.

Map of Romania — SP9
Stephen the Great — SP10

Michael the Brave — SP11
Kings Carol I and Ferdinand — SP12

Adam Clisi Monument — SP13

1927, Mar. 15 Typo. Perf. 13½

B21	SP9	1l +9l lt vio	1.50	1.00
B22	SP10	2l +8l Prus grn	1.50	1.00
B23	SP11	3l +7l dp rose	1.50	1.00
B24	SP12	5l +5l dp bl	1.50	1.00
B25	SP13	6l +4l ol grn	4.00	1.00

Nos. B21–B25 (5) 10.00 5.00

Issued in commemoration of the fiftieth anniversary of the Royal Geographical Society. The surtax was for the benefit of that society. The stamps were valid for postage only from March 15th to April 14th, 1927.

Boy Scouts in Camp — SP15
The Rescue — SP16

Prince Nicholas Chief Scout — SP18
King Carol II in Scout's Uniform — SP19

Design: 3 l +3 l, Swearing in a Tenderfoot.

Wmkd. Crown over PTT, Multiple. (225)

1931, July 15 Photogravure

B26	SP15	1l +1l car rose	3.75	2.25
B27	SP16	2l +2l dp grn	3.75	2.25
B28	SP15	3l +3l ultra	3.75	2.25
B29	SP18	4l +4l ol gray	3.75	2.25
B30	SP19	6l +6l red brn	3.75	2.25

Nos. B26-B30 (5) 18.75 11.25

The surtax was for the benefit of the Boy Scout organization.

Boy Scout Jamboree Issue.

Scouts in Camp — SP20
Semaphore Signaling — SP21

Trailing — SP22
Camp Fire — SP23

King Carol II — SP24
King Carol II and Prince Michael — SP25

Wmkd. Crowns and Monograms. (230)

1932, June 8

B31	SP20	25b +25b pck grn	4.00	1.50
B32	SP21	50b +50b brt bl	5.00	3.00
B33	SP22	1l +1l ol grn	5.75	4.00
B34	SP23	2l +2l org red	10.00	6.00
B35	SP24	3l +3l Prus bl	20.00	12.00
B36	SP25	6l +6l blk brn	17.50	15.00

Nos. B31-B36 (6) 62.25 41.50

Tuberculosis Sanatorium — SP26

Memorial Tablet to Postal Employees Who Died in World War I — SP27

Carmen Sylva Convalescent Home — SP28

1932, Nov. 1

B37	SP26	4l +1l dk grn	5.00	3.00
B38	SP27	6l +1l choc	5.00	3.00
B39	SP28	10l +1l dp bl	5.00	3.00

The surtax of 1 leu on each stamp of this issue was given to a fund for the employees of the postal and telegraph services.

Philatelic Exhibition Issue.
Souvenir Sheet.

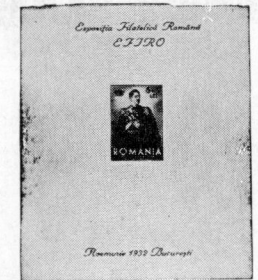

King Carol II — SP29

1932, Nov. 20 Imperf. Unwmkd.

B40	SP29	6l +5l dk ol grn	17.50	17.50

Issued to commemorate the International Philatelic Exhibition at Bucharest, November 20-24, 1932. Each holder of a ticket of admission to the exhibition could buy a copy of the stamp. The ticket cost 20 lei.
Issued in sheets measuring 125 x 100 mm.

Roadside Shrine — SP31
Woman Spinning — SP33

Woman Weaving — SP32

1934, Apr. 16 Perf. 13½ Wmk. 230

B41	SP31	1l +1l dk brn	1.50	1.25
B42	SP32	2l +1l bl	1.50	1.25
B43	SP33	3l +1l sl grn	1.50	1.25

Issued in commemoration of the Weaving Exposition.

Boy Scout Mamaia Jamboree Issue.

Semi-Postal Stamps of 1932 Overprinted in Black or Gold

MAMAIA 1934

1934, July 8

B44	SP20	25b +25b pck grn (Bk)	3.50	2.00

ROMANIA

B45	SP21	50b + 50b brt bl (G)	3.50	2.00
B46	SP22	1 l + 1 l ol grn (Bk)	5.00	3.00
B47	SP23	2 l + 2 l org red (Bk)	5.00	3.50
B48	SP24	3 l + 3 l Prus bl (G)	13.50	11.00
B49	SP25	6 l + 6 l blk brn (G)	22.50	20.00
		Nos. B44-B49 (6)	53.00	41.50

Sea Scout Saluting
SP34

Scout Bugler
SP35

Sea and Land Scouts
SP36

King Carol II
SP37

Sea, Land and Girl Scouts
SP38

1935, June 8

B50	SP34	25b ol blk	1.75	1.25
B51	SP35	1 l violet	3.75	3.25
B52	SP36	2 l green	5.00	4.00
B53	SP37	6 l + 1 l red brn	7.50	4.50
B54	SP38	10 l + 2 l dk ultra	20.00	15.00
		Nos. B50-B54 (5)	38.00	28.00

Fifth anniversary of accession of King Carol II, and a national sports meeting held June 8. Surtax aided the Boy Scouts. Nos. B50-B54 exist imperf.

King Carol II
SP39

1936, May

| B55 | SP39 | 6 l + 1 l rose car | 1.00 | 70 |

Bucharest Exhibition and 70th anniversary of the dynasty. Exists imperf.

Girl of Oltenia
SP40

Girl of Saliste
SP42

Youth from Gorj
SP44

Designs: 1 l + 1 l, Girl of Banat. 3 l + 1 l, Girl of Hateg. 6 l + 3 l, Girl of Neamt. 10 l + 5 l, Youth and girl of Bucovina.

1936, June 8

B56	SP40	50b + 50b brn	90	60
B57	SP40	1 l + 1 l vio	90	60
B58	SP42	2 l + 1 l Prus grn	90	60
B59	SP42	3 l + 1 l car rose	90	60
B60	SP44	4 l + 2 l red org	1.75	1.25
B61	SP40	6 l + 3 l ol gray	1.75	1.50
B62	SP42	10 l + 5 l brt bl	3.25	2.75
		Nos. B56-B62 (7)	10.35	7.90

Sixth anniversary of accession of King Carol II. The surtax was for child welfare. Exist imperf.

Insignia of Boy Scouts
SP47   SP48

Jamboree Emblem
SP49

Submarine "Delfinul"
SP50

1936, Aug. 20

B63	SP47	1 l + 1 l brt bl	4.00	2.50
B64	SP48	3 l + 3 l ol gray	6.00	3.00
B65	SP49	6 l + 6 l car rose	7.50	4.50

Boy Scout Jamboree at Brasov (Kronstadt).

1936, Oct.

Designs: 3 l + 2 l, Training ship "Mircea." 6 l + 3 l, Steamship "S.M.R."

B66	SP50	1 l + 1 l pur	3.75	3.75
B67	SP50	3 l + 3 l ultra	3.75	3.75
B68	SP50	6 l + 3 l car rose	6.00	6.00

Marine Exhibition at Bucharest. Exist imperf.

Soccer—SP53

Swimming—SP54

Throwing the Javelin
SP55

Skiing
SP56

King Carol II Hunting
SP57

Rowing
SP58

Horsemanship
SP59

Founding of the U. F. S. R.
SP60

Wmkd. Crowns and Monograms. (230)

1937, June 8   Perf. 13½

B69	SP53	25b + 25b ol blk	75	50
B70	SP54	50b + 50b brn	75	50
B71	SP55	1 l + 50b vio	75	50
B72	SP56	2 l + 4 l sl grn	75	50
B73	SP57	3 l + 1 l rose lake	1.00	65
B74	SP58	4 l + 1 l red org	1.50	70
B75	SP59	6 l + 2 l dp cl	2.25	1.00
B76	SP60	10 l + 4 l brt bl	3.00	3.00
		Nos. B69-B76 (8)	10.75	7.35

25th anniversary of the Federation of Romanian Sports Clubs (U.F.S.R.); 7th anniversary of the accession of King Carol II. Exist imperf.

Start of Race
SP61

Javelin Thrower
SP62

Designs: 4 l + 1 l, Hurdling. 6 l + 1 l, Finish of race. 10 l + 1 l, High jump.

1937, Sept. 1   Perf. 13½   Wmk. 230

B77	SP61	1 l + 1 l pur	90	90
B78	SP62	2 l + 1 l grn	1.10	1.00
B79	SP61	4 l + 1 l ver	1.50	1.50
B80	SP62	6 l + 1 l mar	2.25	2.25
B81	SP61	10 l + 1 l brt bl	6.00	4.50
		Nos. B77-B81 (5)	11.75	10.15

8th Balkan Games, Bucharest. Exist imperf.

King Carol II
SP66

1938, May 24

| B82 | SP66 | 6 l + 1 l dp mag | 50 | 50 |

Bucharest Exhibition (for local products), May 19-June 19, celebrating 20th anniversary of the union of Rumanian provinces. Exists imperf.

Dimitrie Cantemir
SP67

Maria Doamna
SP68

Mircea the Great
SP69

Constantine Brancoveanu
SP70

Stephen the Great
SP71

Prince Cuza
SP72

Michael the Brave
SP73

Queen Elizabeth
SP74

King Carol II
SP75

King Ferdinand I
SP76

ROMANIA

King Carol I
SP77

1938, June 8 Perf. 13½

B83	SP67	25b +25b ol blk	40	40
B84	SP68	50b +50b brn	40	40
B85	SP69	1 l +1 l blk vio	40	40
B86	SP70	2 l +2 l dk yel grn	40	40
B87	SP71	3 l +2 l dp mag	40	40
B88	SP72	4 l +2 l scar	40	40
B89	SP73	6 l +2 l vio brn	1.00	1.00
B90	SP74	7.50 l gray bl	1.00	1.00
B91	SP75	10 l brt bl	1.00	1.00
B92	SP76	16 l dk sl grn	1.75	1.75
B93	SP77	20 l vermilion	2.25	2.25
	Nos. B83-B93 (11)	9.40	9.40

Eighth anniversary of accession of King Carol II. Surtax was for Straja Tarii, a national organization for boys. Exist imperf.

"The Spring"
SP78

"Escorting Prisoners"
SP79

"Rodica, the Water Carrier" Nicolae Grigorescu
SP81 SP82

Design: 4 l +1 l, "Returning from Market."

1938, June 23 Perf. 13½

B94	SP78	1 l +1 l brt bl	1.10	1.10
B95	SP79	2 l +1 l yel grn	1.10	1.10
B96	SP79	4 l +1 l ver	1.60	1.60
B97	SP81	6 l +1 l lake	1.60	1.60
B98	SP82	10 l +1 l brt bl	2.25	2.25
	Nos. B94-B98 (5)	7.65	7.65

Birth centenary of Nicolae Grigorescu, Romanian painter. Exist imperf.

St. George and the Dragon
SP83

1939, June 8 Photogravure

B99	SP83	25b +25b ol gray	45	45
B100	SP83	50b +50b brn	45	45
B101	SP83	1 l +1 l pale vio	45	45
B102	SP83	2 l +2 l lt grn	45	45
B103	SP83	3 l +2 l red vio	75	45
B104	SP83	4 l +2 l red org	1.00	50
B105	SP83	6 l +2 l car rose	1.10	50
B106	SP83	8 l gray vio	1.25	75
B107	SP83	10 l brt bl	1.35	90
B108	SP83	12 l brt ultra	1.65	1.50
B109	SP83	16 l bl grn	2.00	1.75
	Nos. B99-B109 (11)	10.90	8.15

Ninth anniversary of accession of King Carol II. Exist imperf.

King Carol II
SP87 SP88

SP89

SP90 SP91

Wmkd. Crowns and Monograms. (230)

1940, June 8 Photo. Perf. 13½

B113	SP87	1 l +50b dl pur	25	25
B114	SP88	4 l +1 l fawn	35	35
B115	SP89	6 l +1 l bl	45	45
B116	SP90	8 l rose brn	60	60
B117	SP89	16 l ultra	90	90
B118	SP91	32 l dk vio brn	1.75	1.75
	Nos. B113-B118 (6)	4.30	4.30

10th anniversary of accession of King Carol II. Exist imperf.

King Carol II
SP92 SP93

1940, June 1

B119	SP92	1 l +50b dk grn	30	30
B120	SP92	2.50 l +50b Prus grn	30	30
B121	SP93	3 l +1 l rose car	30	30
B122	SP92	3.50 l +50b choc	30	30
B123	SP93	4 l +1 l org brn	35	35
B124	SP93	6 l +1 l saph	60	60
B125	SP93	9 l +1 l brt bl	90	90
B126	SP93	14 l +1 l dk bl grn	1.25	1.25
	Nos. B119-B126 (8)	4.30	4.30

Surtax was for Romania's air force. Exist imperf.

View of Danube—SP94

Greco-Roman Ruins
SP95

Designs: 3 l +1 l, Hotin Castle. 4 l +1 l, Hurez Monastery. 5 l +1 l, Church in Bucovina. 8 l +1 l, Tower. 12 l +2 l, Village church, Transylvania. 16 l +2 l, Arch in Bucharest.

1940, June 8 Perf. 14½x14, 14x14½

Inscribed:
"Straja Tarii 8 Junie 1940."

B127	SP94	1 l +1 l dp vio	35	35
B128	SP95	2 l +1 l red brn	45	45
B129	SP94	3 l +1 l yel grn	50	50
B130	SP94	4 l +1 l grnsh blk	60	60
B131	SP95	5 l +1 l org ver	75	75
B132	SP95	8 l +1 l brn car	95	95
B133	SP95	12 l +2 l ultra	1.35	1.35
B134	SP95	16 l +2 l dk bl gray	1.90	1.90
	Nos. B127-B134 (8)	6.85	6.85

Issued to honor Straja Tarii, a national organization for boys. Exist imperf.

King Michael Corneliu Codreanu
SP102 SP103

Wmkd. Crowns and Monograms. (230)

1940–42 Photogravure

B138	SP102	1 l +50b yel grn	5	5
B138A	SP102	2 l +50b yel grn ('42)	5	5
B139	SP102	2.50 l +50b dk bl grn	5	5
B140	SP102	3 l +1 l pur	15	15
B141	SP102	3.50 l +50b rose pink	20	20
B141A	SP102	4 l +50b org ver ('42)	10	10
B142	SP102	4 l +1 l brn	10	10
B142A	SP102	5 l +1 l dp plum ('42)	60	60
B143	SP102	6 l +1 l lt ultra	10	10
B143A	SP102	7 l +1 l sl grn ('42)	15	15
B143B	SP102	8 l +1 l dp vio ('42)	20	20
B143C	SP102	12 l +1 l brn vio ('42)	20	20
B144	SP102	14 l +1 l brt bl	40	40
B144A	SP102	19 l +1 l lil rose ('42)	80	80
	Nos. B138-B144A (14)	3.15	3.15

1940, Nov. 8 Perf. 13½ Unwmkd.

| B145 | SP103 | 7 l +30 l dk grn | 3.75 | 3.75 |

Issued to commemorate the 13th anniversary of the founding of the Iron Guard by Corneliu Codreanu.

Vasile Marin
SP104

SP106

Designs: 15 l +15 l, Ion Mota.

1941, Jan. 13

B146	SP104	7 l +7 l rose brn	75	75
B147	SP104	15 l +15 l sl bl	1.50	1.50

Souvenir Sheet
Imperf.

B148	SP106	Sheet of two	35.00	35.00
a.		7 l +7 l Prus grn	7.50	7.50
b.		15 l +15 l Prus grn	7.50	7.50

Issued in honor of Vasile Marin and Ion Mota, Iron Guardists who died in the Spanish Civil War.

No. B148 sold for 300 lei. Size: 88x 56½ mm.

Crown, Leaves and Bible
SP107

Designs: 2 l +43 l, Library shelves. 7 l +38 l, Carol I Foundation, Bucharest. 10 l +35 l, King Carol I. 16 l +29 l, Kings Michael and Carol I.

Perf. 13½

1941, May 9 Photo. Wmk. 230
Inscribed: "1891 1941."

B149	SP107	1.50 l +43.50 l pur	75	75
B150	SP107	2 l +43 l rose brn	75	75
B151	SP107	7 l +38 l rose	75	75
B152	SP107	10 l +35 l ol blk	75	75
B153	SP107	16 l +29 l brn	75	75
	Nos. B149-B153 (5)	3.75	3.75

Issued to commemorate the 50th anniversary of the Carol I Foundation, established to endow research and stimulate the arts.

Same Overprinted **CERNAUTI**
in Red or Black **5 Iulie 1941**

1941, Aug.

B154	SP107	1.50 l +43.50 l pur (R)	1.50	1.50
B155	SP107	2 l +43 l rose brn	1.50	1.50
B156	SP107	7 l +38 l rose	1.50	1.50

ROMANIA

B157	SP107	10 l +35 l ol blk (R)	1.50	1.50
B158	SP107	16 l +29 l brn	1.50	1.50

Occupation of Cernauti, Bucovina.

Same Overprinted **CHISINAU**
in
Red or Black **16 Iulie 1941**
1941, Aug.

B159	SP107	1.50 l +43.50 l pur (R)	1.50	1.50
B160	SP107	2 l +43 l rose brn	1.50	1.50
B161	SP107	7 l +38 l rose	1.50	1.50
B162	SP107	10 l +35 l ol blk (R)	1.50	1.50
B163	SP107	16 l +29 l brn	1.50	1.50
	Nos. B154-B163 (10)		15.00	15.00

Occupation of Chisinau, Bessarabia.

Romanian Red Cross
SP111

SP112

1941, Aug. Perf. 13½

B164	SP111	1.50 l +38.50 l dl pur & car	75	75
B165	SP111	2 l +38 l mag & red	75	75
B166	SP111	5 l +35 l ol gray & car	75	75
B167	SP111	7 l +33 l dl brn & car	75	75
B168	SP111	10 l +30 l brt bl & car	75	75
	Nos. B164-B168 (5)		3.75	3.75

Souvenir Sheet
Imperf.
Without Gum.

B169	SP112	Sheet of two	9.00	9.00
a.		7 l +33 l brn & red	1.75	2.00
b.		10 l +30 l brt bl & red	1.75	2.00

The surtax on Nos. B164-B169 was for the Romanian Red Cross.
No. B169 sold for 200 l. Size: 105x73 mm.

King Michael and
Stephen the Great
SP113

Hotin and Akkerman Castles
SP114

Romanian and German Soldiers
SP115

Soldiers—SP116

1941, Oct. 11 Perf. 14½x13½

B170	SP113	10 l +30 l ultra	75	75
B171	SP114	12 l +28 l dl org red	75	75
B172	SP115	16 l +24 l lt brn	75	75
B173	SP116	20 l +20 l dk vio	75	75

Souvenir Sheet
SP118

B174	SP118	Imperf. Sheet of two	5.50	5.50
a.		16 l bl gray	50	50
b.		20 l brn car	50	50

The sheet measures 105x72 mm. Sold for 200 l. The surtax aided the Anti-Bolshevism crusade.

Nos. B170-B174 **ODESA**
Overprinted **16 Oct. 1941**

1941, Oct. Perf. 14½x13½

B175	SP113	10 l +30 l ultra	75	75
B176	SP114	12 l +28 l dl org red	75	75
B177	SP115	16 l +24 l lt brn	75	75
B178	SP116	20 l +20 l dk vio	75	75
a.		Sheet of 2 (# B174)	7.50	7.50

Occupation of Odessa, Russia.

Types of Regular Issue, 1941.

Designs: 3 l+50 b, Sucevita Monastery, Bucovina. 5.50 l+50 b, Rughi Monastery, Soroca, Bessarabia. 5.50 l+1 l, Tighina Fortress, Bessarabia. 6.50 l+1 l, Soroca Fortress, Bessarabia. 8 l+1 l, St. Nicholas Monastery, Suceava, Bucovina. 9.50 l+1 l, Milisauti Monastery, Bucovina. 10.50 l+1 l, Putna Monastery, Bucovina. 8 l+1 l, Cetatea Alba Fortress, Bessarabia. 25 l+1 l, Hotin Fortress, Bessarabia.

1941, Dec. 1 Perf. 13½ Wmk. 230

B179	A179	3 l +50 b rose brn	15	15
B180	A179	5.50 l +50 b red org	15	15
B181	A179	5.50 l +1 l blk	15	15
B182	A179	6.50 l +1 l dk brn	15	15
B183	A179	8 l +1 l lt bl	15	15
B184	A177	9.50 l +1 l gray bl	40	40
B185	A179	10.50 l +1 l dk bl	30	30
B186	A179	16 l +1 l vio	60	60
B187	A179	25 l +1 l gray blk	90	90
	Nos. B179-B187 (9)		2.95	2.95

Titu Maiorescu
SP128

Statue of Miron
Costin at Jassy
SP130

1942, Oct. 5

B188	SP128	9 l +11 l dl vio	90	90
B189	SP128	20 l +20 l yel brn	90	90
B190	SP128	20 l +30 l bl	90	90

Souvenir Sheet.
Imperf.
Without Gum.

B191	SP128	Sheet of three	6.00	6.00

The surtax aided war prisoners. No. B191 contains one each of Nos. B188-B190, imperf. Size: 127½x81mm. Sold for 200 l.

1942, Dec. Perf. 13½

B192	SP130	6 l +44 l sep	1.25	1.25
B193	SP130	12 l +38 l vio	1.25	1.25
B194	SP130	24 l +26 l bl	1.25	1.25

To commemorate the anniversary of the conquest of Transdniestria, and for use only in this territory which includes Odessa and land beyond the Dniester.

Michael, Antonescu, Hitler, Mussolini and Bessarabia Map
SP131

Michael, Antonescu (inset) Stephen of Moldavia
SP132

Romanian Troops
Crossing Pruth River
to Retake Bessarabia—SP133
Photogravure.

1942 Perf. 13½ Wmk. 230

B195	SP131	9 l +41 l red brn	1.25	1.25
B196	SP132	18 l +32 l ol gray	1.25	1.25
B197	SP133	20 l +30 l brt ultra	1.25	1.25

First anniversary of liberation of Bessarabia.

Bucovina Coats of Arms
SP134   SP135

Design: 20 l+30 l, Bucovina arms with triple-barred cross.

1942, Nov. 1

B198	SP134	9 l +41 l brt ver	1.25	1.25
B199	SP135	18 l +32 l bl	1.25	1.25
B200	SP135	20 l +30 l car rose	1.25	1.25

First anniversary of liberation of Bucovina.

Andrei Muresanu
SP137

1942, Dec. 30

B201	SP137	5 l +5 l vio	60	60

To commemorate the 80th anniversary of the death of the writer, Andrei Muresanu.

Avram Jancu
SP138

1943, Feb. 15

B202	SP138	16 l +4 l brn	90	90

Issued in honor of the national hero, Avram Jancu.

Nurse Aiding Wounded Soldier
SP139

SP140

1943, Mar. 1 Perf. 14½x14

B203	SP139	12 l +8 l red brn & ultra	60	60
B204	SP139	16 l +8 l brt ultra & red	60	60
B205	SP139	20 l +8 l ol gray & red	60	60

Souvenir Sheet
Imperf.

B206	SP140	Sheet of two	3.75	4.50
a.		16 l +8 l brt ultra & red	75	85
b.		20 l +8 l ol gray & red	75	85

Surtax on Nos. B203-B206 aided the Romanian Red Cross.
No. B206 sold for 500 l. Size: 100x60 mm.

Sword Hilt
SP141

Sword Severing Chain
SP142

ROMANIA

Soldier and Family, Guardian Angel
SP143

SP144

Perf. 14x14½

1943, June 22   Wmk. 276

B207	SP141	3 l + 16 l brn	3.00	3.00
B208	SP142	6 l + 13 l brt bl	3.00	3.00
B209	SP143	7 l + 12 l ver	3.00	3.00

Souvenir Sheet.
Imperf.

B210	SP144	Sheet of two	10.00	10.00
a.		6 l + 13 l dp bl	2.00	2.25
b.		7 l + 12 l red org	2.00	2.25

Second anniversary of Romania's entrance into World War II.
No. B210 sold for 600 l. Size: 90x69½ mm.

Petru Maior—SP145

Horia, Closca and Crisan
SP148

Designs: 32 l+11 8 l, Gheorghe Sincal. 36 l+11 4 l, Timotei Cipariu. 91+10 9 l, Gheorghe Cosbuc.

Perf. 13½; 14½x14 (※B214)

1943, Aug. 15   Photo.   Wmk. 276

B211	SP145	16 l + 134 l red org	60	60
B212	SP145	32 l + 118 l lt bl	60	60
B213	SP145	36 l + 114 l vio	60	60
B214	SP148	62 l + 138 l car rose	60	60
B215	SP145	91 l + 109 l dk brn	60	60
		Nos. B211-B215 (5)	3.00	3.00

See also Nos. B219-B223.

King Michael and Ion Antonescu
SP150

1943, Sept. 6

| B216 | SP150 | 16 l + 24 l bl | 1.00 | 1.00 |

To commemorate the third anniversary of the government of King Michael and Marshal Ion Antonescu.

Symbols of Sports
SP151

1943, Sept. 26   **Perf. 13½**

| B217 | SP151 | 16 l + 24 l ultra | 60 | 60 |
| B218 | SP151 | 16 l + 24 l red brn | 60 | 60 |

The surtax was for the benefit of Romanian sports.

Portrait Type of 1943.

1943, Oct. 1

Designs: 16 l+134 l, Samuel Micu. 51 l+99 l, George Lazar. 56 l+144 l, Octavian Goga. 76 l+124 l, Simeon Barnutlu. 77 l+123 l, Andrei Saguna.

B219	SP145	16 l + 134 l red vio	50	50
B220	SP145	51 l + 99 l org	50	50
B221	SP145	56 l + 144 l rose car	50	50
B222	SP145	76 l + 124 l sl bl	50	50
B223	SP145	77 l + 123 l brn	50	50
		Nos. B219-B223 (5)	2.50	2.50

The surtax aided refugees.

Calafat, 1877
SP157

Designs: 2 l+2 l, World War I scene. 3.50 l+3.50 l, Stalingrad, 1943. 4 l+4 l, Theiss, 1919. 5 l+5 l, Odessa, 1941. 6.50 l+6.50 l, Caucasus 1942. 7 l+7 l, Sevastopol, 1942. 20 l+20 l, Prince Bibescu and King Michael.

1943, Nov. 10   Photo.   **Perf. 13½**

B224	SP157	1 l + 1 l red brn	15	15
B225	SP157	2 l + 2 l dl vio	15	15
B226	SP157	3.50 l + 3.50 l lt ultra	15	15
B227	SP157	4 l + 4 l mag	15	15
B228	SP157	5 l + 5 l red org	15	15
B229	SP157	6.50 l + 6.50 l bl	25	25
B230	SP157	7 l + 7 l dp vio	45	45
B231	SP157	20 l + 20 l crim	70	70
		Nos. B224-B231 (8)	2.15	2.15

Centenary of Romanian Artillery.

Emblem of Romanian Engineers' Association
SP165

1943, Dec. 19   **Perf. 14**

| B232 | SP165 | 21 l + 29 l sep | 90 | 90 |

To commemorate the 25th anniversary of the Society of Romanian Engineers.

Motorcycle, Truck and Post Horn
SP166

Post Wagon—SP167

Roman Post Chariot—SP168

Post Rider
SP169

SP170

1944, Feb. 1   **Perf. 14**   Wmk. 276

B233	SP166	1 l + 4 l org red	1.50	1.50
B234	SP167	2 l + 48 l lil rose	1.50	1.50
B235	SP138	4 l + 46 l ultra	1.50	1.50
B236	SP169	10 l + 40 l dl vio	1.50	1.50

Souvenir Sheets.
Perf. 14

B237	SP170	Sheet of three	5.00	7.00
a.		1 l + 49 l org red	1.00	1.00
b.		2 l + 48 l org red	1.00	1.00
c.		4 l + 46 l org red	1.00	1.00

Imperf.

B238	SP170	Sheet of three	5.00	7.00
a.		1 l + 49 l dl vio	1.00	1.00
b.		2 l + 48 l dl vio	1.00	1.00
c.		4 l + 46 l dl vio	1.00	1.00

The surtax aided communications employees.
Nos. B237-B238 each sold for 200 l. Size: 147x84mm.

Nos. B233-B238 Overprinted "1744 1944"

1944, Feb. 28

B239	SP166	1 l + 49 l org red	3.25	3.25
B240	SP167	2 l + 48 l lil rose	3.25	3.25
B241	SP168	4 l + 46 l ultra	3.25	3.25
B242	SP169	10 l + 40 l dl vio	3.25	3.25

Souvenir Sheets.
Perf. 14

| B243 | SP170 | Sheet of three | 9.00 | 10.00 |

Imperf.

| B244 | SP170 | Sheet of three | 9.00 | 10.00 |

Rugby Player
SP171

Dr. N. Cretzulescu
SP172

1944, Mar. 16   **Perf. 15**

| B245 | SP171 | 16 l + 184 l crim | 3.25 | 3.25 |

To commemorate the 30th anniversary of the Romanian Rugby Association. The surtax was used to encourage the sport.

1944, Mar. 1   Photo.   **Perf. 13½**

| B246 | SP172 | 35 l + 65 l brt ultra | 90 | 90 |

Centenary of medical teaching in Romania.

Queen Mother Helen
SP173

1945, Feb. 10

B247	SP173	4.50 l + 5.50 l pur, sep & red	30	30
B248	SP173	10 l + 40 l brn, sep & red	30	30
B249	SP173	15 l + 75 l gray bl, sep & red	30	30
B250	SP173	20 l + 80 l hn brn, sep & red	30	30

The surtax aided the Romanian Red Cross.

Kings Ferdinand and Michael and Map—SP174

1945, Feb.   **Perf. 14**

| B251 | SP174 | 75 l + 75 l dk ol brn | 75 | 50 |

Romania's liberation.

Stefan Tomsa Church, Radaseni
SP175

Municipal Home
SP176

Gathering Fruit
SP177

ROMANIA

School—SP178
Photogravure.

1944		Perf. 14	Wmk. 276	
B252	SP175	5 l +145 l brt bl	50	50
B253	SP176	12 l +138 l car rose	50	50
B254	SP177	15 l +135 l red org	50	50
B255	SP178	32 l +118 l dk brn	50	50

King Michael and Carol I
Foundation, Bucharest
SP179

King Carol I and Foundation
SP180

1945, Feb. 10			Perf. 13	
B256	SP179	20 l +180 l dp org	15	15
B257	SP179	25 l +175 l sl	15	15
B258	SP179	35 l +165 l cl brn	15	15
B259	SP179	75 l +125 l pale vio	15	15

Souvenir Sheet
Imperf.
Without Gum.

B260 SP180 200 l blue 4.50 5.50

The surtax on Nos. B256 to B260 was to aid in rebuilding the Public Library, Bucharest.
Nos. B256–B259 were printed in sheets of four.
No. B260 sold for 1200 lei. Size: 73½x57½.

Ion G. Duca—SP181

SP187

Designs: 16 l+184 l, Virgil Madgearu. 20 l+180 l, Nikolai Jorga. 32 l+168 l, Ilie Pintilie. 35 l+165 l, Bernath Andrei. 36 l+164 l, Filimon Sarbu.

1945, Apr. 30			Perf. 13	
B261	SP181	12 l +188 l dk bl	35	35
B262	SP181	16 l +184 l cl brn	35	35
B263	SP181	20 l +180 l blk brn	35	35
B264	SP181	32 l +168 l brt red	35	35
B265	SP181	35 l +165 l Prus bl	35	35
B266	SP181	36 l +164 l lt vio	35	35
Nos. B261–B266 (6)			2.10	2.10

Souvenir Sheet
Imperf.

B267	SP187	Sheet of two	15.00	17.50
a.		32 l + 168 l mag	3.00	3.50
b.		35 l + 165 l mag	3.00	3.50

Nos. B261–B267 were issued to honor six victims of Nazi terrorism.
No. B267 sold for 1,000 lei. Size: 65x 75mm.

Books and Torch   Flags of Russia
SP188   and Romania
                 SP189

Kremlin,   Tudor
Moscow   Vladimirescu
SP190   and Alexander
             Nevsky
             SP191

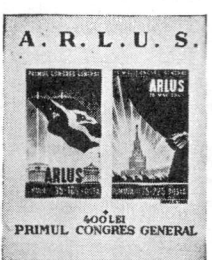

SP192

1945, May 20			Perf. 14	
B268	SP188	20 l +80 l ol grn	30	30
B269	SP189	35 l +165 l brt rose	30	30
B270	SP190	75 l +225 l bl	30	30
B271	SP191	80 l +420 l cl brn	30	30

Souvenir Sheet.
Imperf.
Without Gum.

B272	SP192	Sheet of two	7.50	8.50
a.		35 l + 165 l brt red	1.75	2.00
b.		75 l + 225 l brt red	1.75	2.00

Nos. B268–B272 were issued to commemorate the First Soviet-Romanian Congress, May 20, 1945.
No. B272 sold for 900 lei. Size: 60x70 mm.

Karl Marx
SP193

Designs: 120 l+380 l, Friedrich Engels. 155 l+445 l, Lenin.

1945, June 30			Perf. 13½	
B273	SP193	75 l +425 l car rose	1.25	1.25
B274	SP193	120 l +380 l bl	1.25	1.25
B275	SP193	155 l +445 l dk vio brn	1.25	1.25

Imperf.

B276	SP193	75 l +425 l bl	3.00	3.00
B277	SP193	120 l +380 l dk vio brn	3.00	3.00
B278	SP193	155 l +445 l car rose	3.00	3.00
Nos. B273–B278 (6)			12.75	12.75

Nos. B276–B278 were printed in sheets of 4.

Woman
Throwing
Discus
SP196

Designs: 16 l+184 l, Diving. 20 l+ 180 l, Skiing. 32 l+168 l, Volleyball. 35 l+165 l, Worker athlete.

Photogravure

1945, Aug. 5		Perf. 13	Wmk. 276	
B279	SP196	12 l +188 l ol gray	1.50	1.50
B280	SP196	16 l +184 l lt ultra	1.50	1.50
B281	SP196	20 l +180 l dp grn	1.50	1.50
B282	SP196	32 l +168 l mag	1.50	1.50
B283	SP196	35 l +165 l brt bl	1.50	1.50

Imperf.

B284	SP196	12 l +188 l org red	1.50	1.50
B285	SP196	16 l +184 l vio brn	1.50	1.50
B286	SP196	20 l +180 l dp vio	1.50	1.50
B287	SP196	32 l +168 l yel grn	1.50	1.50
B288	SP196	35 l +165 l dk ol grn	1.50	1.50
Nos. B279–B288 (10)			15.00	15.00

Nos. B279–B288 were printed in sheets of 9 inscribed in top margin.

Scott's editorial staff cannot undertake to identify, authenticate or appraise stamps and postal markings.

Mail Plane and Bird
Carrying Letter—SP201

1945, Aug. 5			Perf. 13½	
B289	SP201	200 l +1000 l bl & dk bl	5.00	5.00
a.		With label	17.50	20.00

The surtax on Nos. B279–B289 was for the Office of Popular Sports.
Issued in sheets of 30 stamps and 10 labels, arranged 10x4 with second and fourth horizontal rows each having five alternating labels.

Agriculture and Industry United
SP202

King Michael—SP203

1945, Aug. 23			Perf. 14	
B290	SP202	100 l +400 l red	15	15
B291	SP203	200 l +800 l bl	20	20

The surtax was for the Farmers' Front.

Political Amnesty
SP204

Military Amnesty
SP205

Agrarian Amnesty
SP206

ROMANIA

Tudor Vladimirescu
SP207

Nicolae Horia
SP208

Reconstruction
SP209

1945, Aug.   Perf. 13

B292	SP204	20 l + 58 0 l choc	6.00	6.00
B293	SP204	20 l + 580 l mag	6.00	6.00
B294	SP205	40 l + 560 l bl	6.00	6.00
B295	SP205	40 l + 560 l sl grn	6.00	6.00
B296	SP106	55 l + 545 l red	6.00	6.00
B297	SP106	55 l + 545 l dk vio brn	6.00	6.00
B298	SP207	60 l + 540 l ultra	6.00	6.00
B299	SP207	60 l + 540 l choc	6.00	6.00
B300	SP208	80 l + 520 l red	6.00	6.00
B301	SP208	80 l + 520 l mag	6.00	6.00
B302	SP209	100 l + 500 l sl grn	6.00	6.00
B303	SP209	100 l + 500 l red brn	6.00	6.00
		Nos. B292-B303 (12)	72.00	72.00

First anniversary of Romania's armistice with Russia. Issued in panes of four.
Nos. B292-B303 also exist on coarse grayish paper, ungummed (same price).

Electric Train
SP210

Coats of Arms
SP211

Truck on Mountain Road
SP212

Oil Field
SP213

"Agriculture"
SP214

1945, Oct. 1   Perf. 14

B304	SP210	10 l + 490 l ol grn	30	30
B305	SP211	20 l + 480 l red brn	30	30
B306	SP212	25 l + 475 l brn vio	30	30
B307	SP213	55 l + 445 l ultra	30	30
B308	SP214	100 l + 400 l brn	30	30

Imperf.

B309	SP210	10 l + 490 l bl	30	30
B310	SP211	20 l + 480 l vio	30	30
B311	SP212	25 l + 475 l bl grn	30	30
B312	SP213	55 l + 445 l gray	30	30
B313	SP214	100 l + 400 l dp mag	30	30
		Nos. B304-B313 (10)	3.00	3.00

Issued to commemorate the 16th Congress of the General Association of Romanian Engineers.

"Brotherhood"—SP215

Designs: 160 l + 1840 l, "Peace." 320 l + 1680 l, Hammer crushing Nazism. 440 l + 2560 l, "World Unity."

1945, Dec. 5   Perf. 14

B314	SP215	80 l + 920 l mag	15.00	15.00
B315	SP215	160 l + 1840 l org brn	15.00	15.00
B316	SP215	320 l + 1680 l vio	15.00	15.00
B317	SP215	440 l + 2560 l yel grn	15.00	15.00

Issued to commemorate the World Trade Union Congress at Paris, September 25 to October 10, 1945.

Nos. B290 and B291 Surcharged in Various Colors.

1946, Jan. 20

B318	SP202	10 l + 90 l on 100 l + 400 l red (Bk)	55	55
B319	SP203	10 l + 90 l on 200 l + 800 l bl (R)	55	55
B320	SP202	20 l + 80 l on 100 l + 400 l red (G)	55	55
B321	SP203	20 l + 80 l on 200 l + 800 l bl (Bk)	55	55
B322	SP202	80 l + 120 l on 100 l + 400 l red (Bl)	55	55
B323	SP203	80 l + 120 l on 200 l + 800 l bl (Bk)	55	55
B324	SP202	100 l + 150 l on 100 l + 400 l red (Bk)	55	55
B325	SP203	100 l + 150 l on 200 l + 800 l bl (R)	55	55
		Nos. B318-B325 (8)	4.40	4.40

Re-distribution of Land
SP219

Sower—SP220

Ox Team Drawing Hay—SP221

Old and New Plowing Methods
SP222

1946, Mar. 6

B326	SP219	50 l + 450 l red	20	20
B327	SP220	100 l + 900 l red vio	20	20
B328	SP221	200 l + 800 l org	20	20
B329	SP222	400 l + 1600 l dk grn	20	20

Issued to commemorate the agrarian reform law of March 23, 1945.

Philharmonic Types of Regular Issue.
Perf. 13, 13½x13

1946, Apr. 26   Photo.   Wmk. 276

B330	A211	200 l + 800 l brt red	85	85
a.		Sheet of 12	20.00	25.00
B331	A213	350 l + 1650 l dk bl	90	90
a.		Sheet of 12	20.00	25.00

Issued to commemorate the 25th anniversary of the Philharmonic Society.

Issued in sheets containing 12 stamps and 4 labels, with bars of music in the margins. Music and labels with No. B330 are slate gray, with No. B331 red orange.

Agriculture
SP223

Dove
SP228

SP229

Designs: 10 l + 200 l, Hurdling. 80 l + 200 l, Research. 80 l + 300 l, Industry. 200 l + 400 l, Workers and flag.

Perf. 11½

1946, July 28   Photo.   Wmk. 276

B332	SP223	10 l + 100 l dk org brn & red	25	25
B333	SP223	10 l + 200 l bl & red brn	25	25
B334	SP223	80 l + 200 l brn vio & brn	25	25
B335	SP223	80 l + 300 l dk org brn & rose lil	25	25
B336	SP223	200 l + 400 l Prus bl & red	25	25
		Nos. B332-B336 (5)	1.25	1.25

Issued in panes of 4 stamps with marginal inscription.

Perf. 13½x13, Imperf.

1946, Oct. 20

B338	SP228	300 l + 1200 l scar	30	35

Souvenir Sheet.
Perf. 14x14½.

B339	SP229	1000 l scarlet	2.50	3.00

Nos. B338 and B339 were issued to publicize Romanian-Soviet friendship.
No. B339 sold for 6000 lei. Size: 69x 64mm.

Skiing
SP230

1946, Sept. 1   Perf. 11½, Imperf.

B340	SP230	160 l + 1340 l dk grn	60	60

Surtax for Office of Popular Sports.

Spinning
SP231

Reaping
SP232

Riding
SP233

Water Carrier
SP234

1946, Nov. 20   Perf. 14

B342	SP231	80 l + 320 l brt red	15	15
B343	SP232	140 l + 360 l dp org	15	15
B344	SP233	300 l + 450 l brn ol	15	15
B345	SP234	600 l + 900 l ultra	15	15

Issued for the Democratic Women's Organization of Romania.

Angel with Food and Clothing
SP235

Bread for Hungry Family
SP236

Care for Needy—SP237

1947, Jan. 15   Perf. 13½x14

B346	SP235	1500 l + 3500 l red org	14	14
B347	SP236	3700 l + 5300 l dp vio	30	30

ROMANIA

Miniature Sheet
Imperf.
Without Gum
B348	SP237	5000 l + 5000 l ultra	1.75	2.50

The surtax on Nos. B346–B348 helped the social relief fund.
No. B348 is miniature sheet of one. Size: 52 x 36 mm.

Student Reciting—SP238

Allegory of Education
SP242

SP243

Designs: 300 l+300 l, Weaving class. 600 l+600 l, Young machinist. 1200 l+1200 l, Romanian school.

Perf. 14x13½
1947, Mar. 5   Photo.   Wmk. 276
B349	SP238	200 l + 200 l vio bl	5	5
B350	SP238	300 l + 300 l red brn	5	5
B351	SP238	600 l + 600 l Prus grn	5	5
B352	SP238	1200 l + 1200 l ultra	5	5
B353	SP242	1500 l + 1500 l dp rose	5	5
		Nos. B349-B353 (5)	25	25

Souvenir Sheet
Imperf.
B354	SP243	3700 l + 3700 l brn & dl bl	1.00	1.25

Nos. B349–B354 were issued to commemorate the 50th anniversary of Romania's vocational schools. Size of No. B354: 66x81mm.

Victor Babes
SP244

Designs: B356, Michael Eminescu. B357, Nicolae Grigorescu. B358, Peter Movila. B359, Aleksander S. Pushkin. B360, Mikhail V. Lomonosov. B361, Peter I. Tchaikovsky. B362, Ilya E. Repin.

1947, Apr. 18   Perf. 14
B355	SP244	1500 l + 1500 l red org	20	20
B356	SP244	1500 l + 1500 l dk ol grn	20	20
B357	SP244	1500 l + 1500 l dk bl	20	20
B358	SP244	1500 l + 1500 l dp plum	20	20
B359	SP244	1500 l + 1500 l scar	20	20
B360	SP244	1500 l + 1500 l rose brn	20	20
B361	SP244	1500 l + 1500 l ultra	20	20
B362	SP244	1500 l + 1500 l choc	20	20
		Nos. B355-B362 (8)	1.60	1.60

Transportation—SP252

Designs: 1500 l+1500 l, Farmer. 2000 l+2000 l, Farm woman. 2500 l+2500 l, Teacher and school. 3000 l+3000 l, Laborer and factory.

1947, May 1
Flag Inscribed; "1 MAI."
B363	SP252	1000 l + 1000 l dk ol brn	15	15
B364	SP252	1500 l + 1500 l red brn	15	15
B365	SP252	2000 l + 2000 l bl	15	15
B366	SP252	2500 l + 2500 l red vio	15	15
B367	SP252	3000 l + 3000 l crim rose	15	15
		Nos. B363-B367 (5)	75	75

Issued to publicize Labor Day, May 1, 1947.

No. 650 Surcharged in Carmine

1947, Sept. 6   Perf. 13½
B368	A234	2 l + 3 on 36,000 vio	75	75

Balkan Games of 1947, Bucharest.

Type of 1947 Surcharged in Carmine

Design: Cathedral of Curtea de Arges.
1947, Oct. 30   Imperf.
B369	A235	5 l + 5 l brt ultra	50	50

Soviet-Romanian Congress, Nov. 1–7.

Plowing
SP257

Perf. 14x14½
1947, Oct. 5   Photo.   Wmk. 276
B370	SP257	1 l + 1 l rose lake	15	15
B371	SP257	2 l + 2 l dk brn		
		(Sawmill)	15	15
B372	SP257	3 l + 3 l pur (Refinery)	15	15

B373	SP257	4 l + 4 l dk sl grn		
		(Steel mill)	20	20
		Nos. B370-B373, CB12 (5)	1.40	1.00

Issued to commemorate the 17th Congress of the General Association of Romanian Engineers.

Allegory of Industry, Science and Agriculture
SP258

Winged Man Holding Hammer and Sickle
SP259

1947, Nov. 10   Perf. 14½x14
B374	SP258	2 l + 10 l rose lake	15	15
B375	SP259	7 l + 10 l bluish blk	25	25

Issued to commemorate the 2nd Trade Union Conference, November 10, 1947.

Convoy of Food for Moldavia
SP260

"Three Years of Action"
SP264

Designs: 2 l+2 l, "Everything for the Front—Everything for Victory." 3 l+3 l, Woman, child and hospital. 4 l+4 l, "Help the Famine-stricken Regions."

1947, Nov. 7   Perf. 14
B376	SP260	1 l + 1 l dk gray bl	15	15
B377	SP260	2 l + 2 l dk brn	15	15
B378	SP260	3 l + 3 l rose lake	15	15
B379	SP260	4 l + 4 l brt ultra	15	15
B380	SP264	5 l + 5 l red	20	20
		Nos. B376-B380 (5)	80	80

Issued in sheets of four.

Discus Thrower
SP265

Labor
SP266

Youths Following Filimon Sarbu Banner
SP269

Designs: 2 l+2 l, Runner. 5 l+5 l, Boy and girl athletes.

Photogravure.
1948, Feb.   Perf. 13½   Wmk. 276
B381	SP265	1 l + 1 l dk brn	30	20
B382	SP265	2 l + 2 l car lake	35	25
B383	SP265	5 l + 5 l bl	65	45
		Nos. B381-B383, CB13-CB14 (5)	4.55	3.05

Balkan Games of 1947.

1948, Mar. 15
Designs: 3 l+3 l, Agriculture. 5 l+5 l, Education.
B384	SP266	2 l + 2 l dk sl bl	20	15
B385	SP266	3 l + 3 l gray grn	30	20
B386	SP266	5 l + 5 l red brn	40	30

Imperf.
B387	SP269	8 l + 8 l dk car rose	60	40
		Nos. B384-B387, CB15 (5)	2.50	1.75

No. B387 issued in triangular sheets of 4.

Gliders
SP270

Sailboat Race—SP271

Designs: No. B389, Early plane. No. B390, Plane over farm. No. B391, Transport plane. B393, Training ship, Mircea. B394, Danube ferry. B395, S.S. Transylvania.

1948, July 26   Perf. 14x14½
B388	SP270	2 l + 2 l bl	1.75	1.75
B389	SP270	5 l + 5 l pur	1.75	1.75
B390	SP270	8 l + 8 l dk car rose	1.75	1.75
B391	SP270	10 l + 10 l choc	1.75	1.75
B392	SP271	2 l + 2 l dk grn	1.50	1.50
B393	SP271	5 l + 5 l sl	1.50	1.50
B394	SP271	8 l + 8 l brt bl	1.50	1.50
B395	SP271	10 l + 10 l ver	1.50	1.50
		Nos. B388-B395 (8)	13.00	13.00

Nos. B388–B395 were issued to publicize Air and Sea Communications Day.

Type of Regular Issue and

Torch, Pen, Ink and Flag
SP272

ROMANIA

Alexandru
Sahia
SP273

Romanian-Soviet
Association
Emblem
SP274

Perf. 14x13½, 13½x14, Imperf.
1948, Sept. 12

B396	A241	5 l + 5 l crim	1.50	1.50
B397	SP272	10 l + 10 l vio	1.75	1.75
B398	SP273	15 l + 15 l bl	1.75	1.75

Issued to publicize the Week of the Democratic Press, Sept. 12–19.

1948, Oct. 29 — *Perf. 14*
Design: 15 l + 15 l, Spasski Tower, Kremlin.

| B399 | SP274 | 10 l + 10 l gray grn | 1.75 | 1.75 |
| B400 | SP274 | 15 l + 15 l dp ultra | 1.75 | 1.75 |

No. B399 was issued in sheets of 50 stamps and 50 labels.

Symbols of United Labor
SP275

Agriculture
SP276

Industry
SP277

Automatic Riflemen
SP278

Soldiers Cutting Barbed Wire
SP279

Perf. 14 x 13½, 13½ x 14
1948, May 1

B401	SP275	8 l + 8 l red	3.00	3.00
B402	SP276	10 l + 10 l ol grn	3.00	3.00
B403	SP277	12 l + 12 l red brn	3.00	3.00

Labor Day, May 1. See No. CB17.

1948, May 9
Flags and Dates:
23 Aug 1944 - 9 Mai 1945

| B404 | SP278 | 1.50 l + 1.50 l rose car | 1.50 | 1.50 |

B405	SP279	2 l + 2 l car lake	1.50	1.50
B406	SP279	4 l + 4 l redsh brn (Field Artillery)	1.50	1.50
B407	SP279	7.50 l + 7.50 l brn blk (Tank)	1.50	1.50
B408	SP279	8 l + 8 l dk vio (Warship)	1.50	1.50

Nos. B404-B408, CB18-CB19 (7) 15.75 15.75

Issued to honor the Romanian Army.

Nicolae Balcescu
SP280

Balcescu and Revolutionists
SP281

Balcescu, Sandor Petöfi and Revolutionists
SP282

Design: No. B412, Balcescu and revolutionists.

1948, June 1 — *Perf. 13x13½*

B409	SP280	2 l + 2 l car lake	1.00	1.00
B410	SP281	5 l + 5 l dk vio	1.00	1.00
B411	SP282	10 l + 10 l dk ol brn	1.00	1.00
B412	SP280	36 l + 18 l dp bl	1.75	1.75

Centenary of Revolution of 1848.

Loading Freighter—SP283

Designs: 3 l + 3 l, Lineman. 11 l + 11 l, Transport plane. 15 l + 15 l, Railroad train.

Photogravure
1948, Dec. 10 — *Perf. 14 Wmk. 289*
Center in Black.

B413	SP283	1 l + 1 l dk grn	1.50	1.50
B414	SP283	3 l + 3 l redsh brn	1.50	1.50
B415	SP283	11 l + 11 l dp bl	1.50	1.50
B416	SP283	15 l + 15 l red	1.50	1.50
a.	Sheet of 4		8.50	9.50

No. B416a contains four imperf. stamps similar to Nos. B413-B416 in changed colors, center in brown. Marginal inscriptions in scarlet. No gum. Size: 110x85mm.

Runners
SP284

Parade of Athletes
SP285

Perf. 13x13½, 13½x13.
1948, Dec. 31

| B421 | SP284 | 5 l + 5 l grn | 3.00 | 3.00 |
| B422 | SP285 | 10 l + 10 l brn vio | 5.50 | 5.50 |

Imperf.

| B423 | SP284 | 5 l + 5 l brn | 3.00 | 3.00 |
| B424 | SP285 | 10 l + 10 l red | 5.50 | 5.50 |

Nos. B421-CB21 (6) 52.00 52.00

Nos. B421 to B424 were issued in sheets of four stamps, with ornamental border and "1948" in contrasting color.

Souvenir Sheet.

SP286

1950, Jan. 27

| B425 | SP286 | 10 l carmine | 2.00 | 75 |

Philatelic exhibition, Bucharest. Label and inscriptions in dark blue and blue. Size: 110x80mm. Sold for 50 lei.

Crossing the Buzau,
by Denis Auguste Marie Raffet
SP287

1967, Nov. 15 Engraved *Perf. 13½*

| B426 | SP287 | 55b + 45b ocher & ind | 75 | 35 |

Stamp Day, 1967.

Old Bucharest, 18th Century Painting—SP288

1968, Nov. 15 Photo. *Perf. 13½*

| B427 | SP288 | 55b + 45b multi | 75 | 35 |

Stamp Day, 1968.

1969, Nov. 15
Design: 55b+45b, Courtyard, by M. Bouquet.

| B428 | SP288 | 55b + 45b multi | 60 | 30 |

Stamp Day, 1969. Se-tenant label at right of stamp carries 45b surtax and initials A F R.

1970, Nov. 15
Design: 55b+45b, Mail Coach in the Snow, by Emil Völkers.

| B429 | SP288 | 55b + 45b multi | 75 | 30 |

Stamp Day 1970. Se-tenant label at right of stamp (imperf. between) carries 45b surtax and initials A F R.

Lady with Letter, by Sava Hentia
SP289

1971, Nov. 15 Photo. *Perf. 13½*

| B430 | SP289 | 1.10 l + 90b multi | 90 | 70 |

Stamp Day 1971. Se-tenant label below stamp carries 90b surtax and shows Romania No. 12.

Stamp Day Type of 1968
Design: 1.10 l+90b, Traveling Gypsies, by Emil Volkers.

1972, Nov. 15 Photo. *Perf. 13½*

| B431 | SP288 | 1.10 l + 90b multi | 1.10 | 70 |

Stamp Day, 1972. Se-tenant label at left of stamp carries 90b surtax and A F R monogram.

Portrait Type of Regular Issue
Designs: 4 l+2 l, Barbat at his Desk, by B. Iscovescu. 6 l+2 l, The Poet Alecsandri with his Family, by N. Livaditti.

1973, June 20 Photo. *Perf. 13½*

| B432 | A728 | 4 l + 2 l multi | 2.00 | 75 |

Souvenir Sheet

| B433 | A728 | 6 l + 2 l multi | 3.00 | 3.00 |

See note after No. 2425. No. B433 contains one stamp (size: 38x500mm.) and green inscription in gold margin. Size: 77x90mm.

Postilion, by A. Verona
SP290

1973, Nov. 15 Photo. *Perf. 13½*

| B434 | SP290 | 1.10 l + 90b multi | 60 | 20 |

Stamp Day 1973.

Map of Europe with Emblem Marking Bucharest
SP291

1974, June 25 Photo. *Perf. 13½*

| B435 | SP291 | 4 l + 3 l multi | 2.00 | 75 |

EUROMAX, European Exhibition of Maximaphily, Bucharest, Oct. 6–13.

Marketplace, Sibiu
SP292

ROMANIA

1974, Nov. 15   Photo.   *Perf. 13½*
B436   SP292   2.10 l + 1.90 l multi   1.50   75

Stamp Day 1974.

No. B436 Overprinted in Red:
"EXPOZITIA FILATELICA 'NATIONALA '74' / 15–24 noiembrie / Bucuresti"

1974, Nov. 15
B437   SP292   2.10 l + 1.90 l multi   3.50   1.30

NATIONALA '74 Philatelic Exhibition, Bucharest, Nov. 15–24.

Post Office, Bucharest
SP293

Design: 2.10 l + 1.90 l, like B438, side view.

1975, Nov. 15   Photo.   *Perf. 13½*
B438   SP293   1.50 l + 1.50 l multi   1.00   30
B439   SP293   2.10 l + 1.90 l multi   1.30   40

Stamp Day.

No. 2612 Surcharged and Overprinted:
"EXPOZITIA FILATELICA / BUCURESTI / 12-19.IX.1976"

1976, Sept. 12   Photo.   *Perf. 13½*
B440   A787   3.60 l + 1.80 l   2.00   1.50

Philatelic Exhibition, Bucharest, Sept. 12–19.

Elena Cuza, by Theodor Aman
SP294

Dispatch Rider Handing Letter to Officer
SP295

1976, Nov. 15   Photo.   *Perf. 13½*
B441   SP294   2.10 l + 1.90 l multi   1.20   75

Stamp Day 1976.

Independence Type of 1977
Design: 4.80 l + 2 l, Battle of Rahova, after etching.

1977, May 9   Photo.   *Perf. 13½*
B442   A806   4.80 l + 2 l multi   1.90   68

1977, Nov.   Photo.   *Perf. 13½*
B443   SP295   2.10 l + 1.90 l multi   1.20   75

Stamp Day 1977.

Dacian Warrior, from Trajan's Column, Rome—SP296

1978, Nov. 5   Photo.   *Perf. 13x13½*
B444   SP296   6 l + 3 l multi   2.50   1.65

NATIONALA '78 Philatelic Exhibition, Bucharest.

Socfilex Type of 1979
Flower Paintings by Luchian: 4 l + 2 l, Field flowers. 10 l + 5 l, Roses.

1979, July 27   Photo.   *Perf. 13½*
B445   A847   4 l + 2 l multi   1.70   60

Souvenir Sheet
B446   A847   10 l + 5 l multi   4.50   1.75

Socfilex, Oct. 26-Nov. 1. International Philatelic Exhibition, Bucharest. No. B446 contains one stamp, size: 50x38mm; black marginal inscription. Size: 81x70½mm.

Stamp Day—SP297

1979, Dec. 12   Photo.   *Perf. 13½*
B447   SP297   2.10 l + 1.90 l multi   1.15   50

Souvenir Sheet

Stamp Day—SP298

1980, July 1   Photo.   *Perf. 13½*
B448   SP298   5 l + 5 l multi   2.50   1.00

Size: 79x91mm.

WE STOCK 267 COUNTRIES
(1840-1970)
PLUS UNITED STATES & POSSESSIONS
AND WE WANT YOUR WANT LIST.
(references or deposit please)
IF IT'S FOR.....
- **UNITED STATES,** Send it to Judy
- **BRITISH EMPIRE,** Send it to Richard
- **BNA & U.S. POSSESSIONS,** Send it to Charles
- **GENERAL FOREIGN,** Send it to George
- **PROOFS & RARITIES,** Send it to Irv
- **SUPPLIES & CATALOGUES,** Send it to Harry
- **AND IF IT'S FOR OUR AUCTION CATALOGUE,** Send it to Bert

Stampazine
EST. 1937
"The stamp store on the fifth floor."

3 East 57th Street,   212-752-5905   New York, NY 10022

ROMANIA

Unused Prices
Catalogue prices for unused stamps through 1960 are for hinged copies in fine condition. Never-hinged unused stamps issued before 1961 often sell above Catalogue prices. Current never-hinged prices for various countries will be found in the Scott StampMarket Update.

See "Special Notices" at the front of this volume for data on the listing methods of this Catalogue, abbreviations, condition, prices and examination.

AIR POST STAMPS.

Capt. C. G. Craiu's Airplane
AP1

Wmkd. Vertical Wavy Lines (95)
1928   Photogravure.   Perf. 13½.

C1	AP1	1 l red brn	3.00	3.00
C2	AP1	2 l brt bl	3.00	3.00
C3	AP1	5 l car rose	3.00	3.00

Wmkd. Horizontal Wavy Lines (95)

C4	AP1	1 l red brn	3.00	3.00
C5	AP1	2 l brt bl	3.00	3.00
C6	AP1	5 l car rose	3.00	3.00

1930
Nos. C4-C6 Overprinted **8 IUNIE 1930**

C7	AP1	1 l red brn	7.50	7.50
C8	AP1	2 l brt bl	7.50	7.50
	a. Vertical pair, imperf. between		300.00	
C9	AP1	5 l car rose	7.50	7.50

Same Overprint on Nos. C1-C3.
Wmkd. Vertical Wavy Lines (95)

C10	AP1	1 l red brn	60.00	60.00
C11	AP1	2 l brt bl	60.00	60.00
C12	AP1	5 l car rose	60.00	60.00

Nos. C7 to C12 commemorated the accession of King Carol II.
Excellent counterfeits are known of Nos. C10-C12.

King Carol II
AP2

1930, Oct. 4
Bluish Paper   Unwmkd.

C13	AP2	1 l dk vio	1.50	60
C14	AP2	2 l gray grn	2.00	60
C15	AP2	5 l red brn	3.50	1.25
C16	AP2	10 l brt bl	5.00	1.50

Junkers Monoplane
AP3

Monoplanes
AP7

Designs: 3 l, Monoplane with biplane behind. 5 l, Biplane. 10 l, Monoplane flying leftward.

1931, Nov. 4
Wmkd. Crowns and Monograms. (230)

C17	AP3	2 l dl grn	1.00	40
C18	AP3	3 l carmine	1.00	40
C19	AP3	5 l red brn	1.25	40
C20	AP3	10 l blue	3.50	75
C21	AP7	20 l dk vio	6.50	1.75
	Nos. C17-C21 (5)		13.25	3.60

Nos. C17 to C21 exist imperforate.

Souvenir Sheets.

Plane over Resita—AP8

Plane over Sinaia—AP9

Photogravure.
1945, Oct. 1   Perf. 13.   Wmk. 276
Without Gum.

| C22 | AP8 | 80 l sl grn | 4.00 | 4.00 |

Imperf.

| C23 | AP9 | 80 l magenta | 5.50 | 5.50 |

Issued in sheets measuring 75 x 55 mm. containing a single stamp, to commemorate the 16th Congress of the General Association of Romanian Engineers.

Plane—AP10

Design: 500 l, Aviator and planes.

1946, Sept. 5   Perf. 13½x13

| C24 | AP10 | 200 l yel grn & bl | 1.25 | 1.00 |
| C25 | AP10 | 500 l org red & dl bl | 1.25 | 1.00 |

Printed in sheets of four with marginal inscription.

Lockheed 12   CGM Congress
Electra   Emblem
AP12   AP13

1946, Oct.   Perf. 11½.

| C26 | AP12 | 300 l crimson | 75 | 75 |
| | a. Se-tenant with No. CB6 | | 2.00 | 2.00 |

Sheet of 16 contains 8 each of Nos. C26 and CB6, arranged so se-tenant or normal pairs are available. Two sheet layouts exist, one with No. C26 in corners and one with No. CB6 in corners.

1947, Mar.   Perf. 13x14   Wmk. 276

| C27 | AP13 | 1000 l blue | 40 | 40 |

Issued to commemorate the Congress of the United Labor Unions ("CGM"). Printed in sheets of 15.

"May 1"   Plane and
Supported by   Conference
Parachutes   Banner
AP14   AP17

Designs: C29, Air Force monument. C30, Plane over rural road.

1947, May 4   Perf. 11½

C28	AP14	3000 l vermilion	20	20
C29	AP14	3000 l grnsh gray	20	20
C30	AP14	3000 l blk brn	20	20

Printed in sheets of four with marginal inscriptions.

1947, Nov. 10   Perf. 14

| C31 | AP17 | 11 l bl & dp car | 40 | 30 |

Issued to commemorate the 2nd Trade Union Conference, November 10, 1947.

Emblem of the Republic
and Factories
AP18

Industry and Agriculture
AP19

Transportation—AP20

Photogravure
1948-50   Perf. 14x13½   Wmk. 289

C32	AP18	30 l cerise	35	8
	a. 30 l car ('50)		45	20
C33	AP19	50 l dk sl grn	55	45
C34	AP20	100 l ultra	1.50	50

Transportation—AP21

Design: 30 l, Agriculture.

1951-52   Perf. 13½   Wmk. 358

| C35 | AP21 | 30 l dk grn ('52) | 3.00 | 2.75 |
| C36 | AP21 | 50 l red brn | 2.25 | 1.75 |

Issued to publicize the 1951-55 Five Year Plan.

Nos. C32-C36 Surcharged with New Values in Blue or Carmine.

1952   Perf. 14x13½   Wmk. 289

| C37 | AP18 | 3b on 30 l cer | 60 | 15 |
| | a. 3b on 30 l car | | 10.00 | 9.00 |

ROMANIA

C38	AP19	3b on 50 l dk sl grn (C)	60	25
C39	AP20	3b on 100 l ultra (C)	60	40

Perf. 13½.
Wmk. 358

C40	AP21	1 l on 30 l dk grn (C)	7.50	3.00
C41	AP21	1 l on 50 l red brn (C)	7.50	3.00
		Nos. C37-C41 (5)	16.80	6.80

Nos. 706 and 707
Surcharged
in Blue
or Carmine

1953   **Perf. 13½, 14**   **Wmk. 289**

C43	A250	3 l on 20 l org brn	12.00	12.00
C44	A251	5 l on 30 l brt bl (C)	17.50	17.50

Plane facing right and surcharge arranged to fit design on No. C44.

Plane over City   **Sputnik 1 and Earth**
AP22   AP23

Designs: 55b, Plane over Mountains. 1.75 l, over Harvest fields. 2.25 l, over Seashore.

1956, Dec. 15   **Photo.**   **Wmk. 358**
Perf. 14½x14

C45	AP22	20b brt bl, org & grn	40	10
C46	AP22	55b brt bl, grn & ocher	70	10
C47	AP22	1.75 l brt bl & red org	1.75	25
C48	AP22	2.55 l brt bl & red org	2.25	25

1957, Nov. 6   **Perf. 14**

Design: 3.75 l, Sputniks 1 and 2 circling globe.

C49	AP23	25b brt ultra	60	20
C50	AP23	25b dk bl grn	60	20
C51	AP23	3.75 l brt ultra	3.00	50
C52	AP23	3.75 l dk bl grn	3.00	50

Nos. C49 and C51 are printed se-tenant with gray label. Nos. C50 and C52 are printed se-tenant with brown label. Each sheet contains 27 triptychs with the center rows arranged tete-beche.
In 1958 Nos. C49-C52 were overprinted: 1.) "Expozitia Universal a Bruxelles 1958") and star. 2.) Large star. 3.) Small star.

Animal Type of Regular Issue, 1957.
Birds: 3.30 l, Black-headed gull (horiz.). 5 l, Sea eagle (horiz.).

Perf. 14x13½

1957, Dec. 27   **Wmk. 358**

C53	A445	3.30 l ultra & gray	4.00	1.00
C54	A445	5 l car & org	6.00	1.50

Armed Forces Type of Regular Issue.
Design: Flier and planes.
Photogravure.

1958, Oct. 2   **Perf. 13½x13**   **Unwmkd.**

C55	A458	3.30 l brt vio	1.75	90

Issued for the Day of the Armed Forces, Oct. 2.

Earth and Sputnik 3 Orbit
AP24

1958, Sept. 20   **Perf. 14x13½**

C56	AP24	3.25 l ind & ocher	3.25	1.00

Launching of Sputnik 3, May 15, 1958.

Souvenir Sheet
Type of Regular Issue, 1958.
Design: Tête bêche pair of 27pa of 1858.
Engraved.

1958, Nov. 15   **Perf. 11½**   **Unwmkd.**

C57	A462	10 l blue	16.50	16.50

No. C57 measures 79x89mm. with marginal inscription in blue. Issued to commemorate the centenary of Romanian postage stamps. A similar sheet, printed in dull red and imperf., exists.
No. C57 was overprinted in 1959 in vermilion to commemorate the 10th anniversary of the State Philatelic Trade.
Prices, $30 and $50.

Lunik I   **Frederic**
Leaving Earth   **Joliot-Curie**
AP25   AP26

1959, Feb. 4   **Photo.**   **Perf. 14**

C58	AP25	3.25 l vio bl, *pnksh*	1.50	1.50

Issued to commemorate the launching of the "first artificial planet of the solar system."

1959, Apr. 25   **Perf. 13½x14**

C59	AP26	3.25 l ultra	3.00	1.00

Issued to honor Frederic Joliot-Curie and the 10th anniversary of the World Peace Movement.

Rock Thrush
AP27

Birds: 20b, European golden oriole. 35b, Lapwing. 40b, Barn swallow. 60, Goldfinch. No. C65, Great spotted woodpecker. No. C66, Great tit. 1 l, Bullfinch. 1.55 l, Long-tailed tit. 5 l, Wall creeper. Nos. C62-C67 vertical.

1959, June 25   **Litho.**   **Perf. 14**
Birds in Natural Colors.

C60	AP27	10b gray, *cr*	10	5
C61	AP27	20b gray, *grysh*	10	5
C62	AP27	35b gray, *grysh*	12	6
C63	AP27	40b gray & red, *pnksh*	15	6
C64	AP27	55b gray, *buff*	30	8
C65	AP27	55b gray, *grnsh*	30	10
C66	AP27	55b gray & ol, *grysh*	30	10
C67	AP27	1 l gray and red, *cr*	1.00	15
C68	AP27	1.55 l gray & red, *pnksh*	1.50	15
C69	AP27	5 l gray, *grnsh*	4.25	75
		Nos. C60-C69 (10)	8.12	1.55

No. C58
Surcharged
in Red

PRIMA RACHETA COSMICA IN LUNA
5 LEI

1959, Sept. 14   **Photo.**   **Unwmkd.**

C70	AP25	5 l on 3.25 l vio bl, *pnksh*	7.50	1.50

Issued to commemorate the first Russian rocket to reach the moon, Sept. 14, 1959.

Prince Vlad Tepes and Document — AP28
Engraved.

1959, Sept. 15   **Perf. 11½x11**

C71	AP28	20 l vio brn	60.00	60.00

Issued to commemorate the 500th anniversary of the founding of Bucharest. Issued in miniature sheets of one. Size: 65½x86mm.

Sport Type of Regular Issue, 1959.
Design: 2.80 l, Boating.

1959, Oct. 5   **Litho.**   **Perf. 13½**

C72	A474	2.80 l multi	2.50	75

Soviet Rocket, Globe, Dog and Rabbit
AP29

Photograph of Far Side of the Moon
AP30

Design: 1.75 l, Trajectory of Lunik 3, which hit the moon.

1959, Dec. Photogravure Wmk. 358
Perf. 14, 13½ (AP30)

C73	AP29	1.55 l dk bl	2.25	50
C74	AP30	1.60 l dk vio bl, *buff*	2.25	50
C75	AP29	1.75 l dk bl	2.25	50

Soviet conquest of space.

Animal Type of Regular Issue, 1960.
Designs: 1.30 l, Golden eagle. 1.75 l, Black grouse. 2 l, Lammergeyer.
Engraved.

1960, Mar. 3   **Perf. 14**   **Unwmkd.**

C76	A480	1.30 l dk bl	1.25	25
C77	A480	1.75 l ol grn	1.75	30
C78	A480	2 l dk car	2.25	35

Aurel Vlaicu and Plane of 1910
AP31

Bucharest Airport and Turbo-Jet
AP32

Designs: 20b, Plane and Aurel Vlaicu. 35b, Amphibian ambulance plane. 40b, Plane spraying crops. 55b, Pilot and planes (vert.). 1.75 l, Parachutes at aviation sports meet.

Lithographed, Unwmkd.: 10b, 20b, 1.60 l, 1.75 l.
Photogravure, Wmk. 358: 35b, 40b, 55b.

1960, June 15   **Perf. 14**

C79	AP31	10b yel & brn	10	8
C80	AP31	20b red org & brn	15	8
C81	AP31	35b crimson	25	8
C82	AP31	40b violet	30	8
C83	AP31	55b blue	35	8
C84	AP32	1.60 l vio bl, yel & emer	1.25	30
C85	AP32	1.75 l bl, red, brn & pale grn	1.75	40
		Nos. C79-C85 (7)	4.15	1.10

Issued to commemorate the 50th anniversary of the first Romanian airplane flight by Aurel Vlaicu.

Bucharest   **Sputnik 4 Flying**
Airport   **into Space**
AP33   AP34

Photogravure

1960   **Perf. 14**   **Wmk. 358**

C86	AP33	3.20 l brt ultra	1.75	25

Type of Regular Issue, 1960
Black Sea Resort: 2 l, Beach at Mamaia.

1960, Aug. 2   **Litho.**   **Unwmkd.**

C87	A491	2 l grn, org & lt bl	1.50	45

New resort towns on Black Sea.

1960, June 8   **Photo.**   **Wmk. 358**

C88	AP34	55b dp bl	1.75	25

Launching of Sputnik 4, May 15, 1960.

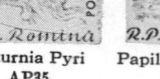
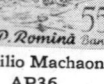

Saturnia Pyri   **Papilio Machaon**
AP35   AP36

ROMANIA 263

Limenitis Populi
AP37

Designs: 40b, Chrisophanus virgaureae. 1.60 l, Acherontia atropos. 1.75 l, Apatura iris (horiz.).

Perf. 13, 14x12½, 14
1960, Oct. 10   Typo.   Unwmkd.

C89	AP35	10b multi	5	5
C90	AP37	20b multi	10	5
C91	AP37	40b multi	20	5
C92	AP36	55b multi	45	15
C93	AP36	1.60 l multi	1.00	20
C94	AP36	1.75 l multi	1.25	35
	Nos. C89-C94 (6)		3.05	85

Compass Rose and Jet
AP38

Perf. 13½x14
1960, Nov. 1   Photo.   Wmk. 358

| C95 | AP38 | 55b brt bl + 45b label | 90 | 30 |

Stamp Day. In sheet, stamps alternate with olive bister label.

Skier—AP39

Slalom   Maj. Yuri
AP40   A. Gagarin
              AP41

Designs: 25b, Skiers going up. 40b, Bobsled. 55b, Ski jump. 1 l, Mountain climber. 1.55 l, Long-distance skier.

Perf. 14x13½, 13½x14
1961, March 18   Litho.   Unwmkd.

C96	AP39	10b ol & gray	10	5
C97	AP40	20b gray & dk red	15	5
C98	AP40	25b gray & bl grn	15	5
C99	AP40	40b gray & pur	20	6
C100	AP39	55b gray & ultra	35	8
C101	AP40	1 l gray & brn lake	75	14
C102	AP39	1.55 l gray & brn	1.35	30
	Nos. C96-C102 (7)		3.05	73

Exist imperf. with changed colors.
Price, set $7.

Perf. 14x14½, 14½x14
1961, Apr. 19   Photo.   Unwmkd.

Design: 3.20 l, Gagarin in space capsule and globe with orbit (horiz.).

| C103 | AP41 | 1.35 l brt bl | 1.00 | 20 |
| C104 | AP41 | 3.20 l ultra | 1.75 | 30 |

No. C104 exists imperf. in dk carmine rose.
Price unused $5, canceled $2.

Eclipse over Republic Palace Place, Bucharest—AP42

Design: 1.75 l, Total Eclipse, Scintela House and telescope.

Perf. 14x13½
1961, June 13   Wmk. 358

| C106 | AP42 | 1.60 l ultra | 1.25 | 15 |
| C107 | AP42 | 1.75 l dk bl | 1.25 | 20 |

Total solar eclipse of Feb. 15, 1961.

Maj. Gherman   Globe
S. Titov   and Stamps
AP43   AP44

Designs: 55b, "Peace" and Vostok 2 rocket. 1.75 l, Yuri A. Gagarin and Gherman S. Titov (horiz.).

Perf. 13½x14
1961, Sept. 11   Unwmkd.

C108	AP43	55b dp bl	45	8
C109	AP43	1.35 l dp pur	1.10	15
C110	AP43	1.75 l dk car	1.35	20

Issued to honor the Russian space navigators Y. A. Gagarin and G. S. Titov.

1961, Nov. 15   Litho.   Perf. 13½x14

| C111 | AP44 | 55b multi + 45b label | 75 | 25 |

Stamp Day. In sheet, stamps alternate with red orange and blue label.

Railroad Station, Constanta
AP45

Buildings: 20b, Tower, RPR Palace place (vert.). 55b, Congress hall, Bucharest. 75b, Mill, Hunedoara. 1 l, Apartment houses, Bucharest. 1.20 l, Circus, Bucharest. 1.75 l, Worker's Club, Mangalia.

Perf. 13½x14, 14x13½
1961, Nov. 20   Typographed

C112	AP45	14b multi	14	5
C113	AP45	40b multi	25	5
C114	AP45	55b multi	25	7
C115	AP45	75b multi	40	10
C116	AP45	1 l multi	50	14
C117	AP45	1.20 l multi	1.00	30
C118	AP45	1.75 l multi	1.50	40
	Nos. C112-C118 (7)		4.04	1.11

Space Exploration Stamps and Dove
AP46

Design: Each stamp shows a different group of Romanian space exploration stamps.

1962, July 27   Perf. 14x13½

C119	AP46	35b yel brn	20	5
C120	AP46	55b green	30	5
C121	AP46	1.35 l blue	60	20
C122	AP46	1.75 l rose red	1.00	20
a.	Sheet of 4		3.50	1.50

Peaceful space exploration.
No. C122a contains four imperf. stamps similar to Nos. C119-C122 in changed colors and with one dove covering all four stamps. Stamps are printed together without space between. Size: 106x79mm.

Andrian G. Nikolayev
AP47

Designs: 1.60 l, Globe and trajectories of Vostoks 3 and 4. 1.75 l, Pavel R. Popovich.

Perf. 13½x14
1962, Aug. 20   Photo.   Unwmkd.

C123	AP47	55b purple	45	6
C124	AP47	1.60 l dk bl	1.25	18
C125	AP47	1.75 l rose cl	1.50	20

Issued to commemorate the first Russian group space flight of Vostoks 3 and 4, Aug. 11–15, 1962.

Exhibition Hall   The Coachmen
AP48   by Szatmary
                    AP49

1962, Oct. 12   Litho.   Perf. 14x13

| C126 | AP48 | 1.60 l bl, vio bl & org | 1.50 | 25 |

4th Sample Fair, Bucharest.

1962, Nov. 15   Perf. 13½x14

| C127 | AP49 | 55b Prus bl & blk + 45b label | 1.00 | 25 |

Stamp Day. Alternating label shows No. 14 on cover.

No. C127
Overprinted
in Violet

1963, Mar. 30

| C128 | AP49 | 55b Prus bl & blk + 45b label | 2.50 | 2.00 |

Issued for the Romanian Philatelists' Association meeting at Bucharest, Mar. 30. The overprint is centered on the stamp and label, about half of it on each.

Sighisoara Glass and Crockery Factory
AP50

Industrial Plants: 40b, Govora soda works. 55b, Tirgul-Jiu wood processing factory. 1 l, Savinesti chemical plant (synthetic fibers). 1.55 l, Hunedoara metal factory. 1.75 l, Brazi thermal power station.

Photogravure
1963, Apr. 10   Perf. 14x13   Unwmkd.

C129	AP50	30b dk bl & red	15	5
C130	AP50	40b sl grn & pur	20	5
C131	AP50	55b brn red & dp bl	25	8
C132	AP50	1 l vio & brn	40	12
C133	AP50	1.55 l ver & dk bl	90	16
C134	AP50	1.75 l dk bl & mag	1.25	20
	Nos. C129-C134 (6)		3.15	66

Industrial achievements.

Lunik 4 Approaching Moon
AP51

1963, Apr. 29   Perf. 13½x14

| C135 | AP51 | 55b dk ultra & red | 60 | 15 |

Imperf.

| C136 | AP51 | 1.75 l vio & red | 1.25 | 25 |

Moon flight of Lunik 4, Apr. 2, 1963.

Steam Locomotive
AP52

Designs: 55b, Diesel locomotive. 75b, Trolley bus. 1.35 l, Passenger ship. 1.75 l, Plane.

1963, July 10   Litho.   Perf. 14½x13

C137	AP52	40b multi	15	5
C138	AP52	55b multi	30	7
C139	AP52	75b multi	45	8
C140	AP52	1.35 l multi	90	30
C141	AP52	1.75 l multi	1.00	40
	Nos. C137-C141 (5)		2.80	90

Valeri Bykovski
AP53

Designs: 1.20 l, Bykovski (vert.). 1.60 l, Tereshkova (vert.). 1.75 l, Valentina Tereshkova.

1963   Photogravure

| C142 | AP53 | 55b blue | 30 | 15 |
| C143 | AP53 | 1.75 l rose red | 1.10 | 35 |

Souvenir Sheet
Perf. 13

C144	AP53	Souv. sheet of 2	3.00	1.00
a.	1.20 l ultra		85	45
b.	1.60 l ultra		85	45

Issued to commemorate the space flights of Valeri Bykovski, June 14–19, and Valentina Tereshkova, first woman cosmonaut, June 16–19, 1963. No. C144 has orange inscription. Size: 118x80mm.

ROMANIA

No. C79 Surcharged and Overprinted:
"1913–1963 50 ani de la moarte"
Lithographed
1963, Sept. 15   Perf. 14   Unwmkd.
C145 AP31   1.75 l on 10b yel & brn   1.75   50

Issued to commemorate the 50th anniversary of the death of Aurel Vlaicu, aviation pioneer.

Centenary Stamp of 1958
AP54

Stamps on Stamps: 40b, Sputnik 2 and Laika, No. 1200. 55b, Yuri A. Gagarin, No. C104a. 1.20 l, Nikolayev and Popovich, Nos. C123 & C125. 1.55 l, Postal Administration Bldg. and letter carrier, No. 965.

1963, Nov. 15   Photo.   Perf. 14x13½
Size: 38x26mm.
C146	AP54	20b lt bl & dk brn	9	5
C147	AP54	40b brt pink & dk bl	21	5
C148	AP54	55b lt ultra & dk car rose	30	6
C149	AP54	1.20 l ocher & pur	75	20
C150	AP54	1.55 l sal pink & ol gray	75	25
		Nos. C146-C150, CB22 (6)	3.85	1.17

15th UPU Congress, Vienna.

Pavel R. Popovich
AP55

Astronauts and flag: 5b, Yuri A. Gagarin. 10b, Gherman S. Titov. 20b, John H. Glenn, Jr. 35b, M. Scott Carpenter. 40b, Andrian G. Nikolayev. 60b, Walter M. Schirra. 75b, Gordon L. Cooper. 1 l, Valeri Bykovski. 1.40 l, Valentina Tereshkova. (5b, 10b, 20b, 35b, 60b and 75b are diamond shaped).

Perf. 13½
1964, Jan. 15   Litho.   Unwmkd.
Light Blue Background
C151	AP55	5b red, yel & vio bl	10	5
C152	AP55	10b red, yel & pur	10	5
C153	AP55	20b red, ultra & ol gray	20	5
C154	AP55	35b red, ultra & sl bl	30	5
C155	AP55	40b red, ultra & ultra	30	5
C156	AP55	55b red, ultra & ultra	45	8
C157	AP55	60b ultra, red & sep	60	8
C158	AP55	75b red, ultra & dk bl	75	12
C159	AP55	1 l red, yel & mar	90	25
C160	AP55	1.40 l red, yel & mar	1.10	30
		Nos. C151-C160 (10)	4.80	1.08

Nos. C151–C160 exist imperf. in changed colors. Price, set $8.
A miniature sheet contains one imperf. horizontal 2 l ultramarine and yellow stamp. Size of stamp: 59½x43mm.; size of sheet: 120x79mm. Price unused $10, canceled $4.

Modern and 19th Century Post Office Buildings
AP56
Engraved and Typographed
1964, Nov. 15   Perf. 13½
C161 AP56   1.60 l ultra + 40b label   1.25   35

Issued for Stamp Day, 1964. Stamp and label are imperf. between. Label is dark red. Inscription between stamp and label is yellow.

Plane Approaching Airport and Coach Leaving Gate
AP57
Engraved and Typographed
1966, Oct. 20   Perf. 13½
C162 AP57   55b sep, ocher & grn + 45b label   75   18

Issued for Stamp Day, 1966. Label is ocher and sepia. Blue inscription between stamp and label.

Space Exploration Type of Regular Issue

U.S. Achievements in Space: 1.20 l, Early Bird satellite and globe. 1.55 l, Mariner 4 transmitting pictures of the moon. 3.25 l, Gemini 6 & 7, rendezvous in space. 5 l, Gemini 8 meeting Agena rocket, and globe.

1967, Feb. 15   Photo.   Perf. 13½
C163	A595	1.20 l sil & multi	50	10
C164	A595	1.55 l sil & multi	75	10
C165	A595	3.25 l sil & multi	1.30	20
C166	A595	5 l sil & multi	3.00	1.00

10 years of space exploration.

Plane Spraying Crops
AP58

Moon, Earth and Path of Apollo 8
AP59

Designs: 55b, Aerial ambulance over river (horiz.). 1 l, Red Cross and plane. 2.40 l, Biplane and Mircea Zorileanu, aviation pioneer.

Perf. 12x12½, 12½x12
1968, Feb. 28   Litho.   Unwmkd.
C167	AP58	40b bl grn, blk & yel brn	20	5
C168	AP58	55b multi	20	8
C169	AP58	1 l ultra, pale grn & red org	45	12
C170	AP58	2.40 l brt rose lil & multi	1.50	50

1969, Jan. 17   Photo.   Perf. 13½
Design: No. C172, Soyuz 4 and 5 over globe with map of Russia.
C171	AP59	3.30 l multi	2.50	50
C172	AP59	3.30 l multi	2.00	50

Issued to commemorate the first manned flight around the Moon, Dec. 21–27, 1968, and the first team flights of the Russian spacecrafts Soyuz 4 and 5, Jan. 16, 1969. See note after Hungary No. C284.
Issued in sheets of 4; decorative margin with silver panels and inscriptions in blue and black.
No. C171 was issued Jan. 17, No. C172, Mar. 28.

Apollo 9 and Lunar Landing Module over Earth
AP60

Design: 2.40 l, Apollo 10 and lunar landing module over moon (vert.).
1969, June 15   Photo.   Perf. 13½
C173	AP60	60b multi	21	7
C174	AP60	2.40 l multi	1.00	35

U.S. space explorations, Apollo 9 and 10.

First Man on Moon
AP61

1969, July 24   Photo.   Perf. 13½
C175 AP61   3.30 l multi   1.75   1.25

Issued to commemorate man's first landing on the moon July 20, 1969, U.S. astronauts Neil A. Armstrong and Col. Edwin E. Aldrin, Jr., with Lieut. Col. Michael Collins piloting Apollo 11. Printed in sheets of 4; decorative margin with portraits of the 3 astronauts and silver panel with commemorative inscription.

1970, June 29
Design: 1.50 l, Apollo 13 capsule splashing down in Pacific.
C176 AP61   1.50 l multi   75   75

Issued to commemorate the flight and safe landing of Apollo 13, Apr. 11–17, 1970. Printed in sheets of 4; decorative margin with portraits of astronauts Capt. James A. Lovell, Jr., Fred W. Haise, Jr., and John L. Swigert, Jr., and silver panel with commemorative inscription.

BAC 1-11 Jet
AP62

Design: 2 l, Fuselage BAC 1-11 and control tower, Bucharest airport.
1970, Apr. 6
C177	AP62	60b multi	30	14
C178	AP62	2 l multi	90	45

Issued to commemorate the 50th anniversary of Romanian civil aviation.

Flood Relief Type of Regular Issue

Design: 60b, Rescue by helicopter.
1970, Sept. 25   Photo.   Perf. 13½
C179 A671   60b bl gray, blk & ol   30   16

Issued to publicize the plight of the victims of the Danube flood. No. C179 printed as a triptych with Nos. 2206–2207.

Henri Coanda's Model Plane
AP63

1970, Dec. 1
C180 AP63   60b multi   35   16

Henri Coanda's first flight, 60th anniversary.

Luna 16 on Moon
AP64

Design: No. C182, Lunokhod 1, unmanned vehicle on moon. No. C183, U.S. astronaut and vehicle on moon.
1971, Mar. 5   Photo.   Perf. 13½
C181	AP64	3.30 l sil & multi	1.50	1.00
C182	AP64	3.30 l sil & multi	1.50	1.00
C183	AP64	3.30 l sil & multi	1.50	1.00

No. C181 commemorates Luna 16 Russian unmanned, automatic moon mission, Sept. 12–24, 1970 (labels are incorrectly inscribed Oct. 12–24). No. C182 commemorates Lunokhod 1 (Luna 17), Nov. 10–17, 1970. Nos. C181–C182 printed in sheets of 4 stamps, arranged checkerwise, and 4 labels. No. C183 commemorates U.S. moon landing, Jan. 31–Feb. 9. Printed in sheets of 4 with 4 labels showing portraits of U.S. astronauts Alan B. Shepard, Edgar D. Mitchell, Stuart A. Roosa, and Apollo 14 emblem.

Souvenir Sheet

Cosmonauts Patsayev, Dobrovolsky and Volkov—AP65

1971, July 26   Litho.   Perf. 13½
C184 AP65   6 l blk & ultra   6.00   6.00

In memory of Russian cosmonauts Viktor I. Patsayev, Georgi T. Dobrovolsky and Vladislav N. Volkov, who died during Soyuz 11 space mission, June 6–30, 1971. No. C184 has gray margin with black inscription, control number and spacecraft design in silver.   Size: 100x80mm.
No. C184 exists imperf. in black & blue green; Size: 130x90mm.

ROMANIA

Lunar Rover on Moon—AP66
1971, Aug. 26   Photogravure
C185 AP66 1.50 l bl & multi   1.25   1.00
U.S. Apollo 15 moon mission, July 26–Aug. 7, 1971. No. C185 printed in sheets of 4 stamps and 4 labels showing astronauts David Scott, James Irwin, Alfred Worden and Apollo 15 emblem with cables.
No. C185 exists imperf. in green & multicolored. The sheet has a control number.

Olympic Souvenir Sheets
Designs: No. C186, Torchbearer and map of Romania. No. C187, Soccer.
1972 Photo. *Perf. 13½*
C186 A699 6 l pale grn & multi   6.00   6.00
C187 A699 6 l bl & multi   6.00   6.00
20th Olympic Games, Munich, Aug. 26–Sept. 11. No. C186 contains one stamp (size: 50x38mm.). Gray margin with multicolored design and greenish gray control number. Size: 100x83mm. No. C187 contains one stamp (size: 48½x37mm.). Blue and multicolored margin with Olympic emblems and green control number. Size: 89x77mm.
Issue dates: No. C186, Apr. 25. No. C187, Sept. 29.
Two imperf. 6 l souvenir sheets exist, one showing equestrian, the other a satellite over globe. Size of sheets: 129x90mm.

Lunar Rover on Moon AP67
1972, May 10 Photo. *Perf. 13½*
C188 AP67 3 l vio bl, rose & gray grn   1.50   75
Apollo 16 U.S. moon mission, Apr. 15–27, 1972. No. C188 printed in sheets of 4 stamps and 4 gray green and black labels showing Capt. John W. Young, Lt. Comdr. Thomas K. Mattingly 2nd, Col. Charles M. Duke, Jr., and Apollo 16 badge.

Aurel Vlaicu and Monoplane AP68
Design: 3 l, Traian Vuja and his flying machine.
1972, Aug. 15
C189 AP68 60b multi   30   10
C190 AP68 3 l multi   1.25   45
Romanian aviation pioneers.

Souvenir Sheet
Olympic Medals Type of Regular Issue
Designs: 6 l, Olympic silver and gold medals (horiz.).
1972, Sept. 29 Litho. *Perf. 13½*
C191 A714 6 l multi   6.00   6.00
Romanian medalists at 20th Olympic Games. No. C191 contains one stamp. Light olive green and lemon margin with black inscription and dark green control number. Size: 90x80mm. An imperf. 6 l souvenir sheet exists showing gold medal. Blue margin with blue design and control number. Size: 129x90mm.

Souvenir Sheet
Apollo Type of Regular Issue
Design: 6 l, Lunar rover, landing module, rocket and astronauts on moon (horiz.).
1972, Dec. 27 Photo. *Perf. 13½*
C192 A715 6 l vio bl, bis & dl grn   5.00   5.00
U.S. Apollo space program. No. C192 contains one stamp (size: 48½x36mm.). Gray and dull green margin with gray control number. Size: 89x78mm.
An imperf. 6 l souvenir sheet exists showing surface of moon with landing sites of last 6 Apollo missions and landing capsule. Violet blue margin with red inscription and blue control number. Size: 104x80mm.

Type of Regular Issue, 1972
Design: 14.60 l, Otopeni Airport (horiz.).
1972, Dec. 20 Photo. *Perf. 13*
Size: 29x21mm.
C193 A710 14.60 l brt bl   4.00   50

Apollo and Soyuz Spacecraft AP69
Design: 3.25 l, Apollo and Soyuz after link-up.
1975, July 14 Photo. *Perf. 13½*
C196 AP69 1.75 l vio bl, red & ol   75   30
C197 AP69 3.25 l vio bl, red & ol   1.25   70
Apollo Soyuz space test project (Russo-American cooperation), launching July 15; link-up, July 17. Nos. C196-C197 printed in sheets of 4 stamps, arranged checkerwise, and 4 rose lilac labels showing Apollo-Soyuz emblem.

European Security and Cooperation Conference—AP70
1975, July 30 Photo. *Perf. 13½*
C198 AP70 Sheet of 4, multi   6.00   6.00
  a. 2.75 l *Map of Europe*   90   90
  b. 2.75 l *Peace doves*   90   90
  c. 5 l *Open book*   1.65   1.65
  d. 5 l *Children playing*   1.65   1.65
European Security and Cooperation Conference, Helsinki, July 30–Aug. 1. No. C198 has blue marginal inscription. No. C198b inscribed "posta aeriana." Size: 110x80mm.
An imperf. 10 l souvenir sheet exists showing Helsinki on map of Europe. Size: 84x114mm.

Red Cross Type of 1976
Design: 3.35 l, Blood donors, Red Cross plane.
1976, Apr. 20 Photo. *Perf. 13½*
C199 A790 3.35 l multi   80   35
Romanian Red Cross centenary.

De Havilland DH-9 AP71

Airplanes: 40b, I.C.A.R.Comercial. 60b, Douglas DC-3. 1.75 l, AN-24. 2.75 l, IL-62. 3.60 l, Boeing 707.
1976, June 24 Photo. *Perf. 13½*
C200 AP71 20b bl & multi   6   5
C201 AP71 40b bl & multi   12   5
C202 AP71 60b multi   12   6
C203 AP71 1.75 l bl & multi   40   20
C204 AP71 2.75 l bl & multi   70   30
C205 AP71 3.60 l multi   1.00   45
  Nos. C200-C205 (6)   2.40   1.11
Romanian Airline, 50th anniversary.

Glider I.C.A.R.-1—AP72
Designs (Gliders): 40b, I.S.-3d. 55b, R.G.-5. 1.50 l, I.S.-11. 3 l, I.S.-29D. 3.40 l, I.S.-28B.
1977, Feb. 20 Photo. *Perf. 13*
C206 AP72 20b multi   5   5
C207 AP72 40b multi   10   5
C208 AP72 55b multi   14   5
C209 AP72 1.50 l bl & multi   30   15
C210 AP72 3 l multi   65   25
C211 AP72 3.40 l multi   80   32
  Nos. C206-C211 (6)   2.04   87

Souvenir Sheet

Boeing 707 over Bucharest Airport and Pioneers—AP73
1977, June 28 Photo. *Perf. 13½*
C212 AP73 10 l multi   3.50   3.50
European Security and Cooperation Conference, Belgrade. No. C212 has blue marginal inscription and black control number. Size: 80x71mm.
An imperf. 10 l souvenir sheet exists showing Boeing 707, map of Europe and buildings; blue marginal inscription and red control number. Size: 90x75mm.

Woman Letter Carrier, Mailbox AP74
Design: 30 l, Plane, newspapers, letters, packages.
1977   Photo. *Perf. 13½*
C213 AP74 20 l multi   4.50   1.50
C214 AP74 30 l multi   7.00   2.25
Issue dates: 20 l, July 25, 30 l, Sept. 10.

LZ-1 over Friedrichshafen, 1900—AP75

Airships: 1 l, Santos Dumont's dirigible over Paris, 1901. 1.50 l, British R-34 over New York and Statue of Liberty, 1919. 2.15 l, Italia over North Pole, 1928. 3.40 l, Zeppelin LZ-127 over Brasov, 1929. 4.80 l, Zeppelin over Sibiu, 1929. 10 l, Zeppelin over Bucharest, 1929.
1978, Mar. 20 Photo. *Perf. 13½*
C215 AP75 60b multi   12   8
C216 AP75 1 l multi   20   10
C217 AP75 1.50 l multi   30   15
C218 AP75 2.15 l multi   45   15
C219 AP75 3.40 l multi   75   25
C220 AP75 4.80 l multi   1.00   30
  Nos. C215-C220 (6)   2.82   1.03

Souvenir Sheet
C221 AP75 10 l multi   3.00   3.00
History of airships. No. C221 contains one stamp (50x37½mm.). Salmon margin with black control number. Size: 80x70mm.

Souvenir Sheet
Soccer Type of 1978
Design: 10 l, Two soccer players and Argentina '78 emblem.
1978, Apr. 15 Photo. *Perf. 13½*
C222 A818 10 l bl & multi   3.00   3.00
11th World Cup Soccer Championship, Argentina, June 1–25. No. C222 contains one stamp (37x50mm.). Multicolored margin shows satellite, stadium and black control number. Size: 80x70mm. A 10 l imperf. souvenir sheet exists showing goalkeeper.

Wilbur and Orville Wright, Flyer A AP76
Aviation History: 1 l, Louis Blériot and his plane over English Channel, 1909. 1.50 l, Anthony Fokker and Fokker F-VII trimotor, 1926. 2.15 l, Andrei N. Tupolev and ANT-25 monoplane, 1937. 3 l, Otto Lilienthal and glider, 1891–96. 3.40 l, Traian Vuia and his plane, Montesson, France, 1906. 4.80 l, Aurel Vlaicu and 1st Romanian plane, 1910. 10 l, Henri Coanda and his "jet," 1910.
1978, Dec. 18 Photo. *Perf. 13½*
C223 AP76 55b multi   10   6
C224 AP76 1 l multi   20   10
C225 AP76 1.50 l multi   30   15
C226 AP76 2.15 l multi   45   15
C227 AP76 3 l multi   65   20
C228 AP76 3.40 l multi   75   20
C229 AP76 4.80 l multi   1.00   35
  Nos. C223-C229 (7)   3.45   1.21

Souvenir Sheet
C230 AP76 10 l multi   3.75   3.75
No. C230 contains one stamp (50x38 mm.); yellow and magenta margin. Size: 78x70mm.

Inter-Europa Type of 1979
Design: 3.40 l, Jet, mail truck and motorcycle.
1979, May 3 Photo. *Perf. 13*
C231 A835 3.40 l multi   95   30
See note after No. 2830.

Animal Type of 1980
Souvenir Sheet
1980, Mar. 25 Photo. *Perf. 13½*
C232 A851 10 l *Pelicans*   3.25   3.25
European Nature Protection Year. No. C232 contains one stamp (38x50mm). Multicolored margin shows birds flying over water; black control number. Size: 89x78mm.

265

ROMANIA

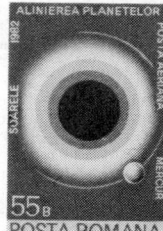

Mercury—AP77

1981, June 30		Photo.	Perf. 13½	
C233	AP77	55b shown	15	6
C234	AP77	1 l Venus, Earth, Mars	20	10
C235	AP77	1.50 l Jupiter	30	15
C236	AP77	2.15 l Saturn	45	20
C237	AP77	3.40 l Uranus	75	25
C238	AP77	4.80 l Neptune, Pluto	1.00	50
		Nos. C233-C238 (6)	2.85	1.26

Souvenir Sheet

| C239 | AP77 | 10 l Earth | 3.00 | 3.00 |

No. C239 contains one stamp (37x50mm.). Multicolored margin shows planets in orbit; black control number. Size: 90x78mm. An imperf. 10 l souvenir sheet exists showing planets in orbit; red control number. Size: 106x80mm.

Romanian-Russian Space Cooperation—AP78

1981		Photo.	Perf. 13½	
C240	AP78	55b Soyuz 40	15	6
C241	AP78	3.40 l Salyut 6, Soyuz 40	75	40

Souvenir Sheet

| C242 | AP78 | 10 l Cosmonauts, spacecraft | 3.00 | 3.00 |

No. C242 contains one stamp (50x39mm.); multicolored margin shows flags, early planes. Size: 78x90mm. Issue dates: 55b, 3.40 l, May 14; 10 l, June 30.

Children's Games Type of 1981

1981, Nov. 25

| C243 | A880 | 4.80 l Flying model planes | 1.00 | 50 |

Standard Glider—AP79

1982, June 20		Photo.	Perf. 13½	
C244	AP79	50b shown	12	5
C245	AP79	1 l Excelsior D	25	12
C246	AP79	1.50 l Dedal I	42	15
C247	AP79	2.50 l Enthusiast	60	25
C248	AP79	4 l AK-22	1.00	45
C249	AP79	5 l Grifrom	1.40	60
		Nos. C244-C249 (6)	3.79	1.62

Agriculture Type of 1982

1982, June 29

| C250 | A888 | 4 l Helicopter spraying insecticide | 1.00 | 50 |

Vlaicu's Glider, 1909—AP80

Aurel Vlaicu (1882-19), Aviator: 1 l, Memorial, Banesti-Prahova (vert.). 2.50 l, Hero Aviators Memorial, by Kotzebue and Fekete (vert.). 3 l, Vlaicu-1 glider, 1910.

1982, Sept. 27		Photo.	Perf. 13½	
C251	AP80	50b multi	12	6
C252	AP80	1 l multi	25	12
C253	AP80	2.50 l multi	62	25
C254	AP80	3 l multi	75	30

25th Anniv. of Space Flight—AP81

Designs: 50b, H. Coanda, reaction motor, 1910. 1 l, H. Oberth, rocket, 1923. 1.50 l, Sputnik I, 1957. 2.50 l, Vostok I, 1961. 4 l, Apollo 11, 1969. 5 l, Columbia space shuttle, 1982. 10 l, Globe.

1983, Jan. 24

C255	AP81	50b multi	12	6
C256	AP81	1 l multi	25	12
C257	AP81	1.50 l multi	38	15
C258	AP81	2.50 l multi	62	25
C259	AP81	4 l multi	1.00	50
C260	AP81	5 l multi	1.25	60
		Nos. C255-C260 (6)	7.24	3.36

Souvenir Sheet

| C261 | AP81 | 10 l multi | 2.50 | 2.50 |

No. C261 contains one stamp (41x53mm.); black control number. Size: 93x80mm.

First Romanian-built Jet Airliner—AP82

1983, Jan. 25		Photo.	Perf. 13½	
C262	AP82	11 l Rombac 1-11	2.75	1.40

World Communications Year—AP83

1983, July 25		Photo.	Perf. 13½	
C263	AP83	2 l Boeing 707, Postal van	1.00	25

ROMANIA

AIR POST SEMI-POSTAL STAMPS.

Corneliu Codreanu
SPAP1
Photogravure.
1940, Dec. 1 *Perf. 14.* **Unwmkd.**
CB1 SPAP1 20 l + 5 l Prus grn 1.25 1.25

Issued as propaganda for the Rome-Berlin Axis.
No. CB1 exists with overprint "1 Mai 1941 Jamboreea Nationala."

Plane over Sinaia—SPAP2
Designs: 200 l+800 l, Plane over Mountains.
1945, Oct. 1 *Imperf.* **Wmk. 276**
CB2 SPAP2 80 l + 420 l gray 1.00 1.00
CB3 SPAP2 200 l + 800 l ultra 1.00 1.00

Issued to commemorate the 16th Congress of the General Association of Romanian Engineers.

Souvenir Sheets.

Re-distribution of Land—SPAP4
1946, May 4 *Photo.* *Perf. 14*
CB4 SPAP4 80 l blue 5.00 6.00

Issued in sheets measuring 74x59 mm. to commemorate the agrarian reform law of March 23, 1945. The sheet sold for 100 lei.

Plane Skywriting—SPAP5
1946, May 1 *Perf. 13*
CB5 SPAP5 200 l bl & brt red 6.00 7.00

Issued to publicize Labor Day, sheets measuring 71x63mm. The sheet sold for 10,000 lei.

Lookheed 12 Electra
SPAP6

1946, Sept. 1 *Perf. 11½*
CB6 SPAP6 300 l + 1200 l dp bl 1.25 1.25

No. CB6 exists se-tenant with No. C26. See note after No. C26.
The surtax was for the Office of Popular Sports.

Miniature Sheet.

Women of Wallachia, Transylvania and Moldavia
SPAP7
1946, Dec. 20 *Imperf.* **Wmk. 276**
CB7 SPAP7 500 l + 9500 l choc & red 3.25 3.50

Issued for the Democratic Women's Organization of Romania. Size: 79x64mm.

SPAP8
1946, Oct. *Imperf.*
CB8 SPAP8 300 l (+1000 l) dp plum 8.00 8.50

The surtax was for the Office of Popular Sports. Sheets of four.

Laborer with Torch
SPAP9
1947, Mar. 1
CB9 SPAP9 300 l + 7000 l choc 50 50

Sheets of four with marginal inscription.

Plane
SPAP10

Plane above Shore Line
SPAP11
1947, June 27 *Imperf.*
CB10 SPAP10 15,000 l + 15,000 l dk Prus grn 50 50

Sheets of four with marginal inscription.

1947, May 1 *Perf. 14x13*
CB11 SPAP11 300 l + 12,000 l bl 35 35

Planes over Mountains
SPAP12

Plane over Athletic Field
SPAP13
1947, Oct. 5 *Perf. 14x14½*
CB12 SPAP12 5 l + 5 l brn 75 35

Issued to commemorate the 17th Congress of the General Association of Romanian Engineers.

Perf. 13½
1948, Feb. 20 *Photo.* **Wmk. 276**
CB13 SPAP13 7 l + 7 l vio 1.50 90

Imperf.
CB14 SPAP13 10 l + 10 l Prus grn 1.75 1.25

Balkan Games. Sheets of four with marginal inscription.

Swallow and Plane
SPAP14
1948, Mar. 15 *Perf. 14x13½*
CB15 SPAP14 12 l + 12 l bl 1.00 70

Bucharest-Moscow Passenger Plane, Douglas DC-3 Dakota
SPAP15
1948, Oct. 29 *Perf. 14*
CB16 SPAP15 20 l + 20 l dp bl 4.50 3.50

Printed in sheets of 8 stamps and 16 small, red brown labels. Sheet yields 8 triptychs, each comprising 1 stamp flanked by label with Bucharest view and label with Moscow view.

Douglas DC-4
SPAP16
1948, May 1 *Perf. 13½x14*
CB17 SPAP16 20 l + 20 l bl 10.00 9.00

Issued to publicize Labor Day, May 1, 1948.

Pursuit Plane and Victim
SPAP17

Launching Model Plane
SPAP18

1948, May 9 *Perf. 13*
CB18 SPAP17 3 l + 3 l dp ultra 3.75 3.75
CB19 SPAP17 5 l + 5 l bl (*Bomber*) 4.50 4.50

Issued to honor the Romanian army.

1948, Dec. 31 *Perf. 13x13½*
CB20 SPAP18 20 l + 20 l dp ultra 17.50 17.50

Imperf.
CB21 SPAP18 20 l + 20 l Prus bl 17.50 17.50

Nos. CB20 and CB21 were issued in sheets of four stamps, with ornamental border and "1948" in contrasting color.

UPU Type of Air Post Issue, 1963
Design: 1.60 l+50b, Globe, map of Romania, planes and UPU monument.
Perf. 14x13½
1963, Nov. 15 *Litho.* **Unwmkd.**
Size: 75x27mm.
CB22 AP54 1.60 l + 50b gray, brt grn & red org 1.75 60

Issued to commemorate the 15th UPU Congress in Vienna. The surtax was for the Romanian Philatelic Federation.

POSTAGE DUE STAMPS.

D1
Perf. 11, 11½, 13½ and Compound.

1881 Typographed. Unwmkd.
J1 D1 2b brown 3.50 1.75
J2 D1 5b brown 15.00 2.75
  a. Tête bêche pair 250.00 100.00
J3 D1 10b brown 17.50 1.75
J4 D1 30b brown 20.00 1.75
J5 D1 50b brown 12.00 3.50
J6 D1 60b brown 10.00 4.00

1885
J7 D1 10b pale red brn 8.00 70
J8 D1 30b pale red brn 8.00 70

1887-90
J9 D1 2b gray grn 3.50 75
J10 D1 5b gray grn 8.00 4.00
J11 D1 10b gray grn 8.00 4.00
J12 D1 30b gray grn 8.00 75

1888
J14 D1 2b grn, *yelsh* 1.00 1.00
J15 D1 5b grn, *yelsh* 3.00 3.00
J16 D1 10b grn, *yelsh* 25.00 3.50
J17 D1 30b grn, *yelsh* 11.00 1.50

Wmkd. Coat of Arms. (163)
1890-96
J18 D1 2b emerald 1.00 40
J19 D1 5b emerald 50 50
J20 D1 10b emerald 1.00 50
J21 D1 30b emerald 1.50 50
J22 D1 50b emerald 5.50 1.00
J23 D1 60b emerald 7.50 3.75

1898 **Wmk. PR (200)**
J24 D1 2b bl grn 40 30
J25 D1 5b bl grn 75 25
J26 D1 10b bl grn 1.00 25
J27 D1 30b bl grn 1.00 25
J28 D1 50b bl grn 4.00 75
J29 D1 60b bl grn 5.00 1.75

1902-10 Unwmkd.
Thin Paper, Tinted Rose on Back.
J30 D1 2b green 50 20
J31 D1 5b green 25 15
J32 D1 10b green 25 15
J33 D1 30b green 45 15
J34 D1 50b green 2.25 50
J35 D1 60b green 5.00 2.50
Nos. J30-J35 (6) 8.70 3.65

ROMANIA

1908-11 White Paper.
J36	D1	2b green	50	30
J37	D1	5b green	50	30
a.		Tête bêche pair	15.00	15.00
J38	D1	10b green	25	15
a.		Tête bêche pair	15.00	15.00
J39	D1	30b green	40	15
a.		Tête bêche pair	15.00	15.00
J40	D1	50b green	2.00	1.00
		Nos. J36-J40 (5)	3.65	1.90

D2   Wmk. 165

1911 Wmkd. PR Interlaced. (165)
J41	D2	2b dk bl	20	12
J42	D2	5b dk bl, *grn*	20	12
J43	D2	10b dk bl, *grn*	20	10
J44	D2	15b dk bl, *grn*	20	15
J45	D2	20b dk bl, *grn*	20	15
J46	D2	30b dk bl, *grn*	40	15
J47	D2	50b dk bl, *grn*	50	20
J48	D2	60b dk bl, *grn*	60	30
J49	D2	1.25l dk bl, *grn*	1.75	70
		Nos. J41-J49 (9)	3.75	1.99

The letters "P.R." appear to be embossed instead of watermarked. They are often faint or entirely invisible.
The 20b, type D2, has two types, differing in the width of the head of the "2." This affects Nos. J45, J54, J58, and J63.

Regular Issue of 1908 Overprinted **TAXA DE PLATA**
1918 Unwmkd.
J50	A46	5b yel grn	1.25	50
a.		Inverted overprint	3.00	3.00
J51	A46	10b rose	1.25	50
a.		Inverted overprint	1.75	1.75

Postage Due Type of 1911. Wmkd. PR Interlaced. (165)
J52	D2	5b blk, *grn*	30	15
J53	D2	10b blk, *grn*	25	15
J54	D2	20b blk, *grn*	6.50	1.00
J55	D2	30b blk, *grn*	1.50	60
J55A	D2	50b blk, *grn*	5.00	1.50
		Nos. J52-J55A (5)	13.55	3.40

1919 Unwmkd.
Perf. 11½, 13½ and Compound.
J56	D2	5b blk, *grn*	20	10
J57	D2	10b blk, *grn*	20	10
J58	D2	20b blk, *grn*	75	25
J59	D2	30b blk, *grn*	60	15
J60	D2	50b blk, *grn*	1.50	60
		Nos. J56-J60 (5)	3.25	1.20

1920-26 White Paper
J61	D2	5b black	15	6
J62	D2	10b black	15	6
J63	D2	20b black	15	6
J64	D2	30b black	40	12
J65	D2	50b black	60	8
J66	D2	60b black	15	8
J67	D2	1l black	50	8
J68	D2	2l black	30	8
J69	D2	3l blk ('26)	30	8
J70	D2	6l blk ('26)	50	8
		Nos. J61-J70 (10)	3.20	78

1923-24
J74	D2	1l blk, *pale grn*	40	20
J75	D2	2l blk, *pale grn*	70	35
J76	D2	3l blk, *pale grn* ('24)	1.75	90
J77	D2	6l blk, *pale grn* ('24)	2.25	90

Postage Due Stamps of 1920-26 Overprinted **8 IUNIE 1930**
1930 Perf. 13½.
J78	D2	1l black	25	10
J79	D2	2l black	30	20
J80	D2	3l black	50	25
J81	D2	6l black	75	40

Accession of King Carol II.

1931 Type of 1911 Issue. Wmkd. Crown over PTT, Multiple. (225)
J82	D2	2l black	1.00	35

D3

Wmkd. Crowns and Monograms. (230)
1932-37
J83	D3	1l black	10	6
J84	D3	2l black	15	6
J85	D3	3l blk ('37)	20	8
J86	D3	6l blk ('37)	25	15

Type of 1911.
1942 Typographed Perf. 13½
J87	D2	50l black	40	30
J88	D2	100l black	60	40

Type of 1932.
1946-47 Perf. 14 Unwmkd.
J89	D3	20l black	1.00	90
J90	D3	100l blk ('47)	75	40
J91	D3	200l black	1.50	90

1946-47 Wmk. 276
J92	D3	20l black	6	6
J93	D3	50l black	10	10
J94	D3	80l black	20	20
J95	D3	100l black	30	30
J96	D3	200l black	60	55
J97	D3	500l black	80	80
J98	D3	5000l blk ('47)	2.00	2.00
		Nos. J92-J98 (7)	4.06	4.01

Crown and King Michael
D3a
Perf. 14½ x 13½

1947 Typographed Wmk. 276
J98A	D3a	2l carmine	50	25
J98B	D3a	4l gray bl	1.00	50
J98C	D3a	5l black	1.50	75
J98D	D3a	10l vio brn	2.50	1.25

Same Overprinted

1948
J98E	D3a	2l carmine	40	25
J98F	D3a	4l gray bl	75	40
J98G	D3a	5l black	1.00	50
J98H	D3a	10l vio brn	1.75	85

In use, Nos. J98A-J106 and following issues were torn apart, one half being affixed to the postage due item and the other half being pasted into the postman's record book. Prices are for unused and canceled-to-order pairs.

Communications Badge and Postwoman
D4

1950 Photogravure. Perf. 14½ x14. Unwmkd.
J99	D4	2l org ver	75	75
J100	D4	4l dp bl	75	75
J101	D4	5l dk gray grn	1.00	1.00
J102	D4	10l org brn	1.25	1.25

Wmk. 358
J103	D4	2l org ver	1.00	75
J104	D4	4l dp bl	1.00	75
J105	D4	5l dk gray grn	1.40	1.00
J106	D4	10l org brn	1.75	1.50
		Nos. J99-J106 (8)	8.90	7.75

Postage Due Stamps of 1950 Surcharged with New Values in Black or Carmine.
1952 Unwmkd.
J107	D4	4b on 2l org ver	40	40
J108	D4	10b on 4l dp bl (C)	40	40
J109	D4	20b on 5l dk gray grn	75	75
J110	D4	50b on 10l org brn	1.25	1.25

Wmk. 358
J111	D4	4b on 2l org ver	35	35
J112	D4	10b on 4l dp bl (C)	55	55
J113	D4	20b on 5l dk gray grn (C)	4.00	2.00
J114	D4	50b on 10l org brn	5.00	2.00
		Nos. J107-J114 (8)	12.70	7.70

See note after No. J98H.

General Post Office and Post Horn
D5

1957 Perf. 14 Wmk. 358
J115	D5	3b black	6	5
J116	D5	5b red org	6	6
J117	D5	10b red lil	10	10
J118	D5	20b brt red	20	10
J119	D5	40b lt bl grn	50	20
J120	D5	1l brt ultra	1.50	35
		Nos. J115-J120 (6)	2.42	86

See note after No. J98H.

General Post Office and Post Horn
D6

1967, Feb. 25 Photo. Perf. 13
J121	D6	3b brt grn	5	5
J122	D6	5b brt bl	5	5
J123	D6	10b lil rose	6	5
J124	D6	20b vermilion	10	5
J125	D6	40b brown	25	9
J126	D6	1l violet	70	20
		Nos. J121-J126 (6)	1.21	49

See note after No. J98H.

1970, Mar. 10 Unwmkd.
J127	D6	3b brt grn	5	5
J128	D6	5b brt bl	5	5
J129	D6	10b lil rose	5	5
J130	D6	20b vermilion	8	5
J131	D6	40b brown	25	6
J132	D6	1l violet	50	15
		Nos. J127-J132 (6)	98	41

See note after No. J98H.

Symbols of Communications—D7
Designs: 10b, Like 5b. 20b, 40b, Pigeons, head of Mercury and post horn. 50b, 1 l, General Post Office, post horn and truck.

1974, Jan. 1 Photo. Perf. 13
J133	D7	5b brt bl	5	5
J134	D7	10b olive	5	5
J135	D7	20b lil rose	6	5
J136	D7	40b purple	12	5
J137	D7	50b brown	25	6
J138	D7	1l orange	50	15
		Nos. J133-J138 (6)	1.03	41

See note after No. J98H.

Postal Symbols—D8

1982, Dec. 23 Photo. Perf. 13½
J139	D8	25b Carrier pigeons	6	5
J140	D8	50b Mailbox	12	6
J141	D8	1l like #J139	25	12
J142	D8	2l Postal headquarters, Bucharest	50	25
J143	D8	3l like #J140	75	30
J144	D8	4l like #J142	1.00	50

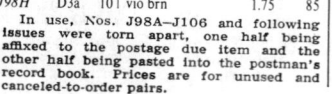

ROMANIA

OFFICIAL STAMPS.

Eagle Carrying
National Emblem
O1

Coat
of Arms
O2

Wmkd. Wavy Lines. (95)
1929 Photogravure. *Perf. 13½.*

O1	O1	25b red org	25	6
O2	O1	50b dk brn	25	6
O3	O1	1 l dk vio	30	5
O4	O1	2 l ol grn	30	5
O5	O1	3 l rose car	50	5
O6	O1	4 l dk ol	50	7
O7	O1	6 l Prus bl	2.50	15
O8	O1	10 l dp bl	85	9
O9	O1	25 l car brn	1.75	1.75
O10	O1	50 l purple	5.00	5.00
	Nos. O1-O10 (10)		12.20	7.33

Type of Official Stamps of 1929

Overprinted **8 IUNIE 1930**

1930 Unwmkd.

O11	O1	25b red org	25	6
O12	O1	50b dk brn	25	10
O13	O1	1 l dk vio	50	9
O14	O1	3 l rose car	70	15

Nos. O11 to O14 were not placed in use without overprint.

Same Overprint on Official Stamps of 1929.
Wmkd. Wavy Lines. (95)

O15	O1	25b red org	30	6
O16	O1	50b dk brn	30	6
O17	O1	1 l dk vio	30	5
O18	O1	2 l dp grn	30	6
O19	O1	3 l rose car	70	15
O20	O1	4 l ol blk	90	15
O21	O1	6 l Prus bl	2.50	5
O22	O1	10 l dp bl	1.00	20
O23	O1	25 l car brn	3.50	3.50
O24	O1	50 l purple	5.00	5.00
	Nos. O15-O24 (10)		14.80	9.28

Nos. O11 to O24 were issued in commemoration of the accession of King Carol II to the throne of Romania.

Typographed.
Wmkd.
Crown over PTT, Multiple. (225)
1931-32 *Perf. 13½, 13½x14½.*

O25	O2	25b black	30	20
O26	O2	1 l lilac	30	25
O27	O2	2 l emerald	50	50
O28	O2	3 l rose	80	80

Wmkd.
Crowns and Monograms. (230)
1932 *Perf. 13½*

O29	O2	25b black	30	30
O30	O2	1 l violet	45	45
O31	O2	2 l emerald	65	65
O32	O2	3 l rose	80	80
O33	O2	6 l red brn	1.25	1.25
	Nos. O29-O33 (5)		3.45	3.45

PARCEL POST STAMPS.

PP1

PP2

Typographed.
1895 Wmkd. Coat of Arms. (163)
Perf. 11½, 13½ and Compound.

Q1	PP1	25b brn red	12.00	2.00

1896

Q2	PP1	25b vermilion	9.00	1.25

1898 Wmkd. RP (200)
Perf. 13½ and 11½x13½.

Q3	PP1	25b brn red	8.00	1.25
a.	Tête bêche pair			
Q4	PP1	25b vermilion	8.00	1.25

Thin Paper.
Tinted Rose on Back.
1905 *Perf. 11½* Unwmkd.

Q5	PP1	25b vermilion	6.00	1.00

1911 White Paper.

Q6	PP1	25b pale red	6.00	1.00

Carmine Surcharge.
1928 *Perf. 13½*

Q7	PP2	5 l on 10b yel grn	1.25	30

POSTAL TAX STAMPS.

Regular Issue of 1908 Overprinted **TIMBRU DE AJUTOR**

Perf. 11½, 13½, 11½x13½.

1915 Unwmkd.

RA1	A46	5b green	30	12
RA2	A46	10b rose	50	15

The "Timbru de Ajutor" stamps represent a tax on postal matter. The money obtained from their sale was turned into a fund for the assistance of soldiers' families.

Until 1923 the only "Timbru de Ajutor" stamps used for postal purposes were the 5b and 10b. Stamps of higher values with this inscription were used to pay the taxes on railway and theatre tickets and other fiscal taxes. In 1923 the postal rate was advanced to 25b.

The Queen Weaving
PT1

1916-18 Typographed.

RA3	PT1	5b gray blk	30	20
RA4	PT1	5b grn ('18)	75	20
RA5	PT1	10b brown	50	30
RA6	PT1	10b gray blk ('18)	75	20

Stamps of 1916 Overprinted in Red or Black

1918 *Perf. 13½.*

RA7	PT1	5b gray blk (R)	60	40
a.	Double overprint		5.00	
c.	Black overprint		75	
RA8	PT1	10b brn (Bk)	75	40
a.	Double overprint		7.50	
b.	Double overprint, one inverted		7.50	
c.	Inverted overprint		7.50	

1919 Same Overprint on RA1 and RA2.

RA11	A46	5b yel grn (R)	25.00	25.00
RA12	A46	10b rose (Bk)	25.00	25.00

Charity
PT3

1921-24 Typographed. Unwmkd.
Perf. 13½, 11½, 13½x11½.

RA13	PT3	10b green	20	5
RA14	PT3	25b blk ('24)	15	5

1928 Type of 1921-24 Issue.
Wmkd.
Wavy Lines Close Together. (95)

RA15	PT3	25b black	1.25	50

Nos. RA13, RA14 and RA15 are the only stamps of type PT3 issued for postal purposes. Other denominations were used fiscally.

Airplane
PT4

Head of Aviator
PT5

1931 Photogravure. Unwmkd.

RA16	PT4	50b Prus bl	50	5
a.	Double impression		25.00	
RA17	PT4	1 l dk red brn	75	8
RA18	PT4	2 l ultra	1.00	25

The use of these stamps, in addition to the regular postage, was obligatory on all postal matter for the interior of the country. The money thus obtained was to augment the National Fund for Aviation. When the stamps were not used to prepay the special tax, it was collected by means of Postal Tax Due stamps Nos. RAJ20 and RAJ21.

Nos. RA17 and RA18 were also used for other than postal tax.

Wmkd. Crowns and Monograms. (230)
1932 *Perf. 14 x 13½*

RA19	PT5	50b Prus bl	35	5
RA20	PT5	1 l red brn	50	5
RA21	PT5	2 l ultra	65	10

The notes after No. RA18 will apply also to Nos. RA19 to RA21.
After 1937 use of Nos. RA20-RA21 was limited to other than postal matter.
Nos. RA19-RA21 exist imperf.
Two stamps similar to type PT5, but inscribed "Fondul Aviatiei," were issued in 1936: 10b sepia and 20b violet.

Aviator
PT6

King Michael
PT7

1937 *Perf. 13½.*

RA22	PT6	50b Prus grn	25	5
RA23	PT6	1 l red brn	35	5
RA24	PT6	2 l ultra	40	15

Stamps overprinted or inscribed "Fondul Aviatiei" other than Nos. RA22, RA23 or RA24 were used to pay taxes on other than postal matters.

Photogravure
1943 *Perf. 14.* Wmk. 276

RA25	PT7	50b org ver	10	10
RA26	PT7	1 l lil rose	10	10
RA27	PT7	2 l brown	10	10
RA28	PT7	4 l lt ultra	10	10
RA29	PT7	5 l dl lil	10	10
RA30	PT7	8 l yel grn	10	10
RA31	PT7	10 l blk brn	10	10
	Nos. RA25-RA31 (7)		70	70

The tax was obligatory on domestic mail.

Protection of Homeless Children
PT8

1945

RA32	PT8	40 l Prus bl	40	30

PT9

"Hope"
PT10

1947 Typographed.
Perf. 14x14½. Unwmkd.
Black Surcharge.

RA33	PT9	1 l on 2 l + 2 l pink	50	25
a.	Inverted surcharge			
RA34	PT9	5 l on 1 l + 1 l gray prn	7.50	6.00

1948 *Perf. 14.*

RA35	PT10	1 l rose	3.00	10
RA36	PT10	1 l rose vio	3.50	20

A 2 lei blue and 5 lei ocher in type PT10 were issued primarily for revenue purposes.

POSTAL TAX DUE STAMPS.

Postage Due Stamps of 1911 Overprinted **TIMBRU DE AJUTOR**

Perf. 11½, 13½, 11½x13½.

1915 Unwmkd.

RAJ1	D2	5b dk bl, grn	50	25
RAJ2	D2	10b dk bl, grn	50	25
	Wmk. 165		7.50	1.00

PTD1

PTD2

1916 Typographed. Unwmkd.

RAJ3	PTD1	5b brn, grn	25	20
RAJ4	PTD1	10b red, grn	25	20

1918

RAJ5	PTD1	5b red, grn	30	20
a.	Wmk. 165		50	35
RAJ6	PTD1	10b brn, grn	30	20
a.	Wmk. 165		50	35

Postal Tax Stamps of 1916, Overprinted in Red, Black or Blue **TAXA DE PLATA**

RAJ7	PT1	5b gray blk (R)	30	20
a.	Inverted overprint			
RAJ8	PT1	10b brn (Bk)	40	25
a.	Inverted overprint			
RAJ9	PT1	10b brn (Bl)	8.00	8.00
a.	Vertical overprint		25.00	25.00

1921 Type of 1916.

RAJ10	PTD1	5b red	50	25
RAJ11	PTD1	10b brown	50	25

1922-25 Typographed.
Greenish Paper.

RAJ12	PTD2	10b brown	15	10
RAJ13	PTD2	20b brown	15	10
RAJ14	PTD2	25b brown	15	10
RAJ15	PTD2	50b brown	15	10

1923-26

RAJ16	PTD2	10b lt brn	15	10
RAJ17	PTD2	20b lt brn	15	10
RAJ18	PTD2	25b brn ('26)	15	15
RAJ19	PTD2	50b brn ('26)	15	15

ROMANIA

J82 and Type of 1911 **TIMBRUL**
Postage Due Stamps **AVIATIEI**
Overprinted in Red
1931   Perf. 13½.   Wmk. 225
RAJ20 D2 1 l black   12   8
RAJ21 D2 2 l black   12   8
When the Postal Tax stamps for the Aviation Fund issue (Nos. RA16 to RA18) were not used to prepay the obligatory tax on letters, etc., it was collected by affixing Nos. RAJ20 and RAJ21.

OCCUPATION STAMPS.
Issued under Austrian Occupation.

Emperor Karl of Austria
OS1   OS2

Engraved.
1917   Perf. 12½.   Unwmkd.
1N1   OS1 3b ol gray   1.40 1.20
1N2   OS1 5b ol grn   1.10   .90
1N3   OS1 6b violet   1.10   .90
1N4   OS1 10b org brn   .20   .10
1N5   OS1 12b dp bl   1.25 1.00
1N6   OS1 15b brt rose   1.10   .90
1N7   OS1 20b red brn   .20   .10
1N8   OS1 25b ultra   .25   .20
1N9   OS1 30b slate   .40   .40
1N10 OS1 40b ol bis   .40   .40
  a.   Perf. 11½   60.00 27.50
  b.   Perf. 11½x12½   65.00 30.00
1N11 OS1 50b dp grn   .40   .40
1N12 OS1 60b rose   .40   .40
1N13 OS1 80b dl bl   .20   .10
1N14 OS1 90b dk vio   .40   .40
1N15 OS2 2 l rose, straw   .60   .40
1N16 OS2 3 l grn, bl   1.00   .60
1N17 OS2 4 l rose, grn   1.00   .60
   Nos. 1N1-1N17 (17)   11.40   9.00
Nos. 1N1 to 1N14 inclusive have "BANI" surcharged in red.
Nos. 1N1 to 1N17 also exist imperforate.
Price, set $30.

OS3   OS4
1918
1N18 OS3 3b ol gray   .20   .18
1N19 OS3 5b ol grn   .24   .12
1N20 OS3 6b violet   .30   .30
1N21 OS3 10b org brn   .35   .35
1N22 OS3 12b dp bl   .24   .24
1N23 OS3 15b brt rose   .18   .18
1N24 OS3 20b red brn   .20   .20
1N25 OS3 25b ultra   .20   .20
1N26 OS3 30b slate   .20   .20
1N27 OS3 40b ol bis   .24   .24
1N28 OS3 50b dp grn   .30   .30
1N29 OS3 60b rose   .30   .30
1N30 OS3 80b dl bl   .18   .15
1N31 OS3 90b dk vio   .24   .27
1N32 OS4 2 l rose, straw .30   .32
1N33 OS4 3 l grn, bl   .40   .40
1N34 OS4 4 l rose, grn   .40   .40
   Nos. 1N18-1N34 (17)   4.47 4.35
Exist. imperf. Price, set $20.
The complete series exists with "BANI" or "LEI" inverted, also with those words and the numerals of value inverted. Neither of these sets was regularly issued.
A set of 13 stamps similar to Austria Nos. M69-M81 was prepared for use in Romania in 1918, but not placed in use there. Denominations are in bani. It is reported that they were on sale after the armistice at the Vienna post office for a few days. Price $1200.

Issued under Bulgarian Occupation.

Bulgarian Stamps
of 1915-16
Overprinted in
Red or Blue

Поща въ Ромъния
1916—1917

1916   Perf. 11½, 14.   Unwmkd.
2N1 A20 1s dk bl grn (R)   15   15
2N2 A22 5s grn & vio brn (R) 2.00 .75
2N3 A24 10s brn & brnsh blk (Bl) 25 15
2N4 A26 25s ind & blk (Bl)   25   15
Nos. 2N1-2N4 were used in the Dobruja district.
Many varieties of overprint exist.

Issued under German Occupation.

German Stamps
of 1905-17
Surcharged

15 Bani
(Black)

Wmkd. Lozenges. (125)
1917   Perf. 14.
3N1 A22 15b on 15pf dk vio (R) 1.00 1.00
3N2 A16 25b on 20pf ultra (Bk) 1.00 1.00
3N3 A16 40b on 30pf org & blk, buff (R) 25.00 25.00

"M.V.i.R." are the initials of "Militär Verwaltung in Rumänien" (Military Administration of Romania).

German Stamps
of 1905-17
Surcharged

M.V.i.R.
25 Bani

1917-18
3N4 A16 10b on 10pf car   40   35
3N5 A22 15b on 15pf dk vio   3.25 3.25
3N6 A16 25b on 20pf ultra   60   60
3N7 A16 40b on 30pf org & blk, buff 75 75
  a.   "40" omitted   75.00 100.00

German Stamps
of 1905-17
Surcharged

Rumänien
25 Bani

1918
3N8   A16 5b on 5pf grn   15   15
3N9   A16 10b on 10pf car   20   20
3N10 A22 15b on 15pf dk vio 15   15
3N11 A16 25b on 20pf bl vio 15   15
  a.   25b on 20pf bl   25   25
3N12 A16 40b on 30pf org & blk, buff 25 25

German Stamps
of 1905-17
Overprinted

Gültig
9. Armee

1918
3N13 A16 10pf carmine   10.00 10.00
3N14 A22 15pf dk vio   15.00 15.00
3N15 A16 20pf blue   1.50   1.50
3N16 A16 30pf org & blk, buff 14.00 14.00

POSTAGE DUE STAMPS.
Issued under German Occupation.

Postage Due Stamps
and Type of Romania
Overprinted in Red

M.V.i.R.

1918   Wmkd. P. R. Interlaced. (165)
Perf. 11½, 13½ and Compound.
3NJ1 D2 5b dk bl, grn   35.00 45.00
3NJ2 D2 10b dk bl, grn   45.00 55.00
The 20b, 30b and 50b with this overprint are fraudulent.

Unwmkd.
3NJ3 D2 5b dk bl, grn   3.00 3.00
3NJ4 D2 10b dk bl, grn   3.00 3.00
3NJ5 D2 20b dk bl, grn   3.00 3.00
3NJ6 D2 30b dk bl, grn   3.00 3.00
3NJ7 D2 50b dk bl, grn   3.00 3.00
   Nos. 3NJ1-3NJ7 (7)   95.00 115.00

OCCUPATION POSTAL TAX STAMPS.
Issued under German Occupation.

Romanian Postal Tax Stamps and Type of 1916.

Overprinted in
Red or Black

M.V.i.R.

1917   Unwmkd.
Perf. 11½, 13½ and Compound.
3NRA1 PT1 5b gray blk (R)   30   30
3NRA2 PT1 10b brn (Bk)   40   30

Same,
Overprinted

M.V.i.R.

1917-18
3NRA3 PT1 5b gray blk (R)   60   60
  a.   Black ovpt.   7.50 7.50
3NRA4 PT1 10b brn (Bk)   60   60
3NRA5 PT1 10b vio (Bk)   50   50

Same,
Overprinted
in Red
or Black

1918
3NRA6 PT1 5b gray blk (R) 15.00
3NRA7 PT1 10b brn (Bk)   15.00

Same,
Overprinted

Gültig
9. Armee

1918
3NRA8 PT1 10b vio (Bk)   25   25

OCCUPATION POSTAL TAX DUE STAMP.
Issued Under German Occupation.

Type of Romanian
Postal Tax Due Stamp
of 1916
Overprinted

M.V.i.R.

1918   Wmkd. P. R. Interlaced. (165)
Perf. 11½, 13½, and Compound.
3NRAJ1 PTD1 10b red, grn   4.00 5.00

Romanian Post Offices in the Turkish Empire.
40 Paras = 1 Piastre

King Carol I
A1   A2
Perf. 11½, 13½ and Compound
1896   Wmkd. P. R. (200)
Black Surcharge.
1 A1 10pa on 5b bl   27.50 27.50
2 A2 20pa on 10b emer   20.00 20.00
3 A1 1pia on 25b vio   20.00 20.00

Violet Surcharge.
4 A1 10pa on 5b bl   15.00 15.00
5 A2 20pa on 10b emer   15.00 15.00
6 A1 1pia on 25b vio   15.00 15.00

Romanian Stamps
of 1908-18
Overprinted in
Black or Red

1919   Typographed.   Unwmkd.
7   A46 5b yel grn   60   60
8   A46 10b rose   80   80
9   A46 15b red brn   80   80
10 A19 25b dp bl (R)   1.00 1.00
11 A19 40b gray brn (R) 2.00 2.00
   Nos. 7-11 (5)   5.20 5.20
All values exist with inverted overprint. Price about $2 each.

POSTAL TAX STAMP.

Romanian
Postal Tax Stamp
of 1918
Overprinted

Perf. 11½, 11½x13½
1919   Unwmkd.
RA1 PT1 5b green   1.75 1.75
  a.   Inverted overprint

ROMAN STATES
See Italian States preceding Italy in Vol. III.

ROUAD, ILE—RUANDA-URUNDI

ROUAD, ILE
(ē'l'rwâd')
(Arwad)

LOCATION—An island in the Mediterranean, off the coast of Latakia, Syria.
GOVT.—French Mandate.

In 1916, while a French post office was maintained on Ile Rouad, stamps were issued by France.

25 Centimes = 1 Piastre

Stamps of French Offices in the Levant, 1902-06, Overprinted

ILE ROUAD

Perf. 14x13½

1916, Jan. 12   Unwmkd.
1	A2	5c green	275.00	135.00
2	A3	10c rose red	275.00	135.00
3	A5	1pi on 25c bl	275.00	135.00

Dangerous counterfeits exist.

Stamps of French Offices in the Levant, 1902-06, Overprinted Horizontally

ILE ROUAD

1916, Dec.
4	A2	1c gray	50	50
5	A2	2c vio brn	50	50
6	A2	3c red org	50	50
a.		Double overprint	47.50	47.50
7	A2	5c green	60	60
8	A3	10c rose	65	65
9	A3	15c pale red	75	75
10	A3	20c brn vio	1.25	1.25
11	A5	1pi on 25c bl	1.25	1.25
12	A3	30c violet	1.25	1.25
13	A4	40c red & pale bl	2.25	2.25
14	A6	2pi on 50c bis brn & lav	3.25	3.25
15	A6	4pi on 1fr cl & ol grn	5.25	5.25
16	A6	20pi on 5fr dk bl & buff	17.50	17.50
		Nos. 4-16 (13)	35.50	35.50

There is a wide space between the two words of the overprint on Nos. 13 to 16 inclusive. Nos. 4, 5 and 6 are on white and coarse, grayish (G. C.) papers. (Note on G. C. paper follows France No. 184.)

RUANDA-URUNDI
(Belgian East Africa)

LOCATION—In central Africa, bounded by Congo, Uganda and Tanganyika.
GOVT.—Former United Nations trusteeship administered by Belgium.
AREA—20,540 sq. mi.
POP.—4,700,000 (est. 1958).
CAPITAL—Usumbura.

See German East Africa in Vol. III for stamps issued under Belgian occupation.

In 1962 the two parts of the trusteeship became independent states, the Republic of Rwanda and the Kingdom of Burundi.

100 Centimes = 1 Franc

Stamps of Belgian Congo, 1923-26, Overprinted

RUANDA URUNDI

1924-26   Perf. 12.
6	A32	5c org yel	18	18
7	A32	10c green	18	18
8	A32	15c ol brn	18	18
9	A32	20c ol grn	18	18
10	A32	20c grn ('26)	18	15
11	A32	25c red brn	30	20
12	A32	30c rose red	25	25
13	A32	30c ol grn ('25)	20	20
14	A32	40c vio ('25)	38	30
15	A32	50c gray bl	25	25
16	A32	50c buff ('25)	38	25
17	A32	75c red org	38	38
18	A32	75c gray bl ('25)	45	30
19	A32	1fr bis brn	50	45
20	A32	1fr dl bl ('26)	30	30
21	A32	3fr gray brn	3.75	2.50
22	A32	5fr gray	7.50	5.00
23	A32	10fr gray blk	18.50	12.00
		Nos. 6-23 (18)	34.29	23.25

Belgian Congo Nos. 112-113 Overprinted in Red or Black

RUANDA-URUNDI

1925-27   Perf. 12½.
| 24 | A44 | 45c dk vio (R) ('27) | 38 | 38 |
| 25 | A44 | 60c car rose (Bk) | 50 | 38 |

RUANDA

Stamps of Belgian Congo, 1923-1927, Overprinted

URUNDI

1927-29
26	A32	10c grn ('29)	25	25
27	A32	15c ol brn ('29)	1.00	75
28	A32	35c green	25	20
29	A32	75c sal rose	35	30
30	A32	1fr rose red	55	40
31	A32	1.25fr dl bl	75	50
32	A32	1.50fr dl bl	65	45
33	A32	1.75fr dl bl	1.40	90

No. 32 Surcharged

1.75

| 34 | A32 | 1.75fr on 1.50fr dl bl ('27) | 65 | 50 |
| | | Nos. 26-34 (9) | 5.85 | 4.25 |

Nos. 30 and 33 Surcharged

2

1931
| 35 | A32 | 1.25fr on 1fr rose red | 3.25 | 1.50 |
| 36 | A32 | 2fr on 1.75fr dl bl | 4.25 | 2.25 |

Porter—A1

Mountain Scene—A2

Designs: 5c, 60c, Porter. 15c, Warrior. 25c, Kraal. 40c, Cattle herders. 50c, Cape buffalo. 75c, Bahutu greeting. 1f, Barundi women. 1.25f, Bahutu mother. 1.50f, 2f, Making wooden vessel. 3.25f, Preparing hides. 4f, Watuba potter. 5f, Mututsi dancer. 10f, Watusi warriors. 20f, Urundi prince.

1931-38   Engraved   Perf. 11½.
37	A1	5c dp lil rose ('38)	12	12
38	A2	10c gray	8	8
39	A2	15c pale red	15	15
40	A2	25c brn vio	8	8
41	A1	40c green	38	38
42	A1	50c gray lil	12	12
43	A1	60c lil rose	12	12
44	A1	75c gray blk	12	12
45	A2	1fr rose red	15	15
46	A1	1.25fr red brn	20	15
47	A1	1.50fr brn vio ('37)	15	15
48	A2	2fr dp bl	30	20
49	A2	2.50fr dp bl ('37)	28	20
50	A1	3.25fr brn vio	30	20
51	A2	4fr rose	40	40
52	A1	5fr gray	45	45
53	A1	10fr brn vio	90	65
54	A1	20fr brown	2.50	2.25
		Nos. 37-54 (18)	6.80	6.05

King Albert Memorial Issue.

King Albert A16

1934   Photogravure.
| 55 | A16 | 1.50fr black | 75 | 75 |

Stamps of 1931-38 Surcharged in Black

0F60   0F60

1941
56	A1	5c on 40c grn	3.75	3.75
57	A1	60c on 50c gray lil	2.50	2.50
58	A2	2.50fr on 1.50fr brn vio	2.50	2.50
59	A2	3.25fr on 2fr dp bl	10.00	10.00

Belgian Congo No. 173 Overprinted in Black

RUANDA URUNDI

Perf. 11.
| 60 | A70 | 10c lt gray | 8.00 | 8.00 |

Belgian Congo Nos. 179, 181 Overprinted in Black

RUANDA URUNDI

1941
| 61 | A70 | 1.75fr orange | 4.25 | 3.75 |
| 62 | A70 | 2.75fr vio bl | 4.25 | 3.75 |

Belgian Congo No. 168 Surcharged in Black

RUANDA URUNDI

5 c.

Perf. 11½.
| 63 | A66 | 5c on 1.50fr dp red brn & blk | 12 | 12 |

Nos. 61-62 Surcharged with New Values and Bars in Black.

1942
| 64 | A70 | 75c on 1.75fr org | 1.75 | 1.75 |
| 65 | A70 | 2.50fr on 2.75fr vio bl | 3.75 | 3.75 |

Belgian Congo Nos. 167, 183 Surcharged in Black:

RUANDA URUNDI 2.50

RUANDA URUNDI 75 c.

1942   Perf. 11, 11½.
66	A65	75c on 90c car & brn	1.10	1.00
a.		Inverted surcharge	14.00	14.00
67	A70	2.50fr on 10fr rose red	1.85	1.50
a.		Inverted surcharge	11.00	11.00

Oil Palms—A17

Oil Palms A18

Watusi Chief A19

Leopard—A20

Askari—A21

Zebra—A22

Askari—A23

Design: 100fr, Watusi chief.

1942-43   Engraved   Perf. 12½
| 68 | A17 | 5c red | 5 | 5 |
| 69 | A18 | 10c ol grn | 8 | 8 |

RUANDA-URUNDI

70	A18	15c brn car	8	8
71	A18	20c dp ultra	8	8
72	A18	25c brn vio	8	8
73	A18	30c dl bl	8	8
74	A18	50c dp grn	10	8
75	A18	60c chestnut	10	8
76	A19	75c dl lil & blk	15	12
77	A19	1fr dk brn & blk	20	12
78	A19	1.25fr rose red & blk	25	20
79	A20	1.75fr dk gray brn	90	50
80	A20	2fr ocher	90	38
81	A20	2.50fr carmine	85	15
82	A21	3.50fr dk ol grn	50	30
83	A21	5fr orange	55	35
84	A21	6fr brt ultra	55	35
85	A21	7fr black	55	45
86	A21	10fr dp brn	90	50
87	A21	20fr org brn & blk	1.75	1.25
88	A21	50fr red & blk ('43)	2.50	1.50
89	A21	100fr grn & blk ('43)	5.00	4.00
	Nos. 68-89 (22)		16.20	10.78

Miniature sheets of Nos. 72, 76, 77 and 83 were printed in 1944 by the Belgian Government in London and given to the Belgian political review, "Message," which distributed them to its subscribers, one a month. Nos. 68–89 exist imperforate, but have no franking value. Price, set $100.
See note after Belgian Congo No. 225.

Baluba Carving of Former King
A25

Carved Figures and Masks of Baluba Tribe: 10c, 50c, 2fr, 10fr, "Ndoha," figure of tribal king. 15c, 70c, 2.50fr, "Tshimanyi," an idol. 20c, 75c, 3.50fr, "Buangakokoma," statue of a kneeling beggar. 25c, 1fr, 5fr, "Mbuta," sacred double cup carved with two faces, Man and Woman. 40c, 1.25fr, 6fr, "Ngadimuashi," female mask. 1.50fr, 50fr, "Buadi-Muadi," mask with squared features (full face). 20fr, 100fr, "Mbowa," executioner's mask with buffalo horns.

1948-50		Perf. 12x12½	Unwmkd.	
90	A25	10c dp org	6	5
91	A25	15c ultra	6	5
92	A25	20c brt bl	12	10
93	A25	25c rose car	25	20
94	A25	40c violet	10	10
95	A25	50c ol brn	10	8
96	A25	70c yel grn	10	10
97	A25	75c magenta	18	18
98	A25	1fr yel org & dk vio	18	8
99	A25	1.25fr lt bl grn & mag	18	15
100	A25	1.50fr ol & mag ('50)	70	50
101	A25	2fr org & mag	20	12
102	A25	2.50fr brn red & bl grn	20	10
103	A25	3.50fr lt bl & blk	30	25
104	A25	5fr bis & mag	45	25
105	A25	6fr brn org & ind	55	18
106	A25	10fr pale vio & red brn	75	30
107	A25	20fr red org & vio brn	1.25	50
108	A25	50fr dp org & blk	3.50	1.25
109	A25	100fr crim & blk brn	6.00	3.25
	Nos. 90-109 (20)		15.23	7.79

Nos. 102 and 105 Surcharged with
New Value and Bars in Black.

1949				
110	A25	3fr on 2.50fr	25	15
111	A25	4fr on 6fr	30	17
112	A25	6.50fr on 6fr	35	30

St. Francis Xavier
A26

1953		Perf. 12½x13.		
113	A26	1.50fr ultra & gray blk	55	55

Issued to commemorate the 400th anniversary of the death of St. Francis Xavier.

Dissotis
A27

Flowers: 15c, Protea. 20c, Vellozia. 25c, Littonia. 40c, Ipomoea. 50c, Angraecum. 60c, Euphorbia. 75c, Ochna. 1fr, Hibiscus. 1.25fr, Protea. 1.50fr, Schizoglossum. 2fr, Ansellia. 3fr, Costus. 4fr, Nymphaea. 5fr, Thunbergia. 7fr, Gerbera. 8fr, Gloriosa. 10fr, Silene. 20fr, Aristolochia.

Photogravure.

1953		Perf. 11½	Unwmkd.	

Flowers in Natural Colors.

114	A27	10c plum & ocher	5	5
115	A27	15c red & yel grn	5	5
116	A27	20c grn & gray	10	5
117	A27	25c dk grn & dl org	10	8
118	A27	40c grn & sal	12	8
119	A27	50c dk car & aqua	15	8
120	A27	60c bl grn & pink	18	10
121	A27	75c dp plum & gray	18	10
122	A27	1fr car & yel	30	8
123	A27	1.25fr dk grn & bl	85	85
124	A27	1.50fr vio & ap grn	30	12
125	A27	2fr ol grn & buff	2.25	25
126	A27	3fr ol grn & pink	65	8
127	A27	4fr choc & lil	65	20
128	A27	5fr dp plum & lt bl grn	1.00	20
129	A27	7fr dk grn & fawn	1.25	45
130	A27	8fr grn & lt yel	1.65	55
131	A27	10fr dp plum & pale ol	2.50	42
132	A27	20fr vio bl & dl sal	4.00	70
	Nos. 114-132 (19)		16.33	4.49

King Baudouin and Tropical Scene
A28

Designs: Various African Views.
Engr.; Portrait Photo. in Black

1955				
133	A28	1.50fr rose car	38	20
134	A28	3fr green	35	18
135	A28	4.50fr ultra	45	25
136	A28	6.50fr dp cl	60	38

Mountain Gorilla
A29

Cape Buffaloes—A30

Animals: 40c, 2fr, Black-and-white colobus (monkey). 50c, 6.50fr, Impalas. 3fr, 8fr, Elephants. 5fr, 10fr, Eland and Zebras. 20fr, Leopard. 50fr, Lions.

Photogravure.

1959-61		Perf. 11½	Unwmkd.	

Granite Paper.
Size: 23x33mm., 33x23mm.

137	A29	10c brn, crim, & blk brn	5	5
138	A30	20c blk, gray & ap grn	5	5
139	A29	40c mag, blk & gray grn	8	5
140	A30	50c grn, org yel & brn	8	5
141	A29	1fr brn, ultra & blk	8	8
142	A30	1.50fr blk, gray & org	22	10
143	A29	2fr grnsh bl, ind & brn	12	10
144	A30	3fr brn, dp car & blk	20	10
145	A30	5fr brn, dl yel, grn & blk	25	20
146	A30	6.50fr red, org yel & brn	40	12
147	A30	8fr bl, mag & blk	65	42
148	A30	10fr multi	65	30

Size: 45x26½mm.

149	A30	20fr multi ('61)	75	60
150	A30	50fr red org, dp bl & brn ('61)	1.75	1.35
	Nos. 137-150 (14)		5.33	3.57

Map of Africa and Symbolic Honeycomb
A31

1960		Perf. 11½	Unwmkd.	

Inscription in French.

| 151 | A31 | 3fr ultra & red | 25 | 18 |

Inscription in Flemish.

| 152 | A31 | 3fr ultra & red | 25 | 20 |

Issued to commemorate the 10th anniversary of the Commission for Technical Co-operation in Africa South of the Sahara (C. C. T. A.)

No. 144 Surcharged with New Value and Bars.

1960				
153	A30	3.50fr on 3fr	38	12

SEMI-POSTAL STAMPS.

Belgian Congo Nos. B10-B11 Overprinted **RUANDA-URUNDI**

1925		Perf. 12½		
B1	SP1	25c +25c car & blk	25	25
B2	SP1	25c +25c car & blk	25	25

No. B2 inscribed "BELGISCH CONGO." Commemorative of the Colonial Campaigns in 1914–1918. Nos. B1 and B2 alternate in the sheet.

RUANDA

Belgian Congo
Nos. B12–B20
Overprinted
in Blue or Red

URUNDI

1930		Perf. 11½		
B3	SP3	10c +5c ver	38	38
B4	SP3	20c +10c dk brn	80	80
B5	SP5	35c +15c grn	1.60	1.60
B6	SP5	60c +30c dl vio	1.85	1.85
B7	SP5	1fr +50c dk car	2.75	2.75
B8	SP5	1.75fr +75c dp bl (R)	3.25	3.25
B9	SP5	3.50fr +1.50fr rose lake	6.25	6.25
B10	SP5	5fr +2.50fr red brn	5.00	5.00
B11	SP5	10fr +5fr gray blk	5.75	5.75
	Nos. B3-B11 (9)		27.63	27.63

On Nos. B3, B4 and B7 there is a space of 26 mm. between the two words of the overprint. The surtax was for native welfare.

Queen Astrid with Native Children
SP1

Lion of Belgium and Inscription "Belgium Shall Rise Again"
SP2

1936		Photogravure.		
B12	SP1	1.25fr +5c dk brn	75	65
B13	SP1	1.50fr +10c dl rose	75	65
B14	SP1	2.50fr +25c dk bl	90	90

Issued in memory of Queen Astrid. The surtax was for the National League for Protection of Native Children.

1942		Engraved	Perf. 12½	
B15	SP2	10fr +40fr bl	2.50	2.50
B16	SP2	10fr +40fr dk red	2.50	2.50

Nos. 74, 78, 79 and 82 Surcharged in Red.

Au profit de la Croix Rouge **+ 50 Fr.** Ten voordeele van het Roode Kruis
a

Ten voordeele van het Roode Kruis **+ 100 Fr.** Au profit de la Croix Rouge
b

Au profit de la Croix Rouge **+ 100 Fr.** Ten voordeele van het Roode Kruis
c

1945		Perf. 12½.	Unwmkd.	
B17	A18 (a)	50c +50fr dp grn	1.65	1.75
B18	A19 (b)	1.25fr +100fr rose red & blk	2.00	2.25
B19	A20 (c)	1.75fr +100fr dk gray brn	1.65	1.75
B20	A21 (b)	3.50fr +100fr dk ol grn	2.00	2.25

RUANDA-URUNDI—RUSSIA 273

Mozart at Age 7
SP3

Queen Elizabeth and
Mozart Sonata
SP4

1956		Engraved	Perf. 11½	
B21	SP3	4.50fr +1.50fr bluish vio	1.25	1.40
B22	SP4	6.50fr +2.50fr cl	2.25	2.25

Issued to commemorate the 200th anniversary of the birth of Wolfgang Amadeus Mozart. The surtax was for the Pro-Mozart Committee.

Nurse and
Children
SP5

Designs: 4.50fr+50c, Patient receiving injection. 6.50fr+50c, Patient being bandaged.

1957		Photogravure.	Perf. 13x10½	
		Cross in Carmine.		
B23	SP5	3fr +50c dk bl	75	75
B24	SP5	4.50fr +50c dk grn	1.00	1.00
B25	SP5	6.50fr +50c red brn	1.25	1.25

The surtax was for the Red Cross.

Soccer—SP6

Sports: 50c+25c, High Jumper. 1.50fr+50c, Hurdlers. 3fr+1.25fr, Javelin thrower. 6.50fr+3.50fr, Discus thrower.

1960		Perf. 13½	Unwmkd.	
B26	SP6	50c +25c int bl & mar	12	12
B27	SP6	1.50fr +50c dk car & blk	25	25
B28	SP6	2fr +1fr blk & dk car	25	25
B29	SP6	3fr +1.25fr org ver & grn	1.25	1.40
B30	SP6	6.50fr +3.50fr ol grn & red	1.25	1.40
		Nos. B26-B30 (5)	3.12	3.42

Issued to commemorate the 17th Olympic Games, Rome, Aug. 25-Sept. 11. The surtax was for the youth of Ruanda-Urundi.

Usumbura
Cathedral
SP7

Designs: 1fr+50c, 5fr+2fr, Cathedral, sideview. 1.50fr+75c, 6.50fr+3fr, Stained glass window.

1961, Dec. 18			Perf. 11½	
B31	SP7	50c +25c brn & buff	8	8
B32	SP7	1fr +50c grn & pale grn	10	10
B33	SP7	1.50fr +75c multi	12	12
B34	SP7	3.50fr +1.50fr lt bl & brt bl	20	20
B35	SP7	5fr +2fr car & sal	38	38
B36	SP7	6.50fr +3fr multi	50	50
		Nos. B31-B36 (6)	1.38	1.38

The surtax went for the construction and completion of the Cathedral at Usumbura.

POSTAGE DUE STAMPS.

Belgian Congo
Nos. J1–J7
Overprinted

RUANDA
URUNDI

1924-27		Perf. 14, 14½.	Unwmkd.	
J1	D1	5c blk brn	18	18
J2	D1	10c dp rose	20	20
J3	D1	15c violet	25	25
J4	D1	30c green	40	38
J5	D1	50c ultra	50	45
J6	D1	50c brt bl ('27)	50	45
J7	D1	1fr gray	60	60
		Nos. J1-J7 (7)	2.63	2.51

Belgian Congo Nos. J8–J12
Overprinted in Carmine

RUANDA
URUNDI

1943		Perf. 14x14½, 12½		
J8	D2	10c ol grn	10	10
J9	D2	20c dk ultra	12	12
J10	D2	50c green	15	15
J11	D2	1fr dk brn	25	25
J12	D2	2fr yel org	32	32
		Nos. J8-J12 (5)	94	94

Nos. J8-J12 prices are for stamps perf. 14x14½. Those perf. 12½ sell for about three times as much.

Belgian Congo
Nos. J13–J19
Overprinted

RUANDA
URUNDI

1959		Engraved	Perf. 11½	
J13	D3	10c ol brn	9	9
J14	D3	20c claret	9	9
J15	D3	50c green	12	12
J16	D3	1fr lt bl	20	20
J17	D3	2fr vermilion	25	25
J18	D3	4fr purple	50	50
J19	D3	6fr vio bl	65	65
		Nos. J13-J19 (7)	1.90	1.90

Both capital and lower-case U's are found in this overprint.

RUSSIA
(rŭsh'á)
(Union of
Soviet Socialist Republics)

LOCATION—Eastern Europe and Northern Asia.
GOVT.—Republic.
AREA—8,647,172 sq. mi.
POP.—258,700,000 (est. 1977).
CAPITAL—Moscow.

An Empire until 1917, the government was in that year overthrown and a socialist union of republics formed under the name of the Union of Soviet Socialist Republics. The U.S.S.R. includes the following autonomous republics which have issued their own stamps: Armenia, Azerbaijan, Georgia and Ukraine.

100 Kopecks = 1 Ruble

Empire.

Coat of Arms
A1   A2   A3

Wmk. 166

Wmkd. Colorless Numerals. (166)

1857, Dec. 10		Typo.	Imperf.	
1	A1	10k brn & bl	4,500.	600.00
		Pen cancellation		175.00
		Penmark & postmark		450.00

Genuine unused copies of No. 1 are exceedingly rare. Most of those offered as used have their pen cancellation removed. The unused price is for a specimen without gum. The very few known stamps with original gum sell for much more.

1858, Jan. 10			Perf. 14½, 15	
2	A1	10k brn & bl	1,500.	75.00
3	A1	20k bl & org	3,000.	1,000.
4	A1	30k car & grn	4,250.	2,000.

Wove Paper.

1858-64		Perf. 12½	Unwmkd.	
5	A2	1k blk & yel ('64)	57.50	30.00
a.		1k blk & org	60.00	27.50
6	A2	3k blk & grn ('64)	80.00	45.00
7	A2	5k blk & lil ('64)	95.00	60.00
8	A1	10k brn & bl	35.00	4.00
9	A1	20k bl & org	150.00	30.00
a.		Half used as 10k on cover		5,000.
10	A1	30k car & grn	160.00	80.00

1863				
11	A3	5k blk & bl	12.00	600.00

No. 11 was issued to pay local postage in St. Petersburg and Moscow. It is known to have been used in other cities. Copies canceled after July, 1864, are worth considerably less.

1865, June 2			Perf. 14½, 15	
12	A2	1k blk & yel	57.50	10.00
a.		1k blk & org	57.50	10.00
13	A2	3k blk & grn	80.00	8.00
14	A2	5k blk & lil	75.00	10.00
15	A1	10k brn & bl	90.00	5.00
a.		Thick paper	150.00	10.00
17	A1	20k bl & org	175.00	30.00
18	A1	30k car & grn	250.00	50.00

Wmk. 168

Wmkd. ЭЗГБ & Wavy Lines (168)

1866-70		Horizontally Laid Paper		
19	A2	1k blk & yel	3.00	50
a.		1k blk & org	3.75	1.00
b.		Imperf.		1,350.
c.		Vertically laid	150.00	30.00
d.		Groundwork inverted	4,500.	1,800.
e.		Thick paper	50.00	30.00
f.		As "c," imperf.	2,800.	2,200.
g.		As "b," "c" & "d"	6,000.	6,000.
20	A2	3k blk & dp grn	6.00	1.00
a.		3k blk & yel grn	6.00	1.00
b.		Imperf.		1,250.
c.		Vertically laid	200.00	50.00
d.		V's in groundwork (error) ('70)	500.00	50.00
22	A2	5k blk & lil	6.00	1.00
a.		5k blk & gray	90.00	15.00
b.		Imperf.	1,500.	850.00
c.		Vertically laid	800.00	150.00
d.		As "c," imperf.		2,500.
23	A1	10k brn & bl	20.00	1.00
a.		Vertically laid	110.00	12.00
b.		Center inverted		5,000.
c.		Imperf.		1,500.
24	A1	20k bl & org	75.00	15.00
a.		Vertically laid	900.00	75.00
25	A1	30k car & grn	100.00	40.00
a.		Vertically laid	700.00	50.00

In Wmk. 168 the initials are those of the State Printing Plant.

Arms
A4

1875-79				
26	A2	2k blk & red	5.00	1.00
a.		Vertically laid	700.00	90.00
b.		Groundwork inverted		7,500.
27	A4	7k gray & rose ('79)	4.00	50
a.		Imperf.		4,000.
b.		Vertically laid	650.00	75.00
c.		Wmk. hexagons ('79)		9,000.
d.		Center inverted		19,000.
e.		Center omitted	300.00	300.00
28	A4	8k gray & rose	6.50	1.00
a.		Vertically laid	600.00	75.00
b.		Imperf.		1,400.
c.		"C" instead of "B" in "Восем"	40.00	40.00
29	A4	10k brn & bl	25.00	5.00
		Center inverted		6,250.
30	A4	20k bl & org	50.00	7.00
a.		Cross-shaped "T" in bottom word	150.00	40.00
b.		Center inverted		7,250.

The hexagon watermark of No. 27c is that of revenue stamps. No. 27c exists with Perm postmark.

Helpful notes abound in the "Information for Collectors" section at the front of this volume.

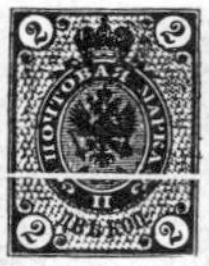
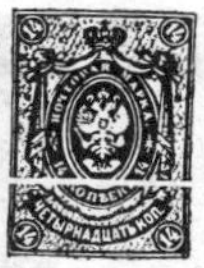

Imperial Eagle and Post Horns
A5 A6

Perf. 14 to 15 and Compound.

1883-88 **Wmk. 168**

Horizontally Laid Paper.

31	A5	1k orange	1.25	35
a.		Imperf.	500.00	500.00
b.		Groundwork inverted	3,500.	3,500.
c.		1k yel	1.50	75
32	A5	2k dk grn	2.00	75
a.		2k yel grn ('88)	2.00	75
b.		Imperf.	500.00	400.00
c.		Wove paper	500.00	300.00
d.		Groundwork inverted		2,500.
33	A5	3k carmine	2.00	50
a.		Imperf.	550.00	500.00
b.		Groundwork inverted		3,500.
c.		Wove paper	500.00	400.00
34	A5	5k red vio	1.75	50
a.		Groundwork inverted		3,500.
35	A5	7k blue	1.75	50
a.		Imperf.	500.00	500.00
b.		Groundwork inverted	750.00	650.00
36	A6	14k bl & rose	4.50	60
a.		Imperf.	725.00	725.00
b.		Center inverted	6,000.	6,000.
c.		Diagonal half surchd. "7" in red, on cover ('84)		22,000.
37	A6	35k vio & grn	20.00	5.00
38	A6	70k brn & org	25.00	5.00

Before 1882 the 1, 2, 3 and 5 kopecks had small numerals in the background; beginning with No. 31 these denominations have a background of network, like the higher values.

No. 36c is handstamped. It is known with cancellations of Tiflis and Kutais, both in Georgia. It is believed to be of philatelic origin.

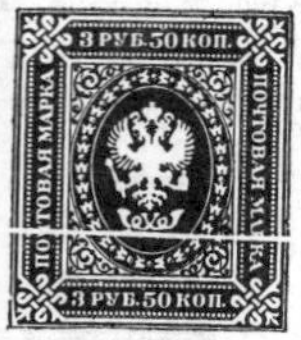

A7

Vertically Laid Paper.

1884 ***Perf. 13½, 13½x11½***

39	A7	3.50r blk & gray	1,000.	650.00
a.		Horiz. laid	6,000.	6,000.
40	A7	7r blk & org	1,000.	650.00

Forgeries exist.

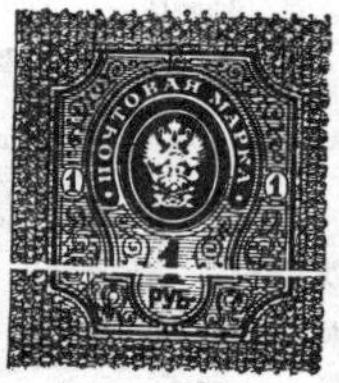

Imperial Eagle and Post Horns with Thunderbolts
A8 A9
With Thunderbolts Across Post Horns.

Perf. 14 to 15 and Compound.

Horizontally Laid Paper

1889, May 14

41	A8	4k rose	75	40
a.		Groundwork invtd.	1,000.	
42	A8	10k dk bl	75	30
43	A8	20k bl & car	2.50	50
44	A8	50k vio & grn	3.50	75

Perf. 13½

45	A9	1r lt brn, brn & org	17.50	3.00
a.		Pair, imperf. between	550.00	550.00
b.		Center omitted	250.00	250.00

See also Nos. 57C, 60, 63, 66, 68, 82, 85, 87, 126, 129, 131.

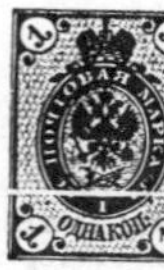
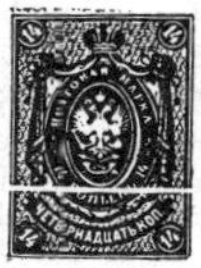

Post Horns with Thunderbolts
A10 A11

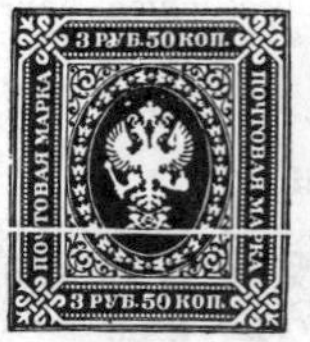

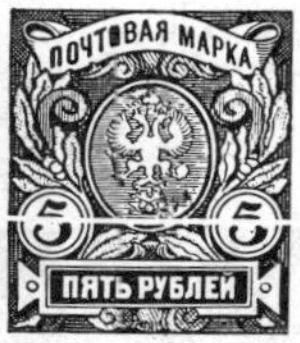

Post Horns with Thunderbolts
A12 A13

Horizontally Laid Paper

1889-92 ***Perf. 14½x15.***

46	A10	1k orange	30	5
a.		Imperf.	500.00	500.00
47	A10	2k green	30	5
a.		Imperf.	350.00	300.00
b.		Groundwork inverted		7,500.
48	A10	3k carmine	40	5
a.		Imperf.	300.00	300.00
49	A10	5k red vio	75	5
b.		Groundwork omitted	800.00	800.00
50	A10	7k dk bl	40	10
a.		Imperf.	600.00	600.00
b.		Groundwork inverted		2,500.
c.		Groundwork omitted	200.00	200.00
51	A11	14k bl & rose	2.00	25
a.		Center inverted	4,500.	4,000.
52	A11	35k vio & grn	7.00	1.00

Perf. 13½.

53	A12	3.50r blk & gray	30.00	10.00
54	A12	7r blk & yel	50.00	20.00
a.		Dbl. impression of blk		300.00

Vertically Laid Paper.

1902-05

Perf. 14 to 15 and Compound.

55	A10	1k orange	25	10
a.		Imperf.	550.00	550.00
b.		Groundwork inverted	900.00	900.00
c.		Groundwork omitted	250.00	250.00
56	A10	2k yel grn	25	10
a.		2k dp grn	10.00	1.00
b.		Groundwork omitted	800.00	400.00
c.		Groundwork inverted	850.00	800.00
d.		Groundwork double	500.00	500.00
57	A10	3k rose red	30	10
a.		Groundwork omitted	400.00	250.00
b.		Dbl. impression	200.00	175.00
d.		Imperf.	150.00	150.00
e.		Groundwork inverted	150.00	150.00
57C	A8	4k rose red ('04)	75	25
f.		Dbl. impression	200.00	200.00
g.		Groundwork inverted	1,500.	600.00
58	A10	5k red vio	75	20
a.		5k dl vio	7.00	4.00
b.		Groundwork inverted	1,000.	1,000.
c.		Imperf.	250.00	250.00
d.		Groundwork omitted	250.00	150.00
59	A10	7k dk bl	60	20
a.		Groundwork omitted	350.00	300.00
b.		Imperf.	400.00	400.00
c.		Groundwork inverted	400.00	400.00
60	A8	10k dk bl ('04)	60	20
a.		Groundwork inverted	20.00	7.50
b.		Groundwork omitted	150.00	30.00
c.		Groundwork double	150.00	30.00
61	A11	14k bl & rose	1.75	25
a.		Center invtd.	4,000.	3,000.
b.		Center omitted	1,500.	1,000.
62	A11	15k brn vio & bl ('05)	2.00	25
a.		Center omitted		
b.		Center inverted	4,500.	3,500.
63	A8	20k bl & car ('04)	1.75	20
64	A11	25k dl grn & lil ('05)	5.00	50
a.		Center inverted	3,000.	3,000.
b.		Center omitted	1,250.	1,250.
65	A11	35k dk vio & grn	6.00	50
a.		Center inverted		20,000.
b.		Center omitted	1,500.	
66	A8	50k vio & grn ('05)	12.00	1.50
67	A11	70k brn & org	15.00	1.50

Perf. 13½.

68	A9	1r lt brn, brn & org	12.00	50
a.		Perf. 11½	500.00	75.00
b.		Perf. 13½x11½, 11½x13½	750.00	700.00
c.		Imperf.	250.00	
d.		Center invtd.	250.00	250.00
e.		Center omitted	250.00	150.00
f.		Horiz. pair, imperf. btwn.	350.00	150.00
69	A12	3.50r blk & gray	12.00	4.00
a.		Center inverted	4,000.	4,000.
b.		Imperf., pair	1,600.	1,600.
70	A12	7r blk & yel	12.00	4.00
a.		Center inverted	4,000.	4,000.
b.		Horizontal pair, imperf. between	1,500.	1,500.
c.		Imperf., pair	1,500.	

1906 ***Perf. 13½.***

71	A13	5r dk bl, grn & pale bl	45.00	5.00
a.		Perf. 11½	250.00	300.00
72	A13	10r car rose, yel & gray	70.00	10.00

The design of No. 72 differs in many details from the illustration. Nos. 71–72 were printed in sheets of 25.

See also Nos. 80–81, 83–84, 86, 108–109, 125, 127–128, 130, 132–135, 137–138.

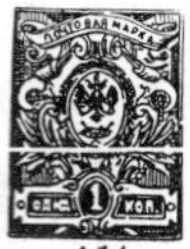
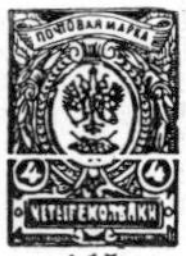

A14 A15

Wove Paper.

Vertical Lozenges of Varnish on Face.

1909-12 ***Perf. 14x14½.*** **Unwmkd.**

73	A14	1k dl org yel	10	20
a.		1k org yel ('09)	35	35
b.		Booklet pane of 6	375.00	
c.		Dbl. impression	100.00	100.00
74	A14	2k dl grn	10	20
a.		2k grn ('09)	40	40
b.		Double impression	37.50	37.50
75	A14	3k carmine	10	20
a.		3k rose red ('09)	40	40
b.		Booklet pane of 6	375.00	
76	A15	4k carmine	10	20
a.		4k car rose ('09)	40	40
77	A14	5k claret	10	20
a.		5k lil ('12)	1.25	1.25
b.		Double impressions	35.00	35.00
78	A14	7k blue	10	20
a.		7k lt bl ('09)	2.50	1.10
b.		Imperf.	300.00	300.00
c.		Booklet pane of 6	600.00	
79	A15	10k dk bl	10	20
a.		10k lt bl ('09)	500.00	30.00
b.		10k pale bl	10.00	2.00
80	A11	14k dk bl & car	20	20
a.		14k bl & rose ('09)	40	40
81	A11	15k red brn & dp bl	10	20
a.		15k dl vio & bl ('09)	1.50	70
c.		Center omitted	150.00	100.00
d.		Center double	50.00	50.00
82	A8	20k dl bl & dk car	10	20
a.		20k bl & car ('10)	1.50	1.00
b.		Groundwork omitted	25.00	15.00
c.		Center double	30.00	30.00
d.		Center and value omitted	100.00	100.00
83	A11	25k dl grn & dk vio	30	30
a.		25k grn & vio ('09)	50	50
b.		Center omitted	150.00	150.00
c.		Center double	30.00	30.00
84	A11	35k red brn & grn	30	30
a.		35k brn vio & yel grn	80	65
b.		35k vio & grn ('09)	80	65
c.		Center double	35.00	35.00
85	A8	50k red brn & grn	10	20
a.		50k vio & grn ('09)	75	60
b.		Groundwork omitted	30.00	30.00
c.		Center double	45.00	45.00
d.		Center and value omitted	160.00	160.00
86	A11	70k brn & red org	10	20
a.		70k lt brn & org ('09)	50	40
b.		Center double	55.00	55.00
c.		Center omitted	160.00	160.00

Perf. 13½

87	A9	1r pale brn, dk brn & org	10	20
a.		1r pale brn, brn & org ('10)	50	40
b.		Perf. 12½	6.00	2.50
c.		Groundwork inverted	30.00	30.00
d.		Pair, imperf. between	35.00	35.00
e.		Center inverted	40.00	40.00
f.		Center double	25.00	25.00

See Nos. 119–124.

No. 87a was issued in sheets of 40 stamps, while Nos. 87 and 87b came in sheets of 50. Nos. 87g–87k are listed below No. 138a.

Nearly all values of this issue are known without the lines of varnish.

The 7k has two types: I. The scroll bearing the top inscription ends at left with three short lines of shading beside the first letter. Four pearls extend at lower left between the leaves and denomination panel. II. Inner lines of scroll at top left end in two curls; three pearls at lower left. Three clichés of type II (an essay) were included by mistake in the plate used for the first printing.

Price of pair, type I with type II, unused $1,500.

SURCHARGES

Russian stamps of types A6-A15 with various surcharges may be found listed under Armenia, Batum, Far Eastern Republic, Georgia, Siberia, South Russia, Transcaucasian Federated Republics and Ukraine.

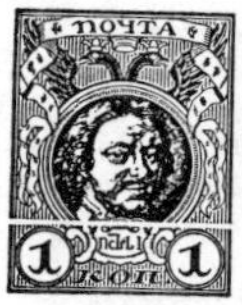
Peter I
A16

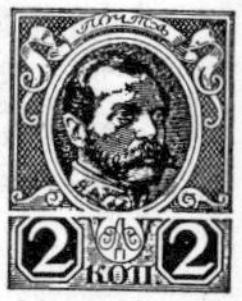
Alexander II
A17

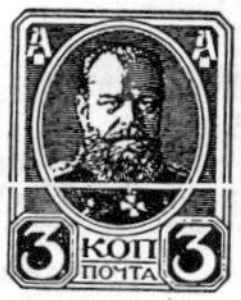
Alexander III
A18

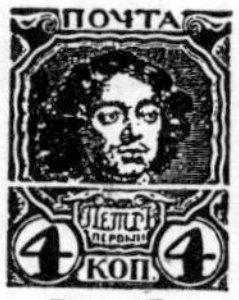
Peter I
A19

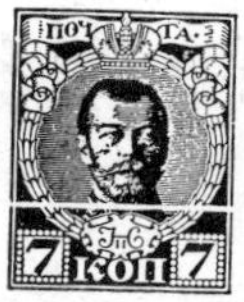
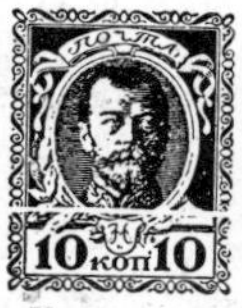
Nicholas II
A20 A21

RUSSIA

Catherine II
A22

Nicholas I
A23

Alexander I
A24

Alexis Mikhailovich
A25

Paul I
A26

Elizabeth Petrovna
A27

Michael Feodorovich
A28

The Kremlin
A29

Winter Palace
A30

Romanov Castle
A31

Nicholas II
A32

Engraved.

101	A29	1r dp grn	15.00	10.00
102	A30	2r red brn	15.00	10.00
	a.	Imperf., pair	1,400.	
103	A31	3r dk vio	35.00	20.00
	a.	Imperf., pair	1,600.	
104	A32	5r blk brn	25.00	35.00
		Nos. 88-104 (17)	111.40	84.75

Issued in commemoration of the tercentenary of the founding of the Romanov dynasty. See also Nos. 105-107, 112-116, 139-141.

Thin Cardboard. Without Gum.
Arms & 5-line Inscription on Back
1915, Nov. Typo. Perf. 13½

105	A21	10k blue	75	9.00
	a.	Imperf.	50.00	
106	A23	15k brown	75	9.00
	a.	Imperf.	50.00	
107	A23	20k ol grn	75	9.00
	a.	Imperf.	50.00	

Nos. 105-107, 112-116 and 139-141 were issued for use as paper money, but contrary to regulations were often used for postal purposes. Back inscription means: "Having circulation on par with silver subsidiary coins."

Types of 1906 Issue.
Vertical Lozenges of Varnish on Face.
1915 Perf. 13½, 13½ x 13.

108	A13	5r ind, grn & lt bl	50	30
	a.	5r dk bl, grn & pale bl ('15)	3.50	1.00
	b.	Perf. 12½	5.00	1.50
	c.	Center double	50.00	
	d.	Pair, imperf. btwn.	325.00	
109	A13	10r car lake, yel & gray	60	40
	a.	10r car, yel & lt gray	75	40
	b.	10r rose red, yel & gray ('15)	1.50	75
	c.	10r car, yel & gray bl (error)	1,600.	
	d.	Groundwork inverted	400.00	
	e.	Center double	60.00	60.00

Nos. 108a and 109b were issued in sheets of 25. Nos. 108, 108b, 109 and 109a came in sheets of 50. Chemical forgeries of No. 109c exist. Genuine copies usually are centered to upper right.

Nos. 92, 94 Surcharged **10 10**

1916

110	A20	10k on 7k brn	25	25
	a.	Invtd. surcharge	50.00	80.00
111	A22	20k on 14k bl grn	25	25
	a.	Invtd. surcharge	50.00	50.00

Types of 1913 Issue.
Thin Cardboard. Without Gum.
Arms, Surcharge & 4-line inscription on Back
Surcharged Large Numerals.
1916-17

112	A16	1 on 1k brn org	50	7.00
113	A17	2 on 2k yel grn	50	7.00

Without Surcharge.

114	A16	1k brn org	15.00	60.00
115	A17	2k yel grn	35.00	100.00
116	A18	3k rose red	75	8.00

See note after No. 107.

Nos. 78a, 80a Surcharged:

коп.10 коп.   к.20к.
a   *b*

1917 Perf. 14 x 14½.

117	A14	10k on 7k lt bl	10	10
	a.	Inverted surcharge	80.00	80.00
	b.	Double surch.	80.00	
118	A11	20k on 14k bl & rose	10	10
	a.	Inverted surcharge	60.00	60.00

Provisional Government.
Civil War.
Types of 1889-1912 Issues.
Wove Paper.
Vertical Lozenges of Varnish on Face.

Two types of 7r:
Type I - Single outer frame line.
Type II - Double outer frame line.

1917 Typographed. Imperf.

119	A14	1k orange	10	10
120	A14	2k gray grn	10	10
121	A14	3k red	10	10
122	A15	4k carmine	20	30
123	A15	5k claret	10	10
124	A15	10k dk bl	6.00	12.00
125	A11	15k red brn & dp bl	10	10
	a.	Center omitted	80.00	
126	A8	20k bl & car	20	50
	a.	Groundwork omitted	20.00	20.00
127	A11	25k grn & gray vio	1.00	1.50
128	A11	35k red brn & grn	15	50
129	A8	50k brn vio & grn	25	40
	a.	Groundwork omitted	20.00	20.00
130	A11	70k brn & org	10	60
	a.	Center omitted	150.00	
131	A9	1r pale brn, brn & red org	10	15
	a.	Center inverted	30.00	30.00
	b.	Center omitted	30.00	30.00
	c.	Center double	25.00	20.00
	d.	Groundwork double	20.00	20.00
	e.	Groundwork inverted	15.00	15.00
	f.	Groundwork omitted	35.00	35.00
	g.	Frame double	25.00	25.00
132	A12	3.50r mar & lt grn	15	40
133	A13	5r dk bl, grn & pale bl	30	50
	a.	5r dk bl, grn & yel (error)	1,000.	
	b.	Groundwork inverted	500.00	
134	A12	7r dk grn & pink (I)	1.00	1.50
	a.	Center invtd.	16,000.	16,000.
135	A13	5r scar, yel & gray	30.00	35.00
	a.	10r scar, grn & gray (error)	1,000.	

Vertical Lozenges of Varnish on Face.
1917 Perf. 13½, 13½ x 13.

137	A12	3.50r mar & lt grn	10	10
138	A12	7r dk grn & pink (II)	10	10
	d.	Type I	3.00	3.00

Perf. 12½.

137a	A12	3.50r mar & lt grn	30	30
138a	A12	7r dk grn & pink (II)	1.50	1.50

Horizontal Lozenges of Varnish on Face.
Perf. 13½ x 13.

87g	A9	1r pale brn, brn & red org	15	15
	h.	Imperforate	15.00	
	i.	As "h", center omitted	35.00	
	j.	As "h", center inverted	35.00	
	k.	As "h", center double	35.00	
137b	A12	3.50r mar & lt grn	25	25
	d.	Imperforate	325.00	
138b	A12	7r dk grn & pink (II)	20	20
	c.	Imperforate	300.00	

Nos. 87g, 137b and 138b often show the eagle with little or no embossing.

Condition is the all-important factor of price. Prices quoted are for stamps in fine condition.

The lack of a price for a listed item does not necessarily indicate rarity.

Types of 1913 Issue.
Thin Cardboard. Without Gum.
Surcharge & 4-line Inscription on Back
Surcharged Large Numerals.

1917

139	A16	1 on 1k brn org	60	7.00
	a.	Imperf.	35.00	35.00
140	A17	2 on 2k yel grn	1.00	7.00
	a.	Imperf.	35.00	35.00
	b.	Surch. omitted, imperf.	70.00	70.00

Without Surcharge.

141	A18	3k rose red	60	7.00

See note after No. 107.
Stamps overprinted with a Liberty Cap on Crossed Swords or with reduced facsimiles of pages of newspapers were a private speculation and without official sanction.

Russian Soviet Federated Socialist Republic.

Severing Chain of Bondage
A33

1918 Typographed Perf. 13½

149	A33	35k blue	15	2.50
	a.	Imperf., pair	150.00	
150	A33	70k brown	15	2.50
	a.	Imperf., pair	500.00	

In 1918-1922 various revenue stamps were permitted to be used for postal duty, sometimes surcharged with new values, more often not.

Symbols of Agriculture
A40

Symbols of Industry
A41

Soviet Symbols of Agriculture and Industry
A42

Science and Arts
A43

1921 Lithographed Imperf. Unwmkd.

177	A40	1r orange	50	1.50
178	A40	2r lt brn	50	1.50
179	A41	5r dl ultra	30	50
180	A42	20r blue	1.20	3.50
	a.	Pelure paper	4.00	4.00
	b.	Dbl. impression	30.00	
181	A40	100r orange	10	10
	a.	Pelure paper	10	20
182	A40	200r lt brn	15	35
	a.	200r ol brn	10.00	10.00

RUSSIA

183	A43	250r dl vio	10	10
a.		Pelure paper	10	10
b.		Chalk surfaced paper	15	15
c.		Tête bêche pair	20.00	20.00
d.		Double impression	30.00	
184	A40	300r green	15	35
a.		Pelure paper	15.00	20.00
185	A41	500r blue	15	50
186	A41	1000r carmine	15	40
a.		Chalk surfaced paper	15	25
b.		Thick paper	15	25
c.		Pelure paper	15	25
		Nos. 177-186 (10)	3.30	8.80

New Russia Triumphant
A44

Wmk. 169
Engraved.

Wmkd. Lozenges. (169)
Type I —37½ mm. by 23½ mm.
Type II—38½ mm. by 23¼ mm.

187	A44	40r sl, type II	30	1.00
a.		Type I	50	1.25

Initials Stand for Russian Soviet Federated Socialist Republic
A45

1921		Lithographed.	Unwmkd.	
188	A45	100r orange	20	50
189	A45	250r violet	20	50
190	A45	1000r car rose	50	1.00

4th anniversary of Soviet Government.
A 200r was not regularly issued. Price $20.

Nos. 177-179 Surcharged in Black
5000 руб.

1922

191	A40	5000r on 1r org	35	1.00
a.		Inverted surcharge	35.00	35.00
b.		Double surcharge, red & black	35.00	35.00
c.		Pair, one without surch.	50.00	
192	A40	5000r on 2r lt brn	60	1.50
a.		Inverted surcharge	25.00	25.00
b.		Double surcharge	30.00	
193	A41	5000r on 5r ultra	35	75
a.		Invtd. surch.	50.00	50.00
b.		Dbl. surch.	50.00	

No. 180 Surcharged
Р.С.Ф.С.Р.
5000 РУБЛЕЙ

194	A42	5000r on 20r bl	75	1.50
a.		Pelure paper	1.50	2.00
b.		Pair, one without surch.	50.00	

Nos. 177-180, 187 Surcharged in Black or Red
РСФСР
10.000 Р.

Wmkd. Lozenges. (169)

195	A44	10,000r on 40r sl, type I	40	75
a.		Invtd. surch.	25.00	25.00
b.		Type II	2.25	3.00
c.		"1.0000" instead of "10.000"	75.00	
d.		Dbl. surch.	50.00	

Red Surcharge.
Unwmkd.

196	A40	5000r on 1r org	65	1.50
a.		Invtd. surch.	25.00	25.00
197	A40	5000r on 2r lt brn	75	2.00
a.		Invtd. surch.	50.00	50.00
198	A41	5000r on 5r ultra	75	2.00
199	A42	5000r on 20r bl	1.25	3.00
a.		Invtd. surch.	60.00	60.00

Wmkd. Lozenges. (169)

200	A44	10,000r on 40r sl, type I (R)	25	35
a.		Invtd. surch.	30.00	30.00
b.		Dbl. surch.	30.00	30.00
c.		With periods after Russian letters	60.00	60.00
d.		Type II		50
e.		As "a," type II	50.00	50.00
f.		As "c," type II	75.00	75.00

No. 183 Surcharged in Black or Blue Black

1922, Mar. **Unwmkd.**

201	A43	7500r on 250r dk vio (BK)	10	15
a.		Pelure paper	10	15
b.		Chalk surfaced paper	20	40
c.		Blue black surch.	15	20
		Nos. 191-201 (11)	6.20	14.50

Nos. 201, 201a and 201b exist with surcharge inverted (price about $15 each), and double (about $25 each).

Type of 1921 and

"Workers of the World Unite"
A46

Wmk. 171

Wmkd. Diamonds. (171)

1922 **Lithographed.**

202	A46	5000r dk vio	50	3.00
203	A42	7500r blue	25	35
204	A46	10,000r blue	2.25	3.00

Unwmkd.

205	A42	7500r bl, buff	25	40
a.		Dbl. impression	25.00	
206	A46	22,500r dk vio, buff	35	50
		Nos. 202-206 (5)	3.60	7.25

No. 183 Surcharged Diagonally
100,000 РУБ.

1922 **Imperf.** **Unwmkd.**

210	A43	100,000r on 250r dl vio	10	15
a.		Invtd. surch.	25.00	25.00
b.		Pelure paper	10	20
c.		Chalk surfaced paper	15	20
d.		As "b," invtd. surcharge	25.00	30.00

Marking 5th Anniversary of October Revolution
A48

1922 **Typographed.**

211	A48	5r ocher & blk	20	25
212	A48	10r brn & blk	20	25
213	A48	25r vio & blk	60	1.00
a.		Pelure paper	25.00	
214	A48	27r rose & blk	1.10	2.00
a.		Pelure paper	25.00	
215	A48	45r bl & blk	75	1.25
a.		Pelure paper	30.00	
		Nos. 211-215 (5)	2.85	4.75

Issued to commemorate the fifth anniversary of the October Revolution. Sold in the currency of 1922 which was valued at 10,000 times that of the preceding years.

Stamps of 1909-18 Surcharged

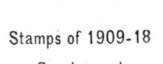

1922-23 **Perf. 14½x15.**

216	A8	5r on 20k bl & car	15	40
a.		Invtd. surcharge	20.00	20.00
b.		Double surcharge	35.00	35.00
217	A11	20r on 15k red brn & bl	25	50
a.		Invtd. surch.	50.00	50.00
218	A11	20r on 70k brn & org	15	25
a.		Inverted surch	15.00	15.00
b.		Double surcharge	25.00	25.00
219	A8	30r on 50k brn red & grn	20	40
a.		Invtd. surcharge	20.00	20.00
c.		Groundwork omitted	25.00	25.00
d.		Double surcharge	20.00	20.00
220	A11	40r on 15k red brn & bl	10	25
a.		Invtd. surch.	25.00	25.00
b.		Double surcharge	25.00	25.00
221	A11	100r on 15k red brn & bl	10	25
a.		Invtd. surch.	25.00	25.00
b.		Double surcharge	20.00	20.00
222	A11	200r on 15k red brn & bl	15	25
a.		Invtd. surch.	20.00	20.00
b.		Double surcharge	15.00	15.00

Nos. 218-220, 222 exist in pairs, one without surcharge; Nos. 221-222 with triple surcharge; No. 221 with double surcharge, one inverted. Price, each $100.

Imperf.

223	A8	5r on 20k bl & car	3.00	7.00
224	A11	20r on 15k red brn & bl	1,200.	1,200.
225	A11	20r on 70k brn & org	30	50
a.		Invtd. surch.	20.00	

226	A8	30r on 50k brn vio & grn	1.50	3.00
227	A11	40r on 15k red brn & bl	10	25
a.		Invtd. surch.	35.00	35.00
b.		Double surch.	25.00	25.00
228	A11	100r on 15k red brn & bl	50	75
a.		Invtd. surch.	60.00	60.00
229	A11	200r on 15k red brn & bl	50	50
a.		Inverted surcharge	60.00	60.00
b.		Dbl. surcharge	40.00	40.00
		Nos. 216-223, 225-229 (13)	7.00	14.30

Worker **Soldier**
A49 A50

1922-23 **Typographed** **Imperf.**

230	A49	10r blue	10	15
231	A50	50r brown	10	15
232	A50	70r brn vio	10	15
233	A50	100r red	20	25

1923 **Perf. 14x14½**

234	A49	10r dp bl, perf. 13½	15	20
a.		Perf. 14	20.00	25.00
b.		Perf.12½	1.00	1.25
235	A50	50r brown	15	20
a.		Perf. 12½	8.00	9.00
b.		Perf. 13½	2.50	3.00
236	A50	70r brn vio	15	20
a.		Perf. 12½	2.50	3.00
237	A50	100r red	20	30
a.		Cliché of 70r in plate of 100r	35.00	45.00

Soldier **Worker** **Peasant**
A51 A52 A53

1923 **Perf. 14½x15.**

238	A51	3r rose	15	40
a.		Imperf.	15.00	30.00
239	A52	4r brown	15	40
a.		Imperf.	20.00	40.00
b.		As "a," dbl. impression	35.00	
240	A53	5r lt bl	15	40
a.		Dbl. impression	12.00	15.00
b.		Imperf.	7.00	10.00
241	A51	10r gray	15	40
d.		Imperf.	7.00	10.00
e.		Dbl. impression	25.00	
f.		As "d," dbl. impression	35.00	
241A	A51	20r brn vio	30	1.25
b.		Double impression	15.00	15.00
c.		Imperf.	60.00	70.00
		Nos. 238-241A (5)	90	2.85

Stamps of 1r buff, type A52, and 2r green, type A53, perf. 12 and imperf. were prepared but not put in use. Price $1 each.

The imperfs of Nos. 238-241A were sold only by the philatelic bureau in Moscow.

Stamps of 20r, type A51, printed in gray black or dull violet are essays. Price $35 each.

The stamps of this and the following issues were sold for the currency of 1923, one ruble of which was equal to 100 rubles of 1922 and 1,000,000 rubles of 1921.

Foreign postal stationery (stamped envelopes, postal cards and air letter sheets) lies beyond the scope of this Catalogue which is limited to adhesive postage stamps.

Union of Soviet Socialist Republics.

Reaping
A54

Sowing
A55

Fordson Tractor—A56

Symbolical of the Exhibition
A57

1923, Aug. 19 Litho. *Imperf.*

242	A54	1r brn & org	1.50	3.00
243	A55	2r dp grn & pale grn	1.50	3.00
244	A56	5r dp bl & pale bl	1.75	4.00
245	A57	7r rose & pink	2.00	5.00

Perf. 12½, 13½.

246	A54	1r brn & org	4.00	5.00
a.		Perf. 12½	30.00	35.00
247	A55	2r dp grn & pale grn, perf. 12½	3.00	3.50
248	A56	5r dp bl & pale bl	3.50	6.00
a.		Perf. 13½	12.00	17.50
249	A57	7r rose & pink	5.00	7.00
a.		Perf. 12½	20.00	25.00
		Nos. 242-249 (8)	22.25	36.50

Issued to commemorate the 1st Agriculture and Craftsmanship Exhibition, Moscow.

Worker
A58

Soldier
A59

Peasant
A60

Lithographed.

1923 *Imperf.* Unwmkd.

250	A58	1k orange	1.00	30
251	A60	2k green	1.25	50
252	A59	3k red brn	1.25	50
253	A58	4k dp rose	1.25	1.00
254	A58	5k lilac	1.25	1.00
255	A60	6k lt bl	1.00	40
256	A59	10k dk bl	1.00	40
257	A58	20k yel grn	4.00	75
258	A60	50k dk brn	6.00	3.00
259	A59	1r red & brn	7.00	3.50
		Nos. 250-259 (10)	25.00	11.35

1924 *Perf. 14½ x15.*

261	A58	4k dp rose	175.00	50.00
262	A59	10k dk bl	175.00	50.00
263	A60	30k violet	40.00	15.00
264	A59	40k sl gray	40.00	15.00

See also Nos. 273-290, 304-321.

Vladimir Ilyich Ulyanov (Lenin)
A61

Worker
A62

1924 *Imperf.*

265	A61	3k red & blk	1.50	1.75
266	A61	6k red & blk	1.50	1.75
267	A61	12k red & blk	1.50	1.75
268	A61	20k red & blk	3.00	2.00

Three printings of Nos. 265-268 differ in size of red frame.

Perf. 13½.

269	A61	3k red & blk	2.00	2.25
270	A61	6k red & blk	2.00	2.25
271	A61	12k red & blk	2.50	3.00
272	A61	20k red & blk	4.00	3.50

Death of Lenin (1870-1924).
Forgeries of Nos. 265-272 exist.

Types of 1923
Typographed

There are small differences between the lithographed stamps of 1923 and the typographed of 1924-25. On a few values this may be seen in the numerals.

Type A58: Lithographed. The two white lines forming the outline of the ear are continued across the cheek. Typographed. The outer lines of the ear are broken where they touch the cheek.

Type A59: Lithographed. At the top of the right shoulder a white line touches the frame at the left. Counting from the edge of the visor of the cap, lines 5, 6 and sometimes 7 touch at their upper ends. Typographed. The top line of the shoulder does not reach the frame. On the cap lines 5, 6 and 7 run together and form a white spot.

Type A60: In the angle above the first letter "C" there is a fan-shaped ornament enclosing four white dashes. On the lithographed stamps these dashes reach nearly to the point of the angle. On the typographed stamps the dashes are shorter and often only three are visible.

On unused copies of the typographed stamps the raised outlines of the designs can be seen on the backs of the stamps.

1924-25 *Imperf.*

273	A59	3k red brn	2.00	2.00
274	A58	4k dp rose	2.00	2.00
275	A59	10k dk bl	3.00	2.00
275A	A60	50k brown	500.00	50.00

Other typographed and imperf. values include: 2k green, 5k lilac, 6k light blue, 20k green and 1r red and brown. Price, unused: $300, $200, $75, $300, and $350.

Nos. 273-275A were regularly issued. The 7k, 8k, 9k, 30k, 40k, 2r, 3r, and 5r also exist imperf. Price, set of 8, $150.

Typographed.
Perf. 14½ x15.

276	A58	1k orange	100.00	10.00
277	A60	2k green	1.00	60
278	A59	3k red brn	1.25	75
279	A58	4k dp rose	1.25	75
280	A58	5k lilac	15.00	2.50
281	A60	6k lt bl	1.25	75
282	A59	7k chocolate	1.50	75
283	A58	8k brn ol	1.75	1.25
284	A60	9k org red	1.75	2.50
285	A59	10k dk bl	2.50	1.00
286	A58	14k sl bl	30.00	5.00
287	A60	15k yellow	*6,000.*	*400.00*
288	A58	20k gray grn	6.00	1.50
288A	A60	30k violet	150.00	5.00
288B	A59	40k sl gray	150.00	10.00
289	A60	50k brown	30.00	7.50
290	A59	1r red & brn	15.00	3.75
291	A62	2r grn & rose	30.00	6.00
		Nos. 276-286, 288-291 (17)	538.25	59.60

See also No. 323.
Forgeries of No. 287 exist.

1925 *Perf. 12.*

276a	A58	1k orange	1.00	30
277a	A60	2k green	12.00	1.75
278a	A59	3k red brn	2.50	1.25
279a	A58	4k dp rose	85.00	6.00
280a	A58	5k lilac	7.00	1.50
282a	A59	7k chocolate	3.50	35
283a	A58	8k brn ol	120.00	7.50
284a	A60	9k org red	20.00	10.00
285a	A59	10k dk bl	4.00	75
286a	A58	14k sl bl	4.00	75
287a	A60	15k yellow	4.00	2.00
288c	A58	20k gray grn	27.50	75
288d	A60	30k violet	30.00	5.00
288e	A59	40k sl gray	25.00	5.00
289a	A60	50k brown	12.00	2.00
290a	A59	1r red & brn	350.00	150.00
		Nos. 276a-290a (16)	707.50	194.90

Soldier
A63

Worker
A64

1924-25 *Perf. 13½.*

292	A63	3r blk brn & grn	20.00	7.50
a.		Perf. 10	450.00	52.50
b.		Perf. 13½x10	350.00	350.00
293	A64	5r dk bl & gray brn	50.00	10.00
a.		Perf. 10½	60.00	60.00

See also Nos. 324-325.

Lenin Mausoleum, Moscow—A65

Wmk. 170

Wmkd. Greek Border and Rosettes. (170)

1925, Jan. Photo. *Imperf.*

294	A65	7k dp bl	4.00	4.00
295	A65	14k dk grn	4.50	4.00
296	A65	20k car rose	4.50	4.00
297	A65	40k red brn	5.00	5.00

Perf. 13½ x14.

298	A65	7k dp bl	4.00	4.00
299	A65	14k dk grn	4.50	4.00
300	A65	20k car rose	4.50	4.00
301	A65	40k red brn	5.00	5.00

First anniversary of Lenin's death.

Nos. 294-301 are found on both ordinary and thick paper. Those on thick paper sell for twice as much, except for No. 301, which is scarcer on ordinary paper.

Lenin
A66

Perf. 13½

1925, July Engr. Wmk. 170

302	A66	5r red brn	35.00	7.50
a.		Perf. 12½	45.00	10.00
b.		Perf. 10½ ('26)	35.00	10.00
303	A66	10r indigo	35.00	15.00
a.		Perf. 12½	200.00	100.00
b.		Perf. 10½ ('26)	25.00	15.00

Imperfs. exist. Price, set $80.
See Nos. 407-408, 621-622

Types of 1923 Issue
Typographed

1925-27 *Perf. 12* Wmk. 170

304	A58	1k orange	75	50
305	A60	2k green	75	30
306	A59	3k red brn	75	50
307	A58	4k dp rose	60	35
308	A58	5k lilac	80	35
309	A60	6k lt bl	80	35
310	A59	7k chocolate	1.00	25
311	A58	8k brn ol	1.00	25
a.		Perf. 14½x15	100.00	30.00
312	A60	9k red	1.50	60
313	A59	10k dk bl	1.50	40
a.		10k pale bl ('27)	2.50	1.50
314	A58	14k sl bl	1.75	50
315	A60	15k yellow	3.00	1.00
316	A59	18k violet	2.00	35
317	A58	20k gray grn	2.50	35
318	A60	30k violet	3.50	35
319	A59	40k sl gray	4.50	50
320	A60	50k brown	6.00	50
321	A59	1r red & brn	6.00	50
a.		Perf. 14½x15	175.00	15.00
323	A62	2r grn & rose red	35.00	6.00
a.		Perf. 14½x15	15.00	3.00

Perf. 13½.

324	A63	3r blk brn & grn	12.50	5.00
a.		Perf. 12½	40.00	15.00
325	A64	5r dk bl & gray brn	25.00	5.00
		Nos. 304-325 (21)	111.20	23.90

Nos. 304-315, 317-325 exist imperf. Price, set $150.

Mikhail V. Lomonosov and Academy of Sciences
A67

1925, Sept. Photo. *Perf. 12½, 13½*

326	A67	3k org brn	8.00	4.00
a.		Perf. 12½x12	12.00	7.50
b.		Perf. 13½x12½	45.00	35.00
c.		Perf. 13½	17.50	10.00
327	A67	15k dk ol grn	8.00	4.00
a.		Perf. 12½	20.00	7.50

Issued to commemorate the bicentenary of the founding of the Russian Academy of Sciences. Exist unwatermarked, on thick paper with yellow gum, Perf. 13½. These are essays, later perforated and gummed.

Prof. A. S. Popov
A68

1925, Oct. *Perf. 13½*

328	A68	7k dp bl	4.00	2.50
329	A68	14k green	6.00	3.00

Issued to commemorate the 20th anniversary of the death of Aleksandr S. Popov (1859-1905), radio pioneer.

RUSSIA

Decembrist
Exiles
A69

Revolutionist
Leaders
A71

Street Rioting in
St. Petersburg
A70

1925, Dec. 28   *Imperf.*
330	A69	3k ol grn	2.50	2.75
331	A70	7k brown	3.00	3.25
332	A71	14k car lake	4.00	4.25

Perf. 13½.
333	A69	3k ol grn	3.50	2.25
a.		Perf. 12½	70.00	50.00
334	A70	7k brown	3.25	2.75
335	A71	14k car lake	4.50	4.00
	Nos. 330-335 (6)		20.75	19.25

Centenary of Decembrist revolution.

Revolters
Parading
A72

Speaker
Haranguing Mob
A73

Street
Barricade,
Moscow
A74

1925, Dec. 20   *Imperf.*
336	A72	3k ol grn	2.50	3.00
337	A73	7k brown	2.75	3.25
338	A74	14k car lake	3.50	4.00

Perf. 12½, 13½, 12x12½
339	A72	3k ol grn	2.50	2.50
a.		Perf. 13½	7.00	7.00
340	A73	7k brown	6.00	6.00
a.		Perf. 13½	17.50	15.00
b.		Horizontal pair, imperf. between	75.00	75.00
341	A74	14k car lake	4.00	4.00
a.		Perf. 13½	35.00	20.00
	Nos. 336-341 (6)		21.25	22.75

20th anniversary of Revolution of 1905.

Lenin
A75

Liberty Monument,
Moscow
A76

Engraved.
1926   *Perf. 10½.*   *Wmk. 170*
342	A75	1r dk brn	8.00	4.00
343	A75	2r blk vio	15.00	7.50
a.		Perf. 12½	65.00	42.50
344	A75	3r dk grn	25.00	7.50

1926, July   *Litho.*   *Perf. 12x12½*
347	A76	7k bl grn & red	4.00	2.50
348	A76	14k bl grn & vio	4.00	2.50

Issued to commemorate the 6th International Esperanto Congress at Leningrad. Exist perf. 11½.

Nos. 282, 282a and
310 Surcharged
in Black

8 КОП

Perf. 14½x15
1927, June   *Unwmkd.*
349	A59	8k on 7k choc	2.00	1.50
a.		Perf. 12	15.00	12.50
b.		Invtd. surch.	200.00	175.00

Perf. 12.   *Wmk. 170*
350	A59	8k on 7k choc	3.00	1.75
a.		Invtd. surch.	75.00	60.00

The surcharge on Nos. 349-350 comes in two types: With space of 2mm. between lines, and with space of 3/4mm. The latter is much scarcer.

Same Surcharge on Stamps of 1925-26 in Black or Red.
Perf. 13½, 12½, 12 x 12½.
353	A68	8k on 7k dp bl (R)	3.50	5.50
a.		Inverted "8"	60.00	60.00
354	A70	8k on 7k brn	9.00	11.00
355	A73	8k on 7k brn	12.00	15.00
356	A76	8k on 7k bl grn & red	10.00	12.50

Imperf.
357	A70	8k on 7k brn	4.00	6.00
358	A73	8k on 7k brn	4.00	6.00
	Nos. 349-350, 353-358 (8)		47.50	59.25

Postage Due Stamps
of 1925
Surcharged

ПОЧТОВАЯ МАРКА КОП. 8 КОП.

Perf. 12, 14½x14
Litho. or Typo.
1927, June   *Unwmkd.*
359	D1	8k on 1k red, typo., perf. 12	1.75	2.25
a.		Litho, perf. 12	27.50	27.50
b.		Invtd. surch.	130.00	130.00
360	D1	8k on 2k vio	2.50	3.50
a.		Invtd. surch.	130.00	130.00
361	D1	8k on 3k lt bl	2.25	3.25
a.		Inverted surcharge	130.00	130.00
362	D1	8k on 7k org	2.50	3.50
a.		Invtd. surch.	130.00	130.00
363	D1	8k on 8k grn	1.75	2.25
a.		Invtd. surch.	130.00	130.00
364	D1	8k on 10k dk bl	2.25	3.25
a.		Invtd. surch.	130.00	130.00
365	D1	8k on 14k brn	1.75	2.25
a.		Inverted surcharge	130.00	130.00
	Nos. 359-365 (7)		14.75	20.25

Typographed.
1927, June   *Perf. 12*   *Wmk. 170*
366	D1	8k on 1k red	2.00	3.50
367	D1	8k on 2k vio	2.00	3.50
368	D1	8k on 3k lt bl	3.50	4.50
369	D1	8k on 7k org	3.50	4.50
370	D1	8k on 8k grn	2.00	3.50
371	D1	8k on 10k dk bl	2.00	3.50
372	D1	8k on 14k brn	2.00	3.50
	Nos. 366-372 (7)		17.00	26.50

#366, 368-372 exist with invtd. surch. Price each, $100.

Dr. L. L. Zamenhof
A77

1927   Photogravure   *Perf. 10½*
373	A77	14k yel grn & brn	4.50	3.00

Unwmkd.
374	A77	14k yel grn & brn	4.50	3.00

40th anniversary of creation of Esperanto.
No. 374 exists perf. 10, 10x10½ and imperf. Price, imperf. pair $200.

Worker, Soldier, Peasant
A78

Worker and Sailor
A81

Lenin in Car Guarded by Soldiers
A79

Smolny Institute, Leningrad
A80

Map of the U. S. S. R.
A82

Men of Various Soviet Republics
A83

Workers of Different Races; Kremlin in Background
A84

Typo. (3k, 8k, 18k), Engr. (7k),
Litho. (14k), Photo. (5k, 28k)
Perf. 13½, 12½x12, 11
1927, Oct.   *Unwmkd.*
375	A78	3k brt rose	1.00	1.50
a.		Imperf. pair	300.00	
376	A79	5k dp brn	5.00	4.00
a.		Imperf.	250.00	250.00
b.		Perf. 12½	40.00	35.00
c.		Perf. 12½x10½	30.00	20.00
377	A80	7k myr grn	6.00	1.00
a.		Perf. 11½	40.00	25.00
b.		Imperf. pair	800.00	
378	A81	8k brn & blk	3.00	1.75
a.		Perf. 10½x12½	6.00	6.00

379	A82	14k dl bl & red	5.00	3.00
380	A83	18k blue	4.00	3.00
a.		Imperf.	175.00	
381	A84	28k ol brn	15.00	10.00
a.		Perf. 10	50.00	50.00
	Nos. 375-381 (7)		40.00	28.25

10th anniversary of October Revolution. The paper of No. 375 has an overprint of pale yellow wavy lines.
No. 377b exists with watermark 170.
Price, $150.00

Worker
A85

Peasant
A86

Lenin
A87

Chalk Surfaced Paper
1927-28   Typographed.   *Perf. 13½.*
382	A85	1k orange	50	40
383	A86	2k ap grn	50	30
385	A85	4k brt bl	50	30
386	A86	5k brown	50	30
388	A85	7k dk red ('28)	3.00	1.00
389	A85	8k green	1.50	30
391	A85	10k lt brn	1.50	30
392	A87	14k dk grn ('28)	2.00	1.00
393	A87	18k ol grn	2.00	50
394	A87	18k dk bl ('28)	3.00	75
395	A86	20k dk gray grn	2.00	50
396	A85	40k rose red	4.00	75
397	A85	50k brt bl	5.00	2.00
399	A85	70k gray grn	6.00	2.00
400	A86	80k orange	8.00	3.00
	Nos. 382-400 (15)		40.00	12.90

The 1k, 2k and 10k exist imperf. Price, each $225.

Soldier and Kremlin
A88

Sailor and Flag
A89

Cavalryman
A90

Aviator
A91

1928, Feb. 6
Chalk Surfaced Paper
402	A88	8k lt brn	1.25	50
a.		Imperf.	125.00	
403	A89	14k dp bl	2.50	1.25
404	A90	18k car rose	2.75	2.25
a.		Imperf.	125.00	
405	A91	28k yel grn	3.50	3.00

10th anniversary of the Soviet Army.

Lenin Types of 1925-26.
Wmkd. Lozenges. (169)
1928-29 Engraved.   *Perf. 10, 10½.*
406	A75	3r dk grn ('29)	10.00	4.00
407	A66	5r red brn	12.00	5.00
408	A66	10r indigo	20.00	8.00

RUSSIA

Bugler Sounding Assembly
A92   A93
Perf. 12½x12

1929, Aug. 18	Photo.	Wmk. 170		
411	A92	10k ol brn	12.00	5.00
a.		Perf. 10½	50.00	30.00
b.		Perf. 12½x12x10½x12	60.00	30.00
412	A93	14k slate	6.00	4.00
a.		Perf. 12½x12x10½x12	80.00	50.00

First All-Soviet Assembly of Pioneers.

Factory Worker A95   Peasant A96   Farm Worker A97

Soldier A98   Worker, Soldier, Peasant A100   Worker A103

Lenin A104   Peasant A107

Factory Worker A109   Farm Worker A111

Perf. 12 x12½

1929-31		Typographed	Wmk. 170	
413	A103	1k orange	25	15
a.		Perf. 10½	22.50	17.50
b.		Perf. 14x14½	75.00	55.00
414	A95	2k yel grn	25	15
415	A96	3k blue	25	15
a.		Perf. 14x14½	70.00	55.00
416	A97	4k claret	50	20
417	A98	5k org brn	50	20
a.		Perf. 10½	45.00	40.00
418	A100	7k scarlet	2.00	1.00
419	A103	10k ol grn	85	15
a.		Perf. 10½	40.00	35.00

Unwmkd.

| 420 | A104 | 14k indigo | 2.00 | 1.00 |
| a. | | Perf. 10½ | 6.00 | 5.00 |

Wmk. 170

421	A100	15k dk ol grn ('30)	1.50	25
422	A107	20k green	1.50	25
a.		Perf. 10½	65.00	35.00
423	A109	30k dk vio	2.50	75
424	A111	50k dp brn	3.50	1.75
425	A98	70k dk red ('30)	3.75	2.00
426	A107	80k red brn ('31)	3.50	2.00
		413-426 (14)	22.85	10.00

Nos. 422, 423, 424 and 426 have a background of fine wavy lines in pale shades of the colors of the stamps.
See Nos. 456–466, 613A–619A, 743.

Symbolical of Industry
A112

Tractors Issuing from Assembly Line
A113

Iron Furnace. Inscription reads, "More Metal More Machines"
A114

Blast Furnace and Chart of Anticipated Iron Production
A115

1929-30			*Perf. 12x12½*	
427	A112	5k org brn	2.50	1.00
428	A113	10k ol grn	2.50	1.50

Perf. 12½x12

| 429 | A114 | 20k dl grn | 6.50 | 3.00 |
| 430 | A115 | 28k vio blk | 4.00 | 2.00 |

Publicity for greater industrial production.
No. 429 exists perf. 10½. Price $150.

Red Cavalry in Polish Town after Battle—A116

Cavalry Charge—A117

Staff Officers of 1st Cavalry Army
A118

Plan of Action for 1st Cavalry Army
A119

1930, Feb.			*Perf. 12x12½*	
431	A116	2k yel grn	2.50	2.00
432	A117	5k lt brn	2.50	2.00
433	A118	10k ol gray	6.00	2.50
434	A119	14k ind & red	2.00	2.00

1st Red Cavalry Army, 10th anniversary.

Students Preparing a Poster Newspaper
A120

1930, Aug. 15				
435	A120	10k ol grn	1.50	1.00

Issued in connection with the Educational Exhibition at Leningrad, July 1 to August 15, 1930.

Telegraph Office, Moscow—A121

Lenin Hydroelectric Power Station on Volchov River
A122

Wmkd. Lozenges. (169)

1930		Photogravure	*Perf. 10½*	
436	A121	1r dp bl	8.00	6.00

Perf. 12½, 12x12½ Wmk. 170

| 437 | A122 | 3r yel grn & blk brn | 8.00 | 4.00 |

See also Nos. 467, 469.

Ironclad "Potemkin"
A123

Inside Presnya Barricade
A124

Moscow Barricades in 1905
A125

Typographed.

1930-31		*Perf. 12x12½, 12½x12*		
438	A123	3k red	2.50	1.00
439	A124	5k blue	2.50	1.25
440	A125	10k dk grn & red	4.50	1.75

Imperf.

452	A123	3k red ('31)	3.00	3.00
453	A124	5k dp bl ('31)	3.50	3.50
454	A125	10k dk grn & red ('31)	4.00	4.00
		Nos. 438-454 (6)	20.00	14.50

Revolution of 1905, 25th anniversary.

Types of 1929–31 Regular Issue.

1931-32			*Imperf.*	
456	A103	1k orange	75	1.00
457	A95	2k yel grn	1.00	1.50
458	A96	3k blue	1.00	2.00
459	A97	4k claret	7.00	10.00
460	A98	5k org brn	2.50	4.00
462	A103	10k ol grn	20.00	30.00
464	A100	15k dk ol grn	25.00	35.00
466	A109	30k dl vio	30.00	55.00
467	A121	1r dk bl	55.00	70.00
		Nos. 456-467 (9)	142.25	208.50

Nos. 459, 462–467 were sold only by the philatelic bureau.

Type of 1930 Issue
1931		*Perf. 12x12½*	*Wmk. 170*	
469	A121	1r dk bl	3.50	2.50

Maxim Gorki
A133

1932-33		Photogravure		
470	A133	15k dk brn	8.00	6.00
a.		Imperf.	150.00	150.00
471	A133	35k dp ultra ('33)	20.00	15.00

40th anniversary of Gorki's literary activity.

Lenin Addressing the People A134   Revolution in Petrograd (Leningrad) A135

Dnieper Hydroelectric Power Station—A136

RUSSIA

Asiatics Saluting the Soviet Flag
A139

Breaking Prison Bars
A140

Designs (dated 1917-1932): 15k, Collective farm. 20k, Magnitogorsk metallurgical plant in Urals. 30k, Radio tower and heads of 4 men.

Perf. 12½x12; 12½ (30k)

1932-33

472	A134	3k dk vio	1.50	.75
473	A135	5k dk brn	1.50	.75
474	A136	10k ultra	3.00	2.00
475	A136	15k dk grn	2.00	1.25
476	A136	20k lake ('33)	2.50	1.75
477	A136	30k dk gray ('33)	8.00	2.25
478	A139	35k gray blk	100.00	50.00
	Nos. 472-478 (7)		118.50	58.75

October Revolution, 15th anniversary.

1932, Nov. Litho. Perf. 12½x12

| 479 | A140 | 50k dk red | 10.00 | 8.00 |

Issued to commemorate the 10th anniversary of the International Revolutionaries' Aid Association.

Trier, Birthplace of Marx
A141

Grave of Marx, Highgate Cemetery, London
A142

Design: 35k, Portrait and signature of Karl Marx.

Perf. 12 x 12½, 12½ x 12.

1933, Mar. Photogravure

480	A141	3k dl grn	6.00	2.00
481	A142	10k blk brn	10.00	4.00
482	A142	35k brn vio	15.00	10.00

Issued to commemorate the 50th anniversary of the death of Karl Marx (1818-1883).

Fine Arts Museum, Moscow
A145

1932, Dec. Perf. 12½

485	A145	15k blk brn	30.00	25.00
486	A145	35k ultra	60.00	45.00
a.	Perf. 10½		80.00	40.00

Moscow Philatelic Exhibition, 1932.
Nos. 485 and 486 were also issued in imperf. sheets of 4 containing 2 of each value, on thick paper for presentation purposes.

Nos. 485 and 486a Surcharged
ЛЕНИНГРАД. 1933 г.
70 коп

1933, Mar. Perf. 12½

| 487 | A145 | 30k on 15k blk brn | 40.00 | 30.00 |

Perf. 10½

| 488 | A145 | 70k on 35k ultra | 60.00 | 40.00 |

Leningrad Philatelic Exhibition, 1933.

Peoples of the Soviet Union.

Kazaks—A146

Lezghians
A147

Tungus
A150

Crimean Tartars—A148

Jews, Birabizhan
A149

Buryats
A151

Yakuts
A156

Chechens—A152

Abkhas—A153

Georgians—A154

Nientzians—A155

Great Russians—A157

Tadzhiks—A158

Transcaucasians—A159

Turkmen
A160

Ukrainians—A161

Uzbeks—A162

Byelorussians—A163

Koryaks
A164

Bashkirs
A165

Chuvashes
A166

Perf. 12, 12x12½, 12½x12, 11x12, 12x11

1933, Apr. Photogravure

489	A146	1k blk brn	2.00	.85
490	A147	2k ultra	2.00	.85
491	A148	3k gray grn	2.00	.85
492	A149	4k gray blk	2.00	.85
493	A150	5k brn vio	2.00	.85
494	A151	6k indigo	2.00	.55
495	A152	7k blk brn	2.00	.55
496	A153	8k rose red	2.00	.75
497	A154	9k ultra	3.50	1.00
498	A155	10k blk brn	3.75	2.50
499	A156	14k ol grn	3.50	1.00
500	A157	15k orange	4.00	1.00
501	A158	15k ultra	3.50	.85
502	A159	15k dk brn	3.50	.85
503	A160	15k rose red	5.00	2.25
504	A161	15k vio brn	4.00	1.00
505	A162	15k gray blk	4.00	1.00
506	A163	15k dl grn	4.00	1.00
507	A164	20k dl bl	12.00	2.25
508	A165	30k brn vio	12.00	2.00
509	A166	35k black	25.00	3.25
	Nos. 489-509 (21)		103.75	26.05

V. V. Vorovsky—A169

Designs: 3k, V. M. Volodarsky. 5k, M. S. Uritzky.

1933, Oct. Perf. 12x12½

514	A169	1k dl grn	1.75	1.00
515	A169	3k bl blk	2.50	1.25
516	A169	5k ol brn	2.50	1.50

No. 514 commemorates the 10th anniversary of the murder of Soviet Representative Vorovsky. No. 515 commemorates the 15th anniversary of the murder of the Revolutionist Volodarsky. No. 516 commemorates the 15th anniversary of the murder of the Revolutionist Uritzky.
See Nos. 531-532, 580-582.

Badge of the Red Banner, Massed Standard Bearers—A173

1933, Nov. 17 Perf. 14 Unwmkd.

| 518 | A173 | 20k blk, red & yel | 1.75 | 1.50 |
| a. | Perf. 9½ | | 250.00 | 150.00 |

Issued to commemorate the 15th anniversary of the Badge of the Red Banner.

RUSSIA

Commissar Schaumyan A174   Commissar Prokofii A. Dzhaparidze A175

Commissars Awaiting Execution A176

Designs: 35k, Monument to the 26 Commissars. 40k, Worker, peasant and soldier dipping flags in salute.

1933, Dec. 1

519	A174	4k brown	15.00	3.00
520	A175	5k dk gray	15.00	3.00
521	A176	20k purple	10.00	3.00
522	A176	35k ultra	50.00	12.00
523	A176	40k carmine	30.00	15.00
	Nos. 519-523 (5)		120.00	36.00

Issued to commemorate the 15th anniversary of the execution of 26 commissars at Baku. No. 521 exists imperf.

Lenin's Mausoleum—A179

1934, Feb. 7 Engraved Perf. 14

524	A179	5k brown	4.00	1.00
a.	Imperf.		250.00	225.00
525	A179	10k sl bl	7.00	4.00
a.	Imperf.		200.00	175.00
526	A179	15k dk car	7.00	2.50
527	A179	20k green	7.00	2.50
528	A179	35k dk brn	12.00	4.50
	Nos. 524-528 (5)		37.00	14.50

10th anniversary of Lenin's death.

Ivan Fedorov—A180

1934, Mar. 5

529	A180	20k car rose	7.00	4.00
a.	Imperf.		250.00	250.00
530	A180	40k indigo	17.50	6.00
a.	Imperf.		275.00	275.00

Issued to commemorate the 350th anniversary of the death of Ivan Fedorov, founder of printing in Russia.

Portrait Type of 1933.
Designs: 10k, Jacob M. Sverdlov. 15k, Victor Pavlovich Nogin.

1934, Mar. Photo. Wmk. 170

531	A169	10k ultra	30.00	12.00
532	A169	15k red	35.00	20.00

15th anniversary of the death of Jacob M. Sverdlov, chairman of the All-Russian Central Executive Committee of the Soviets. 10th anniversary of the death of Victor Pavlovich Nogin, chairman Russian State Textile Syndicate.

Dmitri Ivanovich Mendeleev
A184   A185

1934, Sept. 15 Perf. 14 Wmk. 170

536	A184	5k emerald	7.00	3.00
537	A185	10k blk brn	20.00	6.00
538	A185	15k vermilion	17.50	5.00
539	A184	20k ultra	10.00	5.00

Birth centenary of Prof. D. I. Mendeleev (1834-1907), chemist who discovered the Periodic Law of Classification of the Elements.

Imperfs. exist of 5k (price $100) and 15k (price $150).

Lenin as Child and Youth
A186   A187

Demonstration before Lenin Mausoleum—A190

Designs: 5k, Lenin in middle age. 10k, Lenin the orator. 30k, Lenin and Stalin.

1934, Nov. 23 Perf. 14 Unwmkd.

540	A186	1k ind & blk	3.00	1.50
541	A187	3k ind & blk	4.00	1.75
542	A187	5k ind & blk	6.00	2.50
543	A187	10k ind & blk	4.50	2.50
544	A190	20k brn org & ultra	9.00	4.50
545	A190	30k brn org & car	27.50	11.00
	Nos. 540-545 (6)		53.00	23.75

First decade without Lenin.
See Nos. 931-935, 937.

Bombs Falling on City A192   "Before War and Afterwards" A194

Designs: 10k, Refugees from burning town. 20k, "Plowing with the sword." 35k, "Comradeship."

1935, Jan. 1 Perf. 14 Wmk. 170

546	A192	5k vio blk	8.00	4.00
547	A192	10k ultra	15.00	6.00
548	A194	15k green	25.00	6.00
549	A194	20k dk brn	20.00	8.00
550	A194	35k carmine	50.00	15.00
	Nos. 546-550 (5)		118.00	39.00

Issued as anti-war propaganda, the designs symbolizing the horrors of modern warfare.

Subway Tunnel A197

Subway Station Cross Section A198

Subway Station A199

Train in Station—A200

1935, Feb. 25 Perf. 14 Wmk. 170

551	A197	5k orange	10.00	4.00
552	A198	10k dk ultra	12.00	5.00
553	A199	15k rose car	50.00	20.00
554	A200	20k emerald	20.00	10.00

Completion of Moscow subway.

Friedrich Engels A201

1935, May Perf. 14 Wmk. 170

555	A201	5k carmine	10.00	2.00
556	A201	10k dk grn	5.00	3.00
557	A201	15k dk bl	10.00	4.00
558	A201	20k brn blk	7.00	5.00

Issued to commemorate the 40th anniversary of the death of Friedrich Engels (1820-1895), German socialist and collaborator of Marx.

Running A202

Designs: 2k, Diving. 3k, Rowing. 4k, Soccer. 5k, Skiing. 10k, Bicycling. 15k, Tennis. 20k, Skating. 35k, Hurdling. 40k, Parade of athletes.

1935, Apr. 22 Perf. 14 Unwmkd.

559	A202	1k org & ultra	3.00	1.50
560	A202	2k blk & ultra	3.50	1.50
561	A202	3k grn & blk brn	6.00	3.50
562	A202	4k rose red & ultra	4.00	2.00
563	A202	5k pur & blk brn	4.00	2.00
564	A202	10k rose red & vio	12.50	5.00
565	A202	15k blk & blk brn	25.00	10.00
566	A202	20k blk brn & ultra	20.00	7.00
567	A202	35k ultra & blk brn	30.00	15.00
568	A202	40k blk brn & car	25.00	10.00
	Nos. 559-568 (10)		133.00	57.50

Issued to commemorate the International Spartacist Games at Moscow.

Silver Plate of Sassanian Dynasty A212

1935, Sept. 10 Wmk. 170

569	A212	5k org red	8.00	3.00
570	A212	10k dk yel grn	8.00	3.00
571	A212	15k dk vio	9.00	5.00
572	A212	35k blk brn	15.00	6.00

Issued to commemorate the Third International Exposition of Persian Art held in Leningrad, September 12-18, 1935.

Kalinin, the Worker A213   Mikhail Kalinin A216

Designs: 5k, Kalinin, the farmer. 10k, Kalinin, the orator.

1935, Nov. 20 Perf. 14 Unwmkd.

573	A213	3k rose lil	1.50	1.00
574	A213	5k green	1.50	1.00
575	A213	10k bl sl	2.00	1.50
576	A216	20k brn blk	3.00	2.00

Issued to commemorate the 60th birthday of Mikhail Kalinin, chairman of the Central Executive Committee of the U.S.S.R.
The 20k exists imperf. Price $90.

Leo Tolstoy
A217   A218

Design: 20k, Statue of Tolstoy.

RUSSIA

1935, Dec. 4			Perf. 14	
577	A217	3k ol blk & vio	1.50	75
a.		Perf. 11	3.75	1.00
578	A218	10k vio blk & blk brn	2.25	1.00
a.		Perf. 11	6.50	2.00
579	A217	20k dk grn & blk brn	5.00	2.50
a.		Perf. 11	10.00	3.00

Issued to commemorate the 25th anniversary of the death of Count Leo N. Tolstoy (1828-1910).

Portrait Type of 1933.
Designs: 2k, Mikhail V. Frunze. 4k, N. E. Bauman. 40k, Sergei M. Kirov.

1935, Nov.		Perf. 11	Wmk. 170	
580	A169	2k purple	2.75	5.00
a.		Perf. 14	12.00	1.00
581	A169	4k brn vio	4.50	8.00
a.		Perf. 14	17.00	1.00
582	A169	40k blk brn	10.00	12.00
a.		Perf. 14	40.00	3.00

Death of three revolutionary heroes. Nos. 580-582 exist imperf. but were not regularly issued. Price, set $225.

Pioneers Preventing Theft from Mailbox
A223

Designs: 3k, 5k, Pioneers preventing destruction of property. 10k, Helping recover kite. 15k, Girl Pioneer saluting.

1936, Apr.		Perf. 14	Unwmkd.	
583	A223	1k yel grn	1.25	75
a.		Perf. 11	2.25	75
584	A223	2k cop red	3.25	75
a.		Perf. 11	1.25	75
585	A223	3k sl bl	2.00	1.00
a.		Perf. 11	7.50	1.00
586	A223	5k rose lake	1.75	75
a.		Perf. 11	11.00	1.50
587	A223	10k gray bl	3.25	3.25
a.		Perf. 11	27.50	2.00
588	A223	15k brn ol	17.50	11.00
a.		Perf. 11	5.00	2.00
Nos. 583-588 (6)			29.00	18.50
Nos. 583a-588a (6)			54.50	8.00

N. A. Dobrolyubov
A227

1936, Aug. 13		Typo.	Perf. 11½	
589	A227	10k rose lake	5.00	3.00
a.		Perf. 14	8.00	4.00

Issued to commemorate the centenary of the birth of Nikolai A. Dobrolyubov, writer and critic.

Aleksander Sergeyevich Pushkin
A228

Statue of Pushkin, Moscow
A229

Chalky or Ordinary Paper
Perf. 11 to 14 and Compound

1937, Feb. 1				
590	A228	10k yel brn	50	35
591	A228	20k Prus grn	75	50
592	A228	40k rose lake	1.00	60
593	A229	50k blue	2.00	75
594	A229	80k car rose	2.75	1.00
595	A229	1r green	5.00	2.00
Nos. 590-595 (6)			12.00	5.20

Souvenir Sheet.
Imperf.

596		Sheet of two	5.00	15.00
a.	A228 10k brn		1.00	3.00
b.	A229 50k brn		1.00	3.00

Death centenary of Aleksander Pushkin (1799–1837), writer and poet. No. 596 has marginal inscriptions, top and bottom. Size: 102½x88mm.

Tchaikovsky Concert Hall
A230

Designs: 5k, 15k, Telegraph Agency House. 10k, Tchaikovsky Concert Hall. 20k, 50k, Red Army Theater. 30k, Hotel Moscow. 40k, Palace of the Soviets.

Unwmkd.

1937, June		Photo.	Perf. 12	
597	A230	3k brn vio	1.00	50
598	A230	5k hn brn	1.00	50
599	A230	10k dk brn	1.75	50
600	A230	15k black	1.75	50
601	A230	20k ol grn	1.00	75
602	A230	30k gray blk	1.00	75
a.		Perf. 11	75.00	50.00
603	A230	40k violet	2.00	1.50
a.		Souvenir sheet	10.00	17.50
604	A230	50k dk brn	2.00	1.50
Nos. 597-604 (8)			11.50	6.50

First Congress of Soviet Architects. The 30k is watermarked Greek Border and Rosettes (170). No. 603a contains four copies of No. 603, imperf. with inscriptions in top and bottom margins. Size: 120x93mm. Nos. 597-601, 603-604 exist imperf. Price, each $250.

Feliks E. Dzerzhinski
A235

Shota Rustaveli
A236

1937, July 27		Typo.	Perf. 12	
606	A235	10k yel brn	50	25
607	A235	20k Prus grn	75	60
608	A235	40k rose lake	1.50	1.25
609	A235	80k carmine	1.75	1.50

Issued to commemorate the 10th anniversary of the death of F. E. Dzerzhinski, organizer of Soviet secret police. Exist imperf.

Photogravure

1938, Feb.		Perf. 12	Unwmkd.	
610	A236	20k dp grn	1.50	50

Issued to commemorate the 750th anniversary of the publication of the poem "Knight in the Tiger Skin," by Shota Rustaveli, Georgian poet. Exists imperf. Price $135.

Statue Surmounting Pavilion
A237

Soviet Pavilion at Paris Exposition
A238

1938		Typographed.		
611	A237	5k red	50	30
a.		Imperf.	50.00	
612	A238	20k rose	1.00	50
613	A237	50k dk bl	2.00	75

Issued to commemorate Russia's participation in the 1937 International Exposition at Paris.

Types of 1929–32 and Lenin Types of 1925–26.

1937-52	Perf. 11½x12, 12		Unwmkd.	
613A	A103	1k dl org ('40)	35.00	8.00
614	A95	2k yel grn ('39)	8.00	3.00
615	A97	4k cl ('40)	8.00	1.00
615A	A98	5k org brn ('46)	135.00	30.00
616	A109	10k bl ('38)	75	40
616A	A103	10k ol ('40)	175.00	35.00
616B	A109	10k blk ('52)	75	50
617	A97	20k grn	75	50
617A	A107	20k grn ('39)	125.00	20.00
618	A103	30k cl ('39)	17.50	5.00
619	A104	40k ind ('38)	3.00	1.25
619A	A111	50k dp brn ('40)	1.25	75

Engraved.

620	A75	3r dk grn ('39)	2.75	1.75
621	A66	5r red brn ('39)	4.50	2.50
622	A66	10r ind ('39)	7.50	6.50

Nos. 615 to 619 exist imperforate but were not regularly issued. No. 616B was re-issued in 1954-56 in slightly smaller format, 14½x21 mm., and in gray black. See note after No. 738.

Airplane Route from Moscow to North Pole
A239

Soviet Flag and Airplanes at North Pole
A240

1938, Feb. 25	Lithographed	Perf. 12		
625	A239	10k db & blk	3.00	50
626	A239	20k bl gray & blk	3.50	1.00

Typographed.

627	A240	40k dl grn & car	10.00	3.50
a.		Imperf.	200.00	
628	A240	80k rose car & car	4.00	3.00
a.		Imperf.	150.00	

Soviet flight to the North Pole.

Infantryman
A241

Soldier
A242

Stalin Reviewing Cavalry
A246

Machine Gunners
A247

Designs: 30k, Sailor. 40k, Aviator. 50k, Antiaircraft soldier.

Photogravure

1938, Mar.		Perf. 12	Unwmkd.	
629	A241	10k gray blk & dk red	50	20
630	A242	20k gray blk & dk red	70	30
631	A242	30k gray blk & dk red	1.25	40
632	A242	40k gray blk & dk red	2.00	75
633	A242	50k gray blk & dk red	2.25	1.00
634	A246	80k gray blk & dk red	3.75	1.00

Perf. 12x12½
Typographed.

| 635 | A247 | 1r blk & car | 1.00 | 50 |
| Nos. 629-635 (7) | | | 11.45 | 4.15 |

20th anniversary of Workers' and Peasants' Red Army. No. 635 exists imperf. Price $125.

Aviators Chkalov, Baidukov, Beliakov and Flight Route
A248

Aviators Gromov, Danilin, Yumashev and Flight Route
A249

1938, Apr. 10			Photogravure	
636	A248	10k blk & red	1.25	75
637	A248	20k brn blk & red	1.50	75
638	A248	40k brn & red	2.50	1.25
639	A248	50k brn vio & red	4.00	1.25

Issued to commemorate the first Trans-Polar flight, June 18-20, 1937, from Moscow to Vancouver, Wash. Nos. 636-639 exist imperf. Price $125 each.

1938, Apr. 13				
640	A249	10k claret	2.00	50
641	A249	20k brn blk	2.75	1.00
642	A249	50k dl vio	3.00	1.25

Issued to commemorate the first Trans-Polar flight, July 12–14, 1937, from Moscow to San Jacinto, Calif. Nos. 640-642 exist imperf. Price, each $110.

Arrival of the Rescuing Ice-breakers Taimyr and Murmansk—A250

RUSSIA

Ivan Papanin and His Men
Aboard Ice-breaker Yermak
A251

1938, June 21 Typo. Perf. 12, 12½
| 643 | A250 | 10k vio brn | 5.00 | 1.00 |
| 644 | A250 | 20k dk bl | 5.00 | 1.25 |

Photogravure
645	A251	30k ol brn	10.00	1.50
646	A251	50k ultra	10.00	2.00
a.	Imperf.		175.00	

Rescue of Papanin's North Pole Expedition.

Arms of Uzbek   Arms of U.S.S.R.
A252   A253

Designs: Different arms on each stamp.

Typographed.
1937-38   Perf. 12, 12½   Unwmkd.
647	A252	20k dp bl (Armenia)	2.00	1.00
648	A252	20k dl vio (Azerbaijan)	2.00	1.00
649	A252	20k brn org (White Russia)	2.00	1.00
650	A252	20k car rose (Georgia)	2.00	1.00
651	A252	20k bl grn (Kazak)	2.00	1.00
652	A252	20k emer (Kirghiz)	2.00	1.00
653	A252	20k yel org (Uzbek)	2.00	1.00
654	A252	20k bl (R.S.F.S.R.)	2.00	1.00
655	A252	20k cl (Tadjik)	2.00	1.00
656	A252	20k car (Turkmen)	2.00	1.00
657	A252	20k red (Ukraine)	2.00	1.00

Engraved.
| 658 | A253 | 40k brn red | 3.00 | 3.00 |
| | | Nos. 647-658 (12) | 25.00 | 14.00 |

Constitution of U.S.S.R.
Issue dates: 40k, 1937. Others, 1938.
See also Nos. 841-842.

Nurse Weighing Child
A264

Children at Lenin's Statue   Biology Lesson
A265   A266

Health Camp—A267

Young Model Builders
A268

1938, Sept. 15   Perf. 12   Unwmkd.
659	A264	10k dk bl grn	1.00	30
660	A265	15k dk bl grn	1.00	40
661	A266	20k vio brn	1.25	40
662	A267	30k claret	1.75	75
663	A266	40k lt brn	2.00	1.00
664	A268	50k dp bl	2.75	1.25
665	A268	80k lt grn	4.00	1.25
		Nos. 659-665 (7)	13.75	5.35

Child welfare.

View of Yalta—A269

Crimean Shoreline
A272

Designs: No. 667, View along Crimean shore. No. 668, Georgian military highway. No. 670, View near Yalta. No. 671, "Swallows' Nest" Castle. 20k, Dzerzhinski Rest House for workers. 30k, Sunset in Crimea. 40k, Alupka. 50k, Gursuf. 80k, Crimean Gardens. 1r, "Swallows' Nest" Castle (horiz.).

Photogravure.
1938, Sept. 21   Perf. 12   Unwmkd.
666	A269	5k brown	75	50
667	A269	5k blk brn	75	50
668	A269	10k sl grn	1.00	50
669	A272	10k brown	1.00	50
670	A269	15k blk brn	1.00	50
671	A272	15k dk brn	1.00	50
672	A269	20k dk brn	1.50	50
673	A272	30k blk brn	1.50	50
674	A269	40k brown	2.50	75
675	A272	50k dp sl grn	2.50	1.50
676	A269	80k brown	3.50	1.50
677	A269	1r sl grn	7.50	2.50
		Nos. 666-677 (12)	24.50	10.25

Children Flying Model Plane
A281

Glider—A282

Captive Balloon   Dirigible over Kremlin
A283   A284

Parachute Jumpers
A285

Hydroplane—A286

Balloon in Flight   Balloon Ascent
A287   A288

Four-motor Plane
A289

Typographed.
1938, Oct. 7   Perf. 12   Unwmkd.
678	A281	5k vio brn	1.00	60
679	A282	10k ol gray	1.00	60
680	A283	15k pink	1.75	60
681	A284	20k dp bl	1.75	60
682	A285	30k claret	2.75	1.00
683	A286	40k dk bl	3.50	1.00
684	A287	50k bl grn	7.00	1.50
685	A288	80k brown	6.00	2.50
686	A289	1r bl grn	8.00	2.50
		Nos. 678-686 (9)	32.75	10.40

Mayakovsky Station,
Moscow Subway
A290

Sokol Terminal   Kiev Station
A291   A292

Dynamo Station
A293

Train in Tunnel
A294

Revolution Square Station
A295

Photogravure.
1938, Nov. 7   Perf. 12   Unwmkd.
687	A290	10k dp red vio	2.00	1.00
688	A291	15k dk brn	2.50	1.00
689	A292	20k blk brn	2.50	1.00
690	A293	30k dk red vio	2.50	1.00
691	A294	40k blk brn	2.50	1.50
692	A295	50k dk brn	2.50	2.00
		Nos. 687-692 (6)	14.50	7.50

Issued in connection with the opening of the second line of the Moscow subway.

Girl with Parachute   Young Miner
A296   A297

RUSSIA

Harvesting—A298

Designs: 50k, Students returning from school. 80k, Aviator and sailor.

1938, Dec. 7   Typo.   Perf. 12
693	A296	20k dp bl	1.00	50
694	A297	30k dp cl	1.00	50
695	A296	40k vio brn	1.25	50
696	A296	50k dp rose	1.75	1.00
697	A298	80k dp bl	5.00	1.50
		Nos. 693-697 (5)	10.00	4.00

Issued to commemorate the 20th anniversary of the Young Communist League (Komsomol).

Diving A301

Discus Thrower A302

Tennis A303   Acrobatic Motorcyclists A304

Skier A305

Runners A306

Soccer A307   Physical Culture A308

Photogravure.

1938, Dec. 28   Perf. 12   Unwmkd.
698	A301	5k scarlet	3.50	1.00
699	A302	10k black	3.50	1.00
700	A303	15k brown	4.00	1.00
701	A304	20k green	4.00	1.50
702	A305	30k dl vio	10.00	2.00
703	A306	40k dp grn	12.00	2.50
704	A307	50k blue	10.00	2.00
705	A308	80k dp bl	10.00	3.00
		Nos. 698-705 (8)	57.00	14.00

Gorki Street, Moscow—A309

Dynamo Subway Station A315

Foundryman A316

Designs: 20k, Council House & Hotel Moscow. 30k, Lenin Library. 40k, Crimea Bridge. 50k, Bridge over Moscow River. 80k, Khimki Station.

Paper with network as in parenthesis.

1939, Mar.   Typo.   Perf. 12
706	A309	10k brn (red brn)	1.20	75
707	A309	20k dk sl grn (lt bl)	1.40	75
708	A309	30k brn vio (red brn)	1.40	1.50
709	A309	40k bl (lt bl)	2.75	1.50
710	A309	50k rose lake (red brn)	4.50	2.00
711	A309	80k gray ol (lt bl)	4.75	2.00
712	A315	1r dk bl (lt bl)	8.00	3.00
		Nos. 706-712 (7)	24.00	11.50

Issued as propaganda for "New Moscow." All designs are Moscow scenes. On 30k, denomination is at upper right.

1939, Mar.
713	A316	15k dk bl	80	30
	a.	Imperf.	25.80	

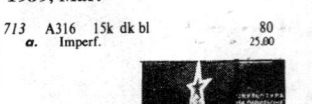
Statue on U.S.S.R. Pavilion A317

U.S.S.R. Pavilion A318

1939-40   Photogravure
714	A317	30k ind & red	60	25
	a.	Imperf. ('40)	1.00	75
715	A318	50k bl & bis brn	80	50
	a.	Imperf. ('40)	5.65	

Issued to commemorate Russia's participation in the New York World's Fair.

Paulina Osipenko A318a

Marina Raskova A318b

Design: 60k, Valentina Grizodubova.

1939, Mar.
718	A318a	15k green	2.00	1.00
719	A318b	30k brn vio	2.00	1.00
720	A318b	60k red	4.00	2.00

Issued to commemorate a non-stop record flight from Moscow to the Far East.

Exist imperf. Price, each $250.

Taras G. Shevchenko, Early Portrait A319

Monument at Kharkov A321

Design: 30k, Shevchenko portrait in later years.

1939, Mar. 9
721	A319	15k blk brn & blk	1.50	75
722	A319	30k dk red & blk	2.00	1.00
723	A321	60k grn & dk brn	4.00	3.00

Issued to commemorate the 125th anniversary of the birth of Taras G. Shevchenko (1814–1861), Ukrainian poet and painter.

 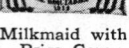
Milkmaid with Prize Cow A322

Tractor-plow at Work on Abundant Harvest A323

Designs: 20k, Shepherd tending sheep. No. 727, Fair pavilion. No. 728, Fair emblem. 45k, Turkmen picking cotton. 50k, Drove of horses. 60k, Symbolizing agricultural wealth. 80k, Kolkhoz girl with sugar beets. 1r, Hunter with Polar foxes.

1939, Aug.
724	A322	10k rose pink	75	15
725	A323	15k red brn	75	15
726	A323	20k sl blk	75	15
727	A323	30k purple	75	15
728	A322	30k red org	75	30
729	A322	45k dk grn	1.00	50
730	A322	50k cop red	1.00	75
731	A322	60k brt pur	1.75	1.00
732	A322	80k dk vio	1.75	1.00
733	A322	1r dk bl	3.50	1.25
		Nos. 724-733 (10)	12.75	5.65

Issued to commemorate the Soviet Agricultural Fair.

Worker A331

Soldier A332

Aviator A333

Arms of U.S.S.R. A334   A335

Typographed

1939-43   Perf. 12   Unwmkd.
734	A331	5k red	25	20
735	A332	15k dk grn	50	50
736	A333	30k dp bl	50	50
737	A334	60k fawn ('43)	1.25	50

Photogravure.

738	A335	60k rose car	1.00	75
		Nos. 734-738 (5)	3.50	2.45

No. 734 was re-issued in 1954–56 in slightly smaller format: 14x21½mm., instead of 14¾x22¼mm. Other values reissued in smaller format: 10k, 15k, 20k, 25k, 30k, 40k and 1r. (See notes following Nos. 622, 1260, 1347 and 1689.)

No. 416 Surcharged with New Value in Black.

1939   Wmk. 170
743	A97	30k on 4k cl	10.00	8.00
	a.	Unwmkd.	50.00	40.00

M. E. Saltykov (N. Shchedrin)
A336   A337

1939, Sept.   Typo.   Unwmkd.
745	A336	15k claret	50	25
746	A337	30k dk grn	75	50
747	A336	45k ol gray	1.25	50
748	A337	60k dk bl	1.50	75

Issued to commemorate the 50th anniversary of the death of Mikhail E. Saltykov (1826–1889), writer and satirist who used pen name of N. Shchedrin.

Sanatorium of the State Bank A338

Designs: 10k, 15k, Soviet Army sanatorium. 20k, Rest home, New Afyon. 30k, Clinical Institute. 50k, 80k, Sanatorium for workers in heavy industry. 60k, Rest home, Sukhum.

1939, Nov.   Photo.   Perf. 12
749	A338	5k dl brn	75	40
750	A338	10k carmine	75	40
751	A338	15k yel grn	75	40
752	A338	20k dk sl grn	75	40
753	A338	30k bluish blk	75	60
754	A338	50k gray blk	1.50	60
755	A338	60k brn vio	1.75	90
756	A338	80k org red	2.25	1.25
		Nos. 749-756 (8)	9.25	4.75

Mikhail Lermontov in 1837 A346

RUSSIA

Portrait in 1838 Portrait in 1841
A347   A348

1939, Dec.

757	A346	15k ind & sep	1.25	60
758	A347	30k dk grn & dl blk	3.50	90
759	A348	45k brick red & ind	2.50	1.25

Issued to commemorate the 125th anniversary of the birth of Mikhail Y. Lermontov (1814–1841), poet and novelist.

Nikolai   Anton
Chernyshevski   Chekhov
A349   A350

1939, Dec. Photogravure

760	A349	15k dk grn	75	30
761	A349	30k dl vio	75	75
762	A349	60k Prus grn	2.00	1.00

Issued to commemorate the 50th anniversary of the death of Nikolai Chernyshevski, scientist and critic.

1940, Feb. Perf. 12 Unwmkd.

Design: 20k, 30k, Portrait with hat.

763	A350	10k dl yel grn	50	25
764	A350	15k ultra	50	25
765	A350	20k violet	1.00	75
766	A350	30k cop brn	2.00	1.00

80th anniversary of birth of Anton Chekhov (1860–1904), playwright.

Welcome to Red Army by
Western Ukraine and
Western Byelorussia
A352

Designs: 30k, Villagers welcoming tank crew. 50k, 60k, Soldier giving newspapers to crowd. 1r, Crowd waving to tank column.

Inscribed: "17 . IX . 1939."

1940, Apr.

767	A352	10k dp rose	75	25
768	A352	30k myr grn	75	25
769	A352	50k gray blk	1.25	50
770	A352	60k indigo	1.25	50
771	A352	1r red	2.00	1.25
	Nos. 767-771 (5)		6.00	2.75

Issued to commemorate the liberation of the people of Western Ukraine and Western Byelorussia.

Ice-breaker "Josef Stalin,"
Captain Beloussov and
Chief Ivan Papanin—A356

Badygin and Papanin
A358

Map of the Drift of the Sedov
and Crew Members
A359

Design: 30k, Icebreaker "George Sedov," Captain Badygin and First Mate Trofimov.

1940, Apr.

772	A356	15k dl yel grn	3.00	1.00
773	A356	30k dl pur	6.00	1.00
774	A358	50k cop brn	5.00	1.00
775	A359	1r dk ultra	10.00	3.00

Issued to commemorate the heroism of the crew of the "George Sedov" which drifted in the Polar Basin for 812 days.

Vladimir V. Mayakovsky
A360   A361

1940, June

776	A360	15k dp red	50	25
777	A360	30k cop brn	80	50
778	A361	60k dk gray bl	1.00	75
779	A361	80k brt ultra	80	75

10th anniversary of the death of V. V. Mayakovsky, poet.

K. A. Timiryasev and
Academy of Agricultural
Sciences—A362

In the Laboratory of
Moscow University
A363

Last Portrait—A364

Monument in Moscow
A365

1940, June

780	A362	10k indigo	75	50
781	A363	15k purple	75	75
782	A364	30k dk vio brn	75	75
783	A365	60k dk grn	3.00	1.50

Issued to commemorate the 20th anniversary of the death of K. A. Timiryasev, scientist and professor of agricultural and biological sciences.

Relay Race—A366

Sportswomen Marching
A367

Children's Sport Badge
A368

Skier—A369

Throwing the Grenade
A370

1940, July 21

784	A366	15k car rose	1.50	40
785	A367	30k sepia	3.00	40
786	A368	50k dk vio bl	3.50	80
787	A369	60k dk vio bl	4.50	1.00
788	A370	1r grysh grn	7.50	2.25
	Nos. 784-788 (5)		20.00	5.05

Issued to mark Russia's second All-Union Physical Culture Day.

Tchaikovsky Museum
at Klin—A371

Tchaikovsky and   Tchaikovsky
Passage from   and Excerpt
his Fourth   from
Symphony   Eugene Onegin
A372   A373

Typographed.

1940, Aug. Perf. 12 Unwmkd.

789	A371	15k Prus grn	1.25	60
790	A372	20k brown	1.25	60
791	A371	30k dk bl	1.25	60
792	A372	50k rose lake	1.25	1.00
793	A373	60k red	1.50	1.50
	Nos. 789-793 (5)		6.50	4.30

Issued to commemorate the centenary of the birth of Peter Ilich Tchaikovsky (1840–1893), composer.

Volga Provinces Pavilion
A374

Northeast Provinces Pavilion
A376

Designs—Pavilions: 15k, Far East Provinces. No. 797, Central Regions. No. 798, Ukrainian. No. 799, Byelorussian. No. 800, Azerbaijan. No. 801, Georgian. No. 802, Armenian. No. 803, Uzbek. No. 804, Turkmen. No. 805, Tadzhik. No. 806, Kirghiz. No. 807, Kazakh. No. 808, Karelian Finnish. 50k, Main Building. 60k, Mechanization Pavilion and Stalin statue.

1940, Oct. Photogravure

794	A374	10k multi	2.00	75
795	A374	15k multi	2.00	75
796	A376	30k grn, gray, buff & dk brn	2.00	1.00
797	A376	30k grn, gray bl, buff & red brn	2.00	1.00
798	A376	30k grn, dp bl, buff, red & blk brn	2.00	1.00
799	A376	30k grn, gray, buff & blk brn	2.00	1.00

RUSSIA

800	A376	30k grn, gray, buff & blk brn	2.00	1.00
801	A374	30k grn, gray bl, buff & bis	2.00	1.00
802	A376	30k grn, gray bl, buff, dk brn & red	2.00	1.00
803	A376	30k grn, gray bl, buff, blk & red	2.00	1.00
804	A374	30k grn, pale gray, buff & brn	2.00	1.00
805	A376	30k grn, gray, buff, org brn & red	2.00	1.00
806	A376	30k grn, gray, buff, bis & dk brn	3.00	2.00
807	A376	30k grn, dp bl, buff, blk brn & red	3.00	2.00
808	A376	30k grn, dp bl, buff, brn, red & blk brn	3.00	2.00
809	A376	50k multi	4.00	2.00
810	A376	60k multi	5.00	2.00
		Nos. 794-810 (17)	42.00	21.50

Issued to commemorate the All-Union Agricultural Fair. Various vertical and horizontal se-tenant combinations of Nos. 796-808 are found because these stamps were printed together in one sheet.

Monument to Red Army Heroes — A391   Map of War Operations and M. V. Frunze — A393

Heroic Crossing of the Sivash — A394

Designs: 15k, Grenade thrower. 60k, Frunze's headquarters, Stroganovka. 1r, Victorious soldier.

1940   *Imperf.*

811	A391	10k dk grn	1.00	40
812	A391	15k org ver	1.00	40
813	A393	30k dl brn & car	1.00	40
814	A394	50k vio brn	1.00	50
815	A394	60k indigo	1.00	75
816	A391	1r gray blk	2.50	75
		Nos. 811-816 (6)	7.50	3.20

20th anniversary of battle of Perekop.
Nos. 811-816 were also issued perf. 12. Set price about 25% more.

Coal Miners A397   Blast Furnace A398

Bridge over Moscow-Volga Canal A399

Three New Type Locomotives A400

Workers on a Collective Farm A401

Automobiles and Planes A402

Oil Derricks A403

1941, Jan.   *Perf. 12*

817	A397	10k dp bl	50	30
818	A398	15k dk vio	50	30
819	A399	20k dp bl	50	30
820	A400	30k dk brn	60	40
821	A401	50k ol brn	60	75
822	A402	60k ol brn	1.00	1.00
823	A403	1r dk bl grn	2.00	1.50
		Nos. 817-823 (7)	5.70	4.55

Issued to publicize Soviet industries.

Troops on Skis A404   Sailor A405

Soldiers with Cannon A406

Designs: 20k, Cavalry. 30k, 3r, Machine gunners. 45k, Army horsemen. 50k, Aviator. 1r, 3r, Marshal's Star.

1941-43

824	A404	5k dk vio	1.00	25
825	A405	10k dp bl	1.00	25
826	A406	15k brt yel grn	40	25
827	A404	20k vermilion	40	25
828	A404	30k dl brn	40	25
829	A406	45k gray grn	1.25	50
830	A404	50k dl bl	75	75
831	A404	1r dl bl grn	1.00	1.00
831A	A404	3r myr grn ('43)	4.00	2.00
		Nos. 824-831A (9)	10.20	5.50

Issued to commemorate the 23rd anniversary of the Army and Navy of the U.S.S.R.

Battle of Ismail A412   Field Marshal Aleksandr Suvorov A413

1941   *Perf. 12*   *Unwmkd.*

832	A412	10k dk grn	75	50
833	A412	15k car rose	1.00	75
834	A413	30k bl blk	1.50	1.00
835	A413	1r ol brn	3.00	1.50

Issued to commemorate the 150th anniversary of the capture of the Turkish fortress, Ismail.

Kirghiz Horse Breeder A414

Kirghiz Miner — A415

1941, Mar.

| 836 | A414 | 15k dl brn | 1.50 | 75 |
| 837 | A415 | 30k dl pur | 2.00 | 1.00 |

Issued to commemorate the 15th anniversary of the Kirghizian Soviet Socialist Republic.

Prof. N. E. Zhukovski A416   Zhukovski Lecturing A418

Military Air Academy A417

1941, Mar.

838	A416	15k dp bl	75	25
839	A417	30k car rose	75	50
840	A418	50k brn vio	1.25	75

Issued to commemorate the 20th anniversary of the death of Prof. N. E. Zhukovski, scientist.

Arms Type of 1938

Design: Arms of Karelian-Finnish Soviet Socialist Republic.

1941, Mar.

| 841 | A252 | 30k rose | 1.00 | 50 |
| 842 | A252 | 45k dk bl grn | 1.50 | 75 |

Issued to commemorate the first anniversary of the Karelian-Finnish Soviet Socialist Republic.

Spasski Tower, Kremlin A420   Kremlin and Moscow River A421

1941, May   *Typo.*   *Unwmkd.*

| 843 | A420 | 1r dl red | 75 | 50 |
| 844 | A421 | 2r brn org | 2.00 | 1.00 |

"Suvorov's March through the Alps, 1799" A422   Vasili Surikov, Self-portrait A424

"Stepan Rasin on the Volga" A423

1941, June   *Photo.*   *Perf. 12*

845	A422	20k black	1.75	75
846	A423	30k scarlet	3.00	1.25
847	A422	50k dk vio brn	6.00	2.25
848	A423	1r gray grn	8.00	2.50
849	A424	2r brown	15.00	3.00
		Nos. 845-849 (5)	33.75	9.75

Issued to commemorate the 25th anniversary of the death of Vasili Ivanovich Surikov (1848-1916), painter.

Mikhail Lermontov A425

1941, July

| 850 | A425 | 15k Prus grn | 5.00 | 2.00 |
| 851 | A425 | 30k dk vio | 7.00 | 3.00 |

Issued to commemorate the centenary of the death of Mikhail Y. Lermontov, poet.

Visitors in Lenin Museum A426

RUSSIA

287

Lenin Museum
A427

1941-42
852	A426	15k rose red	2.00	1.50
853	A427	30k dk vio ('42)	8.00	3.00
854	A426	45k Prus grn	4.00	2.00
855	A427	1r org brn ('42)	4.00	3.00

Fifth anniversary of Lenin Museum.

Mother's Farewell to a Soldier Son ("Be a Hero!")
A428

1941, Aug.
| 856 | A428 | 30k carmine | 20.00 | 15.00 |

Alisher Navoi — A429 People's Militia — A430

1942, Jan.
| 857 | A429 | 30k brown | 3.00 | 2.00 |
| 858 | A429 | 1r dk vio | 5.00 | 3.00 |

Issued to commemorate the 500th anniversary of the birth of Alisher Navoi, Uzbekian poet.

1941, Dec. Typographed
| 859 | A430 | 30k dl bl | 35.00 | 30.00 |

Junior Lieutenant Talalikhin Ramming German Plane in Midair
A431

Captain Gastello and Burning Plane Diving into Enemy Gasoline Tanks
A432

Major General Dovator and Cossack Cavalry in Action
A433

Shura Chekalin Fighting Nazi Soldiers
A434

Nazi Soldiers Leading Zoya Kosmodemjanskaja to her Death
A435

Photogravure.

1942-44 Perf. 12 Unwmkd.
860	A431	20k bluish blk	1.00	35
860A	A431	30k Prus grn ('44)	1.00	35
861	A432	30k bluish blk	1.00	35
861A	A432	30k dp ultra ('44)	1.00	35
862	A433	30k black	1.00	35
863	A434	30k black	1.00	35
863A	A434	30k brt yel grn ('44)	1.00	35
864	A435	30k black	1.00	35
864A	A435	30k rose vio ('44)	1.00	35
865	A434	1r sl grn	4.50	3.00
866	A435	2r sl grn	12.00	6.00
	Nos. 860-866 (11)	20.50	10.15

Issued to honor Soviet heroes.

Anti-tank Artillery
A436

Signal Corps in Action — A437   Defense of Leningrad — A440

Guerrilla Fighters
A438

War Worker — A439

Red Army Scouts
A441

1942-43
867	A436	20k black	40	30
868	A437	30k sapphire	60	30
869	A438	30k Prus grn ('43)	60	30
870	A439	30k dl red brn ('43)	60	30
871	A440	60k bl blk	1.50	1.00
872	A441	1r blk brn	2.75	1.50
	Nos. 867-872 (6)	6.45	3.70

Women Workers and Soldiers
A442

Flaming Tank — A443   Women Preparing Food Shipments — A444

Sewing Equipment for Red Army — A445   Anti-Aircraft Battery in Action — A446

1942-43 Typographed Unwmkd.
873	A442	20k dk bl	75	25
874	A443	20k dl rose vio	75	25
875	A444	30k brn vio ('43)	75	25
876	A445	45k dl rose red	1.50	60
877	A446	45k dp dl bl ('43)	1.50	75
	Nos. 873-877 (5)	5.25	2.10

Manufacturing Explosives
A447

Designs: 10k, Agriculture. 15k, Group of Fighters. 20k, Storming the Palace. 30k, Lenin and Stalin. 60k, Tanks. 1r, Lenin. 2r, Revolution scene.

Inscribed: "1917 XXV 1942".

1943, Jan. Photo. Perf. 12
878	A447	5k blk brn	30	15
879	A447	10k blk brn	30	15
880	A447	15k bl blk	30	15
881	A447	20k bl blk	50	15
882	A447	30k blk brn	50	15
883	A447	60k blk brn	75	30
884	A447	1r dl red brn	1.50	75
885	A447	2r black	3.50	1.25
	Nos. 878-885 (8)	7.65	3.05

25th anniversary of October Revolution.

Mount St. Elias, Alaska
A455

Bering Sea and Bering's Ship
A456

1943, Apr.
886	A455	30k chlky bl	75	30
887	A456	60k Prus grn	1.25	30
888	A455	1r yel grn	2.50	75
889	A456	2r bis brn	5.00	1.25

Issued to commemorate the 200th anniversary of the death of Vitus Bering, explorer.

Medical Corpsmen and Wounded Soldier
A457

Trench Mortar — A458

Army Scouts — A459

Repulsing Enemy Tanks
A460

Snipers — A461

1943
890	A457	30k myr grn	50	30
891	A458	30k brn bis	50	30
892	A459	30k myr grn	50	30
893	A460	60k myr grn	1.50	1.00
894	A461	60k chlky bl	1.50	1.00
	Nos. 890-894 (5)	4.50	2.90

288 RUSSIA

Maxim Gorki—A462

1943, June
| 895 | A462 | 30k green | 75 | 25 |
| 896 | A462 | 60k sl blk | 1.00 | 40 |

Issued to commemorate the 75th anniversary of the birth of Maxim Gorki (1868–1936), writer.

Patriotic War Medal A463   Order of Field Marshal Suvorov A464

1943, July   Engraved
| 897 | A463 | 1r black | 1.25 | 1.25 |
| 898 | A464 | 10r dk ol grn | 4.75 | 3.75 |

Sailors A465

Designs: 30k, Navy gunner and warship. 60k, Soldiers and tank.

1943, Oct.   Photogravure
899	A465	20k gldn brn	25	20
900	A465	30k dk myr grn	30	25
901	A465	60k brt yel grn	60	30
902	A465	3r chlky bl	1.75	75

Issued to commemorate the 25th anniversary of the Red Army and Navy.

Karl Marx A468   Vladimir V. Mayakovsky A469

1943, Sept.
| 903 | A468 | 30k bl blk | 50 | 20 |
| 904 | A468 | 60k dk sl grn | 75 | 25 |

Issued to commemorate the 125th anniversary of the birth of Karl Marx.

1943, Oct.
| 905 | A469 | 30k red org | 50 | 20 |
| 906 | A469 | 60k dp bl | 75 | 25 |

Issued to commemorate the 50th anniversary of the birth of V. V. Mayakovsky, poet.

Flags of U.S., Britain, and Russia A470

1943, Nov.
| 907 | A470 | 30k blk, dp red & dk bl | 1.50 | 75 |
| 908 | A470 | 3r sl bl, red & lt bl | 5.00 | 1.75 |

The Tehran conference.

Ivan Turgenev A471

1943, Oct.
| 909 | A471 | 30k myr grn | 6.00 | 5.00 |
| 910 | A471 | 60k dl pur | 8.00 | 6.00 |

Issued to commemorate the 125th anniversary of the birth of Ivan Turgenev, poet and novelist.

Map of Stalingrad A472

Harbor of Sevastopol and Statue of Lenin A473

Leningrad—A474

Odessa—A475

1944, Mar.   Perf. 12
911	A472	30k dl brn & car	60	25
912	A473	30k dk bl	60	25
913	A474	30k dk sl grn	60	25
914	A475	30k yel grn	60	25

Issued to honor the defenders of Stalingrad, Leningrad, Sevastopol and Odessa. Souvenir sheet of four of No. 913 is listed as No. 959.
No. 911 measures 33x22mm. and also exists in smaller size: 32x21½mm.

Russian War Heroes A476

1944, Apr.
| 915 | A476 | 30k dp ultra | 60 | 25 |

Sailor Loading Gun A477   Tanks A478

Soldier Bayoneting a Nazi A479

Infantryman A480   Soldier Throwing Hand Grenade A481

1943–44   Photogravure
916	A477	15k dp ultra	25	20
917	A478	20k red org ('44)	30	25
918	A479	30k dl brn & dk red ('44)	35	25
919	A480	1r brt yel grn	1.00	60
920	A481	2r Prus grn ('44)	1.50	1.25
	Nos. 916-920 (5)		3.40	2.55

Issued to commemorate the 25th anniversary of the Young Communist League (Komsomol).

Flags of U.S., Russia, Great Britain A482

1944, May 30   Perf. 12   Unwmkd.
| 921 | A482 | 60k blk, red & bl | 1.25 | 60 |
| 922 | A482 | 3r dk bl, red & lt bl | 5.50 | 2.00 |

Issued to commemorate the Day of the Nations United Against Germany, June 14, 1944.

Patriotic War Order A483   Order of Prince Alexander Nevsky A484

Order of Field Marshal Suvorov A485   Order of Field Marshal Kutuzov A486

Paper with network as in parenthesis.

1944   Typo.   Perf. 12, Imperf.
923	A483	15k dl red (rose)	20	20
924	A484	20k bl (lt bl)	25	25
925	A485	30k grn (grn)	30	30
926	A486	60k dl red (rose)	60	60

Order of Patriotic War A487   Order of Prince Alexander Nevski A488

Order of Field Marshal Kutuzov A489   Order of Field Marshal Suvorov A490

Engraved
1944, June   Perf. 12   Unwmkd.
927	A487	1r black	50	30
928	A488	3r bl blk	1.25	75
929	A489	5r dk ol grn	2.00	1.00
930	A490	10r dk red	4.50	1.25

Lenin's Mausoleum—A491

Types of 1934, Inscribed 1924-1944.

Designs: 30k (No. 931), 3r, Lenin and Stalin. 50k, Lenin in middle age. 60k, Lenin, the orator.

1944, June   Photogravure
931	A190	30k org & car	20	15
932	A186	30k sl & blk	20	15
933	A187	45k sl & blk	30	15
934	A187	50k sl & blk	35	20
935	A187	60k sl & blk	40	20
936	A491	1r ind & brn blk	90	30
937	A190	3r bl blk & dl org	2.50	1.00
	Nos. 931-937 (7)		4.85	2.15

Issued to commemorate 20 years without Lenin.

RUSSIA

Nikolai Rimski-Korsakov
A492   A493

1944, June   **Perf. 12. Imperf.**

938	A492	30k gray blk	25	15
939	A493	60k sl grn	50	15
940	A492	1r brt bl	75	25
941	A493	3r purple	1.25	30

Issued to commemorate the centenary of the birth of Nikolai Rimski-Korsakov (1844-1908), composer.

N. A. Shors   V. I. Chapayev
A494   A495

S. G. Lazho   Sergei A. Chaplygin
A496   A497

1944, Sept.   **Perf. 12**

942	A494	30k gray blk	50	20
943	A495	30k dk sl grn	50	20
944	A496	30k brt yel grn	50	20

Issued to honor heroes of the 1918 civil war.

For 60k stamps of types A494 to A496, see Nos. 1209-1211. For 40k stamp of type A495, see No. 1403.

1944, Sept.

945	A497	30k gray	50	15
946	A497	1r lt brn	1.00	30

Issued to commemorate the 75th anniversary of the birth of Sergei A. Chaplygin, scientist and mathematician.

Khanpasha Nuradilov—A498

A. Matrosov—A499

F. Louzan—A500

M. S. Polivanova and N. V. Kovshova
A501

Pilot B. Safonov
A502

1944, July

947	A498	30k sl grn	30	30
948	A499	60k dl pur	60	40
949	A500	60k dl bl	60	40
950	A501	60k brt grn	60	40
951	A502	60k sl blk	80	40
	Nos. 947-951 (5)		2.90	1.90

Issued to honor Soviet war heroes.

Ilya E. Repin   Ivan A. Krylov
A503   A505

"Cossacks' Reply to Sultan Mohammed IV"
A504

1944, Nov.   **Perf. 12½. Imperf.**

952	A503	30k sl grn	50	25
953	A504	50k dk bl grn	75	25
954	A504	60k chlky bl	75	.25
955	A503	1r dk org brn	1.00	30
956	A504	2r dk pur	2.00	40
	Nos. 952-956 (5)		5.00	1.45

Birth centenary of I. E. Repin (1844-1930), painter.

1944, Nov.   **Perf. 12**

957	A505	30k yel brn	25	15
958	A505	1r dk vio bl	60	25

Issued to commemorate the centenary of the death of I. A. Krylov, fable writer.

Souvenir Sheet.

Leningrad—A506

1944, Dec. 6   **Imperf.**

959	A506	30k dk sl grn, sheet of four	4.00	4.00
a.		Single stamp, type A474	40	40

Issued to commemorate the liberation of Leningrad, Jan. 27, 1944. Sheet size, 138x101mm.

Partisan Medal   Order for Bravery
A507   A508

Order of Bogdan Chmielnicki   Order of Victory
A509   A510

Order of Ushakov   Order of Nakhimov
A511   A512

Paper with network as in parenthesis.

Perf. 12½, Imperf.

1945, Jan.   **Typo.**   **Unwmkd.**

960	A507	15k blk (grn)	30	20
961	A508	30k dp bl lt bl	30	20
962	A509	45k dk bl	40	20
963	A510	60k dl rose (pale rose)	50	25
964	A511	1r dl bl (grn)	75	30
965	A512	1r yel grn (bl)	75	30
	Nos. 960-965 (6)		3.00	1.45

Aleksandr S. Griboedov   Red Army Soldier
A513   A514

1945, Jan. Photogravure Perf. 12½

966	A513	30k dk sl grn	60	30
967	A513	60k gray blk	1.10	50

Issued to commemorate the 150th anniversary of the birth of A. S. Griboedov (1795-1829), poet and statesman.

1945, March

968	A514	60k gray blk & hn	1.00	1.00
969	A514	3r gray blk & hn	3.00	2.00

Souvenir Sheet.
Imperf.

970	A514	Sheet of four	40.00	40.00
a.		3r gray brn & hn, single stamp	4.00	4.00

Second anniversary of victory at Stalingrad. No. 970 contains 4 stamps similar to No. 969. Commemorative marginal inscription. Size: 91x138mm.

Order for Bravery   Order of Bogdan Chmielnicki
A516   A517

Order of Victory
A518

1945   **Engraved**   **Perf. 12**

971	A516	1r indigo	80	20
972	A517	2r black	1.50	30
973	A518	3r henna	2.75	60

See also Nos. 1341-1342.

A519   A520

A521

A522

A523

RUSSIA

Battle Scenes
A524

1945, Apr.		Photo.	Perf. 12½	
974	A519	20k sl grn, org red & blk	20	20
975	A520	30k bl blk & dl org	25	20
976	A521	30k bl blk	25	20
977	A522	60k org red	50	20
978	A523	1r sl grn & org red	80	50
979	A524	1r sl grn	80	50
	Nos. 974-979 (6)		2.80	1.80

Issued to commemorate the successes of the Red Army against Germany.

Parade in
Red Square,
Nov. 7,
1941
A525

Designs: 60k, Soldiers and Moscow barricade, Dec. 1941. 1r, Air battle, 1941.

1945, June				
980	A525	30k dk bl vio	20	15
981	A525	60k ol blk	40	25
982	A525	1r blk brn	1.20	40

Issued to commemorate the 3rd anniversary of the victory over the Germans before Moscow.

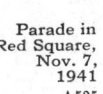 

Elite Guard Badge
and Cannons
A528

Motherhood
Medal
A529

Motherhood Glory
Order
A530

Mother-Heroine
Order
A531

1945, April		Typographed		
983	A528	60k red	60	20

| 1945 | Perf. 12½, Imperf. |
| Paper with network as in parenthesis |
| Size: 22x33¼mm. |

984	A529	20k brn (lt bl)	25	20
985	A530	30k yel brn (grn)	35	25
986	A531	60k dl rose (pale rose)	60	25

Engraved.
Perf. 12½
Size: 20x38mm.

986A	A529	1r blk brn (grn)	70	30
986B	A530	2r dp bl (lt bl)	1.40	60
986C	A531	3r brn red (lt bl)	2.00	1.00
	Nos. 984-986C (6)		5.30	2.60

Academy
Building,
Moscow
A532

Academy at
Leningrad and
M. V. Lomonosov
A533

1945, June		Photo.	Perf. 12½	
987	A532	30k bl vio	70	30
a.	Horiz. pair, imperf. between		5.00	
988	A533	2r grnsh blk	2.25	90

Issued to commemorate the 220th anniversary of the establishment of the Academy of Sciences.

Popov and
his Invention
A534

Aleksandr S.
Popov
A535

1945, July			Unwmkd.	
989	A534	30k dp bl vio	1.00	30
990	A534	60k dk red	2.00	40
991	A535	1r yel brn	3.50	60

Issued to commemorate the 50th anniversary of the "invention of radio" by A. S. Popov.

No. 973
Overprinted
in Blue

ПРАЗДНИК
ПОБЕДЫ

9 мая
1945 года

1945, Aug.			Perf. 12	
992	A518	3r henna	2.00	75

Issued to commemorate the Victory of the Allied Nations in Europe.

Iakovlev Fighter—A536

Petliakov-2
Dive Bombers
A537

Iliushin-2
Bombers
A538

Designs: Nos. 992A, 995, Iakovlev Fighter. Nos. 992B, 1000, Petliakov-2 dive bombers. Nos. 992C, 996, Iliushin-2 bombers. Nos. 992D, 993, Petliakov-8 heavy bomber. Nos. 992E, 1001, Tupolev-2 bombers. Nos. 992F, 997, Iliushin-4 bombers. Nos. 992G, 999, Polikarpov-2 biplane. Nos. 992H, 998, Lavochkin-7 fighters. Nos. 992I, 994, Iakovlev fighter in action.

Photogravure.

1945-46		Perf. 12.	Unwmkd.	
992A	A536	5k dk vio ('46)	40	25
992B	A537	10k hn brn ('46)	40	25
992C	A538	15k hn brn ('46)	50	25
992D	A536	15k Prus grn ('46)	50	25
992E	A538	20k gray brn ('46)	60	30
992F	A538	30k vio ('46)	60	40
992G	A538	30k brn ('46)	60	40
992H	A538	50k bl vio ('46)	1.25	1.00
992I	A536	60k dl bl vio ('46)	1.25	1.00
993	A536	1r gray blk	2.50	1.75
994	A536	1r hn brn	2.50	1.75
995	A536	1r brown	2.50	1.75
996	A538	1r dp brn	2.50	1.75
997	A538	1r int blk	2.50	1.75
998	A538	1r org ver	2.50	1.75
999	A538	1r brt grn	2.50	1.75
1000	A537	1r dp brn	2.50	1.75
1001	A538	1r bl vio	2.50	1.75
	Nos. 992A-1001 (18)		28.60	19.85

Lenin
A545

A546

Various Lenin Portraits.
Dated "1870—1945."

1945, Sept.			Perf. 12½	
1002	A545	30k bluish blk	30	25
1003	A546	50k gray brn	40	25
1004	A546	60k org brn	50	30
1005	A546	1r grnsh blk	80	40
1006	A546	3r sepia	2.50	1.00
	Nos. 1002-1006 (5)		4.50	2.20

Issued to commemorate the 75th anniversary of the birth of Vladimir Ilich Ulyanov (Lenin).

Prince
M. I. Kutuzov
A550

Aleksandr Ivanovich
Herzen
A551

1945, Sept. 16				
1007	A550	30k bl vio	70	25
1008	A550	60k brown	1.20	30

Issued to commemorate the bicentenary of the birth of Field Marshal Prince Mikhail Illarionovich Kutuzov (1745-1813).

1945, Oct. 26				
1009	A551	30k dk brn	60	30
1010	A551	2r grnsh blk	1.75	60

Issued to commemorate the 75th anniversary of the death of A. I. Herzen, author and revolutionist.

Ilya Mechnikov
A552

Friedrich Engels
A553

1945, Nov. 27				
1011	A552	30k brown	40	25
1012	A552	1r grnsh blk	90	45

Issued to commemorate the centenary of the birth of Ilya I. Mechnikov, zoologist and bacteriologist.

1945, Nov.		Perf. 12½	Unwmkd.	
1013	A553	30k dk brn	50	25
1014	A553	60k Prus grn	70	30

Issued to commemorate the 125th anniversary of the birth of Friedrich Engels, collaborator of Karl Marx.

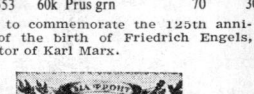

Tank Leaving Assembly Line
A554

Designs: 30k, Harvesting wheat. 60k, Airplane designing. 1r, Moscow fireworks.

1945, Dec. 25			Photogravure	
1015	A554	20k ind & bl	40	25
1016	A554	30k bl blk & org brn	40	25
1017	A554	60k brn & grn	70	30
1018	A554	1r dk bl & org	1.20	40

Artillery Observer and Guns
A558

Heavy Field Pieces—A559

1945, Dec.				
1019	A558	30k brown	60	25
1020	A559	60k sepia	1.20	50

Artillery Day, Nov. 19, 1945.

Victory
Medal
A560

Soldier with
Victory Flag
A561

1946, Jan. 23				
1021	A560	30k dk vio	30	20
1022	A560	30k brown	30	20
1023	A560	60k grnsh blk	60	25
1024	A560	60k henna	60	25
1025	A561	60k blk & dl red	60	25
	Nos. 1021-1025 (5)		2.40	1.15

Arms of U.S.S.R.
A562

Red Square
A563

RUSSIA

1946, Feb. 10

1026	A562	30k henna	40	20
1027	A563	45k henna	50	25
1028	A562	60k grnsh blk	1.00	30

Issued to commemorate the elections to the Supreme Soviet of the U.S.S.R., February 10, 1946.

Artillery in Victory Parade—A564

Victory Parade—A565

1946, Feb. 23

1029	A564	60k dk brn	60	30
1030	A564	2r dl vio	1.20	40
1031	A565	3r blk & red	1.80	60

Issued to publicize the Victory Parade held in Moscow, June 24, 1945.

Order of Lenin — A566   Order of Red Star — A567

Medal of Hammer and Sickle A568   Order of Token of Veneration A569

Gold Star Medal A570   Order of Red Banner A571

Order of the Red Workers' Banner A572

Paper with network as in parenthesis.
Typographed.

1946   Perf. 12½x12   Unwmkd.

1032	A566	60k myr grn (grn)	60	50
1033	A567	60k dk vio brn (brn)	60	50
1034	A568	60k plum (pink)	60	50
1035	A569	60k dp bl (grn)	60	50
1036	A570	60k dk car (sal)	60	50
1037	A571	60k red (sal)	60	50
1038	A572	60k dk brn vio (buff)	60	50
		Nos. 1032-1038 (7)	4.20	3.50

See also Nos. 1650-1654.

Medal for Workers' Achievement of Distinction A573   Medal for Workers' Gallantry A574

Marshal's Star A575   Medal for Defense of Soviet Trans-Arctic Regions A576

Medal for Meritorious Service in Battle A577   Medal for Defense of Caucasus A578

Medal for Defense of Moscow A579   Medal for Bravery A580

Paper with network as in parenthesis.

1946

1039	A573	60k choc (sal)	50	50
1040	A574	60k brn (sal)	50	50
1041	A575	60k bl (pale bl)	50	50
1042	A576	60k dk grn (grn)	50	50
1043	A577	60k dk vio brn (grn)	50	50
1044	A578	60k dk yel grn (grn)	50	50
1045	A579	60k car (pink)	50	50
1046	A580	60k dk vio (bl)	50	50
		Nos. 1039-1046 (8)	4.00	4.00

A581

Maxim Gorki—A582

1946, June 18   Photogravure

1047	A581	30k brown	30	25
1048	A582	60k dk grn	60	40

Issued to commemorate the 10th anniversary of the death of Maxim Gorki (Alexei M. Peshkov).

Mikhail Kalinin A583   Chebyshev A584

1946, June

| 1049 | A583 | 20k sepia | 60 | 30 |

Death of Mikhail Ivanovich Kalinin (1875–1946).

1946, May 25

1050	A584	30k brown	75	20
1051	A584	60k gray brn	1.00	20

125th anniversary of the birth of Pafnuti Lvovich Chebyshev (1821–94), mathematician.

View of Sukhumi A585   Sanatorium at Sochi A587

Designs: 30k, Promenade at Gagri. 45k, New Afyon Sanatorium.

1946, June 18

1052	A585	15k dk brn	30	20
1053	A585	30k dk sl grn	40	20
1054	A587	30k dk grn	40	20
1055	A585	45k chnt brn	60	30

291

All-Union Parade of Physical Culturists A589

1946, July 21

| 1056 | A589 | 30k dk grn | 6.00 | 4.00 |

Tank Divisions in Red Square A590

1946, Sept. 8

1057	A590	30k dk grn	1.00	75
1058	A590	60k brown	1.50	1.00

Issued to honor Soviet tankmen.

Belfry of Ivan the Great, Kremlin A591   Grand Theater, Moscow A592

Hotel Moscow—A593

Red Square—A597

Spasski Tower and Statues of Minin and Pozharski A598

Designs (Moscow scenes): 20k, Grand Theater, Sverdlov Place. 45k, View of Kremlin. 50k, Lenin Museum.

RUSSIA

1946, Sept. 5

1059	A591	5k brown	20	20
1060	A592	10k sepia	25	20
1061	A593	15k chestnut	25	20
1062	A593	20k lt brn	25	20
1063	A593	45k dk grn	40	25
1064	A593	50k brown	40	30
1065	A597	60k bl vio	60	30
1066	A598	1r chnt brn	80	30
		Nos. 1059-1066 (8)	3.15	1.95

Medal for Workers' Achievement of Distinction
A599

Medal for Workers' Gallantry
A600

Medal to the Partisan of the Patriotic War
A601

Medal for Defense of Soviet Trans-Arctic Regions
A602

Medal for Meritorious Service in Battle
A603

Medal for Defense of Caucasus
A604

Medal for Defense of Moscow
A605

Medal for Bravery
A606

1946, Sept. 5   Engraved

1067	A599	1r dk vio brn	80	40
1068	A600	1r dk car	80	40
1069	A601	1r carmine	80	40
1070	A602	1r bl blk	80	40
1071	A603	1r black	80	40
1072	A604	1r blk brn	80	40
1073	A605	1r ol blk	80	40
1074	A606	1r dp cl	80	40
		Nos. 1067-1074 (8)	6.40	3.20

See also Nos. 1650-1654.

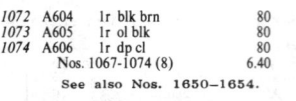
Give the Country Each Year: 127 Million Tons of Grain
A607

60 Million Tons of Oil
A608

60 Million Tons of Steel
A610

500 Million Tons of Coal
A609

50 Million Tons of Cast Iron
A611

Perf. 12½x12

1946, Oct. 6   Photo.   Unwmkd.

1075	A607	5k ol brn	10	15
1076	A608	10k dk sl grn	10	15
1077	A609	15k brown	20	20
1078	A610	20k dk bl vio	25	20
1079	A611	30k brown	60	30
		Nos. 1075-1079 (5)	1.25	1.00

Symbols of Transportation, Map and Stamps
A612

Early Soviet Stamp—A613

Stamps of Soviet Russia—A614

1946, Nov. 6   Perf. 12½

1080	A612	15k blk & dk red	1.25	60
a.		Sheet of 4, imperf.	50.00	50.00
1081	A613	30k dk grn & brn	1.75	60
a.		Sheet of 4, imperf.	75.00	75.00
1082	A614	60k dk grn & blk	2.75	75
a.		Sheet of 4, imperf.	75.00	75.00

Issued to commemorate the 25th anniversary of the first Soviet postage stamp. No. 1080a measures 137x100mm.; No. 1081a measures 131x103mm. and No. 1082a, 140x101mm., with inscriptions in top and bottom margins.

Lenin and Stalin
A615

1946   Photo.   Perf. 12½, Imperf.

1083	A615	30k dp brn org	2.00	2.00
a.		Sheet of 4, imperf.	35.00	35.00
1084	A615	30k dk grn	2.00	2.00

29th anniversary of October Revolution. No. 1083a measures 103x131mm., and contains four of No. 1083. The U.S.S.R. coat of arms appears in top margin, lithographed in dull red.
Issue dates: Nos. 1083-1084 imperf., Nov. 6; perf., Dec. 18. No. 1083a, June, 1947.

Dnieprostroy Dam and Power Station
A616

1946, Dec. 23   Perf. 12½

1085	A616	30k sepia	1.00	75
1086	A616	60k chlky bl	1.50	1.00

A. P. Karpinsky
A617

Nikolai A. Nekrasov
A618

1947, Jan. 17   Unwmkd.

1087	A617	30k dk grn	1.00	50
1088	A617	50k sepia	1.50	75

Centenary of the birth of Aleksandr P. Karpinsky (1847-1936), geologist.

Canceled to Order
Canceled sets of new issues have long been sold by the government. Prices in the second ("used") column are for these canceled-to-order stamps. Postally used copies are worth more.

1946, Dec. 4

1089	A618	30k sepia	50	20
1090	A618	60k brown	65	30

125th anniversary of birth of Nikolai A. Nekrasov (1821-1878), poet.

Lenin's Mausoleum—A619

Lenin—A620

1947, Jan. 21

1091	A619	30k sl bl	1.00	20
1092	A619	30k dk grn	1.00	20
1093	A620	50k dk brn	1.50	20

23rd anniversary of the death of Lenin. See also Nos. 1197-1199.

F. P. Litke and Sailing Vessel
A621

N. M. Przhevalski, Mare and Foal
A622

1947, Jan. 27

1094	A621	20k bl vio	60	25
1095	A621	60k sepia	60	25
1096	A622	60k ol brn	1.25	50
1097	A622	60k sepia	1.25	50

Issued to commemorate the centenary of the Soviet Union Geographical Society.

Nikolai E. Zhukovski
A623

1947, Jan. 17

1098	A623	30k sepia	75	20
1099	A623	60k bl vio	1.00	30

Birth centenary of N. E. Zhukovski (1847-1921), scientist.

Stalin Prize Medal
A624

1946, Dec. 21   Photogravure

1100	A624	30k blk brn	2.00	1.00

RUSSIA

Russian Soldier
A625

Military Instruction
A626

Aviator, Sailor and Soldier
A627

Perf. 12x12½, 12½x12, Imperf. Unwmkd.

1947, Feb. 23

1101	A625	20k sepia	40	30
1102	A626	30k sl bl	40	30
1103	A627	30k brown	40	30

29th anniversary of the Soviet Army.

Arms of:
Russian Socialist Federated Soviet Republic A628 — Armenian Socialist Soviet Republic A629

Azerbaijan S.S.R. A630 — Byelorussian S.S.R. A631

Estonian S.S.R. A632 — Georgian S.S.R. A633

Karelo Finnish S.S.R. A634 — Kazakh S.S.R. A635

Kirghiz S.S.R. A636

Latvian S.S.R. A637

Lithuanian S.S.R. A638

Moldavian S.S.R. A639

Tadjikistan S.S.R. A640

Turkmen S.S.R. A641

Ukrainian S.S.R. A642

Uzbek S.S.R. A643

Soviet Union—A644

Photogravure.

1947 Perf. 12½ Unwmkd.

1104	A628	30k hn brn	50	30
1105	A629	30k chestnut	50	30
1106	A630	30k ol brn	50	30
1107	A631	30k ol grn	50	30
1108	A632	30k vio blk	50	30
1109	A633	30k dk vio brn	50	30
1110	A634	30k dk vio	50	30
1111	A635	30k dp org	50	30
1112	A636	30k vio	50	30
1113	A637	30k yel brn	50	30
1114	A638	30k dk ol grn	50	30
1115	A639	30k dk vio brn	50	30
1116	A640	30k dk grn	50	30
1117	A641	30k gray blk	50	30
1118	A642	30k bl vio	50	30
1119	A643	30k brown	40	30

Lithographed.

1120	A644	1r dk brn, bl, gold & red	1.50	1.00
		Nos. 1104-1120 (17)	9.40	5.80

Aleksander S. Pushkin A645

1947, Feb. Photo. Perf. 12

1121	A645	30k sepia	75	30
1122	A645	50k dk yel grn	1.00	35

Issued to commemorate the 110th anniversary of the death of Aleksander S. Pushkin (1799–1837), poet.

Classroom—A646

Parade of Women A647

1947, Mar. 11

1123	A646	15k brt bl	1.25	80
1124	A647	30k red	1.75	1.20

Issued to commemorate the International Day of Women, March 8, 1947.

Moscow Council Building A648

1947 Perf. 12½

1125	A648	30k sep, gray bl & brick red	1.25	60

Issued to commemorate the 30th anniversary of the Moscow Soviet. Exists imperf. The imperf. exists also with gray blue omitted.
Both perf. and imperf. stamps exist in two sizes: 40x27mm. and 41x27mm.

May Day Parade in Red Square A649

1947, June 10 Perf. 12½

1126	A649	30k scarlet	50	50
1127	A649	1r dk ol grn	1.25	75

Issued to publicize Labor Day, May 1, 1947.

Nos. 1062 and 1064 to 1066 Overprinted in Red

1947, Sept. Perf. 12½x12

1128	A593	20k lt brn	60	30
1129	A593	50k brown	80	40
1130	A597	60k bl vio	1.20	50
1131	A598	1r chnt brn	1.75	60

The overprint is arranged in four lines on No. 1131.

Crimea Bridge, Moscow—A650

Gorki Street, Moscow A651

View of Kremlin, Moscow—A652

Designs: No. 1134, Central Telegraph Building. No. 1135, Kiev Railroad Station. No. 1136, Kazan Railroad Station. No. 1137, Kaluga St. No. 1138, Pushkin Place. 50k, View of Kremlin. No. 1141, Grand Kremlin Palace. No. 1142, "Old Moscow," by Vasnetsov. No. 1143, St. Basil Cathedral. 2r, View of Kremlin. 3r, View of Kremlin. 5r, Hotel Moscow and government building.

1947 Photogravure Perf. 12½
Various Frames, Dated 1147–1947.

1132	A650	5k dk bl & dk brn	40	25
1133	A651	10k red brn & brn blk	40	25
1134	A650	30k brown	50	25
1135	A650	30k dk Prus bl	50	25
1136	A650	30k ultra	50	25
1137	A650	30k dp yel grn	50	25
1138	A651	30k yel grn	50	25
1139	A650	30k dp yel grn	70	35
1140	A652	60k red brn & brn blk	80	35
1141	A651	60k gray bl	80	35
1142	A651	1r dk vio	1.75	75

Typographed.
Colors: Blue, Yellow and Red.

1143	A651	1r multi	1.75	75
1144	A651	2r multi	3.25	1.50
1145	A650	3r multi	6.00	1.50
a.		Sheet of four, imperf.	30.00	30.00
1146	A650	5r multi	10.00	3.00
		Nos. 1132-1146 (15)	28.35	10.30

Nos. 1128 to 1146 were issued to commemorate the 800th anniversary of the founding of Moscow.
Nos. 1143 to 1146 were printed in a single sheet containing a row of each denomination plus a row of labels.
No. 1145a is a souvenir sheet measuring 139½x172½ mm., with national emblem and inscriptions in top and bottom margins.

RUSSIA

Karamyshevsky Dam—A653

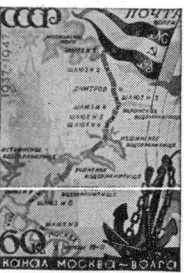

Map Showing
Moscow-Volga Canal
A654

Designs: No. 1148, Direction towers, Yakromsky Lock. 45k, Yakromsky Pumping Station. 50k, Khimki Station. 1r, Lock No. 8.

1947, Sept. 7   Photogravure
1147	A653	30k sepia	1.00	30
1148	A653	30k red brn	1.00	30
1149	A653	45k hn brn	1.00	30
1150	A653	50k brt ultra	1.00	30
1151	A654	60k brt rose	1.00	30
1152	A653	1r violet	1.50	50
		Nos. 1147-1152 (6)	6.50	2.00

Moscow-Volga Canal, 10th anniversary.

Electric Plant
A655

Mayakovsky Station
A656

Planes and Flag
A657

Designs (Moscow Subway scenes): No. 1154, Ismailovsky Station. No. 1155, Sokol Station. No. 1156, Stalinsky Station. No. 1158, Kiev Station.

1947, Sept.
1153	A655	30k sepia	40	25
1154	A655	30k bl blk	40	25
1155	A655	45k yel brn	50	25
1156	A655	45k dp vio	50	25
1157	A656	60k hn brn	75	30
1158	A655	60k dp yel grn	75	30
		Nos. 1153-1158 (6)	3.30	1.60

1947, Sept. 1
1159	A657	30k dp vio	60	25
1160		1r brt ultra	1.25	30

Day of the Air Fleet. See Nos. 1246-1247.

Spasski Tower, Kremlin
A658

Agave Plant at Sukhumi
A659

Gullripsh Sanatorium, Sukhumi
A660

Typographed.

1947, Nov.   Perf. 12½   Unwmkd.
1161	A658	60k dk red	2.75	75

See also No. 1260.

1947, Nov.   Photogravure

Designs (Russian sanatoria): No. 1164, Peasants', Livadia. No. 1165, New Riviera. No. 1166, Abkhasia, New Afyon. No. 1167, Kemeri, near Riga. No. 1168, Kirov Memorial, Kislovodsk. No. 1169, Voroshilov Memorial, Sochi. No. 1170, Riza, Gagri. No. 1171, Zapadugol, Sochi.

1162	A659	30k dk grn	40	20
1163	A660	30k violet	40	20
1164	A660	30k olive	40	20
1165	A660	30k brown	40	20
1166	A660	30k red brn	40	20
1167	A660	30k blk vio	40	20
1168	A660	30k brt ultra	40	20
1169	A660	30k dk brn vio	40	20
1170	A659	30k dk yel grn	40	20
1171	A660	30k sepia	40	20
		Nos. 1162-1171 (10)	4.00	2.00

Blast Furnaces, Constantine
A661

Maxim Gorki Theater, Stalingrad
A666

Designs: 15k, No. 1174, Blast furnaces, Constantine. 20k, No. 1180, Kirov foundry, Makeevka. Nos. 1175, 1179, Agricultural machine plant, Rostov. Nos. 1176, 1181, Tractor plant, Kharkov. Nos. 1177, 1182, Tractor plant, Stalingrad.

1947, Nov.   Perf. 12½, Imperf.
1172	A661	15k yel brn	30	20
1173	A661	20k sepia	30	20
1174	A661	30k vio brn	40	20
1175	A661	30k dk grn	40	20
1176	A661	30k brown	40	20
1177	A661	30k blk vio	40	20
1178	A666	60k vio brn	80	30
1179	A661	60k yel brn	80	30
1180	A661	1r org red	1.30	40
1181	A661	1r red	1.30	40
1182	A661	1r violet	1.30	40
		Nos. 1172-1182 (11)	7.70	3.00

Issued to commemorate the reconstruction of war-damaged cities and factories, and as Five-Year-Plan publicity.

Revolutionists—A667

Designs: 30k, No. 1185, Revolutionists. 50k, 1r, Industry. No. 1186, 2r, Agriculture.

1947, Nov.   Perf. 12½, Imperf.
Frame in Dark Red.
1183	A667	30k grnsh blk	40	20
1184	A667	50k bl blk	60	25
1185	A667	60k brn blk	75	40
1186	A667	30k brown	75	60
1187	A667	1r black	1.25	75
1188	A667	2r grnsh blk	2.50	1.00
		Nos. 1183-1188 (6)	6.25	3.20

30th anniversary of October Revolution.

Palace of the Arts (Winter Palace)
A668

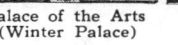
Peter I Monument
A669

Designs (Leningrad in 1947): 60k, Sts. Peter and Paul Fortress. 1r, Smolny Institute.

1948, Jan. 10   Perf. 12½
1189	A668	30k violet	1.00	40
1190	A669	50k dk sl grn	1.40	50
1191	A668	60k sepia	1.50	60
1192	A669	1r dk brn vio	2.75	1.00

Issued to commemorate the 5th anniversary of the liberation of Leningrad from the German blockade.

Government Building, Kiev
A670

Designs: 50k, Dnieprostroy Dam. 60k, Wheat field and granary. 1r, Steel mill and coal mine.

1948, Jan. 25   Perf. 12½
1193	A670	30k indigo	60	30
1194	A670	50k violet	80	40
1195	A670	60k gldn brn	1.20	50
1196	A670	1r sepia	2.00	80

Issued to commemorate the 30th anniversary of the Ukrainian Soviet Socialist Republic.

Lenin Types of 1947.
Inscribed "1924-1948."

1948, Jan. 21   Unwmkd.
1197	A619	30k brn vio	60	40
1198	A619	60k dk gray bl	1.20	50
1199	A620	60k dp yel grn	1.20	50

24th anniversary of the death of Lenin.

Vasili I. Surikov
A672

Soviet Soldier and Artillery
A675

Fliers and Planes
A676

1948, Feb. 15   Photo.   Perf. 12
1201	A672	30k red brn	1.25	40
1202	A672	60k dk brn	2.50	80

Issued to commemorate the centenary of the birth of Vasili Ivanovich Surikov, artist.

1948, Feb. 23
Designs: No. 1206, Soviet sailor. 60k, Military class.
1205	A675	30k brown	70	40
1206	A675	30k gray	70	40
1207	A676	30k vio bl	70	40
1208	A676	60k red brn	1.00	60

Hero Types of 1944
1948, Feb. 23
1209	A494	60k dp grn	1.00	40
1210	A495	60k yel brn	1.00	40
1211	A496	60k vio bl	1.00	40

Nos. 1205 to 1211 were issued to commemorate the 30th anniversary of the Soviet army.

Karl Marx, Friedrich Engels and Communist Manifesto
A677

1948, Apr.
1212	A677	30k black	40	20
1213	A677	50k hn brn	60	30

Centenary of the Communist Manifesto.

Miner
A678

Marine
A679

Aviator
A680

Woman Farmer
A681

Arms of U.S.S.R.
A682

Scientist
A683

Spasski Tower, Kremlin
A684

Soldier
A685

1948   Photogravure
1214	A678	5k sepia	1.50	1.25
1215	A679	10k violet	1.50	1.25

RUSSIA

1216	A680	15k brt bl	2.00	1.75
1217	A681	20k brown	2.25	2.00
1218	A682	30k brn brn	2.50	2.00
1219	A683	45k brn vio	3.50	3.00
1220	A684	50k brt bl	5.50	5.00
1221	A685	60k brt grn	8.50	8.00
		Nos. 1214-1221 (8)	27.25	24.25

See Nos. 1306, 1343-1347, 1689.

May Day Parade in Red Square
A686

1948, June 5   *Perf. 12*

1222	A686	30k dp car rose	50	30
1223	A686	60k brt bl	90	40

Labor Day, May 1, 1948.

Vissarion G. Belinski
A687

1948, June 7   *Perf. 12*   *Unwmkd.*

1224	A687	30k brown	60	40
1225	A687	50k dk grn	90	40
1226	A687	60k purple	1.25	60

Issued to commemorate the centenary of the death of Vissarion G. Belinski (1811-1848), literary critic.

Aleksandr N. Ostrovski
A690   A691

1948, June 10   *Photo.*   *Perf. 12*

1227	A690	30k brt grn	1.00	30
1228	A691	60k brown	1.25	40
1229	A691	1r brn vio	2.00	60

Issued to commemorate the 125th anniversary of the birth of A. N. Ostrovski (1823-1886), playwright.

Exist imperf. Price, set $100.

Ivan I. Shishkin
A692

"Field of Rye," by Shishkin
A693

Design: 60k, "Bears in a Forest," by Shishkin.
Photo. (30k, 1r), Typo. (50k, 60k)

1948, June 12

1230	A692	30k dk grn & vio brn	1.50	1.00
1231	A693	50k multi	2.00	1.00
1232	A693	60k multi	3.00	1.25
1233	A692	1r brn & bl blk	4.50	1.75

Issued to commemorate the 50th anniversary of the death of Ivan I. Shishkin (1832-1898), painter.

Industrial Expansion
A694

Public Gathering at Leningrad
A695

Photo., Frames Litho. in Carmine

1948, June 25

1234	A694	15k red brn	40	30
1235	A695	30k slate	60	40
1236	A694	60k brn blk	1.00	60

Industrial five-year plan.

Planting Crops—A696

Designs: No. 1238, 1r, Gathering vegetables. 45k, No. 1241, Baling cotton. No. 1242, Harvesting grain.

1948, July 12   *Photogravure*

1237	A696	30k car rose	35	25
1238	A696	30k bl grn	35	25
1239	A696	45k red brn	60	35
1240	A696	50k brn blk	75	35
1241	A696	60k dk grn	75	35
1242	A696	60k dk bl grn	75	35
1243	A696	1r purple	1.25	60
		Nos. 1237-1243 (7)	4.80	2.50

Agricultural five-year plan.

Arms and Citizens   **Soviet**
of U. S. S. R.   **Miners**
A697   A698

Photo., Frames Litho. in Carmine

1948, July 25

1244	A697	30k slate	1.50	75
1245	A697	60k grnsh blk	2.00	1.00

Issued to commemorate the 25th anniversary of the Union of Soviet Socialist Republics.

Nos. 1159 and 1160 Overprinted in Red

ИЮЛЬ
1948
года

1948, Aug. 24   *Perf. 12½*

1246	A657	30k dp vio	3.50	1.50
1247	A657	1r brt ultra	5.00	2.50

Air Fleet Day, 1948. On sale one day.

1948, Aug.   *Photo.*   *Perf. 12½x12*

Designs: 60k, Scene in mine. 1r, Miner's badge.

1248	A698	30k blue	30	15
1249	A698	60k purple	60	30
1250	A698	1r green	1.00	40

Miners' Day, August 29th.

A. A. Zhdanov   **Russian Sailor**
A699   A700

1948, Sept. 3

1251	A699	40k slate	1.00	60

Issued in tribute to Andrei A. Zhdanov, statesman, 1896-1948.

1948, Sept. 12   *Perf. 12*

1252	A700	30k bl grn	50	30
1253	A700	60k brt bl	1.00	50

Navy Day, Sept. 12.

Slalom   **Motorcyclist**
A701   A702

Designs: No. 1254, Foot race. 30k, Soccer game. 45k, Motorboat race. 50k, Diving.

1948, Sept. 15   *Perf. 12½x12*

1253A	A701	15k dk bl	1.50	40
1254	A701	15k violet	1.50	40
1254A	A702	20k dk sl bl	1.75	40
1255	A701	30k brown	2.00	40
1256	A701	45k sepia	2.50	40
1257	A702	50k blue	3.50	50
		Nos. 1253A-1257 (6)	12.75	2.50

Tankmen Group
A703

Design: 1r, Tank parade.

1948, Sept. 25

1258	A703	30k sepia	2.00	50
1259	A703	1r rose	5.00	75

Day of the Tankmen, Sept. 25.

Spasski Tower Type of 1947.
1948   *Lithographed*   *Perf. 12x12½*

1260	A658	1r brn red	2.50	60

No. 1260 was re-issued in 1954-56 in slightly smaller format: 14½x21½mm., instead of 14½x22mm., and in a paler shade. See note after No. 738.

Railroad Train—A704

Designs: 60k, Auto and bus at intersection. 1r, Steamships at anchor.

1948, Sept. 30   *Photo.*   *Perf. 12½x12*

1261	A704	30k brown	1.75	1.25
1262	A704	50k dk grn	2.50	1.50
1263	A704	60k blue	4.00	1.50
1264	A704	1r bl vio	5.00	2.50

Transportation five-year plan.

Horses—A705

Design: 60k, Dairy farm.

1948, Sept. 30   *Perf. 12*

1265	A705	30k sl gray	1.75	1.00
1266	A705	60k brt grn	3.00	1.50
1267	A705	1r brown	4.00	2.00

Livestock five-year plan.

Pouring Molten Metal—A706

Designs: 60k, 1r, Iron pipe manufacture.

1948, Oct. 14   *Perf. 12½*

1268	A706	30k purple	1.50	75
1269	A706	50k brown	1.75	1.00
1270	A706	60k carmine	2.25	1.50
1271	A706	1r dl bl	4.50	2.50

Heavy Machinery Plant
A707

Design: 60k, Pump station interior.

1948, Oct. 14

1272	A707	30k purple	1.00	50
1273	A707	50k sepia	1.75	1.25
1274	A707	60k brown	2.50	1.50

Nos. 1268-1274 were issued to publicize the five-year plan for steel, iron and machinery industries.

Khachatur Abovian
A708

1948, Oct. 16   *Perf. 12x12½*

1275	A708	40k purple	2.50	1.50
1276	A708	50k dp grn	3.00	1.50

Issued to commemorate the centenary of the death of Khachatur Abovian (1809-1848), Armenian writer and poet.

RUSSIA

Farkhatz Hydroelectric Station
A709

Design: 60k, Zoulev Hydroelectric Station.

1948, Oct. 24   Perf. 12½
1277	A709	30k green	1.00	75
1278	A709	60k red	2.50	1.25
1279	A709	1r car rose	3.50	2.00

Electrification five-year plan.

Coal Mine
A710

Designs: No. 1282, 1r, Oil field and tank cars.

1948, Oct. 24
1280	A710	30k sepia	1.50	75
1281	A710	60k brown	2.00	1.00
1282	A710	60k red brn	2.00	1.00
1283	A710	1r bl grn	3.00	1.50

Five-year plan of coal mining and oil production.

Flying Model Planes   Pioneers Saluting
A712   A714

Marching Pioneers
A713

Designs: 60k, Pioneer bugler. 1r, Pioneers at campfire.

1948, Oct. 26   Perf. 12½
1284	A712	30k dk bl grn	3.00	2.00
1285	A713	45k dk vio	3.50	2.50
1286	A714	45k dp car	3.50	2.50
1287	A714	60k dp ultra	4.50	3.50
1288	A713	1r dp bl	12.00	6.00
		Nos. 1284-1288 (5)	26.50	16.50

Issued to honor the Young Pioneers, a Russian youth organization, and to publicize governmental supervision of children's summer vacations.

Marching Youths—A715

Farm Girl   League Members and Flag
A716   A717

Designs: 50k, Communist students. 1r, Flag and badges. 2r, Young worker.

Inscribed: "1918 1948 XXX."

1948, Oct. 29   Perf. 12½
1289	A715	20k vio brn	1.00	1.00
1290	A716	25k rose red	1.50	1.25
1291	A717	40k brn & red	2.50	1.50
1292	A715	50k bl grn	3.50	2.00
1293	A717	1r multi	7.00	4.00
1294	A716	2r purple	14.00	8.00
		Nos. 1289-1294 (6)	29.50	17.75

Issued to commemorate the 30th anniversary of the Young Communist League (Komsomol).

Stage of Moscow Art Theater   K. S. Stanislavski V. I. Nemirovich Danchenko
A719   A720

1948, Nov. 1   Perf. 12½
| 1295 | A719 | 40k gray bl | 2.50 | 1.50 |
| 1296 | A720 | 1r vio brn | 3.00 | 2.50 |

Issued to commemorate the 50th anniversary of the establishment of the Moscow Art Theater.

Flag and Moscow Buildings—A721

1948, Nov. 7   Perf. 12½
| 1297 | A721 | 40k red | 2.00 | 1.50 |
| 1298 | A721 | 1r green | 3.00 | 2.50 |

31st anniversary of October Revolution.

House of Unions, Moscow   Player's Badge (Rook and Chessboard)
A722   A723

1948, Nov. 20
1299	A722	30k grnsh bl	1.00	50
1300	A723	40k violet	2.50	60
1301	A722	50k org brn	3.00	75

16th Chess Championship.

Artillery Salute
A724

1948, Nov. 19   Perf. 12½
| 1302 | A724 | 30k blue | 2.00 | 1.50 |
| 1303 | A724 | 1r rose car | 3.00 | 2.50 |

Artillery Day, Nov. 19, 1948.

V. P. Stasov   Stasov and Barracks of Paul's Regiment, Petrograd
A725   A726

1948, Nov. 27   Unwmkd.
| 1304 | A725 | 40k brown | 1.50 | 1.00 |
| 1305 | A726 | 1r sepia | 3.00 | 1.50 |

Issued to commemorate the centenary of the death of Vasili Petrovich Stasov, architect.

Arms Type of 1948

1948   Litho.   Perf. 12x12½
| 1306 | A682 | 40k brn red | 6.00 | 25 |

J. M. Sverdlov Monument
A727

Design: 40k, Lenin Street, Sverdlovsk.

1948   Photogravure   Perf. 12½
1307	A727	30k blue	30	15
1308	A727	40k purple	40	20
1309	A727	1r brt grn	1.00	25

Issued to commemorate the 225th anniversary of the city of Sverdlovsk (before 1924, Ekaterinburg). Exist imperf.

"Swallow's Nest," Crimea   Hot Spring, Piatigorsk
A729   A730

Shoreline, Sukhum   Tree-lined Walk, Sochi
A731   A732

Formal Gardens, Sochi
A733

Stalin Highway, Sochi
A734

Colonnade, Kislovodsk
A735

Seascape, Gagri
A736

1948, Dec. 30   Perf. 12½
1310	A729	40k brown	1.00	30
1311	A730	40k brt red vio	1.00	30
1312	A731	40k dk grn	1.00	30
1313	A732	40k violet	1.00	30
1314	A733	40k dk pur	1.00	30
1315	A734	40k dk bl grn	1.00	30
1316	A735	40k brt bl	1.00	30
1317	A736	40k dk bl grn	1.00	30
		Nos. 1310-1317 (8)	8.00	2.40

Byelorussian S.S.R. Arms
A737

1949, Jan. 4
| 1318 | A737 | 40k hn brn | 2.00 | 1.00 |
| 1319 | A737 | 1r bl grn | 4.00 | 1.75 |

Issued to commemorate the 30th anniversary of the formation of the Byelorussian Soviet Socialist Republic.

Mikhail V. Lomonosov   Lomonosov Museum, Leningrad
A738   A739

1949, Jan. 10
1320	A738	40k red brn	1.50	75
1321	A738	50k green	2.00	75
1322	A739	1r dp bl	4.00	1.50

RUSSIA

Cape Dezhnev (East Cape)
A740

Design: 1r, Map and Dezhnev's ship.

1949, Jan. 30
| 1323 | A740 | 40k ol grn | 3.50 | 1.50 |
| 1324 | A740 | 1r gray | 6.50 | 3.00 |

Issued to commemorate the 300th anniversary of the discovery of the strait between Asia and America by S. I. Dezhnev.

Souvenir Sheet

A741

1949, Dec. Imperf.
1325	A741	Sheet of four, multi	125.00	150.00
a.		40k Stalin's birthplace, Gorki	15.00	20.00
b.		40k Lenin & Stalin, Leningrad, 1917	15.00	20.00
c.		40k Lenin & Stalin, Gorki	15.00	20.00
d.		40k Marshal Stalin	15.00	20.00

70th birthday of Joseph V. Stalin. Border and inscriptions in gold and orange red. Size: 177x221mm.

Lenin Mausoleum—A742

1949, Jan. 21 Perf. 12½
1326	A742	40k ol grn & org brn	2.00	2.00
1327	A742	1r gray blk & org brn	4.00	3.00
a.		Sheet of four	150.00	150.00

25th anniversary of the death of Lenin. No. 1327a measures 175x131mm. and contains four copies of No. 1327, with commemorative inscription at top and the dates "1924–1949" in lower margin.

Sheet exists imperf. Price $750.

Admiral S. O. Makarov
A743

Kirov Military Medical Academy
A744

Professors Botkin, Pirogov and Sechenov
A745

1949, Mar. 15
| 1328 | A743 | 40k blue | 2.50 | 1.50 |
| 1329 | A743 | 1r red brn | 3.50 | 2.50 |

Issued to commemorate the centenary of the birth of Admiral Stepan Osipovich Makarov, shipbuilder.

1949, Mar. 24
1330	A744	40k red brn	2.00	1.50
1331	A745	50k blue	2.50	2.25
1332	A744	1r bl grn	4.50	3.50

Issued to commemorate the 150th anniversary of the foundation of Kirov Military Medical Academy, Leningrad.

Soviet Soldier—A746

1949, Mar. 16 Photogravure
| 1333 | A746 | 40k rose red | 6.00 | 6.00 |

31st anniversary of the Soviet army.

Textile Weaving
A747

Political Leadership
A748

Designs: 25k, Preschool teaching. No. 1337, School teaching. No. 1338, Farm women. 1r, Women athletes.

1949, Mar. 8 Perf. 12½
Inscribed: "8 МАРТА 1949г"
1334	A747	20k dk vio	30	15
1335	A747	25k blue	35	15
1336	A748	40k hn brn	60	20
1337	A747	50k sl gray	90	30
1338	A747	50k brown	90	30
1339	A747	1r green	2.00	50
1340	A748	2r cop red	3.25	1.50
		Nos. 1334-1340 (7)	8.30	3.10

International Women's Day, Mar. 8.

Medal Types of 1945.

1948–49 Engraved
1341	A517	2r grn ('49)	4.00	1.50
1341A	A517	2r vio brn	15.00	15.00
1342	A518	3r brn car ('49)	5.00	1.00

Types of 1948.

1949 Lithographed Perf. 12x12½
1343	A678	15k black	50	25
1344	A681	20k green	50	25
1345	A680	25k dk bl	75	25
1346	A683	30k brown	90	35
1347	A684	50k dp bl	2.25	90
		Nos. 1343-1347 (5)	4.90	2.00

The 20k, 25k and 30k were re-issued in 1954–56 in slightly smaller format. The 20k measures 14x21mm., instead of 15x22 mm.; 25k, 14½x21mm., instead of 14½x 21¾mm., and 30k, 14½x21mm., instead of 15x22mm. The smaller-format 20k is olive green, the 25k, slate blue. The 15k was reissued in 1959 (?) in smaller format: 14x21mm., instead of 14½x22mm. See note after No. 738.
See No. 1709.

V. R. Williams
A749

1949, Apr. 18 Photo. Perf. 12½
| 1348 | A749 | 25k bl grn | 1.00 | 1.00 |
| 1349 | A749 | 50k brown | 1.50 | 1.50 |

Issued to honor Vasili R. Williams (1863–1939), agricultural scientist.

Russian Citizens and Flag
A750

A. S. Popov and Radio
A751

Popov Demonstrating Radio to Admiral Makarov
A752

1949, Apr. 30 Perf. 12½
| 1350 | A750 | 40k scarlet | 1.50 | 1.00 |
| 1351 | A750 | 1r bl grn | 3.00 | 2.00 |

Labor Day, May 1, 1949.

1949, May Unwmkd.
1352	A751	40k purple	2.00	75
1353	A752	1r brown	3.00	1.00
1354	A751	1r gry brn	6.00	2.00

Issued to commemorate the 54th anniversary of Popov's discovery of the principles of radio.

Soviet Publications
A753

Reading Pravda
A754

1949, May 4
| 1355 | A753 | 40k crimson | 2.00 | 1.50 |
| 1356 | A754 | 1r dk vio | 3.50 | 1.75 |

Issued to commemorate Soviet Press Day.

I. V. Michurin
A755

A. S. Pushkin 1822
A756

Pushkin Reading Poem—A757

1949, July 28
| 1357 | A755 | 40k bl gray | 2.00 | 75 |
| 1358 | A755 | 1r brt grn | 4.00 | 1.75 |

Issued to honor Ivan Michurin (1855–1925), agricultural scientist.

1949, June Unwmkd.
Designs: No. 1360, Pushkin portrait by Kiprensky, 1827. 1r, Pushkin Museum, Boldino.

1359	A756	25k ind & sep	75	35
1360	A756	40k org brn & sep	2.00	75
a.		Souvenir sheet of 4	25.00	20.00
1361	A757	40k brn red & dk vio	2.00	1.00
1362	A757	1r choc & sl	4.00	2.00
1363	A757	2r brn & vio bl	7.00	3.00
		Nos. 1359-1363 (5)	15.75	7.10

Issued to commemorate the 150th anniversary of the birth of Aleksander S. Pushkin.

Horizontal rows of Nos. 1361 and 1363 contain alternate stamps and labels. No. 1360a contains two each of Nos. 1359 and 1360, imperf., with marginal inscriptions and floral decorations in brown. Size: 110x142mm. Issued July 20.

River Tugboat—A758

Design: 1r, Freighter, motorship "Bolshaya Volga."

1949, July, 13
| 1364 | A758 | 40k sl bl | 3.00 | 2.00 |
| 1365 | A758 | 1r red brn | 4.50 | 3.00 |

Issued to commemorate the centenary of the establishment of the Sormovo Machine and Boat Works.

VCSPS No. 3, Kislovodsk—A759

State Sanatoria for Workers: No. 1367, Communications, Khosta. No. 1368, Sanatorium No. 3, Khosta. No. 1369, Electric power, Khosta. No. 1370, Sanatorium No. 1, Kislovodsk. No. 1371, State Theater, Sochi. No. 1372, Frunze Sanatorium, Sochi. No. 1373, Sanatorium at Machindzhaury. No. 1374, Clinical, Chaltubo. No. 1375, Sanatorium No. 41, Zheleznovodsk.

1949, Sept. 10 Photo. Perf. 12½
Identical Frames.
1366	A759	40k violet	35	15
1367	A759	40k black	35	15
1368	A759	40k carmine	35	15
1369	A759	40k blue	35	15
1370	A759	40k vio brn	35	15
1371	A759	40k red org	35	15
1372	A759	40k dk brn	35	15
1373	A759	40k green	35	15
1374	A759	40k red brn	35	15
1375	A759	40k bl grn	35	15
		Nos. 1366-1375 (10)	3.50	1.50

Regatta
A760

RUSSIA

Designs (Sports, "1949"): 25k, Kayak race. 30k, Swimming. 40k, Bicycling. No. 1380, Soccer. 50k, Mountain climbing. 1r, Parachuting. 2r, High jump.

1949, Aug. 7

1376	A760	20k brt bl	60	15
1377	A760	25k bl grn	75	15
1378	A760	30k violet	1.00	15
1379	A760	40k red brn	1.25	20
1380	A760	40k green	1.25	20
1381	A760	50k dk bl gray	1.50	20
1382	A760	1r car rose	2.50	60
1383	A760	2r gray blk	5.00	75
		Nos. 1376-1383 (8)	13.85	2.40

V. V. Dokuchayev and Fields
A761

1949, Aug. 8

1384	A761	40k brown	60	50
1385	A761	1r green	1.25	85

Issued to honor Vasili V. Dokuchayev (1846-1903), pioneer soil scientist.

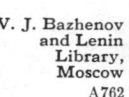 

V. J. Bazhenov and Lenin Library, Moscow
A762

1949, Aug. 14 Photo. Perf. 12½

1386	A762	40k violet	1.25	50
1387	A762	1r red brn	2.25	75

Issued to commemorate the 150th anniversary of the death of Vasili J. Bazhenov, architect.

A. N. Radishchev
A763

Ivan P. Pavlov
A764

1949, Aug. 31

1388	A763	40k bl grn	1.25	75
1389	A763	1r gray	2.75	1.50

Issued to commemorate the 200th anniversary of the birth of Aleksandr N. Radishchev, writer.

1949, Sept. 30 Unwmkd.

1390	A764	40k dp brn	1.00	25
1391	A764	1r gray blk	2.25	50

Issued to commemorate the centenary of the birth of Ivan P. Pavlov (1849-1936), Russian physiologist.

Globe Encircled by Letters
A765

1949, Oct. Perf. 12½

1392	A765	40k org brn & ind	75	30
a.		Imperf.	6.00	5.00
1393	A765	50k ind & gray vio	75	30
a.		Imperf.	6.00	5.00

Issued to commemorate the 75th anniversary of the formation of the Universal Postal Union.

Cultivators—A766

Map of European Russia—A767

Designs: No. 1395, Peasants in grain field. 50k, Rural scene. 2r, Old man and children.

1949, Oct. 18 Perf. 12½

1394	A766	25k green	60	60
1395	A766	40k violet	1.25	1.25
1396	A767	40k gray grn & blk	1.25	1.25
1397	A766	50k dp bl	1.75	1.50
1398	A766	1r gray blk	3.00	2.75
1399	A766	2r dk brn	7.00	6.50
		Nos. 1394-1399 (6)	14.85	13.85

Issued to encourage agricultural development. Nos. 1394, 1398 and 1399 measure 33x19mm. Nos. 1395 and 1397 measure 33x22mm.

Mali (Little) Theater, Moscow
A768

M. N. Ermolova, I. S. Mochalov, A. N. Ostrovski, M. S. Shchepkin and P. M. Sadovsky—A769

1949, Oct. 27

1400	A768	40k green	1.25	30
1401	A768	50k red org	1.50	30
1402	A769	1r dp brn	2.75	60

Issued to commemorate the 125th anniversary of the Mali Theater (State Academic Little Theater).

Chapayev Type of 1944.

1949, Oct. 22 Photogravure

1403	A495	40k brn org	4.00	4.00

Portrait and outer frame same as type A495. Dates "1919 1949" are in upper corners. Other details differ. Issued to commemorate the 30th anniversary of the death of V. I. Chapayev, a hero of the 1918 civil war.

Ivan S. Nikitin
A770

1949, Oct. 24 Unwmkd.

1404	A770	40k brown	1.25	30
1405	A770	1r sl bl	1.75	50

Issued to commemorate the 125th anniversary of the birth of Ivan S. Nikitin, Russian poet.

Spasski Tower and Russian Citizens
A771

1949, Oct. 29 Perf. 12½

1406	A771	40k brn org	1.25	50
1407	A771	1r dp grn	2.25	80

October Revolution 32nd anniversary.

Sheep, Cattle and Farm Woman
A772

1949, Nov. 2

1408	A772	40k chocolate	75	30
1409	A772	1r violet	1.75	50

Issued to encourage better cattle breeding in Russia.

Arms and Flag of U.S.S.R.
A773

1949, Nov. 30 Engraved Perf. 12

1410	A773	40k carmine	6.00	6.00

Issued to commemorate Constitution Day.

Electric Trolley Car
A774

Ski Jump
A775

Designs: 40k, 1r, Diesel train. 50k, Steam train.

1949, Nov. 19 Photo. Perf. 12½

1411	A774	25k red	1.00	15
1412	A774	40k violet	1.25	25
1413	A774	50k brown	1.75	25
1414	A774	1r Prus grn	4.00	50

1949, Nov. 12 Unwmkd.

Designs: 40k, Girl on rings. 50k, Ice hockey. 1r, Weight lifter. 2r, Wolf hunt.

1415	A775	20k dk grn	1.00	25
1416	A775	40k org red	1.75	30
1417	A775	50k dp bl	2.00	30
1418	A775	1r red	3.75	50
1419	A775	2r violet	8.00	1.50
		Nos. 1415-1419 (5)	16.50	2.85

Textile Mills
A776

Designs: 25k, Irrigation system. 40k, 1r, Government buildings, Stalinabad. 50k, University of Medicine.

1949, Dec. 7 Photo. Perf. 12

1420	A776	20k blue	50	20
1421	A776	25k green	60	20
1422	A776	40k red org	75	30
1423	A776	50k violet	1.00	40
1424	A776	1r gray blk	1.75	75
		Nos. 1420-1424 (5)	4.60	1.85

Tahzhik Republic, 20th anniversary.

"Russia" versus "War"
A777

Byelorussians and Flag
A778

1949, Dec. 25

1425	A777	40k rose car	70	25
1426	A777	50k blue	80	35

Issued to portray Russia as the defender of world peace.

1949, Dec. 23 Unwmkd.

Design: No. 1428, Ukrainians and flag.
Inscribed: "1939 1949."

1427	A778	40k org red	3.50	1.00
1428	A778	40k dp org	3.50	1.00

Issued to commemorate the 10th anniversary of the return of western territories to the Byelorussian and Ukrainian Republics.

Teachers College
A779

Designs: 25k, State Theater. No. 1431, Government House. No. 1432, Navoi Street, Tashkent. 1r, Fergana Canal. 2r, Kuigonyarsk Dam.

1950, Jan. 3 Identical Frames

1429	A779	20k blue	35	10
1430	A779	25k gray blk	35	10
1431	A779	40k red org	75	25
1432	A779	40k violet	75	25
1433	A779	1r green	1.75	50
1434	A779	2r brown	3.25	85
		Nos. 1429-1434 (6)	7.20	2.05

Uzbek Republic, 25th anniversary.

Lenin at Razliv—A780

Lenin's Office, Kremlin
A781

Design: 1r, Lenin Museum.

Lithographed.

1950, Jan. *Perf. 12* Unwmkd.

1435	A780	40k	dk grn & dk brn	60	15
1436	A781	50k	dk brn, red brn & grn	1.00	35
1437	A781	1r	dk brn, dk grn & cr	1.75	50

26th anniversary of the death of Lenin.

Textile Factory, Ashkhabad
A782

Designs: 40k, 1r, Power dam and Turkmenian arms. 50k, Rug making.

Identical Frames

1950, Jan. 7 Photogravure

1438	A782	25k	gray blk	50	25
1439	A782	40k	brown	75	35
1440	A782	50k	green	1.00	50
1441	A782	1r	purple	2.25	1.00

Turkmen Republic, 25th anniversary.

Motion Picture Projection
A783

1950, Feb.

1442	A783	25k	brown	6.00	6.00

Issued to commemorate the 30th anniversary of the Soviet motion picture industry.

Voter
A784

Kremlin
A785

1950, Mar. 8

1443	A784	40k	grn, *yel*	2.50	3.00
1444	A785	1r	rose car	4.00	5.00

Issued to publicize the elections to the Supreme Soviet, March 12, 1950.

Pavlik Morozov Monument, Moscow
A786

Globes and Communication Symbols
A787

1950, Mar. 16 *Perf. 12½*

1445	A786	40k	blk brn & red	2.00	3.00
1446	A786	1r	dk grn & red	4.00	5.00

Issued to mark the unveiling of a monument to Pavlik Morozov, Pioneer.

1950, Apr. 1

1447	A787	40k	dp grn	3.00	3.50
1448	A787	50k	dp bl	3.50	3.50

Issued to publicize the meeting of the Post, Telegraph, Telephone and Radio Trade Unions.

State Polytechnic Museum
A788

State Museum of Oriental Cultures
A789

State University Museum
A790

Pushkin Museum—A791

Museums: No. 1451, Tretiakov Gallery. No. 1452, Timiryasev Biologic Museum. No. 1453, Lenin Museum. No. 1454, Museum of the Revolution. No. 1456, State History Museum.

Inscribed:
"МОСКВА 1949" in Top Frame.

1950, Mar. 28 Litho. *Perf. 12½*

Multicolored Centers.

1449	A788	40k	dk bl	70	30
1450	A789	40k	dk bl	70	30
1451	A789	40k	green	70	30
1452	A789	40k	dk brn	70	30
1453	A789	40k	ol brn	70	30
1454	A789	40k	claret	70	30
1455	A790	40k	red	70	30
1456	A790	40k	chocolate	70	30
1457	A791	40k	brn vio	70	30
			Nos. 1449-1457 (9)	6.30	2.70

Russians of Three Races
A792

A. S. Shcherbakov
A793

Design: 1r, Four Russians and communist banner (horiz.).

1950, May 1 Photo. *Perf. 12½*

1458	A792	40k	org red & gray	2.25	2.50
1459	A792	1r	red & gray blk	4.50	5.00

Issued to publicize Labor Day, May 1, 1950.

1950, May Unwmkd.

1460	A793	40k	*pale bl*	1.50	75
1461	A793	1r	dk grn, *buff*	3.00	2.00

Issued to commemorate the fifth anniversary of the death of A. S. Shcherbakov, political leader.

Monument
A794

Victory Medal
A795

Wmk. 293

Wmkd. Hammer and Sickle, Multiple (293)

1950 Photogravure *Perf. 12x12½*

1462	A794	40k	dk brn & red	4.00	4.00

Unwmkd.

1463	A795	1r	car rose	5.00	5.00

Issued to commemorate Russia's 5th International Victory Day, May 9, 1950.

A. V. Suvorov
A796

Farmers Studying Agronomic Techniques
A797

Designs: 50k, Suvorov crossing Alps, 32½x47mm. 60k, Badge, flag and marchers, 24x39½ mm. 2r, Suvorov facing left, 19x33½ mm.

Various Designs and Sizes.
Dated "1800 1950."

1950 *Perf. 12, 12½x12*

1464	A796	40k	bl, *pink*	1.75	75
1465	A796	50k	brn, *pink*	2.00	1.00
1466	A796	60k	gray blk, *pale gray*	2.50	2.00
1467	A796	1r	dk brn, *lem*	4.00	2.00
1468	A796	2r	grnsh bl	7.00	5.00
			Nos. 1464-1468 (5)	17.25	10.75

Issued to commemorate the 150th anniversary of the death of Field Marshal Count Aleksandr V. Suvorov (1730–1800).

1950, June *Perf. 12½*

Designs: No. 1470 & 1r, Sowing on collective farm.

1469	A797	40k	dk grn, *pale grn*	1.50	1.25
1470	A797	40k	gray blk, *buff*	1.50	1.25
1471	A797	1r	bl, *lem*	4.00	3.00

George M. Dimitrov
A798

Opera and Ballet Theater, Baku
A799

1950, July 2

1472	A798	40k	gray blk, *cit*	1.25	1.00
1473	A798	1r	gray blk, *sal*	3.00	2.00

Issued to commemorate the first anniversary of the death of George M. Dimitrov (1882–1949), Bulgarian-born revolutionary leader and Comintern official.

1950, July Photo. *Perf. 12½*

Designs: 40k, Azerbaijan Academy of Science. 1r, Lenin Avenue, Baku.

1474	A799	25k	dp grn, *cit*	50	30
1475	A799	40k	brn, *pink*	1.10	50
1476	A799	1r	gray blk, *buff*	3.25	2.00

Azerbaijan S.S.R., 30th anniversary.

Victory Theater
A800

Lenin Street
A801

Designs: 50k, Gorky Theater. 1r, Monument marking Stalingrad defense line.

1950, June

1477	A800	20k	dk bl	75	50
1478	A801	40k	green	1.25	1.00
1479	A801	50k	red org	2.00	1.50
1480	A801	1r	gray	4.00	3.00

Restoration of Stalingrad.

Moscow Subway Stations: "Park of Culture"
A802

Designs: No. 1482, Kaluzskaya station. No. 1483, Taganskaya. No. 1484, Kurskaya. No. 1485, Paveletskaya. No. 1486, Park of Culture. No. 1487, Taganskaya.

1950, July 30 Size: 33½x23mm.

1481	A802	40k	dp car	1.00	25
1482	A802	40k	dk grn, *buff*	1.00	25
1483	A802	40k	dp bl, *buff*	1.00	25
1484	A802	1r	dk brn, *cit*	2.00	75
1485	A802	1r	purple	2.00	75
1486	A802	1r	dk grn, *cit*	2.00	75

Size: 33x18½ mm.

1487	A802	1r	blk, *pink*	1.85	50
			Nos. 1481-1487 (7)	10.85	3.50

Soviet Citizens and Flags
A803

1950, Aug. 4 *Perf. 12½* Unwmkd.

1488	A803	40k	multi	75	30
1489	A803	50k	multi	1.50	40
1490	A803	1r	multi	1.75	60

RUSSIA

Trade Union Building, Riga — A804
Opera and Ballet Theater, Riga — A805

Designs: 40k, Latvian Cabinet building. 50k, Monument to Jozsef Rainis. 1r, Riga State University. 2r, Latvian Academy of Sciences.

1950   Photogravure   Perf. 12½
1491	A804	25k dk brn	60	25
1492	A804	40k scarlet	75	75
1493	A804	50k dk grn	1.50	75
1494	A805	60k dp bl	1.85	75
1495	A805	1r lilac	2.75	1.50
1496	A804	2r sepia	4.75	2.00
		Nos. 1491-1496 (6)	12.20	6.00

Issued to commemorate the 10th anniversary of the formation of the Latvian Soviet Socialist Republic.

Lithuanian Academy of Sciences — A806
Marite Melnik — A807

Design: 1r, Cabinet building.

1950
1497	A806	25k dp bl, *bluish*	75	50
1498	A807	40k brown	1.50	1.00
1499	A806	1r scarlet	3.00	2.50

Issued to commemorate the 10th anniversary of the formation of the Lithuanian Soviet Socialist Republic.

Stalingrad Square, Tallin — A808
Victor Kingisepp — A809

Designs: 40k, Government building, Tallin. 50k, Estonia Theater, Tallin.

1950
1500	A808	25k dk grn	1.00	75
1501	A808	40k scarlet	1.25	1.00
1502	A808	50k bl, *yel*	1.75	1.50
1503	A809	1r brn, *bl*	3.50	3.00

Issued to commemorate the 10th anniversary of the formation of the Estonian Soviet Socialist Republic.

Citizens Signing Appeal for Peace — A810
Children and Governess — A811

Design: 50k, Peace Demonstration.

1950, Oct. 16   Photogravure
1504	A810	40k red, *sal*	1.00	1.00
1505	A811	40k black	1.00	1.00
1506	A811	50k dk red	1.75	1.50
1507	A810	1r brn, *sal*	3.00	3.00

F. G. Bellingshausen, M. P. Lazarev and Globe — A812
Route of Antarctic Expedition — A813

1950, Oct. 25   Perf. 12½   Unwmkd.
Blue Paper
1508	A812	40k dk car	17.50	12.50
1509	A813	1r purple	35.00	12.50

Issued to commemorate the 130th anniversary of the Bellingshausen-Lazarev expedition to the Antarctic.

M. V. Frunze — A814
M. I. Kalinin — A815

1950, Oct. 31
1510	A814	40k bl, *buff*	2.75	2.50
1511	A814	1r brn, *bl*	5.25	5.50

Issued to commemorate the 25th anniversary of the death of M. V. Frunze, military strategist.

1950, Nov. 20   Engraved
1512	A815	40k dp grn	1.10	1.00
1513	A815	1r redsh brn	2.50	1.75
1514	A815	5r violet	7.00	3.50

Issued to commemorate the 75th anniversary of the birth of M. I. Kalinin, Soviet Russia's first president.

Gathering Grapes — A816
G. M. Sundukian — A818

Armenian Government Building — A817

1950, Nov. 29   Photo.   Perf. 12½
1515	A816	20k dp bl, *buff*	1.00	75
1516	A817	40k red org, *buff*	1.75	1.50
1517	A818	1r ol gray, *yel*	4.00	3.50

Issued to commemorate the 30th anniversary of the formation of the Armenian Republic. The 1 ruble also commemorates the birth of G. M. Sundukian, playwright.

Apartment Building, Koteljnicheskaya Quay — A819
Hotel, Kalanchevkaya Square — A820

Various Buildings.
Inscribed: "*Mockba, 1950*"

1950, Dec. 2   Unwmkd.
1518	A819	1r red brn, *buff*	30.00	40.00
1519	A819	1r gray blk	30.00	40.00
1520	A819	1r brn bl	30.00	40.00
1521	A819	1r dk grn, *bl*	30.00	40.00
1522	A820	1r dp bl, *buff*	30.00	40.00
1523	A820	1r blk, *buff*	30.00	40.00
1524	A820	1r red org	30.00	40.00
1525	A819	1r dk grn, *yel*	30.00	40.00
		Nos. 1518-1525 (8)	240.00	320.00

Skyscrapers planned for Moscow.

Spasski Tower, Kremlin — A821

1950, Dec. 4
1526	A821	1r dk grn, red brn & yel brn	9.00	6.00

October Revolution, 33rd anniversary.

Golden Autumn by Levitan — A822

I. I. Levitan — A823

1950, Dec. 6   Litho.   Perf. 12½
1527	A822	40k multi	4.50	90

Photogravure
Perf. 12.
1528	A823	50k red brn	6.00	90

Issued to commemorate the 50th anniversary of the death of I. I. Levitan, painter.

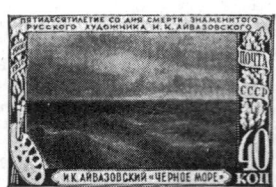

Black Sea by Aivazovsky — A824

I. K. Aivazovsky — A825

Design: 50k, "Ninth Surge."

1950, Dec. 6   Lithographed
Multicolored Centers.
1529	A824	40k chocolate	1.50	25
1530	A824	50k chocolate	1.50	50
1531	A825	1r indigo	2.00	1.25

50th anniversary of the death of Ivan K. Aivazovsky (1817-1900), painter.

Flags and Newspapers Iskra and Pravda — A826
Presidium of Supreme Soviet, Alma-Ata — A827

Design: 1r, Flag and profiles of Lenin and Stalin.

1950, Dec. 23   Photogravure
1532	A826	40k gray blk & red	15.00	17.50
1533	A826	1r dk brn & red	20.00	22.50

50th anniversary of the first issue of the newspaper Iskra.

1950, Dec. 27

Design: 1r, Opera and Ballet Theater.
Inscribed: "АЛМА-АТА."
1534	A827	40k gray blk, *bl*	3.00	4.00
1535	A827	1r red brn, *yel*	4.00	5.00

Kazakh Republic, 30th anniversary.

Decembrists and Senatskaya Square, Leningrad — A828

1950, Dec. 30   Unwmkd.
1536	A828	1r blk brn, *yel*	6.50	5.00

Issued to commemorate the 125th anniversary of the Decembrist revolution of 1825.

Lenin at Razliv — A829

RUSSIA

Design: 1r, Lenin and young communists.
1951, Jan. 21   Litho.   Perf. 12½
Multicolored Centers
1537 A829 40k ol grn   1.20   35
1538 A829 1r indigo   2.00   1.00

27th anniversary of the death of Lenin.

Mountain Pasture
A830

Government Building,
Frunze—A831

1951, Feb. 2   Photo.   Perf. 12½
1539 A830 25k dk brn, bl   1.75   1.25
1540 A831 40k dp grn, bl   2.25   1.75

Issued to commemorate the 25th anniversary of the formation of the Kirghiz Republic.

Government Building, Tirana
A832

1951, Jan. 6   Perf. 12   Unwmkd.
1541 A832 40k grn, bluish   12.00 12.00

Issued to honor the Albanian People's Republic.

Bulgarians
Greeting Russian Troops
A833

Lenin Square, Sofia
A834

Design: 60k, Monument to Soviet soldiers.
1951, Jan. 13
1542 A833 25k gray blk, bluish   1.25   75
1543 A834 40k org red, sal   2.25   1.50
1544 A834 60k blk brn, sal   3.25   2.00

Issued to honor the Bulgarian People's Republic.

Choibalsan State University
A835

State Theater, Ulan Bator
A836

Mongolian Republic
Emblem and Flag
A837

1951, Mar. 12
1545 A835 25k pur, sal   1.00   75
1546 A836 40k dp org, yel   2.00   75
1547 A837 1r multi   5.00   2.50

Issued to honor the Mongolian People's Republic.

D. A.
Furmanov
A838

Furmanov
at Work
A839

1951, Mar. 17   Perf. 12½
1548 A838 40k brown   1.40   85
1549 A839 1r gray blk, buff   2.00   1.25

Issued to commemorate the 25th anniversary of the death of D. A. Furmanov (1891–1926), writer.

Russian War Memorial, Berlin
A840

1951, Mar. 21   Perf. 12
1550 A840 40k dk gray grn & dk red 3.00   2.00
1551 A840 1r brn blk & red   5.00   4.00

Stockholm Peace Conference.

Kirov Machine Works
A841

1951, May 19   Photo.   Perf. 12½
1552 A841 40k brn, cr   3.50   3.00

Issued to commemorate the 150th anniversary of the founding of the Kirov Machine Works.

Bolshoi Theater, Moscow
A842

Russian Composers
A843

1951, May   Unwmkd.
1553 A842 40k multi   5.50   75
1554 A843 1r multi   5.50   75

Issued to commemorate the 175th anniversary of the founding of the Bolshoi Theater, Moscow.

Liberty Bridge,
Budapest
A844

Monument
to Liberators
A845

Budapest Buildings: 40k, Parliament.
60k, National Museum.

1951, June 9   Perf. 12
1555 A844 25k emerald   75   30
1556 A844 40k brt bl   1.25   50
1557 A844 60k sepia   1.75   1.25
1558 A845 1r sep, sal   3.25   2.00

Issued to honor the Hungarian People's Republic.

Harvesting Wheat
A846

Designs: 40k, Apiary. 1r, Gathering citrus fruits. 2r, Cotton picking.

1951, June 25
1559 A846 25k dk grn   75   50
1560 A846 40k grn, bluish   1.00   50
1561 A846 1r brn, yel   2.25   1.25
1562 A846 2r dk grn, sal   5.00   2.00

Kalinin Museum, Moscow
A847

Mikhail I.
Kalinin
A848

F. E.
Dzerzhinski
A849

Design: 1r, Kalinin statue.
1951, Aug. 4   Perf. 12x12½, 12½x12
Inscribed: "1946–1951."
1563 A847 20k org brn & blk   75   50
1564 A848 40k dp grn & choc   1.50   75
1565 A848 1r vio bl & gray   3.00   1.50

Issued to commemorate the 5th anniversary of the death of Mikhail I. Kalinin.

1951, Aug. 4   Engr.   Perf. 12x12½
Design: 1r, Profile of Dzerzhinski.
1566 A849 40k brn red   2.00   1.25
1567 A849 1r gray blk   3.00   2.00

Issued to commemorate the 25th anniversary of the death of F. E. Dzerzhinski.

Aleksandr
M. Butlerov
A850

A. A. Aliabiev
A851

Portraits: No. 1569, A. Kovalevski. No. 1570, Sonya Kovalevskaya. No. 1571, P. K. Kozlov. No. 1572, S. P. Krasheninnikov. No. 1573, N. S. Kurnakov. No. 1574, P. N. Lebedev. No. 1575, N. I. Lobachevski. No. 1576, A. N. Lodygin. No. 1577, D. I. Mendeleev. No. 1578, N. N. Miklukho-Maklai. No. 1579, A. N. Svertzov. No. 1580, A. G. Stoletov. No. 1581, K. A. Timiryasev. No. 1582, K. E. Tsiolkovsky. No. 1583, P. N. Yablochkov.

1951, Aug. 15   Photo.   Perf. 12½
1568 A850 40k org red, bluish   2.00   35
1569 A850 40k dk bl, sal   1.25   25
1570 A850 40k pur, sal   1.25   25
1571 A850 40k org red   1.25   25
1572 A850 40k purple   1.25   25
1573 A850 40k brn, sal   1.25   25
1574 A850 40k blue   1.25   25
1575 A850 40k brown   1.25   25
1576 A850 40k green   1.25   25
1577 A850 40k dp bl   1.25   25
1578 A850 40k org red, sal   1.25   25
1579 A850 40k sep, sal   1.25   25
1580 A850 40k grn, sal   1.25   25
1581 A850 40k brn, sal   1.25   25
1582 A850 40k gray blk, bl   2.00   35
1583 A850 40k sepia   1.25   25
        Nos. 1568-1583 (16)   21.50   4.20

Russian scientists.

RUSSIA

1951, Aug. 28
Design: No. 1585, V. S. Kalinnikov.
| 1584 | A851 | 40k brn, sal | 5.00 | 3.00 |
| 1585 | A851 | 40k gray, sal | 5.00 | 3.00 |

Russian composers.

Opera and Ballet Theater, Tbilisi — A852
Gathering Citrus Fruit — A853

Designs: 40k, Principal street, Tbilisi. 1r, Picking tea.

1951   *Perf. 12½*   Unwmkd.
1586	A852	20k dp grn, yel	75	50
1587	A853	25k pur, org & brn	1.00	50
1588	A853	40k dk brn, bl	2.00	1.00
1589	A853	1r red brn & dk grn	5.00	2.50

Georgian Republic, 30th anniversary.

Emblem of Aviation Society
A854

Planes and Emblem
A855

Designs: 60k, Flying model planes. 1r, Parachutists.

1951, Sept. 19   Litho.   *Perf. 12½*
Dated: "1951"
1590	A854	40k multi	1.00	40
1591	A854	60k emer, lt bl & brn	1.50	60
1592	A854	1r bl, sal & lil	2.50	1.00
1593	A855	2r multi	5.00	1.75

Issued to promote interest in aviation.

Victor M. Vasnetsov
A856

Three Heroes, by Vasnetsov — A857

1951, Oct. 15
| 1594 | A856 | 40k dk bl, brn & buff | 2.00 | 40 |
| 1595 | A857 | 1r multi | 3.00 | 1.75 |

Issued to commemorate the 25th anniversary of the death of V. M. Vasnetsov, painter.

Hydroelectric Station, Lenin and Stalin
A858

Design: 1r, Spasski Tower, Kremlin.

1951, Nov. 6   Photo.   *Perf. 12½*
Dated: "1917-1951"
| 1596 | A858 | 40k bl vio & red | 3.00 | 3.50 |
| 1597 | A858 | 1r dk brn & red | 4.50 | 5.00 |

34th anniversary of October Revolution.

Map, Dredge and Khakhovsky Hydroelectric Station
A859

Map, Volga Dam and Tugboat
A860

Designs (each showing map): 40k, Stalingrad Dam. 60k, Excavating Turkmenian canal. 1r, Kuibyshev dam.

1951, Nov. 28   *Perf. 12½*
1598	A859	20k red brn, brn lil & car	2.00	2.00
1599	A860	30k brn, bl & dk bl	2.75	2.75
1600	A860	40k brn, aqua & red	4.00	4.00
1601	A860	60k dk bl, brn & red	5.00	5.00
1602	A860	1r multi	10.00	10.00
	Nos. 1598-1602 (5)		23.75	23.75

Flag and Citizens Signing Peace Appeal
A861

M. V. Ostrogradski
A862

1951, Nov. 30   *Perf. 12½*
| 1603 | A861 | 40k gray & red | 12.00 | 12.00 |

Third All-Union Peace Conference.

1951, Dec. 10   Unwmkd.
| 1604 | A862 | 40k blk brn, pink | 6.50 | 6.00 |

Issued to commemorate the 150th anniversary of the birth of Mikhail V. Ostrogradski, mathematician.

Monument to Jan Zizka, Prague
A863

Monument to Soviet Liberators
A864

Designs: 25k, Monument to Soviet Soldiers, Ostrava. 40k, Julius Fucik. 60k, Smetana Museum, Prague.

1951, Dec. 10   *Perf. 12½*
1605	A863	20k vio bl, sal	2.00	2.50
1606	A863	25k cop red, yel	2.50	3.00
1607	A863	40k red org, sal	3.00	3.50
1608	A863	60k brnsh gray, buff	4.00	4.00
1609	A864	1r brnsh gray, buff	8.50	10.00
	Nos. 1605-1609 (5)		20.00	24.00

Soviet-Czechoslovakian friendship.

Volkhovski Hydroelectric Station and Lenin Statue — A865

1951, Dec. 19
| 1610 | A865 | 40k dk bl, gray & yel | 1.00 | 35 |
| 1611 | A865 | 1r pur, gray & yel | 2.50 | 1.00 |

Issued to commemorate the 25th anniversary of the opening of the Lenin Volkhovski hydroelectric station.

Lenin as a Schoolboy
A866

Horizontal Designs: 60k, Lenin among children. 1r, Lenin and peasants.

1952, Jan. 24   Photo.   *Perf. 12½*
Multicolored Centers.
1612	A866	40k dk bl grn	1.75	50
1613	A866	60k vio bl	2.25	40
1614	A866	1r org brn	3.25	75

28th anniversary of the death of Lenin.

Pëtr P. Semënov
A867

V. O. Kovalevski
A868

1952, Feb. 1
| 1615 | A867 | 1r sep, bl | 3.00 | 2.25 |

Issued to commemorate the 125th anniversary of the birth of Petr Petrovich Semenov-Tianshanski (1827–1914), traveler and geographer who explored the Tian Shan mountains.

1952, Mar. 3   Unwmkd.
| 1616 | A868 | 40k sep, yel | 3.00 | 2.50 |

Issued to honor V. O. Kovalevski (1843-1883), biologist and palaeontologist.

Skaters — A869

Design: 60k, Skiers.

1952, Mar. 3
| 1617 | A869 | 40k multi | 1.85 | 40 |
| 1618 | A869 | 60k multi | 3.50 | 60 |

N. V. Gogol and Characters from "Taras Bulba"
A870

Designs: 60k, Gogol and V. G. Belinski. 1r, Gogol and Ukrainian peasants.

1952, Mar. 4
Dated: "1852-1952."
1619	A870	40k sep, bl	1.00	10
1620	A870	60k blk, dk brn & brn org	1.50	15
1621	A870	1r multi	2.00	55

Death centenary of N. V. Gogol, writer.

RUSSIA

G. K. Ordzhonikidze A871   Workers and Soviet Flag A872

Workers' Rest Home A873

1952, Apr. 23   Photo.   Perf. 12½

| 1622 | A871 | 40k dp grn, *pink* | 2.00 | 60 |
| 1623 | A871 | 1r sep, *bl* | 3.00 | 90 |

Issued to commemorate the 15th anniversary of the death of Grigori K. Ordzhonikidze, Georgian party worker.

1952, May 15   Unwmkd.

Designs: No. 1626, Aged citizens. No. 1627, Schoolgirl.

1624	A872	40k red & blk, *cr*	4.50	4.50
1625	A873	40k red & dk grn, *pale gray*	4.50	4.50
1626	A873	40k red & brn, *pale gray*	4.50	4.50
1627	A872	40k red & blk, *pale gray*	4.50	4.50

15th anniversary of adoption of Stalin constitution.

A. S. Novikov-Priboy and Ship A874

1952, June 5

| 1628 | A874 | 40k blk, pale cit & bl grn | 60 | 20 |

Issued to commemorate the 75th anniversary of the birth of A. S. Novikov-Priboy, writer.

Victor Hugo A875

1952, June 5   Perf. 12½   Unwmkd.

| 1629 | A875 | 40k brn org, gray & blk | 75 | 20 |

150th anniversary of birth of Victor Hugo (1802–1855), French writer.

Salavat Julaev A876   G. J. Sedov A877

1952, June 28

| 1630 | A876 | 40k rose red, *pink* | 75 | 20 |

Issued to commemorate the 200th anniversary of the birth of Salavat Julaev, Bashkir hero who took part in the insurrection of 1773–75.

1952, July 4

| 1631 | A877 | 40k dk bl, dk brn & bl grn | 7.50 | 4.00 |

Issued to commemorate the 75th anniversary of the birth of George J. Sedov (1877–1914), Arctic explorer.

Arms and Flag of Romania A878   University Square, Bucharest A879

Design: 60k, Monument to Soviet soldiers.

1952, July 26

1632	A878	40k multi	1.10	40
1633	A878	60k dk grn, *pink*	1.65	75
1634	A879	1r brt ultra	2.25	1.50

V. A. Zhukovski A880   N. P. Ogarev A881

Design: No. 1636, K. P. Bryulov.

1952, July 26   Pale Blue Paper.

| 1635 | A880 | 40k gray blk | 1.00 | 50 |
| 1636 | A880 | 40k brt bl grn | 1.00 | 50 |

Issued to commemorate the centenary of the deaths of V. A. Zhukovski, poet, and K. P. Bryulov, painter.

1952, Aug. 29

| 1637 | A881 | 40k dp grn | 60 | 25 |

Issued to commemorate the 75th anniversary of the death of N. P. Ogarev, poet and revolutionary.

G. I. Uspenski A882

1952, Sept. 4

| 1638 | A882 | 40k ind & dk brn | 60 | 20 |

Issued to commemorate the 50th anniversary of the death of Gleb Ivanovich Uspenski (1843–1902), writer.

Admiral P. S. Nakhimov A883

1952, Sept. 9

| 1639 | A883 | 40k multi | 1.25 | 75 |

150th anniversary of birth of Adm. Paul S. Nakhimov (1802–1855).

University Building, Tartu A884

1952, Oct. 2

| 1640 | A884 | 40k blk brn, *sal* | 2.50 | 1.00 |

Issued to commemorate the 150th anniversary of the enlargement of the University of Tartu, Estonia.

Kajum Nasyri A885   A. N. Radishchev A886

1952, Nov. 5

| 1641 | A885 | 40k brn, *yel* | 2.00 | 1.00 |

Issued to commemorate the 50th anniversary of the death of Kajum Nasyri (1825–1902), Tartar educator.

1952, Oct. 23

| 1642 | A886 | 40k blk, brn & dk red | 1.25 | 60 |

Issued to commemorate the 150th anniversary of the death of A. N. Radishchev, writer.

M.S. Joseph Stalin at Entrance to Volga-Don Canal A887

Design: 1r, Lenin, Stalin and red banners.

1952, Nov. 6   Perf. 12½

| 1643 | A887 | 40k multi | 2.50 | 2.00 |
| 1644 | A887 | 1r brn, red & yel | 4.50 | 4.00 |

35th anniversary of October Revolution.

Pavel Fedotov A888   V. D. Polenov A889

"Moscow Courtyard"—A890

1952, Nov. 26

| 1645 | A888 | 40k red brn & blk | 75 | 25 |

Issued to commemorate the centenary of the death of Pavel Andreievitch Fedotov (1815–1852), artist.

1952, Dec. 6

| 1646 | A889 | 40k red brn & buff | 1.25 | 40 |
| 1647 | A890 | 1r multi | 3.00 | 85 |

Issued to commemorate the 25th anniversary of the death of V. D. Polenov, artist.

A. I. Odoyevski A891

1952, Dec. 8

| 1648 | A891 | 40k gray blk & red org | 1.00 | 25 |

Issued to commemorate the 150th anniversary of the birth of A. I. Odoyevski, poet.

D. N. Mamin-Sibiryak A892

1952, Dec. 15

| 1649 | A892 | 40k dp grn, *cr* | 1.00 | 25 |

Issued to commemorate the centenary of the birth of Dimitrii N. Mamin-Sibiryak (1852–1912), writer.

Composite Medal Types of 1946
Frames as A599-A606.
Centers as Indicated.

Medals: 1r, Token of Veneration. 2r, Red Star. 3r, Red Workers' Banner. 5r, Red Banner. 10r, Lenin.

1952–59   Engraved   Perf. 12½

| 1650 | A569 | 1r dk brn | 6.00 | 5.00 |
| 1651 | A567 | 2r red brn | 75 | 35 |

RUSSIA

1652	A572	3r dp bl vio	1.25	60
1653	A571	5r dk car ('53)	1.50	60
1654	A566	10r brt rose	3.00	1.25
a.		10r dl red ('59)	5.00	3.00
		Nos. 1650-1654 (5)	12.50	7.80

V. M. Bekhterev
A893

1952, Dec. 24   Photogravure

1655	A893	40k vio bl, sl & blk	1.00	50

Issued to commemorate the 25th anniversary of the death of Vladimir M. Bekhterev (1857–1927), neuropathologist.

Byelorusskaya Station—A894

Designs (Moscow Subway stations): 40k, Botanical Garden Station. 40k, Novoslobodskaya Station. 40k, Komsomolskaya Station.

1952, Dec. 30
Multicolored Centers.

1656	A894	40k dl vio	1.00	25
1657	A894	40k lt ultra	1.00	25
1658	A894	40k bl gray	1.00	25
1659	A894	40k dl grn	1.00	25

Nos. 1656–1659 were printed together in sheets of 20 (4x5), with each horizontal row consisting of one of each 40k.

USSR Emblem and Flags of 16 Union Republics—A895

1952, Dec. 30

1660	A895	1r grn, dk red & brn	3.50	2.25

Issued to commemorate the 30th anniversary of the Union of Soviet Socialist Republics.

Lenin—A896

1953, Jan. 26   Multicolored Center

1661	A896	40k dk bl	5.00	5.00

Issued to commemorate 29 years without Lenin.

Stalin Peace Medal
A897

1953, Apr. 30   Perf. 12½

1662	A897	40k red brn, bl & dl yel	10.00	13.00

1953, June 6

1663	A898	40k red brn & blk	1.25	1.00

Issued to commemorate the 65th anniversary of the birth of V. V. Kuibyshev (1888–1935), Bolshevik leader.

N. G. Chernyshevski
A899

1953, July 21

1664	A899	40k buff & dk brn	1.25	1.00

Issued to commemorate the 125th anniversary of the birth of Nikolai G. Chernyshevski (1828–1889), writer and radical leader; exiled to Siberia for 24 years.

V. V. Mayakovsky
A900

1953, July 19

1665	A900	40k ver & gray brn	1.25	50

Issued to commemorate the 60th anniversary of the birth of Vladimir V. Mayakovsky, poet.

Lock No. 9, Volga-Don Canal
A901

Designs: No. 1667, Lock 13. No. 1668, Lock 15. No. 1669, Volga River lighthouse. No. 1670, Tsymijanskaja Dam. No. 1671, M. S. "Joseph Stalin" in canal.

1953, Aug. 29   Lithographed
Identical Frames

1666	A901	40k multi	1.25	25
1667	A901	40k multi	1.25	25
1668	A901	40k multi	1.25	25
1669	A901	40k multi	1.25	25
1670	A901	40k multi	1.25	35
1671	A901	1r multi	3.00	75
		Nos. 1666-1671 (6)	9.25	2.10

Issued to publicize the Volga-Don Canal.

V. G. Korolenko
A902

1953, Aug. 29   Photo.   Perf. 12x12½

1672	A902	40k brown	1.00	25

Issued to commemorate the centenary of the birth of V. G. Korolenko (1853–1921), writer.

Leo N. Tolstoy
A903

1953, Sept.   Perf. 12

1673	A903	1r dk brn	3.00	2.00

Issued to commemorate the 125th anniversary of the birth of Count Leo N. Tolstoy, writer.

Moscow University and Two Youths   **Nationalities of the Soviet Union**
A904   A905

Design: 1r, Komsomol badge and four orders.

1953, Oct. 29   Perf. 12½x12

1674	A904	40k multi	3.00	1.50
1675	A904	1r multi	6.00	3.00

Issued to commemorate the 35th anniversary of the Young Communist League (Komsomol).

1953, Nov. 6

Design:
60k, Lenin and Stalin at Smolny monastery.

1676	A905	40k multi	5.00	5.00
1677	A905	60k multi	9.00	9.00

36th anniversary of October Revolution. No. 1676 measures 25½x38mm.; No. 1677, 25½x42mm.

Lenin and His Writings
A906

Design: 1r, Lenin facing left and page of "What to Do."

1953

1678	A906	40k multi	3.00	5.00
1679	A906	1r dk brn, org brn & red	9.00	11.00

The 40k was issued on Nov. 12 to commemorate the 50th anniversary of the formation of the Communist Party. The 1r was issued Dec. 14 to commemorate the 50th anniversary of the 2nd congress of the Russian Socialist Party.

Lenin Statue
A907

Peter I Statue, Decembrists' Square
A908

Leningrad Views: Nos. 1681 & 1683, Admiralty building. Nos. 1685 & 1687, Smolny monastery.

1953, Nov. 23

1680	A907	40k brn blk, yel	2.00	2.00
1681	A907	40k vio brn, yel	2.00	2.00
1682	A907	40k brn blk, pink	2.00	2.00
1683	A907	40k brn blk, cr	2.00	2.00
1684	A908	1r dk brn, pink	5.00	5.00
1685	A908	1r dk grn, pink	5.00	5.00
1686	A908	1r vio, yel	5.00	5.00
1687	A908	1r blk brn, bl	5.00	5.00
		Nos. 1680-1687 (8)	28.00	28.00

See also Nos. 1944–1945, 1943a.

"Pioneers" and Model of Lomonosov Moscow University   **A. S. Griboedov**
A909   A910

1953, Dec. 22   Litho.   Perf. 12

1688	A909	40k dk sl grn, dk brn & red	4.00	4.00

Arms type of 1948

1954-57

1689	A682	40k scarlet	6.00	2.00
a.		7 ribbon turns on wreath at left ('57)	2.00	60

No. 1689 was re-issued in 1954-56 typographed in slightly smaller format: 14½x21¾mm., instead of 14¾x21¾mm., and in a lighter shade. See note after No. 738.

No. 1689 has 8 ribbon turns on left side of wreath.

RUSSIA

1954, Mar. 4   Photogravure
1690 A910 40k dp cl, cr   1.00   35
1691 A910 1r blk, grn   1.75   70

Issued to commemorate the 125th anniversary of the death of Aleksandr S. Griboedov, writer.

Kremlin View
A911

V. P. Chkalov
A912

1954, Mar. 7 Litho.   *Perf. 12½x12*
1692 A911 40k red & gray   1.75   1.75
1954 elections to the Supreme Soviet.

1954, Mar. 16   *Perf. 12*
1693 A912 1r gray, vio bl & dk brn   5.00   1.25

Issued to commemorate the 50th anniversary of the birth of Valeri P. Chkalov (1904–1938), airplane pilot.

Lenin
A913

Lenin at Smolny
A914

Designs: No. 1696, Lenin's home (later museum), Ulyanovsk. No. 1697, Lenin addressing workers. No. 1698, Lenin among students, University of Kazan.

1954, Apr. 16   Photogravure
1694 A913 40k multi   75
    Size: 38x27½mm.
1695 A914 40k multi   2.00   75
1696 A914 40k multi   2.00   75
    Size: 48x35mm.
1697 A914 40k multi   2.00   75
1698 A914 40k multi   2.00   75
   Nos. 1694-1698 (5)   10.00   3.75

30th anniversary of the death of Lenin.
See No. 2060.

Joseph V. Stalin
A915

1954, Apr. 30 *Perf. 12*   Unwmkd.
1699 A915 40k dk brn   3.50   2.75

First anniversary of the death of Stalin.

Supreme Soviet Buildings in Kiev and Moscow—A916

T. G. Shevchenko Statue, Kharkov—A917

Designs: No. 1701, University building, Kiev. No. 1702, Opera, Kiev. No. 1703, Ukranian Academy of Science. No. 1705, Bogdan Chmielnicki statue, Kiev. No. 1706 Flags of Soviet Russia and Ukraine. No. 1707, T. G. Shevchenko statue, Kanev. No. 1708, Chmielnicki proclaming reunion of Ukraine and Russia, 1654.

1954, May 10   Lithographed
Size: 37½x26mm., 26x37½mm.
1700 A916 40k red brn, sal, cr & blk   1.00   20
1701 A916 40k ultra, vio bl & brn   1.00   20
1702 A916 40k red brn, buff, bl & brn   1.00   20
1703 A916 40k org brn, cr & grn   1.00   20
1704 A917 40k rose red, blk, yel & brn   1.25   20
1705 A917 60k multi   1.25   40
1706 A917 1r multi   2.75   65

    Size: 42x28mm.
1707 A916 1r multi   2.00   65
    Size: 45x29½mm.
1708 A916 1r multi, *pink*   2.75   65

300-ЛЕТИЕ

No. 1341
Overprinted
in Carmine

ВОССОЕДИНЕННЯ
УКРАИНЫ
С
РОССИЕЙ

1709 A517 2r green   6.00   2.00
   Nos. 1700-1709 (10)   20.00   5.35

Nos. 1700-1709 were issued to commemorate the 300th anniversary of the union between the Ukraine and Russia.

Sailboat Race—A918

Basketball—A919

Sports: No. 1711, Hurdle race. No. 1712, Swimmers. No. 1713, Cyclists. No. 1714, Track. No. 1715, Skier. No. 1716, Mountain climbing.

1954, May 29
   Frames in Orange Brown
1710 A918 40k bl & blk   1.50   35
1711 A918 40k vio gray & blk   1.50   35
1712 A918 40k dk bl & blk   1.50   35
1713 A918 40k dk brn & buff   1.50   35
1714 A918 40k blk brn & buff   1.50   35
1715 A918 1r bl & blk   3.00   60
1716 A918 1r bl & blk   3.00   60
1717 A919 1r dk brn & brn   3.00   60
   Nos. 1710-1717 (8)   16.50   3.55

See No. 2170.

Cattle—A920

Designs: No. 1719, Potato planting and cultivation. No. 1720, Kolkhoz hydroelectric station.

1954, June 8
1718 A920 40k brn, cr, ind & bl gray   1.75   75
1719 A920 40k gray grn, buff & brn   1.75   75
1720 A920 40k blk, bl grn & vio bl   1.75   75

Anton P. Chekhov
A921

1954, July 15
1721 A921 40k grn & blk brn   75   35

Issued to commemorate the 50th anniversary of the death of Anton P. Chekhov, writer.

F. A. Bredichin, V. J. Struve,
A. A. Belopolski and Observatory
A922

1954, July 26
1722 A922 40k vio bl, blk & bl   8.00   2.50

Restoration of Pulkov Observatory.

Mikhail Glinka
A923

Pushkin and Zhukovsky
Visiting Glinka
A924

1954, July 26
1723 A923 40k dp cl, pink & blk brn   3.00   80
1724 A924 60k multi   4.00   1.25

Issued to commemorate the 150th anniversary of the birth of Mikhail I. Glinka, composer.

Nikolai A.
Ostrovsky
A925

Monument to
Sunken Ships
A926

Defenders of Sevastopol
A927

1954, Sept. 29   *Perf. 12½x12*
1725 A925 40k brn, dk red & yel   1.25   35

Issued to commemorate the 50th anniversary of the birth of N. A. Ostrovsky (1904–1936), blind writer.

1954, Oct. 17   *Perf. 12½*
   Design: 1r, Admiral P. S. Nakhimov.
1726 A926 40k bl grn, blk & ol brn   75   25
1727 A927 60k org brn, blk & brn   1.00   35
1728 A926 1r brn, blk & ol grn   2.00   65

Issued to commemorate the centenary of the defense of Sevastopol during the Crimean War.

RUSSIA

Sculpture at
Exhibition
Entrance
A928

Agriculture Pavilion—A929

Designs: No. 1731, Cattle pavilion. No. 1732, Machinery pavilion. No. 1733, Main entrance. No. 1734, Main pavilion.

Perf. 12½, 12½x12, 12x12½

1954, Nov. 5   Lithographed

Size: 26x37mm.
1729 A928 40k multi   50   25
Size: 40x29mm.
1730 A929 40k multi   50   25
1731 A929 40k multi   50   25
1732 A929 40k multi   50   25
Size: 40½x33mm.
1733 A929 1r multi   1.00   75
Size: 28½x40½mm.
1734 A929 1r multi   1.00   75
     Nos. 1729-1734 (6)   4.00 2.50

Issued to publicize the 1954 Agricultural Exhibition.

Marx, Engels, Lenin and Stalin
A930

1954, Nov. 6 Photo. Perf. 12½x12
1735 A930 1r dk brn, pale org &
            red   5.00 4.50
37th anniversary of October Revolution.

Kazan University Building
A931

1954, Nov. 11   Perf. 12x12½
1736 A931 40k dp bl   1.00   50
1737 A931 60k claret   1.50   75
Issued to commemorate the 150th anniversary of the founding of Kazan University.

Salome Neris—A932

1954, Nov. 17   Perf. 12½x12
1738 A932 40k red org & ol gray 75   15
Issued to commemorate the 50th anniversary of the birth of Salome Neris (1904–1945), Lithuanian poet.

Vegetables and Garden
A933

Cultivating Flax—A934

Designs: No. 1741, Tractor plowing field. No. 1742, Loading ensilage.

1954, Dec. 12 Litho. Perf. 12x12½
1739 A933 40k multi   1.00   25
1740 A934 40k multi   1.00   25
1741 A933 40k multi   1.00   25
1742 A934 60k multi   1.50   50

Joseph Stalin   Anton Rubinstein
   A935   A936

1954, Dec. 21 Engr. Perf. 12½x12
1743 A935 40k rose brn   1.00   75
1744 A935 1r dk bl   2.00 1.00
Issued to commemorate the 75th anniversary of the birth of Joseph V. Stalin.

1954, Dec. 30   Photogravure
1745 A936 40k cl, gray & blk 2.50 60
Issued to commemorate the 125th anniversary of the birth of Anton G. Rubinstein, composer.

V. M. Garshin
A937

Lithographed and Photogravure
1955, Mar. 2   Perf. 12   Unwmkd.
1746 A937 40k buff, blk brn & grn 1.00 30
Issued to commemorate the centenary of the birth of Vsevolod M. Garshin (1855–1888), writer.

K. A. Savitsky and Painting
A938

1955, Mar. 21   Photogravure
1747 A938 40k multi   1.25   50
  a. Sheet of 4, black inscription 30.00 30.00
  b. Sheet of 4, red brn.
      inscription   30.00 30.00
Issued to commemorate the 50th anniversary of the death of K. A. Savitsky (1844–1905), painter. Nos. 1747a and 1747b measure 152x108 mm.

Globe and
Clasped
Hands
A939

1955, Apr. 9   Lithographed
1748 A939 40k multi   50   20
Issued to publicize the International Conference of Public Service Unions, Vienna, April 1955.

Poets Pushkin and Mickiewicz
A940

Brothers in
Arms Monument,
Warsaw
A941

Palace of Culture and Science,
Warsaw—A942

Copernicus, Painting by Jan
Matejko (in Medallion)
A943

Photogravure.
1955, Apr. 22   Perf. 12   Unwmkd.
1749 A940 40k chlky bl, vio & blk 2.00 50
1750 A941 40k vio blk   2.00   50
1751 A942 1r brt red & gray blk 4.00 1.25
1752 A943 1r multi   4.00 1.25
Issued to commemorate the 10th anniversary of the Polish-USSR treaty of friendship.

Lenin at Shushinskoe—A944

Lenin in Secret   Friedrich
Printing House   von Schiller
    A945   A946

Design: 1r, Lenin and Krupskaya with peasants at Gorki, 1921.

1955, Apr. 22
Frame and Inscription in Dark Red.
1753 A944 60k multi   1.00   35
1754 A944 1r multi   1.50   40
1755 A945 1r multi   1.50   40
85th anniversary of the birth of Lenin.

1955, May 10
1756 A946 40k chocolate   65   25
Issued to commemorate the 150th anniversary of the death of Friedrich von Schiller, German poet.

A. G. Venezianov and
"Spring on the Land"
A947

1955, June 21   Photogravure
1757 A947 1r multi   2.50 1.25
  a. Souvenir sheet   15.00 20.00
Issued to commemorate the 175th anniversary of the birth of A. G. Venezianov, painter.
No. 1757a contains four copies of No. 1757, with marginal inscription in bistre brown. Size: 152x107mm.

Anatoli K. Liadov
A948

RUSSIA

1955, July 5   Lithographed
| 1758 | A948 | 40k red brn, blk & lt brn | 1.00 | 20 |

Issued to commemorate the centenary of the birth of Anatoli K. Liadov (1855–1914), composer.

Aleksandr Popov
A949

Lenin
A950

Storming the Winter Palace
A951

1955, Nov. 5   Portraits Multicolored.
| 1759 | A949 | 40k lt ultra | 1.10 | 35 |
| 1760 | A949 | 1r gray brn | 2.00 | 65 |

Issued to commemorate the 60th anniversary of the construction of a coherer for detecting Hertzian electromagnetic waves by A. S. Popov, radio pioneer.

1955, Nov. 6
Design: 1r, Lenin addressing the people.
1761	A950	40k multi	1.10	60
1762	A951	40k multi	1.10	60
1763	A951	1r multi	2.75	1.25

38th anniversary of October Revolution.

Apartment Houses, Magnitogorsk
A952

1955, Nov. 29
| 1764 | A952 | 40k multi | 1.25 | 35 |

Issued to commemorate the 25th anniversary of the founding of the industrial center, Magnitogorsk.

Arctic Observation Post
A953

Design: 1r, Scientist at observation post.

1955, Nov. 29   Perf. 12½x12
1765	A953	40k multi	1.20	40
1766	A953	60k multi	1.80	60
1767	A953	1r multi	2.75	85
a.		Souv. sheet ('58)	17.50	35.00

Issued to publicize the Soviet scientific drifting stations at the North Pole.

No. 1767a contains four copies of No. 1767, with background in ultramarine. Size: 158x116½mm.

In 1962, No. 1767a was overprinted in red "1962" on each stamp and, in the lower sheet margin, a three-line Russian inscription meaning "25 years from the beginning of the work of 'NP-1' station."

Fedor Shubin
A954

1955, Dec. 22   Perf. 12
| 1768 | A954 | 40k grn & multi | 55 | 20 |
| 1769 | A954 | 1r brn & multi | 1.00 | 35 |

Issued to commemorate the 150th anniversary of the death of Fedor Ivanovich Shubin, sculptor.

Federal Socialist Republic Pavilion (R.S.F.S.R.)
A955
Designs: Pavilions.

1955   Lithographed   Unwmkd.
Centers in Natural Colors;
Frames in Blue Green and Olive.
1770	A955	40k shown	35	12
a.		Sheet of four	7.50	12.50
1771	A955	40k Tadzhik	35	12
1772	A955	40k Byelorussian	35	12
a.		Sheet of four	7.50	12.50
1773	A955	40k Azerbaijan	35	12
1774	A955	40k Georgian	35	12
1775	A955	40k Armenian	35	12
1776	A955	40k Turkmen	35	12
1777	A955	40k Uzbek	35	12
1778	A955	40k Ukrainian	35	12
a.		Sheet of four	7.50	12.50
1779	A955	40k Kazakh	35	12
1780	A955	40k Kirghiz	35	12
1781	A955	40k Karelo-Finnish	35	12
1782	A955	40k Moldavian	35	12
1783	A955	40k Estonian	35	12
1784	A955	40k Latvian	35	12
1785	A955	40k Lithuanian	35	12
		Nos. 1770-1785 (16)	5.60	1.92

All-Union Agricultural Fair.
Nos. 1773–1785 were printed in sheets containing various stamps, providing a variety of horizontal se-tenant pairs and strips.
Nos. 1770a, 1772a and 1778a measure 155x106½mm. with marginal inscriptions in dark blue and flags in actual colors. Each souvenir sheet contains a block of four stamps.

Lomonosov Moscow State University
A956

Design: 1r, New University buildings.

1955, June 9   Perf. 12
1786	A956	40k multi	45	25
a.		Sheet of 4 ('56)	3.00	12.50
1787	A956	1r multi	90	50
a.		Sheet of 4 ('56)	6.00	22.50

Issued to commemorate the 200th anniversary of Lomonosov Moscow State University.

Nos. 1786a and 1787a measure 149x109 mm. with marginal inscriptions in light brown.

Vladimir Mayakovsky—A957

1955, May 31
| 1788 | A957 | 40k multi | 80 | 20 |

Issued to commemorate the 25th anniversary of the death of Vladimir V. Mayakovsky, poet.

Race Horse
A958

Trotter—A959

1956, Jan. 9
1789	A958	40k dk brn	65	25
1790	A958	60k Prus grn & bl grn	1.10	35
1791	A959	1r dl pur & bl vio	1.85	60

Issued to commemorate the International Horse Races, Moscow, Aug. 14–Sept. 4, 1955.

Alexei N. Krylov
A960

Symbol of Spartacist Games, Stadium and Factories
A961

1956, Jan. 9
| 1792 | A960 | 40k gray, brn & blk | 65 | 20 |

Issued to commemorate the tenth anniversary of the death of Alexei N. Krylov (1863–1945), mathematician and naval architect.

1956, Jan. 18
| 1793 | A961 | 1r red vio & lt grn | 90 | 25 |

Issued to commemorate the fifth All-Union Spartacist Games of Soviet Trade Union sport clubs, Moscow, Aug. 12–18, 1955.

Atomic Power Station
A962

Design: 60k, Atomic Reactor.

1956, Jan. 31
1794	A962	25k multi	50	12
1795	A962	60k multi	1.50	25
1796	A962	1r multi	2.50	35

Issued to commemorate the establishment of the first Atomic Power Station of the USSR Academy of Science. Inscribed in Russian: "Atomic Energy in the service of the people."

Statue of Lenin, Kremlin and Flags
A963

Khachatur Abovian
A964

1956, Feb.
| 1797 | A963 | 40k multi | 75 | 15 |
| 1798 | A963 | 1r ol, buff & red org | 1.00 | 30 |

Issued to commemorate the 20th Congress of the Communist Party of the Soviet Union.

1956, Feb. 25   Perf. 12   Unwmkd.
| 1799 | A964 | 40k blk brn, bluish | 60 | 20 |

Issued to commemorate the 150th anniversary of the birth of Khachatur Abovian, Armenian writer.

Workers with Red Flag
A965

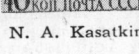
N. A. Kasatkin
A966

1956, Mar. 14
| 1800 | A965 | 40k multi | 60 | 20 |

Revolution of 1905, 50th anniversary.

1956, Apr. 30
| 1801 | A966 | 40k car lake | 50 | 20 |

Issued in honor of Nikolai A. Kasatkin (1859–1930), painter.

"On the Oka River"
A967

1956, Apr. 30   Center Multicolored.
| 1802 | A967 | 40k bis & blk | 1.50 | 20 |
| 1803 | A967 | 1r ultra & blk | 3.00 | 50 |

Issued in honor of A. E. Arkhipov, painter.

I. P. Kulibin
A968

V. G. Perov
A969

RUSSIA

"Birdcatchers"—A970

1956, May 12
1804 A968 40k multi   60   20
Issued to commemorate the 220th anniversary of the birth of I. P. Kulibin, inventor.

1956, May 12
Painting: No. 1807, "Hunters at Rest."
Centers in Multicolor.
1805 A969 40k green   1.50   25
1806 A970 1r brown   3.25   50
1807 A970 1r org brn   3.25   50
Issued in honor of Vassili Grigorievitch Perov (1833–1882), painter.

Ural Pavilion—A971

Designs—Pavilions: No. 1809, Tatar Republic. No. 1810, Volga District. No. 1811, Central Black Earth Area. No. 1812, Northeastern District. No. 1813, Northern Caucasus. No. 1814, Bashkir Republic. No. 1815, Far East. No. 1816, Central Asia. No. 1817, Young Naturalists. No. 1818, Siberia. No. 1819, Leningrad and Northwestern District. No. 1820, Moscow, Tula, Kaluga, Ryazan and Bryansk Districts.

1956, Apr. 25
Multicolored Centers.
1808 A971 1r yel grn & pale yel   1.00 25
1809 A971 1r bl grn & pale yel   1.00 25
1810 A971 1r dk bl grn & pale yel 1.00 25
1811 A971 1r dk bl grn & yel grn   1.00 25
1812 A971 1r dk brn & buff   1.00 25
1813 A971 1r ol gray & pale yel   1.00 25
1814 A971 1r ol & yel   1.00 25
1815 A971 1r ol grn & lem   1.00 25
1816 A971 1r ol brn & lem   1.00 25
1817 A971 1r ol brn & lem   1.00 25
1818 A971 1r brn & yel   1.00 25
1819 A971 1r redsh brn & yel   1.00 25
1820 A971 1r dk red brn & yel   1.00 25
      Nos. 1808-1820 (13)   13.00 3.25

Issued to publicize the All-Union Agricultural Fair, Moscow.
Six of the Pavilion set were printed se-tenant in one sheet of 30 (6x5), the strip containing Nos. 1809, 1816, 1817, 1813, 1818 and 1810 in that order. Two others, Nos. 1819–1820, were printed se-tenant in one sheet of 35.

Lenin   N. I. Lobachevski
A972   A973

1956, May 25
1821 A972 40k lil & multi   2.00 65
86th anniversary of the birth of Lenin.

1956, June 4
1822 A973 40k blk brn   40   15
Issued to commemorate the centenary of the death of Nikolai Ivanovich Lobachevski (1793–1856), mathematician.

Nurse and
Textile
Factory
A974

1956, June 4 Unwmkd.
Design: 40k, First Aid instruction.
1823 A974 40k lt ol grn, grnsh bl & red   45   25
1824 A974 40k red brn, lt bl & red   45   25

Issued in honor of the Red Cross and Red Crescent. No. 1823 measures 37x25 mm.; No. 1824, 40x28mm.

V. K. Arseniev   I. M. Sechenov
A975   A976

1956, June 15 Litho. Perf. 12
1825 A975 40k vio, blk & rose   65   25

V. K. Arseniev (1872–1930), explorer and writer.

1956, June 15
1826 A976 40k multi   65   20
I. M. Sechenov (1829–1905), physiologist.

A. K. Savrasov
A977

1956, June 22
1827 A977 1r dl yel & brn   1.50   35
Issued in honor of A. K. Savrasov, painter.

I. V. Michurin
A978

Design: 60k, I. V. Michurin with Pioneers.
1956, June 22
Center Multicolored.
1828 A978 25k dk brn   75   15
1829 A978 60k grn & lt bl   1.25   25
1830 A978 1r lt bl   2.50   50

Issued to commemorate the centenary of the birth of I. V. Michurin, scientist.
Nos. 1828 and 1830 measure 32x25mm. No. 1829 measures 47x26mm.

Nadezhda K. Krupskaya
A979

1956, June 28
1831 A979 40k brn, lt bl & pale brn   1.75   50
Issued to honor N. K. Krupskaya (1869–1939), teacher and wife of Lenin. See also Nos. 1862, 1886, 1983, 2028.

S. M. Kirov   N. S. Leskov
A980   A981

1956, June 28
1832 A980 40k red, buff & brn   60   20
Issued to commemorate the 70th anniversary of the birth of S. M. Kirov, revolutionary.

1956, July 10
1833 A981 40k ol bis & brn   30   20
1834 A981 1r grn & dk brn   90   35

Issued to commemorate the 125th anniversary of the birth of Nikolai S. Leskov (1831–1895), novelist.

Aleksandr A. Block
A982

1956, July 10
1835 A982 40k ol & brn, cr   45   20
Aleksandr A. Block (1880–1921), poet.

Farm Machinery Factory
A983

1956, July 23   Perf. 12½x12
1836 A983 40k multi   40   20
Issued to commemorate the 25th anniversary of the Rostov Farm Machinery Works.

G. N. Fedotova
A984

1956, July 23   Unwmkd.
1837 A984 40k brn & rose vio   65   30

Issued to commemorate G. N. Fedotova (1846–1925), actress. See also No. 2026.

P. M. Tretiakov and Art Gallery
A985

"The Rooks Have Arrived"
by A. K. Savrasov
A986

1956, July 31   Perf. 12
1838 A985 40k multi   2.00   30
1839 A986 40k multi   2.00   30
Issued to commemorate the centenary of the Tretiakov Art Gallery, Moscow.

Relay Race
A987

Volleyball
A988

Designs: No. 1842, Rowing. No. 1843, Swimming. No. 1844, Medal with heads of man and woman. No. 1845, Tennis. No. 1846, Soccer. No. 1847, Fencing. No. 1848, Bicycle race. No. 1849, Stadium and flag. No. 1850, Diving. No. 1851, Boxing. No. 1852, Gymnast. 1r, Basketball.

1956, Aug. 5
1840 A987 10k car rose   25   5

RUSSIA

1841	A988	25k dk org brn	40	6
1842	A988	25k brt grnsh bl	40	6
1843	A988	25k grn, bl & lt brn	40	6
1844	A988	40k org, pink, bis & yel	60	10
1845	A988	40k org brn	60	10
1846	A987	40k brt yel grn & dk brn	60	10
1847	A987	40k grn, brt grn & dk brn, grnsh	60	10
1848	A988	40k bl grn	60	10
1849	A988	40k brt yel grn & red	60	10
1850	A988	40k grnsh bl	60	10
1851	A988	60k violet	1.00	25
1852	A987	60k brt vio	1.00	25
1853	A987	1r red brn	1.75	45
		Nos. 1840-1853 (14)	9.40	1.88

Issued to commemorate the All-Union Spartacist Games, Moscow, Aug. 5-16.

Parachute Landing A989   **Building under Construction** A990

1956, Aug. 5   **Perf. 12x12½**

1854	A989	40k multi	75	25

Issued to commemorate the third World Parachute Championships, Moscow, July 1956.

1956   **Photogravure**   **Perf. 12**

Designs: 60k, Building a factory. 1r, Building a dam.

1855	A990	40k dp org	30	15
1856	A990	60k brn car	50	20
1857	A990	1r int bl	75	25

Issued in honor of Builders' Day.

Ivan Franko A991   **Makhmud Aivazov** A992

1956, Aug. 27

1858	A991	40k dp cl	60	25
1859	A991	1r brt bl	1.25	35

Issued to commemorate the centenary of the birth of Ivan Franko, writer. See also No. 1896.

1956, Aug. 27

Two types: I. Three lines in panel with "148."
II. Two lines in panel with "148."

1860	A992	40k emer (II)	7.50	2.50
a.		Type I	30.00	30.00

Issued in honor of the 148th birthday of Russia's oldest man, an Azerbaijan collective farmer.

Robert Burns A993

1956-57   **Photogravure**

1861	A993	40k yel brn	2.25	2.00

Engraved.

1861A	A993	40k lt ultra & brn ('57)	2.25	2.00

Issued in honor of the 160th anniversary of the death of Robert Burns, Scottish poet. See also No. 2174.

Portrait Type of 1956
Portrait: Lesya Ukrainka.

1956, Aug. 27   **Lithographed**

1862	A979	40k ol, blk & brn	40	40

Issued in honor of Lesya Ukrainka (1871–1913), Ukrainian writer.

Statue of Nestor A995   **A. A. Ivanov** A996

1956, Sept. 22   **Perf. 12x12½**

1863	A995	40k multi	75	20
1864	A995	1r multi	1.25	35

Issued to commemorate the 900th anniversary of the birth of Nestor, first Russian historian.

1956, Sept. 22   **Unwmkd.**

1865	A996	40k gray & brn	60	20

Issued in honor of the 150th anniversary of the birth of Aleksandr Andreevich Ivanov (1806–1858), painter.

I. E. Repin and "Volga River Boatmen" A997

"Cossacks Writing a Letter to the Turkish Sultan" A998

1956, Aug. 21   **Centers multicolored**

1866	A997	40k org brn & blk	4.00	90
1867	A998	1r chlky bl & blk	9.00	1.10

Issued to honor Ilya E. Repin (1844–1930), painter.

Chicken Farm A999

1956, Oct. 7

Designs: No. 1869, Harvest. 25k, Harvesting corn. No. 1871, Women in corn field. No. 1872, Farm buildings. No. 1873, Cattle. No. 1874, Farm workers, inscriptions and silos.

1868	A999	10k multi	15	15
1869	A999	10k multi	15	15
1870	A999	25k multi	35	15
1871	A999	40k multi	75	20
1872	A999	40k multi	75	20
1873	A999	40k multi	75	20
1874	A999	40k multi	75	20
		Nos. 1868-1874 (7)	3.65	1.25

Nos. 1868, 1872 and 1873 measure 37x25½mm. Nos. 1869-1871 measure 37x27½mm. No. 1874 measures 37x21mm.

Benjamin Franklin A1000

Portraits: No. 1876 Sesshu (Toyo Oda). No. 1877, Rembrandt. No. 1878, George Bernard Shaw. No. 1879, Mozart. No. 1880, Heinrich Heine. No. 1881, Fedor Dostoevski. No. 1882, Henrik Ibsen. No. 1883, Pierre Curie.

1956, Oct. 17   **Photogravure**

Size: 25x37mm.

1875	A1000	40k cop brn	1.50	50
1876	A1000	40k brt org	1.25	25
1877	A1000	40k black	1.50	25
1878	A1000	40k black	1.25	25

Size: 21x32mm.

1879	A1000	40k grnsh bl	1.25	25
1880	A1000	40k violet	1.25	25
1881	A1000	40k green	1.25	25
1882	A1000	40k brown	1.25	25
1883	A1000	40k brt grn	1.50	50
		Nos. 1875-1883 (9)	12.00	2.75

Issued in honor of great personalities of the world.

Antarctic Bases A1001   **G. I. Kotovsky** A1002

1956, Oct. 22 Litho. Perf. 12x12½

1884	A1001	40k sl, grnsh bl & red	1.35	60

Issued to commemorate the Soviet Scientific Antarctic Expedition.

1956, Oct. 30

1885	A1002	40k magenta	85	30

Issued to commemorate the 75th anniversary of the birth of G. I. Kotovsky (1881–1925), military commander.

Portrait Type of 1956
Portrait: Julia A. Zemaite.

1956, Oct. 30   **Perf. 12**

1886	A979	40k lt ol grn & brn	60	60

Julia A. Zemaite (1845–1921), Lithuanian novelist.

F. A. Bredichin—A1004

1956, Oct. 30

1887	A1004	40k sep & ultra	4.00	1.25

Issued to commemorate the 125th anniversary of the birth of Fëdor A. Bredichin (1831–1904), astronomer.

Aleksandr V. Suvorov A1005

1956, Nov. 17   **Engraved**

1888	A1005	40k org & mar	35	20
1889	A1005	1r ol & dk red brn	75	30
1890	A1005	3r lt red brn & blk	2.00	1.25

Issued to commemorate the 225th anniversary of the birth of Field Marshal Count Aleksandr Suvorov (1730–1800).

Shatura Power Station—A1006

1956 Lithographed. Perf. 12½x12

1891	A1006	40k multi	40	10

Issued to commemorate the 30th anniversary of the Shatura power station.

Kryakutni's Balloon, 1731 A1007

1956, Nov. 17

1892	A1007	40k lt brn, sep & yel	50	20

Issued to commemorate the 225th anniversary of the first balloon ascension of the Russian inventor, Kryakutni.

Yuli M. Shokalski A1008

RUSSIA

1956, Dec. 3   *Perf. 12*   Unwmkd.
1893   A1008   40k ultra & brn   50   20

Issued to commemorate the centenary of the birth of Y. M. Shokalski (1856–1940), oceanographer and geodesist.

Vasnetsov and "Winter Scene"
A1009

1956, Dec. 30
1894   A1009   40k multi   75   40

Issued to commemorate the centenary of the birth of Apollinari M. Vasnetsov (1856–1933), painter.

Indian Building and Books   Ivan Franko
A1010   A1011

1956, Dec. 26
1895   A1010   40k dp car   40   20

Issued to commemorate Kalidasa, 5th century Indian poet.

1956, Dec. 26   Engraved
1896   A1011   40k dk sl grn   40   20

Issued to commemorate Ivan Franko, Ukrainian writer. See also Nos. 1858–1859.

Leo N. Tolstoy
A1012

Portraits of Writers: No. 1898, Mikhail V. Lomonosov. No. 1899, Aleksander S. Pushkin. No. 1900, Maxim Gorky. No. 1901, Shota Rustaveli. No. 1902, Vissarion G. Belinski. No. 1903, Mikhail Y. Lermontov, poet, and Darjal Ravine in Caucasus.

1956–57   Litho.   *Perf. 12½x12*
Size: 37½x27½mm.
1897   A1012   40k brt grnsh bl & brn   45   15
1898   A1012   40k dk red, ol & brn ol   45   15

Size: 35½x25½mm.
1899   A1012   40k dk gray bl & brn   45   15
1900   A1012   40k blk & brn car   45   15
1901   A1012   40k ol, brn & ol gray   45   15
1902   A1012   40k bis, dl vio & brn ('57)   45   15
1903   A1012   40k ind & ol ('57)   45   15
Nos. 1897-1903 (7)   3.15   1.05

Issued in honor of famous Russian writers. See also Nos. 1960–1962, 2031, 2112.

Fëdor G. Volkov and Theater
A1013

1956, Dec. 31   Unwmkd.
1904   A1013   40k mag, gray & yel   40   20

Issued to commemorate the 200th anniversary of the founding of the St. Petersburg State Theater.

Vitus Bering and Map of Bering Strait
A1016

1957, Feb. 6
1905   A1016   40k brn & bl   1.25   30

Issued to commemorate the 275th anniversary of the birth of Vitus Bering, Danish navigator and explorer.

Dmitri I. Mendeleev   Mikhail I. Glinka
A1017   A1018

1957, Feb. 6   *Perf. 12x12½*
1906   A1017   40k gray & gray brn   1.00   90

Issued to commemorate the 50th anniversary of the death of D. I. Mendeleev (1834–1907), chemist.

1957, Feb. 23   *Perf. 12*
Design: 1r, Scene from opera Ivan Susanin.
1907   A1018   40k dk red, buff & sep   45   15
1908   A1018   1r multi   75   35

Issued to commemorate the centenary of the death of Mikhail I. Glinka (1804–1857), composer.

Emblem   Emblem
A1019   A1020

1957, Feb. 23
1909   A1019   40k dk bl, red & ocher   40   20

All-Union festival of Soviet Youth, Moscow.

1957, Feb. 24   Photogravure
Designs: 40k, Player. 60k, Goalkeeper.
1910   A1020   25k dp vio   60   20

1911   A1020   40k brt bl   60   25
1912   A1020   60k emerald   60   25

Issued to commemorate the 23rd Ice Hockey World Championship Games in Moscow.

Dove and Festival Emblem   Assembly Line
A1021   A1022

1957   Lithographed   *Perf. 12*
1913   A1021   40k multi   40   20
1914   A1021   60k multi   60   30

6th World Youth Festival, Moscow. Exist imperf. Price, each $25.00

1957, Mar. 15
1915   A1022   40k Prus grn & dp org   60   20

Moscow Machine Works centenary.

Black Grouse—A1023

Axis Deer—A1024

Animals: 10k, Gray partridge. No. 1918, Polar bear. No. 1920, Bison. No. 1921, Mallard. No. 1922, European elk. No. 1923, Sable.

1957, Mar. 28
Center in Natural Colors.
1916   A1024   10k yel brn   50   25
1917   A1023   15k brown   50   25
1918   A1023   15k sl bl   65   35
1919   A1024   20k red org   60   25
1920   A1023   30k ultra   60   25
1921   A1023   30k dk ol grn   60   25
1922   A1023   40k dk ol grn   1.50   50
1923   A1024   40k vio bl   1.50   50
Nos. 1916-1923 (8)   6.45   2.60

See also Nos. 2213–2219, 2429–2431.

Wooden Products, Hohloma
A1025

National Handicrafts: No. 1925, Lace maker, Vologda. No. 1926, Bone carver, North Russia. No. 1927, Woodcarver, Moscow area. No. 1928, Rug weaver, Turkmenistan. No. 1929, Painting.

1957–58   Unwmkd.
1924   A1025   40k red org, yel & blk   75   25
1925   A1025   40k brt car, yel & brn   75   25
1926   A1025   40k ultra, buff & gray   75   25
1927   A1025   40k brn, pale yel & hn brn   75   25
1928   A1025   40k buff, brn, bl & org ('58)   1.00   50
1929   A1025   40k multi ('58)   1.00   50
Nos. 1924-1929 (6)   5.00   2.00

Alexis N. Bach   G. V. Plekhanov
A1026   A1027

1957, Apr. 6   Litho.   *Perf. 12*
1930   A1026   40k ultra, brn & buff   60   20

Birth centenary of Alexis Nikolaievitch Bach (1857–1946), blochemist.

1957, Apr. 6   Engraved
1931   A1027   40k dl pur   50   20

Issued to commemorate the centenary of the birth of Georgi Valentinovich Plekhanov (1856–1918), political philosopher.

Leonhard Euler—A1028

1957, Apr. 17   Lithographed
1932   A1028   40k lil & gray   1.00   40

Issued to commemorate the 250th anniversary of the birth of Leonhard Euler (1707–1783), Swiss mathematician and physicist.

Lenin   Youths of All Races Carrying Festival Banner
A1029   A1030

Designs: No. 1934, Lenin talking to soldier and sailor. No. 1935, Lenin building barricades.

1957, Apr. 22
Centers in Multicolor.
1933   A1029   40k mag & bis   40   15
1934   A1029   40k mag & bis   40   15
1935   A1029   40k mag & bis   40   15

87th anniversary of the birth of Lenin.

RUSSIA

1957, May 27   Perf. 12x12½

Design: 20k, Sculptor with motherhood statue. 40k, Young couples dancing. 1r, Festival banner and fireworks over Moscow University.

1936	A1030	10k emer, pur & yel	10	5
1937	A1030	20k multi	15	10
1938	A1030	25k emer, pur & yel	25	10
1939	A1030	40k rose, bl grn & bis brn	35	10
1940	A1030	1r multi	60	25
		Nos. 1936-1940 (5)	1.45	60

Issued to publicize the 6th World Youth Festival in Moscow. The 10k, 20k, and 1r exist imperf. Price each about $25.00

Marine Museum Place and Neva — A1031   Henry Fielding — A1032

Designs: No. 1942, Lenin monument. No. 1943, Nevski Prospect and Admiralty.

1957, May 27   Photo.   Perf. 12

1941	A1031	40k bl grn	30	10
1942	A1031	40k redsh brn	30	10
1943	A1031	40k bluish vio	30	10
	a.	Souvenir sheet of 3	3.50	3.50

250th anniversary of Leningrad.

No. 1943a contains three imperf. stamps similar to Nos. 1941, 1680 (in reddish brown) and 1943. This red-bordered sheet commemorates the 40th anniversary of the October Revolution, and shows a battleship in Leningrad Harbor. Size: 144x98mm. Issued Nov. 7, 1957. A similar sheet is listed as No. 2002a.

Type of 1953 Overprinted in Red
250 лет Ленинграда

Designs: No. 1944, Peter I Statue, Decembrists' Square. No. 1945, Smolny Monastery.

1957, May 27   Perf. 12½x12

| 1944 | A908 | 1r blk brn, *grnsh* | 70 | 20 |
| 1945 | A908 | 1r grn, *pink* | 70 | 20 |

250th anniversary of Leningrad. The overprint is in one line on No. 1945.

1957, June 20   Lithographed

| 1946 | A1032 | 40k multi | 40 | 20 |

250th anniversary of the birth of Henry Fielding (1707-1754), English playwright and novelist.

William Harvey — A1033   M. A. Balakirev — A1034

1957, May 20   Photogravure

| 1947 | A1033 | 40k brown | 30 | 20 |

Issued to commemorate the 300th anniversary of the death of the English physician William Harvey, discoverer of the blood circulation.

1957, May 20   Engraved

| 1948 | A1034 | 40k bluish blk | 40 | 20 |

120th anniversary of the birth of M. A. Balakirev, composer.

A. I. Herzen and N. P. Ogarev — A1035

1957, May 20   Lithographed

| 1949 | A1035 | 40k blk vio & dk ol gray | 50 | 20 |

Centenary of newspaper Kolokol (Bell).

Kazakhstan Workers' Medal — A1036   A. M. Liapunov — A1037

1957, May 20

| 1950 | A1036 | 40k lt bl, blk & yel | 65 | 20 |

1957   Photogravure

Portraits: No. 1952, V. Mickevicius, writer. No. 1953, G. Bashindchagian, Armenian painter. No. 1954, Yakub Kolas, Byelorussian poet. No. 1955, Carl von Linné, Swedish botanist.

Various Frames

1951	A1037	40k dl red brn	1.25	1.25
1952	A1037	40k sepia	1.25	1.25
1953	A1037	40k sepia	1.25	1.25
1954	A1037	40k gray	1.25	1.25
1955	A1037	40k brn blk	1.25	1.25
		Nos. 1951-1955 (5)	6.25	6.25

See also Nos. 2036-2038, 2059.

Bicyclist — A1038

1957, June 20   Lithographed

| 1956 | A1038 | 40k cl & vio bl | 40 | 20 |

10th Peace Bicycle Race.

Telescope — A1039

Designs: No. 1958, Comet and observatory. No. 1959, Rocket leaving earth.

1957, July 4

Size: 25½x37mm.

| 1957 | A1039 | 40k brn, ocher & bl | 1.25 | 40 |
| 1958 | A1039 | 40k ind, lt bl & yel | 1.25 | 40 |

Size: 14½x21mm.

| 1959 | A1039 | 40k bl vio | 1.25 | 40 |

Issued to publicize the International Geophysical Year, 1957-58. See also Nos. 2089-2091.

Folksinger — A1040

1957, May 20

| 1960 | A1040 | 40k multi | 40 | 20 |

Issued in honor of "The Song of Igor's Army," Russia's oldest literary work.

Taras G. Shevchenko — A1041

Design: No. 1962, Nikolai G. Chernyshevski.

1957, June 20

| 1961 | A1041 | 40k grn & dk red brn | 35 | 15 |
| 1962 | A1041 | 40k org brn & grn | 35 | 15 |

Issued in honor of T. C. Shevchenko, Ukrainian poet. (No. 1961), and N. G. Chernyshevski, writer and politician (No. 1962).

Woman Gymnast — A1043

Designs: 25k, Wrestling. No. 1965, Stadium. No. 1966, Youths of three races. 60k, Javelin thrower.

1957, July 15   Litho.   Perf. 12

1963	A1043	20k bluish vio & org brn	15	10
1964	A1043	25k brt grn & cl	20	15
1965	A1043	40k Prus bl, ol & red	30	15
1966	A1043	40k crim & vio	30	15
1967	A1043	60k ultra & brn	40	25
		Nos. 1963-1967 (5)	1.35	80

Third International Youth Games, Moscow.

Javelin Thrower — A1044

Designs: No. 1969, Sprinter. 25k, Somersault. No. 1971, Boxers. No. 1972, Soccer players (horiz.). 60k, Weight lifter.

1957, July 20   Unwmkd.

1968	A1044	20k lt ultra & ol blk	25	10
1969	A1044	20k brt grn, red vio & blk	25	10
1970	A1044	25k org, ultra & blk	25	15
1971	A1044	40k rose vio & blk	50	20
1972	A1044	40k dp pink, bl, buff & blk	50	20
1973	A1044	60k lt vio & brn	1.00	30
		Nos. 1968-1973 (6)	2.75	1.05

Issued to commemorate the success of Soviet athletes at the 16th Olympic Games, Melbourne.

Yanka Kupala — A1045   Kremlin — A1046

1957, July 27   Photogravure

| 1974 | A1045 | 40k dk gray | 1.00 | 1.00 |

Issued to commemorate the 75th anniversary of the birth of Yanka Kupala (1882-1942), poet.

1957, July 27   Lithographed

Moscow Views: No. 1976, Stadium. No. 1977, University. No. 1978, Bolshoi Theater.

Center in Black.

1975	A1046	40k dl red brn	40	15
1976	A1046	40k brn vio	40	15
1977	A1046	1r red	1.00	20
1978	A1046	1r brt vio bl	1.00	20

Sixth World Youth Festival, Moscow.

Lenin Library — A1047

1957, July 27   Photogravure

| 1979 | A1047 | 40k brt grnsh bl | 40 | 20 |
| | a. | Souvenir sheet | 8.00 | 15.00 |

Issued to commemorate the International Philatelic Exhibition, Moscow, July 29-Aug. 11. No. 1979a exists imperf. Price $12.

No. 1979a measures 142x101mm. and contains two imperf. copies of No. 1979 in light blue. The sheet is pale green, with inscriptions and Youth Festival emblem in light blue.

Pierre Jean de Beranger — A1048   Globe, Dove and Olive Branch — A1049

1957, Aug. 9

| 1980 | A1048 | 40k brt bl grn | 40 | 20 |

Death centenary of Pierre Jean de Beranger (1780-1857), French song writer.

RUSSIA — 312

1957, Aug. 8   Lithographed
1981 A1049 40k bl, grn & bis brn   60   60
1982 A1049 1r vio, grn & brn   1.40   90

Publicity for world peace.

Portrait Type of 1956
1957, Aug. 9
Portrait: 40k, Clara Zetkin.
1983 A979 40k gray bl, brn & blk   65   35

Birth centenary of Clara Zetkin (1857–1933), German communist.

Krenholm Factory, Narva
A1050

1957, Sept. 8   Photogravure
1984 A1050 40k blk brn   55   20

Issued to commemorate the centenary of Krenholm textile factory, Narva, Estonia.

Carrier Pigeon and Globes
A1051

1957, Sept. 26   Perf. 12   Unwmkd.
1985 A1051 40k blue   25   15
1986 A1051 60k lilac   50   20

Issued to publicize International Letter Writing Week, Oct. 6–12.

Wyborshez Factory, Lenin Statue
A1052

1957, Sept. 23   Lithographed
1987 A1052 40k dk bl   45   15

Centenary of Krasny Wyborshez factory, Leningrad.

Vladimir V. Stasov
A1053

1957, Sept. 23   Engraved
1988 A1053 40k brown   50   10
1989 A1053 1r bluish blk   1.00   20

Issued to commemorate the 50th anniversary of the death of Vladimir Vasilievich Stasov (1824–1906), art and music critic.

Congress Emblem
A1054

1957, Oct. 7   Litho.   Perf. 12
1990 A1054 40k gray bl & blk, *bluish*   40   15

Issued to publicize the fourth International Trade Union Congress, Leipzig, Oct. 4–15.

Konstantin E. Tsiolkovsky
and Rockets—A1055

1957, Oct. 7
1991 A1055 40k dk bl & pale brn   2.00   90

Centenary of the birth of Konstantin E. Tsiolkovsky (1857–1935), rocket and astronautics pioneer. See No. 2021.

Sputnik 1   Turbine Wheel,
Circling   Kuibyshev Hydro-
Globe   electric Station
A1056   A1057

1957   Photogravure
1992 A1056 40k ind, *bluish*   1.00   60
1993 A1056 40k brt bl   1.00   60

Launching of first artificial earth satellite, Oct. 4. Issue dates: No. 1992, Nov. 5; No. 1993, Dec. 28.

1957, Nov. 20   Lithographed
1994 A1057 40k red brn   40   15
All-Union Industrial Exhibition. See No. 2030.

Meteor   Lenin
A1058   A1059

1957, Nov. 20
1995 A1058 40k multi   90   25

Issued to commemorate the 10th anniversary of the falling of the Sihote Alinj meteor.

1957, Oct. 30   Engraved
Design: 60k, Lenin reading *Pravda* (horiz.).
1996 A1059 40k blue   40   10
1997 A1059 60k rose red   50   10

40th anniversary of October Revolution.

Students and   Worker and Railroad
Moscow
University
A1060   A1061

Designs: No. 1999, Red flag and Lenin. No. 2000, Lenin addressing workers and peasants. 60k, Harvester.

Perf. 12½x12, 12x12½, 12½
1957, Oct. 15   Lithographed
1998 A1060 10k buff, sep & red   10   5
1999 A1060 40k buff, red, sep & yel   35   10
2000 A1060 40k red, blk & yel   35   10
2001 A1061 40k red, yel & grn   35   10
2002 A1061 60k red, ocher & vio brn   50   15
  a. Souvenir sheet of 3   3.00   3.00
     Nos. 1998-2002 (5)   1.65   50

Issued to commemorate the 40th anniversary of the October Revolution. No. 2002a measures 144x98mm. and contains one each of Nos. 2000–2002 imperf. The sheet shows night view of Moscow and red ribbon. A similar sheet is listed as No. 1943a. Nos. 1998–2002 exist imperf.

Federal Socialist   Uzbek
Republic   Republic
A1062   A1063

Designs (Republic): No. 2005, Tadzhik (Building and peasant girl). No. 2006, Byelorussia (Truck). No. 2007, Azerbaijan (Buildings). No. 2008, Georgia (Valley, palm and couple). No. 2009, Armenia, (Fruit, power line and mountains). No. 2010, Turkmen (couple and lambs). No. 2011, Ukraine (Farmers). No. 2012, Kazakh (Harvester and combine). No. 2013, Kirghiz, (Horseback rider and building). No. 2014, Moldavia (Automatic sorting machine). No. 2015, Estonia (Girl in national costume). No. 2016, Latvia (Couple, sea and field). No. 2017, Lithuania (Farm and farmer couple).

1957, Oct. 25
2003 A1062 40k multi   50   13
2004 A1063 40k multi   50   13
2005 A1062 40k multi   50   13
2006 A1062 40k multi   50   13
2007 A1062 40k multi   50   13
2008 A1062 40k multi   50   13
2009 A1062 40k multi   50   13
2010 A1062 40k multi   50   13
2011 A1063 40k multi   50   13
2012 A1062 40k multi   50   13
2013 A1062 40k multi   50   13
2014 A1062 40k multi   50   13
2015 A1063 40k multi   50   13
2016 A1062 40k multi   50   13
2017 A1062 40k multi   50   13
     Nos. 2003-2017 (15)   7.50   1.95

40th anniversary of the October Revolution.

Artists and   Red Army
Academy of Art   Monument, Berlin
A1064   A1065

Monument: 1r, Worker and Peasant monument, Moscow.

1957, Dec. 16
2018 A1064 40k blk, *pale sal*   30   15

2019 A1065 60k black   40   20
2020 A1065 1r blk, *pink*   65   25

200th anniversary of the Academy of Arts, Leningrad. Artists on 40k are K. P. Bryulov, Ilya Repin and V. I. Surikov.

No. 1991
Overprinted
in Black
1957, Nov. 28
2021 A1055 40k dk bl & pale brn   10.00   7.00

Launching of Sputnik 1.

Ukrainian Arms,
Symbolic Figures—A1066

1957, Dec. 24
2022 A1066 40k yel, red & bl   35   15

Issued to commemorate the 40th anniversary of the Ukrainian Soviet Republic.

Edvard Grieg   Giuseppe Garibaldi
A1067   A1068

1957, Dec. 24   Photogravure
2023 A1067 40k buff   40   20

50th anniversary of the death of Edvard Grieg, Norwegian composer.

1957, Dec. 24   Lithographed
2024 A1068 40k plum, lt grn & blk   40   15

150th anniversary of birth of Giuseppe Garibaldi, (1807–1882) Italian patriot.

V. L.   Kuibyshev
Borovikovsky   Hydroelectric Station
A1069   and Dam
    A1070

1957, Dec. 24   Photogravure
2025 A1069 40k brown   40   15

Issued to commemorate the 200th anniversary of the birth of Vladimir Lukich Borovikovsky (1757–1825), painter.

Portrait Type of 1956
Portrait: 40k, Mariya Nikolayevna Ermolova (1853–1928), actress.

1957, Dec. 28   Lithographed
2026 A984 40k red brn & brt vio   30   20

1957, Dec. 28
2027 A1070 40k dk bl, *buff*   40   15

Type of 1956.
1958, Jan. 8
Portrait: 40k, Rosa Luxemburg (1870–1919), German socialist.

2028 A979 40k bl & brn   75   75

RUSSIA

Chi Pai-shih
A1070a

Flag and Symbols of Industry
A1070b

1958, Jan. 8   Photogravure
2029   A1070a   40k dp vio   40   15

Issued to honor Chi Pai-shih (1860–1957), Chinese painter.

1958, Jan. 8   Lithographed
2030   A1070b   60k gray vio, red & blk   60   15

All-Union Industrial Exhibition. Exists imperf.

Aleksei N. Tolstoi
A1071

1958, Jan. 28   Photo.   Perf. 12
2031   A1071   40k brn ol   35   15

Issued in honor of Aleksei Nikolaevich Tolstoi, novelist and dramatist. See also Nos. 2112, 2175–2178C.

Symbolic Figure Greeting Sputnik 2—A1072

1957–58   Lithographed
Figure in Buff
2032   A1072   20k blk & rose   40   10
2033   A1072   40k blk & grn ('58)   60   25
2034   A1072   60k blk & lt brn ('58)   1.00   35
2035   A1072   1r blk & bl   1.25   50

Launching of Sputnik 2, Nov. 3, 1957.

Small Portrait Type of 1957.
Portraits: No. 2036, Henry W. Longfellow, American poet. No. 2037, William Blake, English artist, poet, mystic. No. 2038, E. Sharents, Armenian poet.

1958, Mar.   Perf. 12   Unwmkd.
Various Frames
2036   A1037   40k gray blk   50   40
2037   A1037   40k gray blk   50   40
2038   A1037   40k sepia   50   40

Victory at Pskov
A1073

Soldier and Civilian
A1074

Designs: No. 2040, Airman, sailor and soldier. No. 2042, Sailor and soldier. 60k, Storming of Berlin Reichstag building.

1958, Feb. 21
2039   A1073   25k multi   15   5
2040   A1074   40k multi   25   10
2041   A1074   40k multi   25   10
2042   A1074   40k multi   25   10
2043   A1073   60k multi   50   15
     Nos. 2039-2043 (5)   1.40   50

40th anniversary of Red Armed Forces.

Peter Ilich Tchaikovsky
A1075

Swan Lake Ballet
A1076

Design: 1r, Tchaikovsky, pianist and violinist.

1958, Mar. 18
2044   A1075   40k grn, bl, brn & red   35   15
2045   A1076   40k grn, ultra, red & yel   35   15
2046   A1075   1r lake & emer   1.00   40

Issued to honor Tchaikovsky and publicize the Tchaikovsky competitions for pianists and violinists. Exist imperf. Price, set $8.

Nos. 2044–2045 were printed in sheets of 30, including 15 stamps of each value and 5 se-tenant pairs.

V. F. Rudnev
A1077

Maxim Gorki
A1078

1958, Mar. 25   Unwmkd.
2047   A1077   40k grn, blk & ocher   60   15

Issued in honor of V. F. Rudnev, naval commander.

1958, Apr. 3   Litho.   Perf. 12
2048   A1078   40k multi   30   15

Issued to commemorate the 90th anniversary of the birth of Maxim Gorki, writer.

Spasski Tower and Emblem
A1079

Russian Pavilion, Brussels
A1080

1958, Apr. 9
2049   A1079   40k dp vio, pnksh   30   10
2050   A1079   40k rose red   40   15

Issued to publicize the 13th Congress of the Young Communist League (Komsomol).

1958, Apr.
2051   A1080   10k multi   10   8
2052   A1080   40k multi   30   12

Issued for the Universal and International Exhibition at Brussels. Exist imperf. Price $2.

Lenin
A1081

Jan A. Komensky (Comenius)
A1082

1958, Apr. 22   Engraved
2053   A1081   40k dk bl gray   40   15
2054   A1081   60k dk rose brn   60   20
2055   A1081   1r brown   1.00   25

88th anniversary of the birth of Lenin.

1958, May 5
Portrait: Nos. 2056–2058, Karl Marx.
2056   A1081   40k brown   30   10
2057   A1081   60k dk bl   50   15
2058   A1081   1r dk red   1.00   25

140th anniversary of the birth of Marx.

1958, Apr. 17   Photogravure
2059   A1082   40k green   65   60

No. 1695 Overprinted in Blue

200 лет Академии художеств СССР. 1957

1958, Apr. 22
2060   A914   40k multi   1.75   60

Issued to commemorate the 200th anniversary of the Academy of Arts, Moscow.

Lenin Order
A1083

Carlo Goldoni
A1084

1958, Apr. 30   Lithographed
2061   A1083   40k brn, yel & red   40   10

1958, Apr. 28   Photogravure
2062   A1084   40k bl & dk gray   40   10

Issued in honor of Carlo Goldoni, Italian dramatist.

Radio Tower, Ship and Planes
A1085

1958, May 7
2063   A1085   40k bl grn & red   1.20   30

Issued for Radio Day, May 7.

Globe and Dove
A1086

Ilya Chavchavadze
A1087

1958, May 6   Lithographed
2064   A1086   40k bl & blk   25   15
2065   A1086   60k ultra & blk   35   15

Issued to publicize the 4th Congress of the International Democratic Women's Federation, June, 1958, at Vienna.

1958, May 12   Photogravure
2066   A1087   40k blk & bl   35   15

Issued to commemorate the 50th anniversary of the death of Ilya Chavchavadze, Georgian writer.

Flags and Communication Symbols
A1088

1958–59   Lithographed.
2067   A1088   40k bl, red, yel & blk   4.00   1.25
  a.   Red half of Czech flag at bottom   4.00   1.25

Issued to commemorate a communist ministers' meeting on social problems in Moscow, Dec. 1957.

On No. 2067, the Czech flag (center flag in vertical row of five) is incorrectly pictured with red stripe on top. This error is corrected on No. 2067a.

Bugler
A1089

Children of Three Races
A1090

Design: 25k, Boy with model plane.

1958, May 29   Perf. 12   Unwmkd.
2068   A1089   10k ultra, red & red brn   15   5
2069   A1089   25k ultra, yel & red brn   20   10

Issued to honor the Pioneers.

1958, May 29
Design: No. 2071, Child and bomb.
2070   A1090   40k car, ultra & brn   30   10
2071   A1090   40k car & brn   30   10

Issued for the International Day for the Protection of Children.

Soccer Players and Globe
A1091

Nikolai A. Rimski-Korsakov
A1092

RUSSIA

1958, June 5

2072	A1091	40k bl, red & buff	25	15
2073	A1091	60k bl, red & buff	50	20

Issued to commemorate the 6th World Soccer Championships, Stockholm, June 8–29. Exist imperf. Price $2.50.

1958, June 5   Photogravure

| 2074 | A1092 | 40k bl & brn | 50 | 15 |

Issued to commemorate the 50th anniversary of the death of Nikolai Andreevich Rimski-Korsakov (1844–1908), composer.

Girl Gymnast—A1093

Design: No. 2076, Gymnast on rings and view.

1958, June 24   Lithographed

| 2075 | A1093 | 40k ultra, red & buff | 40 | 15 |
| 2076 | A1093 | 40k bl, red, buff & grn | 40 | 15 |

14th World Gymnastic Championships, Moscow, July 6–10.

Bomb, Globe, Atom, Sputniks, Ship
A1094

1958, July 1

| 2077 | A1094 | 60k dk bl, blk & org | 75 | 20 |

Issued to publicize a conference for peaceful uses of atomic energy, held at Stockholm.

Street Fighters   Congress Emblem
A1095   A1097

Moscow State University
A1096

1958, July 5

| 2078 | A1095 | 40k red & vio blk | 35 | 20 |

Issued to commemorate the 40th anniversary of the Communist Party in the Ukraine.

1958, July 8   Perf. 12

2079	A1096	40k red & bl	40	10
2080	A1097	60k lt grn, bl & red	60	15
a.		Souv. sheet	4.00	5.00

Issued to commemorate the fifth Congress of the International Architects' Organization, Moscow.

No. 2080a contains one each of Nos. 2079–2080, imperf., with background design in yellow, brown, blue and red. Size 94½x144mm. Issued Sept. 8, 1958.

Young Couple
A1098

1958, June 25

| 2081 | A1098 | 40k bl & ocher | 30 | 10 |
| 2082 | A1098 | 60k yel grn & ocher | 45 | 15 |

Issued for the Day of Soviet Youth.

Sputnik 3   Sadriddin
Leaving Earth   Aini
A1099   A1100

1958, June 16

| 2083 | A1099 | 40k vio bl, grn & rose | 1.00 | 20 |

Launching of Sputnik 3, May 15. Printed in sheets with alternating labels, giving details of launching.

1958, July 15

| 2084 | A1100 | 40k rose, blk & buff | 50 | 20 |

Issued to commemorate the 80th birthday of Sadriddin Aini, Tadzhik writer.

Emblem—A1101

1958, July 21   Typo.   Perf. 12

| 2085 | A1101 | 40k lil & bl | 40 | 20 |

Issued to publicize the first World Trade Union Conference of Working Youths, Prague, July 14–20.

Type of 1958–59 and

TU-104 and Globe
A1102

Design: 1r, Turbo-propeller liner AN-10.

1958, Aug.   Lithographed

| 2086 | A1102 | 60k bl, red & bis | 40 | 15 |
| 2087 | A1123 | 1r yel, red & blk | 75 | 20 |

Issued to honor Russian civil aviation. Exist imperf. Price, set $5.50. See also Nos. 2147–2151.

L. A. Kulik—A1103

1958, Aug. 12

| 2088 | A1103 | 40k sep, bl, yel & cl | 1.00 | 20 |

Issued to commemorate the 50th anniversary of the falling of the Tungus meteor and the 75th anniversary of the birth of L. A. Kulik, meteorist.

IGY Type of 1957

1958, July 29

Designs: No. 2089, Aurora borealis and camera. No. 2090, Schooner "Zarja" exploring earth magnetism. No. 2091, Weather balloon and radar.

Size: 25½ x 37mm.

2089	A1039	40k bl & brt yel	65	20
2090	A1039	40k bl & blk	65	20
2091	A1039	40k brt ultra	65	20

International Geophysical Year, 1957–58.

Crimea   Moscow University
Observatory   A1105
A1104

Design: 1r, Telescope.

1958, Aug.   Photogravure

2092	A1104	40k brn & brt grnsh bl	60	15
2093	A1105	60k lt bl, vio & yel	75	20
2094	A1104	1r dp bl & org brn	90	25

Issued to publicize the 10th Congress of the International Astronomical Union, Moscow.

Postilion, 16th Century
A1106

Designs: No. 2095, 15th century letter writer. No. 2097, A. L. Ordyn-Natshokin and sleigh mail coach, 17th century. No. 2098, Mail coach and post office, 18th century. No. 2099, Troika, 19th century. No. 2100, Lenin stamp, ship and Moscow University. No. 2101, Jet plane and postilion. No. 2102, Leningrad Communications Museum (vert.). No. 2103, V. N. Podbielski and letter carriers. No. 2104, Mail train. No. 2105, Loading mail on plane. No. 2106, Ship, plane, train and globe.

Lithographed.

1958, Aug.   Perf. 12   Unwmkd.

2095	A1106	10k red, blk, yel & lil	10	5
2096	A1106	10k multi	10	5
2097	A1106	25k ultra & sl	25	5
2098	A1106	25k blk & ultra	25	5
2099	A1106	40k car lake & brn blk	35	10
2100	A1106	40k blk, mag & brn	35	10
2101	A1106	40k red, org & gray	35	10
2102	A1106	40k sal & brn	35	10
2103	A1106	60k grnsh bl & red lil	50	15
2104	A1106	60k grnsh bl & lil	50	15
2105	A1106	1r multi	75	25

| 2106 | A1106 | 1r multi | 75 | 25 |
| Nos. 2095-2106 (12) | | | 4.60 | 1.40 |

Centenary of Russian postage stamps. Two imperf. souvenir sheets exist, measuring 155x106mm. One contains one each of Nos. 2095–2099, with background design in red, ultramarine, yellow and brown. The other contains one each of Nos. 2100, 2103–2106, with background design in blue, gray, ochre, pink and brown. Price for both, $10 unused, $5 canceled. Nos. 2096, 2100–2101 exist imperf. Price each $3.50.

M. I. Chigorin   Golden Gate,
A1107   Vladimir
  A1108

1958, Aug. 30   Photogravure

| 2107 | A1107 | 40k blk & emer | 50 | 20 |

Issued to commemorate the 50th anniversary of the death of M. I. Chigorin, chess player.

1958, Aug. 23   Lithographed

Design: 60k, Gorki Street with trolley bus and truck.

| 2108 | A1108 | 40k multi | 25 | 10 |
| 2109 | A1108 | 60k lt vio, yel & blk | 50 | 15 |

Issued to commemorate the 850th anniversary of the city of Vladimir.

Nurse
Bandaging
Man's Leg
A1109

Design: No. 2111, Hospital and people of various races.

1958, Sept. 15

| 2110 | A1109 | 40k multi | 35 | 20 |
| 2111 | A1109 | 40k ol, lem & red | 35 | 20 |

Issued to honor 40 years of Red Cross-Red Crescent work.

Portrait Type of 1958

1958, Sept. 15

Portrait: M. E. Saltykov (Shchedrin).

| 2112 | A1071 | 40k brn blk & mar | 50 | 15 |

Issued to honor Mikhail E. Saltykov (Shchedrin), writer.

Rudagi   V. V. Kapnist
A1110   A1111

1958, Oct. 10   Litho.   Perf. 12

| 2113 | A1110 | 40k multi | 30 | 15 |

Issued to commemorate the 1100th anniversary of the birth of Rudagi, Persian poet.

1958, Sept. 30

| 2114 | A1111 | 40k bl & gray | 30 | 15 |

Issued to commemorate the 200th anniversary of the birth of V. V. Kapnist, poet and dramatist.

RUSSIA

Book, Torch, Lyre, Flower
A1112

1958, Oct. 4
2115 A1112 40k red org, ol & blk   30   15

Issued to commemorate the Conference of Asian and African Writers, Tashkent.

Tcheliabinsk Tractor Factory
A1113

Designs: No. 2117, Zaporozstal foundry. No. 2118, Ural machine building plant.

1958, Oct. 20 Photogravure
2116 A1113 40k grn & yel   25   10
2117 A1113 40k brn red & yel   25   10
2118 A1113 40k blue   25   10

Issued to honor pioneers of Russian Industry.

Ancient Georgian on Horseback
A1114

1958, Oct. 18 Lithographed
2119 A1114 40k ocher, ultra & red   60   15

Issued to commemorate the 1500th anniversary of Tbilisi, capital of Georgia.

Red Square, Moscow—A1115

Cities: No. 2121, Lenin Square, Alma Ata. No. 2122, Lenin statue, Ashkhabad. No. 2123, Lenin statue, Tashkent. No. 2124, Lenin Square, Stalinabad. No. 2125, Rustaveli Ave., Tbilisi. No. 2126, View from Dvina River, Riga. No. 2127, University Square, Frunze. No. 2128, View, Yerevan. No. 2129, Communist Street, Baku. No. 2130, Lenin Prospect, Kishinev. No. 2131, Round Square, Minsk. No. 2132, Viru Gate, Tallinn. No. 2133, Main Street, Kiev. No. 2134, View, Vilnius.

1958 Engraved
2120 A1115 40k violet   30   12
2121 A1115 40k brt bl grn   30   12
2122 A1115 40k grnsh gray   30   12
2123 A1115 40k dk gray   30   12
2124 A1115 40k blue   30   12
2125 A1115 40k vio bl   30   12
2126 A1115 40k brn red   30   12
2127 A1115 40k dk bl gray   30   12
2128 A1115 40k brown   30   12
2129 A1115 40k purple   30   12
2130 A1115 40k olive   30   12
2131 A1115 40k gray brn   30   12
2132 A1115 40k emerald   30   12
2133 A1115 40k lil rose   30   12
2134 A1115 40k org ver   30   12
Nos. 2120-2134 (15)   4.50   1.80

Capitals of Soviet republics. See also No. 2836.

Young Civil War Soldier, 1919
A1116

Designs: 20k, Industrial brigade. 25k, Youth in World War II. 40k, Girl farm worker. 60k, Youth building new towns. 1r, Students, fighters for culture.

1958, Oct. 25 Lithographed
2135 A1116 10k multi   10   5
2136 A1116 20k multi   15   5
2137 A1116 25k multi   20   10
2138 A1116 40k multi   25   10
2139 A1116 60k multi   40   15
2140 A1116 1r multi   1.00   40
Nos. 2135-2140 (6)   2.10   85

Issued to commemorate the 40th anniversary of the Young Communist League (Komsomol).

Marx and Lenin   Lenin, Intellectual,
A1117   Peasant and Miner
                     A1118

1958, Oct. 31
2141 A1117 40k multi   40   15
2142 A1118 1r multi   75   25

41st anniversary of Russian Revolution.

Torch, Wreath   Sergei Esenin
and Family   A1120
A1119

1958, Nov. 5
2143 A1119 60k blk, beige & dl bl   40   15

Issued to commemorate the tenth anniversary of the Universal Declaration of Human Rights.

1958, Nov. 29
2144 A1120 40k multi   40   15

Sergei Esenin (1895-1925), poet.

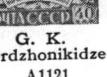

G. K.   Kuan Han-ching
Ordzhonikidze   A1122
A1121

1958, Dec. 12 Perf. 12
2145 A1121 40k multi   30   15

G. K. Ordzhonikidze (1886-1937), Georgian party worker.

1958, Dec. 5
2146 A1122 40k dk bl & gray   30   15

Issued to commemorate the 700th anniversary of the theater of Kuan Han-ching, Chinese dramatist.

Airliner IL-14 and Globe
A1123

Designs: No. 2148, Jet liner TU-104. No. 2149, Turbo-propeller liner TU-114. 60k, Jet liner TU-110. 2r, Turbo-propeller liner IL-18.

1958-59
2147 A1123 20k ultra, blk & red   25   5
2148 A1123 40k bl grn, blk & red   35   10
2149 A1123 40k brt bl, blk & red   35   10
2150 A1123 60k rose car & blk   40   15
2151 A1123 2r plum, red & blk ('59)   1.00   35
Nos. 2147-2151 (5)   2.35   75

Issued to honor Russian civil aviation. Exist imperf.; price $8.50. See Nos. 2086-2087.

Eleonora Duse   John Milton
A1124   A1125

1958, Dec. 26
2152 A1124 40k bl grn & gray   35   15

Issued to commemorate the centenary of the birth of Eleonora Duse, Italian actress.

1958, Dec. 17
2153 A1125 40k brown   35   15

350th birth anniversary of John Milton (1608-1674), English poet.

K. F. Rulye   Fuzuli
A1126   A1127

1958, Dec. 26
2154 A1126 40k ultra & blk   35   15

Issued to commemorate the centenary of the death of K. F. Rulye, educator.

1958, Dec. 23 Photogravure
2155 A1127 40k grnsh bl & brn   35   15

Issued to commemorate the 400th anniversary of the death of Fuzuli (Mehmet Suleiman Oglou), Turkish poet.

Census Emblem   Lunik and
and Family   Sputniks
A1128   over Kremlin
                    A1129

Design: No. 2157, Census emblem.

1958, Dec. Lithographed
2156 A1128 40k multi   35   15
2157 A1128 40k yel, gray, bl & red   35   15

Issued to publicize the 1959 Russian census.

1959, Jan. Perf. 12 Unwmkd.

Designs: 40k, Lenin and view of Kremlin. 60k, Workers and Lenin power plant on Volga.

2158 A1129 40k multi   50   20
2159 A1129 60k multi   75   25
2160 A1129 1r red, yel & vio bl   2.00   50

Issued to commemorate the 21st Congress of the Communist Party and to mark "the conquest of the cosmos by the Soviet people."

Lenin Statue,   Atomic Icebreaker
Minsk   "Lenin"
Buildings   A1131
A1130

1958, Dec. 20
2161 A1130 40k red, buff & brn   40   20

Issued to commemorate the 40th anniversary of the Byelorussian Republic.

1958, Dec. 31
Design: 60k, Diesel Locomotive "TE-3."
2162 A1131 40k multi   50   25
2163 A1131 60k multi   75   35

Shalom   Evangelista
Aleichem   Torricelli
A1132   A1133

1959, Feb. 10
2164 A1132 40k chocolate   40   20

Issued to commemorate the centenary of the birth of Shalom Aleichem, Yiddish writer.

1959, Feb.
Scientists: No. 2166, Charles Darwin, English biologist. No. 2167, N. F. Gamaleya, microbiologist.

Various Frames
2165 A1133 40k bl grn & blk   40   15
2166 A1133 40k chlky bl & brn   40   15
2167 A1133 40k dk red & blk   35   15

Issued to honor famous scientists.

RUSSIA

Woman Skater A1134   Frederic Joliot-Curie A1135

1959, Feb. 5

| 2168 | A1134 | 25k ultra, blk & ver | 35 | 15 |
| 2169 | A1134 | 40k ultra & blk | 50 | 15 |

Women's International Ice Skating Championships, Sverdlovsk.

No. 1717 Overprinted in Orange Brown
Победа баскетбольной команды СССР. Чили 1959 г.

1959, Feb. 12

| 2170 | A919 | 1r org brn, dk brn & brn | 3.50 | 1.75 |

Issued to commemorate the "Victory of the U.S.S.R. Basketball Team—Chile 1959." However, the 3rd World Basketball Championship honors went to Brazil when the Soviet team was disqualified for refusing to play Nationalist China.

1959, Mar. 3   *Litho.*   *Perf. 12*

| 2171 | A1135 | 40k turq bl & gray brn, beige | 50 | 30 |

Frederic Joliot-Curie (1900–1958), French scientist.

Selma Lagerlöf A1136   Peter Zvirka A1137

1959, Feb. 26

| 2172 | A1136 | 40k red brn & blk | 45 | 15 |

Issued to commemorate the centenary of the birth of Selma Lagerlöf (1858–1940), Swedish writer.

1959, Mar. 3

| 2173 | A1137 | 40k hn brn & blk, yel | 35 | 15 |

Issued to commemorate the 50th anniversary of the birth of Peter Zvirka (1909–1947), Lithuanian writer.

No. 1861A Overprinted in Red:
"1759   1959"

1959, Feb. 26   *Engraved*

| 2174 | A993 | 40k lt ultra & brn | 6.50 | 6.00 |

Issued to honor the 200th anniversary of the birth of Robert Burns, Scottish poet.

Type of 1958.

Russian Writers: No. 2175, A. S. Griboedov. No. 2176, A. N. Ostrovski. No. 2177, Anton Chekhov. No. 2178, I. A. Krylov. No. 2178A, Nikolai V. Gogol. No. 2178B, S. T. Aksakov. No. 2178C, A. V. Koltzov, poet and reaper.

1959   *Lithographed*

2175	A1071	40k buff, cl, blk & vio	40	25
2176	A1071	40k vio & brn	40	25
2177	A1071	40k sl & hn brn	40	25
2178	A1071	40k ol bis & brn	40	25
2178A	A1071	40k ol, gray & bis	40	25
2178B	A1071	40k brn, vio & bis	40	25
2178C	A1071	40k vio & blk	40	25
		Nos. 2175-2178C (7)	2.80	1.75

No. 2178A commemorates the sesquicentennial of the birth of Nikolai V. Gogol, writer. No. 2178B commemorates the centenary of the death of S. T. Aksakov, writer.

A. S. Popov and Rescue from Ice Float A1138

1959, Mar. 13

| 2179 | A1138 | 40k brn, blk & dk bl | 50 | 20 |
| 2180 | A1138 | 60k multi | 75 | 30 |

Issued to commemorate the centenary of the birth of A. S. Popov, pioneer in radio research.

M.S. Rossija at Odessa A1139

Ships: 10k, Steamer, Vladivostok-Petropavlovsk-Kamchatka line. 20k, M.S. Feliks Dzerzhinski, Odessa-Latakia line. No. 2184, M.S. Murmansk-Tyksi line. 60k, Ship, Murmansk-Tyksi line. 1r, M.S. Mikhail Kalinin at Leningrad. 1r, M.S. Baltika, Leningrad-London line.

1959   *Lithographed.*   *Unwmkd.*

2181	A1139	10k multi	10	5
2182	A1139	20k red, lt grn & dk bl	25	10
2183	A1139	40k multi	30	10
2184	A1139	40k bl, buff & red	30	10
2185	A1139	60k bl grn, red & buff	50	10
2186	A1139	1r ultra, red & yel	75	15
		Nos. 2181-2186 (6)	2.20	60

Issued to honor the Russian fleet.

Globe and Luna 1 A1140

Design: No. 2188, Globe and route of Luna 1.

1959, Apr. 13

| 2187 | A1140 | 40k red brn & rose | 60 | 25 |
| 2188 | A1140 | 40k ultra & bl | 60 | 25 |

Luna 1, launched Jan. 2, 1959.

Saadi and "Gulistan" A1141

1959, Mar. 20   *Photogravure*

| 2189 | A1141 | 40k dk bl & blk | 40 | 35 |

Issued to honor the Persian poet Saadi (Muslih-ud-Din) and to commemorate the 700th anniversary of his book, "Gulistan" (1258).

Suahan S. Orbeliani A1142   Drawing by Korin A1143

1959, Apr. 2

| 2190 | A1142 | 40k dl rose & blk | 35 | 30 |

Suahan S. Orbeliani (1658–1725), Georgian writer.

1959, Apr. 10   *Lithographed*

| 2191 | A1143 | 40k multi | 35 | 35 |

Issued to honor Ogata Korin (1653?–1716), Japanese artist.

Lenin A1144   Marcel Cachin A1146

1959, Apr. 17   *Engraved*

| 2192 | A1144 | 40k sepia | 35 | 30 |

89th anniversary of the birth of Lenin.

1959, Apr. 27   *Photogravure*

| 2194 | A1146 | 40k dk brn | 35 | 30 |

Issued to commemorate Marcel Cachin (1869–1958), French Communist Party leader.

Joseph Haydn A1147   Alexander von Humboldt A1148

1959, May 8

| 2195 | A1147 | 40k dk bl, gray & brn blk | 35 | 15 |

Issued to commemorate the sesquicentennial of the death of Joseph Haydn, Austrian composer.

1959, May 6

| 2196 | A1148 | 40k vio & brn | 40 | 15 |

Issued to commemorate the centenary of the death of Alexander von Humboldt, German naturalist and geographer.

Three Races Carrying Flag of Peace A1149   Mountain Climber A1150

1959, Apr. 30   *Lithographed*

| 2199 | A1149 | 40k multi | 25 | 15 |

10th anniversary of World Peace Movement.

1959, May 15

Designs: No. 2201, Tourists reading map. No. 2202, Canoeing (horiz.). No. 2203, Skiers.

2200	A1150	40k multi	35	10
2201	A1150	40k multi	35	10
2202	A1150	40k multi	35	10
2203	A1150	40k multi	35	10

Issued to publicize sports and travel.

I. E. Repin Statue, Moscow A1151   N. Y. Coliseum and Spasski Tower A1152

Statues: No. 2205, Lenin, Ulyanovsk. 20k, V. V. Mayakovsky, Moscow. 25k, Alexander Pushkin, Leningrad. 60k, Maxim Gorki, Moscow. 1r, Tchaikovsky, Moscow.

1959   *Photogravure*   *Unwmkd.*

2204	A1151	10k ocher & sep	10	10
2205	A1151	10k red & blk	10	10
2206	A1151	20k vio & sep	15	10
2207	A1151	25k grnsh bl & blk	20	10
2208	A1151	60k lt grn & sl	35	15
2209	A1151	1r lt ultra & gray	60	20
		Nos. 2204-2209 (6)	1.50	75

1959, June 25   *Litho.*   *Perf. 12*

2210	A1152	20k multi	25	10
2211	A1152	40k multi	35	15
a.		Souvenir sheet	3.50	1.75

Issued to publicize the Soviet Exhibition of Science, Technology and Culture, New York, June 20–Aug. 10.
No. 2211a contains one imperf. copy of No. 2211. Size: 62x77mm. Issued July 20.

Animal Types of 1957.

Animals: 20k, Hare. No. 2214, Siberian horse. No. 2215, Tiger. No. 2216, Red squirrel. No. 2217, Pine marten. No. 2218, Hazel hen. No. 2219, Mute swan.

1959-60   *Lithographed*   *Perf. 12*

Center in Natural Colors

2213	A1023	20k vio bl ('60)	25	15
2214	A1023	25k bl blk	25	15
2215	A1023	25k brown	25	15
2216	A1023	40k dp grn	35	15
2217	A1023	40k dk grn	35	15
2218	A1024	60k dk grn	40	15
2219	A1023	1r brt bl	50	35
		Nos. 2213-2219 (7)	2.35	1.25

Louis Braille A1153   Musa Djalil A1154

1959, July 16

| 2220 | A1153 | 60k bl grn, bis & brn | 40 | 20 |

Issued to commemorate the 150th anniversary of the birth of Louis Braille, French educator of the blind.

RUSSIA

1959, July 16   Photogravure
2221   A1154   40k vio & blk   30   15
Issued to honor Musa Djalil, Tartar poet.

Sturgeon
A1155
Design: 60k, Chum salmon.

1959, July 16
2222   A1155   40k bl grn & blk   30   10
2223   A1155   60k vio bl & blk   40   15

See also Nos. 2375–2377.

Gymnast
A1156

Athletes Holding Trophy   Globe and Hands
A1157   A1158
Designs: 25k, Runner. 60k, Water polo.

1959, Aug. 7
2224   A1156   15k lil rose & gray   20   5
2225   A1156   25k yel grn & red brn   25   10
2226   A1157   30k brt red & gray   30   10
2227   A1156   60k bl & org yel   40   20

2nd National Spartacist Games.

1959, Aug. 12   Lithographed
2228   A1158   40k yel, bl & red   30   20

Issued to publicize the 2nd International Conference of Public Employees Unions.

Cathedral and Modern Building   Schoolboys in Workshop
A1159   A1160

1959, Aug. 21   Perf. 12   Unwmkd.
2229   A1159   40k bl, ol, yel & red   30   15

Issued to commemorate the 1100th anniversary of the city of Novgorod.

1959, Aug. 27   Photogravure
Design: 1r, Workers in night school.
2230   A1160   40k dk pur   25   10
2231   A1160   1r dk bl   75   20

Issued to stengthen the connection between school and life.

Glacier Survey   Rocket and Observatory
A1161   A1162

Designs: 25k, Oceanographic ship "Vityaz" and map. 40k, Plane over Antarctica, camp and emperor penguin.

1959
2232   A1161   10k bl grn   15   6
2233   A1161   25k brt bl & red   25   10
2234   A1161   40k ultra & red   40   10
2235   A1162   1r ultra & buff   1.10   50

Issued to commemorate the International Geophysical Year. No. 2235 commemorates the first Russian rocket to reach the moon, Sept. 14, 1959.

Workers and Farmers Holding Atom Symbol
A1163

1959, Sept. 23   Lithographed
2236   A1163   40k red org & bis   35   15

All-Union Economic Exhibition, Moscow.

Russian and Chinese Students
A1164
Design: 40k, Russian miner and Chinese steel worker.

1959, Sept. 25   Litho.   Perf. 12
2237   A1164   20k multi   20   10
2238   A1164   40k multi   25   15

Issued to commemorate the 10th anniversary of the People's Republic of China.

Letter Carrier   Makhtumkuli
A1165   A1166

1959, Sept.
2239   A1165   40k dk car rose & blk   25   8
2240   A1165   60k bl & blk   40   12

Issued to publicize International Letter Writing Week, Oct. 4-10.

1959, Sept. 30   Photogravure
2241   A1166   40k brown   35   15

Issued to commemorate the 225th anniversary of the birth of Makhtumkuli, Turkmen writer.

East German Emblem and Workers
A1167

City Hall, East Berlin
A1168

1959, Oct. 6   Lithographed
2242   A1167   40k multi   30   8

Photogravure.
2243   A1168   60k dp cl & buff   50   12

Nos. 2242-43 issued to commemorate the 10th anniversary of the German Democratic Republic.

Steel Production
A1169

Designs (Industries): No. 2244, Chemicals. No. 2245, Spasski Tower, hammer and sickle. No. 2246, Home building. No. 2247, Meat production, woman with farm animals. No. 2248, Machinery. No. 2249, Grain production, woman tractor driver. No. 2250, Oil. No. 2251, Textiles. No. 2252, Steel. No. 2253, Coal. No. 2254, Iron. No. 2255, Electric power.

1959–60   Lithographed.
2244   A1169   10k vio, grnsh bl & mar   10   5
2245   A1169   10k org & dk car   10   5
2246   A1169   15k brn, yel & red   15   6
2247   A1169   15k brn, grn & mar   15   6
2248   A1169   20k bl grn, yel & red   20   8
2249   A1169   20k grn, yel & red   20   8
2250   A1169   30k lil, sal & red   20   7
2251   A1169   30k gldn brn, lil, red & grn ('60)   30   10
2252   A1169   40k vio bl, yel & org   30   10
2253   A1169   40k dk bl, pink & dp rose   30   10
2254   A1169   60k org red, yel, bl & mar   40   12
2255   A1169   60k ultra, buff & red   40   12
Nos. 2244–2255 (12)   2.80   99

Seven-Year Production Plan.

Arms of Tadzhikistan   Path of Luna 3 and Electronics Laboratory
A1170   A1171

1959, Oct. 13
2258   A1170   40k red, emer, ocher & blk   25   15

Tadzhikistan statehood, 30th anniversary.

1959, Oct. 12
2259   A1171   40k violet   75   40

Flight of Luna 3 around the moon, Oct. 4, 1959.

Red Square, Moscow
A1172

1959, Oct. 26   Engraved
2260   A1172   40k dk red   30   15

42nd anniversary of October Revolution.

U. S. Capitol, Globe and Kremlin
A1173

1959, Oct. 27   Photogravure
2261   A1173   60k bl & yel   40   15

Issued to commemorate the visit of Premier Nikita Khrushchev to the United States, September, 1959.

Helicopter—A1174

Designs: 25k, Diver. 40k, Motorcyclist. 60k, Parachutist.

1959, Oct. 28
2262   A1174   10k vio bl & mar   10   10
2263   A1174   25k bl & brn   20   10
2264   A1174   40k red brn & ind   30   15
2265   A1174   60k bl & ol bis   40   15

Issued to honor the voluntary aides of the army.

Moon, Earth and Path of Rocket
A1175

RUSSIA

Design: No. 2267, Kremlin and diagram showing rocket and positions of moon and earth.

1959, Nov. 1 Lithographed
2266 A1175 40k bl, dk bl, red & bis 60 25
2267 A1175 40k gray, pink & red 60 25

Issued to commemorate the landing of the Soviet cosmic rocket on the moon, Sept. 14, 1959.

Sandor Petöfi   Victory Statue and View of Budapest
A1176   A1177
Perf. 12x12½, 12½x12

1959, Nov. 9
2268 A1176 20k gray & ol bis 15 8
2269 A1177 40k multi 25 12

Soviet-Hungarian friendship. See No. 2308.

Manolis Glezos   A. A.
and Acropolis   Voskresensky
A1178   A1179

1959, Nov. 12 Photo. Perf. 12x12½
2270 A1178 40k ultra & brn 7.50 8.00

Issued to honor Manolis Glezos, Greek communist.

1959, Dec. 7 Perf. 12½x12
2271 A1179 40k ultra & brn 30 15

Issued to commemorate the 150th anniversary of the birth of A. A. Voskresensky, chemist.

Chusovaya River, Ural
A1180

Designs: No. 2273, Lake Ritza, Caucasus. No. 2274, Lena River, Siberia. No. 2275, Seashore, Far East. No. 2276, Lake Iskander, Central Asia. No. 2277, Lake Baikal, Siberia. No. 2278, Belucha Mountain, Altai range. No. 2279, Gursuf region, Crimea. No. 2280, Crimea.

1959, Dec. Engraved Perf. 12½
2272 A1180 10k purple 10 5
2273 A1180 10k rose car 10 5
2274 A1180 25k dk bl 20 10
2275 A1180 25k olive 20 10
2276 A1180 25k dk red 20 10
2277 A1180 40k claret 30 10
2278 A1180 60k Prus bl 50 15
2279 A1180 1r ol grn 60 30
2280 A1180 1r dp org 60 30
Nos. 2272-2280 (9) 2.80 1.25

"Trumpeters of 1st   Farm
Cavalry" by M. Grekov Woman
A1181   A1182

1959, Dec. 30 Litho. Perf. 12½x12
2283 A1181 40k multi 50 40

40th anniversary of the 1st Cavalry.

1958-60 Engraved Perf. 12½
Designs: 25k, Architect. 60k, Steel worker.
2286 A1182 20k sl grn ('59) 2.50 1.00
2287 A1182 25k sep ('59) 2.50 1.50
2288 A1182 60k carmine 25.00 7.50

Lithographed
Perf. 12x12½
2290 A1182 20k grn ('60) 25 15
2291 A1182 25k sep ('60) 30 15
2292 A1182 60k ver ('59) 75 30
2293 A1182 60k bl ('60) 40 30

M. V. Frunze   G. N. Gabrichevski
A1183   A1184

1960, Jan. 25 Photo. Perf. 12½
2295 A1183 40k dk red brn 35 15

Issued to commemorate the 75th anniversary of the birth of Mikhail V. Frunze (1885-1925), revolutionary leader.

Perf. 12½x12
1960, Jan. 30 Unwmkd.
2296 A1184 40k brt vio & brn 35 15

Issued to commemorate the centenary of the birth of G. N. Gabrichevski, microbiologist.

Anton Chekhov and Moscow Home
A1185

Design: 40k, Chekhov in later years, and Yalta home.

1960, Jan. 20 Litho. Perf. 12x12½
2297 A1185 20k red, gray & vio bl 15 10
2298 A1185 40k dk bl, buff & brn 35 15

Birth centenary of Anton P. Chekhov (1860-1904), playwright.

Vera Komis-   Ice Hockey
sarzhevskaya   A1187
A1186

1960, Feb. 5 Photo. Perf. 12½x12
2299 A1186 40k chocolate 30 15

Issued to honor Vera Komissarzhevskaya (1864-1910), actress.

1960, Feb. 18 Litho. Perf. 11½
Sports: 25k, Speed skating. 40k, Skier. 60k, Woman figure skater. 1r, Ski jumper.
2300 A1187 10k ocher & vio bl 15 10
2301 A1187 25k multi 25 10
2302 A1187 40k org, rose lil & vio bl 35 15
2303 A1187 60k vio, grn & buff 50 20
2304 A1187 1r bl, grn & brn 75 30
Nos. 2300-2304 (5) 2.00 85

Issued to commemorate the 8th Olympic Winter Games, Squaw Valley, Calif., Feb. 18-29.

Sword-into-Plowshare Statue,
United Nations, N. Y.
A1188

1960 Perf. 12½x12
2305 A1188 40k grnsh bl, yel & brn 50 20
a. Souvenir sheet 1.25 75

No. 2305a issued to commemorate Premier Nikita Khrushchev's visit to the 15th General Assembly of the U.N. in New York City. No. 2305a contains one stamp with simulated perforation. Blue, yellow and brown background shows Kremlin, olive branch and quotation by Khrushchev. Size: 78x115mm.

Women of Various Races
A1189

1960, Mar. 8
2306 A1189 40k multi 30 20

Issued to commemorate 50 years of International Woman's Day, March 8.

Planes in Combat and
Timur Frunze
A1190

1960, Feb. 23 Perf. 12½x12
2307 A1190 40k multi 30 20

Issued to honor Lieutenant Timur Frunze, World War II hero.

No. 2269 Overprinted in Red

15 лет освобождения Венгрии

1960, Apr. 4
2308 A1177 40k vio, bl, yel & brn 2.00 1.75

15th anniversary of Hungary's liberation from the Nazis.

Lunik 3 Photographing Far
Side of Moon—A1191

1960 Photogravure Perf. 12x12½
Design: 60k, Far side of the moon.
2309 A1191 40k pale bl, dk bl & yel 75 30

Lithographed
2310 A1191 60k lt bl, dk bl & cit 75 30

Issued to commemorate the photographing of the far side of the moon, Oct. 7, 1959.

Lenin as Child—A1192

Various Lenin Portraits and: 20k, Lenin with children and Christmas tree. 30k, Flag, workers and ship. 40k, Kremlin, banners and marchers. 60k, Map of Russia, buildings and ship. 1r, Peace proclamation and globe.

1960, Apr. 10 Litho. Perf. 12½x12
2311 A1192 10k multi 8 6
2312 A1192 20k red, grn & blk 15 6
2313 A1192 30k multi 25 8
2314 A1192 40k multi 30 10
2315 A1192 60k multi 50 30
2316 A1192 1r red, vio bl & brn 80 30
Nos. 2311-2316 (6) 2.08 90

90th anniversary of the birth of Lenin.

Steelworker   Government
A1193   House, Baku
                A1194

1960, Apr. 30 Photogravure
2317 A1193 40k brn & red 30 20

Issued to publicize the industrial overproduction by 50,000,000r during the first year of the 7-year plan.

1960, Apr. Litho. Perf. 12x12½
2318 A1194 40k bis & brn 45 45

Issued to commemorate the 40th anniversary of Azerbaijan. See also No. 2898.

Brotherhood Monument, Prague
A1195

RUSSIA

1960, Apr. 29 Photo. Perf. 12½x12
Design: 60k, Charles Bridge, Prague.
| 2319 | A1195 | 40k brt bl & blk | 30 | 10 |
| 2320 | A1195 | 60k blk brn & yel | 45 | 15 |

Issued to commemorate the 15th anniversary of the Czechoslovak Republic.

Radio Tower and Popov Central Museum of Communications, Leningrad—A1196

1960, May 6   **Lithographed**
| 2321 | A1196 | 40k bl, ocher & brn | 35 | 20 |

Issued for Radio Day.

Gen. I. D. Tcherniakovski and Soldiers—A1197

1960, May 4
| 2322 | A1197 | 1r multi | 85 | 20 |

Issued to honor Gen. I. D. Tcherniakovski, World War II hero and his military school.

Robert Schumann A1198   Jacob M. Sverdlov A1199

1960, May 20 Photo. Perf. 12½x12
| 2323 | A1198 | 40k ultra & blk | 30 | 20 |

Issued to commemorate the 150th anniversary of the birth of Robert Schumann, German composer.

1960, May 24   **Perf. 12½x12**
| 2324 | A1199 | 40k dk brn & org brn | 30 | 20 |

Issued to commemorate the 75th anniversary of the birth of J. M. Sverdlov (1885–1919), first President of the U.S.S.R.

Stamp of 1957 Under Magnifying Glass A1200

1960, May 28 Litho. Perf. 11½
| 2325 | A1200 | 60k grnsh bl & bis brn | 60 | 30 |

Issued for Stamp Day.

Karl Marx Project, Petrozavodsk, Karelian Autonomous Republic
A1201

Capitals, Soviet Autonomous Republics: No. 2327, Lenin street, Batum, Adzhar. No. 2328, Cultural Palace, Izhevsk, Udmurt. No. 2329, August street, Grozny, Chechen-Ingush. No. 2330, Soviet House, Cheboksary, Chuvash. No. 2331, Bulnak Street, Makhachkala, Dagestan. No. 2332, Soviet street, Ioshkar Ola, Mari. No. 2333, Chkalov street, Dzaudzhikau, North Ossetia. No. 2334, October street, Yakutsk, Yakut. No. 2335, House of Ministers, Nukus, Kara-Kalpak.

1960   **Engraved**   **Perf. 12½**
2326	A1201	40k Prus grn	45	20
2327	A1201	40k vio bl	45	20
2328	A1201	40k green	45	20
2329	A1201	40k maroon	45	20
2330	A1201	40k dl red	45	20
2331	A1201	40k carmine	45	20
2332	A1201	40k dk brn	45	20
2333	A1201	40k org brn	45	20
2334	A1201	40k dk bl	45	20
2335	A1201	40k brown	45	20
		Nos. 2326-2335 (10)	4.50	2.00

See Nos. 2338-2344C.

No. 2326 Overprinted in Red   40 лет КАССР 8.VI.1960

1960, June 4
| 2336 | A1201 | 40k Prus grn | 3.50 | 1.50 |

Issued to commemorate the 40th anniversary of the Karelian Autonomous Republic.

No. 2328 Overprinted in Red   40 лет Удмуртской АССР 4/XI 1960.

1960, Nov. 4
| 2337 | A1201 | 40k green | 3.50 | 1.50 |

Issued to commemorate the 40th anniversary of the Udmurt Autonomous Republic.

1961-62   **Perf. 12½, 12½x12**

Capitals, Soviet Autonomous Republics: No. 2338, Rustaveli Street, Sukhumi, Abkhazia. No. 2339, House of Soviets, Nalchik, Kabardino-Balkar. No. 2340, Lenin Street, Ulan-Ude, Buriat. No. 2341, Soviet Street, Syktyvkar, Komi. No. 2342, Lenin Street, Nakhichevan, Nakhichevan. No. 2343, Elista, Kalmyk. No. 2344, Ufa, Bashkir. No. 2344A, Lobachevsky Square, Kazan, Tartar. No. 2344B, Kizil, Tuvinia. No. 2344C, Saransk, Mordovia.

2338	A1201	4k org ver	35	20
2339	A1201	4k dk vio	35	20
2340	A1201	4k dk bl	35	20
2341	A1201	4k gray	35	20
2342	A1201	4k dk car rose	35	20
2343	A1201	4k ol grn	35	20
2344	A1201	4k dl pur	35	20
2344A	A1201	4k grnsh blk ('62)	35	20
2344B	A1201	4k cl ('62)	35	20
2344C	A1201	4k dp grn ('62)	35	20
		Nos. 2338-2344C (10)	3.50	2.00

Denominations of Nos. 2338-2344C are in the revalued currency.

Children's Friendship A1202

Drawings by Children: 20k, Collective farm (vert.). 25k, Winter joys. 40k, "In the Zoo."

Perf. 12x12½, 12½x12
1960, June 1   **Lithographed**
2345	A1202	10k multi	10	10
2346	A1202	20k multi	15	10
2347	A1202	25k multi	20	10
2348	A1202	40k multi	25	15

Lomonosov University and Congress Emblem
A1203

1960, June 17 Photo. Perf. 12½x12
| 2349 | A1203 | 60k yel & dk brn | 40 | 30 |

Issued to commemorate the first congress of the International Federation for Automation Control, Moscow.

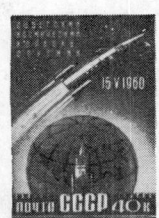

Sputnik 4 and Globe
A1204

1960, June 17   **Perf. 12x12½**
| 2350 | A1204 | 40k vio bl & dp org | 85 | 50 |

Launching on May 15, 1960, of Sputnik 4, which orbited the earth with a dummy cosmonaut.

Kosta Hetagurov
A1205

1960, June 20 Litho. Perf. 12½
| 2351 | A1205 | 40k gray bl & brn | 35 | 35 |

Kosta Hetagurov (1859–1906), Ossetian poet.

Flag and Tallinn
A1206

Designs: No. 2353, Flag and Riga. No. 2354, Flag and Vilnius.

Perf. 12x12½, 12½ (※1253)
1960   **Photogravure**
2352	A1206	40k red & ultra	30	15
		Typographed		
2353	A1206	40k bl, gray & red	30	15
		Lithographed		
2354	A1206	40k bl, red & grn	30	15

Issued to commemorate the 20th anniversary of the Soviet Republics of: No. 2352, Estonia. No. 2353, Latvia. No. 2354, Lithuania.

Cement Factory, Belgorod
A1207

Design: 40k, Factory, Novy Krivoi.

1960, June 28   **Perf. 12½x12**
| 2355 | A1207 | 25k ultra & blk | 20 | 8 |
| 2356 | A1207 | 40k rose brn & blk | 25 | 12 |

Issued to show "New buildings of the first year of the seven-year plan."

Automatic Production Line and Roller Bearing
A1208

Design: No. 2358, Automatic production line and gear.

1960, June 13   **Perf. 11½**
| 2357 | A1208 | 40k rose vio | 25 | 10 |
| 2358 | A1208 | 40k Prus grn | 25 | 10 |

Issued to publicize mechanization and automation of factories.

Running
A1209

Sports: 10k, Wrestling. 15k, Basketball. 20k, Weight lifting. 25k, Boxing. No. 2364, Fencing. No. 2365, Diving. No. 2366, Women's gymnastics. 60k, Canoeing. 1r, Steeplechase.

1960, Aug. 1   **Litho.**   **Perf. 11½**
2359	A1209	5k multi	10	10
2360	A1209	10k brn, bl & yel	10	10
2361	A1209	15k multi	15	10
2362	A1209	20k blk, crim & sal	20	10
2363	A1209	25k lake, sl & rose	25	10
2364	A1209	40k vio bl, bl & bis	25	15
2365	A1209	40k vio, gray & pink	25	15
2366	A1209	40k multi	25	15
2367	A1209	60k multi	50	20
2368	A1209	1r brn, lil & pale grn	1.00	30
		Nos. 2359-2368 (10)	3.05	1.45

Issued to commemorate the 17th Olympic Games, Rome, Aug. 25–Sept. 11.

No. 2365 Overprinted in Red   Международная ярмарка в Риччоне

1960, Aug. 23
| 2369 | A1209 | 40k vio, gray & pink | 3.50 | 3.50 |

12th San Marino-Riccione Stamp Fair.

RUSSIA

Kishinev, Moldavian Republic
A1210

1960, Aug. 2		Perf. 12x12½		
2370	A1210	40k multi	35	20

20th anniversary of Moldavian Republic.

Tractor and Factory
A1211

Book Museum, Hanoi—A1212

Perf. 12x12½, 12½x12
1960, Aug. 25

| 2371 | A1211 | 40k grn, ocher & blk | 25 | 15 |
| 2372 | A1212 | 60k lil & brn | 40 | 15 |

15th anniversary of North Viet Nam.

G. N. Minkh
A1213

1960, Aug. 25 Photo. Perf. 12½x12
2373 A1213 60k bis brn & dk brn   50   15

Issued to commemorate the 125th anniversary of the birth of Gregory N. Minkh, microbiologist.

"March," by I. I. Levitan
A1214

1960, Sept. 3
2374 A1214 40k ol bis & blk   60   15

Issued to commemorate the centenary of the birth of I. I. Levitan, painter.

Fish Type of 1959
Perf. 12½
Designs: 20k, Pikeperch. 25k, Fur seals. 40k, Ludogan whitefish.

2375	A1155	20k bl & blk	15	10
2376	A1155	25k vio gray & red brn	20	10
2377	A1155	40k rose lil & pur	25	15

Forest by I. I. Shishkin—A1215

1960, Aug. 29   Engraved
2378 A1215 1r red brn   1.10   30

Issued to commemorate the 5th World Forestry Congress, Seattle, Wash., Aug. 29–Sept. 10.

Globe with USSR and Letter
A1216

1960, Sept. 10 Litho. Perf. 12x12½
| 2379 | A1216 | 40k multi | 20 | 10 |
| 2380 | A1216 | 60k multi | 40 | 15 |

Issued for International Letter Writing Week, Oct. 3–9.

Farmer, Worker, Scientist
A1217

1960, Oct. 4   Typo.   Perf. 12½
2381 A1217 40k multi   30   15

Issued to commemorate the 40th anniversary of the Kazakh Soviet Socialist Republic.

Globes and Olive Branch
A1218

1960, Sept. 29 Litho. Perf. 12½x12
2382 A1218 60k pale vio, bl & gray   40   15

Issued to commemorate the 15th anniversary of the World Federation of Trade Unions.

Kremlin, Sputnik 5 and Dogs
Belka and Strelka—A1219

1960, Sept. 29   Photogravure
| 2383 | A1219 | 40k brt pur & yel | 75 | 20 |
| 2384 | A1219 | 1r bl & sal | 1.25 | 40 |

Flight of Sputnik 5, Aug. 19–20, 1960.

Passenger Ship "Karl Marx"
A1220

Ships: 40k, Turbo-electric ship "Lenin." 60k, Speedboat "Raketa" (Rocket).

1960, Oct. 24 Litho. Perf. 12x12½
2385	A1220	25k bl, blk, red & yel	20	10
2386	A1220	40k bl, blk & red	30	15
2387	A1220	60k bl, blk & rose	40	20

A. N. Voronikhin and
Kasansky Cathedral, Leningrad
A1221

1960, Oct. 24   Photogravure
2388 A1221 40k gray & brn blk   30   15

Issued to commemorate the 200th anniversary of the birth of A. N. Voronikhin, architect.

J. S. Gogebashvili
A1222

1960, Oct. 29
2389 A1222 40k dk gray & mag   35   15

Issued to commemorate the 120th anniversary of the birth of J. S. Gogebashvili, Georgian teacher and publicist.

Red Flag, Electric Power Station
and Factory—A1223

1960, Oct. 29   Lithographed
2390 A1223 40k red, yel & brn   40   15

43rd anniversary of October Revolution.

Leo Tolstoy—A1224

Designs: 40k, Tolstoy in Yasnaya Polyana. 60k, Portrait (vert.).

Perf. 12x12½, 12½x12
1960, Nov. 14
2391	A1224	20k vio & brn	15	10
2392	A1224	40k bl & lt brn	25	10
2393	A1224	60k dp cl & sep	50	15

Issued to commemorate the 50th anniversary of the death of Count Leo Tolstoy, writer.

Yerevan, Armenian Republic
A1225

1960, Nov. 14   Perf. 12x12½
2394 A1225 40k bl, red, buff & brn   30   15

Issued to commemorate the 40th anniversary of the Armenian Soviet Republic.

Friedrich Engels   Badge of Youth
A1226   Federation
                     A1227

1960, Nov. 25 Engraved Perf. 12½
2395 A1226 60k slate   50   50

Issued to commemorate the 140th anniversary of the birth of Friedrich Engels.

1960, Nov. 2   Lithographed
2396 A1227 60k brt pink, blk & yel   50   25

Issued to commemorate the 15th anniversary of the International Youth Federation.

40-ton Truck MAL-530
A1228

Designs: 40k, "Volga" car. 60k, "Moskvitch 407" car. 1r, "Tourist LAS-697" Bus.

1960, Oct. 29 Photo. Perf. 12x12½
2397	A1228	25k ultra & gray	20	10
2398	A1228	40k ol bis & ultra	25	10
2399	A1228	60k Prus grn & dp car	35	15

Lithographed
2400 A1228 1r multi   75   30
Automotive industry.

N. I. Pirogov   Friendship
A1229   University and
                   Students
                   A1230

1960, Dec. 13 Photo. Perf. 12½x12
2401 A1229 40k grn & brn blk   35   20

Issued to commemorate the 125th anniversary of the birth of N. I. Pirogov, surgeon.

RUSSIA

1960, Nov.   Perf. 12x12½
2402   A1230   40k brn car   35   20

Issued to publicize the completion of Friendship of Nations University in Moscow. See No. 2462.

Mark Twain
A1231

1960, Nov. 30   Perf. 12½x12
2403   A1231   40k dp org & brn   60   60

Issued to commemorate the 125th anniversary of the birth of Mark Twain.

Dove and Globe   Akaki Zeretely
A1232   A1233

1960, Oct. 29   Photogravure
2404   A1232   60k mar & gray   50   35

Issued to commemorate the 15th anniversary of the International Democratic Women's Federation.

1960, Dec. 27
2405   A1233   40k vio & blk brn   50   35

Issued to commemorate the 120th anniversary of the birth of Akaki Zeretely, Georgian poet.

Frederic Chopin,
after Delacroix—A1234

1960, Dec. 24   Perf. 12x11½
2406   A1234   40k bis & brn   40   20

Issued to commemorate the 150th anniversary of the birth of Frederic Chopin, Polish composer.

North Korean   Crocus
Flag and   A1236
Flying Horse
A1235

1960, Dec. 24 Litho.   Perf. 12½x12
2407   A1235   40k multi   35   15

Issued to commemorate the 15th anniversary of "the liberation of the Korean people by the Soviet army."

1960   Perf. 12x12½
Asiatic Flowers: No. 2409, Tulip. No. 2410, Trollius. No. 2411, Tulip. No. 2412, Ginseng. No. 2413, Iris. No. 2414, Hypericum. 1r, Dog rose.
Flowers in Natural Colors
2408   A1236   20k grn & vio   15   5
2409   A1236   20k vio bl & blk   15   5
2410   A1236   25k gray   20   5
2411   A1236   40k ol bis & blk   25   10
2412   A1236   40k grn & blk, wmkd.   25   10
2413   A1236   60k yel, grn & red   30   15
2414   A1236   60k bluish grn & blk   30   15
2415   A1236   1r sl grn & blk   60   20
Nos. 2408-2415 (8)   2.20   85

The watermark on No. 2412 consists of vertical rows of chevrons.

Lithuanian Costumes
A1237

Regional Costumes: 60k, Uzbek.
Perf. 12½ (10k), 11½ (60k)
1960, Dec. 24   Typo.   Unwmkd.
2416   A1237   10k multi   15   10
Lithographed.
2417   A1237   60k multi   60   20

Currency Revalued.
1961-62   Litho.   Perf. 11½
Regional Costumes: No. 2418, Moldavia. No. 2419, Georgia. No. 2420, Ukrainia. No. 2421, White Russia. No. 2422, Kazakhstan. No. 2422A, Latvia. 4k, Koryak. 6k, Russia. 10k, Armenia. 12k, Estonia.
2418   A1237   2k buff, brn & ver   20   15
2419   A1237   2k red, brn, ocher & blk   20   15
2420   A1237   3k ultra, buff, red & brn   25   20
2421   A1237   3k red org, ocher & blk   25   20
2422   A1237   3k buff, brn, grn & red   25   20
2422A   A1237   3k org red, gray ol & blk ('62)   25   20
2423   A1237   4k multi   50   20
2424   A1237   6k multi   65   30
2425   A1237   10k brn, ol bis & ver   1.00   40
2426   A1237   12k red, ultra & blk   1.25   50
Nos. 2418-2426 (10)   4.80   2.50

See also Nos. 2723-2726.

Lenin and Map
Showing Electrification
A1238

1961   Perf. 12½x12
2427   A1238   4k bl, buff & brn   25   25

2428   A1238   10k red org & bl blk   50   50

Issued to publicize the 40th anniversary (in 1960) of the State Electrification Plan.

Animal Types of 1957
1961, Jan. 7   Perf. 12½
Animals: 1k, Brown bear. 6k, Beaver. 10k, Roe deer.
Centers in Natural Colors
2429   A1024   1k dk brn   20   20
2430   A1023   6k black   60   50
2431   A1023   10k black   85   75

Georgian Flag and Views
A1239

1961, Feb. 15   Perf. 12½x12
2432   A1239   4k multi   25   25

Issued to commemorate the 40th anniversary of the Georgian Autonomous Republic.

Nikolai D.   N. A.
Zelinski   Dobrolyubov
A1240   A1241

1961, Feb. 6 Photo.   Perf. 12x12½
2433   A1240   4k rose vio   20   25

Issued to commemorate the centenary of the birth of N. D. Zelinski, chemist.

1961, Feb. 5   Perf. 11½x12
2434   A1241   4k brt bl & brn   25   25

Issued to commemorate the 125th anniversary of the birth of Nikolai A. Dobrolyubov, journalist and critic.

Mechanization of   "Labor"
Grain Harvest   Holding
A1242   Peace Flag
   A1243

Designs: 3k, Cattle. 4k, Tractor in cornfield. 10k, Women picking apples.

1961   Perf. 12x12½, 12x11½
2435   A1242   3k bl & mag   20   10
2436   A1242   4k grn & dk gray   25   10
2437   A1242   6k vio bl & brn   35   15
2438   A1242   10k mar & ol grn   50   25

Agricultural development.
Perf. 12x12½; 12x11½ (Nos. 2439A, 2442 & 12½)
1961-65   Unwmkd.
Designs: 2k, Harvester and silo. 3k, Space rockets. 4k, Arms and flag of U.S.S.R. 6k, Spasski tower. 10k, Workers' monument. 12k, Minin and Pozharsky Monument and Spasski tower. 16k, Plane over power station and dam.
Engraved
2439   A1243   1k ol bis   1.25   1.25
Lithographed
2439A   A1243   1k ol bis   50   20

2440   A1243   2k green   20   20
2441   A1243   3k dk vio   1.75   20
Engraved
2442   A1243   3k dk vio   3.00   1.50
Lithographed
2443   A1243   4k red   60   20
2443A   A1243   4k org brn ('65)   75   50
2444   A1243   6k vermilion   5.00   1.00
2445   A1243   6k dk car rose   1.50   20
2446   A1243   10k orange   2.50   25
Photogravure
2447   A1243   12k brt mag   2.50   35
Lithographed
2448   A1243   16k ultra   4.00   1.75
Nos. 2439-2448 (12)   23.55   6.65

V. P.
Miroshnitchenko
A1244

1961, Feb. 23 Photo.   Perf. 12½x12
2449   A1244   4k vio brn & sl   30   30

Issued to honor a soldier hero of World War II. See also Nos. 2570-2571.

Taras G.
Shevchenko
and
Birthplace
A1245

Shevchenko   Andrei Rubljov
Statue, Kharkov   A1247
A1246

Design: 6k, Book, torch and Shevchenko with beard.

Lithographed; Photogravure (4k)
1961, Mar.   Perf. 12½, 11½x12
2450   A1245   3k brn & vio   50   25
2451   A1246   4k red org & gray   1.00   15
2452   A1245   6k blk, grn & red brn   1.50   40

Issued to commemorate the centenary of the death of Taras G. Shevchenko, Ukrainian poet.
No. 2452 was printed with alternating green and black label, containing a quotation.
See No. 2852.

1961, Mar. 13 Litho.   Perf. 12½x12
2453   A1247   4k ultra, bis & brn   25   15

Issued to commemorate the 600th anniversary of the birth of Andrei Rubljov, painter.

 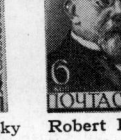

N. V. Sklifosovsky   Robert Koch
A1248   A1249

RUSSIA

1961, Mar. 26 Photo. *Perf. 11½x12*

2454 A1248 4k ultra & blk 30 20

Issued to commemorate the 125th anniversary of the birth of N. V. Sklifosovsky, surgeon.

1961, March 26

2455 A1249 6k dk brn 30 20

Issued to commemorate the 50th anniversary of the death of Robert Koch, German microbiologist.

Globe and Sputnik 8
A1250
Design: 10k, Space probe and its path to Venus.

1961, Apr. *Litho.* *Perf. 11½*

2456 A1250 6k dk & lt bl & org 75 40

Photogravure

2457 A1250 10k vio bl & yel 1.00 60

Issued to commemorate the launching of the Venus space probe, Feb. 12, 1961.

Open Book and Globe
A1251

1961, Apr. 7 *Litho.* *Perf. 12½x12*

2458 A1251 6k ultra & sep 60 20

Issued to commemorate the centenary of the children's magazine "Around the World."

Musician, Dancers and Singers
A1252

1961, Apr. 7 *Unwmkd.*

2459 A1252 4k yel, red & blk 20 20

Issued to commemorate the 50th anniversary of the Russian National Choir.

African Breaking Chains and Map—A1253
Design: 6k, Globe, torch and black and white handshake.

1961, Apr. 15 *Perf. 12½*

2460 A1253 4k multi 20 10
2461 A1253 6k bl, pur & org 30 10

Issued for Africa Day and to commemorate the 3rd Conference of Independent African States, Cairo, March 25–31.

No. 2402
Surcharged
in Red

4 КОП. имени Патриса Лумумбы 1961 г.

1961, Apr. 15 Photo. *Perf. 12x12½*

2462 A1230 4k on 40k brn car 60 35

Issued to publicize the naming of Friendship University, Moscow, in memory of Patrice Lumumba, Premier of Congo.

Maj. Yuri A. Gagarin
A1254

Designs: 6k, Kremlin, rockets and radar equipment. 10k, Rocket, Gagarin with helmet and Kremlin.

1961, Apr. *Perf. 11½ (3k), 12½x12*

2463 A1254 3k Prus bl 30 20

Lithographed

2464 A1254 6k bl, vio & red 50 30
2465 A1254 10k red, bl grn & brn 1.00 50

Issued to commemorate the first man in space, Yuri A. Gagarin, Apr. 12, 1961. No. 2464 printed with alternating light blue label with hammer and sickle emblem and quotation by Khrushchev in red. Nos. 2463–2465 exist imperf. Price $1.75.

Lenin   Rabindranath Tagore
A1255   A1256

1961, Apr. 22 *Litho.* *Perf. 12x12½*

2466 A1255 4k dp car, sal & blk 25 20

91st anniversary of Lenin's birth.

1961, May 8 *Engr.* *Perf. 11½x12*

2467 A1256 6k bis, mar & blk 30 25

Issued to commemorate the birth centenary of Rabindranath Tagore, Indian poet.

The Hunchbacked Horse
A1257

Fairy Tales: 1k, The Geese and the Swans. 3k, Fox, Hare and Cock. 6k, The Peasant and the Bear. 10k, Ruslan and Ludmilla.

1961 *Lithographed* *Perf. 12½*

2468 A1257 1k multi 15 15
2469 A1257 3k multi 40 30
2470 A1257 4k multi 20 25
2471 A1257 6k multi 45 40
2472 A1257 10k multi 60 50
Nos. 2468-2472 (5) 1.80 1.60

"Man Conquering Space"
A1258
Design: 6k, Giuseppe Garibaldi.

1961, May 24 *Photogravure*

2481 A1258 4k org brn 25 15
2482 A1258 6k lil & sal 50 25

International Labor Exposition, Turin.

Lenin   Patrice Lumumba
A1259   A1260

Various Portraits of Lenin
1961 *Photo.* *Perf. 12½x12*

Olive Bistre Frame

2483 A1259 20k dk grn 1.25 1.25
2484 A1259 30k dk bl 2.50 2.50
2485 A1259 50k rose red 3.75 3.75

1961, May 29 *Lithographed*

2486 A1260 2k yel & brn 15 15
Patrice Lumumba (1925–1961), premier of Congo.

Kindergarten
A1261

Designs: 3k, Young Pioneers in camp. 4k, Young Pioneers (vert.).

Perf. 12½x12, 12x12½

1961, May 31 *Photogravure*

2487 A1261 2k org & ultra 12 10
2488 A1261 3k ol bis & pur 18 15
2489 A1261 4k red & gray 25 15

Issued for Children's Day, 1961.

Dog Zvezdochka and Sputnik 10
A1263
Design: 4k, Dog Chernushka and Sputnik 9 (vert.).

1961, June 8 Litho. *Perf. 12½, 11½*

2491 A1263 2k vio, Prus bl & blk 25 20

Photogravure

2492 A1263 4k Prus bl & brt grn 30 30

Sputniks 9 and 10.

Vissarion G. Belinski
A1265

Lt. Gen. D. M. Karbishev
A1266

Engraved and Photogravure

1961, June 13 *Perf. 11½x12*

2493 A1265 4k car & blk 25 20

Issued to commemorate the 150th anniversary of the birth of Vissarion G. Belinski, author and critic.

1961, June 22 *Litho.* *Perf. 12½*

2494 A1266 4k blk, red & ver 15 10

Issued to honor Lt. Gen. D. M. Karbishev, who was tortured to death in the Nazi prison camp at Mauthausen, Austria.

Hydro-meteorological Map and Instruments
A1267

Gliders
A1268

1961, June 21 *Perf. 12x12½*

2495 A1267 6k ultra & grn 30 20

Issued to commemorate the 40th anniversary of hydro-meteorological service in Russia.

1961, July 5 *Photo.* *Perf. 12½*

Designs: 6k, Motorboat race. 10k, Motorcycle race.

2497 A1268 4k dk sl grn & crim 25 10

Lithographed

2498 A1268 6k sl & ver 30 15
2499 A1268 10k sl & ver 50 30

USSR Technical Sports Spartakiad.

Javelin Thrower—A1269

1961, Aug. 8 Photo. *Perf. 12½x12*

2500 A1269 6k dp car & pink 30 20

7th Trade Union Spartacist Games.

S. I. Vavilov   Vazha Pshavela
A1270   A1271

RUSSIA

1961, July 25

| 2501 | A1270 | 4k lt grn & sep | 20 | 20 |

Issued to honor S. I. Vavilov, president of Academy of Science.

1961   Photo.   Perf. 11½x12

| 2502 | A1271 | 4k dk brn & cr | 20 | 20 |

Issued to commemorate the centenary of the birth of Vazha Pshavela, Georgian poet.

Scientists at Control Panel for Rocket—A1272

Globe and Youth Activities
A1273

Design: 2k, Men pushing tank into river.

1961   Perf. 11½   Unwmkd.

2503	A1273	2k org & sep	15	8
2504	A1272	4k lil & dk grn	35	15
2505	A1273	6k ultra & cit	50	17

International Youth Forum, Moscow.

Arms of Mongolian Republic and Sukhe Bator Statue—A1274

1961, July 25   Litho.   Perf. 12½x12

| 2506 | A1274 | 4k multi | 20 | 20 |

Issued to commemorate the 40th anniversary of the Mongol national revolution.

Knight Kalevipoeg   Symbols of Biochemistry
A1275   A1276

1961, July 31

| 2507 | A1275 | 4k blk, bl & yel | 20 | 20 |

Issued to commemorate the centenary of the first publication of "Kalevipoeg," Estonian national saga, recorded by R. K. Kreutzwald, Estonian writer.

1961, July 31

| 2508 | A1276 | 6k multi | 30 | 20 |

Issued to publicize the 5th International Biochemistry Congress, Moscow.

Major Titov and Vostok 2
A1277

Design: 4k, Globe with orbit and cosmonaut.

1961, Aug.   Photo.   Perf. 11½

| 2509 | A1277 | 4k vio bl & dp plum | 35 | 20 |
| 2510 | A1277 | 6k brn, grn & org | 50 | 30 |

Issued to commemorate the first manned space flight around the world, Maj. Gherman S. Titov, Aug. 6–7, 1961. Nos. 2509-2510 exist imperf. Price, set $3.

A. D. Zacharov and Admiralty Building, Leningrad
A1278

1961, Aug. 8   Perf. 12x11½

| 2511 | A1278 | 4k bl, dk brn & buff | 15 | 15 |

Issued to commemorate the 200th anniversary of the birth of A. D. Zacharov (1761–1811), architect.

Defense of Brest, 1941
A1279

Designs: No. 2512, Defense of Moscow. No. 2514, Defense of Odessa. No. 2514A, Defense of Sevastopol. No. 2514B, Defense of Leningrad. No. 2514C, Defense of Kiev. No. 2514D, Battle of the Volga (Stalingrad).

1961–63   Photo.   Perf. 12½x12

| 2512 | A1279 | 4k blk & red brn (*Moscow*) | 45 | 25 |

Lithographed

2513	A1279	4k multi (*Brest*)	45	25
2514	A1279	4k multi (*Odessa*)	45	25
2514A	A1279	4k multi, (*Sevastopol*; '62)	45	25
2514B	A1279	4k brn, dl bl & bis (*Leningrad*; '63)	45	25
2514C	A1279	4k blk & multi (*Kiev*; '63)	45	25
2514D	A1279	4k dl org & multi (*Volga*; '63)	45	25
		Nos. 2512-2514D (7)	3.15	1.75

Issued to commemorate the "War of Liberation," 1941–45. See also Nos. 2757-2758.

Students' Union Emblem
A1280

1961, Aug. 8   Litho.   Perf. 12½

| 2515 | A1280 | 6k ultra & red | 20 | 20 |

Issued to commemorate the 15th anniversary of the founding of the International Students' Union.

Soviet Stamps—A1281
Stamps and Background Different on each Denomination.

1961, Aug.   Perf. 12½x12

2516	A1281	2k multi	20	20
2517	A1281	4k multi	30	30
2518	A1281	6k multi	40	40
2519	A1281	10k multi	60	50

40 years of Soviet postage stamps.

Nikolai A. Schors Statue, Kiev
A1282

Statue: 4k, Gregori I. Kotovski, Kishinev.

1961   Photogravure   Perf. 11½x12

| 2520 | A1282 | 2k lt ultra & sep | 18 | 15 |
| 2521 | A1282 | 4k rose vio & sep | 18 | 15 |

Letters and Means of Transportation
A1283

1961, Sept. 15   Perf. 11½

| 2522 | A1283 | 4k dk car & blk | 35 | 15 |

International Letter Writing Week.

Angara River Bridge, Irkutsk
A1284

1961, Sept. 15   Litho.   Perf. 12½x12

| 2523 | A1284 | 4k ol bis, lil & blk | 30 | 15 |

300th anniversary of Irkutsk.

Lenin, Marx, Engels and Marchers
A1285

Designs: 3k, Obelisk commemorating conquest of space and Moscow University. No. 2526, Harvester combine. No. 2527, Industrial control center. No. 2528, Worker pointing to globe.

1961   Lithographed

2524	A1285	2k ver, yel & brn	10	10
2525	A1285	3k org & dp bl	40	40
2526	A1285	4k mar, bis & red brn	25	30
2527	A1285	4k car rose, brn, org & bl	25	30
2528	A1285	4k red & dk brn	25	30
		Nos. 2524-2528 (5)	1.25	1.25

Issued to commemorate the 22nd Congress of the Communist Party of the USSR, Oct. 17–31.

Soviet Soldier Monument, Berlin
A1286

1961, Sept. 28   Photo.   Perf. 12x12½

| 2529 | A1286 | 4k red & gray vio | 20 | 15 |

Issued to commemorate the 10th anniversary of the International Federation of Resistance, FIR.

Workers Studying Mathematics
A1287

Designs: 2k, Communist labor team. 4k, Workers around piano.

1961, Sept. 28   Litho.   Perf. 12½x12

2530	A1287	2k plum & red, cr	10	10
2531	A1287	3k brn & red, yel	15	10
2532	A1287	4k vio bl & red, cr	20	15

Issued to publicize the Communist labor teams in their efforts for labor, education and relaxation.

Rocket and Stars—A1288
Engraved on Aluminum Foil

1961, Oct. 17   Perf. 12½

| 2533 | A1288 | 1r blk & red | 9.00 | 10.00 |

Issued to commemorate Soviet scientific and technical achievements in exploring outer space.

Overprinted in Red   XXII съезд КПСС

1961, Oct. 23

| 2534 | A1288 | 1r blk & red | 9.00 | 10.00 |

Issued to commemorate the 22nd Congress of the Communist Party of the USSR.

RUSSIA

Amangaldi Imanov A1289 **Franz Liszt** A1290

1961, Oct. 25 Photo. Perf. 11½x12
2535 A1289 4k grn, buff & brn 20 15

Issued to honor Amangaldi Imanov (1873–1919), champion of Soviet power in Kazakhstan.

1961, Oct. 31 Perf. 12x11½
2536 A1290 4k mar, dk brn & ocher 25 15

Issued to commemorate the 150th anniversary of the birth of Franz Liszt, composer.

Flags and Slogans A1291
1961, Nov. 4 Perf. 11½
2537 A1291 4k red, yel & dk red 20 15

44th anniversary of October Revolution.

Hand Holding Hammer A1292 **Congress Emblem** A1293

Designs: Nos. 2538, 2542, Congress emblem. Nos. 2539, 2543, African breaking chains. No. 2541, Three hands holding globe.

1961, Nov. Perf. 12, 12½, 11½
2538 A1293 2k scar & bis 6 5
2539 A1293 2k dk pur & gray 5 5
2540 A1292 4k plum, org & bl 23 8
2541 A1292 4k blk, lt bl & pink 15 10
2542 A1293 6k grn, bis & red 40 10
2543 A1293 6k ind, dl yel & red 30 10
  Nos. 2538-2543 (6) 1.20 50

Issued to publicize the Fifth World Congress of Trade Unions, Moscow, Dec. 4–16.

Lomonosov Statue A1294 **Hands Holding Hammer and Sickle** A1295

Designs: 6k, Lomonosov at desk. 10k, Lomonosov, his birthplace and Leningrad Academy of Science (horiz.).

Photogravure and Engraved
Perf. 11½x12, 12x11½
1961, Nov. 19
2544 A1294 4k Prus bl, yel grn & brn 20 15
2545 A1294 6k grn, yel & blk 30 20

Photogravure
2546 A1294 10k mar, sl & brn 60 40

Issued to commemorate the 250th anniversary of the birth of M. V. Lomonosov, scientist and poet.

1961, Nov. 27 Litho. Perf. 12x12½
2547 A1295 4k red & yel 30 20

Issued to commemorate the 25th anniversary of the constitution of the USSR.

Romeo and Juliet Ballet A1296 **Linemen** A1297

1961–62 Perf. 12x12½
Ballets: 2k, Red Flower. 3k, Paris Flame. 10k, Swan Lake.
2548 A1296 2k brn, car & lt grn ('62) 15 10
2549 A1296 3k multi ('62) 20 10
2550 A1296 6k dk brn, bis & vio 30 10
2551 A1296 10k bl, pink & dk brn 50 15

Issued to honor the Russian Ballet.

1961 Perf. 12½
Designs: 4k, Welders. 6k, Surveyor.
2552 A1297 3k red, red brn & sl 10 5
2553 A1297 4k red, bl & brn 15 7
2554 A1297 6k red, gldn brn & sl 20 8

Issued to honor the self-sacrificing work of youth in the 7-year plan.

Andrejs Pumpurs A1298

1961, Dec. 20 Perf. 12x11½
2555 A1298 4k gray & cl 25 20

Issued to honor Andrejs Pumpurs (1841–1902), Latvian poet and satirist.

Bulgarian Couple, Flag, Emblem and Building A1299

1961, Dec. 28 Perf. 12½x12
2556 A1299 4k multi 25 20

Issued to commemorate the 15th anniversary of the proclamation of the Bulgarian People's Republic.

Fridtjof Nansen—A1300

1961, Dec. 30 Photo. Perf. 11½
2557 A1300 6k dk bl & brn 1.00 90

Issued to commemorate the centenary of the birth of Fridtjof Nansen, Norwegian Polar explorer.

Mihael Ocipovich Dolivo-Dobrovolsky A1301

1962, Jan. 25 Perf. 12x11½
2558 A1301 4k bis & dk bl 20 10

Issued to commemorate the centenary of the birth of Mihael Ocipovich Dolivo-Dobrovolsky, scientist and electrical engineer.

Woman and Various Activities A1302

1962, Jan. 26 Perf. 11½
2559 A1302 4k bis, blk & dp org 20 10

Issued to honor Russian Women.

Aleksander S. Pushkin A1303

1962, Jan. 26 Litho. Perf. 12½x12
2560 A1303 4k buff, dk brn & ver 20 10

Issued to commemorate the 125th anniversary of the death of A. S. Pushkin, poet.

Dancers—A1304
1962, Feb. 6 Perf. 12x12½
2561 A1304 4k bis & ver 20 10

Issued to commemorate the 25th anniversary of the State ensemble of folk dancers.

Speed Skating, Luzhniki Stadium A1305
Photogravure
1962, Feb. 17 Perf. 11½ Unwmkd.
2562 A1305 4k org & ultra 60 15

Issued to publicize the International Winter Sports Championships, Moscow, 1962.

No. 2562 Overprinted СОВЕТСКИЕ КОНЬКОБЕЖЦЫ— ЧЕМПИОНЫ МИРА

1962, March 3
2563 A1305 4k org & ultra 1.00 60

Issued to commemorate the victories of I. Voronina and V. Kosichkin, world speed skating champions, 1962.

Ski Jump—A1305a
Design: 10k, Woman long distance skier (vert.).

1962, May 31 Perf. 11½
2564 A1305a 2k ultra, brn & red 10 10
2565 A1305a 10k org, ultra & blk 50 15

Issued to commemorate the International Winter Sports Championships, Zakopane, 1962.

Hero Type of 1961
Designs: 4k, V. S. Shalandin. 6k, Magomet Gadjiev.
1962, Feb. 22 Perf. 12½x12
2570 A1244 4k dk bl & brn 1.75 1.25
2571 A1244 6k brn & sl grn 1.75 1.25

Soldier heroes of World War II.

Skier—A1306
Designs: 6k, Ice hockey. 10k, Ice skating.
1962, March 3 Perf. 11½
2572 A1306 4k pur & car 15 10
2573 A1306 6k Prus bl & plum 25 15
2574 A1306 10k bl, gray & red 50 20

First People's Winter Games, Sverdlovsk.

Aleksandr Ivanovich Herzen A1307
1962, Mar. 28 Litho. Perf. 12x12½
2575 A1307 4k ultra, blk & buff 35 15

Issued to commemorate the sesquicentennial of the birth of A. I. Herzen (1812–70), political writer.

RUSSIA

 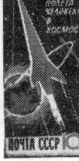

Lenin — A1308   Vostok 1 — A1309

Design: 6k, Lenin (horiz.).
Perf. 12x12½, 12½x12

1962, Mar. 28
2576 A1308 4k brn, red & yel   15   8
2577 A1308 6k bl, org & brn   20   12

Issued to publicize the 14th congress of the Young Communist League (Komsomol).

1962, Apr. Perf. 11x11½ Unwmkd.
2578 A1309 10k multi   1.25   75

Issued to commemorate the first anniversary of Yuri A. Gagarin's flight into space.

No. 2578 was printed in sheets of 20 stamps alternating with 20 labels. Label shows globe with orbit, date and Gagarin's signature, and comes with blue or lilac background.

No. 2578 was also issued imperf. Price $2.50.

Bust of Tchaikovsky — A1310
Photogravure

1962, Apr. 19   Perf. 11½x12
2579 A1310 4k bl, blk & bis   20   15

Issued to commemorate the Second International Tchaikovsky Competition in Moscow.

Youths of 3 Races, Broken Chain, Globe
A1311

1962, Apr. 19   Perf. 11½
2580 A1311 6k blk, brn & yel   25   15

Issued for the International Day of Solidarity of Youth against Colonialism.

Ulyanov (Lenin) Family Portrait
A1312

Lenin — A1313

1962-64   Perf. 12x11½
2581 A1312 4k gray, red & dk brn   20 12

Typographed and Embossed
Perf. 12½
2582 A1313 10k dk red, gray & blk 50 18
 a. Souv. sheet of 2 ('64)   1.50 1.00

92nd anniversary of the birth of Lenin. No. 2582a issued to commemorate the 94th anniversary of the birth of Lenin. The sheet contains two 10k stamps and has gray, dark red and gold ornamental border with "1964" date in gold. Perf. 12. Size: 144x106mm. Issued Nov. 6, 1964. (Nos. 2581-2582 issued Apr. 21, 1962.)

See No. 3024.

Kosmos 3 Satellite — A1314

1962, Apr. 26 Litho. Perf. 12½x12
2586 A1314 6k blk, lt bl & vio   55   25

Issued to commemorate the launching of the Kosmos 3 earth satellite, Apr. 24.

Charles Dickens   Karl Marx Monument, Moscow
A1315   A1316

Portrait: No. 2589, Jean Jacques Rousseau.

1962, Apr. 29
2588 A1315 6k bl, brn & pur   25   15

Photogravure
Perf. 11½x12
2589 A1315 6k gray, lil & brn   25   15

Issued to commemorate the 150th anniversary of the birth of Charles Dickens, English writer, and the 250th anniversary of the birth of Jean Jacques Rousseau, French writer.

1962, Apr. 29   Perf. 12x12½
2590 A1316 4k dp ultra & gray   20   20

Issued to honor Karl Marx.

Pravda, Lenin,   Lenin Reading
Revolutionists   Pravda
A1317   A1318

Designs: No. 2592, Pravda, Lenin and rocket.

1962, May 4   Lithographed
2591 A1317 4k blk, bis & red   15   10
2592 A1317 4k red, blk & ocher   25   10

Photogravure
Perf. 11½
2593 A1318 4k ocher, dp cl & red 15 10

Issued to commemorate the 50th anniversary of Pravda, Russian newspaper founded by Lenin.

Malaria Eradication Emblem and Mosquito — A1319

1962
2594 A1319 4k Prus bl, red & blk 20   10
2595 A1319 6k ol grn, red & blk   30   10

World Health Organization drive to eradicate malaria. Issue dates: 4k, May 6; 6k, June 23.
No. 2595 exists imperf. Price $1.25.

Pioneers Taking Oath before Lenin and Emblem — A1320

Designs (Emblem and): 3k, Lenja Goliokov and Valja Kotik. No. 2598, Pioneers building rocket model. No. 2599, Red Cross, Red Crescent and nurse giving health instruction. 6k, Pioneers of many races and globe.

1962, May 19 Litho. Perf. 12½x12
2596 A1320 2k grn, red & brn   10   10
2597 A1320 3k multi   15   15
2598 A1320 4k multi   20   15
2599 A1320 4k multi   20   15
2600 A1320 6k multi   35   20
 Nos. 2596-2600 (5)   1.00 75

Issued to commemorate the 40th anniversary of the All-Union Lenin Pioneers.

Mesrob   Ivan A. Goncharov
A1321   A1322

1962, May 27 Photo. Perf. 12½x12
2601 A1321 4k yel & dk brn   15   15

Issued to commemorate the "1600th" anniversary of the birth of Bishop Mesrob (350?-439), credited as author of the Armenian and Georgian alphabets.

1962, June 18
2602 A1322 4k gray & brn   20   15

Issued to commemorate the 150th anniversary of the birth of Ivan Aleksandrovich Goncharov (1812-1891), novelist.

Volleyball   Louis Pasteur
A1323   A1324

Designs: 2k, Bicyclists (horiz.). 10k, Eight-man shell. 12k, Goalkeeper, soccer (horiz.). 16k, Steeplechase.

1962, June 27   Perf. 11½
2603 A1323 2k lt brn, blk & ver 10   10
2604 A1323 4k brn org, blk & buff 15 10
2605 A1323 10k ultra, blk & yel 40   15
2606 A1323 12k lt bl, brn & yel 50   20
2607 A1323 16k lt grn, blk & red 60   25
 Nos. 2603-2607 (5)   1.75 80

Issued to commemorate the International Summer Sports Championships, 1962.

1962, June 30   Perf. 12½x12
2608 A1324 6k blk & brn org   30   15

Issued to commemorate the centenary of the invention of the sterilization process by Louis Pasteur, French chemist.

Library, 1862
A1325

1962, June 30   Photogravure
2609 A1325 4k sl & blk   18   10
2610 A1325 4k sl & blk   18   10

Design: No. 2610, New Lenin Library.

Issued to commemorate the centenary of the Lenin Library, Moscow. Nos. 2609-2610 are printed se-tenant in the sheet.

Auction Building and Ermine
A1326

1962, June 30   Lithographed
2611 A1326 6k multi   30   15

International Fur Auction, Leningrad.

RUSSIA

Young Couple, Lenin, Kremlin
A1327

Workers of Three Races and Dove
A1328

1962, June 30　　Perf. 12x12½
2612　A1327　2k multi　　10　6
2613　A1328　4k multi　　20　8

Issued to publicize the program of the Communist Party of the Soviet Union for Peace and Friendship among all people.

Hands Breaking Bomb
A1329

1962, July 7　　Perf. 11½
2614　A1329　6k bl, blk & ol　20　15

Issued to commemorate the World Congress for Peace and Disarmament, Moscow, July 9–14.

Yakub Kolas and Yanka Kupala
A1330

1962, July 7　Photo.　Perf. 12½x12
2615　A1330　4k hn brn & buff　20　10

Issued to commemorate the 80th anniversary of the births of the Byelorussian poets, Yakub Kolas (1882–1956), and Yanka Kupala (1882–1942).

Alepker Sabir
A1331

Cancer Congress Emblem
A1332

1962, July 16　　Perf. 11½
2616　A1331　4k buff, dk brn & bl　20　10

Issued to commemorate the centenary of the birth of the Azerbaijan poet and satirist, Alepker Sabir (1862–1911).

1962, July 16　Litho.　Perf. 12½
2617　A1332　6k grnsh bl, blk & red　30　10

Issued to commemorate the Eighth Anti-Cancer Congress, Moscow, July 1962.

N. N. Zinin
A1333

1962, July 16　Photo.　Perf. 12x11½
2618　A1333　4k vio & dk brn　20　10

Issued to commemorate the 150th anniversary of the birth of N. N. Zinin, chemist.

I. M. Kramskoy, Painter
A1334

I. D. Shadr, Sculptor
A1335

M. V. Nesterov, Painter
A1336

Perf. 11½x12, 12x12½
1962, July 28
2619　A1334　4k gray, mar & dk brn　20　10
2620　A1335　4k blk & red brn　20　10

Lithographed
2621　A1336　4k multi　20　10

Vostok 2 Going into Space
A1337

Photogravure
1962, Aug. 7　Perf. 11½　Unwmkd.
2622　A1337　10k blk, lil & bl　75　35
2623　A1337　10k blk, org & bl　75　35

Issued to commemorate the first anniversary of Gherman Titov's space flight. Issued imperf. on Aug. 6. Price, set $3.

Friendship House, Moscow
A1338

1962, Aug. 15　　Perf. 12x12½
2624　A1338　6k ultra & gray　25　10

Kremlin and Atom Symbol
A1339

Design: 6k, Map of Russia, atom symbol and "Peace" in 10 languages.

1962, Aug. 15　Litho.　Perf. 12½x12
2625　A1339　4k multi　20　10
2626　A1339　6k multi　30　15

Use of atomic energy for peace.

Andrian G. Nikolayev
A1340

Cosmonauts in Space Helmets
A1341

"To Space" Monument by G. Postnikov
A1342

Design: No. 2628, Pavel R. Popovich, with inscription at left and dated "12–15–VIII, 1962."

1962　Photogravure　Perf. 11½
2627　A1340　4k bl, brn & red　20　10
2628　A1340　4k bl, brn & red　20　20

Lithographed
Perf. 12½x12
2629　A1341　6k dk bl, lt bl, org & yel　60　25

Photogravure
Perf. 11½
2630　A1342　6k brt bl & multi　50　15
2631　A1342　10k vio & multi　60　20
Nos. 2627-2631 (5)　2.10　1.00

Souvenir Sheet
Design: 1r, Monument and portraits of Gagarin, Titov, Nikolayev and Popovich.

1962, Nov. 27　Litho.　Perf. 12½
2631A　A1342　1r brt bl, blk & sil　7.00　8.00

Nos. 2627-2631A honor the four Russian "conquerors of space," with Nos. 2627-2629 commemorating the first group space flight, by Vostoks 3 and 4, Aug. 11-15, 1962. Nos. 2627-2631A were also issued imperf.
Size of No. 2631A: 150x71mm.
See also No. 2662.

Carp and Bream
A1343

Design: 6k, Freshwater salmon.

1962, Aug. 28　Photo.　Perf. 11½x12
2632　A1343　4k bl & org　25　8
2633　A1343　6k bl & org　35　12

Fish preservation in USSR.

Feliks E. Dzerzhinski
A1344

1962, Sept. 6　Litho.　Perf. 12½x12
2634　A1344　4k ol grn & dk bl　20　12

Issued to commemorate the 85th anniversary of the birth of Feliks E. Dzerzhinski (1877–1926), organizer of Soviet secret police.

O. Henry and New York Skyline
A1345
Photogravure
1962, Sept. 10　Perf. 12x11½
2635　A1345　6k yel, red brn & blk　30　15

Issued to commemorate the centenary of the birth of O. Henry (William Sidney Porter, 1862–1910), American writer.

Barclay de Tolly, Mikhail I. Kutuzov, Petr I. Bagration
A1346

Designs: 4k, Denis Davidov leading partisans. 6k, Battle of Borodino. 10k, Wasilisa Kozhina and partisans.

1962, Sept. 25　　Perf. 12½x12
2636　A1346　3k org brn　20　10
2637　A1346　4k ultra　25　12
2638　A1346　6k bl gray　35　18
2639　A1346　10k violet　50　25

Issued to commemorate the 150th anniversary of the War of 1812 against the French.

Street in Vinnitsa
A1347

RUSSIA

1962, Sept. 25   Photogravure
2640   A1347   4k yel bis & blk   15   10

Issued to commemorate the 600th anniversary of the town of Vinnitsa, Ukraine.

"Mail and Transportation"
A1348

1962, Sept. 25   Perf. 11½
2641   A1348   4k bl grn, blk & lil   20   12

Issued for International Letter Writing Week, Oct. 7–13.

Cedar   Construction Worker
A1349   A1350

Plants: 4k, Canna. 6k, Arbutus. 10k, Chrysanthemum.

1962, Sept. 27   Engr. & Photo.
2642   A1349   3k ver, blk & grn   15   10
2643   A1349   4k multi   18   10
2644   A1349   6k multi   25   10
2645   A1349   10k multi   50   20

Issued to commemorate the 150th anniversary of the Nikitsky Botanical Gardens.

1962, Sept. 29 Litho. Perf. 12x12½
Designs: No. 2647, Hiker. No. 2648, Surgeon. No. 2649, Worker and lathe. No. 2650, Farmer's wife. No. 2651, Textile worker. No. 2652, Teacher.

2646   A1350   4k org, gray & vio bl   20   7
2647   A1350   4k yel, gray, grn & bl   20   7
2648   A1350   4k grn, gray & lil rose   20   7
2649   A1350   4k ver, gray & lil   20   7
2650   A1350   4k bl, gray & emer   20   7
2651   A1350   4k brt pink, gray & vio   20   7
2652   A1350   4k yel, gray, dp vio, red & brn   20   7
Nos. 2646-2652 (7)   1.40   49

Sputnik and Stars
A1351

1962, Oct. 4   Perf. 12½x12
2653   A1351   10k multi   75   25

5th anniversary, launching of Sputnik 1.

M. F. Ahundov
A1352

1962, Oct. 2   Photogravure
2654   A1352   4k lt grn & dk brn   18   8

Issued to commemorate the 150th anniversary of the birth of M. F. Ahundov, Azerbaijan poet and philosopher.

Farm and Young Couple with Banner
A1353

Designs: No. 2656, Tractors, map and surveyor. No. 2657, Farmer, harvester and map.

1962, Oct. 18 Litho. Perf. 12½x12
2655   A1353   4k multi   50   50
2656   A1353   4k multi   50   50
2657   A1353   4k brn, yel & red   50   50

Issued to honor the pioneer developers of virgin soil.

N. N. Burdenko   V. P. Filatov
A1354   A1355

1962, Oct. 20   Perf. 12½x12
2658   A1354   4k red brn, lt brn & blk   18   10
2659   A1355   4k multi   18   10

Issued to honor N. N. Burdenko and V. P. Filatov, scientists and academicians.

Lenin Mausoleum, Red Square
A1356

1962, Oct. 26   Lithographed
2660   A1356   4k multi   22   10

92nd anniversary of Lenin's birth.

Worker, Flag and Factories
A1357

1962, Oct. 29   Perf. 12x12½
2661   A1357   4k multi   23   10

Issued to commemorate the 45th anniversary of the October Revolution.

No. 2631 Overprinted in Dark Violet

1962, Nov. 3   Photo.   Perf. 11½
2662   A1342   10k vio & multi   1.75   1.50

Launching of a rocket to Mars.

Togolok Moldo
A1358

Sajat Nova
A1359

1962, Nov. 17   Perf. 12x12½
2663   A1358   4k brn red & blk   23   8
2664   A1359   4k ultra & blk   25   8

No. 2663 issued to commemorate the 20th anniversary of the death of Togolok Moldo (1860–1942), Kirghiz poet. No. 2664 commemorates the 250th anniversary of the birth of the Armenian poet, Sajat Nova (1712–1795).

Arms, Hammer & Sickle and Map of USSR—A1360

1962, Nov. 17   Perf. 11½
2665   A1360   4k red, org & dk red   18   8

Issued to commemorate the 40th anniversary of the founding of the U.S.S.R.

Space Rocket, Earth and Mars
A1361

1962, Nov. 17   Perf. 12½x12
Size: 73x27mm.
2666   A1361   10k pur & org red   1.00   35

Issued to commemorate the launching of a space rocket to Mars, Nov. 1, 1962.

Electric Power Industry
A1362

Designs: No. 2668, Machines. No. 2669, Chemicals and oil. No. 2670, Factory construction. No. 2671, Transportation. No. 2672, Telecommunications and space. No. 2673, Metals. No. 2674, Grain farming. No. 2675, Dairy, poultry and meat.

Lithographed
1962, Nov.–Dec.   Perf. 12½x12
2667   A1362   4k ultra, red, blk & gray   20   7
2668   A1362   4k ultra, gray, yel & cl   20   7
2669   A1362   4k yel, pink, blk, gray & brn   20   7
2670   A1362   4k yel, bl, red brn & gray   20   7
2671   A1362   4k mar, yel, red & bl   20   7
2672   A1362   4k brt yel, bl & brn   20   7
2673   A1362   4k lil, org, yel & dk brn   20   7
2674   A1362   4k vio, bis, org red & dk brn   20   7
2675   A1362   4k emer, dk brn, brn & gray   20   7
Nos. 2667-2675 (9)   1.80   63

Issued to publicize "great decisions of the 22nd Communist Party Congress" and to show the Russian people at work.

Queen, Rook and Knight
A1363

Photogravure
1962, Nov. 24 Perf. 12½ Unwmkd.
2676   A1363   4k org yel & blk   35   10

30th Russian Chess Championships.

Gen. Vasili Blucher—A1364

1962, Nov. 27   Perf. 11½
2677   A1364   4k multi   18   8

Issued to honor General Vasili Konstantinovich Blucher (1889–1938).

V. N. Podbelski—A1365

1962, Nov. 27   Perf. 12½x12
2678   A1365   4k red brn, gray & blk   18   8

Issued to commemorate the 75th anniversary of the birth of V. N. Podbelski (1887–1920), minister of posts.

A. Makharenko   A. Gaidar
A1366   A1367

RUSSIA

1962, Nov. 30		Perf. 11½x12		
2679	A1366	4k multi	18	8
2680	A1367	4k multi	18	8

Issued to honor the writers A. S. Maknarenko (1888-1939) and Arkadi Gaidar (1904-1941).

Dove and Globe—A1368

1962, Dec. 22	Litho.	Perf. 12½x12		
2681	A1368	4k multi	25	12

Issued for New Year 1963 with alternating label inscribed "Happy New Year!" Issued imperf. on Dec. 20. Price 75 cents.

D. N. Prjanishnikov
A1369

Rose-colored Starlings
A1370

1962, Dec. 22		Perf. 12x12½		
2682	A1369	4k multi	18	10

Issued to honor D. N. Prjanishnikov, founder of Russian agricultural chemistry.

1962, Dec. 26	Photo.	Perf. 11½		
Birds: 4k, Red-breasted geese. 6k, Snow geese. 10k, White storks. 16k, Greater flamingos.
2683	A1370	3k grn, blk & pink	15	7
2684	A1370	4k brn, blk & dp org	20	10
2685	A1370	6k gray, blk & red	25	13
2686	A1370	10k bl, blk & red	40	25
2687	A1370	16k lt bl, rose & blk	75	35
		Nos. 2683-2687 (5)	1.75	90

FIR Emblem
A1371

1962, Dec. 26		Perf. 12x12½		
2688	A1371	4k vio & red	15	6
2689	A1371	6k grnsh bl & red	20	9

Issued to commemorate the 4th Congress of the International Federation of Resistance, FIR.

Map of Russia, Bank Book and Number of Savings Banks
A1372

Design: 6k, as 4k, but with depositors.

1962, Dec. 30	Litho.	Perf. 12½x12		
2690	A1372	4k multi	15	6
2691	A1372	6k multi	30	9

Issued to commemorate the 40th anniversary of Russian savings banks.

Rustavsky Fertilizer Plant
A1373

Hydroelectric Power Stations: No. 2693, Bratskaya. No. 2964, Volzhskaya.

1962, Dec. 30	Photo.	Perf. 12½		
2692	A1373	4k ultra, lt bl & blk	20	7
2693	A1373	4k yel grn, bl grn & blk	20	7
2694	A1373	4k gray bl, brt bl & blk	20	7

Stanislavski
A1374

Serafimovich
A1375

Engraved

1963, Jan. 15	Perf. 12½ Unwmkd.		
2695	A1374	4k sl grn	18	7

Issued to commemorate the centenary of the birth of Stanislavski, professional name of Konstantin Sergeevich Alekseev (1863-1938), actor, producer and founder of the Moscow Art Theater.

1963, Jan. 19	Photo.	Perf. 11½		
2696	A1375	4k mag, dk brn & gray	18	7

Issued to commemorate the centenary of the birth of A. S. Serafimovich (1863-1949), writer.

Children in Nursery
A1376

Designs: No. 2698, Kindergarten. No. 2699, Pioneers marching and camping. No. 2700, Young people studying and working.

1963, Jan. 31				
2697	A1376	4k brn org, org red & blk	20	10
2698	A1376	4k bl, mag & org	20	10
2699	A1376	4k brt grn, red & brn	20	10
2700	A1376	4k multi	20	10

Wooden Dolls and Toys, Russia
A1377

National Handicrafts: 6k, Pottery, Ukraine. 10k, Bookbinding, Estonia. 12k, Metalware, Dagestan.

1963, Jan. 31	Litho.	Perf. 12x12½		
2701	A1377	4k multi	20	8
2702	A1377	6k multi	30	10
2703	A1377	10k multi	55	12
2704	A1377	12k ultra, org & blk	75	20

Gen. Mikhail N. Tukhachevski
A1378

Designs: No. 2706, U. M. Avetisian. No. 2707, A. M. Matrosov. No. 2708, J. V. Panfilov. No. 2709, Y. F. Fabricius.

1963, Feb.	Photo.	Unwmkd.		
2705	A1378	4k bl grn & sl grn	15	10
2706	A1378	4k org brn & blk	15	10
2707	A1378	4k ultra & dk brn	15	10
2708	A1378	4k dp rose & blk	15	10
2709	A1378	4k rose lil & vio bl	15	10
		Nos. 2705-2709 (5)	75	50

Issued to commemorate the 45th anniversary of the Soviet Army and to honor its heroes. No. 2705 commemorates the 70th anniversary of the birth of Gen. Mikhail Nikolaevich Tukhachevski (1893-1937).

M. A. Pavlov
A1379

E. O. Paton and Dnieper Bridge, Kiev
A1379a

Portraits: No. 2711, I. V. Kurchatov. No. 2712, V. I. Vernadski. No. 2713, Aleksei N. Krylov. No. 2714, V. A. Obrutchev, geologist.

1963		Perf. 11½x12		
		Size: 21x32mm.		
2710	A1379	4k gray, buff & dk bl	15	7
2711	A1379	4k sl & brn	15	7
		Perf. 12		
2712	A1379	4k lil gray & lt brn	15	7
		Perf. 11½		
		Size: 23x34½mm.		
2713	A1379	4k dk bl, sep & red	15	7
2714	A1379	4k brn ol, gray & red	15	7
2715	A1379a	4k grnsh bl, blk & red	15	7
		Nos. 2710-2715 (6)	90	42

Nos. 2710-2715 issued to honor members of the Russian Academy of Science. No. 2715 commemorates the 10th anniversary of the death of Eugene Oskarovich Paton (1870-1953), bridge building engineer.

Winter Sports
A1380

1963, Feb. 28		Perf. 11½		
2716	A1380	4k brt bl, org & blk	30	12

Issued to commemorate the 5th Trade Union Spartacist Games. Printed in sheets of 50 (5x10) with every other row inverted.

No. 2573 Overprinted

Советские хоккеисты— чемпионы мира и Европы Стокгольм 1963 г.

1963, Mar. 20				
2717	A1306	6k Prus bl & plum	1.00	40

Issued to commemorate the victory of the Soviet ice hockey team in the World Championships, Stockholm. See No. 3612.

Victor Kingisepp
A1381

Rudolfs Blaumanis
A1382

1963, Mar. 24		Perf. 12x12½		
2718	A1381	4k bl gray & choc	23	10

Issued to commemorate the 75th anniversary of the birth of Victor Kingisepp, communist party leader.

1963, Mar. 24		Perf. 12½x12		
2719	A1382	4k ultra & dk red brn	23	10

Issued to commemorate the centenary of the birth of Rudolfs Blaumanis (1863-1908), Latvian writer.

Flower and Globe
A1383

Designs: 6k, Atom diagram and power line. 10k, Rocket in space.

1963, Mar. 26		Perf. 11½		
2720	A1383	4k red, ultra & grn	18	10
2721	A1383	6k red, grn & lil	30	12
2722	A1383	10k red, vio & lt bl	35	18

Publicity for a "World without Arms and Wars."
The 10k exists imperf. Price $1.50. See No. 2754.

Costume Type of 1960-62

Regional Costumes: 3k, Tadzhik. No. 2724, Kirghiz. No. 2725, Azerbaijan. No. 2726, Turkmen.

1963, Mar. 31	Litho.	Perf. 11½		
2723	A1237	3k blk, red, ocher & org	20	5
2724	A1237	4k brn, ver, ocher & ultra	25	7
2725	A1237	4k blk, ocher & grn	25	7
2726	A1237	4k red, lil, ocher & blk	25	7

RUSSIA

Lenin
A1384

Lunik 4 Approaching Moon
A1385

1963, Mar. 30   Engraved   Perf. 12

2727   A1384   4k red & brn   25   8

93rd anniversary of the birth of Lenin.

1963, Apr. 2   Photogravure

2728   A1385   6k blk, lt bl & red   50   20

Issued to commemorate Russia's rocket to the moon, Apr. 2, 1963. Exists imperforate. Price $1.25. See No. 3160.

Woman and Beach Scene
A1386

Designs: 4k, Young man's head and factory. 10k, Child's head and kindergarden.

1963, Apr. 7   Litho.   Perf. 12½x12

2729   A1386   2k multi   10   6
2730   A1386   4k multi   17   5
2731   A1386   10k multi   42   15

15th anniversary of World Health Day.

Sputnik and Earth—A1387

Designs: No. 2733, Vostok 1, earth and moon. No. 2734, Rocket and Sun.

1963, Apr. 12

2732   A1387   10k blk, bl & lil rose   60   40
   a.   "10k" bl   60   40
2733   A1387   10k lil rose, bl & blk   60   40
   a.   "10k" lil rose   60   40
2734   A1387   10k blk, red & yel   60   40
   a.   "10k" yel   60   50

Issued for Cosmonauts' Day. Nos. 2732-2734 and 2732a-2734a printed se-tenant. Alternate rows in sheets have colorless "10k."

Demian Bednii
A1388

Soldiers on Horseback and Cuban Flag
A1389

1963, Apr. 13   Photogravure

2735   A1388   4k brn & blk   25   8

Issued to commemorate the 80th anniversary of the birth of Demian Bednii, poet.

1963, Apr. 25   Perf. 11½

Designs: 6k, Cuban flag, hands with gun and book. 10k, Cuban and Russian flags and crane lifting tractor.

2736   A1389   4k blk, red & ultra   20   8
2737   A1389   6k blk, red & ultra   30   12
2738   A1389   10k red, ultra & blk   50   18

Soviet-Cuban friendship.

Karl Marx
A1390

Jaroslav Hasek
A1391

1963, May 9   Perf. 12x12½

2739   A1390   4k dk red brn & blk   20   8

145th anniversary of the birth of Marx.

1963, Apr. 29   Perf. 11½x12

2740   A1391   4k black   20   8

Issued to commemorate the 80th anniversary of the birth of Jaroslav Hasek (1883–1923), Czech writer.

Moscow P.O. for Foreign Mail
A1392

1963, May 9   Perf. 11½

2741   A1392   6k brt vio & red brn   30   10

Issued to commemorate the 5th Conference of Communications Ministers of Socialist countries, Budapest.

King and Pawn—A1393

Designs: 6k, Queen and bishop. 16k, Rook and knight.

1963, May 22   Photogravure

2742   A1393   4k multi   20   6
2743   A1393   6k ultra, brt pink & grnsh bl   30   10
2744   A1393   16k brt plum, brt pink & blk   75   25

Issued to commemorate the 25th Championship Chess Match, Moscow. Imperforates exist, issued May 18. Price $2.

Richard Wagner
A1394

Boxers
A1395

Design: No. 2745A, Giuseppe Verdi.

1963   Perf. 11½x12   Unwmkd.

2745   A1394   4k blk & red   15   10
2745A   A1394   4k red & vio brn   20   10

Issued to commemorate the 150th anniversaries of the births of Richard Wagner and Giuseppe Verdi, German and Italian composers.

1963, May 29   Litho.   Perf. 12½

Design: 6k, Referee proclaiming victor.

2746   A1395   4k multi   20   8
2747   A1395   6k multi   30   12

Issued to commemorate the 15th European Boxing Championships, Moscow.

Valeri Bykovski—A1396

Valentina Tereshkova—A1397

Designs: No. 2749, Tereshkova. No. 2751, Bykovski. No. 2752, Symbolic man and woman fliers. No. 2753, Tereshkova (vert.).

**1963   Litho. (A1396); Photo. (A1397)
Perf. 12½x12, 12½x12½**

2748   A1396   4k multi   30   25
2749   A1396   4k multi   30   25
2750   A1397   6k grn & dk car rose   30   15
2751   A1397   6k pur & brn   30   15
2752   A1397   10k bl & red   55   30
2753   A1396   10k multi   1.20   15
    Nos. 2748-2753 (6)   2.95   1.45

Issued to commemorate the space flights of Valeri Bykovski, June 14–19, and Valentina Tereshkova, first woman cosmonaut, June 16–19, 1963, in Vostoks 5 and 6. Nos. 2750–2753 exist imperf. Price $3.

No. 2720 Overprinted in Red

Всемирный
конгресс
женщин.

1963, June 24   Photo.   Perf. 11½

2754   A1383   4k red, ultra & grn   50   15

Issued to publicize the International Women's Congress, Moscow, June 24–29.

Globe, Camera and Film
A1398

1963, July 7   Photo.   Perf. 11½

2755   A1398   4k gray & ultra   22   8

3rd International Film Festival, Moscow.

Vladimir V. Mayakovsky—A1399

Design: No. 2745A, Giuseppe Verdi.

1963, July 19   Engraved   Perf. 12½

2756   A1399   4k red brn   30   10

Issued to commemorate the 70th anniversary of the birth of Vladimir V. Mayakovsky, poet.

Tanks and Map
A1400

Design: 6k, Soldier, tanks and flag.

1963, July   Litho.   Perf. 12½x12

2757   A1400   4k sep & org   18   9
2758   A1400   6k org, sl grn & blk   27   10

Issued to commemorate the 20th anniversary of the Battle of Kursk in the "War of Liberation," 1941–45.

Bicyclist—A1401

Sports: 4k, Long jump. 6k, Women divers (horiz.). 12k, Basketball. 16k, Soccer.

Perf. 12½x12, 12½x12½

1963, July 27

2759   A1401   3k multi   15   10
2760   A1401   4k multi   22   10
2761   A1401   6k multi   35   15
2762   A1401   12k multi   60   15
2763   A1401   16k multi   75   20
    a.   Souv. sheet of 4   2.75   90
    Nos. 2759-2763 (5)   2.07   70

3rd Spartacist Games. Exist imperf. Price $2.50.

No. 2763a contains 4 imperf. stamps similar to the 3k, 4k, 12k and 16k, with colors changed. Bright green, orange and gray margin. Size: 155x104mm. Issued Dec. 22.

Ice Hockey
A1402

1963, July 27   Photogravure

2764   A1402   6k red & gray bl   25   12

Issued to commemorate the World Ice Hockey Championship, Stockholm. See also No. 3012.

Lenin
A1403

1963, July 29

2765   A1403   4k red & blk   20   6

Issued to commemorate the 60th anniversary of the 2nd Congress of the Social Democratic Labor Party.

RUSSIA

Freighter and Relief Shipment
A1404

Design: 12k, Centenary emblem.

1963, Aug. 8   **Perf. 12½**
| 2766 | A1404 | 3k Prus grn & red | 30 | 10 |
| 2767 | A1404 | 12k dk bl & red | 60 | 20 |

Centenary of International Red Cross.

Lapp Reindeer Race
A1405

Designs: 4k, Pamir polo (vert.). 6k, Burjat archery. 10k, Armenian wrestling (vert.).

1963, Aug. 8   **Perf. 11½**
2768	A1405	3k lt vio bl, brn & red	15	7
2769	A1405	4k bis brn, red & blk	20	8
2770	A1405	6k yel, blk & red	30	10
2771	A1405	10k sep, blk & dk red	40	15

A. F. Mozhaisky (1825–1890), Pioneer Airplane Builder
A1406

Designs: 10k, P. N. Nesterov (1887–1914), pioneer stunt flyer. 16k, N. E. Zhukovski (1847–1921), aerodynamics pioneer, and pressurized air tunnel.

Engraved and Photogravure
1963, Aug. 18
2772	A1406	6k blk & brt bl	30	5
2773	A1406	10k blk & brt bl	40	10
2774	A1406	16k blk & brt bl	60	15

Issued to honor aviation pioneers.

Alexander S. Dargomyzhski and Scene from "Rusalka"
A1408

S. S. Gulak-Artemovsky and Scene from "Cossacks on the Danube"
A1409

Design: No. 2777, Georgi O. Eristavi and theater.

Perf. 11½x12, 12x12½
1963, Sept. 10   **Photogravure**
2776	A1408	4k vio & blk	20	8
2777	A1408	4k gray vio & brn	20	8
2778	A1409	4k red & blk	20	8

Issued to commemorate the 150th anniversaries of the births of A. S. Dargomyzhski, Ukrainian composer; Georgi O. Eristavi, Georgian writer, and S. S. Gulak-Artemovsky, Ukrainian composer.

Map of Antarctica, Penguins, Research Ship and Southern Lights
A1410

Designs: 4k, Map, southern lights and snocats (trucks). 6k, Globe, camp and various planes. 12k, Whaler and whales.

1963, Sept. 16   **Litho.**   **Perf. 12½x12**
2779	A1410	3k multi	15	8
2780	A1410	4k multi	20	10
2781	A1410	6k vio, bl & red	30	12
2782	A1410	12k multi	60	20

"The Antarctic—Continent of Peace."

Letters, Globe, Plane, Train and Ship—A1411

1963, Sept. 20   **Photo.**   **Perf. 11½**
| 2783 | A1411 | 4k vio, blk & org | 20 | 6 |

International Letter Writing Week.

Denis Diderot
A1412

1963, Oct. 10   **Perf. 11½**   **Unwmkd.**
| 2784 | A1412 | 4k dk bl, brn & yel bis | 20 | 10 |

Issued to commemorate the 250th anniversary of the birth of Denis Diderot (1713–84), French philosopher and encyclopedist.

Gleb Uspenski
A1414

1963, Oct. 10

Portraits: No. 2787, N. P. Ogarev. No. 2788, V. Brusov. No. 2789, F. Gladkov.

2786	A1414	4k buff, red brn & dk brn	25	6
2787	A1414	4k blk & pale grn	15	6
2788	A1414	4k car, brn & gray	15	6
2789	A1414	4k car, ol brn & gray	15	6

No. 2786 commemorates the 120th anniversary of the birth of Gleb Ivanovich Uspenski (1843–1902), historian and writer; No. 2787 the 150th anniversary of the birth of N. P. Ogarev, politician; No. 2788 the 90th anniversary of the birth of V. Brusov, poet, and No. 2789 the 80th anniversary of the birth of Fyodor Gladkov (1883–1958), writer.

"Peace" Worker, Student, Astronaut and Lenin
A1415

Kirghiz Academy and Spasski Tower
A1416

Designs: No. 2794, "Labor," automatic controls. No. 2795, "Liberty," painter, lecturer, newspaper man. No. 2796, "Equality," elections, regional costumes. No. 2797, "Brotherhood," Recognition of achievement. No. 2798, "Happiness," Family.

1963, Oct. 15   **Litho.**   **Perf. 12½x12**
2793	A1415	4k dk red, red & blk	20	8
2794	A1415	4k red, dk red & blk	20	8
2795	A1415	4k red, dk red & blk	20	8
2796	A1415	4k red, dk red & blk	20	8
2797	A1415	4k red, dk red & blk	20	8
2798	A1415	4k dk red, red & blk	20	8
a.		Strip of 6	1.35	80
		Nos. 2793-2798 (6)	1.20	48

Issued to proclaim Peace, Labor, Liberty, Equality, Brotherhood and Happiness. Nos. 2793–2798 are printed se-tenant forming complete row in sheet.

1963, Oct. 22   **Perf. 12x12½**
| 2799 | A1416 | 4k red, yel & vio bl | 20 | 7 |

Centenary of Russia's annexation of Kirghizia.

Lenin and Young Workers
A1417

Olga Kobylyanskaya
A1418

Design: No. 2801, Lenin and Palace of Congresses, the Kremlin.

1963, Oct. 24   **Photo.**   **Perf. 11½**
| 2800 | A1417 | 4k crim & blk | 15 | 7 |
| 2801 | A1417 | 4k car & blk | 15 | 7 |

Issued to commemorate the 13th Congress of Soviet Trade Unions, held at Moscow.

1963, Oct. 24   **Perf. 11½x12**
| 2802 | A1418 | 4k tan & dk car rose | 20 | 7 |

Issued to commemorate the centenary of the birth of Olga Kobylyanskaya, Ukrainian novelist.

Elie Metchnikoff
A1419

Cruiser Aurora and Rockets
A1420

Designs: 6k, Louis Pasteur. 12k, Albert Calmette.

1963, Oct. 28   **Perf. 12**
2803	A1419	4k grn & bis	18	5
2804	A1419	6k pur & bis	30	10
2805	A1419	12k bl & bis	60	15

Issued to commemorate the 75th anniversary of the Pasteur Institute, Paris; the 12k commemorates the centenary of the birth of Albert Calmette (1863–1933), bacteriologist.

1963, Nov. 1
| 2806 | A1420 | 4k mar, blk, gray & red org | 30 | 10 |
| 2807 | A1420 | 4k mar, blk, gray & brt rose red | 30 | 10 |

Issued to publicize the development of the Armed Forces, and to commemorate the 46th anniversary of the October Revolution. The bright rose red ink of No. 2807 is fluorescent.

Mausoleum Gur Emi, Samarkand
A1421

Proclamation, Spasski Tower and Globe
A1422

Designs (Architecture in Samarkand, Uzbekistan): No. 2809, Shahi-Zind Mosque. 6k, Registan Square.

1963, Nov. 14 Lithographed Perf. 12

Size: 27½x27½mm.
| 2808 | A1421 | 4k bl, yel & red brn | 20 | 10 |
| 2809 | A1421 | 4k bl, yel & red brn | 20 | 10 |

Size: 55x27½mm.
| 2810 | A1421 | 6k bl, yel & red brn | 40 | 15 |

Photogravure
1963, Nov. 15   **Perf. 12x11½**
| 2811 | A1422 | 6k pur & lt bl | 30 | 20 |

Issued to commemorate the signing of the Nuclear Test Ban Treaty between the U.S.A. and the U.S.S.R.

Pushkin Monument, Kiev
A1423

M. S. Shchepkin
A1424

Portrait: No. 2814, V. L. Durov (1863–1934), circus clown.

1963   **Engraved**   **Perf. 12x12½**
2812	A1423	4k dk brn	15	7
2813	A1424	4k brown	15	7
2814	A1424	4k brn blk	20	10

No. 2813 commemorates the 175th anniversary of the birth of M. S. Shchepkin, actor.

RUSSIA 331

Yuri M. Steklov
A1425

1963, Nov. 17   **Photo.**   **Perf. 11½**
2815   A1425   4k blk & lil rose   18   6

Issued to commemorate the 90th anniversary of the birth of Yuri M. Steklov, first editor of Izvestia.

Vladimir G. Shuhov
and Moscow Radio Tower
A1426

1963, Nov. 17   **Perf. 12½x12**
2816   A1426   4k grn & brk   20   10

Issued to commemorate the 110th anniversary of the birth of Vladimir G. Shuhov, scientist.

Russian and Czech Flags,
Kremlin and Hradčany
A1427

1963, Nov. 25   **Perf. 11½**
2817   A1427   6k red, ultra & brn   30   12

Issued to commemorate the 20th anniversary of the Russo-Czechoslovakian Treaty.

Fyodor A. Poletaev—A1428

1963, Nov. 25   **Litho.**   **Perf. 12½x12**
2818   A1428   4k multi   23   8

Issued to honor F. A. Poletaev, Hero of the Soviet Union, National Hero of Italy, and holder of the Order of Garibaldi.

Julian Grimau and Worker
Holding Flag—A1429

1963, Nov. 29   **Photo.**   **Perf. 11½**
Flag and Name Panel Embossed
2819   A1429   6k vio blk, red & buff   27   12

Issued to honor the Spanish anti-fascist fighter Julian Grimau.

Rockets,   "Happy
Sky and Tree   New Year!"
A1430   A1431

1963, Dec. 12   **Litho.**   **Perf. 12x12½**
2820   A1430   6k multi   30   12

Photogravure and Embossed
1963, Dec. 20   **Perf. 11½**
2821   A1431   4k grn, dk bl & red   18   8
2822   A1431   6k grn, dk bl & fluor. rose red   27   12

Nos. 2820-2822 issued for New Year 1964.

Mikas J. Petrauskas
A1432

1963, Dec. 20   **Photo.**   **Perf. 11½x12**
2823   A1432   4k brt grn & brn   18   8

Issued to commemorate the 90th anniversary of the birth of M. J. Petrauskas, Lithuanian composer.

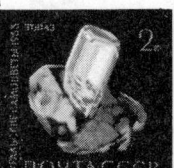

Topaz   Coat of Arms
A1433   and Sputnik
          A1434

Precious stones of the Urals: 4k, Jasper. 6k, Amethyst. 10k, Emerald. 12k, Rhodonite. 16k, Malachite.

1963, Dec. 26   **Litho.**   **Perf. 12**
2824   A1433   2k brn, yel & bl   15   10
2825   A1433   4k multi   30   10
2826   A1433   6k red & pur   35   10
2827   A1433   10k multi   50   15
2828   A1433   12k multi   65   15
2829   A1433   16k multi   90   20
       Nos. 2824-2829 (6)   2.85   80

Lithographed and Embossed
1963, Dec. 27

Rockets: No. 2831, Lunik I. No. 2832, Rocket around the moon. No. 2833, Vostok I, first man in space. No. 2834, Vostok, III & IV. No. 2835, Vostok VI, first woman astronaut.

2830   A1434   10k red, gold & gray   50   25
2831   A1434   10k red, gold & gray   50   25
2832   A1434   10k red, gold & gray   50   25
2833   A1434   10k red, gold & gray   50   25
2834   A1434   10k red, gold & gray   50   25
2835   A1434   10k red, gold & gray   3.25   1.75
    a.   Strip of 6   3.00   1.50
       Nos. 2830-2835 (6)

Issued to publicize Russian achievements in space. Nos. 2830-2835 are printed setenant forming complete vertical row in sheet.

Dyushambe, Tadzhikistan—A1435
1963, Dec. 30   **Engraved**
2836   A1435   4k dl bl   20   8

No. 2836 was issued after Stalinabad was renamed Dyushambe. See No. 2943.

Flame, Broken
Chain and
Rainbow
A1436

1963, Dec. 30   **Lithographed**
2837   A1436   6k multi   27   15

Issued to commemorate the 15th anniversary of the Universal Declaration of Human Rights.

F. A. Sergeev
A1437
1963, Dec. 30   **Photo.**   **Perf. 12x12½**
2838   A1437   4k gray & red   18   6

Issued to commemorate the 80th anniversary of the birth of the revolutionist Artjem (F. A. Sergeev).

Sun and Radar—A1438

Designs: 6k, Sun and Earth (vert.). 10k, Earth and Sun.

1964, Jan. 1   **Photo.**   **Perf. 11½**
2839   A1438   4k brt mag, org & blk   30   15
2840   A1438   6k org yel, red & bl   40   20
2841   A1438   10k bl, vio & org   50   30

International Quiet Sun Year, 1964-65.

Christian Donalitius
A1439
1964, Jan. 1   **Perf. 12**   **Unwmkd.**
2842   A1439   4k grn & blk   18   10

Issued to commemorate the 250th anniversary of the birth of the Lithuanian poet Christian Donalitius (Donelaitis).

Women's Speed Skating
A1440

Designs: 4k, Women's cross country skiing. 6k, 1964 Olympic emblem and torch. 10k, Biathlon. 12k, Figure skating pair.

1964, Feb. 4   **Perf. 11½**   **Imperf.**
2843   A1440   2k ultra, blk & lil rose   12   10
2844   A1440   4k lil rose, blk & ultra   20
2845   A1440   6k dk bl, red & blk   27   15
2846   A1440   10k grn, lil & blk   50   15
2847   A1440   12k lil, blk & grn   55   25
       Nos. 2843-2847 (5)   1.64   75

Issued to commemorate the 9th Winter Olympic Games, Innsbruck Jan. 29-Feb. 9, 1964. See Nos. 2865, 2867-2870.

Anna S. Golubkina
A1441
1964, Feb. 4   **Photogravure**
2848   A1441   4k gray, brn & buff   22   7

Issued to commemorate the centenary of the birth of Anna S. Golubkina (1864-1927), sculptor.

No. 2450
Overprinted
in Red:

150 років з дня
народження.
1964 р.

Taras G.
Shevchenko
A1443

Designs: 4k, Shevchenko statue, Kiev. 10k, Shevchenko by Ilya Repin. (Portrait on 6k by I. Kremsko.)

Lithographed
1964, Feb. 22-Mar. 1   **Perf. 12**
2852   A1245(a)3k brn & vio   18   7
       Engraved
2853   A1443   4k magenta   18   8
2854   A1443   4k dp grn   18   8
2855   A1443   6k red brn   27   12
2856   A1443   6k indigo   27   12
       Photogravure
2857   A1443   10k bis & vio   40   18
2858   A1443   10k buff & dl vio   40   18
       Nos. 2852-2858 (7)   1.88   83

Issued to commemorate the 150th anniversary of the birth of Taras G. Shevchenko, Ukrainian poet.

K. S. Zaslonov—A1444

Soviet Heroes: No. 2860, N. A. Vilkov. No. 2861, J. V. Smirnov. No. 2862, V. S. Khorujaia (heroine). No. 2862A, I. M. Sivko. No. 2862B, I. S. Polbin.

1964-65   **Photogravure**
2859   A1444   4k hn brn & brn blk   18   10
2860   A1444   4k Prus bl & vio blk   18   10
2861   A1444   4k brn red & ind   18   10
2862   A1444   4k bluish gray & dk brn   18   10
2862A A1444   4k lil & blk ('65)   18   10
2862B A1444   4k bl & dk brn ('65)   18   10
       Nos. 2859-2862B (6)   1.08   60

RUSSIA

Printer Inking Form, 16th Century
A1445

Design: 6k, Statue of Ivan Fedorov, first Russian printer.

1964, Mar. 1   Litho.   Unwmkd.

| 2863 | A1445 | 4k multi | 15 | 10 |
| 2864 | A1445 | 6k multi | 20 | 10 |

Issued to commemorate the 400th anniversary of book printing in Russia.

Nos. 2843-2847 Overprinted and

Ice Hockey
A1446

Olympic Gold Medal, "11 Gold, 8 Silver, 6 Bronze"
A1447

1964, Mar. 9   Photo.   Perf. 11½

2865	A1440	2k ultra, blk & lil rose	15	8
2866	A1446	3k blk, bl grn & red	25	10
2867	A1440	4k lil rose, blk & ultra	25	10
2868	A1440	6k dk bl, red & blk	33	12
2869	A1440	10k grn, lil & blk	45	12
2870	A1440	12k lil, blk & grn	50	25

Perf. 12

| 2871 | A1447 | 16k org red & gldn brn | 80 | 35 |
| | Nos. 2865-2871 (7) | | 2.68 | 1.10 |

Issued to commemorate the Russian victories at the 9th Winter Olympic Games. On Nos. 2865, 2867-2870 the black overprints commemorate victories in various events and are variously arranged in 3 to 6 lines, with "Innsbruck" in Russian added below "1964" on 2k, 4k, 10k and 12k.

Rubber Industry   Regular and Volunteer Militiamen
A1448   A1449

Designs: No. 2873, Textile industry. No. 2874, Cotton, wheat, corn and helicopter spraying land.

1964   Litho.   Perf. 12x12½

2872	A1448	4k org, lil, ultra & blk	18	7
2873	A1448	4k org, blk, grn & ultra	18	7
2874	A1448	4k dl yel, ol, red & bl	18	7

Issued to publicize the importance of the chemical industry for Russian economy. Issue dates: No. 2872, Feb. 10. Nos. 2873-2874, Mar. 27.

1964, March 27   Photo.   Perf. 12

| 2875 | A1449 | 4k red & dp ultra | 18 | 7 |

Issued for the Day of the Militia.

Sailor and Odessa Lighthouse
A1450

Liberation Monument, Minsk
A1451

Design: No. 2877, Lenin statue and Leningrad.

Perf. 12½x12

1964, Apr. 10-June 30   Litho.

2876	A1450	4k red, lt grn, ultra & blk	18	7
2877	A1450	4k red, yel, grn, brn & blk	18	7
2878	A1451	4k bl, gray, red & emer	18	7

Issued to commemorate the 20th anniversary of the liberation of Odessa (No. 2876), Leningrad (No. 2877) and Byelorussia (No. 2878).

First Soviet Sputniks
A1452

F. A. Tsander   Lenin
A1453   A1454

Designs: 6k, Mars 1 spacecraft. No. 2886, Konstantin E. Tsiolkovsky. No. 2887, N. I. Kibaltchitch. No. 2888, Statue honoring 3 balloonists killed in 1934 accident. 12k, Gagarin and Kosmos 3.

Photogravure

1964, Apr.   Perf. 11½, Imperf.

2883	A1452	4k red org, blk & bl grn	25	10
2884	A1452	6k dk brn & org red	35	15
2885	A1453	10k grn, blk & fluor. pink	40	30
2886	A1453	10k dk bl grn, blk & fluor. pink	40	30
2887	A1453	10k lil, blk & lt grn	40	30
2888	A1453	10k bl & blk	40	30
2889	A1452	12k bl grn, org brn & blk	50	40
	Nos. 2883-2889 (7)		2.70	1.85

Issued to honor leaders in rocket theory and technique.

Engraved and Photogravure

1964-65   Perf. 12x11½

| 2890 | A1454 | 4k blk, buff & lil rose | 20 | 10 |
| a. | Re-engraved ('65) | | 75 | 25 |

94th anniversary of the birth of Lenin. On No. 2890a, the portrait shading is much heavier. Lines on collar are straight and unbroken, rather than dotted.

William Shakespeare
A1455

1964, Apr. 23   Perf. 11½

| 2891 | A1455 | 10k gray & red brn | 55 | 25 |

Issued to commemorate the 400th anniversary of the birth of William Shakespeare. See also Nos. 2985-2986.

"Irrigation"—A1456

1964, May 12   Litho.   Perf. 12x12½

| 2892 | A1456 | 4k multi | 18 | 7 |

Y. B. Gamarnik
A1457

Photogravure

1964, May 12   Perf. 12½x11½

| 2893 | A1457 | 4k bl & gray brn | 18 | 7 |

Issued to commemorate the 70th anniversary of the birth of Y. B. Gamarnik, army commander.

D. I. Gulia—A1458

Portraits: No. 2895, Hamza Hakim-Zade Nijazi. No. 2896, Saken Seifullin. No. 2896A, M. M. Kotsyubinsky. No. 2896B, Stepanos Nazaryan. No. 2896C, Toktogil Satylganov.

Engraved and Photogravure

1964   Perf. 12x11½   Unwmkd.

2894	A1458	4k grn, buff & blk	18	7
2895	A1458	4k red, buff & blk	18	7
2896	A1458	4k brn, ocher, buff & blk	18	7
2896A	A1458	4k brn lake & buff	18	7
2896B	A1458	4k bl, pale bl, blk & buff	18	7
2896C	A1458	4k red brn & blk	22	7
	Nos. 2894-2896C (6)		1.12	42

No. 2894 commemorates the 90th anniversary of the birth of the Abkhazian poet Gulia; No. 2895 the 75th anniversary of the birth of the Uzbekian writer and composer Nijazi; No. 2896 the 70th anniversary of the birth of the Kazakian poet Seifullin; No. 2896A, birth centenary of Ukrainian writer M. M. Kotsyubinsky (1864-1913); No. 2896B, the 150th anniversary of the birth of Armenian writer Stefanos Nazaryan (1814-1879); No. 2896C, birth centenary of Kirghiz poet Toktogil Satylganov (1864-1933).

Arkadi Gaidar—A1459

Design: No. 2897A, Nikolai Ostrovsky and battle scene (portrait at left).

1964   Photogravure   Perf. 12

| 2897 | A1459 | 4k red org & gray | 18 | 7 |

Engraved

| 2897A | A1459 | 4k brn lake & blk | 18 | 7 |

Issued to commemorate the 60th anniversaries of the birth of writers Arkadi Gaidar (1904-1941) and Nikolai A. Ostrovsky (1904-1936).

No. 2318 Surcharged:

1964, May 27   Litho.   Perf. 12

| 2898 | A1194 | 4k on 40k bis & brn | 60 | 20 |

Issued to commemorate the 150th anniversary of Azerbaijan's joining Russia.

"Romania"   Elephant
A1460   A1461

Designs: No. 2900, "Poland," (map, Polish eagle, industrial and agricultural symbols). No. 2901, "Bulgaria," (flag, rose, industrial and agricultural symbols). No. 2902, Russian and Jugoslav soldiers and embattled Belgrade. No. 2903, "Czechoslovakia" (view of Prague, arms, Russian soldier and woman). No. 2903A, Map and flag of Hungary, Liberty statue. No. 2904, Buildings under construction, Warsaw; Polish flag and medal.

1964-65   Lithographed   Perf. 12

2899	A1460	6k gray & multi	25	10
2900	A1460	6k ocher, red & brn	25	10
2901	A1460	6k tan, grn & red	25	10
2902	A1460	6k gray, blk, dl bl, ol & red	25	10
2903	A1460	6k ultra, blk & red ('65)	25	10
2903A	A1460	6k brn, red & grn ('65)	25	10
2903B	A1460	6k dp org, gray bl & blk ('65)	25	10

RUSSIA

2904 A1460 6k bl, red, yel & bis ('65) 25 10
Nos. 2899-2904 (8) 2.00 80

Issued to commemorate the 20th anniversary of liberation from German occupation of Romania, Poland, Bulgaria, Belgrade, Czechoslovakia, Hungary, Vienna and Warsaw.

Perf. 12x12½, 12½x12, Imperf.
1964 Photogravure
Designs: 2k, Giant panda (horiz.). 4k, Polar bear. 6k, European elk. 10k, Pelican. 12k, Tiger. 16k, Lammergeier.
Size: 25x36mm., 36x25mm.

2905 A1461 1k red & blk 5 5
2906 A1461 2k tan & blk 10 5

Perf. 12
Size: 26x28mm.

2907 A1461 4k grnsh gray, blk & tan 15 6

Perf. 12x12½
Size: 25x36mm.

2908 A1461 6k ol, dk brn & tan 20 10

Perf. 12
Size: 26x28mm.

2909 A1461 10k ver, gray & blk 30 15

Perf. 12½x12, 12x12½
Size: 36x25mm., 25x36mm.

2910 A1461 12k brn, ocher & blk 40 20
2911 A1461 16k ultra, blk, bis & yel 50 25
Nos. 2905-2911 (7) 1.70 86

300th anniversary of the Moscow Zoo.
Issue dates: Perf. set June 18. Imperf. set in May.

Leningrad Post Office
A1462

1964, June 30 Litho. Perf. 12
2912 A1462 4k cit, blk & red 20 6

Issued to commemorate the 250th anniversary of Leningrad postal service.

Corn — A1463
Maurice Thorez — A1464

Designs: 3k, Wheat. 4k, Potatoes. 6k, Beans. 10k, Beets. 12k, Cotton. 16k, Flax.

Photogravure
1964 **Perf. 11½, Imperf.**
2913 A1463 2k ultra, yel & brn 9 5
2914 A1463 3k emer, yel & red brn 15 5
2915 A1463 4k brn, sl grn & lil 18 10
2916 A1463 6k ol bis, bis & grn 25 10
2917 A1463 10k dk car, grn, blk & tan 35 15
2918 A1463 12k lil, ap grn & blk 42 20
2919 A1463 16k lt bl, ol & red brn 60 25
Nos. 2913-2919 (7) 2.04 90

Issue dates: Perf. set July 10. Imperf. set June 25.

1964, July 31
2920 A1464 4k blk & red 50 20

Issued in memory of Maurice Thorez, chairman of the French Communist party.

Equestrian and Russian Olympic Emblem
A1465

Designs: 4k, Weight lifter. 6k, High jump. 10k, Canoeing. 12k, Girl gymnast. 16k, Fencing.

1964, July Perf. 11½, Imperf.
2921 A1465 3k lt yel grn, red, brn & blk 10 5
2922 A1465 4k yel, blk & red 15 6
2923 A1465 6k lt bl, blk & red 20 10
2924 A1465 10k bl grn, red & blk 30 14
2925 A1465 12k gray, blk & red 35 20
2926 A1465 16k lt ultra, blk & red 50 25
Nos. 2921-2926 (6) 1.60 80

Issued for the 18th Olympic Games, Tokyo, Oct. 10-25, 1964.
Two 1r imperf. souvenir sheets exist, showing emblem, woman gymnast and stadium. Size: 91x71mm.
Price, red sheet, $7 unused, $5 canceled; green sheet, $250 unused, $300 canceled.

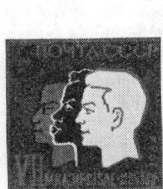 
Three Races — A1466
Jawaharlal Nehru — A1467

1964, Aug. 8 Photogravure Perf. 12
2929 A1466 6k org & blk 25 6

Issued to commemorate the International Congress of Anthropologists and Ethnographers, Moscow.

1964, Aug. 20 Perf. 11½
2930 A1467 4k brn & blk 25 6

Issued in memory of Prime Minister Jawaharlal Nehru of India (1889-1964).

Conquest of Space

A souvenir sheet, issued Aug. 20, 1964, celebrates the Conquest of Space. It carries six perforated, interlocking 10k stamps with different, interlocking designs picturing Soviet rockets and spacecraft. Size of sheet, 141x110mm. Price, $4 unused, $2 canceled. Sheet also exists on glossy paper. Price, $8 unused, $6 canceled.

Karl Marx and Friedrich Engels
A1468
A. V. Vishnevsky
A1469

Designs: No. 2932 Lenin and title page of "CPSS Program." No. 2933, Worker breaking chains around the globe. No. 2934, Title pages of "Communist Manifesto" in German and Russian. No. 2935, Globe and banner inscribed "Workers of the World Unite."

1964, Aug. 27 Photo. Perf. 11½x12
2931 A1468 4k red, dk red & brn 18 10
2932 A1468 4k red, brn & sl 18 10
2933 A1468 4k bl, fluor. brt rose & blk 18 10

Lithographed
Perf. 12½x12
2934 A1468 4k ol blk, blk & red 18 10
2935 A1468 4k bl, red & ol bis 18 10
Nos. 2931-2935 (5) 90 50

Centenary of First Socialist International.

1964 Photogravure Perf. 11½
Portraits: No. 2937, N. A. Semashko. No. 2938, D. Ivanovsky.
Size: 23½x35mm.

2936 A1469 4k gray & brn 15 8
2937 A1469 4k buff, sep & red 15 8

Lithographed
Size: 22x32½mm.

2938 A1469 4k tan, gray & brn 15 8

Issued to commemorate the 90th anniversaries of the birth of A. V. Vishnevsky, surgeon, and N. A. Semashko, founder of the Russian Public Health Service; the centenary of the birth of D. Ivanovsky (1864-1920), physician.

Palmiro Togliatti
A1470

1964, Sept. 15 Perf. 12½x12
2939 A1470 4k blk & red 20 15

Issued to honor Palmiro Togliatti (1893-1964), General Secretary of the Italian Communist Party.

Letter, Aerogram and Globe
A1471

1964, Sept. 20 Lithographed
2940 A1471 4k tan, lil rose & ultra 18 10

Issued for International Letter Writing Week, Oct. 5-11.

Arms of German Democratic Republic, Factories, Ship and Train — A1472

1964, Oct. 7 Perf. 12
2942 A1472 6k blk yel, red & bis 25 15

Issued to commemorate the 15th anniversary of the German Democratic Republic.

No. 2836
Overprinted in Red

40 лет Советскому Таджикистану
1964 год

1964, Oct. 7 Engraved
2943 A1435 4k dl bl 50 65

40th anniversary of Tadzhik Republic.

Woman Holding Bowl of Grain and Fruit — A1473

Uzbek Farm Couple and Arms
A1474
Turkmen Woman Holding Arms
A1475

1964, Oct. 7, 26 Lithographed
2944 A1473 4k red, grn & brn 18 15
2945 A1474 4k red yel & cl 18 15
2946 A1475 4k red, blk & red brn 18 15

Issued to commemorate the 40th anniversaries of the Moldavian, Uzbek and Turkmen Socialist Republics.

Soldier and Flags
A1476

1964, Oct. 14
2947 A1476 4k red, bis, dk brn & bl 20 10

Issued to commemorate the 20th anniversary of the liberation of the Ukraine.

Mikhail Y. Lermontov
A1477

Designs: 4k, Birthplace of Tarchany. 10k, Lermontov and Vissarion G. Belinski.

1964, Oct. 14 Engr.; Litho. (10k)
2948 A1477 4k vio blk 15 6
2949 A1477 6k black 25 10
2950 A1477 10k dk red brn & buff 42 14

Issued to commemorate the 150th anniversary of the birth of Mikhail Y. Lermontov (1814-41), poet.

RUSSIA

Hammer and Sickle
A1478

1964, Oct. 14   Lithographed
2951   A1478   4k dk bl, red, ocher & yel   25   10

47th anniversary of October Revolution.

Col. Vladimir M. Komarov
A1479

Komarov, Feoktistov and Yegorov
A1480

Designs: No. 2953, Boris B. Yegorov, M.D. No. 2954, Konstantin Feoktistov, scientist. 10k, Spacecraft Voskhod I and cosmonauts. 50k, Red flag with portraits of Komarov, Feoktistov and Yegorov, and trajectory around earth.

Photogravure
1964   Perf. 11½ (A1479), 12½x12
2952   A1479   4k bl grn, blk & org   20   15
2953   A1479   4k bl grn, blk & org   20   15
2954   A1479   4k bl grn, blk & org   20   15

Size: 73x23mm.
2955   A1480   6k vio & dk brn   35   20
2956   A1480   10k dp ultra & pur   60   25

Miniature Sheet
Lithographed
Imperf.
Size: 90x45½mm.
2957   A1480   50k vio, red & gray   3.50   1.75
    Nos. 2952-2957 (6)   5.05   2.65

Issued to commemorate the three-men space flight of Vladimir M. Komarov, Boris B. Yegorov and Konstantin Feoktistov, Oct. 12–13. Dates of issue: Nos. 2952-2954, Oct. 19; No. 2955, Oct. 17; No. 2956, Oct. 13; No. 2957, Nov. 20.

A. I. Yelizarova-Ulyanova
A1482

Portrait: No. 2961, Nadezhda K. Krupskaya.

1964, Nov. 6   Photo.   Perf. 11½
2960   A1482   4k brn, org & ind   18   8
2961   A1482   4k ind, red & brn   18   8

Issued to commemorate the centenary of the birth of A. I. Yelizarova-Ulyanova, Lenin's sister and the 95th anniversary of the birth of Nadezhda Krupskaya, Lenin's wife.

Farm Woman, Sheep, Flag of Mongolia
A1483
Mushrooms
A1484

1964, Nov. 20   Litho.   Perf. 12
2962   A1483   6k multi   25   8

Issued to commemorate the 40th anniversary of the Mongolian People's Republic.

1964, Nov. 25   Litho.   Perf. 12
Designs: Various Mushrooms.
2963   A1484   2k ol grn, red brn & yel   20   10
2964   A1484   4k grn & yel   20   10
2965   A1484   6k bluish grn, brn & yel   30   10
2966   A1484   10k grn, org red & brn   40   15
2967   A1484   12k ultra, yel & grn   70   20
    Nos. 2963-2967 (5)   1.80   65

Nos. 2963-2967 exist varnished, printed in sheets of 25 with 10 labels in outside vertical rows. Issued Nov. 30. Price, set $2.50.

A. P. Dovzhenko
A1485

Design: 6k, Scene from "Tchapaev" (man and boy with guns).

1964, Nov. 30 Photogravure   Perf. 12
2968   A1485   4k gray & dp ultra   15   7
2968A   A1485   6k pale ol & blk   20   8

Issued to commemorate the 70th anniversary of the birth of A. P. Dovzhenko (1894–1956), film producer, and the 30th anniversary of the production of the film "Tchapaev."

"Happy New Year"
A1486
V. J. Struve
A1487

Photogravure and Engraved
1964, Nov. 30   Perf. 11½
2969   A1486   4k multi   23   7

Issued for New Year 1965. The bright rose ink is fluorescent.

1964–65   Photo.   Perf. 12½x11½
Portraits: No. 2971, N. P. Kravkov. No. 2971A, P. K. Sternberg. No. 2971B, Ch. Valikhanov. No. 2971C, V. A. Kistjakovlski.
2970   A1487   4k sl bl & dk brn   33   12

Lithographed
2971   A1487   4k brn, red & blk ('65)   18   12

Photogravure
Perf. 11½
2971A   A1487   4k dk bl & blk ('65)   18   12

Perf. 12
2971B   A1487   4k rose vio & blk ('65)   18   12

Lithographed
2971C   A1487   4k brn vio, blk & cit ('65)   18   12
    Nos. 2970-2971C (5)   1.05   60

Issued to commemorate the death centenary of astronomer V. J. Struve (1793–1864), founder of Pulkov Observatory; birth centenary of N. P. Kravkov (1865–1924), pharmacologist; birth centenary of P. K. Sternberg (1865–1920), astronomer; death centenary of Ch. Valikhanov (1835–1865), Kazakh scientist; birth centenary of V. A. Kistjakovski (1865–1952), chemist.

S. V. Ivanov and Skiers
A1488

1964, Dec. 22 Engraved   Perf. 12½
2972   A1488   4k blk & brn   25   10

Issued to commemorate the centenary of the birth of the painter S. V. Ivanov (1864–1910).

Chemical Industry: Fertilizers and Pest Control—A1489
Design: 6k, Synthetics factory.

1964, Dec. 25 Photogravure   Perf. 12
2973   A1489   4k ol & lil rose   15   8
2974   A1489   6k dp ultra & blk   25   12

Issued to publicize the importance of the chemical industry for national economy.

European Cranberries
A1490

Wild Berries: 3k, Huckleberries. 4k, Mountain ash. 10k, Blackberries. 16k, Cranberries.

1964, Dec. 25   Perf. 11½x12
2975   A1490   1k pale grn & car   15   5
2976   A1490   3k gray, vio bl & grn   15   5
2977   A1490   4k gray, org red & brn   22   10
2978   A1490   10k grn, dk vio bl & cl   33   15
2979   A1490   16k gray, brt grn & car rose   45   25
    Nos. 2975-2979 (5)   1.33   60

Academy of Science Library
A1491

1964, Dec. 25 Typo.   Perf. 12x12½
2980   A1491   4k blk, pale grn & red   18   8

Issued to commemorate the 250th anniversary of the founding of the Academy of Science Library, Leningrad.

Congress Palace, Kremlin
A1492

Khan Tengri
A1493

1964, Dec. 25
2981   A1492   1r dk bl   2.75   1.30

1964, Dec. 29   Photo.   Perf. 11½
Mountains: 6k, Kazbek (horiz.). 12k, Twin peaks of Ushba.
2982   A1493   4k grnsh bl, vio bl & buff   10   10
2983   A1493   6k yel, dk brn & ol   25   15
2984   A1493   12k lt yel, grn & pur   50   20

Development of mountaineering in Russia.

Portrait Type of 1964
Design: 6k, Michelangelo. 12k, Galileo.
Engraved and Photogravure
1964, Dec. 25   Perf. 11½
2985   A1455   6k sep, red brn & org   25   10
2986   A1455   12k dk brn & grn   50   20

Issued to commemorate the 400th anniversary of the death of Michelangelo Buonarotti, artist, and the 400th anniversary of the birth of Galileo Galilei, astronomer and physicist.

Helmet
A1494

Treasures from Kremlin Treasury: 6k, Saddle. 10k, Jeweled fur crown. 12k, Gold ladle. 16k, Bowl.

1964, Dec. 30   Lithographed
2987   A1494   4k multi   15   5
2988   A1494   6k multi   20   10
2989   A1494   10k multi   30   15
2990   A1494   12k multi   40   15
2991   A1494   16k multi   45   20
    Nos. 2987-2991 (5)   1.50   65

Dante
A1495

Blood Donor
A1496

1965, Jan. 29   Photo.   Perf. 11½
2995   A1495   4k dk red brn & ol bis   20   8

Issued to commemorate the 700th anniversary of the birth of Dante Alighieri (1265–1321), Italian poet.

RUSSIA

1965, Jan. 31 Lithographed Perf. 12

Design: No. 2997, Hand holding carnation, and donors' emblem.

| 2996 | A1496 | 4k dk car, red, vio bl & bl | 15 | 10 |
| 2997 | A1496 | 4k brt grn, red & dk grn | 15 | 10 |

Issued to honor the blood donors.

Bandy
A1497

Police Dog
A1498

Design: 6k, Figure skaters and Moscow Sports Palace.

1965, Feb. Photo. Perf. 11½x12

| 2998 | A1497 | 4k bl, red & yel | 20 | 10 |
| 2999 | A1497 | 6k grn, blk & red | 25 | 10 |

The 4k was issued Feb. 21, to commemorate the victory of the Russian team in the World Bandy Championship, Moscow, Feb. 21–27; the 6k was issued, Feb. 12, to commemorate the European Figure Skating Championship. See No. 3017.

Photogravure,
Perf. 12x11½, 11½x12;
Lithographed (1k, 10k, 12k, 16k),
Perf. 12x12½, 12½x12.

1965, Feb. 26

Dogs: 1k, Russian hound. 2k, Irish setter. No. 3003, Pointer. No. 3004, Fox terrier. No. 3005, Sheepdog. No. 3006, Borzoi. 10k, Collie. 12k, Husky. 16k, Caucasian sheepdog. (1k, 2k, 4k, 12k and 16k horizontal.)

3000	A1498	1k blk, yel & mar	6	5
3001	A1498	2k ultra, blk & red brn	10	5
3002	A1498	3k blk, ocher & org red	12	5
3003	A1498	4k org, yel grn & blk	18	6
3004	A1498	4k brn, blk & lt grn	18	6
3005	A1498	6k chlky bl, sep & red	25	10
3006	A1498	6k chlky bl, org brn & blk	25	10
3007	A1498	10k yel grn, ocher & red	35	14
3008	A1498	12k gray, blk & ocher	40	20
3009	A1498	16k multi	45	26
Nos. 3000-3009 (10)			2.34	1.07

Richard Sorge
A1499

1965, Mar. 6 Photo. Perf. 12x12½

| 3010 | A1499 | 4k hn brn & blk | 20 | 10 |

Issued to commemorate the 70th anniversary of the birth of Richard Sorge (1895–1944), Russian spy and Hero of the Soviet Union.

Communications Symbols—A1500

1965, Mar. 6 Perf. 12½x12

| 3011 | A1500 | 6k grnsh bl, vio & brt pur | 25 | 10 |

Centenary of the International Telecommunication Union.

No. 2764 Overprinted ТАМПЕРЕ 1965 г.

1965, Mar. 20 Photogravure Perf. 12

| 3012 | A1402 | 6k red & gray bl | 50 | 25 |

Issued to commemorate the Russian victory in the European and World Ice Hockey Championships.

Lt. Col. Alexei Leonov Taking Movies in Space—A1501

Design: 1r, Leonov walking in space and Voskhod 2.

1965, Mar. 23 Photogravure Perf. 12
Size: 73x23mm.

| 3015 | A1501 | 10k brt ultra, org & gray | 50 | 25 |

First man walking in space, Lt. Col. Alexei Leonov, Mar. 17, 1965 ("18 March" on stamp).

Exists imperf. Price 75 cents.

Souvenir Sheet

1965, Apr. 12 Lithographed

| 3016 | A1501 | 1r multi | 4.50 | 2.25 |

Issued to commemorate the space flight of Voskhod 2. No. 3016 contains one stamp (size: 81x27mm.), inscriptions and portraits of Lt. Col. Alexei Leonov and Col. Pavel Belyayev in margin. Size: 142x58mm.

No. 2999 Overprinted Советские фигуристы— чемпионы мира в парном катании

1965, Mar. 26 Perf. 11½x12

| 3017 | A1497 | 6k grn, blk & red | 50 | 25 |

Issued to commemorate the Russian victory in the World Figure Skating Championships.

Flags of USSR and Poland
A1502

1965, Apr. 12 Photo. Perf. 12

| 3018 | A1502 | 6k bis & red | 20 | 8 |

Issued to commemorate the 20th anniversary of the signing of the Polish-Soviet treaty of friendship, mutual assistance and postwar cooperation.

Tsiolkovsky Monument, Kaluga; Globe and Rockets
A1503

Rockets, Radio Telescope, TV Antenna
A1504

Designs: 12k, Space monument, Moscow. 16k, Cosmonauts' monument, Moscow. No. 3023, Globe with trajectories, satellite and astronauts.

1965, Apr. 12 Perf. 11½

3019	A1503	4k pale grn, blk & brt rose	25	10
3020	A1503	12k vio, pur & brt rose	50	20
3021	A1503	16k multi	70	25

Lithographed on Aluminum Foil
Perf. 12½x12

3022	A1504	20k blk & red	3.00	75
3023	A1504	20k blk, bl & red	3.00	75
Nos. 3019-3023 (5)			7.45	2.05

Issued to publicize National Cosmonauts' Day. On Nos. 3019-3021 the bright rose is fluorescent.

Lenin—A1505

1965, Apr. 16 Engraved Perf. 12

| 3024 | A1505 | 10k tan & ind | 35 | 20 |

Issued to commemorate the 95th anniversary of the birth of Lenin. For souvenir sheet see No. 2582a.

Poppies
A1506

Russian Flag, Broken Swastikas, Fighting in Berlin
A1507

Flowers: 3k, Daisies. 4k, Peony. 6k, Carnation. 10k, Tulips.

1965, Apr. 23 Photo. Perf. 11

3025	A1506	1k mar, red & grn	5	5
3026	A1506	3k dk brn, yel & grn	10	5
3027	A1506	4k blk, grn & lil	15	6
3028	A1506	6k dk sl grn, grn & red	20	10
3029	A1506	10k dk plum, yel & grn	30	9
Nos. 3025-3029 (5)			80	44

1965
Designs: 2k, "Fatherland Calling!" (woman with proclamation) by I. Toidze. 3k, Attack on Moscow by V. Gogatkin. No. 3033, Rest after the Battle by Y. Neprintsev. No. 3034, "Mother of Partisan" by S. Gerasimov. 6k, "Our Flag—Symbol of Victory" (soldiers with banner) by V. Ivanov. 10k, "Tribute to the Hero" (mourners at bier) by F. Bogorodsky. 12k, "Invincible Nation and Army" (worker and soldier holding shell) by V. Koretsky. 16k, Victory celebration on Red Square by K. Yon. 20k, Soldier and symbols of war.

Perf. 11½

3030	A1507	1k red, blk & gold	5	5
3031	A1507	2k crim, blk & gold	10	6
3032	A1507	3k ultra & gold	15	8
3033	A1507	4k grn & gold	20	10
3034	A1507	4k vio & gold	20	10
3035	A1507	6k dp cl & gold	25	10
3036	A1507	10k plum & gold	35	15
3037	A1507	12k blk, red & gold	40	15
3038	A1507	16k lil rose & gold	50	20
3039	A1507	20k red, blk & gold	75	35
Nos. 3030-3039 (10)			2.95	1.34

Issued to commemorate the 20th anniversary of the end of World War II. Issued Apr. 25–May 1.

Souvenir Sheet

From Popov's Radio to Space Telecommunications—A1508

1965, May 7 Litho. Perf. 11½

| 3040 | A1508 | 1r bl & multi | 5.00 | 4.00 |

Issued to commemorate the 70th anniversary of Aleksandr S. Popov's radio pioneer work. No. 3040 contains 6 labels without denominations or country name. Size of sheet: 145x102mm.

Marx, Lenin and Crowd with Flags
A1509

1965, May 9 Photo. Perf. 12x12½

| 3041 | A1509 | 6k red & blk | 25 | 10 |

Issued to commemorate the 6th conference of Postal Ministers of Communist Countries, Peking, June 21–July 15.

Bolshoi Theater, Moscow—A1510

1965, May 20 Perf. 11x11½

| 3042 | A1510 | 6k grnsh bl, bis & blk | 25 | 10 |

Issued for the International Theater Day.

Col. Pavel Belyayev
A1511

RUSSIA

Design: No. 3044, Lt. Col. Alexei Leonov.
1965, May 23   Perf. 12x11½

| 3043 | A1511 | 6k mag & sil | 23 | 10 |
| 3044 | A1511 | 6k pur & sil | 23 | 10 |

Issued to commemorate the space flight of Voskhod 2, March 18–19, 1965, and the first man walking in space, Lt. Col. Alexei Leonov.

Jacob M. Sverdlov   A1512
Otto Grothewohl   A1513

Portrait: No. 3046, Juldash Akhunbabaev.

Photogravure and Engraved
1965, May 30   Perf. 11½x12

| 3045 | A1512 | 4k org brn & blk | 18 | 8 |
| 3046 | A1512 | 4k lt vio & blk | 18 | 8 |

Issued to honor Jacob M. Sverdlov, 1885–1919, first president of U.S.S.R., and J. Akhunbabaev, 1885–1943, president of Uzbek Republic.

1965, June 12   Photo.   Perf. 12

| 3051 | A1513 | 4k blk & mag | 23 | 8 |

Issued in memory of Otto Grothewohl, 1894–1964, prime minister of the German Democratic Republic.

Maurice Thorez   A1514
Communication by Satellite   A1515

1965, June 12

| 3052 | A1514 | 6k brn & red | 25 | 12 |

Issued to commemorate the 65th anniversary of the birth of Maurice Thorez, 1900–1964, chairman of the French Communist party.

1965, June 15   Lithographed

Designs: No. 3054, Pouring ladle, steel mill and map of India. No. 3055, Stars, satellites and names of international organizations.

3053	A1515	3k ol, blk & gold	15	5
3054	A1515	6k emer, dk grn & gold	30	10
3055	A1515	6k vio bl, gold & blk	30	10

Issued to emphasize international cooperation through communication, economic cooperation and international organizations.

Symbols of Chemistry   A1516

1965, June 15   Photo.   Perf. 11½

| 3056 | A1516 | 4k blk, brt rose & brt bl | 20 | 12 |

Issued to publicize the 20th Congress of the International Union of Pure and Applied Chemistry (IUPAC), held at Moscow. The bright rose ink is fluorescent.

V. A. Serov   A1517

Design: 6k, Full-length portrait of Feodor Chaliapin, the singer, by Serov.

1965, June 25   Typo.   Perf. 12½

| 3057 | A1517 | 4k red brn, buff & blk | 20 | 10 |
| 3058 | A1517 | 6k ol bis & blk | 30 | 15 |

Issued to commemorate the centenary of the birth of V. A. Serov (1865–1911), historical painter.

Abay Kunanbaev, Kazakh Poet   A1518

Designs (writers and poets): No. 3060, Vsevolod Ivanov (1895–1963). No. 3060A, Eduard Vilde, Estonian writer. No. 3061, Mark Kropivnitsky, Ukrainian playwright. No. 3062, Manuk Apeghyan, Armenian writer and critic. No. 3063, Musa Djalil, Tartar poet. No. 3064, Hagop Hagopian, Armenian poet. No. 3064A, Djalil Mamedkulizade, Azerbaijan writer.

1965–66   Photo.   Perf. 12½x12

3059	A1518	4k lt vio & blk	20	10
3060	A1518	4k rose lil & blk	20	10
3060A	A1518	4k gray & blk	20	10
3061	A1518	4k blk & org brn	20	10

Typographed Perf. 12½

| 3062 | A1518 | 4k crim, bl grn & blk | 20 | 10 |

Photogravure and Engraved Perf. 11½

| 3063 | A1518 | 4k blk & org brn ('66) | 20 | 10 |
| 3064 | A1518 | 4k grn & blk ('66) | 20 | 10 |

Photogravure

| 3064A | A1518 | 4k Prus grn & blk ('66) | 20 | 10 |
| Nos. 3059–3064A (8) | | | 1.60 | 80 |

Size: Nos. 3059–3062, 38x25mm. Nos. 3063–3064A, 35x23mm.

Jan Rainis   A1518a

1965, Sept. 8   Photo.   Perf. 12½x12

| 3064B | A1518a | 4k dl bl & blk | 20 | 10 |

Issued to commemorate the birth centenary of Jan Rainis (1865–1929), Latvian playwright. "Rainis" was pseudonym of Jan Plieksans.

Film, Screen, Globe and Star   A1519

1965, July 5   Litho.   Perf. 12

| 3065 | A1519 | 6k brt bl, gold & blk | 20 | 10 |

Issued to commemorate the Fourth International Film Festival, Moscow: "For Humanism in Cinema Art, for Peace and Friendship among Nations."

Concert Bowl, Tallinn   A1520

"Lithuania"   A1521

"Latvia"   A1522

1965, July   Perf. 12x11½, 11½x12

3066	A1520	4k ultra, blk, red & ocher	18	8
3067	A1521	4k red & brn	18	8
3068	A1522	4k yel, red & bl	18	8

Nos. 3066–68 commemorate the 25th anniversaries of Estonia, Lithuania and Latvia as Soviet Republics. Issue dates: No. 3066, July 7; No. 3067, July 14; No. 3068, July 16.

"Keep Peace"   A1523
Protesting Women and Czarist Eagle   A1524

1965, July 10   Photo.   Perf. 11x11½

| 3069 | A1523 | 6k yel, blk & bl | 23 | 8 |

1965, July 20   Litho.   Perf. 11½

Designs: No. 3071, Soldier attacking distributor of handbills. No. 3072, Fighters on barricades with red flag. No. 3073, Monument for sailors of warship "Potemkin," Odessa.

3070	A1524	4k blk, red & ol grn	15	8
3071	A1524	4k red, ol grn & blk	15	8
3072	A1524	4k red, blk & brn	15	8
3073	A1524	4k red & vio bl	15	8

60th anniversary of the 1905 revolution.

Gheorghe Gheorghiu-Dej   A1525

1965, July 26   Photo.   Perf. 12

| 3074 | A1525 | 4k blk & red | 20 | 12 |

Issued in memory of Gheorghe Gheorghiu-Dej (1901–65), President of Romanian State Council (1961–65).

Relay Race   A1526

Sport: No. 3076, Bicycle race. No. 3077, Gymnast on vaulting horse.

1965, Aug. 5   Litho.   Perf. 12½x12

3075	A1526	4k vio bl, bis brn & red brn	15	8
3076	A1526	4k buff, red brn, gray & mar	15	8
3077	A1526	4k bl, mar, buff & lt brn	15	8

8th Trade Union Spartacist Games.

Electric Power   A1527

Designs: 2k, Metals in modern industry. 3k, Modern chemistry serving the people. 4k, Mechanization, automation and electronics. 6k, New materials for building industry. 10k, Mechanization and electrification of agriculture. 12k, Technological progress in transportation. 16k, Application of scientific discoveries to industry.

1965, Aug. 5   Photo.   Perf. 12x11½

3078	A1527	1k ol, bl & blk	10	5
3079	A1527	2k org, blk & yel	10	5
3080	A1527	3k yel, vio & bis	10	5
3081	A1527	4k ultra, ind & red	15	10
3082	A1527	6k ultra & bis	20	10
3083	A1527	10k yel, org & red brn	30	15
3084	A1527	12k Prus bl & red	40	25
3085	A1527	16k rose lil, blk & vio bl	60	30
Nos. 3078–3085 (8)			1.95	1.05

Issued to publicize the creation of the material and technical basis of communism.

Gymnast   A1528
Javelin and Running   A1529

Design: 6k, Bicycling.

1965, Aug. 12   Perf. 11½

| 3086 | A1528 | 4k ultra & red | 15 | 8 |

RUSSIA

| 3087 | A1528 | 6k grnsh bl, red & brn | 20 | 12 |

9th Spartacist Games for school children.

1965, Aug. 27

Designs: 6k, High jump and shot put. 10k, Hammer throwing and hurdling.

3088	A1529	4k brn, lil & red	15	6
3089	A1529	6k brn, yel grn & red	20	12
3090	A1529	10k brn, chlky bl & red	35	18

Issued to commemorate the United States-Russian Track and Field Meet, Kiev.

Worker and Globe — A1530

Flag of North Viet Nam, Factory and Palm — A1531

Designs: No 3092, Heads of three races and torch. No. 3093, Woman with dove.

1965, Sept. 1

3091	A1530	6k dk pur & tan	20	10
3092	A1530	6k brt bl, brn & red org	20	10
3093	A1530	6k Prus grn & tan	20	10

Issued to commemorate the 20th anniversary of the International Federation of Trade Unions (No. 3091); the Federation of Democratic Youth (No. 3092); the Democratic Women's Federation (No. 3093).

1965, Sept. 1 Litho. Perf. 12

| 3094 | A1531 | 6k red, yel, brn & gray | 20 | 10 |

Issued to commemorate the 20th anniversary of the Republic of North Viet Nam.

Scene from Film "Potemkin" — A1532

Film Scenes: 6k, "Young Guard." 12k, "Ballad of a Soldier."

1965, Sept. 29 Litho. Perf. 12½x12

3095	A1532	4k bl, blk & red	15	6
3096	A1532	6k multi	20	10
3097	A1532	12k multi	40	15

Post Rider, 16th Century — A1533

History of the Post: No. 3099, Mail coach, 17th–18th centuries. 2k, Train, 19th century. 4k, Mail truck, 1920. 6k, Train, ship and plane. 12k, New Moscow post office, helicopter, automatic sorting and cancelling machines. 16k, Lenin, airport and map of USSR.

Perf. 11½x12

1965 Photo. Unwmkd.

3098	A1533	1k org brn, dk gray & dk grn	10	5
3099	A1533	1k gray, ocher & dk brn	10	5
3100	A1533	2k dl lil, brt bl & brn	10	7
3101	A1533	4k bis, rose lake & blk	15	7
3102	A1533	6k pale brn, Prus grn & blk	20	10
3103	A1533	12k lt ultra, lt brn & blk	40	20
3104	A1533	16k gray, rose red & vio blk	50	25
		Nos. 3098-3104 (7)	1.55	79

See also No. 3175.

Atomic Ice-breaker "Lenin" — A1534

Designs: No. 3106, Icebreakers "Taimir" and "Vaigitch." 6k, Dickson Settlement. 10k, Sailing ships, "Vostok" and "Mirni," Bellingshausen-Lazarov expedition, and icebergs. 16k, Vostok South Pole station.

1965, Oct. 23 Litho. Perf. 12

Size: 37x25mm.

3106	A1534	4k bl, blk & org	25	10
3107	A1534	4k bl, blk & org	25	10
3108	A1534	6k sep & dk vio	33	15

Size: 33x33mm.

| 3109 | A1534 | 10k red, blk & buff | 42 | 15 |

Size: 37x25mm.

| 3110 | A1534 | 16k vio blk & red brn | 60 | 25 |
| | | Nos. 3106-3110 (5) | 1.85 | 75 |

Issued to commemorate the scientific conquests of the Arctic and Antarctic. Nos. 3106–3107 printed se-tenant.

Souvenir Sheet

Basketball, Map of Europe and Flags — A1535

1965, Oct. 29 Litho. Imperf.

| 3111 | A1535 | 1r multi | 4.50 | 2.00 |

Issued to commemorate the 14th European Basketball Championship, Moscow. Size: 65x89mm.

Timiryazev Agriculture Academy, Moscow — A1536

1965, Oct. 30 Photo. Perf. 11

| 3112 | A1536 | 4k brt car, gray & vio bl | 20 | 12 |

Issued to commemorate the centenary of the Agriculture Academy, Moscow.

Souvenir Sheet

Lenin

1965, Oct. 30 Litho. & Engr. Imperf.

| 3113 | A1537 | 10k sil, blk & dp org | 1.25 | 50 |

Issued to commemorate the 48th anniversary of the October Revolution. No. 3113 has deep orange margin with silver emblem. Size: 64x93mm.

Nicolas Poussin — A1538   Kremlin — A1539

1965, Nov. 16 Photo. Perf. 11½

| 3114 | A1538 | 4k gray bl, dk bl & dk brn | 25 | 12 |

Issued to commemorate the 300th anniversary of the death of Nicolas Poussin (1594–1665), French painter.

1965, Nov. 16 Perf. 12x11½

| 3115 | A1539 | 4k blk, ver & sil | 20 | 12 |

Issued for New Year 1966.

Mikhail Ivanovich Kalinin — A1540

1965, Nov. 19 Perf. 12½

| 3116 | A1540 | 4k dp cl & red | 20 | 12 |

Issued to commemorate the 90th anniversary of the birth of Mikhail I. Kalinin (1875–1946), president of U.S.S.R. (1923–46).

Klyuchevskaya Sopka — A1541

Kamchatka Volcanoes: 12k, Karumski erupting (vert.). 16k, Koryakski snow-covered.

1965, Nov. 30 Litho. Perf. 12

3117	A1541	4k multi	20	8
3118	A1541	12k multi	50	15
3119	A1541	16k multi	75	22

Octobreska Subway Station, Moscow — A1542

Subway Stations: No. 3121, Leninski Prospect, Moscow. No. 3122, Moscow Gate, Leningrad. No. 3123, Zavod Bolshevik, Kiev.

1965, Nov. 30 Engraved

3120	A1542	6k indigo	20	10
3121	A1542	6k brown	20	10
3122	A1542	6k gray brn	20	10
3123	A1542	6k sl grn	20	10

Buzzard — A1543

Birds: 2k, Kestrel. 3k, Tawny eagle. 4k, Red kite. 10k, Peregrine falcon. 12k, Golden eagle (horiz.). 14k, Lammergeier (horiz.). 16k, Gyrfalcon.

Perf. 11½x12

1965, Nov.–Dec. Photogravure

3124	A1543	1k gray grn & blk	10	5
3125	A1543	2k pale brn & blk	15	5
3126	A1543	3k lt ol grn & blk	20	5
3127	A1543	4k lt gray brn & blk	25	10
3128	A1543	10k lt vio brn & blk	50	15
3129	A1543	12k bl & blk	60	20
3130	A1543	14k bluish gray & blk	70	25
3131	A1543	16k dl red brn & blk	75	35
		Nos. 3124-3131 (8)	3.25	1.20

Red Star Medal, War Scene and View of Kiev — A1544

Red Star Medal, War Scene and View of: No. 3133, Leningrad. No. 3134, Odessa. No. 3135, Moscow. No. 3136, Brest Litovsk. No. 3137, Volgograd (Stalingrad). No. 3138, Sebastopol.

1965, Dec. 20–30 Perf. 11½

| 3132 | A1544 | 10k red, gold & brn | 35 | 15 |

RUSSIA

3133	A1544	10k red, gold & dk bl	35	15
3134	A1544	10k red, gold & Prus bl	35	15
3135	A1544	10k red, gold & dk vio	35	15
3136	A1544	10k red, gold & dk brn	35	15
3137	A1544	10k red, gold & blk	35	15
3138	A1544	10k red, gold & gray	35	15
		Nos. 3132-3138 (7)	2.45	1.05

Issued to honor the heroism of various cities during World War II.

Map and Flag of Jugoslavia, and National Assembly Building — A1545

1965, Dec. 30 Litho. *Perf. 12*
| 3139 | A1545 | 6k vio bl, red & bis | 20 | 10 |

Issued to commemorate the 20th anniversary of the Republic of Jugoslavia.

Collective Farm Watchman by S.V. Gerasimov — A1547

Painting: 16k, "Major's Courtship" by Pavel Andreievitch Fedotov (horiz.).

1965, Dec. 31 Engraved
| 3145 | A1547 | 12k red & sep | 50 | 25 |
| 3146 | A1547 | 16k red & dk bl | 70 | 30 |

No. 3145 commemorates the 80th anniversary of the birth of the painter S. V. Gerasimov; No. 3146 commemorates the 150th anniversary of the birth of the painter Pavel A. Fedotov (1815-52).

Microscope and Moscow University — A1548

Congress Emblems: No. 3148, Turkeys, geese, chicken and globe. No. 3149, Crystals. No. 3150, Oceanographic instruments and ship No. 3151, Mathematical symbols.

1966 Photo. *Perf. 11½*
3147	A1548	6k dl bl, blk & red	25	10
3148	A1548	6k gray, pur & blk	25	10
3149	A1548	6k ol bis, blk & bl	25	10
3150	A1548	6k grnsh bl & blk	20	10

| 3151 | A1548 | 6k dl yel, red brn & blk | 23 | 10 |
| | | Nos. 3147-3151 (5) | 1.18 | 50 |

Issued to publicize international congresses to be held in Moscow: 9th Congress of Microbiology (No. 3147); 13th Congress on Poultry Raising (No. 3148); 7th Congress on Crystallography (No. 3149); 2nd International Congress of Oceanography (No. 3150); International Congress of Mathematicians (No. 3151). See also Nos. 3309-3310.

Mailman and Milkmaid, 19th Century Figurines — A1549

Design: 10k, Tea set.

1966, Jan. 28 Lithographed
| 3152 | A1549 | 6k multi | 23 | 13 |
| 3153 | A1549 | 10k gray, rose red & vio bl | 40 | 17 |

Bicentenary of Dimitrov Porcelain Works.

Romain Rolland — A1550

Portrait: No. 3155, Eugène Pottier.

1966 Photo. & Engr. *Perf. 11½*
| 3154 | A1550 | 4k dk bl & brn org | 18 | 8 |
| 3155 | A1550 | 4k sl, red & dk red brn | 15 | 8 |

Issued to commemorate the birth centenary of Romain Rolland (1866-1944), French writer (No. 3154); the 150th anniversary of the birth of Eugène Pottier (1816-1887), French poet and author of the "International" (No. 3155).

Horseback Rider, and Flags of Mongolia and Russia — A1551

1966, Jan. 31 Litho. *Perf. 12½x12*
| 3159 | A1551 | 4k red, ultra & vio brn | 20 | 10 |

Issued to commemorate the 20th anniversary of the signing of the Mongolian-Soviet treaty of friendship and mutual assistance.

No. 2728 Overprinted in Silver

ЛУНА-9 — НА ЛУНЕ!
3.2. 1966

1966, Feb. 5 Photo. *Perf. 12*
| 3160 | A1385 | 6k blk, lt bl & red | 1.50 | 50 |

Issued to commemorate the first soft landing on the moon by Luna 9, Feb. 3, 1966.

Map of Antarctica With Soviet Stations — A1552

Diesel Ship "Ob" and Emperor Penguins — A1553

Design: No. 3164, Snocat tractors and aurora australis.

1966, Feb. 14 Photo. *Perf. 11*
3162	A1552	10k sky bl, sil & dk car	50	18
3163	A1553	10k sil & dk car	50	18
3164	A1553	10k dk car, sil & sky bl	50	18

Issued to publicize ten years of Soviet explorations in Antarctica. Nos. 3162-3164 are printed in one sheet with Nos. 3163-3164 se-tenant at the base. No. 3162 has horizontal rows of perforation extending from either mid-side up to the map.

Lenin — A1554

1966, Feb. 22 Photo. *Perf. 12x11½*
| 3165 | A1554 | 10k grnsh blk & gold | 40 | 15 |
| 3166 | A1554 | 10k dk red & sil | 35 | 15 |

96th anniversary of the birth of Lenin.

N.Y. Iljin, Guardsman — A1555

Kremlin Congress Hall — A1556

Portrait: No. 3168, Lt. Gen. G. P. Kravchenko. No. 3169, Pvt. Anatoli Uglovsky.

1966 *Perf. 11½x12*
3167	A1555	4k dp org & vio blk	15	8
3168	A1555	4k grnsh bl & dk pur	15	8
3169	A1555	4k grn & brn	15	8

Issued to honor Soviet heroes.

1966, Feb. 28 Typo. *Perf. 12*
| 3172 | A1556 | 4k gold, red & lt ultra | 20 | 12 |

23rd Communist Party Congress.

Hamlet and Queen from Film "Hamlet" — A1557

Film Scene: 4k, Two soldiers from "The Quick and the Dead."

1966, Feb. 28 Lithographed
| 3173 | A1557 | 4k red, blk & ol | 15 | 8 |
| 3174 | A1557 | 10k ultra & blk | 30 | 12 |

No. 3104 Overprinted Учредительная конференция Всесоюзного общества филателистов. 1966

1966, Mar. 10 Photo. *Perf. 11½x12*
| 3175 | A1533 | 16k gray, rose red & vio blk | 1.50 | 1.00 |

Issued to commemorate the constituent assembly of the All-Union Society of Philatelists, 1966.

Emblem and Skater — A1558

Designs: 6k, Emblem and ice hockey. 10k, Emblem and slalom skier.

1966, March 11 *Perf. 11*
3176	A1558	4k ol, brt ultra & red	15	10
3177	A1558	6k bluish lil, red & dk brn	25	12
3178	A1558	10k lt bl, red & dk brn	40	15

Issued to commemorate the Second Winter Spartacist Games, Sverdlovsk. The label-like upper halves of Nos. 3176-3178 are separated from the lower halves by a row of perforation.

Electric Locomotive — A1559

Designs: 6k, Map of the Lenin Volga-Baltic Waterway, Admiralty, Leningrad, and Kremlin. 10k, Ship passing through lock in waterway (vert.). 12k, M.S. Aleksander Pushkin. 16k, Passenger liner and globe.

1966 Litho. *Perf. 12½x12, 12x12½*
| 3179 | A1559 | 4k multi | 15 | 10 |
| 3180 | A1559 | 6k gray, ultra, red & blk | 20 | 10 |

RUSSIA

3181	A1559	10k Prus bl, gray brn & blk	50	15
3182	A1559	12k bl, ver & blk	45	20
3183	A1559	16k bl & multi	65	25
		Nos. 3179-3183 (5)	1.95	80

Issued to publicize modern transportation. Dates of Issue: Nos. 3179-3181, Aug. 6; Nos. 3182-3183, March 25.

Supreme Soviet Building, Frunze A1560

Sergei M. Kirov A1561

1966, March 25 Photo. Perf. 12

| 3184 | A1560 | 4k dp red | 20 | 8 |

Issued to commemorate the 40th anniversary of the Kirghiz Republic.

1966 Engraved Perf. 12

Portraits: No. 3186, Grigori Ordzhonikidze. No. 3187, Ion Yakir.

3185	A1561	4k dk red brn	15	8
3186	A1561	4k sl grn	15	8
3187	A1561	4k dk gray vio	15	8

No. 3185 issued to commemorate the 80th anniversary of the birth of Sergei M. Kirov (1886-1934), revolutionist and Secretary of the Communist Party Central Committee; No. 3186, the 80th anniversary of the birth of Grigori Ordzhonikidze (1886-1937), a political leader of the Red Army and government official; No. 3187, the 70th anniversary of the birth of Ion Yakir, military leader in October Revolution.

Issue dates: No. 3185, Mar. 27. No. 3186, June 22. No. 3187, July 30.

Souvenir Sheet

Lenin—A1563

Embossed and Typographed

1966, March 29 Imperf.

| 3188 | A1563 | 50k red & sil | 2.25 | 1.00 |

Issued to commemorate the 23rd Communist Party Congress. No. 3188 contains one stamp with simulated perforations; dark red and silver margin. Size: 119x80mm.

Aleksandr E. Fersman (1883-1945), Mineralogist A1564

Portraits: No. 3190, D. K. Zabolotny (1866-1929), microbiologist. No. 3191, M. A. Shatelen (1866-1957), physicist. No. 3191A, Otto Yulievich Schmidt (1891-1956), scientist and arctic explorer.

1966, March 30 Litho. Perf. 12½x12

3189	A1564	4k vio bl & multi	15	8
3190	A1564	4k red brn & multi	15	8
3191	A1564	4k lil & multi	15	8
3191A	A1564	4k Prus bl & brn	15	8

Issued to honor Soviet scientists.

Luna 10 Automatic Moon Station A1565

Overprinted in Red:

„Луна-10"—XXIII съезду КПСС

1966, Apr. 8 Typo. Imperf.

| 3192 | A1565 | 10k gold, blk, brt bl & brt rose | 50 | 25 |

Issued to commemorate the launching of the first artificial moon satellite, Luna 10. The bright rose ink is fluorescent on Nos. 3192-3194.

Type A1565 Without Overprint

1966, Apr. 12 Perf. 12

Design: 12k, Station on moon.

| 3193 | A1565 | 10k multi | 40 | 18 |
| 3194 | A1565 | 12k multi | 50 | 22 |

Day of Space Research, Apr. 12, 1966.

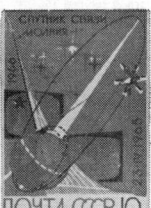 

Lightning 1 and Television Screens A1566

Ernst Thälmann A1567

1966, Apr. 12 Litho. Perf. 12½

| 3195 | A1566 | 10k gold, blk, brt bl & red | 40 | 20 |

Issued to commemorate the launching of the communications satellite "Lightning 1," Apr. 23, 1965.

1966-67 Engraved Perf. 12½x12

Portraits: No. 3197, Wilhelm Pieck. No. 3198, Sun Yat-sen. No. 3199, Sen Katayama.

3196	A1567	6k rose cl	20	10
3197	A1567	6k bl vio	20	10
3198	A1567	6k redsh brn	20	10

Photogravure

| 3199 | A1567 | 6k gray grn ('67) | 20 | 10 |

No. 3196 commemorates the 80th anniversary of the birth of Ernst Thälmann (1886-1944), German Communist leader; No. 3197, the 90th anniversary of the birth of Wilhelm Pieck (1876-1960), President of the German Democratic Republic; No. 3198, the centenary of the birth of Dr. Sun Yat-sen (1866-1925), leader of the Chinese revolution. No. 3199 honors Sen Katayama (1859-1933), who founded the Social Democratic Party in Japan in 1901. Issue dates: No. 3196, Apr. 16, 1966. Nos. 3197-3198, June 22, 1966. 3199, Nov. 2, 1967.

Soldier, 1917, and Astronaut A1568

1966, Apr. 30 Litho. Perf. 11½

| 3200 | A1568 | 4k brt rose & b k | 20 | 8 |

Issued to commemorate the 15th Congress of the Young Communist League (Komsomol).

Ice Hockey Player A1569

1966, Apr. 30

| 3201 | A1569 | 10k red, ultra, gold & blk | 35 | 20 |

Issued to commemorate the Soviet victory in the World Ice Hockey Championships. For souvenir sheet see No. 3232. See also No. 3315.

Nicolai Kuznetsov A1570

Portrait: No. 3203, Imant Sudmalis. No. 3204, Anya Morozova. No. 3205, Filipp Strelets. No. 3206, Tikhon Rumazhkov. (All designs include the Gold Star of Hero of the Soviet Union.)

1966, May 9 Photo. Perf. 12x12½

3202	A1570	4k grn & blk	15	8
3203	A1570	4k ocher & blk	15	8
3204	A1570	4k bl & blk	15	8
3205	A1570	4k brt rose & blk	15	8
3206	A1570	4k vio & blk	15	8
		Nos. 3202-3206 (5)	75	40

Issued to honor heroes of guerrilla warfare during World War II.

Peter I. Tchaikovsky A1571

Designs: 4k, Moscow State Conservatory and Tchaikovsky monument. 16k, Tchaikovsky House, Klin.

1966, May 26 Typo. Perf. 12½

3207	A1571	4k red, yel & blk	10	8
3208	A1571	6k yel, red & blk	15	12
3209	A1571	16k red, bluish gray & blk	40	20

Issued to commemorate the Third International Tchaikovsky Contest, Moscow, May 30-June 29.

Runners—A1572

Designs: 6k, Weight lifters. 12k, Wrestlers.

1966, May 26 Photo. Perf. 11x11½

3210	A1572	4k emer, ol & brn	15	8
3211	A1572	6k org, blk & lt brn	25	12
3212	A1572	12k grnsh bl, brn ol & blk	40	15

Issued to publicize: No. 3210, Znamensky Brothers International Track Competitions; No. 3211, International Weightlifting Competitions; No. 3212, International Wrestling Competitions for Ivan Poddubny Prize.

Jules Rimet World Soccer Cup, Ball and Laurel A1573

Chessboard, Gold Medal, Pawn and King A1574

Designs: No. 3214, Soccer. 12k, Fencers. 16k, Fencer, mask, foil and laurel branch.

1966, May 31 Litho. Perf. 11½

3213	A1573	4k rose red, gold & blk	15	8
3214	A1574	6k emer, tan, blk & red	20	12
3215	A1574	6k brn, gold, blk & white	20	12
3216	A1573	12k brt bl, ol & blk	35	15
3217	A1573	16k multi	50	25
		Nos. 3213-3217 (5)	1.40	70

Nos. 3213-3214 commemorate the World Cup Soccer Championship, Wembley, England, July 11-30; No. 3215 the World Chess Title Match between Tigran Petrosyan and Boris Spassky; Nos. 3216-3217 the World Fencing Championships. For souvenir sheet see No. 3232.

Sable and Lake Baikal, Map of Barguzin Game Reserve A1575

Design: 6k, Map of Lake Baikal region and Game Reserve, brown bear on lake shore.

RUSSIA

1966, June 25   Photo.   *Perf. 12*

| 3218 | A1575 | 4k stl bl & blk | 18 | 8 |
| 3219 | A1575 | 6k rose lake & blk | 27 | 10 |

Issued to commemorate the 50th anniversary of the Barguzin Game Reserve.

Pink Lotus
A1576

Designs: 6k, Palms and cypresses. 12k, Victoria cruziana.

1966, June 30   *Perf. 11½*

3220	A1576	3k grn, pink & yel	12	8
3221	A1576	6k grnsh bl, ol brn & dk brn	25	12
3222	A1576	12k multi	35	15

Issued to commemorate the 125th anniversary of the Sukhum Botanical Garden.

Dogs Ugolek and Veterok after Space Flight
A1577

Designs: No. 3224, Diagram of Solar System, globe and medal of Venus 3 flight. No. 3225, Luna 10, earth and moon.

1966, July 15   *Perf. 12x11½*

| 3223 | A1577 | 6k ocher, ind & org brn | 30 | 12 |
| 3224 | A1577 | 6k crim, blk & sil | 30 | 12 |

Perf. 12x12½

| 3225 | A1577 | 6k dk bl & bis brn | 30 | 12 |

Russian achievements in space.

Itkol Hotel, Mount Cheget and Map of Russia
A1578

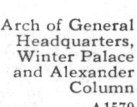

Arch of General Headquarters, Winter Palace and Alexander Column
A1579

Resort Areas: 4k, Ship on Volga River and Zhigul Mountain. 10k, Castle, Kislovodsk. 12k, Ismail Samani Mausoleum, Bukhara, Uzbek. 16k, Hotel Caucasus, Sochi.

Perf. 12½x12, 12½ (6k)

1966   Lithographed

3226	A1578	1k multi	5	5
3227	A1578	4k multi	15	8
3228	A1578	6k multi	20	10
3229	A1578	10k multi	30	12
3230	A1578	12k multi	45	16
3231	A1578	16k multi	60	20
		Nos. 3226-3231 (6)	1.75	71

Issue dates: 10k, Sept. 14. Others, July 20.

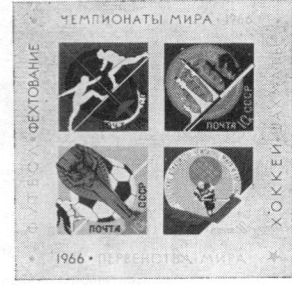

Souvenir Sheet
A1580

1966, July 26   Litho.   *Perf. 11½*

3232	A1580	Souv. sheet of 4	2.25	80
a.		10k red, brnz & blk (fencers)	50	20
b.		10k blk, sil & bl (chess)	50	20
c.		10k bl, sil & blk (soccer cup)	50	20
d.		10k red, blk, gold & bl (ice hockey)	50	20

Issued to commemorate the World Fencing, chess, soccer and ice hockey championships. No. 3232 has marginal inscription in red, blue, gold & black. Size: 109x109mm.

See Nos. 3201, 3213-3217.

Congress Emblem, Congress Palace and Kremlin Tower
A1581

1966, Aug. 6   Photo.   *Perf. 11½x12*

| 3233 | A1581 | 4k brn & yel | 20 | 8 |

Issued to commemorate the 7th Congress of Consumers' Cooperative Societies.

Dove, Crane, Russian and Japanese Flags
A1582

1966, Aug. 9   *Perf. 12½x11½*

| 3234 | A1582 | 6k gray & red | 25 | 12 |

Issued to publicize Soviet-Japanese friendship, and the second meeting of Russian and Japanese delegates at Khabarovsk.

"Knight Fighting with Tiger" by Rustaveli
A1583

Designs: 4k, Shota Rustaveli, bas-relief. 6k, "Avtandil at a Mountain Spring." 50k, Shota Rustaveli Monument and design of 3k stamp.

1966, Aug. 31   Engraved   *Perf. 11½x12½*

3235	A1583	3k ol grn	15	5
3236	A1583	4k brn, yel	15	8
3237	A1583	6k bluish blk, lt ultra	35	12

Souvenir Sheet
Engraved and Photogravure
Imperf.

| 3238 | A1583 | 50k sl grn & bis | 2.50 | 90 |

Issued to commemorate the 800th anniversary of the birth of Shota Rustaveli, Georgian poet, author of "The Knight in the Tiger's Skin." No. 3238 contains one stamp (size: 32x49mm.); dark green margin with design of 6k stamp. Size: 97½x67mm.

Coat of Arms and Fireworks over Moscow
A1584

Lithographed (Lacquered)

1966, Sept. 14   *Perf. 11½*

| 3239 | A1584 | 4k multi | 20 | 8 |

49th anniversary of October Revolution.

Grayling
A1585

Designs (Fish and part of design of 6k stamp): 4k, Sturgeon. 6k, Trawler, net and map of Lake Baikal (vert.). 10k, Two Baikal cisco. 12k, Two Baikal whitefish.

1966, Sept. 25   Photo. & Engr.

3240	A1585	2k multi	10	5
3241	A1585	4k multi	12	8
3242	A1585	6k multi	18	12
3243	A1585	10k multi	30	15
3244	A1585	12k gray, dk grn & red brn	35	20
		Nos. 3240-3244 (5)	1.05	60

Fish resources of Lake Baikal.

Map of Russia and Symbols of Transportation and Communication
A1586

Designs (map of Russia and): No. 3246, Technological education. No. 3247, Agriculture and mining. No. 3248, Increased productivity through five-year plan. No. 3249, Technology and inventions.

1966, Sept. 29   Photo.   *Perf. 11½x12*

3245	A1586	4k ultra & sil	15	8
3246	A1586	4k car & sil	15	8
3247	A1586	4k red brn & sil	15	8
3248	A1586	4k red & sil	15	8
3249	A1586	4k dp grn & sil	15	8
		Nos. 3245-3249 (5)	75	40

Issued to publicize decisions of the 23rd Communist Party Congress.

Government House, Kishinev, and Moldavian Flag
A1587

1966, Oct. 8   Litho.   *Perf. 12½x12*

| 3250 | A1587 | 4k multi | 65 | 8 |

500th anniversary of Kishinev.

Symbolic Water Cycle
A1588

1966, Oct. 12   *Perf. 11½*

| 3251 | A1588 | 6k multi | 20 | 12 |

Hydrological Decade (UNESCO), 1965-74.

Nikitin Monument in Kalinin, Ship's Prow and Map
A1589

1966, Oct. 12   Photogravure

| 3252 | A1589 | 4k multi | 20 | 8 |

Issued to commemorate the 500th anniversary of Afanasii Nikitin's trip to India.

Scene from Opera "Nargiz" by M. Magomayev
A1590

Design: No. 3254, Scene from opera "Kerogli" by Y. Gadjubekov (knight on horseback and armed men).

1966, Oct. 12

| 3253 | A1590 | 4k blk & ocher | 20 | 10 |
| 3254 | A1590 | 4k blk & bl grn | 20 | 10 |

Issued to publicize Azerbaijan opera. Nos. 3253-3254 are printed se-tenant in checkerboard arrangement.

Fighters
A1591

1966, Oct. 26

| 3255 | A1591 | 6k red, blk & ol bis | 23 | 12 |

30th anniversary of Spanish Civil War.

National Militia   Protest Rally
A1592   A1592a

1966, Oct. 26   Litho.   *Perf. 12x12½*

| 3256 | A1592 | 4k red & dk brn | 15 | 8 |

Issued to commemorate the 25th anniversary of the National Militia.

RUSSIA

1966, Oct. 26 Perf. 12
3256A A1592a 6k yel, blk & red 30 15

Issued to proclaim: "Hands off Viet Nam!"

Soft Landing on Moon, Luna 9
A1593

Symbols of Agriculture and Chemistry
A1594

Designs: 1k, Congress Palace, Moscow, and map of Russia. 3k, Boy, girl and Lenin banner. 4k, Flag. 6k, Plane and Ostankino Television Tower. 10k, Soldier and Soviet star. 12k, Steel worker. 16k, "Peace," woman with dove. 20k, Demonstrators in Red Square, flags, carnation and globe. 50k, Newspaper, plane, train and Communications Ministry. 1r, Lenin and industrial symbols.

1966 Lithographed Perf. 12
Inscribed "1966"
3257 A1593 1k dk red brn 5 5
3258 A1593 2k violet 10 5
3259 A1593 3k red lil 10 5
3260 A1593 4k brt red 15 5
3261 A1593 6k ultra 20 5
3262 A1593 10k olive 30 7
3263 A1593 12k red brn 50 9
3264 A1593 16k vio bl 50 15

Photogravure
Perf. 11½
3265 A1594 20k bis, red & dk bl 1.00 25
3266 A1594 30k dp grn & grn 1.25 25
3267 A1594 50k bl & vio bl 2.25 60
3268 A1594 1r blk & red 4.00 1.00
Nos. 3257-3268 (12) 10.40 2.73

No. 3260 was issued on fluorescent paper in 1969.
See also Nos. 3470-3481.

Ostankino Television Tower, Molniya 1 Satellite and Kremlin
A1595

1966, Nov. 19 Litho. Perf. 12
3273 A1595 4k multi 20 8

Issued for New Year, 1967, the 50th anniversary of the October Revolution.

Diagram of Luna 9 Flight
A1596

Arms of Russia and Pennant Sent to Moon
A1597

Design: No. 3276, Luna 9 and photograph of moonscape.

1966, Nov. 25 Typo. Perf. 12
3274 A1596 10k blk & sil 33 15
3275 A1597 10k red & sil 33 15
3276 A1596 10k blk & sil 33 15
   a. Strip of 3 1.00 45

Issued to commemorate the soft landing on the moon by Luna 9, Jan. 31, 1966, and the television program of moon pictures on Feb. 2. Nos. 3274-3276 are printed se-tenant.

Battle of Moscow, 1941—A1598

Details from "Defense of Moscow" Medal and Golden Star Medal
A1599

Design: 10k, Sun rising over Kremlin. Ostankino Tower, chemical plant and rockets.

Perf. 12, 11½ (A1599)
1966, Dec. 1 Photogravure
3277 A1598 4k red brn 15 8
3278 A1599 6k bis & brn 25 12
3279 A1598 10k dp bis & yel 40 15

25th anniversary of Battle of Moscow.

Cervantes and Don Quixote
A1600

1966, Dec. 15 Photo. Perf. 11½
3280 A1600 6k gray & brn 23 12

Issued to commemorate the 350th anniversary of the death of Miguel Cervantes Saavedra (1547-1616), Spanish writer.

Bering's Ship and Map of Voyage to Commander Islands—A1601

Far Eastern Territories: 2k, Medny Island and map. 4k, Petropavlosk-Kamchatski Harbor. 6k, Geyser, Kamchatka (vert.). 10k, Avachinskaya Bay, Kamchatka. 12k, Fur seals, Bering Island. 16k, Guillemots in bird sanctuary, Kurile Islands.

1966, Dec. 25 Litho. Perf. 12
3281 A1601 1k bis & multi 5 5
3282 A1601 2k bis & multi 10 5
3283 A1601 4k dp bl & multi 15 5
3284 A1601 6k multi 20 10
3285 A1601 10k dp bl & multi 30 15
3286 A1601 12k ol & multi 40 18
3287 A1601 16k lt bl & multi 50 20
Nos. 3281-3287 (7) 1.70 83

Communications Satellite, Molniya 1
A1602

Design: No. 3289, Luna 11 moon probe, moon, earth and Soviet emblem.

1966, Dec. 29 Photo. Perf. 12x11½
3288 A1602 6k blk, vio bl & brt rose 35 15
3289 A1602 6k blk & brt rose 35 15

Issued to publicize space explorations. The bright rose is fluorescent.

Golden Stag, Scythia, 6th Century B.C.—A1603

Treasures from the Hermitage, Leningrad: 6k, Silver jug, Persia, 5th Century A.D. 10k, Statue of Voltaire by Jean Antoine Houdon. 12k, Malachite vase, Ural, 1840. 16k, "The Lute Player," by Michelangelo de Caravaggio. (6k, 10k, 12k are vertical).

1966, Dec. 29 Engraved Perf. 12
3290 A1603 4k yellow 18 8
3291 A1603 6k gray 27 12
3292 A1603 10k dl vio 35 15
3293 A1603 12k emerald 45 25
3294 A1603 16k ocher 55 25
Nos. 3290-3294 (5) 1.80 85

Sea Water Converter and Pavilion at EXPO '67
A1604

Designs (Pavilion and): 6k, Splitting atom (vert.). 10k, "Proton" space station. 30k, Russian pavilion.

1967, Jan. 25 Litho. Perf. 12
3295 A1604 4k multi 15 8
3296 A1604 6k multi 25 12
3297 A1604 10k multi 33 15

Souvenir Sheet
3298 A1604 30k multi 1.25 65

Issued to commemorate EXPO '67, International Exhibition, Montreal, Apr. 28-Oct. 27. No. 3298 contains one stamp. Light blue and silver margin shows map of EXPO '67; black and red inscription. Size: 126½x75mm.

1st Lieut. B. I. Sizov
A1605

Design: No. 3300, Sailor V. V. Khodyrev.

1967, Feb. 16 Photo. Perf. 12x11½
3299 A1605 4k dl yel & ocher 15 10
3300 A1605 4k gray & dk gray 15 10

Issued to honor heroes of World War II.

Woman's Head and Pavlov Shawl
A1606

1967, Feb. 16 Perf. 11
3301 A1606 4k vio, red & grn 20 12

International Woman's Day, Mar. 8.

Movie Camera and Film
A1607

1967, Feb. 16 Photo. Perf. 11½
3302 A1607 6k multi 23 10

Issued to publicize the 5th International Film Festival, Moscow, July 5-20.

Trawler Fish Factory and Fish
A1608

Designs: No. 3304, Refrigeration ship. No. 3305, Crab canning ship. No. 3306, Fishing trawler. No. 3307, Black Sea seiner.

1967, Feb. 28 Litho. Perf. 12x11½
Ships in Black and Red
3303 A1608 6k bl & gray 30 10
3304 A1608 6k bl & gray 30 10
3305 A1608 6k bl & gray 30 10
3306 A1608 6k bl & gray 30 10
3307 A1608 6k bl & gray 30 10
Nos. 3303-3307 (5) 1.50 50

Issued to publicize the Russian fishing industry. Nos. 3303-3307 printed in vertical strips of five in sheets of 20 (4x5).

Newspaper Forming Hammer and Sickle, Red Flag
A1609

1967, March 13 Litho. Perf. 12x12½
3308 A1609 4k cl brn, red, yel & brn 18 8

50th anniversary of newspaper Izvestia.

RUSSIA

Congress Type of 1966
Congress Emblems and: No. 3309, Moscow State University, construction site and star. No. 3310, Pile driver, mining excavator, crossed hammers, globe and "V."

1967, March 10   Photo.   Perf. 11½

| 3309 | A1548 | 6k ultra, brt bl & blk | 20 | 10 |
| 3310 | A1548 | 6k blk, org red & bl | 20 | 10 |

Issued to publicize international congresses to be held in Moscow: 7th General Assembly Session of the International Standards Association (No. 3309); 5th International Mining Congress (No. 3310).

International Tourist Year Emblem and Travel Symbols—A1610

1967, March 10   Perf. 11

| 3314 | A1610 | 4k blk, sky bl & sil | 20 | 8 |

International Tourist Year, 1967.

No. 3201 Overprinted: "BeHa-1967"

1967, March 29   Litho.   Perf. 11½

| 3315 | A1569 | 10k multi | 40 | 20 |

Issued to commemorate the victory of the Russian team in the Ice Hockey Championships, Vienna, March 18–29. Overprint reads: "Vienna-1967."

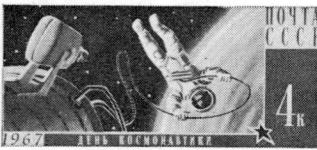

Space Walk—A1611

Designs: 10k, Rocket launching from satellite. 16k, Spaceship over moon, and earth.

1967, March 30   Litho.   Perf. 12

3316	A1611	4k bis & multi	18	10
3317	A1611	10k blk & multi	40	20
3318	A1611	16k lil & multi	60	30

National Cosmonauts' Day.

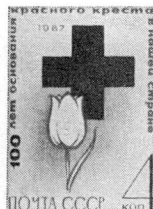

Lenin as Student, by V. Tsigal   A1612

Sculptures of Lenin: 3k, Monument at Ulyanovsk by M. Manizer. 4k, Lenin in Razliv, by V. Pinchuk (horiz.). 6k, Head, by G. Neroda. 10k, Lenin as Leader, statue, by N. Andreyev.

1967   Perf. 12x11½, 11½x12   Photogravure

3319	A1612	2k ol grn, sep & buff	10	5
3320	A1612	3k mar & brn	15	5
3321	A1612	4k ol blk & gold	20	8
3322	A1612	6k dk bl, sil & blk	25	10
3323	A1612	10k sil, gray & blk	50	15

| 3323A | A1612 | 10k gold, gray & blk | 35 | 15 |
| Nos. 3319-3323A (6) | | | 1.55 | 58 |

97th anniversary of the birth of Lenin. Issue dates: No. 3323A, Oct. 25. Others, Apr. 22.

Lt. M. S. Kharchenko and Battle Scenes   A1613

Designs: No. 3325, Maj. Gen. S. V. Rudnev. No. 3326, M. Shmyrev.

1967, Apr. 24   Perf. 12x11½

3324	A1613	4k brt pur & ol bis	15	8
3325	A1613	4k ultra & ol bis	15	8
3326	A1613	4k org brn & ol bis	15	8

Issued to honor partisan heroes of World War II.

Marshal S. S. Biryuzov   A1614

1967, May 9   Photo.   Perf. 12

| 3327 | A1614 | 4k ocher & sl grn | 20 | 8 |

Issued to honor Marshal S. S. Biryuzov, Hero of the Soviet Union.

Driver Crossing Lake Ladoga   A1615

1967, May 9   Perf. 11½

| 3328 | A1615 | 4k plum & bl gray | 20 | 8 |

25th anniversary of siege of Leningrad.

Views of Old and New Minsk   A1616

1967, May 9

| 3329 | A1616 | 4k sl grn & blk | 20 | 8 |

900th anniversary of Minsk.

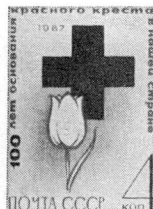

Red Cross and Tulip   A1617

1967, May 15   Perf. 12

| 3330 | A1617 | 4k yel brn & red | 20 | 8 |

Centenary of the Russian Red Cross.

Stamps of 1918 and 1967   A1618

1967   Photo.   Perf. 11½

| 3331 | A1618 | 20k bl & blk | 75 | 35 |
| a. | Souv. sheet of 2 | | 2.00 | 1.00 |

Issued to publicize the All-Union Philatelic Exhibition "50 Years of the Great October," Moscow, Oct. 1–10. Printed se-tenant with light brown label showing exhibition emblem.

No. 3331a contains two black, imperf. stamps similar to No. 3331; red and gold margin with commemorative inscription. Size: 91x76mm.

Issue dates: 20k, May 25. Sheet, Oct. 1.

On Oct. 3 No. 3331 was re-issued with "Oct. 1–10" printed in blue on the label. Price 90 cents.

Komsomolsk-on-Amur and Map of Amur River   A1619

1967, June 12   Perf. 12x12½

| 3332 | A1619 | 4k red & brn | 25 | 8 |

Issued to commemorate the 35th anniversary of the Soviet youth town, Komsomolsk-on-Amur. Printed with red and brown label showing boy and girl of Young Communist League and tents.

Souvenir Sheet

Sputnik Orbiting Earth—A1620

1967, June 24   Litho.   Perf. 13x12

| 3333 | A1620 | 30k blk & multi | 4.00 | 1.00 |

Issued to commemorate the 10th anniversary of the launching of Sputnik 1, the first artificial satellite, Oct. 4, 1957. No. 3333 contains one perforated stamp (size: 73x25mm). Multicolored sheet margin shows trajectory, planetary system, galaxy and commemorative inscription. Size: 104x131mm.

Motorcyclist   A1621

Photogravure and Engraved

1967, June 24   Perf. 12x11½

| 3334 | A1621 | 10k multi | 30 | 18 |

Issued to publicize the International Motor Rally, Moscow, July 19.

G. D. Gai   A1622

1967, June 30   Photo.   Perf. 12

| 3335 | A1622 | 4k red & blk | 20 | 7 |

Issued in memory of G. D. Gai (1887–1937), Corps Commander of the First Cavalry, 1920.

Children's Games Emblem and Trophy   A1623

1967, July 8   Perf. 11½

| 3336 | A1623 | 4k sil, red & blk | 18 | 12 |

Issued to commemorate the 10th National Athletic Games of School Children, Leningrad, July, 1967.

Games Emblem and Trophy   A1624

Designs: No. 3338, Cup and dancer. No. 3339, Cup and bicyclists. No. 3340, Cup and diver.

1967, July 20

3337	A1624	4k sil, red & blk	15	8
3338	A1624	4k sil, red & blk	15	8
3339	A1624	4k sil, red & blk	15	8
3340	A1624	4k sil, red & blk	15	8

Issued to commemorate the 4th National Spartacist Games, celebrating the 50th anniversary of the USSR. Nos. 3337–3338 and Nos. 3339–3340 are printed se-tenant in 2 sheets of 50, in checkerboard arrangement.

V. G. Klochkov   A1625

1967, July 20   Perf. 12½x12

| 3341 | A1625 | 4k red & blk | 20 | 7 |

Issued to honor V. G. Klochkov (1911–41), Hero of the Soviet Union. Printed with alternating red and black label showing citation.

Soviet Flag, Arms and Moscow Views   A1626

Arms of U.S.S.R. and Laurel   A1627

Flag, Crest and Capital of Republic of: No. 3343, Armenia. No. 3344, Azerbaijan. No. 3345, Byelorussia. No. 3346, Estonia. No. 3347, Georgia. No. 3348, Kazakhstan. No. 3349, Kirghizia. No. 3350, Latvia. No. 3351, Lithuania. No. 3352, Moldavia. No. 3353, Tadzhikistan. No. 3354, Turkmenistan. No. 3355, Ukraine. No. 3356, Uzbekistan.

1967, Aug. 4   Litho.   Perf. 12½x12

3342	A1626	4k multi	14	7
3343	A1626	4k multi	14	7
3344	A1626	4k multi	14	7

RUSSIA

3345	A1626	4k multi	14	7
3346	A1626	4k multi	14	7
3347	A1626	4k multi	14	7
3348	A1626	4k multi	14	7
3349	A1626	4k multi	14	7
3350	A1626	4k multi	14	7
3351	A1626	4k multi	14	7
3352	A1626	4k multi	14	7
3353	A1626	4k multi	14	7
3354	A1626	4k multi	14	7
3355	A1626	4k multi	14	7
3356	A1626	4k multi	14	7
3357	A1627	4k red, gold & blk	14	7
		Nos. 3342-3357 (16)	2.24	1.12

50th anniversary of October Revolution.

Communication Symbols
A1628

1967, Aug. 16   Photo.   Perf. 12

| 3358 | A1628 | 4k crim & sil | 50 | 25 |

Development of communications in USSR.

Flying Crane, Dove and Anniversary Emblem
A1629

1967, Aug. 20   Perf. 12½x12

| 3359 | A1629 | 16k sil, red & blk | 55 | 25 |

Issued to commemorate the 3rd Russo-Japanese Friendship Meeting, held at Khabarovsk. Emblem is for 50th anniversary of October Revolution.

Karl Marx and Title Page of "Das Kapital"—A1630

1967, Aug. 22 Engr. Perf. 12½x12

| 3360 | A1630 | 4k sep & dk red | 20 | 12 |

Issued to commemorate the centenary of the publication of "Das Kapital" by Karl Marx.

Russian Checkers Players
A1631

Design: 6k, Woman gymnast.

Photogravure and Engraved

1967, Sept. 9   Perf. 12x11½

| 3361 | A1631 | 1k lt brn, dp brn & sl | 10 | 5 |
| 3362 | A1631 | 6k ol bis & mar | 25 | 10 |

Issued to commemorate the World Championship of Russian Checkers (Shashki) at Moscow (1k), and the World Championship of Rhythmic Gymnastics (6k).

Javelin
A1632

Sport: 3k, Running. 4k, Jumping.

1967, Sept. 9 Engr. Perf. 12x12½

3363	A1632	2k brn red	10	5
3364	A1632	3k dp bl	15	5
3365	A1632	4k Prus bl	20	8

Issued to commemorate the Europa Cup Championships held at Kiev, Sept. 15–17.

Ice Skating and Olympic Emblem
A1633

Designs: 3k, Ski jump. 4k, Emblem of Winter Olympics (vert.). 10k, Ice hockey. 12k, Long-distance skiing.

Photogravure and Engraved

1967, Sept. 20   Perf. 11½

3366	A1633	2k gray, blk & bl	8	5
3367	A1633	3k bis, ocher, blk & grn	12	5
3368	A1633	4k gray, bl, red & blk	16	6
3369	A1633	10k bis, brn, bl & blk	40	10
3370	A1633	12k gray, blk, lil & grn	50	15
		Nos. 3366-3370 (5)	1.26	41

Issued to publicize the 10th Winter Olympic Games, Grenoble, France, Feb. 6–18, 1968.

Silver Fox
A1634

Young Guards Memorial
A1635

Fur-bearing Animals: 2k, Arctic blue fox (horiz.). 6k, Red fox (horiz.). 10k, Muskrat (horiz.). 12k, Ermine. 16k, Sable. 20k, Mink (horiz.).

1967, Sept. 20   Photogravure

3371	A1634	2k brn, blk & gray bl	12	5
3372	A1634	4k tan, dk brn & gray bl	18	6
3373	A1634	6k gray grn, ocher & blk	25	8
3374	A1634	10k yel grn, dk brn & ocher	33	15
3375	A1634	12k lil, blk & bis	42	18
3376	A1634	16k red, brn & blk	45	20
3377	A1634	20k gray bl, blk & dk brn	60	30
		Nos. 3371-3377 (7)	2.35	1.02

International Fur Auctions in Leningrad.

1967, Sept. 23

| 3378 | A1635 | 4k mag, org & blk | 20 | 8 |

Issued to commemorate the 25th anniversary of the fight of the Young Guards at Krasnodon against the Germans.

Map of Cedar Valley Reservation and Snow Leopard—A1636

1967, Oct. 14   Perf. 12

| 3379 | A1636 | 10k ol bis & blk | 35 | 15 |

Far Eastern Cedar Valley Reservation.

Planes and Emblem
A1637

1967, Oct. 14   Perf. 11½

| 3380 | A1637 | 6k dp bl, red & gold | 25 | 12 |

Issued to commemorate the 25th anniversary of the French Normandy-Neman aviators, who fought on the Russian Front.

Militiaman and Soviet Emblem
A1638

1967, Oct. 14   Perf. 12½x12

| 3381 | A1638 | 4k ver & ultra | 20 | 8 |

50th anniversary of the Soviet Militia.

Space Station Orbiting Moon
A1639

Science Fiction: 6k, Explorers on the moon (horiz.). 10k, Rocket flying to the stars. 12k, Landscape on Red Planet (horiz.). 16k, Satellites from outer space.

1967, Oct. 25 Perf. 12x12½, 12½x12

3382	A1639	4k multi	15	8
3383	A1639	6k multi	25	12
3384	A1639	10k multi	35	15
3385	A1639	12k multi	45	20
3386	A1639	16k multi	50	25
		Nos. 3382-3386 (5)	1.70	80

Emblem of U.S.S.R. and Red Star
A1640

Lenin Addressing 2nd Congress of Soviets, by V. A. Serov
A1641

Paintings: No. 3389, Lenin pointing to Map, by L. A. Schmatjko. No. 3390, The First Cavalry Army, by M. B. Grekov. No. 3391, Working Students on the March, by B. V. Yoganson. No. 3392, Russian Friendship for the World, by S. M. Karpov. No. 3393, Five-Year Plan Morning, by Y. D. Romas. No. 3394, Farmers' Holiday, by S. V. Gerasimov. No. 3395, Victory in the Great Patriotic War, by Y. K. Korolev. No. 3396, Builders of Communism, by L. M. Merpert and Y. N. Skripkov.

Lithographed and Embossed

1967, Oct. 25   Perf. 11½

3387	A1640	4k gold, yel, red & dk brn	18	8
3388	A1641	4k gold & multi	18	8
3389	A1641	4k gold & multi	18	8
3390	A1641	4k gold & multi	18	8
3391	A1641	4k gold & multi	18	8
3392	A1641	4k gold & multi	18	8
3393	A1641	4k gold & multi	18	8
3394	A1641	4k gold & multi	18	8
3395	A1641	4k gold & multi	18	8
3396	A1641	4k gold & multi	18	8
	a.	Souv. sheet of 2	3.00	1.25
		Nos. 3387-3396 (10)	1.80	80

50th anniversary of October Revolution. No. 3396a contains two 40k imperf. stamps similar to Nos. 3388 and 3396. Red margin contains Lenin portrait and first documents of the Soviet state. Size: 92x132mm. Issued Nov. 5.

Souvenir Sheet

Hammer, Sickle and Sputnik
A1642

1967, Nov. 5 Engr. Perf. 12½x12

| 3397 | A1642 | 1r lake | 3.50 | 2.00 |

Issued to commemorate the 50th anniversary of the October Revolution. No. 3397 contains one stamp. Marginal inscription and design in lake and gray blue; margin also contains "50" as a watermark. Size: 128½x80mm.

Ostankino Television Tower
A1643

1967, Nov. 5   Litho.   Perf. 11½

| 3398 | A1643 | 16k gray, org & blk | 60 | 20 |

Jurmala Resort and Hepatica
A1644

Health Resorts: 6k, Narva-Joesuu and Labrador tea. 10k, Druskininkai and cranberry blossoms. 12k, Zelenogradsk and Scotch heather (vert.). 16k, Svetlogorsk and club moss (vert.).

RUSSIA

Perf. 12½x12, 12x12½
1967, Nov. 30 Lithographed
Flowers in Natural Colors
3399	A1644	4k bl & blk	15	10
3400	A1644	6k ocher & blk	22	10
3401	A1644	10k grn & blk	30	15
3402	A1644	12k gray ol & blk	35	20
3403	A1644	16k brn & blk	50	20
		Nos. 3399-3403 (5)	1.52	75

Health resorts of Baltic region.

Emergency Commission Emblem
A1645

1967, Dec. 11 Photo. **Perf. 11½**
3404	A1645	4k ultra & red	18	8

Issued to commemorate the 50th anniversary of the All-Russia Emergency Commission (later the State Security Commission).

Hotel Russia and Kremlin
A1646

1967, Dec. 14
3405	A1646	4k sil, dk brn & brt pink	18	7

New Year 1968. The pink is fluorescent.

Soldiers, Sailors, Congress Building, Kharkov, and Monument to the Men of Arsenal—A1647

Designs: 6k, Hammer and sickle and scenes from industry and agriculture. 10k, Ukrainians offering bread and salt, monument of the Unknown Soldier, Kiev, and Lenin monument in Zaporozhye.

1967, Dec. 20 Litho. **Perf. 12½**
3406	A1647	4k multi	15	7
3407	A1647	6k multi	23	8
3408	A1647	10k multi	30	15

Issued to commemorate the 50th anniversary of the Ukrainian Socialist Soviet Republic.

Three Kremlin Towers
A1648

Kremlin: 6k, Cathedral of the Annunciation (horiz.). 10k, Konstantin and Elena, Nabatnaya and Spasski towers. 12k, Ivan the Great bell tower. 16k, Kutafya and Troitskaya towers.

Perf. 12x11½, 11½x12
1967, Dec. 25 Engr. and Photo.
3409	A1648	4k dk brn & cl	18	6
3410	A1648	6k dk brn, yel & grn	25	8
3411	A1648	10k mar & sl	40	12
3412	A1648	12k sl grn, yel & vio	48	14
3413	A1648	16k brn, pink & red	50	20
		Nos. 3409-3413 (5)	1.81	60

Coat of Arms, Lenin's Tomb and Rockets—A1649

Designs: No. 3415, Agricultural Progress: Wheat, reapers and silo. No. 3416, Industrial Progress: Computer tape, atom symbol, cogwheel and factories. No. 3417, Scientific Progress: Radar, microscope, university buildings. No. 3418, Communications progress: Ostankino TV tower, railroad bridge, steamer and Aeroflot emblem (vert.).

1967, Dec. 25 Engr. **Perf. 12½**
3414	A1649	4k maroon	15	5
3415	A1649	4k green	15	5
3416	A1649	4k red brn	15	5
3417	A1649	4k vio bl	15	5
3418	A1649	4k dk bl	15	5
		Nos. 3414-3418 (5)	75	25

Issued to publicize the material and technical basis of Russian Communism.

Monument to the Unknown Soldier, Moscow
A1650

1967, Dec. 25
3419	A1650	4k carmine	15	6

Issued to commemorate the dedication of the Monument of the Unknown Soldier of World War II in the Kremlin Wall.

Seascape by Ivan Aivazovsky
A1651

Paintings: 3k, Interrogation of Communists by B. V. Yoganson. No. 3422, The Lacemaker, by V. A. Tropinin (vert.). No. 3423, Bread-makers, by T. M. Yablonskaya. No. 3424, Alexander Nevsky, by P. D. Korin (vert.). No. 3425, The Boyar Morozov Going into Exile by V. I. Surikov. No. 3426, The Swan Maiden, by M. A. Vrubel (vert.). No. 3427, The Arrest of a Propagandist by Ilya E. Repin. 16k, Moscow Suburb in February by G. G. Nissky.

Perf. 12½x12, 12x12½, 12, 11½
1967, Dec. 29 Lithographed
Size: 47x33mm., 33x47mm.
3420	A1651	3k multi	15	5
3421	A1651	4k multi	15	5
3422	A1651	4k multi	15	5

Size: 60x35mm., 35x60mm.
3423	A1651	6k multi	20	8
3424	A1651	6k multi	20	8
3425	A1651	6k multi	20	8

Size: 47x33mm., 33x47mm.
3426	A1651	10k multi	40	12
3427	A1651	10k multi	40	12
3428	A1651	16k multi	50	18
		Nos. 3420-3428 (9)	2.35	81

Tretiakov Art Gallery, Moscow.

Globe, Wheel and Workers of the World
A1652

1968, Jan. 18 Photo. **Perf. 12**
3429	A1652	6k ver & grn	23	10

14th Trade Union Congress.

Lt. S. Baikov and Velikaya River Bridge
A1653

(War Memorial and) No. 3431. Lt. A. Pokalchuk. No. 3432, P. Gutchenko.

1968, Jan. 20 **Perf. 12½x12**
3430	A1653	4k bl gray & blk	18	6
3431	A1653	4k rose & blk	18	6
3432	A1653	4k gray grn & blk	18	6

Issued to honor heroes of World War II.

Thoroughbred and Horse Race
A1654

Horses: 6k, Arab mare and dressage (vert.). 10k, Orlovski trotters. 12k, Altekin horse performing (vert.). 16k, Donskay race horse.

1968, Jan. 23 **Perf. 11½**
3433	A1654	4k ultra, blk & red lil	15	6
3434	A1654	6k crim, blk & ultra	25	10
3435	A1654	10k grnsh bl, blk & org	35	14
3436	A1654	12k org brn, blk & ap grn	45	18
3437	A1654	16k ol grn, blk & red	60	22
		Nos. 3433-3437 (5)	1.80	70

Issued to publicize horse breeding.

Maria I. Ulyanova
A1655

1968, Jan. 30 **Perf. 12x12½**
3438	A1655	4k ind & pale grn	15	7

Issued in memory of Maria I. Ulyanova (1878-1937), Lenin's sister.

Soviet Star and Flags of Army, Air Force and Navy
A1656

Lenin Addressing Troops in 1919
A1657

Designs: No. 3441, Dneprostroi Dam and sculpture "On Guard." No. 3442, 1918 poster and marching volunteers. No. 3443, Red Army entering Vladivostok, 1922, and soldiers' monument in Primorie. No. 3444, Poster "Red Army as Liberator," Western Ukraine. No. 3445, Poster "Westward," defeat of German army. No. 3446, "Battle of Stalingrad" monument and German prisoners of war. No. 3447, Victory parade on Red Square, May 24, 1945, and Naval War Memorial, Berlin. Nos. 3448-3449, Modern weapons and Russian flag.

1968, Feb. 20 Typo. **Perf. 12x12½**
3439	A1656	4k gold & multi	14	6

Photogravure **Perf. 11½x12**
3440	A1657	4k blk, red, pink & sil	14	6
3441	A1657	4k gold, blk & red	14	6

Lithographed **Perf. 12½x12**
3442	A1657	4k yel grn, blk, red & buff	14	6
3443	A1657	4k grn, dk brn, red & bis	14	6
3444	A1657	4k grn & multi	14	6
3445	A1657	4k yel grn & multi	14	6

Photogravure **Perf. 11½x12, 12x11½**
3446	A1657	4k blk, sil & red	14	6
3447	A1657	4k gold, blk, pink & red	14	6
3448	A1656	4k blk, red & sil	14	6
		Nos. 3439-3448 (10)	1.40	60

Souvenir Sheet
1968, Feb. 23 Litho. **Imperf.**
3449	A1656	1r blk, sil & red	3.50	1.75

Issued to commemorate the 50th anniversary of the Armed Forces of the USSR. No. 3449 contains one stamp (size: 25x37½mm.) with simulated perforations. Ultramarine and multicolored margin shows Victory Order. Size: 71½x98mm.

Maxim Gorki
A1658

RUSSIA

1968, Feb. 29 Photo. *Perf. 12*
3450 A1658 4k gray ol & dk brn 15 6

Birth centenary of Maxim Gorki (1868–1936), writer.

Fireman, Fire Truck and Boat
A1659

1968, Mar. 30 Photo. *Perf. 12x12½*
3451 A1659 4k red & blk 15 6

50th anniversary of Soviet Fire Guards.

Link-up of Kosmos 186 and 188 Satellites
A1660

1968, Mar. 30 *Perf. 11½*
3452 A1660 6k blk, dp lil rose & gold 23 8

First link-up in space of two satellites, Kosmos 186 and Kosmos 188, Oct. 30, 1967.

N. N. Popudrenko
A1661

Design: No. 3453, P. P. Vershigora.

1968, Mar. 30 *Perf. 12½x12*
3453 A1661 4k gray grn & blk 12 6
3454 A1661 4k lt pur & blk 12 6

Issued to honor partisan heroes of World War II.

Globe and Hand Shielding from War
A1662

1968, Apr. 11 *Perf. 11½*
3455 A1662 6k sil, mar, ver & blk 23 8

Issued to publicize the emergency session of the World Federation of Trade Unions and to express solidarity with the people of Vietnam.

Space Walk
A1663

Designs: 6k, Docking operation of Kosmos 186 and Kosmos 188. 10k, Exploration of Venus.

1968, Apr. 12 Lithographed
3456 A1663 4k multi 20 6
3457 A1663 6k multi 30 8
3458 A1663 10k multi 55 15

Issued to publicize National Astronauts' Day. Nos. 3456-3458 are printed in same sheet with alternating commemorative labels.

Lenin, 1919
A1664

Lenin Portraits: No. 3460, Addressing crowd on Red Square, Nov. 7, 1918. No. 3461, Full-face portrait, taken in Petrograd, Jan. 1918.

Engraved and Photogravure
1968, Apr. 16 *Perf. 12x11½*
3459 A1664 4k gold, brn & red 15 6
3460 A1664 4k gold, red & blk 15 6
3461 A1664 4k gold, brn, buff & red 15 6

98th anniversary of the birth of Lenin.

Alisher Navoi
A1665

1968, Apr. 29 Photo. *Perf. 12x12½*
3462 A1665 4k dp brn 15 6

Issued to commemorate the 525th anniversary of the birth of Alisher Navoi, Uzbek poet.

Karl Marx
A1666

1968, May 5 Engr. *Perf. 11½x12*
3463 A1666 4k blk & red 18 6

Issued to commemorate the 150th anniversary of the birth of Karl Marx (1818–1883), political philosopher and writer.

Frontier Guard
A1667

Jubilee Badge
A1668

1968, May 22 Photo. *Perf. 11½*
3464 A1667 4k sl grn, ocher & red 15 6
3465 A1668 6k sl grn, blk & red brn 23 8

Issued to commemorate the 50th anniversary of the Russian Frontier Guards.

Crystal and Congress Emblem
A1669

Congress Emblems and: No. 3467, Power lines and factories. No. 3468, Ground beetle. No. 3469, Roses and carbon rings.

1968, May 30
3466 A1669 6k bl, dk bl & grn 20 8
3467 A1669 6k org, gold & dk brn 20 8
3468 A1669 6k red brn, gold & blk 20 8
3469 A1669 6k lil rose, org & blk 20 8

International congresses to be held in Leningrad: 8th Congress for Mineral Research (No. 3466); 7th World Power Conference (No. 3467); 13th Entomological Congress (No. 3468); 4th Congress for the Study of Volatile Oils (No. 3469).

Types of 1966
Designs as Before
1968, June 20 Engr. *Perf. 12*
3470 A1593 1k dk red brn 12 5
3471 A1593 2k dp vio 12 5
3472 A1593 3k plum 15 5
3473 A1593 4k brt red 18 6
3474 A1593 6k blue 27 7
3475 A1593 10k olive 38 10
3476 A1593 12k red brn 45 12
3477 A1593 16k vio bl 55 16

Perf. 12½
3478 A1594 20k red 75 17
3479 A1594 30k brt grn 1.05 30
3480 A1594 50k vio bl 1.85 50

Perf. 12x12½
3481 A1594 1r gray, red brn & blk 4.00 1.00
Nos. 3470-3481 (12) 9.87 2.63

Sadriddin Aini
A1670

1968, June 30 Photo. *Perf. 12½x12*
3482 A1670 4k ol bis & mar 15 6

Issued to commemorate the 90th anniversary of the birth of Sadriddin Aini (1878–1954), Tadzhik poet.

Post Rider and C.C.E.P. Emblem
A1671

Design: No. 3484, Modern means of communications (train, ship, planes and C.C.E.P. emblem).

1968, June 30
3483 A1671 6k gray & red brn 22 8

3484 A1671 6k org brn & bis 22 8

Issued to publicize the annual session of the Council of the Consultative Commission on Postal Investigation of the Universal Postal Union (C.C.E.P.), Moscow, Sept. 20–Oct. 5.

Bolshevik Uprising, Kiev
A1672

1968, July 5 *Perf. 11½*
3485 A1672 4k gold, red & plum 20 6

Issued to commemorate the 50th anniversary of the Ukrainian Communist Party.

Athletes
A1673

1968, July 9
3486 A1673 4k yel, dp car & bis 20 6

Issued to publicize the First Youth Summer Sports Games celebrating the 50th anniversary of the Leninist Young Communists League.

Field Ball
A1674

Table Tennis
A1675

Designs: 6k, 20th Baltic Regatta. 10k, Soccer player and cup. 12k, Scuba divers.

Perf. 12x12½, 12½x12½
1968, July 18 Lithographed
3487 A1674 2k red & multi 12 5
3488 A1675 4k pur & multi 15 5
3489 A1674 6k bl & multi 20 7
3490 A1674 10k multi 30 11
3491 A1675 12k grn & multi 42 14
Nos. 3487-3491 (5) 1.19 42

Issued to publicize various European youth sports competitions.

Rhythmic Gymnast
A1676

Olympic Sports: 6k, Weight lifting. 10k, Rowing. 12k, Women's hurdling. 16k, Fencing. 40k, Running.

RUSSIA

1968, July 31 Photo. Perf. 11½
Gold Background
3492	A1676	4k bl & grn	18	5
3493	A1676	6k dp rose & pur	25	7
3494	A1676	10k yel grn & grn	40	10
3495	A1676	12k org & red brn	45	13
3496	A1676	16k ultra & pink	55	18
	Nos. 3492-3496 (5)		1.83	53

Souvenir Sheet
Lithographed and Photogravure
Perf. 12½x12
| 3497 | A1676 | 40k gold, grn, org & gray | 1.50 | 50 |

Issued to publicize the 19th Olympic Games, Mexico City, Oct. 12-27. No. 3497 contains one stamp; margin decorated with Aztec calendar stone, Olympic torch runner and Olympic rings and inscriptions. Size: 91x66mm.

Gediminas Tower, Vilnius
A1677
1968, Aug. 14 Photo. Perf. 11½
| 3498 | A1677 | 4k mag, tan & red | 20 | 5 |

Issued to commemorate the 50th anniversary of Soviet power in Lithuania.

Tbilisi State University
A1678
1968, Aug. 14 Perf. 12
| 3499 | A1678 | 4k sl grn & lt brn | 20 | 5 |

50th anniversary of Tbilisi State University, Georgia.

Laocoon
A1679
1968, Aug. 16 Perf. 11½
| 3500 | A1679 | 6k sep, blk & mar | 3.00 | 3.00 |

Issued to "promote solidarity with Greek democrats."

Red Army Man, Cavalry Charge and Order of the Red Banner of Battle—A1680

Designs: 3k, Young man and woman, Dneprostroi Dam and Order of the Red Banner of Labor. 4k, Soldier, storming of the Reichstag, Berlin, and Order of Lenin. 6k, "Restoration of National Economy" (workers), and Order of Lenin. 10k, Young man and woman cultivating virgin land and Order of Lenin. 50k, like 2k.

1968, Aug. 25 Litho. Perf. 12½x12
3501	A1680	2k gray, red & ocher	10	3
3502	A1680	3K multi	10	5
3503	A1680	4k org, ocher & rose car	15	5
3504	A1680	6k multi	20	7
3505	A1680	10k ol & multi	30	10
	Nos. 3501-3505 (5)		85	32

Souvenir Sheet
Imperf.
| 3506 | A1680 | 50k ultra, red & bis | 1.75 | 75 |

Nos. 3501-3506 issued to commemorate the 50th anniversary of the Lenin Young Communist League, Komsomol. No. 3506 contains one stamp. Orange margin with Komsomol medal. Size: 77x100mm.

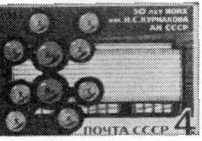

Chemistry Institute and Dimeric Molecule
A1681
1968, Sept. 3 Photo. Perf. 11½
| 3507 | A1681 | 4k vio bl, dp lil rose & blk | 20 | 12 |

50th anniversary of Kurnakov Institute for General and Inorganic Chemistry.

Letter, Compass Rose, Ship and Plane
A1682

Compass Rose and Stamps of 1921 and 1965
A1683
1968, Sept. 16 Photo. Perf. 11½
| 3508 | A1682 | 4k dk car rose, brn & brt red | 15 | 6 |
| 3509 | A1683 | 4k dk bl, blk & bis | 15 | 6 |

No. 3508 issued for Letter Writing Week, Oct. 7-13, and No. 3509 for Stamp Day and the Day of the Collector.

The 26 Baku Commissars, Sculpture by Merkurov
A1684
1968, Sept. 20
| 3510 | A1684 | 4k multi | 20 | 6 |

Issued to commemorate the 50th anniversary of the shooting of the 26 Commissars, Baku, Sept. 20, 1918.

Toyvo Antikaynen
A1685
1968, Sept. 30 Perf. 12
| 3511 | A1685 | 6k gray & sep | 25 | 12 |

Issued to commemorate the 70th anniversary of the birth of Toyvo Antikaynen (1898-1941), Finnish workers' organizer.

Russian Merchant Marine Emblem
A1686
1968, Sept. 30 Perf. 12x11½
| 3512 | A1686 | 6k bl, red & ind | 25 | 12 |

Issued to honor the Russian Merchant Marine.

Order of the October Revolution
A1687

Pavel P. Postyshev
A1688
Typographed and Embossed
1968, Sept. 30 Perf. 12½x12
| 3513 | A1687 | 4k gold & multi | 18 | 12 |

Issued to commemorate the 51st anniversary of the October Revolution. Printed with alternating label showing Supreme Soviet and Kremlin Senate Tower.

Engr. Perf. 12½x12
Designs: No. 3515, Stepan G. Shaumyan (1878-1918). No. 3516, Akmal Ikramov. (1898-1938). No. 3516A, N. G. Markin (1893-1918). No. 3516B, P. E. Dybenko (1889-1938). No. 3516C, S. V. Kosior (1889-1939). No. 3516D, Vasili Kikvidze (1895-1919).

Size: 21½x32½mm.
3514	A1688	4k bluish blk	20	5
3515	A1688	4k bluish blk	20	5
3516	A1688	4k gray blk	20	5
3516A	A1688	4k black	20	5
3516B	A1688	4k dk car ('69)	20	5
3516C	A1688	4k ind ('69)	20	5
3516D	A1688	4k dk brn ('70)	20	5
	Nos. 3514-3516D (7)		1.40	35

Issued to honor outstanding workers for the Communist Party and the Soviet State.
Issue dates: Nos. 3514-3516, Sept. 30, 1968. No. 3516A, Dec. 31, 1968. No. 3516D, Sept. 24, 1970. Others, May 15, 1969. See also No. 3782.

American Bison and Zebra
A1689

Designs: No. 3518, Purple gallinule and lotus. No. 3519, Great white egrets (vert.). No. 3520, Ostrich and golden pheasant (vert.). No. 3521, Eland and guanaco. No. 3522, European spoonbill and glossy ibis.

Perf. 12½x12, 12x12½
1968, Oct. 16 Lithographed
3517	A1689	4k ocher, brn & blk	18	6
3518	A1689	4k ocher & multi	18	6
3519	A1689	6k ol & blk	22	8
3520	A1689	6k gray & multi	22	8
3521	A1689	10k dp grn & multi	38	12
3522	A1689	10k emer & multi	38	12
	Nos. 3517-3522 (6)		1.56	52

Issued to publicize the Askania Nova and Astrakhan state reservations.

Ivan S. Turgenev
A1690

Warrior, 1880 B.C. and Mt. Ararat
A1691
1968, Oct. 10 Engr. Perf. 12x12½
| 3523 | A1690 | 4k green | 1.00 | 5 |

Issued to commemorate the 150th anniversary of the birth of Ivan S. Turgenev (1818-1883), writer.

Engraved and Photogravure
1968, Oct. 18 Perf. 11½
Design: 12k, David Sasountsi monument, Yerevan, and Mt. Ararat.
| 3524 | A1691 | 4k blk & dk bl, gray | 12 | 6 |
| 3525 | A1691 | 12k dk brn & choc, bis | 35 | 14 |

2,750 anniversary of Yerevan, capital of Armenia.

First Radio Tube Generator and Laboratory
A1692
1968, Oct. 26 Photo. Perf. 11½
| 3526 | A1692 | 4k dk bl, dp bis & blk | 15 | 5 |

50th anniversary of Russia's first radio laboratory at Gorki (Nizhni Novgorod).

Prospecting Geologist and Crystals
A1693

Designs: 6k, Prospecting for metals: seismographic test apparatus with shock wave diagram, plane and truck. 10k, Oil derrick in the desert.

1968, Oct. 31 Litho. Perf. 11½
3527	A1693	4k bl & multi	22	10
3528	A1693	6k multi	15	15
3529	A1693	10k multi	33	25

Issued for Geology Day. No. 3527 printed with alternating label with commemorative inscription, showing crystals, compass rose and geologist's hammer.

Borovoe, Kazakhstan
A1694

Landscapes: No: 3531, Djety-Oguz, Kirghizia (vert.). No. 3532, Issyk-kul Lake, Kirghizia. No. 3533, Borovoe, Kazakhstan (vert.).

1968, Nov. 20 Typographed
| 3530 | A1694 | 4k dk red brn & multi | 12 | 5 |
| 3531 | A1694 | 4k gray & multi | 12 | 5 |

RUSSIA

| 3532 | A1694 | 6k dk red brn & multi | 22 | 6 |
| 3533 | A1694 | 6k blk & multi | 22 | 6 |

Issued to publicize recreational areas in the Kazakh and Kirghiz Republics.

Medals and Cup, Riccione, 1952, 1961 and 1965
A1695

Designs: 4k, Medals, Eiffel Tower and Arc de Triomphe, Paris, 1964. 6k, Porcelain plaque, gold medal and Brandenburg Gate, Debria, Berlin, 1950, 1959. 12k, Medal and prize-winning stamp No. 2888, Buenos Aires. 16k, Cups and medals, Rome, 1952, 1954. 20k, Medals, awards and views, Vienna, 1961, 1965. 30k, Trophies, Prague, 1950, 1955, 1962.

1968, Nov. 27   Photo.   Perf. 11½x12

3534	A1695	4k dp cl, sil & blk	18	5
3535	A1695	6k dl bl, gold & blk	25	6
3536	A1695	10k lt ultra, gold & blk	33	10
3537	A1695	12k bl, sil & blk	40	12
3538	A1695	16k red, gold & blk	45	18
3539	A1695	20k brt bl, gold & blk	55	23
3540	A1695	30k org brn, gold & blk	85	33
	Nos. 3534-3540 (7)		3.01	1.07

This issue recalls awards to Russian post office at foreign stamp exhibitions.

Worker with Banner
A1696

V. K. Lebedinsky and Radio Tower
A1697

1968, Nov. 29   Perf. 12x12½

| 3541 | A1696 | 4k red & blk | 15 | 12 |

Issued to commemorate the 50th anniversary of the Estonian Workers' Commune.

1968, Nov. 29   Perf. 11½x12

| 3542 | A1697 | 4k gray grn, blk & gray | 15 | 12 |

Issued to commemorate the centenary of the birth of V. K. Lebedinsky (1868–1937), scientist.

Souvenir Sheet

Communication via Satellite
A1698

1968, Nov. 29   Lithographed   Perf. 12

3543	A1698	Souv. sheet of 3	2.25	90
a.	16k Molniya I		50	25
b.	16k Map of Russia		50	25
c.	16k Ground Station "Orbite"		50	25

Issued to publicize television transmission throughout Russia with the aid of the earth satellite Molniya I. No. 3543 is printed in gray, olive, orange and red. Three stamps and 3 labels with commemorative inscriptions are arranged checkerwise. Size: 95x75mm.

Sprig, Spasski Tower, Lenin Univ. and Library
A1699

1968, Dec. 1   Perf. 11½

| 3544 | A1699 | 4k ultra, sil, grn & red | 12 | 12 |

Issued for New Year 1969.

Maj. Gen. Georgy Beregovoi
A1700

1968, Dec. 14   Photo.   Perf. 11½

| 3545 | A1700 | 10k Prus bl, blk & red | 30 | 12 |

Flight of Soyuz 3, Oct. 26–30.

Rail-laying and Casting Machines
A1701

Design: 4k, Railroad map of the Soviet Union and train.

1968, Dec. 14   Perf. 12½x12

| 3546 | A1701 | 4k rose mag & org | 12 | 5 |
| 3547 | A1701 | 10k brn & emer | 27 | 10 |

Russian railroad transportation.

Newspaper Banner and Monument
A1702

1968, Dec. 23   Perf. 11½

| 3548 | A1702 | 4k tan, red & dk brn | 15 | 12 |

Issued to commemorate the 50th anniversary of the communist party of Byelorussia.

The Reapers, by A. Venetzianov
A1703

Knight at the Crossroads, by Viktor M. Vasnetsov
A1704

Paintings: 2k, The Last Day of Pompeii, by Karl P. Bryullov. 4k, Capture of a Town in Winter, by Vasili I. Surikov. 6k, The Lake, by I. I. Levitan. 10k, Alarm, 1919 (family) by K. Petrov-Vodkin. 16k, Defense of Sebastopol, 1942, by A. Deineka. 20k, Sculptor with a Bust of Homer, by G. Korzhev. 30k, Celebration on Uritsky Square, 1920, by B. Koustodiev. 50k, Duel between Peresvet and Chelubey, by M. Avilov.

Lithographed

1968, Dec. 25   Perf. 12x12½, 12½

3549	A1703	1k multi	10	5
3550	A1704	2k multi	15	5
3551	A1704	3k multi	18	5
3552	A1704	4k multi	20	5
3553	A1704	6k multi	30	5
3554	A1703	10k multi	42	10
3555	A1704	16k multi	50	18
3556	A1703	20k multi	55	22
3557	A1704	30k multi	75	33
3558	A1704	50k multi	1.35	50
	Nos. 3549-3558 (10)		4.50	1.59

Russian State Museum, Leningrad.

House, Zaoneje, 1876
A1705

Russian Architecture: 4k, Carved doors, Gorki Oblast, 1848. 6k, Castle, Kizhi, 1714. 10k, Fortress wall, Rostov-Yaroslav, 16th–17th centuries. 12k, Gate, Tsaritsino, 1785. 16k, Architect Rossi Street, Leningrad.

1968, Dec. 27   Engr.   Perf. 12x12½

3559	A1705	3k dp brn, ocher	15	5
3560	A1705	4k grn, yel	18	5
3561	A1705	6k vio, gray vio	20	10
3562	A1705	10k dk bl, grnsh gray	30	10
3563	A1705	12k car, gray	35	10
3564	A1705	16k blk, yel	45	15
	Nos. 3559-3564 (6)		1.63	55

Banners of Young Communist League, October Revolution Medal—A1707

1968, Dec. 31   Litho.   Perf. 12

| 3566 | A1707 | 12k red, yel & blk | 35 | 12 |

Award of Order of October Revolution to the Young Communist League on its 50th anniversary.

Soldiers on Guard
A1708

1969, Jan. 1   Perf. 12x12½

| 3567 | A1708 | 4k org & cl | 15 | 7 |

Issued to commemorate the 50th anniversary of the Latvian Soviet Republic.

Revolutionaries and Monument
A1709

Designs: 4k, Partisans and sword. 6k, Workers and Lenin Medals.

1969, Jan. Photogravure   Perf. 11½

3568	A1709	2k ocher & rose cl	6	5
3569	A1709	4k ocher & red	12	5
3570	A1709	6k dk ol, mag & red	18	6

Issued to commemorate the 50th anniversary of the Byelorussian Soviet Republic.

Souvenir Sheet

Vladimir Shatalov, Boris Volynov, Alexei S. Elisseyev, Evgeny Khrunov—A1710

1969, Jan. 22   Imperf.

| 3571 | A1710 | 50k dp bis & dk brn | 1.75 | 65 |

Issued to commemorate the first team flights of Soyuz 4 and 5, Jan. 16, 1969. No. 3571 contains one stamp with simulated perforations. Commemorative inscription in margin and drawing of linked spacecraft. Size: 95x68mm.

Leningrad University
A1711

1969, Jan. 23   Photo.   Perf. 12½x12

| 3572 | A1711 | 10k blk & mar | 30 | 10 |

Issued to commemorate the 150th anniversary of the University of Leningrad.

RUSSIA

Ivan A. Krylov   Nikolai Filchenkov
A1712   A1713

1969, Feb. 13 Litho. Perf. 12x12½
3573 A1712 4k blk & multi   15 6

Issued to commemorate the bicentenary of the birth of Ivan A. Krylov (1769?–1844), fable writer.

1969   **Photogravure**

Designs: No. 3575, Alexander Kosmodemiansky. No. 3575A, Otakar Yarosh, member of Czechoslovak Svoboda Battalion.

3574 A1713 4k dl rose & blk   10 5
3575 A1713 4k emer & dk brn 10 5
3575A A1713 4k bl & blk   10 5

Issued to honor heroes of World War II. Issue dates: No. 3575A, May 9. Others, Feb. 23.

"Shoulder to the Wheel," Parliament, Budapest
A1714

Design: "Shoulder to the Wheel" is a sculpture by Zigmond Kisfaludi-Strobl.

1969, Mar. 21 Typo. Perf. 11½
3576 A1714 6k blk, ver & lt grn 18 6

Issued to commemorate the 50th anniversary of the Hungarian Soviet Republic.

Oil Refinery and Salavat Tualeyev Monument
A1715

1969, Mar. 22 Litho. Perf. 12
3577 A1715 4k multi   15 6

Issued to commemorate the 50th anniversary of the Bashkir Soviet Socialist Republic.

Sergei P. Korolev, Sputnik 1, Space Monument, Moscow
A1716

Vostok on Launching Pad
A1717

Designs: No. 3579, Zond 2 orbiting moon, and photograph of earth made by Zond 5. 80k, Spaceship Soyuz 3.

Perf. 12½x12, 12x12½
1969, Apr. 12   **Lithographed**
3578 A1716 10k blk, vio & grn 30 10
3579 A1716 10k dk brn, yel & brn red 30 10
3580 A1717 10k multi   30 10

Souvenir Sheet
Perf. 12
3581 A1716 80k vio, grn & red 2.50 1.10

Issued for National Cosmonauts' Day. No. 3581 contains one stamp (size: 37x 24mm.); olive bister decorative margin with green inscription. Size: 90x67mm.

Lenin University, Kazan, and Kremlin
A1718

Designs (Places Connected with Lenin): No. 3583, Lenin House, Kuibyshev. No. 3584, Lenin House, Pskov. No. 3585, Lenin House, Shushensko. No. 3586, Straw Hut, Razliv. No. 3587, Lenin Museum, Gorki. No. 3588, Smolny Institute, Leningrad. No. 3589, Lenin's room, Kremlin. No. 3590, Lenin Museum, Ulyanovsk. No. 3591, Lenin House, Ulyanovsk.

1969   **Photogravure**   **Perf. 11½**
3582 A1718 4k pale rose & multi 15 5
3583 A1718 4k beige & multi   15 5
3584 A1718 4k bis & multi   15 5
3585 A1718 4k gray vio & multi   15 5
3586 A1718 4k vio & multi   15 5
3587 A1718 4k bl & multi   15 5
3588 A1718 4k brick red & multi 15 5
3589 A1718 4k rose red & multi   15 5
3590 A1718 4k lt red brn & multi 15 5
3591 A1718 4k dl grn & multi   15 5
        Nos. 3582-3591 (10) 1.50 50

99th anniversary of the birth of Lenin.

Telephone, Transistor Radio and Trademark
A1719

1969, Apr. 25   **Perf. 12½x12**
3592 A1719 10k sep & dp org 25 12

50th anniversary of VEF Electrical Co.

ILO Emblem and Globe
A1720

1969, May 9   **Perf. 11**
3593 A1720 6k car ro e & gold 15 12

Issued to commemorate the 50th anniversary of the International Labor Organization.

Suleiman Stalsky
A1721

1969, May 15 Photo. Perf. 12½x12
3595 A1721 4k tan & ol grn 12 12

Birth centenary of Suleiman Stalsky (1869–1937), Dagestan poet.

Yasnaya Polyana Rose
A1722

Flowers: 4k, "Stroynaya" lily. 10k, Cattleya orchid. 12k, "Listopad" dahlia. 14k, "Ural Girl" gladioli.

1969, May 15 Litho. Perf. 11½
3596 A1722 2k gray & multi   10 5
3597 A1722 4k gold & multi   12 5
3598 A1722 10k gold & multi 27 10
3599 A1722 12k gold & multi 33 12
3600 A1722 14k gold & multi 35 15
        Nos. 3596-3600 (5) 1.17 47

Issued to publicize the work of the Botanical Gardens of the Academy of Sciences.

Ukrainian Academy of Sciences
A1723

1969, May 22 Photo. Perf. 12½x12
3601 A1723 4k brn & yel   12 6

Issued to commemorate the 50th anniversary of the Ukrainian Academy of Sciences.

Film, Camera and Medal
A1724

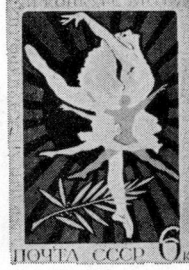

Ballet Dancers
A1725

1969, June 3 Litho. Perf. 12x12½
3602 A1724 6k rose car, blk & gold 25 10
3603 A1725 6k dk brn & multi   25 10

No. 3602 commemorates the International Film Festival in Moscow. No. 3603 commemorates the 1st International Young Ballet Artists' Competitions.

Congress Emblem and Cell Division   Estonian Singer and Festival Emblem
A1726   A1727

1969, June 10 Photo. Perf. 11½
3605 A1726 6k dp cl, lt bl & yel 18 12

Issued to publicize the 3rd International Congress of Protozoologists, Leningrad.

1969, June 14   **Perf. 12x12½**
3606 A1727 4k ver & bis   12 12

Centenary of the Estonian Song Festival.

Mendeleev and Formula with Author's Corrections
A1728

Design: 30k, Dmitri Ivanovich Mendeleev (vert.).

Engraved and Lithographed
1969, June 20   **Perf. 12**
3607 A1728 6k brn & rose   30 15

RUSSIA

Souvenir Sheet

3608 A1728 30k car rose   1.25 60

Issued to commemorate the centenary of the Periodic Law (classification of elements), formulated by Dimitri I. Mendeleev (1834–1907). No. 3608 contains one engraved stamp (size: 29x37mm). Draft of Periodic Table from Mendeleev's workbook in gray on buff in margin. Size: 76½x102½ mm.

Hand Holding Peace Banner and World Landmarks
A1729

1969, June 20 Photo. Perf. 11½

3609 A1729 10k bl, dk brn & gold   27   10

20th anniversary of the Peace Movement.

Laser Beam Guiding Moon Rocket
A1730

1969, June 20

3610 A1730 4k sil, blk & red   12   12

Issued to commemorate the 50th anniversary of Soviet scientific inventions.

Ivan Kotlyarevski
A1731

Typographed and Photogravure
1969, June 25 Perf. 12½x12

3611 A1731 4k blk, ol & lt brn   12   6

Issued to commemorate the 200th anniversary of the birth of Ivan Kotlyarevski (1769–1838), Ukrainian writer.

No. 2717 Overprinted in Vermilion   Стокгольм. 1969

1969, June 25 Photo. Perf. 11½

3612 A1306 6k Prus bl & plum   1.50   80

Issued to commemorate the Russian victory in the Ice Hockey World Championships, Stockholm, 1969.

"Hill of Glory" Monument and Minsk Battle Map
A1732

1969, July 3 Litho. Perf. 12½x12

3613 A1732 4k red & ol   12   6

Issued to commemorate the 25th anniversary of the liberation of White Russia from the Germans.

Eagle, Flag and Map of Poland
A1733

Design: No. 3615, Hands holding torch, flags of Bulgaria and Russia, and Bulgarian coat of arms.

1969, July 10 Photo. Perf. 12

3614 A1733 6k red & bis   18   6

Lithographed

3615 A1733 6k bis, red, grn & blk   18   6

No. 3614 issued to commemorate the 25th anniversary of the Polish Republic; 3615 commemorates the liberation of Bulgaria from the Germans.

Monument to 68 Heroes
A1734

1969, July 15 Photo. Perf. 12

3616 A1734 4k red & mar   12   12

25th anniversary of the liberation of Nikolayev from the Germans.

Old Samarkand
A1735

Design: 6k, Intourist Hotel, Samarkand.

1969, July 15 Typographed

3617 A1735 4k multi   10   6
3618 A1735 6k multi   15   8

2500th anniversary of Samarkand.

Volleyball
A1736

Munkascy and "Woman Churning Butter"
A1737

Design: 6k, Kayak race.

Photogravure and Engraved
1969, July 20 Perf. 11½

3619 A1736 4k dp org & red brn   12   6
3620 A1736 6k multi   18   8

Issued to publicize the European Junior Volleyball Championships (4k) and the European Rowing Championships (6k).

1969, July 20 Photogravure

3621 A1737 6k dk brn, blk & org   20   12

Issued to commemorate the 125th anniversary of the birth of Mihaly von Munkascy (1844–1900), Hungarian painter.

Miners' Monument
A1738

1969, July 30

3622 A1738 4k sil & mag   20   12

Issued to commemorate the centenary of the founding of the city of Donetsk, in the Donets coal basin.

Machine Gun Cart, by Mitrofan Grekov—A1739

1969, July 30 Engr. Perf. 12½x12

3623 A1739 4k red brn & brn red   15   12

Issued to commemorate the 50th anniversary of the First Mounted Army.

Barge Pullers Along the Volga, by Repin—A1740

Ilya E. Repin, Self-portrait
A1741

Repin Paintings: 6k, "Not Expected." 12k, Confession. 16k, Dnieper Cossacks.

Perf. 12½x12, 12x12½
1969, Aug. 5 Lithographed

3624 A1740 4k multi   20   5
3625 A1740 6k multi   27   6
3626 A1741 10k bis, red brn & blk   35   10
3627 A1740 12k multi   45   12
3628 A1740 16k multi   50   16
Nos. 3624-3628 (5)   1.77   49

Issued to commemorate the 125th anniversary of the birth of Ilya E. Repin (1844–1930), painter.

Runner **V. L. Komarov**
A1742   A1743

Designs: 10k, Athlete on rings. 20k, Like 4k.

1969, Aug. 9 Perf. 12x12½

3629 A1742 4k red, bis & blk   12   5
3630 A1742 10k grn, lt bl & blk   30   10

Souvenir Sheet
Imperf.

3631 A1742 20k red, bis & blk   80   40

9th Trade Union Spartakiad, Moscow. No. 3631 contains one stamp with simulated perforations. Gray and multicolored margin with commemorative inscription. Size: 68x94mm.

1969, Aug. 22 Photo. Perf. 12x11½

3632 A1743 4k ol & brn   15   12

V. L. Komarov (1869–1945), botanist.

Hovannes Tumanian, Armenian Landscape
A1744

1969, Sept. 1 Typo. Perf. 12½x12

3633 A1744 10k blk & pck bl   25   12

Birth centenary of Hovannes Tumanian (1869–1923), Armenian poet.

Turkmenian Wine Horn, 2nd Century
A1745

Mahatma Gandhi
A1746

Designs: 6k, Persian Simurg vessel (giant anthropomorphic bird), 13th century. 12k, Head of goddess Kannon, Korea, 8th century. 16k, Bodhisattva, Tibet, 7th century. 20k, Statue of Ebisu and fish (tai), Japan, 17th century.

1969, Sept. 3 Litho. Perf. 12x12½

3634 A1745 4k bl & multi   18   5
3635 A1745 6k lil & multi   25   6
3636 A1745 12k red & multi   40   12
3637 A1745 16k bl vio & multi   45   16
3638 A1745 20k pale grn & multi   60   20
Nos. 3634-3638 (5)   1.88   59

Issued to show treasures from the State Museum of Oriental Art.

1969, Sept. 10 Engraved

3639 A1746 6k dp brn   25   6

Issued to commemorate the centenary of the birth of Mohandas K. Gandhi (1869–1948), leader in India's fight for independence.

350　　　　　　　　　　　　　　　　　　　　RUSSIA

Black Stork Feeding Young
A1747

Designs: 6k, Doe and fawn (red deer). 10k, Fighting bison. 12k, Lynx and cubs. 16k, Wild pig and piglets.

1969, Sept. 10　Photo.　Perf. 12
Size: 75x23mm. (10k); 35x23mm. (others).

3640	A1747	4k blk, yel grn & red	10	6
3641	A1747	6k bl grn, dk brn & ocher	15	8
3642	A1747	10k dk brn, dl org & dp org	30	10
3643	A1747	12k dk & yel grn, brn & gray	30	12
3644	A1747	16k gray, yel grn & dk brn	35	16
		Nos. 3640-3644 (5)	1.20	52

Belovezhskaya Forest reservation.

Komitas
A1748

1969, Sept. 18　Typo.　Perf. 12½x12
| 3645 | A1748 | 6k blk, gray & sal | 18 | 12 |

Birth centenary of Komitas (S. N. Sogomonian (1869–1935)), Armenian composer.

Lisa Chaikina
A1749

A. Cheponis, J. Aleksonis and G. Borisa
A1750

Design: No. 3647, Major S. I. Gritsevets and fighter planes.

1969, Sept. 20　Photo.　Perf. 12½x12
| 3646 | A1749 | 4k ol & brt grn | 15 | 6 |
| 3647 | A1749 | 4k gray & blk | 15 | 6 |

Perf. 11½
| 3648 | A1750 | 4k hn brn, brn & buff | 15 | 12 |

Heroes of the Soviet Union.

 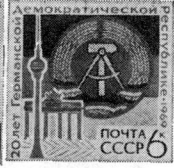

Ivan P. Pavlov　　East German Arms, TV Tower and Brandenburg Gate
A1751　　　　A1752

1969, Sept. 26
| 3649 | A1751 | 4k multi | 12 | 12 |

Issued to commemorate the 120th anniversary of the birth of Ivan Petrovich Pavlov (1849–1936), physiologist.

1969, Oct. 7　　Lithographed
| 3650 | A1752 | 6k red, blk & gold | 20 | 12 |

Issued to commemorate the 20th anniversary of the German Democratic Republic.

Aleksei V. Koltsov　National Emblem
A1753　　　　A1754

1969, Oct. 14　Photo.　Perf. 12x12½
| 3652 | A1753 | 4k lt bl & brn | 12 | 12 |

Issued to commemorate the 160th anniversary of the birth of Aleksei Vasilievich Koltsov (1809–1842), poet.

1969, Oct. 14　　Perf. 12x11½
| 3653 | A1754 | 4k gold & red | 12 | 12 |

Issued to commemorate the 25th anniversary of the liberation of the Ukraine from the Nazis.

Stars, Hammer and Sickle
A1755

1969, Oct. 21　Typo.　Perf. 11½
| 3654 | A1755 | 4k vio bl, gold, yel & red | 15 | 12 |

52nd anniversary of October Revolution.

Georgy Shonin and Valery Kubasov
A1756

Designs: No. 3656, Anatoly Filipchenko, Vladislav Volkov and Viktor Gorbatko. No. 3657, Vladimir Shatalov and Alexey Eliseyev.

1969, Oct. 22　Photo.　Perf. 12½x12
3655	A1756	10k blk & gold	30	10
3656	A1756	10k blk & gold	30	10
3657	A1756	10k blk & gold	30	10

Issued to commemorate the group flight of the space ships Soyuz 6, Soyuz 7 and Soyuz 8, Oct. 11–13. Nos. 3655–3657 are printed se-tenant.

Lenin as a Youth
A1757

1969, Oct. 25　Engraved　Perf. 11½
| 3658 | A1757 | 4k dk red, pink | 12 | 12 |

Issued to publicize the First Russian Youth Philatelic Exhibition, Kiev, dedicated to Lenin's 100th birthday.

Emblem of Communications Unit of Army
A1758

1969, Oct. 30　　Photogravure
| 3659 | A1758 | 4k dk red, red & bis | 12 | 12 |

Issued to commemorate the 50th anniversary of the Communications Troops of Soviet Army.

Souvenir Sheet

Lenin and Quotation—A1759
Lithographed and Embossed

1969, Nov. 6　　Imperf.
| 3660 | A1759 | 50k red, gold & pink | 1.75 | 60 |

Issued to commemorate the 52nd anniversary of the October Revolution. Size: 98x59mm.

Cover of "Rules of the Kolkhoz" and Farm Woman's Monument
A1760

1969, Nov. 18　Photo.　Perf. 12½x12
| 3661 | A1760 | 4k brn & gold | 12 | 12 |

Issued to publicize the 3rd All Union Collective Farmers' Congress, Moscow, Nov.–Dec.

Vasilissa, the Beauty, by Ivan Y. Bilibin
A1761

Designs (Book Illustrations by Ivan Y. Bilibin): 10k, Marya Morevna. 16k, Finist, the Fine Fellow (horiz.). 20k, The Golden Cock. 50k, The Sultan and the Czar. The inscriptions on the 16k and 20k are transposed. 4k, 10k, 16k are fairy tales; 20k and 50k are tales by Pushkin.

1969, Nov. 20　Litho.　Perf. 12
3662	A1761	4k gray & multi	18	10
3663	A1761	10k gray & multi	35	20
3664	A1761	16k gray & multi	50	25

3665	A1761	20k gray & multi	60	25
3666	A1761	50k gray & multi	1.35	50
		Nos. 3662-3666 (5)	2.98	1.30

Issued to honor the illustrator and artist Ivan Y. Bilibin.
Nos. 3662–3666 were printed se-tenant in strips of 5 with 16k turned sideways.

USSR Emblems Dropped on Venus, Radar Installation and Orbits
A1762

Design: 6k, Interplanetary station, space capsule and orbits.

1969, Nov. 25　Photo.　Perf. 12x11½
| 3667 | A1762 | 4k bis, blk & red | 12 | 5 |
| 3668 | A1762 | 6k gray, lil rose & blk | 18 | 6 |

Issued to commemorate the completion of the flights of the space stations Venera 5 and Venera 6.

Flags of Russia　　Russian State
and Afghanistan　　Emblem and Star
A1763　　　　A1764

1969, Nov. 30　Photo.　Perf. 11½
| 3669 | A1763 | 6k red, blk & grn | 18 | 6 |

Issued to commemorate the 50th anniversary of diplomatic relations between Russia and Afghanistan.

Coil Stamp
1969, Nov. 13　　Perf. 11x11½
| 3670 | A1764 | 4k red | 18 | 12 |

MiG Jet and First MiG Fighter Plane—A1765

1969, Dec. 15　　Perf. 11½x12
| 3671 | A1765 | 6k red, blk & gray | 25 | 12 |

Issued to honor Soviet aircraft builders.

Lenin and Flag
A1766

Typographed and Lithographed
1969, Dec. 25　　Perf. 11½
| 3672 | A1766 | 4k gold, bl, red & blk | 12 | 12 |

Issued for "Happy New Year 1970, birth centenary of Lenin."

RUSSIA

Antonov 2—A1767
Aircraft: 3k, PO-2. 4k, ANT-9. 6k, TsAGI 1-EA. 10k, ANT-20 "Maxim Gorki." 12k, Tupolev-104. 16k, MIG-10 helicopter. 20k, Ilyushin-62. 50k, Tupolev-144.

Photogravure and Engraved
1969 *Perf. 11½x12*

3673	A1767	2k bis & multi	10	5
3674	A1767	3k multi	12	5
3675	A1767	4k multi	12	5
3676	A1767	6k multi	18	6
3677	A1767	10k lt vio & multi	27	10
3678	A1767	12k multi	33	12
3679	A1767	16k multi	45	16
3680	A1767	20k multi	50	20
		Nos. 3673-3680 (8)	2.07	79

Souvenir Sheet
Imperf.

| 3681 | A1767 | 50k bl & multi | 2.10 | 75 |

Issued to publicize the history of national aeronautics and aviation. No. 3681 contains one stamp. In the margin is a quotation by N. E. Zhukovsky and the signs of the zodiac, partly overlapping the stamp. Size: 91x65mm.
Issue dates: Nos. 3679 and 3681, Dec. 31; others Dec. 25.

Photograph of Earth by Zond 7
A1768

Designs: No. 3683a, same as 10k. No. 3683b, Photograph of moon.

1969, Dec. 26 *Photo.* *Perf. 12x11½*

| 3682 | A1768 | 10k blk & multi | 35 | 10 |

Souvenir Sheet
Imperf. *Litho.*

3683	A1768	Sheet of 2	3.25	1.25
a.		50k ind & multi	1.50	50
b.		50k dk brn & multi	1.50	50

Issued to publicize the space explorations of the automatic stations Zond 6, Nov. 10-17, 1968, and Zond 7, Aug. 8-14, 1969. No. 3683 contains 2 imperf. stamps (size: 27x40 mm.) with simulated perforations. Light blue margin showing trajectories around earth and moon and black commemorative inscription. Size: 116x 79mm.

Model Aircraft—A1769
Technical Sports: 4k, Motorboats. 6k, Parachute jumping.

1969, Dec. 26 *Engr.* *Perf. 12½x12*

3684	A1769	3k brt mag	12	5
3685	A1769	4k dl bl grn	14	5
3686	A1769	6k red org	20	6

Romanian Arms and Soviet War Memorial, Bucharest
A1770

1969, Dec. 31 *Photo.* *Perf. 11½*

| 3687 | A1770 | 6k rose red & brn | 22 | 6 |

Issued to commemorate the 25th anniversary of Romania's liberation from fascist rule.

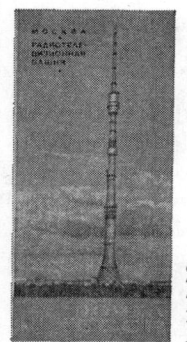

Ostankino Television Tower, Moscow
A1771

1969, Dec. 31 *Typo.* *Perf. 12*

| 3688 | A1771 | 10k multi | 30 | 10 |

Lenin, by N. Andreyev—A1772
Paintings: No. 3690, Lenin at Marxist Meeting, St. Petersburg, by A. Moravov. No. 3691, Lenin at Second Party Day, by Y. Vinogradov. No. 3692, First Day of Soviet Power, by F. Modorov. No. 3693, Conversation with Lenin, by A. Shirokov. No. 3694, Farmers' Delegation Meeting Lenin, by Modorov. No. 3695, With Lenin, by V. A. Serov. No. 3696, Lenin on May 1, 1920, by I. Brodsky. No. 3697, Builder of Communism, by a group of painters. No. 3698, Mastery of Space, by A. Deyneka.

1970, Jan. 1 *Litho.* *Perf. 12*

3689	A1772	4k multi	12	5
3690	A1772	4k multi	12	5
3691	A1772	4k multi	12	5
3692	A1772	4k multi	12	5
3693	A1772	4k multi	12	5
3694	A1772	4k multi	12	5
3695	A1772	4k multi	12	5
3696	A1772	4k multi	12	5
3697	A1772	4k multi	12	5
3698	A1772	4k multi	12	5
		Nos. 3689-3698 (10)	1.20	50

Centenary of birth of Lenin (1870-1924).

Map of Antarctic, "Mirny" and "Vostok"
A1773

Design: 16k, Camp and map of the Antarctic with Soviet Antarctic bases.

1970, Jan. 27 *Photo.* *Perf. 11½*

| 3699 | A1773 | 4k multi | 12 | 6 |
| 3700 | A1773 | 16k multi | 45 | 12 |

Issued to commemorate the 150th anniversary of the Bellingshausen-Lazarev Antarctic expedition.

F. W. Sychkov and "Tobogganing"
A1774

1970, Jan. 27 *Perf. 12½x12*

| 3701 | A1774 | 4k sep & vio bl | 12 | 12 |

Birth centenary of F. W. Sychkov (1870-1958), painter.

Col. V. B. Borsoyev
A1775

Design: No. 3703, Sgt. V. Peshekhonov.

1970, Feb. 10 *Perf. 12x12½*

| 3702 | A1775 | 4k brn ol & brn | 12 | 6 |
| 3703 | A1775 | 4k dk gray & plum | 12 | 6 |

Issued to honor heroes of the Soviet Union.

Geographical Society Emblem and Globes Torch of Peace
A1776   A1777

1970, Feb. 26 *Photo.* *Perf. 11½*

| 3704 | A1776 | 6k bis, Prus bl & dk brn | 18 | 12 |

Issued to commemorate the 125th anniversary of the Russian Geographical Society.

1970, Mar. 3 *Litho.* *Perf. 12*

| 3705 | A1777 | 6k bl grn & tan | 18 | 12 |

Issued to publicize International Women's Solidarity Day, March 8.

Symbols of Russian Arts and Crafts
A1778

Lenin
A1780

Lenin—A1779
Designs: 6k, Russian EXPO '70 pavilion. 10k, Boy holding model ship.

1970, Mar. 10 *Photo.* *Perf. 11½*

3706	A1778	4k dk bl grn, red & blk	12	5
3707	A1778	6k blk, sil & red	18	6
3708	A1778	10k vio bl, sil & red	30	10

Souvenir Sheet
Engraved *Perf. 12x12½*

| 3709 | A1779 | 50k dk red | 1.75 | 75 |

Issued to publicize EXPO '70 International Exhibition, Osaka, Japan, Mar. 15-Apr. 13. No. 3709 has lithographed red margin with USSR pavilion in tan and brown. Size: 71x97mm.

1970, Mar. 14 *Photo.* *Perf. 11½*

| 3710 | A1780 | 4k red, blk & gold | 12 | 12 |

Souvenir Sheet
Photo. and Embossed *Imperf.*

| 3711 | A1780 | 20k red, blk & gold | 75 | 30 |

Issued to publicize the USSR Philatelic Exhibition dedicated to the centenary of the birth of Lenin. No. 3711 contains one stamp with simulated perforations. Dark red margin with gold inscription. Size: 72x91mm.

Friendship Tree, Sochi
A1781

1970, Mar. 18 *Litho.* *Perf. 11½*

| 3712 | A1781 | 10k multi | 35 | 10 |

Issued to publicize friendship among people. Printed with alternating yellow label with black inscription.

National Emblem, Hammer and Sickle, Oil Derricks
A1782

1970, Mar. 18 *Photo.* *Perf. 11½*

| 3713 | A1782 | 4k dk car rose & gold | 12 | 6 |

Azerbaijan Republic, 50th anniversary.

RUSSIA

Ice Hockey Players
A1783

1970, Mar. 18
3714 A1783 6k bl & sl grn 25 12

Issued to commemorate the World Ice Hockey Championships in Sweden.

No. 3714 Overprinted in Upper Right Corner with Orange Cyrillic Inscription in 5 Vertical Lines.

1970, Apr. 1   Photo.   Perf. 11½
3715 A1783 6k bl & sl grn 25 12

Issued to honor Soviet hockey players as the tenfold world champions.

D. N. Medvedev   Hungarian Arms,
A1784   Budapest
                    Landmarks
                    A1786

Worker, Books, Globes and UNESCO Symbol
A1785

Portrait: No. 3717, K. P. Orlovsky.

1970, Mar. 26   Engr.   Perf. 12x12½
3716 A1784 4k chocolate 12 6
3717 A1784 4k dk redsh brn 12 6

Heroes of the Soviet Union.

1970, Mar. 26   Photo.   Perf. 12½x12
3718 A1785 6k car lake & ocher 18 12

Issued to publicize the UNESCO-sponsored Lenin Symposium, Tampere, Finland, Apr. 6–10.

1970, Apr. 4   Typo.   Perf. 11½
3719 A1786 6k multi 20 12

Issued to commemorate the 25th anniversary of the liberation of Hungary. See also No. 3738.

Cosmonauts' Emblem
A1787

1970, Apr. 12   Litho.   Perf. 11½
3720 A1787 6k buff & multi 18 12

Issued for Cosmonauts' Day.

Lenin, 1891   Order of Victory
A1788   A1789

Designs: Various portraits of Lenin.

Lithographed and Typographed

1970, Apr. 15   Perf. 12x12½
3721 A1788 2k grn & gold 5 5
3722 A1788 2k ol gray & gold 5 5
3723 A1788 4k vio bl & gold 12 5
3724 A1788 4k lake & gold 12 5
3726 A1788 6k lake & gold 18 6
3727 A1788 10k dk brn & gold 30 10
3728 A1788 10k dk rose brn & gold 30 10
3729 A1788 12k blk, sil & gold 35 12

Photogravure
3730 A1788 12k red & gold 35 12
Nos. 3721-3730 (10) 1.82 70

Souvenir Sheet

1970, Apr. 22   Litho. & Typo.
3731 A1788 20k blk, sil & gold 75 30

Issued to commemorate the centenary of the birth of Lenin. Issued in sheets of 8 stamps surrounded by 16 labels showing Lenin-connected buildings, books, coats of arms and medals. No. 3731 contains one stamp in same design as No. 3729. Red margin inscribed "Lenin" and gold commemorative inscription. Size: 66x102mm.

1970, May 8   Photo.   Perf. 11½
Designs: 2k, Monument to the Unknown Soldier, Moscow. 3k, Victory Monument, Berlin-Treptow. 4k, Order of the Great Patriotic War. 10k, Gold Star of the Order of Hero of the Soviet Union and Medal of Socialist Labor. 30k, Like 1k.

3732 A1789 1k red lil, gold & gray 6 5
3733 A1789 2k dk brn, gold & red 6 5
3734 A1789 3k dk brn, gold & red 10 5
3735 A1789 4k dk brn, gold & red 12 5
3736 A1789 10k red lil, gold & red 27 10
Nos. 3732-3736 (5) 61 30

Souvenir Sheet
Imperf.

3737 A1789 30k dk red, gold & gray 1.35 50

Issued to commemorate the 25th anniversary of victory in World War II. No. 3737 contains one stamp with simulated perforations. Gold and dark red margin with commemorative inscription and soldiers on parade. Size: 65x96mm.

Arms-Landmark Type of 1970

Design: Czechoslovakia arms and view of Prague.

1970, May 8   Typo.   Perf. 12½
3738 A1786 6k dk brn & multi 18 12

Issued to commemorate the 25th anniversary of the liberation of Czechoslovakia from the Germans.

Young Fighters, and Youth Federation Emblem
A1791

1970, May 20   Litho.   Perf. 12
3739 A1791 6k bl & blk 18 12

Issued to commemorate the 25th anniversary of the World Federation of Democratic Youth.

Lenin
A1792

1970, May 20   Photo.   Perf. 11½
3740 A1792 6k red 18 12

Issued to commemorate the International Youth Meeting dedicated to the centenary of the birth of Lenin, United Nations, N.Y., June 1970.

Komsomol Emblem with Lenin
A1793

1970, May 20   Litho.   Perf. 12
3741 A1793 4k red, yel & pur 18 12

Issued to publicize the 16th Congress of the Young Communist League, May 26–30.

Hammer and Sickle Emblem and Building of Supreme Soviet in Kazan
A1794

Designs (Hammer-Sickle Emblem and Supreme Soviet Building in): No. 3743, Petrozavodsk. No. 3744, Cheboksary. No. 3744A, Elista. No. 3744B, Izhevsk. No. 3744C, Yoshkar-Ola.

1970   Engraved   Perf. 12x12½
3742   A1794 4k vio bl 12 5
3743   A1794 4k green 12 5
3744   A1794 4k dk car 12 5
3744A A1794 4k red 12 5
3744B A1794 4k dk grn 12 5
3744C A1794 4k dk car 12 5
Nos. 3742-3744C (6) 72 30

Issued to commemorate the 50th anniversaries of the Tatar (No. 3742), Karelian (No. 3743), Chuvash (No. 3744), Kalmyk (No. 3744A), Udmurt (No. 3744B) and Mari (No. 3744C) autonomous Soviet Socialist Republics. Issue Dates: No. 3742, May 27; No. 3743, June 5; No. 3744, June 24; Nos. 3744A-3744B, Oct. 22; No. 3744C, Nov. 4.

See also Nos. 3814–3823, 4286.

Soccer   Sword into Plow-
A1795   share Statue,
                     United Nations,
                     N.Y.
                     A1796

Design: 10k, Woman athlete on balancing bar.

1970, May 31   Photo.   Perf. 11½
3745 A1795 10k lt gray & brt rose 25 12
3746 A1795 16k dk grn & org brn 40 18

No. 3745 commemorates the 17th World Gymnastics Championships, Ljubljana, Oct. 22–27; No. 3746 the 9th World Soccer Championships for the Jules Rimet Cup, Mexico City, May 29–June 21.

1970, June 1   Litho.   Perf. 12x12½
3747 A1796 12k gray & lake 35 12

25th anniversary of the United Nations.

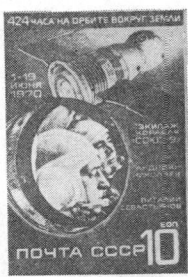

Soyuz 9, Andrian Nikolayev, Vitaly Sevastyanov
A1797

1970, June 7   Photo.   Perf. 12x11½
3748 A1797 10k multi 35 12

Issued to commemorate the space flight of Soyuz 9, June 1–19, which lasted 424 hours.

Friedrich Engels
A1798

1970, June 16   Engr.   Perf. 12x12½
3749 A1798 4k choc & ver 12 6

Issued to commemorate the sesquicentennial of the birth of Friedrich Engels (1820–1895), German socialist, collaborator with Karl Marx.

Armenian Woman and Symbols of Agriculture and Industry
A1799

Design: No. 3751, Kazakh woman and symbols of agriculture and industry.

1970, June 16   Photo.   Perf. 11½
3750 A1799 4k red brn & sil 12 5
3751 A1799 4k brt rose lil & gold 12 5

Issued to commemorate the 50th anniversaries of the Armenian (No. 3750) and the Kazakh (No. 3751) Soviet Socialist Republics.

RUSSIA

Missile Cruiser "Grozny"
A1800

Soviet Warships: 3k, Cruiser "Aurora." 10k, Cruiser "October Revolution." 12k, Missile cruiser "Varyag." 20k, Atomic submarine "Leninsky Komsomol."

1970, July 26 Photo. Perf. 11½x12

3752	A1800	3k lil, pink & blk	10	5
3753	A1800	4k yel & blk	15	6
3754	A1800	10k rose & blk	30	12
3755	A1800	12k buff & dk brn	30	15
3756	A1800	20k bl grn, dk brn & vio bl	40	22
		Nos. 3752-3756 (5)	1.25	60

Issued for Navy Day.

Russian and Polish Workers and Flags
A1801

"History," Petroglyphs, Sputnik and Emblem
A1802

1970, July 26   Perf. 12

3757	A1801	6k red & sl	18	10

Issued to commemorate the 25th anniversary of the Treaty of Friendship, Collaboration and Mutual Assistance between Russia and Poland.

1970, Aug. 16   Perf. 11½

3758	A1802	4k red brn, buff & bl	12	6

Issued to publicize the 13th International Congress of Historical Sciences in Moscow.

Mandarin Ducks
A1803

Animals from the Sikhote-Alin Reserve: 6k, Pine marten. 10k, Asiatic black bear (vert.). 16k, Red deer. 20k, Ussurian tiger.

Perf. 12½x12, 12x12½

1970, Aug. 19   Lithographed

3759	A1803	4k multi	15	6
3760	A1803	6k multi	20	6
3761	A1803	10k multi	25	12
3762	A1803	16k ultra & multi	35	18
3763	A1803	20k gray & multi	50	22
		Nos. 3759-3763 (5)	1.45	64

Magnifying Glass over Stamp, and Covers
A1804

1970, Aug. 31 Photo. Perf. 12x12½

3764	A1804	4k red & sil	12	6

Issued to publicize the 2nd All-Union Philatelists' Congress in Moscow.

Pioneers' Badge—A1805

Designs: 2k, Lenin and Children, monument. 4k, Star and scenes from play "Zarnitsa."

1970, Sept. 24 Photo. Perf. 11½

3765	A1805	1k gray, red & gold	5	5
3766	A1805	2k brn red & sl grn	5	5
3767	A1805	4k lt ol, car & gold	15	6

Soviet general education.

Yerevan University
A1806

1970, Sept. 24 Photo. Perf. 12½x12

3768	A1806	4k ultra & sal pink	15	12

Issued to commemorate the 50th anniversary of Yerevan State University.

Library Bookplate, Vilnius University
A1807

Woman Holding Flowers
A1808

1970, Oct. Typo. Perf. 12x12½

3772	A1807	4k sil, gray & blk	12	6

Issued to commemorate the 400th anniversary of the Vilnius University Library.

1970, Oct. 30   Photogravure

3773	A1808	6k bl & lt brn	18	12

Issued to commemorate the 25th anniversary of the International Democratic Federation of Women.

Farm Woman, Cattle Farm—A1809

Designs: No. 3775, Farmer and mechanical farm equipment. No. 3776, Farmer, fertilization equipment and plane.

1970, Oct. 30   Perf. 11½x12

3774	A1809	4k ol, yel & red	12	6
3775	A1809	4k ocher, yel & red	12	6
3776	A1809	4k lt vio, yel & red	12	6

Aims of the new agricultural 5-year plan.

Lenin—A1810

1970, Nov. 3 Lithographed and Embossed   Perf. 12½x12

3777	A1810	4k red & gold	12	6

Souvenir Sheet

3778	A1810	30k red & gold	1.10	40

Issued to commemorate the 53rd anniversary of the October Revolution. No. 3778 contains one stamp, buff margin with gold hammer and sickle emblem and red inscription. Size: 106x73mm.

No. 3389 Overprinted in Gold
50 лет ленинскому плану ГОЭЛРО • 1970

1970, Nov. 3   Perf. 11½

3779	A1641	4k gold & multi	18	12

Issued to commemorate the 50th anniversary of the GOELRO Plan for the electrification of Russia.

Spasski Tower and Fir Branch
A1811

1970, Nov. 23 Litho. Perf. 12x12½

3780	A1811	6k multi	18	12

Issued for New Year, 1971.

A. A. Baykov
A1812

1970, Nov. 25 Photo. Perf. 12½x12

3781	A1812	4k sep & gldn brn	15	12

Issued to commemorate the centenary of the birth of A. A. Baykov (1870-1946), metallurgist and academician.

Portrait Type of 1968
Portrait: No. 3782, A. D. Tsyurupa.

1970, Nov. 25 Photo. Perf. 12x12½

3782	A1688	4k brn & sal	15	12

Issued to commemorate the centenary of the birth of A. D. Tsyurupa (1870-1928), First Vice Chairman of the Soviet of People's Commissars.

Vasily Blazhenny Church, Red Square
A1813

Designs: 6k, Performance of Swan Lake. 10k, Two deer. 12k, Folk art. 14k, Sword into Plowshare statue, by E. Vouchetich, and museums. 16k, Automobiles and woman photographer.

Photogravure and Engraved

1970, Nov. 29   Perf. 12x11½
Frame in Brown Orange

3783	A1813	4k multi	12	6
3784	A1813	6k multi	18	8
3785	A1813	10k brn org & sl grn	30	12
3786	A1813	12k multi	35	14
3787	A1813	14k multi	38	16
3788	A1813	16k multi	50	18
		Nos. 3783-3788 (6)	1.83	74

Tourist publicity.

Daisy
A1814

Flowers: 6k, Dahlia. 10k, Phlox. 12k, Aster. 16k, Clematis.

1970, Nov. 29 Litho. Perf. 11½

3789	A1814	4k grn & multi	10	6
3790	A1814	6k multi	15	6
3791	A1814	10k yel & multi	25	12
3792	A1814	12k multi	30	14
3793	A1814	16k multi	50	18
		Nos. 3789-3793 (5)	1.30	58

U.N. Emblem, African Mother and Child, Broken Chain
A1815

1970, Dec. 10 Photo. Perf. 12x12½

3794	A1815	10k bl & dk brn	35	12

United Nations Declaration on Colonial Independence, 10th anniversary.

Ludwig van Beethoven
A1816

RUSSIA

1970, Dec. 16 Engr. Perf. 12½x12
3795 A1816 10k dp cl, pink 35 12

Bicentenary of the birth of Ludwig van Beethoven (1770–1827), composer.

Skating Luna 16
A1817 A1818

Design: 10k, Skiing.

1970, Dec. 18 Photo. Perf. 11½
3796 A1817 4k lt gray, ultra & dk red 15 6
3797 A1817 10k lt gray, brt grn & brn 30 12

Publicity for the 1971 Trade Union Winter Games.

1970, Dec. Photo. Perf. 11½
Designs: No. 3799, 3801b, Luna 16 leaving moon. No. 3800, 3801c, Capsule landing on earth. No. 3801a, like No. 3798.
3798 A1818 10k gray bl 30 15
3799 A1818 10k dk pur 30 15
3800 A1818 10k gray bl 30 15

Souvenir Sheet
3801 A1818 Sheet of 3 2.00 1.00
  a. 20k bl 50 25
  b. 20k dk pur 50 25
  c. 20k bl 50 25

Luna 16 unmanned, automatic moon mission, Sept. 12–24, 1970.
Nos. 3801a–c have attached labels (no perf. between vignette and label). Marginal inscription in purple. Size: 100x75 mm. Issue dates: No. 3801, Dec. 18; Nos. 3798–3800, Dec. 28.

The Conestabile Madonna, by Raphael
A1819

Paintings: 4k, Apostles Peter and Paul, by El Greco. 10k, Perseus and Andromeda, by Rubens (horiz.). 12k, The Prodigal Son, by Rembrandt. 16k, Family Portrait, by van Dyck. 20k, The Actress Jeanne Samary, by Renoir. 30k, Woman with Fruit, by Gauguin. 50k, The Litte Madonna, by da Vinci. All paintings from the Hermitage in Leningrad, except 20k from Pushkin Museum, Moscow.

Perf. 12x12½, 12½x12
1970, Dec. 23 Lithographed
3802 A1819 3k gray & multi 10 5
3803 A1819 4k gray & multi 15 10
3804 A1819 10k gray & multi 30 10
3805 A1819 12k gray & multi 30 15
3806 A1819 16k gray & multi 40 20
3807 A1819 20k gray & multi 50 20
3808 A1819 30k gray & multi 1.00 30
  Nos. 3802-3808 (7) 2.75 1.10

Souvenir Sheet
Imperf.
3809 A1819 50k gold & multi 1.50 75

No. 3809 has gold-embossed and gray frame and black marginal inscription. Size: 73x101mm.

Harry Pollyt and Shipyard
A1820

1970, Dec. 31 Photo. Perf. 12
3810 A1820 10k mar & brn 35 12

80th anniversary of the birth of Harry Pollyt (1890–1960), British labor leader.

International Cooperative Alliance
A1821

1970, Dec. 31 Perf. 11½x12
3811 A1821 12k yel grn & red 35 12

International Cooperative Alliance, 75th anniversary.

Lenin—A1822

1971, Jan. 1 Perf. 12
3812 A1822 4k red & gold 12 6

Year of the 24th Congress of the Communist Party of the Soviet Union.

Georgian Republic Flag
A1823

1971, Jan. 12 Litho. Perf. 11½
3813 A1823 4k ol bis & multi 12 6

Georgian Soviet Socialist Republic, 50th anniversary.

Republic Anniversaries Type of 1970

Designs (Hammer-Sickle Emblem and): No. 3814, Supreme Soviet Building, Makhachkala. No. 3815, Fruit, ship, mountain, conveyor. No. 3816, Grapes, refinery, ship. No. 3817, Supreme Soviet Building, Nalchik. No. 3818, Supreme Soviet Building, Syktyvkar, and lumber industry. No. 3819, Natural resources, dam, mining. No. 3820, Industrial installations and natural products. No. 3821, Ship, "industry." No. 3822, Grapes, pylons and mountains. No. 3823, Kazbek Mountain, industrial installations, produce.

1971–74 Engraved Perf. 12x12½
3814 A1794 4k dk bl grn 10 6
3815 A1794 4k rose red 10 6
3816 A1794 4k red 10 6
3817 A1794 4k blue 10 6
3818 A1794 4k green 10 6
3819 A1794 4k brt bl 10 6
3820 A1794 4k car rose 10 7
3821 A1794 4k brt ultra 10 8
3822 A1794 4k gldn brn 10 8

Lithographed
3823 A1794 4k dk red 10 8
  Nos. 3814-3823 (10) 1.00 68

Fiftieth anniversaries of Dagestan (No. 3814), Abkazian (No. 3815), Adzhar (No. 3816), Kabardino-Balkarian (No. 3817), Komi (No. 3818), Yakut (No. 3819), Checheno-Ingush (No. 3820), Buryat (No. 3821), Nakhichevan (No. 3822), and North Ossetian (No. 3823) autonomous Soviet Socialist Republics.
No. 3823 also commemorates the bicentenary of Ossetia's union with Russia.
Issue dates: No. 3814, Jan. 20. No. 3815, Mar. 3. No. 3816, June 16. Nos. 3817–3818, Aug. 17, 1971. No. 3819, Apr. 20. No. 3820, Nov. 22, 1972. No. 3821, May 24, 1973. No. 3822, Feb. 6, 1974. No. 3823, July 7, 1974.

Tower of Genoa, Cranes, Hammer and Sickle
A1824

Palace of Culture, Kiev
A1825

1971, Jan. 28 Typo. Perf. 12
3824 A1824 10k dk red, gray & yel 27 12

2500th anniversary of the founding of Feodosiya in the Crimea.

1971, Feb. 16 Photo. Perf. 11½
3825 A1825 4k red, bis & bl 12 12

24th Congress of the Ukrainian Communist Party.

N. Gubin, I. Chernykh, S. Kosinov
A1826

1971, Feb. 16 Perf. 12½x12
3826 A1826 4k sl grn & vio brn 12 12

Heroes of the Soviet Union.

"Industry and Agriculture"
A1827

Lesya Ukrayinka
A1828

1971, Feb. 16 Perf. 12x12½
3827 A1827 6k ol bis & red 18 8

50th anniversary of the State Planning Organization.

1971, Feb. 25
3828 A1828 4k org red & bis 12 6

Birth centenary of Lesya Ukrayinka (1871–1913), Ukrainian poet.

"Summer" Dance—A1829

Dancers of Russian Folk Dance Ensemble: No. 3830, "On the Skating Rink." No. 3831, Ukrainian dance "Hopak." No. 3832, Adzharian dance. No. 3833, Gypsy dance.

1971, Feb. 25 Photo. Perf. 12½x12
3829 A1829 10k bis & multi 30 12
3830 A1829 10k ol & multi 30 12
3831 A1829 10k ol bis & multi 30 12
3832 A1829 10k gray & multi 30 12
3833 A1829 10k grnsh gray & mul;i 30 12
  Nos. 3829-3833 (5) 1.50 60

Luna 17 on Moon
A1830

Designs: No. 3835, Ground control. No. 3836, Separation of Lunokhod 1 and carrier. 16k, Lunokhod 1 in operation.

1971, March 16 Photo. Perf. 11½
3834 A1830 10k dp vio & sep 25 12
3835 A1830 12k dk bl & sep 30 14
3836 A1830 12k dk bl & sep 30 14
3837 A1830 16k dp vio & sep 40 18
  a. Souvenir sheet of 4 1.50 75

Luna 17 unmanned, automated moon mission, Nov. 10–17, 1970. No. 3837a contains one each of Nos. 3834–3837. Sepia marginal inscription. Size: 91x68 mm.

Paris Commune
A1831

1971, March 18 Litho. Perf. 12
3838 A1831 6k red & blk 15 12

Centenary of the Paris Commune.

Industry, Science, Culture
A1832

1971, March 29 Perf. 11½
3839 A1832 6k bis, brn & red 15 12

24th Communist Party Congress, March 30–Apr. 3.

Yuri Gagarin Medal
A1833

RUSSIA

1971, March 30 Photo. *Perf. 11½*
3840 A1833 10k brn & lem   35   12
Tenth anniversary of man's first flight into space.

Space Research
A1834

1971, March 30
3841 A1834 12k sl bl & vio brn   35   12

Cosmonauts' Day, Apr. 12.

E. Birznieks-Upitis—A1835   Bee and Blossom A1836

1971, Apr. 1 *Perf. 12x12½*
3842 A1835 4k red brn & gray   12   12
Centenary of the birth of E. Birznieks-Upitis (1871–1960), Latvian writer.

1971, Apr. 1 *Perf. 11½*
3843 A1836 6k ol & multi   15   10
23rd International Beekeeping Congress, Moscow, Aug. 22–Sept. 2.

Souvenir Sheet

Cosmonauts and Spacecraft—A1837

1971, Apr. 12 Litho. *Perf. 12*
Designs: 10k, Vostok. No. 3844b, Yuri Gagarin. No. 3844c, First man walking in space. 16k, First orbital station.

3844 A1837 Sheet of 4   1.75 75
  a. 10k vio brn   22   15
  b. 12k Prus grn   27   18
  c. 12k Prus grn   27   18
  d. 16k vio brn   35   22

Tenth anniversary of man's first flight into space. No 3844 has gray margin and commemorative inscription. Size of stamp: 26x19mm. Size of souvenir sheet: 91x76mm.

Lenin Memorial, Ulyanovsk—A1838

1971, Apr. 16 Photo. *Perf. 12*
3845 A1838 4k cop red & ol bis   12   12
Lenin's birthday. Memorial was built for centenary celebration of his birth.

Lt. Col. Nikolai I. Vlasov   Khafiz Shirazi
A1839   A1840

1971, May 9 Photo. *Perf. 12x12½*
3846 A1839 4k gray ol & brn   15   12
Hero of the Soviet Union.

1971, May 9 Lithographed
3847 A1840 4k ol, brn & blk   15   12
650th anniversary of the birth of Khafiz Shirazi, Tadzhik-Persian poet.

GAZ-66—A1841
Soviet Cars: 3k, BelAZ-540 truck. No. 3850, Moskvich-412. No. 3851, ZAZ-968. 10k, Volga.

1971, May 12 Photo. *Perf. 11x11½*
3848 A1841 2k yel & multi   5   5
3849 A1841 3k lt bl & multi 8   5
3850 A1841 4k lt lil & multi 10   6
3851 A1841 4k lt gray & multi 10 6
3852 A1841 10k lt lil & multi 25 12
Nos. 3848-3852 (5)   58   34

A. A. Bogomolets   Satellite
A1842   A1843

1971, May 24 Photo. *Perf. 12*
3853 A1842 4k org & blk   12   12
90th anniversary of the birth of A. A. Bogomolets, physician.

1971, June 9 *Perf. 11½*
3854 A1843 6k bl & multi   17   12
15th General Assembly of the International Union of Geodesics and Geophysics.

Symbols of Science and History
A1844

1971, June 9 *Perf. 12*
3855 A1844 6k grn & gray   17   12
13th Congress of Science History.

Oil Derrick & Symbols
A1845

1971, June 9 *Perf. 11½*
3856 A1845 6k multi   20   12
8th World Oil Congress.

Sukhe Bator Monument—A1846

1971, June 16 Typo *Perf. 12*
3857 A1846 6k red, gold & blk   20   12
50th anniversary of Mongolian revolution.

Monument of Defenders of Liepaja
A1847

1971, June 21 Photogravure
3858 A1847 4k gray, blk & brn   12   12
30th anniversary of the defense of Liepaja (Libau) against invading Germans.

Map of Antarctica and Station   Weather Map, Plane, Ship and Satellite
A1848   A1849

Engraved and Photogravure
1971, June 21 *Perf. 11½*
3859 A1848 6k blk, grn & ultra   25   12
Tenth anniversary of the Antarctic Treaty pledging peaceful uses of and scientific cooperation in Antarctica.

1971, June 12
3860 A1849 10k blk, red & ultra   35   12
50th anniversary of Soviet Hydrometeorological service.

FIR Emblem, "Homeland" by E. Vouchetich
A1850

1971, June 21 Photo. *Perf. 12x12½*
3861 A1850 6k dk red & sl   14   8
International Federation of Resistance Fighters (FIR), 20th anniversary.

Discus and Running
A1851

Designs: 4k, Archery (women). 6k, Dressage. 10k, Basketball. 12k, Wrestling.

Lithographed & Engraved
1971, June 24 *Perf. 11½*
3862 A1851 3k vio bl, *rose*   10   5
3863 A1851 4k sl grn, *pale pink* 15 6
3864 A1851 6k red brn, *ap grn*   20 8
3865 A1851 10k dk pur, *gray bl*   30 12
3866 A1851 12k red brn, *yel*   35 14
Nos. 3863-3866 (5)   1.10   45

5th Summer Spartakiad.

Benois Madonna, by da Vinci
A1852

Paintings: 4k, Mary Magdalene, by Titian. 10k, The Washerwoman, by Jean Simeon Chardin (horiz.). 12k, Portrait of a Young Man, by Frans Hals. 14k, Tancred and Arminia, by Nicolas Poussin (horiz.). 16k, Girl with Fruit, by Murillo. 20k, Girl with Ball, by Picasso.

Lithographed
1971, July 7 *Perf. 12x12½, 12½x12*
3867 A1852 2k bis & multi   10   5
3868 A1852 4k bis & multi   15   6
3869 A1852 10k bis & multi   30   12
3870 A1852 12k bis & multi   35   14
3871 A1852 14k bis & multi   40   18
3892 A1852 16k bis & multi   50   18
3873 A1852 20k bis & multi   60   22
Nos. 3867-3873 (7)   2.40   95
Foreign master works in Russian museums.

Kazakhstan Flag, Lenin Badge
A1853

1971, July 7 Photo. *Perf. 11½*
3874 A1853 4k bl, red & brn   12   12
50th anniversary of the Kazakh Communist Youth League.

Star Emblem and Letters
A1854

1971, July 14
3875 A1854 4k ol, bl & blk   12   12
International Letter Writing Week.

356 RUSSIA

Nikolai A. Nekrasov, by Ivan N. Kramskoi
A1855

Portraits: No. 3877, Aleksandr Spendiarov, by M. S. Saryan. 10k, Fëdor M. Dostoevski, by Vassili G. Perov.

1971, July 14 Litho. Perf. 12x12½

3876	A1855	4k cit & multi	12	6
3877	A1855	4k gray bl & multi	12	6
3878	A1855	10k multi	30	12

Sesquicentennial of the births of Nikolai Alekseevitch Nekrasov (1821–1877), poet, and of Fëdor Mikhailovich Dostoevski (1821–1881), novelist; centenary of the birth of A. Spendiarov (1871–1928), Armenian composer (No. 3877). See Nos. 4056–4057.

Z. Paliashvili and Score
A1856

1971, Aug. 3 Photo. Perf. 12x12½

3879 A1856 4k brown 12 6

Centenary of the birth of Zachary Paliashvili (1871–1933), Georgian composer.

Gorki Kremlin, Stag and Hydrofoil
A1857

1971, Aug. 3 Litho. Perf. 12

3880 A1857 16k multi 45 18

750th anniversary of the founding of Gorki (formerly Nizhni Novgorod). See also Nos. 3889, 3910–3914.

Federation Emblem and Students
A1858

1971, Aug. 3 Photo. Perf. 11½

3881 A1858 6k ultra & multi 20 8

25th anniversary of the International Students Federation.

Common Dolphins
A1859

Sea Mammals: 6k, Sea otter. 10k, Narwhals. 12k, Walrus. 14k, Ribbon seals.

Photogravure and Engraved

1971, Aug. 12 Perf. 11½

3882	A1859	4k sil & multi	15	5
3883	A1859	6k sil & multi	20	6
3884	A1859	10k sil & multi	30	10
3885	A1859	12k sil & multi	35	15
3886	A1859	14k sil & multi	40	15
	Nos. 3882-3886 (5)		1.40	51

Miner's Star of Valor
A1860

1971, Aug. 17 Photo. Perf. 11½

3887 A1860 4k bis, blk & red 12 12

250th anniversary of the discovery of coal in the Donets Basin.

Ernest Rutherford and Diagram of Movement of Atomic Particles
A1861

1971, Aug. 24 Photo. Perf. 12

3888 A1861 6k mag & dk ol 20 12

Centenary of the birth of Ernest Rutherford (1871–1937), British physicist.

Gorki and Gorki Statue
A1862

1971, Sept. 14 Perf. 11½

3889 A1862 4k stl bl & multi 12 12

750th anniversary of the founding of Gorki (Nizhni Novgorod).

Troika and Spasski Tower
A1863

1971, Sept. 14

3890 A1863 10k blk, red & gold 27 12

Issued for New Year 1972.

Automatic Production Center
A1864

Designs: No. 3892, Agricultural development. No. 3893, Family in shopping center. No. 3894, Hydro-generators, thermoelectric station. No. 3895, Marchers, flags, books inscribed Marx and Lenin.

1971, Sept. 29 Photo. Perf. 12x11½

3891	A1864	4k pur, red & blk	12	6
3892	A1864	4k ocher, red & brn	12	6
3893	A1864	4k yel, ol & red	12	6
3894	A1864	4k bis, red & brn	12	6
3895	A1864	4k ultra, red & sl	12	6
	Nos. 3891-3895 (5)		60	30

Resolutions of 24th Soviet Union Communist Party Congress.

The Meeting, by Vladimir Y. Makovsky
A1865

Ivan N. Kramskoi, Self-portrait
A1866

Paintings: 4k, Woman Student, by Nikolai A. Yaroshenko. 6k, Woman Miner, by Nikolai A. Kasatkin. 10k, Harvest, by G. G. Myasoyedov (horiz.). 16k, Country Road, by A. K. Savrasov. 20k, Pine Forest, by I. I. Shishkin (horiz.).

Perf. 12x12½, 12½x12

1971, Oct. 14 Lithographed
Frame in Light Gray

3896	A1865	2k multi	5	5
3897	A1865	4k multi	10	6
3898	A1865	6k multi	15	8
3899	A1865	10k multi	30	12
3900	A1865	16k multi	40	18
3901	A1865	20k multi	60	24
	Nos. 3896-3901 (6)		1.60	73

Souvenir Sheet
Lithographed and Gold Embossed

3902 A1866 50k dk grn & multi 1.50 60

History of Russian painting. No. 3902 contains one stamp, gold margin with black inscription commemorating the centenary of Russian Artists' Organization. Size: 93x67mm.

V. V. Vorovsky
A1867

1971, Oct. 14 Engraved Perf. 12

3903 A1867 4k red brn 12 12

Centenary of the birth of V. V. Vorovsky, Bolshevik party leader and diplomat.

Cosmonauts Dobrovolsky, Volkov and Patsayev—A1868

1971, Oct. 20 Photo. Perf. 11½x12

3904 A1868 4k blk, lil & org 12 12

In memory of cosmonauts Lt. Col. Georgi T. Dobrovolsky, Vladislav N. Volkov and Viktor I. Patsayev, who died during the Soyuz 11 space mission, June 6–30, 1971.

Order of October Revolution
A1869

1971, Oct. 20 Litho. Perf. 12

3905 A1869 4k red, yel & blk 12 12

54th anniversary of October Revolution.

E. Vakhtangov and "Princess Turandot"
A1870

Dzhambul Dzhabayev
A1871

Designs: No. 3907, Boris Shchukin and scene from "Man with Rifle (Lenin)" (horiz). No. 3908, Ruben Simonov and scene from "Cyrano de Bergerac" (horiz.).

Perf. 12x12½, 12½x12

1971, Oct. 26 Photogravure

3906	A1870	10k mar & red brn	27	10
3907	A1891	10k brn & dl yel	27	10
3908	A1891	10k red brn & ocher	27	10

50th anniversary of Vakhtangov Theater, Moscow.

1971, Nov. 16 Perf. 12x12½

3909 A1871 4k org & brn 12 12

125th anniversary of the birth of Dzhambul Dzhabayev (1846–1945), Kazakh poet.

Gorki Kremlin Type, 1971

Designs: 3k, Pskov Kremlin and Velikaya River. 4k, Novgorod Kremlin and eternal flame memorial. 6k, Smolensk Fortress and liberation monument. 10k, Kolomna Kremlin and buses. 50k, Moscow Kremlin.

1971, Nov. 16 Litho. Perf. 12

3910	A1857	3k multi	10	5
3911	A1857	4k multi	10	6
3912	A1857	6k gray & multi	15	8
3913	A1857	10k ol & multi	30	10

Souvenir Sheet
Perf. 11½
Engraved and Lithographed

3914 A1857 50k yel & multi 1.50 60

Historic buildings. No. 3914 contains one stamp (21½x32mm.), red commemorative inscription and gray and yellow tower design in margin. Size: 66x87mm.

RUSSIA

William Foster,
View of New York
A1872

1971   **Litho.**   *Perf. 12*
| 3915 | A1872 | 10k brn & blk ("-1961") | 50 | 20 |
| a. | | "-1964" | 15.00 | 16.00 |

William Foster (1881-1961), chairman of Communist Party of U.S.A.
No. 3915a was issued Nov. 16 with incorrect death date (1964). No. 3915, with corrected date (1961), was issued Dec. 8.

Aleksandr
Fadeyev
and
Cavalrymen
A1873

1971, Nov. 25   **Photo.**   *Perf. 12½x12*
| 3916 | A1873 | 4k sl & org | 15 | 7 |

70th anniversary of the birth of Aleksandr Fadeyev (1901-1956), writer.

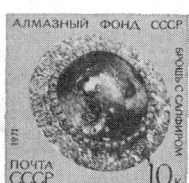

Amethyst
and
Diamond
Brooch
A1874

Precious Jewels: No. 3918, Engraved Shakh diamond, India, 16th century. No. 3919, Diamond daffodils, 18th century. No. 3920, Amethyst and diamond pendant. No. 3921, Diamond rose made for centenary of Lenin's birth. 30k, Diamond and pearl pendant.

1971, Dec. 8   **Litho.**   *Perf. 11½*
3917	A1874	10k brt bl & multi	25	10
3918	A1874	10k dk red & multi	25	10
3919	A1874	10k grnsh blk & multi	25	10
3920	A1874	20k grnsh blk & multi	50	25
3921	A1874	20k rose red & multi	50	25
3922	A1874	30k blk & multi	75	40
		Nos. 3917-3922 (6)	2.50	1.20

Souvenir Sheet

Workers with Banners, Congress Hall and Spasski Tower—A1875

1971, Dec. 15   **Photo.**   *Perf. 11x11½*
| 3923 | A1875 | 20k red, pale grn & brn | 60 | 30 |

See note after No. 3895. No. 3923 contains one partially perforated stamp because the flag continues from the stamp into the margin. Pale green margin with brown inscription. Size: 90x65mm.

Vanda
Orchid
A1876

Flowers: 2k, Anthurium. 4k, Flowering crab cactus. 12k, Amaryllis. 14k, Medinilla magnifica.

1971, Dec. 15   **Litho.**   *Perf. 12x12½*
3924	A1876	1k ol & multi	5	5
3925	A1876	2k grn & multi	5	5
3926	A1876	4k bl & multi	10	10
3927	A1876	12k multi	35	15
3928	A1876	14k multi	40	20
		Nos. 3924-3928 (5)	95	55

Miniature Sheet
Perf. 12
3929	A1876	Sheet of 4	1.50	75
a.		10k like 12k	35	15
b.		10k like 10k	35	15
c.		10k like 4k	35	15
d.		10k like 14k	35	15

Nos. 3929a-3929d have white background, black frame line and inscription. Size of stamps 19x57mm. No. 3929 has pale violet margin with floral design. Size: 81x95mm.
Issue dates: Nos. 3924-3928, Dec. 15; No. 3929, Dec. 30.

Peter I Reviewing Fleet,
1723—A1877

History of Russian Fleet: 4k, Oriol, first ship built in Eddinovo, 1668 (vert.). 10k, Battleship Poltava, 1712 (vert.). 12k, Armed ship Ingermanland, 1715 (vert.). 16k, Frigate Vladimir, 1848.

Engraved and Photogravure
Perf. 11½x12, 12x11½
1971, Dec. 15
3930	A1877	1k multi	5	5
3931	A1877	4k brn & multi	10	7
3932	A1877	10k multi	25	10
3933	A1877	12k multi	25	12
3934	A1877	16k lt grn & multi	40	17
		Nos. 3930-3934 (5)	1.05	51

Ice
Hockey
A1878

1971, Dec. 15   **Litho.**   *Perf. 12½*
| 3935 | A1878 | 6k multi, grn | 25 | 12 |

25th anniversary of Soviet ice hockey.

Oil Rigs and Causeway in
Caspian Sea—A1879

1971, Dec. 30   *Perf. 11½*
| 3936 | A1879 | 4k dp bl, org & blk | 13 | 12 |

Baku oil industry.

G. M.
Krzhizhanovsky
A1880

1972, Jan. 5   **Engraved**   *Perf. 12*
| 3937 | A1880 | 4k yel brn | 13 | 12 |

Centenary of the birth of G. M. Krzhizhanovsky (1872-1959), scientist and co-worker with Lenin.

Alexander   Bering's
Scriabin   Cormorant
A1881   A1882

1972, Jan. 6   **Photo.**   *Perf. 12x12½*
| 3938 | A1881 | 4k ind & ol | 13 | 12 |

Centenary of the birth of Alexander Scriabin (1872-1915), composer.

1972, Jan. 12   *Perf. 11½*
Birds: 6k, Ross' gull (horiz.). 10k, Barnacle geese. 12k, Spectacled eiders (horiz.). 16k, Mediterranean gull.

3939	A1882	4k dk grn, blk & yel	15	5
3940	A1882	6k ind, pink & blk	20	10
3941	A1882	10k grnsh bl, blk & brn	30	15
3942	A1882	12k multi	35	15
3943	A1882	16k ultra, gray & red	50	25
		Nos. 3939-3943 (5)	1.50	70

Waterfowl of Russia.

Speed Skating   Heart, Globe
A1883   and Exercising
            Family
            A1884

Designs (Olympic Rings and): 6k, Women's figure skating. 10k, Ice hockey. 12k, Ski jump. 16k, Long-distance skiing. 50k, Sapporo '72 emblem.

1972, Jan. 20   **Litho.**   *Perf. 12x12½*
3944	A1883	4k bl grn, red & brn	10	5
3945	A1883	6k yel brn, bl & dp org	15	10
3946	A1883	10k vio, bl & dp org	30	10
3947	A1883	12k lt bl, bl & brick red	40	15
3948	A1883	16k gray, bl & brt rose	60	25
		Nos. 3944-3948 (5)	1.55	65

Souvenir Sheet
| 3949 | A1883 | 50k multi | 1.50 | 80 |

11th Winter Olympic Games, Sapporo, Japan, Feb. 3-13. No. 3949 contains one stamp; greenish bl. & gold decorative margin. Size: 66x92mm.

1972, Feb. 9   Photogravure
| 3950 | A1884 | 4k brt grn & rose red | 13 | 12 |

Heart Week sponsored by the World Health Organization.

Leipzig Fair   Hammer, Sickle and
Emblem and   Cogwheel Emblem
Russian Pavilion
A1885   A1886

1972, Feb. 22   *Perf. 11½*
| 3951 | A1885 | 16k red & gold | 50 | 20 |

50th anniversary of the participation of the USSR in the Leipzig Trade Fair.

1972, Feb. 29   *Perf. 12x12½*
| 3952 | A1886 | 4k rose red & lt brn | 13 | 7 |

15th USSR Trade Union Congress, Moscow, March 1972.

Aloe   Aleksandra
A1887   Kollontai
         A1888

Medicinal Plants: 2k, Horn poppy. 4k, Groundsel. 6k, Orthosiphon stamineus. 10k, Nightshade.

1972, Mar. 14   **Litho.**   *Perf. 12x12½*
Flowers in Natural Colors
3953	A1887	1k ol bis	5	5
3954	A1887	2k sl grn	5	5
3955	A1887	4k brt pur	15	5
3956	A1887	6k vio bl	15	10
3957	A1887	10k dk brn	30	15
		Nos. 3953-3957 (5)	70	40

1972, Mar. 20   **Engr.**   *Perf. 12½x12*
Portraits: No. 3959, Georgy Chicherin. No. 3960, Kamo (pseudonym of S.A. Ter-Petrosyan).

3958	A1888	4k red brn	15	7
3959	A1888	4k claret	15	7
3960	A1888	4k ol bis	15	7

Outstanding workers of the Communist Party of the Soviet Union and for the State.

Souvenir Sheet
No. 3949 Overprinted in Margin

СОВЕТСКИЕ СПОРТСМЕНЫ
ЗАВОЕВАЛИ
8 ЗОЛОТЫХ
МЕДАЛЕЙ,
5 СЕРЕБРЯНЫХ,
3 БРОНЗОВЫХ.

1972, Mar. 20   **Litho.**   *Perf. 12x12½*
| 3961 | A1883 | 50k multi | 3.00 | 1.00 |

To commemorate the victories of Russian athletes in the 11th Winter Olympic Games. (8 gold, 5 silver and 3 bronze medals).

RUSSIA

Orbital Station Salyut and Spaceship
Soyuz Docking Above
Earth—A1889

Designs: No. 3963, Mars 2 approaching Mars, and emblem dropped on Mars. 16k, Mars 3, which landed on Mars, Dec. 2, 1971.

1972, Apr. 5   Photo.   Perf. 11½x12

3962	A1889	6k vio, bl & sil	20	6
3963	A1889	6k pur, ocher & sil	20	6
3964	A1889	16k pur, bl & sil	60	25

Cosmonauts' Day.

Shield and Products of Izhory Factory
A1890

1972, Apr. 20   Perf. 12½x12

| 3965 | A1890 | 4k pur & sil | 15 | 10 |

250th anniversary of Izhory Factory, founded by Peter the Great.

Leonid Sobinov in "Eugene Onegin," by Tchaikovsky
A1891

1972, Apr. 5

| 3966 | A1891 | 10k dp brn & buff | 30 | 12 |

Centenary of the birth of Leonid Sobinov (1872–1934), opera singer.

Book, Torch, Children and Globe
A1892

1972, May 5   Perf. 11½

| 3967 | A1892 | 6k brn, grnsh bl & buff | 20 | 8 |

International Book Year 1972.

Girl in Laboratory and Pioneers
A1893

Designs: 1k, Pavlic Morosov (Pioneer hero), Pioneers saluting and banner. 3k, Pioneers with wheelbarrow, Chukchi boy, and Chukotka Pioneer House. 4k, Pioneer honor guard and parade. 30k, Pioneer honor guard (vert.).

1972, May 10

3968	A1893	1k red & multi	5	5
3969	A1893	2k multi	8	5
3970	A1893	3k multi	5	5
3971	A1893	4k gray & multi	15	5

Souvenir Sheet
Perf. 12x12½

| 3972 | A1893 | 30k multi | 1.00 | 50 |

50th anniversary of the Lenin Pioneer Organization of the USSR. No. 3972 contains one stamp. Multicolored margin with vignettes depicting Pioneer activities. Bister border and red inscription. Size: 101x81mm.

Pioneer Bugler
A1894

1972, May 27   Photo.   Perf. 11½

| 3973 | A1894 | 4k red, ocher & plum | 12 | 12 |

2nd Youth Philatelic Exhibition, Minsk, and 50th anniversary of Lenin Pioneer Organization.

 M. S. Ordubady
A1895

1972, May 25   Perf. 12½x12½

| 3974 | A1895 | 4k org & rose brn | 12 | 12 |

Centenary of the birth of M. S. Ordubady (1872–1950), Azerbaijan writer and social worker.

Globe
A1896

1972, May 25   Perf. 11½

| 3975 | A1896 | 6k multi | 25 | 12 |

European Safety and Cooperation Conference, Brussels.

 Cossack Leader, by Ivan Nikitin
A1897

Paintings: 4k, Fedor G. Volkov (actor), by Anton Losenko. 6k, V. Majkov (poet), by Fedor Rokotov. 10k, Nikolai I. Novikov (writer), by Dimitri Levitsky. 12k, Gavriil R. Derzhavin (poet, civil servant), by Vladimir Borovikovsky. 16k, Peasants' Supper, by Mikhail Shibanov (horiz.). 20k, View of Moscow, by Fedor Alexeyev (horiz.).

Perf. 12x12½, 12½x12

1972, June 7   Lithographed

3976	A1897	2k gray & multi	10	5
3977	A1897	4k gray & multi	15	5
3978	A1897	6k gray & multi	20	10
3979	A1897	10k gray & multi	30	10
3980	A1897	12k gray & multi	35	15
3981	A1897	16k gray & multi	50	25
3982	A1897	20k gray & multi	75	30
		Nos. 3976-3982 (7)	2.35	1.00

History of Russian painting. See Nos. 4036-4042, 4074-4080, 4103-4109.

George Dimitrov   Fencing, Olympic Rings
A1898   A1899

1972, June 15   Photo.   Perf. 12½x12

| 3983 | A1898 | 6k brn & ol bis | 20 | 12 |

90th anniversary of the birth of George Dimitrov (1882–1949), Bulgarian Communist Party leader and Premier.

1972, July 1   Perf. 12½x11½

Designs (Olympic Rings and): 6k, Women's gymnastics. 10k, Canoeing. 14k, Boxing. 16k, Running. 50k, Weight lifting.

3984	A1899	4k brt mag & gold	15	5
3985	A1899	6k dp grn & gold	20	6
3986	A1899	10k brt bl & gold	40	10
3987	A1899	14k Prus bl & gold	50	15
3988	A1899	16k red & gold	60	25
		Nos. 3984-3988 (5)	1.85	61

Souvenir Sheet
Perf. 11½

| 3989 | A1899 | 50k gold & multi | 1.75 | 75 |

20th Olympic Games, Munich, Aug. 26–Sept. 11. No. 3989 contains one stamp (25x35mm.), gray green and gold margin with Olympic rings and inscription. Size: 66x85½mm.

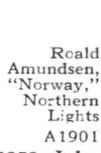

Congress Palace, Kiev
A1900

1972, July 1   Photo. and Engr.

| 3990 | A1900 | 6k Prus bl & bis | 20 | 12 |

9th World Gerontology Congress, Kiev, July 2–7.

Roald Amundsen, "Norway," Northern Lights
A1901

1972, July 13   Photo.   Perf. 11½

| 3991 | A1901 | 6k vio bl & dp bis | 20 | 12 |

Centenary of the birth of Roald Amundsen (1872–1928), Norwegian polar explorer.

17th Century House, Chernigov
A1902

Designs: 4k, Market Square, Lvov (vert.). 10k, Kovnirov Building, Kiev. 16k, Fortress, Kamenets-Podolsky (vert.).

Perf. 12x12½, 12½x12

1972, July 18   Lithographed

3992	A1902	4k cit & multi	15	5
3993	A1902	6k gray & multi	20	6
3994	A1902	10k ocher & multi	30	10
3995	A1902	16k sal & multi	50	17

Historic and architectural treasures of the Ukraine.

Asoka Pillar, Indian Flag, Red Fort, New Delhi
A1903

1972, July 27   Photo.   Perf. 11½

| 3996 | A1903 | 6k dk bl, emer & red | 20 | 12 |

25th anniversary of India's independence.

Miners' Emblem
A1904

1972, Aug. 10

| 3997 | A1904 | 4k vio gray & red | 15 | 12 |

25th Miners' Day.

Far East Fighters' Monument
A1905

Designs: 4k, Monument for Far East Civil War heroes, industrial view. 6k, Vladivostok rostral column, Pacific fleet ships.

1972, Aug. 10

3998	A1905	3k red org, car & blk	10	5
3999	A1905	4k yel, sep & blk	15	5
4000	A1905	6k pink, dk car & blk	20	10

50th anniversary of the liberation of the Far Eastern provinces.

Boy with Dog, by Murillo
A1906

Perf. 12½x12, 12x12½

**1972, Aug. 15   Lithographed
Bister and Multicolored**

4001	A1906	4k Breakfast, Velazquez (horiz.)	15	5
4002	A1906	6k Milkmaid's Family, Louis Le Nain (horiz.)	20	6
4003	A1906	10k shown	30	10
4004	A1906	16k Sad Woman, Watteau	50	17
4005	A1906	20k Moroccan Saddling Steed, Delacroix	75	22
		Nos. 4001-4005 (5)	1.95	60

RUSSIA

Souvenir Sheet
Perf. 12

| 4006 | A1906 | 50k Self-portrait, Van Dyck | 1.75 | 75 |

Paintings from the Hermitage, Leningrad. No. 4006 has gray margin with gold and black inscription. Size: 72½x97mm.

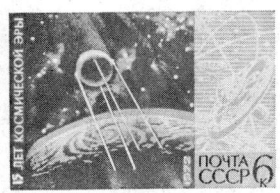

Sputnik 1—A1907

1972, Sept. 14   Litho.   Perf. 12x11½

4007	A1907	6k shown	20	6
4008	A1907	6k Launching of Vostok 2	20	6
4009	A1907	6k Lenov floating in space	20	6
4010	A1907	6k Lunokhod on moon	20	6
4011	A1907	6k Venera 7 descending to Venus	20	6
4012	A1907	6k Mars 3 descending to Mars	20	6
		Nos. 4007-4012 (6)	1.20	36

15 years of space era.   Sheets of 6.

Kontantin Mardzhanishvili A1908

1972, Sept. 20   Engr.   Perf. 12x12½

| 4013 | A1908 | 4k sl grn | 15 | 12 |

Centenary of the birth of Konstantin Aleksandrovich Mardzhanishvili (1872–1933), theatrical producer.

Museum Emblem, Communications Symbols A1909

1972, Sept. 20   Photo.   Perf. 11½

| 4014 | A1909 | 4k sl grn & multi | 15 | 12 |

Centenary of the A. S. Popov Central Museum of Communications.

"Stamp" and Topical Collecting Symbols A1910

1972, Oct. 4   Engr. & Litho.   Perf. 12

| 4015 | A1910 | 4k yel, blk & red | 15 | 12 |

Philatelic Exhibition in honor of 50th anniversary of the U.S.S.R.

Lenin A1911

1972, Oct. 12   Photo.   Perf. 11½

| 4016 | A1911 | 4k gold & red | 15 | 12 |

55th anniversary of October Revolution.

Militia Badge A1912

1972, Oct. 12

| 4017 | A1912 | 4k gold, red & dk brn | 15 | 7 |

55th anniversary of the Militia of the U.S.S.R.

Arms of U.S.S.R. A1913

1972, Oct. 28   Perf. 12x11½

Gold and Multicolored

4018	A1913	4k shown	10	7
4019	A1913	4k Arms and industrial scene	10	7
4020	A1913	4k Arms, Supreme Soviet, Kremlin	10	7
4021	A1913	4k Lenin	10	7
4022	A1913	4k Arms, worker, book (Constitution)	10	7
		Nos. 4018-4022 (5)	50	35

Souvenir Sheet
Lithographed; Embossed   Perf. 12

| 4023 | A1913 | 30k red & gold | 1.25 | 45 |

50th anniversary of the Union of Soviet Socialist Republics. No. 4023 contains one horizontal stamp showing coat of arms and Spasski Tower. Multicolored margin with flags of the Republics. Size: 127x102 mm.

Kremlin and Snowflake A1914   **Savings Bank Book A1915**

Engraved and Photogravure

1972, Nov. 15   Perf. 11½

| 4024 | A1914 | 6k multi | 25 | 8 |

New Year 1973.

1972, Nov. 15   Photo.   Perf. 12x12½

| 4025 | A1915 | 4k lil & sl | 20 | 7 |

50th anniversary of savings banks in the USSR.

Soviet Olympic Emblem and Laurel A1916

Design: 30k, Soviet Olympic emblem and obverse of gold, silver and bronze medals.

1972, Nov. 15   Perf. 11½

| 4026 | A1916 | 20k brn ol, red & gold | 50 | 28 |
| 4027 | A1916 | 30k dp car, gold & brn | 75 | 40 |

Souvenir Sheet
No. 3989 Overprinted in Red

СЛАВА
СОВЕТСНИМ ОЛИМПИЙЦАМ,
ЗАВОЕВАВШИМ
50 ЗОЛОТЫХ, 27 СЕРЕБРЯНЫХ
И 22 БРОНЗОВЫЕ НАГРАДЫ!

| 4028 | A1899 | 50k gold & multi | 3.00 | 1.00 |

Soviet medalists at 20th Olympic Games.

Battleship Peter the Great, 1872 A1917

History of Russian Fleet: 3k, Cruiser Varyag, 1899. 4k, Battleship Potemkin, 1900. 6k, Cruiser Ochakov, 1902. 10k, Mine layer Amur, 1907.

Engraved and Photogravure

1972, Nov. 22   Perf. 11½x12

4029	A1917	2k multi	10	5
4030	A1917	3k multi	10	5
4031	A1917	4k multi	15	7
4032	A1917	6k multi	20	8
4033	A1917	10k multi	40	15
		Nos. 4029-4033 (5)	95	40

Grigory S. Skovoroda A1918   **Child Reading Traffic Rules A1919**

1972, Dec. 7   Engraved   Perf. 12

| 4034 | A1918 | 4k dk vio bl | 15 | 7 |

250th anniversary of the birth of Grigory S. Skovoroda (1722–1794), Ukrainian philosopher and humanist.

1972, Dec. 7   Photo.   Perf. 11½

| 4035 | A1919 | 4k Prus bl, blk & red | 15 | 7 |

Traffic safety campaign.

Russian Painting Type of 1972

Paintings: 2k, Meeting of Village Party Members, by E. M Cheptsov (horiz.). 4k, Pioneer Girl, by Nicolai A. Kasatkin. 6k, Woman Delegate, by G. G. Ryazhsky. 10k, Winter's End, by K. F. Yuon (horiz.). 16k, The Partisan A. G. Lunev, by N. I. Strunnikov. 20k, Igor E. Grabar, self-portrait. 50k, Blue Space (seascape with flying geese), by Arcadi A. Rylov (horiz.).

Perf. 12x12½, 12½x12

1972, Dec. 7   Lithographed

4036	A1897	2k ol & multi	10	6
4037	A1897	4k ol & multi	10	7
4038	A1897	6k ol & multi	15	10
4039	A1897	10k ol & multi	30	14
4040	A1897	16k ol & multi	50	20
4041	A1897	20k ol & multi	75	25
		Nos. 4036-4041 (6)	1.90	82

Souvenir Sheet
Perf. 12

| 4042 | A1897 | 50k multi | 1.75 | 75 |

History of Russian painting. No. 4042 contains one stamp, margin with black inscription simulates picture frame. Size: 91x71mm.

Symbolic of Theory and Practice A1920

Engraved and Photogravure

1972, Dec. 7   Perf. 11½

| 4043 | A1920 | 4k sl grn, yel & red brn | 15 | 10 |

Centenary of Polytechnic Museum, Moscow.

Venus 8 and Parachute A1921

Designs: No. 4045a, Venus 8. No. 4045b, Mars 3.

1972, Dec. 28   Photo.   Perf. 11½

| 4044 | A1921 | 6k dl cl, bl & blk | 25 | 10 |

Souvenir Sheet
Imperf.

4045	A1921	Sheet of 2	5.00	5.00
a.		50k brn	1.75	1.10
b.		50k brn	1.75	1.10

Soviet space research. No. 4045 contains 2 stamps with simulated perforations (size of stamps: 40x20mm.). Olive gray and blue decorative margin with red control number. Size: 90x70mm.

Globe, Torch and Palm—A1922

1973, Jan. 5   Perf. 11x11½

| 4046 | A1922 | 10k tan, vio bl & red | 40 | 18 |

15th anniversary of Afro-Asian Peoples' Solidarity Organization (AAPSO).

RUSSIA

I. V. Babushkin
A1923

"30," Map and Admiralty Tower, Leningrad
A1924

1973, Jan. 10 Engraved Perf. 12
4047 A1923 4k grnsh blk 20 7
Centenary of the birth of I. V. Babushkin (1873–1906), revolutionary.

1973, Jan. 10 Photo. Perf. 11½
4048 A1924 4k pale brn, ocher & blk 20 7
30th anniversary of the breaking of the Nazi blockade of Leningrad.

TU-154 Turbojet Passenger Plane—A1925

1973, Jan. 10 Litho. Perf. 12
4049 A1925 6k multi 20 8
50th anniversary of Soviet Civil Aviation.

Gediminas Tower, Flag, Modern Vilnius
A1926

1973, Jan. 10 Photo. Perf. 11½
4050 A1926 10k gray, red & grn 35 14
650th anniversary of Vilnius.

Heroes' Memorial, Stalingrad—A1927

Designs (Details from Monument): 3k, Man with rifle and "Mother Russia" (vert.). 10k, Mourning mother and child. 12k, Arm with torch (vert.). No. 4055a, Red star, hammer and sickle emblem and statuary like 3k. No. 4055b, "Mother Russia" (vert.).

1973, Feb. 1 Litho. Perf. 11½
4051 A1927 3k dp org & blk 10 5
4052 A1927 4k dp yel & blk 10 7
4053 A1927 10k ol & multi 25 12
4054 A1927 12k dp car & blk 30 15

Souvenir Sheet
Perf. 12x12½, 12½x12
4055 Sheet of 2, multi 1.50 65
a. 20k multi 60 25
b. 20k multi 60 25
30th anniversary of the victory over the Germans at Stalingrad. No. 4055 contains 2 stamps (size: 40x18), blue margin with black inscription and gold and red ornaments. Size: 94x75mm.

Large Portrait Type of 1971
Designs: 4k, Mikhail Prishvin. 10k, Fedor Chaliapin, by K. Korovin.

1973 Lithographed Perf. 11½x12
4056 A1855 4k pink & multi 15 7
4057 A1855 10k lt bl & multi 30 17
Birth centenaries of Mikhail Prishvin (1873–1954), author (4k) and Fedor Chaliapin (1873–1938), opera singer (10k). Issue dates: 4k, Feb. 1; 10k, Feb. 8.

"Mayakovsky Theater" "Mossovet Theater"
A1928 A1929

1973, Feb. 1 Photo. Perf. 11½
4058 A1928 10k red, gray & ind 30 14
4059 A1929 10k red, mag & gray 30 14
50th anniversary of the Mayakovsky and Mossovet Theaters in Moscow.

Copernicus and Solar System
A1930

1973, Feb. 8 Engr. & Photo.
4060 A1930 10k ultra & sep 35 20
500th anniversary of the birth of Nicolaus Copernicus (1473–1543), Polish astronomer.

Ice Hockey
A1931

Design: 50k, Two players (vert.).

1973, Mar. 14 Photo. Perf. 11½
4061 A1931 10k gold, bl & sep 35 12

Souvenir Sheet
4062 A1931 50k bl grn, gold & sep 2.00 75
European and World Ice Hockey Championships, Moscow. No. 4062 contains one stamp. Multicolored decorative margin. Size: 66½x85mm.

Athletes and Banners of Air, Land and Naval Forces
A1932

Tank, Red Star and Map of Battle of Kursk
A1933

1973, Mar. 14
4063 A1932 4k brt bl & multi 15 7
50th anniversary of the Sports Society of Soviet Army.

1973, Mar. 14
4064 A1933 4k gray, blk & red 15 7
30th anniversary of Soviet victory in the Battle of Kursk during World War II.

Nikolai E. Bauman
A1934

1973, Mar. 20 Engr. Perf. 12½x12
4065 A1934 4k brown 15 7
Centenary of the birth of Nikolai E. Bauman (1873–1905), Bolshevist revolutionary.

Red Cross and Red Crescent—A1935

Designs: 6k, Theater curtain and mask. 16k, Youth Festival emblem and young people.

1973, Mar. 20 Photo. Perf. 11
4066 A1935 4k gray grn & red 15 5
4067 A1935 6k vio bl & red 20 10
4068 A1935 16k multi 50 20
50th anniversary of the Union of Red Cross and Red Crescent Societies of the USSR (4k); 15th Congress of the International Theater Institute (6k); 10th World Festival of Youth and Students, Berlin (16k).

Aleksandr N. Ostrovsky, by V. Perov
A1936

1973, Apr. 5 Litho. Perf. 12½x12
4069 A1936 4k tan & multi 15 7
Sesquicentennial of the birth of Aleksandr N. Ostrovsky (1823–1886), dramatist.

Earth Satellite "Interkosmos"
A1937

Lunokhod 2 on Moon and Lenin Moon Plaque
A1938

1973, Apr. 12 Photo. Perf. 11½
4070 A1937 6k brn ol & dl cl 20 10
4071 A1938 6k vio bl & multi 20 10

Souvenir Sheets
Perf. 12x11½
Size: 75x100mm.
4072 A1938 Sheet of 3, pur & multi 2.00 90
a. 20k Lenin plaque 60 25
b. 20k Lunokhod 2 60 25
c. 20k Telecommunications 60 25
4073 A1938 Sheet of 3, sl grn & multi 2.00 90
a. 20k Lenin plaque 60 25
b. 20k Lunokhod 2 60 25
c. 20k Telecommunications 60 25
Cosmonauts' Day. No. 4070 commemorates cooperation in space research by European communist countries.
The souvenir sheets contain 3 horizontal stamps each (size: 50x21mm.). Gold and maroon border. Size: 75x100mm.

Russian Painting Type of 1972

Paintings: 2k, Guitarist, V. A. Tropinin. 4k, Young Widow, by P. A. Fedotov. 6k, Self-portrait, by O. A. Kiprensky. 10k, Woman with Grapes ("An Afternoon in Italy") by K. P. Bryullov. 12k, Boy with Dog ("That was my Father's Dinner") by A. Venetsianov. 20k, Soldiers ("Conquest of Siberia"), by V. I. Surikov (horiz.).

Perf. 12x12½, 12½x12
1973, Apr. 18 Lithographed
4074 A1897 2k gray & multi 10 10
4075 A1897 4k gray & multi 15 10
4076 A1897 6k gray & multi 20 10
4077 A1897 10k gray & multi 30 20
4078 A1897 12k gray & multi 40 20
4079 A1897 16k gray & multi 50 25
4080 A1897 20k gray & multi 60 30
Nos. 4074-4080 (7) 2.25 1.25

Athlete, Ribbon of Lenin Order
A1939

1973, Apr. 18 Photo. Perf. 11½
4081 A1939 4k bl, red & ocher 15 8
50th anniversary of Dynamo Sports Society.

No. 4062 with Blue Green Inscription and Ornaments Added in Margin.

Souvenir Sheet
1973, Apr. 26 Photo. Perf. 11½
4082 A1931 50k bl grn, gold & sep 1.50 75
Russian victory in European and World Ice Hockey Championships, Moscow. Size: 66½x85mm.

"Mikhail Lermontov," Route Leningrad to New York
A1940

1973, May 20 Photo. Perf. 11½
4083 A1940 16k multi 60 25
Inauguration of transatlantic service Leningrad to New York.

Krenkel, Polar Stations and Ship Chelyuskin
A1941

1973, May 20 Litho. & Engraved
4084 A1941 4k dl bl & ol 15 6
70th anniversary of birth of Ernest E. T. Krenkel (1903–1971), polar explorer.

RUSSIA

Emblem and Sports	Singers
A1942	A1943

1973, May 20   Litho.   Perf. 12x12½

| 4085 | A1942 | 4k multi | 15 | 6 |

Sports Association for Labor and Defense.

1973, May 24

| 4086 | A1943 | 10k multi | 35 | 15 |

Centenary of Latvian Song Festival.

Throwing the Hammer
A1944

Designs: 3k, Athlete on rings. 4k, Woman diver. 16k, Fencing. 50k, Javelin.

1973, June 14   Litho.   Perf. 11½

4087	A1944	2k lem & multi	8	5
4088	A1944	3k bl & multi	12	5
4089	A1944	4k cit & multi	15	8
4090	A1944	16k lil & multi	60	20

Souvenir Sheet

| 4091 | A1944 | 50k gold & multi | 1.85 | 80 |

Universiad, Moscow, 1973.
No. 4091 has light green margin with stadium and Kremlin. Size: 70x89mm.

Souvenir Sheet

Valentina Nikolayeva-Tereshkova
A1945

1973, June 14   Photo.   Perf. 12x11½
Multicolored

4092	A1945	Sheet of 3 + label	4.00	1.25
a.		20k as cosmonaut	1.00	35
b.		20k with Indian and African women	1.00	35
c.		20k with daughter	1.00	35

10th anniversary of the flight of the first woman cosmonaut. No. 4092 contains 3 stamps and label with blue and gold inscription. Size: 91½x71mm.

European Bison—A1946

1973, July 26   Photo.   Perf. 11x11½
Multicolored

4093	A1946	1k shown	5	5
4094	A1946	3k Ibex	12	5
4095	A1946	4k Caucasian snowcock	15	10
4096	A1946	6k Beaver	22	10
4097	A1946	10k Deer and fawns	38	15
		Nos. 4093-4097 (5)	92	45

Caucasus and Voronezh wildlife reserves.

Party Membership Card with Lenin Portrait—A1947

1973, July 26   Litho.   Perf. 11½

| 4098 | A1947 | 4k multi | 20 | 10 |

70th anniversary of 2nd Congress of the Russian Social Democratic Workers' Party.

al-Biruni
A1948

1973, Aug. 9   Engr.   Perf. 12x12½

| 4099 | A1948 | 6k red brn | 22 | 10 |

1000th anniversary of birth of abu-al-Rayhan al-Biruni (973-1048), Arabian (Persian) scholar and writer.

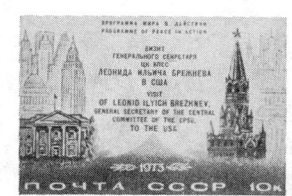

White House, Spasski Tower, Hemispheres—A1949

Designs: No. 4101, Eiffel Tower, Spasski Tower, globe. No. 4102, Schaumburg Palace, Bonn, Spasski Tower, globe. Stamps show representative buildings of Moscow, Washington, New York, Paris and Bonn.

1973, Aug. 10   Photo.   Perf. 11½x12

4100	A1949	10k mag & multi	35	12
4101	A1949	10k brn & multi	35	12
4102	A1949	10k dp car & multi	35	12
a.		Souvenir sheet of 3	1.60	85

Visit of General Secretary Leonid I. Brezhnev to Washington, Paris and Bonn. Nos. 4100-4102 each printed with se-tenant label with different statements by Brezhnev in Russian and English, French and German, respectively.
No. 4102a contains 4k stamps stimilar to Nos. 4100-4102 in changed colors, and 3 labels. Size: 133x138mm. Issued Nov. 26.
See Nos. 4161-4162.

Russian Painting Type of 1972
Paintings: 2k, S. T. Konenkov, sculptor, by P. D. Korin. 4k, Tractor Operators at Supper, by A. A. Plastov. 6k, Letter from the Front, by A. I. Laktionov. 10k, Mountains, by M. S. Saryan. 16k, Wedding on a Future Street, by Y. I. Pimenov. 20k, Ice Hockey, mosaic by A. A. Deineka. 50k, Lenin at 3rd Congress of Young Communist League, by B. V. Yoganson.

1973, Aug. 22   Litho.   Perf. 12x12½
Frame in Light Gray

4103	A1897	2k multi	8	5
4104	A1897	4k multi	12	6
4105	A1897	6k multi	15	8
4106	A1897	10k multi	30	12
4107	A1897	16k multi	50	18
4108	A1897	20k multi	60	27
		Nos. 4103-4108 (6)	1.75	76

Souvenir Sheet
Perf. 12

| 4109 | A1897 | 50k multi | 1.75 | 75 |

History of Russian Painting. No. 4109 contains one stamp, gray and ocher margin. Size: 72½x91mm.

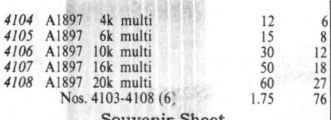

Museum, Tashkent	Y. M. Steklov
A1950	A1951

1973, Aug. 23   Photo.   Perf. 12x12½

| 4110 | A1950 | 4k multi | 20 | 10 |

Lenin Central Museum, Tashkent branch.

1973, Aug. 27   Photo.   Perf. 11½x12

| 4111 | A1951 | 4k multi | 20 | 10 |

Centenary of the birth of Y. M. Steklov (1873-1941), party worker, historian, writer.

Book, Pen and Torch	Echinopanax Elatum
A1952	A1953

1973, Aug. 31   Perf. 11½

| 4112 | A1952 | 6k multi | 20 | 10 |

Conference of Writers of Asia and Africa, Alma-Ata.

1973, Sept. 5   Litho.   Perf. 12x12½
Medicinal Plants: 2k, Ginseng. 4k, Orchis maculatus. 10k, Arnica montana. 12k, Lily of the valley.

4113	A1953	1k yel & multi	5	5
4114	A1953	2k lt bl & multi	8	5
4115	A1953	4k gray & multi	15	5
4116	A1953	10k sep & multi	30	10
4117	A1953	12k grn & multi	40	15
		Nos. 4113-4117 (5)	98	40

Imadeddin Nasimi
A1954

1973, Sept. 5   Engraved

| 4118 | A1954 | 4k sepia | 15 | 8 |

600th anniversary of the birth of Imadeddin Nasimi, Azerbaijani poet.

Cruiser Kirov—A1955

Soviet Warships: 4k, Battleship October Revolution. 6k, Submarine Krasnogvardeyets. 10k, Torpedo boat Soobraziteiny. 16k, Cruiser Red Caucasus.

Engraved and Photogravure

1973, Sept. 12   Perf. 11½x12

4119	A1955	3k vio & multi	13	5
4120	A1955	4k grn & multi	15	5
4121	A1955	6k multi	23	10
4122	A1955	10k bl grn & multi	38	15
4123	A1955	16k multi	60	25
		Nos. 4119-4123 (5)	1.49	60

Globe and Red Flag Emblem
A1956

1973, Sept. 25   Photo.   Perf. 11½

| 4124 | A1956 | 6k gold, buff & red | 23 | 10 |

15th anniversary of the international communist review "Problems of Peace and Socialism," published in Prague.

Emelyan I. Pugachev and Peasant Army—A1957

Engraved and Photogravure

1973, Sept. 25   Perf. 11½x12

| 4125 | A1957 | 4k brn, bis & red | 20 | 10 |

Bicentenary of peasant revolt of 1773-75 led by Emelyn Ivanovich Pugachev.

Crystal, Institute Emblem and Building
A1958

1973, Oct. 5   Perf. 11½

| 4126 | A1958 | 4k blk & multi | 20 | 10 |

Bicentenary of the Leningrad Mining Institute.

Palm, Globe, Flower	Elena Stasova
A1959	A1960

RUSSIA

1973, Oct. 5   Photogravure
4127 A1959 6k red, gray & dk bl   23   10
World Congress of Peace-loving Forces, Moscow.

1973, Oct. 5   Perf. 11½x12
4128 A1960 4k dp cl   20   10
Centenary of the birth of Elena Dmitriyevna Stasova (1873–1966), communist party worker.
See Nos. 4228–4229.

Order of Friendship
A1961

1973, Oct. 5   Litho.   Perf. 12
4129 A1961 4k red & multi   20   10
56th anniversary of the October Revolution. Printed se-tenant with coupon showing Arms of USSR and proclamation establishing Order of Friendship of People, in 1972, on the 50th anniversary of the USSR.

Marshal Malinovsky Ural Man, Red Guard, Worker
A1962   A1963

1973, Oct. 5   Engraved
4130 A1962 4k slate   20   10
75th anniversary of the birth of Marshal Rodion Y. Malinovsky (1898–1967).
See Nos. 4203–4205.

1973, Oct. 17   Photo.   Perf. 11½
4131 A1963 4k red, gold & blk   20   10
250th anniversary of the city of Sverdlovsk.

Dimitri Cantemir
A1964

1973, Oct. 17   Engr.   Perf. 12x12½
4132 A1964 4k rose cl   20   10
300th anniversary of the birth of Dimitri Cantemir (1673–1723), Prince of Moldavia, writer.

Salvador Allende
A1965

1973, Nov. 26   Photo.   Perf. 11½
4133 A1965 6k rose brn & blk   23   10
Salvador Allende (1908–1973), President of Chile.

Spasski Tower, Kremlin   Nariman Narimanov
A1966   A1967

1973, Nov. 30   Litho.   Perf. 12x12½
4134 A1966 6k brt bl & multi   23   10
New Year 1974.

1973, Nov. 30   Engraved   Perf. 12
4135 A1967 4k sl grn   20   10
Nariman Narimanov (1870–1925), Chairman of Executive Committee of USSR.

Russo-Balt, 1909—A1968

1973, Nov. 30   Photo.   Perf. 12x11½
4136 A1968 2k pur & multi   8   5
4137 A1968 3k ol & multi   13   5
4138 A1968 4k ocher & multi   15   10
4139 A1968 12k vio bl & multi   45   15
4140 A1968 16k red & multi   60   15
Nos. 4136-4140 (5)   1.41   50
Development of Russian automotive industry. See Nos. 4216–4220, 4325–4329, 4440–4444.

Still Life, by Frans Snyders—A1969

Paintings: 6k, Woman Trying on Earrings, by Rembrandt (vert.). 10k, Sick Woman and Physician, by Jan Steen (vert.). 12k, Still Life with Sculpture, by Jean-Baptiste Chardin. 14k, Lady in Garden, by Claude Monet. 16k, Young Love, by Jules Bastien-Lepage (vert.). 20k, Girl with Fan, by Auguste Renoir (vert.). 50k, Flora, by Rembrandt (vert.).

Perf. 12x11½, 11½x12
1973, Dec. 12   Lithographed
4141 A1969 4k bis & multi   13   8
4142 A1969 6k bis & multi   20   10
4143 A1969 10k bis & multi   35   10
4144 A1969 12k bis & multi   40   15
4145 A1969 14k bis & multi   45   20
4146 A1969 16k bis & multi   50   22
4147 A1969 20k bis & multi   65   25
Nos. 4141-4147 (7)   2.68   1.10

Souvenir Sheet
Perf. 12
4148 A1969 50k multi   1.75   75
Foreign paintings in Russian museums. No. 4148 contains one stamp. Multicolored margin shows extension of painting and frame. Size: 78x102mm.

Pablo Picasso
A1970

1973, Dec. 20 Photo.   Perf. 12x11½
4149 A1970 6k gold, sl grn & red   23   10
Pablo Picasso (1881–1973), painter.

Organ Pipes and Dome, Riga
A1971

Designs: No. 4151, Small Trakai Castle, Lithuania. No. 4152, Great Sea Gate, Tallinn, Estonia. 10k, Town Hall and "Old Thomas" weather vane, Tallinn.

1973, Dec. 20   Engr.   Perf. 12x12½
4150 A1971 4k blk, red & sl grn   15   6
4151 A1971 4k gray, red & buff   15   6
4152 A1971 4k blk & grn   15   6
4153 A1971 10k sep, grn, red & blk   38   15
Architecture of the Baltic area.

I. G. Petrovsky   L. A. Artsimovich
A1972   A1973

Portraits: No. 4154, I. G. Petrovsky (1901–1973), mathematician, rector of Moscow State University. No. 4155, L. A. Artsimovich (1909–1973), physician, academician. No. 4156, K. D. Ushinsky (1824–1871), teacher. No. 4157, M. D. Millionschikov (1913–1973), vice president of Academy of Sciences.

1973-74   Photo.   Perf. 11½
4154 A1972 4k org & multi   15   8
4155 A1973 4k blk brn & ol   15   8

Engr.   Perf. 12½x12
4156 A1973 4k multi   15   8

Litho.   Perf. 12
4157 A1973 4k multi   15   8
Issue dates: No. 4154, Dec. 28, 1973. Others, Feb. 6, 1974.

Flags of India and USSR, Red Fort, Taj Mahal and Kremlin—A1974

Design: No. 4162, Flags of Cuba and USSR, José Marti Monument, Moncada Barracks and Kremlin.

1973-74   Litho.   Perf. 12
4161 A1974 4k lt ultra & multi   15   10
4162 A1974 4k lt grn & multi ('74)   15   10
Visit of General Secretary Leonid I. Brezhnev to India and Cuba. Nos. 4161-4162 each printed with se-tenant label with different statements by Brezhnev in Russian and Hindi, and Russian and Spanish respectively.

Red Star, Soldier, Newspaper
A1975

1974, Jan. 1   Photo.   Perf. 11x11½
4166 A1975 4k gold, red & blk   20   10
50th anniversary of the Red Star newspaper.

Victory Monument, Peter-Paul Fortress, Statue of Peter I—A1976

1974, Jan. 16   Litho.   Perf. 11½
4167 A1976 4k multi   20   10
30th anniversary of the victory over the Germans near Leningrad.

Oil Workers, Refinery   Comecon Building
A1977   A1978

1974, Jan. 16   Photo.   Perf. 11½
4168 A1977 4k dl bl, red & blk   20   10
10th anniversary of the Tyumen oilfields.

1974, Jan. 16   Photo.   Perf. 11½
4169 A1978 16k red brn, ol & red   40   20
25th anniversary of the Council for Mutual Economic Assistance.

Skaters and Rink, Medeo
A1979

1974, Jan. 28
4170 A1979 6k sl, brn red & bl   23   10
European Women's Skating Championships, Medeo, Alma-Ata.

RUSSIA

Art Palace, Leningrad, Academy, Moscow
A1980

1974, Jan. 30   Photo. & Engr.
4171   A1980   10k multi   38   20

25th anniversary of the Academy of Sciences of the USSR.

3rd Winter Spartiakad Emblem A1981   Young People and Emblem A1982

1974, Mar. 20   Photo.   *Perf. 11½*
4172   A1981   10k gold & multi   38   20
Third Winter Spartiakad.

1974, Mar. 20   Photo. & Engr.
4173   A1982   4k multi   20   10
Youth scientific-technical work.

Azerbaijan Theater A1983

1974, Mar. 20   Photo.   *Perf. 11½*
4174   A1983   6k org, red brn & brn   23   10
Centenary of Azerbaijan Theater.

Meteorological Satellite "Meteor" A1984

Cosmonauts V. G. Lazarev and O. G. Makarov and Soyuz 12—A1985

Design: No. 4177, Cosmonauts P. I. Klimuk and V. V. Lebedev, and Soyuz 13.

1974, Mar. 27   *Perf. 11½*
4175   A1984   6k vio & multi   23   8
     Perf. 12x11½
4176   A1985   10k grnsh bl & multi   38   12
4177   A1985   10k dl yel & multi   38   12

Cosmonauts' Day.

Odessa by Moonlight, by Aivazovski—A1986

Seascapes by Aivazovski: 4k, Battle of Chesma, 1848 (vert.). 6k, St. George's Monastery. 10k, Stormy Sea. 12k, Rainbow (shipwreck). 16k, Shipwreck. 50k, Portrait of Aivazovski, by Kramskoy (vert.).

Perf. 12x11½, 11½x12

1974, Mar. 30   Lithographed
4178   A1986   2k gray & multi   8   3
4179   A1986   4k gray & multi   15   6
4180   A1986   6k gray & multi   23   8
4181   A1986   10k gray & multi   38   12
4182   A1986   12k gray & multi   45   18
4183   A1986   16k gray & multi   60   22
   Nos. 4178-4183 (6)   1.89   71

Souvenir Sheet
4184   A1986   50k gray & multi   1.75   75

Ivan Konstantinovich Aivazovski (1817-1900), marine painter. Sheets of Nos. 4178-4183 each contain 2 labels with commemorative inscriptions. No. 4184 has gold border and black marginal inscription. Size: 67x91mm. See Nos. 4230-4234.

Young Man and Woman, Banner A1987

1974, Mar. 30   Litho.   *Perf. 12½x12*
4185   A1987   4k red, yel & brn   15   10
17th Congress of the Young Communist League.

Lenin, by V. E. Tsigal A1988

1974, Mar. 30
4186   A1988   4k yel, red & brn   15   10
50th anniversary of naming the Komsomol (Young Communist League) after Lenin.

Souvenir Sheet

Lenin at the Telegraph, by Igor E. Grabar—A1989

1974, Apr. 16   Litho.   *Perf. 12*
4187   A1989   50k multi   1.80   75
104th anniversary of the birth of Lenin. No. 4187 has black inscription on lemon panel and gray marginal inscription and border. Size: 108x82mm.

Rainbow, Swallow over Clouds A1990   Congress Emblem and Clover A1991

Designs (EXPO '74 Emblem and): 6k, Fish in water. 10k, Crystal. 16k, Rose. 20k, Fawn. 50k, Infant.

1974, Apr. 24   Photo.   *Perf. 11½*
4188   A1990   4k lil & multi   15   10
4189   A1990   6k multi   22   10
4190   A1990   10k multi   38   15
4191   A1990   16k bl & multi   60   20
4192   A1990   20k cit & multi   70   25
   Nos. 4188-4192 (5)   2.05   80

Souvenir Sheet
Lithographed   *Perf. 12x12½*
4193   A1990   50k bl & multi   1.80   75

EXPO '74 World's Fair, theme "Preserve the Environment," Spokane, Washington, May 4–Nov. 4. No. 4193 contains one stamp. Blue and green ornamental margin and inscription. Size: 73x93mm.

1974, May 7   Photo.   *Perf. 11½*
4194   A1991   4k grn & multi   15   10
12th International Congress on Meadow Cultivation, Moscow, 1974.

"Cobblestones, Weapons of the Proletariat," by I. D. Shadra—A1992

1974, May 7
4195   A1992   4k gold, red & ol   15   10
50th anniversary of the Lenin Central Revolutionary Museum of the USSR.

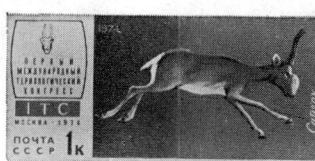

Saiga—A1993

Fauna of USSR: 3k, Koulan (wild ass). 4k, Desman. 6k, Sea lion. 10k, Greenland whale.

1974, May 22   Litho.   *Perf. 11½*
4196   A1993   1k ol & multi   5   5
4197   A1993   3k grn & multi   12   5
4198   A1993   4k multi   15   10
4199   A1993   6k multi   25   10
4200   A1993   10k multi   40   10
   Nos. 4196-4200 (5)   97   40

Peter Ilich Tchaikovsky A1994

1974, May 22   Photo.   *Perf. 11½*
4201   A1994   6k multi   23   10
5th International Tchaikovsky Competition, Moscow.

Souvenir Sheet

Aleksander S. Pushkin, by O. A. Kiprensky—A1995

1974, June 4   Litho.   *Imperf.*
4202   A1995   50k multi   1.80   75
175th anniversary of the birth of Aleksander S. Pushkin (1799-1837). No. 4202 has simulated perforations and multicolored margin. Size: 100x81mm.

Marshal Type of 1973
1974   Engraved   *Perf. 12*
4203   A1962   4k ol grn   15   6
4204   A1962   4k indigo   15   6
4205   A1962   4k sl grn   15   6

Marshal F. I. Tolbukhin (1894-1949) (No. 4203). Admiral I. S. Isakov (1894-1967) (No. 4204); Marshal S. M. Budenny (1883-1973) (No. 4205).
Issue dates: No. 4203, June 5; No. 4204, July 18; No. 4205, Aug. 20.

Stanislavski and Nemirovich-Danchenko A1996

1974, June 12   Litho.   *Perf. 12*
4211   A1996   10k yel, blk & dk red   38   15
75th anniversary of the Moscow Arts Theater.

Runner, Track, Open Book A1997

1974, June 12   Photo.   *Perf. 11½*
4212   A1997   4k multi   15   8
13th National School Spartakiad. Alma-Ata.

Railroad Car A1998

1974, June 12
4213   A1998   4k multi   15   8
Centenary of the Egorov Railroad Car Factory.

Victory Monument, Minsk A1999   Liberation Monument, Poltava A2000

RUSSIA

Design: No. 4215, Monument and Government House, Kiev.

1974, June 20
| 4214 | A1999 | 4k vio, blk & yel | 15 | 8 |
| 4215 | A1999 | 4k bl, blk & yel | 15 | 8 |

30th anniversary of liberation of Byelorussia (No. 4214), and of Ukraine (No. 4215).

Issue dates: No. 4214, June 20; No. 4215, July 18.

Automotive Type of 1973

Designs: 2k, GAZ AA truck, 1932. 3k, GAZ 03-30 bus, 1933. 4k, Zis 5 truck, 1933. 14k, Zis 8 bus, 1934. 16k, Zis 101 car, 1936.

1974, June 20   *Perf. 12x11½*
4216	A1968	2k brn & multi	8	5
4217	A1968	3k multi	13	5
4218	A1968	4k org & multi	15	10
4219	A1968	14k multi	50	15
4220	A1968	16k multi	55	20
	Nos. 4216-4220 (5)	1.41	55

Russian automotive industry.

1974, July 7   *Perf. 11½*
| 4221 | A2000 | 4k dl red & sep | 20 | 10 |

800th anniversary of city of Poltava.

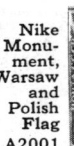

Nike Monument, Warsaw and Polish Flag
A2001

1974, July 7 *Litho.* *Perf. 12½x12*
| 4222 | A2001 | 6k ol & red | 23 | 10 |

Polish People's Republic, 30th anniversary.

Mine Layer—A2002

Soviet Warships: 4k, Landing craft. 6k, Anti-submarine destroyer and helicopter. 16k, Anti-submarine cruiser.

Engraved and Photogravure
1974, July 25   *Perf. 11½x12*
4223	A2002	3k multi	13	5
4224	A2002	4k multi	15	10
4225	A2002	6k multi	27	10
4226	A2002	16k multi	60	25

Pentathlon
A2003

1974, Aug. 7 *Photo.* *Perf. 11½*
| 4227 | A2003 | 16k gold, bl & brn | 55 | 35 |

World Pentathlon Championships, Moscow.

Portrait Type of 1973

Portraits: No. 4228, Dimitri Ulyanov (1874–1943). Soviet official and Lenin's brother. No. 4229, V. Menzhinsky (1874–1934), Soviet official.

1974, Aug. 7 *Engr.* *Perf. 12½x12*
| 4228 | A1960 | 4k sl grn | 15 | 8 |

Lithographed *Perf. 12x11½*
| 4229 | A1960 | 4k rose lake | 15 | 8 |

Painting Type of 1974

Designs: 4k, Lilac, by W. Kontchalovski. 6k, "Towards the Wind" (sailboats), by E. Kalnins. 10k, "Spring" (girl and landscape), by O. Zardarjan. 16k, Northern Harbor, G. Nissky. 20k, Kirghiz Girl, by S. Tchnikov (vert.).

Perf. 12x11½, 11½x12
1974, Aug. 20   *Lithographed*
4230	A1986	4k gray & multi	15	10
4231	A1986	6k gray & multi	23	10
4232	A1986	10k gray & multi	38	15
4233	A1986	16k gray & multi	55	20
4234	A1986	20k gray & multi	75	25
	Nos. 4230-4234 (5)	2.06	80

Russian paintings. Printed in sheets of 18 stamps and 2 labels.

Page of First Russian Primer
A2004

Monument, Russian and Romanian Flags
A2005

1974, Aug. 20   *Photo.* *Perf. 11½*
| 4235 | A2004 | 4k blk, red & gold | 20 | 10 |

400th anniversary of the first printed Russian primer.

1974, Aug. 23
| 4236 | A2005 | 6k dk bl, red & yel | 23 | 10 |

Romania's liberation from Fascist rule, 30th anniversary.

Vitebsk
A2006

1974, Sept. 4 *Lithographed* *Perf. 12*
| 4237 | A2006 | 4k dk car & ol | 20 | 10 |

Millennium of city of Vitebsk.

Kirgiz Republic
A2007

Designs: Flags, industrial and agricultural themes of various Republics. No. 4239, Moldavia. No. 4240, Turkmen. No. 4241, Uzbek. No. 4242, Tadzhik.

1974, Sept. 4   *Perf. 11½x11*
4238	A2007	4k vio bl & multi	15	6
4239	A2007	4k mar & multi	15	6
4240	A2007	4k yel & multi	15	6
4241	A2007	4k grn & multi	15	6
4242	A2007	4k lt bl & multi	15	6
	Nos. 4238-4242 (5)	75	30

50th anniversary of the founding of the Kirgiz, Moldavian, Turkmenian, Uzbek and Tadzhik Soviet Socialist Republics.

Arms and Flag of Bulgaria
A2008

Photogravure and Engraved
1974, Sept. 4   *Perf. 11½*
| 4243 | A2008 | 6k gold & multi | 23 | 10 |

30th anniversary of the Bulgarian revolution.

Arms of DDR and Soviet War Memorial, Treptow
A2009

1974, Sept. 4   *Photogravure*
| 4244 | A2009 | 6k multi | 23 | 10 |

25th anniversary of the German Democratic Republic.

Souvenir Sheet

Russian Stamps and Exhibition Poster—A2010

1974, Sept. 4 *Litho.* *Perf. 12x12½*
| 4245 | A2010 | 50k multi | 2.00 | 2.00 |

3rd Congress of the Philatelic Society of the USSR. No. 4245 has blue gray and greenish gray margin and red control number. Size: 111x71mm.

Maly State Theater
A2011

1974, Oct. 3 *Photo.* *Perf. 11x11½*
| 4246 | A2011 | 4k red, blk & gold | 20 | 10 |

150th anniversary of the Lenin Academic Maly State Theater, Moscow.

"Guests from Overseas," by N. K. Roerich—A2012

1974, Oct. 3 *Litho.* *Perf. 12*
| 4247 | A2012 | 6k multi | 23 | 10 |

Birth centenary of Nicholas Konstantin Roerich (1874–1947), painter and sponsor of Roerich Pact and Banner of Peace.

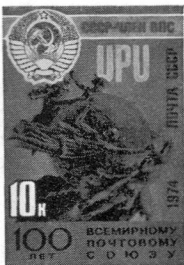

UPU Monument, Bern, and Arms of USSR
A2013

Development of Postal Service
A2014

Designs: No. 4248, Ukrainian coat of arms, letters, UPU emblem and headquarters, Bern. No. 4249, Arms of Byelorussia, UPU emblem, letters, stagecoach and rocket.

Photogravure and Engraved
1974, Oct. 9   *Perf. 12x11½*
4248	A2013	10k red & multi	38	20
4249	A2013	10k red & multi	38	20
4250	A2013	10k red & multi	38	20

Souvenir Sheet
Typographed *Perf. 11½x12*
4251	A2014	Sheet of 3, multi	5.00	2.00
a.	30k Jet and UPU emblem	1.10	60
b.	30k Mail coach and UPU emblem	1.10	60
c.	40k UPU emblem	1.50	60

Centenary of Universal Postal Union. No. 4251 has multicolored margin and red control number. Size: 122x76mm.

Order of Labor, 1st, 2nd and 3rd Grade
A2015

KAMAZ Truck Leaving Kama Plant
A2016

Design: No. 4254, Nurek Hydroelectric Plant.

1974, Oct. 16 *Litho.* *Perf. 12½x12*
4252	A2015	4k multi	15	6
4253	A2016	4k multi	15	6
4254	A2016	4k multi	15	6

RUSSIA

Space Stations Mars 4-7 over Mars A2017
P. R. Popovitch, Y. P. Artyukhin and Soyuz 14 A2018

Design: No. 4257, Cosmonauts G. V. Sarafanov and L. S. Demin, Soyuz 15, (horiz.).

1974, Oct. 28   *Perf. 12x11½, 11½*   Photogravure

4255	A2017	6k multi	20	10
4256	A2018	10k multi	30	20
4257	A2018	10k multi	30	20

Russian explorations of Mars (6k); flight of Soyuz 14 (No. 4256) and of Soyuz 15, Aug. 26-28 (No. 4257).

The Fishmonger, by Pieters A2023

Paintings: 4k, The Marketplace, by Beukelaer, 1564 (horiz.). 10k, A Drink of Lemonade, by Gerard Terborch. 14k, Girl at Work, by Gabriel Metsu. 16k, Saying Grace, by Jean Chardin. 20k, The Spoiled Child, by Jean Greuze. 50k, Self-portrait, by Jacques Louis David.

1974, Nov. 20   *Perf. 12x12½, 12½x12*   Lithographed

4262	A2023	4k bis & multi	15	10
4263	A2023	6k bis & multi	23	10
4264	A2023	10k bis & multi	38	15
4265	A2023	14k bis & multi	50	20
4266	A2023	16k bis & multi	55	25
4267	A2023	20k bis & multi	75	30
		Nos. 4262-4267 (6)	2.56	1.10

Souvenir Sheet
Perf. 12

| 4268 | A2023 | 50k multi | 1.75 | 75 |

Foreign paintings in Russian museums. Printed in sheets of 16 stamps and 4 labels. No. 4268 contains one stamp, light yellow green margin with black inscription. Size: 76x103mm.

Mozhaisky Plane, 1882—A2027

Early Russian Aircraft: No. 4277, Grizidubov-N biplane, 1910. No. 4278, Russia-A, 1910. No. 4279, Russian Vityaz (Sikorsky), 1913. No. 4280, Grigorovich flying boat, 1914.

1974, Dec. 25   Photo.   *Perf. 11½x12*

4276	A2027	6k ol & multi	23	10
4277	A2027	6k ultra & multi	23	10
4278	A2027	6k mag & multi	23	10
4279	A2027	6k red & multi	23	10
4280	A2027	6k brn & multi	23	10
		Nos. 4276-4280 (5)	1.15	50

Russian aircraft history, 1882-1914.

Souvenir Sheet

Sports and Sport Buildings, Moscow—A2028

1974, Dec. 25   *Perf. 11½*

4281	A2028	Sheet of 4, multi	1.75	75
a.		10k Woman gymnast	35	15
b.		10k Running	35	15
c.		10k Soccer	35	15
d.		10k Canoeing	35	15

Moscow preparing for Summer Olympic Games, 1980. No. 4281 has olive green margin and inscription. Size: 94x73mm.

Rotary Press, Pravda Masthead A2029

1975, Jan. 20

| 4282 | A2029 | 4k multi | 15 | 8 |

50th anniversary of the newspaper Pravda.

1975, Jan. 20

| 4284 | A2031 | 4k bl & multi | 15 | 8 |

8th Winter Spartakiad of USSR Trade Unions.

Games' Emblem, Hockey Player and Skier A2032

1975, Jan. 20

| 4285 | A2032 | 16k multi | 60 | 30 |

5th Winter Spartakiad of Friendly Armies, Feb. 23-Mar. 1.

Republic Anniversaries Type of 1970

Design (Hammer-Sickle Emblem and): No. 4286, Landscape and produce.

1975, Jan. 24   Engr.   *Perf. 12½x12*

| 4286 | A1794 | 4k green | 15 | 8 |

50th anniversary of Karakalpak Autonomous Soviet Socialist Republic.

David, by Michelangelo—A2033

Mongolian Flag and Arms A2019

1974, Nov. 14   Photo.   *Perf. 11½*

| 4258 | A2019 | 6k gold & multi | 23 | 10 |

Mongolian People's Republic, 50th anniversary.

Guards' Ribbon, Estonian Government Building, Tower A2020

1974, Nov. 14

| 4259 | A2020 | 4k multi | 15 | 8 |

Liberation of Estonia, 30th anniversary.

Tanker, Passenger and Cargo Ships A2021

1974, Nov. 14   Typo.   *Perf. 12½x12*

| 4260 | A2021 | 4k multi | 15 | 8 |

USSR Merchant Marine, 50th anniversary.

Spasski Tower Clock A2022

1974, Nov. 14   Lithographed   *Perf. 12*

| 4261 | A2022 | 4k multi | 15 | 8 |

New Year 1975.

Morning Glory A2024   **Ivan Nikitin** A2025

Designs: Flora of the USSR.

1974, Nov. 20   *Perf. 12x12½*

4269	A2024	1k red brn & multi	5	5
4270	A2024	2k grn & multi	8	5
4271	A2024	4k multi	15	10
4272	A2024	10k brn & multi	38	15
4273	A2024	12k dk bl & multi	45	20
		Nos. 4269-4273 (5)	1.11	55

1974, Dec. 11   Photo.   *Perf. 11½*

| 4274 | A2025 | 4k gray grn, grn & blk | 15 | 8 |

Sesquicentennial of the birth of Ivan Savvich Nikitin (1824-1861), poet.

Leningrad Mint—A2026
Photogravure and Engraved

1974, Dec. 11   *Perf. 11*

| 4275 | A2026 | 6k sil & multi | 23 | 10 |

250th anniversary of the Leningrad Mint.

Masthead and Pioneer Emblems A2030   **Spartakiad Emblem and Skiers** A2031

1975, Jan. 20

| 4283 | A2030 | 4k red, blk & sil | 15 | 8 |

50th anniversary of the newspaper Pioneers' Pravda.

Michelangelo, Self-portrait A2034

Designs (Works by Michelangelo): 6k, Squatting Boy. 10k, Rebellious Slave. 14k, The Creation of Adam. 20k, Staircase, Laurentian Library, Florence. 30k, The Last Judgment.

Lithographed and Engraved

1975, Feb. 27   *Perf. 12½x12*

4296	A2033	4k sl grn & grn	15	10
4297	A2033	6k red brn & bis	23	10
4298	A2033	10k sl grn & grn	38	15
a.		Miniature sheet of 6	1.65	75
4299	A2033	14k red brn & bis	50	15
4300	A2033	20k sl grn & grn	70	25
4301	A2033	30k red brn & bis	1.10	35
a.		Miniature sheet of 6	5.00	2.00
		Nos. 4296-4301 (6)	3.06	1.10

Souvenir Sheet
Perf. 12x11½

| 4302 | A2034 | 50k gold & multi | 2.00 | 75 |

500th birth anniversary of Michelangelo Buonarroti (1475-1564), Italian sculptor, painter and architect. Nos. 4296-4301 were issued only in miniature sheets of 6 with green and brown margins and inscriptions. No. 4298a contains 2 each of Nos. 4296-4298; No. 4301a contains 2 each of Nos. 4299-4301.

No. 4302 contains one stamp. Gold and brown margin shows ceiling from Sistine Chapel; white commemorative inscription. Size: 165x74mm.

RUSSIA

366

Mozhajski, Early Plane and Supersonic Jet TU-144—A2035

1975, Feb. 27 Photo. Perf. 12x11½

4303 A2035 6k vio bl & ocher   23   10

A. F. Mozhajski (1825–1890), pioneer aircraft designer, birth sesquicentennial.

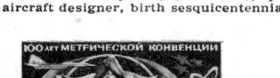

"Metric System"
A2036

1975, Mar. 14   Perf. 11½

4304 A2036 6k blk, vio bl & org   23   10

Centenary of International Meter Convention, Paris, 1875.

Spartakiad Emblem and Sports
A2037

1975, Mar. 14

4305 A2037 6k red, sil & blk   23   10

6th Summer Spartakiad.

Liberation Monument, Parliament, Arms **Charles Bridge Towers, Arms and Flags**
A2038   A2039

1975, Mar. 14

4306 A2038 6k gold & multi   23   10
4307 A2039 6k gold & multi   23   10

30th anniversary of liberation from fascism, Hungary (No. 4306) and Czechoslovakia (No. 4307).

Flags of France and USSR **Yuri A. Gagarin, by L. Kerbel**
A2040   A2041

A.V. Filipchenko, N.N. Rukavishnikov, Russo-American Space Emblem, Soyuz 16—A2042

1975, Mar. 25 Litho. Perf. 12

4308 A2040 6k lil & multi   23   10

50th anniversary of the establishment of diplomatic relations between France and USSR, first foreign recognition of Soviet State.

Perf. 11½x12, 12x11½

1975, Mar. 28   Photogravure

Design: 10k, A. A. Gubarev, G. M. Grechko aboard Soyuz 17 and orbital station Salyut 4.

4309 A2041 6k bl, sil & red   20   7
4310 A2042 10k blk, sil & red   35   12
4311 A2042 16k multi   50   18

Cosmonauts' Day.

Warsaw Treaty Members' Flags
A2043

1975, Apr. 16 Litho. Perf. 12

4312 A2043 6k multi   23   10

20th anniversary of the signing of the Warsaw Treaty (Bulgaria, Czechoslovakia, German Democratic Rep., Hungary, Poland, Romania, USSR).

Lenin on Steps of Winter Palace, by V. G. Zyplakov
A2044

1975, Apr. 22   Perf. 12x12½

4313 A2044 4k multi   20   10

105th anniversary of the birth of Lenin.

Communications Emblem and Exhibition Pavilion—A2045

1975, Apr. 22   Perf. 11½

4314 A2045 6k ultra, red & sil   23   10

International Communications Exhibition, Sokolniki Park, Moscow, May 1975.

Lenin and Red Flag **War Memorial, Berlin-Treptow**
A2046   A2048

Order of Victory—A2047

1975, Apr. 22   Typo.   Perf. 12
Bister, Red and Black

4315 A2046 4k shown   15   8
4316 A2046 4k Eternal Flame and guard   15   8
4317 A2046 4k Woman munitions worker 15   8
4318 A2046 4k Partisans   15   8
4319 A2046 4k Soldier destroying swastika   15   8
4320 A2046 4k Soldier with gun and banner   15   8
Nos. 4315-4320 (6)   90   48

Souvenir Sheet
Litho., Typo. and Photo.   Imperf.
4321 A2047 50k multi   1.75   85

World War II victory, 30th anniversary. No. 4321 has multicolored margin with Russia No. 992 and ribbon. Size: 110x56 mm.

1975, Apr. 25 Litho. Perf. 12x12½

4322 A2048 6k buff & multi   23   12

Souvenir Sheet
4323 A2048 50k dl bl & multi   1.75   85

Socfilex 75 International Philatelic Exhibition commemorating 30th anniversary of WW II victory, Moscow, May 8–18. No. 4323 contains one stamp; multicolored margin shows raising of Soviet flag on Reichstag Building, Berlin. Size: 68x95 mm.

Soyuz-Apollo Docking Emblem and Painting by Cosmonaut A. A. Leonov—A2049

1975, May 8 Photo. Perf. 12x11½

4324 A2049 20k multi   75   40

Russo-American space cooperation.

Automobile Type of 1973

Designs: 2k, GAZ-M-I car, 1936. 3k, 5-ton truck, YAG-6, 1936. 4k, ZIZ-16, autobus, 1938. 12k, KIM-10 car, 1940. 16k, GAZ-67B jeep, 1943.

1975, May 23 Photo. Perf. 12x11½

4325 A1968 2k dp org & multi   8   5
4326 A1968 3k grn & multi   13   5
4327 A1968 4k dk grn & multi   15   10
4328 A1968 12k mar & multi   45   15
4329 A1968 16k ol & multi   60   20
Nos. 4325-4329 (5)   1.41   55

Canal, Emblem, Produce
A2050

1975, May 23   Perf. 11½

4330 A2050 6k multi   23   12

9th International Congress on Irrigation and Drainage, Moscow, and 25th anniversary of International Commission on Irrigation and Drainage.

Flags and Arms of Poland and USSR, Factories
A2051

1975, May 23

4331 A2051 6k multi   23   12

Treaty of Friendship, Cooperation and Mutual Assistance between Poland and USSR, 30th anniversary.

Man in Space and Earth
A2052

1975, May 23

4332 A2052 6k multi   23   12

First man walking in space, Lt. Col. Alexei Leonov, 10th anniversary.

Yakov M. Sverdlov
A2053

1975, June 4

4333 A2053 4k multi   20   12

Yakov M. Sverdlov (1885–1919), organizer and early member of Communist party, 90th anniversary of birth.

Congress, Emblem, Forest and Field
A2054

1975, June 4

4334 A2054 6k multi   23   12

8th International Congress for Conservation of Plants, Moscow.

Symbolic Flower with Plants and Emblem
A2055

RUSSIA

1975, June 20   Litho.   Perf. 11½
4335 A2055 6k multi   23   12
12th International Botanical Congress.

Souvenir Sheet

U.N. Emblem—A2056
1975, June 20 Photo. Perf. 11½x12
4336 A2056 50k gold & bl   1.75   90
30th anniversary of United Nations. No. 4336 has gold inscription and U.N. Headquarters engraved in sepia in margin. Size: 65x80mm.

Globe and Film
A2057
1975, June 20   Photo.   Perf. 11½
4337 A2057 6k multi   23   12
9th International Film Festival, Moscow, 1975.

Russian and American Astronauts and Flags—A2058

Apollo and Soyuz After Link-up and Earth—A2059

Soyuz Launch
A2060

1975, July 15   Litho.   Perf. 11½
4338 A2058 10k multi   30   15
4339 A2059 12k multi   50   20
4340 A2059 12k multi   50   20
4341 A2060 16k multi   48   30

Souvenir Sheet
Photogravure   Perf. 12x11½
4342 A2058 50k multi   2.00 1.00

Apollo-Soyuz space test project (Russo-American space cooperation), launching, July 15; link-up July 17. Nos. 4339-4340 printed se-tenant vertically in sheets of 12 (3x4). See U.S. Nos. 1569-1570.
No. 4342 contains one stamp (50x21 mm.); multicolored margin with Apollo-Soyuz project emblem. Portraits of participating U.S.S.R. and U.S. crews: Aleksei A. Leonov, Valery N. Kubasov, Thomas P. Stafford, Vance D. Brand and Donald K. Slayton. Size: 84x120mm.

Sturgeon, Caspian Sea, Oceanexpo 75 Emblem—A2061

Designs (Oceanexpo 75 Emblem and): 4k, Salt-water shell, Black Sea. 6k, Eel, Baltic Sea. 10k, Sea duck, Arctic Sea. 16k, Crab, Far Eastern waters. 20k, Chrisipther (fish), Pacific Ocean.

1975, July 22   Photo.   Perf. 11
4343 A2061 3k multi   12   5
4344 A2061 4k multi   15   10
4345 A2061 6k grn & multi   23   10
4346 A2061 10k dk bl & multi   38   15
4347 A2061 16k pur & multi   60   20
4348 A2061 20k multi   70   30
       Nos. 4343-4348 (6)   2.18   90

Souvenir Sheet
Perf. 12x11½
4349 A2061 Sheet of 2, multi   2.25 1.00
 a.   30k Dolphin rising   90   30
 b.   30k Dolphin diving   90   30

Oceanexpo 75, First International Oceanographic Exhibition, Okinawa, July 20, 1975-Jan. 1976. No. 4349 contains 2 stamps (size: 55x25mm.). Bright blue marginal design and inscription. Size: 83x121mm.

Parade, Red Square, 1941, by K. F. Yuon—A2062

Paintings: 2k, Morning of Industrial Moscow, by K. F. Yuon. 6k, Soldiers Inspecting Captured Artillery, by Y. Y. Lansere. 10k, Excavating Metro Tunnel, by Y. Y. Lansere. 16k, Pushkin and His Wife at Court Ball, by N. P. Ulyanov (vert.). 20k, De Lauriston at Kutuzov's Headquarters, by N. P. Ulyanov.

1975, July 22 Litho. Perf. 12½x11½
4350 A2062 1k gray & multi   5   5
4351 A2062 2k gray & multi   8   5
4352 A2062 6k gray & multi   23   10
4353 A2062 10k gray & multi   38   15
4354 A2062 16k gray & multi   60   25

4355 A2062 20k gray & multi   70   30
       Nos. 4350-4355 (6)   2.04   90
Birth centenaries of Russian painters: Konstantin F. Yuon (1875-1958), Yevgeni Y. Lansere (1875-1946), Nikolai P. Ulyanov (1875-1949).

Finlandia Hall,   M. K. Chuyrlenis,
Map of Europe,   Waves and
Laurel   Lighthouse
A2063   A2064

1975, Aug. 18   Photo.   Perf. 11½
4356 A2063 6k brt bl, gold & blk 20   10

European Security and Cooperation Conference, Helsinki, July 30-Aug. 1. Printed se-tenant with label with quotation by Leonid I. Brezhnev, first secretary of Communist party.

1975, Aug. 20   Photo. & Engr.
4357 A2064 4k grn, ind & gold   20   10

M. K. Chuyrlenis, Lithuanian composer, birth centenary.

Avetik Isaakyan, by Martiros Sar'yan
A2065
1975, Aug. 20 Litho. Perf. 12½x12½
4358 A2065 4k multi   20   10
Avetik Isaakyan (1875-1957), Armenian poet, birth centenary.

Jacques Duclos   al-Farabi
A2066   A2067
1975, Aug. 20 Photo. Perf. 11½x12
4359 A2066 6k mar & sil   20   10
Jacques Duclos (1896-1975), French labor leader.

1975, Aug. 20   Perf. 11½
4360 A2067 6k grnsh bl, brn & bis 20 10
Nasr al-Farabi (870 ?-950), Arab philosopher.

Male Ruffs
A2068
1975, Aug. 25 Litho. Perf. 12½x12
Multicolored
4361 A2068 1k shown   5   5
4362 A2068 4k Altai roebuck   15   10
4363 A2068 6k Siberian marten   23   10
4364 A2068 10k Old squaw (duck) 38   15
4365 A2068 16k Badger   60   25
       Nos. 4361-4365 (5)   1.41   65
Berezina River and Stolby wildlife reservations, 50th anniversary.

 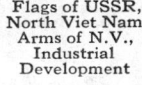

Flags of USSR,   Flags of USSR,
North Korea,   North Viet Nam,
Arms of N. K.,   Arms of N.V.,
Liberation   Industrial
Monument,   Development
Pyongyang
A2069   A2070
1975, Aug. 28   Perf. 12
4366 A2069 6k multi   20   12
4367 A2070 6k multi   20   12
Liberation of North Korea from Japanese occupation (№ 4366); and establishment of Democratic Republic of Viet Nam (№ 4367), 30th anniversaries.

P. Klimuk and V. Sevastyanov, Soyuz 18 and Salyut 4 Docking—A2071
1975, Sept. 12 Photo. Perf. 12½x11½
4368 A2071 10k ultra, blk & dp org 25 12
Docking of space ship Soyuz 18 and space station Salyut 4.

S. A. Esenin and Birches
A2072
Photogravure and Engraved
1975, Sept. 12   Perf. 11½
4369 A2072 6k brn & ocher   23   12
Sergei A. Esenin (1895-1925), poet, 50th death anniversary.

Standardization Symbols
A2073
1975, Sept. 12   Photo.   Perf. 11½
4370 A2073 4k red & multi   20   12
USSR Committee for Standardization of Communications Ministry, 50th anniversary.

368 RUSSIA

Karakul Lamb
A2074

1975, Sept. 22 Photo. Perf. 11½

4371 A2074 6k blk, yel & grn   23   12

3rd International Symposium on astrakhan production, Samarkand, Sept. 22–27.

M. P. Konchalovsky
A2075

Exhibition Emblem
A2076

1975, Sept. 30 Perf. 11½x12

4372 A2075 4k brn & red   20   12

Dr. M. P. Konchalovsky (1875–1942), physician, birth centenary.

1975, Sept. 30 Perf. 11½

4373 A2076 4k dp bl & red   20   12

3rd All-Union Youth Philatelic Exhibition, Erevan.

IWY Emblem and Rose
A2077

Jugoslavian Flag and Parliament
A2078

1975, Sept. 30 Litho. Perf. 12x11½

4374 A2077 6k multi   23   12

International Women's Year 1975.

1975, Sept. 30 Photo. Perf. 11½

4375 A2078 6k gold, red & bl   23   12

30th anniversary of the proclamation of the Republic of Jugoslavia.

Illustration from 1938 Edition, by V. A. Favorsky
A2079

Mikhail Ivanovich Kalinin
A2080

1975, Oct. 20 Typo. Perf. 12

4376 A2079 4k buff, red & blk   20   12

175th anniversary of the 1st edition of the old Russian saga "Slovo o polku Igoreve."

1975, Oct. 20 Engr. Perf. 12

Portrait: No. 4378, Anatoli Vasilievich Lunacharski.

4377 A2080 4k sepia   15   6
4378 A2080 4k sepia   15   6

Birth Centenaries: M. I. Kalinin (1875–1946), chairman of Central Executive Committee and Presidium of Supreme Soviet; A. V. Lunacharski (1875–1933), writer, commissar for education.

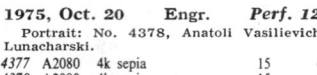

Hand Holding Torch and Lenin Quotation—A2081

1975, Oct. 20 Engraved

4379 A2081 4k red & ol   15   8

70th anniversary of First Russian Revolution (1905).

Building Baikal-Amur Railroad
A2082

Novolipetsk Metallurgical Plant
A2083

Nevynomyssk Chemical Plant, Fertilizer Formula
A2084

1975, Oct. 30 Photo. Perf. 11½

4380 A2082 4k gold & multi   15   8
4381 A2083 4k red, gray & sl grn   15   8
4382 A2084 4k red, bl & sil   15   8

58th anniversary of October Revolution.

Bas-relief of Decembrists and "Decembrists at the Senate Square," by D. N. Kardovsky—A2085

1975, Nov. 12 Litho. & Engr.

4383 A2085 4k gray & multi   15   8

Sesquicentennial of Decembrist rising.

Star and "1976"
A2086

1975, Nov. 12 Litho. Perf. 12x12½

4384 A2086 4k grn & multi   15   8

New Year 1976.

Village Street, by F. A. Vasilev
A2087

Paintings by Vasilev: 4k, Road in Birch Forest. 6k, After the Thunderstorm. 10k, Swamp (horiz.). 12k, In the Crimean Mountains. 16k, Meadow (horiz.). 50k, Self-portrait.

Perf. 12x12½, 12½x12

1975, Nov. 25

4385 A2087 2k gray & multi   8   5
4386 A2087 4k gray & multi   15   6
4387 A2087 6k gray & multi   23   10
4388 A2087 10k gray & multi   38   15
4389 A2087 12k gray & multi   45   18
4390 A2087 16k gray & multi   60   25
Nos. 4385-4390 (6)   1.89   79

Souvenir Sheet
Perf. 12

4391 A2087 50k gray & multi   1.80   85

Fedor Aleksandrovich Vasilev (1850–1873), landscape painter, 125th birth anniversary. Nos. 4385–4390 printed in sheets of 7 stamps and one label with commemorative inscription. No. 4391 has black marginal inscription. Size: 63x93½ mm.

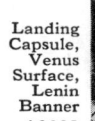 

Landing Capsule, Venus Surface, Lenin Banner
A2088

1975, Dec. 8 Photo. Perf. 11½

4392 A2088 10k multi   38   15

Flights of Soviet interplanetary stations Venus 9 and Venus 10.

Gabriel Sundoukian
A2089

1975, Dec. 8 Litho. Perf. 12

4393 A2089 4k multi   15   8

Gabriel Sundoukian (1825–1912), Armenian playright, birth sesquicentennial.

Polar Poppies, Taiga
A2090

Regional Flowers: 6k, Globeflowers, tundra. 10k, Buttercups, oak forest. 12k, Wood anemones, steppe. 16k, Eminium Lehmannii, desert.

Photogravure & Engraved
1975, Dec. 25 Perf. 12x11½

4394 A2090 4k blk & multi   15   10
4395 A2090 6k blk & multi   23   10
4396 A2090 10k blk & multi   38   15
4397 A2090 12k blk & multi   45   20
4398 A2090 16k blk & multi   60   25
Nos. 4394-4398 (5)   1.81   80

A. L. Mints
A2091

1975, Dec. 31 Photo. Perf. 11½x12

4399 A2091 4k dp brn & gold   15   8

A. L. Mints (1895–1974), academician.

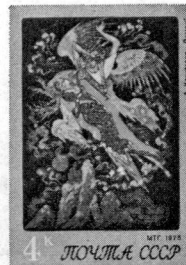

Demon, by A. Kochupalov
A2092

Paintings: 6k, Vasilisa the Beautiful, by I. Vakurov. 10k, Snow Maiden, by T. Zubkova. 16k, Summer, by K. Kukulieva. 20k, The Fisherman and the Goldfish, by I. Vakurov (horiz.).

1975, Dec. 31 Litho. Perf. 12

4400 A2092 4k bis & multi   15   6
4401 A2092 6k bis & multi   23   7
4402 A2092 10k bis & multi   38   12
4403 A2092 16k bis & multi   55   18
4404 A2092 20k bis & multi   65   27
Nos. 4400-4404 (5)   1.96   70

Palekh Art State Museum, Ivanov Region. Nos. 4400–4404 printed se-tenant in sheets of 20 (5x4).

Wilhelm Pieck
A2093

1976, Jan. 3 Engr. Perf. 12½x12

4405 A2093 6k bluish blk   23   12

Wilhelm Pieck (1876–1960), president of German Democratic Republic, birth centenary.

M. E. Saltykov-Shchedrin, by I.N. Kramskoi
A2094

RUSSIA

1976, Jan. 14 Litho. Perf. 12x12½
4406 A2094 4k multi   15   10
Mikhail Evgrafovich Saltykov-Shchedrin (1826–1889), writer and revolutionist, birth sesquicentennial.

Congress Emblem
A2095

Lenin Statue, Kiev
A2096

1976, Feb. 2 Photo. Perf. 11½
4407 A2095 4k red, gold & mar   15   10

Souvenir Sheet Perf. 11½x12
4408 A2095 50k red, gold & mar   1.75   85

25th Congress of the Communist Party of the Soviet Union. No. 4408 contains one stamp, red and gold margin with gray Lenin portrait. Size: 107x74mm.

1976, Feb. 2 Perf. 11½
4409 A2096 4k red, blk & bl   20   12
25th Congress of the Ukrainian Communist Party.

Ice Hockey, Games' Emblem
A2097

Designs (Winter Olympic Games' Emblem and): 4k, Cross-country skiing. 6k, Figure skating, pairs. 10k, Speed skating. 20k, Luge. 50k, Winter Olympic Games' emblem (vert.).

1976, Feb. 4 Litho. Perf. 12½x12
4410 A2097 2k multi   8   5
4411 A2097 4k multi   15   10
4412 A2097 6k multi   23   10
4413 A2097 10k multi   38   15
4414 A2097 20k multi   75   30
      Nos. 4410-4414 (5)   1.59   70

Souvenir Sheet Perf. 12x12½
4415 A2097 50k vio bl, org & red   1.75   85

12th Winter Olympic Games, Innsbruck, Austria, Feb. 4–15. No. 4415 contains one stamp; silver and violet blue margin showing designs of Nos. 4410–4414. Size: 90x80mm.

**Souvenir Sheet
No. 4415 Overprinted in Red.**
1976, Mar. 24
4416 A2097 50k multi   2.75 1.50
Successful participation of Soviet athletes in 12th Winter Olympic Games. Translation of overprint: "Glory to Soviet Sport! The athletes of the USSR have won 13 gold, 6 silver and 8 bronze medals."

K.E. Voroshilov
A2098

1976, Feb. 4 Engr. Perf. 12
4417 A2098 4k sl grn   15   10
Kliment Efremovich Voroshilov (1881–1969), president of revolutionary military council and commander of Leningrad front, 1941. See Nos. 4487–4488.

Flag over Kremlin Palace of Congresses, Spasski Tower
A2099
Photogravure on Gold Foil

1976, Feb. 24 Perf. 12x11½
4418 A2099 20k gold, grn & red   2.00 1.00
25th Congress of the Communist Party of the Soviet Union (CPSU).

Lenin on Red Square, by P. Vasiliev—A2100

1976, Mar. 10 Litho. Perf. 12½x12
4419 A2100 4k yel & multi   20   12
106th anniversary of the birth of Lenin.

Atom Symbol and Dubna Institute
A2101

1976, Mar. 10 Photo. Perf. 11½
4420 A2101 6k vio bl, red & sil   23   12
Joint Institute of Nuclear Research, Dubna, 20th anniversary.

Bolshoi Theater—A2102

1976, Mar. 24 Litho. Perf. 11x11½
4421 A2102 10k yel, bl & dk brn   25   12
Bicentenary of Bolshoi Theater.

Back from the Fair, by Konchalovsky—A2103

Paintings by P. P. Konchalovsky: 2k, The Green Glass. 6k, Peaches. 16k, Meat, Game and Vegetables. 20k, Self-portrait, 1943 (vert.).

1976, Apr. 6 Perf. 12½x12, 12x12½
4422 A2103 1k yel & multi   5   5
4423 A2103 2k yel & multi   8   5
4424 A2103 6k yel & multi   23   10
4425 A2103 16k yel & multi   60   25
4426 A2103 20k yel & multi   75   30
      Nos. 4422-4426 (5)   1.71   75
Birth centenary of P. P. Konchalovsky.

Vostok, Apollo-Soyuz Link-up
A2104

Yuri A. Gagarin—A2105

Designs: 6k, Meteor and Molniya Satellites, Orbita Ground Communications Center. 10k, Cosmonauts on board Salyut space station and Mars planetary station. 12k, Interkosmos station and Apollo-Soyuz linking.

Lithographed and Engraved
1976, Apr. 12 Perf. 11½
4427 A2104 4k multi   15   10
4428 A2104 6k multi   25   10
4429 A2104 10k multi   40   20
4430 A2104 12k multi   45   25

**Souvenir Sheet
Engraved Perf. 12**
4431 A2105 50k black   4.50 1.25
First manned flight in space, 15th anniversary. No. 4431 has multicolored lithographed margin showing "Pilot-Cosmonaut of the USSR" medal and red control number. Size: 65x100mm.

I. A. Dzhavakhishvili
A2106

1976, Apr. 20 Photo. Perf. 11½x12
4432 A2106 4k multi   15   8
I. A. Dzhavakhishvili (1876–1940), scientist, birth centenary.

Samed Vurgun and Derrick
A2107

1976, Apr. 20 Perf. 11½
4433 A2107 4k multi   15   8
Samed Vurgun (1906–1956), national poet of Azerbaijan, 70th birth anniversary.

USSR Flag, Worker and Farmer Monument
A2108

1976, May 12 Litho. Perf. 11½x12
4434 A2108 4k multi   15   8
1st All-Union Festival of Amateur Artists.

FIP Emblem
A2109

1976, May 12 Photo. Perf. 11½
4435 A2109 6k ultra & car   20   8
International Federation of Philately, 50th anniversary.

Souvenir Sheet

V. A. Tropinin, Self-portrait—A2110

1976, May 12 Litho. Perf. 12
4436 A2110 50k multi   1.50 1.00
Vasily Andreevich Tropinin (1776–1857), painter, 200th birth anniversary. No. 4436 has black ornamental margin. Size: 71x92mm.

RUSSIA

Emblem, Dnieper Bridge
A2111

Dr. N. N. Burdenko
A2112

1976, May 20   Photo.   Perf. 11½

| 4437 | A2111 | 4k Prus bl, gold & blk | 12 | 8 |

Bicentenary of Dnepropetrovsk.

1976, May 20   Perf. 11½x12

| 4438 | A2112 | 4k dp brn & red | 12 | 8 |

N. N. Burdenko (1876–1946), neurosurgeon, birth centenary.

K. A. Trenev
A2113

1976, May 20   Perf. 11½

| 4439 | A2113 | 4k blk & multi | 12 | 8 |

K. A. Trenev (1876–1945), playwright, birth centenary.

Automobile Type of 1973

Designs: 2k, ZIS-110 passenger car. 3k, GAZ-51 Gorky truck. 4k, GAZ-M-20 Pobeda passenger car. 12k, ZIS-150 Moscow Motor Works truck. 16k, ZIS-154 Moscow Motor Works bus.

1976, June 15   Photo.   Perf. 12x11½

4440	A1968	2k grnsh bl & multi	6	5
4441	A1968	3k bis & multi	9	5
4442	A1968	4k dk bl & multi	12	6
4443	A1968	12k brn & multi	36	20
4444	A1968	16k dp car & multi	48	25
		Nos. 4440-4444 (5)	1.11	.61

Canoeing
A2114

Designs (USSR National Olympic Committee Emblem and): 6k, Basketball (vert.). 10k, Greco-Roman wrestling. 14k, Women's discus (vert.). 16k, Target shooting. 50k, Olympic medal, obverse and reverse.

Perf. 12½x12, 12½x12½

1976, June 23   Lithographed

4445	A2114	4k red & multi	12	6
4446	A2114	6k red & multi	18	10
4447	A2114	10k red & multi	30	15
4448	A2114	14k red & multi	42	22
4449	A2114	16k red & multi	48	25
		Nos. 4445-4449 (5)	1.50	.78

Souvenir Sheet

| 4450 | A2114 | 50k red & multi | 1.50 | 1.00 |

21st Olympic Games, Montreal, Canada, July 17–Aug. 1. No. 4450 has multi-colored margin with black inscription. Size: 65x86mm.

Electric Trains, Overpass
A2115

1976, June 23   Photo.   Perf. 11½

| 4451 | A2115 | 4k multi | 12 | 8 |

Electrification of USSR railroads, 50th anniversary.

L. Emilio Rekabarren
A2116

1976, July 6

| 4452 | A2116 | 6k gold, red & blk | 18 | 10 |

Luis Emilio Rekabarren (1876–1924), founder of Chilean Communist Party, birth centenary.

L. M. Pavlichenko
A2117

1976, July 6

| 4453 | A2117 | 4k dp brn, sil & yel | 12 | 8 |

Ljudmilla Mikhajlovna Pavlichenko (1916–1974), WWII heroine, Komsomol, War Veterans and Women's Committee member.

New Partner, by P. A. Fedotov
A2118

Paintings: 4k, The Fastidious Fiancée (horiz.). 6k, Aristocrat's Breakfast. 10k, Gamblers (horiz.). 16k, The Outing. 50k, Self-portrait.

Perf. 12x12½, 12½x12

1976, July 15   Lithographed

4454	A2118	2k blk & multi	6	5
4455	A2118	4k blk & multi	12	10
4456	A2118	6k blk & multi	18	10
4457	A2118	10k blk & multi	30	15
4458	A2118	16k blk & multi	48	25
		Nos. 4454-4458 (5)	1.14	.65

Souvenir Sheet
Perf. 12

| 4459 | A2118 | 50k multi | 1.75 | 1.00 |

Pavel Andreevich Fedotov (1815–1852), painter. Nos. 4454–4458 each printed in sheets of 20 stamps and center label with black commemorative inscription. No. 4459 has brown and buff margin with brown inscription. Size: 70x90mm.

S. S. Nametkin
A2119

1976, July 20   Photo. Perf. 11½x12

| 4460 | A2119 | 4k bl, blk & buff | 12 | 8 |

Sergei Semenovich Nametkin (1876–1950), organic chemist, birth centenary.

Squacco Heron
A2120

Waterfowl: 3k, Arctic loon. 4k, European coot. 6k, Atlantic puffin. 10k, Slender-billed gull.

1976, Aug. 18   Litho.   Perf. 12x12½

4465	A2120	1k dk grn & multi	5	5
4466	A2120	3k ol grn & multi	9	5
4467	A2120	4k org & multi	12	6
4468	A2120	6k pur & multi	18	9
4469	A2120	10k brt bl & multi	30	15
		Nos. 4465-4469 (5)	.74	.40

Nature protection.

Peace Dove
A2121

1976, Aug. 25   Photo.   Perf. 11½

| 4470 | A2121 | 4k sal, gold & bl | 12 | 8 |

2nd Stockholm appeal and movement to stop arms race.

Resistance Movement Emblem
A2122

1976, Aug. 25

| 4471 | A2122 | 6k dk bl, blk & gold | 18 | 9 |

International Resistance Movement Federation, 25th anniversary.

Souvenir Sheet
1976, Aug. 25   Litho.   Perf. 12½x12½

| 4472 | A2114 | 50k red & multi | 1.75 | 1.00 |

Victories of Russian athletes in 21st Olympic Games (47 gold, 43 silver and 35 bronze medals).

No. 4450 Overprinted in Gold in Margin Similar to No. 3961

Flags of India and USSR
A2123

1976, Sept. 8   Perf. 12

| 4473 | A2123 | 4k multi | 12 | 8 |

Friendship and cooperation between USSR and India.

UN and UNESCO Emblems, Open Book
A2124

1976, Sept. 8   Engr.   Perf. 12x12½

| 4474 | A2124 | 16k multi | 48 | 25 |

U.N. Educational and Scientific Organization, 30th anniversary.

B. V. Volynov, V. M. Zholobov, Star Circling Globe—A2125

1976, Sept. 8   Photo.   Perf. 12x11½

| 4475 | A2125 | 10k brn, bl & blk | 40 | 25 |

Exploits of Soyuz 21 and Salyut space station.

"Industry"—A2126

1976, Sept. 17

Multicolored

4476	A2126	4k shown	12	8
4477	A2126	4k Farm industry	12	8
4478	A2126	4k Science	12	8
4479	A2126	4k Transport & communications	12	8
4480	A2126	4k International cooperation	12	8
		Nos. 4476-4480 (5)	.60	.40

25th Congress of the Communist Party of the Soviet Union.

Au (woman), by I. V. Markichev
A2127

Paintings: 2k, Plower, by I. I. Golikov (horiz.). 12k, Firebird, by A. V. Kotuhin (horiz.). 14k, Festival, by A. I. Vatagin. 20k, Victory, by I. I. Vakurov.

RUSSIA

	Perf. 12½x12, 12x12½			
1976, Sept. 22		Lithographed		
4481	A2127	2k blk & multi	6	5
4482	A2127	4k blk & multi	12	6
4483	A2127	12k blk & multi	36	20
4484	A2127	14k blk & multi	42	22
4485	A2127	20k blk & multi	60	30
	Nos. 4481-4485 (5)		1.56	83

Palekh Art State Museum, Ivanov Region.

Shostakovich, Score from 7th Symphony, Leningrad — A2128

1976, Sept. 25 Engr. Perf. 12½x12
4486 A2128 6k dk vio bl   18   12

Dimitri Dimitrievich Shostakovich (1906-1975), composer, 70th birth anniversary.

Voroshilov Type of 1976
No. 4487, Georgi K. Zhukov.
No. 4488, Konstantin K. Rokossovsky.

1976, Oct. 7 Engr. Perf. 12
4487 A2098 4k sl grn   12   10
4488 A2098 4k brown   12   10

Marshal Georgi Konstantinovich Zhukov (1896-1974), commander at Stalingrad and Leningrad and Deputy of Supreme Soviet; Marshal Konstantin K. Rokossovsky (1896-1968), commander at Stalingrad.

Interkosmos-14 A2129

Designs: 10k, India's satellite Arryabata. 12k, Soyuz-19 and Apollo before docking. 16k, French satellite Aureole and Northern Lights. 20k, Docking of Soyuz-Apollo, Interkosmos-14 and Aureole.

1976, Oct. 15 Photo. Perf. 11½
4489 A2129 6k blk & multi   15   10
4490 A2129 10k blk & multi 25   15
4491 A2129 12k blk & multi 30   15
4492 A2129 14k blk & multi 40   20
4493 A2129 20k blk & multi 50   25
Nos. 4489-4493 (5) 1.60 85

Interkosmos Program for Scientific and Experimental Research.

Vladimir I. Dahl A2130 Photogravure and Engraved

1976, Oct. 15 Perf. 11½
4494 A2130 4k grn & dk grn   12   12

Vladimir I. Dahl (1801-1872), physician, writer, compiled Russian Dictionary.

Electric Power Industry A2131

Designs: No. 4496, Balashovo textile mill. No. 4497, Laying of drainage pipes and grain elevator.

1976, Oct. 20 Photo. Perf. 11½
4495 A2131 4k dk bl & multi   12   8

4496 A2131 4k rose brn & multi   12   8
4497 A2131 4k sl grn & multi   12   8

59th anniversary of the October Revolution.

Petrov Tumor Research Institute A2132

M. A. Novinski A2133

1976, Oct. 28
4498 A2132 4k vio bl & gold   12   10

Perf. 11½x12
4499 A2133 4k dk brn, buff & bl   16   10

Petrov Tumor Research Institute, 50th anniversary, and 135th birth anniversary of M. A. Novinski, cancer research pioneer.

Aviation Emblem, Gakkel VII A2134

Designs (Russian Aviation Emblem and): 6k, Gakkel IX, 1912. 12k, I. Steglau No. 2, 1912. 14k, Dybovski's Dolphin, 1913. 16k, Iliya Muromets, 1914.

1976, Nov. 4 Lithographed and Engraved
Perf. 12x12½
4500 A2134 3k multi   10   5
4501 A2134 6k multi   18   10
4502 A2134 12k multi 36   20
4503 A2134 14k multi 42   22
4504 A2134 16k multi 48   25
Nos. 4500-4504 (5) 1.54 82

Russian aircraft, 1911-1914. See Nos. C109-C120.

Saffron A2135

Flowers of the Caucasus: 2k, Pasque-flowers. 3k, Gentian. 4k, Columbine. 6k, Checkered lily.

1976, Nov. 17 Perf. 12x11½
4505 A2135 1k multi   5   5
4506 A2135 2k multi   6   5
4507 A2135 3k multi   10   5
4508 A2135 4k multi   12   6
4509 A2135 6k multi   18   10
Nos. 4505-4509 (5)   51   31

Spasski Tower Clock, Greeting Card A2136

1976, Nov. 25 Litho. Perf. 12½x12
4510 A2136 4k multi   12   12

New Year 1977.

Parable of the Workers in the Vineyard, by Rembrandt — A2137

Rembrandt Paintings in Hermitage: 6k, birth anniversary. Nos. 4511 and 4515. 14k, Holy Family (vert.). 20k, Rembrandt's brother Adrian 1654 (vert.). 50k, Artaxerxes, Esther and Haman.

1976, Nov. 25 Perf. 12½x12, 12x12½ Photogravure
4511 A2137 4k multi   12   6
4512 A2137 6k multi   18   10
4513 A2137 10k multi 30   15
4514 A2137 14k multi 42   22
4515 A2137 20k multi 60   30
Nos. 4511-4515 (5) 1.62 83

Souvenir Sheet
4516 A2137 50k multi 5.00 1.50

Rembrandt van Rijn (1606-1669), 370th birth anniversary. Nos. 4511 and 4515 printed in sheets of 7 stamps and decorative label. No. 4516 has dark brown and multicolored margin with self-portrait and gold control number. Size: 127x65mm.

Armed Forces Order A2138

Worker and Farmer, by V. I. Muhina A2139

Marx and Lenin, by Fridman and Belostotsky A2140

Council for Mutual Economic Aid Building A2141

Lenin, 1920 Photograph A2142

Globe and Sputnik Orbits A2143

Designs: 2k, Golden Star and Hammer and Sickle medals. 4k, Coat of arms and "CCCP." 6k, TU-154 plane, globe and airmail envelope. 10k, Order of Labor. 12k, Space exploration medal with Gagarin portrait. 16k, Lenin Prize medal.

1976 Engraved Perf. 12
4517 A2138 1k grnsh blk   5   5
4518 A2138 2k brt mag   5   5
4519 A2139 3k red   10   5
4520 A2139 4k brick red   12   5
4521 A2139 6k Prus bl   18   5
4522 A2138 10k ol grn   30   5
4523 A2139 12k vio bl   35   5
4524 A2139 16k dp grn   40   5

Perf. 12½x12
4525 A2140 20k brn red   50   6
4526 A2141 30k brick red 75   10
4527 A2142 50k brown   1.50 15
4528 A2143 1r dk bl   3.00 20
Nos. 4517-4528 (12) 7.31 91

Issue dates: Nos. 4517-4524, Dec. 17.
Nos. 4525-4528, Aug. 10.
See Nos. 4596-4607.

Luna 24 Emblem and Moon Landing A2144

1976, Dec. 17 Photo. Perf. 11½
4531 A2144 10k multi   30   15

Moon exploration of automatic station Luna 24.

Icebreaker "Pilot" — A2145

Icebreakers: 6k, Ermak. 10k, Fedor Litke. 16k, Vladimir Ilich (vert.). 20k, Krasin.

1976, Dec. 22 Perf. 12x11½, 11½x12 Litho. and Engr.
4532 A2145 4k multi   12   6
4533 A2145 6k multi   18   10
4534 A2145 10k multi   30   15
4535 A2145 16k multi   48   25
4536 A2145 20k multi   60   30
Nos. 4532-4536 (5) 1.68 86
See Nos. 4579-4585.

Soyuz 22 Emblem, Cosmonauts V. F. Bykofsky and V. V. Aksenov — A2146

1976, Dec. 28 Photo. Perf. 12x11½
4537 A2146 10k multi   30   15

Soyuz 22 space flight, Sept. 15-23.

Society Emblem A2147

RUSSIA

1977, Jan. 1   *Perf. 11½*

4538   A2147   4k multi   12   6

Red Banner Voluntary Society, supporting Red Army, Navy and Air Force, 50th anniversary.

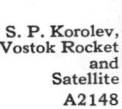 

S. P. Korolev, Vostok Rocket and Satellite
A2148

1977, Jan. 12

4539   A2148   4k multi   12   6

Sergei Pavlovich Korolev (1907–1966), creator of first Soviet rocket space system.

Globe and Palm
A2149

1977, Jan. 12

4540   A2149   4k multi   12   6

World Congress of Peace Loving Forces, Moscow, Jan. 1977.

R. J. Sedov and "St. Foka"
A2150

1977, Jan. 25   Photo.   *Perf. 11½*

4541   A2150   4k multi   12   6

R. J. Sedov (1877–1914), polar explorer and hydrographer, birth centenary.

 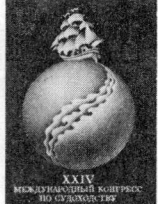

Worker and Farmer Monument and Izvestya Front Page
A2151

Ship Sailing Across the Oceans
A2152

1977, Jan. 25

4542   A2151   4k sil, blk & red   12   6

60th anniversary of newspaper Izvestya.

1977, Jan. 25

4543   A2152   6k dp bl & gold   18   10

24th International Navigation Congress, Leningrad.

Congress Hall and Spasski Tower, Kremlin
A2153

Marshal Leonid A. Govorov (1897–1955)
A2154

1977, Feb. 9   Photo.   *Perf. 11½*

4544   A2153   4k red, gold & blk   12   12

16th Congress of USSR Trade Unions.

1977   Engraved   *Perf. 12*

Portraits: No. 4546, Ivan S. Koniev. No. 4547, K. A. Merezhkov. No. 4548, W. D. Sokolovsky.

4545   A2154   4k brown   12   6
4546   A2154   4k sl grn   12   6
4547   A2154   4k brown   12   6
4548   A2154   4k black   12   6

Marshals of the Soviet Union.
Issue dates: No. 4545, Feb. 9. Nos. 4546–4548, June 7.

Academy, Crest, Anchor and Ribbons
A2155

Photogravure and Engraved

1977, Feb. 9   *Perf. 11½*

4549   A2155   6k multi   18   12

A. A. Grechko Naval Academy, Leningrad, sesquicentennial.

Jeanne Labourbe
A2156

Queen and Knights
A2157

1977, Feb. 25   Photo.   *Perf. 11½*

4550   A2156   4k multi   12   6

Jeanne Labourbe (1877–1919), leader of French communists in Moscow.

1977, Feb. 25

4551   A2157   4k multi   18   12

4th European Chess Championships.

Cosmonauts V. D. Zudov and V. I. Rozhdestvensky—A2158

1977, Feb. 25   *Perf. 12x11½*

4552   A2158   10k multi   20   15

Soyuz 23 space flight, Oct. 14–16, 1976.

A. S. Novikov-Priboy
A2159

1977, Mar. 16   Photo.   *Perf. 11½*

4553   A2159   4k multi   12   12

A. S. Novikov-Priboy (1877–1944), writer, birth centenary.

Welcome, by M. N. Soloninkin
A2160

Paintings: 6k, Along the Street, by V. D. Antonov (horiz.). 10k, Northern Song, by J. V. Karapaev. 12k, Tale of Czar Saltan, by A. I. Kozlov. 14k, Summer Troika, by V. A. Nalimov (horiz.). 16k, Red Flower, by V. D. Lipitsky.

Perf. 12x12½, 12½x12

1977, Mar. 16   Lithographed

4554   A2160   4k blk & multi   12   5
4555   A2160   6k blk & multi   18   10
4556   A2160   10k blk & multi   30   15
4557   A2160   12k blk & multi   36   15
4558   A2160   14k blk & multi   42   20
4559   A2160   16k blk & multi   48   20
Nos. 4554–4559 (6)   1.86   85

Folk tale paintings from Fedoskino artists' colony.

Lenin on Red Square, by K.V. Filatov—A2161

1977, Apr. 12   Litho.   *Perf. 12½x11½*

4560   A2161   4k multi   12   12

107th anniversary of the birth of Lenin.

Electricity Congress Emblem
A2162

1977, Apr. 12   Photo.   *Perf. 11½*

4561   A2162   6k bl, red & gray   18   12

World Electricity Congress, Moscow 1977.

Yuri Gagarin, Sputnik, Soyuz and Salyut—A2163

1977, Apr. 12   *Perf. 12x11½*

4562   A2163   6k multi   18   12

Cosmonauts' Day.

N. I. Vavilov
A2164

Feliks E. Dzerzhinski
A2165

1977, Apr. 26   Photo.   *Perf. 11½*

4563   A2164   4k multi   12   12

N. I. Vavilov (1887–1943), agricultural geneticist, 90th birth anniversary.

1977, May 12   Engr.   *Perf. 12½x12*

4564   A2165   4k black   12   12

Feliks E. Dzerzhinski (1877–1926), organizer and head of secret police (OGPU).

Saxifraga Sibirica
A2166

Siberian Flowers: 3k, Dianthus repena. 4k, Novosieversia glactalis. 6k, Cerasticum maxinicem. 16k, Golden rhododendron.

1977, May 12   Litho.   *Perf. 12x12½*

4565   A2166   2k multi   6   5
4566   A2166   3k multi   10   5
4567   A2166   4k multi   12   6
4568   A2166   6k multi   18   10
4569   A2166   16k multi   48   25
Nos. 4565–4569 (5)   94   51

V. V. Gorbatko, Y. N. Glazkov, Soyuz 24 Rocket
A2167

1977, May 16   Photo.   *Perf. 12x11½*

4570   A2167   10k multi   30   15

Space explorations of cosmonauts on Salyut 5 orbital station, launched with Soyuz 24 rocket.

Film and Globe
A2168

1977, June 21   Photo.   *Perf. 11½*

4571   A2168   6k multi   18   12

10th International Film Festival, Moscow 1977.

RUSSIA

Lion Hunt, by Rubens—A2169

Rubens Paintings, Hermitage, Leningrad: 4k, Lady in Waiting (vert.). 10k, Workers in Quarry. 12k, Alliance of Water and Earth (vert.). 20k, Landscape with Rainbow. 50k, Self-portrait.

Perf. 12x12½, 12½x12

1977, June 24 Lithographed

4572	A2169	4k yel & multi	12	6
4573	A2169	6k yel & multi	18	10
4574	A2169	10k yel & multi	30	15
4575	A2169	12k yel & multi	36	18
4576	A2169	20k yel & multi	60	30
		Nos. 4572-4576 (5)	1.56	79

Souvenir Sheet

| 4577 | A2169 | 50k yel & multi | 2.00 | 1.00 |

Peter Paul Rubens (1577-1640), painter, 400th birth anniversary. Sheets of No. 4575 contain 2 labels with commemorative inscriptions and Atlas statue from Hermitage entrance. No. 4577 has multicolored margin showing cherubs from Ceres painting by Rubens. Size: 105x75mm.

Judith, by Giorgione A2170

1977, July 15 Litho. Perf. 12x12½

| 4578 | A2170 | 50k multi | 1.50 | 1.00 |

Il Giorgione (1478-1511), Venetian painter. No. 4578 contains detail from painting in Hermitage, Leningrad. Brown and gold frame with black and white inscription. Size: 78x106mm.

Icebreaker Type of 1976

Icebreakers: 4k, Aleksandr Sibiryakov. 6k, Georgi Sedov. 10k, Sadko. 12k, Dezhnev. 14k, Siberia. 16k, Lena. 20k, Amguyema.

Lithographed and Engraved

1977, July 27 Perf. 12x11½

4579	A2145	4k multi	12	6
4580	A2145	6k multi	18	10
4581	A2145	10k multi	30	15
4582	A2145	12k multi	36	20
4583	A2145	14k multi	42	22
4584	A2145	16k multi	48	25
4585	A2145	20k multi	60	30
		Nos. 4579-4585 (7)	2.46	1.28

Souvenir Sheet

Icebreaker Arctica—A2171

Lithographed and Engraved

1977, Sept. 15 Perf. 12½x12

| 4586 | A2171 | 50k multi | 5.00 | 5.00 |

Arctica, first ship to travel from Murmansk to North Pole, Aug. 9-17. No. 4586 has multicolored margin with Russian flag and map of Arctica's route; red control number. Size: 108x80mm.

View and Arms of Stavropol A2172 — Stamps and Exhibition Emblem A2173

1977, Aug. 16 Photo. Perf. 11½

| 4587 | A2172 | 6k multi | 18 | 12 |

200th anniversary of Stavropol.

1977, Aug. 16

| 4588 | A2173 | 4k multi | 12 | 12 |

October Revolution Anniversary Philatelic Exhibition, Moscow.

Yuri A. Gagarin and Spacecraft A2174

Designs: No. 4590, Alexei Leonov floating in space. No. 4591, Orbiting space station, cosmonauts at control panel. Nos. 4592-4594, Various spacecraft: No. 4592, International cooperation for space research; No. 4593, Interplanetary flights; No. 4594, Exploring earth's atmosphere. 50k, "XX," laurel, symbolic Sputnik with Red Star.

1977, Oct. 4 Photo. Perf. 11½x12

4589	A2174	10k sep & multi	25	15
4590	A2174	10k gray & multi	25	15
4591	A2174	10k gray grn & multi	25	15
4592	A2174	20k grn & multi	50	30
4593	A2174	20k vio bl & multi	50	30
4594	A2174	20k bis & multi	50	30
		Nos. 4589-4594 (6)	2.25	1.35

Souvenir Sheet

| 4595 | A2174 | 50k cl & gold | 8.00 | 8.00 |

20th anniversary of space research. No. 4595 contains one stamp (22x32mm.); blue and claret margin showing firmament and spacecraft, black control number. Size: 65x87mm.

Types of 1976

Designs: 15k, Communications emblem and globes; others as before.

1977-78 Lithographed Perf. 12

4596	A2138	1k ol grn	5	5
4597	A2138	2k lil rose	6	5
4598	A2139	3k brick red	10	5
4599	A2138	4k vermilion	12	5
4600	A2139	6k Prus bl	18	5
4601	A2138	10k gray grn	30	5
4602	A2139	12k vio bl	36	5
4602A	A2139	15k bl ('78)	45	5
4603	A2139	16k sl grn	48	5
4604	A2140	20k brn red	60	6
4605	A2141	30k dl brick red	90	10
4606	A2142	50k brown	1.50	15
4607	A2143	1r dk bl	3.00	20
		Nos. 4596-4607 (13)	8.10	96

Nos. 4596-4602A, 4604-4607 were printed on dull and shiny paper.

Bas-relief, 12th Century, Cathedral of St. Dimitri, Vladimir—A2175

Designs: 6k, Necklace, Ryazan excavations, 12th century. 10k, Mask, Cathedral of the Nativity, Suzdal, 13th century. 12k, Archangel Michael, 15th century icon. 16k, Chalice by Ivan Fomin, 1449. 20k, St. Basil's Cathedral, Moscow, 16th century.

1977, Oct. 12 Litho. Perf. 12

4608		Sheet of 6	2.25	1.50
a.	A2175	4k gold & blk	12	
b.	A2175	6k gold & multi	18	
c.	A2175	10k gold & multi	30	
d.	A2175	12k gold & multi	36	
e.	A2175	16k gold & multi	48	
f.	A2175	20k gold & multi	60	

Masterpieces of old Russian culture. No. 4608 has yellow brown and gold margin with gold inscription. Size: 188x108 mm.

Fir, Snowflake, Molniya Satellite A2176

1977, Oct. 12 Perf. 12x12½

| 4609 | A2176 | 4k multi | 12 | 12 |

New Year 1978.

Cruiser Aurora and Torch A2177

60th Anniversary of Revolution Medal A2178

Designs: No. 4611, Lenin speaking at Finland Station (monument), 1917. No. 4612, 1917 Peace Decree, Brezhnev book about Lenin. No. 4613, Kremlin tower with star and fireworks.

1977, Oct. 26 Photo. Perf. 12x11½

4610	A2177	4k gold, red & blk	12	6
4611	A2177	4k gold, red & blk	12	6
4612	A2177	4k gold, red & blk	12	6
4613	A2177	4k gold, red & blk	12	6

Souvenir Sheet Perf. 11½

| 4614 | A2178 | 30k gold, red & blk | 1.50 | 90 |

60th anniversary of October Revolution. No. 4614 has black, red and gold margin showing appeal and front-page of Izvestia, 1917. Size: 106x73mm.

Flag of USSR, Constitution (Book) with Coat of Arms—A2179

Designs: No. 4616, Red banner, people and cover of constitution. 50k, Constitution, Kremlin and olive branch.

1977, Oct. 31 Litho. Perf. 12½x12

| 4615 | A2179 | 4k red, blk & yel | 12 | 6 |
| 4616 | A2179 | 4k red, blk & yel | 12 | 6 |

Souvenir Sheet
Lithographed and Embossed
Perf. 11½x12½

| 4617 | A2179 | 50k red, gold & yel | 1.75 | 1.00 |

Adoption of new constitution. No. 4617 contains one stamp (70x50mm.); red and gold margin shows hammer and sickle and quotes from constitution. Size: 112x82 mm.

Souvenir Sheet

Leonid Brezhnev A2180

Lithographed and Embossed
1977, Nov. 2 Perf. 11½x12

| 4618 | A2180 | 50k gold & multi | 1.75 | 1.00 |

Adoption of new constitution, General Secretary Brezhnev and Constitution Commission. No. 4618 has red and gold margin showing cover of constitution and Brezhnev quotation. Size: 142x75mm.

Postal Official and Postal Code—A2181

Designs (Woman Postal Official and): No. 4620, Mail collection and Moskvich 430 car. No. 4621, Automatic letter sorting machine. No. 4622, Mail transport by truck, train, ship and planes. No. 4623, Mail delivery in city and country.

Lithographed and Engraved
1977, Nov. 16 Perf. 12½x12

4619	A2181	4k multi	12	6
4620	A2181	4k multi	12	6
4621	A2181	4k multi	12	6

RUSSIA

| 4622 | A2181 | 4k multi | 12 | 6 |
| 4623 | A2181 | 4k multi | 12 | 6 |

Nos. 4619-4623 (5) 60 30
Mail processing.

Capital, Asoka Pillar, Red Fort
A2182

Proclamation Monument, Charkov
A2183

1977, Dec. 14 Photo. *Perf. 11½*

| 4624 | A2182 | 6k mar, gold & red | 18 | 10 |

30th anniversary of India's independence.

1977, Dec. 14 Litho. *Perf. 12x12½*

| 4625 | A2183 | 6k multi | 18 | 10 |

60th anniversary of Soviet power in the Ukraine.

Lebetina Viper—A2184

Designs: 1k to 12k, Venomous snakes, useful for medicinal purposes. 16k, Polar bear and cub. 20k, Walrus and calf. 30k, Tiger and cub.

Photogravure and Engraved

1977, Dec. 16 *Perf. 11½x12*

4626	A2184	1k blk & multi	5	5
4627	A2184	4k blk & multi	12	6
4628	A2184	6k blk & multi	18	10
4629	A2184	10k blk & multi	30	15
4630	A2184	12k blk & multi	36	18
4631	A2184	16k blk & multi	48	25
4632	A2184	20k blk & multi	60	30
4633	A2184	30k blk & multi	90	45

Nos. 4626-4633 (8) 2.99 1.54
Protected fauna.

Wheat, Combine, Silos
A2185

Congress Palace, Spasski Tower
A2186

1978, Jan. 27 Photo. *Perf. 11½*

| 4634 | A2185 | 4k multi | 12 | 6 |

Gigant collective grain farm, Rostov Region, 50th anniversary.

1978, Jan. 27 Litho. *Perf. 12x12½*

| 4635 | A2186 | 4k multi | 12 | 6 |

Young Communist League, Lenin's Komsomol, 60th anniversary and its 25th Congress.

Liberation Obelisk, Emblem, Dove
A2187

1978, Jan. 27 Photo. *Perf. 11½*

| 4636 | A2187 | 6k multi | 18 | 10 |

8th Congress of International Federation of Resistance Fighters, Minsk, Belorussia.

Soldiers Leaving for the Front
A2188

Designs: No. 4638, Defenders of Moscow Monument, Lenin banner. No. 4639, Soldier as defender of the people.

1978, Feb. 21 Litho. *Perf. 12½x12*

4637	A2188	4k red & multi	12	6
4638	A2188	4k red & multi	12	6
4639	A2188	4k red & multi	12	6

60th anniversary of USSR Military forces.

Morning, by Kustodiev
A2189

Kustodiev Paintings: 4k, Celebration in Village. 6k, Shrovetide (winter landscape). 12k, Merchant's Wife Drinking Tea. 20k, Bolshevik. 50k, Self-portrait (vert.).

1978, Mar. 3 *Perf. 11½*

Size: 70x33mm.

| 4640 | A2189 | 4k lil & multi | 12 | 6 |
| 4641 | A2189 | 6k lil & multi | 18 | 10 |

Size: 47x32mm. *Perf. 12½x12*

4642	A2189	10k lil & multi	30	15
4643	A2189	12k lil & multi	36	18
4644	A2189	20k lil & multi	60	30

Nos. 4640-4644 (5) 1.56 79

Souvenir Sheet
Perf. 11½x12½

| 4644A | A2189 | 50k lil & multi | 1.50 | 1.00 |

Boris Mikhailovich Kustodiev (1878–1927), painter, birth centenary. Nos. 4640–4643 printed with se-tenant label showing museum where painting is kept. No. 4644A has label giving short biography; lilac margin with black inscription. Size: 92x71mm.

Docking in Space, Intercosmos Emblem
A2190

Designs: 6k, Rocket, Russian Cosmonaut Aleksei Gubarev and Czechoslovak Capt. Vladimir Remek on launching pad. 32k, Weather balloon, helicopter, Intercosmos emblem, Russian and Czechoslovakian flags.

1978, Mar. 10 Litho. *Perf. 12x12½*

4645	A2190	6k multi	18	10
4646	A2190	15k multi	45	22
4647	A2190	32k multi	96	48

Intercosmos, Soviet-Czechoslovak cooperative space program.

Festival Emblem
A2191

1978, Mar. 17 Litho. *Perf. 12x12½*

| 4648 | A2191 | 4k bl & multi | 12 | 6 |

11th Youth and Students' Congress, Havana.

Tulip, Bolshoi Theater
A2192

Moscow Flowers: 2k, Rose "Moscow morning" and Lomonosov University. 4k, Dahlia "Red Star" and Spasski Tower. 10k, Gladiolus "Moscovite" and VDNH Building. 12k, Ilich anniversary iris and Lenin Central Museum.

1978, Mar. 17 *Perf. 12½x12*

4649	A2192	1k multi	5	5
4650	A2192	2k multi	6	5
4651	A2192	4k multi	12	6
4652	A2192	10k multi	30	15
4653	A2192	12k multi	36	18

Nos. 4649-4653 (5) 89 49

IMCO Emblem and Waves
A2193

1978, Mar. 17 Litho. *Perf. 12x12½*

| 4654 | A2193 | 6k multi | 18 | 10 |

Intergovernmental Maritime Consultative Organization, 20th anniversary, and World Maritime Day.

   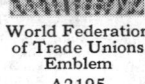

Spaceship, Orbits of Salyut 5, Soyuz 26 and 27
A2194

World Federation of Trade Unions Emblem
A2195

1978, Apr. 12 Photo. *Perf. 12*

| 4655 | A2194 | 6k bl, dk bl & gold | 18 | 10 |

Cosmonauts Day, Apr. 12.

1978, Apr. 16 *Perf. 12*

| 4656 | A2195 | 6k multi | 18 | 10 |

9th World Trade Union Congress, Prague.

2-2-0 Locomotive, 1845, Petersburg and Moscow Stations—A2196

Locomotives: 1k, 1st Russian model by E. A. and M. W. Cherepanov (vert.). 2k, 1-3-0 freight, 1845. 16k, Aleksandrov 0-3-0, 1863. 20k, 2-2-0 passenger and Sergievsk Pustyn platform, 1863.

1978, Apr. 20 Litho. *Perf. 11½*

4657	A2196	1k org & multi	5	5
4658	A2196	2k ultra & multi	6	5
4659	A2196	3k yel & multi	9	5
4660	A2196	16k grn & multi	48	25
4661	A2196	20k rose & multi	60	30

Nos. 4657-4661 (5) 1.28 70

Souvenir Sheet

Lenin, by V. A. Serov—A2197

1978, Apr. 22 *Perf. 12x12½*

| 4662 | A2197 | 50k multi | 1.50 | 1.00 |

108th anniversary of the birth of Lenin. No. 4662 has lemon and gold margin, imitating canvas, black inscription. Size: 72x96mm.

Demand as well as supply determine a stamp's market value. The first is as important as the other.

RUSSIA 375

Soyuz and Salyut 6 Docking in Space
A2198

Y. V. Romanenko and G. M. Grechko
A2199

1978, June 15   **Perf. 12**

| 4663 | A2198 | 15k multi | 45 | 22 |
| 4664 | A2199 | 15k multi | 45 | 22 |

Photographic survey and telescopic observations of stars by crews of Soyuz 26, Soyuz 27 and Soyuz 28, Dec. 10, 1977–March 16, 1978. Nos. 4663–4664 printed se-tenant with label showing schematic pictures of various experiments.

Space Meteorology, Rockets, Spaceship, Earth
A2200

Designs (Intercosmos Emblem and): No. 4666, Natural resources of earth and Soyuz. No. 4667, Space communications, "Orbita" Station and Molniya satellite. No. 4668, Man, earth and Vostok. 50k, Study of magnetosphere, Prognoz over earth.

1978, June 23   **Perf. 12x12½**

4665	A2200	10k grn & multi	30	15
4666	A2200	10k bl & multi	30	15
4667	A2200	10k vio & multi	30	15
4668	A2200	10k rose lil & multi	30	15

Souvenir Sheet
Perf. 11½x12½

| 4669 | A2200 | 50k multi | 1.50 | 1.00 |

Space explorations of the Intercosmos program. No. 4669 contains one stamp (36x51mm.); blue and multicolored margin shows Venus, Mars and spaceships. Size: 102x76mm.

Soyuz Rocket on Carrier—A2201

Designs (Flags of USSR and Poland, Intercosmos Emblem): 15k, Crystal, spaceship (Sirena, experimental crystallogenesis in space). 32k, Research ship "Cosmonaut Vladimir Komarov", spaceship, world map and paths of Salyut 6, Soyuz 29–30.

Perf. 12½x12

1978, June–July   **Lithographed**

4670	A2201	6k multi	18	10
4671	A2201	15k multi	45	22
4672	A2201	32k multi	95	48

Intercosmos, Soviet-Polish cooperative space program.

Lenin, Awards Received by Komsomol
A2202

Kamaz Car, Train, Bridge, Hammer and Sickle
A2203

1978, July 5   **Perf. 12x12½**

| 4673 | A2202 | 4k multi | 12 | 6 |
| 4674 | A2203 | 4k multi | 12 | 6 |

Leninist Young Communist League (Komsomol), 60th anniversary (✶4673); Komsomol's participation in 5-year plan (✶4674).

 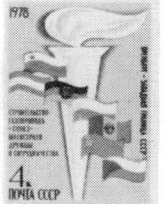

M. V. Zaharov
A2204

Torch, Flags of Participants
A2205

1978, July 5   **Engr.**   **Perf. 12**

| 4675 | A2204 | 4k sepia | 12 | 6 |

M. V. Zaharov (1898–1972), Marshal of the Soviet Union.

1978, July 25 Litho. Perf. 12x12½

| 4676 | A2205 | 4k multi | 12 | 6 |

Construction of Soyuz gas-pipeline (Friendship Line), Orenburg. Flags of participating countries shown: Bulgaria, Hungary, German Democratic Republic, Poland, Romania, USSR, Czechoslovakia.

William Harvey
A2206

N. G. Chernyshevsky
A2207

1978, July 25   **Perf. 12**

| 4677 | A2206 | 6k bl, blk & dp grn | 18 | 10 |

Dr. William Harvey (1578–1657), discoverer of blood circulation, 400th birth anniversary.

1978, July 30 Engr. Perf. 12x12½

| 4678 | A2207 | 4k brn, yel | 12 | 6 |

Nikolai Gavilovich Chernyshevsky (1828–1889), revolutionary, birth sesquicentennial.

White-winged Petrel
A2208

Antarctic Fauna: 1k, Crested penguin (horiz.). 4k, Emperor penguin and chick. 6k, White-blooded pikes. 10k, Sea elephant (horiz.).

Perf. 12x11½, 11½x12

1978, July 30   **Lithographed**

4679	A2208	1k multi	5	5
4680	A2208	3k multi	9	5
4681	A2208	4k multi	12	6
4682	A2208	6k multi	18	10
4683	A2208	10k multi	30	15
		Nos. 4679–4683 (5)	74	41

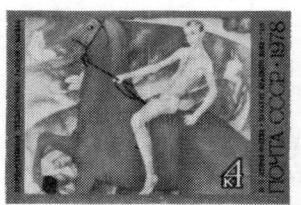

The Red Horse, by Petrov-Votkin
A2209

Paintings by Petrov-Votkin: 6k, Mother and Child, Petrograd, 1918. 10k, Death of the Commissar. 12k, Still-life with Fruit. 16k, Still-life with Teapot and Flowers. 50k, Self-portrait, 1918 (vert.).

1978, Aug. 16 Litho. Perf. 12½x12

4684	A2209	4k sil & multi	12	6
4685	A2209	6k sil & multi	18	10
4686	A2209	10k sil & multi	30	15
4687	A2209	12k sil & multi	36	18
4688	A2209	16k sil & multi	48	25
		Nos. 4684–4688 (5)	1.44	74

Souvenir Sheet
Perf. 11½x12

| 4689 | A2209 | 50k sil & multi | 1.50 | 1.00 |

Kozma Sergeevich Petrov-Votkin (1878–1939), painter. Nos. 4684–4688 have se-tenant silver and black labels with commemorative inscriptions. No. 4689 has label the size of stamp with inscription and silver margin. Size: 93x72mm.

Soyuz 31 in Shop, Intercosmos Emblem, USSR and DDR Flags
A2210

Designs (Intercosmos Emblem, Russian and German Democratic Republic Flags and): 15k, Pamir Mountains photographed from space; Salyut 6, Soyuz 29 and 31 complex and spectrum. 32k, Soyuz 31 docking, photographed from Salyut 6.

Perf. 12x12½

1978, Aug.–Sept.   **Lithographed**

4690	A2210	6k multi	18	10
4691	A2210	15k multi	45	22
4692	A2210	32k multi	95	50

Intercosmos, Soviet-East German cooperative space program.

PRAGA '78 Emblem, Plane, Radar, Spaceship—A2211
Photogravure and Engraved

1978, Aug. 29   **Perf. 11½**

| 4693 | A2211 | 6k multi | 18 | 10 |

PRAGA '78 International Philatelic Exhibition, Prague, Sept. 8–17.

Leo Tolstoi
A2212

1978, Sept. 7 Engr. Perf. 12x12½

| 4694 | A2212 | 4k sl grn | 12 | 6 |

Leo Tolstoi (1828–1910), novelist and philosopher.

Stag, Conference Emblem
A2213

1978   **Photo**   **Perf. 11½**

| 4695 | A2213 | 4k multi | 12 | 6 |

14th General Assembly of the Society for Wildlife Preservation, Ashkhabad.

Bronze Figure, Erebuni, 8th Century
A2214

Armenian Architecture: 6k, Etchmiadzin Cathedral, 4th century. 10k, Stone crosses, Dzaghkatzor, 13th century. 12k, Library, Erevan (horiz.). 16k, Lenin statue, Lenin Square, Erevan (horiz.).

1978 Litho. Perf. 12x12½, 12½x12

4696	A2214	4k multi	12	6
4697	A2214	6k multi	18	10
4698	A2214	10k multi	30	15
4699	A2214	12k multi	36	18
4700	A2214	16k multi	48	25
		Nos. 4696–4700 (5)	1.44	74

Issue dates: 4k, 10k, 16k, Sept. 12; others, Oct. 14.

RUSSIA

Memorial, Messina, Russian Warships
A2215

1978, Sept. 12 Photo. Perf. 11½
4701 A2215 6k multi 18 10
70th anniversary of aid given by Russian sailors during Messina earthquake.

Communications Emblem, Ostankino TV Tower
A2216

1978, Sept. 20 Photo. Perf. 11½
4702 A2216 4k multi 12 6
20th anniversary of Organization for Communication Cooperation of Socialist Countries.

No. 4673 Overprinted

1978, Sept. 20 Litho. Perf. 12x12½
4703 A2202 4k multi 12 6
Philatelic Exhibition of the Leninist Young Communist League.

Souvenir Sheet

Diana, by Paolo Veronese—A2217

1978, Sept. 28 Litho. Perf. 12x11½
4704 A2217 50k multi 1.50 1.00
Paolo Veronese (1528–1588), Italian painter. No. 4704 has multicolored margin showing entire painting of Diana with dog. Size: 77x115mm.

Souvenir Sheet

Kremlin, Moscow
A2218

Lithographed and Embossed
1978, Oct. 7 Perf. 11½x12
4705 A2218 30k gold & multi 1.00
Russian Constitution, 1st anniversary. No. 4705 contains one stamp; multicolored margin shows various coats of arms and page from Constitution. Size: 160x85mm.

S. G. Shauyan
A2219

1978, Oct. 11 Engr. Perf. 12½x12
4706 A2219 4k sl grn 12 6
Stepan Georgevich Shauyan (1878–1918), Communist Party functionary.

Ferry, Russian and Bulgarian Colors
A2220

1978, Oct. 14 Photo. Perf. 11½
4707 A2220 6k multi 18 10
Opening of Ilychovsk-Varna Ferry.

Hammer and Sickle, Flags
A2221

1978, Oct. 26 Photo. Perf. 11½
4708 A2221 4k gold & multi 12 6
61st anniversary of October Revolution.

Silver Gilt Cup, Novgorod, 12th Century—A2222

Old Russian Art: 10k, Pokrowna Nerli Church, 12th century (vert.). 12k, St. George Slaying the Dragon, icon, Novgorod, 15th century (vert.). 16k, The Czar, cannon, 1586.

Perf. 12½x12, 12x12½
1978, Nov. 28 Lithographed
4709 A2222 6k multi 18 10
4710 A2222 10k multi 30 15
4711 A2222 12k multi 36 18
4712 A2222 16k multi 48 25

Lithographed and Embossed

Oncology Institute, Emblem
A2223

Savior Tower, Kremlin
A2224

1978, Dec. 1 Photo. Perf. 11½
4713 A2223 4k multi 12 6
75th anniversary of the P. A. Herzan Tumor Institute.

1978, Dec. 20 Litho. Perf. 12x12½
4714 A2224 4k sil, bl & red 12 6
New Year 1979.

Nestor Pechersky, Chronicler, c. 885—A2225

History of Postal Service: 6k, Birch bark letter and stylus. 10k, Messenger with trumpet and staff, from 14th century Psalm book. 12k, Winter traffic, from 16th century book by Sigizmund Gerberstein. 16k, Prikaz postoffice, from 17th century icon.

Lithographed and Engraved
1978, Dec. 20 Perf. 12½x12
4715 A2225 4k multi 12 6
4716 A2225 6k multi 18 10
4717 A2225 10k multi 30 15
4718 A2225 12k multi 36 18
4719 A2225 16k multi 48 25
Nos. 4715-4719 (5) 1.44 74

Kovalenok and Ivanchenkov, Salyut 6-Soyuz—A2226

1978, Dec. 20 Photo. Perf. 11½x12
4720 A2226 10k multi 30 15
Cosmonauts V. V. Kovalenok and A. S. Ivanchenkov spent 140 days in space, June 15–Nov. 2, 1978.

Vasilii Pronchishchev—A2227

Icebreakers: 6k, Captain Belousov, 1954 (vert.). 10k, Moscow. 12k, Admiral Makarov, 1974. 16k, Lenin, 1959 (vert.). 20k, Nuclear-powered Arctica.

Photogravure and Engraved
Perf. 11½x12, 12x11½
1978, Dec. 20
4721 A2227 4k multi 12 6
4722 A2227 6k multi 18 10
4723 A2227 10k multi 30 15
4724 A2227 12k multi 36 18
4725 A2227 16k multi 48 25
4726 A2227 20k multi 60 30
Nos. 4721-4726 (6) 2.04 1.04

Souvenir Sheet

Mastheads and Globe with Russia—A2228

1978, Dec. 28 Litho. Perf. 12
4727 A2228 30k multi 90 45
Distribution of periodicals through the Post and Telegraph Department, 60th anniversary. No. 4727 has multicolored margin showing a column from Pravda, red carnation and Molniya 1 satellite. Size: 106x82mm.

Cuban Flags Forming Star
A2229

1979, Jan. 1 Photo. Perf. 11½
4728 A2229 6k multi 18 10
Cuban Revolution, 20th anniversary.

Russian and Belorussian Flags, Government Building, Minsk—A2230

1979, Jan. 1
4729 A2230 4k multi 12 6
60th anniversaries of Belorussian Soviet Socialist Republic and Belorussian Communist Party.

Ukrainian and Russian Flags, Reunion Monument
A2231

1979, Jan. 16
4730 A2231 4k multi 12 6
325th anniversary of reunion of Ukraine and Russia.

RUSSIA

377

Old and New Vilnius University Buildings—A2232

1979, Jan. 16 **Photo. & Engr.**

4731 A2232 4k blk & sal   12   6
400th anniversary of University of Vilnius.

Bulgaria No. 1 and Exhibition Hall—A2233

1979, Jan. 25 **Litho.** **Perf. 12½x12**

4732 A2233 15k multi   45   22
Filaserdica '79 Philatelic Exhibition, Sofia, commemorating centenary of Bulgarian postal service.

Sputniks, Soviet Radio Hams Emblem A2234

1979, Feb. 23 **Photo.** **Perf. 11½**

4733 A2234 4k multi   12   6
Sputnik satellites Radio 1 and Radio 2, launched, Oct. 1978.

1-3-0 Locomotive, 1878—A2235

Locomotives: 3k, 1-4-0, 1912. 4k, 2-3-1, 1915. 6k, 1-3-1, 1925. 15k, 1-5-0, 1947.

1979, Feb. 23 **Litho.** **Perf. 11½**

4734 A2235 2k multi   6   5
4735 A2235 3k multi   10   5
4736 A2235 4k multi   12   6
4737 A2235 6k multi   18   10
4738 A2235 15k multi   45   22
    Nos. 4734-4738 (5)   91   48

Souvenir Sheet

Medal for Land Development A2236

Lithographed
1979, Mar. 14 **Perf. 11½x12½**

4739 A2236 50k multi   1.50   1.00
25th anniversary of drive to develop virgin lands. Multicolored margin shows book, grain, elevators and tractor Niva. Size: 99x66mm.

Venera 11 and 12 over Venus A2237

1979, Mar. 16 **Photo.** **Perf. 11½**

4740 A2237 10k multi   30   15
Interplanetary flights of Venera 11 and Venera 12, December 1978.

Albert Einstein, Equation and Signature A2238

1979, Mar. 16

4741 A2238 6k multi   18   10
Albert Einstein (1879-1955), theoretical physicist.

Congress Emblem A2239

1979, Mar. 16

4742 A2239 6k multi   18   10
21st World Veterinary Congress, Moscow.

"To Arms," by R. Berens A2240

1979, Mar. 21

4743 A2240 4k multi   12   6
60th anniversary of proclamation of Soviet Republic of Hungary.

Salyut 6, Soyuz, Research Ship, Letters—A2241

1979, Apr. 12 **Litho.** **Perf. 11½x12**

4744 A2241 15k multi   45   22
Cosmonauts Day.

The indexes in each volume of the Scott Catalogue contain many listings which help to identify stamps.

Souvenir Sheet

Ice Hockey—A2242

1979, Apr. 14 **Photo.** **Perf. 12x11½**

4745 A2242 50k multi   1.50   1.00
World and European Ice Hockey Championships, Moscow, Apr. 14-27. Size: 85x65mm.

Souvenir Sheet

Lenin A2243

1979, Apr. 18

4746 A2243 50k red, gold & brn   1.50   1.00
109th anniversary of the birth of Lenin. Red margin with gold inscription. Size of stamp: 37x52mm.; size of sheet: 90x72mm.

Astronauts' Training Center A2244   Exhibition Emblem A2245

1979, Apr. 12 **Litho.** **Perf. 11½**

4747 A2244 6k multi   18   10
4748 A2244 32k multi   95   48
Joint Soviet-Bulgarian space flight.

1979, Apr. 18 **Photo.** **Perf. 11½**

4749 A2245 15k sil, red & vio bl   45   22
National USSR Exhibition in the United Kingdom. Se-tenant label with commemorative inscription.

Blast Furance, Pushkin Theater, "Tent" Sculpture A2246

1979, May 24 **Photo.** **Perf. 11½**

4750 A2246 4k multi   12   6
50th anniversary of Magnitogorsk City.

Souvenir Sheet

No. 4745 СОВЕТСКИЕ ХОККЕИСТЫ—
Overprinted in ЧЕМПИОНЫ МИРА
Margin in Red И ЕВРОПЫ

1979, May 24 **Perf. 12x11½**

4751 A2242 50k multi   2.00   1.00
Victory of Soviet team in World and European Ice Hockey Championships.

Infant, Flowers, IYC Emblem A2247

1979, June **Litho.** **Perf. 12x12½**

4752 A2247 4k multi   12   6
International Year of the Child.

Horn Player and Bears Playing Balalaika, Bogorodsk Wood Carvings—A2248

Folk Art: 3k, Decorated wooden bowls, Khokhloma. 4k, Tray decorated with flowers, Zhestovo. 6k, Carved bone boxes, Kholmogory. 15k, Lace, Vologda.

1979, June 14 **Litho.** **Perf. 12½x12**

4753 A2248 2k multi   6   5
4754 A2248 3k multi   10   5
4755 A2248 4k multi   12   6
4756 A2248 6k multi   18   10
4757 A2248 15k multi   45   22
    Nos. 4753-4757 (5)   91   48

V. A. Djanibekov, O. G. Makarov, Spacecraft A2249

1979, June **Perf. 12x12½**

4758 A2249 4k multi   12   6
Flights of Soyuz 26-27 and work on board of orbital complex Salyut 26-27.

RUSSIA

COMECON Building, Members' Flags
A2250

Scene from "Potemkin" and Festival Emblem
A2251

1979, June 26   *Perf. 12*
4759 A2250 16k multi 48 25

Council for Mutual Economic Aid of Socialist Countries, 30th anniversary.

Photogravure and Engraved
1979, July   *Perf. 11½*
4760 A2251 15k multi 45 22

11th International Film Festival, Moscow, and 60th anniversary of Soviet film industry.

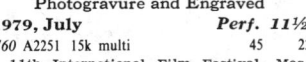

Lenin Square Station, Tashkent
A2252

1979, July   *Litho.*   *Perf. 12*
4761 A2252 4k multi 12 6

Tashkent subway.

Souvenir Sheets

Atom Symbol, Factories, Dam
A2253

USSR Philatelic Society Emblem
A2254

1979, July 23   *Photo.*   *Perf. 11½x12*
4762 A2253 30k multi 90 60

50th anniversary of First Five-Year Plan. No. 4762 has multicolored margin showing flag, rocket and grain. Size: 67x87mm.

1979, July 25   *Litho.*   *Perf. 12x12½*
4763 A2254 50k gray grn & red 1.50 1.00

4th Congress of USSR Philatelic Society, Moscow. No. 4763 has multicolored margin showing space and transportation symbols. Size: 92x66mm.

Exhibition Hall, Scene from "Chapaev"
A2255

1979, Aug. 8   *Photo.*   *Perf. 11½*
4764 A2255 4k multi 12 8

60th anniversary of Soviet Film and Exhibition of History of Soviet Film.

Roses, by P. P. Konchalovsky, 1955
A2256

Russian Flower Paintings: 1k, Flowers and Fruit, by I. F. Khrutsky, 1830. 2k, Phlox, by I. N. Kramskoi, 1884. 3k, Lilac, by K. A. Korovin, 1915. 15k, Bluebells, by S. V. Gerasimov, 1944. 2k, 3k, 15k, vert.

Perf. 12½x12, 12x12½
1979, Aug. 16   Lithographed
4765 A2256 1k multi 5 5
4766 A2256 2k multi 6 5
4767 A2256 3k multi 9 6
4768 A2256 15k multi 45 30
4769 A2256 32k multi 95 65
    Nos. 4765-4769 (5) 1.60 1.11

John McClean
A2257

1979, Aug. 29   *Litho.*   *Perf. 11½*
4770 A2257 4k red & blk 12 8

John McClean (1879-1923), British Communist labor leader.

Soviet Circus Emblem
A2258

1979, Sept.
4771 A2258 4k multi 12 8

Soviet Circus, 60th anniversary.

Friendship—A2259

Children's Drawings: 3k, Children and Horses. 4k, Dances. 15k, The Excursion.

1979, Sept. 10   *Perf. 12½x12*
4772 A2259 2k multi 6 5
4773 A2259 3k multi 9 6
4774 A2259 4k multi 12 8
4775 A2259 15k multi 45 30

International Year of the Child.

See "Special Notices" at the front of this volume for data on the listing methods of this Catalogue, abbreviations, condition, prices and examination.

Oriole—A2260

Birds: 3k, Woodpecker. 4k, Crested titmouse. 10k, Barn owl. 15k, Nightjar.

1979, Sept. 18
4776 A2260 2k multi 6 5
4777 A2260 3k multi 9 6
4778 A2260 4k multi 12 8
4779 A2260 10k multi 30 20
4780 A2260 15k multi 45 30
    Nos. 4776-4780 (5) 1.02 69

German Arms, Marx, Engels, Lenin, Berlin—A2261

1979, Oct. 7   *Photo.*   *Perf. 11½*
4781 A2261 6k multi 18 12

German Democratic Republic, 30th anniversary.

Valery Ryumin, Vladimir Lyakhov, Salyut 6—A2262

Design: No. 4783, Spacecraft.

1979, Oct. 10   *Perf. 12x11½*
4782 A2262 15k multi 45 30
4783 A2262 15k multi 45 30

175 days in space, Feb. 25-Aug. 19. Nos. 4782-4783 printed se-tenant in continuous design.

Star   Hammer and Sickle
A2264   A2265

1979, Oct. 18   *Perf. 11½*
4784 A2263 4k multi 12 8

USSR Armed Forces, 60th anniversary.

1979, Oct. 18
4785 A2264 4k multi 12 8

October Revolution, 62nd anniversary.

Katherina, by T. G. Shevchenko—A2266

Ukrainian Paintings: 3k, Working Girl, by K.K. Kostandi. 4k, Lenin's Return to Petrograd, by A.M. Lopuhov. 10k, Soldier's Return, by N.V. Kostesky. 15k, Going to Work, by M.G. Belsky.

1979, Nov. 18   *Litho.*   *Perf. 12x12½*
4786 A2266 2k multi 6 5
4787 A2266 3k multi 9 6
4788 A2266 4k multi 12 8
4789 A2266 10k multi 30 20
4790 A2266 15k multi 45 30
    Nos. 4786-4790 (5) 1.02 69

Shabolovka Radio Tower, Moscow
A2267

Mischa Holding Stamp
A2268

1979, Nov. 28   *Photo.*   *Perf. 12*
4791 A2267 32k multi 95 65

Radio Moscow, 50th anniversary.

1979, Nov. 28   *Perf. 12x12½*
4792 A2268 4k multi 12 8

New Year 1980.

Hand Holding Peace Message
A2269

Policeman, Patrol Car, Helicopter
A2270

Peace Program in Action: No. 4794, Hands holding cultural symbols. No. 4795, Hammer and sickle, flag.

1979, Dec. 5   *Litho.*   *Perf. 12*
4793 A2269 4k multi 12 8
4794 A2269 4k multi 12 8
4795 A2269 4k multi 12 8

RUSSIA

1979, Dec. 20   *Perf. 12×12½*
Traffic Safety: 4k, Car, girl and ball. 6k, Speeding cars.

4796	A2270	3k multi	9	6
4797	A2270	4k multi	12	8
4798	A2270	6k multi	18	12

Vulkanolog—A2271

Research Ships and Portraits: 2k, Professor Bogorov. 4k, Ernst Krenkel. 6k, Vladislav Volkov. 10k, Cosmonaut Yuri Gagarin. 15k, Academician E.B. Kurchatov.

1979, Dec. 25   *Perf. 12×11½*
Litho. & Engr.

4799	A2271	1k multi	5	5
4800	A2271	2k multi	6	5
4801	A2271	4k multi	12	8
4802	A2271	6k multi	18	12
4803	A2271	10k multi	30	20
4804	A2271	15k multi	45	30
	Nos. 4799-4804 (6)		1.16	80

See Nos. 4881-4886.

Souvenir Sheet

Explorers Raising Red Flag at North Pole—A2272

1979, Dec. 25   **Photo.**   *Perf. 11½×12*

4805	A2272	50k multi	1.50	1.00

Komsomolskaya Pravda North Pole expedition. Size: 66½×85mm.

Type of 1970

Design: 4k, Coat of arms, power line, factories.

1980, Jan. 10   **Litho.**   *Perf. 12×12½*

4806	A1794	4k carmine	12	8

Mordovian Autonomous Soviet Socialist Republic, 50th anniversary.

Freestyle Skating—A2273

1980, Jan. 22   *Perf. 12×12½, 12½×12*
Multicolored

4807	A2273	4k *Speed skating*	12	8
4808	A2273	6k *shown*	18	12
4809	A2273	10k *Ice hockey*	30	20
4810	A2273	15k *Downhill skiing*	45	30
4811	A2273	20k *Luge,* vert.	60	40
	Nos. 4807-4811 (5)		1.65	1.10

Souvenir Sheet

4812	A2273	50k *Cross-country skiing,* vert.	1.75	1.25

13th Winter Olympic Games, Lake Placid, N.Y., Feb. 12-24. Multicolored margin shows cross-country skiers and stars. Size: 63×89½mm.

Nikolai Podvoiski—A2274

1980, Feb. 16   **Engraved**   *Perf. 12½×12*

4813	A2274	4k cl brn	12	8

Nikolai Ilyitch Podvoiski (1880-1948), revolutionary.

Rainbow, by A.K. Savrasov—A2275

Paintings: No. 4815, Summer Harvest, by A.G. Venetsianov (vert.). No. 4816, Old Erevan, by M.S. Saryan.

1980, Mar. 4   **Litho.**   *Perf. 11½*

4814	A2275	6k multi	18	12
4815	A2275	6k multi	18	12
4816	A2275	6k multi	18	12

Souvenir Sheet

Cosmonaut Alexei Leonov—A2276

1980, Mar. 18   **Litho.**   *Perf. 12½×12*

4817	A2276	50k multi	1.50	1.00

Man's first walk in space (Voskhod 2, Mar. 18-19, 1965), 15th anniversary. Multicolored margin shows space craft and sun. Size: 111½×74mm.

Georg Ots, Estonian Artist A2277

Lenin Order, 50th Anniversary—A2278

1980, Mar. 21   **Engraved**

4818	A2277	4k sl bl	12	8

1980, Apr. 6   **Photo.**   *Perf. 11½*

4819	A2278	4k multi	12	8

Souvenir Sheet

Cosmonauts, Salyut 6 and Soyuz—A2279

1980, Apr. 12   **Litho.**   *Perf. 12*

4820	A2279	50k multi	1.50	1.00

Intercosmos cooperative space program. No. 4820 has multicolored margin showing flags of participating countries, hammer and sickle. Size: 117×81½mm.

Flags and Arms of Azerbaijan, Government House A2280

"Mother Russia," Fireworks over Moscow A2282

1980, Apr. 22   **Photo.**

4821	A2280	4k multi	12	8

Azerbaijan Soviet Socialist Republic, Communist Party of Azerbaijan, 60th anniversary.

Souvenir Sheet

1980, Apr. 22   *Perf. 12×11½*

4822	A2281	30k multi	1.00	75

Size: 91½×80mm.

1980, Apr. 25   **Litho.**

Designs: No. 4824, Soviet War Memorial, Berlin, raising of Red flag. No. 4825, Parade, Red Square, Moscow.

4823	A2282	4k multi	12	8
4824	A2292	4k multi	12	8
4825	A2282	4k multi	12	8

35th anniversary of victory in World War II.

Lenin, 110th Birth Anniversary—A2281

Workers' Monument A2283

"XXV" A2284

1980, May 12   **Litho.**   *Perf. 12*

4826	A2283	4k multi	12	8

Workers' Delegates in Ivanovo-Voznesensk, 75th anniversary.

1980, May 14   **Photo.**   *Perf. 11½*

4827	A2284	32k multi	95	65

Signing of Warsaw Pact (Bulgaria, Czechoslovakia, German Democratic Rep., Hungary, Poland, Romania, USSR), 25th anniversary.

YaK-24 Helicopter, 1953—A2285

1980, May 15   **Litho.**   *Perf. 12½×12*

4828	A2285	1k *shown*	5	5
4829	A2285	2k *MI-8, 1962*	6	5
4830	A2285	3k *KA-26, 1965*	10	6
4831	A2285	6k *MI-6, 1957*	20	12
4832	A2285	15k *MI-10*	45	30
4833	A2285	32k *V-12*	95	65
	Nos. 4828-4833 (6)		1.81	1.23

David Anacht, Illuminated Manuscript A2286

Emblem, Training Lab A2287

1980, May 16   *Perf. 12*

4834	A2286	4k multi	12	8

David Anacht, Armenian philosopher, 1500th birth anniversary.

1980, June 4

4835	A2287	6k *shown*	20	12
4836	A2287	15k *Cosmonauts meeting*	45	30
4837	A2287	32k *Press conference*	95	65

Intercosmos cooperative space program (U.S.S.R.-Hungary).

Since the 1860's stamp collectors have been using the Scott Catalogue to identify and evaluate their stamps.

Russia

Polar Fox—A2288

1980, June 25 Litho. Perf. 12x12½
4838	A2288	2k	*Dark silver fox*, vert.	6	5
4839	A2288	4k	*shown*	12	8
4840	A2288	6k	*Mink*	20	12
4841	A2288	10k	*Azerbaijan nutria*, vert.	30	20
4842	A2288	15k	*Black sable*	45	30
	Nos. 4838-4842 (5)			1.13	75

Factory, Buildings, Arms of Tatarskaya—A2289

1980, June 25 Perf. 12
| 4843 | A2289 | 4k multi | 12 | 8 |

Tatarskaya Autonomous Soviet Socialist Republic, 60th anniversary.

Bauman Technological College A2290

Ho Chi Minh A2291

1980, July 1 Photo. Perf. 11½
| 4844 | A2290 | 4k multi | 12 | 8 |

Bauman Technological College, Moscow, 150th anniversary.

1980, July 7
| 4845 | A2291 | 6k multi | 20 | 12 |

Red Flag, Lithuanian Arms, Flag, Red Guards Monument—A2292

1980, July 12 Litho. Perf. 12
| 4846 | A2292 | 4k multi | 12 | 8 |

Lithuanian Soviet Socialist Republic, 40th anniversary.

Russian Flag and Arms, Latvian Flag, Monument, Buildings—A2293

Design: No. 4848, Russian flag and arms, Estonian flag, monument, buildings.

1980, July 21 Litho. Perf. 12
| 4847 | A2293 | 4k multi | 12 | 8 |
| 4848 | A2293 | 4k multi | 12 | 8 |

Restoration of Soviet power.

Cosmonauts Boarding Soyuz—A2294

1980, July 24 Perf. 12x12½
4849	A2294	6k	*shown*	18	12
4850	A2294	15k	*Working aboard spacecraft*	45	30
4851	A2294	32k	*Return flight*	95	65

20th anniv. of Center for Cosmonaut Training.

Avicenna (980-1037), Philosopher and Physician—A2295

Photogravure and Engraved

1980, Aug. 16 Perf. 11½
| 4852 | A2295 | 4k multi | 12 | 8 |

Soviet Racing Car KHADI-7—A2296

1980, Aug. 25 Litho. Perf. 12
4853	A2296	2k	*shown*	6	5
4854	A2296	6k	*KHADI-10*	18	6
4855	A2296	15k	*KHADI-113*	45	30
4856	A2296	30k	*KHADI-133*	90	60

Kazakhstan Republic, 60th Anniversary—A2297

1980, Aug. 26
| 4857 | A2297 | 4k multi | 12 | 8 |

Ingres, Self-portrait, and Nymph—A2298

1980, Aug. 29 Perf. 12x12½
| 4858 | A2298 | 32k multi | 95 | 65 |

Jean Auguste Dominique Ingres (1780-1867), French painter.

Morning on the Field of Kulikovo, by A. Bubnov—A2299

1980, Sept. 6 Litho. Perf. 12
| 4859 | A2299 | 4k multi | 12 | 8 |

Battle of Kulikovo, 600th anniversary.

Town Hall, Tartu A2300

Y.V. Malyshev, V.V. Aksenov A2301

1980, Sept. 15 Photo. Perf. 11½
| 4860 | A2300 | 4k multi | 12 | 8 |

Tartu, 950th anniversary.

1980, Sept. 15 Litho. Perf. 12x12½
| 4861 | A2301 | 10k multi | 30 | 20 |

Soyuz T-2 space flight.

Flight Training, Yuri Gagarin—A2302

1980, Sept. 15 Photo. Perf. 11½x12
4862	A2302	6k	*shown*	18	12
4863	A2302	15k	*Space walk*	45	30
4864	A2302	32K	*Endurance test*	95	62

Gagarin Cosmonaut Training Center, 20th anniversary.

Cosmonauts Training—A2303

Designs (Intercosmos Emblem, Flags of USSR and Cuba and): 15k, Inside weightless cabin. 32k, Landing.

1980, Sept. 15 Litho. Perf. 12x12½
4865	A2303	6k multi	18	6
4866	A2303	15k multi	45	30
4867	A2303	32k multi	95	62

Intercosmos cooperative space program (USSR-Cuba).

October Revolution, 63rd Anniversary—A2304

1980, Sept. 20 Photo. Perf. 11½
| 4868 | A2304 | 4k multi | 18 | 12 |

David Gurumishvily A2305

1980, Sept. 20
| 4869 | A2305 | 6k multi | 18 | 12 |

David Gurumishvily (1705-1792), poet.

Family with Serfs, by N.V. Nevrev—A2305a

Design: No. 4869B. Countess Tarakanova, by K.D. Flavitsky (vert.)

1980, Sept. 25 Litho. Perf. 11½
| 4869A | A2305a | 6k multi | 18 | 12 |
| 4869B | A2305a | 6k multi | 18 | 12 |

N.V. Nevrev (1830-1904) and K.D. Flavitsky (1830-1866).

A.F. Joffe A2306

1980, Sept. 29
| 4870 | A2306 | 4k multi | 12 | 8 |

A.F. Joffe (1880-1960), physicist.

RUSSIA

Siberian Pine—A2307

1980, Sept. 29   Litho.   Perf. 12½x12
4871	A2307	2k	*shown*	6	5
4872	A2307	4k	*Oak*	12	8
4873	A2307	6k	*Lime tree, vert.*	18	12
4874	A2307	10k	*Sea buckthorn*	30	20
4875	A2307	15k	*European ash*	45	30
		Nos. 4871-4875 (5)		1.11	75

A.M. Vasilevsky—A2308

1980, Sept. 30   Engraved   Perf. 12
4876	A2308	4k dk grn	12	8

A.M. Vasilevsky (1895-1977), Soviet marshal.

Souvenir Sheet

Mischa Holding Olympic Torch—A2309

1980, Nov. 24   Perf. 12x12½
4877	A2309	1r multi	4.00	2.00

Completion of 22nd Summer Olympic Games, Moscow, July 19-Aug. 3. Multicolored margin shows route of Olympic torch, Kremlin, Moscow '80 emblem; black control number. Size: 93½x73mm.

A.V. Suvorov (1730-1800), General and Military Theorist—A2310

1980, Nov. 24   Engraved
4878	A2310	4k slate	12	8

Armenian Soviet Socialist Republic and Armenian Communist Party, 60th Anniversary—A2311

1980, Nov. 24   Litho.   Perf. 12
4879	A2311	4k multi	12	8

Alexander Block (1880-1921), Poet—A2312

1980, Nov. 24
4880	A2312	4k multi	12	8

Research Ship Type of 1979

Litho. & Engr.   Perf. 12x11½
1980, Nov. 24
4881	A2271	2k	*Aju Dag, fleetarms*	6	5
4882	A2271	3k	*Valerian Uryvaev*	10	6
4884	A2271	6k	*Sergei Korolev*	18	12
4885	A2271	10k	*Otto Schmidt*	30	20
4886	A2271	15k	*Ustislav Kelgysh*	45	30
		Nos. 4881-4886 (6)		1.09	73

Russian Flag   Soviet Medical
                   College, 50th
A2313   Anniversary
                   A2314

1980, Dec. 1   Engraved   Perf. 12x12½
4887	A2313	3k org red	10	6

1980, Dec. 1   Photo.   Perf. 11½
4888	A2314	4k multi	12	8

New Year 1981—A2315

1980, Dec. 1   Litho.   Perf. 12
4889	A2315	4k multi	12	8

Lenin,   A.N.
Electrical Plant   Nesmeyanov
                    (1899-1980),
A2316   Chemist
                    A2317

1980, Dec. 18
4890	A2316	4k multi	12	8

60th anniversary of GOELRO (Lenin's electro-economic plan).

1980, Dec. 19   Perf. 12½x12
4891	A2317	4k multi	12	8

Nagatinski Bridge, Moscow—A2318

Photo. & Engr.
1980, Dec. 23   Perf. 11½x12
4892	A2318	4k *shown*	12	8
4893	A2318	6k *Luzhniki Bridge*	12	8
4894	A2318	15k *Kalininski Bridge*	45	30

S.K.   Flags of India
Timoshenko   and U.S.S.R.,
                  Government
                  House, New
                  Delhi
A2319   A2320

1980, Dec. 25   Engraved   Perf. 12
4895	A2319	4k rose lake	12	8

S.K. Timoshenko (1895-1970), Soviet marshal.

1980, Dec. 30   Litho.   Perf. 12½x12
4896	A2320	4k multi	12	8

Visit of Pres. Brezhnev to India. Printed se-tenant with inscribed label.

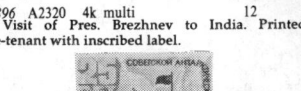

Mirny Base—A2321

1981, Jan. 5   Perf. 12
4897	A2321	4k *shown*	12	8
4898	A2321	6k *Earth station, rocket*	18	12
4899	A2321	15k *Map, supply ship*	45	30

Russian Antarctic research, 25th anniversary.

 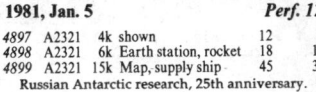

Dagestan Soviet Socialist Republic, 60th Anniversary—A2322

1981, Jan. 20
4900	A2322	4k multi	12	8

Bandy World Championship, Cheborovsk—A2323

1981, Jan. 20
4901	A2323	6k multi	18	12

26th Congress of Ukrainian Communist Party. A2324

1981, Jan. 23   Photo.   Perf. 11½
4902	A2324	4k multi	12	8

Lenin, "XXVI"—A2325

Lenin and Congress Building—A2326

Banner and Kremlin—A2327

1981   Photo.   Perf. 11½
4903	A2325	4k multi	12	8

Photo. & Embossed   Perf. 11½x12
4904	A2326	20k multi	2.00	1.00

Souvenir Sheet
Litho.   Perf. 12x12½
4905	A2327	50k multi	1.50	1.00

26th Communist Party Congress. No. 4905 has multicolored margin showing Lenin and text. Size: 96x74mm. Issue dates: 4k, 20k, Jan. 22; 50k, Feb. 16.

381

RUSSIA

Mstislav V. Keldysh
A2328

Freighter, Flags of USSR and India
A2329

1981, Feb. 10 Photo. & Engr. Perf. 11½x12
4906 A2328 4k multi   12   8
 Mstislav Vsevolodovich Keldysh (1911-1978), mathematician.

1981, Feb. 10 Litho. Perf.12
4907 A2329 15k multi   45   30
 Russian-Indian Shipping Line, 25th anniv.

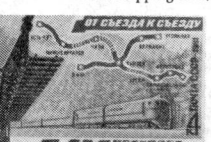

Baikal-Amur Railroad and Map
A2330

10th Five-Year Plan Projects (1976-1980): No. 4909, Gas plant, Urengoi. No. 4910, Enisei River power station. No. 4911, Atomic power plant. No. 4912, Paper mill. No. 4913, Coal mining, Ekibstyi.

1981, Feb. 18   Perf. 12½x12
4908 A2330 4k multi   12   8
4909 A2330 4k multi   12   8
4910 A2330 4k multi   12   8
4911 A2330 4k multi   12   8
4912 A2330 4k multi   12   8
4913 A2330 4k multi   12   8
       Nos. 4908-4913 (6)   72   48

Georgian Soviet Socialist Republic, 60th Anniv.
A2331

1981, Feb. 25   Perf. 12
4914 A2331 4k multi   12   8

Abkhazian Autonomous Soviet Socialist Republic, 60th Anniv.
A2332

1981, Mar. 4
4915 A2332 4k multi   12   8

Communications Institute
A2333

Satellite, Radio Operator
A2334

1981, Mar. 12 Photo.   Perf. 11½
4916 A2333 4k multi   12   8
 Moscow Electrotechnical Institute of Communications, 60th anniv.

1981, Mar. 12
4917 A2334 4k multi   12   8
 30th All-Union Amateur Radio Designers Exhibition.

Cosmonauts L.I. Popov and V.V. Rumin
A2335

1981, Mar. 20 Litho.   Perf. 12
4918 A2335 15k shown   45   30
4919 A2335 15k Spacecraft complex 45   30
 185-day flight of Cosmos 35-Salyut 6-Cosmos 37 complex, Apr. 9-Oct. 11, 1980. Nos. 4918-4919 se-tenant in continuous design and with label showing test and symbols.

Cosmonauts O. Makarov, L. Kizim and G. Strekalov—A2336

1981, Mar. 20   Perf. 12½x12
4920 A2336 10k multi   30   20
 Soyuz T-3 flight, Nov. 27-Dec. 10, 1980.

Lift-Off, Baikanur Base—A2337

1981, Mar. 23
4921 A2337 6k shown   18   12
4922 A2337 15k Mongolians watching flight on TV 45 30
4923 A2337 32k Re-entry   1.00 65
 Intercosmos cooperative space program (USSR-Mongolia).

Vitus Bering
A2338

Yuri Gagarin and Earth
A2339

Yuri Gagarin—A2340

1981, Mar. 25 Engr.   Perf. 12x12½
4924 A2338 4k dk bl   12   8
 Vitus Bering (1680-1741), Danish navigator, 300th birth anniv. (1980).

1981, Apr. 12 Photo.   Perf. 11½x12
4925 A2339 6k shown   18   12
4926 A2339 15k S.P. Korolev (craft designer) 45 30
4927 A2339 32k Monument   1.00 65

Souvenir Sheet
4928 A2340 50k shown   2.00 1.00
 Russian space flights, 20th anniversary. Nos. 4925-4927 each se-tenant with inscribed label. No. 4928 has multicolored margin showing medal; black control number. Size: 102x63mm.

Salyut Orbital Station, 10th Anniv. of Flight—A2341

1981, Apr. 19 Litho.   Perf. 12x12½
4929 A2341 32k multi   1.00 65

Souvenir Sheet

111th Birth Anniv. of Lenin—A2342

1981, Apr. 22   Perf. 11½x12½
4930 A2342 50k multi   1.50 1.00
 No. 4930 has black and gold margin showing Lenin vignettes. Size: 93x92mm.

Serge Prokofiev (1891-1953), Composer
A2343

New Hofburg Palace, Vienna
A2344

1981, Apr. 23 Engr.   Perf. 12
4931 A2343 4k dk pur   12   8

1981, May 5   Litho.
4932 A2344 15k multi   45   30
 WIPA 1981 Philatelic Exhibition, Vienna, May 22-31.

Adzhar Autonomous Soviet Socialist Republic, 60th Anniv.—A2345

1981, May 7
4933 A2345 4k multi   12   8

Centenary of Welding (Invented by N.N. Benardos)—A2346

1981, May 12 Litho. & Engr. Per. 11½
4934 A2346 6k multi   18   12

Intl. Architects Union, 14th Congress, Warsaw
A2347

Albanian Girl, by A.A. Ivanov
A2348

1981, May 12   Photo.
4935 A2347 15k multi   45   30

1981, May 15 Litho.   Perf. 12x12½
 Paintings: No. 4937, Horseman, by F.A. Roubeau. No. 4938, The Demon, by M.A. Wrubel (horiz.). No. 4939, Sunset over the Sea, by N.N. Ge (horiz.).
4936 A2348 10k multi   30   20
4937 A2348 10k multi   30   20
4938 A2348 10k multi   30   20
4939 A2348 10k multi   30   20

Cosmonauts in Training
A2349

1981, May 15
4940 A2349 6k shown   18   12
4941 A2349 15k In space   45   30
4942 A2349 32k Return   1.00 65
 Intercosmos cooperative space program (USSR-Romania).

Dwarf Primrose—A2350

Flowers of the Carpathian Mountains: 6k, Great carline thistle. 10k, Mountain parageum. 15k, Alpine bluebell. 32k, Rhododendron kotschyi.

1981, May 20   Perf. 12
4943 A2350 4k multi   12   8
4944 A2350 6k multi   18   12
4945 A2350 10k multi   30   20
4946 A2350 15k multi   45   30
4947 A2350 32k multi   1.00 65
       Nos. 4943-4947 (5)   2.05 1.35

RUSSIA

Luigi Longo, Italian Labor Leader, 1st Death Anniv.—A2351

1981, May 24   **Photo.**   *Perf. 11½*
4948   A2351   6k multi   18   12

Nizami Gjanshevi (1141-1209), Azerbaijan Poet—A2352

1981, May 25   **Photo. & Engr.**
4949   A2352   4k multi   12   8

Running   Mongolian Revolution, 60th Anniv.
A2353   A2354

1981, June 18   **Litho.**   *Perf. 12*
4950   A2353   4k shown   12   8
4951   A2353   6k Soccer   18   12
4952   A2353   10k Discus throwing   30   20
4953   A2353   15k Boxing   45   30
4954   A2353   32k Diving   1.00   65
     Nos. 4950-4954 (5)   2.05   1.35

1981, July 6
4955   A2354   6k multi   18   12

12th Intl. Film Festival, Moscow—A2355

1981, July 6   **Photo.**   *Perf. 11½*
4956   A2355   15k multi   45   30

River Tour Boat Lenin—A2356

1981, July 9   **Litho.**   *Perf. 12½*
4957   A2356   4k shown   12   8
4958   A2356   6k Cosmonaut Gagarin   18   12
4959   A2356   15k Valerian Kuibyshev   45   30
4960   A2356   32k Freighter Baltijski   1.00   65

Icebreaker Maligin—A2357

1981, July 9   **Photo. & Engr.**   *Perf. 11½x12*
4961   A2357   15k multi   45   30

26th Party Congress Resolutions (Intl. Cooperation)—A2358

1981, July 15   **Photo.**   *Perf. 12x11½*
4962   A2358   4k shown   12   8
4963   A2358   4k Industry   12   8
4964   A2358   4k Energy   12   8
4965   A2358   4k Agriculture   12   8
4966   A2358   4k Communications   12   8
4967   A2358   4k Science   12   8
     Nos. 4962-4967 (6)   72   48

J.N. Ulyanov (Lenin's Father), 150th Anniv. of Birth—A2359

1981, July 25   **Engr.**   *Perf. 11½*
4968   A2359   4k multi   12   8

Leningrad Theater, Sesquicentennial—A2360

1981, Aug. 12   **Photo.**   *Perf. 11½*
4969   A2360   6k multi   18   12

A.M. Gerasimov, Artist, Birth Centenary—A2361

1981, Aug. 12   **Litho.**   *Perf. 12*
4970   A2361   4k multi   12   8

Physical Chemistry Institute, Moscow Academy of Science, 50th Anniv.—A2362

1981, Aug. 12   **Photo.**   *Perf. 11½*
4971   A2362   4k multi   12   8

Siberian Tit A2363

Designs: Song birds.

1981, Aug. 20 Litho.   *Perf. 12½x12, 12x½*
4972   A2363   6k shown   18   12
4973   A2363   10k Tersiphone paradisi, vert.   30   20
4974   A2363   15k Emberiza jankovski   45   30
4975   A2363   20k Sutora webbiana, vert.   60   40
4976   A2363   32k Saxicola torquata, vert.   1.00   65
     Nos. 4972-4976 (5)   2.53   1.67

60th Anniv. of Komi Autonomous Soviet Socialist Republic—A2364

1981, Aug. 22   *Perf. 12*
4977   A2364   4k multi   12   8

Svyaz-'81 Intl. Communications Exhibition A2365

1981, Aug. 22   **Photo. & Engr.**   *Perf. 11½*
4978   A2365   4k multi   12   8

60th Anniv. of Kabardino-Balkar Autonomous Soviet Socialist Republic—A2366

1981, Sept. 1   **Litho.**   *Perf. 12*
4979   A2366   4k multi   12   8

War Veterans' Committee, 25th Anniv. A2367   Schooner Kodor A2368

1981, Sept. 1   **Photo.**   *Perf. 11½*
4980   A2367   4k multi   12   8

1981, Sept. 18 Litho.   *Perf. 12½x12, 12x12½*
Designs: Training ships. 4k, 6k, 15k, 20k horiz.
4981   A2368   4k 4-masted bark Tovarich   12   8
4982   A2368   6k Barkentine Vega I   18   12
4983   A2368   10k shown   30   20
4984   A2368   15k 3-masted bark Tovarich   45   30
4985   A2368   20k 4-masted bark Kruzenstern   60   40
4986   A2368   32k 4-masted bark Sedov   1.00   65
     Nos. 4981-4986 (6)   2.65   1.75

Kazakhstan's Union with Russia, 250th Anniv.
A2369

Mikhail Alekseevich Lavrentiev (1900-1980), Mathematician
A2370

1981, Oct. 10   *Perf. 12*
4987   A2369   4k multi   12   8

1981, Oct. 10   **Photo.**   *Perf. 11½*
4988   A2370   4k multi   12   8

64th Anniv. of October Revolution A2371

1981, Oct. 15   **Litho.**
4989   A2371   4k multi   12   8

Ekran Satellite TV Broadcasting System A2372

1981, Oct. 15   *Perf. 12*
4990   A2372   4k multi   12   8

A2373

A2374

1981, Oct. 15
4991   A2373   10k multi   30   20

Salyut 6-Soyuz flight of V.V. Kovalionok and V.P. Savinykh.

Souvenir Sheet

Birth Centenary of Pablo Picasso—A2375

RUSSIA

1981, Oct. 25   *Perf. 12x12½*
4993   A2375   50k multi   2.00   1.00
Black margin shows drawing of dove; control number. Size: 102x72mm.

Sergei Dmitrievich Merkurov (1881-1952), Artist
A2376

1981, Nov. 5   *Photo. & Engr.*   *Perf. 11½*
4994   A2376   4k multi   12   8

Autumn, by Nino Pirosmanas 1913
A2377

Paintings: 6k, Guriyka, by M.G. Kokodze, 1921. 10k, Fellow Travelers, by U.M. Dzhaparidze, 1936 (horiz.). 15k, Shota Rustaveli, by S.S. Kobuladze, 1938. 32k, Collecting Tea, by V.D. Gudiashvili, 1964 (horiz.).

1981, Nov. 5   *Litho.*   *Perf. 12x12½, 12½x12*
4995   A2377   4k multi   12   8
4996   A2377   6k multi   18   12
4997   A2377   10k multi   30   20
4998   A2377   15k multi   45   30
4999   A2377   32k multi   1.00   65
Nos. 4995-4999 (5)   2.05   1.35

New Year 1982—A2378

1981, Dec. 2   *Litho.*   *Perf. 12*
5000   A2378   4k multi   12   8

Public Transportation 19th-20th Cent.—A2379

1981, Dec. 10 *Photo. & Engr. Perf. 11½x12*
5001   A2379   4k Sled   12   8
5002   A2379   6k Horse-drawn trolley   18   12
5003   A2379   10k Coach   30   20
5004   A2379   15k Taxi, 1926   45   30
5005   A2379   20k Bus, 1926   60   40
5006   A2379   32k Trolley, 1912   1.00   65
Nos. 5001-5006 (6)   2.65   1.75

Souvenir Sheet

Kremlin and New Delhi Parliament—A2380

1981, Dec. 17   *Photo.*
5007   A2380   50k multi   1.50   1.00
First direct telephone link with India. Multicolored labels show Brezhnev and Mrs. Gandhi talking on telephone. Size: 124x67mm.

60th Anniv. of Checheno-Ingush Autonomous Soviet Socialist Republic—A2381

60th Anniv. of Yakutsk Autonomous Soviet Socialist Republic—A2382

1982, Jan. 11   *Litho.*   *Perf. 12*
5008   A2381   4k multi   12   8
5009   A2382   4k multi   12   8

1500th Anniv. of Kiev—A2383

1982, Jan. 12   *Photo.*   *Perf. 11½x12*
5010   A2383   10k multi   30   20

S.P. Korolev (1907-1966), Rocket Designer
A2384

Nazym Khikmet (1902-1963), Turkish Poet
A2385

1982, Jan. 12   *Perf. 11½*
5011   A2384   4k multi   12   8

1982, Jan. 20   *Litho.*   *Perf. 12*
5012   A2385   6k multi   18   12

10th World Trade Union Congress, Havana—A2386

1982, Feb. 1   *Photo.*   *Perf. 11½*
5013   A2386   4k multi   12   8

17th Soviet Trade Union Congress—A2387

1982, Feb. 10   *Litho.*
5014   A2387   15k multi   45   30

Edouard Manet (1832-1883)—A2388

1982, Feb. 10   *Perf. 12x12½*
5015   A2388   32k multi   1.00   65

Equestrian Sports—A2389

1982, Feb. 16   *Photo.*   *Perf. 11½*
5016   A2389   4k Hurdles   12   8
5017   A2389   6k Riding   18   12
5018   A2389   15k Racing   45   30

2nd Death Anniv. of Marshall Tito of Jugoslavia—A2390

1982, Feb. 25   *Litho.*   *Perf. 12*
5019   A2390   6k ol blk   18   12

350th Anniv. of State University of Tartu—A2392

1982, Mar. 4   *Photo.*   *Perf. 11½*
5020   A2392   4k multi   12   8

9th Intl. Cardiologists Congress, Moscow—A2393

1982, Mar. 4
5021   A2393   15k multi   45   30

Souvenir Sheet

Biathlon, Speed Skating—A2394

1982, Mar. 6   *Litho.*   *Perf. 12½x12*
5022   A2394   50k multi   1.50   1.00
5th Natl. Athletic Meet. Size: 96x67mm.

Blueberry Bush
A2395

Venus 13 and Venus 14 Flights
A2396

1982, Mar. 10   *Litho.*   *Perf. 12x12½*
5023   A2395   4k Blackberries   12   8
5024   A2395   6k shown   18   12
5025   A2395   10k Cranberries   30   20
5026   A2395   15k Cherries   45   30
5027   A2395   32k Cranberries, diff.   1.00   65
Nos. 5023-5027 (5)   2.05   1.35

1982, Mar. 10   *Photo.*   *Perf. 11½*
5028   A2396   10k multi   30   20

RUSSIA

Marriage Ceremony, by W.W. Pukirev (1832-1890) A2397

K.I. Tchukovsky (1882-1969), Writer A2398

Paintings: No. 5030, M.I. Lopuchino, by Vladimir Borowikowsky (1757-1825). No. 5031, E.W. Davidov, by O.A. Kiprensky (1782-1836). No. 5032, Landscape.

1982, Mar. 18   *Perf. 12*
5029	A2397	6k multi	18	12
5020	A2397	6k multi	18	12
5031	A2397	6k multi	18	12
5032	A2397	6k multi	18	12

1982, Mar. 31   *Engr.*
| 5033 | A2398 | 4k black | 12 | 8 |

Cosmonauts' Day—A2399

1982, Apr. 12   *Photo.*   *Perf. 12x11½*
| 5034 | A2399 | 6k multi | 18 | 12 |

Souvenir Sheet

112th Birth Anniv. of Lenin—A2400

1982, Apr. 22   *Photo.*   *Perf. 11½x12*
| 5035 | A2400 | 50k multi | 1.50 | 1.00 |

Gold marginal inscription. Size: 67x87mm.

V.P. Soloviev-Sedoi (1907-1979), Composer A2401

G. Dimitrov (1882-1949), 1st Bulgarian Prime Minister A2402

1982, Apr. 25   *Engr.*   *Perf. 12*
| 5036 | A2401 | 4k brown | 12 | 8 |

1982, Apr. 25
| 5037 | A2402 | 6k green | 18 | 12 |

Kremlin Tower, Moscow A2403

70th Anniv. of Pravda Newspaper A2404

1982, Apr. 25   *Litho.*   *Perf. 12½x12*
| 5038 | A2403 | 45k brown | 1.35 | 90 |

1982, May 5   *Photo.*   *Perf. 12x11½*
| 5039 | A2404 | 4k multi | 12 | 8 |

U.N. Conference on Human Environment 10th Anniv. A2405

Pioneers' Org., 60th Anniv. A2406

1982, May 10   *Perf. 11½*
| 5040 | A2405 | 6k multi | 18 | 12 |

1982, May 19
| 5041 | A2406 | 4k multi | 12 | 8 |

Communist Youth Org., 19th Congress A2407

ITU Delegates Conference, Nairobi A2408

1982, May 19
| 5042 | A2407 | 4k multi | 12 | 8 |

1982, May 19
| 5043 | A2408 | 15k multi | 45 | 30 |

TUL-80 Electric Locomotive—A2409

1982, May 20   *Perf. 12x11½*
5044	A2409	4k shown	12	8
5045	A2409	6k TEP-75 diesel	18	12
5046	A2409	10k TEP-7 diesel	30	20
5047	A2409	15k WL-82m electric	45	30
5048	A2409	32k EP-200 electric	1.00	65
		Nos. 5044-5048 (5)	2.05	1.35

1982 World Cup—A2410

1982, June 4   *Perf. 11½x12*
| 5049 | A2410 | 20k ol & pur | 60 | 40 |

Grus Monacha A2411

18th Ornithological Congress, Moscow: Rare birds.

1982, June 10   *Litho.*   *Perf. 12x12½*
5050	A2411	2k shown	6	5
5051	A2411	4k Haliaeetus pelagicus	12	8
5052	A2411	6k Eurynorhynchus pygmeus	18	12
5053	A2411	10k Eulabeia indica	30	20
5054	A2411	15k Chettusia gregaria	45	30
5055	A2411	32k Ciconia boyciana	1.00	65
		Nos. 5050-5055 (6)	2.11	1.40

Komomolsk-on-Amur City, 50th Anniv. A2412

1982, June 10   *Photo. & Engr.*   *Perf. 11½*
| 5056 | A2412 | 4k multi | 12 | 8 |

Tatchanka, by M.B. Grekov (1882-1934)—A2413

1982, June 15   *Litho.*   *Perf. 12½x12*
| 5057 | A2413 | 6k multi | 18 | 12 |

2nd UN Conference on Peaceful Uses of Outer Space, Vienna, Aug. 9-21—A2414

1982, June 15   *Photo.*   *Perf. 11½*
| 5058 | A2414 | 15k multi | 45 | 30 |

Intercosmos Cooperative Space Program (USSR-France)—A2415

1982, June 24   *Litho.*   *Perf 12½x12*
5059	A2415	6k Cosmonauts	18	12
5060	A2415	20k Rocket, globe	60	40
5061	A2415	45k Satellites	1.35	90

Souvenir Sheet
| 5062 | A2415 | 50k Emblem, satellite | 1.50 | 1.00 |

No. 5062 contains one stamp (41x29mm.). Size: 97x69mm.

The Legend of the Goldfish, by P. Sosin, 1968—A2416

Lacquerware Paintings, Ustera: 10k, Minin's Appeal to Count Posharski, by J. Phomitchev, 1953. 15k, Two Peasants, by A. Kotjagin, 1933. 20k, The Fisherman, by N. Klykov, 1933. 32k, The Arrest of the Propagandists, by N. Shishakov, 1968.

1982, July 6   *Litho.*   *Perf. 12½x12*
5063	A2416	6k multi	18	12
5064	A2416	10k multi	30	20
5065	A2416	15k multi	45	30
5066	A2416	20k multi	60	40
5067	A2416	32k multi	1.00	65
		Nos. 5063-5067 (5)	71.63	36.30

Telephone Centenary—A2417

1982, July 13   *Perf. 12*
| 5068 | A2417 | 4k Phone, 1882 | 12 | 8 |

P. Schilling's Electro-magnetic Telegraph Sesquicentennial—A2418

1982, July 16   *Photo. & Engr.*   *Perf. 11½*
| 5069 | A2418 | 6k Voltaic cells | 18 | 12 |

RUSSIA

Intervision Gymnastics Contest—A2419

1982, Aug. 10 Photo.
5070 A2419 15k multi 45 30

Mastjahart Glider, 1923—A2420

Gliders.

1982, Aug. 20 Litho. *Perf. 12½x12*
5071 A2420 4k shown 12 8
5072 A2420 6k Red Star, 1930 18 12
5073 A2420 10k ZAGI-1, 1934 30 20

Size: 60x28mm. *Perf. 11½x12*
5074 A2420 20k Stakhanovets, 1939 60 20
5075 A2420 32k Troop carrier GR-29, 1941 1.00 65
Nos. 5071-5075 (5) 2.20 1.25

Garibaldi (1807-1882)

A2421

Intl. Atomic Energy Authority, 25th Anniv.

A2422

1982, Aug. 25 Photo. *Perf. 11½*
5076 A2421 6k multi 18 12

1982, Aug. 30
5077 A2422 20k multi 60 40

Marshal BM Shaposhnikov (1882-1945)

A2423

World Chess Championship

A2424

1982, Sept. 10 Engr. *Perf. 12*
5078 A2423 4k red brn 12 8

1982, Sept. 10 Photo. *Perf. 11½*
5079 A2424 6k King 18 12
5080 A2424 6k Queen 18 12

African Natl. Congress 70th Anniv.

A2425

SP Botkin (1832-1889), Physician

A2426

1982, Sept. 10
5081 A2425 6k multi 18 12

1982, Sept. 17 Engr. *Perf. 12½x12*
5082 A2426 4k green 12 8

Souvenir Sheet

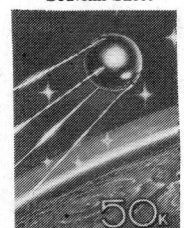

25th Anniv. of Sputnik—A2427

1982, Sept. 17 Litho. *Perf. 12x12½*
5083 A2427 50k multi 1.50 1.00

Multicolored margin continues design; black control number. Size: 93x63mm.

No. 5079 Overprinted in Gold for Karpov's Victory

1982, Sept. 22 Photo. *Perf. 11½*
5084 A2424 6k multi 18 12

World War II Battleships—A2428

Perf. 11½x12

1982, Sept. 22 Photo. & Engr.
5085 A2428 4k Submarine S-56 12 8
5086 A2428 6k Minelayer Gremjashtjay 18 12
5087 A2428 15k Mine sweeper T-205 45 30
5088 A2428 20k Cruiser Red Crimea 60 40
5089 A2428 45k Sebastopol 1.35 90
Nos. 5085-5089 (5) 2.70 1.80

65th Anniv. of October Revolution—A2429

1982, Oct. 12 Litho. *Perf. 12*
5090 A2429 4k multi 12 8

House of the Soviets, Moscow—A2430

60th Anniv. of USSR: No. 5092, Dnieper Dam, Komosomol Monument, Statue of worker. No. 5093, Soviet War Memorial, resistance poster. No. 5094, Worker at podium, decree text. No. 5095, Workers' Monument, Moscow, Rocket, jet. No. 5096, Arms, Kremlin.

1982, Oct. 25 Photo. *Perf. 11½x12*
5091 A2430 10k multi 30 20
5092 A2430 10k multi 30 20
5093 A2430 10k multi 30 20
5094 A2430 10k multi 30 20
5095 A2430 10k multi 30 20
5096 A2430 10k multi 30 20
Nos. 5091-5096 (6) 1.80 1.20

No. 5095 Overprinted in Red for All-Union Philatelic Exhibition, 1984.

1982, Nov. 10
5097 A2430 10k multi 30 20

Portrait of an Actor, by Domenico Fetti—A2431

Paintings from the Hermitage: 10k, St. Sebastian, by Perugino. 20k, The Danae, by Titian (horiz.). 45k, Portrait of a Woman, by Correggio. No. 5102, Portrait of a Young Man, by Capriola. No. 5103, Portrait of a Young Woman, by Melzi.

1982, Nov. 25 Litho. *Perf. 12x12½*
5098 A2431 4k multi 12 8
5099 A2431 20k multi 30 20
5100 A2431 20k multi 60 40
5101 A2431 45k multi 1.35 90
5102 A2431 50k multi 1.50 1.00
Nos. 5098-5102 (5) 3.87 2.58

Souvenir Sheet

5103 Sheet of 2 3.00 2.00
  a. A2431 50k multi 1.50 1.00

No. 5103 has black control number. Size: 145x79mm.

See Nos. 5129-5134, 5199-5204.

New Year 1983—A2432

1982, Dec. 1
5104 A2432 4k multi 12 8

Souvenir Sheet

60th Anniv. of USSR—A2433

1982, Dec. 3 *Perf. 12½x12*
5105 A2433 50k multi 1.50 1.00

Multicolored margin shows flags, arms. Size: 85x96mm.

Souvenir Sheet

Mountain Climbers Reaching Mt. Everest—A2434

1982, Dec. 20 Photo. *Perf. 11½x12*
5106 A2434 50k multi 1.50 1.00

Black control number. Size: 67x87mm.

Lighthouses—A2435

1982, Dec. 29 Litho. *Perf. 12*
5107 A2435 6k grn & multi 18 12
5108 A2435 6k lil & multi 18 12
5109 A2435 6k sal & multi 18 12
5110 A2435 6k lt gldn brn & multi 18 12
5111 A2435 6k L brn & multi 18 12
Nos. 5107-5111 (5) 90 60

See Nos. 5179-5183.

Mail Transport—A2436

1982, Dec. 22 *Perf. 12*
5112 A2436 5k grnsh bl 15 10

1983, May 20 Litho. *Perf. 12*
5113 A2436 5k blue 15 10

RUSSIA

Iskra Newspaper Masthead
A2438

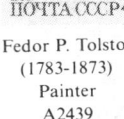
Fedor P. Tolstoi (1783-1873) Painter
A2439

1983, Jan. 5   Litho.   Perf. 12x12½
5114 A2438 4k multi   12   8

80th anniv. of 2nd Social-Democratic Workers' Party.

1983, Jan. 5   Photo.   Perf. 11½
5115 A2439 4k multi   12   8

65th Anniv. of Armed Forces—A2440

1983, Jan. 25   Litho.   Perf. 12
5116 A2440 4k multi   12   8

Souvenir Sheet

60th Anniv. of Aeroflot Airlines—A2441

1983, Feb. 9   Perf. 12x12½
5117 A2441 50k multi   1.50 1.00
Size: 73x98mm.

Glider Type of 1982

1983, Feb. 10   Perf. 12½x12
5118 A2420 2k A-9, 1948   6   5
5119 A2420 4k KAJ-12, 1957 12   8
5120 A2420 6k A-15, 1960   18   12
5121 A2420 20k SA-7, 1970   60   40
5122 A2420 45k LAJ-12, 1979 1.35 90
Nos. 5118-5122 (5)   2.31 1.55

Tashkent Bimillenium—A2442

1983, Feb. 17   Perf. 12½x12
5123 A2442 4k View   12   8

B.N. Petrov (1913-1980), Scientist
A2443

Holy Family, by Raphael
A2444

1983, Feb. 17
5124 A2443 4k multi   12   8

1983, Feb. 17   Perf. 12x12½
5125 A2444 50k multi   1.50 1.00

Soyuz T-7—Salyut 7—Soyuz T-5 Flight—A2445

1983, Mar. 10   Perf. 12x12½
5126 A2445 10k Popov, A.
                  Serebrov, S.
                  Savitskaya   30   20

Souvenir Sheet

World Communications Year—A2446

1983, Mar. 10   Photo.   Perf. 11½
5127 A2446 50k multi   1.50 1.00
Margin shows means of communication. Size: 73x108mm.

A.W. Alexandrov (1883-19), Natl. Anthem Composer—A2447

1983, Mar. 22   Litho.   Perf. 12
5128 A2447 4k multi   12   8

Hermitage Type of 1982

Rembrandt Paintings, Hermitage, Leningrad: 10k, Portrait of a Learned Man. 20k, Old Warrior, 45k, Portrait of Mrs. B. Martens Doomer. No. 5133, Sacrifice of Abraham. No. 5134, Portrait of an Old Man in a Red Garment.

1983, Mar. 25   Perf. 12x12½
5129 A2431 4k multi   12   8
5130 A2431 10k multi   30   20
5131 A2431 20k multi   60   40
5132 A2431 45k multi   1.35 90
5133 A2431 50k multi   1.50 1.00
Nos. 5129-5133 (5)   3.87 2.58

Souvenir Sheet
Litho. & Embossed
5134   50k multi   3.00 2.00
No. 5134 contains 2 stamps; black control number. Size: 146x82mm.

Souvenir Sheet
Cosmonauts' Day—A2449

1983, Apr. 12   Litho.   Perf. 12½x12
5135 A2449 50k Soyuz T   1.50 1.00
Size: 61x92mm.

Souvenir Sheet
113th Birth Anniv. of Lenin—A2450

1983, Apr. 22 Photo. & Engr. Perf. 11½x12
5136 A2450 50k multi   1.50 1.00
Margin shows vignettes. Size: 73x91mm.

A2451

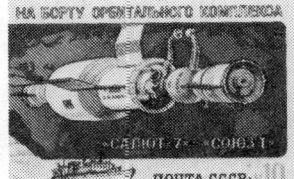
Salyut 7-Soyuz 7 211-Day Flight
A2452

1983, Apr. 25   Litho.   Perf. 12½x12
5137 A2451 10k A. Berezovoy, V.
                  Lebedev   30   20
5138 A2452 10k Spacecraft   30   20

Karl Marx (1818-1883)—A2453

1983, May 5   Perf. 12x12½
5139 A2453 4k multi   12   8

View of Rostov-on-Don—A2454

1983, May 5   Photo.   Perf. 11½
5140 A2454 4k multi   12   8

Buriat Autonomous Soviet Socialist Republic, 60th Anniv.—A2455

1983, May 12   Litho.   Perf. 12
5141 A2455 4k multi   12   8

Kirov Opera and Ballet Theater, Leningrad, 200th Anniv.—A2456

1983, May 12 Photo. & Engr. Perf. 11½x12
5142 A2456 4k multi   12   8

Emblem of Motorcycling, Auto Racing, Shooting, Motorboating, Parachuting Organization—A2457

1983, May 20   Litho.   Perf. 11½
5143 A2457 6k multi   18   12

RUSSIA

A.I. Khachaturian (1903-1978), Composer—A2458

1983, May 25	Engr.	Perf. 12½x12
5144 A2458	4k vio brn	12 8

Chelyabinsk Tractor Plant, 50th Anniv. A2459

1983, June 1	Photo.	Perf. 11½
5145 A2459	4k multi	12 8

Simon Bolivar Bicentenary—A2460

1983, June 10	Photo. & Engr.	Perf. 12
5146 A2460	6k brn & dk brn	18 12

City of Sevastopol, 200th Anniv.—A2461

1983, June 14	Photo.	Perf. 11½x12
5147 A2461	5k multi	15 10

Spring Flowers—A2462

1983, June 14	Litho.	Perf. 12x12½
5148 A2462	4k multi	12 8
5149 A2462	6k multi	18 12
5150 A2462	10k multi	30 20
5151 A2462	15k multi	45 30
5152 A2462	20k multi	60 40
Nos. 5148-5152 (5)		1.65 1.10

Valentina Tereshkova's Spaceflight, 20th Anniv.—A2463

1983, June 16	Litho.	Perf. 12
5153 A2463	10k multi	30 20

P.N. Pospelov (1898-1979), Academician A2464

10th European Congress of Rheumatologists A2465

1983, June 20	Photo. & Engr.	Perf. 11½
5154 A2464	4k multi	12 8

1983, June 21	Photo.	Perf. 11½
5155 A2565	4k multi	12 8

13th International Film Festival, Moscow—A2466

1983, July 7	Litho.	Perf. 12
5156 A2466	20k multi	60 40

Ships of the Soviet Fishing Fleet—A2467

1983, July 20	Photo. & Engr.	Perf. 12x11½
5157 A2467	4k Two trawlers	12 8
5158 A2467	6k Refrigerated trawler	18 12
5159 A2467	10k Large trawler	30 20
5160 A2467	15k Large refrigerated ship	45 30
5161 A2467	20k Base ship	60 40
Nos. 5157-5161 (5)		1.65 1.10

E.B. Vakhtangov (1883-1922), Actor and Producer—A2468

1983, July 20	Photo.	Perf. 11½
5162 A2468	5k multi	15 10

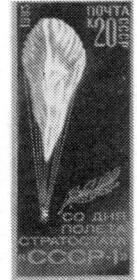
"USSR-1" Stratospheric Flight, 50th Anniv.—A2469

1983, July 25	Photo.	Perf. 12
5163 A2469	20k multi	60 40

Food Fish—A2470

Designs 4k, Oncorhynchus nerka. 6k, Perciformes. 15k, Anarhichas minor. 20k, Neogobius fluviatilis. 45k, Platichthys stellatus.

1983, Aug. 5	Litho.	Perf. 12½x12
5164 A2470	4k multi	12 8
5165 A2470	6k multi	18 12
5166 A2470	15k multi	45 30
5167 A2470	20k multi	60 40
5168 A2470	45k multi	1.35 90
Nos. 5164-5168 (5)		2.70 1.80

SOZPHILEX '83 Philatelic Exhibition—A2471

1983, Aug. 18	Photo.	Perf. 11½
5169 A2471	6k multi	18 12

Souvenir Sheet

Moscow Skyline—A2472

1983, Aug. 18	Photo.	Perf. 12
5170 A2472	50k cob bl	1.50 1.00

SOZPHILEX '83 Philatelic Exhibition. Multicolored margin continues stamp design and shows exhibition emblem. Size: 90x70mm.

Miniature Sheet

First Russian Postage Stamp, 125th Anniv.—A2473

1983, Aug. 25	Photo. & Engr.	Perf. 11½x12
5171 A2473	50k pale yel & blk	1.50 1.00

Decorative marginal border in bister. Size: 78x65mm.

Namibia Day A2474

Palestinian Solidarity A2475

1983, Aug. 26	Photo.	Perf. 11½
5172 A2474	5k multi	15 10

1983, Aug. 29	Photo.	Perf. 11½
5173 A2475	5k multi	15 10

1st European Championship of Radio-Telegraphy, Moscow—A2476

1983, Sept. 1	Photo.	Perf. 11½
5174 A2476	6k multi	18 12

4th UNESCO Council on Communications Development—A2477

1983, Sept. 2	Photo.	Perf. 12x11½
5175 A2477	10k multi	30 20

Muhammad Al-Khorezmi, Uzbek Mathematician, 1200th Birth Anniv. A2478

Marshal A.I. Egorov (1883-1939) A2479

1983, Sept. 6	Photo. & Engr.	Perf. 11½
5176 A2478	4k multi	12 8

1983, Sept. 8	Engr.	Perf. 12
5177 A2479	4k brn vio	12 8

RUSSIA

Union of Georgia and Russia, 200th Anniv.—A2480

1983, Sept. 8   Photo.   *Perf. 11½*
5178   A2480   6k multi   18   12

Lighthouse Type of 1982

Baltic Sea lighthouses.

1983, Sept. 19   Litho.   *Perf. 12*
5179   A2435   1k Kipu   5   5
5180   A2435   5k Keri   15   10
5181   A2435   10k Stirsudden   30   20
5182   A2435   12k Tahkun   36   24
5183   A2435   20k Tallinn   60   40
    Nos. 5179-5183 (5)   1.46   99

Early Spring, by V.K. Bjalynitzky-Birulja, 1912—A2481

Paintings by White Russians: 4k, Portrait of the Artist's Wife with Fruit and Flowers, by J.F. Krutzky, 1838. 15k, Young Partisan, by E.A. Zaitsev, 1943. 20k, Partisan Madonna, by M.A. Savitsky, 1967. 45k, Harvest, by V.K. Tsvirko, 1972. 15k, 20k vert.

1983, Sept. 28   *Perf. 12½x12, 12x12½*
5184   A2481   4k multi   12   8
5185   A2481   6k multi   18   12
5186   A2481   15k multi   45   30
5187   A2481   20k multi   60   40
5188   A2481   45k multi   1.35   90
    Nos. 5184-5188 (5)   2.70   1.80

Hammer and Sickle Steel Mill, Moscow, Centenary—A2482

1983, Oct. 1   Photo.   *Perf. 11½*
5189   A2482   4k multi   12   8

Natl. Food Program—A2483

1983, Oct. 10
5190   A2483   5k Wheat production   15   10
5191   A2483   5k Cattle, dairy products   15   10
5192   A2483   5k Produce   15   10

October Revolution, 66th Anniv.
A2484

1983, Oct. 12   Litho.   *Perf. 12*
5193   A2484   4k multi   12   8

1983, Oct. 12   Engr.   *Perf. 12x12½*
5194   A2485   4k dk brn   12   8

Ivan Fedorov, first Russian printer (Book of the Apostles), 400th death anniv.

Urengoy-Uzgorod Transcontinental Gas Pipeline Completion—A2486

1983, Oct. 12   Photo.   *Perf. 12x11½*
5195   A2486   5k multi   15   10

A.W. Sidorenko (1917-1982), Geologist
A2487

Campaign Against Nuclear Weapons
A2488

1983, Oct. 19   Litho.   *Perf. 12*
5196   A2487   4k multi   12   8

1983, Oct. 19   Photo.   *Perf. 11½*
5197   A2488   5k Demonstration   15   10

Machtumkuli, Turkmenistan Poet, 250th Birth Anniv.—A2489

1983, Oct. 27
5198   A2489   5k multi   15   10

Hermitage Painting Type of 1982

Paintings by Germans: 4k, Madonna and Child with Apple Tree, by Lucas Cranach the Elder. 10k, Self-portrait, by Anton R. Mengs. 20k, Self-portrait, by Jurgen Owen. 45k, Sailboat, by Caspar David Friedrich. No. 5203, Rape of the Sabines, by Johann Schoenfeld (horiz.). No. 5204, Portrait of a Young Man, by Hans Holbein.

1983, Nov. 10   Litho.   *Perf. 12x12½, 12½x12*
5199   A2431   4k multi   12   8
5200   A2431   10k multi   30   20
5201   A2431   20k multi   60   40
5202   A2431   45k multi   1.35   90
5203   A2431   50k multi   1.50   1.00
    Nos. 5199-5203 (5)   3.87   2.58

Souvenir Sheet
5204   Sheet of 2   3.00   2.00
  a.   A2431 50k, multi   1.50   1.00

No. 5204 has black control number. Size: 146x80mm.

Physicians Against Nuclear War Movement—A2490

1983, Nov. 17   Photo.   *Perf. 11½*
5205   A2490   5k Baby, dove, sun   15   10

Sukhe Bator (1893-1923), Mongolian People's Rep. Founder—A2491

1983, Nov. 17
5206   A2491   5k Portrait   15   10

New Year 1984—A2492

1983, Dec. 1
5207   A2492   5k Star, snowflakes   15   10

Newly Completed Buildings, Moscow—A2493

1983, Dec. 15   Engr.   *Perf. 12½x12, 12x12½*
5208   A2493   3k Children's Musical Theater   10   6
5209   A2493   4k Tourist Hotel, vert.   12   8
5210   A2493   6k Council of Ministers   18   12
5211   A2493   20k Ismaelovo Hotel   60   40
5212   A2493   45k Novosti Press Agency   1.35   90
    Nos. 5208-5212 (5)   2.35   1.56

Souvenir Sheet

Environmental Protection Campaign
A2494

1983, Dec. 20   Photo.   *Perf. 11½*
5213   A2494   50k multi   1.50   1.00

Black control number. Size: 82x65mm.

Moscow Local Broadcasting Network, 50th Anniv.
A2495

European Women's Skating Champ.,
A2496

1984, Jan. 1
5214   A2495   4k multi   12   8

1984, Jan. 1   *Perf. 12x11½*
5215   A2496   5k multi   15   10

Cuban Revolution, 25th Anniv.—A2497

1984, Jan. 1   *Perf. 11½*
5216   A2497   5k Flag, "25"   15   10

World War II Tanks—A2498

1984, Jan. 25   Litho.   *Perf. 12½x12*
5217   A2498   10k KW   30   20
5218   A2498   10k IS-2   30   20
5219   A2498   10k T-34   30   20
5220   A2498   10k ISU-152   30   20
5221   A2498   10k SU-100   30   20
    Nos. 5217-5221 (5)   1.50   1.00

1984 Winter Olympics—A2499

1984, Feb. 8   Photo.   *Perf. 11½x12*
5222   A2499   5k Biathlon   15   10
5223   A2499   10k Speed skating   30   20
5224   A2499   20k Hockey   60   40
5225   A2499   45k Figure skating   1.35   90

RUSSIA

Moscow Zoo, 120th Anniv.—A2500

1984, Feb. 16   Litho.   *Perf. 12½x12*

5226	A2500	2k Mandrill	6	5
5227	A2500	3k Gazelle	10	6
5228	A2500	4k Snow leopard	12	8
5229	A2500	5k Crowned crane	15	10
5230	A2500	20k Macaw	60	40
	Nos. 5226-5230 (5)		1.03	69

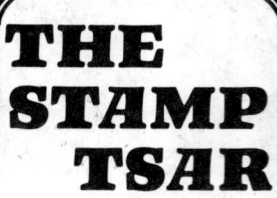

Quality Russian Area

Stamps Bought and Sold
send for free list
or submit want lists

     Rossica

THE STAMP TSAR
P.O. BOX 15652
HARRISBURG, PA 17105
(717) 234-3065

British + Foreign (no U.S.)
also sought. Write or call;
describe before sending
any material.

RUSSIA

SEMI-POSTAL STAMPS
Empire.

Admiral Kornilov Monument, Sevastopol
SP1

Pozharski and Minin Monument, Moscow
SP2

Statue of Peter the Great, Leningrad
SP3

Alexander II Memorial and Kremlin, Moscow
SP4

Perf. 11½ to 13½ and Compound.

1905		Typographed	Unwmkd.	
B1	SP1	3k red, brn & grn	5.00	5.00
a.		Perf. 13½x 11½	275.00	225.00
b.		Perf. 13½	40.00	40.00
c.		Perf. 11½x13½	500.00	500.00
B2	SP2	5k lil, vio & straw	4.00	4.00
B3	SP3	7k lt bl, dk bl & pink	5.00	5.00
a.		Perf. 13½	90.00	90.00
B4	SP4	10k lt bl, dk bl & yel	7.50	7.50

These stamps were sold for 3 kopecks over face value. The surtax was donated to a fund for the orphans of soldiers killed in the Russo-Japanese war.

Ilya Murometz Legendary Russian Hero
SP5

Don Cossack Bidding Farewell to His Sweetheart
SP6

Symbolical of Charity SP7 — St. George Slaying the Dragon SP8

1914		Perf. 11½, 12½, 13½.		
B5	SP5	1k red brn & dk grn, *straw*	40	60
a.		Perf. 13½	50	75
B6	SP6	3k mar & gray grn, *pink*	40	60
		Perf. 13½	40.00	50.00
B7	SP7	7k dk brn & dk grn, *buff*	40	60
		Perf. 13½	40	60
B8	SP8	10k dk bl & brn, *bl*	1.75	2.75
		Perf. 13½	9.00	

1915		White Paper.		
B9	SP5	1k org brn & gray	40	60
B10	SP6	3k car & gray blk	50	75
B12	SP7	7k dk brn & dk grn	7.00	
B13	SP8	10k dk bl & brn	30	60

These stamps were sold for 1 kopeck over face value. The surtax was donated to charities connected with the war of 1914–17.

No. B12 not regularly issued.

#B5-B13 exist imperf. Price each, $50 unused, $75 canceled.

Russian Soviet Federated Socialist Republic.
Volga Famine Relief Issue.

Relief Work on Volga River
SP9

Administering Aid to Famine Victim
SP10

1921		Lithographed	Imperf.	
B14	SP9	2250r green	5.00	12.00
a.		Pelure paper	80.00	110.00
B15	SP9	2250r dp red	4.00	8.50
a.		Pelure paper	10.00	20.00
B16	SP9	2250r brown	4.00	8.00
B17	SP10	2250r dk bl	10.00	25.00

Counterfeits of Nos. B14 to B17 are plentiful.

Stamps of type A33 with this overprint were not charity stamps nor did they pay postage in any form. They represent taxes paid on stamps exported from or imported into Russia. In 1925 the semi-postal stamps of 1914-15 were surcharged for the same purpose. Stamps of the regular issues 1918 and 1921 have also been surcharged with inscriptions and new values, to pay the importation and exportation taxes.

Regular Issue of 1918 Surcharged in Various Colors

Р. С. Ф. С. Р.
ГОЛОДАЮЩИМ
250 р.+250 р

1922, Feb.			Perf. 13½	
B18	A33	100r +100r on 70k brn (Bk)	1.00	2.00
a.		"100 p. + p. 100"	85.00	100.00
B19	A33	100r +100r on 70k brn (R)	1.00	2.00
B20	A33	100r +100r on 70k brn (Bl)	50	1.00
B21	A33	250r +250r on 35k bl (Bk)	50	1.00
B22	A33	250r +250r on 35k bl (R)	1.00	2.00
B23	A33	250r +250r on 35k bl (O)	2.00	4.00
		Nos. B18-B23 (6)	6.00	12.00

Issued to raise funds for Volga famine relief.

Nos. B18-B22 exist with surcharge inverted. Prices $20 to $40.

Regular Issues of 1909-18 Overprinted

РСФСР
Филателия
—Детям—
19-8-22

1922, Aug. 19			Perf. 14	
B24	A14	1k orange	300.00	300.00
B25	A14	2k green	25.00	40.00
B26	A14	3k red	20.00	30.00
B27	A14	5k claret	20.00	30.00
B28	A15	10k dk bl	20.00	30.00

Imperf.

B29	A14	1k orange	300.00	350.00
		Nos. B24-B29 (6)	685.00	780.00

The overprint on Nos. B24 to B29 means "Philately for the Children". The stamps were sold at five million times their face values and eighty per cent of the amount received was devoted to child welfare. The stamps were sold only at Moscow and for one day.

Nos. B24-B29 exist with overprint reading up. Counterfeits of Nos. B24-B29 exist including those with overprint reading up.

Worker and Peasant (Industry and Agriculture)
SP11

Allegory: Agriculture Will Help End Distress
SP12

Star of Hope, Wheat and Worker-Peasant Handclasp
SP13

Sower
SP14

1922		Lithographed Without Gum.	Imperf.	
B30	SP11	2t (2000r) grn	15.00	50.00
B31	SP12	2t (2000r) rose	25.00	80.00
B32	SP13	4t (4000r) rose	25.00	80.00
B33	SP14	6t (6000r) grn	25.00	80.00

Nos. B30-B33 exist with double impression. Price, each $100.

Counterfeits of Nos. B30-B33 exist.

Automobile SP15

Steamship SP16

Railroad Train SP17

Airplane SP18

1922			Imperf.	
B34	SP15	lt vio	15	20
B35	SP16	violet	15	20
B36	SP17	gray bl	15	20
B37	SP18	bl gray	2.00	6.00

Inscribed "For the Hungry." Each stamp was sold for 200,000r postage and 50,000r charity.

RUSSIA

Regular Issues of 1921-23 Surcharged in Bronze, Gold or Silver

1 мая 1923 г.

Филателия—
трудящимся.

2 р. + 2 р.

1923 *Imperf.*

B38	A48	1r + 1r on 10r brn & blk (Bz)	25.00	50.00
a.		Invtd. surch.	400.00	400.00
B39	A48	1r + 1r on 10r brn & blk (G)	25.00	50.00
a.		Invtd. surch.	400.00	400.00
B40	A43	2r + 2r on 250r dl vio (Bz)	30.00	60.00
a.		Pelure paper	25.00	35.00
b.		Invtd. surch.	275.00	275.00
c.		Double surcharge		

Wmkd. Diamonds. (171)

B41	A46	4r + 4r on 5000r dl vio (Bz)	25.00	40.00
a.		Date spaced "1 923"	200.00	200.00
B42	A46	4r + 4r on 5000r dl vio (S)	350.00	350.00
			400.00	400.00
a.		Invtd. surch.	1,000.	1,000.
b.		Date spaced "1 923"	1,000.	1,000.
c.		As "b," invtd. surch.	5,000.	
		Nos. B38-B42 (5)	505.00	600.00

The inscriptions mean "Philately's Contribution to Labor." The stamps were on sale only at Moscow and for one day. The surtax was for charitable purposes. Counterfeits of No. B42 exist.

Leningrad Flood Issue.

С.С.С.Р.
пострадавшему
от наводнения
Ленинграду.

Regular Issue of 1921 Surcharged

7 к. + 20 к.

1924 *Imperf. Unwmkd.*

B43	A40	3k + 10k on 100r org	1.25	1.75
a.		Pelure paper	4.50	6.50
		Invtd. surcharge	125.00	125.00
B44	A40	7k + 20k on 200r brn	1.25	1.75
a.		Invtd. surch.	165.00	165.00
B45	A40	14k + 30k on 300r grn	1.50	3.50
a.		Pelure paper	325.00	325.00

Similar Surcharge in Red or Black.

B46	A41	14k + 40k on 500r bl (R)	2.50	3.50
a.		Double surch.	175.00	175.00
b.		Invtd. surch.	175.00	175.00
B47	A41	20k + 50k on 1000r rose red	1.75	3.50
a.		Thick paper	20.00	30.00
b.		Pelure paper	35.00	45.00
c.		Chalk surface paper	17.50	22.50
		Nos. B43-B47 (5)	8.25	14.00

The surcharge on Nos. B43 to B45 reads: "S.S.S.R. For the sufferers by the inundation at Leningrad." That on Nos. B46 and B47 reads: "S.S.S.R. For the Leningrad Proletariat, 23, IX, 1924."
No. B46 is surcharged vertically, reading down, with the value as the top line.

Orphans
SP19

Lenin as a Child
SP20

1926 *Typographed. Perf. 13½.*

B48	SP19	10k brown	1.50	1.75
B49	SP20	20k dp bl	2.00	2.75

Wmkd. Greek Border and Rosettes. (170)

B50	SP19	10k brown	1.50	1.75
B51	SP20	20k dp bl	2.00	2.75

Two kopecks of the price of each of these stamps was donated to organizations for the care of indigent children.

1927 Types of 1926 Issue.

B52	SP19	8k + 2k yel grn	75	75
B53	SP20	18k + 2k dp rose	2.00	2.50

The surtax was for child welfare.

Industrial Training
SP21

Agricultural Training
SP22

Perf. 10, 10½, 12½

1929-30 Photogravure Unwmkd.

B54	SP21	10k + 2k ol brn & org brn	3.50	3.50
a.		Perf. 10½	80.00	80.00
B55	SP21	10k + 2k ol grn ('30)	2.00	1.75
B56	SP22	20k + 2k blk brn & bl, perf. 10½	3.00	3.00
a.		Perf. 12½	55.00	55.00
b.		Perf. 10	15.00	15.00
B57	SP22	20k + 2k bl grn ('30)	3.00	3.00

Surtax was for child welfare.

"Montreal Passing Torch to Moscow"
SP23

Moscow '80 Olympic Games Emblem
SP24

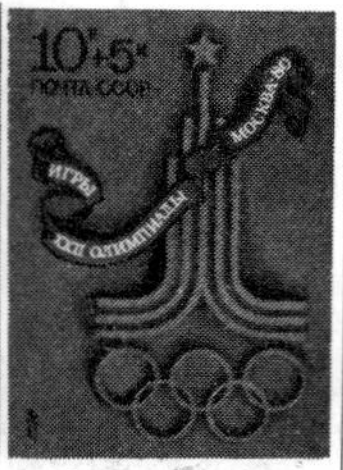

Designs: 16k+6k, like 10k+5k. 60k+30k, Aerial view of Kremlin and Moscow '80 emblem.

1976, Dec. 28 Litho. Perf. 12x12½

B58	SP23	4k + 2k multi	25	20
B59	SP24	10k + 5k multi	50	40
B60	SP24	16k + 6k multi	1.00	50

Souvenir Sheet
Photogravure Perf. 11½

B61	SP23	60k + 30k multi	4.00	3.00

22nd Olympic Games, Moscow, 1980. No. B61 contains one stamp with design extending into red brown margin; gold marginal inscription. Size: 63x83mm.

Greco-Roman Wrestling
SP25

Designs (Moscow '80 Emblem and): 6k+3k, Free-style wrestling. 10k+5k, Judo. 16k+6k, Boxing. 20k+10k, Weight lifting.

1977, June 21 Litho. Perf. 12½x12

B62	SP25	4k + 2k multi	25	15
B63	SP25	6k + 3k multi	35	25
B64	SP25	10k + 5k multi	45	35
B65	SP25	16k + 6k multi	75	50
B66	SP25	20k + 10k multi	1.00	60
		Nos. B62-B66 (5)	2.85	1.85

22nd Olympic Games, Moscow, July 19–Aug. 3, 1980.

Perf. 12½x12, 12x12½

1977, Sept. 22

Designs (Moscow '80 Emblem and): 4k+2k, Bicyclist. 6k+3k, Woman archer (vert.). 10k+5k, Sharpshooting. 16k+6k, Equestrian. 20k+10k, Fencer. 50k+25k, Equestrian and fencer.

B67	SP25	4k + 2k multi	25	15
B68	SP25	6k + 3k multi	35	25
B69	SP25	10k + 5k multi	50	35
B70	SP25	16k + 6k multi	75	50
B71	SP25	20k + 10k multi	1.00	60
		Nos. B67-B71 (5)	2.85	1.85

Souvenir Sheet
Perf. 12½x12

B72	SP25	50k + 25k multi	5.00	3.00

22nd Olympic Games, Moscow, July 19–Aug. 3, 1980. No. B72 has design extending into margin; gold marginal inscription and black control number. Size: 92x72mm.

1978, Mar. 24 Perf. 12½x12

Designs (Moscow '80 Emblem and): 4k+2k, Swimmer at start. 6k+3k, Woman diver (vert.). 10k+5k, Water polo. 16k+6k, Canoeing. 20k+10k, Canadian single. 50k+25k, Start of double scull race.

B73	SP25	4k + 2k multi	20	10
B74	SP25	6k + 3k multi	30	15
B75	SP25	10k + 5k multi	45	25
B76	SP25	16k + 6k multi	65	35
B77	SP25	20k + 10k multi	90	50
		Nos. B73-B77 (5)	2.50	1.35

Souvenir Sheet

B78	SP25	50k + 25k grn & blk	2.50	

22nd Olympic Games, Moscow, July 19–Aug. 3, 1980. No. B78 has green and black margin showing sculls, paddles and laurel; black control number. Size: 92x71mm.

Star-class Yacht
SP26

Women's Gymnastics
SP27

Keel Yachts and Moscow '80 Emblem: 6k+3k, Soling class. 10k+5k, Centerboarder 470. 16k+6k, Finn class. 20k+10k, Flying Dutchman class. 50k+25k, Catamaran Tornado (horiz.).

1978, Oct. 26 Litho. Perf. 12x12½

B79	SP26	4k + 2k multi	20	10
B80	SP26	6k + 3k multi	30	15
B81	SP26	10k + 5k multi	45	25
B82	SP26	16k + 6k multi	65	35
B83	SP26	20k + 10k multi	90	50
		Nos. B79-B83 (5)	2.50	1.35

Souvenir Sheet
Perf. 12½x12

B84	SP26	50k + 25k multi	2.50	1.75

22nd Olympic Games, Moscow, July 19–Aug. 3, 1980. No. B84 has blue marginal inscription and red control number. Size: 70x94mm.

1979, Mar. 21 Litho. Perf. 12x12½

Designs (Moscow '80 Emblem and): 6k+3k, Man on parallel bars. 10k+5k, Man on horizontal bar. 16k+6k, Woman on balance beam. 20k+10k, Woman on uneven bars. 50k+25k, Man on rings.

B85	SP27	4k + 2k multi	20	10
B86	SP27	6k + 3k multi	30	15
B87	SP27	10k + 5k multi	45	25
B88	SP27	16k + 6k multi	65	35
B89	SP27	20k + 10k multi	90	50
		Nos. B85-B89 (5)	2.50	1.35

Souvenir Sheet
Perf. 12½x12

B90	SP25	50k + 25k multi	2.50	1.75

22nd Olympic Games, Moscow, July 19–Aug. 3, 1980. No. B90 has buff and brown margin showing torch, laurel and tracks. Red control number. Size: 91x71mm.

Olympic Type of 1977-79

Designs (Moscow '80 Emblem and): 4k+2k, Soccer. 10k+5k, Basketball. 16k+6k, Women's volleyball. 16k+6k, Handball. 20k+10k, Field hockey.

Perf. 12½x12, 12x12½

1979, June Lithographed

B91	SP25	4k + 2k multi	18	10
B92	SP27	6k + 3k multi	28	15
B93	SP27	10k + 5k multi	45	25
B94	SP25	16k + 6k multi	65	35
B95	SP25	20k + 10k multi	90	48
		Nos. B91-B95 (5)	2.46	1.33

22nd Olympic Games, Moscow, July 19–Aug. 3, 1980.

Running, Moscow '80 Emblem–SP27a

1980 Litho. Perf. 12½x12, 12x12½

B96	SP27a	4k + 2k shown	18	10
B97	SP27a	4k + 2k Pole vault	18	10
B98	SP27a	6k + 3k Discus	28	15
B99	SP27a	6k + 3k Hurdles	28	15
B100	SP27a	10k + 5k Javelin	45	25
B101	SP27a	10k + 5k Walking, vert.	45	25
B102	SP27a	16k + 6k Hammer throw	65	35
B103	SP27a	16k + 6k High jump	65	35
B104	SP27a	20k + 10k Shot put	90	48
B105	SP27a	20k + 10k Long jump	90	48
		Nos. B96-B105 (10)	4.92	2.66

Souvenir Sheet

B106	SP27a	50k + 25k Relay race	2.50	1.50

22nd Olympic Games, Moscow, July 19-Aug. 3. No. B106 has multicolored margin showing Olympic bear, Mischa and runners; red control number. Size: 92x72mm. Issue dates: Nos. B96, B99, B101, B103, B105: Feb. 6; others, Mar. 12.

RUSSIA

Moscow '80 Emblem, Relief from St. Dimitri's Cathedral, Arms of Vladimir—SP28

Designs (Moscow '80 Olympic Games Emblem and): No. B108, Bridge over Klyazma River and Vladimir Hotel. No. B109, Relief from Nativity Cathedral and coat of arms (falcon), Suzdal. No. B110, Tourist complex and Pozharski Monument, Suzdal. No. B111, Frunze Monument, Ivanovo, torch and spindle. No. B112, Museum of First Soviets, Fighters of the Revolution Monument, Ivanovo.

Photogravure and Engraved

1977, Dec. 30   *Perf. 11½x12*

B107	SP28	1r +50k multi	3.00	1.50
B108	SP28	1r +50k multi	3.00	1.50
B109	SP28	1r +50k multi	3.00	1.50
B110	SP28	1r +50k multi	3.00	1.50
B111	SP28	1r +50k multi	3.00	1.50
B112	SP28	1r +50k multi	3.00	1.50
	Nos. B107-B112 (6)		18.00	9.00

"Tourism around the Golden Ring."

Fortifications and Arms of Zagorsk SP29

Designs (Moscow '80 Olympic Games Emblem, Coat of Arms and): No. B114, Gagarin Palace of Culture and new arms of Zagorsk. No. B115, Rostov Kremlin with St. John the Divine Church. No. B116, View of Rostov from Nero Lake. No. B117, Alexander Nevski and WWII soldiers' monuments, Pereyaslav. No. B118, Peter the Great monument, Pereyaslav. No. B119, Tower and wall of Monastery of the Transfiguration, Jaroslaw. No. B120, Dock and monument for Soviet heroes, Jaroslaw.

1978   *Perf. 12x11½*

B113	SP29	1r +50k multi	3.00	1.50
B114	SP29	1r +50k multi	3.00	1.50
B115	SP29	1r +50k multi	3.00	1.50
B116	SP29	1r +50k multi	3.00	1.50
B117	SP29	1r +50k multi	3.00	1.50
B118	SP29	1r +50k multi	3.00	1.50
B119	SP29	1r +50k multi	3.00	1.50
B120	SP29	1r +50k multi	3.00	1.50
	Nos. B113-B120 (8)		24.00	12.00

Issue dates: Nos. B113–B116, Oct. 16; Nos. B117–B120, Dec. 25.

1979   *Perf. 12x11½*

Designs (Moscow '80 Emblem and): No. B121, Narikaly Fortress, Tbilisi, 4th century. No. B122, Georgia Philharmonic Concert Hall, "Muse" sculpture, Tbilisi. No. B123, Chir-Dor Mosque, 17th century, Samarkand. No. B124, Peoples Friendship Museum, "Courage" monument, Tachkent. No. B125, Landscape, Erevan. B126, Armenian State Opera and Ballet Theater, Erevan.

B121	SP29	1r +50k sil & multi	4.50
B122	SP29	1r +50k gold & multi	4.50
B123	SP29	1r +50k sil & multi	4.50
B124	SP29	1r +50k gold & multi	4.50
B125	SP29	1r +50k multi	4.50
B126	SP29	1r +50k multi	4.50
	Nos. B121-B126 (6)		27.00

Issue dates: Nos. B121–B124, Sept. 5; Nos. B125–B126, Oct.

1980, Feb. 28   *Perf. 12x11½*

Designs (Moscow '80 Emblem, Coat of Arms and): No. B127, Kremlin. No. B128, Kalinin Prospect, Moscow.

B127	SP29	1r +50k gold & multi	4.50
B128	SP29	1r +50k gold & multi	4.50

1980   *Perf. 12x11½*

Designs (Moscow '80 Emblem and): No. B129, Admiralteistvo, St. Isaak Cathedral, Leningrad. No. B130, World War II Defense Monument, Leningrad. No. B131, Bogdan Khmelnitisky monument, St. Sophia's Monastery Kiev. No. B132, Metro Bridge, Dnieper River, Kiev. No. B133, Palace of Sports, obelisk, Minsk. No. B134, Republican House of Cinematography, Minsk. No. B135, Vyshgorodsky Castle, Town Hall, Tallinn. No. B136, Viru Hotel, Tallinn.

B129	SP29	1r +50k gold & multi	4.50
B130	SP29	1r +50k gold & multi	4.50
B131	SP29	1r +50k gold & multi	4.50
B132	SP29	1r +50k gold & multi	4.50
B133	SP29	1r +50k gold & multi	4.50
B134	SP29	1r +50k gold & multi	4.50
B135	SP29	1r +50k sil & multi	4.50
B136	SP29	1r +50k sil & multi	4.50
	Nos. B129-B136 (8)		36.00

Tourism. Issue dates: Nos. B129–B130, Mar. 25; Nos. B131–B136, Apr. 30.

See "Special Notices" at the front of this volume for data on the listing methods of this Catalogue, abbreviations, condition, prices and examination.

RUSSIA

AIR POST STAMPS

AP1

Fokker F-111
AP2

Plane Overprint in Red

1922 *Imperf.* **Unwmkd.**

C1	AP1	45r grn & blk	10.00	35.00

5th anniversary of October Revolution.
No. C1 was on sale only at the Moscow General Post Office. Counterfeits exist.

1923 Photogravure

C2	AP2	1r red brn		5.00
C3	AP2	3r dp bl		5.50
C4	AP2	5r green		5.50
a.		Wide "5"		1,500.
C5	AP2	10r carmine		4.00

Nos. C2 to C5 were not placed in use.

Nos. C2–C5 Surcharged **10 КОП. ЗОЛ.**

1924

C6	AP2	5k on 3r dp bl	2.00	2.00
C7	AP2	10k on 5r grn	2.00	2.00
a.		Wide "5"	750.00	750.00
b.		Invtd. surcharge	1,000.	1,000.
C8	AP2	15k on 1r red brn	2.00	2.00
a.		Inverted surch.	1,000.	1,000.
C9	AP2	20k on 10r car	2.00	2.00
a.		Invtd. surcharge	1,000.	1,000.

Airplane over Map of World
AP3

1927, Sept. 1 *Litho.* *Perf. 13x12*

C10	AP3	10k dk bl & yel brn	12.00	8.50
C11	AP3	15k dp red & ol grn	15.00	15.00

Commemorative of the first International Air Post Congress at The Hague, initiated by the U.S.S.R.

Graf Zeppelin and "Call to Complete 5-Year Plan in 4 Years"
AP4

Wmk. 226

Wmkd. Diamonds Enclosing Four Dots. (226)

1930 Photogravure. *Perf. 12½.*

C12	AP4	40k dk bl & dl bl	30.00	20.00
a.		Perf. 10½	40.00	30.00
b.		Imperf.	1,500.	1,750.
C13	AP4	80k dk car & rose	35.00	25.00
a.		Perf. 10½	35.00	25.00
b.		Imperf.	1,500.	1,750.

Issued in connection with the flight of the Graf Zeppelin from Friedrichshafen to Moscow and return.

Symbolical of Airship Communication from the Tundra to the Steppes
AP5

Airship over Dneprostroi Dam
AP6

Airship over Lenin Mausoleum
AP7

Airship Exploring Arctic Regions
AP8

Constructing an Airship
AP9

1931-32 *Imperf.* **Wmk. 170**

Photogravure.

C15	AP5	10k dk vio	15.00	15.00

Lithographed.

C16	AP6	15k gray bl	15.00	15.00

Typographed.

C17	AP7	20k dk car	15.00	20.00

Photogravure.

C18	AP8	50k blk brn	15.00	20.00
C19	AP9	1r dk grn	15.00	20.00
		Nos. C15-C19 (5)	75.00	95.00

Perf. 10½, 12, 12½ and Compound.

C20	AP5	10k dk vio	10.00	7.50

Lithographed.

C21	AP6	15k gray bl	20.00	10.00

Typographed.

C22	AP7	20k dk car	15.00	6.00
a.		20k lt red	15.00	6.00

Photogravure.

C23	AP8	50k blk brn	10.00	6.00
a.		50k gray bl (error)	350.00	400.00
C24	AP9	1r dk grn	12.00	6.00

Engraved.

Perf. 12½. **Unwmkd.**

C25	AP6	15k gray blk ('32)	2.00	1.50
a.		Perf. 10½	800.00	200.00
b.		Perf. 14	75.00	50.00
c.		Imperf.	450.00	
		Nos. C20-C25 (6)	69.00	37.00

The 11½ perforation on Nos. C20–C25 is of private origin.

North Pole Issue.

Graf Zeppelin and Icebreaker "Malygin" Transferring Mail—AP10

1931 *Imperf.* **Wmk. 170**

C26	AP10	30k dk vio	20.00	15.00
C27	AP10	35k dk grn	20.00	15.00
C28	AP10	1r gray blk	20.00	15.00
C29	AP10	2r dp ultra	25.00	20.00

Perf. 12x12½

C30	AP10	30k dk vio	40.00	40.00
C31	AP10	35k dk grn	40.00	40.00
C32	AP10	1r gray blk	40.00	40.00
C33	AP10	2r dp ultra	40.00	40.00

Map of Polar Region, Airplane and Icebreaker "Sibiryakov"—AP11

1932 *Perf. 12, 10½.* **Wmk. 170**

C34	AP11	50k car rose	50.00	35.00
a.		Perf. 10½	900.00	900.00
b.		Perf. 10½x12		1,500.
C35	AP11	1r green	50.00	30.00
a.		Perf. 12	175.00	60.00

Issued to commemorate the second International Polar Year in connection with flight to Franz-Josef Land.

Stratostat "U.S.S.R."
AP12

Furnaces of Kuznetsk
AP13

1933 Photogravure. *Perf. 14.*

C37	AP12	5k ultra	100.00	20.00
a.		Vertical pair, imperf. between		1,000.
C38	AP12	10k carmine	100.00	20.00
a.		Horizontal pair, imperf. between		1,000.
C39	AP12	20k violet	50.00	20.00

Commemorating the ascent into the stratosphere by Soviet aeronauts on September 30th, 1933.

1933 *Perf. 14.* **Wmk. 170**

Designs: 10k, Oil wells. 20k, Collective farm. 50k, Map of Moscow-Volga Canal project. 80k, Arctic cargo ship.

C40	AP13	5k ultra	15.00	8.00
C41	AP13	10k green	15.00	8.00
C42	AP13	20k carmine	30.00	15.00
C43	AP13	50k dl bl	40.00	15.00
C44	AP13	80k purple	30.00	15.00
		Nos. C40-C44 (5)	130.00	61.00

Unwmkd.

C45	AP13	5k ultra	20.00	6.00
C46	AP13	10k green	20.00	6.00
a.		Horizontal pair, imperf. between	500.00	300.00
C47	AP13	20k carmine	30.00	10.00
C48	AP13	50k dl bl	50.00	20.00
C49	AP13	80k purple	40.00	10.00
		Nos. C45-C49 (5)	160.00	52.00

Issued to commemorate the 10th anniversary of Soviet civil aviation and airmail service. Counterfeits exist.

I. D. Usyskin
AP18

Designs: 10k, A. B. Vasenko. 20k, P. F. Fedoseinko.

1934 *Perf. 11.* **Wmk. 170**

C50	AP18	5k vio brn	20.00	6.00
a.		Perf. 14	150.00	125.00
C51	AP18	10k brown	60.00	6.00
a.		Perf. 14	250.00	250.00
C52	AP18	20k ultra	60.00	8.00
a.		Perf.14	300.00	300.00

Issued to honor victims of the stratosphere disaster. See also Nos. C77–C79.

Airship "Pravada"
AP19

Airship Landing
AP20

Airship "Voroshilov"
AP21

RUSSIA

Sideview of Airship
AP22

Airship "Lenin"—AP23

1934			Perf. 14.	
C53	AP19	5k red org	20.00	4.00
C54	AP20	10k claret	20.00	6.00
C55	AP21	15k brown	20.00	8.00
C56	AP22	20k black	50.00	12.00
C57	AP23	30k ultra	90.00	12.00
	Nos. C53-C57 (5)		200.00	42.00

Capt. V. Voronin
and "Chelyuskin"—AP24

Prof. Otto Y. Schmidt—AP25

A. V. Lapidevsky   S. A. Levanevsky
AP26   AP27

"Schmidt Camp"—AP28

Designs: 15k, M. G. Slepnev. 20k, I. V. Doronin. 25k, M. V. Vodopianov. 30k, V. S. Molokov. 40k, N. P. Kamanin.

1935			Perf. 14.	
C58	AP24	1k red org	10.00	5.00
C59	AP25	3k rose car	12.00	5.00
C60	AP26	5k emerald	10.00	5.00
C61	AP27	10k dk brn	12.00	5.00
C62	AP27	15k black	15.00	5.00
C63	AP27	20k dp cl	20.00	10.00
C64	AP27	25k indigo	50.00	15.00
C65	AP27	30k dl grn	70.00	25.00
C66	AP27	40k purple	50.00	15.00
C67	AP28	50k dk ultra	50.00	20.00
	Nos. C58-C67 (10)		299.00	115.00

Aerial rescue of ice-breaker Chelyuskin crew and scientific expedition.

No. C61 Surcharged in Red

Перелет Москва— Сан-Франциско через Сев. полюс 1935   **1р.**

1935, Aug.

C68	AP27	1r on 10k dk brn	350.00	375.00
a.	Invtd. surch.		4,500.	4,500.
b.	Small ф		500.00	500.00

Issued in commemoration of the Moscow-San Francisco flight. Counterfeits exist.

Single-Engined Monoplane
AP34

Five-Engined Transport—AP35

Designs: 20k, Twin-engined cabin plane. 30k, Four-motored transport. 40k, Single-engined amphibian. 50k, Twin-motored transport. 80k, Eight-motored transport.

1937		Perf. 12.	Unwmkd.	
C69	AP34	10k yel brn & blk	2.00	1.25
	a.	Imperf.	225.00	
C70	AP34	20k gray grn & blk	2.00	1.25
C71	AP34	30k red brn & blk	2.50	1.25
C72	AP34	40k vio brn & blk	3.50	1.75
C73	AP34	50k dk vio & blk	6.00	2.75
C74	AP35	80k bl vio & brn	5.00	2.75
C75	AP35	1r blk, brn & buff	15.00	5.50
	a.	Sheet of four, imperf.	50.00	80.00
	Nos. C69-C75 (7)		36.00	16.50

Jubilee Aviation Exhibition, Moscow, Nov. 15-20.
Vertical pairs, imperf. between, exist for No. C71, price $100; No. C73, price $90.
No. C75a measures 165x89mm.

Types of 1938 Regular Issue Overprinted in Various Colors

18 АВГУСТА ДЕНЬ АВИАЦИИ СССР

1939		Typographed.		
C76	A282	10k red (C)	3.00	1.00
C76A	A285	30k bl (R)	3.00	1.00
C76B	A286	40k dl grn (Br)	3.00	1.00
C76C	A287	50k dl vio (R)	5.00	1.50
C76D	A289	1r brn (Bl)	6.00	4.00
	Nos. C76-C76D (5)		20.00	8.50

Soviet Aviation Day, Aug. 18, 1939.

Types of 1934 with "30.1.1944" Added at Lower Left.

Designs: No. C77, P. F. Fedoseinko. No. C78, I. D. Usyskin. No. C79, A. B. Vasenko.

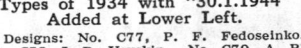

1944		Photogravure.	Perf. 12.	
C77	AP18	1r dp bl	5.00	2.00
C78	AP18	1r sl grn	5.00	2.00
C79	AP18	1r brt yel grn	5.00	2.00

Issued to commemorate the 10th anniversary of the 1934 stratosphere disaster.

Nos. 860A and 861A Surcharged in Red

АВИАПОЧТА 1944 г. 1 РУБЛЬ

1944, May 25

C80	A431	1r on 30k Prus grn	1.00	50
C81	A432	1r on 30k dp ultra	1.00	50

Planes and Soviet Flag
AP42

1948, Dec. 10		Litho.	Perf. 12½	
C82	AP42	1r dk bl	4.00	2.00

Air Force Day.

Plane over Zages, Caucasus
AP43

Plane over Farm Scene
AP44

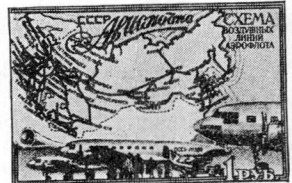

Map of Russian Air Routes and Transport Planes
AP45

Designs: No. C85, Sochi, Crimea. No. C86, Far East. No. C87, Leningrad. No. 2r, Moscow. 3r, Arctic.

Perf. 12x12½

1949, Nov. 9		Photo.	Unwmkd.	
C83	AP43	50k red brn, lem	2.00	1.50
C84	AP44	60k sep, pale buff	4.00	3.00
C85	AP44	1r org brn, yelsh	4.00	3.00
C86	AP43	1r bl, bluish	4.00	3.00
C87	AP43	1r red brn, pale fawn	4.00	3.00
C88	AP45	1r blk, ultra & red, gray	8.00	5.00
C89	AP43	2r org brn, bluish	12.00	7.00
C90	AP43	3r dk grn, bluish	20.00	12.00
	Nos. C83-C90 (8)		58.00	37.50

Plane and Mountain Stream
AP46

Globe and Plane
AP47

Design: 1r, Plane over the Don.

1955		Lithographed.	Perf. 12½x12	
C91	AP46	1r multi	3.00	75
C92	AP46	2r blk & yel grn	4.50	1.00

1955, May 31			Photogravure	
C93	AP47	2r chocolate	4.00	1.00
C94	AP47	2r dp bl	4.00	1.00

Nos. C91 and C92 Overprinted in Red

"Сев. полюс" — Москва 1955 г.

Perf. 12x12½

1955, Nov. 22		Litho.	Unwmkd.	
C95	AP46	1r multi	4.00	4.00
C96	AP46	2r blk & yel grn	6.00	6.00

Issued for use at the scientific drifting stations North Pole-4 and North Pole-5. The inscription reads "North Pole—Moscow, 1955."

Arctic Camp—AP48

1956, June 8			Perf. 12½x12	
C97	AP48	1r bl, grn, brn, yel & red	2.50	1.00

Issued to commemorate the opening of scientific drifting station North Pole-6.

Helicopter over Kremlin
AP49

Air Force Emblem and Arms of Normandy
AP50

1960, Mar. 5		Photo.	Perf. 12	
C98	AP49	60k ultra	1.25	50

Surcharged with New Value, Bars and "1961."

1961, Dec. 20				
C99	AP49	6k on 60k ultra	1.00	50

1962, Dec. 30	Perf. 11½	Unwmkd.		
C100	AP50	6k bl grn, ocher & car	75	25

Issued to commemorate the 20th anniversary of the French Normandy-Neman Escadrille, which fought on the Russian front.
Exists with "6" omitted.

RUSSIA

Jet over Map Showing Airlines in USSR—AP51

Designs: 12k, Aeroflot emblem and globe. 16k, Jet over map showing Russian international airlines.

1963, Feb.

C101	AP51	10k red, blk & tan	75	20
C102	AP51	12k bl, red, tan & blk	1.00	25
C103	AP51	16k bl, blk & red	1.35	50

Issued to commemorate the 40th anniversary of Aeroflot, the civil air fleet.

Tupolev 134 at Sheremetyevo Airport, Moscow—AP52

Designs: 10k, An-24 (Antonov) and Vnukovo Airport, Moscow. 12k, Mi-10 (Mil helicopter) and Central Airport, Moscow. 16k, Be-10 (Beriev) and Chinki Riverport, Moscow. 20k, Antei airliner and Domodedovo Airport, Moscow.

1965, Dec. 31

C104	AP52	6k org, red & vio	40	15
C105	AP52	10k lt grn, org red & gray	60	15
C106	AP52	12k lil, dk sep & lt grn	60	20
C107	AP52	16k lil, lt brn, red & grn	1.00	25
C108	AP52	20k org red, pur & gray	1.25	30
	Nos. C104-C108 (5)		3.85	1.05

Issued to publicize civil aviation.

Aviation Type of 1976

Designs (Russian Aviation Emblem and): 4k, P-4 BIS biplane, 1917. 6k, AK-1 monoplane, 1924. 10k, R-3 (ANT-3) biplane, 1925. 12k, TB-1 (ANT-4) monoplane, 1925. 16k, R-5 biplane, 1929. 20k, Scha-2 amphibian, 1930.

Lithographed and Engraved

1977, Aug. 16   *Perf. 12x11½*

C109	A2134	4k multi	20	15
C110	A2134	6k multi	25	15
C111	A2134	10k multi	35	20
C112	A2134	12k multi	40	25
C113	A2134	16k multi	60	30
C114	A2134	20k multi	75	40
	Nos. C109-C114 (6)		2.55	1.45

Russian Aviation 1917-1930.

1978, Aug. 10

Designs: 4k, PO-2 biplane, 1928. 6k, K-5 passenger plane, 1929. 10k, TB-3 cantilever monoplane, 1930. 12k, Stal-2, 1931. 16k, MBR-2 hydroplane, 1932. 20k, I-16 fighter plane, 1934.

C115	A2134	4k multi	20	10
C116	A2134	6k multi	25	15
C117	A2134	10k multi	35	15
C118	A2134	12k multi	40	20
C119	A2134	16k multi	55	25
C120	A2134	20k multi	65	30
	Nos. C115-C120 (6)		2.40	1.15

Russian aviation 1928-1934.

Jet and Compass Rose AP53

1978, Aug. 4   *Litho.*   *Perf. 12*

C121	AP53	32k dk bl	1.00	50

Aeroflot Plane AH-28—AP54

Designs: Various Aeroflot planes.

Photogravure and Engraved

1979   *Perf. 11½x12*

C122	AP54	2k shown	10	10
C123	AP54	3k YAK-42	15	10
C124	AP54	10k T4-154	30	15
C125	AP54	15k IL76 transport	50	25
C126	AP54	32k IL86 jet liner	1.00	60
	Nos. C122-C126 (5)		2.05	1.20

AIR POST OFFICIAL STAMPS

Used on mail from Russian embassy in Berlin to Moscow. Surcharged on Consular Fee stamps. Currency: the German mark.

OA1

Surcharge in Carmine

1922, July   *Litho.*   *Perf. 13½*

Bicolored Burelage in Parenthesis

CO1	OA1	12m on 2.25r dp bl (grn & org)	100.00	
CO2	OA1	24m on 3r dk grn (pink & grn)	100.00	
CO3	OA1	120m on 2.25r dp bl (grn & org)	150.00	
CO4	OA1	600m on 3r dk grn (pink & grn)	200.00	
CO5	OA1	1200m on 10k brn (grn & org)	350.00	
CO6	OA1	1200m on 50k grn (red & yel)	4,000.	
CO7	OA1	1200m on 2.25r dp bl (grn & org)	700.00	
CO8	OA1	1200m on 3r dk grn (pink & grn)	1,100.	

Three types of each denomination, distinguished by shape of "C" in surcharge and length of second line of surcharge. Used copies have pen or crayon cancel.

SPECIAL DELIVERY STAMPS.

Motorcycle Courier   Express Truck
SD1   SD2

Design: 80k, Locomotive.

Perf. 12½x12, 12x12½.

1932   *Photogravure.*   *Wmk. 170*

E1	SD1	5k dl brn	12.50	10.00
E2	SD2	10k vio brn	17.50	10.00
E3	SD2	80k dl grn	40.00	25.00

POSTAGE DUE STAMPS.

Доплата
3 коп.
золотом

Regular Issue of 1918 Surcharged in Red or Carmine

1924-25   *Perf. 13½*   *Unwmkd.*

J1	A33	1k on 35k bl	15	60
J2	A33	3k on 35k bl	15	60
J3	A33	5k on 35k bl	15	60
a.	Imperf.		90.00	
J4	A33	8k on 35k bl ('25)	35	60
a.	Imperf.		60.00	
J5	A33	10k on 35k bl	25	75
	Pair, one without surcharge	40.00		
J6	A33	12k on 70k brn	20	60
J7	A33	14k on 35k bl ('25)	20	60
a.	Imperf.		100.00	
J8	A33	32k on 35k bl	20	70
J9	A33	40k on 35k bl	20	70
a.	Imperf.		90.00	
	Nos. J1-J9 (9)		1.85	5.75

Surcharge is found inverted on Nos. J1-J2, J4, J6-J9; price $25-$50. Double on Nos. J2, J4-J6; price, $40-$50.

Regular Issue of 1921 Surcharged in Violet

Доплата
1 коп.
Imperf.

1924

J10	A40	1k on 100r org	4.00	7.00
a.	1k on 100r yel	5.00	9.00	
b.	Pelure paper	5.00	9.00	
c.	Invtd. surch.	80.00		

D1

1925   *Litho. or Typo.*   *Perf. 12*

J11	D1	1k red	3.00	1.00
J12	D1	2k violet	1.50	1.50
J13	D1	3k lt bl	1.50	1.50
a.	Perf. 14½x14	6.00	6.00	
J14	D1	7k orange	1.50	1.50
a.	Perf. 14½x14	12.50	12.50	
J15	D1	8k green	1.50	2.00
J16	D1	10k dk bl	2.50	3.00
a.	Perf. 14½x14	50.00	40.00	
J17	D1	14k brown	3.00	3.00
a.	Perf. 14½x14	3.50	3.50	
	Nos. J11-J17 (7)		14.50	13.50

1925   *Typographed.*

   Perf. 12   *Wmk. 170*

J18	D1	1k red	60	75
J19	D1	2k violet	60	75
J20	D1	3k lt bl	75	1.00
J21	D1	7k orange	75	1.00
J22	D1	8k green	75	1.00
J23	D1	10k dk bl	1.00	1.50
J24	D1	14k brown	1.50	2.00
	Nos. J18-J24 (7)		5.95	8.00

BINGO!

Want more from an advertiser? Use our handy Reader Service Card at the back of this book and hit the jackpot.

A well-informed dealer has services to offer that would be helpful toward building your collection.

RUSSIA—Offices in China 397

Wenden (Livonia.)
(vĕn'dĕn [lĭ·vō'nĭ·ȧ])

A former district of Livonia, a province of the Russian Empire, which became part of Latvia, under the name of Vidzeme.

Used prices for Nos. L2–L12 are for pen-canceled copies. Postmarked specimens sell for considerably more.

	A1		
1862		Imperf.	Unwmkd.
L1	A1	(2k) blue	5.00
a.		Tête bêche pair	25.00

No. L1 was never put in use.

 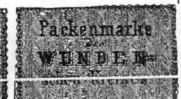

	A2		A3	
1863				
L2	A2	(2k) rose & blk	200.00	200.00
a.		Background inverted	400.00	400.00
L3	A3	(4k) bl grn & blk	100.00	100.00
a.		(4k) yel grn & blk	200.00	200.00
b.		Half used as 2k on cover		2,000.
c.		Background inverted	200.00	200.00
d.		As "a," background inverted	300.00	300.00

The official imitations of Nos. L2 and L3 have a single instead of a double hyphen after "WENDEN".

	A4	A5		A6
1863–71				
L4	A4	(2k) rose & grn	40.00	20.00
a.		Yellowish paper		
b.		Grn frame around central oval	50.00	30.00
c.		Tête bêche pair	2,000.	
L5	A5	(2k) rose & grn ('64)	100.00	75.00
L6	A6	(2k) rose & grn	30.00	30.00

Official imitations of Nos. L4b and L5 have a rosa instead of a greenish line around the central oval. The first official imitation of No. L6 has the central oval 5½ instead of 6¾ mm. wide; the second imitation is less clearly printed than the original and the top of the "f" of "Briefmarke" is too much hooked.

	A7		A8
1872–75			Perf. 12½
L7	A7	(2k) red & grn	35.00	30.00

	L8	A8	2k yel grn & red ('75)	10.00	10.00
a.			Numeral in upper right corner resembles an inverted "3"	40.00	40.00

Reprints of No. L8 have no horizontal lines in the background. Those of No. L8a have the impression blurred and only traces of the horizontal lines.

	A9		A10
1878–80			
L9	A9	2k grn & red	10.00	10.00
a.		Imperf.		
L10	A9	2k blk, grn & red ('80)	10.00	10.00
a.		Imperf. pair	40.00	

No. L9 has been reprinted in blue green and yellow green with perforation 11½ and in gray green with perforation 12½ or imperforate.

1884			Perf. 11½
L11	A9	2k blk, grn & red	3.00	3.00
a.		Grn arm omitted	30.00	
b.		Arm inverted	30.00	
c.		Arm double	40.00	
d.		Imperf. pair	30.00	

1901			Engraved
L12	A10	2k dk grn & brn	5.00	5.00
a.		Tête bêche pair		
b.		Imperf. pair	25.00	

OCCUPATION STAMPS.
Issued under Finnish Occupation.

Finnish Stamps of 1917-18 Overprinted **Aunus**

1919		Perf. 14.	Unwmkd.
N1	A19	5p green	15.00	15.00
N2	A19	10p rose	15.00	15.00
N3	A19	20p buff	15.00	15.00
N4	A19	40p red vio	15.00	15.00
N5	A19	50p org brn	125.00	125.00
N6	A19	1m dl rose & blk	135.00	135.00
N7	A19	5m vio & blk	500.00	500.00
N8	A19	10m brn & blk	875.00	875.00
		Nos. N1-N8 (8)	1,695.	1,695.

"Aunus" is the Finnish name for Olonets, a town of Russia.
Counterfeits exists of overprints on Nos. N1–N8.

Issued under German Occupation.

Germany Nos. 506 to 523 Overprinted in Black **OSTLAND** Typographed.

1941-43		Perf. 14.	Unwmkd.
N9	A115	1pf gray blk	5	5
N10	A115	3pf lt brn	5	5
N11	A115	4pf slate	5	5
N12	A115	5pf dp yel grn	5	5
N13	A115	6pf purple	5	5
N14	A115	8pf red	5	5
N15	A115	10pf dk brn ('43)	20	1.50
N16	A115	12pf car ('43)	20	1.50

Engraved.

N17	A115	10pf dk brn	30	35
N18	A115	12pf brt car	30	35
N19	A115	15pf brn lake	5	5
N20	A115	16pf pck grn	5	5
N21	A115	20pf blue	5	5
N22	A115	24pf org brn	5	5
N23	A115	25pf brt ultra	5	10
N24	A115	30pf ol grn	5	10
N25	A115	40pf brt red vio	5	10
N26	A115	50pf myr grn	5	10
N27	A115	60pf dk red brn	5	10
N28	A115	80pf indigo	10	15
		Nos. N9-N28 (20)	1.85	4.85

Issued for use in Estonia, Latvia and Lithuania.

Same Overprinted in Black **UKRAINE**
Typographed.

N29	A115	1pf gray blk	5	5
N30	A115	3pf lt brn	5	5
N31	A115	4pf slate	5	5
N32	A115	5pf dp yel grn	5	5
N33	A115	6pf purple	5	5
N34	A115	8pf red	5	5
N35	A115	10pf dk brn ('43)	15	1.50
N36	A115	12pf car ('43)	15	1.50

Engraved.

N37	A115	10pf dk brn	35	50
N38	A115	12pf brt car	35	50
N39	A115	15pf brn lake	5	5
N40	A115	16pf pck grn	5	5
N41	A115	20pf blue	5	5
N42	A115	24pf org brn	5	5
N43	A115	25pf brt ultra	5	10
N44	A115	30pf ol grn	5	10
N45	A115	40pf brt red vio	5	10
N46	A115	50pf myr grn	5	10
N47	A115	60pf dk red brn	5	10
N48	A115	80pf indigo	10	25
		Nos. N29-N48 (20)	1.85	5.25

Army of the Northwest
(Gen. Nicolai N. Yudenich)

Russian Stamps of 1909-18 Overprinted in Black or Red **Сѣв. Зап. Армія**

On Stamps of 1909–12
Perf. 14 to 15 and Compound.

1919, Aug. 1				
1	A14	2k green	3.50	6.00
2	A14	5k claret	3.50	6.00
3	A15	10k dk bl (R)	4.00	7.00
4	A11	15k red brn & bl	4.00	7.00
5	A8	20k bl & car	7.00	11.00
6	A11	25k grn & gray vio	12.00	17.00
7	A8	50k brn vio & grn	7.00	9.00

Perf. 13½.

8	A9	1r pale brn, dk brn & org	15.00	20.00
9	A13	10r scar, yel & gray	45.00	75.00

On Stamps of 1917
Imperf.

10	A14	3k red	2.00	5.00
11	A12	3.50r mar & lt grn	25.00	40.00
12	A13	5r dk bl, grn & pale bl	20.00	35.00
13	A12	7r dk grn & pink	110.00	175.00

No. 2 Surcharged
Perf. 14, 14½ x 15.

14	A14	10k on 5k cl	3.00	5.50
		Nos. 1-14 (14)	261.00	418.50

Nos. 1–14 exist with inverted overprint or surcharge. The 1, 3½, 5, 7 and 10 rubles with red overprint are trial printings (price $40 each). The 20k on 14k, perforated, and the 1, 2, 5, 15, 70k and 1r imperforate were overprinted but never placed in use. Price: $80, $30, $40, $40, $40, $40 and $40.

These stamps were in use from Aug. 1 to Oct. 15, 1919.
Counterfeits of Nos. 1–14 abound.

Army of the North

A1 A2

	A3	A4	A5
1919, Sept.		Typo.	Imperf.
1	A1	5k brn vio	25	1.00
2	A2	10k blue	25	1.00
3	A3	15k yellow	25	1.00
4	A4	20k rose	25	1.00
5	A5	50k green	25	1.00
		Nos. 1-5 (5)	1.25	5.00

The letters OKCA are the initials of Russian words meaning "Special Corps, Army of the North". The stamps were in use from about the end of September to the end of December, 1919.

(General Miller)

A set of seven stamps of this design was prepared in 1919, but not issued.

RUSSIAN OFFICES ABROAD.

For various reasons the Russian Empire maintained Post Offices to handle its correspondence in several foreign countries. These were similar to the Post Offices in foreign countries maintained by other world powers.

Offices in China

100 Kopecks = 1 Ruble
100 Cents = 1 Dollar (1917)

Russian Stamps Overprinted in Blue or Red **КИТАЙ**

On Issues of 1889-92.
Horizontally Laid Paper.
1899-1904 Perf. 14½x15 Wmk. 168

1	A10	1k org (Bl)	75	1.00
2	A10	2k yel grn (R)	75	1.00
3	A10	3k car (Bl)	75	1.00
4	A10	5k red vio (Bl)	75	1.00
5	A7	7k dk bl (R)	2.00	3.00
6	A8	10k dk bl (R)	2.00	3.00
7	A8	50k vio & grn (Bl) ('04)	6.00	7.00

Perf. 13½.

8	A9	1r lt brn, brn & org (Bl) ('04)	32.50	35.00
		Nos. 1-8 (8)	45.50	52.00

1904-08

On Issues of 1902-05.
Vertically Laid Paper.
Perf. 14½ to 15 and Compound.
Overprinted in Black, Red or Blue.

9	A8	4k rose red (Bl)	2.00	3.00
10	A10	7k dk bl (R)	12.00	17.50
11	A8	10k dk bl (R)	900.00	1,000.
a.		Groundwork inverted	3,000.	1,200.
12	A11	14k bl & rose (R)	3.00	5.00
13	A11	15k brn vio & bl (Bl) ('08)	5.00	7.00
14	A8	20k bl & car (Bl)	1.50	3.00
15	A11	25k dl grn & lil (R) ('08)	7.50	10.00
16	A11	35k dk vio & grn (Bl)	3.00	5.00
17	A8	50k vio & grn (Bl)	65.00	85.00
18	A11	70k brn & org (Bl)	9.00	17.50

RUSSIA—Offices in China—Offices in the Turkish Empire

Perf. 13½.

19	A9	1r lt brn, brn & org (Bl)	14.00	17.50
20	A12	3.50r blk & gray (R)	17.50	22.50
21	A13	5r dk bl, grn & pale bl (R) ('07)	10.00	12.00
22	A12	7r blk & yel (Bl)	17.50	20.00
23	A13	10r scar, yel & gray (Bl) ('07)	55.00	75.00
		Nos. 9-10, 12-23 (14)	222.00	300.00

On Issues of 1909-12.
Wove Paper.
Lozenges of Varnish on Face.
1910-16 Perf. 14x14½. Unwmkd.

24	A14	1k org yel (Bl)	40	50
25	A14	1k org yel (Bl Bk)	5.50	7.50
26	A14	2k grn (Bk)	40	50
27	A14	2k grn (Bl)	6.50	9.50
a.		Double overprint (Bk and Bl)		
28	A14	3k rose red (Bl)	40	50
29	A14	3k rose red (Bk)	11.00	15.00
30	A15	4k car (Bl)	40	50
31	A15	4k car (Bk)	8.00	11.00
32	A14	7k lt bl (Bk)	40	50
33	A15	10k bl (Bk)	40	50
34	A11	14k bl & rose (Bk)	85	1.00
35	A11	14k bl & rose (Bl)	5.00	7.00
36	A11	15k dl vio & bl (Bk)	50	1.00
37	A8	20k bl & car (Bk)	50	1.00
38	A11	25k grn & vio (Bl)	3.50	5.00
39	A11	25k grn & vio (Bk)	85	2.50
40	A11	35k vio & grn (Bk)	40	50
42	A8	50k grn & vio (Bl)	40	50
43	A8	50k brn vio & grn (Bk)	17.50	25.00
44	A11	70k lt brn & org (Bl)	40	50

Perf. 13½.

45	A9	1r pale brn, brn & org (Bl)	1.50	1.75
47	A13	5r dk bl, grn & pale bl (R)	11.00	13.00
		Nos. 24-47 (22)	75.80	104.75

Russian Stamps of 1902-12 Surcharged:

a   b

c

1917
On Stamps of 1909-12.
Perf. 11½, 13½, 14, 14½x15.

50	A14(a)	1c on 2k dl org yel	75	6.00
51	A14(a)	2c on 2k dl grn	75	6.00
52	A14(a)	3c on 3k car	75	6.00
a.		Invtd. surch.	100.00	
b.		Dbl. surch.	225.00	
53	A15(a)	4c on 4k car	1.50	5.00
54	A14(a)	5c on 5k cl	1.50	17.50
55	A15(b)	10c on 10k dk bl	1.50	17.50
a.		Invtd. surch.	125.00	125.00
b.		Dbl. surch.	175.00	
56	A11(b)	14c on 14k dk bl & car	1.50	12.50
a.		Imperf.	9.00	
b.		Invtd. surch.	150.00	
57	A11(a)	15c on 15k brn lil & dp bl	1.50	17.50
58	A8(b)	20c on 20k bl & car	1.50	17.50
59	A11(a)	25c on 25k grn & vio	1.50	17.50
60	A11(a)	35c on 35k brn vio & grn	2.00	17.50
a.		Invtd. surch.	40.00	
61	A8(a)	50c on 50k brn vio & grn	1.75	17.50
62	A11(a)	70c on 70k brn & red org	1.75	17.50
63	A9(c)	$1 on 1r pale brn, brn & org	1.75	17.50
		Nos. 50-63 (14)	20.00	193.00

On Stamps of 1902-05.
Vertically Laid Paper.
Perf. 11½, 13, 13½, 13½x11½.

64	A12(c)	$3.50 on 3.50r blk & gray	12.50	50.00
65	A13(c)	$5 on 5r dk bl, grn & pale bl	12.50	50.00
66	A12(c)	$7 on 7r blk & yel	12.50	50.00

On Stamps of 1915.
Wove Paper.
Perf. 13½. Unwmkd.

68	A13(c)	$5 on 5r ind, grn & lt bl	20.00	65.00
a.		Invtd. surch.	250.00	
70	A13(c)	$10 on 10r car lake, yel & gray	25.00	150.00
		Nos. 64-70 (5)	82.50	365.00

The surcharge on Nos. 64-70 is in larger type than the $1.

On Stamps of 1909-12.
1920   Perf. 14, 14½x15.

72	A14	1c on 1k dl org yel	60.00	90.00
73	A14	2c on 2k dl grn (R)	30.00	60.00
74	A14	3c on 3k car	30.00	60.00
75	A15	4c on 4k car	40.00	75.00
a.		Inverted surcharge	150.00	
76	A14	5c on 5k cl	40.00	75.00
77	A15	10c on 10k dk bl (R)	125.00	250.00
78	A14	10c on 10k on 7k bl (R)	125.00	250.00

On Stamps of 1917-18.
Imperf.

79	A14	1c on 1k org	35.00	70.00
a.		Inverted surcharge	40.00	90.00
80	A14	5c on 5k cl	50.00	175.00
a.		Invtd. surch.	175.00	
b.		Double surcharge	250.00	
c.		Surcharged "Cent" only	100.00	
		Nos. 72-80 (9)	535.00	1,000.

Offices in the Turkish Empire

Various powers maintained post offices in the Turkish Empire before World War I by authority of treaties which ended with the signing of the Treaty of Lausanne in 1923. The foreign post offices were closed Oct. 27, 1923.

100 Kopecks = 1 Ruble
40 Paras = 1 Piastre (1900)

Coat of Arms
A1

Typographed.
1863   Imperf.   Unwmkd.

1	A1	6k blue	450.00	1,375.
a.		6k lt bl, thin paper	400.00	1,750.
b.		6k dk bl, chlky paper	150.00	

A2   A3

1865   Lithographed

2	A2	(2k) brn & bl	1,250.	1,100.
3	A3	(20k) bl & red	1,600.	1,350.

Twenty-eight varieties of each.

A4   A5

1866   Horizontal Network.

4	A4	(2k) rose & pale bl	50.00	75.00
5	A5	(20k) dp bl & rose	90.00	160.00

1867   Vertical Network.

6	A4	(2k) rose & pale bl	125.00	165.00
7	A5	(20k) dp bl & rose	200.00	325.00

The initials inscribed on Nos. 2 to 7 are those of the Russian Company of Navigation and Trade. Stamps of Russian Offices in the Turkish Empire overprinted with these initials were used in the Ukraine and are listed under that country.

The official imitations of Nos. 2 to 7 are on yellowish white paper. The colors are usually paler than those of the originals and there are minor differences in the designs.

A6

Horizontally Laid Paper.
Wmkd. Wavy Lines. (168)
1868   Typographed.   Perf. 11½.

8	A6	1k brown	55.00	30.00
9	A6	3k green	50.00	30.00
10	A6	5k blue	50.00	30.00
11	A6	10k car & grn	50.00	30.00

Colors of Nos. 8-11 dissolve in water.

1872-90   Perf. 14½x15

12	A6	1k brown	12.50	6.00
a.		Vertically laid	75.00	
13	A6	3k green	40.00	4.00
a.		Vertically laid	75.00	30.00
14	A6	5k blue	7.50	2.00
a.		Vertically laid	75.00	30.00
15	A6	10k car & grn	25.00	7.50
a.		Vertically laid	175.00	75.00
b.		10k pale red & grn ('90)	2.00	1.50

Nos. 12-15 exist imperf.

No. 15 Surcharged in Black or Blue:

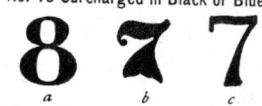
a   b   c

1876

16	A6(a)	8k on 10k car & grn (Bk)	135.00	100.00
a.		Vertically laid		
b.		Inverted surcharge	600.00	
17	A6(a)	8k on 10k car & grn (Bl)	140.00	125.00
a.		Vertically laid		
b.		Inverted surcharge		

1879

18	A6(b)	7k on 10k car & grn (Bk)	150.00	125.00
a.		Vertically laid		
b.		Inverted surcharge		
19	A6(b)	7k on 10k car & grn (Bl)	200.00	165.00
a.		Vertically laid		
b.		Inverted surcharge		
19C	A6(c)	7k on 10k car & grn (Bl)	1,250.	900.00
19D	A6(c)	7k on 10k car & grn (Bk)	900.00	750.00

Nos. 16-19D have been extensively counterfeited.

1879   Perf. 14½x15

20	A6	1k blk & yel	4.50	2.50
a.		Vertically laid	13.50	12.50
21	A6	2k blk & rose	7.00	7.00
a.		Vertically laid	15.00	10.00
22	A6	7k car & gray	10.00	3.00
a.		Vertically laid	40.00	25.00

1884

23	A6	1k orange	50	50
24	A6	2k green	75	75
25	A6	5k pale red vio	3.00	1.75
26	A6	7k blue	1.50	75

Nos. 23-26 Imperforate are believed to be proofs.

No. 23 surcharged "40 PARAS" is bogus, though some copies are postally used.

A7   A8   A9

A10   A11

1900
Surcharged in Blue, Black or Red.
Horizontally Laid Paper.

27	A7	4pa on 1k org (Bl)	25	25
a.		Invtd. surcharge	45.00	45.00
28	A7	4pa on 1k org (Bk)	25	25
29	A7	10pa on 2k grn (R)	45.00	45.00
a.		Inverted surcharge	35	35
30	A8	1pi on 10k dk bl (R)	75	90
a.		Inverted surcharge		

1903-05
Vertically Laid Paper.

31	A7	10pa on 2k yel grn (R)	45	65
a.		Invtd. surcharge	100.00	
32	A8	20pa on 4k rose red (Bl)	45	65
a.		Invtd. surcharge	35.00	
33	A8	1pi on 10k dk bl (R)	45	60
a.		Groundwork inverted	80.00	25.00
34	A8	2pi on 20k bl & car (Bk)	1.00	1.25
35	A8	5pi on 50k brn vio & grn (R)	2.50	2.75
36	A9	7pi on 70k brn & org (Bl)	3.00	4.00

Perf. 13½.

37	A10	10pi on 1r lt brn, brn & org (Bl)	4.50	6.00
38	A11	35pi on 3.50r blk & gray (R)	14.00	17.50

RUSSIA—Offices in the Turkish Empire

39	A11	70pi on 7r blk & yel (R)	16.00	20.00
		Nos. 31-39 (9)	42.35	53.40

A12

A13 **A14**

Wove Paper.
Lozenges of Varnish on Face.
1909   Perf. 14½x15.   Unwmkd.

40	A12	5pa on 1k org	40	50
41	A12	10pa on 2k grn	50	75
a.		Invtd. surcharge	12.00	12.00
42	A12	20pa on 4k car	1.00	1.25
43	A12	1pia on 10k bl	1.10	1.50
44	A12	5pia on 50k vio & grn	2.25	2.50
45	A12	7pia on 70k brn & org	3.50	4.00

Perf. 13½.

46	A13	10pia on 1r brn & org	5.00	7.00
47	A14	35pia on 3.50r mar & lt grn	17.50	20.00
48	A14	70pia on 7r dk grn & pink	30.00	35.00
		Nos. 40-48 (9)	61.25	72.50

Nos. 40 to 48 were issued to commemorate the 50th anniversary of the establishing of the Russian Post Offices in the Levant.

Stamps of 1909
Overprinted with Names of Various Cities.
Overprinted "Constantinople".
Black Overprint.
1909-10   Perf. 14½x15.

61	A12	5pa on 1k org	20	40
a.		"Consnantinople"	2.50	
b.		"Constantinople"	2.50	
62	A12	10pa on 2k grn	20	40
a.		"Constantinople"	2.00	
b.		"Constantinople"	3.00	
63	A12	20pa on 4k car	45	65
a.		"Constantinople"	3.00	
b.		"Constantinople"	3.00	
64	A12	1pia on 10k bl	50	75
a.		"Constantinople"	4.00	
b.		"Constantinople"	4.00	
65	A12	5pia on 50k vio & grn	1.00	1.25
a.		"Constantinople"	4.00	
b.		"Constantinople"	4.00	
66	A12	7pia on 70k brn & org	2.25	3.00
a.		"Constantinople"	7.50	
b.		"Constantinople"	7.50	

Perf. 13½.

67	A13	10pia on 1r brn & org	9.00	12.50
a.		"Constanttnople"	22.50	
68	A14	35pia on 3.50r mar & lt grn	27.50	40.00
a.		"Constautinople"	50.00	
b.		"Constantjnople"	50.00	
69	A14	70pia on 7r dk grn & pink	50.00	60.00
a.		"Constautinople"	90.00	
b.		"Constantjnople"	90.00	

Blue Overprint.
Perf. 14½x15.

70	A12	5pa on 1k org	4.00	5.00
a.		"Consnantinople"	12.00	
		Nos. 61-70 (10)	95.10	123.95

Overprinted "Jaffa".
Black Overprint.

71	A12	5pa on 1k org	2.25	3.50
a.		Invtd. overprint	17.50	
72	A12	10pa on 2k grn	3.00	4.00
a.		Invtd. overprint	17.50	
73	A12	20pa on 4k car	3.50	5.00
a.		Invtd. overprint	40.00	
74	A12	1pia on 10k bl	4.00	5.00
a.		Double overprint	50.00	
75	A12	5pia on 50k vio & grn	10.00	10.00
76	A12	7pia on 70k brn & org	12.00	14.00

Perf. 13½.

77	A13	10pia on 1r brn & org	40.00	55.00
78	A14	35pia on 3.50r mar & lt grn	100.00	125.00
79	A14	70pia on 7r dk grn & pink	135.00	175.00

Blue Overprint.
Perf. 14½x15.

80	A12	5pa on 1k org	6.50	9.00
		Nos. 71-80 (10)	316.25	405.50

Overprinted "Ierusalem".
Black Overprint.

81	A12	5pa on 1k org	2.00	3.00
a.		Inverted overprint	20.00	
b.		"erusalem"	12.50	
82	A12	10pa on 2k grn	3.00	4.00
a.		Inverted overprint	20.00	
b.		"erusalem"	12.50	
83	A12	20pa on 4k car	4.00	5.00
a.		Inverted overprint	20.00	
b.		"erusalem"	12.50	
84	A12	1pia on 10k bl	4.00	5.00
a.		"erusalem"	17.50	
85	A12	5pia on 50k vio & grn	7.00	10.00
a.		"erusalem"	35.00	
86	A12	7pia on 70k brn & org	15.00	17.50
a.		"erusalem"	35.00	

Perf. 13½.

87	A13	10pia on 1r brn & org	55.00	70.00
88	A14	35pia on 3.50r mar & lt grn	120.00	150.00
89	A14	70pia on 7r dk grn & pink	150.00	200.00

Blue Overprint.
Perf. 14½x15.

90	A12	5pa on 1k org	7.50	11.00
		Nos. 81-90 (10)	367.50	475.50

Overprinted "Kerassunde".
Black Overprint.

91	A12	5pa on 1k org	40	60
a.		Inverted overprint	12.50	
92	A12	10pa on 2k grn	40	65
a.		Inverted overprint	12.50	
93	A12	20pa on 4k car	60	90
a.		Inverted overprint	15.00	
94	A12	1pia on 10k bl	75	1.00
95	A12	5pia on 50k vio & grn	1.50	1.75
96	A12	7pia on 70k brn & org	2.00	3.00

Perf. 13½.

97	A13	10pia on 1r brn & org	8.00	11.00
98	A14	35pia on 3.50r mar & lt grn	25.00	30.00
99	A14	70pia on 7r dk grn & pink	35.00	45.00

Blue Overprint.
Perf. 14½x15.

100	A12	5pa on 1k org	5.50	8.00
		Nos. 91-100 (10)	79.15	101.90

Overprinted "Mont Athos".
Black Overprint.

101	A12	5pa on 1k org	60	1.25
a.		"Mont Atho"	20.00	
b.		Inverted overprint	22.50	
102	A12	10pa on 2k grn	60	1.25
a.		"Mont Atho"	20.00	
b.		Inverted overprint	22.50	
103	A12	20pa on 4k car	70	1.35
a.		"Mont Atho"	22.50	
b.		Inverted overprint	27.50	
104	A12	1pia on 10k bl	1.25	1.75
a.		"Mont Atho"	30.00	
b.		Double ovpt.	35.00	
c.		Same as "a," double overprint	125.00	
105	A12	5pia on 50k vio & grn	4.00	5.00
a.		"Mont Atho"	40.00	
106	A12	7pia on 70k brn & org	6.00	8.50
a.		"Mont Atho"	60.00	
b.		Pair, one without "Mont Athos"	25.00	

Perf. 13½.

107	A13	10pia on 1r brn & org	20.00	25.00
108	A14	35pia on 3.50r mar & lt grn	45.00	55.00
109	A14	70pia on 7r dk grn & pink	80.00	110.00

Blue Overprint.
Perf. 14½x15.

110	A12	5pa on 1k org	7.00	12.50
a.		"Mont Atho"	17.50	
		Nos. 101-110 (10)	165.15	221.60

Overprinted G. Лоонz

111	A12	5pa on 1k org	60	85
112	A12	10pa on 2k grn	60	85
113	A12	20pa on 4k car	75	1.25
114	A12	1pia on 10k bl	1.50	2.50
115	A12	5pia on 50k vio & grn	3.00	4.00
116	A12	7pia on 70k brn & org	5.00	7.00

Perf. 13½.

117	A13	10pia on 1r brn & org	30.00	35.00
		Nos. 111-117 (7)	41.45	51.45

The overprint is larger on No. 117.

Overprinted "Salonique".
Black Overprint.
Perf. 14½x15.

131	A12	5pa on 1k org	50	1.00
a.		Inverted overprint	10.00	
b.		Pair, one without overprint		
132	A12	10pa on 2k grn	75	1.50
a.		Inverted overprint	15.00	
133	A12	20pa on 4k car	1.00	1.50
a.		Invtd. overprint	20.00	
134	A12	1pia on 10k bl	1.00	1.50
135	A12	5pia on 50k vio & grn	2.00	3.00
136	A12	7pia on 70k brn & org	4.00	5.00

Perf. 13½.

137	A13	10pia on 1r brn & org	20.00	25.00
138	A14	35pia on 3.50r mar & lt grn	45.00	55.00
139	A14	70pia on 7r dk grn & pink	65.00	85.00

Blue Overprint.
Perf. 14½x15.

140	A12	5pa on 1k org	10.00	12.00
		Nos. 131-140 (10)	149.25	190.50

Overprinted "Smyrne".
Black Overprint.

141	A12	5pa on 1k org	40	75
a.		Double overprint	7.50	
b.		Invtd. overprint	5.00	6.00
		"Smyrn"	5.00	
142	A12	10pa on 2k grn	40	75
a.		Inverted ovpeint	12.50	
		"Smyrn"	5.00	6.00
143	A12	20pa on 4k car	75	1.00
a.		Invtd. overprint	15.00	
		"Smyrn"	5.00	6.00
144	A12	1pia on 10k bl	75	1.25
		"Smyrn"	7.00	8.00
145	A12	5pia on 50k vio & grn	1.50	2.50
		"Smyrn"	7.00	8.00
146	A12	7pia on 70k brn & org	3.00	5.00
a.		"Smyrn"	10.00	10.00

Perf. 13½.

147	A13	10pia on 1r brn & org	15.00	17.50
148	A14	35pia on 3.50r mar & lt grn	30.00	35.00
149	A14	70pia on 7r dk grn & pink	45.00	55.00

Blue Overprint.
Perf. 14½x15.

150	A12	5pa on 1k org	5.50	8.00
		Nos. 141-150 (10)	102.30	126.75

Overprinted "Trebizonde".
Black Overprint.

151	A12	5pa on 1k org	40	75
a.		Invtd. ovpt.	7.00	
152	A12	10pa on 2k grn	40	75
a.		Invtd. ovpt.	10.00	
b.		Pair, one without "Trebizonde"		
153	A12	20pa on 4k car	75	1.00
a.		Invtd. overprint	15.00	
154	A12	1pia on 10k bl	75	1.25
a.		Pair, one without "Trebizonde"	40.00	
155	A12	5pia on 50k vio & grn	1.50	2.50
156	A12	7pia on 70k brn & org	3.00	5.00

Perf. 13½.

157	A13	10pia on 1r brn & org	15.00	17.50
158	A14	35pia on 3.50r mar & lt grn	30.00	35.00
159	A14	70pia on 7r dk grn & pink	45.00	55.00

Blue Overprint.
Perf. 14½x15.

160	A12	5pa on 1k org	5.50	8.00
		Nos. 151-160 (10)	102.30	126.75

On Nos. 158 and 159 the overprint is spelled "Trebisonde".

1910
Overprinted "Beyrouth".
Black Overprint.

161	A12	5pa on 1k org	40	75
162	A12	10pa on 2k grn	40	75
a.		Invtd. ovpt.	30.00	
163	A12	20pa on 4k car	75	1.00
164	A12	1pia on 10k bl	75	1.25
165	A12	5pia on 50k vio & grn	1.50	2.50
166	A12	7pia on 70k brn & org	3.00	5.00

Perf. 13½.

167	A13	10pia on 1r brn & org	15.00	17.50
168	A14	35pia on 3.50r mar & lt grn	30.00	35.00
169	A14	70pia on 7r dk grn & pink	45.00	55.00
		Nos. 161-169 (9)	96.80	118.75

Overprinted "Dardanelles".
Perf. 14½x15.

171	A12	5pa on 1k org	40	75
172	A12	10pa on 2k grn	40	75
a.		Pair, one without overprint		
173	A12	20pa on 4k car	75	1.00
a.		Invtd. ovpt.	15.00	
174	A12	1pia on 10k bl	75	1.25
175	A12	5pia on 50k vio & grn	1.50	2.50
176	A12	7pia on 70k brn & org	3.00	5.00

Perf. 13½.

177	A13	10pia on 1r brn & org	15.00	17.50
178	A14	35pia on 3.50r mar & lt grn	30.00	35.00
a.		Center and overprint inverted		
179	A14	70pia on 7r dk grn & pink	45.00	55.00
		Nos. 171-179 (9)	96.80	118.75

RUSSIA—Offices in the Turkish Empire

Overprinted "Metelin".
Perf. 14½x15.

181	A12	5pa on 1k org	50	1.00
a.		Invtd. ovpt.	15.00	
182	A12	10pa on 2k grn	50	1.00
a.		Invtd. ovpt.	20.00	
183	A12	20pa on 4k car	1.00	1.50
a.		Invtd. ovpt.	20.00	
184	A12	1pia on 10k bl	1.00	1.50
185	A12	5pia on 50k vio & grn	2.00	3.00
186	A12	7pia on 70k brn & org	4.00	6.00

Perf. 13½.

187	A13	10pia on 1r brn & org	20.00	25.00
188	A14	35pia on 3.50r mar & lt grn	45.00	55.00
189	A14	70pia on 7r dk grn & pink	65.00	75.00
		Nos. 181-189 (9)	139.00	169.00

Overprinted "Rizeh".
Perf. 14½x15.

191	A12	5pa on 1k org	40	75
a.		Invtd. ovpt.	11.00	
192	A12	10pa on 2k grn	40	75
a.		Invtd. ovpt.	15.00	
193	A12	20pa on 4k car	75	1.00
a.		Invtd. ovpt.	15.00	
194	A12	1pia on 10k bl	75	1.00
195	A12	5pia on 50k vio & grn	1.50	2.50
196	A12	7pia on 70k brn & org	3.00	5.00

Perf. 13½.

197	A13	10pia on 1r brn & org	15.00	18.00
198	A14	35pia on 3.50r mar & lt grn	30.00	35.00
199	A14	70pia on 7r dk grn & pink	45.00	55.00
		Nos. 191-199 (9)	96.80	119.00

Nos. 61 to 199 were issued to commemorate the 50th anniversary of the establishing of Russian Post Offices in the Levant.

A15   A16   A17

Vertically Laid Paper.
Wmkd. Wavy Lines. (168)

1910   Perf. 14½x15.

200	A15	20pa on 5k red vio (Bl)	75	85

Wove Paper.
Vertical Lozenges of Varnish on Face.

1910   Perf. 14x14½.   Unwmkd.

201	A16	5pa on 1k org yel (Bl)	25	35
202	A16	10pa on 2k grn (R)	25	35
203	A17	20pa on 4k car rose (Bl)	25	35
204	A17	1pia on 10k bl (R)	25	35
205	A8	5pia on 50k vio & grn (Bl)	75	1.00
206	A9	7pia on 70k lt brn & org (Bl)	85	1.10

Perf. 13½.

207	A10	10pa on 1r pale brn, brn & org (Bl)	1.00	1.25
		Nos. 201-207 (7)	3.60	4.75

Russian Stamps of 1909-12 Surcharged in Black:

20 PARA   **1½ PIASTRE**
a   b

1912   Perf. 14x14½.

208	A14 (a)	20pa on 5k cl	25	30
209	A11 (b)	1½pia on 15k dl vio & bl	35	35
210	A8 (b)	2pia on 20k bl & car	35	45
211	A11 (b)	2½pia on 25k grn & vio	50	60
a.		Double surch.	75.00	75.00
212	A11 (b)	3½pia on 35k vio & grn	75	85
		Nos. 208-212 (5)	2.20	2.55

Russian Stamps of 1913 Surcharged:

PARA 5   **PARA 10**   **PARA 10**
c   d

1 PIASTRE   **1 PIAS**   **1½ TRE**
e   f

30 PIASTRES
g

1913   Perf. 13½.

213	A16 (c)	5pa on 1k brn org	20	20
214	A17 (d)	10pa on 2k yel grn	20	20
215	A18 (c)	15pa on 3k rose red	20	20
216	A19 (c)	20pa on 4k dl red	25	25
217	A21 (e)	1pi on 10k dp bl	30	30
218	A23 (f)	1½pia on 15k yel brn	75	75
219	A24 (f)	2pi on 20k ol grn	75	75
220	A25 (f)	2½pi on 25k red vio	1.00	1.00
221	A26 (f)	3½pi on 35k gray vio & dk grn	2.00	2.00
222	A27 (e)	5pi on 50k brn & sl	2.50	2.50
223	A28 (f)	7pi on 70k yel grn & brn	10.00	10.00
224	A29 (e)	10pi on 1r dp grn	10.00	10.00
225	A30 (e)	20pi on 2r red brn	2.00	2.00
226	A31 (g)	30pi on 3r dk vio	3.00	3.00
227	A32 (e)	50pi on 5r blk brn	85.00	90.00
		Nos. 213-227 (15)	118.15	123.75

Romanov dynasty tercentenary.
Forgeries exist of overprint on No. 227.

Russian Stamps of 1905-18 Surcharged:

15 PARA   **PIAS 50**   **TRES**
h   i

Wove Paper.
Perf. 14x14½.

228	A14 (h)	15pa on 3k car	15	15

Perf. 13, 13½.

230	A13 (i)	50pi on 5r dk bl, grn & pale bl	7.50	15.00

Vertically Laid Paper.
Wmkd. Wavy Lines. (168)

231	A13 (i)	100pi on 10r scar, yel & gray	15.00	30.00
a.		Double surcharge	40.00	60.00

No. 228 has lozenges of varnish on face but No. 230 has not.

Wrangel Issues.

For the Posts of Gen. Peter Wrangels army and civilian refugees from South Russia, interned in Turkey, Serbia, etc.

Russian Stamps of 1902-18 Surcharged in Blue, Red or Black

ПОЧТА РУССКОЙ АРМІИ

1.000 РУБЛЕЙ

On Stamps of 1902-04.
Vertically Laid Paper.
Wmkd. Wavy Lines. (168)

1921   Perf. 13½.

232	A12	10,000r on 3.50r blk & gray	12.50	12.50
233	A12	10,000r on 7r blk & yel	10.00	10.00
234	A12	20,000r on 3.50r blk & gray	20.00	20.00
235	A12	20,000r on 7r blk & yel	10.00	10.00

On Stamps of 1909-18.
Wove Paper.
Unwmkd.
Perf. 14 x 14½, 13½.

236	A14	1000r on 1k dl org grn	30	30
237	A14	1000r on 2k dl grn (R)	30	30
237A	A14	1000r on 2k dl grn (Bk)	4.00	4.00
238	A14	1000r on 3k car	5	6
239	A15	1000r on 4k car	5	6
a.		Inverted surcharge	1.00	1.00
240	A14	1000r on 5k dl cl	5	6
a.		Inverted surcharge	1.00	1.00
241	A14	1000r on 7k bl	5	6
a.		Inverted surcharge	1.00	1.00
242	A15	1000r on 10k dk bl	6	9
a.		Inverted surcharge	1.00	1.00
243	A14	1000r on 10k on 7k bl	6	8
244	A14	5000r on 3k car	5	7
245	A11	5000r on 14k dk bl & car	1.00	1.25
246	A11	5000r on 15k red brn & dp bl	5	5
a.		"PYCCKIN"	2.00	2.00
247	A8	5000r on 20k dl bl & dk car	35	40
a.		"PYCCKIN"	2.00	2.00
248	A11	5000r on 20k on 14k dk bl & car	35	40
249	A11	5000r on 25k dl grn & dk vio	10	15
250	A11	5000r on 35k red brn & grn	6	8
b.		New value omitted	1.00	1.00
251	A8	5000r on 50k brn vio & grn	6	8
a.		Inverted surcharge	1.00	1.00
252	A11	5000r on 70k brn & red org	6	6
a.		Inverted surcharge	1.50	1.50
253	A9	10,000r on 1r pale brn, brn & org (Bl)	10	15
254	A9	10,000r on 1r pale brn, brn & org (Bk)	75	1.00
255	A12	10,000r on 3.50r mar & lt grn	30	35
256	A13	10,000r on 5r dk bl, grn & pale bl	4.50	4.50
257	A13	10,000r on 10r scar, yel & gray	40	50
258	A9	20,000r on 1r pale brn, brn & org	25	30
259	A12	20,000r on 3.50r mar & lt grn	25	30
a.		Inverted surcharge	5.00	5.00
b.		New value omitted	40.00	40.00
260	A12	20,000r on 7r dk grn & pink	9.00	9.00
261	A13	20,000r on 10r car lake, yel & gray	30	40
		Nos. 236-261 (27)	22.85	24.05

On Stamp of 1913.

261A	A32	20,000r on 5r blk brn	250.00	

On Stamps of 1917-18.
Imperf.

262	A14	1000r on 1k org	35	40
263	A14	1000r on 2k gray grn (R)	35	40
263A	A14	1000r on 2k gray grn (Bk)	40	50
264	A14	1000r on 3k red	35	40
265	A15	1000r on 4k car	10.00	10.00
266	A14	1000r on 5k cl	40	45
267	A14	5000r on 3k red	35	40
268	A14	5000r on 15k red brn & dp bl	40	45
268A	A8	5000r on 20k bl & car	15.00	
268B	A11	5000r on 25k grn & gray vio	15.00	
269	A11	5000r on 35k red brn & grn	75	85
270	A11	5000r on 50k brn vio & grn	75	85
271	A11	5000r on 70k brn & org	30	35
272	A9	10,000r on 1r pale brn, brn & org (Bl)	5	10
a.		Invtd. surcharge	1.50	1.00
273	A9	10,000r on 1r pale brn, brn & org (Bk)	35	40
274	A12	10,000r on 3.50r mar & lt grn	35	40
275	A13	10,000r on 5r dk bl, grn & pale bl	1.25	1.50
276	A12	10,000r on 7r dk grn & pink	8.00	8.00
276A	A13	10,000r on 10r scar, yel & gray	50.00	
277	A9	20,000r on 1r pale brn, brn & org (Bl)	10	10
a.		Invtd. surcharge	1.50	1.50
278	A9	20,000r on 1r pale brn, brn & org (Bk)	35	40
279	A12	20,000r on 3.50r mar & lt grn	1.25	1.50
280	A13	20,000r on 5r dk bl, grn & lt bl	25	30
281	A12	20,000r on 7r dk grn & pink	6.50	6.50
281A	A13	20,000r on 10r scar, yel & gray	50.00	
		Nos. 262-268, 269-276, 277-281 (21)	32.85	34.25

A18   A19

On Postal Savings Stamps.
Wmkd. Diamonds. (171)
Perf. 14½x15.

282	A18	10,000r on 1k red, buff	25	30
283	A19	10,000r on 5k grn, buff	5	5
a.		Inverted surcharge	4.00	
284	A19	10,000r on 10k brn, buff	5	5
a.		Inverted surcharge	4.00	

On Stamps of Russian Offices in Turkey.
On Issue of 1903-05.
Vertically Laid Paper.
Wmkd. Wavy Lines. (168)

284B	A11	20,000r on 35pi on 3.50r blk & gray	50.00	
284C	A11	20,000r on 70pi on 7r blk & yel	50.00	

On Issue of 1910.
Vertically Laid Paper.

284D	A15	1000r on 20pa on 5k red vio	1.00	1.25

RUSSIA—Offices in the Turkish Empire—RWANDA

Wove Paper.
Unwmkd.

285	A16	1000r on 5pa on 1k org yel	30	35
286	A16	1000r on 10pa on 2k grn	30	35
287	A17	1000r on 20pa on 4k car rose	25	30
288	A17	1000r on 1pi on 10k bl	30	35
289	A8	5000r on 5pi on 50k vio & grn	35	40
290	A9	5000r on 7pi on 70k lt brn & org	35	40
291	A10	10,000r on 10pi on 1r pale brn, brn & org	1.25	1.50
a.		Invtd. surcharge	4.00	4.00
b.		Pair, one without surcharge	4.00	4.00
292	A10	20,000r on 10pi on 1r pale brn, brn & org	25	30
a.		Invtd. surcharge	4.00	4.00
b.		Pair, one without surcharge	4.00	5.20
		Nos. 284D-292 (9)	4.35	5.20

On Issue of 1912.

293	A14	1000r on 20pa on 5k cl	35	40
294	A11	5000r on 1½pi on 15k dl vio & bl	35	40
295	A8	5000r on 2pi on 20k bl & car	35	40
296	A11	5000r on 2½pi on 25k grn & vio	35	40
297	A11	5000r on 3½pi on 35k vio & grn	50	60
		Nos. 293-297 (5)	1.90	2.20

On Issue of 1913.

298	A14	1000r on 15pa on 3k car	35	40
299	A13	10,000r on 50pi on 5r dk bl, grn & pale bl	10.00	10.00
300	A13	10,000r on 100pi on 10r scar, yel & gray	12.00	12.00
301	A13	20,000r on 50pi on 5r dk bl, grn & pale bl	35	40
302	A13	20,000r on 100pi on 10r scar, yel & gray	12.00	12.00
		Nos. 298-302 (5)	34.70	34.80

On Stamps of South Russia.
Denikin Issue.
Imperf.

303	A5	5000r on 5k org	5	6
a.		Inverted surcharge		
304	A5	5000r on 10k grn	5	6
305	A5	5000r on 15k red	5	6
306	A5	5000r on 35k lt bl	5	6
307	A5	5000r on 70k dk bl	5	6
307A	A5	10,000r on 70k dk bl	8.00	8.00
308	A6	10,000r on 1r brn & red	25	30
309	A6	10,000r on 2r gray vio & yel	40	50
a.		Inverted surcharge	2.00	2.00
310	A6	10,000r on 3r dl rose & grn	65	75
311	A6	10,000r on 5r sl & vio	75	85
312	A6	10,000r on 7r gray grn & rose	15.00	15.00
313	A6	10,000r on 10r red & gray	65	75
314	A6	20,000r on 1r brn & red	15	20
315	A6	20,000r on 2r gray vio & yel (Bl)	5.00	5.00
a.		Inverted surcharge	7.50	7.50
315B	A6	20,000r on 2r gray vio & yel (Bk)	30	35
316	A6	20,000r on 3r dl rose & grn (Bl)	8.00	8.00
316A	A6	20,000r on 3r dl rose & grn (Bk)	4.00	4.00
317	A6	20,000r on 5r sl & vio	30	35
318	A6	20,000r on 7r gray grn & rose	10.00	10.00
319	A6	20,000r on 10r red & gray	30	35
		Nos. 303-319 (20)	54.00	54.70

Trident Stamps of Ukraine Surcharged in Blue, Red, Black or Brown

1921 *Perf. 14, 14½x15.*

320	A14	10,000r on 1k org	5	6
321	A14	10,000r on 2k grn	1.00	1.25
322	A14	10,000r on 3k red	5	5
a.		Inverted surcharge	2.00	2.00
323	A15	10,000r on 4k car	5	5
324	A14	10,000r on 5k cl	30	35
325	A14	10,000r on 7k lt bl	5	6
a.		Inverted surcharge	2.00	2.00
326	A15	10,000r on 10k dk bl	5	6
a.		Inverted surcharge		
327	A14	10,000r on 10k on 7k lt bl	10	12
328	A8	20,000r on 20k bl & car (Br)	5	5
a.		Inverted surcharge		
329	A8	20,000r on 20k bl & car (Bk)	20	25
a.		Inverted surcharge		
330	A11	20,000r on 20k on 14k bl & rose	13	20
331	A11	20,000r on 35k red brn & grn	15.00	15.00
332	A8	20,000r on 50k brn vio & grn	5	5
a.		Inverted surcharge	2.00	2.00
		Nos. 320-332 (13)	17.08	17.55

Imperf.

333	A14	10,000r on 1k org	5	8
a.		Inverted surcharge	2.50	
334	A14	10,000r on 2k grn	35	40
335	A14	10,000r on 3k red	10	12
336	A8	10,000r on 20k bl & car	20	25
337	A11	10,000r on 35k red brn & grn	4.00	4.00
338	A8	10,000r on 50k brn vio & grn	35	40
		Nos. 333-338 (6)	5.05	5.25

There are several varieties of the trident surcharge on Nos. 320 to 338.

Same Surcharge on Russian Stamps.
On Stamps of 1909-18.
Perf. 14x14½.

338A	A14	10,000r on 1k dl org yel	40	40
339	A14	10,000r on 2k dl grn	40	40
340	A14	10,000r on 3k car	10	12
341	A15	10,000r on 4k car	10	12
342	A14	10,000r on 5k dk cl	12	15
343	A14	10,000r on 7k bl	15	18
344	A15	10,000r on 10k dk bl	40	45
344A	A14	10,000r on 10k on 7k bl	75	85
344B	A11	20,000r on 14k bl & car	4.00	4.00
345	A11	20,000r on 15k red brn & dp bl	15	20
346	A8	20,000r on 20k bl & dk car	12	15
347	A11	20,000r on 20k on 14k bl & car	75	85
348	A11	20,000r on 35k red brn & grn	30	35
349	A8	20,000r on 50k brn vio & grn	16	18
349A	A11	20,000r on 70k brn & red org	40	50
		Nos. 338A-349A (15)	8.30	8.90

On Stamps of 1917-18.
Imperf.

350	A14	10,000r on 1k org	25	30
351	A14	10,000r on 2k gray grn	25	30
352	A14	10,000r on 3k red	25	30
353	A15	10,000r on 4k car	8.00	8.00
354	A14	10,000r on 5k cl	25	30
355	A11	20,000r on 15k red brn & dp bl	25	30
356	A8	20,000r on 50k brn vio & grn	75	85
357	A11	20,000r on 70k brn & org	40	50
		Nos. 350-357 (8)	10.40	10.85

Same Surcharge on Stamps of Russian Offices in Turkey
On Stamps of 1909.
Perf. 14½x15.

358	A12	10,000r on 5pa on 1k org	2.50	2.50
359	A12	10,000r on 10pa on 2k grn	2.50	2.50
360	A12	10,000r on 20pa on 4k car	2.50	2.50
361	A12	10,000r on 1pi on 10k bl	2.50	2.50
362	A12	10,000r on 5pi on 50k vio & grn	2.50	2.50
363	A12	20,000r on 7pi on 70k brn & org	2.50	2.50
		Nos. 358-363 (6)	15.00	15.00

On Stamps of 1910.

364	A16	10,000r on 5pa on 1k yel org	50	50
365	A16	10,000r on 10pa on 2k grn	50	50
366	A17	10,000r on 20pa on 4k car rose	50	50
367	A17	10,000r on 1pi on 10k bl	50	50
368	A8	5000r on 5pi on 50k vio & grn	50	50
369	A9	20,000r on 7pi on 70k lt brn & org	50	50
		Nos. 364-369 (6)	3.00	3.00

On Stamps of 1912-13.

370	A14	10,000r on 15pa on 3k car	30	30
371	A14	10,000r on 20pa on 5k cl	50	50
372	A11	20,000r on 1½pi on 15k dl vio & bl	60	
373	A8	20,000r on 2pi on 20k bl & car	60	
374	A11	20,000r on 2½pi on 25k grn & vio	60	
375	A11	20,000r on 3½pi on 35k vio & grn	60	

Same Surcharge on Stamp of South Russia, Crimea Issue.

376	A8	20,000r on 5r on 20k bl & car	25.00	
		Nos. 370-376 (7)	28.10	

RUSSIAN TURKESTAN

Russian stamps of 1917-18 surcharged as above are frauds.

Foreign postal stationery (stamped envelopes, postal cards and air letter sheets) lies beyond the scope of this Catalogue which is limited to adhesive postage stamps.

RWANDA
(rōō-än′də)
(Rwandaise Republic)

LOCATION—Central Africa, adjoining the ex-Belgian Congo Republic, Tanganyika, Uganda and Burundi.
GOVT.—Republic
AREA—10,166 sq. mi.
POP.—4,460,000 (est. 1977).
CAPITAL—Kigali

Rwanda was established as an independent republic on July 1, 1962. With Burundi, it had been a United Nations trusteeship territory administered by Belgium.

100 Centimes = 1 Franc

Gregoire Kayibanda and Map of Africa—A1
Design: 40c, 1.50fr, 6.50fr, 20fr, Rwanda map spotlighted, "R" omitted.

Photogravure
1962, July 1 *Perf. 11½ Unwmkd.*

1	A1	10c brn & gray grn	5	5
2	A1	40c brn & rose lil	5	5
3	A1	1fr brn & bl	90	45
4	A1	1.50fr brn & org	10	6
5	A1	3.50fr brn & dp org	17	8
6	A1	6.50fr brn & lt vio bl	27	10
7	A1	10fr brn & cit	30	12
8	A1	20fr brn & rose	65	25
		Nos. 1-8 (8)	2.49	1.16

Map of Africa and Symbolic Honeycomb—A2
Ruanda-Urundi Nos. 151-152 Overprinted with Metallic Frame Obliterating Previous Inscription and Denomination. Black Commemorative Inscription and "REPUBLIQUE RWANDAISE." Surcharged with New Value.

1963, Jan. 28 *Perf. 11½ Unwmkd.*

9	A2	3.50fr sil, blk, ultra & red	15	15
10	A2	6.50fr brnz, blk, ultra & red	1.10	1.10
11	A2	10fr stl bl, blk, ultra & red	30	30
12	A2	20fr sil, blk, ultra & red	55	55

Rwanda's admission to U.N., Sept. 18, 1962.

Stamps of Ruanda-Urundi, 1953, Overprinted

Littonia A3
Designs as Before
1963, Mar. 21 *Perf. 11½ Unwmkd.*
Flowers in Natural Colors; Metallic and Black Overprint

13	A3	25c dk grn & dl org	8	8

RWANDA

14	A3	40c grn & sal	8	8
15	A3	60c bl grn & pink	8	8
16	A3	1.25fr dk grn & bl	1.00	1.00
17	A3	1.50fr vio & ap grn	85	85
18	A3	2fr on 1.50fr vio & ap grn	1.25	1.25
19	A3	4fr on 1.50fr vio & ap grn	1.25	1.25
20	A3	5fr dp plum & lt bl grn	1.25	1.25
21	A3	7fr dk grn & fawn	1.25	1.25
22	A3	10fr dp plum & pale ol	1.25	1.25
		Nos. 13-22 (10)	8.34	8.34

The overprint consists of silver panels with black lettering. The panels on No. 19 are bluish gray.

Imperforates

exist of practically every issue, starting with Nos. 23-26, except Nos. 36, 55-69, 164-169.

Wheat Emblem, Bow, Arrow, Hoe and Billhook—A4

1963, July 1   Photo.   Perf. 13½

23	A4	2fr brn & yel	8	6
24	A4	4fr mag & ultra	15	8
25	A4	7fr red & gray	22	10
26	A4	10fr ol grn & yel	80	55

Issued for the "Freedom from Hunger" campaign of the U.N. Food and Agriculture Organization.

The 20fr leopard and 50fr lion stamps of Ruanda-Urundi, Nos. 149-150, overprinted "Republique Rwandaise" at top and "Contre la Faim" at bottom, were intended to be issued Mar. 21, 1963, but were not placed in use.

Coffee
A5

Designs: 10c, 40c, 4fr, Coffee. 20c, 1fr, 7fr, Bananas. 30c, 2fr, 10fr, Tea.

1963, July 1   Perf. 11½

27	A5	10c vio bl & brn	5	5
28	A5	20c sl & yel	5	5
29	A5	30c ver & grn	5	5
30	A5	40c dp grn & brn	5	5
31	A5	1fr mar & yel	5	5
32	A5	2fr dk bl & grn	85	65
33	A5	4fr red & brn	12	8
34	A5	7fr yel grn & yel	20	12
35	A5	10fr vio & grn	30	17
		Nos. 27-35 (9)	1.72	1.27

First anniversary of independence.

African Postal Union Issue
Common Design Type

1963, Sept. 8   Perf. 12½   Unwmkd.

36	CD114	14fr blk, ocher & red	85	35

Post Horn and Pigeon
A6

1963, Oct. 25   Photo.   Perf. 11½

37	A6	50c ultra & rose	6	6
38	A6	1.50fr brn & bl	75	60
39	A6	3fr dp plum & gray	10	8
40	A6	20fr grn & yel	50	28

Issued to commemorate Rwanda's admission to the U.P.U., Apr. 6, 1963.

Scales, U.N. Emblem and Flame
A7

1963, Dec. 10   Perf. 11½   Unwmkd.

41	A7	5fr crimson	20	10
42	A7	6fr brt pur	65	45
43	A7	10fr brt red	35	20

Issued to commemorate the 15th anniversary of the Universal Declaration of Human Rights.

Children's Clinic
A8

Designs: 20c, 7fr, Laboratory examination (horiz.). 30c, 10fr, Physician examining infant. 40c, 20fr, Litter bearers (horiz.).

1963, Dec.   Photogravure

44	A8	10c yel org, red & brn blk	5	5
45	A8	20c grn, red & brn blk	5	5
46	A8	30c bl, red & brn blk	5	5
47	A8	40c red lil, red & brn	5	5
48	A8	2fr bl grn, red brn & blk	80	70
49	A8	7fr ultra, red & blk	25	17
50	A8	10fr red brn, red & brn blk	33	20
51	A8	20fr dp org, red & blk	65	25
		Nos. 44-51 (8)	2.23	1.52

Centenary of the International Red Cross.

Map of Rwanda and Woman at Water Pump—A9

1964, May 4   Perf. 11½   Unwmkd.

52	A9	3fr grn, dk brn & ultra	10	10
53	A9	7fr pink, dk brn & ultra	40	25
54	A9	10fr yel, dk brn & ultra	55	40

Souvenir Sheet
Imperf.

54A	A9	25fr lil, bl, brn & blk	4.50	4.50

Issued to commemorate the United Nations Fourth World Meteorological Day, March 23.

No. 54A contains a single stamp with brown marginal inscriptions. Size: 72x51mm.

Common Design Types
pictured in section at front of book.

Buffaloes
A10

Designs: 10c, 20c, 30c, Buffaloes. 40c, 2fr, 7.50fr, Impalas. 1fr, Mountain gorilla. 3fr, 4fr, 8fr, African elephants. 5fr, 10fr, Eland and zebras. 20fr, Leopard. 50fr, Lions. 40c, 1fr and 2fr are vertical.

1964, June 29   Photo.   Perf. 11½
Size: 33x23mm., 23x33mm.

55	A10	10c on 20c gray, ap grn & blk	7	5
56	A10	20c blk, gray & ap grn	7	5
57	A10	30c on 1.50fr blk, gray & org	7	5
58	A10	40c mag, blk & ap grn	7	5
59	A10	50c grn, org yel & brn	7	5
60	A10	1fr ultra, blk & brn	10	5
61	A10	2fr grnsh bl, ind & brn	10	5
62	A10	3fr brn, dp car & blk	12	5
63	A10	4fr on 3.50fr on 3fr brn, dp car & blk	25	5
64	A10	5fr brn, dl yel, grn & blk	22	8
65	A10	7.50fr on 6.50fr red, org yel & brn	45	12
66	A10	8fr bl, mag & blk	3.25	2.50
67	A10	10fr brn, dl yel, brt pink & blk	60	17

Size: 45x26½mm.

68	A10	20fr hn brn, ocher & blk	1.00	50
69	A10	50fr dp bl & brn	1.75	1.25
		Nos. 55-69 (15)	8.19	5.07

Boy with Crutch and Gatagara Home
A11

Basketball
A12

Designs: 40c, 8fr, Girls with sewing machines (horiz.). 4fr, 10fr, Girl on crutches, map of Rwanda and Gatagara Home.

1964, Nov. 10   Photo.   Perf. 11½

70	A11	10c lil blk brn	5	5
71	A11	40c bl & blk brn	6	6
72	A11	4fr org red & blk brn	15	12
73	A11	7.50fr yel grn & blk brn	30	22
74	A11	8fr bis & blk brn	1.50	1.00
75	A11	10fr mag & blk brn	45	27
		Nos. 70-75 (6)	2.51	1.72

Gatagara Home for handicapped children.

1964, Dec. 8   Litho.   Perf. 13½

Sport: 10c, 4fr, Runner (horiz.). 30c, 20fr, High jump (horiz.). 40c, 50fr, Soccer.

Size: 26x38mm.

76	A12	10c gray, sl & dk gray	5	5
77	A12	20c pink, sl & rose blk	5	5
78	A12	30c lt grn, sl & grn	5	5
79	A12	40c buff, sl & brn	5	5
80	A12	4fr vio gray, sl & vio	10	8
81	A12	5fr pale grn, sl & yel grn	1.90	1.90
82	A12	20fr pale lil, sl & red lil	50	45
83	A12	50fr gray, sl & dk gray	1.15	1.00
	a.	Souv. sheet of 4	6.00	6.00
		Nos. 76-83 (8)	3.85	3.63

Issued to commemorate the 18th Olympic Games, Tokyo, Oct. 10-25. No. 83a contains 4 stamps (10fr, soccer; 20fr, basketball; 30fr, high jump; 40fr, runner). Orange margin with slate inscription. Size of stamps: 28x38mm. Size of sheet: 134x99mm.

Quill, Books, Radical and Retort
A13

Medical School and Student with Microscope—A14

Designs: 30c, 10fr, Scales, hand, staff of Mercury and globe. 40c, 12fr, View of University.

1965, Feb. 22   Engraved   Perf. 11½

84	A13	10c multi	5	5
85	A14	20c multi	5	5
86	A14	30c multi	5	5
87	A14	40c multi	5	5
88	A13	5fr multi	15	7
89	A14	7fr multi	20	13
90	A13	10fr multi	1.25	1.10
91	A14	12fr multi	35	20
		Nos. 84-91 (8)	2.15	1.70

National University of Rwanda at Butare.

Abraham Lincoln—A15

1965, Apr. 15   Photo.   Perf. 13½

92	A15	10c emer & dk red	6	6
93	A15	20c red brn & dk bl	6	5
94	A15	30c brt vio & red	6	5
95	A15	40c brt grnsh bl & red	6	5
96	A15	9fr org brn & pur	25	20
97	A15	40fr blk & brt grn	2.35	90
		Nos. 92-97 (6)	2.84	1.30

Souvenir Sheet

98	A15	50fr red lil & red	2.75	2.75

Issued to commemorate the centenary of the death of Abraham Lincoln. No. 98 contains one stamp, red marginal inscription. Size: 65x78mm.

RWANDA 403

	Marabous A16		Zebras A17	

Designs: 30c, Impalas. 40c, Crowned cranes, hippopotami and cattle egrets. 1fr, Cape buffalos. 3fr, Cape hunting dogs. 5fr, Yellow baboons. 10fr, Elephant and map of Rwanda with location of park. 40fr, Anhinga, great anad reed cormorants. 100fr, Lions.

1965, Apr. 28   Photo.   Perf. 11½

Size: 32x23mm.

99	A16	10c multi	5	5
100	A17	20c multi	5	5
101	A17	30c multi	6	5
102	A17	40c multi	6	5
103	A16	1fr multi	6	5
104	A16	3fr multi	10	6
105	A16	5fr multi	4.00	1.35
106	A17	10fr multi	25	10

Size: 45x26mm.

107	A17	40fr multi	1.00	38
108	A17	100fr multi	2.50	30
	Nos. 99-108 (10)		8.13	2.44

Kagera National Park publicity.

Telstar and ITU Emblem
A18

Design: 40c, 50fr, Syncom satellite. 60fr, old and new communications equipment.

1965   Perf. 13½   Unwmkd.

109	A18	10c red brn, ultra & yel	5	5
110	A18	40c vio, emer & yel	5	5
111	A18	4.50fr blk, car & dk bl	1.50	55
112	A18	50fr dk brn, yel grn & brt grn	1.25	25

Souvenir Sheet

| 113 | A18 | 60fr blk brn, org brn & bl | 3.25 | 3.25 |

Issued to commemorate the centenary of the International Telecommunication Union. No. 113 contains one stamp; light blue margin with orange brown and black brown inscription. Size: 84x65mm.
Issue dates: No. 113, July 19. Others, May 17.

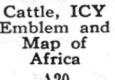

Papilio Bromius Chrapkowskii Suffert
A19

Cattle, ICY Emblem and Map of Africa
A20

Various Butterflies and Moths in Natural Colors

1965–66   Photo.   Perf. 12½

114	A19	10c blk & yel	5	5
115	A19	15c blk & dp org ('66)	5	5
116	A19	20c blk & lil	5	5
117	A19	30c blk & red lil	5	5
118	A19	35c dk brn & dk bl ('66)	5	8
119	A19	40c blk & Prus bl	5	5
120	A19	1.50fr blk & grn ('66)	8	8
121	A19	3fr dk brn & ol grn ('66)	2.10	80
122	A19	4fr blk & red brn	1.25	60
123	A19	10fr blk & pur ('66)	30	15
124	A19	50fr blk & brn	90	35
125	A19	100fr dk brn & bl ('66)	2.50	80
	Nos. 114-125 (12)		7.43	3.11

The 15c, 20c, 40c, 1.50fr, 10fr and 50fr are horizontal.

1965, Oct. 25   Perf. 12   Unwmkd.

ICY Emblem, Map of Africa and: 40c, Tree and lake. 4.50fr, Gazelle under tree. 45fr, Mount Ruwenzori.

126	A20	10c ol bis & bl grn	6	6
127	A20	40c lt ultra, red brn & grn	8	5
128	A20	4.50fr brt grn, yel & brn	1.25	60
129	A20	45fr rose cl	1.10	40

International Cooperation Year, 1965.

John F. Kennedy—A21

1965, Nov. 22   Photo.   Perf. 11½

130	A21	10c brt grn & dk brn	5	5
131	A21	40c brt pink & dk brn	8	8
132	A21	50c dk bl & dk brn	8	8
133	A21	1fr gray ol & dk brn	8	8
134	A21	8fr vio & dk brn	1.75	1.35
135	A21	50fr gray & blk	1.35	1.10
	Nos. 130-135 (6)		3.39	2.74

Souvenir Sheet

136	A21	Sheet of two	10.00	10.00
a.		40fr org & dk brn	4.00	4.00
b.		60fr ultra & dk brn	4.00	4.00

Issued in memory of Pres. John F. Kennedy (1917–1963). No. 136 has ultramarine marginal inscription and various satellites in brown in margin. Size: 92x 99½mm.

Madonna
A22

1965, Dec. 20

137	A22	10c gold & dk grn	5	5
138	A22	40c gold & dk brn red	8	8
139	A22	50c gold & dk bl	8	8
140	A22	4fr gold & sl	1.00	95
141	A22	6fr gold & vio	15	15
142	A22	30fr gold & brn	85	80
	Nos. 137-142 (6)		2.21	2.11

Christmas, 1965.

Father Joseph Damien and Lepers
A23

Designs: 40c, 45fr, Dr. Albert Schweitzer and Hospital, Lambarene.

1966, Jan. 31   Perf. 11½

143	A23	10c ultra & red brn	8	5
144	A23	40c dk red & vio bl	10	8
145	A23	4.50fr sl & brt grn	33	13
146	A23	45fr brn & hn brn	2.25	1.25

Issued for World Leprosy Day.

Pope Paul VI, St. Peter's, U.N. Headquarters and Statue of Liberty
A24

Design: 40c, 50fr, Pope Paul VI, Papal arms and U. N. emblem.

1966, Feb. 28   Photo.   Perf. 12

147	A24	10c hn brn & sl	5	5
148	A24	40c brt bl & sl	8	8
149	A24	4.50fr lil & sl	1.65	1.25
150	A24	50fr brt grn & sl	1.35	50

Issued to commemorate the visit of Pope Paul VI to the United Nations, New York City, Oct. 4, 1965.

Globe Thistle—A25

Flowers: 20c, Blood lily. 30c, Everlasting. 40c, Natal lily. 1fr, Tulip tree. 3fr, Rendle orchid. 5fr, Aloe. 10fr, Ammocharis tinneana. 40fr, Coral tree. 100fr, Caper. (20c, 40c, 1fr, 3fr, 5fr, 10fr are vertical).

1966, March 14   Perf. 11½

Granite Paper

151	A25	10c lt bl & multi	5	5
152	A25	20c org & multi	5	5
153	A25	30c car rose & multi	5	5
154	A25	40c grn & multi	5	5
155	A25	1fr multi	5	5
156	A25	3fr ind & multi	10	8
157	A25	5fr multi	4.00	2.50
158	A25	10fr bl grn & multi	30	20
159	A25	40fr red brn & multi	1.00	50
160	A25	100fr dk bl grn & multi	2.50	1.50
a.		Min. sheet	5.50	4.00
	Nos. 151-160 (10)		8.15	5.03

No. 160a contains one 100fr stamp in changed color, bright blue and multicolored, with bright blue marginal inscriptions. Size: 85x60mm.

WHO Headquarters, Geneva
A26

1966, May 1   Litho.   Perf. 12½x12

161	A26	2fr lt ol grn	8	8
162	A26	3fr vermilion	25	25
163	A26	5fr vio bl	12	12

Issued to commemorate the opening of World Health Organization Headquarters, Geneva.

Soccer
A27

Mother and Child, Planes Dropping Bombs
A28

Designs: 20c, 9fr, Basketball. 30c, 50fr, Volleyball.

1966, May 30   Photo.   Perf. 15x14

164	A27	10c dl grn, litho, & blk	6	6
165	A27	20c crim, grn & blk	6	6
166	A27	30c bl, brt rose lil & blk	6	6
167	A27	40c yel bis, grn & blk	6	6
168	A27	9fr gray, red lil & blk	25	20
169	A27	50fr rose lil, Prus bl & blk	1.35	1.25
	Nos. 164-169 (6)		1.84	1.69

National Youth Sports Program.

1966, June 29   Perf. 13½

Design and Inscription Black and Red

170	A28	20c rose lil	6	6
171	A28	30c yel grn	6	6
172	A28	50c lt ultra	6	6
173	A28	6fr yellow	12	10
174	A28	15fr bl grn	85	30
175	A28	18fr lilac	75	50
	Nos. 170-175 (6)		1.90	1.08

Campaign against nuclear weapons.

Global Soccer Ball
A29

1966, July   Perf. 11½

176	A29	20c org & ind	6	6
177	A29	30c lil & ind	6	6
178	A29	50c brt grn & ind	8	6
179	A29	6fr brt rose & ind	33	12

RWANDA

180	A29	12fr lt vio brn & ind	1.00	38
181	A29	25fr ultra & ind	1.20	75
		Nos. 176-181 (6)	2.73	1.43

Issued to commemorate the World Soccer Cup Championship, Wembley, England, July 11–30.

Nyamilanga Falls—A30

Designs: 10c, Mikeno Volcano and crested shrike (horiz.). 4.50fr, Gahinga and Muhabura volcanoes and lobelias (horiz.). 55fr, Rusumu Falls.

1966, Oct. 24   Engraved   Perf. 14

182	A30	10c green	5	5
183	A30	40c brn car	5	5
184	A30	4.50fr vio bl	70	50
185	A30	55fr red lil	75	50

UNESCO Emblem, African Artifacts and Musical Clef—A31

Designs (UNESCO Emblem and): 30c, 10fr, Hands holding primer showing giraffe and zebra. 50c, 15fr, Atom symbol and power drill. 1fr, 50fr, Submerged sphinxes and sailboat.

1966, Nov. 4   Photo.   Perf. 12

186	A31	20c brt rose & dk bl	5	5
187	A31	30c grnsh bl & blk	5	5
188	A31	50c ocher & bl	5	5
189	A31	1fr vio & blk	6	6
190	A31	5fr yel grn & blk	10	10
191	A31	10fr brn & blk	25	15
192	A31	15fr red lil & dk blk	75	45
193	A31	50fr dl bl & blk	80	70
		Nos. 186-193 (8)	2.11	1.61

Issued to commemorate the 20th anniversary of UNESCO (United Nations Educational, Cultural and Scientific Organization).

Rock Python—A32

Snakes: 20c, 20fr, Jameson's mamba. 30c, 3fr, Rock python. 50c, Gabon viper. 1fr, Black-lipped spitting cobra. 5fr, African sand snake. 70fr, Egg-eating snake. (20c, 50c, 3fr and 20fr are horizontal.)

1967, Jan. 30   Photo.   Perf. 11½

194	A32	20c red & blk	5	5
195	A32	30c bl, dk brn & yel	5	5
196	A32	50c yel grn & multi	6	6
197	A32	1fr lt lil, blk & bis	6	6
198	A32	3fr lt vio, dk brn & yel	15	10
199	A32	5fr yel & multi	25	15
200	A32	20fr pale pink & multi	1.20	90
201	A32	70fr pale vio, brn & blk	1.75	1.00
		Nos. 194-201 (8)	3.57	2.37

Ntaruka Hydroelectric Station and Tea Flowers—A33

Designs: 30c, 25fr, Transformer and chrysanthemums (pyrethrum). 50c, 50fr, Sluice and coffee.

1967, Mar. 6   Photo.   Perf. 13½

202	A33	20c mar & dp bl	5	5
203	A33	30c blk & red brn	5	5
204	A33	50c brn & vio	5	5
205	A33	4fr dk grn & dp plum	8	8
206	A33	25fr vio & sl grn	45	45
207	A33	50fr dk bl & brn	1.30	1.30
		Nos. 202-207 (6)	1.98	1.98

Ntaruka Hydroelectric Station.

Souvenir Sheets

Cogwheels—A34

1967, Apr. 15   Engraved   Perf. 11½

| 208 | A34 | 100fr dk red brn | 3.00 | 3.00 |
| 209 | A34 | 100fr brt rose lil | 3.00 | 3.00 |

Issued to commemorate the 7th "Europa" Philatelic Exhibition and the Philatelic Salon of African States, Naples, Apr. 8–16. Nos. 208–209 have emerald and red typographed marginal inscription and Bay of Naples engraved in color of stamps. Size: 90½x66½mm.

Souvenir Sheet

African Dancers and EXPO '67 Emblem—A35

1967, Apr. 28   Perf. 11½

| 210 | A35 | 180fr dk pur | 4.25 | 4.25 |

Issued to commemorate EXPO '67, International Exhibition, Montreal, Apr. 28–Oct. 27. No 210 has vermilion and ultramarine typographed marginal inscriptions. Size: 74½x90mm.
A similar imperf. sheet has the stamp in violet brown.

St. Martin, by Van Dyck and Caritas Emblem—A36

Paintings: 40c, 15fr, Rebecca at the Well, by Murillo (horiz.). 60c, 18fr, St. Christopher, by Dierick Bouts. 80c, 26fr, Job and his Friends, by Il Calabrese (Mattia Preti) (horiz.).

Perf. 13x11, 11x13

1967, May 8   Photogravure
Black Inscription on Gold Panel

211	A36	20c dk pur	6	6
212	A36	40c bl grn	6	6
213	A36	60c rose car	6	6
214	A36	80c dp bl	8	6
215	A36	9fr redsh brn	1.00	58
216	A36	15fr org ver	35	20
217	A36	18fr dk ol grn	45	20
218	A36	26fr dk car rose	55	38
		Nos. 211-218 (8)	2.61	1.57

Issued to publicize the work of Caritas-Rwanda, Catholic welfare organization.

Round Table Emblem and Zebra—A37

Designs (Round Table Emblem and): 40c, Elephant. 60c, Cape buffalo. 80c, Antelope. 18fr, Wheat. 100fr, Palm tree.

1967, July 31   Photo.   Perf. 14

219	A37	20c gold & multi	5	5
220	A37	40c gold & multi	5	5
221	A37	60c gold & multi	5	5
222	A37	80c gold & multi	5	5
223	A37	18fr gold & multi	42	25
224	A37	100fr gold & multi	2.50	1.00
		Nos. 219-224 (6)	3.12	1.45

Issued to publicize the Rwanda Table No. 9 of Kigali, a member of the International Round Tables Association.

EXPO '67 Emblem, Africa Place and Dancers and Drummers—A38

Designs (EXPO '67 Emblem, Africa Place and): 30c, 3fr, Drum and vessels. 50c, 40fr, Two dancers. 1fr, 34fr, Spears, shields and bow.

1967, Aug. 10   Photo.   Perf. 12

225	A38	20c brt bl & sep	5	5
226	A38	30c brt rose lil & sep	5	5
227	A38	50c org & sep	5	5
228	A38	1fr grn & sep	6	6
229	A38	3fr vio & sep	7	7
230	A38	15fr emer & sep	25	15
231	A38	34fr rose red & sep	75	50
232	A38	40fr grnsh bl & sep	1.00	55
		Nos. 225-232 (8)	2.28	1.48

Issued for EXPO '67, International Exhibition, Montreal, Apr. 28–Oct. 27, 1967.

Lions Emblem, Globe and Zebra—A39

1967, Oct. 16   Photo.   Perf. 13½

233	A39	20c lil, bl & blk	5	5
234	A39	80c lt grn, bl & blk	5	5
235	A39	1fr rose car, bl & blk	6	6
236	A39	8fr bis, bl & blk	18	18
237	A39	10fr ultra, bl & blk	20	20
238	A39	50fr yel grn, bl & blk	1.35	1.00
		Nos. 233-238 (6)	1.89	1.54

50th anniversary of Lions International.

Woodland Kingfisher—A40

Birds: 20c, Red bishop (vert.). 60c, Red-billed quelea (vert.). 80c, Double-toothed barbet. 2fr, Pin-tailed whydah (vert.). 3fr, Solitary cuckoo. 18fr, Green wood hoopoe (vert.). 25fr, Blue-collared bee-eater. 80fr, Regal sunbird (vert.). 100fr, Red-shouldered widowbird.

1967, Dec. 18   Perf. 11½

239	A40	20c multi	5	5
240	A40	40c multi	5	5
241	A40	60c multi	5	5
242	A40	80c multi	8	5
243	A40	2fr multi	10	5
244	A40	3fr multi	12	5
245	A40	18fr multi	60	20
246	A40	25fr multi	70	25
247	A40	80fr multi	1.85	90
248	A40	100fr multi	2.65	1.10
		Nos. 239-248 (10)	6.25	2.75

Souvenir Sheet

Ski Jump, Speed Skating—A41

RWANDA

1968, Feb. 12   *Photo.*   *Perf. 11½*

249	A41	Souv. sheet of 2	2.50	2.50
a.		50fr bl, blk & grn (skier)	1.00	1.00
b.		50fr grn, blk & bl (skater)	1.00	1.00
c.		Souv. sheet of 2, #249a at right	2.50	2.50

10th Winter Olympic Games, Grenoble, France, Feb. 6–18. Black marginal inscription. Size: 129x90mm.

Runner, Mexican Sculpture and Architecture—A42

Designs (Sport and Mexican Art): 40c, Hammer throw, pyramid and animal head. 60c, Hurdler and sculptures. 80c, Javelin and sculptures.

1968, May 27   *Photo.*   *Perf. 11½*

250	A42	20c ultra & multi	5	5
251	A42	40c multi	5	5
252	A42	60c lil & multi	5	5
253	A42	80c org & multi	5	5

Issued to publicize the 19th Olympic Games, Mexico City, Oct. 12–27.

Souvenir Sheet

19th Olympic Games, Mexico City
A43

Designs: 8fr, Soccer. 10fr, Mexican horseman and cactus. 12fr, Field hockey. 18fr, Cathedral, Mexico City. 20fr, Boxing. 30fr, Modern buildings, musical instruments and vase.

1967, May 27   *Photo.*   *Perf. 11½*
Granite Paper

254	A43	Souv. sheet of 6	3.25	3.25
a.		8fr multi	20	20
b.		10fr multi	25	25
c.		12fr multi	30	30
d.		18fr multi	50	50
e.		20fr multi	60	60
f.		30fr multi	90	90

Issued to publicize the 19th Olympic Games, Mexico City, Oct. 12–27. No. 254 has gray marginal inscription and light green ornaments. Size: 178x160mm.

Three sets of circular gold "medal" overprints with black inscriptions were applied to the six stamps of No. 254 to honor 18 Olympic winners. Issued Dec. 12, 1968. Price $10.

Since 1867 American stamp collectors have been using the Scott Catalogue to identify their stamps and Scott Albums to house their collections.

Souvenir Sheet

Martin Luther King, Jr.—A44

1968, July 29   *Engr.*   *Perf. 13½*

255	A44	100fr sepia	3.00	2.00

Issued in memory of the Rev. Dr. Martin Luther King, Jr. (1929–1968), American civil rights leader. No. 255 has emerald marginal inscription. Size: 80x80mm. See No. 406.

Diaphant Orchid
A45

Flowers: 40c, Pharaoh's scepter. 60c, Flower of traveler's-tree. 80c, Costus afer. 2fr, Banana tree flower. 3fr, Flower and fruit of papaw tree. 18fr, Clerodendron. 25fr, Sweet potato flowers. 80fr, Baobab tree flower. 100fr, Passion flower.

1968, Sept. 9   *Litho.*   *Perf. 13*

256	A45	20c lil & multi	5	5
257	A45	40c multi	5	5
258	A45	60c bl grn & multi	5	5
259	A45	80c multi	5	5
260	A45	2fr brt yel & multi	6	6
261	A45	3fr multi	8	8
262	A45	18fr multi	38	20
263	A45	25fr gray & multi	50	25
264	A45	80fr multi	2.00	85
265	A45	100fr multi	2.50	1.10
		Nos. 256-265 (10)	5.72	2.74

Equestrian and "Mexico 1968"
A46

Designs: 40c, Wrestling and "Tokyo 1964." 60c, Fencing and "Rome 1960." 80c, High jump and "Berlin 1936." 38fr, Women's diving and "London 1908 and 1948." 60fr, Weight lifting and "Paris 1900 and 1924."

1968, Oct. 24   *Litho.*   *Perf. 14x13*

266	A46	20c org & sep	5	5
267	A46	40c grnsh bl & sep	5	5
268	A46	60c car rose & sep	5	5
269	A46	80c ultra & sep	5	5
270	A46	38fr red & sep	85	38
271	A46	60fr emer & sep	1.50	75
		Nos. 266-271 (6)	2.55	1.33

Issued to commemorate the 19th Olympic Games, Mexico City, Oct. 12–27.

Tuareg, Algeria
A47

African National Costumes: 40c, Musicians, Upper Volta. 60c, Senegalese women. 70c, Girls of Rwanda going to market. 8fr, Young married couple from Morocco. 20fr, Nigerian officials in state dress. 40fr, Man and women from Zambia. 50fr, Man and woman from Kenya.

1968, Nov. 4   *Litho.*   *Perf. 13*

272	A47	30c multi	5	5
273	A47	40c multi	5	5
274	A47	60c multi	5	5
275	A47	70c multi	5	5
276	A47	8fr multi	15	15
277	A47	20fr multi	45	25
278	A47	40fr multi	90	50
279	A47	50fr multi	1.15	75
		Nos. 272-279 (8)	2.85	1.85

Christmas Issue
Souvenir Sheet

Nativity, by Giorgione—A48

1968, Dec. 16   *Engr.*   *Perf. 11½*

280	A48	100fr green	3.00	3.00

No. 280 has marginal inscription in dark brown and green. Size: 85x85mm.
See Nos. 309, 389, 422, 494, 564, 611, 713, 787, 848, 894.

Singing Boy, by Frans Hals
A49

Paintings and Music: 20c, Angels' Concert, by van Eyck. 40c, Angels' Concert, by Matthias Grunewald. 60c, #283a, Singing Boy, by Frans Hals. 80c, Lute Player, by Gerard Terborch. 2fr, The Fifer, by Manet. 6fr, #286a, Young Girls at the Piano, by Renoir.

1969, Mar. 31   *Photo.*   *Perf. 13*

281	A49	20c gold & multi	5	5
282	A49	40c gold & multi	5	5
283	A49	60c gold & multi	5	5
a.		Souv. sheet, 75fr	2.00	2.00
284	A49	80c gold & multi	5	5
285	A49	2fr gold & multi	10	8
286	A49	6fr gold & multi	20	15
a.		Souv. sheet, 75fr	2.00	2.00
		Nos. 281-286, C6-C7 (8)	4.60	2.08

Nos. 283 and 286a contain one stamp each with decorative margin and inscription. Size: 90x80mm.

Tuareg Men
A50

African Headdresses: 40c, Ovambo woman. South West Africa. 60c, Guinean man and Congolese woman. 80c, Dagger dancer, Guinean forest area. 8fr, Mohammedan Nigerians. 20fr, Luba dancer, Kabondo, Congo. 40fr, Senegalese and Gambian women. 80fr, Rwanda dancer.

1969, May 29   *Litho.*   *Perf. 13*

287	A50	20c multi	5	5
288	A50	40c multi	5	5
289	A50	60c multi	5	5
290	A50	80c multi	5	5
291	A50	8fr multi	20	12
292	A50	20fr multi	45	25
293	A50	40fr multi	1.00	50
294	A50	80fr multi	2.00	90
		Nos. 287-294 (8)	3.85	1.97

See also Nos. 398-405.

The Moneylender and his Wife, by Quentin Massys—A51

Design: 70fr, The Moneylender and his Wife, by Marinus van Reymerswaele.

1969, Sept. 10   *Photo.*   *Perf. 13*

295	A51	30fr sil & multi	90	65
296	A51	70fr gold & multi	2.00	1.50

Issued to publicize the 5th anniversary of the African Development Bank. Printed in sheets of 20 stamps and 20 labels with commemorative inscription.

Souvenir Sheet

First Man on the Moon—A52

RWANDA

1969, Oct. 9   Engraved   Perf. 11½

297 A52 100fr bl gray   3.00 3.00

See note after Mali No. C80. Size of No. 297: 94x109mm. See No. 407.

Camomile and Health Emblem
A53

Worker with Pickaxe and Flag
A54

Medicinal Plants and Health Emblem: 40c, Aloe. 60c, Cola. 80c, Coca. 3fr, Hagenia abissinica. 75fr, Cassia. 80fr, Cinchona. 100fr, Tephrosia.

1969, Nov. 24   Photo.   Perf. 13

Flowers in Natural Colors

298	A53	20c gold, bl & blk	5	5
299	A53	40c gold, yel grn & blk	5	5
300	A53	60c gold, pink & blk	5	5
301	A53	80c gold, grn & blk	6	6
302	A53	3fr gold, org & blk	10	6
303	A53	75fr gold, yel & blk	2.00	.85
304	A53	80fr gold, lil & blk	2.25	1.00
305	A53	100fr gold, dl yel & blk	2.85	1.25
		Nos. 298-305 (8)	7.41	3.37

1969, Nov.   Photo.   Perf. 11½

306	A54	6fr brt pink & multi	10	10
307	A54	18fr ultra & multi	55	30
308	A54	40fr brn & multi	1.10	65

10th anniversary of independence.

Christmas Issue
Souvenir Sheet
Christmas Type of 1968

Design: 100fr, "Holy Night" (detail), by Correggio.

1969, Dec. 15   Engraved   Perf. 11½

309 A48 100fr ultra   3.25 3.25

Marginal inscription in rose magenta. Size: 85x85mm.

The Cook, by Pierre Aertsen
A55

Napoleon Crossing St. Bernard, by Jacques L. David
A56

Paintings: 20c, Quarry Worker, by Oscar Bonnevalle (horiz.). 40c, The Plower, by Pierre Brueghel (horiz.) 60c, Fisherman, by Constantin Meunier. 80c, Slipway, Ostende, by Jean van Noten (horiz.). 10fr, The Forge of Vulcan, by Velasquez (horiz.). 50fr, "Hiercheuse" (woman shoveling coal), by Meunier. 70fr, Miner, by Pierre Paulus.

1969, Dec. 22   Photo.   Perf. 13½

310	A55	20c gold & multi	5	5
311	A55	40c gold & multi	5	5
312	A55	60c gold & multi	5	5
313	A55	8fr gold & multi	8	6
314	A55	8fr gold & multi	30	6
315	A55	10fr gold & multi	35	16
316	A55	50fr gold & multi	1.50	80
317	A55	70fr gold & multi	2.10	1.15
		Nos. 310-317 (8)	4.48	2.44

Issued to commemorate the 50th anniversary of the International Labor Organization.

1969, Dec. 29

Paintings of Napoleon: 40c, Decorating Soldier before Tilsit, by Jean Baptiste Debret. 60c, Addressing Troops at Augsburg, by Claude Gautherot. 80c, First Consul, by Jean Auguste Ingres. 8fr, Battle of Marengo, by Jacques Auguste Pajou. 20fr, Napoleon Meeting Emperor Francis II, by Antoine Jean Gros. 40fr, Genl. Bonaparte at Arcole, by Gros. 80fr Coronation, by David.

318	A56	20c gold & multi	5	5
319	A56	40c gold & multi	5	5
320	A56	60c gold & multi	5	5
321	A56	80c gold & multi	8	5
322	A56	8fr gold & multi	28	12
323	A56	20fr gold & multi	55	30
324	A56	40fr gold & multi	1.10	65
325	A56	80fr gold & multi	2.25	1.25
		Nos. 318-325 (8)	4.41	2.52

Issued to commemorate the bicentenary of the birth of Napoleon Bonaparte (1769-1821).

Epsom Derby, by Gericault
A57

Paintings of Horses: 40c, Horses Emerging from the Sea, by Delacroix. 60c, Charles V at Muhlberg, by Titian (vert.). 80c, Amateur Jockeys, by Edgar Degas. 8fr, Horsemen at Rest, by Philips Wouwerman. 20fr, Imperial Guards Officer, by Géricault (vert.). 40fr, Friends of the Desert. by Oscar Bonnevalle. 80fr, Two Horses (detail from the Prodigal Son), by Rubens.

1970, Mar. 31   Photo.   Perf. 13½

326	A57	20c gold & multi	5	5
327	A57	40fr gold & multi	5	5
328	A57	60fr gold & multi	5	5
329	A57	80fr gold & multi	6	6
330	A57	8fr gold & multi	22	12
331	A57	20fr gold & multi	60	25
332	A57	40fr gold & multi	1.10	50
333	A57	80fr gold & multi	2.10	1.00
		Nos. 326-333 (8)	4.23	2.08

Souvenir Sheet

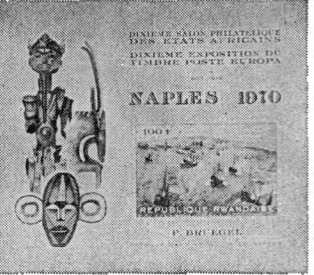

Fleet in Bay of Naples, by Peter Brueghel, the Elder—A58

1970, May 2   Engraved   Perf. 11½

334 A58 100fr brt rose lil   3.25 3.25

Issued to publicize the 10th Europa Philatelic Exhibition, Naples, Italy, May 2-10. No. 334 has blue gray and bright rose lilac marginal inscriptions and blue gray African decorations. Size: 109x 96mm.

Copies of No. 334 were trimmed to 68x 58mm. and overprinted in silver or gold "NAPLES 1973" on the stamp, and "Salon Philatelique des Etats Africaines / Exposition du Timbre-Poste Europa" in October, 1973.

Soccer and Mexican Decorations
A59

Tharaka Meru Woman, East Africa
A60

Designs: Various scenes from soccer game and pre-Columbian decorations.

1970, June 15   Photo.   Perf. 13

335	A59	20c gold & multi	5	5
336	A59	30c gold & multi	5	5
337	A59	50c gold & multi	5	5
338	A59	1fr gold & multi	6	6
339	A59	6fr gold & multi	18	5
340	A59	18fr gold & multi	60	25
341	A59	30fr gold & multi	95	60
342	A59	90fr gold & multi	2.65	1.10
		Nos. 335-342 (8)	4.59	2.22

Issued to publicize the 9th World Soccer Championships for the Jules Rimet Cup, Mexico City, May 30–June 21.

1970, June 1   Lithographed

African National Costumes: 30c, Musician with wooden flute, Niger. 50c, Woman water carrier, Tunisia. 1fr, Ceremonial costumes, North Nigeria. 3fr, Strolling troubadour "Griot," Mali. 5fr, Quipongos women, Angola. 50fr, Man at prayer, Mauritania. 90fr, Sinehatiali dance costumes, Ivory Coast.

343	A60	20c multi	5	5
344	A60	30c multi	5	5
345	A60	50c multi	5	5
346	A60	1fr multi	6	6
347	A60	3fr multi	8	6
348	A60	5fr multi	12	12
349	A60	50fr multi	1.35	65
350	A60	90fr multi	2.50	1.10
		Nos. 343-350 (8)	4.26	2.14

Flower Arrangement, Peacock, EXPO '70 Emblem—A61

Designs (EXPO Emblem and): 30c, Torii and Camellias, by Yukihiko Yasuda. 50c, Kabuki character and Woman Playing Samisen, by Nampu Katayama. 1fr, Tower of the Sun, and Warrior Riding into Water. 3fr, Pavilion and Buddhist deity. 5fr, Pagoda and modern painting by Shuho Yamakawa. 20fr, Japanese inscription "Omatsuri" and Osaka Castle. 70fr, EXPO '70 emblem and Warrior on Horseback.

1970, Aug. 24   Photo.   Perf. 13

351	A61	20c gold & multi	5	5
352	A61	30c gold & multi	5	5
353	A61	50c gold & multi	5	5
354	A61	1fr gold & multi	6	6
355	A61	3fr gold & multi	10	6
356	A61	5fr gold & multi	15	6
357	A61	20fr gold & multi	65	50
358	A61	70fr gold & multi	2.00	1.00
		Nos. 351-358 (8)	3.11	1.83

Issued to commemorate EXPO '70 International Exhibition, Osaka, Japan, Mar. 15–Sept. 13.

Young Mountain Gorillas
A62

Designs: Various Gorillas. 40c, 80c, 2fr, 100fr are vertical.

1970, Sept. 7

359	A62	20c ol & blk	5	5
360	A62	40c brt rose lil & blk	5	5
361	A62	60c bl, brn & blk	5	5
362	A62	80c org brn & blk	5	5
363	A62	1fr dk grn & blk	6	5
364	A62	2fr blk & multi	6	5
365	A62	15fr sep & blk	45	25
366	A62	100fr brt bl & blk	2.75	1.60
		Nos. 359-366 (8)	3.52	2.25

Pierre J. Pelletier and Joseph B. Caventou
A63

Designs: 20c, Cinchona flower and bark. 80c, Quinine powder and pharmacological vessels. 1fr, Anopheles mosquito. 3fr, Malaria patient and nurse. 25fr, "Malaria" (mosquito).

1970, Oct. 27   Photo.   Perf. 13

367	A63	20c sil & multi	5	5
368	A63	80c sil & multi	5	5
369	A63	1fr sil & multi	5	5
370	A63	3fr sil & multi	10	5
371	A63	25fr sil & multi	75	38
372	A63	70fr sil & multi	2.00	90
		Nos. 367-372 (6)	3.00	1.48

Issued to commemorate the 150th anniversary of the discovery of quinine by Pierre Joseph Pelletier (1788-1842) and Joseph Bienaimé Caventou (1795-1877), French pharmacologists.

Apollo Spaceship
A64

Apollo Spaceship: 30c, Second stage separation. 50c, Spaceship over moon surface. 1fr, Landing module and astronauts on moon. 3fr, Take-off from moon. 5fr, Return to earth. 10fr, Final separation of nose cone. 80fr, Splashdown.

1970, Nov. 23   Photo.   Perf. 13

373	A64	20c sil & multi	5	5
374	A64	30c sil & multi	5	5
375	A64	50c sil & multi	5	5
376	A64	1fr sil & multi	6	6
377	A64	3fr sil & multi	10	5
378	A64	5fr sil & multi	18	10
379	A64	10fr sil & multi	30	16
380	A64	80fr sil & multi	2.50	1.35
		Nos. 373-380 (8)	3.32	1.86

Conquest of space.

RWANDA

Franklin D. Roosevelt and Brassocattleya Olympia Alba
A65

Designs: Various portraits of Franklin D. Roosevelt and various orchids.

1970, Dec. 21   Photo.   Perf. 13

381	A65	20c bl, blk & brn	5	5
382	A65	30c car rose, blk & brn	5	5
383	A65	50c dp org, blk & brn	5	5
384	A65	1fr grn, blk & brn	5	5
385	A65	2fr mar, blk & grn	6	4
386	A65	6fr lil & multi	12	6
387	A65	30fr bl, blk & sl grn	90	45
388	A65	60fr lil rose, blk & sl grn	1.90	75
		Nos. 381-388 (8)	3.18	1.51

Pres. Franklin D. Roosevelt, 25th anniversary of his death.

Christmas Issue
Souvenir Sheet
Christmas Type of 1968

Design: 100fr, Adoration of the Shepherds, by José de Ribera (vert.).

1970, Dec. 24   Engraved   Perf. 11½

| 389 | A48 | 100fr Prus bl | 3.25 | 3.25 |

Marginal inscription in rose magenta and Prussian blue. Size: 71x84mm.

Pope Paul VI
A66

Portraits of Popes: 20c, John XXIII, 1958–1963. 30c, Pius XII, 1939–1958. 40c, Pius XI, 1922–39. 1fr, Benedict XV, 1914–22. 18fr, St. Pius X, 1903–14. 20fr, Leo XIII, 1878–1903. 60fr, Pius IX, 1846–78.

1970, Dec. 31   Photo.   Perf. 13

390	A66	10c gold & dk brn	5	5
391	A66	20c gold & dk grn	5	5
392	A66	30c gold & dp cl	5	5
393	A66	40c gold & ind	5	5
394	A66	1fr gold & dk pur	6	6
395	A66	18fr gold & pur	50	25
396	A66	20fr gold & org brn	65	38
397	A66	60fr gold & blk brn	1.65	90
		Nos. 390-397 (8)	3.06	1.79

Centenary of Vatican I, Ecumenical Council of the Roman Catholic Church, 1869–70.

Headdress Type of 1969

African Headdresses: 20c, Rendille woman. 30c, Young Toubou woman, Chad. 50c, Peul man, Niger. 1fr, Young Masai man, Kenya. 5fr, Young Peul girl, Niger. 18fr, Rwanda woman. 25fr, Man, Mauritania. 50fr, Rwanda women with pearl necklaces.

1971, Feb. 15   Litho.   Perf. 13

398	A50	20c multi	5	5
399	A50	30c multi	5	5
400	A50	50c multi	5	5
401	A50	1fr multi	5	5
402	A50	5fr multi	10	6
403	A50	18fr multi	45	30
404	A50	25fr multi	70	40
405	A50	50fr multi	1.50	75
		Nos. 398-405 (8)	2.95	1.71

Souvenir Sheet
M. L. King Type of 1968

Design: 100fr, Charles de Gaulle.

1971, Mar. 15   Engraved   Perf. 13½

| 406 | A44 | 100fr ultra | 3.50 | 2.50 |

In memory of Charles de Gaulle (1890–1970), President of France.

Souvenir Sheet

Astronaut Type of 1969 Inscribed in Dark Violet with Emblem and: "APOLLO / 14 / SHEPARD / ROOSA / MITCHELL"

1971, Apr. 15   Engraved   Perf. 11½

| 407 | A52 | 100fr brn org | 4.50 | 4.00 |

Apollo 14 U.S. moon landing, Jan. 31–Feb. 9. Size of No. 407: 94x109mm.

Beethoven, by Christian Horneman
A67

Beethoven Portraits: 30c, Joseph Stieler. 50c, by Ferdinand Schimon. 3fr, by H. Best. 6fr, by W. Fassbender. 90fr, Beethoven's Funeral Procession, by Leopold Stöber.

1971, July 5   Photo.   Perf. 13

408	A67	20c gold & multi	5	5
409	A67	30c gold & multi	5	5
410	A67	50c gold & multi	5	5
411	A67	3fr gold & multi	10	5
412	A67	6fr gold & multi	20	6
413	A67	90fr gold & multi	2.75	1.50
		Nos. 408-413 (6)	3.20	1.76

Bicentenary of the birth of Ludwig van Beethoven (1770–1827), composer.

Equestrian
A68

Olympic Sports: 30c, Runner at start. 50c, Basketball. 1fr, High jump. 8fr, Boxing. 10fr, Pole vault. 20fr, Wrestling. 60fr, Gymnastics (rings).

1971, Oct. 25   Photo.   Perf. 13

414	A68	20c gold & blk	5	5
415	A68	30c gold & dp rose lil	5	5
416	A68	50c gold & vio bl	5	5
417	A68	1fr gold & dp grn	5	5
418	A68	8fr gold & hn brn	25	13
419	A68	10fr gold & pur	32	18
420	A68	20fr gold & dp brn	60	35
421	A68	60fr gold & Prus bl	1.75	75
		Nos. 414-421 (8)	3.12	1.61

20th Summer Olympic Games, Munich, Aug. 26–Sept. 10, 1972.

Christmas Type of 1968
Souvenir Sheet

Design: 100fr, Nativity, by Anthony van Dyck (vert.).

1971, Dec. 20   Engr.   Perf. 11½

| 422 | A48 | 100fr indigo | 3.25 | 3.25 |

Marginal inscription in rose magenta and indigo. Size: 63x84mm.

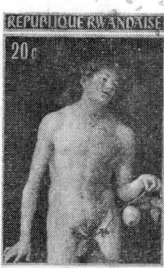

Adam by Dürer
A69

Paintings by Dürer: 30c, Eve. 50c, Hieronymus Holzschuher, Portrait. 1fr, Lamentation of Christ. 3fr, Madonna with the Pear. 5fr, St. Eustace. 20fr, Sts. Paul and Mark. 70fr, Self-portrait, 1500.

1971, Dec. 31   Photo.   Perf. 13

423	A69	20c gold & multi	5	5
424	A69	30c gold & multi	5	5
425	A69	50c gold & multi	5	5
426	A69	1fr gold & multi	5	5
427	A69	3fr gold & multi	10	5
428	A69	5fr gold & multi	15	9
429	A69	20fr gold & multi	65	35
430	A69	70fr gold & multi	2.10	1.40
		Nos. 423-430 (8)	3.20	2.09

Dürer paintings. 500th anniversary of the birth of Albrecht Dürer (1471–1528), German painter and engraver.

A 600fr on gold foil honoring Apollo 15 was issued Jan. 15, 1972.

Guardsmen Exercising
A70

Designs (National Guard Emblem and): 6fr, Loading supplies. 15fr, Helicopter ambulance. 25fr, Health Service for civilians. 50fr, Guardsman and map of Rwanda (vert.).

Perf. 13½x14, 14x13½

1972, Feb. 7

431	A70	4fr dp org & multi	10	7
432	A70	6fr yel & multi	12	10
433	A70	15fr lt bl & multi	35	22
434	A70	25fr red & multi	70	40
435	A70	50fr multi	1.35	90
		Nos. 431-435 (5)	2.62	1.69

"The National Guard serving the nation."

Ice Hockey, Sapporo Olympics Emblem
A71

1972, Feb. 12   Perf. 13x13½
Multicolored

436	A71	20c shown	5	5
437	A71	30c Speed skating	5	5
438	A71	50c Ski jump	5	5
439	A71	1fr Men's figure skating	5	5
440	A71	6fr Cross-country skiing	12	10
441	A71	12fr Slalom	30	20
442	A71	20fr Bobsledding	55	35
443	A71	60fr Downhill skiing	1.75	1.10
		Nos. 436-443 (8)	2.92	1.95

11th Winter Olympic Games, Sapporo, Japan, Feb. 3–13.

Antelopes and Cercopithecus—A72

1972, Mar. 20   Photo.   Perf. 13
Gold and Multicolored

444	A72	20c shown	5	5
445	A72	30c Buffaloes	5	5
446	A72	50c Zebras	5	5
447	A72	1fr Rhinoceroses	5	5
448	A72	2fr Wart hogs	5	5
449	A72	6fr Hippopotamuses	15	10
450	A72	18fr Hyenas	50	30
451	A72	32fr Guinea fowl	90	55
452	A72	60fr Antelopes	1.75	1.10
453	A72	80fr Lions	2.40	1.50
		Nos. 444-453 (10)	5.95	3.80

Akagera National Park.

Family Raising Flag of Rwanda
A73

1972, Apr. 4   Perf. 13x12½

454	A73	6fr dk red & multi	12	10
455	A73	18fr grn & multi	50	30
456	A73	60fr brn & multi	1.65	1.10

10th anniversary of the Referendum establishing Republic of Rwanda.

Common Waxbills and Hibiscus
A74

Birds: 30c, Collared sunbird. 50c, Variable sunbird. 1fr, Greater double-collared sunbird. 4fr, Ruwenzori puff-back flycatcher. 6fr, Red-billed fire finch. 10fr, Scarlet-chested sunbird. 18fr, Red-headed quelea. 60fr, Black-headed gonolek. 100fr, African golden oriole.

1972, May 17   Photo.   Perf. 13

457	A74	20c dl grn & multi	5	5
458	A74	30c buff & multi	5	5
459	A74	50c yel & multi	5	5
460	A74	1fr lt bl & multi	5	5
461	A74	4fr dl rose & multi	10	6
462	A74	6fr lil rose & multi	12	10
463	A74	10fr pink & multi	25	15
464	A74	18fr gray & multi	50	30
465	A74	60fr multi	1.80	1.10
466	A74	100fr vio & multi	2.85	1.80
		Nos. 457-466 (10)	5.82	3.71

Belgica '72 Emblem, King Baudouin, Queen Fabiola, Pres. and Mrs. Kayibanda—A75

RWANDA

1972, June 24 Photo. Perf. 13
Gold and Multicolored
Size: 37x34mm.
| 467 | A75 | 18fr | Rwanda landscape | 55 | 30 |
| 468 | A75 | 22fr | Old houses, Bruges | 70 | 35 |

Size: 50x34mm.
| 469 | A75 | 40fr | shown | 1.25 | 60 |

Belgica '72 International Philatelic Exhibition, Brussels, June 24-July 9. Printed se-tenant in sheets of 15 (3x5).

Pres. Kayibanda Addressing Meeting
A76

Designs (Pres. Grégoire Kayibanda): 30c, promoting officers of National Guard. 50c, with wife and children. 6fr, casting vote. 10fr, with wife and dignitaries at Feast of Justice. 15fr, with Cabinet and members of Assembly. 18fr, taking oath of office. 50fr, Portrait (vert.).

1972, July 4
470	A76	20c	gold & sl grn	5	5
471	A76	30c	gold & dk pur	5	5
472	A76	50c	gold & choc	5	5
473	A76	6fr	gold & Prus bl	15	10
474	A76	10fr	gold & dk pur	30	15
475	A76	15fr	gold & dk bl	45	20
476	A76	18fr	gold & brn	65	30
477	A76	50fr	gold & Prus bl	1.50	90
		Nos. 470-477 (8)		3.20	1.80

10th anniversary of independence.

Equestrian, Olympic Emblems
A77

Designs (Olympic Emblems, Stadium, TV Tower and): 30c, Hockey. 50c, Soccer. 1fr, Broad jump. 6fr, Bicycling. 18fr, Yachting. 30fr, Hurdles. 44fr, Gymnastics, women's.

1972, Aug. 16 Photo. Perf. 14
478	A77	20c	dk brn & gold	5	5
479	A77	30c	vio bl & gold	5	5
480	A77	50c	dk grn & gold	5	5
481	A77	1fr	dp cl & gold	5	5
482	A77	6fr	blk & gold	15	10
483	A77	18fr	brn & gold	45	30
484	A77	30fr	dk vio & gold	90	45
485	A77	44fr	Prus bl & gold	1.25	60
		Nos. 478-485 (8)		2.95	1.65

20th Olympic Games, Munich, Aug. 26-Sept. 11.

Relay (Sport) and U.N. Emblem
A78

1972, Oct. 23 Photo. Perf. 13
Gold and Multicolored
486	A78	20c	shown	5	5
487	A78	30c	Musicians	5	5
488	A78	50c	Dancers	5	5
489	A78	1fr	Operating room	5	5
490	A78	6fr	Weaver & painter	15	10
491	A78	18fr	Classroom	25	30
492	A78	24fr	Laboratory	80	40
493	A78	50fr	Hands of 4 races reaching for equality	1.50	90
		Nos. 486-493 (8)		2.90	1.90

Fight against racism.

Christmas Type of 1968
Souvenir Sheet
Design: 100fr, Adoration of the Shepherds, by Jacob Jordaens (vert.).
1972, Dec. 11 Perf. 11½
| 494 | A48 | 100fr | red brn | 3.25 | 3.25 |

Marginal inscription in green and red brown. Size: 89½x106mm.

Phymateus Brunneri—A79

Designs: Various insects. 30c, 1fr, 6fr, 22fr, 100fr, vertical.

1973, Jan. 31 Photogravure Perf. 13
495	A79	20c	multi	5	5
496	A79	30c	multi	5	5
497	A79	50c	multi	5	5
498	A79	1fr	multi	5	5
499	A79	2fr	multi	5	5
500	A79	6fr	multi	15	10
501	A79	18fr	multi	50	30
502	A79	22fr	multi	65	30
503	A79	70fr	multi	2.00	1.20
504	A79	100fr	multi	3.25	1.80
		Nos. 495-504 (10)		6.80	3.95

Souvenir Sheet
Perf. 14
| 505 | A79 | 80fr | like 20c | 2.75 | 2.75 |

No. 505 contains one stamp (size 43½x 33½mm.); gold marginal inscription and border. Size of sheet: 100x80mm.

Emile Zola, by Edouard Manet
A80

Paintings Connected with Reading, and Book Year Emblem: 30c, Rembrandt's Mother. 50c, St Jerome Removing Thorn from Lion's Paw, by Colantonio. 1fr, Apostles Peter and Paul, by El Greco. 2fr, Virgin and Child with Book, by Roger van der Weyden. 6fr, St. Jerome in his Cell, by Antonella de Messina. 40fr, St. Barbara, by Master of Flemalle. No. 513, Don Quixote, by Otto Bonevalle. No. 514, Pres. Kayibanda reading book.

1973, Mar. 12 Photo. Perf. 13
506	A80	20c	gold & multi	5	5
507	A80	30c	gold & multi	5	5
508	A80	50c	gold & multi	5	5
509	A80	1fr	gold & multi	5	5
510	A80	2fr	gold & multi	5	5
511	A80	6fr	gold & multi	18	10
512	A80	40fr	gold & multi	1.35	65
513	A80	100fr	gold & multi	3.25	1.50
		Nos. 506-513 (8)		5.03	2.50

Souvenir Sheet
Perf. 14
| 514 | A80 | 100fr | gold, bl & ind | 3.25 | 2.50 |

International Book Year 1972. No. 514 has multicolored ornamental border. Size: 70x80mm.

Longombe Rubens and Isabella Brandt, by Rubens
A81 A82

Designs: Musical instruments of Central and West Africa.

1973, Apr. 9 Photo. Perf. 13½
Gray and Multicolored
515	A81	20c	shown	5	5
516	A81	30c	Horn	5	5
517	A81	50c	Xylophone	5	5
518	A81	1fr	Harp	5	5
519	A81	4fr	Alur horns	5	5
520	A81	6fr	Drum, bells and horn	15	10
521	A81	18fr	Large drums (Ngoma)	45	25
522	A81	90fr	Toba	2.50	1.20
		Nos. 515-522 (8)		3.40	1.80

1973, May 11
Paintings from Old Pinakothek, Munich (IBRA Emblem and): 30c, Young Man, by Cranach. 50c, Woman Peeling Turnips, by Chardin. 1fr, The Abduction of Leucippa's Daughters, by Rubens. 2fr, Virgin and Child, by Filippo Lippi. 6fr, Boys Eating Fruit, by Murillo. 40fr, The Lovesick Woman, by Jan Steen. No. 530, Jesus Stripped of His Garments, by El Greco. No. 531, Oswalt Krehl, by Dürer.

523	A82	20c	gold & multi	5	5
524	A82	30c	gold & multi	5	5
525	A82	50c	gold & multi	5	5
526	A82	1fr	gold & multi	5	5
527	A82	2fr	gold & multi	6	5
528	A82	6fr	gold & multi	15	10
529	A82	40fr	gold & multi	1.10	50
530	A82	100fr	gold & multi	2.75	1.25
		Nos. 523-530 (8)		4.26	2.10

Souvenir Sheet
| 531 | A82 | 100fr | gold & multi | 3.00 | 2.50 |

IBRA München 1973 International Philatelic Exhibition, Munich, May 11-20. No. 531 contains one stamp (Size: 40x56 mm.), multicolored margin. Size: 75x90 mm.

Map of Africa and Peace Doves
A83

Design: 94fr, Map of Africa and hands.

1973, July 23 Photo. Perf. 13½
| 532 | A83 | 6fr | gold & multi | 25 | 15 |
| 533 | A83 | 94fr | gold & multi | 2.75 | 2.25 |

Organization for African Unity, 10th anniversary.

Nos. 298-303 Overprinted in Blue, Black, Green or Brown:
"SECHERESSE/SOLIDARITE AFRICAINE"
1973, Aug. 23 Photo. Perf. 13
534	A53	20c	multi (Bl)	5	5
535	A53	40c	multi (Bk)	5	5
536	A53	60c	multi (Bl)	5	5
537	A53	80c	multi (G)	5	5
538	A53	3fr	multi (G)	8	5
539	A53	75fr	multi (Br)	2.25	1.35
		Nos. 534-539, B1 (7)		7.28	5.77

African solidarity in drought emergency.

African Postal Union Issue
Common Design Type
1973, Sept. 12 Engraved Perf. 13
| 540 | CD137 | 100fr | dp brn, bl & brn | 3.00 | 2.50 |

Six-lined Distichodus
A84

African Fish: 30c, Little triggerfish. 50c, Spotted upside-down catfish. 1fr, Nile mouthbreeder. 2fr, African lungfish. 6fr, Pareutropius mandevillei. 40fr, Congo characin. 100fr, Like 20c. 150fr, Julidochromis ornatus.

1973, Sept. 3 Photo. Perf. 13
541	A84	20c	gold & multi	5	5
542	A84	30c	gold & multi	5	5
543	A84	50c	gold & multi	5	5
544	A84	1fr	gold & multi	5	5
545	A84	2fr	gold & multi	8	5
546	A84	6fr	gold & multi	15	10
547	A84	40fr	gold & multi	1.15	60
548	A84	150fr	gold & multi	4.25	2.25
		Nos. 541-548 (8)		5.83	2.65

Souvenir Sheet
| 549 | A84 | 100fr | gold & multi | 3.00 | 3.00 |

No. 549 contains one stamp (48x29mm.); gold margin and inscription. Size: 90x 70mm.

Nos. 398-405 Overprinted in Black, Silver, Green or Blue

1973, Sept. 15 Lithographed
550	A50	20c	multi (Bk)	5	5
551	A50	30c	multi (S)	5	5
552	A50	50c	multi (Bk)	5	5
553	A50	1fr	multi (G)	5	5
554	A50	5fr	multi (S)	18	6
555	A50	18fr	multi (Bk)	50	30
556	A50	25fr	multi (G)	75	40
557	A50	50fr	multi (Bl)	1.75	80
		Nos. 550-557 (8)		3.38	1.76

Africa Weeks, Brussels, Sept. 15-30, 1973. On the 30c, 1fr and 25fr the text of the overprint is horizontal.

Nos. 431-435 Overprinted in Gold

Perf. 13½x14, 14x13½
1973, Oct. 31 Photogravure
559	A70	4fr	dp org & multi	10	7
560	A70	6fr	yel & multi	15	10
561	A70	15fr	lt bl & multi	42	27
562	A70	25fr	red & multi	70	40
563	A70	50fr	multi	1.50	80
		Nos. 559-563 (5)		2.87	1.64

25th Anniversary of the Universal Declaration of Human Rights.

Christmas Type of 1968
Souvenir Sheet
Design: 100fr, Adoration of the Shepherds, by Guido Reni.
1973, Dec. 15 Engraved Perf. 11½
| 564 | A48 | 100fr | brt vio | 3.00 | 3.00 |

Marginal inscription in green and bright violet. Size: 102x86mm.

RWANDA

Copernicus and Astrolabe A85 — Pres. Juvénal Habyarimana A86

Designs: 30c, 18fr, 100fr, Portrait. 50c, 80fr, Copernicus and heliocentric system. 1fr, like 20c.

1973, Dec. 26   Photo.   Perf. 13

565	A85	20c sil & multi	5	5
566	A85	30c sil & multi	5	5
567	A85	50c sil & multi	5	5
568	A85	1fr gold & multi	5	5
569	A85	18fr gold & multi	45	30
570	A85	80fr gold & multi	2.25	1.20
		Nos. 565-570 (6)	2.90	1.70

Souvenir Sheet

| 571 | A85 | 100fr gold & multi | 3.00 | 1.80 |

500th anniversary of the birth of Nicolaus Copernicus (1473-1543), Polish astronomer. No. 571 contains one stamp, black and gold margin. Size: 81x85mm.

1974, Apr. 8   Photo.   Perf. 11½
Black Inscriptions

572	A86	1fr bis & sep	5	5
573	A86	2fr ultra & sep	5	5
574	A86	5fr rose red & sep	12	5
575	A86	6fr grnsh bl & sep	15	5
576	A86	26fr lil & sep	70	45
577	A86	60fr ol grn & sep	1.80	1.00
		Nos. 572-577 (6)	2.87	1.65

Souvenir Sheet

Christ Between the Thieves (Detail), by Rubens—A87

1974, Apr. 12   Engr.   Perf. 11½

| 578 | A87 | 100fr sepia | 4.00 | 4.00 |

Easter 1974. No. 578 has orange and sepia marginal inscription. Size: 91x77 mm.

Jugoslavia-Zaire Soccer Game A88

Designs: Games' emblem and soccer games.

1974, July 6   Photo.   Perf. 13½
Multicolored

579	A88	20c shown	5	5
580	A88	40c Netherlands-Sweden	5	5
581	A88	60c Germany (Fed.)-Australia	5	5
582	A88	80c Haiti-Argentina	5	5
583	A88	2fr Brazil-Scotland	5	5
584	A88	6fr Bulgaria-Uruguay	15	10
585	A88	40fr Italy-Poland	1.05	60
586	A88	50fr Chile-Germany (DDR)	1.50	1.00
		Nos. 579-586 (8)	2.95	1.95

World Cup Soccer Championship, Munich, June 13–July 7.

Marconi's Laboratory Yacht "Elletra"—A89

Designs: 30c, Marconi and steamer "Carlo Alberto." 50c, Marconi's wireless apparatus and telecommunications satellites. 4fr, Marconi and globes connected by communications waves. 35fr, Marconi's radio, and radar. 60fr, Marconi and transmitter at Poldhu, Cornwall. 50fr, like 20c.

1974, Aug. 19   Photo.   Perf. 13½

587	A89	20c vio, blk & grn	5	5
588	A89	30c grn, blk & vio	5	5
589	A89	50c yel, blk & lil	5	5
590	A89	4fr sal, blk & bl	10	6
591	A89	35fr lil, blk & yel	90	60
592	A89	60fr bl, blk & brnz	1.75	1.10
		Nos. 587-592 (6)	2.90	1.91

Souvenir Sheet

| 593 | A89 | 50fr gold, blk & lt bl | 1.75 | 1.75 |

Birth centenary of Guglielmo Marconi (1874–1937), Italian electrical engineer and inventor. No. 593 contains one stamp, black and gold margin. Size: 95x70mm.

The Flute Player, by J. Leyster A90 — Messenger Monk A91

Paintings: 20c, Diane de Poitiers, Fontainebleau School. 50c, Virgin and Child, by David. 1fr, Triumph of Venus, by Boucher. 10fr, Seated Harlequin, by Picasso. 18fr, Virgin and Child, 15th century. 20fr, Beheading of St. John, by Hans Fries. 50fr, Daughter of Andersdotter, by J. F. Höckert.

1974, Sept. 23   Photo.   Perf. 14x13

594	A90	20c gold & multi	5	5
595	A90	30c gold & multi	5	5
596	A90	50c gold & multi	5	5
597	A90	1fr gold & multi	5	5
598	A90	10fr gold & multi	25	15
599	A90	18fr gold & multi	45	25
600	A90	20fr gold & multi	50	35
601	A90	50fr gold & multi	1.50	90
		Nos. 594-601 (8)	2.90	1.85

INTERNABA 74 International Philatelic Exhibition, Basel, June 7–10, and Stockholmia 74, International Philatelic Exhibition, Stockholm, Sept. 21–29.

Six multicolored souvenir sheets exist containing two 15fr stamps each in various combinations of designs of Nos. 594–601. Size: 85x73mm. One souvenir sheet of four 25fr stamps exists with designs of Nos. 595, 597, 599 and 601. Size: 85x117mm.

1974, Oct. 9   Perf. 14

Designs (UPU Emblem and Messengers): 30c, Inca. 50c, Morocco. 1fr, India. 18fr, Polynesia. 80fr, Rwanda.

602	A91	20c gold & multi	5	5
603	A91	30c gold & multi	5	5
604	A91	50c gold & multi	5	5
605	A91	1fr gold & multi	5	5
606	A91	18fr gold & multi	65	55
607	A91	80fr gold & multi	2.50	2.40
		Nos. 602-607 (6)	3.35	3.15

Centenary of Universal Postal Union.

Nos. 306-308 Overprinted

1974, Dec. 16   Photo.   Perf. 11½

608	A54	6fr brt pink & multi	5.00	5.00
609	A54	18fr ultra & multi	5.00	5.00
610	A54	40fr brn & multi	5.50	5.50

15th anniversary of independence.

Christmas Type of 1968
Souvenir Sheet

Design: 100fr, Adoration of the Kings, by Joos van Cleve.

1974, Dec. 23   Engr.   Perf. 11½

| 611 | A48 | 100fr sl grn | 5.00 | 5.00 |

No. 611 has slate green picture frame around stamp and orange marginal inscription. Size: 107x91mm.

Nos. 295-296 Overprinted:
"1974 / 10e Anniversaire"

1974, Dec. 30   Photo.   Perf. 13

| 612 | A51 | 30fr sil & multi | 1.10 | 1.10 |
| 613 | A51 | 70fr gold & multi | 2.10 | 2.10 |

African Development Bank, 10th anniversary.

Uganda Kob A92

Antelopes: 30c, Bongos (horiz.). 50c, Rwanda antelopes. 1fr, Young sitatungas (horiz.). 4fr, Greater kudus. 10fr, Impalas (horiz.). 34fr, Waterbuck. 40fr, Impalas. 60fr, Greater kudu. 100fr, Derby's elands (horiz.).

1975, Mar. 17   Photo.   Perf. 13

614	A92	20c multi	5	5
615	A92	30c multi	5	5
616	A92	50c multi	5	5
617	A92	1fr multi	5	5
618	A92	4fr multi	10	6
619	A92	10fr multi	25	15
620	A92	34fr multi	95	50
621	A92	100fr multi	3.25	1.50
		Nos. 614-621 (8)	4.75	2.41

Miniature Sheets

| 622 | A92 | 40fr multi | 2.75 | 2.75 |
| 623 | A92 | 60fr multi | 2.75 | 2.75 |

Nos. 622-623 contain one stamp each with designs continuing into margins. Size: 130x90mm.

Miniature Sheets

The Burial of Jesus, by Raphael—A93

1975, Apr. 1   Photo.   Perf. 13x14
Gold and Multicolored

624	A93	20fr shown	1.50	1.50
625	A93	30fr Pieta, by Cranach the Elder	1.75	1.75
626	A93	50fr by van der Weyden	1.75	1.75
627	A93	100fr by Bellini	1.75	1.75

Easter 1975. Size of stamps: 40x52 mm.; of sheets: 130x89mm.

Souvenir Sheets

Prince Balthazar Charles, by Velazquez—A94

Paintings: 30fr, Infanta Margaret of Austria, by Velazquez. 50fr, The Divine Shepherd, by Murillo. 100fr, Francisco Goya, by V. Lopez y Portana.

1975, Apr. 4   Photo.   Perf. 13

628	A94	20fr multi	1.50	1.50
629	A94	30fr multi	1.75	1.75
630	A94	50fr multi	1.75	1.75
631	A94	100fr multi	1.75	1.75

España 75 International Philatelic Exhibition, Madrid, Apr. 4–13. Nos. 628–631 have gold border and España 75 emblem. Size of stamps: 38x48mm.; sheets, 89x130mm. See also Nos. 642–643.

Pyrethrum (Insect Powder) A95

1975, Apr. 14   Perf. 13
Gold and Multicolored

632	A95	20c shown	5	5
633	A95	30c Tea	5	5
634	A95	50c Coffee (beans and pan)	5	5
635	A95	4fr Bananas	10	6
636	A95	10fr Corn	25	15
637	A95	12fr Sorghum	30	16
638	A95	26fr Rice	70	35
639	A95	47fr Coffee (workers and beans)	1.60	70
		Nos. 632-639 (8)	3.10	1.60

RWANDA

Souvenir Sheets
Perf. 13½

| 640 | A95 | 25fr like 50c | 1.00 | 1.00 |
| 641 | A95 | 75fr like 47fr | 2.40 | 2.40 |

Year of Agriculture. Nos. 632–641 commemorate 10th anniversary of Office for Industrialized Cultivation. Nos. 640–641 have gold and purple margin. Size: 55x77mm.

Souvenir Sheets
Painting Type of 1975
Paintings: 75fr, Louis XIV, by Hyacinthe Rigaud. 125fr, Cavalry Officer, by Jean Gericault.

1975, June 6 Photo. Perf. 13

| 642 | A94 | 75fr multi | 2.50 | 2.50 |
| 643 | A94 | 125fr multi | 4.25 | 4.25 |

ARPHILA 75, International Philatelic Exhibition, Paris, June 6–16. Nos. 642–643 have gold border and ARPHILA 75 emblem. Size of stamps: 38x48mm.; sheets: 89x130 mm.

Nos. 390–397 Overprinted:
"1975 / ANNEE / SAINTE"

1975, June 23 Photo. Perf. 13

644	A66	10c gold & dk brn	5	5
645	A66	20c gold & dk grn	5	5
646	A66	30c gold & dp cl	5	5
647	A66	40c gold & ind	5	5
648	A66	1fr gold & dk pur	5	5
649	A66	18fr gold & pur	45	12
650	A66	20fr gold & org brn	60	30
651	A66	60fr gold & blk brn	2.25	1.25
		Nos. 644-651 (8)	3.55	1.92

Holy Year 1975.

White Pelicans—A96
Designs: African birds.

1975, June 20 Multicolored

652	A96	20c shown	5	5
653	A96	30c Malachite kingfisher	5	5
654	A96	50c Goliath herons	5	5
655	A96	1fr Saddle-billed storks	5	5
656	A96	4fr African jacana	10	6
657	A96	10fr African anhingas	30	15
658	A96	34fr Sacred ibis	90	50
659	A96	80fr Hartlaub ducks	2.50	1.20
		Nos. 652-659 (8)	4.00	2.11

Miniature Sheets

| 660 | A96 | 40fr Flamingoes | 1.75 | 1.75 |
| 661 | A96 | 60fr Crowned cranes | 2.50 | 2.50 |

Nos. 660–661 contain one stamp each with designs continuing into margins. Size: 130x90mm.

Globe Representing Races and WPY Emblem
A97

The Bath, by Mary Cassatt and IWY Emblem
A98

Designs: 26fr, Population graph and emblem. 34fr, Globe with open door and emblem.

1975, Sept. 1 Photo. Perf. 13½x13

662	A97	20fr dp bl & multi	55	30
663	A97	26fr dl red brn & multi	75	40
664	A97	34fr yel & multi	1.10	50

World Population Year 1974.

1975, Sept. 15 Perf. 13

Designs (IWY Emblem and): 30c, Mother and Infant Son, by Julius Gari Melchers. 50c, Woman with Milk Jug, by Jan Vermeer. 1fr, Water Carrier, by Goya. 8fr, Rwanda woman cotton picker. 12fr, Scientist with microscope. 18fr, Mother and child. 25fr, Empress Josephine, by Pierre-Paul Prud'hon. 40fr, Madame Vigee-Lebrun and Daughter, self-portrait. 60fr, Woman carrying child on back and water jug on head.

665	A98	20c gold & multi	5	5
666	A98	30c gold & multi	5	5
667	A98	50c gold & multi	5	5
668	A98	1fr gold & multi	5	5
669	A98	8fr gold & multi	20	12
670	A98	12fr gold & multi	30	18
671	A98	18fr gold & multi	45	26
672	A98	60fr gold & multi	1.75	90
		Nos. 665-672 (8)	2.90	1.66

Souvenir Sheets
Perf. 13½

| 673 | A98 | 25fr multi | 2.50 | 2.50 |
| 674 | A98 | 40fr multi | 2.50 | 2.50 |

International Women's Year 1975. Nos. 673–674 each contain one stamp (37x49 mm.); design extends into margin which has gold border and IWY emblem. Size: 88x130mm.

Owl, Quill and Book
A99

Designs: 30c, Hygiene emblem. 1.50fr, Kneeling woman holding scales of Justice. 18fr, Chemist in laboratory. 26fr, Symbol of commerce and chart. 34fr, University Building.

1975, Sept. 29 Perf. 13

675	A99	20c pur & multi	5	5
676	A99	30c ultra & multi	5	5
677	A99	1.50fr lil & multi	5	5
678	A99	18fr bl & multi	45	20
679	A99	26fr ol & multi	70	40
680	A99	34fr bl & multi	1.10	50
		Nos. 675-680 (6)	2.40	1.25

National University of Rwanda, 10th anniversary.

Souvenir Sheets
Painting Type of 1975
Designs (Paintings by Vermeer): 20fr, Man and Woman Drinking Wine. 30fr, Young Woman Reading Letter. 50fr, Painter in his Studio. 100fr, Young Woman Playing Virginal.

1975, Oct. 13 Photo. Perf. 13x14

681	A93	20fr multi	60	60
682	A93	30fr multi	90	90
683	A93	50fr multi	1.50	1.50
684	A93	100fr multi	3.00	3.00

Jan Vermeer (1632–1675), painter, 300th death anniversary. Size of stamps: 40x52mm.; of sheets: 130x89mm.

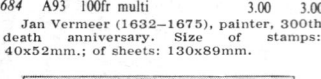

Waterhole and Impatiens Stuhlmannii—A100

Designs: 30c, Antelopes, zebras, candelabra cactus. 50c, Brush fire, and tapinanthus prunifolius. 5fr, Bulera Lake and Egyptian white lotus. 8fr, Erosion prevention and protea madiensis. 10fr, Marsh and melanthera brownei. 26fr, Landscape, lobelias and senecons. 100fr, Sabyinyo Volcano and polystachya kermesina.

1975, Oct. 25 Perf. 13

685	A100	20c blk & multi	5	5
686	A100	30c blk & multi	5	5
687	A100	50c blk & multi	5	5
688	A100	5fr blk & multi	12	8
689	A100	8fr blk & multi	20	12
690	A100	10fr blk & multi	25	15
691	A100	26fr blk & multi	75	38
692	A100	100fr blk & multi	2.75	1.50
		Nos. 685-692 (8)	4.22	2.38

Nature protection.

Nos. 343–348 Overprinted
SECHERESSE SOLIDARITE 1975

1975, Nov. 10 Litho. Perf. 13

693	A60	20c multi	5	5
694	A60	30c multi	5	5
695	A60	50c multi	5	5
696	A60	1fr multi	5	5
697	A60	3fr multi	10	5
698	A60	5fr multi	15	5
		Nos. 693-698, B2-B3 (8)	5.70	4.08

African solidarity in drought emergency.

Fork-lift Truck on Airfield
A101

Designs: 30c, Coffee packing plant. 50c, Engineering plant. 10fr, Farmer with hoe (vert.). 35fr, Coffee pickers (vert.). 54fr, Mechanized harvester.

Wmkd. JEZ Multiple (368)
1975, Dec. 1 Photo. Perf. 14x13½

699	A101	20c gold & multi	5	5
700	A101	30c gold & multi	5	5
701	A101	50c gold & multi	5	5
702	A101	10fr gold & multi	25	15
703	A101	35fr gold & multi	90	50
704	A101	54fr gold & multi	1.50	80
		Nos. 699-704 (6)	2.80	1.60

Basket Carrier and Themabelga Emblem
A102

Designs (Themabelga Emblem and): 30c, Warrior with shield and spear. 50c, Woman with beads. 1fr, Indian woman. 5fr, Male dancer with painted body. 7fr, Woman carrying child on back. 35fr, Male dancer with spear. 51fr, Female dancers.

1975, Dec. 8 Perf. 13½ Unwmkd.

705	A102	20c blk & multi	5	5
706	A102	30c blk & multi	5	5
707	A102	50c blk & multi	5	5
708	A102	1fr blk & multi	5	5
709	A102	5fr blk & multi	15	8
710	A102	7fr blk & multi	20	10
711	A102	35fr blk & multi	90	50
712	A102	51fr blk & multi	1.35	75
		Nos. 705-712 (8)	2.80	1.63

THEMABELGA International Topical Philatelic Exhibition, Brussels, Dec. 13–21.

Christmas Type of 1968
Design: 100fr, Adoration of the Kings, by Peter Paul Rubens.

1975, Dec. 22 Engr. Perf. 11½

| 713 | A48 | 100fr brt rose lil | 3.50 | 3.50 |

Marginal inscription in blue. Size: 105x90mm.

Dr. Schweitzer, Keyboard, Score
A103

Designs (Albert Schweitzer and): 30c, Lambaréné Hospital. 50c, 10fr, Organ pipes from Strassbourg organ, and score. 1fr, 80fr, Dr. Schweitzer's house, Lambaréné. 3fr, like 20c.

1976, Jan. 30 Photo. Perf. 13½

714	A103	20c mar & pur	5	5
715	A103	30c grn & pur	5	5
716	A103	50c brn org & pur	5	5
717	A103	1fr red lil & pur	5	5
718	A103	3fr vio bl & pur	10	5
719	A103	5fr brn & pur	15	8
720	A103	10fr bl & pur	30	15
721	A103	80fr red & pur	2.10	1.20
		Nos. 714-721 (8)	2.85	1.68

World Leprosy Day.

Surrender at Yorktown
A104

Paintings: 30c, Instruction at Valley Forge. 50c, Presentation of Captured Colors at Yorktown. 1fr, Washington at Fort Lee. 18fr, Washington Boarding British Warship. 26fr, Washington Studying Battle Plans at Night. 34fr, Washington Firing Cannon. 40fr, Washington Crossing the Delaware. 100fr, Sailing Ship "Bonhomme Richard" (vert.).

1976, Mar. 22 Photo. Perf. 13x13½

722	A104	20c gold & multi	5	5
723	A104	30c gold & multi	5	5
724	A104	50c gold & multi	5	5
725	A104	1fr gold & multi	5	5
726	A104	18fr gold & multi	50	25
727	A104	26fr gold & multi	65	35
728	A104	34fr gold & multi	90	50
729	A104	40fr gold & multi	1.00	60
		Nos. 722-729 (8)	3.25	1.90

Souvenir Sheet
Perf. 13½

| 730 | A104 | 100fr gold & multi | 3.00 | 3.00 |

American Bicentennial. Design of No. 730, stamp and margin, show naval battle between Bonhomme Richard and Serapis. Size: 108x90mm.

Sister Yohana, First Nun
A105

Yachting
A106

RWANDA

Designs: 30c, Abdon Sabakati, one of first converts. 50c, Father Alphonse Brard, first Superior of Save Mission. 4fr, Abbot Balthazar Gafuku, one of first priests. 10fr, Msgr. Bigirumwami, first bishop. 25fr, Save Church (horiz.). 60fr, Kabgayi Cathedral (horiz.).

Perf. 13x13½, 13½x13

1976, Apr. 26   Photogravure

731	A105	20c multi	5	5
732	A105	30c multi	5	5
733	A105	50c multi	5	5
734	A105	4fr multi	18	10
735	A105	10fr multi	30	15
736	A105	25fr multi	70	38
737	A105	60fr multi	1.50	90
		Nos. 731-737 (7)	2.83	1.68

50th anniversary of the Roman Catholic Church of Rwanda.

1976, May 24   Photo.   *Perf. 13x13½*

Designs (Montreal Games Emblem and): 30c, Steeplechase. 50c, Long jump. 1fr, Hockey. 10fr, Swimming. 18fr, Soccer. 29fr, Boxing. 51fr, Vaulting.

738	A106	20c gray & dk car	5	5
739	A106	30c gray & Prus bl	5	5
740	A106	50c gray & blk	5	5
741	A106	1fr gray & pur	5	5
742	A106	10fr gray & ultra	38	15
743	A106	18fr gray & dk brn	50	25
744	A106	29fr gray & blk	90	45
745	A106	51fr gray & sl grn	1.35	75
		Nos. 738-745 (8)	3.33	1.75

21st Olympic Games, Montreal, Canada, July 17–Aug. 1.

First Message, Manual Switchboard A107

Designs: 30c, Telephone, 1876 and interested crowd. 50c, Telephone c. 1900, and woman making a call. 1fr, Business telephone exchange, c. 1905. 4fr, "Candlestick" phone, globe and A. G. Bell. 8fr, Dial phone and Rwandan man making call. 26fr, Telephone, 1976, satellite and radar. 60fr, Push-button telephone, Rwandan international switchboard operator.

1976, June 21   Photo.   *Perf. 14*

746	A107	20c dl red & ind	5	5
747	A107	30c grnsh bl & ind	5	5
748	A107	50c brn & ind	5	5
749	A107	1fr org & ind	5	5
750	A107	4fr lil & ind	15	8
751	A107	8fr grn & ind	30	15
752	A107	26fr dl red & ind	75	38
753	A107	60fr vio & ind	1.65	90
		Nos. 746-753 (8)	3.05	1.71

Centenary of first telephone call by Alexander Graham Bell, Mar. 10, 1876.

Type of 1976 Overprinted in Silver with Bicentennial Emblem and "Independence Day"

Designs as before.

1976, July 4   *Perf. 13x13½*

754	A104	20c sil & multi	5	5
755	A104	30c sil & multi	5	5
756	A104	50c sil & multi	5	5
757	A104	1fr sil & multi	5	5
758	A104	18fr sil & multi	50	28
759	A104	26fr sil & multi	75	38
760	A104	34fr sil & multi	90	50
761	A104	40fr sil & multi	1.00	60
		Nos. 754-761 (8)	3.35	1.96

Independence Day.

Soccer, Montreal Olympic Emblem A108

Designs (Montreal Olympic Games Emblem and): 30c, Shooting. 50c, Woman canoeing. 1fr, Gymnast. 10fr, Weight lifting. 12fr, Diving. 26fr, Equestrian. 50fr, Shot put.

1976, Aug. 1   Photo.   *Perf. 13½x13*

762	A108	20c multi	5	5
763	A108	30c multi	5	5
764	A108	50c multi	5	5
765	A108	1fr multi	5	5
766	A108	10fr multi	25	15
767	A108	12fr multi	30	18
768	A108	26fr multi	65	38
769	A108	50fr multi	1.50	75
		Nos. 762-769 (8)	2.90	1.66

Souvenir Sheet

Designs: Various phases of hurdles race (horiz.).

770	A108	Sheet of 4	4.25	4.25
a.		20fr Start	50	50
b.		30fr Sprint	85	85
c.		40fr Hurdle	1.10	1.10
d.		60fr Finish	1.50	1.50

21st Olympic Games, Montreal, Canada, July 17–Aug. 1. Margin of No. 770 shows Montreal Olympic Games emblem in blue, multiple. Size: 190x60mm.

Apollo and Soyuz Take-offs, Project Emblem A109

Designs: 30c, Soyuz in space. 50c, Apollo in space. 1fr, Apollo. 2fr, Spacecraft before docking. 12fr, Spacecraft after docking. 30fr, Astronauts visiting in docked spacecraft. 54fr, Apollo splashdown.

1976, Oct. 29   Photo.   *Perf. 13½x14*

771	A109	20c multi	5	5
772	A109	30c multi	5	5
773	A109	50c multi	5	5
774	A109	1fr multi	5	5
775	A109	2fr multi	12	5
776	A109	12fr multi	38	18
777	A109	30fr multi	90	45
778	A109	54fr multi	1.35	80
		Nos. 771-778 (8)	2.95	1.68

Apollo Soyuz space test program (Russo-American cooperation), July 1975.

Eulophia Cucullata A110

Orchids: 30c, Eulophia streptopetala. 50c, Disa Stairsii. 1fr, Aerangis kotschyana. 10fr, Eulophia abyssinica. 12fr, Bonatea steudneri. 26fr, Ansellia gigantea. 50fr, Eulophia angolensis.

1976, Nov. 22   Photo.   *Perf. 14x13½*

779	A110	20c multi	5	5
780	A110	30c multi	5	5
781	A110	50c multi	5	5
782	A110	1fr multi	5	5
783	A110	10fr multi	25	15
784	A110	12fr multi	38	18
785	A110	26fr multi	75	38
786	A110	50fr multi	1.50	75
		Nos. 779-786 (8)	3.08	1.66

Souvenir Sheet
Christmas Type of 1968

Design: 100fr, Nativity, by François Boucher.

1976, Dec. 20   Engr.   *Perf. 11½*

| 787 | A48 | 100fr brt ultra | 3.25 | 3.25 |

Marginal inscription in magenta. Size: 108x90mm.

Nos. 714-721 Overprinted:
"JOURNEE / MONDIALE / 1977"

1977, Jan. 29   Photo.   *Perf. 13½*

788	A103	20c mar & pur	5	5
789	A103	30c grn & pur	5	5
790	A103	50c brn org & pur	5	5
791	A103	1fr red lil & pur	12	6
792	A103	3fr vio bl & pur	25	10
793	A103	5fr brn & pur	38	15
794	A103	10fr bl & pur	2.10	1.20
795	A103	80fr ver & pur	3.05	1.71
		Nos. 788-795 (8)		

World Leprosy Day.

Hands and Symbols of Learning A111

Designs: 26fr, Hands and symbols of science. 64fr, Hands and symbols of industry.

1977, Feb. 7   Litho.   *Perf. 12½*

796	A111	10fr multi	38	15
797	A111	26fr multi	90	38
798	A111	64fr multi	1.75	90

10th Summit Conference of the African and Malagasy Union, Kigali, 1976.

Souvenir Sheets

Descent from the Cross, by Rubens—A112

Design: 25fr, Crucifixion, by Rubens.

1977, Apr. 27   Photo.   *Perf. 13*

799	A112	25fr multi	90	90
800	A112	75fr multi	2.25	2.25

Easter 1977. Size of stamp: 40x40mm.; size of sheet: 89x127mm.

For well over a century collectors have been identifying their stamps with the Scott Catalogue and housing their collections in Scott Albums.

Nos. 685-692 Overprinted

CONFERENCE MONDIALE DE L'EAU

1977, May 2

801	A100	20c blk & multi	5	5
802	A100	30c blk & multi	5	5
803	A100	50c blk & multi	5	5
804	A100	5fr blk & multi	20	10
805	A100	8fr blk & multi	30	15
806	A100	10fr blk & multi	30	15
807	A100	26fr blk & multi	85	45
808	A100	100fr blk & multi	3.25	1.75
		Nos. 801-808 (8)	5.05	2.75

World Water Conference.

Roman Fire Tower, African Tom-tom A113

Designs (ITU Emblem and): 30c, Chappe's optical telegraph and postilion. 50c, Morse telegraph and code. 1fr, Tug Goliath laying cable in English Channel. 4fr, Telephone, radio, television. 18fr, Kingsport (U.S. space exploration ship) and Marots communications satellite. 26fr, Satellite tracking station and O.T.S. satellite. 50fr, Mariner II, Venus probe.

1977, May 23   Litho.   *Perf. 12½*

809	A113	20c multi	5	5
810	A113	30c multi	5	5
811	A113	50c multi	5	5
812	A113	1fr multi	5	5
813	A113	4fr multi	15	6
814	A113	18fr multi	55	28
815	A113	26fr multi	75	38
816	A113	50fr multi	1.50	75
		Nos. 809-816 (8)	3.15	1.67

World Telecommunications Day.

Souvenir Sheets

Amsterdam Harbor, by Willem van de Velde, the Younger A114

Design: 40fr, The Night Watch, by Rembrandt.

1977, May 26   Photo.   *Perf. 13½*

817	A114	40fr multi	1.20	1.20
818	A114	60fr multi	1.80	1.80

AMPHILEX '77 International Philatelic Exhibition, Amsterdam, May 27–June 5. Sheet margins show entire painting. Size of stamp: 38x49mm.; size of sheet: 128x89mm.

Road to Calvary, by Rubens A115

RWANDA

Paintings by Rubens: 30c, Judgment of Paris (horiz.). 50c, Marie de Medicis. 1fr, Heads of Black Men (horiz.). 4fr, 26fr, Details from St. Ildefonso triptych. 8fr, Helene Fourment and her Children (horiz.). 60fr, Helene Fourment.

1977, June 13   *Perf. 14*

819	A115	20c gold & multi	5	5
820	A115	30c gold & multi	5	5
821	A115	50c gold & multi	5	5
822	A115	1fr gold & multi	5	5
823	A115	4fr gold & multi	15	6
824	A115	8fr gold & multi	32	15
825	A115	26fr gold & multi	75	38
826	A115	60fr gold & multi	1.75	90
	Nos. 819-826 (8)		3.17	1.69

Peter Paul Rubens (1577-1640), Flemish painter, 400th birth anniversary.

Souvenir Sheet

Viking on Mars
A116

1977, June 27   Photo.   *Perf. 13*

| 827 | A116 | 100fr multi | 3.75 | 3.75 |

U.S. Viking landing on Mars, first anniversary. No. 827 contains one stamp; dark blue and gold margin shows dish antenna. Size: 128x88½mm.

Crested Eagle
A117

Birds of Prey: 30c, Snake eagle. 50c, Fish eagle. 1fr, Monk vulture. 3fr, Redtailed buzzard. 5fr, Yellow-beaked kite. 20fr, Swallow-tailed kite. 100fr, Bateleur.

1977, Sept. 12   Litho.   *Perf. 14*

828	A117	20c multi	5	5
829	A117	30c multi	5	5
830	A117	50c multi	5	5
831	A117	1fr multi	5	5
832	A117	3fr multi	10	5
833	A117	5fr multi	15	8
834	A117	26fr multi	65	35
835	A117	100fr multi	3.00	1.50
	Nos. 828-835 (8)		4.10	2.18

Nos. 771-778 Overprinted:
"in memoriam / WERNHER VON BRAUN / 1912-1977"

1977, Sept. 19   Photo.   *Perf. 13½x14*

836	A109	20c multi	5	5
837	A109	30c multi	5	5
838	A109	50c multi	5	5
839	A109	1fr multi	5	5
840	A109	2fr multi	10	5
841	A109	12fr multi	45	18
842	A109	30fr multi	1.10	45
843	A109	54fr multi	2.00	90
	Nos. 836-843 (8)		3.85	1.78

Wernher von Braun (1912-1977), space and rocket expert.

Souvenir Sheets

Nos. 628-631 Gold Embossed "ESPAMER '77" and ESPAMER Emblem.

1977, Oct. 3   Photo.   *Perf. 13*

844	A94	20c multi	60	60
845	A94	30c multi	90	90
846	A94	50c multi	1.50	1.50
847	A94	100fr multi	3.00	3.00

ESPAMER '77, International Philatelic Exhibition, Barcelona, Oct. 7-13.

Souvenir Sheet
Christmas Type of 1968

Design: 100fr, Nativity, by Peter Paul Rubens.

1977, Dec. 12   Engr.   *Perf. 13½*

| 848 | A48 | 100fr vio bl | 3.25 | 3.25 |

Marginal inscription typographed in red. Size: 87x87mm.

Boy Scout
Playing Flute
A118

Chimpanzees
A119

Designs: 30c, Campfire. 50c, Bridge building. 1fr, Scouts with unit flag. 10fr, Map reading. 18fr, Boating. 26fr, Cooking. 44fr, Lord Baden-Powell.

1978, Feb. 20   Litho.   *Perf. 12½*

849	A118	20c yel grn & multi	5	5
850	A118	30c bl & multi	5	5
851	A118	50c lil & multi	5	5
852	A118	1fr bl & multi	5	5
853	A118	10fr pink & multi	30	18
854	A118	18fr lt grn & multi	55	28
855	A118	26fr org & multi	80	38
856	A118	44fr sal & multi	1.35	70
	Nos. 849-856 (8)		3.20	1.74

10th anniversary of Rwanda Boy Scouts.

Designs: 30c, Gorilla. 50c, Colobus monkey. 3fr, Galago. 10fr, Cercopithecus monkey (mone). 26fr, Potto. 60fr, Cercopithecus monkey (griuet). 150fr, Baboon.

1978, Mar. 20   Photo.   *Perf. 13½x13*

857	A119	20c multi	5	5
858	A119	30c multi	5	5
859	A119	50c multi	5	5
860	A119	3fr multi	10	5
861	A119	10fr multi	30	18
862	A119	26fr multi	80	38
863	A119	60fr multi	1.80	80
864	A119	150fr multi	4.25	2.25
	Nos. 857-864 (8)		7.40	3.81

Euporus Strangulatus—A120

Coleoptera: 30c, Rhina afzelii (vert.). 50c, Pentalobus palini. 3fr, Corynodes dejeani (vert.). 10fr, Mecynorhina torquata. 15fr, Mecocerus rhombeus (vert.). 20fr, Macrotoma serripes. 25fr, Neptunides stanleyi (vert.). 26fr, Petrognatha gigas. 100fr, Eudicella gralli (vert.).

1978, May 22   Litho.   *Perf. 14*

865	A120	20c multi	5	5
866	A120	30c multi	5	5
867	A120	50c multi	5	5
868	A120	3fr multi	10	5
869	A120	10fr multi	30	20
870	A120	15fr multi	45	30
871	A120	20fr multi	60	40
872	A120	25fr multi	75	42
873	A120	26fr multi	78	45
874	A120	100fr multi	3.00	2.00
	Nos. 865-874 (10)		6.13	3.97

Crossing
"River of
Poverty"
A121

M.R.N.D.

Designs (Emblem and): 10fr, 60fr, Men poling boat, facing right. 26fr, like 4fr.

1978, May 29   *Perf. 12½*

875	A121	4fr multi	12	6
876	A121	10fr multi	30	20
877	A121	26fr multi	78	45
878	A121	60fr multi	1.80	1.20

National Revolutionary Development Movement (M.R.N.D.).

Soccer, Rimet Cup, Flags of
Netherlands and Peru—A122

11th World cup, Argentina, June 1-25. (Various Soccer Scenes and Flags of): 30c, Sweden & Spain. 50c, Scotland & Iran. 2fr, Germany & Tunisia. 3fr, Italy & Hungary. 10fr, Brazil and Austria. 34fr, Poland & Mexico. 100fr, Argentina & France.

1978, June 19   *Perf. 13*

879	A122	20c multi	5	5
879A	A122	30c multi	5	5
879B	A122	50c multi	5	5
880	A122	2fr multi	5	5
881	A122	3fr multi	10	5
882	A122	10fr multi	30	20
883	A122	34fr multi	1.00	65
884	A122	100fr multi	3.00	2.00
	Nos. 879-884 (8)		4.60	3.10

Wright
Brothers,
Flyer I
A123

History of Aviation: 30c, Santos Dumont and Canard 14, 1906. 50c, Henry Farman and Voisin No. 1, 1908. 1fr, Jan Olieslaegers and Bleriot, 1910. 3fr, Marshal Balbo and Savoia S-17, 1919. 10fr, Charles Lindbergh and Spirit of St. Louis, 1927. 55fr, Hugo Junkers and Junkers JU52/3, 1932. 60fr, Igor Sikorsky and Sikorsky VS 300, 1939. 130fr, Concorde over New York.

1978, Oct. 30   Litho.   *Perf. 13½x14*

885	A123	20c multi	5	5
886	A123	30c multi	5	5
887	A123	50c multi	5	5
888	A123	1fr multi	5	5
889	A123	3fr multi	10	5
890	A123	10fr multi	30	20
891	A123	55fr multi	1.65	1.10
892	A123	60fr multi	1.80	1.20
	Nos. 885-892 (8)		4.05	2.75

Souvenir Sheet

Perf. 13x13½

| 893 | A123 | 130fr multi | 4.00 | 4.00 |

No. 893 contains one stamp (47x35mm). Multicolored margin shows sky and experimental jet. Size: 78x95mm.

Souvenir Sheet
Christmas Type of 1968

Design: 200fr, Adoration of the Kings, by Albrecht Dürer (vert.).

1978, Dec. 11   Engr.   *Perf. 11½*

| 894 | A48 | 200fr brown | 6.00 | 6.00 |

Christmas 1978. No. 894 has marginal inscription in bright green and ocher. Size: 65x84mm.

Nos. 532-533, Overprinted
"1963   1978" in Black or Blue

1978, Dec. 18   Photo.   *Perf. 13½*

| 895 | A83 | 6fr multi (Bk) | 25 | 10 |
| 896 | A83 | 94fr multi (Bl) | 2.85 | 1.85 |

Organization for African Unity, 15th anniversary.

Goats
A124

Designs: 20c, Ducks (vert.). 50c, Cock and chickens (vert.). 4fr, Rabbits. 5fr, Pigs (vert.). 15fr, Turkey. 50fr, Sheep and cattle (vert.). 75fr, Bull.

1978, Dec. 28   Litho.   *Perf. 14*

897	A124	20c multi	5	5
898	A124	30c multi	5	5
899	A124	50c multi	5	5
900	A124	4fr multi	12	6
901	A124	5fr multi	15	10
902	A124	15fr multi	45	30
903	A124	50fr multi	1.50	1.00
904	A124	75fr multi	2.25	1.50
	Nos. 897-904 (8)		4.62	3.12

Husbandry Year.

Papilio
Demodocus
A125

Butterflies: 30c, Precis octavia. 50c, Charaxes smaragdalis. 4fr, Charaxes guderiana. 15fr, Colotis evippe. 30fr, Danaus limniace. 50fr, Byblia acheloia. 150fr, Utetheisa pulchella.

1979, Feb. 19   Photo.   *Perf. 14½*

905	A125	20c multi	5	5
906	A125	30c multi	5	5
907	A125	50c multi	5	5
908	A125	4fr multi	12	6
909	A125	15fr multi	45	30
910	A125	30fr multi	90	60
911	A125	50fr multi	1.50	1.00
912	A125	150fr multi	4.50	3.00
	Nos. 905-912 (8)		7.62	5.13

Euphorbia
Grantii,
Weavers
A126

Design: 60fr, Drummers and Intelsat IV-A.

1979, June 8   Photo.   *Perf. 13*

| 913 | A126 | 40fr multi | 1.20 | 80 |
| 914 | A126 | 60fr multi | 1.80 | 1.20 |

Philexafrique II, Libreville, Gabon, June 8-17.

Entandrophragma
Excelsum
A127

Trees and Shrubs: 20c, Polyscias fulva. 50c, Ilex mitis. 4fr, Kigelia africana. 15fr, Ficus thonningi. 20fr, Acacia Senegal. 50fr, Symphonia globulifera. 110fr, Acacia sieberana. 20c, 50c, 15fr, 50fr, vertical.

1979, Aug. 27   *Perf. 14*

915	A127	20c multi	5	5
916	A127	30c multi	5	5
917	A127	50c multi	5	5
918	A127	4 fr multi	12	8
919	A127	15fr multi	45	30
920	A127	20fr multi	60	40
921	A127	50fr multi	1.50	1.00
922	A127	110fr multi	3.25	2.20
	Nos. 915-922 (8)		6.07	4.13

RWANDA

Black and White Boys, IYC Emblem
A128

Designs: 26fr, 100fr, Children of various races, diff. (vert.).

Perf. 13½×13, 13×13½

			1979, Nov. 19	Photo.	
923	A128		Block of 8 multi	6.75	4.50
a.		26fr, any single		80	55
924	A128		42fr multi	1.25	85

Souvenir Sheet

925	A128	100fr multi	3.25	2.25

International Year of the Child. Size: 62×76mm. No. 923 printed in sheets of 16 (4×4).

Basket Weaving—A129

Perf. 12½×13, 13×12½

1979, Dec. 3		Multicolored		Litho.	
926	A129	50c	shown	5	5
927	A129	1.50fr	Wood carving, vert.	5	5
928	A129	2fr	Metal working	6	5
929	A129	10fr	Jewelry, vert.	30	15
930	A129	20fr	Straw plaiting	60	30
931	A129	26fr	Wall painting, vert.	80	40
932	A129	40fr	Pottery	1.20	60
933	A129	100fr	Smelting, vert.	3.00	1.50
		Nos. 926-933 (8)		6.06	3.10

Souvenir Sheet

Children of Different Races, Christmas Tree—A130

1979, Dec. 24		Engraved	Perf. 12	
934	A130	200fr ultra & dp mag	6.25	3.00

Christmas 1979; International Year of the Child. No. 934 has magenta margin; inscription. Size: 85×65mm.

German East Africa No. N5, Hill—A131

Hill and Stamps of Ruanda-Urundi or: 30c, German East Africa No. N23. 50c, German East Africa No. NB9. 3fr, No. 25. 10fr, No. 42. 26fr, No. 123. 100fr, No. B28.

1979, Dec. 31		Litho.	Perf. 14	
935	A131	20c multi	5	5
936	A131	30c multi	5	5
937	A131	50c multi	5	5
938	A131	3fr multi	10	5
939	A131	10fr multi	30	15
940	A131	26fr multi	80	40
941	A131	60fr multi	1.80	90
942	A131	100fr multi	3.00	1.50
		Nos. 935-942 (8)	6.15	3.15

Sir Rowland Hill (1795-1879), originator of penny postage.

Sarothrura Pulchra—A132

Birds of the Nyungwe Forest: 20c Ploceus alienus (vert.). 30c, Regal sunbird (vert.). 3fr, Tockus alboterminatus. 10fr, Pygmy owl (vert.). 26fr, Emerald cuckoo. 60fr, Finch (vert.). 100fr, Stepanoaetus coronatus (vert.).

Perf. 13½×13, 13×13½

1980, Jan. 7			Photo.	
943	A132	20c multi	5	5
944	A132	30c multi	5	5
945	A132	50c multi	5	5
946	A132	3fr multi	10	5
947	A132	10fr multi	30	15
948	A132	26fr multi	80	40
949	A132	60fr multi	1.80	90
950	A132	100fr multi	3.00	1.50
		Nos. 943-950 (8)	6.15	3.15

First Footstep on Moon, Spacecraft—A133

Spacecraft and Moon Exploration: 1.50fr, Descent onto lunar surface. 8fr, American flag. 30fr, Solar panels. 50fr, Gathering soil samples. 60fr, Adjusting sun screen. 200fr, Landing craft.

1980, Jan. 31		Photo.	Perf. 13x13½	
951	A133	50c multi	5	5
952	A133	1.50fr multi	5	5
953	A133	8fr multi	24	12
954	A133	30fr multi	90	45
955	A133	50fr multi	1.50	75
956	A133	60fr multi	1.80	90
		Nos. 951-956 (6)	4.54	2.32

Souvenir Sheet

957	A133	200fr multi	6.00	3.00

Apollo 11 moon landing, 10th anniversary (1979). No. 957 has multicolored margin showing Apollo 11 crew and emblem. Size: 70×58½mm.

Globe, Butare and 1905 Chicago Club Emblems—A134

Rotary International, 75th Anniversary (Globe, Emblems of Butare or Kigali Clubs and): 30c, San Francisco, 1908. 50c, Chicago, 1910. 4fr, Buffalo, 1911. 15fr, London, 1911. 20fr, Glasgow, 1912. 50fr, Bristol, 1917. 60fr, Rotary International, 1980.

1980, Feb. 23		Litho.	Perf. 13	
958	A134	20c multi	5	5
959	A134	30c multi	5	5
960	A134	50c multi	5	5
961	A134	4fr multi	12	6
962	A134	15fr multi	45	22
963	A134	20fr multi	60	30
964	A134	50fr multi	1.50	75
965	A134	60fr multi	1.80	90
		Nos. 958-965 (8)	4.62	2.38

Gymnast, Moscow '80 Emblem—A135

1980, Mar. 10			Perf. 12½	
966	A135	20c shown	5	5
967	A135	30c Basketball	5	5
968	A135	50c Bicycling	5	5
969	A135	3fr Boxing	10	5
970	A135	20fr Archery	60	30
971	A135	26fr Weight lifting	80	40
972	A135	50fr Javelin	1.50	75
973	A135	100fr Fencing	3.00	1.50
		Nos. 966-973 (8)	6.15	3.15

22nd Summer Olympic Games, Moscow, July 19-Aug. 3.

Souvenir Sheet

Amalfi Coast, by Giacinto Gigante—A136

1980, Apr. 28		Photo.	Perf. 13½	
974	A136	200fr multi	6.00	3.00

20th International Philatelic Exhibition, Europa '80, Naples, Apr. 26-May 4. Multicolored margin shows entire painting. Size: 118½×89mm.

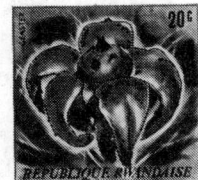

Geaster Mushroom—A137

1980, July 21		Photo.	Perf. 13½	
975	A137	20c shown	5	5
976	A137	30c Lentinus atrobrunneus	5	5
977	A137	50c Gomphus stereoides	5	5
978	A137	4fr Cantharellus cibarius	12	6
979	A137	10fr Stilbothamnium dybowskii	30	15
980	A137	15fr Xeromphalina tenuipes	45	22
981	A137	70fr Podoscypha elegans	2.10	1.05
982	A137	100fr Mycena	3.00	1.50
		Nos. 975-982 (8)	6.12	3.13

Still Life, by Renoir—A138

Impressionist Painters: 30c, 26fr, At the Theater, by Toulouse-Lautrec (vert.). 50c, 10fr, Seaside Garden, by Monet. 4fr, Mother and Child, by Mary Cassatt (vert.). 5fr, Starry Night, by Van Gogh. 10fr, Dancers at their Toilet, by Degas (vert.). 50fr, The Card Players, by Cezanne. 70fr, Tahitian Women, by Gauguin (vert.). 75fr, like 20c. 100fr, In the Park, by Seurat.

1980, Aug. 4		Litho.	Perf. 14	
983	A138	20c multi	5	5
984	A138	30c multi	5	5
985	A138	50c multi	5	5
986	A138	4fr multi	12	6
a.		Sheet of 2 (4fr, 26fr)	90	90
987	A138	5fr multi	15	8
a.		Sheet of 2 (5fr, 75fr)	2.40	2.40
988	A138	10fr multi	30	15
a.		Sheet of 2 (10fr, 70fr)	2.40	2.40
989	A138	50fr multi	1.50	75
a.		Sheet of 2 (50fr, 10fr)	1.80	1.80
990	A138	70fr multi	2.10	1.05
991	A138	100fr multi	3.00	1.50
		Nos. 983-991 (9)	7.32	3.74

Souvenir sheets have black marginal inscription. Size: 138×100mm.

Souvenir Sheet

Virgin of the Harpies, by Andrea Del Sarto—A139

1980, Dec. 22		Photo. & Engr.	Perf. 11½	
992	A139	200fr multi	6.00	3.00

Christmas 1980. Violet and red marginal inscription. Size: 65×85mm.

Belgian War of Independence, Engraving—A140

Belgian Independence Sesquicentennial: Engravings of War of Independence.

1980, Dec. 29		Litho.	Perf. 12½	
993	A140	20c pale grn & brn	5	5
994	A140	30c brn org & brn	5	5
995	A140	50c lt bl & brn	5	5
996	A140	9fr yel & brn	28	14
997	A140	10fr brt lil & brn	30	15
998	A140	20fr ap grn & brn	60	30
999	A140	70fr pink & brn	2.10	1.05
1000	A140	90fr lem & brn	2.70	1.35
		Nos. 993-1000 (8)	6.13	3.14

RWANDA

Swamp Drainage—A141

1980, Dec. 31		Photo.		Perf. 13½	
1001	A141	20c	shown	5	5
1002	A141	30c	Fertilizer shed	5	5
1003	A141	1.50fr	Rice fields	5	5
1004	A141	8fr	Tree planting	24	14
1005	A141	10fr	Terrace planting	30	15
1006	A141	40fr	Farm buildings	1.20	60
1007	A141	90fr	Bean cultivation	2.70	1.35
1008	A141	100fr	Tea cultivation	3.00	1.50
	Nos. 1001-1008 (8)			7.59	3.87

Soil Conservation Year.

Pavetta Rwandensis—A142

1981, Apr. 6		Photo.		Perf. 13x13½	
1009	A142	20c	shown	5	5
1010	A142	30c	Cyrtorchis praetermissa	5	5
1011	A142	50c	Pavonia urens	5	5
1012	A142	4fr	Cynorkis kassnerana	12	6
1013	A142	5fr	Gardenia ternifolia	15	8
1014	A142	10fr	Leptactina platyphylla	30	15
1015	A142	20fr	Lobelia petiolata	60	30
1016	A142	40fr	Tapinanthus brunneus	1.20	60
1017	A142	70fr	Impatiens niamniamensis	2.10	1.05
1018	A142	150fr	Dissotis rwandensis	4.50	2.25
	Nos. 1009-1018 (10)			9.12	4.64

Girl Knitting A143

SOS Children's Village: Various children.

1981, Apr. 27				Perf. 13	
1019	A143	20c	multi	5	5
1020	A143	30c	multi	5	5
1021	A143	50c	multi	5	5
1022	A143	1fr	multi	5	5
1023	A143	8fr	multi	24	12
1024	A143	10fr	multi	30	15
1025	A143	70fr	multi	2.10	1.05
1026	A143	150fr	multi	4.50	2.25
	Nos. 1019-1026 (8)			7.34	3.77

Carolers, by Norman Rockwell—A144

Designs: Saturday Evening Post covers by Norman Rockwell.

1981, May 11		Litho.		Perf. 13½x14	
1027	A144	20c	multi	5	5
1028	A144	30c	multi	5	5
1029	A144	50c	multi	5	5
1030	A144	1fr	multi	5	5
1031	A144	8fr	multi	24	12
1032	A144	20fr	multi	60	30
1033	A144	50fr	multi	1.50	75
1034	A144	70fr	multi	2.10	1.05
	Nos. 1027-1034 (8)			4.69	2.47

Cerval A145

Designs: Meat-eating animals.

1981, June 29		Photo.		Perf. 13½x14	
1035	A145	20c	shown	5	5
1036	A145	30c	Jackals	5	5
1037	A145	2fr	Genet	6	5
1038	A145	2.50fr	Banded mongoose	8	5
1039	A145	10fr	Zorille	30	15
1040	A145	15fr	White-cheeked otter	45	22
1041	A145	70fr	Golden wild cat	2.10	1.05
1042	A145	200fr	Hunting dog, vert.	6.00	3.00
	Nos. 1035-1042 (8)			9.09	4.62

Drummer Sending Message—A146

1981, Sept. 1		Litho.		Perf. 13	
1043	A146	20c	shown	5	5
1044	A146	30c	Map, communication waves	5	5
1045	A146	2fr	Jet, radar screen	6	5
1046	A146	2.50fr	Satellite, teletape	8	5
1047	A146	10fr	Dish antenna	30	15
1048	A146	15fr	Ship, navigation devices	45	22
1049	A146	70fr	Helicopter	2.10	1.05
1050	A146	200fr	Satellite with solar panels	6.00	3.00
	Nos. 1043-1050 (8)			9.09	4.62

1500th Birth Anniv. of St. Benedict—A147

Paintings and Frescoes of St. Benedict: 20c, Leaving his Parents, Mt. Oliveto Monastery, Maggiore. 30c, Oldest portrait, 10th cent., St. Chrisogone Church, Rome (vert.). 50c, Portrait, Virgin of the Misericord polyptich, Borgo San Sepolcro. 4fr, Giving the Rules of the order to his Monks, Mt. Oliveto Monastery. 5fr, Monks at their Meal, Mt. Oliveto Monastery. 20fr, Portrait, 13th cent., Lower Chruch of the Holy Spirit, Subiaco (vert.). 70fr, Our Lady in Glory with Sts. Gregory and Benedict, San Gimigniao (vert.). 100fr, Priest Carrying Easter Meal to St. Benedict, by Jan van Coninxloo, 16th cent.

Perf. 13½x13, 13x13½

1981, Nov. 30		Photo.			
1051	A147	20c	multi	5	5
1052	A147	30c	multi	5	5
1053	A147	50c	multi	5	5
1054	A147	4fr	multi	12	6
1055	A147	5fr	multi	15	8
1056	A147	20fr	multi	60	30
1057	A147	70fr	multi	2.10	1.00
1058	A147	100fr	multi	3.00	3.00
	Nos. 1051-1058 (8)			6.12	4.59

Intl. Year of the Disabled—A148

1981, Dec. 7		Litho.		Perf. 13	
1059	A148	20c	Painting	5	5
1060	A148	30c	Soccer	5	5
1061	A148	4.50fr	Crocheting	14	8
1062	A148	5fr	Painting vase	15	8
1063	A148	10fr	Sawing	30	16
1064	A148	60fr	Sign language	1.80	1.00
1065	A148	70fr	Doing puzzle	2.10	1.20
1066	A148	100fr	Juggling	3.00	1.60
	Nos. 1059-1066 (8)			7.59	4.22

Souvenir Sheet

1067	A149	200fr	Adoration of the Kings, by van der Goes	6.00	3.00

Christmas 1981—A149

No. 1067 has olive green and lilac marginal inscription. Size: 85x85mm.

Natl. Rural Water Supply Year—A150

1981, Dec. 28		Litho.		Perf. 12½	
1068	A150	20c	Deer drinking	5	5
1069	A150	30c	Women carrying water, vert.	5	5
1070	A150	50c	Pipeline	5	5
1071	A150	10fr	Filling pan, vert.	30	16
1072	A150	19fr	Drinking	60	35
1073	A150	70fr	Mother, child, vert.	2.10	1.00
1074	A150	100fr	Lake pumping station, vert.	3.00	1.50
	Nos. 1068-1074 (7)			6.15	3.16

World Food Day (Oct. 16, 1981)—A151

1982, Jan. 25		Litho.		Perf. 13	
1075	A151	20c	Cattle	5	5
1076	A151	30c	Bee	5	5
1077	A151	50c	Fish	5	5
1078	A151	1fr	Avocados	5	5
1079	A151	8fr	Boy eating banana	24	14
1080	A151	20fr	Sorghum	60	32
1081	A151	70fr	Vegetables	2.10	1.00
1082	A151	100fr	Balanced diet	3.00	1.50
	Nos. 1075-1082 (8)			6.14	3.16

Hibiscus Berberidifolius—A152

1982, June 14		Litho.		Perf. 13	
1083	A152	20c	shown	5	5
1084	A152	30c	Hypericum lanceolatum, vert.	5	5
1085	A152	50c	Canarina eminii	5	5
1086	A152	4fr	Polygala ruwenxoriensis	12	6
1087	A152	10fr	Kniphofia grantii, vert.	30	16
1088	A152	35fr	Euphorbia candelabrum, vert.	1.05	50
1089	A152	70fr	Disa erubescens, vert.	2.10	1.00
1090	A152	80fr	Gloriosa simplex	2.40	1.40
	Nos. 1083-1090 (8)			6.12	3.27

20th Anniv. of Independence—A153

1982, June 28					
1091	A153	10fr	Flags	30	16
1092	A153	20fr	Hands releasing doves	60	30
1093	A153	30fr	Flag, handshake	90	45
1094	A153	50fr	Govt. buildings	1.50	75

1982 World Cup—A154

Designs: Various soccer players.

1982, July 6				Perf. 14x14½	
1095	A154	20c	multi	5	5
1096	A154	30c	multi	5	5
1097	A154	1.50fr	multi	5	5
1098	A154	8fr	multi	24	14
1099	A154	10fr	multi	30	15
1100	A154	20fr	multi	60	30
1101	A154	70fr	multi	2.10	1.05
1102	A154	90fr	multi	2.75	1.35
	Nos. 1095-1102 (8)			6.14	3.10

TB Bacillus Centenary—A155

1982, Nov. 22		Litho.		Perf. 14½	
1103	A155	10fr	Microscope, slide	30	16
1104	A155	20fr	Serum, slide	60	30
1105	A155	70fr	Lungs, slide	2.10	1.00
1106	A155	100fr	Koch	3.00	1.50

RWANDA

Madam Recamier, by David—A156

PHILEXFRANCE '82 Intl. Stamp Exhibition, Paris, June 11-21: No. 1108, St. Anne and Virgin and Child with Franciscan Monk, by H. van der Goes. No. 1109, Liberty Guiding the People, by Delacroix. No. 1110, Pygmalion, by P. Delvaux. Sizes: 130x90mm.

1982, Dec. 11			Perf. 13½	
		Souvenir Sheets		
1107	A156	40fr multi	1.25	65
1108	A156	40fr multi	1.25	65
1109	A156	60fr multi	1.75	85
1110	A156	60fr multi	1.75	85

Souvenir Sheet

Rest During the Flight to Egypt, by Murillo—A157

1982, Dec. 20		Photo. & Engr.		
1111	A157	200fr car rose	6.00	3.00

Christmas 1982. Size: 85x85mm.

10th Anniv. of UN Conference on Human Environment—A158

1982, Dec. 27		Litho.	Perf. 14	
1112	A158	20c Elephants	5	5
1113	A158	30c Lion	5	5
1114	A158	50c Flower	5	5
1115	A158	4fr Bull	12	6
1116	A158	5fr Deer	15	8
1117	A158	10fr Flower, diff.	30	15
1118	A158	20fr Zebras	60	30
1119	A158	40fr Crowned cranes	1.20	60
1120	A158	50fr Bird	1.50	75
1121	A158	70fr Woman pouring coffee beans	2.90	1.00

Scouting Year—A159

1983, Jan. 17		Photo.	Perf. 13½x14½	
1122	A159	20c Animal first aid	5	5
1123	A159	30c Camp	5	5
1124	A159	1.50fr Campfire	5	5
1125	A159	8fr Scout giving sign	24	14
1126	A159	10fr Knot	30	15
1127	A159	20fr Camp, diff.	60	30
1128	A159	70fr Chopping wood	2.10	1.00
1129	A159	90fr Sign, map	2.75	1.35
		Nos. 1122-1129 (8)	6.14	3.09

Nectar-sucking Birds A160	Soil Erosion Prevention A161

1983, Jan. 31 Litho.		Perf. 14x14½, 14½x14		
1130	A160	20c Angola nectar bird	5	5
1131	A160	30c Royal nectar birds	5	5
1132	A160	50c Johnston's nectar bird	5	5
1133	A160	4fr Bronze nectar birds	12	6
1134	A160	5fr Collared souimangas	15	8
1135	A160	10fr Blue-headed nectar bird	30	15
1136	A160	20fr Purple-bellied nectar bird	60	30
1137	A160	40fr Copper nectar birds	1.20	60
1138	A160	50fr Olive-bellied nectar birds	1.50	75
1139	A160	70fr Red-breasted nectar bird	2.10	1.00

30c, 4fr, 10fr, 40fr, 70fr horiz. Inscribed 1982.

1983, Feb. 14			Perf. 14½	
1140	A161	20c Driving cattle	5	5
1141	A161	30c Pineapple field	5	5
1142	A161	50c Interrupted ditching	5	5
1143	A161	9fr Hedges, ditches	28	14
1144	A161	10fr Reafforestation	30	15
1145	A161	20fr Anti-erosion barriers	60	30
1146	A161	30fr Contour planting	90	45
1147	A161	50fr Terracing	1.50	75
1148	A161	60fr Protection of river banks	1.80	90
1149	A161	70fr Fallow, planted strips	2.10	1.00

Cardinal Cardijn (1882-1967) A162	Gorilla A163

Young Catholic Workers Movement Activities. Inscribed 1982.

1983, Feb. 22			Perf. 12½x13	
1150	A162	20c Feeding ducks	5	5
1151	A162	30c Harvesting tobacco	5	5
1152	A162	50c Carrying melons	5	5
1153	A162	10fr Teacher	30	15
1154	A162	19fr Shoemakers	58	28
1155	A162	20fr Growing millet	60	30
1156	A162	70fr Embroidering	2.10	1.00
1157	A162	80fr Cardinal Cardijn	2.40	1.20
		Nos. 1150-1157 (8)	6.13	3.08

1983, Mar. 14			Perf. 14	
		Various gorillas. Nos. 1158-1163 horiz.		
1158	A163	20c multi	5	5
1159	A163	50c multi	5	5
1160	A163	9.50fr multi	28	14
1161	A163	10fr multi	30	20
1162	A163	20fr multi	60	30
1163	A163	30fr multi	90	45
1164	A163	60fr multi	1.80	90
1165	A163	70fr multi	2.10	1.00
		Nos. 1158-1165 (8)	6.08	3.09

SEMI-POSTAL STAMPS

No. 305 Surcharged in Black and Overprinted in Brown: "SECHERESSE/SOLIDARITE AFRICAINE"

1973, Aug. 23		Photo.	Perf. 13	
B1	A53	100fr + 50fr multi	4.75	4.25

African solidarity in drought emergency.

Nos. 349-350 Surcharged and Overprinted Like Nos. 693-698.

1975, Nov. 10		Litho.	Perf. 13	
B2	A60	50fr + 25fr multi	2.25	1.50
B3	A60	90fr + 25fr multi	3.00	2.25

African solidarity in drought emergency.

AIR POST STAMPS

African Postal Union Issue, 1967
Common Design Type

1967, Sept. 18		Engraved	Perf. 13	
C1	CD124	6fr brn, rose cl & gray	18	12
C2	CD124	18fr brt lil, ol brn & plum	60	45
C3	CD124	30fr grn, dp bl & red	1.00	80

PHILEXAFRIQUE Issue

Alexandre Lenoir, by Jacques L. David AP1

1968, Dec. 30		Photo.	Perf. 12½	
C4	AP1	100fr emer & multi	3.00	1.25

Issued to publicize PHILEXAFRIQUE, Philatelic exhibition in Abidjan, Feb. 14-23, 1969. Printed with alternating emerald label.

2nd PHILEXAFRIQUE Issue

Ruanda-Urundi No. 123, Cowherd and Lake Victoria—AP2

1969, Feb. 14		Litho.	Perf. 14	
C5	AP2	50fr multi	1.35	1.25

Issued to commemorate the opening of PHILEXAFRIQUE, Abidjan, Feb. 14.

Painting Type of Regular Issue

Paintings and Music: 50fr, The Music Lesson, by Fragonard. 100fr, Angels' Concert, by Memling (horiz.).

1969, Mar. 31		Photo.	Perf. 13	
C6	A49	50fr gold & multi	1.25	55
C7	A49	100fr gold & multi	2.85	1.10

African Postal Union Issue, 1971
Common Design Type

Design: 100fr, Woman and child of Rwanda and UAMPT Building, Brazzaville, Congo.

1971, Nov. 13			Perf. 13x13½	
C8	CD135	100fr bl & multi	3.00	1.75

No. C8 Overprinted in Red

1973, Sept. 17		Photo.	Perf. 13x13½	
C9	AP24(a)	100fmulti	3.00	1.75
C10	AP24(b)	100fmulti	3.00	1.75

3rd Conference of French-speaking countries, Liège, Sept. 15-Oct. 14. Overprints alternate checkerwise in same sheet.

Sassenage Castle, Grenoble—AP3

1977, June 20		Litho.	Perf. 12½	
C11	AP3	50fr multi	1.50	75

10th anniversary of International French Language Council.

Philexafrique II—Essen Issue
Common Design Types

Designs: No. C12, Okapi and Rwanda No. 239. No. C13, Woodpecker and Oldenburg No. 4.

1978, Nov. 1		Litho.	Perf. 12½	
C12	CD138	30fr multi	90	60
C13	CD139	30fr multi	90	60

Nos. C12-C13 printed se-tenant.

RYUKYU ISLANDS

Serving The Collector & Dealer Since 1955

JOHN B. HEAD

P.O. Drawer 7
Bethel, ME. 04217
207-824-2462

RYUKYU ISLANDS
(rē·ōō′kyōō)

LOCATION—Chain of 63 islands between Japan and Formosa, separating the East China Sea from the Pacific Ocean.
GOVT.—Semi-autonomous under United States administration.
AREA—848 sq. mi.
POP.—945,465 (1970).
CAPITAL—Naha, Okinawa.

The Ryukyus were part of Japan until American forces occupied them in 1945. The islands reverted to Japan May 15, 1972.

Before the general issue of 1948, a number of provisional stamps were used. These included a mimeographed-handstamped adhesive for Kume Island, and various current stamps of Japan handstamped with the personal chops of the postmasters of Okinawa, Miyako and Yaeyama. Although authorized by American authorities, these provisionals were local in nature, so are omitted in the listings that follow.

100 Sen = 1 Yen
100 Cents = 1 Dollar (1958).

Cycad
A1

Lily
A2

Sailing Ship
A3

Farmer
A4

Wmk. 257

Typographed.

1948		Perf. 13	Wmk. 257

Second Printing.

1	A1	5s magenta	1.50	1.60
2	A2	10s yel grn	3.75	4.00
3	A1	20s yel grn	2.75	3.00
4	A3	30s vermilion	2.00	2.00
5	A2	40s magenta	1.40	1.50
6	A3	50s ultra	3.50	3.50
7	A4	1y ultra	3.50	3.50
		Nos. 1-7 (7)	18.40	19.10

First Printing.

1a	A1	5s magenta	2.75	3.50
2a	A2	10s yel grn	1.50	1.75
3a	A1	20s yel grn	1.50	1.75
4a	A3	30s vermilion	2.75	3.50
5a	A2	40s magenta	37.50	40.00
6a	A3	50s ultra	3.00	3.50
7a	A4	1y ultra	275.00	175.00
		Nos. 1a-7a (7)	324.00	229.00

First printing: thick yellow gum, dull colors, rough perforations, grayish paper. Second printing: white gum, sharp colors, cleancut perforations, white paper.

Roof Tiles
A5

Ryukyu University
A6

Designs: 1y, Ryukyu girl. 2y, Shuri Castle. 3y, Guardian dragon. 4y, Two women. 5y, Sea shells.

Photogravure

1950		Perf. 13x13½	Unwmkd.
8	A5	50s dk car rose	25	25
9	A5	1y dp bl	3.50	1.00
10	A5	2y rose vio	9.00	3.50
11	A5	3y car rose	22.50	4.50
12	A5	4y grnsh gray	8.00	3.50
13	A5	5y bl grn	6.50	3.25
		Nos. 8-13 (6)	49.75	16.00

A 1958 printing of No. 8 is on whiter paper with colorless gum and has an 8-character imprint in the sheet margin. The original 1950 printing is on toned paper with yellowish gum and has a 5-character imprint.

1951, Feb. 12   Perf. 13½x13
14	A6	3y red brn	40.00	15.00

Opening of Ryukyu University, Feb. 12.

Pine Tree
A7

1951, Feb. 19   Perf. 13
15	A7	3y dk grn	35.00	15.00

Reforestation Week, Feb. 18–24.

Nos. 8 and 10 Surcharged in Black

Three types of 10y surcharge:
I. Narrow-spaced rules, "10" normal spacing.
II. Wide-spaced rules, "10" normal spacing.
III. Rules and "10" both wide-spaced.

1952   Perf. 13x13½
16	A5	10y on 50s dk car rose		
		(II)	10.00	12.50
a.		Type I	30.00	32.50
b.		Type III	35.00	37.50
17	A5	100y on 2y rose vio	1,750.	1,350.

There are two types of surcharge on No. 17.

Dove, Bean Sprout and Map
A8

Madanbashi Bridge
A9

1952, Apr. 1   Perf. 13½x13
18	A8	3y dp plum	80.00	22.50

Issued to commemorate the establishment of the Government of the Ryukyu Islands (GRI), April 1, 1952.

1952–53

Designs: 2y, Main Hall, Shuri Castle. 3y, Shurei Gate. 6y, Stone Gate, Sogenji temple, Naha. 10y, Benzaiten-do temple. 30y, Sonohan Utaki (altar) at Shuri Castle. 50y, Tamaudun (royal mausoleum), Shuri. 100y, Stone Bridge, Hosho Pond.

19	A9	1y red	30	25
20	A9	2y green	40	35
21	A9	3y aqua	50	45
22	A9	6y blue	2.00	2.00
23	A9	10y crim rose	2.00	45
24	A9	30y ol grn	8.50	4.50
a.		30y lt ol grn ('58)	40.00	
25	A9	50y rose vio	9.50	5.00
26	A9	100y claret	12.50	6.00
		Nos. 19-26 (8)	35.70	19.00

Issue dates: 1y, 2y and 3y, Nov. 20, 1952. Others, Jan. 20, 1953.

Reception at Shuri Castle
A10

Perry and American Fleet
A11

Perf. 13½x13, 13x13½

1953, May 26
27	A10	3y dp mag	12.00	4.00
28	A11	6y dl bl	75	85

Issued to commemorate the centenary of the arrival of Commodore Matthew Calbraith Perry at Naha, Okinawa.

Chofu Ota and Pencil-shaped Matrix
A12

Shigo Toma and Pen
A13

1953, Oct. 1   Perf. 13½x13
29	A12	4y yel brn	10.00	3.00

Issued to publicize the third Newspaper Week.

1954, Oct. 1
30	A13	4y blue	12.00	4.00

Issued to publicize the fourth Newspaper Week.

Ryukyu Pottery
A14

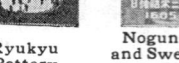
Noguni Shrine and Sweet Potato Plant
A15

Designs: 15y, Lacquerware. 20y, Textile design.

1954-55   Photogravure.   Perf. 13
31	A14	4y brown	75	50
32	A14	15y ver ('55)	3.00	1.50
33	A14	20y yel org ('55)	2.50	1.50

1955, Nov. 26
34	A15	4y blue	12.00	4.00

Issued to commemorate the 350th anniversary of the introduction of the sweet potato to the Ryukyu Islands.

Stylized Trees
A16

Willow Dance
A17

1956, Feb. 18   Unwmkd.
35	A16	4y bluish grn	10.00	3.50

Arbor Week, Feb. 18–24.

1956, May 1   Perf. 13

Design: 8y, Straw hat dance. 14y, Dancer in warrior costume with fan.

36	A17	5y rose lil	85	60
37	A17	8y vio bl	2.25	1.50
38	A17	14y redsh brn	2.75	2.10

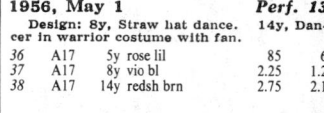
Telephone—A18

1956, June 8
39	A18	4y vio bl	15.00	4.00

Establishment of dial telephone system.

Garland of Pine, Bamboo and Plum
A19

Map of Okinawa and Pencil Rocket
A20

1956, Dec. 1   Perf. 13½x13
40	A19	2y multi	1.75	75

Issued for the New Year, 1957.

1957, Oct. 1   Photo.   Perf. 13½x13
41	A20	4y dp vio bl	65	75

7th annual Newspaper Week, Oct. 1–7.

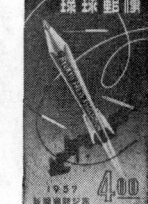
Phoenix—A21

1957, Dec. 1   Perf. 13   Unwmkd.
42	A21	2y multi	20	20

Issued for New Year, 1958.

RYUKYU ISLANDS

417

Ryukyu Stamps—A22

1958, July 1   **Perf. 13½**
43   A22   4y multi   1.00   75
10th anniversary of first Ryukyu stamps.

Yen Symbol and Dollar Sign
A23

1958, Sept. 16 Typographed Perf. 11
Without Gum.
44   A23   ½c orange   40   40
   a. Imperf., pair   1,250.
45   A23   1c yel grn   50   50
46   A23   2c dk bl   60   60
47   A23   3c dp car   50   50
48   A23   4c brt grn   80   80
49   A23   5c orange   2.50   2.50
50   A23   10c aqua   4.00   4.00
51   A23   25c brt vio bl   5.00   4.50
   a. Gummed paper ('61)   9.00
52   A23   50c gray   14.00   6.00
   a. Gummed paper ('61)   9.00
53   A23 $1 rose lil   12.00   4.00
   Nos. 44-53 (10)   40.30   23.80

Printed locally. Perforation, paper and shade varieties exist.

Gate of Courtesy—A24

1958, Oct. 15   **Photo.**   **Perf. 13½**
54   A24   3c multi   1.35   1.00
Issued to commemorate the restoration of Shureimon, Gate of Courtesy, on road leading to Shuri City.

Lion Dance   Trees and
A25   Mountains
               A26

1958, Dec. 10 Perf. 13½ Unwmkd.
55   A25   1½c multi   25   25
Issued for New Year, 1959.

1959, Apr. 30 Litho. Perf. 13½x13
56   A26   3c bl, yel grn & red   1.00   50
   a. Red omitted
Issued to publicize the "Make the Ryukyus Green" movement.

Yonaguni Moth
A27

1959, July 23 Photogravure Perf. 13
57   A27   3c multi   1.25   50
Issued to commemorate the meeting of the Japanese Biological Education Society in Okinawa.

Hibiscus   Toy (Yakaji)
A28   A29

Designs: 3c, Fish (Moorish idol). 8c, Sea shell (Phallum bandatum). 13c, Butterfly (Kallima Inachus Eucerca), denomination at left, butterfly going up. 17c, Jellyfish (Dactylometra pacifera Goette).

Inscribed: 琉球郵便
1959, Aug. 10   **Perf. 13½x13½**
58   A28   ½c multi   30   25
59   A28   3c multi   1.00   40
60   A28   8c lt ultra, blk & ocher   8.00   5.00
61   A28   13c lt bl, gray & org   3.00   1.50
62   A28   17c vio bl, red & yel   17.00   7.00
   Nos. 58-62 (5)   29.30   14.15

Four-character inscription measures 10x2 mm. on ½c; 12x3mm. on 3c, 8c; 8½x2 mm. on 13c, 17c. See also Nos. 76-80.

1959, Dec. 1   **Lithographed**
63   A29   1½c gold & multi   75   40
Issued for the New Year, 1960.

University Badge
A30

1960, May 22 Photogravure Perf. 13
64   A30   3c multi   1.10   55
10th anniversary of the opening of Ryukyu University.

Dancer
A31

Designs: Various Ryukyu Dances.
1960, Nov. 1 Photogravure Perf. 13
Dark Gray Background
65   A31   1c yel, red & vio   1.25   60
66   A31   2½c crim, bl & yel   2.50   1.10
67   A31   5c dk bl, yel & red   75   75
68   A31   10c dk bl, yel & car   1.00   90

See also Nos. 81-87, 220.

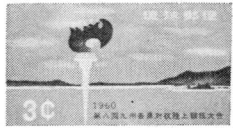
Torch and Nago Bay
A32

Runners at Starting Line
A33

1960, Nov. 8
72   A32   3c lt bl, grn & red   6.50   2.00
73   A33   8c org & sl grn   75   70
Issued to commemorate the 8th Kyushu Inter-Prefectural Athletic Meet, held at Nago, Northern Okinawa, Nov. 6–7.

Little Egret and Rising Sun
A34

1960, Dec. 1   **Perf. 13 Unwmkd.**
74   A34   3c redsh brn   6.50   1.25
Issued to publicize the national census.

Okinawa Bull Fight
A35

1960, Dec. 10   **Perf. 13½**
75   A35   1½c bis, dk bl & red brn   1.75   60
Issued for New Year, 1961.

Type of 1959 With Japanese Inscription Redrawn:
琉球郵便
1960–61 Photo. Perf. 13½x13½
76   A28   ½c multi ('61)   35   25
77   A28   3c multi ('61)   1.25   40
78   A28   8c lt ultra, blk & ocher   1.20   50
79   A28   13c lt bl, brn & red   1.40   80
80   A28   17c vio bl, red & yel   8.00   3.50
   Nos. 76-80 (5)   12.20   5.45

Size of Japanese inscription on Nos. 78–80 is 10½x1½mm. On No. 79 the denomination is at right, butterfly going down.

Dancer Type of 1960 with "RYUKYUS" Added.
1961–64   **Perf. 13**
81   A31   1c multi   20   15
82   A31   2½c multi ('62)   25   15
83   A31   5c multi ('62)   40   30
84   A31   10c multi ('62)   90   40
84A   A31   20c multi ('64)   1.50   1.00
85   A31   25c multi ('62)   1.75   1.00
86   A31   50c multi   3.50   1.00
87   A31 $1 multi   5.50   50
   Nos. 81-87 (8)   14.00   4.50

Pine Tree
A36

1961, May 1 Photogravure Perf. 13
88   A36   3c yel grn & red   1.75   1.00
Issued to publicize the "Make the Ryukyus Green" movement.

Naha, Steamer and Sailboat
A37

1961, May 20
89   A37   3c aqua   2.25   1.00
40th anniversary of Naha.

White Silver   Books and Bird
Temple   A39
A38

Typographed
1961, Oct. 1   **Perf. 11 Unwmkd.**
90   A38   3c red brn   2.00   1.50
   a. Horiz. pair, imperf. between   300.00
   b. Vert. pair, imperf. between   350.00

Issued to commemorate the merger of townships Takamine, Kanegushiku and Miwa with Itoman.

1961, Nov. 12   **Litho. Perf. 13**
91   A39   3c multi   1.50   1.00
Issued for Book Week.

Rising Sun and   Symbolic Steps,
Eagles   Trees and
A40   Government
                 Building
                 A41

1961, Dec. 10   **Photo. Perf. 13½**
92   A40   1½c gold, ver & blk   2.50   1.50
Issued for New Year, 1962.

1962, Apr. 1 Perf. 13½ Unwmkd.
Design: 3c, Government Building.
93   A41   1½c multi   75   80
94   A41   3c brt grn, red & gray   1.00   70

Issued to commemorate the 10th anniversary of the Government of the Ryukyu Islands (GRI).

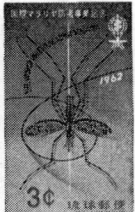
Anopheles Hyrcanus Sinensis
A42

Design: 8c, Malaria eradication emblem and Shurei gate.
1962, Apr. 7   **Perf. 13½x13**
95   A42   3c multi   65   80
96   A42   8c multi   90   1.00
Issued for the World Health Organization drive to eradicate malaria.

RYUKYU ISLANDS

Dolls and Toys A43 **Linden or Sea Hibiscus** A44

1962, May 5 **Litho.** **Perf. 13½**
97 A43 3c red, blk, bl & buff 1.50 1.00

Issued for Children's Day, 1962.

1962, June 1 **Photogravure**
Flowers: 3c, Indian coral tree. 8c, Iju (Schima liukiuensis Nakai). 13c, Touch-me-not (garden balsam). 17c, Shell flower (Alpinia speciosa).

98	A44	½c multi	15	15
99	A44	3c multi	35	15
100	A44	8c multi	45	40
101	A44	13c multi	70	55
102	A44	17c multi	1.20	80
		Nos. 98-102 (5)	2.85	2.05

See Nos. 107 and 114 for 1½c and 15c flower stamps.

Earthenware A45

1962, July 5 **Perf. 13½x13**
103 A45 3c multi 4.00 2.50

Issued for Philatelic Week.

Japanese Fencing (Kendo)—A46

1962, July 25 **Perf. 13**
104 A46 3c multi 5.00 1.00

Issued to commemorate the All-Japan Kendo Meeting in Okinawa, July 25, 1962.

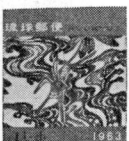

Rabbit Playing near Water, Bingata Cloth Design A47 **Young Man and Woman, Stone Relief** A48

1962, Dec. 10 **Perf. 13½x13**
105 A47 1½c gold & multi 70 60

Issued for New Year, 1963.

1963, Jan. 15 **Photo.** **Perf. 13½**
106 A48 3c gold, blk & bl 1.25 60

Issued for Adult Day.

 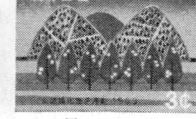

Gooseneck Cactus A49 **Trees and Wooded Hills** A50

1963, Apr. 5 **Perf. 13x13½**
107 A49 1½c dk bl, grn, yel & pink 15 15

1963, Mar. 25 **Perf. 13½x13**
108 A50 3c ultra, grn & red brn 1.25 80

Issued to publicize the "Make the Ryukyus Green" movement.

Map of Okinawa A51 **Hawks over Islands** A52

1963, Apr. 30 **Perf. 13½ Unwmkd.**
109 A51 3c multi 1.50 1.00

Opening of the Round Road on Okinawa.

1963, May 10 **Photogravure**
110 A52 3c multi 1.25 1.00

Issued for Bird Day, May 10.

Shioya Bridge A53

1963, June 5
111 A53 3c multi 1.25 1.00

Opening of Shioya Bridge over Shioya Bay.

Tsuikin-wan Lacquerware Bowl A54

1963, July 1 **Perf. 13½ Unwmkd.**
112 A54 3c multi 3.00 1.50

Issued for Philatelic Week.

Map of Far East and JCI Emblem A55

1963, Sept. 16 **Photo.** **Perf. 13½**
113 A55 3c multi 1.10 55

Issued to commemorate the meeting of the International Junior Chamber of Commerce (JCI), Naha, Okinawa, Sept. 16–19.

Mamaomoto A56 **Site of Nakagusuku Castle** A57

1963, Oct. 15 **Perf. 13½x13**
114 A56 15c multi 85 40

1963, Nov. 1 **Perf. 13½x13**
115 A57 3c multi 85 60

Issued to publicize protection of national cultural treasures.

Flame A58 **Dragon (Bingata Pattern)** A59

1963, Dec. 10 **Perf. 13½**
116 A58 3c red, dk bl & yel 1.00 55

Issued to commemorate the 15th anniversary of the Universal Declaration of Human Rights.

1963, Dec. 10 **Photogravure**
117 A59 1½c multi 30 25

Issued for New Year, 1964.

Carnation A60 **Pineapples and Sugar Cane** A61

1964, May 10 **Perf. 13½**
118 A60 3c bl, yel, blk & car 55 40

Issued for Mother's Day.

1964, June 1
119 A61 3c multi 55 40

Agricultural census.

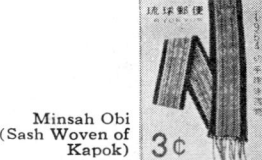

Minsah Obi (Sash Woven of Kapok) A62

1964, July 1 **Perf. 13½ Unwmkd.**
120 A62 3c dp grn, rose pink & ocher 65 50
  a. 3c dp bl, dp car & ocher 85 65

Issued for Philatelic Week.

Girl Scout and Emblem A63

1964, Aug. 31 **Photogravure**
121 A63 3c multi 40 30

10th anniversary of Ryukyuan Girl Scouts.

Shuri Relay Station A64 **Parabolic Antenna and Map** A65

1964, Sept. 1 Perf. 13½ Unwmkd.
Black Overprint
122 A64 3c dp grn 1.10 1.00
  a. Figure "1" invtd. 30.00 30.00
123 A65 8c ultra 1.25 1.00

Issued to commemorate the opening of the Ryukyu Islands–Japan microwave system carrying telephone and telegraph messages between the Ryukyus and Japan. Nos. 122–123 not issued without overprint.

Gate of Courtesy, Olympic Torch and Emblem A66

1964, Sept. 7 **Photo.** **Perf. 13½x13**
124 A66 3c ultra, yel & red 35 25

Issued to commemorate the relaying of the Olympic torch on Okinawa en route to Tokyo.

"Naihanchi," Karate Stance A67

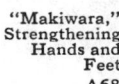 

"Makiwara," Strengthening Hands and Feet A68

"Kumite," Simulated Combat A69

1964–65 **Photo.** **Perf. 13½**
125 A67 3c dl cl, yel & blk 75 50
126 A68 3c yel & multi ('65) 60 40
127 A69 3c gray, red & blk ('65) 60 40

Karate, Ryukyuan self-defense sport.

RYUKYU ISLANDS

Miyara Dunchi	Snake and Iris (Bingata)
A70	A71

1964, Nov. 1   *Perf. 13½*

128   A70   3c multi   40   30

Issued to publicize protection of national cultural treasures. Miyara Dunchi was built as a residence by Miyara-pechin Toen in 1819.

1964, Dec. 10   Photogravure

129   A71   1½c multi   20   15

Issued for New Year, 1965.

Boy Scouts
A72

1965, Feb. 6   *Perf. 13½*

130   A72   3c lt bl & multi   75   50

10th anniversary of Ryukyuan Boy Scouts.

Main Stadium, Onoyama
A73

1965, July 1   *Perf. 13x13½*

131   A73   3c multi   30   20

Issued to commemorate the inauguration of the main stadium of the Onoyama athletic facilities.

Samisen of King Shoko
A74

1965, July 1   Photo.   *Perf. 13½*

132   A74   3c buff & multi   60   40

Issued for Philatelic Week.

Kin Power Plant	ICY Emblem, Ryukyu Map
A75	A76

1965, July 1

133   A75   3c grn & multi   30   20

Completion of Kin power plant.

1965, Aug. 24   Photo.   *Perf. 13½*

134   A76   3c multi   30   20

Issued to commemorate the 20th anniversary of the United Nations and for International Cooperation Year, 1964–65.

Naha City Hall
A77

1965, Sept. 18   *Perf. 13½*   Unwmkd.

135   A77   3c bl & multi   30   20

Completion of Naha City Hall.

Chinese Box Turtle	Horse (Bingata)
A78	A79

Turtles: No. 137, Hawksbill turtle (denomination at top, country name at bottom). No. 138, Asian terrapin (denomination and country name on top).

1965–66   Photo.   *Perf. 13½*

136   A78   3c gldn brn & multi   40   30
137   A78   3c blk, yel & brn ('66)   30   30
138   A78   3c gray & multi ('66)   30   30

Issue dates: No. 136, Oct. 20, 1965. No. 137, Jan. 20, 1966. No. 138, Apr. 20, 1966.

1965, Dec. 10   Photo.   *Perf. 13½*

139   A79   1½c multi   20   15
   a. Gold omitted   1,000.   1,000.

Issued for New Year, 1966.

Nature Conservation Issue

Noguchi's Okinawa Woodpecker	Sika Deer
A80	A81

Design: No. 142, Dugong.

1966   Photo.   *Perf. 13½*

140   A80   3c bl grn & multi   25   25
141   A81   3c bl, red, blk, brn & grn   30   30
142   A81   3c bl, yel grn, blk & red   30   30

Issue dates: No. 140, Feb. 15. No. 141, Mar. 15. No. 142, Apr. 20.

Ryukyu Bungalow Swallow
A82

1966, May 10   Photo.   *Perf. 13½*

143   A82   3c sky bl, blk & brn   20   20

Issued for the 4th Bird Week, May 10–16.

Lilies and Ruins
A83

1966, June 23   *Perf. 13x13½*

144   A83   3c multi   20   20

Issued for Memorial Day, commemorating the end of the Battle of Okinawa, June 23, 1945.

University of the Ryukyus
A84

1966, July 1

145   A84   3c multi   20   20

Issued to commemorate the transfer of the University of the Ryukyus from United States' authority to the Ryukyu Government.

Lacquerware, 18th Century	Tile-Roofed House and UNESCO Emblem
A85	A86

1966, Aug. 1   *Perf. 13½*

146   A85   3c gray & multi   25   25

Issued for Philatelic Week.

1966, Sept. 20   Photo.   *Perf. 13½*

147   A86   3c multi   25   25

Issued to commemorate the 20th anniversary of the United Nations Educational, Scientific and Cultural Organization (UNESCO).

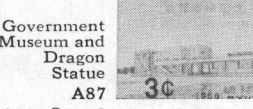

Government Museum and Dragon Statue
A87

1966, Oct. 6

148   A87   3c multi   20   20

Issued to commemorate the completion of the GRI (Government of the Ryukyu Islands) Museum, Shuri.

Tomb of Nakasone-Tuimya Genga, Ruler of Miyako
A88

1966, Nov. 1   Photo.   *Perf. 13½*

149   A88   3c multi   20   20

Issued to publicize the protection of national cultural treasures.

Ram in Iris Wreath (Bingata)	Clown Fish
A89	A90

1966, Dec. 10   Photo.   *Perf. 13½*

150   A89   1½c dk bl & multi   20   20

Issued for New Year, 1967.

1966–67

Fish: No. 152, Young boxfish (white numeral at lower left). No. 153, Forceps fish (pale buff numeral at lower right). No. 154, Spotted triggerfish (orange numeral). No. 155, Saddleback butterflyfish (carmine numeral, lower left).

151   A90   3c org red & multi   25   20
152   A90   3c org yel & multi ('67)   25   20
153   A90   3c multi ('67)   30   20
154   A90   3c multi ('67)   30   20
155   A90   3c multi ('67)   30   20
     Nos. 151–155 (5)   1.40   1.00

Issue dates: No. 151, Dec. 20, 1966. No. 152, Jan. 10, 1967. No. 153, Apr. 10, 1967. No. 154, May 25, 1967. No. 155, June 10, 1967.

Tsuboya Urn	Episcopal Miter
A91	A92

1967, Apr. 20

156   A91   3c yel & multi   25   20

Issued for Philatelic Week, 1967.

1967–68   Photo.   *Perf. 13½*

Seashells: No. 158, Venus comb murex. No. 159, Chiragra spider. No. 160, Green turban. No. 161, Euprotomus bulla.

157   A92   3c lt grn & multi   25   20
158   A92   3c grnsh bl & multi   25   20
159   A92   3c emer & multi ('68)   25   20
160   A92   3c lt bl & multi ('68)   35   20
161   A92   3c brt bl & multi ('68)   75   45
     Nos. 157–161 (5)   1.85   1.25

Issue dates: 1967, No. 157, July 20; No. 158, Aug. 30. 1968, No. 159, Jan. 18; No. 160, Feb. 20; No. 161, June 5.

Red-tiled Roofs and ITY Emblem
A93

1967, Sept. 11   Photo.   *Perf. 13½*

162   A93   3c multi   30   20

Issued for International Tourist Year, 1967.

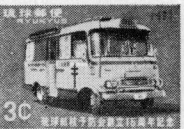

Mobile TB Clinic
A94

1967, Oct. 13   Photo.   *Perf. 13½*

163   A94   3c lil & multi   30   20

Issued to commemorate the 15th anniversary of the Anti-Tuberculosis Society.

Hojo Bridge, Enkaku Temple, 1498
A95

1967, Nov. 1

164   A95   3c bl grn & multi   30   20

Protection of national cultural treasures.

420 RYUKYU ISLANDS

Monkey (Bingata) A96 — TV Tower and Map A97

1967, Dec. 11 Photo. Perf. 13½
165 A96 1½c sil & multi 25 15
Issued for New Year 1968.

1967, Dec. 22
166 A97 3c multi 35 20
Issued to commemorate the opening of Miyako and Yaeyama television stations.

Dr. Kijin Nakachi and Helper A98 — Pill Box (Inro) A99

1968, Mar. 15 Photo. Perf. 13½
167 A98 3c multi 35 20
Issued to commemorate the 120th anniversary of the first vaccination in the Ryukyu Islands, performed by Dr. Kijin Nakachi.

1968, Apr. 18
168 A99 3c gray & multi 60 45
Issued for Philatelic Week, 1968.

Young Man, Library, Book and Map of Ryukyu Islands A100

1968, May 13
169 A100 3c multi 45 35
10th International Library Week.

Mailmen's Uniforms and Stamp of 1948—A101

1968, July 1 Photo. Perf. 13x13½
170 A101 3c multi 45 35
20th anniversary of first Ryukyuan postage stamps.

Main Gate, Enkaku Temple A102

Photogravure and Engraved
1968, July 15 Perf. 13½
171 A102 3c multi 45 35
Issued to commemorate the restoration of the main gate of the Enkaku Temple, built 1492–1495, and destroyed during World War II.

Old Man's Dance A103

1968, Sept. 15 Photo. Perf. 13½
172 A103 3c gold & multi 45 35
Issued for Old People's Day.

Mictyris Longicarpus A104

Crabs: No. 174, Uca dubia stimpson. No. 175, Baptozius vinosus. No. 176, Cardisoma carnifex. No. 177, Ocypode ceratophthalma pallas.

1968–69 Photogravure Perf. 13½
173 A104 3c bl, ocher & blk 75 50
174 A104 3c lt bl grn & multi ('69) 75 50
175 A104 3c lt grn & multi ('69) 75 50
176 A104 3c lt ultra & multi ('69) 90 55
177 A104 3c lt ultra & multi ('69) 90 55
Nos. 173-177 (5) 4.05 2.60

Issue dates: No. 173, Oct. 21, 1968. No. 174, Feb. 5, 1969. No. 175, Mar. 5, 1969. No. 176, May 15, 1969; No. 177, June 2, 1969.

Saraswati Pavilion A105

1968, Nov. 1 Photo. Perf. 13½
178 A105 3c multi 45 30
Issued to commemorate the restoration of the Saraswati Pavilion (in front of Enkaku Temple), destroyed during World War II.

Tennis Player A106 — Cock and Iris (Bingata) A107

1968, Nov. 3 Photo. Perf. 13½
179 A106 3c grn & multi 45 30
Issued to publicize the 35th All-Japan East-West Men's Soft-ball Tennis Tournament, Naha City, Nov. 23–24.

1968, Dec. 10
180 A107 1½c org & multi 20 20
Issued for New Year, 1969.

Boxer A108 — Ink Slab Screen A109

1969, Jan. 3
181 A108 3c gray & multi 45 35
Issued to commemorate the 20th All-Japan Amateur Boxing Championships held at the University of the Ryukyus, Jan. 3–5.

1969, Apr. 17 Photo. Perf. 13½
182 A109 3c sal, ind & red 50 35
Issued for Philatelic Week, 1969.

Box Antennas and Map of Radio Link A110 — Gate of Courtesy and Emblems A111

1969, July 1 Photo. Perf. 13½
183 A110 3c multi 25 20
Issued to commemorate the opening of the UHF (radio) circuit system between Okinawa and the outlying Miyako-Yaeyama Islands.

1969, Aug. 1 Photo. Perf. 13½
184 A111 3c Prus bl, gold & ver 25 20
Issued to commemorate the 22nd All-Japan Formative Education Study Conference, Naha, Aug. 1–3.

Folklore Issue

Tug of War Festival A112

Hari Boat Race A113

Izaiho Ceremony, Kudaka Island A114

Mortar-drum Dance A115

Sea God Dance A116

1969–70 Photogravure Perf. 13
185 A112 3c multi 55 40
186 A113 3c multi 50 40
187 A114 3c multi 50 40
188 A115 3c multi ('70) 1.00 65
189 A116 3c multi ('70) 1.00 65
Nos. 185-189 (5) 3.55 2.50

Issue dates: No. 185, Aug. 1; No. 186, Sept. 5; No. 187, Oct. 3; No. 188, Jan. 20, 1970; No. 189, Feb. 27, 1970.

No. 99 Surcharged 改訂 ½¢

1969, Oct. 15 Photo. Perf. 13½
190 A44 ½c on 3c multi 20 15

Nakamura-ke Farm House, Built 1713-51 A117

1969, Nov. 1 Photo. Perf. 13½
191 A117 3c multi 25 20
Issued to publicize the protection of national cultural treasures.

Statue of Kyuzo Toyama, Maps of Hawaiian and Ryukyu Islands A118

1969, Dec. 5 Photo. Perf. 13½
192 A118 3c lt ultra & multi 45 40
  a. Without overprint 2,000.
  b. Wide-spaced bars 600.00
Ryukyu-Hawaii emigration led by Kyuzo Toyama, 70th anniversary.
The overprint—"1969" at lower left and bars across "1970" at upper right—was applied before No. 192 was issued.

Dog and Flowers (Bingata) A119 — Sake Flask Made from Coconut A120

1969, Dec. 10
193 A119 1½c pink & multi 20 20
Issued for New Year, 1970.

1970, Apr. 15 Photo. Perf. 13½
194 A120 3c multi 50 40
Issued for Philatelic Week, 1970.

Classic Opera Issue

"The Bell" (Shushin Kaneiri) A121

RYUKYU ISLANDS

Child and Kidnapper (Chu-nusudu)
A122

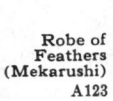

Robe of Feathers (Mekarushi)
A123

Vengeance of Two Young Sons (Nidotichiuchi)
A124

The Virgin and the Dragon (Kokonomaki)
A125

1970		Photo.	Perf. 13½	
195	A121	3c dl bl & multi	75	60
196	A122	3c lt bl & multi	75	60
197	A123	3c bluish grn & multi	75	60
198	A124	3c dl bl grn & multi	75	60
199	A125	3c multi	75	60
	Nos. 195-199 (5)		3.75	3.00
195a-199a	5 sheets of 4		25.00	30.00

Underwater Observatory and Tropical Fish
A126

1970, May 22
200 A126 3c bl grn & multi 40 35
Issued to commemorate the completion of the underwater observatory at Busena-Misaki, Nago.

Noboru Jahana (1865–1908), Politician
A127

Map of Okinawa and People
A128

Portraits: No. 202, Saion Gushichan Bunjaku (1682–1761), statesman. No. 203, Choho Giwan (1823–1876), regent and poet.

1970–71		Engraved	Perf. 13½	
201	A127	3c rose cl	70	50
202	A127	3c dl bl grn	1.60	1.10
203	A127	3c blk ('71)	70	50

Issue dates: No. 201, Sept. 25, 1970. No. 202, Dec. 22, 1970. No. 203, Jan. 22, 1971.

1970, Oct. 1   Photogravure
204 A128 3c red & multi 25 20
The 1970 census, Oct. 1, 1970.

Great Cycad of Une
A129

1970, Nov. 2   Photo.   Perf. 13½
205 A129 3c gold & multi 30 25
Protection of national treasures.

Japanese Flag, Diet and Map of Ryukyus
A130

Wild Boar and Cherry Blossoms (Bingata)
A131

1970, Nov. 15   Photo.   Perf. 13½
206 A130 3c ultra & multi 1.00 75
Citizens' participation in national administration according to Japanese law of Apr. 24, 1970.

1970, Dec. 10
207 A131 1½c multi 25 20
New Year, 1971.

Low Hand Loom (Jibata)
A132

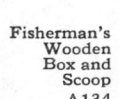 

Farmer Wearing Palm Bark Raincoat and Kuba Leaf Hat
A133

Fisherman's Wooden Box and Scoop
A134

Designs: No. 209, Woman running a filature (reel). No. 211, Woman hulling rice with cylindrical "Shiri-ushi."

1971		Photogravure	Perf. 13½	
208	A132	3c lt bl & multi	40	35
209	A132	3c pale grn & multi	40	35
210	A133	3c lt bl & multi	45	35
211	A132	3c yel & multi	75	50
212	A134	3c gray & multi	50	35
	Nos. 208-212 (5)		2.50	1.90

Issue dates: No. 208, Feb. 16; No. 209, Mar. 16; No. 210, Apr. 13; No. 211, May 20; No. 212, June 15.

Water Carrier (Taku)
A135

1971, Apr. 15   Photo.   Perf. 13½
213 A135 3c bl grn & multi 50 35
Philatelic Week, 1971.

Old and New Naha, and City Emblem—A136

1971, May 20   Perf. 13
214 A136 3c ultra & multi 30 25
50th anniversary of Naha as a municipality.

Caesalpinia Pulcherrima
A137

Design: 2c, Madder (Sandanka).

1971		Photogravure	Perf. 13	
215	A137	2c gray & multi	20	15
216	A137	3c gray & multi	20	15

Issue dates: 2c, Sept. 30; 3c, May 10.

Government Park Series

View from Mabuni Hill
A138

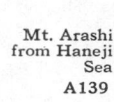 

Mt. Arashi from Haneji Sea
A139

Yabuchi Island from Yakena Port
A140

1971–72				
217	A138	3c grn & multi	40	30
218	A139	3c bl & multi	40	30
219	A140	4c multi ('72)	50	30

Issue dates: No. 217, July 30; No. 218, Aug. 30, 1971; No. 219, Jan. 20, 1972.

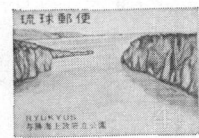

Dancer
A141

Deva King, Torinji Temple
A142

1971, Nov. 1   Photo.   Perf. 13
220 A141 4c Prus bl & multi 20 15

1971, Dec. 1
221 A142 4c dp bl & multi 25 25
Protection of national cultural treasures.

Rat and Chrysanthemums
A143

Student Nurse
A144

1971, Dec. 10
222 A143 2c brn org & multi 20 20
New Year 1972.

1971, Dec. 24
223 A144 4c lil & multi 35 25
Nurses' training, 25th anniversary.

Birds on Seashore
A145

Sun over Islands
A147

Coral Reef
A146

1972		Photo.	Perf. 13	
224	A145	5c brt bl & multi	60	40
225	A146	5c gray & multi	60	40
226	A147	5c ocher & multi	60	40

Issue dates: No. 224, Apr. 14; No. 225, Mar. 30; No. 226, Mar. 21.

Dove, U.S. and Japanese Flags
A148

1972, Apr. 17   Photo.   Perf. 13
227 A148 5c brt bl & multi 1.00 75
Ratification of the Reversion Agreement with U.S. under which the Ryukyu Islands were returned to Japan.

Antique Sake Pot (Yushibin)
A149

1972, Apr. 20
228 A149 5c ultra & multi 80 50
Philatelic Week.
Ryukyu stamps were replaced by those of Japan after May 15, 1972.

RYUKYU ISLANDS—SAAR

AIR POST STAMPS.

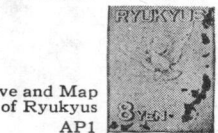

Dove and Map
of Ryukyus
AP1

Photogravure.

1950   Perf. 13x13½   Unwmkd.
C1	AP1	8y brt bl	80.00	40.00
C2	AP1	12y green	20.00	17.50
C3	AP1	16y rose car	15.00	12.50

Heavenly
Maiden
AP2

1951-54
C4	AP2	13y blue	2.50	1.50
C5	AP2	18y green	3.50	2.00
C6	AP2	30y cerise	5.00	1.00
C7	AP2	40y red vio ('54)	8.00	5.00
C8	AP2	50y yel org ('54)	12.00	6.50
	Nos. C4-C8 (5)		31.00	16.00

Heavenly
Maiden
Playing
Flute
AP3

1957, Aug. 1 Engraved Perf. 13½
C9	AP3	15y bl grn	3.00	2.00
C10	AP3	20y rose car	5.00	3.00
C11	AP3	35y yel grn	10.00	5.00
C12	AP3	45y redsh brn	18.00	10.00
C13	AP3	60y gray	24.00	12.00
	Nos. C9-C13 (5)		60.00	32.00

Same Surcharged
in Brown Red or
Light Ultramarine

1959, Dec. 20
C14	AP3	9c on 15y bl grn (BrR)	2.50	1.50
a.	Inverted surch.		550.00	
C15	AP3	14c on 20y rose car (LU)	2.50	2.00
C16	AP3	19c on 35y yel grn (BrR)	6.00	2.00
C17	AP3	27c on 45y redsh brn (LU)	14.00	7.50
C18	AP3	35c on 60y gray (BrR)	20.00	8.00
	Nos. C14-C18 (5)		45.00	21.00

Nos. 31-33, 36 and
38 Surcharged in
Black, Brown, Red,
Blue or Green

1960, Aug. 3   Photo.   Perf. 13
C19	A14	9c on 4y brn	10.00	12.500
a.	Invtd. surch.			
C20	A14	14c on 5y rose lil (Br)	2.25	1.50
C21	A14	19c on 15y ver (R)	1.75	1.50
C22	A17	27c on 14y redsh brn (Bl)	6.50	4.50
C23	A14	35c on 20y yel org (G)	7.50	4.50
	Nos. C19-C23 (5)		21.00	14.00

Wind God
AP4

Designs: 9c, Heavenly Maiden (as on AP2). 14c, Heavenly Maiden (as on AP3). 27c, Wind God at right. 35c, Heavenly Maiden over treetops.

Photogravure
1961, Sept. 21 Perf. 13½ Unwmkd.
C24	AP4	9c multi	45	25
C25	AP4	14c multi	75	50
C26	AP4	19c multi	80	65
C27	AP4	27c multi	1.75	75
C28	AP4	35c multi	2.25	1.10
	Nos. C24-C28 (5)		6.00	3.25

Jet over Gate
of Courtesy
AP5

Jet Plane
AP6

Photogravure
1963, Aug. 28 Perf. 13x13½
| C29 | AP5 | 5½c multi | 20 | 20 |
| C30 | AP6 | 7c multi | 25 | 30 |

SPECIAL DELIVERY STAMP

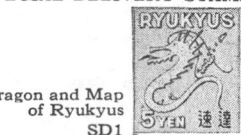

Dragon and Map
of Ryukyus
SD1

Photogravure.
1950   Perf. 13x13½   Unwmkd.
| E1 | SD1 | 5y brt bl | 27.50 | 15.00 |

SAAR
(zär)

LOCATION—On the Franco-German border southeast of Luxembourg.
GOVT.—A German state.
POP.—1,400,000 (1959).
AREA—991 sq. mi.
CAPITAL—Saarbrücken.

A former German territory, the Saar was administered by the League of Nations 1920–35. After a January 12, 1935, plebiscite, it returned to Germany, and the use of German stamps was resumed. After World War II, France occupied the Saar and later established a protectorate. The provisional semi-independent State of Saar was established Jan. 1, 1951. France returned the Saar to the German Federal Republic Jan. 1, 1957. Saar stamps were discontinued in 1959 and replaced by stamps of the German Federal Republic.

100 Pfennig = 1 Mark
100 Centimes = 1 Franc (1921)

German Stamps
of 1906-19
Overprinted

Sarre

Perf. 14, 14½
1920, Jan. 30   Wmk. 125
1	A22	2pf gray	1.25	2.75
a.	Inverted overprint		95.00	130.00
b.	Double overprint		550.00	550.00
2	A22	2½pf gray	2.00	4.00
a.	Inverted ovpt.		135.00	175.00
3	A16	3pf brown	90	2.00
a.	Inverted overprint		120.00	160.00
4	A16	5pf green	25	30
a.	Inverted overprint		160.00	210.00
b.	Double overprint		175.00	250.00
5	A22	7½pf orange	45	85
a.	Invtd. overprint		150.00	200.00
6	A16	10pf carmine	15	30
a.	Inverted overprint		160.00	210.00
b.	Double overprint		250.00	400.00
7	A22	15pf dk vio	15	20
a.	Double overprint		225.00	350.00
8	A16	20pf bl vio	15	20
a.	Double overprint		200.00	300.00
9	A16	25pf org & blk, yel	12.50	14.00
a.	Inverted overprint		300.00	475.00
10	A16	30pf org & blk, buff	25.00	25.00
11	A22	35pf red brn	25	32
a.	Invtd. overprint		140.00	200.00
12	A16	40pf lake & blk	40	50
a.	Invtd. overprint		160.00	210.00
13	A16	50pf pur & blk, buff	30	55
a.	Inverted ovpt.		160.00	250.00
14	A16	60pf red vio	45	60
15	A16	75pf grn & blk	35	50
a.	Inverted overprint		75.00	120.00
16	A16	80pf lake & blk, rose	225.00	250.00

Three types of overprint exist on Nos. 1–5, 12, 13; two types on Nos. 6–11, 14–16.

Overprinted

17	A17	1m car rose	25.00	32.50
a.	Inverted ovpt.		325.00	500.00
b.	Double overprint		300.00	450.00
	Nos. 1-17 (17)		294.55	334.57

The 3m type A19 exists with this overprint but was not issued.
Overprint forgeries exist.

Bavarian Stamps
of 1914-16
Overprinted

Perf. 14x14½
1920, Mar. 1   Wmk. 95
19	A10	2pf gray	1,650.	4,000.
20	A10	3pf brown	165.00	500.00
21	A10	5pf yel grn	65	1.40
a.	Double ovpt.		425.00	550.00
22	A10	7½pf green	75.00	200.00
23	A10	10pf car rose	65	1.60
a.	Double ovpt.		250.00	325.00
24	A10	15pf vermilion	10.00	15.00
a.	Double ovpt.		285.00	375.00
25	A10	15pf carmine	65	1.60
26	A10	20pf blue	65	1.60
a.	Double ovpt.		250.00	325.00
27	A10	25pf gray	6.75	14.00
28	A10	30pf orange	6.00	10.00
29	A10	40pf ol grn	8.50	14.00
30	A10	50pf red brn	85	1.60
a.	Double ovpt.		150.00	200.00
32	A10	60pf dk grn	1.20	2.85

Overprinted

Perf. 11½.
35	A11	1m brown	13.00	25.00
a.	1m dk brn		17.50	30.00
36	A11	2m violet	80.00	135.00
37	A11	3m scarlet	110.00	185.00

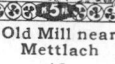

Overprinted

38	A12	5m dp bl	1,000.	1,000.
39	A12	10m yel grn	125.00	210.00
a.	Double ovpt.		4,250.	6,000.

Nos. 19, 20 and 22 were not officially issued, but were available for postage. Examples are known legitimately used on cover. The 20m type A12 was also overprinted in small quantity.
Overprint forgeries exist.

German Stamps
of 1906-20
Overprinted

SAARGEBIET

Perf. 14, 14½
1920, Mar. 26   Wmk. 125
41	A16	5pf green	25	28
a.	Inverted ovpt.		22.50	
42	A16	5pf red brn	45	50
43	A16	10pf carmine	25	28
a.	Inverted ovpt.		22.50	
44	A16	10pf orange	32	32
a.	Inverted ovpt.		13.00	
45	A22	15pf dk vio	25	28
a.	Inverted ovpt.		22.50	
46	A16	20pf bl vio	25	28
a.	Inverted ovpt.		22.50	
47	A16	20pf green	50	50
48	A16	30pf org & blk, buff	30	28
a.	Double ovpt.		90.00	
b.	Inverted ovpt.			
49	A16	30pf dl bl	65	80
50	A16	40pf lake & blk	30	28
51	A16	40pf car rose	1.00	80
52	A16	50pf pur & blk, buff	35	32
a.	Double ovpt.		90.00	
b.	Inverted ovpt.			
53	A16	60pf red vio	60	50
a.	Inverted ovpt.		75.00	
54	A16	75pf grn & blk	60	50
a.	Dbl. overprint		150.00	
55	A17	1.25m green	1.60	1.40
a.	Inverted ovpt.		120.00	
56	A17	1.50m yel brn	1.60	1.40
a.	Inverted ovpt.		100.00	
57	A21	2.50m lil rose	5.00	10.00
58	A16	4m blk & rose	8.00	17.50
a.	Double ovpt.		22.50	
	Nos. 41-58 (18)		22.27	36.22

On No. 57 the overprint is placed vertically at each side of the stamp.

Germany Nos. 90, 120
Surcharged in Black

1921, Feb.
65	A16	20pf on 75pf grn & blk	60	1.25
a.	Inverted surcharge		27.50	40.00
b.	Double surcharge		70.00	110.00

Mark 5 Mark

Surcharged

1920
| 66 | A22 | 5m on 15pf vio brn | 6.00 | 11.50 |
| 67 | A22 | 10m on 15pf vio brn | 7.50 | 14.00 |

Forgeries exist of Nos. 66-67.

Old Mill near
Mettlach
A3

Miner at Work
A4

SAAR

Entrance to Reden Mine
A5

Saar River Traffic
A6

Saar River near Mettlach
A7

Slag Pile at Völklingen
A8

Signal Bridge, Saarbrücken
A9

Church at Mettlach
A10

"Old Bridge," Saarbrücken
A11

Cable Railway at Ferne
A12

Colliery Shafthead
A13 / Saarbrücken City Hall A14

Pottery at Mettlach A15 / St. Ludwig's Cathedral A16

Presidential Residence, Saarbrücken
A17

Burbach Steelworks, Dillingen
A18

Typographed.

1921   Perf. 12½   Unwmkd.

68	A3	5pf ol grn & vio	5	20
a.		Tête Bêche pair	4.50	14.00
b.		Imperf., pair	25.00	32.50
c.		Center inverted	85.00	
69	A4	10pf org & ultra	25	20
a.		Imperf., pair	45.00	60.00
70	A5	20pf grn & sl	35	25
a.		Tête bêche pair	7.50	24.00
b.		Imperf., pair	32.50	45.00
c.		Perf. 10½	22.50	60.00
d.		As "c," tête bêche pair	90.00	300.00
71	A6	25pf brn & dk bl	40	28
a.		Tête bêche pair	9.00	27.50
b.		Imperf., pair	55.00	75.00
72	A7	30pf gray grn & brn	35	32
a.		Tête bêche pair	7.50	24.00
b.		Imperf., pair	50.00	80.00
c.		30pf ol grn & blk	2.00	70.00
d.		As "c", tête bêche pair	14.00	45.00
e.		As "c," imperf., pair	150.00	250.00
73	A8	40pf vermilion	35	32
a.		Tête bêche pair	19.00	60.00
b.		Imperf., pair	90.00	145.00

74	A9	50pf gray & blk	80	1.75
a.		Imperf., pair	25.00	40.00
75	A10	60pf red & dk brn	1.75	1.75
a.		Imperf., pair	35.00	55.00
76	A11	80pf dp bl	70	90
a.		Tête bêche pair	25.00	80.00
b.		Imperf., pair	32.50	52.50
77	A12	1m lt red & blk	70	75
a.		1m grn & blk	800.00	
b.		Imperf., pair	45.00	72.50
78	A13	1.25m lt brn & dk grn	1.00	1.25
a.		Imperf., pair	175.00	275.00
79	A14	2m red & blk	3.25	3.50
a.		Imperf., pair	110.00	175.00
80	A15	3m brn & dk ol	4.00	8.00
a.		Center inverted	125.00	
b.		Imperf., pair	27.50	45.00
81	A16	5m yel & vio	8.00	18.50
a.		Imperf., pair	110.00	175.00
82	A17	10m grn & red brn	13.00	22.50
a.		Imperf., pair	175.00	275.00
83	A18	25m ultra, red & blk	35.00	65.00
a.		Imperf., pair	250.00	400.00
		Nos. 68-83 (16)	70.15	125.47

Prices for tête bêche are for vertical pair. Horizontal pairs sell for about twice as much.
The ultramarine ink on No. 69 appears to be brown where it overlays the orange.

Preceding Issue Surcharged in Red, Blue or Black

5 cent. *a*   1 Fr. *b*

5 FRANKEN *c*

1921, May 1

85	A5(a)	3c on 20pf grn & sl (R)	30	20
a.		Tête bêche pair	5.00	16.00
c.		Imperf., pair	22.50	27.50
d.		Perf. 10½	5.00	17.50
e.		As "d," tête bêche pair	20.00	60.00
86	A6(a)	5c on 25pf brn & dk bl (R)	25	45
a.		Tête bêche pair	90.00	300.00
b.		Imperf., pair	27.50	35.00
87	A7(a)	10c on 30pf gray grn & brn (Bl)	32	35
a.		Tête bêche pair	5.00	16.00
b.		Invtd. surch.	135.00	350.00
c.		Imperf., pair	32.50	45.00
88	A8(a)	15c on 40pf ver (Bk)	55	35
a.		Tête bêche pr.	80.00	300.00
b.		Inverted surcharge	135.00	350.00
c.		Imperf., pair	150.00	200.00
89	A9(a)	20c on 50pf gray & blk (R)	30	18
a.		Imperf., pair	20.00	27.50
90	A10(a)	25c on 60pf red & dk brn (Bl)	45	22
91	A11(a)	30c on 80pf dp bl (Bk)	1.00	50
a.		Tête bêche pair	12.50	40.00
b.		Imperf., pair	90.00	145.00
c.		Inverted surcharge	135.00	350.00
d.		Dbl. surch.		100.00
92	A12(a)	40c on 1m lt red & blk	2.25	50
a.		Inverted surcharge	135.00	350.00
93	A13(a)	50c on 1.25m lt brn & dk grn (Bk)	3.50	90
a.		Imperf., pair	65.00	100.00
b.		Perf. 10½		
94	A14(a)	75c on 2m rec & blk (Bl)	3.50	1.25
95	A15(b)	1fr on 3m brn & dk ol	3.50	2.00
96	A16(b)	2fr on 5m yel & vio (Bl)	10.00	5.50
97	A17(b)	3fr on 10m grn & red brn (Bk)	14.00	16.00
a.		Imperf., pair	125.00	200.00
b.		Dbl. surch.		275.00
98	A18(c)	5fr on 25m ultra, red & blk (Bl)	22.50	30.00
a.		Imperf., pair	300.00	475.00
		Nos. 85-98 (14)	62.42	58.40

In these surcharges the period is occasionally missing and there are various wrong font and defective letters.
Prices for tête bêche are for vertical pairs. Horizontal pairs sell for about twice as much.

Cable Railway, Ferne
A19

Miner at Work
A20

Mettlach Church
A28

"Old Bridge," Saarbrücken
A21

Saarbrücken City Hall
A22

Slag Pile at Völklingen
A23

Pottery at Mettlach
A24

Saar River Traffic
A25

St. Ludwig's Cathedral
A26

Colliery Shafthead
A27

Burbach Steelworks, Dillingen
A29

Perf. 12½x13½, 13½x12½
1922-23   Typographed.

99	A19	3c ol grn & straw	30	32
100	A20	5c org & blk	30	7
a.		Booklet pane of 8		
101	A21	10c bl grn	30	7
102	A19	15c dp brn	45	12
103	A19	15c org ('23)	2.50	45

SAAR

104	A22	20c dk bl & lem	1.75	12
105	A22	20c brt bl & yel ('23)	2.50	45
a.		Booklet pane of 8		
106	A22	25c red & yel	4.00	2.00
107	A22	25c mag & straw ('23)	1.50	25
a.		Booklet pane of 8		
108	A23	30c car & yel	45	60
109	A24	40c brn & yel	75	10
110	A25	50c dk bl & straw	75	10
111	A24	75c dp grn & straw	12.50	22.50
112	A24	75c blk & straw ('23)	15.00	2.50
113	A26	1fr brn red	2.00	45
114	A27	2fr dp vio	3.50	2.25
115	A28	3fr org & dk grn	2.75	2.25
116	A29	5fr brn & red brn	22.50	52.50
		Nos. 99-116 (18)	73.80	87.10

Nos. 99 to 116 exist imperforate but were not regularly issued in that condition.

Madonna of Blieskastel
A30

Size: 23x27mm.

1925, Apr. 9 Photo. Perf. 13½x12½

118	A30	45c lake brn	3.50	2.75

Size: 31½x36mm.

Perf. 12.

119	A30	10fr blk brn	13.00	27.50

Nos. 118-119 exist imperf. Price for set, $300.

Market Fountain, St. Johann
A31

View of Saar Valley
A32

Colliery Shafthead
A35

Burbach Steelworks
A36

Designs: 15c, 75c, View of Saar Valley. 20c, 40c, 90c, Scene from Saarlouis fortifications. 25c, 50c, Tholey Abbey.

1927-32   Perf. 13½.

120	A31	10c dp brn	80	12
121	A32	15c ol blk	55	80
122	A32	20c brn org	50	12
123	A32	25c bluish sl	65	30
124	A31	30c ol grn	90	20
125	A32	40c ol brn	70	12
126	A32	50c magenta	90	10
127	A35	60c red org ('30)	7.00	10
128	A32	75c brn vio	70	15
129	A35	80c red org	3.50	6.00
130	A32	90c dp red ('32)	10.00	22.50
131	A35	1fr violet	3.00	28
132	A36	1.50fr sapphire	3.75	28
133	A36	2fr brn red	3.75	28
134	A36	3fr dk ol grn	8.00	80
135	A36	5fr dp brn	10.00	6.75
		Nos. 120-135 (16)	54.70	38.92

60 cent.

Nos. 126 and 129 Surcharged

1930-34

136	A32	40c on 50c mag ('34)	1.25	1.40
137	A35	60c on 80c red org	1.25	2.50

Plebiscite Issue.
Stamps of 1925-32
Overprinted **VOLKSABSTIMMUNG** in Various Colors **1935**
Perf. 13½, 13½x13, 13x13½.
1934, Nov. 1

139	A31	10c brn (Br)	65	70
140	A32	15c blk grn (G)	65	70
141	A32	20c brn org (O)	55	50
142	A32	25c bluish sl (Bl)	95	1.40
143	A31	30c ol grn (G)	50	60
144	A32	40c ol brn (Br)	55	65
145	A32	50c mag (R)	1.10	1.40
146	A35	60c red org (O)	55	55
147	A32	75c brn vio (V)	1.10	1.60
148	A32	90c dp red (R)	1.10	1.50
149	A35	1fr vio (V)	1.25	1.60
150	A36	1.50fr saph (Bl)	2.25	4.00
151	A36	2fr brn red (R)	3.25	6.00
152	A36	3fr dk ol grn (G)	5.75	8.75
153	A36	5fr dp brn (Br)	25.00	35.00

Size: 31½x36 mm.
Perf. 12.

154	A30	10fr blk brn (Br)	30.00	62.50
		Nos. 139-154 (16)	75.20	127.45

French Administration

Miner
A37

Steel Workers
A38

Harvesting Sugar Beets
A39

Mettlach Abbey
A40

Marshal Ney
A41

Saar River near Mettlach
A42

Photogravure.

1947   Perf. 14   Unwmkd.

155	A37	2pf gray	5	20
156	A37	3pf orange	6	50
157	A37	6pf dk Prus grn	5	25
158	A37	8pf scarlet	5	25
159	A37	10pf rose vio	5	25
160	A38	15pf brown	6	50
161	A38	16pf ultra	5	25
162	A38	20pf brn rose	5	25
163	A38	24pf dp brn org	5	25
164	A39	25pf cerise	30	8.00
165	A39	30pf lt ol grn	10	50
166	A39	40pf org brn	10	50
167	A39	50pf bl vio	30	8.00
168	A40	60pf violet	30	8.00
169	A40	80pf dp org	5	35
170	A41	84pf brown	5	35
171	A42	1m gray grn	6	50
		Nos. 155-171 (17)	1.73	

Nos. 155-162, 164-171 exist imperf.

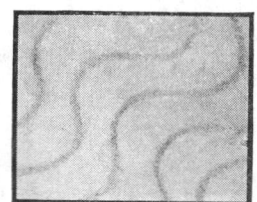

Wmk. 285
Types of 1947
Wmkd. Marbleized Pattern. (285)
1947

172	A37	12pf ol grn	5	25
173	A39	45pf crimson	30	5.50
174	A40	75pf brt bl	6	32

Nos. 172-174 exist imperf.

Types of 1947 Surcharged with New Value, Bars and Ornament in Black or Red.

1947, Nov. 27   Unwmkd.
Printing II: White Paper, Colorless Gum.

175	A37	10c on 2pf gray	6	40
176	A37	60c on 3pf org	6	40
177	A37	1fr on 10pf rose vio	6	40
178	A37	2fr on 12pf ol grn	5	40
179	A38	3fr on 15pf brn	5	40
180	A38	4fr on 16pf ultra	10	2.00
181	A38	5fr on 20pf brn rose	8	40
182	A38	6fr on 24pf dp brn org	8	40
183	A39	9fr on 30pf lt ol grn	15	3.25
184	A39	10fr on 50pf bl vio (R)	20	6.00
185	A40	14fr on 60pf vio	25	3.75
186	A41	20fr on 84pf brn	18	2.75
187	A42	50fr on 1m gray grn	65	9.50
		Nos. 175-187 (13)	1.97	

Printing I: Toned Paper, Grayish Gum.

175a	A37	10c on 2pf gray	75.00	250.00
176a	A37	60c on 3pf org	60.00	600.00
177a	A37	1fr on 10pf rose vio	5.00	13.00
178a	A37	2fr on 12pf ol grn, wmk. 285	45	1.25
179a	A38	3fr on 15pf brn	525.00	1,250.
180a	A38	4fr on 16pf ultra	15.00	75.00
181a	A38	5fr on 20pf brn rose	400.00	1,600.
182a	A38	6fr on 24pf dp brn org	45	1.75
183a	A39	9fr on 30pf lt ol grn	65.00	400.00
184a	A39	10fr on 50pf bl vio (R)	575.00	3,750.
185a	A40	14fr on 60pf vio	135.00	550.00
186a	A41	20fr on 84pf brn	3.50	6.00
187a	A42	50fr on 1m gray grn	60.00	275.00
		Nos. 175a-187a (13)	1,579.40	

Printing I was surcharged on the toned-paper stamps of the earlier 1947 series (Nos. 155-171). The crossbar of the A's in SAAR is high on the 10c, 60c, 1fr, 2fr, 9fr and 10fr; numeral "1" has no base serif on the 3fr and 4fr; wide space between vignette and SAAR panel; 1m inscribed "1M."

Printing II was surcharged on a special printing of the basic stamps, with white paper, colorless gum and details of design that differ on each denomination. The "A" crossbar is low on 10c, 60c, 1fr, 2fr, 9fr, 10fr; numeral "1" has base serif on 3fr and 4fr; narrow space between vignette and SAAR panel; 1m inscribed "1SM."

Surcharge varieties exist, mostly in Printing II.

French Protectorate

Clasped Hands
A43

Colliery Shafthead
A44

Designs: 2fr, 3fr, Worker. 4fr, 5fr, Girl gathering wheat. 6fr, 9fr, Miner. 14fr, Smelting. 20fr, Reconstruction. 50fr, Mettlach Abbey portal.

Perf. 14x13, 13
1948, Apr. 1   Engr.   Unwmkd.

188	A43	10c hn brn	45	1.75
189	A43	60c dk Prus grn	45	1.75
190	A43	1fr brn blk	15	12
191	A43	2fr rose car	15	6
192	A43	3fr blk brn	20	6
193	A43	4fr red	20	6
194	A43	5fr red vio	20	10
195	A43	6fr hn brn	45	10
196	A43	9fr dk Prus grn	3.50	20
197	A44	10fr dk bl	2.00	35
198	A44	14fr dk vio brn	2.50	90
199	A44	20fr hn brn	4.50	90
200	A44	50fr bl blk	11.00	2.75
		Nos. 188-200 (13)	26.25	9.10

Map of the Saar
A45

Caduceus, Microscope, Bunsen Burner and Book
A46

1948, Dec. 15 Photo. Perf. 13½x13

201	A45	10fr dk red	1.10	2.25
202	A45	25fr dp bl	1.75	4.75

Issued to commemorate the first anniversary of the establishment of the French Protectorate.

SAAR

1949, Apr. 2   Perf. 13x13½
203   A46   15fr carmine   3.00   20
Issued to honor Saar University.

Ludwig van Beethoven
A47

Laborer Using Spade
A51

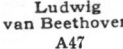
Saarbrücken
A52

Designs: 10c, Building trades. 1fr, 3fr, Gears, factories. 5fr, Dumping mine waste. 6fr, 15fr, Coal mine interior. 8fr, Communications symbols. 10fr, Emblem of printing. 12fr, 18fr, Pottery. 25fr, Blast furnace worker. 45fr, Rock formation "Great Boot." 60fr, Reden Colliery, Landsweiler. 100fr, View of Weibelskirchen.

1949-51   Perf. 13x13½.   Unwmkd.
204   A47   10c vio brn   12   1.75
205   A47   60c gray ('51)   12   1.75
206   A47   1fr car lake   80   10
207   A47   3fr brn ('51)   5.00   30
208   A47   5fr dp vio ('50)   1.40   10
209   A47   6fr Prus grn ('51)   8.00   28
210   A47   8fr ol grn ('51)   45   28
211   A47   10fr org ('50)   3.00   10
212   A47   12fr dk grn   9.00   10
213   A47   15fr red ('50)   5.00   10
214   A47   18fr brn car ('51)   2.00   4.75

   Perf. 13½.
215   A51   20fr gray ('50)   90   20
216   A51   25fr vio bl   13.00   20
217   A52   30fr red brn ('51)   10.00   45
218   A52   45fr rose lake ('51)   3.50   45
219   A51   60fr dp grn ('51)   3.50   1.50
220   A51   100fr brown   5.00   2.25
Nos. 204-220 (17)   70.79   14.66

Peter Wust
A54

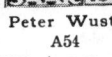
St. Peter
A55

1950, Apr. 3
221   A54   15fr car rose   3.00   5.25
10th anniversary of death of Peter Wust (1884-1940), Catholic philosopher.

1950, June 29   Engr.   Perf. 13
222   A55   12fr dp grn   2.75   7.75
223   A55   15fr red brn   3.25   7.75
224   A55   25fr blue   5.75   16.00
Holy Year, 1950.

Street in Ottweiler
A56

   Perf. 13x13½
1950, July 10   Photogravure
225   A56   10fr org brn   2.50   7.75
Issued to commemorate the 400th anniversary of the founding of Ottweiler.

Symbols of the Council of Europe
A57

1950, Aug. 8   Perf. 13½
226   A57   25fr dp bl   37.50   7.00
Issued to commemorate the Saar's admission to the Council of Europe. See No. C12.

Post Rider and Guard
A62

1951, Apr. 29   Engr.   Perf. 13
227   A62   15fr dk vio brn   4.50   12.00
Issued to publicize Stamp Day, 1951.

"Agriculture and Industry" and Fair Emblem
A63

Tower of Mittelbexbach and Flowers
A67

1951, May 12 Photo.   Perf. 13x13½
228   A63   15fr dk gray grn   1.75   5.25
Issued to publicize the 1951 fair at Saarbrücken.

1951, June 9   Engraved   Perf. 13
229   A67   15fr dk grn   1.75   1.00
Issued to publicize the Exhibition of Gardens and Flowers, Bexbach, 1951.

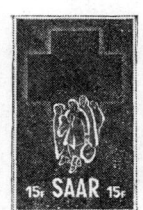
Refugees
A68

Globe and Stylized Fair Building
A69

1952, May 2   Perf. 13   Unwmkd.
230   A68   15fr brt red   1.25   1.00
Issued to honor the Red Cross.

1952, Apr. 26
231   A69   15fr red brn   1.25   1.00
Issued to publicize the 1952 fair at Saarbrücken.

Mine Shafts—A70

Ludwig's Gymnasium
A71

General Post Office
A72

Reconstruction of St. Ludwig's Cathedral
A73

"SM" Monogram
A74

Designs: 3fr, 18fr, Bridge building. 6fr, Transporter bridge, Mettlach. 30fr, Saar University Library.

1952-55   Engraved.
232   A70   1fr dk bl ('53)   9   6
233   A71   2fr pur ('53)   9   6
234   A72   3fr dk car rose ('53)   9   6
235   A72   5fr dk grn (no inscription)   3.75   10
236   A72   5fr dk grn ("Hauptpostamt Saarbrücken") ('54)   9   6
237   A72   6fr vio brn ('53)   20   6
238   A71   10fr BR ol ('53)   25   6
239   A72   12fr grn ('53)   25   6
240   A70   15fr blk brn (no inscription)   5.00   10
241   A70   15fr blk brn ("Industrie-Landschaft") ('53)   2.50   10
242   A70   15fr dp car ('55)   14   6
243   A72   18fr dk rose brn ('55)   1.75   3.50
244   A72   30fr ultra ('53)   50   70
245   A73   500fr brn car ('53)   9.00   35.00
Nos. 232-245 (14)   23.70   39.98

1953, Mar. 23
246   A74   15fr dk ultra   1.25   1.25
Issued to publicize the 1953 fair at Saarbrücken.

Bavarian and Prussian Postilions
A75

1953, May 3
247   A75   15fr dp bl   2.00   7.75
Stamp Day.

Fountain and Fair Buildings
A76

1954, Apr. 10
248   A76   15fr dp grn   1.00   90
1954 International Fair at Saarbrücken.

Post Coach and Post Bus of 1920
A77

1954, May 9   Engraved
249   A77   15fr red   2.00   7.00
Stamp Day, May 9, 1954.

Madonna and Child, Holbein
A78

Designs: 10fr, Sistine Madonna, Raphael. 15fr, Madonna and Child with pear, Durer.

1954, Aug. 14
250   A78   5fr dp car   40   1.75
251   A78   10fr dk grn   55   2.25
252   A78   15fr dp vio bl   80   3.25
Issued to commemorate the centenary of the promulgation of the Dogma of the Immaculate Conception.

Cyclist and Flag
A79

Symbols of Industry and Rotary Emblem
A80

1955, Feb. 28 Photo.   Perf. 13x13½
253   A79   15fr multi   20   45
Issued to publicize the world championship cross country bicycle race.

SAAR

1955, Feb. 28

| 254 | A80 | 15fr org brn | 20 | 45 |

Rotary International, 50th anniversary.

Flags of Participating Nations
A81

1955, Apr. 18 Photo. Perf. 13x13½

| 255 | A81 | 15fr multi | 20 | 45 |

1955 International Fair at Saarbrücken.

Postman at Illingen
A82

Engraved.

1955, May 8 Perf. 13 Unwmkd.

| 256 | A82 | 15fr dp cl | 40 | 1.75 |

Issued to publicize Stamp Day, 1955.

Nos. 242–244 Overprinted
"VOLKSBEFRAGUNG 1955."

1955, Oct. 22

257	A70	15fr dp car	10	35
258	A72	18fr dk rose brn	12	40
259	A72	30fr ultra	20	75

Plebiscite, Oct. 23, 1955.

Symbols of Industry and the Fair   Radio Tower, Saarbrücken
A83   A84

1956, Apr. 14 Photo. Perf. 11½

| 260 | A83 | 15fr dk brn red & yel grn | 12 | 35 |

Issued to publicize the International Fair at Saarbrücken, April 14–29, 1956.

1956, May 6 Granite Paper

| 261 | A84 | 15fr grn & grnsh bl | 12 | 35 |

Stamp Day.

German Administration

Arms of Saar   Pres. Theodor Heuss
A85   A86

1957, Jan. 1 Litho. Wmk. 304

| 262 | A85 | 15fr brick red & bl | 10 | 35 |

Return of the Saar to Germany.

1957 Typographed. Perf. 14

Size: 18x22 mm.

263	A86	1(fr) brt grn	8	10
264	A86	2(fr) brt vio	8	10
265	A86	3(fr) bis brn	8	10
266	A86	4(fr) red vio	12	55
267	A86	5(fr) lt ol grn	8	10
268	A86	6(fr) vermilion	10	45
269	A86	10(fr) gray	8	25
270	A86	12(fr) dp org	10	10
271	A86	15(fr) lt bl grn	12	10
272	A86	18(fr) lt car rose	50	1.50
273	A86	25(fr) brt lil	20	65

Engraved

274	A86	40(fr) pale pur	25	70
275	A86	45(fr) gray ol	95	2.50
276	A86	50(fr) vio brn	95	1.10
277	A86	60(fr) dl rose	1.40	2.75
278	A86	70(fr) red org	2.25	4.50
279	A86	80(fr) ol grn	95	2.75
280	A86	90(fr) dk gray	2.00	5.25

Size: 24x29 mm.

281	A86	100(fr) dk car	2.00	7.75
282	A86	200(fr) violet	5.25	21.00
		Nos. 263–282 (20)	17.54	52.30

See also Nos. 289–308.

Steel Industry   Merzig Arms and St. Peter's Church
A87   A88

Perf. 13x13½

1957, Apr. 20 Litho. Wmk. 304

| 284 | A87 | 15fr gray & mag | 10 | 28 |

The 1957 Fair at Saarbrücken.

1957, May 25 Perf. 14

| 285 | A88 | 15fr blue | 10 | 28 |

Centenary of the town of Merzig.

Europa Issue, 1957

"United Europe"
A89

Perf. 14x13½

Lithographed; Tree Embossed.

1957, Sept. 16 Unwmkd.

| 286 | A89 | 20fr org & yel | 25 | 90 |
| 287 | A89 | 35fr vio & pink | 40 | 95 |

Issued to publicize a united Europe for peace and prosperity.

Carrier Pigeons
A90

Lithographed.

1957, Oct. 5 Perf. 14 Wmk. 304

| 288 | A90 | 15fr dp car & blk | 10 | 28 |

Issued for International Letter Writing Week, Oct. 6–12.

Redrawn Type of 1957;
"F" added after denomination

Lithographed.

1957 Perf. 14 Wmk. 304

Size: 18x22mm.

289	A86	1fr gray grn	8	14
290	A86	3fr blue	8	14
291	A86	5fr olive	8	14
292	A86	6fr lt brn	15	45
293	A86	10fr violet	15	25
294	A86	12fr brn org	15	25
295	A86	15fr dl grn	25	25
296	A86	18fr gray	1.50	4.50
297	A86	20fr lt ol grn	95	2.50
298	A86	25fr org brn	40	45
299	A86	30fr rose lil	75	45
300	A86	35fr brown	1.75	2.75
301	A86	45fr lt bl grn	1.25	3.50
302	A86	50fr dk red brn	75	1.75
303	A86	70fr brt grn	3.25	4.50
304	A86	80fr chlky bl	2.25	4.50
305	A86	90fr rose car	4.25	6.00

Engraved

Size: 24x29mm.

306	A86	100fr orange	3.50	7.00
307	A86	200fr brt grn	6.25	19.00
308	A86	300fr blue	8.75	21.00
		Nos. 289–308 (20)	36.54	79.52

"Max and Moritz"
A91

Design: 15fr, Wilhelm Busch.

Perf. 13½x13

1958, Jan. 9 Litho. Wmk. 304

| 309 | A91 | 12fr lt ol grn & blk | 10 | 20 |
| 310 | A91 | 15fr red & blk | 12 | 35 |

Issued to commemorate the 50th anniversary of the death of Wilhelm Busch, humorist.

"Prevent Forest Fires"
A92

1958, Mar. 5 Perf. 14

| 311 | A92 | 15fr brt red & blk | 10 | 28 |

Issued to aid in the prevention of forest fires.

Rudolf Diesel
A93

1958, Mar. 18 Engraved

| 312 | A93 | 12fr dk bl grn | 10 | 28 |

Issued to commemorate the centenary of the birth of Rudolf Diesel, inventor.

Fair Emblem and City Hall, Saarbrücken   View of Homburg
A94   A95

1958, Apr. 10 Litho. Perf. 14

| 313 | A94 | 15fr dl rose | 10 | 28 |

1958 Fair at Saarbrücken.

1958, June 14 Engr. Wmk. 304

| 314 | A95 | 15fr gray grn | 10 | 28 |

400th anniversary of Homburg.

Turner Emblem   Herman Schulze-Delitzsch
A96   A97

1958, July 21 Litho. Perf. 13½x14

| 315 | A96 | 12fr gray, blk & dl grn | 10 | 28 |

Issued to commemorate 150 years of German turners and on the occasion of the 1958 Turner Festival.

1958, Aug. 29 Engr. Wmk. 304

| 316 | A97 | 12fr yel grn | 10 | 28 |

Issued to commemorate the 150th anniversary of the birth of Hermann Schulze-Delitzsch, founder of German trade organizations.

Europa Issue, 1958
Common Design Type

1958, Sept. 13 Lithographed

Size: 24½x30mm.

| 317 | CD1 | 12fr yel grn & bl | 35 | 85 |
| 318 | CD1 | 30fr lt bl & red | 55 | 1.10 |

Issued to show the European Postal Union at the service of European integration.

Jakob Fugger
A98

Perf. 13x13½

1959, Mar. 6 Wmk. 304

| 319 | A98 | 15fr dk red & blk | 10 | 28 |

Issued to commemorate the 500th anniversary of the birth of Jakob Fugger the Rich, businessman and banker.

Common Design Types
pictured in section at front of book.

SAAR

Old and New City Hall and Burbach Mill
A99

1959, Apr. 1   Engr.   Perf. 14x13½

| 320 | A99 | 15fr lt bl | 10 | 28 |

Greater Saarbrucken, 50th anniversary.

Hands Holding Merchandise
A100

1959, Apr. 1   Lithographed

| 321 | A100 | 15fr dp rose | 12 | 30 |

Issued to publicize the 1959 Fair at Saarbrucken.

Alexander von Humboldt
A101

1959, May 6   Engr.   Perf. 13½x14

| 322 | A101 | 15fr blue | 12 | 30 |

Issued to commemorate the centenary of the death of Alexander von Humboldt, naturalist and geographer.

SEMI-POSTAL STAMPS

Red Cross Dog Leading Blind Man — SP1
Nurse and Invalid — SP2

Children Getting Drink at Spring — SP3
Maternity Nurse with Child — SP4

Perf. 13½

1926, Oct. 25   Photo.   Unwmkd.

B1	SP1	20c +20c dk ol grn	7.50	14.00
B2	SP2	40c +40c dk brn	9.50	16.00
B3	SP3	50c +50c red org	9.50	14.00
B4	SP4	1.50fr +1.50fr brt bl	17.50	35.00

Nos. B1-B4 Overprinted   1927-28

1927, Oct. 1

B5	SP1	20c +20c dk ol grn	15.00	16.00
B6	SP2	40c +40c dk brn	13.00	21.00
B7	SP3	50c +50c red org	12.00	14.00
B8	SP4	1.50fr +1.50fr brt bl	17.50	45.00

"The Blind Beggar" by Dyckmans — SP5
"Almsgiving" by Schiestl — SP6

"Charity" by Raphaël — SP7

1928, Dec. 23   Photogravure

B9	SP5	40c (+40c) blk brn	11.00	21.00
B10	SP5	50c (+50c) brn rose	11.00	21.00
B11	SP5	1fr (+1fr) dl vio	11.00	21.00
B12	SP6	1.50fr (+1.50fr) cob bl	11.00	21.00
B13	SP6	2fr (+2fr) red brn	13.00	25.00
B14	SP6	3fr (+3fr) dk ol grn	13.00	25.00
B15	SP7	10fr (+10fr) dk brn	500.00	3,400.
		Nos. B9-B15 (7)	570.00	

"Orphaned" by Kaulbach — SP8

"St. Ottilia" by Feuerstein — SP9
"Madonna" by Ferruzzio — SP10

1929, Dec. 22

B16	SP8	40c (+15c) ol grn	2.75	4.25
B17	SP8	50c (+20c) cop red	5.75	7.00
B18	SP8	1fr (+50c) vio brn	5.75	8.50
B19	SP9	1.50fr (+75c) Prus bl	5.75	8.50
B20	SP9	2fr (+1fr) brn car	5.75	8.50
B21	SP9	3fr (+2fr) sl grn	9.50	19.00
B22	SP10	10fr (+8fr) blk brn	60.00	100.00
		Nos. B16-B22 (7)	95.25	155.75

"The Safety-Man" — SP11
"The Good Samaritan" — SP12

"In the Window" — SP13

1931, Jan. 20

B23	SP11	40c (+15c) org brn	12.00	23.00
B24	SP11	60c (+20c) org red	12.00	23.00
B25	SP12	1fr (+50c) rose car	12.00	40.00
B26	SP11	1.50fr (+75c) sl bl	16.00	40.00
B27	SP12	2fr (+1fr) brn	16.00	40.00
B28	SP12	3fr (+2fr) ol grn	24.00	40.00
B29	SP13	10fr (+10fr) org brn	110.00	275.00
		Nos. B23-B29 (7)	202.00	

St. Martin of Tours — SP14

"Charity" — SP15
"The Widow's Mite" — SP16

1931, Dec. 23

B30	SP14	40c (+15c) blk brn	20.00	30.00
B31	SP14	60c (+20c) org red	20.00	30.00
B32	SP14	1fr (+50c) vio brn	25.00	52.50
B33	SP15	1.50fr (+75c) dp bl	27.50	52.50
B34	SP15	2fr (+1fr) rose car	30.00	52.50
B35	SP15	3fr (+2fr) ol grn	40.00	100.00
B36	SP16	5fr (+5fr) org brn	125.00	350.00
		Nos. B30-B36 (7)	287.50	

Ruins at Kirkel — SP17
Illingen Castle, Kerpen — SP23

Designs: 60c, Church at Blie. 1fr, Castle Ottweiler. 1.50fr, Church of St. Michael, Saarbrucken. 2fr, Statue of St. Wendel. 3fr, Church of St. John, Saarbrucken.

1932, Dec. 20

B37	SP17	40c (+15c) blk brn	14.00	27.50
B38	SP17	60c (+20c) brn org	14.00	27.50
B39	SP17	1fr (+50c) dp vio	20.00	45.00
B40	SP17	1.50fr (+75c) dp bl	30.00	55.00
B41	SP17	2fr (+1fr) car rose	30.00	55.00
B42	SP17	3fr (+2fr) ol grn	75.00	175.00
B43	SP23	5fr (+5fr) red brn	125.00	300.00
		Nos. B37-B43 (7)	308.00	

Scene of Neunkirchen Disaster — SP24

1933, June 1

B44	SP24	60c (+60c) org red	20.00	17.50
B45	SP24	3fr (+3fr) ol grn	47.50	45.00
B46	SP24	5fr (+5fr) org brn	52.50	70.00

The surtax was for the aid of victims of the explosion at Neunkirchen, Feb. 10.

"Love" — SP25
"Anxiety" — SP26

"Peace" — SP27
"Solace" — SP28

SAAR

"Welfare" SP29 "Truth" SP30

Figure on Tomb of Duchess Elizabeth of Lorraine SP31

1934, Mar. 15   Photogravure

B47	SP25	40c (+15c) blk brn	8.00	16.00
B48	SP26	60c (+20c) red org	8.00	16.00
B49	SP27	1fr (+50c) dl vio	11.00	20.00
B50	SP28	1.50fr (+75c) bl	20.00	35.00
B51	SP29	2fr (+1fr) car rose	19.00	32.50
B52	SP30	3fr (+2fr) ol grn	20.00	35.00
B53	SP31	5fr (+5fr) red brn	42.50	80.00
		Nos. B47-B53 (7)	128.50	

Nos. B47–B53 Overprinted in Various Colors

VOLKSABSTIMMUNG 1935

1934, Dec. 1   Perf. 13x13½

B54	SP25	40c (+15c) blk brn (Br)	6.00	13.00
B55	SP26	60c (+20c) red org (R)	6.00	13.00
B56	SP27	1fr (+50c) dl vio (V)	12.00	22.50
B57	SP28	1.50fr (+75c) bl (Bl)	12.00	22.50
B58	SP29	2fr (+1fr) car rose (R)	16.00	30.00
B59	SP30	3fr (+2fr) ol grn (G)	14.00	27.50
B60	SP31	5fr (+5fr) red brn (Br)	24.00	42.50
		Nos. B54-B60 (7)	90.00	

French Protectorate

SP32   SP33

Perf. 13½x13, 13x13½

1948, Oct. 12   Photogravure
Various Flood Scenes.
Inscribed "Hochwasser-Hilfe 1947–48"

B61	SP32	5fr +5fr dl grn	3.25	8.50
B62	SP33	6fr +4fr dk vio	3.25	8.50
B63	SP32	12fr +8fr red	4.00	10.00
B64	SP33	18fr +12fr bl	5.75	14.00
	a.	Souvenir sheet of 4, imperf.	450.00	2,500.
		Nos. B61-B64, CB1 (5)	41.25	126.00

The surtax was for flood relief.
No. B64a measures 147x104½mm. and contains one each of Nos. B61 to B64. Inscriptions and ornaments in dark brown.

Hikers and Ludweiler Hostel SP34

Designs: No. B66, Hikers approaching Weisskirchen Hostel.

1949, Jan. 11   Perf. 13½x13

B65	SP34	8fr +5fr dk grn	2.25	5.25
B66	SP34	10fr +7fr dk grn	2.50	4.25

The surtax aided youth hostels.

Mare and Foal—SP35
Design: No. B68, Jumpers.

1949, Sept. 25   Perf. 13½

B67	SP35	15fr +5fr brn red	11.00	25.00
B68	SP35	25fr +15fr bl	14.00	28.00

Day of the Horse, Sept. 25, 1949.

Detail from "Moses Striking the Rock" SP36

Designs: No. B70, "Christ at the Pool of Bethesda." No. B71, "The Sick Child." No. B72, "St. Thomas of Villeneuve." No. B73, Madonna of Blieskastel.

1949, Dec. 20   Engr.   Perf. 13

B69	SP36	8fr +2fr ind	7.50	35.00
B70	SP36	12fr +3fr dk grn	9.00	40.00
B71	SP36	15fr +5fr brn lake	12.50	67.50
B72	SP36	25fr +10fr dp vio	19.00	100.00
B73	SP36	50fr +20fr choc	32.50	150.00
		Nos. B69-B73 (5)	80.50	

Adolph Kolping SP37   Relief for the Hungry SP38

1950, Apr. 3   Photo.   Perf. 13x13½

B74	SP37	15fr +5fr car rose	25.00	60.00

Engraved and Typographed.

1950, Apr. 28   Perf. 13

B75	SP38	25fr +10fr brn car & red	22.50	50.00

Stagecoach—SP39

1950, Apr. 22   Engraved

B76	SP39	15fr +15fr brn red & dk brn	52.50	100.00

Issued to commemorate "Stamp Day," April 27, 1950. Sold at the exhibition and to advance subscribers.

Lutwinus Seeking Admission to Abbey—SP40

Designs: 12fr+3fr, Lutwinus Building Mettlach Abbey. 15fr+5fr, Lutwinus as Abbot. 25fr+10fr, Bishop Lutwinus at Rheims. 50fr+20fr, Aid to the poor and sick.

1950, Nov. 10   Perf. 13   Unwmkd.

B77	SP40	8fr +2fr dk brn	6.00	20.00
B78	SP40	12fr +3fr dk grn	6.00	20.00
B79	SP40	15fr +5fr red brn	6.50	27.50
B80	SP40	25fr +10fr bl	10.00	45.00
B81	SP40	50fr +20fr brn car	14.00	67.50
		Nos. B77-B81 (5)	42.50	

The surtax was for public assistance.

Mother and Child SP41   John Calvin and Martin Luther SP42

1951, Apr. 28

B82	SP41	25fr +10fr dk grn & car	20.00	50.00

The surtax was for the Red Cross.

1951, Apr. 28

B83	SP42	15fr +5fr blk brn	1.25	5.00

Issued to commemorate the 375th anniversary of the Reformation in Saar.

"Mother" SP43   Runner with Torch SP44

Paintings: 15fr+5fr, "Before the Theater." 18fr+7fr, "Sisters of Charity." 30fr+10fr, "The Good Samaritan." 50fr+20fr, "St. Martin and Beggar."

1951, Nov. 3

B84	SP43	12fr +3fr dk grn	4.00	12.00
B85	SP43	15fr +5fr pur	4.00	12.00
B86	SP43	18fr +7fr red	4.50	16.00
B87	SP43	30fr +10fr dp bl	7.50	24.00
B88	SP43	50fr +20fr blk brn	17.50	57.50
		Nos. B84-B88 (5)	37.50	

1952, Mar. 29 Perf. 13 Unwmkd.
Design: 30fr+5fr, Hand with olive branch, and globe.
Inscribed: "Olympische Spiele 1952."

B89	SP44	15fr +5fr dp grn	2.50	8.00
B90	SP44	30fr +5fr dp grn	3.25	11.50

XV Olympic Games, Helsinki, 1952.

Postrider Delivering Mail SP45

1952, Mar. 30

B91	SP45	30fr +10fr dk bl	7.50	16.00

Issued to publicize Stamp Day, March 29, 1952.

Count Stroganoff as a Boy SP46   Henri Dunant SP47

Portraits: 18fr+7fr, The Holy Shepherd by Murillo. 30fr+10fr, Portrait of a Boy by Georg Melchior Kraus.

1952, Nov. 3

B92	SP46	15fr +5fr dk brn	3.00	8.00
B93	SP46	18fr +7fr brn lake	3.75	11.50
B94	SP46	30fr +10fr dp bl	4.50	12.50

The surtax was for child welfare.

1953, May 3   Cross in Red

B95	SP47	15fr +5fr blk brn	1.50	5.00

Clarice Strozzi by Titian SP48

Children of Rubens SP49

SAAR

Portrait: 30fr+10fr, Rubens' son.
1953, Nov. 16
B96	SP48	15fr +5fr pur	1.50	4.00
B97	SP49	18fr +7fr dp cl	1.50	4.25
B98	SP48	30fr +10fr dp ol grn	2.75	7.00

The surtax was for child welfare.

St. Benedict Blessing St. Maurus — SP50   Child and Cross — SP51

1953, Dec. 18 Lithographed
| B99 | SP50 | 30fr +10fr blk | 1.75 | 6.25 |

The surtax was for the abbey at Tholey.

1954, May 10 Engraved
| B100 | SP51 | 15fr +5fr choc | 1.75 | 5.25 |

The surtax was for the Red Cross.

Street Urchin with Melon, Murillo — SP52   Nurse Holding Baby — SP53

Paintings: 10fr+5fr, Maria de Medici, Bronzino. 15fr+7fr, Baron Emil von Maucler, Dietrich.

1954, Nov. 15
B101	SP52	5fr +3fr red	22	75
B102	SP52	10fr +5fr dk grn	28	90
B103	SP52	15fr +7fr pur	32	1.10

The surtax was for child welfare.

Perf. 13x13½
1955, May 5 Photo. Unwmkd.
| B104 | SP53 | 15fr +5fr blk & red | 20 | 60 |

The surtax was for the Red Cross.

Dürer's Mother, Age 63 — SP54

Etchings by Dürer: 10fr+5fr, Praying hands. 15fr+7fr, Old man of Antwerp.

1955, Dec. 10 Engr. Perf. 13
B105	SP54	5fr +3fr dk grn	30	70
B106	SP54	10fr +5fr dk grn	50	1.50
B107	SP54	15fr +7fr ol bis	65	1.90

The surtax was for public assistance.

First Aid Station, Saarbrücken, 1870 — SP55

1956, May 7
| B108 | SP55 | 15fr +5fr dk brn | 15 | 35 |

The surtax was for the Red Cross.

"Victor of Benevent" — SP56   Winterberg Monument — SP57

1956, July 25 Perf. 13 Unwmkd.
| B109 | SP56 | 12fr +3fr dk yel grn & bl grn | 15 | 45 |
| B110 | SP56 | 15fr +5fr brn vio & brn | 15 | 45 |

Issued to publicize the forthcoming 16th Olympic Games at Melbourne, Nov. 22-Dec. 8, 1956.

1956, Oct. 29
B111	SP57	5fr +2fr grn	10	18
B112	SP57	12fr +3fr red lil	12	35
B113	SP57	15fr +5fr brn	12	35

The surtax was for the rebuilding of monuments.

"La Belle Ferronnière" by da Vinci — SP58

Designs: 10fr +5fr, "Saskia" by Rembrandt. 15fr+7fr, "Family van Berchem," by Frans Floris. (Detail: Woman playing Spinet.)

1956, Dec. 10
B114	SP58	5fr +3fr dp bl	8	15
B115	SP58	10fr +5fr dp cl	15	35
B116	SP58	15fr +7fr dk grn	20	65

The surtax was for charitable works.

German Administration

Miner with Drill — SP59   "The Fox who Stole the Goose" — SP60

Designs: 6fr+4fr, Miner and conveyor. 15fr+7fr, 30fr+10fr, Miner and coal elevator.

Lithographed.
1957, Oct. 1 Perf. 14 Wmk. 304
B117	SP59	6fr +4fr bis brn & blk	8	20
B118	SP59	12fr +6fr blk & yel grn	10	20
B119	SP59	15fr +7fr bl & red	15	35
B120	SP59	30fr +10fr blk & bl	20	50

The surtax was for independent welfare organizations.

1958, Apr. 1 Perf. 14 Wmk. 304
Design: 15fr+7fr, "A Hunter from the Palatinate."
| B121 | SP60 | 12fr +6fr brn red, grn & blk | 8 | 25 |
| B122 | SP60 | 15fr +7fr grn, red, blk & gray | 12 | 35 |

The surtax was to finance young peoples' study trip to Berlin.

Friedrich Wilhelm Raiffeisen — SP61   Dairy Maid — SP62

Designs: 15fr+7fr, Girl picking grapes. 30fr+10fr, Farmer with pitchfork.

1958, Oct. 1 Perf. 14 Wmk. 304
B123	SP61	6fr +4fr gldn brn & dk brn	8	18
B124	SP62	12fr +6fr grn, red & yel	10	22
B125	SP62	15fr +7fr red, yel & bl	20	45
B126	SP62	30fr +10fr bl & ocher	25	60

The surtax was for independent welfare organizations.

AIR POST STAMPS.

Airplane over Saarbrücken — AP1
Photogravure.
1928, Sept. 19 Perf. 13½ Unwmkd.
| C1 | AP1 | 50c brn red | 3.50 | 2.75 |
| C2 | AP1 | 1fr dk vio | 4.50 | 3.50 |

Saarbrücken Airport and Church of St. Arnual — AP2

1932, April 30
| C3 | AP2 | 60c org red | 6.50 | 4.75 |
| C4 | AP2 | 5fr dk brn | 45.00 | 110.00 |

Nos. C1 to C4 Overprinted in Various Colors
VOLKSABSTIMMUNG 1935

1934, Nov. 1 Perf. 13½, 13½x13
C5	AP1	50c brn red (R)	6.00	8.75
C6	AP1	60c org red (O)	4.00	3.50
C7	AP1	1fr dk vio (V)	8.00	11.50
C8	AP2	5fr dk brn (Br)	12.00	16.00

French Protectorate

Shadow of Plane over Saar River — AP3

Engraved.
1948, April 1 Perf. 13. Unwmkd.
C9	AP3	25fr red	4.50	4.25
C10	AP3	50fr dk Prus grn	2.50	2.25
C11	AP3	200fr rose car	21.00	35.00

Symbols of the Council of Europe — AP4
1950, Aug. 8 Photo. Perf. 13½
| C12 | AP4 | 200fr red brn | 165.00 | 275.00 |

Issued to commemorate the Saar's admission to the Council of Europe.

AIR POST SEMI-POSTAL STAMPS.
French Protectorate

Flood Scene — SPAP1
Perf. 13½x13
1948, Oct. 12 Photo. Unwmkd.
| CB1 | SPAP1 | 25fr +25fr sep | 25.00 | 85.00 |
| a. | | Souv. sheet | 375.00 | 1,800. |

The surtax was for flood relief.
No. CB1a measures 90x60mm., and contains a single stamp. Inscriptions and ornaments in dark brown.

OFFICIAL STAMPS.
Regular Issue of 1922-1923
Overprinted Diagonally in Red or Blue

DIENSTMARKE

1922-23 Unwmkd.
Perf. 12½x13½, 13½x12½.
O1	A19	3c ol grn & straw (R)	90	20.00
O2	A20	5c org & blk (R)	38	25
O3	A21	10c bl grn (R)	38	18
O4	A19	15c dp brn (Bl)	38	20
O5	A19	15c org (Bl) ('23)	2.00	40
O6	A22	20c dk bl & lem (R)	38	18
O7	A22	20c brt bl & straw (R) ('23)	2.00	40
O8	A22	25c red & yel (Bl)	3.75	1.20
O9	A22	25c mag & straw (Bl) ('23)	2.00	40
O10	A23	30c car & yel (Bl)	38	18
O11	A24	40c brn & yel (Bl)	60	20
O12	A25	50c dk bl & straw (R)	60	20
O13	A24	75c dp grn & straw (R)	16.00	23.00
O14	A24	75c blk & straw (R) ('23)	4.00	2.00
O15	A26	1fr brn red (Bl)	6.50	2.50
		Nos. O1-O15 (15)	40.25	51.29

Inverted overprints exist on 10c, 20c, 30c, 50c and 1fr; price, each $65. Double overprints exist on Nos. O4, O6 and 1fr; price, each $110.

Regular Issue of 1927-30 Overprinted in Various Colors

DIENSTMARKE

1927-34 Perf. 13½
| O16 | A31 | 10c dp brn (Bl) ('34) | 1.75 | 1.75 |

O17	A32	15c ol blk (Bl) ('34)	2.75	6.00
O18	A32	20c brn org (Bk) ('31)	1.75	1.25
O19	A32	25c bluish sl (Bl)	2.75	4.25
O20	A31	30c ol grn (C)	2.50	20
O21	A32	40c ol brn (C)	1.75	20
O22	A32	50c mag (Bl)	1.75	20
O23	A35	60c red org (Bk) ('30)	1.25	20
O24	A32	75c brn vio (C)	1.50	60
O25	A35	1fr vio (RO)	2.75	20
O26	A36	2fr brn red (Bl)	2.75	35
		Nos. O16-O26 (11)	23.25	15.20

The overprint exists at 23 to 25-degree angle on Nos. O16–O26, and also at 32-degree angle on Nos. O20–O22, O24–O26. The overprint on Nos. O16 and O20 is known only inverted. Nos. O21–O26 exist with double overprint.

French Protectorate

Arms
O1
Engraved.

1949, Oct. 1 Perf. 14x13 Unwmkd.

O27	O1	10c dp car	30	25.00
O28	O1	30c bl blk	20	25.00
O29	O1	1fr Prus grn	20	20
O30	O1	2fr org red	1.10	1.00
O31	O1	5fr blue	40	30
O32	O1	10fr black	55	60
O33	O1	12fr red vio	4.75	7.00
O34	O1	15fr indigo	55	25
O35	O1	20fr green	1.40	1.00
O36	O1	30fr vio rose	1.50	4.00
O37	O1	50fr purple	1.50	3.50
O38	O1	100fr brn brn	75.00	160.00
		Nos. O27-O38 (12)	87.45	

STE.-MARIE DE MADAGASCAR
(sănt'-mä'rē' dē mä'dȧ'gȧs'kȧr')

LOCATION—An island off the east coast of Madagascar.
GOVT.—French Possession.
AREA—64 sq. mi.
POP.—8,000 (approx.)

In 1896 Ste.-Marie de Madagascar was attached to the colony of Madagascar for administrative purposes.

100 Centimes = 1 Franc

Navigation and Commerce
A1
Typographed.

1894 Perf. 14x11½ Unwmkd.
Name of Colony in Blue or Carmine.

1	A1	1c lil bl	60	60
2	A1	2c brn, buff	75	75
3	A1	4c cl, lav	3.00	2.75
4	A1	5c grn, grnsh	6.00	4.50
5	A1	10c lavender	7.00	5.00
6	A1	15c blue	15.00	13.00
7	A1	20c red, grn	13.00	9.50
8	A1	25c rose	9.50	8.00
9	A1	30c brn, bis	6.75	6.00
10	A1	40c red, straw	7.50	6.00
11	A1	50c car, rose	25.00	19.00
12	A1	75c vio, org	45.00	22.50
13	A1	1fr brnz grn, straw	24.00	16.00
		Nos. 1-13 (13)	163.10	113.60

These stamps were replaced by those of Madagascar.

ST. PIERRE & MIQUELON
(sȧnt pyâr' & mĭk'ē·lŏn')

LOCATION — Two small groups of islands off the southern coast of Newfoundland.
GOVT.—Former French overseas territory.
AREA—93 sq. mi.
POP.—5,450 (est. 1974).
CAPITAL—St. Pierre.

The territory of St. Pierre and Miquelon became a Department of France in July 1976.

100 Centimes = 1 Franc

Stamps of French Colonies Handstamp Surcharged in Black

05

SPM

1885 Imperf. Unwmkd.

1	A8	05c on 40c ver, straw	52.50	22.50
2	A8	10c on 40c ver, straw	12.50	11.00
a.		"M" inverted	90.00	80.00
3	A8	15c on 40c ver, straw	12.50	11.00

Nos. 2 and 3 exist with "SPM" 17mm. wide instead of 15½mm.
Nos. 1–3 exist with surcharge inverted and with it doubled.

Handstamp Surcharged in Black:

05
SPM
b

25 **25**
SPM **SPM**
c *d*

1885

4	A8 (b)	05c on 35c blk, yel	62.50	45.00
5	A8 (b)	05c on 75c car, rose	175.00	110.00
6	A8 (b)	05c on 1fr brnz grn, straw	12.00	11.00
7	A8 (c)	25c on 1fr brnz grn, straw	4,500.	1,650.
8	A8 (d)	25c on 1fr brnz grn, straw	2,000.	1,250.

Nos. 7 and 8 exist with surcharge inverted, and with it vertical. No. 7 exists with "S P M" above "25" (the handstamping was done in two steps).

1885 Perf. 14x13½

9	A9 (c)	5c on 2c brn, buff	3,250.	1,650.
10	A9 (d)	5c on 4c cl, lav	250.00	200.00
11	A9 (b)	05c on 20c red, grn	12.50	11.00

No. 9 surcharge is always inverted. No. 10 exists with surcharge inverted.

Surcharged in Black:

P D
5
A15

1886 Typographed. Imperf.

12	A15	5c white		700.00
13	A15	10c white		850.00
14	A15	15c white		600.00

"P D" are the initials for "Payé à destination."
Excellent forgeries of Nos. 12 to 14 exist.

Stamps of French Colonies Surcharged in Black:

15 c. **15 c.**
SPM **SPM**
e *f*

1891 Perf. 14x13½.

15	A9 (e)	15c on 30c brn, bis	19.00	15.00
a.		Inverted surcharge	110.00	90.00
16	A9 (e)	15c on 35c org	375.00	250.00
a.		Inverted surcharge	375.00	325.00
17	A9 (f)	15c on 35c org	900.00	525.00
a.		Inverted surcharge	1,000.	675.00
18	A9 (e)	15c on 40c red, straw	45.00	32.50
a.		Inverted surcharge	95.00	90.00

Nos. 7, 8, 10, 16 and 17 have been reprinted. Originals are surcharged in dull black, the reprints in deep or glossy black.

Stamps of French Colonies Overprinted in Black or Red

1891

19	A9	1c lil bl	6.00	4.75
a.		Inverted overprint	11.00	11.00
20	A9	1c lil bl (R)	5.25	5.25
a.		Inverted overprint	9.00	9.00
21	A9	2c brn, buff	6.00	4.75
a.		Inverted overprint	12.00	12.00
22	A9	2c brn, buff (R)	12.50	12.50
a.		Inverted overprint	30.00	30.00
23	A9	4c cl, lav	6.00	4.75
a.		Inverted overprint	14.00	14.00
24	A9	4c cl, lav (R)	10.00	10.00
a.		Inverted overprint	22.50	22.50
25	A9	5c grn, grnsh	6.00	4.75
a.		Double surch.	45.00	
26	A9	10c lavender	19.00	15.00
a.		Inverted overprint	32.50	32.50
27	A9	10c lav (R)	9.00	9.00
a.		Inverted overprint	22.50	22.50
28	A9	15c blue	12.00	8.00
29	A9	20c red, grn	37.50	32.50
30	A9	25c rose	15.00	12.00
31	A9	30c brn, bis	55.00	47.50
32	A9	35c vio, org	265.00	225.00
a.		Inverted overprint	375.00	375.00
33	A9	40c red, straw	40.00	32.50
a.		Double surch.	100.00	
34	A9	75c car, rose	60.00	47.50
a.		Inverted overprint	100.00	95.00
35	A9	1fr brnz grn, straw	37.50	32.50
a.		Inverted overprint	90.00	90.00

Numerous varieties of mislettering occur in the preceding overprint: "S," "ST," "P," "M," "ON," or "··" missing; "·" instead of "ON"; "—" instead of "·-" These varieties command prices double or triple those of normal stamps.

Surcharged in Black

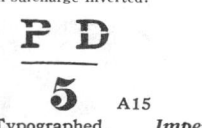

1891-92

36	A9	1c on 5c grn, grnsh	4.00	4.00
37	A9	1c on 10c lav	6.00	4.75
38	A9	1c on 25c rose ('92)	4.00	3.25
39	A9	2c on 10c lav	4.00	3.25
a.		Double surcharge	45.00	
40	A9	2c on 15c bl	3.00	3.00
41	A9	2c on 25c rose ('92)	3.00	3.00
42	A9	4c on 20c red, grn	3.00	3.00
43	A9	4c on 25c rose ('92)	3.00	3.00
44	A9	4c on 30c brn, bis	10.00	9.00
45	A9	4c on 40c red, straw	12.50	7.50

See note after No. 35.

Surcharged:

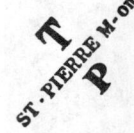
j *k*

1892

46	A9 (j)	1c on 5c grn, grnsh	6.00	5.25
47	A9 (j)	2c on 5c grn, grnsh	6.00	5.25
48	A9 (j)	4c on 5c grn, grnsh	6.00	5.25
49	A9 (k)	1c on 25c rose	3.00	3.00
50	A9 (k)	2c on 25c rose	3.00	3.00
51	A9 (k)	4c on 25c rose	3.00	3.00

See note after No. 35.

Postage Due Stamps of French Colonies Overprinted in Red

1892 Imperf.

52	D1	10c black	18.00	18.00
53	D1	20c black	12.00	12.00
54	D1	30c black	12.50	12.50
55	D1	40c black	12.50	12.50
56	D1	60c black	60.00	60.00

Black Overprint.

57	D1	1fr brown	80.00	80.00
58	D1	2fr brown	150.00	150.00
59	D1	5fr brown	265.00	265.00

See note after No. 35.

Navigation and Commerce
A16

1892-1908 Typo. Perf. 14x13½

60	A16	1c lil bl	45	45
61	A16	2c brn, buff	45	45
62	A16	4c cl, lav	90	80
63	A16	5c grn, grnsh	1.25	1.00
64	A16	5c yel grn ('08)	1.75	1.40
65	A16	10c lavender	3.00	2.60
66	A16	10c red ('00)	2.50	90
67	A16	15c bl, quadrillé paper	3.75	1.75
68	A16	15c gray, lt gray ('00)	40.00	25.00
69	A16	20c red, grn	9.50	8.00
70	A16	25c rose	4.50	1.25
71	A16	25c bl ('00)	8.00	5.25
72	A16	30c brn, bis	4.50	2.25
73	A16	35c yel ('06)	3.75	3.00
74	A16	40c red, straw	3.75	2.25
75	A16	50c car, rose	25.00	18.00
76	A16	50c brn, az ('00)	17.50	15.00
77	A16	75c vio, org	13.00	11.00
78	A16	1fr brnz grn, straw	12.00	6.75
		Nos. 60-78 (19)	155.55	107.10

ST. PIERRE & MIQUELON

Fisherman—A17

Fulmar Petrel—A18

Fishing Schooner—A19

1909-30				
79	A17	1c org red & ol	5	5
80	A17	2c ol & dp bl	6	5
81	A17	4c vio & ol	5	5
82	A17	5c bl grn & ol grn	22	12
83	A17	5c bl & blk ('22)	6	6
84	A17	10c car rose & red	22	22
85	A17	10c bl grn & ol grn ('22)	12	12
86	A17	10c bis & mag ('25)	22	22
86A	A17	15c dl vio & rose ('17)	22	12
87	A17	20c bis brn & vio brn	45	45
88	A18	25c dp bl & bl	75	50
89	A18	25c ol brn & bl grn ('22)	28	28
90	A18	30c org & vio brn	45	45
91	A18	30c rose & dl red ('22)	15	15
92	A18	30c red brn & bl ('25)	5	5
93	A18	30c gray grn & bl grn ('26)	28	28
94	A18	35c org brn & vio brn	22	22
95	A18	40c vio brn & ol grn	1.10	75
96	A18	45c vio & ol grn	30	30
97	A18	50c ol & ol grn	50	50
98	A18	50c bl & pale bl	38	38
99	A18	50c yel brn & mag ('25)	22	22
100	A18	60c dk bl & ver ('25)	28	28
101	A18	65c vio & org brn ('28)	50	50
102	A18	75c brn & ol	50	50
103	A18	90c brn red & org red ('30)	9.00	9.00
104	A18	1fr ol grn & dp bl	1.25	1.00
105	A19	1.10fr bl grn & org red ('28)	1.00	1.00
106	A19	1.50fr bl & dp bl ('30)	4.50	4.50
107	A19	2fr vio & brn	1.40	1.25
108	A19	3fr red vio ('30)	4.50	4.50
109	A19	5fr vio brn & ol grn	4.50	3.00
		Nos. 79-109 (32)	33.78	31.07

Stamps of 1892-1906 Surcharged in Carmine or Black

05 **10**
 n   o

1912

110	A16	5c on 2c brn, buff	75	75
111	A16	5c on 4c cl, lav (C)	18	18
112	A16	5c on 15c bl (C)	18	18
113	A16	5c on 20c red, grn	18	18
114	A16	5c on 25c rose (C)	18	18
115	A16	5c on 30c brn, bis (C)	28	28
116	A16	5c on 35c yel (C)	32	32
117	A16	10c on 40c red, straw	18	18
118	A16	10c on 50c car, rose	28	28
119	A16	10c on 75c dp vio, org	65	65
120	A16	10c on 1fr brnz grn, straw	75	75
		Nos. 110-120 (11)	3.93	3.93

Two spacings between the surcharged numerals are found on Nos. 110 to 120.

Stamps and Types of 1909-17 Surcharged with New Value and Bars in Black, Blue (Bl) or Red.

1924-27

121	A17	25c on 15c dl vio & rose ('25)	22	22
a.		Double surch.	67.50	
b.		Triple surch.	67.50	
122	A19	25c on 2fr vio & lt brn (Bl)	22	22
123	A19	25c on 5fr brn & ol grn (Bl)	22	22
a.		Triple surch.	60.00	
124	A18	65c on 45c vio & ol grn ('25)	50	50
125	A18	85c on 75c brn & ol ('25)	50	50
126	A18	90c on 75c brn red & dp org ('27)	90	90
127	A19	1.25fr on 1fr dk bl & ultra (R) ('26)	80	80
128	A19	1.50fr on 1fr ultra & dk bl ('27)	1.25	1.25
129	A19	3fr on 5fr ol brn & red vio ('27)	90	90
130	A19	10fr on 5fr ver & ol grn ('27)	7.50	7.50
131	A19	20fr on 5fr vio & ver ('27)	10.00	10.00
		Nos. 121-131 (11)	23.01	23.01

Colonial Exposition Issue.
Common Design Types
1931 Engraved Perf. 12½
Name of Country in Black.

132	CD70	40c dp grn	1.10	1.10
133	CD71	50c violet	1.10	1.10
134	CD72	90c red org	1.10	1.10
135	CD73	1.50fr dl bl	1.10	1.10

Map and Fishermen
A20

Common Design Types pictured in section at front of book.

Lighthouse and Fish—A21

Fishing Steamer and Sea Gulls
A22
Perf. 13½ x 14, 14 x 13½.

1932-33 Typographed.

136	A20	1c red brn & ultra	6	6
137	A21	2c blk & dk grn	8	8
138	A22	4c mag & ol brn	12	12
139	A21	5c vio & dk brn	12	12
140	A21	10c red brn & blk	15	15
141	A21	15c blk & dl vio	38	38
142	A20	20c blk & red org	38	38
143	A20	25c lt vio & lt grn	38	38
144	A22	30c vio grn & bl grn	38	38
145	A22	40c dp bl & dk brn	50	50
146	A21	45c ver & dp grn	50	50
147	A21	50c dk brn & dk grn	50	50
148	A22	65c ol brn & org	60	60
149	A22	75c red & org	60	60
150	A20	90c dl red & red	65	65
151	A20	1fr org brn & org red	50	50
152	A20	1.25fr dp bl & lake ('33)	65	65
153	A20	1.50fr dp bl & ol	65	65
154	A22	1.75fr blk & dk brn ('33)	90	90
155	A22	2fr bl blk & Prus bl	3.25	3.25
156	A21	3fr dp grn & dk brn	4.75	4.75
157	A21	5fr brn red & dk brn	10.00	10.00
158	A21	10fr dk grn & vio	27.50	27.50
159	A20	20fr ver & dp grn	27.50	27.50
		Nos. 136-159 (24)	81.10	81.10

Cartier Issue.
Stamps of 1932-33 Overprinted in Black, Red or Blue:

JACQUES CARTIER

JACQUES CARTIER
1534 - 1934   1534-1934
       p   q
1934

160	A21(p)	50c dk brn & dk grn (Bk)	65	65
161	A20(p)	75c grn & red org (Bk)	65	65
162	A20(q)	1.50fr dp bl & bl (Bk)	1.10	1.10
163	A22(p)	1.75fr blk & dk brn (R)	1.25	1.25
164	A21(p)	5fr brn red & dk brn (Bl)	10.00	10.00
		Nos. 160-164 (5)	13.65	13.65

Issued in commemoration of the four hundredth anniversary of the landing of Jacques Cartier.

Paris International Exposition Issue.
Common Design Types
1937 Perf. 13.

165	CD74	20c dp vio	75	75
166	CD75	30c dk grn	75	75
167	CD76	40c car rose	75	75
168	CD77	50c dk brn & bl	75	75
169	CD78	90c red	75	75
170	CD79	1.50fr ultra	75	75
		Nos. 165-170 (6)	4.50	4.50

Colonial Arts Exhibition Issue.
Souvenir Sheet.
Common Design Type
1937 Imperf.

| 171 | CD78 | 3fr dk ultra | 2.50 | 2.50 |

Issued in sheets measuring 118x99mm. containing one stamp.

Dog Team—A23

Port St. Pierre—A24

Tortue Lighthouse
A25

Soldiers' Bay at Langlade
A26

1938-40 Photo. Perf. 13½x13

172	A23	2c dk bl grn	5	5
173	A23	3c brn vio	6	6
174	A23	4c dk red vio	6	6
175	A23	5c car lake	8	8
176	A23	10c bis brn	6	6
177	A23	15c red vio	6	6
178	A23	20c bl vio	12	12
179	A23	25c Prus bl	85	85
180	A24	30c dk red vio	12	12
181	A24	35c dp grn	22	22
182	A24	40c sl bl ('40)	8	8
183	A24	45c dp grn ('40)	22	22
a.		Value omitted	30.00	
184	A24	50c car rose	8	8
185	A24	55c Prus bl	1.10	1.10
186	A24	60c vio ('39)	22	22
187	A24	65c brown	1.50	1.50
188	A24	70c org yel ('39)	22	22
189	A24	80c violet	38	38
190	A25	90c ultra ('39)	22	22
191	A25	1fr brt pink	3.75	3.75
192	A25	1fr pale ol grn ('40)	22	22
193	A25	1.25fr brt rose ('39)	45	45
194	A25	1.40fr dk brn ('40)	18	18
195	A25	1.50fr bl grn	22	22
196	A25	1.60fr rose vio ('40)	22	22
197	A25	1.75fr dp bl	60	60
198	A26	2fr rose vio	15	15
199	A26	2.25fr brt bl ('39)	28	28
200	A26	2.50fr org red ('40)	38	38
201	A26	3fr gray brn	18	18
202	A26	5fr hn brn	38	38

ST. PIERRE & MIQUELON

203	A26	10fr dk bl, *bluish*	50	50
204	A26	20fr sl grn	60	60
		Nos. 172-204 (33)	13.81	13.81

New York World's Fair Issue.
Common Design Type
1939 Engraved Perf. 12½x12

205	CD82	1.25fr car lake	45	45
206	CD82	2.25fr ultra	45	45

Lighthouse on Cliff
A27
1941 Engraved Perf. 12½x12

206A	A27	1fr dl lil	28	
206B	A27	2.50fr blue	28	

Nos. 206A–206B were issued by the Vichy government and were not placed on sale in the colony.
Stamps of types A23 and A26 without "RF" monogram were issued in 1941-1944 by the Vichy government, but were not sold in the colony.

Free French Administration.
The circumstances surrounding the overprinting and distribution of these stamps were most unusual. Practically all of the stamps issued in small quantities, with the exception of Nos. 260 to 299, were obtained by speculators within a few days after issue. At a later date, the remainders were taken over by the Free French Agency in Ottawa, Canada, by whom they were sold at a premium for the benefit of the Syndicat des Oeuvres Sociales.
Excellent counterfeits of these surcharges and overprints are known.

Nos. 86 and 92 Overprinted in Black FRANCE LIBRE F. N. F. L.
a

1942 Perf. 14 x 13½ Unwmkd.

206C	A17	10c bis & mag	675.00	675.00
206D	A18	30c red brn & bl	675.00	675.00

The letters "F. N. F. L." are the initials of "Forces Navales Francaises Libres" or "Free French Naval Forces."

Same Overprint in Black on Stamps of 1932-33.

207	A21	2c blk & Prus bl	135.00	135.00
208	A22	4c mag & ol brn	22.50	22.50
208A	A22	5c vio & dk brn	525.00	525.00
209	A22	40c dp bl & lake	8.00	8.00
a.		Inverted overprint		125.00
210	A21	45c ver & dp grn	95.00	95.00
211	A21	50c dk brn & dp grn	4.75	4.75
212	A22	65c ol brn & vg	18.00	18.00
213	A21	1fr org brn & org red	225.00	225.00
214	A22	1.75fr blk & dk brn	4.75	4.75
215	A22	2fr bl blk & Prus bl	4.75	4.75
216	A21	5fr brn red & dk brn	210.00	210.00

Stamps of 1932-33 Overprinted in Black FRANCE LIBRE F N F L
Perf. 13½ x 14

216A	A20	20c blk & red org	165.00	165.00
217	A20	75c grn & red org	8.00	8.00
218	A20	1.25fr dp bl & lake	8.00	8.00
218A	A20	1.50fr dp bl & bl	225.00	225.00

Same Surcharged with New Value and Bars

219	A20	10fr on 1.25fr dp bl & lake	20.00	20.00
220	A20	20fr on 75c grn & red org	30.00	30.00

No. 154 Surcharged in Red 5 fr FRANCE LIBRE F. N. F. L.
Perf. 14 x 13½

221	A22	5fr on 1.75fr blk & dk brn	4.50	4.50

Stamps of 1938-40 Overprinted type "a" in Black.
Perf. 13½ x 13.

222	A23	2c dk bl grn	300.00	300.00
223	A23	3c brn vio	75.00	75.00
224	A23	4c dk red vio	60.00	60.00
225	A23	5c car lake	600.00	600.00
226	A23	10c bis brn	7.50	7.50
227	A23	15c red vio	1,000.	1,000.
228	A23	20c bl vio	110.00	110.00
229	A23	25c Prus bl	7.50	7.50
230	A24	35c dp grn	475.00	475.00
a.		Double overprint		
231	A24	40c sl bl	7.50	7.50
232	A24	45c dp grn	7.50	7.50
233	A24	55c Prus bl	4,750.	4,750.
234	A24	60c violet	350.00	350.00
235	A24	65c brown	11.00	11.00
236	A24	70c org yel	16.00	16.00
237	A25	80c violet	250.00	250.00
238	A25	90c ultra	10.00	10.00
a.		Inverted overprint		100.00
239	A25	1fr pale ol grn	8.00	8.00
240	A25	1.25fr brt rose	8.00	8.00
241	A25	1.40fr dk brn	8.00	8.00
a.		Inverted overprint		100.00
242	A25	1.50fr brt bl	525.00	525.00
243	A25	1.60fr rose vio	7.50	7.50
244	A26	2fr rose vio	30.00	30.00
245	A26	2.25fr brt bl	7.50	7.50
246	A26	2.50fr org yel	8.00	8.00
247	A26	3fr gray brn	5,500.	5,500.
248	A26	5fr hn brn	1,500.	1,500.
248A	A26	20fr sl grn	675.00	675.00

Stamps of 1938-39 Surcharged in Black FRANCE LIBRE F. N. F. L. 20 c

249	A23	20c on 10c bis brn	3.25	3.25
250	A23	30c on 10c bis brn	3.25	3.25
251	A25	60c on 90c ultra	4.00	4.00
252	A25	1.50fr on 90c ultra	7.50	7.50
253	A25	2.50fr on 90c ultra	7.50	7.50
254	A23	10fr on 10c bis brn	30.00	30.00
255	A25	20fr on 90c ultra	32.50	32.50

New York World's Fair Issue Overprinted type "a" in Black.
Perf. 12½ x 12.

256	CD82	1.25fr car lake	5.25	5.25
257	CD82	2.25fr ultra	5.25	5.25
a.		Inverted overprint		200.00

Same, Surcharged 2 fr 50 FRANCE LIBRE F. N. F. L.

258	CD82	2.50fr on 1.25fr car lake	8.00	8.00
259	CD82	3fr on 2.25fr ultra	8.00	8.00

Stamps of 1938-40 Overprinted in Carmine Noël 1941 FRANCE LIBRE F. N. F. L.
1941 Perf. 13½ x 13

260	A23	10c bis brn	22.50	22.50
261	A23	20c bl vio	22.50	22.50
262	A23	25c Prus bl	22.50	22.50
263	A24	40c sl bl	22.50	22.50
264	A24	45c dp grn	22.50	22.50
265	A24	65c brown	22.50	22.50
266	A24	70c org yel	22.50	22.50
267	A25	80c violet	22.50	22.50
268	A25	90c ultra	22.50	22.50
269	A25	1fr pale ol grn	22.50	22.50
270	A25	1.25fr brt rose	22.50	22.50
271	A25	1.40fr dk brn	22.50	22.50
272	A25	1.60fr rose vio	25.00	25.00
273	A25	1.75fr brt bl	25.00	25.00
274	A26	2fr rose vio	25.00	25.00
275	A26	2.25fr brt bl	25.00	25.00
276	A26	2.50fr org yel	25.00	25.00
277	A26	3fr gray brn	25.00	25.00

Same Surcharged in Carmine with New Values.

278	A23	10fr on 10c bis brn	47.50	47.50
279	A25	20fr on 90c ultra	47.50	47.50
		Nos. 260-279 (20)	515.00	515.00

Stamps of 1938-40 Overprinted in Black.

280	A23	10c bis brn	30.00	30.00
281	A23	20c bl vio	30.00	30.00
282	A23	25c Prus bl	30.00	30.00
283	A24	40c sl bl	30.00	30.00
284	A24	45c dp grn	30.00	30.00
285	A24	65c brn	30.00	30.00
286	A24	70c org yel	30.00	30.00
287	A25	80c violet	30.00	30.00
288	A25	90c ultra	30.00	30.00
289	A25	1fr pale ol grn	30.00	30.00
290	A25	1.25fr brt rose	30.00	30.00
291	A25	1.40fr dk brn	30.00	30.00
292	A25	1.60fr rose vio	30.00	30.00
293	A25	1.75fr brt bl	525.00	525.00
294	A26	2fr rose vio	30.00	30.00
295	A26	2.25fr brt bl	30.00	30.00
296	A26	2.50fr org yel	30.00	30.00
297	A26	3fr gray brn	30.00	30.00

Same Surcharged in Black with New Values.

298	A23	10fr on 10c bis brn	67.50	67.50
299	A25	20fr on 90c ultra	67.50	67.50
		Nos. 280-299 (20)	1,170.	1,170.

Nos. 260 to 299 were issued to commemorate the Christmas Day plebiscite ordered by Vice Admiral Emile Henri Muselier, commander of the Free French naval forces.

St. Malo Fishing Schooner
A28
1942 Photogravure. Perf. 14x14½.

300	A28	5c dk bl	6	6
301	A28	10c dl pink	6	6
302	A28	25c brt blk	6	6
303	A28	30c sl blk	6	6
304	A28	40c brt grnsh bl	6	6
305	A28	60c brn red	6	6
306	A28	1fr dk vio	22	22
307	A28	1.50fr brt red	38	38
308	A28	2fr brown	22	22
309	A28	2.50fr brt ultra	38	38
310	A28	4fr dk org	22	22
311	A28	5fr dp plum	22	22
312	A28	10fr lt ultra	50	50
313	A28	20fr dk grn	75	75
		Nos. 300-313 (14)	3.25	3.25

Stamps o 1942 Surcharged in Carmine or Black 50c
1945

314	A28	50c on 5c dk bl (C)	10	10
315	A28	70c on 5c dk bl (C)	6	6
316	A28	1fr on 5c dk bl (C)	18	18
317	A28	1.20fr on 5c dk bl (C)	12	12
318	A28	2.40fr on 25c brt grn	18	18
319	A28	3fr on 25c brt grn	18	18
320	A28	4.50fr on 25c brt grn	30	30
321	A28	15fr on 2.50fr brt ultra (C)	60	60
		Nos. 314-321 (8)	1.66	1.66

Eboue Issue.
Common Design Type
1945 Engraved Perf. 13

322	CD91	2fr black	30	30
323	CD91	25fr Prus grn	50	50

Nos. 322 and 323 exist imperforate.

Soldiers' Bay
A29

Fishing Industry Symbols
A30

Fishermen
A31

Weighing the Catch
A32

ST. PIERRE & MIQUELON 433

Fishing Boat and Dinghy—A33

Storm-swept Coast—A34

1947		Engraved	Perf. 12½	
324	A29	10c chocolate	5	5
325	A29	30c violet	6	6
326	A29	40c rose lil	6	6
327	A29	50c int bl	5	5
328	A30	60c carmine	15	15
329	A30	80c brt ultra	15	15
330	A30	1fr dk grn	15	15
331	A31	1.20fr bl grn	22	22
332	A31	1.50fr black	22	22
333	A31	2fr red brn	22	22
334	A32	3fr rose vio	65	65
335	A32	3.60fr dp brn org	45	45
336	A32	4fr sepia	45	45
337	A32	5fr orange	38	38
338	A33	6fr blue	50	50
339	A33	10fr Prus grn	65	65
340	A34	15fr dk sl grn	90	90
341	A34	20fr vermilion	75	75
342	A34	25fr dk bl	90	90
	Nos. 324-342 (19)		6.96	6.96

Imperforates
Most stamps of St. Pierre and Miquelon from 1947 onward exist imperforate in issued and trial colors, and also in small presentation sheets in issued colors.

Silver Fox—A35

1952		Perf. 13	Unwmkd.	
343	A35	8fr dk brn	75	60
344	A35	17fr blue	90	75

Military Medal Issue.
Common Design Type

1952		Engraved and Typographed		
345	CD101	8fr multi	2.50	2.50

Fish Freezing Plant—A36

1955-56		Engraved		
346	A36	30c ultra & dk bl ('56)	15	15
347	A36	50c gray, blk & sep ('56)	15	15
348	A36	3fr pur ('56)	22	22
349	A36	40fr Prus bl	95	95

FIDES Issue

Fish Freezer "Le Galantry"—A37

1956		Perf. 13x12½	Unwmkd.	
350	A37	15fr blk brn & chnt	75	45

See note in Common Design section after CD103.

Codfish A38

Design: 4fr, 10fr, Lighthouse and fishing fleet.

1957		Perf. 13		
351	A38	40c dk brn & grnsh bl	12	12
352	A38	1fr brn & grn	12	12
353	A38	2fr ind & dl bl	18	15
354	A38	4fr mar, car & pur	28	22
355	A38	10fr grnsh bl, dk bl & brn	50	38
	Nos. 351-355 (5)		1.20	99

Human Rights Issue.
Common Design Type

1958		Engraved	Perf. 13	
356	CD105	20fr red brn & dk bl	95	80

Universal Declaration of Human Rights, 10th anniversary.

Flower Issue.
Common Design Type
Design: Spruce.

1959		Photogravure	Perf. 12½x12	
357	CD104	5fr red, yel grn & vio	60	45

Ice Hockey—A39

Mink—A40

1959		Engraved	Perf. 13	
358	A39	20fr multi	90	75
359	A40	25fr ind, yel grn & brn	1.40	1.00

Cypripedium Acaule A41

Eider Ducks A42

Flower: 50fr, Calopogon pulchellus.

1962, Apr. 24		Perf. 13	Unwmkd.	
360	A41	25fr grn, org & car rose	75	60
361	A41	50fr grn & car lake	1.60	1.25

See No. C24.

1963, Mar. 4			Perf. 13	
Birds: 1fr, Rock ptarmigan. 2fr, Ringed plovers. 6fr, Blue-winged teal.
362	A42	50c blk, ultra & ocher	18	15
363	A42	1fr red brn, ultra & rose	22	18
364	A42	2fr blk, dk bl & bis	35	30
365	A42	6fr multi	75	55

Albert Calmette—A43

1963, Aug. 5		Engraved		
366	A43	30fr dk brn & dk bl	1.00	80

Issued to commemorate the centenary of the birth of Albert Calmette, bacteriologist.

Red Cross Centenary Issue
Common Design Type

1963, Sept. 2		Perf. 13	Unwmkd.	
367	CD113	25fr ultra, gray & car	1.25	1.10

Centenary of the International Red Cross.

Human Rights Issue
Common Design Type

1963, Dec. 10		Perf. 13	Unwmkd.	
368	CD117	20fr org, bl & dk brn	90	75

Philatec Issue
Common Design Type

1964, Apr. 4		Engraved		
369	CD118	60fr choc, grn & dk bl	2.75	2.75

Rabbits A44

Designs: 4fr, Fox. 5fr, Roe deer. 34fr, Charolais bull.

1964, Sept. 28			Perf. 13	
370	A44	3fr grn, dk brn & red brn	28	22
371	A44	4fr bl, dk brn & grn	28	22
372	A44	5fr dk brn, dk bl & red brn	45	38
373	A44	34fr grn, bl & red brn	1.25	1.00

Airport and Map of St. Pierre and Miquelon A45

Designs: 40fr, Television tube and tower, and map. 48fr, Map of new harbor of St. Pierre.

1967		Engraved	Perf. 13	
374	A45	30fr ind, bl & dk red	90	60
375	A45	40fr sl grn, ol & dk red	1.10	75
376	A45	48fr dk red, brn & sl bl	1.10	90

Issue dates: 30fr, Oct. 23; 40fr, Nov. 20; 48fr, Sept. 25.

WHO Anniversary Issue
Common Design Type

1968, May 4		Engraved	Perf. 13	
377	CD126	10fr multi	1.00	60

Issued for the 20th anniversary of the World Health Organization.

René de Chateaubriand and Map of Islands—A46

Designs: 4fr, J. D. Cassini and map. 15fr, Prince de Joinville, Francois F. d'Orleans (1818-1900), ships and map. 25fr, Admiral Gauchet, World War I warship and map.

1968, May 20		Photo.	Perf. 12½x13	
378	A46	4fr multi	75	60
379	A46	6fr multi	90	75
380	A46	15fr multi	1.25	1.10
381	A46	25fr multi	1.65	1.40

Human Rights Year Issue
Common Design Type

1968, Aug. 10		Engraved	Perf. 13	
382	CD127	20fr bl, ver & org yel	65	50

Belle Rivière, Langlade A47

Design: 15fr, Debon Brook, Langlade.

1969, Apr. 30		Engraved	Perf. 13	
		Size: 36x22mm.		
383	A47	5fr bl, sl grn & brn	60	45
384	A47	15fr brn, bl & dl grn	75	60

See Nos. C41-C42.

Treasury A48

Designs: 25fr, Scientific and Technical Institute of Maritime Fishing. 30fr, Monument to seamen lost at sea. 60fr, St. Christopher College.

1969, May 30		Engraved	Perf. 13	
385	A48	10fr brt bl, cl & blk	45	28
386	A48	25fr dk bl, brt bl & brn red	80	60
387	A48	30fr bl, grn & gray	90	60
388	A48	60fr brt bl, brn red & blk	1.50	1.25

Ringed Seals A49

Designs: 3fr, Sperm whales. 4fr, Pilot whales. 6fr, Common dolphins.

1969, Oct. 6		Engraved	Perf. 13	
389	A49	1fr lil, vio brn & red brn	60	45
390	A49	3fr bl grn, ind & red	60	45
391	A49	4fr ol, gray grn & mar	75	60
392	A49	6fr brt grn, pur & red	1.00	75

ST. PIERRE & MIQUELON

L'Estoile and Granville, France
A50

Designs: 40fr, "La Jolie" and St. Jean de Luz, France, 1750. 48fr, "Le Juste" and La Rochelle, France, 1860.

	1969, Oct. 13	Engraved	*Perf. 13*	
393	A50	34fr grn, mar & sl grn	1.10	90
394	A50	40fr brn red, lem & sl grn	1.50	1.40
395	A50	48fr multi	2.25	1.75

Issued to commemorate historic ships connecting St. Pierre and Miquelon with France.

ILO Issue
Common Design Type

	1969, Nov. 24			
396	CD131	20fr org, gray & ocher	80	60

U.P.U. Headquarters Issue
Common Design Type

	1970, May 20	Engraved	*Perf. 13*	
397	CD133	25fr dk car, brt bl & brn	1.00	90
398	CD133	34fr mar, brn & gray	1.50	1.10

Rowers and Globe
A51

	1970, Oct. 13	Photo.	*Perf. 12½x12*	
399	A51	20fr lt grnsh bl & brn	60	45

Issued to publicize the World Rowing Championships, St. Catherine.

Blackberries
A52

Fruit: 4fr, Strawberries. 5fr, Raspberries. 6fr, Blueberries.

	1970, Oct. 20	Engraved	*Perf. 13*	
400	A52	3fr brn org & multi	45	30
401	A52	4fr red & multi	55	38
402	A52	5fr pur & multi	65	50
403	A52	6fr brt pink & multi	80	65

Ewe and Lamb
A53

Designs: 30fr, Animal quarantine station. 34fr, Charolais bull. 48fr, Refrigeration ship and slaughterhouse.

	1970	Engraved	*Perf. 13*	
404	A53	15fr plum, grn & ol	90	50
405	A53	30fr sl, bis brn & ap grn	95	50
406	A53	34fr red lil, org brn & emer	1.50	90
407	A53	48fr multi	90	75

Issue dates: 48fr, Nov. 10; others, Dec. 8.

Saint François d'Assise 1900
A54

Ships: 35fr, Sainte Jehanne, 1920. 40fr, L'Aventure, 1950. 80fr, Commandant Bourdais, 1970.

	1971, Aug. 25			
408	A54	30fr Prus bl & hn brn	80	60
409	A54	35fr Prus bl, lt grn & ol brn	1.00	75
410	A54	40fr sl grn, bl & dk brn	1.25	90
411	A54	80fr dp grn, bl & blk	2.25	1.50

Deep-sea fishing fleet.

"Aconit" and Map of Islands—A55

Ships: 25fr, Alysse. 50fr, Mimosa.

	1971, Sept. 27	Engraved	*Perf. 13*	
412	A55	22fr bl, blk & brt grn	1.10	60
413	A55	25fr bl & multi	1.75	1.40
414	A55	50fr vio bl, blk & Prus bl	2.25	2.00

30th anniversary of the rallying of the Free French forces.

Ship's Bell
A56

Design: 45fr, Old chart and sextants (horiz.).

	1971, Oct. 25	Photo.	*Perf. 12½x13*	
415	A56	20fr gray & multi	75	60
416	A56	45fr red brn & multi	1.10	90

St. Pierre Museum.

De Gaulle Issue
Common Design Type

Designs: 35fr, Gen. de Gaulle, 1940. Pres. de Gaulle, 1970.

	1971, Nov. 9	Engraved	*Perf. 13*	
417	CD134	35fr ver & blk	1.50	1.10
418	CD134	45fr ver & blk	2.25	2.00

First anniversary of the death of Charles de Gaulle (1890–1970), president of France.

Haddock
A57

Fish: 3fr, Hippoglossoides platessoides. 5fr, Sebastes mentella. 10fr, Codfish.

	1972, Mar. 7			
419	A57	2fr vio bl, ind & pink	45	30
420	A57	3fr grn & gray ol	55	45
421	A57	5fr Prus bl & brick red	60	55
422	A57	10f grn & sl grn	85	65

Oldsquaws
A58

Birds: 10c, 70c, Puffins. 20c, 90c, Snow owl. 40c, Like 6c. Identification of birds on oldsquaw and puffin stamps transposed.

	1973, Jan. 1	Engraved	*Perf. 13*	
423	A58	6c Prus bl, pur & brn	15	15
424	A58	10c Prus bl, blk & org	22	22
425	A58	20c ultra, bis & dk vio	22	22
426	A58	40c pur, sl grn & brn	45	30
427	A58	70c brt grn, blk & org	60	45
428	A58	90c Prus bl, bis & pur	1.40	90
	Nos. 423-428 (6)		3.04	2.24

Indoor Swimming Pool
A59

Design: 1fr, Cultural Center of St. Pierre.

	1973, Sept. 25	Engraved	*Perf. 13*	
429	A59	60c brn, brt bl & dk car	60	45
430	A59	1fr bl grn, ocher & choc	90	75

Opening of Cultural Center of St. Pierre.

Map of Islands, Weather Balloon and Ship, WMO Emblem—A60

	1974, Mar. 23	Engraved	*Perf. 13*	
431	A60	1.60fr multi	1.25	90

World Meteorological Day.

Gannet Holding Letter—A61

	1974, Oct. 9	Engraved	*Perf. 13*	
432	A61	70c bl & multi	75	60
433	A61	90c red & multi	90	75

Centenary of Universal Postal Union.

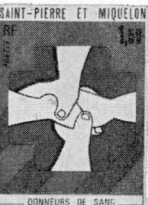

Clasped Hands over Red Cross
A62

Hands Putting Money into Fish-shaped Bank
A63

	1974, Oct. 15	Photo.	*Perf. 12½x13*	
434	A62	1.50fr multi	1.00	90

Honoring blood donors.

	1974, Nov. 15	Engraved	*Perf. 13*	
435	A63	50c ocher & vio bl	60	45

St. Pierre Savings Bank centenary.

Church of St. Pierre and Seagulls
A64

Designs: 10c, Church of Miquelon and fish. 20c, Church of Our Lady of the Sailors, and fishermen.

	1974, Dec. 9	Engraved	*Perf. 13*	
436	A64	6c multi	22	22
437	A64	10c multi	22	22
438	A64	20c multi	45	45

Danaus Plexippus
A65

Design: 1fr, Vanessa atalanta (vert.).

	1975, July 17	Litho.	*Perf. 12½*	
439	A65	1fr bl & multi	75	60
440	A65	1.20fr grn & multi	90	75

Pottery
A66

Mother and Child, Wood Carving
A67

	1975, Oct. 20	Engr.	*Perf. 13*	
441	A66	50c ol, brn & choc	60	45
442	A67	60c bl & dl yel	60	45

Local handicrafts.

Pointe Plate Lighthouse and Murres
A68

Designs: 10c, Galantry lighthouse and Atlantic puffins. 20c, Cap Blanc lighthouse, whale and squid.

ST. PIERRE & MIQUELON

1975, Oct. 21

443	A68	6c vio bl, blk & lt grn	15	15
444	A68	10c lil rose, blk & dk ol	22	22
445	A68	20c bl, ind & brn	30	30

Pompidou Type of Wallis and Futuna Islands

1976, Feb. 17   Engr.   *Perf. 13*

| 446 | A11 | 1.10fr brn & sl | 90 | 60 |

Georges Pompidou (1911–1974), President of France.

Washington and Lafayette, American Flag—A69

1976, July 12   Photo.   *Perf. 13*

| 447 | A69 | 1fr multi | 80 | 60 |

American Bicentennial.

Woman Swimmer and Maple Leaf—A70

Design: 70c, Basketball and maple leaf (vert.).

1976, Aug. 10   Engr.   *Perf. 13*

| 448 | A70 | 70c multi | 60 | 55 |
| 449 | A70 | 2.50fr multi | 2.00 | 1.40 |

21st Olympic Games, Montreal, Canada, July 17–Aug. 1.

Vigie Dam—A71

1976, Sept. 7   Engr.   *Perf. 13*

| 450 | A71 | 2.20fr multi | 1.75 | 1.40 |

Croix de Lorraine—A72

Design: 1.40fr, Goelette.

1976, Oct. 5   Photo.   *Perf. 13*

| 451 | A72 | 1.20fr multi | 1.10 | 75 |
| 452 | A72 | 1.40fr multi | 1.25 | 90 |

Fishing vessels.

ST. PIERRE & MIQUELON

SEMI-POSTAL STAMPS.
Regular Issue of 1909-17
Surcharged in Red ✚ 5c

1915-17 Perf. 14x13½. Unwmkd.
B1	A17	10c + 5c car rose & red	30	30
B2	A17	15c + 5c dl vio & rose	45	45
		('17)		

Curie Issue
Common Design Type
1938 Engraved. Perf. 13.
| B3 | CD80 | 1.75fr + 50c brt ultra | 6.00 | 6.00 |

French Revolution Issue.
Common Design Type
Name and Value Typo. in Black
1939 Photogravure
B4	CD83	45c + 25c grn	3.00	3.00
B5	CD83	70c + 30c brn	3.00	3.00
B6	CD83	90c + 35c red org	3.00	3.00
B7	CD83	1.25fr + 1fr rose pink	3.00	3.00
B8	CD83	2.25fr + 2fr bl	3.00	3.00
	Nos. B4-B8 (5)	15.00	15.00

Common Design Type and

Sailor of Landing Force SP1

Dispatch Boat "Ville d'Ys" SP2

1941 Photogravure Perf. 13½
B8A	SP1	1fr + 1fr red	60
B8B	CD86	1.50fr + 3fr mar	60
B8C	SP2	2.50fr + 1fr bl	60

Nos. B8A-B8C were issued by the Vichy government, and were not placed on sale in the colony.

Nos. 206A-206B were surcharged "OEUVRES COLONIALES" and surtax (including change of denomination of the 2.50fr to 50c). These were issued in 1944 by the Vichy government and not placed on sale in the colony.

Regular Stamps of 1942
With Additional Surcharge in Carmine
✚ 50 c

ŒUVRES SOCIALES

1942 Perf. 13½x13. Unwmkd.
| B9 | A25 | 1fr + 50c pale ol grn | 19.00 | 19.00 |
| B10 | A26 | 2.50fr + 1fr org yel | 19.00 | 19.00 |

Red Cross Issue
Common Design Type
1944 Perf. 14½x14.
| B13 | CD90 | 5fr + 20fr dp ultra | 45 | 45 |

The surtax was for the French Red Cross and national relief.

Tropical Medicine Issue
Common Design Type
1950 Engraved Perf. 13
| B14 | CD100 | 10fr + 2fr red brn & red | 2.25 | 2.25 |

The surtax was for charitable work.

AIR POST STAMPS.
Common Design Type
Perf. 14½x14.
1942, Aug. 17 Photo. Unwmkd.
C1	CD87	1fr dk org	15	15
C2	CD87	1.50fr brt red	18	18
C3	CD87	5fr brn red	22	22
C4	CD87	10fr black	30	30
C5	CD87	25fr ultra	32	32
C6	CD87	50fr dk grn	50	50
C7	CD87	100fr plum	80	80
	Nos. C1-C7 (7)	2.47	2.47

Victory Issue
Common Design Type
1946, May 8 Engraved. Perf. 12½.
| C8 | CD92 | 8fr dp cl | 45 | 45 |

Issued to commemorate the European victory of the Allied Nations in World War II.

Chad to Rhine Issue
Common Design Types
1946, June 6
C9	CD93	5fr brn red	50	50
C10	CD94	10fr lil rose	50	50
C11	CD95	15fr gray blk	65	65
C12	CD96	20fr violet	65	65
C13	CD97	25fr chocolate	95	95
C14	CD98	50fr grnsh blk	95	95
	Nos. C9-C14 (6)	4.20	4.20

Plane, Sailing Vessel and Coast AP2

AP3

AP4

1947, Oct. 6
C15	AP2	50fr yel grn & rose	2.25	1.50
C16	AP3	100fr dk bl grn	3.25	2.50
C17	AP4	200fr bluish blk & brt rose	6.25	3.75

U.P.U. Issue
Common Design Type
1949, July 4 Engraved Perf. 13
| C18 | CD99 | 25fr dp bl, grn, dk brn & red | 5.25 | 5.25 |

Issued to commemorate the 75th anniversary of the formation of the Universal Postal Union.

Liberation Issue.
Common Design Type
1954, June 6
| C19 | CD102 | 15fr sep & red | 2.25 | 2.25 |

10th anniversary of the liberation of France.

Plane over St. Pierre Harbor AP6

1956, Oct. 22
| C20 | AP6 | 500fr ultra & ind | 30.00 | 15.00 |

Dog and Village—AP7
Design: 100fr, Caravelle over archipelago.

1957, Nov. 4 Perf. 13 Unwmkd.
| C21 | AP7 | 50fr gray, brn blk & bl | 10.00 | 7.50 |
| C22 | AP7 | 100fr blk & gray | 5.25 | 5.25 |

Anchors and Torches—AP8
1959, Sept. 14 Engraved Perf. 13
| C23 | AP8 | 200fr dk pur, grn & cl | 6.25 | 4.00 |

Issued to commemorate the approval of the constitution and the vote which confirmed the attachment of the islands to France.

Pitcher Plant—AP9
1962, Apr. 24 Perf. 13 Unwmkd.
| C24 | AP9 | 100fr grn, org & car | 3.25 | 1.75 |

Gulf of St. Lawrence and Submarine "Surcouf"—AP10
Photogravure
1962, July 24 Perf. 13½x12½
| C25 | AP10 | 500fr dk red & bl | 67.50 | 60.00 |

Issued to commemorate the 20th anniversary of St. Pierre & Miquelon's Joining the Free French.

Telstar Issue
Common Design Type
1962, Nov. 22 Engraved Perf. 13
| C26 | CD111 | 50fr Prus grn & bis | 3.00 | 2.25 |

Arrival of Governor Dangeac, 1763 AP11
1963, Aug. 5 Perf. 13 Unwmkd.
| C27 | AP11 | 200fr dk bl, sl grn & brn | 5.50 | 3.75 |

Issued to commemorate the bicentenary of the arrival of the first French governor.

Jet Plane and Map of Maritime Provinces and New England AP12
1964, Sept. 28 Engraved Perf. 13
| C28 | AP12 | 100fr choc & Prus bl | 4.50 | 3.00 |

Issued to commemorate the inauguration of direct airmail service between St. Pierre and New York City.

ITU Issue
Common Design Type
1965, May 17
| C29 | CD120 | 40fr org brn, dk bl & lil rose | 5.25 | 3.75 |

French Satellite A-1 Issue
Common Design Type
Designs: 25fr, Diamant rocket and launching installations. 30fr, A-1 satellite.
1966, Jan. 24 Engraved Perf. 13
C30	CD121	25fr dk brn, dk bl & rose cl	3.00	2.25
C31	CD121	30fr dk bl, rose cl & dk brn	3.00	2.25
a.	Strip of 2 + label	6.50	5.25

Issued to commemorate the launching of France's first satellite, Nov. 26, 1965. No. C31a contains one each of Nos. C30-C31 and dark brown label with commemorative inscription. Each sheet contains 16 triptychs (2x8).

French Satellite D-1 Issue
Common Design Type
1966, May 23 Engraved Perf. 13
| C32 | CD122 | 48fr brt grn, ultra & rose cl | 3.00 | 2.25 |

Arrival of Settlers—AP13
1966, June 22 Photo. Perf. 13
| C33 | AP13 | 100fr multi | 2.50 | 1.75 |

Issued to commemorate the 150th anniversary of the return of the islands of St. Pierre and Miquelon to France.

ST. PIERRE & MIQUELON

Front Page of
Official Journal
and
Printing Presses
AP14

1966, Oct. 20 Engraved Perf. 13

C34 AP14 60fr dk bl, lake & dk pur 2.00 1.40

Issued to commemorate the centenary of the Government Printers and the Official Journal.

Map of Islands, Old and New Fishing Vessels—AP15

Design: 100fr, Cruiser Colbert, maps of Brest, St. Pierre and Miquelon.

1967, July 20 Engraved Perf. 13

| C35 | AP15 | 25fr dk bl, gray & crim | 10.00 | 7.50 |
| C36 | AP15 | 100fr multi | 20.00 | 15.00 |

Visit of President Charles de Gaulle.

Speed Skater and Olympic Emblem
AP16

Design: 60fr, Ice hockey goalkeeper and Olympic emblem.

1968, Apr. 22 Photo. Perf. 13

| C37 | AP16 | 50fr ultra & multi | 1.75 | 1.10 |
| C38 | AP16 | 60fr grn & multi | 2.00 | 1.50 |

Issued to publicize the 10th Winter Olympic Games, Grenoble, France, Feb. 6–18.

War Memorial, St. Pierre
AP17

1968, Nov. 11 Photo. Perf. 12½

C39 AP17 500fr multi 14.00 10.00

Issued for the 50th anniversary of the World War I armistice.

Concorde Issue
Common Design Type

1969, Apr. 17 Engraved Perf. 13

C40 CD129 34fr dk brn & ol 7.00 4.75

Scenic Type of Regular Issue, 1969.

Designs: 50fr, Grazing horses, Miquelon. 100fr, Gathering driftwood on Mirande Beach, Miquelon.

1969, Apr. 30 Engraved Perf. 13
Size: 47½x27mm.

| C41 | A47 | 50fr ultra, brn & ol | 3.25 | 2.25 |
| C42 | A47 | 100fr dk brn, bl & sl | 6.00 | 4.50 |

L'Esperance Leaving Saint-Malo, 1600—AP18

1969, June 16 Engraved Perf. 13

C43 AP18 200fr blk, grn & dk red 4.75 2.25

Pierre Loti and Sailboats—AP19

1969, June 23

C44 AP19 300fr lem, choc & Prus bl 8.00 6.00

Issued in memory of Pierre Loti (1850–1923), French novelist and naval officer.

EXPO Emblem and "Mountains" by Yokoyama Taikan—AP20

Design: 34fr, Geisha, rocket and EXPO emblem (vert.).

1970, Sept. 8 Engraved Perf. 13

| C45 | AP20 | 34fr dp cl, ol & ind | 1.50 | 1.10 |
| C46 | AP20 | 85fr org, ind & car | 3.00 | 2.00 |

EXPO '70 International Exposition, Osaka, Japan, Mar. 15–Sept. 13.

Etienne François Duke of Choiseul and his Ships—AP21

Designs: 50fr, Jacques Cartier, ship and landing party. 60fr, Sebastien Le Gonard de Sourdeval, ships and map of islands.

1970, Nov. 25 Portrait in Lake

C47	AP21	25fr lil & Prus bl	1.25	75
C48	AP21	50fr sl grn & red lil	2.25	1.40
C49	AP21	60fr red lil & sl grn	3.25	1.75

De Gaulle, Cross of Lorraine, Sailor, Soldier, Coast Guard—AP22

1972, June 18 Engraved Perf. 13

C50 AP22 100fr lil, brn & grn 4.00 2.50

Charles de Gaulle (1890–1970), president of France.

Louis Joseph de Montcalm—AP23

Designs: 2fr, Louis de Buade Frontenac (vert.). 4fr, Robert de La Salle.

1973, Jan. 1

C51	AP23	1.60fr Prus bl, blk & pur	1.25	75
C52	AP23	2fr vio, sl grn & dp mag	1.75	1.00
C53	AP23	4fr sl grn, brn ol & rose cl	3.75	2.25

Transall C 160 over St. Pierre
AP24

1973, Oct. 16 Engraved Perf. 13

C54 AP24 10fr multi 9.50 6.00

Arms and Map of Islands, Fish and Bird—AP25

1974, Nov. 5 Photo. Perf. 13

C55 AP25 2fr gold & multi 1.75 1.25

Copernicus, Galileo, Newton and Einstein
AP26

1974, Nov. 26 Engraved

C56 AP26 4fr multi 3.75 2.25

500th anniversary of the birth of Nicolaus Copernicus (1473–1543), Polish Astronomer.

Type of 1909, Cod and ARPHILA Emblem
AP27

1975, Aug. 5 Engraved Perf. 13

C57 AP27 4fr ultra, red & ind 4.00 2.50

ARPHILA 75, International Philatelic Exhibition, Paris, June 6–16.

Judo, Maple Leaf, Olympic Rings
AP28

1975, Nov. 18 Engr. Perf. 13

C58 AP28 1.90fr red, bl & vio 1.75 1.10

Pre-Olympic Year 1975.

Concorde—AP29

1976, Jan. 21 Engr. Perf. 13

C59 AP29 10fr red, blk & sl 9.50 6.00

First commercial flight of supersonic jet Concorde from Paris to Rio de Janeiro, Jan. 21.

A. G. Bell, Telephone and Satellite
AP30

1976, June 22 Litho. Perf. 12½

C60 AP30 5fr vio bl, org & red 4.00 3.00

Centenary of first telephone call by Alexander Graham Bell, Mar. 10, 1876.

AIR POST SEMI-POSTAL STAMPS.

V4

Stamps of the design shown above and stamp of Cameroun type V10 inscribed "St. Pierre-et-Miquelon" were issued in 1942 by the Vichy Government, but were not placed on sale in the Colony.

POSTAGE DUE STAMPS

Postage Due Stamps of French Colonies Overprinted in Red

ST. PIERRE M—on

1892 Imperf. Unwmkd.

J1	D1	5c black	25.00	25.00
J2	D1	10c black	7.25	7.25
J3	D1	15c black	7.25	7.25
J4	D1	20c black	7.25	7.25
J5	D1	30c black	7.25	7.25
J6	D1	40c black	7.25	7.25
J7	D1	60c black	32.50	32.50

Black Overprint.

J8	D1	1fr brown	67.50	67.50
J9	D1	2fr brown	67.50	67.50

These stamps exist with and without hyphen. See note after No. 59.

Postage Due Stamps of France, 1893-1924, Overprinted

SAINT-PIERRE
-ET-
MIQUELON

1925-27 Perf. 14 x 13½.

J10	D2	5c blue	22	22
J11	D2	10c dk brn	22	22
J12	D2	20c ol grn	28	28
J13	D2	25c rose	28	28
J14	D2	30c red	38	38
J15	D2	45c bl grn	38	38
J16	D2	50c brn vio	75	75
J17	D2	1fr red brn, *straw*	90	90
J18	D2	3fr mag ('27)	3.25	3.25

SAINT-PIERRE
-ET-MIQUELON
Surcharged
**2
francs
à percevoir**

J19	D2	60c on 50c buff	75	75
J20	D2	2fr on 1fr red	1.10	1.25
		Nos. J10-J20 (11)	8.51	8.66

Newfoundland Dog   Codfish
D3   D4

1932 Typographed.

J21	D3	5c dk bl & blk	50	50
J22	D3	10c grn & blk	50	50
J23	D3	20c red & blk	65	65
J24	D3	25c red vio & blk	65	65
J25	D3	30c org & blk	1.40	1.40
J26	D3	45c lt bl & blk	1.50	1.50
J27	D3	50c bl grn & blk	2.50	2.50
J28	D3	60c brt rose & blk	3.25	3.25
J29	D3	1fr yel brn & blk	9.00	9.00
J30	D3	2fr dp vio & blk	12.50	12.50
J31	D3	3fr dk brn & blk	12.50	12.50
		Nos. J21-J31 (11)	44.95	44.95

1938 Photogravure. Perf. 13.

J32	D4	5c gray blk	8	8
J33	D4	10c dk red vio	8	8
J34	D4	15c sl grn	8	8
J35	D4	20c dp bl	8	8
J36	D4	30c rose car	12	12
a.		"30c" omitted		
J37	D4	50c dk bl grn	12	12
J38	D4	60c dk bl	18	18
J39	D4	1fr hn brn	28	28
J40	D4	2fr gray brn	1.10	1.10
J41	D4	3fr dl vio	1.50	1.50
		Nos. J32-J41 (10)	3.62	3.62

Type of Postage Due Stamps of 1932 Overprinted in Black

**FRANCE LIBRE
F. N. F. L.**

1942 Perf. 14 x 13½. Unwmkd.

J42	D3	25c red vio & blk	135.00	135.00
J43	D3	30c org & blk	135.00	135.00
J44	D3	50c bl grn & blk	525.00	525.00
J45	D3	2fr dp vio & bl blk	22.50	22.50

Same Surcharged in Black

**3 fr
FRANCE LIBRE
F. N. F. L.**

J46	D3	3fr on 2fr dp vio & blk	9.00	9.00
a.		"F.N.F.L." omitted	3.75	3.75
		Nos. J42-J46 (5)	826.50	826.50

Postage Due Stamps of 1938 Overprinted in Black

**NOËL 1941
F N F L**

1942 Perf. 13.

J48	D4	5c gray blk	11.00	11.00
J49	D4	10c dk red vio	11.00	11.00
J50	D4	15c sl grn	11.00	11.00
J51	D4	20c dp bl	11.00	11.00
J52	D4	30c rose car	11.00	11.00
J53	D4	50c dk bl grn	18.00	18.00
J54	D4	60c dk bl	45.00	45.00
J55	D4	1fr hn brn	55.00	55.00
J56	D4	2fr gray brn	60.00	60.00
J57	D4	3fr dl vio	62.50	62.50
		Nos. J48-J57 (10)	295.50	295.50

Issued to commemorate the Christmas Day plebiscite ordered by Vice Admiral Emile Henri Muselier, commander of the Free French naval forces.

Postage Due Stamps of 1938 Overprinted in Black

**FRANCE
LIBRE
F N F L**

1942

J58	D4	5c gray blk	21.00	21.00
J59	D4	10c dk red vio	2.50	2.50
J60	D4	15c sl grn	2.50	2.50
J61	D4	20c dp bl	2.50	2.50
J62	D4	30c rose car	2.50	2.50
J63	D4	50c dk bl	2.50	2.50
J64	D4	60c dk bl	7.50	7.50
J65	D4	1fr hn brn	7.50	7.50
J66	D4	2fr gray brn	7.50	7.50
J67	D4	3fr dl vio	275.00	275.00
		Nos. J58-J67 (10)	326.00	326.00

Arms and
Fishing
Schooner   Newfoundland Dog
D5   D6

1947 Engraved. Perf. 13.

J68	D5	10c dp org	5	5
J69	D5	30c dp ultra	6	6
J70	D5	50c dk bl grn	12	12
J71	D5	1fr dp car	18	18
J72	D5	2fr dk grn	18	18
J73	D5	3fr violet	30	30
J74	D5	4fr chocolate	38	38
J75	D5	5fr yel org	38	38
J76	D5	10fr blk brn	45	45
J77	D5	20fr org red	50	50
		Nos. J68-J77 (10)	2.60	2.60

1973, Jan. 1 Engraved Perf. 13

J78	D6	2c brn & blk	12	12
J79	D6	10c pur & blk	15	15
J80	D6	20c grnsh bl & blk	32	32
J81	D6	30c dk car & blk	45	45
J82	D6	1fr bl & blk	1.25	1.25
		Nos. J78-J82 (5)	2.29	2.29

PARCEL POST STAMPS.

No. 65
Overprinted   **COLIS
               POSTAUX**

1901 Perf. 14 x 13½. Unwmkd.

Q1	A16	10c lavender	30.00	30.00
a.		Inverted overprint		

No. 66
Overprinted   **Colis Postaux**

Q2	A16	10c red	7.50	7.50

Nos. 84 and 87 Overprinted

Colis Postaux

1917-25

Q3	A17	10c car rose & red	90	90
a.		Double overprint	15.00	
Q4	A17	20c bis brn & vio brn ('25)	75	75
a.		Double overprint	40.00	40.00

No. Q4 with Additional Overprint in Black

**FRANCE LIBRE
F. N. F. L.**

1942

Q5	A17	20c bis brn & vio brn	325.00	325.00

A particular stamp may be scarce, but if few want it, its market potential may remain relatively low.

Scott's editorial staff cannot undertake to identify, authenticate or appraise stamps and postal markings.

ST. THOMAS AND PRINCE ISLANDS
Democratic Republic of São Tomé and Principe

LOCATION — Two islands in the Gulf of Guinea, 125 miles off the west coast of Africa.
GOVT. — Republic.
AREA — 372 sq. mi.
POP. — 80,000 (est. 1977).
CAPITAL — St. Thomas.

This colony of Portugal became a province, later an overseas territory, and achieved independence July 12, 1975, taking the name Democratic Republic of São Tomé and Principe.

1000 Reis = 1 Milreis
100 Centavos = 1 Escudo (1913)
100 Cents = 1 Dobra (1978)

Portuguese Crown   King Luiz
A1   A2

Typographed

FIVE, TWENTY-FIVE, FIFTY REIS:
  Type I. "5" is upright.
  Type II. "5" is slanting.
TEN REIS:
  Type I. "1" has short serif at top.
  Type II. "1" has long serif at top.
FORTY REIS:
  Type I. "4" is broad.
  Type II. "4" is narrow.

1869-75   Unwmkd.
Perf. 12½, 13½

1	A1	5r blk, I	2.75	2.00
a.		Type II	2.75	2.00
2	A1	10r yel, I	17.50	10.00
a.		Type II	17.50	10.00
3	A1	20r bister	4.25	3.00
4	A1	25r rose, I	2.00	1.50
		25r red	4.00	
5	A1	40r bl ('75) I	6.00	4.25
		Type II	6.00	4.25
6	A1	50r gray grn, II	12.00	10.50
		Type I	17.50	16.50
7	A1	100r gray lil	9.00	6.50
8	A1	200r red org ('75)	10.00	6.50
9	A1	300r choc ('75)	10.00	6.50

1881-85

10	A1	10r gray grn, I	9.00	6.50
a.		Type II	9.00	6.50
b.		Perf. 13½	10.00	7.50
11	A1	20r car rose ('85)	4.50	3.00
12	A1	25r vio ('85) II	3.00	1.75
13	A1	40r yel buff, II	6.00	5.50
a.		Perf. 13½	7.50	6.00
14	A1	50r dk bl, I	2.75	2.50
a.		Type II	2.75	2.50

Nos. 1 to 14 inclusive have been reprinted on stout white paper, ungummed, with rough perforation 13½, also on ordinary paper with shiny white gum and clean-cut perforation 13½ with large holes. Price of lowest-cost reprint, $1.

Typo., Head Embossed.
1887 Perf. 12½, 13½.

15	A2	5r black	4.50	3.00
16	A2	10r green	6.50	3.00
17	A2	20r brt rose	6.50	4.00
a.		Perf. 12½	62.50	62.50
18	A2	25r violet	5.50	2.25
19	A2	40r brown	5.50	3.25
20	A2	50r blue	5.50	2.75
21	A2	100r yel brn	5.50	2.50
22	A2	200r gray lil	17.50	10.00
23	A2	300r orange	17.50	10.00

Nos. 15, 16, 19, 21, 22, and 23 have been reprinted in paler colors than the originals, with white gum and clean-cut perforation 13½. Price $1.50 each.

ST. THOMAS AND PRINCE ISLANDS

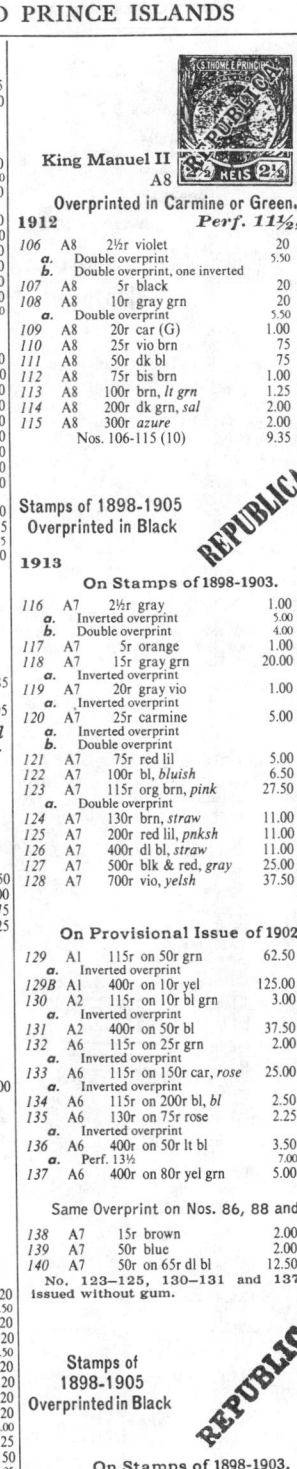

Nos. 16–17, 19 Surcharged:

5 réis *a* **cinco réis** *b* **Rs.50** *c*

1889–91

Without Gum

24	A2(a)	5r on 10r grn	30.00	20.00
25	A2(b)	5r on 20r rose	30.00	20.00
26	A2(c)	50r on 40r brn ('91)	90.00	70.00

Varieties of Nos. 24-26, including inverted and double surcharges, "5" inverted, "Cinco" and "Cinco," were deliberately made and unofficially issued.

King Carlos
A6   A7

1895   Typo.   Perf. 11½, 12½

27	A6	5r yellow	90	65
28	A6	10r red lil	1.25	1.00
29	A6	15r red brn	1.75	1.50
30	A6	20r lavender	1.75	1.50
31	A6	25r green	1.75	80
32	A6	50r lt bl	2.25	80
a.		Perf. 13½	2.50	1.50
33	A6	75r rose	4.50	3.75
34	A6	80r yel grn	9.00	7.75
35	A6	100r brn, yel	4.50	3.50
36	A6	150r car, rose	6.25	5.50
37	A6	200r dk bl, bl	7.50	6.00
38	A6	300r dk bl, sal	8.75	7.50

1898–1903   Perf. 11½
Name and Value in Black except 500r.

39	A7	2½r gray	25	25
40	A7	5r orange	25	20
41	A7	10r lt grn	25	20
42	A7	15r brown	2.00	1.75
43	A7	15r gray grn ('03)	1.25	1.25
44	A7	20r gray vio	1.00	50
45	A7	25r sea grn	60	30
46	A7	25r car ('03)	1.25	35
47	A7	50r blue	75	40
48	A7	50r brn ('03)	5.00	5.00
49	A7	65r dl bl ('03)	8.50	8.50
50	A7	75r rose	10.00	5.50
51	A7	75r red lil ('03)	2.00	1.50
52	A7	80r brt vio	5.50	5.50
53	A7	100r dk bl, bl	2.75	2.00
54	A7	115r org brn, pink ('03)	7.50	7.50
55	A7	130r brn, straw ('03)	7.50	7.50
56	A7	150r brn, buff	3.25	2.75
57	A7	200r red lil, pnksh	4.50	2.00
58	A7	300r dk bl, rose	6.00	6.00
59	A7	400r dl bl, straw ('03)	11.00	11.00
60	A7	500r blk & red, bl ('01)	6.50	4.25
61	A7	700r vio, yelsh ('01)	12.50	10.00
		Nos. 39-61 (23)	100.10	84.20

Stamps of 1869–95 Surcharged in Red or Black

65 RÉIS

1902
On Stamp of 1887.

62	A2	130r on 5r blk (R)	6.25	4.50
a.		Perf. 13½	32.50	32.50

On Stamps of 1869

63	A1	115r on 50r grn	10.00	6.25
64	A1	400r on 10r yel	37.50	25.00
a.		Double surcharge		

On Stamps of 1887.

65	A2	65r on 20r rose	6.25	4.00
		Perf. 13½	8.75	7.50
66	A2	65r on 25r vio	5.00	4.50
a.		Inverted surcharge		
67	A2	65r on 100r yel brn	5.00	4.50
68	A2	115r on 10r bl grn	5.00	4.50
69	A2	115r on 300r org	5.00	4.50
70	A2	130r on 200r gray lil	7.50	4.50
71	A2	400r on 40r brn	11.00	8.50
72	A2	50r on 50r bl	15.00	15.00
a.		Perf. 13½	110.00	90.00

On Stamps of 1895.

73	A6	65r on 5r yel	4.50	4.50
74	A6	65r on 10r red vio	4.50	4.50
75	A6	65r on 15r choc	4.50	4.50
76	A6	65r on 20r lav	4.50	4.50
77	A6	115r on 25r grn	4.50	4.50
78	A6	115r on 150r car, rose	4.50	4.50
79	A6	115r on 200r bl, bl	4.50	4.50
80	A6	130r on 75r rose	4.50	4.50
81	A6	130r on 100r brn, yel	4.50	4.50
a.		Double surcharge		
82	A6	130r on 300r bl, sal	4.50	4.50
83	A6	400r on 50r lt bl	1.25	85
		Perf. 13½	2.50	1.75
84	A6	400r on 80r yel grn	2.25	1.50

On Newspaper Stamp No. P12

85	N3	400r on 2½r brn	1.25	85
a.		Double surcharge		
		Nos. 62-85 (24)	163.25	133.95

Reprints of Nos. 63, 64, 67, 71, and 72 have shiny white gum and clean-cut perf. 13½. Price $1 each.

Stamps of 1898 Overprinted **PROVISORIO**

1902   Perf. 11½

86	A7	15r brown	2.00	1.50
87	A7	25r sea grn	2.00	1.00
88	A7	50r blue	2.25	1.75
89	A7	75r rose	5.00	4.25

No. 49 Surcharged 50 in Black RÉIS

1905

90	A7	50r on 65r dl bl	3.75	3.00

Stamps of 1898–1903 Overprinted in Carmine or Green **REPUBLICA**

1911

91	A7	2½r gray	25	20
a.		Inverted overprint	6.00	4.50
92	A7	5r orange	25	20
93	A7	10r lt grn	30	20
a.		Inverted overprint	5.00	4.50
94	A7	15r gray grn	30	20
95	A7	20r gray vio	30	20
96	A7	25r car (G)	75	20
97	A7	50r brown	30	20
a.		Inverted overprint	6.00	6.00
98	A7	75r red lil	30	25
99	A7	100r dk bl, bl	75	50
a.		Inverted overprint	4.75	3.25
100	A7	115r org brn, pink	1.25	80
101	A7	130r brn, straw	1.50	80
102	A7	200r red lil, pnksh	6.25	3.75
103	A7	400r dl bl, straw	1.50	1.00
104	A7	500r blk & red, bl	1.50	1.00
105	A7	700r vio, yelsh	1.50	1.00
		Nos. 91-105 (15)	16.75	10.50

King Manuel II   A8

Overprinted in Carmine or Green.
1912   Perf. 11½, 12.

106	A8	2½r violet	20	20
a.		Double overprint	5.50	5.50
b.		Double overprint, one inverted		
107	A8	5r black	20	20
108	A8	10r gray grn	20	20
a.		Double overprint	5.50	5.50
109	A8	20r car (G)	1.00	65
110	A8	25r vio brn	75	60
111	A8	50r dk bl	75	60
112	A8	75r bis brn	1.00	60
113	A8	100r brn, lt grn	1.25	60
114	A8	200r dk grn, sal	2.00	1.50
115	A8	300r azure	2.00	1.50
		Nos. 106-115 (10)	9.35	6.65

Stamps of 1898-1905 Overprinted in Black **REPUBLICA**

1913

On Stamps of 1898–1903.

116	A7	2½r gray	1.00	1.00
a.		Inverted overprint	5.00	5.00
b.		Double overprint	4.00	4.00
117	A7	5r orange	1.00	1.00
118	A7	15r gray grn	20.00	15.00
a.		Inverted overprint		
119	A7	20r gray vio	1.00	1.00
a.		Inverted overprint		
120	A7	25r carmine	5.00	5.00
a.		Inverted overprint		
b.		Double overprint		
121	A7	75r red lil	5.00	5.00
122	A7	100r bl, bluish	6.50	5.50
123	A7	115r org brn, pink	27.50	27.50
a.		Double surcharge		
124	A7	130r brn, straw	11.00	11.00
125	A7	200r red lil, pnksh	11.00	11.00
126	A7	400r dl bl, straw	11.00	11.00
127	A7	500r blk & red, gray	25.00	25.00
128	A7	700r vio, yelsh	37.50	37.50

On Provisional Issue of 1902.

129	A1	115r on 50r grn	62.50	55.00
		Inverted overprint		
129B	A2	115r on 10r yel	125.00	125.00
130	A2	115r on 10r bl grn	3.00	2.50
a.		Inverted overprint		
131	A2	400r on 50r bl	37.50	32.50
132	A6	115r on 25r grn	2.00	1.75
a.		Inverted overprint		
133	A6	115r on 150r car, rose	25.00	20.00
a.		Inverted overprint		
134	A6	115r on 200r bl, bl	2.50	2.25
135	A6	130r on 75r rose	2.25	2.00
a.		Inverted overprint		
136	A6	400r on 50r lt bl	3.50	3.00
		Perf. 13½	7.00	5.00
137	A6	400r on 80r yel grn	5.00	3.75

Same Overprint on Nos. 86, 88 and 90

138	A7	15r brown	2.00	2.00
139	A7	50r blue	2.00	2.00
140	A7	50r on 65r dl bl	12.50	12.50

No. 123–125, 130–131 and 137 were issued without gum.

Stamps of 1898–1905 Overprinted in Black **REPUBLICA**

On Stamps of 1898–1903.

141	A7	2½r gray	80	60
a.		Inverted overprint	4.50	
b.		Double overprint	4.50	4.50
c.		Double overprint inverted		
142	A7	5r orange	25.00	17.50
143	A7	5r gray vio	1.75	1.50
a.		Inverted overprint		
144	A7	20r gray vio	45.00	32.50
a.		Inverted overprint		
145	A7	25r carmine	25.00	17.50
a.		Inverted overprint		1.50
146	A7	75r red lil	2.00	1.50
a.		Inverted overprint		
147	A7	100r bl, bl	2.50	1.75
148	A7	115r org brn, pink	6.50	6.50
149	A7	130r brn, straw	8.00	8.00
150	A7	200r red lil, pnksh	2.50	1.75
151	A7	400r dl bl, straw	8.00	7.00
152	A7	500r blk & red, gray	7.50	6.50
153	A7	700r vio, yelsh	7.50	7.00

On Provisional Issue of 1902.

154	A1	115r on 50r grn	90.00	90.00
155	A2	115r on 10r bl grn	2.50	2.25
156	A2	115r on 300r org	90.00	75.00
157	A2	130r on 5r blk	90.00	75.00
158	A2	400r on 50r bl	60.00	50.00
159	A6	115r on 25r grn	2.00	1.50
160	A6	115r on 150r car, rose	2.50	2.25
a.		"REPUBLICA" inverted		
161	A6	115r on 200r bl, bl	2.50	2.25
162	A6	130r on 75r rose	2.50	2.25
a.		Inverted surcharge		
163	A6	130r on 100r brn, yel	175.00	175.00
164	A6	400r on 50r lt bl	2.50	2.25
		Perf. 13½	20.00	6.50
165	A6	400r on 80r yel grn	2.50	2.25
166	N3	400r on 2½r brn	2.25	2.00

Same Overprint on Nos. 86, 88 and 90

167	A7	15r brown	1.50	1.25
a.		Inverted overprint		
168	A7	50r blue	1.50	1.25
a.		Inverted overprint		
169	A7	50r on 65r dl bl	2.50	1.50

Most of Nos. 141-169 were issued without gum.

Vasco da Gama Issue of Various Portuguese Colonies Surcharged as **REPUBLICA S.TOMÉ E PRINCIPE ¼ C.**

On Stamps of Macao.

170	CD20	¼c on ½a bl grn	2.25	2.25
171	CD21	½c on 1a red	2.25	2.25
172	CD22	1c on 2a red vio	2.25	2.25
173	CD23	2½c on 4a yel grn	2.25	2.25
174	CD24	5c on 8a dk bl	2.25	2.25
175	CD25	7½c on 12a vio brn	3.00	3.00
176	CD26	10c on 16a bis brn	2.25	2.25
177	CD27	15c on 24a bis	2.25	2.25
		Nos. 170-177 (8)	18.75	18.75

On Stamps of Portuguese Africa.

178	CD20	¼c on 2½r bl grn	1.50	1.50
179	CD21	½c on 5r red	1.50	1.50
180	CD22	1c on 10r red vio	1.50	1.50
181	CD23	2½c on 25r yel grn	1.50	1.50
182	CD24	5c on 50r dk bl	1.50	1.50
183	CD25	7½c on 75r vio brn	2.00	2.00
184	CD26	10c on 100r bis brn	1.50	1.50
185	CD27	15c on 150r bis	1.50	1.50
		Nos. 178-185 (8)	12.50	12.50

On Stamps of Timor.

186	CD20	¼c on ½a bl grn	2.00	2.00
187	CD21	½c on 1a red	2.00	2.00
188	CD22	1c on 2a red vio	2.00	2.00
a.		Double surcharge		
189	CD23	2½c on 4a yel grn	2.00	2.00
190	CD24	5c on 8a dk bl	2.00	2.00
191	CD25	7½c on 12a vio brn	2.50	2.50
192	CD26	10c on 16a bis brn	2.00	2.00
193	CD27	15c on 24a bis	2.00	2.00
		Nos. 186-193 (8)	16.50	16.50

Ceres
A9

A10

Typographed

1914-26 ***Perf. 12x11½, 15x14.***

Name and Value in Black.

194	A9	¼c ol brn	5	5
195	A9	½c black	15	15
196	A9	1c bl grn	60	60
197	A9	1c yel grn ('22)	15	15
198	A9	1½c lil brn	15	15
199	A9	2c carmine	15	15
200	A9	2c gray ('26)	30	30
201	A9	2½c lt vio	20	20
202	A9	3c org ('22)	25	25
203	A9	4c rose ('22)	25	25
204	A9	4½c gray ('22)	25	25
205	A9	5c dp bl	60	40
206	A9	5c brt bl ('22)	25	25
207	A9	6c lil ('22)	25	25
208	A9	7c ultra ('22)	25	25
209	A9	7½c yel brn	30	30
210	A9	8c slate	30	30
211	A9	10c org brn	25	25
212	A9	12c bl grn ('22)	60	50
213	A9	15c plum	1.75	1.75
214	A9	15c brn rose ('22)	25	25
215	A9	20c yel grn	2.00	1.25
216	A9	24c ultra ('26)	4.00	4.00
217	A9	25c choc ('26)	4.00	4.00
218	A9	30c brn, *grn*	1.75	1.75
219	A9	30c gray grn ('22)	60	60
220	A9	40c brn, *pink*	2.00	2.00
221	A9	40c turq bl ('22)	60	60
222	A9	50c org, *sal*	4.50	4.50
223	A9	50c lt vio ('26)	75	75
224	A9	60c dk bl ('22)	1.50	1.50
225	A9	60c rose ('26)	2.00	2.00
226	A9	80c brt rose ('22)	1.75	60
227	A9	1e grn, *bl*	4.50	4.50
228	A9	1e pale rose ('22)	2.50	1.50
229	A9	1e bl ('26)	2.00	2.00
230	A9	2e dk vio ('22)	3.00	1.75
231	A9	5e buff ('26)	17.50	10.00
232	A9	10e pink ('26)	30.00	20.00
233	A9	20e pale turq ('26)	60.00	50.00
		Nos. 194-233 (40)	152.25	120.30

Perforation and paper variations command a premium for some of Nos. 194-233.

Preceding Issues Overprinted in Carmine

REPUBLICA

1915

On Provisional Issue of 1902.

234	A2	115r on 10r grn	2.50	2.00
235	A2	115r on 300r org	2.50	2.00
236	A2	130r on 5r blk	4.50	3.00
237	A2	130r on 200r gray lil	1.75	1.50
238	A6	115r on 25r grn	75	50
239	A6	115r on 150r car, *rose*	75	50
240	A6	115r on 200r bl, *bl*	75	50
241	A6	130r on 75r rose	75	50
242	A6	130r on 100r brn, *yel*	1.50	1.50
243	A6	130r on 300r bl, *sal*	1.25	1.00

Same Overprint on Nos. 88 and 90

244	A7	50r blue	1.00	75
245	A7	50r on 65r dl bl	1.00	75
		Nos. 234-245 (12)	19.00	14.50

1919

246	A10	2½c on 15r brn	75	75

No. 91 Surcharged in Black ½ C.

247	A7	½c on 2½r gray	3.75	3.75
248	A7	1c on 2½r gray	2.50	2.00
249	A7	2½c on 2½r gray	1.25	75

No. 194 Surcharged in Blue ½

250	A9	½c on ¼c ol brn	2.50	2.00
251	A9	2c on ¼c ol brn	2.50	2.00
252	A9	2½c on ¼c ol brn	7.50	6.25

No. 201 Surcharged in Black $04 Centavos

253	A9	4c on 2½c lt vio	1.00	75
		Nos. 246-253 (8)	21.75	18.25

Nos. 246-253 were issued without gum.

Stamps of 1898-1905 Overprinted in Green or Red

REPUBLICA

1920

On Stamps of 1898-1903

255	A7	75r red lil (G)	65	55
256	A7	100r bl, *bl* (R)	75	75
257	A7	115r org brn, *pink* (G)	1.75	1.75
258	A7	130r brn, *straw* (G)	22.50	22.50
259	A7	200r red lil, *pnksh* (G)	1.75	1.25
260	A7	500r blk & red, *gray* (G)	1.25	1.25
261	A7	700r vio, *yelsh* (G)	1.75	1.25

On Stamps of 1902.

262	A6	115r on 25r grn (R)	1.00	60
263	A6	115r on 200r bl, *bl* (R)	1.25	1.00
264	A6	130r on 75r rose (G)	1.75	1.25

On Nos. 88-89

265	A7	50r bl (R)	1.50	1.25
266	A7	75r rose (G)	8.50	8.50

On No. 90

267	A7	50r on 65r dl bl (R)	8.50	8.50
		Nos. 255-267 (13)	52.90	50.40

Provisional Issue of 1915 Surcharged in Blue or Red

DEZ CENTAVOS

1923

Without Gum

268	A6	10c on 115r on 25r grn (Bl)	60	40
269	A6	10c on 115r on 150r car, *rose* (Bl)	60	40
270	A6	10c on 115r on 200r bl, *bl* (R)	60	40
271	A6	10c on 130r on 75r rose (Bl)	60	40
272	A6	10c on 130r on 100r brn, *yel* (Bl)	60	40
273	A6	10c on 130r on 300r bl, *sal* (R)	60	40
		Nos. 268-273 (6)	3.60	2.40

Nos. 268-273 are usually stained and discolored.

Nos. 84-85 Surcharged

República

40 C.

1925

274	A6	40c on 400r on 80r yel grn	1.00	60
275	N3	40c on 400r on 2½r brn	1.00	60

Nos. 228 and 230 Surcharged

70 C.

1931

281	A9	70c on 1e pale rose	2.00	1.25
282	A9	1.40e on 2e dk vio	3.00	3.00

Ceres
A11

Wmkd. Maltese Cross. (232)

1934 Typographed. ***Perf. 12x11½.***

283	A11	1c bister	20	20
284	A11	5c ol brn	20	20
285	A11	10c violet	20	20
286	A11	15c black	25	20
287	A11	20c gray	25	20
288	A11	30c dk grn	35	30
289	A11	40c red org	35	30
290	A11	45c brt bl	40	30
291	A11	50c brown	40	30
292	A11	60c ol grn	40	30
293	A11	70c brn org	40	30
294	A11	80c emerald	40	30
295	A11	85c dp rose	2.50	1.75
296	A11	1e maroon	75	60
297	A11	1.40e dk bl	2.00	1.25
298	A11	2e dk vio	2.50	2.25
299	A11	5e ap grn	8.50	5.00
300	A11	10e ol bis	15.00	8.00
301	A11	20e orange	55.00	27.50
		Nos. 283-301 (19)	90.05	49.45

Common Design Types
Inscribed "S. Tomé".

1938 ***Perf. 13½x13.*** **Unwmkd.**

Name and Value in Black.

302	CD34	1c gray grn	20	20
303	CD34	5c org brn	30	30
304	CD34	10c dk car	35	35
305	CD34	15c dk vio brn	35	35
306	CD34	20c slate	35	35
307	CD35	30c rose vio	40	40
308	CD35	35c brt grn	75	75
309	CD35	40c brown	75	75
310	CD35	50c brt red vio	75	75
311	CD36	60c gray blk	75	75
312	CD36	70c brn vio	75	75
313	CD36	80c orange	75	75
314	CD36	1e red	1.75	80
315	CD37	1.75e blue	2.00	1.75
316	CD37	2e brn car	17.50	8.00
317	CD37	5e ol grn	14.00	7.50
318	CD38	10e bl vio	20.00	7.50
319	CD38	20e red brn	35.00	9.00
		Nos. 302-319 (18)	96.70	41.00

Marble Column and Portuguese Arms with Cross
A12

1938 ***Perf. 12½***

320	A12	80c bl grn	2.00	1.75
321	A12	1.75e dp bl	10.00	5.00
322	A12	20e brown	40.00	25.00

Issued to commemorate the visit of the President of Portugal to this province in 1938.

Common Design Types

pictured in section at front of book.

Common Design Types
Inscribed "S. Tomé e Principe".

1939 ***Perf. 13½x13.***

Name and Value in Black.

323	CD34	1c gray grn	15	15
324	CD34	5c org brn	15	15
325	CD34	10c dk car	25	25
326	CD34	15c dk vio brn	25	25
327	CD34	20c slate	25	25
328	CD35	30c rose vio	30	25
329	CD35	35c brt grn	30	25
330	CD35	40c brown	30	25
331	CD35	50c brt red vio	30	25
332	CD36	60c gray blk	30	25
333	CD36	70c brn vio	50	40
334	CD36	80c orange	50	40
335	CD36	1e red	90	45
336	CD37	1.75e blue	1.25	55
337	CD37	2e brn car	2.50	1.50
338	CD37	5e ol grn	5.50	3.50
339	CD38	10e bl vio	13.00	4.00
340	CD38	20e red brn	17.50	7.50
		Nos. 323-340 (18)	44.20	20.60

Cola Nuts
A13

U.P.U. Symbols
A14

1948 Lithographed ***Perf 14½***

Designs: 10c, Breadfruit. 30c, Annona. 50c, Cacao pods. 1e, Coffee. 1.75e, Dendem. 2e, Avocado. 5e, Pineapple. 10e, Mango. 20e, Coconuts.

341	A13	5c blk & yel	40	30
342	A13	10c blk & buff	50	35
343	A13	30c ind & gray	1.75	1.50
344	A13	50c brn & yel	1.75	1.50
345	A13	1e red & rose	3.75	2.00
346	A13	1.75e bl & gray	5.25	4.00
347	A13	2e blk & grn	4.00	2.50
348	A13	5e brn & lil rose	1.00	7.50
349	A13	10e blk & pink	14.00	12.50
350	A13	20e blk & gray	45.00	25.00
a.		Sheet of ten	100.00	100.00
		Nos. 341-350 (10)	77.40	57.15

No. 350a measures 149x136 mm., and contains one each of Nos. 341 to 350. Marginal inscriptions in black. The sheet sold for 42.50 escudos.

Lady of Fatima Issue.

Common Design Type

1948, Dec. **Unwmkd.**

351	CD40	50c purple	5.50	5.00

Visit of the statue of Our Lady of Fatima.

U. P. U. Issue.

1949 ***Perf. 14.*** **Unwmkd.**

352	A14	3.50e blk & gray	8.50	6.00

Universal Postal Union, 75th anniversary.

Holy Year Issue.

Common Design Types

1950 ***Perf. 13x13½.***

353	CD41	2.50e blue	3.00	1.75
354	CD42	4e orange	5.50	4.50

Holy Year Extension Issue.

Common Design Type

1951 ***Perf. 14.***

355	CD43	4e ind & bl gray	2.75	2.00

Extension of the Holy Year into 1951.

Medical Congress Issue.

Common Design Type

Design: Clinic.

1952 ***Perf. 13½.***

356	CD44	10c choc & bl	40	30

National Congress of Tropical Medicine, Lisbon.

ST. THOMAS AND PRINCE ISLANDS

| | João de Santarem A15 | Jeronymos Convent A16 |

Portraits: 30c, Pero Escobar. 50c, Fernao de Po Je, Alvaro Esteves. 2e, Lopo Goncalves. 3.50e, Martim Fernandes.

Lithographed.

1952   Perf. 14.   Unwmkd.

Centers Multicolored.

357	A15	10c cr & choc	10	6
358	A15	30c pale grn & dk grn	10	6
359	A15	50c gray & dk gray	10	6
360	A15	1e gray bl & dk bl	80	7
361	A15	2e lil gray & vio brn	60	15
362	A15	3.50e buff & choc	80	25
		Nos. 357-362 (6)	2.50	65

1953   Perf. 13x13½

363	A16	10c dk brn & gray	20	15
364	A16	50c brn org & org	75	40
365	A16	3e bl blk & gray blk	2.25	80

Exhibition of Sacred Missionary Art held at Lisbon in 1951.

Stamp Centenary Issue.

Stamp of Portugal and Arms of Colonies
A17

1953   Photogravure.   Perf. 13.

Stamp and Arms Multicolored.

| 366 | A17 | 50c buff & org brn | 80 | 60 |

Centenary of Portugal's first postage stamps.

Presidential Visit Issue

Map and Plane
A18

Typographed and Lithographed

1954   Perf. 13½

| 367 | A18 | 15c blk, bl, red & grn | 25 | 20 |
| 368 | A18 | 5c brn, grn & red | 1.25 | 80 |

Visit of Pres. Francisco H. C. Lopes.

Sao Paulo Issue
Common Design Type

1954   Lithographed

| 369 | CD46 | 2.50e bl, gray bl & blk | 70 | 35 |

Sao Paulo, 400th anniversary.

Brussels Fair Issue

Fair Emblem, Globe and Arms—A19

1958   Perf. 12x11½   Unwmkd.

| 370 | A19 | 2.50e multi | 85 | 60 |

World's Fair at Brussels.

Tropical Medicine Congress Issue
Common Design Type

Design: Cassia occidentalis.

1958   Perf. 13½

| 371 | CD47 | 5e pale grn, brn, yel, grn & red | 2.50 | 1.75 |

6th International Congress of Tropical Medicine and Malaria, Lisbon, Sept. 1958.

| Compass Rose A20 | Going to Church A21 |

1960   Lithographed   Perf. 13½

| 372 | A20 | 10e gray & multi | 1.00 | 50 |

Issued to commemorate the 500th anniversary of the death of Prince Henry the Navigator.

1960   Perf. 14½

| 373 | A21 | 1.50e multi | 50 | 30 |

Issued to commemorate the 10th anniversary of the Commission for Technical Co-operation in Africa South of the Sahara (C.C.T.A.).

Sports Issue
Common Design Type

Sports: 50c, Angling. 1e, Gymnast on rings. 1.50e, Handball. 2e, Sailing. 2.50e, Sprinting. 20e, Skin diving.

1962, Jan. 18   Litho.   Perf. 13½

Multicolored Design

374	CD48	50c gray grn	5	5
a.		"$50 CORREIOS" omitted		
375	CD48	1e lt lil	75	25
376	CD48	1.50e salmon	40	25
377	CD48	2e blue	80	40
378	CD48	2.50e gray grn	1.00	60
379	CD48	20e dk bl	2.75	2.00
		Nos. 374-379 (6)	5.75	3.55

On No. 374a, the blue impression, including imprint, is missing.

Anti-Malaria Issue
Common Design Type

Design: Anopheles gambiae.

1962   Perf. 13½   Unwmkd.

| 380 | CD49 | 2.50e multi | 1.15 | 80 |

Issued for the World Health Organization drive to eradicate malaria.

Airline Anniversary Issue
Common Design Type

1963   Perf. 14½   Unwmkd.

| 381 | CD50 | 1.50e pale bl & multi | 60 | 50 |

Issued to commemorate the 10th anniversary of Transportes Aéreos Portugueses.

National Overseas Bank Issue
Common Design Type

Design: 2.50e, Francisco de Oliveira Chamico.

1964, May 16   Perf. 13½

| 382 | CD51 | 2.50e multi | 70 | 50 |

Issued to commemorate the centenary of the National Overseas Bank of Portugal.

ITU Issue
Common Design Type

1965, May 17   Litho.   Perf. 14½

| 383 | CD52 | 2.50e tan & multi | 1.50 | 1.00 |

Issued to commemorate the centenary of the International Telecommunication Union.

Infantry Officer, 1788
A22

Designs: 35c, Sergeant with lance, 1788. 40c, Corporal with pike, 1788. 1e, Private with musket, 1788. 2.50e, Artillery officer, 1806. 5e, Private, 1811. 7.50e, Private, 1833. 10e, Lancer officer, 1834.

1965, Aug. 24   Litho.   Perf. 13½

384	A22	20c multi	20	15
385	A22	35c multi	20	15
386	A22	40c multi	25	20
387	A22	1e multi	1.25	60
388	A22	2.50e multi	1.25	60
389	A22	5e multi	2.00	1.50
390	A22	7.50e multi	2.50	2.25
391	A22	10e multi	3.00	2.50
		Nos. 384-391 (8)	10.65	7.95

National Revolution Issue
Common Design Type

Design: 4e, Arts and Crafts School and Anti-Tuberculosis Dispensary.

1966, May 28   Litho.   Perf. 11½

| 392 | CD53 | 4e multi | 75 | 50 |

40th anniversary of National Revolution.

Navy Club Issue
Common Design Type

Designs: 1.50e, Capt. Campos Rodrigues and ironclad corvette Vasco da Gama. 2.50e, Dr. Aires Kopke, microscope and tsetse fly.

1967, Jan. 31   Litho.   Perf. 13

| 393 | CD54 | 1.50e multi | 80 | 50 |
| 394 | CD54 | 2.50e multi | 1.25 | 75 |

Centenary of Portugal's Navy Club.

| Valinhos Shrine, Children and Apparition A23 | Cabral Medal, from St. Jerome's Convent A24 |

1967, May 13   Litho.   Perf. 12½x13

| 395 | A23 | 2.50e multi | 30 | 25 |

Issued to commemorate the 50th anniversary of the apparition of the Virgin Mary to 3 shepherd children, Lucia dos Santos, Francisco and Jacinta Marto, at Fatima.

Cabral Issue

1968, Apr. 22   Litho.   Perf. 14

| 396 | A24 | 1.50e bl & multi | 40 | 30 |

500th anniversary of the birth of Pedro Alvares Cabral, navigator who took possession of Brazil for Portugal.

Admiral Coutinho Issue
Common Design Type

Design: 2e, Adm. Coutinho, Gago Coutinho Island and monument (vert.).

1969, Feb. 17   Litho.   Perf. 14

| 397 | CD55 | 2e multi | 50 | 35 |

| Vasco da Gama's Fleet A25 | Manuel Portal of Guarda Episcopal See A26 |

Vasco da Gama Issue

1969, Aug. 29   Litho.   Perf. 14

| 398 | A25 | 2.50e multi | 75 | 50 |

Issued to commemorate the 500th anniversary of the birth of Vasco da Gama (1469-1524), navigator.

Administration Reform Issue
Common Design Type

1969, Sept. 25   Litho.   Perf. 14

| 399 | CD56 | 2.50e multi | 50 | 35 |

King Manuel I Issue

1969, Dec. 1   Litho.   Perf. 14

| 400 | A26 | 4e multi | 65 | 35 |

Issued to commemorate the 500th anniversary of the birth of King Manuel I.

| Pero Escobar, João de Santarem and Map of Islands A27 | Pres. Américo Rodrigues Thomaz A28 |

1970, Jan. 25   Litho.   Perf. 14

| 401 | A27 | 2.50e lt bl & multi | 35 | 30 |

Issued to commemorate the 500th anniversary of the discovery of St. Thomas and Prince Islands.

1970   Lithographed   Perf. 12½

| 402 | A28 | 2.50e multi | 35 | 30 |

Issued to commemorate the visit of President Américo Rodrigues Thomaz of Portugal.

Marshal Carmona Issue
Common Design Type

Design: 5e, Antonio Oscar Carmona in dress uniform.

1970, Nov. 15   Litho.   Perf. 14

| 403 | CD57 | 5e multi | 75 | 55 |

Birth centenary of Marshal Antonio Oscar Carmona de Fragoso (1869-1951), president of Portugal.

Coffee Plant and Stamps
A29

Designs: 1.50e, Postal Administration Building and stamp No. 1 (horiz.). 2.50e, Cathedral of St. Thomas and stamp No. 2.

1970, Dec.   Perf. 13½

404	A29	1e multi	20	10
405	A29	1.50e multi	30	15
406	A29	2.50e multi	50	20

Centenary of St. Thomas and Prince Islands postage stamps.

ST. THOMAS AND PRINCE ISLANDS

Lusiads Issue

Descent from the Cross
A30

1972, May 25   Litho.   Perf. 13

| 407 | A30 | 20e lil & multi | 2.00 | 1.75 |

4th centenary of publication of The Lusiads by Luiz Camoëns.

Olympic Games Issue
Common Design Type

Design: 1.50e, Track and javelin, Olympic emblem.

1972, June 20   Perf. 14x13½

| 408 | CD59 | 1.50e multi | 35 | 25 |

20th Olympic Games, Munich, Aug. 26–Sept. 11.

Lisbon-Rio de Janeiro Flight Issue
Common Design Type

Design: 2.50e, "Lusitania" flying over warship at St. Peter Rocks.

1972, Sept. 20   Litho.   Perf. 13½

| 409 | CD60 | 2.50e multi | 35 | 25 |

WMO Centenary Issue
Common Design Type

1973, Dec. 15   Litho.   Perf. 13

| 410 | CD61 | 5e dl grn & multi | 60 | 50 |

Centenary of international meteorological cooperation.

Republic

Flags of Portugal and St. Thomas & Prince
A31

1975, July 12   Litho.   Perf. 13½

411	A31	3e gray & multi	40	40
412	A31	10e yel & multi	1.00	30
413	A31	20e lt bl & multi	2.00	50
414	A31	50e sal & multi	3.50	2.25

Argel Agreement, granting independence, Argel, Sept. 26, 1974.

Man and Woman with St. Thomas & Prince Flag
A32

1975, Dec. 21

415	A32	1.50e pink & multi	15	10
416	A32	4e multi	40	20
417	A32	7.50e org & multi	75	40
418	A32	20e bl & multi	1.75	1.00
419	A32	50e ocher & multi	4.00	2.00
		Nos. 415-419 (5)	7.05	3.70

Proclamation of Independence, Dec. 7, 1975.

Chart and Hand
A33

1975, Dec. 21   Litho.   Perf. 13½

420	A33	1e ocher & multi	16	10
421	A33	1.50e multi	20	12
422	A33	2.50e org & multi	30	15

National Reconstruction Fund.

✱✱✱✱✱✱✱✱✱✱✱✱

Stamps of 1952–1973 Overprinted

Rep. Democr.

12-7-75

Lithographed

1977   Perf. 13½, 14, 13

423	A15	10c multi (#357)		
424	A22	20c multi (#384)		
425	A15	30c multi (#358)		
426	A22	35c multi (#385)		
427	A22	40c multi (#386)		
428	A15	50c multi (#359)		
429	A15	1e multi (#360)		
430	CD56	2.50e multi (#399)		
431	A27	2.50e multi (#401)		
432	A15	3.50e multi (#362)		
433	A26	4e multi (#400)		
434	CD61	5e multi (#410)		
435	A22	7.50e multi (#390)		
436	A20	10e multi (#372)		
		Nos. 423-436 (14)	12.50	

The 10c, 30c, 50c, 1e, 3.50e, 10e issued with glassine interleaving stuck to back.

Pres. Manuel Pinto da Costa and Flag
A34

Designs: 3.50e, 4.50e, Portuguese Governor handing over power. 12.50e, like 2e.

1977, Jan.   Perf. 13½

437	A34	2e yel & multi	20	10
438	A34	3.50e bl & multi	25	12
439	A34	4.50e red & multi	35	15
440	A34	12.50e multi	90	35

1st anniversary of independence.

Pairs of Nos. 358–359, 357, 362, 384–386 Overprinted Alternately in Black

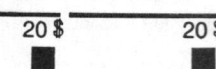

a   *b*

1977, Oct. 19   Litho.   Perf. 14, 13½

442	A15 (a)	3e on 30c multi		
443	A15 (b)	3e on 30c multi		
444	A15 (a)	5e on 50c multi		
445	A15 (b)	5e on 50c multi		
446	A15 (a)	10e on 10c multi		
447	A15 (b)	10e on 10c multi		
448	A15 (a)	15e on 3.50e multi		
449	A15 (b)	15e on 3.50e multi		
450	A22 (a)	20e on 20c multi		
451	A22 (b)	20e on 20c multi		
452	A22 (a)	35e on 35c multi		
453	A22 (b)	35e on 35c multi		
454	A22 (a)	40e on 40c multi		
455	A22 (b)	40e on 40c multi		
		Nos. 442-455 (14)		

Centenary of membership in Universal Postal Union. Overprints "a" and "b" alternate in sheets. Nos. 442–449 issued with glassine interleaving stuck to back.

These overprints exist in red on Nos. 444–445, 450–455, and on 1e on 10c, 3.50e and 30e on 30c.

Mao Tse-tung
A36

1977, Dec.   Litho.   Perf. 13½x14

| 461 | A36 | 50d multi | 4.00 | |
| a. | | Souvenir sheet | 4.50 | |

Mao Tse-tung (1893–1976), Chairman, People's Republic of China, first death anniversary. No. 461a contains one stamp, multicolored margin shows Chinese painting of tree, bird and insect. Size: 135x115 mm.

Lenin
A37

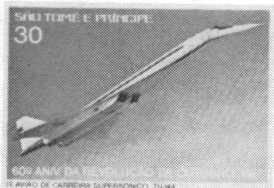

Russian Supersonic Plane—A38

Designs: 40d, Rowing crew. 50d, Cosmonaut Yuri A. Gagarin.

1977, Dec.   Perf. 13½x14, 14x13½

462	A37	15d multi	75	
463	A38	30d multi	1.50	
464	A38	40d multi	2.00	
465	A37	50d red & blk	2.50	

60th anniversary of Russian October Revolution.

Flag of St. Thomas and Prince Islands—A39

Designs: Nos. 479, 479a, Map of Islands (vert.). No. 480, Coat of arms (vert.).

Perf. 14x13½, 13½x14

1978, July 12

478	A39	5d multi	40	
479	A39	5d multi	40	
a.		Souvenir sheet, 50d	4.25	
480	A39	5d multi	40	

Third anniversary of independence. Nos. 478–480 printed se-tenant in sheets of 9. No. 479a contains one imperf. stamp; multicolored margin shows map of Gulf of Guinea, flags and coat of arms. Size: 122x134mm.

ST. THOMAS AND PRINCE ISLANDS

AIR POST STAMPS.
Common Design Type
Inscribed "S. Tomé".

1938   *Perf. 13½x13*
Name and Value in Black.

C1	CD39	10c scarlet	70.00	70.00
C2	CD39	20c purple	40.00	40.00
C3	CD39	50c orange	1.75	1.50
C4	CD39	1e ultra	3.00	2.25
C5	CD39	2e lil brn	4.25	3.50
C6	CD39	3e dk grn	6.50	4.50
C7	CD39	5e red brn	8.50	8.50
C8	CD39	9e rose car	8.50	8.50
C9	CD39	10e magenta	8.50	8.50
	Nos. C1-C9 (9)		151.00	147.25

Common Design Type
Inscribed "S. Tomé e Principe".

1939   Engraved.   Unwmkd.
Name and Value Typo. in Black.

C10	CD39	10c scarlet	40	40
C11	CD39	20c purple	40	40
C12	CD39	50c orange	40	40
C13	CD39	1e dp ultra	40	40
C14	CD39	2e lil brn	1.50	1.25
C15	CD39	3e dk grn	2.00	1.75
C16	CD39	5e red brn	3.75	2.50
C17	CD39	9e rose car	6.00	3.75
C18	CD39	10e magenta	6.00	3.75
	Nos. C10-C18 (9)		20.85	14.60

No. C16 exists with overprint "Exposicao Internacional de Nova York, 1939-1940" and Trylon and Perisphere.

POSTAGE DUE STAMPS.

D1   "S. Thomé"

1904   Typographed.   Perf. 12.   Unwmkd.

J1	D1	5r yel grn	75	75
J2	D1	10r slate	1.00	1.00
J3	D1	20r yel brn	1.00	1.00
J4	D1	30r orange	1.00	1.00
J5	D1	50r gray brn	2.00	2.00
J6	D1	60r red brn	2.25	2.25
J7	D1	100r red lil	3.00	3.00
J8	D1	130r dl bl	4.50	4.50
J9	D1	200r carmine	4.50	4.50
J10	D1	500r gray vio	6.50	6.50
	Nos. J1-J10 (10)		26.50	26.50

Overprinted in Carmine or Green

1911

J11	D1	5r yel grn	20	20
J12	D1	10r slate	20	20
J13	D1	20r yel brn	20	20
J14	D1	30r orange	25	25
J15	D1	50r gray brn	25	25
J16	D1	60r red brn	65	65
J17	D1	100r red lil	80	80
J18	D1	130r dl bl	80	80
J19	D1	200r car (G)	80	80
J20	D1	500r gray vio	1.00	1.00
	Nos. J11-J20 (10)		5.10	5.10

Nos. J1-J10
Overprinted in Black

1913   Without Gum

J21	D1	5r yel grn	3.00	3.00
J22	D1	10r slate	4.00	4.00
J23	D1	20r yel brn	3.00	3.00
J24	D1	30r orange	3.00	3.00
J25	D1	50r gray brn	3.00	3.00
J26	D1	60r red brn	3.75	3.75
J27	D1	100r red lil	6.00	6.00
J28	D1	130r dl bl	15.00	15.00
a.		Inverted overprint		
J29	D1	200r carmine	22.50	20.00
J30	D1	500r gray vio	30.00	22.50
	Nos. J21-J30 (10)		93.25	83.25

Nos. J1-J10
Overprinted in Black

1913   Without Gum

J31	D1	5r yel grn	3.50	3.50
a.		Inverted overprint		
J32	D1	10r slate	2.00	2.00
J33	D1	20r yel brn	2.00	2.00
J34	D1	30r orange	2.00	2.00
a.		Inverted overprint		
J35	D1	50r gray brn	3.50	3.50
J36	D1	60r red brn	3.50	3.50
J37	D1	100r red lil	3.50	3.50
J38	D1	130r dl bl	3.50	3.50
J39	D1	200r carmine	4.50	4.50
J40	D1	500r gray vio	12.50	12.50
	Nos. J31-J40 (10)		40.50	40.50

No. J5 Overprinted "Republica" in Italic Capitals like Regular Issue in Green

1920   Without Gum

J41	D1	50r gray brn	40.00	40.00

D2   "S. Tomé"

1921   Typographed.   *Perf. 11½.*

J42	D2	½c yel grn	18	15
J43	D2	1c slate	18	15
J44	D2	2c org brn	18	15
J45	D2	3c orange	18	15
J46	D2	5c gray brn	18	15
J47	D2	6c lt brn	18	15
J48	D2	10c red vio	18	15
J49	D2	13c dl bl	30	20
J50	D2	20c carmine	30	30
J51	D2	50c gray	40	40
	Nos. J42-J51 (10)		2.26	1.95

In each sheet one stamp is inscribed "S. Thomé" instead of "S. Tomé." Price, set of 10, $60.

Common Design Type
Photogravure and Typographed

1952   *Perf. 14.*   Unwmkd.
Numeral in Red, Frame Multicolored

J52	CD45	10c chocolate	10	10
J53	CD45	30c red brn	10	10
J54	CD45	50c dk bl	10	10
J55	CD45	1e dk bl	25	25
J56	CD45	2e ol grn	60	60
J57	CD45	5e blk brn	1.25	1.25
	Nos. J52-J57 (6)		2.40	2.40

NEWSPAPER STAMPS.

N1   N2

Perf. 11½, 12½ and 13½.

1892   Without Gum   Unwmkd.
Black Surcharge.

P1	N1	2½r on 10r grn	45.00	35.00
P2	N1	2½r on 20r rose	55.00	35.00
P3	N2	2½r on 10r grn	55.00	40.00
P4	N2	2½r on 20r rose	55.00	40.00

Green Surcharge.

P5	N1	2½r on 5r blk	42.50	30.00
P6	N1	2½r on 20r rose	55.00	35.00
P7	N1	2½r on 5r blk	80.00	40.00
P8	N2	2½r on 20r rose	55.00	40.00
P9	N2	2½r on 10r grn	55.00	40.00
P10	N2	2½r on 20r rose	65.00	50.00

Both surcharges exist on No. 18 in green.

N3   d

1893   Typographed   *Perf. 11½, 13½*

P12	N3	2½r brown	60	50

No. P12 Overprinted Type "d" in Blue

1899   Without Gum

P13	N3	2½r brown	30.00	12.50

POSTAL TAX STAMPS.
Pombal Issue.
Common Design Types

1925   *Perf. 12½.*   Unwmkd.

RA1	CD28	15c org & blk	60	60
RA2	CD29	15c org & blk	60	60
RA3	CD30	15c org & blk	60	60

Certain revenue stamps (5e, 6e, 7e, 8e and other denominations) were surcharged in 1946 "Assistencia", 2 bars and new values (1e or 1.50e) and used as postal tax stamps.

PT1

1948-58   Typographed   *Perf. 12x11½*   Unwmkd.
Denomination in Black.

RA4	PT1	50c yel grn	3.00	3.00
RA5	PT1	1e car rose	4.50	4.50
RA6	PT1	1e emer ('58)	3.00	3.00
RA7	PT1	1.50e bis brn	4.50	4.50

Denominations of 2e and up were issued only for revenue purposes. No. RA6 lacks "Colonia de" below coat of arms.

Type of 1958 Surcharged

um escudo
Um escudo
1$00   1$00

   m   n

1964-65   Typo.   *Perf. 12x11½*

RA8	PT1 (m)	1e on 5e org yel	10.00	10.00
RA9	PT1 (n)	1e on 5e org yel ('65)	4.50	4.50

The basic 5e orange yellow does not carry the words "Colonia de."

No. RA6 Surcharged: "Um escudo"

1$00

1965

RA10	PT1	1e emerald	2.50	2.50

Type of 1948 Surcharged

Um ESCUDO

1965   Typographed   *Perf. 12x11½*

RA11	PT1	1e emerald	50	50

POSTAL TAX DUE STAMPS.
Pombal Issue.
Common Design Types

1925   *Perf. 12½.*   Unwmkd.

RAJ1	CD31	30c org & blk	75	75
RAJ2	CD32	30c org & blk	75	75
RAJ3	CD33	30c org & blk	75	75

Want more information from an advertiser? Use the handy Reader Service Card in back of the yellow pages.

For all your Philatelic needs, see the yellow pages.

SALVADOR, EL

(ĕl säl'vä·thôr' ; säl'vȧ·dôr)

LOCATION—On the Pacific Coast of Central America, between Guatemala, Honduras and the Gulf of Fonseca.
GOVT.—Republic.
AREA—8,236 sq. mi.
POP.—4,120,000 (est. 1976).
CAPITAL—San Salvador.

8 Reales = 100 Centavos = 1 Peso
100 Centavos = 1 Colón

Volcano San Miguel
A1

Engraved

		1867	Perf. 12	Unwmkd.	
1	A1	½r blue		1.25	1.50
2	A1	1r red		1.25	1.25
3	A1	2r green		3.00	4.00
4	A1	4r bister		7.00	6.00

Nos. 1 to 4 when overprinted "Contra Sello" and shield with 14 stars, are telegraph stamps.

Nos. 1–4
Handstamped

1874

5	A1	½r blue	10.00	7.00
6	A1	1r red	10.00	7.00
7	A1	2r green	10.00	7.00
8	A1	4r bister	37.50	35.00

Nos. 1–4
Handstamped

9	A1	½r blue	5.00	4.00
10	A1	1r red	5.00	4.00
11	A1	2r green	5.00	4.00
12	A1	4r bister	15.00	12.50

The overprints on Nos. 5–12 exist double. Counterfeits are plentiful.

Coat of Arms
A2   A3

A4   A5

A6

1879 Lithographed. Perf. 12½

13	A2	1c green	2.25	1.75
a.		Inverted "V" for second "A" in "SALVADOR"		
b.		Inverted "V" for "A" in "REPUBLICA"	4.00	3.50
c.		Inverted "V" for "A" in "UNIVERSAL"	3.00	3.50
			3.00	3.50
14	A3	2c rose	3.50	3.00
a.		Inverted scroll in upper left corner	10.00	8.00
15	A4	5c blue	6.00	2.50
a.		5c ultra	11.00	8.00
16	A5	10c black	12.50	7.00
17	A6	20c violet	30.00	20.00
		Nos. 13-17 (5)	54.25	34.25

There are fifteen varieties of the 1c and 2c, twenty-five of the 5c and five each of the 10 and 20c.
In 1881 the 1c, 2c and 5c were redrawn, the 1c in fifteen varieties and the 2c and 5c in five varieties each.
These stamps, when overprinted "Contra sello" and arms, are telegraph stamps.

Allegorical Figure   Volcano
of El Salvador
A7   A8

1887 Engraved. Perf. 12.

18	A7	3c brown	75	35
a.		Imperf. pair	5.00	5.00
19	A8	10c orange	5.00	1.75

El Salvador
A9

1888   *Rouletted.*

| 20 | A9 | 5c dp bl | 60 | 50 |

A10   A11

1889   Perf. 12

21	A10	1c green	25	
22	A10	2c scarlet	25	
23	A11	1c green	60	50
24	A11	2c scarlet	60	

Nos. 21, 22 and 24 were never placed in use.

A12

Type I, thick numerals, heavy serifs.
Type II, thin numerals, straight serifs.

25	A12	1c on 3c brn, type II	1.25	75
a.		Double surcharge	3.00	
b.		Triple surcharge	7.00	
c.		Type I	1.25	

The 1c on 2c scarlet is bogus.

Handstamped 1889.

1889

Violet Handstamp.

25D	A2	1c green	25.00	25.00
25E	A6	20c violet	60.00	60.00
26	A11	1c green	2.00	1.75
26C	A12	1c on 3c brn	40.00	40.00
27	A7	3c brown	2.00	1.75
28	A8	10c orange	10.00	8.00

Black Handstamp.

28A	A2	1c green	30.00	27.50
28B	A3	2c rose	35.00	35.00
28C	A6	20c violet	60.00	60.00
29	A11	1c green	1.75	1.50
30	A7	3c brown	2.00	1.75
31	A12	1c on 3c brn	35.00	35.00
32	A8	10c orange	9.00	7.00

Rouletted.
Black Handstamp.

| 35 | A9 | 5c dp bl | 1.75 | 1.50 |

Violet Handstamp.

| 36 | A9 | 5c dp bl | 1.75 | 1.50 |

The 1889 handstamps as usual, are found double, inverted, etc. Counterfeits are plentiful.

A13   A14

1890   Engraved   Perf. 12

38	A13	1c green	25	25
39	A13	2c bis brn	25	25
40	A13	3c yellow	25	25
41	A13	5c blue	25	25
42	A13	10c violet	25	25
43	A13	20c orange	25	40
44	A13	25c red	25	60
45	A13	50c claret	25	1.25
46	A13	1p carmine	25	3.00
		Nos. 38-46 (9)	2.25	6.50

The issues of 1890 to 1898 inclusive were printed by the Hamilton Bank Note Co., New York, to the order of N. F. Seebeck, who held a contract for stamps with the government of El Salvador. This contract gave the right to make reprints of the stamps and such were subsequently made in some instances, as will be found noted in italic type.
Used prices of 1890–1898 issues are for stamps with genuine cancellations applied while the stamps were valid. Various counterfeit cancellations exist.

1891

47	A14	1c vermilion	25	25
48	A14	2c yel grn	25	25
49	A14	3c violet	25	25
50	A14	5c car lake	25	25
51	A14	10c blue	25	25
52	A14	11c violet	25	25
53	A14	20c green	25	65
54	A14	25c yel brn	25	75
55	A14	50c dk bl	25	1.75
56	A14	1p dk brn	25	3.00
		Nos. 47-56 (10)	2.50	7.65

Nos. 47 and 56 have been reprinted in thick toned paper with dark gum.

A15

Nos. 48, 49 Surcharged in Black or Violet:

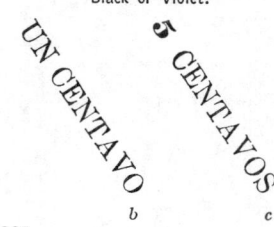

b   c

1891

57	A15	1c on 2c yel grn	4.00	3.50
a.		Inverted surch.	6.00	
58	A14 (b)	1c on 2c yel grn	3.00	2.75
59	A14 (c)	5c on 3c vio	7.00	6.00

Landing of Columbus
A18

1892   Engraved

60	A18	1c bl grn	25	25
61	A18	2c org brn	25	25
62	A18	3c ultra	25	25
63	A18	5c gray	25	25
64	A18	10c vermilion	25	25
65	A18	11c brown	25	75
66	A18	20c orange	25	75
67	A18	25c maroon	25	90
68	A18	50c yellow	25	1.75
69	A18	1p car lake	25	2.50
		Nos. 60-69 (10)	2.50	7.90

Issued to commemorate the 400th anniversary of the discovery of America by Columbus.

A19   A20

Surcharged in Black, Red or Yellow.

1892

70	A19	1c on 5c gray (Bk) (down)	1.50	1.25
a.		Surcharge reading up	2.50	2.25
72	A19	1c on 5c gray (R) (up)	1.50	1.25
a.		Surcharge reading down		
73	A20	1c on 20c org (Bk)	1.75	1.50
a.		Inverted surcharge	5.00	5.00
b.		"V" of "CENTAVO" inverted	5.00	5.00

Similar Surcharge in Yellow or Blue, "centavo" in lower case letters.

74	A20	1c on 25c mar (Y)	3.00	2.00
a.		Inverted surcharge	5.00	5.00
75	A20	1c on 25c mar (Bl)	300.00	300.00
a.		Double surcharge (Bl + Bk)	350.00	350.00

Counterfeits exist of Nos. 75 and 75a.

Gen.
Carlos
Ezeta
A21

1893   Engraved

76	A21	1c blue	25	25
77	A21	2c brn red	25	25
78	A21	3c purple	25	25
79	A21	5c dp brn	25	25

80	A21	10c org brn	25	25
81	A21	11c vermilion	25	*45*
82	A21	20c green	25	*55*
83	A21	25c dk ol gray	25	*75*
84	A21	50c red org	25	*1.00*
85	A21	1p black	25	*1.50*
		Nos. 76-85 (10)	2.50	*5.50*

Founding City of Isabela
A22

Columbus Statue, Genoa
A23

Departure from Palos
A24

1893

86	A22	2p green	1.50
87	A23	5p violet	1.50
88	A24	10p orange	1.50

Nos. 86 to 88 commemorated the discoveries by Columbus. No. 86 is known on cover, but experts are not positive that Nos. 87 and 88 were postally used.

No. 77 Surcharged "UN CENTAVO"

1893

89	A21	1c on 2c brn red	1.00	85
a.		"CENTNVO"	6.00	6.00

Liberty
A26

Columbus before Council of Salamanca
A27

Columbus Protecting Indian Hostages
A28

Columbus Received by Ferdinand and Isabella
A29

1894, Jan.

91	A26	1c brown	25	25
92	A26	2c blue	25	25
93	A26	3c maroon	25	25
94	A26	5c org brn	25	25
95	A26	10c violet	25	25
96	A26	11c vermilion	25	*50*
97	A26	20c dk bl	25	*65*
98	A26	25c orange	25	*75*
99	A26	50c black	25	*1.25*
100	A26	1p sl bl	25	*1.75*
101	A27	2p dp bl	1.50	
102	A28	5p car lake	1.50	
103	A29	10p dp brn	1.50	
		Nos. 91-103 (13)	7.00	

Nos. 101 to 103 commemorated the discoveries by Columbus. Experts are not positive that these were postally used.

Liberty
A30

Coat of Arms
A31

1894, Dec.

104	A30	1c on 11c ver	2.00	1.25
a.		"Ccntavo"	4.00	4.00
b.		Double surcharge		

Arms Overprint in Second Color.

Various Frames

1895, Jan. 1

105	A31	1c ol & grn	25	25
106	A31	2c dk grn & bl	25	25
a.		2c dk grn & grn	1.50	1.20
107	A31	3c brn & brn	25	25
108	A31	5c bl & brn	25	25
109	A31	10c org & brn	25	*35*
110	A31	12c mag & brn	25	*60*
111	A31	15c ver & ver	25	*70*
112	A31	20c yel & brn	25	*85*
a.		Inverted overprint	3.00	
113	A31	24c vio & brn	*20*	*90*
114	A31	30c dp bl & bl	25	*1.00*
115	A31	50c car & brn	25	*1.25*
116	A31	1p blk & brn	25	*1.75*
		Nos. 105-116 (12)	*2.95*	*8.40*

As printed, Nos. 105–116 portrayed Pres. Antonio Ezeta, brother of Gen. Carlos Ezeta. Before issuance, Ezeta's overthrow caused the government to obliterate his features with the national arms overprint. The stamps exist without overprint. Price 15c each.

Reprints of 2c are in dark yellow green on thick paper. Price 15 cents.

Coat of Arms
A32

1895 Engraved. *Perf. 12*

117	A32	1c olive	85	1.00
118	A32	2c dk bl grn	30	25
119	A32	3c brown	30	25
120	A32	5c blue	30	25
121	A32	10c orange	1.25	60
122	A32	12c claret	1.25	60
123	A32	15c vermilion	25	*60*
124	A32	20c dp grn	35	*1.00*
125	A32	24c violet	35	*1.00*
126	A32	30c dp bl	25	*90*
127	A32	50c car lake	2.00	*2.50*
128	A32	1p gray blk	2.50	*3.50*
		Nos. 117-128 (12)	9.95	*12.45*

The reprints are on thicker paper than the originals, and many of the shades differ. Price 15c each.

Nos. 122, 124–126 Surcharged in Black or Red:

UN

centavo

"Peace"
A45

1895

129	A32	1c on 12c cl (Bk)	2.00	1.75
130	A32	1c on 24c vio	2.00	1.75
131	A32	1c on 30c dp bl	2.00	1.75
132	A32	2c on 20c dp grn	2.00	1.75
133	A32	3c on 30c dp bl	2.50	2.25
a.		Double surcharge	9.00	
		Nos. 129-133 (5)	10.50	9.25

1896, Jan. 1 Engr. Unwmkd.

134	A45	1c blue	25	25
135	A45	2c dk brn	25	25
136	A45	3c bl grn	25	30
137	A45	5c brn ol	25	25
138	A45	10c yellow	25	40
139	A45	12c dk bl	1.50	1.75
140	A45	15c bl vio	20	*40*
141	A45	20c magenta	1.25	1.00
142	A45	24c vermilion	25	*50*
143	A45	30c orange	25	*85*
144	A45	50c blk brn	25	*1.00*
145	A45	1p rose lake	25	*1.75*
		Nos. 134-145 (12)	5.20	*8.70*

The frames of Nos. 134 to 145 differ slightly on each denomination.

Wmk. 117

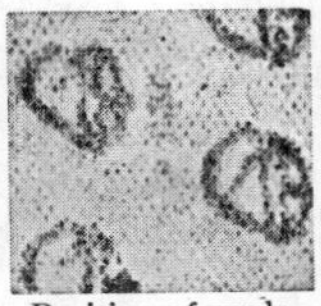

Position of wmk. on reprints

Wmkd. Liberty Cap. (117)

145B	A45	2c dk brn	25	25

The 1c, 2c, 12c, 20c, 30c, 50c and 1p on unwatermarked paper and the 2c on watermarked have been reprinted. The paper is thicker than that of the originals and the shades are different. The watermark is always upright on original stamps of Salvador, sideways on the reprints. Price 15c each.

Coat of Arms
A46

"White House"
A47

Locomotive
A48

Mt. San Miguel
A49

Ocean Steamship
A50 A51

Post Office
A52

Lake Ilopango
A53

Atehausillas Waterfall
A54

Coat of Arms
A55

Coat of Arms
A56

Columbus
A57

1896

146	A46	1c emerald	25	25
147	A47	2c lake	25	25
148	A48	3c yel brn	25	25
149	A49	5c dp bl	25	25
150	A50	10c brown	25	25
151	A51	12c slate	25	*30*
152	A52	15c bl grn	25	*50*
153	A53	20c car rose	25	*60*
154	A54	24c violet	*20*	*75*
155	A55	30c dp grn	25	75
156	A56	50c orange	25	*75*
157	A57	100c dk bl	25	*1.75*
		Nos. 146-157 (12)	*2.95*	*6.65*

Unwmkd.

157B	A46	1c emerald	25	25
157C	A47	2c lake	25	25
157D	A48	3c yel brn	25	25
157E	A49	5c dp bl	25	25
157F	A50	10c brown	35	35
157G	A51	12c slate	25	*35*
157I	A52	15c bl grn	45	*50*
157J	A53	20c car rose	25	*75*
157K	A54	24c violet	1.00	*1.75*
157M	A55	30c dp grn	25	*1.25*
157N	A56	50c orange	25	*1.25*
157O	A57	100c dk bl	25	*2.25*
		Nos. 157B-157O (12)	4.05	*9.45*

The 15c, 30c, 50c and 100c have been reprinted on watermarked and the 1c, 2c, 3c, 5c, 12c, 20c, 24c and 100c on unwatermarked paper. The papers of the reprints are thicker than those of the originals and the shades are different. Price 10c each.

A58

Black Surcharge on Nos. 154, 157K

1896 Wmk. 117

158	A58	15c on 24c vio	6.00	6.00
a.		Double surcharge		
b.		Inverted surch.	12.50	

Unwmkd.

158D	A58	15c on 24c vio	6.00	6.00

Types of 1896.

1897 Engraved Wmk. 117

159	A46	1c scarlet	25	25
160	A47	2c yel grn	25	25
161	A48	3c bis brn	25	25
162	A49	5c orange	25	25
163	A50	10c bl grn	25	25
164	A51	12c blue	85	60
165	A52	15c black	5.00	4.00
166	A53	20c slate	25	45
167	A54	24c yellow	25	50
168	A55	30c rose	25	40
169	A56	50c violet	35	1.00
170	A57	100c brn lake	5.00	4.00
		Nos. 159-170 (12)	13.20	12.20

Unwmkd.

170A	A46	1c scarlet	25	25
170B	A47	2c yel grn	25	25

170C	A48	3c bis brn	25	25
170D	A49	5c orange	25	25
170E	A50	10c bl grn	1.50	1.00
170F	A51	12c blue	1.50	1.50
170G	A52	15c black	4.00	4.00
170H	A53	20c slate	25	*50*
170I	A54	24c yellow	25	*1.00*
170J	A55	30c rose	3.75	2.50
170K	A56	50c violet	1.75	1.75
170L	A57	100c brn lake	12.50	12.50
		Nos. 170A-170L (12)	26.50	*25.75*

The 1c, 2c, 3c, 5c, 12c, 15c, 50c and 100c have been reprinted on watermarked and the entire issue on unwatermarked paper. The papers of the reprints are thicker than those of the originals. Price 10c each.

Surcharged in Red or Black **TRECE centavos**

1897 **Wmk. 117**

171	A54	13c on 24c yel (R)	5.00	4.50
172	A55	13c on 30c rose (Bk)	5.00	4.50
173	A56	13c on 50c vio (Bk)	5.00	4.50
174	A57	13c on 100c brn lake (Bk)	5.00	4.50

Unwmkd.

174A	A54	13c on 24c yel (R)	5.00	4.00
174B	A55	13c on 30c rose (Bk)	5.00	4.00
174C	A56	13c on 50c vio (Bk)	5.00	4.00

Coat of Arms of "Republic of Central America"
A59

ONE CENTAVO.

Originals: The mountains are outlined in red and blue. The sea is represented by short red and dark blue lines on a light blue background.

Reprints: The mountains are outlined in red only. The sea is printed in green and dark blue, much blurred.

FIVE CENTAVOS.

Originals: The sea is represented by horizontal and diagonal lines of dark blue on a light blue background.

Reprints: The sea is printed in green and dark blue, much blurred. The inscription in gold is in thicker letters.

1897 **Lithographed.**

175	A59	1c bl, gold, rose & grn	1.00	*2.00*
176	A59	5c rose, gold, bl & grn	1.00	*3.00*

Issued to commemorate the forming of the "Republic of Central America".

Stamps of type A59 formerly listed as "Type II" are now known to be reprints.

Allegory of Central American Union
A60

1898 **Engraved.** **Wmk. 117**

177	A60	1c org ver	25	25
178	A60	2c rose	25	25
179	A60	3c pale yel grn	25	25
180	A60	5c bl grn	20	20
181	A60	10c gray bl	25	25
182	A60	12c violet	30	40
183	A60	13c brn lake	25	25
184	A60	20c dp bl	25	*35*
185	A60	24c dp ultra	25	*45*
186	A60	26c bis brn	25	*60*
187	A60	50c orange	25	*1.25*
188	A60	1p yellow	25	*1.50*
		Nos. 177-188 (12)	3.00	*6.00*

The entire set has been reprinted on unwatermarked paper and all but the 12c and 20c on watermarked paper. The shades of the reprints are not the same as those of the originals, and the paper is thicker. Price 10c each.

No. 180 Overprinted Vertically, up or down in Black, Violet, Red, Magenta and Yellow **Transito Territorial**

1899

189	A60	5c bl grn (Bk)	15.00	12.50
a.		Italic 3rd "r" in "Territorial"	25.00	25.00
b.		Dbl. ovpt. (Bk + Y)	75.00	75.00
190	A60	5c bl grn (V)	*150.00*	*150.00*
191	A60	5c bl grn (R)	*125.00*	*125.00*
191A	A60	5c bl grn (M)	*125.00*	*125.00*
191B	A60	5c bl grn (Y)	*135.00*	*135.00*

Counterfeits exist.

Nos. 177–184 Overprinted in Black 

1899

192	A60	1c org ver	1.50	75
193	A60	2c rose	2.00	1.50
194	A60	3c pale yel grn	2.00	75
195	A60	5c bl grn	2.25	75
196	A60	10c gray bl	3.00	2.00
197	A60	12c violet	5.00	4.00
198	A60	13c brn lake	5.00	4.00
198A	A60	20c dp bl	150.00	125.00
		Nos. 192-198A (8)	170.75	138.75

Counterfeits exist of the "wheel" overprint used in 1899–1900.

Ceres ("Estado")
A61

Inscribed: "Estado de El Salvador".

Lithographed

1899 ***Perf. 12.*** **Unwmkd.**

199	A61	1c brown	20
200	A61	2c gray grn	20
201	A61	3c blue	20
202	A61	5c brn org	20
203	A61	10c chocolate	20
204	A61	12c dk grn	20
205	A61	13c dp rose	20
206	A61	24c lt bl	20
207	A61	26c car rose	20
208	A61	50c org red	20
209	A61	100c violet	20
		Nos. 199-209 (11)	2.20

Nos. 208–209 were probably not placed in use.

Same, Overprinted 

Red Overprint.

210	A61	1c brown	75.00	65.00

Blue Overprint.

211	A61	1c brown	75	30
212	A61	5c brn org	75	40
212A	A61	10c chocolate	10.00	7.00

Black Overprint.

213	A61	1c brown	75	30
214	A61	2c gray grn	1.00	25
215	A61	3c blue	1.00	35
216	A61	5c brn org	50	25
217	A61	10c chocolate	75	30
218	A61	12c dk grn	2.00	1.00
219	A61	13c dp rose	1.50	1.25
220	A61	24c lt bl	20.00	17.50
221	A61	26c car rose	5.00	4.00
222	A61	50c org red	5.00	4.00
223	A61	100c violet	5.00	4.00
		Nos. 213-223 (11)	42.50	33.20

No. 177 Handstamped **1900**

1900 **Wmk. 117**

224	A60	1c org ver	2.00	1.50

No. 177 Overprinted **1900**

225	A60	1c org ver	25.00	22.50

Stamps of 1898 Surcharged in Black **1900** **1 centavo**

1900

226	A60	1c on 10c gray bl	7.00	6.00
a.		Inverted surcharge	10.00	9.00
227	A60	1c on 13c brn lake	*400.00*	
228	A60	2c on 12c vio	27.50	20.00
a.		"eentavo"		
b.		Inverted surcharge		
c.		"centavos"	50.00	
d.		Same as "c", double surcharge		
e.		Vertical surcharge		
229	A60	2c on 13c brn lake	3.00	2.75
a.		"eentavo"	5.00	4.00
b.		Inverted surcharge	7.00	6.00
c.		"1900" omitted		
230	A60	2c on 20c dp bl	3.00	3.00
a.		Inverted surcharge	5.00	5.00
230B	A60	2c on 26c bis brn	*250.00*	*250.00*
231	A60	3c on 12c vio	*75.00*	*75.00*
a.		"eentavo"		
b.		Inverted surcharge	*70.00*	*70.00*
c.		Double surcharge		
232	A60	3c on 50c org	25.00	25.00
a.		Inverted surcharge	25.00	25.00
233	A60	5c on 12c vio		
234	A60	5c on 24c ultra	22.50	22.50
a.		"eentavo"		
b.		"centavos"	22.50	
235	A60	5c on 26c bis brn	*75.00*	*75.00*
a.		Inverted surcharge	*70.00*	*70.00*
236	A60	5c on 1p yel	30.00	30.00
a.		Inverted surcharge	30.00	30.00

With Additional Overprint in Black 

237	A60	2c on 12c vio	3.50	3.50
a.		Inverted surcharge	3.50	3.50
b.		"eentavo"	12.00	
c.		"centavos"		
d.		"1900" omitted		
237H	A60	2c on 13c brn lake		
238	A60	3c on 12c vio	85.00	85.00
a.		"eentavo"	70.00	70.00
239	A60	5c on 26c bis brn	125.00	125.00
a.		Inverted surcharge		

Vertical Surcharge. "Centavos" in the Plural.

240	A60	2c on 12c vio	175.00	175.00
b.		Without wheel		
240A	A60	5c on 24c dp ultra	175.00	175.00

With Additional Overprint in Black 

241	A60	5c on 12c vio	35.00	35.00
a.		Surcharge reading downward		

Counterfeits exist of the surcharges on Nos. 226–241 and the "wheel" overprint on Nos. 237–239, 241.

Same Surcharge on Stamps of 1898

Without Wheel.

1900 **Unwmkd.**

242	A61	1c on 13c dp rose	60	60
a.		Inverted surcharge	1.10	1.10
b.		"eentavo"	1.10	1.10
c.		"ecntavo"	1.75	1.10
d.		"1 centavo 1"	6.00	4.00
e.		Double surcharge		
243	A61	2c on 12c dk grn	2.50	2.50
a.		Inverted surcharge	3.50	3.50
b.		"eentavo"		
244	A61	2c on 13c dp rose	1.25	1.00
a.		"eentavo"	1.50	1.50
b.		"ecntavo"	1.75	1.75
c.		Inverted surcharge		
245	A61	3c on 12c dk grn	1.25	1.00
a.		Inverted surcharge	3.00	2.25
b.		"eentavo"	6.00	6.00
c.		Double surcharge	3.00	

With Additional Overprint in Black 

246	A61	1c on 2c gray grn	35	25
a.		"eentavo"	1.25	1.25
b.		Inverted surcharge	6.00	6.00
247	A61	1c on 13c dp rose	1.50	1.25
a.		"eentavo"	6.00	
b.		"1 centavo 1"		
248	A61	2c on 12c dk grn	2.00	1.50
a.		"eentavo"	6.00	
b.		Inverted surcharge	1.75	1.75
c.		Double surcharge	3.00	
249	A61	2c on 13c dp rose	85.00	
a.		"eentavo"		
b.		Double surcharge		
250	A61	3c on 12c dk grn	2.00	1.25
a.		Inverted surcharge	2.25	1.75
b.		"eentavo"	3.75	3.50
c.		Date double	6.00	
251	A61	5c on 24c lt bl	3.75	1.75
a.		"eentavo"	6.00	6.00
252	A61	5c on 26c car rose	1.50	1.25
a.		Inverted surcharge	6.00	3.50
b.		"eentavo"	2.50	2.25
252D	A61	5c on 1c on 26c car rose		
		Nos. 246-248, 250-252 (6)	11.10	7.25

Counterfeits exist of the surcharges on Nos. 242–252D and the "wheel" overprint on Nos. 246–252D.

Ceres ("Republica")
A63

There are two varieties of the 1c, type A63, one with the word "centavo" in the middle of the label, the other with "centavo" nearer the left end than the right.

The stamps of type A63 are found in a great variety of shades. Stamps of type A63 without handstamp were not regularly issued.

Handstamped in Violet or Black 

Inscribed: "Republica de El Salvador"

1900

253	A63	1c bl grn	25	25
a.		1c yel grn	25	25
254	A63	2c rose	35	25
255	A63	3c gray blk	25	25
256	A63	5c pale bl	75	50
a.		5c dp bl	75	50
257	A63	10c dp bl	85	60
258	A63	12c yel grn	85	60
259	A63	13c yel brn	75	60
260	A63	24c gray	6.00	5.00
261	A63	26c yel brn	2.50	2.25
262	A63	50c rose red	2.50	2.25
		Nos. 253-262 (10)	15.05	12.55

Handstamped in Violet or Black 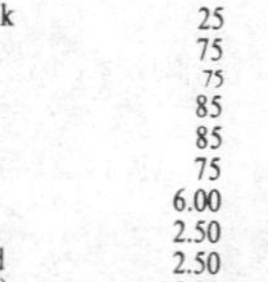

263	A63	1c lt grn	2.25	1.50
264	A63	2c pale rose	2.25	75
265	A63	3c gray blk	2.25	75
266	A63	5c sl bl	2.25	50
267	A63	10c dp bl	100.00	85.00
268	A63	13c yel brn	25.00	17.50
269	A63	50c dl rose	2.50	2.25
		Nos. 263-269 (7)	136.50	108.25

SALVADOR

Handstamped on 1898 Stamps.
Wmkd. Liberty Cap. (117)

| 269A | A60 | 2c rose | 60.00 | 60.00 |
| 269B | A60 | 10c gray bl | 60.00 | 60.00 |

The overprints on Nos. 253 to 269B are handstamped and, as usual with that style of overprint, are to be found double, inverted, omitted, etc.

Stamps of Type A63 Overprinted in Black

1900   Unwmkd.

270	A63	1c lt grn	25	25
271	A63	2c rose	25	25
272	A63	3c gray blk	25	25
273	A63	5c pale bl	25	25
a.		5c dk bl	25	25
274	A63	10c dp bl	50	30
a.		10c pale bl	40	30
275	A63	12c lt grn	50	40
276	A63	13c yel brn	25	25
277	A63	24c gray	60	50
278	A63	26c yel brn	75	60
	Nos. 270-278 (9)		3.60	3.05

This overprint is known double, inverted, etc.

Nos. 271–273 Surcharged in Black

1902

280	A63	1c on 2c rose	4.00	3.00
281	A63	1c on 3c blk	3.00	2.00
282	A63	1c on 5c bl	2.00	1.50

Morazán Monument A64   Wmk. 173

Wmkd. S. (173)

1903   Engraved   Perf. 14, 14½

283	A64	1c green	40	30
284	A64	2c carmine	40	30
285	A64	3c orange	1.25	1.00
286	A64	5c dk bl	40	30
287	A64	10c dl vio	40	30
288	A64	12c slate	50	30
289	A64	13c red brn	50	35
290	A64	24c scarlet	3.00	1.75
291	A64	26c yel brn	3.00	1.50
292	A64	50c bister	1.75	1.00
293	A64	100c grnsh bl	6.50	3.00
	Nos. 283-293 (11)		18.10	10.10

Stamps of 1900 with Shield in Black Overprinted:

1905 (5¾x13½mm.) *a*

1905 (5x14¾mm.) *b*   **1905** (4½x16mm.) *c*

1905 (4½x13½mm.) *d*   **1905** (5x14½mm.) *e*

1905–06   Perf. 12   Unwmkd.
Blue Overprint.

293A	A63 (a)	2c rose		
294	A63 (a)	3c gray blk	6.00	4.00
a.		Without shield		
295	A63 (a)	5c blue	7.00	4.00

Purple Overprint.

296	A63 (b)	3c gray blk (Shield in purple)	7.00	6.00
296A	A63 (b)	5c bl (Shield in purple)	5.00	4.00
297	A63 (b)	3c gray blk	9.00	7.00
298	A63 (b)	5c blue	6.00	4.00

Black Overprint.
| 298A | A63 (b) | 5c blue | | |

Blue Overprint.
299	A63 (c)	1c green	7.00	4.00
299B	A63 (c)	2c rose	60	50
c.		"1905" vert.	1.25	
300	A63 (c)	5c blue	1.75	75
301	A63 (c)	10c dp bl	1.00	75

Black Overprint.
302	A63 (c)	2c rose	4.00	1.50
303	A63 (c)	5c blue	20.00	16.00
304	A63 (c)	10c dp bl	6.00	5.00

Blue Overprint.
305	A63 (d)	1c green	8.00	5.00
306	A63 (d)	2c rose (ovpt. vert.)	4.00	2.00
a.		Ovpt. horiz.		
306B	A63 (d)	3c gray blk	7.50	2.50
307	A63 (d)	5c blue	3.50	1.75

Blue Overprint.
| 311 | A63 (e) | 2c rose | 3.50 | 2.50 |
| a. | | Without shield | 6.00 | 4.50 |

Black Overprint.
| 311B | A63 (e) | 5c blue | 40.00 | 37.50 |

These overprints are found double, inverted, omitted, etc. Counterfeits exist.

Regular Issue of 1903 Surcharged with New Values:

UN CENTAVO *f*

5 CENTAVOS *g*

1 1

1 CENTAVO 1 *h*

1905–06 Perf. 14, 14½   Wmk. 173
Black Surcharge.
| 312 | A64 (f) | 1c on 2c car | 60 | 50 |
| a. | | Double surcharge | 6.00 | |

Red Surcharge.
312B	A64 (g)	5c on 12c sl	1.25	1.00
c.		Double surcharge		
d.		Invtd. overprint		
e.		Blk. surcharge	7.00	7.00
		As "d", double surcharge		

Blue Handstamped Surcharge.
313	A64 (h)	1c on 2c car	35	30
314	A64 (h)	1c on 10c vio	35	30
315	A64 (h)	1c on 12c sl ('06)	1.25	1.00
316	A64 (h)	1c on 13c red brn	6.00	5.00

No. 271 with Handstamped Surcharge in Blue.
Unwmkd.
| 317 | A63 (h) | 1c on 2c rose | 75.00 | 65.00 |

The "h" is handstamped in strips of four stamps each differing from the others in the size of the upper figures of value and in the letters of the word "CENTAVO", particularly in the size of the "N" and the "O" of that word. The surcharge is known inverted, double, etc.

Regular Issue of 1903 with Handstamped Surcharge:

5 *i*   **5**

5   **5**

5 5

5 5 5 5 *j*   *k*

Red Handstamped Surcharge.
Wmk. 173
318	A64 (i)	5c on 12c sl	3.00	1.75
319	A64 (j)	5c on 12c sl	3.00	2.25
a.		Blue surcharge		

Blue Handstamped Surcharge.
| 320 | A64 (k) | 5c on 12c sl | 4.00 | 3.50 |

One or more of the numerals in the handstamped surcharges on Nos. 318, 319 and 320 are frequently omitted, inverted, etc.

Surcharged:

1 1

6 6

6 CENTAVOS 6 *l*   *m*

Blue Handstamped Surcharge.
| 321 | A64 (l) | 6c on 12c sl | 75 | 60 |
| 322 | A64 (l) | 6c on 13c red brn | 1.25 | 85 |

Red Handstamped Surcharge.
| 323 | A64 (l) | 6c on 12c sl | 25.00 | 20.00 |

Type "l" is handstamped in strips of four varieties, differing in the size of the numerals and letters. The surcharge is known double and inverted.

Black Surcharge.
324	A64 (m)	1c on 13c red brn	2.00	2.00
a.		Double surcharge	6.00	6.00
b.		Right "1" & dot omitted		
c.		Both numerals omitted		
325	A64 (m)	3c on 13c red brn	75	75

Stamps of 1900, with Shield in Black, Overprinted

01905 *n*

1905   Perf. 12.   Unwmkd.
Blue Overprint.
326	A63 (n)	1c green	6.00	5.00
a.		Double surcharge		
327	A63 (n)	2c rose	5.00	5.00
a.		Vertical overprint	9.00	8.00
327B	A63 (n)	3c black	40.00	37.50
327C	A63 (n)	5c blue	17.50	13.50
328	A63 (n)	10c dp bl	9.00	7.00

Black Overprint.
| 328A | A63 (n) | 10c dp bl | 9.00 | 6.00 |

Counterfeits of Nos. 326–335 abound.

Condition is the all-important factor of price. Prices quoted are for stamps in fine condition.

The lack of a price for a listed item does not necessarily indicate rarity.

Stamps of 1900, with Shield in Black Surcharged or Overprinted:

1906   **1906** *p*

● ●

2 2   **1906** *o*   *q*

1906 Blue and Black Surcharge.
329	A63 (o)	2c on 26c brn org	60	50
a.		"2" & dot double	11.00	11.00
330	A63 (o)	3c on 26c brn org	6.00	5.00
a.		"3" & dot double		

Black Surcharge or Overprint.
331	A63 (o)	3c on 26c brn org	4.00	3.50
a.		Disks and numerals omitted		
b.		"3" and disks double		
c.		"1906" omitted		
333	A63 (q)	10c dp bl	2.50	2.00
334	A63 (q)	26c brn org	1.75	1.50
334A	A63 (q)	26c brn org	30.00	27.50
b.		"1906" in blue		

No. 257 Overprinted in Black.
| 335 | A63 (q) | 10c dp bl (Shield in violet) | 25.00 | 22.50 |
| a. | | Overprint type "p" | | |

There are numerous varieties of these surcharges and overprints.

Pres. Pedro José Escalón A65

Glazed Paper.

1906   Engraved   Perf. 11½

336	A65	1c grn & blk	20	20
a.		Thin paper	1.50	30
337	A65	2c red & blk	20	20
338	A65	3c yel & blk	20	20
339	A65	5c ultra & blk	20	20
a.		5c dk bl & blk	20	20
340	A65	6c car & blk	20	20
341	A65	10c vio & blk	20	20
342	A65	12c vio & blk	20	20
343	A65	13c dk brn & blk	20	20
345	A65	24c car & blk	50	50
346	A65	26c choc & blk	50	50
347	A65	50c yel & blk	50	75
348	A65	100c bl & blk	1.50	1.50
	Nos. 336-348 (12)		4.60	4.85

All values of this set are known imperforate but are not believed to have been issued in this condition.

The entire set has been reprinted. The shades of the reprints differ from those of the originals, the paper is thinner, the gum whiter and the perforation 12. Price 10c each.

Nos. 336–338 Overprinted in Black

1907
349	A65	1c grn & blk	35	30
a.		Shield in red	5.00	
350	A65	2c red & blk	35	30
a.		Shield in red	5.00	
351	A65	3c yel & blk	35	30

Reprints of Nos. 349 to 351 have the same characteristics as the reprints of the preceding issue. Price 5c each.

SALVADOR

Stamps of 1906
Surcharged with
Shield and **1**

352	A65	1c on 5c ultra & blk	15	15
a.		1c on 5c dk bl & blk	20	15
b.		Inverted surcharge		
c.		Double surcharge		
352D	A65	1c on 6c rose & blk	30	25
e.		Double surcharge	2.00	2.00
353	A65	2c on 6c rose & blk	3.00	1.25
354	A65	10c on 6c rose & blk	75	50

The above surcharges are frequently found with the shield double, inverted, or otherwise misplaced.

National Palace
A66

Paper with or without colored dots.
Overprinted with Shield in Black.

1907 Engraved. Unwmkd.

355	A66	1c grn & blk	20	12
356	A66	2c red & blk	20	15
357	A66	3c yel & blk	20	15
358	A66	5c bl & blk	20	12
a.		5c ultra & blk	20	12
359	A66	6c ver & blk	20	15
a.		Shield in red	5.00	
360	A66	10c vio & blk	20	15
361	A66	12c vio & blk	20	15
362	A66	13c sep & blk	20	12
363	A66	24c rose & blk	20	15
364	A66	26c yel brn & blk	50	25
365	A66	50c org & blk	75	40
a.		50c yel & blk	5.00	
366	A66	100c turq bl & blk	1.50	75
		Nos. 355-366 (12)	4.55	2.66

Most values exist without shield, also with shield inverted, double, and otherwise misprinted. Many of these were never sold to the public.
See also Nos. 369-373.

No. 356
With Additional
Surcharge in Black.
UN CENTAVO

1908

367	A66	1c on 2c red & blk	50	40
a.		Double surcharge	2.00	2.00
b.		Inverted surcharge	1.00	1.00
c.		Double surcharge, one inverted	1.00	1.00
d.		Red surcharge		

Same
Surcharged
in Black or Red **UN CENTAVO**

368	A66	1c on 2c red & blk	35.00	32.50
368A	A66	1c on 2c red & blk (R)	50.00	45.00

Counterfeits exist of the surcharges on Nos. 368-368A.

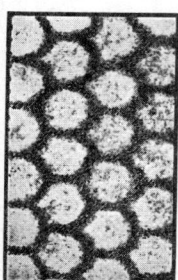

Wmk. 172

Type of 1907.
Wmkd. Honeycomb. (172)

1909 Engraved

369	A66	1c grn & blk	20	20
370	A66	2c rose & blk	20	20
371	A66	3c yel & blk	30	20
372	A66	5c bl & blk	30	20
373	A66	10c vio & blk	35	30
		Nos. 369-373 (5)	1.35	1.10

The note after No. 366 will apply here also.

1821
15 septiembre
1909

Nos. 355, 369
Overprinted
in Red

1909, Sept. Unwmkd.

374	A66	1c grn & blk	3.00	2.25
a.		Inverted overprint		

Wmkd. Honeycomb. (172)

375	A66	1c grn & blk	2.50	2.25
a.		Inverted overprint		

88th anniversary of El Salvador's independence.

2 CENTAVOS

Nos. 362, 364
Surcharged

1909 Unwmkd.

376	A66	2c on 13c sep & blk	2.00	1.75
a.		Inverted surcharge		
377	A66	3c on 26c yel brn & blk	2.50	2.00
a.		Inverted surcharge		

Pres. Fernando
Figueroa
A67

1910 Engraved. Wmk. 172

378	A67	1c sep & blk	20	15
379	A67	2c dk grn & blk	20	18
380	A67	3c org & blk	20	18
381	A67	4c car & blk	20	18
a.		4c scar & blk	30	30
382	A67	5c pur & blk	20	18
383	A67	6c scar & blk	20	18
384	A67	10c pur & blk	30	25
385	A67	12c dp bl & blk	30	25
386	A67	17c ol grn & blk	30	25
387	A67	19c brn red & blk	30	25
388	A67	29c choc & blk	30	25
389	A67	50c yel & blk	20	18
390	A67	100c turq bl & blk	30	25
		Nos. 378-390 (13)	3.20	2.73

José Matías
Delgado
A68

Manuel José
Arce
A69

Centenary
Monument
A70

1912 Perf. 12 Unwmkd.

402	A71	1c dp bl & blk	25	20
403	A72	2c bis brn & blk	30	20
404	A73	5c scar & blk	20	20
405	A74	6c dk grn & blk	25	20
406	A75	12c ol grn & blk	1.25	35

Paper with colored dots.

1911 Unwmkd.

391	A68	5c dp bl & brn	20	20
392	A69	6c org & brn	20	20
393	A70	12c vio & brn	20	20

Wmkd. Honeycomb. (172)

394	A68	5c dp bl & brn	15	15
395	A69	6c org & brn	15	15
396	A70	12c vio & brn	15	15
		Nos. 391-396 (6)	1.05	1.05

Centenary of the insurrection of 1811.

Palace Type of 1907 without Shield.
Paper without colored dots.

1911

397	A66	1c scarlet	10	10
398	A66	2c chocolate	50	50
a.		Paper with brown dots		
399	A66	13c dp grn	20	20
400	A66	24c yellow	30	30
401	A66	50c dk brn	30	30
		Nos. 397-401 (5)	1.40	1.40

José Matías
Delgado
A71

Manuel José
Arce
A72

Francisco Morazán
A73

Rafael Campo
A74

Trinidad
Cabañas
A75

Monument of
Gerardo Barrios
A76

Centenary
Monument
A77

National
Palace
A78

Rosales Hospital
A79

Coat of Arms
A80

407	A76	17c vio & sl	75	30
408	A77	19c scar & sl	1.50	40
409	A78	29c org & sl	1.75	40
410	A79	50c bl & sl	2.25	75
411	A80	1col blk & sl	3.50	60
		Nos. 402-411 (10)	12.10	4.45

Juan Manuel
Rodríguez
A81

Pres. Manuel
E. Araujo
A82

1914 Perf. 11½

412	A81	10c org & brn	3.50	1.50
413	A82	25c pur & brn	3.50	1.50

Type of 1907 without Shield
Overprinted **1915** in Black.
Paper overlaid with colored dots.

1915

414	A66	1c gray grn	20	15
415	A66	2c red	20	15
416	A66	5c ultra	20	12
417	A66	6c pale bl	20	12
418	A66	10c yellow	85	60
419	A66	12c brown	60	30
420	A66	50c violet	30	25
421	A66	100c blk brn	1.80	1.80
		Nos. 414-421 (8)	4.35	3.49

Varieties such as center omitted, center double, center inverted, imperforate exist with or without date, date inverted, date double, etc., but are believed to be entirely unofficial.
Preceding the stamps with the "1915" overprint a quantity of stamps of this type was overprinted with the letter "S". Evidence is lacking that they were ever placed in use. The issue was demonetized in 1916.

National Theater—A83
Various Frames.

1916 Engraved Perf. 12

431	A83	1c dp grn	15	10
432	A83	2c vermilion	20	15
433	A83	5c dp bl	25	15
434	A83	6c gray vio	35	18
435	A83	10c blk brn	35	18
436	A83	12c violet	3.50	1.00
437	A83	17c orange	50	20
438	A83	25c dk brn	1.00	40
439	A83	29c black	7.50	1.50
440	A83	50c slate	2.50	1.25
		Nos. 431-440 (10)	16.30	5.11

Watermarked letters which occasionally appear are from the papermaker's name.

Nos. O324-O325 with "OFICIAL"
Barred out in Black.

1917

441	O3	2c red	60	40
a.		Double bar		
442	O3	5c ultra	75	50
a.		Double bar		

Regular Issue
of 1915
Overprinted
"OFICIAL"
and Re-overprinted
In Red

CORRIENTE

443	A66	6c pale bl	1.00	75
a.		Double bar		
444	A66	12c brown	1.25	1.00
a.		Double bar		
b.		"CORRIENTE" inverted		

SALVADOR

Same Overprint in Red
On Nos. O323-O327

445	O3	1c gray grn	2.50	2.00
a.		"CORRIENTE" inverted		
b.		Double bar		
c.		"CORRIENTE" omitted		
446	O3	2c red	2.50	2.00
a.		Double bar		
447	O3	5c ultra	12.50	10.00
a.		Double bar, both in black		
448	O3	10c yellow	1.50	1.00
a.		"OFICIAL" and bar omitted		
449	O3	50c violet	1.00	75
a.		Double bar		
		Nos. 443-449 (7)	22.25	17.50

Nos. O334-O335
Overprinted or Surcharged in Red:

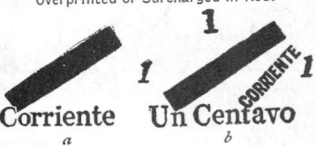

450	A83 (a)	5c dp bl	2.50	2.00
a.		"CORRIENTE" double		
451	A83 (b)	1c on 6c gray vio	1.25	1.00
a.		"CORRIERTE"		
b.		"CORRIENRE"		
c.		"CORRIENTE" double		

A84

1918 Black Surcharge.

452	A84	1c on 6c gray vio	2.50	2.00
a.		Double surcharge		
b.		Inverted surcharge		

No. 434 Surcharged in Black

1 Centavo 1

1918

453	A83	1c on 6c gray vio	2.00	1.50
a.		"Centado"	3.00	3.00
b.		Double surcharge	3.50	3.50
c.		Inverted surcharge		

No. 434 Surcharged in Black or Red

1 CENTAVO 1

454	A83	1c on 6c gray vio	6.00	5.00
a.		Double surcharge		
b.		Inverted surcharge	7.00	7.00
455	A83	1c on 6c gray vio (R)	6.00	5.00
a.		Double surcharge		
b.		Inverted surcharge	7.00	7.00

Counterfeits exist of Nos. 454-455.

Pres. Carlos Meléndez
A85

1919   Engraved
456	A85	1col dk bl & blk	1.00	90

No. 437 Surcharged in Black

1 Centavo 1

1919

457	A83	1c on 17c org	30	15
a.		Inverted surcharge	1.00	1.00
b.		Double surcharge	1.00	1.00

A86   A87

A88   A89

Black or Blue Surcharge.
1920-21

458	A86	1c on 12c vio	25	20
a.		Double surcharge	2.00	2.00
459	A87	2c on 10c dk brn	35	20
460	A88	5c on 50c sl ('21)	60	25
461	A89	6c on 25c dk brn (Bl) ('21)	60	40

Same Surcharge in Black on No. O337
462	A86	1c on 12c vio	1.25	1.25
a.		Double surcharge		

No. 460 surcharged in yellow and 461 surcharged in red are essays.
No. 462 is due to some sheets of Official Stamps being mixed with the ordinary 12c stamps at the time of surcharging. The error stamps were sold to the public and used for ordinary postage.

A90

Surcharged in Red:

15 15 15 15
 I   II   III IV

463	A90	15c on 29c blk (III) ('21)	2.00	75
a.		Double surcharge	4.00	
b.		Type I	3.00	2.00
c.		Type II	2.00	1.50
d.		Type IV	5.00	

A91   A92

Surcharged in Blue or Black.
464	A91	26c on 29c blk (Bl)	1.50	75
a.		Double surcharge		
466	A92	35c on 50c sl (Bk)	1.25	85

One stamp in each row of ten of No. 464 has the "t" of "cts" inverted and one stamp in each row of No. 466 has the letters "c" in "cinco" larger than the normal.
No. 464 surcharged in green or yellow and the 35c on 29c black are essays.

No. 456 Surcharged in Red

467	A85	60c on 1col dk bl & blk	60	50

Setting includes three types of numerals and "CENTAVOS" measuring from 16mm. to 20mm. wide.

A93

1921
468	A93	1c on 1c ol grn	10	10
a.		Double surcharge	1.50	
469	A93	1c on 5c yel	10	10
a.		Inverted surcharge		
b.		Double surcharge		
470	A93	1c on 10c bl	20	15
a.		Double surcharge	1.00	
471	A93	1c on 25c grn	10	10
472	A93	1c on 50c ol	25	25
473	A93	1c on 1p gray blk	35	35
a.		Double surcharge	1.10	1.05
		Nos. 468-473 (6)		

The frame of No. 473 differs slightly from the illustration.
Setting includes many wrong font letters and numerals.

Francisco Menéndez   **Manuel José Arce**
A94   A95

Confederation Coin   **Delgado Addressing Crowd**
A96   A97

Coat of Arms of Confederation   **Francisco Morazán**
A98   A99

Independence Monument   **Columbus**
A100   A101

1921   Engraved   Perf. 12
474	A94	1c green	35	10
475	A95	2c black	40	10
476	A96	5c orange	1.25	15
477	A97	6c car rose	75	15
478	A98	10c dp bl	75	15
479	A99	25c ol grn	3.25	25
480	A100	60c violet	8.00	75
481	A101	1col blk brn	12.00	1.00
		Nos. 474-481 (8)	26.75	2.75

Nos. 474-477 Overprinted in Red, Black or Blue

CENTENARIO a
CENTENARIO b

1921
481A	A94 (a)	1c grn (R)	5.50	4.50
481B	A95 (a)	2c blk (R)	5.50	4.50
481C	A96 (b)	5c org (Bk)	5.50	4.50
481D	A97 (b)	6c car rose (Bl)	5.50	4.50

Centenary of independence.

No. 477 Surcharged:

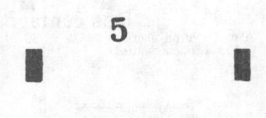

482	A97 (a)	5c on 6c	50	30
483	A97 (b)	5c on 6c	40	30
484	A97 (b)	20c on 6c	50	50

Nos. 482-484 exist with double surcharge.

No. 475 Surcharged in Red

1923
485	A95	10c on 2c blk	75	30

José Simeón Cañas y Villacorta
A102

1923   Engraved   Perf. 11½
486	A102	5c blue	75	50

Centenary of abolition of slavery.

SALVADOR

Nos. 479, 481
Surcharged in
Red or Black

1924   Perf. 12
487   A99   1c on 25c ol grn (R)   25   20
    a. Numeral at right inverted
    b. Double surcharge
488   A99   6c on 25c ol grn (R)   30   25
489   A99   20c on 25c ol grn (R)   70   50
490   A101   20c on 1col blk brn (Bk)   80   75

A103   A104

1924
491   A103   1c on 5c org (Bk)   50   40
492   A104   6c on 10c dp bl (R)   50   40

Nos. 491–492 exist with double surcharge.
A stamp similar to No. 492 but with surcharge "6 centavos 6" is an essay.

No. 476
Surcharged

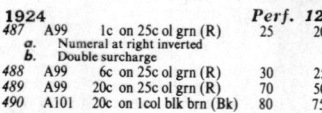

Dos centavos

493   A96   2c on 5c org   50   50
    a. Top ornament omitted   3.00   3.00

A105

1924   Red Surcharge.
494   A105   5c on 60c vio   7.50   6.00
    a. "1781" for "1874"   17.50   17.50
    b. "1934" for "1924"   17.50   17.50

Universal Postal Union, 50th anniversary. This stamp with black surcharge is an essay. Copies have been passed through the post.

Daniel Hernández   National
Monument   Gymnasium
A106   A107

Atlacatl   Conspiracy of 1811
A108   A109

Bridge over   Map of
Lempa River   Central America
A110   A111

Balsam Tree   Tulla Serra
A112   A114

Columbus at   Coat
La Rábida   of Arms
A115   A116

Photo.; Engr. (35c, 1col)
Perf. 12½; 14 (35c, 1col)

1924–25
495   A106   1c red vio   15   10
496   A107   2c dk red   40   15
497   A108   3c chocolate   30   15
498   A109   5c ol blk   30   15
499   A110   6c grnsh bl   40   12
500   A111   10c orange   1.00   30
    a. "ATLANT CO"   10.00   9.00
501   A112   20c dp grn   1.50   50
502   A114   35c scar & grn   3.50   75
503   A115   50c org brn   3.00   60
504   A116   1col grn & vio ('25)   4.50   60
    Nos. 495-504 (10)   15.05   3.42

A117

1925, Aug.   Red Surcharge   Perf. 12
506   A117   2c on 60c vio   2.50   2.25

Issued to commemorate the 400th anniversary of the city of San Salvador.
The variety with dates in black is an essay.

View of San Salvador
A118

1925   Photogravure   Perf. 12½
507   A118   1c blue   1.25   1.25
508   A118   2c org   1.25   1.25
509   A118   3c Mahogany red   1.25   1.25

No. 506 and Nos. 507 to 509 were issued to commemorate the fourth centenary of the founding of the City of San Salvador.

A119   A120
Black Surcharge

1928, July 17
510   A119   3c on 10c org   1.25   1.00
    a. "ATLANT CO"   25.00   25.00

Industrial Exhibition, Santa Ana, July 1928.

Red Surcharge.

1928
511   A120   1c on 5c blk   50   40
    a. Bar instead of top left "1"   75   50

Pres. Pío Romero Bosque, Salvador,
and Pres. Lázaro Chacón, Guatemala
A121

1929   Lithographed.   Perf. 11½.
Portraits in Dark Brown
512   A121   1c dl vio   65   50
    a. Center inverted   20.00   20.00
513   A121   3c bis brn   65   50
    a. Center inverted   60.00   60.00
514   A121   5c gray grn   65   50
515   A121   10c orange   65   50

Issued to celebrate the opening of the international railroad connecting El Salvador and Guatemala.
Nos. 512–515 exist imperforate. No. 512 in the colors of No. 515.

Tomb of Menéndez
A122

1930, Dec. 3
516   A122   1c violet   6.00   5.50
517   A122   3c brown   6.00   5.50
518   A122   5c dk grn   6.00   5.50
519   A122   10c yel brn   6.00   5.50

Issued to commemorate the centenary of the birth of General Francisco Menéndez.

Stamps of 1924-25 Issue
Overprinted   **1932**

1932   Perf. 12½, 14
520   A106   1c dp vio   20   12
521   A107   2c dk red   30   20
522   A108   3c chocolate   40   15
523   A109   5c ol blk   40   12
524   A110   6c dp bl   50   12
525   A111   10c orange   1.25   30
    a. "ATLANT CO"   15.00   12.50
526   A112   20c dp grn   2.25   65
527   A114   35c scar & grn   3.00   1.00
528   A115   50c org brn   4.50   1.50
529   A116   1col grn & vio   6.00   2.50
    Nos. 520-529 (10)   20.80   7.16

Prices are for the overprint measuring 7½x3mm. It is found in two other sizes: 7½x3¼mm. and 8x3mm.

Types of 1924-25.
Surcharged with
New Values in Red or Black

1934   Perf. 12½
530   A109   2(c) on 5c grnsh blk (R)   20   15
    a. Double surcharge
531   A111   3(c) on 10c org   25   15
    a. "ATLANT CO"   8.00   8.00

Stamps of 1924-25
Surcharged with New Values in Black
Perf. 12½, 14½
532   A115   2(c) on 50c org brn   40   25
    a. Double surcharge   6.00
533   A116   8(c) on 1col grn & vio   20   20
534   A114   15(c) on 35c scar & grn   40   35
    Nos. 530-534 (5)   1.45   1.10

Police Barracks   Wmk. 240
A123

Two types of the 2c.
Type I. The clouds have heavy lines of shading.
Type II. The lines of shading have been removed from the clouds.

Wmk.
REPUBLICA DE EL SALVADOR
in Sheet. (240)
Lithographed.

1934-35   Perf. 12½
535   A123   2c gray brn, type I   30   15
    a. 2c brn (type II)   30   15
536   A123   5c car, type II   30   15
537   A123   8c lt ultra, type II   30   15
    Nos. 535-537, C33-C35 (6)   5.65   3.05

Discus
Thrower
A124

1935, Mar. 16   Engr.   Unwmkd.
538   A124   5c carmine   6.00   3.50
539   A124   8c blue   6.25   4.00
540   A124   10c org yel   8.00   4.50
541   A124   15c bister   9.00   6.00
542   A124   37c green   11.50   9.00
    Nos. 538-542 (5)   40.75   27.00

Issued to commemorate the 3rd Central American Games. See Nos. C36-C40.

Same Overprinted   **HABILITADO**
in Black

1935, June 27
543   A124   5c carmine   8.00   6.00
544   A124   8c blue   11.00   6.00
545   A124   10c org yel   11.00   7.00
546   A124   15c bister   11.00   7.00
547   A124   37c green   18.00   11.00
    Nos. 543-547 (5)   59.00   37.00

See also Nos. C41-C45.

Flag of   Tree of
El Salvador   San Vicente
A125   A126

SALVADOR

1935, Oct. 26   Litho.   Wmk. 240

548	A125	1c gray bl	20	10
549	A125	2c blk brn	20	10
550	A125	3c plum	25	15
551	A125	5c rose car	40	15
552	A125	8c ultra	50	40
553	A125	15c fawn	60	25
	Nos. 548-553, C46 (7)		3.05	1.30

1935, Dec. 26
Numerals in Black,
Tree in Yellow Green

554	A126	2c blk brn	50	35
555	A126	3c dk bl grn	60	40
556	A126	5c rose red	80	50
557	A126	8c dk bl	80	60
558	A126	15c brown	1.00	75
	Nos. 554-558 (5)		3.70	2.60

Tercentenary of San Vicente. See Nos. C47-C51.

Volcano of Izalco
A127

Wharf at Cutuco
A128

Doroteo Vasconcelos
A129

Parade Ground
A130

Dr. Tomás G. Palomo
A131

Sugar Mill
A132

Coffee at Pier
A133

Gathering Balsam
A134

Pres. Manuel E. Araujo
A135

1935, Dec.   Engraved   Unwmkd.

559	A127	1c dp vio	20	10
560	A128	2c chestnut	20	10
561	A129	3c green	20	10
562	A130	5c carmine	60	12
563	A131	8c dl bl	25	10
564	A132	10c orange	35	15
565	A133	15c dk ol bis	60	30
566	A134	50c indigo	3.00	1.50
567	A135	1col black	7.50	4.25
	Nos. 559-567 (9)		12.90	6.72

Paper has faint imprint "El Salvador" on face.

Stamps of 1935 Surcharged with New Value in Black.

1938   Perf. 12½

568	A130	1c on 5c car	25	15
569	A132	3c on 10c org	25	15
570	A133	8c on 15c dk ol bis	30	20

No. 486 Surcharged with New Value in Red.

1938   Perf. 11½

| 571 | A102 | 3c on 5c bl | 40 | 45 |

Issued to commemorate the centenary of the death of José Simeón Cañas, liberator of slaves in Latin America.

Map and Flags of U. S. and El Salvador—A136
Engraved & Lithographed

1938, Apr. 21   Perf. 12

| 572 | A136 | 8c multi | 90 | 75 |

150th anniversary of U.S. Constitution. See No. C61.

No. 560 Surcharged with New Value in Black.

1938   Perf. 12½

| 573 | A128 | 1c on 2c chnt | 20 | 18 |

Indian Sugar Mill
A137

Designs; 2c, Indian women washing. 3c, Indian girl at spring. 5c, Indian plowing. 8c, Izote flower. 10c, Champion cow. 20c, Extracting balsam. 50c, Maquilishuat in bloom. 1col, Post Office, San Salvador.

1938-39   Engraved   Perf. 12

574	A137	1c dk vio	25	10
575	A137	2c dk grn	25	10
576	A137	3c dk brn	35	10
577	A137	5c scarlet	35	10
578	A137	8c dk bl	2.00	30
579	A137	10c yel org ('39)	3.50	30
580	A137	20c bis brn ('39)	3.00	40
581	A137	50c dl blk ('39)	4.00	90
582	A137	1col blk ('39)	3.50	1.50
	Nos. 574-582 (9)		17.20	3.80

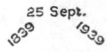

Nos. 566-567, 504
Surcharged in Red

BATALLA
SAN PEDRO PERULAPAN
₡ 0.50

1939, Sept. 25   Perf. 12½, 14

583	A134	8c on 50c ind	50	30
584	A135	10c on 1col blk	75	30
585	A116	50c on 1col grn & vio	5.00	4.00

Issued to commemorate the 100th anniversary of the battle of San Pedro Perulapán.

Sir Rowland Hill
A146

1940, Mar. 1   Perf. 12½

| 586 | A146 | 8c dk bl, lt bl & blk | 6.00 | 1.25 |

Issued to commemorate the centenary of the postage stamp. See Nos. C69-C70.

Statue of Christ and San Salvador Cathedral
A147

Wmk. 269
Wmkd.
REPUBLICA DE EL SALVADOR.
(269)

1942, Nov. 23   Engraved   Perf. 14

| 587 | A147 | 8c dp bl | 1.00 | 40 |

Souvenir Sheet.

A148
Imperf.
Without Gum
Lilac Tinted Paper.

588	A148	Sheet of four	25.00	25.00
a.		8c dp bl	5.00	5.00
b.		30c red org	5.00	5.00

Nos. 587-588 were issued to commemorate the first Eucharistic Congress of Salvador. See No. C85.
No. 588 contains two No. 587 and two No. C85, imperf. The sheet measures 124x122mm.

Cuscatlán Bridge, Pan-American Highway
A149

Arms Overprint at Right in Carmine.
Engraved.
1944, Nov. 24   Perf. 12½   Unwmkd.

| 589 | A149 | 8c dk bl & blk | 30 | 20 |

See also No. C92.

Gen. Juan José Canas
A150

1945, June 9

| 590 | A150 | 8c blue | 20 | 8 |

No. 575
Surcharged in Black
1
a b

1944-46

| 591 | A137(a) | 1(c) on 2c dk grn | 20 | 12 |
| 592 | A137(b) | 1(c) on 2c dk grn ('46) | 20 | 12 |

Lake of Ilopango
A151

Ceiba Tree
A152

Water Carriers
A153

1946-47   Lithographed   Wmk. 240

593	A151	1c bl ('47)	15	15
594	A152	2c lt bl grn ('47)	40	15
595	A153	5c carmine	25	12

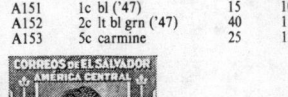
Isidro Menéndez
A154

Designs: 2c, Cristano Salazar. 3c, Juan Bertis. 5c, Francisco Duenas. 8c, Ramon Belloso. 10c, Jose Presentacion Trigueros. 20c, Salvador Rodriguez Gonzalez. 50c, Francisco Castaneda. 1col, David Castro.

Engraved.
1947   Perf. 12   Unwmkd.

596	A154	1c car rose	10	6
597	A154	2c dp org	10	6
598	A154	3c violet	12	10
599	A154	5c sl gray	12	6
600	A154	8c dp bl	15	6
601	A154	10c bis brn	25	15
602	A154	20c green	40	18
603	A154	50c black	1.00	40
604	A154	1col scarlet	2.25	50
	Nos. 596-604 (9)		4.49	1.57

Manuel José Arce—A163

SALVADOR

1948, Feb. 25   *Perf. 12½*

| 605 | A163 | 8c dp bl | 40 | 20 |

See Nos. C108–C110.

President Roosevelt Presenting
Awards for Distinguished Service
A164

President Franklin D. Roosevelt
A165

Designs: 8c, Pres. and Mrs. Roosevelt. 15c, Mackenzie King, Roosevelt and Winston Churchill. 20c, Roosevelt and Cordell Hull. 50c, Funeral of Pres. Roosevelt.

1948, Apr. 12

Various Frames; Center in Black.

606	A164	5c dk bl	20	10
607	A164	8c green	25	15
608	A165	12c violet	35	20
609	A164	15c vermilion	35	20
610	A164	20c car lake	50	50
611	A164	50c gray	1.25	1.00
		Nos. 606-611 (6)	2.90	2.15

Souvenir Sheet.

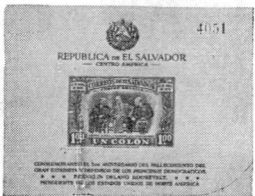

A166

Perf. 13½

| 612 | A166 | 1col ol grn & brn | 3.00 | 3.00 |

Nos. 606–612 commemorate the 3rd anniversary of the death of President Franklin D. Roosevelt. Size of No. 612: 111x 85mm.

See also Nos. C111–C117.

Torch and
Winged
Letter
A167

Engraved.

1949, Oct. 9   *Perf. 12½*   *Unwmkd.*

| 613 | A167 | 8c blue | 75 | 35 |

Issued to commemorate the 75th anniversary of the formation of the Universal Postal Union. See Nos. C122–C124.

Workman   Wreath
and Soldier   and
Holding Torch   Open Book
A168   A169

1949, Dec. 15   Litho.   *Perf. 10½*

| 614 | A168 | 8c blue | 45 | 15 |

Issued to commemorate the 1st anniversary of the Revolution of Dec. 14, 1948.
See Nos. C125–C129.

Perf. 11½

1952, Feb. 14   Photo.   Unwmkd.

Wreath in Dark Green

615	A169	1c yel grn	10	10
616	A169	2c magenta	10	10
617	A169	5c brn red	10	10
618	A169	10c yellow	15	12
619	A169	20c gray grn	30	20
620	A169	1col dp car	1.50	1.00
		Nos. 615-620 (6)	2.25	1.62

Constitution of 1950. See also Nos. C134–C141.

Nos. 598, 600 and 603 Surcharged with
New Values in Various Colors.

1952-53   *Perf. 12½.*

621	A154	2c on 3c vio (C)	15	10
622	A154	2c on 8c dp bl (C)	20	10
623	A154	3c on 8c dp bl (G)	20	10
624	A154	5c on 8c dp bl (O)	20	15
625	A154	8c on 8c dp bl (Bk)	20	15
626	A154	10c on 50c blk (O) ('53)	30	20
		Nos. 621-626 (6)	1.25	80

Nos. C106 and C107 Surcharged and
"AEREO" Obliterated in Various Colors

1952-53   Wmk. 240

627	AP31	2c on 12c choc (Bl) ('53)	25	10
628	AP32	2c on 14c dk bl (R) ('53)	20	10
629	AP31	5c on 12c choc (Bl)	25	15
630	AP32	10c on 14c dk bl (C)	25	20

José
Marti
A170

Perf. 10½

1953, Feb. 27   Litho.   Unwmkd.

631	A170	1c rose red	15	10
632	A170	2c bl grn	20	10
633	A170	10c dk vio	30	15
		Nos. 631-633, C142-C144 (6)	2.45	1.60

Issued to commemorate the centenary of the birth of José Marti, Cuban patriot.

No. 598	"IV Congreso
Overprinted	Médico Social
in Carmine	Panamericano
	15 / 19 Abril,
	1953"

1953, June 19   *Perf. 12½*

| 634 | A154 | 3c violet | 30 | 15 |

Issued to commemorate the 4th Pan-American Congress of Social Medicine, San Salvador, April 16–19, 1953. See No. C146.

Signing of Act   Capt. Gen.
of Independence   Gerardo Barrios
A171   A172

1953, Sept. 15   Litho.   *Perf. 11½*

635	A171	1c rose pink	10	10
636	A171	2c dp bl grn	10	10
637	A171	3c purple	10	10
638	A171	5c dp bl	12	12
639	A171	7c lt brn	15	15
640	A171	10c ocher	30	18
641	A171	20c dp org	40	30
642	A171	50c green	90	40
643	A171	1col gray	1.75	1.50
		Nos. 635-643, C147-C150 (13)	5.71	4.34

Issued to commemorate the 132nd anniversary of the Act of Independence, Sept. 15, 1821.

1953, Dec. 1   *Perf. 11½*

Portrait: 3c, 7c, 10c, 22c, Francisco Morazan, (facing left).

Black Overprint ("C de C").

644	A172	1c green	10	10
645	A172	2c bl green	10	10
646	A172	3c green	10	10
647	A172	5c carmine	15	10
648	A172	7c blue	20	12
649	A172	10c carmine	25	15
650	A172	20c violet	30	25
651	A172	22c violet	40	30
		Nos. 644-651 (8)	1.60	1.22

The overprint "C de C" is a control indicating "Tribunal of Accounts". A double entry of this overprint occurs twice in each sheet of each denomination.

Coastal
Bridge
A173

Motherland and Liberty
A174

Census Allegory   Balboa Park
A175   A176

Designs: Nos. 653 and 664, Fishing boats. Nos. 654 and 655, National Palace. Nos. 658 and 662, Gen. Arce. Nos. 659 and 665, Izalco Volcano. Nos. 660 and 661, Guayabo dam. No. 666, Lake Ilopango. Nos. 667 and 672, ODECA officials and flag. No. 668, Motherland and Liberty. No. 669, Housing development. Nos. 670 and 673, Coast guard boat. No. 671, Modern highway.

Photogravure.

1954, June 1   *Perf. 11½*   Unwmkd.

652	A173	1c car rose & brn	12	10
653	A173	1c ol & bl gray	12	10
654	A173	1c pur & pale lil	12	10
655	A173	2c yel grn & lt gray	20	12
656	A174	2c car lake	20	12
657	A175	2c org red	20	12
658	A173	3c maroon	20	12
659	A173	3c bl grn & bl	25	15
660	A174	3c dk gray & vio	20	12
661	A174	5c red vio & vio	25	12
662	A175	5c emerald	20	12
663	A176	7c mag & buff	25	15
664	A173	7c bl grn & gray bl	25	15
665	A173	7c org brn & org	25	15
666	A174	10c car lake	25	15
667	A174	10c red, dk brn & bl	25	15
668	A174	10c dk bl grn	25	15
669	A174	20c org & cr	50	25
670	A173	22c gray vio	50	50
671	A176	50c dk gray & brn	1.00	55
672	A174	1col brn org, dk brn & bl	1.75	1.00
673	A173	1col brt bl	1.75	1.00
		Nos. 652-673 (22)	9.01	5.46

Capt. Gen.   Coffee
Gerardo Barrios   Picker
A177   A178

Engraved

1955, Dec. 20   *Perf. 12½*   Wmk. 269

674	A177	1c red	15	15
675	A177	2c yel grn	20	15
676	A177	3c vio bl	25	15
677	A177	20c violet	30	25
		Nos. 674-677, C166-C167 (6)	1.55	1.25

Perf. 13½

1956, June 20   Litho.   Unwmkd.

678	A178	3c bis brn	15	10
679	A178	5c red org	18	10
680	A178	10c dk bl	24	18
681	A178	2col dk red	2.50	2.00
		Nos. 678-681, C168-C172 (9)	10.67	8.08

Centenary of Santa Ana Department.

Map of Chalatenango—A179

1956, Sept. 14

682	A179	2c blue	20	10
683	A179	7c rose red	50	35
684	A179	50c yel brn	80	60
		Nos. 682-684, C173-C178 (9)	4.70	3.65

Centenary of Chalatenango Department (in 1955).

Coat of Arms of
Nueva San Salvador—A180

SALVADOR

Engraved
1957, Jan. 3   **Perf. 12½**   **Wmk. 269**

685	A180	1c rose red	10	10
686	A180	2c green	10	10
687	A180	3c violet	10	10
688	A180	7c red org	50	50
689	A180	10c ultra	15	12
690	A180	50c pale brn	60	60
691	A180	1col dl red	1.25	1.25
		Nos. 685-691, C179-C183 (12)	8.05	6.21

Issued to commemorate the centenary of the founding of the city of Nueva San Salvador (Santa Tecla).

Nos. 664-665, 683 and 688 Surcharged with New Value in Black.
Photogravure.

1957   **Perf. 11½**   **Unwmkd.**

692	A173	6c on 7c bl grn & gray bl	35	25
693	A173	6c on 7c org brn & org	35	25

1957   **Lithographed**   **Perf. 13½**

| 694 | A179 | 6c on 7c rose red | 22 | 15 |

Engraved.
1957-58   **Perf. 12½**   **Wmk. 269**

695	A180	5c on 7c red org ('58)	30	20
696	A180	6c on 7c red org	40	25

El Salvador Intercontinental Hotel
A181

Photogravure.
Granite Paper.
1958, June 28   **Perf. 11½**   **Unwmkd.**
Vignette in Green, Dark Blue & Red

697	A181	3c brown	10	10
698	A181	6c crim rose	10	10
699	A181	10c brt bl	15	10
700	A181	15c brt grn	25	15
701	A181	20c lilac	40	25
702	A181	30c brt yel grn	50	35
		Nos. 697-702 (6)	1.50	1.05

Presidents Eisenhower and Lemus and Flags—A182
Granite Paper

1959, Dec. 14
Design in Ultramarine, Dark Brown Light Brown and Red

703	A182	3c pink	20	10
704	A182	6c green	20	10
705	A182	10c crimson	30	10
		Nos. 703-705, C184-C186 (6)	1.80	1.08

Issued to commemorate the visit of Pres. José M. Lemus of El Salvador to the United States, Mar. 9–21.

No. 686 Overprinted: "5 Enero 1960 XX Aniversario Fundacion Sociedad Filatelica de El Salvador"
Engraved.
1960   **Perf. 12½**   **Wmk. 269**

| 706 | A180 | 2c green | 15 | 12 |

Issued to commemorate the 20th anniversary of the Philatelic Association of El Salvador.

Apartment Houses
A183

Photogravure
1960   **Perf. 11½**   **Unwmkd.**
Multicolored Centers; Granite Paper.

707	A183	10c scarlet	12	10
708	A183	15c brt pur	18	12
709	A183	25c brt yel grn	30	20
710	A183	30c Prus bl	35	25
711	A183	40c olive	50	40
712	A183	80c dk bl	1.00	70
		Nos. 707-712 (6)	2.45	1.77

Issued to publicize the erection of multi-family housing projects in 1958.

No. 686 Surcharged with New Value.
Engraved
1960   **Perf. 12½**   **Wmk. 269**

| 713 | A180 | 1c on 2c grn | 15 | 12 |

Poinsettia
A184

Photogravure
1960, Dec.   **Perf. 11½**   **Unwmkd.**
Granite Paper
Design in Slate Green, Red and Yellow

714	A184	3c yellow	15	12
715	A184	6c salmon	22	12
716	A184	10c grnsh bl	30	15
717	A184	15c pale vio bl	40	20
		Nos. 714-717, C188-C191 (8)	4.42	2.29

Miniature Sheet

| 718 | A184 | 40c silver | 75 | 75 |

No. 718 contains one stamp and is inscribed: "Republica de El Salvador, C. A." Size: 99x74mm.

Nos. 718 and C192 exist with overprints for: (1.) First Central American Philatelic Congress, July, 1961. (2.) Death of General Barrios, 96th anniversary. (3.) Centenary of city of Ahuachapan. (4.) Football (soccer) games. (5.) 4th Latin American Congress of Pathological Anatomy and 10th Central American Medical Congress, December, 1963. (6.) Second anniversary of the Alliance for Progress.

Fathers Nicolas, Vicente and Manuel Aguilar—A185

Parish Church, San Salvador, 1808
A186

Designs: 5c, 6c, Manuel José Arce, José Matias Delgado and Juan Manuel Rodriguez. 10c, 20c, Pedro Pablo Castillo, Domingo Antonio de Lara and Santiago José Celis. 50c, 80c, Monument to the Fathers, Plaza Libertad.

Photogravure
1961, Nov. 5   **Perf. 11½**   **Unwmkd.**

719	A185	1c gray & dk brn	10	10
720	A185	2c rose & dk brn	10	10
721	A185	5c pale brn & dk ol grn	20	6
722	A185	6c brt pink & dk brn	20	12
723	A185	10c bl & dk brn	20	10
724	A185	20c vio & dk brn	35	16
725	A186	30c brt bl & vio	50	24
726	A186	40c brn org & sep	75	30
727	A186	50c bl grn & sep	1.00	60
728	A186	80c gray & ultra	1.50	90
		Nos. 719-728 (10)	4.90	2.68

Issued to commemorate the sesquicentennial of the first cry for Independence in Central America.

No. 651 Overprinted: "III Exposición Industrial Centroamericana Diciembre de 1962"
1962, Dec. 21   **Litho.**   **Perf. 11½**

| 729 | A172 | 22c violet | 30 | 22 |

Issued to publicize the 3rd Central American Industrial Exposition. See Nos. C193-C195.

Nos. 708, 726-728 and 673 Surcharged.
1962-63   **Photogravure**

730	A183	6c on 15c brt pur & multi ('63)	35	12
731	A186	6c on 40c brn org & sep ('63)	35	12
732	A186	6c on 50c bl grn & sep ('63)	35	12
733	A183	10c on 15c brt pur & multi ('63)	35	12
734	A186	10c on 50c bl grn & sep ('63)	35	12
735	A186	10c on 80c gray & ultra ('63)	35	12
736	A173	10c on 1col brt bl ('63)	35	12
		Nos. 730-736 (7)	2.45	84

Surcharge includes bars on Nos. 731-734, 736; dot on Nos. 730, 735.

No. 726 Overprinted in Arc: "CAMPAÑA MUNDIAL CONTRA EL HAMBRE"
1963, Mar. 21

| 737 | A186 | 40c brn org & sep | 90 | 60 |

Issued for the "Freedom from Hunger Campaign" of the U.N. Food and Agriculture Organization.

Coyote
A187

Christ on Globe
A188

Designs: 2c, Spider monkey (vert.). 3c, Raccoon. 5c, King vulture (vert.). 6c, Brown coati. 10c, Kinkajou.

1963   **Photogravure**   **Perf. 11½**

738	A187	1c lil, blk, ocher & brn	10	10
739	A187	2c lt grn & blk	10	10
740	A187	3c fawn, dk brn & buff	10	10
741	A187	5c gray grn, ind, red & buff	15	10
742	A187	6c rose lil, blk, brn & buff	15	10
743	A187	10c lt bl, brn & buff	75	60
		Nos. 738-743 (6)		

See also Nos. C200-C207.

1964-65   **Perf. 12x11½**

744	A188	6c bl & brn	12	10
745	A188	10c bl & bis	15	10

Miniature Sheets
Imperf.

746	A188	60c bl & brt pur	90	85
a.		Marginal ovpt. (La Union)	1.75	1.75
b.		Marginal ovpt. (Usulutan)	1.75	1.75
c.		Marginal ovpt. (La Libertad)	1.75	1.75

Issued to commemorate the Second National Eucharistic Congress, San Salvador, Apr. 16-19. No. 746 contains one stamp. Size: 75x100mm. See Nos. C208-C210.

Nos. 746a, 746b and 746c commemorate the centenaries of the Departments of La Union, Usulután and La Libertad. Marginal inscriptions in dull purple (746a), green (746b) and blue (746c).

Issue dates: Nos. 744-746, Apr. 16, 1964. Nos. 746a-746b, June 22, 1965, 746c, Jan. 28, 1965.

Pres. John F. Kennedy
A189

Perf. 11½x12
1964, Nov. 22   **Unwmkd.**

747	A189	6c buff & blk	15	8
748	A189	10c tan & blk	25	10
749	A189	50c pink & blk	75	45
		Nos. 747-749, C211-C213 (6)	2.35	1.53

Miniature Sheet
Imperf.

| 750 | A189 | 70c dp grn & blk | 1.00 | 1.00 |

Issued in memory of President John F. Kennedy (1917-1963). No. 750 contains one stamp; black marginal inscription and control number. Size: 100x76mm.

Water Lily
A190

Flowers: 5c, Maquilishuat. 6c, Cinco negritos. 30c, Hortensia. 50c, Maguey. 60c, Geranium.

1965, Jan. 6   **Photo.**   **Perf. 12x11½**

751	A190	3c dl grn, brn yel & org	6	6
752	A190	5c ol gray & car rose	8	8
753	A190	6c multi	10	10
754	A190	30c ol bis, vio & grn	30	20
755	A190	50c dk bl, yel grn & brn	90	35
756	A190	60c multi	1.00	40
		Nos. 751-756 (6)	2.36	1.11

See also Nos. C215-C220.

ICY Emblem—A191

1965, Apr. 27   **Photo.**   **Perf. 11½x12**
Design in Brown and Gold

757	A191	5c dp yel	8	8
758	A191	6c dp rose	10	8
759	A191	10c gray	15	10
		Nos. 757-759, C221-C223 (6)	1.28	1.03

International Cooperation Year.

No. 728 Overprinted in Red: "Ier. Centenario Muerte / Cap. Gral. Gerardo Barrios / 1865 1965 / 29 de Agosto"
1965   **Perf. 11½**   **Unwmkd.**

| 760 | A186 | 80c gray & ultra | 1.00 | 60 |

Issued to commemorate the centenary of the death of Capt. Gen. Gerardo Barrios.

SALVADOR

 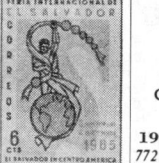

Francisco Antonio Gavidia A192   Fair Emblem A193

Perf. 11½x12

1965, Sept. 24 Photo. Unwmkd.
Portrait in Natural Colors
761	A192	2c blk & rose vio	20	15
762	A192	3c blk & org	25	15
763	A192	6c blk & lt ultra	25	15
	Nos. 761-763, C224-C226 (6)		3.15	1.85

Issued to honor Francisco Antonio Gavidia, philosopher.

No. 759 Overprinted in Carmine:
"1865 / 12 de Octubre / 1965 / Dr. Manuel Enrique Araujo"

1965, Oct. 12
| 764 | A191 | 10c brn, gray & gold | 15 | 10 |

Issued to commemorate the centenary of the birth of Manuel Enrique Araujo, president of Salvador, 1911–1913. See No. C227.

1965, Nov. 5 Photo. Perf. 12x11½
765	A193	6c yel & multi	12	8
766	A193	10c multi	18	10
767	A193	20c pink & multi	30	20
	Nos. 765-767, C228-C230 (6)		6.60	5.63

Issued to publicize the International Fair of El Salvador, Nov. 5-Dec. 4, 1965.

WHO Headquarters, Geneva A194

1966, May 20 Photo. Unwmkd.
| 768 | A194 | 15c beige & multi | 25 | 15 |

Issued to commemorate the inauguration of World Health Organization Headquarters, Geneva. See also No. C231.

No. 728 Overprinted in Red:
"Mes de Conmemoracion / Civica de la Independencia / Centroamericana / 19 Sept. / 1821 1966"

1966, Sept. 19 Photo. Perf. 11½
| 769 | A186 | 80c gray & ultra | 80 | 70 |

Issued to publicize the month of civic commemoration of Central American independence.

UNESCO Emblem A195

1966, Nov. 4 Perf. 12 Unwmkd.
| 770 | A195 | 20c gray, blk & vio bl | 25 | 18 |
| 771 | A195 | 1col emer, blk & vio bl | 1.25 | 80 |

Issued to commemorate the 20th anniversary of UNESCO (United Nations Educational, Scientific and Cultural Organization). See Nos. C233-C234.

Map of Central America, Flags and Cogwheels A196

1966, Nov. 27 Litho. Perf. 12
772	A196	6c multi	12	10
773	A196	10c multi	15	12
	Nos. 772-773, C235-C237 (5)		1.57	1.07

Issued to commemorate the 2nd International Fair of El Salvador, Nov. 5–27.

José Simeon Cañas Pleading for Indian Slaves—A197

1967, Feb. 18 Litho. Perf. 11½
| 774 | A197 | 6c yel & multi | 15 | 8 |
| 775 | A197 | 10c lil rose & multi | 18 | 10 |

Issued to commemorate the bicentenary of the birth of Father José Simeon Cañas y Villacorta, D.D. (1767–1838), emancipator of the Central American slaves. See also No. C239–C240.

No. 726 Overprinted in Red: "XV Convención de Clubes / de Leones, Región de / El Salvador—11 y 12 / de Marzo de 1967"

1967   Photogravure
| 776 | A186 | 40c brn org & sep | 70 | 30 |

Issued to publicize the 15th Convention of Lions Clubs of El Salvador, March 11–12.

Volcano San Miguel A198

1967, Apr. 14 Photo. Perf. 13
| 777 | A198 | 70c lt rose lil & brn | 1.50 | 90 |

Centenary of stamps of El Salvador. See also No. C241.

No. 768 Overprinted in Red: "VIII CONGRESO / CENTROAMERICANO DE / FARMACIA Y BIOQUIMICA / 5 di 11 Noviembre de 1967"

1967, Oct. 26 Photo. Perf. 12x11½
| 778 | A194 | 15c multi | 25 | 15 |

Issued to publicize the 8th Central American Congress for Pharmacy and Biochemistry. See No. C242.

No. 751 Overprinted in Red: "I Juegos / Centroamericanos y del / Caribe de Basquetbol / 25 Nov. al 3 Dic. 1967"

1967, Nov. 15
| 779 | A190 | 3c dl grn, brn, yel & org | 12 | 8 |

Issued to publicize the First Central American and Caribbean Basketball Games, Nov. 25–Dec. 3. See No. C243.

No. 757 Overprinted in Carmine: "1968 / AÑO INTERNACIONAL DE / LOS DERECHOS HUMANOS"

1968, Jan. 2 Photo. Perf. 11½x12
| 780 | A191 | 5c dp yel, brn & gold | 12 | 8 |

Issued for International Human Rights Year 1968. See No. C244.

Weather Map, Satellite and WMO Emblem A199

1968, Mar. 25 Photo. Perf. 11½x12
| 781 | A199 | 1c multi | 15 | 10 |
| 782 | A199 | 30c multi | 45 | 25 |

World Meteorological Day, Mar. 25.

No. 768 Overprinted in Red: "1968 / XX ANIVERSARIO DE LA / ORGANIZACION MUNDIAL / DE LA SALUD"

1968, Apr. 7 Perf. 12x11½
| 783 | A194 | 15c multi | 30 | 15 |

Issued to commemorate the 20th anniversary of the World Health Organization. See also No. C245.

No. 765 Overprinted in Red: "1968 / Año / del Sistema / del Crédito / Rural"

1968, May 6 Photo. Perf. 12x11½
| 784 | A193 | 6c yel & multi | 15 | 8 |

Rural credit system. See also No. C246.

Alberto Masferrer A200   Scouts Helping to Build A201

1968, June 22 Litho. Perf. 12x11½
785	A200	2c multi	10	6
786	A200	6c multi	15	8
787	A200	25c vio & multi	50	20
	Nos. 785-787, C247-C248 (5)		1.10	54

Issued to commemorate the centenary of the birth of Alberto Masferrer, philosopher and scholar.

1968, July 26 Litho. Perf. 12
| 788 | A201 | 25c multi | 35 | 25 |

Issued to publicize the 7th Inter-American Boy Scout Conference, July–Aug., 1968. See also No. C249.

Map of Central America, Flags and Presidents of U.S., Costa Rica, Salvador, Guatemala, Honduras and Nicaragua—A202

1968, Dec. 5 Litho. Perf. 14½
| 789 | A202 | 10c tan & multi | 15 | 8 |
| 790 | A202 | 15c multi | 25 | 12 |

Issued to commemorate the meeting of Pres. Lyndon B. Johnson with the presidents of the Central American republics (J. J. Trejos, Costa Rica; Fidel Sanchez Hernandez, Salvador; J. C. Mendez Montenegro, Guatemala; Osvaldo López Arellano, Honduras; Anastasio Somoza Debayle, Nicaragua), San Salvador, July 5–8, 1968. See Nos. C250–C251.

Heliconius Charithonius A203

Various Butterflies

1969   Lithographed   Perf. 12
791	A203	5c bluish lil, blk & yel	10	5
792	A203	10c beige & multi	15	8
793	A203	30c lt grn & multi	35	20
794	A203	50c tan & multi	60	35
	Nos. 791-794, C252-C255 (8)		16.95	9.85

Red Cross Activities A204

1969   Lithographed   Perf. 12
795	A204	10c lt bl & multi	10	8
796	A204	20c pink & multi	20	12
797	A204	40c lil & multi	40	25
	Nos. 795-797, C256-C258 (6)		7.30	4.10

Issued to commemorate the 50th anniversary of the League of Red Cross Societies.

No. 749 Overprinted in Green: "Alunizaje / Apolo - 11 / 21 Julio / 1969"

1969, Sept. Photo. Perf. 11½x12
| 798 | A189 | 50c pink & blk | 60 | 40 |

Issued to commemorate man's first landing on the moon, July 20, 1969. See note after U.S. No. C76.

The same overprint in red brown and pictures of the landing module and the astronauts on the moon were applied to the margin of No. 750. See C259.

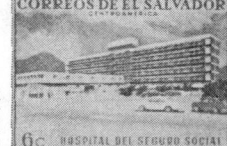

Social Security Hospital A205

1969, Oct. 24 Litho. Perf. 11½
799	A205	6c multi	8	5
800	A205	10c multi	12	8
801	A205	30c multi	40	20
	Nos. 799-801, C260-C262 (6)		10.60	5.68

ILO Emblem A206

1969   Lithographed   Perf. 13
| 802 | A206 | 10c yel & multi | 15 | 10 |

Issued to commemorate the 50th anniversary of the International Labor Organization. See No. C263.

Chorros Spa A207

SALVADOR

Views: 40c, Jaltepeque Bay. 80c, Fountains, Amapulapa Spa.

1969, Dec. 19 Photo. Perf. 12x11½

803	A207	10c blk & multi	12	12
804	A207	40c blk & multi	50	35
805	A207	80c blk & multi	1.00	70
		Nos. 803-805, C264-C266 (6)	3.02	1.89

Tourism.

Euchroma Gigantea—A208

Insects: 25c, Grasshopper. 30c, Digger wasp.

1970, Feb. 24 Litho. Perf. 11½x11

806	A208	5c lt bl & multi	10	8
807	A208	25c dl yel & multi	30	12
808	A208	30c dl rose & multi	40	24
		Nos. 806-808, C267-C269 (6)	12.05	6.36

Map and Arms of Salvador,
National Unity Emblem—A209

1970, Apr. 14 Litho. Perf. 14

| 809 | A209 | 10c yel & multi | 15 | 6 |
| 810 | A209 | 40c pink & multi | 70 | 20 |

Issued to publicize Salvador's support of universal human rights. See Nos. C270-C271.

Soldiers with Flag
A210

Design: 30c, Anti-aircraft gun.

1970, May 7 Perf. 12

811	A210	10c grn & multi	15	8
812	A210	30c lem & multi	45	20
		Nos. 811-812, C272-C274 (5)	2.05	95

Issued for Army Day, May 7.

National Lottery Headquarters
A211

1970, July 15 Litho. Perf. 12

| 813 | A211 | 20c lt vio & multi | 25 | 10 |

National Lottery centenary. See No. C291.

U.N. and Education Year Emblems
A212

1970, Sept. 11 Litho. Perf. 12

| 814 | A212 | 50c multi | 60 | 25 |
| 815 | A212 | 1col multi | 1.25 | 60 |

Issued for International Education Year. See Nos. C292-C293.

Map of Salvador, Globe and Cogwheels
A213

1970, Oct. 28 Litho. Perf. 12

| 816 | A213 | 5c pink & multi | 9 | 5 |
| 817 | A213 | 10c buff & multi | 18 | 6 |

4th International Fair, San Salvador. See Nos. C294-C295.

Beethoven
A214

1971, Feb. 22 Litho. Perf. 13½

| 818 | A214 | 50c ol, brn & yel | 75 | 40 |

Second International Music Festival. See No. C296.

No. 787 Overprinted:
"Año / del Centenario de la / Biblioteca Nacional / 1970"

1970, Nov. 25 Perf. 12x11½

| 819 | A200 | 25c vio & multi | 30 | 25 |

Centenary of the National Library. See No. C297.

Maria Elena Sol   Pietà, by
A215   Michelangelo
                 A216

1971, Apr. 1 Litho. Perf. 14

| 820 | A215 | 10c lt grn & multi | 15 | 6 |
| 821 | A215 | 30c multi | 40 | 20 |

Maria Elena Sol, Miss World Tourism, 1970-71. See Nos. C298-C299.

1971, May 10

| 822 | A216 | 10c sal & vio brn | 12 | 10 |

Mother's Day, 1971. See No. C300.

No. 810 Overprinted in Red

1867
CIV Aniversario*
Fundación de la
Policía Nacional
6-Julio
1971

1971, July 6 Lithographed Perf. 14

| 823 | A209 | 40c pink & multi | 70 | 35 |

104th anniversary of National Police. See No. C301.

Tiger Sharks
A217

Design: 40c, Swordfish.

1971, July 28

| 824 | A217 | 10c multi | 12 | 8 |
| 825 | A217 | 40c grn & multi | 40 | 24 |

See Nos. C302-C303.

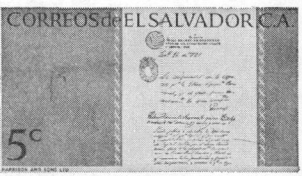

Declaration of Independence—A218

Designs: Various sections of Declaration of Independence of Central America.

1971 Perf. 13½x13

826	A218	5c yel grn & blk	6	5
827	A218	10c brt rose & blk	12	6
828	A218	15c dp org & blk	18	10
829	A218	20c dp red lil & blk	25	12
		Nos. 826-829, C304-C307 (8)	3.36	1.68

Sesquicentennial of Independence of Central America.

Izalco Church
A219

Design: 30c, Sonsonate Church.

1971, Aug. 21 Litho. Perf. 13x13½

| 830 | A219 | 20c blk & multi | 40 | 15 |
| 831 | A219 | 30c pur & multi | 60 | 20 |

See Nos. C308-C309.

No. 821 Overprinted in Carmine: "1972 Año de Turismo / de las Américas"

1972, Nov. 15 Litho. Perf. 14

| 832 | A215 | 30c multi | 40 | 15 |

Tourist Year of the Americas, 1972.

No. 818 Overprinted in Red

III Festival
Internacional de
Música 9-25-
Febrero - 1973.

1973, Feb. 5 Litho. Perf. 13½

| 833 | A214 | 50c ol, brn & yel | 50 | 25 |

3rd International Music Festival, Feb. 9-25. See No. C313.

Lions International Emblem
A220

1973, Feb. 20 Litho. Perf. 13

| 834 | A220 | 10c pink & multi | 8 | 6 |
| 835 | A220 | 25c lt bl & multi | 20 | 12 |

31st Lions International District "D" Convention, San Salvador, May 1972. See Nos. C314-C315.

No. 812 Overprinted:
"1923 1973 / 50 AÑOS
FUNDACION / FUERZA AEREA"

1973, Mar. 20 Litho. Perf. 12

| 836 | A210 | 30c lem & multi | 35 | 15 |

50th anniversary of Salvadorian Air Force.

Hurdling
A221

Designs (Olympic Emblem and): 10c, High jump. 25c, Running. 60c, Pole vault.

1973, May 21 Lithographed Perf. 13

837	A221	5c lil & multi	5	5
838	A221	10c dl org & multi	8	6
839	A221	25c bl & multi	20	12
840	A221	60c ultra & multi	55	30
		Nos. 837-840, C316-C319 (8)	6.33	2.93

20th Olympic Games, Munich, Aug. 26-Sept. 11, 1972.

No. 777 Surcharged:

 10 CTS.

1973, Dec. Photogravure Perf. 13

| 841 | A198 | 10c on 70c multi | 8 | 6 |

See No. C320.

Nos. 774, C240 Surcharged with New Value and Overprinted "1823 - 1973 / 150 Aniversario Liberación / Esclavos en Centroamérica"

1973-74 Litho. Perf. 11½

| 841A | A197 | 5c on 6c multi ('74) | 5 | 5 |
| 842 | A197 | 10c on 45c multi | 8 | 6 |

Sesquicentennial of the liberation of the slaves in Central America. On No. 841A two bars cover old denomination. On No. 842 "Aereo" is obliterated with a bar and old denomination with two bars.

Nos. 747 and 786 Surcharged:

 5 CTS.

1974 Photogravure Perf. 11½x12

| 843 | A189 | 5c on 6c buff & blk | 15 | 10 |

Lithographed Perf. 12x11½

| 843A | A200 | 5c on 6c multi | 15 | 10 |

No. 843A has one obliterating rectangle and sans-serif "5".
Issue dates: No. 843, Apr. 22. No. 843A, June 21.

Rehabilitation Institute Emblem
A222

1974, Apr. 30 Litho. Perf. 13

| 844 | A222 | 10c multi | 8 | 6 |

10th anniversary of the Salvador Rehabilitation Institute. See No. C324.

SALVADOR

INTERPOL Headquarters, Saint-Cloud, France
A223

1974, Sept. 2   Litho.   Perf. 12½
845 A223   10c multi   8   6
50th anniversary of International Criminal Police Organization (INTERPOL). See No. C341.

UN and FAO Emblems
A224

1974, Sept. 2   Litho.   Perf. 12½
846 A224   10c bl, dk bl & gold   8   6
World Food Program, 10th anniversary. See No. C342.

25c Silver Coin, 1914
A225

Coins: 15c, 50c silver, 1953. 25c, 25c silver, 1943. 30c, 1c copper, 1892.

1974, Nov. 19   Litho.   Perf. 12½x13
848 A225   10c multi   8   6
849 A225   15c multi   12   9
850 A225   25c multi   20   15
851 A225   30c multi   24   18
  Nos. 848-851, C343-C346 (8) 2.00 1.50

No. 763 Surcharged

XII Serie Ajedrez de Centro America y del Caribe Oct. 1974   **5 cts.**

1974, Oct. 14   Photo. Perf. 11½x12
852 A192   5c on 6c multi   12   8
12th Central American and Caribbean Chess Tournament, Oct. 1974.

No. 762 and 771 Surcharged

₡ 0.10

1974-75   Perf. 11½x12, 12
853   A192 10c on 3c multi   12   8
853A A195 25c on 1col multi ('75) 20 10
Bar and surcharge on one line on No. 853A. Issue dates: No. 853, Dec. 19, 1974. No. 853A, Jan. 13, 1975.

UPU Emblem
A226

1975, Jan. 22   Litho.   Perf. 13
854 A226   10c bl & multi   8   6
855 A226   60c bl & multi   48   35
Centenary of Universal Postal Union. See Nos. C356-C357.

Acajutla Harbor
A227

1975, Feb. 17
856 A227   10c bl & multi   8   6
See No. C358.

No. 799 Surcharged

₡ 0.05

1975   Lithographed   Perf. 11½
857 A205   5c on 6c multi   12   8

Central Post Office, San José
A228

1975, Apr. 25   Litho.   Perf. 13
858 A228   10c bl & multi   8   6
See No. C359.

Map of Americas and El Salvador, Trophy
A229

1975, June 25   Litho.   Perf. 12½
859 A229   10c red org & multi 15   10
860 A229   40c bl & multi   50   35
El Salvador, site of 1975 Miss Universe Contest. See Nos. C360-C361.

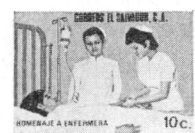

Claudia Lars, Poet, and IWY Emblem
A230

1975, Sept. 4   Litho.   Perf. 12½
861 A230   10c yel & bl blk   8   6
International Women's Year 1975. See Nos. C362-C363.

Nurses Attending Patient
A231

1975, Oct. 24   Litho.   Perf. 12½
862 A231   10c lt grn & multi 15   10
Nurses' Day. See No. C364.

Congress Emblem
A232

1975, Nov. 19   Litho.   Perf. 12½
863 A232   10c yel & multi   8   6
15th Congress of Inter-American Security Printers Association, San Salvador, Nov. 16-20. See No. C365.

No. 768 Overprinted in Red:
"XVI / CONGRESO MEDICO / CENTRO-AMERICANO / SAN SALVADOR, / EL SALVADOR, / DIC. 10-13, 1975"

1975, Nov. 26   Photo. Perf. 12x11½
864 A194   15c beige & multi 25   15
16th Central American Medical Congress, San Salvador, Dec. 10-13.

Flags of Participants, Arms of Salvador
A233

1975, Nov. 28   Litho.   Perf. 12½
865 A233   15c blk & multi   12   8
866 A233   50c brn & multi   40   30
8th Ibero-Latin-American Dermatological Congress, San Salvador, Nov. 28-Dec. 3. See Nos. C366-C367.

Jesus and Caritas Emblem
A234

1975, Dec. 18   Litho.   Perf. 13½
867 A234   10c dl red & mar   8   6
7th Latin American Charity Congress, San Salvador, Nov. 1971. See No. C368.

No. 862 Overprinted:
"III CONGRESO / ENFERMERIA / CENCAMEX 76"

1976, May 10   Litho.   Perf. 12½
868 A231   10c lt grn & multi 12   8
CENCAMEX 76, 3rd Nurses' Congress.

Map of El Salvador
A235

1976, May 18
869 A235   10c vio bl & multi 8   6
10th Congress of Revenue Collectors (Centro Interamericano de Administradores Tributarios, CIAT), San Salvador, May 16-22. See No. C382.

Flags of Salvador and U.S., Torch, Map of Americas—A236

The Spirit of '76, by Archibald M. Willard—A237

1976, June 30   Litho.   Perf. 12½
870 A236   10c yel & multi   8   6
871 A237   40c multi   32   24
American Bicentennial. See Nos. C383-C384.

American Crocodile—A238

Reptiles: 20c, Green iguana. 30c, Iguana.

1976, Sept. 23   Litho.   Perf. 12½
872 A238   10c multi   8   6
873 A238   20c multi   16   12
874 A238   30c multi   24   18
  Nos. 872-874, C385-C387 (6) 1.28 96

Post-classical Vase, San Salvador
A239

Pre-Columbian Art: 15c, Brazier with classical head, Tazumal. 40c, Vase with classical head, Tazumal.

1976, Oct. 11   Litho.   Perf. 12½
875 A239   10c multi   8   6
876 A239   15c multi   12   8
877 A239   40c multi   32   24
  Nos. 875-877, C388-C390 (6) 1.60 1.22

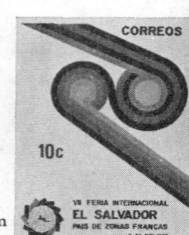

Fair Emblem
A240

SALVADOR

1976, Oct. 25   Litho.   Perf. 12½

| 878 | A240 | 10c multi | 8 | 6 |
| 879 | A240 | 30c gray & multi | 23 | 18 |

7th International Fair, Nov. 5–22. See Nos. C391–C392.

Child under Christmas Tree
A241

1976, Dec. 16   Litho.   Perf. 11

880	A241	10c yel & multi	8	6
881	A241	15c buff & multi	12	9
882	A241	30c vio & multi	24	18
883	A241	40c pink & multi	32	24
		Nos. 880–883, C393–C396 (8)	2.44	1.83

Christmas 1976.

Rotary Emblem, Map of Salvador
A242

1977, June 20   Litho.   Perf. 11

| 884 | A242 | 10c multi | 15 | 10 |
| 885 | A242 | 15c multi | 20 | 15 |

San Salvador Rotary Club, 50th anniversary. See Nos. C397–C398.

Cerron Grande Hydroelectric Station
A243

Designs: No. 887, 15c, Central sugar refinery, Jiboa. 30c, Radar station, Izalco (vert.).

1977, June 29   Perf. 12½

886	A243	10c multi	8	6
887	A243	10c multi	8	6
888	A243	15c multi	12	10
889	A243	30c multi	24	18
		Nos. 886–889, C399–C401 (7)	1.72	1.30

Industrial development. Nos. 886–889 have colorless overprint in multiple rows: GOBIERNO DEL SALVADOR.

Nos. 785 and 774 Surcharged with New Value and Bar

1977, June 30   Perf. 12x11½, 11½

| 890 | A200 | 15c on 2c multi | 12 | 10 |
| 891 | A197 | 25c on 6c multi | 20 | 16 |

Microphone, ASDER Emblem
A244

1977, Sept. 14   Litho.   Perf. 14

| 892 | A244 | 10c multi | 15 | 10 |
| 893 | A244 | 15c multi | 20 | 15 |

Broadcasting in El Salvador, 50th anniversary (Asociacion Salvadoreño de Empresa Radio). See Nos. C404–C405.

The index in each Catalogue volume contains many listings which help to identify stamps.

Wooden Drum
A245

Design: 10c, Flute and recorder.

1978, Aug. 29   Litho.   Perf. 12½

894	A245	5c multi	5	5
895	A245	10c multi	8	6
		Nos. 894–895, C433–C435 (5)	1.38	1.04

"Man and Engineering"
A246

1978, Sept. 12   Litho.   Perf. 13½

| 896 | A246 | 10c multi | 8 | 6 |

4th National Engineers' Congress, San Salvador, Sept. 18–23. See No. C436.

Izalco Station
A247

1978, Sept. 14   Perf. 12½

| 897 | A247 | 10c multi | 8 | 6 |

Inauguration of Izalco satellite earth station, Sept. 15, 1978. See No. C437.

Fair Emblem
A248

1978, Oct. 30   Litho.   Perf. 12½

| 898 | A248 | 10c multi | 8 | 6 |
| 899 | A248 | 20c multi | 16 | 12 |

8th International Fair, Nov. 3–20. See Nos. C440–C441.

Henri Dunant, Red Cross Emblem
A249

1978, Oct. 30   Perf. 11

| 900 | A249 | 10c multi | 8 | 6 |

Henri Dunant (1828–1910), founder of the Red Cross. See No. C442.

World Map and Cotton Boll
A250

1978, Nov. 22   Perf. 12½

| 901 | A250 | 15c multi | 12 | 8 |

International Cotton Consulting Committee, 37th Meeting, San Salvador, Nov. 27–Dec. 2. See No. C443.

Nativity, Stained-glass Window
A251

1978, Dec. 5   Litho.   Perf. 12½

| 902 | A251 | 10c multi | 8 | 6 |
| 903 | A251 | 15c multi | 12 | 8 |

Christmas 1978. See Nos. C444–C445.

Athenaeum Coat of Arms
A252

1978, Dec. 20   Litho.   Perf. 14

| 904 | A252 | 5c multi | 5 | 5 |

Millennium of Castilian language. See No. C446.

Postal Service and UPU Emblems
A253

1979, Apr. 2   Litho.   Perf. 14

| 905 | A253 | 10c multi | 8 | 6 |

Centenary of Salvador's membership in Universal Postal Union. See No. C447.

"75," Health Organization and WHO Emblems
A254

1979, Apr. 7   Perf. 14x14½

| 906 | A254 | 10c multi | 8 | 6 |

Pan-American Health Organization, 75th anniversary. See No. C448.

Flame and Pillars
A255

1979, May 25   Litho.   Perf. 12½

| 907 | A255 | 10c multi | 8 | 6 |
| 908 | A255 | 15c multi | 12 | 10 |

Social Security 5-year plan, 1978–1982. See Nos. C449–C450.

Pope John Paul II, Map of Americas
A256

1979, July 12   Litho.   Perf. 14½x14

| 909 | A256 | 10c multi | 8 | 6 |
| 910 | A256 | 20c multi | 16 | 12 |

See Nos. C454–C455.

Mastodon—A257

1979, Sept. 7   Litho.   Perf. 14

911	A257	10c shown	8	6
912	A257	20c Saber-toothed tiger	16	12
913	A257	30c Toxodon	24	18
		Nos. 911–913, C458–C460 (6)	2.40	1.82

Salvador Flag, José Aberiz and Proclamation—A258

1979, Sept. 14   Perf. 14½x14

| 914 | A258 | 10c multi | 8 | 6 |

National anthem centenary. See No. C461.

Cogwheel around Map of Americas—A259

458 SALVADOR

1979, Oct. 19	Litho.	Perf. 14½×14
915	A259	10c multi	8	6

8th COPIMERA Congress (Mechanical, Electrical and Allied Trade Engineers), San Salvador, Oct. 22-27. See No. C462.

Children of Various Races, IYC Emblem — A260

Children and Nurses, IYC Emblem — A261

1979, Oct. 29   Perf. 14×14½, 14½×14
916 A260 10c multi   8   6
917 A261 15c multi   12   10

International Year of the Child.

Map of Central and South America, Congress Emblem — A262

1979, Nov. 1   Litho.   Perf. 14½×14
918 A262 10c multi   8   6

5th Latin American Clinical Biochemistry Congress, San Salvador, Nov. 5-10. See No. C465.

Coffee Bushes in Bloom, Coffee Association Emblem — A263

Salvador Coffee Association, 50th Anniversary: 30c, Planting coffee bushes (vert.). 40c, Coffee berries.

1979, Dec. 18   Perf. 14×14½, 14½×14
919 A263 10c multi   8   6
920 A263 30c multi   24   18
921 A263 40c multi   32   24
    Nos. 919-921, C466-C468 (6) 2.44 1.83

Children, Dove and Star — A264

1979, Dec. 18   Perf. 14½×14
922 A264 10c multi   8   6

Christmas 1979.

Hoof and Mouth Disease Prevention — A265

1980, June 3   Litho.   Perf. 14½×14
923 A265 10c multi   8   6

See No. C469.

Anadara Grandis — A266

1980, Aug. 12   Perf. 14×14½
924 A266 10c shown   8   6
925 A266 30c Ostrea iridescens 24 18
926 A266 40c Turritello leucostoma 32 24
    Nos. 924-926, C470-C473 (7) 2.36 1.78

Quetzal (Pharomachrus mocino) — A267

1980, Sept. 10   Litho.   Perf. 14x14½
927 A267 10c shown   8   6
928 A267 20c Penelopina nigra 16 12
    Nos. 927-928, C474-C476 (5) 1.44 1.08

Local Snakes — A268

1980, Nov. 12   Litho.   Perf. 14x14½
929 A268 10c Tree snake   8   6
930 A268 20c Water snake 16   12

See Nos. C477-C478.

Corporation of Auditors, 50th Anniv. — A269

1980, Nov. 26   Litho.   Perf. 14
931 A269 15c multi   12   10
932 A269 20c multi   16   12

See Nos. C479-C480.

Christmas 1980 — A270

1980, Dec. 5   Litho.   Perf. 14
933 A270 5c multi   5   5
934 A270 10c multi   8   6

See Nos. C481-C482.

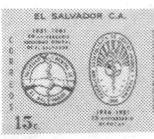

Dental Association Emblems — A271

1981, June 18   Litho.   Perf. 14
935 A271 15c lt yel grn & blk 12 10

Dental Society of Salvador, 50th anniv.; Odontological Federation of Central America and Panama, 25th anniv. See No. C494.

Hands Reading Braille Book — A272

1981, Aug. 14   Litho.   Perf. 14x14½
936 A272 10c multi   8   6
    Nos. 936, C495-C498 (5) 2.08 1.56

Intl. Year of the Disabled.

Roberto Quinonez Natl. Agriculture College, 25th Anniv. — A273

1981, Aug. 28   Litho.   Perf. 14x14½
937 A273 10c multi   8   6

See No. C499.

World Food Day — A274

1981, Sept. 16   Litho.   Perf. 14x14½
938 A274 10c multi   8   6

See No. C500.

1981 World Cup Preliminaries — A275

1981, Nov. 27   Litho.   Perf. 14x14½
939 A275 10c shown   8   6
940 A275 40c Cup, soccer ball, flags 32 24

See Nos. C505-C506.

Salvador Lyceum (High School), 100th Anniv. — A276

1981, Dec. 17   Litho.   Perf. 14
941 A276 10c multi   8   6

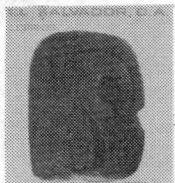

Pre-Columbian Stone Sculptures — A277

1982, Jan. 22   Litho.   Perf. 14
942 A277 10c Axe with bird's head 8 6
943 A277 20c Sun disc   16   12
944 A277 40c Steel carving with effigy 32 24
    Nos. 942-944, C508-C510 (6) 1.64 1.23

Scouting Year — A278

1982, Mar. 17   Litho.   Perf. 14½×14
945 A278 10c Flag, globe   8   6
946 A278 30c Girl Scout helping woman 24 18

See Nos. C511-C512.

SALVADOR

Armed Forces—A279

1982, May 7   Litho.   *Perf. 14x13½*
947   A279   10c multi   8   6
See No. C514.

1982 World Cup—A280

1982, July 14   *Perf. 14x14½*
948   A280   10c Team, emblem   8   6
See Nos. C518-C520.

10th International Fair—A281

1982, Oct. 14   Litho.   *Perf. 14*
949   A281   10c multi   8   6
See No. C524.

Christmas 1982—A282

1982, Dec. 14   Litho.   *Perf. 14*
950   A282   5c multi   5   5
See No. C528.

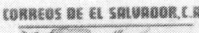

Dancers, Pre-Colombian Ceramic Design—A283

1983, Feb. 18   Litho.   *Perf. 14*
951   A283   10c shown   8   6
952   A283   20c Sower   16   12
953   A283   25c Flying Man   20   15
954   A283   60c Hunters   50   40
955   A283   60c Hunters, diff.   50   40
956   A283   1col Procession   80   60
957   A283   1col Procession, diff.   80   60
Nos. 951-957 (7)   3.04   2.33

Nos. 953-957 airmail. Stamps of same denomination se-tenant.

Visit of Pope John Paul II—A284

1983, Mar. 4   Litho.   *Perf. 14*
958   A284   25c shown   20   15
959   A284   60c Monument to the Divine Savior, Pope   50   40

Salvadoran Air Force, 50th Anniv.—A285

1983, Mar. 24   Litho.   *Perf. 14*
960   A285   10c Ricardo Aberle   8   6
961   A285   10c Air Force Emblem   8   6
962   A285   10c Enrico Massi   8   6
   a.   Strip of 3 (#960-962)   24   18
963   A285   10c Juan Ramon Munes   8   6
964   A285   10c American Air Force Cooperation Emblem   8   6
965   A285   10c Belisario Salazar   8   6
   a.   Strip of 3 (#963-965)   24   18

Arranged se-tenant horizontally with two Nos. 960 or 963 at left and two Nos. 962 or 965 at right.

Local Butterflies—A286

1983, May 31   Litho.   *Perf. 14*
966   Pair   10   10
   a.   A273 5c Papilio torquatus   5   5
   b.   A273 5c Metamorpha steneles   5   5
967   Pair   16   12
   a.   A273 10c Papilio torquatus, diff.   8   6
   b.   A273 10c Anaea marthesia   8   6
968   Pair   25   20
   a.   A273 15c Prepona brooksiana   12   10
   b.   A273 15c Caligo atreus   12   10
969   Pair   40   30
   a.   A273 25c Morpho peleides   20   15
   b.   A273 25c Dismorphia praxinoe   20   15
970   Pair   80   60
   a.   A273 50c Morpho polyphemus   40   30
   b.   A273 50c Metamorphia epaphus   40   30
Nos. 966-970 (10)   1.71   1.32

Simon Bolivar, 200th Birth Anniv.—A287

1983, June 23   Litho.   *Perf. 14*
971   A287   75c multi   60   45

Salvador Medical College, 40th Anniv.—A288

1983, July 21   Litho.   *Perf. 14*
972   A288   10c Dr. Jose Mendoza, college emblem   8   6

Centenary of David J. Guzman National Museum—A289

1983, Oct. 30   Litho.   *Perf. 13½x14, 14x13½*
973   A289   10c multi   8   6
974   A289   50c multi, horiz.   40   30

50c airmail.

World Communications Year—A290

Designs: 10c, Gen. Juan Jose Canas, Francisco Duenas (organizers of First natl. telegraph service), Morse key, 1870. 25c, Mailman delivering letters (vert.). 50c, Post Office sorting center, San Salvador. 25c, 50c airmail.

Perf. 14x13½, 13½x14
1983, Nov. 23   Litho.
975   A290   10c multi   8   6
976   A290   25c multi   20   15
977   A290   50c multi   40   30

Christmas 1983—A291

1983, Nov. 30   *Perf. 13½x14, 14x13½*
978   A291   10c Dove over globe   8   6
979   A291   25c Creche figures, horiz.   20   15

25c airmail.

Environmental Protection—A292

1983, Dec. 13
980   A292   10c Vehicle exhaust   8   6
981   A292   15c Fig tree   12   8
982   A292   25c Rodent   20   16

15c, 25c airmail.

Philatelists' Day—A293

1984, Jan. 5   *Perf. 14x13½*
983   A293   10c No. 1   8   6

Corn—A294

1984, Feb. 21   Litho.   *Perf. 14½x14*
984   A294   10c shown   8   6
985   A294   15c Cotton   12   8
986   A294   25c Coffee beans   20   15
987   A294   50c Sugar cane   40   30
988   A294   75c Beans   60   45
989   A294   1 col Agave   80   60
990   A294   5 col Balsam   4.00   3.00
Nos. 984-990 (7)   16.75   8.19

Caluco Church, Sonsonate—A295

1984, Mar. 30   *Perf. 14x13½*
991   A295   5c shown   5   5
992   A295   10c Salcoatitan, Sonsonate   8   6
993   A295   15c Huizucar, La Libertad   12   8
994   A295   25c Santo Domingo, Sonsonate   20   15
995   A295   50c Pilar, Sonsonate   40   30
996   A295   75c Nahuizalco, Sonsonate   60   45
Nos. 991-996 (6)   1.45   1.09

Nos. 993-996 airmail.

SALVADOR

AIR POST STAMPS.
Regular Issue of 1924-25
Overprinted in Black or Red **Servicio Aéreo**

First Printing.
15c on 10c: "15 QUINCE 15" measures 22½ mm.
20c: Shows on the back of the stamp an albino impression of the 50c surcharge.
25c on 35c: Original value cancelled by a long and short bar.
40c on 50c: Only one printing.
50c on 1col: Surcharge in dull orange red.

Perf. 12½, 14

1929, Dec. 28   Unwmkd.

C1	A112	20c dp grn (Bk)	7.50	6.00
a.		Red overprint	700.00	700.00

Counterfeits exist of No. C1a.

With Additional Surcharge of New Values and Bars in Black or Red.

C3	A111	15c on 10c org	1.25	1.25
a.		"ALTANT CO"	35.00	35.00
C4	A114	25c on 35c scar & grn	3.00	3.00
a.		Bars inverted	15.00	15.00
C5	A115	40c on 50c org brn	1.25	80
C6	A116	50c on 1col grn & vio (R)	17.50	12.50

Second Printing.
15c on 10c: "15 QUINCE 15" measures 20½ mm.
20c: Has not the albino impression on the back of the stamp.
25c on 35c: Original value cancelled by two bars of equal length.
50c on 1col: Surcharge in carmine rose.

1930, Jan. 10

C7	A112	20c dp grn	1.00	1.00
C8	A111	15c on 10c org	1.00	1.00
a.		"ATLANT CO"	35.00	
b.		Double surcharge	20.00	
c.		As "a" double surcharge	150.00	
d.		Pair, one without surch.	350.00	
C9	A114	25c on 35c scar & grn	85	85
C10	A116	50c on 1col grn & vio (C)	2.00	2.00
a.		Without bars over "UN COLON"	5.00	
b.		As "a" and without block over "1"	5.00	

Numerous wrong font and defective letters exist in both printings of the surcharges.
No. C10 with black surcharge is bogus.

Mail Plane over San Salvador
AP1

1930, Sept. 15   Engr.   Perf. 12½

C11	AP1	15c dp red	30	15
C12	AP1	20c emerald	40	15
C13	AP1	25c brn vio	40	15
C14	AP1	40c ultra	75	12

Simón Bolívar
AP2

1930, Dec. 17   Litho.   Perf. 11½

C15	AP2	15c dp red	10.00	7.50
a.		"15" double	125.00	
C16	AP2	20c emerald	10.00	7.50
C17	AP2	25c brn vio	10.00	7.50
b.		Vert. pair, imperf. between	175.00	
		Imperf., pair		
C18	AP2	40c dp ultra	10.00	7.50

Centenary of death of Simón Bolívar.
Counterfeits of Nos. C15-C18 exist.

No. 504 Overprinted in Red

1931, June 29   Engraved.   Perf. 14

C19	A116	1col grn & vio	6.00	5.00

Tower of La Merced Church
AP3

1931, Nov. 5   Litho.   Perf. 11½

C20	AP3	15c dk red	7.00	6.00
a.		Imperf., pair	100.00	
C21	AP3	20c bl grn	7.00	6.00
C22	AP3	25c dl vio	7.00	6.00
a.		Vertical pair, imperf. between	175.00	
C23	AP3	40c ultra	7.00	6.00
a.		Imperf. (pair)	100.00	

Issued in commemoration of the 120th anniversary of the first movement toward the political independence of El Salvador. In the tower of La Merced Church (AP3) hangs the bell which José Matías Delgado—called the Father of his Country—rang to initiate the movement for liberty.

José Matías Delgado   Airplane and Caravels of Columbus
AP4   AP5

Wmkd. Wavy Lines. (271)

1932, Nov. 12   Perf. 12½

C24	AP4	15c dl red & vio	2.00	2.00
C25	AP4	20c bl grn & bl	3.00	3.00
C26	AP4	25c dl vio & brn	3.00	3.00
C27	AP4	40c ultra & grn	3.50	3.50

Issued in commemoration of the first centenary of the death of Father José Matías Delgado, who is known as the Father of El Salvadoran Political Emancipation.
Nos. C24 to C27 show cheek without shading in the 72nd stamp of each sheet.

1933, Oct. 12   Perf. 13   Wmk. 240

C28	AP5	15c red org	2.00	2.00
C29	AP5	20c bl grn	4.00	4.00
C30	AP5	25c lilac	4.00	4.00
C31	AP5	40c ultra	4.00	4.00
C32	AP5	1col black	4.00	4.00
		Nos. C28-C32 (5)	18.00	18.00

Commemorative of the 441st anniversary of the sailing of Chistopher Columbus from Palos, Spain, for the New World.

Police Barracks
AP6

1934, Dec. 16   Perf. 12½

C33	AP6	25c lilac	75	35
C34	AP6	30c brown	1.00	75
a.		Imperf. (pair)	85.00	
C35		1col black	3.00	1.50

Runner—AP7

1935, Mar. 16   Engraved.   Unwmkd.

C36	AP7	15c carmine	7.50	7.50
C37	AP7	25c violet	7.50	7.50
C38	AP7	30c brown	6.50	6.00
C39	AP7	55c blue	32.50	30.00
C40	AP7	1col black	25.00	22.50
		Nos. C36-C40 (5)	79.00	73.50

Issued in commemoration of the Third Central American Games.

Same Overprinted in Black
HABILITADO

1935, June 27

C41	AP7	15c carmine	7.50	3.25
C42	AP7	25c violet	7.50	3.25
C43	AP7	30c brown	7.50	3.25
C44	AP7	55c blue	55.00	45.00
C45	AP7	1col black	16.50	2.50
		Nos. C41-C45 (5)	94.00	57.25

Flag of   Tree of
El Salvador   San Vicente
AP8   AP9

1935, Oct. 26   Litho.   Wmk. 240

C46	AP8	30c blk brn	90	35

1935, Dec. 26   Perf. 12½
Numerals in Black, Tree in Yellow Green.

C47	AP9	10c yellow	2.00	1.75
C48	AP9	15c brown	2.00	1.75
C49	AP9	20c dk bl grn	2.00	1.75
C50	AP9	25c dk pur	2.00	1.75
C51	AP9	30c blk brn	2.00	1.75
		Nos. C47-C51 (5)	10.00	8.75

Tercentenary of San Vicente.

No. 565 Overprinted in Red

1937   Engraved   Unwmkd.

C52	A133	15c dk ol bis	60	40
a.		Double ovpt.	50.00	

No. C44 Surcharged in Red   **30**

C53	AP7	30c on 55c bl	4.00	1.75

Panchimalco Church
AP10

1937, Dec. 3   Engraved.   Perf. 12

C54	AP10	15c org yel	35	25
C55	AP10	20c green	35	20
C56	AP10	25c violet	35	20
C57	AP10	30c brown	30	10
C58	AP10	40c blue	55	50
C59	AP10	1col black	1.50	50
C60	AP10	5col rose car	6.00	4.75
		Nos. C54-C60 (7)	9.40	6.50

U.S. Constitution Type of Regular Issue

1938, Apr. 22   Engr. & Litho.

C61	A136	30c multi	1.75	1.50

150th anniversary of U.S. Constitution.

José Simeón Cañas Villacorta
AP12

1938, Aug. 18   Engraved.

C62	AP12	15c orange	2.00	2.00
C63	AP12	20c brt grn	2.50	2.00
C64	AP12	30c redsh brn	2.50	1.50
C65	AP12	1col black	9.00	7.50

Issued to commemorate the centenary of the death of José Simeón Cañas y Villacorta (1767–1838), liberator of slaves in Central America.

Golden Gate Bridge, San Francisco Bay—AP13

1939, Apr. 14   Perf. 12½

C66	AP13	15c dl yel & blk	50	25
C67	AP13	30c dk brn & blk	60	25
C68	AP13	40c dk bl & blk	90	50

Golden Gate International Exposition, San Francisco.

Sir Rowland Hill
AP14

1940, Mar. 1   Engraved

C69	AP14	30c dk brn, buff & blk	10.00	4.00
C70	AP14	80c org red & blk	25.00	22.50

Issued to commemorate the centenary of the postage stamp. Covers postmarked Feb. 29 were predated. Actual first day was Mar. 1.

Map of the Americas, Figure of Peace, Plane—AP15

1940, May 22   Perf. 12

C71	AP15	30c brn & bl	60	55
C72	AP15	80c dk rose & blk	1.50	1.35

Pan American Union, 50th anniversary.

SALVADOR

Coffee Tree
in Bloom
AP16

Coffee Tree
with Ripe Berries
AP17

1940, Nov. 27

C73	AP16	15c yel org	1.75	35
C74	AP16	20c dp grn	2.00	20
C75	AP16	25c dk vio	3.00	75
C76	AP17	30c cop brn	3.50	35
C77	AP17	1col black	12.50	90
		Nos. C73-C77 (5)	22.75	2.55

Juan Lindo, Gen. Francisco
Mallespin and New National
University of El Salvador
AP18

Designs (portraits changed): 40c, 80c, Narciso Monterey and Antonio José Canas. 60c, 1col, Isidro Menéndez and Chrisanto Salazar.

1941, Feb. 16   Perf. 12½

C78	AP18	20c dk grn & rose lake	1.75	1.35
C79	AP18	40c old rose & brn org	1.75	1.35
C80	AP18	60c dl pur & brn	1.75	1.35
C81	AP18	80c hn brn & dk bl grn	4.75	4.25
C82	AP18	1col blk & org	4.75	4.25
C83	AP18	2col yel org & rose vio	4.75	4.25
a.		Miniature sheet, perf. 11½	25.00	25.00
		Nos. C78-C83 (6)	19.50	16.80

Centenary of University of El Salvador.
No. C83a measures 178x183mm. and contains one each of Nos. C78-C83 with no marginal inscriptions.
Stamps from No. C83a, perf. 11½, sell for about the same prices as the perf. 12½ stamps.

Map of El Salvador—AP20
Engraved.

1942, Nov. 25   Perf. 14   Wmk. 269

| C85 | AP20 | 30c red org | 1.00 | 85 |
| a. | | Horiz. pair, imperf. between | 150.00 | |

First Eucharistic Congress of El Salvador.
See No. 588.

Nos. C66 to C68
Surcharged with New Values
in Dark Carmine **15**

1943   Perf. 12½   Unwmkd.

C86	AP13	15c on 15c dl yel & blk	60	45
C87	AP13	20c on 30c dk brn & blk	70	45
C88	AP13	25c on 40c bl & blk	1.25	80

Nos. C66 to C68
Surcharged with
New Values in Dark Carmine **15**

1944

C89	AP13	15c on 15c dl yel & blk	65	60
C90	AP13	20c on 30c dk brn & blk	1.00	60
C91	AP13	25c on 40c dk bl & blk	1.50	75

Bridge Type of Regular Issue
Arms Overprint at Right in
Blue Violet.

1944, Nov. 24   Engraved

| C92 | A149 | 30c crim rose & blk | 70 | 35 |

No. C92 exists without overprint, but was not issued in that form.

Presidential Palace
AP22

National Theater—AP23

National Palace
AP24

1944, Dec. 22   Perf. 12½

C93	AP22	15c red vio	25	15
C94	AP23	20c dk bl grn	35	15
C95	AP24	25c dl vio	40	18

No. 582
Overprinted in Red **Aéreo**

1945, Aug. 23   Perf. 12

| C96 | A137 | 1col black | 1.25 | 60 |

Juan Ramon Uriarte
AP25
Typographed.

1946, Jan. 1   Perf. 12½   Wmk. 240

| C97 | AP25 | 12c dk bl | 35 | 18 |
| C98 | AP25 | 14c dp org | 35 | 12 |

Mayan Pyramid,
St. Andrés Plantation
AP26

Municipal Children's Garden,
San Salvador—AP27

Civil Aeronautics School,
Ilopango Airport—AP28

1946, May 1   Unwmkd.

C99	AP26	30c rose car	35	15
C100	AP27	40c dp ultra	55	40
C101	AP28	1col black	1.65	90

Alberto Masferrer
AP29

1946, July 19   Litho.   Wmk. 240

C102	AP29	12c carmine	40	20
C103	AP29	14c dl grn	40	15
a.		Imperf., pair	25.00	

Souvenir Sheets.

AP30

Designs: 40c, Charles I of Spain. 60c, Juan Manuel Rodriguez. 1col, Arms of San Salvador. 2col, Flag of El Salvador.

Perf. 12, Imperf.

1946, Nov. 8   Engr.   Unwmkd.

C104	AP30	Sheet of four	4.00	4.00
a.		40c brn	75	75
b.		60c car	75	75
c.		1col grn	75	75
d.		2col ultra	75	75

Issued in sheets measuring 118 x 162 mm., to commemorate the 4th centenary of San Salvador's city charter. The imperforate sheets are without gum.

Felipe Soto   Alfredo Espino
AP31   AP32
Lithographed.

1947, Sept. 11   Perf. 12½   Wmk. 240

| C106 | AP31 | 12c chocolate | 40 | 20 |
| C107 | AP32 | 14c dk bl | 30 | 15 |

Arce Type of Regular Issue

1948, Feb. 25   Engraved   Unwmkd.

C108	A163	12c green	30	20
C109	A163	14c rose car	40	20
C110	A163	1col violet	4.00	3.50

Issued to commemorate the centenary of the death of Manuel José Arce (1783–1847), "Father of Independence" and first president of the Federation of Central America.

Roosevelt Types of Regular Issue

Designs: 12c, Pres. Franklin D. Roosevelt. 14c, Pres. Roosevelt presenting awards for distinguished service. 20c, Pres. Roosevelt and Cordell Hull. 25c, Pres. and Mrs. Roosevelt. 1col, Mackenzie King, Roosevelt and Winston Churchill. 2col, Funeral of Pres. Roosevelt. 4col, Pres. and Mrs. Roosevelt.

1948, Apr. 12   Engr.   Perf. 12½
Various Frames; Center in Black.

C111	A165	12c green	60	40
C112	A164	14c olive	60	40
C113	A164	20c chocolate	60	50
C114	A164	25c carmine	60	50
C115	A164	1col vio brn	2.50	2.00
C116	A164	2col bl vio	4.50	3.00
		Nos. C111-C116 (6)	9.40	6.90

Souvenir Sheet.
Perf. 13½.

| C117 | A166 | 4col gray & brn | 7.00 | 7.00 |

Issued in sheets measuring 111 x 85 mm. Nos. C111 to C117 commemorate the 3rd anniversary of the death of President Franklin D. Roosevelt.

Nos. 599, 601 and 604
Overprinted
in Carmine or Black **Aéreo**

1948, Sept. 7   Perf. 12½

C118	A154	5c sl gray	15	10
C119	A154	10c bis brn	20	12
C120	A154	1col scar (Bk)	2.00	1.10

No. C99 Surcharged in Black

1949, July 23

| C121 | AP26 | 10(c) on 30c rose car | 30 | 12 |

UPU Type of Regular Issue

1949, Oct. 9   Engr.   Perf. 12½

C122	A167	5c brown	20	15
C123	A167	10c black	35	10
C124	A167	1col purple	12.50	12.50

Issued to commemorate the 75th anniversary of the formation of the Universal Postal Union.

Flag and Arms
of El Salvador
AP38

1949, Dec. 15   Perf. 10½
Flag and Arms in Blue,
Yellow and Green.

C125	AP38	5c ocher	25	10
C126	AP38	10c dk grn	35	12
a.		Yellow omitted	40.00	
C127	AP38	15c violet	45	12
C128	AP38	1col rose	1.00	90
C129	AP38	5col red vio	8.50	8.00
		Nos. C125-C129 (5)	10.55	9.24

Issued to commemorate the 1st anniversary of the Revolution of Dec. 14, 1948.

Isabella I
of Spain
AP39

Flag, Torch
and Scroll
AP40

SALVADOR

1951, Apr. 28   Litho.   Unwmkd.
Background in Ultramarine,
Red and Yellow.

C130	AP39	10c green	60	15
C131	AP39	20c purple	60	30
a.		Horiz. pair, imperf. between	50.00	
C132	AP39	40c rose car	60	30
C133	AP39	1col blk brn	2.00	1.10

Issued to commemorate the 500th anniversary of the birth of Queen Isabella I of Spain.
Nos. C130-C133 exist imperforate.

1952, Feb. 14   Photo.   Perf. 11½
Flag in Blue.

C134	AP40	10c brt bl	15	10
C135	AP40	15c chocolate	30	15
C136	AP40	20c dp bl	30	12
C137	AP40	25c gray	30	15
C138	AP40	40c purple	60	45
C139	AP40	1col red org	1.25	90
C140	AP40	2col org brn	4.00	3.50
C141	AP40	5col vio bl	4.00	1.75
		Nos. C134-C141 (8)	10.90	7.12

Constitution of 1950.

**Marti Type of Regular Issue
Inscribed "Aereo"
1953, Feb. 27   Litho.   Perf. 10½**

C142	A170	10c dk pur	30	20
C143	A170	20c dl brn	30	20
C144	A170	1col dl org	1.25	85

Issued to commemorate the centenary of the birth of José Marti, Cuban patriot.

No. C95 Surcharged "C 0.20"
and Obliterations in Red.
1953, Mar. 20   Perf. 12½

| C145 | AP24 | 20c on 25c dl vio | 40 | 30 |

No. C95
Overprinted
in Carmine
"IV Congreso Medico
Social Panamericano
16 / 19 Abril, 1953"
1953, June 19

| C146 | AP24 | 25c dl vio | 60 | 35 |

See note after No. 634.

Bell Tower, La Merced Church—AP42
1953, Sept. 15   Perf. 11½

C147	AP42	5c rose pink	12	12
C148	AP42	10c dp bl grn	12	12
C149	AP42	20c blue	30	25
C150	AP42	1col purple	4.00	90

Issued to commemorate the 132nd anniversary of the Act of Independence, September 15, 1821.

Fishing Boats—AP43

Gen. Manuel
José Arce
AP44

Balboa
Park
AP45

ODECA Officials and Flag
AP46

Designs: No. C152, Census allegory. No. C155, National Palace. No. C157, Coast guard boat. No. C158, Lake Ilopango. No. C159, Coastal bridge. No. C160, Guayabo dam. No. C161, Housing development. No. C162, Modern highway. No. C163, and C165, Motherland and Liberty. No. C164, Izalco volcano.

Photogravure.
1954, June 1   Perf. 11½   Unwmkd.

C151	AP43	5c org brn & cr	30	10
C152	AP44	5c brt car	30	10
C153	AP44	10c gray bl	35	10
C154	AP45	10c pur & lt brn	35	10
C155	AP43	10c ol & bl gray	35	10
C156	AP46	10c bl grn, dk grn & bl	35	10
C157	AP43	10c rose car	45	12
C158	AP43	15c dk gray	55	20
C159	AP43	20c pur & gray	65	22
C160	AP46	25c bl grn & bl	65	28
C161	AP46	30c mag & sal	70	28
C162	AP45	40c brt org & brn	1.10	50
C163	AP46	80c red brn	2.25	1.85
C164	AP43	1col mag & sal	2.50	1.85
C165	AP46	2col orange	5.00	2.00
		Nos. C151-C165 (15)	15.85	7.90

Barrios Type of Regular Issue, 1955
Engraved.
1955, Dec. 20   Perf. 12½   Wmk. 269

C166	A177	20c brown	25	20
C167	A177	30c dp red lil	40	35

Santa Ana
Type of Regular Issue, 1956.
Lithographed.
1956, June 20   Perf. 13½   Unwmkd.

C168	A178	5c org brn	10	10
C169	A178	10c green	10	10
C170	A178	40c red lil	40	35
C171	A178	80c emerald	1.00	85
C172	A178	5col gray bl	6.00	4.25
		Nos. C168-C172 (5)	7.60	5.70

Centenary of Santa Ana Department.

Chalatenango
Type of Regular Issue, 1956.
1956, Sept. 14

C173	A179	10c brt rose	15	12
C174	A179	15c orange	25	15
C175	A179	20c lt ol grn	25	18
C176	A179	25c dl pur	50	35
C177	A179	50c org brn	80	55
C178	A179	1col brt vio bl	1.25	1.25
		Nos. C173-C178 (6)	3.20	2.60

Centenary of Chalatenango Department (in 1955).

Nueva San Salvador
Type of Regular Issue, 1957
Engraved.
1957, Jan. 3   Perf. 12½   Wmk. 269

C179	A180	10c pink	20	12
C180	A180	20c dl red	30	12
C181	A180	50c pale org red	50	45
C182	A180	1col lt grn	1.25	90
C183	A180	2col org red	3.00	1.85
		Nos. C179-C183 (5)	5.25	3.44

Issued to commemorate the centenary of the founding of the city of Nueva San Salvador (Santa Tecla).

Lemus' Visit
Type of Regular Issue, 1959.
Photogravure.
1959, Dec. 14   Perf. 11½   Unwmkd.
Granite Paper
Design in Ultramarine, Dark Brown
Light Brown and Red.

C184	A182	15c red	30	18
C185	A182	20c green	35	25
C186	A182	30c carmine	45	35

Visit of Pres. José M. Lemus to the United States, Mar. 9-21.

No. C169 Overprinted in Red: "ANO MUNDIAL DE LOS REFUGIADOS 1959-1960."
1960, Apr. 7   Lithographed   Perf. 13½

| C187 | A178 | 10c green | 35 | 30 |

Issued to publicize World Refugee Year, July 1, 1959-June 30, 1960.

Type of Regular Issue, 1960
Poinsettia
Photogravure
1960, Dec. 17   Perf. 11½   Unwmkd.
Granite Paper
Design in Slate Green,
Red and Yellow

C188	A184	20c rose lil	50	25
C189	A184	30c gray	60	40
C190	A184	40c lt gray	1.00	50
C191	A184	50c sal pink	1.25	55

Miniature Sheet
Imperf.

| C192 | A184 | 60c gold | 1.75 | 1.75 |

No. C192 contains one stamp and is inscribed: "REPUBLICA DE EL SALVADOR, C.A." Size: 99x74mm.
See note after No. 718.

Nos. 672, 691 and C183 Overprinted: "III Exposición Industrial Centroamericana Diciembre de 1962" with "AEREO" Added on Nos. 672, 691.
1962, Dec. 21   Perf. 11½, 12½

C193	A174	10c brn org, dk brn & bl	75	65
C194	A180	1col dl red	75	65
C195	A180	2col org red	1.50	1.25

Issued to publicize the 3rd Central American Industrial Exposition.

Nos. C189, C194, C182 and C195
Surcharged
1963

C196	A184	10c on 30c multi	25	15
C197	A180	10c on 1col dl red	25	18
C198	A180	10c on 1col lt grn	1.65	18
C199	A180	10c on 2col org red	1.65	15

Surcharges include: "X" on No. C196; two dots and bar at bottom on No. C197. Heavy bar at bottom on No. C198. On No. C199, the four-line "Exposicion" overprint is lower than on No. C195.

Turquoise-
browed
Motmot
AP49

Birds: 5c, King vulture (vert., like No. 741). 6c, Yellow-headed parrot (vert.). 10c, Spotted-breasted oriole. 30c, Great-tailed grackle. 40c, Great curassow (vert.). 50c, Magpie-jay. 80c, Golden-fronted woodpecker (vert.).

Photogravure
1963   Perf. 11½   Unwmkd.
Birds in Natural Colors

C200	AP49	5c gray grn & blk	10	10
C201	AP49	6c tan & bl	12	12
C202	AP49	10c lt bl & blk	18	18
C203	AP49	20c gray & brn	35	18
C204	AP49	30c ol bis & blk	50	30
C205	AP49	40c pale & dk vio	75	40
C206	AP49	50c lt grn & blk	85	50
C207	AP49	80c vio bl & blk	1.50	80
		Nos. C200-C207 (8)	4.35	2.52

Type of Regular Issue, 1964
(Eucharistic Congress)
1964-65   Perf. 12x11½

C208	A188	10c sl grn & bl	15	10
C209	A188	25c red & bl	30	25

Miniature Sheets
Imperf.

C210	A188	80c bl & grn	1.00	1.00
a.		Marginal ovpt. (La Union)	1.25	1.25
b.		Marginal ovpt. (Usulutan)	1.25	1.25
c.		Marginal ovpt. (La Libertad)	1.25	1.25

Issued to commemorate the Second National Eucharistic Congress, San Salvador, Apr. 16-19. No. C210 contains one stamp. Size: 75x100mm.
Nos. C210a, C210b and C210c commemorate the centenaries of the Departments of La Union, Usulatán and La Libertad respectively. Marginal inscriptions in dull purple (C210a), green (C210b), and blue (C210c).
Issue dates: Nos. C208-C210, Apr. 16, 1964. Nos. C210a-C210b, June 22, 1965, 210c, Jan. 28, 1965.

Kennedy Type of Regular Issue
1964, Nov. 22   Perf. 11½x12

C211	A189	15c gray & blk	25	20
C212	A189	20c sage grn & blk	35	25
C213	A189	40c yel & blk	60	45

Miniature Sheet
Imperf.

| C214 | A189 | 80c grnsh bl & blk | 1.50 | 1.50 |

Issued in memory of President John F. Kennedy (1917-1963). No. C214 contains one stamp; black marginal inscription and control number. Size: 100x76mm.

Flower Type of Regular Issue
Flowers: 10c, Rose. 15c, Platanillo. 25c, San Jose. 40c, Hibiscus. 45c, Veranera. 70c, Fire flower.
1965, Jan. 6   Photo.   Perf. 12x11½

C215	A190	10c lt grn, ol & dp grn	15	10
C216	A190	15c multi	20	15
C217	A190	25c bl, yel & grn	30	25
C218	A190	40c gray, car rose & grn	40	35
C219	A190	45c sl, lil & grn	60	40
C220	A190	70c multi	85	65
		Nos. C215-C220 (6)	2.50	1.90

ICY Type of Regular Issue
Perf. 11½x12
1965, Apr. 27   Photo.   Unwmkd.
Design in Brown and Gold

C221	A191	15c lt bl	15	15
C222	A191	30c dl lil	30	20
C223	A191	50c ocher	50	45

Gavidia Type of Regular Issue
1965, Sept. 24   Photo.   Unwmkd.
Portraits in Natural Colors

C224	A192	10c blk & grn	25	15
C225	A192	20c blk & bis	40	25
C226	A192	1col blk & rose	1.75	1.00

Issued to honor Francisco Antonio Gavidia, philosopher.

No. C223 Overprinted in Green:
"1865 / 12 de Octubre / 1965 /
Dr. Manuel Enrique Araujo"
1965, Oct. 12   Perf. 11½x12

| C227 | A191 | 50c brn, ocher & gold | 65 | 45 |

See note after No. 764.

Fair Type of Regular Issue, 1965
1965, Nov. 5   Perf. 12x11½

| C228 | A193 | 20c bl & multi | 25 | 15 |

SALVADOR

C229	A193	80c multi		1.00	85
C230	A193	5col multi		4.75	4.25

Issued to publicize the International Fair of El Salvador, Nov. 5–Dec. 4, 1965.

WHO Type of Regular Issue
1966, May 20 Photo. **Unwmkd.**

C231	A194	50c multi	65	45

Issued to commemorate the inauguration of World Health Organization Headquarters, Geneva.

No. C209 Overprinted in Dark Green:
"1816 1966 / 150 años / Nacimiento / San Juan Bosco"

1966, Sept. 3 Photo. **Perf. 12x11½**

C232	A188	25c red & bl	50	35

Issued to commemorate the 150th anniversary of the birth of St. John Bosco (1815–1888), Italian priest, founder of the Salesian Fathers and Daughters of Mary.

UNESCO Type of Regular Issue
1966, Nov. 4 Photo. **Perf. 12**

C233	A195	30c tan, blk & vio bl	50	25
C234	A195	2col emer, blk & vio bl	2.50	1.65

See note after No. 771.

Fair Type of Regular Issue, 1966
1966, Nov. 27 Litho. **Perf. 12**

C235	A196	15c multi	25	15
C236	A196	20c multi	30	20
C237	A196	60c multi	75	50

Issued to commemorate the 2nd International Fair of El Salvador, Nov. 5–27.

No. C209 Overprinted:
"IX-Congreso / Interamericano / de Educación / Católica / 4 Enero 1967"

1967, Jan. 4 Photo. **Perf. 12x11½**

C238	A188	25c red & bl	50	30

Issued to publicize the 9th Inter-American Congress for Catholic Education.

Cañas Type of Regular Issue
1967, Feb. 18 Litho. **Perf. 11½**

C239	A197	5c multi	15	10
C240	A197	45c lt bl & multi	85	50

See note after No. 775.

Volcano Type of Regular Issue
1967, Apr. 14 Photo. **Perf. 13**

C241	A198	50c ol gray & brn	75	45

Centenary of stamps of El Salvador.

No. C231 Overprinted in Red:
"VIII CONGRESO / CENTROAMERICANO DE / FARMACIA & BIOQUIMICA / 5 di 11 Noviembre de 1967"

1967, Oct. 26 Photo. **Perf. 12x11½**

C242	A194	50c multi	65	45

Issued to publicize the 8th Central American Congress for Pharmacy and Biochemistry.

No. C217 Overprinted in Red:
"I Juegos / Centroamericanos y del / Caribe de Basquetbol / 25 Nov. al 3 Dic. 1967"

1967, Nov. 15

C243	A190	25c bl, yel & grn	35	25

First Central American and Caribbean Basketball Games, Nov. 25–Dec. 3.

No. C222 Overprinted in Carmine:
"1968 / AÑO INTERNACIONAL DE / LOS DERECHOS HUMANOS"

1968, Jan. 2 Photo. **Perf. 11½x12**

C244	A191	30c dl lil, brn & gold	60	35

International Human Rights Year 1968.

No. C231 Overprinted in Red:
"1968 / XX ANIVERSARIO DE LA / ORGANIZACION MUNDIAL / DE LA SALUD"

1968, Apr. 7 **Perf. 12x11½**

C245	A194	50c multi	75	40

Issued to commemorate the 20th anniversary of the World Health Organization.

No. C229 Overprinted in Red:
"1968 / Año / del Sistema / del Crédito / Rural"

1968, May 6 Photo. **Perf. 12x11½**

C246	A193	80c multi	1.00	60

Rural credit system.

Masferrer Type of Regular Issue
1968, June 22 Litho. **Perf. 12x11½**

C247	A200	5c brn & multi	15	8
C248	A200	15c grn & multi	20	12

Issued to commemorate the centenary of the birth of Alberto Masferrer, philosopher and scholar.

Scouts Hiking
AP50

1968, July 26 Litho. **Perf. 12**

C249	AP50	10c multi	15	10

Issued to publicize the 7th Inter-American Boy Scout Conference, July–Aug., 1968.

Presidents' Meeting Type of Regular Issue
1968, Dec. 5 Litho. **Perf. 14½**

C250	A202	20c sal & multi	20	12
C251	A202	1col lt bl & multi	1.10	75

See note after No. 790.

Butterfly Type of Regular Issue
Designs: Various butterflies.

1969 Lithographed **Perf. 12**

C252	A203	20c multi	25	12
C253	A203	1col multi	1.00	70
C254	A203	2col multi	2.50	1.35
C255	A203	10col gray & multi	12.00	7.00

Red Cross, Crescent and Lion and Sun Emblems
AP51

1969 Lithographed **Perf. 11**

C256	AP51	30c yel & multi	35	20
C257	AP51	1col multi	1.25	70
C258	AP51	4col multi	5.00	2.75

Issued to commemorate the 50th anniversary of the League of Red Cross Societies.

No. C213 Overprinted in Green:
"Alunizaje / Apolo - 11 / 21 Julio / 1969"

1969, Sept. Photo. **Perf. 11½x12**

C259	A189	40c yel & blk	45	30

Issued to commemorate man's first landing on the moon, July 20, 1969. See note after U.S. No. C76.
The same overprint in red brown and pictures of the landing module and the astronauts on the moon were applied to the margin of No. C214.

Hospital Type of Regular Issue
Design: Benjamin Bloom Children's Hospital.

1969, Oct. 24 Litho. **Perf. 11½**

C260	A205	1col multi	1.25	70
C261	A205	2col multi	2.50	1.40
C262	A205	5col multi	6.25	3.25

ILO Type of Regular Issue
1969 Lithographed **Perf. 13**

C263	A206	50c lt bl & multi	60	35

Issued to commemorate the 50th anniversary of the International Labor Organization.

Tourist Type of Regular Issue
Views: 20c, Devil's Gate. 35c, Ichanmichen Spa. 60c, Aerial view of Acajutla Harbor.

1969, Dec. 19 Photo. **Perf. 12x11½**

C264	A207	20c blk & multi	25	12
C265	A207	35c blk & multi	40	20
C266	A207	60c blk & multi	75	40

Insect Type of Regular Issue, 1970
Insects: 2col, Bee. 3col, Elaterida. 4col, Praying mantis.

1970, Feb. 24 Litho. **Perf. 11½x11**

C267	A208	2col multi	2.50	1.40
C268	A208	3col multi	3.75	2.00
C269	A208	4col org & multi	5.00	2.75

Human Rights Type of Regular Issue
Design: 20c, 80c, Map and arms of Salvador and National Unity emblem similar to A209, but vertical.

1970, Apr. 14 Litho. **Perf. 14**

C270	A209	20c bl & multi	25	12
C271	A209	80c bl & multi	1.15	55

Issued to publicize El Salvador's support of universal human rights.

Army Type of Regular Issue
Designs: 20c, Fighter plane. 40c, Gun and crew. 50c, Patrol boat.

1970, May 7 **Perf. 12**

C272	A210	20c gray & multi	25	12
C273	A210	40c grn & multi	55	25
C274	A210	50c bl & multi	65	30

Issued for Army Day, May 7.

Brazilian Team, Jules Rimet Cup
AP52

Designs: Soccer teams and Jules Rimet Cup.

1970, May 25 Litho. **Perf. 12**
Multicolored

C275	AP52	1col Belgium	1.50	1.35
C276	AP52	1col Brazil	1.50	1.35
C277	AP52	1col Bulgaria	1.50	1.35
C278	AP52	1col Czechoslovakia	1.50	1.35
C279	AP52	1col Germany (Fed. Rep.)	1.50	1.35
C280	AP52	1col Britain	1.50	1.35
C281	AP52	1col Israel	1.50	1.35
C282	AP52	1col Italy	1.50	1.35
C283	AP52	1col Mexico	1.50	1.35
C284	AP52	1col Morocco	1.50	1.35
C285	AP52	1col Peru	1.50	1.35
C286	AP52	1col Romania	1.50	1.35
C287	AP52	1col Russia	1.50	1.35
C288	AP52	1col Salvador	1.50	1.35
C289	AP52	1col Sweden	1.50	1.35
C290	AP52	1col Uruguay	1.50	1.35
		Nos. C275-C290 (16)	24.00	21.60

Issued to publicize the 9th World Soccer Championships for the Jules Rimet Cup, Mexico City, May 30–June 21, 1970.

Lottery Type of Regular Issue
1970, July 15 Litho. **Perf. 12**

C291	A211	80c multi	1.00	50

Centenary of the National Lottery.

Education Year Type of Regular Issue
1970, Sept. 11 Litho. **Perf. 12**

C292	A212	20c pink & multi	25	12
C293	A212	2col buff & multi	2.50	1.25

Issued for International Education Year.

Fair Type of Regular Issue
1970, Oct. 28 Litho. **Perf. 12**

C294	A213	20c multi	35	12
C295	A213	30c yel & multi	50	18

4th International Fair, San Salvador.

Music Type of Regular Issue
Design: 40c, Johann Sebastian Bach, harp, horn and music.

1971, Feb. 22 Litho. **Perf. 13½**

C296	A214	40c gray & multi	75	35

Second International Music Festival.

No. C247 Overprinted:
"Año / del Centenario de la / Biblioteca Nacional / 1970"

1970, Nov. 25 **Perf. 12x11½**

C297	A200	5c brn & multi	8	5

Miss Tourism Type of Regular Issue
1971, Apr. 1 Litho. **Perf. 14**

C298	A215	20c lil & multi	25	15
C299	A215	60c gray & multi	90	35

Maria Elena Sol, Miss World Tourism, 1970–71.

Pietà Type of Regular Issue
1971, May 10

C300	A216	40c lt yel grn & vio brn	65	30

Mother's Day, 1971.

No. C270 Overprinted in Red Like No. 823
1971, July 6 Lithographed **Perf. 14**

C301	A209	20c bl & multi	35	15

104th Anniversary of National Police.

Fish Type of Regular Issue
Designs: 30c, Smalltooth sawfish. 1col, Atlantic sailfish.

1971, July 28

C302	A217	30c lil & multi	36	18
C303	A217	1col multi	1.25	60

Independence Type of Regular Issue
Designs: Various sections of Declaration of Independence of Central America.

1971 Lithographed **Perf. 13½x13**

C304	A218	30c bl & blk	40	20
C305	A218	40c brn & blk	60	30
C306	A218	50c yel & blk	75	35
C307	A218	60c gray & blk	1.00	50
a.		Souvenir sheet of 8	3.50	3.25

Sesquicentennial of independence of Central America. No. C307a contains 8 stamps with simulated perforations similar to Nos. 826–829, C304–C307. Gray margin with white commemorative inscription. Size: 172x190mm.

Church Type of Regular Issue
Designs: 15c, Metapan Church. 70c, Panchimalco Church.

1971, Aug. 21 Litho. **Perf. 13x13½**

C308	A219	15c ol & multi	25	9
C309	A219	70c multi	1.10	42

No. C274 Overprinted in Red
1951-12 Octubre-1971
XX Aniversario
MARINA NACIONAL

1971, Oct. 12 Litho. **Perf. 12**

C310	A210	50c bl & multi	75	30

National Navy, 20th anniversary.

No. C229 Overprinted: "V Feria / Internacional / 3-20 Noviembre / de 1972"

1972, Nov. 3 Photo. **Perf. 12x11½**

C311	A193	80c multi	1.75	60

5th International Fair, El Salvador, Nov. 3–20.

SALVADOR

No. C223 Overprinted in Red
1972 - XXX Aniversario Creacion Instituto Interamericano de Ciencias Agricolas
1972, Nov. 30 Photo. Perf. 11½x12
C312 A191 50c ocher, brn & gold 85 40
30th anniversary of the Inter-American Institute for Agricultural Sciences.

No. C296 Overprinted
III Festival Internacional de Música 9 - 25 - Febrero - 1973.
1973, Feb. 5 Litho. Perf. 13½
C313 A214 40c gray & multi 60 30
3rd International Music Festival, Feb. 9-29.

Lions Type of Regular Issue
Designs: 20c, 40c, Map of El Salvador and Lions International Emblem.
1973, Feb. 20 Litho. Perf. 13
C314 A220 20c gray & multi 30 12
C315 A220 40c multi 60 24
31st Lions International District "D" Convention, San Salvador, May 1972.

Olympic Type of Regular Issue
Designs: 20c, Javelin, women's. 80c, Discus, women's. 1col, Hammer throw. 2col, Shot put.
1973, May 21 Lithographed Perf. 13
C316 A221 20c lt grn & mult. 25 12
C317 A221 80c sal & multi 1.10 48
C318 A221 1col ultra & multi 1.35 60
C319 A221 2col multi 2.75 1.20
20th Olympic Games, Munich, Aug. 26-Sept. 11, 1972.

No. C241 Surcharged Like No. 841
1973, Dec. Photogravure Perf. 13
C320 A198 25c on 50c multi 20 15

Souvenir Sheet
No. C307a Overprinted:
"Centenario / Cuidad / Santiago de Maria / 1874 1974"
1974, Mar. 7 Litho. Imperf.
C321 A218 Sheet of 8 2.00
Centenary of the City Santiago de Maria. The overprint is so arranged that each line appears on a different pair of stamps. Size of sheet: 172x190mm.

No. C231 Surcharged in Red
25 cts.

1974, Apr. 22 Photo. Perf. 12x11½
C322 A194 25c on 50c multi 25 15

No. C229 Surcharged
10 CTS.
1974, Apr. 24
C323 A193 10c on 80c multi 15 10

Rehabilitation Type of 1974
1974, Apr. 30 Litho. Perf. 13
C324 A222 25c multi 20 15
10th anniversary of the Salvador Rehabilitation Institute.

Nos. C275-C290 Overprinted
ALEMANIA 1974
1974, June 4 Litho. Perf. 12
Multicolored
C325 AP52 1col Belgium 1.25 75
C326 AP52 1col Brazil 1.25 75
C327 AP52 1col Bulgaria 1.25 75
C328 AP52 1col Czechoslovakia 1.25 75
C329 AP52 1col Germany 1.25 75
C330 AP52 1col Britain 1.25 75
C331 AP52 1col Israel 1.25 75
C332 AP52 1col Italy 1.25 75
C333 AP52 1col Mexico 1.25 75
C334 AP52 1col Morocco 1.25 75
C335 AP52 1col Peru 1.25 75
C336 AP52 1col Romania 1.25 75
C337 AP52 1col Russia 1.25 75
C338 AP52 1col Salvador 1.25 75
C339 AP52 1col Sweden 1.25 75
C340 AP52 1col Uruguay 1.25 75
Nos. C325-340 (16) 20.00 12.00
World Cup Soccer Championship, Munich, June 13-July 7.

INTERPOL Type of 1974
1974, Sept. 2 Litho. Perf. 12½
C341 A223 25c multi 20 15
50th anniversary of International Criminal Police Organization (INTERPOL).

FAO Type of 1974
1974, Sept. 2 Litho. Perf. 12½
C342 A224 25c bl, dk bl & gold 20 15
World Food Program, 10th anniversary.

Coin Type of 1974
1974, Nov. 19 Litho. Perf. 12½x13
Coins: 20c, 1p silver, 1892. 40c, 20c, silver, 1828. 50c, 20p gold, 1892. 60c, 20col gold, 1925.
C343 A225 20c multi 16 12
C344 A225 40c multi 32 24
C345 A225 50c multi 40 30
C346 A225 60c multi 48 36

Souvenir Sheet
No. C307a Overprinted: " X ASAMBLEA GENERAL DE LA CONFERENCIA / INTERAMERICANA DE SEGURIDAD SOCIAL Y XX / REUNION DEL COMITE PERMANENTE INTERAMERICANO / DE SEGURIDAD SOCIAL, 24 —— 30 NOVIEMBRE 1974"
1974, Nov. 18 Litho. Imperf.
C347 A218 Sheet of 8 3.50
Social Security Conference, El Salvador, Nov. 24-30. The overprint is so arranged that each line appears on a different pair of stamps. Size: 172x190mm.

Issues of 1965-69 Surcharged

₡ 0.10
₡ 0.10
a *b*
₡ 0.25
c
₡ 0.25

d
Photo., Litho.
Perf. 12x11½, 13, 12, 11, 11½
1974-75
C348 A190(a) 10c on 45c #C219 15 10
C349 A190(a) 10c on 70c #C220 15 10
C350 A198(b) 10c on 50c #C241 10 8
C351 AP51(d) 25c on 1col #C257 30 20
C352 AP195(c) 25c on 2col #C234 ('75) 65 35
C353 A203(d) 25c on 2col #C254 ('75) 30 20
C354 AP51(d) 25c on 4col #C258 30 20
C355 A205(d) 25c on 5col #C262 30 20
Nos. C348-C355 (8) 2.25 1.43
No. C353 has new value at left and 6 vertical bars.
No. C355 has 7 vertical bars.

UPU Type of 1975
1975, Jan. 22 Litho. Perf. 13
C356 A226 25c bl & multi 20 15
C357 A226 30c bl & multi 24 18
Centenary of Universal Postal Union.

Acajutla Harbor Type of 1975
1975, Feb. 17
C358 A227 15c bl & multi 12 9

Post Office Type of 1975
1975, Apr. 25 Litho. Perf. 13
C359 A228 25c bl & multi 20 15

Miss Universe Type of 1975
1975, June 25 Perf. 12½
C360 A229 25c multi 35 20
C361 A229 60c lil & multi 75 50
El Salvador, site of 1975 Miss Universe Contest.

Women's Year Type and IWY Emblem AP53

1975, Sept. 4 Litho. Perf. 12½
C362 A230 15c bl & bl blk 12 9
C363 AP53 25c yel grn & bl blk 20 15
International Women's Year 1975.

Nurse Type of 1975
1975, Oct. 24 Litho. Perf. 12½
C364 A231 25c lt bl & multi 35 20
Nurses' Day.

Printers' Congress Type of 1975
1975, Nov. 19 Litho. Perf. 12½
C365 A232 30c grn & multi 24 18
15th Congress of Inter-American Security Printers Association, San Salvador, Nov.16-20.

Dermatologists' Congress Type, 1975
1975, Nov. 28
C366 A233 20c bl & multi 16 12
C367 A233 30c red & multi 24 18
8th Ibero-Latin-American Dermatological Congress, San Salvador, Nov. 28-Dec. 3.

Caritas Type of 1975
1975, Dec. 18 Litho. Perf. 13½
C368 A234 20c bl & vio bl 16 12
7th Latin American Charity Congress, San Salvador, Nov. 1971.

UNICEF Emblem AP54

1975, Dec. 18
C369 AP54 15c lt grn & sil 15 10

C370 AP54 20c dl rose & sil 20 15
UNICEF (United Nations International Children's Fund), 25th anniversary (in 1971).

Nos. C267-C269 Surcharged
25c. 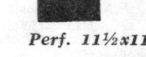
1976, Jan. 14 Perf. 11½x11
C371 A208 25c on 2col multi 25 15
C372 A208 25c on 3col multi 25 15
C373 A208 25c on 4col multi 25 15

Caularthron Bilamellatum AP55
Designs: Orchids.
1976, Feb. 19 Litho. Perf. 12½
Multicolored
C374 AP55 25c shown 30 15
C375 AP55 25c Oncidium oligmanthum 30 15
C376 AP55 25c Epidendrum radicans 30 15
C377 AP55 25c Epidendrum vitellinum 30 15
C378 AP55 25c Cyrtopodium punctatum 30 15
C379 AP55 25c Pleurothallis schiedei 30 15
C380 AP55 25c Lycaste cruenta 30 15
C381 AP55 25c Spiranthes speciosa 30 15
Nos. C374-C381 (8) 2.40 1.20

CIAT Type of 1976
1976, May 18 Litho. Perf. 12½
C382 A235 50c org & multi 40 30
10th Congress of Revenue Collectors (CIAT), San Salvador, May 16-22.

Bicentennial Types of 1976
1976, June 30 Litho. Perf. 12½
C383 A236 25c multi 20 15
C384 A237 5col multi 4.00 3.00
American Bicentennial.

Reptile Type of 1976
Reptiles: 15c, Green fence lizard. 25c, Basilisk. 60c, Star lizard.
1976, Sept. 23 Litho. Perf. 12½
C385 A238 15c multi 12 9
C386 A238 25c multi 20 15
C387 A238 60c multi 48 36

Archaeology Type of 1976
Pre-Columbian Art: 25c, Brazier with pre-classical head, El Trapiche. 50c, Kettle with pre-classical head, Atiquizaya. 70c, Classical whistling vase, Tazumal.
1976, Oct. 11 Litho. Perf. 12½
C388 A239 25c multi 20 14
C389 A239 50c multi 40 28
C390 A239 70c multi 48 42

Fair Type of 1976
1976, Oct. 25 Litho. Perf. 12½
C391 A240 25c multi 20 15
C392 A240 70c yel & multi 55 42
7th International Fair, Nov. 5-22.

Christmas Type of 1976
1976, Dec. 16 Litho. Perf. 11
C393 A241 25c bl & multi 20 15
C394 A241 50c multi 40 30
C395 A241 60c multi 48 36
C396 A241 75c red & multi 60 45
Christmas 1976.

SALVADOR

Rotary Type of 1977
1977, June 20   Litho.   Perf. 11

C397	A242	25c multi	35	20
C398	A242	1col multi	1.25	75

San Salvador Rotary Club, 50th anniversary.

Industrial Type of 1977
Designs: 25c, Radar station, Izalco (vert.). 50c, Central sugar refinery, Jiboa. 75c, Cerron Grande hydroelectric station.

1977, June 29   Perf. 12½

C399	A243	25c multi	20	15
C400	A243	50c multi	40	30
C401	A243	75c multi	60	45

Industrial development. Nos. C399-C401 have colorless overprint in multiple rows: GOBIERNO DEL SALVADOR.

Nos. C271 and C239 Surcharged with New Value and Bar
1977   Perf. 14, 11½

C402	A209	25c on 80c multi	45	25
C403	A197	30c on 5c multi	30	20
C404	A197	40c on 5c multi	35	25
C405	A197	60c on 5c multi	40	30

Broadcasting Type of 1977
1977, Sept. 14   Litho.   Perf. 14

C406	A244	20c multi	30	15
C407	A244	30c multi	40	20

Broadcasting in El Salvador, 50th anniversary.

Symbolic Chessboard and Emblem
AP56

1977, Oct. 20   Litho.   Perf. 11

C408	AP56	25c multi	20	16
C409	AP56	50c multi	40	32

El Salvador's victory in International Chess Olympiad, Tripoli, Libya, Oct. 24–Nov. 15, 1976.

Soccer
AP57

Boxing
AP58

1977, Nov. 16   Litho.   Perf. 16
Multicolored

C410	AP57	10c shown	8	6
C411	AP57	10c Basketball	8	6
C412	AP57	15c Javelin	12	10
C413	AP57	15c Weight lifting	12	10
C414	AP57	20c Volleyball	16	12
C415	AP58	20c shown	16	12
C416	AP57	25c Baseball	20	15
C417	AP58	25c Softball	20	15
C418	AP58	30c Swimming	24	18
C419	AP58	30c Fencing	24	18
C420	AP58	40c Bicycling	32	24
C421	AP58	50c Rifle shooting	40	30
C422	AP58	50c Women's tennis	40	30
C423	AP57	60c Judo	48	35
C424	AP58	75c Wrestling	60	45
C425	AP58	1col Equestrian hurdles	80	60
C426	AP58	1col Woman gymnast	80	60
C427	AP58	2col Table tennis	1.60	1.20
		Nos. C410-C427 (18)	7.00	5.26

Imperf.
Size: 100x119mm.

C428	AP57	5col Games' poster	4.00	

2nd Central American Olympic Games, San Salvador, Nov. 25–Dec. 4.

No. C390 Overprinted in Red:
"CENTENARIO / CIUDAD DE / CHALCHUAPA / 1878–1978"

1978, Feb. 13   Litho.   Perf. 12½

C429	A239	70c multi	48	42

Centenary of Chalchuapa.

Map of South America, Argentina '78 Emblem
AP59

1978, Aug. 15   Litho.   Perf. 11

C430	AP59	25c multi	20	15
C431	AP59	60c multi	48	35
C432	AP59	5col multi	4.00	3.00

11th World Cup Soccer Championship, Argentina, June 1–25.

Musical Instrument Type of 1978
Designs: 25c, Drum (vert.). 50c, Hollow rattles. 80c, Xylophone.

1978, Aug. 29   Perf. 12½

C433	A245	25c multi	20	15
C434	AP59	50c multi	40	30
C435	AP59	80c multi	65	48

Engineering Type of 1978
1978, Sept. 12   Litho.   Perf. 13½

C436	A246	20c multi	20	15

4th National Engineers' Congress, San Salvador, Sept. 18–23.

Izalco Station Type of 1978
1978, Sept. 14   Perf. 12½

C437	A247	75c multi	60	45

Inauguration of Izalco satellite earth station, Sept. 15, 1978.

Softball, Bat and Globes
AP60

1978, Oct. 17   Litho.   Perf. 12½

C438	AP60	25c pink & multi	20	15
C439	AP60	1col yel & multi	80	60

4th World Softball Championship for Women, San Salvador, Oct. 13–22.

Fair Type, 1978
1978, Oct. 30   Litho.   Perf. 12½

C440	A248	15c multi	12	8
C441	A248	25c multi	20	15

8th International Fair, Nov. 3–20.

Red Cross Type, 1978
1978, Oct. 30   Litho.   Perf. 11

C442	A249	25c multi	20	15

Henri Dunant (1828–1910), founder of the Red Cross.

Cotton Conference Type, 1978
1978, Nov. 22   Perf. 12½

C443	A250	40c multi	32	25

International Cotton Consulting Committee, 37th Meeting, El Salvador, Nov. 27–Dec. 2.

Christmas Type, 1978
1978, Dec. 5   Litho.   Perf. 12½

C444	A251	25c multi	20	15
C445	A251	1col multi	80	60

Athenaeum Type 1978
1978, Dec. 20   Litho.   Perf. 14

C446	A252	25c multi	20	15

Millennium of Castilian language.

UPU Type of 1979
1979, Apr. 2   Litho.   Perf. 14

C447	A253	75c multi	60	45

Centenary of Salvador's membership in Universal Postal Union.

Health Organization Type of 1979
1979, Apr. 7   Perf. 14x14½

C448	A254	25c multi	20	15

Pan-American Health Organization, 75th anniversary.

Social Security Type of 1979
1979, May 25   Litho.   Perf. 12½

C449	A255	25c multi	20	15
C450	A255	1col multi	80	60

Social Security 5-year plan 1978–1982.

Games Emblem
AP61

1979   Litho.   Perf. 14½x14

C451	AP61	25c multi	20	15
C452	AP61	40c multi	32	25
C453	AP61	70c multi	56	40

8th Pan American Games, Puerto Rico, July 1–15.

Pope John Paul II Type of 1979
Design: 60c, 5col, Pope John Paul II and pyramid (horiz.).

1979, July 12

C454	A256	60c multi	48	35
C455	A256	5col multi	4.00	3.00

"25," Family and Map of Salvador
AP62

1979, May 14   Litho.   Perf. 14x14½

C456	AP62	25c blk & bl	20	15
C457	AP62	60c blk & lil rose	48	35

Social Security, 25th anniversary.

Pre-Historic Animal Type, 1979
1979, Sept. 7   Litho.   Perf. 14
Multicolored

C458	A257	15c Mammoth	12	10
C459	A257	25c Giant anteater (vert.)	20	16
C460	A257	2 col Hyenas	1.60	1.20

National Anthem Type, 1979
1979, Sept. 14   Perf. 14½x14
Multicolored

C461	A258	40c José Aberiz, score	32	24

COPIMERA Type, 1979
1979, Oct. 19   Litho.   Perf. 14½x14

C462	A259	50c multi	40	30

8th COPIMERA Congress (Mechanical, Electrical and Allied Trade Engineers), San Salvador, Oct. 22-27.

Circle Dance, IYC Emblem—AP63

Children's Village and IYC Emblems
AP64

1979, Oct. 29   Perf. 14½×14, 14×14½

C463	AP63	25c multi	20	16
C464	AP64	30c vio & blk	24	18

International Year of the Child.

Biochemistry Type of 1979
1979, Nov. 1   Litho.   Perf. 14½×14

C465	A262	25c multi	20	15

5th Latin American Clinical Biochemistry Congress, San Salvador, Nov. 5-10.

Coffee Type of 1979
50c, Picking coffee. 75c, Drying coffee beans. 1col, Coffee export.

1979, Dec. 18   Perf. 14×14½, 14½×14

C466	A263	50c multi	40	30
C467	A263	75c multi	60	45
C468	A263	1 col multi	80	60

Hoof and Mouth Disease Type of 1980
1980, June 3   Litho.   Perf. 14½x14

C469	A265	60c multi	48	35

Shell Type of 1980
1980, Aug. 12   Perf. 14x14½

C470	A266	15c Hexaplex regius	12	10
C471	A266	25c Polinices helicoides	20	15
C472	A266	75c Jenneria pustulata	60	45
C473	A266	1 col Pitar lupanaria	80	60

Birds Type
1980, Sept. 10   Litho.   Perf. 14x14½

C474	A267	25c Aulacorhynchus prasinus	20	15
C475	A267	50c Strix varia fulvescens	40	30
C476	A267	75c Myadestes unicolor	60	45

SALVADOR

Snake Type of 1980
1980, Nov. 12 Litho. *Perf. 14x14½*
C477	A268	25c Rattlesnake	20	15
C478	A268	50c Coral snake	40	30

Auditors Type
1980, Nov. 26 Litho. *Perf. 14*
C479	A269	50c multi	40	30
C480	A269	75c multi	60	45

Christmas Type
1980, Dec. 5 Litho. *Perf. 14*
C481	A270	25c multi	20	15
C482	A270	60c multi	48	36

Intl. Women's Decade, 1976-85—AP65

1981, Jan. 30 *Perf. 14½x14*
C483	AP65	25c org & blk	20	15
C484	AP65	1 col ol grn & blk	80	60

Protected Animals—AP66

1981, Mar. 20 Litho. *Perf. 14x14½*
C485	AP66	25c Ateles geoffroyi	20	15
C486	AP66	40c Lepisosteus tropicus	32	24
C487	AP66	50c Iguana iguana	40	30
C488	AP66	60c Eretmochelys imbricata	48	36
C489	AP66	75c Spizaetus ornatus	60	45
		Nos. C485-C489 (5)	2.00	1.50

Heinrich von Stephan, 150th Birth Anniv.—AP67

1981, May 18 Litho. *Perf. 14½x14*
C490	AP67	15c multi	12	10
C491	AP67	2 col multi	1.60	1.20

Nos. C435, C453 Surcharged
1981, May 18 Litho. *Perf. 12½, 14½x14*
C492	AP59	50c on 80c, #C435	40	30
C493	AP61	1 col on 70c, #C453	80	60

Dental Associations Type
1981, June 18 Litho. *Perf. 14*
C494	A271	5 col bl & blk	4.00	3.00

IYD Type of 1981
1981, Aug. 14 *Perf. 14x14½*
C495	A272	25c like #936	20	15
C496	A272	50c Emblem	40	30
C497	A272	75c like #936	60	45
C498	A272	1 col like #C496	80	60

Quinonez Type
1981, Aug. 28 Litho. *Perf. 14x14½*
C499	A273	50c multi	40	30

World Food Day Type
1981, Sept. 16 Litho. *Perf. 14x14½*
C500	A274	25c multi	20	15

Land Registry Office, 100th Anniv.—AP68

1981, Oct. 30 Litho. *Perf. 14x14½*
C501	AP68	1 col multi	80	60

TACA Airlines, 50th Anniv.—AP69

1981, Nov. 10 Litho. *Perf. 14*
C502	AP69	15c multi	12	10
C503	AP69	25c multi	20	15
C504	AP69	75c multi	60	45

World Cup Preliminaries Type
1981, Nov. 27 Litho. *Perf. 14x14½*
C505	A275	25c Like No. 939	20	15
C506	A275	75c Like No. 940	60	45

Lyceum Type
1981, Dec. 17 Litho. *Perf. 14*
C507	A276	25c multi	20	15

Sculptures Type
1982, Jan. 22 Litho. *Perf. 14*
C508	A277	25c Palm leaf with effigy	20	15
C509	A277	30c Jaguar mask	24	18
C510	A277	80c Mayan flint carving	64	48

Scouting Year Type of 1982
1982, Mar. 17 Litho. *Perf. 14½x14*
C511	A278	25c Baden-Powell	20	15
C512		50c Girl Scout, emblem	40	30

TB Bacillus Centenary—AP70

1982, Mar. 24 *Perf. 14*
C513		50c multi	40	30

Armed Forces Type of 1982
1982, May 7 Litho. *Perf. 14x13½*
C514	A279	25c multi	20	15

Symbolic Design
AP71

14th World Telecommunications Day
AP72

1982, May 14 *Perf. 14*
C515	AP71	75c multi	60	45

25th anniv. of Latin-American Tourist Org. Confederation (COTAL).

1982, May 17 *Perf. 14x14½*
C516	AP72	15c multi	12	8
C517	AP72	2 col multi	1.60	1.25

World Cup Type of 1982
1982, July 14
C518	A280	25c Team, emblem	20	15
C519	A280	60c Map, cup	50	35

Size: 67x47mm. *Perf. 11½*
C520	A280	2 col Team, emblem, diff.	1.60	1.25

1982 World Cup—AP73

Flags or Arms of Participating Countries: C521a, C522a, Italy. C521b, C522c, Germany. C521c, C522e, Argentina. C521d, C522m, England. C521e, C522o, Spain. C521f, C522g, Brazil. C521g, C522b, Poland. C521h, C522d, Algeria. C521i, C522f, Belgium. C521j, C522n, France. C521k, C522p, Honduras. C521l, C522r, Russia. C521m, C522q, Peru. C521s, C522i, Chile. C521o, C522k, Hungary. C521p, C522s, Czechoslovakia. C521q, C522u, Jugoslavia. C521r, C522w, Scotland. C521s, C522h, Cameroun. C521t, C522j, Austria. C521u, C522l, Salvador. C521v, C522t, Kuwait. C521w, C522v, Ireland. C521x, C522x, New Zealand.

1982, Aug. 26
C521		Sheet of 24	3.00	
a-x.		15c Flags	12	8
C522		Sheet of 24	5.00	
a-x.		25c Arms	20	15

Salvador Team, Cup, Flags—AP74

1982, Aug. 26 Litho. *Perf. 11½*
C523	AP74	5 col multi	4.00	3.00

International Fair Type
1982, Oct. 14 Litho. *Perf. 14*
C524	A281	15c multi	12	10

World Food Day—AP75

1982, Oct. 21 Litho. *Perf. 14*
C525	AP75	25c multi	20	15

St. Francis of Assisi, 800th Birth Anniv.—AP76

1982, Nov. 10 Litho. *Perf. 14*
C526	AP76	1 col multi	80	60

National Labor Campaign—AP77

1982, Nov. 30 Litho. *Perf. 14x14½*
C527	AP77	50c multi	40	30

Christmas Type
1982, Dec. 14 Litho. *Perf. 14*
C528	A282	25c multi, horiz.	20	15

Salvadoran Paintings—AP78

Designs: No. C529, The Pottery of Paleca, by Miguel Ortiz Villacorta. No. C530, The Rural School, by Luis Caceres Madrid. No. C531, To the Wash, by Julia Diaz. No. C532, "La Pancha" by Jose Mejia Vides. No. C533, Boats Near The Beach, by Raul Elas Reyes. No. C534, The Muleteers, by Canjura.

1983, Oct. 18 Litho. *Perf. 14x13½, 13½x14*
C529	AP78	25c multi	20	15
C530	AP78	25c multi	20	15
C531	AP78	75c multi, vert.	60	45
C532	AP78	75c multi, vert.	60	45
C533	AP78	1 col multi, vert.	80	60
C534	AP78	1 col multi, vert.	80	60
		Nos. C529-C534 (6)	3.20	2.40

Stamps of the same denomination are se-tenant.

Fishing Industry—AP79

1983, Dec. 20	Litho.		Perf. 14½x14	
C535	AP79	25c Fisherman	20	15
C536	AP79	75c Feeding fish	60	45

WE STOCK OVER 267 COUNTRIES!

If you need stamps issued before 1960 to complete your collection

SEND US YOUR WANTLIST OR CALL TODAY!

(References Please)

EST. 1937

**Stampazine Inc.
3 E. 57th St.
N.Y., N.Y. 10022
(212) PL2-5905**

REGISTRATION STAMPS.

Gen. Rafael
Antonio Gutiérrez
R1

Wmkd. Liberty Cap. (117)

1897		Engraved	Perf. 12	
F1	R1	10c dk bl	200.00	
F2	R1	10c brn lake		30

Unwmkd.

| F3 | R1 | 10c dk bl | 40 | |
| F4 | R1 | 10c brn lake | | 30 |

Nos. F1 and F3 were probably not placed in use without the overprint "FRANQUEO OFICIAL" (Nos. O127-O128).

The reprints are on thick unwatermarked paper. Price 8c each.

ACKNOWLEDGMENT OF RECEIPT STAMPS.

AR1

Wmkd. Liberty Cap. (117)

1897		Engraved	Perf. 12	
H1	AR1	5c dk grn		15

Unwmkd.

| H2 | AR1 | 5c dk grn | | 20 |

No. H2 has been reprinted on thick paper. Price 8c.

POSTAGE DUE STAMPS.

D1

Engraved.

1895		Perf. 12	Unwmkd.	
J1	D1	1c ol grn	20	20
J2	D1	2c ol grn	20	20
J3	D1	3c ol grn	20	20
J4	D1	5c ol grn	20	20
J5	D1	10c ol grn	20	20
J6	D1	15c ol grn	20	25
J7	D1	25c ol grn	20	35
J8	D1	50c ol grn	30	50
		Nos. J1-J8 (8)	1.70	2.10

1896		Wmkd. Liberty Cap. (117)		
J9	D1	1c red	20	20
J10	D1	2c red	20	20
J11	D1	3c red	20	25
J12	D1	5c red	25	25
J13	D1	10c red	25	25
J14	D1	15c red	30	30
J15	D1	25c red	20	30
J16	D1	50c red	35	35
		Nos. J9-J16 (8)	1.95	2.10

Unwmkd.

J17	D1	1c red	20	20
J18	D1	2c red	20	20
J19	D1	3c red	20	20
J20	D1	5c red	20	20
J21	D1	10c red	20	20
J22	D1	15c red	20	30
J23	D1	25c red	20	30
J24	D1	50c red	20	35
		Nos. J17-J24 (8)	1.60	1.95

Nos. J17 to J24 exist imperforate.

SALVADOR

1897

J25	D1	1c dp bl	20	20
J26	D1	2c dp bl	20	20
J27	D1	3c dp bl	20	20
J28	D1	5c dp bl	20	20
J29	D1	10c dp bl	20	25
J30	D1	15c dp bl	20	25
J31	D1	25c dp bl	20	30
J32	D1	50c dp bl	20	40
		Nos. J25-J32 (8)	1.60	2.00

1898

J33	D1	1c violet	20	
J34	D1	2c violet	20	
J35	D1	3c violet	20	
J36	D1	5c violet	20	
J37	D1	10c violet	35	
J38	D1	15c violet	20	
J39	D1	25c violet	20	
J40	D1	50c violet	40	
		Nos. J33-J40 (8)	1.95	

Reprints of Nos. J1 to J40 are on thick paper, often in the wrong shades and usually with the impression somewhat blurred. They exist on both watermarked and unwatermarked paper. Price 5c each.

Wmkd. Liberty Cap Sideways. (117)

1899

J41	D1	1c orange	20
J42	D1	2c orange	20
J43	D1	3c orange	20
J44	D1	5c orange	20
J45	D1	10c orange	20
J46	D1	15c orange	20
J47	D1	25c orange	20
J48	D1	50c orange	20
		Nos. J41-J48 (8)	1.60

Unwmkd. Thick Porous Paper.

J49	D1	1c orange	20
J50	D1	2c orange	20
J51	D1	3c orange	20
J52	D1	5c orange	20
J53	D1	10c orange	20
J54	D1	15c orange	20
J55	D1	25c orange	20
J56	D1	50c orange	20
		Nos. J49-J56 (8)	1.60

Nos. J41-J56 were probably not put in use without the wheel overprint.

Nos. J49–J56 Overprinted in Black

1900

J57	D1	1c orange	75
J58	D1	2c orange	75
J59	D1	3c orange	75
J60	D1	5c orange	1.00
J61	D1	10c orange	1.50
J62	D1	15c orange	1.50
J63	D1	25c orange	1.75
J64	D1	50c orange	2.25
		Nos. J57-J64 (8)	10.25

See note after No. 198A.

Morazán Monument
D2
Wmkd. S. (173)

1903 Engraved. Perf. 14, 14½.

J65	D2	1c yel grn	2.50	1.50
J66	D2	2c carmine	4.00	2.50
J67	D2	3c orange	4.00	2.50
J68	D2	5c dk bl	4.00	2.50
J69	D2	10c dl vio	4.00	2.50
J70	D2	25c bl grn	4.00	2.50
		Nos. J65-J70 (6)	22.50	14.00

Nos. 355, 356, 358 and 360 Overprinted **DEFICIENCIA DE FRANQUEO**

1908 Perf. 11½. Unwmkd.

J71	A66	1c grn & blk	75	60
J72	A66	2c red & blk	60	50
J73	A66	5c bl & blk	1.50	1.00
J74	A66	10c vio & blk	2.25	2.00

Same Overprint on No. O275

J75	O3	3c yel & blk	1.50	1.25
		Nos. J71-J75 (5)	6.60	5.35

Nos. 355–358, 360 Overprinted **Deficiencia de franqueo**

J76	A66	1c grn & blk	50	50
J77	A66	2c red & blk	60	60
J78	A66	3c yel & blk	70	70
J79	A66	5c bl & blk	1.00	1.00
J80	A66	10c vio & blk	2.00	2.00
		Nos. J76-J80 (5)	4.80	4.80

It is now believed that stamps of type A66, on paper with Honeycomb watermark, do not exist with genuine overprints of the types used for Nos. J71 to J80.

Pres. Fernando Figueroa
D3
Wmkd. Honeycomb. (172)

1910 Engraved.

J81	D3	1c sep & blk	18	18
J82	D3	2c dk grn & blk	18	18
J83	D3	3c org & blk	18	18
J84	D3	4c scar & blk	18	18
J85	D3	5c pur & blk	18	18
J86	D3	12c dp bl & blk	18	18
J87	D3	24c brn red & blk	18	18
		Nos. J81-J87 (7)	1.26	1.26

OFFICIAL STAMPS.

Regular Issues Overprinted

1896 Perf. 12 Unwmkd.

O1	A45	1c blue	20
O2	A45	2c dk brn	20
a.		Double overprint	
O3	A45	3c bl grn	60
O4	A45	5c brn ol	20
O5	A45	10c yellow	20
O6	A45	12c dk bl	20
O7	A45	15c bl vio	20
O8	A45	20c magenta	60
O9	A45	24c vermilion	20
O10	A45	30c orange	60
O11	A45	50c blk brn	35
O12	A45	1p rose lake	20
		Nos. O1-O12 (12)	3.75

The 1c has been reprinted on thick unwatermarked paper. Price 10c.

Wmkd. Liberty Cap. (117)

O13	A46	1c emerald	20
O14	A47	2c lake	20
O15	A48	3c yel brn	20
a.		Inverted overprint	1.25
O16	A49	5c dp bl	25
O17	A50	10c brown	20
a.		Inverted overprint	2.50
O18	A51	12c slate	30
O19	A52	15c bl grn	30
O20	A53	20c car rose	30
a.		Inverted overprint	
O21	A54	24c violet	30
O22	A55	30c dp grn	30
O23	A56	50c orange	30
O24	A57	100c dk bl	40
		Nos. O13-O24 (12)	3.15

Unwmkd.

O25	A46	1c emerald	20
a.		Double overprint	
O26	A47	2c lake	20
O27	A48	3c yel brn	20
O28	A49	5c dp bl	1.65
O29	A50	10c brown	25
a.		Inverted overprint	
O30	A51	12c slate	30
O31	A52	15c bl grn	45
O32	A53	20c car rose	30
a.		Inverted overprint	
O33	A54	24c violet	85
O34	A55	30c dp grn	25
O35	A56	50c orange	1.65
O36	A57	100c dk bl	2.25
		Nos. O25-O36 (12)	8.55

The 3, 5, 10, 12, 15, 20, 24, 30 and 100c have been reprinted on thick unwatermarked paper and the 15c, 50c and 100c on thick watermarked paper. Price 10c each.

Nos. 134–145 Handstamped in Black or Violet

1896

O37	A45	1c blue	15.00
O38	A45	2c dk brn	15.00
O39	A45	3c bl grn	15.00
O40	A45	5c brn ol	15.00
O41	A45	10c yellow	17.50
O42	A45	12c dk bl	22.50
O43	A45	15c bl vio	22.50
O44	A45	20c magenta	22.50
O45	A45	24c vermilion	22.50
O46	A45	30c orange	22.50
O47	A45	50c blk brn	30.00
O48	A45	1p rose lake	30.00
		Nos. O37-O48 (12)	250.00

Reprints of the 1c and 2c on thick paper exist with this handstamp. Price 10c each.

Forged overprints exist of Nos. O37–O78, O103–O126 and of the higher priced stamps of Nos. O141–O214.

Same Overprint Handstamped on Nos. 146–157 in Black or Violet

1896 Wmk. 117

O49	A46	1c emerald	12.50
O50	A47	2c lake	12.50
O51	A48	3c yel brn	12.50
O52	A49	5c dp bl	12.50
O53	A50	10c brown	12.50
O54	A51	12c slate	20.00
O55	A52	15c bl grn	22.50
O56	A53	20c car rose	22.50
O57	A54	24c violet	22.50
O58	A55	30c dp grn	22.50
O59	A56	50c orange	22.50
O60	A57	100c dk bl	22.50
		Nos. O49-O60 (12)	217.50

Unwmkd.

O61	A46	1c emerald	12.50
O62	A47	2c lake	12.50
O63	A48	3c yel brn	12.50
O64	A49	5c dp bl	12.50
O65	A50	10c brown	17.50
O66	A51	12c on 24c vio	22.50
O67	A52	15c bl grn	22.50
O68	A53	20c car rose	22.50
O69	A54	24c violet	22.50
O70	A55	30c dp grn	22.50
O71	A56	50c orange	25.00
O72	A57	100c dk bl	25.00
		Nos. O61-O72 (12)	230.00

Nos. 175–176 Overprinted in Black

1897

O73	A59	1c bl, gold, rose & grn	40
O74	A59	5c rose, gold, bl & grn	40

These stamps were probably not officially issued.

Nos. 175–176 Handstamped in Black or Violet

1900

O75	A59	1c bl, gold, rose & grn	35.00
O76	A59	5c rose, gold, bl & grn	35.00

Nos. 159–170L Overprinted in Black

1897 Wmk. 117

O79	A46	1c scarlet	20	
O80	A47	2c yel grn	2.50	
O81	A48	3c bis brn	75	
O82	A49	5c orange	20	20
O83	A50	10c bl grn	35	
O84	A51	12c blue	35	
O85	A52	15c black	35	50
O86	A53	20c slate	25	
O87	A54	24c yellow	35	
a.		Inverted overprint		
O88	A55	30c rose	75	
O89	A56	50c violet	2.50	2.00
O90	A57	100c brn lake	3.50	
		Nos. O79-O90 (12)	11.95	

Unwmkd.

O91	A46	1c scarlet	10	
O92	A47	2c yel grn	60	
O93	A48	3c bis brn	25	
O94	A49	5c orange	25	35
O95	A50	10c bl grn	1.25	
O96	A51	12c blue	1.25	
O97	A52	15c black	1.50	
O98	A53	20c slate	25	75
O99	A54	24c yellow	25	75
O100	A55	30c rose	25	75
O101	A56	50c violet	1.25	
O102	A57	100c brn lake	75	2.00
		Nos. O91-O102 (12)	7.95	

All values have been reprinted on thick paper without watermark and the 1c, 12c, 15c and 100c on thick paper with watermark. Price 10c each.

Nos. 159–170L Handstamped in Violet or Black

1897 Wmk. 117

O103	A46	1c scarlet	15.00	
O104	A47	2c yel grn	15.00	
O105	A48	3c bis brn	15.00	
O106	A49	5c orange	15.00	
O107	A50	10c bl grn	17.50	
O108	A51	12c blue		
O109	A52	15c black		
O110	A53	20c slate	30.00	
O111	A54	24c yellow	35.00	
O112	A55	30c rose		
O113	A56	50c violet		
O114	A57	100c brn lake		

Unwmkd.

O115	A46	1c scarlet	15.00
O116	A47	2c yel grn	15.00
O117	A48	3c bis brn	15.00
O118	A49	5c orange	15.00
O119	A50	10c bl grn	15.00
O120	A51	12c blue	
O121	A52	15c black	
O122	A53	20c slate	
O123	A54	24c yellow	
O124	A55	30c rose	30.00
O125	A56	50c violet	
O126	A57	100c brn lake	35.00

Forged overprints on Nos. O103–O126 exist.

Reprints of the 1 and 15c on thick watermarked paper and the 12, 30, 50 and 100c on thick unwatermarked paper are known with this overprint. Price 10c each.

SALVADOR

Registration Stamps
Overprinted
in Red

Wmkd. Liberty Cap. (117)
O127 R1 10c dk bl   20
Unwmkd.
O128 R1 10c dk bl   30

The reprints are on thick paper. Price 10c.

Originals of the 10c brown lake Registration Stamp and the 5c Acknowledgment of Receipt stamp are believed not to have been issued with the "FRANQUEO OFICIAL" overprint. They are believed to exist only as reprints.

Nos. 177–188
Overprinted

1898   **Wmk. 117**
O129 A60 1c org ver   20
O130 A60 2c rose   20
O131 A60 3c pale yel grn 2.75
O132 A60 5c bl grn   20
O133 A60 10c gray bl   20
O134 A60 12c violet   2.75
O135 A60 13c brn lake   20
O136 A60 20c dp bl   20
O137 A60 24c ultra   20
O138 A60 26c bis brn   20
O139 A60 50c orange   20
O140 A60 1p yellow   20
  Nos. O129-O140 (12)   7.50

Reprints of the above set are on thick paper with and without watermark. Price 10c each.

No. 177
Handstamped
in Violet

O141 A60 1c org ver   60.00

Same, with Additional
Overprint in Black

O142 A60 1c org ver
Counterfeits exist of the "wheel" overprint.

Nos. 204–205,
207 and 209
Overprinted

1899   **Unwmkd.**
O143 A61 12c dk grn
O144 A61 13c dp rose
O145 A61 26c car rose
O146 A61 100c violet

Nos. 204–205
Overprinted
and Punched with
12 small holes

O147 A61 12c dk grn
O148 A61 13c dp rose
Official stamps punched with twelve small holes were issued and used for ordinary postage.

Nos. 199–209
Overprinted

1899   **Blue Overprint.**
O149 A61 1c brown   20
O150 A61 2c gray grn   20
O151 A61 3c blue   20
O152 A61 5c brn org   20
O153 A61 10c chocolate   20
O154 A61 13c dp rose   20
O155 A61 26c car rose   20
O156 A61 50c org red   20
O157 A61 100c violet   20
  Nos. O149-O157 (9)   1.80

Black Overprint.
O158 A61 3c blue   20
O159 A61 12c dk grn   20
O160 A61 24c lt bl   20
Nos. O149 to O160 were probably not placed in use.

With Additional
Overprint in Black

O161 A61 1c brown   60   50
O162 A61 2c gray grn   90   75
O163 A61 3c blue   60   50
O164 A61 5c brn org   60   50
O165 A61 10c chocolate   75   60
O166 A61 12c dk grn
O167 A61 13c dp rose   1.50 1.25
O168 A61 24c lt bl   25.00 22.50
O169 A61 26c car rose   75   60
O170 A61 50c org red   1.50 1.25
O171 A61 100c violet   1.50 1.25

Regular Issue
of 1899
Overprinted

and Punched

Blue Overprint.
O172 A61 1c brown   1.25   30
O173 A61 2c gray grn   1.50   30
O174 A61 3c blue   2.00 1.75
O175 A61 5c brn org   2.50   90
O176 A61 10c chocolate   3.50 2.50
O177 A61 13c dp rose   3.50 1.25
O177A A61 24c lt bl
O178 A61 26c car rose   40.00 17.50
  Nos. O172-O177, O178 (7) 54.25 24.50

It is stated that Nos. O172–O214 inclusive were issued for ordinary postage and not for use as official stamps.

O179 A61 12c dk grn   2.50 1.75

With Additional
Overprint in Black

O180 A61 1c brown   2.00 1.75
O180A A61 2c gray grn
O181 A61 3c blue
O182 A61 5c brn org   1.75
O182A A61 10c chocolate
O182B A61 12c dk grn
O183 A61 13c dp rose   6.00 2.50
O184 A61 26c car rose

Overprinted in Black

 and

O185 A61 100c violet

Postage Due Stamps of
1899 Issue, Nos. J49 to
J56 Overprinted in Black
1900
O186 D1 1c orange   30.00
O187 D1 2c orange   30.00
O188 D1 3c orange   30.00
O189 D1 5c orange   30.00
O190 D1 10c orange   30.00
O191 D1 15c orange   65.00
O192 D1 25c orange   65.00
O193 D1 50c orange   65.00
  Nos. O186-O193 (8)   345.00

With Additional
Overprint in Black

O194 D1 1c orange
O195 D1 2c orange   15.00
O196 D1 3c orange
O197 D1 5c orange
O198 D1 15c orange   15.00
O199 D1 25c orange   17.50
O200 D1 50c orange   165.00

Overprinted
in Black

and Punched

O201 D1 1c orange   30.00
O202 D1 2c orange   30.00
O203 D1 3c orange   30.00
O204 D1 5c orange   30.00

With Additional
Overprint in Black

O205 D1 1c orange   11.00 8.00
O206 D1 2c orange   8.00
O207 D1 3c orange   8.00
O208 D1 5c orange   11.00 7.00

Overprinted  in Violet

and in Black.

O209 D1 2c orange   25.00
  a. Inverted overprint
O210 D1 3c orange
O211 D1 10c orange   6.00

With Additional
Handstamp in Violet

O212 D1 1c orange   15.00 10.00
O213 D1 2c orange   15.00 11.00
O214 D1 3c orange   15.00 11.00
See note after No. O48.

Type of Regular
Issue of 1900
Overprinted in Black

O223 A63 1c lt grn   50   50
  a. Inverted overprint
O224 A63 2c rose   60   50
  a. Inverted overprint   3.50
O225 A63 3c gray blk   40   40
  a. Overprint vertical
O226 A63 5c blue   40   40
O227 A63 10c blue   1.00   1.00
  a. Inverted overprint
O228 A63 12c yel grn   1.00   1.00
O229 A63 13c yel brn   1.00   1.00
O230 A63 24c gray blk   75   1.00
O231 A63 26c yel brn   35.50 30.00
  a. Inverted overprint
O232 A63 50c dl rose
  a. Inverted overprint
  Nos. O223-O231 (9)   41.15 35.80

With Additional
Overprint in Violet

O233 A63 1c lt grn   7.00   6.00
O234 A63 2c rose
  a. "FRANQUEO OFICIAL" inverted
O235 A63 26c yel rose   75   75
O236 A63 50c dl rose   1.00   85

Overprinted in Black

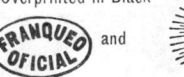 and

O237 A63 1c lt grn   7.00   7.00
O238 A63 3c gray blk
O239 A63 5c blue
O240 A63 10c blue
O241 A63 12c yel grn

Violet Overprint.

O242 A63 50c dl rose   20.00
The shield overprinted on No. O242 is of the type on No. O212.

Wmkd. S. (173)
1903   **Perf. 14, 14½**
O243 O1 1c yel grn   50   35
O244 O1 2c carmine   50   25
O245 O1 3c orange   1.50 1.20
O246 O1 5c dk bl   50   25
O247 O1 10c dl vio   75   50
O248 O1 13c red brn   75   50
O249 O1 15c yel brn   5.00 2.50
O250 O1 24c scarlet   50   50
O251 O1 50c bister   75   35
O252 O1 100c grnsh blk   75   1.20
  Nos. O243-O252 (10)   11.50 7.60

No. 285
Handstamped
in Black

1904
O253 A64 3c orange   60.00

2 **2**

Nos. O246-O248
Surcharged in Black

● ●

1905
O254 O1 2c on 5c dk bl   5.00 4.00
O255 O1 3c on 5c dk bl
  a. Double surcharge
O256 O1 3c on 10c dl vio 11.00 9.00
O257 O1 3c on 13c red brn 1.25 1.00
A 2c surcharge of this type exists on No. O247.

No. O225 Overprinted in Blue

1905   **1905**
  a   *b*
1905   **Unwmkd.**
O258 A63(a) 3c gray blk 3.00 2.50
O259 A63(b) 3c gray blk 2.50 2.00

Nos. O224-O225 Overprinted in Blue

1906   **1906**
  c   *d*
1906
O260 A63(c) 2c rose   20.00 17.50
O261 A63(c) 3c gray blk 1.75 1.50
  a. Overprint "1906" in blk
O262 A63(d) 3c gray blk 2.00 1.75

Escalón   National Palace
  O2   O3
1906 Engraved **Perf. 11½**
O263 O2 1c grn & blk   20   13
O264 O2 2c car & blk   20   13
O265 O2 3c yel & blk   20   12
O266 O2 5c bl & blk   20   65
O267 O2 10c vio & blk   20   13
O268 O2 13c dk brn & blk 20   15
O269 O2 15c red org & blk 30   15
O270 O2 24c car & blk   35   33
O271 O2 50c org & blk   35   1.35

SALVADOR

O272	O2	100c dk bl & blk	40	*4.00*
		Nos. O263-O272 (10)	2.60	*7.14*

The centers of these stamps are also found in blue black.

Nos. O263 to O272 have been reprinted. The shades differ, the paper is thinner, the gum whiter and the perforation 12. Price 5c each.

1908

O273	O3	1c grn & blk	15	15
O274	O3	2c red & blk	15	15
O275	O3	3c yel & blk	15	15
O276	O3	5c bl & blk	15	15
O277	O3	10c vio & blk	15	15
O278	O3	13c vio & blk	20	20
O279	O3	15c pale brn & blk	20	20
O280	O3	24c rose & blk	20	20
O281	O3	50c yel & blk	20	20
O282	O3	100c turq bl & blk	40	40
		Nos. O273-O282 (10)	1.95	1.75

Same Overprinted in Black

O283	O3	1c grn & blk		1.25
O284	O3	2c red & blk		1.50
O285	O3	3c yel & blk		1.50
O286	O3	5c bl & blk		2.00
O287	O3	10c vio & blk		2.00
O288	O3	13c vio & blk		2.25
O289	O3	15c pale brn & blk		2.50
O290	O3	24c rose & blk		2.75
O291	O3	50c yel & blk		3.00
O292	O3	100c turq & blk		3.50
		Nos. O283-O292 (10)		22.25

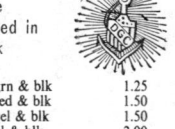

Pres. Figueroa
O4
Wmkd. Honeycomb. (172)

1910 Engraved.

O293	O4	2c dk grn & blk	18	18
O294	O4	3c org & blk	18	18
O295	O4	4c scar & blk	18	18
a.		4c car & blk		
O296	O4	5c pur & blk	18	18
O297	O4	6c scar & blk	18	18
O298	O4	10c pur & blk	18	18
O299	O4	12c dp bl & blk	18	18
O300	O4	17c ol grn & blk	18	18
O301	O4	19c brn red & blk	18	18
O302	O4	29c choc & blk	18	18
O303	O4	50c yel & blk	18	18
O304	O4	100c turq & blk	18	18
		Nos. O293-O304 (12)	2.16	2.16

Regular Issue, Type A63, Overprinted or Surcharged:

OFICIAL
a

OFICIAL
3
b

UN COLON
c

1911 Unwmkd.

O305	A63(a)	1c lt grn	15	15
O306	A63(b)	3c on 13c yel brn	15	15
O307	A63(b)	5c on 10c dp bl	15	15
O308	A63(a)	10c dp bl	15	15
O309	A63(a)	12c lt grn	15	15
O310	A63(b)	13c yel brn	15	15
O311	A63(b)	50c on 10c dp bl	15	15
O312	A63(c)	1col on 13c yel brn	25	25
		Nos. O305-O312 (8)	1.30	1.30

O5

O6

Typographed.
Background in Green, Shield and "Provisional" in Black.

1914 Perf. 12.

O313	O5	2c yel brn	15	15
O314	O5	3c yellow	15	15
O315	O5	5c dk bl	15	15
O316	O5	10c red	15	15
O317	O5	12c green	15	15
O318	O5	17c violet	15	15
O319	O5	50c brown	15	15
O320	O5	100c dl rose	15	15
		Nos. O313-O320 (8)	1.20	1.20

Stamps of this issue are known imperforate or with parts of the design omitted or misplaced. These varieties were not regularly issued.

1914 Typographed.

O321	O6	2c bl grn	15	15
O322	O6	3c orange	15	15

Type of Official Stamps of 1908 Overprinted

1915 and OFICIAL

1915

O323	O3	1c gray grn	40	30
a.		"1915" double		
b.		"OFICIAL" inverted		
O324	O3	2c red	40	30
O325	O3	5c ultra	40	30
O326	O3	10c yellow	40	35
a.		Date omitted		
O327	O3	50c violet	90	75
O328	O3	100c blk brn	1.75	1.75
		Nos. O323-O328 (6)	4.25	3.75

Same Overprint on Nos. 414, 417, 419.

O329	A66	1c gray grn	2.50	2.50
O330	A66	6c pale bl	75	60
a.		6c ultra		
O331	A66	12c brown	90	90

Nos. O323 to O331, except No. O328, exist imperforate.
No. O329-O331 exist with "OFICIAL" inverted and double. See note after No. 421.

Nos. 431–440 Overprinted in Blue or Red

1916

O332	A83	1c dp grn	15	12
O333	A83	2c vermilion	50	30
O334	A83	5c dp bl (R)	35	30
O335	A83	6c gray vio (R)	15	12
O336	A83	10c blk brn	15	12
O337	A83	12c violet	60	50
O338	A83	17c orange	15	12
O339	A83	25c dk brn	15	12
O340	A83	29c blk (R)	15	12
O341	A83	50c sl (R)	15	12
		Nos. O332-O341 (10)	2.50	1.94

Nos. 474-481 Overprinted

OFICIAL
a

OFICIAL
b

1921

O342	A94(a)	1c green	20	15
O343	A95(a)	2c black	20	15
a.		Invtd. ovpt.		
O344	A96(b)	5c orange	30	25
O345	A97(a)	6c car rose	25	15
O346	A98(a)	10c dp bl	40	30
O347	A99(a)	25c ol grn	1.00	50
O348	A100(a)	60c violet	1.25	75
O349	A101(a)	1col blk brn	1.25	90
		Nos. O342-O349 (8)	4.85	3.15

Nos. 498 and 500 Overprinted in Black or Red OFICIAL

1925

O350	A109	5c ol blk	50	20
O351	A111	10c org (R)	1.00	25
a.		"ATLANT CO"	15.00	12.50

Inverted overprints exist.

Regular Issue of 1924-25 Overprinted OFICIAL in Black or Red

1927

O352	A106	1c red vio	25	15
O353	A107	2c dk red	50	15
O354	A109	5c ol blk (R)	50	18
O355	A110	6c dp bl (R)	5.00	4.00
O356	A111	10c orange	50	25
a.		"ATLANT CO"	25.00	22.50
O357	A116	1col orn & vio (R)	2.50	1.50
		Nos. O352-O357 (6)	9.25	6.23

Inverted overprints exist on 1c, 2c, 5c and 10c.

Regular Issue of 1924-25 Overprinted OFICIAL in Black

1932 Perf. 12½.

O358	A106	1c dp vio	25	12
O359	A107	2c dk red	50	12
O360	A109	5c ol blk	25	10
O361	A111	10c orange	1.00	25
a.		"ATLANT CO"	27.50	25.00

Regular Issue of 1947 Overprinted OFICIAL in Black or Red

1948 Engraved. Perf. 12 Unwmkd.

O362	A154	1c car rose	60.00	35.00
O363	A154	2c dp org	60.00	35.00
O364	A154	5c sl gray (R)	60.00	35.00
O365	A154	10c bis brn (R)	60.00	35.00
O366	A154	20c grn (R)	60.00	35.00
O367	A154	50c blk (R)	60.00	35.00
		Nos. O362-O367 (6)	360.00	210.00

No. 602 Surcharged In Carmine and Black

1 CTS

 X X

OFICIAL

1964(?)

O368	A154	1c on 20c grn		

The X's are black, the rest carmine.

PARCEL POST STAMPS.

Mercury
PP1
Engraved

1895 Perf. 12 Unwmkd.

Q1	PP1	5c brn org		35
Q2	PP1	10c dk bl		35
Q3	PP1	15c red		35
Q4	PP1	20c orange		35
Q5	PP1	50c bl grn		35
		Nos. Q1-Q5 (5)		1.75

POSTAL TAX STAMPS.

Nos. 503, 501 Surcharged

EDIFICIOS POSTALES 1

1931 Perf. 12½ Unwmkd.

RA1	A115	1c on 50c org brn	25	15
a.		Double surcharge	3.00	3.00
RA2	A112	2c on 20c dp grn	25	20

Nos. 501, 503 Surcharged

EDIFICIOS POSTALES ₡ 0.01

RA3	A112	1c on 20c dp grn	25	20
RA4	A115	2c on 50c org brn	25	20
a.		Without period in "0.02"	1.50	

The use of these stamps was obligatory, in addition to the regular postage, on letters and other postal matter. The money obtained from their sale was to be used to erect a new post office in San Salvador.

SAMOA

SAMOA
(sä·mō'ā)

LOCATION—An archipelago in the South Pacific Ocean, east of Fiji.
GOVT.—Former monarchy and (partially) former German possession.
AREA—1,130 sq. mi.
POP.—39,000 (est. 1910).
CAPITAL—Apia.

In 1861–99, Samoa was an independent kingdom under the influence of the United States, to which the harbor of Pago Pago had been ceded, and that of Great Britain and Germany. In 1898 a disturbance arose, resulting in the withdrawal of Great Britain, and the partitioning of the islands between Germany and the United States. Early in World War I the islands under German domination were occupied by New Zealand troops and in 1920 the League of Nations declared them a mandate to New Zealand. See Vol. I for British issues.

```
12 Pence  = 1 Shilling
20 Shillings = 1 Pound
100 Pfennig = 1 Mark (1900)
```

Issues of the Kingdom.

A1

Type I. Line above "X" is usually unbroken. Dots over "SAMOA" are uniform and evenly spaced. Upper right serif of "M" is horizontal.

Type II. Line above "X" is usually broken. Small dot near upper right serif of "M".

Type III. Line above "X" roughly retouched. Upper right serif of "M" bends down.

Type IV. Speck of color on curved line below center of "M".

Perf. 12, 12½

		1877–82 Lithographed.	Unwmkd.	
1	A1	1p bl (III) ('79)	32.50	34.00
a.		1p ultra (III) ('79)	35.00	37.50
b.		1p ultra (I) ('78)	70.00	75.00
c.		1p ultra (I) ('77)	140.00	75.00
2	A1	2p lil rose (IV) ('82)	32.50	
3	A1	3p ver (III) ('79)	37.50	40.00
a.		3p brt scar (III) ('79)	37.50	40.00
b.		3p scar (II)	160.00	125.00
c.		3p dp scar (I) ('77)	160.00	125.00
4	A1	6p vio (III) ('79)	37.50	40.00
a.		6p vio (II) ('78)	125.00	95.00
b.		6p vio (I) ('77)	125.00	95.00
5	A1	9p yel brn (IV) ('80)	55.00	57.50
a.		9p org brn (IV) ('80)	55.00	57.50
6	A1	1sh org yel (II) ('78)	57.50	60.00
a.		1sh dl yel (I) ('78)	57.50	60.00
7	A1	2sh dp brn (III) ('79)	140.00	150.00
a.		2sh red brn (II) ('78)	140.00	150.00
b.		2sh brn (II) ('78)	140.00	150.00
8	A1	5sh yel grn (III) ('79)	425.00	425.00
a.		5sh dp grn (III) ('79)	425.00	450.00
b.		5sh gray grn (II) ('78)	500.00	525.00

The 1p often has a period after "PENNY." The 2p was never placed in use.
Imperforates of this issue are proofs.
Sheets of the first issue were not perforated around the outer sides. All values except the 2p were printed in sheets of 10 (2x5). The 1p, 3p and 6p type I and the 1p type III were also printed in sheets of 20 (4x5), and six stamps on each of these sheets were perforated all around. The 2p was printed in sheets of 21 (3x7) and five stamps in the second row were perforated all around. These are the only varieties of the original stamps which have not one or two imperforate edges.
Reprints are of type IV and nearly always perforated on all sides. They have a spot of color at the edge of the panel below the "M". This spot is not on any originals except the 2p, which may be distinguished by its color, and the 9p which may be distinguished by having a rough blind perf. 12.

Palms — King Malietoa Laupepa
A2 — A3

Wmk. 62
Wmkd.
N. Z. and Star Wide Apart. (62)
1895–99 Typographed Perf. 11

9	A2	½p brn vio ('95)	30	30
10	A2	½p grn ('99)	70	90
11	A2	1p grn ('95)	70	65
12	A2	1p red brn ('99)	65	85
13	A3	2p brt yel ('95)	1.50	1.50
14	A3	2½p rose ('92)	1.25	1.25
15	A3	2½p blk perf. 10x11 ('96)	1.75	1.75
a.		Perf. 11 ('95)		
16	A2	4p bl ('95)	1.60	1.60
17	A2	6p mar ('95)	1.75	1.75
18	A2	1sh rose ('95)	2.25	2.25
19	A2	2sh6p red vio ('95)	5.25	5.25
c.		Vert. pair, imperf. between	750.00	
		Nos. 9-19 (11)	17.70	18.05

1886–92 Perf. 12½

9a	A2	½p brn vio	2.25	1.25
11a	A2	1p green	2.25	1.25
13a	A2	2p orange	2.25	1.10
14a	A3	2½p rose ('92)	1.75	1.75
16a	A2	4p blue	9.00	6.25
17a	A2	6p maroon	375.00	
18a	A2	1sh rose	22.50	14.00
c.		Diagonal half used as 6p on cover		525.00
19a	A2	2sh6p purple	37.50	22.50
		Nos. 9a-16a, 18a-19a (7)	77.50	48.10

1887–92 Perf. 12x11½

9b	A2	½p brn vio	30	30
11b	A2	1p green	75	60
13b	A2	2p brn org	1.00	85
14b	A3	2½p rose ('92)	1.25	1.10
16b	A2	4p blue	5.00	1.75
17b	A2	6p maroon	3.25	3.25
18b	A2	1sh rose	15.00	2.25
19b	A2	2sh6p red vio	16.00	2.50
		Nos. 9b-19b (8)	42.55	12.60

Three forms of watermark 62 are found on stamps of type A2: 1. Wide "N Z" and wide star, 6mm. apart (used 1886–87). 2. Wide "N Z" and narrow star, 4mm. apart (1890). 3. Narrow "NZ" and narrow star, 7mm. apart (1890–1900). The 2½p has only the last form.

No. 14a Handstamp Surcharged in Black or Red:

1893 Perf. 12x11½

20	A2(a)	5p on 4p bl (bar 16mm)	50.00	50.00
21	A2(b)	5p on 4p bl	125.00	125.00
22	A2(c)	5p on 4p bl (R)	20.00	20.00

As the surcharges on Nos. 20–21 were handstamped in two steps and on No. 22 in three steps, various varieties exist.

Flag Design
A7

1894–95 Typo. Perf. 11½x12

23	A7	5p vermilion	1.50	1.50
a.		Perf. 11 ('95)	1.50	1.50

Types of 1887–1895
Surcharged in Blue, Black, Red or Green:

Surcharged 1½d.   R 3d.

1895 Perf. 11

24	A2(d)	1½p on 2p org (Bl)	1.50	1.50
a.		1½p on 2p brn org, perf. 12x11½ (Bl)	3.00	3.00
b.		1½p on 2p yel, "2" ends with vertical stroke	1.50	1.50
25	A2(e)	3p on 2p brn org (Bk)	3.00	3.25
a.		3p on 2p brn org, perf. 12x11½ (Bk)	4.50	4.50
b.		3p on 2p yel, perf. 11 (Bk)	57.50	57.50
c.		Vert. pair, imperf. btwn.	450.00	

1898–1900 Perf. 11

26	A2(d)	2½p on 1sh rose (Bk)	1.75	1.75
a.		Double surcharge	425.00	
27	A2(d)	2½p on 2sh6p vio (Bk)	6.75	6.75
28	A2(d)	2½p on 1p bl grn (R)	75	75
a.		Inverted surcharge	400.00	
29	A2(d)	2½p on 1sh rose (R)	10.00	11.00
30	A2(e)	3p on 2p org (G)	1.10	

No. 30 was a re-issue, available for postage.

Stamps of 1886–99 Overprinted in Red or Blue

PROVISIONAL GOVT.

1899

31	A2	½p grn (R)	35	40
32	A2	1p red brn (Bl)	35	40
33	A2	2p org (R)	60	75
a.		2p yel	75	90
34	A2	4p bl (R)	60	75
35	A7	5p scar (Bl)	90	1.10
36	A2	6p mar (Bl)	1.25	1.75
37	A2	1sh rose (Bl)	3.00	3.50
38	A2	2sh6p vio (R)	5.50	6.00
		Nos. 31-38 (8)	12.55	14.65

In 1900 the Samoan islands were partitioned between the United States and Germany. The part which became American has since used U.S. stamps.

Issued under German Dominion.

A10    A11

Stamps of Germany Overprinted in Black.
1900 Perf. 13½x14½. Unwmkd.

51	A10	3pf dk brn	11.50	16.00
52	A10	5pf green	16.00	20.00
53	A11	10pf carmine	11.50	20.00
54	A11	20pf ultra	22.50	35.00
55	A11	25pf orange	55.00	62.50
56	A11	50pf red brn	55.00	62.50
		Nos. 51-56 (6)	171.50	216.00

Kaiser's Yacht "Hohenzollern"
A12   A13

1900 Typographed Perf. 14

57	A12	3pf brown	1.10	1.10
58	A12	5pf green	1.40	1.10
59	A12	10pf carmine	1.40	1.10
60	A12	20pf ultra	90	2.25
61	A12	25pf org & blk, yel	1.50	16.00
62	A12	30pf org & blk, sal	1.40	16.00
63	A12	40pf lake & blk	1.40	16.00
64	A12	50pf pur & blk, sal	1.75	16.00
65	A12	80pf lake & blk, rose	3.50	35.00

Engraved. Perf. 14½x14

66	A13	1m carmine	4.00	72.50
67	A13	2m blue	5.50	115.00
68	A13	3m blk vio	8.00	160.00
69	A13	5m sl & car	180.00	625.00
		Nos. 57-69 (13)	211.85	

Typographed. Perf. 14
1915 Wmkd. Lozenges. (125)

70	A12	3pf brown	1.10	
71	A12	5pf green	1.50	
72	A12	10pf carmine	1.50	

Engraved. Perf. 14½x14

| 73 | A13 | 5m sl & car | 20.00 | |

Nos. 70-73 were never put in use.

Stamps issued under British dominion and those of Western Samoa are listed in Volume I.

A particular stamp may be scarce, but if few want it, its market potential may remain relatively low.

SAN MARINO

SAN MARINO
(sän mä·rē'nō)

LOCATION—In eastern Italy, about 20 miles inland from the Adriatic Sea.
GOVT.—Republic.
AREA—24 sq. mi.
POP.—20,000 (est. 1977).
CAPITAL—San Marino.

100 Centesimi = 1 Lira

Prices of San Marino Nos. 1-28, 72 are for specimens in fine condition with original gum. Very fine to superb stamps sell at higher prices. Copies without gum or with perforations cutting into the design sell at lower prices, depending on the condition of the individual specimen.

Coat of Arms
A1   A2

Wmk. 140
Wmkd. Crown. (140)

	1877-99	Typographed.	*Perf. 14.*	
1	A1	2c green	5.50	2.50
2	A1	2c bl ('94)	4.50	3.00
3	A1	2c cl ('95)	5.50	3.00
4	A2	5c org ('90)	30.00	7.50
5	A2	5c ol grn ('92)	2.50	1.25
6	A2	5c grn ('99)	2.75	1.25
7	A2	10c ultra	45.00	7.50
a.		10c bl ('90)	165.00	27.50
8	A2	10c dk grn ('92)	2.75	1.75
9	A2	10c cl ('99)	2.75	1.50
10	A2	15c cl ('94)	70.00	21.00
11	A2	20c vermilion	8.50	2.50
12	A2	20c lil ('95)	4.50	2.75
13	A2	25c mar ('90)	45.00	10.00
14	A2	25c bl ('99)	2.75	2.25
15	A2	30c brown	250.00	35.00
16	A2	30c org yel ('92)	3.75	3.00
17	A2	40c violet	250.00	35.00
18	A2	40c dk brn ('92)	2.75	3.00
19	A2	45c gray grn ('95)	3.25	3.00
20	A2	65c red brn ('92)	3.25	3.00
21	A2	1 l car & yel ('92)	1,000.	300.00
22	A2	1 l lt bl ('95)	1,000.	300.00
23	A2	2 l brn & yel ('94)	35.00	32.50
24	A2	5 l vio & grn ('94)	80.00	90.00

See Nos. 911-915.

Nos. 7a, 15, 11 Surcharged in Black **C mi. 5**

1892
25	A2	5c on 10c bl	30.00	8.50
a.		Inverted surcharge	30.00	8.50
b.		5c on 10c ultra	5,000.	1,350.
c.		As "b," invtd. surcharge	5,000.	1,350.
26	A2	5c on 30c brn	250.00	40.00
a.		Inverted surch.	250.00	40.00
b.		Double surcharge, one inverted	250.00	90.00
c.		Dbl. invtd. surcharge	250.00	65.00

27	A2	10c on 20c ver	22.50	2.50
a.		Inverted surcharge	30.00	4.50
b.		Double surcharge, one inverted	30.00	15.00
c.		Dbl. surcharge	30.00	15.00

Ten to twelve varieties of each surcharge.

No. 11 Surcharged **10   10**
| 28 | A2 | 10c on 20c ver | 125.00 | 3.25 |

Government Palace and Portraits of Regents, Tonnini and Marcucci
A6   A7

Portraits of Regents and View of Interior of Palace
A8   Wmk. 174
Wmkd. Coat of Arms. (174)

	1894, Sept. 30	Litho.	*Perf. 15½*	
29	A6	25c bl & dk brn	2.50	80
30	A7	50c dl red & dk brn	9.50	1.75
31	A8	1 l grn & dk brn	9.50	2.50

Issued in commemoration of the opening of the new Government Palace and the installation of the new Regents.

Statue of Liberty
A9
Typographed

	1899-1922	*Perf. 14.*	Wmk. 140	
32	A9	2c brown	1.85	90
33	A9	2c cl ('22)	12	12
34	A9	5c brn org	2.65	2.10
35	A9	5c ol grn ('22)	12	12
36	A9	10c brn org ('22)	12	12
37	A9	20c dp brn ('22)	35	30
38	A9	25c ultra ('22)	50	45
39	A9	45c red brn ('22)	1.75	1.35
		Nos. 32-39 (8)	7.46	5.46

Numeral of Value   Mt. Titano
A10   A11

	1903-25	*Perf. 14, 14½x14*		
40	A10	2c violet	9.00	1.00
41	A10	2c org brn ('21)	8	7
42	A11	5c bl grn	2.75	50
43	A11	5c ol grn ('21)	12	12
44	A11	5c red brn ('25)	10	18
45	A11	10c claret	2.75	65
46	A11	10c brn org ('21)	12	12
47	A11	10c ol grn ('25)	10	18
48	A11	15c brn ('22)	12	18
49	A11	15c brn vio ('25)	18	35
50	A11	20c brn org	9.00	12.50
51	A11	20c brn ('21)	12	18
52	A11	20c bl grn ('25)	18	35
53	A11	25c blue	7.25	2.00
54	A11	25c gray ('21)	15	25
55	A11	25c vio ('25)	18	35
56	A11	30c brn red	3.75	4.00
57	A11	30c cl ('21)	5.75	70
58	A11	30c org ('25)	6.00	4.75
59	A11	40c org red	6.00	3.50
60	A11	40c dp rose ('21)	22	30
61	A11	40c brn ('25)	25	50
62	A11	45c yellow	6.00	5.00
63	A11	50c brn vio ('23)	30	50
64	A11	50c gray blk ('25)	25	38
65	A11	60c brn red ('25)	40	80
66	A11	65c chocolate	6.00	4.00
67	A11	80c bl ('21)	40	60
68	A11	90c brn ('23)	40	60
69	A11	1 l org	13.00	5.75
70	A11	1 l ultra ('21)	60	60
71	A11	1 l lt bl ('25)	45	90
72	A11	2 l violet	475.00	150.00
73	A11	2 l org ('21)	13.00	12.00
74	A11	2 l lt grn ('25)	1.50	1.50
75	A11	5 l slate	60.00	65.00
76	A11	5 l brn red ('25)	9.00	9.00
		Nos. 40-76 (37)	661.47	290.36

1905
No. 50 Surcharged **15**

	1905, Sept. 1			
77	A11	15c on 20c brn org	4.50	2.25
a.		Large "5" in "1905"	17.50	10.00

Coat of Arms
A12   A13

Two types:
I. Width 18½mm.
II. Width 19mm.

Engraved.
	1907-10	*Perf. 12*	Unwmkd.	
78	A12	1c brn, II ('10)	1.50	1.10
a.		Type I	3.75	1.40
79	A13	15c gray, I	11.50	2.00
a.		Type II ('10)	120.00	10.00

No. 79a Surcharged in Brown **Cent. 20**

1918
	1918, Mar. 15			
80	A13	20c on 15c gray	1.75	1.25

St. Marinus
A14
Wmkd. Crowns (140)
Perf. 14½x14, 14x14½
	1923, Aug. 11	Typographed		
81	A14	30c dk grn	45	45

Commemorative of the San Marino International Exhibition of 1923. Proceeds from the sale of this stamp went to a mutual aid society.

Italian Flag and Views of Arbe and Mt. Titano
A15

	1923, Aug. 6			
82	A15	50c ol grn	45	45

Issued to commemorate the presentation to San Marino of the Italian flag which had flown over the island of Arbe, the birthplace of the founder of San Marino. Inscribed on back: "V. Moraldi dis. Blasi inc. Petiti impr.—Roma".

Mt. Titano and Sword
A16
	1923, Sept. 29		*Perf. 14x14½*	
83	A16	1 l dk brn	7.25	7.25

Issued in honor of the San Marino Volunteers who were killed or wounded in World War I.

Giuseppe Garibaldi   Allegory—San Marino Sheltering Garibaldi
A17   A18

	1924, Sept. 25		*Perf. 14*	
84	A17	30c dk vio	45	45
85	A17	50c ol brn	45	45
86	A17	60c dl red	1.50	1.50
87	A18	1 l dp bl	2.25	2.25
88	A18	2 l gray grn	3.00	3.00
		Nos. 84-88 (5)	7.65	7.65

Commemorating the 75th anniversary of Garibaldi's taking refuge in San Marino.

Semi-Postal Stamps of 1918 Surcharged with New Values and Bars

Cmi 30

	1924, Oct. 9			
89	SP1	30c on 45c yel brn & blk	30	30

Surcharged
LIRE   UNA

90	SP2	60c on 1 l bl grn & blk	5.25	4.75
91	SP2	1 l on 2 l vio & blk	9.00	9.00
92	SP2	2 l on 3 l red brn & blk	7.25	7.25

Nos. 67 and 68 Surcharged in Black or Red **Lire 1,20**

	1926, July 1			
93	A11	75c on 80c bl	60	60
94	A11	1.20 l on 90c brn	60	60

SAN MARINO

95	A11	1.25 l on 90c brn (R)	2.25	1.75
96	A11	2.50 l on 80c bl (R)	3.25	3.00

Antonio Onofri
A19

A20

Engraved.
1926, July 29   Perf. 11   Unwmkd.

97	A19	10c dk bl & blk	12	12
98	A19	20c ol grn & blk	90	80
99	A19	45c dk vio & blk	45	45
100	A19	65c grn & blk	45	45
101	A19	1 l org & blk	2.75	2.50
102	A19	2 l red vio & blk	2.75	2.50
	Nos. 97-102 (6)		7.42	6.82

Wmkd. Crowns. (140)
1926, Nov. 25   Perf. 14½ x 14

| 103 | A20 | 1.85 l on 60c vio | 70 | 70 |

Nos. 101 and 102 Surcharged **1,25**

1927, Mar. 10   Perf. 11   Unwmkd.

104	A19	1.25 l on 1 l org & blk	2.00	2.00
105	A19	2.50 l on 2 l red vio & blk	5.50	5.50
106	A19	5 l on 2 l red vio & blk	37.50	37.50

Type of Special Delivery Stamp of 1923 Surcharged **L. 1,75**

1927, Sept. 15   Perf. 14   Wmk. 140

| 107 | A11 | 1.75 l on 50c on 25c vio | 1.10 | 1.10 |

The 50c on 25c violet was not issued without 1.75-lire surcharge.

War Memorial
A21

Engraved.
1927, Sept. 28   Perf. 12   Unwmkd.

108	A21	50c brn vio	90	90
109	A21	1.25 l blue	1.75	1.75
110	A21	10 l gray	20.00	20.00

Issued in commemoration of the erection of a cenotaph in memory of the San Marino volunteers in World War I.

Capuchin Church and Convent
A22

Design: 2.50 l, 5 l, Death of St. Francis.

1928, Jan. 2

111	A22	50c red	11.50	2.50
112	A22	1.25 l dp grn	2.00	2.00
113	A22	2.50 l dk brn	2.00	2.00
114	A22	5 l dl vio	14.00	14.00

Issued in commemoration of the seventh centenary of the death of Saint Francis of Assisi.

The Rocca (State Prison) A24
Government Palace A25

Statue of Liberty
A26   Wmk. 217

Wmkd. Three Plumes. (217)
1929-35

115	A24	5c vio brn & ultra	6	12
116	A24	10c bl gray & red vio	60	7
117	A24	15c dp org & emer	6	12
118	A24	20c dk bl & org red	6	7
119	A24	25c grn & gray blk	6	12
120	A24	30c gray brn & red	6	13
121	A24	50c red vio & ol gray	6	8
122	A24	75c dp red & gray blk	6	12
123	A25	1 l dk brn & emer	6	13
124	A25	1.25 l dk bl & blk	6	12
125	A25	1.75 l grn & org	30	30
126	A25	2 l bl gray & red	18	18
127	A25	2.50 l car rose & ultra	18	18
128	A25	3 l dp org & bl	18	18
129	A25	3.70 l ol blk & red brn ('35)	75	50
130	A26	5 l dk vio & dk grn	45	45
131	A26	10 l bis brn & dk bl	2.25	2.25
132	A26	15 l grn & red vio	17.50	17.50
133	A26	20 l dk bl & red	250.00	175.00
	Nos. 115-133 (19)		272.93	197.62

General Post Office A27
San Marino-Rimini Electric Railway A28

1932, Feb. 4

134	A27	20c bl grn	3.00	1.50
135	A27	50c dk red	5.00	3.25
136	A27	1.25 l dk bl	150.00	80.00
137	A27	1.75 l dk brn	45.00	35.00
138	A27	2.75 l dk vio	17.50	17.50
	Nos. 134-138 (5)		220.50	117.25

Opening of new General Post Office.

1932, June 11

139	A28	20c dp grn	90	90
140	A28	50c dk red	1.40	1.40
141	A28	1.25 l dk bl	2.25	2.25
142	A28	5 l dp brn	32.50	32.50

Issued in celebration of the opening of the new electric railway between San Marino and Rimini.

Giuseppe Garibaldi
A29

Garibaldi's Arrival at San Marino
A30

1932, July 30

143	A29	10c vio brn	90	90
144	A29	20c violet	40	40
145	A29	25c green	70	70
146	A29	50c yel green	2.50	2.50
147	A30	75c dk red	2.50	2.50
148	A30	1.25 l dk bl	3.75	3.75
149	A30	2.75 l brn org	18.00	18.00
150	A30	5 l ol grn	225.00	200.00
	Nos. 143-150 (8)		253.75	228.75

Issued to commemorate the 50th anniversary of the death of Giuseppe Garibaldi (1807-1882), Italian patriot.

Nos. 138 and 137 Surcharged **50 CENT 28 MAGGIO 1933 CONVEGNO FILATELICO**

1933, May 27

151	A27	25c on 2.75 l dk vio	1.40	1.40
152	A27	50c on 1.75 l dk brn	3.50	3.50
153	A27	75c on 1.75 l dk brn	14.00	14.00
154	A27	1.25 l on 1.75 l dk brn	240.00	225.00

Issued in commemoration of a convention of philatelists at San Marino, May 28th, 1933.

Nos. 134-137 Surcharged in Black

1934, Apr. 12

155	A27	25c on 1.25 l dk bl	90	90
156	A27	50c on 1.75 l dk brn	4.00	4.00
157	A27	75c on 50c dk red	4.00	4.00
158	A27	1.25 l on 20c bl grn	35.00	35.00

Issued to publicize San Marino's participation (with a philatelic pavilion) in the 15th annual Trade Fair at Milan, April 12-27.

Nos. 136 and 138 Surcharged Wheel and New Value.

1934, Apr. 12

159	A27	3.70 l on 1.25 l dk bl	90.00	90.00
160	A27	3.70 l on 2.75 l dk vio	90.00	90.00

Ascent to Mt. Titano
A31

Engraved.
1935, Feb. 7   Perf. 14   Unwmkd.

161	A31	5c choc & blk	10	10
162	A31	10c dk vio & blk	10	10
163	A31	20c org & blk	10	10
164	A31	25c grn & blk	10	10
165	A31	50c ol bis & blk	35	35
166	A31	75c brn red & blk	2.25	2.25
167	A31	1.25 l bl & blk	5.00	5.00
	Nos. 161-167 (7)		8.00	8.00

Issued in commemoration of the 12th anniversary of the founding of the Fascist Movement.

Melchiorre Delfico A32
Statue of Delfico A33

1935, Apr. 15   Perf. 12   Wmk. 217

Center in Black.

169	A32	5c brn lake	10	10
170	A32	7½c lt brn	10	10
171	A32	10c dk bl grn	10	10
172	A32	15c rose car	7.00	1.50
173	A32	20c orange	10	10
174	A32	25c green	18	10
175	A32	30c dl vio	18	18
176	A33	50c ol grn	1.25	1.00
177	A33	75c red	6.00	6.00
178	A33	1.25 l dk bl	1.50	1.50
179	A33	1.50 l dk brn	18.00	18.00
180	A33	1.75 l brn org	25.00	22.50
	Nos. 169-180 (12)		59.51	51.18

Issued to commemorate the centenary of the death of Melchiorre Delfico (1744-1835), historian.

Nos. 99-100 Surcharged in Black **80**

1936, Apr. 14   Perf. 11   Unwmkd.

181	A19	80c on 45c dk vio & blk	4.50	4.50
182	A19	80c on 65c grn & blk	4.50	4.50

Nos. 112-113 Surcharged in Black **L. 2,05**

1936, Aug. 23   Perf. 12

183	A22	2.05 l on 1.25 l dp bl	8.00	8.00
184	A22	2.75 l on 2.50 l dk brn	40.00	48.00

Souvenir Sheet

Design from Base of Roman Column—A34

1937, Aug. 23   Engr.   Wmk. 217

| 185 | A34 | 5 l stl bl | 11.00 | 11.00 |

Issued to commemorate the unveiling of the Roman Column at San Marino. The date "1636 d. F. R." means the 1,636th year since the founding of the republic. Sheet size: 125x105mm.

No. 185 was privately surcharged "+ 10 L 1941."

SAN MARINO

Souvenir Sheets.

Abraham Lincoln—A35
1938, Apr. 7   Perf. 13   Wmk. 217
| 186 | A35 | 3 l dk bl | 1.50 | 1.50 |
| 187 | A35 | 5 l rose red | 15.00 | 15.00 |

Issued to commemorate the dedication of a Lincoln bust, Sept. 3, 1937. Sheet size: 124x104½mm.

No. 49 and Type of 1925 Surcharged with New Value in Black.
1941   Perf. 14.   Wmk. 140
| 188 | A11 | 10c on 15c brn vio | 18 | 18 |
| 189 | A11 | 10c on 30c brn org | 70 | 70 |

Flags of Italy and San Marino
A36

Harbor of Arbe
A37

1942   Photogravure.
190	A36	10c yel brn & brn org	6	8
191	A36	15c brn & red brn	6	8
192	A36	20c gray grn & gray blk	6	8
193	A36	25c grn & bl	6	8
194	A36	50c brn red & brn	6	8
195	A36	75c red & gray blk	6	8
196	A37	1.25 l bl & gray bl	18	18
197	A37	1.75 l brn & grnsh blk	22	22
198	A37	2.75 l bis brn & gray bl	60	60
199	A37	5 l grn & brn	10.00	10.00
		Nos. 190-199 (10)	11.36	11.48

Return of the Italian flag to Arbe.

No. 190 Surcharged in Black

1942, July 30
| 200 | A36 | 30c on 10c yel brn & brn org | 35 | 35 |

Rimini-San Marino Stamp Day, Aug. 3.

No. 192 Surcharged with New Value and Bars in Black.
1942, Sept. 14
| 201 | A36 | 30c on 20c gray grn & gray blk | 50 | 50 |

No. 177 Surcharged with New Value in Black.
1942, Sept. 28   Perf. 12   Wmk. 217
| 202 | A33 | 20 l on 75c red & blk | 16.00 | 16.00 |

Printing Press and Newspaper
A38

Newspapers
A39

Photogravure.
1943, Apr. 12   Perf. 14   Wmk. 140
203	A38	10c dp grn	6	8
204	A38	15c bister	6	8
205	A38	20c dk org brn	6	8
206	A38	30c dk rose vio	6	8
207	A38	50c bl blk	6	8
208	A38	75c red org	6	8
209	A39	1.25 l blue	6	8
210	A39	1.75 l dp vio	22	22
211	A39	5 l slate	60	60
212	A39	10 l dk brn	7.00	7.00
		Nos. 203-212 (10)	8.24	8.38

Nos. 206 and 207 Overprinted in Red

1943, July 1
| 213 | A38 | 30c dk rose vio | 10 | 10 |
| 214 | A38 | 50c bl blk | 10 | 10 |

Rimini-San Marino Stamp Day, July 5.

A40

A41

Overprinted in Black:
"28 LVGLIO 1943 1642 F. R."
1943, Aug. 27
215	A40	5c brown	6	8
216	A40	10c org red	6	8
217	A40	20c ultra	6	8
218	A40	25c dp grn	6	8
219	A40	30c brn car	6	8
220	A40	50c dp vio	6	8
221	A40	75c car rose	6	8
222	A41	1.25 l sapphire	6	8
223	A41	1.75 l red org	20	20
224	A41	2.75 l dk red org	25	25
225	A41	5 l green	85	85
226	A41	10 l violet	1.50	1.50
227	A41	20 l sl bl	3.50	3.50
		Nos. 215-227 (13)	6.78	6.94

This series was prepared to commemorate the 20th anniversary of fascism, but as Mussolini was overthrown July 25, 1943, it was converted by overprinting to commemorate the downfall of fascism.
Overprint on Nos. 222-227 adds "d." before "F.R."
Nos. 215-227 exist without overprint (not regularly issued). Price of set $55.
See Nos. C26–C33.

A42

A43

Overprinted "Governo Provvisorio" in Black
1943, Aug. 27
228	A42	5c brown	6	8
229	A42	10c org red	6	8
230	A42	20c ultra	6	8
231	A42	25c dp grn	6	8
232	A42	30c brn car	6	8
233	A42	50c dp vio	6	8
234	A42	75c car rose	6	8
235	A43	1.25 l sapphire	6	8
236	A43	1.75 l red org	35	35
237	A43	5 l green	1.25	1.25
238	A43	20 l sl bl	3.25	3.25
		Nos. 228-238 (11)	5.33	5.49

See Nos. C34–C39.

Souvenir Sheets.

A44

Perf. 14, Imperf.
1945, Mar. 15   Photo.   Unwmkd.
239	A44	Sheet of three	55.00	55.00
a.		10 l dl bl	12.50	12.50
b.		15 l dl grn	12.50	12.50
c.		25 l dl red brn	12.50	12.50

The sheets measure 183x125mm. Marginal inscriptions are printed in red brown. Sheets contain a papermaker's watermark, "Hammermill Bond, Made in U. S. A."
Nos. 239, 241 and C40 were issued to commemorate the 50th anniversary of the reconstruction of the Government Palace.

Government Palace
A45

1945, Mar. 15   Perf. 14   Wmk. 140
| 241 | A45 | 25 l brn vio | 12.00 | 12.00 |

Coats of Arms

Faetano A46   Montegiardino A47   San Marino A48

Fiorentino A49

Borgomaggiore A50

Serravalle A51

Wmk. 277

Wmkd. Winged Wheel. (277)
1945-46
242	A46	10c dk bl	8	8
243	A47	20c vermilion	8	8
244	A47	40c dp org	8	8
245	A47	60c sl blk	8	8
246	A49	80c dk grn	8	8
247	A46	1 l dk car rose	8	8
248	A46	1.20 l dp vio	10	10
249	A49	2 l chestnut	18	10
250	A49	3 l dp bl ('46)	10	10
250A	A49	4 l red org ('46)	15	25
251	A48	5 l dk brn	10	10
251A	A46	15 l dp bl ('46)	1.75	2.00

Unwmkd.
Lithographed and Engraved.
252	A50	10 l brt red & brn	2.75	2.00
253	A51	20 l brt red & ultra	4.00	3.00
254	A51	20 l org brn & ultra ('46)	3.50	3.00
a.		Vert. pair, imperf. between	250.00	
255	A47	25 l hn brn & ultra ('46)	3.50	3.25

Size: 22x27 mm.

| 256 | A48 | 50 l ol brn & ultra ('46) | 10.00 | 10.00 |
| | | Nos. 242-256 (17) | 26.61 | 24.38 |

Nos. 252-256 are in sheets of 10 (2x5). Prices: Nos. 252, 254-255, $80 each. No. 253, $110, No. 256, $250.

"Dawn of New Hope"—A52
Engraved and Lithographed.
1946   Perf. 14   Unwmkd.
| 257 | A52 | 100 l dl yel & brn vio | 7.00 | 7.00 |
| j. | | Vertical pair, imperf. betwn. | 225.00 | |

Issued to honor the United Nations Relief and Rehabilitation Administration. Sheets of 10 with blue coat of arms in top margin.

Franklin D. Roosevelt and Flags of San Marino and U.S.—A52a

Designs: 1 l, 50 l, Quotation on Liberty, from Franklin D. Roosveelt. 2 l, 100 l, Roosevelt portrait (vert.). 5 l, 15 l, Roosevelt and flags (as shown).

SAN MARINO

Photogravure
1947, May 3   Perf. 14   Wmk. 277

257A	A52a	1 l bis & brn	6	10
257B	A52a	2 l bl & sep	6	10
257C	A52a	5 l vio & multi	6	10
257D	A52a	15 l grn & multi	18	18
257E	A52a	50 l ver & brn	75	65
257F	A52a	100 l vio & sep	1.75	1.25
	Nos. 257A-257F (6)		2.86	2.38

In memory of Franklin D. Roosevelt (1882–1945), 32nd president of the U.S.A. See Nos. C51A–C51H.

Nos. 257A–257C Surcharged with New Value
1947, June 16

257G	A52a	3 l on 1 l bis & brn	50	50
257H	A52a	4 l on 2 l bl & sep	50	50
257I	A52a	6 l on 5 l vio & multi	50	50
	Nos. 257G-257I, C51I-C51K (6)	3.00	3.00

No. 250A Surcharged with New Value in Black.
1947, June 16   Wmk. 277

| 258 | A49 | 6(l) on 4 l red org | 30 | 30 |

No. 250A Surcharged in Black

| 259 | A49 | 21 l on 4 l red org | 1.50 | 1.50 |

"St. Marinus Raising the Republic" by Girolamo Batoni
A53

Perf. 12

1947, July 18   Engraved   Wmk. 217

260	A53	1 l brt grn & vio	5	10
261	A53	2 l pur & ol	5	10
262	A53	4 l vio brn & dk bl grn	5	10
263	A53	10 l org & bl blk	15	15
264	A53	25 l car & pur	1.10	1.00
265	A53	50 l dk bl grn & brn	20.00	20.00
	Nos. 260-265, C52-C53 (8)	30.40	30.45

United States 1847 Stamp
A54

United States Stamps of 1847 and 1869
A55

A56

Photogravure.
1947, Dec. 24   Perf. 14   Wmk. 277

266	A54	2 l red vio & dk brn	6	8
267	A55	3 l sl gray, dp ultra & car	6	8
268	A54	6 l dp bl & dk gray grn	6	8
269	A56	15 l vio, dp ultra & car	50	50
270	A55	35 l dk brn, dp ultra & car	1.40	1.40
271	A56	50 l sl grn, dp ultra & car	2.00	2.00
	Nos. 266-271, C55 (7)	15.08	14.14

Centenary of the first United States postage stamps.

Laborer and San Marino Flag
A57

1948, June 3

272	A57	5 l brown	12	18
273	A57	8 l green	20	30
274	A57	30 l crimson	40	60
275	A57	50 l red brn & rose lil	2.75	3.50

Engraved.

| 276 | A57 | 100 l dk bl & dp vio | 40.00 | 40.00 |
| | Nos. 272-276 (5) | 43.47 | 44.58 |

See Nos. 373–374.

No. 172 Surcharged with New Value and Ornaments in Black.
1948   Perf. 12.   Wmk. 217

| 277 | A32 | 100 l on 15c rose car & blk | 50.00 | 50.00 |

Government Palace
A58

Mt. Titano, Distant View
A59

Various Views of San Marino.

Photogravure.
1949-50   Perf. 14.   Wmk. 277

278	A58	1 l blk & bl	6	6
279	A58	2 l vio & car	6	6
280	A58	3 l vio & ultra	6	6
281	A58	4 l blk & vio	7	7
282	A58	5 l vio & brn	6	6
283	A58	6 l dp bl & sep	18	35
284	A59	8 l blk brn & yel brn	28	45
285	A59	10 l brn blk & bl	28	30
286	A58	12 l brt rose & vio	65	1.00
287	A58	15 l vio & brt rose	1.10	1.50
288	A58	20 l dp bl & brn ('50)	6.50	2.00
289	A58	35 l grn & vio	3.75	3.50
290	A58	50 l brt rose & yel brn	1.75	2.00
291	A58	55 l dp bl & dl grn ('50)	21.00	22.50

Engraved
Perf. 14x13½.

| 292 | A59 | 100 l blk brn & dk grn | 100.00 | 45.00 |

| 293 | A59 | 200 l dp bl & brn | 110.00 | 62.50 |
| | Nos. 278-293 (16) | 245.80 | 141.41 |

Nos. 260 and 261 Overprinted in Black
Giornata Filatelica San Marino-Riccione 28-6-1949

1949, June 28   Wmk. 217

| 294 | A53 | 1 l brt grn & vio | 25 | 25 |
| 295 | A53 | 2 l pur & ol | 25 | 25 |

San Marino-Riccione Stamp Day, June 28.

Francesco Nullo
A60

Designs: 1 l, 20 l, Francesco Nullo. 2 l, 5 l, Anita Garibaldi. 3 l, 50 l, Giuseppe Garibaldi. 4 l, 15 l, Ugo Bassi.

Perf. 14
1949, July 31   Photo.   Wmk. 277

Size: 22x28mm.

296	A60	1 l blk & car lake	8	10
297	A60	2 l red brn & bl	8	10
298	A60	3 l car lake & dk grn	8	10
299	A60	4 l vio & dk brn	8	10

Size: 26½x36½mm.

300	A60	5 l pur & dk brn	18	30
301	A60	15 l car lake & gray bl	1.10	1.50
302	A60	20 l vio & car lake	1.40	2.00
303	A60	50 l red brn & vio	27.50	22.50
	Nos. 296-303 (8)	30.50	26.70

Issued to commemorate the centenary of Garibaldi's escape to San Marino. See also Nos. C57–C61, 404–410.

Stagecoach on Road from San Marino
A61

1949, Dec. 29   Engraved

| 304 | A61 | 100 l bl & gray vio | 20.00 | 18.50 |
| | Sheet of 6 | | 175.00 | 175.00 |

Issued to commemorate the 75th anniversary of the formation of the Universal Postal Union.

A62   A63a

A63

Perf. 13½x14, 14x13½
1951, Mar. 15   Engraved   Wmk. 277

Sky and Cross in Carmine.

305	A62	25 l dk brn & red vio	5.00	4.75
306	A63	75 l org brn & dk brn	7.50	7.50
307	A63a	100 l dk brn & gray blk	12.50	12.00

Issued to honor the San Marino Red Cross.

Christopher Columbus
A64

Designs: 2 l, 25 l, Columbus on his ship. 3 l, 10 l, 20 l, Landing of Columbus. 4 l, 15 l, 80 l, Pioneers trading with Indians. 5 l, 200 l, Columbus and map of Americas.

1952, Jan. 28   Photo.   Perf. 14

308	A64	1 l brn org & dk grn	8	8
309	A64	2 l dk brn & vio	8	8
310	A64	3 l vio & dk brn	8	8
311	A64	4 l bl & org brn	8	8
312	A64	5 l grn & dk brn	8	8
313	A64	10 l dk brn & blk	28	45
314	A64	15 l car & blk	42	60

Engraved.

315	A64	20 l dp bl & dk bl grn	70	1.00
316	A64	25 l vio brn & blk brn	2.75	2.00
317	A64	60 l choc & vio bl	5.50	6.50
318	A64	80 l gray & blk	12.00	12.00
319	A64	200 l Prus grn & dp ultra	27.50	27.50
	Nos. 308-319, C80 (13)	72.05	72.95

Issued to honor Christopher Columbus.

Type of 1952 in New Colors Overprinted FIERA DI TRIESTE in Black or Red   1952
1952, June 29   Photogravure

320	A64	1 l vio & dk brn	8	8
321	A64	2 l car & blk	8	8
322	A64	3 l grn & dk bl grn (R)	8	8
323	A64	4 l dk brn & blk	8	8
324	A64	5 l pur & vio	20	40
325	A64	10 l bl & org brn (R)	2.50	2.50
326	A64	15 l org brn & bl	7.00	7.00
	Nos. 320-326, C81 (8)	22.02	28.22

Issued to publicize the 4th International Sample Fair of Trieste.

Discobolus—A65

Tennis
A66

SAN MARINO

Model Airplane
A67

Designs: 3 l, Runner. 4 l, Cyclist. 5 l, Soccer. 25 l, Shooting. 100 l, Roller skating.

1953, Apr. 20   **Perf. 14**   **Wmk. 277**
327	A65	1 l dk brn & blk	8	8
328	A66	2 l blk & brn	8	8
329	A65	3 l blk & grnsh bl	8	8
330	A66	4 l blk & brt bl	8	8
331	A66	5 l dk brn & sl grn	12	20
332	A67	10 l dp bl & crim	35	50
333	A67	25 l blk & dk brn	2.75	3.00
334	A66	100 l dk brn & sl	6.75	6.00
		Nos. 327-334, C90 (9)	85.29	85.02

See also No. 438.

Type of 1953 in New Colors
Overprinted GIORNATA FILATELICA
in Black S. MARINO - RICCIONE
24 AGOSTO 1953

1953, Aug. 24
| 335 | A66 | 100 l grn & dk bl grn | 30.00 | 30.00 |

San Marino-Riccione Stamp Day, Aug. 24.

Narcissus—A68

Flowers: 2 l, Tulips. 3 l, Oleanders. 4 l, Cornflowers. 5 l, Carnations. 10 l, Irises. 25 l, Cyclamen. 80 l, Geraniums. 100 l, Roses.

1953, Dec. 28   **Photogravure**
336	A68	1 l multi	8	8
337	A68	2 l multi	8	8
338	A68	3 l multi	8	8
339	A68	4 l multi	8	8
340	A68	5 l multi	8	8
341	A68	10 l multi	22	50
342	A68	25 l multi	3.75	4.00
343	A68	80 l multi	20.00	22.50
344	A68	100 l multi	25.00	25.00
		Nos. 336-344 (9)	49.37	52.40

Walking Racer
A69

Fencing—A70

Sports: 3 l, Boxing. 4 l, 200 l, 250 l, Gymnastics. 5 l, Motorcycling. 8 l, Javelin-throwing. 12 l, Automobiling. 25 l, Wrestling. 80 l, Walking racer.

1954-55   **Photogravure**   **Wmk. 277**
345	A69	1 l vio & cer	8	8
346	A70	2 l dk grn & vio	8	8
347	A70	3 l brn & brn org	8	8
348	A69	4 l dk bl & brt bl	8	8
349	A70	5 l dk grn & dk brn	8	8
350	A70	8 l lil rose & pur	22	35
351	A70	12 l blk & crim	22	35
352	A69	25 l bl & dk bl grn	45	50
353	A69	80 l dk bl & bl grn	90	1.00
354	A69	200 l vio & brn	4.25	4.00

Engraved.
Perf. 12½ x 13
355	A69	250 l multi ('55)	62.50	57.50
		Sheet of 4 (#355)	350.00	325.00
		Nos. 345-355 (11)	68.94	64.10

Liberty Statue and Government Palace
A71

1954, Dec. 16   **Perf. 13 x 13½**
| 356 | A71 | 20 l choc & bl | 35 | 50 |
| 357 | A71 | 60 l car & dk grn | 2.75 | 2.50 |

See also No. C92.

Sailboat—A72   Wmk. 303
Wmkd. Multiple Stars. (303)

1955, Aug. 27   **Perf. 14**
| 358 | A72 | 100 l gray blk & bl | 10.00 | 10.00 |

Issued to commemorate the 7th San Marino-Riccione Stamp Fair. See also No. 385.

Murata Nuova Bridge View of La Rocca
A73 A74

Design: 15 l, Government Palace.

1955, Nov. 15   **Perf. 14**
Size: 22x27½mm.; 27½x22mm.
359	A73	5 l bl & brn	8	8
360	A74	10 l org & bl grn	8	8
361	A74	15 l Prus grn & car	18	10
362	A73	25 l dk brn & vio	22	20
363	A74	35 l vio & red car	50	45
		Nos. 359-363 (5)	1.06	.91

See also Nos. 386-388, 636-638.

Ice Skater—A75

Skier
A76

Designs: 3 l, 50 l, Tobogganing. 4 l, Skier going downhill. 5 l, 100 l, Ice Hockey player. 10 l, Girl ice skater.

1955, Dec. 15   **Perf. 14**   **Wmk. 303**
364	A75	1 l brn & yel	8	8
365	A76	2 l brt bl & red	8	8
366	A76	3 l blk brn & lt brn	8	8
367	A76	4 l bl & grn	8	8
368	A76	5 l ultra & sal pink	8	8
369	A75	10 l ultra & pink	25	30
370	A76	25 l gray blk & red	1.25	1.40
371	A76	50 l bl & ind	2.75	3.50
372	A76	100 l blk & Prus grn	7.50	9.00
		Nos. 364-372, C95 (10)	33.15	35.52

Issued to publicize the seventh Winter Olympic Games at Cortina d'Ampezzo, Jan. 26-Feb. 5, 1956.

Type of 1948 Inscribed:
"50th Anniversario Arengo 25 Marzo 1906"

1956, Mar. 24   **Perf. 14**   **Wmk. 303**
| 373 | A57 | 50 l sapphire | 16.50 | 17.50 |

Issued to commemorate the 50th anniversary of the meeting of the heads of families (Arengo), the beginning of the democratic era in San Marino.

Type of 1948 inscribed:
"Assistenza Invernale"

1956, Mar. 24   **Photogravure**
| 374 | A57 | 50 l dk grn | 16.50 | 17.50 |

Issued to publicize the Winterhelp charity.

Pointer and Arms—A77

Dogs: 2 l, Russian greyhound. 3 l, Sheep dog. 4 l, English greyhound. 5 l, Boxer. 10 l, Great Dane. 25 l, Irish setter. 60 l, German shepherd. 80 l, Scotch collie. 100 l, Hunting hound.

1956, June 8   **Perf. 14**   **Wmk. 303**
375	A77	1 l ultra & brn	8	8
376	A77	2 l car lake & bl gray	8	8
377	A77	3 l ultra & brn	8	8
378	A77	4 l grnsh bl & gray vio	8	8
379	A77	5 l car lake & dk brn	8	8
380	A77	10 l ultra & brn	20	25
381	A77	25 l dk bl & multi	32	35
382	A77	60 l car lake & multi	2.75	3.00
383	A77	80 l dk bl & multi	4.00	4.00
384	A77	100 l car lake & multi	5.75	6.00
		Nos. 375-384 (10)	13.42	14.00

Sailboat Type of 1955.
1956   **Perf. 14**   **Wmk. 303**
| 385 | A72 | 100 l brn & bl grn | 5.25 | 5.00 |

8th San Marino-Riccione Stamp Fair.
Types of 1955 with added inscription: "Congresso Internaz. Periti Filatelici San Marino-Salsomaggiore 6-8 Ottobre 1956."
Designs: 20 l, La Rocca. 80 l, Murata Nuova Bridge. 100 l, Government palace.

1956, Oct. 6   **Perf. 14**
Size: 26x36mm.; 36x26mm.
386	A74	20 l bl & brn	65	50
387	A73	80 l vio & red car	3.50	3.00
388	A74	100 l org & bl grn	5.00	5.00

Issued to publicize the International Philatelic Congress, San Marino, Oct. 6-8.

Street and Borgo Maggiore Church Hospital Street
A78 A79

Views: 3 l, Gate tower. 20 l, Covered Market of Borgo Maggiore. 125 l, View from South Bastion.

1957, May 9   **Photo.**   **Wmk. 303**
389	A78	2 l dk grn & rose red	8	8
390	A78	3 l bl & brn	8	8
391	A78	20 l dk bl grn	20	18
392	A79	60 l brn & bl vio	2.00	2.00

Engraved.
| 393 | A78 | 125 l dk bl & blk | 60 | 60 |
| | | Nos. 389-393 (5) | 2.96 | 2.94 |

See also Nos. 473-476, 633-635.

Daisies and View of San Marino
A80

Flowers: 2 l, Primrose. 3 l, Lily. 4 l, Orchid. 5 l, Lily of the Valley. 10 l, Poppy. 25 l, Pansy. 60 l, Gladiolus. 80 l, Wild Rose. 100 l, Anemone.

Photogravure.
1957, Aug. 31   **Perf. 14**   **Wmk. 303**
Flowers in Natural Colors.
394	A80	1 l dk vio bl	8	8
395	A80	2 l dk vio bl	8	8
396	A80	3 l dk vio bl	8	8
397	A80	4 l dk vio bl	8	8
398	A80	5 l dk vio bl	8	8
399	A80	10 l bl, buff & lil	8	8
400	A80	25 l bl, yel & lil	12	18
401	A80	60 l bl, yel & dl red brn	60	70
402	A80	80 l bl & dl red brn	1.00	1.00
403	A80	100 l bl, yel & dl red brn	2.75	2.50
		Nos. 394-403 (10)	4.95	4.86

Type of 1949 Inscribed: "Commemorazione 150 Nascita G. Garibaldi."
Portraits: 2 l, 50 l, Anita Garibaldi. 3 l, 25 l, Francesco Nullo. 5 l, 100 l, Giuseppe Garibaldi. 15 l, Ugo Bassi.

1957, Dec. 12   **Perf. 14**   **Wmk. 303**
Size: 22x28mm.
404	A60	2 l vio & dl bl	6	6
405	A60	3 l lake & dk grn	6	6
406	A60	5 l brn & ol gray	6	6

SAN MARINO

Size: 26½x37mm.
407	A60	15 l bl & vio	18	25
408	A60	25 l grn & dk gray	32	50
409	A60	50 l vio & brn	3.50	3.50
410	A60	100 l brn & vio	3.50	3.50
		Nos. 404-410 (7)	7.68	7.93

Nos. 409–410 are printed se-tenant.
Issued to commemorate the 150th anniversary of the birth of Giuseppe Garibaldi.

Panoramic View—A81

1958, Feb. 27   Engraved   Perf. 14
| 411 | A81 | 500 l grn & blk | 85.00 | 85.00 |
| | | Sheet of 6 | 725.00 | 600.00 |

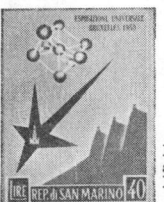

Fair Emblem and San Marino Peaks
A82

1958, Apr. 12   Photo.   Perf. 14
| 412 | A82 | 40 l yel grn & brn | 50 | 50 |
| 413 | A82 | 60 l brt bl & mar | 80 | 80 |

World's Fair, Brussels, Apr. 17–Oct. 19.

Madonna and Fair Entrance
A83

Design: 60 l, View of Fair Grounds.

1958, Apr. 12
| 414 | A83 | 15 l yel, grn & bl | 35 | 30 |
| 415 | A83 | 60 l grn & rose red | 1.75 | 1.75 |

Issued to commemorate San Marino's 10th participation in the Milan Fair. See No. C97.

Wheat—A84

Designs: 2 l, 125 l, Corn. 3 l, 80 l, Grapes. 4 l, 25 l, Peaches. 5 l, 40 l, Plums.

1958, Aug. 30   Perf. 14   Wmk. 303
416	A84	1 l dk bl & yel org	6	6
417	A84	2 l dk grn & red org	6	6
418	A84	3 l bl & ocher	6	6
419	A84	4 l grn & rose car	6	6
420	A84	5 l bl, yel & grn	8	8
421	A84	15 l ultra & brn org	18	20
422	A84	25 l multi	18	20
423	A84	40 l multi	50	50
424	A84	80 l multi	1.00	1.00
425	A84	125 l bl, grn & org ver	4.25	4.00
		Nos. 416-425 (10)	6.43	6.22

Bay and Stamp of Naples—A85

1958, Oct. 8   Photogravure
| 426 | A85 | 25 l bl & red brn | 65 | 50 |

Issued to commemorate the centenary of the stamps of Naples. See No. C100.

Pierre de Coubertin
A86

Portraits: 3 l, Count Alberto Bonacossa. 5 l, Avery Brundage. 30 l, Gen. Carlo Montu. 60 l, J. Sigfrid Edstrom. 80 l, Henri de Baillet-Latour.

1959, May 19   Perf. 14   Wmk. 303
427	A86	2 l brn org & blk	5	6
428	A86	3 l lil & gray brn	5	5
429	A86	5 l bl & dk grn	5	6
430	A86	30 l vio & blk	8	8
431	A86	60 l dk grn & gray brn	25	25
432	A86	80 l car rose & dp grn	25	25
		Nos. 427-432, C106 (7)	5.72	5.01

Issued to honor leaders of the Olympic movement and to publicize the 1960 Olympic Games in Rome.

Lincoln and his Praise of San Marino, May 7, 1861
A87

Lincoln Portraits and: 10 l, Map of San Marino. 15 l, Government palace. 70 l, San Marino peaks (vert.).

1959, July 1   Perf. 14
433	A87	5 l brn & blk	7	7
434	A87	10 l bl grn & ultra	7	7
435	A87	15 l gray & grn	25	35

Engraved   Perf. 13x13½
| 436 | A87 | 70 l violet | 2.50 | 2.50 |

Issued to commemorate the sesquicentennial of the birth of Abraham Lincoln. See No. C108.

Arch of Augustus, Rimini, and Romagna ½ b Stamp
A88

1959, Aug. 29   Photo.   Perf. 14
| 437 | A88 | 30 l blk & brn | 35 | 35 |

Issued to commemorate the centenary of the first stamps of Romagna. See No. C109.

Type of 1953 Inscribed: "Universiade Torino"
1959, Aug. 29   Perf. 14   Wmk. 303
| 438 | A65 | 30 l red org | 1.35 | 1.35 |

Issued to publicize the Turin University Sports Meet, Aug. 27–Sept. 6.

Messina Cathedral Portal and Stamp of Sicily 1859
A89

Stamp of Sicily and: 2 l, Greek temple, Selinus. 3 l, Erice Church. 4 l, Temple of Concordia, Agrigento. 5 l, Ruins of Castor and Pollux Temple, Agrigento. 25 l, San Giovanni degli Eremiti Church. 60 l, Greek theater, Taormina (horiz.).

1959, Oct. 16
439	A89	1 l ocher & dk brn	5	6
440	A89	2 l ol & dk red	5	5
441	A89	3 l bl & sl	5	6
442	A89	4 l red & brn	5	5
443	A89	5 l dl bl & rose lil	5	6
444	A89	25 l multi	50	50
445	A89	60 l multi	50	50
		Nos. 439-445, C110 (8)	4.25	4.30

Centenary of stamps of Sicily.

Golden Oriole
A90

Nightingale   Shot Put
A91   A92

Birds: 3 l, Woodcock. 4 l, Hoopoe. 5 l, Red-legged partridge. 10 l, Goldfinch. 25 l, European Kingfisher. 60 l, Ring-necked pheasant. 80 l, Green woodpecker. 110 l, Red-breasted flycatcher.

1960, Jan. 28   Photo.   Perf. 14
Centers in Natural Colors.
446	A90	1 l blue	7	7
447	A91	2 l grn & red	7	7
448	A90	3 l grn & red	7	7
449	A91	4 l dk grn & red	7	7
450	A90	5 l dk grn	7	7
451	A91	10 l bl & red	10	10
452	A91	25 l grnsh bl	60	40
453	A90	60 l bl & red	3.25	2.25
454	A91	80 l Prus bl & red	5.75	3.50
455	A91	110 l bl & red	6.75	4.50
		Nos. 446-455 (10)	16.80	11.70

1960, May 23   Perf. 14   Wmk. 303

Sports: 2 l, Gymnastics. 3 l, Walking. 4 l, Boxing. 5 l, Fencing (horiz.). 10 l, Bicycling. 15 l, Hockey (horiz.). 25 l, Rowing (horiz.). 60 l, Soccer. 110 l, Equestrian (horiz.).
456	A92	1 l car rose & vio	6	6
457	A92	2 l gray & org	6	6
458	A92	3 l brn ol & pur	6	6
459	A92	4 l rose red & brn	6	6
460	A92	5 l brn & bl	6	6
461	A92	10 l red brn & bl	6	6
462	A92	15 l emer & lil	6	6
463	A92	25 l bl grn & org	18	18
464	A92	60 l dp grn & org	90	65
465	A92	110 l emer, red & blk	1.10	90
		Set of 3 souvenir sheets	15.00	
		Nos. 456-465, C111-C114 (14)	5.40	4.57

Issued to commemorate the 17th Olympic Games, Rome, Aug. 25–Sept. 11.
Souvenir sheets are: (1.) Sheet of 4, one each of 1 l, 2 l, 3 l and 60 l, all printed in deep green and brown. Size: 91x126mm. (2.) Sheet of 4, one each of 4 l and 10 l plus a 20 l and 40 l in designs of Nos. C111-C112 but without "Posta Aerea" inscribed—all 4 printed in rose red and brown. Size: 90x125mm. (3.) Sheet of 6, one each of 5 l, 15 l, 25 l and 110 l plus an 80 l and 125 l in designs of Nos. C113-C114 but without "Posta Aerea"—all 6 printed in emerald and brown. Size: 146x99½mm.

Mt. Titano
A93

Founder Melvin Jones and Lions Headquarters
A94

Designs (Lions Emblem and): 60 l, Government Palace and statue of Liberty. 115 l, Clarence L. Sturm, president. 150 l, Finis E. Davis, vice president.

1960, July 1   Photo.   Wmk. 303
466	A93	1 l red brn & dk bl	28	28
467	A94	45 l bl vio & bis brn	90	45
468	A93	60 l dl rose & bl	28	28
469	A94	115 l grn & blk	90	65
470	A94	150 l brn & dk bl	6.75	4.00
		Nos. 466-470, C115 (6)	22.11	14.66

Issued in honor of Lions International and to commemorate the founding of the Lions Club of San Marino.

Beach of Riccione and San Marino Peaks
A95

1960, Aug. 27   Perf. 14
| 471 | A95 | 30 l multi | 1.00 | 75 |

Issued to commemorate the 12th San Marino-Riccione Stamp Day, Aug. 27. See No. C116.

SAN MARINO

Boy with Basket of Fruit, by Caravaggio
A96

1960, Dec. 29 Perf. 14 Wmk. 303

| 472 | A96 | 200 l multi | 20.00 | 13.00 |

Issued to commemorate the 350th anniversary of the death of Michelangelo da Caravaggio (Merisi), painter.

Types of 1957

Views: 1 l, Hospital street. 4 l, Government building. 80 l, Gate tower. 115 l, Covered market of Borgo Maggiore.

1961, Feb. 16 Perf. 14

473	A79	1 l dk bl grn	5	5
474	A78	4 l dk bl & blk	7	7
475	A78	30 l brt vio & brn	2.50	70
476	A78	115 l brn & bl	1.75	1.50

Hunting Roebuck—A97

Hunting Scenes (16th–18th century): 2 l, Falconer (vert.). 3 l, Wild boar hunt. 4 l, Duck shooting with crossbow. 5 l, Stag hunt. 10 l, Mounted falconer (vert.). 30 l, Hunter with horn and dogs. 60 l, Hunter with rifle and dog (vert.). 70 l, Hunter and beater. 115 l, Duck hunt.

Photogravure
1961, May 4 Perf. 14 Wmk. 303

477	A97	1 l lil rose & vio bl	7	7
478	A97	2 l gray, dk red & blk	7	7
479	A97	3 l red org, brn & blk	7	7
480	A97	4 l lt bl, red & blk	7	7
481	A97	5 l yel grn & brn	7	7
482	A97	10 l org, blk, brn & vio	18	18
483	A97	30 l yel bl & dk grn	22	22
484	A97	60 l ocher, brn, blk & red	65	45
485	A97	70 l grn, blk & car	90	65
486	A97	115 l brt pink, blk & dk bl	2.25	2.00
		Nos. 477-486 (10)	4.55	3.85

Mt. Titano and Cancelled Stamp of Sardinia, 1862
A98

Photogravure and Embossed
1961, Sept. 5 Perf. 13 Wmk. 303

487	A98	30 l multi	3.50	2.25
488	A98	70 l multi	7.25	4.50
489	A98	200 l multi	2.75	2.25

Issued to commemorate the Centenary of Independence Philatelic Exhibition, Turin, 1961.

Europa Issue, 1961.

View of San Marino
A99

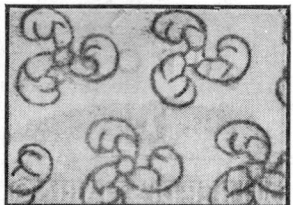

Wmk. 339
1961, Oct. 20 Photogravure Perf. 13

| 490 | A99 | 500 l brn & bl grn | 25.00 | 18.50 |
| | | Sheet of 6 | 150.00 | 110.00 |

King Enzo's Palace and Neptune Fountain, Bologna
A100

Views of Bologna: 70 l, Loggia del Mercanti. 100 l, Two Towers.

1961, Nov. 25 Perf. 14 Wmk. 339

491	A100	30 l grnsh bl & blk	20	20
492	A100	70 l dk ol grn & blk	60	60
493	A100	100 l red brn & blk	1.20	1.20

Bophilex, philatelic exhibition, Bologna.

Duryea, 1892
A101

Automobiles (pre-1910): 2 l, Panhard-Levassor. 3 l, Peugeot. 4 l, Daimler. 5 l, Fiat (vert.). 10 l, Decauville. 15 l, Wolseley. 20 l, Benz. 25 l, Napier. 30 l, White (vert.). 50 l, Oldsmobile. 70 l, Renault (vert.). 100 l, Isotta Fraschini. 115 l, Bianchi. 150 l, Alfa.

1962, Jan. 23 Perf. 14 Wmk. 303

494	A101	1 l red brn & bl	7	7
495	A101	2 l ultra & org brn	7	7
496	A101	3 l blk, brn & org	7	7
497	A101	4 l gray & dk red	7	7
498	A101	5 l vio & org	7	7
499	A101	10 l blk & org	7	7
500	A101	15 l blk & ver	7	7
501	A101	20 l blk & ultra	12	12
502	A101	25 l gray & org	12	12
503	A101	30 l blk & ocher	12	12
504	A101	50 l blk & brt pink	20	20
505	A101	70 l blk, gray & grn	25	25
506	A101	100 l blk, yel & car	25	25
507	A101	115 l blk, org & bl grn	25	25
508	A101	150 l multi	60	60
		Nos. 494-508 (15)	2.40	2.40

Wright Plane, 1904
A102

Historic Planes (1907–1910): 2 l, Ernest Archdeacon. 3 l, Albert and Emile Bonnet-Labranche. 4 l, Glenn Curtiss. 5 l, Farman. 10 l, Louis Bleriot. 30 l, Hubert Latham. 60 l, Alberto Santos Dumont. 70 l, Alliott Verdon Roe. 115 l, Faccioli.

Photogravure
1962, Apr. 4 Perf. 14 Wmk. 339

509	A102	1 l blk & dl yel	7	7
510	A102	2 l red brn & grn	7	7
511	A102	3 l red brn & gray grn	7	7
512	A102	4 l brn & blk	7	7
513	A102	5 l mag & bl	7	7
514	A102	10 l ocher & bl grn	7	7
515	A102	30 l ocher & ultra	12	12
516	A102	60 l blk & ocher	35	35
517	A102	70 l dp org & blk	35	35
518	A102	115 l blk, grn & ocher	1.10	1.10
		Nos. 509-518 (10)	2.34	2.34

Mountaineer Descending—A103

Designs: 2 l, View of Sassolungo. 3 l, Mt. Titano. 4 l, Three Peaks of Javaredo. 5 l, Matterhorn. 15 l, Skier on downhill run. 30 l, Climbing an overhang. 40 l, Cutting steps in ice. 85 l, Giant's Tooth. 115 l, Mt. Titano.

1962, June 14 Perf. 14 Wmk. 339

519	A103	1 l bis brn & blk	5	5
520	A103	2 l Prus grn & blk	5	5
521	A103	3 l lil & blk	5	5
522	A103	4 l brt bl & blk	5	5
523	A103	5 l dp org & blk	5	5
524	A103	15 l org yel & blk	20	20
525	A103	30 l car & blk	20	20
526	A103	40 l grnsh bl & blk	20	20
527	A103	85 l lt grn & blk	65	65
528	A103	115 l vio bl & blk	1.50	1.50
		Nos. 519-528 (10)	3.00	3.00

Hunter with Dog
A104

Modern Hunting Scenes: 2 l, Hound master on horseback (vert.). 3 l, Duck hunt. 4 l, Stag hunt. 5 l, Partridge hunt. 15 l, Lapwing (hunt). 50 l, Wild duck hunt. 70 l, Duck hunt from boat. 100 l, Boar hunt. 150 l, Pheasant hunt (vert.).

1962, Aug. 25 Photo. Perf. 14

529	A104	1 l brn & yel grn	6	6
530	A104	2 l dk bl & org	6	6
531	A104	3 l blk & Prus bl	6	6
532	A104	4 l blk & brn	6	6
533	A104	5 l brn & yel grn	6	6
534	A104	15 l blk & org brn	12	12
535	A104	50 l brn, dp grn & blk	30	30
536	A104	70 l grn, sal pink & blk	40	40
537	A104	100 l blk, brick red & sep	70	70
538	A104	150 l grn lil & blk	1.50	1.50
		Nos. 529-538 (10)	3.32	3.32

Europa Issue, 1962

Mt. Titano and "Europa"
A105

1962, Oct. 25 Wmk. 339

| 539 | A105 | 200 l gray & car | 6.25 | 4.75 |
| | | Sheet of 6 | 42.50 | 30.00 |

Egyptian Cargo Ship
A106

Ancient Ships: 2 l, Greece, 2nd Cent. B.C. 3 l, Roman galley. 4 l, Vikings, 10th Cent. 5 l, "Santa Maria," 1492. 10 l, Cypriote galleon (vert.). 30 l, Galley, 1600. 60 l, "Sovereign of the Seas," 1637 (vert.). 70 l, Danish ship, 1750 (vert.). 115 l, Frigate, 1850.

1963, Jan. 10

540	A106	1 l bl & org yel	7	7
541	A106	2 l mag, tan & brn	7	7
542	A106	3 l brn & lil rose	7	7
543	A106	4 l vio brn & gray	7	7
544	A106	5 l brn & yel	7	7
545	A106	10 l brn & brt yel grn	12	12
546	A106	30 l blk bl & sep	1.50	75
547	A106	60 l lt vio bl & yel grn	75	75
548	A106	70 l blk, gray & dl red	75	75
549	A106	115 l blk, brn & gray bl	4.00	3.25
		Nos. 540-549 (10)	7.47	5.97

SAN MARINO

Lady with Veil, by Raphael
A107

Jousting with "Saracen," Arezzo
A108

Paintings by Raphael: 70 l, Self-portrait. 100 l, St. Barbara from Sistine Madonna. 200 l, Portrait of a Young Woman (Maddalena Strozzi).

Photogravure
1963, Mar. 28 Perf. 14 Wmk. 339
Size: 26½x37mm.
550	A107	30 l multi	1.10	1.10
551	A107	70 l multi	12	12
552	A107	100 l multi	30	30

Size: 26½x44mm.
| 553 | A107 | 200 l multi | 90 | 90 |

1963, June 22 Perf. 14 Wmk. 339
Medieval "Knightly Games": 2 l, French knights (horiz.). 3 l, Crossbow contest. 4 l, English knight receiving lance (horiz.). 5 l, Tournament, Florence. 10 l, Jousting with "Quintana," Ascoli Piceno. 30 l, "Quintana," Foligno (horiz.). 60 l, Race through Siena. 70 l, Tournament, Malpaga (horiz.). 115 l, Knights challenging.

554	A108	1 l lil rose	8	8
555	A108	2 l slate	8	8
556	A108	3 l black	8	8
557	A108	4 l violet	8	8
558	A108	5 l rose vio	8	8
559	A108	10 l dl grn	8	8
560	A108	30 l red brn	8	8
561	A108	60 l Prus grn	25	10
562	A108	70 l brown	20	20
563	A108	115 l black	35	35
Nos. 554-563 (10)			1.36	1.21

Butterfly
A109

Designs: Various Butterflies (70 l, 115 l, horiz.).

Photogravure
1963, Aug. 31 Perf. 14 Wmk. 339
564	A109	25 l multi	8	8
565	A109	30 l multi	12	12
566	A109	60 l multi	25	25
567	A109	70 l multi	35	35
568	A109	115 l multi	50	50
Nos. 564-568 (5)			1.30	1.30

St. Marinus Statue, Government Palace
A110

Design: No. 570, Modern fountain.
1963, Aug. 31
| 569 | A110 | 100 l blk & bl | 1.25 | 1.25 |
| 570 | A110 | 100 l sep & bl | 1.00 | 1.00 |
San Marino-Riccione Stamp Fair.

Europa Issue, 1963

Flag and "E"—A111
1963, Sept. 21 Perf. 14 Wmk. 339
| 571 | A111 | 200 l bl & brn org | 1.25 | 1.25 |

Women's Hurdles
A112

Sports: 2 l, Pole vaulting (vert.). 3 l, Women's relay race. 4 l, Men's high jump. 5 l, Soccer. 10 l, Women's high jump. 30 l, Women's discus throw (vert.). 60 l, Women's javelin throw. 70 l, Water polo. 115 l, Hammer throw.

1963, Sept. 21
572	A112	1 l org & red brn	5	5
573	A112	2 l lt grn & dk brn	5	5
574	A112	3 l bl & dk brn	5	5
575	A112	4 l dp bl & dk brn	5	5
576	A112	5 l red & dk brn	5	5
577	A112	10 l lil rose & cl	5	5
578	A112	30 l gray & red brn	10	10
579	A112	60 l brt yel & dk brn	12	12
580	A112	70 l brt bl & dk brn	12	12
581	A112	115 l grn & dk brn	20	20
Nos. 572-581 (10)			84	84

Publicity for 1964 Olympic Games.

Modern Pentathlon
A113

Designs: 1 l, Runner (vert.). 2 l, Woman gymnast (vert.). 3 l, Basketball (vert.). 5 l, Dual rowing. 15 l, Broad jumper. 30 l, Swimmer in racing dive. 70 l, Woman sprinter. 120 l, Bicycle racers (vert.). 150 l, Fencers (vert.).

Inscribed "Tokio, 1964"
1964, June 25 Perf. 14 Wmk. 339
582	A113	1 l brn & yel grn	9	9
583	A113	2 l blk & red brn	9	9
584	A113	3 l blk & brn	9	9
585	A113	4 l blk & org red	9	9
586	A113	5 l blk & brt bl	9	9
587	A113	15 l dk brn & org	9	9
588	A113	30 l dk vio & bl	10	10
589	A113	70 l red brn & grn	12	12
590	A113	120 l brn & brt bl	12	12
591	A113	150 l blk & crim	45	45
Nos. 582-591 (10)			1.33	1.33

18th Olympic Games, Tokyo, Oct. 10–25.

Same Inscribed "Verso Tokio"
1964, June 25 Photogravure
| 592 | A113 | 30 l ind & lil | 30 | 30 |
| 593 | A113 | 70 l brn & Prus grn | 45 | 45 |
Issued for the "Verso Tokyo" Stamp Exhibition at Rimini, Italy, June 25–July 6.

Murray-Blenkinsop Locomotive, 1812
A114

History of Locomotive: 2 l, Puffing Billy, 1813. 3 l, Locomotion I, 1825. 4 l, Rocket, 1829. 5 l, Lion, 1838. 15 l, Bayard, 1839. 20 l, Crampton, 1849. 50 l, Little England, 1851. 90 l, Spitfire, c. 1860. 110 l, Rogers, c. 1865.

1964, Aug. 29 Perf. 14 Wmk. 339
594	A114	1 l blk & buff	8	8
595	A114	2 l blk & grn	8	8
596	A114	3 l blk & rose lil	8	8
597	A114	4 l blk & yel	8	8
598	A114	5 l blk & sal	8	8
599	A114	15 l blk & yel grn	8	8
600	A114	20 l blk & dp pink	8	8
601	A114	50 l blk & pale bl	12	12
602	A114	90 l blk & yel org	50	50
603	A114	110 l blk & brt bl	85	85
Nos. 594-603 (10)			2.03	2.03

Baseball Players
A115

Design: 70 l, Pitcher.
1964, Aug. 29 Photogravure
| 604 | A115 | 30 l blk, dp grn & gray | 45 | 45 |
| 605 | A115 | 70 l blk & dp car | 65 | 65 |

Issued to commemorate the Eighth European Baseball Championship, Milan.

Europa Issue, 1964

"E" and Globe
A116
1964, Oct. 15 Perf. 14 Wmk. 339
| 606 | A116 | 200 l dk bl & red | 1.75 | 1.75 |

President John F. Kennedy
A117

Design: 130 l, John F. Kennedy and American flag (vert.).
1964, Nov. 22 Photo. Perf. 14
| 607 | A117 | 70 l multi | 25 | 25 |
| 608 | A117 | 130 l multi | 35 | 35 |
Issued in memory of President John F. Kennedy (1917–63).

Start of Bicycle Race from Government Palace
A118

Designs: 70 l, Cyclists (going right) and view of San Marino. 200 l, Cyclists (going left) and view of San Marino.

1965, May 15 Photo. Wmk. 339
609	A118	30 l sepia	20	20
610	A118	70 l dp cl	20	20
611	A118	200 l rose red	35	35
48th Bicycle Tour of Italy.

Brontosaurus—A119

Dinosaurs: 2 l, Brachiosaurus (vert.). 3 l, Pteranodon. 4 l, Elasmosaurus. 5 l, Tyrannosaurus. 10 l, Stegosaurus. 75 l, Thaumatosaurus victor. 100 l, Iguanodon. 200 l, Triceratops.

1965, June 30 Perf. 14 Wmk. 339
612	A119	1 l dk brn & emer	7	7
613	A119	2 l blk & sl bl	7	7
614	A119	3 l sl grn, ol grn & yel	7	7
615	A119	4 l brn & sl bl	7	7
616	A119	5 l cl & grn	7	7
617	A119	10 l cl & grn	10	10
618	A119	75 l dk bl & bl grn	55	55
619	A119	100 l grn & cl	80	80
620	A119	200 l brn & grn	1.25	1.25
Nos. 612-620 (9)			3.05	3.05

Europa Issue, 1965

Rooks on Chessboard
A120
1965, Aug. 28 Photo. Perf. 14
| 621 | A120 | 200 l brn & multi | 50 | 50 |

Dante by Gustave Doré
A121

Doré's Illustrations for Divina Commedia: 90 l, Charon ferrying boat across Acheron. 130 l, Eagle carrying Dante from Purgatory to Paradise. 140 l, Dante with Beatrice examined by Sts. Peter, James and John on faith.

Perf. 14x14½
1965, Nov. 20 Engr. Wmk. 339
Center in Brown Black
622	A121	40 l indigo	22	22
623	A121	90 l car rose	22	22
624	A121	130 l red brn	22	22
625	A121	140 l ultra	32	30
Issued to commemorate the 700th anniversary of the birth of Dante Alighieri (1265–1321), poet.

SAN MARINO

Stylized Peaks, Flags of Italy and San Marino—A122

1965, Nov. 25   Photo.   *Perf. 14*

| 626 | A122 | 115 l grn, red, ocher & bl | 30 | 30 |

Issued to commemorate the visit of Giuseppe Saragat, president of Italy.

Trotter
A123

Horses: 20 l, Cross Country (vert.). 40 l, Hurdling. 70 l, Gallop. 90 l, Steeplechase. 170 l, Polo (vert.).

Perf. 14x13, 13x14

1966, Feb. 28   Photo.   Wmk. 339

627	A123	10 l multi	8	8
628	A123	20 l multi	8	8
629	A123	40 l multi	8	8
630	A123	70 l multi	12	12
631	A123	90 l multi	20	20
632	A123	170 l multi	30	30
		Nos. 627-632 (6)	86	86

Scenic Types of 1955-57

Designs: 5 l, Hospital Street. 10 l, Gate tower. 15 l, View from South Bastion. 40 l, Murata Nuova Bridge. 90 l, View of La Rocca. 140 l, Government Palace.

1966, Mar. 29   *Perf. 14*   Wmk. 339

633	A79	5 l bl & brn	6	6
634	A78	10 l dk sl grn & bl grn	6	6
635	A78	15 l dk brn & vio	6	6
636	A73	40 l dk pur & brick red	10	10
637	A74	90 l blk & dl bl	20	20
638	A74	140 l vio & org	35	35
		Nos. 633-638 (6)	83	83

"Bella" by Titian
A124

Titian Paintings: 90 l, 100 l, Details from "The Education of Love." 170 l, Detail from "Sacred and Profane Love."

1966, June 16   *Perf. 14*   Wmk. 339

639	A124	40 l multi	12	12
640	A124	90 l multi	25	25
641	A124	100 l multi	25	25
642	A124	170 l multi	40	40

Stone Bass
A125

Fish: 2 l, Cuckoo wrasse. 3 l, Dolphin. 4 l, John Dory. 5 l, Octopus (vert.). 10 l, Orange scorpionfish. 40 l, Electric ray (vert.). 90 l, Jellyfish (vert.). 115 l, Sea Horse (vert.). 130 l, Dentex.

Perf. 14x13½, 13½x14

1966, Aug. 27   Photo.   Wmk. 339

643	A125	1 l multi	7	7
644	A125	2 l multi	7	7
645	A125	3 l multi	7	7
646	A125	4 l multi	7	7
647	A125	5 l multi	7	7
648	A125	10 l multi	7	7
649	A125	40 l multi	12	12
650	A125	90 l multi	12	12
651	A125	115 l multi	20	20
652	A125	130 l multi	25	25
		Nos. 643-652 (10)	1.11	1.11

Europa Issue, 1966

Our Lady of Europe
A126

1966, Sept. 24   *Perf. 14*   Wmk. 339

| 653 | A126 | 200 l multi | 50 | 50 |

Peony and Mt. Titano
A127

Flowers and Various Views of Mt. Titano: 10 l, Bell flowers. 15 l, Pyrenean poppy. 20 l, Purple nettle. 40 l, Day lily. 140 l, Gentian. 170 l, Thistle.

Photogravure

1967, Jan. 12   *Perf. 14*   Wmk. 339

654	A127	5 l multi	8	8
655	A127	10 l multi	8	8
656	A127	15 l multi	8	8
657	A127	20 l multi	8	8
658	A127	40 l multi	8	8
659	A127	140 l multi	30	30
660	A127	170 l multi	30	30
		Nos. 654-660 (7)	1.00	1.00

St. Marinus
A128

The Return of the Prodigal Son
A129

Design: 170 l, St. Francis. The paintings are by Giovanni Francesco Barbieri (1591-1666).

Photogravure

1967, March 16   *Perf. 14*   Wmk. 339

661	A128	40 l multi	12	12
662	A128	170 l multi	30	30
663	A129	190 l multi	40	40
		Strip of 3, #661-663	85	85

Nos. 661-663 printed as triptychs. Each sheet contains 10 triptychs (2x5).

Map Showing Members of CEPT
A130

Amanita Caesarea
A131

Europa Issue, 1967

1967, May 5   *Perf. 14*   Wmk. 339

| 664 | A130 | 200 l sl grn & brn org | 45 | 45 |

Conference of European Postal and Telecommunications Administrations.

1967, June 15   Photo.   *Perf. 14*
Various Mushrooms

665	A131	5 l multi	8	8
666	A131	15 l multi	8	8
667	A131	20 l multi	8	8
668	A131	40 l multi	12	12
669	A131	50 l multi	12	12
670	A131	170 l multi	30	30
		Nos. 665-670 (6)	78	78

Amiens Cathedral
A132

Designs: 40 l, Siena Cathedral. 80 l, Toledo Cathedral. 90 l, Salisbury Cathedral. 170 l, Cologne Cathedral.

Engraved

1967, Sept. 21   *Perf. 14*   Wmk. 339

671	A132	20 l dk vio, bis	8	8
672	A132	40 l sl grn, bis	8	8
673	A132	80 l sl bl, bis	20	20
674	A132	90 l sep, bis	20	20
675	A132	170 l dp plum, bis	30	30
		Nos. 671-675 (5)	86	86

Crucifix of Santa Croce, by Cimabue
A133

1967, Dec. 5   *Perf. 15*   Wmk. 339

| 676 | A133 | 300 l brn & vio bl | 60 | 60 |

The Crucifix of Santa Croce by Giovanni Cimabue (1240-1302), was severely damaged in the Florentine flood of November 1966.

Coat of Arms
A134

Coats of Arms: 3 l, Penna Rossa. 5 l, Fiorentino. 10 l, Montecerreto. 25 l, Serravalle. 35 l, Montegiardino. 50 l, Faetano. 90 l, Borgo Maggiore. 180 l, Montelupo. 500 l, State arms of San Marino.

Perf. 13x13½

1968, Mar. 14   Litho.   Wmk. 339

677	A134	2 l multi	6	6
678	A134	3 l multi	6	6
679	A134	5 l multi	6	6
680	A134	10 l multi	6	6
681	A134	25 l multi	6	6
682	A134	35 l multi	12	12
683	A134	50 l multi	15	15
684	A134	90 l multi	20	20
685	A134	180 l multi	30	30
686	A134	500 l multi	80	80
		Nos. 677-686 (10)	1.87	1.87

Europa Issue, 1968
Common Design Type

1968, Apr. 29   Engr.   *Perf. 14x13½*
Size: 37x27½mm.

| 687 | CD11 | 250 l cl brn | 60 | 60 |

"Battle of San Romano" (Detail), by Paolo Uccello—A135

Designs: Details from "The Battle of San Romano," by Paolo Uccello (1397-1475). 90 l is vertical.

Photogravure and Engraved

1968, June 14   *Perf. 14*   Wmk. 339

688	A135	50 l pale pink & blk	10	10
689	A135	90 l pale lil & blk	12	12
690	A135	130 l pale lil & blk	25	25
691	A135	230 l pale pink & blk	45	45

The Mystic Nativity, by Botticelli, Detail—A136

Perf. 14

1968, Dec. 5   Engraved   Wmk. 339

692	A136	50 l dk bl	12	12
693	A136	90 l dp cl	20	20
694	A136	180 l sepia	40	40

Christmas 1968.

SAN MARINO

"Peace" by Lorenzetti
A137

Designs: 8 l, "Justice." 9 l, "Moderation." 18 l, View of Siena, 14th century (horiz.). All designs are from the "Good Government" frescoes by Ambrogio Lorenzetti in the Town Hall of Siena.

Engraved
1969, Feb. 13   Perf. 14   Wmk. 339

695	A137	5 0 l	dk bl	10	10
696	A137	8 0 l	brown	20	20
697	A137	9 0 l	dk bl vio	20	20
698	A137	180 l	magenta	40	40

Young Soldier, by Bramante
A138

Designs: 90 l, Old Soldier, by Bramante. Designs are from murals in the Pinakotheke of Brear, Milan.

1969, Apr. 28   Photo.   Perf. 14

699	A138	5 0 l	multi	10	10
700	A138	9 0 l	multi	20	20

Issued to commemorate the 525th anniversary of the birth of Bramante (1444–1514), Italian architect and painter.

Europa Issue, 1969
Common Design Type
1969, Apr. 28   Engr.   Perf. 14x13
Size: 37x27mm.

701	CD12	5 0 l	dl grn	25	25
702	CD12	180 l	rose cl	35	35

Charabanc
A139

Coaches, 19th Century: 10 l, Barouche. 25 l, Private drag. 40 l, Hansom cab. 50 l, Curricle. 90 l, Wagonette. 1.80 l, Spider phaeton.

Unwmkd.
1969, June 25 Photo. Perf. 14½x14

703	A139	5 l	blk, ocher & dk bl	6	6
704	A139	10 l	blk, grn & pur	6	6
705	A139	25 l	dk grn, pink & brn	6	6
706	A139	40 l	ind, lil & lt brn	12	12
707	A139	50 l	blk, dl yel & dk bl	12	12
708	A139	90 l	blk, yel grn & brn	15	15
709	A139	180 l	multi	20	20
	Nos. 703-709 (7)			77	77

Pier at Rimini
A140

Paintings by R. Viola: 20 l, Mt. Titano. 200 l, Pier at Riccione (horiz.).

1969, Sept. 17 Perf. 14 Unwmkd.

710	A140	20 l	multi	8	8
711	A140	180 l	multi	30	30
712	A140	200 l	multi	40	40

"Faith" by Raphael
A141

Designs: 180 l, "Hope" by Raphael. 200 l, "Charity" by Raphael.

Perf. 13½x14
1969, Dec. 10   Engr.   Wmk. 339

713	A141	20 l	dl pur & sal	8	8
714	A141	180 l	dl pur & lt grn	30	30
715	A141	200 l	dl pur & bis	40	40

Aries
A142

Signs of the Zodiac: 2 l, Taurus. 3 l, Gemini. 4 l, Cancer. 5 l, Leo. 10 l, Virgo. 15 l, Libra. 20 l, Scorpio. 70 l, Sagittarius. 90 l, Capricorn. 100 l, Aquarius. 180 l, Pisces.

Perf. 14x13½
1970, Feb. 18   Photo.   Unwmkd.

716	A142	1 l	blk & yel	7	7
717	A142	2 l	blk & pink	7	7
718	A142	3 l	blk & lil	7	7
719	A142	4 l	blk & dp yel grn	7	7
720	A142	5 l	blk & bl	7	7
721	A142	10 l	blk & sal	7	7
722	A142	15 l	blk & dl yel	7	7
723	A142	20 l	blk & ocher	7	7
724	A142	70 l	blk & bis	12	12
725	A142	90 l	blk & brt pink	15	15
726	A142	100 l	blk & rose	15	15
727	A142	180 l	blk & gray bl	1.00	1.00
	Nos. 716-727 (12)			1.98	1.98

Fleet in Bay of Naples, by Peter Brueghel, the Elder—A143

Photogravure
1970, Apr. 30   Perf. 14   Unwmkd.

728	A143	230 l	multi	50	50

Issued to publicize the 10th Europa Philatelic Exhibition, Naples, May 2-10.

Europa Issue, 1970
Common Design Type
1970, Apr. 30   Perf. 14x13½
Size: 36x27mm.

729	CD13	90 l	brt yel grn & red	25	25
730	CD13	180 l	ocher & red	35	35

St. Francis' Gate and Rotary Emblem
A144

Woman with Mandolin, by Tiepolo
A145

Design: 220 l, Rocca (State Prison) and Rotary emblem.

1970, June 25   Photo.   Perf. 13½x14

731	A144	180 l	multi	40	40
732	A144	220 l	multi	45	45

Issued to commemorate the 65th anniversary of Rotary International and the 10th anniversary of the San Marino Rotary Club.

1970, Sept. 10   Perf. 14   Unwmkd.
Paintings by Tiepolo: 180 l, Woman with Parrot. 220 l, Rinaldo and Armida Surprised (horiz.).
Size: 26½x37½mm.

733	A145	50 l	multi	20	20
734	A145	180 l	multi	35	35

Size: 56x37½mm.

735	A145	220 l	multi	45	45
	Strip of 3, #733-735			1.10	1.10

Issued to commemorate the 200th anniversary of the death of Giambattista Tiepolo (1696–1770), Venetian painter. Nos. 733-735 printed as triptychs. Each sheet contains 10 triptychs (2x5).

Black Pete
A146

Walt Disney and Jungle Book Scene
A147

Disney Characters: 2 l, Gyro Gearloose. 3 l, Pluto. 4 l, Minnie Mouse. 5 l, Donald Duck. 10 l, Goofy. 15 l, Scrooge McDuck. 50 l, Huey, Louey and Dewey. 90 l, Mickey Mouse.

Photogravure
1970, Dec. 22   Perf. 13x14, 14x13

736	A146	1 l	multi	7	7
737	A146	2 l	multi	7	7
738	A146	3 l	multi	7	7
739	A146	4 l	multi	7	7
740	A146	5 l	multi	7	7
741	A146	10 l	multi	7	7
742	A146	15 l	multi	7	7
743	A146	50 l	multi	30	30
744	A146	90 l	multi	1.00	1.00
745	A146	220 l	multi	11.50	11.50
	Nos. 736-745 (10)			13.29	13.29

Honoring Walt Disney (1901–1966), cartoonist and film maker.

Customhouse Dock, by Canaletto—A148

Paintings by Canaletto: 180 l, Grand Canal between Balbi Palace and Rialto Bridge. 200 l, St. Mark's and Doges' Palace.

1971, March 23 Perf. 14 Unwmkd.

746	A148	20 l	multi	8	8
747	A148	180 l	multi	35	35
748	A148	200 l	multi	35	35

Save Venice campaign.

Europa Issue, 1971
Common Design Type
1971, May 29   Perf. 13½x14
Size: 27½x23mm.

749	CD14	50 l	org & bl	25	25
750	CD14	90 l	bl & org	45	45

Congress Emblem and Hall, San Marino Flag—A149

Design: 90 l, Detail from Government Palace door, Congress and San Marino emblems (vert.).

1971, May 29   Photo.   Perf. 12

751	A149	20 l	vio & multi	7	7
752	A149	90 l	ol & multi	12	12
753	A149	180 l	multi	35	35

Italian Philatelic Press Union Congress, San Marino, May 29–30.

Duck-shaped Jug with Flying Lasa
A150

Etruscan Art, 6th-3rd Centuries B.C.: 80 l, Head of Mercury (vert.). 90 l, Sarcophagus of a married couple (vert.). 180 l, Chimera.

Photogravure and Engraved
1971, Sept. 16   Perf. 14

754	A150	50 l	blk & org	12	12
755	A150	80 l	blk & lt grn	18	18
756	A150	90 l	blk & lt bl	18	18
757	A150	180 l	blk & org	30	30

Common Design Types
pictured in section at front of book.

SAN MARINO

Tiger Lily
A151

Venus, by Botticelli
A152

Flowers: 2 l, Phlox. 3 l, Carnations. 4 l, Globe flowers. 5 l, Thistles. 10 l, Peonies. 15 l, Hellebore. 50 l, Anemones. 90 l, Gaillardia. 220 l, Asters.

Photogravure
1971, Dec. 2 Perf. 11½ Unwmkd.

758	A151	1 l brt yel & multi	5	5
759	A151	2 l lt bl & multi	5	5
760	A151	3 l yel & multi	5	5
761	A151	4 l multi	5	5
762	A151	5 l multi	5	5
763	A151	10 l gray & multi	5	5
764	A151	15 l pink & multi	5	5
765	A151	50 l pale bl & multi	12	12
766	A151	90 l tan & multi	12	12
767	A151	220 l multi	35	35
		Nos. 758-767 (10)	94	94

Perf. 14, 13x14 (180 l)
1972, Feb. 23

Details from La Primavera, by Sandro Botticelli: 180 l, Three Graces. 220 l, Spring.

Sizes: 50 l, 220 l, 21x37mm.; 180 l, 27x37mm.

768	A152	50 l gold & multi	20	20
769	A152	180 l gold & multi	40	40
770	A152	220 l gold & multi	65	65

Europa Issue 1972
Common Design Type
1972, Apr. 27 Perf. 11½
Granite Paper
Size: 22½x33mm.

771	CD15	50 l org & multi	20	20
772	CD15	90 l lt bl & multi	20	20

St. Marinus Taming Bear
A153

Designs: 55 l, Donna Felicissima asking St. Marinus for mercy for her sons. 100 l, St. Marinus turning archers to stone. 130 l, Felicissima giving mountains to St. Marinus to establish Republic.

Photogravure & Engraved
1972, Apr. 27 Perf. 14

773	A153	25 l dl yel & blk	12	12
774	A153	55 l sal pink & blk	12	12
775	A153	100 l dl bl & blk	20	20
776	A153	130 l cit & blk	25	25

Allegories of San Marino after 16th century paintings.

Italian House Sparrow
A154

1972, June 30 Photo. Perf. 11½
Granite Paper
Black Frame and Inscription, Birds in Natural Colors

777	A154	1 l shown	5	5
778	A154	2 l Firecrest	5	5
779	A154	3 l Blue tit	5	5
780	A154	4 l Ortolan bunting	5	5
781	A154	5 l White-spotted bluethroat	5	5
782	A154	10 l Bullfinch	5	5
783	A154	25 l Linnet	5	5
784	A154	50 l Black-eared wheatear	12	12
785	A154	90 l Sardinian warbler	12	12
786	A154	220 l Greenfinch	30	30
		Nos. 777-786 (10)	89	89

Young Man, Heart, Emblem
A155

Italian Philatelic Federation Emblem
A156

Design: 90 l, Heart disease victim (horiz.).

Perf. 13½x14, 14x13½
1972, Aug. 26

787	A155	50 l lt bl & multi	15	15
788	A155	90 l ocher & multi	20	20

World Heart Month.

1972, Aug. 26 Perf. 13½x14

| 789 | A156 | 25 l gold & ultra | 20 | 20 |

Honoring veterans of Philately.

5c Coin, 1864
A157

Coins: 10 l, 10c coin, 1935. 15 l, 1 lira, 1906. 20 l, 5 lire, 1898. 25 l, 5 lire, 1937. 50 l, 10 lire, 1932. 55 l, 20 lire, 1938. 220 l, 20 lire, 1925.

Perf. 12½x13
1972, Dec. 15 Litho. Unwmkd.

790	A157	5 l gray, blk & brn	5	5
791	A157	10 l org, blk & sil	5	5
792	A157	15 l brt rose, blk & sil	7	7
793	A157	20 l lil, blk & sil	7	7
794	A157	25 l vio, blk & sil	7	7
795	A157	50 l brt bl, blk & sil	10	10
796	A157	55 l ocher, blk & sil	15	15
797	A157	220 l emer, blk & gold	35	35
		Nos. 790-797 (8)	91	91

New York, 1673 — A158

Design: 300 l, View of New York from East River, 1973.

1973, Mar. 9 Photo. Perf. 11½
Granite Paper

798	A158	200 l bis, ocher & ol grn	50	50
799	A158	300 l bl, lil & blk	70	70
		Pair, #798-799	1.25	1.25

300 years New York. Nos. 798-799 printed se-tenant checkerwise in sheets of 50.

Rotary Press, San Marino Towers
A159

Gymnasts and Olympic Rings
A160

Perf. 13x14
1973, May 10 Photo. Unwmkd.

| 800 | A159 | 50 l multi | 25 | 25 |

Tourist Press Congress, San Marino, May 10.

1973, May 10

| 801 | A160 | 100 l grn & multi | 30 | 30 |

5th Youth Games.

Europa Issue 1973
Common Design Type
1973, May 10 Perf. 11½
Size: 32½x23mm.

802	CD16	20 l sal & multi	45	45
803	CD16	180 l lt bl & multi	2.25	2.25

Grapes
A161

1973, July 11 Photo. Perf. 11½
Multicolored

804	A161	1 l shown	5	5
805	A161	2 l Tangerines	5	5
806	A161	3 l Apples	5	5
807	A161	4 l Plums	5	5
808	A161	5 l Strawberries	5	5
809	A161	10 l Pears	6	6
810	A161	25 l Cherries	7	7
811	A161	50 l Pomegranate	12	12
812	A161	90 l Apricots	12	12
813	A161	220 l Peaches	25	25
		Nos. 804-813 (10)	87	87

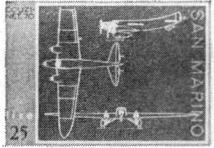

Arc-en-Ciel, France
A162

Famous Aircraft: 55 l, Macchi Castoldi, Italy. 60 l, Antonov, USSR. 90 l, Spirit of St. Louis, USA. 220 l, Handley Page, Great Britain.

1973, Aug. 31 Photo. Perf. 14x13½

814	A162	25 l ocher, vio bl & gold	12	12
815	A162	55 l gray, vio bl & gold	12	12
816	A162	60 l rose, vio bl & gold	12	12
817	A162	90 l lem, vio bl & gold	20	20
818	A162	220 l org, vio bl & gold	35	35
		Nos. 814-818 (5)	91	91

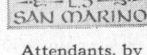

Crossbowman, Serravalle Castle
A163

Attendants, by Gentile Fabriano
A164

Designs: 10 l, Crossbowman, Pennarossa Castle. 15 l, Drummer, Montegiardino Castle. 20 l, Trumpeter, Fiorentino Castle. 30 l, Crossbowman, Borga Maggiore Castle. 50 l, Trumpeter, Guaita Castle. 80 l, Crossbowman, Faetano Castle. 200 l, Crossbowman, Montelupo Castle.

1973, Nov. 7 Photo. Perf. 13½

819	A163	5 l blk & multi	5	5
820	A163	10 l blk & multi	6	6
821	A163	15 l blk & multi	6	6
822	A163	20 l blk & multi	7	7
823	A163	30 l blk & multi	10	10
824	A163	40 l blk & multi	10	10
825	A163	50 l blk & multi	25	25
826	A163	80 l blk & multi	25	25
827	A163	200 l blk & multi	40	40
		Nos. 819-827 (9)	1.34	1.34

San Marino victories in the Crossbow Tournament, Massa Marittima, July 15, 1973.

1973, Dec. 19 Photo. Perf. 11½

Designs: Details from Adoration of the Kings, by Gentile Fabriano (1370-1427).

Multicolored

828	A164	5 l shown	5	5
829	A164	30 l King	9	9
830	A164	115 l King	20	20
831	A164	250 l Horses	35	35

Christmas 1973.

Shield, 16th Century
A165

Designs (16th Century Armor): 5 l, Round shield. 10 l, German full armor. 15 l, Helmet with intricate etching. 20 l, Horse's head armor "Massimiliano." 30 l, Decorated helmet with Sphinx statuette on top. 50 l, Pommeled sword and gauntlets. 80 l, Sparrow-beaked helmet. 250 l, Sforza round shield.

Engraved & Lithographed
1974, Mar. 12 Perf. 13

832	A165	5 l blk, lt grn & buff	5	5
833	A165	10 l blk, buff & bl	6	6
834	A165	15 l blk, bl & ultra	6	6
835	A165	20 l blk, tan & blk	8	8
836	A165	30 l blk & lt bl	8	8
837	A165	50 l blk, rose & ultra	12	12
838	A165	80 l blk, gray & grn	12	12
839	A165	250 l blk & yel	30	30
		Nos. 832-839 (8)	87	87

SAN MARINO

Europa Issue 1974

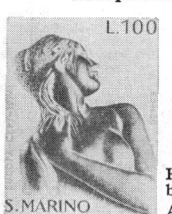
Head of Woman, by Emilio Greco
A166

Design: 200 l, Nude, by Emilio Greco (head shown on 100 l).

Engraved & Lithographed
1974, May 9   Perf. 13x14

840	A166	100 l buff & blk	30	30
841	A166	200 l pale grn & blk	50	50

Yachts at Riccione and San Marino Peaks
A167

1974, July 18   Photo.   Perf. 11½
Granite Paper

842	A167	50 l ultra & multi	32	32

26th San Marino-Riccione Stamp Day.

Arms of San Sepolcro
A168

Designs: Coats of arms of participating cities.

1974, July 18   Perf. 12
Gold & Multicolored

843	A168	15 l shown	2.50	2.50
844	A168	20 l Massa Marittima	2.50	2.50
845	A168	50 l San Marino	2.50	2.50
846	A168	115 l Gubbio	2.50	2.50
847	A168	300 l Lucca	2.50	2.50
		Strip of 5, #843-847	13.50	13.50
		Nos. 843-847 (5)	12.50	12.50

9th Crossbow Tournament, San Marino. Nos. 843-847 printed se-tenant in sheets of 25 (5x5).

UPU Emblem—A169

1974, Oct. 9   Photo.   Perf. 11½
Granite Paper

848	A169	50 l multi	12	12
849	A169	90 l grn & multi	20	20

Centenary of Universal Postal Union.

Mt. Titano and Hymn by Tommaseo
A170

Niccolo Tommaseo
A171

Death centenary of Niccolo Tommaseo (1802–74), Italian writer.

1974, Dec. 12   Photo.   Perf. 13½x14

850	A170	50 l lt grn, blk & red	8	8
851	A171	150 l yel, grn & blk	32	32

Virgin and Child, 14th Century Wood Panel
A172

1974, Dec. 12   Perf. 11½

852	A172	250 l gold & multi	55	55

Christmas 1974.

"Refuge in San Marino"
A173

1975, Feb. 20   Photo.   Perf. 13½x14

853	A173	50 l multi	22	22

Flight of 100,000 refugees from Romagna to San Marino, 30th anniversary.

Musicians, from Leopard Tomb, Tarquinia—A174

Etruscan Art: 30 l, Chariot race, from Tomb on the Hill, Chiusi. 180 l, Achilles and Troilus, from Bulls' Tomb, Tarquinia. 220 l, Dancers, from Triclinium Tomb, Tarquinia.

Lithographed and Engraved
1975, Feb. 20   Perf. 14

854	A174	20 l multi	8	8
855	A174	30 l multi	10	10
856	A174	180 l multi	30	30
857	A174	220 l multi	50	50

Europa Issue 1975

St. Marinus, by Guercino (Francesco Barbieri)
A175   A176

1975, May 14   Photo.   Perf. 11½
Granite Paper

858	A175	100 l multi	30	30
859	A176	200 l multi	40	40

The Lamentation, by Giotto
A177

Frescoes by Giotto (details): 40 l, Mary and Jesus (Flight into Egypt). 50 l, Heads of four angels (Flight into Egypt). 100 l, Mary Magdalene (Noli Me Tangere) (horiz.). 500 l, Angel and the elect (Last Judgment) (horiz.).

1975, July 10   Photo.   Perf. 11½
Granite Paper

860	A177	10 l gold & multi	5	5
861	A177	40 l gold & multi	20	20
862	A177	50 l gold & multi	20	20
863	A177	100 l gold & multi	25	25
864	A177	500 l gold & multi	70	70
		Nos. 860-864 (5)	1.40	1.40

Holy Year 1975.

Tokyo, 1835, Woodcut by Hiroshige
A178

Design: 300 l, Tokyo Business District, 1975.

1975, Sept. 5   Photo.   Perf. 11½
Granite Paper

865	A178	200 l multi	45	45
866	A178	300 l multi	55	55

Nos. 865-866 printed se-tenant checkerwise in sheets of 50.

Aphrodite
A179

1975, Sept. 19   Photo.   Perf. 11½

867	A179	50 l vio, blk & gray	25	25

Europa '75 Philatelic Exhibition, Naples.

Multiple Crosses
A180

1975, Sept. 19

868	A180	100 l blk, dp org & vio	30	30

EUROCOPHAR International Pharmaceutical Congress.

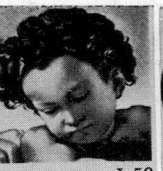 
Angel   Doni Madonna
A181   A182

Design: 100 l, Head of Virgin, from Doni Madonna by Michelangelo.

1975, Dec. 3   Photo.   Perf. 11½
Granite Paper

869	A181	50 l multi	20	20
870	A181	100 l multi	25	25
871	A182	250 l multi	40	40
		Strip of 3	90	90

Christmas 1975. Nos. 869-871 printed se-tenant in sheets of 30 (6x5).

Woman on Balcony, by Gentilini
A183

Two Women, by Gentilini
A184

Design: 230 l, Woman (same as right head on 150 l) and IWY emblem, by Franco Gentilini.

1975, Dec. 3   Granite Paper

872	A183	70 l bl & multi	12	12
873	A184	150 l multi	35	35
874	A183	230 l multi	50	50

International Women's Year 1975.

Modesty, by Emilio Greco   Capitol, Washington, D.C.
A185   A186

Designs ("Civic Virtues"): 20 l, Temperance. 50 l, Fortitude. 100 l, Altruism. 150 l, Hope. 220 l, Prudence. 250 l, Justice. 300 l, Faith. 500 l, Honesty. 1000 l, Industry. Designs show drawings of women's heads by Emilio Greco.

1976, Mar. 4   Photo.   Perf. 11½
Granite Paper

875	A185	10 l buff & blk	5	5
876	A185	20 l pink & blk	5	5
877	A185	50 l grnsh & blk	8	8
878	A185	100 l sal & blk	25	25
879	A185	150 l lil & blk	30	30
880	A185	220 l gray & blk	40	40
881	A185	250 l yel & multi	50	50
882	A185	300 l gray & blk	60	60
883	A185	500 l yel & blk	90	90
884	A185	1000 l gray & blk	1.75	1.75
	Nos. 875-884 (10)		4.88	4.88

See Nos. 900-905, 931-933.

1976, May 29   Photo.   Perf. 11½
Designs (Arms of San Marino and): 150 l, Statue of Liberty. 180 l, Independence Hall, Philadelphia.

885	A186	70 l multi	20	20
886	A186	150 l multi	30	30
887	A186	180 l multi	35	35

American Bicentennial.

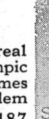

Montreal Olympic Games Emblem
A187

1976, May 29

| 888 | A187 | 150 l crim & blk | 40 | 40 |

21st Olympic Games, Montreal, Canada, July 17-Aug. 1.

Europa Issue 1976

Decorated Plate
A188

Design: 180 l, Seal of San Marino.

1976, July 8   Photo.   Perf. 11½
Granite Paper

| 889 | A188 | 150 l multi | 35 | 35 |
| 890 | A188 | 180 l bl, sil & blk | 35 | 35 |

"Unity"   "Peaks of
A189   San Marino"
                A190

1976, July 8   Perf. 13½x14

| 891 | A189 | 150 l vio blk, yel & red | 40 | 40 |

United Mutual Aid Society, centenary.

1976, Oct. 14   Photo.   Perf. 13x14

| 892 | A190 | 150 l blk & multi | 40 | 40 |

ITALIA 76 International Philatelic Exhibition, Milan, Oct. 14-24.

Children and UNESCO Emblem
A191

1976, Oct. 14   Perf. 11½
Granite Paper

| 893 | A191 | 180 l multi | 40 | 40 |
| 894 | A191 | 220 l multi | 45 | 45 |

U.N. Educational, Scientific and Cultural Organization, 30th anniversary.

Annunciation (detail), by Titian
A192

Design: 300 l, Virgin and Child, by Titian.

Lithographed and Engraved
1976, Dec. 15   Perf. 13x14

| 895 | A192 | 150 l multi | 40 | 40 |
| 896 | A192 | 300 l multi | 60 | 60 |

Christmas 1976. Nos. 895-896 printed se-tenant.

Exhibition Emblem
A193

1977, Jan. 28   Photo.   Perf. 11½
Granite Paper

897	A193	80 l multi	20	20
898	A193	170 l multi	30	30
899	A193	200 l multi	40	40

San Marino 77 Philatelic Exhibition. See No. C133.

Civic Virtues Type of 1976
Designs: 70 l, Fortitude. 90 l, Prudence. 120 l, Altruism. 160 l, Temperance. 170 l, Hope. 320 l, Faith.

1977, Apr. 14   Photo.   Perf. 11½
Granite Paper

900	A185	70 l pink & blk	10	10
901	A185	90 l buff & blk	20	20
902	A185	120 l lt bl & blk	25	25
903	A185	160 l lt grn & blk	35	35
904	A185	170 l cr & blk	40	40
905	A185	320 l lil & blk	65	65
	Nos. 900-905 (6)		1.95	1.95

Europa Issue 1977

San Marino, after Ghirlandaio
A194

Design: 200 l, San Marino, detail from painting by Guercino.

1977, Apr. 14   Granite Paper

| 906 | A194 | 170 l multi | 40 | 40 |
| 907 | A194 | 200 l multi | 40 | 40 |

Vertical Flying Machine, by da Vinci
A195

Lithographed and Engraved
1977, June 6   Perf. 13x14

| 908 | A195 | 120 l multi | 35 | 35 |

Centenary of Enrico Forlanini's experiments with vertical flight.

University Square, Bucharest, 1877
A196

Design: 400 l, National Theater and Intercontinental Hotel, 1977.

1977, June 6   Photo.   Perf. 11½
Granite Paper

| 909 | A196 | 200 l bis & multi | 50 | 50 |
| 910 | A196 | 400 l lt bl & multi | 75 | 75 |

Centenary of Romanian independence. Nos. 909-910 printed checkerwise in sheets of 50.

Type A2 of 1877
A197

1977, June 15   Engr.   Perf. 15x14½

911	A197	40 l sl grn	6	6
912	A197	70 l dp bl	20	20
913	A197	170 l red	35	35
914	A197	500 l brown	1.00	1.00
915	A197	1000 l purple	1.50	1.50
	Nos. 911-915 (5)		3.11	3.11

Centenary of San Marino stamps.

St. Marinus,   Medicinal
by Retrosi   Plants
A198   A199

Souvenir Sheet
1977, Aug. 28   Photo.   Perf. 11½
Granite Paper
Multicolored

| 916 | A198 | Sheet of 5 | 18.00 | 16.00 |
| | a. 1000 l single stamp | | 3.00 | 2.75 |

Centenary of San Marino stamps, and San Marino '77 Philatelic Exhibition, Aug. 28-Sept. 4. No. 916 has multicolored margin with San Marino coat of arms and exhibition emblem. Size: 165x116mm.

1977, Oct. 19   Photo.   Perf. 11½

| 917 | A199 | 170 l multi | 38 | 38 |

Congress of Italian Pharmacists' Union. Design is from illustrations in old herbal showing high mallow, tilia, camomile, borage, centaury and juniper.

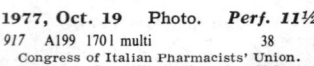

Woman Attacked by Octopus, Emblem
A200

1977, Oct. 19

| 918 | A200 | 200 l multi | 42 | 42 |

World Rheumatism Year.

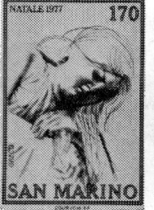

Virgin   San Francisco
Mary   Gate
A201   A202

Designs: 230 l, Palm, olive and star. 300 l, Angel.

1977, Dec. 5   Photo.   Perf. 11½

919	A201	170 l sil, gray & blk	35	35
920	A201	230 l sil, gray & blk	45	45
921	A201	300 l sil, gray & blk	55	55

Christmas 1977. Nos. 919-921 printed se-tenant.

Europa Issue 1978
Design: 200 l, Ripa Gate.

1978, May 30   Photo.   Perf. 11½

| 922 | A202 | 170 l lt bl & dk bl | 55 | 55 |
| 923 | A202 | 200 l buff & brn | 55 | 55 |

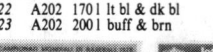

Baseball Player   Feather,
and Diamond   WHO Emblem
A203   A204

1978, May 30

| 924 | A203 | 90 l multi | 18 | 18 |
| 925 | A203 | 120 l multi | 25 | 25 |

World Baseball Championships.

1978, May 30

| 926 | A204 | 320 l multi | 60 | 60 |

Fight against hypertension.

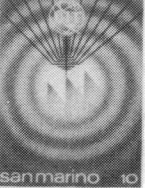

ITU Emblem, Waves Coming from 3 Peaks
A205

SAN MARINO

1978, July 26		Photo.	Perf. 11½
927	A205	10 l car & yel	5 5
928	A205	200 l vio bl & lt bl	32 32

Membership in International Telecommunications Union (ITU).

Seagull and Falcon, 3 Peaks
A206

1978, July 26

929	A206	120 l multi	25 25
930	A206	170 l multi	35 35

30th San Marino-Riccione Stamp Day.

Civic Virtues Type of 1976
Drawings by Emilio Greco: 5 l, Wisdom. 35 l, Love. 2000 l, Faithfulness.

1978, Sept. 28		Photo.	Perf. 11½
		Granite Paper	
931	A185	5 l lt vio & blk	5 5
932	A185	35 l gray & blk	20 20
933	A185	2000 l yel & blk	3.75 3.75

Holly Leaves
A207

Designs: 120 l, Stars. 170 l, Snowflakes.

1978, Dec. 6   Photo.   Perf. 14x13½

941	A207	10 l multi	5 5
942	A207	120 l multi	20 20
943	A207	170 l multi	30 30

Christmas 1978.

Globe and Woman Holding Torch
A208

1978, Dec. 6   Perf. 11½x12

944	A208	200 l multi	42 42

Universal Declaration of Human Rights, 30th anniversary.

Europa Issue 1979

First San Marino Autobus, 1915
A209

Design: 220 l, Mail coach, 1895.

1979, Mar. 29 Photo. Perf. 11½x12

945	A209	170 l multi	50 50
946	A209	220 l multi	50 50

Albert Einstein
A210

1979, Mar. 29			Perf. 11½
947	A210	120 l gray, lt & dk brn	30 30

Albert Einstein (1879–1955), theoretical physicist.

San Marino Crossbow Federation Emblem
A211

Maigret
A212

1979, July 12		Litho.	Perf. 14x13
948	A211	120 l multi	50 50

14th Crossbow Tournament.

Lithographed and Engraved

1979, July 12   Perf. 13x14

Fictional Detectives: 80 l, Perry Mason. 150 l, Nero Wolfe. 170 l, Ellery Queen. 220 l, Sherlock Holmes.

949	A212	10 l multi	5 5
950	A212	80 l multi	20 20
951	A212	150 l multi	30 30
952	A212	170 l multi	30 30
953	A212	220 l multi	42 42
		Nos. 949-953 (5)	1.27 1.27

Girl Holding Bird
A213

IYC Emblem, Paintings by Marina Busignani: 120 l, 170 l, 220 l, Children and birds (diff.). 350 l, Mother nursing child.

1979, Sept. 6   Litho.   Perf. 11½

954	A213	20 l multi	6 6
955	A213	120 l multi	25 25
956	A213	170 l multi	35 35
957	A213	220 l multi	40 40
958	A213	350 l multi	60 60
		Nos. 954-958 (5)	1.66 1.66

International Year of the Child.

St. Apollonia, 15th Century Woodcut
A214

1979, Sept. 6   Photogravure

| 959 | A214 | 170 l multi | 42 42 |

13th Biennial International Congress of Stomatology.

Waterskier
A215

1979, Sept. 6			
960	A215	150 l multi	38 38

European Waterskiing Championship.

Chestnut Tree, Deer—A216

Protected Trees and Animals or Birds: 10 l, Cedar of Lebanon, falcon. 35 l, Dogwood, racoon. 50 l, Banyan, tiger. 70 l, Umbrella pine, hoopoe. 90 l, Siberian spruce, marten. 100 l, Eucalyptus, koala bear. 120 l, Date palm, camel. 150 l, Sugar maple, beaver. 170 l, Adansonia, elephant.

1979, Oct. 25   Photo.   Perf. 11½

961	A216	5 l multi	5 5
962	A216	10 l multi	5 5
963	A216	35 l multi	6 6
964	A216	50 l multi	10 10
965	A216	70 l multi	12 12
966	A216	90 l multi	20 20
967	A216	100 l multi	20 20
968	A216	120 l multi	25 25
969	A216	150 l multi	30 30
970	A216	170 l multi	35 35
		Nos. 961-970 (10)	1.68 1.68

Holy Family, by Antonio Alberto de Ferrara, 15th Century Fresco—A217

Christmas 1979 (de Ferrara Fresco): 80 l, St. Joseph. 170 l, Infant Jesus. 220 l, One of the Three Kings.

1979, Dec. 6   Photo.   Perf. 12

971	A217	80 l multi	25 25
972	A217	170 l multi	40 40
973	A217	220 l multi	50 50
974	A217	320 l multi	60 60

Disturbing Muses, by Giorgio de Chirico—A218

Chirico Paintings:

1979, Dec.

975	A218	40 l shown	12 12
976	A218	150 l Ancient horses	35 35
977	A218	170 l Self-portrait	40 40

Giorgio de Chirico, Italian surrealist painter.

St. Benedict, 15th Century Fresco
A219

Fight Against Cigarette Smoking
A220

1980, Mar. 27   Photo.   Perf. 12x11½
Granite Paper

| 978 | A219 | 170 l multi | 42 42 |

St. Benedict of Nursia, 1500th birth anniversary.

1980, Mar. 27

Designs: Sketches of smokers and cigarettes by Giuliana Consilivio.

979	A220	120 l multi	25 25
980	A220	170 l multi	50 50
981	A220	520 l multi	1.00 1.00

Naples, 17th Century Engraving—A221

1980, Mar. 27   Perf. 14x13½

| 982 | A221 | 170 l multi | 40 40 |

20th International Philatelic Exhibition, Europa '80, Naples, Apr. 26-May 4.

View of London, 1850—A222

1980, May 8   Perf. 11½x12

983	A222	200 l shown	50 50
984	A222	400 l London, 1980	85 85

London 1980 International Stamp Exhibition, May 6-14. Nos. 983-984 printed se-tenant checkerwise in sheets of 50.

Europa Issue 1980

Giovanbattista Belluzzi (1506-1554), Military Architect—A223

Designs: 220 l, Antonio Orafo (1460-1552), goldsmith and jeweler.

1980, May 8   Perf. 11½

985	A223	170 l multi	60 60
986	A223	220 l multi	60 60

485

Bicycling—A224
1980, July 7		Photo.		Perf. 11½
		Granite Paper		
987	A224	70 l	shown	20	20
988	A224	90 l	Basketball	20	20
989	A224	170 l	Running	40	40
990	A224	350 l	Gymnast	80	80
991	A224	450 l	High jump	1.00	1.00
		Nos. 987-991 (5)		2.60	2.60

22nd Summer Olympic Games, Moscow, July 19-Aug. 3.

Ancient Fortifications A225 — Weight Lifting A226

Photogravure & Engraved
1980, Sept. 18   Perf. 13½x14
992   A225   220 l   multi   50   50
World Tourism Conference, Manila, Sept. 27.

1980, Sept. 18   Photo.   Perf. 14x13½
993   A226   170 l   multi   40   40
European Junior Weight Lifting Championship, Sept.

Robert Stolz, "Philatelic Waltz" Score—A227
Photogravure & Engraved
1980, Sept. 18   Perf. 14
994   A227   120 l   lt bl & blk   30   30
Robert Stolz (1880-1975) composer.

Madonna of the Harpies, by Andrea Del Sarto—A228

Annunciation by Del Sarto (Details): 250 l, Virgin Mary. 500 l Angel.

1980, Dec. 11   Perf. 13½
995   A228   180 l   multi   50   50
996   A228   250 l   multi   75   75
997   A228   500 l   multi   1.25   1.25

Christmas 1980 and 450th death anniversary of Andrea Del Sarto.

St. Joseph's Eve Bonfire—A229
1981, Mar. 24   Photo.   Perf. 12
       Granite Paper
998   A229   200 l   shown   60   60
999   A229   300 l   San Marino Day fireworks   60   60

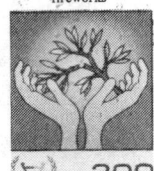

International Year of the Disabled—A230

1981, May 15   Photo.   Perf. 11½
       Granite Paper
1000   A230   300 l   multi   70   70

St. Charle's Square, Vienna, by Jakob Alt, 1817—A231

1981, May 15   Granite Paper
1001   A231   200 l   shown   50   50
1002   A231   300 l   Vienna, 1981   60   60

WIPA '81 International Philatelic Exhibition, Vienna, May 22-31. Nos. 1001-1002 se-tenant.

Woman Playing Flute A232 — Grand Prix Motorcycle Race A233

Designs: Drawings based on Roman sculptures.

1981, July 10   Photo.   Perf. 11½
       Granite Paper
1003   A232   300 l   shown   50   50
1004   A232   550 l   Soldier   1.00   1.00
1005   A232   1500 l   Shepherd   2.00   2.00
    a.   Souvenir sheet of 3   14.00   14.00

Virgil's birth bimillennium. Nos. 1003-1005 in continuous design. Nos. 1005a contains Nos. 1003-1005; gray marginal inscription. Size: 128x100mm.

1981, July 10   Litho.   Perf. 14x15
1006   A233   200 l   multi   50   50

Natl. Urban Development Plan (Housing)—A234

1981, Sept. 22   Photo.
       Granite Paper
1007   A234   20 l   shown   5   5
1008   A234   80 l   Parks   20   20
1009   A234   400 l   Energy plants   1.00   1.00

European Junior Judo Championship, Oct. 30-Nov. 1—A235

1981, Sept. 22   Photo.   Perf. 11½
       Granite Paper
1010   A235   300 l   multi   85   85

World Food Day—A236

1981, Oct. 23   Granite Paper
1011   A236   300 l   multi   80   80

Child Holding a Dove, by Pablo Picasso (1881-1973)—A237

Designs: 200 l, Homage to Picasso, by Renato Guttuso.

1981, Oct. 23   Granite Paper
1012   A237   150 l   multi   35   35
1013   A237   200 l   multi   55   55

One of the Three Kings with Goblet, by Garafalo—A238

Christmas 1981 and 500th Birth Anniv. of Benvenuto Tisi da Garafalo (Adoration of the Kings and St. Bartholomew): 300 l, King with a Jar. 600 l, Virgin and Child.

1981, Dec. 15   Photo. & Engr.   Perf. 13½
1014   A238   200 l   multi   50   50
1015   A238   300 l   multi   65   65
1016   A238   600 l   multi   1.25   1.25

Postal Cover Centenary—A239

1982, Feb. 19   Photo.   Perf. 12
1017   A239   200 l   multi   35   35

Savings Bank Centenary—A240
1982, Feb. 19
1018   A240   300 l   multi   50   50

Europa 1982 A241

Designs: 300 l, Convocation of the Assembly of Heads of Families, 1906. 450 l, Napoleons's Treaty of Friendship offer, 1797.

1982, Apr. 21   Photo.   Perf. 11½
       Granite Paper
1019   A241   300 l   multi   75   75
1020   A241   450 l   multi   90   90

Archimedes A242

1982, Apr. 21   Perf. 14x13½
1021   A242   20 l   shown   5   5
1022   A242   30 l   Copernicus   5   5
1023   A242   40 l   Newton   8   8
1024   A242   50 l   Lavoisier   10   10
1025   A242   60 l   Marie Curie   12   12
1026   A242   100 l   Robert Koch   12   12
1027   A242   200 l   Thomas Edison   30   30
1028   A242   300 l   Guglielmo Marconi   45   45
1029   A242   450 l   Hippocrates   70   70
1030   A242   5000 l   Galileo   7.50   7.50
       Nos. 1021-1030 (10)   9.47   9.47

Nos. 1021-1026, Photo.; Nos. 1027-1029, Litho. & Engr.; No. 1030, Engraved. See Nos. 1041-1046.

800th Birth Anniv. of St. Francis of Assisi—A243

SAN MARINO

1982, June 10 Photo.
1031 A243 200 l multi 35 35

Notre Dame, 1806—A244

1982, June 10
1032 A244 300 l shown 45 45
1033 A244 450 l 1982 75 75

PHILEXFRANCE '82 Stamp Exhibition, Paris, June 11-21. Nos. 1032-1033 se-tenant.

Visit of Pope   Natl. Flags of
John Paul II   ASCAT
                Members
A245   A246

1982, Aug. 29 Litho. Perf. 13½x14
1034 A245 900 l multi 1.40 1.40

          Wmk.
1982, Sept. 1 Photo. Perf. 11½
     Granite Paper
1035 A246 300 l multi 45 45

Inaugural Meeting of ASCAT (Assoc. of Editors of Philatelic Catalogues), 1977.

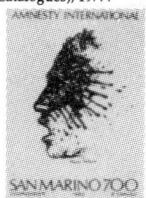
15th Amnesty Intl. Congress, Rimini, Italy, Sept. 9-15—A247

1982, Sept. 1 Unwmkd.
1036 A247 700 l blk & red 1.10 1.10

Christmas 1982—A248
Paintings by Gregorio Sciltian (b. 1900).

1982, Dec. 15 Photo. & Engr. Perf. 13½
1037 A248 200 l Angel 30 30
1038 A248 300 l Virgin and Child 45 45
1039 A248 450 l Angel, diff. 70 70

Secondary School Centenary—A249

1983, Feb. 24 Photo. Perf. 13½x14
1040 A249 300 l Begni Building 55 55

    Scientist Type of 1982

1983, Apr. 21 Perf. 14x13½
1041 A242 150 l Alexander Fleming
                  (1881-1955) 28 28
1042 A242 250 l Alessandro Volta
                  (1745-1827) 45 45
1043 A242 350 l Evangelista
                  Torricelli
                  (1608-1647) 65 65
1044 A242 400 l Carolus Linnaeus
                  (1707-1778) 70 70
1045 A242 1000 l Pitagora (6th cent.
                  BC) 1.80 1.80
1046 A242 1400 l Leonardo da Vinci
                  (1452-1519) 2.50 2.50
     Nos. 1041-1046 (6) 6.38 6.38

3rd Grand Prix Formula One—A250

1983, Apr. 20 Photo. Perf. 14x13½
1047 A250 50 l multi 10 10
1048 A250 350 l multi 65 65

Europa 1983—A251
Auguste Piccard (1884-1962), Swiss scientist.

1983, Apr. 20 Granite Paper Perf. 12x11½
1049 A251 400 l Aerostat 70 70
1050 A251 500 l Bathyscaph 90 90

World Communications Year—A252

1983, Apr. 28 Engr. Perf. 14x13
1051 A252 400 l Ham radio operator 70 70
1052 A252 500 l Mailman 90 90

Manned Flight Bicentenary—A253

1983, May 22 Litho. & Engr. Perf. 13½x14
1053 A253 500 l Montgolfiere, 1783 90 90

Botafogo Bay and Monte Corcovado,
Rio de Janeiro—A254

1983, July 29 Photo. Perf. 11½x12
     Granite Paper
1054 A254 400 l 1845 70 70
1055 A254 1400 l 1983 2.50 2.50

Se-tenant. BRASILIANA '83 Intl. Stamp Show, Rio de Janeiro, July 29-Aug. 7.

20th Anniv. of World Food
Program—A255

1983, Sept. 29 Photo. Perf. 14x13½
1056 A255 500 l multi 90 90

Christmas 1983—A256

Paintings, Raffello Sanzio (1483-1520): 300 l, Our Lady of the Grand Duke. 400 l, Our Lady of the Goldfinch. 500 l, Our Lady of the Chair.

1983, Dec. 1 Photo. & Engr. Perf. 13½
1057 A256 300 l multi 55 55
1058 A256 400 l multi 70 70
1059 A267 500 l multi 90 90

    Olympic Type of 1959

IOC Presidents: 300 l, Demetrius Vikelas, 1894-96. 400 l, Lord Killanin. 500 l, Antonio Samaranch, 1984.

1984, Feb. 8 Photo. Perf. 14x13½
1060 A86 300 £ multi 55 55
1061 A86 400 £ multi 70 70
1062 A86 550 £ multi 1.00 1.00

Flag-wavers Group, 2nd Anniv.—A257

1984, Apr. 27 Litho. & Engr. Perf. 13x14
1063 A257 300 l Flags 55 55
1064 A257 400 l Flags 70 70

Europa (1959-84)—A258

1984, Apr. 27 Photo. Perf. 11½
     Granite Paper
1065 A258 400 l multi 70 70
1066 A258 550 l multi 1.00 1.00

SAN MARINO

SEMI-POSTAL STAMPS.
Regular Issue of 1903 Surcharged:

1917   **1917**

Pro combattenti   **Pro combattenti**

= 25 Cent.   **50**
    a   *b*

1917, Dec. 15   Perf. 14   Wmk. 140
B1	A10 (a)	25c on 2c vio	2.00	2.00
B2	A11 (b)	50c on 2 l vio	27.50	27.50

Statue of Liberty
SP1

View of San Marino
SP2

1918, June 1   Typographed
B3	SP1	2c dl vio & blk	22	22
B4	SP1	5c bl grn & blk	22	22
B5	SP1	10c lake & blk	22	22
B6	SP1	20c brn org & blk	22	22
B7	SP1	25c ultra & blk	45	45
B8	SP1	45c yel brn & blk	45	45
B9	SP2	1 l bl grn & blk	11.50	11.50
B10	SP2	2 l vio & blk	9.00	9.00
B11	SP2	3 l cl & blk	9.00	9.00
		Nos. B3-B11 (9)	31.28	31.28

These stamps were sold at an advance of 5c each over face value, the receipts from that source being devoted to the support of a hospital for Italian soldiers.

3 Novembre 1918

Nos. B6-B8 Overprinted

1918, Dec. 12
B12	SP1	20c brn org & blk	1.40	1.40
B13	SP1	25c ultra & blk	90	90
B14	SP1	45c yel brn & blk	90	90

Overprinted **3 Novembre 1918**
B15	SP2	1 l bl grn & blk	1.40	1.40
B16	SP2	2 l vio & blk	9.00	9.00
B17	SP2	3 l cl & blk	9.00	9.00
		Nos. B12-B17 (6)	22.60	22.60

Celebration of Italian Victory over Austria. Inverted overprints were privately produced.

Coat of Arms
SP3

Liberty
SP4

1923, Sept. 20   Engraved
B18	SP3	5c +5c ol grn	25	25
B19	SP3	10c +5c org	25	25
B20	SP3	15c +5c dk grn	25	25
B21	SP3	25c +5c brn lake	75	75
B22	SP3	40c +5c vio brn	1.75	1.75
B23	SP3	50c +5c gray	1.00	50
B24	SP4	1 l +5c blk & bl	3.25	3.25
		Nos. B18-B24 (7)	7.50	7.00

St. Marinus
SP5

Perf. 14

1944, Apr. 25   Photo.   Wmk. 140
B25	SP5	20 l +10 l gldn brn	1.50	1.50
		Sheet of 8	50.00	50.00

The surtax was used for workers' houses. See also No. CB1.

No. 256   "L. 10"
Surcharged in Red

1946, Aug. 24   Unwmkd.
B26	A48	50 l +10 l ol brn & ultra	15.00	15.00
		Sheet of 10	750.00	750.00

Third Philatelic Day, Rimini. The surtax was for the exhibition.

Air Post Types of 1946
Surcharged "CONVEGNO FILATELICO / 30 NOVEMBRE 1946 / + LIRE 25" (or "LIRE 50") in Red or Violet

1946, Nov. 30   Wmk. 277
B26A	AP7	3 l +25 l dk brn (R)	30	50
B26B	AP8	5 l +25 l red org (V)	30	50
B26C	AP6	10 l +50 l ultra (R)	15.00	15.00

Inscription "Posta Aerea" does not appear on these stamps.

No. 260   "+ 1"
Surcharged in Black

1947, Nov. 13   Perf. 12   Wmk. 217
B27	A53	1 l +1 l brt grn & vio	12	12
B28	A53	1 l +2 l brt grn & vio	12	12
B29	A53	1 l +3 l brt grn & vio	12	12
B30	A53	1 l +4 l brt grn & vio	12	12
B31	A53	1 l +5 l brt grn & vio	12	12

Surcharged on No. 261.
B32	A53	2 l +1 l pur & ol	12	12
B33	A53	2 l +2 l pur & ol	12	12
B34	A53	2 l +3 l pur & ol	12	12
B35	A53	2 l +4 l pur & ol	12	12
B36	A53	2 l +5 l pur & ol	12	12

Surcharged on No. 262.
B37	A53	4 l +1 l vio brn & dk bl grn	6.50	6.50
B38	A53	4 l +2 l vio brn & dk bl grn	6.50	6.50
		Nos. B27-B38 (12)	14.20	14.20

Surcharges on Nos. B27-B38 are arranged consecutively, changing from ascending to descending order of denomination on alternate rows in the sheet.

AIR POST STAMPS.

View of San Marino
AP1

Wmkd. Three Plumes. (217)

1931, June 11   Engraved   Perf. 12
C1	AP1	50c bl grn	90	90
C2	AP1	80c red	1.40	1.40
C3	AP1	1 l bis brn	1.40	1.40
C4	AP1	2 l brt vio	1.75	1.75
C5	AP1	2.60 l Prus bl	13.00	13.00
C6	AP1	3 l dk gray	13.00	13.00
C7	AP1	5 l ol grn	3.50	3.50
C8	AP1	7.70 l ol brn	4.50	4.50
C9	AP1	9 l dp org	5.50	5.50
C10	AP1	10 l dk bl	275.00	275.00
		Nos. C1-C10 (10)	319.95	319.95

Nos. C1 to C10 exist imperforate.

Graf Zeppelin Issue.
Stamps of type AP1
Surcharged in Blue or Black

1933, Apr. 28
C11	AP1	3 l on 50c org (Bl)	2.00	90.00
C12	AP1	5 l on 80c grn (Bl)	40.00	90.00
C13	AP1	10 l on 1 l dk bl (Bk)	40.00	110.00
C14	AP1	12 l on 2 l yel brn (Bl)	40.00	135.00
C15	AP1	15 l on 2.60 l dl red (Bk)	40.00	160.00
C16	AP1	20 l on 3 l bl grn (Bk)	40.00	175.00
		Nos. C11-C16 (6)	202.00	760.00

Nos. C11 to C16 exist imperforate.

Nos. C1 and C2 Surcharged

1936, Apr. 14
C17	AP1	75c on 50c bl grn	4.50	4.50
C18	AP1	75c on 80c red	19.00	19.00

Nos. C5 and C6 Surcharged with New Value and Bars.

1941, Jan. 12
C19	AP1	10 l on 2.60 l Prus bl	140.00	140.00
C20	AP1	10 l on 3 l dk gray	35.00	35.00

View of Arbe
AP2

Perf. 14

1942, Mar. 16   Photo.   Wmk. 140
C21	AP2	25c brn & gray blk	20	20
C22	AP2	50c grn & brn	25	25
C23	AP2	75c gray bl & red brn	30	30
C24	AP2	1 l ocher & brn	50	50
C25	AP2	5 l bis brn & bl	17.50	17.50
		Nos. C21-C25 (5)	18.75	18.75

Return of the Italian flag to Arbe.

San Marino Map,   Fasces and Wing
AP3   AP4

Overprinted
"28 LVGLIO 1943 1642 d. F. R."
in Black.

1943, Aug. 27
C26	AP3	25c yel org	8	12
C27	AP3	50c car rose	8	12
C28	AP3	75c dk brn	8	12
C29	AP3	1 l dk rose vio	8	12
C30	AP3	2 l sapphire	8	12
C31	AP3	5 l org red	50	50
C32	AP3	10 l dp grn	1.25	1.25
C33	AP3	20 l black	5.00	5.00
		Nos. C26-C33 (8)	7.15	7.35

See footnote after No. 227. Nos. C26-C33 exist without overprint (not regularly issued). Price $2,750.

Overprinted "GOVERNO PROVVISORIO"
1943, Aug. 27
C34	AP4	25c yel org	8	12
C35	AP4	50c car rose	8	12
C36	AP4	75c dk brn	8	12
C37	AP4	1 l dk rose vio	8	12
C38	AP4	5 l org red	90	90
C39	AP4	20 l black	3.50	3.50
		Nos. C34-C39 (6)	4.72	4.88

Government Palace
AP5

Planes over Mt. Titano
AP8

Gulls and San Marino Skyline
AP6

Plane and View of San Marino
AP7

Plane over Globe
AP9

1945, Mar. 15   Photogravure
C40	AP5	25 l bis brn	12.50	12.50
		See note after No. 239.		

SAN MARINO

Photo., Engr. (20 l, 50 l)
1946-47   *Perf. 14*   Unwmkd.

C41	AP6	25c bl blk	8	8
C42	AP7	75c red org	8	8
C43	AP6	1 l brown	8	8
C44	AP7	2 l dl grn	8	8
C45	AP7	3 l violet	8	8
C46	AP8	5 l vio bl	15	25
C47	AP6	10 l crimson	22	35
C48	AP8	20 l brn lake	3.00	4.00
C49	AP8	35 l org red	7.25	6.50
C50	AP8	75 l dk yel org	7.25	6.50
C51	AP9	100 l sep ('47)	2.75	2.75
		Nos. C41-C51 (11)	21.02	20.75

Some values exist imperforate.
Issue dates: 35 l, Nov. 3, 1946; 100 l,
Mar. 27, 1947; others, Aug. 8, 1946.

Roosevelt Type of Regular Issue, 1947
Designs (F. D. Roosevelt and): 1 l, 31 l, 50 l, Eagle. 2 l, 20 l, 100 l, San Marino arms. 5 l, 200 l, Flags of San Marino and U.S. (vert.).

Photogravure
1947, May 3   *Perf. 14*   Wmk. 277

C51A	A52a	1 l dp ultra & sep	8	12
C51B	A52a	2 l org red & sep	8	12
C51C	A52a	5 l multi	8	12
C51D	A52a	20 l choc & sep	8	12
C51E	A52a	31 l org & sep	18	25
C51F	A52a	50 l dk car & sep	45	40
C51G	A52a	100 l bl & sep	1.50	1.20
C51H	A52a	200 l multi	18.00	16.00
		Nos. C51A-C51H (8)	20.45	18.33

In memory of Franklin D. Roosevelt (1882-1945), 32nd President of the U.S.A.
Nos. C51A-C51E, C51H exist imperf.
Price, set $175.

Nos. C51A-C51C Surcharged
1947, June 16

C51I	A52a	3 l on 1 l dp ultra & sep	50	50
C51J	A52a	4 l on 2 l org red & sep	50	50
C51K	A52a	6 l on 5 l multi	50	50

St. Marinus Type of Regular Issue, 1947
Engraved.
1947, July 18   *Perf. 12*   Wmk. 217
Center in Bright Blue.

C52	A53	25 l dp org	3.00	3.00
C53	A53	50 l red brn	6.00	6.00

No. C51 Overprinted in Red
Giornata Filatelica Rimini - San Marino
18 Luglio 1947

1947, July 18   *Perf. 14*   Unwmkd.

C54	AP9	100 l sepia	2.50	2.50
a.		Double ovpt.	40.00	
b.		Invtd. ovpt.	125.00	

Issued to commemorate the Rimini Philatelic Exhibition, July 18-20, 1947.

U.S. No. 1 and Mt. Titano
AP11
Engraved.
1947, Dec. 24   *Perf. 14*   Wmk. 277

C55	AP11	100 l dk pur & dk brn	11.00	10.00
a.		Imperf.	100.00	
		Sheet of 10	1,500.	

Issued to commemorate the centenary of the first United States postage stamps.

No. 264 Surcharged "POSTA AEREA" and New Value in Black.
1948, Oct. 9   *Perf. 12*   Wmk. 217

C56	A53	200 l on 25 l car & pur	25.00	25.00

Giuseppe and Anita Garibaldi
Entering San Marino
AP12
Photogravure.
1949, June 28   *Perf. 14*   Wmk. 277
Size: 27½x22mm.

C57	AP12	2 l brn red & ultra	12	18
C58	AP12	3 l dk grn & sep	12	18
C59	AP12	5 l dk bl grn & ultra	22	35

Size: 37x22mm.

C60	AP12	25 l dk grn & vio	5.25	5.00
C61	AP12	65 l grnsh blk & gray blk	20.00	20.00
		Nos. C57-C61 (5)	25.71	25.71

Issued to commemorate the centenary of Garibaldi's escape to San Marino.

Stagecoach on Road from San Marino
AP13
1950, Feb. 9   Engraved   *Perf. 14*

C62	AP13	200 l dp bl	4.00	4.00
a.		Perf. 13½x14 ('51)	6.00	6.00
		As "a," sheet of 6	50.00	50.00
b.		Imperf ('51)	27.50	27.50
		As "b," sheet of 6	225.00	225.00

Issued to commemorate the 75th anniversary of the Universal Postal Union. No. C62 was issued in sheets of 25; Nos. C62a and C62b in sheets of 6. See also No. C75.

AP14   AP15

AP16
Various Views of San Marino.
1950, Apr. 12   Photo.   *Perf. 14*
Size: 27½x21½mm. (Horiz.)
21½x27½mm. (Vert.)

C63	AP14	2 l vio & dp grn	5	5
C64	AP14	3 l bl & brn	5	5
C65	AP15	5 l brn blk & rose red	5	5
C66	AP14	10 l grnsh blk & bl	30	50
C67	AP14	15 l grnsh blk & vio	35	60

Size: 36x26½mm. (Horiz.)
26½x36mm. (Vert.)

C68	AP15	55 l dp bl & dp grn	21.00	25.00
C69	AP14	100 l car & gray	2.50	3.50
C70	AP15	250 l vio & brn	18.00	21.00

Engraved.

C71	AP16	500 l bl, dk grn & vio brn	120.00	120.00
		Nos. C63-C71 (9)	162.30	170.75

See also No. C78.

Types of 1950 Overprinted in Black, Blue or Brown

XXVIII FIERA INTERNAZIONALE DI MILANO APRILE 1950

1950, Apr. 12   Photogravure
New Colors; Sizes as Before.

C72	AP15	5 l dp bl & dp grn	18	25
C73	AP14	15 l car & gray (Bl)	2.00	1.75
C74	AP15	55 l vio & brn (Br)	10.00	10.00

The overprint is arranged differently on each denomination.
Issued to publicize San Marino's participation in the 28th International Fair of Milan, April, 1950.

Stagecoach Type of 1950
1951, Jan. 31   Engr.   *Perf. 13½x14*

C75	AP13	300 l cl, brn & dk brn	18.50	18.50
a.		Imperf.	500.00	
		Sheet of 6	175.00	175.00

No. C71 Surcharged in Black
"Giornata Filatelica San Marino-Riccione 20-8-1951," New Value and Bars.
1951, Aug. 20   *Perf. 14*

C76	AP16	300 l on 500 l bl, dk grn & vio brn	47.50	47.50

Flag and Plane
AP17
Perf. 13½x14
1951, Nov. 22   Engraved   Wmk. 277

C77	AP17	1000 l blk brn, bl & vio brn	525.00	425.00
		Sheet of 6	6,750.	5,500.

Type of 1950.
1951, Apr. 28   Photo.   *Perf. 14*
Size: 36x26½mm.

C78	AP16	500 l dk grn & brn	140.00	140.00
		Sheet of 6	1,650.	1,500.

Pro-alluvionati italiani 1951

No. C70 Surcharged in Black

100 ≡

1951, Dec. 6

C79	AP15	100 l on 250 l vio & brn	9.00	9.00

Issued to raise funds for flood victims in northern Italy.

Columbus, Globe, Statue of Liberty and Buildings
AP18
1952, Jan. 28   Engraved

C80	AP18	200 l dk bl & blk	22.50	22.50

Issued to honor Christopher Columbus.

Type of 1952 Overprinted in Red
FIERA DI TRIESTE 1952

1952, June 29

C81	AP18	200 l blk brn & choc	18.00	18.00

4th International Sample Fair of Trieste.

Cyclamen—AP19

Flowers and Seacoast—AP20
Designs: 2 l, As Nos. C85 to C87 with flowers omitted. 3 l, Rose.
1952, Aug. 25   Photo.   *Perf. 10x14*

C82	AP19	1 l pur & lil rose	8	12
C83	AP19	2 l bl & bl grn	8	12
C84	AP19	3 l dk brn & red	8	12

Perf. 14

C85	AP20	5 l rose lil & brn	8	12
C86	AP20	25 l vio & bl grn	42	60

Engraved.
Perf. 13

C87	AP20	200 l multi	47.50	47.50
		Sheet of 6 (C87)	800.00	725.00
		Nos. C82-C87 (6)	48.24	48.58

Issued to publicize the Riccione Philatelic Exhibition, Aug. 25, 1952.

Plane Making Photographic Survey
AP21
Design: 75 l, Aerial survey, seen through window.
1952, Nov. 17   Photo.   *Perf. 14*

C88	AP21	25 l ol grn	3.75	4.00
C89	AP21	75 l red brn & pur	9.50	9.50

Issued to publicize the aerial photographic survey of San Marino, 1952.

Skier
AP22

490 SAN MARINO

1953, Apr. 20 Engraved
C90 AP22 200 l bl grn & dk grn 75.00 75.00
    Sheet of 6 850.00 850.00

Plane and Arms of San Marino
AP23

1954, April 5
C91 AP23 1000 l dk bl & brn 125.00 125.00
    Sheet of 6 1,100. 900.00

Type of Regular Issue, 1954
1954, Dec. 16 Photo. Perf. 13
C92 A71 120 l dp bl & red brn 3.50 3.50

Hurdler—AP25
Design: 120 l, Relay.

1955, June 26 Perf. 14 Wmk. 303
C93 AP25 80 l brn red & gray blk 2.50 2.50
C94 AP25 120 l dk bl grn & brn red 3.25 3.50

Issued to publicize San Marino's first International Exhibition of Olympic Stamps, June 1955.

Ski Jumper—AP26

1955, Dec. 15
C95 AP26 200 l blk & red org 21.00 21.00

Issued to publicize the seventh Winter Olympic Games at Cortina d'Ampezzo, Jan. 26-Feb. 5, 1956.

No. 372 Overprinted in Upper Right Corner with Plane and "Posta Aerea."
1956, Dec. 10
C96 A76 100 l blk & Prus grn 5.00 5.00

Helicopter, Plane and Modernistic Building
AP27
Photogravure.
1958, April 12 Perf. 14 Wmk. 303
C97 AP27 125 l lt bl & brn 7.50 7.50

San Marino's 10th participation in Milan Fair.

View of San Marino
AP28
Design: 300 l, Road from Mt. Titano.
Engraved.
1958, June 23 Perf. 13 Wmk. 303
C98 AP28 200 l brn & dk bl 6.50 8.50
C99 AP28 300 l mag & vio 6.50 8.50
  a. Strip, Nos. C98, C99 + label 13.00 17.50

Printed in sheets containing 20 each of Nos. C98 and C99 flanking a center label with San Marino coat of arms. Nos. C98 and C99 also come se-tenant in sheet.

Type of Regular Issue, 1958.
Design: Bay of Naples and 50g stamp of Naples.
1958, Oct. 8 Photo. Perf. 14
C100 A85 125 l brn & red brn 8.50 8.50

Centenary of stamps of Naples.

Sea Gull—AP29
Birds: 10 l, Falcon. 15 l, Mallard. 120 l, Stock dove. 250 l, Barn swallow.
1959, Feb. 12 Perf. 14
C101 AP29 5 l grn & gray 8 8
C102 AP29 10 l bl & org brn 8 8
C103 AP29 15 l red & multi 12 18
C104 AP29 120 l rose red, yel & gray blk 85 1.00
C105 AP29 250 l dp grn, yel & blk 3.75 3.75
  Nos. C101-C105 (5) 4.88 5.09

Pierre de Coubertin—AP30
Engraved.
1959, May 19 Perf. 13 Wmk. 303
C106 AP30 120 l sepia 5.00 4.25

Issued to honor Pierre de Coubertin and to publicize the 1960 Olympic Games in Rome.

Alitalia Viscount Over San Marino
AP31
1959, June 3 Photo. Perf. 14
C107 AP31 120 l brt vio 4.00 4.00
First flight San Marino-Rimini-London.

Type of Regular Issue, 1959.
Design: Abraham Lincoln and San Marino peaks.
1959, July 1 Engraved Perf. 14x13
C108 A87 200 l dk bl 14.00 12.50
Issued to commemorate the sesquicentennial of the birth of Abraham Lincoln.

Type of Regular Issue, 1959.
Design: Bologna view; 3 b, Romagna stamp.
Photogravure.
1959, Aug. 29 Perf. 14. Wmk. 303
C109 A88 120 l blk & bl grn 4.50 4.50

Centenary of stamps of Romagna.

Type of Regular Issue, 1959.
Design: Fishing boats, Monte Pellegrino and 50g stamp of Sicily (horiz.).
1959, Oct. 16
C110 A89 200 l multi 3.00 3.00
Centenary of stamps of Sicily.

Olympic Games Issue
Type of Regular Issue, 1960
Sports: 20 l, Basketball. 40 l, Sprint race. 80 l, Swimming (horiz.). 125 l, Target shooting (horiz.).
1960, May 23 Perf. 14 Wmk. 303
C111 A92 20 l lilac 20 12
C112 A92 40 l bis brn & dk red 30 20
C113 A92 80 l ultra & buff 90 90
C114 A92 125 l ver & dk brn 1.40 1.20

Issued to commemorate the 17th Olympic Games, Rome, Aug. 25-Sept. 11.
Souvenir sheets are priced and described below No. 465.

Lions International Issue
Type of Regular Issue, 1960
Design: 200 l, Globe and Lions emblem.
1960, July 1 Photogravure
C115 A94 200 l ol grn, brn & ultra 13.00 9.00
Issued in honor of Lions International and to commemorate the founding of the Lions Club of San Marino.

Type of Regular Issue, 1960
1960, Aug. 27 Perf. 14 Wmk. 303
C116 A95 125 l multi 5.00 3.50
12th San Marino-Riccione Stamp Fair.

Helicopter and Mt. Titano
AP32
1961, July 6 Engraved Perf. 14
C117 AP32 1000 l rose car 90.00 57.50
    Sheet of 6 600.00 425.00

Tupolev TU-104A
AP33
Planes: 10 l, Boeing 707 (vert.). 15 l, Douglas DC-8. 25 l, Boeing 707. 50 l, Vickers Viscount 837. 75 l, Caravelle (vert.). 120 l, Vickers VC10. 200 l, D. H. Comet 4C. 300 l, Boeing 727. 500 l, Rolls Royce Dart turbo-prop. 1000 l, Boeing 707.
Photogravure
1963-65 Perf. 14 Wmk. 339
C118 AP33 5 l bl & vio brn 8 8
C119 AP33 10 l org & dk bl 8 8
C120 AP33 15 l vio & red 8 8
C121 AP33 25 l vio & car 12 12
C122 AP33 50 l grnsh bl & red 12 12
C123 AP33 75 l emer & dp org 12 12
C124 AP33 120 l vio bl & red 50 50
C125 AP33 200 l brt yel & blk 35 35
C126 AP33 300 l org & blk 45 45

Perf. 13
C127 AP33 500 l multi ('65) 10.00 7.25
    Sheet of 4 40.00 30.00
C128 AP33 1000 l lil rose, ultra & yel ('64) 9.00 6.75
    Sheet of 4 50.00 40.00
    Nos. C118-C128 (11) 20.90 15.90

Dates of issue: Nos. C118-C126, Dec. 5, 1963. No. C127, Mar. 4, 1965. No. C128, Mar. 12, 1964.

Mt. Titano and Flight Symbolized
AP34
1972, Oct. 25 Perf. 11½ Unwmkd.
Granite Paper
C129 AP34 1000 l multi 2.25 2.25

Glider—AP35
Designs: Each stamp shows a different type of air current in background.
1974, Oct. 9 Photo. Perf. 11½
Granite Paper
C130 AP35 40 l multi 12 12
C131 AP35 120 l multi 30 30
C132 AP35 500 l multi 90 90
50th anniversary of gliding in Italy.

San Marino 77 Type of 1977
1977, Jan. 28 Photo. Perf. 11½
C133 A193 200 l multi 45 45
San Marino 77 Philatelic Exhibition.

Wright Brothers' Flyer A
AP36
1978, Sept. 28 Photo. Perf. 11½
C134 AP36 10 l multi 5 5
C135 AP36 50 l multi 8 8
C136 AP36 200 l multi 30 30
75th anniversary of first powered flight.

SAN MARINO

AIR POST SEMI-POSTAL STAMP.

View of San Marino APSP1

Photogravure.
1944, Apr. 25   Perf. 14   Wmk. 140

CB1	APSP1	20 l + 10 l ol grn	1.50	1.50
		Sheet of 8	50.00	50.00

The surtax was used for workers' houses.

SPECIAL DELIVERY STAMPS.

SD1

Engraved.
1907, Apr. 25   Perf. 12   Unwmkd.

| E1 | SD1 | 25c carmine | 8.00 | 4.00 |

Type of Regular Issue of 1903
Overprinted **ESPRESSO**
Wmkd. Crowns. (140)
1923, May 30   Perf. 14½x14

| E2 | A11 | 60c violet | 45 | 45 |

Type of 1907 Issue Surcharged
Cent. 60
1923, July 26   Perf. 14

| E3 | SD1 | 60c on 25c car | 60 | 60 |
| a. | Vert. pair, imperf. btwn. | 30.00 | |

No. E2 Surcharged **Lire 1,25**
1926, Nov. 25   Perf. 14½x14

| E4 | A11 | 1.25 l on 60c vio | 1.00 | 1.00 |

No. E3 Surcharged
L 1,25
1927, Sept. 15

E5	SD1	1.25 l on 60c on 25c brn car	75	75
a.	Inverted surch.	10.00	
b.	Vert. pair, imperf. btwn.	50.00	
c.	Double surch.	110.00	

Statue of Liberty and View of San Marino—SD2

Engraved.
1929, Aug. 29   Perf. 12   Wmk. 217

| E6 | SD2 | 1.25 l green | 30 | 30 |

Overprinted in Red UNIÓN POSTALE UNIVERSELLE

| E7 | SD2 | 2.50 l dp bl | 1.75 | 1.75 |

Arms of San Marino SD3

Photogravure.
1943, Sept.   Perf. 14   Wmk. 140

| E8 | SD3 | 1.25 l green | 15 | 15 |
| E9 | SD3 | 2.50 l redsh org | 15 | 15 |

View of San Marino SD4

Pegasus SD5

1945-46   Photo.   Wmk. 140

| E12 | SD4 | 2.50 l dp grn | 15 | 15 |
| E13 | SD4 | 5 l dp org | 20 | 20 |

Unwmkd.

| E14 | SD4 | 5 l car rose | 90 | 50 |

Wmk. 277

| E15 | SD4 | 10 l saph ('46) | 3.75 | 4.00 |

Unwmkd. Engraved

| E16 | SD5 | 30 l dp red ('46) | 8.00 | 8.00 |
| | Nos. E12-E16 (5) | 13.00 | 12.85 |

See also Nos. E22-E23.

Nos. E14 and E15 Surcharged in Black
L. 15

1947   Perf. 14.   Unwmkd.

| E17 | SD4 | 15 l on 5 l car rose | 60 | 50 |

Wmk. 277

| E18 | SD4 | 15 l on 10 l saph | 60 | 50 |

No. E16 Surcharged with New Value and Bars in Carmine
1947-48   Unwmkd.

E19	SD5	35 l on 30 l dp ultra ('48)	37.50	35.00
E20	SD5	60 l on 30 l dp ultra	5.25	5.00
E21	SD5	80 l on 30 l dp ultra ('48)	18.00	20.00

Types of 1945-46.
1950, Dec. 11   Photo.   Wmk. 277

| E22 | SD4 | 60 l rose brn | 13.00 | 12.50 |
| E23 | SD5 | 80 l dp bl | 16.00 | 18.00 |

Nos. E22-E23 Surcharged with New Value and Three Bars.
1957, Dec. 12   Perf. 14

| E24 | SD4 | 75 l on 60 l rose brn | 4.00 | 4.00 |
| E25 | SD5 | 100 l on 80 l dp bl | 4.00 | 4.00 |

Crossbow SD6

Design: No. E27, "Espresso" at left; crossbow casts two shadows.
1965, Aug. 28   Photo.   Wmk. 339

| E26 | SD6 | 120 l on 75 l blk, gray & yel | 25 | 25 |
| E27 | SD6 | 135 l on 100 l blk & org | 30 | 30 |

Without Surcharge

Design: 80 l, 100 l, "Espresso" at left; crossbow casts two shadows.
1966, March 29

E28	SD6	75 l blk, gray & yel	12	12
E29	SD6	80 l blk & lil	18	18
E30	SD6	100 l blk & org	18	18

SEMI-POSTAL SPECIAL DELIVERY STAMP.

SPSD1

Wmkd. Crowns. (140)
1923, Sept. 20   Engraved   Perf. 14

| EB1 | SPSD1 | 60c + 5c brn red | 1.50 | 1.50 |

POSTAGE DUE STAMPS.

D1   D2

D3   D4

D5

Wmkd. Crown. (140)
1897-1920   Typographed   Perf. 14

J1	D1	5c bl grn & dk brn	8	12
J2	D2	10c bl grn & dk brn	18	18
a.	Numerals inverted	15.00	15.00
J3	D1	30c bl grn & dk brn	28	28
J4	D2	50c bl grn & dk brn	90	90
a.	Numerals inverted	15.00	15.00
J5	D2	60c bl grn & dk brn	3.50	3.50
J6	D3	1 l cl & dk brn	2.25	1.75
J7	D4	3 l cl & brn ('20)	6.25	6.25
J8	D4	5 l cl & dk brn	32.50	20.00
J9	D5	10 l cl & dk brn	9.00	9.00
	Nos. J1-J9 (9)	54.94	41.98

1924

J10	D1	5c rose & brn	10	12
J11	D1	10c rose & brn	10	12
J12	D2	30c rose & brn	15	15
J13	D2	50c rose & brn	15	15
J14	D2	60c rose & brn	2.00	2.00
J15	D3	1 l grn & brn	2.50	2.50
J16	D4	3 l grn & brn	9.50	9.50
J17	D4	5 l grn & brn	9.50	9.50
J18	D5	10 l grn & brn	160.00	160.00
	Nos. J10-J18 (9)	184.00	184.04

1925-39   Perf. 14.

J19	D1	5c bl & brn	5	5
a.	Numerals inverted	18.00	18.00
J20	D2	10c bl & brn	5	5
a.	Numerals inverted	18.00	18.00
J21	D2	15c bl & brn ('39)	10	10
J22	D2	20c bl & brn ('39)	10	10
J23	D2	25c bl & brn ('39)	28	28
J24	D2	30c bl & brn	10	10
J25	D2	40c bl & brn ('39)	2.75	1.85
J26	D2	50c bl & brn	22	22
a.	Numerals inverted	18.00	18.00
J27	D2	60c bl & brn	90	90
J28	D3	1 l buff & brn	3.25	90
J29	D4	2 l buff & brn ('39)	1.40	1.40
J30	D4	3 l buff & brn	45.00	22.50
J31	D4	5 l buff & brn	11.50	4.50
J32	D5	10 l buff & brn	20.00	6.75
J33	D4	15 l buff & brn ('28)	90	90
J34	D4	25 l buff & brn ('28)	35.00	17.50
J35	D4	30 l buff & brn ('28)	8.00	8.00
J36	D4	50 l buff & brn ('28)	9.00	9.00
	Nos. J19-J36 (18)	138.60	75.10

Postage Due Stamps of 1925 Surcharged in Black and Silver

1931, May 18

J37	D1	15c on 5c bl & brn	15	15
J38	D2	15c on 10c bl & brn	15	15
J39	D2	15c on 30c bl & brn	15	15
J40	D1	20c on 10c bl & brn	8	12
J41	D2	20c on 10c bl & brn	8	12
J42	D2	20c on 30c bl & brn	8	12
J43	D1	25c on 5c bl & brn	70	40
J44	D2	25c on 10c bl & brn	70	40
J45	D2	25c on 30c bl & brn	9.50	4.75
J46	D2	40c on 10c bl & brn	50	25
J47	D2	40c on 10c bl & brn	60	25
J48	D2	40c on 30c bl & brn	60	25
J49	D1	2 l on 5c bl & brn	27.50	17.50
J50	D1	2 l on 10c bl & brn	55.00	27.50
J51	D2	2 l on 30c bl & brn	35.00	22.50
	Nos. J37-J51 (15)	130.79	74.61

Postage Due Stamps of 1925-39 Surcharged in Black
Lire 1
Perf. 14, 14½x14
1936-40   Wmk. 140

J52	D1	10c on 5c bl & brn ('38)	90	90
J53	D2	25c on 30c bl & brn ('38)	9.00	9.00
J54	D1	50c on 5c bl & brn ('37)	9.00	8.00
J55	D2	1 l on 30c bl & brn	27.50	5.50
J56	D2	1 l on 40c bl & brn ('40)	9.00	4.50
J57	D4	1 l on 3 l buff & brn ('37)	22.50	1.75
J58	D4	1 l on 25 l buff & brn ('39)	67.50	9.00
J59	D4	2 l on 15 l buff & brn ('38)	27.50	11.00
J60	D4	3 l on 20c bl & brn ('40)	25.00	21.00
	Nos. J52-J60 (9)	197.90	70.65

Coat of Arms

D6   D7

1939 Typographed. *Perf. 14.*

J61	D6	5c bl & brn	6	6

Nos. J61 and J36 Surcharged with New Values and Bars.

1940–43

J62	D6	10c on 5c bl & brn	45	45
J63	D6	50c on 5c bl & brn	1.75	90
J64	D4	25 l on 50 l buff & brn ('43)	3.50	3.50

Photogravure.

1945, June 7 *Perf. 14* Unwmkd.

J65	D7	5c dk grn	5	5
J66	D7	10c org brn	5	5
J67	D7	15c rose red	6	5
J68	D7	20c dp ultra	6	5
J69	D7	25c dk pur	6	5
J70	D7	30c rose lake	6	5
J71	D7	40c bister	6	5
J72	D7	50c sl blk	6	5
J73	D7	60c chestnut	6	5
J74	D7	1 l dp org	6	5
J75	D7	2 l carmine	12	20
J76	D7	5 l dl vio	15	25
J77	D7	10 l dk bl	25	38
J78	D7	20 l dk grn	12.50	12.00
J79	D7	25 l red org	12.50	12.00
J80	D7	50 l dk brn	12.50	12.00
		Nos. J65-J80 (16)	38.60	37.33

PARCEL POST STAMPS.

These stamps were used by affixing them to the way bill so that one half remained on it following the parcel, the other half staying on the receipt given the sender. Most used halves are right halves. Complete stamps were and are obtainable canceled, probably to order.

Both unused and used prices are for complete stamps.

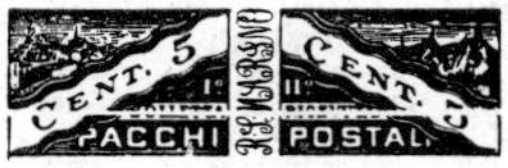

PP1

Engraved, Values Typographed.

1928, Nov. 22 *Perf. 12* Unwmkd.

Pairs are imperforate between.

Q1	PP1	5c blk brn & bl	20	20
a.		Imperf.	15.00	
Q2	PP1	10c dk bl & bl	20	20
Q3	PP1	20c gray blk & bl	20	20
a.		Imperf.	15.00	
Q4	PP1	25c car & bl	20	20
Q5	PP1	30c ultra & bl	20	20
Q6	PP1	50c org & bl	20	20
Q7	PP1	60c rose & bl	20	20
Q8	PP1	1 l vio & brn	20	20
a.		Imperf.	15.00	
Q9	PP1	2 l grn & brn	30	30
Q10	PP1	3 l bis & brn	40	40
Q11	PP1	4 l gray & brn	50	50
Q12	PP1	10 l rose lil & brn	1.00	1.00
Q13	PP1	12 l red brn & brn	5.00	5.00
Q14	PP1	15 l ol grn & brn	10.00	10.00
a.		Imperf.	15.00	
Q15	PP1	20 l brn vio & brn	12.00	12.00
		Nos. Q1-Q15 (15)	30.80	30.80

Halves Used

Q1-Q7	5
Q8	5
Q9-Q10	10
Q11	15
Q12	40
Q13	65
Q14	3.00
Q15	5.00

1945–46 *Perf. 14* Wmk. 140

Pairs are perforated between.

Q16	PP1	5c rose vio & red org	5	5
Q17	PP1	10c red org & blk	5	5
Q18	PP1	20c dk red & grn	5	5
Q19	PP1	25c yel & blk	5	5
Q20	PP1	30c red vio & org red	5	5
Q21	PP1	50c dl pur & blk	5	5
Q22	PP1	60c rose lake & blk	5	5
Q23	PP1	1 l brn & dp bl	5	5
Q24	PP1	2 l dk brn & dk bl	5	5
Q25	PP1	3 l ol brn & brn	5	5
Q26	PP1	4 l bl grn & brn	5	5
Q27	PP1	10 l bl blk & brt pur	10	10
Q28	PP1	12 l myr grn & dl bl	4.50	4.50
Q29	PP1	15 l grn & pur	3.75	3.50
Q30	PP1	20 l rose lil & brn	2.75	2.50
Q31	PP1	25 l dp car & ultra ('46)	42.50	40.00
Q32	PP1	50 l yel & dp org ('46)	47.50	50.00
		Nos. Q16-Q32 (17)	101.65	101.15

Halves Used

Q16-Q26	5
Q27	5
Q28	8
Q29	10
Q30	15
Q31	25
Q32	50

Nos. Q32 and Q31 Surcharged with New Value and Wavy Lines in Black.

1948-50

Q33	PP1	100 l on 50 l yel & dp org	90.00	65.00
		Half, used		1.00
Q34	PP1	200 l on 25 l dp car & ultra ('50)	150.00	135.00
		Half, used		1.00

1953, Mar. 5 *Perf. 13½* Wmk. 277

Pairs Perforated Between

Q35	PP1	10 l dk grn & rose lil	55.00	10.00
		Half, used		1.00
Q36	PP1	300 l pur & lake	225.00	190.00
		Half, used		1.00

1956 *Perf. 13½* Wmk. 303

Q37	PP1	10 l gray & brt pur	1.00	1.50
		Half, used		5
Q38	PP1	50 l yel & dp org	2.00	2.00
		Half, used		10

No. Q38 Surcharged with New Value and Wavy Lines In Black.

Q39	PP1	100 l on 50 l yel & dp org	3.00	3.50
		Half, used		25

1960–61

Q40	PP1	300 l vio & brn	110.00	85.00
		Half, used		50
Q41	PP1	500 l dk brn & car ('61)	10.00	8.00
		Half, used		5

1965–72 *Perf. 13½* Wmk. 339

Pairs Perforated Between

Q42	PP1	10 l gray & brt pur	12	12
Q43	PP1	50 l yel & red org	12	12
Q44	PP1	100 l on 50 l yel & red org	4.00	4.00
Q45	PP1	300 l vio & brn	1.50	1.50
Q46	PP1	500 l brn & red ('72)	27.50	27.50
Q47	PP1	1000 l bl grn & lt red brn ('67)	2.50	2.50
		Nos. Q42-Q47 (6)	35.74	35.74

Halves Used

Q42-Q43	5
Q44-Q45	10
Q46	20
Q47	90

SARDINIA

See Italian States preceding Italy in Vol. III.

SASENO

(sä'sȧ·nō)

LOCATION—An island in the Adriatic Sea, lying at the entrance of Valona Bay, Albania.

GOVT.—Former Italian possession.

AREA—2 sq. mi.

Italy occupied this Albanian islet in 1914, and returned it to Albania in 1947.

100 Centesimi = 1 Lira

Italian Stamps of 1901-22 Overprinted SASENO

1923 Wmkd. Crown. (140) *Perf. 14.*

1	A48	10c claret	2.50	6.00
2	A48	15c slate	2.50	6.00
3	A50	20c brn org	2.50	6.00
4	A49	25c blue	2.50	6.00
5	A49	30c yel brn	2.50	6.00
6	A49	50c violet	2.50	6.00
7	A49	60c carmine	2.50	6.00
8	A46	1 l brn & grn	2.50	6.00
a.		Double ovpt.	50.00	
		Nos. 1-8 (8)	20.00	48.00

Nos. 1 to 8 were superseded by postage stamps of Italy.

SAUDI ARABIA

(sȧ·ōō'dĭ)

LOCATION—Southwestern Asia, on the Arabian Peninsula between the Red Sea and the Persian Gulf.

GOVT.—Kingdom.

AREA—870,000 sq. mi (approx).

POP.—9,520,000 (est. 1977).

CAPITAL—Riyadh.

In 1916 the Grand Sherif of Mecca declared the Sanjak of Hejaz independent of Turkish rule. In 1925, Ibn Saud, then Sultan of the Nejd, captured the Hejaz after a prolonged siege of Jedda, the last Hejaz stronghold.

The resulting Kingdom of the Hejaz and Nejd was renamed Saudi Arabia in 1932.

40 Paras = 1 Piaster = 1 Guerche (Garch, Grouche or Qirsh)
11 Guerche = 1 Riyal (1928)
110 Guerche = 1 Sovereign (1931)
440 Guerche = 1 Sovereign (1952)
20 Piasters (Guerche) = 1 Riyal (1960)
100 Halalas = 1 Riyal (1976)

Hejaz

Sherifate of Mecca

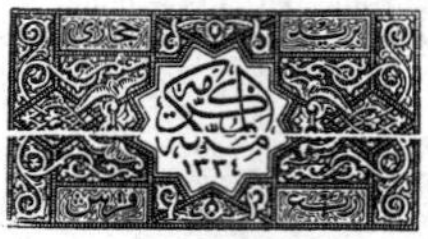

Adapted from Carved Door Panels of Mosque El Salih Talay, Cairo

A1

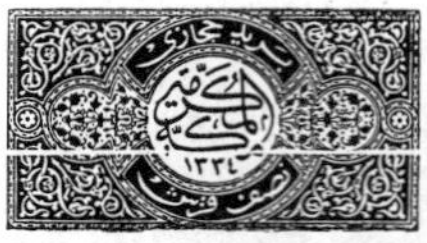

Taken from Page of Koran in Mosque of El Sultan Barquq, Cairo

A2

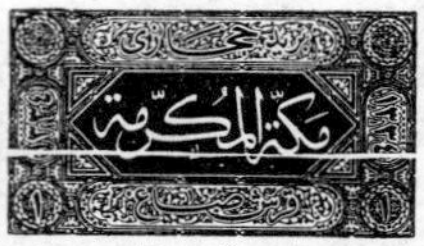

Taken from Details of an Ancient Prayer Niche in the Mosque of El Amri at Qus in Upper Egypt

A3

Typographed

1916 *Perf. 10, 12.* Unwmkd.

L1	A1	¼pi green	40.00	30.00
L2	A2	½pi red	50.00	40.00
a.		Perf. 10	120.00	100.00
L3	A3	1pi blue	10.00	10.00
a.		Perf. 12	150.00	150.00
b.		Perf. 10x12	850.00	

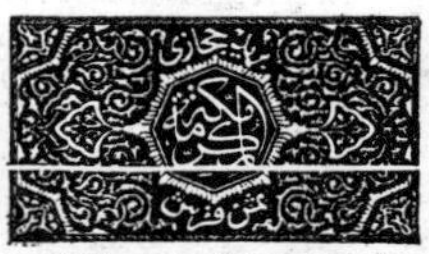

Central Design Adapted from a Koran Design for a Tomb. Background is from Stone Carving on Entrance Arch to the Ministry of Wakfs

A4

1917 *Roulette 20*

L4	A4	⅛pi orange	3.00	2.50
L5	A1	¼pi green	3.00	2.50
L6	A2	½pi red	3.00	2.50
L7	A3	1pi blue	3.00	2.50

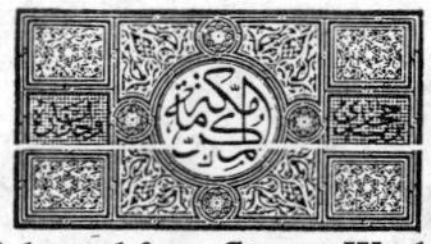

Adapted from Stucco Work above Entrance to Cairo R. R. Station

A5

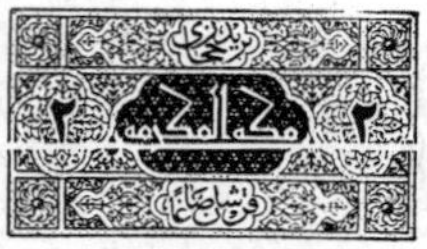

Adapted from First Page of the Koran of Sultan Farag

A6

1917–18 *Serrate Roulette 13*

L8	A5	1pa lil brn	2.00	1.50
L9	A4	⅛pi orange	2.00	1.50
L10	A1	¼pi green	2.00	1.50
L11	A2	½pi red	2.00	1.50
L12	A3	1pi blue	2.00	1.50
L13	A6	2pi magenta	15.00	10.00
		Nos. L8-L13 (6)	25.00	17.50

Designs A1–A6 are inscribed "Hejaz Postage."

Kingdom of the Hejaz

Stamps of 1917-18 Overprinted in Black, Red or Brown:

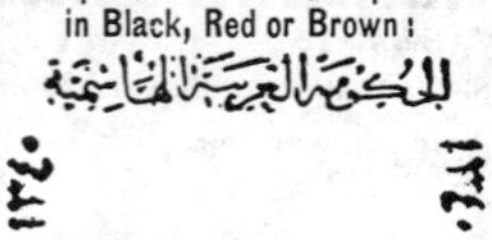

1921, Dec. 21 *Serrate Roulette 13*

L14	A5	1pa lil brn	12.50	12.50
L15	A4	⅛pi orange	17.50	17.50
a.		Inverted overprint	50.00	
b.		Double overprint	150.00	
c.		Roulette 20	500.00	
d.		As "c", invtd. overprint		*1,000.*
L16	A1	¼pi green	5.00	5.00
a.		Invtd. overprint	50.00	
b.		Double overprint	125.00	
c.		Roulette 20	500.00	

L17 A2 ½pi red 5.00 5.00
a. Inverted overprint 85.00 85.00
b. Roulette 20 500.00
L18 A3 1pi bl (R) 6.00 6.00
a. Brown ovpt. 20.00 20.00
b. Black ovpt. 30.00 30.00
c. As "b", invtd. ovpt. 60.00
d. Roulette 20 600.00
L19 A6 2pi magenta 6.00 6.00
Nos. L14-L19 (6) 52.00 52.00

Nos. L15–L17, L18b and L19 exist with date (1340) omitted at one or both sides.

With Additional Surcharge:

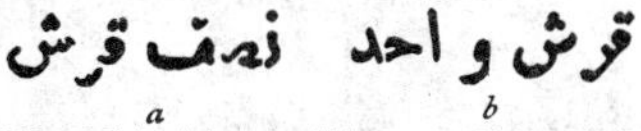

L22 A5(a) ½pi on 1pa lil brn 100.00 100.00
L23 A5(b) 1pi on 1pa lil brn 100.00 100.00

Stamps of 1917–18 Overprinted in Black

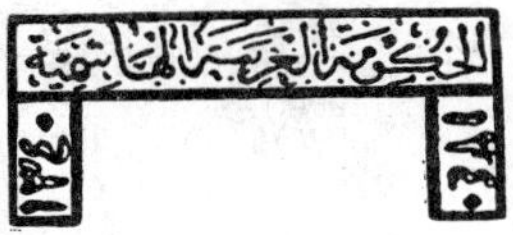

1922, Jan. 7

L24 A5 1pa lil brn 3.00 3.00
a. Inverted ovpt. 50.00
b. Double overprint 50.00
c. Double overprint, one inverted 60.00
L25 A4 ⅛pi orange 10.00 7.00
a. Inverted ovpt. 45.00
b. Double overprint, one inverted 60.00
L26 A1 ¼pi green 3.00 3.00
a. Inverted ovpt. 45.00
b. Double overprint, one inverted 75.00
L27 A2 ½pi red 2.00 2.00
a. Inverted ovpt. 40.00
b. Double overprint, one inverted 60.00
L28 A3 1pi blue 2.00 50
a. Double overprint 60.00
b. Inverted ovpt. 60.00
L29 A6 2pi magenta 5.00 5.00
a. Double overprint 150.00

With Additional Surcharge of New Value.

L30 A5(a) ½pi on 1pa lil brn 15.00 10.00
L31 A5(b) 1pi on 1pa lil brn 2.00 50
a. Inverted surch. 70.00
b. Double surch.
c. Double surcharge, one inverted
Nos. L24-L31 (8) 42.00 31.00

The 1921 and 1922 overprints read: The Government of Hashemite Arabia, 1340."
The overprint on Nos. L24–L31 in red is bogus.

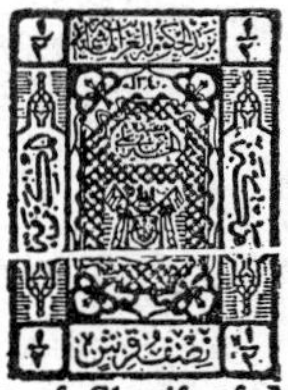

Arms of Sherif of Mecca
A7

1922 Typographed. *Perf. 11½*

L32 A7 ⅛pi red brn 1.25 30
L34 A7 ½pi red 1.25 30
L35 A7 1pi dk bl 1.25 30
L36 A7 1½pi violet 1.25 30
L37 A7 2pi orange 1.25 30
L38 A7 3pi ol brn 1.25 30
L39 A7 5pi ol grn 1.25 60
Nos. L32-L39 (7) 8.75 2.40

Numerous shades exist.
Nos. L32, L34–L36, L39 exist imperf.

Stamps of 1922 Surcharged with New Values in Arabic:

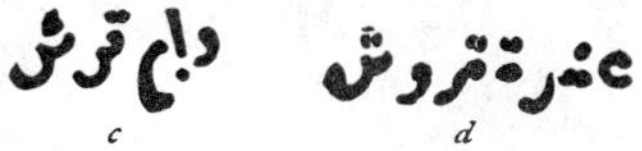

1923

L40 A7(c) ¼pi on ½pi org brn 5.00 5.00
a. Double surcharge
b. Double inverted surcharge
c. Double surcharge, one inverted
d. Invtd. surch.
L41 A7(d) 10pi on 5pi ol grn 10.00 10.00
a. Double surcharge, one inverted
b. Inverted surch.

Caliphate Issue.

Stamps of 1922 Overprinted in Gold

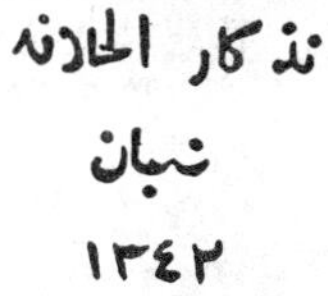

1924

L42 A7 ⅛pi org brn 2.25 1.75
L43 A7 ½pi red 2.25 1.75
L44 A7 1pi dk bl 2.25 1.75
L45 A7 1½pi violet 2.25 1.75
L46 A7 2pi orange 2.25 1.75
L47 A7 3pi ol brn 2.25 1.75
L48 A7 5pi ol grn 2.25 1.75
Nos. L42-L48 (7) 15.75 12.25

The overprint reads "In commemoration of the Caliphate, Shaaban, 1342." The issue commemorates the assumption of the Caliphate by King Hussein in March, 1924.
The overprint was typographed in black and dusted with "gold" powder while wet. It exists inverted on all denominations. The several settings differ in spacing and alignment. Forgeries exist.

Type of 1922 and

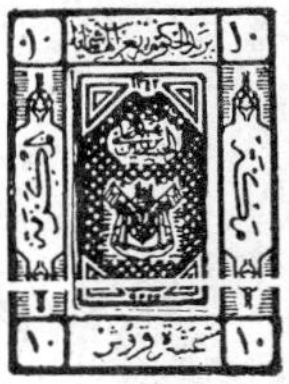

Arms of Sherif of Mecca
A8

1924 *Perf. 11½*

L48A A7 ¼pi yel grn 1.50 90
b. Tête bêche pair 5.00
L49 A7 3pi brn red 2.00 2.00
a. 3pi dl red 2.00 2.00
L50 A8 10pi vio & dk brn 4.00 4.00
a. Center inverted 20.00 15.00
b. Center omitted 15.00
c. 10pi pur & sep 4.00 4.00

Nos. L48A, L50, L50a exist imperf.

See Jordan for various overprints on 1922–25 issues of Hejaz.

Jedda Issues

Stamps of 1917-18 Overprinted

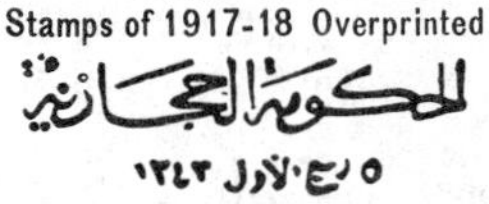

The control overprints on Nos. L51–L185 read: "Hukumat al Hageziet, 5 Rabi al'awwal 1343" (The Hejaz Government, October 4, 1924). This is the date of the accession of King Ali.
Counterfeits exist of all Jedda overprints.

Red Overprint.

1925, Jan. *Roulette 20*

L51 A4 ⅛pi orange 6.00 6.00
a. Inverted overprint 60.00
b. Overprinted on face and back 90.00
L52 A1 ¼pi green 6.00 6.00
a. Inverted overprint 30.00
b. Double overprint 30.00
c. Double overprint, one invtd. 100.00
L53 A2 ½pi red 30.00 30.00
a. Inverted overprint 75.00
L54 A3 1pi blue 15.00 15.00
a. Inverted overprint 60.00
b. Double overprint, one inverted 80.00

Serrate Roulette 13.

L55 A5 1pa lil brn 5.00 5.00
a. Inverted overprint 35.00
b. Double overprint 35.00
c. Overprinted on face and back 75.00
L56 A4 ⅛pi orange 12.50 12.50
a. Inverted overprint 40.00
L57 A1 ¼pi green 10.00 10.00
a. Pair, one without overprint 100.00
b. Inverted overprint 25.00
c. Double overprint, one inverted 100.00
L58 A2 ½pi red 10.00 10.00
a. Inverted overprint 25.00
L59 A3 1pi blue 12.50 12.50
a. Inverted overprint 40.00
L60 A6 2pi magenta 8.00 8.00
a. Inverted overprint 35.00

Gold Overprint.
Roulette 20

L61 A1 ¼pi green 1,000. *1,500.*

Serrate Roulette 13.

L62 A1 ¼pi green 15.00 15.00
a. Inverted overprint 40.00

The overprint on No. L61 was typographed in red or blue (No. L62 only in red) and dusted with "gold" powder while wet.

Blue Overprint.
Roulette 20

L63 A1 ¼pi green 9.00 9.00
a. Inverted overprint 40.00
b. Overprinted on face and back 60.00
L64 A2 ½pi red, invtd. ovpt. 75.00 75.00
a. Upright overprint 100.00

Serrate Roulette 13.

L65 A1 ¼pi green 15.00 15.00
a. Inverted overprint 35.00
b. Vertical overprint
L66 A2 ½pi red 9.00 9.00
a. Inverted overprint 50.00
L66B A6 2pi mag, invtd. ovpt. 500.00

Blue overprint on No. L55 is bogus.

Same Overprint in Blue on Provisional Stamps of 1922, Overprinted on No. L17.

L67 A2 ½pi red 1,000.

Overprinted on Nos. L24–L29.

L68 A5 1pa lil brn 32.50 27.50
a. Inverted overprint
L69 A4 ⅛pi orange 1,000. 750.00
L70 A1 ¼pi green 35.00 22.50
a. Inverted overprint 300.00
L71 A2 ½pi red 35.00 25.00
a. Inverted overprint 500.00
L72 A3 1pi blue 50.00 32.50
L73 A6 2pi magenta 45.00 45.00
a. Inverted overprint 400.00

Same Overprint on Nos. L30 and L31

L74 A5(a) ½pi on 1pa lil brn 60.00 60.00
L75 A5(b) 1pi on 1pa lil brn 50.00 50.00
a. Inverted overprint 250.00

Same Overprint in Blue Vertically, Reading Up or Down, on Stamps of 1922–24.

Perf. 11½.

L76 A7 ½pi red 125.00 125.00
L76A A8 10pi vio & dk brn 150.00 175.00

Nos. L5, L10 Overprinted in Blue or Red

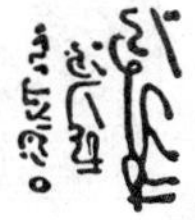

Roulette 20

L77 A1 ¼pi grn (Bl) 75.00 75.00
L78 A1 ¼pi grn (R) 50.00 50.00

Serrate Roulette 13.

L79 A1 ¼pi grn (Bl) 60.00 60.00
L80 A1 ¼pi grn (R) 20.00 30.00

Nos. L77–L80 exist with overprint reading up or down. It reads up in illustration.

No. L10 and Stamps of 1922–24 Overprinted

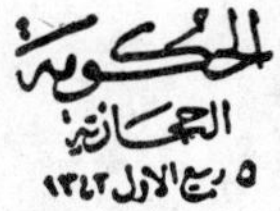

Serrate Roulette 13.

Red Overprint (vertical).

L81 A1 ¼pi green 300.00

Overprint on No. L81 also exists horizontal and inverted.

Perf. 11½.

Blue Overprint.

L82 A7 ⅛pi red brn 3.00 2.00
a. Inverted overprint 10.00
L83 A7 ½pi red 3.00 3.00
a. Double overprint 20.00
b. Inverted overprint 12.50 10.00
c. Double overprint, one inverted 25.00
d. Vertical overprint
L84 A7 1pi dk bl 75.00 75.00
a. Inverted overprint 75.00 75.00
L85 A7 1½pi violet 6.00 5.00
a. Inverted overprint 15.00 10.00
L86 A7 2pi orange 4.00 3.00
a. Double overprint, one inverted 25.00
b. Inverted overprint 12.50
c. Double overprint 20.00
L87 A7 3pi ol brn 3.00 2.00
a. Inverted overprint 12.50
b. Double overprint, one inverted 25.00
c. Vertical overprint 150.00
d. Dbl. ovpt., both invtd. 25.00
L88 A7 3pi dl red 4.00 3.00
a. Inverted overprint 12.50
b. Double overprint, one inverted 25.00
L89 A7 5pi ol grn 6.00 5.00
a. Inverted overprint 25.00

Black Overprint.

L90 A7 ⅛pi red brn 4.00 3.00
a. Inverted overprint 12.50
L91 A7 ½pi red 4.00 3.00
a. Inverted overprint 12.50
L92 A7 1pi dk bl 65.00 60.00
a. Inverted overprint 65.00
L93 A7 1½pi violet 4.00 4.00
a. Inverted overprint 12.50
L94 A7 2pi orange 3.00 2.00
a. Inverted overprint 12.50
L95 A7 3pi ol brn 6.00 5.00
a. Inverted overprint 17.50 15.00
L96 A7 3pi dl red 6.00 5.00
a. Inverted overprint 20.00
L97 A7 5pi ol grn 7.50 6.00
a. Inverted overprint 25.00

Red Overprint.

L98 A7 ⅛pi red brn, invtd. 50.00 40.00
L99 A7 ¼pi yel grn 6.00 5.00
a. Tête bêche pair 20.00
b. Inverted overprint 10.00
L100 A7 ½pi red 40.00 35.00
a. Inverted overprint 40.00
L101 A7 1pi dk bl 3.00 2.50
a. Inverted overprint 15.00
b. Double overprint, one invtd. 25.00
L102 A7 1½pi violet 3.00 2.50
a. Inverted overprint 15.00
L103 A7 2pi orange 3.00 2.50
a. Inverted overprint 10.00
b. Vertical overprint 175.00
L104 A7 3pi ol brn 5.00 4.00
a. Inverted overprint 15.00
L105 A7 3pi dl red, invtd. 75.00 70.00
L106 A7 5pi ol grn 4.00 3.00
a. Inverted overprint 20.00
b. Vertical overprint
L107 A8 10pi vio & dk brn 12.50 10.00
a. Inverted overprint 25.00
b. Center inverted 20.00
c. As "b," invtd. ovpt. *125.00*

Double overprint is also found on Nos. L87-L88, L94-L95, L100, L103-L105.

Gold Overprint.

L108 A7 ½pi red brn 20.00 20.00
a. Inverted overprint 30.00
L109 A7 ½pi red 20.00 20.00
L110 A7 1pi dk bl 20.00 20.00
L111 A7 1½pi violet 20.00 20.00
L112 A7 2pi orange 25.00 25.00
L113 A7 3pi ol brn 25.00 25.00
L114 A7 3pi dl red 25.00 25.00
L115 A7 5pi ol grn 25.00 25.00

Same Overprint on Nos. L42–L48

Blue Overprint.

L116 A7 ⅛pi red brn 8.00 8.00
a. Double ovpt., one inverted 50.00
b. Inverted overprint 25.00

L117	A7	½pi red	15.00	15.00
a.		Inverted overprint	25.00	
L118	A7	1pi dk bl	10.00	10.00
L119	A7	1½pi violet	12.00	12.00
L120	A7	2pi orange	18.00	18.00
a.		Inverted overprint	30.00	
L121	A7	3pi ol brn	20.00	20.00
a.		Inverted overprint	35.00	
L122	A7	5pi ol grn	8.00	8.00
a.		Inverted overprint	40.00	

Black Overprint

L123	A7	⅛pi red brn	8.00	8.00
a.		Inverted overprint	15.00	
L124	A7	½pi red	6.00	6.00
a.		Inverted overprint	15.00	
L125	A7	1½pi violet	12.00	12.00
a.		Inverted overprint	20.00	
L127	A7	3pi ol brn	10.00	10.00
a.		Inverted overprint	35.00	
L128	A7	5pi ol grn	10.00	10.00
a.		Inverted overprint	25.00	

Red Overprint.

L129	A7	1pi dk bl	20.00	20.00
L130	A7	1½pi violet	20.00	20.00
L131	A7	2pi orange	20.00	20.00

Experts question the authenticity of the ½pi red and 3pi brown with red overprint.

Stamps of 1922–24 Surcharged

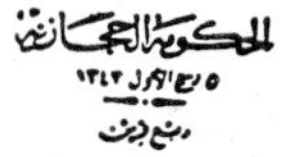

a

and Handstamped

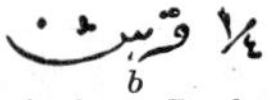

b

1925 Lithographed *Perf. 11½*

L135	A7	¼pi on ¼pi on ⅛pi red brn	8.00	8.00
b.		1 pi on ¼ pi on ⅛ pi red brn		
L136	A7	¼pi on ¼pi on ½pi red	8.00	8.00
a.		¼pi on 1pi on ½ pi, surch. invtd.	20.00	
L137	A7	1pi on ¼pi on ½pi red	60.00	60.00
L138	A7	1pi on 1pi on 2pi org	12.00	12.00
a.		¼pi on ¼pi on 2pi org		
b.		10pi on 1pi on 2pi org	100.00	
c.		¼pi on 1pi on 2pi org	50.00	
d.		1pi on ¼pi on 2pi org	*100.00*	
L139	A7	1pi on 1pi on 3pi ol brn	10.00	10.00
L140	A7	1pi on 1pi on 3pi dl red	10.00	10.00
b.		¼ pi on 1 pi on 3 pi dl red		
L141	A7	10pi on 10pi on 5pi ol grn	10.00	10.00
b.		on 10 pi on 5 pi		
		Nos. L135-L141 (7)	118.00	118.00

The printed surcharge (a) reads "The Hejaz Government. October 4, 1924." with new denomination in third line. This surcharge alone was used for the first issue (Nos. L135a—L141a). The new denomination was so small and indistinct that its equivalent in larger characters was soon added by handstamp (b) at bottom of each stamp for the second issue (Nos. L135—L141).

The handstamped surcharge (b) is found double, inverted, etc. It is also known in dark violet.

Without Handstamp "b"

L135a	A7	¼pi on ⅛pi red brn	25.00	25.00
L136b	A7	¼pi on ½pi red	25.00	25.00
L138e	A7	1pi on 2pi org	25.00	25.00
L139a	A7	1pi on 3pi ol brn	25.00	25.00
L140a	A7	1pi on 3pi dl red	25.00	25.00
L141a	A7	10 pi on 5pi ol grn	25.00	25.00

Stamps of 1922–24 Surcharged

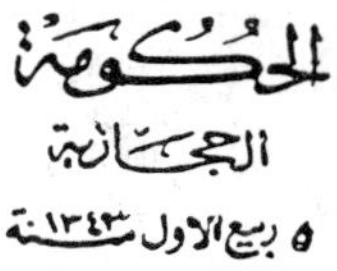

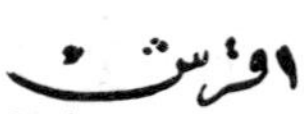

Black Surcharge

L142	A7	⅛pi on ½pi red	5.00	5.00
a.		Inverted surcharge	25.00	
L143	A7	¼pi on ½pi red	5.00	5.00
a.		Inverted surcharge	25.00	
L144	A7	1pi pi red	5.00	5.00
a.		Inverted surcharge	15.00	
L145	A7	1pi on 1½pi vio	5.00	5.00
a.		Inverted surcharge	15.00	
L146	A7	1pi on 2pi org	5.00	5.00
a.		"10pi"	75.00	
b.		Inverted surcharge	25.00	
L147	A7	1pi on 3pi ol brn	5.00	5.00
a.		"10pi"	75.00	
b.		Inverted surcharge	35.00	
L148	A7	10pi on 5pi ol grn	12.00	10.00
a.		Inverted surcharge	25.00	

Blue Surcharge.

L149	A7	⅛p on ½pi red	5.00	5.00
a.		Inverted surcharge	25.00	
L150	A7	¼pi on ½pi red	5.00	5.00
a.		Inverted surcharge	25.00	
L151	A7	1pi on ½pi red	5.00	5.00
a.		Inverted surcharge	25.00	
b.		Double surcharge		
L152	A7	1pi on 1½pi vio	5.00	5.00
a.		Inverted surcharge	25.00	
L153	A7	1pi on 2pi org	5.00	5.00
a.		"10pi"	30.00	
b.		Inverted surcharge	25.00	
L154	A7	1pi on 3pi ol brn	8.00	6.00
a.		"10pi"	45.00	
b.		Inverted surcharge	25.00	
L155	A7	10pi on 5pi ol grn	10.00	8.00
a.		Inverted surcharge	25.00	

Red Surcharge.

L156	A7	1pi on 1½pi vio	5.00	5.00
a.		Inverted surcharge	20.00	
L157	A7	1pi on 2pi org	5.00	5.00
a.		"10pi"	25.00	
b.		Inverted surcharge	20.00	
L158	A7	1pi on 3pi ol brn	6.00	5.00
a.		"10pi"	25.00	
b.		Inverted surcharge	20.00	
L159	A7	10pi on 5pi ol grn	6.00	5.00
a.		Inverted surcharge	25.00	

The "10pi" surcharge is found inverted on Nos. L146a, L147a, L153a, L154a, L157a and L158a.

King Ali Issue

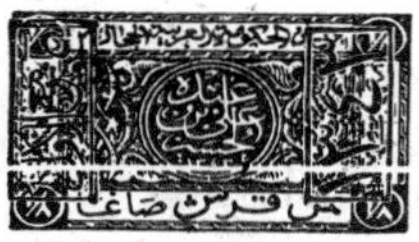

A9

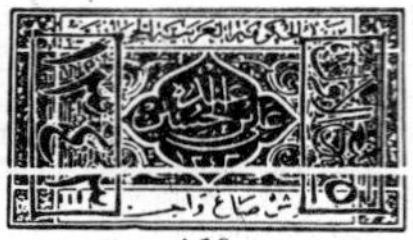

A10

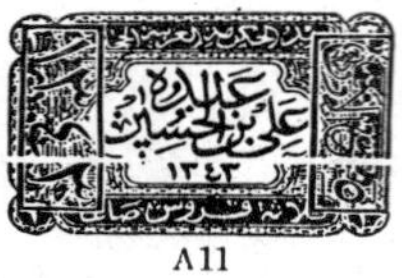

A11

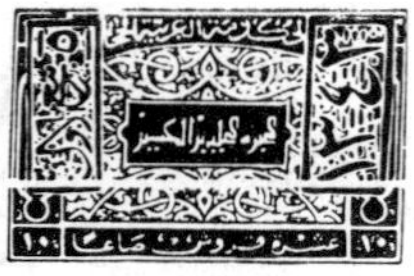

A12

1925, May–June *Perf. 11½*

Black Overprint.

L160	A9	⅛pi chocolate	60	60
L161	A9	¼pi ultra	60	60
L162	A9	½pi car rose	60	60
L163	A10	1pi yel grn	75	75
L164	A10	1½pi orange	75	75
L165	A10	2pi blue	90	90
L166	A11	3pi dk grn	1.00	1.00
L167	A11	5pi org brn	1.00	1.00
L168	A12	10pi red & grn	2.00	2.00
a.		Center inverted	25.00	

Red Overprint.

L169	A9	⅛pi chocolate	60	60
L170	A9	¼pi ultra	60	60
L171	A10	1pi yel grn	75	75
L172	A10	1½pi orange	75	75
L173	A10	2pi dp bl	90	90
L174	A11	3pi dk grn	1.00	1.00
a.		Imperf. vertically		
L175	A11	5pi org brn	1.00	1.00
L176	A12	10pi red & grn	2.00	2.00

Blue Overprint

L177	A9	⅛pi chocolate	60	60
L179	A9	½pi car rose	60	60
L180	A10	1pi yel grn	75	75
L181	A10	1½pi orange	75	75
L182	A11	3pi dk grn	90	90
L183	A11	5pi org brn	1.00	1.00
L184	A12	10pi red & grn	2.00	2.00
L185	A12	10pi red & org	100.00	*150.00*

Without Overprint.

L186	A12	10pi red & grn	2.00	2.00
a.		Double impression of center	*100.00*	

The overprint in the tablets on Nos. L160–L185 reads: "5 Rabi al' awwal, 1343" (Oct. 5, 1924), the date of the accession of King Ali.

The tablet overprints vary slightly in size. Each is found reading upward or downward and at either side of the stamp. These control overprints were first applied in Jedda by the government press. They were later made from new plates by the stamp printer in Cairo. In the Jedda overprint, the bar over the "0" figure extends to the left. The lines of the Cairo overprinting are generally heavier and the bar is at center right. Imperforates exist.

Nos. L160–L168 are known with the overprints spaced as on type D3 and aligned horizontally.

Copies of these stamps (perforated or imperforate) without the overprint, except No. L186 were not regularly issued and not available for postage.

No. L185 without overprint is a proof. Two sheets were overprinted by error and were put on sale with the ordinary stamps.

The ¼ pi with blue overprint is bogus.

Nejd

Handstamped in Blue, Red, Black or Violet

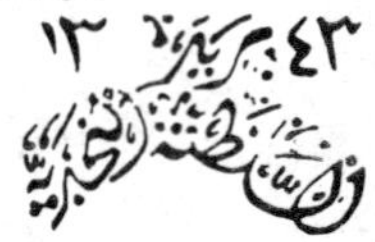

The overprint reads: "1343. Barid al Sultanat at Nejdia" (1925. Post of the Sultanate of Nejd).

The overprints on this and succeeding issues are handstamped and, as usual, are found double, inverted, etc. These variations are scarce.

Perf. 12

1925, March–April Unwmkd.

On Stamp of Turkey, 1915, With Crescent and Star in Red.

1	A22	5pa ocher (Bl)	30.00	30.00
2	A22	5pa ocher (R)	12.00	12.00
3	A22	5pa ocher (Bk)	12.00	12.00
4	A22	5pa ocher (V)	12.00	12.00

On Stamp of Turkey, 1913.

5	A28	10pa grn (Bl)	15.00	15.00
6	A28	10pa grn (R)	15.00	15.00

On Stamps of Hejaz, 1922-24.
Perf. 11½.

7	A7	⅛pi red brn (R)	17.50	17.50
8	A7	⅛pi red brn (Bk)	17.50	17.50
9	A7	⅛pi red brn (V)	17.50	17.50
10	A7	⅛pi car (R)	17.50	17.50
11	A7	⅛pi car (Bk)	17.50	17.50
12	A7	⅛pi car (V)	17.50	17.50
13	A7	½pi red (Bl)	10.00	10.00
14	A7	½pi red (V)	10.00	10.00
15	A7	1½pi vio (R)	17.50	17.50
16	A7	2pi yel buff (R)	35.00	35.00
a.		2pi org (R)	40.00	
17	A7	2pi yel buff (V)	35.00	35.00
a.		2pi org (V)	40.00	40.00
18	A7	3pi brn red (Bl)	17.50	17.50
19	A7	3pi brn red (R)	15.00	15.00
20	A7	3pi brn red (V)	12.00	15.00

Many Hejaz stamps of the 1922 type were especially printed for this and following issues. The re-impressions are usually more clearly printed, in lighter shades than the 1922 stamps, and some are in new colors.

Counterfeits exist.

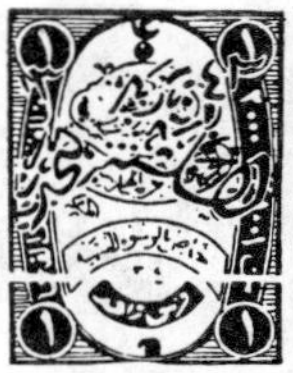

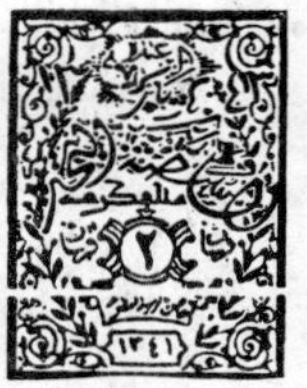

Arabic Inscriptions

R1 R2

On Hejaz Bill Stamp.

22	R1	1pi vio (R)	10.00	10.00

On Hejaz Notarial Stamps.

23	R2	1pi vio (R)	15.00	15.00
24	R2	2pi bl (R)	15.00	15.00
25	R2	2pi bl (V)	15.00	15.00

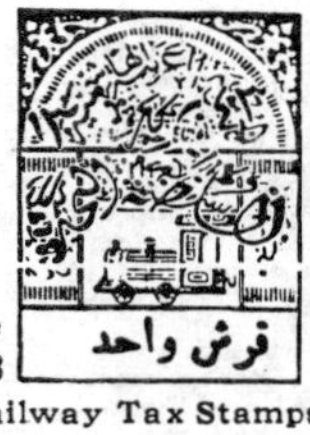

Locomotive

R3

On Hejaz Railway Tax Stamps

26	R3	1pi bl (R)	10.00	10.00
27	R3	2pi ocher (R)	15.00	15.00
28	R3	2pi ocher (V)	15.00	15.00
29	R3	3pi lil (R)	20.00	20.00
		Nos. 1-20, 22-29 (28)	468.00	471.00

There are two types of basic stamps.

Pilgrimage Issue.

Various Stamps Handstamp Surcharged in Blue and Red:

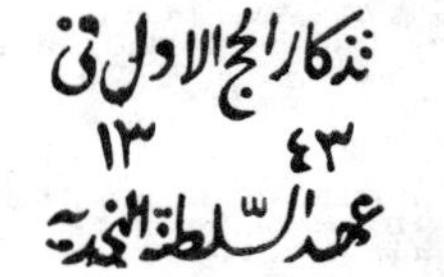

a

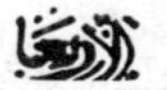

b

and Tablets with New Values.

Surcharge "a" reads: "Tezkar al Hajj al Awwal Fi 'ahd al Sultanat al Nejdia, 1343". (Commemorating the first pilgrimage under the Nejdi Sultanate, 1925).

Surcharge "b" reads: "Al Arba" (Wednesday.)

1925, July 1 *Perf. 12*

On Stamps of Turkey, 1913.
Perf. 12.

30	A28	1pi on 10pa grn (Bl & R)	45.00	45.00
31	A30	5pi on 1pi bl (Bl & R)	45.00	40.00

On Stamps of Hejaz, 1917-18.
Serrate Roulette 13.

32	A5	2pi on 1pa lil brn (R & Bl)	85.00	75.00
33	A4	4pi on ⅛pi org (R & Bl)	350.00	350.00

On Hejaz Railway Tax Stamp.
Perf. 11½.

34	R3	3pi lil (Bl & R)	45.00	40.00
		Nos. 30-34 (5)	570.00	550.00

Handstamped in Blue, Red, Black or Violet

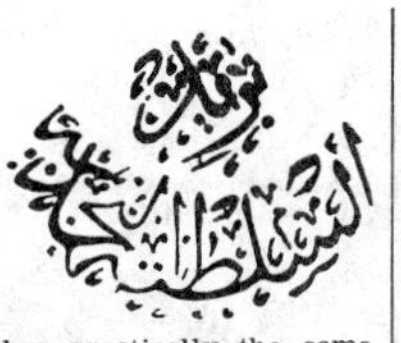

This overprint has practically the same meaning as that described over No. 1. The Mohammedan year (1343) is omitted.

1925, July-Aug. *Perf. 12*

On Stamp of Turkey, 1915, with Crescent and Star in Red.

35	A22	5pa ocher (Bl)	12.00	12.00

On Stamps of Turkey, 1913.

36	A28	10pa grn (Bl)	17.50	17.50
a.		Black ovpt.	80.00	

On Stamps of Hejaz, 1922. (Nos. L28–L29)

Serrate Roulette 13.

37	A3	1pi bl (R)	60.00	75.00
38	A6	2pi mag (Bl)	60.00	75.00

On Stamps of Hejaz, 1922-24.

Perf. 11½.

38A	A7	⅛pi red brn (Bk)	1,100.	
38B	A7	⅛pi red brn (Bl)	1,400.	
39	A7	½pi red (Bl)	10.00	10.00
a.		Imperf., pair	17.50	17.50
39B	A7	½pi red (Bk)	10.00	10.00
c.		Imperf., pair	17.50	17.50
40	A7	1pi gray vio (R)	15.00	15.00
a.		1pi blk vio (R)	15.00	
b.		Imperf., pair	50.00	
41	A7	1½pi dk red (Bk)	15.00	15.00
a.		1½pi brick red (Bk)	22.50	
42	A7	2pi yel buff (Bl)	35.00	35.00
a.		2pi org (Bl)	35.00	35.00
43	A7	2pi dp vio (Bl)	35.00	35.00
a.		Imperf., pair		
44	A7	3pi brn red (Bl)	12.00	12.00
a.		Imperf., pair		
45	A7	5pi scar (Bl)	17.50	17.50
a.		Imperf., pair		
		Nos. 35-38, 39-45 (12)	299.00	329.00

With Additional Surcharge of New Value Typographed in Black:

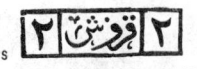

قرش واحد

c

قرش ونصف   قرشان ،

d   e

Color in parenthesis is that of overprint on basic stamp.

46	A7 (c)	1pi on ½pi red (Bl)	8.00	2.00
a.		Imperf., pair	17.00	
b.		Ovpt. & surch. invtd.		
47	A7 (d)	1½pi on ½pi red (Bl)	10.00	8.00
a.		Imperf., pair	30.00	
b.		Black ovpt.	14.00	
48	A7 (e)	2pi on 3pi brn red (Bl)	8.00	8.00

Several variations in type settings of "c," "d" and "e" exist, including inverted letters and values.

On Hejaz Notarial Stamp.

49	R2	2pi bl (Bk)	8.00	8.00

On Hejaz Railway Tax Stamps.

50	R3	1pi bl (R)	6.00	6.00
51	R3	1pi bl (Bk)	10.00	10.00
52	R3	2pi ocher (Bl)	8.00	8.00
53	R3	3pi lil (Bl)	15.00	15.00
54	R3	5pi grn (Bl)	10.00	10.00

Hejaz Railway Tax Stamp Handstamped in Black

السعوديه

السلطنه النجديه

This overprint reads: "Al Saudia.—Al Sultanat al Nejdia." (The Saudi Sultanate of Nejd.)

1925–26

55	R3	1pi blue	100.00	100.00

On Nos. L34, L36–L37, L41

55A	A7	½ pi red	500.00	
56	A7	1½pi violet	500.00	
a.		Violet overprint	500.00	
57	A7	2pi orange	500.00	
57A	A7	10pi on 5pi ol grn	500.00	

On Nos. L95 and L97

Color in parentheses is that of rectangular overprint on basic stamp.

58	A7	3pi ol brn (Bk)	500.00	
58A	A7	5pi ol grn (Bk)	500.00	

On Nos. L162–L163, L173

Perf. 11½

58B	A9	½pi car rose (Bk)	500.00	
58C	A10	1pi yel grn (Bk)	300.00	
58D	A10	2pi bl (R)	500.00	

Nos. 55–58D were provisionally issued at Medina after its capitulation.

Specialists question the status of unused examples of Nos. 55A-58D.

This overprint exists on Nos. L160–L161, L164–L172, L174–L175, L180–L183. These 17 are known as bogus items, but may exist genuine.

No. L161 (¼pi) is known with a similar but larger overprint.

Lithographed overprints are forgeries. The illustrated overprint is not genuine.

Medina Issue.

Hejaz Railway Tax Stamps Handstamped

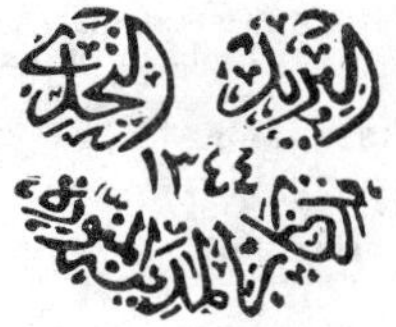

and Handstamp Surcharged in Various Colors

٢ قروش ٢

The large overprint reads: "The Nejdi Posts—1344—Commemorating Medina, the Illustrious". The tablet shows the new value.

1925

59	R3	1pi on 10pi vio (Bk & V)	40.00	50.00
60	R3	2pi on 50pi lt bl (R & Bl)	40.00	50.00
61	R3	3pi on 100pi red brn (Bl & Bk)	40.00	50.00
62	R3	4pi on 500pi dl red (Bl & Bk)	40.00	50.00
63	R3	5pi on 1000pi dp red (Bl & Bk)	40.00	50.00
		Nos. 59-63 (5)	200.00	250.00

Jedda Issue

Hejaz Railway Tax Stamps Handstamped and Tablet with New Value in Various Colors

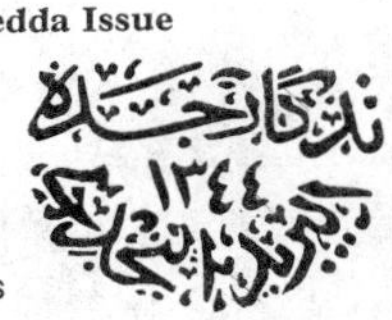

This handstamp reads: "Commemorating Jedda—1344—The Nejdi Posts".

1925

64	R3	1pi on 10pi vio (Bk & Bl)	30.00	35.00
65	R3	2pi on 50pi lt bl (R & Bk)	30.00	35.00
66	R3	3pi on 100pi red brn (R & Bl)	30.00	35.00
67	R3	4pi on 500pi dl red (Bk & Bl)	30.00	35.00
68	R3	5pi on 1000pi dp red (Bk & Bl)	30.00	35.00
		Nos. 64-68 (5)	150.00	175.00

Nos. 59–63 and 64–68 were prepared in anticipation of the surrender of Medina and Jedda.

Kingdom of Hejaz-Nejd

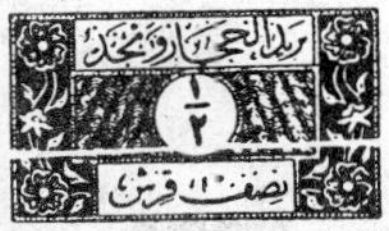

Arabic Inscriptions and Value

A1

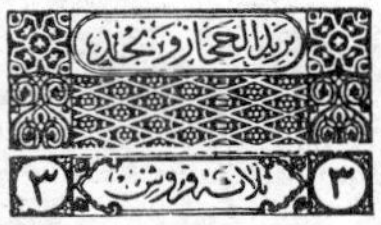

A2

Inscriptions in upper tablets: "Barid al Hejaz wa Nejd" (Posts of the Hejaz and Nejd)

Perf. 11

1926, Feb. Typographed Unwmkd.

69	A1	¼pi violet	4.00	4.00
70	A1	½pi gray	4.00	4.00
71	A1	1pi dp bl	6.50	5.00
72	A2	2pi bl grn	5.00	4.00
73	A2	3pi carmine	6.50	5.00
74	A2	5pi maroon	3.00	3.00
		Nos. 69-74 (6)	29.00	25.00

#69-71, 74 exist imperf. Price, each $25.

1926, Mar. *Perf. 11*

75	A1	¼pi orange	1.25	1.25
76	A1	½pi bl grn	75	75
77	A1	1pi carmine	60	60
78	A2	2pi violet	75	75
79	A2	3pi dk bl	75	75
80	A2	5pi lt brn	1.25	1.25
a.		5pi ol brn		
		Nos. 75-80 (6)	5.35	5.35

Nos. 75–80 also exist with perf. 14, 14x11, 11x14 and imperf. All of these sell for 10 times the prices quoted.

Counterfeits of types A1 and A2 are perf. 11½. They exist with and without overprints.

Types A1 and A2 in colors other than listed are proofs.

Pan-Islamic Congress Issue.

Stamps of 1926 Handstamped

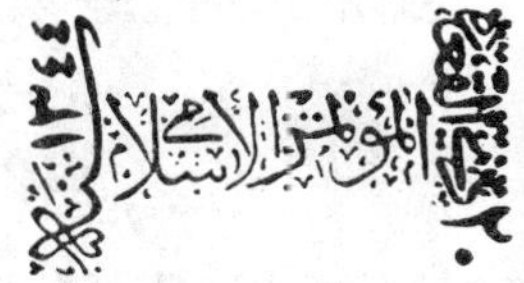

1926 *Perf. 11*

92	A1	¼pi orange	2.25	2.25
93	A1	½pi bl grn	2.25	2.25
94	A1	1pi carmine	2.25	2.25
95	A2	2pi violet	2.25	2.25
96	A2	3pi dk bl	2.25	2.25
97	A2	5pi lt brn	2.25	2.25
		Nos. 92-97 (6)	13.50	13.50

The overprint reads: "al Mootamar al Islami 20 Zilkada, Sanat 1344". (The Islamic Congress, June 1, 1926.)

See counterfeit note after No. 80.

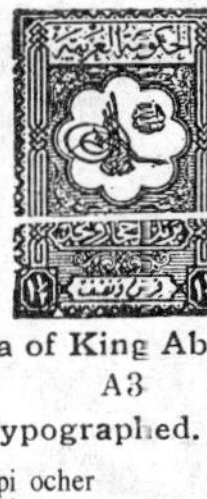

Tughra of King Abdul Aziz

A3

1926-27 Typographed. *Perf. 11½.*

98	A3	⅛pi ocher	3.50	50
99	A3	¼pi gray grn	3.50	50
100	A3	½pi dl red	3.50	50
101	A3	1pi dp vio	3.50	50
102	A3	1½pi gray bl	10.00	75
103	A3	3pi ol grn	9.00	1.25
104	A3	5pi brn org	15.00	1.75
105	A3	10pi dk brn	45.00	2.50
		Nos. 98-105 (8)	93.00	8.25

Inscription at top reads: "Al Hukumat al Arabia" (The Arabian Government). Inscription below tughra reads: "Barid al Hejaz wa Nejd" (Post of the Hejaz and Nejd).

Stamps of 1926-27 Handstamped in Black or Red

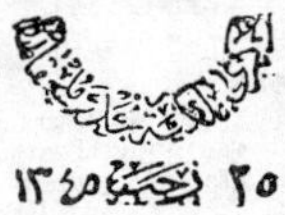

1927

107	A3	⅛pi ocher	10.00	10.00
108	A3	¼pi gray grn	10.00	10.00
109	A3	½pi dl red	10.00	10.00
110	A3	1pi dp vio	10.00	10.00
111	A3	1½pi gray bl (R)	10.00	10.00
112	A3	3pi ol grn	10.00	10.00
113	A3	5pi brn org	10.00	10.00
114	A3	10pi dk brn	10.00	10.00
		Nos. 107-114 (8)	80.00	80.00

The overprint reads: "In commemoration of the Kingdom of Nejd and Dependencies, 25th Rajab 1345".

Turkey No. 258 Surcharged in Violet

قرش واحد

1927 (?) *Perf. 12*

115	A28	1g on 10pa grn	175.00	

Similar surcharges of 6g and 20g were made in red, but were not known to have been issued.

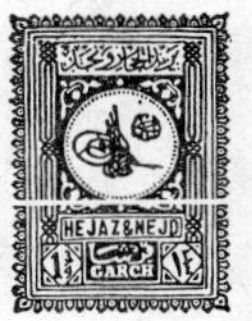

A4

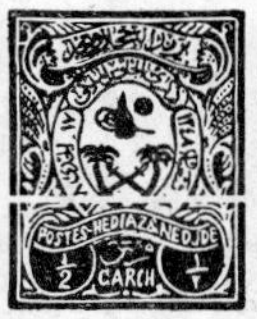

A5

1929–30 Typo. *Perf. 11½*

117	A4	1¾g gray bl	20.00	1.00
119	A4	20g violet	25.00	3.00
120	A4	30g green	40.00	5.00

1930 *Perf. 11, 11½*

125	A5	½g rose	10.00	3.00
126	A5	1½g violet	10.00	2.00
127	A5	1¾g ultra	10.00	2.50
128	A5	3½g emerald	10.00	4.00
129	A5	5g blk brn	15.00	6.00
		Nos. 125-129 (5)	55.00	17.50

Issued in commemoration of the anniversary of King Ibn Saud's accession to the throne of the Hejaz, January 8, 1926.

SAUDI ARABIA

A6   A7

1931-32			Perf. 11½	
130	A6	⅛g ocher ('32)	5.00	1.00
131	A6	¼g bl grn	5.00	75
133	A6	1¾g ultra	6.00	1.00

1932			Perf. 11, 11½	
135	A7	¼g bl grn	4.00	60
136	A7	½g scarlet	12.50	1.00
137	A7	2¼g ultra	25.00	1.25

Kingdom of Saudi Arabia

A8

1934, Jan.		Typo.	Perf. 11½, Imperf.	
138	A8	¼g yel grn	10.00	8.00
139	A8	½g red	10.00	8.00
140	A8	1½g lt bl	20.00	15.00
141	A8	3g bl grn	20.00	15.00
142	A8	3½g ultra	40.00	6.00
143	A8	5g yellow	50.00	30.00
144	A8	10g red org	100.00	
145	A8	20g brt vio	125.00	
146	A8	¼s claret	150.00	
147	A8	30g dl vio	150.00	
148	A8	½s chocolate	550.00	
149	A8	1s vio brn	1,100.	
Nos. 138-149 (12)			2,325.	

Proclamation of Emir Saud as Heir Apparent of Arabia. Perf. and imperf. stamps were issued in equal quantities.

Tughra of King Abdul Aziz
A9

1934-57			Perf. 11, 11½	
159	A9	⅛g yellow	2.00	6
160	A9	¼g yel grn	2.00	10
161	A9	½g dk car	2.00	8
a.		½g rose red ('43)	2.00	
162	A9	⅞g lt bl ('56)	3.00	8
163	A9	1g bl grn	2.00	8
164	A9	2g ol grn ('57)	2.00	8
a.		2g ol bis ('57)		
165	A9	2⅞g vio ('57)	3.00	15
166	A9	3g ultra ('38)	5.00	10
a.		3g lt bl	6.00	
167	A9	3½g lt ultra	11.00	75
168	A9	5g orange	5.00	12
169	A9	10g violet	12.50	50
170	A9	20g pur brn	9.00	40
a.		20g pur blk	17.50	2.00
171	A9	100g red vio ('42)	45.00	3.00
172	A9	200g vio brn ('42)	90.00	4.00
Nos. 159-172 (14)			193.50	9.50

The ½g has two types differing in position of the tughra.
No. 162 measures 31x22mm. No. 164 measures 30½x21½mm.; No. 165, 30½x22mm. No. 166 measures 30x21mm.; No. 171, 31x22mm.; No. 172, 30½x21½mm.; rest of set, 29x20½mm.

Grayish paper was used in 1946-49 printings.

Yanbu Harbor near Radwa
A10

1945		Typographed	Perf. 11½	
173	A10	½g brt car	6.00	25
174	A10	3g lt ultra	7.50	1.00
175	A10	5g purple	22.50	1.25
176	A10	10g dk brn vio	50.00	3.00

Meeting of King Abdul Aziz and King Farouk of Egypt at Jebal Radwa, Saudi Arabia, Jan. 24, 1945.

Type I   Type II
Map of Saudi Arabia
A11

Type I: Flag inscriptions intact.
Type II: Flag inscriptions scratched out.

1946		Perf. 11½	Unwmkd.	
177	A11	½g mag (II)	10.00	1.00
a.	Type I		15.00	
b.	Type I, perf. 11		20.00	6.00
c.	Type II, perf. 11		15.00	

Return of King Ibn Saud from Egypt.

Arms of Saudi Arabia and Afghanistan
A12

1950, Mar.			Perf. 11	
178	A12	½g carmine	1.00	1.00
179	A12	3g vio bl	7.50	1.50

Visit of Zahir Shah of Afghanistan, March 1950. One 3g in each sheet inscribed POSTFS, price $15.

Old City Walls, Riyadh
A13

1950   Center in Red Brown

180	A13	½g magenta	1.00	10
181	A13	1g lt bl	2.00	10
182	A13	3g violet	3.00	50
183	A13	5g vermilion	6.00	1.00
184	A13	10g green	10.00	2.50
a.	Singular "guerche" in Arabic		50.00	40.00
Nos. 180-184 (5)			22.00	4.20

Issued to commemorate the 50th lunar anniversary of King Ibn Saud's capture of Riyadh, Jan. 16, 1902.
No. 184a: On the 3g, 5g and 10g the currency is expressed in the plural in both French (grouche) and Arabic. One stamp in each sheet of 20 (4x5), position 11, of the 10g shows the Arabic characters in the singular form of "guerche," as on the ½g and 1g.

Arms of Saudi Arabia and Jordan
A14

1951, Nov.			Perf. 11	
185	A14	½g carmine	3.00	1.00
a.	"BOYAUME"		75.00	
186	A14	3g vio bl	5.00	1.50
a.	"BOYAUME"		75.00	

Visit of King Tallal of Jordan, Nov. 1951.

Bedouins and Train
A15

1952, June		Engraved	Perf. 12	
187	A15	½g redsh brn	2.50	75
188	A15	1g dp grn	2.50	75
189	A15	3g violet	5.00	50
190	A15	10g rose pink	10.00	3.50
191	A15	20g blue	20.00	7.50
Nos. 187-191 (5)			40.00	13.00

Issued to commemorate the inaugural trip over the Saudi Government Railroad between Riyadh and Dammam.

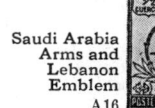 

Saudi Arabia Arms and Lebanon Emblem
A16

1953, Feb.		Typographed	Perf. 11	
192	A16	½g carmine	4.00	1.00
193	A16	3g vio bl	6.00	1.50

Issued to commemorate the visit of President Camille Chamoun of Lebanon.

Arms of Saudi Arabia and Emblem of Pakistan
A17

1953, Mar.				
194	A17	½g dk car	4.00	1.00
195	A17	3g vio bl	8.00	1.50

Visit of Gov.-Gen. Ghulam Mohammed of Pakistan.

Arms of Saudi Arabia and Jordan
A18

1953, July			Unwmkd.	
196	A18	½g carmine	3.00	1.00
a.	"GOERCHE"		75.00	
197	A18	3g vio bl	7.00	1.50

Visit of King Hussein of Jordan, July, 1953.

Globe
A18a

1955, July		Lithographed		
198	A18a	½g emerald	1.50	50
199	A18a	3g violet	5.00	1.00
200	A18a	4g orange	8.00	2.50

Issued to commemorate the founding of the Arab Postal Union, July 1, 1954.

Ministry of Communications Building, Riyadh—A19

1960, Apr. 12		Photo.	Perf. 13	
201	A19	2p brt bl	50	15
202	A19	5p dp cl	1.00	20
203	A19	10p dk grn	2.50	50

Arab Postal Union Conference, at Riyadh, Apr. 11. Imperfs. exist.

Arab League Center, Cairo
A20

1960, Mar. 22			Perf. 13x13½	
204	A20	2p dl grn & blk	40	20

Issued to commemorate the opening of the Arab League Center and the Arab Postal Museum in Cairo. Exists imperf.

Radio Tower and Waves
A21

1960, June 4				
205	A21	2p red & blk	1.25	25
206	A21	5p brn blk & mar	2.00	30
207	A21	10p bluish blk & ultra	3.50	70

Issued to commemorate the first international radio station in Saudi Arabia.

Map of Palestine, Refugee Camp and WRY Emblem
A22

1960, Oct. 30		Litho.	Perf. 13	
208	A22	2p dk bl	15	8
209	A22	8p lilac	35	12
210	A22	10p green	1.00	20

World Refugee Year, July 1, 1959—June 30, 1960. Imperfs. exist.

Wadi Hanifa Dam, near Riyadh   Gas-Oil Separating Plant, Buqqa
A23   A24

Type I (Saud Cartouche)
(Illustrated over No. 300)

Photogravure

1960-62		Perf. 14	Unwmkd.	
Size: 27½x22mm.				
211	A23	½p bis brn & org	1.00	10
211A	A23	1p ol bis & pur	1.00	10
212	A23	2p bl & sep	1.00	8
213	A23	3p sep & bl	1.00	6
214	A23	4p sep & ocher	1.00	8
215	A23	5p blk & dk vio	1.00	10

SAUDI ARABIA

216	A23	6p brn blk & car rose ('62)	1.00	20
a.		6p blk & car rose	1.25	35
217	A23	7p red & gray ol	1.00	15
217A	A23	8p dk bl & brn blk	1.00	30
217B	A23	9p org brn & scar	1.00	30
c.		9p yel brn & metallic red	1.25	50
218	A23	10p emer grn & mar ('62)	1.25	35
a.		10p bl grn & mar	1.50	75
219	A23	20p brn & grn	3.00	35
220	A23	50p blk & brn	15.00	1.00
221	A23	75p brn & gray	45.00	2.25
222	A23	100p dk bl & grn bl	35.00	2.50
223	A23	200p lil & grn	60.00	6.50
		Nos. 211-223 (16)	169.25	14.42

1960-61

224	A24	½p mar & org	1.00	10
225	A24	1p bl & red org	1.00	10
226	A24	2p ver & bl	1.00	10
227	A24	3p lil & brt grn	1.00	10
228	A24	4p yel grn & lil	1.00	8
229	A24	5p dk gray & brn red	1.00	10
230	A24	6p brn org & dk vio	1.00	10
231	A24	7p vio & dl grn	1.00	12
232	A24	8p brn & gray	1.00	20
233	A24	9p ultra & sep	3.00	20
234	A24	10p dk bl & rose	1.75	35
235	A24	20p org brn & blk	6.00	40
236	A24	50p red & brn grn	17.50	1.50
237	A24	75p red & blk brn	27.50	3.00
238	A24	100p dk bl & rose	40.00	2.75
239	A24	200p dk gray & ol grn	70.00	6.50
		Nos. 224-239 (16)	174.75	15.80

Nos. 211-211A, 213-218, 224-227, 230-239 exist imperf.; probably not regularly issued.
See also Nos. 255-270, 300-343D, 393-420A, 431-452.

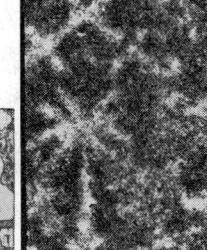

Dammam Port Wmk. 337
A25
Watermarked Crossed Swords and Palm Tree. (337)
1961, Aug. 16   Litho.   Perf. 13

240	A25	3p lilac	1.00	20
241	A25	6p lt bl	2.00	30
242	A25	8p dk grn	3.00	40

Expansion of the port of Dammam.
Imperf min. sheets of 4 exist. Set price, $75.

Globe, Radio and Telegraph
A26

Unwmkd.
1961, Aug. 7   Photo.   Perf. 13x13½

243	A26	3p dl pur	30	15
244	A26	6p gray blk	75	30
245	A26	8p brown	1.00	50

Arab Union of Telecommunications. Imperfs. exist.

Arab League Building, Cairo   **Malaria Eradication Emblem**
A27   **A28**
1962, Apr. 22   Perf. 13   Wmk. 337

246	A27	3p ol grn	50	20
247	A27	6p car rose	1.00	30
248	A27	8p sl bl	1.50	40

Arab League Week, Mar. 22-28.

Imperforate or missing-color varieties of Nos. 246-299 and 344-353 were not regularly issued, except No. 252a.

1962, May 7   Litho.   Wmk. 337

249	A28	3p red org & bl	50	15
250	A28	6p emer & Prus bl	75	25
251	A28	8p blk & lil rose	1.00	40
a.		Souv. sheet of 3	10.00	10.00

Issued for the World Health Organization drive to eradicate malaria.
No. 251a contains one each of Nos. 249-251, imperf., with marginal inscriptions in lilac rose. Size: 90x110mm.
Nos. 249-251 are known unofficially overprinted with new dates only, or with "AIR MAIL" and two plane silhouettes.
A 4p exists as an essay.

Koran
A29
1963, Mar. 12 Perf. 11 Wmk. 337

252	A29	2½p lil rose & pink	50	15
a.		Pink background omitted	150.00	
253	A29	7½p vio & pale grn	1.00	35
254	A29	9½p grn & gray	1.25	40

A 3p exists as an essay.
First anniversary of the Islamic Institute, Medina.

Dam Type of 1960 Redrawn
Type I (Saud Cartouche)
Lithographed
1963-65 Perf. 13½x13   Wmk. 337
Size: 28½x23mm.

255	A23	½p bis brn & org	5.00	15

Nos. 255 and 261-262 are widely spaced in the sheet, producing large margins.

Photogravure
Perf. 14
Size: 27½x22mm.

256	A23	½p bis brn & org ('65)	4.00	50
257	A23	3p sep & bl	5.00	50
258	A23	4p sep & ocher ('64)	6.00	1.00
259	A23	5p blk & dk vio	6.00	1.00
260	A23	20p dk car & grn	12.00	1.00
		Nos. 255-260 (6)	38.00	4.15

A 1p was prepared but not issued. It is known only imperf.

Gas-Oil Plant Type of 1960 Redrawn
Type I (Saud Cartouche)
Lithographed
1963-65   Perf. 13½x13   Wmk. 337
Size: 28½x23mm.

261	A24	½p mar & org	3.00	1.00
262	A24	1p bl & red crg ('64)	2.50	75

Photo.   Perf. 14
Size: 27½x22mm.

263	A24	½p mar & org ('64)	1.50	50
264	A24	1p bl & red crg	1.00	30
265	A24	3p lil & brt grn	2.50	30
266	A24	4p yel grn & lil	2.50	30
267	A24	5p dk gray & brn red	2.50	50
268	A24	6p brn org & dk vio ('65)	4.00	50
269	A24	8p dk bl & blk	5.00	75
270	A24	9p bl & sep	6.00	1.00
		Nos. 261-270 (10)	30.50	5.90

The 3p, 4p and 6p exist imperf.

Hands Holding Wheat Emblem
A30
1963, Mar. 21   Litho.   Perf. 11

287	A30	2½p lil rose & rose	25	10
288	A30	7½p brt lil & pink	75	30
289	A30	9p red brn & lt bl	1.00	35

Issued for the "Freedom from Hunger" campaign of the U.N. Food and Agriculture Organization. The 3p imperf. in this design is an essay.

Jet over Dhahran Airport   **Flame**
A31   **A32**
1963, July 27 Lithographed Perf. 13

290	A31	1p bl gray & ocher	50	10
291	A31	3½p ultra & emer	1.50	20
292	A31	6p emer & rose	1.75	25
a.		"Thahran" for "Dhahran" in Arabic	6.00	
293	A31	7½p lil rose & lt bl	1.75	30
294	A31	9½p ver & dl vio	2.50	40
		Nos. 290-294 (5)	8.00	1.25

Issued to commemorate the opening of the U.S.-financed terminal building at Dhahran Airport and the inauguration of international jet air service.
On No. 292a the misspelling consists of an omitted dot over character near top left in one horizontal row of five.

1964, Apr. Perf. 13x13½ Wmk. 337

296	A32	3p lil, pink & Prus bl	1.50	15
297	A32	6p yel grn, lt bl & Prus bl	2.00	25
298	A32	9p brn, buff & Prus bl	4.00	40

Issued to commemorate the 15th anniversary of the signing of the Universal Declaration of Human Rights.

King Faisal and Arms of Saudi Arabia—A33

1964, Nov.   Litho.   Perf. 13

299	A33	4p dk bl & emer	1.75	15

Issued to commemorate the installation of Prince Faisal ibn Abdul Aziz as King, Nov. 2, 1964.

King Saud's Cartouche Type I   **King Faisal's Cartouche Type II**

Redrawn Dam Type of 1960
Type I (Saud Cartouche)
Unwmkd.
1965-70   Lithographed   Perf. 14
Size: 27x22mm.

300	A23	1p ol bis & pur	3.00	10
301	A23	2p dk bl & sep ('66)	35	10
302	A23	3p sep & bl	60	10
303	A23	4p sep & ocher ('66)	60	15
304	A23	5p blk & dk vio	75	15
305	A23	6p blk & car rose ('68)	1.00	20
305A	A23	7p brn & gray ('68)	1.00	25
305B	A23	8p dk bl & gray ('68)	5.00	25
306	A23	9p org brn & scar ('68)	1.00	35
307	A23	10p bl grn & mar ('66)	65.00	30
308	A23	11p red & yel grn ('66)	2.00	40
309	A23	12p org & dk bl ('66)	2.00	40
310	A23	13p dk ol & rose ('66)	2.00	40
311	A23	14p org brn & yel grn ('66)	2.00	50
312	A23	15p sep & gray grn ('66)	2.00	50
313	A23	16p red & dl vio ('66)	3.00	75
314	A23	17p rose lil & dk bl ('66)	3.00	75
315	A23	18p grn & brt bl ('66)	3.00	75
316	A23	19p blk & bis ('66)	4.00	75
316A	A23	20p brn & ocher ('66)	4.00	75
317	A23	23p mar & lil	4.00	75
318	A23	24p ver & bl	4.00	60
319	A23	26p ol & yel	5.00	75
320	A23	27p ultra & red brn	5.00	1.00
321	A23	31p gray & dl bl	5.00	1.00
322	A23	33p ol grn & lil	5.00	1.00
322C	A23	100p dk bl & grnsh bl ('70)	55.00	3.00
322D	A23	200p dl lil & grn ('70)	55.00	3.50
		Nos. 300-322D (28)	243.30	19.35

Redrawn Gas-Oil Plant Type of 1960
1964-70   Lithographed   Unwmkd.
Type I (Saud Cartouche)
Size: 27x22mm.

323	A24	1p bl & red org ('66)	75	10
324	A24	2p ver & bl ('66)	75	10
325	A24	3p lil & brt grn	50	10
326	A24	4p yel grn & lil ('65)	60	15
326A	A24	5p dl gray vio & dk red brn ('66)	10.00	20
326B	A24	6p brn org & dk vio ('68)	1.50	20
326C	A24	7p vio & dl grn ('68)	1.00	25
327	A24	8p bl grn & gray ('65)	1.00	25
328	A24	9p ultra & sep ('65)	3.50	25
329	A24	10p dk bl & rose	75.00	60
330	A24	11p ol & org ('66)	1.50	50
331	A24	12p bis & grn ('66)	1.50	50
332	A24	13p rose red & dk bl ('66)	1.50	50
333	A24	14p vio & lt brn ('66)	2.00	50

497

SAUDI ARABIA

333A	A24	15p rose red & sep ('67)	2.50	50
334	A24	16p grn & rose red ('66)	2.50	50
335	A24	17p car rose & red brn ('66)	2.50	50
336	A24	18p gray & ultra ('66)	2.50	60
337	A24	19p brn & yel ('66)	2.50	70
337A	A24	20p dl org & dk gray ('66)	3.00	35
338	A24	23p org & car ('65)	4.00	30
339	A24	24p emer & org yel ('65)	4.00	60
340	A24	26p lil & red brn ('65)	5.00	75
341	A24	27p ver & dk gray ('65)	7.00	75
342	A24	31p dl grn & car ('65)	7.00	1.00
343	A24	33p red brn & gray ('65)	9.00	1.00
343A	A24	50p red brn & dl grn ('69)	80.00	1.25
343D	A24	200p dk gray & ol gray ('70)	27.50	2.50
		Nos. 323-343D (28)	260.10	15.50

Holy Kaaba, Mecca
A34

1965, Apr. 17   Perf. 13   Wmk. 337

344	A34	4p sal & blk	2.00	20
345	A34	6p brt pink & blk	4.00	25
346	A34	10p yel grn & blk	5.00	40

Issued to commemorate the Mecca Conference of the Moslem World League.

Arms of Saudi Arabia and Tunisia
A35

1965, Apr.   Lithographed

347	A35	4p car rose & sil	2.00	20
348	A35	8p red lil & sil	3.00	35
349	A35	10p ultra & sil	4.00	40

Issued to commemorate the visit of Pres. Habib Bourguiba of Tunisia, Feb. 22–26.

Highway, Hejaz Mountains
A36

1965, June 2   Perf. 13   Wmk. 337

350	A36	2p red & blk	1.00	30
351	A36	4p bl & blk	2.00	40
352	A36	6p lil & blk	2.50	50
353	A36	8p brt grn & blk	3.00	60

Opening of highway from Mecca to Tayif.

ICY Emblem—A37

1965, Nov. 13   Perf. 13   Unwmkd.

354	A37	1p yel & dk brn	1.00	5
355	A37	2p org & ol grn	1.00	10
356	A37	3p lt bl & gray	1.00	10
357	A37	4p yel grn & dk sl grn	1.00	20

358	A37	10p org & mag	2.00	50
		Nos. 354-358 (5)	6.00	95

International Cooperation Year, 1965.

ITU Emblem, Old and New Communication Equipment
A38

1965, Dec. 22   Litho.   Perf. 13

359	A38	3p bl & blk	1.00	10
360	A38	4p lil & blk	1.00	10
361	A38	8p emer & dk brn	1.00	35
362	A38	10p dl org & dk grn	1.00	40

Issued to commemorate the centenary of the International Telecommunication Union.

Library Aflame and Lamp
A39

1966, Jan.   Litho.   Perf. 12x12½

363	A39	1p orange	25	15
364	A39	2p dk red	25	15
365	A39	3p red vio	75	15
366	A39	4p violet	1.25	20
367	A39	5p lil rose	1.50	35
368	A39	6p vermilion	2.50	50
		Nos. 363-368 (6)	6.50	1.50

Issued to commemorate the burning of the Library of Algiers, June 2, 1962. Nos. 363-368 were withdrawn from sale Jan. 26, 1966, due to incorrect Arabic inscriptions. Later some values were inadvertently again placed in use.

Arab Postal Union Emblem
A40

Dagger in Map of Palestine
A41

1966, Mar. 15   Litho.   Perf. 14

369	A40	3p dl pur & ol	50	15
370	A40	4p dp bl & ol	50	15
371	A40	6p mar & ol	1.00	25
372	A40	7p dp grn & ol	1.00	35

Issued to commemorate the 10th anniversary (in 1964) of the Arab Postal Union. Printed in sheets of two panes, so horizontal gutter pairs exist.

1966, March 19   Litho.   Perf. 13

373	A41	2p yel grn & blk	1.00	15
374	A41	4p lt brn & blk	2.00	15
375	A41	6p dl bl & blk	3.00	25
376	A41	8p ocher & blk	4.00	35

Deir Yassin massacre, Apr. 9, 1948.

Emblems of World Boy Scout Conference and Saudi Arabian Scout Association
A42

1966, Mar. 23   Unwmkd.

377	A42	4p yel, blk, grn & gray	1.50	50
378	A42	8p yel, blk, org & lt bl	1.50	50
379	A42	10p yel, blk, sal & bl	2.00	75

Arab League Rover Moot (Boy Scout Jamboree).

WHO Headquarters, Geneva, and Flag
A43

1966, May   Litho.   Perf. 13

380	A43	4p aqua & multi	25	15
381	A43	6p yel brn & multi	75	25
382	A43	10p pink & multi	1.00	40

Issued to commemorate the inauguration of the World Health Organization Headquarters, Geneva.

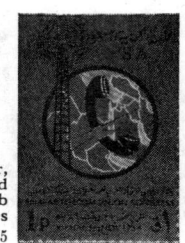

UNESCO Emblem
A44

1966, Sept.   Perf. 12   Unwmkd.

383	A44	1p ap grn & multi	25	5
384	A44	2p dl org & multi	25	10
385	A44	3p lil rose & multi	50	10
386	A44	4p pale grn & multi	50	15
387	A44	10p gray & multi	1.50	40
		Nos. 383-387 (5)	3.00	80

Issued to commemorate the 20th anniversary of UNESCO (United Nations Educational, Scientific and Cultural Organization).

Radio Tower, Telephone and Map of Arab Countries
A45

1966, Nov. 7   Litho.   Perf. 12½

Design in Black, Carmine & Yellow

388	A45	1p vio bl	25	10
389	A45	2p bluish lil	25	15
390	A45	4p rose lil	50	15
391	A45	6p lt ol grn	50	30
392	A45	7p gray grn	1.50	40
		Nos. 388-392 (5)	3.00	1.10

Issued to publicize the 8th Congress of the Arab Telecommunications Union, Riyadh.

**Redrawn Dam Type of 1960
Type II (Faisal Cartouche)**

(Illustrated over No. 300)

Unwmkd.

1966–76   Lithographed   Perf. 14

Size: 27x22mm.

393	A23	1p ol bis & pur	125.00	5
394	A23	2p dk bl & sep ('67)	30	10
395	A23	3p blk & dk bl ('68)	50	10
396	A23	4p sep & ocher ('68)	40	10
397	A23	5p blk & dk vio ('69)	17.50	20
398	A23	6p blk & car rose ('68)	17.50	20
399	A23	7p sep & gray ('68)	50	20
400	A23	8p dk bl & gray ('69)	1.50	30
400A	A23	9p org brn & scar ('70?)	2.00	30
401	A23	10p bl grn & mar ('67)	2.00	30
401A	A23	11p red & yel grn ('73)	2.00	35
401B	A23	12p org & dk bl ('72)	2.00	35
401C	A23	13p blk & rose ('75)	2.00	40
401D	A23	14p org brn & yel grn ('75)	1.50	35
401E	A23	15p sep & gray grn ('72)	3.00	50
401F	A23	16p dk red & dl vio ('72)	2.00	35
401G	A23	17p rose lil & dk bl ('74)	2.00	45
401H	A23	18p grn & brt bl ('76)	3.00	50
401I	A23	19p blk & bis ('75)	3.00	50
402	A23	20p brn & grn ('68)	22.50	35
402A	A23	23p mar & lil ('70)	90.00	35
402B	A23	24p ver & bl ('75)	22.50	35
402C	A23	26p ol & yel ('75)	5.00	60
402D	A23	27p ultra & red brn ('75)	5.00	60
402E	A23	33p ol grn & lil ('75)	5.00	60
402G	A23	50p blk & brn ('74)	8.00	1.00
402H	A23	100p dk bl & grnsh bl ('74)	70.00	2.00
402I	A23	200p dl lil & grn ('74)	80.00	3.00
		Nos. 393-402I (28)	495.70	14.45

A 31p has been reported.

**Redrawn Gas-Oil Plant Type of 1960
Type II (Faisal Cartouche)**

1966–78   Unwmkd.

Size: 27x22mm.

403	A24	1p bl & red org	10.00	5
404	A24	2p ver & dl bl	15	10
405	A24	3p lil & brt grn ('68)	15	10
406	A24	4p grn & dl lil	25	10
407	A24	5p dl gray vio & dk red brn ('68)	30	20
408	A24	6p brn org & dl pur ('68)	10.00	20
409	A24	7p vio & dl grn ('68)	50	20
410	A24	8p bl grn & grnsh gray ('68)	50	30
411	A24	9p ultra & sep ('68)	50	30
412	A24	10p dk bl & rose	1.50	30
413	A24	11p ol & org ('70)	10.00	35
413A	A24	12p bis & grn ('75)	2.00	35
413B	A24	13p rose red & dk bl ('73)	2.00	40
414	A24	14p vio & lt brn ('70)	2.00	40
415	A24	15p car & sep ('68)	2.00	35
416	A24	16p grn & rose red ('68)	2.00	60
416A	A24	17p car rose & red brn ('75)	2.00	50
417	A24	18p gray & ultra ('73)	2.00	50
417A	A24	19p brn & yel ('74)	2.00	50
418	A24	20p brn org & gray ('67)	2.00	50
418A	A24	23p org & car	10.00	40
419	A24	24p emer & org yel ('73)	3.00	50
419A	A24	26p lil & red brn ('78?)	100.00	
419B	A24	27p ver & dk gray ('75)	6.00	75
419C	A24	31p grn & rose car ('75)	6.00	60
419D	A24	33p brn & gray ('75)	6.00	60
419E	A24	50p red brn & dl grn ('74)	90.00	1.00
420	A24	100p dk bl & red brn ('69)	70.00	2.00
420A	A24	200p dk gray & ol gray ('70)	135.00	2.50
		#403-419, 419B-420A (28)	377.85	14.75

SAUDI ARABIA

Emblem of Saudi Arabian Scout Association	Meteorological Instruments and WMO Emblem
A46	A47

1967, Mar. 28 Litho. Perf. 13½
Emblem in Green, Red, Yellow & Black

421	A46	1p dk bl & blk	1.00	15
422	A46	2p bl grn & blk	1.00	15
423	A46	3p lt bl & blk	1.00	15
424	A46	4p rose brn & blk	2.00	15
425	A46	10p brn & blk	4.00	50
		Nos. 421-425 (5)	9.00	1.10

2nd Arabic League Rover Moot, Mecca, March 13–28.

1967, July Perf. 13 Unwmkd.

426	A47	1p brt mag	1.00	5
427	A47	2p violet	1.00	10
428	A47	3p olive	1.00	10
429	A47	4p bl grn	1.00	10
430	A47	10p blue	2.00	35
		Nos. 426-430 (5)	6.00	70

Issued for World Meteorological Day.

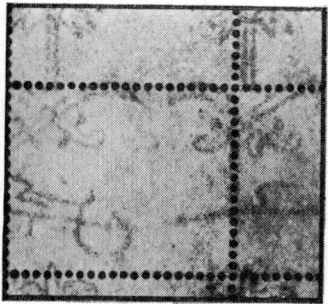

Wmk. 361
Watermarked Crossed Swords, Palm Tree and Arabic Inscription (361)
Redrawn Dam Type of 1960
Type II (Faisal Cartouche)
Lithographed

1968-76 Perf. 14 Wmk. 361

431	A23	1p ol bis & pur ('71)	225.00	150.00
432	A23	2p dk bl & sep	6.00	5
433	A23	3p blk & dk bl ('69)	5.00	5
434	A23	4p sep & ocher ('73)	17.50	10
435	A23	5p blk & dk vio ('71)	7.00	12
436	A23	6p blk & car rose ('71)	4.00	15
437	A23	7p sep & gray ('72)	4.00	16
438	A23	8p bl bl & gray ('71)	4.00	25
438A	A23	9p org brn & ver ('76)	4.00	25
439	A23	10p bl grn & mar	8.00	30
440	A23	11p red & yel grn ('72)	17.50	
441	A23	12p org & sl bl ('72)	9.00	35
441A	A23	13p blk & rose ('74)	8.00	35
		Nos. 432-441A (12)	95.00	

Redrawn Gas-Oil Plant Type of 1960
1968-76 Type II Perf. 14

442	A24	1p bl & red org	15	5
443	A24	2p ver & dl bl	15	5
445	A24	4p grn & dl lil	17.50	5
446	A24	5p dk brn & red brn ('73)	1.25	15
447	A24	6p brn org & dk vio ('73)	1.25	17
448	A24	9p dk bl & sep ('76)	3.00	25
449	A24	10p dk bl & rose	1.50	30
450	A24	11p ol & org ('72)	1.25	32
451	A24	12p bis & grn ('72)	1.25	35
452	A24	23p org & car ('74)	2.00	45
		Nos. 442-452 (10)	29.30	2.14

Map Showing Dammam to Jedda Road, and Dates
A48
Lithographed

1968, Aug. Perf. 14 Wmk. 361

453	A48	1p yel & multi	25	5
454	A48	2p org & multi	25	10
455	A48	3p multi	50	10
456	A48	4p multi	50	10
457	A48	10p multi	1.50	40
		Nos. 453-457 (5)	3.00	75

Issued to commemorate the completion of the trans-Saudi Arabia highway in 1967.

Prophet's Mosque, Medina—A49	New Arcade, Mecca Mosque A50

Perf. 13½x14
1968-76 Litho. Wmk. 361

458	A49	1p org & grn wmk. 337 ('70)	1.50	10
459	A49	2p red brn & grn ('72)	1.50	10
a.		Wmk. 337 ('71)	1.50	10
460	A49	3p vio & grn ('72)	1.50	15
a.		Wmk. 337 ('70)	1.50	15
461	A49	4p ocher & grn	1.50	15
a.		Wmk. 337 ('71)	1.50	15
462	A49	5p dp lil rose & grn wmk. 337 ('71)	7.50	15
463	A49	6p blk & grn ('73)	7.50	1.00
a.		6p gray & grn ('76)	7.50	25
467	A49	10p brn & grn	7.50	50
477	A49	20p dk brn & grn ('70)	7.50	75
484	A49	50p sep & grn ('75)	10.00	1.00
485	A49	100p dk bl & grn ('75)	20.00	1.00
486	A49	200p red & grn ('75)	30.00	3.50
		Nos. 458-486 (11)	96.00	8.40

1968-69

489	A50	3p dp org & gray ('69)	125.00	25.00
490	A50	4p grn & gray	1.50	15
496	A50	10p mag & gray	6.00	1.00

Expansion of Prophet's Mosque—A51	Madayin Saleh A52

1968-76

507	A51	1p org & grn ('72)	1.50	10
a.		Wmk. 337	1.50	10
508	A51	2p brn & grn ('72)	1.50	10
a.		Wmk. 337 ('73)	1.50	15
509	A51	3p blk & grn ('69)	1.50	25
a.		Wmk. 337 ('71)	1.50	10
b.		3p gray & grn ('76)	1.50	10
510	A51	4p vio & grn ('70)	1.50	10
a.		Wmk. 337 ('72)	1.50	10
511	A51	5p red & grn ('74)	1.50	35
a.		Wmk. 337 ('70)	1.50	25
512	A51	6p Prus bl & grn ('72)	1.50	40
a.		Wmk. 337 ('72)	1.50	40
514	A51	8p rose red & grn ('76)	2.00	30
516	A51	10p brn red & grn ('70)	3.00	60
a.		Wmk. 337	4.00	1.00
b.		10p org & grn ('76)	3.00	80
524	A51	20p vio & grn ('74)	5.00	90
a.		Wmk. 337 ('72)	5.00	80
		Nos. 507-524(9)	20.50	3.30

1968-75

528	A52	2p ultra & bis brn ('70)	12.00	10
530	A52	4p dk & lt brn	1.50	15
533	A52	7p org & lt brn ('75)	20.00	25
536	A52	10p sl grn & lt brn	7.50	40
546	A52	20p lil rose & brn ('71)	6.00	50

 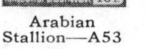

Arabian Stallion—A53	Camels and Oil Derrick A54

550	A53	4p mag & org brn	1.50	15
556	A53	10p blk & org brn	4.00	50
560	A53	14p bl & ocher ('71)	5.00	50
566	A53	20p ol grn & ocher ('71)	6.00	60

1969-71

571	A54	4p dk pur & redsh brn ('71)	5.00	10
577	A54	10p ultra & hn brn	6.00	40

Holy Kaaba, Mecca
A55
Numeral & "Postage" on Gray Background, 8p on White

1969-75

591	A55	4p dp grn & blk ('70)	3.00	25
a.		Value corner white ('74)	1.50	15
593	A55	6p dp lil rose & blk ('71)	1.50	20
a.		Value corner white ('74)	1.50	20
595	A55	8p red & blk ('75)	1.50	35
597	A55	10p org & blk ('69)	7.50	1.25
a.		Value corner white ('74)	1.00	40

Some of Nos. 458-597 were issued in two types differing in a redrawing of the border inscriptions (value numerals, "P." or "P", thin or thick lettering, "AB" of "ARABIA" joined, etc.).

Rover Moot Badge—A56

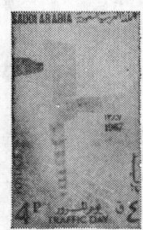

Traffic Light and Intersection
A57

Perf. 13½x14
1969, Feb. 19 Litho. Wmk. 337

607	A56	1p org & multi	50	10
608	A56	4p dl pur & multi	1.50	20
609	A56	10p org brn & multi	5.00	60

3rd Arab League Rover Moot, Mecca, Feb. 19–Mar. 3.

1969, Feb. Perf. 13½ Wmk. 361

610	A57	3p dl bl, red & brt bl grn	50	15
a.		3p dl bl, red & gray grn		
611	A57	4p org brn, red & gray grn	50	15
612	A57	10p dl pur, red & gray grn	1.00	50

Issued for Traffic Day.

WHO Emblem
A58

1969 Perf. 14 Wmk. 337

| 613 | A58 | 4p lt bl, vio bl & yel | 3.00 | 15 |

20th anniversary (in 1968) of World Health Organization.

Islamic Conference Emblem
A59

1970, Mar. Litho. Wmk. 361

614	A59	4p bl & blk	50	15
615	A59	10p yel bis & blk	1.00	45

Islamic Conference of Foreign Ministers, Jedda, March 1970.

A well informed dealer can help the collector build his collection. He is the one to turn to when philatelic property must be sold.

A little time given to study of the arrangement of the Scott Catalogue can make it easier to use effectively.

SAUDI ARABIA

Open Book and Satellite Earth Receiving Station
A60

Wmk. 337

1970, Aug. 1   Litho.   Perf. 14x13½
616 A60   4p vio bl & multi   50   15
617 A60   10p grn & multi   1.00   50
World Telecommunications Day.

Steel Rolling Mill, Jedda
A61

1970, Oct. 26 Perf. 13½ Wmk. 337
618 A61   3p yel org & multi   50   10
619 A61   4p vio & multi   1.00   15
620 A61   10p brt grn & multi   1.50   50
Inauguration of first steel mill in Saudi Arabia.

Rover Moot Emblem
A62

1971, Feb.   Litho.   Perf. 14
621 A62   10p brt bl & multi   2.00   75
4th Arab League Rover Moot, 1971.

Telecommunications Symbol
A63

1971, May 17 Perf. 14 Wmk. 337
622 A63   4p bl & blk   50   15
623 A63   10p lil & blk   1.00   40
World Telecommunications Day.

University Minaret
A64

Arab League Emblem
A65

Wmk. 337; Wmk. 361 (4p)
1971, Aug.   Litho.   Perf. 14
624 A64   3p brt grn & blk   50   10
625 A64   4p brn & blk   75   15
626 A64   10p bl & blk   2.00   50
King Abdul Aziz National University.

1971, Nov.   Perf. 13½   Wmk. 337
627 A65   10p multi   1.00   40
Arab League Week.

Education Year Emblem
A66

OPEC Emblem
A67

1971, Nov.   Lithographed
628 A66   4p ap grn & brn red   30   15
International Education Year 1970.

1971, Dec.   Perf. 14
629 A67   4p lt bl   75   15
10th anniversary of OPEC (Organization of Petroleum Exporting Countries).

Globe
A63

1972, Aug.   Perf. 14   Wmk. 361
630 A68   4p multi   1.00   12
4th World Telecommunications Day.

Telephone
A69

1972, Oct.   Wmk. 337, 361 (5p)
631 A69   1p red, blk & grn   50   5
632 A69   4p dk grn, blk & grn   50   15
633 A69   5p lil, blk & grn   1.00   20
634 A69   10p tan, blk & grn   2.00   50
Inauguration of automatic telephone system (1969).

Writing Hand
A70

1972, Sept. 8   Litho.   Wmk. 361
635 A70   10p multi   1.00   35
World Literacy Day, Sept. 8.

Holy Kaaba and Grand Mosque, Mecca
A71

Designs (Rover Moot Emblem and): 4p, Prophet's Mosque, Medina. 10p, Plains of Arafat.

1973
636 A71   4p lt bl & multi   1.00   20
637 A71   6p lil & multi   2.00   30
638 A71   10p sal & multi   3.00   60
5th Arab League Rover Moot.

Globe and Map of Palestine—A71a

1973   Litho.   Perf. 14   Wmk. 361
639 A71a 4p blk, yel & red   50   15
640 A71a 10p bl, yel & red   1.00   40
Palestine Week.

Leaf and Emblem
A72

1973
641 A72   4p yel & multi   1.00   25
International Hydrological Decade 1965–74.

Arab Postal Union Emblem
A73

1973, Dec.   Lithographed   Perf. 14
642 A73   4p sep & multi   1.00   25
643 A73   10p pur & multi   2.00   50
25th anniversary (in 1971) of the Conference of Sofar, Lebanon, establishing the Arab Postal Union.

Balloons and Pacifier
A74

1973, Dec.
644 A74   4p lt bl & multi   50   15
Universal Children's Day (stamp dated 1971).

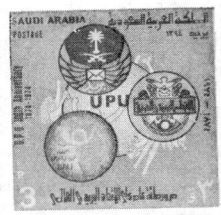

Arab Postal and UPU Emblems
A75

1974, July 7   Perf. 14   Wmk. 361
645 A75   3p yel & multi   10.00 2.50
646 A75   4p rose & multi   15.00 5.00
647 A75   10p lt grn & multi   20.00 7.50
Centenary of the Universal Postal Union.

Handshake and UNESCO Emblem—A76

1974, May 21   Perf. 13½
648 A76   4p org & multi   1.50   25
649 A76   10p grn & multi   3.50   75
International Book Year, 1972.

Desalination Plant
A77

1974, Sept. 3   Perf. 14   Wmk. 361
650 A77   4p dp org & bl   50   15
651 A77   6p emer & vio   1.00   25
652 A77   10p rose red & blk   1.50   50
Opening (in 1971) of sea water desalination plant, Jedda.

INTERPOL Emblem
A78

SAUDI ARABIA

1974, Nov. 1

653	A78	4p ocher & ultra	50	20
654	A78	10p emer & ultra	1.00	50

50th anniversary (in 1973) of International Criminal Police Organization.

APU Emblem, Tower and Letter — A79

1974, Oct. 26 Litho. Wmk. 361

| 655 | A79 | 4p multi | 35 | 15 |

Arab Consultative Council for Postal Studies, 3rd session.

UPU Headquarters, Bern — A80

1974, Nov. 15 Perf. 13½

656	A80	3p org & multi	1.00	25
657	A80	4p lil & multi	2.00	50
658	A80	10p bl & multi	5.00	1.25

Opening of new Universal Postal Union Headquarters, Bern, May 1970.

Tank, Planes, Rockets and Flame — A81

1974, Dec. 15 Perf. 14

659	A81	3p sl & multi	30	15
660	A81	4p brn & multi	50	25
661	A81	10p lil & multi	1.50	75

King Faisal Military Cantonment, 1971.

Red Crescent Flower — A82

1974, Dec. 17 Perf. 14x14½

662	A82	4p gray & multi	50	25
663	A82	6p lt gn & multi	1.00	50
664	A82	10p lt bl & multi	2.25	1.00

Saudi Arabian Red Crescent Society, 10th anniversary (in 1973).

Saudi Arabian Scout Emblem and Minarets — A83

1974, Dec. 23 Perf. 14 Wmk. 361

665	A83	4p brn & multi	50	20
666	A83	6p bl blk & multi	1.00	30
667	A83	10p pur & multi	1.50	60

6th Arab League Rover Moot, Mecca.

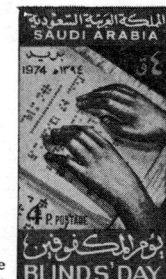

Reading Braille — A84

1975, Mar. 31 Perf. 14x13½

| 668 | A84 | 4p multi | 50 | 25 |
| 669 | A84 | 10p multi | 1.00 | 50 |

Day of the Blind.

Anemometer and Weather Balloon with UN Emblem — A85

Perf. 13½x14

1975, May 8 Litho. Wmk. 361

| 670 | A85 | 4p multi | 50 | 25 |

Centenary (in 1973) of International Meteorological Cooperation.

King Faisal — A86 Conference Emblem — A87

1975, July 6 Perf. 14 Unwmkd.

671	A86	4p grn & rose brn	50	25
672	A86	16p vio & grn	1.50	75
673	A86	23p dk grn & vio	2.50	1.25

Miniature Sheet

Imperf.

| 674 | A86 | 40p Prus bl & ocher | 350.00 |

King Faisal ibn Abdul-Aziz Al Saud (1906–1975). Size of No. 674: 71x80 mm.

1975, July 11 Perf. 14

| 675 | A87 | 10p rose brn & blk | 1.00 | 50 |

6th Islamic Conference of Foreign Ministers, Jedda, July 12.

Wheat and Sun — A88

1975, Sept. 17 Litho. Wmk. 361

| 676 | A88 | 4p lil & mu ti | 40 | 20 |
| 677 | A88 | 10p bl & mu ti | 75 | 40 |

Charity Society, 20th anniversary.

Holy Kaaba, Globe, Clasped Hands — A89

1975, Sept. 17 Perf. 14

| 678 | A89 | 4p ol bis & multi | 30 | 15 |
| 679 | A89 | 10p org & multi | 70 | 35 |

Conference of Moslem Organizations, Mecca, Apr. 6–10, 1974.

Saudia Tri-Star and DC-3 — A90

1975, Sept. Litho. Unwmkd.

| 680 | A90 | 4p buff & multi | 50 | 25 |
| 681 | A90 | 10p lt bl & multi | 1.00 | 50 |

Saudia, Saudi Arabian Airline, 30th anniversary.

Conference Centers in Mecca and Riyadh — A91

1975, Sept. Perf. 14

| 682 | A91 | 10p multi | 1.10 | 50 |

Friday Mosque, Medina, and Juwatha Mosque, al-Hasa — A92

1975, Oct. 26 Litho. Unwmkd.

| 683 | A92 | 4p grn & multi | 50 | 25 |
| 684 | A92 | 10p ver & multi | 1.25 | 50 |

Ancient Islamic holy places.

FAO Emblem — A93

1975, Oct. 26

| 685 | A93 | 4p gray & multi | 40 | 20 |
| 686 | A93 | 10p buff & multi | 1.00 | 50 |

World Food Program, 10th anniversary (in 1973). Stamps are dated 1973.

Conference Emblem — A94

1976, Mar. 20 Perf. 14 Unwmkd.

| 687 | A94 | 4p multi | 50 | 25 |

Islamic Solidarity Conference of Science and Technology.

Saudi Arabia Map, Transmission Tower, TV Screen — A95

1976, May 26 Litho. Perf. 14

| 688 | A95 | 4p multi | 50 | 25 |

Saudi Arabian television, 10th anniversary.

Grain, Atom Symbol, Graph — A96

1976, June 28 Litho. Perf. 14

| 689 | A96 | 20h yel & multi | 50 | 25 |
| 690 | A96 | 50h yel & multi | 1.00 | 50 |

Second Five-year Plan.

Holy Kaaba — A97

Two types:
I. "White" minarets. Gray vignette.
II. Black minarets and vignette. Design redrawn, strengthened, darkened, clarified.

Wmk. 361

1976–79 Lithographed Perf. 14
Type II

| 691 | A97 | 5h lil & blk ('78) | 10 | 5 |
| 692 | A97 | 10h lt vio & blk ('78) | 20 | 10 |

SAUDI ARABIA

693	A97	15h sal & blk ('78)		50	15
a.		Type I		15	8
694	A97	20h lt bl & blk, I ('77)		50	15
a.		Type II		50	15
695	A97	25h yel & blk ('78)		50	20
696	A97	30h gray grn & blk ('78)		60	25
697	A97	35h bis & blk ('78)		35	18
698	A97	40h lt grn & blk ('78)		1.50	50
a.		Type I ('77)		40	20
b.		Imperf, pair, II			
699	A97	45h dl rose & blk ('78)		45	22
700	A97	50h pink & blk ('78)		50	25
703	A97	65h gray bl & blk ('79)		65	32
710	A97	1r lt yel grn & blk ('78)		1.00	50
711	A97	2r grn & blk ('79)		2.00	1.00
		Nos. 691-711 (13)		8.85	3.87

Imperfs of Nos. 691—711 other than No. 698b were not regularly issued.

Quba Mosque, Medina, built 622 — A98

1976-77
719	A98	20h org & blk	30	15
720	A98	50h emer & lil ('77)	70	30

Reissued in 1978 in different shades.

Globe, Telephones 1876 and 1976 — A100

1976, July 17 Perf. 13½ Unwmkd.
721	A100	50h multi	50	30

Centenary of first telephone call by Alexander Graham Bell, Mar. 10, 1876.

Arab Leaders — A101

1976, Oct. 30 Litho. Perf. 14
722	A101	20h ultra & emer	50	25

Arab Summit Conference, Riyadh, October. Leaders pictured: Pres. Elias Sarkis, Lebanon; Pres. Anwar Sadat, Egypt; Pres. Hafez al Assad, Syria; King Khalid, Saudi Arabia; Amir Sabah, Kuwait; Yasir Arafat, Palestine Liberation Organization chairman.

WHO Emblem and Eye — A102

1976, Nov. 28 Litho. Perf. 14
723	A102	20h multi	35	15

World Health Day; Prevention of Blindness.

Holy Kaaba — A103

1976, Nov. 28 Unwmkd.
724	A103	20h multi	40	20

50th anniversary of installation of new covering of Holy Kaaba, Mecca.

Conference Emblem — A104

Perf. 14
1977, Feb. 18 Litho. Unwmkd.
725	A104	20h multi	30	15

Islamic Jurisprudence Conference, Riyadh, Oct. 24–Nov. 2, 1976.

Sharia College Emblem — A105

1977, Feb. 25 Perf. 14
726	A105	4p multi	30	15

25th anniversary (in 1974) of the founding of Sharia (Islamic Law) College, Mecca.

King Khalid ibn Abdul-Aziz — A106

1977
727	A106	20h dk brn & brt grn	30	15
a.		Incorrect date	40.00	
728	A106	80h bl blk & brt grn	1.00	50
a.		Incorrect date	40.00	

2nd anniversary of installation of King Khalid ibn Abdul-Aziz. Nos. 727a–728a (illustrated), issued Mar. 3, have incorrect Arabic date in bottom panel, last characters of 2nd and 3rd rows identical "ir." Stamps withdrawn after a few days and replaced Aug. 14 with corrected date, last characters in 3rd row changed to "ro."

Diesel Train and Map of Route — A107

1977, May 23 Litho. Perf. 14
729	A107	20h multi	30	15

Dammam-Riyadh railroad, 25th anniversary.

Arabic Ornament and Names — A108

Designs (Names from Left to Right): UL, Malik Ben Anas (715–795). UR, Mohammad Ben Idris Al-Shafi'i (767–820). LL, Abu Hanifa an-Nu'man (699–767). LR, Ahmed Ben Hanbel (780–855).

1977, Aug. 15 Litho. Perf. 14
730	A108	Block of 4, multi	1.25	65
a.		20h, single stamp	20	10

Famous Imams (7th–9th centuries), founders of traditional schools of Islamic jurisprudence. Sheets of 60.

Al Khafji Oil Rig — A109

Wmk. 361
1976 Lithographed Perf. 14
731	A109	5h vio bl & org	10	5
732	A109	10h yel grn & org	15	5
733	A109	15h brn & org	20	8
734	A109	20h grn & org	30	10
735	A109	25h dk pur & org	35	12
736	A109	30h bl & org	40	15
737	A109	35h sep & org	50	18
a.		Imperf, pair		
738	A109	40h mag & org	50	20
a.		40h dl pur & org		
739	A109	45h vio & org	60	22
740	A109	50h rose & org	75	25
a.		50h dl org & org (error)	10.00	
741	A109	55h grnsh bl & org	10.00	50
743	A109	65h sep & org	1.00	35
750	A109	1r gray & org	1.25	60
751	A109	2r dk vio & org ('80)	2.00	1.00
		Nos. 731-751 (14)	18.10	3.85

All values exist with an extra dot in Arabic "Al-khafji." Some were retouched to remove extra dot.
Color of flame varies from light orange to vermilion.

Mohenjo-Daro Ruins — A110

1977, Oct. 23 Litho. Unwmkd.
761	A110	50h multi	60	30

UNESCO campaign to save Mohenjo-Daro excavations in Pakistan.

Idrisi's World Map, 1154 — A111

1977, Nov. 1 Litho. Perf. 14
762	A111	20h multi	30	15
763	A111	50h multi	70	35

First International Symposium on Studies in the History of Arabia at the University of Riyadh, Apr. 23–26, 1977.

King Faisal Specialist Hospital, Riyadh — A112

1977, Nov. 13 Litho. Unwmkd.
764	A112	20h multi	40	20
765	A112	50h multi	75	35

Conference Emblem — A113

1977 Lithographed Perf. 14
766	A113	20h vio bl & yel	30	15

First World Conference on Moslem Education.

APU Emblem, Members' Flags — A114

1977
767	A114	20h multi	25	15
768	A114	80h multi	1.00	50

25th anniversary of Arab Postal Union.

Taif-Abha-Gizan Highway — A115

1978, Oct. 15 Litho. Perf. 14
769	A115	20h multi	20	10
770	A115	80h multi	80	40

Inauguration of Taif-Abha-Gizan highway.

SAUDI ARABIA

Pilgrims, Mt. Arafat and
Holy Kaaba—A116
Perf. 14

1978, Nov.		Litho.	Unwmkd.	
771	A116	20h multi	20	10
772	A116	80h multi	80	40

Pilgrimage to Mecca.

Gulf Postal
Organization
Emblem
A117

1979, Feb. 6		Litho.	Perf. 14	
773	A117	20h multi	20	10
774	A117	50h multi	50	25

First Conference of Gulf Postal Organization, Baghdad.

Saudi Arabia No. 129, King Abdul
Aziz ibn Saud—A118
Perf. 14

1979, June 4		Litho.	Unwmkd.	
775	A118	20h multi	20	10
776	A118	50h multi	50	25
777	A118	115h multi	1.15	58

Souvenir Sheet
Imperf.

778	A118	100h multi		75.00

First commemorative stamp, 50th anniversary. No. 778 contains one stamp with simulated perforations; marginal inscription and portrait of King. Size: 101x76mm.

Crown
Prince
Fahd
A119

1979, June 25			Perf. 14	
779	A119	20h multi	20	10
780	A119	50h multi	50	25

Crown Prince Fahd ibn Abdul Aziz.

Dome of
the Rock,
Jerusalem
A120

1979, July 2			Wmk. 361	
781	A120	20h multi (shades)	20	10

Gold Door, Holy Ka'aba—A121

1979, Oct. 13		Litho.	Perf. 14	
782	A121	20h multi	20	10
783	A121	80h multi	80	40

Installation of new gold doors.

Pilgrims at Holy Ka'aba,
Mecca Mosque—A122

1979, Oct. 27				
784	A122	20h multi	20	10
785	A122	50h multi	50	25

Pilgrimage to Mecca.

Birds in Trees, IYC Emblem—A123
IYC Emblem and: 50h, Child's drawing.

1980, Feb. 19		Litho.	Perf. 14	
786	A123	20h multi	20	10
787	A123	50h multi	50	25

International Year of the Child (1979).

King Abdul Aziz ibn Saud on
Horseback, Saudi Flag—A124

1980, Apr. 5		Litho.	Perf. 14	
788	A124	20h multi	20	10
789	A124	80h multi	80	40

Saudi Arabian Army, 80th anniversary (1979).

COLORS
Please refer to page v for a complete list of color abbreviations used in this book.

Arab League,
35th Anniversary
A125

Smoke Entering
Lungs, WHO
Emblem
A127

International Bureau of Education, 50th
Anniversary—A126

1980, Apr. 27		Litho.	Perf. 14	
790	A125	20h multi	20	10

1980, May 4
| 791 | A126 | 50h multi | 50 | 25 |

1980, May 20
| 792 | A127 | 20h shown | 20 | 10 |
| 793 | A127 | 50h Cigarette, horiz. | 50 | 25 |

Anti-smoking campaign.

20th Anniversary of OPEC—A128

Design: 50h, Workers holding OPEC emblem (Organization of Petroleum Exporting Countries, vert.).

1980, Sept. 1		Litho.	Perf. 14	
794	A128	20h multi	20	10
795	A128	50h multi, vert.	50	25

Pilgrims Arriving at Jeddah
Airport—A129

1980, Oct. 18				
796	A129	20h multi	20	10
797	A129	50h multi	50	25

Pilgrimage to Mecca.

Conference
Emblem
A130

Holy Ka'aba,
Mecca Mosque
A131

1981, Jan. 25		Litho.	Perf. 14	
798	A130	20h shown	20	10
799	A131	20h shown	20	10
800	A131	20h Prophet's Mosque, Medina	20	10
801	A131	20h Dome of the Rock, Jerusalem	20	10

Third Islamic Summit Conference, Mecca.

Hegira, 1500th Anniv.—A132

1981, Jan. 26				
802	A132	20h multi	20	10
803	A132	50h multi	50	25
804	A132	80h multi	80	40

Souvenir Sheet
| 805 | A132 | 300h multi | | |

Industry Week—A133

1981, Feb. 21				
806	A133	20h multi	20	10
807	A133	80h multi	80	40

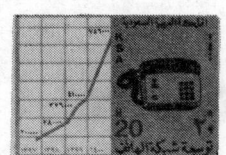

Line Graph and Telephone—A134

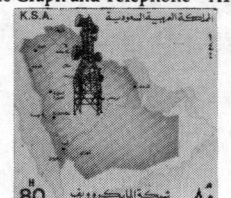

Map of Saudi Arabia, Microwave
Tower—A135

1981, Feb. 28				
808	A134	20h shown	20	10
809	A135	80h shown	80	40
810	A134	115h Earth satellite station	1.15	55

Souvenir Sheets
811	A134	100h like #808		
812	A135	100h like #809		
813	A134	100h like #810		

Ministry of Posts and Telecommunications achievements.

SAUDI ARABIA

Arab City Day—A135

1981, Apr. 2   Litho.   Perf. 14
814	A135	20h multi	20	10
815	A135	65h multi	65	32
816	A135	80h multi	80	40
817	A135	115d multi	1.15	60

Jeddah Airport Opening—A136

1981, Apr. 12
| 818 | A136 | 20h shown | 20 | 10 |
| 819 | A136 | 80h Plane over airport, diff. | 80 | 40 |

1982 World Cup Soccer Preliminary Games A137   Intl. Year of the Disabled A138

1981, July 26   Litho.   Perf. 14
| 820 | A137 | 20h multi | 20 | 10 |
| 821 | A137 | 80h multi | 80 | 40 |

1981, Aug. 5
| 822 | A138 | 20h Reading braille | 20 | 10 |
| 823 | A138 | 50h Man weaving rug | 50 | 25 |

3rd Five-year Plan (1981-1985) A139

1981, Sept. 5
| 824 | A139 | 20h multi | 20 | 10 |

King Khalil and Map of Saudi Arabia—A140

1981, Sept. 23   Litho.   Perf. 14
825	A140	5h multi	5	5
826	A140	10h multi	10	5
827	A140	15h multi	15	8
828	A140	20h multi	20	10
829	A140	50h multi	50	25
830	A140	65h multi	65	32
831	A140	80h multi	80	40
832	A140	115h multi	1.15	58
		Nos. 825-832 (8)	3.60	1.83

Souvenir Sheet
Imperf.
| 833 | A140 | 10r multi | 20.00 | |

50th anniv. of kingdom. No. 833 shows king, map, document. Size: 100x75mm.

Pilgrimage to Mecca A141

1981, Oct. 7
| 834 | A141 | 20h multi | 20 | 10 |
| 835 | A141 | 65h multi | 65 | 32 |

World Food Day—A142

1981, Oct. 16
| 836 | A142 | 20h multi | 20 | 10 |

2nd Session of the Gulf Cooperative Council Summit Conference, Riyadh, Nov. 10—A143

1981, Nov. 10   Litho.   Perf. 14
| 837 | A143 | 20h multi | 20 | 10 |
| 838 | A143 | 80h multi | 80 | 40 |

King Saud University, 25th Anniv.—A144

1982, Mar. 10   Litho.   Perf. 14
| 839 | A144 | 20h multi | 20 | 10 |
| 840 | A144 | 50h multi | 50 | 25 |

New Regional Postal Centers—A145

1982, July 14   Litho.   Perf. 14
841	A145	20h Riyadh P.O.	20	10
842	A145	65h Jeddah	65	32
843	A145	80h Dammam	80	40
844	A145	115h Automated sorting	1.15	58

Four 300h souvenir sheets exist in same designs as Nos. 841-844 respectively.

Riyadh Television Center—A146

1982, Sept. 4
| 845 | A146 | 20h multi | 20 | 10 |

25th Anniv. of King's Soccer Cup—A147

1982, Sept. 8
| 846 | A147 | 20h multi | 20 | 10 |
| 847 | A147 | 65h multi | 65 | 32 |

30th Anniv. of Arab Postal Union—A148

1982, Sept. 8
| 848 | A148 | 20h Emblem | 20 | 10 |
| 849 | A148 | 65h Map, vert. | 65 | 32 |

Pilgrimage to Mecca—A149

1982, Sept. 26
| 850 | A149 | 20h multi | 20 | 10 |
| 851 | A149 | 50h multi | 50 | 25 |

World Standards Day—A150

1982, Oct. 14
| 852 | A150 | 20h multi | 20 | 10 |

World Food Day—A151

1982, Oct. 16
| 853 | A151 | 20h multi | 20 | 10 |

Coronation of King Fahd, June 14, 1982—A152

Installation of Crown Prince Abdullah, June 14, 1982—A153

1983, Feb. 12   Litho.   Perf. 14
854	A152	20h multi	20	10
855	A153	20h multi	20	10
856	A152	50h multi	50	25
857	A153	50h multi	50	25
858	A152	65h multi	65	32
859	A153	65h multi	65	32
860	A152	80h multi	80	40
861	A153	80h multi	80	40
862	A152	115h multi	1.15	60
863	A153	115h multi	1.15	60
		Nos. 854-863 (10)	6.60	3.34

Two one-stamp souvenir sheets contain Nos. 862-863, perf. 12½.

6th Anniv. of United Arab Shipping Co.—A154

Various freighters.

1983, Aug. 9   Litho.   Perf. 14
| 864 | A154 | 20h multi | 12 | 6 |
| 865 | A154 | 65h multi | 40 | 20 |

Dome of the Rock, Jerusalem—A155

Wmk. 361
1983, Sept.   Litho.   Perf. 13½x12
| 866 | A155 | 20h multi | 12 | 6 |

Pilgrimage to Mecca—A156

1983, Sept. 16   Litho.   Perf. 14
| 867 | A156 | 20h brt bl & multi | 12 | 6 |
| 868 | A156 | 65h blk & multi | 40 | 20 |

SAUDI ARABIA

World Communications Year—A157

1983, Oct. 8		Litho.	Perf. 14
869	A157	20h Post and UPU emblems	12 6
870	A157	80h Telephone and ITU emblems	48 24

SAUDI ARABIA
العربية السعودية

Buying - Selling - Appraisals - of Collections/Stocks/Rarities

- *Full Color Album*
- *Binders*
- *Accessories*
- *Certification*
- *Price Lists*

Filatco

P.O. Box 1461

Appleton, WI 54913

Telephone (414) 735-0701

Telex 260355 ED TECH APLE

AIR POST STAMPS

Airspeed Ambassador Airliner
AP1
Typographed

1949-58		Perf. 11	Unwmkd.	
C1	AP1	1g bl grn	1.25	10
C2	AP1	3g ultra	2.00	10
	a.	3g bl ('58)	7.50	75
C3	AP1	4g orange	2.00	10
C4	AP1	10g purple	4.00	15
C5	AP1	20g chocolate	12.50	25
	a.	20g brn vio ('58?)	5.00	20
C6	AP1	100g vio rose	35.00	4.00
		Nos. C1-C6 (6)	56.75	4.70

Imperfs. exist.

Saudi Airlines Convair 440
AP2
Type I (Saud Cartouche)
(Illustrated over No. 300)

1960-61		Photogravure	Perf. 14	
C7	AP2	1p dl pur & grn	60	5
C8	AP2	2p grn & dl pur	60	5
C9	AP2	3p brn red & bl	60	5
C10	AP2	4p bl & dl pur	60	10
C11	AP2	5p grn & rose red	60	10
C12	AP2	6p ocher & sl	1.00	20
C13	AP2	8p rose & gray ol	1.25	20
C14	AP2	9p pur & red brn	1.75	20
C15	AP2	10p blk & dl red brn	4.00	45
C16	AP2	15p bl & bis brn	4.00	20
C17	AP2	20p bis brn & emer	4.00	40
C18	AP2	30p sep & Prus grn	10.00	1.00
C19	AP2	50p grn & ind	22.50	75
C20	AP2	100p gray & dk brn	45.00	2.00
C21	AP2	200p dk vio & blk	65.00	3.00
		Nos. C7-C21 (15)	161.50	8.75

The 5p, 9p, 10p, 15p and 20p exist imperf; probably not regularly issued.

1963-64		Photo.	Wmk. 337	
		Size: 27½x22mm.		
C24	AP2	1p lil & grn	1.25	10
C25	AP2	2p grn & dl pur	1.25	10
C26	AP2	4p bl & dl pur	2.50	15
C27	AP2	6p ocher & sl	5.00	25
C28	AP2	8p rose & gray ol	10.00	50
C29	AP2	9p pur & red brn ('64)	5.00	40
		Nos. C24-C29 (6)	25.00	1.50

Redrawn
Lithographed

1964		Perf. 13½x13	Wmk. 337	
		Size: 28½x23mm.		
C30	AP2	3p brn red & dl bl	2.50	50
C31	AP2	10p blk & dk red brn	5.00	1.00
C32	AP2	20p bis brn & emer	10.00	1.50

Nos. C30–C32 are widely spaced in the sheet, producing large margins.

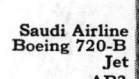

Saudi Airline
Boeing 720-B
Jet
AP3

Type I (Saud Cartouche)
(Illustrated over No. 300)
Lithographed

1965-70		Perf. 14	Unwmkd.	
C33	AP3	1p lil & grn ('66)	20.00	5.00
C33A	AP3	2p grn & dl pur ('70)	85.00	35.00
C34	AP3	3p rose lil & dl bl ('66)	25	5
C35	AP3	4p bl & dl pur	30	5
C35A	AP3	5p ol & rose red ('69)		
			150.00	75.00
C35B	AP3	6p ocher & sl ('70)	35	15
C36	AP3	7p rose & ol gray ('66)	40	20
C37	AP3	8p rose & gray ol ('70)	40	25
C38	AP3	9p pur & red brn	90	40
C39	AP3	10p blk & dk red brn ('66)		
			15.00	30
C40	AP3	11p grn & bis ('69)	15.00	
C41	AP3	12p org & gray ('66)	75	30
C42	AP3	13p dk grn & yel grn ('66)	75	40
C43	AP3	14p dk bl & org ('66)	75	40
C43A	AP3	15p bl & bis brn ('70?)	90	50
C44	AP3	16p blk & ult-a ('66)	90	50
C45	AP3	17p bis & sep ('66)	90	50
C46	AP3	18p bl & yel grn ('66)	90	50
C47	AP3	19p car & dp org ('66)	1.25	60
C47A	AP3	20p bis brn & emer ('70)		
			20.00	1.50
C48	AP3	23p ol & bis	17.50	65
C49	AP3	24p dk bl & sep	1.50	50
C50	AP3	26p ver & bl grn	2.00	50
C51	AP3	27p ol brn & ap grn	2.00	50
C52	AP3	31p car rose & rose red	2.50	55
C53	AP3	33p red & dl pur	2.75	80

Type II (Faisal Cartouche)
(Illustrated over No. 300)
Lithographed

1966-78		Perf. 14	Unwmkd.	
C54	AP3	1p dl pur & grn	20	5
C55	AP3	2p grn & dl pur	20	5
C56	AP3	3p brn red & dl bl	20	10
C57	AP3	4p bl & dl pur ('68)	20	7
C57A	AP3	5p ol & rose red	150.00	75.00
C57B	AP3	6p ocher & sl ('71)	60.00	15
C58	AP3	7p rose & ol gray ('71)		
			17.50	20
C59	AP3	8p rose & gray ol ('70)		
			17.50	25
C60	AP3	9p pur & red brn ('70)	90	25
C61	AP3	10p blk & dl red brn	90	30
C62	AP3	11p grn & bis	50	30
C62A	AP3	12p org & gray ('75)	60	30
C63	AP3	13p dk grn & yel grn ('71)		
			1.50	40
C64	AP3	14p dk bl & org ('75)	90	45
C65	AP3	15p bl & bis brn ('75)	2.00	50
C66	AP3	16p blk & ultra ('71)	75	50
C67	AP3	17p bis & sep ('75)	75	50
C67A	AP3	18p dk bl & yel grn ('76)	75	55
C67B	AP3	19p car & org ('75)	2.25	60
C68	AP3	20p brn & brt grn ('70)	45.00	65
C69	AP3	23p ol & bis	1.75	40
C69A	AP3	24p dk bl & blk ('75)	1.00	50
C69B	AP3	31p car rose & rose red ('78)		175.00
C70	AP3	33p red & dl pur ('68)	2.00	1.05
C70A	AP3	50p emer & ind ('74)	85.00	1.00
C70B	AP3	100p gray & dk brn ('78)	90.00	
C70C	AP3	200p dk vio & blk ('74)	100.00	2.50

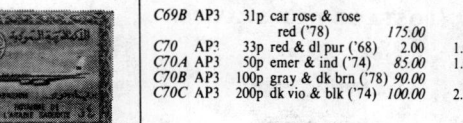

The existence of 26p and 27p denominations has been reported.

Lithographed

1968-71		Perf. 14	Wmk. 361	
C71	AP3	1p lil & grn	4.00	5
C72	AP3	2p grn & lil	4.00	5
C73	AP3	3p rose lil & dl bl ('69)		
			20.00	10
C74	AP3	4p bl & dl pur ('70)	2.50	10
C76	AP3	7p rose & gray ('71)	2.50	20
C77	AP3	8p red & gray ol ('71)	4.00	25
C78	AP3	9p pur & red brn ('71)	5.00	25
C79	AP3	10p blk & dl red brn ('69)		
			5.00	30
		Nos. C71-C79 (8)	45.50	1.30

Falcon
AP4

Perf. 13½x14

1968-71		Lithographed	Wmk. 361	
C96	AP4	1p grn & red brn	1.00	10
C97	AP4	4p dk red & red brn	.10.00	1.00
C98	AP4	10p bl & red brn	2.00	50
C99	AP4	20p grn & red brn ('71)	20.00	2.50

Nine other denominations were printed but are not known to have been issued.

SAUDI ARABIA

For the advanced collector.
We buy and sell
specialized material.

George
Alevizos

2716 Ocean Park Blvd. Ste. 1020
Santa Monica, CA 90405
Telephone: 213/450-2543

POSTAGE DUE STAMPS.

Hejaz

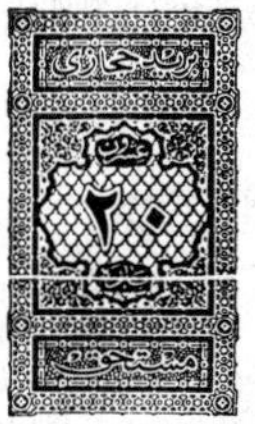

From Old Door at El Ashraf Barsbai in Shari el Ashrafiya, Cairo
D1

Serrate Roulette 13

1917, June 27 Typo. Unwmkd.

LJ1	D1	20pa red	2.50	2.25
LJ2	D1	1pi blue	2.50	2.25
LJ3	D1	2pi magenta	2.50	2.25

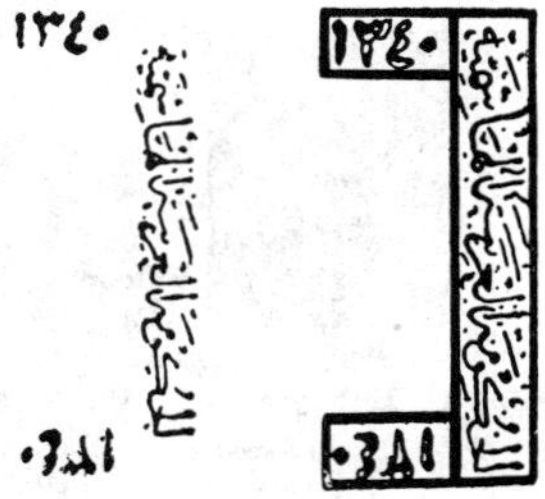

a *b*

Nos. LJ1–LJ3 Overprinted Type "a" in Black or Red

1921, Dec.

LJ4	D1	20pa red	12.00	3.00
a.		Double overprint, one at left	80.00	
b.		Ovpt. at left	12.50	20.00
LJ5	D1	1pi bl (R)	2.00	2.00
LJ6	D1	1pi bl, ovpt. at left	15.00	20.00
a.		Ovpt. at right	17.50	35.00
LJ7	D1	2pi magenta	3.00	3.00
a.		Double overprint, one at left	70.00	
b.		Ovpt. at left	7.50	

Nos. LJ1–LJ3 Overprinted Type "b" in Black

1922, Jan.

LJ8	D1	20pa red	20.00	30.00
a.		Ovpt. at left	25.00	
LJ9	D1	1pi blue	1.50	3.00
a.		Ovpt. at left	20.00	
LJ10	D1	2pi magenta	1.50	3.00
a.		Ovpt. at left	35.00	

Regular issue of 1922 Overprinted

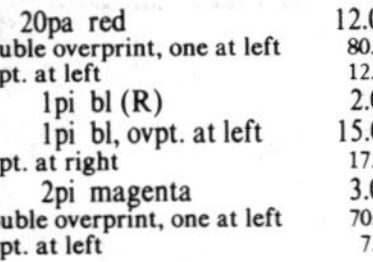

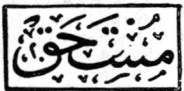

Black Overprint.

1923 ***Perf. 11½***

LJ11	A7	½pi red	1.50	1.50
LJ12	A7	1pi dk bl	1.50	1.50
LJ13	A7	2pi orange	2.00	2.00

1924 Blue Overprint.

LJ14	A7	½pi red	3.00	3.00
LJ15	A7	1pi dk bl	3.00	3.00
LJ16	A7	2pi orange	5.00	5.00

This overprint reads "Mustahaq" (Due).

Jedda Issues

Nos. LJ1–LJ3 Overprinted in Red or Blue (Overprint reads up in illustration)

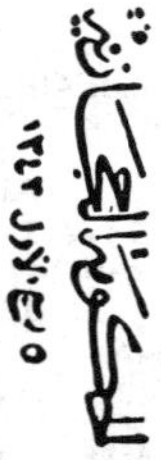

1925, Jan. ***Serrate Roulette 13.***

LJ17	D1	20pa red (R)	200.00	200.00
a.		Ovpt. reading down	300.00	300.00
LJ18	D1	20pa red, ovpt. reading down (Bl)	400.00	
LJ19	D1	1pi bl (R)	15.00	20.00
a.		Ovpt. reading down	12.00	20.00
LJ20	D1	1pi bl (Bl)	10.00	10.00
a.		Ovpt. reading down	60.00	90.00
LJ21	D1	2pi mag (Bl)	6.00	10.00
a.		Ovpt. reading down	50.00	50.00

Nos. LJ1–LJ3 Overprinted in Blue or Red

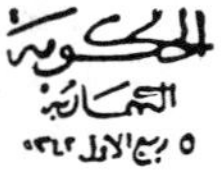

1925

LJ22	D1	20pa red (Bl)	250.00	300.00
a.		Inverted overprint	250.00	250.00
LJ24	D1	1pi bl (R)	20.00	30.00
a.		Inverted overprint	20.00	30.00
LJ25	D1	2pi mag (Bl)	12.00	20.00
a.		Inverted overprint	25.00	50.00
b.		Double overprint	200.00	

No. LJ2 with this overprint in blue is bogus.

Regular Issues of 1922–24 Overprinted

a

and Handstamped

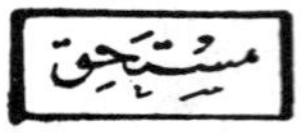

b

1925 ***Perf. 11½.***

LJ26	A7	⅛pi red brn	5.00	5.00
LJ27	A7	½pi red	5.00	5.00
LJ28	A7	1pi dk bl	6.00	6.00
LJ29	A7	1½pi violet	6.00	6.00
LJ30	A7	2pi orange	9.00	9.00
LJ31	A7	3pi ol brn	8.00	8.00
LJ32	A7	3pi dl red	6.00	6.00
LJ33	A7	5pi ol grn	6.00	6.00
LJ34	A7	10pi vio & dk brn	9.00	9.00
		Nos. LJ26-LJ34 (9)	60.00	60.00

The printed overprint (*a*), consisting of the three top lines of Arabic, was used alone for the first issue (Nos. LJ26a–LJ34a). The "postage due" box was so small and indistinct that its equivalent in larger characters was added by boxed handstamp (*b*) at bottom of each stamp for the second issue (Nos. LJ26–LJ34).

The handstamped overprint (*b*) is found double, inverted, etc.

Counterfeits exist of both overprint and handstamp.

Without Boxed Handstamp "b"

LJ26a	A7	⅛pi red brn	8.00	8.00
LJ27a	A7	½pi red	8.00	8.00
LJ28a	A7	1pi dk bl	8.00	8.00
LJ29a	A7	1½pi violet	8.00	8.00
LJ30a	A7	2pi orange	8.00	8.00
LJ31a	A7	3pi ol brn	9.00	9.00
LJ32a	A7	3pi dl red	9.00	9.00
LJ33a	A7	5pi ol grn	12.00	12.00
LJ34a	A7	10pi vio & dk brn	15.00	15.00
		Nos. LJ26a-LJ34a (9)	85.00	85.00

Regular Issue of 1922 Overprinted

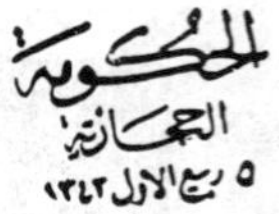

and Handstamped

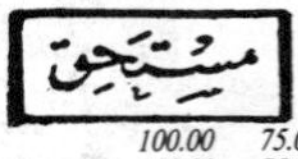

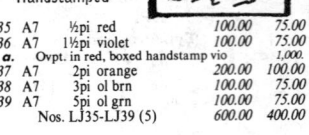

LJ35	A7	½pi red	100.00	75.00
LJ36	A7	1½pi violet	100.00	75.00
a.		Ovpt. in red, boxed handstamp vio		1,000.
LJ37	A7	2pi orange	200.00	100.00
LJ38	A7	3pi ol brn	100.00	75.00
LJ39	A7	5pi ol grn	100.00	75.00
		Nos. LJ35-LJ39 (5)	600.00	400.00

Counterfeits exist of Nos. LJ4–LJ39.

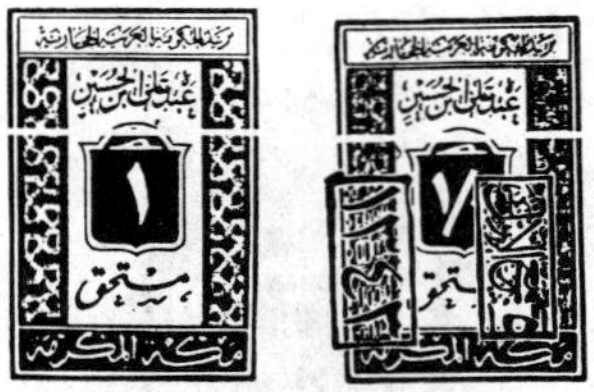

Arabic Numeral of Value
D2 D3

1925, May–June ***Perf. 11½***

LJ40	D2	½pi lt bl	75	75
LJ41	D2	1pi orange	75	75
LJ42	D2	2pi lt brn	75	75
LJ43	D2	3pi pink	75	75

Nos. LJ40–LJ43 exist imperforate.

Impressions in colors other than issued are trial color proofs.

1925

Black Overprint.

LJ44	D3	½pi lt bl	1.00	1.00
LJ45	D3	1pi orange	1.00	1.00
LJ46	D3	2pi lt brn	1.00	1.00
LJ47	D3	3pi pink	1.00	1.00

Nos. LJ44–LJ47 exist imperforate.

Red Overprint.

LJ48	D3	½pi lt bl	1.00	1.00
LJ49	D3	1pi orange	1.00	1.00
LJ50	D3	2pi lt brn	1.00	1.00
LJ51	D3	3pi pink	1.00	1.00

Blue Overprint.

LJ52	D3	½pi lt bl	1.00	1.00
LJ53	D3	1pi orange	1.00	1.00
LJ54	D3	2pi lt brn	1.00	1.00
LJ55	D3	3pi pink	1.00	1.00
		Nos. LJ40-LJ55 (16)	15.00	15.00

Nos. LJ44–LJ55 exist with either Jedda or Cairo overprints and the tablets normally read upward. Prices are for Cairo overprints; Jedda overprints, especially the red and blue, sell for more.

Nejd

Handstamped in Blue, Red, Black or Violet

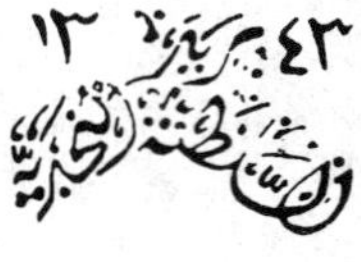

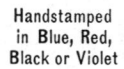

On Hejaz Postage Due Stamps.

Typographed or Handstamped in Black

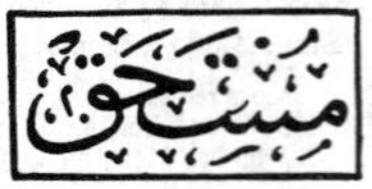

Unwmkd.

1925, April–June ***Perf. 11½***

J1	A7	½pi red (Bl)	8.00	8.00
J2	A7	1pi lt bl (R)	8.00	8.00
a.		1pi dk bl (R)	15.00	15.00
J3	A7	2pi yel buff (Bl)	10.00	10.00
a.		2pi org (Bl)	15.00	15.00

Same, with Postage Due Overprint in Blue.

J4	A7	½pi red (Bl)	25.00	
J5	A7	1pi dk bl (R)	100.00	
J6	A7	2pi org (Bl)	75.00	

On Hejaz Stamps of 1922-24.

Handstamped in Blue

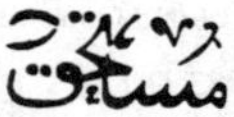

J7	A7	½pi red (Bl & Bl)	10.00	10.00
J8	A7	3pi brn red (Bl & Bl)	10.00	10.00

Handstamped in Blue, Black or Violet

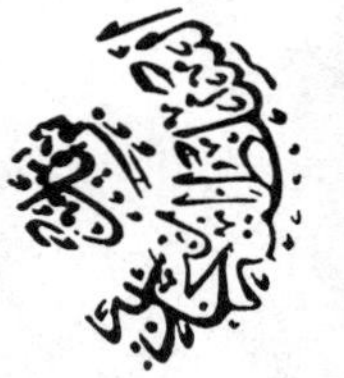

On Hejaz No. LJ9

Serrate Roulette 13½.

J9	D1	1pi bl (V)	40.00	30.00

Same Overprint on Hejaz Stamps of 1924 with additional Handstamp in Black, Blue or Red

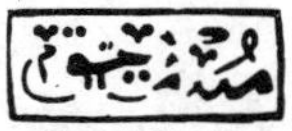

Perf. 11½.

J10	A7	3pi brn red (Bl & Bk)	8.00	8.00
J11	A7	3pi brn red (Bk & Bl)	8.00	8.00

Same Handstamps on Hejaz Railway Tax Stamps.

J12	R3	1pi bl (Bk & R)	6.00	6.00
J13	R3	2pi ocher (Bl & Bk)	6.00	6.00
J14	R3	5pi grn (Bk & R)	10.00	10.00
J15	R3	5pi grn (V & BK)	10.00	10.00

The second handstamp, which is struck on the lower part of the Postage Due Stamps, is the word Mustahaq (Due) in various forms.

No. J13 exists with second handstamp in blue.

Hejaz-Nejd

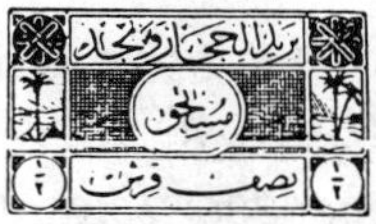

D1

1926 Typographed. ***Perf. 11.***

J16	D1	½pi carmine	1.50	75
J17	D1	2pi orange	1.50	75
J18	D1	6pi lt brn	1.50	75

Nos. J16–J18 exist with perf. 14, 14x11 and 11x14, and imperf. These sell for six times the prices quoted.

Nos. J16–J18 in colors other than listed (both perf. and imperf.) are proofs.

Counterfeit note after No. 80 also applies to Nos. J16–J21.

Pan-Islamic Congress Issue.

Postage Due Stamps of 1926 Handstamped like Regular Issue

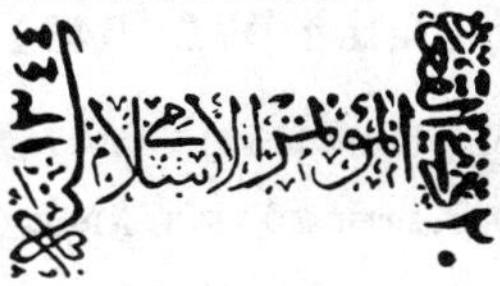

J19	D1	½pi carmine	2.25	2.25
J20	D1	2pi orange	2.25	2.25
J21	D1	6pi lt brn	2.25	2.25

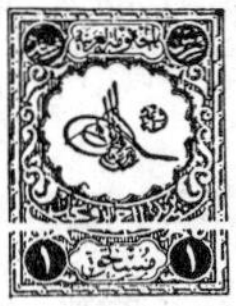

D2

1927 ***Perf. 11½.***

J22	D2	1pi slate	7.50	50
a.		Inscription reads "2 piastres" in upper right circle	40.00	40.00
J23	D2	2pi dk vio	3.00	50

There are two types of No. J22.

Saudi Arabia

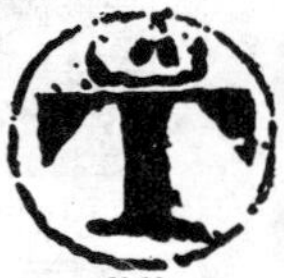

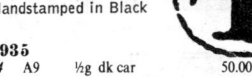

Saudi Arabia No. 161 Handstamped in Black

1935

J24	A9	½g dk car	50.00

Two types of overprint.

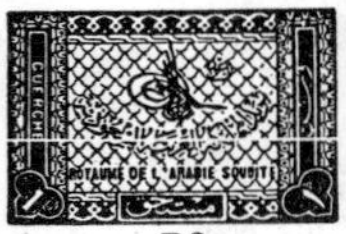

D3

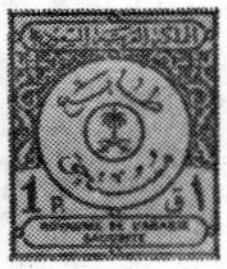

D4

1937–39 **Unwmkd.**

J25	D3	½g org brn ('39)	3.00	1.50
J26	D3	1g lt bl	3.00	1.50
J27	D3	2g rose vio ('39)	6.00	2.50

1961 Lithographed ***Perf. 13x13½***

J28	D4	1p purple	1.00	1.00
J29	D4	2p green	2.00	1.00
J30	D4	4p rose red	5.00	2.00

The use of Postage Due stamps ceased in 1963.

OFFICIAL STAMPS.

Official stamps were normally used only on external correspondence.

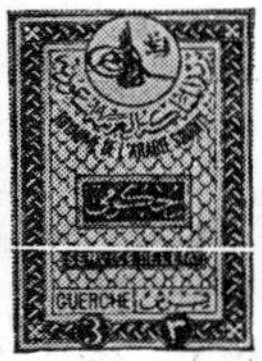

O1

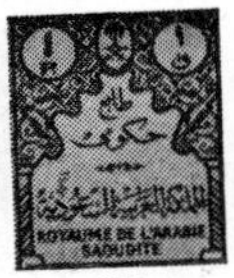

O2

Typographed.

1939 ***Perf. 11, 11½*** **Unwmkd.**

O1	O1	3g dp ultra	1.00	1.00
O2	O1	5g red vio	2.00	2.00
O3	O1	20g brown	3.00	3.00
O4	O1	50g bl grn	8.00	7.00
O5	O1	100g ol grn	60.00	50.00
O6	O1	200g purple	40.00	35.00
		Nos. O1-O6 (6)	114.00	98.00

1961 Lithographed ***Perf. 13x13½***

Size: 18x22–22½mm.

O7	O2	1p black	50	10
O8	O2	2p dk grn	75	20
O9	O2	3p bister	1.00	30
O10	O2	4p dk bl	1.25	40
O11	O2	5p rose red	1.50	50
O12	O2	10p maroon	2.00	1.00
O13	O2	20p vio bl	6.00	1.50
O14	O2	50p dl brn	17.50	3.50
O15	O2	100p dl grn	30.00	7.00
		Nos. O7-O15 (9)	60.50	14.50

Nos. O11–O15 exist imperf.

1964–65 ***Perf. 13½x13*** **Wmk. 337**

Size: 21x26mm.

O16	O2	1p black	50	25
O17	O2	2p grn ('65)	1.00	50
O18	O2	3p bister	3.00	1.00
O19	O2	4p dk bl	2.00	75
O20	O2	5p rose red	2.00	75
		Nos. O16-O20 (5)	8.50	3.25

Typographed

1965–70 ***Perf. 11*** **Wmk. 337**

Size: 21x26mm.

O21	O2	1p dk brn	25	10
O22	O2	2p green	1.00	10
O23	O2	3p bister	1.00	10
O24	O2	4p dk bl	1.00	15
O25	O2	5p dp org	2.00	40
O26	O2	6p red lil	2.00	40
O27	O2	7p emerald	1.50	25
O28	O2	8p car rose	1.50	30
O29	O2	9p red	1.50	35
O30	O2	10p red brn	1.50	35
O31	O2	11p pale grn	5.00	75
O32	O2	12p violet	5.00	75
O33	O2	13p blue	2.50	50
O34	O2	14p purple	4.00	60
O35	O2	15p orange	6.00	1.00
O36	O2	16p black	6.00	
a.		"19" instead of "16"	50.00	
O37	O2	17p gray grn	10.00	
O38	O2	18p yellow	10.00	
O39	O2	19p dp red lil	10.00	
O40	O2	23p ultra	10.00	
O41	O2	24p yel grn	10.00	
O42	O2	26p bister	10.00	
O43	O2	27p pale lil	12.00	
O44	O2	31p pale sal	15.00	
O45	O2	33p yel grn	15.00	
O46	O2	50p ol bis	20.00	
O47	O2	100p ol gray ('70)	40.00	
		Nos. O21-O47 (27)	203.75	

Nos. O21–O30 and O33–O34 were released to the philatelic trade in 1964. Nos. O21–O46 were printed from new plates; lines of the design are heavier. The numerals have been enlarged and the P's are smaller. Head of "P" 2mm. wide on 1964–65 issue, 1 mm. wide on 1965–70 issue.

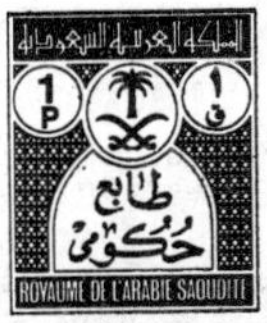

O3

Wmk. 361, 337 (7p, 8p, 9p, 11p)

1970–71 Litho. ***Perf. 13½x14***

O48	O3	1p red brn	15	5
O49	O3	2p dp grn	30	10
O50	O3	3p rose red	40	15
O51	O3	4p brt bl	50	20
O52	O3	5p brick red	50	25
O53	O3	6p orange	60	30
a.		Wmk. 337		
O54	O3	7p dp sal	75.00	
O55	O3	8p violet		
O56	O3	9p dk bl grn		
O57	O3	10p blue	1.00	50
O58	O3	11p ol grn		
O59	O3	20p gray vio	1.50	75
a.		Wmk. 337		
O60	O3	31p dp plum	2.00	1.00
O61	O3	50p lt brn		
O62	O3	100p green		

Nos. O48–O62 were not regularly available unused to the public.

Use of official stamps ceased in 1974.

NEWSPAPER STAMPS

Nos. 8, 9 and 14 with Additional Overprint.

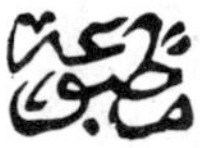

1925 ***Perf. 11½*** **Unwmkd.**

P1	A7	⅛pi red brn (Bk+Bk)	*1,500.*	*1,500.*
P2	A7	⅛pi red brn (V & Bk)	*1,000.*	*750.00*
P3	A7	½pi red (V & Bk)	*2,500.*	*1,500.*

Overprint reads: "Matbu'a" (Newspaper), but these stamps were normally used for regular postage. Counterfeits exist.

POSTAL TAX STAMPS.

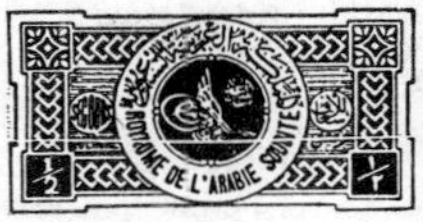

PT1

1934, June ***Perf. 11½*** **Unwmkd.**

RA1	PT1	½g scarlet	*100.00*	1.50

No. RA1 collected a "war tax" to aid wounded of the 1934 Saudi-Yemen war.

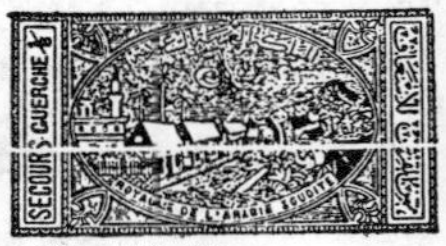

General Hospital, Mecca PT2

1936, Oct. **Size: 37x20mm.**

RA2	PT2	⅛g scarlet	*350.00*	3.00

Nos. RA2–RA7 raised funds for public health purposes.

Type of 1936 Redrawn.

1937-42 **Size: 30½x18 mm.**

RA3	PT2	⅛g scarlet	*45.00*	15
a.		⅛g rose ('39)	*100.00*	15
b.		⅛g rose car, perf. 11 ('42)	*100.00*	10

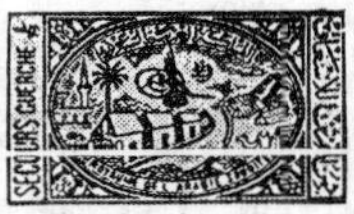

General Hospital, Mecca PT3

1943 Typo. ***Perf. 11½, 11***

Grayish Paper.

RA4	PT3	⅛g car rose	*25.00*	10
a.		⅛g scar	*25.00*	

Type of 1943 Redrawn.

1948–53 Litho. ***Perf. 11x10***

RA5	PT3	⅛g rose brn	20.00	10
a.		⅛g car, perf. 10 ('53)	10.00	10
b.		⅛g rose, perf. 10 ('53)	5.00	
c.		As RA5, perf. 10 ('53)	5.00	5

1950 ***Rouletted***

RA6	PT3	⅛g red brn	4.00	10
a.		⅛g rose	2.00	10
b.		⅛g car	2.00	10

All lines in lithographed design considerably finer; some shading in center eliminated.

Type of 1943

1955–56 Typo. ***Perf. 11***

RA7	PT3	⅛g rose car	4.00	10
RA8	PT3	¼g car rose ('56)	1.25	10

Nos. RA4–RA8 exist imperf., part perf. and in various shades.

The tax on postal matter was discontinued in May, 1964.

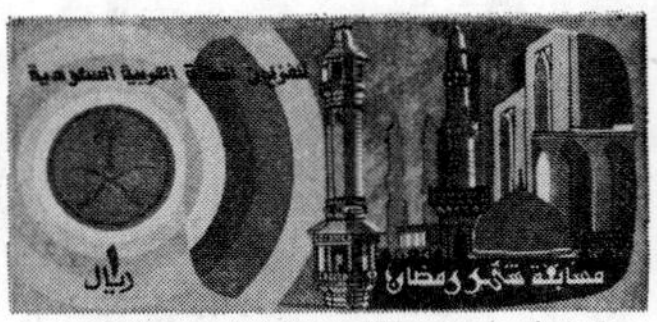

Coat of Arms, Waves and View—PT4

Perf. 14

1974, Oct. Litho. **Wmk. 361**

RA9	PT4	1r bl & multi	*25.00*

Obligatory on all mailed entries in a government television contest during month of Ramadan in 1974 and 1975. The tax aided a benevolent society.

SAUDI ARABIA
Buying
Saudi Arabia
All Mint-NH-LH

Sets and Singles Wanted. Write for Free Buying List. High values used also purchased.

All errors, specialized material, covers and postal history especially desired.

Write with details
Henry Gitner Philatelists, Inc.
P.O. Box 3077
(35 Mountain Ave.)
Middletown, N.Y. 10940
(914) 343-5151

SAXONY

See German States group preceding Germany in Vol. III.

SCHLESWIG
(shlās'vĭk)

LOCATION — In the northern part of the former Schleswig-Holstein Province, in northern Germany. Schleswig was divided into North and South Schleswig after the Versailles Treaty, and plebiscites were held in 1920. North Schleswig (Zone 1) voted to join Denmark, South Schleswig to stay German.

100 Pfennig = 1 Mark
100 Öre = 1 Krone

Plebiscite Issue.

| | Arms A11 | View of Schleswig A12 |

Wmk. 114

Wmkd. Multiple Crosses. (114)

1920, Jan. 25   Typo.   **Perf. 14x15.**

1	A11	2½pf gray	8	8
2	A11	5pf green	8	8
3	A11	7½pf yel brn	15	12
4	A11	10pf dp rose	22	18
5	A11	15pf red vio	12	10
6	A11	20pf dp bl	25	20
7	A11	25pf orange	40	32
8	A11	35pf brown	60	50
9	A11	40pf violet	32	28
10	A11	75pf grnsh bl	60	50
11	A11	1m dk brn	60	50
12	A12	2m dp bl	85	70
13	A12	5m green	1.25	1.00
14	A12	10m red	2.25	1.75
	Nos. 1-14 (14)		7.77	6.31

The colored portions of type A11 are white, and the white portions are colored, on Nos. 7-10.

Types of 1920 Overprinted in Blue

1920, May 20

15	A11	1ő dk gray	10	85
16	A11	5ő green	8	45
17	A11	7ő yel brn	8	65
18	A11	10ő rose red	15	85
19	A11	15ő lil rose	15	85
20	A11	20ő dk bl	10	1.15
21	A11	25ő orange	28	4.00
22	A11	35ő brown	1.10	9.00
23	A11	40ő violet	40	3.00
24	A11	75ő grnsh bl	60	6.00
25	A11	1k dk brn	80	6.00
26	A12	2k dp bl	6.00	30.00
27	A12	5k green	3.75	30.00
28	A12	10k red	8.00	62.50
	Nos. 15-28 (14)		21.59	

OFFICIAL STAMPS.

Regular Issue of 1920 Overprinted

C·I·S

Wmkd. Multiple Crosses. (114)

1920   **Perf. 14x15.**

O1	A11	2½pf gray	95.00	100.00
O2	A11	5pf green	95.00	110.00
O3	A11	7½pf yel brn	95.00	100.00
O4	A11	10pf dp rose	90.00	110.00
O5	A11	15pf red vio	60.00	60.00
O6	A11	20pf dp bl	85.00	72.50
O7	A11	25pf orange	185.00	150.00
a.	Inverted overprint		1,500.	
O8	A11	35pf brown	185.00	170.00
O9	A11	40pf violet	150.00	100.00
O10	A11	75pf grnsh bl	170.00	240.00
O11	A12	1m dk brn	170.00	240.00
O12	A12	2m dp bl	275.00	260.00
O13	A12	5m green	375.00	425.00
O14	A12	10m red	700.00	600.00
	Nos. O1-O14 (14)		2,635.00	2,737.50

The letters "C.I.S." are the initials of "Commission Interalliée Slesvig," under whose auspices the plebiscites took place. Counterfeit overprints exist.

SCHLESWIG-HOLSTEIN

See German States group preceding Germany in Vol. III.

SENEGAL
(sĕn'ē-gôl')

LOCATION — On the west coast of Africa, bordering on the Atlantic Ocean.

GOVT. — Republic; former French Colony.

AREA — 76,000 sq. mi.

POP. — 5,090,000 (est. 1976).

CAPITAL — Dakar (St. Louis was capital of the colony).

The former French colony of Senegal became part of French West Africa in 1943. The Republic of Senegal was established Nov. 25, 1958. From Apr. 4, 1959, to June 20, 1960, the Republic of Senegal and the Sudanese Republic together formed the Mali Federation. After its breakup, Senegal resumed issuing its own stamps in 1960.

100 Centimes = 1 Franc

French Colonies Nos. 48, 49, 51, 52, 55, type A9, Surcharged:

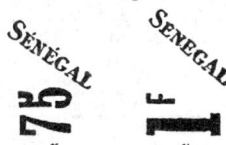

| a | b | c | d | e |

1887   **Perf. 14x13½**   **Unwmkd.**

Black Surcharge

1	(a)	5c on 20c red, grn	110.00	110.00
a.	Double surcharge			
2	(b)	5c on 20c red, grn	200.00	200.00
3	(c)	5c on 20c red, grn	675.00	675.00
4	(d)	5c on 20c red, grn	135.00	135.00
5	(e)	5c on 20c red, grn	250.00	250.00
6	(a)	5c on 30c brn, bis	200.00	200.00
7	(b)	5c on 30c brn, bis	800.00	800.00
8	(d)	5c on 30c brn, bis	275.00	275.00

| f | g | h | i |
| j | k | l | m |

9	(f)	10c on 4c cl, lav	75.00	75.00
10	(g)	10c on 4c cl, lav	100.00	100.00
11	(h)	10c on 4c cl, lav	45.00	45.00
12	(i)	10c on 4c cl, lav	400.00	400.00
a.	"1" without top stroke			
13	(h)	10c on 20c red, grn	400.00	400.00
14	(g)	10c on 20c red, grn	400.00	400.00
15	(h)	10c on 20c red, grn	375.00	375.00
16	(i)	10c on 20c red, grn	2,500.	2,500.
17	(j)	10c on 20c red, grn	400.00	400.00
18	(k)	10c on 20c red, grn	400.00	400.00
19	(l)	10c on 20c red, grn	400.00	400.00
20	(m)	10c on 20c red, grn	400.00	400.00

15 15 15 15 15
n o p q r

15 15 15 15
s t u v

15
w

21	(n)	15c on 20c red, grn	45.00	45.00
22	(o)	15c on 20c red, grn	42.50	42.50
23	(p)	15c on 20c red, grn	30.00	30.00
24	(q)	15c on 20c red, grn	67.50	67.50
25	(r)	15c on 20c red, grn	37.50	37.50
26	(s)	15c on 20c red, grn	37.50	37.50
27	(t)	15c on 20c red, grn	125.00	125.00
28	(u)	15c on 20c red, grn	30.00	30.00
29	(v)	15c on 20c red, grn	52.50	52.50
30	(w)	15c on 20c red, grn	250.00	250.00

Counterfeits exist of Nos. 1-34.

Surcharged:

Sénégal 75   Sénégal 1F
x   y

1892   **Black Surcharge.**

| 31 | A9 | 75c on 15c bl | 250.00 | 110.00 |
| 32 | A9 | 1fr on 5c grn, grnsh | 250.00 | 120.00 |

"SENEGAL" in Red.

| 33 | A9 | 75c on 15c bl | 7,000. | 2,500. |
| 34 | A9 | 1fr on 5c grn, grnsh | 3,250. | 800.00 |

Navigation and Commerce—A24

1892-1900   **Typographed**

Name of Colony in Blue or Carmine.

35	A24	1c lil bl	32	32
36	A24	2c brn, buff	1.00	90
37	A24	4c cl, lav	80	60
38	A24	5c grn, grnsh	80	60
39	A24	5c yel grn ('00)	75	50
40	A24	10c lavender	3.75	3.50
41	A24	10c red ('00)	2.00	50
42	A24	15c bl, quadrille paper	3.75	75
43	A24	15c gray ('00)	1.80	1.20
44	A24	20c red, grn	5.25	3.75
45	A24	25c rose	8.00	3.25
46	A24	25c bl ('00)	17.50	15.00
47	A24	30c brn, bis	8.00	3.25
48	A24	40c red, straw	10.00	9.50
49	A24	50c car, rose	17.50	13.00
50	A24	50c red, az ('00)	22.50	20.00
51	A24	75c vio, org	9.00	7.50
52	A24	1fr brnz grn, straw	9.00	7.50
	Nos. 35-52 (18)		121.72	91.62

Stamps of 1892 Surcharged:

1903

53	A24	5c on 40c red, straw	7.50	7.50
54	A24	10c on 50c car, rose	11.00	11.00
55	A24	10c on 75c vio, org	11.00	11.00
56	A24	10c on 1fr brnz grn, straw	45.00	40.00

General Louis Faidherbe—A25

Oil Palms A26

Dr. Noël Eugène Ballay A27

1906   Typographed

SÉNÉGAL in Red or Blue

57	A25	1c slate	32	32
a.	"SENEGAL" omitted	52.50	52.50
58	A25	2c choc (R)	50	50
58A	A25	2c choc (Bl)	1.00	1.00
59	A25	4c choc, gray bl	65	65
60	A25	5c green	60	32
61	A25	10c car (Bl)	3.00	32
a.	"SENEGAL" omitted	150.00	150.00
62	A25	15c violet	3.25	2.25
63	A26	20c blk, az	4.00	2.25
64	A26	25c bl, pnksh	1.00	70
65	A26	30c choc, pnksh	3.25	2.25
66	A26	35c yellow	10.00	1.25
67	A26	40c car, az (Bl)	5.25	4.25
67A	A26	45c choc, grnsh	10.00	8.00
68	A26	50c dp vio	4.50	3.75
69	A26	75c bl, org	3.75	2.25
70	A27	1fr blk, az	13.00	10.00
71	A27	2fr bl, pink	20.00	15.00
72	A27	5fr car, straw (Bl)	37.50	30.00
	Nos. 57-72 (18)		121.57	85.06

Stamps of 1892-1900 Surcharged in Carmine or Black

1912

73	A24	5c on 15c gray (C)	30	30
74	A24	5c on 20c red, grn	45	45
75	A24	5c on 30c brn, bis (C)	30	30
76	A24	10c on 40c red, straw	45	45
77	A24	10c on 50c car, rose	1.40	1.40
78	A24	10c on 75c vio, org	3.00	3.00
	Nos. 73-78 (6)		5.90	5.90

Two spacings between the surcharged numerals found on Nos. 73 to 78.

SENEGAL

Senegalese Preparing Food
A28

1914-33 Typographed.

79	A28	1c ol brn & vio	5	5
80	A28	2c blk & bl	5	5
81	A28	4c gray & brn	5	5
82	A28	5c yel grn & bl grn	12	12
83	A28	5c blk & rose ('22)	6	5
84	A28	10c org red & rose	12	12
a.		Booklet pane of 4	3.00	
85	A28	10c yel grn & bl grn ('22)	12	12
a.		Booklet pane of 4	2.00	
86	A28	10c red brn & bl ('25)	6	6
87	A28	15c red org & brn vio ('17)	6	6
a.		Booklet pane of 4	2.75	
88	A28	20c choc & blk	6	6
89	A28	20c grn & bl grn ('26)	6	6
90	A28	20c db & lt bl ('27)	15	15
91	A28	25c ultra & bl	12	12
92	A28	25c red & blk ('22)	8	8
93	A28	30c blk & rose	12	8
94	A28	30c red org & rose ('22)	12	12
95	A28	30c gray & bl ('26)	15	15
96	A28	30c dl grn & dp grn ('28)	22	8
97	A28	35c org & vio	8	6
98	A28	40c vio & grn	30	12
99	A28	45c bl & ol brn	50	50
100	A28	45c rose & bl ('22)	15	15
101	A28	45c rose & ver ('25)	15	15
102	A28	45c ol brn & org ('28)	1.75	1.75
103	A28	50c vio brn & bl	30	12
104	A28	50c ultra & bl ('22)	95	80
105	A28	50c red org & grn ('26)	15	12
106	A28	60c vio, pnksh ('26)	15	15
107	A28	65c rose red & dp grn ('28)	75	75
108	A28	75c gray & rose	38	22
109	A28	75c dk bl & lt bl ('25)	22	15
110	A28	75c rose & gray bl ('26)	75	22
111	A28	90c brn red & rose ('30)	3.00	2.75
112	A28	1fr vio & blk	45	18
113	A28	1fr bl ('26)	22	15
114	A28	1fr blk & gray bl ('26)	45	15
115	A28	1.10fr bl grn & blk ('28)	1.75	1.75
116	A28	1.25fr dp grn & dp org ('33)	38	38
117	A28	1.50fr dk bl & bl ('30)	1.25	1.25
118	A28	1.75fr dk brn & Prus bl ('33)	3.75	50
119	A28	2fr car & bl	90	75
120	A28	2fr lt bl & brn ('22)	95	25
121	A28	3fr red vio ('30)	2.50	1.00
122	A28	5fr grn & vio	2.25	60
		Nos. 79-122 (44)	26.20	16.62

Nos. 79, 82, 84 and 97 are on both ordinary and chalky paper.

Stamps and Type of 1914 Surcharged

≡ 60 ≡ 60

1922-25

123	A28	60c on 75c vio, pnksh	32	32
124	A28	65c on 15c red org & dl vio ('25)	45	45
125	A28	85c on 15c red org & dl vio ('25)	45	45
126	A28	85c on 75c gray & rose ('25)	55	55

No. 87 Surcharged

≡ 0,01 ≡ 0,01

in Various Colors.

1922

127	A28	1c on 15c (Bk)	15	15
128	A28	2c on 15c (Bl)	15	15
129	A28	4c on 15c (G)	15	15
130	A28	5c on 15c (R)	15	15
		Nos. 123-130 (8)	2.37	2.37

Stamps and Type of 1914 Surcharged with New Value and Bars in Black or Red

1924-27

131	A28	25c on 5fr grn & vio	25	25
132	A28	90c on 75c brn red & cer ('27)	50	45
a.		Double surch.	52.50	52.50
133	A28	1.25fr on 1fr bl & lt bl (R) ('26)	25	25
134	A28	1.50fr on 1fr dk bl & ultra ('27)	38	30
135	A28	3fr on 5fr mag & ol brn ('27)	1.00	45
136	A28	10fr on 5fr dk bl & red org ('27)	3.50	1.00
137	A28	20fr on 5fr vio & ol bis ('27)	4.50	3.00
		Nos. 131-137 (7)	10.38	5.70

Colonial Exposition Issue.
Common Design Types
Name of Country Typographed in Black.

1931 Engraved. Perf. 12½.

138	CD70	40c dp grn	1.25	1.25
139	CD71	50c violet	1.25	1.25
140	CD72	90c red org	1.25	1.25
a.		"SENEGAL" double	47.50	
141	CD73	1.50fr dl bl	1.25	1.25

Faidherbe Bridge, St. Louis
A29

Diourbel Mosque—A30

1935-40 Perf. 12½x12

142	A29	1c vio bl	5	5
143	A29	2c brown	5	5
144	A29	3c vio ('40)	6	5
145	A29	4c gray bl	6	5
146	A29	5c org red	6	5
147	A29	10c violet	6	5
148	A29	15c black	6	6
149	A29	20c dk car	6	6
150	A29	25c blk brn	10	10
151	A29	30c green	10	10
152	A29	40c rose lake	10	10
153	A29	45c dk bl grn	10	10
154	A30	50c red org	6	6
155	A30	60c vio ('40)	12	12
156	A30	65c dk vio	15	15
157	A30	70c red brn ('40)	28	28
158	A30	75c brown	38	38
159	A30	90c rose car	1.25	1.00
160	A30	1fr violet	4.50	1.25
161	A30	1.25fr redsh brn	60	38
162	A30	1.25fr rose car ('39)	40	40
163	A30	1.40fr dk bl grn ('40)	28	28
164	A30	1.50fr dk bl	15	15
165	A30	1.60fr pck bl ('40)	30	30
166	A30	1.75fr dk bl grn	15	15
167	A30	2fr blue	15	15
168	A30	3fr green	15	15
169	A30	5fr blk brn	45	30
170	A30	10fr rose lake	60	45
171	A30	20fr grnsh s	60	45
		Nos. 142-171 (30)	11.43	7.22

Nos. 143, 148 and 56 surcharged with new values are listed under French West Africa.

Paris International Exposition Issue.
Common Design Types

1937 Perf. 13

172	CD74	20c dp vio	50	50
173	CD75	30c dk grn	50	50
174	CD76	40c car rose	50	50
175	CD77	50c dk brn	65	65
176	CD78	90c red	65	65
177	CD79	1.50fr ultra	95	95
		Nos. 172-177 (6)	3.75	3.75

Colonial Arts Exhibition Issue.
Souvenir Sheet.
Common Design Type

1937 Imperf Unwmkd.

178	CD76	3fr rose vio	2.25	2.25

Sheet size: 1.8x99mm.

Senegalese Woman
A31

1938-40 Perf. 12x12½, 12½x12

179	A31	35c green	38	22
180	A31	55c chocolate	38	30
181	A31	80c violet	50	22
182	A31	90c lt rose vio ('39)	15	15
183	A31	1fr car lake	1.10	65
184	A31	1fr cop brn ('40)	12	12
185	A31	1.75fr ultra	38	22
186	A31	2.25fr ultra ('39)	30	30
187	A31	2.50fr blk ('40)	45	45
		Nos. 179-187 (9)	3.76	2.63

Caillié Issue
Common Design Type

1939 Engraved Perf. 12½x12

188	CD81	90c org brn & org	28	28
189	CD81	2fr brt vio	38	38
190	CD81	2.25fr ultra & dk bl	38	38

Centenary of the death of René Caillié (1799-1838), French explorer.
For No. 188 surcharged 20fr and 50fr, see French West Africa.

New York World's Fair Issue.
Common Design Type
Perf. 12½x12

191	CD82	1.25fr car lake	35	35
192	CD82	2.25fr ultra	35	35

Common Design Types
pictured in section at front of book.

Diourbel Mosque and Marshal Pétain
A32

1941 Engraved.

193	A32	1fr green	28	
194	A32	2.50fr blue	28	

Nos. 193-194 were issued by the Vichy government, but it is doubtful whether they were placed on sale in Senegal.

Stamps of types A29, A30 and A31, without "RF", were issued in 1943 by the Vichy Government, but were not placed on sale in the colony.

Republic

Roan Antelope
A33

Animals: 10fr, Savannah buffalo (horiz.). 15fr, Wart hog. 20fr, Giant eland. 25fr, Bushbuck (horiz.). 85fr, Defassa waterbuck.

Engraved
1960 Perf. 13 Unwmkd.

195	A33	5fr brn, grn & cl	15	8
196	A33	10fr grn & brn	25	12
197	A33	15fr blk, cl & org brn	30	15
198	A33	20fr brn, grn, ocher & sal	40	15
199	A33	25fr brn, lt grn & org	50	25
200	A33	85fr brn, grn, ol & bis	1.60	75
		Nos. 195-200 (6)	3.20	1.50

Imperforates

Most Senegal stamps from 1960 onward exist imperforate in issued and trial colors, and also in small presentation sheets in issued colors.

Allegory of Independent State
A34

1961, Apr. 4

201	A34	25fr bl, choc & grn	35	20

Issued for Independence Day, Apr. 4.

Wrestling
A35

Designs: 1fr, Pirogues racing. 2fr, Horse race. 30fr, Male tribal dance. 45fr, Lion game.

1961, Sept. 30 Perf. 13

202	A35	50c ol, bl & choc	5	5
203	A35	1fr grn, bl & mar	5	5

510 SENEGAL

204	A35	2fr ultra, bis & sep	8	5
205	A35	30fr car & cl	45	28
206	A35	45fr ind & brn org	60	40
		Nos. 202-206 (5)	1.23	83

U.N. Headquarters, New York and Flag—A36

1962, Jan. 6 Engraved *Perf. 13*

207	A36	10fr grn, ocher & car	20	15
208	A36	30fr car, ocher & grn	45	32
209	A36	85fr grn, ocher & car	1.10	65

Issued to commemorate the first anniversary of Senegal's admission to the United Nations, Sept. 28, 1960.

Map of Africa, ITU Emblem and Man with Telephone A37

1962, Jan. 22 Photo. *Perf. 12½x12*

| 210 | A37 | 25fr blk, grn, red & ocher | 40 | 30 |

Issued to publicize the meeting of the Commission for the Africa Plan of the International Telecommunication Union, Dakar.

African and Malgache Union Issue
Common Design Type

1962, Sept. 8 Unwmkd.

| 211 | CD110 | 30fr bluish grn, red & gold | 60 | 50 |

Issued to commemorate the first anniversary of the African and Malgache Union.

Boxing A38

Designs: 15fr, Diving (horiz.). 20fr, High jump (horiz.). 25fr, Soccer. 30fr, Basketball. 85fr, Running.

1963, Apr. 11 Engraved *Perf. 13*
Athletes in Dark Brown

212	A38	10fr ver & emer	20	12
213	A38	15fr dk bl & bis	25	15
214	A38	20fr ver & dk bl	35	20
215	A38	25fr grn & dk bl	40	25
216	A38	30fr ver & grn	50	32
217	A38	85fr vio bl	1.30	90
		Nos. 212-217 (6)	3.00	1.94

Friendship Games, Dakar, Apr. 11–21.

UPU Monument, Bern A39

1963, June 14 *Perf. 13* Unwmkd.

218	A39	10fr grn & ver	25	20
219	A39	15fr dk bl & red brn	30	25
220	A39	30fr red brn & dk bl	50	35

Issued to commemorate the second anniversary of Senegal's admission to the Universal Postal Union.

Charaxes Varanes A40

Butterflies: 45fr, Papilio nireus. 50fr, Colotis danae. 85fr, Epiphora bauhinlae. 100fr, Junonia hierta. 500fr, Danaus chrysippus.

1963, July 20 Photo. *Perf. 12½x13*
Butterflies in Natural Colors

221	A40	30fr bl gray & blk	60	25
222	A40	45fr org & blk	85	35
223	A40	50fr brt yel & blk	1.00	45
224	A40	85fr red & blk	1.50	80
225	A40	100fr bl & blk	1.65	1.00
226	A40	500fr emer & blk	6.50	3.50
		Nos. 221-226 (6)	12.10	6.35

Gaston Berger and Owl A41

1963, Nov. 13 *Perf. 12½x12*

| 227 | A41 | 25fr multi | 35 | 20 |

Issued to honor Prof. Gaston Berger (1896–1960), philosopher.

Scales, Globe, Flag and UNESCO Emblem—A42

1963, Dec. 10

| 228 | A42 | 60fr multi | 80 | 45 |

Issued to commemorate the 15th anniversary of the Universal Declaration of Human Rights.

Flag, Mother and Child A43

1963, Dec. 21 *Perf. 12x12½*

| 229 | A43 | 25fr multi | 45 | 35 |

Issued for the Senegalese Red Cross.

Dredging of Titanium-bearing Sand A44

Designs: 10fr, Titanium extraction works. 15fr, Cement works at Rufisque. 20fr, Phosphate quarry at Pallo. 25fr, Extraction of phosphate ore at Taiba. 85fr, Mineral dock, Dakar.

Engraved

1964, July 4 *Perf. 13* Unwmkd.

230	A44	5fr grnsh bl, car & dk brn	10	8
231	A44	10fr ocher, grn & ind	15	6
232	A44	15fr dk bl, brt grn & dk brn	20	10
233	A44	20fr ultra, ol & pur	25	15
234	A44	25fr dk bl, yel & blk	40	8
235	A44	85fr bl, red & brn	1.25	65
		Nos. 230-235 (6)	2.35	1.12

Cooperation Issue
Common Design Type

1964, Nov. 7 Engraved *Perf. 13*

| 236 | CD119 | 100fr dk grn, dk brn & car | 1.35 | 85 |

St. Theresa's Church, Dakar A45

Designs: 10fr, Mosque, Touba. 15fr, Mosque, Dakar (vert.).

1964, Nov. 28 *Perf. 13* Unwmkd.

237	A45	5fr bl, grn & red brn	12	10
238	A45	10fr dk bl, ocher & blk	18	12
239	A45	15fr brn, bl & sl grn	25	18

Leprosy Examination—A46

Leprosarium, Peycouk Village A47

1965, Jan. 30 Engraved *Perf. 13*

| 240 | A46 | 20fr brn red, grn & blk | 35 | 30 |
| 241 | A47 | 65fr org, dk bl & grn | 1.00 | 60 |

Issued to publicize the fight against leprosy.

Upper Casamance Region A48

Views: 30fr, Sangalkam. 45fr, Forest along Senegal River.

1965, Feb. 27 *Perf. 13* Unwmkd.
Size: 36x22mm.

242	A48	25fr red brn, sl bl & grn	35	20
243	A48	30fr ind & lt brn	40	20
244	A48	45fr yel grn, red brn & dk brn	60	35

Abdoulaye Seck A49 **Berthon-Ader Telephone A51**

General Post Office, Dakar A50

1965, Apr. 24 *Perf. 13* Unwmkd.

| 245 | A49 | 10fr dk brn & blk | 15 | 10 |
| 246 | A50 | 15fr brn & dk sl grn | 25 | 13 |

1965, May 17 Engraved

Designs: 60fr, Cable laying ship "Alsace." 85fr, Picard's cable relay for submarine telegraph.

247	A51	50fr bl grn & org brn	75	45
248	A51	60fr mag & dk bl	90	55
249	A51	85fr ver, bl & red brn	1.35	75

Issued to commemorate the centenary of the International Telecommunication Union.

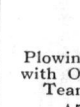 

Plowing with Ox Team A52

Designs: 60fr, Harvesting millet (vert.). 85fr, Men working in rice field.

1965, July 3 *Perf. 13* Unwmkd.

250	A52	25fr dk ol grn, brn & pur	40	25
251	A52	60fr ind, sl grn & dk brn	80	35
252	A52	85fr dp car, sl grn & brt grn	1.25	55

Gorée Sailboat A53 **Cashew A54**

Designs: 20fr, Large Seumbedlou canoe. 30fr, Fadiouth one-man canoe. 45fr, One-man canoe on Senegal River.

1965, Aug. 7 Photo. *Perf. 12½x13*

253	A53	10fr multi	15	10
254	A53	20fr multi	25	15
255	A53	30fr multi	45	25
256	A53	45fr multi	65	40

SENEGAL

1965	Photogravure		Perf. 12½	
		Multicolored		
257	A54	10fr shown	20	10
258	A54	15fr Papaya	25	15
259	A54	20fr Mango	30	18
260	A54	30fr Peanuts	45	12

Dates of issue: Nov. 6, 10fr, 15fr, 20fr. Dec. 18, 30fr.

"Elegant Man" Doll
A55

Drummer and Map of Africa
A56

Dolls of Gorée: 2fr, "Elegant Woman." 3fr, Woman peddling fruit. 4fr, Woman pounding grain.

1966, Jan. 22	Engraved		Perf. 13	
261	A55	1fr brn, rose car & ultra	8	6
262	A55	2fr brn, bl & org	8	6
263	A55	3fr brn, red & bl	8	8
264	A55	4fr brn, lil & emer	12	12

1966

Designs: 15fr, Sculpture; mother and child. No. 267, Music; stringed instrument. 75fr, Dance; carved antelope headpiece (Bambara). 90fr, Ideogram.

265	A56	15fr dk red brn, bl & ocher	20	20
266	A56	30fr brn, red & grn	45	27
267	A56	30fr dk red brn, bl & yel	45	27
268	A56	75fr dk red brn, bl & blk	1.10	65
269	A56	90fr dk red brn, org & sl grn	1.35	80
a.		Souv. sheet of 4	3.75	3.75
		Nos. 265-269 (5)	3.55	2.19

Issued to commemorate the International Negro Arts Festival, Dakar, Apr. 1–24. No. 269a contains one each of Nos. 265, 267–269; marginal inscription in black and red. Size: 139x110mm.
Dates of issue: No. 266, Feb. 5. Others, Apr. 2. See also No. 364.

Tuna—A57

Fish: 30fr, Merou. 50fr, Girella. 100fr, Parrot fish.

1966, Feb. 26 Photo.		Perf. 12½x13	
270	A57	20fr multi, pale grn	35	20
271	A57	30fr multi, bl	50	25
272	A57	50fr multi, pink	85	45
273	A57	100fr multi, buff	1.65	75

Arms of Senegal
A58

Mexican Poppy
A59

1966, July 2 Litho.		Perf. 13x12½	
274	A58	30fr multi	40	12

1966, Nov. 19 Photo.		Perf. 11½	

Flowers: 55fr, Mimosa. 60fr, Haemanthus. 90fr, Baobab.

Flowers in Natural Colors

275	A59	45fr dp brn & brt grn	65	28
276	A59	55fr yel grn & brt pur	75	32
277	A59	60fr grnsh bl	90	35
278	A59	90fr dp bl & lt ultra	1.20	55

Harbor, Gorée Island
A60

Designs: 25fr, S.S. France in roadstead, Dakar and seagulls. 30fr, Hotel and tourist village, N'Gor. 50fr, Hotel and bay, N'Gor.

1966, Dec. 25	Engraved		Perf. 13	
279	A60	20fr mar & vio bl	30	20
280	A60	25fr red, grn & blk	35	20
281	A60	30fr dk red & dp bl	40	25
282	A60	50fr brn, sl grn & emer	70	30

Laying Urban Water Pipes
A61

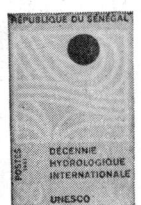
Symbolic Water Cycle
A62

Designs: 20fr, Cattle at water trough. 50fr, Village well.

1967, March 25 Engraved		Perf. 13	
283	A61	10fr org brn, grn & dk bl	20	15
284	A61	20fr grn, brt bl & org brn	40	30

	Typographed		Perf. 13x14	
285	A62	30fr sky bl, blk & org	50	15

	Engraved		Perf. 13	
286	A62	50fr brn red, brt bl & bis	85	30

Issued to publicize the International Hydrological Decade (UNESCO), 1965–74.

Lions Emblem
A63

1967, May 27 Photo.		Perf. 12½x13	
287	A63	30fr lt ultra & multi	45	25

50th anniversary of Lions International.

Blaise Diagne
A64

1967, June 10 Engraved		Perf. 13	
288	A64	30fr ocher, sl grn & dk red brn	45	30

Issued in memory of Blaise Diagne (1872–1934), member of French Chamber of Deputies and Colonial Minister.

City Hall and Arms, Dakar
A65

1967, June 10				
289	A65	90fr bl, dk grn & blk	1.20	55

Eagle and Antelope Carvings
A66

Design: 150fr, Flags, maple leaf and EXPO '67 emblem.

1967, Sept. 2 Photo.		Perf. 13x12½	
290	A66	90fr red & blk	1.20	60
291	A66	150fr red & multi	2.00	1.00

Issued to commemorate EXPO '67 International Exhibition, Montreal, Apr. 28–Oct. 27.

International Tourist Year Emblem
A67

Tourist Photographing Hippopotamus and Siminti Hotel—A68

1967, Oct. 7 Typo.		Perf. 14x13	
292	A67	50fr blk & bl	85	50

	Engraved		Perf. 13	
293	A68	100fr blk, sl grn & ocher	1.65	75

International Tourist Year, 1967

Monetary Union Issue
Common Design Type

1967, Nov. 4	Engraved		Perf. 13	
294	CD125	30fr multi	40	15

Issued to commemorate the 5th anniversary of the West African Monetary Union.

Lyre-shaped Megalith, Kaffrine
A69

Design: 70fr, Ancient covered bowl, Bandiala.

1967, Dec. 2	Engraved		Perf. 13	
295	A69	30fr grn, grnsh bl & red brn	40	15
296	A69	70fr red brn, ocher & brt bl	90	40

Nurse Feeding Child
A70

Human Rights Flame
A71

1967, Dec. 23				
297	A70	50fr bl grn, red & red brn	70	35

Issued for the Senegalese Red Cross.

Parliament, Dakar
A72

1968, Jan. 20 Photo.		Perf. 13x12½	
298	A71	30fr brt grn & gold	45	20

International Human Rights Year 1968.

1968, Apr. 16 Photo.		Perf. 12½x13	
299	A72	30fr car rose	40	20

Issued to commemorate the Inter-Parliamentary Union Meeting, Dakar.

Pied Kingfisher
A73

Goose Barnacles
A74

Designs: 10fr, Green lobster. 15fr, African jacana. 20fr, Sea cicada. 35fr, Shrimp. African anhinga.

1968-69	Photogravure		Perf. 11½	

Dated "1968" or (70fr) "1969."

Granite Paper

300	A73	5fr brn & multi	10	7
301	A74	10fr red & multi	15	10
302	A73	15fr yel & multi	25	13
303	A74	20fr ultra & multi	30	15
304	A74	35fr car rose & ol grn	45	20
305	A73	70fr Prus bl & multi ('69)	1.00	50
306	A74	100fr yel & multi	1.35	75
		Nos. 300-306 (7)	3.60	2.00

Dates of issue: 5fr, July 13, 1968; 15fr, Dec. 21, 1968; 70fr, Apr. 26, 1969; others May 18, 1968. See also Nos. C53–C57.

SENEGAL

Steer and Hypodermic Syringe
A75

1968, Aug. 17	Engraved	*Perf. 13*		
307	A75	30fr dk grn, dp bl & brn red	35	25

Campaign against cattle plague.

Boy and WHO		Bambara Antelope
Emblem		Symbol
A76		A77

1968, Nov. 16	Engraved	*Perf. 13*		
308	A76	30fr blk, grn & car	40	20
309	A76	45fr red brn, grn & blk	60	30

Issued to commemorate the 20th anniversary of the World Health Organization.

1969, Jan. 13 Engraved *Perf. 13*

Design: 30fr, School of Medicine and Pharmacology, Dakar (horiz.).

| 310 | A77 | 30fr emer, brt bl & ind | 40 | 25 |
| 311 | A77 | 50fr red, gray ol & bl grn | 60 | 30 |

6th Medical Meeting, Dakar, Jan. 13–18.

Panet, Camels and Mogador-
St. Louis Route
A78

1969, Feb. 15	Engraved	*Perf. 13*		
312	A78	75fr ultra, Prus bl & brn	90	40

Issued to commemorate the 150th anniversary of the birth of Leopold Panet (1819–1859), first explorer of the Mauritanian Sahara.

ILO Emblem
A79

1969, May 3	Photo.	*Perf. 12½x13*		
313	A79	30fr blk & grnsh bl	35	15
314	A79	45fr blk & dp car	60	28

Issued to commemorate the 50th anniversary of the International Labor Organization.

Arms of Casamance
A80

Design: 20fr, Arms of Gorée Island.

1969, July 26	Litho.	*Perf. 13½*		
315	A80	15fr rose & multi	15	6
316	A80	20fr bl & multi	20	10

Development Bank Issue
Common Design Type

1969, Sept. 10	Engraved	*Perf. 13*		
317	CD130	30fr gray, grn & ocher	40	25
318	CD130	45fr brn, grn & ocher	60	30

Issued to commemorate the 5th anniversary of the African Development Bank.

Mahatma Gandhi
A81

1969, Oct. 2	Engraved	*Perf. 13*		
319	A81	50fr multi	65	30
a.	Min. sheet of 4		2.75	2.75

Issued to commemorate the centenary of the birth of Mohandas K. Gandhi (1869–1948), leader in India's fight for independence. No. 319a contains 4 No. 319. Size: 99x129mm.

Rotary Emblem and Symbolic Ship
A82

1969, Nov. 29	Photo.	*Perf. 12½x13*		
320	A82	30fr ultra, yel & blk	50	30

Dakar Rotary Club, 30th anniversary.

ASECNA Issue
Common Design Type

1969, Dec. 12	Engraved	*Perf. 13*		
321	CD132	100fr dk gray	1.00	50

Tourist Issue

Niokolo-Koba Campsite
A83

Designs: 20fr, Cape Skiring, Casamance. 35fr, Elephants at Niokolo-Koba National Park. 45fr, Millet granaries, pigs and boats, Fadiouth Island.

1969, Dec. 27

322	A83	20fr bl, red brn & ol	25	15
323	A83	30fr bl, red brn & ocher	40	15
324	A83	35fr grnsh bl, blk & ocher	45	25
325	A83	45fr vio bl & hn brn	50	25

| Bottle-nosed Dolphins | Lenin |
| A84 | A85 |

1970, Feb. 21	Photo.	*Perf. 12x12½*		
326	A84	50fr dl bl, blk & red	60	30

1970, Apr. 22	Photo.	*Perf. 11½*		
327	A85	30fr brn, buff & ver	35	25
a.	50fr souvenir sheet		2.50	

Issued to commemorate the centenary of the birth of Lenin (1870–1924), Russian communist leader. No. 327a contains one 50fr stamp (size: 32x48mm., perf. 12x 11½) in same design and colors as No. 327; red and dark brown sheet margin. Size: 66½x95mm.

U.P.U. Headquarters Issue
Common Design Type

1970, May 20	Engraved	*Perf. 13*		
328	CD133	30fr dk red, ind & dp cl	35	20
329	CD133	45fr dl brn, dk car & bl grn	60	28

Textile Plant, Thies—A86

Design: 45fr, Fertilizer plant, Dakar.

1970, Nov. 21	Engraved	*Perf. 13*		
330	A86	30fr grn, brt bl & brn red	40	20
331	A86	45fr brn red & brt bl	60	28

Industrialization of Senegal.

Boy Scouts	Three Heads
A87	and Sun
	A88

Design: 100fr, Lord Baden-Powell, map of Africa with Dakar, and fleur-de-lis.

1970, Dec. 11	Photo.	*Perf. 11½*		
332	A87	30fr multi	35	20
333	A87	100fr multi	1.25	55

First African Boy Scout Conference, Dakar, Dec. 11–14.

1970, Dec. 19	Engraved	*Perf. 13*		
Design: 40fr, African man and woman, globe with map of Africa.				
334	A88	25fr ultra, org & vio brn	40	20
335	A88	40fr brn ol, dk brn & org	70	30

International Education Year.

Senegal	Refugees and U.N.
Arms	Emblem—A90
A89	

1970-76	Photo.	*Perf. 12*		
336	A89	30fr yel grn & multi	30	15
336A	A89	35fr brt pink & multi ('71)	35	15
b.	Bklt. pane of 10 ('72)		3.75	
336C	A89	50fr bl & multi ('75)	40	15
336D	A89	65fr lil rose & multi ('76)	50	15

The booklet pane has a control number in the margin.

1971, Jan. 16		*Perf. 12½x12*		
337	A90	40fr ver, blk, yel & grn	50	25

High Commissioner for Refugees, 20th anniversary. See No. C94.

Mare "Mbayang"
A91

Horses: 25fr, Mare Madjiguene. 100fr, Stallion Pass. 125fr, Stallion Pepe.

1971	Photo.	*Perf. 11½*		
338	A91	25fr multi	30	15
339	A91	40fr multi	50	25
340	A91	100fr multi	1.10	60
341	A91	125fr multi	1.40	60

Improvements in horse breeding.

U.N. Emblem,
Black and
White
Children
A92

U.N. Emblem, Four Races
A93

Perf. 13x12½, 12½x11

1971, March 21		Lithographed		
342	A92	30fr multi	35	15
343	A93	50fr multi	60	30

International Year against Racial Discrimination.

Globe and Telephone
A94

SENEGAL

Design: 40fr, Radar, satellite, orbits.

1971, May 17	Engraved	Perf. 13
344 A94	30fr pur, grn & brn	35 20
345 A94	40fr Prus bl, dk brn & red brn	45 20

3rd World Telecommunications Day.

Drummer (Hayashida)—A95

Designs (Jamboree Emblem and): 50fr, Dwarf Japanese quince and grape hyacinth. 65fr, Judo. 75fr, Mt. Fuji.

1971, Aug. 7	Photo.	Perf. 13½
346 A95	35fr lt ultra & multi	40 20
347 A95	50fr yel & multi	60 30
348 A95	65fr dp org & multi	75 35
349 A95	75fr grn & multi	90 50

13th Boy Scout World Jamboree, Asagiri Plain, Japan, Aug. 2–10.

Map of West Africa with Senegal, UNICEF Emblem A97

Design: 100fr, Nurse, children and UNICEF emblem.

1971, Oct. 30		Perf. 12½
352 A97	35fr dl bl, org & blk	40 20
353 A97	100fr multi	1.20 55

25th anniversary of United Nations International Children's Fund (UNICEF).

Basketball and Games' Emblem A98

Designs: 40fr, Basketball and emblem. 75fr, Games' emblem.

1971, Dec. 24	Photo.	Perf. 13½x13
354 A98	35fr lt vio & multi	45 25
355 A98	40fr emer & multi	50 28
356 A98	75fr ocher & multi	1.00 55

6th African Basketball Championships, Dakar, Dec. 25, 1971–Jan. 2, 1972.

"The Exile of Albouri"—A99

Design: 40fr, "The Merchant of Venice."

1972, Mar. 25		Perf. 13x12½
357 A99	35fr dk red & multi	45 25
358 A99	40fr dk red & multi	55 30

International Theater Day. See No. C112.

WHO Emblem and Heart A100

Design: 40fr, Physician with patient, WHO emblem and electrocardiogram.

1972, Apr. 7	Engraved	Perf. 13
359 A100	35fr brt bl & red brn	40 20
360 A100	40fr sl grn & brn	45 25

"Your heart is your health," World Health Month.

Containment of the Desert, Environment Emblem—A101

1972, June 3	Photo.	Perf. 13x12½
361 A101	35fr multi	45 25

U.N. Conference on Human Environment, Stockholm, June 5–16. See No. C113.

Tartarin Shooting the Lion—A102

Design: 100fr, Alphonse Daudet.

1972, June 24	Engraved	Perf. 13
362 A102	40fr brt grn, rose car & brn	50 20
363 A102	100fr Prus bl, bl & brn	1.20 50

75th anniversary of the death of Alphonse Daudet (1840–1897), French novelist, and centenary of the publication of his "Tartarin de Tarascon."

Souvenir Sheet

Stringed Instrument—A103

1972, July 1	Engr.	Perf. 11½
364 A103	150fr rose red	2.50 2.00

Belgica 72, International Philatelic Exhibition, Brussels, June 24–July 9. No. 364 contains one stamp in design similar to No. 267. View of Grand-Place, Brussels, in violet blue; rose red and violet blue inscription in margin. Size: 110x95 mm.

Wrestling, Olympic Rings A104

1972, July 22	Photo.	Perf. 14x13½

Gold and Multicolored

365 A104	15fr shown	20 12
366 A104	20fr 100-meter dash	25 15
367 A104	100fr Basketball	1.00 50
368 A104	125fr Judo	1.20 60

Souvenir Sheet

Perf. 13½x14½

| 369 A104 | 240fr Torchbearer and Munich | 3.25 2.50 |

20th Olympic Games, Munich, Aug. 26–Sept. 11. No. 369 contains one stamp, Olympic and motion emblems in multicolored margin. Size: 90x70mm.

Book Year Emblem, Children Reading A105

Senegalese Fashion A106

1972, Sept. 16	Photo.	Perf. 13
370 A105	50fr gray & multi	55 25

International Book Year 1972.

1972–76		Engraved
371 A106	25fr black	25 8
a.	Bklt. pane of 5	2.50
b.	Bklt. pane of 10	5.00
372 A106	40fr brt ultra	40 8
a.	Bklt. pane of 5	4.00
b.	Bklt. pane of 10	8.00
372C A106	60fr brt grn ('76)	50 8
372D A106	75fr lil rose	75 32

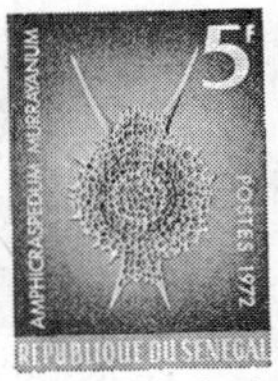

Aleksander Pushkin A107

Amphicrasphedum Murrayanum A108

1972, Oct. 28	Photo.	Perf. 11½
373 A107	100fr sal & pur	1.20 60

135th anniversary of the death of Aleksander Pushkin (1799–1837), Russian writer.

West African Monetary Union Issue
Common Design Type

Design: 40fr, African couple, city, village and commemorative coin.

1972, Nov. 2	Engraved	Perf. 13
374 CD136	40fr ol brn, bl & gray	45 25

10th anniversary of West African Monetary Union.

1972–73	Photo.	Perf. 11½

Marine Life: 10fr, Pterocanium tricolpum. 15fr, Ceratospyris polygona. 20fr, Cortiniscus typicus. 30fr, Theopera cortina.

375 A108	5fr multi	8 5
376 A108	10fr multi	12 7
377 A108	15fr multi	20 8
378 A108	20fr multi ('73)	20 10
379 A108	30fr multi ('73)	20 10
Nos. 375-379, C115-C118 (9)		4.00 1.98

Issue dates: Nos. 375–377, Nov. 25, 1972. Nos. 378–379, July 28, 1973.

1872-1972

No. 288 Surcharged in Vermilion **100F**

1972, Dec. 9	Engraved	Perf. 13
380 A64	100fr on 30fr multi	90 45

Centenary of the birth of Blaise Diagne (1872–1934), member of French Chamber of Deputies, and Colonial Minister.

Melchior A109

Black and White Men Carrying Emblem A110

1972, Dec. 23	Photo.	Perf. 13x13½

Multicolored

381 A109	10fr shown	15 10
382 A109	15fr Caspar	20 10
383 A109	40fr Balthasar	45 25
384 A109	60fr Joseph	60 40
385 A109	100fr Virgin and Child	1.00 65
Nos. 381-385 (5)		2.40 1.50

Christmas 1972. Nos. 381–385 printed se-tenant with continuous design, showing traditional Gorée dolls.

Europafrica Issue

1973, Jan. 20	Engraved	Perf. 13
386 A110	65fr blk & grn	65 35

Radar Station, Gandoul A111

1973, May 17	Engraved	Perf. 13
387 A111	40fr multi	40 25

Phases of Solar Eclipse A112

Designs: 65fr, Moon between earth and sun casting shadow on earth. 150fr, Diagram of areas of partial and total eclipse, satellite in space.

SENEGAL

1973, June 30   Photo.   Perf. 13x14
388	A112	35fr dk bl & multi	35	20
389	A112	65fr dk bl & multi	55	40
390	A112	150fr dk bl & multi	1.35	90

Total solar eclipse over Africa, June 30, 1973.

Men Holding Torch over Africa — A113

1973, July 7   Perf. 12½x13
| 391 | A113 | 75fr multi | 65 | 45 |

Organization for African Unity, 10th anniversary.

No. 338 Surcharged with New Value, 2 Bars, and Overprinted in Ultramarine: "SECHERESSE / SOLIDARITE AFRICAINE"

1973, July 21   Photo.   Perf. 11½
| 392 | A91 | 100fr on 25fr multi | 90 | 60 |

African solidarity in drought emergency.

African Postal Union Issue
Common Design Type

1973, Sept. 12   Engraved   Perf. 13
| 393 | CD137 | 100fr dk grn, vio & dk red | 90 | 45 |

Child, Map of Senegal, WMO Emblem — A114

1973, Sept. 22
| 394 | A114 | 50fr multi | 45 | 15 |

Centenary of international meteorological cooperation.

INTERPOL Headquarters, Paris — A115

1973, Oct. 6   Engraved   Perf. 13
| 395 | A115 | 75fr ultra, bis & sl grn | 65 | 40 |

50th anniversary of International Criminal Police Organization.

Souvenir Sheet

John F. Kennedy — A116

1973, Nov. 22   Engraved   Perf. 13
| 396 | A116 | 150fr ultra | 1.50 | 1.50 |

10th anniversary of the death of Pres. John F. Kennedy (1917–1963). No. 396 contains one stamp. Lilac marginal inscription. Size: 91x105mm.

Amilcar Cabral — A117   Victorious Athletes and Flag — A118

1973, Dec. 15   Photo.   Perf. 12½x13
| 397 | A117 | 75fr multi | 65 | 50 |

Amilcar Cabral (1924–1973), leader of anti-Portuguese guerrilla movement in Portuguese Guinea.

1974, Apr. 6   Photo.   Perf. 12½x13

Design: 40fr, Folk theater.
| 398 | A118 | 35fr multi | 35 | 20 |
| 399 | A118 | 40fr multi | 45 | 30 |

National Youth Week.

Soccer Cup, Jugoslavia-Brazil Game, Our Lady's Church, Munich — A119

Designs (Soccer Cup and Games): 40fr, Australia-Germany (Fed. Rep.) and Belltower, Hamburg. 65fr, Netherlands-Uruguay and Tower, Hanover. 70fr, Zaire-Italy and Church, Stuttgart.

1974, June 29   Photo.   Perf. 13x14
400	A119	25fr car & multi	25	12
401	A119	40fr car & multi	40	25
402	A119	65fr car & multi	60	25
403	A119	70fr car & multi	65	28

World Cup Soccer Championship, Munich, June 13–July 7.

UPU Emblem, Envelopes and Means of Transportation — A120

1974, Oct. 9   Engraved   Perf. 13
| 404 | A120 | 100fr multi | 90 | 60 |

Centenary of Universal Postal Union.

Fair Emblem — A121

1974, Nov. 28   Engr.   Perf. 12½x13
| 405 | A121 | 100fr bl, org & dk brn | 80 | 50 |

Dakar International Fair.

No. 401 Surcharged in Black on Gold

1975, Feb. 1   Photo.   Perf. 13x14
| 406 | A119 | 200fr on 40fr multi | 1.60 | 1.00 |

World Cup Soccer Championships, 1974, victory of German Federal Republic.

Pres. Senghor and King Baudouin — A122

1975, Feb. 28   Photo.   Perf. 13x13½
| 407 | A122 | 65fr lil & dk bl | 50 | 30 |
| 408 | A122 | 100fr org & grn | 80 | 50 |

Visit of King Baudouin of Belgium to Senegal.

International Labor Organization Emblem — A123

1975, Apr. 30   Photo.   Perf. 13½x13½
| 409 | A123 | 125fr multi | 1.00 | 55 |

International Labor Festival.

Globe, Stamp, Letters, España 75 Emblem — A124

1975, June 6   Engr.   Perf. 13
| 410 | A124 | 55fr ind, grn & red | 45 | 30 |

España 75 International Philatelic Exhibition, Madrid, Apr. 4–13.

Apollo of Belvedere, Arphila 75 Emblem, Stamps — A125

1975, June 6
| 411 | A125 | 95fr dk brn, brn & bis | 75 | 50 |

Arphila 75 International Philatelic Exhibition, Paris, June 6–16.

Professional Instruction — A126

1975, June 28   Engr.   Perf. 13
| 412 | A126 | 85fr multi | 70 | 40 |

Dr. Schweitzer, Lambarene Hospital — A127

1975, July 5
| 413 | A127 | 85fr grn & vio brn | 70 | 40 |

Dr. Albert Schweitzer (1875–1965), medical missionary, birth centenary.

Senegalese Soldier, Batallion Flag, Map of Sinai — A128

1975, July 10   Litho.   Perf. 12½
| 414 | A128 | 100fr multi | 80 | 40 |

Senegalese Battalion of the United Nations' Sinai Service, 1973–1974.

Women and Child — A129

Design: 55fr, Women pounding grain, IWY emblem (vert.).

1975, Oct. 18   Photo.   Perf. 13½
| 415 | A129 | 55fr sil & multi | 45 | 22 |
| 416 | A129 | 75fr sil & multi | 60 | 30 |

International Women's Year 1975.

Staff of Aesculapius and African Mask — A130

1975, Dec. 1   Photo.   Perf. 12½x13
| 417 | A130 | 50fr multi | 40 | 15 |

40th French Medical Congress, Dakar, Dec. 1–3.

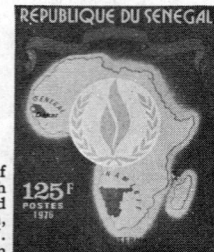

Map of Africa with Senegal and Namibia, U.N. Emblem — A131

SENEGAL

1976, Jan. 5	Photo.	Perf. 13
418 A131 125fr vio bl & multi	1.00	50

International Human Rights and Namibia Conference, Dakar, Jan. 5-8.

Sailfish Fishing
A132

Design: 200fr, Racing yachts and Oceanexpo 75 emblem.

1976, Jan. 28	Photo.	Perf. 13½x13
419 A132 140fr multi	1.10	55
420 A132 200fr multi	1.65	80

Oceanexpo 75, First International Oceanographic Exhibition, Okinawa, July 20, 1975-Jan. 1976.

Servals—A133

Designs: 3fr, Black-tailed godwits. 4fr, River hogs. 5fr, African fish eagles. No. 425, Okapis. No. 426, Sitatungas.

1976, Feb. 26	Photo.	Perf. 13
421 A133 2fr gold & multi	5	5
422 A133 3fr gold & multi	5	5
423 A133 4fr gold & multi	5	5
424 A133 5fr gold & multi	5	5
425 A133 250fr gold & multi	2.00	1.00
426 A133 250fr gold & multi	2.00	1.00
Strip of 2 + label	4.25	
Nos. 421-426 (6)	4.20	2.20

Basse Casamance National Park. Nos. 425-426 printed se-tenant and with label showing map with location of park. See Nos. 473-478.

A. G. Bell, Telephone, ITU Emblem—A134

1976, Mar. 31	Litho.	Perf. 12½x13
427 A134 175fr multi	1.40	65

Centenary of first telephone call by Alexander Graham Bell, Mar. 10, 1876.

Map of African French-speaking Countries
A135

1976, Apr. 12	Litho.	Perf. 13½
428 A135 60fr yel grn & multi	50	30

Scientific and Cultural Meeting of the African Dental Association, Dakar, Apr. 12-17.

Family and Graph
A136

1976, Apr. 26		
429 A136 65fr multi	50	30

First population census in Senegal, Apr. 1976.

Thomas Jefferson and 13-star Flag
A137

1976, June 19	Engr.	Perf. 13
430 A137 50fr bl, red & blk	40	20

American Bicentennial.

Planting Seedlings—A138

1976, Aug. 21	Litho.	Perf. 12
431 A138 60fr yel & multi	50	25

Reclamation of Sahel region.

Campfire
A139

Jamboree Emblem, Map of Africa
A140

1976, Aug. 30	Litho.	Perf. 12½
432 A139 80fr multi	65	50
433 A140 100fr multi	80	60

1st All Africa Scout Jamboree, Sherehills, Jos, Nigeria, Apr. 2-8, 1977.

Mechanized Tomato Harvest
A141

1976, Oct. 23	Photo.	Perf. 13
434 A141 180fr multi	1.50	65

Map of Dakar and Gorée
A142

Designs: 60fr, Star over Africa. 70fr, Students in laboratory and library. 200fr, Handshake over world map, Pres. Senghor.

1976, Oct. 9	Litho.	Perf. 13½x14
435 A142 40fr multi	35	18
436 A142 60fr multi	50	25
437 A142 70fr multi	55	30
438 A142 200fr multi	1.65	80

70th birthday of Pres. Leopold Sedar Senghor.

Scroll with Map of Africa, Senegalese People
A143

1977, Jan. 8		Perf. 12½
439 A143 60fr multi	50	25

Day of the Black People.

Joe Frazier and Mohammed Ali
A144

Design: 60fr, Ali and Frazier in ring (vert.).

1977, Jan. 7	Photo.	Perf. 13x13½
440 A144 60fr bl & blk	50	25
441 A144 150fr emer & blk	1.25	60

World boxing champion Mohammed Ali.

Dancer and Musician
A145

Designs (Festival Emblem and): 75fr, Wood carving and masks. 100fr, Dancers and ancestor statuette.

1977, Feb. 10	Litho.	Perf. 12½
442 A145 50fr yel & multi	40	20
443 A145 75fr grn & multi	60	30
444 A145 100fr rose & multi	85	40

2nd World Black and African Festival, Lagos, Nigeria, Jan. 15-Feb. 12.

Cogwheels and Symbols of Industry
A146

1977, Mar. 28	Engr.	Perf. 13
445 A146 70fr yel grn & ocher	55	28

Dakar Industrial Zone, 1st anniversary.

Burning Match and Burnt Trees
A147

Design: 60fr, Burnt trees and house, firetruck (horiz.).

1977, Apr. 30	Litho.	Perf. 12½
446 A147 40fr grn & multi	30	15
447 A147 60fr sl & multi	50	25

Prevention of forest fires.

Drummer, Telephone, Agriculture and Industry—A148

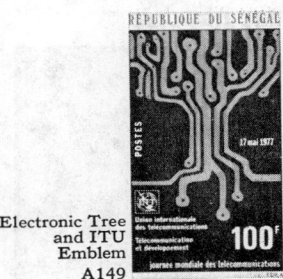

Electronic Tree and ITU Emblem
A149

1977, May 17	Litho.	Perf. 13
448 A148 80fr multi	65	35
449 A149 100fr multi	80	40

World Telecommunications Day.

Symbol of Language Studies
A150

Sassenage Castle, Grenoble—A151

Perf. 12x12½, 12½

1977, May 21		Lithographed
450 A150 65fr multi	50	28
451 A151 250fr multi	2.00	1.00

10th anniversary of International French Language Council.

SENEGAL

Woman in Boat, Wooden Shoe
A152

Design: 125fr, Senegalese woman, symbolic tulip and stamp (vert.).

1977, June 4 Perf. 13½x14, 14x13½

| 452 | A152 | 50fr bl grn & multi | 40 | 20 |
| 453 | A152 | 125fr ocher & multi | 1.00 | 50 |

Amphilex '77 International Philatelic Exhibition, Amsterdam, May 26–June 5.

Adult Reading Class
A153

Design: 65fr, Man learning to read.

1977, Sept. 10 Litho. Perf. 12½

| 454 | A153 | 60fr multi | 50 | 25 |
| 455 | A153 | 65fr multi | 55 | 35 |

National Literacy Week, Sept. 8–14.

Mercury, by Rubens
A154

Paintings: 25fr, Daniel in the Lions' Den, by Rubens. 40fr, The Empress, by Titian. 60fr, Flora, by Titian. 65fr, Jo, the Beautiful Irish Woman, by Courbet. 100fr, The Painter's Studio, by Courbet.

1977, Nov. Photo. Perf. 13x13½

456	A154	20fr multi	15	8
457	A154	25fr multi	20	10
458	A154	40fr multi	30	15
459	A154	60fr multi	45	25
460	A154	65fr multi	50	25
461	A154	100fr multi	85	40
		Nos. 456-461 (6)	2.45	1.26

Peter Paul Rubens (1577–1640), 400th birth anniversary; Titian (1477–1576), 500th birth anniversary; Gustave Courbet (1819–1877), death centenary.

Adoration by People of Various Races
A155

Designs: 25fr, Decorated arch and procession. 40fr, Christmas tree, mother and child. 100fr, Adoration of the Kings (horiz.).

1977, Dec. 22 Litho. Perf. 12½

462	A155	20fr multi	15	8
463	A155	25fr multi	20	10
464	A155	40fr multi	30	15
465	A155	100fr multi	85	40

Christmas 1977.

Regatta at Soumbedioun
A156

Designs: 10fr, Senegalese wrestlers. 65fr, Regatta at Soumbedioun (horiz.). 100fr, Dancers (horiz.).

1978, Jan. 7 Litho. Perf. 12½

466	A156	10fr multi	10	5
467	A156	30fr multi	25	12
468	A156	65fr multi	50	28
469	A156	100fr multi	85	40

Tourist publicity.

Acropolis, Athens, and African Buildings
A157

1978, Jan. 30

| 470 | A157 | 75fr multi | 60 | 30 |

UNESCO campaign to save world's cultural heritage.

Solar-powered Pump, Field and Sheep
A158

Design: 95fr, Pylon bringing electricity to villages and factories.

1978, Feb. 25

| 471 | A158 | 50fr multi | 40 | 20 |
| 472 | A158 | 95fr multi | 75 | 40 |

Energy in Senegal.

Park Type of 1976

Designs: 5fr, Caspian terns in flight, royal terns on ground. 10fr, Pink-backed pelicans. 15fr, Wart hog and gray heron. 20fr, Greater flamingoes, nests, eggs and young. No. 477, Gray heron and royal terns. No. 478, Abyssinian ground hornbill and wart hog.

1978, Apr. 22 Photo Perf. 13

473	A133	5fr gold & multi	5	5
474	A133	10fr gold & multi	10	5
475	A133	15fr gold & multi	15	6
476	A133	20fr gold & multi	20	8
477	A133	150fr gold & multi	1.50	1.00
478	A133	150fr gold & multi	1.50	1.00
		Strip of 2 + label	3.00	
		Nos. 473-478 (6)	3.50	2.24

Saloum Delta National Park. Nos. 477–478 printed se-tenant and with label showing map with location of park.

Dome of the Rock, Jerusalem
A159

1978, May 15 Litho. Perf. 12½

| 479 | A159 | 60fr multi | 60 | 22 |

Palestinian fighters and their families.

Vaccination, Dr. Jenner, WHO Emblem
A160

1978, June 3

| 480 | A160 | 60fr multi | 60 | 22 |

Eradication of smallpox.

Soccer, Flags: Argentina, Hungary, France, Italy
A161

Mahatma Gandhi
A162

Soccer, Cup, Argentina '78 Emblem and Flags of: 40fr, ✱486a, Poland, German Democratic Rep., Tunisia, Mexico. 65fr, 125fr, Austria, Spain, Sweden, Brazil. 75fr, ✱484, Netherlands, Iran, Peru, Scotland. 150fr, like 25fr.

1978, June 24 Photo. Perf. 13

481	A161	25fr multi	25	10
482	A161	40fr multi	40	16
483	A161	65fr multi	65	28
484	A161	100fr multi	1.00	42

Souvenir Sheets

485		Sheet of 2	2.25	
a.		A161 75fr multi	75	
b.		A161 125fr multi	1.25	
486		Sheet of 2	2.75	
a.		A161 100fr multi	1.00	
b.		A161 150fr multi	1.50	

11th World Cup Soccer Championship, Argentina, June 1–25. No. 485 has red and gray margin, No. 486, blue and gray. Size: 100x82mm.

1978, June 27 Perf. 12

Design: 150fr, No. 489a, Martin Luther King. No. 489b, like 125fr.

| 487 | A162 | 125fr multi | 1.25 | 50 |
| 488 | A162 | 150fr multi | 1.50 | 60 |

Souvenir Sheet

489		Sheet of 2	4.25	
a.		A162 200fr multi	2.00	
b.		A162 200fr multi	2.00	

Mahatma Gandhi and Martin Luther King, advocates of non-violence. No. 489 has gray marginal inscription. Size: 85x73 mm.

Homes and Industry—A163

1978, Aug. 5 Litho. Perf. 12½

| 490 | A163 | 110fr multi | 1.10 | 45 |

3rd International Fair, Dakar, Nov. 28–Dec. 10.

A little time given to study of the arrangement of the Scott Catalogue can make it easier to use effectively.

Wright Brothers and Flyer—A164

Designs: 150fr, like 75fr. 100fr, 250fr, Yuri Gagarin and spacecraft. 200fr, 300fr, U.S. astronauts Frank Borman, William Anders, James Lovell Jr. and spacecraft.

1978, Sept. 25 Litho. Perf. 13½x14

491	A164	75fr multi	75	32
492	A164	100fr multi	1.00	42
493	A164	200fr multi	2.00	85

Souvenir Sheet

494		Sheet of 3, multi	7.50	
a.		A164 150fr multi	1.50	
b.		A164 250fr multi	2.50	
c.		A164 300fr multi	3.50	

75th anniversary of 1st powered flight; 10th anniversary of the death of Yuri Gagarin, first man in space; 10th anniversary of Apollo 8 flight around moon. No. 494 has black marginal inscription. Size: 95x160mm.

Henri Dunant, Patients, Red Cross
A165

Design: 20fr, Henri Dunant, First Aid station, Red Cross flag.

1978, Oct. 28 Photo. Perf. 11½

| 495 | A165 | 5fr brt bl & red | 5 | 5 |
| 496 | A165 | 20fr multi | 20 | 8 |

Henri Dunant (1828–1910), founder of Red Cross.

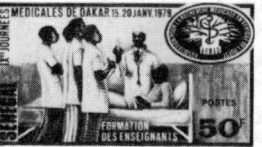

Bedside Lecture and Emblem—A166

Design: 100fr, Pollution, fish and mercury bottles.

1979, Jan. 15 Litho. Perf. 13½x13

| 497 | A166 | 50fr multi | 50 | 20 |
| 498 | A166 | 100fr multi | 1.00 | 40 |

9th Medical Days, Dakar, Jan. 15–20.

Map of Senegal with Shortwave Stations—A167

Designs: 60fr, Children on vacation, ambulance, soccer player. 65fr, Rural mobile post office.

1978, Dec. 27 Litho. Perf. 13½x13

499	A167	50fr multi	50	20
500	A167	60fr multi	60	25
501	A167	65fr multi	65	28

Achievements of postal service.

Farmer
A168

SENEGAL

Design: 150fr, Factories, communication, transportation, fish, physician and worker.

1979, Feb. 17   Litho.   Perf. 12½
| 502 | A168 | 30fr multi | 30 | 12 |
| 503 | A168 | 150fr multi | 1.50 | 60 |

Pride in workmanship.

Children's Village and Children
A169

Design: 60fr, Different view of village.

1979, Mar. 30   Perf. 12x12½
| 504 | A169 | 40fr multi | 40 | 15 |
| 505 | A169 | 60fr multi | 60 | 25 |

Children's SOS villages.

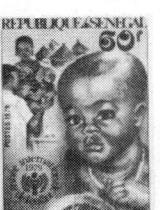

Infant, Physician Vaccinating Child, IYC Emblem
A170

Design: 65fr, Boys with book and globe, IYC emblem.

1979, Apr. 24   Litho.   Perf. 13½x13
| 506 | A170 | 60fr multi | 60 | 25 |
| 507 | A170 | 65fr multi | 65 | 28 |

International Year of the Child.

Drum, Carrier Pigeon, Satellite
A171

Design: 60fr, Baobab tree and flower, Independence monument with lion (vert.).

1979, June 8   Perf. 12½x13
Size: 36x48mm.
| 508 | A171 | 60fr multi | 60 | 25 |

Perf. 12½
Size: 36x36mm.
| 509 | A171 | 150fr multi | 1.50 | 60 |

Philexafrique II, Libreville, Gabon, June 8–17. Nos. 508, 509 each printed with labels showing UAPT '79 emblem.

People Walking through Open Book
A172

1979, Sept. 15   Photo.   Perf. 11½x12
| 510 | A172 | 250fr multi | 2.50 | 1.00 |

International Bureau of Education, Geneva, 50th anniversary.

Hill, Type AP3 with Exhibition Cancel
A173

1979, Oct. 9   Perf. 11½
| 511 | A173 | 500fr multi | 5.00 | 2.00 |

Sir Rowland Hill (1795-1879), originator of penny postage.

Black Trees, by Hundertwasser—A174
Lithographed and Engraved

1979, Dec. 10   Perf. 13½x14
Multicolored
512	A174	60fr shown	60	24
a.		Souvenir sheet of 4	2.75	1.25
513	A174	100fr Head of a man	1.00	40
a.		Souvenir sheet of 4	4.25	1.75
514	A174	200fr Rainbow windows	2.00	80
a.		Souvenir sheet of 4	8.25	3.50

Paintings by Friedensreich Hundertwasser, pseudonym of Friedrich Stowasser (b. 1928). Nos. 512a-514a have decorative margins with control numbers. Size: 190x259mm.

Running, Championship Emblem
A175

1980, Jan. 14   Litho.   Perf. 13
Multicolored
515	A175	20fr shown	20	8
516	A175	25fr Javelin	25	10
517	A175	50fr Relay race	50	20
518	A175	100fr Discus	1.00	40

1st African Athletic Championships.

Musicians—A176

1980, Mar. 22   Photo.   Perf. 14
519	A176	50fr shown	50	20
520	A176	100fr Dancers, festival building	1.00	40
521	A176	200fr Drummer, dancers	2.00	80

Mudra Afrique Arts Festival.

Lions Emblem, Map of Dakar Harbor—A177

1980, May 17   Litho.   Perf. 13
| 522 | A177 | 100fr multi | 1.00 | 40 |

22nd Congress, Lions International District 403, Dakar.

Chimpanzees—A178

1980, June 2   Photo.   Perf. 13½
523	A178	40fr shown	40	15
524	A178	60fr Elephants	60	25
525	A178	65fr Derby's elands	65	28
526	A178	100fr Hyenas	1.00	40
527		Pair	4.00	1.60
a.	A178	200fr Herd	2.00	80
b.	A178	200fr Guest house	2.00	80
		Nos. 523-527 (6)	6.65	2.68

Souvenir Sheet
528		Sheet of 4	5.00	2.00
a.	A178	125fr like #523	1.25	50
b.	A178	125fr like #524	1.25	50
c.	A178	125fr like #525	1.25	50
d.	A178	125fr like #526	1.25	50

Niokolo Koba National Park. No. 527 printed in continuous design with label showing location of park. No. 528 has multicolored decorative margin. Size: 133½x98mm.

Tree Planting Year—A179

1980, June 27   Litho.   Perf. 13
| 529 | A179 | 60fr multi | 60 | 25 |
| 530 | A179 | 65fr multi | 65 | 28 |

Rural Women Workers—A180

1980, July 19
Designs: Rural women workers. 50fr, 200fr, horiz.
531	A180	50fr multi	50	20
532	A180	100fr multi	1.00	40
533	A180	200fr multi	2.00	80

Wrestling, Moscow '80 Emblem—A181

1980, Aug. 21   Perf. 14½
534	A181	60fr shown	60	25
535	A181	65fr Running	65	28
536	A181	70fr Sports, map showing Moscow	70	30
537	A181	100fr Judo	1.00	40
538	A181	200fr Basketball	2.00	80
		Nos. 534-538 (5)	4.95	2.03

Souvenir Sheet
539		Sheet of 2	2.00	
a.	A181	75fr like #534	75	35
b.	A181	125fr like #535	1.25	50
540		Sheet of 2	2.00	
a.	A181	75fr like #537	75	35
b.	A181	125fr like #538	1.25	50

22nd Summer Olympic Games, Moscow, July 19-Aug. 3. Nos. 539-540 have black marginal inscription. Size: 77x62mm.

Caspian Tern and Sea Gulls, Kalissaye Bird Sanctuary—A182

National Park Wildlife: 70fr, Laughing gulls and Hansel's tern, Barbarie Spit. 85fr, Turtle and crab, Madeleine Islands. 150fr, Cormorant, Madeleine Islands.

1981, Jan. 31   Litho.   Perf. 14½x14
541	A182	50fr multi	50	20
542	A182	70fr multi	70	30
543	A182	85fr multi	85	35
544	A182	150fr multi	1.50	60

Souvenir Sheet
545		Sheet of 4	5.00	2.00
a.	A182	125fr like #541	1.25	50
b.	A182	125fr like #542	1.25	50
c.	A182	125fr like #543	1.25	50
d.	A182	125fr like #544	1.25	50

No. 545 has blue decorative margin. Size: 128x115mm.

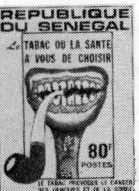

Anti-Tobacco Campaign—A183

1981, June 20   Litho.   Perf. 13
| 546 | A183 | 75fr Healthy people | 75 | 32 |
| 547 | A183 | 80fr shown | 80 | 35 |

SENEGAL

4th Intl. Dakar Fair, Nov. 25-Dec. 7—A184

1981, Sept. 19	Litho.		Perf. 12½	
548	A184	80fr multi	80	35

Natl. Hero Lat Dior—A185

1982, Jan. 11	Photo.		Perf. 14	
549	A185	80fr Portrait, vert.	80	35
550	A185	500fr Battle	5.00	2.00

Local Flora—A186

1982, Feb. 1			Perf. 11½	
551	A186	50fr Nymphaea lotus	50	20
552	A186	75fr Strophanthus sarmentosus	75	30
553	A186	200fr Crinum moorei	2.00	80
554	A186	225fr Cochlospermum tinctorium	2.25	90

Inscribed 1981.

Euryphrene Senegalensis—A187

1982, Feb. 27	Litho.		Perf. 14	
555	A187	45fr shown	45	15
556	A187	55fr Hypolimnas salmacis	55	22
557	A187	75fr Cymothoe caenis	75	30
558	A187	80fr Precis cebrene	80	35

Souvenir Sheet
Perf. 14½

559		Sheet of 4	7.00	3.00
a.	A187	100fr like 45fr	1.00	40
b.	A187	150fr like 55fr	1.50	60
c.	A187	200fr like 75fr	2.00	80
d.	A187	250fr like 80fr	2.50	1.00

No. 559 has multicolored margin showing butterflies. Size: 124x96mm.

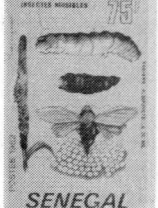

Destructive Insects
A188

Banner and Stamp
A189

Various insects. 80fr, 100fr horiz.

1982, Apr. 7	Litho.		Perf. 14	
560	A188	75fr multi	75	30
561	A188	80fr multi	80	35
562	A188	100fr multi	1.00	40

Fashion Type of 1972

1982, Apr. 30	Engr.		Perf. 13	
563	A106	5fr Prus bl	5	5
564	A106	10fr dl red	10	5
565	A106	15fr orange	15	6
566	A106	20fr dk pur	20	8
567	A106	30fr hn brn	30	12
		Nos. 563-567 (5)	80	36

1982, Dec. 30	Photo.		Perf. 13	
575	A189	100fr shown	1.00	40
576	A189	500fr Stamp, arrows	5.00	2.00

PHILEXFRANCE Intl. Stamp Exhibition, Paris, June 11-21.

Senegambia Confederation, Feb. 1—A190

1982, Nov. 15	Litho.		Perf. 12½	
577	A190	225fr Map, flags	2.25	1.00
578	A190	350fr Arms	3.50	1.50

Local Birds
A191

1982 World Cup
A192

1982, Dec. 1	Photo.		Perf. 11½	
		Granite Paper		
579	A191	45fr Godwit	45	18
580	A191	75fr Jabiru	75	32
581	A191	80fr Francolin	80	35
582	A191	500fr Eagle	5.00	2.00

1982, Dec. 11	Litho.		Perf. 12½x13	
583	A192	30fr Player	30	12
584	A192	50fr Player, diff.	50	20
585	A192	75fr Ball	75	32
586	A192	80fr Cup	80	35

Souvenir Sheets
Perf. 12½

587	A192	75fr like 30fr	75	40
588	A192	100fr like 50fr	1.00	50
589	A192	150fr like 75fr	1.50	75
590	A192	200fr like 80fr	2.00	1.00

Sizes: 90x80mm.

Dakar '82 Stamp Exhibition—A193

Designs: 60fr, Exhibition poster, viewers, horiz. 70fr, Simulated butterfly stamps. 90fr, Simulated stamps under magnifying glass. 95fr, Coat of Arms over Exhibition Building.

1983, Aug. 6	Litho.		Perf. 12½	
591	A193	60fr multi	30	15
592	A193	70fr multi	35	18
593	A193	90fr multi	45	22
594	A193	95fr multi	48	24

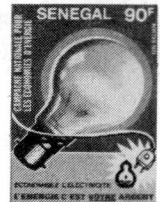

Energy Conservation—A194

1983, Oct. 25	Litho.		Perf. 12½x13	
595	A194	90fr Electricity	45	22
596	A194	95fr Gasoline	48	24
597	A194	260fr Coal, wood	1.30	65

SENEGAL

SEMI-POSTAL STAMPS.

No. 84 Surcharged +5c in Red

1915 Perf. 14x13½. Unwmkd.
B1 A28 10c +5c org red & rose 45 45

No. B1 is on both ordinary and chalky paper.

Same Surcharge on No. 87

1918
B2 A28 15c +5c red org & brn vio 50 50

Curie Issue
Common Design Type
1938 Engraved. Perf. 13.
B3 CD80 1.75fr +50c brt ultra 5.50 5.50

French Revolution Issue.
Common Design Type
1939 Photogravure.
Name and Value Typo. in Black.
B4 CD83 45(c) +25(c) grn 3.75 3.75
B5 CD83 70(c) +30(c) brn 3.75 3.75
B6 CD83 90(c) +35(c) red org 3.75 3.75
B7 CD83 1.25fr +1fr rose pink 3.75 3.75
B8 CD83 2.25fr +2fr bl 3.75 3.75
Nos. B4-B8 (5) 18.75 18.75

Stamps of 1935-38 SECOURS
Surcharged +1 fr.
in Red or Black NATIONAL

1941 Perf. 12x12½, 12.
B9 A30 50c +1fr red org (Bk) 50 50
B10 A31 80c +2fr vio (R) 2.25 2.25
B11 A30 1.50fr +2fr dk bl (Bk) 2.75 2.75
B12 A30 2fr +3fr bl (Bk) 2.75 2.50

Common Design Type and

Bambara Sharpshooter SP1
Colonial Soldier SP2

1941 Photogravure Perf. 13½
B13 SP1 1fr +1fr red 50
B14 CD86 1.50fr +3fr mar 50
B15 SP2 2.50fr +1fr bl 50

The surtax was for the defense of the colonies.
Nos. B13-B15 were issued by the Vichy government, but it is doubtful whether they were placed in use in Senegal. Stamps of 1935 A32 surcharged "OEUVRES COLONIALES" and new values were issued in 1944 by the Vichy Government, but were not placed on sale in the colony.

Republic
Anti-Malaria Issue
Common Design Type
Perf. 12½x12
1962, Apr. 7 Engraved Unwmkd.
B16 CD108 25fr +5fr brt grn 70 70

Issued for the World Health Organization drive to eradicate malaria.

Freedom from Hunger Issue
Common Design Type
1963, Mar. 21 Perf. 13
B17 CD112 25fr +5fr dp vio, grn & brn 60 60

AIR POST STAMPS.

Landscape—AP1

Caravan—AP2

Perf. 12½x12, 12x12½.
1935 Engraved. Unwmkd.
C1 AP1 25c dk brn 15 15
C2 AP1 50c red org 30 28
C3 AP1 1fr rose lil 15 15
C4 AP1 1.25fr yel grn 15 15
C5 AP1 2fr blue 15 15
C6 AP1 3fr ol grn 15 15
C7 AP1 3.50fr violet 15 15
C8 AP2 4.75fr orange 30 30
C9 AP2 6.50fr dk bl 50 45
C10 AP2 8fr black 75 60
C11 AP2 15fr rose lake 50 45
Nos. C1-C11 (11) 3.25 2.98

No. C8, surcharged "ENTR' AIDE FRANCAIS + 95f 95" in green, red violet or blue, was never issued in this colony.

Common Design Type
1940 Engraved Perf. 12½x12
C12 CD85 1.90fr ultra 22 22
C13 CD85 2.90fr dk red 22 22
C14 CD85 4.50fr dk gray grn 30 30
C15 CD85 4.90fr yel bis 30 30
C16 CD85 6.90fr dp org 32 32
Nos. C12-C16 (5) 1.36 1.36

Common Design Types
1942
C17 CD88 50c car & bl 8
C18 CD88 1fr brn & blk 22
C19 CD88 2fr dk grn & red brn 22
C20 CD88 3fr dk bl & scar 60
C21 CD88 5fr vio & brn red 32

Frame Engraved,
Center Typographed.
C22 CD89 10fr ultra, ind & hn 32
C23 CD89 20fr rose car, mag & choc 38
C24 CD89 50fr yel grn, dl grn & yel 80 1.10

Engraved and Photogravure.
Size: 47x26 mm.
C25 CD88 100fr dk red & bl 1.50 1.50
Nos. C17-C25 (9) 4.44

There is doubt whether Nos. C17 to C23 were officially placed in use.

Republic

Abyssinian Roller—AP3

Designs: 50fr, Carmine bee-eater (vert.). 200fr, Violet touraco (vert.). 250fr, Red bishop (vert.). 500fr, Fish eagle (vert.).

Perf. 12½x13, 13x12½
1960-63 Photo. Unwmkd.
Birds in Natural Colors
C26 AP3 50fr blk & gray bl ('61) 1.00 32
C27 AP3 100fr blk, yel & lil 2.00 70
C28 AP3 200fr blk, grn & bl ('61) 4.00 2.25
C29 AP3 250fr blk & pale grn ('63) 5.00 2.75
C30 AP3 500fr blk & bl 8.00 3.75
Nos. C26-C30 (5) 20.00 9.77

Air Afrique Issue
Common Design Type
1962, Feb. 17 Engr. Perf. 13
C31 CD107 25fr vio brn, sl grn & ocher 45 25

Issued to commemorate the founding of Air Afrique (African Airlines).

African Postal Union Issue
Common Design Type
1963, Sept. 8 Photo. Perf. 12½
C32 CD114 85fr choc, ocher & red 1.00 65

Air Afrique Issue, 1963
Common Design Type
1963, Nov. 19 Perf. 13x12 Unwmkd.
C33 CD115 50fr multi 1.10 75

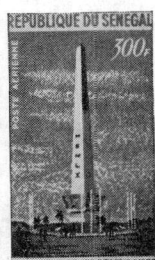
Independence Monument—AP4

1964, Apr. 4 Photo. Perf. 12x13
C34 AP4 300fr ultra, tan, ocher & grn 4.00 2.00

Symbolic European and African Cities—AP5

1964, Apr. 18 Engraved Perf. 13
C35 AP5 150fr grn, brn red & blk 2.40 1.50

Issued to commemorate the Congress of the International Federation of Twin Cities, Dakar.

Europafrica Issue, 1964

Peanuts, Globe, Factory, Figures of "Africa," and "Europe"—AP6

1964, July 20 Photo. Perf. 13x12
C36 AP6 50fr multi 1.00 75
See note after Madagascar No. 357.

Basketball AP7
Launching of Syncom 2 AP8

Design: 100fr, Pole vault.

1964, Aug. 22 Engraved Perf. 13
C37 AP7 85fr org brn & bl 1.25 85
C38 AP7 100fr dk grn, red brn & dk brn 1.75 1.00

18th Olympic Games, Tokyo, Oct. 10-25.

1964, Oct. 24 Perf. 13 Unwmkd.
C39 AP8 150fr grn, red brn & ultra 2.25 1.10

Communication through space.

President John F. Kennedy AP9
Mother and Child, Globe and Emblems AP10

1964, Dec. 5 Photo. Perf. 13
C40 AP9 100fr brt yel, dk grn & brn red 1.75 1.50
a. Souv. sheet of 4 7.00 7.00

Issued in memory of Pres. John F. Kennedy (1917-63). No. C40a has dark green marginal inscription. Size: 90x 130mm.

Scenic Type of Regular Issue, 1965
View: 100fr, Shore of Gambia River in Eastern Senegal.

1965, Feb. 27 Engraved Perf. 13
Size: 48x27mm.
C41 A48 100fr brn blk, grn & bis 1.50 65

1965, Sept. 25 Perf. 13 Unwmkd.
C42 AP10 50fr choc, brt bl & grn 70 40

International Cooperation Year, 1965.

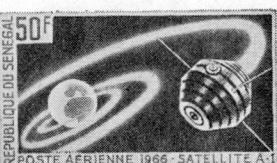
A-1 Satellite and Earth AP11

Designs: No. C44, Diamant rocket. 90fr, Scout rocket and FR-1 satellite.

1966, Feb. 19 Engraved Perf. 13
C43 AP11 50fr yel brn, dk grn & blk 75 40

520 SENEGAL

C44	AP11	50fr Prus bl, lt red brn & car rose	75	40
C45	AP11	90fr dk red brn, dk gray & Prus bl	1.60	85

French achievements in space.

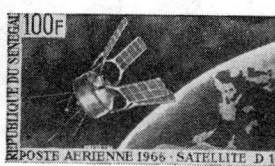

D-1 Satellite over Globe—AP12

1966, June 11 Engraved Perf. 13

C46	AP12	100fr dk car, sl & vio	1.50	85

Issued to commemorate the launching of the D-1 satellite at Hammaguir, Algeria, Feb. 17, 1966.

Air Afrique Issue, 1966
Common Design Type

1966, Aug. 31 Photo. Perf. 13

C47	CD123	30fr red brn, blk & lem	45	20

Issued to commemorate the introduction of DC-8F planes by Air Afrique.

Mermoz Plane "Arc-en-Ciel"
AP13

Jean Mermoz
AP14

Designs: 35fr, Latecoère 300 "Croix du Sud." 100fr, Map showing last flight from Dakar to Brazil.

1966, Dec. 7 Engraved Perf. 13

C48	AP13	20fr bl, rose lil & ind	35	25
C49	AP13	35fr sl, brn & grn	55	30
C50	AP13	100fr grn, lt grn & mar	1.50	65
C51	AP14	150fr blk, ultra & mar	2.25	1.10

Issued in memory of Jean Mermoz (1901–36), French aviator, on the 30th anniversary of his last flight.

Dakar-Yoff Airport—AP15

1967, Apr. 22 Engraved Perf. 13

C52	AP15	200fr red brn, ind & brt bl	2.25	75

Knob-billed Goose—AP16

Flowers and Birds: 100fr, Mimosa. 150fr, Flowering cactus. 250fr, Village weaver. 500fr, Bateleur.

Granite Paper
1967–69 Photogravure Perf. 11½

Dated "1967"

C53	AP16	100fr gray, yel & grn	1.60	70
C54	AP16	150fr multi	2.40	1.00

Dated "1969"

C55	AP16	250fr gray & multi	3.25	1.50

Dated "1968"

C56	AP16	300fr brt bl & multi	4.50	1.85
C57	AP16	500fr org & multi	6.50	2.75
		Nos. C53–C57 (5)	18.25	7.80

Issue dates: 100fr, 150fr, June 24, 1967; 500fr, July 13, 1968; 300fr, Dec. 21, 1968; 250fr, Apr. 26, 1969.

The Girls from Avignon, by Picasso
AP17

1967, July 22   Perf. 12x13

C59	AP17	100fr multi	1.75	1.25

African Postal Union Issue, 1967
Common Design Type

1967, Sept. 9 Engraved Perf. 13

C60	CD124	100fr brt grn, vio & car lake	1.40	70

Konrad Adenauer
AP18

Weather Balloon, Vegetation and WMO Emblem
AP19

1968, Feb. 17 Photo. Perf. 12½

C61	AP18	100fr dk red, ol & blk	1.60	80
a.		Souv. sheet of 4	6.50	6.50

Issued in memory of Konrad Adenauer (1876–1967), chancellor of West Germany (1949–63). No. C61a contains 4 No. C61. Margin with black inscription and 1967 CEPT (Europa) emblem. Size: 120½x170 mm.

1968, Mar. 23 Engraved Perf. 13

C62	AP19	50fr blk, ultra & bl grn	70	35

8th World Meteorological Day, Mar. 23.

Hurdling
AP20

Designs: 30fr, Javelin. 50fr, Wrestling. 75fr, Basketball.

1968, Oct. 12 Engraved Perf. 13

C63	AP20	20fr dp brn, bl gray & grn	30	12
C64	AP20	30fr dk brn, lt lil & ocher	35	25
C65	AP20	50fr mar, bl & ol brn	65	28
C66	AP20	75fr brn, grn & gray brn	90	35

Issued to commemorate the 19th Olympic Games, Mexico City, Oct. 12–27.

PHILEXAFRIQUE Issue

Young Woman Reading Letter, by Jean Raoux—AP21

1968, Oct. 26 Photo. Perf. 12½

C67	AP21	100fr buff & multi	1.60	1.50

Issued to publicize PHILEXAFRIQUE, Philatelic Exhibition in Abidjan, Feb. 14–23, 1969. Printed with alternating buff label.

2nd PHILEXAFRIQUE Issue
Common Design Type

Design: 50fr, Senegal No. 160 and Boulevard, Dakar.

1969, Feb. 14 Engraved Perf. 13

C68	CD128	50fr grn, gray & pur	90	75

Issued to commemorate the opening of PHILEXAFRIQUE, Abidjan, Feb. 14.

Tourist Emblem with Map of Africa and Dove—AP22

1969 Photogravure Perf. 13

C69	AP22	100fr red, lt grn & lt bl	1.15	50

Year of African Tourism, 1969.

Pres. Lamine Gueye
AP23

Design: 45fr, Pres. Gueye wearing fez.

1969, June 10 Photo. Perf. 12½

C70	AP23	30fr brn, org & blk	35	20
C71	AP23	45fr brn, lt grnsh bl & blk	50	25
a.		Min. sheet of 4	1.85	1.85

Issued in memory of Pres. Lamine Gueye (1891–1968). No. C71a contains 2 each of Nos. C70–C71. Size: 120x159mm.

"Transmission of Thought" Tapestry
by Ousmane Faye
AP24

Fari, Tapestry by Allaye N'Diaye
AP25

1969, Oct. 25 Photo. Perf. 12½

C72	AP24	25fr multi	35	20
		Perf. 12x12½		
C73	AP25	50fr multi	70	35

SENEGAL

Europafrica Issue

Baila Bridge—AP26
1969, Nov. 15 Photo. Perf. 13x12
C74 AP26 100fr multi 1.15 55

Emile Lécrivain, Plane and
Toulouse-Dakar Route—AP27
1970, Jan. 31 Engraved Perf. 13
C75 AP27 50fr grn, sl & rose brn 60 35

Issued to commemorate the 50th anniversary of the disappearance of the aviator Emile Lécrivain (1897–1929).

René Maran, Martinique
AP28
Portraits: 45fr, Marcus Garvey, Jamaica. 50fr, Dr. Price Mars, Haiti.
1970, Mar. 21 Photo. Perf. 12½
C76 AP28 30fr red brn, lt grn & blk 35 15
C77 AP28 45fr bl, pink & blk 55 25
C78 AP28 50fr grn, buff & blk 60 25

Issued to honor prominent Negro leaders.

"One People, One Purpose, One Faith"
AP29
1970, Apr. 3 Photo. Perf. 11½
C79 AP29 500fr gold & multi 6.00 2.75
a. Souvenir sheet 7.00 7.00

Issued to commemorate the 10th anniversary of independence. No. C79 contains one stamp. Black marginal inscriptions with signature of Pres. Senghor and gray control number. Size: 72x102½mm. Sold for 600fr.

Bay of Naples and
Dakar Post Office—AP30
1970, May 2 Photo. Perf. 13x12½
C80 AP80 100fr multi 1.20 80

Issued to publicize the 10th Europa Philatelic Exhibition, Naples, May 2–10.

Blue Cock, by
Mamadou Niang
AP31
Tapestries: 45fr, Fairy. 75fr, "Lunaris," by Jean Lurçat.
1970, June 20 Photo. Perf. 12½x12
C81 AP31 30fr blk & multi 40 25
C82 AP31 45fr dk red brn & multi 70 30
C83 AP31 75fr yel & multi 1.00 60

Head of the Courtesan Nagakawa,
by Chobunsai Yeishi, and Mt.
Fuji, by Hokusai
AP32
Designs (EXPO Emblem and): 25fr, Woman Playing Guitar, by Hokusai, and Sun Tower (vert.). 150fr, "One of the Present-day Beauties of Nanboku" by Katsukawa Shuncho (vert.).
1970, July 18 Engraved Perf. 13
C84 AP32 25fr red & grn 30 20
C85 AP32 75fr yel grn, dk bl & red brn 85 35
C86 AP32 150fr bl, red brn & ocher 1.65 85

Issued to publicize EXPO '70 International Exhibition, Osaka, Japan, Mar. 15–Sept. 13.

Tuna, Processing Plant and Ship
AP33

Urban Development in Dakar
AP34
1970, Aug. 22 Engraved Perf. 13
C87 AP33 30fr dl red, blk & brt bl 35 20
C88 AP34 100fr choc & grn 1.15 60

Issued to publicize progress in industrialization and urbanization in Dakar.

Beethoven; Napoleon and
Allegory of Eroica Symphony
AP35
Design: 100fr, Ludwig van Beethoven holding quill.
1970, Sept. 26 Engraved Perf. 13
C89 AP35 50fr ol, brn & ocher 65 35
C90 AP35 100fr Prus grn & dp cl 1.25 75

Issued to commemorate the bicentenary of the birth of Ludwig van Beethoven (1770–1827), composer.

Globe, Scales and Women of
Four Races—AP36
1970, Oct. 24 Engraved Perf. 13
C91 AP36 100fr grn, ocher & red 1.40 80

25th anniversary of United Nations.

De Gaulle,
Map of Africa,
Symbols
AP37
Design: 100fr, Charles de Gaulle and map of Senegal.
1970, Dec. 31 Photo. Perf. 12½
C92 AP37 50fr multi 70 50
C93 AP37 100fr bl & multi 1.50 1.00

Honoring Pres. Charles de Gaulle as liberator of the colonies.

"A Roof for Every Refugee"—AP38
1971, Jan. 16
C94 AP38 100fr multi 1.25 65

High Commissioner for Refugees, 20th anniversary.

Phillis
Wheatley,
American
Poet
AP39
Portraits: 40fr, James E. K. Aggrey, Methodist missionary, Ghana. 60fr, Alain Le Roy Locke, American educator. 100fr, Booker T. Washington, American educator.
1971, Apr. 10 Photo. Perf. 12½
C95 AP39 25fr multi 25 15
C96 AP39 40fr blk, bl & bis 45 25
C97 AP39 60fr blk, bl & emer 70 28
C98 AP39 100fr blk, bl & red 1.10 55

Prominent blacks.

Napoleon
as First
Consul, by
Ingres
AP40
Designs: 25fr, Napoleon in 1809, by Robert Lefevre. 35fr, Napoleon on his death bed, by Georges Rouget. 50fr, Awakening into Immortality, sculpture by Francois Rude.
1971, June 19 Photo. Perf. 13
C99 AP40 15fr gold & multi 40 30
C100 AP40 25fr gold & multi 60 40
C101 AP40 35fr gold & multi 70 50
C102 AP40 50fr gold & multi 1.00 85

Sesquicentennial of the death of Napoleon Bonaparte (1769–1821).

Gamal Abdel
Nasser
AP41

Alfred Nobel
AP41a

522 SENEGAL

1971, July 17   *Perf. 12½*
C103 AP41 50fr multi 60 30
In memory of Gamal Abdel Nasser (1918–1970), President of Egypt.

1971, Sept. 25 Photo. *Perf. 13½x13*
C103A AP41a 100fr multi 1.20 70
75th anniversary of the death of Alfred Nobel (1833–1896), who invented dynamite and established the Nobel Prizes.

Iranian Flag and Senegal Coat of Arms—AP42

1971, Oct. 15   *Perf. 13x12½*
C104 AP42 200fr multi 2.25 1.00
2500th anniversary of the founding of the Persian empire by Cyrus the Great.

African Postal Union Issue, 1971
Common Design Type
Design: 100fr, Arms of Senegal and UAMPT Building, Brazzaville, Congo.

1971, Nov. 13   *Perf. 13x13½*
C105 CD135 100fr bl & multi 1.10 45

Louis Armstrong
AP43

1971, Nov. 27 Photo. *Perf. 12½*
C106 AP43 150fr gold & dk brn 1.80 1.20

Louis Armstrong (1900–1971), American jazz musician.

Sapporo Olympic Emblem and Speed Skating—AP44
Designs (Sapporo '72 Emblem and): 10fr, Bobsledding. 125fr, Skiing.

1972, Jan. 22   *Perf. 13*
C107 AP44 5fr multi 8 5
C108 AP44 10fr multi 12 8
C109 AP44 125fr multi 1.35 55
11th Winter Olympic Games, Sapporo, Japan, Feb. 3–13.

Fonteghetto della Farina, by Canaletto—AP45
Design: 100fr, San Giorgio Maggiore, by Giovanni Antonio Guardi (vert.).

1972, Feb. 26
C110 AP45 50fr gold & multi 60 30
C111 AP45 100fr gold & multi 1.20 60
UNESCO campaign to save Venice.

Theater Type of Regular Issue
Design: 150fr, Daniel Sorano as Shylock (vert.).

1972, Mar. 25 Photo. *Perf. 12½x13*
C112 A99 150fr multi 2.00 1.10
International Theater Day.

Environment Type of Regular Issue
Design: 100fr, Protection of the ocean (oil slick).

1972, June 3 Photo. *Perf. 13x12½*
C113 A101 100fr multi 1.20 70
U.N. Conference on Human Environment, Stockholm, June 5–16.

Emperor Haile Selassie, Ethiopian and Senegalese Flags
AP46

1972, July 23 Photo. *Perf. 13½x13*
C114 AP46 100fr gold & multi 1.20 60
80th birthday of Emperor Haile Selassie of Ethiopia.

Swordfish—AP47
Designs: 65fr, Killer whale. 75fr, Rhincodon. 125fr, Common rorqual (whale).

1972–73 Photo. *Perf. 11½*
C115 AP47 50fr multi 50 15
C116 AP47 65fr multi ('73) 60 27
C117 AP47 75fr multi ('73) 70 35
C118 AP47 125fr multi 1.35 80
Issue dates: Nos. C115, C118, Nov. 25, 1972. Nos. C116–C117, July 28, 1973.

Palace of the Republic—AP48
1973, Apr. 3 Photogravure *Perf. 13*
C119 AP48 100fr multi 90 50

Hotel Teranga, Dakar—AP49
1973, May 26 Photo. *Perf. 13*
C120 AP49 100fr multi 90 50

Emblem of African Lions Club
AP50

1973, June 2
C121 AP50 150fr multi 1.50 1.00
15th Congress of Lions International, District 403, Dakar, June 1–2.

"Couple with Mimosa," by Marc Chagall
AP51

1973, Aug. 11 Photo. *Perf. 13*
C122 AP51 200fr multi 2.40 1.35

Map of Italy with Riccione
AP52

1973, Aug. 25   Engraved
C123 AP52 100fr dk grn, red & pur 90 55
International Philatelic Exhibition, Riccione 1973.

Raoul Follereau and World Map—AP53
Design: 100fr, Dr. Armauer G. Hansen and leprosy bacilli.

1973, Dec. 22 Engr. *Perf. 13*
C124 AP53 40fr sl grn, pur & red brn 40 20
C125 AP53 100fr sl grn, mag & plum 1.00 60
Centenary of the discovery of the Hansen bacillus, the cause of leprosy.

Human Rights Flame and People
AP54
Design: 65fr, Human Rights flame and drummer.

1973, Dec. 15 Photo. *Perf. 13½*
C126 AP54 35fr grn & multi 30 20
C127 AP54 65fr org & multi 40 35
25th anniversary of the Universal Declaration of Human Rights.

Men of Four Races, Arms of Dakar, Congress Emblem—AP55
Design: 50fr, Key joining twin cities and emblem (vert.).

1973, Dec. 26   Photogravure
C128 AP55 50fr org & multi 50 30
C129 AP55 125fr red & multi 1.20 70
8th Congress of the World Federation of Twin Cities, Dakar, Dec. 26–29.

Finfoots—AP56
1974, Feb. 9 Photogravure *Perf. 13*
Gold and Multicolored
C130 AP56 1fr shown 5 5
C131 AP56 2fr Spoonbills 5 5
C132 AP56 3fr Crested cranes 6 5
C133 AP56 4fr Egrets 6 5
C134 AP56 250fr Flamingos 2.00 1.40
C135 AP56 250fr Flamingos 2.00 1.40
Strip of 2 + label 4.25
Nos. C130-C135 (6) 4.22 3.00
Djoudj Park bird sanctuary. Nos. C134–C135 printed se-tenant with label showing map of Senegal. Denomination in gold on No. C134, in black on No. C135.

Tiger Attacking Wild Horse, by Delacroix—AP57
Design: 200fr, Tiger Hunt, by Eugène Delacroix.

1974, Mar. 23 Photo. *Perf. 13*
C136 AP57 150fr gold & multi 1.40 90

SENEGAL

C137 AP57 200fr gold & multi 1.85 1.00

Paintings by Eugène Delacroix (1798–1863).

A Dakar Fair set of 2 was issued in 1974.

Soyuz and Apollo, Space Docking Emblem—AP58

1975, May 23 Engraved Perf. 13

C138 AP58 125fr multi 1.00 50

Russo-American space cooperation.

Senegal Type D6, Tuscany Type A1, Map of Italy—AP59

1975, Aug. 23 Engr. Perf. 13

C139 AP59 125fr org, vio & dk red 1.00 50

International Philatelic Exhibition, Riccione 1975.

No. C138 Overprinted:
"JONCTION / 17 Juil. 1975"

1975, Oct. 21 Engr. Perf. 13

C140 AP58 125fr multi 1.00 50

Apollo-Soyuz link-up in space, July 17, 1975.

Boston Massacre—AP60

Design: 500fr, Lafayette, Washington, Rochambeau and Battle of Yorktown.

1975, Dec. 20 Engr. Perf. 13

C141 AP60 250fr ultra, red & brn 2.00 1.00
C142 AP60 500fr bl & ver 4.00 2.00

American Bicentennial.

Concorde and Map—AP61

1976, Jan. 21 Litho. Perf. 13

C143 AP61 300fr multi 2.40 1.20

First commercial flight of supersonic jet Concorde, Paris to Rio de Janeiro, Jan. 21.

Spaceship and Control Room AP62

1977, June 25 Litho. Perf. 12½

C144 AP62 300fr multi 2.40 1.20

Viking space mission to Mars.

No. C143 Overprinted in Red:
"22.11.77 / PARIS NEW-YORK"

1977, Nov. 22 Perf. 13

C145 AP61 300fr multi 2.40 1.20

Concorde, first commercial flight, Paris to New York.

Philexafrique II—Essen Issue
Common Design Types

Designs: No. C146, Lion and Senegal No. C28. No. C147, Capercaillie and Schleswig-Holstein No. 1.

1978, Nov. 1 Litho. Perf. 12½

C146 CD138 100fr multi 1.00 42
C147 CD139 100fr multi 1.00 42

Nos. C146–C147 printed se-tenant.

J. Dabry, L. Gimie, and J. Mermoz, Airplane, Map of Route (St. Louis-Natal)—AP63

1980, Dec. Photo. Perf. 13

C148 AP63 300fr multi 3.00 1.20

1st airmail crossing of South Atlantic, 50th anniversary.

Scott
First in the Field

- Buying
- Selling
- Estate Appraisals
- Auction Consignments

ALL SERVICES AVAILABLE FROM THE RECOGNIZED PHILATELIC EXPERTS

TO PLACE YOUR NAME ON OUR LIST TO RECEIVE INFORMATION ABOUT SERVICES ON OUR UPCOMING SALES, WRITE TO:

The Scott Auction Galleries
3 EAST 57TH ST.
NEW YORK, N.Y. 10022

SENEGAL—SENEGAMBIA & NIGER—SERBIA

AIR POST SEMI-POSTAL STAMPS.
Common Design Type
Photogravure.
1939 Perf. 13. Unwmkd.
Name and Value Typo. in Orange.

CB1	CD83	4.75 +4fr brn blk	6.00	6.00

Issued to commemorate the 150th anniversary of the French Revolution. The surtax was used for the defense of the colonies.

Stamps of types of Dahomey V1, V2, V3, and V4 inscribed "Sénégal" were issued in 1942 by the Vichy Government, but were not placed on sale in the colony.

Republic

Nile Gods Uniting Upper and Lower Egypt (Abu Simbel)
SPAP1

1964, Mar. 7 Engraved Perf. 13

CB2	SPAP1	25fr +5fr Prus bl, red brn & sl grn	1.25	90

UNESCO campaign to save historic monuments in Nubia.

POSTAGE DUE STAMPS.

Postage Due Stamps of French Colonies Surcharged **10**

1903 Imperf. Unwmkd.

J1	D1	10c on 50c lil	52.50	52.50
J2	D1	10c on 60c brn, *buff*	52.50	52.50
J3	D1	10c on 1fr rose, *buff*	225.00	225.00

D2   D3

Typographed.
1906 Perf. 14x13½.

J4	D2	5c grn, *grnsh*	2.50	2.50
J5	D2	10c red brn	3.25	3.25
J6	D2	15c dk bl	3.75	3.75
J7	D2	20c *yellow*	4.50	3.75
J8	D2	30c red, *straw*	4.75	4.50
J9	D2	50c violet	4.75	4.50
J10	D2	60c blk, *buff*	6.00	6.00
J11	D2	1fr *pinkish*	11.00	10.00
		Nos. J4-J11 (8)	40.50	38.25

1914

J12	D3	5c green	15	15
J13	D3	10c rose	22	22
J14	D3	15c gray	22	22
J15	D3	20c brown	45	30
J16	D3	30c blue	60	50
J17	D3	50c black	75	60
J18	D3	60c orange	90	75
J19	D3	1fr violet	90	75
		Nos. J12-J19 (8)	4.19	3.49

Type of 1914 Issue Surcharged **2F.**

1927

J20	D3	2fr on 1fr lil rose	2.25	1.75
J21	D3	3fr on 1fr org brn	2.25	1.75

D4

1935 Engraved Perf. 12½x12

J22	D4	5c yel grn	7	7
J23	D4	10c red org	7	7
J24	D4	15c violet	8	8
J25	D4	20c ol grn	8	8
J26	D4	30c redsh brn	12	12
J27	D4	50c rose lil	35	35
J28	D4	60c orange	60	60
J29	D4	1fr black	40	40
J30	D4	2fr dk bl	40	40
J31	D4	3fr dk car	50	50
		Nos. J22-J31 (10)	2.67	2.67

Republic

D5   Lion
                  D6
Perf. 14x13½
1961, Feb. 20 Typo. Unwmkd.

J32	D5	1fr org & red	8	8
J33	D5	2fr ultra & red	12	12
J34	D5	5fr brn & red	15	15
J35	D5	20fr grn & red	45	45
J36	D5	25fr red lil & red	50	50
		Nos. J32-J36 (5)	1.30	1.30

1966, Dec. 1 Typo. Perf. 14x13
Lion in Gold

J37	D6	1fr red & blk	5	5
J38	D6	2fr yel brn & blk	10	10
J39	D6	5fr red lil & blk	12	12
J40	D6	10fr brt bl & blk	25	25
J41	D6	20fr emer & blk	38	38
J42	D6	30fr gray & blk	60	60
		Nos. J37-J42 (6)	1.50	1.50

OFFICIAL STAMPS

Arms   Baobab Tree
O1   O2
Perf. 14x13½
1961, Sept. 18 Typo. Unwmkd.
Denominations in Black

O1	O1	1fr sep & bl	5	5
O2	O1	2fr dk bl & org	12	12
O3	O1	5fr mar & grn	12	12
O4	O1	10fr ver & bl	15	15
O5	O1	25fr vio bl & ver	50	50
O6	O1	50fr ver & gray	90	45
O7	O1	85fr lil & org	1.50	75
O8	O1	100fr ver & yel grn	2.25	1.25
		Nos. O1-O8 (8)	5.59	3.04

1966-77 Typo. Perf. 14x13

O9	O2	1fr blk & blk	6	5
O10	O2	5fr org & blk	12	6
O11	O2	10fr red & blk	12	12
O12	O2	20fr dp red lil & blk	18	12
O13	O2	25fr dp lil & blk ('75)	15	8
O14	O2	30fr bl & blk	35	15
O15	O2	35fr bl & blk ('73)	45	45
O16	O2	40fr grnsh bl & blk ('75)	28	8
O17	O2	55fr emer & blk	65	45
O18	O2	60fr emer & blk ('77)	40	8
O19	O2	90fr dk bl grn & blk	1.00	28
O20	O2	100fr brn & blk	1.25	28
		Nos. O9-O20 (12)	5.01	1.90

No. O17 Surcharged with New Value and Two Bars

1969

O21	O2	60fr on 55fr emer & blk	90	15

SENEGAMBIA & NIGER
(sĕn′ĕ·găm′bĭ·à & nī′jẽr)

A French Administrative unit for the Senegal and Niger possessions in Africa during the period when the French possessions in Africa were being definitely divided into colonies and protectorates. The name was dropped in 1904 when this territory was consolidated with part of French Sudan, under the name Upper Senegal and Niger.

100 Centimes = 1 Franc

Navigation and Commerce—A1
Typographed.
1903 Perf. 14x13½ Unwmkd.
Name of Colony in Blue or Carmine.

1	A1	1c *lil bl*	1.00	1.00
2	A1	2c brn, *buff*	1.25	1.25
3	A1	4c cl, *lav*	2.25	2.25
4	A1	5c yel grn	2.25	2.25
5	A1	10c red	3.00	3.00
6	A1	15c gray	6.00	6.00
7	A1	20c red, *grn*	6.00	6.00
8	A1	25c blue	8.00	8.00
9	A1	30c brn, *bis*	8.00	8.00
10	A1	40c red, *straw*	12.00	12.00
11	A1	50c brn, *az*	25.00	25.00
12	A1	75c dp vio, *org*	27.50	27.50
13	A1	1fr brnz grn, *straw*	32.50	32.50
		Nos. 1-13 (13)	134.75	134.75

SERBIA
(sûr′bĭ·à)

LOCATION — In southeastern Europe, bounded by Romania and Bulgaria on the east, the former Austro-Hungarian Empire on the north, Greece on the south, and Albania and Montenegro on the west.
GOVT.—A former Kingdom.
AREA—18,650 sq. mi.
POP.—2,911,701 (1910).
CAPITAL—Belgrade.

Following World War I, Serbia united with Montenegro, Bosnia and Herzegovina, Croatia, Dalmatia and Slovenia to form the kingdom (later republic) of Jugoslavia.

100 Paras = 1 Dinar

Coat   Prince Michael
of Arms   (Obrenovich III)
A1   A2

Typographed.
Paper colored Through
1866 Imperf. Unwmkd.

1	A1	1p dk grn, *dk vio rose*	60.00	

Surface Colored Paper, Thin or Thick

2	A1	1p dk grn, *lil rose*	75.00	
a.		1p ol grn, *rose*	75.00	
b.		1p yel grn, *pale rose* (thick paper)	450.00	
3	A1	2p red brn, *lil*	85.00	
a.		2p red brn, *lil gray* (thick paper)	300.00	
b.		2p dl grn, *lil gray* (thick paper)	1,200.	

Vienna Printing.
Perf. 12.

4	A2	10p orange	1,000.	700.00
5	A2	20p rose	700.00	30.00
6	A2	40p blue	750.00	200.00
a.		Half used as 20p on cover		

Belgrade Printing.
Perf. 9½.

7	A2	1p green	22.50	
8	A2	2p bis brn	35.00	
9	A2	20p rose	20.00	12.50
a.		Pair, imperf. between		
10	A2	40p ultra	250.00	250.00
a.		Half used as 20p on cover		

Pelure Paper.

11	A2	10p orange	100.00	100.00
12	A2	20p rose	60.00	13.50
a.		Pair, imperf. between		
13	A2	40p ultra	60.00	32.50
a.		Pair, imperf. between		
b.		Half used as 20p on cover		

Nos. 1-3, 7-8, 14-16, 25-26 were used only as newspaper tax stamps.

1868-69 Ordinary Paper. Imperf.

14	A2	1p green	50.00	
a.		1p ol grn ('69)	2,500.	
15	A2	2p brown	65.00	
a.		2p bis brn ('69)	250.00	

Counterfeits of type A2 are common.

Prince Milan (Obrenovich IV)
A3   A4
Perf. 9½, 12 and Compound.
1869-78

16	A3	1p yellow	4.00	60.00
17	A3	10p red brn	6.50	3.25
a.		10p yel brn	250.00	40.00
18	A3	10p org ('78)	2.00	3.50
19	A3	15p orange	70.00	17.50
20	A3	20p gray bl	1.00	1.40
a.		20p ultra	4.00	2.00
b.		Half used as 10p on cover		
21	A3	25p rose	1.60	5.00
22	A3	35p lt grn	3.25	3.75
23	A3	40p violet	1.40	2.75
a.		Half used as 20p on cover		
24	A3	50p bl grn	4.50	4.00
		Nos. 16-24 (9)	94.25	101.15

The first setting, which included all values except No. 18, had the stamps 2-2½ mm. apart. A new setting, introduced in 1878, had the stamps 3-4 mm. apart, providing wider margins. Only Nos. 17, 18, 20 and 21 exist in this new setting, which differs also in shades from the earlier setting. The narrow-spaced Nos. 17, 20 and 21 are rarer, especially those in the earlier shades of Nos. 23 and 24. All values except Nos. 19 and 24 are known in various partly perforated varieties.

Counterfeits exist.

1872-79 Imperf.

25	A3	1p yellow	6.00	10.00
a.		Tête bêche pair		

SERBIA

26	A4	2p blk, thin paper ('79)	70	70
a.		Thick paper ('73)	1.50	8.00

Used price of No. 26 is for canceled-to-order.

King Milan I King Alexander
A5 (Obrenovich V)
  A6

1880 Perf. 13x13½

27	A5	5p green	60	20
a.		5p ol grn	175.00	2.00
28	A5	10p rose	60	20
29	A5	20p orange	50	20
a.		20p yel	3.00	1.00
30	A5	25p ultra	60	25
a.		25p bl	4.00	1.00
31	A5	50p brown	60	1.25
a.		50p brn vio	95.00	3.00
32	A5	1d violet	9.00	8.50
		Nos. 27-32 (6)	11.90	10.60

1890

33	A6	5p green	20	15
34	A6	10p rose red	50	15
35	A6	15p red vio	50	15
36	A6	20p orange	40	15
37	A6	25p blue	60	20
38	A6	50p brown	2.50	1.50
39	A6	1d dl lil	13.00	11.00
		Nos. 33-39 (7)	17.70	13.30

King Alexander
A7

1894-96 Perf. 13x13½
Granite Paper.

40	A7	5p green	3.50	15
a.		Perf. 11½	3.00	50
41	A7	10p car rose	3.25	15
b.		Perf. 11½	45.00	1.00
42	A7	15p violet	4.25	15
43	A7	20p orange	50.00	40
a.		Half used as 10p on cover		450.00
44	A7	25p blue	10.00	30
45	A7	50p brown	11.00	60
46	A7	1d dk grn	1.50	2.25
47	A7	1d red brn, bl ('96)	11.00	3.50
		Nos. 40-47 (8)	94.50	7.50

1898-1900 Perf. 13x13½, 11½
Ordinary Paper.

48	A7	1p dl red	20	20
49	A7	5p green	1.50	15
50	A7	10p rose	40.00	15
51	A7	15p violet	7.00	15
52	A7	20p orange	6.00	20
53	A7	25p dp bl	6.00	25
54	A7	50p brown	10.00	1.50
		Nos. 48-54 (7)	70.70	2.60

Nos. 49-54 exist imperf. Nos. 49-51, 53 and 56-57 exist with perf. 13x13½x11½x13½.

Type of 1900 Stamp Surcharged 10 ПАРА

1900

| 56 | A7 | 10p on 20p rose | 1.25 | 15 |

Same, Surcharged 10 ПАРА

1901

57	A7	10p on 20p rose	2.50	15
58	A7	15p on 1d red brn, bl	5.00	1.50
a.		Invtd. surch.	150.00	175.00

King Alexander (Obrenovich V)
A8 A9

1901-03 Typographed Perf. 11½

59	A8	5p green	15	10
60	A8	10p rose	15	10
61	A8	15p red vio	15	10
62	A8	20p orange	15	10
63	A8	25p ultra	15	10
64	A8	50p bister	20	15
65	A9	1d brown	1.00	1.00
66	A9	3d brt rose	12.50	7.50
67	A9	5d dp vio	9.50	7.50
		Nos. 59-67 (9)	23.95	16.65

Counterfeits of Nos. 66-67 exist. Nos. 59-67 imperf., price of set of pairs, $60.

Arms of Serbia on Head
of King Alexander
A10

Two Types of the Overprint.

Type I. Overprint 12mm. wide. Bottom of mantle defined by a single line. Wide crown above shield.
Type II. Overprint 10mm. wide. Double line at bottom of mantle. Smaller crown above shield.

Arms Overprinted in Blue, Black, Red and Red Brown.

1903-04 Type I. Perf. 13½

68	A10	1p red lil & blk (Bl)	70	75
a.		Inverted overprint	10.00	
69	A10	5p yel grn & blk (Bl)	40	10
70	A10	10p car & blk (Bk)	25	10
a.		Double overprint	12.50	
71	A10	15p ol gray & blk (Bk)	25	10
a.		Double overprint	12.50	
72	A10	20p org & blk (Bk)	40	25
73	A10	50p bl & blk (Bk)	40	25
a.		Double overprint	15.00	
74	A10	50p gray & blk (R)	1.25	1.25

There were two printings of the type I overprint on Nos. 68-74, one typographed and one lithographed.

Type II.

| 75 | A10 | 1d bl grn & blk (Bk) | 10.00 | 3.00 |

Nos. 68-75 with overprint omitted, price, set $60.

Perf. 11½.

Type I.

75A	A10	5p yel grn & blk (Bl)	30	50
75B	A10	50p gray & blk (R)	80	3.00
75C	A10	1d bl grn & blk (Bk)	2.00	5.50

Type II.

76	A10	3d vio & blk (R Br)	2.25	2.50
a.		Perf. 13½	125.00	125.00
77	A10	5d lt brn & blk (Bl)	2.25	2.50

Type I.

With Additional Surcharge 1 ПАРА 1

78	A10	1p on 5d lt brn & blk (R)	1.25	2.00
a.		Perf. 13½	350.00	350.00
		Nos. 68-78 (14)	23.75	21.80

Karageorge and Peter I—A11

Insurgents, 1804
A12

1904 Typographed.

79	A11	5p yel grn	10	10
80	A11	10p rose red	10	10
81	A11	15p red vio	10	10
82	A11	25p blue	10	10
83	A11	50p gray brn	35	35
84	A12	1d bister	1.75	2.25
85	A12	3d bl grn	1.75	2.50
86	A12	5d violet	2.75	3.00
		Nos. 79-86 (8)	7.00	8.50

Centenary of the Karageorgevich dynasty and the coronation of King Peter. Counterfeits of Nos. 79-86 exist.

King Peter I Karageorgevich
A13 A14

1905 Wove Paper.
Perf. 11½, 12x11½

87	A13	1p gray & blk	20	10
88	A13	5p yel grn & blk	30	10
89	A13	10p red & blk	1.00	10
90	A13	15p red lil & blk	1.40	10
91	A13	20p yel & blk	2.00	15
92	A13	25p ultra & blk	3.25	15
93	A13	30p sl grn & blk	3.00	15
94	A13	50p dk brn & blk	4.00	30
95	A13	1d bis & blk	60	40
96	A13	3d bl grn & blk	60	75
97	A13	5d vio & blk	2.50	1.25
		Nos. 87-97 (11)	18.85	3.55

Counterfeits of Nos. 87-97 abound.
The stamps of this issue may be found on both thick and thin paper.

1908 Laid Paper.

98	A13	1p gray & blk	30	10
99	A13	5p yel grn & blk	1.00	10
100	A13	10p red & blk	3.00	10
101	A13	15p red lil & blk	3.00	20
102	A13	20p yel & blk	3.50	20
103	A13	25p ultra & blk	3.00	20
104	A13	30p gray grn & blk	6.50	20
105	A13	50p dk brn & blk	7.00	60
		Nos. 98-105 (8)	27.30	1.70

Nos. 90, 98-100, 102-104 are known imperforate but are not believed to have been issued in this condition.
Prices of Nos. 98-105 are for horizontally laid paper. Four values also exist on vertically laid paper (1p, 5p, 10p, 30p).

1911-14 Thick Wove Paper

108	A14	1p sl grn	5	5
109	A14	2p dk vio	5	5
110	A14	5p green	10	5
111	A14	5p pale yel grn ('14)	5	
112	A14	10p carmine	10	5
113	A14	10p red ('14)	5	
114	A14	15p red vio	20	10
115	A14	15p sl blk ('14)	15	10
a.		15p red (error)		
116	A14	20p yellow	30	10
117	A14	20p brn ('14)	50	30
118	A14	25p dp bl	45	5
119	A14	25p ind ('14)	5	5
120	A14	30p bl grn	20	5
121	A14	30p ol grn ('14)	5	5
122	A14	50p dk brn	25	5
123	A14	50p brn red ('14)	10	5
124	A14	1d orange	20.00	35.00
125	A14	1d sl ('14)	1.75	4.00
126	A14	3d lake	40.00	110.00
127	A14	3d ol yel ('14)	110.00	650.00
128	A14	5d violet	32.50	60.00
129	A14	5d dk vio ('14)	1.75	20.00
		Nos. 108-129 (22)	208.65	

Counterfeits exist.

King Peter and Military Staff
A15

1915 Perf. 11½

132	A15	5p yel grn	15	1.50
133	A15	10p scarlet	15	1.50
134	A15	15p slate	3.00	
135	A15	20p brown	75	
136	A15	25p blue	6.50	
137	A15	30p ol grn	4.00	
138	A15	50p org brn	30.00	
		Nos. 132-138 (7)	44.55	

Nos. 134-138 were prepared but not issued for postal use. Instead they were permitted to be used as wartime emergency currency. Some are known imperf. The 15p exists also in blue; price $200.

POSTES SERBES

Stamps of France, 1900-1907, with this handstamped control were issued in 1916-1918 by the Serbian Postal Bureau, in the Island of Corfu, during a temporary shortage of Serbian stamps. On the 1c to 35c, the handstamp covers 2 or 3 stamps. It was applied after the stamps were on the cover, and frequently no further cancellation was used.

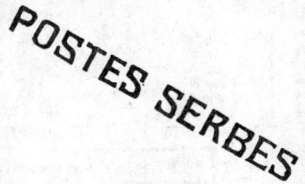

King Peter and Prince Alexander
A16

1918-20 Typographed Perf. 11, 11½

155	A16	1p black	10	7
156	A16	2p ol brn	10	7
157	A16	5p ap grn	10	7
158	A16	10p red	10	7
159	A16	15p blk brn	10	7
160	A16	20p red brn	12	10
161	A16	20p vio ('20)	2.50	1.25
162	A16	25p dp bl	12	10
163	A16	30p ol grn	12	10
164	A16	50p violet	12	10
165	A16	1d vio brn	35	15
166	A16	3d lt grn	1.25	1.00
167	A16	5d red brn	2.00	1.25
		Nos. 155-167 (13)	7.08	4.35

Nos. 157-160, 164 exist imperf. Price each $6.

1920 Pelure Paper Perf. 11½

169	A16	1p black	10	15
170	A16	2p ol brn	10	15

SERBIA

POSTAGE DUE STAMPS.

Coat of Arms
D1   D2
Typographed.

1895   *Perf. 13 x 13½.*   Unwmkd.
Granite Paper.

J1	D1	5p red lil	2.00	90
J2	D1	10p blue	2.00	90
J3	D1	20p org brn	35.00	4.00
J4	D1	30p green	30	50
J5	D1	50p rose	40	60
a.		Cliché of 5p in plate of 50p	40.00	50.00

No. J1 exists imperf.   Price $35.

1898–1904   Ordinary Paper.

J6	D1	5p mag ('04)	1.00	1.00
J7	D1	20p brown	4.00	1.00
a.		Tête bêche pair	125.00	125.00
J8		20p dp brn ('04)	4.00	1.00

1906   Granite Paper.   *Perf. 11½.*

J9	D1	5p magenta	4.75	1.00

1909   Laid Paper

J10	D1	5p magenta	80	80
J11	D1	10p pale bl	3.00	2.00
J12	D1	20p pale brn	50	50

1914   White Wove Paper.

J13	D1	5p rose	40	50
J14	D1	10p dp bl	2.25	3.50

1918–20   *Perf. 11.*

J15	D2	5p red	25	50
J16	D2	5p red brn ('20)	25	50
J17	D2	10p yel grn	25	50
J18	D2	20p ol brn	25	50
J19	D2	30p sl grn	25	50
J20	D2	50p chocolate	50	75
		Nos. J15-J20 (6)	1.75	3.25

NEWSPAPER STAMPS.

N1
Typographed
Overprinted with Crown-topped Shield in Black

1911   *Perf. 11½.*   Unwmkd.

P1	N1	1p gray	60	60
P2	N1	5p green	60	60
P3	N1	10p orange	60	60
a.		Cliché of 1p in plate of 10p	300.00	
P4	N1	15p violet	60	60
P5	N1	20p yellow	60	60
a.		Cliché of 5p in plate of 20p	60.00	125.00
P6	N1	25p blue	60	60
P7	N1	30p slate	6.00	6.00
P8	N1	50p brown	5.25	5.25
P9	N1	1d bister	5.25	5.25
P10	N1	3d rose red	5.25	5.25
P11	N1	5d gray vio	5.25	5.25
		Nos. P1-P11 (11)	30.60	30.60

OCCUPATION STAMPS.

Issued under
Austrian Occupation.

100 Heller = 1 Krone

Stamps of Bosnia,
1912–14,
Overprinted

SERBIEN

1916   *Perf. 12½.*   Unwmkd.

1N1	A23	1h ol grn	3.00	2.50
1N2	A23	2h brt bl	3.00	2.25
1N3	A23	3h claret	2.75	2.00
1N4	A23	5h green	55	50
1N5	A23	6h dk gray	1.75	1.50
1N6	A23	10h rose car	55	50
1N7	A23	12h dp ol grn	1.75	1.50
1N8	A23	20h org brn	75	75
1N9	A23	25h ultra	55	55
1N10	A23	30h org red	55	55
1N11	A24	35h myr grn	55	55
1N12	A24	40h dk vio	55	55
1N13	A24	45h ol brn	55	55
1N14	A24	50h sl bl	55	55
1N15	A24	60h brn vio	55	55
1N16	A24	72h dk bl	55	55
1N17	A25	1k brn vio, *straw*	1.00	90
1N18	A25	2k dk gray, *bl*	1.00	90
1N19	A25	3k car, *grn*	1.00	90
1N20	A26	5k dk vio, *gray*	1.00	90
1N21	A25	10k dk ultra, *gray*	18.50	17.50
		Nos. 1N1-1N21 (21)	41.00	37.00

Stamps of Bosnia, 1912–14, Overprinted
"SERBIEN" Horizontally at Bottom.

1916

1N22	A23	1h ol grn	9.00	9.00
1N23	A23	2h brt bl	9.00	9.00
1N24	A23	3h claret	9.00	9.00
1N25	A23	5h green	80	80
1N26	A23	6h dk gray	9.00	9.00
1N27	A23	10h rose car	80	80
1N28	A23	12h dp ol grn	9.00	9.00
1N29	A23	20h org brn	9.00	9.00
1N30	A23	25h ultra	9.00	9.00
1N31	A23	30h org red	9.00	9.00
1N32	A24	35h myr grn	9.00	9.00
1N33	A24	40h dk vio	9.00	9.00
1N34	A24	45h ol brn	9.00	9.00
1N35	A24	50h sl bl	9.00	9.00
1N36	A24	60h brn vio	9.00	9.00
1N37	A24	72h dk bl	9.00	9.00
1N38	A25	1k brn vio, *straw*	22.50	22.50
1N39	A25	2k dk gray, *bl*	22.50	22.50
1N40	A26	3k car, *grn*	22.50	22.50
1N41	A26	5k dk vio, *gray*	37.50	37.50
1N42	A25	10k dk ultra, *gray*	52.50	52.50
		Nos. 1N22-1N42 (21)	285.10	285.10

Nos. 1N22 to 1N42 were prepared in 1914, at the time of the first Austrian occupation of Serbia. They were not issued at that time because of the retreat. The stamps were put on sale in 1916, at the same time as Nos. 1N1 to 1N21.

Issued under German Occupation.

In occupied Serbia, authority was ostensibly in the hands of a government created by the former Jugoslav General, Milan Nedich, supported by the Chetniks, a nationalist organization which turned fascist. Actually, however, the German military ran the country.

Types of Jugoslavia,
1939–40,
Overprinted in Black

SERBIEN

Typographed.

1941   *Perf. 12½.*   Unwmkd.

Paper with colored network.

2N1	A16	25p blk (*lt grn*)	20	40
2N2	A16	50p org (*pink*)	20	25
2N3	A16	1d yel grn (*lt grn*)	20	25
2N4	A16	1.50d red (*pink*)	20	25
2N5	A16	2d dp mag (*pink*)	20	25
2N6	A16	3d dl red brn (*pink*)	1.40	3.00
2N7	A16	4d ultra (*lt grn*)	30	45
2N8	A16	5d dk bl (*lt grn*)	80	1.10
2N9	A16	5.50d dk vio brn (*pink*)	80	1.10
2N10	A16	6d sl bl (*lt grn*)	80	1.10
2N11	A16	8d sep (*lt grn*)	1.25	1.75
2N12	A16	12d brt vio (*lt grn*)	1.25	1.75
2N13	A16	16d dl vio (*pink*)	2.00	3.75
2N14	A16	20d bl (*lt grn*)	2.00	4.50
2N15	A16	30d brt pink (*lt grn*)	9.00	25.00
		Nos. 2N1-2N15 (15)	20.60	44.90

Double overprints exist on 50p, 1d, 2d, 5d, 5.50d and 12d. Price, each $100.

Stamps of Jugoslavia,
1939–40,
Overprinted in Black

SERBIEN

Paper with colored network.

2N16	A16	25p blk (*lt grn*)	20	45
2N17	A16	50p org (*pink*)	20	45
2N18	A16	1d yel grn (*lt grn*)	25	45
2N19	A16	1.50d red (*pink*)	25	45
2N20	A16	2d dp mag (*pink*)	25	45
2N21	A16	3d dl red brn (*pink*)	60	2.00
2N22	A16	4d ultra (*lt grn*)	40	45
2N23	A16	5d dk bl (*lt grn*)	40	1.25
2N24	A16	5.50d dk vio brn (*pink*)	80	2.00
2N25	A16	6d sl bl (*lt grn*)	80	2.00
2N26	A16	8d sep (*lt grn*)	1.25	2.00
2N27	A16	12d brt vio (*lt grn*)	1.60	2.75
2N28	A16	16d dl vio (*pink*)	1.60	3.25
2N29	A16	20d bl (*lt grn*)	1.60	3.50
2N30	A16	30d brt pink (*lt grn*)	8.75	16.00
		Nos. 2N16-2N30 (15)	18.95	37.45

Lazaritza Monastery
OS1

Ruins of Manassia Monastery
OS4

Designs: 1d, Kalenica Monastery. 1.50d, Ravanica Monastery. 3d, Ljubostinja Monastery. 4d, Sopocane Monastery. 7d, Tsitsa Monastery. 12d, Gorlak Monastery. 16d, Studenica Monastery.

1942–43   Typographed   *Perf. 11½*

2N31	OS1	50p brt vio	10	25
2N32	OS1	1d red	10	15
2N33	OS1	1.50d red brn	1.00	1.25
2N34	OS1	1.50d grn ('43)	10	60
2N35	OS4	2d dl rose vio	10	20
2N36	OS4	3d brt bl	10	1.25
2N37	OS4	3d rose pink ('43)	10	20
2N38	OS4	4d ultra	10	25
2N39	OS4	7d dk sl grn	10	25
2N40	OS1	12d lake	30	1.00
2N41	OS1	16d grnsh blk	90	1.50
		Nos. 2N31-2N41 (11)	3.90	6.90

Post Rider—OS10

Post Wagon
OS11

Designs: 9d, Mail train. 30d, Mail truck. 50d, Mail plane.

1943, Oct. 15   Photo.   *Perf. 12½*

2N42	OS10	3d cop red & gray lil	45	90
2N43	OS11	8d vio rose & gray	45	90
2N44	OS10	9d dk bl grn & sep	45	90
2N45	OS10	30d chnt & sl grn	45	90
2N46	OS10	50d dp bl & red brn	45	90
		Nos. 2N42-2N46 (5)	2.25	4.50

Centenary of postal service in Serbia. Printed in sheets of 24 containing 4 of each stamp and 4 labels.

OCCUPATION SEMI-POSTAL STAMPS.

Smederevo Fortress
on the Danube
OSP1

Refugees—OSP2
Perf. 11½ x 12½

1941, Sept. 22   Typo.   Unwmkd.

2NB1	OSP1	50p +1d dk brn	25	60
2NB2	OSP2	1d +2d dk gray grn	30	80
2NB3	OSP2	1.50d +3d dp cl	60	1.25
a.		Perf. 12½	5.25	6.50
2NB4	OSP1	2d +4d dk bl	80	1.75

The surtax aided victims of an explosion at Smederevo.

Souvenir Sheets.

OSP3

SERBIA

	Perf. 11½ x 12½.			
2NB5	OSP3	Sheet of two	47.50	65.00
a.		1d + 49d rose lake	14.00	25.00
b.		2d + 48d gray	14.00	25.00
	Imperf.			
2NB6	OSP3	Sheet of two	47.50	65.00
a.		1d + 49d gray	14.00	25.00
b.		2d + 48d rose lake	14.00	25.00

The sheets measure 150x110mm. The surtax was used for the reconstruction of Smederevo.

Christ and Virgin Mary
OSP4

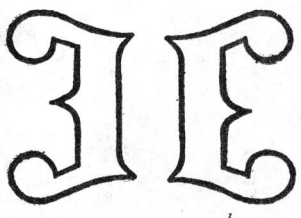

a   *b*

1941, Dec. 5   Photo.   *Perf. 11½*

With Rose Burelage.

2NB7	OSP4	50p + 1.50d brn red	35	1.00
a.		With symbol (a) outlined in cerise	12.00	20.00
b.		With symbol (b) outlined in cerise	12.00	20.00
c.		Without burelage	1.75	4.00
2NB8	OSP4	1d + 3d sl grn	35	1.00
a.		With symbol (a) outlined in cerise	12.00	20.00
b.		With symbol (b) outlined in cerise	12.00	20.00
c.		Without burelage	1.75	4.00
2NB9	OSP4	2d + 6d dp red	35	1.00
a.		With symbol (a) outlined in cerise	12.00	20.00
b.		With symbol (b) outlined in cerise	12.00	20.00
c.		Without burelage	1.75	4.00
2NB10	OSP4	4d + 12d dp bl	35	1.00
a.		With symbol (a) outlined in cerise	12.00	20.00
b.		With symbol (b) outlined in cerise	12.00	20.00
c.		Without burelage	1.75	4.00

These stamps were printed in sheets of 50, divided into two panes of 25. In these panes, Nos. 8, 12, 13, 14 and 18, forming a cross, are without burelage. Nos. 7 and 17 are of type *a*. Nos. 9, and 19 are of type *b*. Sixteen of the 25 units have the over-all burelage.
The surtax aided prisoners of war.

Thicker Paper, Without Burelage

1942, Mar. 26

2NB11	OSP4	50p + 1.50d brn	1.00	2.00
2NB12	OSP4	1d + 3d bl grn	1.00	2.00
2NB13	OSP4	2d + 6d mag	1.00	2.00
2NB14	OSP4	4d + 12d ultra	1.00	2.00

OSP5

OSP6

OSP7   OSP8

Designs: Anti-Masonic symbolisms.

1942, Jan. 1

2NB15	OSP5	50p + 50p yel brn	20	40
2NB16	OSP6	1d + 1d dk grn	20	40
2NB17	OSP7	2d + 2d rose car	50	1.00
2NB18	OSP8	4d + 4d ind	50	1.00

To commemorate the Anti-Masonic Exposition of October 22, 1941. The surtax was used for anti-Masonic propaganda.

Mother and Children
OSP9

1942

2NB19	OSP9	2d + 6d brt pur	1.75	2.75
2NB20	OSP9	4d + 8d dp bl	1.75	2.75
2NB21	OSP9	7d + 13d dk bl grn	1.75	2.75
2NB22	OSP9	20d + 40d dp rose lake	1.75	2.75

Nos. 2NB19–2NB22 were issued in sheets of 16 consisting of a block of four of each denomination. The surtax aided war orphans.

Broken Sword
OSP10

Wounded Flag-bearer
OSP11

Designs: 3d+5d, Wounded soldier. 4d+10d, Tending casualty.

1943

2NB23	OSP10	1.50d + 1.50d dk brn	70	1.25
2NB24	OSP11	2d + 3d dk bl grn	70	1.25
2NB25	OSP11	3d + 5d dp rose vio	95	2.00
2NB26	OSP10	4d + 10d dp bl	1.50	2.50

The surtax aided war victims.

Souvenir Sheets.

OSP14

OSP15

Thick Paper.

2NB27	OSP14	Sheet of two	47.50	85.00
a.		1.50d + 48.50d dk brn	12.50	25.00
b.		4d + 46d dp bl	12.50	25.00
2NB28	OSP15	Sheet of two	47.50	85.00
a.		2d + 48d bl grn	12.50	25.00
b.		3d + 47d dp rose vio	12.50	25.00

The sheets measure 150x110mm. The surtax aided war victims.

Stamps of 1942-43 Surcharged in Black

За пострадале
од англо-америчког
терор. бомбардовања
Ниша — 20-X-1943

+ 9

1943, Dec. 11   Pale Green Burelage

2NB29	OS1	50p + 2d brt vio	18	40
2NB30	OS1	1d + 3d red	18	45
2NB31	OS1	1.50d + 4d dp grn	18	45
2NB32	OS4	2d + 5d dl rose vio	25	75
2NB33	OS4	3d + 7d rose pink	25	75
2NB34	OS4	4d + 9d ultra	25	1.00
2NB35	OS4	7d + 15d dk sl grn	50	1.25
2NB36	OS1	12d + 25d lake	50	2.00
2NB37	OS1	16d + 33d grnsh blk	1.00	3.00
		Nos. 2NB29-2NB37 (9)	3.29	10.05

The surtax aided victims of the bombing of Nisch.

Scott's International Album provides spaces for an extensive representative collection of the world's postage stamps.

AIR POST STAMPS.

Types of Air Post Stamps of Jugoslavia, 1937-40, Overprinted in Carmine or Maroon

a

b

1941   *Perf. 12½*   Unwmkd.

Paper with colored network.

2NC1	AP6(a)	50p brn (C)	5.00	8.00
2NC2	AP7(a)	1d yel grn (C)	5.00	8.00
2NC3	AP8(a)	2d bl gray (C)	5.00	8.00
2NC4	AP9(b)	2.50d rose red (M)	5.00	8.00
2NC5	AP6(a)	5d brn vio (C)	5.00	8.00
2NC6	AP7(a)	10d brn lake (M)	5.00	8.00
2NC7	AP8(a)	20d dk grn (C)	5.00	8.00
2NC8	AP9(b)	30d ultra (C)	8.50	13.50
2NC9	AP10(a)	40d Prus grn & pale grn (C)	12.00	16.50
2NC10	AP11(b)	50d sl bl & gray bl (C)	13.50	22.50
		Nos. 2NC1-2NC10 (10)	69.00	108.50

Nos. 2NC1–2NC2 exist without network.

Same Surcharged in Maroon or Carmine with New Values and Bars.

Without colored network.

2NC11	AP7	1d on 10d brn lake (M)	3.00	4.50
2NC12	AP8	3d on 20d dk grn (C)	3.00	4.50
2NC13	AP9	6d on 30d ultra (C)	3.00	4.50
2NC14	AP10	8d on 40d Prus grn & pale grn (C)	3.75	6.00
2NC15	AP11	12d on 50d sl bl & gray bl (C)	6.50	12.00
		Nos. 2NC11-2NC15 (5)	19.25	31.50

Regular Issue of Jugoslavia, 1939-40, Surcharged in Black

1942   **Green Network.**

2NC16	A16	2d on 2d dp mag	20	60
2NC17	A16	4d on 4d ultra	20	60
2NC18	A16	10d on 12d brt vio	20	60
2NC19	A16	14d on 20d bl	20	60
2NC20	A16	20d on 30d brt pink	70	3.00
		Nos. 2NC16-2NC20 (5)	1.50	5.40

OCCUPATION POSTAGE DUE STAMPS.

OD1   OD2

Typographed.

1941   *Perf. 12½*   *Unwmkd.*

2NJ1	OD1	50p violet	90	1.50
2NJ2	OD1	1d lake	90	1.50
2NJ3	OD1	2d dk bl	90	1.50
2NJ4	OD1	3d red	1.25	2.25
2NJ5	OD2	4d lt bl	1.60	3.00
2NJ6	OD2	5d orange	1.60	3.00
2NJ7	OD2	10d violet	3.50	7.50
2NJ8	OD2	20d green	10.00	25.00
	Nos. 2NJ1-2NJ8 (8)		20.65	45.25

OD3   OD4

1942   *Perf. 12½.*

2NJ9	OD3	1d mar & grn	20	60
2NJ10	OD3	2d dk bl & red	20	60
2NJ11	OD3	3d ver & bl	35	1.25
2NJ12	OD4	4d bl & red	35	1.25
2NJ13	OD4	5d org & bl	40	1.50
2NJ14	OD4	10d vio & red	45	2.25
2NJ15	OD4	20d grn & red	1.60	6.00
	Nos. 2NJ9-2NJ15 (7)		3.55	13.45

OD5

2NJ16	OD5	50p black	25	60
2NJ17	OD5	3d violet	25	60
2NJ18	OD5	4d blue	25	60
2NJ19	OD5	5d dk sl grn	25	60
2NJ20	OD5	6d orange	45	1.50
2NJ21	OD5	10d red	80	2.75
2NJ22	OD5	20d ultra	1.50	5.25
	Nos. 2NJ16-2NJ22 (7)		3.75	11.90

OCCUPATION OFFICIAL STAMP.

OOS1

Typographed.

1943   *Perf. 12½*   *Unwmkd.*

2NO1	OOS1	3d red lil	70	1.10

SHANGHAI
(shăng′hī′)

LOCATION—A city on the Whangpoo River, Kiangsu Province, China.

POP.—3,489,998.

A British settlement was founded there in 1843 and by agreement with China settlements were established by France and the United States. Special areas were set aside for the foreign settlements and a postal system independent of China was organized which was continued until 1898.

16 Cash = 1 Candareen
100 Candareens = 1 Tael
100 Cents = 1 Dollar (1890)

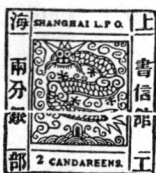

Dragon
A1

Typographed.

1865-66   *Imperf.*   *Unwmkd.*

Antique Numerals.
Roman "I" in "I6".
"Candareens" in the Plural.
Wove Paper.

1	A1	2ca black	110.00
a.		Pelure paper	100.00
2	A1	4ca yellow	70.00
a.		Pelure paper	65.00
b.		Double impression	
3	A1	8ca green	85.00
a.		8ca yel grn	85.00
4	A1	16ca scarlet	70.00
a.		16ca ver	70.00
b.		Pelure paper	70.00

Antique Numerals.
"Candareens" in the Plural.
Pelure Paper.

5	A1	2ca black	110.00
a.		Wove paper	70.00
6	A1	4ca yellow	110.00
7	A1	8ca dp grn	110.00

Antique Numerals.
"Candareen" in the Singular
Laid Paper.

8	A1	1ca blue	110.00
a.		1ca dk bl	120.00
9	A1	2ca black	1,100.
10	A1	4ca yellow	350.00

Wove Paper.

11	A1	1ca blue	110.00
12	A1	2ca black	130.00
13	A1	4ca yellow	110.00
14	A1	8ca ol grn	110.00
15	A1	16ca vermilion	110.00
a.		"1" of "16" omitted	3,500.

Only one copy of No. 15a is known.

Antique Numerals.
Roman "I".
"Candareens" in the Plural
Wove Paper.

16	A1	1ca blue	225.00
17	A1	12ca fawn	135.00
18	A1	12ca chocolate	135.00

Antique Numerals.
"Candareens" in the Plural
Except on 1ca.
Wove Paper.

19	A1	1ca indigo	110.00
a.		Pelure paper	85.00
20	A1	3ca org brn	70.00
a.		Pelure paper	70.00
21	A1	6ca red brn	65.00
22	A1	6ca fawn	300.00
23	A1	6ca vermilion	90.00
24	A1	12ca org brn	65.00
25	A1	16ca vermilion	65.00
a.		"1" of "16" omitted	225.00

Antique Numerals.
Roman "I".
"Candareens" in the Plural
Except on 1ca.
Laid Paper.

26	A1	1ca blue	10,000.
27	A1	2ca black	1,100.
28	A1	3ca red brn	7,000.

Modern Numerals.
"Candareen" in the Singular

29	A1	1ca dk bl	65.00
		1ca sl bl	65.00
30	A1	3ca red brn	65.00

"Candareens" in the Plural
Except the 1c.

31	A1	2ca black	45.00
32	A1	3ca red brn	45.00

Coarse Porous Wove Paper.

33a	A1	1ca blue	35.00
34a	A1	2ca black	40.00
b.		grysh paper	40.00
35a	A1	3ca red brn	40.00
36a	A1	4ca yellow	40.00
37a	A1	6ca ol grn	40.00
38a	A1	8ca emerald	40.00
39a	A1	12ca org ver	40.00
40a	A1	16ca red	45.00
41a	A1	16ca red brn	45.00

Nos. 1, 2, 11 and 32 exist on thicker paper, usually toned. Most authorities consider these four stamps and Nos. 33a-41a to be official reprints made to present sample sets to other post offices. The tone in this paper is an acquired characteristic, due to various causes. Many shades and minor varieties exist of Nos. 1-41a.

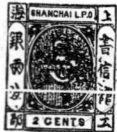 

Dragon
A2   A3

A4   A5

1866   *Lithographed*   *Perf. 12*

42	A2	2c rose	10.00	6.00
43	A3	4c lilac	22.50	17.50
44	A4	8c gray bl	25.00	17.50
a.		Defective "8" like a "3"	60.00	55.00
45	A5	16c green	50.00	35.00

Nos. 42-45 imperforate are proofs.

A6   A7

A8   A9

1866   *Perf. 15.*

46	A6	1ca brown	5.50	4.50
a.		"CANDS"	37.50	35.00
47	A7	3ca orange	17.50	15.00
a.		Defective "3" like a "6"	110.00	
48	A8	6ca slate	20.00	15.00
49	A9	12ca ol gray	45.00	35.00

1872

50	A2	2c rose	45.00	40.00

Handstamp
Surcharged in Blue,
Red or Black

a

1873   *Perf. 12.*

51	A2	1ca on 2c rose	15.00	11.00
52	A3	1ca on 4c lil (Bl)	12.50	10.00
53	A3	1ca on 4c lil (R)	900.00	900.00
54	A3	1ca on 4c lil (Bk)	11.00	10.00
55	A4	1ca on 8c gray bl (Bl)	17.50	15.00
56	A4	1ca on 8c gray bl (R)	2,000.	2,000.
57	A5	1ca on 16c grn (Bl)	750.00	750.00
58	A5	1ca on 16c grn (R)	2,000.	2,000.

Perf. 15.

59	A2	1ca on 2c rose (Bl)	15.00	12.50

1875   *Perf. 12*

60	A2	3ca on 2c rose (Bl)	40.00	35.00
61	A5	3ca on 16c grn (Bl)	800.00	750.00

Perf. 15.

62	A7	1ca on 3ca org (Bl)	2,500.	2,500.
63	A8	1ca on 6ca sl (Bl)	125.00	100.00
64	A8	1ca on 6ca sl (R)	1,500.	1,500.
65	A9	1ca on 12ca ol gray (Bl)	150.00	135.00
66	A9	1ca on 12ca ol gray (R)	1,500.	1,250.
67	A2	3ca on 2c rose (Bl)	125.00	100.00
68	A9	3ca on 12ca ol gray (Bl)	1,000.	1,000.

Counterfeits exist of Nos. 51-68.

Types of 1866.

1875   *Perf. 15*

69	A6	1ca yel, *yel*	22.50	15.00
70	A7	3ca rose, *rose*	22.50	15.00

Perf. 11½

71	A6	1ca yel, *yel*	150.00	125.00

1876   *Perf. 15.*

72	A6	1ca yellow	6.00	4.50
73	A7	3ca rose	30.00	27.50
74	A8	6ca green	55.00	40.00
75	A9	9ca blue	65.00	50.00
76	A9	12ca lt brn	90.00	70.00

1877   *Engraved*   *Perf. 12½*

77	A6	1ca rose	500.00	450.00

Stamps of 1875-76 Surcharged type "a" in Blue or Red

1877   *Lithographed*   *Perf. 15*

78	A7	1ca on 3ca rose, *rose* (Bl)	125.00	115.00
79	A7	1ca on 3ca rose (Bl)	27.50	27.50

SHANGHAI

80	A8	1ca on 6ca grn (Bl)	35.00	30.00
81	A9	1ca on 9ca bl (Bl)	125.00	125.00
82	A9	1ca on 12ca lt brn (Bl)	600.00	600.00
83	A9	1ca on 12ca lt brn (R)	2,250.	2,000.

Counterfeits exist of Nos. 78–83.

A11   A12

A13   A14

1877   *Perf. 15.*

84	A11	20 cash vio	6.00	4.00
a.		20 cash bl vio	6.00	4.00
85	A12	40 cash rose	8.00	6.00
86	A13	60 cash grn	11.00	9.00
87	A14	80 cash bl	17.50	12.50
88	A14	100 cash brn	17.50	12.50

Handstamp Surcharged in Blue

b

1879   *Perf. 15.*

89	A12	20 cash on 40c rose	11.00	11.00
90	A14	60 cash on 80c bl	17.50	17.50
91	A14	60 cash on 100c brn	17.50	17.50

Types of 1877

1880   *Perf. 11½*

92	A11	20 cash vio	5.50	5.00
93	A12	40 cash rose	2.75	2.50
94	A13	60 cash grn	2.75	2.50
95	A14	80 cash bl	8.50	7.50
96	A14	100 cash brn	8.50	7.50

Perf. 15 x 11½.

97	A11	20 cash lil	22.50	20.00

Surcharged type "b" in Blue.

1884   *Perf. 11½*

98	A12	20 cash on 40c rose	6.00	6.00
99	A14	60 cash on 80c bl	12.50	12.50
100	A14	60 cash on 100c brn	15.00	15.00

Types of 1877

1884

101	A11	20 cash grn	4.00	3.50

1885   *Perf. 15.*

102	A11	20 cash grn	3.00	2.50
103	A12	40 cash brn	4.00	3.50
104	A13	60 cash vio	7.00	6.00
a.		60 cash red vio	12.00	11.00
105	A14	80 cash buff	6.00	5.00
106	A14	100 cash yel	6.00	5.00

Perf. 11½ x 15.

107	A11	20 cash grn	3.00	2.50
108	A13	60 cash red vio	6.00	5.00

Surcharged type "b" in Blue.

1886   *Perf. 15.*

109	A14	40 cash on 80c buff	3.50	3.50
110	A14	60 cash on 100c yel	5.00	5.00

Types of 1877

1888   *Perf. 15.*

111	A11	20 cash gray	2.25	2.00
112	A12	40 cash blk	3.50	3.00
113	A13	60 cash rose	3.50	3.00
a.		Third character at left lacks dot at top	7.00	6.00
114	A14	80 cash grn	5.00	4.00
115	A14	100 cash lt bl	7.00	6.00

Handstamp Surcharged in Blue or Red:

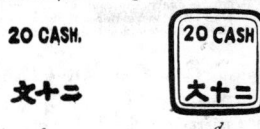

c   d

1888   *Perf. 15.*

116	A14(b)	40 cash on 100c yel (Bl)		
117	A14(b)	40 cash on 100c yel (R)	4.00	4.00
118	A12(c)	20 cash on 40c brn (Bl)	5.00	5.00
119	A14(c)	20 cash on 80c buff (Bl)	9.00	9.00
120	A12(d)	20 cash on 40c brn (Bl)	2.50	2.50
			9.00	9.00

Inverted surcharges exist on Nos. 116–120; double on Nos. 118, 119, 120; omitted surcharges paired with normal stamp on Nos. 116, 119.

Handstamp Surcharged in Black and Red or Red

e

1889   *Unwmkd.*

121	A14(e)	100 cash on 20c on 100c yel	20.00	20.00
a.		Without the surcharge "100 cash"	125.00	
b.		Blue & red surcharge		
122	A14(c)	20 cash on 80c grn (R)	5.00	5.00
123	A14(c)	20 cash on 80c bl (R)	5.00	5.00

Counterfeits exist of Nos. 116–123.

Kung Pu (Municipal Council)
Wmk. 175   A20

Wmkd. Chinese Characters. (175)

1889   *Perf. 15.*

124	A11	20 cash gray	1.75	1.50
125	A12	40 cash blk	3.00	2.50
126	A13	60 cash rose	3.50	3.00
a.		Third character at left lacks dot at top	7.00	6.00

Perf. 12.

127	A14	80 cash grn	4.50	4.00
128	A14	100 cash dk bl	8.50	7.50

Nos. 124-126 are sometimes found without watermark. This is caused by the sheet being misplaced in the printing press, so that the stamps are printed on the unwatermarked margin of the sheet.

Lithographed.

1890   *Perf. 15*   *Unwmkd.*

129	A20	2c brown	1.50	1.00
130	A20	5c rose	4.50	4.00
131	A20	15c blue	4.50	4.00

Nos. 129–131 imperforate are proofs.

Wmkd. Chinese Characters. (175)

132	A20	10c black	5.00	4.00
133	A20	15c blue	10.00	9.00
134	A20	20c violet	5.00	4.00

1891   *Perf. 12.*

135	A20	2c brown	1.75	1.25
136	A20	5c rose	3.50	3.00

1892

137	A20	2c green	.90	.75
138	A20	5c red	1.75	1.50
139	A20	10c orange	3.00	2.50
140	A20	15c violet	5.00	4.00
141	A20	20c brown	5.00	4.00

No. 130 Handstamp Surcharged in Blue

f

1892   *Perf. 15.*   *Unwmkd.*

142	A20	2c on 5c rose	17.50	14.00

Counterfeits exist of Nos. 142–152.

Stamps of 1892 Handstamp Surcharged in Blue:

g   h

1893   *Perf. 12.*   *Wmk. 175*

143	A20	½c on 15c vio	5.00	3.00
144	A20	1c on 20c brn	4.00	3.50
a.		½c on 20c brn (error)	1,750.	

Surcharged in Blue or Red on Halves of Stamps:

i   j   k   m

145	A20(i)	½c on half of 5c rose	4.00	2.00
146	A20(j)	½c on half of 5c rose	4.00	3.00
147	A20(k)	½c on half of 5c rose	40.00	
148	A20(i)	½c on half of 5c red	4.00	2.00
149	A20(j)	½c on half of 5c red	4.00	
150	A20(k)	½c on half of 5c red	40.00	
151	A20(m)	1c on half of 2c brn	1.50	1.25
c.		Dbl. surch., one in green	250.00	
d.		Double surcharge, one in blk	250.00	
152	A20(m)	1c on half of 2c grn (R)	9.00	7.00

The ½c surcharge setting of 20 (2x10) covers a vertical strip of 10 unsevered stamps, with horizontal gutter midway. This setting has 11 of type "i", 8 of type "j" and 1 of type "k". Nos. 145-152 are perforated vertically down the middle.

Inverted surcharges exist on Nos. 145-151. Double surcharges, one inverted, are also found in this issue.

Handstamped provisionals somewhat similar to Nos. 145–152 were issued in Foochow by the Shanghai Agency.

Coat of Arms
A24

Mercury
A26

1893   Litho.   *Perf. 13½x14*

Frame Inscriptions in Black

153	A24	½c org, typo.	.25	.25
a.		½c org, litho.	2.00	2.00
154	A24	1c brn, typo.	.25	.25
a.		1c brn, litho.	2.00	2.00
155	A24	2c vermilion	.50	.50
a.		Imperf.		
156	A24	5c blue	.25	.25
a.		Black inscriptions inverted	275.00	
157	A24	10c org, typo. & litho.	.35	.35
a.		10c grn, litho.	1.75	1.75
158	A24	15c yellow	.40	.40
159	A24	20c lil, typo. & litho.	.50	.50
a.		20c lil, litho.	2.00	2.00
		Nos. 153-159 (7)	2.50	2.50

On Nos. 157 and 159, frame inscriptions are lithographed, rest of design typographed.

Stamps of 1893 Overprinted in Black

1893, Dec. 14

160	A24	½c org & blk	.50	.50
161	A24	1c brn & blk	.60	.60
a.		Double overprint	9.00	
162	A24	2c ver & blk	.75	.75
a.		Inverted ovpt.	35.00	
163	A24	5c bl & blk	2.50	2.50
a.		Inverted overprint		
164	A24	10c grn & blk	3.50	3.00
165	A24	15c yel & blk	3.50	3.00
166	A24	20c lil & blk	6.00	5.00
		Nos. 160-166 (7)	17.35	15.35

Nos. 160-167 commemorate the 50th anniversary of the first foreign settlement in Shanghai.

1893, Nov. 11   Litho.   *Perf. 13½*

167	A26	2c ver & blk	.75	.75

Nos. 158 and 159 Handstamp Surcharged in Black

1896   *Perf. 13½x14*

168	A24	4c on 15c yel & blk	5.00	5.00
169	A24	6c on 20c lil & blk	5.00	5.00

Surcharge occurs inverted or double on Nos. 168–169.

Arms Type of 1893

1896

170	A24	2c scar & blk	.40	.40
a.		Black inscriptions inverted	60.00	
171	A24	4c org & blk, yel	.50	.50
172	A24	6c car & blk rose	1.00	1.00

POSTAGE DUE STAMPS.

Postage Stamps of 1890-92 Handstamped in Black, Red or Blue

1892   *Perf. 15.*   *Unwmkd.*

J1	A20	2c brn (Bk)	100.00	75.00
J2	A20	5c rose (Bk)	3.00	3.00
J3	A20	15c bl (Bk)	17.50	17.50

Wmkd. Chinese Characters. (175)

J4	A20	10c blk (R)	7.50	7.50
J5	A20	15c bl (Bk)	6.00	6.00
J6	A20	20c vio (Bk)	3.00	3.00

1892-93   *Perf. 12.*

J7	A20	2c brn (Bk)	.75	.50
J8	A20	2c brn (Bl)	.75	.50
J9	A20	5c rose (Bl)	1.50	1.50
J10	A20	10c org (Bk)	50.00	40.00
J11	A20	10c org (Bl)	2.00	2.00

SIBERIA—SOMALIA

J12	A20	15c vio (R)	5.00	5.00
J13	A20	20c brn (R)	5.00	5.00

D2

Lithographed
1893   *Perf. 14x13½, 13½ (½c)*

J14	D2	½c org & blk	30	25
J15	D2	1c brn & blk	30	25
J16	D2	2c ver & blk	30	25
J17	D2	5c bl & blk	30	30
J18	D2	10c grn & blk	50	40
J19	D2	15c yel & blk	50	40
J20	D2	20c vio & blk	50	40
		Nos. J14-J20 (7)	2.70	2.25

Stamps of Shanghai were discontinued in 1898.

SIAM
See Thailand.

SIBERIA
(sī·bēr'ĭ·ȧ)

LOCATION — A vast territory of Russia lying between the Ural Mountains and the Pacific Ocean. The anti-Bolshevist provisional government set up at Omsk by Adm. Aleksandr V. Kolchak issued Nos. 1-10 in 1919. The monarchist, anti-Soviet government in Priamur province issued Nos. 51-118 in 1921-22. (Stamps of the Czechoslovak Legion are listed under Czechoslovakia.)

100 Kopecks = 1 Ruble

Russian Stamps of 1909-18 Surcharged

Wove Paper.
Lozenges of Varnish on Face.
On Stamps of 1909-12.
1919   *Perf. 14x14½   Unwmkd.*

1	A14(a)	35k on 2k dl grn	75	1.75
	a.	Invtd. surch.	50.00	
2	A14(a)	50k on 3k car	75	2.00
	a.	Invtd. surch.	50.00	
3	A14(a)	70k on 1k dl org yel	1.50	5.00
	a.	Invtd. surch.	50.00	
4	A15(b)	1r on 4k car	1.50	3.00
	a.	Dbl. surch., one inverted	80.00	
	b.	Invtd. surch.	80.00	
5	A14(b)	3r on 7k bl	2.50	6.00
	a.	Double surch.	40.00	
	b.	Invtd. surch.	30.00	
6	A11(b)	5r on 14k dk bl & car	4.00	9.00
	a.	Double surch.	40.00	
	b.	Invtd. surch.	35.00	

On Stamps of 1917.
Imperf.

7	A14(a)	35k on 2k gray grn	1.50	3.00
8	A14(a)	50k on 3k red	1.50	3.00
	a.	Invtd. surch.	150.00	
9	A14(a)	70k on 1k org	1.25	2.25
	a.	Invtd. surcharge	40.00	
10	A15(b)	1r on 4k car	7.50	13.00
		Nos. 1-10 (10)	22.75	48.00

Nos. 1-10, were first issued in Omsk during the regime of Admiral Kolchak. Later they were used along the line of the Trans-Siberian railway to Vladivostok. Some experts question the postal use of most off-cover canceled copies of Nos. 1-10.

Similar surcharges, handstamped as above are bogus.

Priamur Government Issues.

Nikolaevsk Issue.

A5   A6

A7

Russian Stamps Handstamp Surcharged or Overprinted

On Stamps of 1909-12.
Perf. 14x14½, 13½.
1921   Unwmkd.

51	A5	10k on 4k car	100.00	50.00
52	A5	10k on 10k dk bl	1,000.	2,000.
53	A6	15k on 14k dk bl & car	125.00	75.00
54	A6	15k on 15k red brn & dp bl	100.00	35.00
55	A6	15k on 35k red brn & grn	100.00	35.00
56	A6	15k on 50k brn vio & grn	70.00	30.00
57	A6	15k on 70k brn & red org	200.00	90.00
58	A6	15k on 1r brn & org	650.00	400.00
59	A5	20k on dl bl & dk car	200.00	90.00
60	A5	20k on 14k dk bl & car	225.00	115.00
	a.	15k on 20k on 14k dk bl & car (error)	550.00	
61	A7	20k on 3½r mar & lt grn	200.00	90.00
62	A7	20k on 5r ind, grn & lt bl	700.00	400.00
63	A7	20k on 7r dk grn & pink	375.00	200.00

Nos. 59-60 are overprinted with initials but original denominations remain.
A 10k on 5k claret (Russia No. 77) and a 15k on 20k blue & carmine (Russia No. 82a) were not officially issued. Some authorities consider them bogus.

On Semi-Postal Stamp of 1914.

64	SP6	20k on 3k mar & gray grn, *pink*	600.00	300.00

On Stamps of 1917.
Imperf.

65	A5	10k on 1k org	50.00	25.00
66	A5	10k on 2k gray grn	65.00	25.00
67	A5	10k on 3k red	65.00	30.00
68	A5	10k on 5k cl	450.00	300.00
69	A6	15k on 1r pale brn, brn & red org	70.00	45.00
70	A7	20k on 1r pale brn, brn & red org	125.00	75.00
71	A7	20k on 3½r mar & lt grn	275.00	125.00

72	A7	20k on 7r dk grn & pink	400.00	250.00

The letters of the overprint are the initials of the Russian words for "Nikolaevsk on Amur Priamur Provisional Government". As the surcharges on Nos. 51-72 are handstamped, a number exist inverted or double.
A 20k blue & carmine (Russia No. 126) with Priamur overprint and a 15k on 20k (Russia No. 126) were not officially issued. Some authorities consider them bogus.

Priamur Commemorative Issue.

Stamps of Far Eastern Republic Overprinted

1922

78	A2	2k gray grn	30.00	40.00
	a.	Invtd. overprint	200.00	
79	A2a	4k rose	25.00	30.00
	a.	Invtd. overprint	175.00	
80	A2	5k claret	30.00	40.00
81	A2a	10k blue	30.00	40.00

This issue was to commemorate the anniversary of the overthrow of the Bolshevik power in the Priamur district.
The letters of the overprint are the initials of "Vremeno Priamurski Pravitel'stvo" i. e. Provisional Priamur Government, 26th May.

Priamur Issue.

Russian Stamps of 1909-21 Overprinted in Dark Blue or Vermilion

On Stamps of 1909-18.
1922   *Perf. 14x14½.*

85	A14	1k dl org yel	70.00	80.00
86	A14	2k dl grn	115.00	150.00
87	A14	3k carmine	40.00	50.00
88	A15	4k carmine	15.00	15.00
89	A14	5k dk cl	40.00	55.00
90	A14	7k bl (V)	40.00	50.00
91	A15	10k dk bl (V)	50.00	60.00
92	A11	14k dk bl & car	90.00	100.00
93	A11	15k red brn & dp bl	15.00	20.00
94	A8	20k dl bl & dk car	15.00	20.00
95	A11	20k on 14k dk bl & car	120.00	150.00
96	A11	25k dl grn & dk vio (V)	40.00	60.00
97	A11	35k red brn & grn	7.50	10.00
	a.	Invtd. ovpt.	110.00	
98	A8	50k brn vio & grn	15.00	15.00
99	A11	70k brn & red org	40.00	50.00

On Stamps of 1917.
Imperf.

100	A14	1k orange	7.50	10.00
	a.	Invtd. ovpt.	125.00	150.00
101	A14	2k gray grn	11.00	15.00
102	A14	3k red	17.50	25.00
103	A15	4k carmine	90.00	120.00
104	A14	5k claret	30.00	40.00
105	A11	15k red brn & dp bl	175.00	250.00
106	A8	20k bl & car	70.00	90.00
107	A9	1r pale brn, brn & red org	25.00	40.00

On Stamps of Siberia, 1919.
Perf. 14½x15.

108	A14	35k on 2k gray grn	75.00	90.00

Imperf.

109	A14	70k on 1k org	95.00	130.00

On Stamps of Far Eastern Republic, 1921.

110	A2	2k gray grn	8.00	9.00
111	A2a	4k rose	8.00	9.00
112	A2	5k claret	8.00	9.00
	a.	Invtd. overprint	150.00	
113	A2a	10k bl (R)	5.00	6.00

Same, Surcharged with New Values

114	A2	1k on 2k gray grn	5.00	6.00
115	A2a	3k on 4k rose	5.00	6.00

The overprint is in a rectangular frame on stamps of 1k to 10k and 1r; on the other values the frame is omitted. It is larger on the 1 ruble than on the smaller stamps.
The overprint reads "Priamurski Zemski Krai", Priamur Rural Province.

Far Eastern Republic

Nos. 30-32 Overprinted in Blue

Perf. 14½ x15.

116	A14	35k on 2k grn	10.00	15.00

Imperf.

117	A14	35k on 2k gray grn	125.00	150.00
118	A14	70k on 1k org	20.00	20.00

Counterfeits of Nos. 51-118 abound.

SLOVAKIA
(Listed under Czechoslovakia in Vol. II.)

SOMALIA
(sō·mä'lē·ȧ)
(Somali Democratic Republic)
(Italian Somaliland)
(Benadir)

LOCATION — In eastern Africa, bordering on the Indian Ocean and the Gulf of Aden.
GOVT.—Republic.
AREA—262,000 sq. mi.
POP.—3,350,000 (est. 1977).
CAPITAL—Mogadishu (Mogadiscio).

This former Italian colony which included the territory west of the Juba River known as Oltre Giuba (Trans-Juba), was absorbed into Italian East Africa in 1936. It was under British military administration 1941-49. Italian trusteeship took effect in 1950, with a United Nations Advisory Council helping the administrator. On July 1, 1960, the former Italian colony merged with Somaliland Protectorate (British) to form the independent Republic of Somalia.

4 Besas = 1 Anna
16 Annas = 1 Rupee
100 Besas = 1 Rupee (1922)
100 Centesimi = 1 Lira (1905, 1925)
100 Centesimi = 1 Somalo (1950)
100 Centesimi = 1 Somali Shilling (1961)

Italian Somaliland

Elephant—A1

Lion—A2

Wmk. 140

SOMALIA

Wmkd. Crown. (140)
1903, Oct. Typo. Perf. 14
1	A1	1b brown	32.50	5.50
2	A1	2b bl grn	1.75	1.75
3	A1	1a claret	2.25	2.75
4	A2	2a org brn	4.50	13.00
5	A2	2½a blue	2.25	3.50
6	A2	5a orange	4.50	13.00
7	A2	10a lilac	4.50	13.00
	Nos. 1-7 (7)		52.25	52.50

Surcharged **Centesimi 15**

1905, Dec. 29
8	A2	15c on 5a org	1,350.	275.00
9	A2	40c on 10a lil	250.00	75.00

Surcharged **C. 2**

1906-07
10	A1	2c on 1b brn	1.40	6.75
11	A1	5c on 2b bl grn	1.40	3.50

Surcharged **C. 10**
12	A2	10c on 1a cl	1.40	2.75
13	A2	15c on 2a brn org ('06)	1.40	3.25
14	A2	25c on 2½a bl	2.75	3.50
15	A2	50c on 5a yel	7.50	6.75

Surcharged **1 LIRA 1**
16	A2	1 l on 10a lil	6.75	9.00
	Nos. 10-16 (7)		22.60	35.50

Nos. 15 and 16 Surcharged **C. 5** and bars over former Surcharge.

1916, May
18	A2	5c on 50c on 5a yel	8.25	9.00
19	A2	20c on 1 l on 10a dl lil	3.00	4.50

No. 4 Surcharged **C. 20**
20	A2	20c on 2a org brn	4.50	1.25

Stamps of 1906-07 Surcharged:
3 3 a **6 BESA 6** b

1922, Feb. 1
22	A1(a)	3b on 5c on 2b bl grn	2.75	9.00
23	A2(b)	6c on 10c on 1a cl	2.25	4.50
24	A2(b)	9b on 15c on 2a brn org	2.75	4.50
25	A2(b)	15b on 25c on 2½a bl	3.50	5.50
26	A2(b)	30b on 50c on 5a yel	5.75	10.00
27	A2(b)	60b on 1 l on 10a lil	10.00	20.00
	Nos. 22-27 (6)		27.00	53.50

Victory Issue.
Italy Nos. 136-139 Surcharged **SOMALIA ITALIANA BESA 3**

1922, Apr.
28	A64	3b on 5c ol grn	45	1.75
29	A64	6b on 10c red	45	1.75
30	A64	9b on 15c sl grn	70	5.25
31	A64	15b on 25c ultra	70	4.50

Stamps of 1906-07 Surcharged with Bars and **2 2** c **5 BESA 5** d

1923, July 1
40	A1	1b brown	1.75	9.00
41	A1(c)	2b on 2c on 1b brn	1.75	9.00
42	A1(c)	3b on 2c on 1b brn	1.75	9.00
43	A2(c)	5b on 50c on 5a yel	1.75	6.75
44	A2(c)	6b on 5c on 2b bl grn	2.75	3.50
45	A2(d)	18b on 10c on 1a rose red	2.75	3.50
46	A2(d)	20b on 15c on 2a brn org	3.25	3.50
47	A2(d)	25b on 15c on 2a brn org	3.25	3.50
48	A2(d)	30b on 25c on 2½a bl	4.50	5.50
49	A2(d)	60b on 1 l on 10a lil	5.50	17.50
50	A2(d)	1r on 1 l on 10a lil	7.25	22.50
	Nos. 40-50 (11)		36.25	93.25

No. 40 is No. 10 with bars over the 1907 surcharge.

Propaganda of the Faith Issue.
Italy Nos. 143-146 Surcharged **SOMALIA ITALIANA besa 6**

1923, Oct. 24 Wmk. 140
51	A68	6b on 20c ol grn & brn org	1.50	6.25
52	A68	13b on 30c cl & brn org	1.50	6.25
53	A68	20b on 50c vio & brn org	1.10	5.00
54	A68	30b on 1 l bl & brn org	1.10	5.00

Fascisti Issue.
Italy Nos. 159-164 Surcharged **SOMALIA ITALIANA** in Red or Black **BESA 30**

1923, Oct. 29 Perf. 14 Unwmkd.
55	A69	8b on 10c dk grn (R)	1.50	5.25
56	A69	13b on 30c dk vio (R)	1.50	5.25
57	A69	20b on 50c brn car	1.50	5.25

Wmkd. Crowns. (140)
58	A70	30b on 1 l bl	1.50	5.25
59	A70	1r on 2 l brn	1.50	5.25
60	A71	3r on 5 l blk & bl (R)	3.50	17.50
	Nos. 55-60 (6)		11.00	43.75

Manzoni Issue.
Italy Nos. 165-170 Surcharged in Red **SOMALIA ITALIANA besa 9**

1924, Apr. 1
61	A72	6b on 10c brn red & blk	45	2.25
62	A72	9b on 15c bl grn & blk	45	2.25
63	A72	13b on 30c blk & sl	45	2.25
64	A72	20b on 50c org brn & blk	45	2.25

Surcharged **SOMALIA ITALIANA rupie 3**
65	A72	30b on 1 l bl & blk	9.00	35.00
66	A72	3r on 5 l vio & blk	210.00	525.00
	Nos. 61-66 (6)		220.80	569.00

Victor Emmanuel Issue.
Italy Nos. 175-177 Overprinted **SOMALIA ITALIANA**

1925-26 Perf. 13½ Unwmkd.
67	A78	60c brn car	28	1.75
a.	Perf. 11		10.00	30.00
68	A78	1 l dk bl, perf. 11	45	2.75
a.	Perf. 13½		2.25	13.00
69	A78	1.25 l dk bl ('26)	40	4.50
a.	Perf. 11		85.00	150.00

Stamps of 1907-16 with Bars over Original Values.
1926, Mar. 1 Perf. 14 Wmk. 140
70	A1	2c on 1b brn	8.00	22.50
71	A1	5c on 2b bl grn	6.25	16.00
72	A2	10c on 1a rose red	2.25	2.75
73	A2	15c on 2a org brn	2.25	3.50
74	A2	20c on 2a org brn	2.75	4.50
75	A2	25c on 2½a bl	2.75	6.75
76	A2	50c on 5a yel	3.25	9.00
77	A2	1 l on 10a dl lil	4.00	13.00
	Nos. 70-77 (8)		31.50	78.00

Saint Francis of Assisi Issue.
Italy Nos. 178-180 Overprinted **SOMALIA ITALIANA**

1926, Apr. 12 Perf. 14
78	A79	20c gray grn	65	2.25
79	A80	40c dk vio	65	2.25
80	A81	60c red brn	65	2.25

Italy Nos. 182 and Type of 1926 Overprinted in Red **Somalia**
Perf. 11 Unwmkd.
81	A82	1.25 l dk bl	65	2.25

Perf. 14
82	A83	5 l + 2.50 l ol grn	2.75	9.00
	Nos. 78-82 (5)		5.35	18.00

Italian Stamps of 1901-26 Overprinted **SOMALIA ITALIANA**
1926-30 Wmkd. Crown. (140)
83	A43	2c org brn	90	1.40
84	A48	5c green	1.10	1.10
85	A48	10c claret	28	32
86	A49	20c rose brn	35	45
87	A46	25c grn & pale grn	28	28
88	A49	30c gray ('30)	2.25	5.50
89	A49	60c brn & grn	40	45
90	A46	75c dk red & rose	17.50	4.50
91	A46	1 l brn & grn	45	28
92	A46	1.25 l bl & ultra	1.40	90
93	A46	2 l dk grn & org	1.85	1.75
94	A46	2.50 l dk grn & org	2.25	2.25
95	A46	5 l bl & rose	14.00	8.00
96	A51	10 l gray grn & red	14.00	9.00
	Nos. 83-96 (14)		57.01	36.18

Volta Issue
Type of Italy, 1927, Overprinted **Somalia Italiana**
1927, Oct. 10
97	A84	20c purple	1.75	5.25
98	A84	50c dp org	1.75	3.50
a.	Double ovpt.		12.00	
99	A84	1.25 l brt bl	3.25	9.00

Italian Stamps of 1927-28 Overprinted in Black or Red **SOMALIA ITALIANA**
1928-30
100	A86	7½c lt brn (Bk)	4.50	13.00
a.	Double overprint		60.00	
101	A85	50c brn & sl (R)	1.75	1.75
102	A86	50c brt vio (Bk) ('30)	3.50	5.25

Perf. 11 Unwmkd.
103	A85	1.75 l dp brn	4.50	2.75

Monte Cassino Issue.
Types of Monte Cassino Issue of Italy Overprinted in Red or Blue **SOMALIA ITALIANA**
Wmkd. Crowns. (140)
1929, Oct. 14 Perf. 14
104	A96	20c dk grn (R)	1.10	4.50
105	A96	25c red org (Bl)	1.10	4.50
106	A96	50c + 10c crim (R)	1.10	4.50
107	A98	75c + 15c ol brn (R)	1.10	4.50
108	A96	1.25 l + 25c dk vio (R)	1.10	4.50
109	A98	5 l + 1 l saph (R)	3.25	9.00

Overprinted in Red **Somalia Italiana**
Unwmkd.
110	A100	10 l + 2 l gray brn	3.25	9.00
	Nos. 104-110 (7)		12.00	40.50

Royal Wedding Issue
Type of Italian Royal Wedding Stamps of 1930 Overprinted **SOMALIA ITALIANA**
1930, Mar. 17 Wmk. 140
111	A101	20c yel grn	45	1.75
112	A101	50c + 10c dp org	55	3.00
113	A101	1.25 l + 25c rose red	60	4.00

Ferrucci Issue.
Types of Italian Stamps of 1930 Overprinted in Red or Blue **SOMALIA ITALIANA**
1930, July 26
114	A102	20c vio (R)	55	1.50
115	A103	25c dk grn (R)	55	1.50
116	A103	50c blk (R)	55	1.50
117	A103	1.25 l dp bl (R)	55	1.50
118	A104	5 l + 2 l dp car (bl)	1.40	2.75
	Nos. 114-118 (5)		3.60	8.75

Virgil Issue.
Types of Italian Stamps of 1930 Overprinted in Red or Blue **SOMALIA**
1930, Dec. 4 Photo. Wmk. 140
119	A106	15c vio bl	25	1.75
120	A106	20c org brn	25	1.75
121	A106	25c dk grn	25	1.25
122	A106	30c lt brn	25	1.75
123	A106	50c dl vio	25	1.25
124	A106	75c rose red	25	1.75
125	A106	1.25 l gray bl	25	1.75

Engraved Unwmkd.
126	A106	5 l + 1.50 l dk vio	1.75	5.25
127	A106	10 l + 2.50 l ol grn	1.75	5.25
	Nos. 119-127 (9)		5.25	21.75

Saint Anthony of Padua Issue.
Types of Italian Stamps of 1931 Overprinted in Blue or Red **SOMALIA**
1931, May 7 Wmkd. Crowns (140)
129	A116	20c brn (Bl)	45	2.25
130	A116	25c grn (R)	45	2.25
131	A118	30c gray brn (Bl)	45	2.25
132	A118	50c dl vio (Bl)	45	1.25
133	A120	1.25 l sl bl (R)	45	2.25

Overprinted in Red or Black **Somalia**
Engraved Unwmkd.
134	A121	75c blk (R)	45	2.25
135	A122	5 l + 2.50 l dk brn (Bk)	2.75	10.00
	Nos. 129-135 (7)		5.45	22.50

SOMALIA

Italy Nos. 218, 221 Overprinted in Red — SOMALIA ITALIANA

1931   Wmkd. Crown. (140)
136	A94	25c dk grn (R)	2.25	1.75
137	A95	50c pur (R)	2.25	.70

Lighthouse at Cape Guardafui — A3

Tower at Mnara Ciromo — A4

Governor's Palace at Mogadishu — A5

Termite Nest — A6

Ostrich — A7

Hippopotamus — A8

Greater Kudu — A9

Lion — A10

Photogravure.

1932   *Perf. 12*   Wmk. 140
138	A3	5c dp brn	1.50	45
139	A3	7½c violet	2.00	4.50
140	A3	10c gray blk	2.75	28
141	A3	15c ol grn	90	28
142	A4	20c carmine	22.50	28
143	A4	25c dp grn	90	18
144	A4	30c dk brn	2.75	32
145	A5	35c dk bl	2.25	1.50
146	A5	50c violet	27.50	8
147	A5	75c carmine	1.10	45
148	A6	1.25 l dk bl	1.10	35
149	A6	1.75 l red org	1.75	35
150	A6	2 l carmine	90	45
151	A7	2.55 l indigo	9.00	17.50
152	A7	5 l carmine	3.00	1.40
153	A8	10 l violet	10.00	5.75
154	A9	20 l dk grn	27.50	20.00
155	A10	25 l dk bl	40.00	28.50
		Nos. 138-155 (18)	157.40	82.62

1934-37   *Perf. 14*
138a	A3	5c dp brn	22	18
139a	A3	7½c violet	22	1.25
140a	A3	10c gray blk	22	18
141a	A3	15c ol grn	22	28
142a	A4	20c carmine	22	5
143a	A4	25c dp grn	22	5
144a	A4	30c dk brn	32	28
145a	A5	35c dk bl	45	1.25
146a	A5	50c violet	3.25	5
147a	A5	75c carmine	1.10	18
148a	A6	1.25 l dk bl	7.50	35
149a	A6	1.75 l red org	27.50	28
150a	A6	2 l carmine	9.00	35
151a	A7	2.55 l indigo	160.00	110.00
152a	A7	5 l carmine	1.75	90
153a	A8	10 l violet	27.50	8.00
154a	A9	20 l dk vio	4,500.	350.00
155a	A10	25 l dk bl	75.00	90.00
		Nos. 138a-153a, 155a (17)	314.69	213.63

Eleven denominations in the foregoing series exist perf. 12x14 or 14x12.

Types of 1932 Issue Overprinted in Black or Red — ONORANZE AL DUCA DEGLI ABRUZZI

1934, May   *Perf. 14*
156	A3	10c brn (Bk)	1.25	4.50
157	A4	25c green	1.25	4.50
158	A5	50c dl vio (Bk)	1.25	4.50
159	A6	1.25 l blue	1.25	4.50
160	A7	5 l brn blk	2.75	6.75
161	A8	10 l car rose (Bk)	2.75	6.75
162	A9	20 l dl bl	2.75	6.75
163	A10	25 l dk grn	2.75	6.75
		Nos. 156-163 (8)	16.00	45.00

Issued in tribute to the Duke of the Abruzzi (Luigi Amadeo, 1873-1933).

Mother and Child — A11

1934, Oct.
164	A11	5c ol grn & brn	1.50	4.00
165	A11	10c yel brn & blk	1.50	4.00
166	A11	20c scar & blk	1.50	4.00
167	A11	50c dk vio & brn	1.50	4.00
168	A11	60c org brn & blk	1.50	4.00
169	A11	1.25 l dk bl & grn	1.50	4.00
		Nos. 164-169 (6)	9.00	24.00

Second Colonial Arts Exhibition, Naples.

Somalia

Tower at Mnara Ciromo — A12

Governor's Palace, Mogadishu — A13

Design: 5c, 20c, 60c, Ostrich.

Photogravure

1950, Mar. 24   *Perf. 14*   Wmk. 277
170	A12	1c gray blk	12	10
171	A12	5c car rose	10	5
172	A13	6c violet	18	10
173	A12	8c Prus grn	18	10
174	A13	10c dk grn	18	5
175	A12	20c bl grn	18	6
176	A12	35c red	35	28
177	A13	55c brt bl	40	18
178	A12	60c purple	45	18
179	A13	65c brown	55	18
180	A13	1s dp org	1.10	18
		Nos. 170-180, E8-E9 (13)	6.54	3.43

Council in Session — A14

1951, Oct. 4
181	A14	20c dk grn & brn	3.00	45
182	A14	55c brn & vio	6.00	5.75

Meeting of First Territorial Council. See Nos. C27A-C27B.

Somali Tiger, Palm Tree and Minaret — A16

Mother and Child — A17

1952, Sept. 14   *Perf. 14*   Wmk. 277
185	A16	25c red & dk brn	2.50	3.25
186	A16	55c bl & dk brn	2.50	3.25

Issued to publicize the first Somali Fair, Mogadishu, Sept. 14-28. See No. C28.

1953, May 27
Center in Dark Brown
187	A17	5c rose vio	12	18
188	A17	25c rose	20	28
189	A17	50c blue	1.00	1.40

Anti-tuberculosis campaign. See No. C29.

Laborer at Fair Entrance — A18

Perf. 11½

1953, Sept. 28   Unwmkd.
190	A18	25c dk grn & gray	35	45
191	A18	60c bl & gray	70	90

Issued to publicize the 2nd Somali Fair, Mogadishu, Sept. 28-Oct. 12. See Nos. C30-C31.

Map and Stamps of 1903 — A19

Perf. 13x13½

1953, Dec. 16   Engr.   Wmk. 277
"Stamps" in Brown and Rose Carmine
192	A19	25c dp mag	35	45
193	A19	35c dk grn	35	45
194	A19	60c orange	35	45
		Nos. 192-194, C32-C33 (5)	2.95	2.65

Issued to commemorate the 50th anniversary of the first Somali postage stamps.

Somalia Brushwood — A20

Perf. 12½x13½

1954, June 1   Photo.   Unwmkd.
195	A20	25c dp bl & dk gray	35	45

196	A20	60c org brn & brn	35	45

Issued to publicize the convention of Nov. 11, 1953, with the Sovereign Military Order of Malta, providing for the care of lepers. See Nos. C37-C38.

Somali Flag — A21

Adenium Somalense — A22

Perf. 13½x13

1954, Oct. 12   Litho.   Wmk. 277
197	A21	25c blk, grn, bl, red & yel	35	45

Adoption of a Somali flag. See No. C39.

1955, Feb.   Photo.   *Perf. 13*

Flowers: 5c, Haemanthus multiflorus martyn. 10c, Grinum scabrum. 25c, Poinciana elata. 60c, Calatropis procera. 1s, Pancratium. 1.20s, Sesamothamnus bussernus.
198	A22	1c bl, dp rose & dk ol brn	10	18
199	A22	5c bl, rose lil & grn	8	18
200	A22	10c lil & grn	40	18
201	A22	25c vio brn, yel & grn	60	28
202	A22	60c blk, car & grn	12	28
203	A22	1s red brn & grn	20	35
204	A22	1.20s dk brn, yel & grn	22	35
		Nos. 198-204 (7)	1.72	1.80

See also Nos. 216-220, E10-E11.

Weaver at Loom — A23

Design: 30c, Cattle fording stream.

Perf. 13½x14

1955, Sept. 24   Wmk. 303
205	A23	25c dk brn	35	45
206	A23	30c dk grn	35	45

Issued to publicize the 3rd Somali Fair, Mogadishu, September, 1955. See Nos. C46-C47.

Casting Ballots — A24

Arms of Somalia — A25

1956, Apr. 30   *Perf. 14*
207	A24	5c brn & gray grn	12	18
208	A24	10c brn & ol bis	12	18
209	A24	35c brn & brn red	12	18
		Nos. 207-209, C48-C49 (5)	76	1.14

Issued in honor of the opening of the territory's first democratically elected Legislative Assembly.

SOMALIA

1957, May 6 Perf. 13½ Wmk. 303
Coat of Arms in Dull Yellow, Blue and Black.

210	A25	5c lt red brn	8	8
211	A25	25c carmine	20	28
212	A25	60c bluish vio	22	32
		Nos. 210-212, C50-C51 (5)	1.00	1.35

Issued in honor of the new coat of arms.

Dam at Falcheiro—A26

Designs: 10c, Juba River Bridge. 25c, Silos at Margherita.

1957, Sept. 28 Photo. Perf. 14

213	A26	5c brn & pur	8	10
214	A26	10c bis & bl grn	12	18
215	A26	25c car & bl	20	28
		Nos. 213-215, C52-C53 (5)	1.05	1.46

Fourth Somali Fair and Film Festival.

Flower Type of 1955.

Flowers: 1c, Adenium Somalense. 10c, Grinum scabrum. 15c, Adansonia digitata. 25c, Poinciana elata. 50c, Gloriosa virescens.

Photogravure.

1956-59 Perf. 13 Wmk. 303

216	A22	1c bl, dp rose & dk ol brn	8	8
217	A22	10c lil, grn & yel ('59)	18	22
218	A22	15c red, grn & yel ('58)	22	32
219	A22	25c dl lil, grn & yel ('59)	18	22
220	A22	50c bl, grn, red & yel ('58)	35	45
		Nos. 216-220 (5)	1.01	1.29

Runner—A27

Soccer Player—A28

Designs: 5c, Discus thrower. 6c, Motorcyclist. 8c, Fencer. 10c, Archer. 25c, Boxers.

1958, Apr. 28 Perf. 14 Wmk. 303

221	A27	2c violet	6	8
222	A28	4c green	6	8
223	A27	5c vermilion	6	8
224	A28	6c gray	6	8
225	A27	8c vio bl	6	8
226	A28	10c orange	6	8
227	A28	25c dk grn	10	10
		Nos. 221-227, C54-C56 (10)	1.16	1.50

Book and Assembly Palace A29

White Stork A30

1959, June 19

| 228 | A29 | 5c grn & ultra | 18 | 22 |
| 229 | A29 | 25c ocher & ultra | 18 | 22 |

Opening of Somalia's Constituent Assembly.
See Nos. C59-C60 and souvenir sheet No. C60a.

1959, Sept. 4 Photo. Perf. 14

Birds: 10c, Saddle-billed stork. 15c, Sacred ibis. 25c, Pink-backed pelican.

230	A30	5c yel, blk & red	12	18
231	A30	10c brn, red & yel	12	18
232	A30	15c org & blk	12	18
233	A30	25c dk car, blk & org	12	18
		Nos.230-233, C61-C62 (6)	92	3.04

Incense Bush A31

Arms of University Institute A32

Design: 60c, Girl burning incense.

1959, Sept. 28 Wmk. 303

| 234 | A31 | 20c org & blk | 20 | 28 |
| 235 | A31 | 60c blk, org & dk red | 30 | 40 |

Issued to publicize the 5th Somali Fair, Mogadishu. See Nos. C63-C64.

1960, Jan. 14 Photo. Perf. 14

Designs: 50c, Map of Africa and arms (horiz.). 80c, Arms of University Institute.

236	A32	5c brn & sal	8	8
237	A32	50c lt vio bl, brn & blk	28	28
238	A32	80c brt red & blk	35	35
		Nos. 236-238, C65-C66 (5)	1.61	1.61

Issued to commemorate the opening of the University Institute of Somalia.

Globe and Uprooted Oak Emblem A33

Palm—A34

Design: 60c, Like 10c but with inscription and emblem rearranged.

1960, Apr. 7 Perf. 14

239	A33	10c yel brn, grn & blk	8	8
240	A33	60c dp bis & blk	18	18
241	A34	80c pink, grn & blk	18	18

Issued to publicize World Refugee Year, July 1, 1959—June 30, 1960. See No. C67.

Republic

Somaliland

No. 217 Overprinted **Independence 26 June 1960**

Perf. 13

1960, June 26 Photo. Wmk. 303

| 242 | A22 | 10c lil, grn & yel | 9.00 | 10.00 |

Nos. 242, C68-C69 were issued in Hargeisa on June 26, 1960, to commemorate the independence of British Somaliland, which became part of the Republic of Somalia.

Gazelle and Map of Africa A36

Design: 25c, New York skyline, U.N. Building and U.N. flag.

1960, July 1 Perf. 14

| 243 | A36 | 5c lil & brn | 15 | 7 |
| 244 | A36 | 25c blue | 25 | 18 |

Somalia independence. See Nos. C70-C71.

Boy Drawing Giraffe A37

Designs: 15c, Zebra. 25c, Black rhinoceros.

1960, Nov. 24

245	A37	10c bl grn, blk & brn	8	5
246	A37	15c dp car, blk & yel grn	10	6
247	A37	25c multi	10	8

See No. C72.

Olympic Torch, Somalia Flag A38

Girl Harvesting Papaya A39

Designs: 10c, Runners, flag and Olympic rings.

1960 Perf. 14 Wmk. 303

| 248 | A38 | 5c grn & bl | 8 | 5 |
| 249 | A38 | 10c yel & bl | 8 | 6 |

Issued to commemorate the 17th Olympic Games, Rome, Aug. 25—Sept. 11. See Nos. C73-C74.

1961, July 5 Photogravure

Girl harvesting: 10c, Durrah (sorghum). 20c, Cotton. 25c, Sesame. 40c, Sugar cane. 50c, Bananas. 75c, Peanuts (horiz.). 80c, Grapefruit (horiz.).

250	A39	5c multi	6	5
251	A39	10c multi	6	5
252	A39	20c multi	8	6
253	A39	25c multi	12	8
254	A39	40c multi	12	8
255	A39	50c multi	25	12
256	A39	75c multi	30	12
257	A39	80c multi	50	12
		Nos. 250-257 (8)	1.49	68

Shield, Bow and Quiver A40

Pomacanthus Semicirculatus A41

Design: 45c, Pottery and incense jug.

1961, Sept. 28

| 258 | A40 | 25c blk, car & ocher | 8 | 8 |
| 259 | A40 | 45c blk, bl grn & ocher | 18 | 12 |

Issued to publicize the 6th Somali Fair, Mogadishu. See Nos. C82-C83.

1962, Apr. 26 Photogravure

Fish: 15c, Girl embroidering fish on cloth. 40c, Novaculichthys taeniourus.

260	A41	15c brn, blk & pink	12	12
261	A41	25c org, blk & ultra	18	12
262	A41	40c grn, blk & rose	42	25

See No. C84.

Mosquito Trapped by Sprays A42

Design: 25c, Man with spray gun and malaria eradication emblem (vert.).

1962, Oct. 25 Perf. 14 Wmk. 303

| 263 | A42 | 10c org red & grn | 12 | 8 |
| 264 | A42 | 25c rose lil, brn & blk | 18 | 8 |

Issued for the World Health Organization drive to eradicate malaria. See Nos. C85-C86.

Police Auxiliary Woman A43

Designs: 10c, Army auxiliary woman. 25c, Radio police car. 75c, First aid army auxiliary (vert.).

1963, May 15 Perf. 14 Wmk. 303

265	A43	5c multi	5	5
266	A43	10c blk & org	12	12
267	A43	25c multi	18	8
268	A43	75c multi	38	18
		Nos. 265-268, C87-C88 (6)	2.13	91

Women's auxiliary forces.

SOMALIA

Carved Fork and Spoon
and Wheat Emblem
A44

1963, June 25   Photogravure
269   A44   75c grn & red brn   30   18

Issued for the "Freedom from Hunger" campaign of the U.N. Food and Agriculture Organization. See No. C89.

Pres. Aden Abdulla Osman
A45

1963, Sept. 15   *Perf. 14*   Wmk. 303
270   A45   25c bl, dk brn, org & lt bl   30   18

Issued to commemorate the 3rd anniversary of independence. See Nos. C90–C91.

Dunes Theater—A46

Design: 55c, African Merchants' and Artisans' Exhibit.

1963, Sept. 28   Photogravure
271   A46   25c bl grn   18   12
272   A46   55c car rose   25   18

Issued to publicize the 7th Somali Fair, Mogadishu. See No. C92.

Somali Credit Bank Building
A47

1964, May 16   *Perf. 14*   Wmk. 303
273   A47   60c ind, red lil & yel   42   18

Issued to commemorate the 10th anniversary of the Somali Credit Bank. See Nos. C93–C94.

Running—A48
Design: 25c, High jump.

1964, Oct. 10   *Perf. 14*   Wmk. 303
274   A48   10c org brn & bl   12   8
275   A48   25c org brn & bl   30   18

18th Olympic Games, Tokyo, Oct. 10–25. See Nos. C95–C96.

DC-3
A49

Design: 20c, Passengers leaving DC-3.

1964, Nov. 8   Photo.   *Perf. 14*
276   A49   5c dk bl & lil rose   12   5
277   A49   20c bl & org   50   12

Issued to commemorate the establishment of Somali Air Lines. See Nos. C97–C98.

ITU Emblem and
Map of Africa
A50

1965, May 17   *Perf. 14*   Wmk. 303
278   A50   25c dp bl & dp org   30   6

Issued to commemorate the centenary of the International Telecommunication Union. See Nos. C99–C100.

Tanning
Industry
A51

Designs: 25c, Meat industry; cannery and cattle. 35c, Fishing industry; cannery and fishing boats.

1965, Sept. 28   Photo.   *Perf. 14*
279   A51   10c sep & buff   8   5
280   A51   25c sep & pink   12   7
281   A51   35c sep & lt bl   18   12
Nos. 279-281, C101-C102 (5)   2.13   87

8th Somali Fair, Mogadishu.

Hottentot
Fig and
Gazelle
A52

Designs: 60c, African tulip and giraffes. 1sh, Ninfea and flamingos. 1.30sh, Pervincia and ostriches. 1.80sh, Bignonia and zebras.

1965, Nov. 1   *Perf. 14*   Wmk. 303
Flowers in Natural Colors
282   A52   20c blk & brt bl   8   5
283   A52   60c blk & dk gray   18   12
284   A52   1sh blk, sl grn & ol grn   38   18
285   A52   1.30sh blk & dp grn   75   25
286   A52   1.80sh blk & brt bl   1.10   38
Nos. 282-286 (5)   2.49   98

Narina's
Trogon
A53

Birds: 35c, Bateleur eagle (vert.). 50c, Vulture. 1.30sh, European roller. 2sh, Vulturine guinea fowl (vert.).

1966, June 1   Photo.   Wmk. 303
287   A53   25c multi   12   6
288   A53   35c brt bl & multi   12   8
289   A53   50c multi   18   12
290   A53   1.30sh multi   50   30
291   A53   2sh multi   75   38
Nos. 287-291 (5)   1.67   94

Globe and
U.N. Emblem
A54

Designs (U.N. emblem and): 1sh, Map of Africa. 1.50sh, Map of Somalia.

1966, Oct. 24   Litho.   *Perf. 13x12½*
292   A54   35c bl, pur & brt bl   12   12
293   A54   1sh brn, yel & brick red   25   25
294   A54   1.50sh grn, blk, bl & yel   42   42

21st anniversary of United Nations.

Woman
Sitting on
Crocodile
A55

Paintings: 1sh, Woman and warrior. 1.50sh, Boy leading camel. 2sh, Women pounding grain.

Photogravure
1966, Dec. 1   *Perf. 14*   Wmk. 303
295   A55   25c multi   8   7
296   A55   1sh multi   18   18
297   A55   1.50sh multi   30   25
298   A55   2sh multi   38   30

Issued to publicize Somali art, exhibited in the Garesa Museum, Mogadishu.

UNESCO
Emblem
A56

1966, Dec. 20   *Perf. 14*   Wmk. 303
299   A56   35c blk, dk red & gray   8   8
300   A56   1sh blk, emer & yel   18   18
301   A56   1.80sh blk, ultra & red   42   38

Issued to commemorate the 20th anniversary of UNESCO (United Nations Educational, Scientific and Cultural Organization).

Haggard's Oribi   Dancers
A57   A58

Gazelles: 60c, Long-snouted dik-dik. 1sh, Gerenuk. 1.80s, Soemmering's gazelle.

1967, Feb. 20   Photo.   *Perf. 14*
302   A57   35c blk, ultra & bis   8   8

---

303   A57   60c blk, org & brn   12   12
304   A57   1sh blk, red & brn   18   18
305   A57   1.80sh, yel grn & brn   42   38

Lithographed
1967, July 15   *Perf. 13*   Unwmkd.
Designs: Various Folk Dances.
306   A58   25c multi   8   8
307   A58   50c multi   12   12
308   A58   1.30sh multi   30   30
309   A58   2sh multi   38   38

Boy Scout
Giving
Scout Sign
A59

Designs: 50c, Boy Scouts with flags. 1sh, Boy Scout cooking and tent. 1.80sh, Jamboree emblem.

1967, Aug. 15
310   A59   35c multi   12   12
311   A59   50c multi   12   12
312   A59   1sh multi   38   18
313   A59   1.80sh multi   80   50

Issued to commemorate the 12th Boy Scout World Jamboree, Farragut State Park, Idaho, Aug. 1–9.

Pres. Abdirascid Ali Scermarche and
King Faisal—A60

Designs: 1sh, Clasped hands, flags of Somalia and Saudi Arabia.

Photogravure
1967, Sept. 21   *Perf. 14*   Wmk. 303
314   A60   50c blk & lt bl   12   12
315   A60   1sh multi   25   18

Issued to commemorate the visit of King Faisal of Saudi Arabia. See No. C103.

Gaterin Gaterinus
A61

Tropical Fish: 50c, Chaetodon semilarvatus. 1sh, Priacanthus hamrur. 1.80sh, Epinephelus summana.

1967, Nov. 15   Litho.   *Perf. 14*
316   A61   35c dk bl, yel & blk   8   8
317   A61   50c brt bl, ocher & blk   12   12
318   A61   1sh emer, org, brn & blk   38   25
319   A61   1.80sh pur, yel & blk   75   65

Physician
Treating
Infant
A62

SOMALIA

Designs: 1sh, Physician examining boy, and nurse. 1.80sh, Physician and nurse treating patient.

Photogravure
1968, Mar. 20 Perf. 14 Wmk. 303

320	A62	35c blk, scar, bl & brn	8	8
321	A62	1sh blk, grn & brn	18	18
322	A62	1.80sh blk, org & brn	50	38

Issued to commemorate the 20th anniversary of the World Health Organization.

Woman and Basket with Lemons
A63

Waterbuck
A64

Designs: 10c, Oranges. 25c, Coconuts. 35c, Papayas. 40c, Limes. 50c, Grapefruit. 1sh, Bananas. 1.30sh, Cotton bolls. 1.80sh, Speke's gazelle. 2sh, Lesser kudu. 5sh, Hunter's hartebeest. 10sh, Clark's gazelle (dibatag).

1968 Litho. Perf. 11½

323	A63	5c lt bl & multi	5	5
324	A63	10c yel & multi	5	5
325	A63	25c lt lil & multi	7	5
326	A63	35c sal & multi	7	7
327	A63	40c buff & multi	12	12
328	A63	50c multi	12	12
329	A63	1sh lt bl & multi	25	25
330	A63	1.30sh gray & multi	38	38
331	A64	1.50sh lt bl & multi	30	25
332	A64	1.80sh multi	42	38
333	A64	2sh pink & multi	50	38
334	A64	5sh multi	1.50	1.20
335	A64	10sh multi	4.00	2.00
	Nos. 323-335 (13)		7.83	5.30

Issue dates: Nos. 323-330, Apr. 25; Nos. 331-335, May 10.

Javelin
A65

Woman Grinding Grain, Statuette
A66

Sports: 50c, Running. 80c, High jump. 1.50sh, Basketball.

Photogravure
1968, Oct. 12 Perf. 14 Wmk. 303

336	A65	35c blk, yel & brn	8	8
337	A65	50c blk, rose red & brn	12	12
338	A65	80c blk, brt rose lil & brn	18	12
339	A65	1.50sh blk, brt grn & brn	38	25
a.	Souv. sheet of 4		1.10	.90

Issued to commemorate the 19th Olympic Games, Mexico City, Oct. 12-27. No. 339a contains one each of Nos. 336-339. Black marginal inscription and design. Size: 160x180mm. Sold for 3.65sh.

Perf. 11½x12
1968, Dec. 1 Litho. Unwmkd.

Statuettes: 35c, Woman potter. 2.80sh, Woman mat maker.

340	A66	25c rose lil, blk & brn	8	5
341	A66	35c brick red, blk & brn	8	8
342	A66	2.80sh grn, blk & brn	80	55

Cornflower and Rhinoceros
A67

Flowers: 80c, Sunflower and elephant. 1sh, Oleander and antelopes. 1.80sh, Chrysanthemums and storks.

Perf. 13x12½
1969, Mar. 25 Litho. Unwmkd.

343	A67	40c red & multi	8	8
344	A67	80c vio & multi	18	12
345	A67	1sh lil & multi	25	18
346	A67	1.80sh yel & multi	42	38

ILO Emblem and Blacksmiths
A68

Designs: 1sh, Oxdrawn plow. 1.80sh, Drawing water from well.

Photogravure
1969, May 10 Perf. 14 Wmk. 303

347	A68	25c dk red, dp bis & blk	7	5
348	A68	1sh car rose, brn & blk	25	18
349	A68	1.80sh multi	42	38

Issued to commemorate the 50th anniversary of the International Labor Organization.

Mahatma Gandhi
A69

Designs: 1.50sh, Gandhi, globe and hands releasing dove (horiz.). 1.80sh, Gandhi seated.

Photogravure
1969, Oct. 2 Perf. 13 Unwmkd.

Size: 25x35½mm.

| 350 | A69 | 35c brn vio | 8 | 8 |

Perf. 14½x14

Size: 37½x20mm.

| 351 | A69 | 1.50sh bis brn | 30 | 30 |

Perf. 13

Size: 25x35½mm.

| 352 | A69 | 1.80sh ol gray | 38 | 38 |

Issued to commemorate the centenary of the birth of Mohandas K. Gandhi (1869-1948), leader in India's fight for independence.

A Space Exploration (US) set of 7, plus souvenir sheet, was issued Feb. 14, 1970.

Nivprale Vevanes
A70

Butterflies: 50c, Leschenault. 1.50sh, Papilio (ornytoptera) aeacus. 2sh, Urania riphaeus.

Perf. 12½x13
1970, Mar. 25 Litho. Unwmkd.

353	A70	25c multi	7	7
354	A70	50c multi	12	12
355	A70	1.50sh org & multi	30	30
356	A70	2sh yel & multi	42	42

Somali Democratic Republic

Lenin Addressing Crowd
A71

Designs: 25c, Lenin walking with children. 1.80sh, Lenin in his study (horiz.).

Perf. 12x12½, 12½x12
1970, Apr. 22 Litho. Unwmkd.

357	A71	25c multi	7	5
358	A71	1sh multi	32	22
359	A71	1.80sh multi	35	28

Issued to commemorate the centenary of the birth of Lenin (1870-1924), Russian communist leader.

Bird Feeding Young
A72

Designs: 35c, Monument and Battle of Dagahtur. 1sh, Arms of Somalia and U.N. emblem (vert.). 2.80sh, Boy milking camel, and star (vert.).

Perf. 14x13½, 13½x14
1970, July 28 Photo. Wmk. 303

360	A72	25c bl & multi	9	7
361	A72	35c sl & multi	10	10
362	A72	1sh vio & multi	32	30
363	A72	2.80sh bl & multi	1.00	75

10th anniversary of independence.

"Agriculture"
A73

Designs: 40c, Soldier and flag. 1sh, Hand on open book. 1.80sh, Grain, scales of justice and dove.

Perf. 14x13½
1970, Oct. 21 Photo. Wmk. 303

364	A73	35c grn & multi	10	8
365	A73	40c ultra & blk	12	8
366	A73	1sh red brn & blk	32	18
367	A73	1.80sh multi	65	35

First anniversary of Oct. 21st Revolution.

Snake Strangling Black Man, Map of South Africa—A74

Design: 1.80sh, Concentration camp and symbols of justice holding scales.

Perf. 14x13½
1971, June 20 Photo. Wmk. 303

| 368 | A74 | 1.50sh multi | 45 | 22 |
| 369 | A74 | 1.80sh gray, red & blk | 70 | 50 |

Against racial discrimination in South Africa.

Waves
A75

Design: 2.80sh, Waves and globe.

1971, June 30

| 370 | A75 | 25c blk & bl | 8 | 7 |
| 371 | A75 | 2.80sh blk, grn & bl | 95 | 70 |

3rd World Telecommunications Day, May 17.

Map of Africa and Telecommunications System
A76

Design: 1.50sh, Map of Africa and telecommunications system (different design).

1971, July 25

| 372 | A76 | 1sh blk, lt bl & grn | 32 | 22 |
| 373 | A76 | 1.50sh blk & yel | 50 | 40 |

Pan-African Telecommunications system.

White Rhinoceros
A77

Wild Animals: 1sh, Cheetahs. 1.30sh, Zebras. 1.80sh, Lion attacking camel.

1971, Aug. 25

374	A77	40c ocher & multi	18	8
375	A77	1sh vio & multi	35	22
376	A77	1.30sh vio & multi	65	30
377	A77	1.80sh multi	80	40

Headquarters, Mogadishu, Flag, Map of Africa
A78

Design: 1.30sh, Desert Fort.

SOMALIA

1971, Oct. 18
| 378 | A78 | 1.30sh blk & red org | 35 | 35 |
| 379 | A78 | 1.50sh blk, bl & yel | 45 | 40 |

East and Central African Summit Conference.

Revolution Monument A79

Designs: 1sh, Field workers. 1.35sh, Building workers.

1971, Oct. 21
380	A79	10c blk & bl	5	5
381	A79	1sh blk, yel brn & grn	28	28
382	A79	1.35sh blk, dp brn & yel	55	32

2nd anniversary of 1969 revolution.

Vaccination of Cow A80

Design: 1.80sh, Veterinarian vaccinating cow.

Perf. 14x13½
1971, Nov. 28 Photo. Wmk. 303
| 383 | A80 | 40c blk, red & bl | 60 | 8 |
| 384 | A80 | 1.80sh lt grn & multi | 70 | 55 |

Rinderpest campaign.

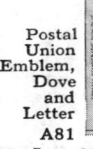 

Postal Union Emblem, Dove and Letter A81

1972, Jan. 25 Unwmkd.
| 385 | A81 | 1.50sh multi | 80 | 70 |

10th anniversary of African Postal Union. See No. C108.

Children and UNICEF Emblem A82

1972, Mar. 30 *Perf. 13x14, 13x13*
| 386 | A82 | 50c blk, bis brn & dk brn | 18 | 18 |
| 387 | A82 | 2.80sh lt bl & multi | 1.10 | 80 |

25th anniversary (in 1971) of the United Nations International Children's Fund (UNICEF).

Camel A83

Designs: 10c, Cattle and cargo ship. 20c, Bull. 40c, Sheep. 1.70sh, Goat.

1972, Apr. 10 *Perf. 14x13*
388	A83	5c grn & multi	6	5
389	A83	10c multi	10	6
390	A83	20c multi	12	10
391	A83	40c org red & blk	22	12
392	A83	1.70sh dl grn & blk	1.25	70
		Nos. 388-392 (5)	1.75	1.03

Hands Holding Infant A84

Designs: 1sh, Youth Corps emblem, marchers with flags. 1.50sh, Woman, man, tent and tractor.

1972, Oct. 21 Photo. *Perf. 14x13½*
393	A84	70c yel & multi	28	18
394	A84	1sh red & multi	35	28
395	A84	1.50sh lt bl & multi	55	45

3rd anniversary of October 21 Revolution.

Folk Dance A85

Folk Dances: 40c, Man and woman (vert.). 1sh, Group dance (vert.). 2sh, Two men and a woman.

1973 Photo. *Perf. 14x13½, 13½x14*
396	A85	5c dl bl & multi	5	5
397	A85	40c brn & multi	12	8
398	A85	1sh yel & multi	35	25
399	A85	2sh brick red & multi	70	45

Hand Writing Somali Script A86

Designs: 40c, Flame and "FAR SOMALI" inscription (vert.). 1sh, Woman and sunburst with Somali script.

Perf. 13½x14, 14x13½
1973, Oct. 21 Photogravure
400	A86	40c red & multi	12	8
401	A86	1sh blk & multi	32	22
402	A86	2sh yel & multi	70	45

Publicity for use of Somali script.

Map of Africa and Emblem A87

Map of Africa with Target on Somalia A88

1974, June 12 *Perf. 13½x14*
| 403 | A87 | 40c multi | 18 | 6 |
| 404 | A88 | 2sh multi | 80 | 45 |

Organization of African Unity (OAU) Meeting, Mogadishu.

Hurdler A89

Designs: 1sh, Runners. 1.40sh, Netball (vert.).

1974, Aug. 1 *Perf. 14x13, 13x14*
405	A89	50c blk & org	18	12
406	A89	1sh blk & grn	35	28
407	A89	1.40sh blk & ol	55	35

Victory Pioneers A90 Pioneers Helping Woman A91

1974, Aug. 25 Photo. *Perf. 13x14*
| 408 | A90 | 40c multi | 12 | 8 |
| 409 | A91 | 2sh multi | 60 | 45 |

Victory Pioneers, founded Aug. 24, 1972, to defend Socialist Revolution.

Map of Arab Countries A92

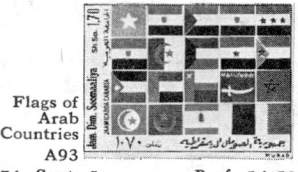

Flags of Arab Countries A93

1974, Sept. 1 *Perf. 14x13*
| 410 | A92 | 1.50sh multi | 55 | 32 |
| 411 | A93 | 1.70sh multi | 65 | 35 |

Somalia's admission to the Arab League, Feb. 14, 1974.

Tank Tracks in Desert A94

Somalis Reading Books A95

Perf. 14x13½, 13½x14
1974, Oct. 21 Lithographed
| 412 | A94 | 40c multi | 18 | 12 |
| 413 | A95 | 2sh multi | 80 | 45 |

5th anniversary of the Oct. 21st Revolution.

Carrier Pigeons A96

Design: 3sh, Postrider.

1975, Feb. 15 Litho. *Perf. 14x13½*
| 414 | A96 | 50c bl & multi | 35 | 18 |
| 415 | A96 | 3sh multi | 2.00 | 70 |

Centenary (in 1974) of Universal Postal Union.

Africa A97

Design: 1.50sh, Carrier pigeons.

1975, Apr. 10
| 416 | A97 | 1sh multi | 45 | 22 |
| 417 | A97 | 1.50sh multi | 75 | 35 |

African Postal Union.

Somali Warrior A98

Designs: Traditional costumes of Somali men (1sh, 10sh) and women (40c, 50c, 5sh).

1975, Oct. 27 Photo. *Perf. 13½*
418	A98	10c yel & multi	5	5
419	A98	40c lt bl & multi	12	6
420	A98	50c multi	18	8
421	A98	1sh grn & multi	35	20
422	A98	5sh cl & multi	2.00	1.00
423	A98	10sh rose & multi	4.00	2.75
		Nos. 418-423 (6)	6.70	4.14

Monument A99

IWY Emblem A100

1975, Dec. 10 Litho. *Perf. 13½x14*
| 424 | A99 | 50c blk & red org | 18 | 12 |
| 425 | A100 | 2.30sh blk, pink & mag | 75 | 60 |

International Women's Year 1975.

SOMALIA

Abdulla Hassan Monument — A101

Abdulla Hassan with Warriors — A102

Designs: 1.50sh, Abdulla Hassan speaking to his men. 2.30sh, Attacking horsemen (horiz.).

Perf. 14x13½, 13½x14

1976, Nov. 30   Photogravure

426	A101	50c multi	16	10
427	A102	60c multi	18	12
428	A102	1.50sh multi	45	35
429	A102	2.30sh multi	75	55

Sayid Mohammed Abdulla Hassan (1864–1920), poet and military leader.

Cypraea Gracilis — A103

Sea Shells: 75c, Charonia bardayi. 1sh, Chlamys townsendi. 2sh, Cymatium ranzanii. 2.75sh, Conus argillaceus. 2.90sh, Strombus oldi.

1976, Dec. 15   **Photo.**   **Perf. 14x13½**

430	A103	50c bl & multi	18	12
431	A103	75c bl & multi	22	15
432	A103	1sh bl & multi	32	22
433	A103	2sh bl & multi	70	50
434	A103	2.75sh bl & multi	1.00	70
435	A103	2.90sh bl & multi	1.15	70
a.	Souvenir sheet of 6		4.50	4.50
	Nos. 430-435 (6)		3.57	2.39

No. 435a contains one each of Nos. 430-435; pink margin with black inscription and blue coat of arms. Size: 148x218mm. Sold for 11sh.

Benin Head and Hunters — A104

Designs (Benin Head and): 75c, Handicrafts. 2sh, Dancers. 2.90sh, Musicians.

1977, Aug. 30   **Photo.**   **Perf. 14x13½**

436	A104	50c multi	18	12
437	A104	75c multi	22	15
438	A104	2sh multi	70	50
439	A104	2.90sh multi	90	65

2nd World Black and African Festival, FESTAC '77, Lagos, Nigeria, Jan. 15-Feb. 12.

Arms of Somalia — A105

Designs: 75c, Somali flags (vert.). 1.50sh, Pres. Mohammed Siad Barre and globe. 2sh, Arms over rising sun and flags (vert.).

Perf. 13½x14, 14x13½

1977, Sept. 30   Photogravure

440	A105	75c multi	28	18
441	A105	1sh multi	32	22
442	A105	1.50sh multi	40	32
443	A105	2sh multi	70	55

Somali Socialist Revolutionary Party, established July 1, 1976.

Licaon Pictus — A106

Protected Animals: 75c, Bush baby. 1sh, Somali ass. 1.50sh, Aardwolf. 2sh, Greater kudu. 3sh, Giraffe.

1977, Nov. 25   **Photo.**   **Perf. 14x13½**

444	A106	50c multi	18	12
445	A106	75c multi	22	18
446	A106	1sh multi	35	28
447	A106	1.50sh multi	55	40
448	A106	2sh multi	75	55
449	A106	3sh multi	1.10	90
a.	Souvenir sheet of 6		4.00	4.00
	Nos. 444-449 (6)		3.15	2.43

No. 449a contains one each of Nos. 444-449; green and multicolored margin shows leopard. Size: 178x118mm.

Leonardo da Vinci's Flying Machine — A107

Designs (ICAO Emblem and): 1.50sh, Montgolfier's balloon. 2sh, Wright brothers' plane. 2.90sh, Somali Airlines' turbojet.

1977, Dec. 23   **Photo.**   **Perf. 14x13½**

450	A107	1sh multi	35	28
451	A107	1.50sh multi	55	35
452	A107	2sh multi	70	60
453	A107	2.90sh multi	1.10	70
a.	Souvenir sheet of 4		3.50	3.50

International Civil Aviation Organization (ICAO), 30th anniversary. No. 453a contains one each of Nos. 450-453; blue, black and bright lilac margin showing Mogadiscio Airport. Size: 170x100mm. Sold for 10sh.

Dome of the Rock — A108

Lithographed and Engraved

1978, Apr. 30   **Perf. 13x14**

454	A108	75c multi	28	18
455	A108	2sh multi	70	55

Palestinian fighters and their families.

Stadium and Soccer Player — A109

Designs: 4.90sh, Stadium and goalkeeper. 5.50sh, Stadium and player.

1978, Aug. 5   **Litho.**   **Perf. 14x13½**

456	A109	1.50sh multi	55	35
457	A109	4.90sh multi	1.75	1.40
458	A109	5.50sh multi	2.00	1.75
a.	Souvenir sheet of 3		5.75	5.75

11th World Cup Soccer Championship, Argentina, June 1-25. No. 458a contains Nos. 456-458; silver and multicolored margin. Size: 155x105mm. Sold for 14sh.

Acacia Tortilis — A110

Trees: 50c, Ficus sycomorus (vert.). 75c, Terminalia catapa (vert.). 2.90sh, Baobab.

1978, Sept. 5   **Photo.**   **Perf. 14**

459	A110	40c multi	18	12
460	A110	50c multi	22	18
461	A110	75c multi	32	22
462	A110	2.90sh multi	70	55

Forest conservation.

Hibiscus — A111

Flowers of Somalia: 1sh, Cassia baccarinii. 1.50sh, Kigelia somalensis. 2.30sh, Dichrostachys glomerata.

1978, Dec. 15   **Photo.**   **Perf. 13½x14**

463	A111	50c multi	18	12
464	A111	1sh multi	35	28
465	A111	1.50sh multi	45	40
466	A111	2.30sh multi	80	55
a.	Souvenir sheet of 4		3.00	3.00

No. 466a contains Nos. 463-466, perf. 14; multicolored margin shows water lilies. Size: 124x99mm.

Huri and Siganus Rivulatus — A112

Fishery Development: 80c, Sail fry, gaterin gaterinus. 2.30sh, Fishing boats, hypacanthus amia. 2.50sh, Motorized fishing boat, mackerel.

1979, Sept. 1   **Photo.**   **Perf. 14x13½**

467	A112	75c multi	18	18
468	A112	80c multi	22	22
469	A112	2.30sh multi	65	65
470	A112	2.50sh multi	70	70

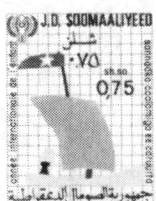

Sailing, IYC Emblem — A113

IYC Emblem, Children's Drawings: 50c, Schoolboy. 1.50sh, Houses. 3sh, Bird and flower.

1979, Sept. 10   **Photo.**   **Perf. 13½x14**

471	A113	50c multi	10	10
472	A113	75c multi	22	22
473	A113	1.50sh multi	40	40
474	A113	3sh multi	80	80
a.	Souvenir sheet of 4		2.75	2.75

No. 474a contains Nos. 471-474. Multicolored margin shows sheep; gold embossed inscription. Size: 137½x92mm.

International Year of the Child.

University Students, Outdoor Classrooms — A114

Flower and: 50c, Housing construction. 75c, Children's recreation. 1sh, Doctor examining child, woman and man carrying grain and fish. 2.40sh, Woman and children carrying produce over bridge. 3sh, Dish antenna.

1979, Nov. 30   **Litho.**   **Perf. 14x13½**

475	A114	20c multi	6	5
476	A114	50c multi	18	12
477	A114	75c multi	22	12
478	A114	1sh multi	28	18
479	A114	2.40sh multi	70	40
480	A114	3sh multi	80	50
	Nos. 475-480 (6)		2.24	1.37

Oct. 21 revolution, 10th anniversary.

Barbopsis Devecchii — A115

Freshwater Fish: 90c, Phreatichthys andruzzii. 1sh, Uegitglanis zammaranoi. 2.50sh, Pardi's catfish.

1979, Dec. 12

481	A115	50c multi	22	12
482	A115	90c multi	28	18
483	A115	1sh multi	32	18
484	A115	2.50sh multi	80	50
a.	Souvenir sheet of 4		3.25	3.25

No. 484a contains Nos. 481-484; multicolored decorative margin. Size: 139½x92½mm. Sold for 10sh.

Taleh Fortress, Congress Emblem — A116

1980, June 1   **Photo.**   **Perf. 14x13½**

485	A116	2.25sh multi	72	55
486	A116	3.50sh multi	1.15	85

1st International Congress of Somalian Studies, Mogadishu, July 6-13.

Scott's International Album provides spaces for an extensive representative collection of the world's postage stamps.

SOMALIA

View of Marka—A117

		1980, July 1	Litho.	Perf. 14	
487	A117	75c shown		24	18
488	A117	1sh Gandersee		32	24
489	A117	2.30sh Afgooye		75	55
490	A117	3.50sh Muqdisho		1.15	85

Nos. 487-490 each se-tenant with label showing regional map. See Nos. 502-505.

Batis Perkeo—A118

		1980, July 30	Photo.	Perf. 13½x14	
491	A118	1sh shown		32	24
492	A118	2.25sh Rynchostruthus socotranus louisae		72	55
493	A118	5sh Laniarius ruficeps		1.60	1.20
a.		Souvenir sheet of 3		2.75	2.00

No. 493a contains Nos. 491-493; multicolored margin shows bird. Size: 141x96mm.

World Food Day A119   13th World Telecommunications Day A120

		1981, Oct. 16	Litho.	Perf. 13½x14, 14x13½	
494	A119	75c Globe, grain		24	18
495	A119	3.25sh Emblem, horiz.		1.05	80
496	A119	5.50sh like #494		1.80	1.35

		1981, Oct. 10		Perf. 13½x14	
497	A120	1sh Shepherdess, sheep, dish antenna		32	24
498	A120	3sh Emblems		1.00	75
499	A120	4.60sh like #498		1.10	80

Hegira, 1500th Anniv.—A121

		1981, Oct.	Photo.	Perf. 13½x14	
500	A121	1.50sh multi		48	36
501	A121	3.80sh multi		1.30	1.00

View Type of 1980

		1982, May 31	Litho.	Perf. 13½x14	
502	A117	2.25sh Balcad		72	55
503	A117	4sh Jowhar		1.35	1.00
504	A117	5.50sh Golaleey		1.80	1.35
505	A117	8.30sh Muqdisho		2.75	2.00

Nos. 502-505 each se-tenant with label showing regional map.

1982 World Cup—A122

Designs: Various soccer players.

		1982, June 13			
506	A122	1sh multi		32	24
507	A122	1.50sh multi		50	36
508	A122	3.25sh multi		1.05	80
a.		Souvenir sheet of 3		1.50	

No. 508a contains Nos. 506-508; multicolored margin shows player, map of Spain. Size: 137x94mm.

ITU Plenipotentiaries Conference, Nairobi, Sept.—A123

		1982, Oct. 15	Photo.	Perf. 14x13½	
509	A123	75c grn & multi		25	18
510	A123	3.25sh org & multi		1.05	80
511	A123	5.50sh bl & multi		1.80	1.35

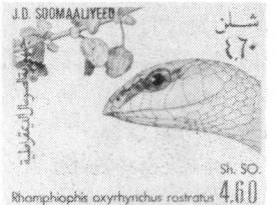
Local Snakes—A124

		1982, Dec. 20	Photo.	Perf. 14	
512	A124	2.80sh Bitis arietans		90	65
513	A124	3.20sh Psammophis punctulatus		1.00	75
514	A124	4.60sh Rhamphiophis oxyrhynchus		1.50	1.00

Souvenir Sheet

515	A124	8.60sh Sphalerosophis josephscorteccii		3.00	2.25

Nos. 515 has multicolored margin continuing design. Size: 125x105mm.

Somali Woman—A125

		1982, Dec. 30		Perf. 14x13½	
516	A125	1sh yel & multi		32	24
517	A125	5.20sh lil & multi		1.70	1.25
518	A125	5.80sh org & multi		1.85	1.40
519	A125	6.40sh bl & multi		2.05	1.55
520	A125	9.40sh lt brn & multi		3.00	2.25
521	A125	25sh grn & multi		8.00	6.00
		Nos. 516-521 (6)		16.92	12.69

World Communications Year—A126

		1983, July 20		Perf.	
522	A126	5.20sh multi		1.70	1.25
523	A126	6.40sh multi		2.05	1.55

2nd Intl. Congress of Somali Studies, Hamburg—A127

Various views of Hamburg.

		1983, Aug. 1		Perf.	
524	A127	5.20sh multi		1.70	1.25
525	A127	6.40sh multi		2.05	1.55

SOMALIA

SEMI-POSTAL STAMPS.
Italy Nos. B1-B4
Overprinted **SOMALIA**
1916 Wmkd. Crown. (140) *Perf. 14.*

B1	SP1	10c +5c rose	1.75	2.75
B2	SP2	15c +5c sl	3.50	10.00
B3	SP2	20c +5c org	1.75	4.50
B4	SP2	20c on 15c +5c sl	3.50	10.00

Holy Year Issue.
Italy Nos. B20-B25
Surcharged in Black or Red
SOMALIA ITALIANA

Besa = 13

Besa = 6

1925, June 1 *Perf. 12*

B5	SP4	6b +3b on 20c+10c dk grn & brn	90	3.50
B6	SP4	13b +6b on 30c+15c dk brn & brn	90	3.50
B7	SP4	15b +8b on 50c+25c vio & brn	90	3.50
B8	SP4	18b +9b on 60c+30c dp rose & brn	90	3.50
B9	SP8	30b +15b on 1l+50c (R)	90	3.50
B10	SP8	1r +50b on 5l+2.50l (R)	90	3.50
		Nos. B5-B10 (6)	5.40	21.00

Colonial Institute Issue.

"Peace" Substituting Spade for Sword — SP10

1926, June 1 Typo. *Perf. 14*

B11	SP10	5c +5c brn	20	1.50
B12	SP10	10c +5c ol grn	20	1.50
B13	SP10	20c +5c bl grn	20	1.50
B14	SP10	40c +5c brn red	20	1.50
B15	SP10	60c +5c org	20	1.50
B16	SP10	1l +5c bl	20	1.50
		Nos. B11-B16 (6)	1.20	9.00

The surtax of 5c on each stamp was for the Italian Colonial Institute.

Types of Italian Semi-Postal Stamps of 1926
Overprinted **SOMALIA ITALIANA**
Perf. 11½

1927, Apr. 21 Unwmkd.

B17	SP10	40c +20c dk brn & blk	90	3.50
B18	SP10	60c +30c brn red & ol brn	90	3.50
B19	SP10	1.25l +60c dp bl & blk	90	3.50
B20	SP10	5l +2.50l dk grn & blk	1.40	7.25

The surtax was for the charitable work of the Voluntary Militia for Italian National Defense.

Allegory of Fascism and Victory — SP11

1928, Oct. 15 *Perf. 14* Wmk. 140

B21	SP11	20c +5c bl grn	55	2.10
B22	SP11	30c +5c red	55	2.10
B23	SP11	50c +10c pur	55	2.10
B24	SP11	1.25l +20c dk bl	55	2.10

Issued to commemorate the 46th anniversary of the Societa Africana d'Italia. The surtax aided that society.

Types of Italian Semi-Postal Stamps of 1928
Overprinted **SOMALIA ITALIANA**

1929, Mar. 4 *Perf. 11* Unwmkd.

B25	SP10	30c +10c red & blk	90	3.50
B26	SP10	50c +20c vio & blk	90	3.50
B27	SP10	1.25l +50c brn & bl	1.40	5.25
B28	SP10	5l +2l ol grn & bl	1.40	5.25

The surtax was for the charitable work of the Voluntary Militia for Italian National Defense.

Types of Italian Semi-Postal Stamps of 1926
Overprinted in Black or Red
SOMALIA ITALIANA

1930, Oct. 20 *Perf. 14*

B29	SP10	30c +10c dk grn & bl grn (Bk)	2.25	9.00
B30	SP10	50c +10c dk grn & vio (R)	2.25	9.00
B31	SP10	1.25l +30c ol brn & red brn (R)	2.75	13.00
B32	SP10	5l +1.50l ind & grn (R)	9.00	35.00

The surtax was for the charitable work of the Voluntary Militia for Italian National Defense.

Irrigation Canal — SP14

1930, Nov. 27 Photo. Wmk. 140

B33	SP14	50c +20c ol brn	90	3.50
B34	SP14	1.25l +20c dp bl	90	3.50
B35	SP14	1.75l +20c grn	90	3.50
B36	SP14	2.55l +50c pur	1.40	5.75
B37	SP14	5l +1l dp car	1.40	5.75
		Nos. B33-B37 (5)	5.50	22.00

Issued in commemoration of the 25th anniversary of the Italian Colonial Agricultural Institute. The surtax was for the aid of that institution.

SP15

King Victor Emmanuel III — SP16

1935, Jan. 1

B38	SP15	5c +5c blk brn	65	2.50
B39	SP15	7½c +7½c vio	65	2.50
B40	SP15	15c +10c ol blk	65	2.50
B41	SP15	20c +10c rose red	65	2.50
B42	SP15	25c +10c dp grn	65	2.50
B43	SP15	30c +10c brn	65	2.50
B44	SP15	50c +10c pur	65	2.50
B45	SP15	75c +15c rose car	65	2.50
B46	SP15	1.25l +15c dp bl	65	2.50
B47	SP15	1.75l +25c red org	65	2.50
B48	SP15	2.75l +25c gray	8.50	32.50
B49	SP15	5l +1l dp cl	8.50	32.50
B50	SP15	10l + 1.80 l red brn	8.50	35.00
B51	SP16	25l + 2.75 l brn & red	35.00	65.00
		Nos. B38-B51 (14)	67.00	190.00

Visit of King Victor Emmanuel III.

Somalia

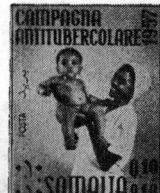

Nurse Holding Infant — SP17

1957, Nov. 30 *Perf. 14* Wmk. 303

B52	SP17	10c +10c red & brn	20	28
B53	SP17	25c +10c grn & brn	20	28

The surtax was for the fight against tuberculosis. See Nos. CB11-CB12.

Refugees — SP18

1964, Dec. 12 Photo. *Perf. 14*

B54	SP18	25c +10c vio bl & red	38	12

The surtax was to help refugees. See Nos. CB13-CB14.

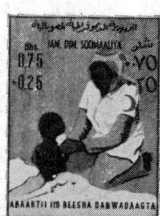

Red Cross Nurse Feeding Child — SP19

Designs: 80c+20c, Nomad in parched land (horiz.). 2.40sh+10c, Family with fish and produce. 2.90sh+10c, Physician and Aid Society emblem (horiz.).

1976, Dec. 10 *Perf. 13x14, 14x13*

B55	SP19	75c +25c multi	40	40
B56	SP19	80c +20c multi	40	40
B57	SP19	2.40sh +10c multi	80	80
B58	SP19	2.90sh +10c multi	1.10	1.10

Famine relief.

Refugees — SP20

1981, Dec. 15 Photo. *Perf. 13½x14*

B59	SP20	2sh +50c multi	80	60
B60	SP20	6.80sh +50c multi	2.35	95
a.		Souvenir sheet of 2	3.25	1.75

No. B60a contains Nos. B59-B60; multicolored margin shows map. Size: 91x137mm.

TB Bacillus Centenary — SP31

1982, Dec. 30 Photo. *Perf. 14*

B61	SP31	4.60sh +60c multi	1.70	1.25
B62	SP31	5.80sh +60c multi	2.05	1.55

SOMALIA

AIR POST STAMPS.

View of Coast—AP1

Cheetahs—AP2

		Photogravure		
1934, Oct.		Perf. 14	Wmk. 140	
C1	AP1	25c sl bl & red org	1.50	4.00
C2	AP1	50c dk grn & blk	1.50	4.00
C3	AP1	75c brn & red org	1.50	4.00
	a.	Imperf.		
C4	AP2	80c org brn & blk	1.50	4.00
C5	AP2	1 l scar & blk	1.50	4.00
C6	AP2	2 l dk bl & brn	1.50	4.00
		Nos. C1-C6 (6)	9.00	24.00

2nd Colonial Arts Exhibition, Naples.

Banana Tree and Airplane—AP3

Designs: 25c, 1.50 l, Banana tree and plane. 50c, 2 l, Plane over cotton field. 60c, 5 l, Plane over orchard. 75c, 10 l, Plane over field workers. 1 l, 3 l, Small girl watching plane.

1936			Photogravure	
C7	AP3	25c sl grn	65	1.25
C8	AP3	50c brown	22	22
C9	AP3	60c red org	1.10	4.00
C10	AP3	75c org brn	45	45
C11	AP3	1 l dp bl	8	5
C12	AP3	1.50 l purple	55	28
C13	AP3	2 l sl bl	1.40	65
C14	AP3	3 l cop red	4.00	1.50
C15	AP3	5 l yel grn	4.50	2.50
C16	AP3	10 l dp rose red	5.00	9.00
		Nos. C7-C16 (10)	17.95	19.90

Somalia

AP8

1950-51			Wmk. 277	
C17	AP8	30c yel brn	15	22
C18	AP8	45c dk car	15	15
C19	AP8	65c dk bl vio	15	28
C20	AP8	70c dl bl	20	28
C21	AP8	90c ol brn	15	28
C22	AP8	1s lil rose	22	22
C23	AP8	1.35s violet	35	65
C24	AP8	1.50s bl grn	35	55
C25	AP8	3s blue	3.25	1.75
C26	AP8	5s chocolate	4.50	3.25
C27	AP8	10s red org ('51)	6.25	1.75
		Nos. C17-C27 (11)	15.67	9.45

Scene in Mogadishu
AP8a

1951, Oct. 4				
C27A	AP8a	1s vio & Prus bl	2.75	1.80
C27B	AP8a	1.50s ol grn & chnt brn	5.50	5.50

First Territorial Council meeting.

Plane, Palm Tree and Minaret Mother and Child
AP9   AP10

1952, Sept. 14				
C28	AP9	1.20s ol bis & dp bl	2.25	3.25

1st Somali Fair, Mogadishu, Sept. 14-28.

1953, May 27				
C29	AP10	1.20s dk grn & dk brn	1.00	1.40

Somali anti-tuberculosis campaign.

Fair Entrance—AP11
Perf. 11½

1953, Sept. 28			Unwmkd.	
C30	AP11	1.20s brn car & pink	50	65
C31	AP11	1.50s yel brn & buff	50	65

Issued to publicize the second Somali Fair, Mogadishu, Sept. 28–Oct. 12, 1953.

Plane over Map and Stamps of 1903
AP12
Perf. 13x13½

1953, Dec. 16	Engr.		Wmk. 277	
Early Stamps in Brown and Rose Carmine				
C32	AP12	60c org brn	50	65
C33	AP12	1s grnsh blk	50	65

Issued to commemorate the 50th anniversary of the first Somali postage stamps.

"UPU" among Constellations
AP13
Perf. 11½

1953, Dec. 16	Photo.		Unwmkd.	
C34	AP13	1.20s red & cr	40	55
C35	AP13	1.50s brn & cr	60	80
C36	AP13	2s grn & lt bl	70	90

Issued to commemorate the 75th anniversary (in 1949) of the formation of the Universal Postal Union.

Alexander Island Somali
Juba River   Flag
AP14   AP15

1954, June 1			Perf. 13½x12½	
C37	AP14	1.20s dk grn & brn	50	65
C38	AP14	2s dk car & pur	80	1.10

See note after No. 196.

Perf. 13½x13

1954, Oct. 12	Litho.		Wmk. 277	
C39	AP15	1.20s multi	35	45

Adoption of Somali flag.

Haggard's Oribi
AP16

Designs: 45c, Phillip's dik-dik. 50c, Speke's gazelle. 75c, Gerenuk. 1.20s, Soemmering's gazelle. 1.50s, Waterbuck.

Photogravure.

1955, Apr. 12 Perf. 13½ Wmk. 277
Antelopes in Natural Colors
Size: 22x33mm.

C40	AP16	35c gray grn & blk	35	35
C41	AP16	45c lil & blk	80	65
C42	AP16	50c rose lil & blk	35	35
C43	AP16	75c red	50	45
C44	AP16	1.20s dk gray grn	50	45
C45	AP16	1.50s brt bl	80	90
		Nos. C40-C45 (6)	3.30	3.15

See Nos. C57-C58.

Caravan at Water Hole
AP17

Design: 1.20s, Village well.

1955, Sept. 24		Perf. 13½x14	Wmk. 303	
C46	AP17	45c brn & org	35	45
C47	AP17	1.20s saph & pink	50	65

Issued to publicize the third Somali Fair, Mogadishu, September, 1955.

Ballot Type of Regular Issue.

1956, Apr. 30	Photo.		Perf. 14	
C48	A24	60c brn & ultra	20	28
C49	A24	1.20s brn & org	20	32

Issued in honor of the opening of the territory's first democratically elected Legislative Assembly.

Arms Type of Regular Issue.

1957, May 6   Perf. 13½   Wmk. 303
Coat of Arms in Dull Yellow
Blue and Black.

C50	A25	45c blue	22	32
C51	A25	1.20s bluish grn	28	35

Issued in honor of the new coat of arms.

Type of Regular Issue, 1957 and

Oil Well—AP18

Design: 60c, Irrigation canal construction.

1957, Sept. 28			Perf. 14	
C52	A26	60c bl & brn	35	45
C53	AP18	1.20s blk & ver	35	45

Fourth Somali Fair and Film Festival.

Sport Type of Regular Issue

Designs: 60c, Runner. 1.20s, Bicyclist. 1.50s, Basketball player.

1958, Apr. 28	Perf. 14		Wmk. 303	
C54	A27	60c brown	20	28
C55	A27	1.20s blue	22	32
C56	A27	1.50s rose car	22	32

Animal Type of 1955

Designs: 3s, Lesser kudu. 5s, Hunter's hartebeest.

1958-59		Photogravure		
		Size: 20½x36½mm.		
C57	AP16	3s ocher & sep	1.00	1.40
C58	AP16	5s gray, blk & yel ('59)	1.00	1.40

See No. CE1.

Police Bugler
AP19

1959, June 19			Photogravure.	
C59	AP19	1.20s ocher & ultra	35	45
C60	AP19	1.50s ol grn & ultra	35	45
	a.	Souvenir sheet of 4	2.00	2.75

Issued to commemorate the opening of the Constituent Assembly of Somalia. No. C60a measures 149x195mm, and contains one each of Nos. 228–229 and C59–C60 with brown marginal inscription.

SOMALIA

Marabou
AP20

Design: 2s, Great egret.

1959, Sept. 4   Wmk. 303
C61	AP20	1.20s vio, blk & red	30	40
C62	AP20	2s bl, gray & red	38	50

Incense Shipment,
15th Century B.C.
AP21

Design: 2s, Incense burner and view of Mogadishu harbor.

1959, Sept. 28   Perf. 14
C63	AP21	1.20s red & blk	35	45
C64	AP21	2s bl, blk & org	50	65

5th Somali Fair, Mogadishu.

University Institute and Arms
AP22

Design: 1.20s, Front view of Institute.

1960, Jan. 14
C65	AP22	45c grn, blk & org brn	35	35
C66	AP22	1.20s bl, ultra & blk	55	55

Issued to commemorate the opening of the University Institute of Somalia.

Stork and Uprooted Oak Emblem
AP23

1960, Apr. 7   Perf. 14   Wmk. 303
C67	AP23	1.50s lt grn, bl & red	40	40

Issued to publicize World Refugee Year, July 1, 1959–June 30, 1960.

Republic

Nos. C42 and C44 Overprinted
Like No. 242
Photogravure

1960, June 26   Perf. 13½   Wmk. 277
Antelopes in Natural Colors
C68	AP16	50c rose lil & blk	9.00	8.50
C69	AP16	1.20s dk gray grn	16.00	8.50

See note after No. 242.

Parliament and Italian Flag
AP25

Design: 1.80s, Somali flag and assembly building.

1960, July 1   Perf. 14   Wmk. 303
C70	AP25	1s org red, grn & red	42	25
C71	AP25	1.80s red org, ultra & blk	90	50

Somalia's independence.

Animal Type of Regular Issue
Design: 3s, Leopard.

1960, Nov. 24
C72	A37	3s multi	90	75

Type of Regular Issue
(Olympic Games)

Designs: 45c, Runner, flag and Olympic rings. 1.80s, Long distance runner, flag & Olympic rings.

1960, Nov. 24
C73	A38	45c lil & bl	25	25
C74	A38	1.80s org ver & bl	50	50

Issued to commemorate the 17th Olympic Games, Rome, Aug. 25–Sept. 11.

Amauris Fenestrata and Jet Plane
AP26

Various Butterflies.

1961, Sept. 9
C75	AP26	60c bl, brn & yel	18	18
C76	AP26	90c yel, blk & grn	25	18
C77	AP26	1s multi	2.50	18
C78	AP26	1.80s org, blk & red	60	38
C79	AP26	3s multi	80	60
C80	AP26	5s ver, blk & brt bl	1.80	1.10
C81	AP26	10s multi	3.75	1.85
		Nos. C75–C81 (7)	9.88	4.47

Wooden Headrest, Comb and Cap
AP27

Design: 1.80s, Camel, metal sculpture.

1961, Sept. 28   Perf. 14   Wmk. 303
C82	AP27	1s blk, ultra & ocher	38	25
C83	AP27	1.80s blk, yel & brn	60	42

6th Somali Fair, Mogadishu.

Fish Type of Regular Issue
Fish: 2.70sh, Lutianus sebae.

1962, Apr. 26
C84	A41	2.70s ultra, brn & rose brn	1.40	60

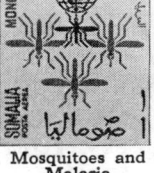 

Mosquitoes and Malaria Eradication Emblem
AP28

Police Auxiliary Women
AP29

Photogravure

1962, Oct. 25   Perf. 14   Wmk. 303
C85	AP28	1sh bis brn & blk	42	25
C86	AP28	1.80sh lt grn & blk	90	42

Issued for the World Health Organization drive to eradicate malaria.

1963, May 15   Perf. 14   Wmk. 303
Design: 1.80sh, Army auxiliary women with flag.
C87	AP29	1sh dk bl, yel & org	50	18
C88	AP29	1.80sh multi	90	30

Women's auxiliary forces.

Freedom from Hunger Issue
Type of Regular Issue
Design: 1sh, Sower and wheat.

1963, June 25
C89	A44	1sh dk brn, yel & bl	65	30

Issued for the "Freedom from Hunger" campaign of the U.N. Food and Agriculture Organization.

Type of Regular Issue, 1963
(President Osman)

1963, Sept. 15   Perf. 14   Wmk. 303
C90	A45	1sh multi	55	30
C91	A45	1.80sh multi	80	42

Third anniversary of Independence.

Type of Regular Issue, 1963.
(Somali Fair)
Design: 1.80sh, Government Pavilion.

1963, Sept. 28   Photogravure
C92	A46	1.80sh blue	1.25	60

7th Somali Fair, Mogadishu.

Map of Somalia, Animals and Globe
AP30

Design: 1.80sh, Somali Credit Bank emblem.

1964, May 16   Perf. 14   Wmk. 303
C93	AP30	1sh multi	50	25
C94	AP30	1.80sh blk, bl & yel	1.10	50

10th anniversary of Somali Credit Bank.

Olympic Type of Regular Issue, 1964
Designs: 90c, Diving. 1.80sh, Soccer.

1964, Oct. 10   Photogravure
C95	A48	90c org brn & bl	55	30
C96	A48	1.80sh org brn & bl	80	50

18th Olympic Games, Tokyo, Oct. 10–25.

Elephants and DC-3
AP31

Design: 1.80sh, Plane over Mogadishu.

1964, Nov. 8   Photo.   Perf. 14
C97	AP31	1sh brn & grn	90	38
C98	AP31	1.80sh blk & bl	1.85	60

Establishment of Somali Air Lines.

ITU Type of Regular Issue

1965, May 17   Perf. 14   Wmk. 303
C99	A50	1sh dp grn & blk	60	18
C100	A50	1.80sh rose lil & brn	1.20	60

Issued to commemorate the centenary of the International Telecommunication Union.

Type of Regular Issue, 1965
(Somali Fair)

Designs: 1.50sh, Sugar industry; harvesting sugar cane and refinery. 2sh, Dairy industry; bottling plant and milk cow.

1965, Sept. 28   Photo.   Perf. 14
C101	A51	1.50sh sep & pale bl	60	25
C102	A51	2sh sep & rose	1.15	38

8th Somali Fair, Mogadishu.

Faisal Type of Regular Issue
Design: 1.80sh, Kaaba, Mecca, Pres. Abdirascid Ali Scermarche and King Faisal.

1967, Sept. 21   Perf. 14   Wmk. 303
C103	A60	1.80sh blk, dp rose & org	42	30

Visit of King Faisal of Saudi Arabia.

Egret
AP32

Birds: 1sh, Southern carmine bee-eater. 1.30sh, Bruce's green pigeon. 1.80sh, Broad-tailed paradise whydah.

Lithographed

1968, Nov. 1   Perf. 11½   Unwmkd.
C104	AP32	35c bl & multi	8	8
C105	AP32	1sh grn & multi	30	18
C106	AP32	1.30sh vio bl & multi	38	30
C107	AP32	1.80sh yel & multi	42	38

Somali Democratic Republic

Postal Union Type of Regular Issue
Design: 1.30sh, Postal Union emblem and letter.

Perf. 14x13½
1972, Jan. 25   Photo.   Unwmkd.
C108	A81	1.30sh multi	65	55

10th anniversary of African Postal Union.

SOMALIA

AIR POST SEMI-POSTAL STAMPS.

King Victor Emmanuel III
SPAP1
Wmkd. Crowns. (140)

		1934, Nov. 5	Photo.	Perf. 14	
CB1	SPAP1	25c +10c gray grn		1.35	4.25
CB2	SPAP1	50c +10c brn		1.35	4.25
CB3	SPAP1	75c +15c rose red		1.35	4.25
CB4	SPAP1	80c +15c blk brn		1.35	4.25
CB5	SPAP1	1 l +20c red brn		1.35	4.25
CB6	SPAP1	2 l +20c brt bl		1.35	4.25
CB7	SPAP1	3 l +25c pur		13.00	40.00
CB8	SPAP1	5 l +25c org		13.00	40.00
CB9	SPAP1	10 l +30c rose vio		13.00	40.00
CB10	SPAP1	25 l +2 l dp grn		13.00	40.00
		Nos. CB1-CB10 (10)		60.10	185.50

Issued in commemoration of the 65th birthday of King Victor Emmanuel III and for the non-stop flight from Rome to Mogadishu.

Somalia
Type of Semi-Postal Stamps, 1957
1957, Nov. 30 Perf. 14 Wmk. 303

CB11	SP17	55c +20c dk bl & brn		25	35
CB12	SP17	1.20s +20c vio & brn		35	45

The surtax was for the fight against tuberculosis.

Type of Semi-Postal Issue, 1964
Designs: 75c+20c, Destroyed Somali village. 1.80sh+50c, Soldier aiding children, and map of Somalia (vert.).

1964, Dec. 12 Photo. Perf. 14

CB13	SP18	75c +20c blk, red & brn		60	25
CB14	SP18	1.80sh +50c blk, ol bis & sl		1.40	50

AIR POST SPECIAL DELIVERY STAMP

Antelopes
APSD1
Photogravure.
1958, Oct. 4 Perf. 14 Wmk. 303

CE1	APSD1	1.70s org ver & blk		1.00	1.40

AIR POST OFFICIAL STAMP
No. C1 Overprinted

**11 NOV. 1934-XIII
SERVIZIO AEREO
SPECIALE**

Photogravure
1934, Nov. 11 Perf. 14 Wmk. 140

CO1	AP1	25c sl bl & red org		575.00	900.00

Forgeries of this overprint exist.

AIR POST SEMI-POSTAL OFFICIAL STAMP.
Type of Air Post Semi-Postal Stamps, 1934
Overprinted Crown and
"SERVIZIO DI STATO" in Black.
1934, Nov. 5 Perf. 14 Wmk. 140

CBO1	SPAP1	25 l +2 l cop red		1,500.

SPECIAL DELIVERY STAMPS.
Italy No. E3 Surcharged
BESA 30 Somalia Italiana
1923, July 16 Perf. 14 Wmk. 140

E1	SD1	30b on 60c dl red		8.50	11.00

Italy, type of 1908
Special Delivery Stamp Surcharged
60 BESA 60 SOMALIA ITALIANA

E2	SD2	60b on 1.20 l bl & red		8.50	11.00

"Italia"—SD3

1924, June Engr. Unwmkd.

E3	SD3	30b dk red & brn		3.50	6.25
E4	SD3	60b dk bl & red		3.50	6.25

Nos. E3–E4 Surcharged
CENT 70 [Arabic] and Bars, in Black or Red

1926, Oct.

E5	SD3	70c on 30b dk red & brn (Bk)		3.25	5.50
E6	SD3	2.50 l on 60b dk bl & red (R)		4.00	7.25
	a.	Imperf., pair		140.00	

Same Surcharge on No. E3.
1927 Perf. 11

E7	SD3	1.25 l on 30b dk red & brn		2.75	4.00
	a.	Perf. 14		160.00	275.00
	b.	Imperf., pair		150.00	

Somalia

Bananas, Grant's gazelles
SD4
Photogravure.
1950, Apr. 24 Perf. 14 Wmk. 277

E8	SD4	40c bl grn		1.25	65
E9	SD4	80c violet		1.50	1.50

Gardenias—SD5
Design: 1s, Eryrhina melanocantha.
1955, Feb. Perf. 13

E10	SD5	50c lil & grn		35	45
E11	SD5	1s bl, rose brn & grn		70	90

AUTHORIZED DELIVERY STAMP.
Italy No. EY2
Overprinted in Black **SOMALIA ITALIANA**
1941 Perf. 14. Wmk. 140

EY1	AD2	10c dk brn		15

No. EY1 was prepared but not issued.

POSTAGE DUE STAMPS.
Somalia Italiana
Postage Due Stamps of Italy Overprinted **Meridionale**

1906–08 Perf. 14 Wmk. 140

J1	D3	5c buff & mag		2.25	4.50
J2	D3	10c buff & mag		16.00	13.00
J3	D3	20c org & mag		6.75	13.00
J4	D3	30c buff & mag		5.50	13.00
J5	D3	40c buff & mag		6.75	13.00
J6	D3	50c buff & mag		6.75	13.00
J7	D3	60c buff & mag ('08)		11.00	13.00
J8	D3	1 l bl & mag		225.00	55.00
J9	D3	2 l bl & mag		185.00	67.50
J10	D3	5 l bl & mag		185.00	75.00
J11	D3	10 l bl & mag		45.00	90.00
		Nos. J1-J11 (11)		695.00	370.00

Postage Due Stamps of Italy Overprinted at Top of Stamps **Somalia Italiana**
1909–19

J12	D3	5c buff & mag		1.25	2.75
J13	D3	10c buff & mag		1.25	2.75
J14	D3	20c org & mag		2.25	4.50
J15	D3	30c buff & mag		4.50	9.00
J16	D3	40c buff & mag		4.50	9.00
J17	D3	50c buff & mag		4.50	9.00
J18	D3	60c buff & mag ('19)		4.50	9.00
J19	D3	1 l bl & mag		13.50	22.50
J20	D3	2 l bl & mag		22.50	35.00
J21	D3	5 l bl & mag		27.50	45.00
J22	D3	10 l bl & mag		4.50	17.50
		Nos. J12-J22 (11)		90.75	166.00

Same with Overprint at Bottom of Stamps
1920

J12a	D3	5c buff & mag		27.50	22.50
J13a	D3	10c buff & mag		27.50	22.50
J14a	D3	20c org & mag		32.50	32.50
J15a	D3	30c buff & mag		17.50	22.50
J16a	D3	40c buff & mag		17.50	22.50
J17a	D3	50c buff & mag		17.50	22.50
J18a	D3	60c buff & mag		27.50	22.50
J19a	D3	1 l bl & mag		32.50	22.50
J20a	D3	2 l bl & mag		32.50	22.50
J21a	D3	5 l bl & mag		40.00	22.50
		Nos. J12a-J21a (10)		272.50	235.00

D4   D5

1923, July 1

J23	D4	1b buff & blk		30	1.25
J24	D4	2b buff & blk		30	1.25
	a.	Invtd. ovpt.		32.50	
J25	D4	3b buff & blk		30	1.25
J26	D4	5b buff & blk		45	1.25
J27	D4	10b buff & blk		45	1.25
J28	D4	20b buff & blk		45	1.25
J29	D4	40b buff & blk		45	1.25
J30	D4	1r bl & blk		1.75	2.75
		Nos. J23-J30 (8)		4.45	11.50

Type of Postage Due Stamps of Italy
Overprinted **Somalia Italiana**
1926, Mar. 1

J31	D3	5c buff & blk		8.50	4.25
J32	D3	10c buff & blk		5.50	2.75
	a.	Numerals and overprint inverted		15.00	
J33	D3	20c buff & blk		3.25	2.75
	a.	Numerals and overprint inverted		125.00	
J34	D3	30c buff & blk		3.25	2.75
	a.	Numerals and overprint inverted		15.00	
J35	D3	40c buff & blk		3.25	2.75
	a.	Numerals and overprint inverted		15.00	
J36	D3	50c buff & blk		6.75	2.75
	a.	Numerals and overprint inverted		15.00	
J37	D3	60c buff & blk		6.75	2.75
	a.	Numerals and overprint inverted			
J38	D3	1 l bl & blk		11.00	4.50
J39	D3	2 l bl & blk		16.00	4.50
J40	D3	5 l bl & blk		16.00	4.50
J41	D3	10 l bl & blk		16.00	4.50
		Nos. J31-J41 (11)		96.25	38.75

Postage Due Stamps of Italy, 1934, Overprinted in Black **SOMALIA ITALIANA**
1934, May 12

J42	D6	5c brown		65	1.25
J43	D6	10c blue		65	1.25
J44	D6	20c rose red		1.25	1.85
J45	D6	25c green		1.25	1.85
J46	D6	30c red org		2.25	4.50
J47	D6	40c blk brn		2.25	6.75
J48	D6	50c violet		3.50	1.75
J49	D6	60c black		4.50	9.00
J50	D7	1 l red org		9.00	4.50
J51	D7	2 l green		13.00	17.50
J52	D7	5 l violet		15.00	30.00
J53	D7	10 l blue		17.50	35.00
J54	D7	20 l carmine		20.00	40.00
		Nos. J42-J54 (13)		90.80	155.20

Somalia
Photogravure.
1950 Perf. 14. Wmk. 277

J55	D5	1c dk gray vio		18	22
J56	D5	2c dp bl		18	22
J57	D5	5c bl grn		18	22
J58	D5	10c rose lil		18	22
J59	D5	40c violet		70	90
J60	D5	1s dk brn		1.50	2.25
		Nos. J55-J60 (6)		2.92	4.03

PARCEL POST STAMPS.

These stamps were used by affixing them to the way bill so that one half remained on it following the parcel, the other half staying on the receipt given the sender. Most used halves are right halves. Complete stamps were and are obtainable canceled, probably to order.

Both unused and used prices are for complete stamps.

Parcel Post Stamps of Italy, 1914-17,
Overprinted **SOMALIA ITALIANA**
1917–19 Perf. 13½ Wmk. 140

Q1	PP2	5c brown		90	2.25
	a.	Double ovpt.		60.00	
Q2	PP2	10c blue		90	2.25
Q3	PP2	20c blk ('19)			75.00
Q4	PP2	25c red		1.75	3.50
	a.	Double ovpt.		150.00	
Q5	PP2	50c orange		20.00	35.00
Q6	PP2	1 l lilac		11.00	17.50
Q7	PP2	2 l green		13.00	22.50
Q8	PP2	3 l bister		16.00	27.50
Q9	PP2	4 l slate		17.50	32.50
		Nos. Q1-Q9 (9)			218.00

Halves Used

Q1,Q4		15
Q2		10
Q3, Q5		4.00
Q6-Q7		50
Q8		80
Q9		2.00

Nos. Q5–Q9 were overprinted in 1922 with a slightly different type in which the final "A" of SOMALIA is directly over the final "A" of ITALIANA. They were not regularly issued. Price for set, $400.

Parcel Post Stamps of Italy, 1914-17,
1923 Overprinted **SOMALIA**

Q10	PP2	25c red		22.50	55.00
Q11	PP2	50c orange		13.00	27.50
Q12	PP2	1 l violet		17.50	27.50
Q13	PP2	2 l green		17.50	32.50
Q14	PP2	3 l bister		22.50	40.00
Q15	PP2	4 l slate		27.50	45.00
		Nos. Q10-Q15 (6)		120.50	227.50

SOMALIA—SOMALI COAST

Halves Used

Q10		1.75
Q11, Q12		.50
Q13		.60
Q14		1.25
Q15		2.50

Parcel Post Stamps of Italy, 1914-17, Surcharged

BESA	SOMALIA ITALIANA		SOMALIA ITALIANA	BESA 5

1928

Q16	PP2	3b on 5c brn	1.25	2.75
Q17	PP2	5b on 5c brn	1.25	2.75
Q18	PP2	10b on 10c bl	2.25	4.50
Q19	PP2	25c on 25c red	2.75	5.50
Q20	PP2	50b on 50c org	5.50	11.00
Q21	PP2	1r on 1 l lil	6.75	13.00
Q22	PP2	2r on 2 l grn	11.00	21.00
Q23	PP2	3r on 3 l bis	16.00	32.50
Q24	PP2	4r on 4 l sl	21.00	42.50
		Nos. Q16-Q24 (9)	67.75	135.50

Halves Used

Q16-Q17		.20
Q18-Q19		.30
Q20-Q21		.50
Q22		.90
Q23		1.75
Q24		2.50

No. Q16 has the numeral "3" at the left also.

Parcel Post Stamps of Italy, 1914-22 Overprinted SOMALIA ITALIANA

1926-31 Red Overprint.

Q25	PP2	5c brown	10.00	13.00
Q26	PP2	10c blue	10.00	13.00
Q27	PP2	20c black	16.00	27.50
Q28	PP2	25c red	16.00	27.50
Q29	PP2	50c orange	16.00	27.50
Q30	PP2	1 l violet	16.00	27.50
Q31	PP2	2 l green	22.50	27.50
Q32	PP2	3 l yellow	2.75	4.50
Q33	PP2	4 l slate	2.75	4.50
Q34	PP2	10 l vio brn ('30)	5.50	13.00
Q35	PP2	12 l red brn ('31)	5.50	13.00
Q36	PP2	15 l ol ('31)	5.50	13.00
Q37	PP2	20 l dl vio ('31)	5.50	13.00
		Nos. Q25-Q37 (13)	134.00	224.50

Halves Used

Q25-Q26	.50
Q27-Q28, Q33	1.10
Q29, Q34	1.35
Q30-Q31	.80
Q32	.60
Q35-Q36	1.75
Q37	2.00

Nos. Q25-Q31 come with two types of overprints: I. The first "I" and last "A" of ITALIANA extend slightly at both sides of SOMALIA. II. Only the "I" extends. These seven stamps with type I overprint were not regularly issued, and Nos. Q27-Q31 (type I) sell for less than with type II overprint.

Black Overprint.

Q38	PP2	10 l vio brn	17.50	8.50
Q39	PP2	12 l red brn	9.00	8.50
Q40	PP2	15 l olive	9.00	8.50
Q41	PP2	20 l dl vio	9.00	8.50

Halves Used

Q38	.70
Q39-Q41	.45

Same Overprint on Parcel Post Stamps of Italy, 1927-38.

Black Overprint.

1928-39

Q42	PP3	25c red ('31)	40.00	72.50
Q43	PP3	30c ultra	.32	1.75
Q43A	PP3	50c orange	6,750.	3,000.
Q44	PP3	60c red	.32	1.75
Q45	PP3	1 l lil ('31)	6.75	13.00
Q46	PP3	2 l grn ('31)	6.75	13.00
Q47	PP3	3 l bister	.35	2.75
Q48	PP3	4 l gray blk	.55	3.50
Q49	PP3	10 l rose lil ('34)	67.50	110.00
Q50	PP3	20 l lil brn ('34)	67.50	120.00
		Nos. Q42-Q43, Q44-Q50 (9)	190.04	338.25

Halves Used

Q42, Q50	1.50
Q43, Q44	.30
Q43A	40.00
Q45-Q48	.50
Q49	3.25

The 25c, 1 l and 2 l come with both types of overprint (see note below No. Q37). Both types were regularly issued. Prices are for type I on 25c, type II on 1 l and 2 l.

Red Overprint.

Q51	PP3	5c brn ('39)	9.00	
Q52	PP3	3 l bis ('30)	6.25	13.00
		Half stamp		.50
Q53	PP3	4 l gray blk ('30)	6.25	13.00
		Half stamp		.50

Same Overprint in Black on Italy Nos. Q24-Q25

1940 Perf. 13.

Q54	PP3	5c brown	.90	1.75
		Half stamp		.10
Q55	PP3	10c dp bl	1.40	3.50
		Half stamp		.15

Somalia

PP1

1950 Photogravure. Perf. 14. Wmk. 277

Q56	PP1	1c cerise	.20	.32
Q57	PP1	3c dk gray vio	.20	.32
Q58	PP1	5c rose lil	.20	.32
Q59	PP1	10c red org	.20	.32
Q60	PP1	20c dk brn	.20	.32
Q61	PP1	50c bl grn	.40	.65
Q62	PP1	1s violet	2.00	2.75
Q63	PP1	2s brown	3.25	3.50
Q64	PP1	D blue	4.00	5.00
		Nos. Q56-Q64 (9)	10.65	13.50

Halves Used

Q56-Q58	5
Q59-Q60	8
Q61	15
Q62	20
Q63	45
Q64	75

SOMALI COAST
(sô-mä′lê kōst)
(Djibouti)

LOCATION — In eastern Africa, bordering on the Gulf of Aden.
GOVT. — French Overseas Territory.
AREA — 8,500 sq. mi.
POP. — 86,000 (est. 1963).
CAPITAL — Djibouti (Jibuti).

The port of Obock, which issued postage stamps in 1892-1894, was included in the territory and began to use stamps of Somali Coast in 1902. See Obock in Vol. III.

On Mar. 19, 1967, the territory changed its name to the French Territory of the Afars and Issas. The Republic of Djibouti was proclaimed June 27, 1977.

100 Centimes = 1 Franc

Navigation and Commerce
A1   A2

A3

Camel and Rider—A4

Obock Nos. 32–33, 35, 45 with Overprint or Surcharge Handstamped in Black, Blue or Red

1894 Perf. 14x13½. Unwmkd.

1	A1	5c grn & red, grnsh (with bar)	90.00	85.00
1A	A1	5c grn & red, grnsh	750.00	400.00
2	A1	25c on 2c brn & bl, buff (Bl & Bk)	210.00	125.00
a.		"25" omitted	600.00	475.00
b.		"DJIBOUTI" omitted	600.00	475.00
c.		"DJIBOUTI" inverted	625.00	600.00
3	A3	50c on 1c blk & red, bl (R & Bl)	250.00	150.00
a.		"5" instead of "50"	750.00	525.00
b.		"0" instead of "50"	750.00	525.00
c.		"DJIBOUTI" omitted	750.00	525.00

Imperf.

4	A4	1fr on 5fr car	450.00	325.00
5	A4	5fr carmine	1,100.	950.00

The overprint on No. 1 includes a bar to obliterate "OBOCK." "DJIBOUTI" is in blue on No. 2, in red on No. 3.

Counterfeits exist of Nos. 4–5.

View of Djibouti, Somali Warriors
A5

French Gunboat—A7

Crossing Desert—A8

Size: 66mm. wide, including simulated perfs.

Designs: 15c, 25c, 30c, 40c, 50c, 75c, Different views of Djibouti. 1fr, 2fr, Djibouti quay.

Imperf. (Simulated Perforations in Frame Color)

Quadrille Lines Printed on Paper

1894-1902 Typographed.

6	A5	1c blk & cl	1.50	1.50
7	A5	2c cl & blk	1.50	1.50
8	A5	4c vio brn & bl	5.25	3.75
9	A5	5c bl grn & red	5.25	3.75
10	A5	5c grn & yel grn ('02)	4.75	4.75
11	A5	10c brn & grn	7.50	3.75
a.		Half used as 5c on cover		67.50
12	A5	15c vio & grn	6.75	3.75
13	A5	25c rose & bl	11.00	6.00
14	A5	30c gray brn & rose	8.00	6.00
a.		Half used as 15c on cover		275.00
15	A5	40c org & bl ('00)	32.50	26.50
16	A5	50c bl & rose	11.00	8.00
a.		Half used as 25c on cover		750.00
17	A5	75c vio & org	26.00	21.00
18	A5	1fr vio & blk	11.00	8.00
19	A5	2fr gray brn & rose	55.00	45.00
20	A7	5fr rose & bl	100.00	75.00
21	A8	25fr red & bl	700.00	700.00
22	A8	50fr bl & rose	525.00	525.00

High values are found with the overprint "S" (Specimen) erased and, usually, a cancellation added.

A9

1899 Black Surcharge.

23	A9	40c on 4c brn & bl	2,250.	12.00
a.		Double surch.	3,250.	600.00

Surcharged **0-05**

1902 Blue Surcharge.

24	A5	0.05c on 75c vio & org	32.50	22.50
a.		Inverted surcharge	325.00	275.00
25	A5	0.10c on 1fr ol grn & blk	45.00	37.50
a.		Inverted surcharge	325.00	225.00
26	A5	0.40c on 2fr gray brn & rose	325.00	250.00

Black Surcharge.

27	A7	0.75c on 5fr rose & bl	375.00	300.00
a.		Inverted surcharge	1,500.	1,250.

Obock No. 57 Surcharged in Blue.

27B	A7	0.05c on 75c gray lil & org	1,000.	600.00

A10

Nos. 15–16 Surcharged in Black.

28	A10	5c on 40c org & bl	3.00	2.75
a.		Double surcharge	60.00	60.00
29	A10	10c on 50c bl & rose	13.00	13.00
a.		Inverted surch.	275.00	275.00

Surcharged on Stamps of Obock

Group of Warriors—A11

SOMALI COAST

Black Surcharge.

30	A11	5c on 30c bis & yel grn	6.00	4.50
a.		Inverted surcharge	135.00	100.00
b.		Double surcharge	125.00	110.00

A12

Red Surcharge.

31	A12	10c on 25c blk & bl	6.75	6.00
a.		Inverted surcharge	150.00	135.00
b.		Double surch.	165.00	135.00
c.		Triple surcharge	750.00	750.00

A13

Black Surcharge.

32	A13	10c on 10fr org & red vio	18.00	15.00
a.		Double surch.	150.00	125.00
b.		Triple surcharge, one inverted	575.00	575.00

A14

Black Surcharge.

33	A14	10c on 2fr dl vio & org	32.50	26.00
a.		"DJIBOUTI" inverted	175.00	150.00
b.		Large "0" in "10"	70.00	60.00
c.		Double surcharge	750.00	600.00

Same Surcharge on Obock No. 53 in Red

| 33D | A7 | 10c on 25c blk & bl | 24,000. | 12,000. |

A14a

Black Surcharge on Obock Nos. 63-64.

33E	A14a	5c on 25fr brn & bl	32.50	30.00
33F	A14a	10c on 50fr red vio & grn	40.00	32.50
g.		"01" instead of "10"	125.00	110.00
h.		"CENTIMES" inverted	1,750.	1,750.
i.		Double surch.	1,500.	1,500.

Tadjoura Mosque
A15

Somalis on Camel
A16

Warriors
A17

1902 Engraved. Perf. 11½.

34	A15	1c brn vio & org	45	38
35	A15	2c yel brn & yel grn	45	38
36	A15	4c bl & car	1.25	75
37	A15	5c bl grn & yel grn	90	60
38	A15	10c car & red org	4.00	2.25
39	A15	15c brn org & bl	3.25	2.25
40	A16	20c vio & grn	5.25	4.50
41	A16	25c blue	8.00	7.25
a.		25c ind & bl ('03)	10.00	9.00
42	A16	30c red & blk	3.25	2.35
43	A16	40c org & bl	6.75	5.25
44	A16	50c grn & red org	25.00	21.00
45	A16	75c org & vio	2.75	2.25
46	A17	1fr red org & vio	8.00	7.50
47	A17	2fr yel grn & car	17.50	15.00
a.		Without names of designer and engraver at bottom	75.00	75.00
48	A17	5fr org & bl	10.00	7.50
		Nos. 34-48 (15)	96.80	79.21

1903

49	A15	1c brn vio & blk	38	38
50	A15	2c yel brn & blk	50	50
51	A15	4c lake & blk	65	50
a.		4c red & blk	70	55
52	A15	5c bl grn & blk	1.50	1.25
53	A15	10c car & blk	3.75	1.50
54	A15	15c org brn & blk	7.50	4.75
55	A16	20c dl vio & blk	10.00	9.50
56	A16	25c ultra & blk	4.50	3.75
57	A16	40c org & blk	4.50	3.75
58	A16	50c grn & blk	8.00	6.75
60	A16	75c buff & blk	6.00	5.25
a.		75c brn org & blk	32.50	30.00
61	A17	1fr org & blk	7.50	6.00
62	A17	2fr yel grn & blk	4.00	3.25
a.		Without names of designer and engraver at bottom	24.00	24.00
63	A17	5fr red org & blk	7.50	6.00
a.		5fr ocher & blk	8.00	8.00
		Nos. 49-63 (14)	65.28	53.73

Imperforates, transposed colors and inverted centers exist in the 1902 and 1903 issues. Most of these were issued from Paris and some are said to have been fraudulently printed.

Tadjoura Mosque
A18

Somalis on Camel
A19

Warriors
A20

1909 Typographed. Perf. 14x13½.

64	A18	1c mar & brn	45	38
65	A18	2c vio & ol gray	45	38
66	A18	4c ol gray & bl	60	50
67	A18	5c grn & gray grn	75	38
68	A18	10c car & ver	1.75	75
69	A18	20c blk & red brn	3.25	3.00
70	A19	25c bl & pale bl	2.25	2.00
71	A19	30c brn & scar	3.00	2.50
72	A19	35c vio & grn	3.25	2.75
73	A19	40c rose & vio	3.25	2.50
74	A19	45c brn & bl grn	3.75	3.00
75	A19	50c mar & brn	3.75	3.50
76	A19	75c scar & grn	7.50	6.00
77	A20	1fr vio & brn	10.00	9.50
78	A20	2fr brn & rose	18.00	16.00
79	A20	5fr vio brn & bl grn	30.00	25.00
		Nos. 64-79 (16)	92.00	78.14

Drummer
A21

Somali Girl
A22

Djibouti-Addis Ababa Railroad Bridge
A23

Chalky Paper.

1915-33 Perf. 13½x14

80	A21	1c brt vio & red brn	6	6
81	A21	2c ocher & ind	6	6
82	A21	4c dk brn & red	12	12
83	A21	5c yel grn & grn	30	30
84	A21	5c org & dl red ('22)	28	28
85	A22	10c car & dk red	38	38
86	A22	10c ap grn & grn ('22)	38	38
87	A22	10c ver & grn ('25)	12	12
88	A22	15c brn vio & car	28	28
89	A22	20c org & blk brn	18	18
90	A22	20c dp grn & bl grn ('25)	12	12
91	A22	20c dk grn & red ('27)	22	18
92	A22	25c ultra & dl bl	28	28
93	A22	25c blk & bl grn ('22)	40	40
94	A22	30c blk & bl grn	55	50
95	A22	30c rose & red brn ('22)	40	40
96	A22	30c vio & ol grn ('25)	15	15
97	A22	30c grn & dl grn ('27)	15	15
98	A22	35c lt grn & dl rose	30	30
99	A22	40c bl & brn vio	30	30
100	A22	45c red brn & dk bl	45	38
101	A22	50c car rose & blk	4.50	3.25
102	A22	50c ultra & ind ('24)	55	55
103	A22	50c dk brn & red vio ('25)	15	12
104	A22	60c ol grn & red vio ('25)	15	15
105	A22	65c car rose & ol grn ('25)	18	15
106	A22	75c dl vio & choc	50	32
107	A22	75c ind & ultra ('25)	15	15
108	A22	75c brt vio & ol brn ('27)	75	50
109	A22	85c vio brn & bl grn ('25)	60	40
110	A22	90c brn red & brt red ('30)	3.75	2.75
111	A23	1fr bis brn & red	75	45
112	A23	1.10fr lt brn & ultra ('28)	2.75	2.75
113	A23	1.25fr dk bl & blk brn ('33)	4.50	3.85
114	A23	1.50fr lt bl & dk bl ('30)	55	50
115	A23	1.75fr gray grn & lt red ('33)	3.00	2.75
116	A23	2fr bl vio & blk	1.50	1.00
117	A23	3fr red vio ('30)	4.50	3.25
118	A23	5fr rose red & blk	3.00	1.50
		Nos. 80-118 (39)	37.31	29.71

No. 99 is on ordinary paper.

Stamps of 1915 Surcharged in Green or Blue

1922

119	A21	10c on 5c yel grn & grn (G)	30	30
a.		Double surch.	37.50	37.50
120	A22	50c on 25c ultra & bl (Bl)	30	30

Type of 1915
Surcharged **0,01** in Various Colors.

1922

121	A22	0,01c on 15c vio & rose (Bk)	15	15
122	A22	0,02c on 15c vio & rose (Bl)	15	15
123	A22	0,04c on 15c vio & rose (G)	15	15
124	A22	0,05c on 15c vio & rose (R)	15	15

Stamps and Type of 1915 Surcharged 60

1923-27

125	A22	60c on 75c ol grn & vio	15	15
126	A22	65c on 15c brn vio & car ('25)	45	45
127	A22	85c on 40c bl & brn vio ('25)	50	50
128	A22	90c on 75c brn red & red ('27)	2.25	2.25

Stamps and Type of 1915-17 Surcharged with New Value and Bars in Black or Red.

1924-27

| 129 | A23 | 25c on 5fr rose red & blk | 45 | 45 |

SOMALI COAST

130	A23	1.25fr on 1fr dk bl & ultra (R) ('26)	45	45
131	A23	1.50fr on 1fr lt bl & dk bl ('27)	60	60
132	A23	3fr on 5fr ver & red vio ('27)	1.75	1.75
133	A23	10fr on 5fr brn red & ol brn ('27)	3.75	3.75
134	A23	20fr on 5fr gray grn & lil rose ('27)	6.25	6.25
		Nos. 129-134 (6)	13.25	13.25

Colonial Exposition Issue.
Common Design Types
Name of Country Typo. in Black
1931 Engraved. *Perf. 12½.*

135	CD70	40c dp grn	2.50	2.50
136	CD71	50c violet	2.50	2.50
137	CD72	90c red org	2.50	2.50
138	CD73	1.50fr dl bl	2.50	2.50

Paris International Exposition Issue.
Common Design Types
1937 Engraved. *Perf. 13.*

139	CD74	20p dp vio	60	60
140	CD75	30c dk grn	65	65
141	CD76	40c car rose	60	60
142	CD77	50c dk brn & bl	65	65
143	CD78	90c red	85	85
144	CD79	1.50fr ultra	85	85
		Nos. 139-144 (6)	4.20	4.20

Colonial Arts Exhibition Issue.
Souvenir Sheet.
Common Design Type
1937 *Imperf.*

145	CD75	3fr dl vio	2.50	2.50

Issued in sheets measuring 18x99mm, containing one stamp.

Mosque of Djibouti
A24

Somali Warriors
A25

Governor Léonce Lagarde
A26

View of Djibouti—A27

1938-40 *Perf. 12x12½, 12½*

146	A24	2c dl red vio	5	5
147	A24	3c sl grn	6	6
148	A24	4c dl red brn	5	5
149	A24	5c carmine	6	5
150	A24	10c bl gray	6	6
151	A24	15c sl blk	12	12
152	A24	20c dk org	12	12
153	A25	25c dk brn	18	15
154	A25	30c dk bl	15	15
155	A25	35c ol grn	32	28
156	A24	40c org grn ('40)	8	8
157	A24	45c dl grn ('40)	12	12
158	A25	50c red	15	15
159	A25	55c dl red vio	32	25
160	A25	60c blk ('40)	30	30
161	A25	65c org brn	30	30
162	A25	70c lt vio ('40)	60	60
163	A26	80c gray blk	75	60
164	A25	90c rose vio ('39)	75	75
165	A26	1fr carmine	90	60
166	A26	1fr blk ('40)	28	28
167	A26	1.25fr mag ('39)	45	45
168	A26	1.40fr pck bl ('40)	45	45
169	A26	1.50fr dl grn	38	32
170	A26	1.60fr brn car ('40)	45	45
171	A26	1.75fr ultra	38	30
172	A26	2fr dk org	38	30
173	A26	2.25fr ultra ('39)	60	60
174	A26	2.50fr org brn ('40)	80	80
175	A26	3fr dl vio	38	32
176	A27	5fr brn & pale cl	90	75
177	A27	10fr ind & pale bl	90	90
178	A27	20fr car lake & gray	1.25	1.25
		Nos. 146-178 (33)	13.04	11.92

New York World's Fair Issue.
Common Design Type
1939 Engraved. *Perf. 12½x12.*

179	CD82	1.25fr car lake	50	50
180	CD82	2.25fr ultra	50	50

Mosque of Djibouti and Marshal Pétain
A28

1941 Engraved. *Perf. 12x12½*

181	A28	1fr yel brn	32	
182	A28	2.50fr blue	32	

Nos. 181-182 were issued by the Vichy government, but it is doubtful whether they were placed in use in Somali Coast. Stamps of types A24, A25 and A26, without "RF", were issued in 1944 by the Vichy Government, but were not placed on sale in the colony.

Stamps of 1915-33 Overprinted in Black or Red

FRANCE LIBRE
a

Perf. 13½x14, 14x13½.
1943 Unwmkd.

183	A21	1c brt vio & red brn	45	45
184	A21	2c ocher & ind	60	60
185	A21	4c dk brn & red	12.50	12.50
186	A21	5c org & dl red	60	60
187	A22	15c brn vio & car	2.50	2.50
188	A22	20c dk grn & red	60	60
189	A22	30c grn & dl grn	60	60
190	A22	40c red & red	45	45
191	A22	65c car rose & ol grn	65	65
192	A23	1.50fr lt bl & dk bl (R)	65	65
193	A23	1.75fr gray grn & lt red	3.25	3.25
		Nos. 183-193 (11)	22.85	22.85

Common Design Types
pictured in section at front of book.

Stamps of 1938-40 Overprinted in Black or Red

FRANCE
France
Libre **LIBRE**
b *c*
France
Libre
d
FRANCE LIBRE
e

1943 *Perf. 12x12½, 12½*

194	A24 (b)	2c dl red vio	75	75
195	A24 (b)	3c sl grn (R)	75	75
196	A24 (b)	4c dl red brn	75	75
197	A24 (b)	5c carmine	75	75
198	A24 (b)	10c bl gray (R)	38	38
199	A24 (b)	15c sl blk (R)	75	75
200	A24 (b)	20c dk org	75	75
201	A25 (c)	25c dk brn (R)	1.25	1.25
202	A25 (c)	30c dk bl (R)	30	30
203	A25 (c)	35c ol (R)	90	90
204	A24 (b)	40c brn org	30	30
205	A24 (b)	45c dl grn	75	75
206	A25 (b)	55c dl red vio (R)	75	75
207	A25 (b)	60c blk (R)	38	38
208	A25 (b)	70c lt vio (R)	32	32
a.		Inverted ovpt.	80.00	80.00
209	A26 (d)	80c gray blk (R)	45	45
210	A26 (d)	90c rose vio (R)	32	32
211	A26 (d)	1.25fr magenta	45	45
212	A26 (d)	1.40fr pck bl (R)	30	30
213	A26 (d)	1.50fr dl grn	45	45
214	A26 (d)	1.60fr brn car	55	55
215	A26 (d)	1.75fr ultra (R)	4.75	4.75
216	A26 (d)	2fr dk org	30	30
217	A26 (d)	2.25fr ultra (R)	60	60
218	A26 (d)	2.50fr chestnut	60	60
219	A26 (d)	3fr dl vio (R)	70	70
220	A27 (e)	5fr brn & pale cl	4.25	4.25
221	A27 (e)	10fr ind & pale bl	75.00	75.00
222	A27 (e)	20fr car lake & gray	3.00	3.00

The space between surcharge on Nos. 206 and 208 measures 10½ mm.

FRANCE LIBRE
No. 161 Surcharged in Black
= **50c.**

223	A25	50c on 65c org brn	30	30
		Nos. 194-223 (30)	101.85	101.85

Locomotive and Palms
A29

Photogravure.
1943 *Perf. 14½x14.* Unwmkd.

224	A29	5c ryl bl	6	
225	A29	10c pink	6	6
226	A29	25c emerald	15	15
227	A29	30c gray blk	12	12
228	A29	40c violet	12	12
229	A29	80c red brn	15	15
230	A29	1fr aqua	18	18
231	A29	1.50fr scarlet	15	15
232	A29	2fr brown	22	22
233	A29	2.50fr ultra	28	28
234	A29	4fr brt org	32	32
235	A29	5fr dp rose lil	32	32
236	A29	10fr lt ultra	45	45
237	A29	20fr green	65	65
		Nos. 224-237 (14)	3.23	3.23

Eboue Issue.
Common Design Type
1945 Engraved. *Perf. 13.*

238	CD91	2fr black	30	30
239	CD91	25fr Prus grn	75	75

Nos. 238 and 239 exist imperforate.

Nos. 224, 226 and 233 Surcharged with New Values and Bars in Carmine or Black

1945 *Perf. 14½x14.*

240	A29	50c on 5c ryl bl (C)	30	30
241	A29	60c on 5c ryl bl (C)	15	15
242	A29	70c on 5c ryl bl (C)	15	15
a.		Inverted surch.	80.00	
243	A29	1.20fr on 5c ryl bl	30	30
244	A29	2.40fr on 25c emer	38	38
a.		Inverted surch.	67.50	
245	A29	3fr on 25c emer	30	30
246	A29	4.50fr on 25c emer	38	38
a.		Inverted surch.	67.50	
247	A29	15fr on 2.50fr ultra (C)	50	50
		Nos. 240-247 (8)	2.46	2.46

Danakil Tent
A30

Khor-Angar Outpost
A31

Obock-Tadjouran Road
A32

Somali Woman—A33

SOMALI COAST

Somali Village—A34

Djibouti Mosque—A35

Photogravure

1947		Perf. 13	Unwmkd.	
248	A30	10c vio bl & org	5	5
249	A30	30c ol brn & org	5	5
250	A30	40c dp plum & org	5	5
251	A31	50c bl grn & org	5	5
252	A31	60c choc & dp yel	12	12
253	A31	80c vio bl & org	15	15
254	A32	1fr bl & choc	15	15
255	A32	1.20fr bl grn & ol grn	32	32
256	A32	1.50fr org & vio bl	18	18
257	A33	2fr red lil & bl gray	35	30
258	A33	3fr dp bl & brn org	38	30
259	A33	3.60fr car rose & cop red	90	75
260	A33	4fr choc & bl gray	75	45
261	A34	5fr org & choc	38	30
262	A34	6fr gray bl & int bl	50	32
263	A34	10fr gray bl & red lil	50	32
264	A35	15fr choc, gray bl & pink	75	45
265	A35	20fr dk bl, gray bl & org	1.00	50
266	A35	25fr vio brn, lil rose & gray bl	1.50	1.40
		Nos. 248-266 (19)	8.13	6.21

Military Medal Issue.
Common Design Type

1952		Engr. & Typo.	
267	CD101	15fr blk, grn, yel & dk pur	2.50	2.50

Imperforates

Most stamps of Somali Coast from 1956 onward exist imperforate in issued and trial colors, and also in small presentation sheets in issued colors.

FIDES Issue
Common Design Type and

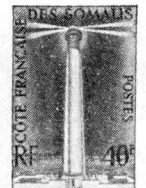

Lighthouse, Ras-Bir
A36

Design: 15fr, Loading ship and map, Djibouti.

Engraved.

1956		Perf. 13	Unwmkd.	
268	CD103	15fr purple	75	42
269	A36	40fr dp ultra & gray	1.75	1.10

Flower Issue
Common Design Type

Design: 10fr, Haemanthus (horiz.).

1958		Photogravure.	Perf. 12½x12	
270	CD104	10fr grn, red & yel	1.20	60

Wart Hog
A37

Designs: 40c, Cheetah. 50c, Gerenuk (vert.).

1958		Engraved.	Perf. 13	
271	A37	30c red brn & sep	22	12
272	A37	40c brn & ol	22	18
273	A37	50c brn, grn & gray	30	22
		See No. C21.		

Human Rights Issue.
Common Design Type

1958			Unwmkd.	
274	CD105	20fr brt pur & dk bl	1.50	1.50

Universal Declaration of Human Rights, 10th anniversary.

Parrotfish
A38

Designs: Various Tropical Fish.

1959		Engraved.	Perf. 13	
275	A38	1fr brt bl, brn & red org	30	30
276	A38	2fr blk, lt bl, yel & grn	35	30
277	A38	3fr vio & blk brn	35	30
278	A38	4fr brt grnsh bl, org & lt brn	60	45
279	A38	5fr brt grnsh bl & blk	70	42
280	A38	20fr brt bl, dl red brn & rose	1.50	1.00
281	A38	25fr red, grn & ultra	2.10	1.10
282	A38	60fr bl & dk grn	4.75	2.50
		Nos. 275-282 (8)	11.05	6.37

No. 276 is vertical.

Flamingo
A39

Birds: 15fr, Bee-eater (horiz.). 30fr, Sacred ibis (horiz.). 75fr, Pink-backed pelican.

1960		Perf. 13	Unwmkd.	
283	A39	10fr bluish grn, bis & cl	90	65
284	A39	15fr rose lil, grn & yel	1.10	80
285	A39	30fr bl, blk, org & brn	3.00	1.75
286	A39	75fr grn, sl grn & yel	6.75	3.75

Dragon Tree—A40

Klipspringer
A41

Meleagrina Margaritifera
A42

Designs: 4fr, Cony. 6fr, Large flatfish. 25fr, Fennecs. 40fr, Griffon vulture.

Engraved

1962, Mar. 24		Perf. 13	Unwmkd.	
287	A40	2fr grn, yel, org & brn	1.10	60
288	A40	4fr ocher & choc	1.10	60
289	A40	6fr brn, mar, grn & yel	2.25	1.20
290	A40	25fr red brn, ocher & grn	3.75	2.40
291	A40	40fr dk bl, brn & gray	3.75	3.00
292	A41	50fr bis, bl & lil	6.75	4.50
		Nos. 287-292 (6)	18.70	12.30

1962, Nov. 24			Photogravure

Sea Shells: 10fr, Tridacna squamosa (horiz.). 25fr, Strombus tricornis (horiz.). 30fr, Trochus dentatus.

Shells in Natural Colors

293	A42	8fr red & blk	60	45
294	A42	10fr car rose & blk	60	45
295	A42	25fr dp bl & brn	1.75	1.00
296	A42	30fr rose lil & brn	1.50	90

See Nos. C28-C29.

Red Cross Centenary Issue
Common Design Type

1963, Sept. 2		Engraved	Perf. 13	
297	CD113	50fr org brn, gray & car	3.75	3.75

Centenary of International Red Cross.

Astraea Coral
A43

Design: 6fr, Organ-pipe coral.

1963, Nov. 30		Photo.	Perf. 13x13½	
298	A43	5fr multi	60	50
299	A43	6fr multi	60	50

See Nos. C26-C27, C30.

Human Rights Issue
Common Design Type

1963, Dec. 20		Engraved	Perf. 13	
300	CD117	70fr dk brn & ultra	5.25	5.25

Philatec Issue
Common Design Type

1964, Apr. 7		Perf. 13	Unwmkd.	
301	CD118	80fr dp lil rose, grn & brn	5.25	5.25

Houri (Somali Sailboats)
A44

Design: 25fr, Sambouk (Somali sailboats).

1964, June 9			Engraved	
302	A44	15fr multi	75	70
303	A44	25fr multi	1.25	90

View of Dadwayya and Map of Somali Coast—A45

Design: 20fr, View of Tadjourah and map of Somali Coast.

1965, Oct. 20		Engraved	Perf. 13	
304	A45	6fr ultra, sl grn & red brn	60	45
305	A45	20fr ultra, org brn & brt grn	60	50

Senna
A46

Designs: 8fr, Poinciana. 25fr, Aloe.

1966		Engraved	Perf. 13	
306	A46	5fr red brn, sl grn & org	60	45
307	A46	8fr brn, dk grn & org	60	45
308	A46	25fr sl grn, ver & ind	90	75

See No. C41.

Desert Monitor
A47

1967, May 8		Engraved	Perf. 13	
309	A47	20fr red brn, ocher & sep	1.50	1.10

Stamps of Somali Coast were replaced in 1967 by those of the French Territory of the Afars and Issas.

SEMI-POSTAL STAMPS.

Somali Girl
SP1

SOMALI COAST

Chalky Paper.
1915 *Perf. 13½x14* Unwmkd.
B1 SP1 10c +5c car & dk red 4.50 4.50

Curie Issue
Common Design Type
1938 Engraved *Perf. 13*
B2 CD80 1.75fr +50c brt ultra 3.75 3.75

French Revolution Issue.
Common Design Type
1939 Photogravure
Name and Value Typo. in Black.
B3 CD83 45(c) +25(c) brn 3.75 3.75
B4 CD83 70(c) +30(c) brn 3.75 3.75
B5 CD83 90(c) +35(c) red org 3.75 3.75
B6 CD83 1.25fr +1fr rose pink 3.75 3.75
B7 CD83 2.25fr +2fr bl 3.75 3.75
Nos. B3-B7 (5) 18.75 18.75

Common Design Type and

Somali Guard SP2

Local Police SP3

1941 Photogravure *Perf. 13½*
B8 SP2 1fr +1fr red 60
B9 CD86 1.50fr +3fr mar 60
B10 SP3 2.50fr +1fr bl 60

Nos. B8-B10 were issued by the Vichy government, but were not placed in use in the colony.
Nos. 181-182 surcharged "OEUVRES COLONIALES" and surtax were issued in 1944 by the Vichy Government, but were not placed on sale in the colony.

Red Cross Issue
Common Design Type
Inscribed "Djibouti".
1944 *Perf. 14½x14.*
B13 CD90 5fr +20fr emer 90 90
The surtax was for the French Red Cross and national relief.

Tropical Medicine Issue
Common Design Type
1950 Engraved. *Perf. 13.*
B14 CD100 10fr +2fr red brn & red 2.50 2.50
The surtax was for charitable work.

Anti-Malaria Issue
Common Design Type
1962, Apr. 7 *Perf. 13* Unwmkd.
B15 CD108 25fr +5fr aqua 5.50 5.50
Issued for the World Health Organization drive to eradicate malaria.

Infant, Sun, Chest and Skulls SP4

1965, Dec. 10 Engraved *Perf. 13*
B16 SP4 25fr +5fr ocher, sl & brt grn 1.60 1.60
Campaign against tuberculosis.

AIR POST STAMPS.

V1

Stamps of the design shown above were issued in 1943 by the Vichy Government, but were not placed on sale in the colony.

Common Design Type
Inscribed "Djibouti".
Photogravure.
1944 *Perf. 14½x14.* Unwmkd.
C1 CD87 1fr dk org 38 38
C2 CD87 1.50fr brt red 38 38
C3 CD87 5fr brn red 50 50
C4 CD87 10fr black 65 65
C5 CD87 25fr ultra 95 95
C6 CD87 50fr dk grn 90 90
C7 CD87 100fr plum 1.40 1.40
Nos. C1-C7 (7) 5.16 5.16

Victory Issue
Common Design Type
1946 Engraved. *Perf. 12½.*
C8 CD92 8fr dp bl 65 65
Issued to commemorate the European victory of the Allied Nations in World War II.

Chad to Rhine Issue
Common Design Types
1946
C9 CD93 5fr gray blk 80 80
C10 CD94 10fr dp org 65 65
C11 CD95 15fr vio brn 65 65
C12 CD96 20fr brt vio 65 65
C13 CD97 25fr bl grn 1.25 1.25
C14 CD98 50fr lt ultra 1.50 1.50
Nos. C9-C14 (6) 5.50 5.50

Somali Gazing Skyward AP1

Frontier Post, Loyada—AP2

Governor's Mansion, Djibouti AP3

Perf. 12½x13, 13x12½.
1947 Photogravure. Unwmkd.
C15 AP1 50fr gray bl & choc 2.75 90
C16 AP2 100fr ol grn, org yel & gray bl 3.00 1.75
C17 AP3 200fr gray bl, org yel & ol grn 5.25 3.00

U. P. U. Issue.
Common Design Type
1949 Engraved *Perf. 13*
C18 CD99 30fr bl, dp bl, brn red & grn 4.25 4.25
Issued to commemorate the 75th anniversary of the formation of the Universal Postal Union.

Liberation Issue
Common Design Type
1954, June 6
C19 CD102 15fr ind & pur 3.75 3.75
10th anniversary, Liberation of France.

Somali Woman and Map of Djibouti AP4

1956, Feb. 20 Unwmkd.
C20 AP4 500fr dk vio & rose vio 35.00 27.50

Mountain Reedbucks—AP5

1958, July 7 Engraved. *Perf. 13*
C21 AP5 100fr ultra, lt grn & dk red brn 2.75 2.00

Albert Bernard, Flag and Troops AP6

1960, Jan. 18
C22 AP6 55fr ultra, sep & car 1.50 1.50
Issued to commemorate the 25th anniversary of the death of Administrator Albert Bernard at Moraito.

Great Bustard—AP7

1960, Oct. 24 *Perf. 13* Unwmkd.
C23 AP7 200fr brn, org & sl 7.00 4.50

Salt Dealers' Caravan at Assal Lake—AP8

1962, Jan. 6 Engraved *Perf. 13*
C24 AP8 500fr dk bl, red brn, pink & blk 10.00 6.00

Obock—AP9

1962, Mar. 11 *Perf. 13* Unwmkd.
C25 AP9 100fr bl & org brn 2.75 1.75
Centenary of the founding of Obock.

Rostellaria Magna—AP10

Designs: 40fr, Millepore coral. 55fr, Brain coral. 100fr, Lambis bryonia (seashell). 200fr, Branch coral.
1962-63 Photo. *Perf. 13½x12½*
C26 AP10 40fr multi ('63) 1.00 90
C27 AP10 55fr multi ('63) 1.75 90
C28 AP10 60fr multi 1.75 90
C29 AP10 100fr multi 2.25 1.50
C30 AP10 200fr multi ('63) 3.75 2.25
Nos. C26-C30 (5) 10.50 6.15

Telstar Issue
Common Design Type
1963, Feb. 9 Engraved *Perf. 13*
C31 CD111 20fr dp cl & dk grn 60 60

Zaroug (Somali Sailboats)—AP11

Designs: 85fr, Sambouk (boat) building. 300fr, Zeima sailboat.
1964-65 Engraved *Perf. 13*
C32 AP11 50fr bl, ocher & choc 1.65 1.00
C33 AP11 85fr Prus grn, dk brn & mag 2.10 1.65
C34 AP11 300fr ultra, lt brn & bl grn ('65) 6.75 4.00

547

SOMALI COAST—SOUTH RUSSIA

Discus Thrower AP12

1964, Oct. 10   Engraved
C35   AP12   90fr rose lil, red brn & blk   5.25   4.50

18th Olympic Games, Tokyo, Oct. 10–25.

ITU Issue
Common Design Type

C36   CD120   95fr lil rose, brt bl & lt brn   8.50   5.50

Issued to commemorate the centenary of the International Telecommunication Union.

Camels in Ghoubet Kharab and Map of Somali Coast—AP13

Design: 45fr, Abbé Lake.

1965   Engraved   Perf. 13
C37   AP13   45fr Prus bl, bl & red brn   1.40   70
C38   AP13   65fr bl, choc & yel   1.50   1.10

Issue dates: 45fr, Oct. 20; 65fr, July 16.

French Satellite A-1 Issue
Common Design Type

Designs: 25fr, Diamant rocket and launching installations. 30fr, A-1 satellite.

1966, Jan. 28   Engraved   Perf. 13
C39   CD121   25fr reddish brn, ol brn & dl red   1.40   1.40
C40   CD121   30fr ol brn, dl red & redsh brn   1.40   1.40
   a.   Strip of 2 + label   2.75   2.75

Issued to commemorate the launching of France's first satellite, Nov. 26, 1965. No. C40a contains one each of Nos. C39–C40 and reddish brown label with commemorative inscription. Each sheet contains 16 triptychs (2x8).

Stapelia—AP14

1966   Engraved   Perf. 13
C41   AP14   55fr sl grn, dl mag & emer   1.75   1.10

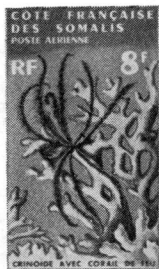

Feather Starfish and Coral AP15

Fish: 25fr, Regal angelfish. 40fr, Pomocanthops filamentosus. 50fr, Amphiprion ephippium. 70fr, Squirrelfish. 80fr, Surgeonfish. 100fr, Pterois lunulatus.

1966   Photogravure   Perf. 13
C42   AP15   8fr multi   60   60
C43   AP15   25fr multi   1.20   1.20
C44   AP15   40fr multi   1.75   1.75
C45   AP15   50fr multi   2.75   2.75
C46   AP15   70fr multi   3.50   3.50
C47   AP15   80fr multi   3.75   3.75
C48   AP15   100fr multi   4.50   4.50
Nos. C42–C48 (7)   18.05   18.05

French Satellite D-1 Issue
Common Design Type

1966, June 10   Engraved   Perf. 13
C49   CD122   48fr dk brn, brt bl & grn   1.75   1.25

AIR POST SEMI-POSTAL STAMPS.

Stamps of the design shown above and stamp of Cameroun type V10 inscribed "Côte Frcs. des Somalis" were issued in 1942 by the Vichy Government, but were not placed on sale in the colony.

Pharaoh Sacrificing before Horus and Hathor—SPAP1
Engraved

1964, Aug. 28   Perf. 13   Unwmkd.
CB1   SPAP1   25fr + 5fr Prus grn, dk red & brn   4.50   4.50

Issued to publicize the UNESCO world campaign to save historic monuments in Nubia.

POSTAGE DUE STAMPS.

D1   D2

Typographed.
Chalky Paper.

1915   Perf. 14x13½   Unwmkd.
J1   D1   5c dp ultra   15   15
J2   D1   10c brn red   22   22
J3   D1   15c black   22   22
J4   D1   20c purple   38   38
J5   D1   30c orange   50   50
J6   D1   50c maroon   1.00   1.00
J7   D1   60c green   1.75   1.75
J8   D1   1fr dk bl   2.50   2.50
Nos. J1–J8 (8)   6.72   6.72

Type of 1915 Issue Surcharged **2 F.**

1927
J9   D1   2fr on 1fr lt red   3.00   3.00
J10   D1   3fr on 1fr lil rose   3.00   3.00

Type of 1915.

1938   Engraved   Perf. 12½x13
J11   D1   5c lt ultra   5   5
J12   D1   10c dk car   5   5
J13   D1   15c brn blk   8   8
J14   D1   20c violet   12   12
J15   D1   30c org yel   30   30
J16   D1   50c brown   22   22
J17   D1   60c emerald   30   30
J18   D1   1fr indigo   80   80
J19   D1   2fr red   28   28
J20   D1   3fr dk brn   38   38
Nos. J11–J20 (10)   2.58   2.58

Nos. J11 to J20 are inscribed "Inst de Grav" below design.

FRANCE
Postage Due Stamps of 1915 Overprinted in Red or Black

LIBRE

1943   Perf. 14x13½   Unwmkd.
J21   D1   5c ultra (R)   40   40
J22   D1   10c brn red   40   40
J23   D1   15c blk (R)   40   40
J24   D1   20c purple   40   40
J25   D1   30c orange   40   40
J26   D1   50c maroon   40   40
J27   D1   60c green   40   40
J28   D1   1fr dk bl (R)   2.75   2.75
Nos. J21–J28 (8)   5.55   5.55

France
Postage Due Stamps of 1938 Overprinted in Red or Black

Libre

1943   Perf. 12½x13
J29   D1   5c lt ultra (R)   30   30
J30   D1   10c dk car   30   30
J31   D1   15c brn blk (R)   30   30
J32   D1   20c violet   30   30
J33   D1   30c org yel   45   45
J34   D1   50c brown   45   45
J35   D1   60c emerald   40   40
J36   D1   1fr ind   40   40
J37   D1   2fr red   2.50   2.50
J38   D1   3fr dk brn (R)   3.50   3.50
Nos. J29–J38 (10)   8.90   8.90

In 1944 the Vichy Government issued five stamps of type D1, but without "RF," which were not placed on sale in the colony. The stamps were engraved, with the value numerals typographed, done in different color inks. Denominations: 30c, 50c, 60c, 2fr, 3fr.

1947   Photo.   Perf. 13½x13
J39   D2   10c purple   5   5
J40   D2   30c brown   5   5
J41   D2   50c green   5   5
J42   D2   1fr dp org   12   12
J43   D2   2fr lil rose   18   18
J44   D2   3fr dk org brn   18   18
J45   D2   4fr blue   30   30
J46   D2   5fr org red   30   30
J47   D2   10fr ol grn   32   32
J48   D2   20fr bl vio   60   60
Nos. J39–J48 (10)   2.15   2.15

SOUTH BULGARIA
See Eastern Rumelia in Vol. II.

SOUTH KASAI

This part of a Congo province declared itself an autonomous state and in 1961 issued several series of stamps, some of which were overprints on Congo (ex-Belgian) stamps. Established nations did not recognize South Kasai as an independent state.

SOUTH MOLUCCAS
(Republik Maluku Selatan)

On the basis of information received from the Republic of Indonesia, it appears that stamps of the so-called republic of South Moluccas were privately issued and had no postal use. Accordingly, they are not recognized as postage stamps.

SOUTH RUSSIA
(south rŭsh'à)

LOCATION — An area in southern Russia bordering on the Caspian and Black Seas.

A provisional government set up and maintained by General Denikin in opposition to the Bolshevik forces in Russia following the downfall of the Empire. The stamps were used in the field postal service established for carrying on communication between the various armies united in the revolt. These armies included the Don Cossacks, the Kuban Cossacks, and also the neighboring southern Russian people in favor of the counter-revolution against the Bolsheviks.

100 Kopecks = 1 Ruble

Prices for used stamps are for canceled to order copies. Postally used specimens sell for considerably more.

Don Government.
(Novocherkassk.)
Rostov Issue.
Russian Stamps of 1909-17 Surcharged **25**

1918   Perf. 14x14½.   Unwmkd.
1   A14   25k on 1k dl org yel   2.00   2.75
   a.   Inverted surcharge   30.00   60.00
2   A14   25k on 2k dl grn   75   1.00
   a.   Inverted surcharge   25.00   55.00
3   A14   25k on 3k car   75   1.25
   a.   Double surcharge   45.00   85.00
4   A15   25k on 4k car   3.00   4.00
   a.   Inverted surcharge   25.00   55.00
5   A14   50k on 7k bl   5.00   7.00

Imperf.

6   A14   25k on 1k org   75   1.00
   a.   Inverted surch.   25.00   60.00
7   A14   25k on 2k gray grn   8.00   11.00
8   A14   25k on 3k red   2.25   3.25
Nos. 1–8 (8)   22.50   31.25
Counterfeits exist of Nos. 1–8.

Ermak, Cossack Leader
A1
Inscription on Back.

1919   Perf. 11½
10   A1   20k green   50.00   75.00
This stamp was available for both postage and currency.

Novocherkassk Issue.
25   **1P.**   **1P.**

Russian stamps with these surcharges are bogus.

Kuban Government.
Ekaterinodar Issues.
Russian Stamps of 1909-17 Surcharged:

—25 —70 к. —1 р.
 d   e   f

—1 р. —3— 10
         рубля рублей
 g   h   i

1918-20 *Perf. 14x14½.* *Unwmkd.*

20	A14 (d)	25k on 1k dl org yel	75	1.00
a.		Inverted surcharge	30.00	40.00
b.		Double surcharge, one inverted	25.00	40.00
21	A14 (d)	50k on 2k dl grn	7.00	9.00
a.		Inverted surcharge	25.00	40.00
b.		Double surcharge	16.00	20.00
		Double surcharge inverted	16.00	20.00
22	A14 (e)	70k on 5k dk cl	1.00	1.25
23	A14 (f)	1r on 3k car	2.25	3.00
a.		Inverted surcharge	17.50	25.00
b.		Double surcharge	8.00	15.00
c.		Pair, one without surcharge	8.00	15.00
24	A14 (g)	1r on 3k car	1.00	1.50
a.		Inverted surcharge	12.00	20.00
b.		Double surcharge	12.00	20.00
c.		Pair, one without surcharge	17.50	20.00
25	A15 (h)	3r on 4k rose	15.00	17.50
b.		Double surcharge	40.00	75.00
c.		Double surcharge	45.00	80.00
		Double surcharge inverted	45.00	80.00
26	A15 (i)	10r on 4k rose	5.00	6.00
a.		10r on 4k car	12.00	20.00
b.		Inverted surcharge	50.00	75.00
27	A11 (i)	10r on 15k red brn & dp bl	1.75	1.50
a.		Surcharged on face and back	20.00	20.00
b.		Double surcharge, one inverted	45.00	90.00
28	A14 (i)	25r on 3k car	3.50	2.50
a.		Inverted surcharge	7.00	15.00
29	A14 (i)	25r on 7k bl	35.00	40.00
a.		Inverted surcharge	60.00	80.00
30	A11 (i)	25r on 14k dk bl & car	75.00	100.00
a.		Inverted surcharge	80.00	110.00
31	A11 (i)	25r on 25k dl grn & dk vio	50.00	65.00
a.		Inverted surcharge	80.00	110.00

Imperf.

35	A14 (d)	25d on 1k org	1.75	3.00
36	A14 (d)	50k on 2k gray grn	35	50
a.		Invtd. surch.	30.00	30.00
b.		Dbl. surch.	30.00	35.00
c.		Pair, one without surcharge	30.00	40.00
37	A14 (e)	70k on 5k cl	3.50	5.00
38	A14 (f)	1r on 3k red	2.25	3.00
a.		Inverted surcharge	20.00	25.00
b.		Double surcharge	11.00	17.50
c.		Pair, one without surcharge	6.00	12.00
39	A14 (g)	1r on 3k red	60	1.00
a.		Double surcharge	11.00	25.00
b.		Pair, one without surch.	11.00	25.00
c.		As "a," invtd.	32.50	60.00
40	A11 (i)	10r on 15k red brn & dp bl	3.50	5.00
41	A14 (i)	25r on 3k red	8.00	5.00
a.		Inverted surcharge	65.00	

Russian Stamps of 1909-17 Surcharged
—70 коп.
 k

1919 *Perf. 14, 14½x15.*

45	A14	70k on 1k dl org yel	2.00	2.00

Imperf.

46	A14	70k on 1k org	2.00	2.00
a.		Inverted surcharge	16.00	22.50
b.		Double surch., one inverted	22.50	30.00

The 1k postal savings stamp with this surcharge inverted is a proof.
Counterfeits exist of Nos. 20-46.

Postal Savings Stamps Surcharged for Postal Use.

A2 Wmk. 171
Wmkd. Diamonds. (171)

1919 *Perf. 14½x15*

47	A2	10r on 1k red, buff	22.50	32.50
a.		Invtd. surch.	110.00	
48	A2	10r on 5k grn, buff	50.00	60.00
a.		Dbl. surch.	165.00	
49	A2	10r on 10k brn, buff	120.00	150.00

Counterfeits exist of Nos. 47-49.

Crimea.
Russian Stamp of 1917 Surcharged
—35 коп.

1919 *Imperf.* *Unwmkd.*

51	A14	35k on 1k org	50	1.50
a.		Comma, instead of period in surch.		1.25

A3
Paper with Buff Network. Inscription on Back.

1919 *Imperf.*

52	A3	50k brown	60.00	60.00

Available for both postage and currency.

Russian Stamps of 1909-17 Surcharged
5 ПЯТЬ рублей.

1920 *Perf. 14x14½.*

53	A14	5r on 5k dk cl	2.25	4.00
a.		Inverted surch.	55.00	
b.		Double surch.	65.00	
54	A8	5r on 20k dl bl & dk car	2.25	4.00
a.		Invtd. surcharge	22.50	
b.		Double surcharge	55.00	
c.		"5" omitted	22.50	

Imperf.

55	A14	5r on 5k cl	2.25	4.00
a.		Double surcharge	22.50	

Same Surcharge on Stamp of Denikin Issue.

57	A5	5r on 35k lt bl	14.00	20.00
a.		Double surcharge	100.00	

A4

1920 *Perf. 14x14½*

58	A4	100r on 1k dl org yel	5.00	
a.		"10" in place of "100"	75.00	
b.		Invtd. surch.	35.00	
c.		Double surch.	75.00	

Imperf.

59	A4	100r on 1k org		4.00

Nos. 53-57 were issued at Sevastopol during the occupation by General Wrangel's army. Nos. 58-59 were prepared but not used.

Denikin Issue.

A5 St. George A6

1919 *Imperf.* *Unwmkd.*

61	A5	5k orange	20	40
62	A5	10k green	20	40
63	A5	15k red	30	60
64	A5	35k lt bl	20	40
65	A5	70k dk bl	20	60
		Tête bêche pair	100.00	
66	A6	1r brn & red	60	85
67	A6	2r gray vio & yel	60	1.25
68	A6	3r dl rose & grn	60	1.25
a.		Perf. 11½	2.00	2.00
69	A6	5r sl & vio	1.25	1.75
a.		Perf. 11½	3.00	3.00
70	A6	7r gray grn & rose	1.75	4.50
71	A6	10r red & gray	1.25	3.50
a.		Perf. 11½		
		Nos. 61-71 (11)	7.15	15.50

Nos. 61-71 were issued at Ekaterinodar and used in all parts of South Russia that were occupied by the People's Volunteer Army under Gen. Anton Ivanovich Denikin. The inscription on the stamps reads "United Russia".

Stamps of type A6 with rosettes instead of numerals in the small circles at the sides are private and fraudulent. So are perforated copies of Nos. 61-67 and 70.

Foreign postal stationery (stamped envelopes, postal cards and air letter sheets) lies beyond the scope of this Catalogue which is limited to adhesive postage stamps.

SPAIN
(spān)

LOCATION—Southwestern Europe, Iberian Peninsula.
GOVT.—Monarchy.
AREA—194,883 sq. mi.
POP.—36,350,000 (est. 1977).
CAPITAL—Madrid.

Spain was a monarchy until 1931, when a republic was set up. After the Civil War (1936-1939), the Spanish State (Estado Español) of Gen. Francisco Franco was recognized. The monarchy was restored in 1975.

32 Maravedis = 8 Cuartos = 1 Real
1000 Milesimas = 100 Centimos = 1 Escudo (1866)
100 Milesimas = 1 Real
4 Reales = 1 Peseta
100 Centimos = 1 Peseta (1872)

> Prices of early Spanish stamps vary according to condition. Quotations for Nos. 1-73 are for fine copies. Very fine to superb specimens sell at much higher prices, and inferior or poor copies sell at reduced prices, depending on the condition of the individual specimen.
> Stamps punched with a small round hole have done telegraph service. In this condition they sell for 5 cents to $1.00 apiece.
> Stamps of 1854 to 1882 cancelled with three parallel horizontal bars are remainders. Most of these are priced through No. 101.

Kingdom.

Queen Isabella II
A1   A2

6 CUARTOS.
Type I. "T" and "O" of CUARTOS separated.
Type II. "T" and "O" joined.

Lithographed.

1850, Jan. 1 *Imperf.* *Unwmkd.*

1	A1	6c blk (II)	300.00	15.00
		Thin paper	400.00	32.50
		6c blk (I)	350.00	17.50
2	A2	12c lilac	2,250.	250.00
a.		Thin paper	3,250.	275.00
3	A2	5r red	1,750.	200.00
4	A2	6r blue	3,000.	800.00
5	A2	10r green	3,250.	1,900.

Stamps of types A2, A3, A4, A6, A7a and A8 are inscribed "FRANCO" on the cuarto values and "CERTIFICADO," "CERTIFO" or "CERT DO" on the reales values.

A3   A4

Typographed.

1851, Jan. 1 Thin Paper

6	A3	6c black	225.00	3.25
a.		Thick paper	500.00	14.00
7	A3	12c lilac	3,000.	190.00
8	A3	2r red	13,500.	6,500.
9	A3	5r rose	2,250.	250.00
		5r red brn (error)	15,000.	7,500.
10	A3	6r blue	3,250.	950.00
a.		Cliché of 2r in plate of 6r	135,000.	110,000.
11	A3	10r green	2,350.	525.00

SPAIN

1852, Jan. 1 — Thick Paper
12	A4	6c rose	265.00	2.75
a.		Thin paper	325.00	4.75
13	A4	12c lilac	1,500.	160.00
a.		12c gray lil	2,100.	210.00
14	A4	2r pale red	12,000.	4,500.
15	A4	5r green	1,650.	150.00
16	A4	6r grnsh bl	2,850.	525.00
a.		6r bl	3,500.	650.00

A5 Arms of Madrid
A6 Queen Isabella II

1853, Jan. 1 — Thin Paper
17	A5	1c bronze	2,100.	575.00
18	A5	3c bronze	11,000.	5,750.
19	A6	6c car rose	325.00	2.00
a.		Thick paper	475.00	13.00
b.		bluish thick paper	650.00	22.50
20	A6	12c red vio	1,650.	135.00
21	A6	2r vermilion	9,000.	2,850.
22	A6	5r lt grn	1,650.	135.00
23	A6	6r dp bl	2,400.	450.00

Nos. 17–18 were issued for use on Madrid city mail only. They were reprinted on thin white paper in duller colors.

A7   A7a   A8
Coat of Arms of Spain

1854 — Thin White Paper.
24	A7	2c green	1,750.	475.00
25	A7a	4c carmine	300.00	2.50
a.		Thick paper	325.00	6.25
		Bar cancellation		7.50
26	A8	6c carmine	275.00	2.00
a.		Thick paper	700.00	17.50
		Bar cancellation		2.00
27	A7a	1r indigo	2,000.	300.00
		Bar cancellation		17.50
28	A7a	2r scarlet	1,250.	130.00
a.		2r ver	1,500.	175.00
		Bar cancellation		7.50
29	A8	5r green	1,250.	130.00
		Bar cancellation		12.50
30	A8	6r blue	1,900.	350.00
		Bar cancellation		17.50

See boxed note on bar cancellation below country heading.

Thick Bluish Paper.
31	A7	2c green	13,000.	2,000.
32	A7a	4c carmine	325.00	6.25
33	A7a	1r pale bl	25,000.	8,500.
		Bar cancellation		200.00
34	A8	2r dl red	5,250.	800.00

The 2c on paper watermarked loops is a proof.

Queen Isabella II
A9

Wmk. 104   Wmk. 105

1855, Apr. 1   Wmkd. Loops. (104)
Blue Paper.
36	A9	2c green	2,500.	130.00
a.		2c yel grn	3,000.	175.00
		Bar cancellation		7.50
37	A9	4c brn red	225.00	1.00
a.		4c car	300.00	2.25
b.		4c lake	300.00	2.25
		Bar cancellation		1.50
38	A9	1r grn bl	900.00	16.00
a.		1r bl	1,000.	19.00
b.		Cliché of 2r in plate of 1r	16,500.	3,000.
		Bar cancellation		4.00
39	A9	2r brn vio	625.00	15.00
a.		2r red vio	850.00	17.50
		Bar cancellation		4.00

Wmkd. Crossed Lines. (105)
1856, Jan. 1
Rough Yellowish Paper.
40	A9	2c green	2,850.	225.00
		Bar cancellation		12.50
41	A9	4c rose	11.00	2.50
		Bar cancellation		1.50
42	A9	1r grnsh bl	2,750.	200.00
a.		1r dl bl	3,500.	265.00
		Bar cancellation		7.50
43	A9	2r brn vio	425.00	15.00
a.		2r redsh vio	525.00	45.00
		Bar cancellation		6.00

1856, Apr. 11   Unwmkd.
White Smooth Paper.
44	A9	2c bl grn	385.00	40.00
a.		2c yel grn	475.00	45.00
		Bar cancellation		6.00
45	A17	4c rose	5.00	45
a.		4c car	55.00	26.00
46	A9	1r blue	21.00	13.00
a.		1r grnsh bl	30.00	20.00
		Bar cancellation		3.00
47	A9	2r dl lil	65.00	22.50
a.		2r dl lil	80.00	30.00
		Bar cancellation		4.00

Three types of No. 45.

1859
48	A9	12c orange	175.00	
		Bar cancellation		35.00

No. 48 was never put in use.

A10   A11

1860-61   Tinted Paper.
49	A10	2c grn, grn	275.00	21.00
		Bar cancellation		2.00
50	A10	4c org, grn	37.50	90
51	A10	12c car, buff	275.00	13.00
		Bar cancellation		4.00
52	A10	19c brn, buff ('61)	2,250.	1,250.
53	A10	1r bl, grn	185.00	11.50
		Bar cancellation		3.50
54	A10	2r lil, lil	240.00	11.00
		Bar cancellation		3.50

1862, July 16
55	A11	2c dp bl, yel	35.00	12.00
56	A11	4c dk brn, redsh buff	2.50	60
a.		4c brn, white	4.75	1.50
57	A11	12c bl, pnksh	45.00	10.00
		Bar cancellation		3.00
58	A11	19c car, lil	175.00	200.00
a.		19c car, white	275.00	285.00
59	A11	1r brn, yel	55.00	25.00
		Bar cancellation		3.50
60	A11	2r grn, pnksh	35.00	14.00
		Bar cancellation		3.00

A12   A13

1864, Jan. 1
61	A12	2c dk bl, lil	40.00	17.50
62	A12	4c rose, redsh buff	2.50	60
		4c car, redsh buff	20.00	
63	A12	12c grn, pnksh	45.00	15.00
64	A12	19c vio, pnksh	200.00	200.00
65	A12	1r brn, grn	175.00	90.00
		Bar cancellation		5.00
66	A12	2r dp bl, pnksh	40.00	13.00
		Bar cancellation		4.00

1865, Jan. 1   Imperf.
67	A13	2c rose	240.00	27.50
68	A13	4c blue	3,000.	
69	A13	12c bl & rose	375.00	22.50
a.		Frame invtd.	10,000.	1,000.
		Bar cancellation		5.00
70	A13	19c brn & rose	1,500.	650.00
		Bar cancellation		75.00
71	A13	1r yel grn	400.00	62.50
		Bar cancellation		10.00
72	A13	2r red lil	375.00	35.00
		Bar cancellation		7.50
73	A13	2r rose	500.00	67.50
a.		2r sal	500.00	75.00
		Bar cancellation		15.00

No. 68 may not have been regularly issued.

1865, Jan. 1   Perf. 14
74	A13	2c rose red	425.00	90.00
		Bar cancellation		10.00
75	A13	4c blue	40.00	1.00
76	A13	12c bl & rose	525.00	55.00
		Bar cancellation		7.50
a.		Frame invtd.	17,500.	2,500.
		As "a," bar cancel		700.00
77	A13	19c brn & rose	3,250.	2,250.
78	A13	1r yel grn	1,500.	400.00
		Bar cancellation		20.00
79	A13	2r violet	1,000.	225.00
		Bar cancellation		15.00
80	A13	2r rose	1,250.	325.00
a.		2r sal	1,250.	325.00
b.		2r dl org		325.00
		Bar cancellation		25.00

A14   A14a

1866, Jan. 1
81	A14	2c rose	225.00	22.50
		Bar cancellation		4.00
82	A14	4c blue	35.00	1.00
83	A14	12c orange	200.00	12.50
a.		12c org yel	275.00	30.00
84	A14	19c brown	850.00	350.00
		Bar cancellation		35.00

1866
85	A14	10c green	265.00	22.50
		Bar cancellation		2.50
86	A14	20c lilac	185.00	21.00
		Bar cancellation		2.50
87	A14a	20c dl lil	725.00	57.50
		Bar cancellation		3.00

A15   A15a

A15b   A15c

1867-68
88	A15	2c yel brn	325.00	32.50
89	A15a	4c blue	27.50	1.00
90	A15b	12c org yel	200.00	7.50
a.		12c dk org	285.00	11.00
b.		12c red org ('68)	900.00	70.00
91	A15c	19c rose	1,250.	400.00
		Bar cancellation		35.00

A15d   A15e

92	A15d	10c lilac	225.00	22.50
		Bar cancellation		2.00
93	A15e	20c lilac	100.00	10.00
		Bar cancellation		2.00

A16   A17

A18   A19

94	A16	5m green	40.00	13.00
		Bar cancellation		2.00
95	A17	10m brown	40.00	11.50
a.		Tête bêche pair	16,000.	5,250.
96	A18	25m bl & rose	225.00	21.00
		Frame inverted		13,500.
		Bar cancellation		5.00
97	A18	50m bis brn	20.00	85

1868-69
98	A18	25m blue	250.00	15.00
		Bar cancellation		3.00
99	A19	50m violet	21.00	65
100	A15b	100m brown	475.00	65.00
		Bar cancellation		2.00
101	A15c	200m green	165.00	11.50
		Bar cancellation		1.50
102	A15c	19c brown	1,900.	500.00

Provisional Government.
Excellent counterfeits exist of the provisional and provincial overprints.

Regular Issues Handstamped in Black

HABILITADO POR LA NACION.

1868-69
116	A15d	10c green	32.50	12.00
117	A15e	20c lilac	25.00	10.00
118	A16	5m green	18.50	6.25
119	A17	10m brown	15.00	5.00
120	A18	25m bl & rose	42.50	15.00
121	A18	25m blue	40.00	12.50
122	A18	50m bis brn	7.50	5.00
123	A19	50m violet	7.50	5.00
124	A15b	100m brown	90.00	30.00
125	A15c	200m green	27.50	10.00
126	A15b	12c orange	45.00	10.00
127	A15c	19c rose	400.00	150.00
128	A15c	19c brown	750.00	200.00

Nos. 116-128 exist with handstamp in blue, a few in red. These sell for more.

For Andalusian Provinces.

Regular Issues Handstamped Vertically in Blue

HABILITADO POR LA NACION.

114a	A15	2c brown	80.00	42.50
115a	A15a	4c blue	37.50	17.00
116a	A15d	10c green	45.00	14.00
117a	A15e	20c lilac	32.50	15.00
118a	A16	5m green	22.50	8.00
119a	A17	10m brown	15.00	6.25
120a	A18	25m bl & rose	47.50	15.00
b.		Frame inverted		
121a	A18	25m blue	45.00	15.00
122a	A18	50m bis brn	10.00	5.50
123a	A19	50m violet	10.00	5.00
124a	A15b	100m brown	75.00	37.50
125a	A15c	200m green	30.00	15.00
126a	A15b	12c orange	55.00	20.00
127a	A15c	19c rose	475.00	250.00
128a	A15c	19c brown	900.00	300.00

SPAIN 551

For Valladolid Province.

Regular Issues Handstamped in Black

HABILITADO POR LA NACION.

(Two types of overprint)

116c	A15d	10c green	47.50	22.50
117c	A15e	20c lilac	42.50	17.50
120c	A18	25m bl & rose	55.00	15.00
121c	A18	25m blue	60.00	20.00
122c	A18	50m bis brn	18.50	10.00
123c	A19	50m violet	18.50	12.00
124c	A15b	100m brown	95.00	42.50
125c	A15c	200m green	45.00	20.00
126c	A15b	12c orange	55.00	22.50
127c	A15c	19c rose	*500.00*	*250.00*
128c	A15c	19c brown	*1,000.*	*350.00*

For Asturias Province.

Regular Issues Handstamped in Black

Habilitado por la Junta Revolucionaria

117d	A15e	20c lilac	200.00	125.00
122d	A18	50m bis brn	200.00	125.00

For Teruel Province.

Regular Issues Handstamped in Black

117e	A15e	20c lilac	130.00	95.00
120e	A18	25m bl & rose	150.00	95.00
122e	A18	50m bis brn	110.00	45.00
123e	A19	50m violet	110.00	45.00
124e	A15b	100m brown	200.00	110.00
125e	A15c	200m green	150.00	57.50
126e	A15b	12c orange	150.00	110.00

For Salamanca Province.

Regular Issues Handstamped in Blue

117f	A15e	20c lilac	130.00	80.00
119f	A17	10m brown	110.00	70.00
122f	A18	50m bis brn	130.00	80.00

Duke de la Torre Regency.

"España"
A20

1870, Jan. 1 Typographed

159	A20	1m brn lil, *buff*	9.00	7.00
a.		1m brn lil, *buff*	11.00	8.00
b.		1m brn lil, *pnksh buff*	11.00	8.00
161	A20	2m *pinkish*	10.00	8.00
a.		2m *buff*	11.50	9.00
163	A20	4m bis brn	17.50	15.00
164	A20	10m rose	21.00	7.50
a.		10m car	25.00	8.00
165	A20	25m gray lil	52.50	10.00
a.		25m lil	50.00	10.00
b.		25m anil vio	85.00	11.00
166	A20	50m ultra	12.50	50
a.		50m dl bl	150.00	7.50
167	A20	100m red brn	32.50	8.00
a.		100m cl	37.50	11.00
b.		100m org brn	37.50	11.00
168	A20	200m pale brn	32.50	8.00
169	A20	400m green	265.00	32.50
170	A20	1e 600m dl lil	1,250.	525.00
171	A20	2e blue	1,000.	300.00
172	A20	12c red brn	250.00	10.00
173	A20	19c yel grn	325.00	210.00

Kingdom.

A21 A22

King Amadeo
A23 A24

1872, Oct. 1 *Imperf.*

174	A21	¼c ultra	3.25	3.25
a.		Complete 1c (block four ¼c)	67.50	47.50

See also No. 221A.

1872–73 *Perf. 14*

176	A22	2c gray lil	25.00	11.00
a.		2c vio	37.50	18.00
b.		Imperf.		85.00
177	A22	5c green	135.00	52.50
a.		Imperf., pair	400.00	
178	A23	5c rose ('73)	25.00	7.50
179	A23	6c blue	135.00	21.00
180	A23	10c brn lil	300.00	120.00
181	A23	10c ultra ('73)	7.50	50
182	A23	12c gray lil	15.00	2.10
183	A23	20c gray vio ('73)	125.00	42.50
184	A23	25c brown	45.00	10.00
185	A23	40c pale red brn	65.00	10.00
186	A23	50c dp grn	100.00	11.00
187	A24	1p lilac	100.00	35.00
188	A24	4p red brn	500.00	325.00
189	A24	10p dp grn	1,750.	135.00

First Republic.

Mural Crown "España"
A25 A26

1873, July 1 *Imperf.*

190	A25	¼c green	1.50	1.25
a.		Complete 1c (block four ¼c)	42.50	21.00

1873, July 1 *Perf. 14*

191	A26	2c orange	16.00	7.50
192	A26	5c claret	37.50	7.50
193	A26	10c green	10.00	50
a.		Tête bêche pair		*24,000.*
194	A26	20c black	85.00	25.00
195	A26	25c dp brn	37.50	10.00
196	A26	40c brn vio	42.50	10.00
197	A26	50c ultra	16.00	10.00
198	A26	1p gray lil	50.00	22.50
199	A26	4p red brn	575.00	350.00
200	A26	10p vio brn	1,850.	1,400.

"Justice" Coat of Arms
A27 A28

1874, July 1

201	A27	2c yellow	26.00	11.50
202	A27	5c violet	37.50	9.50
a.		5c red vio	37.50	12.00
203	A27	10c ultra	12.50	50
a.		Imperf., pair	32.50	
204	A27	20c dk grn	160.00	42.50
205	A27	25c red brn	37.50	9.50
a.		25c lil (error)	300.00	350.00
b.		Imperf., pair		125.00
206	A27	40c violet	400.00	11.00
a.		40c brn (error)	265.00	
b.		Imperf., pair	475.00	
207	A27	50c yellow	110.00	11.00
a.		Imperf., pair	240.00	
208	A27	1p yel grn	80.00	22.50
a.		1p emer	90.00	32.50
b.		Imperf., pair	325.00	
209	A27	4p rose	600.00	325.00
a.		4p car	750.00	425.00
210	A27	10p black	2,250.	1,400.

1874, Oct. 1

211	A28	10c red brn	21.00	1.00
a.		10c brn	21.00	1.00
b.		Imperf., pair	350.00	

Kingdom.

King Alfonso XII
A29

1875, Aug. 1

Blue Framed Numbers on Back, 1 to 100 on Each Sheet.

212	A29	2c org brn	21.00	10.00
a.		2c choc brn	27.50	13.00
b.		Imperf., pair	125.00	125.00
213	A29	5c lilac	62.50	12.50
a.		Imperf., pair	175.00	175.00
214	A29	10c blue	9.50	50
a.		Imperf., pair	50.00	50.00
215	A29	20c brn org	265.00	90.00
216	A29	25c rose	57.50	8.00
217	A29	40c dp brn	110.00	40.00
a.		Imperf., pair	400.00	400.00
218	A29	50c gray lil	150.00	26.00
219	A29	1p black	185.00	52.50
220	A29	4p dk grn	400.00	250.00
221	A29	10p ultra	1,350.	1,100.

1876, June 1 *Imperf.*

221A	A21	¼c green	30	10
b.		Complete 1c (block four ¼c)	1.25	50
c.		Block of four with two ¼c sideways	185.00	185.00
d.		Tête bêche (block 4 with both upper ¼c invtd.)	185.00	185.00
e.		Tête bêche (block 4 with upper left ¼c invtd.)	*1,400.*	*700.00*

King Alfonso XII
A30 A31

Wmk. 178

ONE PESETA:

Type I. Thin figures of value and "PESETA" in thick letters.

Type II. Thick figures of value and "PESETA" in thin letters.

Wmkd. Castle. (178)

1876, June 1 Engr. *Perf. 14*

222	A30	5c yel brn	11.00	2.75
a.		Imperf.	15.00	
223	A30	10c blue	5.00	50
a.		Imperf.	7.50	
224	A30	20c dk grn	21.00	11.00
225	A30	25c brown	10.00	4.00
a.		Imperf.	15.00	
226	A30	40c blk brn	70.00	35.00
227	A30	50c green	16.00	6.00
a.		Imperf.	22.50	
228	A30	1p dp bl, I	21.00	10.00
a.		1p ultra, II	27.50	11.00
b.		Imperf.	30.00	
229	A30	4p brn vio	50.00	38.50
a.		Imperf.	110.00	
230	A30	10p vermilion	130.00	125.00
a.		Imperf.	250.00	

Two plates each were used for the 5c, 10c, 25c, 50c, 1p and 10p. The 1p plates are most easily distinguished.

Typographed.

1878, July 1 *Perf. 14* **Unwmkd.**

232	A31	2c lilac	27.50	10.00
a.		Imperf.	70.00	
233	A31	5c orange	42.50	10.00
234	A31	10c brown	10.00	50
235	A31	20c black	140.00	85.00
a.		Imperf.	300.00	
236	A31	25c ol bis	25.00	3.00
237	A31	40c red brn	160.00	100.00
238	A31	50c bl grn	90.00	10.00
239	A31	1p gray	72.50	22.50
240	A31	4p violet	185.00	110.00
241	A31	10p blue	325.00	325.00
a.		Imperf.	425.00	

A32 A33

1879, May 1

242	A32	2c black	10.00	1.25
243	A32	5c gray grn	12.50	1.25
244	A32	10c rose	11.50	50
245	A32	20c red brn	120.00	13.00
246	A32	25c bluish gray	13.50	50
247	A32	40c brown	27.50	5.50
248	A32	50c dl buff	110.00	5.50
a.		50c yel	150.00	8.50
249	A32	1p brt rose	110.00	2.50
250	A32	4p lil gray	500.00	27.50
251	A32	10p ol bis	1,500.	250.00

1882, Jan. 1

252	A33	15c salmon	9.00	50
a.		15c org	30.00	1.00
253	A33	30c red lil	240.00	6.25
254	A33	75c gray lil	240.00	6.25
a.		Imperf.	37.50	

King Alfonso XIII
A34 A35

1889–99

255	A34	2c bl grn	5.25	50
256	A34	2c blk ('99)	30.00	5.25
257	A34	5c blue	10.00	22
258	A34	5c bl grn ('99)	90.00	1.25
259	A34	10c red brn	15.00	22
260	A34	10c red ('99)	185.00	4.00
261	A34	15c vio brn	4.00	22
262	A34	20c yel grn	35.00	4.00
263	A34	25c blue	13.00	22
264	A34	30c ol gray	55.00	2.75
265	A34	40c brown	55.00	2.25
266	A34	50c rose	55.00	1.00
267	A34	75c orange	140.00	3.25
268	A34	1p dk vio	42.50	50
269	A34	4p car rose	575.00	32.50
270	A34	10p org red	850.00	72.50

The 15c yellow, type A34 is an official stamp listed as No. O9.

Nos. 256–261, 263–264, 266–268 exist imperf.

Control Number on Back

1900-05 **Engraved.** **Unwmkd.**

272	A35	2c bis brn	3.50	25
a.		Imperf.	25.00	

552 SPAIN

273	A35	5c dk grn	7.50	25
a.		Imperf.	30.00	
274	A35	10c rose red	10.00	25
a.		Imperf.	30.00	
275	A35	15c bl blk	16.00	25
a.		Imperf.	70.00	
276	A35	15c dl lil ('02)	10.00	25
a.		Imperf.	27.50	
277	A35	15c pur ('05)	7.50	25
a.		Imperf.	20.00	
278	A35	20c grnsh blk	35.00	1.50
a.		Imperf.	75.00	
279	A35	25c blue	6.50	25
a.		Imperf.	20.00	
b.		25c grn (error)	3,750.	
280	A35	30c bl grn	37.50	50
a.		30c dp grn	37.50	50
b.		Imperf.	70.00	
281	A35	40c ol bis	125.00	5.00
a.		Imperf.	250.00	
282	A35	40c rose ('05)	250.00	2.25
a.		Imperf.	450.00	
283	A35	50c sl bl	40.00	50
a.		Imperf.	90.00	
b.		50c bl grn (error)	1,750.	1,350.
284	A35	1p lake	40.00	50
a.		Imperf.	65.00	
285	A35	4p dk vio	250.00	20.00
a.		Imperf.	400.00	
286	A35	10p brn org	240.00	72.50
a.		Imperf.	350.00	
		Nos. 272-286 (15)	1,071.	104.25

Don Quixote Starts Forth—A36

Designs: 10c, Don Quixote attacks windmill. 15c, Meets country girls. 25c, Sancho Panza tossed in blanket. 30c, Don Quixote knighted. 40c, Tilting at sheep. 50c, On wooden horse. 1p, Adventure with lions. 4p, In bullock cart. 10p, The Enchanted Lady.

Control Number on Back

1905, May 1 **Typographed**

287	A36	5c dk grn	2.25	1.50
a.		Imperf.	40.00	
288	A36	10c org red	4.00	1.50
289	A36	15c violet	4.00	1.50
a.		Imperf.	50.00	
290	A36	25c dk bl	10.00	2.00
291	A36	30c dk bl grn	50.00	7.50
292	A36	40c brt rose	100.00	21.00
293	A36	50c slate	20.00	4.00
294	A36	1p rose red	300.00	80.00
295	A36	4p dk vio	115.00	75.00
296	A36	10p brn org	200.00	120.00
		Nos. 287-296 (10)	805.25	314.00

300th anniversary of the publication of Cervantes' "Don Quixote".

Counterfeits exist of Nos. 287–296.

Six stamps picturing King Alfonso XIII and Queen Victoria Eugenia were issued Oct. 1, 1907, at the Madrid Industrial Exhibition. They were not valid for postage.

King Alfonso XIII

A46 A47

Blue Control Number on Back

1909–22 **Engraved**

Perf. 13x12½, 13, 13½x13, 14.

297	A46	2c dk brn	1.00	5
a.		No control number	1.00	12
298	A46	5c green	2.00	5
299	A46	10c carmine	2.00	5
300	A46	15c violet	10.00	5
301	A46	20c ol grn	55.00	45
302	A46	25c dp bl	5.00	5
303	A46	30c bl grn	10.00	18
304	A46	40c rose	16.00	38
305	A46	50c sl bl	13.00	30
a.		50c bl ('22)	20.00	45
306	A46	1p lake	35.00	30
307	A46	4p dp vio	100.00	7.50
309	A46	10p orange	110.00	16.00
		Nos. 297-309 (12)	359.00	25.36

Nos. 297–309 exist imperforate.

The 5c exists in carmine (price $300); the 15c in blue (price $525); the 4p in lake (price $1,250). The 4p lake is known only with perfin "B.H.A." (Banco Hispano-Americano).

Control Number on Back in Red or Orange.

1917

310	A46	15c yel ocher	5.00	7
a.		Control number in bl	18.00	1.50

Control Number on Back in Blue.

1918

313	A46	40c lt red	150.00	7.50

1920 **Typographed.** ***Imperf.***

314	A47	1c bl grn	50	20

Lithographed.

Perf. 13x12½, 14.

315	A46	2c bister	6.00	20
316	A46	20c violet	60.00	6

Nos. 314–315 have no control number on back.

1921 Engraved.

317	A46	20c violet	50.00	18

Madrid Post Office

A48

1920, Oct. 1 **Typo.** ***Perf. 13½***

Center and Portrait in Black.

318	A48	1c bl grn	75	25
319	A48	2c ol bis	75	25

Control Number on Back

320	A48	5c green	1.50	1.50
321	A48	10c red	1.50	1.00
322	A48	15c yellow	2.25	1.50
323	A48	20c violet	3.00	1.50
324	A48	25c gray bl	3.00	3.00
325	A48	30c dk grn	7.50	5.00
326	A48	40c rose	32.50	7.50
327	A48	50c brt bl	37.50	22.50
328	A48	1p brn red	42.50	20.00
329	A48	4p brn vio	115.00	80.00
330	A48	10p orange	225.00	160.00
		Nos. 318-330 (13)	472.75	304.00

Universal Postal Union Congress, Madrid, Oct. 10–Nov. 30.

Nos. 318–330 exist imperforate. Prices: 3 times those of perforated stamps.

King Alfonso XIII

A49 A49a

FIFTEEN CENTIMOS.
Die I. Narrow "5".
Die II. Wide "5".

TWENTY FIVE CENTIMOS.
Die I. "25" is 2¾mm. high. Vertical stroke of "5" is 1 mm long.
Die II. "25" is 3 mm. high. Vertical stroke of "5" is 1½ mm. long.

Perf. 11 to 14, Compound

1922-26 **Engraved.** **Unwmkd.**

331	A49	2c ol grn	45	5
a.		2c dp org (error)	125.00	150.00

Control Number on Back

332	A49	5c red vio	4.75	5
333	A49	5c claret	2.25	5
334	A49	10c carmine	2.25	1.25
335	A49	10c yel grn	3.00	5
a.		10c bl grn ('23)	5.00	20
336	A49	15c sl bl (I)	9.00	5
a.		15c blk grn (II)	55.00	2.00
337	A49	20c violet	4.50	7
338	A49	25c car (I)	4.50	5
a.		25c rose red (II)	6.75	15
b.		25c lil rose (error)	100.00	125.00
339	A49	30c blk brn ('26)	13.00	30
340	A49	40c dp bl	5.50	7
341	A49	50c orange	21.00	8
a.		50c org red	55.00	3.25
342	A49a	1p bl blk	18.00	8
343	A49a	4p lake	80.00	5.00
344	A49a	10p brown	37.50	11.00
		Nos. 331-344 (14)	205.70	18.15

Nos. 331, 334, 336–344 exist imperf.

The 5c exists in vermilion (price $120); the 25c in dark blue (price $180). The 50c exists in red brown, the 4p in brown and 10p in lake; price, each $125. These five were not regularly issued.

"Santa Maria" and View of Seville

A50

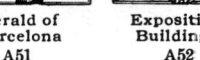

Herald of Barcelona **Exposition Buildings**

A51 A52

King Alfonso XIII and View of Barcelona—A53

1929, Feb. 15 ***Perf. 11***

345	A50	1c grnsh bl	35	35
346	A51	2c pale yel grn	35	35
347	A52	5c rose lake	65	65

Control Number on Back

348	A53	10c green	1.00	75
349	A50	15c Prus bl	65	35
350	A51	20c purple	1.00	75
351	A50	25c brt rose	1.00	75
352	A52	30c blk brn	5.00	4.00
353	A53	40c dk bl	6.75	5.00
354	A51	50c dp org	5.00	4.00
355	A52	1p bl blk	10.00	7.50
356	A53	4p dp rose	30.00	25.00
357	A53	10p brown	67.50	50.00
		Nos. 345-357, E2 (14)		

Perf. 14

345a	A50	1c grnsh bl	50	45
348a	A53	10c green	22.50	22.50
350a	A51	20c purple	27.50	27.50
351a	A50	25c brt rose	32.50	32.50
352a	A52	30c blk brn	32.50	32.50
353a	A53	40c dk bl	70.00	70.00
354a	A51	50c dp org	32.50	32.50
355a	A52	1p bl blk	32.50	32.50
356a	A53	4p dp rose	32.50	32.50
357a	A53	10p brown	125.00	125.00
		Nos. 345a-357a, E2a (11)		

Seville and Barcelona Exhibitions.

Nos 345–357 exist imperf. Prices about 6 times those of perf. stamps.

See note after No. 432.

Stamps of 1920-26 Overprinted in Red or Blue

Sociedad de las Naciones LV reunión del Consejo Madrid.

1929, June 10 ***Imperf.***

358	A47	1c bl grn	60	50

Perf. 13½x12½.

359	A49	2c ol grn	60	50
360	A49	5c cl (Bl)	60	50
361	A49	10c yel grn	60	50
362	A49	15c sl bl	60	50
363	A49	20c violet	60	50
364	A49	25c car (Bl)	45	35
365	A49	30c blk brn	2.75	1.75
366	A49	40c dp bl	2.75	1.75
367	A49	50c org (Bl)	2.75	1.75
368	A49a	1p bl blk	13.00	11.00
369	A49a	4p lake (Bl)	13.00	11.00
370	A49a	10p brn (Bl)	45.00	40.00
		Nos. 358-370, E4 (14)	97.30	84.60

55th assembly of League of Nations at Madrid June 10–16. The stamps were available for postal use only on those days.

Exposition Building

A54

1930 **Lithographed.** ***Perf. 11.***

371	A54	5c dk bl & sal	7.50	6.25
372	A54	5c dk vio & bl	7.50	6.25

Barcelona Philatelic Congress and Exhibition. "C. F. y E. F." are the initials of "Congreso Filatelico y Exposicion Filatelica". For each admission ticket, costing 2.75 pesetas, the holder was allowed to buy one of each of these stamps.

Locomotives

A55 A56

1930, May 10 ***Perf. 14***

373	A55	1c lt bl	50	45
374	A55	2c ap grn	50	45

Control Number on Back

375	A55	5c lake	50	45
376	A55	10c yel grn	50	45
377	A55	15c bluish gray	50	45
378	A55	20c purple	50	45
379	A55	25c brt rose	35	25
380	A55	30c ol gray	2.00	1.25
381	A55	40c dk bl	1.75	1.40
382	A55	50c dl org	4.00	3.00
383	A56	1p dk gray	5.25	4.50
384	A56	4p dp rose	60.00	52.50
385	A56	10p bis brn	350.00	300.00
		Nos. 373-385, E6 (14)	481.35	418.10

11th International Railway Congress, Madrid, 1930.

These stamps were on sale May 10–21, 1930, exclusively at the Palace of the Senate in Madrid and at the Barcelona and Seville expositions.

See Nos. C12–17, E6.

SPAIN

Francisco de Goya at 80
("1746 1828") A57   ("1828 1928") A59

"La Maja Desnuda"
A58

1930, June 15   Litho.   Perf. 12½
Inscribed "Correos Espana"

386	A57	1c yellow	10	10
387	A57	2c bis brn	10	10
388	A57	5c lil rose	10	10
389	A57	10c green	30	18

Engraved.

390	A57	15c lt bl	20	15
391	A57	20c brn vio	20	15
392	A57	25c red	20	15
393	A57	30c brown	6.75	5.50
394	A57	40c dk bl	6.75	5.50
395	A57	50c vermilion	6.75	5.50
396	A57	1p black	9.00	6.50
397	A58	1p dk vio	1.25	1.00
398	A58	4p sl gray	90	75
399	A58	10p red brn	18.00	15.00

Inscribed "1828 Goya 1928"
Lithographed

400	A59	2c ol grn	10	10
401	A59	5c gray vio	10	10

Engraved.

402	A59	25c rose car	50	50
		Nos. 386-402, E7 (18)	51.70	41.73

Nos. 386–402 commemorate the death of Francisco de Goya y Lucientes, painter and engraver.
Nos. 386–399 were issued in connection with the Spanish-American Exposition at Seville.
Nos. 386–402 exist imperf. Prices about 6 times those of perf. stamps.
See also Nos. C18–C30, CE1.
See note after No. 432.

King Alfonso XIII
A61

Two types of the 40c:

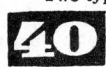
Type I   Type II

1930   Perf. 11½, 12 x 11½

406	A61	2c red brn	30	5

Control Number on Back

407	A61	5c blk brn	9.00	5
408	A61	10c green	4.50	5
409	A61	15c sl grn	15.00	5
410	A61	20c dk vio	6.00	75
411	A61	25c carmine	90	5
412	A61	30c brn lake	16.00	1.50
413	A61	40c dk bl (I)	25.00	1.25
a.		Type II	32.50	1.25
414	A61	50c orange	25.00	1.85
		Nos. 406-414 (9)	93.60	5.60

Nos. 406–414 exist imperf. Price for set, $325.

Bow of "Santa Maria"
A63

Stern of "Santa Maria"
A64

"Santa Maria," "Niña," "Pinta"
A65

Columbus Leaving Palos—A66

Columbus Arriving in America
A67

1930, Sept. 29   Litho.   Perf. 12½

418	A63	1c ol gray	20	15
419	A64	2c ol grn	20	15
420	A63	2c ol grn	20	15
421	A64	5c red brn	20	15
422	A63	5c red brn	20	15
423	A64	10c bl grn	1.00	75
424	A64	15c ultra	1.00	75
425	A64	20c violet	1.25	1.10

Engraved.

426	A65	25c dk red	1.25	1.10
427	A66	30c bis brn, bl & blk brn	5.75	5.50
428	A65	40c ultra	4.75	3.25
429	A66	50c dk vio, bl & vio brn	5.75	5.50
430	A65	1p black	5.75	5.50
431	A67	4p blk & dk bl	6.00	5.50
432	A67	10p red brn & dk brn	30.00	30.00
		Nos. 418-432, E8 (16)	65.20	61.10

Christopher Columbus tribute.
Nos. 418 to 432 were privately produced. Their promoters presented a certain quantity of these labels to the Spanish Postal Authorities, who placed them on sale and allowed them to be used for three days, retaining the money obtained from the sale.
This note will also apply to Nos. 345–357, 386–402, 433–448, 557–571, B1–B105, C18–C57, C73–C87, CB1–CB5, CE1, E2, E7–E9, E15 and EB1.
Many so-called "errors" of color and perforation are known.
Nos. 418–432 exist imperf. Prices about 5 times those of perf. stamps.

Arms of Spain, Bolivia, Paraguay—A68

Pavilion and Map of Central America A69   Exhibition Pavilion of Ecuador A70

Colombia Pavilion—A71

Dominican Republic Pavilion—A72

Uruguay Pavilion—A73

Argentina Pavilion—A74

Chile Pavilion—A75

Brazil Pavilion—A76

Mexico Pavilion—A77

Cuba Pavilion—A78

Peru Pavilion—A79

U.S. Pavilion—A80

553

SPAIN

Exhibition Pavilion of Portugal
A81

King Alfonso XIII and Queen Victoria
A82

Photogravure.
1930, Oct. 10 *Perf. 14* Unwmkd.

433	A68	1c bl grn	30	35
434	A69	2c bis brn	30	35
435	A70	5c ol grn	30	35
436	A71	10c dk grn	60	38
437	A72	15c indigo	60	38
438	A73	20c violet	60	38
439	A74	25c car rose	60	38
440	A75	25c car rose	60	38
441	A76	30c rose lil	2.00	2.00
442	A77	40c sl bl	1.10	1.50
443	A78	40c sl bl	1.10	1.50
444	A79	50c brn org	2.00	2.25
445	A80	1p ultra	3.00	3.25
446	A81	4p brn vio	15.00	13.00
447	A82	10p brown	2.00	2.00

Engraved.
Perf. 11, 14.

448	A82	10p org brn	42.50	30.00
		Nos. 433-448, E9 (17)	72.95	59.70

Spanish-American Union Exhibition, Seville. See Nos. C50–C57.
The note after No. 432 will also apply to Nos. 433 to 448. All values exist imperforate.
Reprints of Nos. 433–448 have blurred colors, yellowish paper and an inferior, almost invisible gum. They sell for 5c to 10c each.

Revolutionary Issues.
Madrid Issue.
Regular Issues of 1920-30
Overprinted
in Black, Green
or Red   REPUBLICA
On No. 314

1931 *Imperf.*

449	A47	1c bl grn	15	15

On Nos. 406–411
Perf. 11½.

450	A61	2c red brn (G)	35	35
451	A61	5c blk brn (R)	35	35
452	A61	10c green	70	70
453	A61	15c sl grn (R)	1.50	1.50
454	A61	20c dk vio (R)	1.50	1.50
455	A61	25c car (G)	2.00	2.00
		Nos. 449-455 (7)	6.55	6.55

First Barcelona Issue.
Regular Issues of 1920-30
Overprinted in
Black or Red   REPUBLICA
On No. 314

1931 *Imperf.*

457	A47	1c bl grn	15	15

On Nos. 406–414
Perf. 11½.

458	A61	2c red brn	15	15
459	A61	5c blk brn	15	15
460	A61	10c green	60	60
461	A61	15c sl grn (R)	75	75
462	A61	20c dk vio (R)	75	75
463	A61	25c carmine	75	75
464	A61	30c brn lake	5.75	5.75
465	A61	40c dk bl (R)	1.50	1.50
466	A61	50c orange	1.50	1.50

On Stamp of 1922-26.

467	A49a	1p bl blk (R)	9.00	9.00
		Nos. 457-467 (11)	21.05	21.05

Nos. 457 to 467 are known both with and without accent over "U".

Second Barcelona Issue.
Regular Issues
of 1920-30
Overprinted in
Black or Red   REPUBLICA

On No. 314
Imperf.

468	A47	1c bl grn	15	15

On Nos. 406–414
Perf. 11½.

469	A61	2c red brn	15	15
470	A61	5c blk brn (R)	30	30
471	A61	10c green	30	30
472	A61	15c sl grn (R)	1.50	1.50
473	A61	20c dk vio (R)	40	40
474	A61	25c carmine	40	40
475	A61	30c brn lake	8.00	8.00
476	A61	40c dk bl (R)	1.50	1.50
477	A61	50c orange	7.25	7.25
		Nos. 468-477 (10)	19.95	19.95

General Issue of the Republic.
Nos. 406–414, 342
Overprinted in
Blue or Red   República Española.

1931, May 27

478	A61	2c red brn	30	5
479	A61	5c blk brn (R)	45	5
480	A61	10c grn (R)	45	5
481	A61	15c sl grn (R)	4.00	22
482	A61	20c dk vio (R)	2.00	75
483	A61	25c carmine	30	8
484	A61	30c brn lake	6.00	1.20
485	A61	40c dk bl (R)	6.00	75
486	A61	50c orange	11.00	75
487	A49a	1p bl blk (R)	62.50	1.25
		Nos. 478-487 (10)	93.00	5.15

The setting contained 18 repetitions of "Republica Española" for each vertical row of 10 stamps. According to its sheet position, a stamp received different parts of the overprinted words.
Overprint position varieties include: reading down on 25c, 30c, 40c and 50c; double on 1p; double, both reading down, on 25c, 40c and 50c.

Fountain of Lions, The Alhambra, Granada
A84

Interior of Mosque, Córdoba
A85

Alcántara Bridge and Alcazar, Toledo
A86

Francisco García y Santos
A87

Puerta del Sol, Madrid, on April 14, 1931 as Republic Was Proclaimed
A88

Engraved
1931, Oct. 10 *Perf. 12½* Unwmkd.

491	A84	5c vio brn	15	12
492	A85	10c bl grn	50	45
493	A86	15c dk vio	50	45
494	A85	25c dp red	50	45
495	A87	30c ol grn	50	45
496	A85	40c indigo	1.10	80
497	A85	50c org red	1.10	80
498	A86	1p black	2.00	1.75
499	A88	4p red vio	10.00	8.00
500	A88	10p red brn	32.50	27.50
		Nos. 491-500 (10)	48.85	40.77

Third Pan-American Postal Union Congress, Madrid. See Nos. C62–C67, CO1–CO6.
Nos. 491-500 exist imperforate. Prices about 5 times those of perforated stamps.

Symbolical of Montserrat Cut With a Saw
A89

Abbott Oliva and Monastery Workman
A90

"Black Virgin"
A91

A92

Montserrat Monastery
A93

1931, Dec. 9 *Perf. 11, 14*

501	A89	1c myr grn	2.25	2.00
a.	A89	Perf. 14	26.00	26.00
502	A89	2c red brn	1.10	90
a.		Perf. 14	20.00	20.00

Control Number on Back

503	A89	5c blk brn	1.40	1.10
a.		Perf. 14	20.00	20.00
504	A89	10c yel grn	1.40	1.10
a.		Perf. 14	20.00	20.00
505	A90	15c myr grn	2.00	1.40
a.		Perf. 14	26.00	25.00
506	A91	20c dk vio	4.00	3.00
a.		Perf. 11	165.00	165.00
507	A92	25c lake	5.50	4.50
a.		Perf. 14	8.00	8.00
508	A91	30c dp red	57.50	50.00
a.		Perf. 14	52.50	52.50
509	A93	40c dl bl	32.50	22.50
a.		Perf. 11	225.00	225.00
510	A90	50c dk org	70.00	57.50
a.		Perf. 14	95.00	95.00
511	A92	1p gray blk	70.00	57.50
a.		Perf. 11	135.00	135.00
512	A93	4p lil rose	600.00	500.00
a.		Perf. 14	1,000.	1,000.
513	A92	10p dp brn	500.00	525.00
a.		Perf. 14	925.00	925.00
		Nos. 501-513, E13 (14)	1,376.15	1,255.

Commemorative of the building of the old Monastery at Montserrat, started in 1031, and of the image of the Black Virgin (said to have been carved by St. Luke) which was crowned by Pope Leo XIII in 1881.
Nos. 501-513 exist imperforate. Prices about 3 times those of perforated stamps.
See Nos. C68–C72.

Francisco Pi y Margall
A95

Joaquín Costa
A96

Nicolás Salmerón
A97

Pablo Iglesias
A99

Emilio Castelar
A100

1931-32 *Perf. 11½.*

Control Number on Back

516	A95	5c brnsh blk	3.50	25
517	A96	10c yel grn	7.50	25
518	A97	15c sl grn	5.75	10
520	A99	25c lake	27.50	60
b.		Imperf.	60.00	
521	A99	30c car rose	9.00	6
c.		Imperf.	60.00	
522	A100	40c dk bl	50.00	3.50
523	A97	50c orange	60.00	6.50
		Nos. 516-523 (7)	163.25	11.26

See Nos. 532, 538, 550, 579, 579a.

Without Control Number

516a	A95	5c brnsh blk ('32)	6.25	8
b.		Imperf.	11.00	

SPAIN 555

517a	A96	10c	yel grn ('32)	5.75	8
b.			Imperf.	15.00	
518a	A97	15c	sl grn ('32)	90	6
b.			Imperf.	8.50	
520a	A99	25c	lake	45.00	10
c.			Imperf.	90.00	
521a	A99	30c	car rose	2.50	15
b.			Imperf.	8.50	
522a	A100	40c	dk bl ('32)	12	12
b.			Imperf.	16.00	
523a	A97	50c	org ('32)	37.50	50
b.			Imperf.	100.00	
			Nos. 516a-523a (7)	98.02	1.09

Blasco Ibáñez
A103

Manuel Ruiz-Zorrilla
A104

Without Control Number

1931–34 ***Perf. 11½***

526	A103	2c	red brn ('32)	12	5
a.			Imperf.	15.00	
528	A103	5c	choc ('34)	10	10
a.			Imperf.	3.50	
532	A95	20c	dk vio	40	8
a.			Imperf.	8.50	
534	A104	25c	lake ('34)	1.00	5
a.			Imperf.	3.00	
538	A100	60c	ap grn ('32)	12	12
a.			Imperf.	8.50	
			Nos. 526-538 (5)	1.74	40

Cliff Houses, Cuenca
A105

Alcázar of Segovia
A106

Gate of the Sun at Toledo
A107

1932–38 ***Perf. 10***

539	A105	1p	gray blk ('38)	12	10
a.			Imperf.	7.00	7.00
b.			Perf. 11½	25	15
540	A106	4p	mag ('38)	45	40
a.			Imperf.	12.00	12.00
b.			Perf. 11½	1.00	1.00
541	A107	10p	dp brn ('38)	75	70
a.			Perf. 11½	2.75	2.75
b.			Imperf.	8.50	8.50

Numeral
A108

Santiago Ramón y Cajal
A109

Typographed.

1933 ***Imperf.*** **Unwmkd.**

542	A108	1c	bl grn	10	10

Perf. 11½.

543	A108	2c	buff	35	10
a.			Perf. 13½x13	75	18

See also Nos. 592–597.

1934 **Engraved.** ***Perf. 11½ x11.***

545	A109	30c	blk brn	10.00	75
a.			Perf. 14	30.00	32.50
b.			Imperf.	40.00	

Type of 1931 and

Mariana Pineda
A110

Concepción Arenal
A111

Gumersindo de Azcarate
A112

Gaspar Melchor de Jovellanos
A113

1935

546	A110	10c	green	16	6
a.			Imperf.	2.00	
547	A111	15c	green	80	10
a.			Imperf.	3.50	
548	A112	30c	car rose	11.00	25
a.			Imperf.	37.50	
549	A113	30c	rose red	8	8
a.			Imperf.	2.00	
550	A97	50c	dk bl	1.50	50
a.			Imperf.	60.00	
			Nos. 546-550 (5)	13.54	99

Shades exist.

Lope's Bookplate
A116

Lope de Vega
A117

Alcántara and Alcázar, Toledo
A118

Perf. 11½x11, 11x11½

1935, Oct. 12

552	A116	15c	myr grn	9.00	35
a.			Imperf.	225.00	
553	A117	30c	rose red	3.50	25
a.			Imperf.	11.50	
b.			Perf. 14	10.00	10.00
554	A117	50c	dk bl	18.00	2.75
a.			Imperf.	60.00	
b.			Perf. 14	40.00	40.00
555	A118	1p	bl blk	30.00	2.00
a.			Imperf.	47.50	
b.			Perf. 14	40.00	40.00

Issued in commemoration of the 300th anniversary of the death of Lope Felix de Vega Carpio (1562–1635), Spanish dramatist and poet.

Map of Amazon by Bartolomeo Oliva, 16th Century
A119

1935, Oct. 12 ***Perf. 11½***

556	A119	30c	rose red	3.00	1.00
a.			Perf. 14	26.00	26.00
b.			Imperf.	35.00	

Issued in commemoration of the proposed Iglesias Amazon Expedition.

Miguel Moya
A120

Torcuato Luca de Tena
A121

José Francos Rodríguez
A122

Alejandro Lerroux
A123

Nazareth School and Rotary Press
A124

1936, Feb. 14 **Photo.** ***Perf. 12½***

Size: 22x26mm.

557	A120	1c	crimson	10	10
558	A121	2c	org brn	10	10
559	A122	5c	blk brn	10	10
560	A123	10c	emerald	10	10

Size: 24x28½mm.

561	A120	15c	bl grn	20	10
562	A121	20c	violet	20	10
563	A122	25c	red vio	20	10
564	A123	30c	crimson	10	10

Size: 25½x30½mm.

565	A120	40c	orange	65	12
566	A121	50c	ultra	35	12
567	A122	60c	ol grn	70	18
568	A123	1p	gray blk	70	18
569	A124	2p	lt bl	9.50	3.00
570	A124	4p	lil rose	9.50	5.00
571	A124	10p	red brn	24.00	12.50
			Nos. 557-571,E15 (16)	46.90	22.25

Madrid Press Association, 40th anniversary.

Nos. 557–571 exist imperf. Prices about 7 times those of perf. stamps.

See note after No. 432. See Nos. C73–C87.

Arms of Madrid
A125

1936, Apr. 2 **Engr.** ***Imperf.***

572	A125	10c	brn blk	52.50	52.50
573	A125	15c	dk grn	52.50	52.50

Issued in commemoration of the first National Philatelic Exhibition which opened in Madrid, April 2nd, 1936.

"Republica Espanola"
A126

Gregorio Fernández
A127

1936 **Litho.** ***Perf: 11½, 13½x13***

574	A126	2c	org brn	10	5

1936, Mar. 10 **Engr.** ***Perf. 11½***

576	A127	30c	carmine	1.75	1.00
a.			Perf. 14	13.00	13.00
b.			Imperf.	20.00	

Issued to commemorate the tercentenary of the death of Gregorio Fernandez, sculptor.

Type of 1931 and

Pablo Iglesias
A128 A129

Velázquez
A130

Fermín Salvoechea
A131

1936-38 ***Perf. 11, 11½, 11½x11.***

577	A128	30c	rose red	10	7
578	A129	30c	car rose	1.75	50
579	A100	40c	car rose ('37)	1.75	50
580	A129	45c	car ('37)	15	10
581	A130	50c	dk bl	15	6
582	A131	60c	ind ('37)	1.10	1.00
583	A131	60c	dp org ('38)	7.25	6.00
			Nos. 577-583 (7)	12.25	8.23

Perf. 14

577a	A128	30c	rose red	10.00	
578a	A129	30c	car rose	10.00	
579a	A100	40c	car rose	9.00	
580a	A129	45c	carmine	9.00	
582a	A131	60c	indigo	9.00	
583a	A131	60c	dp org	14.00	
			Nos. 577a-583a (6)	61.00	

Nos. 577–583 exist imperf. Price, set $70.

Statue of Liberty, Spanish and U.S. Flags—A132

1938, June 1 **Photo.** ***Perf. 11½***

585	A132	1p	multi	17.50	17.50
a.			Imperf., pair	100.00	100.00
b.			Imperf.vert., pair	110.00	110.00
c.			Souv. sheet of 1	30.00	30.00
d.			As "c," imperf.	250.00	250.00

Issued in commemoration of the 150th anniversary of the Constitution of the United States of America.

Nos. 585c, 585d have control numbers on front. Size: 102x104mm.

556 SPAIN

No. 289 Surcharged in Black

**14 ABRIL 1938
VII Aniversario de la República
45 cts.**

1938   Perf. 14.
586   A36   45c on 15c vio   17.50   17.50
7th anniversary of the Republic.

No. 289 Surcharged in Black:

a

**Fiesta del Trabajo
1 MAYO
1938
1 Peseta**
b

1938, May 1
587   A36   45c on 15c vio   4.00   4.00
588   A36   1p on 15c vio   6.50   6.50
Issued to commemorate Labor Day.

No. 507 Surcharged in Black

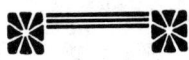

1938, Nov. 10   Perf. 11½
589   A92   2.50p on 25c lake   20   25
b.   Perf. 14   5.75   5.75

Types of 1933-36 Surcharged in Blue or Red

45 céntimos.

1938

Perf. 10, 11, 13½x13, 13x14.
590   A108   45c on 1c grn (R)   85   50
b.   Imperf.   7.50
590A   A108   45c on 2c buff (Bl)   20.00   20.00
591   A126   45c on 2c org brn (Bl)   15   5

Numeral Type of 1933.
1938-39   Litho.   Perf. 11½, 13
White or Gray Paper.
592   A108   5c gray brn   10   6
593   A108   10c yel grn   10   6
594   A108   15c sl grn   10   6
595   A108   20c vio, gray paper   10   6
596   A108   25c red vio   10   6
597   A108   30c scarlet   10   6
Nos. 592-597 (6)   60   36

"Republic"
A133

1938   Perf. 11½
598   A133   40c rose red   10   5
599   A133   45c car rose   10   5
a.   Printed on both sides   15.00   15.00
600   A133   50c ultra   10   5
601   A133   60c dp ultra   60   45
Nos. 598-601 exist imperf. Price for set $16.50.

Machine Gunners
A134

Infantry—A135

Perf. 11½x11, 11x11½, Imperf.
1938, Sept. 1   Photogravure
602   A134   25c dk grn   11.50   11.50
603   A135   45c red brn   11.50   11.50
Issued in commemoration of the 43rd Division of the Republican Army. Sold only at the Philatelic Agency and for foreign exchange.

Blast Furnace
A136

Steel Mill and Sculpture, "Defenders of Numantia"
A137

1938, Aug. 9   Perf. 16
604   A136   45c black   20   25
605   A137   1.25p dk bl   20   25
Issued in honor of the workers of Sagunto.

'Correo Submarino'
A set of six stamps and souvenir sheet inscribed "Correo Submarino" was issued Aug. 11, 1938. It was sold at double face value and only at the Philatelic Agency. The stamps and sheet were used on 300 agency-prepared covers carried on a single submarine voyage from Barcelona to Mahon, Minorca. Price for set of six, $1,000; souvenir sheet, $800.

Riflemen
A138

Machine Gunners
A139

Bomb Throwing
A140

1938, Nov. 25   Engr.   Perf. 10
606   A138   5c sepia   4.50   4.00
607   A138   10c dp vio   4.50   4.00
608   A138   25c bl grn   4.50   4.00
609   A139   45c rose red   4.50   4.00
610   A139   60c dk bl   8.00   6.75
611   A139   1.20p black   165.00   150.00
612   A140   2p orange   50.00   47.50
613   A140   5p dk brn   275.00   225.00
614   A140   10p dk bl grn   55.00   47.50
Nos. 606-614 (9)   571.00   492.75
Issued in honor of the Militia. Sold only at the Philatelic Agency and for foreign exchange. Exist imperf.

Spanish State.

Arms of Spain—A141

1936   Litho.   Imperf.
Thin Transparent Paper.
615   A141   30c blue   325.00
616   A141   30c pale grn   325.00

Perf. 11.
Thick Wove Paper.
617   A141   30c dk bl   750.00   125.00
Issued in Granada during siege. After the city was liberated, these stamps were used throughout the province of Granada.

A143

Cathedral of Burgos
A145

"La Giralda," Seville
A148

University of Salamanca
A146

Cathedral del Pilar, Zaragoza
A147

Xavier Castle, Navarre
A149

Court of Lions, Alhambra at Granada
A150

Mosque, Córdoba
A151

Alcántara Bridge and Alcázar, Toledo
A152

Soldier Carrying Flag
A153

Troops Landing at Algeciras
A154

Two types of 30c:
Type I: Imprint 12 mm. long; "3" does not touch frame.
Type II: Imprint 8 mm. long; "3" touches frame.

Lithographed.
1936   Imperf.   Unwmkd.
623   A143   1c green   7.50   7.50

Perf. 11½.
624   A143   2c org brn   1.00   75
625   A145   5c gray brn   1.00   1.00
626   A146   10c green   1.00   50
627   A147   15c dl grn   1.00   50
628   A148   25c rose lake   1.20   50
629   A149   30c car (I)   1.50   1.00
a.   Type II   1.75   1.25
630   A150   50c dp bl   20.00   15.00
631   A151   60c yel grn   1.50   1.00
632   A152   1p black   8.00   4.00
633   A153   4p rose vio, red & yel   70.00   45.00
634   A154   10p lt brn   75.00   37.50
Nos. 623-634 (12)   188.70   114.25

Nos. 624-634 exist imperf. Price, set $375.
Nos. 625-631, 633-634 were privately overprinted "VIA AEREA" and plane, supposedly for use in Ifni.

Nos. 542-543 Surcharged "Habilitado 0'05 ptas." in Two Lines.
1936   Imperf., Perf. 11½.
634A   A108   5c on 1c bl grn   4.25   4.25
634B   A108   5c on 2c buff   4.25   4.25
634C   A108   10c on 1c bl grn   4.25   4.25
634D   A108   15c on 2c buff   4.25   4.25
Issued in the Balearic Islands to meet a shortage of these values. Nos. 634A and 634C are imperf., Nos. 634B and 634D are perf. 11½.

St. James of Compostela
A155

St. James Cathedral
A156

SPAIN

Pórtico de la Gloria
A157

Two types of 30c:
 I. No dots in "1937".
 II. Dot before and after "1937".

1937		Perf. 11½, 11x11½		
635	A155	15c vio brn	1.80	2.00
636	A156	30c rose red (I)	6.00	75
a.		Type II	12.00	11.00
637	A157	1p bl & org	18.00	4.00
a.		Center invtd.	475.00	250.00

Holy Year of Compostela.
Nos. 635–637 exist imperf. Price for set $140.

"Estado Espanol"
A159   A160

"El Cid"   Queen Isabella I
A161   A162

Two types of 5c, 30c and 10p:
 5 Centimos.
 Type I Imprint 9½ mm. long.
 Type II Imprint 14 mm. long.
 30 Centimos.
 Type I Imprint, "Hija De B. Fournier Burgos".
 Type II Imprint, "Fournier Burgos".
 10 Pesetas.
 Type I "10" 2½ mm. high.
 Type II "10" 3 mm. high.

With Imprint

1936-40			Imperf.	
638	A159	1c green	10	5

Perf. 11.

| 639 | A159 | 1c green | 10 | 10 |
| 640 | A160 | 2c brown | 10 | 5 |

Perf. 11, 11½, 11½x11, 11½x10½.

641	A161	5c brn (I)	75	15
642	A161	5c brn (II)	20	5
643	A161	10c green	12	5

Perf. 11, 11x11½.

644	A162	15c gray blk	25	5
645	A162	20c dk vio	45	12
646	A162	25c brn lake	35	5
647	A162	30c rose (I)	60	5
648	A162	30c rose (II)	21.00	3.00
649	A162	40c orange	2.50	12
650	A162	50c dk bl	2.50	12
651	A162	60c yellow	40	12
652	A162	1p blue	21.00	50
653	A162	4p magenta	27.50	6.50
654	A161	10p dk bl (I) ('37)	90.00	45.00
655	A161	10p dp bl (II) ('40)	37.50	67.50
		Nos. 638-655 (18)	205.42	123.58

No. 639 is said to have been privately perforated. See also Nos. 662–667.

A particular stamp may be scarce, but if few want it, its market potential may remain relatively low.

Ferdinand   Emblem
the Catholic   of the Falange
A163   A164

1938   **Perf. 10½, 11½x11**

Imprint: "Lit Fournier Vitoria".

| 656 | A163 | 15c dp grn | 3.00 | 10 |
| 657 | A163 | 30c dp red | 6.50 | 10 |

Imprint: "Fournier Vitoria".

Perf. 10

658	A163	15c dp grn	2.00	7
659	A163	20c purple	12.50	2.25
660	A163	25c brn car	1.00	7
661	A163	30c dp red	6.00	7
		Nos. 656–661 (6)	31.00	2.66

Nos. 656–661 exist imperf.; price for set, $60. Part-perf. varieties exist.

Without Imprint.

1938-48   **Perf. 11, 13½**

Two types of the 15 Centimos.
 Type I. Medieval style numerals with diagonal line through "5".
 Type II. Modern numerals. Narrower "5" without diagonal line.

662	A159	1c green, Imperf.	12	12
663	A160	2c brn (size 18½ x 22mm) ('40)	12	12
a.		2c bis brn (size 17½ x 21 mm) ('48)	12	12
664	A161	5c gray brn ('39)	30	12
665	A161	10c dk car	45	12
a.		10c rose	1.10	15
666	A161	15c dk grn (I)	1.50	12
666A	A161	15c dk grn (II)	1.50	12
667	A162	70c dk bl ('39)	90	18
		Nos. 662–667 (7)	4.89	90

1938, July 17   **Perf. 10**

668	A164	15c bl grn & lt grn	6.50	5.50
669	A164	25c rose red & rose	6.50	5.50
670	A164	30c bl & lt bl	3.00	2.50
671	A164	1p brn & yel	110.00	85.00

Second anniversary of the Civil War.

Queen   General
Isabella I   Francisco Franco
A165   A166

1938-39   **Lithographed**   **Perf. 10**

672	A165	20c brt vio ('39)	1.00	25
673	A165	25c brn car	10.00	90
674	A165	30c rose red	65	25
675	A165	40c dl vio	65	6
676	A165	50c ind ('39)	37.50	4.00
677	A165	1p dp bl	12.00	1.25
		Nos. 672–677 (6)	61.80	6.71

Imprint: "Sanchez Toda".

1939-40   **Perf. 10.**

678	A166	20c brt vio	50	8
679	A166	25c rose lake	50	8
680	A166	30c rose car	40	8
681	A166	40c sl grn	45	8
682	A166	45c ver ('40)	3.00	2.75
683	A166	50c indigo	45	8
684	A166	60c orange	4.50	4.00
685	A166	70c blue	55	8
686	A166	1p black	18.00	8
687	A166	2p dk brn	26.00	1.75
688	A166	4p dk vio	140.00	20.00
689	A166	10p lt brn	72.50	47.50
		Nos. 678–689 (12)	266.85	76.56

Nos. 686 to 689 have value and "Pta." on one line while Nos. 702 to 705 have value and "Pta." on two lines.

Without Imprint.

Perf. 9½x10½, 12½x13

1939-51   **Lithographed**   **Unwmkd.**

690	A166	5c dl brn vio ('40)	50	18
691	A166	10c brn org	2.50	80
692	A166	15c lt grn	60	18
693	A166	20c brt vio	50	7
694	A166	25c dp cl	50	7
695	A166	30c blue	50	5
696	A166	35c aqua ('51)	50	5
697	A166	40c Prus grn ('40)	50	7
a.		40c grnsh blk	55	
698	A166	45c ultra ('41)	60	12
699	A166	50c ind ('40)	50	7
a.		Perf. 11½ ('47)	10.00	3.25
700	A166	60c dl org ('40)	75	18
701	A166	70c bl ('40)	1.00	7
702	A166	1p gray blk ('40)	8.00	7
703	A166	2p dl brn ('40)	10.00	25
704	A166	4p dl rose ('40)	35.00	25
705	A166	10p lt brn ('40)	185.00	4.00
		Nos. 690–705 (16)	246.95	6.55

The 40c exists in three types, with variations in the value tablet: I. "CTS" does not touch bottom line. II. Light background in tablet. III. As type I, but with well defined lines of white and color around rectangle.

The 60c exists in two types: I. Top and left side of value tablet touch rest of design. II. Tablet separated from rest of design by white lines.

Five values exist with perf. 10: 5c, 10c, 45c, 4p and 10p. The imperforate 10c dull claret, type A166, without imprint, is a postal tax stamp, RA14.

1944   **Redrawn**

| 706 | A166 | 1p gray | 75.00 | 75 |

"PTS" instead of "PTA" as No. 702.
Nos. 690–706 exist imperforate.

The value reads "PTAS"
instead of "PTS".

1944   **Perf. 9½x10½, 13,**   **Unwmkd.**

| 709 | A166 | 10p brown | 22.50 | 30 |

General   St. John
Franco   of the Cross
A167   A168

1942-48   **Engraved**   **Perf. 12½x13**

712	A167	40c chestnut	40	20
713	A167	75c dk bl, perf. 9½x10½ ('46)	4.00	50
714	A167	90c dk grn ('48)	30	8
a.		Perf. 9½x10½ ('47)	1.25	20
715	A167	1.35p pur ('48)	25	8
a.		Perf. 9½x10½ ('46)	1.00	40

1942   **Lithographed**   **Perf. 9½x10½**

721	A168	20c violet	1.00	18
722	A168	40c salmon	2.00	45
723	A168	75c ultra	2.50	2.50

400th birth anniversary of St. John of the Cross (1542–1591).
Nos. 721 to 723 exist imperforate.

Holy Year Issues.

Statue in St. James Cathedral
A169

St. James of   Incense
Compostela   Burner
A170   A171

Perf. 9½x10½

1943, Oct.   **Litho.**   **Unwmkd.**

724	A169	20c dp bl	32	20
725	A170	40c dk red brn	80	28
726	A171	75c dp bl	3.25	2.75

Carvings in St. James Cathedral
A172   A174

St. James   St. James' Casket
A173   A175

East Portal   St. James
of Cathedral   Cathedral
A176   A177

1943-44   **Perf. 9½x10½, 10½x9½**

727	A172	20c rose red ('44)	32	20
728	A173	40c dl grn	65	28
729	A174	75c dk bl ('44)	4.00	3.00

1944

730	A175	20c red vio	32	20
731	A176	40c dl brn	85	28
732	A177	75c brt bl	42.50	37.50

Millenium of Castile Issues.

Arms of Soria   Arms of Castile
A178   A179

Arms of Avila   Fortress
A180   A181

SPAIN

Arms of Segovia
A182

Arms of Fernan González
A183

Arms of Avila
A184

Arms of Burgos
A185

Arms of Santander
A186

Lithographed.
1944 Perf. 9½x10½ Unwmkd.

733	A178	20c violet	28	22
734	A179	40c dl brn	4.50	55
735	A180	75c blue	4.50	4.00

1944

736	A181	20c rose vio	28	28
737	A182	40c dl brn	4.50	55
738	A183	75c dl bl	4.00	4.00

1944

739	A184	20c red vio	28	28
740	A185	40c dl brn	3.25	60
741	A186	75c blue	4.75	4.00

Francisco de Quevedo
A187

1945, Sept. 8 Engr. Perf. 10

| 742 | A187 | 40c dk brn | 90 | 65 |

Issued to commemorate the 300th anniversary of the death of Francisco Gomez de Quevedo y Villegas (1580–1645), writer.

Type of Semi-Postal Stamp, 1940, Without Imprint at Lower Left and Right.

1946, Jan. 1 Litho. Perf. 11

| 743 | SP20 | 50c (40c+10c) sl grn & rose vio | 2.00 | 20 |

No. 743 was used as an ordinary postage stamp of 50c denomination.

Elio Antonio de Nebrija
A188

University of Salamanca and Signature of Francisco de Vitoria
A189

1946, Oct. 12 Engr. Perf. 9½x10

| 744 | A188 | 50c dp plum | 55 | 25 |
| 745 | A189 | 75c dp bl | 65 | 50 |

Issued in connection with Stamp Day and the Day of the Race, Oct. 12, 1946. See also No. C121.

Francisco de Goya
A190

Benito Jeronimo Feijoo y Montenegro
A191

1946, Oct 26

746	A190	25c dp plum	10	10
747	A190	50c green	10	10
748	A190	75c dk bl	90	90

Issued to commemorate the bicentenary of the birth of Francisco de Goya.

1947, June 1 Unwmkd.

| 749 | A191 | 50c dp grn | 60 | 55 |

Don Quixote Reading
A192

"Don Quixote" by Zuloaga
A193

Engraved.

1947, Oct. 9 Perf. 9½x10½

| 750 | A192 | 50c sepia | 30 | 25 |
| 751 | A193 | 75c dk bl | 60 | 50 |

Issued to commemorate Stamp Day and the 400th anniversary of the birth of Miguel de Cervantes Saavedra. See also No. C122.

General Franco
A194 A195

1948 Lithographed Perf. 12½x13

| 752 | A194 | 15c green | 20 | 10 |
| 753 | A195 | 50c rose vio | 1.40 | 10 |

See Nos. 760–768, 780, 801–803.

Hernando Cortez
A196

Mateo Aleman
A197

Perf. 12½x13, 9½x10½.

1948, June 15 Engraved

| 754 | A196 | 35c black | 20 | 20 |
| 755 | A197 | 70c dk vio brn | 3.00 | 2.75 |

Ferdinand III (The Saint)
A198

Grandson of Adm. Ramon de Bonifaz
A199

1948, Sept. 20 Litho. Perf. 12½x13

| 756 | A198 | 25c rose vio | 35 | 10 |
| 757 | A199 | 30c scarlet | 20 | 10 |

Issued to commemorate the 700th anniversary of the Spanish navy and of the capture of Seville by Ferdinand the Saint.

José de Salamanca y Mayol
A200

Train Crossing Pancorbo Viaduct
A201

Perf. 12½x13, 13x12½.

1948, Oct. 9 Unwmkd.

| 758 | A200 | 50c brown | 60 | 10 |
| 759 | A201 | 5p dp grn | 2.00 | 12 |

Issued to commemorate the centenary of Spanish railroads. See also No. C125.

Franco Types of 1948.
1948–49 Litho. Perf. 12½x13

760	A194	5c brown	10	10
761	A195	25c vermilion	10	10
762	A195	35c bl grn	10	10
763	A195	40c red brn	80	10
764	A195	45c car rose ('49)	60	12
765	A194	50c bister	30	15
766	A195	70c pur ('49)	2.25	25
767	A195	75c dk vio bl	2.00	25
768	A195	1p rose pink	7.25	10
Nos. 760-768 (9)			13.50	1.27

No. 761 exists imperforate.

Symbols of U.P.U.
A202

1949, Oct. 9

| 769 | A202 | 50c red brn | 60 | 10 |
| 770 | A202 | 75c vio bl | 55 | 50 |

Issued to commemorate the 75th anniversary of the formation of the Universal Postal Union. See also No. C126.

St. John of God
A203

Pedro Calderon de la Barca
A204

1950, Mar. 8 Engr. Unwmkd.

| 771 | A203 | 1p dk vio | 17.50 | 5.00 |

Issued to commemorate the 400th anniversary of the death of St. John of God, humanitarian.

1950–53 Photo. Perf. 12½

Designs: 10c Lope de Vega. 15c, Tirso de Molina. 20c, Juan Ruiz de Alarcon, dramatist. 50c, St. Antonio Maria Claret y Clara.

772	A204	5c brn ('51)	10	8
773	A204	10c dp rose brn ('51)	10	8
773A	A204	15c dk sl grn ('53)	35	8
774	A204	20c violet	30	8

Engraved. Perf. 12½x13.

| 775 | A204 | 50c dk bl ('51) | 6.00 | 3.00 |
| Nos. 772-775 (5) | | | 6.85 | 3.32 |

Stamp of 1850
A205

Queen Isabella I
A206

1950, Oct. 12 Engraved. Imperf.

776	A205	50c purple	9.00	9.00
777	A205	75c ultra	9.00	9.00
778	A205	10p dk sl grn	165.00	165.00
779	A205	15p red	165.00	165.00
Nos. 776-779, C127-C130 (8)			696.00	696.00

Centenary of Spain's stamps.

Franco Type of 1948.
1950 Lithographed Perf. 12½x13

| 780 | A195 | 45c red | 1.50 | 15 |

1951, Apr. 22 Photo. Perf. 12½

781	A206	50c brown	1.00	65
782	A206	75c blue	1.25	65
783	A206	90c rose	70	40
784	A206	1.50p orange	14.00	10.00
785	A206	2.80p ol grn	37.50	37.50
Nos. 781-785 (5)			54.45	49.20

Issued to commemorate the 500th anniversary of the birth of Queen Isabella I. See Nos. C132–C136.

Ferdinand, the Catholic
A210

Maria Michaela Dermaisiéres
A211

1952, May 10 Photo. Perf. 13

787	A210	50c green	90	50
788	A210	75c indigo	6.00	2.50
789	A210	90c rose brn	70	50
790	A210	1.50p orange	14.00	11.50
791	A210	2.80p brown	25.00	25.00
Nos. 787-791 (5)			46.60	40.00

Issued to commemorate the 500th anniversary of the birth of Ferdinand the Catholic of Spain. See Nos. C139–C143.

1952, May 26 Perf. 12½x13

| 792 | A211 | 90c claret | 15 | 10 |

Issued to publicize the 35th International Eucharistic Congress, Barcelona, 1952. See also No. C137.

Dr. Santiago Ramon y Cajal
A212

Portrait: 4.50p, Dr. Jaime Ferran y Clua.

1952, July 8 Photogravure

| 793 | A212 | 2p brt bl | 30.00 | 35 |
| 794 | A212 | 4.50p red brn | 70 | 70 |

Issued to commemorate the centenary of the births of Dr. Santiago Ramon y Cajal and Dr. Jaime Ferran y Clua.

SPAIN

University Seal
A213

Luis de Leon
A214

Cathedral of Salamanca
A215

Perf. 12½x13, 13x12½

1953, Oct. 12
795	A213	50c dp mag	60	15
796	A214	90c dk ol gray	3.50	3.50
797	A215	2p brown	25.00	4.50

Issued in connection with Stamp Day, Oct. 12, 1953, to commemorate the 700th anniversary of the founding of the University of Salamanca.

The Magdalene
A216

1954, Jan. 10   Perf. 12½x13
| 798 | A216 | 1.25p dp mag | 10 | 10 |

Issued to commemorate the 300th anniversary of the death of José de Ribera, painter.

St. James of Compostela
A217

St. James Cathedral
A218

1954, Mar. 1
| 799 | A217 | 50c dk brn | 15 | 12 |
| 800 | A218 | 3p blue | 45.00 | 4.00 |

Holy Year of Compostela, 1954.

Franco Types of 1948
1954   Lithographed.   Perf. 12½
801	A194	5c ol gray	10	5
802	A195	30c dp grn	15	12
803	A194	80c dl car rose	4.75	15

Virgin by Alonso Cano
A219

Marcelino Menendez y Pelayo
A220

Virgins: 15c, Begoña. 25c, Of the Abandoned. 30c, Black. 50c, Of the Pillar. 60c, Covadonga. 80c, Kings'. 1p, Almudena. 2p, Africa. 3p, Guadalupe.

1954, July 18   Photo.   Perf. 12½x13
804	A219	10c dk car rose	10	10
805	A219	15c ol grn	10	10
806	A219	25c purple	15	10
807	A219	30c brown	20	10
808	A219	50c brn ol	80	10
809	A219	60c gray	20	10
810	A219	80c grnsh gray	4.75	10
811	A219	1p lil gray	4.75	10
812	A219	2p red brn	1.25	10
813	A219	3p brt bl	1.40	1.40
	Nos. 804-813 (10)	13.70	2.30

Issued to publicize the Marian Year.

1954, Oct. 12
| 814 | A220 | 80c dk gray grn | 8.00 | 25 |

Issued to publicize Stamp Day, October 12, 1954.

Gen. Franco
A221

Imprint: "F.N.M.T."

1954-56   Perf. 12½x13
815	A221	10c dk car lake	10	5
816	A221	15c bister	10	5
817	A221	20c dk ol grn ('55)	10	5
818	A221	25c bl vio	10	5
819	A221	30c brown	10	5
820	A221	40c rose vio ('55)	10	5
821	A221	50c dk brn ol	10	5
822	A221	60c dk vio brn	12	5
823	A221	70c dk grn	20	5
824	A221	80c dk bl grn	10	5
825	A221	1p dp org	10	5
826	A221	1.40p lil rose ('56)	20	15
827	A221	1.50p lt bl grn ('56)	10	5
828	A221	1.80p emer ('56)	20	5
829	A221	2p red	28.50	1.40
830	A221	2p red lil ('56)	10	5
831	A221	3p Prus bl	10	5
832	A221	5p dk red brn	16	5
833	A221	6p dk gray ('55)	18	8
834	A221	8p brt vio ('56)	18	10
835	A221	10p yel grn ('55)	25	10
	Nos. 815-835 (21)	31.19	2.73

Coils: The 1.50p, No. 830, the 3p and the 6p were issued in coils in brighter tones (the 3p in 1974, others in 1973). Every fifth stamp has a black control number on the back.
See also Nos. 937-938, 1852-1855.

St. Ignatius of Loyola
A222

St. Ignatius and Loyola Palace
A223

Perf. 13x12½, 12½x13

1955, Oct. 12   Photo.   Unwmkd.
836	A222	25c dl pur	15	10
837	A223	60c bister	90	30
838	A222	80c Prus grn	3.75	20

Issued to mark the fourth centenary of the death of St. Ignatius of Loyola, founder of the Jesuit Order and to publicize the Day of the Stamp, 1955.

Symbols of Telegraph and Radio Communication
A224

St. Vincent Ferrer
A225

1955, Dec. 8   Perf. 13x12½
839	A224	15c dk ol bis	40	20
840	A224	80c Prus grn	9.00	35
841	A224	3p brt bl	16.00	1.50

Spanish telegraph system centenary.

1955, Dec. 20   Perf. 13
| 842 | A225 | 15c ol bis | 40 | 30 |

Canonization of St. Vincent Ferrer, fifth centenary.

"Holy Family" by El Greco
A226

Marching Soldiers and Dove
A227

1955, Dec. 24   Perf. 13x12½
| 843 | A226 | 80c dk grn | 4.25 | 65 |

1956, July 17   Unwmkd.
844	A227	15c ol bis & brn	10	10
845	A227	50c lt ol grn & ol	60	60
846	A227	80c mag & grnsh blk	6.75	30
847	A227	3p ultra & dp bl	6.75	2.50

20th anniversary of Civil War.

Ciudad de Toledo—A228

1956, Aug. 3   Perf. 12½x13
| 848 | A228 | 3p blue | 4.50 | 2.00 |

Issued to publicize the voyage of the S. S. Ciudad de Toledo to Central and South America carrying the First Floating (Industrial) Exposition.

Black Virgin of Montserrat
A229

Archangel Gabriel by Fra Angelico
A230

Design: 60c, Monastery of Montserrat, mountains and crucifix.

1956, Sept. 11   Perf. 13x12½
849	A229	15c bister	10	10
850	A229	60c vio blk	40	40
851	A229	80c bl grn	60	50

Issued to commemorate the 75th anniversary of the coronation of the Black Virgin of Montserrat.

1956, Oct. 12   Engraved
| 852 | A230 | 80c dl grn | 90 | 70 |

Stamp Day, Oct. 12.

Statistical Chart—A231

1956, Nov. 3   Perf. 12½x13
853	A231	15c dk ol bis	35	35
854	A231	80c green	4.50	75
855	A231	1p red org	4.50	75

Centenary of Spanish Statistics.

Hermitage and Monument—A232

1956, Dec. 4
| 856 | A232 | 80c dl bl grn | 4.50 | 45 |

Issued to commemorate the 20th anniversary of the nomination of Gen. Franco as chief of state and commander in chief of the army.

Hungarian Children
A233

St. Marguerite Alacoque's Vision of Jesus
A234

1956, Dec. 17   Perf. 13x12½
857	A233	10c brn lake	10	10
858	A233	15c dk bis	15	10
859	A233	50c ol grn	30	25
860	A233	80c dk bl grn	2.75	20
861	A233	1p red org	2.75	20
862	A233	3p brt bl	9.00	2.75
	Nos. 857-862 (6)	15.05	3.60

Issued in sympathy to the children of Hungary.

1957, Oct. 12   Photo.   Unwmkd.
863	A234	15c dk ol bis	10	10
864	A234	60c vio blk	45	15
865	A234	80c dk bl grn	45	15

Issued to commemorate the centenary of the feast of the Sacred Heart of Jesus and for Stamp Day 1957.

Gonzalo de Cordoba
A235

SPAIN

1958, Feb. 28   Engr.   Perf. 13x12½

| 866 | A235 | 1.80p yel grn | 12 | 10 |

Issued in honor of El Gran Capitan, 15th century military leader.

"The Parasol," by Goya   A236

"Wife of the Bookseller of Carretas Street"   A237

Goya Paintings: 50c, Duke of Fernan-Nunez. 60c, The Crockery Seller. 70c, Isabel Cobos de Porcel. 80c, Goya by Vicente Lopez. 1p, "El Pelele" (Carnival Doll). 1.80p, Goya's grandson Marianito. 2p, The Vintage. 3p, The Drinker.

1958, Mar. 24   Photo.   Perf. 13
Gold Frame.

867	A236	15c bister	8	6
868	A237	40c plum	10	6
869	A237	50c ol gray	10	6
870	A237	60c vio gray	10	6
871	A237	70c dp yel grn	10	10
872	A237	80c dk sl grn	10	10
873	A237	1p org red	12	10
874	A237	1.80p brt grn	10	10
875	A237	2p red lil	40	40
876	A237	3p brt bl	70	70
		Nos. 867-876 (10)	1.90	1.74

Issued to honor Francisco Jose de Goya and for the "Day of the Stamp," March 24. See also Nos. 1111-1114.

Exhibition Emblem and Globe
A238

1958, June 7   Perf. 13x12½

877	A238	80c car, dk brn & gray	25	15
a.		Souvenir sheet, imperf.	60.00	50.00
878	A238	3p car, vio blk & bl	1.25	1.15
a.		Souvenir sheet, imperf.	60.00	50.00

Nos. 877a, 878a have control number on front and are inscribed: "Exposition Filatelica Nacional. Madrid junio de 1958." No. 877a is printed in carmine, brown & green, with marginal inscription in green. It sold for 2p. No. 878a is printed in orange vermilion, violet black & violet, with marginal inscription in violet. It sold for 5p. Size: 49x83½mm.

Issued for the Universal and International Exposition at Brussels.

Charles V
A239

Various Portraits of Charles V: 50c, 1.80p, with helmet. 70c, 2p, facing left. 80c, 3p, with beret.

1958, July 30   Photo.   Perf. 13

879	A239	15c buff & brn	10	10
880	A239	50c lt grn & ol brn	10	10
881	A239	70c gray, grn & blk	25	25
882	A239	80c pale brn & Prus grn	15	10
883	A239	1p bis & brick red	35	10
884	A239	1.80p pale grn & brt grn	25	25
885	A239	2p gray & lil	85	85
886	A239	3p pale brn & brt bl	1.75	1.75
		Nos. 879-886 (8)	3.80	3.50

Issued to commemorate the 400th anniversary of the death of Charles V (Carlos I of Spain.)

Escorial and Streamlined Train
A240

Designs: 60c, 2p, Railroad bridge at Despeñaperros (vert.). 80c, 3p, Train and Castle of La Mota.

1958, Sept. 29   Perf. 12½x13

887	A240	15c dk ol bis	10	10
888	A240	60c dk pur	10	10
889	A240	80c dk bl grn	15	10
890	A240	1p red org	50	10
891	A240	2p red lil	50	10
892	A240	3p blue	1.75	1.25
		Nos. 887-892 (6)	3.10	1.75

International Railroad Congress, Madrid, Sept. 28–Oct. 7.

Velazquez Self-portrait
A240a

Velazquez Paintings: 15c, The Drinkers (horiz.). 40c, The Spinners. 50c, Surrender of Breda. 60c, The Little Princesses. 70c, Prince Balthazar. 1p, The Coronation of Our Lady. 1.80p, Aesop. 2p, Vulcan's Forge. 3p, Menippus.

1959, Mar. 24   Photo.   Perf. 13
Gold Frame

893	A240a	15c dk brn	10	10
894	A240a	40c rose vio	10	10
895	A240a	50c olive	10	10
896	A240a	60c blk brn	10	10
897	A240a	70c dp yel grn	10	10
898	A240a	80c dk sl grn	15	10
899	A240a	1p org red	20	10
900	A240a	1.80p emerald	10	10
901	A240a	2p red lil	35	30
902	A240a	3p brt bl	65	65
		Nos. 893-902 (10)	1.95	1.75

Issued to honor Diego de Silva Velazquez (1599–1660) and for Stamp Day, Mar. 24.

Civil War Memorial
A241

1959, Apr. 1   Litho.   Unwmkd.

| 903 | A241 | 80c yel grn & dk sl grn | 15 | 12 |

Issued to commemorate the inauguration of the war memorial at the monastery of the Holy Cross in the Valley of the Fallen.

Louis XIV and Philip II
A242

1959, Oct. 24   Photo.   Perf. 13x12½

| 904 | A242 | 1p gold & rose brn | 15 | 12 |

Issued to commemorate the 300th anniversary of the signing of the Treaty of the Pyrenees. Design shows the French-Spanish meeting at Isle des Faisans in 1659, as pictured in the Lebrun Tapestry, Versailles.

Monastery of Guadalupe
A243

Designs: 80c, Monastery, different view. 1p, Portals.

1959, Nov. 16   Engr.   Perf. 12½x13

905	A243	15c lt red brn	10	10
906	A243	80c slate	20	15
907	A243	1p rose red	20	15

Issued to commemorate the 50th anniversary of the entrance of the Franciscan Brothers into Guadalupe monastery.

Holy Family, by Goya
A244

1959, Dec. 10   Photo.   Perf. 13x12½

| 908 | A244 | 1p org brn | 25 | 12 |

Lidian Bull—A245

Bullfighter, 19th Century
A246

Designs: 20c, Rounding up bulls. 25c, Running with the bulls, Pamplona. 30c, Bull entering arena. 50c, Bullfighting with cape. 70c, Bullfighting with banderillas. 80c, 1p, 1.40p, 1.50p, Fighting with muleta, various poses. 1.80p, Mounted bullfighter placing banderillas.

Perf. 12½x13, 13x12½
1960, Feb. 29   Engraved   Unwmkd.

909	A245	15c sep & bis	12	10
910	A245	20c vio & bl vio	12	10
911	A246	25c gray	12	10
912	A246	30c sep & bis	12	10
913	A246	50c dl vio & sep	25	10
914	A246	70c sep & sl grn	30	20
915	A246	80c bl grn & grn	12	10
916	A246	1p red & brn	55	10
917	A246	1.40p brn & lake	12	10
918	A246	1.50p grnsh bl & grn	12	10
919	A245	1.80p brn & dk grn	12	10
920	A246	5p brn & brn car	1.10	85
		Nos. 909-920, C159-C162 (16)	4.98	3.05

Murillo Self-portrait   A246a

Christ of Lepanto   A247

Murillo Paintings: 25c, The Good Shepherd. 40c, Rebecca and Eliezer. 50c, Virgin of the Rosary. 70c, Immaculate Conception. 80c, Children with Shell. 1.50p, Holy Family with Bird (horiz.). 2.50p, Children Playing Dice. 3p, Children Eating. 5p, Children counting Money.

1960, Mar. 24   Photo.   Perf. 13
Gold Frame

921	A246a	25c dl vio	12	10
922	A246a	40c plum	12	10
923	A246a	50c ol gray	20	10
924	A246a	70c dp yel grn	20	15
925	A246a	80c dp grn	20	10
926	A246a	1p vio brn	20	10
927	A246a	1.50p bl grn	20	10
928	A246a	2.50p rose car	25	10
929	A246a	3p brt bl	1.75	1.00
930	A246a	5p dp red brn	60	35
		Nos. 921-930 (10)	3.84	2.20

Issued to honor Bartolome Esteban Murillo (1617–1682) and for Stamp Day, Mar. 24.

1960, Mar. 27   Perf. 13x12½

Designs: 80c, 2.50p, 10p, Holy Family Church, Barcelona.

931	A247	70c brn car & grn	3.00	2.25
932	A247	80c blk & ol grn	3.00	2.25
933	A247	1p cl & brt red	3.00	2.25
934	A247	2.50p brt vio & gray vio	3.00	2.25
935	A247	5p sep & bis	3.00	2.25
936	A247	10p sep & bis	3.00	2.25
		Nos.931-936, C163-C166 (10)	45.00	32.50

Issued to commemorate the First International Congress of Philately, Barcelona, March 26–Apr. 5. Nos. 931-936 could be bought at the exhibition upon presentation of 5p entrance ticket.

Franco Type of 1954-56.
Imprint: "F.N.M.T.-B"

1960, Mar. 31   Photo.   Perf. 13

| 937 | A221 | 1p dp org | 2.50 | 1.75 |
| 938 | A221 | 5p dk red brn | 5.00 | 1.75 |

Printed and issued at the International Congress of Philately in Barcelona.

SPAIN

	St. Juan de Ribera A248	St. Vincent de Paul A249		

1960, Aug. 16 Photo. Perf. 13

| 939 | A248 | 1p org red | 70 | 14 |
| 940 | A248 | 2.50p lil rose | 18 | 12 |

Canonization of St. Juan de Ribera.

Europa Issue, 1960
Common Design Type

1960, Sept. 19 Perf. 12½x13
Size: 38½x21½mm.

| 941 | CD3 | 1p sl grn & ol bis | 3.75 | 25 |
| 942 | CD3 | 5p choc & sal | 3.75 | 50 |

1960, Sept. 27 Perf. 13 Unwmkd.

| 943 | A249 | 25c violet | 12 | 10 |
| 944 | A249 | 1p org red | 75 | 10 |

Issued to commemorate the 3rd centenary of the death of St. Vincent de Paul.

	Pedro Menendez de Aviles A250	Runner A251		

Portraits: 70c, 2.50p, Hernando de Soto. 80c, 3p, Juan Ponce de León. 1p, 5p, Alvar Nunez Cabeza de Vaca.

1960, Oct. 12 Perf. 13x12½

945	A250	25c vio bl, *bl*	15	10
946	A250	70c sl grn, *pink*	15	10
947	A250	80c dk grn, *pale brn*	15	10
948	A250	1p org brn, *yel*	20	10
949	A250	2p dk car rose, *pink*	40	10
950	A250	2.50p lil rose, *buff*	75	10
951	A250	3p dk brn, *grnsh*	3.25	60
952	A250	5p dk brn, *cit*	2.50	1.10
		Nos. 945-952 (8)	7.55	2.30

Issued to commemorate the fourth centenary of Florida's discovery and colonization.

Perf. 13x12½, 12½x13

1960, Oct. 31 Photogravure

Sports: 40c, 2p, Bicycling (horiz.). 70c, 2.50p, Soccer (horiz.). 80c, 3p, Athlete with rings. 1p, 5p, Hockey on roller skates (horiz.).

953	A251	25c dk vio, brn & blk	12	10
954	A251	40c pur, org & blk	12	10
955	A251	70c brt & red	40	12
956	A251	80c dp grn, car & blk	30	10
957	A251	1p red org, brt grn & blk	90	10
958	A251	1.50p Prus grn, brn & blk	40	10
959	A251	2p red lil, emer & blk	1.10	10
960	A251	2.50p lil rose & grn	40	10
961	A251	3p ultra, red & blk	65	20
962	A251	5p red brn, bl & blk	1.10	40
		Nos. 953-962, C167-C170 (14)	8.99	3.11

Isaac Albeniz
A252

1960, Nov. 7 Perf. 13

| 963 | A252 | 25c dk gray | 12 | 10 |
| 964 | A252 | 1p org red | 55 | 12 |

Issued to commemorate the centenary of the birth of Isaac Albeniz, composer.

Courtyard of Samos Monastery
A253

Designs: 1p, Fountain (vert.). 5p, Facade (vert.).

Perf. 12½x13, 13x12½

1960, Nov. 21 Engraved

965	A253	80c bl grn & Prus grn	18	6
966	A253	1p org brn & car rose	2.75	15
967	A253	5p sep & ocher	1.75	70

Issued in honor of the reconstructed Benedictine monastery at Samos, Lugo.

Adoration, by Velazquez
A254

1960, Dec. 1 Photo. Perf. 13x12½

| 968 | A254 | 1p org red | 50 | 10 |

Flight into Egypt by Francisco Bayeu
A255

1961, Jan. 23 Perf. 12½x13

| 969 | A255 | 1p cop red | 65 | 10 |
| 970 | A255 | 5p dl red brn | 1.25 | 15 |

World Refugee Year.

Common Design Types
pictured in section at front of book.

	Leandro F. de Moratin, by Goya A256	St. Peter by El Greco A257		

1961, Feb. 13 Perf. 13

| 971 | A256 | 1p hn brn | 45 | 10 |
| 972 | A256 | 1.50p dk bl grn | 25 | 10 |

Issued to commemorate the 200th anniversary of the birth of Leandro Fernandez de Moratin (1760–1823), poet and dramatist.

1961, March 24 Perf. 13

El Greco Paintings: 40c, Virgin Mary. 70c, Head of Christ. 80c, Knight with Hand on Chest. 1p, Self-portrait. 1.50p, Baptism of Christ. 2.50p, Holy Trinity. 3p, Burial of Count Orgaz. 5p, Christ Stripped of His Garments. 10p, St. Mauritius and the Theban Legion.

Gold Frame

973	A257	25c vio blk	20	15
974	A257	40c lilac	15	10
975	A257	70c green	25	25
976	A257	80c Prus grn	25	10
977	A257	1p chocolate	2.50	10
978	A257	1.50p grnsh bl	25	10
979	A257	2.50p dk car rose	35	10
980	A257	3p brt bl	1.25	1.00
981	A257	5p blk brn	3.00	2.50
982	A257	10p purple	50	60
		Nos. 973-982 (10)	8.70	5.00

Issued in honor of El Greco and for Stamp Day, March 24.

	Diego Velazquez A258	Canceled Stamp A259		

Velazquez Paintings: 1p, Duke de Olivares. 2.50p, Infant Margarita. 10p, Detail from The Spinners (horiz.).

Engraved

1961, Apr. 17 Perf. 13 Unwmkd.

983	A258	80c dk bl & s grn	1.50	25
a.		Souvenir sheet	15.00	10.00
984	A258	1p brn red & choc	3.50	25
a.		Souvenir sheet	15.00	10.00
985	A258	2.50p vio bl & bl	85	45
a.		Souvenir sheet	15.00	10.00
986	A258	10p grn & yel grn	3.00	1.25
a.		Souvenir sheet	15.00	10.00

Issued to commemorate the 300th anniversary (in 1960) of the death of Velazquez, painter.

Each souvenir sheet contains one imperf. stamp with marginal inscriptions and red control numbers. Size: 73x86mm. The colors of the stamps have been changed: 80c, red brown & slate; 1p, blue & violet; 2.50p, green & blue; 10p, slate blue & greenish blue. The sheets were sold at a premium.

1961, May 6 Photo. Perf 13x12½

987	A259	25c gray & red	15	10
988	A259	1p org & blk	2.25	10
989	A259	10p ol grn & brn	2.25	60

Issued for International Stamp Day.

	Juan Vazquez de Mella A260	Flag, Angel and Peace Doves A261		

1961, June 8 Perf. 13 Unwmkd.

| 990 | A260 | 1p hn brn | 1.25 | 8 |
| 991 | A260 | 2.30p red lil | 30 | 25 |

Issued to commemorate the centenary of the birth of Juan Vazquez de Mella y Fanjul, politician and writer.

1961, July 10

Designs: 80c, Ships and Strait of Gibraltar. 1p, Alcazar and horseman. 1.50p, Ruins and triumphal arch. 2p, Horseman over Ebro. 2.50p, Victory parade. 2.50p, Ship building. 3p, Steel industry. 5p, Map of Spanish irrigation dams and statue (horiz.). 6p, Dama de Elche statue and power station. 8p, Mining development. 10p, General Franco.

992	A261	70c multi	10	10
993	A261	80c multi	10	10
994	A261	1p multi	30	10
995	A261	1.50p gold, pink & brn	15	10
996	A261	2p gold, gray & bl	18	10
997	A261	2.30p multi	20	15
998	A261	2.50p multi	20	10
999	A261	3p gold, red & dk gray	45	45
1000	A261	5p bl grn, ol gray & pink	3.50	1.75
1001	A261	6p multi	1.75	1.50
1002	A261	8p gold, ol & sep	1.10	80
1003	A261	10p gold, gray & grn	85	80
		Nos. 992-1003 (12)	8.88	6.05

25th anniversary of national uprising.

	Christ, San Clemente, Tahull A262	Luis de Argote y Gongora A263		

1961, July 24 Perf. 13 Unwmkd.
Gold Frame

Designs: 25c, Bas-relief, Compostela Cathedral. 1p, Cloister of Silos. 2p, Virgin of Irache.

1004	A262	25c bl vio	40	10
1005	A262	1p org brn	45	10
1006	A262	2p dp plum	65	10
1007	A262	3p grnsh bl, sal & blk	1.10	10

Issued to publicize the Seventh Exposition of the Council of Europe dedicated to Romanesque art, Barcelona-Santiago de Compostela, July 10–Oct. 10, 1961.

1961, Aug. 10 Photo. Perf. 13

| 1008 | A263 | 25c vio blk | 10 | 10 |
| 1009 | A263 | 1p hn brn | 70 | 12 |

Issued to commemorate the 400th anniversary of the birth of Luis de Argote y Gongora, poet.

Europa Issue, 1961
Common Design Type

1961, Sept. 18 Perf. 12½x13
Size: 37½x21½mm.

| 1010 | CD4 | 1p brt ver | 40 | 10 |
| 1011 | CD4 | 5p brown | 1.40 | 40 |

561

SPAN

Cathedral at Burgos	Sebastian de Belalcazar
A264	A265

1961, Oct. 1   Perf. 13

| 1012 | A264 | 1p gold & ol grn | 25 | 12 |

Issued to commemorate the 25th anniversary of the nomination of Gen. Francisco Franco as Head of State.

Builders of the New World

1961, Oct. 12 Photo. *Perf. 13x12½*

Portraits: 70c, 2.50p, Blas de Lezo. 80c, 3p, Rodrigo de Bastidas. 1p, 5p, Nuflo de Chaves.

1013	A265	25c ind, *grn*	15	10
1014	A265	70c grn, *cr*	20	10
1015	A265	80c sl grn, *pnksh*	20	10
1016	A265	1p dk bl, *sal*	85	15
1017	A265	2p dk car, *bluish*	5.25	15
1018	A265	2.50p lil, *pale lil*	1.25	50
1019	A265	3p bl, *grysh*	2.50	85
1020	A265	5p brn, *yel*	2.75	1.10
		Nos. 1013-1020 (8)	13.15	3.05

Issued to honor the discoverers and conquerors of Colombia and Bolivia.
See also Nos. 1131–1138, 1187–1194, 1271–1278, 1316–1323, 1377–1384, 1489–1496, 1548, 1550, 1587–1588, 1632–1633.

Patio of the Kings, Escorial
A266

Views of Escorial: 80c, Patio. 1p, Garden of the Monks and Escorial (horiz.). 2.50p, Staircase. 5p, General view of Escorial (horiz.). 6p, Main altar.

Perf. 13x12½, 12½x13

1961, Oct. 31 Engraved Unwmkd.

1021	A266	70c bl grn & ol grn	25	10
1022	A266	80c Prus grn & ind	25	10
1023	A266	1p ocher & dk red	1.00	10
1024	A266	2.50p cl & dl vio	70	15
1025	A266	5p bis & dk brn	2.50	80
1026	A266	6p sl bl & dl pur	3.00	2.00
		Nos. 1021-1026 (6)	7.70	3.25

Alfonso XII Monument, Retiro Park	Church of St. Mary, Naranco
A267	A268

Designs: 1p, King Philip II. 2p, Town hall (horiz.). 2.50p, Cibeles fountain (horiz.). 3p, Alcala gate (horiz.). 5p, Cervantes memorial, Plaza de Espagna.

Photogravure (25c, 2p, 5p)
Engraved (1p, 2.50p, 3p)

1961, Nov. 13 *Perf. 13* Unwmkd.

1027	A267	25c gray & dl pur	10	10
1028	A267	1p bis brn & gray	50	10
1029	A267	2p cl & gray	50	10
1030	A267	2.50p blk & lil	30	10
1031	A267	3p sl & ind	90	55
1032	A267	5p Prus grn & beige	2.25	80
		Nos. 1027-1032 (6)	4.55	1.75

Issued to commemorate the 400th anniversary of Madrid as capital of Spain.

1961, Nov. 27

Designs: 1p, King Fruela I, founder of Oviedo. 2p, Cross of the Angels. 2.50p, King Alfonso II. 3p, King Alfonso III. 5p, Apostles from Oviedo Cathedral (sculpture).

1033	A268	25c pur & gray grn	10	10
1034	A268	1p bis brn & brn	50	10
1035	A268	2p dk brn & pale pur	1.10	10
1036	A268	2.50p cl & ind	25	10
1037	A268	3p sl & ind	1.10	55
1038	A268	5p ol & ol grn	1.75	85
		Nos. 1033-1038 (6)	4.80	1.80

Issued to commemorate the 1200th anniversary of the founding of Oviedo, capital of Asturia.

Nativity Sculptured by José Gines	"La Cierva" Autogiro
A269	A270

1961, Dec. 1 Photo. *Perf. 13x12½*

| 1039 | A269 | 1p dl pur | 55 | 10 |

1961, Dec. 11 *Perf. 13* Unwmkd.

Designs: 2p, Hydroplane "Plus Ultra." (horiz.). 3p, "Jesus del Gran Poder," plane of Madrid-Manila flight (horiz.). 5p, Bustard hunt by plane. 10p, Madonna of Loretto, patron saint of Spanish airmen.

1040	A270	1p ind & bl	25	10
1041	A270	2p grn, dl pur & blk	50	20
1042	A270	3p blk & ol grn	2.50	60
1043	A270	5p dl pur, gray bl & blk	4.75	1.40
1044	A270	10p blk, lt bl & ol gray	2.50	75
		Nos. 1040-1044 (5)	10.50	3.05

50th anniversary of Spanish aviation.

Provincial Arms Issue

Arms of Alava Province	Arms of Spain
A271	A271a

1962–66 Photogravure *Perf. 13*
Arms in Original Colors

1045	A271	5p blk (*Alava*)	20	15
1046	A271	5p blk (*Albacete*)	20	15
1047	A271	5p blk (*Alicante*)	35	35
1048	A271	5p blk (*Almeria*)	35	35
1049	A271	5p blk (*Avila*)	35	15
1050	A271	5p blk (*Badajoz*)	20	15
1051	A271	5p blk (*Baleares*)	20	15
1052	A271	5p blk (*Barcelona*)	20	15
1053	A271	5p blk (*Burgos*)	1.40	40
1054	A271	5p blk (*Caceres*)	80	25
1055	A271	5p blk (*Cadiz*)	1.10	35
1056	A271	5p blk (*Castellon de la Plana*)	9.00	2.50
		Nos. 1045-1056 (12)	14.35	5.30

(1963)

1057	A271	5p blk (*Ciudad Real*)	1.10	35
1058	A271	5p blk (*Cordoba*)	7.50	2.25
1059	A271	5p blk (*Coruña*)	1.10	40
1060	A271	5p blk (*Cuenca*)	1.10	40
1061	A271	5p blk (*Fernando Po*)	1.75	1.40
1062	A271	5p blk (*Gerona*)	20	15
1063	A271	5p blk (*Gran Canaria*)	20	15
1064	A271	5p blk (*Granada*)	40	30
1065	A271	5p blk (*Guadalajara*)	1.10	35
1066	A271	5p blk (*Guipuzcoa*)	20	15
1067	A271	5p blk (*Huelva*)	20	15
1068	A271	5p blk (*Huesca*)	20	15
		Nos. 1057-1068 (12)	15.05	6.20

(1964)

1069	A271	5p blk (*Ifni*)	20	15
1070	A271	5p blk (*Jaen*)	20	15
1071	A271	5p blk (*Leon*)	30	22
1072	A271	5p blk (*Lerida*)	20	15
1073	A271	5p blk (*Logrono*)	20	15
1074	A271	5p blk (*Lugo*)	20	15
1075	A271	5p blk (*Madrid*)	20	15
1076	A271	5p blk (*Malaga*)	20	15
1077	A271	5p blk (*Murcia*)	20	15
1078	A271	5p blk (*Navarra*)	20	15
1079	A271	5p blk (*Orense*)	20	15
1080	A271	5p blk (*Oviedo*)	20	15
		Nos. 1069-1080 (12)	2.50	1.87

(1965)

1081	A271	5p blk (*Palencia*)	20	15
1082	A271	5p blk (*Pontevedra*)	20	15
1083	A271	5p blk (*Rio Muni*)	20	15
1084	A271	5p blk (*Sahara*)	20	15
1085	A271	5p blk (*Salamanca*)	20	15
1086	A271	5p blk (*Santander*)	20	15
1087	A271	5p blk (*Segovia*)	20	15
1088	A271	5p blk (*Seville*)	20	15
1089	A271	5p blk (*Soria*)	20	15
1090	A271	5p blk (*Tarragona*)	20	15
1091	A271	5p blk (*Tenerife*)	20	15
1092	A271	5p blk (*Teruel*)	20	15
		Nos. 1081-1092 (12)	2.40	1.80

(1966)

1093	A271	5p blk (*Toledo*)	15	12
1094	A271	5p blk (*Valencia*)	15	12
1094A	A271	5p blk (*Valladolid*)	15	12
1094B	A271	5p blk (*Vizcaya*)	15	12
1094C	A271	5p blk (*Zamora*)	15	12
1094D	A271	5p blk (*Zaragoza*)	15	12
1094E	A271	5p blk (*Ceuta*)	15	12
1094F	A271	5p blk (*Melilla*)	15	12
1094G	A271a	10p black	35	15
		Nos. 1093-1094G (9)	1.55	1.11
		Nos. 1045-1094G (57)	35.55	16.69

Zurbaran Self-portrait
A272

Zurbaran Paintings: 25c, Martyr (horiz.). 40c, Burial of St. Catherine. 70c, St. Casilda. 80c, Jesus crowning St. Joseph. 1.50P, St. Jerome. 70c, Virgin of Grace. 3p, The Apotheosis of St. Thomas Aquinas. 5p, The Virgin as a child. 10p, The Immaculate Virgin.

Photogravure

1962, March 24 *Perf. 13* Unwmkd.
Gold Frame

1095	A272	25c ol gray	10	10
1096	A272	40c purple	10	10
1097	A272	70c green	25	12
1098	A272	80c Prus grn	20	10
1099	A272	1p chocolate	5.25	10
1100	A272	1.50p brt bl grn	55	10
1101	A272	2.50p dk car rose	55	10
1102	A272	3p brt bl	55	50
1103	A272	5p dp brn	1.75	10
1104	A272	10p ol grn	1.75	1.25
		Nos. 1095-1104 (10)	11.05	3.57

Issued to honor Francisco de Zurbaran (1598–1664) and for Stamp Day, March 24.

San Jose Convent, Avila
A272a

St. Theresa (by Velázquez?)	Mercury
A273	A274

Design: 1p, St. Theresa by Bernini.

1962, Apr. 10 *Perf. 13*

| 1105 | A272a | 25c bluish blk | 10 | 10 |
| 1106 | A272a | 1p brown | 25 | 15 |

Perf. 13x12½

| 1107 | A273 | 3p brt bl | 2.50 | 30 |

Issued to commemorate the 4th centenary of St. Theresa's reform of the Carmelite order.

1962, May 7

1108	A274	25c vio, rose & mag	10	10
1109	A274	1p brn, org & lt brn	25	10
1110	A274	10p dp grn, ol grn & brt grn	3.25	85

International Stamp Day, May 7.

Painting Type of 1958

Rubens Paintings: 25c, Ferdinand of Austria. 1p, Self-portrait. 3p, Philip II. 10p, Duke of Lerma on horseback.

1962, May 28 *Perf. 13*
Gold Frame
Size: 25x30mm.

1111	A237	25c vio blk	45	20
1112	A237	1p chocolate	4.00	10
1113	A237	3p blue	3.50	1.50

Perf. 13x12½
Size: 26x38mm.

| 1114 | A237 | 10p sl grn | 2.75 | 1.75 |

SPAIN

St. Benedict	El Cid, Statue by Cristobal
A275	A276

Berruguete Sculptures: 80c, Apostle. 1p, St. Peter. 2p, St. Christopher carrying Christ Child. 3p, Ecce Homo (Christ). 10p, St. Sebastian.

1962, July 9   *Perf. 13x12½*

1115	A275	25c lt bl & plum	15	10
1116	A275	80c sal & ol gray	35	10
1117	A275	1p gray & red	70	10
1118	A275	2p gray & mag	5.50	10
1119	A275	3p brn pink & dk bl	2.00	1.10
1120	A275	10p rose & brn	2.00	75
		Nos. 1115-1120 (6)	10.70	2.25

Issued to commemorate the 400th anniversary of the death of Alonso Berruguete (1486-1561), architect, sculptor and painter.

Perf. 13x12½, 12½x13

1962, July 30   Engraved

Designs: 2p, Equestrian statue by Anna Huntington. 3p, El Cid's treasure chest (horiz.). 10p, Oath-taking ceremony at Santa Gadea (horiz.).

1121	A276	1p lt grn & gray	20	10
1122	A276	2p brn & choc	2.00	10
1123	A276	3p bl & sl grn	5.50	1.75
1124	A276	10p lt grn & sl grn	2.75	1.10

Issued to commemorate El Cid Campeador (Rodrigo Diaz de Vivar, 1040-99), Spain's national hero.

Europa Issue, 1962

Bee and Honeycomb
A277

1962, Sept. 13   Photo.   *Perf. 12½x13*

| 1125 | A277 | 1p dp rose | 75 | 10 |
| 1126 | A277 | 5p dl grn | 3.00 | 35 |

Discus Thrower	UPAE Emblem
A278	A279

Sports: 80c, Runner. 1p, Hurdler. 3p, Sprinter at start.

1962, Oct. 7   *Perf. 13x12½*

1127	A278	25c pale pink & vio blk	15	10
1128	A278	80c pale yel & dk grn	55	10
1129	A278	1p pale rose & brn	25	10
1130	A278	3p pale bl & dk bl	40	20

Issued to commemorate the Second Spanish-American Games, Madrid, Oct. 7-12.

Builders of the New World
Portrait Type of 1961

1962, Oct. 12   Unwmkd.

Portraits: 25c, 2p, Alonso de Mendoza. 70c, 2.50p, Jiménez de Quesada. 80c, 3p, Juan de Garay. 1p, 5p, Pedro de la Gasca.

1131	A265	25c rose lil, gray	10	10
1132	A265	70c grn, pale pink	1.00	15
1133	A265	80c dk grn, pale yel	80	15
1134	A265	1p red brn, gray	1.40	15
1135	A265	2p car, lt bl	3.75	15
1136	A265	2.50p dk vio, pnksh	80	25
1137	A265	3p dp bl, pale pink	8.50	1.10
1138	A265	5p brn, pale yel	4.00	1.50
		Nos. 1131-1138 (8)	20.35	3.55

1962, Oct. 20   Engraved   *Perf. 13*

| 1139 | A279 | 1p sep & grn | 25 | 10 |

Issued to commemorate the 50th anniversary of the founding of the Postal Union of the Americas and Spain, UPAE.

The Annunciation, by Murillo	Holy Family by Pedro de Mena
A280	A281

1962, Oct. 26

Mysteries of the Rosary: 70c, The Visitation, Correa. 80c, Nativity, Murillo. 1p, The Presentation, Pedro de Campaña. 1.50p, The Finding in the Temple, (unknown painter). 2p, The Agony in the Garden, Gianquinto. 2.50p, The Scourging at the Pillar, Alonso Cano. 3p, The Crowning with Thorns, Tiepolo. 5p, Carrying of the Cross, El Greco. 8p, The Crucifixion, Murillo. 10p, The Resurrection, Murillo.

1140	A280	25c lil & brn	10	10
1141	A280	70c grn & dk bl grn	10	10
1142	A280	80c ol & dk bl grn	10	10
1143	A280	1p grn & gray	4.50	90
1144	A280	1.50p grn & dk bl	15	10
1145	A280	2p brn & vio	1.00	15
1146	A280	2.50p dk brn & rose cl	25	20
1147	A280	3p lil & gray	25	20
1148	A280	5p brn & dk car	50	50
1149	A280	8p vio brn & blk	50	45
1150	A280	10p grn & yel grn	75	40
		Nos. 1140-1150, C171-C174 (15)	10.30	5.05

1962, Dec. 6   Photo.   *Perf. 13x12½*

| 1151 | A281 | 1p ol gray | 85 | 15 |

Malaria Eradication Emblem
A282

1962, Dec. 21   *Perf. 12½x13*

| 1152 | A282 | 1p blk, yel grn & yel | 60 | 10 |

Issued for the World Health Organization drive to eradicate malaria.

Pope John XXIII and St. Peter's, Rome—A283

1962, Dec. 29   Engraved

| 1153 | A283 | 1p dp plum & blk | 60 | 20 |

Issued to commemorate Vatican II, the 21st Ecumenical Council of the Roman Catholic Church. See also No. 1199.

St. Paul, by El Greco	Courtyard, Poblet Monastery
A284	A285

1963, Jan. 25   *Perf. 13*

| 1154 | A284 | 1p brn, blk & ol | 75 | 25 |

Issued to commemorate the 1,900th anniversary of St. Paul's visit to Spain.

Perf. 12½x13, 13x12½

1963, Feb. 25   Unwmkd.

Designs: 1p, Royal sepulcher. 3p, View of monastery (horiz.). 5p, Gothic arch.

1155	A285	25c choc & sl grn	15	8
1156	A285	1p org ver & rose car	70	15
1157	A285	3p vio bl & dk bl	1.75	25
1158	A285	5p brn & ocher	3.25	1.50

Issued in honor of the Cistercian monastery of Santa Maria de Poblet.

José de Ribera, Self-portrait	Coach
A285a	A286

Ribera Paintings: 25c, Archimedes. 40c, Jacob's Flock. 70c, Triumph of Bacchus. 80c, St. Christopher. 1.50p, St. Andrew. 2.50p, St. John the Baptist. 3p, St. Onofre. 5p, St. Peter. 10p, The Immaculate Virgin.

Photogravure

1963, Mar. 24   *Perf. 13*   Unwmkd.

Gold Frame

1159	A285a	25c violet	10	10
1160	A285a	40c red lil	10	10
1161	A285a	70c green	35	10
1162	A285a	80c dk grn	35	10
1163	A285a	1p brown	35	10
1164	A285a	1.50p bl grn	35	10
1165	A285a	2.50p car rose	1.75	20
1166	A285a	3p dk bl	1.75	45
1167	A285a	5p olive	6.75	2.00
1168	A285a	10p dl red brn	1.75	1.00
		Nos. 1159-1168 (10)	13.60	4.25

Issued to honor José de Ribera (1588-1652) and for Stamp Day, Mar. 24.

1963, May 3   *Perf. 13x12½*

| 1169 | A286 | 1p multi | 15 | 10 |

Issued to commemorate the centenary of the first International Postal Conference, Paris, 1863.

Globe
A287

1963, May 8   *Perf. 12½x13*

1170	A287	25c multi	10	10
1171	A287	1p multi	20	10
1172	A287	10p multi	2.25	50

Issued for International Stamp Day, 1963.

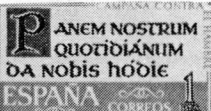

"Give us this Day our Daily Bread . . ."
A288

1963, June 1   Unwmkd.

| 1173 | A288 | 1p multi | 12 | 10 |

Issued for the "Freedom from Hunger" campaign of the U.N. Food and Agriculture Organization.

"Pillars of Hercules" and Globes	Seal of Council of San Sebastian
A289	A290

Designs: 80c, Fleet of Columbus. 1p, Columbus and compass rose.

1963, June 4   *Perf. 13*

1174	A289	25c multi	10	10
1175	A289	80c brn, lt grn & gold	18	10
1176	A289	1p sl grn, sep & gold	18	10

Issued to publicize the Congress of Institutions of Spanish Culture, June 5-15.

1963, June 27   Photogravure

Designs: 80c, Burning of city, 1813. 1p, View, 1836.

1177	A290	25c vio, grn & blk	10	10
1178	A290	80c dk brn, gray & red	18	10
1179	A290	1p dk grn, grn & ol	18	10

150th anniversary of the rebuilding of San Sebastian.

Europa Issue, 1963

Our Lady of Europe
A291

SPAIN

1963, Sept. 16 — Perf. 13x12½ — Engraved
1180	A291	1p bis brn & choc	30	10
1181	A291	5p bluish grn & blk	1.50	40

Arms of Order of Mercy
A292

King James I
A293

Designs: 1p, Our Lady of Mercy. 1.50p, St. Pedro Nolasco. 3p, St. Raimundo de Peñafort.

1963, Sept. 24 Photo. Perf. 13
1182	A292	25c blk, car rose & gold	10	10

Engraved
1183	A293	80c sep & grn	10	10
1184	A293	1p gray vio & brn vio	10	20
1185	A293	1.50p dl bl & blk	10	20
1186	A293	3p gray & blk	35	20
		Nos. 1182-1186 (5)	85	70

Issued to commemorate the 75th anniversary of the coronation of Our Lady of Mercy.

Builders of the New World
Portrait Type of 1961.
1963, Oct. 12 — Perf. 13x12½

Portraits: 25c, 2p, Father Junipero Serra. 70c, 2.50p, Vasco Nuñez de Balboa. 80c, 3p, José de Galvez. 1p, 5p, Diego Garcia de Paredes.

1187	A265	25c vio bl, bl	20	10
1188	A265	70c grn, pale rose	20	10
1189	A265	80c dk grn, yel	70	10
1190	A265	1p dk bl, pale rose	70	10
1191	A265	2p mag, lt bl	2.50	10
1192	A265	2.50p vio blk, dl vio	1.50	10
1193	A265	3p brt bl, pink	3.00	70
1194	A265	5p brn, yel	3.75	2.00
		Nos. 1187-1194 (8)	12.55	3.30

The Good Samaritan
A294

1963, Oct. 28 — Unwmkd.
1195	A294	1p gold, pur & brt car	12	10

Centenary of International Red Cross.

Holy Family by Alonso Berruguete (1486–1561)
A295

Father Raymond Lully
A296

1963, Dec. 2 Photo. Perf. 13x12½
1196	A295	1p dk grn	12	10

Christmas 1963. See also No. 1279.

1963, Dec. 5 — Engraved
Portrait: 1.50p, Cardinal Luis Antonio de Belluga (1662–1743).

1197	A296	1p dk vio & blk	35	5
1198	A296	1.50p sep & dl vio	20	5

See also Nos. C175–C176.

Papal Type of 1962
Design: 1p, Pope Paul VI and St. Peter's, Rome.

1963, Dec. 30 — Perf. 12½x13
1199	A283	1p dk grn & blk	18	10

Issued to commemorate the second session of Vatican II, the 21st Ecumenical Council of the Roman Catholic Church.

Tourist Issue, 1964

Alcazar, Segovia
A297

Dragon Caves, Majorca
A298

Designs: 40c, Potes, Santander. 50c, Leon Cathedral. No. 1202, Crypt of San Isidro at Leon. No. 1203, Costa Brava. 80c, Christ of the Lanterns, Cordova. No. 1206, Court of Lions, Alhambra, Granada. No. 1208, Interior of La Mezquita, Cordova. 1.50p, View of Gerona.

1964 — Engraved — Perf. 13
1200	A297	40c sep & bl	10	8
1201	A298	50c gray & sep	10	8
1202	A297	70c ind & dk bl grn	10	8
1203	A298	70c vio & brn	10	8
1204	A298	80c dp ultra & blk	20	8
1205	A297	1p vio bl & pur	10	8
1206	A297	1p rose red & dl pur	10	8
1207	A298	1p dk grn & blk	10	8
1208	A298	1p brn vio & rose	10	8
1209	A297	1.50p gray grn, brn & blk	10	8
		Nos. 1200-1209 (10)	1.10	80

See also Nos. 1280–1289.

Santa Maria de Huerta Monastery
A299

Joaquin Sorolla, Self-portrait
A300

Designs: 1p, Great Hall. 5p, View of monastery with apse (horiz.).

Perf. 13x12½, 12½x13
1964, Feb. 24
1212	A299	1p gray grn & grn	10	10
1213	A299	2p grnsh bl & sep	10	10
1214	A299	5p dk bl	2.85	55

8th century of Santa Maria Monastery, Huerta.

1964, Mar. 24 Photo. Perf. 13
Sorolla Paintings: 25c, The Jug (woman and child). 40c, Oxen and Driver (horiz.). 70c, Man and Woman from La Mancha. 80c, Fisher Woman of Valencia. 1p, Self-portrait. 1.50p, Round up (horiz.). 2.50p, Fishermen (horiz.). 3p, Children at the Beach (horiz.). 5p, Unloading the Boat. 10p, Man and Woman on Horseback, Valencia.

Gold Frame
1215	A300	25c violet	10	10
1216	A300	40c purple	10	10
1217	A300	70c dp yel grn	10	10
1218	A300	80c bluish grn	10	10
1219	A300	1p brown	10	10
1220	A300	1.50p Prus bl	10	10
1221	A300	2.50p dk car rose	20	10
1222	A300	3p vio bl	55	30
1223	A300	5p chocolate	1.50	1.10
1224	A300	10p dp grn	90	25
		Nos. 1215-1224 (10)	3.75	2.35

Issued to honor Joaquin Sorolla y Bastida (1863–1923) and for Stamp Day, March 24.

"Peace"
A301

"Sport"
A302

Designs: 40c, Radio and television. 50c, New apartments. 70c, Agriculture. 80c, Reforestation. 1p, Economic development. 1.50p, Modern architecture. 2p, Transportation. 2.50p, Hydroelectric development. 3p, Electrification. 5p, Scientific achievements. 6p, Buildings, tourism. 10p, Generalissimo Franco.

1964, Apr. 1
1225	A301	25c blk, emer & gold	10	10
1226	A302	30c blk, bl & sal pink	10	10
1227	A301	40c gold & blk	10	10
1228	A301	50c multi	10	10
1229	A301	70c multi	10	10
1230	A301	80c multi	10	10
1231	A302	1p multi	35	10
1232	A302	1.50p multi	20	10
1233	A301	2p multi	20	10
1234	A302	2.50p multi	20	12
1235	A301	3p gold, blk & red	1.40	1.10
1236	A302	5p gold, grn & red	40	40
1237	A301	6p multi	1.00	85
1238	A302	10p multi	1.00	85
		Nos. 1225-1238 (14)	5.35	4.22

Issued to commemorate 25 years of peace.

Bullfight and Unisphere
A303

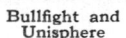
Stamp of 1850 and Modern Stamps
A304

Designs: 1p, Spanish pavilion (horiz.). 2.50p, La Mota castle, Medina de Campo. 5p, Spanish dancer. 50p, Jai alai.

Perf. 12½x13, 13x12½
1964, Apr. 23 — Engraved
1239	A303	1p bl grn & yel grn	50	10
1240	A303	1.50p car, bl & brn	12	10
1241	A303	2.50p dk bl & sl grn	20	10
1242	A303	5p car & dk car rose	65	65
1243	A303	50p vio bl & dk bl	2.25	60
		Nos. 1239-1243 (5)	3.72	1.55

New York World's Fair, 1964–65.

1964, May 6 — Perf. 13x12½
1244	A304	25c dk car rose & dl pur	10	10
1245	A304	1p yel grn & blk	45	10
1246	A304	10p org & rose red	1.40	45

Issued for International Stamp Day, 1964.

Virgin of Hope (La Macarena)
A305

Santa Maria
A306

1964, May 31 Photo. Perf. 13x12½
1247	A305	1p dk grn	12	10

Issued to commemorate the canonical coronation of the Virgin of Hope (La Macarena) in St. Gil's Church, Seville, May 31.

1964, July 16 — Perf. 13
Designs (ships): 15c, 13th century ship of King Alfonso X, from medieval manuscript (vert.). 25c, Carrack, from 15th century engraving (vert.). 50c, Galley. 70c, Galleon. 80c, Xebec. 1p, Warship, Santisima Trinidad (vert.). 1.50p, 18th century corvette, Atrevida (vert.). 2p, Steamer, Isabel II. 2.50p, Frigate, Numancia, Spain's first armored ship. 3p, Destroyer. 5p, Submarine of Isaac Peral. 6p, Cruiser, Baleares. 10p, Training ship, Juan Sebastian Elcano.

1248	A306	15c dp rose & vio blk	10	10
1249	A306	25c org yel & gray grn	10	10
1250	A306	40c ultra & dk bl	10	10
1251	A306	50c sl grn & dk bl	10	10
1252	A306	70c vio & dk bl	10	10
1253	A306	80c dl bl grn & ultra	10	10
1254	A306	1p org & vio brn	10	10
1255	A306	1.50p car & sep	10	10
1256	A306	2p blk & sl grn	1.25	10
1257	A306	2.50p rose car & dl vio	15	10
1258	A306	3p sep & ind	15	12
1259	A306	5p dk bl, lt grn & vio	1.40	85
1260	A306	6p lt grn & vio	70	70
1261	A306	10p org yel & rose red	55	40
		Nos. 1248-1261 (14)	5.00	3.07

Issued to honor the Spanish Navy.

Europa Issue, 1964
Common Design Type
1964, Sept. 14 Photo. Perf. 12½x13
Size: 21½x39mm.

1262	CD7	1p bis, red & grn	75	10
1263	CD7	5p brt bl, mag & grn	2.25	50

Madonna of Alcazar
A307

Shot Put
A308

SPAIN

1964, Oct. 9		Photo.	Perf. 13	
1264	A307	25c bis & brn	10	5
1265	A307	1p gray & ind	10	5

700th anniversary of the reconquest of Jerez de la Frontera.

1964, Oct. 10
Sport: 80c, Broad jump. 1p, Slalom. 3p, Judo. 5p, Discus.

Gold Olympic Rings

1266	A308	25c org red & blk	10	10
1267	A308	80c emer & blk	10	10
1268	A308	1p brt bl & ind	10	10
1269	A308	3p bis & ind	35	20
1270	A308	5p lil & ind	45	20
		Nos. 1266-1270 (5)	1.10	70

1964 Olympic Games.

Builders of the New World
Portrait Type of 1961

1964, Oct. 12			Perf. 13x12½	

Portraits: 25c, Diego de Almagro. 70c, 2.50p, Francisco de Toledo. 80c, 3p, Archbishop Toribio de Mogrovejo. 1p, 5p, Francisco Pizarro.

1271	A265	25c pale grn & vio	10	10
1272	A265	70c pink & ol gray	10	10
1273	A265	80c buff & Prus grn	45	25
1274	A265	1p buff & gray vio	10	10
1275	A265	2p pale bl & ol gray	45	10
1276	A265	2.50p pale grn & cl		25	20
1277	A265	3p gray & dk bl	3.00	85
1278	A265	5p yel & brn	2.00	1.10
		Nos. 1271-1278 (8)	6.80	2.80

Christmas Type of 1963
Design: Nativity by Francisco de Zurbaran (1598–1664).

1964, Dec. 4			Photogravure	
1279	A295	1p ol blk	12	10

Tourist Issue, 1965
Types of 1964

Designs: 25c, Columbus monument, Barcelona. 30s, Facade of Santa Maria, Burgos. 50c, Santa Maria la Blanca (medieval synagogue), Toledo. 70c, Bridge, Zamora. 80c, La Giralda (tower) and Cathedral of Seville. 1p, Boat and nets in Cudillero harbor. No. 1286, Cathedral of Burgos, interior. No. 1287, View of Mogrovejo, Santander. 3p, Bridge, Cambados, Pontevedra. 6p, Silk merchants' hall (Lonja), Valencia, interior.

1965		Engraved	Perf. 13	
1280	A298	25c dk bl & blk	10	5
1281	A298	30c dl grn & sep	10	5
1282	A298	50c cl & rose car	10	5
1283	A297	70c vio bl & ind	10	5
1284	A298	80c rose cl & dk pur	10	5
1285	A298	1p dp cl, car & blk	10	5
1286	A298	2.50p brn vio & bis	10	5
1287	A297	2.50p dl bl & gray	10	5
1288	A298	3p rose car & dk brn	10	5
1289	A298	6p sl & blk	20	8
		Nos. 1280-1289 (10)	1.10	53

Alfonso X, the Wise (1232–84)
A309

Julio Romero de Torres, Self-portrait
A310

Portraits: 25c, Juan Donoso-Cortes (1809–53). 2.50p, Gaspar M. Jovellanos (1744–1810). 5p, St. Dominic de Guzman (1170–1221).

			Perf. 13x12½	
1965, Feb. 25			Engraved	
1292	A309	25c sl bl & blk	10	7
1293	A309	70c bl & ind	25	10
1294	A309	2.50p sl grn & sep	25	8
1295	A309	5p dl grn & sl grn	60	15

1965, Mar. 24		Photo.	Perf. 13	

De Torres Paintings: 25c, Girl with Jar. 40c, "The Song" (girl with guitar). 70c, Madonna of the Lanterns. 80c, Girl with guitar. 1.50p, "The Poem of Cordova" (pensive woman). 2.50p, Martha and Mary. 3p, "The Poem of Cordova" (two women holding statue of angel). 5p, Girl with the Charcoal. 10p, Back of woman's head.

Gold Frame

1296	A310	25c dl pur	10	10
1297	A310	40c purple	10	10
1298	A310	70c ol grn	10	10
1299	A310	80c sl grn	10	10
1300	A310	1p dk red brn	15	10
1301	A310	1.50p bl grn	10	10
1302	A310	2.50p lil rose	10	10
1303	A310	3p dk bl	20	10
1304	A310	5p brown	40	15
1305	A310	10p sl grn	60	20
		Nos. 1296-1305 (10)	1.95	1.15

Issued to honor Julio Romero de Torres (1880–1930) and for Stamp Day, March 24.

Bull and Symbolic Stamps
A311

1965, May 6			Perf. 13x12½	
1306	A311	25c multi	10	10
1307	A311	1p org & multi	30	10
1308	A311	10p multi	1.25	40

Issued for International Stamp Day, 1965.

ITU Emblem, Old and New Communication Equipment
A312

1965, May 17			Perf. 12½x13	
1309	A312	1p sal, blk & red	12	10

Issued to commemorate the centenary of the International Telecommunication Union.

Pilgrim
A313

Design: 2p, Pilgrim (profile).

Explorer, Royal Flag of Spain and Ships
A314

1965, July 25		Photo.	Perf. 13	
1310	A313	1p multi	10	6
1311	A313	2p multi	10	10

Issued to commemorate the Holy Year of St. James of Compostela, patron saint of Spain.

1965, Aug. 28			Perf. 13x12½	
1312	A314	3p red, blk & yel	15	10

Issued to commemorate the 400th anniversary of the settlement of Florida, and the first permanent European settlement in the continental United States, St. Augustine, Fla. See also United States No. 1271.

St. Benedict
A315

Sports Palace, Madrid
A316

Europa Issue, 1965

			Perf. 13x12½	
1965, Sept. 27			Engraved	
1313	A315	1p yel grn & sl grn	25	10
1314	A315	5p lil & vio	1.40	15

1965, Oct. 9		Photo.	Perf. 13	
1315	A316	1p gray, gold & dk brn	12	8

Issued to commemorate the meeting of the International Olympic Committee in Madrid.

Builders of the New World
Portrait Type of 1961

Portraits: 25c, 2p, Don Fadrique de Toledo. 70c, 2.50p, Father José de Anchieta. 80c, 3p, Francisco de Orellana. 1p, 5p, St. Luis Beltran.

1965, Oct. 12		Photo.	Perf. 13x12½	
1316	A265	25c pale grn & dp pur	10	8
1317	A265	70c pink & brn	10	8
1318	A265	80c cr & Prus grn	10	8
1319	A265	1p buff & dk vio	10	8
1320	A265	2p lt bl & dk ol gray	15	8
1321	A265	2.50p lt bl & pur	15	8
1322	A265	3p gray & dk bl	1.10	20
1323	A265	5p yel & brn	1.10	30
		Nos. 1316-1323 (8)	2.90	98

Chamber of Charles V, Yuste Monastery
A317

Stamp of 1865 (No. 78)
A318

Yuste Monastery: 1p, Courtyard (horiz.). 5p, View of monastery (horiz.).

		Perf. 12½x13, 13x12½	
1965, Nov. 15			Engraved
1324	A317	1p bl gray & blk	10	10
1325	A317	2p red brn & brn blk	35	10
1326	A317	5p grysh bl & grn	50	25

Monastery of Yuste, Estremadura.

1965, Nov. 22			Perf. 13x12½	

Designs: 1p, Stamp of 1865 (No. 77). 5p, Stamp of 1865 (No. 80).

1327	A318	80c blk & yel grn	10	5
1328	A318	1p plum, brn & rose	10	7
1329	A318	5p sep & org brn	10	10

Issued to commemorate the centenary of the first Spanish perforated postage stamps.

Nativity
A319

1965, Dec. 1		Photo.	Perf. 12½x13	
1330	A319	1p brt grn	12	10

Virgin of Peace, Antipolo
A320

Globe and Four Beasts of Apocalypse
A321

Design: 3p, Father Andres de Urdaneta.

1965, Dec. 3			Perf. 13x12½	
1331	A320	1p pale sal & ol brn	20	10
1332	A320	3p gray & dp bl	30	10

Issued to commemorate the 400th anniversary of the Christianization of the Philippines.

1965, Dec. 29		Photo.	Perf. 13x12½	
1333	A321	1p grnsh bl, yel & brn	12	10

Issued to commemorate Vatican II, the 21st Ecumenical Council of the Roman Catholic Church, Oct. 11, 1962–Dec. 8, 1965.

Admiral Alvaro de Bazan (1526–1588)
A322

Exhibition Emblem; Type Block "P"
A323

Portrait: 2p, Daza de Valdes, scientist (17th century).

1966, Feb. 26		Engr.	Perf. 13x12½	
1334	A322	25c dl bl & gray	10	5
1335	A322	2p mag & vio	20	5

See also Nos. C177–C178.

1966, March 4		Photo.	Perf. 13	
1336	A323	1p red, grn & vio bl	12	10

Issued to publicize the Graphic Arts and Advertising Packaging Exhibition "Graphispack," Barcelona, March 4–13.

SPAIN

José Maria Sert,　Santa Maria
Self-portrait　Church, Guernica
A324　A325

Sert Paintings: 25c, The Magic Ball. 40c, Evocation of Toledo (horiz.). 70c, Christ on the Cross. 80c, Parachutists. 1.50p, "Audacity." 2.50p, "Justice." 3p, Jacob Wrestling with the Angel. 5p, "The Five Continents." 10p, Sts. Peter and Paul.

1966, March 24 Gold Frame

1337	A324	25c dk pur	10	6
1338	A324	40c dp mag	10	6
1339	A324	70c green	10	5
1340	A324	80c dk ol grn	10	5
1341	A324	1p cl brn	10	5
1342	A324	1.50p dl bl	10	5
1343	A324	2.50p dk red	12	6
1344	A324	3p dp bl	12	10
1345	A324	5p sepia	18	10
1346	A324	10p black	30	15
		Nos. 1337-1346 (10)	1.32	73

Issued to honor José Maria Sert (1876-1945) and for Stamp Day, March 24.

1966, Apr. 28 Photo. Perf. 13

Designs: 1p, Arms of Guernica and Luno. 3p, Tree of Guernica.

1347	A325	80c bl, sep & grn	10	6
1348	A325	1p yel grn & multi	10	8
1349	A325	3p bl, grn & vio brn	10	8

Issued to commemorate the 6th centenary of the founding of Guernica and Luno.

Cover with
Stamp of
1850
(No. 1)
A326

Designs (covers): 1p, 5r (No. 3). 10p, 10r (No. 5).

1966, May 6 Perf. 12½x13

1350	A326	25c rose vio, blk & red	10	5
1351	A326	1p red brn, org & blk	10	5
1352	A326	10p ol grn, grn & org	50	20

Issued for International Stamp Day, 1966.

Tourist Issue, 1966

Bohi Valley　Torla, Huesca
A327　A328

Designs: 40c, Portal of Sigena Monastery, Huesca. 50c, Santo Domingo Church, Soria. 80c, Torre del Oro, Seville. 1p, Palm and view, Pico de Teyde, Santa Cruz de Tenerife. 1.50p, Monastery of Guadalupe, Caceres. 2p, Alcala de Henares University. 3p, Seo Cathedral, Lerida. 10p, Courtyard of St. Gregorio, Valladolid.

1966 Engraved Perf. 13

1353	A327	10c gray grn & bl grn	6	5
1354	A328	15c gray grn & brn	6	5
1355	A327	40c bis brn & grn	6	5
1356	A327	50c car rose & dp cl	6	5
1357	A327	80c lil & rose vio	6	5
1358	A327	1p vio bl & bl grn	6	5
1359	A328	1.50p dk bl & blk	6	5
1360	A328	2p sl bl & sep	6	5
1361	A328	3p ultra & blk	6	6
1362	A327	10p brt bl & grnsh bl	20	5
		Nos. 1353-1362 (10)	74	51

Tree and
Globe
A329

1966, June 6 Photo. Perf. 12½x13

1363	A329	1p brn & dk grn	12	10

Issued to commemorate the 6th International Forestry Congress, Madrid, June 6-18.

Navy Emblem
A330

1966, July 1 Photo. Perf. 13

1364	A330	1p gray & dk bl	12	10

Naval Week, Barcelona, July 1-3.

Guadamur
Castle
A331

Castles: 25c, Alcazar, Segovia. 40c, La Mota. 50c, Olite. 70c, Monteagudo. 80c, Butron (vert.). 1p, Manzanares. 3p, Almansa (vert.).

1966, Aug. 13 Engraved Perf. 13

1365	A331	10c grysh bl & sep	6	5
1366	A331	25c vio & pur	6	5
1367	A331	40c grnsh bl & bl grn	6	5
1368	A331	50c grnsh bl & ultra	6	5
1369	A331	70c vio bl & ind	6	5
1370	A331	80c vio & sl grn	6	5
1371	A331	1p ol bis & gray	8	5
1372	A331	3p rose & red lil	8	5
		Nos. 1365-1372 (8)	52	40

Don Quixote, Dulcinea
and Aldonza Lorenzo
A332

1966, Sept. 5 Photo. Perf. 13

1373	A332	1.50p sal, lt grn & blk	12	10

4th World Congress of Psychiatry, Madrid.

Europa Issue, 1966

The
Rape of
Europa
A333

1966, Sept. 28 Photo. Perf. 12½x13

1374	A333	1p multi	35	10
1375	A333	5p multi	85	10

Don Quixote　Title Page of
and Sancho　"Dotrina
Panza on　Christiana"
Clavileno
A334　A335

1966, Oct. 9 Perf. 13x12½

1376	A334	1.50p sl bl, red brn & dk brn	12	10

Issued to commemorate the 17th Congress of the International Astronautical Federation.

Builders of the New World
Types of 1961 and A335

Designs: 30c, Antonio de Mendoza. 1p, José A. Manso de Velasco. 1.20p, Coins of Lima, 1699. 1.50p, Manuel de Castro y Padilla. 3p, Portal of Oruro Convent, Bolivia. 3.50p, Manuel de Amat. 6p, Inca courier, El Chasqui.

1966, Oct. 12

1377	A265	30c pale pink & brn	8	6
1378	A335	50c pale bis & brn	8	6
1379	A265	1p gray & vio	8	6
1380	A335	1.20p gray & sl	8	6
1381	A265	1.50p pale grn & dp grn	8	6
1382	A335	3p pale gray & dp bl	8	6
1383	A265	3.50p pale lil & pur	8	6
1384	A265	6p buff & sep	30	6
		Nos. 1377-1384 (8)	86	48

Ramon del Valle
Inclan
A336

Portraits: 3p, Carlos Arniches. 6p, Jacinto Benavente y Martinez.

1966, Nov. 7 Photo. Perf. 13

1385	A336	1.50p bl & grn	12	10
1386	A336	3p blk & gray vio	10	8
1387	A336	6p blk & sl	15	10

Issued to honor Spanish writers.

Carthusian
Monastery,
Jerez
A337

St. Mary Carthusian Monastery: 1p, Portal (vert.). 5p, Entrance gate.

Perf. 13x12½, 12½x13
1966, Nov. 24 Engraved

1388	A337	1p grnsh bl & sl bl	10	7
1389	A337	2p grn & yel grn	25	10
1390	A337	5p lil & cl	25	12

Nativity, Sculpture by Pedro Duque Cornejo
A338

1966, Dec. 5 Photo. Perf. 12½x13

1391	A338	1.50p multi	12	10

Regional Costumes Issue

Woman from
Alava
A339

1967		Photogravure	Perf.	13
1392	A339	6p multi	18	12
1393	A339	6p multi (*Albacete*)	18	12
1394	A339	6p multi (*Alicante*)	18	12
1395	A339	6p multi (*Almeria*)	18	12
1396	A339	6p multi (*Avila*)	18	12
1397	A339	6p multi (*Badajoz*)	18	12
1398	A339	6p multi (*Baleares*)	18	12
1399	A339	6p multi (*Barcelona*)	18	12
1400	A339	6p multi (*Burgos*)	18	12
1401	A339	6p multi (*Caceres*)	18	12
1402	A339	6p multi (*Cadiz*)	18	12
1403	A339	6p multi (*Castellon de la Plana*)	12	12
		Nos. 1392-1403 (12)	2.16	1.44

(1968)

1404	A339	6p multi (*Ciudad Real*)	18	12
1405	A339	6p multi (*Cordoba*)	18	12
1406	A339	6p multi (*Coruña*)	18	12
1407	A339	6p multi (*Cuenca*)	18	12
1408	A339	6p multi (*Fernando Po*)	18	12
1409	A339	6p multi (*Gerona*)	18	12
1410	A339	6p multi (*Gran Canaria, Las Palmas*)	18	12
1411	A339	6p multi (*Granada*)	18	12
1412	A339	6p multi (*Guadalajara*)	18	12
1413	A339	6p multi (*Guipuzcoa*)	18	12
1414	A339	6p multi (*Huelva*)	18	12
1415	A339	6p multi (*Huesca*)	18	12
		Nos. 1404-1415 (12)	2.16	1.44

(1969)

1416	A339	6p multi (*Ifni*)	18	12
1417	A339	6p multi (*Jaen*)	18	12
1418	A339	6p multi (*Leon*)	18	12
1419	A339	6p multi (*Lerida*)	18	12
1420	A339	6p multi (*Logroño*)	18	12
1421	A339	6p multi (*Lugo*)	18	12
1422	A339	6p multi (*Madrid*)	18	12
1423	A339	6p multi (*Malaga*)	18	12
1424	A339	6p multi (*Murcia*)	18	12
1425	A339	6p multi (*Navarra*)	18	12
1426	A339	6p multi (*Orense*)	18	12
1427	A339	6p multi (*Oviedo*)	18	12
		Nos. 1416-1427 (12)	2.16	1.44

(1970)

1428	A339	6p multi (*Palencia*)	18	12
1429	A339	6p multi (*Pontevedra*)	18	12
1430	A339	6p multi (*Sahara*)	18	12
1431	A339	6p multi (*Salamanca*)	18	12

SPAIN

1432	A339	6p multi (Santa Cruz de Tenerife)	18	12
1433	A339	6p multi (Santander)	18	12
1434	A339	6p multi (Segovia)	18	12
1435	A339	6p multi (Seville)	18	12
1436	A339	6p multi (Soria)	18	12
1437	A339	6p multi (Tarragona)	20	12
1438	A339	6p multi (Teruel)	20	12
1439	A339	6p multi (Toledo)	20	12
		Nos. 1428-1439 (12)	2.22	1.44

(1971)

1440	A339	6p multi (Valencia)	25	15
1441	A339	8p multi (Valladolid)	35	15
1442	A339	8p multi (Vizcaya)	35	15
1443	A339	8p multi (Zamora)	35	15
1444	A339	8p multi (Zaragoza)	35	15
		Nos. 1440-1444 (5)	1.65	75
		Nos. 1392-1444 (53)	10.17	6.39

Archers
A340

Ornament
A341

Designs: 50c, Boar hunt. 1.20p, Bison. 1.50p, Hands. 2p, Warrior. 2.50p, Deer. 3.50p, Archers. 4p, Hunters and gazelle. 6p, Hunters and deer herd.

1967, Mar. 27   Photo.   Perf. 13
Gold Frame

1449	A340	40c ocher & car rose	8	5
1450	A340	50c gray & dk red	8	5
1451	A341	1p ocher & org ver	12	5
1452	A340	1.20p gray & rose brn	8	5
1453	A340	1.50p gray & red	8	5
1454	A341	2p lt brn & dk car rose	8	5
1455	A341	2.50p sky bl & rose brn	8	5
1456	A340	3.50p yel & blk	25	8
1457	A341	4p cit & red	8	12
1458	A341	6p ol & red	20	18
		Nos. 1449-1458 (10)	1.13	73

Issued for Stamp Day, 1967. The designs are from paleolithic and mesolithic wall paintings found in Spanish caves.

Palma Cathedral and
Conference Emblem—A342

1967, March 28

| 1459 | A342 | 1.50p brt bl grn | 12 | 10 |

Issued to publicize the Congress of the Interparliamentary Union, Palma de Mallorca.

W. K. Röntgen, X-ray Tube
and Atom—A343

1967, Apr. 3   Photo.   Perf. 13

| 1460 | A343 | 1.50p green | 12 | 10 |

Issued to publicize the 7th Congress of Latin Radiologists and the 1st Congress of European Radiologists, Barcelona, Apr. 2–8.

Averroës
(1120–1198),
Physician and
Philosopher
A344

Portraits: 3.50p, José de Acosta (1539–1600), Jesuit, historian, poet. 4p, Moses ben Maimonides (1135–1204), Jewish philosopher and physician. 25p, Andres Laguna, 16th century physician.

1967, Apr. 6 Engraved Perf. 13x12½

1461	A344	1.20p lil & dl vio	10	5
1462	A344	3.50p mag & dl pur	15	7
1463	A344	4p brn & sep	15	8
1464	A344	25p dl bl & blk	45	12

Europa Issue, 1967
Common Design Type

1967, May 2   Photo.   Perf. 13
Size: 25x31mm.

| 1465 | CD10 | 1.50p sl grn, red brn & dl red | 50 | 10 |
| 1466 | CD10 | 6p vio, brt bl & brn | 45 | 15 |

Exhibition Building and Fountain,
Valencia—A345

1967, May 3

| 1467 | A345 | 1.50p gray grn | 12 | 10 |

Issued to commemorate the 50th anniversary of the International Fair at Valencia.

Numeral
Postmark
No. 3 of 1850
A346

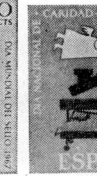
Guardian Angel
Over Indigent
Sleeper
A347

Designs: 1.50p, No. 2, 12c stamp of 1850 with crowned M postmark of Madrid. 6p, No. 4, 6r stamp of 1850 with 1r postmark.

1967, May 6

1468	A346	40c brn org, dl bl & blk	10	5
1469	A346	1.50p brn, grn & blk	10	5
1470	A346	6p bl, red & blk	15	10

International Stamp Day, 1967.
See Nos. 1527–1528.

1967, May 16   Perf. 13

| 1471 | A347 | 1.50p bl, blk, brn & red | 12 | 10 |

Issued for National Caritas Day to honor Caritas, Catholic welfare organization.

Tourist Issue, 1967

Betanzos Church,
Coruña
A348

International
Tourist Year
Emblem
A349

Designs: 1p, Tower of St. Miguel Church, Palencia. 1.50p, Human pyramid (Castellers). 2.50p, Columbus monument, Huelva. 5p, The Enchanted City, Cuenca. 6p, Church of Our Lady, Sanlucar, Cadiz.

1967, July 26 Engraved   Perf. 13

1472	A348	10c ultra & blk	10	6
1473	A348	1p dl bl & blk	10	6
1474	A348	1.50p lt brn & blk	10	6
1475	A348	2.50p grnsh bl & dk bl	10	6
1476	A349	3.50p dl pur & dk bl	15	6
1477	A348	5p yel grn & dk grn	15	6
1478	A348	6p red lil & dl lil	25	6
		Nos. 1472-1478 (7)	95	42

Balsareny
Castle
A350

Castles: 1p, Jarandilla. 1.50p, Almodovar. 2p, Ponferrada (vert.). 2.50p, Peniscola. 5p, Coca. 6p, Loarre. 10p, Belmonte.

1967, Aug. 11   Engraved

1479	A350	50c gray & lt brn	10	8
1480	A350	1p bl gray & dl pur	15	8
1481	A350	1.50p bl gray & sage grn	10	8
1482	A350	2p brick red & bis brn	10	8
1483	A350	2.50p grnsh bl & sep	10	8
1484	A350	5p rose vio & vio bl	25	8
1485	A350	6p bis brn & gray brn	25	10
1486	A350	10p aqua & sl	35	10
		Nos. 1479-1486 (8)	1.40	68

Globe, Snow-
flake and
Thermometer
A351

Galleon, Map of
Americas, Spain
and Philippines
A352

1967, Aug. 30   Photogravure

| 1487 | A351 | 1.50p brt bl | 12 | 10 |

Issued to publicize the 12th International Refrigeration Congress, Madrid, Sept. 4–8.

1967, Oct. 10   Photo.   Perf. 13

| 1488 | A352 | 1.50p red lil | 12 | 10 |

Issued to commemorate the 4th Congress of Spanish, Portuguese, American and Philippine Municipalities, Barcelona, Oct. 6-12.

Builders of the New World
Type of 1961 and

Nootka Settlement
A353

Designs: 40c, Francisco de la Bodega. 50c, Old map of Nootka coast (vert.). 1p, Francisco Antonio Mourelle. 1.50p, Esteban José Martinez. 3p, Old maps of coast of Northern California. 3.50p, Cayetano Valdes. 6p, Ships, San Elias, Alaska.

1967, Oct. 12

1489	A265	40c pink & grnsh gray	10	5
1490	A353	50c dk brn	10	5
1491	A265	1p pale bl & red lil	12	5
1492	A353	1.20p dk ol grn	10	5
1493	A265	1.50p pale pink & bl grn	10	5
1494	A353	3p buff & vio blk	10	8
1495	A265	3.50p pale pink & bl	15	12
1496	A353	6p red brn, bluish	30	8
		Nos. 1489-1496 (8)	1.07	53

Issued to honor the explorers of the Northwest coast of North America.

Roman Statue
and Gate
A354

José
Bethencourt
A355

Designs: 3.50p, Ancient plower with ox team (horiz.). 6p, Roman coins of Caceres.

1967, Oct. 31   Photo.   Perf. 13

1497	A354	1.50p multi	15	10
1498	A354	3.50p multi	15	10
1499	A354	6p multi	20	10

Issued to commemorate the 2000th anniversary of the founding of Caceres by the Romans.

1967, Nov. 15

Portraits: 1.50p, Enrique Granados (composer). 3.50p, Ruben Dario (poet). 6p, St. Ildefonso.

1500	A355	1.20p gray & red brn	10	6
1501	A355	1.50p blk & grn	10	6
1502	A355	3.50p brn & pur	12	6
1503	A355	6p blk & sl	15	8

Issued to honor famous Spanish men.

SPAIN

Santa Maria de Veruela Monastery
A356

St. José Receiving Last Unction, by Goya
A357

Designs: 3.50p, Aerial view of monastery (horiz.). 6p, Inside view (horiz.).

1967, Nov. 24 Engraved Perf. 13

1504	A356	1.50p ultra & ind	10	8
1505	A356	3.50p grn & blk	15	10
1506	A356	6p rose vio & bis brn	45	10

1967, Nov. 27 Photogravure

| 1507 | A357 | 1.50p multi | 12 | 10 |

Issued to commemorate the 200th anniversary of the canonization of St. José de Calasanz (1556-1648), founder of the first Christian Schools in Rome.

Nativity, by Francisco Salzillo
A358

1967, Dec. 5

| 1508 | A358 | 1.50p multi | 12 | 10 |

Christmas, 1967.

Slalom—A359

Designs: 3.50p, Bobsled (vert.). 6p, Ice hockey.

1968, Feb. 6 Photo. Perf. 13

1509	A359	1.50p multi	10	10
1510	A359	3.50p multi	20	10
1511	A359	6p multi	30	12

Issued to commemorate the 10th Winter Olympic Games, Grenoble, France, Feb. 6-18.

Mariano Fortuny, Self-portrait
A360

Fortuny Paintings: 40c, The Vicariate (horiz.). 50c, "Fantasy" (pianist). 1p, "Idyll" (piper and sheep). 1.20p, The Print Collector (horiz.). 2p, Old Man in the Sun. 2.50p, Calabrian Man. 3.50p, Lady with Fan. 4p, Battle of Tetuan, 1860. 6p, Queen Christina in Carriage (horiz.).

1968, Mar. 25 Photo. Perf. 13
Gold Frame

1512	A360	40c dp red lil	6	6
1513	A360	50c dk bl grn	6	6
1514	A360	1p brown	6	5
1515	A360	1.20p dp vio	6	6
1516	A360	1.50p dp brn	6	6
1517	A360	2p org brn	6	5
1518	A360	2.50p car rose	8	6
1519	A360	3.50p dk red brn	40	12
1520	A360	4p dk ol	15	6
1521	A360	6p brt bl	25	10
		Nos. 1512-1521 (10)	1.24	67

Issued to honor Mariano Fortuny y Carbo (1838-74), and for Stamp Day.

Beatriz Galindo
A361

Famous Women: 1.50p, Agustina de Aragon. 3.50p, Maria Pacheco. 6p, Rosalia de Castro.

1968, Apr. 8 Engr. Perf. 12½x13

1522	A361	1.20p yel brn & blk brn	10	9
1523	A361	1.50p bl grn & dk bl	10	8
1524	A361	3.50p lt vio & dk vio	20	10
1525	A361	6p gray bl & blk	25	10

Europa Issue, 1968
Common Design Type

1968, Apr. 29 Photo. Perf. 13
Size: 38x22mm.

| 1526 | CD11 | 3.50p brt bl, gold & brn | 30 | 10 |

Spain No. 1 with Galicia Puebla Postmark
A362

Map of León and Seal
A363

Design: 3.50p, Spain No. 4 with Serena postmark.

1968, May 6 Photo. Perf. 13

| 1527 | A362 | 1.50p blk, bl & ocher | 10 | 10 |
| 1528 | A362 | 3.50p bl, dk grn & blk | 12 | 10 |

Issued for Stamp Day, 1968. See Nos. 1568-1569, 1608, 1677, 1754.

Perf. 13x12½, 12½x13
1968, June 15 Photogravure
Size: 25x38½mm.

Designs: 1.50p, Roman legionary. 3.50p, Emperor Galba coin (horiz.).

| 1529 | A363 | 1p lil, red brn & yel | 10 | 10 |

Size: 25x47½mm.

| 1530 | A363 | 1.50p brn, dk brn & buff | 10 | 10 |

Size: 37½x26mm.

| 1531 | A363 | 3.50p ocher & sl grn | 45 | 12 |

Issued to commemorate the 1900th anniversary of the founding of León by the Roman Legion VII Gemina.

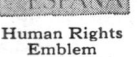

Human Rights Emblem
A364

Benavente Palace, Baeza
A365

1968, June 25 Photo. Perf. 13x12½

| 1532 | A364 | 3.50p bl, red & grn | 15 | 10 |

International Human Rights Year, 1968.

Tourist Issue, 1968

1968, July 15 Engraved Perf. 13

Designs: 1.20p, View of Salamanca with Tormes River Bridge (horiz.). 1.50p, Statuary group from St. Vincent's Church, Avila (The Adoration of the Magi). 2p, Tomb of Martin Vazquez de Arce, Cathedral of Sigüenza (horiz.). 3.50p, Portal of St. Mary's Church, Sangüesa, Navarre.

1533	A365	50c dp rose & brn	10	6
1534	A365	1.20p emer & sl grn	10	6
1535	A365	1.50p dp grn & ind	10	6
1536	A365	2p lil rose & blk	25	6
1537	A365	3.50p brt lil & rose lil	20	6
		Nos. 1533-1537 (5)	75	30

Escalona Castle, Toledo
A366

Castles: 1.20p, Fuensaldaña, Valladolid. 1.50p, Peñafiel, Valladolid. 2.50p, Villasobroso, Pontevedra. 6p, Frias, Burgos (vert.).

1968, July 29 Engraved Perf. 13

1538	A366	40c dk bl & sep	15	10
1539	A366	1.20p vio brn & vio blk	10	8
1540	A366	1.50p ol & blk	10	6
1541	A366	2.50p ol grn & blk	15	5
1542	A366	6p vio bl & bl grn	30	10
		Nos. 1538-1542 (5)	80	39

Rifle Shooting
A367

Designs: 1.50p, Horse jumping. 3.50p, Bicycling. 6p, Sailing (vert.).

Perf. 12½x13, 13x12½
1968, Sept. 24 Photogravure

1543	A367	1p multi	10	6
1544	A367	1.50p multi	15	8
1545	A367	3.50p multi	30	9
1546	A367	6p multi	20	10

Issued to publicize the 19th Olympic Games, Mexico City, Oct. 12-27.

Builders of the New World
Type of 1961 and

Map of Capuchin Missions along Orinoco River, 1732—A368

Designs: 1p, Diego de Losada. 1.50p, Losada family coat of arms. 3.50p, Diego de Henares. 6p, Map of Caracas, drawn by Diego de Henares, 1578 (horiz.).

1968, Oct. 12 Photo. Perf. 13

1547	A368	40c grnsh bl, bluish	10	6
1548	A265	1p red lil, gray	12	6
1549	A368	1.50p sl, pale rose	12	15
1550	A265	3.50p dk bl, pnksh	35	15
1551	A368	6p dk ol bis	45	30
		Nos. 1547-1551 (5)	1.14	72

Issued to commemorate the Christianization of Venezuela and the founding of Caracas.

St. Maria del Parral Monastery, Segovia—A369

Designs: 3.50p, Monastery, inside view. 6p, Madonna and Child, statue from main altar.

1968, Nov. 25 Engraved Perf. 13

1552	A369	1.50p gray bl & rose vio	6	6
1553	A369	3.50p brn & red brn	70	15
1554	A369	6p rose cl & brn	70	15

Nativity, by Federico Fiori da Urbino
A370

Alonso Cano by Velázquez
A371

1968, Dec. 2 Photo. Perf. 13x12½

| 1555 | A370 | 1.50p gold & multi | 12 | 10 |

Christmas, 1968.

1969, Mar. 24 Photo. Perf. 13

Cano Paintings: 40c, St. Agnes. 50c, St. John. 1p, Jesus and Angel. 2p, Holy Family. 2.50p, Madonna and Child. 3p, Jesus and the Samaritan Woman. 3.50p, Madonna and Child. 4p, Sts. John Capistrano and Bernardino (horiz.). 6p, Vision of St. John the Baptist.

Gold Frame

| 1556 | A371 | 40c dp plum | 10 | 10 |

SPAIN

1557	A371	50c green	10	10
1558	A371	1p sepia	12	10
1559	A371	1.50p sl grn	10	10
1560	A371	2p red brn	20	10
1561	A371	2.50p dp red lil	12	10
1562	A371	3p ultra	15	10
1563	A371	3.50p dk rose brn	15	10
1564	A371	4p dl lil	15	10
1565	A371	6p sl bl	30	12
		Nos. 1556-1565 (10)	1.49	1.02

Issued to honor Alonso Cano (1601–1667), and for Stamp Day.

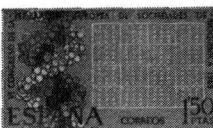

DNA (Genetic Code)
Molecule and Chart
A372

1969, Apr. 7   Photo.   Perf. 13

| 1566 | A372 | 1.50p gray & multi | 12 | 10 |

Issued to publicize the 6th European Congress of Biochemistry, Madrid, Apr. 7–11.

Europa Issue, 1969
Common Design Type

1969, Apr. 28   Size: 38x22mm.

| 1567 | CD12 | 3.50p multi | 35 | 12 |

Stamp Day Type of 1968

Design: 1.50p, Spain No. 6 with crowned M postmark. 3.50p, Spain No. 11 with Corvera postmark.

1969, May 6   Photo.   Perf. 13

| 1568 | A362 | 1.50p blk, red & grn | 10 | 10 |
| 1569 | A362 | 3.50p grn, bl & red | 15 | 10 |

Issued for Stamp Day, 1969.

Spectrum
A373

1969, May 26

| 1570 | A373 | 1.50p blk & multi | 12 | 10 |

Issued to publicize the 15th International Spectroscopy Colloquium, Madrid, May 26–30.

World Map, Red Crescent, Cross, Lion and Sun Emblems
A374

1969, May 30

| 1571 | A374 | 1.50p multi | 12 | 10 |

Issued to commemorate the 50th anniversary of the League of Red Cross Societies.

Last Supper,
Finial from Lugo
Cathedral
A375

1969, June 4

| 1572 | A375 | 1.50p grn, brn & blk | 12 | 10 |

Issued to commemorate the 300th anniversary of the dedication of Galicia Province to the reign of Jesus.

Turegano Castle, Segovia
A376

Father Junipero Serra
A377

Castles: 1.50p, Villalonso, Zamora. 2.50p, Velez Blanco, Almeria. 3.50p, Castilnovo, Segovia. 6p, Torrelobaton, Valladolid.

1969, June 24   Engraved   Perf. 13

1573	A376	1p dl grn & sl	12	10
1574	A376	1.50p bluish lil & dk bl	25	10
1575	A376	2.50p bl vio & bluish lil	18	10
1576	A376	3.50p red brn & ol grn	25	10
1577	A376	6p gray grn & dl brn	25	10
		Nos. 1573-1577 (5)	1.05	50

1969, July 16   Photo.   Perf. 13

| 1578 | A377 | 1.50p multi | 12 | 10 |

Bicentenary of San Diego, Calif.

Rock of Gibraltar
A378

Dama de Elche
A379

Design: 2p, View of Gibraltar across the Bay of Algeciras.

1969, July 18

| 1579 | A378 | 1.50p bl grn | 30 | 10 |
| 1580 | A378 | 2p brt rose lil | 20 | 10 |

Tourist Issue, 1969

Designs: 1.50p, Alcañiz Castle, Teruel (horiz.). 3p, Murcia Cathedral. 6p, St. Maria de la Redonda, Logroño.

1969, July 23   Engraved   Perf. 13

1581	A379	1.50p dl grn & blk	30	10
1582	A379	3p yel grn & bl grn	25	10
1583	A379	3.50p gray bl & dk bl	30	10
1584	A379	6p yel grn & vio blk	35	10

Builders of the New World
Type of 1961 and

Santo Domingo
Church, Santiago,
Chile
A380

Designs: 1.50p, Casa de Moneda de Chile (horiz.). 2p, Ambrosio O'Higgins. 3.50p, Pedro de Valdivia. 6p, First large bridge over Mapocho River (horiz.).

1969, Oct. 12   Photo.   Perf. 13

1585	A380	40c lt bl & dk red brn	10	10
1586	A380	1.50p pale rose & dk vio	15	10
1587	A265	2p pale pink & ol	35	10
1588	A265	3.50p pale yel & dk Prus grn	45	10
1589	A380	6p pale yel & blk brn	60	15
		Nos. 1585-1589 (5)	1.65	55

Exploration and development of Chile. See also Nos. 1630–1631, 1634.

Adoration of the Magi, by Juan
Bautista Mayno
A381

Design: 2p, Nativity, bas-relief from altar of Cathedral of Gerona.

1969, Nov. 3

| 1590 | A381 | 1.50p multi | 10 | 8 |
| 1591 | A381 | 2p multi | 15 | 8 |

Christmas, 1969.

Tomb of Alfonso VIII and Wife,
Las Huelgas Monastery, Burgos
A382

Designs: 1.50p, Las Huelgas Monastery. 6p, Inside view (vert.).

1969, Nov. 22   Engraved

1592	A382	1.50p lt bl grn & ind	50	10
1593	A382	3.50p ultra & vio bl	40	15
1594	A382	6p ol & yel grn	65	15

See also Nos. 1639–1641.

St. Juan de
Avila, by
El Greco
A383

St. Stephen,
by Luis
de Morales
A384

Design: 50p, Bishop Rodrigo Ximenez de Rada, Juan de Borgona mural.

1970, Feb. 25   Engraved   Perf. 13

| 1595 | A383 | 25p pale pur & ind | 4.75 | 15 |
| 1596 | A383 | 50p brn org & brn | 3.75 | 40 |

1970, Mar. 24   Photo.   Perf. 13

Morales Paintings: 1p, Annunciation. 1.50p, Madonna and Child with St. John. 2p, Madonna and Child. 3p, Presentation at the Temple. 3.50p, St. Jerome. 4p, St. John de Ribera. 5p, Ecce Homo. 6p, Pieta. 10p, St. Francis of Assisi.

1597	A384	50c gold & multi	10	10
1598	A384	1p gold & multi	15	10
1599	A384	1.50p gold & multi	25	10
1600	A384	2p gold & multi	25	10
1601	A384	3p gold & multi	10	10
1602	A384	3.50p gold & multi	10	10
1603	A384	4p gold & multi	30	10
1604	A384	5p gold & multi	25	10
1605	A384	6p gold & multi	25	20
1606	A384	10p gold & multi	40	30
		Nos. 1597-1606 (10)	2.15	1.30

Issued to honor Luis de Morales, "El Divino" (1509–1586), and for Stamp Day.

Europa Issue, 1970
Common Design Type

1970, May 4   Photo.   Perf. 13x12½
Size: 37½x22mm.

| 1607 | CD13 | 3.50p brt bl & gold | 25 | 10 |

Stamp Day Type of 1968

Design: 2p, Spain No. 51 with "Ferro Carril de Langreo" postmark.

1970, May 4   Perf. 13x12½

| 1608 | A362 | 2p dl red, grn & blk | 15 | 10 |

Issued for Stamp Day, 1969.

Barcelona
Fair
Building
A385

1970, May 27   Perf. 13

| 1609 | A385 | 15p multi | 65 | 15 |

Barcelona Trade Fair, 50th anniversary.

Miguel Primo
de Rivera
A386

1970, June 6   Photo.   Perf. 13

| 1610 | A386 | 2p buff, brn & ol grn | 18 | 10 |

Issued to commemorate the centenary of the birth of Gen. Miguel Primo de Rivera (1870–1930), Spanish dictator, 1923–1930.

Valencia
de Don
Juan Castle
A387

Castles: 1.20p, Monterrey. 3.50p, Mombeltran. 6p, Sadaba. 10p, Bellver.

1970, June 24   Engraved

1611	A387	1p blk & dl bl	75	10
1612	A387	1.20p lt grnsh bl & vio	30	10
1613	A387	3.50p pale grn & brn	75	10
1614	A387	6p sep & dl pur	75	10
1615	A387	10p fawn & sep	2.25	15
		Nos. 1611-1615 (5)	4.80	55

569

SPAIN

Tourist Issue, 1970

Alcazaba Castle, Almeria
A388

Designs: 1p, Malaga Cathedral. 1.50p, St. Mary of the Assumption, Lequeitio (vert.). 2p, Cloister of St. Francis of Orense. 3.50p, Market (Lonja), Zaragoza (vert.). 5p, The Gate of Vitoria (vert.).

1970, July 23   Engraved   Perf. 13

1616	A388	50c bluish gray & dl pur	10	10
1617	A388	1p red brn & ocher	35	10
1618	A388	1.50p bluish gray & sl grn	25	10
1619	A388	2p sl & dk bl	1.25	10
1620	A388	3.50p pur & vio bl	50	12
1621	A388	5p gray grn & red brn	1.75	10
		Nos. 1616-1621 (6)	4.20	62

Tailor, from Book Published in Madrid, 1589
A389

1970, Aug. 18   Photo.   Perf. 13

| 1622 | A389 | 2p mag, brn & dl vio | 12 | 10 |

Issued to publicize the 14th International Tailoring Congress, Madrid.

Diver and Map of Europe
A390

1970, Aug. 25

| 1623 | A390 | 2p grn & brt bl | 12 | 10 |

Issued to publicize the 12th European Championships in Swimming, Diving and Water Polo, Barcelona.

Concha Espina
A391

Portraits: 1p, Guillen de Castro. 1.50p, Juan Ramon Jimenez. 2p, Gustavo Adolfo Becquer. 2.50p, Miguel de Unamuno. 3.50p, José M. Gabriel y Galan.

1970, Sept. 21   Photo.   Perf. 13x12½

1624	A391	50c brn, vio bl & pale rose	10	8
1625	A391	1p sl grn, dp rose lil & gray	15	8
1626	A391	1.50p dk bl, brt grn & gray	20	8
1627	A391	2p dk ol & buff	35	8
1628	A391	2.50p pur, rose lake & buff	25	8
1629	A391	3.50p brn, dk red & gray	30	8
		Nos. 1624-1629 (6)	1.35	48

Issued to honor Spanish writers.

Builders of the New World
Portrait Type of 1961 and Building Type of 1969.

Designs: 40c, Ecala House, Queretaro, Mexico. 1.50p, Mexico Cathedral (horiz.). 2p, Vasco de Quiroga. 3.50p, Brother Juan de Zumarraga. 6p, Cathedral Towers, Morelia, Mexico.

1970, Oct. 12   Photo.   Perf. 13

1630	A380	40c lt bl & ol gray	10	8
1631	A380	1.50p lt bl & brn	35	8
1632	A265	2p buff & dk vio	90	8
1633	A265	3.50p pale grn & dk grn	50	10
1634	A380	6p pale pink & Prus bl	70	10
		Nos. 1630-1634 (5)	2.55	44

Exploration and development of Mexico.

Map of Western Mediterranean
A392

1970, Oct. 20   Photo.   Perf. 13

| 1635 | A392 | 2p multi | 18 | 10 |

Issued to commemorate the centenary of the Geographical and Statistical Institute.

Adoration of the Shepherds, by El Greco
A393

Design: 2p, Adoration of the Shepherds, by Murillo.

1970, Oct. 30

| 1636 | A393 | 1.50p multi | 10 | 8 |
| 1637 | A393 | 2p multi | 15 | 8 |

Christmas 1970.

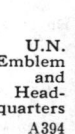

U.N. Emblem and Headquarters
A394

1970, Nov. 3

| 1638 | A394 | 8p multi | 30 | 10 |

25th anniversary of the United Nations.

Monastery Type of 1969

Ripoll Monastery: 2p, Portal. 3.50p, View of monastery. 5p, Inside court.

1970, Nov. 12   Engraved

1639	A382	2p vio & pur	1.40	10
1640	A382	3.50p org & mar	65	15
1641	A382	5p Prus grn & yel grn	2.25	15

Map with Main European Pilgrimage Routes
A395

Cathedral of St. David, Wales
A396

Designs: No. 1643, Map of main pilgrimage routes. No. 1644, St. Bridget statue, Vadstena, Sweden. No. 1645, Santiago Cathedral. No. 1646, Tower of St. Jacques, Paris. No. 1647, Pilgrim before entering Santiago de Compostela. No. 1648, St. James statue, Pistoia, Italy. No. 1649, Lugo Cathedral. 2.50p, Villafranca del Bierzo church. No. 1652, Astorga Cathedral. 3.50p, San Marcos de León. No. 1654, Charlemagne, bas-relief, Aachen Cathedral, Germany. No. 1655, San Tirso de Sahagun. 5p, San Martín de Fromista. 6p, Bas-relief, King's Hospital, Burgos. 7p, Portal of Santo Domingo de la Calzada. 7.50p, Cloister, Najera. 8p, Puente de la Reina (Christ on the Cross and portal). 9p, Santa Maria de Eunate. 10p, Cross of Roncesvalles.

1971   Engraved   Perf. 13

1642	A395	50c grnsh bl & sep	10	8
1643	A396	50c bl & dl vio	12	10
1644	A395	1p brn & sl grn	20	8
1645	A395	1p grn & sl brn	40	10
1646	A395	1.50p dl grn & dp plum	45	8
1647	A395	1.50p vio bl & lil	30	10
1648	A395	2p dk pur & blk	35	8
1649	A395	2p sl grn & dk bl	1.50	10
1650	A396	2.50p vio brn & dl vio	40	10
1651	A396	3p ultra & dk bl	45	8
1652	A395	3p dl red & rose lil	65	10
1653	A396	3.50p dp org & gray grn	50	12
1654	A396	4p ol grn	75	8
1655	A396	4p grnsh bl & brn	50	10
1656	A396	5p lt grn & blk	1.00	10
1657	A395	6p lt ultra	45	10
1658	A396	7p lil & dl vio	60	10
1659	A396	7.50p car lake & dl vio	35	25
1660	A396	8p grn & vio blk	35	15
1661	A396	9p grn & vio	35	25
1662	A395	10p grn & brn	80	15
		Nos. 1642-1662 (21)	10.57	2.40

Ignacio Zuloaga, Self-portrait
A397

Amadeo Vives, Composer
A398

Zuloaga Paintings: 50c, "My Uncle Daniel." 1p, View of Segovia (horiz.). 1.50p, Countess of Alba. 3p, Juan Belmonte. 4p, Countess of Noailles. 5p, Pablo Uranga. 8p, Cobblers' Houses at Lerma (horiz.).

1971, March 24   Photo.   Perf. 13

1663	A397	50c gold & multi	10	10
1664	A397	1p gold & multi	12	10
1665	A397	1.50p gold & multi	15	10
1666	A397	2p gold & multi	35	10
1667	A397	3p gold & multi	40	10
1668	A397	4p gold & multi	20	10
1669	A397	5p gold & multi	45	10
1670	A397	8p gold & multi	40	10
		Nos. 1663-1670 (8)	2.07	85

Ignacio Zuloaga (1870–1945). Stamp Day.

1971, Apr. 20

Portraits: 2p, St. Teresa of Avila. 8p, Benito Perez Galdos, writer. 15p, Ramon Menendez Pidal, writer.

1671	A398	1p multi	50	10
1672	A398	2p multi	50	10
1673	A398	8p multi	50	10
1674	A398	15p multi	65	12

Europa Issue, 1971
Common Design Type

1971, Apr. 29   Photo.   Perf. 13
Size: 37x26mm.

| 1675 | CD14 | 2p lt bl, brn & vio bl | 2.25 | 10 |
| 1676 | CD14 | 8p lt grn, dk brn & dk grn | 90 | 20 |

Stamp Day Type of 1968

Design: 2p, Spain No. 1 with blue "A" cancellation.

1971, May 6

| 1677 | A362 | 2p blk, bl & ol | 18 | 10 |

Stamp Day, 1971.

Gymnast
A399

Design: 2p, Gymnast on bar.

1971, May 14

| 1678 | A399 | 1p ocher & multi | 30 | 8 |
| 1679 | A399 | 2p lt bl & multi | 30 | 8 |

9th European Gymnastic Championships for Men, Madrid, May 14–15.

Great Bustard
A400

Designs: 2p, Pardine lynx. 3p, Brown bear. 5p, Red-legged partridge (vert.). 8p, Spanish ibex (vert.).

1971, May 24

1680	A400	1p multi	35	10
1681	A400	2p multi	65	10
1682	A400	3p multi	65	10
1683	A400	5p multi	1.00	12
1684	A400	8p multi	80	15
		Nos. 1680-1684 (5)	3.45	57

Legionnaires
A401

Designs: 2p, Legionnaires on dress parade. 5p, Memorial service. 8p, Desert fighter and tank column.

1971, June 21   Photo.   Perf. 13

1685	A401	1p multi	12	12
1686	A401	2p multi	80	12
1687	A401	3p multi	80	12
1688	A401	8p multi	50	25

50th anniversary of the Legion, a voluntary military organization.

SPAIN

UNICEF Emblem,
Children of Various
Races
A402

1971, Sept. 10
1689 A402   8p multi   25   10

25th anniversary of United Nations International Children's Fund (UNICEF).

Don Juan of Austria, Fleet Commander
A403

Hockey Players, Hockey League and Games Emblems
A404

Designs: 5p, Battle of Lepanto (horiz.). 8p, Holy League banner in Cathedral.

1971, Oct. 7   Engraved   *Perf. 13*
1690 A403   2p sep & sl grn   1.50   10
1691 A403   5p chocolate   1.50   10
1692 A403   8p rose car & vio brn 2.00 35

400th anniversary of the Battle of Lepanto against the Turks.

1971, Oct. 15   Photogravure
1693 A404   5p multi   1.40   15

First World Hockey Cup, Barcelona, Oct. 15–24.

De Havilland DH-9 over Seville
A405

Design: 15p, Boeing 747 over Plaza de la Cibeles, Madrid.

1971, Oct. 25
1694 A405   2p multi   75   10
1695 A405   15p multi   75   25

50th anniversary of Spanish air mail service.

Nativity, Avia Altarpiece
A406

Emilia Pardo Bazan
A407

Design: 8p, Nativity, Sagas altarpiece.

1971, Nov. 4   *Perf. 12½x13*
1696 A406   2p multi   30   8
1697 A406   8p multi   30   15

Christmas 1971.

1972, Jan. 27   Engraved   *Perf. 13*
Portraits: 25p, José de Espronceda. 50p, King Fernan Gonzalez.
1698 A407   15p brn & sl grn 40   10
1699 A407   25p lt grn & sl grn 45   15
1700 A407   50p cl & dp brn   70   25

Honoring Emilia Pardo Bazan (1852–1921), novelist (15p); José de Espronceda (1808–1842), poet (25p); Fernan Gonzalez (910–970), first King of Castile (50p).

Figure Skating
A408

Don Quixote Title Page, 1605
A409

Design: 2p, Ski jump and Sapporo Olympic emblem (horiz.).

1972, Feb. 10   Photogravure
1701 A408   2p gray & multi   80   8
1702 A408   15p bl & multi   60   25

11th Winter Olympic Games, Sapporo, Japan, Feb. 3–13.

1972, Feb. 24   Engr.   *Perf. 13x12½*
1703 A409   2p brn & cl   15   10

International Book Year 1972.

José Gutierrez Solana with Wife and Child
A410

Gutierrez Solana Paintings: 1p, Clowns (horiz.). 3p, Balladier. 4p, Fisherman. 5p, Mask makers. 7p, The book collector. 10p, Merchant marine captain. 15p, After-dinner speaker (horiz.).

1972, Mar. 24   Photo.   *Perf. 13*
1704 A410   1p gold & multi   35   10
1705 A410   2p gold & multi   85   10
1706 A410   3p gold & multi   85   10
1707 A410   4p gold & multi   60   10
1708 A410   5p gold & multi   1.75 10
1709 A410   7p gold & multi   65   10
1710 A410   10p gold & multi 1.10 12
1711 A410   15p gold & multi 85   12
       Nos. 1704-1711 (8)   7.00 84

José Gutierrez Solana (1886–1945). Stamp Day 1972.

Fir
A411

1972, Apr. 21
Multicolored
1712 A411   1p shown   50   10
1713 A411   2p Strawberry tree 70 10
1714 A411   3p Cluster pine   70   10
1715 A411   5p Evergreen oak 75   12
1716 A411   8p Juniper   75   15
       Nos. 1712-1716 (5)   3.40 57

Europeans Interlocking
A412

Pre-stamp Cordoba Postmark (1824–42)—A413

Common Design Type and Type A412

1972, May 2
1717 A412   2p dl grn & ocher 4.50   10

Size: 25x38mm.
1718 CD15 8p multi   2.50   30

1972, May 6   *Perf. 12½x13*
1719 A413   2p dl yel, blk & car 15   10

Stamp Day 1972.

Santa Catalina Castle, Jaén
A414

Castles: 1p, Sajazarra, Rioja (vert.). 3p, Biar, Alicante. 5p, San Servando, Toledo. 10p, Pedraza, Segovia.

1972, June 22   Engraved   *Perf. 13*
1720 A414   1p dl bl grn & brn 75   10
1721 A414   2p gray cl & brn   1.50 10
1722 A414   3p rose car & red brn 1.50 15
1723 A414   5p vio bl & dl grn 1.50 20
1724 A414   10p sl & lil   4.00   20
       Nos. 1720-1724 (5)   9.25   75

Weight Lifting, Olympic Emblems
A415

1972, Aug. 26   Photo.   *Perf. 13*
Multicolored
1725 A415   1p Olympic emblems, fencing, horiz. 25 10
1726 A415   2p shown   50   10
1727 A415   5p Sculling   50   15
1728 A415   8p Pole vaulting 50   20

20th Olympic Games, Munich, Aug. 26–Sept. 11.

Egyptian Mongoose
A416

1972, Sept. 14
Multicolored
1729 A416   1p Aquatic mole, vert. 20 10
1730 A416   2p Chamois   50   10
1731 A416   3p Wolf   75   12

1732 A416   5p shown   1.10   10
1733 A416   7p Spotted genet 90   15
       Nos. 1729-1733 (5)   3.45   59

Brigadier M.A. de Ustariz
A417

San Juan, 1870
A418

1972, Oct. 12   Photo.   *Perf. 13*
Multicolored
1734 A417   1p shown   30   10
1735 A418   2p shown   50   10
1736 A418   5p San Juan, 1625 65   10
1737 A418   8p Map of Plaza and Bay, 1792 85 25

450th anniversary of San Juan.

St. Tomas Monastery, Avila
A419

Designs: 8p, Inside view. 15p, Cloister (horiz.).

1972, Oct. 26   Engraved
1738 A419   2p Prus bl & gray grn 1.75 10
1739 A419   8p gray & cl   1.25   15
1740 A419   15p vio & red lil 2.00 20

Teatro del Liceo, Barcelona
A420

1972, Nov. 7   *Perf. 12½x13*
1741 A420   8p ultra & sep   75   18

125th anniversary of the Gran Teatro del Liceo in Barcelona.

Annunciation
A421

Design: 8p, Angel and shepherds. Designs are from Romanesque murals in the Collegiate Basilica of San Isidro, Leon.

1972, Nov. 14   Photo.   *Perf. 13*
1742 A421   2p gold & multi   25   8
1743 A421   8p gold & multi   20   8

Christmas 1972.

SPAIN

Juan de Herrera and Escorial
A422

Designs: 10p, Juan de Villanueva and Prado. 15p, Ventura Rodriguez and Apollo Fountain.

1973, Jan. 29 Engr. Perf. 12½x13

1744	A422	8p sep & sl grn	1.40	15
1745	A422	10p blk brn & bluish blk	2.75	20
1746	A422	15p brt grn & ind	85	10

Great Spanish architects.

Myrica Faya
A423

Europa, Roman Mosaic
A424

Designs: Flora of Canary Islands.

1973, Mar. 21 Photo. Perf. 13
Multicolored

1747	A423	1p *Apollonias canariensis*, horiz.	40	10
1748	A423	2p shown	1.25	10
1749	A423	4p Palms	40	10
1750	A423	5p Holly	1.25	10
1751	A423	15p *Dracaena draco*	60	15
		Nos. 1747-1751 (5)	3.90	55

Europa Issue
Common Design Type and A424

1973, Apr. 30 Photo. Perf. 13

| 1752 | A424 | 2p multi | 1.50 | 10 |

Size: 37x26mm.

| 1753 | CD16 | 8p lt bl, blk & red | 1.10 | 15 |

Stamp Day Type of 1968

Design: 2p, Spain No. 23 with red Madrid, 1853, cancellation.

1973, May 5

| 1754 | A362 | 2p blk, bl & red | 15 | 10 |

Stamp Day 1973.

Iznajar Dam on Genil River
A425

1973, June 9 Photo. Perf. 12½x13

| 1755 | A425 | 8p multi | 25 | 15 |

11th Congress of the International Commission on High Dams, Madrid, June 11-15.

Oñate University, Guipuzcoa
A426

Designs: 2p, Plaza del Campo and fountain, Lugo. 3p, Plaza de Llerena and fountain, Badajoz (vert.). 5p, House of Columbus, Las Palmas. 8p, Windmills, La Mancha.

1973, June 11 Engr. Perf. 13

1756	A426	1p gray & sep	40	10
1757	A426	2p brt grn & sl grn	1.25	10
1758	A426	3p dk brn & org brn	1.00	10
1759	A426	5p dk gray & vio blk	2.25	10
1760	A426	8p dk gray & car	1.75	30
		Nos. 1756-1760 (5)	6.65	70

Azure-winged Magpie
A427

Knight, Holy Fraternity of Castile, 1488
A428

Birds: 1p, Black-bellied sand grouse (horiz.). 2p, Black stork (horiz.). 7p, Imperial eagle (horiz.). 15p, Red-crested pochard.

1973, July 3 Photogravure Perf. 13

1761	A427	1p multi	20	10
1762	A427	2p multi	75	10
1763	A427	5p multi	1.00	10
1764	A427	7p multi	1.20	10
1765	A427	15p multi	75	30

1973, July 17

Uniforms: 2p, Knight, Castile, 1493 (horiz.). 3p, Harquebusier, 1534. 7p, Mounted rifleman, 1560. 8p, Infantry sergeants, 1567.

1766	A428	1p multi	35	15
1767	A428	2p multi	1.10	10
1768	A428	3p multi	90	15
1769	A428	7p multi	90	10
1770	A428	8p multi	1.10	20
		Nos. 1766-1770 (5)	4.35	70

See Nos. 1794-1798, 1824-1828, 1869-1873, 1902-1906, 1989-1993, 2020-2024, 2051-2055, 2078-2082.

Fish in Net
A429

1973, Sept. 12 Photo. Perf. 13

| 1771 | A429 | 2p multi | 15 | 10 |

6th International Fishing Exhibition, Vigo, Sept. 12-19.

Conference Hall
A430

1973, Sept. 14

| 1772 | A430 | 2p multi | 20 | 10 |

Plenipotentiary Conference of the International Telecommunications Union, Torremolinos, Sept. 1973.

Vicente López, Self-portrait
A431

Paintings by Vicente López: 1p, King Ferdinand VII. 3p, Señora de Carvallo. 4p, Marshal Castelldosrrius. 5p, Queen Isabella II. 7p, Francisco Goya. 10p, Maria Amalia de Sajonia. 15p, The organist Felix López.

1973, Sept. 29 Photo. Perf. 13

1773	A431	1p gold & multi	15	10
1774	A431	2p gold & multi	40	10
1775	A431	3p gold & multi	40	10
1776	A431	4p gold & multi	30	10
1777	A431	5p gold & multi	30	10
1778	A431	7p gold & multi	30	10
1779	A431	10p gold & multi	30	12
1780	A431	15p gold & multi	40	20
		Nos. 1773-1780 (8)	2.55	92

Vicente López y Portaña (1772-1850), painter. Stamp Day 1973.

Leon Cathedral, Nicaragua
A432

Designs: 2p, Subtiava Church. 5p, Portal of Governor's House (vert.). 8p, Rio San Juan Castle.

1973, Oct. 12

1781	A432	1p multi	15	10
1782	A432	2p multi	50	10
1783	A432	5p multi	65	10
1784	A432	8p multi	50	15

Hispanic-American buildings in Nicaragua.

Pope Gregory XI and Pedro Fernandez Pecha
A433

1973, Oct. 26

| 1785 | A433 | 2p multi | 15 | 10 |

600th anniversary of the founding of the Order of the Hermites of St. Jerome by Pedro Fernandez Pecha.

St. Domingo de Silos Monastery
A434

Nativity, Column Capital, Silos Church
A435

Designs: 8p, Cloister walk (horiz.). 15p, Three saints, sculpture.

Perf. 13x12½, 12½x13

1973, Oct. 26 Engraved

1786	A434	2p brn & rose mag	55	10
1787	A434	8p dk bl & pur	55	15
1788	A434	15p Prus grn & ind	80	15

St. Domingo de Silos Monastery, Burgos.

1973, Nov. 6 Photogravure Perf. 13

Design: 8p, Adoration of the Kings, Butrera Church (horiz.).

| 1789 | A435 | 2p multi | 25 | 10 |
| 1790 | A435 | 8p multi | 20 | 15 |

Christmas 1973.

Map of Spain and Americas with Dates of First Printings—A436

Designs: 7p, Teacher and Pupils, woodcut from "Libros de los Suenos," Valencia, 1474 (vert.). 15p, Title page from "Los Sinodales," Segovia, 1472.

1973, Dec. 11 Engraved Perf. 13

1791	A436	1p ind & sl grn	70	10
1792	A436	7p vio bl & pur	45	12
1793	A436	15p pur & blk	70	20

500 years of Spanish printing.

Uniform Type of 1973

Uniforms: 1p, Harquebusier on horseback, 1603. 2p, Harquebusiers, 1632. 3p, Cuirassier, 1635. 5p, Mounted drummer of the Dragoons, 1677. 9p, Two Musketeers, 1694.

1974, Jan. 5 Photogravure Perf. 13

1794	A428	1p multi	20	10
1795	A428	2p multi	1.10	10
1796	A428	3p multi	1.50	10
1797	A428	5p multi	1.75	25
1798	A428	9p multi	1.10	25
		Nos. 1794-1798 (5)	5.65	70

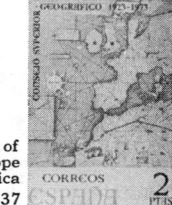

Nautical Chart of Western Europe and North Africa
A437

1974, Jan. 26

| 1799 | A437 | 2p multi | 15 | 10 |

50th anniversary of the Superior Geographical Council of Spain. The chart is from a 14th century Catalan atlas.

M. Biada and Steam Engine
A438

1974, Apr. 2 Photo. Perf. 13

| 1800 | A438 | 2p multi | 15 | 10 |

125th anniversary of Barcelona-Mataro Railroad.

Young Collector, Album, Magnifier
A439

Exhibition Emblem
A440

Design: 8p, Emblem, globe and arrows.

SPAIN

1974, Apr. 4		Perf. 13	
1801	A439	2p lil rose & multi	15 10

Perf. 12½

1802	A440	5p buff, blk & dl bl	65 10
1803	A440	8p dl grn & multi	45 20

Espana 75, International Philatelic Exhibition, Madrid, Apr. 4–13, 1975.

Europa Issue 1974

Woman with Offering
A441

Design: 8p, Woman from Baza, painted sculpture.

1974, Apr. 29	Photo.	Perf. 13	
1804	A441	2p multi	1.75 10
1805	A441	8p multi	85 20

No. 28 and 1854 "Sevilla" Cancel
A442

1974, May 6			
1806	A442	2p blk, bl & red	15 10

World Stamp Day.

Father Jaime Balmes
A443

Designs: 10p, Father Pedro Poveda. 15p, Jorge Juan y Santacilla.

1974, May 28	Engraved	Perf. 13	
1807	A443	8p bl gray & sep	45 15
1808	A443	10p red brn & dk brn	1.75 10
1809	A443	15p brn & sl	55 15

Famous Spaniards: Jaime Balmes (1810–1848), mathematician; death centenary of Pedro Poveda, pedagogue; Don Jorge Juan (1712–1773), explorer and writer.

Templeto, by Bramante, Rome
A444

1974, June 4		Photogravure	
1810	A444	5p multi	50 12

Centenary of the Spanish Academy of Fine Arts, Rome.

Aqueduct, Segovia
A445

Designs: 2p, Tajo Bridge, Alcantara. 3p, Marcus Valerius Martial lecturing. 4p, Triumphal Arch, Tarragona (vert.). 5p, Theater, Merida. 7p, Bishop Ossius of Cordoba preaching. 8p, Tribunal Arch, Talavera Forum (vert.). 9p, Emperor Trajan (vert.).

1974, June 25		Engraved	
1811	A445	1p brn & blk	15 10
1812	A445	2p gray grn & sep	75 10
1813	A445	3p lt & dk brn	20 10
1814	A445	4p grn & ind	20 10
1815	A445	5p gray bl & choc	30 10
1816	A445	7p gray grn & lil	30 15
1817	A445	8p dk brn & grn	30 15
1818	A445	9p brt red lil & cl	30 20
		Nos. 1811-1818 (8)	2.50 1.00

Roman architecture and history in Spain.

Greek Tortoise
A446

Reptiles: 2p, Common chameleon. 5p, Wall gecko. 7p, Emerald lizard. 15p, Blunt-nosed viper.

1974, July 3		Photogravure	
1819	A446	1p multi	12 10
1820	A446	2p multi	55 10
1821	A446	5p multi	1.00 15
1822	A446	7p multi	80 20
1823	A446	15p multi	60 20
		Nos. 1819-1823 (5)	3.07 75

Uniform Type of 1973

Uniforms: 1p, Hussar and horse, 1705. 2p, Artillery officers, 1710. 3p, Piper and drummer, Granada Regiment, 1734. 7p, Mounted standard-bearer, Numancia Dragoons, 1737. 8p, Standard-bearer and soldier, Zamora Regiment, 1739.

1974, July 17			
1824	A428	1p multi	15 10
1825	A428	2p multi	70 10
1826	A428	3p multi	1.25 12
1827	A428	7p multi	70 15
1828	A428	8p multi	1.00 20
		Nos. 1824-1828 (5)	3.80 67

Life Saving
A447

1974, Sept. 5	Photo.	Perf. 13	
1829	A447	2p multi	15 10

18th World Life Saving Championships, Barcelona, Sept. 1974.

Eduardo Rosales, by Federico Madrazo
A448

Eduardo Rosales Paintings: 1p, Tobias and the Angel. 3p, The Last Will of Isabella the Catholic (horiz.). 4p, Nena (little girl). 5p, Presentation of John of Austria to Charles I (horiz.). 7p, The First Step (horiz.). 10p, St. John the Evangelist. 15p, St. Matthew.

1974, Sept. 29	Photo.	Perf. 13	
1830	A448	1p gold & multi	15 10
1831	A448	2p gold & multi	15 10
1832	A448	3p gold & multi	25 10
1833	A448	4p gold & multi	18 10
1834	A448	5p gold & multi	35 10
1835	A448	7p gold & multi	25 10
1836	A448	10p gold & multi	50 15
1837	A448	15p gold & multi	50 25
		Nos. 1830-1837 (8)	2.33 1.00

Eduardo Rosales (1836–1873). Stamp Day 1974.

"International Mail" A449   UPU Monument, Bern A450

1974, Oct. 9			
1838	A449	2p dk bl & multi	30 15
1839	A450	8p red & multi	25 25

Centenary of Universal Postal Union.

Sobremonte House, Cordoba, Argentina
A451

Ruins of San Ignacio de Mini, 18th Century A452   The Gaucho Martin Fierro A453

Design: 2p, Municipal Council Building, Buenos Aires, 1829.

1974, Oct. 12			
1840	A451	1p multi	15 10
1841	A451	2p multi	60 10
1842	A452	5p multi	60 10
1843	A453	10p multi	45 12

Cultural ties with Latin America.

Nativity, Valdavia Church
A454

Adoration of the Kings, Valcobero Church
A455

1974	Photogravure	Perf. 13	
1844	A454	2p multi	15 10
1845	A455	3p lt bl & multi	25 10
1846	A455	8p ol & multi	20 10

Christmas 1974.
Issue dates: 2p, 8p, Nov. 4; 3p, Dec. 2.

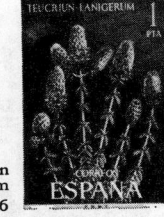

Teucriun Lanigerum
A456

Flowers: 2p, Hypericum ericoides. 4p, Thymus longiflorus. 5p, Anthyllis onobrychioides. 8p, Helianthemun paniculatum.

1974, Nov. 8			
1847	A456	1p multi	15 10
1848	A456	2p multi	50 10
1849	A456	4p multi	20 10
1850	A456	5p multi	50 10
1851	A456	8p multi	50 12
		Nos. 1847-1851 (5)	1.85 52

Franco Type of 1954–56
Imprint: "F.N.M.T."

1974–1975		Perf. 12½x13	
1852	A221	4p rose car ('75)	12 5
1853	A221	7p brt ultra	12 6
1854	A221	12p bl grn	15 6
1855	A221	20p rose car	40 12

Leyre Monastery
A457

Designs: 8p, Column and bas-relief (vert.). 15p, Crypt.

1974, Dec. 10	Engr.	Perf. 12½x13	
1862	A457	2p slate	1.10 10
1863	A457	8p carmine	35 15
1864	A457	15p grnsh blk	60 12

Leyre Monastery, Navarre.

Spain Nos. 1 and 1802
A458

Mail Coach, 1850
A459

Designs: 8p, Mail ship of Indian Service. 10p, Chapel of St. Mark.

Perf. 12½x13, 13x12½

1975, Jan. 2		Engraved	
1865	A458	2p sl bl	25 10
1866	A459	3p ol & brn	80 10
1867	A459	8p lil & sl bl	80 15
1868	A458	10p brn & sl grn	90 20

125th anniversary of Spanish postage stamps.

SPAIN

Uniform Type of 1973
Uniforms: 1p, Sergeant and grenadier, Toledo Regiment, 1750. 2p, Royal Artillery, 1762. 3p, Queen's Regiment, 1763. 5p, Fusiliers, Vitoria Regiment, 1766. 10p, Dragoon, Sagunto Regiment, 1775.

1975, Jan. 7   Photo.   *Perf. 13*

1869	A428	1p multi	50	10
1870	A428	2p multi	1.25	10
1871	A428	3p multi	2.50	15
1872	A428	5p multi	1.25	15
1873	A428	10p multi	2.50	15
		Nos. 1869-1873 (5)	8.00	65

Antonio Gaudi   A460

Designs: 10p, Antonio Palacios and Casa Guell, Barcelona. 15p, Secundino Zuazo.

1975, Feb. 25   Engraved   *Perf. 13*

1874	A460	8p grn & blk	60	15
1875	A460	10p car & dp cl	60	12
1876	A460	15p brn & blk	80	15

Contemporary Spanish architects.

Souvenir Sheets

Spanish Goldsmiths' Works—A461

Designs: 2p, Agate box, 9th century. 3p, Votive crown of Recesvinto. 8p, Cover of Evangelistary, Roncesvalles Collegiate Church, 12th century. 10p, Chalice of Infanta Donna Urraca, 11th century. 12p, Processional monstrance, St. Domingo de Silos, 16th century. 15p, Sword of Boabdil, 15th century. 25p, Sword and head of Charles V (Carlos I of Spain). 50p, Earring and bracelet from Aliseda, 6th–4th centuries B.C. 3p, 10p, 25p vertical (No. 1878).

1975, Apr. 4   Engraved   *Perf. 13*

1877	A461	Sheet of 4	21.00	21.00
a.		2p gray & Prus bl	2.50	2.50
b.		8p brn & Prus bl	3.75	3.75
c.		15p gray & dk car	3.75	3.75
d.		50p dk car & gray	11.00	11.00
1878	A461	Sheet of 4	21.00	21.00
a.		3p sl grn & gray	2.50	2.50
b.		10p sep & sl	3.75	3.75
c.		12p gray & bluish blk	3.75	3.75
d.		25p sep & bluish blk	7.50	7.50

España 75 International Philatelic Exhibition, Madrid, Apr. 4–13. Nos. 1877-1878 have black and brown marginal inscriptions, España 75 emblem and black control numbers. Size of No. 1877: 121x85mm., of No. 1878, 85x121mm.

Pomegranates
A462

Woman Gathering Honey, Arana Cave
A463

1975, Apr. 21   Photogravure   Multicolored

1879	A462	1p Almonds, nuts and blossoms (horiz.)	15	8
1880	A462	2p shown	65	8
1881	A462	3p Oranges	65	8
1882	A462	4p Chestnuts	30	8
1883	A462	5p Apples	35	8
		Nos. 1879-1883 (5)	2.10	40

Europa Issue 1975

Design: 12p, Horse (horiz.), wall painting from Tito Bustillo Cave.

1975, Apr. 28   Photo.   *Perf. 13*

1884	A463	3p brn & multi	1.40	10
1885	A463	12p brn & multi	90	15

Pre-stamp León Cancellation
A464

1975, May 6   *Perf. 12½x13*

1886	A464	3p multi	15	10

World Stamp Day.

World Tourism Organization Emblem
A465

1975, May 12   Photo.   *Perf. 13*

1887	A465	3p dk bl	15	10

First General Assembly of the World Tourism Organization, Madrid, May 1975.

Fair Emblem, Agricultural Symbols
A466

1975, May 14

1888	A466	3p multi	15	10

25th Agricultural Fair.

Equality Between Men and Women
A467

1975, June 3

1889	A467	3p multi	15	10

International Women's Year.

Virgin of Cabeza Sanctuary
A468

1975, June 18   Photo.   *Perf. 13*

1890	A468	3p multi	15	10

Virgin of Cabeza Sanctuary, site of siege during Civil War, 1937.

Cervantes' Prison Cell, Argamasilla de Alba
A469

Designs: 2p, Bridge of St. Martin, Toledo. 3p, Church of St. Peter, Tarrasa. 4p, Arch, Alhambra, Granada (vert.). 5p, Street, Mijas, Malaga (vert.). 7p, Church of St. Mary, Tarrasa (vert.).

1975, June 25   Engr.   *Perf. 13*

1891	A469	1p pur & blk	10	8
1892	A469	2p red brn & brn	25	8
1893	A469	3p sl & sep	25	8
1894	A469	4p org & cl	15	8
1895	A469	5p sl grn & ind	45	8
1896	A469	7p vio bl & ind	90	10
		Nos. 1891-1896 (6)	2.10	50

Salamander
A470

Designs: 2p, Newt. 3p, Tree toad. 6p, Midwife toad. 7p, Leaf frog.

1975, July 9   Photo.   *Perf. 13*

1897	A470	1p ol & multi	15	10
1898	A470	2p lt bl & multi	70	10
1899	A470	3p gray & multi	70	10
1900	A470	6p vio bl & multi	35	12
1901	A470	7p bl grn & multi	60	12
		Nos. 1897-1901 (5)	2.50	54

Uniform Type of 1973
Uniforms: 1p, Cavalry officer, 1788. 2p, Fusilier, Asturias Regiment, 1789. 3p, Infantry Colonel, 1802. 4p, Artillery standard-bearer, 1803. 7p, Sapper, 1809.

1975, July 17

1902	A428	1p multi	20	8
1903	A428	2p multi	80	8
1904	A428	3p multi	40	8
1905	A428	4p multi	25	12
1906	A428	7p multi	60	12
		Nos. 1902-1906 (5)	2.25	48

Infant and Children Playing
A471

1975, Sept. 9   Photo.   *Perf. 13*

1907	A471	3p multi	12	10

"Defend Life."

Scroll and Emblem
A472

1975, Sept. 25

1908	A472	3p multi	15	10

13th International Congress of Latin Notaries, Barcelona, Sept. 26–Oct. 4.

Blessing of the Birds
A473

Designs (Scenes from Apocalypse): 2p, Angel at River of Life. 3p, Angel Guarding Gate of Paradise. 4p, Fox carrying cock. 6p, Daniel with wild bulls. 7p, The Last Judgment. 10p, Four horsemen of the Apocalypse. 12p, Bird holding snake. 2p, 3p, 7p, 10p, 12p are vertical.

1975, Sept. 29

1909	A473	1p gold & multi	10	8
1910	A473	2p gold & multi	35	8
1911	A473	3p gold & multi	35	8
1912	A473	4p gold & multi	15	8
1913	A473	6p gold & multi	15	8
1914	A473	7p gold & multi	35	8
1915	A473	10p gold & multi	35	8
1916	A473	12p gold & multi	40	12
		Nos. 1909-1916 (8)	2.20	68

Millenium Gerona Cathedral.

Symbols of Industry
A474

1975, Oct. 7   Engr.   *Perf. 13*

1917	A474	3p vio & lil	15	10

Spanish industrialization.

Pioneers' Covered Wagon
A475

Designs: 1p, El Cabildo, meeting house of 1st Uruguayan Government. 3p, Fort St. Theresa over River Plate. 8p, Montevideo Cathedral (vert.).

1975, Oct. 12   Photogravure

1918	A475	1p multi	12	8
1919	A475	2p multi	35	8
1920	A475	3p multi	35	8
1921	A475	8p multi	25	12

Cultural ties with Latin America; sesquicentennial of Uruguay's independence.

Ruined Columns, San Juan de la Peña
A476

Madonna, Mosaic, Navarra Cathedral
A477

Designs: 3p, Monastery (horiz.). 8p, Cloister (horiz.).

Perf. 13x12½, 12½x13

1975, Oct. 28   Engraved

1922	A476	3p sl grn & brn	40	10
1923	A476	8p vio & brt lil	20	10
1924	A476	10p dp mag & car	65	15

San Juan de la Peña Monastery.

1975, Nov. 4   Photo.   *Perf. 13*

Design: 12p, Flight into Egypt, carved capital, Navarra Cathedral (horiz.).

1925	A477	3p multi	25	7
1926	A477	12p multi	20	10

Christmas 1975.

SPAIN

King Juan Carlos I — A478
Queen Sofia and King — A479

Designs: No. 1928, Queen Sofia, like No. 1929.

1975, Dec. 29 Photo. Perf. 13x12½

| 1927 | A478 | 3p multi | 30 | 6 |
| 1928 | A478 | 3p multi | 30 | 6 |

Perf. 12½

| 1929 | A479 | 3p multi | 30 | 6 |
| 1930 | A479 | 12p multi | 45 | 8 |

King Juan Carlos I, accession to the throne.

Pilgrim Virgin, Pontevedra — A480
Mountains and Center Emblem — A481

1976, Jan. 2 Engr. Perf. 13

| 1931 | A480 | 3p rose & brn | 30 | 10 |

Holy Year of St. James of Compostela, patron saint of Spain.

1976, Feb. 10 Photogravure

| 1932 | A481 | 6p multi | 18 | 10 |

Catalunya Excursion Center, centenary.

Cosme Damian Churruca — A482

Navigators: 12p, Luis de Requesens. 50p, Juan Sebastian Elcano (horiz.).

1976, Mar. 1 Engr. Perf. 13

1933	A482	7p vio brn & grnsh blk	1.50	20
1934	A482	12p lt bl & vio	65	15
1935	A482	50p dp brn & gray ol	1.25	20

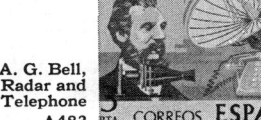

A. G. Bell, Radar and Telephone — A483

1976, Mar. 10 Photogravure

| 1936 | A483 | 3p multi | 20 | 10 |

Centenary of first telephone call by Alexander Graham Bell, March 10, 1876.

"Watch at Street Crossings" — A484

Designs: 3p, "Don't pass when in doubt" (vert.). 5p, "Wear seat belts."

1976, Apr. 6 Photo. Perf. 13

1937	A484	1p org & multi	28	5
1938	A484	3p gray & multi	85	6
1939	A484	5p lil & multi	75	6

Road safety.

St. George, Alcoy Cathedral — A485

1976, Apr. 23

| 1940 | A485 | 3p multi | 15 | 10 |

7th centenary of the apparition of St. George in Alcoy.

Europa Issue 1976

Talavera Pottery — A486

Design: 12p, Lace making.

1976, May 3 Photo. Perf. 13

| 1941 | A486 | 3p multi | 1.50 | 10 |
| 1942 | A486 | 12p multi | 2.00 | 15 |

17th Conference of European Postal and Telecommunications Administrations.

6r Stamp of 1851 with Coruna Cancel — A487

1976, May 6

| 1943 | A487 | 3p bl, org & blk | 18 | 10 |

World Stamp Day.

Coin of Caesar Augustus — A488

Designs: 7p, Map of Roman camp on banks of Ebro, and coin. 25p, Orpheus, mosaic from Roman era (vert.).

1976, May 26 Engr. Perf. 13

1944	A488	3p dk brn & mar	3.75	8
1945	A488	7p dk brn & bl	1.50	15
1946	A488	25p brn & blk	1.75	10

2000th anniversary of the founding of Saragossa.

Spanish-made Rifle, 1757 — A489

Designs (Bicentennial Emblem and): 3p, Bernardo de Galvez, Spanish governor. 5p, Dollar bank note, Richmond, 1861. 12p, Spanish capture of Pensacola from English.

1976, May 29

1947	A489	1p dk brn & vio bl	40	10
1948	A489	3p sl grn & dk brn	2.00	10
1949	A489	5p dk brn & sl grn	85	10
1950	A489	12p sl grn & dk brn	1.00	15

American Bicentennial.

Old Customs House, Cadiz — A490

Customs Houses: 3p, Madrid. 7p, Barcelona.

1976, June 9

1951	A490	1p blk & ma―	30	8
1952	A490	3p sep & grn	1.00	10
1953	A490	7p red brn & vio brn	2.00	10

Postal Savings Box with Symbols — A491
Railroad Post Office — A492

Rural Mailman in Winter — A493

Design: 10p, Automatic letter sorting machine.

1976, June 16 Photogravure

1954	A491	1p multi	25	10
1955	A492	3p multi	80	10
1956	A493	6p multi	30	10
1957	A493	10p multi	1.00	15

Postal service.

King and Queen, Map of Americas — A494

1976, June 25

| 1958 | A494 | 12p multi | 45 | 15 |

Visit of King Juan Carlos I and Queen Sofia to the Americas, June 1976.

San Marcos, León — A495
Greco-Roman Wrestling — A496

Tourist Issue, 1976

Designs (Famous Hotels): 2p, Las Cañadas, Tenerife. 3p, Portal of R. R. Catolicos, Santiago (vert.). 4p, Cruz de Tejeda, Las Palmas. 7p, Gredos, Avila. 12p, La Arruzafa, Cordoba.

1976, June 30 Engr. Perf. 13

1959	A495	1p sl & sep	20	8
1960	A495	2p grn & ind	70	8
1961	A495	3p brn & red brn	65	8
1962	A495	4p sep & sl	25	8
1963	A495	7p sl & sep	70	8
1964	A495	12p rose brn & pur	1.10	15
	Nos. 1959-1964 (6)		3.60	55

1976, July 9 Photogravure

Designs (Montreal Olympic Emblem and): 1p, Men's rowing (horiz.). 2p, Boxing (horiz.). 12p, Basketball.

1965	A496	1p multi	15	8
1966	A496	2p lil & multi	35	8
1967	A496	3p multi	55	8
1968	A496	12p multi	55	10

21st Olympic Games, Montreal, Canada, July 17—Aug. 1.

King Juan Carlos I — A497

1976–77 Photo. Perf. 13

1969	A497	10c org ('77)	5	5
1970	A497	25c ap grn ('77)	5	5
1971	A497	30c dp bl ('77)	5	5
1972	A497	50c pur ('77)	5	5
1973	A497	1p emer ('77)	5	5
1974	A497	1.50p scarlet	7	5
1975	A497	2p dp bl	7	5
1976	A497	3p dp grn	9	5
1977	A497	4p lt grn ('77)	15	5
1978	A497	5p dp car rose	15	5
1979	A497	6p brt grn ('77)	18	5
1980	A497	7p olive	15	5
1982	A497	8p brt bl ('77)	12	5
1983	A497	10p lil rose ('77)	15	10
1984	A497	12p gldn brn	18	5
1985	A497	15p vio bl ('77)	28	8
1986	A497	20p brt red lil ('77)	28	8
	Nos. 1969-1986 (17)		2.09	96

See Nos. 2191-2196, 2261-2264.

Uniform Type of 1973

Uniforms: 1p, Trumpeter, Alcantara Regiment, 1815. 2p, Sapper, 1821. 3p, Engineer in dress uniform, 1825. 7p, Artillery infantry, 1828. 25p, Infantry riflemen, 1830.

1976, July 17

1989	A428	1p multi	20	10
1990	A428	2p multi	1.25	10
1991	A428	3p multi	60	10
1992	A428	7p multi	35	10
1993	A428	25p multi	70	25
	Nos. 1989-1993 (5)		3.10	65

SPAIN

Blood Donors A498   Mosaic, Batitales A499

1976, Sept. 7   Engr.   *Perf. 13*
1994 A498   3p car & blk   15   10
Give blood, save a life!

1976, Sept. 22
Designs: 3p, Lugo city wall. 7p, Obverse and reverse of Roman 1st Legion coin.
1995 A499   1p blk & pur   35   7
1996 A499   3p blk & dp brn   75   7
1997 A499   7p grn & mag   1.00   8
2000th anniversary of Lugo City.

Parliament, Madrid A500

1976, Sept. 23
1998 A500   12p grn & sep   35   10
63rd Conference of Inter-parliamentary Union, Madrid.

Still Life, by L. E. Menendez A501   St. Christopher Carrying Christ Child A502

Luis Eugenio Menendez Paintings: 2p, Peaches and jar. 3p, Pears, melon and barrel. 4p, Brace of pigeons and basket. 6p, Sea bream and oranges (horiz.). 7p, Water melon and bread (horiz.). 10p, Figs, bread and jug (horiz.). 12p, Various fruits (horiz.).

1976, Sept. 29   Photo.   *Perf. 13*
1999 A501   1p gold & multi   10   5
2000 A501   2p gold & multi   12   5
2001 A501   3p gold & multi   25   5
2002 A501   4p gold & multi   12   5
2003 A501   6p gold & multi   15   8
2004 A501   7p gold & multi   15   10
2005 A501   10p gold & multi   40   10
2006 A501   12p gold & multi   40   12
Nos. 1999-2006 (8)   1.69   60
Luis Eugenio Menendez (1716–1780). Stamp Day 1976.

1976, Oct. 8
Design: 3p, Nativity (horiz.). Both designs after painted wood carvings.
2007 A502   3p multi   90   8
2008 A502   12p multi   85   8
Christmas 1976.

Nicoya Church, Costa Rica A503   Juan Vazquez de Coronado A504

Designs: 3p, Orosi Mission, Costa Rica (horiz.). 12p, Tomas de Acosta.

1976, Oct. 12
2009 A503   1p multi   10   8
2010 A504   2p multi   25   8
2011 A503   3p multi   35   8
2012 A504   12p multi   45   10
Spain's link with Costa Rica.

Map of South and Central America, Santa Maria, King and Queen—A505

1976, Oct. 12
2013 A505   12p multi   40   15
Visit of King Juan Carlos I and Queen Sofia to Latin America.

St. Peter of Alcantara Monastery—A506

Tomb of Peter of Alcantara A507   St. Peter of Alcantara A508

1976, Oct. 29   Engr.   *Perf. 13*
2014 A506   3p dp brn & sep   35   10
2015 A507   7p dk pur & blk   30   20
2016 A508   20p brn & dk brn   65   20
St. Peter of Alcantara (1499–1562), Franciscan reformer.

Hand Releasing Doves A509

1976, Nov. 23   Litho.   *Perf. 13*
2017 A509   3p multi   15   8
11th Philatelic Exhibition of the National Association of the Handicapped.

Casals and Cello A510

Design: 5p, Manuel de Falla and Fire Dance from El Amor Brujo.

1976, Dec. 29   Engr.   *Perf. 13*
2018 A510   3p blk & vio bl   15   8
2019 A510   5p sl grn & car   20   10
Birth centenaries of Pablo Casals (1876–1973), cellist and composer, and of Manuel de Falla (1876–1946), composer.

Uniform Type of 1973
Uniforms: 1p, Outrider, Calatrava Lancers, 1844. 2p, Sapper, 1850. 3p, Corporal, Light Infantry, 1861. 4p, Drum Major, 1861. 20p, Artillery Captain, Mounted, 1862.

1977, Jan. 5   Photo.   *Perf. 13*
2020 A428   1p multi   10   5
2021 A428   2p multi   45   5
2022 A428   3p multi   30   5
2023 A428   4p multi   15   10
2024 A428   20p multi   80   12
Nos. 2020-2024 (5)   1.80   37

King James I A511

1977, Feb. 10   Engr.   *Perf. 13*
2025 A511   4p pur & ocher   12   7
James I, El Conquistador (1208–1276), King of Aragon, 700th death anniversary.

Jacinto Verdaguer A512

Portraits: 7p, Miguel Servet. 12p, Pablo Sarasate. 50p, Francisco Tarrega.

1977, Feb. 22
2026 A512   5p pur & dk red   45   6
2027 A512   7p ol & sl grn   35   8
2028 A512   12p dk bl & bl grn   45   10
2029 A512   50p lt grn & brn   1.10   20
Honoring Jacinto Verdaguer (1845–1902), Catalan poet; Miguel Servet (1511–1553), physician and theologian; Pablo Sarasate (1844–1908), violinist and composer; Francisco Tarrega (1854–1909), creator of modern Spanish guitar music.

Marquis de Penaflorida A513

1977, Feb. 24   Engr.   *Perf. 13*
2030 A513   4p dl grn & brn   12   8
Bicentenary of the Economic Society of the Friends of the Land (agricultural improvements).

Trout A514

Fish: 1p, Salmon (vert.). 3p, Eel. 4p, Carp. 6p, Barbel.

1977, Mar. 8   Photogravure
2031 A514   1p multi   10   5
2032 A514   3p multi   25   5
2033 A514   3p multi   20   5
2034 A514   4p multi   15   10
2035 A514   6p multi   25   10
Nos. 2031-2035 (5)   95   35

Slalom A515

1977, Mar. 24   Engr.   *Perf. 13*
2036 A515   5p multi   15   8
World Ski Championships, Granada, Sierra Nevada, Mar. 24–27.

La Cuadra, 1900 A516

Spanish Pioneer Automobiles: 4p, Hispano Suiza, 1916. 5p, Elizalde, 1915. 7p, Abadal, 1914.

1977, Apr. 23   Photo.   *Perf. 13*
2037 A516   2p multi   15   5
2038 A516   4p multi   10   5
2039 A516   5p multi   18   8
2040 A516   7p multi   25   10

Europa Issue 1977

Ordesa National Park A517

Design: 3p, Tree in Doñana National Park.

1977, May 2   Lithographed
2041 A517   3p multi   30   5
2042 A517   12p multi   85   10

Plaza Mayor, Spanish Stamps, Tongs A518

SPAIN

1977, May 7   Engraved   *Perf. 13*

2043   A518   3p multi   12   5

50th anniversary of Philatelic Market on Plaza Mayor, Madrid.

Enrique de Osso, St. Theresa and Book — A519

1977, June 7   Photo.   *Perf. 13*

2044   A519   8p multi   20   10

Centenary of the founding by Enrique de Osso of the Society of St. Theresa of Jesus.

Tourist Issue 1977

Toledo Gate, Ciudad Real — A520

Designs: 2p, Roman aqueduct, Almuñecar. 3p, Cathedral, Jaen (vert.). 4p, Ronda Gorge, Malaga (vert.). 7p, Ampudia Castle, Palencia. 12p, Bisagra Gate, Toledo.

1977, June 24   Engr.   *Perf. 13*

2045   A520   1p org & brn   10   5
2046   A520   2p sep & sl   10   5
2047   A520   3p vio & pur   10   5
2048   A520   4p brt & dk grn   10   5
2049   A520   7p brn & blk   25   8
2050   A520   12p vio org & brn   30   12
    Nos. 2045-2050 (6)   95   40

Uniform Type of 1973

Uniforms: 1p, Military Administration official, 1875. 2p, Cavalry lancers, 1883. 3p, General Staff Commander, 1884. 7p, Trumpeter, Divisional Artillery, 1887. 25p, Medical Corps official, 1895.

1977, July 16   Photogravure

2051   A428   1p multi   10   5
2052   A428   2p multi   30   5
2053   A428   3p multi   30   5
2054   A428   7p multi   20   10
2055   A428   25p multi   45   15
    Nos. 2051-2055 (5)   1.35   40

St. Emilian Cuculatus and Earliest Known Catalan Manuscript — A521

1977, Sept. 9   Engr.   *Perf. 13*

2056   A521   5p vio, grn & brn   15   5

Millennium of Catalan language.

The Boy Florez, by Madrazo — A522

Federico Madrazo Portraits: 2p, Duke of San Miguel. 3p, Senora Coronado. 4p, Campoamor. 6p, Marquesa de Montelo. 7p, Rivadeneyra. 10p, Countess de Vilches. 15p, Senora Gomez de Avellaneda.

1977, Sept. 29   Photo.   *Perf. 13*

2057   A522   1p gold & multi   10   8
2058   A522   2p gold & multi   15   8
2059   A522   3p gold & multi   15   8
2060   A522   4p gold & multi   10   8
2061   A522   6p gold & multi   10   10
2062   A522   7p gold & multi   12   10
2063   A522   10p gold & multi   20   10
2064   A522   15p gold & multi   40   12
    Nos. 2057-2064 (8)   1.32   74

Federico Madrazo (1815-1894).

Sailing Ship and Mail Routes, 18th Century — A523

1977, Oct. 7   Engraved

2065   A523   15p blk, brn & grn   75   75

ESPAMER '77 Philatelic Exhibition, Barcelona, Oct. 7-13, and for the Bicentenary for regular mail routes to the Indies (Central and South America). No. 2065 issued in sheets of 8 stamps and 8 labels showing exhibition emblem.

Church of St. Francis, Guatemala City — A524

Designs (Guatemala City): 3p, Modern buildings. 7p, Government Palace. 12p, Columbus Square and monument.

1977, Oct. 12   Photo.   *Perf. 13*

2066   A524   1p multi   10   5
2067   A524   3p multi   10   5
2068   A524   7p multi   15   8
2069   A524   12p multi   25   10

Spain's link with Guatemala.

San Pedro Monastery, Cardeña — A525

Designs: 7p, Cloister. 20p, Tomb of El Cid and Dona Gimena.

1977, Oct. 28   Engraved

2070   A525   3p vio bl & sl   25   5
2071   A525   7p brn & mar   15   10
2072   A525   20p grn & sl   35   12

San Pedro Monastery, Cardeña, Burgos.

Adoration of the Kings — A526

Design: 12p, Flight into Egypt (vert.). Designs from Romanesque paintings in Jaca Cathedral Museum.

1977, Nov. 3   Photogravure

2073   A526   5p multi   18   5
2074   A526   12p multi   20   8

Christmas 1977.

Old and New Iberia Planes — A527

1977, Nov. 3

2075   A527   12p multi   25   10

IBERIA, Spanish Airlines, 50th anniversary.

Felipe de Borbon, Prince of Asturias — A528   Judo, Games Emblem — A529

1977, Dec. 22   Photo.   *Perf. 13*

2076   A528   5p multi   15   6

Felipe de Borbon, Spanish crown prince.

1977, Dec. 29

2077   A529   3p multi   12   5

10th World Judo Championships, Taiwan.

Uniform Type of 1973

Uniforms: 1p, Flag bearer, 1908. 2p, Lieutenant Colonel, Hussar, 1909. 3p, Mounted artillery lieutenant, 1912. 5p, Engineers' captain, 1921. 12p, Captain General, 1925.

1978, Jan. 5

2078   A428   1p multi   10   5
2079   A428   2p multi   12   5
2080   A428   3p multi   20   6
2081   A428   5p multi   20   8
2082   A428   12p multi   20   10
    Nos. 2078-2082 (5)   82   34

Hilarión Eslava and Score — A530

Designs: 8p, José Clara and sculpture. 25p, Pio Baroja and farm. 50p, Antonio Machado Ruiz and castle.

1978, Feb. 20   Engr.   *Perf. 13*

2083   A530   5p blk & dk pur   20   5
2084   A530   8p bl grn & blk   15   6
2085   A530   25p yel grn & blk   50   15
2086   A530   50p dk pur & dk brn   85   25

Miguel Hilarión Eslava (1807-1878), composer; José Clara, sculptor; Pio Baroja (1872-1956), author and physician; Antonio Machado Ruiz (1875-1939), poet and playwright.

Burial of Christ, by de Juni — A531

Detail from Burial of Christ — A532

Designs: No. 2089, Juan de Juni. No. 2090, Rape of Sabine Women, by Rubens. No. 2091, Rape (detail) and Rubens portrait. No. 2092, Rubens signature and palette. No. 2093, Judgment of Paris, by Titian. No. 2094, Judgment and Titian portrait. No. 2095, Initial "TF" and palette.

1978, Mar. 28   Engr.   *Perf. 12½x13*

2087   A532   3p multi   8   5
2088   A531   3p multi   8   5
2089   A532   3p multi   8   5
2090   A531   5p multi   8   6
2091   A531   5p multi   8   6
2092   A532   5p multi   8   6
2093   A532   8p multi   15   8
2094   A531   8p multi   15   8
2095   A532   8p multi   15   8
    Nos. 2087-2095 (9)   93   57

Juan de Juni (1507-1577), sculptor, 400th death anniversary (3p); Peter Paul Rubens (1577-1640), painter, 400th birth anniversary (5p); Titian (1477-1576), painter, 500th birth anniversary (8p). Stamps of same denomination printed setenant.

Edelweiss in Pyrenees — A533

Designs: 5p, Fish and duck, wetlands. 7p, Forest, and forest destroyed by fire. 12p, Waves, oil rig, tanker and city. 20p, Sea gulls and seals (vert.).

1978, Apr. 4   Photo.   *Perf. 13*

2096   A533   3p multi   10   5
2097   A533   5p multi   10   6
2098   A533   7p multi   15   8
2099   A533   12p multi   20   10
2100   A533   20p multi   32   12
    Nos. 2096-2100 (5)   87   41

Protection of the environment.

Europa Issue 1978

Palace of Charles V, Granada — A534

Design: 12p, The Lonja, Seville.

1978, May 2   Engr.   *Perf. 13*

2101   A534   5p dl grn & sl grn   20   5
2102   A534   12p dl grn & car rose   35   10

"España" — A535

1978, May 5   Photo.   *Perf. 12½*

2103   A535   12p multi   20   10

Spain's admission to the Council of Europe.

SPAIN

1978, June 27   Engr.   *Perf. 13*
2104   A536   5p sl grn   12   5
Stamp Day.

Symbols and Emblems of Postal Service A536

Map of Las Palmas, 16th Century A537

Designs: 5p, Hermitage of Columbus Church (vert.). 12p, View of Las Palmas, 16th century.

1978, June 23   Photogravure
2105   A537   3p multi   8   5
2106   A537   10p multi   10   5
2107   A537   12p multi   30   10
500th anniversary of the founding of Las Palmas.

Pablo Picasso, Self-portrait A538

Picasso Paintings: 3p, Señora Canals. 8p, Jaime Sabartes. 10p, End of the Act (actress). 12p, Science and Charity (woman patient, doctor, nurse and child; horiz.). 15p, "Las Mennas" (blue period; horiz.). 20p, The Sparrows. 25p, The Painter and his Model (horiz.).

1978, Sept. 29   Photo.   *Perf. 13*
2108   A538   3p gold & multi   10   6
2109   A538   5p gold & multi   10   6
2110   A538   8p gold & multi   18   10
2111   A538   10p gold & multi   20   10
2112   A538   12p gold & multi   20   10
2113   A538   15p gold & multi   25   12
2114   A538   20p gold & multi   30   12
2115   A538   25p gold & multi   40   15
Nos. 2108-2115 (8)   1.73   .81
Pablo Picasso (1881–1972). Stamp Day 1978.

José de San Martín A539

Design: 12p, Simon Bolivar.

1978, Oct. 12   Engr.   *Perf. 13*
2116   A539   7p sep & car   15   6
2117   A539   12p vio & car   25   10
José de San Martín (1778–1850) and Simon Bolivar (1783–1830), South American liberators.

Flight into Egypt, Capital from St. Mary de Nieva—A540

Design: 12p, Annunciation, capital from St. Mary de Nieva.

1978, Nov. 3   Photo.   *Perf. 13*
2118   A540   5p multi   10   6
2119   A540   12p multi   20   10
Christmas 1978.

Mexican Calendar Stone A541

Designs (King Juan Carlos I, Queen Sofia and): No. 2121, Machu Picchu. No. 2122, Calchaqui jars from Tucuman and Angalgala.

1978
2120   A541   5p multi   12   6
2121   A541   5p multi   12   6
2122   A541   5p multi   12   6
Royal visits to Mexico, Peru and Argentina.
Issue dates: No. 2120 (Mexico), Nov. 17; No. 2121 (Peru), Nov. 22; No. 2122 (Argentina), Nov. 26.

King Philip V A542

Rulers of Spain: No. 2124, Louis I. 8p, Ferdinand VI. 10p, Carlos III. 12p, Carlos IV. 15p, Ferdinand VII. 20p, Isabella II. 25p, Alfonso XII. 50p, Alfonso XIII. 100p, Juan Carlos I.

1978, Nov. 22   Engr.   *Perf. 13*
2123   A542   5p dk bl & rose red   12   6
2124   A542   5p ol & dl grn   12   6
2125   A542   8p vio bl & red brn   20   10
2126   A542   10p bl grn & blk   20   10
2127   A542   12p brn & mar   25   12
2128   A542   15p blk & ind   30   15
2129   A542   20p ol & ind   35   15
2130   A542   25p ultra & vio brn   40   20
2131   A542   50p ver & brn   75   35
2132   A542   100p ultra & vio blk   1.75   60
Nos. 2123-2132 (10)   4.44   1.89

Spanish Flag, Preamble to Constitution, Parliament—A543

1978, Dec.   Photo.   *Perf. 13*
2133   A543   5p multi   12   6
Proclamation of New Constitution.

A well informed dealer can help the collector build his collection. He is the one to turn to when philatelic property must be sold.

Illuminated Pages from Bible and Codex—A544

1978, Dec. 27
2134   A544   5p multi   12   6
Millennium of the consecration of the Basilica of Santa Maria de Ripoll.

Car and Drop of Oil A545

Designs: 8p, Insulated house and thermometer. 10p, Hand pulling plug.

1979, Jan. 24   Photo.   *Perf. 13*
2135   A545   5p multi   10   6
2136   A545   8p multi   12   6
2137   A545   10p multi   15   6
Energy conservation.

De La Salle, Students A546

1979, Feb. 14   Photo.   *Perf. 13*
2138   A546   5p multi   10   6
Institute of Christian Brothers, founded by Jean-Baptiste de la Salle, centenary.

Jorge Manrique A547

Portraits: 8p, Fernan Caballero (pen name of Cecilia Böhl de Faber). 10p, Francisco Villaespesa. 20p, Gregorio Marañon.

1979, Feb. 28   Engraved
2139   A547   5p grn & brn   6   6
2140   A547   8p dk red & bl   15   6
2141   A547   10p brn & pur   15   8
2142   A547   20p grn & ol   40   10
Jorge Manrique, poet, 500th death anniversary; Fernan Caballero, Francisco Villaespesa, and Gregorio Marañon, writers, birth centenaries.

Running and Jumping A548

Sport for All: 8p, Children kicking ball and skipping rope, men jogging and bicycling. 10p, Family jogging and dog.

1979, Mar. 14   Photo.   *Perf. 13*
2143   A548   5p multi   10   6
2144   A548   8p multi   12   6
2145   A548   10p multi   15   6

Children in Library A549

1979, Apr. 27   Photo.   *Perf. 13*
2146   A549   5p multi   10   6
International Year of the Child.

Europa Issue 1979

Manuel Ysasi (1810–1855) Postal Reformer A550

Design: 5p, Mounted messenger and postilion, 1761 engraving (vert.).

1979, Apr. 30   Engraved
2147   A550   5p brn & sep   10   6
2148   A550   12p red brn & sl grn   20   8

Radar and Satellite A551

Design: 5p, Symbolic people and cables (vert.).

1979, May 17   Photo.   *Perf. 13*
2149   A551   5p multi   10   6
2150   A551   8p multi   15   6
World Telecommunications Day, May 17.

Bulgaria No. 1, Sofia Opera House, Housing Development—A552

1979, May 18
2151   A552   12p multi   20   10
Philaserdica '79, International Philatelic Exhibition, Sofia, Bulgaria, May 18–27.

Tank, Jet and Destroyer A553

1979, May 25
2152   A553   5p multi   10   6
Armed Forces Day.

See "Special Notices" at the front of this volume for data on the listing methods of this Catalogue, abbreviations, condition, prices and examination.

SPAIN

Messenger Handing Letter to King A554

1979, June 15		Litho. and Engr.		
2153	A554	5p multi	10	6

Stamp Day 1979.

Daroca Gate, Zaragoza A555

Architecture: 8p, Gerona Cathedral. 10p, Interior, Carthusian Monastery Church, Granada. 20p, Portal, Palace of the Marques de Dos Aguas, Valencia.

1979, June 27		Engraved		
2154	A555	5p vio bl & lil brn	10	6
2155	A555	8p dk bl & sep	12	8
2156	A555	10p blk & grn	15	8
2157	A555	20p brn & sep	30	8

Turkey Sponge A556

Fauna: 7p, Crayfish. 8p, Scorpion. 20p, Starfish. 25p, Sea anemone.

1979, July 11		Photo.	Perf. 13	
2158	A556	5p multi	8	6
2159	A556	7p multi	10	6
2160	A556	8p multi	12	6
2161	A556	20p multi	30	10
2162	A556	25p multi	40	15
	Nos. 2158-2162 (5)		1.00	43

Gen. Antonio Gutierrez and Battle A557

1979, Aug.		Engraved		
2163	A557	5p multi	10	8

Naval defense of Tenerife, 18th century.

Immaculate Conception, by Juanes A558

Juan de Juanes Paintings: 10p, Holy Family. 15p, Ecce Homo. 20p, St. Stephen in the Synagogue. 25p, The Last Supper (horiz.). 50p, Adoration of the Mystic Lamb (horiz.).

1979, Sept. 28		Photo.	Perf. 13×13½	
2164	A558	8p multi	15	8
2165	A558	10p multi	18	10
2166	A558	15p multi	30	10
2167	A558	20p multi	35	10
2168	A558	25p multi	45	15
2169	A558	50p multi	90	22
	Nos. 2164-2169 (6)		3.85	1.55

Zaragoza Cathedral, Mother and Child Statue—A559

1979, Oct. 3		Photo.	Perf. 13×13½	
2170	A559	5p multi	10	6

8th Mariology and 15th International Marianist Congresses, Zaragoza, Oct. 3-12.

Felipe de Borbon, Hospital—A560

1979, Oct.		Perf. 13½×13		
2171	A560	5p multi	10	6

Hospital of the Child Jesus, centenary.

St. Bartholomew College, Bogota—A561

Design: 12p, University of St. Mark, Lima, coat of arms.

1979, Oct. 12		Engr.	Perf. 13	
2172	A561	7p multi	12	6
2173	A561	12p multi	20	10

Hispanidad 79.

Clasped Hands, Badge, Governor's Palace—A562

Design: No. 2175, Statute book (vert.).

1979, Oct. 27		Litho. & Engr.	Perf. 13	
2174	A562	8p multi	15	6
2175	A562	8p multi	15	6

Catalonian and Basque autonomy statute.

Type A54, Barcelona Coat of Arms A563

Perf. 13½×13

1979, Nov. 6		Photo. & Engr.		
2176	A563	5p multi	10	6

Barcelona Philatelic Congress and Exhibition, 50th anniversary.

Nativity, Capital from St. Peter the Elder A564

Christmas 1979: 19p, Flilght into Egypt, column from St. Peter the Elder, Huesca.

1979, Nov. 14		Photo.		
2177	A564	8p multi	12	6
2178	A564	19p multi	32	10

Carlos I, Coat of Arms—A565

Kings of the House of Austria (Hapsburg Dynasty): 20p, Philip II. 25p, Philip III. 50p, Philip IV. 100p, Carlos II.

1979, Nov. 22		Engr.	Perf. 13	
2179	A565	15p sl grn & dk bl	25	10
2180	A565	20p dk bl & mag	30	10
2181	A565	25p vio & yel bis	40	15
2182	A565	50p brn & sl grn	75	25
2183	A565	100p mag & brn	1.50	50
	2179-2183 (5)		3.20	1.10

2nd International Olive Oil Year—A566

1979, Dec. 4		Photo.	Perf. 13½×13	
2184	A566	8p multi	15	6

King Juan Carlos I Type of 1976

1980, Feb.		Photo.	Perf. 13	
2191	A497	13p dk red brn ('81)	22	10
2192	A497	16p sepia	32	10
2194	A497	19p orange	50	10
2196	A497	30p dk grn ('81)	6	5

Train and People—A567

Public Transportation: 4p, Bus. 5p, Subway.

1980, Feb. 20		Engraved	Perf. 13½	
2200	A567	3p car rose & brn	8	5
2201	A567	4p dk bl & brn	8	5
2202	A567	5p sl & brn	10	6

Steel Export—A568

1980, Mar. 15		Photo.	Perf. 13½×13	
2203	A568	5p shown	10	6
2204	A568	8p Ships	15	6
2205	A568	13p Shoes	22	10
2206	A568	19p Machinery	32	10
2207	A568	25p Technology	45	35
	Nos. 2203-2207 (5)		1.24	67

Europa Issue 1980

Federico Garcia Lorca (1899-1936)—A569

Design: 19p, José Ortega y Gasset (1883-1955), philosopher and statesman.

1980, Apr. 28		Engraved	Perf. 13½	
2208	A569	8p vio & ol grn	15	6
2209	A569	19p brn & dk grn	32	10

Armed Forces Day—A570

1980, May 24		Photo.	Perf. 13½×13	
2210	A570	8p multi	15	6

Soccer Players—A571

1980, May 23				
2211	A571	8p shown	15	10
2212	A571	19p Soccer ball, flags	35	12

World Soccer Cup 1982.

SPAIN

Bourbon Arms, Ministry of Finance—A572

1980, June 9 **Engraved** *Perf. 13½*
2213 A572 8p dk brn 15 6
Public Finances in Bourbon Spain Exhibition.

Helen Keller, Sign Language—A573

1980, June 27
2214 A573 19p dk yel grn & rose lake 30 10
Helen Keller (1880-1968), deaf mute writer and lecturer.

Mounted Postman, 12th Century Panel, Barcelona—A574

1980, June 28 Litho. & Engr. Perf. 13x12½
2215 A574 8p multi 15 6
Stamp Day.

King Alfonso and Count of Maceda at 1930 National Exhibition—A575

1980, July 1 **Photo.** *Perf. 13½*
2216 A575 8p multi 15 6
1st National Stamp Exhibition, Barcelona, 50th anniversary.

Altar of the Virgin, La Palma Cathedral—A576

1980, July 12 **Engraved** *Perf. 13*
2217 A576 8p blk & brn 15 6
Appearance of the Virgin of the Snow at La Palma, 300th anniversary.

Perez de Ayala—A577

1980, Aug. 9 **Engraved** *Perf. 13*
2218 A577 100p sl & sep 1.65 30
Ramon Perez de Ayala (1881-1962), novelist and diplomat.

Souvenir Sheet

La Atlantida Ruins, Mexican Bonampak Musicians—A578

Designs: No. 2219b, Sun Gate, Tiahuanaco; Roman arch, Medinaceli. No. 2219c, Alonso de Ercilla, Garcilaso de la Vega; title pages from La Arauca and Commentario Reales. No. 2219d, Virgin of Quito, Virgin of Seafarers.

1980, Oct. 3 **Engraved** *Perf. 13*
2219 Sheet of 4 3.75 3.25
 a. A578 25p multi 45 45
 b. A578 25p multi 45 45
 c. A578 50p multi 90 60
 d. A578 100p multi 2.00 1.50
ESPAMER '80 Stamp Exhibition, Madrid, Oct. 3-12. No. 2219 has 2 labels showing exhibition emblem; black control number. Size: 150½x100mm.

400th Anniversary of Buenos Aires—A579

1980, Oct. 24
2220 A579 19p multi 32 10

Miniature Sheet

The Creation, Tapestry, Gerona Cathedral—A580

1980, Nov. **Litho.** *Perf. 13½x13*
2221 Sheet of 6 3.75 3.75
 a. A580 25p multi 40 15
 b. A580 25p multi 40 15
 c. A580 25p multi 40 15
 d. A580 50p multi 75 30
 e. A580 50p multi 75 30
 f. A580 50p multi 75 30
No. 2221 has black marginal inscription and control number. Size: 132x107mm.

Conference Building, Flags of Participants A581

Holy Family Church of Santa Maria, Cuina A582

1980, Nov. 11 **Photo.** *Perf. 13½*
2222 A581 22p multi 35 10

1980, Nov. 12
Christmas 1980, 22p, Adoration of the Kings, portal, Church of Santa Maria, Cuina (horiz.).
2223 A582 10p multi 18 5
2224 A582 22p multi 38 10

Pedro Vives and His Airplane—A583

Designs: Aviation pioneers.

1980, Dec. 10
2225 A583 5p shown 10 6
2226 A583 10p Benito Loygorri 18 6
2227 A583 15p Alfonso De Orleans 28 10
2228 A583 22p Alfredo Kindelan 38 10

Winter University Games—A584

1981, Mar. 4 *Perf. 13½x13*
2229 A584 30p multi 55 10

Picasso's Birth Centenary Emblem, by Joan Miro—A585

1981, Mar. 27 *Perf. 13*
2230 A585 100p multi 1.75 30
Pablo Picasso (1881-1972).

Galician Autonomy—A586

1981, Mar. 27 **Photo. & Engr.** *Perf. 13*
2231 A586 12p multi 22 10

Homage to the Press A587

1981, Apr. 8 **Photo.** *Perf. 13½x13*
2232 A587 12p multi 22 10

International Year of the Disabled—A588

1981, Apr. 29 **Litho.**
2233 A588 30p multi 55 10

Soccer Players A589

1981, May 2 **Photo.**
2234 A589 12p Soccer players, diff., vert. 25 8
2235 A589 30p shown 55 10
1982 World Cup Soccer.

Europa Issue 1981

La Jota Folkdance A590

1981, May 4 **Engr.**
2236 A590 12p shown 22 6
2237 A590 30p Virgin of Rocio procession 55 10

SPAIN

Armed Forces Day — A591

Gabriel Miro (1879-1930), Writer A592

1981, May 29 Photo. *Perf. 13x13½*
2238 A591 12p multi   35 10

Famous Men: 12p, Francisco de Quevedo (1580-1645), writer. 30p, St. Benedict (480-543), patron saint of Europe.

1981, June 17 Engr.
2239 A592 6p pur & dk grn   10   5
2240 A592 12p brn & pur   22   5
2241 A592 30p dk grn & brn 55 10

Mail Messenger, 14th Cent., Woodcut — A593

1981, June 19 Photo. & Engr. *Perf. 12½x13*
2242 A593 12p multi   22 10
Stamp Day

Map of Balearic Islands, Diego Homem's Atlas, 1563 — A594

1981, July 8 Photo. *Perf. 13x12½*
2243 A594 7p shown   12   6
2244 A594 12p Canary Islds., Prunes map, 1563   22   6

Kings Alfonso XII and Juan Carlos, Advocates Arms — A595

1981, July 27 Engr. *Perf. 13½x13*
2245 A595 50p multi   90 10
Chamber of Advocates of State (Public Prosecutor) centenary.

King Sancius VI of Navarre with City Charter, 12th Cent. Miniature — A596

1981, Aug. 5 Photo. *Perf. 12½x13*
2246 A596 12p multi   32 10
Vitoria, 800th anniv.

Exports A597

1981, Sept. 30 Photo. *Perf. 13½x13*
2247 A597 6p Fruit   10   5
2248 A597 12p Wine   22   8
2249 A597 30p Vehicles 55 10

Congress Palace, Buenos Aires — A598

1981, Oct. 12 Engr. *Perf. 13½x13*
2250 A598 12p dk bl & car rose   22 10
ESPAMER '81 Intl. Stamp Exhibition, Buenos Aires, Nov. 13-22.

World Food Day A599

1981, Oct. 16
2251 A599 30p multi   55 10

Souvenir Sheet

Guernica, by Pablo Picasso (1881-1973) — A600

1981, Oct. 25 Photo.
2252 A600 200p multi   3.50 1.25
No. 2252 has multicolored margin; black control number. Size: 163x105mm.

Adoration of the Kings, Cervera de Pisuerga, Palencia — A601

1981, Nov. 18 Litho. *Perf. 13*
2253 A601 12p shown   20   8
2254 A601 30p Nativity, Paredes de Nava 45 10
Christmas 1981.

King Type of 1976 and

King Juan Carlos I — A602

1981, Oct. 21 Photo. *Perf. 13*
2261 A497 50p org ver   90   8
2262 A497 60p blue   1.10   8
2263 A497 75p brt yel grn 1.25   8
2264 A497 85p gray   1.40   8

Engr. *Perf. 13x12½*
2268 A602 100p brown   1.75   15
2269 A602 200p dk grn 3.50   25
2270 A602 500p dk bl   9.00   60
Nos. 2261-2270 (7)   18.90 1.32

Postal Museum, Madrid — A603

1981, Nov. 30 Engr. *Perf. 13*
2275   Sheet of 4   3.00 2.75
  a. A603 7p Telegraph operator   12
  b. A603 12p Coach   22
  c. A603 50p Emblem   90
  d. A603 100p Cap, posthorn, pouch   1.75
No. 2275 has dark green marginal inscription; black control number. Size: 135x100mm.

Royal Mint Building, Seville A604

1981, Dec. 4 Engr. *Perf. 13*
2276 A604 12p blk & brn   22 10
Spanish Administration of the Bourbons in the Indies.

Iparraguirre (1820-1881) — A605

Designs: 30p, Juan Ramon Jimenez (1881-1958), writer. 50p, Pedro Calderon (1600-1681), playwright.

1981, Dec. 16
2277 A605 12p blk & dk bl   22 10

1982, Mar. 10
2278 A605 30p dk bl & dk grn   55 10
2279 A605 50p blk & vio   90 20

Espana '82 World Cup Soccer A606

Andres Bello (1782-1865), Writer A607

1982, Feb. 24 Photo.
2280 A606 14p Poster by Juan Miro   25   8
2281 A606 33p Cup, emblem   60 15

1982, Mar. 10 Engr.
2282 A607 30p grn & dk grn   90 10

Holy Year of Compostelo — A608

1982, Mar. 31 Photo. *Perf. 13*
2283 A608 14p St. John of Compostelo   25   10

SPAIN

Manuel Fernandez Caballero
(1835-1906) and Scene from his
Gigantes and Cabezudos
A609   A610

Designs: Operetta composers and scenes from their works. Stamps of same denomination se-tenant.

1982, Apr. 28   Litho. & Engr.   Perf. 13
2284	A609	3p shown	5	5
2285	A610	3p shown	5	5
2286	A609	6p Amadeo Vives Roig (1871-1932)	10	6
2287	A610	6p Dona Francisquita	10	6
2288	A609	8p Tomas Breton Hernandez (1850-1923)	15	6
2289	A610	8p Verbena of Paloma	15	6
		Nos. 2284-2289 (6)	60	34

Europa 1982—A611

1982, May 3   Engr.   Perf. 12½
2290	A611	14p Unification, 1512	25	8
2291	A611	33p Discovery of New World, 1492	60	15

Armed Forces Day—A612

1982, May 28   Photo.   Perf. 13
2292	A612	14p multi	25	8

1982 World Cup—A613

Designs: Soccer players.

1982, June 13   Perf. 13
2293	A613	14p multi	25	10
2294	A613	33p multi	60	20

Souvenir Sheets
2295	Sheets of 4 (#2293-2294, 9p, 100p)	2.75	2.50
a.	A613 9p Captains' handshake	15	10
b.	A613 100p Player holding cup	1.80	60

No. 2295 has two types of multicolored margin, each showing seven arms of the 14 host cities. Size: 164x106mm.

One sheet has 3 blue coats of arms, the other has 2.

Stamp Day—A614

1982, July 16   Litho. & Engr.   Perf. 12½
2296	A614	14p Map, postal code	25	10

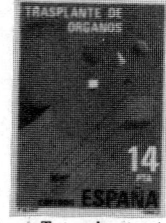

Organ Transplants—A615

1982, July 28   Photo.   Perf. 13
2297	A615	14p Symbolic organs	25	10

Storks and Express Train—A616

Locomotive, 1850—A617

1982, Sept. 27   Photo.   Perf. 12½, 13 (A617)
2298	A616	9p shown	15	8
2299	A617	14p shown	25	10
2300	A617	33p Santa Fe locomotive	60	15

23rd Intl. Railways Congress, Malaga.

ESPAMER '82 Intl. Stamp Exhibition, San Juan, Oct. 12-17—A618

1982, Oct. 12   Engr.   Perf. 13½x13
2301	A618	33p dk bl & pur	60	15

St. Teresa of Avila (1515-1582)—A619

1982, Oct. 15
2302	A619	33p Statue by Gregorio Hernandez	60	15

Visit of Pope John Paul II, Oct. 31-Nov. 9—A620

1982, Oct. 31   Engr.   Perf. 12½
2303	A620	14p multi	25	10

Water Wheel, Alcantarilla—A621

Landscapes and Monuments. 6p horiz.

1982, Nov. 5   Perf. 13x12½, 12½x13
2304	A621	4p shown	8	6
2305	A621	6p Bank of Spain, 19th cent.	10	6
2306	A621	9p Crucifixion	18	10
2307	A621	14p St. Martin's Tower, Teruel	25	10
2308	A621	33p St. Andrew's Gate, Zamora	60	15
		Nos. 2304-2308 (5)	1.21	47

Christmas 1982—A622

1982, Nov. 17   Photo.   Perf. 13½
2309	A622	14p Nativity, wood carving, by Gil de Siloe	25	8
2310	A622	33p Flight into Egypt	60	15

Pablo Gargallo, Sculpture, Birth Centenary
A623

Salesian Fathers in Spain Centenary
A624

1982, Dec. 9   Engr.   Perf. 13
2311	A623	14p bl & dk grn	25	8

1982, Dec. 16   Photo.   Perf. 12½x13
2312	A624	14p multi	25	8

Arms of King Juan Carlos I—A625

1983, Feb. 9   Photo.   Perf. 12½
2313	A625	14p multi	42	14

Andalusia Autonomy Statute—A626

1983   Litho. & Engr.   Perf. 13½
2314	A626	14p shown	42	14
2315	A626	14p Cantabria	42	14

Issue dates: No. 2314, Feb. 28; No. 2315, Mar. 15.

State Security Forces—A627

1983, Mar. 23   Photo.
2316	A627	9p Natl. Police Force	28	10
2317	A627	14p Civil Guard	42	14
2318	A627	33p Superior Police Corps	1.00	35

Operetta Type of 1982

Designs: 4p, Francisco Alonso Lopez (1887-1948), La Parranda. 6p, Jacinto Guerrero y Torres (1895-1951), La Rosa del Azafran. 9p, Jesus de Guridi Bidaola (1886-1961), El Caserio.

1983, Apr. 22   Litho. & Engr.   Perf. 13
2319	A609	4p multi	6	5
2320	A610	4p multi	6	5
2321	A609	6p multi	10	5
2322	A610	6p multi	10	5
2323	A609	9p multi	14	5
2324	A610	9p multi	14	5
		Nos. 2319-2324 (6)	60	30

Europa 1983—A628

Designs: 16p, Scene from Don Quixote, by Miguel Cervantes. 38p, L. Torres Quevedo's Niagara Spanish aerocar.

1983, May 5   Engr.   Perf. 13x12½
Granite Paper
2325	A628	16p dk grn & brn red	22	6
2326	A628	38p brown	52	15

SPAIN

Francisco
Salzillo Alvarez
(1707-1783),
Painter
A629

Designs: 38p, Antonio Soler Ramos (1729-1783), composer. 50p, Joaquin Turina Perez (1882-1949), composer. 100p, St. Isidro Labrador (1082-1170), patron saint of Madrid.

1983, May 14   *Perf. 13*
2327	A629	16p pur & dk grn	22	6
2328	A629	38p bl & brn	52	15
2329	A629	50p bl grn & dk brn	70	20
2330	A629	100p red brn & pur	1.40	30

1983, May 17   Photo.   *Perf. 13*
| 2331 | A630 | 38p multi | 52 | 15 |

World
Communications
Year
A630

Rioja Autonomous Region—A631

1983, May 25   Litho. & Engr.   *Perf. 13*
| 2332 | A631 | 16p multi | 22 | 6 |

Armed Forces Day—A632

1983, May 26   Photo.
| 2333 | A632 | 16p multi | 22 | 6 |

Intl. Canine Exhibition, Madrid, June 1984—A633

1983, June 8   Litho. & Engr.   *Perf. 13½*
2334	A633	10p Pointer	14	5
2335	A633	16p Mastiff	22	6
2336	A633	26p Iberian hound	36	12
2337	A633	38p Navarro pointer	52	15

Discovery of Tungsten
Bicentenary—A634

Scouting Year—A635

400th Anniv. of University of Zaragoza—A636

1983, June 22   Photo.   *Perf. 13*
2338	A634	16p Elhuyar brothers	22	6
2339	A635	38p multi	52	18
2340	A636	50p multi	70	20

Murcia Autonomous Region—A637

1983, July 8   Photo. & Engr.   *Perf. 13½*
| 2341 | A637 | 16p Arms | 22 | 6 |

Asturias Autonomous Region—A638

1983, Sept. 8   Litho. & Engr.   *Perf. 13*
| 2342 | A638 | 14p Victory Cross, Covadonga Basilica | 18 | 5 |

Intl. Institute of Statistics, 44th Congress, Madrid, Sept. 12-22—A639

1983, Sept. 12   Photo.   *Perf. 13*
| 2343 | A639 | 38p Institute building | 50 | 15 |

Stamp Day—A640

1983, Oct. 8   Litho. & Engr.   *Perf. 13x12½*
| 2344 | A640 | 16p Roman mail cart | 22 | 6 |

No. 2344 se-tenant with label publicizing ESPANA '84 Philatelic Exhibition, April 27-May 6, 1984.

Valencia Automony Statute, 1st Anniv.—A641

1983, Oct. 10   Litho. & Engr.   *Perf. 13*
| 2345 | A641 | 16p multi | 22 | 6 |

View of Sevilla, 16th cent.—A642

1983, Oct. 12   Engraved   *Perf. 12½x13*
| 2346 | A642 | 38p multi | 50 | 15 |

Spanish-American trade in 17th century.

Stained Glass Windows—A643

Designs: 10p King, Leon Cathedral. 16p, Epiphany, Gerona Cathedral. 38p, Apostle Santiago, Royal Hospital Chapel, Santiago.

1983, Oct. 28   Litho. & Engr.   *Perf. 12½x13*
2347	A643	10p multi	14	5
2348	A643	16p multi	22	6
2349	A643	38p multi	50	15

Church at Llivia, Gerona—A644

Designs: 6p, Temple, Santa Maria del Mar, Barcelona. 16p, Cathedral, Ceuta. 38p, Gate of the Santiago Bridge, Melila. 50p, Charity Hospital, Sevilla.

1983, Nov. 9   Engr.   *Perf. 13x12½*
2350	A644	3p dk bl gray & grn	5	5
2351	A644	6p dk bl gray	8	5
2352	A644	16p red brn & dl vio	22	6
2353	A644	38p bis brn & rose car	50	15
2354	A644	50p brn & org red	70	18
		Nos. 2350-2354	1.55	49

Christmas 1983
A645

1983, Nov. 23   Photo.   *Perf. 13x13½*
| 2355 | A645 | 16p The Nativity, Tortosa | 22 | 6 |
| 2356 | A645 | 38p The Adoration, Vich | 50 | 15 |

Indalecia Prieto (1883-1962),
Patriot—A646

1983, Dec. 14   Engr.   *Perf. 13*
| 2357 | A646 | 16p red brn & blk | 22 | 6 |

Industrial Accident Prevention—A647

1984, Jan. 25   Photo.   *Perf. 13½*
2358	A647	7p Construction worker	10	5
2359	A647	10p Fire	14	5
2360	A647	16p Electrical plug, pliers	22	6

Extremadura Statute of Autonomy, First Anniv.—A648

1984, Feb. 25   Litho. and Engr.   *Perf. 13*
| 2361 | A648 | 16p multi | 22 | 6 |

1500th Anniv. of City of Burgos—A649

1984, Mar. 1   Engr.
| 2362 | A649 | 16p multi | 22 | 6 |

Carnivals—A650

1984   Photo.   *13½x13*
| 2363 | A650 | 16p Santa Cruz de Tenerife | 22 | 6 |
| 2364 | A650 | 16p Valencia Fallas | 22 | 6 |

Issue dates: No. 2363, Mar. 5; No. 2364, Mar. 16.

SEMI-POSTAL STAMPS.
Red Cross Issue.

Princesses María Cristina and Beatrice SP1

Queen as a Nurse SP2

Queen Victoria Eugénia SP3

Prince of Asturias SP4

King Alfonso XIII SP5

Engraved.

1926, Sept. 15 Perf. 12½ Unwmkd.

B1	SP1	1c black	2.25	2.00
B2	SP2	2c ultra	2.25	2.00
B3	SP3	5c vio brn	5.00	4.00
B4	SP4	10c green	4.00	4.00
B5	SP1	15c indigo	1.75	1.50
B6	SP2	20c dl vio	1.75	2.00
a.		20c vio brn (error)	300.00	
B7	SP3	25c rose red	40	85
B8	SP1	30c bl grn	32.50	40.00
B9	SP2	40c dk bl	22.50	20.00
B10	SP3	50c red org	21.00	17.50
B11	SP4	1p slate	1.75	2.50
B12	SP3	4p magenta	45	85
B13	SP5	10p brown	80	1.25
		Nos. B1-B13, EB1 (14)	104.90	106.10

The 20c was printed in violet brown for use in three colonies (Cape Juby, Spanish Guinea and Spanish Sahara). No. B6a, the missing overprint error, is listed here because it is not known to which colony it belongs.

Airplane and Map of Madrid-Manila Flight—SP6

1926, Sept. 15

B14	SP6	15c dp ultra & org	28	40
B15	SP6	20c car & yel grn	28	40
B16	SP6	30c dk brn & ultra	28	40
B17	SP6	40c dk grn & brn org	28	40
B18	SP6	4p mag & yel	80.00	72.50
		Nos. B14-B18 (5)	81.12	74.10

Madrid to Manila flight of Captains Eduardo G. Gallarza and Joaquim Loriga y Taboada.

Nos. B1–B18, CB1–CB5 and EB1 were used for regular postage on Sept. 15, 16, 17, 1926. Subsequently the unsold stamps were given to the Spanish Red Cross Society, by which they were sold uncancelled but they then had no franking power.

Coronation Silver Jubilee Issue.
Red Cross Stamps of 1926 Overprinted "ALFONSO XIII", Dates and Ornaments in Various Colors

1927, May 27

B19	SP1	1c blk (R)	5.00	4.50
B20	SP2	2c ultra (Bl)	9.00	7.00
B21	SP3	5c vio brn (R)	2.25	2.25
a.		Double overprint	40.00	
B22	SP4	10c grn (Bl)	50.00	45.00
B23	SP1	15c ind (R)	1.75	1.50
B24	SP2	20c dl vio (Bl)	3.25	2.75
B25	SP5	25c rose red (Bl)	50	45
B26	SP1	30c bl grn (Bl)	1.00	80
B27	SP3	40c dk bl (R)	1.00	80
B28	SP4	50c red org (Bl)	1.00	80
B29	SP4	1p sl (R)	1.75	1.50
B30	SP3	4p mag (Bl)	9.00	7.50
B31	SP5	10p brn (G)	32.50	32.50
		Nos. B19-B31 (13)	118.00	107.35

Same with Additional Surcharges of New Values.

B32	SP2	3c on 2c ultra (G)	10.00	9.50
B33	SP5	4c on 2c ultra (Bk)	10.00	9.50
B34	SP5	10c on 25c rose red (Bk)	50	20
B35	SP5	25c on 25c rose red (Bl)	50	20
B36	SP2	55c on 2c ultra (R)	1.00	90
B37	SP4	55c on 10c grn (Bk)	60.00	55.00
B38	SP4	55c on 20c dl vio (Bk)	60.00	55.00
B39	SP1	75c on 15c ind (R)	35	35
B40	SP1	75c on 30c bl grn (R)	185.00	175.00
B41	SP3	80c on 5c vio brn (R)	52.50	50.00
B42	SP3	2p on dk bl (G)	85	65
B43	SP4	2p on 1p sl (R)	85	65
B44	SP2	5p on 50c red org (R)	2.25	1.75
B45	SP3	5p on 4p mag (Bk)	3.00	2.25
B46	SP5	10p on 10p brn (G)	22.50	21.50
		Nos. B32-B46 (15)	409.30	382.45

Gallarza Flight Stamps Overprinted

✤✤✤✤✤✤✤ ✤✤✤✤✤✤✤
17 MAYO 17
1902   1927
✤✤✤✤✤✤✤ ✤✤✤✤✤✤✤

ALFONSO XIII.

B47	SP6	15c ultra & org (Br)	30	18
a.		Double overprint	35.00	
B48	SP6	20c car & yel grn (Bl)	30	18
a.		Brown overprint (error)	80.00	
b.		Inverted overprint	35.00	
B50	SP6	30c dk brn & ultra (R)	30	18
a.		Blue overprint (error)	80.00	
b.		Dbl. ovpt.	35.00	
B52	SP6	40c dk grn & brn org (Br)	30	18
a.		Invtd. ovpt.	35.00	
b.		Double overprint (Bl + Br)	135.00	
B53	SP6	4p mag & yel (Bl)	90.00	75.00
a.		Inverted overprint	235.00	

Semi-Postal Special Delivery Stamp of 1926 Overprinted "ALFONSO XIII", Dates and Ornaments in Violet.

B54	SPSD1	20c red vio & vio brn	6.50	5.50
		Nos. B47-B54 (6)	97.70	81.22

Semi-Postal Air Post Stamps of 1926 Overprinted

17-V-1902   17-V-1927
A   A
XIII   XIII

in Various Colors.

B55	SPAP1	5c blk & vio (R)	2.00	1.75
a.		Inverted overprint	35.00	
B56	SPAP1	10c ultra & blk (R)	2.25	1.75
a.		Inverted overprint	35.00	
B57	SPAP1	25c car & blk (Bl)	30	18
B58	SPAP1	50c red org & blk (Bl)	30	18
a.		Double overprint, one inverted	80.00	
B59	SPAP1	1p blk & grn (R)	2.75	2.00
a.		Inverted overprint	100.00	

Same with Additional Surcharges of New Values.

B60	SPAP1	75c on 5c blk & vio (R)	5.25	4.25
a.		Inverted surcharge	35.00	
B61	SPAP1	75c on 10c ultra & blk (R)	24.00	17.50
a.		Inverted surcharge	35.00	
B62	SPAP1	75c on 25c car & blk (Bl)	40.00	32.50
a.		Double surcharge	60.00	
B63	SPAP1	75c on 50c red org & blk (Bl)	20.00	17.50
		Nos. B55-B63 (9)	96.85	77.61

Nos. B54 to B63 inclusive were available for ordinary postage.

Stamps of Spanish Offices in Morocco and Spanish Colonies, 1926
(Spain Types SP3, SP5)
Surcharged with New Values and

17-V-1902   17-V-1927

in Various Colors.

On Spanish Morocco.

B64	SP3	55c on 4p bis (Bl)	10.00	9.00
B65	SP5	80c on 10p vio (Br)	10.00	9.00

On Spanish Tangier.

B66	SP5	1p on 10p vio (Br)	42.50	40.00
B67	SP3	4p bis (G)	17.50	15.00

On Cape Juby.

B68	SP3	5p on 4p bis (R)	27.50	25.00
B69	SP5	10p on 10p vio (R)	17.50	17.00

On Spanish Guinea.

B70	SP5	1p on 10p vio (Bl)	10.00	9.00
B71	SP3	2p on 4p bis (G)	10.00	9.00

On Spanish Sahara.

B72	SP5	80c on 10p vio (R)	15.00	14.00
B73	SP3	2p on 4p bis (R)	10.00	9.00
		Nos. B64-B73 (10)	170.00	156.00

Nos. B64 to B73 inclusive were available for postage in Spain only.
Nos. B19 to B73 were issued to commemorate the 25th year of the reign of King Alfonso XIII.

Catacombs Restoration Issues.

Pope Pius XI and King Alfonso XIII—SP7

1928, Dec. 23 Engraved Perf. 12½

Santiago Issue.

B74	SP7	2c vio & blk	32	28
B75	SP7	2c lake & blk	55	45
B76	SP7	3c bl blk & vio	32	28
B77	SP7	3c dl bl & vio	55	45
B78	SP7	5c ol grn & vio	1.10	55
B79	SP7	10c yel grn & blk	1.75	1.40
B80	SP7	15c bl grn & vio	6.75	5.75
B81	SP7	25c dp rose & vio	6.75	5.75
B82	SP7	40c ultra & blk	22	22
B83	SP7	55c ol brn & vio	22	22
B84	SP7	80c red & blk	22	22
B85	SP7	1p gray blk & vio	22	22
B86	SP7	2p red brn & blk	7.50	7.50
B87	SP7	3p pale rose & vio	7.50	7.50
B88	SP7	4p vio brn & blk	7.50	7.50
B89	SP7	5p grnsh blk & vio	7.50	7.50

Toledo Issue.

B90	SP7	2c bl blk & car	32	28
B91	SP7	2c ultra & car	55	45
B92	SP7	3c bis brn & ultra	32	28
B93	SP7	3c ol grn & ultra	55	45
B94	SP7	5c red vio & car	1.10	55
B95	SP7	10c yel grn & ultra	1.75	1.40
B96	SP7	15c sl bl & car	6.75	5.75
B97	SP7	25c red brn & ultra	6.75	5.75
B98	SP7	40c ultra & car	22	22
B99	SP7	55c dk brn & ultra	22	22
B100	SP7	80c blk & car	22	22
B101	SP7	1p yel & car	22	22
B102	SP7	2p dk gray & ultra	7.50	7.50
B103	SP7	3p vio & car	7.50	7.50
B104	SP7	4p vio brn & car	7.50	7.50
B105	SP7	5p bis & ultra	7.50	7.50
		Nos. B74-B105 (32)	97.94	91.58

Nos. B74 to B105 inclusive replaced the stamps of the regular series from Dec. 24, 1928 to Jan. 6, 1929 inclusive. The proceeds from their sale were given to a fund to restore the catacombs of Saint Damasus and Saint Praetextatus at Rome.

Issues of the Republic.

SP13

1938, Apr. 15 Perf. 11½

B106	SP13	45c + 2p bl & grnsh bl	75	85
a.		Imperf., pair	12.50	12.50
b.		Souv. sheet	25.00	27.50
c.		Souvenir sheet, imperf.	250.00	250.00

The surtax was used to benefit the defenders of Madrid.
Nos. B106b and B106c contain one of No. B106. Size: 119x104½mm.
See No. CB6.

SPAIN

Nurse and Orderly
Carrying Wounded Soldier
SP14

1938, June 1   Engr.   Perf. 10

B107	SP14	45c + 5p cop red	1.00	90
a.		Imperf., pair	55.00	

See also No. CB7.

No. B106 Overprinted in Black

SEGUNDO ANIVERSARIO DE LA

7 NOV. 1938

HEROICA DEFENSA DE MADRID

1938, Nov. 7   Perf. 11½

B108	SP13	45c + 2p bl & grnsh bl	3.75	3.75

Defense of Madrid, 2nd anniversary.
A similar but larger overprint was applied to cover blocks of four. Price $17.50.

Spanish State.
Souvenir Sheets

Alcazar, Toledo—SP15

Design: No. B108C, A patio of Alcazar after Civil War fighting.

Photogravure.

1937   Perf. 11½   Unmwkd.

Control Numbers on Back

B108A	SP15	2p org brn	20.00	20.00
b.		Imperf.	450.00	450.00
B108C	SP15	2p dk grn	20.00	20.00
d.		Imperf.	450.00	450.00

Nos. B108A–B108C contain one stamp. Marginal inscription of No. B108A: "Primer Aniversario del Alzamiento Nacional—Julio 1936." Of No. B108C: "Liberacion de Toledo—Setiembre 1936." Size: 139x 100mm. Sold for 4p each.

SP16

Designs: 20c, Covadongas Cathedral. 30c, Palma Cathedral, Majorca. 50c, Alcazar of Segovia. 1p, Leon Cathedral.

Engraved.

1938   Perf. 12½   Unmwkd.

Control Numbers on Back

B108E	SP16	Sheet of four	60.00	60.00
f.		20c dl vio	8.50	8.50
g.		30c rose red	8.50	8.50
h.		50c brt bl	8.50	8.50
i.		1p grnsh gray	8.50	8.50
j.		Imperf. sheet	100.00	100.00

Sheets measure 140x100mm. Marginal inscription: "Monumentos Historicos de Espana." Each sheet sold for 4p.

SP17

Designs, alternating in sheet: Flag bearer. Battleship "Admiral Cervera." Soldiers in trenches. Moorish guard.

1938, July 1   Perf. 13   Unmwkd.

Control Numbers on Back

B108K	SP17	Sheet of 20	40.00	40.00
l.		Imperf. sheet	200.00	200.00

Sheet measures 175x132mm. Consists of five vertical rows of four 2c violet, 3c deep blue, 5c olive gray, 10c deep green and 30c red orange, with each denomination appearing in two different designs. Marginal inscription: "Homenaje al Ejercito y a la Marina" (Honoring the Army and Navy). Sold for 4p, or double face value.

Souvenir Sheets

Don Juan
of Austria
SP18

Battle of
Lepanto
SP19

Engraved.

1938, Dec. 15   Perf. 12½   Unmwkd.

Control Numbers on Back

B108M	SP18	30c dk car	15.00	15.00
B108N	SP19	50c bl blk	15.00	15.00

Imperf.

B108O	SP18	30c blk vio	400.00	425.00
B108P	SP19	50c dk sl grn	400.00	400.00

Issued to commemorate the victory over the Turks in the Battle of Lepanto, 1571.
Nos. B108M–B108P contain one stamp. The dates "1571–1938" appear in the lower sheet margin. Size: 89x74mm. Sold for 10p a pair.

Ruins of Belchite
SP20

Miracle of Calanda—SP21

Designs: 10c+5c, 70c—20c, Ruins of Belchite. 15c+10c, 80c+20c, The Rosary. 20c+10c, 1.50p+50c, El Pilar Cathedral. 25c+10c, 1p+30c, Mother Raffols praying. 40c+10c, 2.50p+50c, The Little Chamber. 45c+15c, 1.40p+40c, Oath of the Besieged. 10p+4p, The Apparition.

Perf. 10½, 11½x10½, 11½.

1940, Jan. 29   Litho.   Unmwkd.

B109	SP20	10c +5c dp bl & vio brn	15	12
B110	SP20	15c +10c rose vio & dk grn	22	15
B111	SP20	20c +10c vio & dp bl	22	15
B112	SP20	25c +10c dp rose & vio brn	22	18
B113	SP20	40c +10c sl grn & rose vio	15	12
B114	SP20	45c +15c vio & dp rose	45	28
B115	SP20	70c +20c multi	45	28
B116	SP20	80c +20c dp rose & vio	55	40
B117	SP20	1p +30c dk sl grn & pur	55	40
B118	SP20	1.40p +40c pur & gray blk	50.00	42.50
B119	SP20	1.50p +50c lt bl & brn vio	65	55
B120	SP20	2.50p +50c choc & bl	65	55
B121	SP21	4p +1p rose lil & sl grr	17.00	13.00
a.		4p +1p vio & sl grn	75.00	75.00
B122	SP21	10p +4p ultra & chnt	235.00	225.00
a.		10p+4p ultra & brn vio	75.00	75.00

Nos. B109–B122, EB2 (15) 306.66 284.03

19th centenary of the Virgin of the Pillar.
The surtax was used to help restore the Cathedral at Zaragoza, damaged during the Civil War.
Nos. B109–B122 exist imperf. Price, 1½ times that of perf. set.
See No. 743, CB8–CB17.

General
Franco
SP23

Knight and
Lorraine Cross
SP24

1940, Dec. 23   Perf. 10   Unmwkd.

B123	SP23	20c +5c dk grn & red	60	60
B124	SP23	40c +10c dk bl & red	80	30

The surtax was for the tuberculosis fund.
See also Nos. RA15, RAC1.
Stamps of 10c denomination, types SP23 to SP28, are postal tax issues.

1941, Dec. 23

B125	SP24	20c +5c bl vio & red	65	45
B126	SP24	40c +10c sl grn & red	65	40

The surtax was used to fight tuberculosis.
See also Nos. RA16, RAC2.

Cross of Lorraine
SP25   SP26

1942, Dec. 23   Lithographed

B127	SP25	20c +5c pale brn & rose red	1.75	1.75
B128	SP25	40c +10c lt bluish grn & rose red	1.25	30

The surtax was used to fight tuberculosis.
See also Nos. RA17, RAC3.

1943, Dec. 23   Photo.   Perf. 11½

B129	SP26	20c +5c dl sl grn & dl red	5.00	2.25
B130	SP26	40c +10c brt bl & dl red	3.25	1.75

The surtax was used to fight tuberculosis.
See also Nos. RA18, RAC4.

Dragon   St. George Slaying
Slaying   the Dragon
SP27   SP28

Perf. 9½x10

1944, Dec. 23   Litho.   Unmwkd.

B131	SP27	20c +5c sl grn & red	40	40
B132	SP27	40c +10c dl vio & red	75	25
B133	SP27	80c +10c ultra & rose	12.50	12.00

The surtax was used to fight tuberculosis.
See also Nos. RA19, RAC5.

1945, Dec. 23

Lorraine Cross in Red

B134	SP28	20c +5c dl gray grn	35	25
B135	SP28	40c +10c vio	40	25
B136	SP28	80c +10c ultra	12.50	12.00

The surtax was used to fight tuberculosis.
See also Nos. RA20, RAC6.

**VISITA
DEL
CAUDILLO
A CANARIAS
OCTUBRE 1950
SOBRETASA:
DIEZ CTS**

Nos. 753
and 768
Surcharged
in Blue

1950, Oct. 23

B137	A195	50c +10c rose vio	60.00	60.00
a.		"Caudillo" 14¾mm wide	140.00	140.00
B138	A195	1p +10c rose pink	60.00	60.00
a.		"Caudillo" 14¾mm wide	140.00	140.00

Visit of General Franco to Canary Islands. First printing was issued in Canary Islands. Second printing was issued in Madrid Feb. 22, 1951. See No. CB18.

LOCAL CHARITY STAMPS.

Hundreds of different charity stamps were issued by local organizations and cities during the Civil War, 1936–39. Some had limited franking value, but most were simply charity labels. They are of three kinds: 1. Local semipostals. 2. Obligatory surtax stamps. 3. Propaganda or charity labels.

SPAIN

AIR POST STAMPS.

Regular Issue of 1909-10 Overprinted **CORREO AEREO** in Red or Black
Unwmkd.

1920, Apr. 4   Perf. 13x12½, 14

C1	A46	5c grn (R)	1.40	.75
a.		Imperf. (pair)	110.00	110.00
b.		Double overprint	25.00	25.00
c.		Inverted ovpt.	80.00	80.00
d.		Double overprint, one inverted	27.50	27.50
e.		Triple overprint	27.50	27.50
C2	A46	10c car (Bk)	2.00	1.00
a.		Imperf. (pair)	110.00	110.00
b.		Double overprint	25.00	25.00
d.		Double overprint, one inverted	27.50	27.50
C3	A46	25c dp bl (R)	3.00	1.40
a.		Invtd. ovpt.	95.00	95.00
b.		Double overprint	30.00	30.00
C4	A46	50c sl bl (R)	13.00	5.25
a.		Imperf. (pair)	110.00	110.00
C5	A46	1p lake (Bk)	40.00	20.00
a.		Imperf. (pair)	400.00	400.00
		Nos. C1-C5 (5)	59.40	28.40

The overprint and its varieties have been counterfeited.
A 30c green was authorized, but not issued. Price $1,100.

"Spirit of St. Louis" over Coast of Europe — AP1

Plane and Congress Seal — AP2

Seville-Barcelona Exposition Issue.
Control Numbers on Back.

1929, Feb. 15   Engraved   Perf. 11

C6	AP1	5c brown	7.00	6.00
C7	AP1	10c rose	7.00	7.00
C8	AP1	25c dk bl	8.50	7.50
C9	AP1	50c purple	11.00	10.00
C10	AP1	1p green	52.50	40.00
C11	AP1	4p black	40.00	30.00
		Nos.C6 to C11 (6)	126.00	100.50

Nos. C6 to C11 exist imperforate. Prices about four times those of perforated stamps.

The so-called errors of color of Nos. C10, C18-C21, C23-C24, C28-C31, C37, C40, C42, C44, C46, C48, C50, C52, C55, C62-C67 are believed to have been irregularly produced.

Railway Congress Issue.
Control Numbers on Back.

1930, May 10   Litho.   Perf. 14

C12	AP2	5c bis brn	6.25	6.25
a.		Imperf., pair	100.00	
C13	AP2	10c rose	6.25	6.25
C14	AP2	25c dk bl	6.25	6.25
C15	AP2	50c purple	16.00	13.00
a.		Vert.pair, imperf. between	250.00	
C16	AP2	1p yel grn	32.50	25.00
C17	AP2	4p black	35.00	27.50
		Nos.C12-C17 (6)	102.25	84.25

The note after No. 385 will apply here also. Dangerous counterfeits exist.

Goya Issue.

Fantasy of Flight — AP3

1930, June 15   Engr.   Perf. 12½

C18	AP3	5c brn red & yel	12	12
C19	AP3	15c blk & red org	22	18
C20	AP3	25c brn car & dp red	32	18

Asmodeus and Cleofas — AP4

C21	AP4	5c ol grn & grnsh bl	12	12
C22	AP4	10c sl grn & yel grn	22	18
C23	AP4	20c ultra & rose red	22	18
C24	AP4	40c vio bl & lt bl	60	50

Fantasy of Flight — AP5

C25	AP5	30c brn & vio	60	50
C26	AP5	50c ver & grn	60	50
C27	AP5	4p brn car & blk	4.00	2.75

Fantasy of Flight — AP6

C28	AP6	1p vio brn & vio	60	50
C29	AP6	4p bl blk & sl grn	4.00	2.75
C30	AP6	10p blk brn & bis brn	15.00	14.00
		Nos. C18-C30, CE1 (14)	27.07	22.86

Nos. C18-C30 exist imperf. Price for set, $250.

Christopher Columbus Issue.

La Rábida Monastery — AP7

Martín Alonso Pinzón — AP8

Vicente Yanez Pinzón — AP9

Columbus in His Cabin — AP10

1930, Sept. 29   Lithographed

C31	AP7	5c lt red brn	15	10
C32	AP7	5c ol bis	15	10
C33	AP7	10c bl grn	25	18
C34	AP7	15c dk vio	25	18
C35	AP7	20c ultra	25	18

Engraved.

C36	AP8	25c car rose	25	18
C37	AP9	30c dp red brn	2.10	2.00
C38	AP9	40c indigo	2.10	2.00
C39	AP9	50c orange	2.10	2.00
C40	AP8	1p dl vio	2.10	2.00
C41	AP10	4p ol grn	2.10	2.00
C42	AP10	10p lt brn	12.50	12.50
		Nos. C31-C42 (12)	24.30	23.42

Nos. C31-C42 exist imperf. Price for set, $210.

Spanish-American Issue.

AP11

Columbus — AP12

Columbus and Pinzón Brothers — AP13

1930, Sept. 29   Lithographed

C43	AP11	5c lt red	12	12
C44	AP11	10c dl grn	22	18

Engraved

C45	AP12	25c scarlet	22	18
C46	AP12	50c sl gray	2.75	2.25
C47	AP12	1p fawn	2.75	2.25
C48	AP13	4p sl bl	2.75	2.25
C49	AP13	10p brn vio	12.50	11.00
		Nos. C43-C49 (7)	21.31	18.23

Nos. C43-C49 exist imperf. Price for set, $225.

Spanish-American Exhibition Issue.

Santos-Dumont and First Flight of His Airplane — AP14

Teodoro Fels and His Airplane — AP15

Dagoberto Godoy and Pass over Andes — AP16

Sacadura Cabral and Gago Coutinho and Their Airplane — AP17

Sidar of Mexico and Map of South America — AP18

Ignacio Jiménez and Francisco Iglesias — AP19

SPAIN

Charles A. Lindbergh, Statue of
Liberty, Spirit of St. Louis
and Cat
AP20

Santa Maria, Plane and
Torre del Oro, Seville
AP21

1930, Oct. 10 — Photo. — Perf. 14

C50	AP14	5c gray blk	40	20
C51	AP15	10c dk ol grn	40	20
C52	AP16	25c ultra	40	20
C53	AP17	50c bl gray	90	75
C54	AP18	50c black	90	75
C55	AP19	1p car lake	1.75	1.50
a.		1p brn vio	50.00	42.50
C56	AP20	1p dp grn	1.75	1.50
C57	AP21	4p sl bl	4.50	5.00
	Nos. C50–C57 (8)		11.00	10.10

Exist imperf. Price, set $165.
Note after No. 432 also applies to Nos.
C31–C57.

Reprints of Nos. C50–C57 have
blurred impressions, yellowish paper.
Price, one-tenth of originals.

Nos. C1–C4
Overprinted **REPUBLICA**
in Red or Black

1931 — Perf. 13x12½

C58	A46	5c grn (R)	13.00	13.00
C59	A46	10c car (Bk)	13.00	13.00
C60	A46	25c dp bl (R)	20.00	20.00
C61	A46	50c sl bl (R)	35.00	35.00

Counterfeits of overprint exist.

Plane and Royal Palace, Madrid
AP22

Madrid Post Office and
Cibeles Fountain
AP23

Plane over Calle de Alcalá,
Madrid—AP24

1931, Oct. 10 — Engraved — Perf. 12

C62	AP22	5c brn vio	15	10
C63	AP22	10c dp grn	15	10
C64	AP22	25c dl red	15	10
C65	AP23	50c dp bl	55	50
C66	AP23	1p dp vio	90	75
C67	AP24	4p black	12.50	11.50
	Nos. C62–C67 (6)		14.40	13.05

Issued to commemorate the 3rd Pan-
American Postal Union Congress, Madrid.
Exist imperf. Price, set $60.

Montserrat Issue.

Plane over Montserrat Pass
AP25

1931, Dec. 9 — Perf. 11½
Control Number on Back

C68	AP25	5c blk brn	60	50
a.	Perf. 14		7.00	7.00
C69	AP25	10c yel grn	3.25	3.00
a.	Perf. 14		60.00	60.00
C70	AP25	25c dp rose	12.50	11.00
a.	Perf. 14		100.00	100.00
C71	AP25	50c orange	45.00	35.00
a.	Perf. 14		100.00	100.00
C72	AP25	1p gray blk	30.00	24.00
f.	Perf. 14		100.00	100.00
	Nos. C68–C72 (5)		91.35	73.50

Issued to commemorate the 900th anniversary of Montserrat Monastery.
Nos. C68–C72 exist imperf. Prices
about 7 times those quoted for perf. 11½
stamps.

Autogiro over Seville
AP26

1935–39 — Perf. 11½

C72A	AP26	2p gray bl	30.00	6.00
g.	Imperf., pair		275.00	

Re-engraved.

C72B	AP26	2p dk bl ('38)	30	30
c.	Imperf., pair		35.00	
d.	Perf. 10 ('39)		1.50	1.50
e.	Perf. 14		10.00	10.00

The sky has heavy horizontal lines of
shading. Entire design is more heavily
shaded than No. C72A.

Eagle and Newspapers—AP27

Press Building, Madrid
AP28

Don Quixote and Sancho Panza
Flying on the Wooden Horse
AP29

Design: 15c, 30c, 50c, 1p, Autogiro over
House of Nazareth.

1936, Mar. 11 — Photo. — Perf. 12½

C73	AP27	1c rose car	10	10
C74	AP28	2c dk brn	10	10
C75	AP28	5c blk brn	10	10
C76	AP28	10c dk yel grn	10	10
C77	AP28	15c Prus bl	20	10
C78	AP28	20c violet	20	10
C79	AP28	25c magenta	10	10
C80	AP28	30c red org	10	10
C81	AP27	40c orange	65	40
C82	AP28	50c lt bl	40	40
C83	AP28	60c ol grn	90	40
C84	AP28	1p brnsh blk	90	40
C85	AP29	2p brt ultra	6.50	3.00
C86	AP29	4p lil rose	6.50	5.00
C87	AP29	10p vio brn	17.50	10.00
	Nos. C73–C87 (15)		34.45	20.40

Madrid Press Association, 40th anniver-
sary.
Exist imperf. Price, set $525.
See note after No. 432.

Types of
Regular Postage
of 1936
Overprinted
in Blue or Red

1936 — Imperf.

C88	A125	10c dk red (Bl)	200.00	175.00
C89	A125	15c dk red (R)	200.00	175.00

Issued in commemoration of the first National Philatelic Exhibition which opened in
Madrid, April 2nd, 1933.

VUELO :-:-:
:-: MANILA
No. 577 **MADRID :-:**
Overprinted in Black **1936**
ARNAIZ -:-:
:-:-: CALVO

1936, Aug. 1 — Perf. 11½

C90	A128	30c rose red	6.50	3.50
a.	Perf. 14		65.00	65.00
b.	Imperf., pair		150.00	

Issued in commemoration of the flight of
aviators Antonio Arnaiz and Juan Calvo
from Manila to Spain.

No. 288 Surcharged in Black
CORREO AÉREO
14 Abril 1938
VII Aniversario
de la República
2'50 pts.

1938, Apr. 13 — Perf. 14

C91	A36	2.50p on 10c org red	120.00	120.00

7th anniversary of the Republic.

No. 507
Surcharged
in
Various
Colors

CORREO AÉREO
CORREO AÉREO
50 CTS.

1938, Aug. — Perf. 11½

C92	A92	50c on 25c lake (Bk)	30.00	27.50
C93	A92	1p on 25c lake (G)	1.50	1.00
C94	A92	1.25p on 25c lake (R)	1.50	1.00
C95	A92	1.50p on 25c lake (Bl)	1.50	1.00
C96	A92	2p on 25c lake (Bk & R)	30.00	27.50

No. 585 Surcharged **AEREO + 5 Pts.**

1938, June 1 — Perf. 11½

C97	A132	5p on 1p multi	265.00	250.00
a.	Imperf., pair		700.00	700.00
b.	Inverted surcharge		350.00	350.00
c.	Souv. sheet		900.00	900.00
d.	Souvenir sheet, imperf.		3,500.	3,500.
e.	Dbl. surch.		450.00	450.00

Type of 1938–39 **correo**
Overprinted in **aereo**
Red or Carmine

1938, May — Perf. 10, 10½

C98	A163	50c ind (R)	1.25	60
C99	A163	1p dk bl (C)	4.00	60

Exist imperf. Price, each $80.
Exist without overprint. Price, each
$100.

Juan de la Cierva and his
Autogiro over Madrid—AP30
Lithographed.

1939, Jan. — Perf. 11 — Unwmkd.

C100	AP30	20c red org	75	50
C101	AP30	25c dk car	60	22
C102	AP30	35c brt vio	75	30
C103	AP30	50c dk brn	85	30
C105	AP30	1p blue	85	30
C107	AP30	2p green	4.75	2.40
C108	AP30	4p dl bl	7.25	3.75
	Nos. C100–C108 (7)		15.80	7.97

Exist imperf. Price, set $600.

1941–47 — Perf. 10.

C109	AP30	20c dk red org	25	8
C110	AP30	25c redsh brn	25	7
C111	AP30	35c lil rose	2.00	75
C112	AP30	50c brown	50	5
C113	AP30	1p chlky bl	1.75	5
C114	AP30	2p lt gray grn	2.00	5

587

588 SPAIN

C115	AP30	4p gray bl	6.75	50
C116	AP30	10p brt pur ('47)	4.75	90
		Nos. C109-C116 (8)	18.25	2.48

Issued in honor of Juan de la Cierva (1895–1936), inventor of the autogiro.
Exist imperf. Price, set $75.
The overprint "EXPOSICION NACIONAL DE FILATELIA 1948 SAN SEBASTIAN" multiple, in parallel horizontal lines, on Nos. C109 to C113 and other airmail stamps, was privately applied.

Correo Aéreo

Nos. 625–634, 660, 676 and 677 with either of these overprints have not been established as issues of the Spanish government.

Mariano Pardo de Figueroa (Dr. Thebussem)—AP31

1944, Oct. 12 Engr. Perf. 10

C117	AP31	5p brt ultra	22.50	20.00

Issued to commemorate "Stamp Day" and "Day of the Race," October 12, 1944. Valid for franking air mail correspondence one day only.

Mail Coach, Plane and Count of St. Louis
AP32

1945, Oct. 12 Unwmkd.

C118	AP32	10p yel grn	25.00	20.00

Issued to commemorate "Stamp Day" and "Day of the Race," October 12, 1945, and to honor Luis José Sartorius, Count of St. Louis, who issued the decree for Spain's first postage stamps. No. C118 was valid for franking air mail correspondence one day only.

Maj. Joaquin Garcia Morato
AP33

1945, Nov. 27

C119	AP33	10p dp cl	32.50	10.00

Capt. Carlos Haya Gonzalez **Bartolomé de las Casas**
AP34 **AP35**

1945, Dec. 14

C120	AP34	4p red	13.00	8.00

1946, Oct. 12 Perf. 11½x11

C121	AP35	5.50p green	3.00	3.00

Stamp Day and Day of the Race. Exists imperf. Price $15.

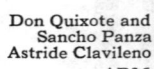

Don Quixote and Sancho Panza Astride Clavileno
AP36

1947, Oct. 9 Perf. 10

C122	AP36	5.50p purple	6.00	6.00

Issued to commemorate Stamp Day and the 400th anniversary of the birth of Miguel de Cervantes Saavedra.

Manuel de Falla **Ignacio Zuloaga**
AP37 **AP38**

1947, Dec. 1 Perf. 9½x10½
Control Number on Back

C123	AP37	25p dk vio & brn	57.50	25.00
C124	AP38	50p dk car	210.00	37.50

Train and Plane
AP39

1948, Oct. 9 Litho. Perf. 13x12½

C125	AP39	2p scarlet	2.50	2.00

Issued to commemorate the centenary of Spanish railroads and Stamp Day.

U.P.U. Type of Regular Issue with Pedestal and Propeller Added.

1949, Oct. 9 Perf. 12½x13

C126	A202	4p dk ol grn	40	40

Issued to commemorate Stamp Day and the 75th anniversary of the formation of the Universal Postal Union.

Stamp of 1850 **Map of Western Hemisphere**
AP40 **AP41**

1950, Oct. 12 Engraved Imperf.

C127	AP40	1p rose brn	9.00	9.00
C128	AP40	2.50p brn org	9.00	9.00
C129	AP40	20p dk bl	165.00	165.00
C130	AP40	25p green	165.00	165.00

Centenary of Spanish postage stamps.

1951, Apr. 16 Photo. Perf. 12½

C131	AP41	1p blue	8.50	2.50

Issued to commemorate the 6th Congress of the Postal Union of the Americas and Spain.

Queen Isabella I
AP42

1951, Oct. 12 Engraved. Perf. 13

C132	AP42	60c dk gray grn	8.00	75
C133	AP42	90c orange	8.00	1.00
C134	AP42	1.30p plum	8.00	8.00
C135	AP42	1.90p sepia	8.00	8.00
C136	AP42	2.30p dk bl	4.25	4.25
		Nos. C132-C136 (5)	29.15	22.00

Issued to publicize Stamp Day, Oct. 12, 1951, and to commemorate the 500th anniversary of the birth of Queen Isabella I.

"The Eucharist" by Tiepolo **St. Francis Xavier**
AP43 **AP44**

1952, May 26 Photo. Perf. 12½x13

C137	AP43	1p gray grn	6.25	65

Issued to publicize the 35th International Eucharistic Congress, Barcelona, 1952.

1952, July 3 Engraved.

C138	AP44	2p dp bl	55.00	32.50

Issued to commemorate the 400th anniversary of the death of St. Francis Xavier.

Ferdinand the Catholic and Columbus Presenting Natives
AP45

1952, Oct. 12

C139	AP45	60c dl grn	30	25
C140	AP45	90c orange	30	25
C141	AP45	1.30p plum	65	25
C142	AP45	1.90p sepia	5.00	4.00
C143	AP45	2.30p dp bl	17.00	17.00
		Nos. C139-C143 (5)	23.25	21.75

Issued to commemorate the 500th anniversary of the birth of Ferdinand the Catholic and to publicize Stamp Day.

Joaquin Sorolla y Bastida **Miguel Lopez de Legazpi**
AP46 **AP47**

1953, Oct. 9 Perf. 13x12½

C144	AP46	50p dk vio	500.00	35.00

Issued to honor Joaquin Sorolla y Bastida (1863–1923), impressionist painter.

1953, Nov. 5

C145	AP47	25p gray blk	125.00	50.00

Issued to commemorate the Spanish-Philippine Postal Convention of 1951.

Leonardo Torres Quevedo
AP48

Perf. 13x12½.

1955, Sept. 6 Engraved Unwmkd.

C146	AP48	50p bluish gray & blk	7.50	1.75

Issued in honor of Leonardo Torres Quevedo (1852–1939), mathematician and inventor.

Plane and Caravel
AP49

1955-56 Photogravure. Perf. 12½x13

C147	AP49	20c gray grn ('56)	12	12
C148	AP49	25c gray vio	12	12
C149	AP49	50c ol gray ('56)	12	12
C150	AP49	1p red org	12	12
C151	AP49	1.10p emer ('56)	12	12
C152	AP49	1.40p rose car	15	10
C153	AP49	3p brt bl ('56)	15	10
C154	AP49	4.80p yellow	15	10
C155	AP49	5p redsh brn	75	10
C156	AP49	7p lil ('56)	30	25
C157	AP49	10p lt ol grn ('56)	42	35
		Nos. C147-C157 (11)	2.52	1.60

Mariano Fortuny
AP50

1956, Jan. 10 Engr. Perf. 13x12½

C158	AP50	25p grnsh blk	20.00	1.10

Issued in honor of Mariano Fortuny y Carbo (1838–1874), painter.

Bullfight Type of Regular Issue

Designs: 25c, Small town arena. 50c, Fighting with cape. 1p, Dedication of the bull. 5p, Bull ring.

Perf. 13x12½, 12½x13

1960, Feb. 29 Engraved Unwmkd.

C159	A246	25c brn car & dl lil	12	10
C160	A245	50c blue	12	10
C161	A246	1p red & dl red	50	10
C162	A245	5p red lil & vio	1.10	70

Jai Alai—AP51

1960, Mar. 27 Photo. Perf. 12½x13

C163	AP51	1p brt red & dk brn	6.75	4.75
C164	AP51	5p dp brn & mag	6.75	4.75
C165	AP51	6p vio blk & mag	6.75	4.75
C166	AP51	10p grn, mag & dk brn	6.75	4.75

Issued to commemorate the first International Congress of Philately, Barcelona, March 26–Apr. 5. Nos. C163–C166 could be bought at the exhibition upon presentation of 5p entrance ticket.

SPAIN

Sport Type of Regular Issue, 1960
Sports: 1.25p, 6p, Steeplechase (horiz.). 1.50p, 10p, Basque ball game.

Perf. 12½x13, 13x12½

1960, Oct. 31   Unwmkd.

C167	A251	1.25p choc & car	50	12
C168	A251	1.50p pur, brn & blk	50	12
C169	A251	6p vio blk & car	1.10	65
C170	A251	10p ol grn, red & blk	1.40	80

Rosary Type of Regular Issue, 1962
Mysteries of the Rosary: 25c, The Ascension, Bayeu. 1p, The Descent of the Holy Ghost, El Greco. 5p, The Assumption, Mateo Cerezo. 10p, The Coronation of the Virgin Mary, El Greco.

1962, Oct. 26   Engraved   Perf. 13

C171	A280	25c vio & dl gray vio	10	10
C172	A280	1p ol & brn	25	20
C173	A280	5p brn & rose cl	50	35
C174	A280	10p bluish grn & yel grn	1.25	80

Recaredo I, Visigothic King, 586–601 — AP52

Portrait: 50p, Francisco Cardinal Jimenez de Cisneros (1436–1517).

1963, Dec. 5   Engr.   Perf. 13x12½

C175	AP52	25c dl pur	1.75	35
C176	AP52	50p grn & blk	1.50	60

1966, Feb. 26

Portraits: 25p, Seneca (4 B.C.–65 A.D.). 50p, Pope St. Damasus I (304?–384).

C177	AP52	25p yel grn & dk grn	2.50	25
C178	AP52	50p sky bl & gray bl	3.50	45

Plaza de Espana, Seville — AP53

1981, Nov. 26   Engr.   Perf. 13

C179	AP53	13p shown	20	6
C180	AP53	20p Rande River Bridge, Pontevedra	30	6

St. Thomas, by El Greco — AP54

1982, July 7   Photo.   Perf. 13

C181	AP54	13p Sts. Andrew and Francis	24	5
C182	AP54	20p shown	35	8

Bowling — AP55

1983, Apr. 13   Photo.   Perf. 13

C183	AP55	13p Bicycling, vert.	20	6
C184	AP55	20p shown	30	10

AIR POST SEMI-POSTAL STAMPS.
Red Cross Issue.

Ramon Franco's Plane Plus Ultra
SPAP1

Perf. 12½, 13

1926, Sept. 15   Engr.   Unwmkd.

CB1	SPAP1	5c blk & vio	1.75	1.50
CB2	SPAP1	10c ultra & blk	2.00	1.50
CB3	SPAP1	25c car & blk	25	20
CB4	SPAP1	50c red org & blk	25	20
CB5	SPAP1	1p blk & grn	2.50	2.00
		Nos. CB1-CB5 (5)	6.75	5.40

No. B106 Surcharged in Black    AEREO + 5 Pts.

1938, Apr. 15   Perf. 11½

CB6	SP13	45c + 2p + 5p	300.00	285.00
a.		Imperf. (pair)	900.00	900.00
b.		Souvenir sheet	3,000.	3,000.
c.		Souvenir sheet, imperf.	3,500.	3,500.
d.		Souvenir sheet, surch. invtd.	3,250.	3,250.

The surtax was used to benefit the defenders of Madrid.

No. B107 Surcharged

1938, June 1   Perf. 10

CB7	SP14	45c + 5p + 3p cop red	10.00	10.00

Monument   Caravel Santa Maria
SPAP2   SPAP3

Dome Fresco by Goya, Cathedral of Zaragoza
SPAP6

Designs: SPAP4, The Ascension. SPAP5, The Coronation. SPAP7, Bombardment of Cathedral of Zaragoza.

Perf. 10½, 11½x10½, 11½.

1940, Jan. 29   Litho.   Unwmkd.

CB8	SPAP2	25c + 5c rose vio & sl grn	35	25
CB9	SPAP3	50c + 5c brt rose & vio	35	25
CB10	SPAP4	65c + 15c vio & bl	35	25
CB11	SPAP2	70c + 15c sl grn & rose vio	35	25
CB12	SPAP4	90c + 20c choc & rose	35	25
CB13	SPAP5	1.20p + 30c dl vio & sl grn	35	25
CB14	SPAP3	1.40p + 40c dp bl & vio brn	35	40
CB15	SPAP5	2p + 50c rose vio & vio	50	45
CB16	SPAP6	4p + 1p sl grn & rose lil	12.50	9.00
a.		4p + 1p sl grn & vio	75.00	75.00
CB17	SPAP7	10p + 4 chnt & ultra	250.00	240.00
a.		10p + 4p red vio & ultra	75.00	75.00
		Nos. CB8-CB17 (10)	265.45	251.35

Issued in commemoration of the 19th centenary of the Pillar Virgin. The surtax was used to help restore the Cathedral at Zaragoza, damaged during the Civil War.
Exist imperf. Price, set $575.

No. C123 Surcharged in Black

Correspondencia
por avión
VISITA DEL
CAUDILLO
A CANARIAS
OCTUBRE 1950
Sobretasa:
DIEZ CTS

1950-51   Perf. 9½x10½

CB18	AP37	25p + 10c dk vio brn ('51)	475.00	375.00
a.		Without control number	2,000.	375.00

Issued to commemorate the visit of General Franco to the Canary Islands, October, 1950.
No. CB18a is from the first printing of the surcharge issued Oct. 23, 1950. The control number was printed on the gum, and regummed copies of No. CB18 are frequently offered as No. CB18a.
No. CB18 was issued Feb. 22, 1951.

AIR POST SPECIAL DELIVERY STAMP.
Goya Commemorative Issue.
Type of Air Post Stamp of 1930

Overprinted **URGENTE**

1930   Perf. 12½   Unwmkd.

CE1	AP4	20c bl blk & lt brn (Bk)	45	40
a.		Blue overprint	17.50	17.50
b.		Ovpt. omitted	30.00	30.00

See note after No. 432.

AIR POST OFFICIAL STAMPS.
Pan-American Postal Union Congress Issue.
Types of Air Post Stamps of 1931
Overprinted in Red or Blue **OFICIAL**

1931   Perf. 12.   Unwmkd.

CO1	AP22	5c red brn (R)	15	10
CO2	AP22	10c bl grn (Bl)	15	10
CO3	AP22	25c rose (Bl)	15	10
CO4	AP23	50c lt bl (R)	15	10
a.		50c dp bl (R)	30.00	30.00
CO5	AP23	1p vio (R)	15	10
CO6	AP24	4p gray blk (R)	5.50	4.75
		Nos. CO1-CO6 (6)	6.25	5.25

SPECIAL DELIVERY STAMPS.

Pegasus and Coat of Arms
SD1

Typographed.

1905–25   *Perf. 14*   Unwmkd.
Control Number on Back.

E1	SD1	20c dp red	50.00	45
a.		20c rose red, litho. ('25)	45.00	40
b.		Imperf. pair	200.00	
c.		As "a", imperf., pair	160.00	

Gazelle   Pegasus
SD2   SD3

1929   Engraved.   *Perf. 11*
Control Number on Back

E2	SD2	20c dl red	18.50	12.50
a.		Perf. 14	32.50	32.50

Seville and Barcelona Exhibitions. See note after No. 432.

1929–32   *Perf. 13½ x 12½, 11½*
Control Number on Back

E3	SD3	20c red	20.00	1.00
a.		Imperf., pair	110.00	
b.		Without control number, perf. 11½ ('32)	80.00	1.00
		As "b", imperf., pair	475.00	

No. E3 Overprinted like Nos. 358-370

| E4 | SD3 | 20c red (Bl) | 14.00 | 14.00 |

League of Nations 55th assembly.

No. E3 Overprinted in Blue **URGENCIA**

1930   *Perf. 13½ x 12½, 11½*

| E5 | SD3 | 20c red | 17.00 | 70 |

Railway Congress Issue.

Electric Loco-motive
SD4

1930, May 10   Litho.   *Perf. 14*
Control Number on Back

| E6 | SD4 | 20c brn org | 55.00 | 52.50 |

The note after No. 385 will apply here also.

Goya Issue.
Type of Regular Issue of 1930
Overprinted **URGENTE**

1930   *Perf. 12½*

| E7 | A57 | 20c lil rose | 40 | 35 |

Christopher Columbus Issue.
Type of Regular Issue of 1930
Overprinted **URGENTE**

1930, Sept. 29

| E8 | A64 | 20c brn vio | 1.75 | 1.50 |

Spanish-American Exhibition Issue.

View of Seville Exhibition
SD5

1930, Oct. 10   Photo.   *Perf. 14*

| E9 | SD5 | 20c orange | 35 | 25 |

The note after No. 432 will apply to Nos. E8 and E9, also to No. E15.

Madrid Issue.
No. E5 Overprinted in Green **REPUBLICA**

1931   *Perf. 11½*

| E10 | SD3 | 20c red | 5.00 | 5.00 |

Barcelona Issue.
No. E3 Overprinted **REPUBLICA**

| E11 | SD3 | 20c red | 5.75 | 5.75 |

No. E11 also exists with accent over "U".

No. E3 Overprinted in Blue
República Española.

| E12 | SD3 | 20c red | 8.00 | 80 |

Montserrat Issue.

Pegasus
SD6

1931   Engraved   *Perf. 11*
Control Number on Back.

E13	SD6	20c vermilion	28.50	28.50
a.		Perf. 14	62.50	62.50

SD7

1934   *Perf. 10*

E14	SD7	20c vermilion	10	10
a.		Imperf., pair	5.00	

Newsboy   Pegasus
SD8   SD9

1936   Photogravure   *Perf. 12½*

| E15 | SD8 | 20c rose car | 40 | 35 |

Issued in commemoration of the 40th anniversary of the Madrid Press Association. See note after No. 432.

Spanish State

Lithographed.

1937–38   *Perf. 11.*   Unwmkd.
With imprint "Hija. deB Fournier-Burgos".

E16	SD9	20c vio brn	9.50	4.00
a.		Imperf., pair	75.00	

Without Imprint

E17	SD9	20c dk vio brn ('38)	1.50	20
a.		Imperf., pair	52.50	

No. 645 Overprinted in Black CORRESPONDENCIA URGENTE

1937

| E18 | A162 | 20c dk vio | 12.00 | 12.00 |

Pegasus
SD10

1939–42   *Perf. 10½*
Imprint: "SANCHEZ TODA".

E19	SD10	25c carmine	6.75	65
a.		Imperf., pair	45.00	

Without Imprint.
Perf. 10.

E20	SD10	25c car ('42)	25	15
a.		Imperf., pair	8.50	

"Flight"
SD11

Centaur
SD12

Perf. 12½ x 13, 13 x 12½

1956, Feb. 12   Photo.   Unwmkd.

E21	SD11	2p scarlet	8	8
E22	SD12	4p blk & mag	12	12

1965–66

E23	SD11	3p dp car	12	10
E24	SD11	5p dp org ('66)	20	10
E25	SD12	6.50p dk vio & rose brn ('66)	15	10
		Nos. E21-E25 (5)	67	50

Chariot
SD13

Mail Circling Globe
SD14

1971, June 1   Photo.   *Perf. 13*

E26	SD13	10p red & yel grn	15	10
E27	SD14	15p red, bl & blk	25	10

SEMI-POSTAL SPECIAL DELIVERY STAMPS.
Red Cross Issue.

Royal Family Group
SPSD1

Engraved.

1926   *Perf. 12½, 13.*   Unwmkd.

| EB1 | SPSD1 | 20c red vio & vio brn | 8.50 | 8.50 |

See notes after Nos. 432 and B18.

Motorcyclist and Zaragoza Cathedral
SPSD2

1940   Lithographed.   *Perf. 11½*

| EB2 | SPSD2 | 25c + 5c rose red & buff | 40 | 35 |

Issued in commemoration of the 19th centenary of the Pillar Virgin. The surtax was used to help restore the Cathedral at Zaragoza, damaged during the Civil War.

DELIVERY TAX STAMPS.

D1

Lithographed.

1931   *Perf. 11½*   Unwmkd.

| ER1 | D1 | 5c black | 7.50 | 15 |

No. ER1 Overprinted in Red REPUBLICA

1931

| ER2 | D1 | 5c black | 2.00 | 2.00 |

No. ER2 also exists with accent over "U".

No. ER1 Overprinted in Red REPUBLICA

| ER3 | D1 | 5c black | 4.50 | 4.50 |

These stamps were originally issued for Postage Due purpose but were later used as regular postage stamps.

WAR TAX STAMPS.

These stamps did not pay postage but represented a fiscal tax on mail matter in addition to the postal fees. Their use was obligatory.

Coat of Arms
WT1   WT2

SPAIN

Typographed.
1874, Jan. 1   *Perf. 14*   *Unwmkd.*

MR1	WT1	5c black	6.25	80
a.		Imperf. pair	18.00	
MR2	WT1	10c pale bl	14.00	2.75
a.		Imperf., pair	80.00	

1875, Jan. 1

MR3	WT2	5c green	6.25	90
a.		Imperf., pair	37.50	
MR4	WT2	10c lilac	15.00	3.75
a.		Imperf., pair	70.00	

King Alfonso XII
WT3   WT4

1876, June 1

MR5	WT3	5c pale grn	2.75	80
MR6	WT3	10c blue	2.75	80
		Cliché of 5c in plate of 10c	20.00	20.00
MR7	WT3	25c black	35.00	11.00
MR8	WT3	1p lilac	300.00	55.00
MR9	WT3	5p rose	425.00	165.00

Nos. MR5–MR9 exist imperforate.

1877, Sept. 1

MR10	WT4	15c claret	11.00	65
a.		Imperf., pair	115.00	
MR11	WT4	50c yellow	375.00	52.50

King Alfonso XII   Numeral of Value
WT5   WT6

1879

MR12	WT5	5c blue	50.00	
MR13	WT5	10c rose	30.00	
MR14	WT5	15c violet	17.00	
MR15	WT5	25c brown	30.00	
MR16	WT5	50c ol grn	20.00	
MR17	WT5	1p bister	30.00	
MR18	WT5	5p gray	100.00	

Nos. MR12–MR18 were never placed in use.

Inscribed "1897 A 1898"

1897   *Perf. 14*

MR19	WT6	5c green	3.75	50
MR20	WT6	10c green	3.75	50
MR21	WT6	15c green	375.00	150.00
MR22	WT6	20c green	8.50	1.40

Nos. MR19–MR22 exist imperf. Price for set $600.

Inscribed "1898–99"

1898

MR23	WT6	5c black	1.25	35
MR24	WT6	10c black	1.50	35
MR25	WT6	15c black	50.00	11.00
MR26	WT6	20c black	3.75	1.40

Nos. MR23–MR26 exist imperf. Price about $150 a pair.

King Alfonso XIII
WT7

1898

MR27	WT7	5c black	8.00	25
a.		Imperf., pair	90.00	

OFFICIAL STAMPS.

Coat of Arms
O1   O2

Typographed
1854, July 1   *Imperf.*   *Unwmkd.*

O1	O1	½o yellow	2.75	1.00
O2	O1	1o rose	4.00	1.40
a.		1o bl	42.50	
O3	O1	4o green	10.00	2.50
O4	O1	1l blue	75.00	52.50

1855-63

O5	O2	½o yellow	2.00	1.00
a.		½o straw ('63)	3.25	1.10
O6	O2	1o rose	2.00	1.00
a.		1o sal rose	3.25	1.10
O7	O2	4o green	4.50	2.00
a.		4o yel green	6.00	4.00
O8	O2	1l gray bl	20.00	12.50

The "value indication" on Nos. O1–O8 actually is the weight of the mail in onzas (ounces, "o") and libras (pounds, "l") for which they were valid.

Type of Regular Issue of 1889.

1895   *Perf. 14*

O9	A34	15c yellow	6.25	1.25
a.		Imperf., pair	110.00	

Coat of Arms
O5

1896-98

O10	O5	rose	7.25	1.10
O11	O5	dk bl ('98)	17.50	5.25
a.		Imperf., pair	75.00	

Cervantes Issue.

Chamber of Deputies
O6

National Library
O8

Statue of Cervantes   Cervantes
O7   O9

1916, Apr. 22   *Engraved*   *Perf. 12*

For the Senate.

O12	O6	grn & blk	1.25	1.25
O13	O7	brn & blk	1.25	1.25
O14	O8	car & blk	1.25	1.25
O15	O9	brn & blk	1.25	1.25

For the Chamber of Deputies.

O16	O6	vio & blk	1.25	1.25
O17	O7	car & blk	1.25	1.25
O18	O8	grn & blk	1.25	1.25
O19	O9	vio & blk	1.25	1.25
		Nos. O12–O19 (8)	10.00	10.00

Nos. O12–O19 exist imperf. Price $300 for set of pairs.
Nos. O12–O19 exist with centers inverted. Price for set, $100.

Pan-American Postal Union Congress Issue.
Types of Regular Issue of 1931
Overprinted in Red or Blue **Oficial.**

1931   *Perf. 12½*

O20	A84	5c dk brn (R)	25	20
O21	A85	10c brt grn (Bl)	25	20
O22	A86	15c dl vio (R)	25	20
O23	A85	25c dp rose (Bl)	25	20
O24	A87	30c ol grn (R)	25	20
O25	A84	40c ultra (R)	50	50
O26	A85	50c dp org (Bl)	50	50
O27	A86	1p bl blk (R)	50	50
O28	A88	4p mag (Bl)	8.00	7.25
O29	A88	10p lt brn (R)	21.00	20.00
		Nos. O20–O29 (10)	31.75	29.75

Nos. O22–O29 exist imperf. Prices about 5 times those quoted.

POSTAL TAX STAMPS.

PT5   PT6

Lithographed.
1937, Dec. 23   *Perf. 10½x11½*

RA11	PT5	10c blk, pale bl & red	6.25	1.75
a.		Imperf. pair	80.00	

The tax was for the tuberculosis fund.

1938, Dec. 23   *Perf. 11½*

RA12	PT6	10c multi	2.00	2.00
a.		Imperf. pair	55.00	

The tax was for the tuberculosis fund.

"Spain" Holding Wreath of Peace over Marching Soldiers—PT7

1939, July 18   *Perf. 11*

RA13	PT7	10c blue	20	15
a.		Imperf. pair	100.00	

Type of Regular Issue, 1939. Without Imprint. Lithographed.

1939, Dec. 23   *Imperf.*   *Unwmkd.*

RA14	A166	10c dl cl	20	15

Tuberculosis Fund Issues.
Types of Corresponding Semi-Postal Stamps.

1940, Dec. 23   *Perf. 10*

RA15	SP23	10c vio & red	10	8

1941, Dec. 23

RA16	SP24	10c blk & red	20	8

1942, Dec. 23

RA17	SP25	10c dl sal & rose red	20	15

1943, Dec. 23   *Photo.*   *Perf. 11*

RA18	SP26	10c pur & dl red	40	35

Perf. 9½x10
1944, Dec. 23   *Litho.*   *Unwmkd.*

RA19	SP27	10c sal & rose	20	15

1945, Dec. 23

RA20	SP28	10c sal & car	20	8

Mother and Child
PT8

Lithographed.
1946, Dec. 22   *Perf. 9½x10½*

RA21	PT8	5c vio & red	10	10
RA22	PT8	10c grn & red	10	10

See also No. RAC7.

Lorraine Cross   Tuberculosis Sanatorium
PT9   PT10

Perf. 9½x10½
1947, Dec. 22   *Unwmkd.*

RA23	PT9	5c dk brn & red	10	10
RA24	PT10	10c vio bl & red	10	10

See also No. RAC8.

Aesculapius   "El Cid"
PT11   PT11a

Photogravure; Cross Engraved.
1948, Dec. 22   *Perf. 12½*   *Unwmkd.*

RA25	PT11	5c brn & red	10	10
RA26	PT11	10c dp grn & car	10	10

The tax on Nos. RA15–RA26 was used to fight tuberculosis. See also Nos. RAB1, RAC9.

1949, Feb. 1   *Litho.*   *Perf. 10½x9½*

RA27	PT11a	5c violet	25	12

The tax aided displaced children. Valid for ordinary postage after Dec. 24, 1949.

Tuberculosis Fund Issues

Galleon and Lorraine Cross   Pine Branch and Candle
PT12   PT13

SPAIN

Photogravure; Cross Engraved.
1949, Dec. 22 Perf. 12½
| RA28 | PT12 | 5c vio & red | 10 | 10 |
| RA29 | PT12 | 10c yel grn & red | 10 | 10 |

See also Nos. RAB2, RAC10.

1950, Dec. 22 Cross in Carmine.
| RA30 | PT13 | 5c rose vio | 10 | 5 |
| RA31 | PT13 | 10c dp grn | 10 | 5 |

See also Nos. RAB3, RAC11.

Children at Seashore	Nurse and Baby
PT14	PT15

1951, Oct. 1 Cross in Carmine.
| RA32 | PT14 | 5c rose brn | 12 | 10 |
| RA33 | PT14 | 10c dl grn | 60 | 10 |

See also No. RAC12.

1953, Oct. 1 Cross in Carmine.
| RA34 | PT15 | 5c car lake | 50 | 10 |
| RA35 | PT15 | 10c gray bl | 1.40 | 10 |

See also No. RAC13.
The tax on RA28–RA35 was used to fight tuberculosis.

POSTAL TAX SEMI-POSTAL STAMPS.

Types of Corresponding Postal Tax Stamps.

Photogravure; Cross Engraved.
1948 Perf. 12½ Unwmkd.
| RAB1 | PT11 | 50c +10c red brn & car | 1.25 | 1.10 |

1949
| RAB2 | PT12 | 50c +10c dk ol bis & red | 70 | 40 |

1950
| RAB3 | PT13 | 50c +10c brn & car | 3.00 | 2.00 |

The surtax on Nos. RAB1–RAB3 was used to fight tuberculosis. Combines domestic letter rate and tax obligatory from December 22 until January 3.

POSTAL TAX AIR POST STAMPS.
Tuberculosis Fund Issues.

General Franco	Knight and Lorraine Cross
PTAP1	PTAP2

Lithographed.
1940, Dec. 23 Perf. 10 Unwmkd.
| RAC1 | PTAP1 | 10c brt pink & red | 70 | 60 |

1941, Dec. 23
| RAC2 | PTAP2 | 10c bl & red | 35 | 30 |

Lorraine Cross and Doves
PTAP3

1942, Dec. 23
| RAC3 | PTAP3 | 10c dl sal & rose | 1.10 | 40 |

Cross of Lorraine	Tuberculosis Sanatorium
PTAP4	PTAP5

1943, Dec. 23 Photo. Perf. 11
| RAC4 | PTAP4 | 10c vio & dl red | 1.25 | 1.25 |

1944, Dec. 23 Litho. Perf. 10x9½
| RAC5 | PTAP5 | 25c sal & rose | 5.00 | 5.00 |

Lorraine Cross and Eagle
PTAP6

1945, Dec. 23 Perf. 10
| RAC6 | PTAP6 | 25c red & car | 2.00 | 1.75 |

Eagle—PTAP7

1946, Dec. 22
| RAC7 | PTAP7 | 25c red & car | 25 | 25 |

Tuberculosis Sanatorium	Plane over Sanatorium
PTAP8	PTAP9

1947, Dec. 22 Perf. 11½
| RAC8 | PTAP8 | 25c red vio | 25 | 25 |

Photogravure; Cross Engraved.
1948, Dec. 22 Perf. 12½
| RAC9 | PTAP9 | 25c ultra & car | 40 | 40 |

Bell and Lorraine Cross	Dove and Flowers
PTAP10	PTAP11

1949, Dec. 22
| RAC10 | PTAP10 | 25c mar & red | 25 | 20 |

1950, Dec. 22
| RAC11 | PTAP11 | 25c dk bl & car | 60 | 1.00 |

Mother and Child	Tobias and Archangel
PTAP12	PTAP13

1951, Oct. 1
| RAC12 | PTAP12 | 25c brn & car | 90 | 18 |

1953, Oct. 1
| RAC13 | PTAP13 | 25c brn & car | 6.25 | 4.50 |

FRANCHISE STAMPS.

| F1 | F2 |

Lithographed.
1869 Imperf. Unwmkd.
| S1 | F1 | blue | 60.00 | 47.50 |
| a. | | Tête bêche pair | 165.00 | 165.00 |

The franchise of No. S1 was granted to Diego Castell to use in distributing his publications on Spanish postal history.

1881
| S2 | F2 | blk, buff | 40.00 | 17.50 |

The franchise of No. S2 was granted to Antonio Fernandez Duro for his book, "Reseña histórico—descriptiva de los sellos correos de España."
Reprints of No. S2 have been made on carmine, blue, gray, fawn and yellow paper.

CARLIST STAMPS.

From the beginning of the Civil War (April 21, 1872) until separate stamps were issued on July 1, 1873, stamps of France were used on all mail from the provinces under Carlist rule.

	Tilde on N
King Carlos VII	
A1	A1a

Lithographed.
1873, July 1 Imperf. Unwmkd.
| X1 | A1 | 1r blue | 650.00 | 650.00 |
| X2 | A1a | 1r blue | 400.00 | 400.00 |

These stamps were reprinted three times in 1881 and once in 1887. The originals have 23 white lines and dots in the lower right spandrel. They are thin and of even width and spacing. The first reprint has 17 to 20 lines in the spandrel, most of them thick and of irregular width and length. The second and third reprints have 21 very thin lines, the second from the bottom being almost invisible. In the fourth reprint the lower right spandrel is an almost solid spot of color.
Originals of type A1 have the curved line above "ESPAÑA" broken at the left of the "E." All reprints of this type have the curved line continuous. The reprints exist in various shades of blue, rose, red, violet and black.

| King Carlos VII | |
| A2 | A3 |

| A4 | A5 |

1874
X3	A2	1r violet	275.00	275.00
X4	A3	16m rose	5.25	100.00
X5	A4	½r rose	120.00	120.00

Nos. X3 and X6–X7 were for use in the Basque Provinces and Navarra; No. X4 in Catalonia, and No. X5 in Valencia.
Two types of No. X5, alternating in each sheet. No. X4 with favor cancellation (lozenge of dots) sells for same price as unused.

1875 White Paper
X6	A5	50c green	11.00	80.00
a.		bluish paper	27.50	100.00
b.		bluish paper	65.00	
X7	A5	1r brown	11.00	80.00
a.		bluish paper	65.00	

Fake cancellations exist on Nos. X1–X7.

REVOLUTIONARY OVERPRINTS.
Issued by the Nationalist (Revolutionary) Forces.

Many districts or cities made use of the stamps of the Republic overprinted in various forms. Most such overprinting was authorized by military or postal officials but some were without official sanction. These overprints were applied in patriotic celebration and partly as a protection from the use of unoverprinted stamps seized or stolen by soldiers.

Burgos Issue.
AIR POST STAMPS.

RAP1

SPAIN

Revenue Stamps Overprinted in Red, Blue or Black.

1936, Dec. 1 *Perf. 11½* Unwmkd. Control Number on Face of Stamp.

7LC1	RAP1	25c gray grn & blk (R)	25.00	25.00
a.		Blue ovpt.	35.00	35.00
7LC2	RAP1	1.50p bl & blk (R)	5.00	5.00
7LC3	RAP1	3p rose & blk (Bl)	5.00	5.00

RAP2   RAP4

Perf. 13½.
Blue Control Number on Back.

7LC4	RAP2	15c grn (R)	3.50	3.50
7LC5	RAP2	25c bl (R)	30.00	30.00

Perf. 11½.
Without Control Number. Overprint in Black

7LC6	RAP4	1.50p dk bl	6.00	6.00
7LC7	RAP4	3p carmine	6.00	6.00

RAP5   RAP6

Overprint in Black
Perf. 13½, 11½.

7LC8	RAP5	1.20p green	25.00	25.00

Perf. 14
Control Number on Back

7LC9	RAP6	1.20p green	25.00	25.00
7LC10	RAP6	2.40p green	25.00	25.00

No. 7LC9 is inscribed "CLASE 8a".

RAP7

1937 *Perf. 11½* Unwmkd. Control Number on Back.

7LC11	RAP7	25c ultra (R)	275.00	275.00

¡VIVA ESPAÑA!
Stamps of Spain, 1931-36, Overprinted in Red

Correo Aéreo

Perf. 11, 11½, 11x11½.
1937, Apr. 1 Unwmkd.
Overprint 15 mm. high

7LC12	A100	40c blue	1.00	1.00
7LC13	A97	50c dk bl	1.00	1.00
7LC14	AP26	2p gray bl	25.00	25.00

1937, May 1
Overprint 13 mm. high

7LC15	A100	40c dk bl	1.00	1.00
7LC16	A97	50c dk bl	1.50	1.50
7LC17	A130	50c dk bl	1.50	1.50
7LC18	A100	60c ap grn	2.00	2.00
7LC19	AP26	2p gray bl	30.00	30.00

Spain No. 576 Overprinted in Black or Blue

¡VIVA ESPAÑA!
CORREO AÉREO

1937, May *Perf. 11½x11*

7LC20	A127	30c car (Bk)	2.00	2.00
7LC21	A127	30c car (Bl)	1.00	1.00

Spain No. 578 Overprinted in Black or Blue

¡VIVA ESPAÑA!
CORREO AÉREO

Perf. 11x11½.

7LC22	A129	30c car rose (Bk)	2.00	2.00
7LC23	A129	30c car rose (Bl)	1.00	1.00

SPECIAL DELIVERY STAMPS
Pair of Spain No. 546 Overprinted in Black

Correspondencia URGENTE

1936 *Perf. 11½x11.* Unwmkd.

7LE3	A110	20c (10c + 10c) emer	5.00	5.00
a.		Overprint invtd.	15.00	

Type of Regular Stamp of 1931 Overprinted in Red

CORRESPONDENCIA URGENTE

7LE4	A95	20c dk vio	12.00	12.00

Type of Delivery Tax Stamp of 1931 Overprinted in Red on four 5c stamps

HABILITADO PARA LA CORRESPONDENCIA URGENTE

Perf. 11½.

7LE5	D1	20c black	11.00	11.00

Same Overprinted in Red on four 5c stamps

Habilitado para la correspond urgente

7LE6	D1	20c black	22.50	22.50

SD1

1936 *Perf. 11½.* Unwmkd.

7LE7	SD1	20c grn & blk	7.50	7.50
7LE8	SD1	20c grn & red	7.50	7.50

Nos. 7LE7-7LE8 exist with control number on back. Price $37.50 each.

Cadiz Issue.
(kā'dĭz ; kä'thĕth)

SEMI-POSTAL STAMPS.

Stamps of Spain, 1931-36, Surcharged in Black or Red

VIVA ESPAÑA +5CTS / AGOSTO 1936. AYUNTAMIENTO DE CADIZ

1936 *Imperf.* Unwmkd.

8LB1	A108	1c + 5c bl grn	22	22

Perf. 11½x11, 11½.

8LB2	A108	2c + 5c org brn	22	22
8LB3	A103	5c + 5c choc (R)	50	50
8LB4	A110	10c + 5c grn	50	50
8LB5	A111	15c + 5c Prus grn (R)	3.00	3.00
8LB6	A95	20c + 5c dk vio (R)	5.25	5.25
8LB7	A104	25c + 5c lake	3.00	3.00
8LB8	A113	30c + 5c rose red	75	75
8LB9	A100	40c + 5c dk bl (R)	3.50	3.50
8LB10	A97	50c + 5c dk bl (R)	7.50	7.50
		Nos. 8LB1-8LB10 (10)	24.44	24.44

Canary Islands.
(kă-nâr'ĭ ī'lăndz)

AIR POST STAMPS.
Issued for Use via the Lufthansa Service.

Stamps of Spain, 1932-34, Surcharged in Blue

VIVA ESPAÑA 18 JULIO 1936 HABILITADO AVION Pts. 0'50

1936, Oct. 27 *Imperf.* Unwmkd.

9LC1	A108	50c on 1c bl grn	25.00	12.00

Perf. 11½x11.

9LC2	A108	80c on 2c buff	12.00	4.50
9LC3	A103	1.25p on 5c choc	35.00	18.00

The date July 18, 1936, in the overprints of Nos. 9LC1–9LC22 marks the beginning of the Franco regime.

Spain Nos. 542, 543, 528 and 641 Surcharged in Black, Red or Green

VIVA ESPAÑA 18 JULIO 1936 HABILITADO AVION CANARIAS 50 Cts.

1936-37 *Imperf.*

9LC4	A108	50c on 1c bl grn	4.25	2.75
9LC5	A108	50c on 1c bl grn (R) ('37)	6.50	3.25

Perf. 11, 11½x11.

9LC6	A108	80c on 2c buff	2.25	1.75
9LC7	A108	80c on 2c buff (G) ('37)	4.75	2.25
9LC8	A103	"1.25 Pts" on 5c choc (R)	6.00	4.00
9LC9	A103	"Pts 1.25" on 5c choc (R) ('37)	12.50	7.00
9LC10	A161	1.25p on 5c brn (G) ('37)	4.75	1.75
		Nos. 9LC4-9LC10 (7)	41.00	22.50

Spain Nos. 542, 543 and 641 Surcharged in Blue

CANARIAS FRANCO 18 JULIO 1936 AVION 50 Cts.

1937, Mar. 31 *Imperf.*

9LC11	A108	50c on 1c bl grn	5.25	2.50

Perf. 11.

9LC12	A108	80c on 2c buff	3.75	1.25
9LC13	A161	1.25p on 5c brn	4.25	1.25

Stamps of Spain, 1931-1936, Surcharged in Blue or Red

VIVA ESPAÑA 18 JULIO 1936 AVION CANARIAS + 80

1937

9LC14	A104	25c + 50c lake	45.00	14.00
9LC15	A162	30c + 80c rose	16.00	9.00
9LC16	A162	30c + 1.25p rose	20.00	11.00
9LC17	A97	50c + 1.25p dp bl (R)	30.00	15.00
9LC18	A100	60c + 80c ap grn	21.00	11.50
9LC19	A105	1p + 1.25p bl blk (R)	50.00	20.00
		Nos. 9LC14-9LC19 (6)	182.00	80.50

The surcharge represents the airmail rate and the basic stamp the postage rate.

Spain Nos. 542, 624 and 641 Surcharged in Black

ARRIBA ESPAÑA 18 JULIO 1936 CANARIAS AVION 50 Cts.

1937, May 25 *Imperf.* Unwmkd.

9LC20	A108	50c on 1c bl grn	5.75	1.75

Perf. 11½, 11½x11.

9LC21	A143	80c on 2c org brn	4.25	1.10
9LC22	A161	1.25p on 5c gray brn	4.25	1.10

Stamps of Spain, 1933-36, Surcharged in Black

CANARIAS CORREO AÉREO 50 Cts.

1937, July *Perf. 13½x13, 11, 11½*

9LC23	A143	50c on 2c org brn	1.40	60
9LC24	A126	80c on 2c org brn	300.00	150.00
9LC25	A161	80c on 5c gray brn	1.75	90
9LC26	A108	1.25p on 1c bl grn	2.00	1.00
9LC27	A161	2.50p on 10c grn	10.00	4.50

Spain Nos. 647, 650 and 652 Surcharged in Black or Red

CANARIAS CORREO AÉREO + 80

Perf. 11.

9LC28	A162	30c + 80c rose	1.25	60
9LC29	A162	50c + 1.25p dk bl (R)	6.00	3.25
9LC30	A162	1p + 1.25p bl (R)	11.00	5.50

See note after No. 9LC19.

594 SPAIN

Wmk. 116

AP1

Wmkd. Crosses and Circles. (116)
1937, July 16   Perf. 14x13½
Surcharge in Various Colors.
9LC31	AP1	50c on 5c ultra (Br)	4.75	3.25
9LC32	AP1	80c on 5c ultra (G)	2.50	2.50
9LC33	AP1	1.25p on 5c ultra (V)	3.25	2.50

Spain
Nos. 641, 643 and 640
Surcharged in
Green or Orange

50 Cts.
CORREO AEREO
CANARIAS

1937, Oct. 29   Perf. 11   Unwmkd.
9LC34	A161	50c on 5c brn (G)	12.00	4.75
9LC35	A161	80c on 10c grn (O)	4.25	2.50
9LC36	A160	1.25p on 2c brn (G)	15.00	7.50

Spain
Nos. 638, 640
and 643
Surcharged in
Red, Blue or Violet

CANARIAS
50 Cts.
Correo Aéreo

1937, Dec. 23   Imperf.
9LC37	A159	50c on 1c grn (R)	12.00	4.75

Perf. 11, 11x11½.
9LC38	A160	80c on 2c brn (Bl)	4.25	2.50
9LC39	A161	1.25p on 10c grn (V)	12.00	4.75

Spain
Nos. 647, 650 to 652
Surcharged in
Black, Green or Brown

CANARIAS
Correo Aereo
+30 C

1937, Dec. 29
9LC40	A162	30c + 30c rose	2.75	1.75
9LC41	A162	50c + 2.50p dk bl (G)	32.50	18.00
9LC42	A162	60c + 2.30p yel (G)	32.50	18.00
9LC43	A162	1p + 5p bl (Br)	37.50	18.00

See note after No. 9LC19.

Stamps of Spain,
1936,
Surcharged in
Black, Green, Blue
or Red

CANARIAS
Vía Aérea
50 C

1938, Feb. 2   Perf. 11, 11½, 11x11½
9LC44	A160	50c on 2c brn	3.25	1.50
9LC45	A103	80c on 5c brn (G)	2.75	1.40
9LC46	A162	80c on 30c rose (Bl)	2.75	1.40
9LC47	A161	1.25p on 10c grn (Bl)	3.25	1.50
9LC48	A162	1.25p on 50c dk bl (R)	3.75	1.50
		Nos. 9LC44-9LC48 (5)	15.75	7.30

Spain
Nos. 645, 646
and 649
Surcharged in
Brown, Green
or Violet

Vía Aérea
CANARIAS
2'50 Pts.

1938, Feb. 14
9LC51	A162	2.50p on 20c dk vio (Br)	52.50	27.50
9LC52	A162	5p on 25c brn lake (G)	52.50	27.50
9LC53	A162	10p on 40c org (V)	52.50	27.50

Malaga Issue.
(mä′lä-gä ; mäl′á-gá)

¡Arriba España!
Málaga
Liberada
8-2-1937

Stamps of 1920-36
Overprinted
in Black or Red

1937   Imperf.   Unwmkd.
10L1	A47	1c bl grn (Bk)	15	15
10L2	A108	1c bl grn (Bk)	15	15
10L3	A108	1c lt grn (R)	15	15

Perf. 13½, 13½x13, 11, 11½x11.
10L4	A108	2c org brn (Bk)	7.50	7.50
10L5	A126	2c org brn (Bk)	15	15
10L6	A103	5c choc (R)	15	15
10L7	A96	10c yel grn (Bk)	15.00	15.00
10L8	A110	10c emer (Bk)	15	15
10L9	A111	15c Prus grn (R)	50	50
10L10	A97	15c bl grn (R)	50	50
10L11	A95	20c dk vio (R)	30	30
10L12	A99	25c lake (Bk)	1.50	1.50
10L13	A104	25c lake (Bk)	30	30
10L14	A113	30c car (Bk)	15	15
10L15	A129	30c car rose (Bk)	1.20	1.20
10L16	A100	40c bl (R)	15	15
10L17	A97	50c dk bl (R)	1.50	1.50
10L18	A100	60c ap grn (Bk)	1.00	1.00
10L19	A105	1p blk (R)	1.50	1.50
		Nos. 10L1-10L19 (19)	32.00	32.00

Stamps of 1932-35
Overprinted in Red or Black
in panes of 25, reading down.
"8.2.37" and "¡Arriba Espana!"
form the lower half of all overprints.
The upper half varies.

First and second rows "MALAGA AGRADE-
CIDA A TRANQUILLO-BIANCHI".
Third row "MALAGA A SU SALVADOR
QUEIPO DE LLANO".
Fourth and fifth rows "MALAGA A SU
CAUDILLO FRANCO".

1937   Perf. 11½.
10L20	A111	15c Prus grn (R)	1.50	1.50
10L21	A113	30c rose red (R)	1.50	1.50
10L22	A97	50c dk bl (R)	2.75	2.75
10L23	A100	60c ap grn (Bk)	2.75	2.75

SPECIAL DELIVERY STAMP.
Same Overprint on
Type of Special Delivery Stamp of 1934.
1936   Perf. 10.
10LE1	SD7	20c rose red (Bk)	60	60

Orense Issue.

Stamps of 1931-36
Overprinted in
Red, Blue or Black

¡VIVA
ESPAÑA!

1936   Imperf.
11L1	A108	1c bl grn (Bl)	60	60

Perf. 11½, 13½x13.
11L2	A108	2c org brn (Bk)	3.75	3.75
11L3	A126	2c org brn (Bk)	60	60
11L4	A103	5c brn (R)	1.25	1.25
11L5	A110	10c lt grn (Bl)	2.50	2.50
11L6	A111	15c Prus grn (R)	2.50	2.50
11L7	A95	20c vio (Bl)	2.50	2.50
11L8	A104	25c lake (Bk)	3.75	3.75
11L9	A113	30c rose red (Bl)	2.85	2.85
11L10	A100	40c bl (R)	4.00	4.00
a.		Imperf., pair	12.00	12.00
11L11	A97	50c dk bl (R)	7.00	7.00
11L12	A100	60c ap grn (Bk)	5.75	5.75
a.		Imperf., pair	10.00	10.00
		Nos. 11L1-11L12 (12)	37.05	37.05

SEMI-POSTAL STAMPS.
Stamps of Spain,
1931-36,
Surcharged in Blue
on front and on
back of stamp

¡VIVA
ESPAÑA!
+ 5 cts.

1936-37   Imperf.   Unwmkd.
11LB1	A47	1c + 5c bl grn	1.00	1.00
11LB2	A108	1c + 5c bl grn	50	50

Perf. 13½x13, 11½, 11½x11.
11LB3	A108	2c + 5c org brn	60	60
11LB4	A126	2c + 5c red brn	60	60
11LB5	A103	5c + 5c choc	90	90
11LB6	A110	10c + 5c emer	90	90
11LB7	A111	15c + 5c Prus grn	1.25	1.25
11LB8	A95	20c + 5c vio	90	90
11LB9	A104	25c + 5c lake	1.25	1.25
11LB10	A113	30c + 5c rose red	3.00	3.00
11LB11	A113	30c + 5c rose red	45.00	45.00
		Nos. 11LB1-11LB11 (11)	55.90	55.90

SPECIAL DELIVERY STAMPS
Type of Special Delivery Stamp of 1934
Overprinted "¡VIVA ESPANA!"
in Blue or Black.
1936   Perf. 10.
11LE1	SD7	20c rose red (Bl)	2.65	2.65
11LE2	SD7	20c rose red (Bk)	5.75	5.75

Same with Surcharge "+ 5 cts."
11LE3	SD7	20c + 5c rose red	1.35	1.35

Same Surcharge, Overprint
Repeated at Right.
11LE4	SD7	20c + 5c rose red	1.50	1.50

San Sebastian Issue.
(sän sȧ-bäs′tyän′)
For Use in Province of Guipuzcoa

Stamps of 1931-36
Overprinted
in Red or Blue

¡¡ARRIBA
ESPAÑA!!
1936

1937   Imperf.   Unwmkd.
12L1	A108	1c bl grn (R)	65	65

Perf. 11, 13½.
12L2	A108	2c buff (Bl)	1.00	1.00
12L3	A126	2c org brn (Bl)	1.00	1.00
12L4	A95	5c choc (R)	6.00	6.00
12L5	A103	5c choc (R)	1.00	1.00
12L6	A110	10c emer (R)	1.50	1.50
12L7	A111	15c Prus grn (R)	1.75	1.75
12L8	A95	20c dk vio (R)	2.25	2.25
12L9	A104	25c car lake (Bl)	2.25	2.25
12L10	A113	30c rose red (Bl)	1.50	1.50
12L11	A100	40c bl (R)	4.50	4.50
12L12	A97	50c dk bl (R)	4.50	4.50
		Nos. 12L1-12L12 (12)	27.90	27.90

Scott's editorial staff cannot undertake to identify,
authenticate or appraise
stamps and postal markings.

Santa Cruz de Tenerife Issue.
Stamps of Spain,
1931-36
Overprinted
in Black or Red

Viva España
18 Julio
1936

1936   Imperf.   Unwmkd.
13L1	A108	1c bl grn (Bk)	1.10	1.10
13L2	A108	1c bl grn (Bk)	3.00	3.00

Perf. 11, 13½.
13L3	A108	2c buff (Bk)	7.50	7.50
13L4	A126	2c org brn (Bk)	1.10	1.10
13L5	A103	5c choc (R)	4.00	4.00
13L6	A110	10c grn (R)	3.75	3.75
13L7	A104	25c lake (Bk)	7.50	7.50
13L8	A100	40c dk bl (R)	3.00	3.00
13L9	A107	10p dp brn (R)	300.00	300.00
		Nos. 13L1-13L9 (9)	330.95	330.95

Seville Issue.
(sĕv′ĭl ; sĕ·vĭl′)

Stamps of Spain,
1931-36,
Overprinted
in Black or Red

Sevilla
"VIVA
ESPAÑA"
Julio-1936

1936   Imperf.
14L1	A108	1c bl grn (Bk)	30	30

Perf. 13½x13, 11, 11½x11.
14L2	A126	2c org brn (Bk)	30	30
14L3	A103	5c choc (R)	50	50
14L4	A110	10c emer (Bk)	65	65
14L5	A111	15c Prus grn (R)	1.25	1.25
14L6	A95	20c vio (R)	1.25	1.25
14L7	A104	25c lake (Bk)	1.25	1.25
14L8	A113	30c car (Bk)	1.25	1.25
14L9	A128	30c rose red (Bk)	9.50	9.50
14L10	A100	40c dk bl (R)	6.75	6.75
14L11	A97	50c dk bl (R)	6.75	6.75
14L12	A100	60c ap grn (Bk)	8.25	8.25
		Nos. 14L1-14L12 (12)	38.00	38.00

Stamps of Spain,
1931-36,
Handstamped
in Black

SEVILLA
"VIVA
ESPAÑA"
JULIO-1936

Imperf.
14L13	A108	1c bl grn	30	30

Perf. 13½x13, 11, 11x11½,
11½x11.
14L14	A126	2c org brn	50	50
14L15	A103	5c chocolate	50	50
14L16	A110	10c emerald	50	50
14L17	A111	15c Prus grn	65	65
14L18	A95	20c violet	50	50
14L19	A104	25c lake	50	50
14L20	A113	30c carmine	50	50
14L21	A128	30c rose red	3.00	3.00
14L22	A100	40c blue	1.10	1.10
14L23	A97	50c dk bl	3.00	3.00
14L24	A100	60c ap grn	1.10	1.10
14L25	A105	1p black	3.00	3.00
14L26	AP26	2p gray bl	16.50	16.50
14L27	A106	4p magenta	6.25	6.25
14L28	A107	10p dp brn	12.50	12.50
		Nos. 14L13-14L28, 14LE1 (17)	62.50	62.50

The date "Julio-1936" in the overprints
of Nos. 14L1-14L28 and 14LE1 marks the
beginning of the Franco regime.

SPECIAL DELIVERY STAMP.
Same Overprint on
Type of Special Delivery Stamp of 1934.
1936   Perf. 10.
14LE1	SD7	20c rose red	2.10	2.10

SPANISH GUINEA

(spăn'ish gĭn'ĭ)

LOCATION — In western Africa, bordering on the Gulf of Guinea.

GOVT.—Spanish Colony.

AREA—10,852 sq. mi.

POP.—212,000 (est. 1957).

CAPITAL—Santa Isabel.

Spanish Guinea Nos. 1–84 were issued for and used only in the continental area later called Rio Muni. From 1909 to 1960, Spanish Guinea also included Fernando Po, Elobey, Annobon and Corisco.

Fernando Po and Rio Muni united in 1968 to become the Republic of Equatorial Guinea.

100 Centimos = 1 Peseta

King Alfonso XIII

A1 A2

Typographed.

1902 ***Perf. 14*** **Unwmkd.**

Blue Control Numbers on Back.

1	A1	5c dk grn	9.50	1.50
2	A1	10c indigo	9.50	1.50
3	A1	25c claret	67.50	12.50
4	A1	50c dp brn	67.50	11.50
5	A1	75c violet	67.50	11.50
6	A1	1p car rose	100.00	11.50
7	A1	2p ol grn	120.00	16.50
8	A1	5p dl red	200.00	52.50
		Nos. 1-8 (8)	641.50	119.00

Revenue Stamps Surcharged

HABILITADO

PARA

CORREOS

10 cen de peseta

1903 ***Imperf.***

Blue or Black Control Numbers on Back.

8A	10c on 25c blk (R)	575.00	240.00
8B	10c on 50c org (Bl)	135.00	42.50
8D	10c on 1p 25c car (Bk)	675.00	400.00
8F	10c on 2p cl (Bk)	900.00	625.00
g.	Blue surcharge	1,350.	900.00
8H	10c on 2p 50c red brn (Bl)	1,350.	750.00
8J	10c on 5p ol blk (R)	1,350.	525.00

Nos. 8A–8J are surcharged on stamps inscribed "Posesiones Espanolas de Africa Occidental" and "1903," with arms at left. This surcharge was also applied to revenue stamps of 10, 15, 25, 50, 75 and 100 pesetas.

See also Nos. 98–101C.

1903 Typographed. ***Perf. 14.***

Blue Control Numbers on Back.

9	A2	¼c black	1.00	25
10	A2	½c bl grn	1.00	25
11	A2	1c claret	1.00	20
12	A2	2c dk ol	1.00	20
13	A2	3c dk brn	1.00	20
14	A2	4c vermilion	1.00	20
15	A2	5c blk brn	1.00	20
16	A2	10c red brn	1.50	25
17	A2	15c dk bl	5.50	1.50
18	A2	25c org buff	5.50	2.25
19	A2	50c car lake	9.50	3.50
20	A2	75c violet	14.00	3.50
21	A2	1p bl grn	20.00	5.25
22	A2	2p dk grn	20.00	5.25
23	A2	3p scarlet	55.00	6.25
24	A2	4p dl bl	70.00	10.00
25	A2	5p dk vio	120.00	17.50
26	A2	10p car rose	200.00	21.00
		Nos. 9-26 (18)	528.00	77.75

1905 Same, Dated "1905".

Blue Control Numbers on Back.

27	A2	1c black	20	10
28	A2	2c bl grn	20	10
29	A2	3c claret	20	10
30	A2	4c brnz grn	20	10
31	A2	5c dk brn	20	10
32	A2	10c red	1.00	50
33	A2	15c blk brn	3.50	1.50
34	A2	25c chocolate	3.50	1.50
35	A2	50c dk bl	7.25	3.25
36	A2	75c org buff	8.00	3.25
37	A2	1p car rose	8.00	3.25
38	A2	2p violet	17.50	6.50
39	A2	3p bl grn	40.00	14.00
40	A2	4p dk grn	40.00	19.00
40A	A2	5p vermilion	70.00	20.00
41	A2	10p dl bl	110.00	60.00
		Nos. 27-41 (16)	309.75	133.25

Stamps of Elobey, 1905, Overprinted in Violet or Blue

1906

42	A1	1c rose	5.00	2.40
43	A1	2c dp vio	5.00	2.40
44	A1	3c black	5.00	2.40
45	A1	4c org red	5.00	2.40
46	A1	5c dp grn	5.00	2.40
47	A1	10c bl grn	11.00	6.50
48	A1	15c violet	19.00	9.50
49	A1	25c rose lake	19.00	9.50
50	A1	50c org buff	26.00	12.00
51	A1	75c dk bl	32.50	14.00
52	A1	1p red brn	60.00	26.00
53	A1	2p blk brn	85.00	19.00
54	A1	3p vermilion	120.00	40.00
55	A1	4p dk brn	450.00	140.00
56	A1	5p brnz grn	450.00	140.00
57	A1	10p claret	*2,000.*	*800.00*
		Nos. 42-54 (13)	397.50	148.50

King Alfonso XIII

A3 A4

1907 Typographed.

Blue Control Numbers on Back

58	A3	1c dk grn	60	15
59	A3	2c dl bl	60	15
60	A3	3c violet	60	15
61	A3	4c yel grn	60	15
62	A3	5c car lake	60	15
63	A3	10c orange	3.00	65
64	A3	15c brown	2.25	40
65	A3	25c dk bl	2.25	40
66	A3	50c blk brn	2.25	40
67	A3	75c bl grn	2.25	45
68	A3	1p red	4.00	75
69	A3	2p dk brn	7.00	2.50
70	A3	3p ol gray	7.00	2.50
71	A3	4p maroon	8.50	2.50
72	A3	5p green	9.50	3.75
73	A3	10p red vio	15.00	4.50
		Nos. 58-73 (16)	66.00	19.55

Issue of 1907 Surcharged in Black or Red

1908-09

74	A3	05c on 1c dk grn (R)	3.25	2.00
75	A3	05c on 2c bl (R)	3.25	2.00
76	A3	05c on 3c vio	3.25	2.00
77	A3	05c on 4c yel grn	3.25	2.00
78	A3	05c on 10c org	3.25	2.00
a.		Red surcharge	9.00	4.25
84	A3	15c on 10c org	15.00	8.50
		Nos. 74-84 (6)	31.25	18.50

Many stamps of this issue are found with the surcharge inverted, sideways, double and in both black and red. Other stamps of the 1907 issue are known with this surcharge but are not believed to have been put in use. Price, each $15.

1909 Typographed. ***Perf. 14½.***

Blue Control Numbers on Back.

85	A4	1c org brn	15	6
86	A4	2c rose	15	6
87	A4	5c dk grn	1.25	15
88	A4	10c vermilion	40	10
89	A4	15c dk brn	40	10
90	A4	20c violet	65	25
91	A4	25c dl bl	70	25
92	A4	30c chocolate	75	20
93	A4	40c lake	50	15
94	A4	50c dk vio	50	15
95	A4	1p bl grn	13.00	3.75
96	A4	4p orange	3.25	2.50
97	A4	10p red	3.25	2.50
		Nos. 85-97 (13)	24.95	10.22

Revenue Stamps Surcharged like Nos. 8A–8J in Black

1909 ***Imperf.***

With or Without Control Numbers on Back

98	10c on 50c bl grn	100.00	67.50
a.	Red or vio surcharge	125.00	90.00
99	10c on 1p 25c violet	125.00	80.00
100	10c on 2p dk brn	750.00	475.00
100A	10c on 5p dk vio	750.00	475.00
101	10c on 25p red brn	*1,000.*	*675.00*
101A	10c on 50p brn lil	*2,500.*	*1,850.*
101B	10c on 75p carmine	*2,500.*	*1,850.*
101C	10c on 100p orange	*2,500.*	*1,850.*

Nos. 98–101C are surcharged on undated stamps, arms centered. Stamps inscribed: "Territorios Espanoles del Africa Occidental." Basic revenue stamps similar to Rio de Oro type A3.

Stamps of 1909 Overprinted with Handstamp in Black, Blue, Green or Red

1911

102	A4	1c org brn (Bl)	30	20
103	A4	2c rose (G)	30	20
104	A4	5c dk grn (R)	1.00	20
105	A4	10c vermilion	80	30
106	A4	15c dk brn (R)	1.00	50
107	A4	20c violet	1.50	70
108	A4	25c dl bl (R)	1.75	1.25
109	A4	30c choc (Bl)	2.25	1.50
110	A4	40c lake (Bl)	2.50	1.75
111	A4	50c dk vio	3.50	3.00
112	A4	1p bl grn (R)	35.00	7.25
113	A4	4p org (G)	16.00	6.50
114	A4	10p red (G)	21.00	11.00
		Nos. 102-114 (13)	86.90	34.35

The date "1911" is missing from the overprint on the first stamp in each row, or ten times in each sheet of 100 stamps. This variety occurs on all stamps of the series.

King Alfonso XIII

A5 A6

1912 Typographed. ***Perf. 13½***

Blue Control Numbers on Back.

115	A5	1c black	15	6
116	A5	2c dk brn	15	6
117	A5	5c dp grn	15	6
118	A5	10c red	25	12
119	A5	15c claret	30	12
120	A5	20c red	45	12
121	A5	25c dl bl	30	12
122	A5	30c lake	2.75	1.25
123	A5	40c car rose	1.75	75
124	A5	50c brn org	1.40	30
125	A5	1p dk vio	1.75	80
126	A5	4p lilac	3.75	1.75
127	A5	10p bl grn	8.50	5.25
		Nos. 115-127 (13)	21.65	10.76

1914 ***Perf. 13.***

Blue Control Numbers on Back

128	A6	1c dl vio	25	15
129	A6	2c car rose	25	20
130	A6	5c dp grn	25	15
131	A6	10c vermilion	25	20
132	A6	15c dk vio	25	20
133	A6	20c dk brn	75	30
134	A6	25c dk bl	35	25
135	A6	30c brn org	1.25	35
136	A6	40c bl grn	1.25	35
137	A6	50c dp cl	60	25
138	A6	1p vermilion	1.25	1.00
139	A6	4p maroon	5.25	2.50
140	A6	10p ol blk	6.00	4.00
		Nos. 128-140 (13)	17.95	9.90

Stamps with these or similar overprints are unauthorized and fraudulent.

Stamps of 1912 Overprinted

1917

1917 ***Perf. 13½.***

141	A5	1c black	57.50	15.00
142	A5	2c dk brn	57.50	15.00
143	A5	5c dp grn	50	25
144	A5	10c red	50	25
145	A5	15c claret	50	25
146	A5	20c red	50	20
147	A5	25c dl bl	20	20
148	A5	30c lake	50	25
149	A5	40c car rose	70	40
150	A5	50c brn org	40	25
151	A5	1p dk vio	70	40
152	A5	4p lilac	8.00	3.00
153	A5	10p bl grn	8.00	3.00
		Nos. 141-153 (13)	135.50	38.45

Nos. 143–153 exist with overprint double, inverted, in dark blue, reading "9117" and in pairs one without overprint.

Stamps of 1917 Surcharged

HTADO

15 Cents.

1918

154	A5	5c on 40c car rose	32.50	10.00
155	A5	10c on 4p lil	32.50	10.00
156	A5	15c on 20c red	60.00	17.50
157	A5	25c on 10p bl grn	60.00	17.50
a.		"52" for "25"	400.00	350.00

The varieties "Gents" and "Censt" occur on Nos. 154–157. Prices 50 percent more.

King Alfonso XIII

A7 A8

1919 Typographed. ***Perf. 13.***

Blue Control Numbers on Back.

158	A7	1c lilac	1.00	25
159	A7	2c rose	1.00	25
160	A7	5c vermilion	1.00	25

SPANISH GUINEA

161	A7	10c violet	1.50	25
162	A7	15c brown	1.50	30
163	A7	20c blue	1.50	60
164	A7	25c green	1.50	60
a.		25c bl (error)	75.00	
165	A7	30c orange	1.50	60
166	A7	40c orange	4.00	50
167	A7	50c red	4.00	50
168	A7	1p lt brn	4.00	1.00
169	A7	4p claret	9.00	4.00
170	A7	10p brown	17.00	6.50
		Nos. 158-170 (13)	48.50	15.60

1920
Blue Control Numbers on Back.

171	A8	1c brown	20	6
172	A8	2c dl rose	20	6
173	A8	5c gray grn	25	20
174	A8	10c dl rose	25	6
175	A8	15c orange	25	20
176	A8	20c yellow	25	20
177	A8	25c dl bl	60	20
178	A8	30c grnsh bl	32.50	9.50
179	A8	40c lt brn	50	20
180	A8	50c lilac	1.50	20
181	A8	1p lt red	1.50	20
182	A8	4p brt rose	5.00	2.50
183	A8	10p gray lil	7.00	4.75
		Nos. 171-183 (13)	50.00	18.33

1922
Blue Control Numbers on Back.

184	A9	1c dk brn	50	10
185	A9	2c claret	50	10
186	A9	5c bl grn	50	10
187	A9	10c pale red	3.25	50
188	A9	15c orange	50	10
189	A9	20c lilac	2.00	45
190	A9	25c dk bl	3.50	50
191	A9	30c violet	3.25	60
192	A9	40c turq bl	2.25	30
193	A9	50c dp rose	2.25	30
194	A9	1p myr grn	2.25	35
195	A9	4p red brn	9.00	4.75
196	A9	10p yellow	18.00	8.00
		Nos. 184-196 (13)	47.75	16.15

1924
Blue Control Numbers on Back.

197	A10	5c choc & bl	25	15
198	A10	10c gray grn & bl	25	15
199	A10	15c rose & blk	30	25
200	A10	20c vio & blk	25	15
201	A10	25c org red & blk	50	35
202	A10	30c org & blk	50	25
203	A10	40c dl bl & blk	50	25
204	A10	50c cl & blk	50	25
205	A10	60c red brn & blk	50	25
206	A10	1p dk vio & blk	2.00	25
a.		Center inverted	250.00	110.00
207	A10	4p brt bl & blk	5.00	2.00
208	A10	10p bl grn & blk	11.00	4.75
		Nos. 197-208 (12)	21.55	9.05

Seville-Barcelona Exhibition Issue.
Seville-Barcelona Issue of Spain, 1929, Overprinted GUINEA in Red or Blue.

1929 Perf. 11

209	A52	5c rose lake	10	10
210	A53	10c grn (R)	10	10
211	A50	15c Prus bl (R)	10	10
212	A51	20c pur (R)	10	10
213	A50	25c brt rose	10	10
214	A52	30c blk brn	10	10
215	A53	40c dk bl (R)	20	10
216	A51	50c dp org	15	15
217	A52	1p bl blk (R)	1.25	1.25
218	A53	4p dp rose	3.00	2.75
219	A53	10p brown	4.75	4.00
		Nos. 209-219 (11)	9.95	8.95

Porter A11

Drummers A12

King Alfonso XIII and Queen Victoria A13

1931 Engraved. Perf. 14.

220	A11	1c bl grn	10	6
221	A11	2c red brn	10	6

Blue Control Numbers on Back

222	A11	5c brn blk	15	6
223	A11	10c lt grn	15	6
224	A11	15c dk grn	25	10
225	A11	20c dp vio	25	10
226	A12	25c carmine	25	10
227	A12	30c lake	30	10
228	A12	40c dk bl	75	50
229	A12	50c red org	1.75	1.00
230	A13	80c bl vio	3.00	1.50
231	A13	1p black	5.00	3.50
232	A13	4p vio rose	32.50	13.00
233	A13	5p dk brn	14.00	11.00
		Nos. 220-233 (14)	58.55	31.14

Exist imperf. Price for set, $400.

Stamps of 1931 Overprinted REPUBLICA ESPAÑOLA

1931

234	A11	1c bl grn	15	10
235	A11	2c red brn	15	10
236	A11	5c brn blk	20	10
237	A11	10c lt grn	20	10
238	A11	15c dk grn	20	10
239	A11	20c dp vio	20	10
240	A12	25c carmine	20	10
241	A12	30c lake	50	25
242	A12	40c dk bl	1.50	50
243	A12	50c red org	9.00	5.00
244	A13	80c bl vio	3.00	1.50
245	A13	1p black	10.00	3.00
246	A13	4p vio rose	17.50	9.00
247	A13	5p dk brn	17.50	9.00
		Nos. 234-247 (14)	60.30	28.95

Stamps of 1931 Overprinted in Red or Blue República Española

1933

248	A11	1c bl grn (R)	15	10
249	A11	2c red brn (Bl)	15	10
250	A11	5c brn blk (R)	20	10
251	A11	10c lt grn (Bl)	20	10
252	A11	15c dk grn (R)	20	10
253	A11	20c dp vio (R)	50	10
254	A12	25c car (Bl)	40	25
255	A12	30c lake (Bl)	40	25
256	A12	40c dk bl (R)	3.00	75
257	A12	50c red org (R)	10.00	3.75
258	A12	80c bl vio (R)	5.50	3.25
259	A13	1p blk (R)	11.50	3.50
260	A13	4p vio rose (Bl)	40.00	16.00
261	A13	5p dk brn (Bl)	40.00	16.00
		Nos. 248-261 (14)	112.20	44.35

Types of 1931. Without Control Number.
1934-35 Engraved. Perf. 10.

262	A11	1c bl grn ('35)	8.00	20
263	A11	2c red brn ('35)	8.00	20
264	A11	5c blk brn	1.50	80
265	A11	10c lt grn	1.50	10
266	A11	15c dk grn	3.00	10
267	A12	30c rose red	3.75	10
268	A12	50c ind ('35)	8.50	75
		Nos. 262-268 (7)	34.25	1.65

Types of 1931.
1941 Lithographed. Unwmkd.

269	A11	5c ol gray	1.75	10
270	A11	20c violet	1.75	10
271	A12	40c gray grn	80	10

Stamps of 1931-33 Surcharged in Black
HABILITADO 1 30 Cts. peseta.
a *b*

1936-37 Perf. 10, 14.

272	A12	30c on 40c dk bl (#228)	3.75	2.25
273	A12	30c on 40c dk bl (#242)	15.00	3.50
274	A12	30c on 40c dk bl (#256)	57.50	16.00

The surcharge on Nos. 272-274 exists in two types, differing in the "3" which is scarcer in italic.

No. 268 Surcharged Type "b" in Red.

275	A12	1p on 50c ind	21.00	
276	A12	4p on 50c ind	80.00	
277	A12	5p on 50c ind	42.50	

Stamps of Spain, 1936, Overprinted in Black or Carmine
Territorios Españoles del Golfo de Guinea

1938 Perf. 11

278	A161	10c gray grn	2.00	50
279	A162	15c gray blk (C)	2.00	50
280	A162	20c dk vio	4.25	1.40
281	A162	25c brn lake	4.25	1.40

Stamps of 1931-33, Surcharged in Black Habilitado
1939 40 cts.

282	A13	40c on 80c bl vio (#244)	12.00	6.00
283	A13	40c on 80c bl vio (#258)	12.00	4.00

A14

A15

Revenue Stamps Surcharged in Black.
1940-41 Perf. 11½.

284	A14	5c on 35c pale grn	10.00	3.50
285	A14	25c on 60c org brn	10.00	4.00
286	A14	50c on 75c blk brn	13.00	4.75

Red Surcharge

287	A15	10c on 75c blk brn	13.00	4.75
288	A15	15c on 1.50p lt vio	10.00	4.00
289	A15	25c on 60c org brn	17.50	6.00

A16

A17

Black or Carmine Surcharge.
Perf. 11.

290	A16	1p on 17p dp red	80.00	25.00
291	A17	1p on 40p yel grn (C)	20.00	7.00

A18 — A19

Black Surcharge.
Perf. 11, 13 x 12½.

292	A18	5c carmine	8.50	3.00
293	A19	1p yellow	160.00	60.00

General Francisco Franco A20 — A21

Black Surcharge.

294	A20	1p on 15c gray grn	20.00	7.00

1940 Perf. 11½, 13½.

295	A21	5c ol brn	3.00	50
296	A21	40c blue	4.00	50
297	A21	50c green	5.00	50
a.		50c grnsh gray	18.00	8.50

Nos. 295-297 exist imperf. Prices twice those quoted.

Habilitado
No. 270 Surcharged in Black 3 Pesetas

1942

298	A11	3p on 20c vio	12.50	1.75

Spain, Nos. 702 and 704 Overprinted in Carmine or Black Golfo de Guinea.

1942 Perf. 9½x10½.

299	A166	1p gray blk (C)	50	25
300	A166	4p dl rose (Bk)	5.75	75

The overprint on No. 299 exists in two types: Spacing between lines of 2mm., and spacing of 3mm. The 3mm. spacing sells for about twice as much.

Spain, No. 703 Overprinted in Carmine
Territorios españoles del Golfo de Guinea

1943

301	A166	2p dl brn	1.25	25

Nos. 299 and 301 Surcharged in Green Habilitado para quince cts.

1949 Perf. 9½x10½. Unwmkd.

302	A166	5c (cinco) on 1p gray blk	25	10
303	A166	15c on 2p dl brn	25	10

The two types of No. 299, described in footnote, also exist on No. 302.

Men Poling Canoe—A22

Nipa House A10

A9

SPANISH GUINEA

1949, Oct. 9   Litho.   Perf. 12½x13

| 304 | A22 | 4p dk vio | 2.25 | 75 |

Issued to commemorate the 75th anniversary of the formation of the Universal Postal Union.

San Carlos Bay—A23
Designs: Various Views

1949-50   Perf. 12½x13.

305	A23	2c brown	25	6
306	A23	5c rose vio	25	6
307	A23	10c Prus bl	25	6
308	A23	15c dp ol gray	30	6
309	A23	25c red brn	30	6
309A	A23	30c brt yel ('50)	25	6
310	A23	40c ol gray	25	6
311	A23	45c rose lake	25	6
312	A23	50c brn org	25	6
312A	A23	75c ultra ('50)	25	6
313	A23	90c dl bl grn	30	6
314	A23	1p gray	1.75	25
315	A23	1.35p violet	7.00	1.25
316	A23	2p sepia	17.50	2.00
317	A23	5p lil rose	25.00	5.25
318	A23	10p lt brn	90.00	22.50
	Nos. 305-318 (16)		144.15	31.91

Surveyor—A24

1951, Dec. 5

| 319 | A24 | 5c orange | 40 | 5 |
| 320 | A24 | 5p indigo | 12.50 | 1.75 |

Issued to publicize the International Conference of West Africans 1951.

Drummer—A25

1952, Mar. 10

321	A25	5c red brn	6	5
322	A25	50c ol gray	6	6
323	A25	5p violet	3.75	6

Musician—A26
Design: 60c, Musician facing right.

1953, July 1   Photogravure

324	A26	15c sepia	6	6
325	A26	60c brown	10	6
	See also Nos. B25-B26.			

Woman and Dove   Drummer
A27   A28

1953, Sept. 5   Perf. 13x12½

326	A27	5c orange	6	5
327	A27	10c brt lil rose	6	5
328	A27	60c brown	15	5
329	A28	1p dl pur	1.50	6
330	A28	1.90p grnsh blk	3.75	40
	Nos. 326-330 (5)		5.52	61

Tragocephala Nobilis
A29
Butterfly: 60c, Papilio antimachus.

1953, Nov. 23

| 331 | A29 | 15c dk grn | 40 | 25 |
| 332 | A29 | 60c brown | 40 | 25 |

Colonial Stamp Day. See Nos. B27-B28.

Hunter—A30
Design: 60c, Hunter and elephant.

1954, June 10   Perf. 12½x13

| 333 | A30 | 15c dk gray grn | 6 | 6 |
| 334 | A30 | 60c dk brn | 35 | 15 |

See also Nos. B29-B30.

Swimming Turtle—A31
Design: 60c, Shark.

1954, Nov. 23

| 335 | A31 | 15c gray grn | 6 | 6 |
| 336 | A31 | 60c org brn | 35 | 15 |

Colonial Stamp Day. See Nos. B31-B32.

Manuel Iradier y Bulfy—A32

1955, Jan. 18

| 337 | A32 | 60c org brn | 25 | 12 |
| 338 | A32 | 1p dk vio | 5.25 | 45 |

Issued to commemorate the centenary (in 1954) of the birth of Manuel Iradier y Bulfy.

Priest Saying Mass—A33

1955, June 1   Photo.   Perf. 13x12½

| 339 | A33 | 50c ol gray | 20 | 6 |

Issued to commemorate the centenary of the establishment of an Apostolic Prefecture at Fernando Po. See also Nos. B33-B34.

Palace of Pardo—A34

1955, July 18   Perf. 12½x13

340	A34	5c ol brn	5	5
341	A34	15c brn lake	5	5
342	A34	80c Prus grn	12	5

Treaty of Pardo, 1778.

Red-eared Guenons   Orchid
A35   A36

1955, Nov. 23   Perf. 13x12½

| 343 | A35 | 70c gray grn & bl | 30 | 25 |

Colonial Stamp Day. See Nos. B35-B36.

1956, June 1   Unwmkd.

Flower: 50c, Strophantus Kombe.

| 344 | A36 | 50c bluish grn | 20 | 8 |
| 345 | A36 | 50c brown | 20 | 8 |

See Nos. 360-361, B37-B38, B53-B54.

Arms of   African
Santa Isabel   Gray Parrot
A37   A38

1956, Nov. 23   Perf. 13x12½

| 346 | A37 | 70c lt ol grn | 8 | 5 |

Colonial Stamp Day. See Nos. B39-B40.

1957, June 1   Photogravure

| 347 | A38 | 70c ol grn | 25 | 8 |

See also Nos. B41-B42.

Elephants—A39
Design: 70c, Elephant (vertical).

Perf. 12½x13, 13x12½

1957, Nov. 23

| 348 | A39 | 20c bl grn | 10 | 8 |
| 349 | A39 | 70c emerald | 20 | 10 |

Colonial Stamp Day. See Nos. B43-B44.

Boxing
A40

Basketball   Preaching Missionary
A41   A42

Various Sports: 15c, 2.30p, Jumping. 80c, 3p, Runner at finish line.

1958, Apr. 10   Photo.   Unwmkd.

350	A40	5c vio brn	5	5
351	A41	10c org brn	5	5
352	A40	15c brown	5	5
353	A41	80c green	6	5
354	A40	1p org red	6	5
355	A41	2p rose lil	30	5
356	A40	2.30p dl vio	50	6
357	A41	3p brt bl	1.57	6
	Nos. 350-357 (8)		2.64	42

1958, June 1   Perf. 13x12½

Design: 70c, Crucifix and missal.

| 358 | A42 | 20c bl grn | 5 | 5 |
| 359 | A42 | 70c green | 15 | 5 |

75th anniversary of Catholic missions in Spanish Guinea. See Nos. B48-B49.

Type of 1956 Inscribed:
"Pro-Infancia 1959."
Plants: 20c, Castor bean. 70c, Digitalis.

1959, June 1   Perf. 13x12½

| 360 | A36 | 20c bl grn | 6 | 6 |
| 361 | A36 | 70c green | 10 | 8 |

Issued to promote child welfare. See also Nos. B53-B54.

Stamps of Spanish Guinea were succeeded by those of Fernando Po and Rio Muni in 1960.

SEMI-POSTAL STAMPS.
Red Cross Issue.

Types of Semi-Postal Stamps of Spain, 1926, Overprinted in Black or Blue   **CUINEA ESPAÑOLA**

1926   Perf. 12½, 13   Unwmkd.

B1	SP3	5c blk brn	2.00	1.25
B2	SP4	10c dk grn	2.00	1.25
B3	SP1	15c dk vio (Bl)	70	50
B4	SP4	20c vio brn	70	50
B5	SP5	25c dp car	70	50
B6	SP5	30c ol grn	70	50
B7	SP3	40c ultra	20	15
B8	SP2	50c red brn	20	15
B9	SP5	60c myr grn	20	15
B10	SP4	1p vermilion	20	15
B11	SP3	4p bister	60	40
B12	SP5	10p lt vio	90	70
	Nos. B1-B12 (12)		9.10	6.20

Allegory   Leopard
SP1   SP2

1950, Dec. 1   Photo.   Perf. 13x12½

B13	SP1	50c +10c ultra	40	25
B14	SP1	1p +25c dk grn	20.00	5.50
B15	SP1	6.50p +1.65p dp org	5.00	2.50

The surtax was to help the native population.

SPANISH GUINEA

1951, Nov. 23
B16	SP2	5c +5c brn	6	6
B17	SP2	10c +5c red org	6	6
B18	SP2	60c +15c ol brn	40	25

Colonial Stamp Day, Nov. 23.

Love Lily — SP3
Brown-cheeked Hornbill — SP4

1952, June 1
B19	SP3	5c +5c brn	6	6
B20	SP3	50c +10c gray	6	6
B21	SP3	2p +30c bl	2.25	1.00

The surtax was to help the native population.

1952, Nov. 23 — Perf. 12½
B22	SP4	5c +5c brn	10	6
B23	SP4	10c +5c brn car	30	20
B24	SP4	60c +15c dk grn	70	35

Colonial Stamp Day, Nov. 23.

Music Type of Regular Issue.
Designs: 5c+5c, Musician facing left. 10c+5c, Musician facing right.

1953, July 1 — Perf. 12½x13
B25	A26	5c +5c lt rose brn	6	6
B26	A26	10c +5c red vio	6	6

The surtax was to help the native population.

Insect Type of Regular Issue.
Designs: 5c+5c, Beetle. 10c+5c, Butterfly.

1953, Nov. 23 — Perf. 13x12½
B27	A29	5c +5c dk bl	6	6
B28	A29	10c +5c brt red vio	6	6

Colonial Stamp Day, Nov. 23.

Hunter Type of Regular Issue.
Designs: 5c+5c, Hunter with bow and arrow. 10c+5c, Hunter and elephant.

1954, June 10 — Perf. 12½x13
B29	A30	5c +5c rose brn	6	6
B30	A30	10c +5c vio	6	6

The surtax was to help the native population.

Type of Regular Issue
1954, Nov. 23
Designs: 5c+5c, Turtle. 10c+5c, Shark.

B31	A31	5c +5c org ver	6	6
B32	A31	10c +5c mag	6	6

Colonial Stamp Day, Nov. 23.

Type of Regular Issue and

Baptism — SP5
Design: 10c+5c, Priest.

Perf. 13x12½

1955, June 1 — Photo. Unwmkd.
B33	A33	10c +5c red vio	6	6
B34	A33	25c +10c vio	6	6

Issued to commemorate the centenary of the establishment of an Apostolic Prefecture at Fernando Po.

Type of Regular Issue and

Red-eared Guenons — SP6
Design: 5c+5c, Talapoin monkeys (vert.).

Perf. 13x12½, 12½x13

1955, Nov. 23
B35	A35	5c +5c redsh brn & rose car	20	15
B36	SP6	15c +5c rose car & blk brn	20	15

Issued to publicize Colonial Stamp Day.

Flower Type of Regular Issue.
Design: 15c+5c, Strophantus Kombe.

1956, June 1 — Perf. 13x12½
B37	A36	5c +5c grnsh gray	6	6
B38	A36	15c +5c bis	6	6

The tax was for native welfare work.

Type of Regular Issue and

Drummers and Arms of Bata — SP7
Design: 5c+5c, Arms of Santa Isabel.

Perf. 13x12½, 12½x13

1956, Nov. 23
B39	A37	5c +5c red brn	10	6
B40	SP7	15c +5c bl vio	10	6

Issued for Colonial Stamp Day.

Type of Regular Issue and

African Gray Parrot — SP8
Design: 5c+5c, African gray parrot (vert.).

Perf. 13x12½, 12½x13

1957, June 1 — Photo. Unwmkd.
B41	A38	5c +5c brn car	6	6
B42	SP8	15c +5c bis	6	6

The surtax was for child welfare.

Type of Regular Issue, 1957.
Designs: 10c+5c, Elephants (horizontal). 15c+5c, Elephant (vertical).

Perf. 12½x13, 13x12½

1957, Nov. 23
B43	A39	10c +5c lil rose	6	6
B44	A39	15c +5c bis	6	6

Stamp Day, 1957.

Type of Regular Issue and

Pigeons and Arms of Valencia and Santa Isabel — SP9

1958, Mar. 6 — Perf. 12½x13
B45	SP9	10c +5c org brn	6	6
B46	SP9	15c +10c bis	6	6
B47	SP9	50c +10c ol gray	15	10

The surtax was to aid the victims of the Valencia flood, Oct., 1957.

Type of Regular Issue, 1958.
Designs: 10c+5c, Preaching missionary. 15c+5c, Crucifix and missal.

1958, June 1 — Photo. Perf. 13x12½
B48	A42	10c +5c red brn	5	5
B49	A42	15c +5c dp bis	5	5

The surtax was to help the native population.

Butterflies — SP10
Early Bicycle — SP11

1958, Nov. 23 — Unwmkd.
Various Butterflies.
B50	SP10	10c +5c brn red	5	5
B51	SP10	25c +10c brt pur	6	6
B52	SP10	50c +10c gray ol	15	6

Stamp Day, 1958.

Type of Regular Issue 1956 Inscribed: "Pro-Infancia 1959"
Plants: 10c+5c, Digitalis. 15c+5c, Castor bean.

1959, June 1 — Photo. Perf. 13x12½
B53	A36	10c +5c rose brn	5	5
B54	A36	15c +5c bis	5	5

The surtax was for child welfare.

1959, Nov. 23
Designs: 20c+5c, Bicycle race. 50c+20c, Bicyclist winning race.

B55	SP11	10c +5c lt rose brn	5	5
B56	SP11	20c +5c turq bl	5	5
B57	SP11	50c +20c ol gray	12	6

Stamp Day, 1959.

AIR POST STAMPS.

AP1
Revenue Stamp Surcharged
"Habilitado para / Correo Aéreo / Intercolonial / Una Peseta"
Type I: "Correo Aereo," 20½ mm.
Type II: "Correo Aereo," 22 mm.

1941 — Perf. 11. Unwmkd.
C1	AP1	1p on 17p dp red, I	55.00	6.00
a.		Type II	60.00	14.00

Spain No. C113 Overprinted in Red

Golfo de Guinea.

1942, June 23
C2	AP30	1p chlky bl	2.00	25

No. 300 Overprinted in Green — **Correo Aéreo Viaje Ministerial 10-19 Enero 1948**

1948, Jan. 15 — Perf. 10½x9½
C3	A166	4p dl rose	11.00	3.25

The overprint exists in two types: I. The numeral 1's are lower case L's. II. The numeral 1's are actual ones.

Count of Argelejo and Frigate Catalina at Fernando Po, 1778 — AP2

1949, Nov. 23 — Photo. Perf. 12½x13
C4	AP2	5p dk sl grn	2.25	75

Stamp Day, Nov. 23, 1949.

Manuel Iradier and Native Products — AP3

1950, Nov. 23 — Perf. 12½x13 Unwmkd.
C5	AP3	5p dk brn	3.75	80

Stamp Day, Nov. 23, 1950.

Benito Rapids — AP4
Various Views.

1951, Mar. 1 — Litho. Perf. 12½x13
C6	AP4	25c ocher	6	5
C7	AP4	50c lil rose	6	5
C8	AP4	1p green	6	5
C9	AP4	2p brt bl	30	6
C10	AP4	3.25p rose lil	1.00	15
C11	AP4	5p gray brn	6.50	2.00
C12	AP4	10p rose red	27.50	4.75
		Nos. C6-C12(7)	35.48	7.11

Woman Holding Dove — AP5

1951, Apr. 22 — Engraved Perf. 10
C13	AP5	5p dk bl	30.00	3.75

Issued to commemorate the 500th anniversary of the birth of Queen Isabella I.

Ferdinand the Catholic — AP6
Soccer Players — AP7

SPANISH GUINEA—SPANISH MOROCCO

Photogravure
1952, July 18   Perf. 13x12½
C14	AP6	5p red brn	45.00	7.00

Issued to commemorate the 500th anniversary of the birth of Ferdinand the Catholic of Spain.

1955-56   Unwmkd.
C15	AP7	25c bl vio ('56)	6	6
C16	AP7	50c ol ('56)	6	6
C17	AP7	1.50p brn ('56)	1.50	6
C18	AP7	4p rose car ('56)	4.50	30
C19	AP7	10p yel grn	2.75	30
		Nos. C15-C19 (5)	8.87	78

Planes and Arm Holding Spear
AP8

1957, Sept. 19   Perf. 13x12½
C20	AP8	25p bis & sep	12.00	1.25

Issued to commemorate the 30th anniversary of the Atlantida Squadron flight to Spanish Guinea.

SPECIAL DELIVERY STAMP.

View of Fernando Po—SD1
Perf. 12½x13

1951, Mar. 1   Litho.   Unwmkd.
E1	SD1	25c rose car	30	20

SPANISH MOROCCO
(spăn'ĭsh mô·rŏk'ō)

LOCATION—Northwest coast of Africa.
GOVT.—Former Spanish Protectorate
AREA—17,398 sq. mi. (approx.).
POP.—1,010,117 (1950).
CHIEF TOWN—Tetuán.

Spanish Morocco was a Spanish Protectorate until 1956 when it, along with the French and Tangier zones of Morocco, became the independent country, Morocco.

100 Centimos = 1 Peseta

Spanish Offices in Morocco

Spain No. 221A Overprinted in Carmine

1903-09   Imperf.   Unwmkd.
1	A21	¼c bl grn	45	15

Stamps of Spain Overprinted in Carmine or Blue

On Stamps of 1900.
Perf. 14.
2	A35	2c bis brn	90	45
3	A35	5c green	1.15	25
4	A35	10c rose red (Bl)	1.40	15
5	A35	15c brt vio	1.75	30
6	A35	20c grnsh blk	5.50	1.10
7	A35	25c blue	70	30
8	A35	30c bl grn	4.00	1.10
9	A35	40c rose (Bl)	6.75	1.75
10	A35	50c sl grn	4.00	1.50
11	A35	1p lake (Bl)	8.00	2.50
12	A35	4p dl vio	18.00	4.00
13	A35	10p brn org (Bl)	18.00	7.50
		Nos. 1-13 (13)	70.60	21.05

Many varieties of overprint exist. Nos. 7-13 exist imperf.

On Stamps of 1909-10.
Perf. 13 x 12½, 14.
14	A46	2c dk brn	40	10
15	A46	5c green	1.75	10
16	A46	10c car (Bl)	2.00	10
17	A46	15c violet	4.75	20
18	A46	20c ol grn	9.50	35
19	A46	25c dp bl	150.00	
20	A46	30c bl grn	4.00	20
21	A46	40c rose (Bl)	4.00	20
22	A46	50c sl bl	6.75	2.75
23	A46	1p lake (Bl)	12.50	5.50
24	A46	4p dp vio	150.00	
25	A46	10p org (Bl)	150.00	
		Nos. 14-18, 20-23 (9)	45.65	9.50

The stamps overprinted "Correo Espanol Marruecos" were used in all Morocco until the year 1914. After the issue of special stamps for the Protectorate the "Correo Espanol" stamps were continued in use solely in the city of Tangier.
Many varieties of overprint exist.
Nos. 19, 24 and 25 were not regularly issued.

Spanish Morocco.

Spain No. 221A Overprinted in Carmine

1914   Imperf.
26	A21	¼c green	10	10

Stamps of Spain 1909-10 Overprinted in Carmine or Blue
Perf. 13 x 12½, 14.
27	A46	2c dk brn (C)	10	10
28	A46	5c grn (C)	30	20
29	A46	10c car (Bl)	30	20
30	A46	15c vio (C)	90	65
31	A46	20c ol grn (C)	1.75	1.00
32	A46	25c dp bl (C)	1.75	75
33	A46	30c bl grn (C)	3.25	1.40
34	A46	40c rose (Bl)	7.00	1.75
35	A46	50c sl bl (C)	4.00	1.40
36	A46	1p lake (Bl)	4.00	1.75
37	A46	4p dp vio (C)	17.50	11.00
38	A46	10p org (Bl)	25.00	12.50
		Nos. 26-38, E1 (14)	68.95	34.05

Many varieties of overprint exist, including inverted. Nos. 27-38 exist imperf. Price for set, $475.

Stamps of Spain 1876 and 1909-10 Overprinted in Red or Blue

1915   Imperf.
39	A21	¼c bl grn (R)	30	10

Perf. 13 x 12½, 14.
40	A46	2c dk brn (R)	15	6
41	A46	5c grn (R)	35	10
42	A46	10c car (Bl)	35	5
43	A46	15c vio (R)	40	12
44	A46	20c ol grn (R)	1.00	20
45	A46	25c dp bl (R)	1.00	20
46	A46	30c bl grn (R)	1.25	25
47	A46	40c rose (Bl)	1.75	25
48	A46	50c sl bl (R)	3.00	20
49	A46	1p lake (R)	3.00	25
50	A46	4p dp vio (R)	18.00	10.00
51	A46	10p org (Bl)	27.50	11.50
		Nos. 39-51, E2 (14)	60.30	24.08

One stamp in the setting on Nos. 39-51 has the first "R" of "PROTECTORADO" inverted. Many other varieties of overprint exist, including double and inverted.
Nos. 40-51 exist imperf. Price, set $700.

Stamps of Spain 1877 and 1909-10 Overprinted in Red or Blue

1916-18   Imperf.
52	A21	¼c bl grn (R)	90	15

Perf. 13 x 12½, 14.
53	A46	2c dk brn (R)	90	15
54	A46	5c grn (R)	3.50	15
55	A46	10c car (R)	4.50	15
56	A46	15c vio (R)	210.00	
57	A46	20c ol grn (R)	210.00	
58	A46	25c dp bl (R)	13.00	1.00
59	A46	30c bl grn (R)	18.00	6.50
60	A46	40c rose (R)	17.50	45
61	A46	50c sl bl (R)	10.00	20
62	A46	1p lake (R)	22.50	1.40
63	A46	4p dp vio (R)	35.00	13.00
64	A46	10p org (Bl)	75.00	30.00
		Nos. 52-55, 58-64 (11)	200.80	53.15

Nos. 56-57 were not regularly issued.
Varieties of overprint, including double and inverted, exist for several denominations.
The 5c exists in olive brown. Price $475.

Same Overprint on Spain No. 310
1920
65	A46	15c ocher (Bl)	4.50	22

Exists imperf.; also with overprint inverted.

Stamps of 1915
Perforated through the middle and each half Surcharged "10 céntimos" in Red.

1920
66	A46	10c on half of 20c ol grn	5.00	2.00
67	A46	15c on half of 30c bl grn	11.50	8.00

No. E2 Divided and Surcharged in Black
68	SD1	10c on half of 20c red	14.00	8.00
a.		"10/cts." surch. added	90.00	25.00

Prices of Nos. 66-68 are for pairs, both halves of the stamp. Varieties were probably made deliberately.

"Justice"
A1

Revenue Stamps Perforated through the Middle and each half Surcharged with New Value in Red or Green

1920   Perf. 11½
69	A1	5c on 5p lt ol (R)	11.00	2.00
70	A1	5c on 10p grn (R)	30	15
71	A1	10c on 25p dk grn (R)	30	15
a.		Inverted surch.	14.00	12.50
72	A1	10c on 50p ind (R)	60	40
73	A1	15c on 100p red (G)	60	40
74	A1	15c on 500p cl (G)	15.00	6.50
		Nos. 69-74 (6)	27.80	9.60

Prices of Nos. 69-74 are for pairs, both halves of the stamp.

Stamps of Spain 1917-20 Overprinted Type "a" in Blue or Red.
1921-24   Perf. 13.
75	A46	15c ocher (Bl)	1.75	10
76	A46	20c vio (R)	3.00	10

Stamps of Spain 1920-21 Overprinted Type "b" in Red.
Imperf.
77	A47	1c bl grn	1.40	10

Engraved.
Perf. 13.
78	A46	20c violet	8.50	10

Stamps of Spain, 1922 Overprinted Type "a" in Red or Blue
1923-28   Perf. 13½ x 12½
79	A49	2c ol grn (R)	2.75	10
80	A49	5c red vio (Bl)	2.75	10
81	A49	10c yel grn (R)	3.25	10
82	A49	20c vio (R)	5.00	50

Same Overprinted Type "b."
1923-25
83	A49	2c ol grn (R)	65	6
84	A49	5c red vio (Bl)	65	5
85	A49	10c yel grn (R)	2.25	5
86	A49	15c bl (R)	2.25	10
87	A49	20c vio (R)	4.50	5
88	A49	25c car (Bl)	8.00	65
89	A49	40c dp bl (R)	9.50	2.00
90	A49	50c org (Bl)	22.50	2.50
91	A49a	1p bl blk (R)	32.50	2.00
		Nos. 83-91 (9)	82.80	7.46

Spain No. 314 Overprinted Type "a" in Red.
1927   Imperf.
92	A47	1c bl grn	38	10

Mosque of Alcazarquivir
A2

Moorish Gateway at Larache
A3

Well at Alhucemas
A4

View of Xauen—A5

View of Tetuan—A6

Engraved.
1928-32   Perf. 14, 14½
93	A2	1c red ("Cs")	12	7
94	A2	1c car rose ("Ct") ('32)	30	20

SPANISH MOROCCO

95	A2	2c dk vio	10	7
96	A2	5c dp bl	10	7
97	A2	10c dk grn	10	7
98	A3	15c org brn	40	7
99	A3	20c ol grn	40	7
100	A3	25c cop red	40	7
102	A3	30c blk brn	1.25	10
103	A3	40c dl bl	1.75	10
104	A3	50c brn vio	3.00	6
105	A4	1p yel grn	5.00	25
106	A5	2.50p red vio	16.00	3.00
107	A6	4p ultra	11.50	2.00
	Nos. 93-107, E4 (15)		43.42	7.70

Seville-Barcelona Issue of Spain, 1929,
Overprinted **PROTECTORADO MARRUECOS** in Red or Blue

1929   *Perf. 11, 14.*

108	A50	1c grnsh bl	10	10
109	A51	2c pale yel grn	10	10
110	A52	5c rose lake (Bl)	10	10
111	A53	10c green	10	10
112	A50	15c Prus bl	10	10
113	A51	20c purple	10	10
114	A50	25c brt rose (Bl)	10	10
115	A52	30c blk brn (Bl)	30	25
116	A53	40c dk bl	30	25
117	A51	50c dp org (Bl)	30	25
118	A52	1p bl blk	2.00	1.50
119	A53	4p dp rose (Bl)	5.25	3.75
120	A53	10p brn (Bl)	7.50	5.25
	Nos. 108-120 (13)		16.35	11.95

Stamps of Spain, 1922-31,
Overprinted Type "a" in Black, Blue or Red.

1929-34   *Perf. 11½, 13 x 12½.*

121	A49	5c cl (Bk)	2.75	10
122	A61	10c grn (R)	3.00	25
123	A61	15c sl grn (R)	85.00	70
124	A61	20c vio (R)	3.25	35
125	A61	30c brn lake (Bl)	3.50	65
126	A61	40c dk bl (R)	13.00	2.00
127	A49	50c org (Bl)	21.00	1.75
128	A49a	10p brn (Bl)	3.25	3.00
	Nos. 121-128 (8)		134.75	8.80

Stamps of Spain, 1922-26, overprinted diagonally as above, and with no control number, or with "A000,000" on back, were not issued but were presented to the delegates at the 1929 Universal Postal Union Congress in London.

Stamps of Spain 1931-32,
Overprinted in Black **MARRUECOS**

1933-34   *Imperf.*

130	A108	1c bl grn	20	10

Perf. 11½.

131	A108	2c buff	20	10
132	A95	5c brnsh blk	20	10
133	A96	10c yel grn	20	10
134	A97	15c sl grn	20	10
135	A95	20c dk vio	20	10
136	A104	25c lake	20	10
137	A99	30c car rose	37.50	2.25
138	A100	40c dk bl	45	10
139	A97	50c orange	1.00	10
140	A100	60c ap grn	1.00	10
141	A105	1p bl blk	1.00	20
142	A106	4p magenta	2.75	1.25
143	A107	10p dp brn	3.50	2.25
	Nos. 130-143, E7 (15)		50.35	7.30

Street Scene in Tangier
A7

View of Xauen
A8

Gate in Town Wall, Arzila
A9

Street Scene in Tangier
A10

Mosque of Alcazarquivir
A11

Caliph and His Guard
A12

View of Tangier—A13

Green Control Numbers Printed on Gum

1933-35   Photo.   *Perf. 14, 13½*

144	A7	1c brt rose	10	7
145	A8	2c grn ('35)	10	7
146	A9	5c mag ('35)	15	7
147	A10	10c dk grn	30	6
148	A11	15c yel ('35)	1.25	10
149	A7	20c sl grn	50	6
150	A12	25c crim ('35)	13.00	25
151	A10	30c red brn	3.75	5
152	A13	40c dp bl	8.00	15
153	A13	50c red org	22.50	2.50
154	A8	1p sl blk ('35)	9.00	15
155	A9	2.50p brn ('35)	15.00	2.50
156	A11	4p yel grn ('35)	15.00	2.50
157	A12	5p blk ('35)	15.00	2.50
	Nos. 144-157, E5 (15)		107.90	11.18

Mosque—A14

Landscape—A15

Green Control Numbers Printed on Gum

1935

158	A14	25c violet	75	10
159	A15	30c crimson	9.50	10
160	A14	40c orange	5.75	20
161	A15	50c brt bl	5.75	20
162	A14	60c dk bl grn	5.75	20
163	A15	2p brn lake	25.00	4.00
	Nos. 158-163 (6)		52.50	4.80

See also No. 174.

Regular Issue and Special Delivery Stamp of 1928, Surcharged in Blue, Green or Red with New Values and Ornaments.

1936

164	A6	1c on 4p ultra (Bl)	25	10
165	A5	2c on 2.50p red vio (G)	25	10
166	A3	5c on 25c cop red (R)	15	10
167	A4	10c on 1p yel grn (G)	6.25	3.00
168	SD2	15c on 20c blk (Bl)	5.25	1.75
	Nos. 164-168 (5)		12.15	5.05

Caliph and Viziers
A16

View of Bokoia
A17

View of Alcazarquivir
A18

Sidi Saida Mosque
A19

Caliph and Procession
A20

1937   Photogravure.   *Perf. 13½.*

169	A16	1c green	10	7
170	A17	2c red vio	10	7
171	A18	5c orange	20	7
172	A16	15c violet	20	7
173	A19	30c red	50	10
174	A14	1p ultra	4.00	25
175	A20	10p brown	37.50	11.00
	Nos. 169-175 (7)		42.60	11.63

See also Nos. 192–193, souvenir sheets.

Harkeno Rifleman
A21

Troops Marching
A22

Designs: 2c, Legionnaires. 5c, Cavalryman leading his mount. 10c, Moroccan phalanx. 15c, Legion flag-bearer. 20c, Colonial soldier. 25c, Ifni sharpshooters. 30c, Mounted trumpeters. 40c, Cape Juby Dromedary Corps. 50c, Regular infantry. 60c, Caliphate guards. 1p, Orderly on guard. 2p, Sentry. 2.50p, Regular cavalry. 4p, Orderly.

1937   *Perf. 13½*

176	A21	1c dl bl	6	6
177	A21	2c org brn	6	6
178	A21	5c cerise	6	6
179	A21	10c emerald	6	6
180	A21	15c brt bl	6	6
181	A21	20c red brn	6	6
182	A21	25c magenta	6	6
183	A21	30c red org	6	6
184	A21	40c orange	15	15
185	A21	50c ultra	15	15
186	A21	60c yel grn	15	15
187	A21	1p bl vio	15	15
188	A21	2p Prus bl	5.75	3.75
189	A21	2.50p gray blk	5.75	3.75
190	A21	4p dk brn	5.75	3.75
191	A22	10p black	5.75	3.75
	Nos. 176-191, E6 (17)		24.23	16.23

First Year of Spanish Civil War.

Souvenir Sheets

1937   *Perf. 13½*

192		Sheet of 4 (1, 2, 5c, 1p)	16.50	9.00
193		Sheet of 4 (2, 5, 15, 30c)	16.50	9.00

Issued to commemorate the first year of the Spanish Civil War.

No. 192 contains one each of Nos. 169-171 and 174, with marginal inscription in blue.

No. 193 contains one each of Nos. 170-173, with marginal inscription in red. Size of both sheets: 105x95mm.

Nos. 192-193 were privately overprinted "TANGER" in black on each stamp in the sheet for "use" in the International City of Tangier, and "GUINEA" for "use" in Spanish Guinea.

Spanish Quarter
A25

Designs: 10c, Moroccan quarter. 15c, Street scene, Larache. 20c, Tetuan.

Photogravure.

1939   *Perf. 13½.*   Unwmkd.

194	A25	5c orange	25	7
195	A25	10c brt bl grn	25	7
196	A25	15c gldn brn	55	7
197	A25	20c brt ultra	55	7

Postman
A26

Mail Box
A27

SPANISH MOROCCO

Landscape
A28

Street Scene, Alcazarquivir
A29

Spanish War Veterans
A38

Victory Flag Bearers
A39

Market Place, Larache
A44

Vegetable Garden
A51

View of Xauen
A30

Sentry Guarding Palace at Sat
A31

Cavalry
A40   Day of Court
A41

Photogravure.

1940		Perf. 11½x11	Unwmkd.	
198	A26	1c dk brn	10	6
199	A27	2c ol grn	10	6
200	A28	5c dk bl	20	5
201	A29	10c dk red lil	20	5
202	A30	15c dk grn	20	5
203	A31	20c purple	20	5
204	A32	25c blk brn	20	5
205	A33	30c brt grn	20	5
206	A34	40c sl grn	1.75	5
207	A35	45c org ver	70	8
208	A36	50c brn org	70	6
209	A37	70c sapphire	70	6
210	A38	1p ind & brn	2.00	8
211	A39	2.50p choc & dk grn	9.50	2.50
212	A40	5p dk cer & sep	2.00	25
213	A41	10p dk ol grn & brn org	18.00	4.25
		Nos. 198-213, E8 (17)	37.15	8.08

Tangier
A45   A46

Photogravure.

1941		Perf. 10½	Unwmkd.	
230	A42	5c dk brn & brn	10	7
231	A43	10c dp rose & ver	20	6
232	A44	15c sl grn & yel grn	20	5
233	A45	20c vio bl & dp bl	45	6
234	A46	40c dp plum & cl	1.25	6
		Nos. 230-234 (5)	2.20	30

1943		Perf. 12 x 12½.		
234A	A43	5c dk bl	10	5
235	A44	40c dl vio brn	20.00	20

Picking Oranges—A52

Goat Herd—A53

Photogravure.

1944		Perf. 12½	Unwmkd.	
236	A47	1c choc & lt bl	15	6
237	A48	2c sl grn & lt grn	15	6
238	A49	5c dk grn & grnsh blk	15	6
239	A50	10c brt ultra & red org	15	6
240	A51	15c sl grn & lt grn	15	6
241	A52	20c dp cl & blk	15	6
242	A53	25c lt bl & choc	20	6
243	A47	30c yel grn & brt ultra	20	6
244	A48	40c choc & red vio	15	6
245	A49	50c brt ultra & red brn	40	6
246	A50	75c yel grn & brt ultra	50	6
247	A51	1p brt ultra & choc	50	5
248	A52	2.50p blk & brt ultra	5.50	1.75
249	A53	10p sal & gray blk	8.50	3.75
		Nos. 236-249 (14)	16.85	6.21

The Chieftain
A32

Market Place, Larache
A33

"ZONA" printed in black on back.

Stamps of 1937 Overprinted in Various Colors
17-VII-940 4 ANIVERSARIO

1940		Perf. 13½	Unwmkd.	
214	A21	1c dl bl (Bk)	75	75
215	A21	2c org brn (Bk)	75	75
216	A21	5c cer (Bk)	75	75
217	A21	10c emer (Bk)	75	75
218	A21	15c brt bl (Bk)	75	75
219	A21	20c red brn (Bk)	75	75
220	A21	25c mag (Bk)	75	75
221	A21	30c red org (V)	75	75
222	A21	40c org (V)	1.25	1.25
223	A21	50c ultra (Bk)	1.25	1.25
224	A21	60c yel grn (Bk)	1.25	1.25
225	A21	1p bl vio (V)	1.25	1.25
226	A21	2p Prus bl (Bl)	35.00	35.00
227	A21	2.50p gray blk (V)	35.00	35.00
228	A21	4p dk brn (Bl)	35.00	35.00
229	A22	10p blk (R)	35.00	35.00
		Nos. 214-229, E10 (17)	162.00	162.00

4th anniversary of Spanish Civil War.

Plowing—A47

Harvesting—A48

Returning from Work
A49

Transporting Wheat
A50

Potters—A54

Blacksmiths
A56

Tetuán
A34

Ancient Gateway at Xauen
A35

Scene in Alcazarquivir
A36

Post Office
A37

Larache
A42   Alcazarquivir
A43

Dyers—A55

601

SPANISH MOROCCO

Cobblers—A57

Weavers—A58

Metal Workers—A59

Lithographed.

1946 Perf. 10½x10 Unwmkd.

250	A54	1c pur & brn	6	5
251	A55	2c dk Prus grn & vio blk	6	5
252	A55	10c dp org & vio bl	6	5
253	A55	15c dk bl & bl grn	6	5
254	A55	25c yel grn & ultra	6	5
255	A56	40c dk bl & brn, perf. 12½	6	
256	A56	45c blk & rose	60	6
257	A57	1p dk Prus grn & dp bl	75	6
258	A58	2.50p dp org & grnsh gray	2.25	75
259	A59	10p dk bl & gray	3.75	2.00
		Nos. 250-259 (10)	7.71	3.17

Control letter "Z" in circle in black on back.

A60

Sanitarium A61

1946, Sept. 1 Perf. 11½x10½, 10½

260	A60	10c crim & bl grn	10	6
261	A61	25c crim & brn	10	6
		Nos. 260-261, B14-B16 (5)	1.60	73

Issued to aid anti-tuberculosis work.

A62

A63

1947 Perf. 10

262	A62	10c car & bl	10	10
263	A63	25c red & choc	10	10
		Nos. 262-263, B17-B19 (5)	1.50	1.15

Issued to aid anti-tuberculosis work.

Commerce by Railroad—A64

Commerce by Truck—A65

Urban Market—A66

Country Market—A67

Caravan—A68

Maritime Commerce A69

Perf. 10, 10x10½.

1948 Lithographed Unwmkd.

264	A64	2c pur & brn	6	6
265	A65	5c dp cl & vio	6	6
266	A66	15c brt ultra & bl grn	6	6
267	A67	25c blk & Prus grn	6	6
268	A65	35c brt ultra & gray blk	6	6
269	A68	50c red & vio	6	6
270	A66	70c dk gray grn & ultra	6	6
271	A67	90c cer & dk gray grn	15	7
272	A66	1p brt ultra & vio	50	7
273	A64	2.50p vio brn & sl grn	1.25	35
274	A69	10p blk & dp ultra	2.25	1.00
		Nos. 264-274 (11)	4.57	1.91

Emblem of Tuberculosis Association A70

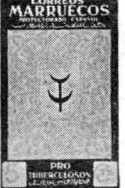
A71

Design: 25c, Plane over sanatorium.

1948, Oct. 1 Perf. 10

275	A70	10c car & grn	6	6
276	A70	25c car & grnsh gray	1.75	85
		Nos. 275-276, B20-B23 (6)	28.31	10.56

1949

Designs: 10c, Road of Health. 25c, Minaret and Palm.

Black Control Number on Back

277	A71	5c car & grn	6	6
278	A71	10c car & dk vio	6	6
279	A71	25c car & blk	70	30
		Nos. 277-279, B25-B26 (5)	2.52	80

Mail Transport, 1890 A72

Herald A73

Designs: 5c, 50c, 90c, Mail transport, 1890. 10c, 45c, 1p, Mail transport, 1906. 15c, 1.50p, Mail transport, 1913. 35c, 75c, 5p, Mail transport, 1914. 10p, Mail transport, 1918.

1950 Lithographed. Perf. 10½.

280	A72	5c choc & vio bl	6	6
281	A72	10c dp bl & sep	6	6
282	A72	15c grnsh blk & emer	6	6
283	A72	35c pur & gray blk	15	12
284	A72	45c dp car & rose lil	20	20
285	A72	50c emer & dk brn	6	6
286	A72	75c dk vio bl & bl	15	12
287	A72	90c grnsh blk & rose car	6	5
288	A72	1p blk brn & gray	10	7
289	A72	1.50p car & bl	50	15
290	A72	5p blk & vio brn	90	20
291	A72	10p pur & ultra	17.50	11.00
		Nos. 280-291, E11 (13)	37.30	23.15

75th anniversary (in 1949) of Universal Postal Union.
Nos. 280–291 exist imperf. Price $350.

1950 Perf. 10 Unwmkd.

Designs: 10c, Old fort. 25c, Sanatorium.

Frame and Device in Carmine
Black Control Number on Back

292	A73	5c gray blk	6	5
293	A73	10c bl grn	6	6
294	A73	25c vio bl	95	50
		Nos. 292-294, B27-B28 (5)	2.21	1.07

Issued to aid anti-tuberculosis work.

Boar Hunt A74

Designs: 10c and 1p, Hunters and hounds. 50c, Boar hunt. 5p, Fishermen. 10p, Moorish fishing boat.

1950, Dec. 30 Perf. 10½x10

Black Control Number on Back

295	A74	5c dk brn & rose vio	6	5
296	A74	10c car & gray	6	5
297	A74	50c grn & sep	6	5
298	A74	1p bl vio & cl	60	5
299	A74	5p dp cl & bl vio	1.00	8
300	A74	10p grnsh blk & dp cl	2.50	50
		Nos. 295-300 (6)	4.28	78

Emblem A75

Designs: 10c, Patients expressing gratitude. 25c, Plane in the Clouds.
Dated "1951"

1951 Lithographed. Perf. 12.
Frame and Device in Carmine
Black Control Number on Back

301	A75	5c green	12	10
302	A75	10c bl vio	12	10
303	A75	25c gray blk	90	50
		Nos. 301-303, B29-B32 (7)	12.64	7.00

Issued to aid anti-tuberculosis work.

Armed Attack—A76

Designs: 10c, Horses on parade. 15c, Holiday procession. 20c, Road to market. 25c, "Brotherhoods." 35c, "Offering." 45c, Soldiers. 50c, On the rooftop. 75c, Teahouse. 90c, Wedding. 1p, Pilgrimage. 5p, Storyteller. 10p, Market corner.

1952 Perf. 11.
Black Control Number on Back

304	A76	5c dk bl & brn	6	6
305	A76	10c dk brn & lil rose	6	6
306	A76	15c blk & emer	6	6
307	A76	20c ol grn & red vio	6	6
308	A76	25c red & lt bl	6	6
309	A76	35c ol & org	6	6
310	A76	45c red & rose red	6	6
311	A76	50c rose car & gray grn	6	6
312	A76	75c pur & ultra	6	6
313	A76	90c dk bl & rose vio	6	6
314	A76	1p dk bl & red brn	6	6
315	A76	5p red & bl	2.00	35
316	A76	10p dk grn & gray blk	3.25	55
		Nos. 304-316, E12 (14)	5.99	1.64

Worship A77

Designs: 10c, Distributing alms. 25c, Prickly pear.

1952, Oct. 1 Dated "1952"
Black Control Number on Back

317	A77	5c car & dk ol grn	6	6
318	A77	10c car & dk brn	6	6
319	A77	25c car & dp bl	45	30
		Nos. 317-319, B33-B37 (8)	8.13	4.63

Semi-Postal Types of 1948–49
Dated "1953"

Designs: 10c, As No. B26. 25c, As No. B23.

1953 Lithographed Perf. 10
Black Control Number on Back

| 320 | SP7 | 5c car & bl grn | 6 | 6 |

SPANISH MOROCCO

321	SP9	10c car & pur	6	6
322	SP7	25c car & grn	80	50
	Nos. 320-322, B38-B42 (8)		12.05	7.62

Issued to aid anti-tuberculosis work.

A78   Mountain Women A79

1953, Nov. 15

Black Control Number on Back

| 323 | A78 | 5c red | 15 | 7 |
| 324 | A78 | 10c gray grn | 15 | 7 |

1953, Dec. 15   Photogravure

Designs: 50c and 2.50p, Water carrier. 90c and 2p, Mountaineers and donkey. 1p and 4.50p, Moorish women and child. 10p, Mounted dignitary.

Black Control Number on Back

334	A79	35c grn & rose vio	6	6
335	A79	50c red & grn	6	6
336	A79	90c dk bl & org	6	6
337	A79	1p dk brn & grn	6	6
338	A79	1.25p dk grn & car rose	15	6
339	A79	2p dk rose vio & bl	30	30
340	A79	2.50p blk & org	70	30
341	A79	4.50p brt car rose & dk grn	3.00	35
342	A79	10p grn & blk	3.50	80
	Nos. 334-342, E13 (10)		8.14	2.30

25th anniversary of Spanish Morocco's first definitive postage stamps.

Zauia   Queen's Gate
A80   A81

Designs: 10c, "The Family." 25c, Plane and Spanish coast.

Dated "1954."

1954, Nov. 1

Black Control Number on Back

343	A80	5c car & bl grn	6	6
344	A80	10c car & dk brn	6	6
345	A80	25c car & bl	20	20
	Nos. 343-345, B43-B45 (6)		9.13	5.38

1955   Lithographed.   *Perf. 11*

Gates: 25c and 1p, Saida. 80c, Queen's. 15p, Ceuta.

Black Control Number on Back
Frames in Black

346	A81	15c green	6	6
347	A81	25c vio rose	6	6
348	A81	80c blue	6	6
349	A81	1p car rose	25	6
350	A81	15p Prus grn	3.75	90
	Nos. 346-350, E14 (6)		4.38	1.29

Honor Guard
A82

Designs: 25c, 80c, 3p, Caliph Moulay Hassan ben el-Medi. 30c, 1p, 5p, Caliph and procession. 15p, Coat of arms.

Perf. 13x12½

1955, Nov. 8   Photo.   Unwmkd.

351	A82	15c ol brn & ol	6	6
352	A82	25c lil & dp rose	6	6
353	A82	30c brn blk & Prus grn	6	6
354	A82	70c Prus grn & yel grn	6	6
355	A82	80c ol & ol brn	6	6
356	A82	1p dk bl & redsh brn	15	6
357	A82	1.80p blk & bl vio	25	6
358	A82	3p bl & gray	25	6
359	A82	5p dk grn & brn	1.75	60

Engraved.

| 360 | A82 | 15p red brn & yel grn | 3.50 | 2.00 |
| | Nos. 351-360 (10) | | 6.20 | 3.08 |

30th anniversary of accession to throne by Caliph Moulay Hassan ben el-Medi ben Ismail.

Succeeding issues, released under the Kingdom, are listed under Morocco.

SEMI-POSTAL STAMPS.
Types of Semi-Postal Stamps of Spain, 1926, Overprinted in Black or Blue

ZONA PROTECTORADO ESPAÑOL

1926   *Perf. 12½, 13.*   Unwmkd.

B1	SP1	1c orange	2.25	2.00
B2	SP2	2c rose	3.25	2.50
B3	SP3	5c blk brn	1.50	1.00
B4	SP4	10c dk grn	1.50	1.00
B5	SP1	15c dk vio (Bl)	40	40
B6	SP4	20c vio brn	40	40
B7	SP5	25c dp car	40	40
B8	SP1	30c ol grn	40	40
B9	SP3	40c ultra	15	15
B10	SP4	50c red brn	15	15
B11	SP4	1p vermilion	15	15
B12	SP4	4p bister	40	40
B13	SP5	10p lt vio	90	75
	Nos. B1-B13, EB1 (14)		12.75	10.45

Tuberculosis Fund Issues.

SP1   SP2

SP3

Perf. 10½, 11½x10½

1946, Sept. 1   Litho.   Unwmkd.

B14	SP1	25c +5c crim & rose vio	10	6
B15	SP2	50c +10c crim & bl	40	20
B16	SP3	90c +10c crim & gray brn	90	35

Medical   Nurse and
Center   Children
SP4   SP5

"Protection"   Herald
SP6   SP7

1947   *Perf. 10*

B17	SP4	25c +5c red & vio	10	10
B18	SP5	50c +10c red & bl	35	25
B19	SP6	90c +10c red & sep	85	60

1948, Oct. 1

Designs: No. B21, Protection. No. B22, Sun bath. No. B23, Plane over Ben Karrich.

B20	SP7	50c +10c car & dk vio	25	15
B21	SP7	90c +10c car & dk gray	1.25	50
B22	SP7	2.50p +50c car & brn	10.00	3.75
B23	SP7	5p +1p car & vio bl	15.00	5.25

Moulay Hassan
ben el-Medi ben   Flag
Ismail   SP9
SP8

1949, May 15

| B24 | SP8 | 50c +10c lil rose | 30 | 25 |

Wedding of the Caliph at Tetuan, June 5.

Tuberculosis Fund Issues.

1949

Design: No. B26, Fight with dragon.

Black Control Numbers on Back

| B25 | SP9 | 50c +10 car & brn | 45 | 8 |
| B26 | SP9 | 90c +10 car & grnsh gray | 1.25 | 30 |

Crowd at
Fountain of Life   Warrior
SP10   SP11

Design: 90c+10c, Mohammedan hermit's tomb.

1950, Oct. 1   Litho.   *Perf. 10*

Black Control Numbers on Back
Frame and Cross in Carmine.

| B27 | SP10 | 50c +10c dk brn | 35 | 6 |
| B28 | SP10 | 90c +10c dk grn | 80 | 40 |

Dated "1951."

1951   *Perf. 12.*   Unwmkd.

Designs: 90c+10c, Fort. 1p+5p, Port of Salvation. 1.10p+25c, Road to market.

Black Control Numbers on Back.

B29	SP11	50c +10c car & brn	10	10
B30	SP11	90c +10c car & bl	40	20
B31	SP11	1p +5p car & gray	7.00	4.00
B32	SP11	1.10p +25c car & gray	4.00	2.00

Pilgrimage   Armed Horseman
                in Action
SP12   SP13

Designs: 60c+25c, Palmettos. 90c+10c, Fort. 1.10p+25c, Agave. 5p+2p, Warrior.

1952   Dated "1952"   *Perf. 11.*

Black Control Numbers on Back

B33	SP12	50c +10c car & gray	6	6
B34	SP12	60c +25c car & dk grn	75	45
B35	SP12	90c +10c car & vio brn	75	45
B36	SP12	1.10p +25p car & pur	1.75	1.00
B37	SP12	5p +2p car & gray	4.25	2.25
	Nos. B33-B37 (5)		7.56	4.21

1953   Dated "1953."   *Perf. 10.*

Designs: 60c+25c, As No. 276. 1.10p+25c, Plane and clouds.

Black Control Numbers on Back

B38	SP13	50c +10c car & vio	8	8
B39	A70	60c +25c car & brn	1.75	1.00
B40	SP11	90c +10c car & blk	55	40
B41	SP13	1.10p +25p car & vio brn	2.50	1.75
B42	A73	5p +2p car & bl	6.25	3.75
	Nos. B38-B42 (5)		11.13	6.98

Stork
SP14

Designs: 50c+10c, Father & Child. 5p+2p, Tomb.

Dated "1954."

1954   Photogravure.

Black Control Numbers on Back.

B43	SP14	5c +5c car & rose vio	6	6
B44	SP14	50c +10c car & gray grn	70	50
B45	SP14	5p +2p car & gray	5.75	4.50

SPANISH MOROCCO

AIR POST STAMPS.

Mosque de Baja and Plane
AP1

View of Tetuán and Plane
AP2

Designs: 10c, Stork of Alcazar. 25c, Shore scene and plane. 40c, Desert tribesmen watching plane. 75c, View of shoreline at Larache. 1p, Arab mailman and plane above. 1.50p, Arab farmers and stork. 2p, Plane at twilight. 3p, Shadow of plane over city.

Photogravure.

		1938	Perf. 13½.	Unwmkd.	
C1	AP1	5c red brn		10	6
C2	AP1	10c emerald		15	10
C3	AP1	25c crimson		10	5
C4	AP1	40c dl bl		2.75	60
C5	AP2	50c cerise		10	5
C6	AP2	75c ultra		10	5
C7	AP1	1p dk brn		15	5
C8	AP1	1.50p purple		90	40
C9	AP1	2p brn lake		60	6
C10	AP1	3p gray blk		2.25	30
		Nos. C1–C10 (10)		7.20	1.72

Nos. C1–C10 exist imperf. Price of set, $275.

Landscape, Ketama
AP3

Mosque, Tangier
AP4

Velez
AP5

Sanjurjo
AP6

Strait of Gibraltar
AP7

AP8

		1942		Perf. 12½.	
C11	AP3	5c dp bl		6	6
C12	AP4	10c org brn		6	6
C13	AP5	15c grnsh blk		6	6
C14	AP6	90c dk rose		6	6
C15	AP7	5p black		1.40	70
		Nos. C11–C15 (5)		1.64	94

Nos. C11–C15 exist imperf. Price of set, $90.

	1949	Lithographed.	Perf. 10.	

Designs: 5c, 1.75p, Strait of Gibraltar. 10c, 20c, 3p, Market day. 30c, 4p, Kebira Fortress. 6.50p, Airmail arrival. 8p, Horseman.

C16	AP8	5c vio brn & brt grn	6	6
C17	AP8	10c blk & rose lil	6	6
C18	AP8	30c dk vio bl & grnsh gray	6	6
C19	AP8	1.75p car & bl vio	15	6
C20	AP8	3p dk bl & gray	25	6
C21	AP8	4p grnsh blk & car rose	50	25
C22	AP8	6.50p brt grn & brn	1.50	30
C23	AP8	8p rose lil & bl vio	2.50	50
		Nos. C16–C23 (8)	5.08	1.35

Nos. C16–C23 exist imperf. Price of set, $150.

Road to Tetuan
AP9

1952 Perf. 11.
Black Frames and Inscriptions.
Black Control Numbers on Back.

C24	AP9	2p brt bl	15	6
C25	AP9	4p scarlet	40	10
C26	AP9	8p dk ol grn	60	35
C27	AP9	16p vio brn	3.00	1.25

Part of the proceeds was used toward the establishment of a postal museum at Tetuan.

Plane over Boat
AP10

Designs: 60c, Mosques, Sidi Saidi. 1.10p, Plowing. 4.50p, Fortress, Xauen.

	1953		Perf. 10.	
C28	AP10	35c dp bl & car rose	20	6
C29	AP10	60c dk car & sl grn	20	6
C30	AP10	1.10p dp bl & blk	35	10
C31	AP10	4.50p dk car & dk brn	1.25	30

Nos. C28–C31 exist imperf. Price of set, $75.

No. C6 Surcharged with New Value in Black

50 Type I   **50** Type II

	1953		Perf. 13½	
C32	AP2	50c on 75c ultra (I)	45	15
a.		50c on 75c ultra (II)	45	15
b.		Vertical gutter pair, types (I) and (II)	2.50	

Sheets of 2 panes, 25 stamps each, with gutter between. Upper pane surcharged type I, lower type II.

AIR POST SEMI-POSTAL STAMPS.

No. 150 Surcharged in Black
18-7-36

= 0′25 + 2′00 =

	1936	Perf. 14.	Unwmkd.	
CB1	A12	25c +2p on 25c crim	13.50	5.25
a.		Bars at right omitted	47.50	47.50
b.		Blue surcharge	35.00	16.00

25c was for postage, 2p for air post.

Nos. C1 to C10 surcharged "Lucha Antituberculosa," a Lorraine cross and surtax are stated to be bogus.

Crowd at Palace
SPAP1

1949, May 15	Perf. 10	Unwmkd.	
CB2	SPAP1	1p +10c gray blk	1.00	45

Wedding of the Caliph at Tetuan, June 5.

SPECIAL DELIVERY STAMPS.

Special Delivery Stamp of Spain Overprinted in Blue

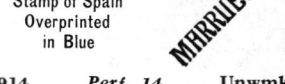

	1914	Perf. 14	Unwmkd.	
E1	SD1	20c red	3.00	1.25

Special Delivery Stamp of Spain Overprinted in Blue

PROTECTORADO ESPAÑOL EN MARRUECOS

	1915			
E2	SD1	20c red	2.25	1.00

Special Delivery Stamp of Spain Overprinted in Blue

ZONA DE PROTECTORADO ESPAÑOL EN MARRUECOS

	1923			
E3	SD1	20c red	6.50	2.75

Mounted Courier
SD2

1928	Engraved.	Perf. 14, 14½.	
E4	SD2	20c black	3.00	1.50

Moorish Postman
SD3

Mounted Courier
SD4

1935	Photogravure.	Perf. 14.

Green Control Number on Back

E5	SD3	20c vermilion	1.25	15

See also No. E9.

1937		Perf. 13½.
E6	SD4	20c brt car	15	15

Issued in commemoration of the First Year of the Spanish Civil War.

Spain No. E14 Overprinted in Black   **MARRUECOS**

1938		Perf. 10.	
E7	SD7	20c vermilion	1.75	30

Arab Postman
SD5

Airmail 1935
SD6

1940	Photo.	Perf. 11½x11	
E8	SD5	25c scarlet	40	25

"ZONA" printed on back in black.

1940	Type of 1935. Lithographed	Perf. 10	
E9	SD3	20c blk brn	1.85	

No. E9 was prepared but not issued.

No. E6 Surcharged with New Value, Bars and **17-VII-940 4º ANIVERSARIO**

1940		Perf. 13½	
E10	SD4	25c on 20c brt car	11.00	11.00

4th anniversary of Spanish Civil War.

1950	Lithographed. Perf. 10½	Unwmkd.	
E11	SD6	25c car & gray	17.50	11.00

Issued to commemorate the 75th anniversary (in 1949) of the formation of the Universal Postal Union.

Moorish Postrider
SD7

1952		Perf. 11	

Black Control Number on Back.

| E12 | SD7 | 25c car & rose car | 8 | 8 |

SPANISH MOROCCO

Rider with Special
Delivery Mail
SD8

Gate of
Tangier
SD9

1953 Photogravure. *Perf. 10.*
Black Control Number on Back
E13 SD8 25c dk bl & car rose 25 25

Issued to commemorate the 25th anniversary of Spanish Morocco's first definitive postage stamps.

1955 Lithographed. *Perf. 11.*
Black Control Number on Back
E14 SD9 2p vio & blk 20 15

SEMI-POSTAL SPECIAL DELIVERY STAMP.

Type of Semi-Postal Special
Delivery Stamp of Spain,
1926, **ZONA PROTECTORADO**
Overprinted **ESPAÑOL**

1926 *Perf. 12½, 13.* Unwmkd.
EB1 SPSD1 20c ultra & blk 90 75

POSTAL TAX STAMPS.

General Francisco Franco—**PT1**
Photogravure.

1937-39		*Perf. 12½.*	Unwmkd.	
RA1	PT1	10c sepia	50	10
a.		Sheet of 4, imperf.	2.75	1.75
RA2	PT1	10c cop brn ('38)	50	10
a.		Sheet of 4, imperf.	2.75	1.75
RA3	PT1	10c bl ('39)	50	10
a.		Sheet of 4, imperf.	2.75	1.75

The tax was used for the disabled soldiers in North Africa.
Nos. RA1a to RA3a have marginal inscriptions in color of stamps. Size: 121x100 mm.

Soldiers—**PT2**

1941		Lithographed	*Perf. 13½*	
RA4	PT2	10c brt grn	2.50	15
RA5	PT2	10c rose pink	2.50	15
RA6	PT2	10c hn brn	2.50	15
RA7	PT2	10c ultra	2.50	15

The tax was used for the disabled soldiers in North Africa.

General Franco
PT3

1943		Photogravure	*Perf. 10*	
RA8	PT3	10c chlky bl	4.50	10
RA9	PT3	10c sl bl	4.50	10
RA10	PT3	10c dl gray brn	4.50	10
RA11	PT3	10c bl vio	4.50	10
1944			*Perf. 12*	
RA12	PT3	10c dp mag & brn	3.75	10
RA13	PT3	10c dp org & dk grn	3.75	10
1946			Lithographed	
RA14	PT3	10c ultra & brn	3.75	10
RA15	PT3	10c gray blk & rose lil	3.75	10

TANGIER

For the International City of Tangier.

Seville-Barcelona Issue of Spain, 1929,
Overprinted TANGER in Blue or Red.

1929			*Perf. 11.*	
L1	A52	5c rose lake	12	10
L2	A53	10c grn (R)	12	10
L3	A50	15c Prus bl (R)	12	10
L4	A51	20c pur (R)	12	10
L5	A52	25c brt rose	12	10
L6	A52	30c blk brn	12	10
L7	A53	40c dk bl (R)	30	25
L8	A51	50c dp org	30	25
L9	A52	1p bl blk (R)	2.25	1.50
L10	A53	4p dp rose	5.25	3.75
L11	A53	10p brown	7.50	5.25
		Nos. L1-L11 (11)	16.32	11.60

Overprints of 1937-39

The following overprints on stamps of Spain exist in black or in red:
"TANGER" vertically on Nos. 517-518, 522-525, 528, 532, 534, 539-543, 549.
"Correo Espanol Tanger" horizontally or vertically in three lines on Nos. 540, 592-597 (gray paper), 598-601.
"Tanger" horizontally on Nos. 539-541, 592-601.
"Correo Tanger" horizontally in two lines on five consular stamps.

Woman
A1

A2

Man
A3

Old Map of Tangier
A4

Tangier Street
A5

Moroccan Women
A6

Head of Moor
A7

Engr., Photo. (1c, 2c)
Perf. 9½x10½, 12½x13 (1c, 2c, 10c, 20c)

1948-51			Unwmkd.	
L12	A1	1c bl grn ('51)	6	6
L13	A1	2c red org ('51)	6	6
L14	A2	5c vio brn ('49)	6	6
L15	A3	10c dp bl ('51)	6	6
L16	A3	20c gray ('51)	10	6
L17	A2	25c grn ('51)	10	6
L18	A4	30c dk sl grn	40	5
L19	A3	45c car rose	40	5
L20	A6	50c dp cl	40	5
L21	A7	75c dp bl	80	5
L22	A7	90c green	60	6
L23	A4	1.35p org ver	2.50	30
L24	A6	2p purple	4.50	30
L25	A5	10p dk grnsh bl ('49)	5.25	55
		Nos. L12-L25, LE1 (15)	16.19	2.06

Nos. L18-L25, LE1 exist imperf. Price, set $250.

SEMI-POSTAL STAMPS.

For the International City of Tangier.

Types of Semi-Postal Stamps of Spain,
1926, **CORREO ESPAÑOL**
Overprinted **TANGER**

1926			*Perf. 12½, 13.*	
LB1	SP1	1c orange	1.75	1.50
LB2	SP2	2c rose	1.75	1.50
LB3	SP3	5c blk brn	1.00	85
LB4	SP4	10c dk grn	1.00	85
LB5	SP1	15c dk vio	50	50
LB6	SP2	20c vio brn	50	50
LB7	SP5	25c dp car	50	50
LB8	SP1	30c ol grn	50	50
LB9	SP3	40c ultra	20	20
LB10	SP2	50c red brn	20	20
LB11	SP4	1p vermilion	20	20
LB12	SP3	4p bister	35	35
LB13	SP5	10p lt vio	1.00	85
		Nos. LB1-LB13, LEB1 (14)	10.25	9.33

AIR POST STAMPS.

Overprints of 1939

The following overprints on stamps of Spain exist in black or in red:
"Correo Aereo Tanger" in two lines on Nos. 539-541, 596 (gray paper), 600, C72B.
"Via Aerea Tanger" in three lines on Nos. 539-540, 592-597 (gray paper), 599, 601, E14.
"Correo Aereo Tanger" in three lines on four consular stamps.
"Correo Espanol Tanger" in three lines on No. C72B.
"Tanger" on No. C72B.

Plane over Shore
AP1

Twin-Engine Plane
AP2

Passenger Plane in Flight
AP3

Perf. 11x11½, 11½.

1949-50		Engraved	Unwmkd.	
LC1	AP1	20c vio brn ('50)	40	6
LC2	AP2	25c brt red	40	6
LC3	AP3	35c dl grn	40	6
LC4	AP1	1p vio ('50)	1.25	5
LC5	AP2	2p dp bl	2.25	35
LC6	AP3	10p brn vio	4.00	1.25
		Nos. LC1-LC6 (6)	8.70	1.83

Nos. LC1, LC4-LC6 exist imperf. Price $50 each.

SPECIAL DELIVERY STAMP.

Arab Postrider
SD1
Engraved.

1949		*Perf. 13.*	Unwmkd.	
LE1	SD1	25c red	90	30

SEMI-POSTAL SPECIAL DELIVERY STAMP

For the International City of Tangier
Type of Semi-Postal Special
Delivery Stamp of Spain,
1926, **CORREO ESPAÑOL**
Overprinted **TANGER**

1926		*Perf. 12½, 13*	Unwmkd.	
LEB1	SPSD1	20c ultra & blk	1.00	85

TETUAN

Stamps of Spanish
Offices in Morocco,
1903-09,
Handstamped
in Black,
Blue or Violet

1908		*Imperf.*	Unwmkd.	
1	A21	¼c bl grn	16.00	10.00
		Perf. 14.		
2	A35	2c bis brn	140.00	75.00
3	A35	5c green	135.00	42.50
4	A35	10c rose red	135.00	42.50
5	A35	20c grnsh blk	325.00	140.00
6	A35	25c blue	115.00	40.00
		Nos. 1-6 (6)	866.00	350.00

Same Handstamp
On Stamps of Spain, 1877 and 1900-05,
in Black, Blue or Violet.

1908			*Imperf.*	
7	A21	¼c dp grn	11.00	4.50

SPANISH MOROCCO—SPANISH SAHARA

		Perf. 14.		
8	A35	2c bis brn	42.50	15.00
9	A35	5c dk grn	52.50	25.00
10	A35	10c rose red	55.00	27.50
11	A35	15c purple	55.00	27.50
12	A35	20c grnsh blk	185.00	140.00
13	A35	25c blue	85.00	45.00
14	A35	30c bl grn	200.00	80.00
15	A35	40c ol bis	265.00	140.00
		Nos. 7-15 (9)	951.00	504.50

Counterfeits of this overprint are plentiful.

SPANISH SAHARA
(Spanish Western Sahara)

LOCATION—Northwest Africa, bordering on the Atlantic.
GOVT.—Former Spanish possession.
AREA—102,703 sq. mi.
POP.—76,425 (1970).
CAPITAL—Aaiún.

Spanish Sahara is a subdivision of Spanish West Africa. It includes the colony of Rio de Oro and the territory of Saguiet el Hamra. Spanish Sahara was formerly known as **Spanish Western Sahara**, which superseded the older title of Rio de Oro.

In 1976, Spanish Sahara was divided between Morocco and Mauritania.

100 Centimos = 1 Peseta

Tuareg and Camel
A1

1924   Perf. 13.   Unwmkd.
Control Number on Back

1	A1	5c bl grn	1.75	40
2	A1	10c gray grn	1.75	40
3	A1	15c turq bl	1.75	40
4	A1	20c dk vio	1.75	50
5	A1	25c red	1.75	50
6	A1	30c red brn	1.75	50
7	A1	40c dk bl	1.75	50
8	A1	50c orange	1.75	50
9	A1	60c violet	1.75	50
10	A1	1p rose	7.50	2.00
11	A1	4p chocolate	37.50	11.50
12	A1	10p claret	75.00	30.00
		Nos. 1-12 (12)	135.75	47.70

Nos. 1-12 were for use in La Aguera and Rio de Oro.

A set of 10, similar to Nos. 3-12, exists with perf. 10 and no control number except on 50c.

Seville-Barcelona Issue of Spain, 1929
Overprinted SAHARA in Blue or Red.

1929   Perf. 11.

13	A52	5c rose lake	10	10
14	A53	10c grn (R)	10	10
15	A50	15c Prus bl (R)	10	10
16	A51	20c pur (R)	10	10
17	A50	25c brt rose	10	10
18	A52	30c blk brn	10	10
19	A53	40c dk bl (R)	20	20
20	A51	50c dp org	20	20
21	A52	1p bl blk (R)	1.00	75
22	A53	4p dp rose	6.00	4.75
23	A53	10p brown	12.00	8.00
		Nos. 13-23 (11)	20.00	14.50

Stamps of 1924 Overprinted in Red or Blue

1931   Perf. 13.

24	A1	5c bl grn (R)	50	30
25	A1	10c gray grn (R)	50	30
26	A1	15c turq bl (R)	50	30
27	A1	20c dk vio (R)	50	30
28	A1	25c red	60	30
29	A1	30c red brn	60	30
30	A1	40c dk bl (R)	2.75	50
31	A1	50c orange	2.75	1.00
32	A1	60c violet	2.75	1.00
33	A1	1p rose	2.75	1.00
34	A1	4p chocolate	27.50	9.50
35	A1	10p claret	50.00	16.00
		Nos. 24-35 (12)	91.70	30.80

The stamps of the 1931 issue exist with the overprint reading upward, downward or horizontally.

Stamps of Spain, 1936-40, Overprinted in Carmine or Blue

SAHARA ESPAÑOL

1941–46   Imperf.   Unwmkd.

36	A159	1c green	1.75	1.25
		Perf. 10 to 11		
37	A160	2c org brn (Bl)	1.75	1.25
38	A161	5c gray brn	50	50
39	A161	10c dk car (Bl)	1.75	1.25
40	A161	15c dk grn	50	50
41	A166	20c brt vio	50	50
42	A166	25c dp cl	1.00	60
43	A166	30c lt bl	1.00	90
44	A166	40c Prus grn	50	50
45	A166	50c indigo	4.75	90
46	A166	70c blue	3.25	1.50
47	A166	1p gray blk	14.00	2.00
48	A166	2p dl brn	75.00	42.50
49	A166	4p dl rose (Bl)	160.00	85.00
50	A166	10p lt brn	450.00	150.00
		Nos. 36-50 (15)	716.25	289.15

Dorcas Gazelles   **Caravan**
A2   A3

Camel Troops
A4

1943   Perf. 12½   Unwmkd.

51	A2	1c brn & lil rose	6	6
52	A3	2c yel grn & sl bl	6	6
53	A4	5c mag & vio	6	6
54	A2	15c sl grn & grn	10	10
55	A3	20c vio & red brn	10	10
56	A2	40c rose vio & vio	15	15
57	A3	45c brn vio & red	25	22
58	A4	75c ind & bl	25	25
59	A2	1p red & brn	1.00	1.00
60	A3	3p bl vio & sl grn	2.00	2.00
61	A4	10p blk brn & blk	25.00	22.50
		Nos. 51-61, E1 (12)	30.03	27.53

Nos. 51-61, E1 exist imperf. Price for set, $100.

Gen. Franco and Desert Scene
A5

1951   Photo.   Perf. 12½x13

62	A5	50c dp org	15	6
63	A5	1p chocolate	50	50
64	A5	5p bl grn	52.50	18.00

Visit of Gen. Francisco Franco, 1950.

Allegorical Figure   **Woman**
and Globe   **Musician**
A6   A7

1953, Mar. 2   Perf. 13x12½

65	A6	5c red org	6	6
66	A6	35c dk sl grn	6	6
67	A6	60c brown	25	10

Issued to commemorate the 75th anniversary of the founding of the Royal Geographical Society.

1953, June 1
Design: 60c, Man musician.

68	A7	15c ol gray	6	6
69	A7	60c brown	20	6

See also Nos. B25-B26.

Orange Scorpionfish—A8
Fish: 60c, Banded sargo.

1953, Nov. 23   Perf. 12½x13

70	A8	15c dk ol grn	15	10
71	A8	60c orange	20	10

Colonial Stamp Day. See Nos. B27-B28.

Hurdlers
A9

Runner—A10

Perf. 12½x13, 13x12½
1954, June 1

72	A9	15c gray grn	15	6
73	A10	60c brown	15	6

See also Nos. B29-B30.

Atlantic Flyingfish—A11
Fish: 60c, Gilthead.

1954, Nov. 23   Perf. 12½x13

74	A11	15c dk ol grn	10	6
75	A11	60c red brn	25	8

Colonial Stamp Day. See Nos. B31-B32.

Emilio Bonelli
A12

1955, June 1   Photo.   Unwmkd.

| 76 | A12 | 50c ol gray | 15 | 6 |

Issued to commemorate the centenary of the birth of Emilio Bonelli, explorer. See also Nos. B33-B34.

Scimitar-horned Oryx
A13

1955, Nov. 23

| 77 | A13 | 70c green | 25 | 6 |

Colonial Stamp Day. See Nos. B35-B36.

Antirrhinum Romosissimum
A14

Design: 50c, Sesivium portulacastrum.

1956, June 1   Perf. 13x12½

78	A14	20c bluish grn	10	6
79	A14	50c brown	15	6

See also Nos. B37-B38.

Arms of Aaiun and Camel Rider
A15

1956, Nov. 23   Perf. 12½x13

| 80 | A15 | 70c ol grn & sep | 15 | 6 |

Colonial Stamp Day. See Nos. B39-B40.

Dromedaries   **Golden Eagle**
A16   A17

Designs: 15c, 80c, Ostrich. 50c, 1.80p, Mountain gazelle.

1957, Apr. 10   Perf. 13x12½

81	A16	5c purple	6	5
82	A16	15c bister	6	5

SPANISH SAHARA

83	A16	50c dk ol	6	5
84	A16	70c yel grn	1.40	15
85	A16	80c bl grn	1.40	15
86	A16	1.80p lil rose	1.40	30
		Nos. 81-86 (6)	4.38	75

1957, June 1 Photo. Unwmkd.

87	A17	70c dk grn	25	10

See also Nos. B41-B42.

Striped Hyena
A18

Design: 70c, Striped Hyena (horizontal).
Perf. 13x12½, 12½x13

1957, Nov. 23

88	A18	20c sl grn	6	5
89	A18	70c yelsh grn	20	8

Stamp Day. See Nos. B43-B44.

Don Quixote and the Lion
A19

Cervantes   Gray Heron
A20   A21

Perf. 12½x13, 13x12½

1958, June 1

90	A19	20c bis brn & grn	6	5
91	A20	70c dk grn & yel grn	15	6

See also Nos. B48-B49.

Cervantes Type of 1958.
Designs: 20c, Actor as "Peribanez," by Lope de Vega. 70c, Lope de Vega.

1959, June Photo. Perf. 13x12½

92	A20	20c lt grn & brn	10	6
93	A20	70c yel grn & sl grn	10	5

Issued to promote child welfare. See also Nos. B53-B54.

Perf. 13x12½

1959, Oct. 15 Unwmkd.
Birds: 50c, 1.50p, 5p, Sparrowhawk. 75c, 2p, 10p, Sea gull. 1p, 3p, As 25c.

94	A21	25c dl vio	7	5
95	A21	50c dk ol	7	5
96	A21	75c dk brn	7	5
97	A21	1p red org	7	5
98	A21	1.50p brt grn	7	5
99	A21	2p brt red lil	1.40	45
100	A21	3p blue	1.40	6
101	A21	5p red brn	2.50	15
102	A21	10p ol grn	11.50	5.25
		Nos. 94-102 (9)	17.15	5.76

Scene from "The Pilferer Don Pablos" by Quevedo
A22

Francisco Gomez de Quevedo
A23

1960, June Perf. 13x12½, 12½x13

103	A22	35c sl grn	10	5
104	A23	80c Prus grn	10	5

Issued to honor Francisco Gomez de Quevedo, writer. See also Nos. B58-B59.

Houbara Bustard   Map of
A24   Spanish Sahara
                 A25

Gen. Franco and Camel Rider
A26

Design: 50c, 1p, 2p, 5p, Doves.

1961, Apr. 18 Photo. Perf. 13x12½

105	A24	25c bl vio	6	5
106	A24	50c ol gray	6	5
107	A24	75c brn vio	6	5
108	A24	1p org ver	6	5
109	A24	1.50p bl grn	6	6
110	A24	2p magenta	1.25	6
111	A24	3p dk bl	1.40	6
112	A24	5p red brn	1.75	50
113	A24	10p olive	4.00	1.50
		Nos. 105-113 (9)	8.70	2.38

Perf. 13x12½, 12½x13

1961, Oct. 1 Unwmkd.
Design: 70c, Chapel of Aaiun.

114	A25	25c gray vio	10	5
115	A26	50c ol brn	10	5
116	A25	70c brt grn	10	5
117	A26	1p red org	12	5

Issued to commemorate the 25th anniversary of the nomination of Gen. Francisco Franco as Chief of State.

The only foreign revenue stamps listed in this Catalogue are those authorized for prepayment of postage.

Neurada   Clock
Procumbres Fish
A27   A28

Designs: 50c, 1.50p, 10p, Anabasis articulata, flower. 70c, 2p, Euphorbia resinifera, cactus.

1962, Feb. 26 Perf. 13x12½

118	A27	25c blk vio	5	5
119	A27	50c dk brn	5	5
120	A27	70c brt grn	5	5
121	A27	1p org ver	6	6
122	A27	1.50p bl grn	60	5
123	A27	2p red lil	2.00	6
124	A27	3p slate	3.25	45
125	A27	10p olive	7.00	1.50
		Nos. 118-125 (8)	13.06	2.27

Perf. 13x12½, 12½x13

1962, July 10 Photogravure
Design: 50c, Avia fish (horiz.).

126	A28	25c vio blk	5	5
127	A28	50c dk grn	6	5
128	A28	1p org brn	18	6

Goats
A29

Design: 35c, Sheep.

1962, Nov. 23 Perf. 12½x13

129	A29	15c yel grn	5	5
130	A29	35c magenta	5	5
131	A29	1p org brn	20	5

Issued for Stamp Day.

Seville Cathedral Tower
A30

1963, Jan. 29 Perf. 13x12½

132	A30	50c olive	10	5
133	A30	1p brn org	12	5

Issued to help Seville flood victims.

Camel   Hands Releasing
Riders   Dove and Arms
A31   A32

Design: 50c, Tuareg and camel.

1963, June 1 Unwmkd.

134	A31	25c dp vio	10	7
135	A31	50c gray	10	7
136	A31	1p org red	15	7

Issued for child welfare.

1963, July 12

137	A32	50c Prus grn	10	5
138	A32	1p org brn	10	5

Issued for Barcelona flood relief.

John Dory
A33

Fish: 50c, Plain bonito (vert.).
Perf. 12½x13, 13x12½

1964, Mar. 6

139	A33	25c purple	5	5
140	A33	50c ol grn	5	5
141	A33	1p brn red	15	5

Issued for Stamp Day 1963.

Moth and Flowers
A34

Design: 50c, Two moths (vert.).
Perf. 12½x13, 13x12½

1964, June 1 Unwmkd.

142	A34	25c dl vio	10	5
143	A34	50c brn blk	10	5
144	A34	1p org red	15	5

Issued for child welfare.

Camel Rider and
Microphone   Squirrel
A35   A36

Designs: 50c, 1.50p, 3p, Boy with flute and camels. 70c, 2p, 10p, Woman with drum.

1964, Sept. Photo. Perf. 13x12½

145	A35	25c dl pur	5	5
146	A35	50c olive	5	5
147	A35	70c green	5	5
148	A35	1p dl red brn	6	6
149	A35	1.50p brt grn	10	6
150	A35	2p Prus grn	25	15
151	A35	3p dk bl	40	15
152	A35	10p car lake	2.25	1.00
		Nos. 145-152 (8)	3.21	1.57

1964, Nov. 23 Unwmkd.
Design: 1p, Squirrel's head (horiz.).

153	A36	50c ol gray	10	5
154	A36	1p brn car	10	5
155	A36	1.50p green	15	6

Issued for Stamp Day, 1964.

SPANISH SAHARA

Tuareg Girl
A37

Wellhead and Camel Rider—A38

Design: 1p, Physician examining patient (horiz.).

Perf. 13x12½, 12½x13

1965, Feb. 22 Photogravure
156	A37	50c blk brn	10	5
157	A38	1p dk red	10	5
158	A38	1.50p dp bl	15	6

Issued to commemorate 25 years of peace.

Anthia Sexmaculata
A39

Design: 1p, 3p, Blepharopsis mendica (vert.).

Perf. 12½x13, 13x12½

1965, June 1 Photo. Unwmkd.
159	A39	50c sl bl	5	5
160	A39	1p bl grn	5	5
161	A39	1.50p brown	6	6
162	A39	3p dk bl	1.75	90

Issued for child welfare.

Basketball
A40

Arms and Camels
A41

1965, Nov. 23 **Perf. 13x12½**
163	A40	50c rose cl	10	5
164	A41	1p dp mag	10	5
165	A40	1.50p sl bl	15	6

Issued for Stamp Day 1965.

Ship "Rio de Oro"
A42

Design: 1.50p, S.S. Fuerte Ventura.

1966, June 1 Photo. **Perf. 12½x13**
166	A42	50c olive	10	5
167	A42	1p dk red brn	10	6
168	A42	1.50p bl grn	15	6

Issued for child welfare.

Ocean Sunfish
A43

A44

Designs: 10c, 1.50p, Bigeye tuna (horiz.).

1966, Nov. 23 Photo. **Perf. 13**
169	A43	10c bl gray & cit	5	5
170	A43	40c sl & pink	5	5
171	A43	1.50p brn & ol	6	6
172	A43	4p rose vio & gray	25	15

Issued for Stamp Day 1966.

1967, June 1 Photo. **Perf. 13**

Designs: 40c, 4p, Flower and leaves.
173	A44	10c blk, ocher & gray grn	5	5
174	A44	40c emer & lil	5	5
175	A44	1.50p dk grn & yel grn	6	6
176	A44	4p brt bl & org	25	15

Issued for child welfare.

Aaiun Harbor
A45

Design: 4p, Villa Cisneros Harbor.

1967, Sept. 28 Photo. **Perf. 12½x13**
| 177 | A45 | 1.50p brt bl & red brn | 6 | 6 |
| 178 | A45 | 4p brt bl & bis brn | 20 | 10 |

Modernization of harbor installations.

Ruddy Sheldrake
A46

Designs: 1.50p, Flamingo (vert.). 3.50p, Rufous bush robin.

1967, Nov. 23 Photo. **Perf. 13**
179	A46	1p bis brn & grn	6	6
180	A46	1.50p brt rose & gray	6	6
181	A46	3.50p brn red & sep	30	20

Issued for Stamp Day 1967.

Scorpio
A47

Mailman
A48

Zodiac Issue

Signs of the Zodiac: 1.50p, Aries. 2.50p, Virgo.

1968, Apr. 25 Photo. **Perf. 13**
182	A47	1p brt mag, lt yel	6	6
183	A47	1.50p brn, pink	6	6
184	A47	2.50p dk vio, yel	30	20

Issued for child welfare.

1968, Nov. Photo. **Perf. 13x12½**

Designs: 1p, Post horn, pigeon, letter and Spain No. 1. 1.50p, Letter, canceller and various stamps of Spain and Ifni.
185	A48	1p dp lil rose & dk bl	6	6
186	A48	1.50p grn & sl grn	6	6
187	A48	2.50p dp org & dk bl	25	15

Issued for Stamp Day.

Dorcas Gazelle
A49

Designs: 1.50p, Doe and fawn. 2.50p, Gazelle and camel. 6p, Leaping gazelle.

1969, June 1 Photo. **Perf. 13**
188	A49	1p gldn brn & blk	5	5
189	A49	1.50p gldn brn & blk	6	6
190	A49	2.50p gldn brn & blk	15	6
191	A49	6p gldn brn & blk	40	25

Child welfare. See Nos. 196–199.

Woman Playing Drum
A50

Designs: 1.50p, Man with flute. 2p, Drum and camel rider (horiz.). 25p, Flute (horiz.).

1969, Nov. 23 Photo. **Perf. 13**
192	A50	50c brn red & lt ol	5	5
193	A50	1.50p dk bl grn & grnsh gray	6	6
194	A50	2p ind & bis brn	6	6
195	A50	25p brn & lt bl grn	1.50	45

Issued for Stamp Day, 1969.

Animal Type of 1969

Fennec: 50c, Sitting. 2p, Running. 2.50p, Head. 6p, Vixen and pups.

1970, June 1 Photo. **Perf. 13**
196	A49	50c dp bis & blk	5	5
197	A49	2p org brn & blk	10	6
198	A49	2.50p dp bis & blk	20	6
199	A49	6p dp bis & blk	35	25

Issued for child welfare.

Grammodes Boisdeffrei
A51

Designs: 1p, like 50c. 2p, 5p, Danaus chrysippus. 8p, Celerio euphorbiae.

1970, Nov. 23 Photo. **Perf. 12½**
200	A51	50c red & multi	5	5
201	A51	1p car & multi	6	6
202	A51	2p grn & multi	6	6
203	A51	5p Prus bl & multi	40	15
204	A51	8p dk bl & multi	55	30
	Nos. 200-204 (5)	1.12	62

Issued for Stamp Day.

Gazelle, Arms of Aaiun—A52

Smara Mosque
A53

Designs: 2p, Inn (horiz.). 5p, Assembly building, Aaiun (horiz.).

Perf. 12½x13, 13x12½

1971, June 1 Photogravure
205	A52	1p multi	6	5
206	A53	2p gray grn & ol	6	6
207	A53	5p lt bl & lt red brn	20	10
208	A53	25p lt bl & grnsh gray	1.40	30

Issued for child welfare.

Trumpeter Bullfinch
A54

Birds: 2p, as 1.50p. 5p, Cream-colored courser. 10p, Lanner (falcon).

1971, Nov. 23 Photo. **Perf. 12½**
209	A54	1.50p blk & multi	6	6
210	A54	2p bl & multi	6	6
211	A54	5p grn & multi	25	10
212	A54	24p blk & multi	1.40	30

Stamp Day.

Saharan Woman
A55

Tuareg Woman
A56

Designs: 1.50p, 2p, Saharan man. 5p, as 1p. 8p, 10p, Man's head. 12p, Woman. 15p, Soldier. 24p, Dancer.

1972, Feb. 18 Photo. **Perf. 13**
213	A55	1p bl, pink & brn	5	5
214	A55	1.50p brn, lil & blk	6	6
215	A55	2p grn, buff & sep	6	6
216	A55	5p grn, pur & vio brn	15	8
217	A55	8p blk, lt grn & vio	35	15
218	A55	10p blk, gray & Prus bl	55	15
219	A55	12p multi	65	30
220	A55	15p multi	80	40
221	A55	24p multi	1.75	60
	Nos. 213-221 (9)	4.42	1.85

SPANISH SAHARA

1972, June 1 Photo. Perf. 13
Design: 12p, Tuareg man.
| 222 | A56 | 8p multi | 40 | 10 |
| 223 | A56 | 12p multi | 60 | 25 |

Child welfare.

Mother and Child
A57

1972, Nov. 23 Photo. Perf. 13
Multicolored
| 224 | A57 | 4p shown | 30 | 6 |
| 225 | A57 | 15p Saharan man| 70 | 30 |

Stamp Day. See No. 229.

Dunes
A58

Design: 7p, Old Market and Gate, Aaiun.

1973, June 1 Photo. Perf. 13
| 226 | A58 | 2p multi | 6 | 6 |
| 227 | A58 | 7p multi | 30 | 15 |

Child welfare.

Type of 1972 and

View of Villa Cisneros
A59

Design: 7p, Tuareg man.

1973, Nov. 23 Photo. Perf. 13
| 228 | A59 | 2p multi | 6 | 6 |
| 229 | A57 | 7p multi | 30 | 15 |

Stamp Day.

UPU Monument, Bern
A60

Gate, Smara Mosque
A61

1974, May Photogravure Perf. 13
| 230 | A60 | 15p multi | 65 | 20 |

Centenary of the Universal Postal Union.

1974, May
Design: 2p, Court and Minaret, Villa Cisneros Mosque.
| 231 | A61 | 1p multi | 10 | 5 |
| 232 | A61 | 2p multi | 10 | 5 |

Child welfare.

Desert Eagle Owl
A62

1974, Nov. Photogravure Perf. 13
Multicolored
| 233 | A62 | 2p shown | 10 | 5 |
| 234 | A62 | 5p Lappet-faced vulture| 20 | 15 |

Stamp Day.

España 75 Emblem, Spain No. 1084
A63

1975, Apr. 4 Photo. Perf. 13
| 235 | A63 | 8p ol, blk & bl | 25 | 10 |

España 75 International Philatelic Exhibition, Madrid, Apr. 4–13.

Children
A64

Design: 3p, Children's village.

1975 Photogravure Perf. 13
| 236 | A54 | 1.50p multi | 10 | 5 |
| 237 | A54 | 3p multi | 10 | 6 |

Child welfare.

Old Man
A65

1975, Nov. 7 Photo. Perf. 13
| 238 | A65 | 3p blk, lt grn & mar | 20 | 6 |

Use the Yellow Pages to fulfill your philatelic requirements.

SPANISH SAHARA

SEMI-POSTAL STAMPS.
Red Cross Issue.
Types of Semi-Postal Stamps of Spain, 1926, Overprinted

SAHARA ESPAÑOL

		1926 Perf. 12½, 13 Unwmkd.		
B1	SP1	5c blk brn	2.50	1.75
B2	SP4	10c dk brn	2.50	1.75
B3	SP1	15c dk vio	1.00	80
B4	SP4	20c vio brn	1.00	80
B5	SP5	25c dp car	1.00	80
B6	SP1	30c ol grn	1.00	80
B7	SP3	40c ultra	10	10
B8	SP2	50c red brn	10	10
B9	SP5	60c myr grn	10	10
B10	SP4	1p vermilion	10	10
B11	SP3	4p bister	80	70
B12	SP5	10p lt vio	1.75	1.25
		Nos. B1-B12 (12)	11.95	9.05

Shepherd and Lamb — SP1
Dromedary and Calf — SP2

Perf. 13x12½

		1950, Oct. 20 Photo. Unwmkd.		
B13	SP1	50c +10c brn	35	25
B14	SP1	1p +25c rose brn	16.00	7.25
B15	SP1	6.50p +1.65p dk gray grn	9.00	2.50

The surtax was for child welfare.

1951, Nov. 23

B16	SP2	5c +5c brn	6	6
B17	SP2	10c +5 red org	6	6
B18	SP2	60c +15c ol grn	40	15

Colonial Stamp Day, Nov. 23.

Child and Protector — SP3
Ostrich — SP4

1952, June 1

B19	SP3	5c +5c brn	15	6
B20	SP3	50c +10c gray	15	20
B21	SP3	2p +30c bl	2.50	1.40

The surtax was for child welfare.

1952, Nov. 23 Perf. 12½

B22	SP4	5c +5c brn	10	10
B23	SP4	10c +5c brn car	10	10
B24	SP4	60c +15c dk grn	40	20

Colonial Stamp Day, Nov. 23.

Musician Type of Regular Issue.
Designs: 5c+5c, Woman musician. 10c+5c, Man musician.

1953, June 1 Perf. 13x12½

B25	A7	5c +5c fawn	6	6
B26	A7	10c +5c dp red vio	6	6

The surtax was for child welfare.

Fish Type of Regular Issue.
Fish: 5c+5c, Orange scorpionfish. 10c+5c, Banded sargo.

1953, Nov. 23 Perf. 12½x13

B27	A8	5c +5c vio	10	10
B28	A8	10c +5c grn	10	10

Colonial Stamp Day, Nov. 23.

Athlete Types of Regular Issue.
Perf. 12½x13, 13x12½

1954, June 1

B29	A9	5c +5c brn org	10	6
B30	A10	10c +5c pur	10	6

The surtax was to help the native population.

Fish Type of Regular Issue.
Designs: 5c+5c, Atlantic flyingfish. 10c+5c, Gilthead.

1954, Nov. 23 Perf. 12½x13

B31	A11	5c +5c ver	6	6
B32	A11	10c +5c plum	6	6

Issued to publicize Colonial Stamp Day.

Type of Regular Issue and

Emilio Bonelli — SP5

Design: 10c+5c, Bonelli's head at right.

1955, June 1 Photo. Unwmkd.

B33	A12	10c +5c red vio	6	6
B34	SP5	25c +10c vio	6	6

Issued to commemorate the centenary of the birth of Emilio Bonelli, explorer. The surtax was for child welfare.

Antelope Type of Regular Issue.
Design: 15c+5c, Head of scimitar-horned oryx.

1955, Nov. 23 Perf. 12½x13

B35	A13	5c +5c org brn	6	6
B36	A13	15c +5c ol bis	6	6

Issued to publicize Colonial Stamp Day.

Flower Type of Regular Issue.
Design: 15c+5c, Sesivium portulacastrum.

1956, June 1 Perf. 12½x13

B37	A14	5c +5c grnsh gray	10	6
B38	A14	15c +5c bis	10	6

The tax was for the children.

Aaiun Type of Regular Issue and

Arms of Villa Cisneros and Man — SP6

Design: 5c+5c, Arms of Aaiun and Camel Rider.

Perf. 12½x13, 13x12½

1956, Nov. 23 Unwmkd.

B39	A15	5c +5c pur & blk	10	6
B40	SP6	15c +5c bis & grn	10	6

Stamp Day.

Eagle Type of Regular Issue.
Design: 15c+5c, Lesser spotted eagle in flight.

1957, June 1

B41	A17	5c +5c red brn	6	6
B42	A17	15c +5c gldn brn	6	6

The surtax was for child welfare.

Hyena Type of Regular Issue.
Designs: 10c + 5c, Striped Hyena (vertical). 15 + 5c, Striped Hyena (horizontal).

Perf. 13x12½, 12½x13

1957, Nov. 23

B43	A18	10c +5c red vio	6	6
B44	A18	15c +5c bis	6	6

Stamp Day, 1957.

Stork and Arms of Valencia and Aaiun — SP7

1958, Mar. 6 Photo. Perf. 12½x13

B45	SP7	10c +5c org brn	6	6
B46	SP7	15c +10c bis	6	6
B47	SP7	50c +10c brn ol	10	10

The surtax was to aid the victims of the Valencia flood, Oct., 1957.

Cervantes Type of Regular Issue.
Designs: 10c+5c, Cervantes. 15c+5c, Don Quixote and Sancho Panza.

1958, June 1 Perf. 13x12½

B48	A20	10c +5c hn brn & chnt brn	5	
B49	A20	15c +5c dp org & sl grn	5	

The surtax was for child welfare.

Hoopoe Lark — SP8
Mailman — SP9

Designs: 25c+10c, Hoopoe larks (horiz.). 50c+10c, Bird.

Perf. 13x12½, 12½x13

1958, Nov. 23 Photo. Unwmkd.

B50	SP8	10c +5c brn red	10	6
B51	SP8	25c +10c brt pur	10	6
B52	SP8	50c +10c ol	12	6

Issued for the Day of the Stamp, 1958.

Cervantes Type of Regular Issue, 1958.
Designs: 10c+5c, Lope de Vega. 15c+5c, Actress from "Star of Seville," by Lope de Vega.

1959, June Perf. 13x12½

B53	A20	10c +5c org brn & ol gray	10	5
B54	A20	15c +5c dp ocher & choc	10	5

The surtax was for child welfare.

1959, Nov. 23 Photogravure

Designs: 20c+5c, Mailman. 50c+20c, Mailman on camel.

B55	SP9	10c +5c rose & brn	7	7
B56	SP9	20c +5c lt grn & brn	7	7
B57	SP9	50c +20c ol gray & sl	14	6

Issued for the Day of the Stamp, 1959.

Quevedo Type of Regular Issue.
Designs: 10c+5c, Francisco Gomez de Quevedo. 15c+5c, Winged wheel and hourglass, symbolic of "Hora de Todas."

Perf. 12½x13, 13x12½

1960, June 1

B58	A23	10c +5c mar	10	5
B59	A23	15c +5c bis brn	10	5

The surtax was for child welfare.

Leopard — SP10
Alonso Fernandez de Lugo — SP11

Designs: 20c+5c, Desert fox. 30c+10c, Eagle and leopard. 50c+20c, Sand fox.

1960, Nov. 23 Photo. Perf. 13x12½

B60	SP10	10c +5c rose lil	5	5
B61	SP10	20c +5c dk sl grn	5	5
B62	SP10	30c +10c choc	6	5
B63	SP10	50c +20c ol gray	20	5

Issued for Stamp Day, 1960.

Animal Type of 1961 inscribed:
"Pro-Infancia 1961"

Designs: Various Mountain Gazelles.

1961, June 21 Unwmkd.

B64	SP10	10c +5c rose brn	5	5
B65	SP10	25c +10c gray vio	5	5
B66	SP10	80c +20c dk grn	15	5

The surtax was for child welfare.

1961, Nov. 23 Perf. 13x12½

Design: 25c+10c, 1p+10c, Diego de Herrera.

B67	SP11	10c +5c org red	10	6
B68	SP11	25c +10c dk pur	10	6
B69	SP11	30c +10c dk red brn	10	6
B70	SP11	1p +10c red org	15	6

Issued for Stamp Day, 1961.

AIR POST STAMPS.

In 1942, seven air post stamps of Spain, Nos. C100 to C108, were overprinted "SAHARA ESPANOL", but satisfactory information regarding its status is not available.

Ostriches — AP1
Desert Scene — AP2

Lithographed.

1943 Perf. 12½ Unwmkd.

C8	AP1	5c cer & vio brn	10	10
C9	AP2	25c yel grn & ol grn	10	10
C10	AP1	50c ind & turq grn	15	15
C11	AP2	1p pur & grnsh bl	15	15
C12	AP1	1.40p gray grn & bl	15	15
C13	AP2	2p mag & org brn	1.25	1.25
C14	AP1	5p brn & pur	1.75	1.50
C15	AP2	6p brt bl & gray grn	25.00	22.50
		Nos. C8-C15 (8)	28.65	25.95

Nos. C8-C15 exist imperf. Price of set $125.

SPANISH SAHARA—SPANISH WEST AFRICA—SURINAM   611

Diego Garcia de Herrera
AP3

1950, Nov. 23   Photogravure

C16 AP3 5p rose vio   4.00   1.25

Issued to publicize Stamp Day, November 23, 1950.

Woman Holding Dove—AP4

1951, Apr. 22 Engr. Perf. 10

C17 AP4 5p dp grn   30.00   6.00

Issued to commemorate the 500th anniversary of the birth of Queen Isabella I.

Helmet and Trappings
AP5

Plane and Camel Rider
AP6

1952, July 18 Photo. Perf. 13x12½

C18 AP5 5p brown   37.50 6.50

Issued to commemorate the 500th anniversary of the birth of Ferdinand the Catholic, of Spain.

1961, May 16   Unwmkd.

C19 AP6 25p gray brn   4.25   1.25

SPECIAL DELIVERY STAMPS
Type A4 Inscribed "URGENTE".

1943 Perf. 12½   Unwmkd.

E1 A4 25c dk grn & car   1.00   1.00

Messenger on Motorcycle—SD1
Photogravure

1971, Sept. 6 Perf. 13   Unwmkd.

E2 SD1 10p brt rose & ol   60   35

SPANISH WEST AFRICA
(spăn'ĭsh wĕst' ăf'rĭ-kà)

LOCATION—Northwest Africa bordering on the Atlantic Ocean.
GOVT.—Spanish administration.
AREA—117,000 sq. mi.
POP.—95,000 (1950).
CAPITAL—Sidi Ifni.

Spanish West Africa was the major political division of Spanish areas in northwest Africa. It included Spanish Sahara (Rio de Oro and Saguiet el Hamra), Ifni, and, for administrative purposes, Southern Morocco. Separate stamp issues have been used for Rio de Oro, Ifni and La Aguera.

Native
A1

Perf. 13x12½

1949, Oct. Litho.   Unwmkd.

1 A1 4p dk gray grn   3.00   1.25

Issued to commemorate the 75th anniversary of the formation of the Universal Postal Union.

Nomad Camp
A2

Designs: 5c, 30c, 75c, 2p, Tinzgarrentz Oasis. 10c, 40c, 90c, 5p, Desert well. 15c, 45c, 1p, Caravan.

1950, June 5   Perf. 12½x13

2	A2	2c brown	5	5
3	A2	5c rose vio	5	5
4	A2	10c Prus bl	5	5
5	A2	15c dp ol gray	20	10
6	A2	25c red brn	20	6
7	A2	30c brt yel	10	6
8	A2	40c ol gray	10	6
9	A2	45c rose lake	10	6
10	A2	50c brn org	10	6
11	A2	75c ultra	20	15
12	A2	90c dl bl grn	6	6
13	A2	1p gray	6	6
14	A2	1.35p violet	90	50
15	A2	2p sepia	1.75	1.00
16	A2	5p lil rose	13.00	2.25
17	A2	10p lt brn	27.50	12.00
		Nos. 2-17 (16)	44.42	16.57

AIR POST STAMPS.

Isabella the Catholic, Queen of Castile
AP1

Perf. 13x12½

1949, Nov. 23 Photo. Unwmkd.

C1 AP1 5p yel brn   2.50   1.25

Stamp Day, Nov. 23, 1949.

Desert Camp
AP2

Designs: Various Desert Scenes.

1951, Mar. 1 Litho. Perf. 12½x13

C2	AP2	25c ocher	25	6
C3	AP2	50c lil rose	15	6
C4	AP2	1p green	30	6
C5	AP2	2p brt bl	80	6
C6	AP2	3.25p rose lil	1.40	50
C7	AP2	5p gray brn	12.50	1.50
C8	AP2	10p rose red	27.50	11.00
		Nos. C2-C8 (7)	42.90	13.24

SPECIAL DELIVERY STAMP.

Tilimenzo Pass and Franco
SD1

Perf. 12½x13

1951, Mar. 1 Litho. Unwmkd.

E1 SD1 25c rose car   50   30

SURINAM
(sōō'rĭ·năm')
(Dutch Guiana)

LOCATION—On the northeast coast of South America, bordering on the Atlantic Ocean.
GOVT.—Republic.
AREA—70,087 sq. mi.
POP.—450,000 (est. 1977).
CAPITAL—Paramaribo.

The Dutch colony of Surinam became an integral part of the Kingdom of the Netherlands under the Constitution of 1954. It became an independent state Nov. 25, 1975.

100 Cents = 1 Gulden

King William III
A1

Numeral of Value
A2

Perf. 11½, 11½x12, 12½x12, 13½, 14.

1873-88 Typographed Unwmkd.

1	A1	1c lil gray ('85)	1.75	1.75
2	A1	2c yel ('85)	60	60
3	A1	2½c rose	60	40
b.		Perf. 14, small holes	10.00	12.50
4	A1	3c green	11.00	8.00
b.		Perf. 14, small holes	12.00	18.00
5	A1	5c dl vio	13.00	4.50
b.		Perf. 14, small holes	14.00	14.00
6	A1	10c bister	2.75	6.00
b.		Perf. 14, small holes	15.00	15.00
7	A1	12½c sl bl ('85)	11.00	4.00
8	A1	15c gray ('88)	13.00	4.50
9	A1	20c grn ('88)	25.00	20.00
10	A1	25c grnsh bl	60.00	6.00
11	A1	25c ultra	210.00	14.00
b.		Perf. 14, small holes	210.00	50.00
12	A1	30c red brn ('88)	25.00	22.50
13	A1	40c dk brn ('88)	21.00	20.00
14	A1	50c brn org	25.00	14.00
b.		Perf. 14, small holes	37.50	37.50

| 15 | A1 | 1g red brn & gray ('88) | 40.00 | 35.00 |
| 16 | A1 | 2.50g grn & org ('79) | 65.00 | 60.00 |

The paper of Nos. 3-6, 11 and 14 sometimes has an accidental bluish tinge of varying strength. During its manufacture a chemical whitener (bluing agent) was added in varying quantities. No particular printing was made on bluish paper.
Nos. 1-16 were issued without gum.

1890   Perf. 11½x11, 12½

17	A2	1c gray	60	70
18	A2	2c yel brn	1.40	1.25
19	A2	2½c carmine	2.00	1.00
20	A2	3c green	4.50	3.25
21	A2	5c ultra	22.50	1.75

A3

1892   Perf. 10½.

22	A3	2½c blk & org	1.00	60
a.		First and fifth vertical words have fancy "F"	30.00	17.50
b.		Imperf.	1.50	
c.		Same as "a" imperf.	30.00	

No. 22 was issued without gum.

No. 14 Surcharged in Black

2½ CENT.

1892, Aug. 1 Perf. 14

23	A1	2½c on 50c brn org	250.00	10.00
a.		Perf. 12½x12	350.00	10.00
b.		Perf. 11½x12	400.00	14.00
c.		Double surch.	350.00	300.00

Nos. 23-23c were issued without gum.

Queen Wilhelmina
A5

1892-93 Typographed Perf. 12½

25	A5	10c bister	35.00	2.00
26	A5	12½c rose lil	37.50	4.00
27	A5	15c gray	1.75	90
28	A5	20c green	2.25	1.40
29	A5	25c blue	9.00	5.75
30	A5	30c red brn	2.50	1.75

Nos. 25-30 were issued without gum.

Nos. 7-12 Surcharged

10 CENT

Perf. 11½x12, 12½x12, 13½

1898

31	A1	10c on 12½c sl bl	25.00	3.00
32	A1	10c on 15c gray	60.00	50.00
33	A1	10c on 20c grn	3.00	2.75
34	A1	10c on 25c grnsh bl	7.00	4.50
34A	A1	10c on 25c ultra	800.00	650.00
b.		Perf. 11½x12	900.00	725.00
35	A1	10c on 30c red brn	3.00	3.00
a.		Dbl. surcharge	275.00	

Nos. 31-35 were issued without gum.
Dangerous counterfeits exist.

Netherlands Nos. 80, 83-84 Surcharged

50 Ct 2.50 2.50

SURINAME c SURINAME d

1900 ***Perf. 11½x11, 12½***

36	A11 (c)	50c on 50c brnz grn & red brn	22.50	7.00
37	A12 (d)	1g on 1g dk grn	20.00	12.00
38	A12 (d)	2.50g on 2½g brn lil	14.00	10.00

Nos. 36-38 were issued without gum.

Nos. 13-16 Surcharged 25 cent

Perf. 11½, 11½x12, 12½x12, 14.

1900

39	A1	25c on 40c dk brn	2.25	3.00
40	A1	25c on 50c brn org	1.40	1.40
a.		Perf. 14, small holes	140.00	140.00
b.		Perf. 11½x12	3.50	4.00
41	A1	50c on 1g red brn & gray	22.50	22.50
42	A1	50c on 2.50g grn & org	140.00	160.00

Nos. 39-42 were issued without gum. Counterfeits of No. 42 exist.

A9

Queen Wilhelmina
A10 A11

1902-08 **Typo.** ***Perf. 11, 12½***

44	A9	½c violet	70	60
45	A9	1c ol grn	1.75	90
46	A9	2c yel brn	10.00	3.00
47	A9	2½c bl grn	3.50	40
48	A9	3c orange	5.00	3.00
49	A9	5c red	6.50	25
50	A9	7½c gray ('08)	16.00	7.00
51	A10	10c slate	11.00	90
52	A10	12½c dp bl	1.75	20
53	A10	15c dp brn	27.50	8.00
54	A10	20c ol grn	27.50	4.50
55	A10	22½c brn & ol grn	18.00	10.00
56	A10	25c violet	20.00	1.25
57	A10	30c org brn	40.00	13.00
58	A10	50c lake brn	27.50	6.00
59	A11	1g violet	50.00	10.00
60	A11	2½g sl bl	50.00	60.00
		Nos. 44-60 (17)	316.70	129.00

Nos. 44-50, and possibly 59-60, were issued without gum.

A12

1909 ***Serrate Roulette 13½***

61	A12	5c red	10.00	9.00
a.		Tête bêche pair	140.00	125.00

Perf. 11½x10½.

62	A12	5c red	12.00	11.00
a.		Tête bêche pair	100.00	90.00

Nos. 61-62 were issued without gum.

Nos. 17-18, 29-30, 38 Surcharged in Red

1/ /2 cent f

15 cent. g

30 cent h

A13

1911 ***Perf. 12½ and 11½x11.***

63	A2 (f)	½c on 1c gray	80	80
64	A2 (f)	½c on 2c yel brn	7.00	8.00
65	A5 (g)	15c on 25c bl	65.00	60.00
66	A5 (g)	20c on 30c red brn	7.00	7.25
67	A12 (h)	30c on 2.50g on 2½g brn lil	115.00	115.00
		Nos. 63-67 (5)	194.80	191.05

Nos. 63-67 were issued without gum.

1912, July **Typeset** ***Perf. 11½***

70	A13	½c lilac	70	70
a.		Horizontal pair, imperf. btwn.	180.00	
71	A13	2½c dk grn	80	70
72	A13	5c pale red	7.75	6.75
a.		Vert. pair, imperf. btwn.	250.00	
73	A13	12½c dp bl	11.00	10.00

Nos. 70-73 were issued without gum.

Numeral of Value
A14

Queen Wilhelmina
A15 A16

Perf. 11x11½, 11½, 12½.

1913-31 **Typographed.**

74	A14	½c violet	25	30
75	A14	1c ol grn	25	15
76	A14	1½c bl ('21)	25	15
77	A14	2c yel brn	1.00	1.25
78	A14	2½c green	50	12
79	A14	3c yellow	60	50
80	A14	3c grn ('26)	2.50	2.50
81	A14	4c chlky bl ('26)	8.00	4.50
82	A14	5c rose	1.10	12
83	A14	5c grn ('22)	1.10	90
84	A14	5c lil ('26)	1.10	15
85	A14	6c bis ('26)	2.50	2.50
86	A14	6c red org ('31)	2.25	25
87	A14	7½c db	80	20
88	A14	7½c org ('27)	1.10	40
89	A14	7½c yel ('31)	9.00	9.00
90	A14	10c vio ('22)	3.25	3.25
91	A14	10c rose ('26)	3.00	40
92	A15	10c car rose	1.40	60
93	A15	12½c blue	1.75	50
94	A15	12½c red ('22)	1.75	2.00
95	A15	15c ol grn	50	50
96	A15	15c lt bl ('26)	6.00	4.75
97	A15	20c green	3.25	3.25
98	A15	20c bl ('22)	2.50	1.75
99	A15	20c ol grn ('26)	3.00	2.25
100	A15	22½c orange	2.00	2.50
101	A15	25c red vio	3.50	40
102	A15	30c slate	4.75	1.10
103	A15	32½c vio & org ('22)	15.00	18.00
104	A15	35c sl & red ('26)	4.75	4.50

Perf. 11, 11½, 11½x11, 12½

Engraved

105	A16	50c green	3.00	50
a.		Perf. 12½ ('32)	13.00	1.25
106	A16	1g brown	4.00	40
a.		Perf. 12½ ('32)	14.00	50
107	A16	1½g dp vio ('26)	35.00	35.00
108	A16	2½g carmine	25.00	25.00
a.		Perf. 11½x11	35.00	32.50
		Nos. 74-108 (35)	155.70	129.64

All stamps issued in 1913 were without gum.

Queen Wilhelmina
A17

1923 ***Perf. 11, 11x11½, 11½.***

109	A17	5c green	60	70
110	A17	10c car rose	1.00	1.50
111	A17	20c indigo	2.50	2.75
112	A17	50c brn org	14.00	21.00
113	A17	1g brn vio	22.50	14.00
114	A17	2½g gray blk	70.00	210.00
115	A17	5g brown	90.00	250.00
		Nos. 109-115 (7)	200.60	499.95

25th anniversary of the assumption of the government of the Netherlands by Queen Wilhelmina, at age 18.

Prices for Nos. 114-115 used are for copies clearly dated before July 15, 1924.

Nos. 83, 93-94, 98 Surcharged in Black or Red:

3 j

= 15

10 CENT k CENT m

1925

116	A14	3c on 5c grn	90	1.00
117	A15	10c on 12½c red	2.00	2.00
118	A15	15c on 12½c bl (R)	1.50	1.40
119	A15	15c on 20c bl	1.50	1.40

No. 100 Surcharged in Blue

12½ Ct.

1926

120	A15	12½c on 22½c org	27.50	27.50

Postage Due Stamps Nos. J14 and J29 Surcharged in Blue or Black:

Frankeerzegel 12½ Cent SURINAME o

Frankeerzegel 12½ CENT SURINAME p

121	D2(o)	12½c on 40c lil & blk (Bl)	2.00	2.00
122	D2 (p)	12½c on 40c lil (Bk)	27.50	27.50

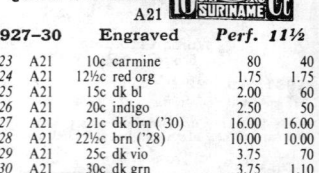

Queen Wilhelmina
A21

1927-30 **Engraved** ***Perf. 11½***

123	A21	10c carmine	80	40
124	A21	12½c red org	1.75	1.75
125	A21	15c dk bl	2.00	60
126	A21	20c indigo	2.50	50
127	A21	21c dk brn ('30)	16.00	16.00
128	A21	22½c brn ('28)	10.00	10.00
129	A21	25c dk vio	3.75	70
130	A21	30c dk grn	3.75	1.10
131	A21	35c blk brn	3.75	3.75
		Nos. 123-131 (9)	44.30	34.80

Types of Netherlands Marine Insurance Stamps Inscribed "SURINAME" and Surcharged

FRANKEER = ZEGEL = 10 CENT

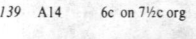

1927, Oct. 26

132	MI 1	3c on 15c dk grn	15	25
133	MI 1	10c on 60c car rose	20	25
134	MI 1	12½c on 75c gray brn	25	15
135	MI 2	15c on 1.50 dk bl	2.25	2.25
136	MI 2	25c on 2.25g org brn	5.00	4.75
137	MI 3	30c on 4½g blk	11.50	9.50
138	MI 3	50c on 7½g red	5.00	4.75
		Nos. 132-138 (7)	24.35	21.90

Nos. 135-137 have "FRANKEERZEGEL" in small capitals in one line. Nos. 135 and 136 have a heavy bar across the top of the stamp.

No. 88 Surcharged 6

1930, Mar. 1 ***Perf. 12½***

139	A14	6c on 7½c org	2.00	1.00

Prince William I (Portrait by Van Key)
A22

SURINAM

1933, Apr. 19   Photogravure
141   A22   6c dp org   7.00   1.75
Issued in commemoration of the 400th anniversary of the birth of Prince William I, Count of Nassau and Prince of Orange, frequently referred to as William the Silent.

Van Walbeeck's Ship Queen Wilhelmina
A23   A24

1936-42   Litho.   Perf. 13½x12½
142   A23   ½c yel brn   20   25
143   A23   1c lt yel grn   35   15
144   A23   1½c brt bl   60   40
145   A23   2c blk brn   70   25
146   A23   2½c green   15   15
  a. Perf. 13 ('41)   15.00   5.00
147   A23   3c dk ultra   65   40
148   A23   4c orange   80   70
149   A23   5c gray   70   20
150   A23   6c red   3.00   2.00
151   A23   7½c red vio   15   15
  a. 7½c plum, perf. 13 ('41) 5.00   50

Engraved.
Perf. 14, 12½
Size: 20x30mm.
152   A24   10c vermilion   80   10
  a. Perf. 12½ ('39)   50.00   10.00
153   A24   12½c dl grn   3.25   15
154   A24   15c dk bl   1.25   60
155   A24   20c yel org   2.00   60
156   A24   21c dk gray   3.00   3.00
  a. Perf. 12½ ('39)   3.00   3.00
157   A24   25c brn lake   2.25   1.00
158   A24   30c brn vio   3.50   10
159   A24   35c ol brn   4.00   3.75

Perf. 12½x14
Size: 22x33mm.
160   A24   50c dl yel grn   4.00   1.75
161   A24   1g dl bl   7.00   2.25
162   A24   1.50g blk brn   20.00   16.00
163   A24   2.50g rose lake   12.00   8.00
  Nos. 142-163 (22)   70.35   43.95

 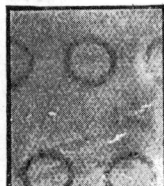

Queen Wilhelmina
A25   Wmk. 202

1938, Aug. 30 Photo. Perf. 12½x12
164   A25   2c dl pur   60   50
165   A25   7½c red org   1.25   1.10
166   A25   15c ryl bl   3.75   3.00
Issued in commemoration of the 40th anniversary of the reign of Queen Wilhelmina.

Van Walbeeck's Ship Queen Wilhelmina
A26   A27
Lithographed.
1941   Perf. 12.   Unwmkd.
168   A26   1c lt yel grn   1.00   75
169   A26   2c blk brn   1.50   1.50
Type A26 is similar to type A23 except for the white side frame lines which extend to the base.

Size: 18x22½mm.
1941-46   Photo.   Perf. 13½x12½
Perf. 12½
174   A27   12½c ryl bl ('46)   30   20
175   A27   15c ultra   20.00   7.00

Royal Family
A28

1943, Nov. 2 Engr. Perf. 13½x13
176   A28   2½c dp org   30   40
177   A28   7½c red   30   20
178   A28   15c black   2.25   1.75
179   A28   40c dp bl   3.00   2.25
Issued in honor of Princess Margriet Francisca of the Netherlands.

Nos. 151, 152 and 168 Surcharged with New Values and Bars in Black.
1945   Perf. 13, 13½, 12.   Unwmkd.
180   A26   ½c on 1c lt yel grn   10   20
181   A23   2½c on 7½c red vio   2.00   2.25
182   A24   5c on 10c ver   70   50
183   A24   7½c on 10c ver   80   50
  a. Double surch.   200.00 210.00

Bauxite Mine, Moengo
A29

Queen Wilhelmina
A30   A31

Designs: 1½c, Bush Negroes on Cottica River near Moengo. 2c, Waterfall in interior. 2½c, Road scene, Coronie District. 3c, Surinam River near Berg en Dahl Plantation. 4c, Government Square, Paramaribo. 5c, Mining gold. 6c, Street in Paramaribo. 7½c, Sugar cane train.

1945   Engraved   Perf. 12
184   A29   1c rose car   30   30
185   A29   1½c rose lake   1.50   1.50
186   A29   2c violet   50   40
187   A29   2½c ol brn   50   40
188   A29   3c dl grn   1.10   60
189   A29   4c brown   1.10   70
190   A29   5c blue   1.10   30
191   A29   6c olive   2.00   1.40
192   A29   7½c dp org   70   30
193   A30   10c blue   1.25   15
194   A30   15c brown   1.40   25
195   A30   20c dl grn   2.50   20
196   A30   22½c gray   3.00   80
197   A30   25c carmine   8.00   4.00
198   A30   30c ol grn   6.50   50
199   A30   35c brt bl grn   15.00   7.50
200   A30   40c rose lake   6.50   30
201   A30   50c red org   6.50   25
202   A30   60c violet   6.50   70
203   A31   1g brn brn   5.50   30
204   A31   1.50g lilac   5.50   70
205   A31   2.50g ol brn   10.00   80
206   A31   5g rose car   25.00   11.00
207   A31   10g red org   40.00   10.00
  Nos. 184-207 (24)   151.95   49.35

Numeral   Queen Wilhelmina
A32   A33

Nos. 151 and 152 Surcharged with New Value and Bar in Blue or Black.
1947   Perf. 13½x12½, 14
209   A23   1½(c) on 7½c red vio (Bl)   10   20
  a. Dbl. surch.   200.00
210   A24   2½c on 10c ver (Bk)   1.00   30

Photogravure.
1948   Perf. 12½x13½.   Unwmkd.
211   A32   1c dk red   10   10
212   A32   1½c plum   15   15
213   A32   2c purple   25   10
214   A32   2½c ol grn   1.40   15
215   A32   3c dk grn   15   12
216   A32   4c red brn   20   15

Perf. 13½x12½
217   A33   5c dk grn   40   15
218   A33   6c dk ol   1.00   70
219   A33   7½c scarlet   40   20
220   A33   10c blue   40   10
221   A33   12½c dk bl   1.10   1.00
222   A33   15c hn brn   1.50   35
223   A33   17½c dk vio brn   1.75   1.40
224   A33   20c dk bl grn   1.40   15
225   A33   22½c sl bl   1.40   70
226   A33   25c crimson   1.40   30
227   A33   27½c car lake   1.40   20
228   A33   30c ol brn   1.75   20
229   A33   37½c ol brn   3.00   2.00
230   A33   40c lil rose   2.00   30
231   A33   50c red org   2.10   30
232   A33   60c purple   2.50   20
233   A33   70c black   2.50   55
  Nos. 211-233 (23)   28.20   9.77

See also Nos. 241-242.

Queen Wilhelmina
A34
Engraved.
1948   Perf. 12½x13½   Unwmkd.
234   A34   7½c vermilion   80   70
235   A34   12½c dp bl   80   70
Issued to commemorate the 50th anniversary of the reign of Queen Wilhelmina.

Queen Juliana
A35
Photogravure.
1948   Perf. 14x13.   Wmk. 202
236   A35   7½c dp org   3.25   3.00
237   A35   12½c ultra   3.25   3.00
Issued to commemorate the investiture of Queen Juliana, September 6, 1948.

Post Horns Entwined
A36

1949   Perf. 11½x12½.   Unwmkd.
238   A36   7½c brn red   6.00   3.00
239   A36   27½c dl bl   5.00   2.00
Issued to commemorate the 75th anniversary of the formation of the Universal Postal Union.

No. 192 Surcharged with New Value, Square and Bar in Black.
1950   Perf. 12.
240   A29   1c on 7½c dp org   70   70

Numeral Type of 1948.
1951   Perf. 12½x13½.
241   A32   5c dp bl   1.40   10
242   A32   7½c dp org   3.00   1.25

Queen Juliana
A37   A38
1951   Perf. 13½x12½
243   A37   10c blue   40   10
244   A37   15c hn brn   1.00   25
245   A37   20c dk bl grn   2.50   12
246   A37   25c crimson   1.75   40
247   A37   27½c car lake   1.50   15
248   A37   30c ol grn   1.50   40
249   A37   35c ol brn   1.75   1.10
250   A37   40c lil rose   2.00   40
251   A37   50c red org   2.75   40

Engraved.
252   A38   1g red brn   27.50   35
  Nos. 243-252 (10)   42.65   3.67

Shooting   Plowing with
Fish   Water Buffalo
A39   A40

Designs: 2½c, Fisherman. 5c, Bauxite mining. 6c, Log raft. 10c, Woman picking fruit. 12½c, Armored catfish. 15c, Macaw. 17½c, Armadillo. 20c, Poling canoe. 25c, Common iguana.

1953-55 Photo. Perf. 14x13, 13x14
253   A40   2c ol grn ('53)   10   10
254   A40   2½c bl grn   30   20
255   A40   5c gray   30   12
256   A40   6c brt bl   1.75   1.25
257   A40   7½c pur ('53)   15   10
258   A40   10c brt red ('53)   20   10
259   A40   12½c dk gray bl   1.75   1.40
260   A40   15c crimson   60   25
261   A40   17½c red brn   3.00   2.00
262   A40   20c Prus grn ('53)   50   10
263   A40   25c ol grn   2.75   80
  a. Miniature sheet of 4 ('55) 37.50 30.00
  Nos. 253-263 (11)   11.40   6.42

No. 263a contains one each of Nos. 259-261 and 263. No marginal inscription. Size: 111x146mm.

SURINAM

Queen Juliana
A41

1954, Dec. 15   *Perf. 13½*
264   A41   7½c dk red brn   90   80
Issued to publicize the Charter of the Kingdom, adopted Dec. 15, 1954.

Harvesting Bananas
A46

Globe and Mercury's Rod
A47

Designs: 7½c, Pounding rice. 10c, Preparing cassava. 15c, Fishing.

1955, May   *Perf. 14x13*
265   A46   2c dk grn   1.75   1.25
266   A46   7½c dl yel   3.00   2.00
267   A46   10c org yel   3.00   2.00
268   A46   15c ultra   3.00   2.00

Issued to commemorate the 4th anniversary of the establishment of the Caribbean Tourist Association.

    Perf. 13x12
1955, Sept. 19   Unwmkd.
269   A47   5c brt ultra   50   35
Issued to publicize the Paramaribo Trade Fair, October, 1955.

Flags and Map of Caribbean
A48

1956, Dec. 6   Litho.   *Perf. 12½x14*
270   A48   10c lt bl & red   55   50
10th anniversary of Caribbean Commission.

No. 247 Surcharged   **8**   **C**

1958   Photo.   *Perf. 13½x12½*
271   A37   8c on 27½c car lake   20   15

Queen Juliana
A49

Symbolic Flowers
A50

    Lithographed.
1959   *Perf. 12½x12*   Unwmkd.
272   A49   1g magenta   1.50   10
273   A49   1.50g ol bis   2.50   70
274   A49   2.50g dk car   4.00   40
275   A49   5g dl bl   8.00   40

1959   *Perf. 12½x13*
276   A50   20c multi   3.25   1.50
Issued to commemorate the 5th anniversary of the constitution. Flowers in design symbolize Netherlands, Surinam and Netherlands Antilles.

Charles Lindbergh's Plane
A51

Designs: 10c, De Snip plane. 15c, Cessna 170B. 20c, Super Constellation. 40c, Boeing 707 Jet.

1960, Mar. 12   Litho.   *Perf. 12½*
277   A51   8c chlky bl   2.25   2.50
278   A51   10c brt grn   3.00   2.00
279   A51   15c rose red   3.00   2.50
280   A51   20c pale vio   3.25   2.50
281   A51   40c lt brn   4.00   4.00
    Nos. 277-281 (5)   15.50   13.50

Issued to commemorate the inauguration of Zanderij Airport, March 12, 1960. Nos. 277–281 show 25 years of Surinam's civil aviation.

Flag of Surinam and Map
A52

Arms of Surinam
A53

1960, July 1   *Perf. 12½x13*
282   A52   10c multi   1.00   1.00
283   A53   15c multi   1.00   1.00
Day of Freedom, July 1.

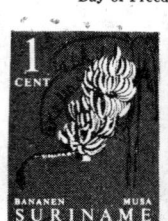 

Bananas
A54

Finance Building
A55

Designs: 2c, Citrus fruit. 3c, Cacao. 4c, Sugar cane. 5c, Coffee. 6c, Coconuts. 8c, Rice.

1961, March 1   Litho.   *Perf. 13½*
284   A54   1c sl, yel & blk   10   10
285   A54   2c bis, grn & blk   10   10
286   A54   3c dl red brn, blk & ocher   10   10
287   A54   4c lt ultra , blk & lem   10   10
288   A54   5c brn, blk & crim   10   10
289   A54   6c yel grn, blk & bis   10   10
290   A54   8c ultra, blk & yel   10   10
    Nos. 284-290 (7)   70   70

1961   *Perf. 13½*   Unwmkd.
Buildings: 15c, Court of Justice. 20c, Concordia Lodge (Masons). 25c, Neve Shalom Synagogue, Paramaribo (horiz.). 30c, Old Dutch lock in New Amsterdam. 35c, Government office (horiz.). 40c, Governor's palace (horiz.). 50c, Legislative Council (horiz.). 60c, Old Dutch Reformed Church (horiz.). 70c, Zeelandia Fortress (horiz.).
291   A55   10c multi   10   10
292   A55   15c multi   20   15
293   A55   20c multi   30   20
294   A55   25c multi   60   35
295   A55   30c multi   2.50   1.40
296   A55   35c multi   2.50   1.50
297   A55   40c multi   90   60
298   A55   50c multi   1.00   30
299   A55   60c multi   1.40   1.10
300   A55   70c multi   1.75   1.10
    Nos. 291-300 (10)   11.25   6.80

Dag Hammarskjold
A56

1962, Jan. 2   Litho.   *Perf. 12, 12½*
301   A56   10c brt bl & blk   15   15
302   A56   20c lil & blk   25   25
Issued in memory of Dag Hammarskjold, Secretary General of the United Nations, 1953–61. Printed in sheets of 12 (3x4) with ornamental borders and inscriptions.
Sheets exist either with or without extension of perforations through the margins.

Queen Juliana and Prince Bernhard
A56a

1962, Jan. 31   Photo.   *Perf. 14x13*
303   A56a   20c ol grn   40   40
Issued to commemorate the silver wedding anniversary of Queen Juliana and Prince Bernhard.

Malaria Eradication Emblem
A57

    Lithographed
1962, Apr. 7   *Perf. 13x14*   Unwmkd.
304   A57   8c brt red   25   25
305   A57   10c blue   30   30
Issued for the World Health Organization drive to eradicate malaria.

Stoelmans Guesthouse
A58

Design: 15c, Torarica Hotel.
1962, July 10   *Perf. 13½*
306   A58   10c multi   60   60
307   A58   15c multi   60   60
Issued to commemorate the opening of the Torarica Hotel in Paramaribo and Stoelmans Guesthouse on Stoelman Island.

Deaconess Residence and Recreation Area
A59

Design: 20c, Deaconess Hospital.
1962, Nov. 30
308   A59   10c multi   50   50
309   A59   20c multi   50   50

Hands Holding Wheat Emblem
A60

Design: 20c, Farmer harvesting and wheat emblem (vert.).

1963, Mar. 21   *Perf. 13½x13, 13x13½*   Photogravure
310   A60   10c dp car   30   30
311   A60   20c dk bl   30   30
Issued for the "Freedom from Hunger" campaign of the U.N. Food and Agriculture Organization.

Broken Chain
A61

1963, July 1   Litho.   *Perf. 13½x13*
312   A61   10c red & blk   30   30
313   A61   20c grn & blk   30   30
Centenary of emancipation of the slaves.

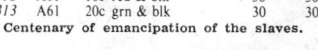

Prince William of Orange Landing at Scheveningen
A61a

Faja Lobbi Wreath
A62

    Photogravure
1963, Nov. 21   *Perf. 13x14*   Unwmkd.
Size: 26x26mm.
314   A61a   10c dl bl, blk & brn   25   25
Issued to commemorate the 150th anniversary of the founding of the Kingdom of the Netherlands.

1964, Dec. 15   Litho.   *Perf. 12½x13*
315   A62   25c multi   50   50
Issued to commemorate the 10th anniversary of the Charter of the Kingdom of the Netherlands.

SURINAM

Abraham Lincoln
A63

1965, Apr. 14 Litho. Perf. 12½x13
316 A63 25c ol bis & brn 30 30

Centenary of death of Abraham Lincoln.

ICY Emblem
A64

1965, May 26 Perf. 13x12½
317 A64 10c org & bl 10 10
318 A64 15c red & vio bl 20 20

International Cooperation Year, 1965.

Bauxite Mine, Moengo — A65   Red-breasted Blackbird — A66

Designs: 15c, Alum Pottery Works, Paranam. 20c, Hydroelectric plant, Afobaka. 25c, Aluminum smeltery, Paranam.

1965, Oct. 9 Photo. Unwmkd.
319 A65 10c ocher 10 10
320 A65 15c dk grn 20 20
321 A65 20c dk bl 30 30
322 A65 25c carmine 30 30

Opening of the Brokopondo Power Station.

1966, Feb. 16 Litho. Perf. 13x14
Birds: 2c, Great kiskadee. 3c, Silver-beaked tanager. 4c, Ruddy ground dove. 5c, Blue-gray tanager. 6c, Glittering-throated emerald (hummingbird). 8c, Turquoise tanager. 10c, Pale-breasted robin.

323 A66 1c brt grn, blk & red 10 10
324 A66 2c lt ultra, yel & brn 10 10
325 A66 3c multi 10 10
326 A66 4c lt ol grn, red brn & blk 10 10
327 A66 5c org, ultra & blk 10 10
328 A66 6c multi 10 10
329 A66 8c gray, vio bl & blk 10 10
330 A66 10c multi 10 10
Nos. 323-330 (8) 80 80

Central Hospital
A67

Design: 15c, Hospital, side view.

1966, Mar. 9 Litho. Perf. 13x12½
331 A67 10c multi 20 20
332 A67 15c multi 25 25

Opening of Central Hospital, Paramaribo.

Father Petrus Donders
A68

Designs: 10c, Church and parsonage, Batavia. 15c, Msgr. Joannes B. Swinkels. 25c, Cathedral, Paramaribo.

1966, Mar. 26 Photo. Perf. 12½x13
333 A68 4c org brn & blk 10 10
334 A68 10c rose brn & blk 20 20
335 A68 15c yel brn & blk 20 20
336 A68 25c lt vio & blk 30 30

Issued to commemorate the centenary of the Redemptorist Mission in Surinam (Congregation of the Most Holy Redeemer).

100-Year-Old Tree
A69

1966, May 9 Litho. Perf. 13x12½
337 A69 25c grn, dp org & blk 30 30
338 A69 30c red org, grn & blk 30 30

Centenary of the Surinam Parliament.

Television Transmitter, Eye and Globe
A70

1966, Oct. 20 Litho. Perf. 12½x13
339 A70 25c dk bl & ver 30 30
340 A70 30c brn & ver 30 30

Inauguration of television service.

Bauxite Industry, 1916
A71

Design: 25c, Bauxite industry, 1966.

1966, Dec. 19 Litho. Perf. 12½x13
341 A71 20c yel, org & blk 30 30
342 A71 25c org, bl & blk 30 30

50th anniversary of bauxite industry.

Central Bank, Paramaribo
A72

Design: 25c, Central Bank, different view.

1967, Apr. 1 Litho. Perf. 13x12½
343 A72 10c dp yel & blk 20 20
344 A72 25c lil & blk 30 30

Issued to commemorate the 10th anniversary of the Central Bank of Surinam.

Amelia Earhart, Lockheed Electra and Paramaribo—A73

1967, June 3 Photo. Perf. 13x12½
345 A73 20c yel & dk car 30 30
346 A73 25c yel & grn 30 30

Issued to commemorate the 30th anniversary of Amelia Earhart's visit to Surinam, June 3-4, 1937.

Siva Nataraja, God of Dance, and Ballerina's Foot
A74

Design: 25c, Drummer's mask "Bashi Lele," and scroll of violin.

1967, June 21 Perf. 12½x13
347 A74 10c yel grn & bl 20 20
348 A74 25c yel grn & blk 30 30

Issued to commemorate the 20th anniversary of the Surinam Cultural Center Foundation.

New Amsterdam, 1660 (New York City)
A75

Designs after 17th Century Engravings: 10c, Fort Zeelandia, Paramaribo, 1670. 25c, Breda Castle, Netherlands, 1667.

1967, July 31 Litho. Perf. 13x12½
349 A75 10c yel, blk & bl 30 30
350 A75 20c red brn, yel & blk 30 30
351 A75 25c bl grn, yel & blk 40 40

Issued to commemorate the 300th anniversary of the Treaty of Breda between Britain, France and the Netherlands.

WHO Emblem
A76

1968, Apr. 7 Litho. Perf. 13x12½
352 A76 10c mag & dk bl 20 20
353 A76 25c bl & dk pur 40 40

Issued to commemorate the 20th anniversary of the World Health Organization.

Chandelier and Christian Symbols
A77

Design: 15c, like 10c, reversed. Brass chandelier from the Reformed Church, Paramaribo.

1968, May 29 Litho. Perf. 13x12½
354 A77 10c dk bl 20 20
355 A77 25c dp yel grn 45 45

Issued to commemorate the 300th anniversary of the Reformed Church of Paramaribo.

Missionary Store, 1768
A78

Designs: 25c, Main Church and store, Paramaribo, 1868. 30c, C. Kersten & Co., 1968.

1968, June 29 Litho. Perf. 13x12½
356 A78 10c yel & blk 20 20
357 A78 25c lt grnsh bl & blk 40 40
358 A78 30c lil rose & blk 50 50

Issued to commemorate the 200th anniversary of C. Kersten & Co., which is partially owned by the Evangelical Brotherhood Missionary Society.

Joden Savanne Synagogue
A79

Designs: 20c, Map of Joden Savanne and Surinam River. 30c, Gravestone, 1733. The Hebrew inscriptions are quotations from the Bible: 20c, Joshua 24:2; 25c, Isaiah 56:7; 30c, Genesis 31:52.

1968, Aug. 28 Perf. 12½x13
359 A79 20c multi 45 45
360 A79 25c multi 55 45
361 A79 30c multi 60 55

Issued to commemorate the founding of the first synagogue in the Western Hemisphere in 1685 in Joden Savanne, Surinam.

Spectacled Caiman
A80

Designs: 20c, Squirrel monkey (vert.). 25c, Armadillo.

Perf. 13x12½, 12½x13
1969, Aug. 20 Lithographed
362 A80 10c grn & multi 60 40
363 A80 20c bl gray & multi 60 60
364 A80 25c vio & multi 60 60

Mahatma Gandhi
A81

1969, Oct. 2 Litho. Perf. 12½x13
365 A81 25c red & blk 60 60

Issued to commemorate the centenary of the birth of Mohandas K. Gandhi (1869-1948), leader in India's fight for independence.

ILO Emblem
A82

SURINAM

1969, Oct. 29 Litho. Perf. 13x12½
| 366 | A82 | 10c brt bl grn & blk | 40 | 40 |
| 367 | A82 | 25c red & blk | 55 | 55 |

Issued to commemorate the 50th anniversary of the International Labor Organization.

Queen Juliana and Rising Sun
A82a

1969, Dec. 15 Photo. Perf. 14x12½
| 368 | A82a | 25c bl & multi | 60 | 60 |

Issued to commemorate the 15th anniversary of the Charter of the Kingdom of the Netherlands. Phosphorescent paper.

"1950–1970"
A83

1970, Apr. 3 Photo. Perf. 13x12½
| 369 | A83 | 10c brn, grn & org | 30 | 30 |
| 370 | A83 | 25c emer, dk bl & org | 40 | 40 |

Issued to commemorate the 20th anniversary of secondary education in Surinam.

U.P.U. Headquarters, Bern
A84

Design: 25c, U.P.U. Headquarters, sideview and U.P.U. emblem.

1970, May 20 Litho. Perf. 13x12½
| 371 | A84 | 10c sky bl & dk pur | 40 | 40 |
| 372 | A84 | 25c red & blk | 50 | 50 |

Issued to commemorate the inauguration of the Universal Postal Union Headquarters in Bern, Switzerland.

"UNO" Plane over Paramaribo
A85   A86

1970, June 26 Litho. Perf. 12x13
| 373 | A85 | 10c ocher & yel | 40 | 40 |
| 374 | A85 | 25c dp bl & ultra | 50 | 50 |

25th anniversary of the United Nations.

1970, July 15

Designs: 20c, Plane over map of Totness. 25c, Plane over Nieuw-Nickerie.

375	A86	10c bl, vio bl & gray	40	40
376	A86	20c yel, red & gray	40	40
377	A86	25c pink, dk red & gray	40	40

Issued to commemorate the 40th anniversary of domestic airmail service.

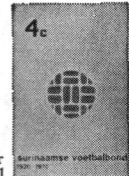

Plan of Soccer Field and Ball
A87

Designs: Plan of soccer field with ball in different positions.

1970, Oct. 1 Litho. Perf. 12x13
378	A87	4c yel, red brn & blk	10	10
379	A87	10c pale lem, red brn & blk	20	20
380	A87	5c lt yel grn, red brn & blk	40	40
381	A87	25c lt grn, red brn & blk	50	50

Issued to commemorate the 50th anniversary of the Soccer Association of Surinam.

Cocoi Heron
A88

Birds in Flight: 20c, Flamingo. 25c, Scarlet macaw.

1971, Feb. 14 Litho. Perf. 13x12½
382	A88	15c gray & multi	50	50
383	A88	20c ultra & multi	50	50
384	A88	25c pale grn & multi	60	60

25th anniversary of regular air service between the Netherlands, Surinam and Netherlands Antilles.

Morse Key Prince Bernhard, Fokker F27, Boeing 747B
A89   A89a

Designs: 20c, Telephone. 25c, Lunar landing module, telescope.

1971, May 17 Litho. Perf. 12½x13
385	A89	15c lt grn & multi	80	50
386	A89	20c bl & multi	80	55
387	A89	25c lil & multi	80	60

3rd World Telecommunications Day.

1971, June 29 Photo. Perf. 13x14
| 388 | A89a | 25c multi | 70 | 70 |

60th birthday of Prince Bernhard.

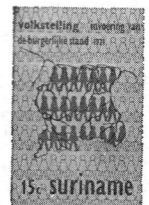

Map of Surinam, Population Chart—A90

Design: 30c, Map of Surinam and individual representing population.

1971, July 31 Litho. Perf. 12½x13
| 389 | A90 | 15c gray bl, blk & ver | 50 | 50 |
| 390 | A90 | 30c ver, gray bl & blk | 50 | 50 |

50th anniversary of the first census and the introduction of civil registration in Surinam.

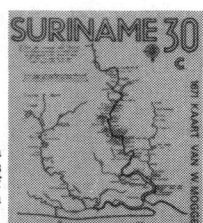

William Mogge's Map of Surinam
A91

1971, Oct. 27 Perf. 11½x11
| 391 | A91 | 30c dl yel & dk brn | 90 | 80 |

300th anniversary of the first map of Surinam.

Map of Albina
A92

August Kappler Drop of Water
A93   A94

Design: 20c, View of Albina from Maroni River.

Perf. 13x12½, 12½x13
1971, Dec. 13
392	A92	15c saph & blk	60	60
393	A92	20c brt grn & blk	60	60
394	A93	25c yel & blk	60	60

125th anniversary of the founding of Albina by August Kappler (1815–1887).

1972, Feb. 2 Perf. 12½x13

Design: 30c, Faucet and water tower.
| 395 | A94 | 15c vio & blk | 70 | 70 |
| 396 | A94 | 30c bl & blk | 70 | 70 |

Surinam water works, 40th anniversary.

Air Mail Envelope
A95

1972, Aug. 2 Litho. Perf. 13x12½
| 397 | A95 | 15c red & bl | 40 | 40 |
| 398 | A95 | 30c bl & red | 40 | 40 |

50th anniversary of the arrival of the first airmail in Surinam, carried by Capt. Dutertre from French Guiana.

Giant Tree
A96

Designs: 20c, Wood transport by air lift. 30c, Hands tending seedling.

1972, Dec. 20 Photo. Perf. 12½x13
399	A96	15c yel & dk brn	35	35
400	A96	20c bl & dp brn	50	50
401	A96	30c brt grn & dp brn	50	50

25th anniversary of the Surinam Forestry Commission.

Hindu Woman in Rice Field
A97

Designs: 25c, J. F. A. Cateau van Rosevelt with map of Surinam and ship "Lalla Rookh." 30c, Symbolic bird, flower, sun, flag and factories.

1973, May 23 Litho. Perf. 13x13½
402	A97	15c pur & yel	40	40
403	A97	25c mar & gray	50	50
404	A97	30c yel & lt bl	50	50

Centenary of the first immigrants from India.

Queen Juliana, Surinam and House of Orange Colors
A97a

Engraved & Lithographed
1973, Sept. 4 Perf. 12½
| 405 | A97a | 30c sil, blk & org | 90 | 60 |

25th anniversary of reign of Queen Juliana.

INTERPOL Emblem Mailman
A98   A99

Design: 30c, INTERPOL emblem, Surinam visa handstamp.

1973, Nov. 7 Litho. Perf. 14x14½
| 406 | A98 | 15c vio bl & multi | 40 | 40 |
| 407 | A98 | 30c lt bl, lil & blk | 40 | 40 |

50th anniversary of International Criminal Police Organization.

1973, Dec. 12 Litho. Perf. 12½

Designs: 15c, Pigeons carrying Letters. 30c, Map of Surinam, plane, ship, train and truck.

408	A99	15c lt yel grn & bl	40	40
409	A99	25c sal, blk & bl	50	50
410	A99	30c ver & multi	55	55

Centenary of stamps of Surinam.

SURINAM

Patient and Blood Transfusion
A100

Design: 30c, Cross section of tissue and oscilloscope.

1974, June 1   Litho.   Perf. 14½x14

| 411 | A100 | 15c red brn & multi | 40 | 40 |
| 412 | A100 | 30c lem & multi | 40 | 40 |

75th anniversary of the Medical College.

Crop Dusting
A101

Design: 30c, Fertilizer plant.

1974, July 17   Litho.   Perf. 13½

| 413 | A101 | 15c multi | 40 | 40 |
| 414 | A101 | 30c multi | 40 | 40 |

25th anniversary of the Foundation for Development of Mechanical Agriculture in Surinam.

Old Title Page
A102

1974, Aug. 12   Perf. 14x14½

| 415 | A102 | 15c multi | 40 | 40 |
| 416 | A102 | 30c multi | 40 | 40 |

Bicentenary of the "Weekly Wednesday Surinam Newspaper." First editor was Beeldsnijder Matroos.

Paramaribo Main Post Office
A103

Design: 30c, Post Office, different view.

1974, Sept. 11   Litho.   Perf. 14½x14

| 417 | A103 | 15c brn & blk | 40 | 40 |
| 418 | A103 | 30c bl & blk | 40 | 40 |

Centenary of Universal Postal Union.

Gold Panner
A104

Design: 30c, Modern excavator.

1975, Feb. 5   Litho.   Perf. 13x12½

| 419 | A104 | 15c brn & ol bis | 40 | 40 |
| 420 | A104 | 30c ver & mar | 45 | 40 |

Centenary of prospecting policy granting concessions for winning of raw materials.

Symbolic Design
A105

1975, June 25   Litho.   Perf. 13x12½

421	A105	15c grn & multi	50	40
422	A105	25c bl & multi	50	50
423	A105	30c red & multi	60	50

Centenary of International Meter Convention, Paris, 1875.

Hands Holding Saw
A106

Designs: 50c, Book with notes and letter "a". 75c, Hands holding ball.

1975, Nov. 25   Litho.   Perf. 13x14

424	A106	25c yel, red & brn	34	34
425	A106	50c yel, red & pur	68	68
426	A106	75c dk bl, org & emer	1.00	1.00

Independence. Sheets of 10 (5x2) with ornamental marins.

Oncidium Lanceanum
A107

Central Bank, Paramaribo
A109

Orchids: 2c, Epidendrum stenopetalum. 3c, Brassia lanceana. 4c, Epidendrum ibaguense. 5c, Epidendrum fragrans.

1975-76   Litho.   Perf. 14½x13½

427	A107	1c multi	5	5
428	A107	2c multi	5	5
429	A107	3c multi	5	5
430	A107	4c multi	5	5
431	A107	5c multi	8	8

Perf. 13½x13

436	A109	1g rose lil & blk	1.35	40
437	A109	1½g brn, dp org & blk	2.00	40
438	A109	2½g red brn, org red & blk	3.50	50
439	A109	5g grn, yel grn & blk	6.75	80
440	A109	10g dk vio bl & blk	13.50	1.60
		Nos. 427-431, 436-440 (10)	27.38	3.95

Issue dates: Nos. 436-439, Nov. 25, 1975. Nos. 427-431, Feb. 18, 1976. No. 440, May 6, 1976.

Flag of Surinam
A110

1976, Mar. 3   Perf. 14x13

Design: 35c, Coat of Arms.

| 445 | A110 | 25c emer & multi | 34 | 34 |
| 446 | A110 | 35c red org & multi | 48 | 48 |

Sheets of 12 (6x2) with ornamental margins.

Pomacanthus Semicirculatus
A111

Fish: 2c, Adioryx diadema. 3c, Pogonoculius zebra. 4c, Balistes vetula. 5c, Myripristis jacobus.

1976, June 2   Litho.   Perf. 12½x13

447	A111	1c multi	5	5
448	A111	2c multi	5	5
449	A111	3c multi	5	5
450	A111	4c multi	5	5
451	A111	5c multi	8	8
		Nos. 447-451, C55-C57 (8)	2.81	2.81

See Nos. 471-475, C72-C74.

19th Century Switchboard and Telephone—A112

Design: 35c, Satellite, globe and 1976 telephone.

1976, Aug. 5   Litho.   Perf. 13x13½

| 452 | A112 | 20c yel & multi | 32 | 32 |
| 453 | A112 | 35c ultra & multi | 56 | 56 |

Centenary of first telephone call by Alexander Graham Bell, Mar. 10, 1876.

Perf. 13x13½, 13½x13

1976, Sept. 29   Photogravure

454	A113	20c multi	32	32
455	A113	30c multi	48	48
456	A113	35c multi	56	56
457	A113	50c multi	80	80

Paintings by Surinam artists.

The Story of Anansi Tori, by A. Baag—A113

Designs: 30c, "Surinam Now" (young people), by R. Chang. 35c, Lamentation, by Nola Hatterman (vert.). 50c, Chess Players, by Q. Jan Telting.

Franklin's Divided Snake Poster, 1754—A114

1976, Nov. 10   Litho.   Perf. 13x13½

| 458 | A114 | 20c grn & blk | 32 | 32 |
| 459 | A114 | 60c org & blk | 96 | 96 |

American Bicentennial.

Ionopsis Utricularioides
A115

Surinam Costume
A116

Orchids: 30c, Rodiguezia secunda. 35c, Oncidium pusillum. 55c, Sobralia sessilis. 60c, Octomeria surinamensis.

1977, Jan. 19   Litho.   Perf. 14½x13

460	A115	20c ver & multi	32	32
461	A115	30c ultra & multi	48	48
462	A115	35c mag & multi	56	56
463	A115	55c yel & multi	88	88
464	A115	60c grn & multi	96	96
		Nos. 460-464 (5)	3.20	3.20

1977, Mar. 2   Photo.   Perf. 14x13½

Designs: Various Surinamese women's costumes.

465	A116	10c brt bl & multi	16	16
466	A116	15c grn & multi	24	24
467	A116	35c vio & multi	55	55
468	A116	60c org & multi	96	96
469	A116	75c ultra & multi	1.20	1.20
470	A116	1g yel & multi	1.60	1.60
		Nos. 465-470 (6)	4.71	4.71

Fish Type of 1976

1977, June 8   Litho.   Perf. 12½x13

Tropical Fish: 1c, Liopropoma carmabi. 2c, Holacanthus ciliaris. 3c, Opistognathus aurifrons. 4c, Anisotremus virginicus. 5c, Gramma loreto.

471	A111	1c multi	5	5
472	A111	2c multi	5	5
473	A111	3c multi	5	5
474	A111	4c multi	6	6
475	A111	5c multi	8	8
		Nos. 471-475, C72-C74 (8)	4.59	4.59

Edison's Phonograph, 1877—A117

Design: 60c, Modern turntable.

1977, Aug. 24   Litho.   Perf. 13½x14

| 475 | A117 | 20c multi | 32 | 32 |
| 477 | A117 | 60c multi | 96 | 96 |

Centenary of the invention of the phonograph.

Packet Curacao, 1827
A118

Designs: 15c, Helvoetsluis Harbor and postmark, 1827. 30c, Sea chart and technical details of packet Curacao. 60c, Logbook and compass rose. 60c, Map of Paramaribo harbor and 1852 postmark. 95c, Modern liner Stuyvesant.

1977, Sept. 28   Litho.   Perf. 14x13½

478	A118	5c grnsh bl & dk bl	8	8
479	A118	15c org & mar	24	24
480	A118	30c lt brn & blk	48	48
481	A118	35c ol & blk	56	56
482	A118	60c lil & blk	96	96
483	A118	95c yel grn & dk grn	1.52	1.52
		Nos. 478-483 (6)	3.84	3.84

Regular steamer connection between the Netherlands and Surinam, 150th anniversary.

Passiflora Quadrangularis
A119

Javanese Costume
A120

SURINAM

Flowers: 30c, Centropogon surinamensis. 55c, Gloxinia perennis. 60c, Hydrocleis nymphoides. 75c, Clusia grandiflora.

1978, Feb. 8		Litho.	Perf. 13x14	
484	A119	20c multi	32	32
485	A119	30c multi	48	48
486	A119	55c multi	85	85
487	A119	60c multi	95	95
488	A119	1g multi	1.15	1.15
		Nos. 484-488 (5)	3.75	3.75

1978, Mar. 1		Photo.	Perf. 14x13	

People of Surinam, Costumes: 20c, Forest black. 35c, Chinese. 60c, Creole. 75c, Aborigine Indian. 1g, Hindustani.

489	A120	10c multi	16	16
490	A120	32c multi	32	32
491	A120	35c multi	52	52
492	A120	60c multi	95	95
493	A120	75c multi	1.15	1.15
494	A120	1g multi	1.60	1.60
		Nos. 489-494 (6)	4.70	4.70

Air Post Stamps of 1972 Surcharged

1978	Lithographed	Perf. 13x13½
	Multicolored	

495	AP6	1c on 25c (#C44)	5	5
496	AP6	4c on 15c (#C42)	5	5
497	AP6	4c on 30c (#C45)	6	6
498	AP6	5c on 40c (#C47)	8	8
499	AP6	10c on 75c (#C54)	16	16
		Nos. 495-499 (5)	41	41

"Luchtpost" obliterated with 2 bars.

Old Municipal Church A121

Johannes King A122

Designs: 55c, New Municipal Church. 60c, Johannes Raillard.

1978, May 31		Litho.	Perf. 14x13	
500	A121	10c bl, blk & gray	16	16
501	A122	20c gray & blk	36	36
502	A122	55c rose lil & blk	85	85
503	A122	60c org & blk	96	96

Evangelical Brothers Community Church, Paramaribo, bicentenary.

Nannacara Anomala A123

Tropical Fish: 2c, Leporinus fasciatus. 3c, Pristella riddlei. 4c, Nannostomus beckfordi. 5c, Rivulus agilae.

1978, June 21			Perf. 12½x13	
504	A123	1c multi	5	5
505	A123	2c multi	5	5
506	A123	3c multi	5	5
507	A123	4c multi	5	5
508	A123	5c multi	6	6
		Nos. 504-508,C85-C87 (8)	4.56	4.56

Souvenir Sheet

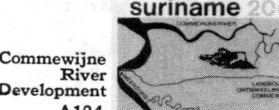

Commewijne River Development A124

Designs: 60c, Map of Surinam and dam. 95c, Planes and world map.

1978, Oct. 18		Litho.	Perf. 13½x14	
509		Sheet of 3	2.50	2.50
a.	A124	20c multi	25	25
b.	A124	60c multi	75	75
c.	A124	95c multi	1.15	1.15

Development. No. 509 has brown margin with white design. Size: 129x85mm.

Coconuts A125

1978, Nov. 8	Photo.	Perf. 13x12½
	Multicolored	

510	A125	5c shown	6	6
a.	Bklt. pane of 12 (4 #510, 3 #511, 5 #515) ('80)		2.75	
511	A125	10c Oranges	12	12
512	A125	15c Papayas	18	18
a.	Bklt. pane of 11 + label (5 #512, 6 #514) ('79)		2.75	
513	A125	20c Bananas	24	24
514	A125	25c Soursop	30	30
515	A125	35c Watermelon	42	42
		Nos. 510-515 (6)	1.32	1.32

Wright Brothers' Flyer 1 A126

Designs: 20c, Daedalus and Icarus (vert.). 95c, DC 8. 125c, Concorde.

	Perf. 13x14, 14x13		
1978, Dec. 13		Lithographed	
516	A126	20c multi	24	24
517	A126	60c multi	75	75
518	A126	95c multi	1.15	1.15
519	A126	125c multi	1.50	1.50

75th anniversary of 1st powered flight.

Rodriguezia Candida A127

Javanese Dancer A128

Flowers: 20c, Stanhopea grandiflora. 35c, Scuticaria steelei. 60c, Bollea violacea.

1979, Feb. 7		Photo.	Perf. 12½x14	
520	A127	10c multi	12	12
521	A127	20c multi	24	24
522	A127	35c multi	42	42
523	A127	60c multi	75	75

1979, Feb. 28

Dancing Costumes: 10c, Forest Negro. 15c, Chinese. 20c, Creole. 25c, Aborigine Indian. 35c, Hindustani.

524	A128	5c multi	6	6
525	A128	12c multi	12	12
526	A128	15c multi	18	18
527	A128	20c multi	24	24
528	A128	25c multi	30	30
529	A128	35c multi	42	42
		Nos. 524-529 (6)	1.32	1.32

Equetus Pulchellus A129

Tropical Fish: 2c, Apogon binotatus. 3c, Anisotremus virginicus. 5c, Bodianus rufus. 35c, Microspathodon chrysurus.

1979, May 30		Photo.	Perf. 14x13	
530	A129	1c multi	5	5
531	A129	2c multi	5	5
532	A129	3c multi	5	5
533	A129	5c multi	6	6
534	A129	35c multi	42	42
		Nos. 530-534, C89-C91 (8)	3.90	3.90

Javanese Wooden Head A130

Folkart: 35c, Head ornament, Indian. 60c, Horse's head, Javanese.

1979, Aug. 29		Litho.	Perf. 14x13	
535	A130	20c multi	24	24
536	A130	35c multi	42	42
537	A130	60c multi	75	75

Sir Rowland Hill—A131

1979, Oct. 3		Litho.	Perf. 13x14	
538	A131	1g yel & ol	1.20	1.20

Sir Rowland Hill (1795-1879), originator of penny postage.

SOS Emblem, House—A132

Design: 60c, SOS emblem and buildings.

1979, Oct. 3			Perf. 14x13	
539	A132	20c multi	25	25
540	A132	60c multi	75	75

International Year of the Child; SOS Children's Villages, 30th anniversary.

Javanese Girl's Costume—A133

1980, Feb. 6		Photo.	Perf. 13x14	
541	A133	10c shown	12	12
542	A133	15c Forest Black boy	18	18
543	A133	25c Chinese girl	30	30
544	A133	60c Creole girl	75	75
545	A133	90c Indian girl	1.10	1.10
546	A133	1g Hindustani boy	1.20	1.20
		Nos. 541-546 (6)	3.65	3.65

Rotary International, 75th Anniversary—A134

Design: 20c, Handshake, Rotary emblem (vert.).

1980, Feb. 23		Litho.	Perf. 13x14, 14x13	
547	A134	20c ultra & yel	25	25
548	A134	60c ultra & yel	75	75

Rowland Hill A135

Weight Lifting A136

1980, May 6		Litho.	Perf. 13x14	
549	A135	50c Mailcoach	60	60
550	A135	1g shown	1.20	1.20
a.		Souvenir sheet	1.20	1.20
551	A135	2g People mailing letters	2.40	2.40

London 1980 International Stamp Exhibition, May 6-14. No. 550a contains No. 550 in changed colors. Blue and black margin shows designs of Nos. 549, 551, London 1980 emblem. Size: 141x90½mm. (No. 550 in lilac rose and multicolored; stamps of No. 550a in light green and multicolored.)

1980, June 17				
552	A136	20c shown	24	24
553	A136	30c Diving	36	36
554	A136	60c Gymnast	60	60
555	A136	75c Basketball	90	90
556	A136	150c Running	1.80	1.80
a.		Souvenir sheet of 3	3.50	3.50
		Nos. 552-556 (5)	3.90	3.90

22nd Summer Olympic Games, Moscow, July 19-Aug. 3. No. 556a contains Nos. 554-556; green margin shows Moscow '80 emblem. Size: 100x72mm.

Fish Type of 1979

Tropical Fish: 10c, Osteoglossum bicirrhosum. 15c, Colossoma species. 25c, Hemigrammus pulcher. 30c, Petitella georgiae. 45c, Copeina guttata.

1980, Sept. 10		Photo.	Perf. 14x13	
557	A129	10c multi	12	12
558	A129	15c multi	18	18
559	A129	25c multi	30	30
560	A129	30c multi	36	36
561	A129	45c multi	55	55
		Nos. 557-561, C92-C94 (8)	4.16	4.16

Souvenir Sheet

Open Hands (Reflection)—A137

1980, Nov. 19		Litho.	Perf. 13x14	
562		Sheet of 3	4.25	4.25
a.	A137	50c shown	60	60
b.	A137	1g Shaking hands (cooperation)	1.20	1.20
c.	A137	2g Victory sign	2.40	2.40

5th anniversary of independence. No. 562 has multicolored margin showing various stamps of Surinam. Size: 91x121mm.

SURINAM

Passiflora Laurifolia—A138

Designs: Flower paintings by Maria Sibylle Merian (1647-1717).

1981, Jan. 14		Litho.	Perf. 13x14	
563	A138	20c shown	24	24
564	A138	30c Aphelandra pectinata	36	36
565	A138	60c Caesalpinia pulcherrima	72	72
566	A138	75c Hibiscus mutabilis	90	90
567	A138	1.25g Hippeastrum puniceum	1.50	1.50
		Nos. 563-567 (5)	3.72	3.72

Renovation of the Economic Order—A139

1981, Feb. 25			Perf. 14x13	
568	A139	30c shown	36	36
569	A139	60c Educational Order	72	72
570	A139	75c Social Order	90	90
571	A139	1g Political Order	1.20	1.20
a.		Souvenir sheet of 2		

Government renovation. No. 571a contains Nos. 569, 571; gold and orange margin. Size: 108x50mm.

Youths—A140

1981, Apr. 29		Litho.	Perf. 13½	
572		Sheet of 2	3.25	3.25
a.	A140	1g shown	1.20	1.20
b.	A140	1.50g Youths, diff.	1.80	1.80

Youth and its future. Entire sheet in continuous design; multicolored margin also shows map of Surinam. Size: 117x70mm.

Souvenir Sheet

No. 424, Exhibition Hall—A141

1981, May 22		Litho.	Perf. 13½x14	
573		Sheet of 3	4.25	4.25
a.	A141	50c shown	60	60
b.	A141	1g Penny Black	1.20	1.20
c.	A141	2g Austria #5	2.40	2.40

WIPA '81 Intl. Philatelic Exhibition, Vienna, May 22-31. No. 573 has multicolored margin showing exhibition emblem and hall. Size: 120x85mm.

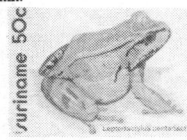

Leptodactylus Pentadactylus—A142

1981, June 24		Photo.	Perf. 14x13	
574	A142	40c Phyllomedusa hypochondrialis	50	50
575	A142	50c shown	60	60
576	A142	60c Hyla boans	72	72
		Nos. 574-576, C95-C97 (6)	5.42	5.42

Child Wearing Earphones A143

1981, Sept. 16		Litho.	Perf. 14x13	
580	A143	50c shown	60	60
581	A143	100c Child reading Braille	1.20	1.20
582	A143	150c Woman in wheelchair	1.80	1.80

Intl. Year of the Disabled.

Planter's House on Parakreek River—A144

Designs: Illustrations from Voyage to Surinam, by P.I. Benoit.

1981, Oct. 21		Photo.	Perf. 14x13	
583	A144	20c shown	25	25
584	A144	30c Saramaca St., Paramaribo	35	35
585	A144	75c Negro Hamlet, Paramaribo	90	90
586	A144	1g Fish Market, Paramaribo	1.20	1.20
a.		Miniature sheet of 4	1.25	1.25
587	A144	1.25g Blaauwe Berg Cascade	1.50	1.50
		Nos. 583-587 (5)	4.20	4.20

Research and Peaceful Uses of Space—A145

1982, Jan. 13		Litho.		
588	A145	35c Satellites	40	40
589	A145	65c Columbia space shuttle	75	75
590	A145	1g Apollo-Soyuz	1.20	1.20

Caretta Caretta—A146

1982, Feb. 17		Photo.	Perf. 14x13	
591	A146	5c shown	6	6
592	A146	10c Chelonia mydas	12	12
593	A146	20c Dermochelys coriacea	25	25
594	A146	25c Eretmochelys imbricata	30	30
595	A146	35c Lepidochelys olivacea	40	40
		Nos. 591-595, C98-C100 (8)	4.28	4.28

25th Anniv. of Lions Intl. in Surinam—A147

1982, May 7		Litho.		
596	A147	35c multi	40	40
597	A147	70c multi	80	80

Beatification of Father Petrus Donders, May 23—A148

1982, May 18		Litho.	Perf. 13x14	
598	A148	35c Helping the sick	40	40
599	A148	65c Birthplace, map	75	75
a.		Souvenir sheet		75

No. 599a contains No. 599; Yellow and black margin. Size: 50x72mm.

PHILEXFRANCE '82 Stamp Exhibition, Paris, June 11-21—A149

1982, June 9		Litho.	Perf. 13x14	
600	A149	50c Stamp designing	60	60
601	A149	100c Printing	1.25	1.25
602	A149	150c Collecting	1.85	1.85
a.		Souvenir sheet of 3	3.75	3.75

Nos. 600-602 in continuous design. No. 602a contains Nos. 600-602; multicolored margin. Size: 100x72mm.

TB Bacillus Centenary—A150

1982, Sept. 15		Litho.	Perf. 14x13	
603	A150	35c Text	40	40
604	A150	65c Microscope	75	75
605	A150	150c Bacillus	1.85	1.85

Marienburg Sugar Co. Centenary—A151

1982, Oct. 20				
606	A151	35c Mill	40	40
607	A151	65c Gathering cane	75	75
608	A151	100c Rail transport	1.20	1.20
609	A151	150c Gears	1.80	1.80

EBG Missionaries, 250th Anniv. in Caribbean
A152 A153

1982, Dec. 13		Litho.	Perf. 14x13, 13x14	
610	A152	35c Municipal Church, horiz.	40	40
611	A152	65c St. Thomas Monastery, horiz.	75	75
612	A152	150c Johan Leonhardt Dober (1706-1766)	1.80	1.80

1983, Jan. 12				

Flower Paintings by Maria Sibylle Merian (1647-1717). Nos. 613-618 horiz.

613	A153	1c Erythrina fusca	5	5
614	A153	2c Ipomoea acuminata	5	5
615	A153	3c Heliconia psittacorum	5	5
616	A153	5c Ipomoea	6	6
617	A153	10c Herba non denominata	12	12
618	A153	15c Anacardium occidentale	18	18
619	A153	20c shown	25	25
620	A153	25c Abelmoschus moschatus	30	30
621	A153	30c Argemone mexicana	36	36
622	A153	35c Costus arabicus	40	40
623	A153	45c Muellera frutescens	52	52
624	A153	65c Punica granatum	75	75

Scouting Year—A154

1983, Feb. 22		Litho.	Perf. 13x14	
625	A154	40c Anniv. emblem	50	50
626	A154	65c Baden-Powell	75	75
627	A154	70c Tent, campfire	80	80
628	A154	80c Ax in log	1.00	1.00

500th Birth Anniv. of Raphael—A155

Crayon sketches.

1983, Apr. 13		Photo.		
629	A155	5c multi	6	6
630	A155	10c multi	12	12
631	A155	40c multi	50	50
632	A155	65c multi	75	75
633	A155	70c multi	80	80
634	A155	80c multi	1.00	1.00
		Nos. 629-634 (6)	3.23	3.23

SURINAM

1982 Coins and Banknotes—A156

1983, June 1		Litho.	Perf. 14x13	
635	A156	5c 1-cent coin	6	6
636	A156	10c 5-cent coin	12	12
637	A156	40c 10-cent coin	50	50
638	A156	65c 25-cent coin	75	75
639	A156	70c 1g note	85	85
640	A156	80c 2.50g note	1.00	1.00
		Nos. 635-640 (6)	3.28	3.28

25th Anniv. of Dept. of Construction—A157

1983, June 15		Litho.	Perf. 13x14	
641	A157	25c Map	30	30
642	A157	50c Map, bulldozers	60	60

Local Butterflies—A158

Drawings by Maria Sibylle Merian (1647-1717). Nos. 643-648 vert.

		Litho.		
1983, Sept. 14		Perf. 13x14, 14x13		
643	A158	1c Papile anchisiades esper	5	5
644	A158	2c Urania leilus	5	5
645	A158	3c Morpho deidamia	5	5
646	A158	5c Thysania aguippina	6	6
647	A158	10c Morpho sp.	12	12
648	A158	15c Metamorpha dido	18	18
649	A158	20c Morpho menelaus	24	24
650	A158	25c Manduca rustica	30	30
651	A158	30c Rothschildia sp.	36	36
652	A158	35c Catopsilia ebule	42	42
653	A158	45c Papilio androgeos	55	55
654	A148	65c Eumorpha vitis	80	80

Manned Ballooning, 200th Anniv.—A159

Designs: 5c, 1783, sheep, cock and duck. 10c, first manned flight, d'Arlandes and Pilatre de Rozier. 40c, first hydrogen balloon, Jacques Charles. 65c, 1870, Paris flight, minister Gambetta. 70c, Double Eagle II, transatlantic flight. 80c, Intl. Balloon Festival, Albuquerque.

1983, Oct. 19		Litho.	Perf. 13x14	
655	A159	5c multi	6	6
656	A159	10c multi	12	12
657	A159	40c multi	50	.50
658	A159	65c multi	75	75
659	A159	70c multi	85	85
660	A159	80c multi	1.00	1.00
		Nos. 655-660 (6)	3.28	3.28

Martin Luther, 500th Birth Anniv.—A160

1983, Dec. 7		Litho.		
661	A160	25c Portrait	30	30
662	A160	50c Engraving	60	60

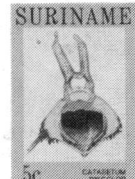

Local Flowers—A161

1984, Jan. 11		Litho.		
663	A161	5c Catasetum discolor	6	6
664	A161	10c Menadenium labiosum	12	12
665	A161	40c Comparettia falcata	50	50
666	A161	50c Rodriquezia decora	75	75
667	A161	70c Oncidium papilio	85	85
668	A161	75c Epidendrum porpax	92	92
		Nos. 663-668 (6)	3.20	3.20

Local Seashells—A162

1984, Feb. 22		Litho.		
669	A162	40c Arca zebra	50	50
670	A162	65c Trachycardium egmontianum	82	82
671	A162	70c Tellina radiata	85	85
672	A162	80c Vermicularia knorrii	1.00	1.00

Intl. Civil Aviation Org., 40th Anniv.—A163

1984, May 16		Litho.	Perf. 14x13	
673	A163	35c Sea plane	42	42
674	A163	65c Surinam Airways jet	82	82

1984 Summer Olympics—A164

Greek Art and Artifacts: Ancient Games.

1984, June 13			Perf. 13x14	
675	A164	2c Running	5	5
676	A164	3c Javelin, discus, long jump	5	5
677	A164	5c Massage	6	6
678	A164	10c Ointment massage	12	12
679	A164	15c Wrestling	18	18
680	A164	20c Boxing	25	25
681	A164	30c Horse racing	38	38
682	A164	35c Chariot racing	42	42
683	A164	45c Temple of Olympia	56	56
684	A164	50c Crypt entrance	62	62
685	A164	65c Olympia Stadium	82	82
686	A164	75c Zeus (bust)	95	95
	a.	Miniature sheet of 3 (#675, 682, 686)	1.50	
		Nos. 675-686 (12)	4.46	4.46

Size of No. 686a: 95x64mm.

Scott
First in the Field

- Buying
- Selling
- Estate Appraisals
- Auction Consignments

ALL SERVICES AVAILABLE FROM THE RECOGNIZED PHILATELIC EXPERTS

TO PLACE YOUR NAME ON OUR LIST TO RECEIVE INFORMATION ABOUT SERVICES ON OUR UPCOMING SALES, WRITE TO:

The Scott Auction Galleries
3 EAST 57TH ST.
NEW YORK, N.Y. 10022

SURINAM

SEMI-POSTAL STAMPS

Green Cross—SP1

SP2   SP3
Photogravure

1927   Perf. 12½   Unwmkd.

B1	SP1	2c (+2c) bl blk & grn	1.25	1.50
B2	SP2	5c (+3c) vio & grn	1.25	1.50
B3	SP3	10c (+3c) ver & grn	2.50	1.75

The money received for the surtax on these stamps was given to the Green Cross Society, an organization similar to the Red Cross Society in other countries.

Nurse and Patient   Good Samaritan
SP4   SP5

1928, Dec. 1   Perf. 11½

B4	SP4	1½c (+1½c) ultra	6.00	6.00
B5	SP4	2c (+2c) bl grn	6.00	6.00
B6	SP4	5c (+3c) vio	6.00	6.00
B7	SP4	7½c (+2½c) ver	6.00	6.00

The surtax on these stamps was for a fund to combat indigenous diseases.

1929, Dec. 1   Perf. 12½

B8	SP5	1½c (+1½c) grn	8.00	8.00
B9	SP5	2c (+2c) scar	8.00	8.00
B10	SP5	5c (+3c) ultra	8.00	8.00
B11	SP5	6c (+4c) blk	8.00	8.00

The surtax on these stamps was for the benefit of the Green Cross Society.

Surinam Mother and Child—SP6

1931, Dec. 14

B12	SP6	1½c (+1½c) blk	6.00	6.00
B13	SP6	2c (+2c) car rose	6.00	6.00
B14	SP6	5c (+3c) ultra	6.00	6.00
B15	SP6	6c (+4c) dp grn	6.00	6.00

The surtax was for Child Welfare Societies.

Designs Symbolical of the Creed
of the Moravians
SP7   SP8

1935, Aug. 1   Perf. 12½x13½

B16	SP7	1c (+½c) dk brn	2.50	2.00
B17	SP7	2c (+1c) dp ultra	4.00	2.00
B18	SP8	3c (+1½c) grn	4.25	3.25
B19	SP8	4c (+2c) red org	4.25	3.25
B20	SP8	5c (+2½c) blk brn	4.25	3.75
B21	SP7	10c (+5c) car	4.25	3.75
		Nos. B16-B21 (6)	23.50	18.00

200th anniversary of the founding of the Moravian Mission in Surinam.

Surinam Child
SP9

1936, Dec. 14   Perf. 12½

B22	SP9	2c (+1c) dk grn	3.75	3.75
B23	SP9	3c (+1½c) dk bl	3.75	3.75
B24	SP9	5c (+2½c) brn blk	4.50	4.50
B25	SP9	10c (+5c) lake	4.50	4.50

"Emancipation"   Surinam Girl
SP10   SP11

1938, June 1   Litho.   Perf. 12½x12

| B26 | SP10 | 2½c (+2c) dk bl grn | 2.25 | 1.75 |

Photogravure

B27	SP11	3c (+2c) vio blk	2.25	1.75
B28	SP11	5c (+3c) dk brn	2.50	2.25
B29	SP11	7½c (+5c) ind	2.50	2.25

Issued in commemoration of the 75th anniversary of the abolition of slavery in Surinam.

Creole Woman   Javanese Woman
SP12   SP13

Hindustani   American Indian
Woman   Woman
SP14   SP15

1940   Engraved.   Perf. 12½x14

B30	SP12	2½c (+2c) dk grn	2.50	2.50
B31	SP13	3c (+2c) red org	2.50	2.50
B32	SP14	5c (+3c) dp bl	2.50	2.50
B33	SP15	7½c (+5c) hn brn	2.50	2.50

Netherlands Coat of Arms
and Inscription,
"Netherlands Shall Rise Again"
SP16

1941, Aug. 30   Typo.   Perf. 12½

B34	SP16	7½c + 7½c dp org, ultra & blk	3.00	3.00
B35	SP16	15c + 15c scar, ultra & blk	3.50	3.50
B36	SP16	1g + 1g gray & ultra	25.00	20.00

The surtax was used to buy bombers for Dutch pilots in the Royal Air Force of Great Britain.

Stamps of 1936-41 Surcharged in Red:

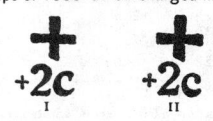

1942, Jan. 2

B37	A23	2c + 2c blk brn, I	2.00	2.00
a.		Type II	2.00	2.00
B38	A26	2c + 2c blk brn, I	52.50	45.00
a.		Type II	52.50	45.00
B39	A23	2½c + 2c grn, I	2.00	2.00
a.		Type II	2.00	2.00
B40	A23	7½c + 5c red vio, III		
a.		Type IV	15.00	15.00
b.		Type V	40.00	40.00

The surtax was for the Red Cross.
In type III, the "c" may be "large," as illustrated, or "small," as in type II. Price is the same.
The distinctive feature of type IV is the pointed ending of the lower part of the "5."

Types of
Regular Issue of 1945
Surcharged in Black

Engraved.

1945, July 23   Perf. 12   Unwmkd.

B41	A29	7½c + 5c dp org	3.50	2.25
B42	A30	15c + 10c brn	3.00	2.25
B43	A30	20c + 15c dl grn	3.00	2.25
B44	A30	22½c + 20c gray	3.00	2.25
B45	A30	40c + 35c rose lake	3.00	2.25
B46	A30	60c + 50c vio	3.00	2.25
		Nos. B41-B46 (6)	18.50	13.50

The surtax was for the National Welfare Fund.

Star   Marie Curie
SP17   SP18

Photogravure.

1947, Dec. 16   Perf. 13½x12½

| B47 | SP17 | 7½c + 12½c red org | 3.00 | 2.50 |
| B48 | SP17 | 12½c + 37½c bl | 3.00 | 2.50 |

The surtax was used to combat leprosy. See also Nos. CB4-CB5.

Inscribed: "Kanker Bestrijding."

1950, May 15   Perf. 14x13
Designs: 7½c+22½c, 27½c+12½c,
William Roentgen.

B49	SP18	7½c + 7½c lil	12.00	8.50
B50	SP18	7½c + 22½c dl bl grn	12.00	8.50
B51	SP18	27½c + 12½c dp gray bl	12.00	8.50
B52	SP18	27½c + 97½c red brn	12.00	8.50

The surtax was used to combat cancer.

Nos. 236-237
Surcharged in
Black or Red
STORMRAMP
NEDERLAND
1953

Perf. 14x13

1953, Feb. 18   Wmk. 202

| B53 | A35 | 12½c + 7½c on 7½c dp org | 3.50 | 3.00 |
| B54 | A35 | 20c + 10c on 17½c ultra (R) | 3.50 | 3.00 |

The surtax was for flood relief in the Netherlands.

Stadium, Paramaribo
SP19

Photogravure

1953, Aug. 29   Perf. 13½   Unwmkd.

B55	SP19	10c + 5c cl	11.00	8.00
B56	SP19	15c + 7½c brn	11.00	8.00
B57	SP19	30c + 15c dk grn	11.00	8.00

Issued to publicize Sport Week, 1953.

Surinam Children   Doves
SP20   SP21

1954, Nov. 1   Perf. 13x14

B58	SP20	7½c + 3c sep	7.50	6.00
B59	SP20	10c + 5c bl grn	7.50	6.00
B60	SP20	15c + 7½c red brn	7.50	6.00
B61	SP20	30c + 15c bl	7.50	6.00

The surtax was for the youth center of the Moravian Church.

1955, May 5   Perf. 14x13

| B62 | SP21 | 7½c + 3½c brt red | 3.75 | 3.00 |
| B63 | SP21 | 15c + 8c ultra | 3.75 | 3.00 |

Issued to commemorate the 10th anniversary of the Netherlands' liberation.

Queen Juliana and
Prince Bernhard
SP22

SURINAM

1955, Oct. 27   Unwmkd.
| B64 | SP22 | 7½c +2½c dk ol | 90 | 60 |

Royal visit to Surinam, 1955.

Theater, 1837
SP23

Designs: 10c+5c, Theater and car, circa 1920. 15c+7½c, Theater and car, circa 1958. 20c+10c, Theater interior.

1958, Feb. 15   Litho.   *Perf. 13x12½*
B65	SP23	7½c +3c lt bl & blk	80	80
B66	SP23	10c +5c rose lil & blk	80	80
B67	SP23	15c +7½c lt grn & blk	80	80
B68	SP23	20c +10c org & blk	80	80

Issued to commemorate the 120th anniversary of the "Thalia" theatrical society.

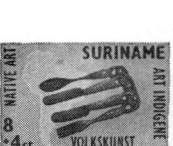

Carved Eating Utensils and Map of South America
SP24

Uprooted Oak Emblem of WRY
SP25

Native Art (Map of So. America and): 10c+5c, Feather headgear. 15c+7c, Clay pottery. 20c+10c, Carved wooden stool.

1960, Jan. 15
B69	SP24	8c +4c multi	1.60	1.40
B70	SP24	10c +5c sal, red & bl	1.60	1.40
B71	SP24	15c +7c red org, grn & sep	1.60	1.40
B72	SP24	20c +10c lt bl, ultra & bis	1.60	1.40

1960, Apr. 7   *Perf. 12½x13½*
| B73 | SP25 | 8c +4c choc & grn | 40 | 40 |
| B74 | SP25 | 10c +5c vio bl & ol grn | 40 | 40 |

Issued to publicize World Refugee Year, July 1, 1959—June 30, 1960. The surtax was for aid to refugees.

Putting the Shot
SP26

Sports: 10c+5c, Basketball. 15c+7c, Runner. 20c+10c, Swimmer. 40c+20c, Soccer.

1960, Aug. 10   Photo.   *Perf. 14x13*
B75	SP26	8c +4c gray, brn & blk	1.25	1.10
B76	SP26	10c +5c red org & blk	1.25	1.25
B77	SP26	15c +7c vio, bis & blk	1.75	1.25
B78	SP26	20c +10c bl, bis & blk	1.75	1.40

| B79 | SP26 | 40c +20c emer, brn & blk | 1.75 | 1.75 |
| Nos. B75–B79 (5) | | | 7.75 | 6.75 |

Issued to commemorate the 17th Olympic Games, Rome, Aug. 25–Sept. 11.

Girl Scout Signaling
SP27

Designs: 10c+3c, Scout Saluting (vert.). 15c+4c, Brownies around toadstool. 20c+5c, Scouts around campfire (vert.). 25c+6c, Scouts cooking outdoors.

Lithographed
1961, Aug. 19   *Perf. 14x13, 13x14*
Multicolored Designs.
B80	SP27	8c +2c bl	70	70
B81	SP27	10c +3c lil	70	70
B82	SP27	15c +4c yel	70	70
B83	SP27	20c +5c brn red	70	70
B84	SP27	25c +6c aqua	70	70
Nos. B80–B84 (5)			3.50	3.50

Caribbean Girl Scout Jamborette.

Hibiscus—SP28

Flowers: 10c+5c, Caesalpinia pulcherrima. 15c+6c, Heliconia psittacorum. 20c+10c, Lochnera rosea. 25c+12c, Ixora macrothyrsa.

1962, Mar. 7   Photo.   *Perf. 14x13½*
Cross in Red.
B85	SP28	8c +4c dk ol & scar	50	50
B86	SP28	10c +5c dk bl & org	50	50
B87	SP28	15c +6c multi	50	50
B88	SP28	20c +10c multi	50	50
B89	SP28	25c +12c dk bl grn, red & yel	50	50
Nos. B85–B89 (5)			2.50	2.50

The surtax was for the Red Cross.

Hands Protecting Duck
SP29

American Indian Girl
SP30

Designs: 8c+2c, Dog. 10c+3c, Donkey. 15c+4c, Horse.

1962, Dec. 15   Litho.   *Perf. 13x14*
B90	SP29	2c +1c chlky bl & red	20	20
B91	SP29	8c +2c blk & red	40	40
B92	SP29	10c +3c dl grn & blk	40	40
B93	SP29	15c +4c red & blk	40	40

The surtax was for the Organization for Animal Protection.

1963, Oct. 30   Photo.   Unwmkd.

Girls: 10c+4c, Negro. 15c+10c, East Indian. 20c+10c, Indonesian. 40c+20c, Caucasian.

B94	SP30	8c +3c Prus grn	20	20
B95	SP30	10c +4c red brn	30	30
a.	Minature sheet of 4		2.50	2.50

B96	SP30	15c +10c dp bl	40	40
B97	SP30	20c +10c brn red	40	40
B98	SP30	40c +20c red vio	50	50
Nos. B94–B98 (5)			1.80	1.80

The surtax was for Child Welfare. No. B95a contains two each of Nos. B94–B95.

X-15
SP31

Designs: 8c+4c, Flag of the Aeronautical and Astronautical Foundation. 10c+5c, 20c+10c, Agena B Ranger rocket.

1964, Apr. 14   *Perf. 13x12½*
B99	SP31	3c +2c blk & rose lake	20	20
B100	SP31	8c +4c blk, ultra & lt ultra	30	30
B101	SP31	10c +5c blk & grn	30	30
B102	SP31	15c +7c blk & yel brn	40	40
B103	SP31	20c +10c blk & vio	40	40
Nos. B99–B103 (5)			1.60	1.60

The surtax was for the benefit of the Aeronautical and Astronautical Foundation of Surinam.

Stylized Campfire amid Trees
SP32

Girls Skipping Rope
SP33

1964, July 29   *Perf. 13x14*
B104	SP32	3c +1c brn ol, yel bis & lem	10	10
B105	SP32	8c +4c bluish blk, vio bl & yel bis	20	20
B106	SP32	10c +5c dk red, red & yel bis	30	30
B107	SP32	20c +10c grnsh blk, ol grn & yel bis	40	40

Issued to commemorate the Jamborette at Paramaribo, Aug. 20–30, marking the 40th anniversary of the Surinam Boy Scout Association.

Designs: 10c+4c, Children on swings. 15c+9c, Girl on scooter. 20c+10c, Boy rolling hoop.

1964, Nov. 30   Photo.   *Perf. 14x13*
B108	SP33	8c +3c dk bl	10	10
B109	SP33	10c +4c red	20	20
a.	Minature sheet of 4		80	80
B110	SP33	15c +9c ol grn	30	30
B111	SP33	20c +10c mag	40	40

Issued for Child Welfare. No. B109a contains 2 each of Nos. B108–B109.

Mother and Child
SP34

Designs: 4c+2c, Pregnant woman. 15c+7c, Child. 25c+12c, Old man.

1965, Feb. 27   Photo.   *Perf. 13x14*
| B112 | SP34 | 4c +2c grn | 10 | 10 |

B113	SP34	10c +5c brn & grn	20	20
B114	SP34	15c +7c Prus bl & grn	30	30
B115	SP34	25c +12c brt pur & grn	40	40

Issued to commemorate the 50th anniversary of the Green Cross Association which promotes public health services.

Girl with Leopard and Spider
SP35

Designs: 10c+5c, Boy with monkey and spider. 15c+7c, Girl with tortoise and spider. 25c+10c, Boy with rabbit and spider.

Perf. 13x12½
1965, Nov. 26   Litho.   Unwmkd.
B116	SP35	4c +4c blk & grn	10	10
B117	SP35	10c +5c ocher & blk	20	20
B118	SP35	15c +7c dp org & blk	30	30
a.	Minature sheet of 4		90	90
B119	SP35	25c +10c lt ultra & blk	30	30

Issued for Child Welfare. No. B118a contains 2 each of Nos. B116 and B118.

"Help them to a safe haven"
SP35a

1966, Jan. 31   Photo.   *Perf. 14x13*
B120	SP35a	10c +5c blk & grn	30	30
B121	SP35a	25c +10c blk & rose brn	30	30
a.	Min. sheet of 3		1.00	1.00

The surtax was for the Intergovernmental Committee for European Migration (ICEM). The message on the stamps was given and signed by Queen Juliana. No. B121a contains two Nos. B120 and one No. B121. Size: 117x43mm.

Mary Magdalene, Disciples and "Round Table" Emblem
SP36

"New Year's Eve" Boys with Bamboo Gun
SP37

Mary Magdalene (John 20:18), and Service Club Emblems: 15c+8c, Toastmasters International. 20c+10c, Junior Chamber, Surinam. 25c+12c, Rotary International. 30c+15c, Lions International.

1966, Apr. 13   Photo.   *Perf. 12½x13*
B122	SP36	10c +5c dp crim, blk & gold	15	15
B123	SP36	15c +8c dp vio, blk & bl	25	25
B124	SP36	20c +10c yel org, blk & ultra	35	35
B125	SP36	25c +12c grn, blk & gold	40	40
B126	SP36	30c +15c ultra, blk & gold	50	50
Nos. B122–B126 (5)			1.65	1.65

Issued for Easter 1966.

SURINAM

1966, Nov. 25 Litho. Perf. 12½x13
Designs: 15c+8c, "The End of Lent," boys pouring paint over each other. 20c+10c, "Liberation Day," parading children. 25c+12c, "Queen's Birthday," children on hobbyhorses. 30c+15c, "Christmas," Children decorating room with star.

B127	SP37	10c +5c multi	10	10
B128	SP37	15c +8c multi	30	30
B129	SP37	20c +10c multi	25	25
a.		Minature sheet of 3	70	
B130	SP37	25c +12c multi	50	50
B131	SP37	30c +15c multi	50	50
		Nos. B127-B131 (5)	1.65	1.65

Issued for child welfare. No. B129a contains two No. B127 and one No. B129. Size: 96x76mm.

Good Samaritan Giving His Coat SP38 — Children Stilt-walking SP39

The Good Samaritan: 15c+8c, Dressing the wounds. 20c+10c, Feeding the poor man. 25c+12c, Poor man riding Samaritan's horse. 30c+15c, Samaritan taking poor man to the inn.

1967, March 22

B132	SP38	10c +5c yel & blk	15	15
B133	SP38	15c +8c lt blk & blk	25	25
B134	SP38	20c +10c buff & blk	35	35
B135	SP38	25c +12c pale rose & blk	45	45
B136	SP38	30c +15c mult	45	45
		Nos. B132-B136 (5)	1.65	1.65

Issued for Easter 1967.

1967, Nov. 27 Litho. Perf. 12½x13
Children's Games: 15c+8c, Boys playing with marbles. 20c+10c, Girl playing dibs (five stones). 25c+12c, Boy making kite. 30c+15c, Girls play-cooking.

B137	SP39	10c +5c multi	15	15
B138	SP39	15c +8c multi	40	40
B139	SP39	20c +10c multi	30	30
a.		Minature sheet of 3	90	90
B140	SP39	25c +12c multi	55	55
B141	SP39	30c +15c multi	55	55
		Nos. B137-B141 (5)	1.95	1.95

Issued for child welfare. No. B139a contains two No. B137 and one No. B139. Size: 96x75mm.

Cross, Ash Wednesday SP40 — Hopscotch SP41

Easter Symbols: 15c+8c, Palms, Palm Sunday. 20c+10c, Bread and Wine, Maundy Thursday. 25c+12c, Cross, Good Friday. 30c+15c, Chrismon, Easter Sunday.

1968, Apr. 10 Litho. Perf. 12½x13

B142	SP40	10c +5c lil & gray	20	20
B143	SP40	15c +8c brick red & grn	30	30
B144	SP40	20c +10c yel & dk grn	40	40
B145	SP40	25c +12c gray & blk	50	50
B146	SP40	30c +15c brt yel & brn	50	50
		Nos. B142-B146 (5)	1.90	1.90

1968, Nov. 22 Photo. Perf. 12½x13
Designs: 15c+8c, Balancing pyramid. 20c+10c, Handball. 25c+12c, Handicraft. 30c+15c, Tug-of-war.

B147	SP41	10c +5c fawn & blk	20	20
B148	SP41	15c +8c lt ultra & blk	30	30
B149	SP41	20c +10c pink & blk	40	40
a.		Min. sheet of 3	1.00	
B150	SP41	25c +12c yel grn & blk	50	50
B151	SP41	30c +15c bluish lil & blk	70	70
		Nos. B147-B151 (5)	2.10	2.10

Issued for child welfare. No. B149a contains two No. B147 and one No. B149. Size: 97x76mm.

Globe with Map of South America SP42 — Pillow Fight SP43

Easter Issue
1969, Apr. 2 Litho. Perf. 12½x13

B152	SP42	10c +5c bl & lt bl	55	55
B153	SP42	15c +8c sl grn & yel	60	60
B154	SP42	20c +10c sl grn & gray grn	65	65
B155	SP42	25c +12c brn & bis	75	75
B156	SP42	30c +15c vio & gray	80	80
		Nos. B152-B156 (5)	3.35	3.35

1969, Nov. 21 Litho. Perf. 12½x13
Designs: 15c+8c, Eating contest. 20c+10c, Pole climbing. 25c+12c, Sack race. 30c+15c, Obstacle race.

B157	SP43	10c +5c lt ultra & mag	30	30
B158	SP43	15c +8c yel & brn	50	50
B159	SP43	20c +10c gray & dp bl	40	40
a.		Min. sheet of 3	1.75	1.40
B160	SP43	25c +12c pink & brt bl	75	75
B161	SP43	30c +15c emer & brn	75	75
		Nos. B157-B161 (5)	2.70	2.70

Issued for child welfare. No. B159a contains two No. B157 and one No. B159. Size: 97x75mm.

Flower SP44 — Ludwig van Beethoven, 1786 SP45

Designs: 15c+8c, Butterfly. 20c+10c, Flying bird. 25c+12c, Sun. 30c+15c, Star.

1970, Mar. 25 Litho. Perf. 12½x13

B162	SP44	10c +5c multi	1.10	1.10
B163	SP44	15c +8c multi	1.10	1.10
B164	SP44	20c +10c multi	1.10	1.10
B165	SP44	25c +12c multi	1.10	1.10
B166	SP44	30c +15c multi	1.25	1.25
		Nos. B162-B166 (5)	5.65	5.65

Easter 1970.

1970, Nov. 25 Litho. Perf. 12½x13
Various Portraits of Beethoven: 15c+8c, In 1804. 20c+10c, In 1812. 25c+12c, In 1814. 30c+15c, In 1827 (death mask).

Portrait and Inscription in Gray and Ocher

B167	SP45	10c +5c grn	90	90
B168	SP45	15c +8c scar	1.10	1.10
B169	SP45	20c +10c bl	1.10	1.10
a.		Minature sheet of 3	3.00	3.00
B170	SP45	25c +12c red org	1.10	1.10
B171	SP45	30c +15c pur	1.25	1.25
		Nos. B167-B171 (5)	5.45	5.45

Issued to commemorate the bicentenary of the birth of Ludwig van Beethoven (1770–1827), composer. The surtax was for child welfare. No. B169a contains 2 No. B167 and one No. B169. Size: 97x77mm.

Donkey and Palm SP46 — Leapfrog, by Peter Brueghel SP47

Designs: 15c+8c, Cock. 20c+10c, Lamb of God. 25c+12c, Cross and Crown of Thorns. 30c+15c, Sun.

1971, Apr. 7 Litho. Perf. 12½x13

B172	SP46	10c +5c multi	1.00	1.00
B173	SP46	15c +8c bl & multi	1.10	1.10
B174	SP46	20c +10c multi	1.10	1.10
B175	SP46	25c +12c multi	1.10	1.10
B176	SP46	30c +15c multi	1.10	1.10
		Nos. B172-B176 (5)	5.40	5.40

Easter 1971.

1971, Nov. 24 Photo. Perf. 13½x14
Children's Games, by Peter Brueghel: 15c+8c, Girl strewing flowers. 20c+10c, Spinning the hoop. 25c+12c, Ball players. 30c+15c, Stilt walker.

B177	SP47	10c +5c multi	1.00	1.00
B178	SP47	15c +8c multi	1.00	1.00
B179	SP47	20c +10c multi	1.00	1.00
a.		Minature sheet of 3	3.00	3.00
B180	SP47	25c +12c multi	1.00	1.00
B181	SP47	30c +15c multi	1.00	1.00
		Nos. B177-B181 (5)	5.00	5.00

Child welfare. No. B179a contains 2 No. B177 and one No. B179. Size: 119x83mm.

Easter Candle SP48 — Toys SP49

Designs: 15c+8c, Christ teaching Apostles, and crosses. 20c+10c, Cup and folded hands. 25c+12c, Fish in net. 30c+15c, Judas' bag of silver.

1972, Mar. 29 Litho. Perf. 12x13

B182	SP48	10c +5c multi	80	80
B183	SP48	15c +8c multi	80	80
B184	SP48	20c +10c multi	80	80
B185	SP48	25c +12c multi	80	80
B186	SP48	30c +15c multi	80	80
		Nos. B182-B186 (5)	4.00	4.00

Easter 1972.

1972, Nov. 29 Litho. Perf. 12½x13
Designs: 15c+8c, Abacus and clock. 20c+10c, Pythagorean theorem. 25c+12c, Model of molecule. 30c+15c, Monkey wrench and drill. Each design represents a different stage of education.

B187	SP49	10c +5c multi	70	70
B188	SP49	15c +8c multi	1.00	1.00
B189	SP49	20c +10c multi	90	90
a.		Minature sheet of 3	2.50	2.50
B190	SP49	25c +12c multi	1.00	1.00
B191	SP49	30c +15c multi	1.00	1.00
		Nos. B187-B191 (5)	4.60	4.60

Child welfare. No. B189a contains 2 No. B187 and one No. B189. Size: 96x 76mm.

Jesus Calming the Waves SP50

Designs: 15c+8c, The washing of the feet. 20c+10c, Jesus carrying Cross. 25c+12c, Cross and "ELI, ELI, LAMA SABACHTHANI?" 30c+15c, on the road to Emmaus.

1973, Apr. 4 Litho. Perf. 12½x13

B192	SP50	10c +5c multi	70	70
B193	SP50	15c +8c multi	70	70
B194	SP50	20c +10c multi	70	70
B195	SP50	25c +12c multi	70	70
B196	SP50	30c +15c multi	70	70
		Nos. B192-B196 (5)	3.50	3.50

Easter 1973.

Red Cross and Florence Nightingale SP51

1973, Oct. 3 Litho. Perf. 15x14

B197	SP51	30c +10c multi	1.25	1.25

30th anniversary of Surinam Red Cross.

Flower SP52 — Bitterwood SP53

1973, Nov. 28 Litho. Perf. 14x14½
Multicolored

B198	SP52	10c +5c shown	40	40
B199	SP52	15c +8c Tree	60	60
B200	SP52	20c +10c Dog	60	60
a.		Minature sheet of 3	1.75	1.40
B201	SP52	25c +12c House	80	80
B202	SP52	30c +15c Girl	80	80
		Nos. B198-B202 (5)	3.20	3.20

Child welfare. No. B200a contains two No. B198 and one No. B200.

1974, Apr. 3 Litho. Perf. 14x14½
Tropical Flowers: 15c+8c, Passion flower. 20c+10c, Wild angelica. 25c+12c, Candlestick senna. 30c+15c, Blood flower.

B203	SP53	10c +5c multi	60	60
B204	SP53	15c +8c multi	70	70
B205	SP53	20c +10c multi	70	70

SURINAM

B206	SP53	25c +12c multi	70	70
B207	SP53	30c +15c multi	70	70
	Nos. B203-B207 (5)		3.40	3.40

Easter charities.

Boy Scout, Tent and Trees
SP54

Designs: 15c+8c, 5th Caribbean Jamboree emblem. 20c+10c, Scouts and emblem.

1974, Aug. 21   Litho.   Perf. 14x14½

B208	SP54	10c +5c multi	50	50
B209	SP54	15c +8c multi	50	50
B210	SP54	20c +10c multi	60	60

50th anniversary of Surinam Boy Scouts.

Fruit
SP55

Designs: 15c+8c, Children, birds and nest (security). 20c+10c, Flower, mother and child (protection). 25c+12c, Child and corn (good food). 30c+15c, Dancing children (child care).

1974, Nov. 27   Litho.   Perf. 14½x14

B211	SP55	10c +5c multi	40	30
B212	SP55	15c +8c multi	50	50
B213	SP55	20c +10c multi	60	55
a.		Miniature sheet of 3	1.40	1.15
B214	SP55	25c +12c multi	70	70
B215	SP55	30c +15c multi	80	80
	Nos. B211-B215 (5)		3.00	2.85

Child welfare. No. B213a contains two No. B211 and one No. B213.

The Good Shepherd
SP56

Woman and IWY Emblem
SP57

Designs: 20c+10c, Peter's denial. 30c+15c, The Women at the Tomb. 35c+20c, Jesus showing His wounds to Thomas.

1975, Mar. 26   Litho.   Perf. 12½x13

B216	SP56	15c +5c yel grn & grn	70	60
B217	SP56	20c +10c org & dk bl	90	80
B218	SP56	30c +15c yel & red	1.00	80
B219	SP56	35c +20c bl & pur	1.00	80

Easter charities.

1975, May 14   Photo.   Perf. 12½x13

B220	SP57	15c +5c multi	90	70
B221	SP57	30c +15c multi	90	70

International Women's Year 1975.

Carib Indian Water Jug
SP58

Designs: 20c+10c, 35c+20c, Indian arrowhead (diff.). 30c+15c, Wayana board with animal figures.

1975, Nov. 12   Litho.   Perf. 12½x13

B222	SP58	15c +5c multi	60	50
B223	SP58	20c +10c multi	70	60
a.		Miniature sheet of 3	1.75	1.50
B224	SP58	30c +15c multi	1.00	90
B225	SP58	35c +20c multi	1.10	1.00

Child welfare. No. B223a contains 2 No. B222 and one No. B223.

Feeding the Hungry
SP59

Paintings: 25c+15c, Visiting the Sick. 30c+15c, Clothing the Naked. 35c+15c, Burying the Dead. 50c+25c, Giving Water to the Thirsty. Designs after panels in Alkmaar Church, 1504.

1976, Apr. 14   Photo.   Perf. 14x13

B226	SP59	20c +10c multi	40	40
B227	SP59	25c +15c multi	50	50
B228	SP59	30c +15c multi	60	60
a.		Souvenir sheet of 3	1.50	1.50
B229	SP59	35c +15c multi	65	65
B230	SP59	50c +25c multi	1.00	1.00
	Nos. B226-B230 (5)		3.15	3.15

Easter 1976. No. B228a contains 2 No. B226 and one No. B228. Black marginal inscription.

Pekingese and Boy's Head
SP60

Designs (Child's Head and): 25c+10c, German shepherd. 30c+15c, Dachshund. 35c+15c, Retriever. 50c+25c, Terrier.

1976   Litho.   Perf. 13½

B231	SP60	20c +10c multi	40	40
B232	SP60	25c +10c multi	55	55
B233	SP60	30c +15c multi	60	60
a.		Miniature sheet of 3	1.50	1.50
B234	SP60	35c +15c multi	65	65
B235	SP60	50c +25c multi	1.00	1.00
	Nos. B231-B235 (5)		3.20	3.20

Surtax was for child welfare. No. B233a contains 2 No. B231 and one No. B233. Size: 139x99mm.

St. Veronica's Veil
SP61

Descent from the Cross
SP62

Designs: Religious scenes, side panels, front and back, from triptych by Jan Mostaert (1473-1555).

1977, Apr. 6   Litho.   Perf. 13½x14

B236	SP61	20c +10c multi	40	40
B237	SP61	25c +15c multi	55	55
B238	SP61	30c +15c multi	60	60
B239	SP62	35c +15c multi	65	65
B240	SP61	50c +25c multi	1.00	1.00
	Nos. B236-B240 (5)		3.20	3.20

Easter 1977.

Dog and Girl's Head
SP63

Crosses, Luke 23:43
SP64

Designs (Child's Head and): 25c+15c, Monkey. 30c+15c, Rabbit. 35c+15c, Cat. 50c+25c, Parrot.

1977, Nov. 23   Litho.   Perf. 13x14

B241	SP63	20c +10c multi	40	40
B242	SP63	25c +15c multi	55	55
B243	SP63	30c +15c multi	60	60
a.		Miniature sheet of 3	1.50	1.50
B244	SP63	35c +15c multi	65	65
B245	SP63	50c +25c multi	1.00	1.00
	Nos. B241-B245 (5)		3.20	3.20

Surtax was for child welfare. No. B243a contains 2 No. B241 and one No. B243. Size: 100x72mm.

1978, Mar. 22   Litho.   Perf. 12½x14

Designs: 25c+15c, Serpent and Cross, John 3:14. 30c+15c, Lamb and blood, Exodus 12:13. 35c+15c, Passover plate, chalice and bread. 60c+30c, Cross and solar eclipse.

B246	SP64	20c +10c multi	48	48
B247	SP64	25c +15c multi	65	65
B248	SP64	35c +15c multi	72	72
B249	SP64	35c +15c multi	80	80
B250	SP64	60c +30c multi	1.45	1.45
	Nos. B246-B250 (5)		4.10	4.10

Easter 1978.

Child's Head and White Cat
SP65

Church, Cross and Chalice
SP66

Designs: Child's head and cats in various positions.

1978, Nov. 22   Litho.   Perf. 14x13

B251	SP65	20c +10c multi	35	35
B252	SP65	25c +15c multi	48	48
B253	SP65	30c +15c multi	55	55
a.		Miniature sheet of 3	1.25	1.25
B254	SP65	35c +15c multi	60	60
B255	SP65	60c +30c multi	1.10	1.10
	Nos. B251-B255 (5)		3.08	3.08

Surtax was for child welfare. No. B253a contains 2 No. B251 and one No. B253. Size: 144x50mm.

1979, Apr. 11   Litho.   Perf. 13x14

Easter: Cross, chalice and various churches.

B256	SP66	20c +10c multi	35	35
B257	SP66	30c +15c multi	55	55
B258	SP66	35c +15c multi	60	60
B259	SP66	40c +20c multi	70	70
B260	SP66	60c +30c multi	1.05	1.05
	Nos. B256-B260 (5)		3.25	3.25

Boy, Bird, Red Cross, Blood Transfusion Bottle—SP67

1979, Nov. 21   Litho.   Perf. 13x14

B261	SP67	20c +10c multi	35	35
B262	SP67	30c +15c multi	55	55
B263	SP67	35c +15c multi	60	60
a.		Miniature sheet of 3	1.50	1.50
B264	SP67	40c +20c multi	70	70
B265	SP67	50c +30c multi	1.05	1.05
	Nos. B261-B265 (5)		3.25	3.25

Surtax was for child welfare. No. B263a contains 2 No. B261 and one No. B263. Size: 99x72mm.

Cross—SP68   Anansi—SP69

Easter: Various symbols.

1980, Mar. 26   Litho.   Perf. 13x14

B266	SP68	20c +10c multi	35	35
B267	SP68	30c +15c multi	55	55
B268	SP68	40c +20c multi	70	70
B269	SP68	50c +25c multi	90	90
B270	SP68	60c +30c multi	1.05	1.05
	Nos. B266-B270 (5)		3.55	3.55

Designs: Characters from Anansi and His Creditors.

1980, Nov. 5   Litho.   Perf. 13x14

B271	SP69	20 +10c shown	35	35
B272	SP69	25 +15c Ba Tigri	42	42
B273	SP69	30 +15c Kakafowroe	55	55
B274	SP69	35 +15c Ontiman	60	60
B275	SP69	60 +30c Mat Kalaka	1.10	1.10
a.		Miniature sheet of 3	2.00	2.00
	Nos. B271-B275 (5)		3.02	3.02

Surtax was for child welfare. No. B275a contains 2 No. B271 and No. B275. Size: 100x72mm.

Woman Reading—SP70

1980, Dec. 10   Perf. 14x13

B276	SP70	25 +10c shown	42	42
B277	SP70	50 +15c Gardening	75	75
B278	SP70	75 +20c With grandchildren	1.15	1.15

Surtax was for the elderly.

Crucifixion—SP71

Easter 1981: Scenes from the Passion of Christ.

SURINAM

1981, Apr. 8   Litho.   *Perf. 13x14*

B279	SP71	20 +10c multi	35	35
B280	SP71	30 +15c multi	55	55
B281	SP71	50 +25c multi	90	90
B282	SP71	60 +30c multi	1.05	1.05
B283	SP71	75 +35c multi	1.15	1.15
	Nos. B279-B283 (5)		4.00	4.00

Surtax was for the elderly.

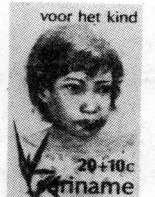 

Indian Girl—SP72   Easter 1982—SP73

1981, Nov. 26   Litho.

B284	SP72	20 +10c shown	35	35
B285	SP72	30 +15c Black	55	55
B286	SP72	50 +25c Hindustani	90	90
B287	SP72	60 +30c Javanese	1.05	1.05
B288	SP72	75 +35c Chinese	1.15	1.15
a.	Souvenir sheet of 3		2.25	2.25
	Nos. B284-B288 (5)		4.00	4.00

Surtax was for child welfare. No. B288a contains 2 No. B285, No. B288.

1982, Apr. 7   Litho.   *Perf. 13x14*

Designs: Stained-glass windows, Sts. Peter and Paul Church, Paramaribo.

B289	SP73	20 +10c multi	35	35
B290	SP73	35 +15c multi	60	60
B291	SP73	50 +25c multi	90	90
B292	SP73	65 +30c multi	1.10	1.10
B293	SP73	75 +35c multi	1.20	1.20
	Nos. B289-B293 (5)		4.15	4.15

Man Pushing Wheelbarrow—SP74   Easter 1983—SP75

Children's Drawings of City Cleaning Activities.

1982, Nov. 17   Litho.

B294	SP74	20 +10c multi	35	35
B295	SP74	35 +15c multi	60	60
B296	SP74	50 +25c multi	90	90
B297	SP74	65 +30c multi	1.10	1.10
B298	SP74	75 +35c multi	1.20	1.20
a.	Souvenir sheet of 3		2.50	2.50
	Nos. B294-B298 (5)		4.15	4.15

Surtax was for child welfare. No. B298a contains 2 No. B295, No. B298.

1983, Mar. 23   Litho.   *Perf. 13x14*

Mosaic Symbols.

B299	SP75	10c +5c Dove	18	18
B300	SP75	15c +5c Bread	22	22
B301	SP75	25c +10c Fish	40	40
B302	SP75	50c +25c Eye	90	90
B303	SP75	65c +30c Wine cup	1.10	1.10
	Nos. B299-B303 (5)		2.80	2.80

Pitcher—SP76

1983, Nov. 16   Litho.   *Perf. 13x14*

B304	SP76	10 +5c shown	18	18
B305	SP76	15 +5c Head-dress	22	22
B306	SP76	25 +10c Medicine rattle	40	40
B307	SP76	50 +25c Sieve	90	90
B308	SP76	65 +30c Basket	1.10	1.10
a.	Miniature sheet of 3 (#B305, B306, B308)		1.75	1.75
	Nos. B304-B308 (5)		2.80	2.80

Easter 1984—SP77

1984, Apr. 4   Litho.   *Perf. 13x14*

B309	SP77	10 +5c Cross, rose	18	18
B310	SP77	15 +15c Cemetery	22	22
B311	SP77	25 +10c Candles	40	40
B312	SP77	50 +25c Cross, crown of thorns	90	90
B313	SP77	65 +30c Candle	1.10	1.10
	Nos. B309-B313 (5)		2.80	2.80

AIR POST STAMPS

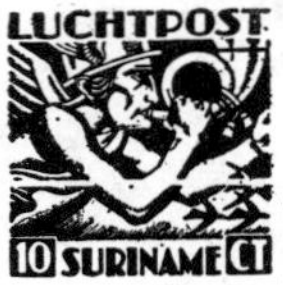

Allegory of Flight
AP1

Engraved.

1930 ***Perf. 12½*** **Unwmkd.**

C1	AP1	10c dl red	4.25	50
C2	AP1	15c ultra	4.00	70
C3	AP1	20c dl grn	10	20
C4	AP1	40c orange	20	35
C5	AP1	60c brn vio	50	40
C6	AP1	1g gray blk	1.40	1.50
C7	AP1	1½g dp brn	1.75	2.00
		Nos. C1-C7 (7)	12.20	5.65

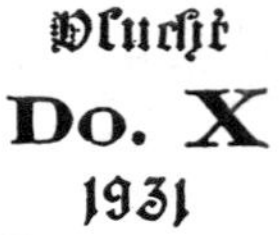

Nos. C1–C7 Overprinted in Black or Red

1931

C8	AP1	10c red (Bk)	20.00	15.00
a.		Double overprint	400.00	
C9	AP1	15c ultra (Bk)	20.00	15.00
C10	AP1	20c dl grn (R)	20.00	15.00
C11	AP1	40c org (Bk)	30.00	20.00
a.		Double overprint	400.00	
C12	AP1	60c brn vio (R)	65.00	55.00
C13	AP1	1g gray blk (R)	75.00	60.00
C14	AP1	1½g dp brn (Bk)	75.00	67.50
		Nos. C8-C14 (7)	305.00	247.50

The variety with period omitted after "Do" occurs twice on each sheet.

Type of 1930.
Thick Paper.

1941 **Lithographed** ***Perf. 13***

C15	AP1	20c lt grn	2.25	90
C16	AP1	40c lt org	11.00	5.00
C17	AP1	2½g yellow	13.00	11.00
C18	AP1	5g bl grn	300.00	300.00
C19	AP1	10g lt bis	32.50	50.00
		Nos. C15-C19 (5)	358.75	366.90

The lines of shading on Nos. C15 and C16 are not as heavy as on Nos. C3 and C4.

Type of 1930.

1941 **Redrawn** ***Perf. 12***

C20	AP1	10c lt red	1.75	30
C21	AP1	60c dl brn vio	1.25	40
C22	AP1	1g black	27.50	20.00

Redrawn stamps have three horizontal lines through post horn and many minor variations.

Nos. C17, C19 and C21 Surcharged with New Values and Bars in Carmine.

1945 ***Perf. 13, 12***

C23	AP1	22½c on 60c dl brn vio	40	60
a.		Inverted surcharge	300.00	300.00
C24	AP1	1g on 2½g yel	10.00	13.00
C25	AP1	5g on 10g lt bis	17.00	21.00

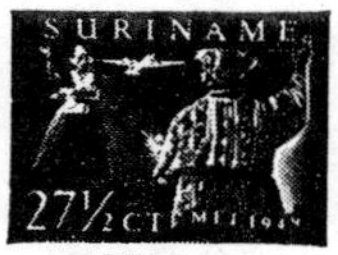

Women of Netherlands and Surinam
AP2

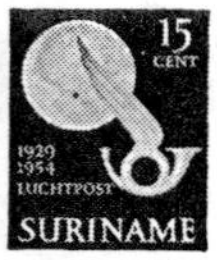

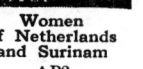

Globe and Winged Post Horn
AP3

Perf. 12x12½

1949, May 10 **Photo.** **Unwmkd.**

C26	AP2	27½c hn brn	6.00	3.00

Valid only on first flight of Paramaribo-Amsterdam service.

1954, Sept. 25 ***Perf. 13½x12½***

C27	AP3	15c dp ultra & ultra	1.75	1.25

Issued to commemorate the 25th anniversary of the establishment of airmail service in Surinam.

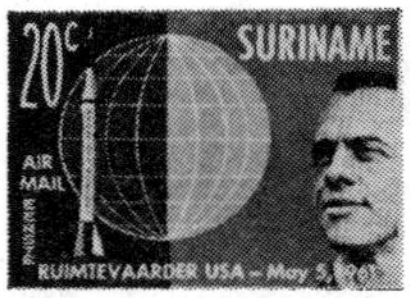

Redstone Mercury Rocket and Comdr. Alan B. Shepard, Jr.
AP4

Design: 15c, Astronaut Gagarin in capsule and globe.

1961, July 3 **Litho.** ***Perf. 12***

C28	AP4	15c multi	1.10	1.40
C29	AP4	20c multi	1.10	1.40

Issued to commemorate "Man in Space," Major Yuri A. Gagarin, USSR, and Comdr. Alan B. Shepard, Jr., USA.

Printed in sheets of 12 (4x3) with ornamental borders and inscriptions.

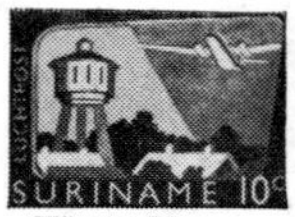

Water Tower
AP5

Eucyane Bicolor
AP6

Designs: 15c, 65c, Brewery. 20c, Boat on lake. 25c, 75c, Wood industry. 30c, Bauxite mine. 35c, 50c, Poelepantje bridge. 40c, Ship in harbor. 45c, Wharf.

1965, July 31 **Photo.** ***Perf. 14x13½***

Size: 25x18mm.

C30	AP5	10c ol grn	10	10
C31	AP5	15c ocher	15	10
C32	AP5	20c sl grn	25	10
C33	AP5	25c vio bl	30	10
C34	AP5	30c bl grn	30	25
C35	AP5	35c red org	40	20
C36	AP5	40c orange	45	20
C37	AP5	45c dk car	50	60
C38	AP5	50c vermilion	55	20
C39	AP5	55c emerald	65	80
C40	AP5	65c bister	70	80
C41	AP5	75c blue	80	60
		Nos. C30-C41 (12)	5.15	4.05

See Nos. C75–C84.

1972, July 26 **Litho.** ***Perf. 13x13½***

Multicolored

C42	AP6	15c *shown*	15	15
C43	AP6	20c *Helicopis cupido*	20	15
C44	AP6	25c *Papilio thoas thoas*	30	25
C45	AP6	30c *Urania leilus*	30	25
C46	AP6	35c *Stalachtis calliope*	40	35
C47	AP6	40c *Stalachtis phlegia*	40	25
C48	AP6	45c *Victorina steneles*	45	30
C49	AP6	50c *Papilio neophilus*	55	35
C50	AP6	55c *Anartia amathea*	60	55
C51	AP6	60c *Adelpha cytherea*	70	95
C52	AP6	65c *Heliconius doris metharmina*	70	55
C53	AP6	70c *Nessaea obrinus*	75	1.25
C54	AP6	75c *Ageronia feronia*	75	50
		Nos. C42-C54 (13)	6.25	5.85

Surinam butterflies. Valid for regular postage also.

Fish Type of 1976

Fish: 35c, Chaetodon unimaculatus. 60c, Centropyge loriculus. 95c, Caetodon collare.

1976, June 2 **Litho.** ***Perf. 12½x13***

C55	A111	35c multi	48	48
C56	A111	60c multi	80	80
C57	A111	95c multi	1.25	1.25

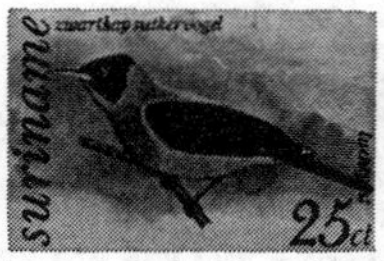

Black-headed Sugarbird
AP7

Birds of Surinam: 20c, Leistes militaris. 30c, Paradise tangara. 40c, Whippoorwill. 45c, Hemitraupis flavicollis. 50c, White-tailed gold-throated hummingbird. 55c, Saberwing. 60c, Blackcap parrot (vert.). 65c, Toucan (vert.). 70c, Manakin (vert.). 75c, Collared parrot (vert.). 80c, Cayenne cotinga (vert.). 85c, Trogon (vert.). 95c, Black-striped tropical tree owl (vert.).

Perf. 14x12½, 12½x14

1977 **Lithographed**

C58	AP7	20c multi	32	32
C59	AP7	25c multi	40	40
C60	AP7	30c multi	48	48
a.		Miniature sheet of 4	1.80	1.80
C61	AP7	40c multi	64	64
C62	AP7	45c multi	72	72
C63	AP7	50c multi	80	80
C64	AP7	55c multi	88	88
C65	AP7	60c multi	95	95
C66	AP7	65c multi	1.05	1.05
C67	AP7	70c multi	1.12	1.12
C68	AP7	75c multi	1.20	1.20
C69	AP7	80c multi	1.28	1.28
C70	AP7	85c multi	1.35	1.35
C71	AP7	95c multi	1.50	1.50
		Nos. C58-C71 (14)	12.69	12.69

No. C60a contains 2 each of Nos. C59–C60, perf. 13½. Size: 108x75mm.

A souvenir sheet of 4 with same stamps and perf. as No. C60a has marginal inscription "Amphilex 77" with magnifier over No. 424. Size: 135x85mm. Sold only canceled in folder at philatelic exhibition in Amsterdam May 26–June 5, 1977.

See No. C88.

Fish Type of 1976

Tropical Fish: 60c, Chaetodon striatus. 90c, Bodianus pulchellus. 120c, Centropyge argi.

1977, June 8 **Litho.** ***Perf. 12½x13***

C72	A111	60c multi	95	95
C73	A111	90c multi	1.45	1.45
C74	A111	120c multi	1.90	1.90

Type of 1965 Redrawn

Designs: 5c, Brewery. 10c, Water tower. 20c, Boat on lake. 25c, Wood industry. 30c, Bauxite mine. 35c, Poelepantje bridge. 40c, Ship in harbor. 60c, Wharf.

1977–78 **Photo.** ***Perf. 12½x13½***

Size: 22x18mm.

C75	AP5	5c ocher ('78)	8	5
a.		Bklt. pane of 7 + label (4 #C75, 3 #C84)	3.25	
C76	AP5	10c ol grn	16	8
a.		Bklt. pane of 5 + label (1 #C76, 4 #C80)	2.25	
C77	AP5	20c sl grn	32	16
a.		Bklt. pane of 6 (2 # C77, 2 #C78, 2 #C79)	2.25	
b.		Bklt. pane of 8 (6 #C77, 2 #C81) ('78)	3.25	
C78	AP5	25c vio bl	35	18
C79	AP5	30c bl grn	40	20
C80	AP5	35c red org	50	25
C81	AP5	40c org ('78)	65	32
C84	AP5	60c dk car ('78)	96	48

Nos. C75–C84 issued in booklets only. Nos. C75a and C77b have inscribed selvage the size of 4 stamps; Nos. C76a and C77a the size of 6 stamps.

Fish Type of 1978

Tropical Fish: 60c, Astyanax species. 90c, Corydoras wotroi. 120c, Gasteropelecus sternicla.

1978, June 21 **Litho.** ***Perf. 12½x13***

C85	A123	60c multi	95	95
C86	A123	90c multi	1.45	1.45
C87	A123	120c multi	1.90	1.90

Bird Type of 1977

Design: 5g, Crested curassow (vert.).

1979, Jan. 10 **Engr.** ***Perf. 13x13½***

C88	AP7	5g violet	6.00	6.00

Fish Type of 1979

Tropical Fish: 60c, Cantherinus macrocerus. 90c, Holocenthrus rufus. 120c, Holacanthus tricolor.

1979, May 30 **Photo.** ***Perf. 14x13***

C89	A129	60c multi	72	72
C90	A129	90c multi	1.10	1.10
C91	A129	120c multi	1.45	1.45

Fish Type of 1979

Tropical Fish: 60c, Symphysodon discus. 75c, Aequidens curviceps. 90c, Catoprion mento.

1980, Sept. 10 **Photo.** ***Perf. 14x13***

C92	A129	60c multi	70	70
C93	A129	75c multi	90	90
C94	A129	90c multi	1.05	1.05

Frog Type

1981, June 24 ***Perf. 13x14***

C95	A142	75c Phyllomedusa burmeisteri, vert.	90	90
C96	A142	1g Dendrobates tinctorius, vert.	1.20	1.20
C97	A142	1.25g Bufo guttatus, vert.	1.50	1.50

Turtle Type of 1982

1982, Feb. 17 **Photo.** ***Perf. 14x13***

C98	A146	65c Platemys platycephala	75	75
C99	A146	75c Phrynops gibba	90	90
C100	A146	125c Rhinoclemys punctularia	1.50	1.50

AIR POST SEMI-POSTAL STAMPS.

No. C20 Surcharged in Red:

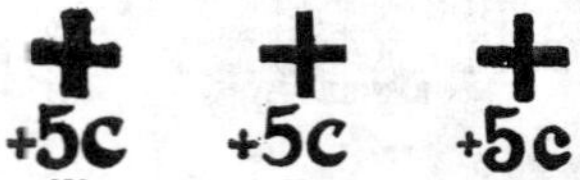

III IV V

1942, Jan. 2 ***Perf. 12*** **Unwmkd.**

CB1	AP1	10c +5c lt red, III	5.00	5.00
a.		Type IV	15.00	15.00
b.		Type V	40.00	40.00

The surtax was for the Red Cross.

See note on types III and IV below No. B4C.

Nos. 193 and 194 Surcharged in Carmine

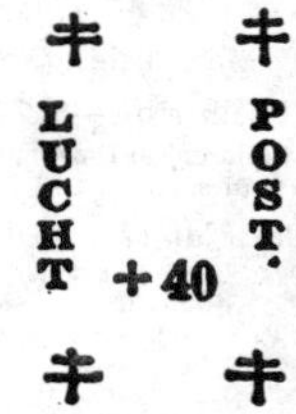

1946

CB2	A30	10c +40c bl	1.75	1.75
CB3	A30	15c +60c brn	1.75	1.75

The surtax was used for the prevention of tuberculosis.

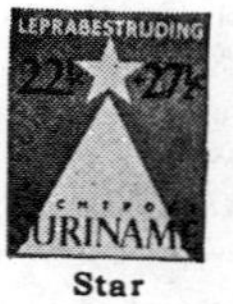

Star
SPAP1

Photogravure

1947 ***Perf. 13½x12½.***

CB4	SPAP1	22½c +27½c gray	3.00	2.50
CB5	SPAP1	27½c +47½c grn	3.00	2.50

The surtax was used to combat leprosy.

SURINAM—SWEDEN 627

POSTAGE DUE STAMPS.

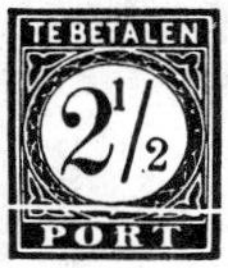

D1

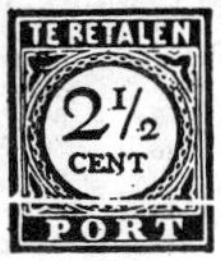

D2

Type I. 34 loops. "T" of "BETALEN" over center of loop; top branch of "E" of "TE" shorter than lower branch.

Type II. 33 loops. "T" of "BETALEN" over space between two loops.

Type III. 32 loops. "T" of "BETALEN" slightly to the left of center of loop; top branch of first "E" of "BETALEN" shorter than lower branch.

Type IV. 37 loops and letters of "PORT" larger than in the other three types.

Perf. 12½x12.

Value in Black.

1886 Typographed. Unwmkd.

J1	D1	2½c lil (III)	2.00	2.00
a.		2½c lil (I)	4.00	4.00
b.		2½c lil (II)	3.00	3.00
J2	D1	5c lil (III)	5.50	5.50
a.		5c lil (I)	6.75	6.75
b.		5c lil (II)	5.75	5.75
J3	D1	10c lil (III)	90.00	60.00
a.		10c lil (I)	100.00	70.00
b.		10c lil (II)	1,350.	1,350.
c.		10c lil (IV)	450.00	250.00
J4	D1	20c lil (III)	5.50	5.50
a.		20c lil (I)	14.00	14.00
b.		20c lil (II)	5.75	5.75
J5	D1	25c lil (III)	8.00	8.00
a.		25c lil (I)	11.00	11.00
b.		25c lil (II)	350.00	350.00
c.		25c lil (IV)	130.00	130.00
J6	D1	30c lil (III)	1.40	1.40
a.		30c lil (I)	14.00	14.00
b.		30c lil (II)	70.00	70.00
J7	D1	40c lil (III)	3.75	3.75
a.		40c lil (I)	8.00	8.00
b.		40c lil (II)	350.00	350.00
c.		40c lil (IV)	130.00	130.00
J8	D1	50c lil (III)	1.75	1.75
a.		50c lil (I)	2.50	2.50
b.		50c lil (II)	3.25	3.25

Nos. J1–J16 were issued without gum.

1892-96 *Perf. 12½.*

Value in Black

J9	D2	2½c lil (III)	25	25
a.		2½c lil (I)	25	25
b.		2½c lil (II)	50	60
J10	D2	5c lil (III)	80	60
a.		5c lil (I)	1.25	1.25
b.		5c lil (II)	1.75	1.75
J11	D2	10c lil (III)	15.00	14.00
a.		10c lil (I)	14.00	12.00
b.		10c lil (II)	30.00	32.50
J12	D2	20c lil (III)	1.50	1.25
a.		20c lil (I)	3.25	3.25
b.		20c lil (II)	80.00	80.00
J13	D2	25c lil (III)	6.00	6.00
a.		25c lil (I)	8.00	8.00
b.		25c lil (II)	90.00	95.00
J14	D2	40c lil (I)	2.00	2.75

Stamps of 1886 Surcharged in Red

10 cent

1911

J15	D1	10c on 30c (III)	80.00	80.00
a.		10c on 30c (I)	190.00	230.00
b.		10c on 30c (II)	2,000.	2,000.
J16	D1	10c on 50c (III)	100.00	100.00
a.		10c on 50c (I)	110.00	110.00
b.		10c on 50c (II)	110.00	110.00

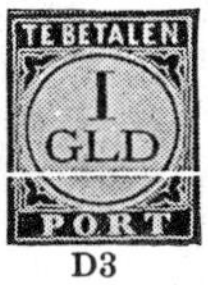

D3

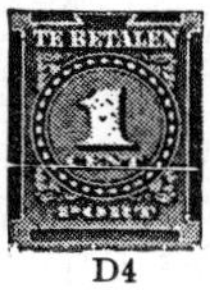

D4

Type I.

Value in Color of Stamp.

1912–31 *Perf. 12½, 13½x12½*

J17	D2	½c lil ('30)	10	10
J18	D2	1c lil ('31)	10	15
J19	D2	2c lil ('31)	20	20
J20	D2	2½c lilac	10	10
J21	D2	5c lilac	10	10
J22	D2	10c lilac	15	12
J23	D2	12c lil ('31)	15	20
J24	D2	12½c lil ('22)	15	10
J25	D2	15c lil ('26)	25	25
J26	D2	20c lilac	50	25
J27	D2	25c lilac	20	10
J28	D2	30c lil ('26)	20	40
J29	D2	40c lilac	10.00	10.00
J30	D2	50c lil ('26)	80	70
J31	D2	75c lil ('26)	90	90
J32	D3	1g lil ('26)	1.10	90
		Nos. J17-J32 (16)	15.00	14.57

1945 Lithographed *Perf. 12*

J33	D4	1c lt brn vio	20	20
J34	D4	5c lt brn vio	3.25	1.25
J35	D4	25c lt brn vio	8.00	20

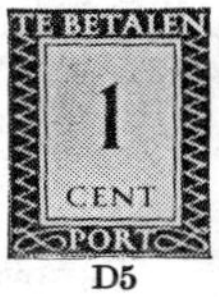

D5

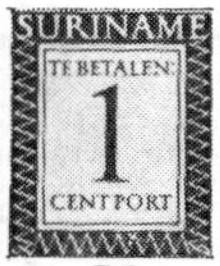

D6

Photogravure

1950 *Perf. 13½x12½* Unwmkd.

J36	D5	1c purple	1.50	1.40
J37	D5	2c purple	2.00	1.25
J38	D5	2½c purple	1.75	1.40
J39	D5	5c purple	3.00	30
J40	D5	10c purple	1.40	30
J41	D5	15c purple	3.50	1.75
J42	D5	20c purple	1.30	2.50
J43	D5	25c purple	7.00	20
J44	D5	50c purple	12.00	1.00
J45	D5	75c purple	35.00	27.50
J46	D5	1g purple	11.00	5.00
		Nos. J36-J46 (11)	79.45	42.60

1956

J47	D6	1c purple	10	10
J48	D6	2c purple	40	20
J49	D6	2½c purple	40	20
J50	D6	5c purple	40	20
J51	D6	10c purple	40	20
J52	D6	15c purple	60	40
J53	D6	20c purple	60	45
J54	D6	25c purple	70	20
J55	D6	50c purple	1.75	25
J56	D6	75c purple	2.50	80
J57	D6	1g purple	3.25	60
		Nos. J47-J57 (11)	11.10	3.60

SWEDEN

(swē'dĕn)

LOCATION — In northern Europe occupying the eastern half of the Scandinavian Peninsula.

GOVT.—Kingdom.

AREA—173,341 sq. mi.

POP.—8,260,000 (est. 1977).

CAPITAL—Stockholm.

48 skilling banco = 1 rixdaler banco (until 1858)

100 öre = 1 rixdaler (1858 to 1874)

100 öre = 1 krona (since 1874)

Prices of early Swedish stamps vary according to condition. Quotations for Nos. 1–38, J1–J11, LX1–LX2 and O1–O11 are for fine copies. Very fine to superb specimens sell at much higher prices, and inferior or poor copies sell at reduced prices, depending on the condition of the individual specimen.

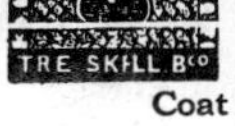

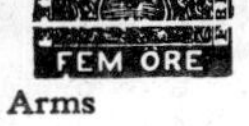

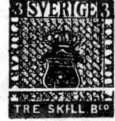

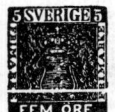

Coat of Arms

A1 A2

Typographed

1855 *Perf. 14* Unwmkd.

1	A1	3s bl grn	*6,250.*	*3,750.*
a.		3s org (error)		
2	A1	4s lt bl	1,200.	100.00
a.		4s gray bl	*6,500.*	*275.00*
3	A1	6s gray	*6,500.*	1,200.
a.		6s gray brn	*8,000.*	1,300.
b.		Imperf.		*9,000.*
4	A1	8s orange	3,750.	600.00
a.		8s yel org	4,000.	600.00
b.		8s lem yel	4,500.	1,100.
c.		Imperf.		
5	A1	24s dl red	*6,250.*	2,000.

Nos. 1–5 were reprinted two or three times with perf. 14, once with perf. 13. Price of the lowest-cost perf. 14 reprints, $300 each. Price of the perf. 13 reprints, $250 each.

The reprints were made after Nos. 1–5 were withdrawn, but before they were demonetized. Used copies are known.

1858-61 *Perf. 14.*

6	A2	5ŏ green	160.00	25.00
a.		5ŏ dp grn	475.00	160.00
7	A2	9ŏ violet	425.00	240.00
a.		9ŏ lil	475.00	260.00
8	A2	12ŏ blue	160.00	4.00
9	A2	12ŏ ultra ('61)	325.00	12.50
10	A2	24ŏ orange	350.00	32.50
a.		24ŏ yel	425.00	50.00
11	A2	30ŏ brown	300.00	35.00
a.		30ŏ red brn	325.00	40.00
12	A2	50ŏ rose	400.00	90.00
a.		50ŏ car	475.00	110.00

Nos. 6 and 8 exist with double impressions. No. 8 is known printed on both sides. No. 11 exists imperf.

Nos. 6–8, 10–12 were reprinted in 1885, perf. 13. Price $100 each. Also reprinted in 1963, perf. 13½, with lines in stamp color crossing denominations, and affixed to book page. Price $17.50 each.

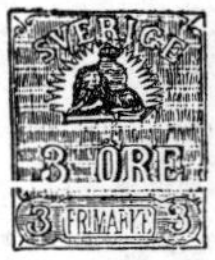

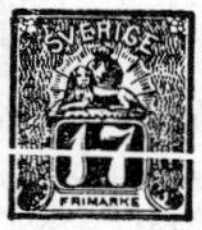

Lion and Arms

A3 A4

1862-69

13	A3	3ŏ bis brn	80.00	25.00
a.		Printed on both sides		*3,000.*
14	A4	17ŏ red vio ('66)	425.00	200.00
15	A4	17ŏ gray ('69)	800.00	800.00
16	A4	20ŏ ver ('66)	160.00	25.00

Nos. 13, 15–16 were reprinted in 1885, perf. 13. Price $100 each.

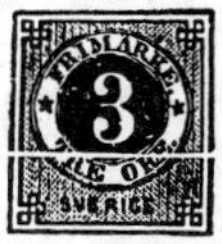

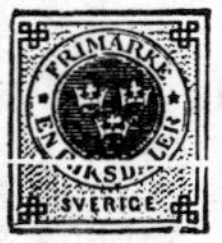

Numeral of Value — A5

Coat of Arms — A6

1872-77 *Perf. 14.*

17	A5	3ŏ bis brn	55.00	9.00
18	A5	4ŏ gray ('76)	225.00	130.00
19	A5	5ŏ bl grn	225.00	5.00
a.		5ŏ emer	225.00	20.00
20	A5	6ŏ violet	180.00	27.50
a.		6ŏ dk vio	180.00	27.50
21	A5	6ŏ gray ('74)	600.00	50.00
22	A5	12ŏ blue	110.00	1.20
23	A5	20ŏ vermilion	350.00	8.00
a.		20ŏ dl org yel ('75)	2,250.	27.50
b.		Dbl. impression, dl yel & ver ('76)	2,250.	27.50
24	A5	24ŏ orange	350.00	30.00
a.		24ŏ yel	375.00	32.50
25	A5	30ŏ pale brn	325.00	9.00
a.		30ŏ blk brn	375.00	9.00
26	A5	50ŏ rose	400.00	45.00
a.		50ŏ car	400.00	45.00
27	A6	1rd bis & bl	500.00	70.00
a.		1rd bis & ultra	500.00	70.00

1877–79 *Perf. 13*

28	A5	3ŏ yel brn	35.00	4.50
a.		Imperf., pair	750.00	
29	A5	4ŏ gray ('79)	110.00	3.50
a.		Imperf., pair	750.00	
30	A5	5ŏ dk grn	100.00	1.20
a.		Imperf., pair	750.00	
31	A5	6ŏ lilac	120.00	6.00
a.		6ŏ red lil	120.00	6.00
b.		Imperf., pair	750.00	
32	A5	12ŏ blue	25.00	60
a.		Imperf., pair	750.00	
33	A5	20ŏ vermilion	140.00	1.50
a.		"TRETIO" instead of "TJUGO" ('79)	5,000.	4,000.
b.		Imperf., pair	750.00	
34	A5	24ŏ org ('78)	42.50	16.00
a.		24ŏ yel	42.50	16.00
b.		Imperf., pair	750.00	
35	A5	30ŏ pale brn	180.00	2.00
a.		30ŏ blk brn	180.00	2.00
b.		Imperf., pair	750.00	
36	A5	50ŏ car ('78)	200.00	8.00
a.		Imperf., pair	750.00	
37	A6	1rd bis & bl	1,300.	475.00
38	A6	1k bis & bl ('78)	375.00	13.00
a.		Imperf., pair ('78)	800.00	

See also Nos. 40–44, 46–49.

No. 37 has been reprinted in yellow brown and dark blue; perforated 13. Price, $100.

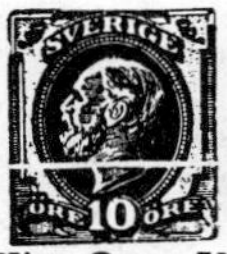

King Oscar II — A7

Coat of Arms — A8

1885 Typographed

39	A7	10ŏ dl rose	250.00	80
a.		Imperf., pair	*2,000.*	

1886-91

Same with Post Horn on Back.

40	A5	2ŏ org ('91)	4.00	4.50
a.		Period before "FRIMARKE"	7.00	7.50
b.		Imperf., pair	600.00	
41	A5	3ŏ yel brn ('87)	15.00	18.00
42	A5	4ŏ gray	35.00	1.25
43	A5	5ŏ green	60.00	80
44	A5	6ŏ red lil ('88)	30.00	35.00
a.		6ŏ vio	32.50	35.00
45	A7	10ŏ pink	110.00	20
a.		10ŏ rose	110.00	20
b.		Imperf.		2,500.
46	A5	20ŏ vermilion	100.00	80
47	A5	30ŏ pale brn	160.00	1.00
48	A5	50ŏ rose	140.00	4.00
49	A6	1k bis & dk bl	100.00	3.00
a.		Imperf., pair	600.00	

Nos. 32, 34 with Blue Surcharge

1889, Oct. 1

50	A8	10ŏ on 12ŏ bl	4.00	5.50
51	A8	10ŏ on 24ŏ org	20.00	*50.00*

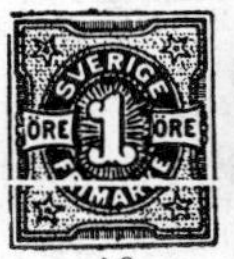

A9

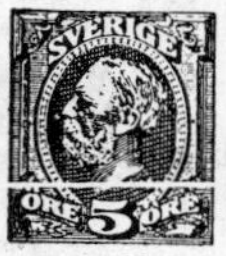

A10

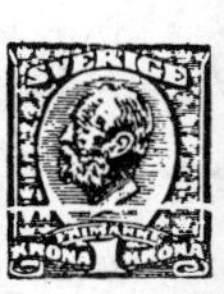

King Oscar II — A11

Wmk. 180

Wmkd. Crown. (180)

1891-1904 Typo. *Perf. 13*

52	A9	1ö brn & ultra ('92)	2.00	40
a.		Imperf., pair ('92)	110.00	
53	A9	2ö bl & yel org	8.00	12
a.		Imperf., pair	*275.00*	
54	A9	3ö brn & org ('92)	1.40	1.40
a.		Imperf., pair	*325.00*	
55	A9	4ö car & ultra ('92)	16.00	10
a.		Imperf., pair ('92)	275.00	

Engraved.

56	A10	5ö yel grn	4.00	5
a.		5ö bl grn	10.00	10
b.		Imperf. 5ö yel grn, pair	100.00	
c.		Imperf. 5ö bl grn, pair	250.00	
d.		5ö brn (error)	*7,000.*	
e.		Booklet pane of 6	55.00	
57	A10	8ö red vio ('03)	8.00	1.00
a.		Imperf., pair	275.00	
58	A10	10ö carmine	10.00	5
b.		Imperf., pair	50.00	
c.		Booklet pane of 6	85.00	
59	A10	15ö red brn ('96)	35.00	10
a.		Imperf., pair	325.00	
60	A10	20ö blue	30.00	10
a.		Imperf., pair	120.00	
61	A10	25ö red org ('96)	45.00	10
a.		Imperf., pair	400.00	
62	A10	30ö brown	70.00	15
a.		Imperf., pair	450.00	
63	A10	50ö slate	90.00	40
a.		Imperf., pair	400.00	
64	A10	50ö ol gray ('04)	85.00	40
a.		Imperf., pair	300.00	
65	A11	1k car & sl ('00)	150.00	2.00
a.		Imperf., pair	350.00	
		Nos. 52-65 (14)	554.40	6.37

See also Nos. 75-76.

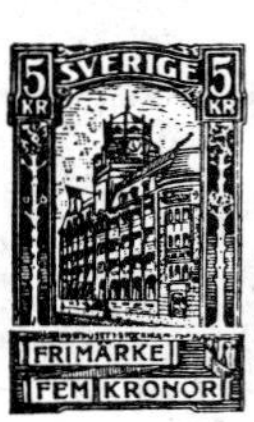

Stockholm Post Office
A12

1903, Oct. 26

66	A12	5k blue	375.00	30.00
a.		Imperf., pair	2,000.	

Opening of the new General Post Office at Stockholm.

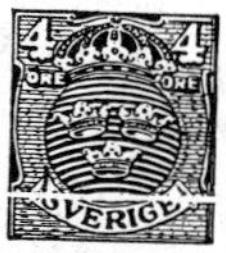

Arms
A13

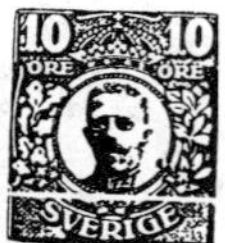

King Gustaf V
A14

Perf. 13, 13x13½.

1910-14 Typographed Wmk. 180

67	A13	1ö blk ('11)	1.00	1.75
68	A13	2ö org ('10)	4.00	3.00
69	A13	4ö vio ('10)	7.00	1.60

Engraved.

70	A14	5ö grn ('11)	12.00	*35.00*
71	A14	10ö car ('10)	25.00	60
72	A14	1k *yel* ('11)	125.00	40
73	A14	5k cl, *yel* ('14)	5.00	3.25
		Nos. 67-73 (7)	179.00	*45.60*

See also Nos. 95-98.

1911 Unwmkd.

75	A10	20ö blue	27.50	11.00
76	A10	25ö red org	35.00	4.50

1910-19

77	A14	5ö grn ('11)	4.00	5
a.		Bklt. pane of 10	225.00	
b.		Bklt. pane of 4	120.00	
78	A14	7ö gray grn ('18)	35	25
a.		Bklt. pane of 10	7.00	
79	A14	8ö mag ('12)	35	40
80	A14	10ö car ('10)	6.00	5
a.		Bklt. pane of 10	225.00	
b.		Bklt. pane of 4	120.00	
81	A14	12ö rose lake ('18)	35	15
a.		Bklt. pane of 10	8.00	
82	A14	15ö red brn ('11)	12.00	5
a.		Bklt. pane of 10	325.00	
83	A14	20ö dp bl ('11)	18.00	5
a.		Bklt. pane of 10	350.00	
84	A14	25ö org red ('11)	60	8
85	A14	27ö pale bl ('18)	1.00	1.25
86	A14	30ö cl brn ('11)	35.00	5
87	A14	35ö dk vio ('11)	35.00	10
88	A14	40ö ol grn ('17)	55.00	10
89	A14	50ö gray ('12)	65.00	10
90	A14	55ö pale bl ('18)	1,500.	2,500.
91	A14	65ö pale ol grn ('18)	1.75	2.50
92	A14	80ö blk ('18)	1,500.	2,500.
93	A14	90ö gray grn ('18)	2.00	60
94	A14	1k *yel* ('19)	110.00	40
		Nos. 77-89, 91, 93-94 (16)	346.40	6.18

Excellent forgeries of Nos. 90 and 92 exist.

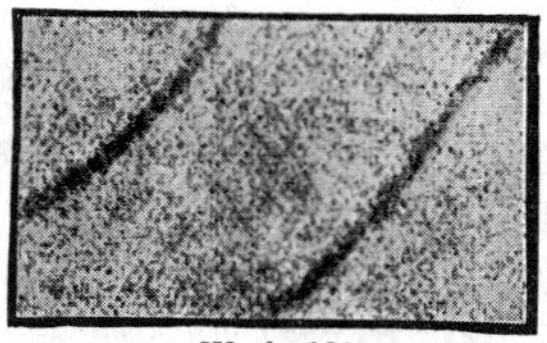

Wmk. 181

Wmkd. Wavy Lines. (181)

1911-19 Typographed *Perf. 13*

95	A13	1ö black	18	18
96	A13	2ö orange	18	18
97	A13	3ö pale brn ('19)	18	18
98	A13	4ö pale vio	18	18

Stamps of these and many later issues are frequently found with watermark showing parts of the words "Kungl Postverket" in double-lined capitals. This watermark is normally located in the margins of the sheets of unwatermarked paper or paper watermarked wavy lines or crown.

Remainders of Nos. 95-98 received various private overprints, mostly as publicity for stamp exhibitions. They were not postally valid.

Stamps of 1910-18 Surcharged:

7 **7** **12** **12**
a *b*

1918 Unwmkd.

99	A14 (a)	7ö on 10ö car	60	40
100	A14 (b)	12ö on 25ö red org	4.00	40
a.		Inverted surcharge	200.00	300.00
101	A14 (a)	12ö on 65ö pale ol grn	3.00	1.20
102	A14 (a)	27ö on 55ö pale bl	1.40	1.80
103	A14 (a)	27ö on 65ö pale ol grn	3.00	3.75
104	A14 (a)	27ö on 80ö blk	1.25	2.00
		Nos. 99-104 (6)	13.25	9.55

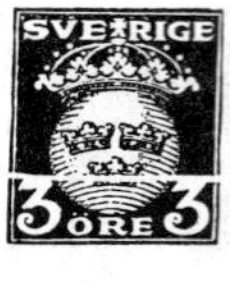

Arms
A15

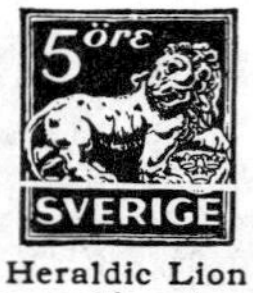

Heraldic Lion Supporting Arms of Sweden
A16

Two types each of 5ö green, 5ö copper red and 10ö violet, type A16.

Perf. 10 Vertically.

1920-25 Engraved Unwmkd.

115	A15	3ö cop red	40	40
116	A16	5ö green	4.75	6
117	A16	5ö cop red ('21)	10.00	15
118	A16	10ö grn ('21)	15.00	15
a.		Tête bêche pair	850.00	1,000.
119	A16	10ö vio ('25)	4.00	6
120	A16	25ö org ('21)	20.00	30
121	A16	30ö brown	70	8

Wmkd. Wavy Lines. (181)

Perf. 10 Vertically.

122	A16	5ö green	1.75	15
123	A16	5ö cop red ('22)	9.00	70
124	A16	10ö grn ('22)	2.00	70
125	A16	30ö brown	6.00	4.00
		Nos. 115-125 (11)	73.60	6.75

Coil Stamps

Unless part of a booklet pane any stamp perforated only horizontally or vertically is a coil stamp.

1920-26 *Perf. 10* Unwmkd.

126	A16	5ö green	5.00	60
a.		Booklet pane of 10	50.00	
127	A16	10ö grn ('21)	12.00	3.00
a.		Booklet pane of 10	120.00	
128	A16	10ö vio ('25)	5.00	40
a.		Booklet pane of 10	60.00	
129	A16	30ö brown	37.50	4.00

Wmkd. Wavy Lines. (181)

Perf. 10.

130	A16	5ö green	12.00	14.00
131	A16	10ö grn ('21)	15.00	20.00
a.		Bklt. pane of 10	150.00	

Unwmkd.

Perf. 13 Vertically

132	A16	5ö grn ('25)	5.00	1.00
133	A16	5ö cop red ('21)	300.00	100.00
134	A16	10ö vio ('26)	11.00	14.00

Wmkd. Wavy Lines. (181)

Perf. 13 Vertically

135	A16	5ö grn ('25)	2.00	1.50
136	A16	5ö cop red ('22)	2.00	2.00
137	A16	10ö grn ('24)	8.50	11.00
138	A16	10ö vio ('25)	5.00	6.50
		Nos. 126-138 (13)	420.00	178.00

The paper used for the earlier printings of types A16, A17, A18, A18a and A20 is usually tinted by the color of the stamp. Printings of 1934 and later are on white paper in slightly different shades.

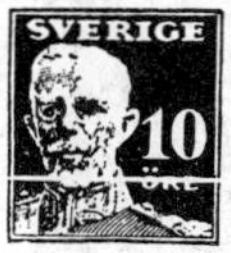

King Gustaf V
A17

Perf. 10 Vertically

1920-21 Unwmkd.

139	A17	10ö rose	25.00	35
140	A17	15ö claret	40	40
141	A17	20ö blue	30.00	40

Perf. 10

142	A17	10ö rose	15.00	4.50
143	A17	20ö bl ('21)	22.50	5.50
a.		Booklet pane of 10	275.00	
		Nos. 139-143 (5)	92.90	11.15

Wmkd. Wavy Lines. (181)

Perf. 10

144	A17	20ö blue	600.00	

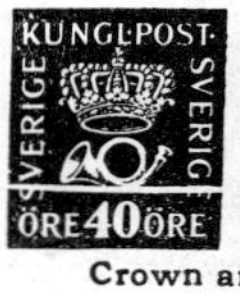

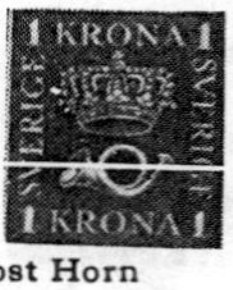

Crown and Post Horn
A18 A18a

1920-34 *Perf. 10 Vert.* Unwmkd.

See note after No. 138 regarding paper. There are two types of the 35ö, 40ö, 45ö and 60ö.

145	A18	35ö yel ('22)	45.00	40
146	A18	40ö ol grn	40.00	40
147	A18	45ö brn ('22)	1.50	50
148	A18	60ö claret	25.00	10
149	A18	70ö red brn ('22)	1.00	1.80
150	A18	80ö dp grn	75	10
151	A18	85ö myr grn ('29)	4.00	40
152	A18	90ö lt bl ('25)	55.00	10
153	A18a	1kr dp org ('21)	12.00	15
154	A18	110ö ultra	1.00	10
155	A18	115ö red brn ('29)	10.00	40
156	A18	120ö gray blk ('25)	80.00	60
157	A18	120ö lil rose ('33)	8.50	60
158	A18	140ö gray blk	1.50	20
159	A18	145ö brt grn ('30)	7.00	80

Wmkd. Wavy Lines. (181)

Perf. 10 Vertically.

160	A18	35ö yel ('23)	62.50	3.00
161	A18	60ö red vio	70.00	90.00
162	A18	80ö bl grn	4.25	3.00
163	A18	110ö ultra	3.25	1.25
		Nos. 145-163 (19)	432.25	103.90

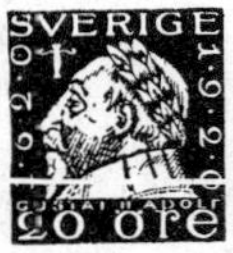

Gustavus Adolphus
A19

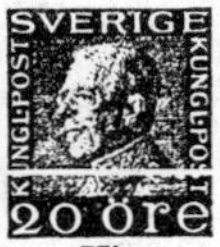

King Gustaf V
A20

Perf. 10 Vertically.

1920, July 28 Unwmkd.

164	A19	20ö dp bl	3.00	40

Wmkd. Wavy Lines. (181)

165	A19	20ö blue	100.00	15.00

Perf. 10

Unwmkd.

166	A19	20ö blue	7.00	1.50
a.		Bklt. pane of 10	80.00	

Tercentenary of Swedish post which first ran between Stockholm and Hamburg.

1921-36 *Perf. 10 Vert.* Unwmkd.

See note after No. 138 regarding paper.
There are two types each of the 15ö rose and 40ö olive green.

167	A20	15ö vio ('22)	25.00	8
168	A20	15ö rose ('25)	10.00	6
169	A20	15ö brn ('36)	7.00	6
170	A20	20ö violet	45	6
171	A20	20ö rose ('22)	25.00	40
172	A20	20ö org ('25)	40	15
174	A20	25ö rose red ('22)	60	1.00
175	A20	25ö dk bl ('25)	25.00	8
176	A20	25ö dk ultra ('34)	25.00	12
177	A20	25ö yel org ('36)	40.00	8
178	A20	30ö bl ('23)	25.00	18
179	A20	30ö brn ('25)	45.00	8
180	A20	30ö lt ultra ('36)	7.00	15
181	A20	35ö red vio ('30)	14.00	6
182	A20	40ö blue	60	80
183	A20	40ö ol grn ('29)	35.00	90
184	A20	45ö brn ('29)	3.00	15
185	A20	50ö gray	2.50	10
186	A20	85ö myr grn ('25)	15.00	1.75
187	A20	115ö brn red ('25)	14.00	1.75
188	A20	145ö ap grn ('25)	10.00	1.75
		Nos. 167-188 (21)	329.55	9.76

Wmkd. Wavy Lines. (181)

Perf. 10 Vertically.

189	A20	15ö vio ('22)	1,800.	600.00
189A	A20	20ö violet		850.00

1922-36 *Perf. 10* Unwmkd.

190	A20	15ö violet	27.50	50
a.		Booklet pane of 10	325.00	
191	A20	15ö rose red ('25)	25.00	12
a.		Booklet pane of 10	250.00	

SWEDEN

192	A20	15ö brn ('36)		7.00	.25
a.		Booklet pane of 10		80.00	
193	A20	20ö vio ('22)		.60	1.00
a.		Booklet pane of 10		7.00	

Gustavus Vasa
A21

1921, June   Perf. 10 Vertically.

194	A21	20ö violet		10.00	18.00
195	A21	110ö ultra		75.00	6.00
196	A21	140ö gray blk		6.00	6.00

400th anniversary of Gustavus Vasa's war of independence from the Danes.

Universal Postal Union Congress Issue

Composite View of Stockholm's Skyline
A22

King Gustaf V
A23

1924, July 4   Perf. 10   Unwmkd.

197	A22	5ö red brn		3.00	3.00
198	A22	10ö green		3.00	3.00
199	A22	15ö dk vio		3.00	3.00
200	A22	20ö rose red		16.00	16.00
201	A22	25ö dp org		25.00	22.50
202	A22	30ö dp bl		22.50	20.00
a.		30ö grnsh bl		100.00	47.50
203	A22	35ö black		30.00	30.00
204	A22	40ö ol grn		37.50	37.50
205	A22	45ö dp brn		40.00	40.00
206	A22	50ö gray		40.00	40.00
207	A22	60ö vio brn		70.00	70.00
208	A22	80ö myr grn		55.00	50.00
209	A23	1k green		100.00	110.00
210	A23	2k rose red		200.00	275.00
211	A23	5k dp bl		400.00	525.00

Wmkd. Wavy Lines. (181)

212	A22	10ö green		27.50	27.50
	Nos. 197-212 (16)			1,072.50	1,272.50

Universal Postal Union Issue.

Postrider Watching Airplane
A24

Carrier Pigeon and Globe
A25

1924, Aug. 16   Engr.   Unwmkd.

213	A24	5ö red brn		4.00	4.00
214	A24	10ö green		4.00	4.00
215	A24	15ö dk vio		4.00	3.00
216	A24	20ö rose red		20.00	20.00
217	A24	25ö dp org		25.00	25.00
218	A24	30ö dp bl		25.00	25.00
a.		30ö grnsh bl		100.00	47.50
219	A24	35ö black		30.00	40.00
220	A24	40ö ol grn		40.00	40.00
221	A24	45ö dp brn		45.00	37.50
222	A24	50ö gray		47.50	47.50
223	A24	60ö vio brn		72.50	72.50
224	A24	80ö myr grn		55.00	42.50
225	A25	1k green		100.00	90.00
226	A25	2k rose red		200.00	125.00
227	A25	5k dp bl		400.00	300.00

Wmkd. Wavy Lines. (181)

228	A24	10ö green		30.00	30.00
	Nos. 213-228 (16)			1,202.	953.50

Royal Palace at Stockholm
A26

Death of Gustavus Adolphus
A27

1931, Nov. 26   Perf. 10   Unwmkd.

229	A26	5k dk grn		150.00	12.00
a.		Bklt. pane of 10		2,000.	

1932, Nov. 1

230	A27	10ö dk vio		4.00	4.00
a.		Booklet pane of 10		50.00	
231	A27	15ö dk red		5.50	1.30
a.		Bklt. pane of 10		100.00	

Perf. 10 Vertically

232	A27	10ö dk vio		4.00	.20
233	A27	15ö dk red		4.00	.20
234	A27	25ö dk bl		11.00	1.00
235	A27	90ö dk grn		35.00	2.75
	Nos. 230-235 (6)			63.50	9.45

Commemorative of the 300th anniversary of the death of King Gustavus Adolphus II who was killed on the battlefield of Lützen, Nov. 6, 1632.

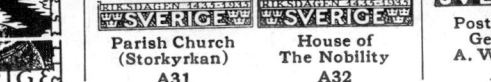

Catching Sunlight in Bowl
A28

1933, Dec. 6   Perf. 10.

236	A28	5ö green		3.50	1.00
a.		Booklet pane of 10		50.00	

There are two types of No. 236.

Perf. 10 Vertically.

237	A28	5ö green		3.50	.20

Perf. 13 Vertically.

238	A28	5ö green		3.50	6.00

50th anniversary of the Swedish Postal Savings Bank.

The Old Law Courts
A29

Stock Exchange
A30

Parish Church (Storkyrkan)
A31

House of The Nobility
A32

House of Parliament
A33

The "Four Estates" and Arms of Engelbrekt
A34

1935, Jan. 10   Perf. 10

239	A29	5ö green		4.00	1.00
a.		Bklt. pane of 10		70.00	
240	A30	10ö dl vio		4.00	4.50
a.		Booklet pane of 10		70.00	
241	A31	15ö carmine		5.00	.80
a.		Booklet pane of 10		90.00	

Perf. 10 Vertically

242	A29	5ö green		2.25	.20
243	A30	10ö dl vio		5.00	.20
244	A31	15ö carmine		3.00	.20
245	A32	25ö ultra		15.00	1.00
246	A33	35ö dp cl		22.50	2.75
247	A34	60ö dp cl		30.00	2.75
	Nos. 239-247 (9)			90.75	13.40

Issued in commemoration of the 500th anniversary of the Swedish Parliament.

Chancellor Axel Oxenstierna
A35

Post Runner
A36

Mounted Courier
A37

Old Sailing Packet
A38

Mail Paddle Steamship
A39

Mail Coach
A40

1855 Stamp Model
A41

Mail Train
A42

Postmaster General A. W. Roos
A43

Mail Truck and Trailer
A44

Modern Swedish Liner
A45

Junkers Plane with Pontoons
A46

1936, Feb. 20   Engr.   Perf. 10.

248	A35	5ö green		3.00	.55
a.		Bklt. pane of 18		125.00	
249	A36	10ö dk vio		3.50	2.75
a.		Bklt. pane of 18		150.00	
250	A37	15ö dk car		5.00	.55
c.		Bklt. pane of 18		200.00	

Perf. 10 Vertically.

251	A35	5ö green		3.00	.20
252	A36	10ö dk vio		3.00	.20
253	A37	15ö dk car		3.00	.20
254	A38	20ö lt bl		16.00	4.50
255	A39	25ö lt ultra		10.00	.55
256	A40	30ö yel brn		37.50	3.75
257	A41	35ö plum		11.00	2.00
258	A42	40ö ol grn		10.00	2.75
259	A43	45ö myr grn		18.00	3.75
260	A44	50ö gray		35.00	3.75
261	A45	60ö maroon		50.00	1.00
262	A46	1k dp bl		16.00	8.50
	Nos. 248-262 (15)			224.00	35.00

Issued in commemoration of the 300th anniversary of the Swedish Postal Service. See also Nos. 946-950, B55-B56.

Airplane over Bromma Airport
A47

Emanuel Swedenborg
A48

1936, May 23   Perf. 10 Vert.

263	A47	50ö ultra		9.00	11.00

Issued to commemorate the opening of Bromma Airport near Stockholm.

Swedish Booklets

Before 1940, booklets were handmade and usually held two panes of 10 stamps (2x5). About every third booklet contained one row of stamps with straight edges at right or left side. Se-tenant pairs may be obtained with one stamp perforated on 4 sides and one perforated on 3 sides. Starting in 1940, booklet stamps have one or more straight edges.

1938, Jan. 29   Perf. 12½.

264	A48	10ö violet		1.50	.20
a.		Perf. on 3 sides		15.00	2.50
b.		Bklt. pane of 10		20.00	

Perf. 12½ Vertically.

266	A48	10ö violet		1.50	.15
267	A48	100ö green		10.00	1.40

Issued in commemoration of the 250th anniversary of the birth of Emanuel Swedenborg, scientist, philosopher and religious writer.

Johann Printz and Indian Chief
A49

"Kalmar Nyckel" Sailing from Gothenburg
A50

SWEDEN

Symbolizing the Settlement of New Sweden
A51

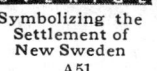
Holy Trinity Church, Wilmington, Del.
A52

Queen Christina
A53

1938, Apr. 8 Perf. 12½ Vert.

268	A49	5ö green	1.00	10
269	A50	15ö brown	1.00	10
270	A51	20ö red	5.00	60
271	A52	30ö ultra	14.00	1.00
272	A53	60ö brn lake	16.00	25

Perf. 12½.

273	A49	5ö green	2.00	30
a.		Perf. on 3 sides	15.00	5.00
b.		Bklt. pane of 18	57.50	
274	A50	15ö brown	3.00	30
a.		Perf. on 3 sides	17.50	6.00
b.		Bklt. pane of 10	70.00	
		Nos. 268-274 (7)	42.00	2.65

Tercentenary of the Swedish settlement at Wilmington, Del. See No. B54.

King Gustaf V
A54

1938, June 16 Perf. 12½ Vert.

275	A54	5ö green	1.00	10
276	A54	15(ö) brown	1.00	10
277	A54	30(ö) ultra	30.00	1.00

Perf. 12½.

278	A54	5ö green	1.50	30
a.		Perf. on 3 sides	20.00	3.50
b.		Bklt. pane of 10	27.50	
279	A54	15(ö) brown	2.25	30
a.		Perf. on 3 sides	25.00	1.50
b.		Bklt. pane of 10	35.00	
		Nos. 275-279 (5)	35.75	1.80

80th birthday of King Gustaf V.

King Gustaf V
A55

Three Crowns
A56

1939 Perf. 12½ Vertically.

280	A55	10ö violet	1.40	15
281	A55	20ö carmine	2.00	50
282	A56	60ö lake	4.50	6
283	A56	85ö dk grn	2.00	30
284	A56	90ö pck bl	4.00	6
285	A56	1k orange	1.10	5
286	A56	1.15k hn brn	1.25	10
287	A56	1.35k brt rose vio	4.50	20
288	A56	1.45k lt yel grn	6.00	80

Perf. 12½.

289	A55	10ö violet	2.50	2.00
a.		Perf. on 3 sides	55.00	30.00
b.		Bklt. pane of 10, perf. on 4 sides	30.00	
		Nos. 280-289 (10)	29.25	4.22

See also Nos. 394-398, 416-417, 425-426, 431, 439-441, 473, 588-591, 656-664.

Per Henrik Ling
A57

1939, Feb. 25 Perf. 12½ Vert.

| 290 | A57 | 5ö green | 25 | 5 |
| 291 | A57 | 25(ö) brown | 2.00 | 15 |

Perf. 12½.

292	A57	5ö green	1.60	30
a.		Perf. on 3 sides	22.50	1.75
b.		Bklt. pane of 10	17.50	

Issued in commemoration of the centenary of the death of P. H. Ling, father of Swedish gymnastics.

J. J. Berzelius
A58

Carl von Linné
A59

Perf. 12½ Vertically.

1939, June 2 Engraved

293	A58	10ö violet	3.00	10
294	A59	15ö fawn	60	8
295	A59	30ö ultra	25.00	40
296	A59	50ö gray	27.50	1.00

Perf. 12½.

297	A58	10ö violet	3.00	60
a.		Perf. on 3 sides	85.00	20.00
b.		Booklet pane of 10	35.00	
298	A59	15ö fawn	6.00	30
a.		Perf. on 3 sides	16.00	12
b.		Booklet pane of 10	65.00	
c.		As "a," bklt. pane of 20	325.00	
		Nos. 293-298 (6)	65.10	2.48

Issued in commemoration of the 200th anniversary of the founding of the Royal Academy of Science at Stockholm.

King Gustaf V
Type A55 Re-engraved.

1939-46 Perf. 12½

299	A60	5ö dp grn ('46)	25	5
a.		Booklet pane of 20, perf. on 4 sides	250.00	
b.		Perf. on 3 sides ('41)	25	5
c.		As "b," bklt. pane of 20	6.00	
300	A60	10(ö) vio ('46)	25	5
a.		Booklet pane of 10, perf. on 4 sides	20.00	
b.		Booklet pane of 20, perf. on 4 sides	250.00	
c.		Bklt. pane of 20	75	15
i.		As "c," bklt. pane of 20	22.50	
300D	A60	15(ö) chnt ('46)	25	12
e.		Booklet pane of 20, perf. on 4 sides	60.00	
f.		Perf. on 3 sides ('45)	50	35
j.		As "f," bklt. pane of 20	10.00	
300G	A60	20(ö) red ('42)	35	5
h.		Booklet pane of 20	7.00	

No. 300 differs slightly from the original due to deeper engraving. No. 300G was issued only in booklets; all copies have one straight edge.

1940-42 Perf. 12½ Vertically

301	A60	5ö dp grn ('41)	25	5
302	A60	10(ö) violet	25	5
302A	A60	15(ö) chnt ('42)	35	5
303	A60	20(ö) red	25	5
304	A60	25(ö) orange	1.50	5
305	A60	30(ö) ultra	70	5
306	A60	35(ö) red vio ('41)	1.50	12
307	A60	40(ö) ol grn	1.20	5
308	A60	45(ö) dk brn	1.20	8

| 309 | A60 | 50(ö) gray blk ('41) | 5.50 | 15 |
| | | Nos. 301-309 (10) | 12.70 | 70 |

Numerals measure 4½ mm. high. Less shading around head gives a lighter effect. Horizontal lines only as background for SVERIGE.
See also Nos. 391-393, 399.

Karl Mikael Bellman
A61

Tobias Sergel
A62

Engraved.

1940, Feb. 4 Perf. 12½ Vert.

| 310 | A61 | 5ö green | 25 | 8 |
| 311 | A61 | 35(ö) rose red | 1.50 | 30 |

Perf. 12½.

312	A61	5ö green	1.75	40
a.		Perf. on 3 sides	12.50	60
b.		Booklet pane of 10	20.00	
c.		As "a," bklt. pane of 20	260.00	

Bicentenary of birth of Karl Mikael Bellman (1740-1795), lyric poet.

Perf. 12½ on 3 Sides.

1940, Sept. 5

| 313 | A62 | 15ö lt brn | 9.00 | 40 |
| a. | | Bklt. pane of 20 | 200.00 | |

Perf. 12½ Vertically.

| 314 | A62 | 15ö lt brn | 3.00 | 12 |
| 315 | A62 | 50ö gray blk | 35.00 | 1.00 |

Bicentenary of birth of Johan Tobias von Sergel (1740-1814), sculptor.

Reformers Presenting Bible to Gustavus Vasa
A63

View of Skansen
A64

Perf. 12½ on 3 Sides

1941, May 11

| 316 | A63 | 15ö brown | 3.00 | 30 |
| a. | | Bklt. pane of 18 | 60.00 | |

Perf. 12½ Vertically.

| 317 | A63 | 15ö brown | 45 | 8 |
| 318 | A63 | 90(ö) ultra | 30.00 | 80 |

Issued to commemorate the 400th anniversary of the first authorized version of the Bible in Swedish.

Perf. 12½ on 3 Sides

1941, June 18

| 319 | A64 | 10ö violet | 3.00 | 40 |
| a. | | Bklt. pane of 20 | 70.00 | |

Perf. 12½ Vertically.

| 320 | A64 | 10ö violet | 2.00 | 15 |
| 321 | A64 | 60(ö) red lil | 20.00 | 40 |

Issued in commemoration of the 50th anniversary of Skansen, an open air extension of the Nordic Museum.

Royal Palace at Stockholm
A65

Artur Hazelius
A66

1941 Perf. 12½ on 3 Sides

322	A65	5k blue	3.50	50
a.		Perf. on 4 sides	50.00	1.75
b.		Bklt. pane 20, perf. 3 sides	90.00	
c.		Bklt. pane of 10, perf. 4 sides	650.00	

For coil stamp see No. 537.

Perf. 12½ on 3 Sides.

1941, Aug. 30

| 323 | A66 | 5ö lt grn | 3.00 | 40 |
| a. | | Bklt. pane of 20 | 70.00 | |

Perf. 12½ Vertically.

| 324 | A66 | 5ö lt grn | 30 | 10 |
| 325 | A66 | 1k lt org | 18.00 | 3.25 |

Issued to honor Artur Hazelius, founder of Skansen, Nordic museum.

St. Bridget
A67

Perf. 12½ on 3 Sides.

1941, Oct. 7 Engraved

| 326 | A67 | 15ö dp brn | 2.00 | 30 |
| a. | | Bklt. pane of 18 | 37.50 | |

Perf. 12½ Horizontally.

| 327 | A67 | 15ö dp brn | 45 | 12 |
| 328 | A67 | 1.20k red vio | 60.00 | 18.00 |

Issued to honor St. Bridget of Sweden.

King Gustavus III
A68

K. G. Tessin, Architect
A69

Perf. 12½ on 3 Sides

1942, June 29

| 329 | A68 | 20ö red | 2.00 | 30 |
| a. | | Bklt. pane of 20 | 40.00 | |

Perf. 12½ Vertically

| 330 | A68 | 20ö red | 50 | 10 |
| 331 | A69 | 40(ö) ol grn | 40.00 | 1.50 |

Issued to commemorate the sesquicentennial of the Swedish National Museum, Stockholm.

Torsten Rudenschöld and Nils Mansson—A70

Perf. 12½ Horizontally

1942, July 1 Engraved

| 332 | A70 | 10ö magenta | 70 | 50 |
| a. | | Booklet pane of 20 | 7.00 | |

Perf. 12½ Vertically

| 333 | A70 | 10ö magenta | 60 | 40 |
| 334 | A70 | 90ö lt bl | 6.00 | 20 |

Issued to commemorate the 100th anniversary of the Swedish Public School System.

SWEDEN

Carl Wilhelm
Scheele
A71

King
Gustaf V
A72

Perf. 12½ on 3 Sides

1942, Dec. 9
335	A71	5ö green	2.00	50
a.		Bklt. pane of 20	40.00	

Perf. 12½ Vertically.
| 336 | A71 | 5ö green | 25 | 8 |
| 337 | A71 | 60ö dp mag | 18.00 | 35 |

Issued in commemoration of the 200th anniversary of the birth of Carl Wilhelm Scheele, chemist.

Perf. 12½ Horizontally.

1943, June 16
338	A72	20ö red	1.10	25
339	A72	30ö ultra	2.50	3.25
340	A72	60ö brt red vio	5.00	5.00

Perf. 12½ on 3 Sides
| 341 | A72 | 20ö red | 12.00 | 85 |
| a. | | Bklt. pane of 20 | 325.00 | |

85th birthday of King Gustaf V, June 16.

Rifle Federation
Emblem
A73

Oscar
Montelius
A74

1943, July 22   **Perf. 12½ Vert.**
| 342 | A73 | 10ö rose vio | 20 | 8 |
| 343 | A73 | 90ö dp ultra | 10.00 | 30 |

Perf. 12½ on 3 Sides
| 344 | A73 | 10ö rose vio | 70 | 50 |
| a. | | Booklet pane of 20 | 14.00 | |

Issued to commemorate the 50th anniversary of the Swedish Voluntary Rifle Associations.

Engraved.

1943, Sept. 9   **Perf. 12½ Vert.**
| 345 | A74 | 5ö green | 20 | 8 |
| 346 | A74 | 1.20k brt red vio | 18.00 | 3.00 |

Perf. 12½ on 3 Sides
| 347 | A74 | 5ö green | 50 | 25 |
| a. | | Booklet pane of 20 | 10.00 | |

Birth centenary of Oscar Montelius (1843–1921), archaeologist.

Johan Månsson's
Chart of Baltic, 1644
A75

Perf. 12½ on 3 Sides

1944, Apr. 15   **Engr.**   **Unwmkd.**
| 348 | A75 | 5ö green | 1.75 | 60 |
| a. | | Bklt. pane of 20 | 35.00 | |

Perf. 12½ Vertically.
| 349 | A75 | 5ö green | 20 | 12 |
| 350 | A75 | 60ö lake | 12.00 | 40 |

Issued to commemorate the tercentenary of the first Swedish Marine Chart.

"The Lion of Smaland"
A76

Clas Fleming
A77

"Kung Karl"
A78

Stern of "Amphion,"
Flagship of
Gustavus III
A79

"Gustaf V"
A80

1944, Oct. 13   **Perf. 12½ Vert.**
351	A76	10ö purple	45	35
352	A77	20ö red	65	8
353	A78	30ö blue	1.10	1.00
354	A79	40ö ol grn	1.40	90
355	A80	90ö gray blk	18.00	2.00

Perf. 12½ on 3 Sides
356	A76	10ö purple	1.40	1.40
a.		Booklet pane of 20	30.00	
357	A77	20ö red	4.50	40
a.		Booklet pane of 20	110.00	
		Nos. 351-357 (7)	27.50	6.13

Issued to honor the Swedish Fleet and mark the tercentenary of the Swedish naval victory at Femern, 1644.
See also Nos. B53, B57–B58.

Red Cross
A81

Torch and
Quill Pen
A82

1945, Feb. 27   **Perf. 12½ Vert.**
| 358 | A81 | 20ö red | 1.00 | 8 |

Perf. 12½ on 3 Sides
| 359 | A81 | 20ö red | 3.00 | 40 |
| a. | | Bklt. pane of 20 | 70.00 | |

Issued to commemorate the 80th anniversary of the Swedish Red Cross Society.

1945, May 29   **Perf. 12½ Vert.**
| 360 | A82 | 5ö green | 20 | 8 |
| 361 | A82 | 60ö car rose | 8.00 | 40 |

Perf. 12½ on 3 Sides
| 362 | A82 | 5ö green | 40 | 30 |
| a. | | Booklet pane of 20 | 8.00 | |

Tercentenary of Swedish press.

Viktor Rydberg
A83

Oak Tree
A84

1945, Sept. 21   **Perf. 12½ Vert.**
| 363 | A83 | 20ö red | 40 | 5 |
| 364 | A83 | 90ö blue | 11.00 | 30 |

Perf. 12½ on 3 Sides.
| 365 | A83 | 20ö red | 1.80 | 25 |
| a. | | Booklet pane of 20 | 36.00 | |

50th anniversary of death of Viktor Rydberg (1828–1895), author.

1945, Oct. 27   **Perf. 12½ Vert.**
| 366 | A84 | 10ö violet | 20 | 20 |
| 367 | A84 | 40ö olive | 1.50 | 1.10 |

Perf. 12½ on 3 Sides.
| 368 | A84 | 10ö violet | 60 | 60 |
| a. | | Booklet pane of 20 | 12.00 | |

Issued to commemorate the 125th anniversary of the Savings Bank movement.

Angel and
Lund Cathedral
A85

View of Lund
Cathedral
A86

1946, May 28   **Unwmkd.**

Perf. 12½ Vertically.
369	A85	15ö org brn	90	40
370	A86	20ö red	30	5
371	A85	90ö ultra	9.00	1.00

Perf. 12½ on 3 Sides.
372	A85	15ö org brn	1.00	1.25
a.		Bklt. pane of 20	20.00	
373	A85	20ö red	2.00	25
a.		Bklt. pane of 20	40.00	
		Nos. 369-373 (5)	13.20	2.95

Lund Cathedral, 800th anniversary.

Mare and Colt
A87

1946, June 8   **Perf. 12½ Vert.**
| 374 | A87 | 5ö green | 15 | 8 |
| 375 | A87 | 60ö car rose | 6.50 | 40 |

Perf. 12½ on 3 Sides
| 376 | A87 | 5ö green | 35 | 30 |
| a. | | Booklet pane of 20 | 7.00 | |

Issued to commemorate the centenary of Swedish agricultural shows.

Esaias Tegner
A88

Perf. 12½ Vertically

1946, Nov. 2   **Engr.**   **Unwmkd.**
| 377 | A88 | 10ö dp vio | 15 | 10 |
| 378 | A88 | 40ö dk ol grn | 1.80 | 35 |

Perf. 12½ on 3 Sides.
| 379 | A88 | 10ö dp vio | 35 | 30 |
| a. | | Booklet pane of 20 | 7.00 | |

Death centenary of Esaias Tegner (1782–1846), poet.

Alfred Nobel
A89

Erik Gustaf Geijer
A90

1946, Dec. 10   **Perf. 12½ Vert.**
| 380 | A89 | 20ö red | 70 | 8 |
| 381 | A90 | 30ö ultra | 2.50 | 90 |

Perf. 12½ on 3 Sides.
| 382 | A89 | 20ö red | 2.25 | 30 |
| a. | | Booklet pane of 20 | 45.00 | |

Issued to commemorate the 50th anniversary of the death of Alfred Nobel, inventor and philanthropist.

1947, Apr. 23   **Perf. 12½ Vert.**
| 383 | A90 | 5ö dk yel grn | 15 | 12 |
| 384 | A90 | 90ö ultra | 5.50 | 25 |

Perf. 12½ on 3 Sides.
| 385 | A90 | 5ö dk yel grn | 35 | 30 |
| a. | | Booklet pane of 20 | 7.00 | |

Issued to commemorate the centenary of the death of Erik Gustaf Geijer, historian, philosopher and poet.

King Gustaf V
A91

Engraved.

1947, Dec. 8   **Perf. 12½ Horiz.**
386	A91	10ö dp vio	20	25
387	A91	20ö red	30	30
388	A91	60ö red vio	2.25	2.25

Perf. 12½ on 3 Sides.
389	A91	10ö dp vio	25	30
a.		Booklet pane of 20	5.00	
390	A91	20ö red	70	50
a.		Booklet pane of 20	14.00	
		Nos. 386-390 (5)	3.70	3.60

Issued to commemorate the 40th anniversary of the reign of King Gustaf V.

King and 3-Crown Types of 1939

Perf. 12½ Vertically.

1948   **Unwmkd.**
391	A60	5ö orange	25	5
392	A60	10ö green	30	5
393	A60	25ö violet	1.00	15
394	A56	55ö org brn	4.50	10
395	A56	80ö org brn	1.50	10
396	A56	1.10k violet	11.00	5
397	A56	1.40k dk bl grn	1.50	8
398	A56	1.75k brt grnsh bl	45.00	10.00

Perf. 12½ on 3 Sides.
399	A60	10ö green	25	20
a.		Booklet pane of 20	7.00	
		Nos. 391-399 (9)	65.30	10.78

Plowman,
Early and
Modern Buildings
A92

August
Strindberg
A93

1948, Apr. 26   **Perf. 12½ Vert.**
400	A92	15ö org brn	30	20
401	A92	30ö ultra	1.10	35
402	A92	1k orange	3.00	40

Perf. 12½ on 3 Sides
| 403 | A92 | 15ö org brn | 60 | 55 |
| a. | | Booklet pane of 20 | 12.00 | |

Issued to commemorate the centenary of the Swedish pioneers' settlement in the United States.

1949, Jan. 22   **Perf. 12½ Vert.**
404	A93	20ö red	30	15
405	A93	30ö blue	1.00	90
406	A93	80ö ol grn	2.75	50

SWEDEN

Perf. 12½ on 3 Sides.
407	A93	20ö red	70	25
a.		Booklet pane of 20	14.00	

Birth centenary of August Strindberg (1849–1912), author and playwright.

Girl and Boy Gymnasts
A94
Engraved

1949, July 27 — Perf. 12½ Horiz.
408	A94	5ö ultra	25	20
409	A94	15ö brown	30	20

Perf. 12½ on 3 Sides.
410	A94	15ö brown	65	65
a.		Bklt. pane of 20	13.00	

Issued to publicize the second Lingiad or World Gymnastics Festival, Stockholm, July–August 1949.

Symbols of UPU
A95   A96

1949, Oct. 9 — Perf. 12½ Vert.
411	A95	10ö green	20	20
412	A95	20ö red	25	15

Perf. 12½ Horizontally.
413	A96	30ö lt bl	60	50

Perf. 12½ on 3 sides.
414	A95	10ö green	25	15
a.		Booklet pane of 20	5.00	
415	A95	20ö red	30	20
a.		Booklet pane of 20	6.00	
		Nos. 411-415 (5)	1.60	1.20

Issued to commemorate the 75th anniversary of the formation of the Universal Postal Union.

Three-Crown Type of 1939.
Perf. 12½ Vertically.
1949, Nov. 11 — Unwmkd.
416	A56	65ö lt yel grn	1.40	20
417	A56	70ö pck bl	8.00	1.75

King Gustaf VI Adolf (Letters in color)
A97

Christopher Polhem
A98

1951, June 6
Without Imprint
418	A97	10ö dl grn	30	5
419	A97	15ö chnt brn	45	10
420	A97	20ö car rose	60	5
421	A97	25ö gray	2.00	5
422	A97	30ö ultra	45	15

Perf. 12½ on 3 sides.
423	A97	10ö dl grn	30	15
a.		Booklet pane of 20	6.00	
424	A97	25ö gray	60	15
a.		Booklet pane of 20	14.00	
		Nos. 418-424 (7)	4.70	80

See also Nos. 435-438, 442-443, 456-461, 502, 505-509, 515-517.

Three-Crown Type of 1939.
1951, June 1 — Perf. 12½ Vert.
425	A56	85ö org brn	11.00	2.00
426	A56	1.70k red	2.00	6

1951, Aug. 30 — Perf. 12½ Vert.
427	A98	25ö gray	50	15
428	A98	45ö brown	55	55

Perf. 12½ on 3 sides.
429	A98	25ö gray	40	25
a.		Booklet pane of 20	8.00	

Issued to commemorate the 200th anniversary of the death of Christopher Polhem, engineer and technician.

Numeral (Lettering in color)
A99

Olaus Petri Preaching
A100

Type A99 and 3-Crown Type of 1939
1951, Nov. — Engr. — Perf. 12½ Vert.
430	A99	5ö rose car	30	6
431	A56	1.50k red vio	2.75	2.00

For other stamps similar to type A99, see type A115a, Nos. 503-504, 513-514, 570, 580, 666-667.

1952, Apr. 19 — Perf. 12½ Horiz.
432	A100	25ö gray blk	30	15
433	A100	1.40k brown	4.00	1.00

Perf. 12½ on 3 sides.
434	A100	25ö gray blk	1.25	1.25
a.		Booklet pane of 20	25.00	

400th anniversary of death of Olaus Petri (1493–1552), Lutheran clergyman, historian and Bible translator.

King and 3-Crown Types of 1951 and 1939.
1952 — Perf. 12½ Vertically.
Without Imprint
435	A97	20ö gray	40	5
436	A97	25ö car rose	2.75	5
437	A97	30ö dk brn	50	35
438	A97	40ö blue	2.00	25
439	A97	50ö green	11.00	20
440	A56	75ö org brn	6.00	80
441	A56	2k red vio	1.60	5

Perf. 12½ on 3 sides
442	A97	20ö gray	60	40
a.		Booklet pane of 20	14.00	
443	A97	25ö car rose	70	25
a.		Bklt pane of 20	14.00	
		Nos. 435-443 (9)	25.55	2.40

Ski Jump
A101

Ice Hockey
A102

Designs: 40(ö), Woman throwing slingball. 1.40kr, Wrestlers.

Perf. 12½ Vert. (V), Horiz. (H)
1953, May 27
444	A101	10ö grn (V)	60	40
445	A102	15ö brn (H)	1.20	60
446	A102	40ö dp bl (H)	1.60	1.75
447	A101	1.40k red vio (V)	4.50	1.50

Perf. 12½ on 3 sides.
448	A101	10ö green	1.00	1.00
a.		Booklet pane of 20	20.00	
		Nos. 444-448 (5)	8.90	5.25

50th anniversary of Swedish Athletic Association.

Old Stockholm
A103

Original and Present Seals of Stockholm
A104

1953, June 17 — Perf. 12½ Vert.
449	A103	25ö blue	35	10
450	A104	1.70k red	4.00	75

Perf. 12½ on 3 sides.
451	A103	25ö blue	60	10
a.		Booklet pane of 20	14.00	

Issued to commemorate the 700th anniversary of the founding of Stockholm.

"Telephone"
A105

Designs: 40(ö), "Radio." 60(ö), "Telegraph."

1953, Nov. 22 — Perf. 12½ Horiz.
452	A105	25ö dp ultra	35	10
453	A105	40ö ol grn	1.40	1.75
454	A105	60ö dp car	1.50	1.75

Perf. 12½ on 3 sides.
455	A105	25ö dp ultra	60	20
a.		Booklet pane of 20	12.00	

Issued to commemorate the centenary of the foundation of the Swedish Telegraph Service.

King Type of 1951.
1954 — Perf. 12½ Vertically
Without Imprint
456	A97	10ö dk brn	15	5
457	A97	25ö ultra	30	5
458	A97	30ö red	30.00	15
459	A97	40ö ol grn	1.00	15

Perf. 12½ on 3 sides
460	A97	10ö dk brn	25	15
a.		Bklt. pane of 10	9.00	
b.		Bklt. pane of 20	6.00	
461	A97	25ö ultra	25	5
a.		Bklt. pane of 4	14.00	
b.		Bklt. pane of 8	100.00	
c.		Bklt. pane of 20	6.00	
		Nos. 456-461 (6)	31.95	60

The booklet pane of 4 contains two copies of No. 461 which are perforated on two adjoining sides.

Skier
A106

Anna Maria Lenngren
A107

Design: 1k, Girl skier.

1954, Feb. 13 — Perf. 12½ Vert.
462	A106	20ö gray	60	40
463	A106	1k blue	13.00	1.50

Perf. 12½ on 3 sides.
464	A106	20ö gray	1.40	1.75
a.		Bklt. pane of 20	32.50	

Issued to publicize the World Ski Championship Matches, 1954.

1954, June 18 — Perf. 12½ Horiz.
465	A107	20ö gray	35	30
466	A107	65ö dk brn	9.00	3.25

Perf. 12½ on 3 sides
467	A107	20ö gray	1.40	1.75
a.		Bklt. pane of 20	32.50	

Issued to commemorate the 200th anniversary of the birth of Anna Maria Lenngren, author.

Rock Carvings
A108

Coat of Arms
A109

1954, Nov. 8 — Perf. 12½ Vert.
468	A108	50ö gray	40	5
469	A108	60ö dp car	40	5
470	A108	65ö dk ol grn	2.00	35
471	A108	75ö dk brn	3.25	35
472	A108	90ö dk bl	1.00	8
		Nos. 468-472 (5)	7.05	88

See also Nos. 510-512, 655.

Three-Crown Type of 1939
1954, Dec. 10 — Perf. 12½ Vert.
473	A56	2.10k dp ultra	13.00	25

1955, May 16 — Perf. 12½ Vert.
474	A109	25ö blue	15	5
475	A109	40ö green	2.25	50

Perf. 12½ on 3 sides
476	A109	25ö blue	20	20
a.		Bklt. pane of 4	14.00	
b.		Bklt. pane of 20	4.00	

Issued to commemorate the centenary of Sweden's first postage stamps.

The booklet pane of 4 contains two copies of No. 476 which are perforated on two adjoining sides.

Crown and Flag
A110
Lithographed.

1955, June 6 — Perf. 12½ Unwmkd.
477	A110	10ö grn, bl & yel	30	25
478	A110	15ö lake, bl & yel	35	30

National Flag Day.

A111    Wmk. 307

Wmkd. Crown and 1955 (307)
1955, July 1 — Typo. — Perf. 13
479	A111	3ö yel grn	4.00	5.00
480	A111	4ö blue	4.00	5.00
481	A111	6ö gray	4.00	5.00
482	A111	8ö org yel	4.00	5.00

SWEDEN

483 A111 20ö salmon   4.00   5.00
     Nos. 479-483 (5)   20.00 25.00

Issued to commemorate the centenary of the first Swedish postage stamps. Nos. 479-483 were printed in sheets of nine. They were sold in complete sets at the Stockholmia Philatelic Exhibition, July 1-10, 1955. A set cost 45 öre (face value) plus 2k (entrance fee). Price for set of 5 sheets, $225 unused, $325 canceled.

Per Atterbom
A112

Greek Horseman
A113

Perf. 12½ Horizontally.
1955, July 21   Engr.   Unwmkd.
484 A112 20ö dk bl   30   15
485 A112 1.40k sepia   4.00   60
Perf. 12½ on 3 sides
486 A112 20ö dk bl   1.20 1.30
  a.   Booklet pane of 20   30.00

Issued to commemorate the centenary of the death of Per Daniel Amadeus Atterbom, poet.

1956, Apr. 16   Perf. 12½ Vert.
487 A113 20ö carmine   30   20
488 A113 25ö ultra   30   20
489 A113 40ö gray grn   2.50 2.00
Perf. 12½ on 3 sides
490 A113 20ö carmine   60   50
  a.   Booklet pane of 20   12.00
491 A113 25ö ultra   60   35
  a.   Booklet pane of 20   12.00
     Nos. 487-491 (5)   4.30 3.25

Issued to publicize the Olympic Equestrian Competitions, Stockholm, June 10-17, 1956.

Northern Countries Issue.

Whooper Swans
A113a

Perf. 12½ Vertically
1956, Oct. 30   Engr.   Unwmkd.
492 A113a 25ö rose red   1.00   15
493 A113a 40ö ultra   3.00   80

See footnote after Norway No. 354.

Railroad Builders
A114

Ship in Distress and Lifeboat
A115

Designs: 25ö, First Swedish locomotive and passenger car. 40ö, Express train crossing Årsta bridge.

1956, Dec. 1   Perf. 12½ Vert.
494 A114 10ö ol grn   60   25
495 A114 25ö ultra   40   20
496 A114 40ö orange   2.75 3.75
Perf. 12½ on 3 sides.
497 A114 10ö ol grn   60   55
  a.   Booklet pane of 20   12.00
498 A114 25ö ultra   60   40
  a.   Booklet pane of 20   12.00
     Nos. 494-498 (5)   4.95 5.10

Centenary of Swedish railroads.

Perf. 12½ Vertically
1957, June 1   Engr.   Unwmkd.
499 A115 30ö blue   7.00   20
500 A115 1.40k dp rose   9.00 1.50
Perf. 12½ on 3 sides
501 A115 30ö blue   1.40 1.00
  a.   Booklet pane of 20   50.00

Issued to commemorate the 50th anniversary of the Swedish Life Saving Society.

King Type of 1951.
1957, June 1   Perf. 12½ Vert.
Without Imprint
502 A97 25ö dk brn   2.00 2.75

Re-engraved Types of 1951 and 1954 with Imprint, and

Numeral (Letters in white)
A115a

1957-64   Perf. 12½ Vertically
503 A115a 5ö red ('61)   10   5
  a.   5ö dk red   25   15
504 A115a 10ö bl ('61)   15   5
  a.   10ö dk bl   35   15
505 A97 15ö dk red   30   5
506 A97 20ö gray   30   5
507 A97 25ö brown   70   5
508 A97 30ö blue   55   5
509 A97 40ö ol grn   1.20   20
510 A108 55ö vermilion   1.30   30
511 A108 70ö orange   1.00   5
512 A108 80ö yel grn   1.00   6
Perf. 12½ on 3 sides
513 A115a 5ö red ('61)   10   5
  a.   Bkit. pane of 20 ('64) 2.00
  b.   5ö dk red   1.50   20
  c.   Bklt. pane of 10 (5 No.
          513b+5 No. 515)   8.50
514 A115a 10ö bl ('61)   15   6
  a.   Bkit. pane of 20   12.00   2.00
  b.   Bkit. pane of 4 (1 No.
          514a+3 No. 517)   35.00
515 A97 15ö dk red   45   20
  a.   Bkit. pane of 20   12.00
516 A97 20ö gray   1.00   55
  a.   Bkit. pane of 20   25.00
517 A97 30ö blue   50   5
  a.   Bkit. pane of 20   20.00
     Nos. 503-517 (15)   8.80 1.97

In the redrawn Numeral type A99, "Sverige, öre" and the "g" tail flourishes are white instead of in color.
Booklet pane including No. 513 is listed as No. 581b.
The booklet pane of 4, No. 514b, contains two copies of No. 517 which are imperf. on two adjoining sides. No. 514a was issued only in booklet pane No. 514b.
See also Nos. 570, 580, 580a, 581b, 584b, 586b-586c, 668a, 669b-669c.

Helicopter Mail Service
A116
Modern and 17th Century Vessels
A117

Perf. 12½ Vertically
1958, Feb. 10   Engr.   Unwmkd.
518 A116 30ö blue   25   10
519 A116 1.40k brown   8.00 1.00
Perf. 12½ on 3 sides
520 A116 30ö blue   70   40
  a.   Booklet pane of 20   14.00

Issued to commemorate the 10th anniversary of helicopter mail service to the Stockholm archipelago, Feb. 10.

1958, Feb. 10   Perf. 12½ Vert.
521 A117 15ö dk red   40   20
522 A117 40ö gray ol   7.00 3.50

Perf. 12½ on 3 sides
523 A117 30ö blue   60   70
  a.   Booklet pane of 20   12.00

Issued to commemorate three centuries of transatlantic mail service.

Soccer Player
A118

1958, May 8   Perf. 12½ Vert.
524 A118 15ö vermilion   25   25
525 A118 20ö yel grn   40   25
526 A118 1.20k dk bl   1.80 1.20
Perf. 12½ on 3 sides.
527 A118 15ö vermilion   60   55
  a.   Bkit. pane of 20   12.00
528 A118 20ö yel grn   60   60
  a.   Bkit. pane of 20   12.00
     Nos. 524-528 (5)   3.65 2.85

Issued to publicize the 6th World Soccer Championships, Stockholm, June 8-29.

Bessemer Converter
A119
Selma Lagerlöf
A120

Perf. 12½ Horizontally
1958, July 18   Engr.   Unwmkd.
529 A119 30ö gray bl   30   15
530 A119 1.70k dl red brn   4.00 1.00
Perf. 12½ on 3 sides
531 A119 30ö gray bl   70   50
  a.   Bkit. pane of 20   14.00

Issued to commemorate the centenary of the first successful Bessemer blow in Sweden, July 18, 1858.

1958, Nov. 20   Perf. 12½ Horiz.
532 A120 20ö dk red   25   25
533 A120 30ö blue   35   20
534 A120 80ö gray ol   1.20 1.60
Perf. 12½ on 3 Sides
535 A120 20ö dk red   60   55
  a.   Bkit. pane of 20   12.00
536 A120 30ö blue   60   55
  a.   Bkit. pane of 20   12.00
     Nos. 532-536 (5)   3.15

Issued to commemorate the centenary of the birth of Selma Lagerlöf, writer.

Palace Type of 1941
1958, Sept. 17   Perf. 12½ Vert.
537 A65 5k blue   3.50   12

Electric Power Line
A121

Hydroelectric Plant and Dam
A122

Perf. 12½ Horiz. (H), Vert. (V)
1959, Jan. 20   Unwmkd.
538 A121 30ö ultra (H)   50   10
539 A122 90ö car rose (V)   4.00 3.00
Perf. 12½ on 3 sides
540 A121 30ö ultra   70   35
  a.   Bkit. pane of 20   14.00

Issued to commemorate the 50th anniversary of the establishment of the State Power Board.

Verner von Heidenstam
A123
Forest
A124

1959, July 6 Engraved. Unwmkd.
Perf. 12½ Horizontally
541 A123 15ö rose car   1.00   20
542 A123 1k slate   6.50   90
Perf. 12½ on 3 sides
543 A123 15ö rose car   90   90
  a.   Bkit. pane of 20   18.00

Issued to commemorate the centenary of the birth of Verner von Heidenstam, poet.

1959, Sept. 4   Perf. 12½ Horiz.
Design: 1.40k, Felling tree.
544 A124 30ö green   1.75   15
545 A124 1.40k brn red   5.00   90
Perf. 12½ on 3 sides
546 A124 30ö green   1.00   90
  a.   Booklet pane of 20   20.00

Centenary of administration of crown lands and forests.

Svante Arrhenius
A125
Anders Zorn
A126

1959, Dec. 10   Engr.   Unwmkd.
Perf. 12½ Horizontally
547 A125 15ö dl red brn   35   20
548 A125 1.70k dk bl   4.50   60
Perf. 12½ on 3 sides
549 A125 15ö dl red brn   60   60
  a.   Bkit. pane of 20   12.00

Birth centenary of Svante Arrhenius (1859-1927), chemist and physicist.

1960, Feb. 18   Perf. 12½ Horiz.
550 A126 30ö gray   35   20
551 A126 80ö sepia   4.50 1.50
Perf. 12½ on 3 sides
552 A126 30ö gray   2.00   35
  a.   Booklet pane of 20   40.00

Birth centenary of Anders Zorn (1860-1920), painter and sculptor.

Uprooted Oak Emblem
A127

SWEDEN

People of Various
Races and
WRY Emblem
A128
Perf. 12½ Vert. (V), Horiz. (H)
1960, Apr. 7   Engr.   Unwmkd.
| 553 | A127 | 20ö red brn (V) | 15 | 15 |
| 554 | A128 | 40ö pur (H) | 60 | 60 |

Perf. 12½ on 3 sides
| 555 | A127 | 20ö red brn | 60 | 55 |
| a. | Booklet pane of 20 | 12.00 | | |

Issued to publicize World Refugee Year, July 1, 1959–June 30, 1960.

Target Shooting   Gustaf Fröding
A129   A130
Design: 903, Parade of riflemen.
1960, June 30   *Perf. 12½ Vert.*
| 556 | A129 | 15ö rose car | 35 | 20 |
| 557 | A129 | 90ö grnsh bl | 3.25 | 1.75 |

Perf. 12½ on 3 sides
| 558 | A129 | 15ö rose car | 60 | 55 |
| a. | Booklet pane of 20 | 12.00 | | |

Issued to commemorate the centenary of the founding of the Voluntary Shooting Organization.

1960, Aug. 22   *Perf. 12½ Horiz.*
| 559 | A130 | 30ö red brn | 35 | 20 |
| 560 | A130 | 1.40k sl grn | 5.00 | 50 |

Perf. 12½ on 3 sides
| 561 | A130 | 30ö red brn | 70 | 35 |
| a. | Booklet pane of 20 | 14.00 | | |

Birth centenary of Gustaf Fröding (1860–1911), poet.

Europa Issue, 1960
Common Design Type
1960, Sept. 19   *Perf. 12½ Vert.*
Size: 27x21mm.
| 562 | CD3 | 40ö blue | 25 | 20 |
| 563 | CD3 | 1k red | 60 | 50 |

Hjalmar Branting
A131
Engraved
1960, Nov. 23   *Perf. 12½ Horiz.*
| 564 | A131 | 15ö rose car | 20 | 20 |
| 565 | A131 | 1.70k sl bl | 5.50 | 70 |

Perf. 12½ on 3 sides
| 566 | A131 | 15ö rose car | 35 | 35 |
| a. | Booklet pane of 20 | 7.00 | | |

Issued to commemorate the centenary of the birth of Hjalmar Branting (1860–1925), Labor Party leader and Prime Minister.

SAS Issue

DC-8 Airliner
A131a
Perf. 12½ Vertically
1961, Feb. 24   Unwmkd.
| 567 | A131a | 40ö blue | 30 | 30 |

Perf. 12½ on 3 sides
| 568 | A131a | 40ö blue | 1.10 | 1.00 |
| a. | Booklet pane of 10 | 11.00 | | |

Issued to commemorate the 10th anniversary of the Scandinavian Airlines System, SAS.

**Numeral Type of 1957,
Three-Crown Type of 1939 and**

King Gustaf   Rune Stone,
VI Adolf   Oland,
(Letters, numerals   11th Century
in white)
A132   A133

Engraved
1961–1965   *Perf. 12½ Vertically*
570	A115a	15ö grn ('62)	25	8
571	A132	15ö red	30	8
572	A132	20ö gray	30	5
573	A132	25ö brown	30	5
574	A132	30ö ultra	4.50	8
575	A132	30ö lil ('62)	55	5
576	A132	35ö lilac	55	5
577	A132	35ö ultra ('62)	1.10	8
578	A132	40ö emerald	1.00	5
579	A132	50ö gray grn ('62)	1.40	8

Perf. 12½ on 3 sides
580	A115a	15ö grn ('65)	25	15
a.	Bklt. pane of 6 (2 each #514, 580, 583)	2.25		
581	A132	15ö red	20	15
a.	Bklt. pane of 20	5.00		
b.	Bklt. pane of 10 (5 each #513, 581)	2.50		
582	A132	20ö gray	80	50
a.	Bklt. pane of 20	16.00		
583	A132	25ö brn ('62)	30	20
a.	Bklt. pane of 20	11.00		
b.	Bklt. pane of 4	2.25		
584	A132	30ö ultra	25	20
a.	Bklt. pane of 20	12.00		
b.	Bklt. pane of 4 (1 No. 514 + 3 No. 584)	5.00		
585	A132	30ö lil ('64)	40	50
a.	Bklt. pane of 20	11.00		
586	A132	35ö ultra ('62)	30	5
a.	Bklt. pane of 5 (3 No. 514 + 2 No. 586 + blank label)	5.00		
b.	Bklt. pane of 5 (3 No. 514 + 2 No. 586 + inscribed label)	3.50		

Perf. 12½ Vertically
588	A56	1.05k Prus grn ('62)	3.50	50
589	A56	1.50k brn ('62)	2.50	20
590	A56	2.15k dk sl grn ('62)	13.00	60
591	A56	2.50k emerald	2.00	10

Perf. 12½ on 3 sides
592	A133	10k dl red brn	14.00	1.00
a.	Bklt. pane of 10 ('68)	140.00		
b.	Bklt. pane of 20	500.00		
	Nos. 570-592 (22)	47.75	5.10

Booklet panes of 4, 5 or 6 (Nos. 580a, 583b, 584b, 586b, 586c) contain one stamps which are imperf. on two adjoining sides.

Combination panes (Nos. 580a, 581b, 584b, 586b, 586c) come in different arrangements of the denominations.

The label of No. 586c is inscribed "ett brev / betyder / så / mycket" ("a letter means so much"). The label inscription "nord 63 / 5–13 oktober / GÖTEBORG" was privately applied to No. 586b by the Gothenburg Philatelic Society to raise funds for Nord 63 Philatelic Exhibition in Gothenburg. The pane was sold for the equivalent of $1 U.S., 5 times face value.

See also Nos. 648–654A, 666a, 668–672D.

K.-G. Pilo,   Jonas
Self-portrait   Alströmer
A134   A135

1961, Apr. 17   *Perf. 12½ Horiz.*
| 594 | A134 | 30ö brown | 30 | 10 |
| 595 | A134 | 1.40k Prus bl | 6.00 | 1.20 |

Perf. 12½ on 3 sides
| 596 | A134 | 30ö brown | 1.10 | 25 |
| a. | Bklt. pane of 20 | 30.00 | | |

25th anniversary of birth of Karl-Gustaf Pilo (1711–1793), painter. Self-portrait from "The Coronation of Gustavus III."

1961, June 2   *Perf. 12½ Vert.*
| 597 | A135 | 15ö dl cl | 25 | 20 |
| 598 | A135 | 90ö grnsh bl | 2.00 | 1.40 |

Perf. 12½ on 3 sides
| 599 | A135 | 15ö dl cl | 40 | 35 |
| a. | Bklt. pane of 20 | 9.00 | | |

Issued to commemorate the 200th anniversary of the birth of Jonas Alströmer, pioneer of agriculture and industry.

17th Century   Roentgen,
Printer and   Prudhomme,
Student in   von Behring,
Library   van't Hoff
A136   A137

Engraved
1961, Sept. 22   *Perf. 12½ Vert.*
| 600 | A136 | 20ö dk red | 25 | 20 |
| 601 | A136 | 1k blue | 15.00 | 1.25 |

Perf. 12½ on 3 sides
| 602 | A136 | 20ö dk red | 45 | 35 |
| a. | Bklt. pane of 20 | 9.00 | | |

Issued to commemorate the 300th anniversary of the regulation requiring copies of all Swedish printed works to be deposited in the Royal Library.

Common Design Types
pictured in section at front of book.

1961, Dec. 9   *Perf. 12½ Vertically*
603	A137	20ö vermilion	25	20
604	A137	40ö blue	40	20
605	A137	50ö green	40	20

Perf. 12½ on 3 sides
| 606 | A137 | 20ö vermilion | 50 | 40 |
| a. | Bklt. pane of 20 | 10.00 | | |

Issued to commemorate the winners of the 1901 Nobel Prize; Wilhelm K. Roentgen, Rene Sully Prudhomme, Emil von Behring, Jacob van't Hoff.

Footsteps and   Voting Tool
Postmen's Badges   (Budkavle),
A138   Codex of Law
                   and Gavel
                   A139

Engraved
1962, Jan. 29   *Perf. 12½ Vert.*
| 607 | A138 | 30ö lilac | 35 | 20 |
| 608 | A138 | 1.70k rose red | 5.50 | 50 |

Perf. 12½ on 3 sides
| 609 | A138 | 30ö lilac | 45 | 35 |
| a. | Bklt. pane of 20 | 10.00 | | |

Issued to commemorate the centenary of local mail delivery service in Sweden.

1962, Mar. 21   *Perf. 12½ Horiz.*
| 610 | A139 | 30ö dk bl | 35 | 15 |
| 611 | A139 | 2k red | 5.50 | 50 |

Perf. 12½ on 3 sides
| 612 | A139 | 30ö dk bl | 60 | 50 |
| a. | Bklt. pane of 20 | 12.00 | | |

Issued to commemorate the centenary of the municipal reform laws.

St. George,   Skokloster Castle
Great Church,   A141
Stockholm
A140

Perf. 12½ Horiz. (H), Vert. (V)
1962, Sept. 24
| 613 | A140 | 20ö rose lake (H) | 30 | 20 |
| 614 | A141 | 50ö dk sl grn (V) | 50 | 20 |

Perf. 12½ on 3 sides
615	A140	20ö rose lake	30	20
a.	Booklet pane of 20	6.00		
616	A141	50ö dk sl grn	1.00	1.00
a.	Booklet pane of 10	10.00		

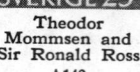

Theodor   Ice Hockey
Mommsen and   A143
Sir Ronald Ross
A142

SWEDEN

Design: 50ö, Hermann Emil Fischer, Pieter Zeeman and Hendrik Antoon Lorentz.

1962, Dec. 10 Perf. 12½ Vert.

| 617 | A142 | 25ö dk red | 45 | 35 |
| 618 | A142 | 50ö blue | 45 | 15 |

Perf. 12½ on 3 sides

| 619 | A142 | 25ö dk red | 90 | 90 |
| a. | Booklet pane of 20 | | 18.00 | |

Issued to commemorate the winners of the 1902 Nobel Prize. See also Nos. 689-692, 710, 712, 769-772, 805, 807.

1963, Feb. 15 Perf. 12½ Horiz.

| 620 | A143 | 25ö green | 25 | 15 |
| 621 | A143 | 1.70k vio bl | 4.50 | 50 |

Perf. 12½ on 3 sides

| 622 | A143 | 25ö green | 50 | 50 |
| a. | Bklt. pane of 20 | | 10.00 | |

1963 Ice Hockey World Championships.

Wheat Emblem and Stylized Hands
A144

Engineering and Industry Symbols
A145

1963, Mar. 21 Perf. 12½ Vertically

| 623 | A144 | 35ö lil rose | 25 | 10 |
| 624 | A144 | 50ö violet | 40 | 20 |

Perf. 12½ on 3 sides

| 625 | A144 | 35ö lil rose | 40 | 40 |
| a. | Bklt. pane of 20 | | 8.00 | |

Issued for the "Freedom from Hunger" campaign of the U.N. Food and Agriculture Organization.

1963, May 27 Perf. 12½ Vertically

| 626 | A145 | 50ö gray | 40 | 40 |
| 627 | A145 | 1.05k orange | 4.50 | 3.00 |

Perf. 12½ on 3 sides

| 628 | A145 | 50ö gray | 3.50 | 3.50 |
| a. | Bklt. pane of 10 | | 35.00 | |

Gregoire François Du Reitz
A146

Hammarby, Home of Carl von Linné (Linnaeus)
A147

1963, Sept. 16 Engraved Unwmkd.

629	A146	25ö brown	40	40
630	A146	35ö dk bl	30	10
631	A146	2k dk red	5.50	70

Perf. 12½ on 3 sides

632	A146	25ö brown	1.00	1.00
a.	Booklet pane of 20		20.00	
633	A146	35ö dk bl	60	20
a.	Bklt. pane of 20		12.00	
	Nos. 629-633 (5)		7.80	2.40

Issued to commemorate the 300th anniversary of the Swedish Board of Health. Dr. Du Reitz (1607-1682) was first president of the "Collegium Medicorum," forerunner of the Board of Health.

1963, Oct. 25 Perf. 12½ Vert.

| 634 | A147 | 20ö org red | 25 | 20 |
| 635 | A147 | 50ö yel grn | 40 | 20 |

Perf. 12½ on 3 sides

| 636 | A147 | 20ö org red | 40 | 25 |
| a. | Bklt. pane of 20 | | 8.00 | |

Svante Arrhenius, Niels Finsen, Björnstjerne Björnson
A148

"The Assumption of Elijah"
A149

Design: 50ö, Antoine Henri Becquerel, Pierre and Marie Curie.

Perf. 12½ Vertically

1963, Dec. 10 Engraved Unwmkd.

| 637 | A148 | 25ö gray ol | 75 | 60 |
| 638 | A148 | 50ö chocolate | 75 | 20 |

Perf. 12½ on 3 sides

| 639 | A148 | 25ö gray ol | 1.25 | 1.25 |
| a. | Bklt. pane of 20 | | 25.00 | |

Issued to commemorate the winners of the 1903 Nobel Prize. See also Nos. 711, 713, 804, 806.

1964, Feb. 3 Perf. 12½ Horiz.

| 640 | A149 | 35ö lt ultra | 1.00 | 15 |
| 641 | A149 | 1.05k dl red | 9.00 | 3.50 |

Perf. 12½ on 3 sides

| 642 | A149 | 35ö lt ultra | 60 | 25 |
| a. | Bklt. pane of 20 | | 12.00 | |

Issued to commemorate the centenary of the birth of the poet Erik Axel Karlfeldt (1864-1931).

Seal of Archbishop Stephen
A150

1964, June 12 Perf. 12½ Horiz.

| 643 | A150 | 40ö sl grn | 35 | 25 |
| 644 | A150 | 60ö org brn | 50 | 45 |

Perf. 12½ Vertically

645	A150	40ö sl grn	35	25
a.	Bklt. pane of 10		3.50	
646	A150	60ö org brn	60	60
a.	Bklt. pane of 10		6.00	

Issued to commemorate the 800th anniversary of the Archbishopric of Uppsala. Nos. 645-646 are from the booklet panes.

Types of Regular Issues, 1939-61, and

Post Horns
A151

Ship Grave, Skane (Bronze Age)
A152

1964-71 Engraved Perf. 12½ Vert.

647	A151	20ö sl bl & org yel ('65)	20	5
648	A132	35ö gray	90	20
649	A132	40ö ultra	1.10	8
650	A132	45ö orange	1.10	8
651	A132	45ö vio bl ('67)	1.10	8
652	A132	50ö grn ('68)	75	5
652A	A132	55ö dk red ('69)	75	5
653	A132	60ö rose car	1.50	75
653A	A132	65ö dl grn ('71)	1.80	8
654	A132	70ö lil rose ('67)	90	10
654A	A132	85ö dp cl ('71)	1.75	35
655	A108	95ö violet	11.00	6.00
656	A56	1.20k lt bl	14.00	3.50
657	A56	1.80c dk bl ('67)	6.00	70
658	A56	1.85c bl ('67)	15.00	1.40
659	A56	2k dp car ('69)	1.00	10
660	A56	2.30c choc ('65)	45.00	35
661	A56	2.55c red	12.50	2.50
662	A56	2.80c red ('67)	7.50	25
663	A56	2.85c org ('65)	10.00	7.00
664	A56	3k brt ultra	3.25	15
665	A152	3.50k grnsh gray ('66)	2.50	25

Perf. 12½ on 3 Sides

666	A115a	10ö brown	30	30
a.	Bklt. pane of 6 (2 each #666, 667, 583)		3.75	
667	A115a	15ö brown	80	80
668	A132	30ö rose red, perf. on 2 adjoining sides ('66)	1.10	1.10
a.	Bklt. pane of 6 (2 each #513, 580, 668)		2.75	
b.	Perf. on 3 sides		2.00	1.50
c.	Bklt. pane of 10 (2 each #513-514, 580, 668b-669)		7.00	
669	A132	40ö ultra	60	8
a.	Bklt. pane of 20		15.00	
b.	Bklt. pane of 4 (2 each #514, 669)		2.75	
670	A132	45ö org ('67)	60	20
a.	Bklt. pane of 20		15.00	
671	A132	45ö vio bl ('67)	75	8
a.	Bklt. pane of 20		16.00	
672	A132	50ö grn ('69)	80	70
a.	Bklt. pane of 20		9.00	
672B	A132	55ö dk red ('69)	70	8
a.	Bklt. pane of 20		9.00	
672D	A132	65ö dl grn ('71)	1.00	25
a.	Bklt. pane of 20		12.00	
672F	A132	85ö dp cl ('71)	1.60	1.25
g.	Bklt. pane of 10		17.00	
	Nos. 647-672F (32)		147.25	28.91

Some combination booklet panes of 4, 6 or 10 contain two stamps which are imperf. on two adjoining sides. Combination panes come in different arrangements of the denominations.

Fluorescent Paper

Starting in 1967, fluorescent paper was used in printing both definitive and commemorative issues. Its use was gradually eliminated starting in 1976. Numerous definitives and a few commemoratives were printed on both ordinary and fluorescent paper.

Echegaray, Mistral and Strutt
A153

Visby Town Wall
A154

Designs: 30ö, José Echegaray y Eizaguirre, Frédéric Mistral and John William Strutt, Lord Rayleigh. 40ö, Sir William Ramsey and Ivan Petrovich Pavlov.

Perf. 12½ Vertically

1964, Dec. 10 Engraved

| 673 | A153 | 30ö blue | 40 | 35 |
| 674 | A153 | 40ö red | 55 | 12 |

Perf. 12½ on 3 Sides

675	A153	30ö blue	60	50
a.	Bklt. pane of 20		12.00	
676	A153	40ö red	80	20
a.	Bklt. pane of 20		16.00	

Winners of the 1904 Nobel Prize.

Since 1867 American stamp collectors have been using the Scott Catalogue to identify their stamps and Scott Albums to house their collections.

1965, Apr. 5 Perf. 12½ Horiz.

| 677 | A154 | 30ö dk car rose | 25 | 8 |
| 678 | A154 | 2k brt ultra | 4.75 | 35 |

Perf. 12½ on 3 Sides

| 679 | A154 | 30ö dk car rose | 50 | 50 |
| a. | Bklt. pane of 20 | | 10.00 | |

Antenna
A155

Prince Eugen
A156

1965, May 17 Perf. 12½ Horiz.

| 680 | A155 | 60ö lilac | 40 | 20 |
| 681 | A155 | 1.40k bluish blk | 5.00 | 1.20 |

Perf. 12½ on 3 Sides

| 682 | A155 | 60ö lilac | 80 | 80 |
| a. | Bklt. pane of 10 | | 8.00 | |

Issued to commemorate the centenary of the International Telecommunication Union.

1965, July 5 Perf. 12½ Horiz.

| 683 | A156 | 40ö black | 25 | 10 |
| 684 | A156 | 1k brown | 2.50 | 40 |

Perf. 12½ on 3 Sides

| 685 | A156 | 40ö black | 45 | 20 |
| a. | Bklt. pane of 20 | | 9.00 | |

Issued to commemorate the centenary of the birth of Prince Eugen (1865-1947), painter and patron of the arts.

Fredrika Bremer
A157

Perf. 12½ Vertically

1965, Oct. 25 Engraved

| 686 | A157 | 25ö violet | 20 | 10 |
| 687 | A157 | 3k gray grn | 10.00 | 60 |

Perf. 12½ on 3 Sides

| 688 | A157 | 25ö violet | 30 | 15 |
| a. | Bklt. pane of 20 | | 6.00 | |

Issued to commemorate the centenary of the death of Fredrika Bremer (1801-1865), novelist.

Nobel Prize Winners Type of 1962.

Designs: 30ö, Philipp von Lenard and Adolf von Baeyer. 40ö, Robert Koch and Henryk Sienkiewicz.

Perf. 12½ Vertically

1965, Dec. 10 Unwmkd.

| 689 | A142 | 30ö ultra | 40 | 25 |
| 690 | A142 | 40ö dk red | 40 | 10 |

Perf. 12½ on 3 Sides

691	A142	30ö ultra	60	50
a.	Booklet pane of 20		12.00	
692	A142	40ö dk red	75	20
a.	Booklet pane of 20		15.00	

Winners of the 1905 Nobel Prize.

Nathan Söderblom
A158

Speed Skater
A159

SWEDEN

1966, Jan. 15 Perf. 12½ Horiz.
693 A158 60ö brown   40 15
694 A158 80ö green   1.10 20

Perf. 12½ on 3 Sides
695 A158 60ö brown   60 60
 a. Bklt. pane of 10   7.00

Issued to commemorate the centenary of the birth of Nathan Soderblom (1866–1931), Protestant theologian, who worked for the union of Christian churches and received 1930 Nobel Peace Prize.

Perf. 12½ on 3 Sides

1966, Feb. 18 Engraved
696 A159 5ö rose red   15 15
697 A159 25ö sl grn   20 20
698 A159 40ö dk bl   65 65
 a. Bklt. pane of 10 (4 #696, 4 #697, 2 #698)   2.75

World Speed Skating Championships for Men, Gothenburg, Feb. 18–20, and 75th anniversary of World Skating Championships.

National Museum, Staircase, 1866
A160

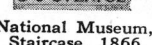

Baron Louis Gerhard De Geer
A161

1966, Mar. 26 Perf. 12½ Vert.
699 A160 30ö violet   25 25
 a. Bklt. pane of 10   2.50
700 A160 2.30k ol grn   1.50 1.50
 a. Bklt. pane of 10   15.00

Issued to commemorate the centenary of the National Gallery, Blasieholmen, Stockholm. The design is from an 1866 woodcut showing the inauguration of the Museum.

Perf. 12½ Vertically

1966, May 12 Engraved
701 A161 40ö dk bl   60 10
702 A161 3k brn car   8.00 90

Perf. 12½ on 3 Sides
703 A161 40ö dk bl   60 35
 a. Bklt. pane of 20   12.00

Issued to commemorate the centenary of the reform of the Representative Assembly under the leadership of Minister of Justice (1858–1870) Baron Louis Gerhard De Geer (1818–1896).

Stage, Drottningholm Court Theater
A162

Carl J. L. Almqvist and Wild Rose
A163

Perf. 12½ on 3 Sides

1966, June 15 Engraved
Salmon Paper
704 A162 5ö vermilion   10 10
705 A162 25ö ol bis   15 15
706 A162 40ö dk pur   85 85
 a. Bklt. pane of 10 (4 #704, 4 #705, 2 #706)   2.75

Issued to commemorate the 200th anniversary of the Drottningholm Court Theater.

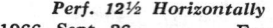

Perf. 12½ Horizontally

1966, Sept. 26
707 A163 25ö magenta   30 8
708 A163 1k green   4.00 35

Perf. 12½ on 3 Sides
709 A163 25ö magenta   40 20
 a. Bklt. pane of 20   8.00

Issued to commemorate the centenary of the death of Carl Jonas Love Almqvist (1793–1866), writer and poet.

Nobel Prize Winner Types of 1962–63

Designs: 30ö, Joseph John Thomson and Giosue Carducci. 40ö, Henri Moissan, Camillo Golgi and Santiago Ramon y Cajal.

Perf. 12½ Vertically

1966, Dec. 10 Engraved
710 A142 30ö rose lake   60 35
711 A148 40ö dk grn   40 10

Perf. 12½ on 3 Sides
712 A142 30ö rose lake   60 40
 a. Bklt. pane of 20   12.00
713 A148 40ö dk grn   60 50
 a. Bklt. pane of 20   12.00

Winners of the 1906 Nobel Prize.

Field Ball Player
A164

Perf. 12½ Horizontally

1967, Jan. 12
714 A164 45ö dk vio bl   35 10
715 A164 2.70k dp rose lil   4.50 1.50

Perf. 12½ on 3 Sides
716 A164 45ö dk vio bl   40 15
 a. Bklt. pane of 20   8.00

Issued to publicize the World Field Ball Championships, Jan. 12–21.

EFTA Emblem
A165

1967, Feb. 15 Perf. 12½ Horiz.
717 A165 70ö orange   60 40

Perf. 12½ on 3 Sides
718 A165 70ö orange   1.50 1.50
 a. Bklt. pane of 10   15.00

European Free Trade Association. Tariffs were abolished Dec. 31, 1966, among EFTA members: Austria, Denmark, Finland, Great Britain, Norway, Portugal, Sweden, Switzerland.

"The Fjeld," by Sixten Lundbohm
A166

Lion Fortress, Gothenburg
A167

Uppsala Cathedral
A168

Gripsholm Castle
A169

1967 Engraved Perf. 12½ Vert.
719 A166 35ö dl bl & blk brn   20 7

Perf. 12½ Horiz.
720 A167 3.70k violet   3.25 20
721 A168 4.50k dl red   4.00 20

Perf. 12½ Vert.
722 A169 7k vio bl & rose red   6.00 60

Perf. 12½ on 3 Sides
723 A166 35ö dl bl & blk brn   25 15
 a. Bklt. pane of 10   2.50
  Nos. 719–723 (5)   13.70 1.22

Issue Dates: Nos. 719, 721, 723, Mar. 15; No. 720, Feb. 15; No. 722, Apr. 11.

Table Tennis
A170

1967, Apr. 11 Perf. 12½ Horiz.
724 A170 35ö brt mag   25 8
725 A170 90ö grnsh bl   1.30 60

Perf. 12½ on 3 Sides
726 A170 35ö brt mag   45 35
 a. Bklt. pane of 20   9.00

Issued to publicize the World Table Tennis Championships, Stockholm.

Man with Axe and Fettered Beast
A171

Double Mortise Corner
A172

Designs: 15ö, Man fighting two bears. 30ö, Warrior disguised as wolf pursuing enemy. 35ö, Two warriors with swords and lances. The designs are taken from 6th century bronze plates (1¾ in. x 2½ in.) used to decorate helmets; now in Swedish Museum of National Antiquities.

Perf. 12½ on 3 Sides

1967, May 17 Engraved
727 A171 10ö dk brn & dp bl   10 10
728 A171 15ö dp bl & dk brn   30 15
729 A171 30ö brt pink & dk brn   35 35
730 A171 35ö dk brn & brt pink   35 20
 a. Bklt. pane of 10 (4 #727, 2 each #728–730)   2.50

Lithographed and Photogravure

1967, June 16 Perf. 12½
731 A172 10ö ol & multi   20 20
732 A172 35ö dk bl multi   35 30
 a. Bklt. pane of 10 (6 #731, 4 #732)   2.60

Issued to honor generations of Finnish settlers in Sweden.

Right-hand Driving as Seen Through Windshield
A173

Perf. 12½ Vert.

1967, Sept. 2 Engraved
733 A173 35ö dp bl, ocher & blk   25 25
734 A173 45ö yel grn, ocher & blk   25 20

Perf. 12½ Horiz.
735 A173 35ö dp bl, ocher & blk   30 30
 a. Bklt. pane of 10   3.00
736 A173 45ö yel grn, ocher & blk   35 30
 a. Bklt. pane of 10   3.50

Issued to publicize the introduction of right-hand driving in Sweden, Sept. 3, 1967.

Postrider
A174

Griffin
A174a

Rocky Isles in Bloom, by Harald Lindberg
A175

Dalsland Canal
A176

Gothenburg Harbor—A176a

Nils Holgersson Riding Wild Goose
A176b

Elk
A177

Mail Coach, by Eigil Schwab
A177a

SWEDEN

Illustration from *Lapponia*,
by Johannes Schefferus
A177b

Blood-money Coins and Old Map of Sweden
A177c

Great Seal, 1439 (St. Erik with Banner and Shield)
A177d

Designs: 10ö, Merchant vessel in Oresund, 1661. 15ö, The Prodigal Son, 13th century, Rada Church. 20ö, St. Stephen as a boy tending horses, medallion from Dädesjö Church. No. 742, Lion, from Grodinge tapestry, 15th century. 45ö, Log roller. 60ö, Horse-drawn timber sled. 75ö, Windmills, Öland Island. 80ö, Steamer Storskar and Royal Palace, Stockholm. 95ö, Roe deer. 1k, Dancing cranes. 2.55k, Seal of Magnus Ladulas, 1285 (King Magnus Birgersson on throne with lily scepter and orb). 3k, Seal of Duke Erik Magnusson, 1306 (Duke on horseback with standard of Folkunga dynasty). 6k, Gustavus Vasa's silver daler.

Perf. 12½ Horiz. or Vert.
1967-72 Engraved

737	A174	5ö red & blk	8	5
738	A174	10ö bl & blk	10	5
739	A177d	15ö sl grn, *grnsh* ('71)	20	8
740	A174	20ö sep, *buff* ('70)	15	8
741	A174a	25ö bis & blk ('71)	25	12
742	A174a	25ö blk & bis ('71)	25	12
743	A175	30ö ultra & ver	20	8
744	A176	40ö blk, dk grn & ultra ('68)	20	6
745	A177	45ö bl & brn blk ('70)	24	8
746	A176a	55ö bl & vio, perf. 12½ vert. ('71)	40	20
747	A176	60ö blk brn ('71)	30	10
747A	A176b	65ö brt bl ('71)	35	10
748	A177	75ö sl grn ('71)	40	5
749	A176	80ö bl & blk ('71)	40	12
750	A177	90ö sep & bl gray	45	15
750A	A175	95ö sep ('72)	50	15
751	A177	1k sl grn ('68)	60	10
751A	A177a	1.20k multi ('71)	60	20
751B	A177d	1.40k lt bl & red ('72)	70	25
752	A177d	2.55k brt bl ('70)	2.00	75
753	A177d	3k dk gray bl ('70)	1.50	20
754	A177c	4k blk ('71)	2.00	20
755	A177c	5k Prus grn ('70)	2.50	30
755A	A177c	6k ind ('72)	3.00	40

Nos. 741-742 printed se-tenant.
Perf. 12½ on 3 Sides

756	A174	5ö red & blk	6	6
a.	Bklt. pane of 20		1.20	
757	A174	10ö bl & blk ('69)	7	6
a.	Bklt. pane of 20		1.40	
758	A175	30ö ultra & ver	25	15
a.	Bklt. pane of 10		3.00	
759	A176	40ö blk, dk grn & ultra ('68)	40	35
a.	Bklt. pane of 10		4.00	
760	A176	45ö bl & brn blk ('70)	40	20
a.	Bklt. pane of 10		4.00	
761	A176a	55ö bl & vio, perf. 12½ horiz. ('71)	40	20
a.	Bklt. pane of 10		4.00	
762	A176b	65ö brt bl ('71)	35	10
a.	Bklt. pane of 10		3.50	
763	A177	75ö sl grn ('72)	1.00	8
a.	Bklt. pane of 10		12.00	
764	A177	90ö sep & bl gray	1.50	1.00
a.	Bklt. pane of 10		15.00	
	Nos. 737-764 (33)		21.80	6.19

King Gustaf VI Adolf
A178

1967, Nov. 11 Perf. 12½ Horiz.
Engraved

765	A178	45ö lt ultra	30	15
766	A178	70ö green	40	20

Perf. 12½ on 3 Sides

767	A178	45ö lt ultra	30	15
a.	Bklt. pane of 20		6.00	
768	A178	70ö green	70	60
a.	Bklt. pane of 10		7.00	

85th birthday of King Gustaf VI Adolf.

Nobel Prize Winners Type of 1962
Designs: 35ö, Eduard Buchner (Chemistry) and Albert A. Michelson (Physics). 45ö, Charles L. A. Laveran (Medicine) and Rudyard Kipling (Literature).

Perf. 12½ Vertically
1967, Dec. 9 Engraved

769	A142	35ö vermilion	90	60
770	A142	45ö dk bl	45	15

Perf. 12½ on 3 Sides

771	A142	35ö vermilion	90	90
a.	Bklt. pane of 10		9.00	
772	A142	45ö dk bl	60	25
a.	Bklt. pane of 10		7.00	

Winners of the 1907 Nobel Prize.

Franz Berwald, Violin and His Music
A179

National Bank Seal
A180

Perf. 12½ Horizontally
1968, Apr. 3 Engraved

773	A179	35ö blk & red	35	30
774	A179	2k blk, vio bl & org yel	4.00	80

Perf. 12½ on 3 Sides

775	A179	35ö blk & red	60	50
a.	Bklt. pane of 10		6.00	

Issued to commemorate the centenary of the death of Franz Berwald (1796-1868), composer. Design includes opening bar of overture to his opera, "The Queen of Golconda."

Perf. 12½ Vertically
1968, May 15 Engraved

776	A180	45ö dl bl	25	12
777	A180	70ö blk, *pink*	40	25

Perf. 12½ on 3 Sides

778	A180	45ö dl bl	40	35
a.	Bklt. pane of 10		4.00	
779	A180	70ö blk, *pink*	80	75
a.	Bklt. pane of 10		8.00	

Issued to commemorate the 300th anniversary of the National Bank of Sweden. Nos. 777 and 779 are on non-fluorescent paper.

Seal of Lund University
A181

Butterfly Orchid
A182

1968, June 4 Perf. 12½ on 3 sides

780	A181	10ö dp bl	15	10
781	A181	35ö red	60	55
a.	Bklt. pane of 10 (6 No. 780 + 4 No. 781)		3.30	

300th anniversary of University of Lund.

1968, June 4
Nordic Wild Flowers: No. 783, Wood anemone. No. 784, Dog rose. No. 785, Prune Cherry. No. 786, Lily of the valley.

782	A182	45ö sl grn	60	35
783	A182	45ö gray grn	60	35
784	A182	45ö sl grn & rose car	60	35
785	A182	45ö gray grn	60	35
786	A182	45ö sl grn	60	35
a.	Bklt. pane of 10 (2 each Nos. 782-786)		10.00	
	Nos. 782-786 (5)		3.00	1.75

World Council of Churches' Emblem
A183

Electron Orbits
A184

1968, July 4 Perf. 12½ Horiz.

787	A183	70ö plum	40	25
788	A183	90ö Prus grn	1.30	20

Perf. 12½ on 3 Sides

789	A183	70ö plum	75	70
a.	Bklt. pane of 10		7.50	

Issued to commemorate the 4th General Assembly of the World Council of Churches, Uppsala, July 4-19.

Perf. 12½ Horizontally
1968, Aug. 9 Engraved

790	A184	45ö rose car	25	8
791	A184	2k dk bl	3.50	40

Perf. 12½ on 3 Sides

792	A184	45ö rose car	40	35
a.	Bklt. pane of 10		4.00	

Issued to commemorate the centenary of the establishment of the first three People's Colleges.

"Orienteer" Finding Way through Forest
A185

"Fingerkrok" by Axel Petersson
A186

Perf. 12½ Horizontally
1968, Sept. 5 Engraved

793	A185	40ö vio & red brn	30	25
794	A185	2.80k grn & vio	5.00	4.00

Perf. 12½ on 3 Sides

795	A185	40ö vio & red brn	75	70
a.	Bklt. pane of 10		7.50	

Issued to publicize the World Championships in Orienteering, Linköping, Sept. 28-29.

Perf. 12½ on 3 Sides
1968, Oct. 28 Engraved

796	A186	5ö green	15	15
797	A186	25ö sepia	1.40	1.40
798	A186	45ö blk brn & red brn	30	30
a.	Bklt. pane of 8 (3 #796, 2 #797, 3 #798)		4.25	

Issued to commemorate the centenary of the birth of Axel Petersson, called "Döderhultarn" (1868-1925), sculptor.

Black-backed Gull
A187

Designs: No. 799, Varying hare. No. 801, Red fox. No. 802, Hooded crows harassing golden eagle. No. 803, Weasel.

Perf. 12½ on 3 Sides
1968, Nov. 9 Engraved

799	A187	30ö blue	60	60
800	A187	30ö black	60	60
801	A187	30ö dk brn	60	60
802	A187	30ö black	60	60
803	A187	30ö blue	60	60
a.	Bklt. pane of 10 (2 each #799-803)		7.00	
	Nos. 799-803 (5)		3.00	3.00

See Nos. 873-877.

Nobel Prize Winners Types of 1962 and 1963
Designs: 35ö, Elie Metchnikoff, Paul Ehrlich and Ernest Rutherford. 45ö, Gabriel Lippmann and Rudolf Eucken.

1968, Dec. 10 Perf. 12½ Vertically

804	A148	35ö maroon	45	30
805	A142	45ö dk grn	45	15

Perf. 12½ on 3 Sides

806	A148	35ö maroon	50	40
a.	Bklt. pane of 10		5.00	
807	A142	45ö dk grn	50	40
a.	Bklt. pane of 10		5.00	

Nordic Cooperation Issue

Five Ancient Ships
A187a

1969, Feb. 28 Engr. Perf. 12½ Vert.

808	A187a	45ö dk gray	35	30
809	A187a	70ö blue	75	75

Perf. 12½ on 3 Sides

810	A187a	45ö dk gray	1.50	1.30
a.	Bklt. pane of 10		15.00	

See footnote after Norway No. 524.

Helpful notes abound in the "Information for Collectors" section at the front of this volume.

SWEDEN

Worker, by Albin Amelin
A188

1969, Mar. 31   *Perf. 12½ Horiz.*   Engraved

811	A188	55ö dk car rose	30	6
812	A188	70ö dk bl	1.00	40

Perf. 12½ on 3 Sides

| 813 | A188 | 55ö dk car rose | 45 | 25 |
| a. | | Bklt. pane of 10 | 4.50 | |

Issued to commemorate the 50th anniversary of the International Labor Organization.

Europa Issue, 1969
Common Design Type

1969, Apr. 28   Photo.   *Perf. 14 Vert.*
Size: 27x22mm.

| 814 | CD12 | 70ö org & multi | 60 | 50 |
| 815 | CD12 | 1k vio bl & multi | 60 | 20 |

Perf. 14 on 3 Sides

| 816 | CD12 | 70ö org & multi | 2.00 | 2.00 |
| a. | | Bklt. pane of 10 | 20.00 | |

Not fluorescent.

Albert Engstrom with Owl, Self-portrait
A189

1969, May 12   Engraved

| 817 | A189 | 35ö blk brn | 25 | 25 |
| 818 | A189 | 55ö bl gray | 30 | 15 |

Perf. 12½ on 3 Sides

819	A189	35ö blk brn	40	30
a.		Bklt. pane of 10	4.00	
820	A189	55ö bl gray	40	35
a.		Bklt. pane of 10	4.00	

Issued to commemorate the centenary of the birth of Albert Engstrom (1869-1940), cartoonist.

Souvenir Sheet

Paintings by Ivan Agueli
A190

1969, June 6   Litho.   *Perf. 13½*

821	A190	Sheet of 6, multi	2.75	3.50
a.		45ö *Landscape*	45	55
b.		45ö *Still life*	45	55
c.		45ö *Near East town*	45	55
d.		55ö *Young woman*	45	55
e.		55ö *Sunny landscape*	45	55
f.		55ö *Street at night*	45	55

Issued to commemorate the centenary of the birth of Ivan Agueli (1869-1917), painter. Size of Nos. 821a-821c: 35x28 mm., Nos. 821d-821e: 28x44mm., No. 821f: 48x44mm. No. 821 has bister marginal inscription. Size: 135x89mm. Not fluorescent.

Tjörn Bridges—A191
Designs: 15ö, 30ö, Various bridges.

Perf. 12½ on 3 Sides

1969, Sept. 3   Engraved
Size: 20x19mm.
Bluish Paper

| 822 | A191 | 15ö dp bl | 3.25 | 60 |
| 823 | A191 | 30ö dk grn & blk | 3.25 | 60 |

Size: 41x19mm.

| 824 | A191 | 55ö blk & dp bl | 3.25 | 80 |
| a. | | Bklt. pane of 6 (2 each #822-824) | 25.00 | |

Issued to publicize the Tjörn highway bridges connecting the Islands of Orust and Tjörn in the Gothenburg Archipelago with the mainland.

Man's Head, Woodcarving
A192

Warship Wasa, 1628
A193

Designs: No. 826, Crowned lion. No. 827, Great Swedish coat of arms. No. 828, Lion, front view. No. 829, Man's head (different from No. 825).

Perf. 12½ on 3 Sides

1969, Sept. 3

825	A192	55ö dk red	40	20
826	A192	55ö brown	40	20
827	A193	55ö dk bl	40	35
828	A192	55ö brown	40	20
829	A192	55ö dk red	40	20
830	A193	55ö dk bl	40	35
a.		Bklt. pane of 10 (#827, #830, 2 each #825-826, 828-829)	4.00	
		Nos. 825-830 (6)	2.40	1.50

Issued to publicize the salvaging of the warship Wasa, sunk on her maiden voyage, Aug. 10, 1628, and salvaged in 1961.

Hjalmar Soderberg
A194

Bo Bergman
A195

Engraved

1969, Oct. 13   *Perf. 12½ Horiz.*

| 831 | A194 | 45ö brn, *buff* | 30 | 20 |

Perf. 12½ Vert.

| 832 | A195 | 55ö grn, *grnsh* | 30 | 20 |

Perf. 12½ on 3 Sides

833	A194	45ö brn, *buff*	60	50
a.		Bklt. pane of 10	6.00	
834	A195	55ö grn, *grnsh*	60	25
a.		Bklt. pane of 10	6.00	

Nos. 831 and 833 commemorate the centenary of the birth of Hjalmar Soderberg (1869-1941), writer; Nos. 832 and 834 of Bo Bergman (1869-1967), poet.

Lever Light, Lightship, Landsort and Svenska Lighthouses
A196

Perf. 12½ Vert.

1969, Nov. 17   Photogravure

| 835 | A196 | 30ö gray, blk & pink | 35 | 30 |
| 836 | A196 | 55ö lt bl, blk & brn | 35 | 15 |

Issued to commemorate the 300th anniversary of Swedish lighthouses.

Pelle's New Suit
A197

The Adventures of Nils
A198

Swedish Fairy Tales: No. 839, Pippi Longstocking (little girl, horse and monkey). No. 840, Vill-Vallareman (boy blowing horn). No. 841, Kattresan (child riding on back of cat).

Perf. 12½ on 3 Sides

1969, Nov. 17   Engraved

837	A197	35ö org, red & dk brn	1.60	1.40
838	A198	35ö dk brn	1.60	1.40
839	A197	35ö org, red & dk brn	1.60	1.40
840	A198	35ö dk brn	1.60	1.40
841	A197	35ö org, red & dk brn	1.60	1.40
a.		Bklt. pane of 10 (2 each #837-841)	17.00	
		Nos. 837-841 (5)	8.00	7.00

Issued for use on Christmas cards.

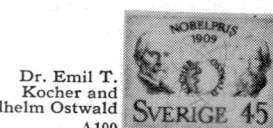

Dr. Emil T. Kocher and Wilhelm Ostwald
A199

Designs: 55ö, Selma Lagerlöf and open book. 70ö, Guglielmo Marconi and Carl Ferdinand Braun.

1969, Dec. 10   *Perf. 12½ Vert.*

842	A199	45ö dl grn	60	50
843	A199	55ö *pale sal*	40	12
844	A199	70ö black	70	70

Perf. 12½ on 3 Sides

845	A199	45ö dl grn	60	60
a.		Bklt. pane of 10	6.00	
846	A199	55ö *pale sal*	60	20
a.		Bklt. pane of 10	6.00	
		Nos. 842-846 (5)	2.90	2.12

Winners of the 1909 Nobel Prize.

Weather Vane, Söderala Church
A200

Door with Iron Fittings, Björksta Church, Vastmanland
A201

Swedish Art Forgings: 10ö, like 5ö, facing right. 30ö, Memorial cross, Ekshärad churchyard, Varmland.

1970, Feb. 9   Engraved
Perf. 12½ on 3 sides

847	A200	5ö sl grn & brn	40	25
848	A200	10ö sl grn & brn	40	25
849	A200	30ö blk & sl grn	60	25

Perf. 12½ Vert.

| 850 | A201 | 55ö brn & sl grn | 60 | 25 |
| a. | | Bklt. pane of 8 (2 each #847-850) | 5.00 | |

Ljusman River Rapids
A202

Perf. 12½ Vert.

1970, May 11   Engraved
Coil Stamps

| 851 | A202 | 55ö blk & multi | 80 | 15 |
| 852 | A202 | 70ö blk & multi | 1.00 | 60 |

Issued to publicize the European Nature Conservation Year, 1970.

Skiing—A203

"Around the Arctic Circle": No. 853, View of Kiruna. No. 855, Boat on mountain lake in Stora Sjofellet National Park. No. 856, Reindeer herd and herdsman. No. 857, Rocket probe under northern lights.

Perf. 12½ Horiz.

1970, June 5   Engraved

853	A203	45ö sepia	60	75
854	A203	45ö vio bl	60	75
855	A203	45ö dl grn	60	75
856	A203	45ö sepia	60	75
857	A203	45ö vio bl	60	75
a.		Bklt. pane of 10 (2 each #853-857)	6.00	
		Nos. 853-857 (5)	3.00	3.75

China Palace, Drottningholm Park, 1769
A204

Perf. 12½ Vert.

1970, Aug. 28   Photogravure

| 858 | A204 | 2k yel, grn & pink | 2.50 | 30 |

SWEDEN

Glimmingehus,
Skane Province,
15th Century
A205

1970, Aug. 28   Perf. 12½ Horiz.   Engraved
859	A205	55ö gray grn	40	10

Perf. 12½ on 3 Sides
860	A205	55ö gray grn	40	25
a.		Booklet pane of 10	4.00	

Timber Industry
A206

Shipping Industry—A207

Miner
A208

Designs: No. 863, Heavy industry (propeller). No. 864, Hydroelectric power (dam and diesel). No. 865, Mining (freight train and mine). No. 866, Technical research.

Perf. 12½ on 3 sides
1970, Sept. 28   Engraved
861	A206	70ö ind & lt brn	7.00	5.00
862	A207	70ö ind, lt brn & dp plum	7.00	5.00
863	A206	70ö ind & dp plum	7.00	5.00
864	A207	70ö ind & dp plum	7.00	5.00
865	A206	70ö ind & dp plum	7.00	5.00
866	A206	70ö dp plum & lt brn	7.00	5.00
a.		Bklt. pane of 6 (#861-866)	45.00	
867	A208	1k blk, *buff*	60	20
a.		Booklet pane of 10	6.00	

Perf. 12½ Vertically
868	A208	1k blk, *buff*	80	15
		Nos. 861-868 (8)	43.40	30.35

Issued to publicize Swedish trade and industry.

"Love, Not War"—A209

Design: 70ö, Four-leaf clovers symbolizing efforts for equality and brotherhood.

Engraved and Lithographed
1970, Oct. 24   Perf. 12½ Horiz.
869	A209	55ö rose red, yel & blk	30	15
a.		Booklet pane of 4	1.60	
870	A209	70ö emer, yel & blk	60	45
a.		Booklet pane of 4	2.40	

Perf. 12½ Vert.
871	A209	55ö rose red, yel & blk	35	15
872	A209	70ö emer, yel & blk	60	35

25th anniversary of the United Nations.

Bird Type of 1968

Birds: No. 873, Blackbird. No. 874, Great titmouse. No. 875, Bullfinch. No. 876, Greenfinch. No. 877, Blue titmouse.

Perf. 12½ on 3 Sides
1970, Nov. 20   Photogravure
873	A187	30ö bl grn & multi	90	90
874	A187	30ö bis & multi	90	90
875	A187	30ö bl & multi	90	90
876	A187	30ö pink & multi	90	90
877	A187	30ö org yel & multi	90	90
a.		Bklt. pane of 10 (2 each #873-877)	11.00	
		Nos. 873-877 (5)	4.50	4.50

Paul Johann
Ludwig Heyse
A210

Kerstin
Hesselgren
A211

Designs: 55ö, Otto Wallach and Johannes Diderik van der Waals. 70ö, Albrecht Kossel.

Perf. 12½ Horiz.
1970, Dec. 10   Engraved
878	A210	45ö violet	60	40
879	A210	55ö sl bl	40	12
880	A210	70ö gray	80	80

Perf. 12½ on 3 Sides
881	A210	45ö violet	70	70
a.		Booklet pane of 10	7.00	
882	A210	55ö sl bl	80	30
a.		Booklet pane of 10	10.00	
		Nos. 878-882 (5)	3.30	2.32

Winners of the 1910 Nobel Prize.

Engraved
1971, Feb. 19   Perf. 12½ Horiz.
883	A211	45ö dp cl, *gray*	40	25
884	A211	1k dp brn, *buff*	80	20

Perf. 12½ on 3 Sides
885	A211	45ö dp cl, *gray*	60	40
a.		Booklet pane of 10	6.00	

50th anniversary of woman suffrage; Kerstin Hesselgren, was first woman member of Swedish Upper House.

Terns in Flight
A212

Abstract Music, by
Ingvar Lidholm
A213

1971, March 26   Perf. 13½ Vert.
886	A212	40ö dk red	40	35
887	A212	55ö vio bl	90	15

Perf. 12½ on 3 Sides
888	A212	55ö vio bl	1.00	25
a.		Booklet pane of 10	10.00	

Joint northern campaign for the benefit of refugees.

Engraved
1971, Aug. 27   Perf. 12½ Horiz.
889	A213	55ö dp lil	40	20
890	A213	85ö green	65	40

Perf. 12½ on 3 Sides
891	A213	55ö dp lil	40	25
a.		Booklet pane of 10	4.00	

The Three Kings,
Grötlingbo Church
A214

Flight
into
Egypt,
Stanga
Church
A215

Designs: 10ö, Adam and Eve, Gammelgarn Church. 55ö, Saint on horseback and Samson with the lion, Hogrän Church.

Perf. 12½ on 3 Sides
1971, Sept. 28   Engraved
892	A214	5ö vio & brn	30	20
893	A214	10ö vio & sl grn	30	20

Perf. 12½ Horiz.
894	A215	55ö sl grn & brn	1.25	40
895	A215	65ö brn & vio blk	60	20
a.		Bklt. pane of 5 (#892-894, 2 #895)	3.50	

Art of medieval stonemasons in Gotland.

Toddler and
Automobile
Wheel
A216

1971, Oct. 20   Perf. 12½ Vert.
896	A216	35ö blk & red	35	30
897	A216	65ö dp bl & multi	35	10

Perf. 12½ on 3 Sides
898	A216	65ö dp bl & multi	90	40
a.		Booklet pane of 10	9.00	

Publicity for road safety.

King Gustavus
Vasa's Sword,
c. 1500
A217

Perf. 12½ on 3 Sides
1971, Oct. 20   Engraved

Swedish Crown Regalia: No. 900, Scepter. No. 901, Crown. No. 902, Orb (Scepter, crown and orb were made in 1561 for Erik XIV). No. 903, Karl IX's anointing horn, 1606.

899	A217	65ö lt bl & multi	60	40
900	A217	65ö lt ol grn & multi	60	40
901	A217	65ö dk bl & multi	60	40
902	A217	65ö lt ol grn & multi	60	40
903	A217	65ö lt bl & multi	60	40
a.		Bklt. pane of 10 (2 each #899-903)	6.00	
		Nos. 899-903 (5)	3.00	2.00

Christmas Elf
and Goat
Bringing Gifts
A218

Christmas Customs (Old Prints): No. 905, Christmas market. No. 906, Dancing children and father playing fiddle. No. 907, Ice-skating on frozen waterways in Stockholm. No. 908, Sleigh ride to church.

1971, Nov. 10
904	A218	35ö dp car	1.60	1.40
905	A218	35ö vio brn	1.60	1.40
906	A218	35ö vio brn	1.60	1.40
907	A218	35ö vio bl	1.60	1.40
908	A218	35ö sl grn	1.60	1.40
a.		Bklt. pane of 10 (2 each #904-908)	17.00	
		Nos. 904-908 (5)	8.00	7.00

Maurice
Maeterlinck
A219

Designs: 65ö, Wilhelm Wien and Allvar Gullstrand. 85ö, Marie Sklodovska Curie.

1971, Dec. 10   Perf. 12½ Horiz.
909	A219	55ö orange	60	30
910	A219	65ö green	60	20
911	A219	85ö dk car	1.20	1.00

Perf. 12½ on 3 Sides
912	A219	55ö orange	90	90
c.		Booklet pane of 10	9.00	
913	A219	65ö green	90	40
c.		Booklet pane of 10	9.00	
		Nos. 909-913 (5)	4.20	2.80

Winners of the 1911 Nobel Prize.

Figure
Skating
A220

Women Athletes: No. 915, Tennis. No. 916, Gymnastics. No. 917, Diving. No. 918, Fencing.

Perf. 12½ on 3 Sides
1972, Feb. 23
914	A220	55ö indigo	80	90
915	A220	55ö lilac	80	90
916	A220	55ö dp grn	80	90
917	A220	55ö vio bl	80	90
918	A220	55ö dp lil	80	90
a.		Bklt. pane of 10 (2 each #914-918)	9.00	
		Nos. 914-918 (5)	4.00	4.50

Lars Johan
Hierta,
by Christian
Eriksson
A221

Frans Michael
Franzen, by
Söderberg and
Hultström
A222

Hugo Alfven, by
Carl Milles
A223

Georg
Stiernhielm,
by David K.
Ehrenstrahl
A224

SWEDEN

Photo., Perf. 12½ Horiz. (35ö, 85ö);
Engr., Perf. 12½ Vert. (50ö, 65ö)

1972, Feb. 23
919	A221	35ö	multi	35	30
920	A222	50ö	violet	40	15
921	A223	65ö	bluish blk	60	15
922	A224	85ö	multi	55	30

Anniversaries of: Lars Johan Hierta (1801–1872), journalist, centenary of death (35ö). Frans Michael Franzen (1772–1847), poet, bicentenary of birth (50ö). Hugo Alfven (1872–1960), composer, centenary of birth (65ö). Georg Stiernhielm (1598–1672), poet, writer, scientist, tricentenary of death (85ö).

Glass Blower—A225

Swedish Glassmaking: No. 923, Lifting molten glass. No. 925, Decorating vase. No. 926, Annealing vase. No. 927, Polishing jug.

Engraved
1972, Mar. 22   Perf. 12½ Horiz.
923	A225	65ö	black	1.30	75
924	A225	65ö	vio bl	1.30	75
925	A225	65ö	carmine	1.30	75
926	A225	65ö	black	1.30	75
927	A225	65ö	vio bl	1.30	75
a.	Bklt. pane of 10 (2 each #923-927)			13.00	
	Nos. 923-927 (5)			6.50	3.75

Horses and Ruin of Borgholm Castle—A226

Designs: No. 929, Oland Island Bridge. No. 930, Kalmar Castle. No. 931, Salmon fishing. No. 932, Schooner Falken, Karlskrona.

1972, May 8   Perf. 12½ Horiz.
928	A226	55ö	chocolate	55	55
929	A226	55ö	dk vio bl	55	55
930	A226	55ö	chocolate	55	55
931	A226	55ö	bl grn	55	55
932	A226	55ö	dk vio bl	55	55
a.	Bklt. pane of 10 (2 each #928-932)			5.50	
	Nos. 928-932 (5)			2.75	2.75

Tourist attractions in Southeast Sweden.

"Only one Earth" Environment Emblem
A227

"Spring," Bror Hjorth
A228

Perf. 12½ Vert.
1972, June 5   Engraved
| 933 | A227 | 65ö | bl & car | 50 | 20 |

Perf. 12½ Horiz.
| 934 | A227 | 65ö | bl & car | 50 | 20 |
| a. | Booklet pane of 10 | | | 5.00 | |

Perf. 12½ Vert.
| 935 | A228 | 85ö | brn & multi | 1.00 | 80 |
| a. | Booklet pane of 4 | | | 4.00 | |

U.N. Conference on Human Environment, Stockholm, June 5–16.

Junkers JU52
A229

Historic Planes: 5ö, Junkers F13. 25ö, Friedrichshafen FF49. 75ö, Douglas DC-3.

Perf. 12½ on 3 Sides
1972, Sept. 8
Size: 20x19mm.
| 936 | A229 | 5ö | lilac | 15 | 15 |

Size: 44x19mm.
937	A229	15ö	blue	30	20
938	A229	25ö	blue	30	20
939	A229	75ö	gray grn	55	25
a.	Bklt. pane of 6 (#937-938, 2 #936, 2 #939)			2.25	

Lady with Veil, by Alexander Roslin
A230

Amphion Figurehead, by Per Ljung
A231

Stockholm from the South, by Johan Fredrik Martin
A232

Designs: No. 941, (Queen) Sofia Magdalena, by Carl Gustaf Pilo. No. 943, Quadriga, by Johan Tobias von Sergel. No. 945, Anchor Forge, by Pehr Hillestrøm.

Perf. 12½ on 2 Sides, or on 3 Sides (#942-943)
1972, Oct. 7   Engraved
940	A230	75ö	dk brn, blk & dk car	60	40
941	A230	75ö	dk brn, blk & dk car	60	40
942	A231	75ö	dk car	60	40
943	A231	75ö	dk car	60	40
944	A232	75ö	dk brn	60	40
945	A232	75ö	grnsh blk	60	40
a.	Bklt. pane of 6 (#940-945)			3.60	
	Nos. 940-945 (6)			3.60	2.40

18th century Swedish art.

Types of 1936
Imprint: "1972"
1972, Oct. 7   Perf. 12½ on 3 Sides
946	A36	10ö	dk car	60	60
947	A37	15ö	yel grn	60	60
948	A42	40ö	dp bl	60	60
949	A44	50ö	dp cl	60	60
950	A45	60ö	dp bl	60	60
a.	Bklt. pane of 10 (2 each #946-950)			6.00	
	Nos. 946-950 (5)			3.00	3.00

Centenary of the birth of Olle Hjortzberg (1872–1959), stamp designer. Price of booklet was 5k of which 1.50k was for "Stockholmia 74," International Philatelic Exhibition, Sept. 21–29, 1973.

Santa Claus
A233

St. Lucia Singers
A234

Design: No. 952, Candles.

Photogravure
1972, Nov. 6   Perf. 14 on 3 Sides
951	A233	45ö	red & multi	45	25
952	A233	45ö	vio bl & multi	45	25
a.	Bklt. pane of 10 (5 each #951-952)			4.50	

Perf. 12½ Vert.
| 953 | A234 | 75ö | gray & multi | 80 | 18 |

Christmas 1972 (children's drawings).

Horse   Viking Ship
A235   A236

Willows, by Peter A. Persson
A237

Trosa, by Reinhold Ljunggren   Spring Birches, by Oskar Bergman
A238   A239

King Gustaf VI Adolf
A240

Perf. 12½ Horiz. or Vert.
1972–73   Engraved
954	A235	5ö	mar ('73)	5	5
955	A236	10ö	dk bl ('73)	5	5
956	A237	40ö	sep ('73)	20	8
957	A238	50ö	blk & brn ('73)	25	8
958	A239	55ö	yel grn ('73)	40	20
959	A240	75ö	indigo	38	8
960	A240	1k	dp car	60	10

1973   Perf. 12½ on 3 Sides
961	A235	5ö	maroon	5	5
a.	Booklet pane of 20			60	
962	A236	10ö	dk bl	5	5
a.	Booklet pane of 20			1.00	
963	A240	75ö	indigo	45	8
a.	Booklet pane of 10			4.50	
	Nos. 954-963 (10)			2.48	82

King Gustaf VI Adolf   Chinese Objects
A245   A246

Designs: No. 983, King opening Parliament. No. 984, Etruscan vase and dish. No. 985, King with flowers.

1972, Nov. 11   Perf. 12½ Vert.
981	A245	75ö	vio bl	4.50	5.50
982	A246	75ö	sl grn	4.50	5.50
983	A245	75ö	maroon	4.50	5.50
984	A246	75ö	vio bl	4.50	5.50
985	A245	75ö	sl grn	4.50	5.50
a.	Bklt. pane of 5 (#981-985)			22.50	
	Nos. 981-985 (5)			22.50	27.50

90th birthday of King Gustaf VI Adolf. Booklet sold for 4.75k of which 1k was for the King Gustaf VI Adolf Foundation for Swedish Cultural Activities.

Paul Sabatier and Victor Grignard   Dr. Alexis Carrel
A247   A248

Designs: 75ö, Nils Gustaf Dalen. 1k, Gerhart Hauptmann.

1972, Dec. 8   Engr.   Perf. 12½ Vert.
| 986 | A247 | 60ö | ol bis | 60 | 60 |

Perf. 12½ Horiz.
987	A248	65ö	dk bl	90	45
988	A248	75ö	violet	1.00	15
989	A248	1k	redsh brn	1.25	25

Winners of the 1912 Nobel Prize.

Mail Coach, 1923
A249

Design: 70ö, Postal autobus, 1972.

Engraved
1973, Jan. 18   Perf. 12½ on 3 Sides
| 990 | A249 | 60ö | blk, yel | 40 | 30 |
| a. | Booklet pane of 10 | | | 4.00 | |

SWEDEN

		Perf. 12½ Vert.		
991	A249	70ö bl, org & grn	35	12

Tintomara, by Lars
Johan Werle
A250

Orpheus and Eurydice,
by Christoph W. Gluck
A251

1973, Jan. 18   *Perf. 12½ Horiz.*

992	A250	75ö green	40	12
		Booklet Stamp		
993	A251	1k red lil	60	35
a.		Booklet pane of 5	3.00	

Bicentenary of the Royal Theater in Stockholm. The 75ö shows a stage setting by Bo-Ruben Hedwall for Tintomara, a new opera, performed for the bicentenary celebration. The 1k shows painting by Pehr Hillström of Orpheus and Eurydice, which was first opera performed in Royal Theater.

Vaasa Ski Race, Dalecarlia
A252

Designs: No. 995, "Going to Church in Mora" (church boats), by Anders Zorn. No. 996, Church stables, Rättvig. No. 997, Falun copper mine. No. 998, Midsummer Dance, by Bengt Nordenberg.

1973, Mar. 2   *Perf. 12½ Horiz.*

994	A252	65ö sl grn	60	50
995	A252	65ö sl grn	60	50
996	A252	65ö black	60	50
997	A252	65ö sl grn	60	50
998	A252	65ö claret	60	50
a.		Bklt. pane of 10 (2 each #994-998)	6.00	
		Nos. 994-998 (5)	3.00	2.50

Tourist attractions in Dalecarlia.

Worker, Confederation Emblem
A253

Observer Reading Temperature
A254

1973, Apr. 26   *Perf. 12½ Vert.*

999	A253	65ö dk car	38	15
1000	A253	1.40k sl bl	90	30

75th anniversary of the Swedish Confederation of Trade Unions (LO).

Engraved

Design: No. 1002, Clouds, photographed by US weather satellite.

1973, May 24   *Perf. 12½ Vert.*

1001	A254	65ö sl grn	2.50	50
1002	A254	65ö blk & ultra	2.50	50

Centenary of the Swedish Weather Organization and of International Meteorological Cooperation. Nos. 1001-1002 printed setenant.

Nordic Cooperation Issue 1973

Nordic House, Reykjavik
A254a

1973, June 26   *Perf. 12½ Vert.*

1003	A254a	75ö multi	80	20
1004	A254a	1k multi	1.00	35

A century of postal cooperation among Denmark, Finland, Iceland, Norway and Sweden and in connection with the Nordic Postal Conference, Reykjavik, Iceland.

Carl Peter Thunberg (1743-1828)
A255

Designs: No. 1006, Anders Sparrman (1748-1820) and Polynesian double canoe. No. 1007, Nils Adolf Erik Nordenskjöld (1832-1901) and ship in pack ice. No. 1008, Salomon August Andrée (1854-1897) and balloon on snow field. No. 1009, Sven Hedin (1865-1952) and camel riders.

1973, Sept. 22   *Perf. 12½ Horiz.*   *Engraved*

1005	A255	1k sl grn, bl & brn	1.60	1.50
1006	A255	1k bl, sl grn & brn	1.60	1.50
1007	A255	1k bl, sl grn & brn	1.60	1.50
1008	A255	1k blk & multi	1.60	1.50
1009	A255	1k blk & multi	1.60	1.50
a.		Bklt. pane of 5 (#1005-1009)	8.00	
		Nos. 1005-1009 (5)	8.00	7.50

Swedish explorers.

Plower with Ox Team
A256

Designs: No. 1011, Woman working flax brake. No. 1012, Farm couple planting potatoes. No. 1013, Women baking bread. No. 1014, Man with horse-drawn sower.

1973, Oct. 24   *Perf. 12½ Horiz.*   *Engraved*

1010	A256	75ö grnsh blk	4.50	40
1011	A256	75ö red brn	4.50	40
1012	A256	75ö grnsh blk	4.50	40
1013	A256	75ö plum	4.50	40
1014	A256	75ö red brn	4.50	40
a.		Bklt. pane of 10 (2 each #1010-1014)	45.00	
		Nos. 1010-1014 (5)	22.50	2.00

Centenary of Nordic Museum, Stockholm.

Gray Seal
A257

King Gustaf VI Adolf
A258

Protected Animals: 20ö, Peregrine falcon. 25ö, Lynx. 55ö, Otter. 65ö, Wolf. 75ö, White-tailed sea eagle.

1973, Oct. 24   *Perf. 12½ on 3 Sides*

1015	A257	10ö sl grn	10	10
1016	A257	20ö violet	10	10
1017	A257	25ö Prus grn	13	10
1018	A257	55ö Prus grn	28	20
1019	A257	65ö violet	32	20
1020	A257	75ö sl grn	40	40
a.		Bklt. pane of 12 (2 each #1015-1020)	2.75	
		Nos. 1015-1020 (6)	1.33	1.10

1973, Oct. 24   *Perf. 12½ Vert.*

1021	A258	75ö dk vio bl	40	20
1022	A258	1k purple	60	30

In memory of King Gustaf VI Adolf (1882-1973).

The Three Kings
A259

Charles XIV John
A260

The Goosegirl, by Josephson
A261

Designs: No. 1024, Merry country dance. No. 1026, Basket with stylized Dalecarlian gourd plant.

1973, Nov. 12 Photo.   *Perf. 14 Horiz.*

1023	A259	45ö multi	80	30
1024	A259	45ö multi	80	30
a.		Bklt. pane of 10 (5 each #1023-1024)	9.00	

Coil Stamps

1025	A260	75ö multi	3.50	18
1026	A260	75ö multi	3.50	18

Christmas 1973. Designs are from Swedish peasant paintings. Nos. 1025-1026 printed se-tenant.

Engraved

1973, Nov. 12   *Perf. 12½ Horiz.*

1027	A261	10k multi	5.00	1.00

Ernst Josephson (1851-1906), painter.

Alfred Werner and Heike Kamerlingh-Onnes
A262

Charles Robert Richet
A263

Design: 1.40k, Rabindranath Tagore.

Engraved

1973, Dec. 10   *Perf. 12½ Vert.*

1028	A262	75ö dk vio	50	15

Perf. 12½ Horiz.

1029	A263	1k dk brn	70	25
1030	A263	1.40k green	90	25

Winners of 1913 Nobel Prize.

Ski Jump
A264

Skiing: No. 1032, Cross-country race. No. 1033, Relay race. No. 1034, Slalom. No. 1035, Women's cross-country race.

1974, Jan. 23   *Perf. 12½ Horiz.*   *Engraved*

1031	A264	65ö sl grn	75	75
1032	A264	65ö vio bl	75	75
1033	A264	65ö sl grn	75	75
1034	A264	65ö dk car	75	75
1035	A264	65ö vio bl	75	75
a.		Bklt. pane of 10 (2 each #1031-1035)	7.50	
		Nos. 1031-1035 (5)	3.75	3.75

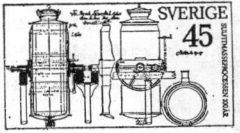

Drawing of First Industrial Digester
A265

Hans Järta and Quotation from 1809 Act
A266

Samuel Owen and 19th Century Factory
A267

Engraved

1974, Mar. 5   *Perf. 12½ Vert.*

1036	A265	45ö sepia	40	12
1037	A266	60ö green	40	25
1038	A267	75ö dl red	50	15

Issued to commemorate: Centenary of sulphite pulp process (45ö); Bicentenary of the birth of Hans Järta (1774-1847), statesman responsible for the Instrument of Government Act of 1809 (60ö); Bicentenary of the birth of Samuel Owen (1774-1854), English-born industrialist who introduced new production methods (75ö).

Stora Sjöfallet (Great Falls)
A268

Street in Ystad
A269

1974, Apr. 2   *Perf. 12½ Horiz.*

1039	A268	35ö bl grn & blk	18	10

Perf. 12½ on 3 Sides

1040	A269	75ö dp cl	40	12
a.		Booklet pane of 10	4.50	

UPU Type of 1924
A270

SWEDEN

1974   *Engr.*   *Perf. 12½ on 3 Sides*

1041	A270	20ö green	25	35
1042	A270	25ö ultra	25	35
1043	A270	30ö dk brn	25	35
1044	A270	35ö dk red	25	35
a.		Bklt. pane of 8 (2 each #1041-1044)	2.00	

Miniature Sheets
Perf. 12½

1045	A270	20ö ocher, sheet of 4	3.00	3.00
a.		Single stamp	75	75
1046	A270	25ö dk vio, sheet of 4	3.00	3.00
a.		Single stamp	75	75
1047	A270	30ö dk red, sheet of 4	3.00	3.00
a.		Single stamp	75	75
1048	A270	35ö yel grn, sheet of 4	3.00	3.00
a.		Single stamp	75	75

Stockholmia 74 philatelic exhibition, Stockholm, Sept. 21-29. Booklet sold for 3k with surtax going toward financing the exhibition.

Nos. 1045-1048 sold during exhibition in folder with 5k entrance ticket. Size of sheets: 120x80mm.

Issue dates: Nos. 1041-1044, Apr. 2. Nos. 1045-1048, Sept. 21.

Europa Issue 1974

"Man in Storm,"
by Bror Marklund
A271

Design: 1k, Sculpture by Picasso, Lake Vanern, Kristinehamn.

Engraved

1974, Apr. 29   *Perf. 12½ Horiz.*

1049	A271	75ö vio brn	60	20
1050	A271	1k sl grn	80	20

King Karl XVI
Gustaf
A272

1974-78   *Engr.*   *Perf. 12½ Vert.*

1068	A272	75ö sl grn	80	5
1069	A272	90ö brt bl ('75)	80	6
1070	A272	1k maroon	50	6
1071	A272	1.10k rose ('75)	55	10
1072	A272	1.30k grn ('76)	65	20
1073	A272	1.40k vio bl ('77)	70	20
1074	A272	1.50k red lil ('80)	75	10
1075	A272	1.70k org ('78)	85	20
1076	A272	2k dk brn ('80)	1.00	30

Perf. 12½ on 3 Sides

1077	A272	75ö sl grn	60	5
a.		Booklet pane of 10	8.00	
1078	A272	90ö brt bl ('75)	60	12
a.		Booklet pane of 10	8.00	
1079	A272	1k mar ('76)	50	5
a.		Booklet pane of 10	5.00	
1080	A272	1.10k rose red ('77)	55	10
a.		Booklet pane of 10	5.50	
1081	A272	1.30k grn ('78)	65	20
a.		Booklet pane of 10	6.50	
1082	A272	1.50k red lil ('80)	75	10
a.		Booklet pane of 10	7.50	
		Nos. 1068-1082 (15)	10.25	1.89

Central Post Office, Stockholm
A273   A274

Mailman, Northernmost
Rural Delivery Route
275

Engraved

1974, June 7   *Perf. 12½ on 3 Sides*

1084	A273	75ö vio brn	1.50	35
1085	A274	75ö vio brn	1.50	35
a.		Bklt. pane of 10 (5 each #1084-1085)	15.00	

Coil Stamp
Perf. 12½ Vert.

1086	A275	1k sl grn	60	25

Centenary of Universal Postal Union.

Regatta
A276

Scenes from Sweden's West Coast: No. 1088, Vinga Lighthouse. No. 1089, Varberg Fortress. No. 1090, Seine fishing. No. 1091, Fishing village Mollosund.

1974, June 7   *Perf. 12½ Horiz.*

1087	A276	65ö crimson	60	40
1088	A276	65ö blue	60	40
1089	A276	65ö dk ol grn	60	40
1090	A276	65ö sl grn	60	40
1091	A276	65ö brown	60	40
a.		Bklt. pane of 10 (2 each #1087-1091)	6.00	
		Nos. 1087-1091 (5)	3.00	2.00

Mr. Simmons, by   Thread and
Axel Fridell   Spool
A277   A278

Perf. 12½ on 3 Sides

1974, Aug. 28   *Engraved*

1092	A277	45ö black	40	25
a.		Booklet pane of 10	4.00	

Perf. 12½ Horiz.

1093	A277	1.40k dp cl	80	20

Swedish Publicists' Club, centenary.

1974, Aug. 28   *Perf. 12½ Horiz.*

Design: No. 1094, Sewing machines (abstract).

1094	A278	85ö dp vio	60	50
1095	A278	85ö blk & org	60	50

Swedish textile and clothing industries. Nos. 1094-1095 printed se-tenant.

Tugs in Stockholm Harbor
A279

Designs: No. 1097, Skane Train Ferry, Trelleborg-Sassnitz. No. 1098, Ice breakers Tor and Atle. No. 1099, Liner "Snow Storm." No. 1100, Tanker.

Engraved

1974, Nov. 16   *Perf. 12½ Horiz.*

1096	A279	1k dk bl	1.00	80
1097	A279	1k dk bl	1.00	80
1098	A279	1k dk bl	1.00	80
1099	A279	1k dk bl	1.00	80
1100	A279	1k dk bl	1.00	80
a.		Bklt. pane of 5 (#1096-1100)	5.00	
		Nos. 1096-1100 (5)	5.00	4.00

Swedish shipping industry.

Miniature Sheet

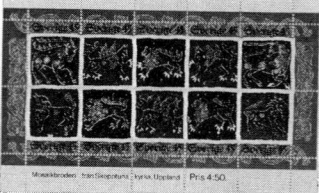

Quilt from Skepptuna Church
A280

Deer, Quilt from
Hog Church
A281

Designs are from woolen quilts, 15th-16th centuries. Motifs shown on No. 1101 are stylized deer, griffins, lions, unicorn and horses.

1974, Nov. 16   *Photo.*   *Perf. 14*

1101	A280	Sheet of 10, grn, red & dk bl	13.00	20.00
a.		45ö, single stamp	1.20	1.00

Perf. 13 Horiz.

1102	A281	75ö bl blk, red & yel	40	20

Max von Laue
A282

Designs: 70ö, Theodore William Richards. 1k, Robert Bárány.

1974, Dec. 10 Engr.   *Perf. 12½ Vert.*

1103	A282	65ö rose red	50	50
1104	A282	70ö slate	50	50
1105	A282	1k indigo	60	20

Winners of 1914 Nobel Prize.

Sven Jerring's   Televising
Children's   Parliamentary
Program   Debate
A283   A284

1974, Dec. 10   *Perf. 12½ Vert.*

1106	A283	75ö dk bl & brn	2.00	25
1107	A284	75ö brn & dk bl	2.00	25

Swedish Broadcasting Corporation, 50th anniversary. Nos. 1106-1107 printed se-tenant.

Account Holder's Envelope
A285

Photogravure and Engraved

1975, Jan. 21   *Perf. 14 Vert.*

1108	A285	1.40k ocher & blk	70	20

Swedish Postal Giro Office, 50th anniversary.

Male and Female   Jenny Lind
Architects, New   (1820-87), by
Parliament   J. O. Sodermark
A286   A287

Perf. 12½ Vert.

1975, Mar. 25   *Engraved*

1109	A286	75ö sl grn	38	15

Perf. 12½ Horiz.

1110	A287	1k claret	60	20

Perf. 12½ on 3 Sides

1111	A286	75ö sl grn	40	15
a.		Booklet pane of 10	4.00	

International Women's Year 1975.

Horseman,
Helmet Decoration   "Gold Men"
A288   A289

Designs: 15ö, Scabbard and hilt. 20ö, Shield buckle. 55ö, Iron helmet.

1975, Mar. 25   *Perf. 12½ Vert.*

1112	A288	10ö dl red	5	5
1113	A288	15ö sl grn	8	5
1114	A288	20ö violet	10	5
1115	A288	55ö vio brn	27	14
a.		Bklt. pane of 8 (2 each #1112-1115)	1.00	

Perf. 12½ Horiz.

1116	A289	25ö dp yel	18	15

Treasures from tombs of the Vendel period (550-800A.D.), and "gold men" (25ö) from Eketorp II excavations (400-700A.D.).

Europa Issue 1975

New Year's Eve at Skansen, by
Eric Hallström
A290

SWEDEN

Inferno,
by August
Strindberg
A291

Perf. 12½ Vert.
1975, Apr. 28   Photogravure
1117 A290 90ö multi   60   40
Perf. 12½ Horiz.
1118 A291 1.10k multi   80   35

Capercaillie
A292

Rök Stone, 9th
Century
A293

1975, May 20
Perf. 12½ Vert.
1119 A292 1.70ö indigo   85   25
Perf. 12½ Horiz.
1120 A293 2k dp cl   1.00 35

Metric Tape
Measure
A294

Folke Filbyter
Statue, by
Milles
A296

Hern-
qvist
by Per
Krafft
the
Younger
A295

1975, May 20   *Perf. 12½ Vert.*
1121 A294 55ö dp bl   40   25
1122 A295 70ö yel brn & dk brn 40 20
Perf. 12½ Horiz.
1123 A296 75ö violet   40   35

Anniversaries: Centenary of International Meter Convention, Paris, 1875; bicentenary of Swedish veterinary medicine, founded by Peter Hernqvist (1726–1808); birth centenary of Carl Milles (1875–1955), sculptor.

Officers'
Mess,
Romme-
hed,
1798
A297

Designs: No. 1125, Falun Mine pithead gear, 1852. No. 1126, Gunpowder Tower, Visby. No. 1127, Foundry and furnace, Engelsberg, 18th century. No. 1128, Skellefteå Church Village, 17th century.

1975, June 13   *Perf. 12½ Horiz.*
1124 A297 75ö vio bl   40   40
1125 A297 75ö dk car   40   40
1126 A297 75ö black   40   40
1127 A297 75ö dk car   40   40
1128 A297 75ö black   40   40
 a. Bklt. pane of 10 (2 each
      #1124-1128)   4.00
      Nos. 1124-1128 (5)   2.00 2.00

European Architectural Heritage Year 1975.

Rescue at Sea: Helicopter over
Ice-covered Tanker—A298

Designs: No. 1130, Hospital Service: patient arriving by ambulance. No. 1131, Police: Officer talking to boy on bridge. No. 1132, Customs narcotics service: trained dogs checking cargo. No. 1133, Fire fighters: firemen fighting fire.

Engraved
1975, Aug. 27   *Perf. 12½ Horiz.*
1129 A298 90ö green   70   40
1130 A298 90ö dk bl   70   40
1131 A298 90ö dk rose   70   40
1132 A298 90ö dk bl   70   40
1133 A298 90ö dk rose   70   40
 a. Bklt. pane of 10 (2 each
      #1129-1133)   7.00
      Nos. 1129-1133 (5)   3.50 2.00

Public service organizations watching, guarding, helping.

"Fryckstad"
A299

"Gotland"
A300

Design: 90ö, "Prins August."

1975, Aug. 27 *Perf. 12½ on 3 Sides*
Size: 20x19mm.
1134 A299 5ö green   20   15
1135 A300 5ö dk bl   20   15
Size: 45x19mm.
1136 A299 90ö sl grn   1.00 25
 a. Bklt. pane of 6 (2 each
      #1134-1136)   3.00

Scouts Around
Campfire
A301

Scouts in Canoes
A302

1975, Oct. 11 *Photo. Perf. 14 Vert.*
1137 A301 90ö multi   1.30 25
1138 A302 90ö multi   1.30 25

Nordjamb 75, 14th World Boy Scout Jamboree, Lillehammer, Norway, July 29–Aug. 7. Nos. 1137–1138 printed se-tenant.

Hedgehog
A303

Old Man Playing
Key Fiddle
A304

Romeo and Juliet
Ballet
A305

1975, Oct. 11 *Engr. Perf. 12½ Vert.*
1139 A303 55ö black   35   10
1140 A304 75ö dk red   38   15
Perf. 12½ Horiz.
1141 A305 7k bl grn   3.00 45
Perf. 12½ on 3 Sides
1142 A303 55ö black   30   25
 a. Booklet pane of 10   3.00

Virgin Mary,
12th Century
Statue
A306

Chariot of the
Sun, from 12th
Century Altar
A307

Mourning Mary,
c. 1280
A308

Jesse at Foot of
Genealogical Tree,
c. 1510
A309

Design: No. 1145, Nativity, from 12th century gilt-copper altar. No. 1148, like No. 1147.

1975, Nov. 11 *Photo. Perf. 14 Horiz.*
1143 A306 55ö multi   40   20
Perf. 12½ on 3 Sides
1144 A307 55ö gold & multi   40   20
1145 A307 55ö gold & multi   40   20
 a. Bklt. pane of 10 (5 each
      #1144-1145)   4.00

Engraved   *Perf. 12½ Horiz.*
1146 A308 90ö brown   60   20
Perf. 12½ on 3 Sides
1147 A309 90ö red   1.40 35
1148 A309 90ö blue   1.40 35
 a. Bklt. pane of 10 (5 each
      #1147-1148)   17.00

Christmas 1975.
No. 1145a was issued with top row of 5 either No. 1144 or No. 1145.

William H. and
William L. Bragg
A310

Designs: 90ö, Richard Willstätter. 1.10k, Romain Rolland.

Engraved   *Perf. 12½ Vert.*
1975, Dec. 10
1149 A310 75ö claret   40   30
1150 A310 90ö vio bl   60   20
1151 A310 1.10k sl grn   60   35

Winners of 1915 Nobel Prize.

Cave of the Winds, by Eric Grate
A311

1976, Jan. 27   *Perf. 12½ Vert.*
1152 A311 1.90k sl grn   95   25

The sculpture by Eric Grate (b. 1896) stands in front of the Town Hall of Västerås.

Razor-billed
Auks and Black
Guillemot
A312

Bobbin Lace
Maker from
Vadstena
A313

Engraved
1976, Mar. 10   *Perf. 12½ Vert.*
1153 A312 85ö dk bl   42   18
Perf. 12½ Horiz.
1154 A313 1k cl brn   50   20
Perf. 12½ on 3 Sides
1155 A312 85ö dk bl   42   18
 a. Booklet pane of 10   4.20
1156 A313 1k cl brn   50   20
 a. Booklet pane of 10

Old and New Telephones,
Relays
A314

1976, Mar. 10   *Perf. 12½ Vert.*
1157 A314 1.30k brt vio   65   25
1158 A314 3.40k red   2.00 70

Centenary of first telephone call by Alexander Graham Bell, March 10, 1876.

Europa Issue 1976

Lapp Elk Horn
Spoon
A315

Tile Stove
A316

1976, May 3 *Photo. Perf. 14½ Horiz.*
1159 A315 1k multi   80   25
1160 A316 1.30k multi   80   50

SWEDEN

Wheat and Cornflower Seeds A317 — Viable and Non-viable Seedlings A318

1976, May 3 Engr. Perf. 12½ Vert.
1161 A317 65ö brown 60 30
1162 A318 65ö choc & grn 60 30
Swedish seed testing centenary. Nos. 1161-1162 printed se-tenant.

King Karl XVI Gustaf and Silvia Sommerlath — A319

Engraved
1976, June 19 Perf. 12½ Vert.
1163 A319 1k rose car 60 10
1164 A319 1.30k sl grn 65 20
Perf. 12½ on 3 Sides
1165 A319 1k rose car 60 20
   a. Booklet pane of 10 6.00
Wedding of King Karl XVI Gustaf and Silvia Sommerlath.

View from Ringkallen, by Helmer Osslund — A320

Views in Angermanland Province: No. 1167, Tugboat pulling timber. No. 1168, Hay-drying racks. No. 1169, Granvagsnipan slope, Angerman River. No. 1170, Seine fishing.

1976, June 19 Perf. 12½ Horiz.
1166 A320 85ö sl grn 42 50
1167 A320 85ö vio bl 42 50
1168 A320 85ö dp brn 42 50
1169 A320 85ö sl bl 42 50
1170 A320 85ö brn red 42 50
   a. Bklt. pane of 10 (2 each #1166-1170) 4.20
   Nos. 1166-1170 (5) 2.10 2.50

Roman Cross and Ship's Wheel A321

1976, June 19 Perf. 12½ Horiz.
1171 A321 85ö brt bl & bl 60 25
Swedish Seamen's Church, centenary.

Torgny Segerstedt and 1917 Page of Gothenburg Journal — A322

1976, June 19 Perf. 12½ Vert.
1172 A322 1.90k brn & blk 95 25
Torgny Segerstedt (1876–1945), editor in chief of the Gothenburg Journal of Commerce and Shipping, birth centenary.

Coiled Snake, Bronze Buckle A323 — Pilgrim's Badge, Adoration of the Magi A324

Drinking Horn, 14th Century A325

Chimney Sweep A326 — Girl's Head, by Bror Hjorth, 1922 A327

Perf. 12½ Horiz., Vert. (30ö)
1976, Sept. 8 Engraved
1173 A323 15ö bister 8 5
1174 A324 20ö green 10 5
1175 A325 30ö dk rose brn 15 6
1176 A326 90ö indigo 45 18
1177 A327 9k yel grn & sl grn 4.00 40
   Nos. 1173-1177 (5) 4.78 74

John Ericsson, Ship Propeller and "Monitor" — A328

Designs: No. 1179, Helge Palmcrantz (1842–1880) and reaper. No. 1180, Lars Magnus Ericsson (1846–1926) and switchboard. No. 1181, Sven Wingquist (1876–1953) and ball bearing. No. 1182, Gustaf de Laval (1845–1913) and milk separator.

Perf. 12½ Horiz.
1976, Oct. 9 Engraved
1178 A328 1.30k multi 1.20 90
1179 A328 1.30k multi 1.20 90
1180 A328 1.30k multi 1.20 90
1181 A328 1.30k multi 1.20 90
1182 A328 1.30k multi 1.20 90
   a. Bklt. pane of 5 (#1178-1182) 6.00
   Nos. 1178-1182 (5) 6.00 4.50
Swedish inventors and their technological inventions.

Hands and Cogwheels A329 — Verner von Heidenstam, Lake Vattern A330

1976, Oct. 9 Perf. 12½ Vert.
1183 A329 85ö org & dk vio 60 30
1184 A329 1k yel grn & brn 60 20
Industrial safety.

1976, Nov. 17 Engr. Perf. 12½ Vert.
1185 A330 1k yel grn 60 20
1186 A330 1.30k blue 75 35
Verner von Heidenstam (1859–1940), Swedish poet, 1916 Nobel Prize winner.

Archangel Michael A331 — Virgin Mary Visiting St. Elizabeth A332

Designs: No. 1189, like No. 1187. No. 1190, St. Nicholas saving 3 children. No. 1191, like No. 1188. No. 1192, Illuminated page, prayer to Virgin Mary. 65ö stamps are from Flemish prayer book, c. 1500. 1k stamps are from Austrian prayer book, late 15th century.

1976, Nov. 17 Photogravure
1187 A331 65ö bl & multi 40 20
1188 A332 1k gold & multi 60 20
Perf. 12½ on 3 Sides
1189 A331 65ö bl & multi 40 20
1190 A331 65ö bl & multi 40 20
   a. Bklt. pane of 10 (5 each #1189-1190) 4.00
Perf. 12½ Vert.
1191 A332 1k gold & multi 60 20
1192 A332 1k gold & multi 60 20
   a. Bklt. pane of 10 (5 each #1191-1192) 6.00
Christmas 1976.

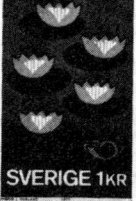 

Five Water Lilies A333 — Tailor A334

Perf. 12½ Horiz.
1977, Feb. 2 Photo. & Engr.
1193 A333 1k brt grn & multi 80 20
1194 A333 1.30k ultra & multi 75 75

Nordic countries cooperation for protection of the environment and 25th Session of Nordic Council, Helsinki, Feb. 19.

1977, Feb. 24 Perf. 12½ Vert.
1195 A334 2.10k red brn 1.05 25

Long-distance Skating A335

Designs: No. 1197, Swimming. No. 1198, Bicycling. No. 1199, Jogging. No. 1200, Badminton.

1977, Mar. 24 Perf. 12½ Horiz.
1196 A335 95ö blue 48 35
1197 A335 95ö sl grn 48 35
1198 A335 95ö red 48 35
1199 A335 95ö sl grn 48 35
1200 A335 95ö blue 48 35
   a. Bklt. pane of 10 (2 each #1196-1200) 4.80
   Nos. 1196-1200 (5) 2.40 1.75
Physical fitness.

Politeness, by "OA," 1905 A336

1977, Mar. 24 Perf. 12½ on 3 Sides
1201 A336 75ö black 40 30
   a. Booklet pane of 10 4.00
Perf. 12½ Horiz.
1202 A336 3.80k red 1.90 70
Oskar Andersson (1877–1906), cartoonist.

Calle Schewen — A337

Designs: No. 1204, Seagull. No. 1205, Dancers and accordionist. No. 1206, Fishermen in boat. No. 1207, Tree on shore at sunset. Designs are illustrations for poem The Calle Schewen Waltz, by Evert Taube, and include bars of music of this song.

Engraved
1977, May 2 Perf. 12½ Horiz.
1203 A337 95ö sl grn 48 40
1204 A337 95ö vio bl 48 40
1205 A337 95ö grn & blk 48 40
1206 A337 95ö dk bl 48 40
1207 A337 95ö red 48 40
   a. Bklt. pane of 10 (2 each #1203-1207) 4.80
   Nos. 1203-1207 (5) 2.40 2.00
Tourist publicity for Roslagen (archipelago) and to honor Evert Taube (1890–1976), poet.

Gustavianum, Uppsala University A338

1977, May 2 Photo. Perf. 12½ Vert.
1208 A338 1.10k multi 55 22
Perf. 12½ on 3 Sides
1209 A338 1.10k multi 55 22
   a. Booklet pane of 10 5.50
Uppsala University, 500th anniversary.

Europa Issue 1977

Forest in Snow A339

SWEDEN

Rapadalen Valley
A340

1977, May 2   *Perf. 12½ Vert.*

| 1210 | A339 | 1.10k multi | 55 | 22 |
| 1211 | A340 | 1.40k multi | 80 | 60 |

Owl
A341

Cast-iron Stove Decoration
A342

Gotland Ponies—A343

1977, Sept. 8 Engr.   *Perf. 12½ Vert.*

| 1212 | A341 | 45ö dk sl grn | 30 | 25 |

Perf. 12½ Horiz.

| 1213 | A342 | 70ö dk vio bl | 35 | 12 |

Booklet Stamp

| 1214 | A343 | 1.40k brown | 70 | 45 |
| a. | Bklt.pane of 5 | | 3.50 | |

Blackberry
A344

Designs: Wild berries.

Photogravure

1977, Sept. 8   *Perf. 14 on 3 Sides*
Multicolored

1215	A344	75ö shown	40	40
1216	A344	75ö Cranberry	40	40
1217	A344	75ö Raspberry	40	40
1218	A344	75ö Whortleberry	40	40
1219	A344	75ö Alpine strawberry	40	40
a.	Bklt. pane of 10 (2 each #1215-1219)		4.00	
	Nos. 1215-1219 (5)		2.00	2.00

Horse-drawn Trolley
A345

Designs: Public transportation.

1977, Oct. 8 Engr.   *Perf. 12½ Horiz.*

1220	A345	1.10k shown	55	40
1221	A345	1.10k Electric trolley	55	40
1222	A345	1.10k Ferry	55	40
1223	A345	1.10k Tandem bus	55	40
1224	A345	1.10k Subway	55	40
a.	Bklt. pane of 5 (#1220-1224)		2.75	
	Nos. 1220-1224 (5)		2.75	2.00

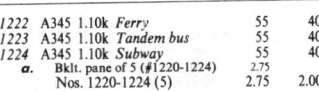

Putting up Sheaf for the Birds
A346

Preparing Dried Soaked Fish
A347

Traditional Christmas Preparations: No. 1227, Children baking ginger snaps. No. 1228, Bringing in Yule tree. No. 1229, Making straw goat. No. 1230, Candle dipping.

1977, Nov. 17 Engr.   *Perf. 12½ horiz.*

| 1225 | A346 | 75ö violet | 40 | 25 |
| 1226 | A347 | 1.10k yel grn | 40 | 25 |

Perf. 12½ on 3 Sides

1227	A346	75ö ocher	40	25
1228	A346	75ö sl grn	40	25
a.	Booklet pane of 10 (5 each #1227-1228)		4.00	
1229	A347	1.10k dk red	55	22
1230	A347	1.10k dk bl	55	22
a.	Booklet pane of 10 (5 each #1229-1230)		5.50	
	Nos. 1225-1230 (6)		2.70	1.44

Christmas 1977.

Henrik Pontoppidan, Karl Adolph Gjellerup
A348

Design: 1.40k, Charles Glover Barkla.

1977, Nov. 17   *Perf. 12½ Vert.*

| 1231 | A348 | 1.10k red brn | 55 | 22 |
| 1232 | A348 | 1.40k yel grn | 80 | 80 |

1917 Nobel Prize winners: Henrik Pontoppidan (1857–1943) and Karl Adolph Gjellerup (1857–1919), Danish writers; Charles Glover Barkla (1877–1944), English X-ray pioneer.

Space Without Affiliation, by Arne Jones
A349

Brown Bear
A350

1978, Jan. 25   *Perf. 12½ Horiz.*

| 1233 | A349 | 2.50k vio bl | 1.25 | 18 |

1978, Apr. 11   *Perf. 12½ Horiz.*

| 1234 | A350 | 1.15k dk brn | 60 | 20 |

The indexes in each volume of the Scott Catalogue contain many listings which help to identify stamps.

Europa Issue 1978

Örebro Castle
A351

Arch and Stairs
A352

1978, Apr. 11   *Perf. 12½ Vert.*

| 1235 | A351 | 1.30k sl grn | 65 | 20 |

Perf. 12½ Horiz.

| 1236 | A352 | 1.70k dl red | 80 | 80 |

Pentecostal Preacher and Congregation
A353

Free Churches: No. 1238, Swedish Missionary Society. No. 1239, Evangelical National Missionary Society. No. 1240, Baptist Society. No. 1241, Salvation Army.

1978, Apr. 11 *Perf. 12½ on 3 sides*

1237	A353	90ö purple	60	50
1238	A353	90ö slate	60	50
1239	A353	90ö violet	60	50
1240	A353	90ö slate	60	50
1241	A353	90ö purple	60	50
a.	Booklet pane of 10 (2 each #1237-1241)		6.00	
	Nos. 1237-1241 (5)		3.00	2.50

Independent Christian Associations.

Brösarp Hills
A354

Grindstone Production
A355

Red Limestone Cliff
A356

Designs: No. 1243, Avocets. No. 1245, Linnaea borealis (Linné's favorite flower.) No. 1247, Linné with Lapp drum, wearing Lapp clothes and Dutch doctor's hat.

1978, May 23 Engr.   *Perf. 12½ Horiz.*

| 1242 | A354 | 1.30k gray grn | 65 | 30 |
| 1243 | A354 | 1.30k vio bl | 65 | 30 |

Perf. 12½ on 3 Sides

1244	A355	1.30k vio brn	65	30
1245	A355	1.30k brn red	65	30
1246	A355	1.30k vio bl	65	30
1247	A356	1.30k vio brn	65	30
a.	Bklt.pane of 6 (#1242-1247)		3.90	
	Nos. 1242-1247 (6)		3.90	1.80

Travels of Carl von Linné (1707–1778), botanist.

Cranes, Lake Hornborgasjon—A357

Designs: No. 1248, Gliding School, Alleberg. No. 1250, Skara Church, Lacko Island. No. 1251, Ancient rock tomb, Luttra. No. 1252, Cloth merchants, sculpture by Nils Sjögren.

1978, May 23   *Perf. 12½ Horiz.*

1248	A357	1.15k dl grn	60	50
1249	A357	1.15k maroon	60	50
1250	A357	1.15k vio bl	60	50
1251	A357	1.15k dk gray grn	60	50
1252	A357	1.15k brn & gray grn	60	50
a.	Booklet pane of 10 (2 each #1284-1252)		6.00	
	Nos. 1248-1252 (5)		3.00	2.50

Tourist publicity for Vastergotland.

Laurel and Scroll
A358

1978, May 23   *Perf. 12½ Vert.*

| 1253 | A358 | 2.50k gray & sl grn | 1.25 | 35 |

Stockholm University, centenary.

Homecoming, by Carl Kylberg
A359

Nude, by Karl Isakson
A360

Self-portrait, by Ivar Arosenius
A361

Engraved

1978, Sept. 5   *Perf. 12½ Vert.*

| 1254 | A359 | 90ö multi | 75 | 30 |

Perf. 12½ Horiz.

| 1255 | A360 | 1.15k multi | 75 | 30 |
| 1256 | A361 | 4.50k multi | 2.25 | 70 |

Swedish painters: Carl Kylberg (1878–1952); Karl Isakson (1878–1922); Ivar Arosenius (1878–1909).

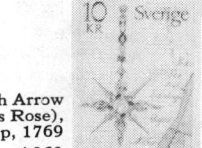

North Arrow (Compass Rose), Map, 1769
A362

1978, Sept. 5   *Perf. 12½ Horiz.*

| 1257 | A362 | 10k lilac | 4.00 | 40 |

SWEDEN

Coronation Coach, 1699
A363

Engraved

1978, Oct. 7   Perf. 12½ Horiz.
1258	A363	1.70k dk red, yel	1.00	75
a.		Booklet pane of 5	5.00	

Orange Russula
A364

Designs: Edible mushrooms.

1978, Oct. 7   Perf. 12½ on 3 Sides
Multicolored
1259	A364	1.15k shown	60	50
1260	A364	1.15k Common puff ball	60	50
1261	A364	1.15k Parasol mushroom	60	50
1262	A364	1.15k Chanterelle	60	50
1263	A364	1.15k Boletus edulis	60	50
1264	A364	1.15k Ramaria botrytis	60	50
a.		Booklet pane of 6 (#1259-1264)	3.60	
		Nos. 1259-1264 (6)	3.60	3.00

Toy Ferris Wheel
A365

Rider Drawing Water Cart
A366

Toys: No. 1266, Teddy bear. No. 1267, Dalecarlian wooden horse. No. 1268, Doll. No. 1270, Spinning tops.

Engraved

1978, Nov. 14   Perf. 12½ Horiz.
1265	A365	90ö dk red & grn	60	20
1266	A365	1.30k brt ultra	65	20

Photogravure
Perf. 12½ on 3 Sides
1267	A365	90ö multi	55	30
1268	A365	90ö multi	55	30
a.		Booklet pane of 10 (5 each #1267-1268)	5.50	
1269	A366	1.30k multi	65	20
1270	A366	1.30k multi	65	20
a.		Booklet pane of 10 (5 each #1269-1270)	6.50	
		Nos. 1265-1270 (6)	3.65	1.40

Christmas 1978.

Fritz Haber
A367

Design: 1.70k, Max Planck.

Engraved

1978, Nov. 14   Perf. 12½ Vert.
1271	A367	1.30k dk brn	65	35
1272	A367	1.70k dk vio bl	85	80

1918 Nobel Prize winners: Fritz Haber (1868–1934), German chemist; Max Planck (1858–1947), German physicist.

Bandy
A368

1979, Jan. 25 Engr.   Perf. 12½ Vert.
1273	A368	1.05k vio bl	55	20
1274	A368	2.50k orange	1.25	30

Child Wearing Gas Mask in Heavy Traffic—A369

Engraved

1979, Mar. 13   Perf. 12½ Vert.
| 1275 | A369 | 1.70k dk bl | 85 | 80 |

International Year of the Child.

Drill-weave Tapestry, c. 1855–1860
A370

Carrier Pigeon, Hand with Quill
A371

1979, Mar. 13   Perf. 12½ Horiz.
| 1276 | A370 | 4k gray & red | 1.50 | 30 |

Perf. 14x14½ on 3 Sides
1979, Apr. 2   **Photogravure**
1277	A371	(1k) ultra & yel	60	18
a.		Booklet pane of 20	12.00	

Every Swedish household received during April, 1979, 2 coupons for the purchase of 2 discount booklets. The stamps were for use on post cards and letters within Sweden. Price of booklet 20k.

Europa Issue 1979

Mail Service by Boat, Grisslehamn to Echero—A372

Design: 1.70k, Hand on telegraph.

1979, May 7 Engr.   Perf. 12½ Vert.
1278	A372	1.30k sl grn & blk	65	20
1279	A372	1.70k ocher & blk	80	80

Woodcutter, Winter
A373

Designs: No. 1281, Sowing, spring. No. 1282, Grazing cattle, summer. No. 1283, Harvester, summer. No. 1284, Plowing, autumn.

1979, May 7   Perf. 12½ Horiz.
1280	A373	1.30k multi	65	20
1281	A373	1.30k sl grn & dk brn	65	20
1282	A373	1.30k dk brn & sl grn	65	20
1283	A373	1.30k sl grn & ocher	65	20
1284	A373	1.30k multi	65	20
a.		Booklet pane of 10 (2 each #1280-1284)	6.50	
		Nos. 1280-1284 (5)	3.25	1.00

Tourist Steamer Juno—A374

Roller Bridge, Hajstorp
A375

Sailing Ship
A376

Göta Canal: No. 1286, Borenshult Lock. No. 1288, Hand-drawn gate. No. 1290, Rowboat in Forsvik lock.

1979, May 7   Perf. 12½ Horiz.
1285	A374	1.15k vio bl	60	50
1286	A374	1.15k sl grn	60	50

Perf. 12½ on 3 Sides
1287	A375	1.15k dl pur	60	50
1288	A375	1.15k carmine	60	50

Perf. 12½ on 2 Sides
1289	A376	1.15k vio bl	60	50
1290	A376	1.15k sl grn	60	50
a.		Booklet pane of 6 (#1285-1290)	3.60	
		Nos. 1285-1290 (6)	3.60	3.00

Strikers and Sawmill
A377

Temperance Movement Banner
A378

Jöns Jacob Berzelius
A379

Johan Olof Wallin
A380

1979, Sept. 6 Engr.   Perf. 12½ Vert.
| 1291 | A377 | 90ö car & dp brn | 45 | 15 |

Perf. 12½ Horiz.
Lithographed
| 1292 | A378 | 1.30k multi | 80 | 20 |

Engraved
1293	A379	1.70k brn & grn	85	70
1294	A380	4.50k sl bl	2.25	70

Centenaries of Sundsvall strike and Swedish Temperance Movement; birth bicentennials of Jöns Jacob Berzelius (1779–1848), physician and chemist; Johan Olof Wallin (1779–1839), Archbishop and poet.

Dragonfly
A381

Green Spotted Toad
A383

Pike
A382

1979, Sept. 6   Perf. 12½ Horiz.
| 1295 | A381 | 60ö violet | 40 | 25 |

Perf. 12½ Vert.
1296	A382	65ö gray	40	25
1297	A383	80ö ol grn	40	30

Potpourri Pot
A384

Portrait, by Johan Henrik Scheffel
A385

Designs: 1.30k, Silver coffeepot. 1.70k, Bust of Carl Johan Cronstedt.

Souvenir Sheet
Engraved and Photogravure

1979, Oct. 6   Perf. 12x12½
1298		Sheet of 4	3.00	3.50
a.	A384	90ö multi	75	85
b.	A385	1.15k multi	75	85
c.	A384	1.30k multi	75	85
d.	A385	1.70k multi	75	85

Swedish Rococo. No. 1298 has marginal inscription. Sold for 6k; surcharge was for philately. Size: 144x63mm.

Herrings, Age Determination
A386

Sea Research: No. 1300, Acoustic survey of sea bottom. No. 1301, Water bloom of algae in Baltic Sea. No. 1302, Computer map of herring distribution in South Baltic Sea. No. 1303, Research ship Argos.

1979, Oct. 6 Engr.   Perf. 12½ Horiz.
1299	A386	1.70k multi	85	75
1300	A386	1.70k sepia	85	75
1301	A386	1.70k multi	85	75
1302	A386	1.70k sepia	85	75
1303	A386	1.70k multi	85	75
a.		Booklet pane of 5 (#1299-1303)	4.25	
		Nos. 1299-1303 (5)	4.25	3.75

SWEDEN   647

Brooch from Jamtland A387

Ljusdal Costume A388

Christmas 1979 (Costumes and Jewelry from): No. 1305, Pendant, Smaland. No. 1307, Osteraker. No. 1308, Goinge. No. 1309, Mora.

1979, Nov. 15   Engraved   Perf. 12½ Horiz.
| 1304 | A387 90ö dk Prus bl | 45 | 15 |
| 1305 | A3871.30kdl red | 65 | 20 |

Photogravure
Perf. 12½ on 3 Sides
Size: 22×27mm.
1306	A388 90ö multi	45	30
1307	A388 90ö multi	45	30
a.	Booklet pane of 10 (5 each #1306-1307)	4.50	

Perf. 12½ Vert.
Size: 26×44mm.
1308	A3881.30kmulti	65	20
1309	A3881.30kmulti	65	20
a.	Booklet pane of 10 (5 each #1308-1309)	6.50	
	Nos. 1304-1309 (6)	3.30	1.35

Nobel Prize Winner Type of 1978
1919 Nobel Prize Winners: 1.30k, Jules Bordet (1870—1961), Belgian bacteriologist. 1.70k, Johannes Stark (1874—1957), German physicist. 2.50k, Carl Spitteler (1845—1924), Swiss poet.

1979, Nov. 15   Engraved   Perf. 12½ Vert.
1310	A3671.30lilac	65	20
1311	A3671.70kultra	65	60
1312	A3672.50kol grn	2.00	38

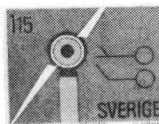
Wind Power—A389

Renewable Energy Sources: No. 1314, Biodegradable material. No. 1315, Solar energy. No. 1316, Geothermal energy. No. 1317, Hydro power.

Perf. 12½ on 3 sides
1980, Jan. 29   Engraved
1313	A3891.15kdk bl	60	50
1314	A3891.15kdk grn & bis	60	50
1315	A3891.15kyel org	60	50
1316	A3891.15kdk grn	60	50
1317	A3891.15kdk bl & dk grn	60	50
a.	Bklt. pane of 10 (2 each #1313-1317)	6.00	
	Nos. 1313-1317 (5)	3.00	2.50

Crown Princess Victoria and King Karl XVI Gustaf—A390

1980, Feb. 26   Perf. 12½ on 3 sides
| 1318 | A3901.30kbrt bl | 65 | 20 |
| a. | Bklt. pane of 10 | 6.50 | |

Perf. 12½ Vert.
| 1319 | A3901.30kbrt bl | 65 | 20 |
| 1320 | A3901.70kcar rose | 85 | 70 |

Child Holding Adult's Hand A391

Hand Holding Cane A392

1980, Apr. 22   Engraved   Perf. 12½ Horiz.
| 1321 | A3911.40kred brn | 70 | 20 |
| 1322 | A3921.60ksl grn | 70 | 30 |

Parents' insurance system; care for the elderly.

Squirrel—A393

Perf. 15 on 3 Sides
1980, May 12   Photo.
| 1323 | A393(1k) ultra & yel | 50 | 15 |
| a. | Bklt. pane of 20 | 10.00 | |

See note after No. 1277.

Europa Issue 1980

Elise Ottesen-Jensen (1886-1973), Journalist—A394

Design: 1.70k, Joe Hill (1879-1915), member of American Workers' Movement and poet.

1980, June 4   Engraved   Perf. 12½ Vert.
| 1324 | A3941.30kgreen | 65 | 20 |
| 1325 | A3941.70kred | 85 | 70 |

Banga Farm, Alfta, Halsingland Province—A395

Tourism (Halsingland Province): No. 1327, Iron Works, Iggesund. No. 1328, Blaxas Ridge, Forsa. No. 1329, Tybling farm, Tyby. No. 1330, Sunds Canal, Hudiksvall.

1980, June 4   Perf. 12½ Horiz.
1326	A3951.15kred	60	50
1327	A3951.15kdk bl	60	50
1328	A3951.15kdk grn	60	50
1329	A3951.15kchocolate	60	50
1330	A3951.15kdk bl	60	50
a.	Bklt. pane of 10 (2 each #1326-1330)	6.00	
	Nos. 1326-1330 (5)	3.00	2.50

Booklet Panes

Panes consisting of blocks, strips or pairs removed from large sheets of regular issue and fastened or enclosed within a cover or folder, often by stapling or sewing in the sheet margin, are no longer being listed. Such panes contain no straight edges and can easily be made privately.

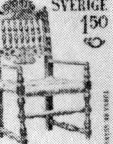
Chair, Scania, 1831 A396

Cradle, North Bothnia, 19th Century A397

1980, Sept. 9   Engraved   Perf. 12½ Horiz.
| 1331 | A3961.50kgrnsh bl | 75 | 22 |

Perf. 12½ Vert.
| 1332 | A397 2k dk red brn | 1.00 | 35 |

Norden 80.

Scene from "Diagonal Symphony," 1924—A398

1980, Sept. 9   Perf. 12½ Horiz.
| 1333 | A398 3k dk bl | 1.50 | 30 |

Viking Eggeling (1880-1925), artist and film maker.

Souvenir Sheet

Gustaf Erikson's Carriage—A399

Vabis, 1909—A400

Swedish Automobile History: 1.30k, Thulin, 1923. 1.40k, Scania, 1903. 1.50k, Tidaholm, 1917. 1.70k, Volvo, 1927.

Photogravure & Engraved
1980, Oct. 11   Perf. 12½
1334	Sheet of 6	4.00	4.50
a.	A399 90ö lt bl & dk brn	65	70
b.	A400 1.15k cr & dk brn	65	70
c.	A399 1.30k lt bl & dk brn	65	70
d.	A399 1.40k lt bl & dk brn	65	70
e.	A400 1.50k cr & dk brn	65	70
f.	A399 1.70k lt bl & dk brn	65	70

No. 1334 has light blue marginal inscription; black control number. Size: 120x67mm. Sold for 9k.

Bamse the Bear—A401

Farmer Kronblom—A402

Christmas 1980 (Comic Strip Characters): No. 1336, Mandel Karlsson (vert.). No. 1337, Adamson (vert.).

1980, Oct. 11   Engraved   Perf. 12½ Vert.
| 1335 | A4011.15kmulti | 45 | 15 |

Photo.   Perf. 12½ on 3 sides
| 1336 | A4011.15kmulti | 45 | 15 |
| a. | 3klt. pane of 10 | 4.50 | |

Engraved
| 1337 | A4011.50kblack | 75 | 22 |

Photo.
| 1338 | A4021.50kmulti | 75 | 22 |
| | Bklt. pane of 10 | 7.50 | |

Angel Blowing Horn—A403

1980, Nov. 18   Engraved   Perf. on 3 Sides
| 1339 | A4031.25kmulti | 60 | 25 |
| a. | Bklt. pane of 12 | 7.20 | |

Christmas 1980.

Necken, by Ernst Josephson—A404

1980, Nov. 18   Perf. 12½ Horiz.
| 1340 | A404 8k multi | 3.25 | 40 |

Nobel Prize Winner Type of 1978
1920 Nobel Prize Winners: No. 1341, Knut Hamsun (1859-1953), Norwegian writer. No. 1342, August Krogh (1874-1949), Danish Physiologist, No. 1343, Charles-Edouard Guillaume (1861-1938), French chemist. No. 1344, Walther Nerns (1864-1941), German physicist.

1980, Nov. 18   Perf. 13 on 3 Sides
1341	A3671.40kdk bl gray	70	35
1342	A3671.40kred	70	35
a.	Bklt. pane of 10 (5 each #1341-1342)	7.00	
1343	A367 2k green	1.00	60
1344	A367 2k brown	1.00	60
a.	Bklt. pane of 10 (5 each #1343-1344)	10.00	

Ernst Wigforss A405

Freya (Fertility Goddess) A406

1981, Jan. 29   Engraved   Perf. 12½ Vert.
| 1345 | A405 5k rose car | 2.00 | 50 |

Ernst Wigforss (1881-1977), politician and writer.

1981, Jan. 29   Perf. 12½ on 3 Sides
Norse Mythological Characters: 10ö, Thor (thunder god). 15ö, Heimdall (rainbow god). 50ö, Frey (god of peace, fertility, weather). 1k, Odin.

1346	A406 10ö bl blk	5	5
1347	A406 15ö dk car	6	5
1348	A406 50ö dk car	20	8
1349	A406 75ö dp grn	30	12
1350	A406 1k bl blk	40	18
a.	Bklt. pane of 10 (2 each #1346-1350)	2.00	
	Nos. 1346-1350 (5)	1.01	48

SWEDEN

Gyrfalcon—A407

1981, Feb. 26   Engraved   Perf. 12½ Vert.
1351 A407 50k multi   17.50   7.00
  a.   Bklt. pane of 4   70.00

Europa Issue 1981

Troll Chasing Boy—A408

Design: 2k, Lady of the Woods.
1981, Apr. 28   Engr.
1352 A408 1.50k dk bl & red   75   22
1353 A408 2k dk grn & red   1.00 35

International Year of the Disabled—A409

1981, Apr. 28
1354 A409 1.50k dk grn   75   22
1355 A409 3.50k purple   1.75 60

Arms of Ostergotland Province — A410   Sail Boat, Bohuslan — A411

1981, May 18 Photo. Perf. 14½ on 3 Sides
1356 A410 1.40k shown   70   20
1357 A410 1.40k Jamtland   70   20
1358 A410 1.40k Dalarna   70   20
1359 A410 1.40k Bohuslan   70   20
  a.   Bklt. pane of 20 (5 each #1356-1359)   14.00

See note after No. 1277. See Nos. 1403-1406, 1456-1459.

1981, May 26   Engr.   Perf. 12½ on 3 Sides
1360 A411 1.65k shown   70   35
1361 A411 1.65k Blekinge   70   35
1362 A411 1.65k Norrbotten   70   35
1363 A411 1.65k Halsingland   70   35
1364 A411 1.65k Gotland   70   35
1365 A411 1.65k Skane   70   35
  a.   Bklt. pane of 6 (#1360-1365)   4.20
        Nos. 1360-1365 (6)   4.20 2.10

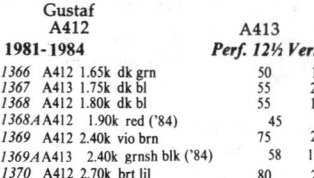

King Karl XVI Gustaf — A412   Queen Silvia — A413

1981-1984   Perf. 12½ Vert.
1366   A412 1.65k dk grn   50   15
1367   A413 1.75k dk bl   55   25
1368   A412 1.80k dk bl   55   15
1368A A412 1.90k red ('84)   45   8
1369   A412 2.40k vio brn   75   25
1369A A413 2.40k grnsh blk ('84)   58   12
1370   A412 2.70k brt lil   80   25
1371   A413 3.20k red   95   30

Day and Night   Scene from Par Lagerkvist's Autobiography Guest of Reality
A414   A415

1981, Sept. 9   Engr.   Perf. 12½ on 3 Sides
1376 A414 1.65k purple   65   25
  a.   Bklt. pane of 10   6.50

1981, Sept. 9
1377 A415 1.50k dk grn   60   22

Conductor Sixten Ehrling and Opera Singer Birgit Nilsson — A416

Bjorn Borg, Tennis Player — A417   Baker's Sign — A418

Designs: No. 1378, Electric locomotive. No. 1379, Trucks. No. 1381, Oil rig. No. 1383, Ingemar Stenmark, Olympic skier.

1981, Sept. 9
1378 A416 2.40k rose car   1.00   80
1379 A416 2.40k red   1.00   80
1380 A416 2.40k rose lil   1.00   80
1381 A416 2.40k dp vio   1.00   80
1382 A417 2.40k dk bl   1.00   80
1383 A417 2.40k dk bl   1.00   80
  a.   Bklt. pane of 6 (4 #1378-1381, #1382-1383)   6.00

1981, Sept. 9   Perf. 12½ Vert.
1384 A418 2.30k shown   1.00   40
1385 A418 2.30k Pewter shop sign   1.00   40

Nos. 1384-1385 se-tenant.

Ingrid Bergman and Gosta Ekman in Intermezzo — A419

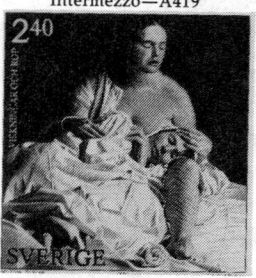

Kari Sylwan and Harriet Andersson in Cries and Whispers — A420

Swedish Films: No. 1386a, Olof Ahs in The Coachman. No. 1386c, Greta Garbo in The Gosta Berling Saga, No. 1386d, Stig Jarrel and Alf Kjellin in Persecution.

1981, Oct. 10   Photo. & Engr.   Perf. 13½
1386   Sheet of 5   4.00 4.50
  a.   A419 1.50k multi   75   85
  b.   A419 1.50k multi   75   85
  c.   A419 1.65k multi   75   85
  d.   A419 1.65k multi   75   85
  e.   A420 2.40k multi   1.00 1.10

No. 1386 has blue marginal inscription; black control number. Size: 135x70mm. Sold for 10k.

Nobel Prize Winner Type of 1978

1921 Winners: 1.35k, Albert Einstein (1879-1955), German physicist 1.65k, Anatole France (1844-1924), French writer. Frederick Soddy (1877-1956), British chemist.

1981, Nov. 24   Engr.   Perf. 12½ Vert.
1387 A367 1.35k red   65   60
1388 A367 1.65k green   65   25
1389 A367 2.70k blue   1.25 80

Christmas 1981 — A421

Designs: Wooden birds.

1981, Nov. 24   Perf. 12½ on 3 Sides
1390 A421 1.40k red   70   30
1391 A421 1.40k green   70   30
  a.   Bklt. pane of 10 (5 each #1390-1391)   7.00

Knight on Horseback, by John Bauer — A422

John Bauer (1882-1918), Fairytale Illustrator: No. 1393, "What a Miserable Little Paleface, said the Troll Mother." No. 1394, Marsh Princess. No. 1395, Now the Dusk of the Night is already Upon Us.

Perf. 12x12½ on 3 sides

1982, Feb. 16   Engr.
1392 A422 1.65k multi   70   30
1393 A422 1.65k multi   70   30
1394 A422 1.65k multi   70   30
1395 A422 1.65k multi   70   30
  a.   Bklt. pane of 4 (#1392-1395) 2.80

Impossible Figures — A423   Newspaper Distributor, by Svenolov Ehren — A424

Graziella, by Carl Larsson — A425

Designs: Geometric figures.

1982, Feb. 16   Perf. 12½ Horiz.
1396 A423 25o vio brn   10   10
1397 A423 50o brn ol   20   10
1398 A423 75o dk bl   30   10

1982, Feb. 16
1399 A424 1.35k dp vio   50   18
1400 A425 5k vio brn   1.50 30

Europa Issue 1982

Land Reform, 19th Cent. — A426

Anders Celsius (1701-1744), Inventor of Temperature Scale — A427

1982, Apr. 26   Engr.   Perf. 12½ Vert.
1401 A426 1.65k dk ol grn   65   25
          Perf. 12½ on 3 Sides
1402 A427 2.40k dk grn   1.00 65
  a.   Bklt. pane of 6   6.00

Provincial Arms Type of 1981

1982, Apr. 26   Photo.   Perf. 14 on 3 Sides
1403 A410 1.40k Dalsland   60   15
1404 A410 1.40k Halsingland   60   15
1405 A410 1.40k Vastmandland   60   15
1406 A410 1.40k Oland   60   15
  a.   Bklt. pane of 20 (5 each #1403-1406)   12.00

See note after No. 1277.

Elin Wagner (1882-1949), Writer — A428

1982, June 3   Engr.   Perf. 12½ Horiz.
1407 A428 1.35k Sketch by Siri Derkert 60   30

SWEDEN

	Burgher House	Embroidered Lace Ribbon, 19th Cent.
	A429	A430

1982, June 3   *Perf. 12½ Vert.*
1408 A429 1.65k brown 60 20
    Perf. 12½ Horiz.
1409 A430 2.70k bister 1.00 45

Centenary of Museum of Cultural History, Lund.

1982 Intl. Buoyage System—A431

Designs: Various buoy signals.

1982, June 3   *Perf. 13 Horiz.*
1410 A431 1.65k shown 60 30
1411 A431 1.65k Ferry 60 30
1412 A431 1.65k Six sailboats 60 30
1413 A431 1.65k One-globed buoy 60 30
1414 A431 1.65k Two-globed buoy 60 30
  a. Bklt. pane of 10 (2 each #1410-1414) 6.00
    Nos. 1410-1414 (5) 3.00 1.50

Vietnamese Workers in Sweden—A432

Living Together: Swedish emigration and immigration.

1982, Aug. 26   *Engr.*   *Perf. 13 Horiz.*
1415 A432 1.65k Leaving Sweden, 1880 60 30
1416 A432 1.65k shown 60 30
1417 A432 1.65k Local voting right 60 30
1418 A432 1.65k Girls 60 30
  a. Bklt. pane of 8 (2 each #1415-1418) 4.80

Early Purple Orchid—A433

1982, Oct. 9   *Photo. & Engr.*   *Perf. 12x13*
1419 Sheet of 4 3.50 4.00
  a. A433 1.65k shown .65 .75
  b. A433 1.65k Lady's slipper .65 .75
  c. A433 2.40k Marsh helleborine 1.00 1.10
  d. A433 2.70k Elder-flowered orchid 1.10 1.10

Wild orchids. Black marginal inscription. Size: 145x63mm. Sold for 10k for benefit of stamp collecting.

Christmas 1982—A434

Stained-glass Windows, Church at Lye, Gotland, 14th cent.

1982, Nov. 24   *Photo.*   *Perf. 13 on 3 Sides*
1420 A434 1.40k Angel 70 40
1421 A434 1.40k Child in the Temple 70 40
1422 A434 1.40k Adoration of the Kings 70 40
1423 A434 1.40k Tidings to the Shepherds 70 40
1424 A434 1.40k Birth of Christ 70 40
  a. Bklt. pane of 10 (2 each #1420-1424) 7.00
    Nos. 1420-1424 (5) 3.50 2.00

Signature, Atomic Model—A435

Nobel Prizewinners in Physics (Quantum Mechanics): Various atomic models.

1982, Nov. 24   *Engr.*   *Perf. 13 Horiz.*
1425 A435 2.40k Niels Bohr, Denmark, 1922 1.00 65
1426 A435 2.40k Erwin Schrodinger, Austria, 1933 1.00 65
1427 A435 2.40k Louis de Broglie, France, 1929 1.00 65
1428 A435 2.40k Paul Dirac, England, 1933 1.00 65
1429 A435 2.40k Werner Heisenberg, Germany, 1932 1.00 65
  a. Bklt. pane of 5 (#1425-1429) 5.00
    Nos. 1425-1429 (5) 5.00 3.25

Fruit A436

1983, Feb. 10   *Engr.*   *Perf. 12½ Vert.*
1430 A436 5o Horse chestnut 5 5
1431 A436 10o Norway maple 5 5
1432 A436 15o Dogrose 8 5
1433 A436 20o Sloe 10 6

Keep your collection
up to date!!
Subscribe to the
Scott Stamp Monthly
with
Chronicle of New Issues
Today!

Peace Movement Centenary A437

1983, Feb. 10
1446 A437 1.35k blue 55 20

Nils Ferlin (1898-1961), Poet—A438

1983, Feb. 10
1447 A438 6k dk grn 1.75 35

500th Anniv. of Printing in Sweden—A439

1983, Feb. 10   *Perf. 13 Horiz.*
1448 A439 1.65k Lead type 60 30
1449 A439 1.65k Dialogus Creaturarum, 1483 60 30
1450 A439 1.65k Carolus XII Bible, 1793 60 30
1451 A439 1.65k ABC Books, 1760s 60 30
1452 A439 1.65k Laser photo composition 60 30
  a. Bklt. pane of 10 (2 each #1448-1452) 6.00
    Nos. 1448-1452 (5) 3.00 1.50

Sweden-US Relations Bicentenary—A440

1983, Mar. 24
1453 A440 2.70k Benjamin Franklin, Swedish Arms 1.10 50
  a. Bklt. pane of 5 5.50

See U.S. No. 2036.

Nordic Cooperation Issue—A441

1983, Mar. 24   *Engr.*   *Perf. 12½ Horiz.*
    Size: 21x27mm.
1454 A441 1.65k Bicycling 65 25
    Perf. 13 Vert.
1455 A441 2.40k Sailing 1.00 45

Provincial Arms Type of 1981

1983, Apr. 25   *Photo.*   *Perf. 14½x14*
1456 A410 1.60k Gotland 60 15
1457 A410 1.60k Gastrikland 60 15
1458 A410 1.60k Medelpad 60 15
1459 A410 1.60k Vastergotland 60 15
  a. Bklt. pane of 20 (5 each #1456-1459) 12.00

See note after No. 1277.

Europa 1983—A442

1983, Apr. 25   *Engr.*   *Perf. 12½ Horiz.*
1460 A442 1.65k Swedish Ballet Co. 60 25
1461 A442 2.70k Sliding-jaw spanner 90 45

STOCKHOLMIA Intl. Stamp Exhibition, Aug. 28-Sept. 7, 1986—A443

Designs: 1k, 3k, 10-ore King Oscar II definitive essays, 1884. 2k, No. 39. 4k, No. 58.

1983, May 25   *Perf. 12½*
1462 A443 1k blue 30 30
1463 A443 2k red 60 60
1464 A443 3k blue 90 90
1465 A443 4k green 1.20 1.20
  a. Bklt. pane of 4 (#1462-1465) 3.00

Red Cross	Greater Karlso
A444	A445

1983, Aug. 24   *Engr.*   *Perf. 12½ Horiz.*
1466 A444 1.50k red 45 30
1467 A445 1.60k dk bl 48 32

Planorbis Snail	Arctic Fox
A446	A447

1983, Aug. 24   *Perf. 12½ on 3 Sides, Horiz.*
1468 A446 1.80k green 55 25
  a. Bklt. pane of 10 5.50
1469 A447 2.10k grnsh blk 65 40

SWEDEN

Hjalmar Bergman (1883-1931), Writer—A448

1983, Aug. 24 **Perf. 13 Horiz.**
| 1470 | A448 | 1.80k Portrait | 55 | 34 |
| 1471 | A448 | 1.80k Jac the Clown illustration by Nisse Skoog | 55 | 34 |

Se-tenant.

View of Helgeandsholmen, Stockholm, by Franz Hogenberg, 1580—A449

1983, Aug. 24 **Perf. 12½ Vert.**
| 1472 | A449 | 2.70k | 85 | 55 |

Wilhelm Stenhammar Composer and Pianist—A450

Hins—Anders, Violinist—A451

1983, Oct. 1 **Photo. & Engr.** **Perf. 13½**
1473		Sheet of 5	3.50	4.00
a.		A450 1.80k shown	60	70
b.		A450 1.80k Aniara (opera)	60	70
c.		A450 1.80k Lars Gullin jazz saxaphonist	60	70
d.		A450 1.80k ABBA pop music group	60	70
e.		A451 2.70k shown	1.00	1.00

Sold for 11.50k.

Christmas 1983—A452

Postcard designs: No. 1474, Christmas Gnomes around the tree. No. 1475, on straw goats. No. 1476, Folk children, Christmas porridge and gingerbread. No. 1477, shown.

1983, Nov. 22 **Photo.** **Perf. 12½ on 3 sides**
1474	A452	1.60k multi	48	32
1475	A452	1.60k multi	48	32
1476	A452	1.60k multi	48	32
1477	A452	1.60k multi	48	32
a.		Bklt. pane of 12 (3 each #1474-1477)	6.00	4.00

Chemistry, Nobel Prize Winners—A453

Designs: No. 1478, Arne Tiselius (1902-1971), Electrophoresis Studies. No. 1479, George De Hevsy (1885-1966), Radioactive isotope tracers. No. 1480 Svante Arrenius (1859-1927), Theory of Electrolytic Dissociation. No. 1481, Theodor Svedberg (1884-1971), Colloid Studies. No. 1482, Hans Von Euler-Chelpin (1873-1964). Enzyme and Vitamin Structures.

1983, Nov. 22 **Photo. & Engr.** **Perf. 12½ horiz.**
1478	A453	2.70k slate	85	55
1479	A453	2.70k dp bl vio	85	55
1480	A453	2.70k grnsh blk	85	55
1481	A453	2.70k bl blk	85	55
1482	A453	2.70K red lil	85	55
a.		Bklt. pane of 5 (#1478-1482)	4.25	2.75
		Nos. 1478-1482 (5)	4.25	2.75

Postal Savings Centenary—A454

Design: 100o, Three crowns.

1984, Feb. 9 **Engr.** **Perf. 12½ vert.**
1483	A454	100o orange	32	32
1484	A454	1.60k purple	50	50
1485	A454	1.80k pink	55	55

Europa 1984—A455

Design: Symbolic bridge of communications exchange.

1984, Feb. 9 **Perf. 12½ horiz.**
1486	A455	1.80k red	55	55
a.		Bklt. pane of 10	5.50	
1487	A455	2.70k dp ultra	85	85

Lemmings A456   Angelica A457

1984, Mar. 27 **Perf. 12½ on 3 Sides**
1488	A456	1.90k shown	45	8
1489	A456	1.90k Musk ox	45	8
a.		Bklt. pane of 10 (5 each #1488-1489)	4.50	
1490	A457	2k shown	50	10
1491	A457	2.25k Alpine birch	55	12

Provincial Arms Type of 1981

1984, Apr. 24 **Photo.** **Perf. 14½x14**
1492	A410	1.60k Skane	40	8
1493	A410	1.60k Blekinge	40	8
1494	A410	1.60k Sodermanland	40	8
1495	A410	1.60k Vasterbotten	40	8
a.		Bklt. pane of 20 (5 each #1492-1495)	8.00	

See note after No. 1277.

Swedish Patent System Centenary—A458

Designs: No. 1496, Paraffin stove, F.W. Lindquist, 1892. No. 1497, Industrial robot ASEA-IRB 6. No. 1498, Fan suction vacuum cleaner, Axel Wennergren, 1912. No. 1499, Inboard-outboard motor, AQ-200, No. 1500, SLIC integrated electronic circuit. No. 1501, Tetrahedron container, 1948, 1951.

1984, June 6 **Engr.** **Perf. 12½ on 3 Sides**
1496	A458	2.70k red	65	12
1497	A458	2.70k sepia	65	12
1498	A458	2.70k green	65	12
1499	A458	2.70k green	65	12
1500	A458	2.70k sepia	65	12
1501	A458	2.70k blue	65	12
a.		Bklt. pane of 6 (#1496-1501)	4.00	
		Nos. 1496-1501 (6)	3.90	72

Famous Letters—A459

Stockholmia '86: 1k, Erik XIV's marriage proposal to Queen Elizabeth I, 1561. 2k, Erik Dahlbergh to Sten Bielke, 1684. 3k, Feather letter, 1834. 4k, August Strindberg to Harriet Bosse, 1905.

Litho. & Engr.

1984, June 6 **Perf. 12½**
1502		Sheet of 4	2.50	2.50
a.	A459	1k multi	25	5
b.	A459	2k multi	50	10
c.	A459	3k multi	75	15
d.	A459	4k multi	1.00	20
e.		Bklt. pane of 4 (1502a-1502d)	2.50	

Size: 145x63mm.

Collectors of Nordic Countries are welcome to try filling your wants from Scandinavia's biggest stamp-stock.

Low prices now in 16% devaluated S.Kr.

Rolf Gummesson AB,
Kungsgatan 55
111 22 Stockholm,
Sweden.

ASDA member since 1946.

SWEDEN

SEMI-POSTAL STAMPS.

Type of 1872-91 Issues Surcharged in Dark Blue

Wmkd. Wavy Lines. (181)

			1916, Dec. 21	Perf. 13x13½.	
B1	A5	5ö +5ö on 2ö org		7.50	8.00
B2	A5	5ö +5ö on 3ö yel brn		7.50	8.00
B3	A5	5ö +5ö on 4ö gray		7.50	8.00
B4	A5	5ö +5ö on 5ö grn		7.50	8.00
B5	A5	5ö +5ö on 6ö lil		7.50	8.00
B6	A5	10ö +10ö on 12ö pale bl		7.50	8.00
B7	A5	10ö +10ö on 20ö red org		7.50	8.00
B8	A5	10ö +10ö on 24ö yel		7.50	8.00
B9	A5	10ö +10ö on 30ö brn		7.50	8.00
B10	A5	10ö +10ö on 50ö rose red		7.50	8.00
		Nos. B1-B10 (10)		75.00	80.00

The surtax on Nos. B1–B31 was for the militia. See note after No. B21.

No. 66 Surcharged in Dark Blue

Wmkd. Two Crowns. (180)

		1916, Dec. 21		Perf. 13	
B11	A12	10ö +4.90k on 5k dl bl		175.00	300.00

Postage Due Stamps of 1877 Surcharged in Dark Blue

	1916, Dec. 21	Perf. 13	Unwmkd.		
B12	D1	5ö +5ö on 1ö blk		8.00	8.00
B13	D1	5ö +5ö on 3ö rose		5.00	6.00
B14	D1	5ö +5ö on 5ö brn		5.00	6.00
B15	D1	5ö +10ö on 6ö yel		6.00	8.00
B16	D1	5ö +15ö on 12ö pale red		27.50	22.50
B17	D1	10ö +20ö on 20ö pale bl		18.00	20.00
B18	D1	10ö +40ö on 24ö lil		75.00	100.00
B19	D1	10ö +20ö on 30ö grn		5.00	8.00
B20	D1	10ö +40ö on 50ö yel brn		40.00	45.00
B21	D1	10ö +90ö on 1kr bl & yel brn		200.00	350.00
		Nos. B12-B21 (10)		389.50	573.50

The surtax on Nos. B12–B21 is indicated not in figures, but in words at bottom of surcharge: Fem, 5; Tio, 10; Femton, 15; Tjugo, 20; Fyrtio, 40; Nittio, 90.

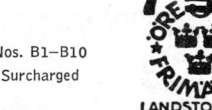

Nos. B1-B10 Surcharged

1918, Dec. 18		Wmk. 181		
B22	A5	7ö +3ö on 5ö on 2ö org	8.00	12.00

B23	A5	7ö +3ö on 5ö on 3ö yel brn	3.50	2.25
B24	A5	7ö +3ö on 5ö on 4ö gray	3.50	2.25
B25	A5	7ö +3ö on 5ö on 5ö grn	3.50	2.25
B26	A5	7ö +3ö on 5ö on 6ö lil	3.50	2.25
B27	A5	12ö +8ö on 10ö on 12ö pale bl	3.50	2.25
B28	A5	12ö +8ö on 10ö on 20ö red org	3.50	2.25
B29	A5	12ö +8ö on 10ö on 24ö yel	3.50	2.25
B30	A5	12ö +8ö on 10ö on 30ö brn	3.50	2.25
B31	A5	12ö +8ö on 10ö on 50ö rose red	3.50	2.25
		Nos. B22-B31 (10)	39.50	32.25

The 12ö+8ö surcharge exists on Nos. B1–B5 and the 7ö+3ö surcharge exists on Nos. B6–B10. Price, each $65.
Nos. B24, B26, B28 and B30 exist with surcharge inverted. Price unused, each $110.

King Gustaf V
SP1 SP2

Unwmkd.

1928, June 16		Engr.	Perf. 10	
B32	SP1	5ö (+5ö) yel grn	6.00	9.00
a.		Booklet pane of 8	100.00	
B33	SP1	10ö (+5ö) dk vio	5.00	9.00
a.		Booklet pane of 8	100.00	
B34	SP1	15ö (+5ö) car	5.00	8.00
a.		Booklet pane of 8	100.00	
B35	SP1	20ö (+5ö) org	10.00	4.50
B36	SP1	25ö (+5ö) dk bl	10.00	4.50
		Nos. B32-B36 (5)	36.00	35.00

70th birthday of King Gustaf V. The surtax was used for anti-cancer work.

1948, June 16		Perf. 12½ Vertically		
B37	SP2	10ö +10ö grn	60	1.00
B38	SP2	20ö +10ö red	90	1.20
B39	SP2	30ö +10ö ultra	70	1.20

Perf. 12½ on 3 Sides.

B40	SP2	10ö +10ö grn	75	1.00
a.		Bklt. pane of 20	15.00	
B41	SP2	20ö +10ö red	90	1.00
a.		Booklet pane of 20	18.00	
		Nos. B37-B41 (5)	3.85	5.40

Issued to commemorate the 90th anniversary of the birth of King Gustaf V. The surtax provided aid for Swedish youth.

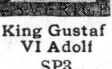

King Gustaf VI Adolf SP3   Henri Dunant SP4

1952, Nov. 11		Perf. 12½ Horiz.		
B42	SP3	10ö +10ö grn	40	40
B43	SP3	25ö +10ö car rose	50	50
B44	SP3	40ö +10ö ultra	60	60

Perf. 12½ on 3 Sides

B45	SP3	10ö +10ö grn	50	50
a.		Booklet pane of 20	10.00	
B46	SP3	25ö +10ö car rose	50	50
a.		Booklet pane of 20	10.00	
		Nos. B42-B46 (5)	2.50	2.50

70th birthday of King Gustaf VI Adolf. The surtax was used to promote Swedish culture.

1959, May 8		Perf. 12½ Horizontally		
B47	SP4	30ö +10ö red	1.10	1.40

Perf. 12½ on 3 Sides

B48	SP4	30ö +10ö red	1.25	1.50
		Bklt. pane of 20	25.00	

Issued to commemorate the centenary of the Red Cross idea. The surtax went to the Swedish Red Cross.

King Gustav VI Adolf SP5

1962, Nov. 10 Engraved Unwmkd.
Perf. 12½ Vertically
Size: 58x24mm.

B49	SP5	20ö +10ö brn	35	65
B50	SP5	35ö +10ö bl	35	65

Perf. 12½ Horizontally

B51	SP5	20ö +10ö brn	50	65
a.		Bklt. pane of 10	5.00	
B52	SP5	35ö +10ö bl	50	65
a.		Bklt. pane of 10	5.00	

Issued to commemorate the 80th birthday of King Gustaf VI Adolf. The surtax went to the King Gustaf VI Adolf 80th anniversary Foundation for Swedish Cultural Activities.

Ship Types of Regular Issues, 1936–44
Imprint: "1966"

Designs (Ships): 10ö, "The Lion of Smaland." 15ö, "Kalmar Nyckel." 20ö, Old Sailing Packet. 25ö, Mail Paddle Steamship. 30ö, "Kung Karl." 40ö, Stern of "Amphion."

Perf. 12½ on 3 Sides

1966, Nov. 15			Engraved	
B53	A76	10ö vermilion	30	45
B54	A50	15ö vermilion	30	45
B55	A38	20ö sl grn	30	45
B56	A39	25ö ultra	20	45
B57	A78	30ö vermilion	30	45
B58	A79	40ö vermilion	30	45
a.		Bklt. pane of 10 (#B53-B54, B57-B58, 2#B55, 4#B56)	2.65	
		Nos. B53-B58 (6)	1.70	2.45

The booklet sold for 3.50k and the surtax of 1.15k went to the National Cancer Fund.

AIR POST STAMPS.

Official Stamps Surcharged in Dark Blue

Wmkd. Wavy Lines. (181)

1920, Sept. 17			Perf. 13	
C1	O3	10ö on 3ö brn	5.50	9.00
a.		Inverted surcharge	150.00	250.00
C2	O3	20ö on 2ö org	11.00	14.00
a.		Inverted surcharge	150.00	250.00
C3	O3	50ö on 4ö vio	45.00	50.00
a.		Inverted surcharge	150.00	325.00

Wmkd. Crown. (180)

C4	O3	20ö on 2ö org	1,500.	1,600.
C5	O3	50ö on 4ö vio	150.00	150.00

Airplane over Stockholm AP2

Perf. 10 Vertically.

1930, May 9		Engraved	Unwmkd.	
C6	AP2	10ö dp bl	50	1.00
C7	AP2	50ö dk vio	75	1.50

Flying Swans AP3

1942-53		Perf. 12½ on 3 Sides		
C8	AP3	20k brt ultra ('53)	7.00	1.00
a.		Bklt. pane of 20 ('53)	600.00	
b.		Bklt. pane of 10 ('68)	70.00	
c.		Perf. on 4 sides	80.00	13.00
d.		As "c", bklt. pane of 10	1,250.	

SWEDEN—SWITZERLAND

POSTAGE DUE STAMPS.

D1

Typographed.

1874			Perf. 14	Unwmkd.	
J1	D1	1ö	black	37.50	30.00
J2	D1	3ö	rose	37.50	30.00
J3	D1	5ö	brown	37.50	30.00
J4	D1	6ö	yellow	80.00	70.00
J5	D1	12ö	pale red	8.50	6.00
J6	D1	20ö	blue	55.00	37.50
J7	D1	24ö	violet	300.00	225.00
J8	D1	24ö	gray	42.50	35.00
J9	D1	30ö	dk grn	42.50	35.00
J10	D1	50ö	brown	75.00	37.50
J11	D1	1k	bl & bis	140.00	65.00

1877–86				Perf. 13	
J12	D1	1ö	blk ('80)	3.50	4.50
J13	D1	3ö	rose	6.50	6.50
J14	D1	5ö	brown	4.50	4.50
J15	D1	6ö	yellow	4.50	4.50
a.		Printed on both sides		650.00	
J16	D1	12ö	pale red ('82)	9.00	13.00
J17	D1	20ö	pale bl ('78)	6.00	4.00
J18	D1	24ö	red lil ('86)	17.00	17.00
a.		24ö	violet ('84)	17.00	17.00
J19	D1	24ö	gray lil ('82)	85.00	75.00
J20	D1	30ö	yel grn	6.00	4.50
J21	D1	50ö	yel brn	9.00	6.00
J22	D1	1k	bl & bis	37.50	30.00

Nos. J12–J17, J19–J22 exist imperf.

Price, pairs, each $300.

STAMPS FOR CITY POSTAGE.

S1

Perf. 14 x 13½

1856–62		Typographed	Unwmkd.	
LX1	S1	(1sk or 3ö) blk	525.00	325.00
LX2	S1	(3ö) bis brn ('62)	400.00	350.00

From 1856 to 1858 No. LX1 was sold at 1sk, from 1858 to 1862 at 3ö.

No. LX1 was reprinted three times with perf. 14, once with perf. 13. No. LX2 was reprinted once with each perforation. Price of lowest-cost Perf. 14 reprints, $200 each. Perf. 13, $160 each.

OFFICIAL STAMPS.

Coat of Arms
O1

Typographed.

1874–77			Perf. 14	Unwmkd.	
O1	O1	3ö	bister	40.00	17.00
a.		Imperf., pair		250.00	
O2	O1	4ö	gray ('77)	175.00	32.50
a.		Imperf., pair		325.00	
O3	O1	5ö	yel grn	175.00	30.00
a.		Imperf., pair		350.00	
O4	O1	6ö	lilac	225.00	40.00
a.		Imperf., pair		300.00	
O5	O1	6ö	gray	325.00	110.00
O6	O1	12ö	blue	90.00	3.50
a.		Imperf., pair		525.00	
O7	O1	20ö	pale red	500.00	65.00
a.		Imperf., pair		625.00	
O8	O1	24ö	yellow	450.00	25.00
a.		24ö org		450.00	25.00
b.		Imperf., pair		700.00	
O9	O1	30ö	pale brn	275.00	30.00
a.		Imperf., pair		500.00	
O10	O1	50ö	rose	400.00	80.00
a.		Imperf., pair		500.00	
O11	O1	1k	bl & bis	1,000.	55.00
a.		Imperf., pair		1,600.	

1881–93				Perf. 13	
O12	O1	2ö	org ('91)	2.50	2.50
a.		Imperf., pair		275.00	
O13	O1	3ö	bis brn	3.25	3.25
O14	O1	4ö	gray blk ('93)	2.75	35
a.		4ö gray ('82)		7.00	70
O15	O1	5ö	grn ('84)	3.50	25
O16	O1	6ö	red lil ('82)	27.50	32.50
a.		6ö lil ('81)		27.50	32.50
O17	O1	10ö	car ('85)	4.00	20
a.		Imperf., pair		275.00	
b.		10ö rose		35.00	1.20
c.		Imperf., pair (rose)		275.00	
O18	O1	12ö	blue	40.00	18.00
O19	O1	20ö	ver ('82)	140.00	2.50
O20	O1	20ö	dk bl ('91)	4.00	35
a.		Imperf., pair		50.00	
O21	O1	24ö	yellow	50.00	17.50
a.		24ö org		50.00	17.50
O22	O1	30ö	brown	22.50	60
O23	O1	50ö	pale rose	160.00	2.50
O24	O1	50ö	pale gray ('93)	20.00	2.50
a.		Imperf., pair		275.00	
O25	O1	1k	dk bl & yel brn	25.00	2.50

Surcharged in Dark Blue

1889

O26	O1	10ö on 12ö bl	18.00	20.00
a.		Invtd. surch.	325.00	450.00
b.		Perf. 14	1,700.	1,500.
O27	O1	10ö on 24ö yel	22.50	25.00
a.		Invtd. surch.	800.00	900.00
b.		Perf. 14	1,600.	1,500.

O3

Typographed

1910–12		Wmkd. Crown. (180)		
O28	O3	1ö	black	30	25
O29	O3	2ö	orange	2.75	3.50
O30	O3	4ö	pale vio	4.00	5.00
O31	O3	5ö	green	1.20	1.20
O32	O3	8ö	claret	1.20	1.20
O33	O3	10ö	red	20.00	1.00
O34	O3	15ö	red brn	1.60	1.00
O35	O3	20ö	dp bl	14.00	1.20
O36	O3	25ö	red org	14.00	2.25
O37	O3	30ö	chocolate	14.00	3.00
O38	O3	50ö	gray	14.00	3.00
O39	O3	1k	yellow	17.50	10.00
O40	O3	5k	cl, yel	22.50	8.00
		Nos. O28–O40 (13)	127.05	40.80

1910–19		Wmkd. Wavy Lines. (181)		
O41	O3	1ö	black	4.00	4.00
O42	O3	2ö	orange	30	15
O43	O3	3ö	pale brn	50	50
O44	O3	4ö	pale vio	30	30
O45	O3	5ö	green	12	10
O46	O3	7ö	gray grn	1.00	1.00
O47	O3	8ö	rose	22.50	30.00
O48	O3	10ö	red	20	10
O49	O3	12ö	rose red	20	20
O50	O3	15ö	org brn	20	20
O51	O3	20ö	dp bl	40	15
O52	O3	25ö	orange	2.00	20
O53	O3	30ö	chocolate	80	35
O54	O3	35ö	dk vio	1.50	70
O55	O3	50ö	gray	4.00	2.00
		Nos. O41–O55 (15)	38.02	40.45

Use of official stamps ceased on July 1, 1920.

PARCEL POST STAMPS.
Regular Issue of 1914
Surcharged **Kr.1.98**

1917	Perf. 13.	Wmkd. Crown. (180)		
Q1	A14	1.98k on 5k cl, yel	4.50	5.50
Q2	A14	2.12k on 5k cl, yel	4.50	5.50

SWITZERLAND
(swit'zẽr·lănd)
(Helvetia)

LOCATION—In central Europe, between France, Germany and Italy.
GOVT.—Republic.
AREA—15,944 sq. mi.
POP.—6,330,000 (estimated 1977).
CAPITAL—Bern.

100 Rappen or Centimes = 1 Franc

Unused prices of Nos. 1L1–3L1 are for stamps without gum.

CANTONAL ADMINISTRATION.
Zurich.
(zōor'ĭk; zū'rĭk)
A Canton of Switzerland.

Numerals of Value
A1 A2

Lithographed.
Red Vertical Lines.

1843		Imperf.	Unwmkd.	
1L1	A1	4r black	13,500.	12,500.
1L2	A2	6r black	2,750.	1,350.

1846 Red Horizontal Lines.

1L3	A1	4r black	12,000.	15,000.
1L4	A2	6r black	1,300.	1,200.

Five varieties of each value.

Reprints of the Zurich stamps show signs of wear and lack the red lines. Prices: 4r, $3,250; 6r, $1,200.

Coat of Arms
A3

1850		Imperf.	Unwmkd.	
1L5	A3	2½r blk & red	4,500.	3,500.

No. 1L5 was formerly attributed to Winterthur.

Geneva.
(jẽ·nē′vȧ)
A Canton of Switzerland

Coat of Arms
A1

Lithographed.

1843		Imperf.	Unwmkd.	
2L1	A1	10c yel grn	42,500.	35,900.
a.		Either half	15,000.	7,000.
b.		Stamp composed of right half at left side and left half at right side	60,000.	58,000.

A2 A3

1845–48				
2L2	A1	5c yel grn	2,000.	1,500.
2L3	A3	5c yel grn ('47)	1,350.	1,300.
2L4	A3	5c dk grn ('48)	3,000.	2,500.

Coat of Arms
A4 A5

1849–50				
2L5	A4	4c blk & red	27,500.	16,000.
2L6	A4	5c blk & red ('50)	1,650.	1,300.

1850
2L7	A5	5c blk & red	7,000.	3,500.

Nos. 2L5 and 2L6 were formerly attributed to Vaud and No. 2L7 to Neuchâtel.

ENVELOPE STAMP USED AS ADHESIVE.

E1

1849		Imperf.	Unwmkd.	
2LU1	E1	5c yel grn		16,500.

Price is for cut-out stamp used on cover. Price of entire envelope (1846), unused $350.00

Basel.
(bä′zĕl)
A Canton of Switzerland.

Dove of Basel
A1
Typo. & Embossed

1845		Imperf.	Unwmkd.	
3L1	A1	2½r blk, crim & bl	8,500.	8,250.

Proofs are black, vermilion and green.
Price $2,250.

FEDERAL ADMINISTRATION.

A10 A11

SWITZERLAND 653

Lithographed.
1850 Imperf. Unwmkd.

Full Black Frame Around Cross.
| 1 | A10 | 2½r blk & red | 1,650. | 1,200. |
| 2 | A11 | 2½r blk & red | 1,350. | 1,150. |

Without Frame Around Cross.
| 3 | A10 | 2½r blk & red | 3,500. | 2,000. |
| 4 | A11 | 2½r blk & red | 35,000. | 19,000. |

Forty types of each.

A12

A13

1850

Full Black Frame Around Cross.
5	A12	5r blk & red, bl	2,750.	1,100.
a.		5r blk & red, dk bl	2,850.	1,200.
6	A13	10r blk & red, yel		60,000.

No. 6 used, with only parts of frame around cross showing, price $120 to $450.

Without Frame Around Cross.
7	A12	5r blk & red lt bl	1,200.	400.00
a.		5r blk & red, dp bl	1,200.	400.00
b.		5r blk & red, pur bl	4,500.	2,000.
c.		5r blk & red, grnsh bl	1,300.	450.00
8	A13	10r blk & red, yel	675.00	100.00
a.		10r blk & red, buff	675.00	100.00
b.		10r blk & red, org	675.00	100.00
c.		Half used as 5r on cover		4,500.

1851

Full Blue Frame Around Cross.
| 9 | A12 | 5r lt bl & red | | 75,000. |

No. 9 used, with only parts of frame around cross showing, price $165 to $4000.

Without Frame Around Cross.
| 10 | A12 | 5r lt bl & red | 400.00 | 110.00 |
| a. | | 5r dk bl & red | 400.00 | 110.00 |

Forty types of each.

A14

A15

A16

1852

Colored Frame Around Cross.
11	A14	15r vermilion	5,500.	600.00
12	A15	15r vermilion	1,400.	110.00
13	A16	15c vermilion	8,250.	850.00

Ten types of each.
On October 1st, 1854, all stamps of the preceding issues were declared obsolete.

Prices of Nos. 14–40 are for copies which show three full frame lines. Those with fewer sell for half price or less. Copies with complete frame bring double the catalogue price or more.

Helvetia A17

1854 Embossed. Unwmkd.
Thin Paper. Fine Impressions.
Emerald Silk Threads.
14	A17	5r org brn	4,500.	1,250.
15	A17	5r red brn	400.00	75.00
16	A17	10r blue	500.00	27.50
17	A17	15r car rose	725.00	110.00
a.		15r pale rose	775.00	120.00
18	A17	40r pale yel grn	5,500.	900.00
19	A17	40r yel grn	800.00	175.00

Emerald Silk Threads.
Medium Thick Paper.
1854-55 Fine Impressions.
20	A17	5r pale yel brn	350.00	55.00
a.		5r bl	4,500.	5,500.
21	A17	10r blue	650.00	45.00
22	A17	15r rose	550.00	50.00
23	A17	20r pale org	850.00	75.00

Some authorities question whether No. 20a is an essay or an error.

1855-57 Mixed Silk Threads.
Medium Thick Paper.
Fine to Rough Impressions.
24	A17	5r yel brn (yel)	300.00	50.00
25	A17	5r dk brn (blk)	190.00	20.00
26	A17	10r mlky bl (red)	200.00	25.00
27	A17	10r bl (car)	160.00	19.00
a.		Thin paper	2,000.	200.00
28	A17	15r rose (bl)	300.00	37.50
29	A17	40r yel grn (mar)	600.00	50.00
30	A17	1fr lav (blk)	675.00	475.00
31	A17	1fr lav (yel)	950.00	475.00
a.		Thin paper		2,750.

Thin (Emergency) Paper.
Rough Impressions.
1857 Green Silk Threads.
32	A17	5r pale gray brn	2,100.	900.00
33	A17	15r pale dl rose	1,500.	225.00
34	A17	20r pale dl rose	1,500.	125.00

Thick Ordinary Paper.
Rough Impressions.
1858-62 Green Silk Threads.
35	A17	2r gray	200.00	300.00
a.		One and one-half used as 3r on newspaper or wrapper		7,500.
36	A17	5r brown	120.00	7.00
a.		5r blk brn	135.00	20.00
b.		Half used as 2½r on wrapper or cover		700.00
37	A17	10r dk bl	135.00	6.00
38	A17	15r dk rose	175.00	25.00
39	A17	20r dk org	275.00	32.50
40	A17	40r dk yel grn	275.00	40.00

Helvetia—A18 Wmk. 182
This is not a true watermark, having been impressed after the paper was manufactured.

Wmkd. Cross in Oval. (182)
1862-63 Embossed Perf. 11½
White Wove Paper.
41	A18	2c gray	42.50	1.75
42	A18	3c black	6.00	57.50
43	A18	5c dk brn	1.40	25
a.		5c bis brn	55.00	35
b.		5c gray brn	17.50	1.00
c.		Double embossing, one inverted	2,000.	350.00
d.		Double impression of lower left "5"		650.00
44	A18	10c blue	190.00	35
a.		Double embossing, one inverted		6,500.
45	A18	20c orange	1.25	1.10
a.		20c yel	35.00	1.10
46	A18	30c vermilion	550.00	16.00
47	A18	40c green	550.00	32.50
48	A18	60c bronze	450.00	125.00
50	A18	1fr gold	13.00	47.50
a.		1fr brnz	600.00	275.00

1867-78
52	A18	2c bis brn	1.40	35
a.		2c red brn	450.00	185.00
53	A18	10c carmine	1.75	25
54	A18	15c lemon	2.25	15.00
55	A18	25c bl grn	1.10	1.40
a.		25c yel grn	6.00	4.00
b.		Double embossing, one inverted		500.00
56	A18	30c ultra	240.00	3.25
a.		30c bl	1,000.	150.00
58	A18	40c gray	1.10	55.00
59	A18	50c violet	30.00	27.50

1881 Granite Paper.
60	A18	2c bister	35	5.00
a.		Dbl. embossing, one inverted	250.00	
61	A18	5c brown	12	2.00
a.		Double embossing, one inverted	20.00	300.00
b.		Double impression of lower left "5"		650.00
62	A18	10c rose	2.50	2.25
63	A18	15c lemon	5.75	175.00
64	A18	20c orange	32	62.50
65	A18	25c green	18	52.50
66	A18	40c gray	25	1,750.
67	A18	50c dp vio	5.75	235.00
b.		Double embossing, one inverted	175.00	2,500.
68	A18	1fr gold	6.50	525.00

The granite paper contains fragments of blue and red silk threads.
Forged cancellations are found frequently on Nos. 42 to 68.
All stamps of the preceding issues were declared obsolete on October 1st, 1883. Some of the remainders of Nos 41-68 were overprinted "AUSSER KURS" (Obsolete) diagonally in black.

Numeral A19

1882-99 Typographed Perf. 11½
69	A19	2c bister	80	35
70	A19	3c gray brn	1.40	3.25
a.		3c gray	16.00	15.00
71	A19	5c maroon	9.00	10
a.		Tête bêche pair		7,500.
72	A19	5c dp grn ('99)	5.75	8
a.		Bklt. pane of 6		
73	A19	10c red	3.75	5
a.		10c car	6.00	25
b.		10c lt rose	250.00	4.50
c.		As #73, bklt. pane of 6		
74	A19	12c ultra	4.50	22
a.		12c chlky bl	11.00	75
b.		12c grnsh bl	550.00	25.00
75	A19	15c yellow	100.00	13.50
76	A19	15c vio ('89)	45.00	1.00

1882 White Paper.
77	A19	2c bister	300.00	250.00
78	A19	5c maroon	325.00	45.00
79	A19	10c rose	1,650.	50.00
80	A19	12c chlky bl	125.00	16.00
81	A19	15c yellow	200.00	225.00

See also Nos. 113–118.

Helvetia (Large numerals) A20

Helvetia (Small numerals) A21

1882-1904 Engraved Perf. 11½
82	A20	20c orange	150.00	2.00
83	A20	25c green	70.00	1.50
84	A20	40c gray	80.00	16.50
85	A21	40c gray ('04)	32.50	7.25
86	A20	50c blue	125.00	8.50
87	A20	1fr claret	225.00	2.50
88	A20	3fr yel brn ('91)	190.00	10.00

1888 Perf. 9½
89	A20	20c orange	600.00	40.00
90	A20	25c yel grn	135.00	6.75
91	A20	40c gray	600.00	425.00
92	A20	50c blue	1,000.	190.00
93	A20	1fr claret	800.00	32.50

1891-99 Perf. 11½x11
82a	A20	20c orange	35.00	1.00
83a	A20	25c green	10.00	60
94	A20	25c bl ('99)	10.00	65
95	A20	30c red brn ('92)	30.00	1.00
84a	A20	40c gray	60.00	2.25
86a	A20	50c blue	32.50	3.00
96	A20	50c grn ('99)	42.50	5.25
87a	A20	1fr claret	37.50	1.75
88a	A20	1fr carmine	72.50	4.50
88	A20	3fr yel brn	150.00	16.50

1901-03 Perf. 11½x12
82b	A20	20c orange	27.50	60
94a	A20	25c blue	10.00	60
95a	A20	30c red brn	40.00	1.00
84b	A20	40c gray	60.00	9.50
96a	A20	50c green	42.50	2.75
87b	A20	1fr claret	1,900.	160.00
97a	A20	1fr car ('03)	450.00	15.00
88b	A20	3fr yel brn	180.00	12.00

Some clichés in the plate of the 25c have been retouched. The retouched stamps are found in both green and blue printings.

UPU Allegory A22

1900 Perf. 11½
98	A22	5c gray grn	30.00	70
99	A22	10c car rose	11.50	60
100	A22	25c blue	17.50	14.00

Re-engraved.
101	A22	5c gray grn	3.50	65
102	A22	10c car rose	40.00	16.50
103	A22	25c blue	1,200.	6,500.

Universal Postal Union, 25th anniversary.
The impression of the re-engraved stamps is much clearer, especially the horizontally lined background. The figures of value are lined instead of being solid.

SWISS STAMPS

(The "Aristocrats" of Philately)

for the

Discriminating Collector

Swiss stamps are a source of great philatelic pleasure to the collector but are also an international investment asset, both for this generation and for those to come. Our stocks have been built up over the past 37 years, during which time we have become the **leading Specialists in the English-speaking world** in everything connected with Swiss stamps.

Although dealing entirely in Swiss stamps, we are a British firm-no need to correspond in a foreign language!

WE PUBLISH OUR OWN SPECIALISED SWITZERLAND CATALOGUE HANDBOOK IN ENGLISH

The 1984/85 Twenty-seventh Edition is now available:
$ 7.00 Seamail Post free
$10.00 Airmail Post free

This superb Catalogue contains much information not available in any other English language catalogue and information not even available in German language catalogues!

Whether you need our services to fill the simplest inexpensive gaps in your collection; whether you are the most advanced specialist; or any shade in between these two extremes: you will find something of interest in our stock, and, this is very important, at very competitive prices.

Our great strength is the ability to supply items other dealers cannot.

To name a few of our specialities: CLASSICS, PROOFS, ESSAYS, HOTEL POSTS, PIONEER AIRMAILS, STAMP BOOKLETS, VARIETIES (retouches, double prints, errors, etc.) MULTIPLES, REVENUES, etc., etc. All are available in our APPROVAL SERVICE, the finest in the world for Swiss stamps!

For your convenience our sendings are fully insured in transit both ways.

American Express, MasterCard, Bankamericard (VISA), or your personal check are accepted.

P.S. Write for your free sample copy of our magazine "THE SWISS PHILATELIST."

H.L. KATCHER

The Amateur Collector Ltd

"The Swiss Specialists"
P.O. Box 242, Highgate, London N6 4LW, England
PTS, BPA, SPA

Efficient
WANT LIST SERVICE
for
SWITZERLAND

Careful and prompt settlement of want-lists at fair market prices.

Extensive price-list available against 2 IRC.

HANS P. WALSER
Wiesriedtweg 3
8630 RUTI
SWITZERLAND

Member of IFSDA - APS

SWITZERLAND

FREE PRICE LIST
of NH, HINGED AND USED SETS
Top quality at realistic prices. Complete stock of singles from sets, covers, 19th Century including Cantonals, and all specialized material at your disposal.
Want lists and inquiries invited

─ SPECIAL OFFER ─
1958-1983 Complete
(w/o Officials) F-VF NH
Scott Nos. 273a-278a, 365-743
371a, B252-B504, C46, CB1
Regularly priced as year sets
$476.00—NET $428.40 ppd.
(Individual years listed on our price list)

SATISFACTION GUARANTEED!
CREDIT CARDS ACCEPTED
NY RESIDENTS ADD SALES TAX

ZUMSTEIN 1982 SPECIALIZED CATALOGUE – Current Edition 950 pages of valuable information on Swiss and Liechtenstein stamps, in German, much not found in *any other* catalogue.
Regularly $45.00. Only $25.00 ppd.! Catalogue FREE with all Swiss orders over $250.00!!!

WE BUY SWITZERLAND! TOP PRICES PAID!
call or write:
Henry Gitner Philatelists, Inc.
formerly Frank Geiger Philatelist, Inc.
P.O. Box 3077
(35 Mountain Ave.)
Middletown, NY 10940
(914) 343-5151

SWITZERLAND 655

Helvetia Types of 1882–1904

Wmk. 183

Wmkd. Greek Cross. (183)

1905 *Perf. 11½x11*

White Paper.

105	A20	20c orange	4.25	1.00
106	A20	25c blue	6.00	3.00
107	A20	30c brown	4.50	1.10
a.		"HELVETTA"	165.00	275.00
108a	A21	40c gray	100.00	55.00
109	A20	50c green	40.00	3.00
110	A20	1fr carmine	110.00	1.50
111	A20	3fr yel brn	325.00	65.00

Some clichés in the plates of the 20c, 25c, 30c, 50c and 3fr have been retouched.

1906 Re-engraved *Perf. 11½x11*

112	A20	25c pale bl	5.50	80

In the re-engraved stamp the stars are larger and the background below "FRANCO" is of horizontal or horizontal and vertical crossed lines, instead of horizontal and curved lines.

1906 *Perf. 11½*

112a	A20	25c pale bl	75.00	3.25
108	A21	40c gray	25.00	4.00

1907 *Perf. 11½x12*

105a	A20	20c orange	6.25	3.00
109a	A20	50c green	40.00	5.00
110a	A20	1fr carmine	95.00	3.75
111a	A20	3fr yel brn	350.00	95.00

Numeral Type of 1882–99

Granite Paper.

1905 Typographed *Perf. 11½*

113	A19	2c dl bis	2.25	70
114	A19	3c gray brn	2.75	*20.00*
115	A19	5c green	2.75	15
a.		Booklet pane of 6		
116	A19	10c scarlet	2.75	15
a.		Booklet pane of 6		
117	A19	12c ultra	3.00	25
118	A19	15c brn vio	62.50	3.75
		Nos. 113-118 (6)	76.00	*25.00*

Helvetia Types of 1882–1904

Granite Paper.

1907 Engraved *Perf. 11½x12*

119	A20	20c orange	2.75	1.50
120	A20	25c blue	9.00	3.25
121	A20	30c red brn	5.00	3.25
122	A21	40c gray	18.50	11.00
a.		Helvetia without diadem	250.00	*500.00*
123	A20	50c gray grn	6.00	3.25
124	A20	1fr carmine	21.00	1.50
125a	A20	3fr yel brn		*11,000.*

There are retouched clichés in the plates of the 20c, 30c, 50c, 1fr and 3fr.

Perf. 11½x11

120a	A20	25c dp bl	9.00	2.50
121a	A20	30c red brn	180.00	*300.00*
122b	A21	40c gray		*11,000.*
124a	A20	1fr carmine		*4,250.*
125	A20	3fr yel brn	140.00	21.00

William Tell's Son
A23

Helvetia
A24

Helvetia
A25

Granite Paper.

1907–25 Typographed *Perf. 11½*

126	A23	2c pale bis	25	25
127	A23	3c lil brn	25	*6.50*
128	A23	5c yel grn	2.75	12
a.		Booklet pane of 6	25.00	
129	A24	10c rose red	1.50	20
a.		Booklet pane of 6	17.50	
130	A24	12c ocher	55	*2.00*
131	A24	15c red vio	2.50	3.75
132	A25	20c red & yel ('08)	2.50	35
133	A25	25c dp bl ('08)	2.25	25
a.		Tête bêche pair	37.50	*100.00*
b.		Booklet pane of 6	20.00	
134	A25	30c yel brn & pale grn ('08)	2.25	15
135	A25	35c yel grn & yel ('08)	2.25	25
136	A25	40c red vio & yel ('08)	13.50	35
a.		Designer's name in full on the rock ('08)	6.50	*40.00*
137	A25	40c dp bl ('21)	4.50	55
a.		40c lt bl ('22)	1.50	10
138	A25	40c red vio & grn ('25)	32.50	15
139	A25	50c dp grn & pale grn ('08)	6.75	12
140	A25	60c brn org & buff ('18)	7.25	10
141	A25	70c dk brn & buff ('08)	135.00	3.75
142	A25	70c vio & buff ('24)	14.00	1.00
143	A25	80c sl & buff ('15)	7.25	30
144	A25	1fr dp cl & pale grn ('08)	9.50	20
145	A25	3fr bis & yel ('08)	525.00	1.10
		Nos. 126-145 (20)	772.30	*21.44*

No. 136 has two leaves and "CL" below sword hilt. No. 136a has three leaves and designer's full name below hilt.

1933 With Grilled Gum

135a	A25	35c yel grn & yel	1.65	3.50
138a	A25	40c red vio & grn	27.50	25
139a	A25	50c dp grn & pale grn	6.50	35
140a	A25	60c brn org & buff	11.50	20
142a	A25	70c vio & buff	16.00	1.65
143a	A25	80c sl & buff	8.00	1.25
144a	A25	1fr dp cl & pale grn	12.00	1.75
		Nos. 135a-144a (7)	83.15	8.95

"Grilled" Gum

In 1930–44 many Swiss stamps were treated with a light grilling process, applied with the gumming to counteract the tendency to curl. It resembles a faint grill of vertical and horizontal ribs covering the entire back of the stamp, and can be seen after the gum has been removed. Listings of the grilled gum varieties begin with No. 135a.

William Tell's Son—A26

Bow-string in front of stock.

1909 *Perf. 11½, 12*

Granite Paper

146	A26	2c bister	35	50
a.		Tête bêche pair	3.25	*15.00*
b.		Bklt. pane of 6	11.00	
147	A26	3c dk vio	20	*7.00*
148	A26	5c green	3.00	15
a.		Tête bêche pair	19.00	32.50
b.		Bklt. pane of 6	27.50	

1910-17 First Redrawing.

Bow-string behind stock. Thin loop above crossbow. Letters of "HELVETIA" without serifs.

Granite Paper

149	A26	2c bis ('10)	6.00	2.00
150	A26	3c dk vio ('10)	10	10
a.		Tête bêche pair	3.50	5.00
b.		Booklet pane of 6	11.50	
151	A26	3c brn org ('17)	10	15
a.		Tête bêche pair	6.50	7.00
152	A26	5c grn ('10)	35.00	2.75
a.		Tête bêche pair	165.00	210.00
b.		Bklt. pane of 6	275.00	

1911-30 Second Redrawing.

Bow-string behind stock. Thick loop above crossbow. Letters of "HELVETIA" have serifs.

7½ CENTIMES.

Type I. Top of "7" is ½mm. thick. The "1" of "½" has only traces of serifs. The two base plates of the statue are of even thickness.

Type II. Top of "7" is 1mm. thick. The "1" of "½" has distinct serifs. The upper base plate is thinner than the lower.

Granite Paper

153	A26	2c bis ('11)	10	12
a.		Tête bêche pair	3.75	5.00
b.		Booklet pane of 6		
154	A26	2½c cl ('18)	10	*60*
155	A26	2½c ol, *buff* ('28)	35	*1.35*
156	A26	3c ultra, *buff* ('30)	1.25	*4.00*
157	A26	5c grn ('11)	90	12
a.		Tête bêche pair	3.75	*7.50*
b.		Bklt. pane of 6	10.00	
158	A26	5c org, *buff* ('21)	12	10
a.		Bklt. pane of 6 (5 No. 158 + 1 No. 168)	10.00	*15.00*
159	A26	5c gray vio, *buff* ('24)	10	10
a.		Bklt. pane of 6 (5 No. 159 + 1 No. 168)	6.00	*10.00*
160	A26	5c red vio, *buff* ('27)	10	10
a.		Bklt. pane 6 (5 No. 160 + 1 No. 168)	17.50	*27.50*
161	A26	5c dk grn, *buff* ('30)	25	15
a.		Bklt. pane 6 (5 No. 161 + 1 No. 169)	15.00	*25.00*
162	A26	7½c gray (I) ('18)	1.00	15
a.		Tête bêche pair	17.50	*40.00*
b.		Booklet pane of 6	11.00	11.00
c.		7½c sl (II)	1.75	60
163	A26	7½c dp grn, *buff* (I) ('28)	15	*1.75*
		Nos. 153-163 (11)	4.42	*8.54*

With Grilled Gum

1933

156a	A26	3c ultra, *buff*	1.50	*4.50*
161b	A26	5c dk grn, *buff*	40	75

Helvetia
A27

William Tell
A28

1909 Granite Paper

164	A27	10c carmine	70	12
a.		Tête bêche pair	3.25	*7.50*
b.		Booklet pane of 6	8.00	
165	A27	12c bis brn	70	15
166	A27	15c red vio	30.00	75

Granite Paper.

1914-30 *Perf. 11½.*

TEN CENTIMES.

Type I. Bust 16½mm. high. "HELVETIA" 15½mm. wide. Cross bar of "H" at middle of the letter.

Type II. Bust 15mm. high. "HELVETIA" 15mm. wide. Cross bar of "H" above middle of the letter.

167	A28	10c red, *buff* (type II)	60	10
a.		10c red, *buff* (type I)	1.75	*17.50*
b.		Tête bêche pair (II)	4.00	6.00
c.		Booklet pane of 6	5.50	5.50
d.		Bklt. pane 6 (5 No. 167 + 1 No. 172)	13.50	13.50
168	A28	10c grn, *buff* (type II) ('21)	12	6
a.		Tête bêche pair	1.50	1.00
b.		Booklet pane of 6	2.75	2.75
168C	A28	10c bl grn, *buff* (type II) ('28)	10	8
d.		Tête bêche pair	2.00	2.00
e.		Booklet pane of 6	2.50	2.50
169	A28	10c vio, *buff* (type II) ('30)	50	8
a.		Tête bêche pair	7.50	2.50
b.		Booklet pane of 6	7.50	7.50
170	A28	12c brn, *buff*	40	*3.00*
171	A28	13c ol grn, *buff* ('15)	1.50	30
172	A28	15c vio, *buff*	2.75	8
a.		Booklet pane of 6	15.00	15.00
b.		15c dk vio, *buff*	17.50	1.00
c.		Tête bêche pair	130.00	120.00
173	A28	15c brn red, *buff* ('28)	2.00	1.40
174	A28	20c red vio, *buff* ('21)	1.75	10
a.		Tête bêche pair	6.00	4.25
b.		Booklet pane of 6	13.50	13.50
175	A28	20c ver, *buff* ('24)	1.25	20
a.		Tête bêche pair	5.00	5.50
b.		Bklt. pane of 6	12.50	12.50
176	A28	20c car, *buff* ('25)	50	8
a.		Tête bêche pair	3.00	2.50
b.		Booklet pane of 6	9.00	9.00
177	A28	25c ver, *buff* ('21)	1.25	1.40
178	A28	25c car, *buff* ('22)	1.00	45
179	A28	25c brn, *buff* ('25)	2.00	80
180	A28	30c dp bl, *buff* ('24)	10.00	10
		Nos. 167-180 (15)	25.72	*8.23*

With Grilled Gum

1932–33

169c	A28	10c vio, *buff*	1.25	15
173a	A28	15c brn red, *buff* ('33)	40.00	12.00
176c	A28	20c car, *buff*	10.00	1.25
179a	A28	25c brn, *buff* ('33)	90.00	14.00
180a	A28	30c dp bl, *buff*	60.00	90

The Mythen—A29

The Rütli—A30

The Jungfrau—A31

1914–30 Engr. Granite Paper

181	A29	3fr dk grn	1,450.	3.50
182	A29	3fr red ('18)	175.00	65
183	A30	5fr dp ultra	40.00	1.50
184	A31	10fr dl vio	190.00	1.75
185	A31	10fr gray grn ('30)	375.00	35.00
		Nos. 181-185 (5)	2,230.	42.40

See also No. 206.

Stamps of 1909-14 Surcharged

1 (a) — 13 (b) — 13 (c)

1915

186	A26 (a)	1c on 2c bis	10	15
187	A27 (b)	13c on 12c bis brn	25	*5.00*
188	A28 (c)	13c on 12c brn, *buff*	25	80

SWITZERLAND

No. 141			
Surcharged		**80**	**80**
189 A25	80c on 70c dk brn & buff	37.50	4.25
a.	Upper loop of right 8 broken	150.00	325.00

Significant of Peace
A32

"Peace"
A33

"Dawn of Peace"
A34

1919, Aug. 1   Typo.   Perf. 11½   Unwmkd.

190	A32	7½c ol db & blk	45	1.25
191	A33	10c red & yel	60	3.00
192	A34	15c vio & yel	1.75	1.10

Commemorating Peace after World War I.

Stamps of 1910–18
Surcharged in Black, Red or Dark Blue

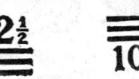

1921   Wmkd. Greek Cross. (183)

193	A26 (e) 2½c on 3c org (Bl)	10	12
a.	Tête bêche pair	85	3.00
b.	Inverted surcharge	550.00	1,250.
c.	Dbl. surch.	425.00	600.00
194	A26 (e) 5c on 2c bis (R)	15	1.25
a.	Dbl. surch.		
195	A26 (e) 5c on 7½c gray (I) (R)	12	15
a.	Tête bêche pair	11.00	42.50
b.	Double surcharge	300.00	350.00
c.	5c on 7½c sl (II)	2,000.	3,000.
d.	Booklet pane of 6	2.25	2.25
196	A28 (f) 10c on 13c ol grn, buff (R)	20	1.00
a.	Double surcharge	300.00	350.00
197	A28 (f) 20c on 15c vio, buff (Bk)	65	1.30
a.	Tête bêche pr.	3.50	40.00
b.	Dbl. surch.	475.00	600.00
c.	Booklet pane of 6	8.00	15.00
198	A28 (f) 20c on 15c vio, buff (Bl)	2.00	2.00
b.	Double surcharge	475.00	600.00
	Nos. 193-198 (6)	3.22	5.82

A35   A36

1921   Red Surcharge.

| 199 | A35 | 20c on 25c dp bl | 25 | 40 |
| a. | Tête bêche pair | 1.65 | 7.00 |

1924   Typographed   Perf. 11½
Granite Paper, Surface Colored.

200	A36	90c grn & red, grn	20.00	70
201	A36	1.20fr brn rose & red, rose	8.00	1.10
b.	"HFLVETIA"	25.00	85.00
202	A36	1.50fr bl & red, bl	22.50	1.25
203	A36	2fr gray blk & red, gray	90.00	1.10

With Grilled Gum
1933

200a	A36	90c grn & red, grn	22.50	55
201a	A36	1.20fr brn rose & red, rose	45.00	55
202a	A36	1.50fr bl & red, bl	25.00	90
203a	A36	2fr gray blk & red, gray	55.00	1.50

Building in Bern, Location of 1st
U.P.U. Congress, 1874
A37   A38

1924, Oct. 9   Engr.   Wmk. 183
Granite Paper.

| 204 | A37 | 20c vermilion | 25 | 60 |
| 205 | A38 | 30c dl bl | 70 | 3.00 |

Issued to commemorate the 50th anniversary of the founding of the Universal Postal Union.

The Rütli
A39

Type of 1914 Issue

1928   Re-engraved.   Perf. 11½

| 206 | A39 | 5fr blue | 185.00 | 2.50 |
| a. | Imperf., pair | | 10,000. |

In the re-engraved stamp the picture is clearer and lighter than on No. 183. "HELVETIA" is in smaller letters. The names at foot of the stamp are "Grasset—J. Sprenger" instead of "E. GRASSET—A. BURKHARD."

Nos. 155 and 163 Surcharged

1930, June   Perf. 11½

| 207 | A26 | 3c on 2½c ol grn, buff | 10 | 1.00 |
| 208 | A26 | 5c on 7½c dp grn, buff | 15 | 3.25 |

The Mythen
A40

1931   Engraved   Granite Paper.

| 209 | A40 | 3fr org brn | 75.00 | 2.25 |

Dove on Broken Sword
A41

"Peace"
A42

1932, Feb. 2   Typo.   Perf. 11½
Granite Paper.

210	A41	5c pck bl	20	20
211	A41	10c orange	25	7
212	A41	20c cerise	30	7
213	A41	30c ultra	2.25	55
214	A41	60c ol brn	22.50	90

Photogravure.
Unwmkd.

| 215 | A42 | 1fr ol gray & bl | 27.50 | 6.50 |
| | Nos. 210-215 (6) | 53.00 | 8.29 |

Issued to commemorate the International Disarmament Conference at Geneva in February, 1932.

Louis Favre   Alfred Escher
A43   A44

Emil Welti
A45

Wmkd. Greek Cross. (183)

1932, May 31   Engr.   Perf. 11½
Granite Paper.

216	A43	10c red brn	10	15
217	A44	20c vermilion	15	15
218	A45	30c dp ultra	30	1.10

Issued in commemoration of the fiftieth anniversary of the completion of the St. Gotthard tunnel. Nos. 216 to 218 exist imperforate.

Staubbach Falls   Mt. Pilatus
A46   A47

Chillon Castle   Rhone Glacier
A48   A49

St. Gotthard   Via Mala   Rhine
Railroad   Gorge   Falls
A50   A51   A52

1934, July 2   Typo.   Perf. 11½
Granite Paper.

219	A46	3c olive	20	1.40
220	A47	5c emerald	20	7
a.	Tête bêche pair	2.00	1.75
b.	Booklet pane of 6	4.00	
221	A48	10c brt vio	30	7
a.	Tête bêche pair	2.00	1.50
b.	Booklet pane of 6	2.50	
222	A49	15c orange	40	1.00
a.	Tête bêche pair	2.50	4.50
b.	Booklet pane of 6	8.00	

223	A50	20c red	60	10
a.	Tête bêche pair	3.75	3.50
b.	Booklet pane of 6	3.50	
224	A51	25c brown	12.00	3.50
225	A52	30c ultra	40.00	60
	Nos. 219-225 (7)	53.70	6.74

Souvenir Sheet.

A52a

1934, Sept. 29

| 226 | A52a | Sheet of four | 675.00 | 850.00 |

No. 226 was issued in connection with the Swiss National Philatelic Exhibition at Zurich, Sept. 29 to Oct. 7, 1934. It contains one each of Nos. 220-223. Size: 62x72mm.

Staubbach Falls   Mt. Pilatus
A53   A54

Chillon Castle   Rhone Glacier
A55   A56

St. Gotthard   Via Mala
Railroad   Gorge
A57   A58

Rhine Falls   Balsthal Pass
A59   A60

Alpine Lake of Säntis
A61

Two types of 10c red violet:
I. Shading inside "0" of 10 has only vertical lines.
II. Shading in "0" includes two diagonal lines.

Engraved.
1936-42   Perf. 11½.   Unwmkd.

| 227 | A53 | 3c olive | 15 | 13 |

SWITZERLAND

228	A54	5c bl grn	15	5
a.		Tête bêche pair	80	80
b.		Booklet pane of 6	1.25	
c.		Bklt. pane of 10	42.50	
229	A55	10c red vio (I)	1.10	15
a.		Tête bêche pair	3.50	4.75
b.		Booklet pane of 6	5.00	
c.		Type II	35	5
230	A55	10c dk red brn ('39)	15	6
a.		Tête bêche pair	2.00	2.00
230B	A55	10c org brn ('42)	15	5
a.		Booklet pane of 6	1.25	
d.		Tête bêche pair	70	90
231	A56	15c orange	40	45
232	A57	20c carmine	5.25	8
a.		Tête bêche pair	25.00	32.50
b.		Bklt. pane of 6	40.00	
233	A58	25c lt brn	60	35
234	A59	30c ultra	1.00	8
235	A60	35c yel grn	1.00	45
236	A61	40c gray	5.25	5
		Nos. 227-236 (11)	15.20	1.87

Three types of the 20c.
See also Nos. 316 to 321.

With Grilled Gum

1936-40

227a	A53	3c olive	20	55
228d	A54	5c bl grn	12	5
229d	A55	10c red vio (I)	65	5
e.		Type II	35	5
230e	A55	10c dk red brn ('40)	1.75	14.00
231a	A56	15c orange	35	20
232c	A57	20c carmine	5.25	5
233a	A58	25c lt brn	60	70
234a	A59	30c ultra	1.10	5
235a	A60	35c yel grn	1.10	55
236a	A61	40c gray	5.75	5
		Nos. 227a-236a (10)	16.87	16.35

Mobile Post Office
A62

1937, Sept. 5   Photogravure
Granite Paper.

237	A62	10c blk & yel	28	20

No. 237 was sold exclusively by the traveling post office. It exists on two kinds of granite paper. See No. 307 for type A62 redrawn.

View of Labor Building from
Lake Geneva
A63

Palace of League of Nations
A64

Main Building,
Palace of League of Nations
A65

Labor Building and
Albert Thomas Monument
A66

1938, May 2   Perf. 11½
Granite Paper

238	A63	20c red & buff	20	10
239	A64	30c bl & lt bl	55	20
240	A65	60c brn & buff	2.25	70
241	A66	1fr blk & buff	9.00	12.00

Issued in commemoration of the opening of Assembly Hall of the Palace of the League of Nations.

Souvenir Sheet.

A67

Engraved and Typographed.
Granite Paper.
Perf. 11½

1938, Sept. 17   Unwmkd.

242	A67	Sheet of 3	50.00	40.00
a.		10c on 65c gray bl & dp bl	27.50	25.00
b.		20c red (A68)	3.50	2.50

Issued to commemorate the National Philatelic Exhibition at Aarau, Sept. 17-25, 1938, and the 25th anniversary of Swiss air mail. The sheet contains two of No. 243 and a 10c on 65c similar to No. C22, with gray marginal inscriptions. Size: 74x 87mm.

No. 242a is type AP4, but redrawn, with wing tips 1½mm. from side frame lines; overall size 37x20½mm.; no watermark. On No. C22, wing tips touch frame lines; size is 36x21½mm.; Wmk. 183.

No. 242b is on granite paper, No. 243 on regular white paper.

Lake Lugano
A68

First Federal Pact, 1291
A69

Diet of Stans, 1481
A70

Citizens Voting—A71

1938, Sept. 17   Engr.   Perf. 11½

243	A68	20c red	15	5
a.		Tête bêche pair	1.00	70
b.		Booklet pane of 6	1.50	
c.		Grilled gum	25	10
d.		As "c", tête bêche pair	16.00	2.75

Granite Paper

244	A69	3fr brn car, *grnsh*	16.00	2.50
245	A70	5fr sl bl, *grnsh*	16.00	2.50
246	A71	10fr grn, *grnsh*	55.00	16.00

No. 243 is printed on ordinary paper. Nos. 244 to 246 are on granite surface-colored paper.

For type A68 in orange brown, see No. 318.

See also Nos. 284 to 286.

Deputation of
Trades and Professions
A72

Swiss Family—A73

Alpine Scenery—A74

1939, Feb. 1   Engr.   Perf. 11½

Inscribed in French.

247	A72	10c dl pur & red	28	10
248	A73	20c lake & red	60	10

Photogravure.

249	A74	30c dp bl & red	3.00	2.50

Engraved

Inscribed in German.

250	A72	10c dl pur & red	28	10
251	A73	20c lake & red	60	10

Photogravure.

252	A74	30c dp bl & red	3.00	1.50

Engraved.

Inscribed in Italian.

253	A72	10c dl pur & red	28	13
254	A73	20c lake & red	1.25	20

Photogravure.

255	A74	30c dp bl & red	3.50	4.50
		Nos. 247-255 (9)	12.79	9.23

National Exposition of 1939, Zurich.

Tree and Crossbow
A75

Granite Paper

1939, May 6   Photo.   Perf. 11½

Inscribed in French.

256	A75	5c dp grn	70	1.50
257	A75	10c gray brn	75	1.65
258	A75	20c brt car	1.20	1.65
259	A75	30c vio bl	3.25	6.50

Inscribed in German.

260	A75	5c dp grn	70	1.50
a.		Booklet pane of 10	52.50	
261	A75	10c gray brn	70	1.25
262	A75	20c brt car	1.25	1.50
263	A75	30c vio bl	2.75	5.00

Inscribed in Italian.

264	A75	5c dp grn	70	2.25
265	A75	10c gray brn	90	1.50
266	A75	20c brt car	1.25	2.00
267	A75	30c vio bl	3.50	6.75
		Nos. 256-267 (12)	17.65	33.05

National Exposition of 1939.
The 5c, 10c and 20c stamps in the three languages exist se-tenant in coils.

View of Geneva—A76
Perf. 11½

1939, Aug. 22   Photo.   Unwmkd.
Granite Paper

268	A76	20c red, car & buff	25	30
269	A76	30c bl, car & gray	50	1.25

Issued in commemoration of the 75th anniversary of the founding of the International Red Cross Society.

"The Three Swiss"   William Tell
A77   A78

Fighting Soldier   Dying Warrior
A79   A80

Standard Bearer   Ludwig Pfyffer
A81   A82

SWITZERLAND

Jürg Jenatsch A83

Francois de Reynold A84

Joachim Forrer A85

1941-59   Engraved   Perf. 11½
Granite Paper

270	A77	50c dp pur, *grnsh*	7.50	12
271	A78	60c red brn, *buff*	8.25	5
272	A79	70c rose vio, *pale lil*	6.00	70
273	A80	80c pale gray	1.75	10
a.		80c *pale lil* ('58)	1.25	5
274	A81	90c dk red, *pale rose*	1.75	5
a.		90c dk red, *buff* ('59)	1.50	30
275	A82	1fr dk grn, *grnsh*	2.00	5
276	A83	1.20fr red vio, *pale gray*	2.50	13
a.		1.20fr red vio, *pale lil* ('58)	1.75	25
277	A84	1.50fr dk bl, *buff*	3.00	22
278	A85	2fr mar, *pale rose*	4.00	12
a.		2fr mar, *buff* ('59)	3.50	30
		Nos. 270-278 (9)	36.75	1.54

Farmer Plowing—A86

1941, Mar. 21   Photogravure
Granite Paper

279	A86	10c brn & buff	10	12

Issued to publicize the National Agriculture Development Plan of 1941.

Masons, Knight and Bern Coat of Arms A87

1941, Sept. 6   Granite Paper

280	A87	10c multi	10	12

750th anniversary of Bern.

"In order to Endure, Reclaim Used Materials" Inscribed in French A88

Inscriptions: No. 282, German. No. 283, Italian.
Perf. 11½

1942, Mar. 21   Unwmkd.

281	A88	10c brn, red & gray bl	40	20
282	A88	10c brn, red & gray bl	8	10
283	A88	10c brn, red & gray bl	5.50	1.75
		Sheet of 25	90.00	300.00

Printed in sheets of 25, containing 8 No. 281, 12 No. 282 and 5 No. 283.

Types of 1938.
1942-55   Engraved
Cream-surfaced Granite Paper

284	A69	3fr brn car ('55)	8.50	25
a.		Cream paper	35.00	40
285	A70	5fr sl bl ('55)	5.00	40
a.		Cream paper	24.00	40
286	A71	10fr grn ('55)	5.00	1.50
a.		Cream paper	35.00	80

The 1955 set is on cream-surfaced granite paper with white back, and blue and red fibers. The 1942 set is on colored-through cream paper with black and red fibers.

Zurich Stamps of 1843 A91

1943, Feb. 26

287	A91	10c blk & sal	10	12

Centenary of postage stamps of Switzerland.
See Nos. B130-B131.

Apollo Statue A94

1944, Mar. 21   Photogravure
Granite Paper

290	A94	10c org yel & gray blk	15	55
291	A94	20c cer & gray blk	25	55
292	A94	30c lt bl & gray blk	60	4.00

Olympic Jubilee.

Numeral of Value A95
Olive Branch—A96

Designs: 60c, Keys of peace. 80c, Horn of plenty. 1fr, Dove of peace. 2fr, Plowing. 3fr, Field of crocus. 5fr, Clasped hands. 10fr, Aged couple.

1945, May 9   Perf. 12   Unwmkd.
Granite Paper

293	A95	5c gray & grn	20	20
294	A95	10c gray & brn	35	20
295	A95	20c gray & car rose	60	20
296	A95	30c gray & ultra	1.25	2.00
297	A95	40c gray & org	1.60	7.50
298	A96	50c dk red	3.75	15.00
299	A96	60c dl gray	3.75	5.00
300	A96	80c sl grn	9.00	60.00
301	A96	1fr blue	18.50	65.00
302	A96	2fr red brn	52.50	120.00
		Engraved.		
303	A96	3fr dk sl grn, *buff*	50.00	45.00
304	A96	5fr brn lake, *buff*	250.00	300.00
305	A96	10fr rose vio, *buff*	250.00	110.00
		Nos. 293-305, B145 (14)	642.00	730.75

End of war in Europe.

Johann Heinrich Pestalozzi A104

1946, Jan. 12   Engr.   Perf. 11½

306	A104	10c rose vio	12	5

Issued to commemorate the 200th anniversary of the birth of J. H. Pestalozzi, educational reformer.

Mobile P.O. Type of 1937.
Redrawn.
1946, July 6   Photogravure
Granite Paper

307	A62	10c blk & yel	1.80	14

The designer's and printer's names are larger on the redrawn stamp. There are many minor differences in the two designs. Sizes: 1937, 37½x21 mm. 1946, 38x22½ mm.

First Swiss Steam Locomotive A105

Modern Steam Locomotive A106

Electric Gotthard Express A107

Electric Trains Passing on Bridge A108

1947, Aug. 6   Photo.   Perf. 11½
Granite Paper

308	A105	5c dk grn, blk & yel	20	40
309	A106	10c dk brn, gray & blk	30	10
310	A107	20c dk red & red	30	10
311	A108	30c dk bl & bl gray	1.20	2.00

Issued to commemorate the centenary of the opening of the first Swiss railroad, between Zurich and Baden.

Johann Rudolf Wettstein A109

Castle at Neuchatel—A110

"Helvetia"—A111

Symbol of Swiss Federal State A112

1948, Feb. 27
Granite Paper

312	A109	5c dp grn	10	27
313	A110	10c gray blk	12	10
314	A111	20c dk red	30	10
315	A112	30c dk bl & red	65	1.25

Issued to commemorate the tercentenary of the acknowledgment of independence of the Swiss Confederation, and the centenaries of the Neuchatel Revolution and the Swiss Federal State.
See Nos. B178a and B178b for 10c and 20c denominations, type A109.

Types of 1936-42 and

Grisons National Park A113

1948, Mar. 1   Engraved

316	A54	5c chocolate	20	7
a.		Tête bêche pair	1.50	1.65
317	A55	10c green	30	5
a.		Tête bêche pair	2.25	2.25
318	A68	20c org brn	60	5
a.		Tête bêche pair	2.75	2.75
319	A113	25c carmine	3.00	1.40
		Bklt. pane of 10	37.50	
320	A59	30c grnsh bl	12.50	1.50
321	A61	40c ultra	20.00	40
		Nos. 316-321 (6)	36.60	3.47

Figures Encircling Globe A114

SWITZERLAND

Designs: 25c, Globe and inscribed ribbon. 40c, Globe and pigeons.

Perf. 11½

1949, May 16   Photo.   Unwmkd.

322	A114	10c green	15	8
323	A114	25c dk red	80	6.00
324	A114	40c brt bl	1.10	2.50

Issued to commemorate the 75th anniversary of the formation of the Universal Postal Union.

Post Horn—A115

Horse Drawn Mail Coach
A116

Design: 30c, Post bus with trailer.

1949, May 16

325	A115	5c gray, yel & pink	10	20
326	A116	20c pur, gray & yel	40	20
327	A116	30c dk org brn, gray & yel	85	3.00

Issued to commemorate the centenary of the establishment of the Federal Post in Switzerland.

High Tension Conductors
A117

Viaducts
A118

Mountain Railway
A119

Rotary Snow Plow
A120

Reservoir, Grimsel
A121

Lake Dam
A122

Dam and Power Station
A123

Alpine Postal Road
A124

Harbor of the Rhine
A125

Suspension Railway
A126

Railway Viaduct
A127

Triangulation Point
A128

Two types of 20c:
I. Crosshatching ends evenly with top of "20." Three lines above curved rock.
II. Crosshatching extends slightly above "20." Two lines above rock.

Perf. 12x11½

1949, Aug. 1   Engr.   Unwmkd.

328	A117	3c gray	4.25	4.50
329	A118	5c orange	20	5
a.		Tête bêche pair	70	25
b.		Booklet pane of 4	1.25	1.25
c.		Booklet pane of 10		
330	A119	10c yel grn	20	5
a.		Tête bêche pair	55	25
b.		Booklet pane of 4	2.00	2.00
331	A120	15c aqua	25	5
332	A121	20c brn car (II)	35	5
a.		Tête bêche pr.	75	70
b.		Booklet pane of 4	2.25	2.25
c.		Type I	3,000.	
333	A122	25c red	45	7
334	A123	30c olive	60	5
335	A124	35c red brn	75	40
336	A125	40c dp bl	2.50	5
337	A126	50c sl gray	2.00	10
338	A127	60c bl grn	4.50	5
339	A128	70c purple	2.75	30
		Nos. 328-339 (12)	18.80	5.72

For use in vending machines, some printings of the 5c, 10c, 20c (II), 25c, 30c and 40c carry a control number on the back of every fifth stamp. The number was applied on top of the gum.

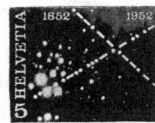
Symbolical of the Telegraph
A129

Symbolical Designs: 10c, Telephone. 20c, Radio. 40c, Television.

1952, Feb. 1   Photo.   Perf. 11½

340	A129	5c org & yel	50	50
341	A129	10c brt grn & pink	65	20
342	A129	20c dp red lil & gray bl	1.20	20
343	A129	40c dp bl & lt bl	3.75	5.25

"A century of telecommunications."

Zurich Airport and Tail of Plane
A130

1953, Aug. 29

344	A130	40c bl red & gray	6.00	7.50

Opening of Zurich-Kloten airport.

Alpine Post Bus, Winter Background
A131

Design: 20c, Same, summer background.

1953, Oct. 8

345	A131	10c dk grn, grn & yel	10	5
346	A131	20c dk red, red brn & yel	20	6

Sold only on Swiss alpine post buses.

Symbols of Agriculture, Forestry and Horticulture
A132

Map and Nautical Emblems
A133

Designs: 20c, Winged spoon. 40c, Football and map.

1954, Mar. 15   Perf. 14

347	A132	10c multi	30	20
348	A132	20c multi	1.50	20
349	A133	25c red, dk ol grn & gray	2.50	3.50
350	A132	40c bl, yel & brn	3.00	2.50

Nos. 347-348 were issued to publicize exhibitions at Lucerne and Bern; No. 349, fifty years of navigation on the Rhine; No. 350, the 1954 World Soccer Championships in Switzerland.

Lausanne Cathedral
A134

Alphorn Blower—A135

Designs: 10c, Vand costume hat. 40c, Automobile steering wheel.

1955, Feb. 15   Perf. 11½

351	A134	5c multi	35	20
352	A134	10c grn, yel & red	40	10
a.		Souvenir sheet of 2	85.00	100.00
353	A135	20c red & sep	1.00	10
354	A134	40c bl, pink & gray	2.75	2.25

No. 352a contains 10c and 20c multicolored, imperf. stamps of Cathedral type A134. Size: 104x52mm. Border inscriptions on olive green ribbons.

Issued to publicize the following: National Philatelic Exhibition (5c and No. 352a), Winegrowers' Festival (10c), Alpine Herdsman and Costume Festival (20c) and 25th International Automobile Show (40c).

First Swiss Post Bus
A136

Designs: 10c, North Gate of Simplon Tunnel and Stockalper Palace. 20c, Children crossing street and road signs. 40c, Planes and emblem of Swissair (vertical).

1956, Mar. 1   Photogravure

Granite Paper.

355	A136	5c ol gray, blk & yel	30	25
356	A136	10c brt grn, gray & red	45	10
357	A136	20c multi	1.10	15
358	A136	40c bl & red	3.25	1.50

Issued to publicize the following: 50th anniversary of the Swiss Motor Coach Service (No. 355); 50th anniversary of the opening of Simplon Tunnel (No. 356); Accident prevention (No. 357); 25th anniversary of the founding of Swissair (No. 358).

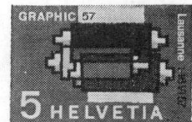
Inking Device, Printing Machine
A137

Designs: 10c, Train on southern ramp of Gotthard Railroad. 20c, Shield of civil defense and coat of arms. 40c, Munatius Plancus and view of Basel.
Two types of 10c:
I. "Black" bottom line on train.
II. Brown bottom line.

1957, Feb. 27   Perf. 11½

Granite Paper

359	A137	5c multi	20	20
360	A137	10c lt bl grn, dk grn & red brn (I)	2.00	10
a.		Type II	1.50	30
361	A137	20c red org & gray	75	15
362	A137	40c multi	2.00	1.50

Issued to publicize the following: International Exhibition for Graphic Arts, Lausanne, June 1-16, 1957 (No. 359). 75th anniversary of St. Gotthard railroad (No. 360). Civil defense (No. 361), 2000th anniversary of Basel (No. 362).

Rope and Symbol of European Unity
A138

1957, July 15   Engr.   Perf. 11½

363	A138	25c lt red	1.00	30
364	A138	40c blue	3.75	18

Issued to emphasize European unity.

Nyon Castle and Corinthian Capital
A139

Designs: 10c, Woman's head and ribbons in Swiss colors. 20c, Crossbow emblem. 40c, Salvation Army hat.

1958, Mar. 5 Photo. Unwmkd.

Granite Paper

365	A139	5c ol bis & dl pur	15	20
366	A139	10c grn, dk grn & red	20	10
367	A139	20c ver, lil & car	55	10
368	A139	40c multi	1.75	1.00

Issued to publicize the following: 2000th anniversary of Nyon (No. 365). Saffa Exhibition, Zurich, July 17-Sept. 15 (No. 366). 25th anniversary of Swiss manufacturing emblem (No. 367). 75th anniversary of the Salvation Army in Switzerland (No. 368).

Symbol of Nuclear Fission

A140

1958, Aug. 25 *Perf. 11½*

Granite Paper

369	A140	40c bl, yel & red	45	80

Issued to publicize the 2nd United Nations Atomic Conference for peaceful uses of atomic power, Geneva, Sept. 1958.

"Transportation"

A141

Designs: 10c, Fasces and post horn. 20c, Owl, rabbit and fish. 50c, Jean Calvin, Theodore de Beze and University of Geneva.

1959, Mar. 9 Photo. Unwmkd.

Granite Paper

370	A141	5c multi	25	12
371	A141	10c emer, yel & lt gray	35	8
a.		Souvenir sheet of 2, imperf.	13.00	18.50
372	A141	20c multi	1.10	12
373	A141	50c multi	1.35	1.25

Issued to publicize the following: Opening of the Swiss House of Transport and Communications (5c). National Philatelic Exhibition, St. Gall, Aug. 21-30 (10c and No. 371a). Protection of animals (20c). 400th anniversary of the University of Geneva (50c).

No. 371a measures 95x58mm., and contains a 10c green, gold and light gray and a 20c deep carmine, gold and light gray in design of the 10c. Light blue margin with indigo inscription. Sold for 2fr; the money went for the St. Gall Philatelic Exhibition.

Chain Symbolizing European Unity

A142

1959, June 22 Engr. *Perf. 11½*

374	A142	30c brick red	45	15
375	A142	50c lt ultra	60	20

Issued to emphasize European Unity.

Overprinted
"REUNION DES PTT D'EUROPE 1959"
in Ultramarine or Red.

376	A142	30c brick red	6.00	7.00
377	A142	50c lt ultra	6.00	7.00

Issued to publicize the European Conference of PTT Administrations, Montreux, June 22–July 31. Nos. 376–377 were on sale only during the conference at a special P. O. in Montreux.

"Cancer Control"

A143

Designs: 20c, Founding charter and scepter of University of Basel. 50c, Uprooted Oak Emblem. 75c, Swissair Jet DC-8.

1960, Apr. 7 Photo. *Perf. 11½*

Granite Paper

378	A143	10c brt grn & red	75	10
379	A143	20c car rose, gray blk & yel	95	12
380	A143	50c ultra & yel	80	1.25
381	A143	75c lt bl, gray & red	2.00	4.00

Issued to publicize the following: 50th anniversary of the Swiss League for Cancer Control (10c). 500th anniversary of the University of Basel (20c). World Refugee Year, July 1, 1959–June 30, 1960 (50c). Swissair's entry into the jet age (75c).

Messenger, Fribourg — A144

Cathedral, Lausanne — A145

Designs: 10c, Messenger, Schwyz. 15c, Messenger and pack animal. 20c, Postilion on horseback. 30c, Grossmünster (church), Zürich. 35c, 1.30fr, Woodcutters' Guildhall, Biel. 40c, Cathedral, Geneva. 50c, Spalen Gate, Basel. 60c, Clock Tower, Berne. 70c, 2.80fr, Sts. Peter and Stephen Church, Bellinzona (tower omitted on 2.80fr). 75c, Bridge and water tower, Lucerne. 80c, Cathedral, St. Gallen. 90c, Munot tower, Schaffhausen. 1fr, Townhall, Fribourg. 1.20fr, Basel gate, Solothurn. 1.50fr, Reding house, Schwyz. 1.70fr, 2fr, 2.20fr, Church, Einsiedeln.

Two types of 5c, 10c, 20c, 50c:

5 Centimes.
- Type I. Four lines on pike at left of hand.
- Type II. Three lines.

10 Centimes.
- Type I. Dot on pike below head.
- Type II. No dot.

20 Centimes.
- Type I. Ten dots on horizontal harness strip.
- Type II. Nine dots.

50 Centimes.
- Type I. Three shading lines at right above arch.
- Type II. Two shading lines.

White Paper except 1.30fr, 1.70fr, 2.20fr, 2.80fr on Granite Paper, Red & Blue Fibers

1960–63 Engraved *Perf. 11½*

382	A144	5c lt ultra (I)	10	5
a.		Bklt. pane of 4	45	45
c.		Tête bêche pair	25	20
h.		Bklt. pane of 10	7.00	
383	A144	10c bl grn (I)	13	5
a.		Bklt. pane of 4	55	55
c.		Tête bêche pair	30	25
i.		Bklt. pane of 10	7.00	
384	A144	15c lt red brn	18	5
385	A144	20c rose pink (I)	20	5
a.		Bklt. pane of 4	1.10	1.10
c.		Tête bêche pair	50	40
386	A145	25c emerald	25	12
387	A145	30c vermilion	50	8
388	A145	35c org red	60	60
389	A145	40c lilac	65	5
390	A145	50c lt vio bl (I)	70	5
a.		Bklt. pane of 4	3.50	3.50
c.		Tête bêche pair	3.50	3.50
391	A145	60c rose red	75	5
392	A145	70c orange	1.75	1.25
393	A145	75c lt bl	1.25	30
394	A145	80c dp cl	1.40	10
395	A145	90c ol grn	1.25	10
396	A144	1fr dl org	1.60	10
397	A144	1.20fr dl red	1.75	50
397A	A145	1.30fr red brn, *pink* ('63)	1.40	25
398	A144	1.50fr brt grn	1.75	45
398A	A144	1.70fr rose lil, *pink* ('63)	1.75	25
399	A144	2fr brt bl	14.00	1.50
399A	A144	2.20fr bl grn, *grn* ('63)	2.00	60
399B	A145	2.80fr org, *buff* ('63)	3.00	55
		Nos. 382-399B (22)	36.96	7.10

See also Nos. 440–455.

Violet Fibers, Fluorescent Paper

1963–76

382d	A144	5c lt ultra (I)	8	5
f.		Bklt. pane of 4 ('68)	35	35
g.		Tête bêche pair ('68)	20	15
383d	A144	10c bl grn (I)	13	5
e.		Bklt. pane of 2+2 labels ('68)	50	50
f.		Bklt. pane of 4 ('68)	55	55
g.		Tête bêche pair ('68)	35	25
384a	A144	15c lt red brn	22	8
385d	A144	20c rose pink (I)	25	5
f.		Bklt. pane of 4 ('68)	1.10	1.10
g.		Tête bêche pair ('68)	55	40
386a	A145	25c emerald	30	10
387a	A145	30c vermilion	40	8
b.		Bklt. pane of 4 ('68)	1.65	1.65
c.		Tête bêche pair ('68)	1.10	90
389a	A145	40c lil ('67)	55	8
b.		Bklt. pane of 4 ('76)	2.25	2.25
c.		Tête bêche pair ('76)	1.10	90
390d	A145	50c lt vio bl (I)	80	8
391a	A145	60c rose red ('67)	70	13
393a	A145	75c lt bl ('68)	95	60
394a	A145	80c dp cl	1.25	15
395a	A145	90c ol grn ('67)	1.25	8
396a	A144	1fr dl org ('67)	2.75	10
397b	A144	1.20fr dl red ('68)	3.25	1.50
398b	A144	1.50fr brt grn ('68)	3.50	1.25
		Nos. 382d-398b (15)	16.38	4.38

Coil Stamps.

1960 White Paper

382b	A144	5c lt ultra (II)	90	90
383b	A144	10c bl grn (II)	75	75
385b	A144	20c rose pink (II)	1.00	1.00
390b	A145	50c lt vio bl (II)	3.25	3.25

The coil stamps were printed in sheets (available to collectors) and pasted into coils. Every fifth stamp has a control number on the back.

Other denominations issued in coils on white paper are: 40c, 60c, 90c, 1fr, 1.30fr, 1.70fr, 2.20fr and 2.80fr.

Denominations issued in coils on granite paper (red & blue fibers) are: 1.30fr, 1.70fr, 2.20fr and 2.80fr.

Coil Stamps

Violet Fibers, Fluorescent Paper

1965–68

382e	A144	5c lt ultra (II)	1.40	1.40
383h	A144	10c bl grn (II)	40	40
385e	A144	20c rose pink (II)	60	60
390e	A145	50c lt vio bl (II)	3.25	3.25

Other denominations issued in coils on violet-fiber paper are: 40c, 60c, 90c and 1fr.

Europa Issue, 1960

Common Design Type

1960, Sept. 19 *Perf. 11½* Unwmkd.

Size: 33x23mm.

400	CD3	30c vermilion	35	15
401	CD3	50c ultra	50	25

Wall under Construction and Globe

A146

Designs: 10c, Symbolic sun (HYSPA Emblem). 20c, Ice hockey stick and puck. 50c, Wiring diagram on map of Switzerland.

1961, Feb. 20 Photo. *Perf. 11½*

Granite Paper

402	A146	5c gray, brick red & grnsh bl	45	13
403	A146	10c aqua & yel	45	8
404	A146	20c multi	1.25	10
405	A146	50c ultra, gray & car rose	2.25	1.75

Issued to publicize the following: Development aid to new nations (5c). HYSPA 1961, Health and Sports Exhibition, Bern, May 18–July 17 (10c). International Ice Hockey Championships, Lausanne and Geneva, March 2–12 (20c). Fully automatic Swiss telephone service (50c).

St. Matthew and Angel

A147

Evangelists: 5fr, St. Mark and winged lion. 10fr, St. Luke and winged ox. 20fr, St. John and eagle.

Engraved

1961, Sept. 18 *Perf. 11½* Unwmkd.

Granite Paper

406	A147	3fr rose car	4.00	12
407	A147	5fr dk bl	4.00	15
408	A147	10fr dk brn	9.25	50
409	A147	20fr red	18.00	2.50

Designs are after 15th century wood carvings from St. Oswald's church, Zug.

Europa Issue, 1961

Common Design Type

1961, Sept. 18

Size: 26x21mm.

410	CD4	30c vermilion	40	17
411	CD4	50c blue	50	28

Trans-Europe Express

A148

Designs: 10c, Rower. 20c, Jungfrau railroad station and Mönch. 50c, W.H.O. Anti-malaria emblem.

1962, Mar. 19 Photo. *Perf. 11½*

412	A148	5c multi	60	15
413	A148	10c brt grn, lem & lil	60	15
414	A148	20c rose lil, pale bl & bis	1.00	15
415	A148	50c ultra, lt grn & rose lil	1.50	1.40

Issued to publicize the following: Introduction of Swiss electric TEE trains (5c). Rowing world championship, Lucerne, Sept. 6–9 (10c). 50th anniversary of the railroad station on the Jungfrau mountain (20c). World Health Organization Anti-Malaria campaign (50c).

Europa Issue, 1962

Common Design Type

1962, Sept. 17 *Perf. 11½* Unwmkd.

Size: 33x23mm.

416	CD5	30c org, yel & brn	70	60
417	CD5	50c ultra, lt grn & brn	1.00	80

Common Design Types

pictured in section at front of book.

SWITZERLAND

Boy Scout—A149

Designs: 10c, Swiss Alpine Club emblem. 20c, Luegelkinn viaduct. 30c, Wheat Emblem. No. 426, 428a, Red Cross Jubilee Emblem. No. 427, Post Office Building, Paris, 1863.

1963, Mar. 21   Photogravure

422	A149	5c gray, dk red & brn	80	15
423	A149	10c dk grn, gray & red	50	10
424	A149	20c dk car, brn & gray	1.25	15
425	A149	30c yel grn, yel & org	1.50	1.40
426	A149	50c bl, sil & red	1.50	1.10
427	A149	50c ultra, pink, yel & gray	1.50	1.10
		Nos. 422-427 (6)	7.05	4.00

Souvenir Sheet
Imperf.

428	A149	Sheet of four	13.00	9.00
a.		50c bl, lt bl, sil & red	2.75	1.90

Issued to publicize the following: 50 years of Swiss Boy Scouts (5c). Centenary of Swiss Alpine Club (10c). 50 years Lötschberg Railroad (20c). "Freedom from Hunger" campaign of U.N. Food and Agriculture Organization (30c). Red Cross Centenary (Nos. 426 and 428). First International Postal Conference, Paris 1863 (No. 427).

No. 428 has blue inscriptions and two red crosses in margin. Size: 100x80mm. Sold for 3fr.

Europa Issue, 1963
Common Design Type

1963, Sept. 16   *Perf. 11½*   Unwmkd.
Granite Paper
Size: 26x21mm.

429	CD6	50c ultra & ocher	1.00	50

EXPO Emblem
A150

Designs: 50c, EXPO emblem on globe and moon ("Outlook"). 75c, EXPO emblem on globe ("Insight").

1963, Sept. 16   *Perf. 11½*   Unwmkd.
Granite Paper

430	A150	10c brt grn & dk grn	45	5
431	A150	20c red & mar	45	5
432	A150	50c ultra & red	70	70
433	A150	75c pur & red	90	70

Issued to publicize the Swiss National Exhibition, Lausanne, Apr. 30–Oct. 25, 1964.

Road Tunnel Through Great St. Bernard
A151

Designs: 10c, Symbolic water god and waves. 20c, Soldiers of 1864 and 1964. 50c, Standards of Swiss Confederation and Geneva.

1964, Mar. 9   Photo.   Granite Paper

434	A151	5c ol, ultra & red	20	8
435	A151	10c Prus bl & grn	20	8
436	A151	20c red, ultra, blk & sal	40	15
437	A151	50c ultra, red, yel & blk	1.25	90

Issued to publicize the following: First Trans-Alpine Automobile route from Switzerland to Italy (5c). "Pro Aqua" water conservation campaign (10c). Centenary of the Swiss Noncommissioned Officers' Association (20c). Sesquicentennial of union of Geneva with Swiss Confederation (50c).

Europa Issue, 1964
Common Design Type

1964, Sept. 14   Engraved   *Perf. 11½*
Size: 21x26mm.
Violet Fibers, Fluorescent Paper

438	CD7	20c vermilion	30	10
439	CD7	50c ultra	80	30

Type of Regular Issue, 1960–63

Designs: 5c, Lenzburg. 10c, Freuler Mansion, Näfels. 15c, St. Mauritius Church, Appenzell. 20c, Planta House, Samedan. 30c, Gabled houses, Gais. 50c, Castle and Abbey Church, Neuchâtel. 70c, Lussy House, Wolfenschiessen. 1fr, Santa Croce Church, Riva San Vitale. 1.20fr, Abbey Church, Payerne. 1.30fr, Church of St. Pierre de Clages. 1.50fr, La Porte de France, Porrentruy. 1.70fr, Frauenfeld Castle. 2fr, A Pro Castle, Seedorf. 2.20fr, Thomas Tower and Gate, Liestal. 2.50fr, St. Oswald's Church, Zug. 3.50fr, Benedictine Abbey, Engelberg.

1964–68   Engraved   *Perf. 11½*
Violet Fibers, Fluorescent Paper

440	A144	5c car rose ('68)	10	5
441	A144	10c vio bl ('68)	10	5
a.		Booklet pane of 4	65	
b.		Tête bêche pair	32	22
c.		Booklet pane of 2 + 2 labels	35	
d.		Booklet pane of 10	3.50	
442	A144	15c brn red ('68)	15	5
a.		Booklet pane of 4	1.10	
b.		Tête bêche pair	55	50
443	A144	20c bl grn ('68)	20	5
a.		Booklet pane of 4	1.40	
b.		Tête bêche pair	65	45
444	A144	30c ver ('68)	35	5
a.		Booklet pane of 4	2.10	
b.		Tête bêche pair	1.00	80
445	A144	50c ultra ('68)	55	12
446	A145	70c brn ('67)	75	10
447	A145	1fr dk grn ('68)	1.00	6
448	A145	1.20fr brn red ('68)	1.25	10
449	A145	1.30fr vio bl ('66)	1.75	80
450	A145	1.50fr grn ('68)	1.50	20
451	A145	1.70fr brn org ('66)	2.25	80
452	A145	2fr org ('67)	2.00	35
453	A145	2.20fr green	3.00	60
454	A145	2.50fr Prus grn ('67)	2.50	40
455	A145	3.50fr pur ('67)	3.00	45
		Nos. 440-455 (16)	20.45	

The 15c was issued in coils in 1972 (?) with control number on the back of every fifth stamp.

Nurse and Patient
A152

Seated Helvetia, 1854
A153

Women's Army Auxiliary
A154

Intercontinental Communications Map
A155

1965, Mar. 8   Photo.   *Perf. 11½*
Violet Fibers, Fluorescent Paper

462	A152	5c lt ultra & red	12	8
463	A153	10c emer, brn & blk	20	6
464	A154	20c red & multi	25	6

Granite Paper, Red and Blue Fibers

465	A155	50c dl bl grn & mar	70	60

Issued to publicize the following: Nursing and auxiliary medical professions (5c). National Postage Stamp Exhibition, NABRA, Bern, Aug. 27–Sept. 5, 1965 (10c). 20th anniversary of Women's Army Auxiliary Corps (20c). Centenary of International Telecommunication Union (50c).

See No. B344.

Swiss Arms, Cantonal Emblems of Valais, Neuchatel, Geneva—A156

1965, June 1   *Perf. 11½*   Unwmkd.
Granite Paper, Red and Blue Fibers

466	A156	20c multi	25	10

Issued to commemorate the 150th anniversary of the entry of the cantons of Valais, Neuchatel and Geneva in the Swiss Confederation.

Matterhorn
A157

Design: 30c, like 10c but inscribed in French "Cervin."

1965, June 1   Photogravure
Granite Paper, Red and Blue Fibers

467	A157	10c grn, sl & dk red	20	10

Violet Fibers, Fluorescent Paper

468	A157	30c dk red, grn & sl	55	55

Issued to commemorate the Year of the Alps; the centenary of the first wintertime visitors to the Alps and the centenary of the first ascent of the Matterhorn. Nos. 467-468 on sale only at Swiss Alpine post buses.

Europa Issue, 1965
Common Design Type

1965, Sept. 14   *Perf. 11½*   Unwmkd.
Violet Fibers, Fluorescent Paper

469	CD8	50c bl, dk bl & grn	50	30

Figure Skating
A159

1965, Sept. 14   Photogravure
Violet Fibers, Fluorescent Paper

470	A159	5c grn, dl bl & blk	10	8

Issued to publicize the World Figure Skating Championships, Davos, Feb. 22–27, 1966.

ITU Emblem and Atom Diagram
A160

Design: 30c, Symbol of communications, waves.

1965, Sept. 14

471	A160	10c ultra & multi	15	10

Granite Paper, Red and Blue Fibers

472	A160	30c org, red & gray	50	50

Nos. 471–472 issued to commemorate the centenary of the International Telecommunication Union.

Violet Fibers, Fluorescent Paper

Paper from No. 473 onward is fluorescent and has violet fibers, unless otherwise noted.

European Kingfisher
A161

Mercury's Helmet and Laurel
A162

Flags of 13 Member Nations and Nuclear Fission
A163

1966, Feb. 21   Photogravure

473	A161	10c emer & multi	20	8
474	A162	20c dp mag, red & brt grn	20	8
475	A163	50c sl bl & multi	55	40

Issued to publicize the following: International Congress for Conservation "Pro Natura," Lucerne (10c). Fiftieth anniversary of Swiss Trade Fair, Basel, Apr. 16–26 (20c). European Organization for Nuclear Research, CERN (50c).

Emblem of Society of Swiss Abroad
A164

Finsteraarhorn
A165

1966, June 1   Photo.   *Perf. 11½*

476	A164	20c ultra & ver	20	7

Issued to commemorate the 50th anniversary of the Society of Swiss Abroad.

Europa Issue, 1966
Common Design Type

1966, Sept. 26   Engraved   *Perf. 11½*
Size: 21x26mm.

477	CD9	20c vermilion	20	5
478	CD9	50c org	55	30

1966, Sept. 26   Photogravure

479	A165	10c lt grnsh bl, dk bl & dk red	10	5

SWITZERLAND

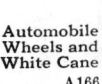
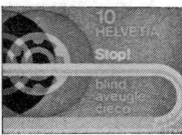

Automobile Wheels and White Cane A166

Flags of EFTA Members A167

1967, March 13   Photo.   Perf. 11½

| 480 | A166 | 10c bl grn, blk & yel | 10 | 5 |
| 481 | A167 | 20c multi | 20 | 10 |

No. 480 issued to publicize the white cane as a distinguishing mark for blind pedestrians. No. 481 publicizes the European Free Trade Association, EFTA. See note after Norway No. 501.

Europa Issue, 1967
Common Design Type
Violet Fibers, Fluorescent Paper

| 482 | CD10 | 30c bl gray | 30 | 15 |

Cogwheel and Swiss Emblem A169

Hourglass and Sun A170

San Bernardino, from North A171

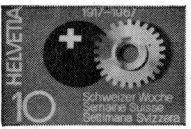

Railroad Wheel A172

1967, Sept. 18   Photo.   Perf. 11½

483	A169	10c multi	8	5
484	A170	20c red, yel & blk	15	5
485	A171	30c multi	35	10
486	A172	50c multi	60	50

Issued to publicize the following: 50th anniversary of Swiss Week (10c). 50th anniversary of the Foundation for the Aged (20c). Opening of the San Bernardino Road Tunnel (30c). 75th anniversary of the Central Office for International Railroad Transportation (50c).

Mountains and Club's Emblem A173

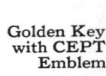

Golden Key with CEPT Emblem A174

Rook and Chessboard A175

Aircraft Tail and Satellites A176

1968, Mar. 14   Photo.   Perf. 11½

487	A173	10c grn, lt ultra & red	12	5
488	A174	20c Prus bl, yel & brn	20	5
489	A175	30c dk ol bis & vio bl	35	8
490	A176	50c dk bl & red	60	50

Issued to publicize the following: 50th anniversary of the Swiss Women's Alpine Club (10c). A unified Europe through postal cooperation (20c). 18th Chess Olympics, Lugano, Oct. 17–Nov. 6 (30c). Inauguration of the new Geneva-Cointrin Air Terminal (50c).

Worker's Protective Helmet A177

Double Geneva and Zurich Stamps of 1843 A178

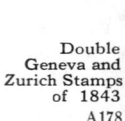

Map Showing Systematic Planning A179

Flag of Rhine Navigation Committee A180

1968, Sept. 12   Photo.   Perf. 11½

491	A177	10c bl grn & yel	10	5
492	A178	20c dp car, blk & yel grn	15	5
493	A179	30c multi	25	10
494	A180	50c bl, yel & blk	55	40

Issued to commemorate the following: 50th anniversary of the Swiss Accident Insurance company, SUVA (10c). 125th anniversary of first Swiss postage stamps (20c). 25th anniversary of the Swiss Society for Systematic Planning (30c). Centenary of the Rhine Navigation Act (50c).

Swiss Girl Scouts' Emblem and Camp A181

Pegasus Constellation A182

Comptoir Suisse Emblem and Beaulieu Building, Lausanne A183

Gymnaestrada Emblem (Man in Circle) A184

Swissair DC-8 and DH-3 A185

1969, Feb. 12   Photo.   Perf. 11½

495	A181	10c multi	10	5
496	A182	20c dk bl	25	8
497	A183	30c red, ocher, grn & gray	25	12
498	A184	50c vio bl, bl, red, grn & sil	55	45
499	A185	2fr bl, dk bl & red	2.50	2.00
		Nos. 495-499 (5)	3.65	2.70

Issued to commemorate the following: 50th anniversary of Swiss Girl Scouts (10c). Opening of first Swiss Planetarium, Lucerne, July 1 (20c). 50th anniversary of the Comptoir Suisse (trade fair, 30c). 5th Gymnaestrada (gymnastic meet), Basel, July 1–5 (50c). 50th anniversary of Swiss airmail service (2fr).

Europa Issue, 1969
Common Design Type
1969, Apr. 28   Size: 32½x23mm.

| 500 | CD12 | 30c brn org & multi | 30 | 10 |
| 501 | CD12 | 50c chlky bl & multi | 55 | 50 |

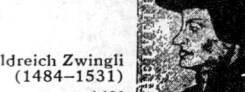

Huldreich Zwingli (1484–1531) A186

Portraits: 20c, Gen. Henri Guisan (1874–1960). 30c, Francesco Borromini, architect (1599–1667). 50c, Othmar Schoeck, musician (1886–1957). 80c, Germaine de Staël, writer (1766–1817).

1969, Sept. 18   Engraved   Perf. 11½

502	A186	10c brt pur	10	5
503	A186	20c green	15	5
504	A186	30c dp car	35	12
505	A186	50c dp bl	75	75
506	A186	80c red brn	1.00	90
		Nos. 502-506 (5)	2.35	1.87

Issued to honor famous Swiss.

Kreuzberge, Alpstein Mountains A187

Children Crossing Street A188

Steelworker A189

1969, Sept. 18   Photogravure

507	A187	20c bl & multi	40	5
508	A188	30c car & multi	30	8
509	A189	50c vio & multi	55	55

No. 508 publicizes the traffic safety campaign; No. 509 commemorates the 50th anniversary of the International Labor Organization.

Telex Tape A190

Fireman Rescuing Child A191

Pro Infirmis Emblem A192

United Nations Emblem A193

New UPU Headquarters A194

1970, Feb. 26   Photo.   Perf. 11½

| 510 | A190 | 20c dk grn, yel & blk | 12 | 6 |

SWITZERLAND

511	A191	30c dk car & multi	25	12
512	A192	30c red & multi	25	12
513	A193	50c dk bl, lt grnsh bl & sil	55	55
514	A194	80c dk pur, sep & tan	90	90
	Nos. 510-514 (5)		2.07	1.75

Issued to commemorate the following: 75th anniversary of the Swiss Telegraph Agency (20c). Centenary of the Swiss Firemen's Association (No. 511). 50th anniversary of the Pro Infirmis Foundation (No. 512). 25th anniversary of the United Nations (50c). New Headquarters of the Universal Postal Union in Bern (80c).

Europa Issue, 1970
Common Design Type
1970, May 4 Engraved Perf. 11½
Size: 21x26mm.

515	CD13	30c vermilion	25	10
516	CD13	50c brt bl	55	40

Soccer A195

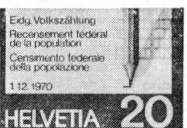
Census Form A196

Piz Palu, Grisons A197

"Nature Conservation"—A198   Numeral A199

1970, Sept. 17 Photo. Perf. 11½

517	A195	10c grn & multi	10	5
518	A196	20c dk grn & multi	15	10
519	A197	30c sl bl & multi	50	12
520	A198	50c dk bl & multi	55	55

Issued to commemorate the following: 75th anniversary of Swiss Soccer Association (10c). Federal Census of 1970 (20c). Swiss Alps (30c). Nature Conservation Year (50c).

Coil Stamps
1970, Sept. 17 Engraved Perf. 11½

521	A199	10c brn lake	10	5
522	A199	20c ol grn	20	5
523	A199	50c ultra	50	40

Control number in stamp's color on back of every fifth stamp. Nos. 521-523 were regularly issued only in coils, but exist in sheets of 50.

Gymnastic Trio A200

Rose A201

Switzerland No. 8 A202

Rising Spiral A203

Intelsat 4 Satellite A204

Adaptation of 1850 Design A205
Design: No. 525, Runners (men).

1971, Mar. 11 Photo. Perf. 11½

524	A200	10c ol, brn & bl	25	5
525	A200	10c gray, brn & yel	25	5
526	A201	20c dk grn & multi	20	10
527	A202	30c dp car & multi	30	10
528	A203	50c dk bl & bis	50	40
529	A204	80c multi	1.10	90
	Nos. 524-529 (6)		2.60	1.60

Souvenir Sheet
Typographed Imperf.

530	A205	2fr bl & multi	4.00	4.00

Issued to commemorate the following: New article on gymnastics and sports in Swiss Constitution (10c); International Child Welfare Organization (20c); NABA National Postage Stamp Exhibition, Basel, June 4-13 (30c, 2fr); Second decade of development aid (50c); International Space Communications Conference, Geneva, June-July, 1971 (80c).

Nos. 524-525 printed se-tenant checkerwise in sheets of 50. No. 530 has gray margin with blue inscription; gray inscription on back; sold for 3fr. Size: 61x75 mm.

Europa Issue, 1971
Common Design Type
1971, May 3 Engraved Perf. 11½
Size: 26x21mm.

531	CD14	30c rose car & org	35	15
532	CD14	50c bl & org	60	40

Les Diablerets, Vaud A206

Telecommunications Symbols A207

1971, Sept. 23 Photo. Perf. 11½

533	A206	30c rose lil & bl gray	50	12
534	A207	40c ultra, yel & brt pink	60	60

No. 534 commemorates the 50th anniversary of Radio-Suisse, which is also in charge of air traffic control.

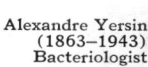
Alexandre Yersin (1863-1943) Bacteriologist A208

Physicians: 20c, Auguste Forel (1848-1931), psychiatrist. 30c, Jules Gonin (1870-1935), ophthalmologist. 40c, Robert Koch (1843-1910), German bacteriologist. 80c, Frederick G. Banting (1891-1941), Canadian physiologist.

1971, Sept. 23 Engraved

535	A208	10c gray ol	10	8
536	A208	20c bluish grn	20	10
537	A208	30c car rose	30	10
538	A208	40c dk bl	80	75
539	A208	80c brt pur	1.00	1.00
	Nos. 535-539 (5)		2.40	2.03

Wrench, Road Sign, Club Emblems A209

Electronic Switch Panel A210

Boy's Head and Radio Waves A211

Symbolic Tree A212

1972, Feb. 17 Photo. Perf. 11½

540	A209	10c multi	15	6
541	A210	20c ol & multi	15	15
542	A211	30c org & mar	38	15
543	A212	40c bl, grn & pur	70	50

Issued to commemorate: 75th anniversary of the touring and automobile clubs of Switzerland (10c). 125th anniversary of Swiss railroads (20c). 50th anniversary of Swiss radio (30c). 50th annual congress of Swiss citizens living abroad, Bern, Aug. 25-27 (40c).

Europa Issue 1972
Common Design Type
1972, May 2
Size: 21x26mm.

544	CD12	30c multi	40	20
545	CD12	40c multi	80	45

Alberto Giacometti (1901-66), Painter and Sculptor A213

Portraits and Signatures: 20c, Charles Ferdinand Ramuz (1878-1947), writer. 30c, Le Corbusier (Charles Edouard Jeanneret; 1887-1965) architect. 40c, Albert Einstein (1879-1955), physicist. 80c, Arthur Honegger (1892-1955), composer.

Engr. & Photo.
1972, Sept. 21 Perf. 11½

546	A213	10c ocher & blk	10	5
547	A213	20c lt ol & blk	20	12
548	A213	30c pink & blk	30	15
549	A213	40c lt bl & blk	80	70
550	A213	80c lil rose & blk	95	80
	Nos. 546-550 (5)		2.35	1.82

Civil Defense Emblem A214

Spannörter A215

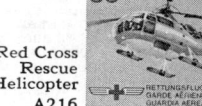
Red Cross Rescue Helicopter A216

Clean Air, Fire, Earth and Water A217

1972, Sept. 21 Photogravure

551	A214	10c org, bl & yel	15	10
552	A215	20c brn & multi	20	15
553	A216	30c lil, red & ind	40	15
554	A217	40c lt bl & multi	65	50

Issued to publicize Civil Defense (10c); Swiss Alps (20c); Air Rescue Service (30c); Nature and environment protection (40c).

SWITZERLAND

Earth Satellite Station, Leuk, World Map
A218

Quill Pen and Arrows in Circle
A219

INTERPOL Emblem
A220

1973, Feb. 15   Photo.   Perf. 11½

555	A218	15c gray, yel & bl	20	13
556	A219	30c multi	30	20
557	A220	40c dp bl, lt bl & gray	55	45

Issued to publicize the opening of the satellite station at Leuk (15c); centenary of the Swiss Association of Commercial Employees (30c); 50th anniversary of the International Criminal Police Organization (INTERPOL).

Sottoceneri
A221

Sign of Inn "Zur Sonne," Toggenburg
A222

Villages: 10c, Graubunden. 15c, Central Switzerland. 25c, Jura. 30c, Simme Valley. 35c, Central Switzerland (2 buildings). 40c, Vaud. 50c, Valais. 60c, Engadine. 70c, Sopraceneri. 80c, Eastern Switzerland.
Designs: 1fr, Rose window, Lausanne Cathedral. 1.10fr, Gallus Portal, Basel Cathedral. 1.20fr, Romanesque capital (eagle), St. Jean Baptiste Church, Grandson. 1.50fr, Ceiling medallion (pelican feeding nestlings), Stein am Rhein Convent. 1.70fr, Romanesque capital (St. George and dragon), St. Jean Baptiste, Grandson. 1.80fr, Gargoyle, Bern Cathedral. 2fr, Bay window, Schaffhausen. 2.50fr, Cock weather vane, St. Ursus Cathedral, Solothurn. 3.50fr, Astronomical clock, Bern clock tower.

1973-80   Engraved   Perf. 11½

Fluorescent, No Violet Fibers

558	A221	5c dl yel & dk bl	6	5
559	A221	10c rose lil & ol grn	10	5
560	A221	15c org & vio bl	15	5
561	A221	25c emer & vio bl	25	5
562	A221	30c brick red & dk bl	30	5
563	A221	35c red org & brt vio ('75)	35	15
564	A221	40c brt bl & blk	40	5
565	A221	50c ol grn & org	50	15
566	A221	60c yel brn & gray	60	20
567	A221	70c sep & blk	70	20
568	A221	80c brt grn & brick red	80	20

Violet Fibers, Fluorescent Paper

569	A222	1fr pur ('74)	1.00	10
570	A222	1.10fr Prus bl ('75)	1.00	20
571	A222	1.20fr rose red ('74)	1.25	1.00
572	A222	1.30fr ocher	2.50	90
573	A222	1.50fr grn ('74)	1.50	30
574	A222	1.70fr gray	1.40	70
575	A222	1.80fr dp org	1.50	40
576	A222	2fr ultra ('74)	1.75	25
577	A222	2.50fr gldn brn ('75)	2.50	90
578	A222	3fr dk car ('79)	2.75	25
579	A222	3.50fr ol grn ('80)	3.00	1.10
		Nos. 558-579 (22)	24.36	8.30

Europa Issue 1973
Common Design Type
1973, Apr. 30   Engr. & Photo.
Size: 38x28mm.

580	CD16	25c brn & yel	35	15
581	CD16	40c ultra & yel	65	40

"Man and Time"
A223

Skier and Championship Emblem
A224

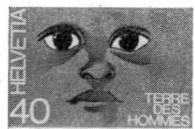

Child
A225

1973, Aug. 30   Photo.   Perf. 11½

582	A223	15c multi	20	12
583	A224	30c pink & multi	30	12
584	A225	40c bl vio & blk	65	50

Issued to publicize the opening of the International Clock Museum, La Chaux-de-Fonds, 1974 (15c); International Alpine Skiing Championships, St. Moritz, Feb. 2-10, 1974 (30c); "Terre des hommes" children's aid program (40c).

Medieval Postal Couriers—A226

1974, Jan. 29   Photo.   Perf. 11½
Multicolored

585	A226		Souvenir sheet of 4	12.00	11.00
a.			30c Basel (with staff)	2.25	2.25
b.			30c Zug (without staff)	2.25	2.25
c.			60c Uri	2.25	2.25
d.			80c Schwyz	2.25	2.25

Centenary of Universal Postal Union and for INTERNABA 74 International Philatelic Exhibition, Basel, June 7-16. No. 585 has plum marginal inscription and ultramarine exhibition emblem. Size: 82x 72mm. Sold for 3 fr.

Pine and Cabin on Globe
A227

Gymnast and Hurdlers
A228

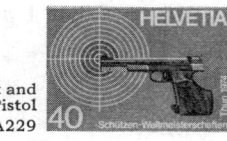

Target and Pistol
A229

1974, Jan. 29

586	A227	15c lt grn & multi	15	10
587	A228	30c red & multi	30	15
588	A229	40c bl & multi	50	40

Issued for: 50th anniversary of Swiss Youth Hostels (15c); Centenary of Swiss Workers' Gymnastic and Sports Association (SATUS) (30c); World Marksmanship Championships, Thun and Bern, Sept. 1974 (40c).

Old Houses, Parliament RR Station, Bern
A230

Eugène Borel
A231

Designs: No. 590, Castle, Town Hall, Chauderon Center, Lausanne. 40c, Heinrich von Stephan. 80c, Montgomery Blair.

1974, Mar. 28   Photo.   Perf. 11½

589	A230	30c org & multi	45	30
590	A230	30c scar & multi	45	30

Engraved

591	A231	30c rose & blk	25	10
592	A231	40c gray & blk	40	40
593	A231	80c lt yel grn & blk	1.00	75

Centenary of the Universal Postal Union. Nos. 589-590 publicize the Centenary Congress, Lausanne, May 22-July 5; Nos. 591-593 honor the founders of the Universal Postal Union.

Europa Issue 1974

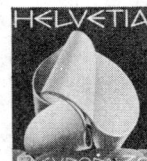

"Continuity," by Max Bill
A232

Design: 40c, "Amazon," bronze sculpture by Carl Burckhardt.

1974, Mar. 28   Photogravure

594	A232	30c red & blk	30	10
595	A232	40c ultra & sep	75	40

Oath of Allegiance, by Werner Witschi
A233

Sports Foundation Emblem
A234

Conveyor Belts, Paths of Mail Transport and Delivery
A235

1974, Sept. 19   Photo.   Perf. 11½

596	A233	15c lil, ol & dk ol	18	15
597	A234	30c sil & multi	38	15
598	A235	30c plum & multi	38	30

Centenary of Swiss Constitution (15c); Swiss Sports Foundation (No. 597); 125th anniversary of Swiss Federal Post (No. 598).

Standard Meter, Krypton Spectrum
A236

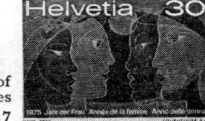

Women of Four Races
A237

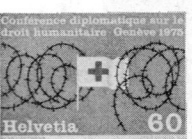

Red Cross Flag, Barbed Wire
A238

"Ville de Lucerne" Dirigible
A239

1975, Feb. 13   Photo.   Perf. 11½

599	A236	15c grn, org & ultra	15	10
600	A237	30c brn & multi	35	15
601	A238	60c ultra, blk & red	75	15
602	A239	90c bl & multi	1.10	90

Centenary of International Meter Convention, Paris, 1875 (15c); International Women's Year 1975 (30c); 2nd Session of Diplomatic Conference on Humanitarian International Law, Geneva, Feb. 1975 (60c); Aviation and Space Travel exhibition in Museum of Transport and Communications, Lucerne (90c).

Europa Issue 1975

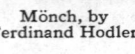

Mönch, by Ferdinand Hodler
A240

Vineyard Worker, by Maurice Barraud
A241

SWITZERLAND

Design: 50c, Still Life with Guitar, by René Auberjonois.

1975, Apr. 28   Photo.   Perf. 12x11½

603	A240	30c gray & multi	30	10
604	A241	50c multi	60	60
605	A241	60c bl gray & multi	80	70

Man Pulling Wheel Chair Upstairs
A242

"The Helping Hand"
A243

Architectural Heritage Year Emblem
A244

Beat Fischer von Reichenbach
A245

1975, Sept. 11   Photogravure

606	A242	15c lil, blk & grn	30	10
607	A243	30c red, blk & car	30	10
608	A244	50c yel brn & mar	55	50
609	A245	60c bl & multi	75	65

Special building features for the handicapped (15c); interdenominational telephone pastoral counseling (30c); European Architectural Heritage Year 1975 (50c); Fischer Post, Bern, tercentenary (60c).

Forest
A246

Fruits and Vegetables
A247

Black Infant
A248

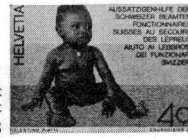

Telephones of 1876 and 1976
A249

1976, Feb. 12   Photo.   Perf. 11½
Fluorescent, No Violet Fibers

610	A246	20c grn & multi	20	15
611	A247	40c car & multi	40	15
612	A248	40c lil rose & multi	40	15

Engraved
Violet Fibers, Fluorescent Paper

| 613 | A249 | 80c lt bl & dk bl | 95 | 80 |

Centenary of Federal forest laws (20c); healthy nutrition to combat alcoholism (No. 611); fight against leprosy (No. 612); telephone centenary (80c).

Europa Issue 1976

Cotton and Gold Lace, St. Gall
A250

Pocket Watch, 18th Century
A251

1976, May 3   Engr.   Perf. 11½

| 614 | A250 | 40c red brn & multi | 45 | 28 |
| 615 | A251 | 80c blk & multi | 95 | 75 |

Both 40c and 80c are on fluorescent paper, the 80c having violet fibers.

Fawn, Frog and Swallow
A252

"Conserve Energy"
A253

St. Gotthard Mountains
A254

Skater
A255

1976, Sept. 16   Photo.   Perf. 11½
Fluorescent, No Violet Fibers

616	A252	20c multi	20	15
617	A253	40c multi	40	12
618	A254	40c multi	50	12
619	A255	80c multi	80	75

Wildlife protection (20c); energy conservation (#617); Pizzo Lucendro to Pizzo Rotondo, seen from Altanca (#618); World Men's Skating Championships, Davos, Feb. 5-6, 1977 (80c).

Oskar Bider, Bleriot Monoplane
A256

Designs: 80c, Eduard Spelterini and balloon gondola. 100c, Armand Dufaux and Dufaux plane. 150c, Walter Mittelholzer and Dornier hydroplane.

1977, Jan. 27   Engr.   Perf. 11½

620	A256	40c multi	40	15
621	A256	80c multi	1.25	1.10
622	A256	100c multi	1.25	90
623	A256	150c multi	1.75	1.50

Swiss aviation pioneers.

Blue Cross
A257

Festival Emblem
A258

Balloons Carrying Letters
A259

1977, Jan. 27   Photogravure

624	A257	20c gray, bl & blk	25	15
625	A258	40c red, gold & brn	45	15
626	A259	80c lt bl & multi	85	85

Blue Cross Society (care of alcoholics and fight against alcoholism), centenary (20c); Vintage Festival, Vevey, July 30-Aug. 14 (40c); JUPHILEX 77 Youth Philatelic Exhibition, Bern, Apr. 7-11 (80c).

Fluorescent Paper

From No. 624 onward the paper lacks violet fibers but is fluorescent, unless otherwise noted.

Europa Issue 1977

St. Ursanne on Doubs River
A260

Design: 80c, Sils-Baselgia on Inn River.

1977, May 2   Engr.   Perf. 11½

| 627 | A260 | 40c multi | 48 | 20 |
| 628 | A260 | 80c multi | 90 | 70 |

Worker and Factories
A261

Ionic Column and Shield
A262

Swiss Cross, Arrow and Butterfly
A263

1977, Aug. 25   Photo.   Perf. 11½

629	A261	20c multi	20	12
630	A262	40c multi	40	25
631	A263	80c multi	90	80

Federal Factories Act, centenary (20c); protection of cultural monuments (40c); Swiss hiking trails (80c).

Star Singer, Bergün
A264

Folk Customs: 10c, Horse race, Zürich. 20c, New Year's Eve costumes, Herisau. 35c, Cutting off the goose, Sursee. 40c, Herald reading proclamation and men scaling wall, Geneva. 50c, Masked men, Laupen. 70c, Procession (horse and masked men), Mendrisio. 80c, Griffins, Basel. 90c, Masked men, Lotschental.

1977, Aug. 25   Engr.   Perf. 11½

632	A264	5c bl grn	8	5
633	A264	10c dk red	13	7
a.	Booklet pane of 2 + 2 labels		30	
635	A264	20c orange	20	10
a.	Booklet pane of 4		1.00	
636	A264	30c grn ('82)	30	20
637	A264	35c olive	40	12
638	A264	40c brn lake	40	10
a.	Booklet pane of 4		2.10	
639	A264	50c red brn	50	20
641	A264	70c purple	70	25
642	A264	80c stl bl	80	30
643	A264	90c dp brn	90	35
	Nos. 632-643 (10)		4.41	1.74

Arms of Vaud Canton
A265

Old Lucerne
A266

Title Page of "Melusine"
A267

Stylized Lens and Bellows
A268

1978, Mar. 9   Photo.   Perf. 11½

652	A265	20c multi	20	15
653	A266	40c multi	40	15
654	A267	70c multi	80	80
655	A268	80c multi	90	45

LEMANEX 78 Philatelic Exhibition, Lausanne, May 26-June 4 (20c); Founding of Lucerne, 800th anniversary (40c); printing in Geneva, 500th anniversary (70c); 2nd International Triennial Photography Exhibition, Fribourg, June 17-Oct. 22 (80c).

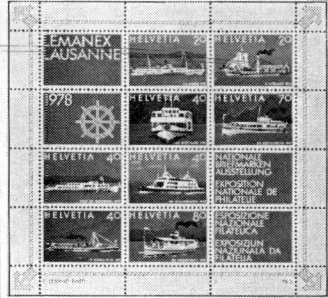

Steamers on Swiss Lakes—A269

SWITZERLAND

1978, Mar. 9   Sheet of 8, multi
656	A269		15.00	15.00
a.		20c La Suisse, 1910	65	65
b.		20c Il Verbano, 1826	65	65
c.		40c MS Gotthard, 1970	1.25	1.25
d.		40c Ville de Neuchatel, 1972	1.25	1.25
e.		40c MS Romanshorn, 1958	1.25	1.25
f.		40c Le Winkelried, 1871	1.25	1.25
g.		70c DS Loetschberg, 1914	1.50	1.50
h.		80c DS Waedenswil, 1895	2.25	2.25

LEMANEX 78 Philatelic Exhibition, Lausanne, May 26–June 4. Size of No. 656: 134x129mm. Sold for 5fr.

Europa Issue 1978

Stockalper Palace, Brig — A270

Design: 80c, Diet Hall, Bern.

1978, May 2   Engr.   Perf. 11½
657	A270	40c multi	45	25
658	A270	80c multi	90	75

Machinist — A271

Joseph Bovet (1879–1951), Composer — A272

Designs: No. 660, Chemical worker (French inscription). No. 661, Construction worker (Italian inscription).

1978, Sept. 14   Photo.   Perf. 11½
659	A271	40c multi	80	45
660	A271	40c multi	80	45
661	A271	40c multi	80	45

Industrial safety. Nos. 659–661 printed se-tenant in sheets of 50.

1978, Sept. 14   Engraved

Portraits: 40c, Henri Dunant (1828–1910), founder of Red Cross. 70c, Carl Gustave Jung (1875–1961), psychologist. 80c, Auguste Piccard (1884–1962), physicist and balloonist.

662	A272	20c dl grn	20	12
663	A272	40c rose lake	40	12
664	A272	70c gray	75	60
665	A272	80c bl gray	90	75

Arms of Switzerland and Jura — A273

1978, Sept. 25   Photo.   Perf. 11½
666	A273	40c buff, red & blk	40	20

Admission of Jura as 23rd Canton.

Rainer Maria Rilke (1875–1926), Poet, Muzot Castle — A274

Designs: 40c, Paul Klee (1879–1940), painter and "heroic roses." 70c, Hermann Hesse (1877–1962), writer, and vines. 80c, Thomas Mann (1875–1955), writer, and Lubeck buildings.

1979, Feb. 21   Engr.   Perf. 11½
667	A274	20c gray grn	20	12
668	A274	40c red	40	12
669	A274	70c brown	75	60
670	A274	80c gray bl	85	65

O. H. Ammann, Verrazano-Narrows Bridge, N.Y. — A275

Target Hit with Pole and Lucerne Flag — A276

Hot Air Balloon — A277

Airport, Swissair and Air France Jets — A278

1979, Feb. 21   Photogravure
671	A275	20c multi	20	12
672	A276	40c multi	40	12
673	A277	70c multi	75	60
674	A278	80c multi	85	65

Othmar H. Ammann (1879–1965), engineer, bridge builder in U.S.; 50th Federal Riflemen's Festival, Lucerne, July 7–22; World Esperanto Congress, Lucerne; new runway at Basel-Mulhouse International Airport.

Europa Issue 1979

Letter Box, 1845, Spalentor, Basel — A279

Design: 80c, Microwave radio relay station on Jungfraujoch.

1979, Apr. 30   Engr.   Perf. 11½
675	A279	40c multi	40	15
676	A279	40c multi	95	80

Helvetian Gold Quarter Stater, 2nd Century B.C. — A280

Three-stage Launcher Ariane — A283

Child and Dove — A281

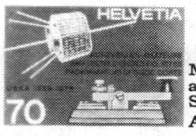

Morse Key and Satellite — A282

1979, Sept. 6   Photogravure
677	A280	20c multi	20	15
678	A281	40c multi	40	25
679	A282	70c multi	70	60
680	A283	80c multi	85	70

Centenary of Swiss Numismatic Society; International Year of the Child; Union of Swiss Radio Amateurs, 50th anniversary; European Space Agency (ESA).

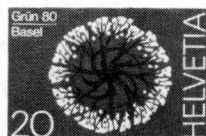

Tree in Bloom — A284

Hand Carved Milk Bucket — A285

Winterthur Town Hall — A286

"Pic-Pic," 1930 — A287

1980, Feb. 21   Photo.
681	A284	20c multi	20	12
682	A285	40c multi	40	20
683	A286	70c multi	65	50
684	A287	80c multi	80	60

Green '80, Swiss Horticultural and Gardening Exposition, Basel, Apr. 12–Oct. 12; Swiss Arts and Crafts Centers, 50th anniversary; Society for Swiss Art History, centenary; 50th International Automobile Show, Geneva, Mar. 16.

Foreign postal stationery (stamped envelopes, postal cards and air letter sheets) lies beyond the scope of this Catalogue which is limited to adhesive postage stamps.

Europa Issue 1980

Johann Konrad Kern (1808–1888), Politician — A288

Design: 80c, Gustav Adolf Hasler (1830–1900), communications pioneer.

1980, Apr. 28   Litho. & Engr.   Granite Paper   Perf. 11½
685	A288	40c multi	40	20
686	A288	80c multi	80	70

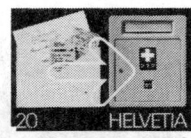

Postal Giro System — A289

Postal Bus System — A290

Security Printing Plant, 50th Anniversary — A291

Swiss Telephone Service Centenary — A292

1980, Sept. 5   Photo., Photo & Engr. (70c)   Perf. 12
687	A289	20c multi	20	20
688	A290	40c multi	40	20
689	A291	70c multi	70	60
690	A292	80c multi	80	70

Swiss Meteorological Office Centenary — A293

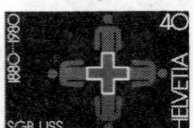

Swiss Trade Union Federation Centenary — A294

SWITZERLAND

Opening of St. Gotthard Tunnel for Year-round Traffic—A295

1980, Sept. 5   Photo.
691	A293	20c multi	20	15
692	A294	40c multi	40	20
693	A295	80c multi	80	75

Granary, Kiesen, 17th Century—A296

International Year of the Disabled—A297

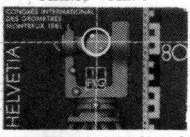
The Parish Clerk, by Albert Anker—A298

Theodolite and Rod—A299

DC-9 (50th Anniversary of Swissair)—A300

1981, Mar. 9   Photo.   Perf. 11½
694	A296	20c multi	20	12
695	A297	40c multi	40	20
696	A298	70c multi	70	60
697	A299	80c multi	80	70
698	A300	110c multi	1.10	1.00
	Nos. 694-698 (5)		3.20	2.62

Ballenberg Open-air Museum of Rural Architecture, Furnishing and Crafts; Albert Anker (1831-1910), artist (70c); 16th Congress of the International Federation of Surveyors, Montreux, Aug. (80c).

Couple Dancing in Native Costumes—A301

1981, May 4   Photo.   Perf. 11½
699	A301	40c shown	40	30
700	A301	80c Stone putting	80	75

Seal of Fribourg—A302

1981, Sept. 3   Photo. & Engr.
701	A302	40c shown	40	35
702	A302	40c Seal of Solothurn	40	35
703	A302	80c Old Town Hall, Stans	75	65

500th anniv. of Diet of Stans and of entry of Fribourg and Solothurn into the Swiss Confederation.

Voltage Regulator—A303

Crossbow Quality Emblem—A304

Youths—A305

Flower Mosaic, St. Peter's Cathedral, Geneva—A306

1981, Sept. 3   Photo.
704	A303	20c multi	20	15
705	A304	40c multi	40	30
706	A305	70c multi	65	55
707	A306	1.10fr multi	1.00	80

Technorama Industrial Fair, Winterthur; Crossbow Quality Emblem, 50th anniv.; Swiss Youth Assoc., 50th anniv.; restoration of St. Peter's Cathedral.

Gotthard Railway Centenary—A307

Designs: Locomotives. Nos. 708-709 se-tenant with label showing workers' monument.

1982, Feb. 18   Photo.
708	A307	40c Steam	40	35
709	A307	40c Electric	40	35

Swiss Hoteliers' Assoc. Centenary—A308

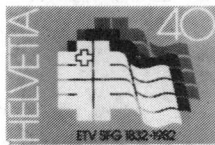
Federal Gymnastic Society Sesquicentennial—A309

Intl. Gas Union, 50th Anniv. Convention, Lausanne—A310

Bern Museum of Natural History Sesquicentennial—A311

Society of Chemical Industries Centenary—A312

1982, Feb. 18
710	A308	20c multi	20	14
711	A309	40c multi	40	35
712	A310	70c multi	70	60
713	A311	80c multi	75	65
714	A312	110c multi	1.10	90
	Nos. 710-714 (5)		3.15	2.64

Europa 1982—A313

1982, May 3   Photo.   Perf. 11½
715	A313	40c Oath of Eternal Fealty	40	40
716	A313	80c Pact of 1291	75	75

Aquarius, Old Bern—A314

Signs of the Zodiac and City Views.

1982, Aug. 23   Photo. & Engr.   Perf. 11½
721	A314	1fr Aquarius, Old Bern	90	90
722	A314	1.10fr Pisces, Nax near Sion	1.00	1.00
723	A314	1.20fr Aries, Graustock	1.10	1.10
724	A314	1.50fr Taurus, Basel Cathedral	1.40	1.40
725	A314	1.60fr Gemini, Schonengrund	1.50	1.50

1983, Feb. 17   Photo. & Engr.   Perf. 11½
726	A314	1.70fr Cancer, Wetterhorn, Grindelwald	1.60	1.60
727	A314	1.80fr Leo, Areuse Gorge, Neuchatel	1.65	1.65
728	A314	2fr Virgo, Jungfrau Monch Eiger Mountains	1.85	1.85

1983, Nov. 24
728A	A314	2fr Virgo, Schwarzee above Zermatt	2.00	75

1984, Feb. 21   Photo. & Engr.   Perf.
728B	A314	4fr Sagittarius	3.75	1.50
728C	A314	4.50fr Capricorn	4.25	1.90

Zurich Tram Centenary—A315

Centenary of Salvation Army in Switzerland—A316

World Dressage Championship, Lausanne, Aug. 25-29—A317

Intl. Water Supply Assoc, 14th World Congress, Zurich, Sept. 6-10—A318

SWITZERLAND

1982, Aug. 23 Photo.
729	A315	20c multi	20	15
730	A316	40c multi	40	40
731	A317	70c multi	65	65
732	A318	80c multi	75	75

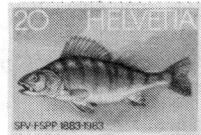
Fishing and Pisciculture Fed. Centenary—A319

Zurich University Sesquicentennial—A320

Journalists' Fed. Centenary—A321

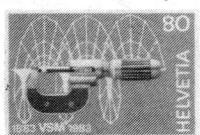
Machine Manufacturers' Assoc. Centenary—A322

1983, Feb. 17 Photo. Granite Paper
733	A319	20c Perch	20	20
734	A320	40c multi	40	40
735	A321	70c Computer print outs	70	70
736	A322	80c Micrometer, cycloidal computer pattern	75	75

Europa 1983   Basel Seal, 1832-48
A323   A324

1983, May 3 Photo. & Engr. Perf. 11½
| 737 | A323 | 40c Celestial globe, 1594 | 40 | 15 |
| 738 | A323 | 80c Cog railway, 1871 | 80 | 50 |

1983, May 26 Photo.
| 739 | A324 | 40c multi | 40 | 15 |

Basel Canton sesquicentennial (land division).

Octodurus Martigny Bimillenium—A325

Swiss Kennel Club Centenary—A326

Bicycle and Motorcycle Federation Centenary—A327

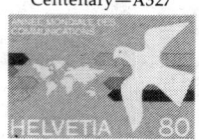
World Communications Year—A328

1983, Aug. 22 Photo.
740	A325	20c multi	25	8
741	A326	40c multi	50	15
742	A327	70c multi	90	25
743	A328	80c multi	1.00	30

NABA-ZURI '84 Natl. Stamp Show, Zurich, June 22-July 1—A329

1100th Anniv. of Saint Imier
A330

Upper City, Lausanne—A331

1984, Feb. 21 Photo. Perf.
744	A329	25c multi	25	8
745	A330	50c multi	50	16
746	A331	80c multi	80	28

Selection of Lausanne as permanent headquarters for the Intl. Olympic Committee (80c).

Europa (1959-84)—A332

1984, May 2 Photo. Perf. 11½
| 747 | A332 | 50c lil rose | 50 | 16 |
| 748 | A332 | 80c ultra | 80 | 28 |

Souvenir Sheet

View of Zurich—A333

1984, May 24
| 749 | | Sheet of 4 | 3.00 | 3.00 |
| a-d. | A333 | 50c, any single | 75 | 75 |

NABA-ZURI '84 Stamp Show. Size: 145x70mm. Sold for 3fr.

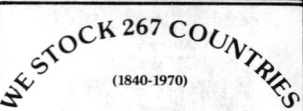

WE STOCK 267 COUNTRIES
(1840-1970)

PLUS
UNITED STATES & POSSESSIONS

AND WE WANT YOUR WANT LIST.
(references or deposit please)

IF IT'S FOR.....

UNITED STATES,
U.S. POSSESSIONS, & BNA
Send it to Charles

BRITISH EMPIRE
Send it to Richard

GENERAL FOREIGN
Send it to John

PROOFS & RARITIES
Send it to Iru

SUPPLIES & CATALOGUES
Send it to Harry

AND IF IT'S FOR OUR
AUCTION CATALOGUE
Send it to Bert

Stampazine
EST. 1937
"The stamp store on the fifth floor."

3 East 57th Street,   New York, NY 10022
212-752-5905

SWITZERLAND

SEMI-POSTAL STAMPS.

Nos. B1–B76, B81–B84 were sold at premiums of 2c, 5c and 10c.

Helvetia and Matterhorn
SP2

Wmkd. Greek Cross. (183)
1913, Dec. 1 Typo. Perf. 11½, 12
Granite Paper
B1 SP2 5c (+5c) grn 4.00 5.00

Boy (Appenzell) SP3   Girl (Lucerne) SP4

1915, Dec. 1 Perf. 11½
B2 SP3 5c (+5c) grn, buff 6.00 5.50
 a. Tête bêche pair 100.00 800.00
 b. Booklet pane of 6
B3 SP4 10c (+5c) red, buff 160.00 80.00

Girl (Fribourg) SP5   Dairy Boy (Bern) SP6   Girl (Vaud) SP7

1916, Dec. 1
B4 SP5 3c (+2c) vio, buff 7.00 27.50
B5 SP6 5c (+5c) grn, buff 16.00 7.25
B6 SP7 10c (+5c) brn red, buff 65.00 65.00

Girl (Valais) SP8   Girl (Unterwalden) SP9   Girl (Ticino) SP10

1917, Dec. 1
B7 SP8 3c (+2c) vio, buff 6.00 35.00
B8 SP9 5c (+5c) grn, buff 10.00 4.50
B9 SP10 10c (+5c) red, buff 27.50 22.50

Arms of Uri SP11   Arms of Geneva SP12
Straw-Surfaced Paper
1918, Dec. 1
B10 SP11 10c (+5c) red, org & blk 9.00 14.00
B11 SP12 15c (+5c) vio, red, org & blk 11.00 8.00

Arms of Nidwalden SP13   Arms of Vaud SP14   Arms of Obwalden SP15
Cream-Surfaced Paper
1919, Dec. 1
B12 SP13 7½c (+5c) gray, red & blk 3.00 8.00
B13 SP14 10c (+5c) lake, grn & blk 3.00 8.00
B14 SP15 15c (+5c) pur, red & blk 3.00 4.00

Arms of Schwyz SP16   Arms of Zürich SP17   Arms of Ticino SP18
Cream-Surfaced Paper
1920, Dec. 1
B15 SP16 7½c (+5c) gray & red 3.50 8.00
B16 SP17 10c (+5c) red & lt bl 4.50 8.00
B17 SP18 15c (+5c) vio, red & bl 3.50 3.00

Arms of Valais SP19   Arms of Bern SP20   Arms of Switzerland SP21
Cream-Surfaced Paper
1921, Dec. 1
B18 SP19 10c (+5c) grn, red & blk 80 2.50
B19 SP20 20c (+5c) vio, red, org & blk 1.00 3.00
B20 SP21 40c (+10c) bl & red 10.00 50.00

Arms of Zug SP22   Arms of Fribourg SP23

Arms of Lucerne SP24   Arms of Switzerland SP25
Cream-Surfaced Paper
1922, Dec. 1
B21 SP22 5c (+5c) org, pale bl & blk 60 4.00
B22 SP23 10c (+5c) ol grn & blk 50 2.00
B23 SP24 20c (+5c) vio, pale bl & blk 70 1.75
B24 SP25 40c (+10c) bl & red 11.50 50.00

Arms of Basel SP26   Arms of Glarus (St. Fridolin) SP27

Arms of Neuchâtel SP28   Arms of Switzerland SP29
Cream-Surfaced Paper
1923, Dec. 1
B25 SP26 5c (+5c) org & blk 35 3.00
B26 SP27 10c (+5c) multi 40 1.60
B27 SP28 20c (+5c) multi 40 1.60
B28 SP29 40c (+10c) dk bl & red 8.00 45.00

Arms of Appenzell SP30   Arms of Solothurn SP31

Arms of Schaffhausen SP32   Arms of Switzerland SP33
Cream-Surfaced Paper
1924, Dec. 1
B29 SP30 5c (+5c) dk vio & blk 20 1.10
B30 SP31 10c (+5c) grn, red & blk 25 90
B31 SP32 20c (+5c) car, yel & blk 30 90
B32 SP33 30c (+10c) bl, red & blk 1.75 7.00

Arms of St. Gallen (Canton) SP34   Arms of Appenzell-Ausser-Rhoden SP35

Arms of Grisons SP36   Arms of Switzerland SP37

Cream-Surfaced Paper
1925, Dec. 1
B33 SP34 5c (+5c) vio, grn & blk 10 1.00
B34 SP35 10c (+5c) grn & blk 25 80
B35 SP36 20c (+5c) multi 30 90
B36 SP37 30c (+10c) dk bl, red & blk 1.50 7.00

Arms of Thurgau SP38   Arms of Basel SP39

Arms of Aargau SP40   Arms of Switzerland SP41
Cream-Surfaced Paper
1926, Dec. 1
B37 SF38 5c (+5c) vio, bis & grn 15 1.00
B38 SF39 10c (+5c) gray grn, red & blk 30 90
B39 SF40 20c (+5c) red, blk & bl 30 90
B40 SF41 30c (+10c) dk bl & red 1.50 7.00

Orphan SP42   Orphan at Pestalozzi School SP43   J. H. Pestalozzi SP44

J. H. Pestalozzi SP45
Granite Paper.
1927, Dec. 1 Typo. Wmk. 183
B41 SP42 5c (+5c) red vio & yel, grysh 20 65
B42 SP43 10c (+5c) grn & fawn, grnsh 25 50

Engraved.
B43 SP44 20c (+5c) red 30 55
Photogravure. Unwmkd.
B44 SP45 30c (+10c) gray bl & blk 1.40 4.25

Nos. B43 and B44 were in commemoration of the centenary of the death of Johann Heinrich Pestalozzi, the Swiss educational reformer.

Arms of Lausanne SP46   Arms of Winterthur SP47

SWITZERLAND

Arms of St. Gallen (City)
SP48

J. H. Dunant
SP49

1928, Dec. 1   Typo.   Wmk. 183
Cream-Surfaced Paper.
B45	SP46	5c (+5c) dk vio, red & blk	15	90
B46	SP47	10c (+5c) bl grn, org red & blk	20	80
B47	SP48	20c (+5c) brn red, blk & yel	20	80

Photogravure.
Unwmkd.
Thick White Paper.
| B48 | SP49 | 30c (+10c) dl bl & red | 1.50 | 4.50 |

No. B48 was issued in commemoration of the centenary of the birth of Jean Henri Dunant, Swiss author, philanthropist and founder of the Red Cross Society.

Lake Lugano and Mt. Salvatore
SP50

Lake Engstlen and Mt. Titlis
SP51

Mt. Lyskamm
SP52

Nicholas von der Flüe
SP53

1929, Dec. 1   Perf. 11x11½
B49	SP50	5c (+5c) dk vio & red org	20	65
B50	SP51	10c (+5c) ol brn & gray bl	30	50
B51	SP52	20c (+5c) brn garnet & bl	35	50
B52	SP53	30c (+10c) dk bl	1.75	5.50

No. B52 was in commemoration of Nicholas von der Flüe, the Swiss patriot. By his advice the Swiss Confederation was continued and Swiss independence was saved.

Arms of Fribourg
SP54

Arms of Altdorf
SP55

Arms of Schaffhausen
SP56

Jeremias Gotthelf
SP57

Cream-Surfaced Paper.
Wmkd. Greek Cross. (183)
1930, Dec. 1   Typo.   Perf. 11½
B53	SP54	5c (+5c) dp grn, dl bl & blk	15	65
B54	SP55	10c (+5c) multi	20	65
B55	SP56	20c (+5c) multi	25	65

Engraved.
White Paper.
| B56 | SP57 | 30c (+10c) sl bl | 1.50 | 4.50 |

No. B56 was commemorative of Jeremias Gotthelf, pen name of Albrecht Bitzius, pastor and author.

Lakes Silvaplana and Sils
SP58

Wetterhorn—SP59

Lake Geneva—SP60

Alexandre Vinet—SP61

Granite Paper.
1931, Dec. 1   Photo.   Unwmkd.
B57	SP58	5c (+5c) dp grn	25	70
B58	SP59	10c (+5c) dk vio	40	50
B59	SP60	20c (+5c) brn red	50	50

Engraved
Wmkd. Greek Cross. (183)
| B60 | SP61 | 30c (+10c) ultra | 6.00 | 11.00 |

No. B60 was commemorative of Alexandre Rudolph Vinet, critic and theologian.

Flag Swinger
SP62

Putting the Stone
SP63

Wrestling
SP64

Eugen Huber
SP65

Granite Paper.
1932, Dec. 1   Typo.   Unwmkd.
B61	SP62	5c (+5c) dk grn & red	55	1.25
B62	SP63	10c (+5c) org	70	1.25
B63	SP64	20c (+5c) scar	70	1.25

Engraved.
Wmkd. Greek Cross. (183)
| B64 | SP65 | 30c (+10c) ultra | 2.75 | 5.25 |

No. B64 was commemorative of Eugen Huber, jurist and author of the Swiss Civil Law Book.

Girl of Vaud
SP66

Girl of Bern
SP67

Girl of Ticino
SP68

Jean Baptiste Girard
(Le Père Grégoire)
SP69

Granite Paper.
1933, Dec. 1   Photo.   Unwmkd.
B65	SP66	5c (+5c) grn & buff	20	80
B66	SP67	10c (+5c) vio & buff	30	50
B67	SP68	20c (+5c) red & buff	40	60

Engraved.
Wmkd. Greek Cross. (183)
| B68 | SP69 | 30c (+10c) ultra | 2.00 | 5.50 |

Girl of Appenzell
SP70

Girl of Valais
SP71

Girl of Grisons
SP72

Albrecht von Haller
SP73

1934, Dec. 1   Photo.   Unwmkd.
B69	SP70	5c (+5c) grn & buff	20	80
B70	SP71	10c (+5c) vio & buff	35	60
B71	SP72	20c (+5c) red & buff	45	60

Engraved
Wmkd. Greek Cross. (183)
| B72 | SP73 | 30c (+10c) ultra | 2.25 | 6.75 |

Girl of Basel
SP74

Girl of Lucerne
SP75

Girl of Geneva
SP76

Stefano Franscini
SP77

Granite Paper.
1935, Dec. 1   Photo.   Unwmkd.
B73	SP74	5c (+5c) grn & buff	25	75
B74	SP75	10c (+5c) vio & buff	40	60
B75	SP76	20c (+5c) red & buff	40	1.00

Engraved
Wmkd. Greek Cross. (183)
| B76 | SP77 | 30c (+10c) ultra | 2.50 | 7.00 |

No. B76 honors Stefano Franscini (1796–1857), political economist and educator.

National Defense Issue.

Alpine Herdsman
SP78

Perf. 11½
1936, Oct. 1   Photo.   Unwmkd.
Granite Paper.
B77	SP78	10c +5c vio	40	55
B78	SP78	20c +10c dk red	80	2.25
B79	SP78	30c +10c ultra	3.50	12.00

A particular stamp may be scarce, but if few want it, its market potential may remain relatively low.

SWITZERLAND

Souvenir Sheet.

SP78a

B80	SP78a	Sheet of three	40.00	210.00
a.		Block of four sheets	275.00	1,000.

Nos. B77–B80 were issued in connection with the Swiss National Defense Fund Drive.
No. B80 contains stamps similar to Nos. B77–B79, but on different granite paper with blue and red fibers instead of black and red. Sold for 2fr. Size: 120x130mm.

Johann Georg Nägeli SP79 — Girl of Neuchâtel SP80

Girl of Schwyz SP81 — Girl of Zurich SP82

Granite Paper.
Wmkd. Greek Cross. (183)
1936, Dec. 1   Engr.   Perf. 11½

B81	SP79	5c (+5c) grn	25	55

Photogravure.
Unwmkd.

B82	SP80	10c (+5c) vio & buff	35	55
B83	SP81	20c (+5c) red & buff	50	80
B84	SP82	30c (+10c) ultra & buff	4.00	14.00

Gen. Henri Dufour SP83 — Nicholas von der Flüe SP84

Boy SP85

Girl—SP86
Engraved.
1937, Dec. 1   Perf. 11½   Unwmkd.

B85	SP83	5c +5c bl grn	15	25
B86	SP84	10c +5c red vio	15	35

Photogravure.
Granite Paper.

B87	SP85	20c +5c red & sil	25	35
B88	SP86	30c +10c ultra & sil	1.75	5.00

Issued to commemorate the 25th anniversary of the Pro Juventute (child welfare) stamps.

Souvenir Sheet.

SP86a
1937, Dec. 20   Imperf.

B89	SP86a	Sheet of two	4.50	55.00
a.		20c +5c red & sil	1.50	16.00
b.		30c +10c ultra & sil	1.50	16.00

Simulated perforation in silver. Size: 105x59mm. Sheet sold for 1fr.

Tell Chapel, Lake Lucerne—SP87
1938, June 15   Perf. 11½
Granite Paper

B90	SP87	10c +5c brt vio & yel	40	50
a.		Grilled gum	20.00	60.00

National Fête Day.

Salomon Gessner SP88 — Girl of St. Gallen SP89

Girl of Uri SP90 — Girl of Aargau SP91

1938, Dec. 1   Engraved   Perf. 11½

B91	SP88	5c +5c dp bl grn	15	20

Photogravure.
Granite Paper.

B92	SP89	10c +5c pur & buff	20	35
B93	SP90	20c +5c red & buff	25	35
B94	SP91	30c +10c ultra	1.50	5.00

Castle at Laupen SP92
1939, June 15

B95	SP92	10c +10c brn, gray & red	35	45

Issued in commemoration of the 600th anniversary of the Battle of Laupen. The surtax was used to aid needy mothers.

Hans Herzog SP93 — Girl of Fribourg SP94

Girl of Nidwalden SP95 — Girl of Basel SP96

Engraved.
1939, Dec. 1   Perf. 11½   Unwmkd.

B96	SP93	5c +5c dk grn	10	30

Photogravure.
Granite Paper

B97	SP94	10c +5c rose vio & buff	20	30
B98	SP95	20c +5c org red	35	35
B99	SP96	30c +10c ultra & buff	1.75	6.75

Sempach, 1386 SP97 — Giornico, 1478 SP98

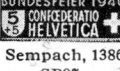 

Calven, 1499 SP99 — World War I Ranger SP100

Granite Paper
1940, Mar. 20   Photogravure

B100	SP97	5c +5c emer, blk & red	25	1.00

B101	SP98	10c +5c brn org, blk & car	30	40
B102	SP99	20c +5c brn red, blk & car	2.00	70
B103	SP100	30c +10c brt bl, brn blk & red	2.50	5.50

Issued in commemoration of the National Fête Day. The surtax was for the National Fund and the Red Cross.

Redrawn.

B104	SP99	20c +5c brn red, blk & car	14.00	5.00
		Nos. B100-B104 (5)	19.05	12.60

The base of statue has been heavily shaded and "Calven 1499" moved nearer to bottom line of base. Top line of base removed.

Souvenir Sheet.

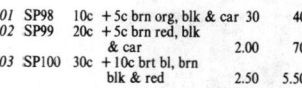

SP101
Granite Paper
Photogravure.
1940, July 16   Imperf.   Unwmkd.

B105	SP101	Sheet of four	350.00	900.00
a.		5c +5c yel grn, blk & red	50.00	85.00
b.		10c +5c org yel, blk & red	50.00	85.00
c.		20c +5c brn red, blk & red	50.00	85.00
d.		30c +10c chlky bl, blk & red	50.00	85.00

Issued in commemoration of National Fête Day.
Sheets measure 125x65mm. and sold for 5fr.

Gottfried Keller SP102 — Girl of Thurgau SP103

Girl of Solothurn SP104 — Girl of Zug SP105

1940, Dec. 1   Engraved   Perf. 11½

B106	SP102	5c +5c dk bl grn	15	30

Photogravure.

B107	SP103	10c +5c brn & buff	20	30
B108	SP104	20c +5c org red & buff	25	35
B109	SP105	30c +10c dp ultra & buff	1.75	5.50

Lake Lucerne, Arms of Cantons SP106

SWITZERLAND

Tell Chapel at Chemin Creux SP107

1941, June 15

| B110 | SP106 | 10c +10c multi | 40 | 65 |
| B111 | SP107 | 20c +10c org, red & lt buff | 40 | 50 |

Issued in commemoration of the National Fête Day and the 650th anniversary of Swiss Independence.

Johann Lavater SP108 — Girl of Schaffhausen SP109

Girl of Obwalden SP110 — Daniel Jean Richard SP111

1941, Dec. 1 Engraved

| B112 | SP108 | 5c +5c dk grn | 20 | 20 |
| B113 | SP111 | 30c +10c dp ultra | 1.50 | 4.50 |

Photogravure.

| B114 | SP109 | 10c +5c chnt & buff | 30 | 35 |
| B115 | SP110 | 20c +5c ver & buff | 30 | 35 |

Souvenir Sheet.

SP112 *Imperf.*

B116	SP112	Sheet of two	65.00	325.00
a.		10c+5c chnt & buff	22.50	135.00
b.		20c+5c ver & buff	22.50	135.00

Issued in sheets measuring 75x70mm. and sold for 2fr. The surtax was used for charity.

Ancient Geneva SP113

Soldiers' Monument, Forch SP114

1942, June 15 Perf. 11½

| B117 | SP113 | 10c +10c gray blk, red & yel | 40 | 55 |
| B118 | SP114 | 20c +10c cop red, red & buff | 40 | 55 |

Issued in commemoration of the National Fête Day, 1942. No. B117 commemorates the 2000th anniversary of the City of Geneva.

Souvenir Sheet.

SP115 *Imperf.*

B119	SP115	Sheet of two	57.50	250.00
a.		10c+10c gray blk, red & yel	16.00	90.00
b.		20c+20c cop red, red & buff	16.00	90.00

Issued in sheets measuring 105 x 63 mm. in commemoration of National Fête and the 2000th anniversary of the City of Geneva. Sold for 2 fr. The surtax was divided between the Swiss Alliance of Samaritans and the National Community Chest.

Niklaus Riggenbach SP116 — Girl of Appenzell SP117

Girl of Glarus SP118 — Konrad Escher von der Linth SP119

1942, Dec. 1 Engr. Perf. 11½

| B120 | SP116 | 5c +5c dp grn | 10 | 35 |
| B121 | SP119 | 30c +10c ryl bl | 1.75 | 4.00 |

Photogravure

| B122 | SP117 | 10c +5c dp brn & buff | 20 | 35 |
| B123 | SP118 | 20c +5c org red | 25 | 35 |

Intragna—SP120

Parliament Buildings, Bern SP121

1943, June 15 Photo. Perf. 11½

| B124 | SP120 | 10c +10c blk brn, buff & dk red | 40 | 55 |
| B125 | SP121 | 20c +10c cop red, buff & dk red | 50 | 60 |

National Fête Day, 1943.

Emanuel von Fellenberg SP122 — Silver Thistle SP123

Lady Slipper SP124 — Gentian SP125

1943, Dec. 1 Engraved

| B126 | SP122 | 5c +5c grn | 10 | 25 |

Photogravure.

B127	SP123	10c +5c sl grn & ocher	20	40
B128	SP124	20c +5c cop red & yel	25	40
B129	SP125	30c +10c ryl bl & lt bl	1.75	6.50

Souvenir Sheets.

SP126

1943 Engraved *Imperf.*

| B130 | SP126 | Sheet of twelve | 42.50 | 75.00 |
| a. | | Single stamp, 10c blk | 1.25 | 3.50 |

Sold for 5 francs. Size: 165x140mm.

SP127

Red Horizontal Lines.

B131	SP127	Sheet of two	40.00	60.00
a.		4c blk & red	14.00	17.50
b.		6c blk & red	14.00	17.50

Sold for 3 francs. Size: 70x75mm.

Arms of Geneva—SP128

| B132 | SP128 | Sheet of two | 37.50 | 50.00 |
| a. | | 5c grn & blk | 8.00 | 16.00 |

Sold for 3fr. Size:72×72mm. Centenary of Swiss postage stamps. The surtax aided the Swiss Red Cross.

Heiden—SP129

St. Jacob—SP130

Mesocco—SP131

Basel—SP132

Perf. 11½

1944, June 15 Photo. Unwmkd.

B133	SP129	5c +5c dk bl grn, red & buff	30	1.25
B134	SP130	10c +10c gray blk, red & buff	30	40
B135	SP131	20c +10c hn, red & buff	30	70
B136	SP132	30c +10c brt ultra & red	3.75	12.00

National Fête Day.

Numa Droz SP133 — Edelweiss SP134

SWITZERLAND

Lilium Martagon SP135 — Aquilegia Alpina SP136

1944, Dec. 1   Engraved
B137 SP133 5c + 5c grn   15   35
Photogravure.
B138 SP134 10c + 5c dk sl grn, yel & gray   20   40
B139 SP135 20c + 5c red, yel & gray   40   40
B140 SP136 30c + 10c bl, gray & lt bl   1.75   6.75

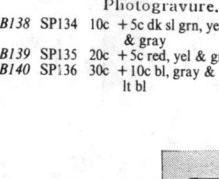

Symbol of Faith, Hope and Love SP137 — Lifeboat Making a Rescue SP138

1945, Feb. 20   Perf. 11½
B141 SP137 10c + 10c sl grn, blk & pale gray   45   55
B142 SP137 20c + 60c cop red, blk & pale gray   1.75   5.00

Souvenir Sheet. Imperf.
B143 SP138 3fr + 7fr bl gray   225.00   300.00
Issued in sheets measuring 70x110mm. The surtax on Nos. B141 to B143 was for the benefit of war victims.

Souvenir Sheet.

Dove of Basel SP139

1945, Apr. 14   Typographed
B144 SP139 Sheet of two   100.00   125.00
   a. 10c gray, mar & blk   30.00   35.00

Issued to commemorate the centenary of the Basel Cantonal Stamp. The sheets measure 71 x 63 mm. and sold for 3 francs. The surtax was for the Pro Juvente Foundation.

Numeral of Value and Red Cross—SP140

1945   Photogravure   Perf. 12
B145 SP140 5c + 10c grn & red   50   65

Weaver—SP141

Farm of Jura—SP142

Farm of Emmental SP143

Frame House, Eastern Switzerland SP144

1945, June 15   Engr.   Perf. 11½
B146 SP141 5c + 5c bl grn & red   50   1.40
Photogravure.
B147 SP142 10c + 10c brn, gray bl & red   50   60
B148 SP143 20c + 10c hn brn, buff & red   60   60
B149 SP144 30c + 10c saph & red   7.25   22.50

The surtax was for needy mothers.

Ludwig Forrer SP145 — Susanna Orelli SP146

Alpine Dog-Rose SP147 — Crocus SP148

1945, Dec. 1   Engraved
B150 SP145 5c + 5c dk grn   25   30
B151 SP146 10c + 10c dk red brn   30   40
Photogravure.
B152 SP147 20c + 10c rose brn, rose & yel org   70   40
B153 SP148 30c + 10c dk bl, gray & lil   2.85   7.25

Cheese Making—SP149

Farm Buildings and Vineyards SP150

House in Appenzell SP151

House in Engadine SP152

1946, June 15   Engraved
B154 SP149 5c + 5c bl grn & red   60   1.75
Photogravure.
B155 SP150 10c + 10c brn, buff & red   60   60
B156 SP151 20c + 10c hn, buff & red   60   60
B157 SP152 30c + 10c saph & red   5.50   9.00

Rodolphe Toepffer SP153 — Narcissus SP154

Mountain Sengreen SP155 — Blue Thistle SP156

1946, Nov. 30   Engraved
B158 SP153 5c + 5c grn   25   30
Photogravure.
B159 SP154 10c + 10c dk sl grn, gray & red org   30   40
B160 SP155 20c + 10c brn car, gray & yel   40   40
B161 SP156 30c + 10c dk bl, gray & pink   2.90   6.00

Railroad Laborers SP157

Railroad Station, Rorschach SP158

Lüen-Castiel Station SP159

Flüelen Station SP160

Perf. 11½
1947, June 14   Engr.   Unwmkd.
B162 SP157 5c + 5c dk grn & red   60   2.00
Photogravure.
B163 SP158 10c + 10c gray blk, cr & red   60   80
B164 SP159 20c + 10c rose lil, cr & red   60   80
B165 SP160 30c + 10c bl, gray & red   5.75   8.00

The surtax was for professional education of invalids and for the fight against cancer.

Jakob Burckhardt SP161 — Alpine Primrose SP162

Red Lily SP163 — Cyclamen SP164

1947, Dec. 1   Engraved
B166 SP161 5c + 5c grn   20   20
Photogravure.
B167 SP162 10c + 10c sl blk, gray & yel   25   40

SWITZERLAND

B168	SP163	20c +10c red brn, gray & cop red	45	40
B169	SP164	30c +10c dk bl, gray & pink	3.00	5.50

Sun and Olympic Emblem
SP165

Snowflake and Olympic Emblem
SP166

Ice-hockey Player
SP167

Ski-runner
SP168

1948, Jan. 15

B170	SP165	5c +5c dk bl grn & yel	45	1.40
B171	SP166	10c +10c choc & bl	45	1.40
B172	SP167	20c +10c dp mag, gray & org yel	90	1.40
B173	SP168	30c +10c dk bl, bl & gray blk	2.00	4.75

Issued to publicize the 5th Olympic Winter Games, St. Moritz, Jan. 30 to Feb. 8, 1948.

Frontier Guard
SP169

House of Fribourg
SP170

House of Valais
SP171

House of Ticino—SP172

1948, June 15 Engraved

B174	SP169	5c +5c dk grn & red	30	60

Photogravure.

B175	SP170	10c +10c sl & gray	30	50
B176	SP171	20c +10c brn red & pink	40	50
B177	SP172	30c +10c bl & gray	4.00	6.25

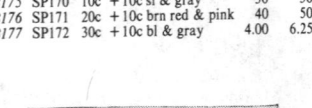

Johann R. Wettstein—SP173

1948, Aug. 21 Perf. 11x12½

B178	SP173	Sheet of 2	75.00	67.50
a.		10c rose lil	25.00	22.50
b.		20c chlky bl	25.00	22.50

Issued in sheets measuring 110x60mm., to commemorate the International Philatelic Exposition, Basel, August 21–29, 1948. Sheet sold for 3 francs, of which the surtax was used for the exhibition and charitable purposes.

Gen. Ulrich Wille
SP174

Foxglove
SP175

Designs: 20c+10c, Alpine rose. 40c+10c, Lily of paradise.

1948, Dec. 1 Engr. Perf. 11½

B179	SP174	5c +5c dk vio brn	25	30

Photogravure.

B180	SP175	10c +10c dk grn, yel grn & yel	50	40
B181	SP175	20c +10c brn, crim & buff	65	40
B182	SP175	40c +10c bl, gray & org	2.65	5.50

Postman
SP176

Mountain Farmhouse
SP177

House of Lucerne—SP178

House of Prattigau
SP179

1949, June 15 Engr. & Photo.
Shield in Carmine

B183	SP176	5c +5c rose vio	55	1.25

Photogravure.

B184	SP177	10c +10c bl grn & cr	60	70
B185	SP178	20c +10c dk brn & cr	75	70
B186	SP179	40c +10c bl & pale bl	5.00	8.50

The surtax was for professional education of Swiss youth.

Niklaus Wengi
SP180

Anemone Sulphureous
SP181

Designs: 20c+10c, Alpine clematis. 40c+10c, Superb pink.

1949, Dec. 1 Engr. Perf. 11½

B187	SP180	5c +5c vio brn	30	20

Photogravure.

B188	SP181	10c +10c grn, gray & yel	45	30
B189	SP181	20c +10c brn, bl & yel	55	40
B190	SP181	40c +10c brt bl, lav & yel	2.65	5.25

Adaptation of 1850 Design
SP182

Putting the Stone
SP183

Designs: 20c+10c, Wrestlers. 30c+10c, Runners. 40c+10c, Target shooting.

1950, June 1 Engr. & Photo.
Shield in Red

B191	SP182	5c +5c blk	50	75

Inscribed: "I. VIII. 1950."

Photogravure.

B192	SP183	10c +10c grn	85	75
B193	SP183	20c +20c brn ol	1.00	1.00
B194	SP183	30c +10c rose lil	7.75	15.00
B195	SP183	40c +10c dl bl	7.75	11.50
		Nos. B191-B195 (5)	17.85	29.00

The surtax was for the Red Cross and the Society of Swiss History of Art.

 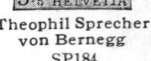

Theophil Sprecher von Bernegg
SP184

Admiral Butterfly
SP185

Designs: 20c+10c, Blue Underwing Butterfly. 30c+10c, Bee. 40c+10c, Sulphur Butterfly.

1950, Dec. 1 Engraved

B196	SP184	5c +5c sep	25	25

Photogravure.

B197	SP185	10c +10c multi	45	30
B198	SP185	20c +10c multi	70	30
B199	SP185	30c +10c rose lil, gray & dk brn	5.75	13.00
B200	SP185	40c +10c bl, dk brn & yel	5.00	9.50
		Nos. B196-B200 (5)	12.15	23.35

Arms of Switzerland and Zurich
SP186

Valaisan Polka
SP187

Designs: 20c+10c, Flag-swinging. 30c+10c, Hornussen (national game). 40c+10c, Blowing alphorn.

1951, June 1 Engraved
Shield in Red.

B201	SP186	5c +5c gray	45	50

Inscribed: "1. VIII. 1951".

Photogravure.

Shield in Red,

Figures Shaded in Gray.

B202	SP187	10c +10c grn	1.00	70
B203	SP187	20c +10c ol bis	1.00	70
B204	SP187	30c +10c red vio	7.00	12.50
B205	SP187	40c +10c brt bl	7.25	13.00
		Nos. B201-B205 (5)	16.70	27.40

The surtax was used primarily for needy mothers.

Souvenir Sheet.

Flag-Swinging
SP188

Photogravure.

1951, Sept. 29 Imperf. Unwmkd.

B206	SP188	40c (+2.60fr) brt bl, sheet	300.00	260.00

Issued in sheets measuring 74x56mm., on the occasion of the National Philatelic Exhibition, LUNABA, Sept. 29–Oct. 7, 1951, at Lucerne. The net proceeds were used for Swiss schools abroad.

Johanna Spyri
SP189

Dragonfly
SP190

Butterflies: 20c+10c, Black-Veined. 30c+10c, Orange-Tip. 40c+10c, Saturnia pyri.

SWITZERLAND

Albrecht
von Haller
SP209

Pansy
SP210

Flowers: 20c+10c, China aster. 30c+10c, Morning glory. 40c+10c, Christmas rose.

1958, Dec. 1 Engraved Perf. 11½

B277	SP209	5c +5c brn car	20	16
a.		Bklt. pane of 4	1.20	1.25

Photogravure.
Granite Paper

B278	SP210	10c +10c grn, yel & brn	20	16
a.		Bklt. pane of 4	1.75	1.75
B279	SP210	20c +10c multi	25	16
a.		Bklt. pane of 4	4.00	4.00
B280	SP210	30c +10c multi	2.25	3.50
B281	SP210	40c +10c dk bl, yel & grn	2.25	3.00
		Nos. B277-B281 (5)	5.15	6.98

See Nos. B287-B291.

Mineral Type of 1958 and

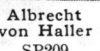

Globe and
Swiss Flags
SP211

Designs: 10c+10+, Agate. 20c+10c, Tourmaline. 30c+10c, Amethyst. 40c+10c, Fossil salamander (andrias).

1959, June 1 Engraved Perf. 11½

B282	SP211	5c +5c dl grn & red	30	40

Photogravure.
Granite Paper

B283	SP208	10c +10c gray, yel grn & ver	45	30
B284	SP208	20c +10c blk, lil rose & bl grn	45	30
B285	SP208	30c +10c blk, lt brn & vio	2.25	3.00
B286	SP208	40c +10c blk, bl & gray	2.25	3.00
		Nos. B282-B286 (5)	5.70	7.00

Types of 1958
Designs: 5c+5c, Karl Hilty. 10c+10c, Marigold. 20c+10c, Poppy. 30c+10c, Nasturtium. 50c+10c, Sweet pea.

1959, Dec. 1 Engraved Perf. 11½

B287	SP209	5c +5c brn car	15	15
a.		Bklt. pane of 4	1.00	1.10

Photogravure.

B288	SP210	10c +10c dk grn, grn & yel	20	20
a.		Bklt. pane of 4	1.60	1.60
B289	SP210	20c +10c mag, red & grn	40	25
a.		Bklt. pane of 4	2.75	2.75
B290	SP210	30c +10c multi	2.00	3.00
B291	SP210	50c +10c multi	2.00	3.50
		Nos. B287-B291 (5)	4.75	7.10

Mineral Type of 1958 and

Owl, T-Square and Hammer
SP212

Designs: 5c+5c, Smoky quartz. 10c+10c, Feldspar. 20c+10c, Gryphaea, fossil. 30c+10c, Azurite.

1960, June 1 Photo. Perf. 11½

Granite Paper

B292	SP208	5c +5c blk, bl & ocher	50	55
B293	SP208	10c +10c blk, yel grn & pink	75	45
B294	SP208	20c +10c blk, lil rose & yel	75	45
B295	SP208	30c +10c multi	3.00	4.00

Engraved

B296	SP212	50c +10c bl & gold	3.00	4.00
		Nos. B292-B296 (5)	8.00	9.45

Souvenir Sheet
Typographed
Imperf.

B297	Sheet of four	35.00	27.50

No. B297 contains four 50c+10c stamps of type SP212 in gold and blue with slate and red marginal inscription. Size: 84x75mm. Sold for 3fr.

Alexandre Calame   Dandelion
SP213   SP214

Flowers: 20c+10c, Phlox. 30c+10c, Larkspur. 50c+10c, Thorn apple.

1960, Dec. 1 Engr. Unwmkd.

B298	SP213	5c +5c grnsh bl	20	20
a.		Bklt. pane of 4	1.10	1.20

Photogravure.
Granite Paper

B299	SP214	10c +10c grn, yel & gray	25	20
a.		Bklt. pane of 4	1.50	1.50
B300	SP214	20c +10c mag, grn & gray	45	20
a.		Bklt. pane of 4	2.25	2.25
B301	SP214	30c +10c org brn, grn & bl	2.50	3.50
B302	SP214	50c +10c ultra & grn	2.75	3.75
		Nos. B298-B302 (5)	6.15	7.85

See also Nos. B308-B312, B329-B333, B339-B343.

Mineral Type of 1958 and

Book of History with Symbols of
Time and Eternity
SP215

Designs: 10c+10c, Fluorite. 20c+10c, Petrified fish. 30c+10c, Lazulite. 50c+10c, Petrified fern.

1961, June 1 Engr. Perf. 11½

B303	SP215	5c +5c lt bl	28	28

Photogravure.
Granite Paper

B304	SP208	10c +10c gray, grn & pink	40	25
B305	SP208	20c +10c gray & car rose	60	25
B306	SP208	30c +10c gray, org & grnsh bl	3.00	3.25
B307	SP208	50c +10c gray, bl & bis	3.00	3.25
		Nos. B303-B307 (5)	7.28	7.28

Types of 1960.
Designs: 5c+5c, Jonas Furrer. 10c+10c, Sunflower. 20c+10c, Lily of the valley. 30c+10c, Iris. 50c+10c, Silverweed.

1961, Dec. 1 Engr. Perf. 11½

B308	SP213	5c +5c dk bl	20	20
a.		Bklt. pane of 4	85	1.00

Photogravure
Granite Paper

B309	SP214	10c +10c grn, yel & org	20	20
a.		Bklt. pane of 4	1.50	1.50
B310	SP214	20c +10c dk red, grn & gray	40	20
a.		Bklt. pane of 4	2.25	2.25
B311	SP214	30c +10c multi	2.00	2.25
B312	SP214	50c +10c dk bl, yel & grn	2.10	2.25
		Nos. B308-B312 (5)	4.90	5.10

Jean Jacques   Half-Thaler,
Rousseau   Obwalden, 1732
SP216   SP217

Coins: 20c+10c, Ducat, Schwyz, ca. 1653. 30c+10c, "Steer Head" Batzen, Uri, 1659. 50c+10c, Nidwalden Batzen.

Engraved

1962, June 1 Perf. 11½ Unwmkd.

B313	SP216	5c +5c dk bl	20	20

Photogravure
Granite Paper

B314	SP217	10c +10c grn & stl bl	40	40
B315	SP217	20c +10c car rose & yel	40	40
B316	SP217	30c +10c org & sl bl	1.75	1.75
B317	SP217	50c +10c ultra & vio bl	1.75	1.75
		Nos. B313-B317 (5)	4.50	4.50

Apple Blossoms   Mother and Child
SP218   SP219

Designs: 10c+10c, Boy chasing duck. 30c+10c, Girl and sunflowers. 50c+10c, Forsythia. 1fr+20c, Mother and child, facing right.

1962, Dec. 1 Perf. 11½

Granite Paper

B318	SP218	5c +5c bl gray, pink, grn & yel	15	15
a.		Bklt. pane of 4	85	1.10
B319	SP218	10c +10c grn, pink & dk grn	15	15
a.		Booklet pane of 4	1.00	1.10
B320	SP219	20c +10c org red, brn, grn & pink	40	25
B321	SP218	30c +10c org, red & yel	1.75	2.25
B322	SP218	50c +10c dp yel, brn & yel	1.75	2.25
		Nos. B318-B322 (5)	4.20	5.05

Souvenir Sheet
Imperf.

B323	SP219	1fr +20c multi, sheet of two	8.00	8.00

Issued to commemorate the 50th anniversary of the Pro Juventute (Youth Aid) Foundation. No. B323 has pale yellow margin showing toys and blue inscription. Size: 81x62mm. Sold for 3fr.

Anna Heer, M.D.   Bandage Roll
SP220   SP221

Designs: 20c+10c, Gift parcel. 30c+10c, Plasma bottles. 50c+10c, Red Cross armband.

1963, June 1 Engraved Perf. 11½

B324	SP220	5c +5c bl	15	20

Photogravure
Granite Paper
Cross in Red

B325	SP221	10c +10c lt & dk grn & gray	25	20
B326	SP221	20c +10c rose, gray & blk	35	20
B327	SP221	30c +10c multi	1.25	1.40
B328	SP221	50c +10c bl, gray & blk	1.40	1.40
		Nos. B324-B328 (5)	3.40	3.40

Types of 1960
Designs: 5c+5c, Portrait of a Boy by Albert Anker. 10c+10c, Daisy. 20c+10c, Geranium. 30c+10c, Cornflower. 50c+10c, Carnation.

1963, Nov. 30 Engraved Perf. 11½

B329	SP213	5c +5c bl	20	30
a.		Bklt. pane of 4	1.10	1.50

Photogravure

B330	SP214	10c +10c grn, gray & yel	25	50
a.		Bklt. pane of 4	1.65	2.25
B331	SP214	20c +10c multi	80	50
a.		Bklt. pane of 4	3.50	3.50
B332	SP214	30c +10c multi	1.40	1.40
B333	SP214	50c +10c ultra, lil rose & grn	1.40	1.40
		Nos. B329-B333 (5)	4.05	4.10

Nos. B329-B331 were printed on two kinds of paper: I. Fluorescent, with violet fibers. II. Non-fluorescent, the 10c+10c and 20c+10c with mixed red and blue fibers. Nos. B332-B333 exist only on violet-fibered, fluorescent paper. The booklet panes, Nos. B329a, B330a and B331a, exist only on non-fluorescent paper.

Johann Georg   Copper Coin,
Bodmer   Zurich
SP222   SP223

Coins: 20c+10c, Doppeldicken, Basel. 30c+10c, Silver taler, Geneva. 50c+10c, Gold half florin, Bern.

Violet Fibers, Fluorescent Paper

1964, June 1 Engraved Perf. 11½

B334	SP222	5c +5c bl	10	10

Photogravure

B335	SP223	10c +10c grn, bis & blk	15	15
B336	SP223	20c +10c rose car, gray & blk	40	40
B337	SP223	30c +10c org, gray & blk	70	70

SWITZERLAND

1951, Dec. 1	Engr.	Perf. 11½		
B207	SP189	5c +5c red brn	20	20

Photogravure.

B208	SP190	10c +10c grn & dk bl	25	30
B209	SP190	20c +10c rose lil, cr & blk	40	30
B210	SP190	30c +10c ol grn, gray & org	4.25	8.25
B211	SP190	40c +10c bl, dk brn & car	4.00	8.00
	Nos. B207-B211 (5)		9.10	17.05

Arms of Switzerland, Glarus and Zug
SP191

Doubs River
SP192

Designs: 20c+10c, Lake of St. Gotthard. 30c+10c, Moesa River. 40c+10c, Lake of Marjelen.

1952, May 31	Engr. & Typo.		
B212	SP191	5c +5c gray & red	40	60

Photogravure.

B213	SP192	10c +10c bl grn	50	40
B214	SP192	20c +10c brn car	50	40
B215	SP192	30c +10c brn	4.00	6.00
B216	SP192	40c +10c bl	4.00	6.00
	Nos. B212-B216 (5)		9.40	13.40

The surtax was used primarily for historical research and popular culture.
See Nos. B233-B236, B243-B246, B253-B256.

Portrait of a Boy, by Albert Anker
SP193

Ladybug
SP194

Designs: 20c+10c, Barred-wing butterfly. 30c+10c, Argus butterfly. 40c+10c, Silkworm moth.

Engraved.

1952, Dec. 1	Perf. 11½	Unwmkd.		
B217	SP193	5c +5c brn car	20	20

Photogravure.

B218	SP194	10c +10c bluish grn, blk & org red	35	30
B219	SP194	20c +10c rose lil, cr & blk	55	30
B220	SP194	30c +10c brn, blk & gray bl	4.25	7.50
B221	SP194	40c +10c pale vio, brn & buff	5.25	7.25
	Nos. B217-B221 (5)		10.60	15.55

See Nos. B227-B231, B234-B241.

Types Similar to 1952.
Designs: 5c+5c, Arms of Switzerland and Bern. 10c+10c, Reuss River. 20c+10c, Sihl Lake. 30c+10c, Bisse River. 40c+10c, Lake of Geneva.

1953, June 1	Engr. & Photo.		
B222	SP191	5c +5c gray & red	40	65

Photogravure.

B223	SP192	10c +10c bl grn	50	45
B224	SP192	20c +10c brn car	65	45
B225	SP192	30c +10c brn	3.75	6.25
B226	SP192	40c +10c bl	3.75	6.25
	Nos. B222-B226 (5)		9.05	14.05

The surtax was used for Swiss nationals abroad and for disabled persons.

Types Similar to 1952, Dated "1953".
Designs: 5c+5c, Portrait of a girl, by Albert Anker. 10c+10c, Nun moth. 20c+10c, Camberwell beauty butterfly. 30c+10c, Purple longicorn beetle. 40c+10c, Self-portrait, Ferdinand Hodler, facing left.

1953, Dec. 1	Engr.	Perf. 11½		
B227	SP193	5c +5c rose brn	25	20
a.	Bklt. pane of 6		2.25	2.75

Photogravure.

B228	SP194	10c +10c bl grn, brn & rose pink	30	20
a.	Booklet pane of 6		4.50	5.25
B229	SP194	20c +10c multi	40	20
a.	Sheet of 24		275.00	1,000.
b.	Booklet pane of 6 (4 No. B229 + 2 No. B230)		35.00	60.00
B230	SP194	30c +10c ol, blk & red	4.50	7.25

Engraved

| B231 | SP193 | 40c +10c bl | 5.25 | 7.25 |
| | Nos. B227-B231 (5) | | 10.70 | 15.10 |

No. B229a consists of 16 No. B229 and 8 No. B230, arranged to include four se-tenant pairs and four pairs which are both se-tenant and tête bêche.

Opening Bars of "Swiss Hymn"
SP195

Jeremias Gotthelf
SP196

Types Similar to 1952, Dated "1954".
Views: 10c + 10c, Neuchatel lake. 20c+10c, Maggia river. 30c+10c, Cascade, Taubenloch gorge. 40c+10c, Sils lake.

1954, June 1	Engr.	Perf. 11½		
B232	SP195	5c +5c dk bl grn	45	40

Photogravure.

B233	SP192	10c +10c bl grn	55	40
B234	SP192	20c +10c dp plum	55	40
B235	SP192	30c +10c dk bl	4.00	6.00
B236	SP192	40c +10c dp bl	4.00	6.00
	Nos. B232-B236 (5)		9.55	13.20

The surtax was used to aid vocational training and home nursing.
No. B232 commemorates the centenary of the death of Alberik Zwyssig, composer of the "Swiss Hymn."

Types Similar to 1952, Dated "1954".
Insects: 10c+10c, Garden tiger. 20c+10c, Bumble bee. 30c+10c, Ascalaphus. 40c+10c, Swallow-tail.

1954, Dec. 1		Engraved		
B237	SP196	5c +5c dk red brn	20	30
a.	Booklet pane of 4		1.50	1.75

Photogravure.

B238	SP194	10c +10c multi	45	30
a.	Booklet pane of 4		2.25	2.00
B239	SP194	20c +10c multi	65	60
a.	Booklet pane of 4		5.00	5.75
B240	SP194	30c +10c rose vio, brn & yel	4.75	6.75
B241	SP194	40c +10c multi	4.75	6.75
	Nos. B237-B241 (5)		10.80	14.70

Type Similar to 1952, Dated "1955", and

Federal Institute of Technology, Zurich—SP197

Views: 10c+10c, Saane river. 20c+10c, Lake of Aegeri. 30c+10c, Grappelen Lake. 40c+10c, Lake of Bienne.

1955, June 1	Engr.	Perf. 11½		
B242	SP197	5c +5c gray	40	60

Photogravure.

| B243 | SP192 | 10c +10c dp grn | 50 | 35 |
| B244 | SP192 | 20c +10c rose brn | 50 | 40 |

B245	SP192	30c +10c brn	4.25	5.00
B246	SP192	40c +10c dp bl	9.90	11.35
	Nos. B242-B246 (5)			

The surtax aided mountain dwellers.
No. B242 was issued to commemorate the centenary of the Federal Institute of Technology in Zurich.

Charles Pictet de Rochemont
SP198

Peacock Butterfly
SP199

Insects: 20c+10c, Great Horntail. 30c+10c, Yellow Bear moth. 40c+10c, Apollo butterfly.

1955, Dec. 1	Engraved	Unwmkd.		
B247	SP198	5c +5c brn car	20	25
a.	Booklet pane of 4		2.00	2.25

Photogravure.

Insects in Natural Colors.

B248	SP199	10c +10c yel grn	35	30
a.	Booklet pane of 4		2.00	2.25
B249	SP199	20c +10c red	50	35
a.	Booklet pane of 4		4.25	4.75
B250	SP199	30c +10c dk ocher	4.75	6.25
B251	SP199	40c +10c ultra	4.50	6.25
	Nos. B247-B251 (5)		10.30	13.40

Types Similar to 1952, Dated "1956", and

"Woman's Work"
SP200

Designs: 10c+10c, Rhone at St. Maurice. 20c+10c, Katzensee. 30c+10c, Rhine at Trin. 40c+10c, Lake Wallen.

1956, June 1	Engr.	Perf. 11½		
B252	SP200	5c +5c turq bl	30	45

Photogravure.

B253	SP192	10c +10c grn	45	45
B254	SP192	20c +10c car	45	45
B255	SP192	30c +10c brn	3.75	5.00
B256	SP192	40c +10c ultra	3.75	5.00
	Nos. B252-B256 (5)		8.70	11.35

The surtax was for the National Day Collection, the National Library and Academy of Arts and Letters. No. B252 was issued in honor of Swiss women.

Carlo Maderno
SP201

Burnet Moth
SP202

Insects: 20c+10c, Purple Emperor. 30c+10c, Blue ground beetle. 40c+10c, Cabbage butterfly.

1956, Dec. 1	Engraved	Perf. 11½		
B257	SP201	5c +5c brn car	35	20
a.	Booklet pane of 4		1.75	1.90

Photogravure.
Granite Paper.

B258	SP202	10c +10c grn, dk grn & car rose	40	25
a.	Bklt. pane of 4		2.10	2.10
B259	SP202	20c +10c multi	60	35
a.	Bklt. pane of 4		2.85	2.85
B260	SP202	30c +10c yel & dp bl	3.00	5.00

| B261 | SP202 | 40c +10c lt ultra, pale yel & sep | 3.75 | 5.00 |
| | Nos. B257-B261 (5) | | 8.10 | 10.80 |

Red Cross and Swiss Emblems
SP203

"Charity"
SP204

Engraved and Photogravure

1957, June 1	Perf. 11½	Unwmkd.		
B262	SP203	5c +5c gray & red	40	50

Photogravure.
Granite Paper.
Cross in Deep Carmine.

B263	SP204	10c +10c brt grn & gray	50	40
B264	SP204	20c +10c red & bl gray	60	40
B265	SP204	30c +10c brn & vio gray	3.25	4.75
B266	SP204	40c +10c brt bl & bis	3.25	4.75
	Nos. B262-B266 (5)		8.00	10.80

The surtax went to the Red Cross for the needs of the sick and to combat cancer.

Leonhard Euler
SP205

Clouded Yellow
SP206

Insects: 20c+10c, Magpie moth. 30c+10c, Rose Chafer. 40c+10c, Red Underwing.

1957, Nov. 30	Engraved	Perf. 11½		
B267	SP205	5c +5c brn car	30	20
a.	Bklt. pane of 4		2.25	2.25

Photogravure.
Granite Paper.

B268	SP206	10c +10c multi	30	20
a.	Bklt. pane of 4		2.00	2.00
B269	SP206	20c +10c lil rose, blk & yel	40	20
a.	Bklt. pane of 4		3.50	3.50
B270	SP206	30c +10c rose brn, ind & brt grn	2.75	4.00
B271	SP206	40c +10c multi	2.75	3.75
	Nos. B267-B271 (5)		6.50	8.35

Mother and Child
SP207

Fluorite
SP208

Designs: 20c+10c, Ammonite. 30c+10c, Garnet. 40c+10c, Rock Crystal.

Engraved.

1958, May 31	Perf. 11½	Unwmkd.		
B272	SP207	5c +5c brn car	30	40

Photogravure
Granite Paper

B273	SP208	10c +10c multi	40	60
B274	SP208	20c +10c blk, red & ol bis	40	60
B275	SP208	30c +10c blk, dl yel & mag	2.75	4.00
B276	SP208	40c +10c blk, chlky bl & sl bl	2.75	3.75
	Nos. B272-B276 (5)		6.60	9.35

The surtax was for needy mothers.
See also Nos. B283-B286, B292-B295, B304-B307.

SWITZERLAND 677

Granite Paper, Red and Blue Fibers

B338	SP223	50c +10c ultra, yel & brn	95	95
		Nos. B334-B338 (5)	2.30	2.30

Fluorescent Paper

Paper of Nos. B334–B425, B427 and B429 is fluorescent and has violet fibers.

Nos. B426, B428 and all semipostals from No. B430 onward are fluorescent but lack violet fibers, unless otherwise noted.

Types of 1960

Designs: 5c+5c, Portrait of a Girl by Albert Anker. 10c+10c, Daffodil. 20c+10c, Rose. 30c+10c, Clover. 50c+10c, Water lily.

1964, Dec. 1 Engraved *Perf. 11½*

B339	SP213	5c +5c grnsh bl	10	10
a.		Bklt. pane of 4	65	90

Photogravure

B340	SP214	10c +10c dp grn, yel & org	15	15
a.		Bklt. pane of 4	1.00	1.00
B341	SP214	20c +10c dp car, rose & grn	30	20
a.		Bklt. pane of 4	1.50	1.50
B342	SP214	30c +10c brn, lil & grn	1.10	75
B343	SP214	50c +10c multi	1.00	80
		Nos. B339-B343 (5)	2.65	2.00

Type of Regular Issue, 1965

Designs: 10c, 20r Seated Helvetia. 20c, 40r Seated Helvetia.

Souvenir Sheet

Granite Paper, Nonfluorescent

1965, March 8 Photo. *Imperf.*

B344	A153	Sheet of two	2.25	2.00
a.		10c grn, pale org & blk	80	80
b.		20c dk red, yel grn & blk	80	80

Issued to publicize the National Postage Stamp Exhibition, NABRA, Bern, Aug. 27-Sept. 5, 1965. No. B344 contains two stamps, light blue margin and dark red inscription. Size: 94x61½mm. Sold for 3fr, the net proceeds were used to cover expenses of the exhibition and to promote philately.

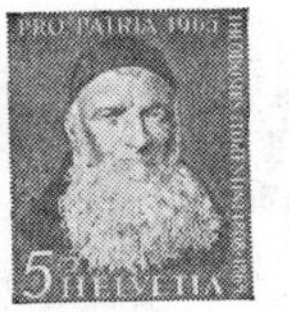

Father Theodosius Florentini

SP224

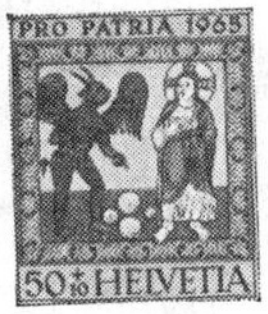

The Temptation of Christ

SP225

Ceiling Paintings from Church of St. Martin at Zillis, 12th century: 10c+10c, Symbol of evil (goose with fishtail). 20c+10c, Magi on horseback. 30c+10c, Fishermen on Sea of Galilee.

1965, June 1 *Perf. 11½* Unwmkd.

Engraved

B345	SP224	5c +5c bl	10	10

Photogravure

B346	SP225	10c +10c ol grn, ocher & bl	15	15
B347	SP225	20c +10c dk brn, red & buff	20	20
B348	SP225	30c +10c dk brn, sep & bl	60	60
B349	SP225	50c +10c vio bl, bl & brn	60	60
		Nos. B345-B349 (5)	1.65	1.65

See also Nos. B355–B359, B365–B369.

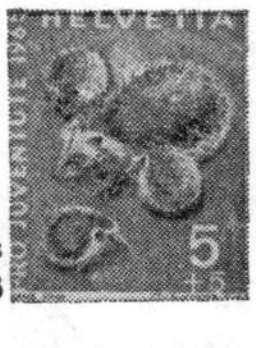

Hedgehogs

SP226

Designs: 10c+10c, Alpine marmots. 20c+10c, Red deer. 30c+10c, European badgers. 50c+10c, Varying hares.

1965, Dec. 1 Photo. *Perf. 11½*

B350	SP226	5c +5c red, brn & bis	10	8
a.		Bklt. pane of 4	50	50
B351	SP226	10c +10c grnsh bl, yel & gray	20	12
a.		Bklt. pane of 4	1.00	1.00
B352	SP226	20c +10c org brn, dk brn & gray	30	20
a.		Bklt. pane of 4	1.50	1.50
B353	SP226	30c +10c yel, blk & gray	55	55
B354	SP226	50c +10c ultra, gray, sep	60	60
		Nos. B350-B354 (5)	1.75	1.55

See also Nos. B360–B364.

Types of 1965

Designs: 5c+5c, Heinrich Federer (1866–1928), writer. 10c+10c, Joseph's dream. 20c+10c, Joseph on his way. 30c+10c, Virgin and Child fleeing to Egypt. 50c+10c, Angel leading the way. Nos. B356–B359 from ceiling paintings, Church of St. Martin at Zillis.

1966, June 1 Engraved *Perf. 11½*

B355	SP224	5c +5c dp bl	10	10

Photogravure

B356	SP225	10c +10c multi	15	15
B357	SP225	20c +10c multi	30	20
B358	SP225	30c +10c multi	45	45
B359	SP225	50c +10c multi	70	70
		Nos. B355-B359 (5)	1.70	1.60

Animal Type of 1965

Designs: 5c+5c, Ermine. 10c+10c, Red squirrel. 20c+10c, Red fox. 30c+10c, Hares. 50c+10c, Two chamois.

1966, Dec. 1 Photo. *Perf. 11½*

Animals in Natural Colors

B360	SP226	5c +5c grnsh bl	10	10
a.		Bklt. pane of 4	55	55
B361	SP226	10c +10c emer	20	15
a.		Bklt. pane of 4	1.00	1.00
B362	SP226	20c +10c ver	25	20
a.		Bklt. pane of 4	1.40	1.40
B363	SP226	30c +10c brt lem	55	45
B364	SP226	50c +10c ultra	60	60
		Nos. B360-B364 (5)	1.70	1.50

Types of 1965

Designs: 5c+5c, Dr. Theodor Kocher. 10c+10c, Annunciation to the Shepherds. 20c+10c, Jesus and the Samaritan Woman at the Well. 30c+10c, Adoration of the Magi. 50c+10c St. Joseph. (Ceiling paintings, St. Martin at Zillis).

1967, June 1 *Perf. 11½* Unwmkd.

Engraved

B365	SP224	5c +5c bl	10	1(

Photogravure

B366	SP225	10c +10c multi	15	
B367	SP225	20c +10c multi	25	
B368	SP225	30c +10c multi	40	
B369	SP225	50c +10c multi	55	
		Nos. B365-B369 (5)	1.45	

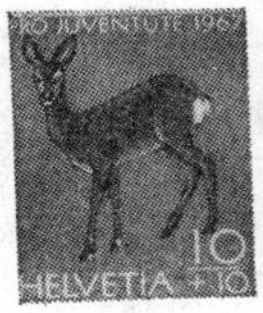

Roe Deer

SP227

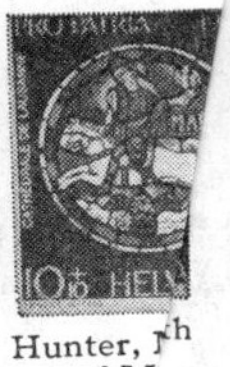

Hunter, ...h of M...

SP...

Designs: 20c+10c, Pine mar... 30c+10c, Alpine ibex. 50c+20c, Ott...

1967, Dec. 1 Photo. ... *11½*

Animals in Natural ...s

B370	SP227	10c +10c yel grn	15	15
a.		Bklt. pane of 4	1.00	1.00
B371	SP227	20c +10c dp car	20	20
a.		Bklt. pane of 4	1.40	1.40
B372	SP227	30c +10c ol bis	55	30
a.		Bklt. pane of 4	2.75	2.10
B373	SP227	50c +20c ultra	60	60

1968, May 30 Photo. *Perf. 11½*

Designs from Rose Window, Lausanne Cathedral: 20c+10c, Leo. 30c+10c, Libra. 50c+20c, Pisces.

B374	SP228	10c +10c multi	15	15
B375	SP228	20c +10c multi	25	20
B376	SP228	30c +10c multi	40	25
B377	SP228	50c +20c multi	80	70

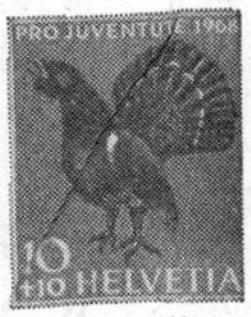

Capercaillie

SP229

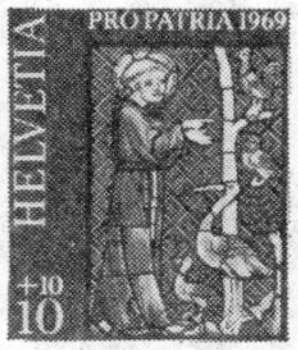

St. Francis

SP230

Birds: 20c+10c, Bullfinch. 30c+10c, Woodchat shrike. 50c+20c, Firecrest.

1968, Nov. 28 Photo. *Perf. 11½*

Birds in Natural Colors

B378	SP229	10c +10c dl yel	15	15
a.		Bklt. pane of 4	1.00	1.00
B379	SP229	20c +10c ol grn	20	20
a.		Bklt. pane of 4	1.40	1.40
B380	SP229	30c +10c lil rose	45	20
a.		Bklt. pane of 4	2.25	2.25
B381	SP229	50c +20c dp vio	70	60

See also Nos. B386–B389.

1969, May 29 Photo. *Perf. 11½*

Designs: 10c+10c, St. Francis Preaching to the Birds, Königsfelden Convent Church. 20c+10c, Israelites Drinking from Spring of Moses, Berne Cathedral. 30c+10c, St. Christopher, Laufelfinger Church (now Basel Museum). 50c+20c, Virgin and Child, Chapel at Grapplang (now National Museum).

B12	SP230	10c +10c multi	20	15
B13	SP230	20c +10c multi	25	20
B14	SP230	30c +10c multi	40	35
B5	SP230	50c +20c multi	60	60

Bird Type of 1968

Birds: 10c+10c, European goldfinch. 20c+10c, Golden oriole. 30c+10c, Wall creeper. 50c+20c, Eurasian jay.

1969, Dec. 1 Photo. *Perf. 11½*

Birds in Natural Colors

B386	SP229	10c +10c gray	15	15
a.		Bklt. pane of 4	1.00	1.00
B387	SP229	20c +10c grn	20	20
a.		Bklt. pane of 4	1.40	1.40
B388	SP229	30c +10c plum	45	25
a.		Bklt. pane of 4	2.25	2.25
B389	SP229	50c +20c ultra	65	65

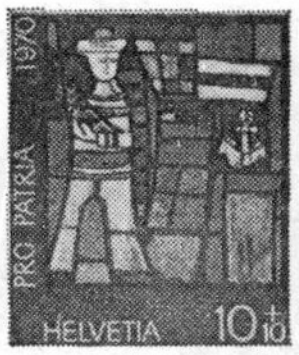

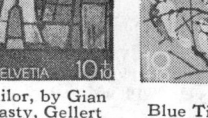

Sailor, by Gian Casty, Gellert Schoolhouse, Basel—SP231

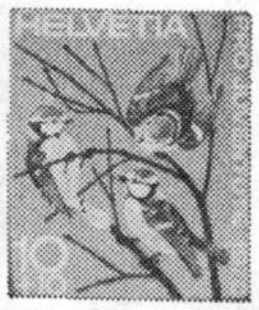

Blue Titmice

SP232

Contemporary Stained Glass Windows: 20c+10c, Abstract composition, by Celestino Piatti. 30c+10c, Bull (Assyrian god Marduk), by Hans Stocker. 50c+20c, Man and Woman, by Max Hunziker and Karl Ganz.

1970, May 29 Photo. *Perf. 11½*

B390	SP231	10c +10c multi	15	15
B391	SP231	20c +10c multi	20	20
B392	SP231	30c +10c multi	40	35
B393	SP231	50c +20c multi	65	60

See also Nos. B398–B401.

1970, Dec. 1 Photo. *Perf. 11½*

Birds: 20c+10c, Hoopoe. 30c+10c, Greater spotted woodpecker. 50c+20c, Crested grebes.

Birds in Natural Colors

B394	SP232	10c +10c org	20	15
a.		Booklet pane of 4	1.10	1.00
B395	SP232	20c +10c emer	30	18
a.		Booklet pane of 4	1.65	1.50
B396	SP232	30c +10c brt rose	40	20
a.		Booklet pane of 4	2.25	2.25
B397	SP232	50c +20c bl	90	90

See Nos. B402–B405.

Art Type of 1970

Contemporary Stained Glass Windows: 10c+10c, "Composition," by Jean-François Comment. 20c+10c, Cock, by Jean Prahin. 30c+10c, Fox, by Kurt Volk. 50c+20c, "Composition," by Bernard Schorderet.

1971, May 27 Photo. *Perf. 11½*

B398	SP231	10c +10c multi	15	15
B399	SP231	20c +10c multi	25	25
B400	SP231	30c +10c multi	40	30
B401	SP231	50c +20c multi	65	65

Bird Type of 1970

Birds: 10c+10c, European redstarts. 20c+10c, White-spotted bluethroats. 30c+10c, Peregrine falcon. 40c+20c, Mallards.

1971, Dec. 1

B402	SP232	10c +10c multi	15	15
a.		Booklet pane of 4	1.10	1.00
B403	SP232	20c +10c multi	20	20
a.		Booklet pane of 4	1.65	1.50
B404	SP232	30c +10c multi	55	20
a.		Booklet pane of 4	4.50	4.00
B405	SP232	40c +20c multi	1.00	90

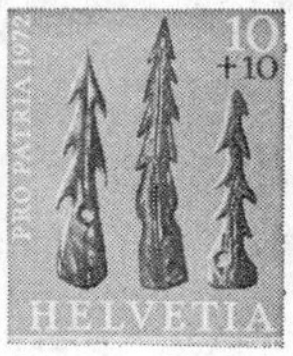

Harpoon Heads, Late Stone Age

SP233

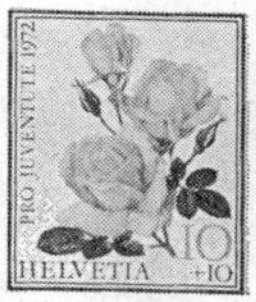

McGredy's Sunset

SP234

Archaeological Treasures: 20c+10c, Bronze hydria, Hallstadt period. 30c+10c, Gold bust of Emperor Marcus Aurelius, Roman period. 40c+20c, Horseback rider (decorative disk), early Middle Ages.

1972, June 1

B406	SP233	10c +10c multi	20	15
B407	SP233	20c +10c multi	30	20
B408	SP233	30c +10c multi	35	25
B409	SP233	40c +20c multi	90	90

1972, Dec. 1 Photo. *Perf. 11½*

Famous Roses: 20c+10c, Miracle. 30c+10c, Papa Meilland. 40c+20c, Madame Dimitriu.

B410	SP234	10c +10c multi	30	25
a.		Booklet pane of 4	1.65	1.50
B411	SP234	20c +10c multi	50	25
a.		Booklet pane of 4	2.50	2.25
B412	SP234	30c +10c multi	60	25
a.		Booklet pane of 4	3.25	3.25
B413	SP234	40c +20c multi	1.40	1.40

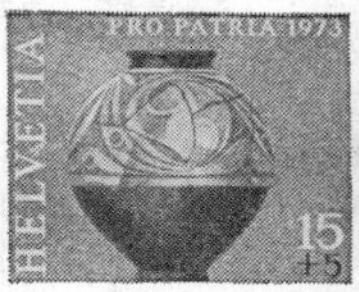

Rauraric (Gallic) Jug

SP235

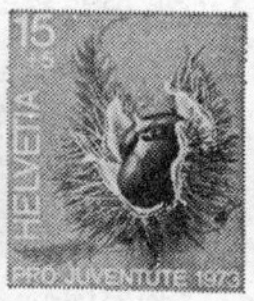

Chestnut

SP236

Archeologic Finds: 30c+10c, Bronze head of a Gaul. 40c+20c, Alemannic dress fasteners (fish), 6th century. 60c+20c, Gold bowl, 6th century B.C.

SWITZERLAND

1973, May 29   Photo.   *Perf. 11½*

B414	SP235	15c +5c multi	18	18
B415	SP235	30c +10c multi	40	25
B416	SP235	40c +20c multi	75	75
B417	SP235	60c +20c multi	1.00	1.00

See Nos. B422–B425.

1973, Nov. 29   Photo.   *Perf. 11½*

Fruits of the Forest: 30c+10c, Sweet cherries. 40c+20c, Blackberries. 60c+20c, Blueberries.

B418	SP236	15c +5c multi	20	15
a.		Booklet pane of 4	1.00	1.00
B419	SP236	30c +10c multi	40	15
a.		Booklet pane of 4	2.00	2.00
B420	SP236	40c +20c multi	90	90
a.		Booklet pane of 4	3.75	3.50
B421	SP236	60c +20c multi	1.10	1.10

Archaeological Type of 1973

Archaeological Finds: 15c+5c, Polychrome glass bowl. 30c+10c, Bull's head. 40c+20c, Gold fibula. 60c+20c, Ceramic bird.

1974, May 30   Photo.   *Perf. 11½*

B422	SP235	15c +5c multi	20	20
B423	SP235	30c +10c multi	40	20
B424	SP235	40c +20c multi	80	30
B425	SP235	60c +20c multi	1.00	1.00

Laurel   Gold Fibula, 6th Century
SP237   SP238

Designs: 30c+20c, Belladonna. 50c+20c, Laburnum. 60c+25c, Mistletoe.

1974, Nov. 29   Photo.   *Perf. 11½*

B426	SP237	15c +10c multi	25	20
a.		Booklet pane of 4	1.35	1.25
B427	SP237	30c +20c multi	50	20
a.		Booklet pane of 4	2.50	2.50
B428	SP237	50c +20c multi	90	90
B429	SP237	60c +25c multi	1.10	1.10

1975, May 30   Photo.   *Perf. 11½*

Archaeological Treasures: 30c+20c, Bronze head of Bacchus, 2nd century. 50c+20c, Bronze daggers, 1800–1600 B.C. 60c+25c, Colored glass bottle, 1st century.

B430	SP238	15c +10c multi	30	25
B431	SP238	30c +20c multi	55	40
B432	SP238	50c +20c multi	90	85
B433	SP238	60c +25c multi	1.00	1.00

Mail Bucket   Hepatica
SP239   SP240

Forest Plants: 30c+20c, Mountain ash berries. 50c+20c, Yellow nettle. 60c+25c, Sycamore maple.

1975, Nov. 27   Photo.   *Perf. 11½*

B434	SP239	10c +5c multi	18	18
a.		Booklet pane of 4	80	80
B435	SP240	15c +10c multi	25	20
a.		Booklet pane of 4	1.25	1.25
B436	SP240	30c +20c multi	50	40
a.		Booklet pane of 4	2.50	2.50
B437	SP240	50c +20c multi	90	90
B438	SP240	60c +25c multi	1.10	1.00
		Nos. B434-B438 (5)	2.93	2.68

See Nos. B443–B446.

SP241

1976, May 28   Photo.   *Perf. 11½*

B439	SP241	20c +10 Kyburg	40	30
B440	SP241	40c +20 Grandson	75	50
B441	SP241	40c +20 Murten	80	50
B442	SP241	80c +40 Bellinzona	1.50	1.35

See Nos. B447–B450, B455–B459, B463–B466.

Plant Type of 1975

Medicinal Forest Plants: 20c+10c, Barberry. No. B444, Black elder. No. B445, Linden. 80+40c, Pulmonaria.

1976, Nov. 29   Photo.   *Perf. 11½*

B443	SP240	20c +10c multi	30	25
a.		Booklet pane of 4	1.50	1.50
B444	SP240	40c +20c multi	55	25
a.		Booklet pane of 4	3.00	3.00
B445	SP240	40c +20c multi	55	25
B446	SP240	80c +20c multi	1.40	1.40

Castle Type of 1976

1977, May 26   Photo.   *Perf. 11½*

B447	SP241	20c +10c Aigle	30	25
B448	SP241	40c +20c Pratteln	65	40
B449	SP241	70c +30c Sargans	1.10	1.10
B450	SP241	80c +40c Hallwil	1.40	1.25

Wild Rose   Communal Arms
SP242   SP243

Designs: Roses.

1977, Nov. 28   Photo.   *Perf. 11½*

B451	SP242	20c +10c multi	30	20
a.		Booklet pane of 4	1.50	1.50
B452	SP242	40c +20c multi	60	20
a.		Booklet pane of 4	3.00	3.00
B453	SP242	70c +30c multi	1.25	1.25
B454	SP242	80c +40c multi	1.40	1.40

See Nos. B492-B496.

Castle Type of 1976

1978, May 26   Photo.   *Perf. 11½*

B455	SP241	20c +10c Hagenwil	30	30
B456	SP241	40c +20c Burgdorf	65	55
B457	SP241	70c +30c Tarasp	1.25	1.00
B458	SP241	80c +40c Chillon	1.40	1.20

1978, Nov. 28   Photo.   *Perf. 11½*

B459	SP243	20c +10c Aarburg	30	30
a.		Booklet pane of 4	1.40	
B460	SP243	40c +20c Gruyeres	55	30
a.		Booklet pane of 4	3.00	
B461	SP243	70c +30c Castasegna	1.00	1.00
B462	SP243	80c +40c Wangen an der Aare	1.10	1.10

Castle Type of 1976

1979, May 25   Photo.   *Perf. 11½*

B463	SP241	20c +10c Oron	30	30
B464	SP241	40c +20c Spiez	60	40
B465	SP241	70c +30c Porrentruy	1.10	1.00
B466	SP241	80c +40c Rapperswil	1.40	1.20

Arms Type of 1978

1979, Nov. 28   Photo.   *Perf. 11*

B467	SP243	20c +10c Cadro	30	20
a.		Bklt. pane of 4	1.30	
B468	SP243	40c +20c Rute	60	25
a.		Bklt. pane of 4	2.60	
B469	SP243	70c +30c Schwamendingen	1.00	1.00
B470	SP243	80c +40c Perroy	1.25	1.25

Masons' and Carpenters' Sign—SP244

1980, May 29   Photo.   *Perf. 11½*

B471	SP244	20c +10c shown	30	30
B472	SP244	40c +20c Barber	60	30
B473	SP244	70c +30c Hat maker	1.00	1.00
B474	SP244	80c +40c Baker	1.25	1.25

Arms Type of 1978

1980, Nov. 26   Photo.   *Perf. 11½*

B475	SP243	20 +10c Cortaillod	30	15
B476	SP243	40 +20c Sierre	60	30
B477	SP243	70 +30c Scuol	1.00	1.00
B478	SP243	80 +40c Wolfenschiessen	1.25	1.25

Icarus in Flight—SP245

1981, Mar. 9   Photo.

B479	SP245	2fr +1fr multi	3.00	3.00

Swissair, 50th Anniversary. Surtax was for Pro Aero Foundation. Issued in sheet of 8.

Post Office Sign, Aarburg, 1685—SP246

Post Office Signs (c. 1849).

1981, May 4   Photo.

B480	SP246	20 +10c shown	30	30
B481	SP246	40 +20c Fribourg	60	40
B482	SP246	70 +30c Gordola	1.00	90
B483	SP246	80 +40c Splungen	1.25	1.00

Communal Arms Type

1981, Nov. 26   Photo.   *Perf. 11½*

B484	SP243	20 +10c Uffikon	30	28
B485	SP243	40 +20c Torre	55	45
B486	SP243	70 +30c Benken	90	85
B487	SP243	80 +40c Preverenges	1.10	1.00

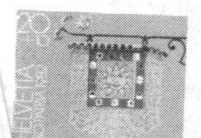

Inn Sign, Willisau—SP247

1982, May 27   Photo.   *Perf. 11½*

B488	SP247	20 +10c shown	30	30
B489	SP247	40 +20c A L'Onde, St. Saphorin	55	55
B490	SP247	70 +30c Three Kings, Rheinfelden	90	90
B491	SP247	80 +40c Krone, Winterthur	1.10	1.10

See Nos. B500

Rose Type of 1977

Designs: 10c+10c, Letter balance. 20c+10c, La Belle Portugaise. 40c+20c, Hugh Dickson. 70c+30c, Mermaid. 80c+40c, Madame Caroline.

1982, Nov. 25   Photo.

B492	SP242	10 +10c multi	20	20
B493	SP242	20 +10c multi	30	30
B494	SP242	40 +20c multi	55	55
B495	SP242	70 +30c multi	90	90
B496	SP242	80 +40c multi	1.10	1.10
		Nos. B492-B496 (5)	3.05	3.05

Inn Sign Type of 1982

1983, May 26   Photo.

B497	SP247	20c +10c Lion Inn, Heimiswil, 1669	30	25
B498	SP247	40c +20c Cross Hotel, Sachseln, 1489	60	50
B499	SP247	70c +30c Tankard Inn, 1830	1.00	80
B500	SP247	80c +40c Au Cavalier Inn, Vaud	1.20	95

Antique Toys—SP248

1983, Nov. 24

B501	SP248	20 +10c Kitchen stove, 1850	30	22
B502	SP248	40 +20c Rocking horse, 1826	60	40
B503	SP248	70 +30c Doll, 1870	1.00	65
B504	SP248	80 +40c Steam locomotive, 1900	1.20	75

Ceramic Tiled Stoves—SP249

1984, May 24   Photo.   *Perf. 11½*

B505	SP249	35 +15c 1566	50	35
B506	SP249	50 +20c 1646	70	45
B507	SP249	70 +30c 1768	1.00	65
B508	SP249	80 +40c 18th cent.	1.20	80

SWITZERLAND

681

OFFICIAL STAMPS.

For General Use.

With Perforated Cross.

In 1935 the government authorized the use of regular postage issues perforated with a nine-hole cross for all government departments. Twenty-seven different stamps were so perforated. These were succeeded in 1938 by the cross overprints.

> Prices for canceled Official Stamps are for those canceled to order. Postally used stamps sell for considerably less. This note does not apply to Nos. 1O1–1O16, 2O27–2O30, 3O23–3O26.

Regular Issues of 1908-36 Overprinted in Black

1938 ***Perf. 11½.*** **Unwmkd.**

O1	A53	3c olive	25	45
O2	A54	5c bl grn	25	20
O3	A55	10c red vio	80	30
O4	A56	15c orange	50	2.00
O5	A68	20c red	60	40
O6	A58	25c brown	60	2.25
O7	A59	30c ultra	60	90
O8	A60	35c yel grn	75	2.25
O9	A61	40c gray	80	1.00

Wmkd. Greek Cross. (183)

With Grilled Gum

O10	A25	50c dp grn & pale grn	1.00	2.25
O11	A25	60c brn org & buff	1.75	2.50
O12	A25	70c vio & buff	1.40	4.50
O13	A25	80c sl & buff	1.50	3.25
O14	A36	90c grn & red, *grn*	2.75	3.75
O15	A25	1fr dp cl & pale grn	2.25	4.00
O16	A36	1.20fr brn rose & red, *rose*	2.50	4.75
O17	A36	1.50fr bl & red, *bl*	3.25	6.00
O18	A36	2fr gray blk & red, *gray*	3.75	6.75
		Nos. O1-O18 (18)	25.30	47.50

Nos. O14, O16, O17 and O18 are on surface-colored paper.

With Grilled Gum

1938 **Unwmkd.**

O1a	A53	3c olive	4.50	45
O2a	A54	5c bl grn	1.40	30
O3a	A55	10c red vio	2.00	45
O4a	A56	15c orange	3.25	2.00
O5a	A68	20c red	2.25	45
O6a	A58	25c brown	55.00	8.00
O7a	A59	30c ultra	3.00	1.00
O8a	A60	35c yel grn	80	2.25
O9a	A61	40c gray	80	1.00
		Nos. O1a-O9a (9)	73.00	15.90

See Grilled Gum note after No. 145.

Postage Stamps of 1936-42 Overprinted in Black *Officiel*

1942-45 ***Perf. 11½.*** **Unwmkd.**

O19	A53	3c olive	60	1.75
O20	A54	5c bl grn	60	25
O21	A55	10c dk red brn	75	60
O21A	A55	10c org brn ('45)	20	35
O22	A56	15c orange	80	2.50
O23	A68	20c red	95	30
O24	A58	25c lt brn	1.25	2.75
O25	A59	30c ultra	1.50	90
O26	A60	35c yel grn	1.75	2.75
O27	A61	40c gray	2.00	90
O28	A77	50c dp pur, *grnsh*	4.75	4.00
O29	A78	60c red brn, *buff*	5.75	3.75
O30	A79	70c rose vio, *pale lil*	5.75	8.50
O31	A80	80c blk, *pale gray*	1.75	1.75
O32	A81	90c dk red, *pale rose*	1.90	2.25
O33	A82	1fr dk grn, *grnsh*	2.00	2.50
O34	A83	1.20fr red vio, *pale gray*	2.50	3.25
O35	A84	1.50fr dk bl, *buff*	3.00	4.50
O36	A85	2fr mar, *pale rose*	4.00	5.50
		Nos. O19-O36 (19)	41.80	49.05

Same Overprint on Nos. 329 to 339.

1950 ***Perf. 12x11½.*** **Unwmkd.**

O37	A118	5(c) orange	60	95
O38	A119	10(c) yel grn	90	95
O39	A120	15(c) aqua	4.75	12.00
O40	A121	20(c) brn car	2.25	95
O41	A122	25(c) red	3.25	8.50
O42	A123	30(c) olive	3.00	3.50
O43	A124	35(c) red brn	4.00	8.50
O44	A125	40(c) dp bl	4.00	3.50
O45	A126	50(c) sl gray	4.50	5.50
O46	A127	60(c) bl grn	6.75	6.00
O47	A128	70(c) purple	16.00	20.00
		Nos. O37-O47 (11)	50.00	70.35

For the War Board of Trade.

Regular Issues of 1908-18 Overprinted **Industrielle Kriegs-wirtschaft**

1918 ***Perf. 11½, 12.*** **Wmk. 183**

1O1	A26	3c brn org	100.00	160.00
1O2	A26	5c green	9.00	22.50
1O3	A26	7½c gray (I)	300.00	400.00
a.		7½c sl (II)	500.00	675.00
1O4	A28	10c red, *buff*	12.00	18.00
1O5	A28	15c vio, *buff*	12.00	30.00
1O6	A25	20c red & yel	110.00	*250.00*
1O7	A25	25c dp bl	110.00	*250.00*
1O8	A25	30c yel brn & pale grn	110.00	*250.00*
		Nos. 1O1-1O8 (8)	763.00	*1,380.50*

Counterfeits exist.

Overprinted **Industrielle Kriegs-wirtschaft**

1918

1O9	A26	3c brn org	4.50	12.00
1O10	A26	5c green	12.50	27.50
1O11	A26	7½c gray	5.00	12.00
1O12	A28	10c red, *buff*	20.00	40.00
1O13	A28	15c vio, *buff*	95.00	
1O14	A25	20c red & yel	10.00	22.50
1O15	A25	25c dp bl	10.00	22.50
1O16	A25	30c yel brn & pale grn	16.00	45.00
		Nos. 1O9-1O16 (8)	173.00	

No. O13 was never placed in use. Fraudulent cancellations are found on Nos. 1O1–1O16.

For the League of Nations.

Regular Issues Overprinted **SOCIÉTÉ DES NATIONS**

1922-31 ***Perf. 11½, 12*** **Wmk. 183**

On 1908-30 Issues.

2O1	A26	2½c ol, *buff* ('28)	175.00	30
2O2	A26	3c ultra, *buff* ('30)	265.00	7.25
2O3	A26	5c org, *buff*	150.00	3.75
2O4	A26	5c gray vio, *buff* ('26)	250.00	2.75
2O5	A26	5c red vio, *buff* ('27)	110.00	1.75
2O6	A26	5c dk grn, *buff* ('31)	285.00	22.50
2O7	A26	7½c dp grn, *buff* ('28)	175.00	45
2O8	A28	10c grn, *buff*	80.00	50
2O9	A28	10c bl grn, *buff* ('28)	225.00	1.50
2O10	A28	10c vio, *buff* ('31)	225.00	1.75
2O11	A28	15c brn red, *buff* ('28)	150.00	1.50
2O12	A28	20c red vio, *buff*	175.00	4.75
2O13	A28	20c car, *buff* ('26)	110.00	2.00
2O14	A28	25c ver, *buff*	135.00	5.25
2O15	A28	25c car, *buff*	135.00	90
2O16	A28	25c brn, *buff* ('27)	150.00	16.00
2O17	A28	30c dp bl, *buff* ('25)	140.00	10.00
2O18	A25	30c yel brn & pale grn	285.00	11.00
2O19	A25	35c yel grn & yel	100.00	4.75
2O20	A25	40c dp bl	90.00	1.50
2O21	A25	40c red vio & grn ('28)	100.00	9.00
2O22	A25	50c dp grn & pale grn	100.00	10.00
2O23	A25	60c brn org & buff	27.50	1.50
2O24	A25	70c vio & buff ('25)	150.00	30.00
2O25	A25	80c sl & buff	110.00	2.50
2O26	A25	1fr dp cl & pale grn	235.00	6.00
2O27	A29	3fr red	210.00	40.00
2O28	A30	5fr ultra	235.00	65.00
2O29	A31	10fr dl vio	350.00	150.00
2O30	A31	10fr gray grn ('30)	375.00	210.00
		Nos. 2O1-2O30 (30)	5,302.50	624.15

With Grilled Gum

1930-44

2O2a	A26	3c ultra, *buff* ('33)	600.00	9.00
2O6a	A26	5c dk grn, *buff* ('33)	600.00	22.50
2O17a	A28	30c dp bl, *buff*	*2,250.*	350.00
2O22a	A25	50c dp grn & pale grn ('35)	1.25	1.75
2O23a	A25	60c brn org & buff ('44)	30.00	*140.00*
2O24a	A25	70c vio & buff ('32)	1.50	3.00
2O25a	A25	80c sl & buff ('42)	3.50	2.00
2O26a	A25	1fr dp cl & pale grn ('42)	100.00	4.00

1925-36

With Grilled Gum

2O31	A36	90c grn & red, *grn* ('36)	140.00	6.50
a.		Ordinary gum ('24)	140.00	14.00
2O32	A36	1.20fr brn rose & red, *rose* ('36)	3.00	4.00
a.		Ordinary gum	140.00	5.25
b.		Invtd. ovpt.		*3,250.*
c.		As "a" "HFLVETIA"	*6,000.*	150.00
2O33	A36	1.50fr bl & red, *bl* ('35)	3.00	4.00
a.		Ordinary gum	140.00	14.50
2O34	A36	2fr gray blk & red, *gray* ('36)	3.75	6.50
a.		Ordinary gum	140.00	12.00

1928

2O35	A39	5fr blue	325.00	115.00

1932 On 1932 Issue.

2O36	A41	5c pck bl	350.00	20.00
2O37	A41	10c orange	350.00	1.50
2O38	A41	20c cerise	350.00	1.50
2O39	A41	30c ultra	350.00	47.50
2O40	A41	60c ol brn	350.00	10.50

Unwmkd.

2O41	A42	1fr ol gray & bl	350.00	13.00
		Nos. 2O36-2O41 (6)	2,100.	94.00

1934-35 On 1934 Issue.

Wmkd. Greek Cross. (183)

2O42	A46	3c olive	385.00	35
2O43	A47	5c emerald	385.00	40
2O44	A49	15c org ('35)	385.00	1.10
2O45	A51	25c brown	385.00	12.00
2O46	A52	30c ultra	385.00	1.40
		Nos. 2O42-2O46 (5)	1,925.	15.25

1937 On 1936 Issue **Unwmkd.**

2O47	A53	3c olive	15	20
2O48	A54	5c bl grn	20	20
2O49	A55	10c red vio	350.00	90
2O50	A56	15c orange	45	60
2O51	A57	20c carmine	350.00	1.25
2O52	A58	25c brown	55	95
2O53	A59	30c ultra	55	80
2O54	A60	35c yel grn	55	80
2O55	A61	40c gray	70	1.10
		Nos. 2O47-2O55 (9)	703.15	6.80

With Grilled Gum

1937

2O47a	A53	3c olive	285.00	30
2O48a	A54	5c bl grn	285.00	40
2O49a	A55	10c red vio	385.00	4.50
2O50a	A56	15c orange	325.00	60
2O51a	A57	20c carmine	385.00	1.40
2O52a	A58	25c brown	325.00	1.10
2O53a	A59	30c ultra	325.00	1.00
2O54a	A60	35c yel grn	325.00	3.00
2O55a	A61	40c gray	325.00	2.00
		Nos. 2O47a-2O55a (9)	2,965.	14.30

On 1931 Issue.

1937 **Wmkd. Greek Cross. (183)**

2O56	A40	3fr org brn	550.00	200.00

On 1938 Issue.

1938 ***Perf. 11½.*** **Unwmkd.**

Granite Paper.

2O57	A63	20c red & buff	300.00	1.50
2O58	A64	30c bl & lt bl	300.00	2.50
2O59	A65	60c brn & buff	300.00	5.00
2O60	A66	1fr blk & buff	300.00	9.50

Regular Issue of 1938 Overprinted in Black or Red **SERVICE DE LA SOCIÉTÉ DES NATIONS**

Granite Paper.

2O61	A63	20c red & buff	300.00	1.75
2O62	A64	30c bl & lt bl	300.00	3.50
2O63	A65	60c brn & buff	300.00	6.50
2O64	A66	1fr blk & buff (R)	300.00	10.00

Regular Issue of 1938 Overprinted in Black **SOCIÉTÉ DES NATIONS**

1939

2O65	A69	3fr brn car, *buff*	3.50	8.00
2O66	A70	5fr sl bl, *buff*	5.50	14.00
2O67	A71	10fr grn, *buff*	12.00	27.50

Same Overprint in Black on Regular Issues of 1939-42.

1942-43

2O68	A55	10c dk red brn	200.00	1.25
2O68A	A55	10c org brn ('43)	25	75
2O69	A68	20c red	40	80

Stamps of 1936-42 Overprinted in Black **COURRIER DE LA SOCIÉTÉ DES NATIONS**

1944

2O70	A53	3c olive	15	30
2O71	A54	5c bl grn	20	30
2O72	A55	10c org brn	25	45
2O73	A56	15c orange	30	60
2O74	A68	20c red	40	70
2O75	A58	25c lt brn	40	70
2O76	A59	30c ultra	50	90
2O77	A60	35c yel grn	60	1.10
2O78	A61	40c gray	65	1.25

Nos. 2O73–2O75 and 2O78 exist with grilled gum. Price each $800 unused, $1,250 used.

Stamps of 1941 Overprinted in Black **COURRIER DE LA SOCIÉTÉ DES NATIONS**

2O79	A77	50c dp pur, *grnsh*	1.25	2.25
2O80	A78	60c red brn, *buff*	1.25	2.25
2O81	A79	70c rose vio, *pale lil*	1.40	2.50
2O82	A80	80c blk, *pale gray*	1.40	2.50
2O83	A81	90c dk red, *pale rose*	1.40	2.50
2O84	A82	1fr dk grn, *grnsh*	1.50	3.00
2O85	A83	1.20fr red vio, *pale gray*	1.75	3.25
2O86	A84	1.50fr dk bl, *buff*	2.00	3.50
2O87	A85	2fr mar, *pale rose*	3.25	5.25

Stamps of 1942 Overprinted in Black **COURRIER DE LA SOCIÉTÉ DES NATIONS**

Perf. 11½ **Unwmkd.**

2O88	A69	3fr brn car, *cr*	6.00	14.00

SWITZERLAND

2089	A70	5fr sl bl, *cr*	10.00	22.50
2090	A71	10fr grn, *cr*	20.00	40.00
	Nos. 2070-2090 (21)		54.65	109.80

For the International Labor Bureau.

Regular Issues Overprinted

S.d.N. Bureau international du Travail

On 1908-30 Issues.
Wmkd. Greek Cross. (183)

1923-30   Perf. 11½, 12

301	A26	2½c ol grn, *buff* ('28)	210.00	40
302	A26	3c ultra, *buff* ('30)	325.00	1.75
303	A26	5c org, *buff*	150.00	50
304	A26	5c red vio, *buff* ('28)	150.00	40
305	A26	7½c dp grn, *buff* ('28)	190.00	50
306	A28	10c grn, *buff*	87.50	40
307	A28	10c bl grn, *buff* ('28)	185.00	1.25
308	A28	15c brn red, *buff* ('28)	225.00	1.40
309	A28	20c red vio, *buff*	180.00	8.50
3010	A28	20c car, *buff* ('27)	130.00	5.00
3011	A28	25c car, *buff*	95.00	1.00
3012	A28	25c brn, *buff* ('28)	150.00	2.75
3013	A28	30c dp bl, *buff* ('25)	130.00	2.50
3014	A25	30c yel brn & pale grn	300.00	60.00
3015	A25	35c yel grn & yel	125.00	5.75
3016	A25	40c dp bl	110.00	1.00
3017	A25	40c red vio & grn	140.00	10.00
3018	A25	50c dp grn & pale grn	95.00	4.50
3019	A25	60c brn org & buff	1.40	2.00
3020	A25	70c vio & buff ('24)	165.00	27.50
3021	A25	80c sl & buff	12.00	2.00
3022	A25	1fr dp cl & pale grn	150.00	2.00
3023	A29	3fr red	225.00	40.00
3024	A30	5fr ultra	250.00	55.00
3025	A31	10fr dl vio	375.00	250.00
3026	A31	10fr gray grn ('30)	350.00	210.00
	Nos. 301-3026 (26)		4,505.90	696.10

With Grilled Gum

1937-44

3018a	A25	50c dp grn & pale grn ('42)	1.40	2.00
3020a	A25	70c vio & buff	1.40	2.75
3021a	A25	80c sl & buff ('44)	22.50	100.00
3022a	A25	1fr dp cl & pale grn ('42)	150.00	3.25

1925-42
With Grilled Gum

3027	A36	90c grn & red, grn ('37)	225.00	12.00
a.		Ordinary gum	120.00	6.00
3028	A36	1.20fr brn rose & red, rose ('42)	12.00	5.75
a.		Ordinary gum	140.00	5.75
b.		As "a," "HFLVETIA"	6,000.	750.00
3029	A36	1.50fr bl & red, *bl* ('37)	2.50	5.00
a.		Ordinary gum	140.00	10.00
3030	A36	2fr gray blk & red, gray ('36)	2.75	6.50
a.		Ordinary gum	140.00	37.50

1928

3031	A39	5fr blue	325.00	140.00

1932   On 1932 Issue.

3032	A41	5c pck bl	325.00	1.40
3033	A41	10c orange	325.00	1.40
3034	A41	20c cerise	325.00	1.40
3035	A41	30c ultra	325.00	9.50
3036	A41	60c ol brn	325.00	10.50

Unwmkd.

3037	A42	1fr ol gray & bl	325.00	15.00
	Nos. 3032-3037 (6)		1,950.	39.20

1937   On 1936 Issue

3038	A53	3c olive	20	25
3039	A54	5c bl grn	20	20
3040	A55	10c red vio	450.00	1.75
3041	A56	15c orange	35	45
3042	A57	20c carmine	375.00	1.50
3043	A58	25c brown	55	70
3044	A59	30c ultra	60	80
3045	A60	35c yel grn	60	1.00
3046	A61	40c gray	80	1.40
	Nos. 3038-3046 (9)		828.30	8.05

With Grilled Gum

1937

3038a	A53	3c olive	300.00	60
3039a	A54	5c bl grn	300.00	40
3040a	A55	10c red vio	385.00	1.00
3041a	A56	15c orange	300.00	75
3042a	A57	20c carmine	400.00	95
3043a	A58	25c brown	325.00	1.50
3044a	A59	30c ultra	325.00	1.50
3045a	A60	35c yel grn	325.00	1.50
3046a	A61	40c gray	325.00	2.00
	Nos. 3038a-3046a (9)		2,985.	10.20

On 1931 Issue.
Wmkd. Greek Cross. (183)

1937

3047	A40	3fr org brn	500.00	225.00

On 1934 Issue.

3048	A46	3c olive	425.00	6.00

On 1938 Issue.

1938   Perf. 11½.   Unwmkd.
Granite Paper.

3049	A63	20c red & buff	350.00	1.25
3050	A64	30c bl & lt bl	350.00	3.75
3051	A65	60c brn & buff	350.00	5.25
3052	A66	1fr blk & buff	350.00	7.00

Regular Issue of 1938
Overprinted in Black or Red

3053	A63	20c red & buff (Bk)	350.00	4.00
3054	A64	30c bl & lt bl (Bk)	350.00	4.00
3055	A65	60c brn & buff (Bk)	350.00	7.25
3056	A66	1fr blk & buff (R)	350.00	9.00

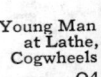

Regular Issue of 1938 Overprinted in Black

1939

3057	A69	3fr brn car, *buff*	3.50	7.00
3058	A70	5fr sl bl, *buff*	6.75	12.00
3059	A71	10fr grn, *buff*	10.00	22.50

Same Overprint in Black on Regular Issues of 1939-42.

1942-43

3060	A55	10c dk red brn	210.00	1.00
3060A	A55	10c org brn ('43)	40	80
3061	A68	20c red	55	1.00

Stamps of 1936-42 Overprinted in Black

COURRIER DU BUREAU INTERNATIONAL DU TRAVAIL

1944

3062	A53	3c olive	20	30
3063	A54	5c bl grn	20	30
3064	A55	10c org brn	25	40
3065	A56	15c orange	40	70
3066	A68	20c red	40	80
3067	A58	25c lt brn	60	1.00
3068	A59	30c ultra	70	1.40
3069	A60	35c yel grn	80	1.50
3070	A61	40c gray	90	1.75

Stamps of 1941 Overprinted

COURRIER DU BUREAU INTERNATIONAL DU TRAVAIL

3071	A77	50c dp pur, *grnsh*	3.75	8.00
3072	A78	60c red brn, *buff*	3.75	8.00
3073	A79	70c rose vio, *pale lil*	3.75	8.00
3074	A80	80c blk, *pale gray*	80	2.50
3075	A81	90c dk red, *pale rose*	90	2.50
3076	A82	1fr dk grn, *grnsh*	1.25	3.25
3077	A83	1.20fr red vio, *pale gray*	1.50	4.00
3078	A84	1.50fr dl bl, *buff*	1.75	4.00
3079	A85	2fr mar, *pale rose*	2.50	5.75

Stamps of 1942 Overprinted

COURRIER DU BUREAU INTERNATIONAL DU TRAVAIL.

3080	A69	3fr brn car, *cr*	5.75	12.00
3081	A70	5fr sl bl, *b*	8.00	16.00
3082	A71	10fr grn, *cr*	20.00	37.50
	Nos. 3062-3082 (21)		58.15	119.65

Nos. 329 to 339 Overprinted in Black

BUREAU INTERNATIONAL DU TRAVAIL

1950   Perf. 12x11½.   Unwmkd.

3083	A118	5c orange	1.75	2.25
3084	A119	10c yel grn	2.00	2.75
3085	A120	15c aqua	2.50	3.25
3086	A121	20c brn car	2.75	4.00
3087	A122	25c red	4.75	7.50
3088	A123	30c olive	6.00	8.50
3089	A124	35c red brn	7.50	11.50
3090	A125	40c dp bl	7.50	8.50
3091	A126	50c sl gray	8.75	13.50
3092	A127	60c bl grn	12.50	16.50
3093	A128	70c purple	12.50	17.50
	Nos. 3083-3093 (11)		68.50	98.25

Miners   Globe, Chimney and Wheel
O1   O2

1956   Engraved.   Perf. 11½   Unwmkd.

3094	O1	5c dk gray	6	6
3095	O1	10c green	12	12
3096	O1	20c vermilion	2.50	2.50
3097	O1	40c blue	2.75	2.75
3098	O2	60c redsh brn	50	50
3099	O2	2fr rose vio	1.40	1.40
	Nos. 3094-3099 (6)		7.33	7.33

1960

30100	O2	20c car rose	20	20
30101	O2	30c org ver	30	30
30102	O1	50c lt ultra	50	50

Type of 1960 Overprinted: "Visite du / Pape Paul VI / Genève / 10 juin 1969"

1969, June 10
Violet Fibers, Fluorescent Paper

30103	O2	30c org ver	40	40

Issued to commemorate the visit of Pope Paul VI to the International Labor Bureau to celebrate its 50th anniversary, Geneva, June 10.

ILO Headquarters, Geneva
O3

1974, May 30   Photo.   Perf. 11½
Violet Fibers, Fluorescent Paper

30104	O3	80c bl, yel & gray	80	80

Inauguration of the new International Labor Organization Building.

Young Man at Lathe, Cogwheels
O4

Designs: 60c, Woman at drilling machine. 100c, Surveyor with theodolite and topographical map.

1975, Feb. 13   Photo.   Perf. 11½

30105	O4	30c red brn & dk brn	30	30
30106	O4	60c ultra & blk	60	60
30107	O4	100c dk grn & blk	1.00	1.00

Professional Education for Youth—O5

1983, Aug. 22   Photo.

30108	O5	120c multi	1.10	1.10

SWITZERLAND

For the International Bureau of Education.

Regular Issues of 1936-42, Overprinted in Black
COURRIER DU BUREAU INTERNATIONAU D'EDUCATION

1944		Perf. 11½.	Unwmkd.	
401	A53	3c olive	50	1.00
402	A54	5c bl grn	65	1.25
403	A55	10c org brn	85	1.65
404	A56	15c orange	1.00	2.25
405	A68	20c red	1.25	3.00
406	A58	25c lt brn	1.50	3.25
407	A59	30c ultra	1.50	3.50
408	A60	35c yel grn	1.50	3.50
409	A61	40c gray	1.50	3.50

Regular Issue of 1941, Overprinted in Black
COURRIER DU BUREAU INTERNATIONAL D'EDUCATION

4010	A77	50c dp pur grnsh	6.00	9.00
4011	A78	60c red brn, buff	6.00	9.00
4012	A79	70c rose vio, pale lil	6.00	9.00
4013	A80	blk, pale gray	85	2.25
4014	A81	90c dk red, pale rose	1.00	2.50
4015	A82	1fr dk grn, grnsh	1.25	3.25
4016	A83	1.20fr red vio, pale gray	2.00	4.50
4017	A84	1.50fr dk bl, buff	2.00	4.50
4018	A85	2fr mar, pale rose	2.75	8.00

Regular Issue of 1942, Overprinted in Black
COURRIER DU BUREAU INTERNATIONAL D'ÉDUCATION

4019	A69	3fr brn car, cr	8.50	22.50
4020	A70	5fr sl bl, cr	11.00	25.00
4021	A71	10fr grn, cr	30.00	52.50
	Nos. 401-4021 (21)		87.60	174.40

1946
No. 306 Overprinted in Carmine — B I E

4022	A104	10c rose vio	20	40

Nos. 316 to 321 Overprinted in Black
BUREAU INTERNATIONAL D'ÉDUCATION

1948		Perf. 11½	Unwmkd.	
4023	A54	5c chocolate	2.65	4.00
4024	A55	10c green	2.65	4.00
4025	A68	20c org brn	2.65	4.00
4026	A113	25c carmine	2.65	4.00
4027	A59	30c grnsh bl	3.50	5.50
4028	A61	40c ultra	3.50	5.50
	Nos. 4023-4028 (6)		17.60	27.00

Same Overprint on Nos. 329 to 339.
1950 Perf. 12 x 11½. Overprint 18 mm. wide.

4029	A118	5c orange	1.25	1.75
4030	A119	10c yel grn	1.25	1.75
4031	A120	15c aqua	2.25	4.00
4032	A121	20c brn car	2.50	4.00
4033	A122	25c red	3.75	6.00
4034	A123	30c olive	3.75	6.00
4035	A124	35c red brn	4.75	8.00
4036	A125	40c dp bl	4.75	8.00
4037	A126	50c sl gray	5.25	8.50
4038	A127	60c bl grn	5.25	9.50
4039	A128	70c purple	6.50	12.00
	Nos. 4029-4039 (11)		41.25	69.50

Globe and Books O1

Designs: 20c, 60c, 2fr, Pestalozzi Monument at Yverdon.

1958		Engraved. Perf. 11½	Unwmkd.	
4040	O1	5c dk gray	6	6
4041	O1	10c green	10	10
4042	O1	20c vermilion	2.50	2.50
4043	O1	40c blue	3.00	3.00
4044	O1	60c redsh brn	50	50
4045	O1	2fr rose vio	1.50	1.50
	Nos. 4040-4045 (6)		7.66	7.66

1960
Designs: 20c, 30c, Pestalozzi Monument at Yverdon. 50c, Globe and books.

4046	O1	20c car rose	20	20
4047	O1	30c org ver	30	30
4048	O1	50c lt ultra	45	45

For the World Health Organization.
No. 316 to 319 and 321 Overprinted in Black
ORGANISATION MONDIALE DE LA SANTÉ

1948		Perf. 11½	Unwmkd.	
501	A54	5c chocolate	3.00	4.50
502	A55	10c green	3.00	4.50
503	A68	20c org brn	3.50	4.50
504	A113	25c carmine	3.50	5.50
505	A61	40c ultra	6.50	10.00
	Nos. 501-505 (5)		19.50	30.00

Regular Issues of 1941, 1942 and 1949 Overprinted in Black
ORGANISATION MONDIALE DE LA SANTÉ
1948-50

506	A118	5c orange	75	80
507	A119	10c yel grn	75	90
508	A120	15c aqua	75	1.20
509	A121	20c brn car	2.25	3.75
5010	A122	25c red	2.25	3.75
5011	A123	30c olive	2.25	3.25
5012	A124	35c red brn	2.75	3.75
5013	A125	40c dp bl	2.75	3.75
5014	A126	50c sl gray	3.25	4.25
5015	A127	60c bl grn	4.25	4.50
5016	A128	70c purple	4.25	5.50
5017	A128	80c blk, pale gray ('48)	2.00	2.75
5018	A81	90c dk red, pale rose	8.50	11.00
5019	A82	1fr dk grn, grnsh ('48)	2.25	3.25
5020	A83	1.20fr red vio, pale gray	9.25	12.00
5021	A84	1.50fr dk bl, buff	12.00	15.00
5022	A85	2fr mar, pale rose ('48)	4.25	6.00
5023	A69	3fr brn car, cr	35.00	50.00
5024	A70	5fr sl bl, cr ('48)	13.00	17.50
5025	A71	10fr grn, cr	65.00	85.00
	Nos. 506-5025 (20)		176.75	238.15

WHO Emblem O2

1957		Engraved Perf. 11½	Unwmkd.	
5026	O2	5c gray	6	6
5027	O2	10c lt grn	10	10
5028	O2	20c vermilion	2.50	2.50
5029	O2	40c blue	3.00	3.00
5030	O2	60c red brn	50	50
5031	O2	2fr rose lil	1.40	1.40
	Nos. 5026-5031 (6)		7.56	7.56

1960

5032	O2	20c car rose	20	20
5033	O2	30c org ver	30	30
5034	O2	50c lt ultra	45	45

No. 5034 Overprinted: "ERADICATION DU PALUDISME"
1962, Apr. 7

5035	O2	50c lt ultra	60	60

Issued for the World Health Organization drive to eradicate malaria.

World Health Organization Emblem—O3

1975, Feb. 13		Typo. Perf. 11½		
5036	O3	30c multi	30	30
5037	O3	60c lt bl & multi	55	55
5038	O3	90c lil & multi	90	90
5039	O3	100c org & multi	1.00	1.00

For the International Organization for Refugees.
Stamps of 1941 and 1949 Overprinted in Black
ORGANISATION INTERNATIONALE POUR LES RÉFUGIÉS
1950 Perf. 12x11½, 11½ Unwmkd.

601	A118	5c orange	13.00	18.00
602	A119	10c yel grn	13.00	18.00
603	A121	20c brn car	13.00	18.00
604	A122	25c red	13.00	18.00
605	A125	40c dp bl	13.00	18.00
606	A80	80c blk, pale gray	13.00	18.00
607	A82	1fr dk grn, grnsh	13.00	18.00
608	A85	2fr mar, pale rose	13.00	18.00
	Nos. 601-608 (8)		104.00	144.00

For the United Nations European Office.
Stamps of 1941-49 Overprinted in Black
NATIONS UNIES OFFICE EUROPÉEN
1950 Perf. 12x11½, 11½ Unwmkd.

701	A118	5c orange	80	1.40
702	A119	10c yel grn	1.00	2.00
703	A120	15c aqua	1.00	3.25
704	A121	20c brn car	1.35	2.50
705	A122	25c red	2.00	5.25
706	A123	30c olive	2.25	5.25
707	A124	35c red brn	3.75	8.00
708	A125	40c dp bl	2.75	7.00
709	A126	50c sl gray	4.50	8.00
7010	A127	60c bl grn	4.50	12.00
7011	A128	70c purple	6.00	13.00
7012	A80	80c blk, pale gray	22.50	37.50
7013	A81	90c dk red, pale rose	22.50	37.50
7014	A82	1fr dk grn, grnsh	22.50	37.50
7015	A83	1.20fr red vio, pale gray	30.00	40.00
7016	A84	1.50fr dk bl, buff	30.00	40.00
7017	A85	2fr mar, pale rose	30.00	40.00
7018	A69	3fr brn car, cr	120.00	200.00
7019	A70	5fr sl bl, cr	160.00	250.00
7020	A71	10fr grn, cr	285.00	375.00
	Nos. 701-7020 (20)		752.40	1,125.15

United Nations Emblem O1

Statue from U. N. Building, Geneva O2

1955		Engraved. Perf. 11½		
7021	O1	5c dk vio brn	6	6
7022	O1	10c green	10	10
7023	O2	20c vermilion	7.25	7.25
7024	O1	40c ultra	7.50	7.50
7025	O2	60c red brn	60	60
7026	O2	2fr lilac	1.90	1.90
	Nos. 7021-7026 (6)		17.41	17.41

See Nos. 7028-7030.

United Nations Emblem O3

1955, Oct. 24		Photogravure		
7027	O3	40c dk bl & bis	4.50	5.00

Issued to commemorate the tenth anniversary of the United Nations, Oct. 24, 1955.

Types of 1955.

1959		Engraved Perf. 11½		
7028	O2	20c car rose	25	25
7029	O2	30c org ver	35	35
7030	O1	50c ultra	60	60

Nos. 7028 and 7030 Overprinted in Black or Red: "ANNÉE MONDIALE DU RÉFUGIÉ 1959 1960"

1960

7031	O2	20c car rose	35	35
7032	O1	50c ultra (R)	45	45

Issued to publicize World Refugee Year, July 1, 1959–June 30, 1960.

Palace of Nations, Geneva O4

1960		Granite Paper Perf. 11½		
7033	O4	5fr blue	5.50	5.00

Types of 1955 Inscribed:
"MUSÉE PHILATELIQUE" (O1) or "ONU MUSÉE PHILATELIQUE" (O2)
Engraved; Inscription Typographed
1962, Oct. 24 Perf. 11½ Unwmkd.

7034	O1	10c grn & red	15	15
7035	O1	30c org ver & ultra	40	40
7036	O1	50c ultra & org	65	65
7037	O2	60c red brn & emer	80	80

Issued to commemorate the opening of the Philatelic Museum, U.N. European Office, Geneva.

UNCSAT Emblem O5

O6

1963, Feb. 4		Engr. Perf. 11½		
7038	O5	50c ultra & car rose	40	40
7039	O6	2fr lil & emer	1.75	1.75

Issued to commemorate the U.N. Conference on the Application of Science and Technology for the Benefit of the Less Developed Areas (UNCSAT), Geneva, Feb. 4–20.

683

SWITZERLAND

Stamps issued, starting Oct. 4, 1969, by the United Nations in Swiss currency for use by U.N. staff members or the public are listed under "United Nations" in Vol. I of this catalogue and in Scott's U.S. Specialized Catalogue. These stamps are on sale in various U.N. post offices, but are valid only in the U.N. enclave in Geneva. They are not inscribed "Helvetia."

For the World Meteorological Organization.

Sun, Cloud, Rain and Snow
O1

Design: 20c, 60c, 2fr, Direction indicator and anemometer.

Engraved.

1956		Perf. 11½	Unwmkd.	
801	O1	5c dk gray	6	6
802	O1	10c green	10	10
803	O1	20c vermilion	3.00	3.00
804	O1	40c blue	3.50	3.50
805	O1	60c redsh brn	50	50
806	O1	2fr rose vio	1.40	1.40
		Nos. 801-806 (6)	8.56	8.56

1960

Designs: 20c, 30c, Direction indicator and anemometer. 50c, Sun, cloud, rain and snow.

807	O1	20c car rose	20	20
808	O1	30c org ver	30	30
809	O1	50c lt ultra	45	45

WMO Emblem
O2

1973, Aug. 30 Engraved *Perf. 11½*
Violet Fibers, Fluorescent Paper

8010	O2	30c carmine	30	30
8011	O2	40c blue	40	40
8012	O2	1fr ocher	75	75

Type O12 Inscribed:
"OMI / OMM / 1873 / 1973"

1973, Aug. 30 Photo. *Perf. 11½*
Violet Fibers, Fluorescent Paper

8013	O2	80c dp vio & gold	85	85

Centenary of international meteorological cooperation.

For the International Bureau of the Universal Postal Union.

UPU Monument, Bern
O1

Design: 10c, 20c, 60c, Pegasus.

Engraved.

1957		Perf. 11½	Unwmkd.	
901	O1	5c gray	6	6
902	O1	10c lt grn	10	10
903	O1	20c vermilion	2.50	2.50
904	O1	40c blue	3.00	3.00
905	O1	60c red brn	50	50
906	O1	2fr rose lil	1.40	1.40
		Nos. 901-906 (6)	7.56	7.56

1960

Designs: 20c, 30c, Pegasus. 50c, UPU Monument, Bern.

907	O1	20c car rose	20	20
908	O1	30c org ver	30	30
909	O1	50c lt ultra	45	45

First Class Mail
O2

Parcel Post
O3

Money Orders
O4

Technical Cooperation
O5

1976, Sept. 16 Photo. *Perf. 11½*
Fluorescent Paper

9010	O2	40c multi	40	40
9011	O3	80c multi	75	75
9012	O4	90c multi	80	80
9013	O5	100c multi	90	90

Intl. Reply and Notication Service—O6

1983, Aug. 22 Photo.

9014	O6	120c multi	1.10	1.10

For the International Telecommunication Union.

Transmitter
O1

ITU Headquarters, Geneva
O2

Designs: 20c, 60c, 2fr, Antenna.

Engraved.

1958		Perf. 11½	Unwmkd.	
1001	O1	5c dk gray	6	6
1002	O1	10c green	10	10
1003	O1	20c vermilion	2.50	2.50
1004	O1	40c blue	3.00	3.00
1005	O1	60c redsh brn	50	50
1006	O1	2fr rose vio	1.40	1.40
		Nos. 1001-1006 (6)	7.56	7.56

1960

Designs: 20c, 30c, Antenna. 50c, Transmitter.

1007	O1	20c car rose	20	20
1008	O1	30c org ver	30	30
1009	O1	50c lt ultra	45	45

1973, Aug. 30 Photo. *Perf. 11½*
Violet Fibers, Fluorescent Paper

10010	O2	80c bl & blk	80	80

Sound Waves, ITU Emblem
O3

Airplane, Ocean Liner
O4

Radio Waves, Face on TV, Microphone
O5

Photogravure and Engraved

1976, Feb. 12 *Perf. 11½*
Violet Fibers, Fluorescent Paper

10011	O3	40c dp org & vio bl	40	40
10012	O4	90c bl, vio bl & yel	85	85
10013	O5	1fr grn & multi	1.00	1.00

ITU activities: world telecommunications, mobile radio and mass media.

SWITZERLAND

For the World Intellectual Property Organization

WIPO Emblem—O1

1982. May 27   Litho.   Perf. 12x11½

1101	O1	40c shown	40	40
1102	O1	80c Headquarters, Geneva	75	75
1103	O1	100c Industrial symbols	90	90
1104	O1	120c Educational and artistic symbols	1.10	1.10

Scott— First in the Field

- Buying
- Selling
- Estate Appraisals
- Auction
- Consignments

ALL SERVICES AVAILABLE FROM THE RECOGNIZED PHILATELIC EXPERTS

The Scott Auction Galleries

TO PLACE YOUR NAME ON OUR LIST TO RECEIVE INFORMATION ABOUT SERVICES ON OUR UPCOMING SALES, WRITE TO:

SCOTT AUCTION GALLERIES
DIRECTOR OF CUSTOMER SERVICES
3 EAST 57TH ST.
NEW YORK, N.Y. 10022

FRANCHISE STAMPS.

These stamps were distributed to many institutions and charitable societies for franking their correspondence.

F1

Control Figures Overprinted in Black   214
Wmkd. Greek Cross. (183)
1911–21   Typo.   Perf. 11½, 12
Blue Granite Paper.

S1	F1	2c ol grn & red	15	25
S2	F1	3c ol grn & red	2.50	40
S3	F1	5c ol grn & red	75	15
S4	F1	10c ol grn & red	1.25	15
S5	F1	15c ol grn & red	17.00	2.75
S6	F1	20c ol grn & red	4.00	60
		Nos. S1-S6 (6)	25.65	4.30

Without Control Figures:

S1a	F1	2c ol grn & red	40	16.00
S2a	F1	3c ol grn & red	35	17.50
S3a	F1	5c ol grn & red	3.50	27.50
S4a	F1	10c ol grn & red	7.00	50.00
S5a	F1	15c ol grn & red	4.00	75.00
S6a	F1	20c ol grn & red	7.50	35.00
		Nos. S1a-S6a (6)	22.75	221.00

Control Figures Overprinted in Black   365
1926

S7	F1	5c ol grn & red	7.50	3.00
S8	F1	10c ol grn & red	4.50	1.75
S9	F1	20c ol grn & red	6.00	2.50

Control Figures Overprinted in Black   806
1927   White Granite Paper

S10	F1	5c grn & red	3.50	25
S11	F1	10c grn & red	2.00	15
b.		Grilled gum	225.00	400.00
S12	F1	20c grn & red	2.50	15

Without Control Figures.

S10a	F1	5c grn & red	14.00	70.00
S11a	F1	10c grn & red	14.00	80.00
c.		Grilled gum	100.00	350.00
S12a	F1	20c grn & red	18.00	90.00

Nurse F2   Nun F3   J. H. Dunant F4

Control Figures Overprinted in Black
1935   Perf. 11½

S13	F2	5c turq grn	1.25	2.75
b.		Grilled gum	3.75	40
S14	F3	10c lt vio	1.25	2.75
b.		Grilled gum	5.00	20
S15	F4	20c scarlet	1.25	2.75
b.		Grilled gum	5.25	40

Without Control Figures.

S13a	F2	5c turq grn	1.25	2.75
c.		Grilled gum	14.00	1.25
S14a	F3	10c lt vio	1.25	2.75
c.		Grilled gum	14.00	1.25
S15a	F4	20c scarlet	1.25	2.75
c.		Grilled gum	14.00	1.25

SYRIA

(sĭr′ĭ-ă)

LOCATION—In Asia Minor, bordering on Turkey, Iraq, Lebanon, Israel and the Mediterranean Sea.
GOVT.—Republic.
AREA—72,234 sq. mi.
POP.—7,840,000 (est. 1977).
CAPITAL—Damascus.

Syria was originally part of the Turkish province of Sourya conquered by British and Arab forces in late 1918 and later partitioned. The British assumed control of the Palestine and Transjordan regions; the French were permitted to occupy the sanjaks of Lebanon, Alaouites and Alexandretta (which see); and the remaining territory, including the vilayets of Damascus and Aleppo, was established as an independent Arab kingdom, under which the first Syrian stamps were issued.

French forces from Beirut deposed King Faisal in July, 1920, and two years of military occupation followed until Syria was mandated to France in July, 1922. Syrian autonomy was substituted for the mandate in 1934, but full independence was not again achieved until 1946.

In 1958 Syria and Egypt merged to form the United Arab Republic. Syria left this union in 1961, adopting the name Syrian Arab Republic.

UAR issues for Syria are listed following Syria's 1919-20 "Issues of the Arabian Government."

10 Milliemes = 1 Piastre
40 Paras = 1 Piastre (Arabian Govt.)
100 Centimes = 1 Piastre (1920)

Issued under French Occupation

T. E. O.

Stamps of France, 1900-07, Surcharged

5 MILLIEMES

Perf. 14x13½

1919, Nov. 21   Unwmkd.

1	A16	1m on 1c gray	135.00	135.00
2	A16	2m on 2c vio brn	300.00	300.00
3	A16	3m on 3c red org	150.00	150.00
4	A20	4m on 15c gray grn	20.00	20.00
5	A22	5m on 5c dp grn	12.00	12.00
6	A22	1p on 10c red	20.00	20.00
7	A22	2p on 25c bl	9.50	9.50
8	A18	5p on 40c red & pale bl	13.00	13.00
9	A18	9p on 50c bis brn & lav	30.00	30.00
10	A18	10p on 1fr cl & ol grn	47.50	47.50
		Nos. 1-10 (10)	737.00	737.00

The letters "T. E. O." are the initials of "Territoires Ennemis Occupés." There are two types of the numerals in the surcharges on Nos. 2, 3, 8 and 9.

Stamps of French Offices in Turkey, 1902-03, Surcharged

T. E. O.

2 MILLIEMES

1919

11	A2	1m on 1c gray	35	30
a.		Inverted surcharge	11.00	11.00
12	A2	2m on 2c vio brn	35	30
a.		Inverted surcharge	11.00	11.00
13	A2	3m on 3c red org	60	45
14	A3	4m on 15c pale red	30	30
a.		Inverted surcharge	11.00	11.00
15	A2	5m on 5c grn	35	28

Overprinted **T. E. O.**

16	A5	1p on 25c bl	35	28
a.		Inverted overprint	11.00	11.00
17	A6	2p on 50c bis brn & lav	60	55
18	A6	4p on 1fr cl & ol grn	1.10	90
19	A6	8p on 2fr gray vio & yel	4.00	3.50
a.		"T.E.O." double	32.50	32.50
20	A6	20p on 5fr dk bl & buff	225.00	150.00
		Nos. 11-20 (10)	233.00	156.86

On Nos. 17-20 "T.E.O." reads vertically up.
Nos. 1-20 were issued in Beirut and mainly used in Lebanon. Nos. 16-20 were also used in Cilicia.

Stamps of France, 1900-07, Surcharged

O. M. F.
Syrie
1
MILLIEME

1920

21	A16	1m on 1c gray	2.50	2.50
a.		Inverted surcharge	18.00	18.00
b.		Double surcharge		
22	A16	2m on 2c vio brn	2.75	2.75
a.		Double surch.		
23	A22	3m on 5c grn	5.50	5.50
a.		Double surcharge		
24	A18	20p on 5fr dk bl & buff	400.00	400.00

The letters "O. M. F." are the initials of "Occupation Militaire Francaise."

Stamps of France, 1900-07, Surcharged in Black or Red

O. M. F.
Syrie
2
MILLIEMES

1920

25	A16	1m on 1c gray	30	30
26	A16	2m on 2c vio brn	60	60
27	A22	3m on 5c grn	45	45
28	A22	5m on 10c red	30	30
a.		Inverted surcharge		
29	A18	20p on 5fr dk bl & buff	55.00	55.00
30	A18	20p on 5fr dk bl & buff (R)	225.00	225.00
		Nos. 25-30 (6)	281.65	281.65

Stamps of France, 1900-21, Surcharged in Black or Red:

O. M. F.   **O. M. F.**
Syrie   or   **Syrie**
50   **3**
CENTIMES   **PIASTRES**

1920-22

31	A16	25c on 1c gray	50	50
32	A16	50c on 2c vio brn	50	50
33	A16	75c on 3c red org	50	50
34	A22	1p on 5c grn (R)	35	35
35	A22	1p on 5c grn	22	22
36	A22	1p on 20c red brn ('21)	12	12
37	A22	1.25p on 25c bl ('22)	60	60
38	A22	1.50p on 30c org ('22)	38	30
39	A22	2p on 10c red	28	28
40	A22	2p on 25c bl (R)	28	28
41	A18	2p on 40c red & pale bl ('21)	45	28
42	A20	2.50p on 50c dl bl ('22)	50	45
a.		Final "S" of "Piastres" omitted	1.75	1.75
43	A22	3p on 25c bl (R)	45	45
44	A18	3p on 60c vio & ultra ('21)	60	45
45	A20	5p on 15c gray grn	45	45
46	A18	5p on 1fr cl & ol grn	1.20	1.00
47	A18	10p on 40c red & pale bl	75	75
48	A18	10p on 2fr org & pale bl ('21)	2.25	1.75
49	A18	25p on 50c bis brn & lav	1.10	1.10
50	A18	25p on 5fr dk bl & buff ('21)	90.00	90.00
51	A18	50p on 1fr cl & ol grn	1.75	1.75
a.		"PIASTRES"	850.00	850.00
52	A18	100p on 5fr dk bl & buff (R)	30.00	30.00
53	A18	100p on 5fr dk bl & buff (Bk)	225.00	225.00
a.		"PIASRTES"	1,250.	1,250.
		Nos. 31-53 (23)	358.23	357.08

In first printing, space between "Syrie" and numeral is 2mm. In second printing, 1mm.
Surcharge is found inverted on Nos. 32, 35-38, 42, 44-45. Price, each $2-$3.
Surcharge is found double on Nos. 31, 37, 40, 42. Price, each $2.

O. M. F.
Syrie
25
CENTIMES

Surcharged in Black or Red

1920-23

54	A16	10c on 2c vio ('23)	30	30
55	A22	10c on 5c org (R) ('23)	22	22
56	A22	10c on 5c dk gray	25	20
a.		50c on 1c dk gray (error)	1.20	1.20
57	A22	25c on 5c grn	20	20
58	A22	25c on 5c org ('22)	30	30
a.		"CENTIEMES" omitted	10.00	10.00
59	A18	50c on 2c vio brn	20	20
60	A22	50c on 10c red ('21)	20	20
61	A22	50c on 10c grn ('22)	45	30
62	A20	75c on 3c red org	30	30
63	A20	75c on 15c sl grn ('21)	30	30
		Nos. 54-63 (10)	2.72	2.52

Surcharge is found inverted on Nos. 54-55, 58-59, 62-63; double on Nos. 60, 62. Price $1.50-$2.

Preceding Issues Overprinted

1920

Black Overprint.

64	A16	25c on 1c sl gray	7.25	7.25
65	A16	50c on 2c vio brn	7.25	7.25
66	A22	1p on 5c grn	5.50	5.50
67	A22	2p on 25c bl	11.00	11.00
68	A20	5p on 15c gray grn	25.00	25.00
69	A18	10p on 40c red & pale bl	35.00	35.00
70	A18	25p on 50c bis brn & lav	100.00	100.00
71	A18	50p on 1fr cl & ol grn	450.00	450.00
72	A18	100p on 5fr dk bl & buff	1,350.	1,350.
		Nos. 64-72 (9)	1,991.	1,991.

Red Overprint.

73	A16	25c on 1c sl gray	6.25	6.25
74	A16	50c on 2c vio brn	4.00	4.00
75	A22	1p on 5c grn	4.50	4.50
76	A22	2p on 25c bl	3.25	3.25
77	A20	5p on 15c gray grn	25.00	25.00
78	A18	10p on 40c red & pale bl	35.00	35.00
79	A18	25p on 50c bis brn & lav	100.00	100.00
80	A18	50p on 1fr cl & ol grn	225.00	225.00
81	A18	100p on 5fr dk bl & buff	900.00	900.00
		Nos. 73-81 (9)	1,303.	1,303.

Nos. 64-81 were used only in the vilayet of Aleppo where Egyptian gold currency was still in use.

A1
Black or Red Surcharge.

1921   *Perf. 11½*

82	A1	25c on 1/10p lt brn	50	45
a.		"25 Centiemes" omitted		
83	A1	50c on 2/10p grn	50	45
84	A1	1p on 3/10p yel	60	45
a.		"2/10" for "3/10"	8.00	8.00
85	A1	1p on 5m rose	80	60
86	A1	2p on 5m rose	90	65
a.		Tête bêche pair	75.00	75.00
87	A1	3p on 1p gray bl	1.10	95
88	A1	5p on 2p bl grn	2.75	2.25
89	A1	10p on 5p vio brn	4.25	3.25
90	A1	10p on 10p gray (R)	5.50	4.25
		Nos. 82-90 (9)	16.90	12.80

Nos. 82-90 are surcharged on stamps of the Arabian Government Nos. 85, 87-93 and have the designs and sizes of those stamps.
Surcharge is found inverted on Nos. 84-88, 90; double on No. 86.

Kilis Issue.

A2
Handstamped
Sewing Machine Perf. 9
1921   Pelure Paper

91	A2	(1p) violet	4.00	5.00

Issued at Kilis to meet a shortage of the regular issue, caused by the sudden influx of a large number of Armenian refugees from Turkey. The Kilis area was restored to Turkey in October, 1923.

Stamps of France, Surcharged

O. M. F.
Syrie
3 **PIASTRES**

1921-22   *Perf. 14x13½*

92	A18	2p on 40c red & pale bl	32	22
93	A18	2.50p on 50c bis brn & lav ('22)	50	45
a.		2p on 50c bis brn & lav (error)	25.00	22.50
94	A18	3p on 60c vio & ultra	65	45
95	A18	5p on 1fr cl & ol grn	4.50	3.50
96	A18	10p on 2fr org & pale bl	7.50	6.75
97	A18	20p on 5fr dk bl & buff	6.25	5.50
		Nos. 92-97 (6)	19.72	16.87

On No. 93 the surcharge reads: "2 PIASTRES 50".
Surcharge is found inverted on Nos. 92-95; double on No. 94. Price $2-$3.

French Mandate

French Stamps of 1900-23, Surcharged

Syrie
Grand Liban
25
CENTIMES

1923

104	A16	10c on 2c vio brn	15	15
105	A22	25c on 5c grn	15	15

SYRIA

106	A22	50c on 10c grn	22	22
a.		25c on 10c grn (error)	75.00	
107	A20	75c on 15c sl grn	30	30
108	A20	1p on 20c red brn	22	22
109	A22	1.25p on 25c bl	30	30
110	A22	1.50p on 30c org	30	30
111	A22	1.50p on 30c red	22	22
112	A20	2.50p on 50c dl bl	22	22

On Pasteur Stamps of 1923.

113	A23	50c on 10c grn	45	45
114	A23	1.50p on 30c red	45	45
115	A23	2.50p on 50c bl	45	45

Surcharge is found inverted on Nos. 104–108, 110, 115; double on Nos. 104, 106. Price $1.50–$2.

Surcharged Syrie - Grand Liban 2 PIASTRES

116	A18	2p on 40c red & pale bl	22	22
a.		Inverted surcharge	9.00	
b.		Double surcharge	10.00	
c.		"Liabn"		
117	A18	3p on 60c vio & ultra	45	45
		"Liabn"		
118	A18	5p on 1fr cl & ol grn	75	75
		"Liabn"		
119	A18	10p on 2fr org & pale bl	3.50	3.50
		"Liabn"		
120	A18	25p on 5fr dk bl & buff	15.00	15.00
		Inverted surcharge	30.00	30.00
		Nos. 104-120 (17)	23.35	23.35

SYRIE
Stamps of France, 1900–21, Surcharged **50 CENTIEMES**

1924   *Perf. 14 x 13½.*

121	A16	10c on 2c vio brn	8	6
a.		Double surcharge		
122	A22	25c on 5c org	10	6
a.		"25" omitted	4.00	
123	A22	50c on 10c grn	20	20
124	A20	75c on 15c sl grn	28	22
125	A22	1p on 20c red brn	30	15
a.		"1 PIASTRES"	5.00	
126	A22	1.25p on 25c bl	45	45
127	A22	1.50p on 30c org	45	45
128	A22	1.50p on 30c red	45	40
129	A20	2.50p on 50c dl bl	45	40

Same on Stamps of France, 1923 (Pasteur).

1924

130	A23	50c on 10c grn	12	12
131	A23	1.50p on 30c red	50	40
132	A23	2.50p on 50c bl	12	12
		Nos. 121-132 (12)	3.50	3.03

Olympic Games Issue.
Stamps of France, 1924, Surcharged "SYRIE" and New Values.

1924

133	A24	50c on 10c gray grn & yel grn	25.00	25.00
134	A25	1.25p on 25c rose & dk rose	25.00	25.00
135	A26	1.50p on 30c brn red & blk	25.00	25.00
136	A27	2.50p on 50c ultra & dk bl	25.00	25.00

SYRIE
Stamps of France 1900–20 Surcharged **2 PIASTRES**

137	A18	2p on 40c red & pale bl	30	22
138	A18	3p on 60c vio & ultra	50	45
139	A18	5p on 1fr cl & ol grn	1.60	1.60
140	A18	10p on 2fr org & pale bl	1.75	1.50
141	A18	25p on 5fr dk bl & buff	3.00	2.75

Syrie 0, P. 25
Stamps of France 1900–21, Surcharged

سوريا
١/٤ القرش

1924-25

143	A16	10c on 2c vio brn	10	10
a.		Double surcharge	10.00	
b.		Inverted surcharge	9.00	
144	A22	25c on 5c org	15	15
a.		Double surcharge	10.00	
145	A22	50c on 10c grn	22	22
a.		Double surcharge	10.00	
b.		Inverted surcharge	9.00	
146	A20	75c on 15c gray grn	22	22
a.		Double surcharge	10.00	
b.		Inverted surcharge	9.00	
147	A22	1p on 20c red brn	10	10
a.		Inverted surcharge	9.00	
148	A22	1p25 on 25c bl	22	22
a.		Inverted surcharge	9.00	
149	A22	1p50 on 30c red	30	30
a.		Double surcharge	10.00	
150	A22	1p50 on 30c org	16.00	16.00

SYRIE
Syrie 2 Piastres
Surcharged

سوريا
غرش ٢

151	A22	2p on 35c vio ('25)	22	22
152	A18	2p on 40c red & pale bl	22	22
a.		Arabic "Piastre" in singular	22	22
153	A18	2p on 45c grn & bl ('25)	1.75	1.75
154	A18	3p on 60c vio & ultra	45	45
155	A20	3p on 60c lt vio ('25)	45	45
156	A20	4p on 85c ver	22	22
157	A18	5p on 1fr cl & ol grn	45	45
158	A18	10p on 2fr org & pale bl	75	75
159	A18	25p on 5fr dk bl & buff	75	75
		Nos. 143-159 (17)	22.57	22.57

On No. 152a, the surcharge is as illustrated. The correct fourth line ("2 Piastres"—plural), as it appears on Nos. 151, 152 and 153, has four characters, the third resembling "9."

Same Surcharge on Stamps of France, (Pasteur).

1924-25

160	A23	50c on 10c grn	30	30
161	A23	75c on 15c grn ('25)	50	50
162	A23	1p50 on 30c red	45	45
163	A23	2p on 45c red ('25)	30	30
164	A23	2p50 on 50c bl	50	50
165	A23	4p on 75c bl	60	60
		Nos. 160-165 (6)	2.65	2.65

Olympic Games Issue.
Stamps of France, 1924, Surcharged "Syrie" and New Values in French and Arabic.

1924

166	A24	50c on 10c gray grn & yel grn	25.00	25.00
167	A25	1p25 on 25c rose & dk rose	25.00	25.00
168	A26	1p50 on 30c brn red & blk	25.00	25.00
169	A27	2p50 on 50c ultra & dk bl	25.00	25.00

Ronsard Issue.
Same Surcharge on France No. 219.

1925

170	A28	4p on 75c bl, *bluish*	45	45

Mosque at Hama   Mosque at Damascus
A3   A5

View of Merkab
A4

Designs: 50c, View of Alexandretta. 75c, View of Hama. 1p, Omayyad Mosque, Damascus. 1.25p, Latakia Harbor. 1.50p, View of Damascus. 2p, View of Palmyra. 2.50p, View of Kalat Yamoun. 3p, Bridge of Daphne. 5p, View of Aleppo. 10p, View of Aleppo. 25p, Columns at Palmyra.

Perf. 12½, 13½

			Litho.	Unwmkd.
173	A3	10c dk vio	6	6
		Photogravure.		
174	A4	25c ol blk	30	30
175	A4	50c yel grn	22	22
176	A4	75c brn org	28	18
177	A5	1p magenta	22	5
178	A4	1p25 dp grn	70	45
179	A4	1p50 rose red	18	5
180	A4	2p dk green	30	18
181	A4	2p50 pck bl	45	45
182	A4	3p org brn	22	12
183	A4	5p violet	60	20
184	A4	10p vio brn	1.00	20
185	A4	25p ultra	1.25	90
		Nos. 173-185 (13)	5.78	3.46

Surcharged in Black or Red

1P.   غ١

1926-30

186	A4	1p on 3pi org brn ('30)	45	32
187	A4	2p on 1p25 dp grn (R) ('28)	32	18
a.		Double surcharge		
188	A4	3p50 on 75c org brn	30	22
a.		Double surch.	5.50	5.50
189	A4	4p on 25c ol blk	45	22
190	A4	4p on 25c ol blk ('27)	70	60
191	A4	4p on 25c ol blk (R) ('28)	32	18

192	A4	4p50 on 75c brn org	30	22
193	A4	6p on 2p50 pck bl	30	22
194	A4	6p on 2p50 pck bl	30	22
195	A4	7p50 on 2p50 pck bl (R) ('28)	65	60
a.		Double surcharge	2.50	
196	A4	12p on 1p25 dp grn	32	25
a.		Surcharge on face and back	25.00	25.00
197	A4	15p on 25p ultra	45	30
198	A4	20p on 1p25 dp grn	40	30
		Nos. 186-198 (13)	5.26	3.83

Size of numerals and arrangement of this surcharge varies on the different denominations. No. 189 has slanting foot on "4". No. 190, foot straight.

No. 173 Surcharged in Red

05 · 0

1928

199	A3	05c on 10c dk vio	6	6

Stamps of 1925 Issue Overprinted in Red or Blue

EXPOSITION INDUSTRIELLE DAMAS 1929
معرض الصناعات الوطنية
دمشق ١٩٢٩

1929   *Perf. 13½*

200	A4	50c yel grn (R)	1.75	1.75
201	A5	1p mag (Bl)	1.75	1.75
202	A4	1p50 rose red (Bl)	1.75	1.75
203	A4	3p org brn (Bl)	1.75	1.75
204	A4	5p vio (R)	1.75	1.75
205	A4	10p vio brn (Bl)	1.75	1.75
206	A4	25p ultra (R)	1.75	1.75
		Nos. 200-206 (7)	12.25	12.25

Issued in connection with an Industrial Exhibition at Damascus, September, 1929.

View of Hama   View of Alexandretta
A6   A9

Citadel at Aleppo
A10

Great Mosque of Damascus
A11

Ruins of Bosra
A13

SYRIA

Mosque at Homs—A15

View of Sednaya—A16

Citadel at Aleppo—A17

Ancient Bridge at Antioch
A18

Mosque at Damascus
A22

Designs: 0p20, Great Mosque, Aleppo. 0p25, Minaret, Hama. 2pi, View of Antioch. 4pi, Square at Damascus. 15pi, Mosque at Hama. 25pi, Monastery of St. Simeon the Stylite (ruins). 50pi, Sun Temple (ruins), Palmyra.

Perf. 12x12½
1930–36   Litho.   Unwmkd.

208	A6	10c red vio	12	12
209	A6	10c vio brn ('33)	12	12
209A	A6	10c vio brn redrawn ('35)	8	8
210	A6	20c dk bl	6	6
211	A6	20c brn org ('33)	6	6
212	A6	25c gray grn	8	8
213	A6	25c dk bl gray ('33)	18	18

Photogravure.
Perf. 13.

214	A9	50c violet	6	6
215	A15	75c org red ('32)	6	6
216	A10	1p green	12	8
217	A10	1p bis brn ('36)	12	8
218	A11	1.50p bis brn	2.25	2.00
219	A11	1.50p dp grn ('33)	32	32
220	A9	2p dk vio	12	12
221	A13	3p yel grn	45	32
222	A10	4p yel org	12	8
223	A15	4.50p rose car	45	32
224	A16	6p grnsh blk	32	28
225	A17	7.50p dl bl	50	38
226	A18	10p dk brn	55	22
227	A10	15p dp grn	70	50
228	A18	25p vio brn	85	60
229	A15	50p ol brn	3.25	2.75
230	A22	100p red org	8.50	7.25
		Nos. 208-230 (24)	19.44	16.06

On No. 209A Arabic inscriptions, upper right, are entirely redrawn with lighter lines. Hyphen added in "Helio-Vaugirard" imprint. Lines in buildings and background more distinct.
On No. 215 the letters of "VAUGIRARD" in the imprint are reversed as in a mirror.

Autonomous Republic

Parliament Building
A23

abu-al-Ala al-Maarri
A24

President Ali Bek el Abed
A25

Saladin
A26

1934, Aug. 2   Engraved   Perf. 12½

232	A23	10c ol grn	75	75
233	A23	20c black	75	75
234	A23	25c red org	75	75
235	A23	50c ultra	75	75
236	A23	75c plum	75	75
237	A24	1p vermilion	2.75	2.75
238	A24	1.50p green	3.50	3.50
239	A24	2p red brn	3.50	3.50
240	A24	3p Prus bl	3.50	3.50
241	A24	4p brt vio	3.50	3.50
242	A24	4.50p carmine	3.50	3.50
243	A24	5p dk bl	3.50	3.50
244	A24	6p dk brn	3.50	3.50
245	A24	7.50p dk ultra	3.50	3.50
246	A25	10p dk brn	5.50	5.50
247	A25	15p dl bl	7.50	7.50
248	A25	25p rose red	11.00	11.00
249	A26	50p dk brn	20.00	20.00
250	A26	100p lake	32.50	32.50
		Nos. 232-250 (19)	111.00	111.00

Issued to commemorate the Proclamation of the Republic. See Nos. C57-C66.

Stamps of 1930-36
Overprinted in Red or Black

1936, Apr. 15

253	A9	50c vio (R)	1.50	1.50
254	A10	1p bis brn (Bk)	1.50	1.50
255	A9	2p dk vio (R)	1.50	1.50
256	A13	3p yel grn (Bk)	1.50	1.50
257	A10	4p yel org (Bk)	1.50	1.50
258	A15	4.50p rose car (Bk)	1.50	1.50
259	A16	6p grnsh blk (R)	1.50	1.50
260	A17	7.50p dl bl (R)	1.50	1.50
261	A18	10p dk brn (Bk)	2.25	2.25
		Nos. 253-261 (9)	14.25	14.25

Issued in connection with an Industrial Exhibition at Damascus, May, 1936. See Nos. C67-C71.

Stamps of 1930 Surcharged in Black

1937-38   Perf. 13½x13

262	A10	2.50p on 4p yel org ('38)	22	22
263	A22	10p on 100p red org	70	70

Stamps of 1930-33
Surcharged in Red or Black

1938   Perf. 13½

264	A15	25c on 75c org red (Bk)	12	12
265	A11	50c on 1.50p dp grn (R)	12	12
266	A17	2p on 7.50p dl bl (R)	18	18
267	A17	5p on 7.50p dl bl (R)	30	30
268	A15	10p on 50p ol brn (Bk)	65	65
		Nos. 264-268 (5)	1.37	1.37

President Hashem Bek el Atassi
A27

1938-43   Photogravure   Unwmkd.

268A	A27	10p dp bl ('43)	32	32
269	A27	12.50p on 10p dp bl (R)	45	45
270	A27	20p dk brn	45	45

The 10pi and 20pi exist imperf.

Columns at Palmyra
A28

1940   Lithographed.   Perf. 11½.

271	A28	5p pale rose	32	25

Exists imperf.

Museum at Damascus
A29

Hotel at Bloudan
A30

Kasr-el-Heir
A31

1940   Typographed   Perf. 13x14

272	A29	10c brt rose	5	5
273	A29	20c lt bl	5	5
274	A29	25c fawn	6	5
275	A29	50c ultra	6	5

Engraved.
Perf. 13.

276	A30	1p pck bl	8	6
277	A30	1.50p chocolate	18	18
278	A30	2.50p dk grn	10	10
279	A31	5p violet	30	12
280	A31	7.50p vermilion	50	42
281	A31	50p sepia	1.10	75
		Nos. 272-281 (10)	2.48	1.83

President Taj Eddin Hassani
A32

1942, Apr. 6   Litho.   Perf. 11½

282	A32	50c sage grn	3.00	3.00
283	A32	1.50p dl gray brn	3.00	3.00
284	A32	6p fawn	3.00	3.00
285	A32	15p lt bl	3.00	3.00
		Nos. 282-285, C96-C97 (6)	16.50	16.50

Issued to commemorate the proclamation of independence by the Allies, September 27, 1941.

President Taj Eddin Hassani
A33

President Hassani and Map of Syria
A34

1942   Photogravure   Unwmkd.

286	A33	6p rose lake & sal rose	1.75	1.75
287	A33	15p dl bl & bl	1.75	1.75

See No. C98. Nos. 286-287 exist imperforate.

1943   Lithographed.

288	A34	1p lt grn	1.50	1.50
289	A34	4p buff	1.50	1.50
290	A34	8p pale vio	1.50	1.50
291	A34	10p salmon	1.50	1.50
292	A34	20p dl chky bl	1.50	1.50
		Nos. 288-292, C99-C102 (9)	13.50	13.50

Proclamation of a United Syria.

Stamps of 1943
Overprinted with Border in Black.
1943

293	A34	1p lt grn	1.50	1.50
294	A34	4p buff	1.50	1.50
295	A34	8p pale vio	1.50	1.50
296	A34	10p salmon	1.50	1.50
297	A34	20p dl chky bl	1.50	1.50
		Nos. 293-297, C103-C106 (9)	13.50	13.50

Mourning for President Hassani.
Nos. 288 to 297 exist imperforate.

SYRIA

Nos. 278 and 280
Overprinted in
Carmine or Black

1944		Perf. 13	Unwmkd.	
298	A30	2.50p dk grn (C)	2.75	2.75
299	A31	7.50p ver (Bk)	2.75	2.75
		Nos. 298-299, C114-C116 (5)	22.50	22.50

Issued to commemorate the 1000th anniversary of the Arab poet and philosopher, abu-al-Ala al-Maarri.

President Shukri
el Kouatly
A35

1945, Mar. 15		Litho.	Perf. 11½	
300	A35	4p pale lil	35	35
301	A35	6p dl bl	35	35
302	A35	10p salmon	35	35
303	A35	15p dk brn	55	55
304	A35	20p sl grn	60	60
305	A35	40p orange	14.46	9.83
		Nos. 300-305, C117-C123 (13)	14.56	9.93

Issued to commemorate the resumption of constitutional government.

A36   A37

A38   A39

Fiscal Stamps Overprinted
or Surcharged in Black.

1945		Typo.	Perf. 11, 11½x11	
306	A36	12½p on 15p yel grn	2.00	2.00
307	A37	25p buff	3.50	3.50
307A	A38	25p on 25s lt vio brn	2.25	2.25
308	A39	50p on 75p brn org	4.25	4.25
309	A39	75p brn org	6.00	6.00
310	A37	100p yel grn	6.75	6.75
		Nos. 306-310 (6)	24.75	24.75

Type of 1945 and
Nos. 308 and 310 Overprinted in Black.

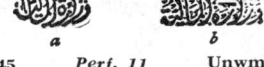
a   b

1945		Perf. 11	Unwmkd.	
311	A37(b)	50p magenta	2.00	2.00
312	A39(a)	50p on 75p brn org	1.50	1.50
313	A37(b)	100p yel grn	2.75	2.75

Independent Republic

A40

Fiscal Stamp Overprinted in Carmine.

1946				
314	A40	200p lt bl	5.00	5.00

Sun and Ears   President Shukri
of Wheat   el Kouatly
A41   A42

1946		Lithographed.	Perf. 13x13½.	
315	A41	50c brn org	10	8
316	A41	1p violet	15	10
317	A41	2.50p bl gray	20	15
318	A41	5p lt bl grn	30	25

Photogravure.
Perf. 13½x13, 13x13½.

319	A42	7.50p dk brn	18	12
320	A42	10p Prus grn	25	12
321	A42	12.50p dp vio	30	7
		Nos. 315-321 (7)	1.48	89

Arab Horse
A44

1946-47			Lithographed	
325	A44	50p ol brn	2.75	70
326	A44	100p dk bl grn ('47)	6.00	1.50
327	A44	200p rose vio ('47)	12.00	4.00

Nos. 320, 321 and 325
Overprinted in Black or Green

1946, Apr. 17				
328	A42	10p Prus grn	50	50
329	A42	12.50p dp vio	75	75
330	A44	50p ol brn (G)	2.00	2.00

Issued to commemorate the evacuation of British and French troops from Syria. See No. C135.

President Shukri el Kouatly
A45
Lithographed.

1946		Perf. 13½x13	Unwmkd.	
331	A45	15p red	25	15
332	A45	20p violet	55	50
333	A45	25p ultra	85	20

No. 333
Overprinted
in Magenta

1946, Aug. 28				
334	A45	25p ultra	1.40	1.20

Issued to commemorate the 8th Arab Medical Congress at Aleppo, Aug. 28–Sept. 4, 1946. See Nos. C136–C138.

Nos. 328 to 330
With Additional
Overprint in Black

Perf. 13½x13, 13x13½
1947, June 10

335	A42(e)	10p Prus grn	50	12
336	A42(e)	12.50p dp vio	85	20
337	A44(f)	50p ol brn	2.00	65

Issued to commemorate the first anniversary of the evacuation of British and French troops from Syria. See No. C139.

Hercules and the Lion—A46

Mosaics from Omayyad
Mosque, Damascus
A47

1947, Nov. 15   Litho.   Perf. 11½

| 338 | A46 | 12.50p sl grn | 65 | 50 |
| 339 | A47 | 25p gray bl | 1.20 | 90 |

Issued to commemorate the first Arab Archaeological Congress, Damascus, Nov. 1947. See Nos. C140–C141 and souvenir sheet No. C141a.

Courtyard of Azem Palace—A48

Telephone Building—A49

1947, Nov. 15

| 340 | A48 | 12.50p dp cl | 65 | 50 |
| 341 | A49 | 25p brt bl | 1.10 | 70 |

Issued to commemorate the 3rd Congress of Arab Engineers, Damascus, Nov. 1947. See Nos. C142–C143 and souvenir sheet No. C143a.

House of Parliament—A50

President Shukri el Kouatly
A51

1948, June 23   Perf. 10½   Unwmkd.

| 342 | A50 | 12.50p blk & org | 55 | 25 |
| 343 | A51 | 25p dp rose | 90 | 50 |

Issued to commemorate the reelection of President Shukri el Kouatly. See Nos. C144–C145 and souvenir sheet No. C145a.

National   Syrian Flag
Emblem   and Soldier
A52   A53

1948, June 23   Lithographed

| 344 | A52 | 12.50p gray & choc | 50 | 30 |
| 345 | A53 | 25p multi | 90 | 50 |

Issued to publicize the inauguration of compulsory military training. See Nos. C146–C147 and souvenir sheet No. C147a.

Nos. 215 and 327 Surcharged
with New Value and Bars in Black.

1948		Perf. 13, 13x13½		
346	A15	50c on 75c org red	12	8
347	A44	25p on 200p rose vio	60	30

Col. Husni Zayim   Palmyra
A54   A56

Ain el Arous—A55

SYRIA

1949, June 20   Litho.   Perf. 11½
348   A54   25p blue   90   45

Issued to commemorate the revolution of Mar. 30, 1949. See No. C153.
A souvenir sheet comprises Nos. 348 and C153, imperf. Size: 137x170mm. Price $80.

1949, June 20
349   A55   12.50p violet   2.00   2.00
350   A56   25p blue   3.00   3.00

Issued to commemorate the 75th anniversary of the formation of the Universal Postal Union.
See Nos. C154–C155 and note after No. C155.

Pres. Husni Zayim and Map
A57

Wmk. 291
Wmkd. National Emblem Multiple. (291)

1949, Aug. 6   Litho.   Perf. 11½
351   A57   25p bl and brn   3.00   2.00

Issued to commemorate the election of President Husni Zayim. See No. C156 and imperf. souvenir sheet No. C156a.

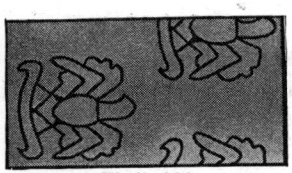

Tel-Chehab Waterfall
A58

Damascus Scene
A59

1949
352   A58   5p gray   12   10
353   A58   7.50p ol gray   25   15
354   A59   12.50p vio brn   50   25
355   A59   25p blue   70   55

See also No. 376.

Nos. 327 and 326 Surcharged with New Value and Bars in Black.

1950   Perf. 13x13½   Unwmkd.
356   A44   2.50p on 200p rose vio   25   20
357   A44   10p on 100p dk bl grn   30   20

National Emblem
A60

Road to Damascus
A61

Postal Administration Building, Damascus
A62

1950-51   Lithographed   Perf. 11½
358   A60   50c org brn   12   10
359   A60   2.50p pink   20   10
360   A61   10p pur ('51)   40   30
361   A61   12.50p sage grn ('51) 70   50
362   A62   25p bl ('51)   1.25 25
363   A62   50p blk ('51)   3.75 70
      Nos. 358-363 (6)   6.42 1.95

Nos. 358 to 363 exist imperforate.

Parliament Building, Damascus
A63

1951, Apr. 14
364   A63   12.50p gray blk   40   20
365   A63   25p blue   70   50

Issued to publicize the new constitution adopted Sept. 5, 1950. See Nos. C162–C163.
Nos. 364–365 exist imperforate.

Water Wheel, Hama
A64

Palace of Justice, Damascus
A65

Perf. 11½

1952, Apr. 22   Litho.   Unwmkd.
366   A64   50c dk brn   10   5
367   A64   2.50p dk bl   15   6

368   A64   5p bl grn   25   9
369   A64   10p red   40   12
370   A65   12.50p gray blk   50   12
371   A65   15p lil rose   90   25
372   A65   25p dp bl   1.00 30
373   A65   100p ol brn   5.75 1.10
      Nos. 366-373 (8)   9.05 2.09

Nos. 366-373 exist imperforate.

Type of 1949 and

Crusaders' Fort
A66

Crusaders' Fort
A67

1953   Photogravure.
374   A67   50c rose red   8   5
375   A66   2.50p dk brn   10   5
376   A58   7.50p green   15   10
377   A67   12.50p dp bl   15   5

Farm Workers
A68

Family Group
A69

Designs: 1pi, 5pi, Farm workers. 10pi, 12½p, Family group. 20pi, 25pi, 50pi, Factory and construction workers.

1954   Perf. 11½.
378   A68   1p olive   7   5
379   A68   2½p brn red   10   5
380   A68   5p dp bl   12   5
381   A69   7½p brn red   18   8
382   A69   10p black   25   8
383   A69   12½p violet   50   12
384   A69   20p dp plum   75   30
385   A69   25p violet   1.40 35
386   A69   50p dk grn   2.75 85
      Nos. 378-386 (9)   6.12 1.93

Nos. 382 and 385 Overprinted in Carmine

1954, Oct. 9
387   A69   10p black   90   40
388   A69   25p violet   1.10 60

Issued to publicize the Cotton Festival, Aleppo, October 1954. See Nos. C185–C186.

Arab Postal Union Issue.

Globe—A69a

1955   Photogravure.   Perf. 13½x13.
389   A69a   12½p green   50   20
390   A69a   25p violet   90   40

Issued to commemorate the founding of the Arab Postal Union, July 1, 1954. Exist imperf.
See No. C191.

Mother and Child—A70

1955, May 13   Litho.   Perf. 11½
391   A70   25p red   45   25

Mother's Day. See Nos. C194–C195.

United Nations Emblem—A71

1955   Photogravure.
392   A71   7½p crimson   50   40
393   A71   12½p Prus grn   90   50

Issued to commemorate the 10th anniversary of the United Nations, Oct. 24, 1955. See Nos. C200–C201.

Aqueduct at Aleppo—A72

1955   Lithographed   Unwmkd.
394   A72   7.50p lilac   25   8
395   A72   12.50p carmine   40   12

Issued to publicize the new aqueduct, bringing water from the Euphrates to Northern Syria. Exist imperf. See No. C202.

Nos. 389–390 Overprinted in Ultramarine or Green

1955   Photo.   Perf. 13½x13
396   A69a   12½p green   30   25
397   A69a   25p vio (G)   80   50

Issued to commemorate the Arab Postal Union Congress held at Cairo, Mar. 15, 1955. See No. C203.

Nos. 389–390 Overprinted in Black

1956
398   A69a   12½p green   45   40
399   A69a   25p violet   75   65

Issued to commemorate the visit of King Hussein of Jordan to Damascus, April, 1956. See No. C207.

SYRIA

Cotton
A73
Lithographed.
1956 *Perf. 11½* Unwmkd.
400 A73 2½p bluish grn 24 10
Issued to publicize a Cotton Festival.

Nos. 392-393
Overprinted in Black

1956 Photogravure *Perf. 11½*
401 A71 7½p crimson 50 40
402 A71 12½p Prus grn 70 50
Issued to commemorate the 11th anniversary of the United Nations. See Nos. C221–C222.

People's Army—A74
1957 Lithographed *Perf. 11½*
403 A74 5p lil rose 20 10
404 A74 20p gray grn 50 25
Issued to commemorate the formation of the Popular Resistance Movement.

Nos. 403-404
Overprinted in Black or Red
1957
405 A74 5p lil rose 25 10
406 A74 20p gray grn (R) 60 40
Issued to commemorate the evacuation of Port Said by British and French troops, Dec. 22, 1956.

Azem Palace, Damascus
A75
1957 Litho. *Perf. 11½*
407 A75 12½p lilac 20 10
408 A75 15p gray 30 15

Map of Near East, Scales and Damascus Skyline — **Cotton, Bale and Ship**
A76 — A77
1957 *Perf. 11½* Wmk. 291
409 A76 12½p brt grn 30 15
Issued for the third Congress of the Union of Arab Lawyers, Damascus, Sept. 21–25. See Nos. C240–C241.

1957
410 A77 12½p lt bl grn & blk 40 25
Issued for the Cotton Festival, Aleppo, Oct. 3–5. See Nos. C242–C243.

Children
A78
1957, Oct. 7
411 A78 12½p olive 50 25
Issued for International Children's Day, Oct. 7. See Nos. C244–C245.
See No. 13A in United Arab Republic (Syria) listings following Syria for "RAU" overprint on No. 411.

Mailing and Receiving Letter
A79
1957 Unwmkd.
412 A79 5p magenta 50 25
Issued for International Letter Writing Week, Oct. 6–12. See No. C246.

Nos. 403-404
Overprinted in Black or Red
1957 *Perf. 11½*
413 A74 5p lil rose 10 10
414 A74 20p gray grn (R) 40 40
Issued to commemorate the digging of fortifications along the Syrian-Israeli frontier.

Scales, Torch and Map
A80
1957, Nov. 8 Wmk. 291
415 A80 20p ol gray 50 25
Issued to commemorate the Congress of Afro-Asian Jurists, Damascus. See Nos. C247–C248.

Glider—A81
1957, Nov. 8 Litho. *Perf. 11½*
416 A81 25p red brn 80 30
417 A81 35p green 1.25 40
418 A81 40p ultra 2.40 60
Issued to commemorate a glider festival.

Khaled ibn el Walid Mosque, Homs
A82

1957 *Perf. 12* Unwmkd.
419 A82 2½p dl brn 15 10

Scroll, Communications Building and Telephone
A83
1958 *Perf. 11½* Wmk. 291
420 A83 25p ultra 40 25
See Nos. C249–C250.

Issues of 1958–61 released by the United Arab Republic are listed following the listings of Syria, Issues of the Arabian Government.

Syrian Arab Republic

Hall of Parliament, Damascus
A83a
Lithographed
1961 *Perf. 12* Unwmkd.
420A A83a 15p magenta 25 10
420B A83a 35p ol gray 65 40
Establishment of Syrian Arab Republic.

Water Wheel, Hama — **Roman Arch of Triumph, Latakia**
A84 — A85

Qalb Lozah Church, Aleppo
A86
Design: 7½p, 10p, Khaled ibn el Walid Mosque, Homs.
Lithographed
1961–62 *Perf. 11½x11* Unwmkd.
421 A84 2½p rose red 5 5
422 A84 5p blue 10 5
423 A84 7½p bl grn ('62) 15 5
424 A84 10p org ('62) 20 5
Perf. 12x11½
425 A85 12½p gray brn 60 5
426 A86 17½p ol gray ('62) 25 10
427 A85 25p dl red brn 90 18
428 A86 35p dl grn ('62) 40 30
Nos. 421-428 (8) 2.65 83

Types of 1961, Regular and Air Post
Designs: 2½p, 5p, 7½p, 10p, Arch, Jupiter Temple. 12½p, 15p, 17½p, 22½p, "The Beauty of Palmyra."
1962 *Perf. 11½x11*
429 A84 2p gray bl 10 5
430 A84 5p brn org 20 5
431 A84 7½p ol bis 25 5
432 A84 10p claret 10 5
Perf. 12x11½
Size: 26x38mm.
433 AP68 12½p gray ol 35 5
434 AP68 15p ultra 40 7
435 AP68 17½p brown 45 12
436 AP68 22½p grnsh bl 50 12
Nos. 429-436 (8) 2.35 56

Martyrs' Memorial — **Pres. Nazem el-Kodsi**
A87 — A88
1962, June 11 Lithographed
440 A87 12½p tan & sep 20 8
441 A87 35p grn & bl grn 50 30
Issued to commemorate the 1925 Revolution.

1962, Dec. 14 *Perf. 12x11½*
442 A88 12½p sep & lt bl 30 8
Issued to commemorate the first anniversary of the election of President Nazem el-Kodsi. See No. C278.

Queen Zenobia
A89

Central Bank of Syria
A90
Designs: 2½p, 5p, "The Beauty of Palmyra." 17½p, Hejaz Railway Station, Damascus. 22½p, Mouassat Hospital, Damascus. 35p, P.T.T. Jalaa Avenue Office, Damascus.
1963 *Perf. 11½x11* Unwmkd.
443 A89 2p dk bl gray 10 5
444 A89 5p rose lil 10 5
445 A89 7½p dl bl 30 5
446 A89 10p ol gray 50 5
447 A89 12½p ultra 90 6
448 A89 15p vio brn 1.25 9
Perf. 11½x12
449 A90 17½p dl vio 20 10
450 A90 22½p brt vio 25 15
451 A90 25p bis brn 30 12
452 A90 35p brt pink 40 20
Nos. 443-452 (10) 4.30 92

Wheat Emblem and Globe
A91

Boy Playing Ball and U.N. Emblem
A92

1963, Mar. 21 Litho. *Perf. 12x11½*

453	A91	12½p ultra & blk	15	10

Issued for the "Freedom from Hunger" Campaign of the U.N. Food and Agriculture Organization.

See No. C291 and souvenir sheet No. C291a.

Cotton Festival
Type of Air Post Issue, 1962, Inscribed "1963"

1963, Sept. 26 *Perf. 12x11½*

455	AP75	17½p multi	15	12
456	AP75	22½p multi	25	20

The 1963 Cotton Festival, Aleppo.

1963, Oct. 24 *Perf. 12x11½*

457	A92	12½p emer & sl grn	15	10
458	A92	22½p rose red & dk grn	25	15

Issued for International Children's Day.

Ugharit Princess
A93

1964 Litho. *Perf. 11½x11*

459	A93	2½p gray	5	5
460	A93	5p brown	5	5
461	A93	7½p rose cl	5	5
462	A93	10p emerald	7	5
463	A93	12½p lt vio	13	6
464	A93	17½p ultra	20	10
465	A93	20p rose car	42	15
466	A93	25p orange	65	15
		Nos.459-466 (8)	1.62	66

Map of North Africa and Middle East, Flag of Syria, and Crowd
A94

1965, Mar. 8 Litho. *Perf. 11½x12*

467	A94	12½p multi	10	6
468	A94	17½p multi	20	8
469	A94	20p multi	30	15

March 8 Revolution, 2nd anniversary.

Weather Map and Anemometer
A95

1965, Mar. 23 Litho. Unwmkd.

470	A95	12½p dl lil & blk	10	8
471	A95	27½p lt bl & blk	24	20

Fifth World Meteorological Day.

"Evacuation of Apr. 17, 1946"
A96

Peasants' Union Emblem
A97

1965, Apr. 17 Litho. *Perf. 12x11½*

472	A96	12½p bl & brt yel grn	10	6
473	A96	27½p rose red & lt lil	30	14

Issued to commemorate the 19th anniversary of the evacuation of British and French troops from Syria.

1965, Aug. *Perf. 11½x11* Unwmkd.

474	A97	2½p bl grn	7	5
475	A97	12½p purple	9	6
476	A97	15p maroon	10	7

Issued to publicize the Peasants' Union.

Torch, Map of Arab Countries and Farmer, Soldier, Woman, Intellectual and Worker
A98

Workers, Factory and Emblem
A99

1965, Nov. 23 *Perf. 12x11½*

477	A98	12½p multi	10	8
478	A98	25p multi	25	14

Issued to publicize the National Council of the Revolution, a legislative body working for a socialist and democratic society.

1966, Jan. Litho. *Perf. 11½x11*

479	A99	12½p blue	8	6
480	A99	15p carmine	12	10
481	A99	20p dl vio	20	12
482	A99	25p ol gray	30	20

Issued to commemorate the establishment of the General Union of Trade Unions.

Roman Lamp
A100

Islamic Vessel, 12th Century
A101

1966 Litho. *Perf. 11½x11*

483	A100	2½p sl grn	5	5
484	A100	5p magenta	20	20
485	A101	7½p brown	6	5
486	A101	10p brt rose lil	8	6

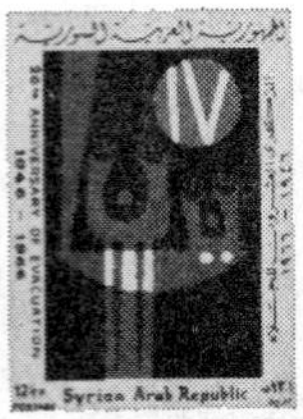

"Evacuation of Troops"
A102

Bust of Core, Terra Cotta Vase
A103

1966, Apr. 17 Litho. *Perf. 12x11½*

487	A102	12½p multi	12	6
488	A102	27½ multi	25	23

Issued to commemorate the 20th anniversary of the evacuation of British and French troops from Syria.

1967 *Perf. 11½x11*

Design: 15p, 20p, 25p, 27½p, Bronze vase in form of seated African woman.

489	A103	2½p brt grn	5	5
490	A103	5p sal pink	6	5
491	A103	10p grnsh bl	8	5
492	A103	12½p dl brn	10	5
493	A103	15p brt pink	12	7
494	A103	20p brt bl	15	9
495	A103	25p green	20	10
496	A103	27½p vio bl	30	15
		Nos. 489-496 (8)	1.06	61

Arab Revolution Monument, Damascus
A104

1968, Mar. 8 Litho. *Perf. 12x12½*

497	A104	12½p blk, yel & brn	8	6
498	A104	25p blk, pink & car rose	30	15
499	A104	27½p blk, lt grn & grn	30	20

March 8 Revolution, 5th anniversary.

Map of Syria
A105

Hands Holding Wrench, Gun and Torch
A106

1968, Apr. 4 Litho. *Perf. 12x12½*

500	A105	12½p pink & multi	10	6
501	A105	60p gray & multi	50	30

Issued to commemorate the 21st anniversary of the Arab Baath Socialist Party.

1968, Apr. 13

502	A106	12½p tan & multi	8	6
503	A106	17½p rose & multi	12	10
504	A106	25p yel & multi	25	15

Issued to publicize the mobilization effort.

Rising Sun, Power Lines and Railroad Tracks
A107

1968, Apr. 17 Litho. *Perf. 12½x12*

505	A107	12½p multi	10	8
506	A107	27½p vio & multi	25	12

Issued to commemorate the 22nd anniversary of the evacuation of British and French troops from Syria.

Oil Wells and Oil Pipe Line on Map—A108

1968, May 1

507	A108	12½p lt & dk grn & ultra	10	8
508	A108	17½p pink, brn & ultra	15	10

Issued to publicize Syrian oil exploitation and the completion of the oil pipe line to Tartus.

Map of Palestine and Torch
A109

Citadel of Aleppo, Wheat and Cogwheel
A110

1968, May Litho. *Perf. 12x12½*

509	A109	12½p ultra, blk & red	8	6
510	A109	25p ol bis, blk & red	20	20
511	A109	27½p gray, blk & red	25	20

Issued for Palestine Day, 1968.

1968, July 18 Litho. *Perf. 12x12½*

512	A110	12½p multi	10	8
513	A110	27½p multi	20	12

Industrial and Agricultural Fair, Aleppo.

Fair Emblem, Globe, Grain, Wheel and Horse
A111

Woman Carrying Cotton, and Castle of Aleppo
A112

Design: 27½p, Syrian flag, hand with torch, fair emblem, globe, grain and wheel.

Perf. 12x12½, 12½x12

1968, Aug. 25 Lithographed

514	A111	12½p dp brn, blk & emer	8	6
515	A111	27½p multi	25	15
516	A111	60p bl gray, blk & dp org	45	40

Issued to publicize the 15th International Damascus Fair, Aug. 25–Sept. 20.

1968, Oct. 3 Litho. Perf. 12x12½

517	A112	12½p multi	10	6
518	A112	27½p multi	20	15

13th Cotton Festival, Aleppo.

Al Jahez — A113

Oil Derrick and Pipe Line — A114

1968, Nov. 9 Litho. Perf. 12x12½

519	A113	12½p blk & buff	8	6
520	A113	27½p blk & gray	25	20

Issued for the 9th Science Week and to commemorate the 1100th anniversary of the death of Al Jahez Abu Uthman Amr ben Bahr (776–868).

1968 Perf. 12x11

521	A114	2½p grnsh bl & dk grn	5	5
522	A114	5p grn & vio bl	5	5
523	A114	7½p lt yel grn & bl	8	5
524	A114	10p brt yel & grn	8	5
525	A114	12½p yel & ver	13	6
526	A114	15p ol bis & dk brn	15	8
527	A114	27½p dl org & dk red brn	25	12
		Nos. 521-527 (7)	79	46

Broken Chains and Sun
A115

1969, Mar. 8 Litho. Perf. 12½x12

Sun in Yellow and Red

528	A115	12½p vio bl & blk	8	6
529	A115	25p gray & blk	25	12
530	A115	27½p dl grn & blk	30	12

March 8 Revolution, 6th anniversary.

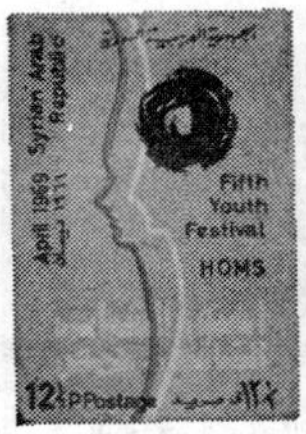

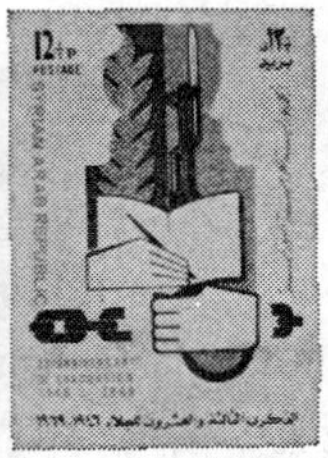

"Sun of Freedom, Young Man and Woman" — A116

Liberation through Knowledge and Construction — A117

1969, Mar. 29 Perf. 12x12½

531	A116	12½p multi	8	6
532	A116	25p multi	20	15

Issued to publicize Youth Week and the 5th Youth Festival, Homs, Apr. 18–24.

1969, Apr. 17 Litho. Perf. 12x12½

533	A117	12½p yel & multi	8	6
534	A117	27½p gray & multi	20	15

Issued to commemorate the 23rd anniversary of the evacuation of British and French troops from Syria.

Mahatma Gandhi — A118

Cotton — A119

1969, Oct. 7 Litho. Perf. 12x12½

535	A118	12½p brn & dl yel	8	6
536	A118	27½p grn & yel	20	15

Issued to commemorate the centenary of the birth of Mohandas K. Gandhi (1869–1948), leader in India's fight for independence.

1969, Oct. 10

537	A119	12½p multi	8	6
538	A119	17½p multi	14	12
539	A119	25p multi	20	17

14th Cotton Festival, Aleppo.

Map of Arab Countries
A120

Designs: 25p, Arab Academy. 27½p, Damascus University.

1969, Nov. 2 Litho. Perf. 12½x12

540	A120	12½p ultra & lt grn	8	6
541	A120	25p dk pur & dp pink	20	20
542	A120	27½p dp bis & yel grn	30	25

Issued to commemorate the 10th Science Week, and the 6th Arab Scientific Conference. No. 541 also commemorates the 50th anniversary of the Arab Academy and No. 542 the 50th anniversary of the Medical School of the Damascus University.

Symbols of Progress
A121

1970, Mar. 8 Litho. Perf. 12½x12

543	A121	12½p brt bl, blk & bis brn	8	8
544	A121	25p red, blk & dp bl	20	15
545	A121	27½p lt grn, blk & tan	25	22

March 8 Revolution, 7th anniversary.

Map of Arab League Countries, Flag and Emblem—A122

1970, Mar. 22

546	A122	12½p multi	8	8
547	A122	25p gray & multi	20	15
548	A122	27½p multi	25	22

25th anniversary of the Arab League.

Sultan Saladin and Battle of Hattin, 1187, between Saracens and Crusaders—A123

1970, Apr. 17 Litho. Perf. 12½x12

549	A123	15p brn & buff	12	10
550	A123	35p lil & buff	25	15

Issued to commemorate the 24th anniversary of the evacuation of British and French troops from Syria.

Development of Agriculture and Industry
A124

1970–71 Litho. Perf. 11x11½

551	A124	2½p brn & red ('71)	5	5
552	A124	5p org & bl	15	15
553	A124	7½p lil & gray ('71)	5	5
554	A124	10p lt & dk brn	6	6
555	A124	12½p bl & org ('71)	8	8
556	A124	15p grn & red lil	9	10
557	A124	20p vio & red brn	17	15
558	A124	22½p red brn & blk ('71)	20	15
559	A124	25p gray & vio bl ('71)	20	17
560	A124	27½p brt grn & dk brn ('71)	20	20
561	A124	35p rose red & emer ('71)	30	25
		Nos. 551-561 (11)	1.55	1.41

Young Man and Woman, Map of Arab Countries
A125

Perf. 12½x12

1970, May 7 **Unwmkd.**

569	A125	15p grn & ocher	9	10
570	A125	25p brn & ocher	20	20

Issued to publicize the First Youth Week, Latakia, Apr. 23–29. Inscribed "Youth's First Weak" (sic.).

Refugee Family
A126

1970, May 15

571	A126	15p multi	9	10
572	A126	25p gray & multi	25	15
573	A126	35p grn & multi	30	25

Issued for Arab Refugee Week.

Cotton—A127

Designs: 10p, Tomatoes. 15p, Tobacco. 20p, Beets. 35p, Wheat.

1970, Aug. 18 Litho. Perf. 12½

574	A127	5p multi	5	5
575	A127	10p yel & multi	8	8
576	A127	15p multi	12	9
577	A127	20p yel grn & multi	18	15
578	A127	35p lil & multi	40	30
		Nos. 574-578 (5)	83	67

Issued to publicize the Industrial and Agricultural Fair, Aleppo. Nos. 574–578 printed se-tenant.

Boy Scout, Tent, Emblem and Map of Arab Countries
A128

1970, Aug. 25 Perf. 12½x12

579	A128	15p gray grn	20	14

Issued to publicize the 9th Pan-Arab Boy Scout Jamboree, Damascus.

Olive Tree and Emblem
A129

1970, Sept. 28 Litho. Perf. 11½x12

580	A129	15p gray grn, yel & blk	12	12
581	A129	25p red brn, yel & blk	25	15

Issued to publicize World Olive Year.

Protection of Industry, Agriculture, Arts and Commerce—A130

1971, March 8 Litho. Perf. 12½x12

582	A130	15p ol, yel & bl	12	9
583	A130	22½p red brn, yel & ol	18	15
584	A130	27½p bl, yel & red brn	30	20

March 8 Revolution, 8th anniversary.

Workers Memorial, Hands with Wrench and Olive Branch
A131

SYRIA

1971, May 1 Litho. Perf. 12½x12

| 585 | A131 | 15p brn vio, yel & bl | 15 | 15 |
| 586 | A131 | 25p dk bl, bl & yel | 25 | 18 |

Labor Day, 1971.

Child and Traffic Lights A132

Design: 25p, Road signs, traffic lights, children (vert.).

1971, May 4 Perf. 11½x12, 12x11½

587	A132	15p blk, red & bl	12	9
588	A132	25p gray & multi	20	18
589	A132	45p blk, red & yel	40	30

World Traffic Day.

Factories, Cogwheel and Cotton A133

1971, July 15 Litho. Perf. 12½x12

| 590 | A133 | 15p lt grn, bl & blk | 12 | 9 |
| 591 | A133 | 30p red & blk | 28 | 25 |

11th Industrial and Agricultural Fair, Aleppo.

Arab Postal Union Emblem A134

Flag, Map of Syria, Egypt and Libya A135

1971, Aug. 13 Perf. 12x12½

| 592 | A134 | 15p cl & multi | 12 | 9 |
| 593 | A134 | 20p vio bl & multi | 25 | 15 |

25th anniversary of the Conference of Sofar, Lebanon, establishing the Arab Postal Union.

1971, Aug. 13 Perf. 12x11½

| 594 | A135 | 15p car, dl grn & blk | 15 | 9 |

Confederation of the Arab states of Syria, Libya and Egypt.

Red Pepper and Chemical Factory (Fertilizer Industry)—A136

Designs: 15p, Electronics industry (TV, telephone, computer). 35p, Glass industry (old lamp and glass manufacture). 50p, Carpet industry (carpet and looms).

1971, Aug. 25 Perf. 12½

595	A136	5p vio & multi	5	5
596	A136	15p dl grn & multi	12	9
597	A136	35p multi	40	25
598	A136	50p yel grn & multi	50	40

18th International Damascus Fair.

Pres. Hafez al Assad and Crowd A137

UNESCO Emblem, Radar, Spacecraft, Telephone A138

1971, Nov.   Litho. Perf. 12x12½

| 599 | A137 | 15p vio bl, blk & car | 12 | 9 |
| 600 | A137 | 20p dk & lt grn, car & blk | 20 | 20 |

1st anniversary of Correctionist Movement of Nov. 16, 1970.

1971, Dec. 8

| 601 | A138 | 15p vio bl & multi | 15 | 9 |
| 602 | A138 | 50p grn & multi | 50 | 40 |

25th anniversary of the United Nations Educational, and Scientific Cultural Organization (UNESCO).

UNICEF Emblem and Playing Children A139

1971, Dec. 21

| 603 | A139 | 15p ultra, dk bl & dp car | 15 | 9 |
| 604 | A139 | 25p grnsh bl, ocher & dk bl | 25 | 20 |

25th anniversary of the United Nations International Children's Fund (UNICEF).

Conference Emblem A140

1971, Dec. Perf. 12½x12

| 605 | A140 | 15p blk, grnsh bl & org | 15 | 9 |

Scholars' Conference.

Book Year Emblem A141

1972, Jan. 2

| 606 | A141 | 15p tan, lt bl & vio | 12 | 9 |
| 607 | A141 | 20p brn, lt grn & grn | 18 | 15 |

International Book Year 1972.

Wheel, "8" and Scales of Justice A142

Baath Party Emblem A143

1972, Mar. 8 Litho. Perf. 12x12½

| 608 | A142 | 15p bl grn & vio | 12 | 9 |
| 609 | A142 | 20p ol bis & car | 18 | 15 |

March 8 Revolution, 9th anniversary.

1972, Apr. 7

| 610 | A143 | 15p dk bl & multi | 12 | 9 |
| 611 | A143 | 20p vio & multi | 18 | 15 |

Arab Baath Socialist Party, 25th anniversary.

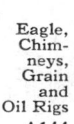 

Eagle, Chimneys, Grain and Oil Rigs A144

1972, Apr. 17 Perf. 12½x12

| 612 | A144 | 15p gold, blk & car | 12 | 9 |

Federation of Arab Republics, 1st anniversary.

Symbolic Flower, Broken Chain A145

Hand Holding Wrench and Spade A146

1972, Apr. 17 Perf. 12x11½

| 613 | A145 | 15p rose red & gray | 12 | 9 |
| 614 | A145 | 50p pale bl grn & gray | 45 | 45 |

26th anniversary of the evacuation of British and French troops from Syria.

1972, May 1

| 615 | A146 | 15p ol grn, bl & blk | 12 | 9 |
| 616 | A146 | 50p vio bl, brn & blk | 50 | 45 |

Labor Day 1972.

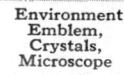

Environment Emblem, Crystals, Microscope A147

Dove over Factory A148

1972, June 5

| 617 | A147 | 15p multi | 15 | 9 |
| 618 | A147 | 50p bl & multi | 50 | 45 |

U.N. Conference on Human Environment, Stockholm, June 5–16.

1972, July 17 Litho. Perf. 12x11½

| 619 | A148 | 15p yel & multi | 12 | 9 |
| 620 | A148 | 20p multi | 18 | 15 |

Agricultural and Industrial Fair, Aleppo.

Folk Dance—A149

1972, Aug. 25 Litho. Perf. 12x12½
Multicolored

621	A149	15p shown	12	9
622	A149	20p Women and tambourine player	18	15
623	A149	50p Men and drummer	50	45

19th International Damascus Fair.

Olympic Rings, Discus, Soccer, Swimming—A150

Warriors on Horseback, Olympic Emblems—A151

Design: 60p, Olympic rings, running, gymnastics, fencing.

1972 Lithographed Perf. 12½x12

| 624 | A150 | 15p ol bis, blk & vio | 15 | 9 |
| 625 | A150 | 60p dl bl, blk & org | 55 | 50 |

Souvenir Sheet
Imperf.

| 626 | A151 | 75p lt grn, bl & blk | 1.00 | 1.00 |

20th Olympic Games, Munich, Aug. 26–Sept. 11, 1972. No. 626 has blue commemorative inscription in margin and multicolored Olympic emblem. Size: 105x80 mm.

Emblem of Revolution and Prancing Horse A152

1973, Mar. 8 Litho. Perf. 11½x12

627	A152	15p brt grn, blk & red	12	9
628	A152	20p dl org, blk & red	16	12
629	A152	25p bl, blk & red	20	15

March 8 Revolution, 10th anniversary.

SYRIA

695

Heart and WHO Emblem
A153

1973, Mar. 21
| 630 | A153 | 15p gray & multi | 15 | 9 |
| 631 | A153 | 50p lt brn & multi | 45 | 30 |

25th anniversary of the World Health Organization.

Cogwheel and Grain Emblem
A154

1973, Apr. 17   *Perf. 12x12½*
| 632 | A154 | 15p bl & multi | 12 | 9 |
| 633 | A154 | 20p multi | 16 | 12 |

27th anniversary of the evacuation of British and French troops from Syria.

Workers and Globe
A155

1973, May 1   *Perf. 11½x12*
| 634 | A155 | 15p rose & multi | 15 | 9 |
| 635 | A155 | 50p bl & multi | 45 | 30 |

Labor Day 1973.

UN, FAO Emblems, People and Symbols
A156
Stock A157

1973, May 7   *Perf. 12x11½*
| 636 | A156 | 15p lt grn & red brn | 12 | 9 |
| 637 | A156 | 50p lil & bl | 40 | 40 |

10th anniversary, world food program.

1973, May 15   Multicolored
638	A157	5p shown	5	5
639	A157	10p *Gardenia*	8	6
640	A157	15p *Jasmine*	15	9
641	A157	20p *Rose*	20	15
642	A157	25p *Narcissus*	25	16
		Nos. 638-642 (5)	73	51

International Flower Show, Damascus. Nos. 638-642 printed se-tenant.

Children and Flame

Designs: 3 children's heads and flame in different arrangements; 25p, 35p, 70p, vertical.

   Perf. 11½x12, 12x11½
1973-74   Lithographed
643	A158	2½p lt ol grn	5	5
644	A158	5p orange	5	5
645	A158	7½p dk brn	5	5
646	A158	10p crimson	6	5
647	A158	15p ultra	9	7
648	A158	25p gray	15	10
649	A158	35p brt bl	25	15
650	A158	55p green	35	20
651	A158	70p rose lil	50	25
		Nos. 643-651 (9)	1.55	97

Children's Day.
Issue dates: 15p, 55p, 70p, May, 1973. Others, Mar. 1974.

Fair Emblem
A159

1973, June 17   *Perf. 11½x12*
| 652 | A159 | 15p multi | 9 | 7 |

13th Agricultural and Industrial Fair, Aleppo.

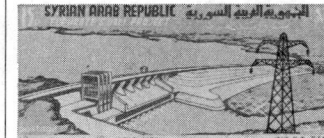

Euphrates Dam and Power Plant
A160

1973, July 5   *Perf. 12½x12*
| 653 | A160 | 15p grn & multi | 15 | 10 |
| 654 | A160 | 50p brn & multi | 35 | 25 |

Euphrates River diversion and dam project.

 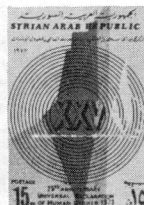

Woman from Deir Ezzor
A161
Map of Palestine, Barbed Wire, Human Rights Emblem
A162

Women's Costumes from: 10p, Hassaké. 20p, As Sahel. 25p, Zakié. 50p, Sarakeb.

1973, July 25   Litho.   *Perf. 12*
655	A161	5p multi	5	5
656	A161	10p multi	6	5
657	A161	20p multi	12	9
658	A161	25p multi	15	13
659	A161	50p multi	33	22
		Nos. 655-659 (5)	71	52

20th International Damascus Fair. Nos. 655-659 printed se-tenant.

1973, Aug. 20   *Perf. 12x11½*
| 660 | A162 | 15p lt grn & multi | 9 | 5 |
| 661 | A162 | 50p lt bl & multi | 33 | 25 |

25th anniversary of the Universal Declaration of Human Rights.

Citadel of Ja'abar
A163

Designs: 15p, Minaret of Meskeneh (vert.). 25p, Statue of Psyche at Anab al Safinah (vert.).

   Perf. 11½x12, 12x11½
1973, Sept. 5   Lithographed
662	A163	10p blk, org & bl	6	5
663	A163	15p blk, org & bl	9	5
664	A163	25p blk, org & bl	15	10

Salvage of monuments threatened by Euphrates Dam.

WMO Emblem
A164

1973, Sept. 12   *Perf. 11½x12*
| 665 | A164 | 70p yel & multi | 50 | 30 |

Centenary of international meteorological cooperation.

Maalula
A165

Design: 50p, Ruins of Afamia.

1973, Oct. 22   Litho.   *Perf. 11½x12*
| 666 | A165 | 15p gray bl & blk | 9 | 5 |
| 667 | A165 | 50p brn & blk | 33 | 25 |

Arab Emigrants' Congress, Buenos Aires.

Workers and Soldiers—A166

1973, Nov. 16   Litho.   *Perf. 12x11½*
| 668 | A166 | 15p ultra & yel | 9 | 5 |
| 669 | A166 | 25p pur & red brn | 20 | 15 |

3rd anniversary of Correctionist Movement of Nov. 16, 1970.

Nicolaus Copernicus
A167

Design: 25p, Abu-al-Rayhan al-Biruni.

1973, Dec. 15   *Perf. 12x11½*
| 670 | A167 | 15p gold & blk | 9 | 5 |
| 671 | A167 | 25p gold & blk | 20 | 15 |

14th Science Week.

Arms of Syria and Emblems
A168

1974, Mar. 8   *Perf. 11x12*
| 672 | A168 | 20p gray & bl | 12 | 8 |
| 673 | A168 | 25p lt grn & vio | 15 | 10 |

11th anniversary of March 8th Revolution.

UPU Emblem
A169

Designs: 20p, Air mail letter and UPU emblem (horiz.). 70p, like 15p.

   Perf. 12x11½, 11½x12
1974, Mar. 15
674	A169	15p gray & multi	9	8
675	A169	20p multi	15	12
676	A169	70p gray & multi	50	40

Centenary of Universal Postal Union.

Arab Postal Institute
A170

1974, Apr. 10   *Perf. 11½x12*
| 677 | A170 | 15p multi | 9 | 5 |

Inauguration of the Higher Arab Postal Institute, Damascus, Apr. 10.

Sun and Monument
A171

1974, Apr. 10
| 678 | A171 | 15p emer, blk & org | 9 | 5 |
| 679 | A171 | 20p dp org, blk & org | 12 | 8 |

28th anniversary of the evacuation of British and French troops from Syria.

Machine Shop Worker
A172
Abulfeda
A173

1974, May 1   *Perf. 12x12½*
| 680 | A172 | 15p blk, yel & bl | 9 | 5 |
| 681 | A172 | 50p blk, buff & bl | 30 | 25 |

Labor Day 1974.

1974   Lithographed   *Perf. 11½x11*

Design: 200p, al-Farabi.

| 682 | A173 | 100p pale grn | 65 | 50 |
| 683 | A173 | 200p lt brn | 1.20 | 1.00 |

Damascus Fair Emblem
A174

SYRIA

Design: 25p, Cog wheel and sun.
1974, July 25 Perf. 11½x11
684 A174 15p multi   9   5
685 A174 25p bl, blk & yel 15   8
21st International Damascus Fair.

Figs
A175

Fruits: 15p, Grapes. 20p, Pomegranates. 25p, Cherries. 35p, Rose hips.
1974, Aug. 21 Perf. 12x12½
686 A175 5p gray & multi   5   5
687 A175 15p gray & multi   9   5
688 A175 20p gray & multi 12   7
689 A175 25p gray & multi 20   10
690 A175 35p gray & multi 25   17
      Nos. 686-690 (5)   71   44
Agricultural and Industrial Fair, Aleppo.
Nos. 686-690 printed se-tenant.

Burning Fuse and Flowers
A176
Rook and Knight
A177

Design: 20p, Bomb and star-shaped holes in target.
1974, Oct. 6 Litho. Perf. 12x12½
691 A176 15p multi   9   5
692 A176 20p multi 12   7
First anniversary of October Liberation War (Yom Kippur War).

1974, Nov. 23
Design: 50p, Knight and chess board.
693 A177 15p bl & blk   15   10
694 A177 20p org, blk & bl 40   25
Chess Federation, 50th anniversary.

WPY Emblem
A178
Ishtup, Ilum
A179

1974, Dec. 4 Litho. Perf. 12x12½
695 A178 50p blk, sl & red 40   25
World Population Year 1974.

1975 Perf. 12x11½
Designs (Ancient Statuettes): 55p, Woman holding pitcher. 70p, Ur-Nina.
696 A179 20p brt grn   12   8
697 A179 50p brown   32   22
698 A179 70p gray bl   50   30

"A," People and Sun
A180
Postal Savings Bank Emblem, Family
A181

1975, Mar. 8 Litho. Perf. 12x11½
699 A180 15p gray & multi 9   5
12th anniversary, March 8th Revolution.

1975, Mar. 17
Design: 20p, Family depositing money, and stamped envelope.
700 A181 15p brt grn & multi 9   5
701 A181 20p org & blk   12   10
Publicity for Savings Certificates and Postal Savings Bank.

"Sun" and Dove
A182

1975, Apr. 17 Litho. Perf. 12x11½
702 A182 15p bis, red & blk   9   5
703 A182 25p bis, grn & blk 17   10
29th anniversary of the evacuation of British and French troops from Syria.

"Worker and Industry"
A183
Camomile
A184

1975, May 1 Litho. Perf. 12x11½
704 A183 15p bl grn & blk   9   5
705 A183 25p brn, yel & blk 15   10
Labor Day 1975.

1975, May 17
Flowers: 10p, Chincherinchi. 15p, Carnation. 20p, Poppy. 25p, Honeysuckle.
706 A184 5p ultra & multi   5   5
707 A184 10p lil & multi   6   5
708 A184 15p bl & multi   9   5
709 A184 20p gray grn & multi 15   10
710 A184 25p vio bl & multi   20   15
      Nos. 706-710 (5)   55   40
International Flower Show, Damascus.
Nos. 706-710 printed se-tenant.

Al-Kuneitra Destroyed and Rebuilt—A185
1975, June 5 Perf. 12½
711 A185 50p blk & multi 40   30
Re-occupation of Al-Kuneitra by Syria.

Apples
A186

Fruit: 10p, Quince. 15p, Apricots. 20p, Grapes. 25p, Figs.
1975, July 7
712 A186 5p lt bl & multi   5   5
713 A186 10p lt bl & multi   6   5
714 A186 15p lt bl & multi   9   7
715 A186 20p lt bl & multi 15   10
716 A186 25p lt bl & multi 20   15
      Nos. 712-716 (5)   55   42
Agricultural and Industrial Fair, Aleppo.
Nos. 712-716 printed se-tenant.

Ornament
A187

1975, July 25 Litho. Perf. 12x11½
717 A187 15p ol grn & multi   9   5
718 A187 35p brn & multi   15   15
22nd International Damascus Fair.

Pres. Hafez al Assad
A188

1975, Nov. 29 Litho. Perf. 11½x12
719 A188 15p grn & multi   9   5
720 A188 50p bl & multi   38   25
5th anniversary of Correctionist Movement of Nov. 16, 1970.

Designs (IWY Emblem and): 15p, Mother. 25p, Student. 50p, Laboratory technician.
1975, Nov. 29 Perf. 12x11½
721 A189 10p buff & multi   6   5
722 A189 15p rose & blk   9   5
723 A189 25p dl grn & blk 20   15
724 A189 50p org & blk   40   30
International Women's Year.

Horse-shaped Bronze Lamp
A190
Man's Head Inkstand
A191

Designs: 10p, 25p, like 20p. 35p, like 30p. 50p, 60p, Nike. 75p, Hera. 100p, Imdugug-Mari (winged animal). 500p, Palmyrene coin of Vasalathus. 1000p, Abraxas coin.
1976 Perf. 11½x12, 12x11½
725 A190 10p brt bluish grn   6   5
726 A190 20p lil rose   12   6
727 A190 25p vio rose   15   8
728 A191 30p brown   18   10
729 A191 35p olive   22   15
730 A191 50p brt bl   30   20
731 A191 60p violet   35   18
732 A191 75p orange   50   38
733 A191 100p lil rose   60   32
734 A191 500p grnsh gray   3.50 2.50
735 A191 1000p dk grn   6.00 4.50
      Nos. 725-735 (11)   11.98 8.52
See Nos. 798-803.

National Theater, Damascus and Pres. al Assad
A192

1976, Mar. 8 Litho. Perf. 11½x12
736 A192 25p brt grn, sil & blk 15   8
737 A192 35p ol, sil & blk   22 20
13th anniversary of March 8 Revolution.

Syria, Arabian Government No. 85—A193
1976, Apr. 12 Perf. 12x12½
738 A193 25p brt grn & multi 20   15
739 A193 35p bl & multi   25   20
Post's Day 1976.

Nurse and Emblem
A194
Eagle and Stars
A195

SYRIA

1976, Apr. 8   *Perf. 12x11½*

| 740 | A194 | 25p bl, blk & red | 20 | 10 |
| 741 | A194 | 100p vio, blk & red | 70 | 60 |

Arab Red Cross and Red Crescent Societies, 8th Conference, Damascus.

1976, Apr. 17

| 742 | A195 | 25p blk, red & brt grn | 20 | 15 |
| 743 | A195 | 35p blk, red & brt grn | 25 | 20 |

30th anniversary of the evacuation of British and French troops from Syria.

Hand Holding Wrench A196   Cotton and Factory A197

Design: 60p, Hand holding globe.

1976, May 1

| 744 | A196 | 25p bl & blk | 20 | 15 |
| 745 | A196 | 60p cit & multi | 50 | 40 |

May Day 1976.

1976, July 1

| 746 | A197 | 25p vio & multi | 20 | 15 |
| 747 | A197 | 35p bl & multi | 25 | 20 |

Agricultural and Industrial Fair, Aleppo.

Tulips—A198

1976, July 26

748	A198	5p shown	5	5
749	A198	15p Yellow daisies	9	5
750	A198	20p Turk's-cap lilies	12	10
751	A198	25p Irises	15	10
752	A198	35p Freesia	25	20
		Nos. 748-752 (5)	66	50

International Flower Show, Damascus. Nos. 748-752 printed se-tenant.

People, Globe and Olive Branch A199

Design: 60p, Symbolic arrow piercing darkness.

1976, Sept. 2   *Perf. 11½x12*

| 753 | A199 | 40p yel & multi | 30 | 25 |
| 754 | A199 | 60p multi | 45 | 35 |

5th Summit Conference of Non-aligned Countries, Colombo, Sri Lanka, Aug. 9-19.

Soccer, Games Emblem A200

Designs (Pan Arab Games Emblem and): 10p, Swimming. 25p, Running. 35p, Basketball. 50p, Javelin. 100p, Steeplechase.

1976, Oct. 6   *Litho.*   *Perf. 12½*

755	A200	5p multi	5	5
756	A200	10p multi	6	5
757	A200	20p multi	20	8
758	A200	35p multi	25	18
759	A200	50p multi	40	30
		Nos. 755-759 (5)	96	66

Souvenir Sheet
Imperf.

| 760 | A200 | 100p yel, blk & brn | 1.25 | 1.25 |

5th Pan Arab Sports Tournament. Nos. 755-759 printed se-tenant. No. 760 has brown Arabic marginal inscription. Size of stamp: 55x35mm.; size of sheet: 75x55mm.

"Development" A201   The Fox and the Crow A202

1976, Nov. 16 Litho. *Perf. 12½x12½*

| 761 | A201 | 35p multi | 22 | 15 |

6th anniversary of Correctionist Movement of Nov. 16, 1970.

Perf. 12x12½, 12½x12

1976, Dec. 7

Fairy Tales: 15p, The Hare and the Tortoise (horiz.). 20p, Little Red Riding Hood. 25p, The Lamb and the Wolf (horiz.). 35p, The Lamb and the Wolf.

762	A202	10p multi	6	5
763	A202	15p multi	9	5
764	A202	20p multi	12	8
765	A202	25p multi	15	12
766	A202	35p multi	25	20
		Nos. 762-766 (5)	67	50

Children's literature. Nos. 762-766 printed se-tenant.

Syrian Airlines Boeing 747—A203

1977, Feb. Litho. *Perf. 12½x12*

| 767 | A203 | 35p multi | 25 | 20 |

Civil Aviation Day.

Muhammad Kurd-Ali A204

1977, Feb.   *Perf. 12x12½*

| 768 | A204 | 25p lt grn & multi | 20 | 15 |

Muhammad Kurd-Ali (1876–1953), philosopher, birth centenary.

Woman Holding Syrian Flag A205

1977, Mar. 8 Litho. *Perf. 12x12½*

| 769 | A205 | 35p multi | 25 | 20 |

14th anniversary of March 8 Revolution.

Warrior on Horseback—A206

1977, Apr. 10 Litho. *Perf. 12½*

| 770 | A206 | 100p multi | 70 | 50 |

31st anniversary of the evacuation of British and French troops from Syria.

APU Emblem A207

1977, Apr. 12 Litho. *Perf. 12x12½*

| 771 | A207 | 35p sil & multi | 25 | 15 |

Arab Postal Union, 25th anniversary.

Tools and Factories A208

1977, May 1   *Perf. 12½x12*

| 772 | A208 | 60p multi | 45 | 35 |

Labor Day.

ICAO Emblem, Plane and Globe A209

1977, May 11

| 773 | A209 | 100p multi | 65 | 55 |

International Civil Aviation Organization, 30th anniversary.

Pioneers A210   Lemon A211

1977, Aug. 15 Litho. *Perf. 12x12½*

| 774 | A210 | 35p multi | 30 | 20 |

Al Baath Pioneer Organization.

1977, Aug. 1

Citrus Fruit: 20p, Lime. 25p, Grapefruit. 35p, Oranges. 60p, Tangerines.

775	A211	10p multi	6	5
776	A211	20p multi	12	6
777	A211	25p multi	15	10
778	A211	35p multi	25	18
779	A211	60p multi	35	22
		Nos. 775-779 (5)	93	61

Agricultural and Industrial Fair, Aleppo. Nos. 775-779 printed se-tenant.

Mallow A212

Flowers: 20p, Coxcomb. 25p, Morning glories. 35p, Almond blossoms. 60p, Lilacs.

1977, Aug. 6 Litho. *Perf. 12½x12*

780	A212	10p sil & multi	6	5
781	A212	20p sil & multi	12	6
782	A212	25p sil & multi	15	10
783	A212	35p sil & multi	25	18
784	A212	60p sil & multi	36	22
		Nos. 780-784 (5)	94	61

International Flower Show, Damascus. Nos. 780-784 printed se-tenant.

Coffeepot and Ornament A213

1977, Sept. 10   *Perf. 12x12½*

| 785 | A213 | 25p blk, bl & red | 15 | 8 |
| 786 | A213 | 60p blk, grn & brn | 35 | 17 |

24th International Damascus Fair.

Blind Man, Globe and Eye A214   Globe and Measures A215

SYRIA

1977, Nov. 17   Litho.   Perf. 12x12½
| 787 | A214 | 55p multi | 32 | 20 |
| 788 | A214 | 70p multi | 45 | 25 |

World Blind Week.

1977, Nov. 5
| 789 | A215 | 15p grn & multi | 10 | 5 |

World Standards Day, Oct. 14.

Microscope, Book, Harp, UNESCO Emblem
A216

1977, Nov. 5   Perf. 12½x12
| 790 | A216 | 25p multi | 15 | 10 |

30th anniversary of UNESCO.

Archbishop Capucci, Map of Palestine, Bars
A217

Fight Cancer Shield, Crab and Surgeon
A218

1977, Nov. 17   Perf. 12x12½
| 791 | A217 | 60p multi | 40 | 25 |

Palestinian Archbishop Hilarion Capucci, jailed by Israel in 1974.

1977, Nov. 17
| 792 | A218 | 100p multi | 60 | 40 |

Fight Cancer Week.

Dome of the Rock, Jerusalem
A219

1977, Dec. 6   Perf. 12
| 793 | A219 | 5p multi | 5 | 5 |
| 794 | A219 | 10p multi | 6 | 5 |

Palestinian fighters and their families.

Mural
A220

Pres. Hafez al Assad
A221

Designs: 10p, 15p, Murals from Dura-Europos, in National Museum, Damascus (15p horiz.).

1978, Jan. 22 Litho.   Perf. 12x11½
795	A220	5p gray grn	5	5
796	A220	10p vio bl	10	5
797	A220	15p brown	9	5

Types of 1976
Designs: 40p, Man's head inkstand. 55p, Nike. 70p, 80p, Hera. 200p, Arab-Islamic astrolabe. 300p, Palmyrene (Herod) coin.

Lithographed
1978   Perf. 12x11½, 11½x12
798	A191	40p pale org	25	10
799	A191	55p brt rose	32	10
800	A191	70p vermilion	45	10
801	A191	80p green	55	20
802	A191	200p lt ultra	1.25	60
803	A190	300p rose lil	2.25	1.00
		Nos. 798-803 (6)	5.07	2.10

1978   Perf. 12x11½
| 805 | A221 | 50p multi | 30 | 16 |

Anniversary of "Correction Movement."

Blood Circulation, WHO Emblem
A222

Factory
A223

1978, Apr. 7   Litho.   Perf. 12x11½
| 806 | A222 | 100p multi | 60 | 35 |

World Health Day, fight against hypertension.

1978, Apr. 17
| 807 | A223 | 35p multi | 22 | 10 |

32nd anniversary of the evacuation of British and French troops from Syria.

Rosette
A224

Map of Arab Countries, Police, Flag and Eye
A225

1978, Apr. 21
| 808 | A224 | 25p blk & grn | 20 | 10 |

14th Arab Engineering Conference, Damascus, Apr. 21–26.

1978, May
| 809 | A225 | 35p multi | 20 | 10 |

6th Conference of Arab Police Commanders.

European Goldfinch
A226

Birds: 20p, Peregrine falcon. 25p, Rock dove. 35p, Eurasian hoopoe. 60p, Old World quail.

1978   Perf. 11½x12
810	A226	10p multi	10	10
811	A226	20p multi	15	10
812	A226	25p multi	15	10
813	A226	35p multi	25	15
814	A226	60p multi	36	25
		Nos. 810-814 (5)	1.01	70

Nos. 810–814 printed se-tenant.

Trout
A227

Designs: Various fish.

1978, July   Litho.   Perf. 11½x12
815	A227	10p multi	10	10
816	A227	20p multi	15	10
817	A227	25p multi	15	10
818	A227	35p multi	25	15
819	A227	60p multi	35	25
		Nos. 815-819 (5)	1.00	70

Nos. 815–819 printed se-tenant.

Miniature Sheet
Pres. Assad Type of Air Post 1978
1978, Sept.   Litho.   Imperf.
| 820 | AP161 | 100p gold & multi | 75 | 60 |

Reelection of President Assad. Size of stamp: 58x80mm.; size of sheet: 80x105 mm.

Flowering Cactus
A228

Fair Emblem
A229

Designs: Flowering cacti.

1978   Litho.   Perf. 12½
821	A228	25p multi	15	10
822	A228	30p multi	18	10
823	A228	35p multi	22	15
824	A228	50p multi	30	16
825	A228	60p multi	36	20
		Nos. 821-825 (5)	1.21	71

International Flower Show, Damascus. Printed se-tenant.

1978   Litho.   Perf. 12x12½
| 826 | A229 | 25p sil & multi | 15 | 10 |
| 827 | A229 | 35p sil & multi | 22 | 10 |

Miniature Sheet
Imperf.
| 828 | A229 | 100p sil & multi | 60 | 60 |

25th International Damascus Fair. No. 828 shows different ornament, yellow margin with black inscription. Size of stamp: 40x46mm.; size of sheet: 105x80mm.

Euphrates Dam and Pres. Assad—A230

1978, Dec.   Litho.   Perf. 12½x12
| 829 | A230 | 60p multi | 36 | 20 |

Inauguration of Euphrates Dam.

Pres. Hafez al Assad
A231

1978, Nov. 16   Litho.   Perf. 12x12½
| 830 | A231 | 60p multi | 36 | 20 |

Nov. 16 Movement.

Racial Equality Emblem
A232

1978, Mar.   Litho.   Perf. 12½
| 831 | A232 | 35p multi | 22 | 12 |

International Year to Combat Racism.

Averroes
A233

1979, Mar.
| 832 | A233 | 100p multi | 60 | 32 |

Averroes (1126–1198), Spanish-Arabian philosopher and physician.

Human Rights Flame and Globe
A234

Symbolic Design
A235

1978, Dec.   Perf. 12x12½
| 833 | A234 | 60p multi | 36 | 30 |

30th anniversary of Universal Declaration of Human Rights (in 1978).

1979, March
| 834 | A235 | 100p multi | 60 | 32 |

16th anniversary of March 8 Revolution.

Princess, 2nd Century Shield
A236

Designs: 20p, Helmet of Homs. 35p, Ishtar.

1979   Litho.   Perf. 11½
836	A236	20p green	12	6
837	A236	25p rose car	15	8
838	A236	35p sepia	22	12

SYRIA

Molar, Emblem
with Mosque
A237

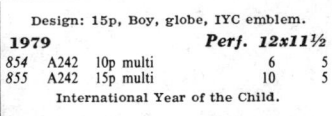

Flame Emblem
A238

1979		Litho.		Perf. 12x11½	
846	A237	35p multi		22	12

International Middle East Dental Congress.

1979					
847	A238	35p multi		22	12

33rd anniversary of evacuation.

Ibn
Assaker
A239

1979				Perf. 11½x12	
848	A239	75p multi		45	25

Ibn Assaker, 900th anniversary.

Telephone
Lineman
A240

1979, May 1		Litho.	Perf. 12x11½	
849	A240	50p multi	30	16
850	A240	75p multi	45	25

May Day 1979.

Wright
Brothers'
Plane
A241

Designs: 75p, Bleriot's plane crossing English Channel. 100p, Spirit of St. Louis.

1979			Perf. 11½x12	
851	A241	50p multi	30	16
852	A241	75p multi	45	25
853	A241	100p multi	60	32

75th anniversary of 1st powered flight.

Girl with
IYC Emblem
A242

Power Plant
A243

Design: 15p, Boy, globe, IYC emblem.

1979			Perf. 12x11½	
854	A242	10p multi	6	5
855	A242	15p multi	10	5

International Year of the Child.

1979			Perf. 11x11½	
856	A243	5p blue	5	5
857	A243	10p lil rose	6	5
858	A243	15p gray grn	10	5

Flags and Pavillion—A244

Design: 75p, Lamppost and flags.

1979		Photo.	Perf. 12x11½	
859	A244	60p multi	36	18
860	A244	75p multi	45	25

26th International Damascus Fair.

Correction Movement, 9th Anniversary
A245

1979		Photo.	Perf. 11½×12	
861	A245	100p multi	60	30

Games Emblem, Running—A246

1979, Nov.			Multicolored	
862	A246	25p shown	15	8
863	A246	35p Diving	24	12
864	A246	50p Soccer	30	16

8th Mediterranean Games, Split, Jugoslavia, Sept. 15-29.

Butterfly—A247

Designs: Various butterflies.

1979, Dec.		Litho.	Perf. 12×11½	
865	A247	20p multi	12	6
866	A247	25p multi	15	8
867	A247	30p multi	18	10
868	A247	35p multi	24	12
869	A247	50p multi	30	16

Nos. 865-869 (5) 99 52

Damascus International Flower Show
A248

Design: Roses.

1980, Feb.		Litho.	Perf. 12½	
870	A248	5p multi	5	5
871	A248	10p multi	6	5
872	A248	15p multi	10	5
873	A248	35p multi	30	16
874	A248	75p multi	45	25
875	A248	100p multi	60	32

Nos. 870-875 (6) 1.56 88

March 8 Revolution, 17th
Anniversary—A249

1980, Mar. 8		Litho.	Perf. 12x11½	
876	A249	40p multi	24	12

Astrolabe—A250

1980, May 2			Perf. 12½	
877	A250	50p violet	30	16
878	A250	100p sepia	60	32
879	A250	1000p gray grn	6.00	3.25

2nd International History of Arabic Sciences Symposium, Apr. 5.

Lit Cigarette,
Skull
A251

Evacuation,
34th
Anniversary
A252

1980, Apr. 17		Photo.	Perf. 12x11½	
880	A251	60p Smoker	35	18
881	A251	100p shown	60	32

World Health Day/anti-smoking campaign.

1980		Litho.		
882	A252	40p multi	24	15
883	A252	60p multi	35	18

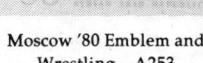

Moscow '80 Emblem and
Wrestling—A253

1980, July		Litho.	Perf. 11½x12	
884	A253	15p shown	10	5
885	A253	25p Fencing	15	8
886	A253	35p Weight lifting	24	12
887	A253	50p Judo	30	15
888	A253	75p Boxing	45	25

Nos. 884-888 (5) 1.24 65

22nd Summer Olympic Games, Moscow, July 19-Aug. 3. Nos. 884-888 se-tenant.

Souvenir Sheet

		Litho.	Imperf.	
888A	A253	300p Discus, running	2.00	80

Multicolored margin shows track. Size: 105x81mm.

Sinbad the Sailor—A254

1980		Litho.	Perf. 11½x12	
889	A254	15p shown	10	5
890	A254	25p Shahrazad and Shahrayar	15	8
891	A254	35p Ali Baba and the Forty Thieves	24	12
892	A254	50p Hassan the Clever	30	15
893	A254	100p Aladdin's Lamp	60	30

Nos. 889-893 (5) 1.39 70

Popular stories. Nos. 889-893 se-tenant.

Savings Certificates—A255

1980				
894	A255	25p multi	15	8

Hegira, 1500th Anniv. —A256

1980			Perf. 12½x12	
895	A256	35p multi	24	12

SYRIA

A257

1980   Perf. 12x11½
896	A257	20p shown	12	5
897	A257	30p Chrysanthemums	20	8
898	A257	40p Clematis	25	12
899	A257	60p Yellow roses	40	14
900	A257	100p Chrysanthemums, diff.	60	28
		Nos. 896-900 (5)	1.57	67

International Flower Show, Damascus. Nos. 896-900 se-tenant.

May Day — A258

Children's Day — A259

1980, May
| 901 | A258 | 35p multi | 24 | 10 |

1980
| 902 | A259 | 25p multi | 15 | 8 |

November 16th Movement, 10th Anniversary — A260

1980   Perf. 11½x12
| 903 | A260 | 100p multi | 60 | 28 |

Steam-powered Passenger Wagon — A261

1980
904	A261	25p shown	15	8
905	A261	35p Benz, 1899	24	10
906	A261	40p Rolls-Royce, 1903	25	12
907	A261	50p Mercedes, 1906	30	15
908	A261	60p Austin, 1915	40	16
		Nos. 904-908 (5)	1.34	61

Nos. 904-908 se-tenant.

Mother's Arms around Infant — A262

1980   Perf. 12x11½
| 909 | A262 | 40p shown | 25 | 12 |
| 910 | A262 | 100p Mother and child | 60 | 28 |

Mother's Day.

27th International Damascus Fair — A263

1981, Jan. 24   Perf. 11½x12
| 911 | A263 | 50p multi | 30 | 15 |
| 912 | A263 | 100p multi | 60 | 28 |

Army Day — A264

1981, Jan. 24   Perf. 12½x12
| 913 | A264 | 50p multi | 30 | 15 |

18th Anniv. of March 8th Revolution — A265

1981, Mar. 8   Litho.   Perf. 12x11½
| 914 | A265 | 50p multi | 30 | 15 |

35th Anniversary of Evacuation — A266

1981, Apr. 17   Litho.   Perf. 12x11½
| 915 | A266 | 50p multi | 30 | 15 |

World Conference on History of Arab and Islamic Civilization, Damascus — A267

1981, May 30   Photo.   Perf. 12½x12
| 916 | A267 | 100p multi | 60 | 30 |

Intl. Workers' Solidarity Day
A268

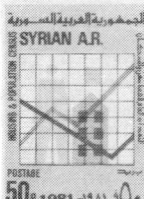
Housing and Population Census
A269

1981, May 30   Litho.   Perf. 12x11½
| 917 | A268 | 100p multi | 60 | 30 |

1981, June 1
| 918 | A269 | 50p multi | 30 | 15 |

Umayyad Window — A270   Abdul Malik Gold Coin — A270a

Designs: 10p, figurine. 15p, Rakkla's cavalier, Abbcid ceramic. 160p, like 5p. 500p, Umar B. Abdul Aziz gold coin.

1981   Perf. 12x11½, 11½x12
919	A270	5p crim rose	5	5
920	A270	10p brt grn	6	5
921	A270	15p dp rose lil	10	5
922	A270a	75p blue	45	20
923	A270	160p dk grn	1.00	45
924	A270a	500p dk brn	3.00	1.35
		Nos. 919-924 (6)	4.66	2.15

Olives
A270b

Designs: 100p, 180p, Harbor.

1982   Perf. 12x11½
925	A270b	50p ol grn	30	15
926	A270b	60p bl gray	40	20
929	A270b	100p lilac	60	30
930	A270b	180p red	1.10	55

Saving Certificates Plan
A271

Avicenna (980-1037), Philosopher and Physician
A272

1981, June 22
| 931 | A271 | 50p gldn brn & blk | 30 | 15 |

1981, Aug.
| 932 | A272 | 100p multi | 60 | 30 |

Syria-P.L.O. Solidarity, Intl. Conference — A273

1981, June 22
| 933 | A273 | 160p multi | 1.00 | 50 |

Grand Mosque, Damascus — A274

1981   Perf. 12½
934	A274	50p Glass lamp, 13th cent.	30	15
935	A274	180p shown	1.10	55
936	A274	180p Hunter	1.10	55

Youth Festival
A275

1981   Perf. 12½
| 937 | A275 | 60p multi | 40 | 20 |

28th Intl. Damascus Fair
A276

Intl. Palestinian Solidarity Day
A277

1981   Perf. 12x11½
| 938 | A276 | 50p Ornament | 30 | 15 |
| 939 | A276 | 160p Emblem | 1.00 | 50 |

1981
| 940 | A277 | 100p multi | 60 | 30 |

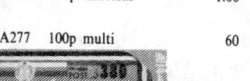
1300th Anniv. of Bulgaria
A278

1981   Perf. 11½x12
| 941 | A278 | 380p multi | 2.30 | 1.15 |

Intl. Children's Day — A279

SYRIA

1981
942 A279 180p multi 1.10 55

World Food Day, Oct. 16 — A280

1981
943 A280 180p multi 1.10 55

9th Intl. Flower Show, Damascus — A281

Designs: Flowers. Nos. 944-948 se-tenant.

1981   *Perf. 12x11½*
944 A281 25p multi   15   8
945 A281 40p multi   25 12
946 A281 50p multi   30 15
947 A281 60p multi   40 20
948 A281 100p multi 60 30
     Nos. 944-948 (5) 1.70 85

Souvenir Sheet

Koran Competition — A282

1981   *Litho.*   *Imperf.*
949 A282 500p multi   3.00 1.50
Size: 104x83mm.

11th Anniv. of Correction Movement — A283

1981, Nov.   *Perf. 12x11½*
950 A283 60p multi   36 18

TB Bacillus Centenary — A284

1982   *Litho.*   *Perf. 11½x12*
951 A284 180p multi   1.10 55

Mothers' Day
A285

1982   *Perf. 11½*
952 A285 40p green   25 12
953 A285 75p brown   45 22
1982, Mar.   *Perf. 12x11½*
954 A286 50p multi   30 15

Intl. Year of the Disabled (1981)
A287

1982
955 A287 90p multi   55 28
1982   *Perf. 11½*
956 A288 150p ultra   90 45

36th Anniv. of Evacuation
A289

1982   *Perf. 12x11½*
957 A289 70p multi   45 22
1982
958 A290 180p multi   1.10 55

Intl. Workers' Solidarity Day — A291

1982
959 A291 180p multi   1.10 55

World Telecommunication Day, May 17 — A292

1982
960 A292 180p multi   1.10 55

Soldier Holding Rifles
A293

Arab Postal Union, 30th Anniv.
A294

1982   *Photo.*   *Perf. 12x11½*
961 A293 50p multi   30 15
1982
962 A294 60p multi   40 20

1982 World Cup — A295

Various soccer players. 300p, Ball.

1982, July   *Perf. 12½*
963 A295 40p multi   25 12
964 A295 60p multi   40 20
965 A295 100p multi   60 30
        Size: 75x55mm.   *Imperf.*
966 A296 300p multi

10th Intl. Flower Show, Damascus — A297

1982   *Perf. 12x11½*
967 A297 50p Honeysuckle 30 15
968 A297 60p Geraniums   40 20

Scouting Year — A298

1982, Nov. 4   *Perf. 11½x12*
969 A298 160p green   1.00 50

Ladybug — A299

1982   *Perf. 12x11½*
970 A299 Strip of 5   80   40
  a. A299 5p Dragonfly   5   5
  b. A299 10p Stag Beetle 6   5
  c. A299 20p shown   12   6
  d. A299 40p Grasshopper 25   12
  e. A299 50p Honeybee   30   15

ITU Plenipotentiaries Conference, Nairobi, Sept — A300

1982   *Perf. 11½x12*
971 A300 50p Map   30   15
972 A300 180p Dish antenna 1.10 55

12th Anniv. of Correction Movement — A301

1982, Nov.
973 A301 50p dk bl & sil   30   15

A302

Designs: Various buildings. 30p, No. 925A, 200p horiz.

1982   *Litho.*   *Perf. 11½*
974 A302 30p brown   20   10
975 A302 50p dk grn   30   15
976 A302 70p green   45   22
977 A302 200p red   1.20 60

Dove and Satellite
A303

Intl. Palestinian Solidarity Day
A304

1982   *Litho.*   *Perf. 12x11½*
978 A303 50p multi   30   15

2ND UN Conference on Peaceful Uses of Outer Space, Vienna, Aug. 9-21.

1982
979 A304 50p multi   30   15

SYRIA

20th Anniv. of March 8th
Revolution—A305

1983   *Perf. 12½x12*
980   A305   60p multi   40   20

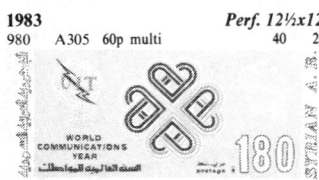
World Communications Year—A306

1983
981   A306   180p multi   1.25   60

9th Anniv. of Liberation of Qnaytra
A306

1983, June 26   *Litho.*   *Perf. 11½*
982   A306   50p View   30   15
983   A306   100p View, diff.   60   30

Arab Pharmacists' Day, Apr. 2—A307

1983, Apr. 2   *Perf. 11½x12*
984   A307   100p multi   60   30

25th Anniv. of Intl. Maritime
Org.—A308

1983, June   *Perf. 12x11½*
985   A308   180p multi   1.25   60

Namibia Day, Aug. 26—A309

1983, Aug. 26   *Perf. 11½x12*
986   A309   180p multi   1.25   60

Eibla Sculpture, 3rd Cent. BC—A310

1983
987   A310   380p ol & brn   2.50   1.25

World Standards Day—A311

1983, Oct. 14   *Photo.*   *Perf. 11½*
988   A311   50p Factory, emblem   30   15
989   A311   100p Measuring equipment   60   30

1983 Intl. Flower Show,
Damascus—A312

1983, Oct. 14   *Litho.*   *Perf. 11½*
990   A312   50p multi   30   15
991   A312   60p multi, diff.   36   18

World Heritage Day—A313

1983, Oct. 14   *Photo.*   *Perf. 11½*
992   A313   60p dk brn   36   18

Waterwheels of   Factory
Hama
A314   A315

1983   *Litho.*   *Perf. 11x11½, 11½x11*
993   A314   5p sepia   5   5
994   A314   10p violet   6   5
995   A314   20p red   12   6
997   A315   50p dk grn   30   15

Statue   View of Aleppo
A316   A317

1983   *Perf. 12*
1003   A316   225p brown   1.35   70

Intl. Symposium on History and Archaeology of Deir Ez-zor.

1983   *Perf. 12x12½*
1004   A317   245p multi   1.50   75

Intl. Symposium on Conservation of Old City of Aleppo, Sept. 26-30.

Mar. 8th Revolution, 21st
Anniv.—A318

1983   *Perf. 12½x12*
1005   A318   60p Alassad Library   36   18

Massacre at Sabra and Shatilla—A319

1983   *Litho.*   *Perf. 11½x12*
1006   A319   225p Victims, mother &
           child   1.15   60

Mothers' Day 1984—A320

1984, Mar. 21   *Perf. 12x11½*
1007   A320   245p Mother & child   1.50   75

12th Intl. Flower Show,
Damascus—A321

Various flowers.

1984, May 25
1008   A321   245p multi   1.50   75
1009   A321   285p multi   1.70   85

AIR POST SEMI-POSTAL STAMPS

Nos. C30-C33 Surcharged
Like Nos. B1-B12 in Black and Red.

1926, Apr. 1   *Perf. 13½*   *Unwmkd.*
CB1   A4   2p + 1p dk brn   1.50   1.50
CB2   A4   3p + 2p org brn   1.50   1.50
CB3   A4   5p + 3p vio   1.50   1.50
CB4   A4   10p + 5p vio brn   1.50   1.50

The surcharged value is in red and rest of the overprint in black on Nos. CB1-CB3. The entire overprint is black on No. CB4. See note following Nos. B1-B12.

Fair Entrance
SPAP1

Industry, Handicraft
and Farming
SPAP2

Design: 70(pi)+10(pi), Fairgrounds.

Perf. 11½, Imperf.

1955   *Lithographed*   *Unwmkd.*
CB5   SPAP1   25p + 5p gray blk   60   60
CB6   SPAP2   35p + 5p ultra   70   70
CB7   SPAP2   40p + 10p rose lil   80   80
CB8   SPAP1   70p + 10p Prus grn   1.60   1.60

Issued to commemorate the International Fair at Damascus, September 1955.

United Nations Refugee Emblem
SPAP3

1966, Dec. 12   *Litho.*   *Perf. 11½x12*
CB9   SPAP3   12½p + 2½p ultra & blk   12   12
CB10   SPAP3   50p + 5p grn & blk   50   40

Issued to commemorate the 21st anniversary of United Nations Day and to commemorate Refugee Week, Oct. 24-31.

SYRIA

SEMI-POSTAL STAMPS
Regular Issue of 1925 Surcharged in Red or Black
Secours aux Réfugiés

اعانات للاجئين

Aff¹
0ᴾ·25 ع ¼

1926 Perf. 12½, 13½. Unwmkd.

B1	A4	25c +25c ol blk (R)	1.50	1.50
B2	A4	50c +25c yel org	1.50	1.50
B3	A4	75c +25c brn org	1.50	1.50
B4	A5	1p +50c mag	1.50	1.50
B5	A4	1p25 +50c dp grn (R)	1.50	1.50
B6	A4	1p50 +50c rose red	1.50	1.50
B7	A4	2p +75c dk brn (R)	1.50	1.50
B8	A4	2p50 +75c pck bl (R)	1.50	1.50
B9	A4	3p +1p org brn (R)	1.50	1.50
B10	A4	5p +1p vio	1.50	1.50
B11	A4	10p +2p vio brn	1.50	1.50
B12	A4	25p +5p ultra (R)	1.50	1.50
		Nos. B1-B12 (12)	18.00	18.00

On No. B4 the surcharge is set in six lines to fit the shape of the stamp.

These stamps were sold for their combined values, original and surcharged. The latter represented their postal franking value and the former was a contribution to the relief of refugees from the Djebel Druze War. See also Nos. CB1-CB4.

Syrian Arab Republic

Jordanian Flags on Map of Israel, and Arabs
SP1

1965, June 12 Litho. Perf. 12x11½

B13	SP1	12½p +5p multi	20	20
B14	SP1	25p +5p multi	25	25

Issued for Palestine Week.

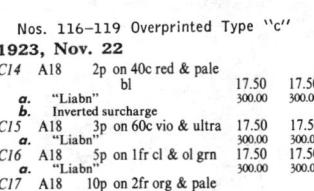

Father with Children and Red Crescent
SP2

1968, May Litho. Perf. 12½x12

B15	SP2	12½p +2½p ultra, rose lil & blk	30	25
B16	SP2	27½p +7½p brt vio, red & blk	30	25

The surtax was for refugees.

The only foreign revenue stamps listed in this Catalogue are those authorized for prepayment of postage.

AIR POST STAMPS.

POSTE PAR AVION
a

AVION
b

Nos. 35, 45, 47 Handstamped Type "a" in Violet

1920, Dec. Perf. 13½ Unwmkd.

C1	A22	1p on 5c grn	100.00	27.50
C2	A20	5p on 15c gray grn	200.00	
C3	A18	10p on 40c red & pale bl	325.00	55.00

Nos. 36, 46, 48 Overprinted Type "a" in Violet

1921, June 12

C4	A22	1p on 20c red brn	50.00	32.50
C5	A18	5p on 1fr cl & ol grn	300.00	100.00
C6	A18	10p on 2fr org & pale bl	300.00	100.00

Excellent counterfeits exist of Nos. C1 to C6.

Nos. 36, 46, 48 Overprinted Type "b"

1921, Oct. 5

C7	A22	1p on 20c red brn	42.50	9.50
C8	A18	5p on 1fr cl & ol grn	100.00	22.50
	a.	Inverted overprint	200.00	165.00
C9	A18	10p on 2fr org & pale bl	135.00	32.50
	a.	Double overprint	250.00	235.00

Nos. 92, 94-96 Overprinted

Poste par Avion
c

1922, May 28

C10	A18	2p on 40c red & pale bl	12.00	12.00
	a.	Inverted overprint		
C11	A18	3p on 60c vio & ultra	12.00	12.00
C12	A18	5p on 1fr cl & ol grn	12.00	12.00
C13	A18	10p on 2fr org & pale bl	12.00	12.00

Nos. 116-119 Overprinted Type "c"

1923, Nov. 22

C14	A18	2p on 40c red & pale bl	17.50	17.50
	a.	"Liabn"	300.00	300.00
	b.	Inverted surcharge		
C15	A18	3p on 60c vio & ultra	17.50	17.50
	a.	"Liabn"	300.00	300.00
C16	A18	5p on 1fr cl & ol grn	17.50	17.50
	a.	"Liabn"	300.00	300.00
C17	A18	10p on 2fr org & pale bl	17.50	17.50
	a.	"Liabn"	300.00	300.00
	b.	Double overprint		

Nos. 137-140 Overprinted Type "c"

1924, Jan. 13

C18	A18	2p on 40c red & pale bl	1.50	1.50
	a.	Double overprint		
C19	A18	3p on 60c vio & ultra	1.50	1.50
	a.	Inverted overprint	27.50	
C20	A18	5p on 1fr cl & ol grn	1.50	1.50
	a.	Double overprint		
C21	A18	10p on 2fr org & pale bl	1.50	1.50

Nos. 152, 154, 157-158 Overprinted

Avion

1924, July 17

C22	A18	2p on 40c red & pale bl	2.25	2.25
	a.	Inverted overprint	22.50	
C23	A18	3p on 60c vio & ultra	2.25	2.25
	a.	Inverted overprint	22.50	
	b.	Double overprint	22.50	
C24	A18	5p on 1fr cl & ol grn	2.25	2.25
C25	A18	10p on 2fr org & pale bl	2.25	2.25
	a.	Inverted overprint	22.50	

AVION
طيارة

Regular Issue of 1925 Overprinted in Green

1925, Mar. 1

C26	A4	2p dk brn	1.10	1.10
C27	A4	3p org brn	1.10	1.10
C28	A4	5p violet	1.10	1.10
C29	A4	10p vio brn	1.10	1.10

Regular Issue of 1925 Overprinted in Red

1926

C30	A4	2p dk brn	60	60
	a.	Inverted overprint	22.50	
C31	A4	3p org brn	70	70
	a.	Inverted overprint	22.50	
C32	A4	5p violet	70	70
	a.	Inverted overprint	22.50	
	b.	Double overprint	22.50	
C33	A4	10p vio brn	70	70
	a.	Inverted overprint	22.50	

Nos. C30-C33 received their first airmail use June 16, 1929, at the opening of the Beirut-Marseille line.

Regular Issue of 1925 Overprinted Type "f" in Red or Black

1929

C34	A4	50c yel grn (R)	40	40
	a.	Inverted overprint	20.00	
	b.	Overprinted on face and back		
	c.	Double overprint	20.00	
	d.	Double overprint, one inverted	40.00	
	e.	Pair, one without overprint		
C35	A5	1p mag (Bk)	50	50
	a.	Reversed overprint		
	b.	Red overprint		
C36	A4	25p ultra (R)	2.50	2.50
	a.	Inverted overprint	37.50	
	b.	Pair, one without overprint		

On No. C35, the overprint is vertical, with plane nose down.

No. 197 Overprinted Type "f" in Red

1929, July 9

C37	A4	15p on 25p ultra	1.20	1.20
	a.	Inverted overprint		

Air Post Stamps of 1926-29 Overprinted in Various Colors

EXPOSITION INDUSTRIELLE
DAMAS 1929
معرض الصناعات الوطنية
دمشق ١٩٢٩

1929, Sept. 5

C38	A4	50c yel grn (R)	1.50	1.50
C39	A5	1p mag (Bl)	1.50	1.50
C40	A4	2p dk brn (V)	1.50	1.50
C41	A4	3p org brn (Bl)	1.50	1.50
	a.	Inverted overprint		
C42	A4	5p vio (R)	1.50	1.50
C43	A4	10p vio brn (R)	1.50	1.50
C44	A4	25p ultra (R)	1.50	1.50
		Nos. C38-C44 (7)	10.50	10.50

Damascus Industrial Exhibition.

AP1
Red Surcharge.

1930, Jan. 30

C45	AP1	2p on 1p25 dp grn	80	80
	a.	Inverted surcharge		
	b.	Double surcharge	27.50	

Plane over Homs
AP2

Designs: 1pi, City Wall, Damascus. 2pi, Euphrates River. 3pi, Temple Ruins, Palmyra. 5pi, Deir-el-Zor. 10pi, Damascus. 15pi, Aleppo Citadel. 25pi, Hama. 50pi, Zebdani. 100pi, Telebisse.

1931-33 Photogravure. Unwmkd.

C46	AP2	50c ocher	22	22
C47	AP2	50c blk brn ('33)	45	42
C48	AP2	1p chnt brn	45	35
C49	AP2	2p Prus bl	1.25	90
C50	AP2	3p bl grn	45	30
C51	AP2	5p red vio	45	30
C52	AP2	10p sl grn	45	30
C53	AP2	15p org red	90	75
C54	AP2	25p org brn	1.00	75
C55	AP2	50p black	1.10	1.00
C56	AP2	100p magenta	1.25	1.10
		Nos. C46-C56 (11)	7.97	6.39

Nos. C46 to C56 exist imperforate.

Village of Bloudan
AP12

1934, Aug. 2 Engraved Perf. 12½

C57	AP12	50c yel brn	1.60	1.60
C58	AP12	1p green	1.60	1.60
C59	AP12	2p pck bl	1.60	1.60
C60	AP12	3p red	1.60	1.60
C61	AP12	5p plum	1.60	1.60
C62	AP12	10p brt vio	17.50	17.50
C63	AP12	15p org brn	17.50	17.50
C64	AP12	25p dk ultra	20.00	20.00
C65	AP12	50p black	27.50	27.50
C66	AP12	100p red brn	50.00	50.00
		Nos. C57-C66 (10)	140.50	140.50

Proclamation of the Republic. Exist imperf.

Air Post Stamps of 1931-33 Overprinted in Red or Black

معرض دمشق
١٩٣٦ - ١٩٣٦
FOIRE DE DAMAS

1936, Apr. 15 Perf. 13½x13, 13½

C67	AP2	50c blk brn (R)	2.25	2.25
C68	AP2	1p chnt brn (Bk)	2.25	2.25
C69	AP2	2p Prus bl (R)	2.25	2.25
C70	AP2	3p bl grn (R)	2.25	2.25
C71	AP2	5p red vio (Bk)	2.25	2.25
		Nos. C67-C71 (5)	11.25	11.25

Issued in connection with an Industrial Exhibition held at Damascus, May, 1936.

SYRIA

Syrian Pavilion at
Paris Exposition
AP13

1937, July 1		Photo.	Perf. 13½
C72	AP13	½p yel grn	1.20 1.20
C73	AP13	1p green	1.20 1.20
C74	AP13	2p lt brn	1.20 1.20
C75	AP13	3p rose red	1.20 1.20
C76	AP13	5p brn org	1.60 1.60
C77	AP13	10p grnsh blk	2.25 2.25
C78	AP13	15p blue	2.50 2.50
C79	AP13	25p dk vio	2.50 2.50
		Nos. C72-C79 (8)	13.65 13.65

Paris International Exposition. Exist imperf.

Ancient Citadel at Aleppo
AP14

Omayyad Mosque and Minaret
of Jesus at Damascus—AP15

1937		Engraved	Perf. 13
C80	AP14	½p dk vio	30 30
C81	AP15	1p black	30 30
C82	AP14	2p dp grn	30 30
C83	AP15	3p dp ultra	30 30
C84	AP15	5p rose lake	75 75
C85	AP15	10p red brn	60 60
C86	AP14	15p lake brn	2.25 2.25
C87	AP15	25p dk bl	2.75 2.75
		Nos. C80-C87 (8)	7.55 7.55

No. C80 to C87 exist imperforate.

Maurice Noguès and
Route of France-Syria Flight
AP16

1938, July		Photo.	Perf. 11
C88	AP16	10p dk grn	2.25 2.25
a.	Souv. sheet of 4, perf. 13½		20.00 20.00
b.	Perf. 13½		4.00 4.00

10th anniversary of first Marseille-Beirut flight, by Maurice Noguès.
No. C88a has marginal inscriptions in French and Arabic. Size: 160x120mm. Exists imperf.; price $200.

Bridge
at Deir-
el-Zor
AP17

1940		Engraved.	Perf. 13.
C89	AP17	25c brn blk	12 12
C90	AP17	50c pck bl	12 12
C91	AP17	1p dp ultra	15 15
C92	AP17	2p dk org brn	22 22
C93	AP17	5p green	45 45

C94	AP17	10p rose car	60 60
C95	AP17	50p dk vio	2.00 2.00
		Nos. C89-C95 (7)	3.66 3.66

No. C89 to C95 exist imperforate.

President
Taj Eddin
Hassani
AP18

1942		Lithographed	Perf. 11½
C96	AP18	10p bl gray	2.25 2.25
C97	AP18	50p gray lil	2.25 2.25

Issued to commemorate the proclamation of Independence by the Allies, September 27, 1941.

 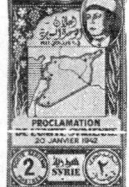

President Taj   President Hassani
Eddin Hassani   and Map of Syria
AP19   AP20

1942		Photogravure.	
C98	AP19	10p sl grn & yel grn	3.25 3.25

No. C98 exists imperforate.

1943		Lithographed.	
C99	AP20	2p dl brn	1.50 1.50
C100	AP20	10p red vio	1.50 1.50
C101	AP20	20p aqua	1.50 1.50
C102	AP20	50p rose pink	1.50 1.50

Proclamation of United Syria.

Same, Overprinted with Black Border.

1943, May 5			
C103	AP20	2p dl brn	1.50 1.50
C104	AP20	10p red vio	1.50 1.50
C105	AP20	20p aqua	1.50 1.50
C106	AP20	50p rose pink	1.50 1.50

Mourning for President Hassani.
Nos. C99-C106 exist imperf.

President Shukri
el Kouatly
AP21

1944			
C107	AP21	200p sepia	6.50 6.50
C108	AP21	500p dl bl	10.00 10.00

Stamps of 1931-44
Overprinted in Black,
Blue or Carmine

1944		Perf. 13, 13½, 11½.	
C109	AP15	10p red brn (Bk)	1.50 1.50
C110	AP2	15p org red (Bl)	1.50 1.50
C111	AP2	25p org brn (Bl)	1.50 1.50
C112	AP2	100p mag (Bl)	5.25 5.25
C113	AP21	200p sep (C)	6.75 6.75
		Nos. C109-C113 (5)	16.50 16.50

Issued to commemorate the first congress of Arab lawyers held in Damascus, September, 1944.

Nos. C53-C54, C108
Overprinted in
Black or Orange

1944			
C114	AP2	15p org red	1.75 1.75
C115	AP2	25p org brn	1.75 1.75
C116	AP21	500p dl bl (O)	13.50 13.50

See note after No. 299.

President Shukri el Kouatly
AP22

1945, Mar. 15		Litho.	Perf. 11½
C117	AP22	5p pale grn	30 42
C118	AP22	10p dl red	38 42
C119	AP22	15p orange	38 42
C120	AP22	25p lt bl	60 42
C121	AP22	50p lt vio	1.00 55
C122	AP22	100p dp brn	2.25 90
C123	AP22	200p fawn	6.25 3.25
		Nos. C117-C123 (7)	11.16 6.38

Issued to commemorate the resumption of constitutional government.

Plane and Flock of Sheep
AP23

Kattineh Dam—AP24

Kanawat, Djebel Druze
AP25

Sultan Ibrahim Mosque
AP26

1946-47			Perf. 13x13½.
C124	AP23	3p rose brn	50 10
C125	AP23	5p lt bl grn ('47)	50 12
C126	AP23	6p dp org ('47)	50 12
C127	AP24	10p sl gray ('47)	15 12
C128	AP24	15p scar ('47)	18 18
C129	AP24	25p blue	30 25
C130	AP25	50p violet	50 25
C131	AP25	100p bl grn	1.50 50
C132	AP25	200p brn ('47)	4.00 1.00
C133	AP26	300p red brn ('47)	7.00 2.50
C134	AP26	500p ol gray ('47)	13.00 4.00
		Nos. C124-C134 (11)	28.13 9.14

No. C129
Overprinted in Red
1946, Apr. 17

| C135 | AP24 | 25p blue | 1.75 1.00 |

Issued to commemorate the evacuation of British and French troops from Syria.

Nos. C129-C131
Overprinted
in Magenta

 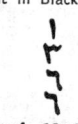

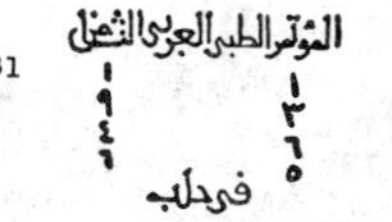

1946, Aug. 28			
C136	AP24	25p blue	1.65 1.00
C137	AP25	50p violet	2.75 1.25
C138	AP25	100p bl grn	5.00 2.35

See note after No. 334.

No. C135
with Additional Overprint in Black

1947, June 10			Perf. 13x13½
C139	AP24	25p blue	1.65 1.00

Issued to commemorate the first anniversary of the evacuation of British and French troops from Syria.

Window at
Kasr El-Heir El-Gharbi
AP27

Ram-headed Sphinxes Carved
in Ivory, from King Hazael's Bed
AP28

1947, Nov. 15		Litho.	Perf. 11½
C140	AP27	12.50p dk vio	1.00 50
C141	AP28	50p brown	3.50 2.00
a.	Souvenir sheet of four		20.00 20.00

Issued to commemorate the first Arab Archaeological Congress, Damascus, November, 1947.
No. C141a measures 138½x189mm. and contains one each of Nos. 338, 339, C140 and C141 with arms and inscriptions in top and bottom margins. The sheet sold for 125 piastres.

Kasr El-Heir El-Charqui
AP29

Congress
Emblem
AP30

SYRIA

1947, Nov. 15

C142	AP29	12.50p ol blk	3.00	40
C143	AP30	50p dl vio	3.25	2.00
a.		Souvenir sheet of 4	30.00	20.00

Issued to commemorate the 3rd Congress of Arab Engineers, Damascus, November, 1947.
No. C143a measures 138½x189mm. and contains one each of Nos. 340, 341, C142 and C143 with arms and inscriptions in top and bottom margins. The sheet sold for 125 plastres.

Kouatly Types of Regular Issue
1948, June 22 Litho. Perf. 10½

C144	A50	12.50p dp bl & vio brn	50	30
C145	A51	50p vio brn & grn	2.50	1.00
a.		Souvenir sheet of 4, imperf.	110.00	110.00

Issued to commemorate the reelection of President Shukri el Kouatly.
C145a measures 139x186mm. and contains one each of Nos. 342, 343, C144 and C145, with national emblem and Arabic inscriptions in black in top and bottom margins.

Military Training Types of Regular Issue
1948, June 22

C146	A52	12.50p bl & dk bl	70	40
C147	A53	50p grn car & blk	3.00	1.00
a.		Souvenir sheet of 4, imperf.	110.00	110.00

Issued to publicize the inauguration of compulsory military training.
No. C147a measures 137x190mm. and contains one each of Nos. 344, 345, C146 and C147, with Arabic inscription in black in lower margin.

Nos. C124, C126 and C132 to C134 Surcharged with New Value and Bars in Black or Carmine.
1948, Oct. 18 Perf. 13x13½

C148	AP23	2.50p on 3p rose brn	7	7
C149	AP23	2.50p on 6p dp org	8	8
C150	AP25	25p on 200p brn (C)	50	20
C151	AP26	50p on 300p red brn	1.40	60
C152	AP26	50p on 500p ol gray	1.40	60
		Nos. C148-C152 (5)	3.45	1.55

Husni Zayim Type of Regular Issue
1949, June 20 Litho. Perf. 11½

C153	A54	50p brown	3.50	2.35

Revolution of March 30, 1949.

Pigeons and Globe
AP36

Husni Zayim and View of Damascus
AP37

1949, June 20 Unwmkd.

C154	AP36	12.50p claret	5.00	5.00
C155	AP37	50p gray blk	14.00	10.00

Issued to commemorate the 75th anniversary of the formation of the Universal Postal Union.
A souvenir sheet contains one each of Nos. 349, 350, C154 and C155, with arms and inscriptions in top and bottom margins in dull blue. Size: 138 x178mm. Price $250.

Election Type of Regular Issue Lithographed.
1949, Aug. 6 Perf. 11½ Wmk. 291

C156	A57	50p car rose & dk grnsh bl	3.50	2.35
a.		Souvenir sheet of two, imperf.	140.00	140.00

Issued to commemorate the election of President Husni Zayim.
No. C156a contains one each of Nos. C156 and 351, with marginal inscriptions and national emblem in gray lilac. The sheets measure 125 x 188 mm.

No. C131 Surcharged with New Value and Bars in Black.
1950 Perf. 13x13½ Unwmkd.

C157	AP25	2.50p on 100p bl grn	10	10

Port of Latakia
AP38

1950, Dec. 25 Perf. 11½

C158	AP38	2.50p dl lil	50	10
C159	AP38	10p grnsh bl	1.00	10
C160	AP38	15p org brn	2.50	15
C161	AP38	25p brt bl	5.50	25

Nos. C158-C161 exist imperf. See No. C173.

Symbolical of Constitution
AP39

1951, Apr. 14 Unwmkd.

C162	AP39	12.50p crim rose	40	20
C163	AP39	50p brn vio	1.25	80

Issued to publicize the new constitution adopted Sept. 5, 1950. Both values exist imperforate.

Ruins, Palmyra
AP40

Citadel at Aleppo
AP41

1952, Apr. 22 Litho. Perf. 11½

C164	AP40	2.50p vermilion	10	6
C165	AP40	5p green	20	8
C166	AP40	15p violet	30	16
C167	AP41	25p dp bl	60	25
C168	AP41	100p lil rose	3.25	55
		Nos. C164-C168 (5)	4.45	1.10

Nos. C164-C168 exist imperforate.

Stamps of 1946-52 Overprinted in Black

1953, Feb. 16 Perf. 13x13½, 11½

C169	AP38	10p grnsh bl	2.00	1.50
C170	AP40	15p violet	2.00	1.30
C171	AP41	25p dp bl	3.00	2.00
C172	AP25	50p violet	9.00	3.00

Issued to commemorate the United Nations Social Welfare Seminar held at Damascus, Dec. 8-20, 1952.

Type of 1950 and

Post Office, Aleppo—AP42

1953, Oct. Photo. Perf. 11½

C173	AP38	10p vio bl	50	15
C174	AP42	50p red brn	1.50	25

Building at Hama and PTT Emblem
AP43

University of Syria, Damascus
AP44

1954

C175	AP43	5p violet	20	7
C176	AP43	10p brown	25	10
C177	AP43	15p dl grn	30	10
C178	AP44	30p dk brn	40	20
C179	AP44	35p blue	60	20
C180	AP44	40p orange	80	40
C181	AP44	50p dp plum	1.10	60
C182	AP44	70p purple	1.60	60
		Nos. C175-C182 (8)	5.25	2.27

Monument, Damascus Square
AP45

Mosque and Syrian Flag
AP46

1954, Sept. 2

C183	AP45	40p car rose	1.00	50
C184	AP46	50p green	1.20	60

Issued to publicize the Damascus Fair, Sept., 1954. Nos. C183-C184 exist imperforate.

Nos. C174 and C168 Overprinted in Blue or Black

1954, Oct. 9

C185	AP42	50p red brn (Bl)	1.00	90
C186	AP41	100p lil rose	2.00	1.65

Cotton Festival, Aleppo, October 1954.

Virgin of Sednaya Convent
AP47

Omayyad Mosque
AP48

1955, Mar. 27 Photo. Perf. 11½

C187	AP47	25p dp pur	50	30
C188	AP47	75p dp bl grn	2.00	1.20

Issued to commemorate the 50th anniversary of the founding of Rotary International. Both values exist imperforate.

1955, March 26

C189	AP48	35p cerise	75	55
C190	AP48	65p dp grn	1.65	60

Issued to publicize the 1955 Regional Congress of Rotary International, Damascus.

Arab Postal Union Type of Regular Issue
1955, Jan. 1 Perf. 13½x13

C191	A69a	5p yel brn	30	15

Issued to commemorate the founding of the Arab Postal Union, July 1, 1954.

Young Couple and View of Damascus
AP49

Design: 60pi, Tank and planes leading advancing troops.

1955, Apr. 16 Litho. Perf. 11½

C192	AP49	40p dk rose lake	60	50
C193	AP49	60p ultra	1.00	60

Issued to commemorate the 9th anniversary of the evacuation of British and French troops from Syria.

Mother's Day Type of Regular Issue
1955, May 13 Unwmkd.

C194	A70	35p violet	1.00	70
C195	A70	40p black	1.40	80

Issued to publicize Mother's Day.

Emigrants under Syrian Flag
AP51

Mother and Child
AP52

1955, July 26 Perf. 11½

Design: 15pi, Airplane over globe and fountain.

C196	AP51	5p magenta	50	25
C197	AP51	15p lt bl	60	40

Emigrants' Congress. Exist imperf.

1955, Oct. 3 Photogravure

C198	AP52	25p dp bl	70	50
C199	AP52	50p plum	1.25	70

International Children's Day.

SYRIA

Globe, Scales and Dove
AP53

1955, Oct. 30
C200 AP53 15p ultra 70 30
C201 AP53 35p brn blk 1.25 50
Issued to commemorate the tenth anniversary of the United Nations, Oct. 24, 1955.

Aqueduct Type of Regular Issue
1955, Nov. 21 Litho. Unwmkd.
C202 A72 30p dk bl 2.00 1.00
Issued to publicize the new aqueduct, bringing water from the Euphrates to Northern Syria.

No. C191 Overprinted in Ultramarine
1955, Dec. 29 Photo. Perf. 13½x13
C203 A69a 5p yel brn 45 20
Issued to commemorate the Arab Postal Union Congress held at Cairo, March 15, 1955.

Liberation Monument
AP54

Designs: 65p, Winged figure with shield and sword. 75pi, President Shukri el Kouatly.
1956, Apr. 17 Litho. Perf. 11½
C204 AP54 35p blk brn 75 60
C205 AP54 65p rose red 1.10 90
C206 AP54 75p dk sl grn 1.50 1.25

Issued to commemorate the tenth anniversary of the evacuation of British and French troops from Syria.

No. C191 Overprinted in Black
1956, Apr. 11 Photo. Perf. 13½x13
C207 A69a 5p yel brn 40 20
Issued to commemorate the visit of King Hussein of Jordan to Damascus, April, 1956.

President Shukri el Kouatly
AP55

Gate of Kasr el Heir, Palmyra
AP56

1956, July 7 Litho. Perf. 11½
C208 AP55 100p black 1.20 75
C209 AP55 200p violet 2.50 1.75
C210 AP55 300p dl rose 3.00 2.25
C211 AP55 500p dk bl grn 6.50 5.00

Nos. CB5-CB8 Overprinted with 3 Bars obliterating surtax.
1956
C212 SPAP1 25p gray blk 50 20
C213 SPAP2 35p ultra 70 30
C214 SPAP2 40p rose lil 1.20 50
C215 SPAP1 70p Prus grn 1.60 1.20

1956, Sept. 1 Unwmkd.
Designs: 20p, Hand loom and modern mill. 30p, Ox-drawn plow and tractor. 35c, Cogwheels and galley. 50p, Textiles and vase.
C216 AP56 15p gray 40 40
C217 AP56 20p brt ultra 50 50
C218 AP56 30p bl grn 70 70
C219 AP56 35p blue 90 90
C220 AP56 50p rose lil 1.00 1.00
Nos. C216-C220 (5) 3.50 3.50
Issued to publicize the 3rd International Fair at Damascus.

Nos. C200-201 Overprinted in Red or Green

1956, Oct. 30 Photo. Perf. 11½
C221 AP53 15p ultra (R) 1.20 50
C222 AP53 35p brn blk (G) 2.50 1.25

United Nations, 11th anniversary.

Clay Tablet with First Alphabet
AP57

Helmet of Syrian Legionary and Ornament—AP58

Design: 50pi, Lintel from Temple of the Sun, Palmyra.
1956, Oct. 8 Typographed.
C223 AP57 20p gray 60 40
C224 AP58 30p magenta 90 60
C225 AP57 50p gray brn 1.50 1.20
Issued to publicize International Museum Week (UNESCO), Oct. 8–14.

Trees and Mosque
AP59

1956, Dec. 27 Litho. Perf. 11½
C226 AP59 10p ol bis 25 10
C227 AP59 40p sl grn 70 70
Day of the Tree, Dec. 27, 1956.
See also United Arab Republic, Syria, No. 36.

Mother and Child
AP60

Sword and Shields
AP61

Design: 60p, Mother holding infant.

1957, Mar. 21 Unwmkd.
C228 AP60 40p ultra 70 60
C229 AP60 60p vermilion 1.20 75
Issued for Mother's Day, 1957.

1957, Apr. 20 Wmk. 291
Designs: 15p, 35p, Map and "Syria" holding torch. 25p, Pres. Kouatly.
C230 AP61 10p redsh brn 15 15
C231 AP61 15p bl grn 25 20
C232 AP61 25p violet 50 25
C233 AP61 35p cerise 70 45
C234 AP61 40p gray 1.10 65
Nos. C230-C234 (5) 2.70 1.70
Issued to commemorate the 11th anniversary of the British-French troop evacuation.

Ship Loading
AP62

Sugar Production—AP63

Design: 30p, 40p, Harvesting grain and cotton.
1957, Sept. 1 Perf. 11½ Unwmkd.
C235 AP62 25p magenta 40 25
C236 AP62 30p lt red brn 50 30
C237 AP63 35p lt bl 80 50
C238 AP62 40p bl grn 1.00 55
C239 AP62 70p ol bis 1.25 85
Nos. C235-C239 (5) 3.95 2.45
4th International Fair, Damascus.

Arab Lawyers Type of Regular Issue, 1957
1957, Sept. 21 Litho. Wmk. 291
C240 A76 17½p red 50 25
C241 A76 40p black 55 50
Issued for the third Congress of the Union of Arab Lawyers, Damascus, Sept. 21–25.

Cotton Festival Type of Regular Issue, 1957
1957, Oct. 17
C242 A77 17½p org & blk 50 30
C243 A77 40p lt bl & blk 1.00 50

Cotton Festival, Aleppo, Oct. 3–5.

Children's Day Type of Regular Issue, 1957
1957, Oct. 3
C244 A78 17½p ultra 1.20 50
C245 A78 20p red brn 1.20 50
International Children's Day, Oct. 7.
For "RAU" overprint on Nos. C244-C245, see Nos. C10-C11 in United Arab Republic (Syria) listings following Syria.

Family Writing and Reading Letters
AP64

1957, Oct. 18 Litho. Unwmkd.
C246 AP64 5p brt grn 30 20
Issued for International Letter Writing Week Oct. 6–12.

Afro-Asian Jurists Type of Regular Issue, 1957
1957, Nov. Perf. 11½ Wmk. 291
C247 A80 30p lt bl grn 50 30
C248 A80 50p lt vio 75 50
Congress of Afro-Asian Jurists, Damascus.

Type of Regular Issue and

Radio, Telegraph and Telephone
AP65

1958, Feb. 12 Perf. 11½
C249 A83 10p brt grn 25 10
C250 AP65 15p brown 35 25

Syrian Arab Republic

Syrian Flag—AP67
Souvenir Sheet
Lithographed
1961 Imperf. Unwmkd.
C253 AP67 50p multi 3.25 3.25
Establishment of Syrian Arab Republic.
No. C253 has green marginal inscription.
Size: 80x80mm.

"The Beauty of Palmyra"
AP68

Archway, Palmyra
AP69

Design: 200p, 300p, 500p, 1000p, Niche, King Zahir Bibar's tomb.

1961-63 Lithographed Perf. 12x11½
C255 AP68 45p citron 50 45
C256 AP68 50p red org 60 50
C257 AP69 85p sepia 1.20 65
C258 AP69 100p lilac 1.60 65
C259 AP69 200p sl grn ('62) 2.50 1.40
C260 AP69 300p dk bl ('62) 3.50 1.60
C261 AP69 500p lil ('63) 6.00 3.00
C262 AP69 1000p dk gray ('63) 11.00 6.00
Nos. C255-C262 (8) 26.90 14.25

See Nos. 433–436.

SYRIA

Arab League Building, Cairo, and Emblem AP70 | Malaria Eradication Emblem AP71

1962, Apr. 1   Perf. 12x11½
C264 AP70 17½p Prus grn & yel grn 20 15
C265 AP70 22½p dk & lt bl 30 25
C266 AP70 50p dk brn & dl org 75 50

Arab League Week, Mar. 22–28.

1962, Apr. 7
C267 AP71 12½p ol, lt bl & pur 25 20
C268 AP71 50p brn, yel & grn 70 50

Issued for the World Health Organization drive to eradicate malaria.

Prancing Horse AP72 | Gen. Yusef al-Azmeh AP73

1962, Apr. 17
C269 AP72 45p vio & org 50 40
C270 AP73 55p vio bl & lt bl 80 50

Evacuation Day, 1962.

Martyrs' Square Memorial, Globe and Handshake AP74 | Cotton and Cogwheel AP75

Design: 40p, 45p, Eastern Gate at Fair.

1962, Aug. 25 Litho. Perf. 12x11½
C271 AP74 17½p rose cl & brn 20 12
C272 AP74 22½p ver & mag 25 18
C273 AP74 40p vio brn & lt brn 40 30
C274 AP74 45p grnsh bl & lt grn 65 40

9th International Damascus Fair.

1962, Sept. 20   Perf. 12x11½
C275 AP75 12½p multi 25 20
C276 AP75 50p multi 55 50

Cotton Festival, Aleppo.
See Nos. 455–456.

President Type of Regular Issue
1962, Dec. 14   Unwmkd.
C278 A88 50p bl gray & tan 65 40

Issued to commemorate the first anniversary of the election of President Nazem el-Kodsi.

Queen Zenobia of Palmyra AP76 | Saad Allah El Jabri AP77

1962, Dec. 28   Perf. 12x11½
C279 AP76 45p violet 60 25
C280 AP76 50p rose red 70 30
C281 AP76 85p bl grn 90 50
C282 AP76 100p rose cl 1.50 65

1962, Dec. 30   Lithographed
C283 AP77 50p dl bl 50 30

Issued to honor Saad Allah El Jabri (1894–1947), a leader in Syria's struggle for independence.

Woman from Mohardé AP78 | Eagle in Flight AP79

Regional Costumes: 40p, Marje Sultan. 45p, Kalamoun. 55p, Jabal-Al-Arab. 60p, Afrine. 65p, Hauran.

1963   Perf. 12
Costumes in Original Colors
C285 AP78 40p pale lil & blk 35 25
C286 AP78 45p pink & blk 40 30
C287 AP78 50p lt grn & blk 60 35
C288 AP78 55p lt bl & blk 70 50
C289 AP78 60p tan & blk 75 50
C290 AP78 65p pale grn & blk 90 60
    Nos. C285-C290 (6) 3.70 2.50

Hunger Type of Regular Issue
Design: 50p, Wheat emblem and bird feeding nestlings.

Perf. 12x11½
1963, Mar. 21   Unwmkd.
C291 AP91 50p ver & blk 50 30
   a. Souv. sheet 2.50 2.50

Issued for the "Freedom from Hunger" campaign of the U.N. Food and Agriculture Organization. No. C291a contains 2 imperf. stamps similar to Nos. 453 and C291. Emerald margin with black inscription. Size: 90x65mm.

1963, Apr. 18   Lithographed
C292 AP79 12½p brt grn 10 10
C293 AP79 50p lil rose 50 40

Revolution of Mar. 8, 1963.

Faris el Khouri AP80 | Arms and Wreath AP81

1963, Apr. 27   Perf. 12x11½
C294 AP80 17½p gray 30 20
C295 AP81 22½p bl grn & blk 30 15

Evacuation Day, 1963.

abu-al-Ala al-Maarri AP82 | Copper Pitcher, Arch and Fair AP83

1963, Aug. 19   Perf. 12x11½
C296 AP82 50p vio bl 50 40

Issued to honor abu-al-Ala al-Maarri (973–1057), poet and philosopher.

1963, Aug. 25
C297 AP83 37½p ultra, yel & brn 50 25
C298 AP83 50p brt bl, yel & brn 55 30

10th International Damascus Fair.

Centenary Emblem AP84 | Abou Feras al Hamadani AP85

Design: 50p, Centenary emblem and globe.

1963, Sept. 19   Lithographed
C299 AP84 15p chlky bl, red & blk 25 25
C300 AP84 50p yel grn, blk & red 50 40

Centenary of the International Red Cross.

1963, Nov. 13   Perf. 12x11½
C301 AP85 50p yel ol & dk brn 50 40

Abou Feras (932–968), poet.

Heads of Three Races and Flame AP86

1964, Jan. 6   Unwmkd.
C302 AP86 17½p multi 15 15
C303 AP86 22½p grn, blk & red 25 15
C304 AP86 50p vio, blk & red 50 30
   a. Souv. sheet of 3 1.00 1.00

Issued to commemorate the 15th anniversary of the Universal Declaration of Human Rights. No. C304a contains 3 imperf. stamps similar to Nos. C302–C304 with simulated perforations; black inscription. Size: 109x70mm.

Flag, Torch and Map of Arab Countries AP87

1964, March 8 Perf. 11½ Unwmkd.
C305 AP87 15p multi 10 10
C306 AP87 17½p multi 20 15
C307 AP87 22½p multi 40 25

Issued to commemorate the first anniversary of the Revolution of March 8, 1963.

Kaaba, Mecca, and Mosque, Damascus—AP88

1964, Mar. 14 Litho. Perf. 11½x12
C308 AP88 12½p bl & blk 10 10
C309 AP88 22½p rose lil & blk 25 15
C310 AP88 50p lt grn & blk 50 30

First Arab Conference of Moslem Wakf Ministers, Damascus.

Young Couple and View of Damascus—AP89

1964, Apr. 17   Unwmkd.
C311 AP89 20p blue 15 12
C312 AP89 25p rose car 25 18
C313 AP89 60p emerald 50 40

Evacuation Day, Apr. 17, 1964.

Abul Kasim (Albucasis) AP90

1964, Apr. 21   Perf. 12x11½
C314 AP90 60p brown 50 40

Issued to commemorate the Fourth Arab Congress of Dental and Oral Surgery, Damascus.

SYRIA

Mosaic, Chahba, Thalassa
AP91

1964, June–July Lithographed
Perf. 11½x12
C315	AP91	27½p car rose	25	15
C316	AP91	45p gray	45	30
C317	AP91	50p brt grn	50	30
C318	AP91	55p sl grn	50	35
C319	AP91	60p ultra	70	40
		Nos. C315-C319 (5)	2.40	1.40

Hanging Lamp,   Globe and
Fair Emblem   Fair Emblem
AP92   AP93

1964, Aug. 28 Perf. 12x11½
C320	AP92	20p multi	40	12
C321	AP93	25p multi	45	18

11th International Damascus Fair.

Industrial and Agricultural Symbols
AP94

1964, Sept. 22 Litho. Unwmkd.
C322	AP94	25p multi	25	15

Same Overprinted with two Red Lines in Arabic

C323	AP94	25p multi	30	20

Issued to publicize the Cotton Festival in Aleppo. Overprint on No. C323 translates: "Market for Industrial and Agricultural Products."

Arms of Syria and
Aero Club Emblem
AP95

1964, Oct. 8 Litho. Perf. 11½x12
C324	AP95	12½p emer & blk	20	8
C325	AP95	17½p crim & blk	25	15
C326	AP95	20p brt bl & blk	60	20

10th anniversary of Syrian Aero Club.

 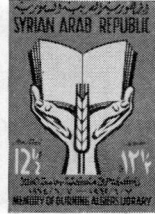

Arab Postal   Grain and
Union Emblem   Hands Holding
AP96   Book
                      AP97

1964, Nov. 12 Litho. Perf. 12x11½
C327	AP96	12½p org & blk	10	10
C328	AP96	20p emer & blk	20	12
C329	AP96	25p dp lil rose & blk	25	20

Issued to commemorate the 10th anniversary of the permanent office of the Arab Postal Union.

1964, Nov. 30 Unwmkd.
C330	AP97	12½p emer & blk	10	8
C331	AP97	17½p mar & blk	20	12
C332	AP97	20p dp bl & blk	24	15

Issued to commemorate the burning of the library of Algiers, June 7, 1962.

Tennis Player
AP98

Designs: 17½p, Wrestlers and drummer. 20p, Weight lifter. 100p, Wrestlers and drummer (horiz.).

1965, Feb. 7 Perf. 12x11½
C333	AP98	12½p multi	15	10
C334	AP98	17½p multi	25	15
C335	AP98	20p multi	40	20

Souvenir Sheet
C336	AP98	100p multi	2.00	2.00

Issued to commemorate the 18th Olympic Games, Tokyo, Oct. 10–25, 1964. No. C336 contains one stamp (size: 45x33mm.); black marginal inscription. Size: 89x68 mm.

Ramses Battling the Hittites
AP99

Design: 50p, Two statues of Ramses II.

1965, Mar. 21 Litho. Perf. 11x12
C337	AP99	22½p emer, ultra & blk	25	20
C338	AP99	50p ultra, emer & blk	50	30

Issued to publicize the UNESCO world campaign to save historic monuments in Nubia.

Al-Sharif Al-Radi   Dagger in
AP100   Map of Palestine
                     AP102

Hippocrates and Avicenna—AP101

1965, Apr. 3 Litho. Perf. 12x11½
C339	AP100	50p gray brn	50	30

Issued to publicize the Fifth Poetry Festival held in Latakia, and to honor Al-Sharif Al-Radi (970–1015), poet.

1965, Apr. 19 Perf. 11½
C340	AP101	60p dl bl grn & blk	50	40

Issued to publicize "Medical Days of the Near and Middle East," a convention held at Damascus Apr. 19–25.

1965, May 15
C341	AP102	12½p multi	20	8
C342	AP102	60p multi	50	40

Deir Yassin massacre, Apr. 9, 1948.

ITU Emblem, Old and New
Communication Equipment
AP103
Perf. 11½x12

1965, May 24 Litho. Unwmkd.
C343	AP103	12½p multi	20	8
C344	AP103	27½p multi	40	20
C345	AP103	60p multi	70	60

Issued to commemorate the centenary of the International Telecommunication Union.

Syrian Welcoming   Bridge and
Immigrant   Gate
AP104   AP105

1965, Aug. Perf. 12x11½ Unwmkd.
C346	AP104	25p pur & multi	25	12
C347	AP104	100p blk & multi	90	50

Issued to welcome Arab immigrants.

1965, Aug. 28 Lithographed
Designs: 27½p, Fair emblem. 60p, Jug and ornaments.
C348	AP105	12½p blk, brt ultra & brn	8	6
C349	AP105	27½p multi	25	15
C350	AP105	60p multi	50	40

12th International Damascus Fair.

Fair Emblem and
Cotton Pickers
AP106

1965, Sept. 30 Perf. 12x11½
C351	AP106	25p ol & multi	25	15

10th Cotton Festival, Aleppo.

Same with Red Overprint in English and Arabic:
"INDUSTRIAL & AGRICULTURAL / PRODUCTION FAIR-ALEPPO / 1965"

1965, Sept. 30
C352	AP106	25p ol & multi	25	15

Industrial and Agricultural Fair, Aleppo.

View of Damascus and ICY Emblem
AP107

1965, Oct. 24 Perf. 11½x12
C353	AP107	25p multi	30	20

International Cooperation Year, 1965.

Radio Trans-   Hand (shaped
mitter, Globe,   like a dove)
Syrian Flag and   Holding Flower
View of Damascus
AP108   AP109

1966, Feb. 16 Litho. Perf. 12x11½
C354	AP108	25p multi	20	12
C355	AP108	60p multi	50	30

Issued to publicize the third Conference of Arab Information Ministers, Damascus, Feb. 14–18.

Perf. 12x11½, 11½x12

1966, March 8
Design: 17½p, Stylized people (horiz.).
C356	AP109	12½p multi	10	8
C357	AP109	17½p multi	15	12
C358	AP109	50p multi	90	30

March 8 Revolution, 3rd anniversary.

SYRIA

Statues of Ramses II from Abu Simbel
AP110

1966, March 15   *Perf. 12x11½*
C359   AP110   25p dk bl   25   12
C360   AP110   60p dk sl grn   50   30

Arab "Save the Nubian Monument Week."

U.N. Headquarters Building and Emblem
AP111

Design: 100p, U.N. Flag.

1966, Apr. 11   *Litho. Perf. 11½x12*
C361   AP111   25p blk & gray   15   12
C362   AP111   50p blk & pale grn   45   28

Souvenir Sheet
Imperf.
C363   AP111   100p yel, brt bl & blk   80   80

Issued to commemorate the 20th anniversary (in 1965) of the United Nations. No. C363 contains one stamp (42x36mm.), black marginal inscription. Size: 90x70 mm.

Marching Workers
AP112

1966, May 1   *Litho. Perf. 11½x12*
C364   AP112   60p multi   50   40

Issued for May Day, 1966.

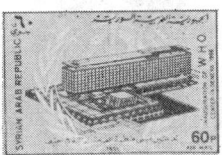

WHO Headquarters, Geneva
AP113

1966, May 3
C365   AP113   60p blk, bl & yel   50   40

Issued to commemorate the inauguration of the World Health Organization Headquarters, Geneva.

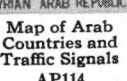

Map of Arab Countries and Traffic Signals
AP114

Astarte and Tyche, 1st-century Bas-relief, Palmyra
AP115

1966, May 4   *Perf. 12x11½*
C366   AP114   25p gray & multi   20   12

Issued to publicize Traffic Day.

1966, July 26   *Litho. Perf. 12x11½*
C367   AP115   50p pale brn   32   25
C368   AP115   60p slate   40   30

Symbolic Flag, Wheat, Globe and Fair Emblem
AP116

Shuttle and Symbols of Agriculture, Industry and Cotton
AP117

1966, Aug. 25   *Litho. Perf. 12x11½*
C369   AP116   12½p gold, blk, red & grn   10   8
C370   AP116   60p sil, blk, red & grn   55   40

Issued to publicize the 13th International Damascus Fair, Aug. 25–Sept. 20.

1966, Sept. 9   *Litho. Perf. 12x11½*
C371   AP117   50p sil, blk & plum   50   30

11th Cotton Festival, Aleppo.

Symbolic Water Cycle
AP118

Abd-el Kader
AP119

1966, Oct. 24   *Litho. Perf. 12x11½*
C372   AP118   12½p emer, blk & org   10   8
C373   AP118   60p ultra, blk & org   55   33

Hydrological Decade (UNESCO), 1965–74.

1966, Nov. 7
C374   AP119   12½p brt grn & blk   25   8
C375   AP119   50p brt grn & red brn   40   33

Issued to commemorate the transfer from Damascus to Algiers of the ashes of Abd-el Kader (1807?–1883), Emir of Mascara.

Clasped Hands over Map of South Arabia
AP120

Pipelines and Pigeons
AP121

1967, Feb. 8   *Litho. Perf. 12x11½*
C376   AP120   20p pink & multi   20   10
C377   AP120   25p multi   25   15

Issued to commemorate the 3rd Congress of Solidarity with the Workers and People of Aden, Damascus, Jan. 15–18.

1967, March 8   *Litho. Perf. 12x11½*
C378   AP121   17½p multi   20   10
C379   AP121   25p multi   25   15
C380   AP121   27½p multi   30   20

4th anniversary of March 8 Revolution.

Soldier, Woman and Man Holding Flag
AP122

Workers' Monument, Damascus
AP123

1967, Apr. 17   *Litho. Perf. 12x11½*
C381   AP122   17½p green   15   10
C382   AP122   25p dp cl   25   15
C383   AP122   27½p vio bl   30   15

Issued to commemorate the 21st anniversary of the evacuation of British and French troops from Syria.

1967, May 1
C384   AP123   12½p bl grn   10   6
C385   AP123   50p brt pink   50   40

Issued for Labor Day, May 1.

Fair Emblem and Gate, Minaret, Omayyad Mosque
AP124

1967, Aug. 25   *Litho. Perf. 12x12½*
C386   AP124   12½p multi   10   8
C387   AP124   60p multi   50   33

Issued to publicize the 14th International Damascus Fair, Aug. 25–Sept. 20.

Statue of Ur-Nina and ITY Emblem
AP125

1967, Sept. 2   *Perf. 12½x12*
C388   AP125   12½p lt bl, brt rose lil & blk   10   6
C389   AP125   25p lt bl, ver & blk   20   12
C390   AP125   27½p lt bl, dk bl & blk   30   15

Souvenir Sheet
Imperf.
C391   AP125   60p lt bl & vio bl   50   50

Issued for International Tourist Year, 1967. No. C391 contains one stamp with black inscription and violet blue design in margin. Size 105x80mm.

Cotton Boll and Cogwheel Segment
AP126

Head of Young Man, Amrith, 4th–5th Century B.C.
AP127

1967, Sept. 28   *Litho. Perf. 12x12½*
C392   AP126   12½p ocher, brn & blk   10   6
C393   AP126   60p ap grn, brn & blk   50   30

12th Cotton Festival, Aleppo.

Same with Red Overprint in English and Arabic "INDUSTRIAL & AGRICULTURAL PRODUCTION FAIR / ALEPPO 1967"

1967, Sept. 28
C394   AP126   12½p multi   10   6
C395   AP126   60p multi   50   30

Issued to commemorate the Industrial and Agricultural Production Fair, Aleppo.

1967, Oct. 7
Design: 100p, 500p, Bronze bust of a Princess, 2nd century.
C396   AP127   45p orange   30   25
C397   AP127   50p brt pink   50   25
C398   AP127   60p grnsh bl   55   30
C399   AP127   100p green   65   50
C400   AP127   500p brn red   3.50   2.75
Nos. C396-C400 (5)   5.50   4.05

Ibn el-Naphis
AP128

1967, Dec. 28   *Litho. Perf. 12x12½*
C401   AP128   12½p grn & org   10   6
C402   AP128   27½p dk bl & lil rose   25   15

Issued to commemorate the 700th anniversary of the death of Ibn el-Naphis (1210–1288), Arab physician.

Human Rights Flame and People
AP129

Design: 100p, Heads of various races and Human Rights flame.

SYRIA

1968, Feb. 21 Litho. Perf. 12½x12
| C403 | AP129 | 12½p lt grnsh bl, bl & blk | 10 | 6 |
| C404 | AP129 | 60p pink, blk & dl red | 50 | 45 |

Souvenir Sheet
Imperf.
| C405 | AP129 | 100p multi | 90 | 90 |

Issued to commemorate the 20th anniversary of the Declaration of Human Rights and for International Human Rights Year. No. C405 contains one stamp, commemorative inscription and design in margin. Size: 105½x80mm.

Old Man and Woman Reading
AP130

Design: 17½p, Torch and book.

1968, Mar. 3 Perf. 12x12½
C406	AP130	12½p rose car, blk & org	8	8
C407	AP130	17½p multi	12	10
C408	AP130	25p grn, blk & org	25	12
C409	AP130	45p bl & multi	40	30

Issued to publicize the literacy campaign.

Euphrates Dam Project
AP131

1968, Apr. 11 Litho. Perf. 12½x12
C410	AP131	12½p multi	8	6
C411	AP131	17½p multi	12	8
C412	AP131	25p multi	25	15

Proposed dam across Euphrates River.

WHO Emblem and Avenzoar (1091–1162)
AP132

Designs (WHO Emblem and): 25p, Rhazes (Razi, 850–923). 60p, Geber (Jabir 721–776).

1968, June 10 Litho. Perf. 12½x12
C413	AP132	12½p brn, grn & sal	10	8
C414	AP132	25p brn, gray & sal	20	12
C415	AP132	60p brn, gray bl & sal	50	30

Issued for the 20th anniversary of the World Health Organization.

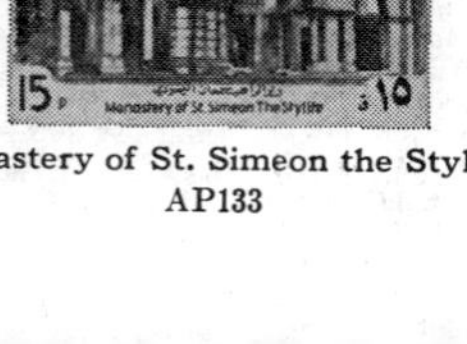

Monastery of St. Simeon the Stylite
AP133

Designs: 17½p, El Tekkieh Mosque, Damascus (vert.). 22½p, Columns, Palmyra (vert.). 45p, Chapel of St. Paul, Bab Kisan. 50p, Theater of Bosra.

1968, Oct. 10 Perf. 12½x12, 12x12½
Lithographed
C416	AP133	15p pale grn & rose brn	9	7
C417	AP133	17½p redsh brn & dk red brn	15	12
C418	AP133	22½p grn gray & dk red brn	20	20
C419	AP133	45p yel & dk red brn	40	25
C420	AP133	50p lt bl & dk red brn	40	30
		Nos. C416-C420 (5)	1.24	.94

Hammer Throw
AP134

Designs: 25p, Discus. 27½pi, Running. 60p, Basketball. 50p, Polo (horiz.).

1968, Dec. 19 Litho. Perf. 12x12½
C421	AP134	12½p brt pink, blk & grn	10	6
C422	AP134	25p red, grn & blk	20	12
C423	AP134	27½p blk, gray & grn	25	20
C424	AP134	60p multi	45	30

Souvenir Sheet
Imperf.
| C425 | AP134 | 50p multi | 70 | 70 |

Issued to commemorate the 19th Olympic Games, Mexico City, Oct. 12–27. No. C425 contains one horizontal stamp (size: 52x80mm.). Dark brown marginal inscription and Olympic emblem. Size: 105x 80mm.

Damascus International Airport
AP135

1969, Jan. 20 Litho. Perf. 12½x12
C426	AP135	12½p yel, brt bl & grn	10	8
C427	AP135	17½p org, pur & lt grn	15	12
C428	AP135	60p car, blk & yel	50	30

Issued to commemorate the construction of Damascus International Airport.

Baal Shamin Temple, Palmyra
AP136

Designs: 45p, Interior of Omayyad Mosque, Damascus (vert.). 50p, Amphitheater, Palmyra. 60p, Khaled bin al-Walid Mosque, Homs (vert.). 100p, Ruins of St. Simeon, Djebel Samaan.

1969, Jan. 20 Photo. Perf. 12x11½
C429	AP136	25p multi	15	12
C430	AP136	45p bl & multi	25	20
C431	AP136	50p multi	35	28
C432	AP136	60p multi	50	30
C433	AP136	100p vio & multi	75	60
		Nos. C429-C433 (5)	2.00	1.50

Workers, ILO Emblem, Cogwheel
AP137

Design: 60p, ILO emblem.

1969, May 1 Litho. Perf. 12½x12
| C434 | AP137 | 12½p multi | 15 | 6 |
| C435 | AP137 | 27½p multi | 25 | 14 |

Miniature Sheet
Imperf.
| C436 | AP137 | 60p multi | 40 | 35 |

Issued to commemorate the 50th anniversary of the International Labor Organization. No. C436 contains one stamp, size: 53½x47mm. Size of sheet: 75x55 mm.

Ballet Dancers
AP138

Designs: 12½p, Russian dancers. 45p, Lebanese singer and dancers. 55p, Egyptian dancer and musicians. 60p, Bulgarian dancers.

1969, Aug. 25 Litho. Perf. 12½x12
C437	AP138	12½p multi	13	10
C438	AP138	27½p bl & multi	25	14
C439	AP138	45p multi	32	25
C440	AP138	55p multi	40	30
C441	AP138	60p multi	50	40
		Nos. C437-C441 (5)	1.60	1.19

Issued to publicize the 16th International Fair, Damascus, Aug. 25–Sept. 20. Nos. C437–C441 are printed se-tenant in sheets of 50 (10x5).

Children Playing   **Fortuna**
AP139   AP140

1969, Oct. 6 Litho. Perf. 12x12½
C442	AP139	12½p aqua, dk bl & emer	10	6
C443	AP139	25p brn red, dk bl & lt vio	20	10
C444	AP139	27½p ultra, dk bl & gray	25	14

Issued for Children's Day.

1969, Oct. 10
Designs: 25p, Seated woman from Palmyra. 60p, Motherhood. All sculptures from Greco-Roman period.
C445	AP140	17½p blk, yel grn & grn	12	10
C446	AP140	25p dk brn, red brn & lt grn	18	14
C447	AP140	60p blk, lt gray & bl gray	40	30

Issued to publicize the 9th International Congress for Classical Archaeology, Oct. 11–20.

Cock—AP141

Designs: 17½p, Cow. 20p, Corn. 50p, Olives.

1969, Dec. 24 Litho. Perf. 12½x12
C448	AP141	12p red & multi	10	8
C449	AP141	17½p red & multi	15	8
C450	AP141	20p red & multi	20	10
C451	AP141	50p red & multi	35	23

Issued to publicize the Damascus Agricultural Museum. Nos. C448–C451 printed se-tenant in strips of 4 with label showing dove and grain.

Weather Satellite Tracking and U.N. Emblem
AP142

1970, Mar. 23 Litho. Perf. 12½x12
| C452 | AP142 | 25p blk, sl grn & yel | 25 | 15 |
| C453 | AP142 | 60p brn, dk bl & yel | 55 | 40 |

10th World Meteorological Day.

Lenin
AP143

1970, Apr. 15 Litho. Perf. 12x12½
| C454 | AP143 | 15p red & dk brn | 15 | 9 |
| C455 | AP143 | 60p red & grn | 48 | 40 |

Issued to commemorate the centenary of the birth of Lenin (1870–1924), Russian communist leader.

Workers' Syndicate Emblem
AP144

1970, May 1 Litho. Perf. 12½x12
| C456 | AP144 | 15p dk brn & brt grn | 12 | 9 |
| C457 | AP144 | 60p dk brn & org | 55 | 40 |

Issued for Labor Day.

SYRIA

Radar and Open Book AP145

1970, May 17
C458 AP145 15p brt pink & blk 12 9
C459 AP145 60p bl & blk 55 40

International Telecommunications Day.

U.P.U. Headquarters, Bern AP146

1970, May 30
C460 AP146 15p multi 12 9
C461 AP146 60p multi 55 40

Issued to commemorate the opening of the new Universal Postal Union Headquarters in Bern.

"Zahier Piebers and Maarouf" AP147

Folk Tales: 10p, Two warriors on horseback. 15p, Two warriors on white horses. 20p, Lady and warrior on horseback. 60p, Warriors, woman and lion.

1970, Aug. 12 Litho. Perf. 12½
C462 AP147 5p lt bl & multi 5 5
C463 AP147 10p lt bl & multi 8 8
C464 AP147 15p lt bl & multi 12 9
C465 AP147 20p lt bl & multi 20 18
C466 AP147 60p lt bl & multi 75 50
  Nos. C462-C466 (5) 1.20 90

Nos. C462–C466 printed se-tenant.

Al Aqsa Mosque on Fire AP148

1970, Aug. 21 Perf. 12½x12
C467 AP148 15p multi 12 9
C468 AP148 60p multi 55 40

Issued to commemorate the first anniversary of the burning of Al Aqsa Mosque, Jerusalem.

Wood Carving—AP149

Handicrafts: 20p, Jewelry. 25p, Glass making. 30p, Copper engraving. 60p, Shellwork.

1970, Aug. 25 Perf. 12½
C469 AP149 15p vio & multi 12 9
C470 AP149 20p ol & multi 16 12
C471 AP149 25p multi 20 15
C472 AP149 30p multi 40 25
C473 AP149 60p multi 65 50
  Nos. C469-C473 (5) 1.53 1.11

Issued to publicize the 17th International Fair in Damascus. Nos. C469–C473 printed se-tenant.

Education Year Emblem AP150

1970, Nov. 2 Litho. Perf. 12
C474 AP150 15p dl grn & dk brn 12 9
C475 AP150 60p vio bl & dk brn 50 40

International Education Year.

U.N. Emblem, Symbols of Progress, Justice and Peace AP151

1970, Nov. 3
C476 AP151 15p lt ultra, red & blk 15 9
C477 AP151 60p bl, yel & blk 55 45

United Nations, 25th anniversary.

Khaled ibn-al-Walid—AP152   **Woman with Garland** AP153

Perf. 12x11½, 12½x12½

1970–71
C478 AP152 45p brt pink 50 27
C479 AP152 50p green 55 30
C480 AP152 60p vio brn 65 35
C481 AP152 100p dk bl 80 60
C482 AP152 200p grnsh gray ('71) 2.00 1.20
C483 AP152 300p lil ('71) 3.00 2.00
C484 AP152 500p gray ('71) 4.00 3.25
  Nos. C478-C484 (7) 11.50 7.97

1971, Apr. 17 Litho. Perf. 12
C485 AP153 15p dl red, blk & grn 12 9
C486 AP153 60p grn, blk & dk red 50 40

25th anniversary of the evacuation of British and French troops from Syria.

People Dancing Around Globe AP154

1971, Apr. 28 Litho. Perf. 12½x12
C487 AP154 15p vio & multi 9 7
C488 AP154 60p grn & multi 40 38

International Year against Racial Discrimination.

Pres. Hafez al Assad and Council Chamber—AP155

1971, Sept. 30 Litho. Perf. 12½x12
C489 AP155 15p grn & multi 12 9
C490 AP155 65p bl & multi 65 38

People's Council and presidential election.

Pres. Nasser AP156

1971, Oct. 17 Perf. 12x12½
C491 AP156 15p lt ol grn & brn 15 9
C492 AP156 20p gray & brn 20 12

In memory of Gamal Abdel Nasser (1918–1970), president of Egypt.

Globe and Arrows AP157

1972, May 17 Litho. Perf. 11½
C493 AP157 15p bl, vio bl & pink 12 9
C494 AP157 50p org, yel & sep 48 40

4th World Telecommunications Day.

Pres. Hafez al Assad AP158   **Airline Emblem, Eastern Hemisphere** AP159

1972, July Litho. Perf. 12x11½
C495 AP158 100p dk grn 90 50
C496 AP158 500p dk brn 5.00 2.50

1972, Sept. 16 Litho. Perf. 12x11½
C497 AP159 15p blk, lt bl & Prus bl 15 9
C498 AP159 50p blk, gray & Prus bl 45 40

Syrianair, Syrian airline, 25th anniversary.

Pottery—AP160

Handicraft Industries: 25p, Rugs. 30p, Metal (weapons). 35p, Straw (baskets, mats). 100p, Wood carving.

1976, July Litho. Perf. 12x12½
C499 AP160 10p multi 6 5
C500 AP160 25p multi 15 8
C501 AP160 30p multi 22 15
C502 AP160 35p multi 25 17
C503 AP160 100p multi 75 60
  Nos. C499-C503 (5) 1.43 1.05

23rd International Damascus Fair. Nos. C499–C503 printed se-tenant.

Pres. Hafez al Assad AP161

1978, Sept. Litho. Perf. 12½x12
C504 AP161 25p sil & multi 15 10
C505 AP161 35p grn & multi 20 15
C506 AP161 60p gold & multi 30 20

Reelection of Pres. Assad. See No. 820.

A well-informed dealer has services to offer that would be helpful toward building your collection.

Use the **Yellow Pages** to fulfill your philatelic requirements.

SYRIA

POSTAGE DUE STAMPS.
Under French Occupation

O. M. F Syrie Ch. taxe 1 PIASTRE

Stamps of French Offices in the Turkish Empire, 1902-03, Surcharged

1920 *Perf. 14x13½.* Unwmkd.
J1	A3	1p on 10c rose red	110.00	110.00
J2	A3	2p on 20c brn vio	110.00	110.00
J3	A3	3p on 30c lil	110.00	110.00
J4	A4	4p on 40c red & pale bl	110.00	110.00

Postage Due Stamps of France, 1893–1920, Surcharged in Black or Red

O. M. F. Syrie 2 PIASTRES

1920
J5	D2	1p on 10c brn	75	75
J6	D2	2p on 20c ol grn (R)	75	75
a.		"PIASTRE"	300.00	300.00
J7	D2	3p on 30c red	75	75
a.		"PIASTRE"		
J8	D2	4p on 50c brn vio	2.75	2.75
a.		3p in setting of 4p	350.00	350.00

1921-22
J9	D2	50c on 10c brn	45	45
a.		"75" instead of "50"	40.00	
b.		"CENTIMES" instead of "CENTIEMES"	5.50	
J10	D2	1p on 20c ol grn	45	45
J11	D2	2p on 30c red	1.50	1.50
J12	D2	3p on 50c brn vio	1.75	1.75
J13	D2	5p on 1fr red brn, straw	3.50	3.50
		Nos. J9-J13 (5)	7.65	7.65

D3   D4

1921 *Red Surcharge.* *Perf. 11½*
J14	D3	50c on 1p blk	1.75	1.75
J15	D3	1p on 1p blk	90	90

1922
J16	D4	2p on 5m rose	2.75	2.75
a.		"AX" of "TAXE" invtd.	90.00	90.00
J17	D4	3p on 1p gray bl	6.25	5.75

French Mandate
Postage Due Stamps of France, 1893-1920, Surcharged

Syrie Grand Liban 2 PIASTRES

1923
J18	D2	50c on 10c brn	50	50
J19	D2	1p on 20c ol grn	85	85
J20	D2	2p on 30c red	60	60
J21	D2	3p on 50c vio brn	60	60
J22	D2	5p on 1fr red brn, straw	2.00	2.00
		Nos. J18-J22 (5)	4.55	4.55

Postage Due Stamps of France, 1893-1920, Surcharged

SYRIE 1 PIASTRE

1924
J23	D2	50c on 10c brn	30	30
J24	D2	1p on 20c ol grn	38	38
J25	D2	2p on 30c red	45	45
J26	D2	3p on 50c vio brn	55	55
J27	D2	5p on 1fr red brn, straw	60	60
		Nos. J23-J27 (5)	2.28	2.28

Postage Due Stamps of France, 1893-1920, Surcharged

Syrie 2 Piastres سوريا غروش ٢

1924
J28	D2	0p.50 on 10c brn	30	30
J29	D2	1p on 20c ol grn	38	38
J30	D2	2p on 30c red	45	45
J31	D2	3p on 50c vio brn	60	60
J32	D2	5p on 1fr red brn, straw	75	75
		Nos. J28-J32 (5)	2.48	2.48

Water Wheel at Hama — D5

Bridge at Antioch — D6

Designs: 2p, The Tartous. 3p, View of Banias. 5p, Chevaliers' Castle.

1925 *Photogravure.* *Perf. 13½.*
J33	D5	50c brn, yel	15	15
J34	D6	1p vio, rose	18	18
J35	D5	2p blue	18	18
J36	D5	3p red org	45	45
J37	D5	5p bl grn	45	45
		Nos. J33-J37 (5)	1.41	1.41

D7

Lion — D8

1931
J38	D7	8p gray bl	2.25	2.25
J39	D8	15p dl rose	3.25	3.25

Syrian Arab Republic

D9

1965 *Lithographed* *Perf. 11½x11* Unwmkd.
J40	D9	2½p vio bl	10	10
J41	D9	5p blk brn	10	10
J42	D9	10p green	15	15
J43	D9	17½p car rose	30	30
J44	D9	25p blue	40	40
		Nos. J40-J44 (5)	1.05	1.05

MILITARY STAMPS.
Free French Administration.
Syria No. 222 Surcharged in Black

1942 *Perf. 13* Unwmkd.
M1	A10	50c on 4p yel org	3.00	3.00

Lebanon Nos. 155 and 142A Surcharged in Carmine

M2	A13	1fr on 5p grnsh bl	3.00	3.00
M3	A25	2.50fr on 12½p dp ultra	3.00	3.00

Camel Corps, Palmyra — M1

1942 *Lithographed.* *Perf. 11½* Unwmkd.
M4	M1	1fr dp rose	22	22
M5	M1	1.50fr brt vio	22	22
M6	M1	2fr orange	22	22
M7	M1	2.50fr brn gray	22	22
M8	M1	3fr Prus bl	22	22
M9	M1	4fr dp grn	35	35
M10	M1	5fr dp cl	35	35
		Nos. M4-M10 (7)	1.80	1.80

Nos. M4 to M10 exist imperforate.

MILITARY SEMI-POSTAL STAMPS.
Free French Administration.

RÉSISTANCE +9F

1943 *Perf. 11½.* Unwmkd.
MB1	M1	1fr +9fr dp rose	2.75	2.75
MB2	M1	5fr +20fr dp cl	2.75	2.75

MILITARY AIR POST STAMPS.
Free French Administration.
Syria Nos. C55–C56 Surcharged in Carmine, Black or Orange

1942 *Perf. 13.* Unwmkd.
MC1	AP2	4fr on 50p blk (C)	1.50	1.50
MC2	AP2	6.50fr on 50p blk (C)	1.50	1.50
MC3	AP2	8fr on 50p blk (O)	1.50	1.50
MC4	AP2	10fr on 100p mag (Bk)	1.50	1.50

Winged Shields and Cross of Lorraine — MAP1

1942 *Lithographed.* *Perf. 11½.*
MC5	MAP1	6.50fr pale pink & rose car	50	50
MC6	MAP1	10fr lt bl & dl vio	50	50

Nos. MC5 and MC6 exist imperforate.

Souvenir Sheets.

MAP2

1942 *Without Gum* *Perf. 11*
MC7	MAP2	Sheet of two	8.00	8.00
a.		6.50fr pale pink & rose car	2.25	2.25
b.		10fr lt bl & dl vio	2.25	2.25

Imperf.
MC8	MAP2	Sheet of two	8.00	8.00
a.		6.50fr pale pink & rose car	2.25	2.25
b.		10fr lt bl & dl vio	2.25	2.25

The sheets measure 106½x149½ mm.

No. MC5 Surcharged in Rose Carmine With New Value and Bars.
Perf. 11½.
MC9	MAP1	4fr on 6.50fr	90	70

Military Stamp of 1942 Surcharged in Black

1943
MC10	M1	4fr on 3fr Prus bl	90	70

SYRIA

MILITARY AIR POST SEMI-POSTAL STAMPS.
Free French Administration.
Military Air Post Stamps of 1942 Surcharged in Black

1943   Perf. 11½.   Unwmkd.

MCB1	MAP1	6.50fr + 48.50fr	11.00	11.00
MCB2	MAP1	10fr + 100fr	11.00	11.00

POSTAL TAX STAMPS.

R1
Revenue Stamps Overprinted in Red or Black

1945   Perf. 10½ x 11½.   Unwmkd.

RA1	R1(a)	5p dk bl (R)	20.00	1.25

On Stamps Overprinted

RA2	R1(a)	5p dk bl (Bk+Bk)	10.00	1.00
RA3	R1(a)	5p dk bl (Bk+Bk)	10.00	1.00
RA4	R1(a)	5p dk bl (R+R)	10.00	1.00
RA5	R1(b)	5p dk bl (R+R)	10.00	1.00

On Stamps Overprinted

RA6	R1(a)	5p dk bl (Bk+Bk)	10.00	1.00
RA7	R1(a)	5p dk bl (Bk+Bk)	10.00	1.00
RA8	R1(a)	5p dk bl (R+R)	10.00	1.00
RA9	R1(a)	5p dk bl (R+R)	10.00	1.00
	Nos. RA1-RA9 (9)		100.00	9.25

The tax was for national defense.

R2
Revenue Stamp Surcharged in Black.

1945   Perf. 11   Unwmkd.

RA10	R2(c)	5p on 25c on 40c rose red	110.00	1.25

The surcharge reads "Tax (postal) for Syrian Army."

Revenue Stamp Surcharged in Black

1945

RA11	R2(d)	5p on 25c on 40c rose red	110.00	1.25

Same, Overprinted in Black

RA12	R2(d)	5p on 25c on 40c rose red	120.00	75

The tax on Nos. RA11 and RA12 was for the army.

ISSUES OF THE ARABIAN GOVERNMENT.

The following issues replaced the British Military Occupation (E.E.F.) stamps (Palestine Nos. 2–14) which were used in central and eastern Syria from Nov. 1918 until Jan. 1920.

Turkish Stamps of 1913–18 Handstamped in Various Colors

Also Handstamp Surcharged with New Values as:

   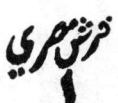

1 millieme   1 Egyptian piaster

The Seal reads: "Hakuma al Arabie" (The Arabian Government).

Perf. 11½, 12, 12½, 13½.

1919–20   Unwmkd.

1	A24	1m on 2pa red lil (254)	1.00	1.00
2	A25	1m on 4pa dk brn (255)	1.00	1.00
3	A26	2m on 5pa vio brn (256)	1.50	1.50
4	A15	2m on 5pa on 10pa gray grn (291)	1.00	1.00
5	A18	2m on 5pa ocher (304)	30.00	25.00
6	A41	2m on 5pa grn (345)	400.00	300.00
7	A18	2m on 5pa ocher (378)	80.00	80.00
8	A28	4m on 10pa grn (258)	8.00	8.00
9	A28	4m on 10pa grn (271)	1.00	1.00
10	A22	4m on 10pa bl grn (329)	2.00	2.00
11	A41	4m on 10pa car (346)	35.00	35.00
12	A23	4m on 10pa grn (415)	8.00	8.00
13	A44	4m on 10pa grn (424)	1.50	1.50
14	A11	4m on 10pa on 20pa vio brn (B38)	1.50	1.50
15	A41	4m on 10pa car (B42)	1.00	1.00
16	SP1	4m on 10pa red vio (B46)	1.50	1.50
17	SP1	4m on 10pa on 20pa car rose (B47)	1.50	1.50
18	A21	5pa ocher (317)		
19	A21	20pa car rose (153)	100.00	200.00
21	A21			
22	A29	20pa red (259)	1.50	1.50
23	A29	20pa red (272)	400.00	400.00
24	A17	20pa car (299)	3.00	3.00
25	A21	20pa car rose (318)	3.00	3.00
26	A22	20pa car rose (330)	15.00	15.00
27	A22	20pa car rose (342)	8.00	8.00
28	A41	20pa ultra (347)	2.50	2.50
29	A16	20pa mag (363)	12.00	12.00
30	A17	20pa car (371)		
31	A18	20pa car (379)	8.00	8.00
32	A45	20pa dp rose (425)	4.00	4.00
33	A22	20pa car rose (B8)	2.50	2.50
34	A22	20pa car rose (B33)	3.00	3.00
35	A22	20pa car rose (B36)	16.00	16.00
36	A41	20pa car (B43)	50	50
37	A16	20pa mag (P140)	4.00	4.00
38	A17	20pa car (P144)	400.00	400.00
39	A30	1pi bl (260)	3.00	3.00
40	A31	1pi on 1½pa car & blk (261)	500.00	500.00
41	A30	1pi bl (273)	80.00	80.00
42	A30	1pi on 1pi bl (273)	120.00	120.00
43	A17	1pi bl (300)	5.00	5.00
44	A18	1pi bl (307)	100.00	100.00
45	A22	1pi ultra (331)	8.00	8.00
46	A21	1pi ultra (343)	15.00	15.00
47	A41	1pi vio & blk (348)	1.50	1.50
48	A18	1pi brt bl (389)	8.00	8.00
49	A46	1pi dl vio (426)	2.50	2.50
50	A47	1pi on 50pa ultra (428)	1.00	1.00
51	A21	1pi ultra (B9)	10.00	10.00
52	A22	1pi ultra (B15)	16.00	16.00
53	A18	1pi brt bl (B21)	10.00	10.00
54	A18	1pi bl (B23)	25.00	25.00
55	A22	1pi ultra (B34)	20.00	20.00
56	A41	1pi vio & blk (B44)	2.50	2.50
57	A33	2pi grn & blk (263)	80.00	70.00
58	A13	2pi brn org (289)	2.00	2.00
59	A18	2pi sl (308)	25.00	25.00
60	A18	2pi sl (314)	25.00	25.00
61	A21	2pi bl blk (320)	5.00	5.00
62	A17	2pi org (373)	5.00	5.00
63	A18	5pi brn (310)	12.00	12.00
64	A22	5pi dl vio (333)	25.00	25.00
65	A41	5pi yel brn & blk (349)	4.00	4.00
66	A41	5pi yel brn & blk (418)	4.00	4.00
67	A53	5pi on 2pa Prus bl (547)	3.00	3.00
68	A21	5pi dk vio (Bl)	350.00	350.00
69	A17	5pi lil rose (B20)	60.00	60.00
70	A41	5pi yel brn & blk (B45)	5.00	5.00
72	A50	10pi dk grn (431)	120.00	120.00
73	A50	10pi dk vio (432)	110.00	110.00
74	A50	10pi dk brn (433)	700.00	
75	A18	10pi org brn (B2)	300.00	300.00
76	A37	25pi ol grn (267)	400.00	400.00
77	A40	25pi on 200pi grn & blk (287)	500.00	500.00
78	A17	25pi brn (303)	400.00	400.00
79	A51	25pi car, *straw* (434)	100.00	100.00
81	A52	50pi ind (438)	250.00	250.00

The variety "surcharge omitted" exists on Nos. 1–5, 12–13, 16, 32, 49–50, 67.
A few copies of No. 377 (50pi) and No. 269 (100pi) were overprinted but not regularly issued.

Overprinted

The Inscription reads "Hakum Soria Arabie" (Syrian-Arabian Government).
On Stamp of 1913.

83	A26	2m on 5pa vio brn (256)	5.00	5.00

On Stamp of 1916–18.

84	A45	20pa dp rose (425)	50	50

A1
Lithographed
Perf. 11½

85	A1	5m rose	50	40
a.		Tête bêche pair	20.00	15.00
b.		Imperf.		

Independence Issue.
Arabic Overprint in Green:
"Souvenir of Syrian Independence March 8, 1920".

86	A1	5m rose	80.00	70.00
a.		Tête bêche pair		
b.		Invtd. ovpt.	200.00	150.00

A2
Lithographed
Size: 22x18 mm.

87	A2	1/10pi lt grn	30	20

Size: 28x22 mm.

88	A2	2/10pi yel grn	50	35
a.		2/10pi yel (error)	12.50	8.00
89	A2	3/10pi yellow	25	20
90	A2	1pi gray bl	25	20
91	A2	2pi bl grn	2.00	75

Size: 31x25 mm.

92	A2	5pi vio brn	3.00	1.50
93	A2	10pi gray	3.00	2.00
	Nos. 86-93 (8)		89.30	75.20

Nos. 86-93 exist imperf.

PF1   PF2

Revenue Stamps Surcharged as on Postage Stamps, for Postal Use

1920   Perf. 11½.   Unwmkd.

94	PF1	5m on 5pa red	50	50
95	PF2	1m on 5pa red	35	25
96	PF2	2m on 5pa red	50	30
97	PF2	1pi on 5pa red	1.00	75

SYRIA

Surcharged
in Syrian
Piasters

98	PF2	2pi on 5pa red	35	35
99	PF2	3pi on 5pa red	35	35
	Nos. 94-99 (6)		3.05	2.50

POSTAGE DUE STAMPS.

Postage Due Stamps of Turkey, 1914, Handstamped and Surcharged with New Value

1920		Perf. 12.	Unwmkd.	
J1	D1	2m on 5pa cl	8.00	8.00
J2	D2	20pa red	8.00	8.00
J3	D3	1pi dk bl	8.00	8.00
J4	D4	2pi slate	8.00	8.00

Type of Regular Issue.
Lithographed.
Perf. 11½.

J5	A2	1pi black	1.50	1.50

United Arab Republic Issues for Syria

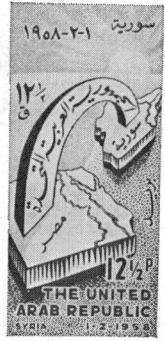

Linked Maps of Egypt
and Syria—A1
Lithographed.

1958		Perf. 11½	Unwmkd.	
1	A1	12½p yel & grn	20	15

Establishment of United Arab Republic.

Freedom Monument
A2

1958, May

2	A2	5p yel & vio	40	20
3	A2	15p yel grn & brn red	60	40

Issued to commemorate the 12th anniversary of the British-French troop evacuation. See also Nos. C2–C3.

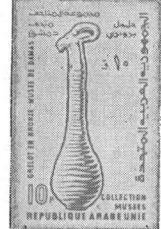

Bronze Rattle—A3

Antique Art: 15p, Goddess. 20p, Lamgi Mari. 30p, Mithras fighting bull. 40p, Aspasia. 60p, Minerva. 75p, Flask. 100p, Enameled Vase. 150p, Mosaic from Omayyad Mosque, Damascus.

1958, Sept. 14   Litho.   Perf. 12

4	A3	10p lt ol grn	15	8
5	A3	15p brn org	20	10
6	A3	20p rose lil	25	12
7	A3	30p lt brn	30	15
8	A3	40p gray	40	20
9	A3	60p green	60	30
10	A3	75p blue	85	40
11	A3	100p brn car	1.25	65
12	A3	150p dl pur	2.00	80
	Nos. 4-12 (9)		6.00	2.80

Issued to publicize archaeological collections and museums.

Hand Holding Torch,
Broken Chain and Flag
A4

1958, Oct. 14   Perf. 11½

13	A4	12.50p car rose	20	15

Establishment of Republic of Iraq.

Syria No. 411
Overprinted

1958, Oct. 6   Perf. 11½   Wmk. 291

13A	A78	12½p olive	52.50	45.00

Issued for International Children's Day, 1958. See Nos. C10–C11.

View of Damascus—A5

1958, Dec. 10   Unwmkd.

14	A5	12½p green	30	15

Issued to publicize the 4th Near East Regional Conference, Damascus, Dec. 10–20. See No. C14.

Secondary School, Damascus—A6

1959, Feb. 26   Litho.   Perf. 12

15	A6	12½p dl grn	15	10

See also No. 26.

Flags of UAR and Yemen
A7
Perf. 13x13½

1959, Mar. 8   Photo.   Wmk. 318

16	A7	12½p grn red & blk	25	20

First anniversary of United Arab States.

Arms of UAR
A8
Perf. 12x11½

1959, Feb. 22   Litho.   Wmk. 291

17	A8	12½p grn blk & red	25	15

United Arab Republic 1st anniversary.

Mother
and
Children
A9

1959, Mar. 21   Perf. 11½

18	A9	15p car rose	20	15
19	A9	25p dk sl grn	30	25

Arab Mother's Day, Mar. 21.

Syria No. 378 Surcharged "U.A.R."
in Arabic and English,
and New Value in Red.

1959, Apr. 6   Photo.   Unwmkd.

20	A68	2½p on 1p ol	12	8

Type of 1959 and

A10

Boys' School, Damascus
A11

Designs: 5p, 7½p, 10p, Various arabesques. 12½p, St. Simeon's Monastery. 17½p, Hittin school. 35p, Normal School for Girls, Damascus.

Lithographed.

1959–61   Perf. 11½   Unwmkd.

21	A10	2½p violet	6	6
22	A10	5p ol bis	6	5
23	A10	7½p ultra	8	5
24	A10	10p bl grn	8	5
25	A11	12½p lt bl ('61)	15	7
26	A6	17½p brt lil ('60)	40	10
27	A11	25p brt grnsh bl	30	20
28	A11	35p brn ('60)	50	25
	Nos. 21-28 (8)		1.63	83

Fair Emblem and Globe—A12

Male Profile and Fair
Emblem
A13
Souvenir Sheet.

1959, Aug. 30   Imperf.   Unwmkd.

30	A12	30p dl yel & grn	2.00	2.00

Perf. 11½.

31	A13	35p gray, grn & vio	50	30

Nos. 30–31 issued to publicize the 6th International Damascus Fair.
No. 30 measures 79x79mm. and has marginal inscription in green.

Shield and Cogwheel
A14
Perf. 13½x13

1959, Oct. 20   Wmk. 328

32	A14	50p sepia	75	45

Issued for Army Day, 1959.

SYRIA

Syria Nos. 408 and 386 with Red Overprint Similar to

الجمهورية العربية المتحدة
U.A.R

Lithographed.
1959   *Perf. 11½*   Unwmkd.
33   A75   15p gray   25   15
         Photogravure.
34   A69   50p dk grn   75   60

The overprints differ in size and lettering: No. 33 is 28x8½mm.; No. 34 is 21x6mm. A period follows "R" on Nos. 33–34. The Arabic overprint means "United Arab Republic."

Cogwheel, Wheat and Cotton   A. R. Kawakbi
A15   A16

1959, Oct. 30   Lithographed
35   A15   35p gray, bl & ocher   50   25

Issued to publicize the Industrial and Agricultural Production Fair, Aleppo. See also No. 46.

Type of Syria Air Post, 1956, Inscribed "U.A.R."

1959, Dec. 31   *Perf. 13½*   Unwmkd.
36   AP59   12½p gray ol & bis   20   15

Issued to publicize the Day of the Tree.

1960, Jan. 11   *Perf. 12x11½*
37   A16   15p dk grn   25   15

Issued to commemorate the 50th anniversary of the death of A. R. Kawakbi, Arabic writer.

Arms and Flag
A17
Perf. 13½x13

1960, Feb. 22   Photo.   Wmk. 328
38   A17   12½p red & dk sl grn   20   15

United Arab Republic, 2nd anniversary.

Diesel Train and Old Town—A18

Perf. 11½x11

1960, Mar. 15   Litho.   Unwmkd.
39   A18   12½p brn & brt bl   25   18

Issued to publicize construction of the Latakia-Aleppo railroad.

Arab League Center, Cairo, and Arms of UAR
A19

Perf. 13x13½

1960, Mar. 22   Photo.   Wmk. 328
40   A19   12½p dl grn & blk   20   12

Issued to commemorate the opening of the Arab League Center and the Arab Postal Museum in Cairo.

Nos. 18–19 Overprinted: "ARAB MOTHERS DAY 1960" in Arabic and English in Black or Magenta.

Lithographed
1960, Apr. 3   *Perf. 11½*   Wmk. 291
41   A9   15p car rose   25   12
42   A9   25p dk sl grn (M)   35   20

Issued for Arab Mother's Day.

Refugees Pointing to Map of Palestine
A20

Perf. 13x13½

1960, Apr. 7   Photo.   Wmk. 328
43   A20   12½p car rose   20   15
44   A20   50p green   50   35

Issued to publicize World Refugee Year, July 1, 1959–June 30, 1960.

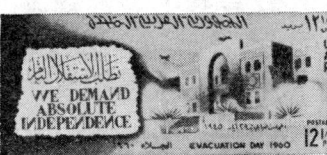

A21
Lithographed
1960, May 12   *Perf. 11½*   Unwmkd.
45   A21   12½p vio, rose & pale grn   25   15

Evacuation Day, 1960.

No. 35 Overprinted "1960" in Red in Arabic and English.

1960
46   A15   35p gray, bl & ocher   40   30

Issued to publicize the 1960 Industrial and Agricultural Production Fair, Aleppo.

Souvenir Sheet

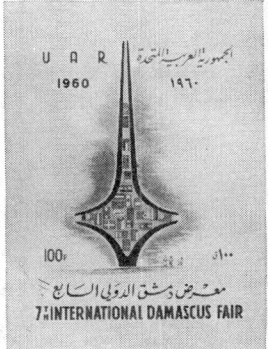

Flags in Symbolic Design
A22
1960   *Imperf.*   Unwmkd.
47   A22   100p gray, brn & lt bl   2.00   2.00

Issued to publicize the 7th International Damascus Fair. Size: 70x100mm.

Child
A23
1960   Lithographed   *Perf. 11½*
48   A23   35p dk grn & fawn   50   30

Issued for Children's Day.

No. 36 Overprinted in Carmine

1960   *Perf. 11½*   Unwmkd.
49   AP59   12½p gray ol & bis   25   15

Issued to publicize the Day of the Tree.

Coat of Arms and Victory Wreath
A24
Perf. 13½x13

1961, Feb. 22   Photo.   Wmk. 328
50   A24   12½p lt vio   20   15
United Arab Republic, 3rd anniversary.

Cogwheel, Retort and Ear of Wheat
A25
Lithographed
1961, June 8   *Perf. 11½*   Unwmkd.
51   A25   12½p multi   25   15
Industrial and Agricultural Fair, Aleppo.

SEMI-POSTAL STAMP

Postal Emblem
SP1
Perf. 13½x13

1959, Jan. 2   Photo.   Wmk. 318
B1   SP1   20p +10p bl grn, red & blk   60   50

Issued for Post Day. The surtax went to the social fund for postal employees.

AIR POST STAMPS

Map Type of Regular Issue
Lithographed.
1958, Apr. 3   *Perf. 11½*   Unwmkd.
C1   A1   17½p ultra & brn   40   25
Establishment of United Arab Republic.

Broken Chain, Dove and Olive Branch—AP1

1958, May 17
C2   AP1   35p rose & blk   1.00   40
C3   AP1   45p bl & brn   1.50   60

Issued to commemorate the 12th anniversary of the British-French troop evacuation.

Scout Putting up Tent—AP2

1958, Aug. 31   *Perf. 12*
C4   AP2   35p dk brn   1.50   1.50
C5   AP2   40p ultra   2.50   2.50
3rd Pan-Arab Boy Scout Jamboree.

SYRIA

View of Damascus Fair
AP3

U. A. R. Flag and Fair Emblem
AP4

Designs: 30p, Minaret, vase and emblem (vert.). 45p, Mosque, chimneys and wheel (vert.).

1958, Sept. 1		Litho.	Perf. 11½	
C6	AP3	25p vermilion	60	40
C7	AP3	30p brt bl grn	90	70
C8	AP3	45p violet	1.00	90

Souvenir Sheet.
Imperf.

| C9 | AP4 | 100p brt grn, car & blk | 75.00 | 75.00 |

Fifth Damascus International Fair. No. C9 measures 80x80mm. with black marginal inscription.

Syria Nos. C244-C245
Overprinted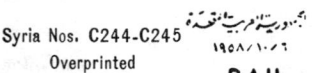

1958, Oct. 6		Perf. 11½	Wmk. 291	
C10	A78	17½p ultra	35.00	35.00
C11	A78	20p red brn	35.00	35.00

International Children's Day.

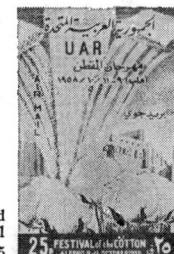

Cotton and Cotton Material
AP5

1958, Oct. 10		Perf. 12	Unwmkd.	
C12	AP5	25p brn & yel	50	40
C13	AP5	35p brn & brick red	90	75

Cotton Festival, Aleppo, Oct. 9–11.

Type of Regular Issue, 1958.
1958, Dec. 10

| C14 | A5 | 17½p brt vio | 30 | 20 |

Issued to publicize the 4th Near East Regional Conference, Damascus, Dec. 10–20.

Children and Glider
AP6

1958, Dec. 1		Lithographed	Perf. 12	
C15	AP6	7½p gray grn	30	20
C16	AP6	12½p olive	1.75	1.25

Issued to publicize the 1958 glider festival.

U. N. Emblem
AP7

1958, Dec. 10

C17	AP7	25p dl pur	30	20
C18	AP7	35p lt bl	40	25
C19	AP7	40p brn red	60	35

Issued to commemorate the tenth anniversary of the signing of the Universal Declaration of Human Rights.

Globe, Radio and Telegraph
AP8

1959, Mar. 1			Perf. 12	
C20	AP8	40p grn & blk	50	25

Issued to publicize the Arab Union of Telecommunications.

Same Overprinted in Red: "2nd Conferance Damascus 1-3-59" and in Arabic Characters.

1959, Mar. 1

| C21 | AP8 | 40p grn & blk | 50 | 25 |

Issued to commemorate the 2nd Conference of the Arab Union of Telecommunications, Damascus.

Laurel and Map of Syria
AP9

Design: 35p, Torch and broken chain.

1959, Apr. 17			Perf. 12x11½	
C22	AP9	15p ocher & grn	20	15
C23	AP9	35p gray & car	50	40

Issued to commemorate the 13th anniversary of the British-French troop evacuation.

"Emigration"—AP10

1959, Aug. 4	Perf. 11½x12.	Unwmkd.	
C24	AP10	80p brt grn, blk & red	90	65

Issued to commemorate the convention of the Association of Arab Emigrants in the United States.

Refinery—AP11

1959, Aug. 12		Lithographed	
C25	AP11	50p bl, blk & car	75	40

Opening of first oil refinery in Syria.

Syria Nos. C246 and C181-C182 Overprinted

1959			Perf. 11½	
C26	AP64	5p brt grn	6	6
C27	AP44	50p dp plum	60	35
C28	AP44	70p purple	1.00	50

The overprints differ in size and lettering: No. C26 is 25½x9½mm.; Nos. C27-C28 are 27x8mm. A period follows "R" on Nos. C27-C28. The Arabic overprint means "United Arab Republic."

Cotton Boll and Thread
AP12

Boy and Building Blocks
AP13

1959, Oct. 1		Litho.	Perf. 11½	
C29	AP12	45p gray bl	50	25
C30	AP12	50p claret	50	30

Issued to publicize the Cotton Festival, Aleppo.

1959, Oct. 5

| C31 | AP13 | 25p dl lil, red & dk bl | 30 | 20 |

Issued for Children's Day, 1959.

Crane and Compass
AP14

1960		Perf. 11½	Unwmkd.	
C32	AP14	50p lt brn, crim & blk	60	40

7th Damascus International Fair.

Nos. C29–C30 Overprinted with Arabic Date and Cotton Boll in Claret or Gray Blue.

1960		Lithographed	Perf. 11½	
C33	AP12	45p gray bl (C)	50	25
C34	AP12	50p cl (GB)	55	35

1960 Cotton Festival, Aleppo.

Basketball
AP15

Globe, Laurel and "UN"
AP16

Sports: 20p, Swimmer. 25p, Fencing. 40p, Horsemanship.

1960, Dec. 27		Perf. 12	Unwmkd.	
C35	AP15	15p bl, blk & bis	30	15
C36	AP15	20p bl, blk & sal	40	20
C37	AP15	25p multi	50	20
C38	AP15	40p car rose, blk & vio	80	50

Issued to commemorate the 17th Olympic Games, Rome, Aug. 25–Sept. 11.

1960, Dec. 31

| C39 | AP16 | 35p multi | 35 | 25 |
| C40 | AP16 | 50p bl, red & yel | 60 | 35 |

United Nations, 15th anniversary.

Ibrahim Hanano
AP17

Soldier with Flag
AP18

1961		Lithographed	Perf. 12x11½	
C41	AP17	50p buff & sl grn	60	35

Issued to honor Ibrahim Hanano, leader of liberation movement.

1961, Apr. 17		Perf. 11½	Wmk. 291	
C42	AP18	40p gray grn	50	30

Issued for Evacuation Day, 1961.

SYRIA—TAHITI—TANNU TUVA

Arab and Map of Palestine — AP19
Abu-Tammam — AP20

1961, May 15   Perf. 12
C43 AP19 50p ultra & blk   60   30
Issued for Palestine Day.

1961, July 20 Perf. 11½ Unwmkd.
C44 AP20 50p brown   60   30
Issued to honor Abu-Tammam (807–?845), Arabian poet.

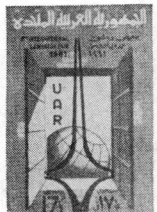

Discus Thrower and Lyre — AP21

1961, Aug. 23 Litho. Perf. 11½
C45 AP21 15p crim & blk   25   12
C46 AP21 35p bl grn & vio   75   25

5th University Youth Festival.
A souvenir sheet contains one each of Nos. C45–C46 imperf. Orange margin with black inscription. Size: 100x63mm.

Fair Emblem — AP22
U.A.R. Pavilion — AP23

1961, Aug. 25
C47 AP22 17½p vio & grn   20   12
C48 AP23 50p brt lil & blk   60   35
  a. Black omitted

8th International Damascus Fair.

St. Simeon's Monastery — AP24

1961, Oct. Litho. Perf. 12
C49 AP24 200p vio bl   2.00   1.25

No. C49 was issued by the Syrian Arab Republic after dissolution of the UAR.

AIR POST SEMI-POSTAL STAMP

Eye, Hand and U.N. Emblem
SPAP1
Perf. 12x11½

1961, Apr. 29 Litho. Wmk. 291
CB1 SPAP1 40p + 10p sl grn & blk   60   50

Issued to publicize the United Nations' welfare program for the blind.

TAHITI
(tä·hē′tē ; tä′ē·tī ; tä′hē·tē)

LOCATION — An island in the South Pacific Ocean, one of the Society group.
GOVT.—A part of the French Oceania Colony.
AREA—600 sq. mi.
POP.—19,029.
CHIEF TOWN—Papeete.

The stamps of Tahiti were replaced by those of French Oceania (see French Polynesia in Vol. II).

100 Centimes = 1 Franc

Stamps of French Colonies Surcharged in Black:

a   b

c   d

1882   Imperf.   Unwmkd.
1   A8 (a) 25c on 35c dk vio, org   165.00 140.00
1A   A8 (b) 25c on 35c dk vio, org   3,000. 3,000.
1B   A8 (a) 25c on 40c ver, straw   3,750. 3,750.

Inverted surcharges on Nos. 1–1B are same price as upright surcharges.
Counterfeits exist of surcharges and overprints on Nos. 1–31.

1884   Perf. 14x13½.
2   A9 (c) 5c on 20c red, grn   110.00   80.00
3   A9 (d) 10c on 20c red, grn   165.00 125.00

Imperf.
4   A8 (b) 25c on 1fr brnz grn, straw   385.00 325.00

Inverted and vertical surcharges on Nos. 2–4 are same price as normally placed surcharges.

Handstamped in Black

e

1893 Perf. 14x13½
5   A9   1c lil bl   450.00 385.00
6   A9   2c brn, buff   1,850. 1,500.
7   A9   4c cl, lav   800.00 625.00
8   A9   5c grn, grnsh   16.00   16.00
9   A9 10c lavender   16.00   16.00
10   A9 15c blue   16.00   16.00
11   A9 20c red, grn   16.00   16.00
12   A9 25c yel, straw   3,750.   3,250.
13   A9 25c rose   16.00   16.00
14   A9 35c vio, org   1,500.   1,500.
15   A9 75c car, rose   22.50   22.50
16   A9   1fr brnz grn, straw 30.00   30.00

Nearly all values of this set are known with overprint inverted, sloping up, sloping down and horizontal. Some occur double.

Overprinted in Black
1893
f

1893
17   A9   1c lil bl   475.00 450.00
  a. Inverted overprint   625.00 625.00
18   A9   2c brn, buff   2,000. 1,750.
  a. Inverted overprint   2,250. 2,250.
19   A9   4c cl, lav   1,000.   900.00
  a. Inverted overprint   1,200. 1,200.
20   A9   5c grn, grnsh   625.00 550.00
  a. Inverted overprint   750.00 750.00
21   A9 10c lavender   185.00 185.00
  a. Inverted overprint   400.00 400.00
22   A9 15c blue   16.00   16.00
  a. Inverted overprint   67.50   67.50
23   A9 20c red, grn   16.00   16.00
  a. Inverted overprint   90.00   90.00
24   A9 25c yel, straw   21,000. 1,500.
25   A9 25c rose   16.00   16.00
  a. Inverted overprint   90.00   90.00
26   A9 35c vio, org   1,650.   1,500.
  a. Inverted overprint   1,750. 1,750.
27   A9 75c car, rose   16.00   16.00
  a. Inverted overprint   90.00   90.00
  b. Double overprint   120.00 120.00
28   A9   1fr brnz grn, straw 17.00 17.00
  a. Inverted overprint   90.00   90.00

Stamps of French Polynesia Surcharged in Black or Carmine:

TAHITI 10 CENTIMES   TAHITI 10 centimes
g   h

1903
29   A1 (g) 10c on 15c bl (Bk)   3.00   3.00
  a. Double surcharge   21.00   21.00
  b. Inverted surcharge   21.00   21.00
30   A1 (h) 10c on 25c rose (C)   3.00   3.00
  a. Dbl. surch.   21.00   21.00
  b. Invtd. surch.   21.00   21.00
31   A1 (h) 10c on 40c red, straw (Bk) 3.00 3.00
  a. Double surch.   21.00   21.00
  b. Invtd surch.   21.00   21.00

In the surcharges on Nos. 29 to 31 there are two varieties of the "1" in "10", i. e. with long and short serif.

SEMI-POSTAL STAMPS.
Stamps of French Polynesia Overprinted in Red

TAHITI

1915 Perf. 14x13½. Unwmkd.
B1   A1   15c blue   90.00   90.00
  a. Invtd. overprint   165.00 165.00
B2   A1   15c gray   10.00   10.00
  a. Inverted overprint   67.50   67.50

Counterfeits exist.

POSTAGE DUE STAMPS.
Postage Due Stamps of French Colonies Handstamped in Black, type "e".

1893   Imperf.   Unwmkd.
J1   D1   1c black   200.00 200.00
J2   D1   2c black   200.00 200.00
J3   D1   3c black   250.00 250.00
J4   D1   4c black   250.00 250.00
J5   D1   5c black   250.00 250.00
J6   D1   10c black   250.00 250.00
J7   D1   15c black   250.00 250.00
J8   D1   20c black   200.00 200.00
J9   D1   30c black   250.00 250.00
J10 D1   40c black   250.00 250.00
J11 D1   60c black   250.00 250.00
J12 D1   1fr brown 550.00 550.00
J13 D1   2fr brown 550.00 550.00

Many values exist with inverted or double overprint.
Counterfeits exist of Nos. J1–J26.

Overprinted in Black, type "f".

1893
J14 D1   1c black   1,350. 1,350.
  a. Inverted ovpt. 1,500. 1,500.
J15 D1   2c black   325.00 325.00
J16 D1   3c black   325.00 325.00
J17 D1   4c black   325.00 325.00
J18 D1   5c black   325.00 325.00
J19 D1   10c black   325.00 325.00
J20 D1   15c black   325.00 325.00
J21 D1   20c black   200.00 200.00
J22 D1   30c black   325.00 325.00
J23 D1   40c black   325.00 325.00
J24 D1   60c black   325.00 325.00
J25 D1   1fr brown 325.00 325.00
J26 D1   2fr brown 325.00 325.00

Nos. J15–J20, J22–J26 exist with overprint inverted, double or both. Price, each $400.

TANNU TUVA
(tăn′nōō tōō·vä′)
(Tuva Autonomous Region.)

LOCATION — In the Tannu Mountains on the Siberian border in northwestern Mongolia.
GOVT.—A former republic closely identified with Soviet Russia in Asia.
AREA—64,000 sq. mi. (approx.).
POP.—65,000 (approx.).
CAPITAL—Kyzyl.

The status of this country which has been under both Chinese and Russian rule at various times, was settled in 1926 by a Mixed Claims Commission. As a republic, its independence was maintained under Soviet protection. Later it became part of the Soviet Union as the Tuva Autonomous Soviet Socialist Republic.

100 Kopecks = 1 Ruble

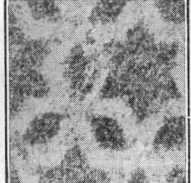

Wheel of Life
A1   Wmk. 204

TANNU TUVA—TETE—THAILAND

Wmkd. Stars and Diamonds. (204)
Size: 20x26mm.

1926 Typographed. *Perf. 13½.*
1	A1	1k red	1.10	1.10
2	A1	2k lt bl	1.10	1.10
3	A1	5k orange	1.10	1.10
4	A1	8k yel grn	1.10	1.10
5	A1	10k violet	1.10	1.10
6	A1	30k dk brn	1.10	1.10
7	A1	50k gray blk	2.25	2.25

Size: 22½x30mm.
Perf. 10½
8	A1	1r bl grn	6.50	5.50
9	A1	3r red brn	9.50	8.00
10	A1	5r dk ultra	13.00	11.00
		Nos. 1-10 (10)	37.85	33.35

Stamps of 1926
Surcharged in
Red or Black

A2

1927 *Perf. 13½, 11*
11	A2	8k on 50k gray blk (R)	12.50	11.00
12	A2	14k on 1r bl grn (R)	15.00	14.00
13	A2	18k on 3r red brn (Bk)	20.00	17.50
14	A2	28k on 5r dk ultra (Bk)	25.00	22.50

Nos. 11–14 exist with surcharge inverted and No. 14 with surcharge double. Price $30 each.

Reprints exist of Nos. 1-14.

Mongol Woman — A3
Map of Tannu Tuva — A8

Sheep Herding—A11

Fording a Stream
A13

Mongols Riding Reindeer—A16

Designs: 2k, Stag. 3k, Mountain goat. 4k, Mongol and tent. 5k, Mongol man. 10k, Bow-and-arrow hunters. 14k, Camel caravan. 28k, Landscape. 50k, Weaving. 70k, Mongol on horseback.

1927 Typo. *Perf. 12½, 12½x12*
15	A3	1k blk, lt brn & red	75	50
16	A3	2k pur, dp brn & grn	1.00	50
17	A3	3k blk, bl grn & yel	1.00	75
18	A3	4k vio bl & choc	1.00	50
19	A3	5k org, blk & dk bl	75	50
20	A8	8k ol brn, pale bl & red brn	1.50	1.25
21	A8	10k blk, grn & brn red	5.50	1.75
22	A8	14k vio bl & red org	14.00	8.50

Perf. 10, 10½
23	A11	18k dk bl & red brn	14.00	8.50
24	A11	28k emer & blk brn	8.00	2.75
25	A13	40k rose & bl grn	5.50	2.75
26	A13	50k blk, grn & red brn	5.50	3.25
27	A13	70k dl red & bis	6.50	5.50
28	A16	1r yel brn & vio	16.00	8.50
		Nos. 15-28 (14)	81.00	45.50

Stamps of 1927
Surcharged "Tuva", "Posta" and
New Values in Various Colors.

1932
29	A13	1k on 40k rose & bl grn (Bk)	11.00	11.00
30	A13	2k on 50k blk, grn & red brn (Br)	11.00	11.00
31	A13	3k on 70k dl red & bis (Bl)	11.00	11.00
a.		Invtd. surch.	400.00	
32	A8	5k on 8k ol brn, pale bl & red brn (Bk)	14.00	14.00
33	A8	10k on 8k grn & brn red (Bk)	14.00	14.00
34	A8	15k on 14k dk bl & org (Bk)	14.00	14.00
		Nos. 29-34 (6)	75.00	75.00

Issued in connection with the Romanization of the alphabet.

A17

A18

Wmkd.
Stars and Diamonds. (204)
1933 Black Surcharge.
35	A17	35k on 18k dk bl & red brn	165.00	150.00
36	A18	35k on 28k emer & blk brn	165.00	150.00

A19
Revenue Stamps
Surcharged "Posta" and New Values.
1933 *Perf. 12x12½*
37	A19	15k on 6k org	325.00	325.00
38	A19	35k on 15k brn	1,400.	1,400.

Various pictorial sets, perf. and imperf., of triangular, diamond, square and oblong shapes, inscribed, "Postage," "Air-Mail" and "Registered," appeared in 1934 and 1935. The editors do not consider them to have been issued primarily for postal purposes.

TETE
(tā'tĕ)

LOCATION—In southeastern Africa between Nyasaland and Southern Rhodesia.
GOVT.—A district of the Portuguese East Africa Colony.
AREA—46,600 sq. mi. (approx.).
POP.—367,000 (approx.).
CAPITAL—Tete.

This district was formerly a part of Zambezia. Stamps of Mozambique replaced those of Tete. See Mozambique.

100 Centavos = 1 Escudo

Vasco da Gama Issue of Various Portuguese Colonies Surcharged as
REPUBLICA
TETE
¼ C.

1913 *Perf. 12½, 16* Unwmkd.
On Stamps of Macao.
1	CD20	¼c on ½a bl grn	2.00	2.00
2	CD21	½c on 1a red	2.00	2.00
3	CD22	1c on 2a red vio	2.00	2.00
4	CD23	2½c on 4a yel grn	2.00	2.00
5	CD24	5c on 8a dk bl	2.00	2.00
6	CD25	7½c on 12a vio brn	3.00	3.00
7	CD26	10c on 16a bis brn	2.00	2.00
8	CD27	15c on 24a bis	2.00	2.00

On Stamps of Portuguese Africa.
9	CD20	¼c on 2½r bl grn	2.00	2.00
10	CD21	½c on 5r red	2.00	2.00
11	CD22	1c on 10r red vio	2.00	2.00
12	CD23	2½c on 25r yel grn	2.00	2.00
13	CD24	5c on 50r dk bl	2.00	2.00
14	CD25	7½c on 75r vio brn	3.00	3.00
15	CD26	10c on 100r bis brn	2.00	2.00
16	CD27	15c on 150r bis	2.00	2.00

On Stamps of Timor.
17	CD20	¼c on ½a bl grn	2.00	2.00
18	CD21	½c on 1a red	2.00	2.00
19	CD22	1c on 2a red vio	2.00	2.00
a.		Invtd. ovpt.	10.00	10.00
20	CD23	2½c on 4a yel grn	2.00	2.00
21	CD24	5c on 8a dk bl	2.00	2.00
22	CD25	7½c on 12a vio brn	3.00	3.00
23	CD26	10c on 16a bis brn	2.00	2.00
24	CD27	15c on 24a bis	2.00	2.00
		Nos. 1-24 (24)	51.00	51.00

Common Design Types
pictured in section at front of book.

Ceres
A1
1914 Typographed. *Perf. 15x14.*
Name and Value in Black.
25	A1	¼c ol brn	1.00	1.00
26	A1	½c black	1.00	1.00
27	A1	1c bl grn	75	75
28	A1	1½c lil brn	1.00	1.00
29	A1	2c carmine	1.00	1.00
30	A1	2½c lt vio	75	75
31	A1	5c dp bl	1.25	1.25
32	A1	7½c yel brn	2.00	2.00
33	A1	8c slate	2.50	2.50
34	A1	10c org brn	2.50	2.50
35	A1	15c plum	5.00	5.00
36	A1	20c yel grn	2.50	2.50
37	A1	30c brn, *grn*	3.00	3.00
38	A1	40c brn, *pink*	3.00	3.00
39	A1	50c org, *sal*	3.00	3.00
40	A1	1e grn, *bl*	3.50	3.50
		Nos. 25-40 (16)	33.75	33.75

Stamps of Tete were replaced by those of Mozambique.

THAILAND
(tī'land)
(Siam)
(sī.ăm'; sī'ăm)

LOCATION—Western part of the Malay peninsula in southeastern Asia.
GOVT.—Kingdom.
AREA—200,148 sq. mi.
POP.—44,160,000 (est. 1977).
CAPITAL—Bangkok.

32 Solot = 16 Atts = 8 Sio = 4 Sik
= 2 Fuang = 1 Salung
4 Salungs = 1 Tical
100 Satangs (1909) = 1 Tical
1 Baht (1912)

King Chulalongkorn
A1   A2

A4
Engraved.
1883 *Perf. 14½, 15* Unwmkd.
1	A1	1sol blue	1.50	1.75
a.		Pair, imperf. vert. or horiz.	200.00	200.00
b.		Imperf., pair	250.00	250.00
2	A1	1att carmine	1.75	1.50
3	A1	1sio vermilion	3.50	3.50
4	A2	1sik yellow	4.50	4.50
5	A4	1sa orange	6.50	5.50
		1sa ocner	7.50	6.50

There are three types of No. 1, differing mainly in the background of the small oval at the top.
A 1 fuang red, of similar design to the foregoing, was prepared but not placed in use.

THAILAND

No. 1 Surcharged in Red:

1 TICAL *a*

1 Tical *b*   **1 Tical** *c*

1 Tical *d*   **1 Tical** *e*

1885

6	A1 (a)	1t on 1 sol bl	225.00	225.00
7	A1 (b)	1t on 1 sol bl	200.00	200.00
a.	Double surcharge			
b.	Double surcharge, red and blk			
c.	"1" inverted		1,250.	1,250.
8	A1 (c)	1t on 1 sol bl	250.00	250.00
9	A1 (d)	1t on 1 sol bl	275.00	275.00
a.	Inverted surcharge			
b.	Double surcharge			
10	A1 (e)	1t on 1 sol bl	200.00	200.00
a.	Inverted surcharge			
b.	Double surcharge		400.00	400.00

Surcharges of Nos. 6–10 have been counterfeited.

King Chulalongkorn
A7   Wmk. 176
Wmkd. Chakra. (176)

1887-91   Typographed.   Perf. 14.

11	A7	1a grn ('91)	90	40
12	A7	2a grn & car	90	50
13	A7	3a grn & bl	1.75	75
14	A7	4a grn & org brn	2.25	1.50
15	A7	8a grn & yel	3.00	1.00
16	A7	12a lil & car	1.50	50
17	A7	24a lil & bl	1.50	60
18	A7	64a lil & org brn	15.00	4.50
	Nos. 11-18 (8)		26.80	9.75

The design of No. 11 has been redrawn and differs from the illustration in many minor details.

No. 3 Surcharged อั๋

1889   Perf. 15.   Unwmkd.

19	A1	1a on 1sio ver	3.00	3.00
a.	Double surcharge		175.00	200.00
b.	Pair, one without surcharge		175.00	
c.	Inverted surch.		300.00	

Nos. 12 and 13 Surcharged ๑ อั๋ 1

Wmkd. Chakra. (176)

1890   Perf. 14.

20	A7	1a on 2a grn & car	1.25	1.25
a.	"1" omitted		150.00	150.00
b.	Pair, one without surcharge		200.00	200.00
c.	First Siamese character inverted			
d.	First Siamese character omitted		175.00	175.00
21	A7	2a on 3a grn & bl	2.25	2.25
a.	Inverted "1"		110.00	110.00
b.	Thick "1"		85.00	

No. 21 exists with large "2" surcharged on top of "1." Price $125.

Surcharged ๑ อั๋ 1

22	A7	1a on 2a grn & car	20.00	17.50

Surcharged ๑ อั๋ 1

24	A7	1a on 2a grn & car	25.00	22.50
a.	Double surcharge			

Surcharged ๑ อั๋ 1

25	A7	1a on 2a grn & car	325.00	325.00

Surcharged ๑ อั๋ 1

26	A7	1a on 3a grn & bl	1,500.	1,250.

Surcharged ๒ อั๋ 2

27	A7	2a on 3a grn & bl	15.00	15.00

Surcharged ๒ อั๋ 2

28	A7	2a on 3a grn & bl	25.00	25.00
a.	Double surcharge		150.00	125.00
b.	"2" omitted		150.00	

Surcharged ๒ อั๋ 2

29	A7	2a on 3a grn & bl	8.00	8.00

Surcharged ๒ อั๋ 2

30	A7	2a on 3a grn & bl	40.00	40.00

Surcharged ๒ อั๋ 2

31	A7	2a on 3a grn & bl	400.00	400.00

No. 17 Handstamp Surcharged:

ราคา๔อั๋ *f*   ราคา๔อั๋ *g*

1892

33	A7 (f)	4a on 24a lil & bl	12.00	10.00
34	A7 (g)	4a on 24a lil & bl	12.00	10.00

Surcharges exist double on Nos. 33-34 and inverted on No. 33.

Stamps of 1887 Surcharged in Siamese and English.

1893-94

Surcharged **4 atts**

35	A7	4a on 24a lil & bl	3.50	3.00
a.	Siamese surcharge double		55.00	55.00
b.	Siamese surcharge omitted		65.00	65.00
c.	Inverted "s"		12.50	12.50
d.	Siamese surcharge inverted		60.00	60.00
e.	English surcharge double		100.00	100.00

Surcharged **4 atts.**

36	A7	4a on 24a lil & bl	5.00	4.00
a.	Inverted "s"		12.00	12.00
b.	Siamese surcharge double		35.00	35.00
c.	Siamese surcharge omitted		85.00	85.00

Surcharged **4 atts**

37	A7	4a on 24a lil & bl	6.00	4.75
a.	Siamese surcharge omitted		75.00	75.00
b.	Pair, one without English surch.			
c.	Siamese surcharge double		60.00	60.00

Surcharged **4 atts.**

38	A7	4a on 24a lil & bl	4.00	4.00
a.	English surcharge double		60.00	60.00
b.	Siamese surcharge double		25.00	25.00
c.	Siamese surcharge omitted		75.00	75.00

1894

Surcharged **1 Atts**

39	A7	1a on 64a lil & org brn	1.50	1.50
a.	Inverted "s"		7.50	7.50
b.	Inverted surch.		50.00	50.00
d.	Italic "s"		7.50	7.50
e.	Italic "1"		7.50	7.50

Surcharged **1 Att.**

40	A7	1a on 64a lil & org brn	75	75
	Inverted capital "S" added to the surcharge		50.00	50.00

Surcharged:

2 Atts. *h*   **2 Atts.** *i*

2 Atts. *j*   **2 Atts.** *k*

2. Atts. *l*   **2 Atts.** *m*

41	A7 (h)	2a on 64a lil & org brn	1.50	1.50
a.	Inverted "s"		7.50	7.50
b.	Double surchage		60.00	60.00
42	A7 (i)	2a on 64a lil & org brn	600.00	600.00
43	A7 (j)	2a on 64a lil & org brn	7.50	6.50
44	A7 (k)	2a on 64a lil & org brn	2.50	2.50
45	A7 (l)	2a on 64a lil & org brn	5.00	5.00
46	A7 (m)	2a on 64a lil & org brn	1.00	75
a.	"Att.s"		17.50	17.50

1895

Surcharged **1 Att.**

47	A7	1a on 64a lil & org brn	85	75
a.	Surcharged on face and back		35.00	
b.	Surcharge on back inverted		50.00	
c.	Double surcharge		90.00	
d.	Invtd. surchage		100.00	
e.	Siamese surcharge omitted		75.00	

Surcharged **2 Atts.**

48	A7	2a on 64a lil & org brn	75	60
a.	"Att"		15.00	12.00
b.	Inverted surcharge		60.00	60.00
c.	Surcharged on face and back		30.00	30.00
d.	Surcharge on back inverted		30.00	30.00
e.	Double surcharge		45.00	45.00
f.	Double surcharge, one inverted		45.00	45.00
g.	Inverted "s"		10.00	10.00

1895   Surcharged **10 Atts.**

49	A7	10a on 24a lil & bl	90	75
a.	Inverted "s"		10.00	10.00
b.	Surcharged on face and back		70.00	70.00
c.	Surcharge on back inverted		60.00	60.00

1896   Surcharged **4 Atts.**

50	A7	4a on 12a lil & car	4.00	1.25
a.	Inverted "s"		22.50	17.50
b.	Surcharged on face and back		45.00	45.00
c.	Double surcharge on back		70.00	70.00

Antique Surcharges

1 Atts. *a*   **1 Att.** *b*   **2 Atts.** *c*

3 Atts. *d*   **4 Atts.** *e*   **10 Atts** *f*

1896-99

51	A7 (a)	1a on 12a lil & car	75.00	75.00
52	A7 (b)	1a on 12a lil & car	6.00	5.00
53	A7 (c)	2a on 64a lil & org brn	15.00	6.00
a.	Dbl. surch.		125.00	125.00
54	A7 (d)	3a on 12a lil & car	2.50	1.75
a.	Double surcharge		150.00	150.00
55	A7 (e)	4a on 12a lil & car	5.00	1.00
a.	Double surcharge		60.00	60.00
56	A7 (e)	4a on 24a lil & bl	10.00	5.00
57	A7 (f)	10a on 24a lil & bl	225.00	225.00

Roman Surcharges:

1 Atts. *g*   **1 Att.** *h*   **2 Atts.** *i*

3 Atts. *j*   **4 Atts.** *k*   **10 Atts.** *l*

58	A7 (g)	1a on 12a lil & car	75.00	75.00
59	A7 (h)	1a on 12a lil & car	10.00	10.00
60	A7 (i)	2a on 64a lil & org brn	9.00	9.00
61	A7 (j)	3a on 12a lil & car	10.00	10.00
62	A7 (k)	4a on 12a lil & car	4.00	2.00
a.	Double surcharge		50.00	50.00
b.	No period after "Atts."		12.50	12.50
63	A7 (k)	4a on 24a lil & bl	12.50	7.50
64	A7 (l)	10a on 24a lil & bl	300.00	300.00

In making the settings to surcharge Nos. 51 to 64 two fonts were mixed. Antique and Roman letters are frequently found on the same stamp.

Surcharged:

1 Att. *m*   **1 Att.** *n*

1 Att. *o*

2 Atts. *p*   **2 Atts.** *r*

1899

65	A7 (m)	1a on 12a lil & car	4.00	3.50
66	A7 (n)	1a on 12a lil & car	7.50	5.00
a.	Inverted "1"		75.00	75.00
b.	Inverted "t"		75.00	75.00
67	A7 (o)	1a on 64a lil & org brn	1.50	1.50

THAILAND

68	A7 (p)	2a on 64a lil & org brn	10.00	6.00
a.		"1Atts."	150.00	150.00
69	A7 (r)	2a on 64a lil & org brn	7.25	4.25

A13   A14

1899   Typographed.   Unwmkd.

70	A13	1a dl grn	75.00	60.00
71	A13	2a dl grn & rose	90.00	65.00
72	A13	3a car & bl	200.00	150.00
73	A13	4a blk & grn	350.00	250.00
74	A13	10a car & grn	500.00	350.00
		Nos. 70-74 (5)	1,215.	875.00

The King rejected Nos. 70-74 in 1897, but some were released by mistake to three post offices in October, 1899. Used prices are for copies canceled to order at Korat in December, 1899. Postally used examples sell for more.

1899-04

75	A14	1a gray grn	50	30
76	A14	2a yel grn	50	25
77	A14	2a scar & bl ('04)	90	40
78	A14	3a red & bl	1.50	50
79	A14	3a grn ('04)	3.00	3.00
80	A14	4a dk rose	1.00	30
81	A14	4a vio brn & rose ('04)	1.50	60
82	A14	6a dk rose ('04)	2.25	2.00
83	A14	8a dk grn & org	1.50	35
84	A14	10a ultra	3.50	35
85	A14	12a brn vio & rose	4.00	35
86	A14	14a ultra ('04)	6.00	4.50
87	A14	24a brn vio & bl	8.00	2.00
88	A14	28a vio brn & bl ('04)	7.00	5.00
89	A14	64a brn vio & org brn	9.00	2.25
		Nos. 75-89 (15)	50.15	22.15

Two types of 1a differ in size and shape of Thai "1" and in drawing of spandrel ornaments.

Nos. 78 and 85 Surcharged With 6 or 7 Siamese Characters (1 line) in Violet

1902   Typewritten

78a	A14	2a on 3a red & bl	650.00	650.00
85a	A14	10a on 12a brn vio & rose	700.00	750.00

Nos. 78a and 85a were authorized provisionals, surcharged and issued by the Battambang postmaster.

1 Att.

Nos. 86 and 88 Surcharged in Black

1905

90	A14	1a on 14a ultra	1.00	85
a.		No period after "Att"	9.00	9.00
91	A14	2a on 28a vio brn & bl	1.35	1.25
a.		Double surcharge	75.00	75.00

King Chulalongkorn
A15   A16

1905-08   Engraved.

92	A15	1a org & grn	50	15
93	A15	2a vio & sl	50	15
94	A15	2a grn ('08)	1.25	40
95	A15	3a green	75	35
96	A15	3a vio & sl ('08)	1.75	60
97	A15	4a gray & red	1.00	15
98	A15	4a car & rose ('08)	1.25	20
99	A15	5a car & rose	1.00	85
100	A15	8a blk & ol bis	1.25	20
101	A15	9a bl ('08)	2.50	90
102	A15	12a blue	1.50	35
103	A15	18a red brn ('08)	8.50	2.50
104	A15	24a red brn	3.00	1.00
105	A15	1t dp bl & brn org	6.00	50
		Nos. 92-105 (14)	30.75	8.30

1907   Black Surcharge.

106	A16	10t gray grn	300.00	90.00
107	A16	20t gray grn	850.00	110.00
108	A16	40t gray grn	750.00	175.00

Counterfeits of Nos. 106-108 exist. In the genuine, the surcharged figures correspond to the Siamese value inscriptions on the basic revenue stamps.

No. 17 Surcharged   **1 att.**

1908

109	A7	1a on 24a lil & bl	60	40
a.		Double surcharge	85.00	85.00

No. 99 Surcharged   **4**

| 110 | A15 | 4a on 5a car & rose | 2.00 | 1.75 |

The No. 110 surcharge is found in two spacings of the numerals: normally 15mm. apart, and a narrow, scarcer spacing of 13½mm.

Nos. 17 and 84 Surcharged in Black:

2 Atts.   9 Atts
      a   b

111	A7	2a on 24a lil & bl	90	75
a.		Inverted surcharge	65.00	65.00
112	A14	9a on 10a ultra	2.50	2.25
a.		Inverted surcharge	85.00	85.00

Jubilee Issue.

รัชมังคลา
ภิเศก
๔๗-๑๒๗.

Stamps of 1906-08 Overprinted in Black or Red

Jubilee 1868-1908

1908, Nov. 11

113	A15	1a org & grn	1.50	1.00
a.		Siamese date "137" instead of "127"	350.00	350.00
b.		Pair, one without ovpt.		
114	A15	3a green	2.00	1.25
115	A15	4a on 5a car & rose	3.50	1.50
a.		Horizontal pair, imperf. between	350.00	
116	A15	8a blk & ol bis (R)	10.00	10.00
117	A15	18a red brn	9.00	8.00
		Nos. 113-117 (5)	26.00	21.75

This issue was in commemoration of the fortieth year of the reign of King Chulalongkorn.

Nos. 113 to 117 exist with a small "i" in "Jubilee."

Statue of King Chulalongkorn
A19

1908   Engraved.   Perf. 13½.

118	A19	1t grn & vio	6.00	75
119	A19	2t red vio & org	7.00	1.75
120	A19	3t pale ol & bl	9.00	2.00
121	A19	5t dl vio & dk grn	17.50	3.00
122	A19	10t bis & car	75.00	15.00
123	A19	20t gray & red brn	100.00	17.50
124	A19	40t sl bl & blk brn	200.00	40.00
		Nos. 118-124 (7)	414.50	80.00

The inscription at the foot of the stamps reads: "Coronation Commemoration—Forty-first year of the reign—1908."

๖ สตางค์
Stamps of 1887-1904 Surcharged   **6 Satang**

1909-10   Perf. 14.

125	A14	6s on 6a dk rose	2.25	1.50
126	A7	14s on 12a lil & car	40.00	40.00
127	A14	14s on 14a ultra	6.00	6.00

Stamps of 1905-08 Surcharged   ๒ สตางค์   **2 Satang and Bar.**

128	A15	2s on 1a org & grn	35	15
129	A15	2s on 2a vio & sl	70.00	80.00
130	A15	2s on 2a grn	35	20
a.		"2" omitted	60.00	
131	A15	3s on 3a grn	85	50
a.		Siamese numeral inverted	85.00	
132	A15	3s on 3a vio & sl	35	25
133	A15	6s on 4a gray & red	7.00	6.50
a.		"6" omitted	85.00	
134	A15	6s on 4a car & rose	40	20
a.		"6" omitted	60.00	
135	A15	6s on 5a car & rose	75	45
136	A15	12s on 8a blk & ol bis	75	30
137	A15	14s on 9a bl	75	15
138	A15	14s on 12a bl	25.00	25.00
		Nos. 125-138 (14)	154.80	161.20

King Chulalongkorn
A20

1910   Engraved   Perf. 14x14½

139	A20	2s org & grn	30	15
140	A20	3s green	40	15
141	A20	6s carmine	40	15
142	A20	12s blk & ol bis	60	15
143	A20	14s blue	90	30
144	A20	28s red brn	2.00	90
		Nos. 139-144 (6)	4.60	1.80

King Vajiravudh
A21   A22

Printed at the Imperial Printing Works, Vienna.

1912   Perf. 14½.

145	A21	2s brn org	20	8
a.		Vertical pair, imperf. between	85.00	85.00
b.		Horiz. pair, imperf. between	85.00	85.00
146	A21	3s yel grn	40	8
a.		Horizontal pair, imperf. between	85.00	85.00
147	A21	6s car rose	60	20
148	A21	12s gray blk & brn	1.00	25
149	A21	14s ultra	1.50	30
150	A21	28s chocolate	2.50	1.00
151	A22	1b bl & blk	4.50	35
a.		Pair, imperf. between	125.00	150.00
152	A22	2b car rose & ol brn	10.00	60
153	A22	3b yel grn & bl blk	11.00	75
154	A22	5b vio & blk	14.00	1.00
155	A22	10b ol grn & vio brn	65.00	15.00
156	A22	20b sl bl & red brn	100.00	12.50
		Nos. 145-156 (12)	210.70	32.11

See also Nos. 164-175.

Nos. 147–150 Surcharged in Red or Blue

๕ สตางค์
5 Satang

1914-15

157	A21	2s on 14s ultra (R)	60	15
a.		Vertical pair, imperf. between	75.00	75.00
b.		Double surch.	50.00	
158	A21	5s on 6s car rose (Bl)	60	15
a.		Horizontal pair, imperf. between	85.00	75.00
b.		Double surch.	80.00	
159	A21	10s on 12s gray blk & brn (R)	75	15
a.		Double surch.	100.00	80.00
160	A21	15s on 28s choc (Bl)	1.10	15

The several settings of the surcharges on Nos. 157 to 160 show variations in the figures and letters.

Nos. 92–93 Surcharged   ๒ สตางค์   **2 Satang**

1915

161	A15	2s on 1a org & grn	85	50
a.		Pair, one without surch.	75.00	75.00
162	A15	2s on 2a vio & sl	85	50

No. 143 Surcharged in Red   ๒ สตางค์   **2 Satang**

1916

| 163 | A20 | 2s on 14s bl | 85 | 50 |

Printed by Waterlow & Sons, London. Types of 1912 Re-engraved.

1917   Perf. 14.

164	A21	2s org brn	25	10
165	A21	3s emerald	25	10
a.		Vert. pair, imperf. between	75.00	75.00
b.		Horiz. pair, imperf. between	150.00	115.00

THAILAND

721

166	A21	5s rose red	35	15
167	A21	10s blk & ol	50	15
168	A21	15s blue	75	15
170	A22	1b bl & gray blk	17.50	1.00
171	A22	2b car rose & brn	22.50	3.50
172	A22	3b yel grn & blk	75.00	60.00
173	A22	5b dp vio & blk	35.00	10.00
174	A22	10b ol gray & vio brn	75.00	4.00
a.		Perf. 12½	300.00	40.00
175		20b sea grn & brn	125.00	20.00
a.		Perf. 12½	325.00	45.00
		Nos. 164-175 (11)	352.10	99.15

The re-engraved design of the satang stamps varies in numerous minute details from the 1912 issue. Four lines of the background appear between the vertical strokes of the "M" of "SIAM" in the 1912 issue and only three lines in the 1917 issue.
The 1912 stamps with value in bahts are 37½ mm. high; those of 1917 are 39 mm. In the latter the king's features, especially the eyes and mouth, are more distinct and the uniform and decorations are more sharply defined.
The 1912 stamps have seven pearls between the earpieces of the crown. On the 1917 stamps there are nine pearls in the same place.
Nos. 174 and 175 exist imperforate.

Nos. 164-173
Overprinted in Red วันชัย VICTORY

1918

176	A21	2s org brn	40	35
a.		Double ovpt.	70.00	
177	A21	3s emerald	40	35
178	A21	5s rose red	45	45
a.		Double ovpt.	70.00	
179	A21	10s blk & ol	1.75	1.50
180	A21	15s blue	2.00	1.75
181	A22	1b bl & gray blk	12.50	12.00
182	A22	2b car rose & brn	20.00	20.00
183	A22	3b yel grn & blk	25.00	25.00
184	A22	5b dp vio & blk	50.00	50.00
		Nos. 176-184 (9)	112.50	111.40

Counterfeits of this overprint exist.

Nos. 147-148 Surcharged in Green or Red

1919

185	A21	5s on 6s car rose (G)	1.00	25
186	A21	10s on 12s gray blk & brn (R)	1.00	25

King Vajiravudh
A24

1920-26 Engr. Perf. 14-15, 12½

187	A23	2s brn, yel	35	15
188	A23	3s grn, grn	70	18
189	A23	3s choc ('24)	85	15
190	A23	5s rose, pale rose	65	12
191	A23	5s grn ('22)	3.50	30
192	A23	5s dk vio, lil ('26)	65	15
193	A23	10s blk & org	1.25	15
194	A23	15s bl, bluish	1.75	30
195	A23	15s car ('22)	2.50	60
196	A23	25s chocolate	3.75	60
197	A23	25s dk bl ('22)	2.50	60
198	A23	50s ocher & blk	7.50	60
		Nos. 187-198 (12)	25.95	3.90

1926 Perf. 12½

199	A24	1t gray vio & grn	5.00	60
200	A24	2t car & org red	15.00	3.00
201	A24	3t ol grn & bl	30.00	15.00
202	A24	5t dl vio & ol grn	17.50	5.50
203	A24	10t red & ol bis	150.00	10.00
204	A24	20t gray bl & brn	125.00	30.00
		Nos. 199-204 (6)	342.50	64.10

This issue was intended to commemorate the fifteenth year of the reign of King Vajiravudh. Because of the King's death the stamps were issued as ordinary postage stamps.

Nos. 195 and 150
with Surcharge similar to 1914-15 Issue
in Black or Red

1928

205	A23	5s on 15s car	3.50	75
206	A21	10s on 28s choc (R)	3.50	75

King Prajadhipok
A25 A26

1928 Engraved. Perf. 12½

207	A25	2s dp red brn	15	10
a.		Booklet pane of 4	150.00	
208	A25	3s dp grn	15	10
a.		Booklet pane of 4	150.00	
209	A25	5s dk vio	15	10
a.		Booklet pane of 4	175.00	
210	A25	10s dp rose	20	10
a.		Booklet pane of 4	175.00	
211	A25	15s dk bl	25	12
212	A25	25s blk & org	40	12
213	A25	50s brn org & blk	75	15
214	A25	80s bl & blk	1.10	35
215	A26	1b dk bl & blk	1.40	35
216	A26	2b car rose & blk brn	3.00	75
217	A26	3b yel grn & blk	5.00	1.00
218	A26	5b dp vio & gray blk	13.50	2.00
219	A26	10b ol grn & red vio	18.50	2.75
220	A26	20b Prus grn & brn	30.00	4.50
221	A26	40b dk grn & ol brn	65.00	20.00
		Nos. 207-222 (15)	139.55	32.49

On the single colored stamps, type A25, the lines in the background are uniform; those of the bicolored values are shaded and do not extend to the frame.

Nos. 142, 144
Surcharged
in Red or Blue

๒๕ สตางค์
25 SATANG

1930 Perf. 14

223	A20	10s on 12s blk & ol brn (R)	45	25
224	A20	25s on 28s red brn (Bl)	90	25

King Prajadhipok and
Chao P'ya Chakri
A27 A28

A29

1932 Engraved Perf. 12½

225	A27	2s dk brn	75	10
226	A27	3s dp grn	1.10	20
227	A27	5s dl vio	1.10	20
228	A29	10s red brn & blk	1.50	25
229	A29	15s dl bl & blk	3.25	25
230	A29	25s vio & blk	4.00	40
231	A29	50s cl & blk	7.25	1.10
232	A28	1b bl blk	22.50	2.50
		Nos. 225-232 (8)	41.45	5.00

This issue commemorates the 150th anniversary of the Chakri dynasty, the founding of Bangkok in 1782, and the opening of the memorial bridge across the Chao Phraya River.

Assembly Hall, Bangkok
A30

Lithographed.

1939 Perf. 11, 12. Unwmkd.

233	A30	2s dl red brn	60	15
234	A30	3s green	1.25	35
235	A30	5s dk vio	1.25	15
236	A30	10s carmine	2.00	60
237	A30	15s dk bl	4.00	60
		Nos. 233-237 (5)	9.10	1.50

Issued in commemoration of the 7th anniversary of the Siamese Constitution.

Chakri Palace,
Bangkok
A31

1940 Typographed Perf. 12½

238	A31	2s dl brn	60	15
239	A31	3s dp yel grn	75	20
a.		Cliché of 5s in plate of 3s	350.00	300.00
240	A31	5s dk vio	1.00	15
241	A31	10s carmine	1.75	20
242	A31	15s dk bl	2.50	50
		Nos. 238-242 (5)	6.60	1.20

King Ananda   Plowing
Mahidol   Rice Field
A32   A33

Royal Pavilion   King Ananda
at Bang-pa-in   Mahidol
A34   A35

1941 Engraved

243	A32	2s brown	20	12
244	A32	3s dp grn	20	12
245	A32	5s violet	20	10
246	A32	10s dk red	20	12
247	A33	15s dp bl & gray blk	50	15
248	A33	25s sl & org	75	35
249	A33	50s red org & gray	85	35
250	A34	1b brt ultra & gray	2.25	40
251	A34	2b dk car rose & gray	4.00	50
252	A34	3b dp grn & gray	5.00	1.00
253	A34	5b blk & rose red	10.00	2.00
a.		Horiz. pair, imperf. between	40.00	
254	A34	10b ol blk & yel	20.00	5.00
		Nos. 243-254 (12)	44.15	10.21

1943 Perf. 11. Unwmkd.

255	A35	1b dk bl	2.25	1.00

See also No. 274.

Indo-China   Bangkhaen
War Monument   Monument
A36   A37

1943 Engraved Perf. 11, 12½

256	A36	3s dk grn	2.50	1.50

Lithographed.
Perf. 12½x11

257	A36	3s dl grn	2.00	1.50

1943, Nov. 25 Perf. 12½, 12½x11

Two types of 10s:
 I. Size 19.5x24mm.
 II. Size 20.75x25.25mm.

258	A37	2s brn org	1.00	30
259	A37	10s car rose (I)	1.10	30
a.		Type II		25

Issued to commemorate the 10th anniversary of the quelling of a counter-revolution led by a member of the royal family on October 11, 1933.
Stamps of similar design, but with values in "cents", are listed in Volume I under Malaya, Occupation Stamps.

King Bhumibol Adulyadej
A38   A39

1947-48 Pin-perf. 12½x11

260	A38	5s orange	1.75	50
261	A38	10s lt brn	1.50	50
a.		10s ol ('48)	1.00	
262	A38	20s blue	1.50	40
263	A38	50s bl grn	1.50	40

Coming of age of King Bhumibol Adulyadej.

Engraved.

1947-49 Perf. 12½ Unwmkd.
Size: 20x25mm.

264	A39	5s violet	15	5
265	A39	10s red ('49)	20	5
266	A39	20s chocolate	35	5
267	A39	50s ol ('49)	60	6

1948 Size: 22x27 mm.

268	A39	1b vio & dp bl	1.25	15
269	A39	2b ultra & grn	2.00	25
270	A39	3b brn red & blk	3.50	30
271	A39	5b bl grn & brn red	6.00	35
272	A39	10b dk brn & pur	9.00	65
273	A39	20b blk & rose brn	17.50	1.25
		Nos. 264-273 (10)	40.55	3.16

THAILAND

Type of 1943.
1948 Litho. Perf. 11½, 12½x11½
274	A35	1b chlky bl	2.75	1.25
a.		Pair, imperf. btwn.	40.00	40.00

King Bhumibol Adulyadej and Palace
A40   A41

Engraved.
1950, May 5 Perf. 12½ Unwmkd.
275	A40	5s red vio	15	6
276	A40	10s red	20	5
277	A40	15s purple	30	5
278	A40	20s chocolate	40	5
279	A40	80s green	60	30
280	A40	1b dp bl	75	12
281	A40	2b org yel	1.50	50
282	A40	3b gray	3.00	60
		Nos. 275-282 (8)	6.90	1.73

Coronation of Bhumibol Adulyadej as Rama IX, May 5, 1950.

1951-60 Perf. 12½, 13x12½
283	A41	5s rose lil	15	10
284	A41	10s dp grn	15	10
285	A41	15s red brn ('52)	15	10
285A	A41	20s choc ('60)	20	10
286	A41	25s carmine	20	10
287	A41	50s gray ol ('56)	30	10
288	A41	1b dp bl	60	12
289	A41	1.15b dp bl ('53)	1.25	30
290	A41	1.25b org brn ('54)	1.00	20
291	A41	2b dl bl grn	1.00	15
292	A41	3b gray	2.00	15
293	A41	5b aqua & red ('55)	2.25	25
294	A41	10b blk brn & vio ('55)	7.50	30
295	A41	20b gry & ol ('55)	22.50	1.00
		Nos. 283-295 (14)	39.25	3.07

United Nations Emblem
A42

1951
296	A42	25s ultra	1.50	1.25

Issued to publicize United Nations Day, Oct. 24, 1951.

Overprinted "1952" in Carmine.
1952
297	A42	25s ultra	1.50	1.00

Overprinted "1953" in Carmine.
1953
298	A42	25s ultra	75	70

Overprinted "1954" in Carmine.
1954
299	A42	25s ultra	75	75

See also Nos. 315 and 320.

Nos. 209 and 210 Overprinted in Black

1955, Jan. 4 Perf. 12½
300	A25	5s dk vio	90	70
301	A25	10s dp rose	90	70

No. 266 Surcharged with New Value in Black or Carmine
302	A39	5s on 20s choc	70	20
303	A39	10s on 20s choc (C)	70	20

King Naresuan on War Elephant
A43

Engraved.
1955, Feb. 15 Perf. 13½ Unwmkd.
304	A43	25s brt car	75	15
305	A43	80s rose vio	1.75	15
306	A43	1.25b dk ol grn	2.50	25
307	A43	2b dp bl	3.50	35
308	A43	3b hn brn	5.00	60
		Nos. 304-308 (5)	13.50	1.50

Issued to commemorate the 400th anniversary of the birth of King Naresuan (1555-1605).

Tao Suranari
A44

1955, Apr. 15 Perf. 12x13½
309	A44	10s purple	20	10
310	A44	25s emerald	50	12
311	A44	1b brown	1.25	30

Issued to honor the memory of Lady Mo, called Tao Suranari (Brave Woman) for her role in stopping an 1826 rebellion.

King Taksin Statue at Thonburi
A45

Don Jedi Monument
A46

1955, May 1 Perf. 12½x12
312	A45	5s vio bl	20	10
313	A45	25s Prus grn	30	10
314	A45	1.25b red	1.00	35

Issued to honor King Somdech P'ya Chao Taksin (1734-1782).

No. 296 Overprinted "1955" in Red.
1955, Oct. 24 Perf. 12½
315	A42	25s ultra	60	40

United Nations Day, Oct. 24, 1955.

1956, Feb. 1 Perf. 13½x13
316	A46	10s emerald	20	10
317	A46	50s redsh brn	50	10
318	A46	75s violet	75	20
319	A46	1.50b brn org	1.25	30

No. 296 Overprinted "1956" in Red Violet
1956, Oct. 24
320	A42	25s ultra	60	35

United Nations Day, Oct. 24, 1956.

Dharmachakra and Deer
A47

Wmk. 329

Designs: 20s, 25s, 50s, Hand of peace and Dharmachakra. 1b, 1.25b, 2b, Pagoda of Nakon Phatom.

Wmkd. Zigzag Lines. (329)
1957, May 13 Photo. Perf. 13½
321	A47	5s dk brn	10	6
322	A47	10s rose lake	15	6
323	A47	15s brt grn	30	7
324	A47	20s orange	30	7
325	A47	25s redsh brn	35	8
326	A47	50s magenta	50	10
327	A47	1b ol brn	90	25
328	A47	1.25b sl bl	1.00	35
329	A47	2b dp cl	1.50	50
		Nos. 321-329 (9)	5.10	1.54

2500th anniversary of birth of Buddha.

U.N. Emblem
A48

Thai Archway
A49

1957, Oct. 24 Perf. 13½
330	A48	25s olive	30	15

United Nations Day, Oct. 24, 1957.

1958, Oct. 24
331	A48	25s brt ocher	25	15

United Nations Day, Oct. 24, 1958.

1959
332	A48	25s indigo	25	15

United Nations Day, Oct. 24, 1959.

1959 Photogravure Perf. 13½
Designs (inscribed "SEAP Games 1959"): 25s, Royal tiered umbrellas. 1.25b, Thai archer, ancient costume. 2b, Wat Arun pagoda and prow of royal barge.
333	A49	10s orange	10	10
334	A49	25s dk car rose	30	10
335	A49	1.25b brt grn	75	30
336	A49	2b lt bl	90	30

Issued to publicize the South-East Asia Peninsula Games, Bangkok, Dec. 12-17.

Wat Arun, WRY Emblem
A50

Wat Arun, Bangkok
A51

1960
337	A50	50s chocolate	45	20
338	A50	2b yel grn	75	40

Issued to publicize World Refugee Year, July 1, 1959-June 30, 1960.

1960 Perf. 13½ Wmk. 329
339	A51	50s car rose	30	15
340	A51	2b ultra	75	45

Anti-leprosy campaign.

Elephants in Teak Forest
A52

Globe and SEATO Emblem
A53

1960 Photogravure Perf. 13½
341	A52	25s emerald	30	12

Issued to commemorate the Fifth World Forestry Congress, Seattle, Washington, Aug. 29-Sept. 10.

1960
342	A53	50s chocolate	30	10

Issued to publicize SEATO Day, Sept. 8 (South-East Asia Treaty Organization).

Siamese Child
A54

Hand with Pen and Globe
A55

1960 Wmk. 329
343	A54	50s magenta	30	10
344	A54	1b orange	60	30

Issued for Children's Day, 1960.

1960
345	A55	50s car rose	30	10
346	A55	2b blue	75	40

Issued for International Letter Writing Week, Oct. 3-9, 1960.

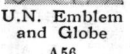

U.N. Emblem and Globe
A56

King Bhumibol Adulyadej
A57

1960 Perf. 13½
347	A56	50s purple	40	15

15th anniversary of the United Nations. See also Nos. 369, 390.

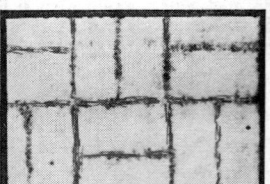

Wmk. 334

Wmkd. Rectangles (334)
1961-68 Engraved Perf. 13½x13
348	A57	5s rose cl ('62)	10	5
349	A57	10s grn ('62)	10	5
350	A57	15s red brn ('62)	10	5
351	A57	20s brn ('62)	10	5
352	A57	25s car ('63)	10	5

THAILAND

353	A57	50s ol ('62)	10	5
354	A57	80s org ('62)	25	6
355	A57	1b vio bl & brn	30	6
355A	A57	1.25b red & cit ('65)	30	6
356	A57	1.50b dk vio & yel grn	40	12
357	A57	2b red & vio	45	20
358	A57	3b brn & bl	75	20
358A	A57	4b ol bis & blk ('68)	90	40
359	A57	5b bl & grn	1.00	50
360	A57	10b red org & blk	3.00	65
361	A57	20b emer & ultra	5.00	1.25
362	A57	25b grn & bl	6.00	2.00
362A	A57	40b yel & blk ('65)	10.00	3.50
		Nos. 348-362A (18)	28.95	9.30

Children in Garden
A58

Pen and Envelope with Map
A59

Photogravure

1961, Oct. 2 Perf. 13½ Wmk. 329

363	A58	20s indigo	20	8
364	A58	2b purple	85	30

Issued for Children's Day.

1961, Oct. 9

Design: 1b, 2b, Pen and letters circling globe.

365	A59	25s gray grn	10	5
366	A59	50s rose lil	20	12
367	A59	1b brt rose	35	15
368	A59	2b ultra	75	35

Issued for International Letter Writing Week, Oct. 2–8.

U.N. Type of 1960.

1961, Oct. 24 Perf. 13½ Wmk. 329

369	A56	50s maroon	30	12

Issued for United Nations Day, Oct. 24.

Scout Emblem
A60

Scouts Saluting and Tents
A61

Design: 2b, King Vajiravudh and Scouts.

1961, Nov. 1 Photogravure

370	A60	50s car rose	35	15
371	A61	1b brt grn	50	20
372	A61	2b brt bl	1.25	45

Thai Boy Scouts, 50th anniversary.

Malaria Eradication Emblem and Siamese Designs
A62   A63

1962, Apr. 7 Perf. 13 Wmk. 329

373	A62	5s org brn	5	5
374	A62	10s sepia	5	5
375	A62	20s blue	10	5
376	A62	50s car rose	20	6
377	A63	1b green	35	12
378	A63	1.50b dk car rose	50	15
379	A63	2b dk bl	90	25
380	A63	3b violet	1.10	40
		Nos. 373-380 (8)	3.25	1.13

Issued for the World Health Organization drive to eradicate malaria.

View of Bangkok and Seattle Fair Emblem
A64

1962 Perf. 13 Wmk. 329

381	A64	50s red lil	25	15
382	A64	2b dp bl	85	40

Issued to publicize the "Century 21" International Exposition, Seattle, Wash., Apr. 21–Oct. 12.

Mother and Child
A65

Globe, Letters, Carrier Pigeons
A66

Photogravure

1962, Oct. 1 Perf. 13 Wmk. 329

383	A65	25s lt bl grn	15	5
384	A65	50s bis brn	20	15
385	A65	2b brt pink	75	30

Issued for Children's Day.

1962, Oct. 8

Design: 1b, 2b, Quill pen and scroll.

386	A66	25s violet	15	5
387	A66	50s red	20	8
388	A66	1b lemon	30	20
389	A66	2b lt bluish grn	60	10

Issued for International Letter Writing Week, Oct. 7–13.

U.N. Type of 1960

1962, Oct. 24 Perf. 13½

390	A56	50s car rose	25	12

United Nations Day, Oct. 24.

Exhibition Emblem
A67

Temple Lion
A69

Woman Harvesting Rice
A68

1962 Unwmkd.

391	A67	50s ol bis	25	12

Students' Exhibition, Bangkok.

Engraved

1963, Mar. 21 Perf. 14 Wmk. 334

392	A68	20s green	20	8
393	A68	50s ocher	35	15

Issued for the "Freedom from Hunger" campaign of the U.N. Food and Agriculture Organization.

1963, Apr. 1 Perf. 13½ Wmk. 329

394	A69	50s grn & bis	25	10

Issued to commemorate the first anniversary of the formation of the Asian-Oceanic Postal Union, AOPU.

New and Old Post and Telegraph Buildings—A70

Engraved

1963, Aug. 4 Perf. 14 Wmk. 334

395	A70	50s org, bluish blk & grn	25	10
396	A70	3b grn, dk red & brn	1.10	40

Issued to commemorate the 80th anniversary of the Post and Telegraph Department.

King Bhumibol Adulyadej
A71

Child with Dolls
A72

Photogravure

1963-71 Perf. 13x13½ Wmk. 329

397	A71	5s dk car rose	5	5
398	A71	10s dk grn	5	5
399	A71	15s red brn	5	5
400	A71	20s blk brn	5	5
401	A71	25s carmine	5	5
402	A71	50s ol gray	10	5
402A	A71	75s brt vio ('71)	25	10
403	A71	80s dl org	15	6
404	A71	1b dk bl & dk brn	30	8
404A	A71	1.25b org brn & ol ('65)	30	15
405	A71	1.50b vio bl & grn	35	10
406	A71	2b dk red & vio	40	15
407	A71	3b brn & dk bl	60	18
407A	A71	4b dp bis & blk ('68)	90	35
408	A71	5b bl & grn	1.25	30
409	A71	10b org & blk	2.25	45
410	A71	20b brt grn & ind	6.00	80
411	A71	25b dk grn & bl	6.00	1.00
411A	A71	40b yel & blk ('65)	12.50	2.25
		Nos. 397-411A (19)	31.60	6.27

Nos. 397-403 were issued in 1963; Nos. 404, 405-407, 408-411 in 1964.

1963, Oct. 7 Litho. Perf. 13½

412	A72	50s rose red	20	8
413	A72	2b dl bl	55	30

Issued for Children's Day.

Garuda Carrying Letter—A73

Design: 2b, 3b, Thai women writing letters.

1963, Oct. 7 Wmk. 329

414	A73	50s lt bl & cl	25	15
415	A73	1b lt grn & vio brn	50	20
416	A73	2b yel brn & turq bl	1.00	40
417	A73	3b org brn & yel grn	1.75	85

Issued for International Letter Writing Week, Oct. 6–12.

U.N. Emblem
A74

1963, Oct. 24 Perf. 13½ Wmk. 329

418	A74	50s brt bl	22	8

Issued for United Nations Day, Oct. 24.

King Bhumibol Adulyadej—A75

Photogravure

1963, Dec. 5 Perf. 13½ Wmk. 329

419	A75	1.50b bl, org & ind	75	20
420	A75	5b brt lil rose, org & blk	2.00	60

King Bhumibol's 36th birthday.

UNICEF Emblem
A76

1964, Jan. 13 Lithographed

421	A76	50s blue	20	7
422	A76	2b dl grn	70	30

Issued to commemorate the 17th anniversary of UNICEF (United Nations International Children's Emergency Fund).

Hand (flags), Pigeon and Globe
A77

Designs: 1b, Girls and world map. 2b, Pen, pencil and unfolded world map. 3b, Globe and hand holding quill.

1964, Oct. 5 Perf. 13½ Wmk. 329

423	A77	50s lil & lt grn	15	8
424	A77	1b red brn & grn	30	10
425	A77	2b yel & vio bl	75	20
426	A77	3b bl & dk brn	1.25	30

Issued for International Letter Writing Week, Oct. 5–11.

U.N. Emblem and Globe
A78

King and Queen
A79

1964, Oct. 24 Photo. Perf. 13½

427	A78	50s gray	25	10

Issued for United Nations Day, Oct. 24.

THAILAND

1965, Apr. 28 *Perf. 13½* **Wmk. 329**
| 428 | A79 | 2b brn & multi | 75 | 30 |
| 429 | A79 | 5b vio & multi | 2.00 | 60 |

15th wedding anniversary of King Bhumibol Adulyadej and Queen Sirikit.

ITU Emblem, Old and New Communications Equipment
A80

1965, May 17 Photogravure
| 430 | A80 | 1b brt grn | 65 | 20 |

Issued to commemorate the centenary of the International Telecommunication Union.

World Map, Letters and Goddess
A81

Designs: 2b, 3b, World map, letters and handshake.

1965, Oct. 3 *Perf. 13½* **Wmk. 329**
431	A81	50s dp plum, gray & sal	15	6
432	A81	1b dk vio bl, lt vio & yel	35	12
433	A81	2b dk gray, bis & dp org	75	25
434	A81	3b multi	1.00	40

Issued for International Letter Writing Week, Oct. 3–9.

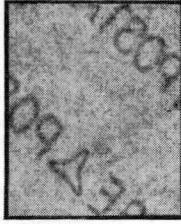 

Wmk. 356   Gates of Royal Chapel of Emerald Buddha
A82

Wmkd. POSTAGE (356)
Engraved and Lithographed
1965, Oct. 24 *Perf. 13½x14*
| 435 | A82 | 50s sl grn, bl & ocher | 22 | 10 |

International Cooperation Year, 1965.

Map of Thailand and UPU Monument, Bern
A83

Lithographed
1965, Nov. 1 *Perf. 13½* **Wmk. 329**
436	A83	20s dk bl & lil	10	5
437	A83	50s gray & bl	25	5
438	A83	1b org brn & vio bl	60	15
439	A83	3b grn & bis	1.75	50

80th anniversary of Thailand's admission to the UPU.

Lotus Blossom and Child
A84

Design: 1b, Boy with book walking up steps.

1966, Jan. 8 *Perf. 13½* **Wmk. 334**
| 440 | A84 | 50s hn brn & blk | 25 | 10 |
| 441 | A84 | 1b grn & blk | 50 | 20 |

Issued for Children's Day, 1966.

Bicycling
A85

Designs: 25s, Tennis. 50s, Running. 1b, Weight lifting. 1.25b, Boxing. 2b, Swimming. 3b, Netball. 5b, Soccer.

1966, Aug. 4 Photo. **Wmk. 329**
442	A85	20s dk car rose	10	5
443	A85	25s purple	10	5
444	A85	50s rose red	12	5
445	A85	1b dp ultra	35	10
446	A85	1.25b gray	40	15
447	A85	2b bl grn	75	25
448	A85	3b red brn	1.25	35
449	A85	5b dk rose brn	2.25	60
Nos. 442-449 (8)			5.32	1.60

5th Asian Games, Bangkok.

Trade Fair Emblem and Temple of Dawn
A86

1966, Sept. 1 Litho. *Perf. 13½*
| 450 | A86 | 50s lilac | 25 | 6 |
| 451 | A86 | 1b brn red | 45 | 20 |

Issued to publicize the first International Asian Trade Fair, Bangkok.

Letter Writer—A87
Design: 50s, 1b, Letters, maps and pen.

1966, Oct. 3 Photo. **Wmk. 329**
452	A87	50s scarlet	15	5
453	A87	1b org brn	35	15
454	A87	2b brt vio	75	25
455	A87	3b brt bl grn	1.25	35

Issued for International Letter Writing Week, Oct. 6–12.

U.N. Emblem   Pra Buddha Bata Monastery and UNESCO Emblem
A88   A90

Rice Field—A89

Lithographed
1966, Oct. 24 *Perf. 13½* **Wmk. 334**
| 456 | A88 | 50s ultra | 25 | 12 |

Issued for United Nations Day, Oct. 24.

1966, Nov. 1 Engr. **Wmk. 329**
| 457 | A89 | 50s dp bl & grnsh bl | 60 | 20 |
| 458 | A89 | 3b plum & pink | 1.75 | 65 |

Issued to publicize the International Rice Year under sponsorship of the U.N. Food and Agricultural Organization.

1966, Nov. 4 Photo. **Wmk. 329**
| 459 | A90 | 50s blk & yel grn | 40 | 10 |

Issued to commemorate the 20th anniversary of UNESCO (United Nations Educational, Scientific and Cultural Organization).

Thai Boxing—A91

Designs: 1b, Takraw (three men playing ball). 2b, Kite fighting. 3b, Cudgel play.

1966, Dec. 9 *Perf. 13½* **Wmk. 329**
460	A91	50s blk, brn & red	20	8
461	A91	1b blk, brn & red	40	12
462	A91	2b blk, brn & red	90	30
463	A91	3b blk, brn & red	1.50	60

5th Asian Games.

Snakehead
A92

Pigmy Mackerel—A93

Fish: 3b, Barb. 5b, Siamese fighting fish.

1967, Jan. 1 Photogravure
464	A92	1b brt bl & multi	35	10
465	A93	2b multi	75	20
466	A93	3b yel grn & multi	1.00	30
467	A92	5b pale grn & multi	2.00	50

Dharmachakra, Globe and Temples—A94

Lithographed
1967, Jan. 15 *Perf. 13½* **Wmk. 329**
| 468 | A94 | 2b blk & yel | 75 | 35 |

Issued to commemorate the establishment of the headquarters of the World Fellowship of Buddhists in Thailand.

Great Hornbill   Ascocentrum Curvifolium
A95   A96

Birds: 25s, Hill myna. 50s, White-rumped shama. 1b, Diard's fireback pheasant. 1.50b, Spotted dove. 2b, Sarus crane. 3b, White-breasted kingfisher. 5b, Asiatic open-bill (stork).

1967, Feb. 1 Photogravure
469	A95	tan & multi	5	5
470	A95	25s lt gray & multi	5	5
471	A95	50s yel grn & multi	10	6
472	A95	1b ol & multi	30	15
473	A95	1.50b dl yel & multi	50	15
474	A95	2b pale sal & multi	60	20
475	A95	3b gray & multi	1.00	40
476	A95	5b multi	1.50	55
Nos. 469-476 (8)			4.10	1.61

1967, Apr. 1 *Perf. 13½* **Wmk. 329**

Orchids: 20s, Vandopsis parishii. 80s, Rhynchostylis retusa. 1b, Rhynchostylus gigantea. 1.50b, Dendrobium falconerii. 2b, Paphiopedilum callosum. 3b, Dendrobium formosum. 5b, Dendrobium primulinum.

477	A96	20s blk & multi	10	5
478	A96	50s brt bl & multi	10	5
479	A96	80s blk & multi	30	10
480	A96	1b bl & multi	35	12
481	A96	1.50b blk & multi	50	15
482	A96	2b ver & multi	75	18
483	A96	3b brn & multi	1.00	30
484	A96	5b multi	1.50	40
Nos. 477-484 (8)			4.60	1.35

Thai Mansion—A97

Thai Architecture: 1.50b, Pagodas. 2b, Bell tower. 3b, Temple.

1967, Apr. 6 Engraved
485	A97	50s dl bl & vio	15	6
486	A97	1.50b bis brn & brn org	50	15
487	A97	2b grnsh bl & vio bl	75	25
488	A97	3b dl yel & gray	1.00	30

THAILAND

Grand Palace and Royal Barge
on Chao Phraya River—A98
1967, Sept. 15 Perf. 13½ Wmk. 329
489 A98 2b ultra & sep 45 24
International Tourist Year, 1967.

Globe, Dove, People and Letters
A99
Design: 2b, 3b, Clasped hands, globe and doves.
1967, Oct. 8 Photogravure
490 A99 50s dk bl & multi 15 5
491 A99 1b multi 35 8
492 A99 2b brt yel grn & blk 80 25
493 A99 3b brn & blk 1.10 30
Issued for International Letter Writing Week, Oct. 6–12.

U.N. Emblem
A100
1967, Oct. 24 Perf. 13½ Wmk. 329
494 A100 50s vio blk, grnsh bl & scar 25 8
Issued for United Nations Day, Oct. 24.

Flag and Map of Thailand—A101
1967, Dec. 5 Photo. Perf. 13½
495 A101 50s grnsh bl, red & vio bl 15 5
496 A101 2b ol gray, red & vio bl 45 22
50th anniversary of the flag.

Elephant Carrying Teakwood
A102
1968, Mar. 1 Engraved Wmk. 329
497 A102 2b rose cl & gray ol 60 25
See also Nos. 537, 566.

Syncom Satellite
over Thai
Tracking Station
A103
1968, Apr. 1 Photo. Perf. 13
498 A103 50s multi 15 8
499 A103 3b multi 1.00 30

Earth Goddess—A104
1968, May 1 Perf. 13 Wmk. 329
500 A104 50s blk, gold, red & bl grn 35 10
Hydrological Decade (UNESCO), 1965–74.

Snake-skinned Gourami—A105
Fish: 20s, Red-tailed black "shark." 25s, Tor tambroides. 50s, Pangasius sanitwongsei. 80s, Bagrid catfish. 1.25b, Vaimosa rambaiae. 1.50b, Catlocarpio siamensis. 4b, Featherback.
1968, June 1 Photo. Perf. 13
501 A105 10s multi 10 5
502 A105 20s multi 10 5
503 A105 25s multi 10 5
504 A105 50s multi 15 8
505 A105 80s multi 25 10
506 A105 1.25b multi 35 12
507 A105 1.50b multi 50 12
508 A105 4b multi 1.25 35
Nos. 501-508 (8) 2.80 92

Arcturus Butterfly—A106
Various Butterflies
1968, July 1 Perf. 13 Wmk. 329
509 A106 50s lt bl & multi 15 5
510 A106 1b multi 35 10
511 A106 3b multi 90 35
512 A106 4b buff & multi 1.25 50

Queen
Sirikit
A107

Designs: Various portraits of Queen Sirikit.
Photogravure and Engraved
Perf. 13½x14
1968, Aug. 12 Wmk. 334
513 A107 50s gold & multi 20 5
514 A107 2b gold & multi 75 25
515 A107 3b gold & multi 1.00 50
516 A107 5b gold & multi 1.75 75
Issued to commemorate Queen Sirikit's 36th birthday, or third 12-year "cycle."

WHO Emblem and Medical
Apparatus—A108
1968, Sept. 1 Photo. Perf. 12½
517 A108 50s ol, blk & gray 35 10
Issued to commemorate the 20th anniversary of the World Health Organization.

Globe, Pen and Envelope—A109
Design: 1b, 3b, Pen nib, envelope and globe.
1968, Oct. 6 Perf. 13½ Wmk. 329
518 A109 50s brn & multi 15 8
519 A109 1b pale brn & multi 35 12
520 A109 2b multi 55 20
521 A109 3b vio & multi 85 35
Issued for International Letter Writing Week, Oct. 7–13.

U.N. Emblem
and Flags
A110
1968, Oct. 24
522 A110 50s multi 20 10
Issued for United Nations Day.

Human Rights Flame
and Bas-relief—A111
Perf. 13½
1968, Dec. 10 Photo. Wmk. 329
523 A111 50s sl grn, red & vio 20 10
International Human Rights Year.

King
Rama II
A112

1968, Dec. 30 Engr. Wmk. 329
524 A112 50s sep & bis 25 10
Issued to commemorate the bicentenary of the birth of King Rama II (1768–1824), who reigned 1809–1824.

National Assembly Building
A113
Photogravure and Engraved
1969, Feb. 10 Perf. 13½ Wmk. 329
525 A113 50s multi 20 10
526 A113 2b multi 55 30
First constitutional election day.

ILO Emblem and Cogwheels
A114
1969, May 1 Photo. Perf. 13½
527 A114 50s rose vio & dk bl 20 10
Issued to commemorate the 50th anniversary of the International Labor Organization.

Ramwong Dance—A115
Designs: 1b, Candle dance. 2b, Krathop Mai dance. 3b, Nohra dance.
1969, July 15 Perf. 13 Wmk. 329
528 A115 50s multi 15 8
529 A115 1b multi 35 12
530 A115 2b multi 60 24
531 A115 3b multi 90 35

Posting and Receiving Letters
A116
Design: 2b, 3b, Writing and posting letters.
1969, Oct. 5 Photo. Wmk. 334
532 A116 50s multi 12 8
533 A116 1b multi 25 14
534 A116 2b multi 50 24
535 A116 3b multi 75 36
International Letter Writing Week.

Hand Holding
Globe
A117

THAILAND

1969, Oct. 24   Perf. 13   Wmk. 329

| 536 | A117 | 50s multi | 20 | 10 |

Issued for United Nations Day.

Teakwood Type of 1968
Design: 2b, Tin mine.

1969, Nov. 18   Engr.   Perf. 13½

| 537 | A102 | 2b choc, bl & ind | 50 | 30 |

Issued to publicize tin export, and the 2nd Technical Conference of the International Tin Council, Bangkok.

Loy Krathong Festival—A118
Designs: 1b, Marriage ceremony. 2b, Khwan ceremony. 5b, Songkran festival.

1969, Nov. 23   Photo.   Wmk. 329

538	A118	50s gray & multi	12	8
539	A118	1b multi	30	10
540	A118	2b multi	60	24
541	A118	5b multi	1.50	60

Biplane, Mailmen and Map of First Thai Airmail Flight, 1919
A119

1969, Dec. 10   Engr.   Perf. 13½

| 542 | A119 | 1b multi | 25 | 15 |

50th anniversary of Thai airmail service.

Phra Rama Shadow Play
A120

Shadow Plays: 2b, Ramasura. 3b, Mekhala. 5b, Ongkhot.

Photogravure and Engraved

1969, Dec. 18   Wmk. 329

543	A120	50s bl & multi	12	6
544	A120	2b grn & multi	50	25
545	A120	3b lil & multi	90	30
546	A120	5b bl & multi	1.50	50

Symbols of Agriculture, Industry and Shipping—A121

1970, Jan. 1   Photogravure

| 547 | A121 | 50s multi | 25 | 10 |

Productivity Year 1970.

World Map, Thai Temples and Emblem—A122

1970, Jan. 31   Lithographed

| 548 | A122 | 50s brt bl & blk | 20 | 10 |

Issued to publicize the 19th triennial meeting of the International Council of Women, Bangkok.

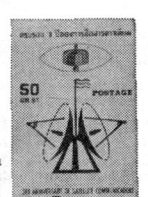

Earth Station Radar and Satellite
A123

Perf. 14½x15

1970, Apr. 1   Litho.   Wmk. 356

| 549 | A123 | 50s multi | 20 | 10 |

Communication by satellite.

Household and Population Statistics
A124

Perf. 13x13½

1970, Apr. 1   Photo.   Wmk. 329

| 550 | A124 | 1b multi | 22 | 12 |

Issued to publicize the 1970 census.

U.P.U. Headquarters, Bern
A125

Lithographed and Engraved

1970, June 15   Perf. 13½   Wmk. 334

| 551 | A125 | 50s lt bl, lt grn & grn | 20 | 10 |

Issued to commemorate the inauguration of the new Universal Postal Union Headquarters in Bern.

Khun Ram Kamhang Teaching (Mural)—A126

1970, July 1   Lithographed

| 552 | A126 | 50s blk & multi | 20 | 10 |

Issued for International Education Year.

Swimming Stadium—A127
Designs: 1.50b, Velodrome. 3b, Subhajalasaya Stadium. 5b, Kittikachorn Indoor Stadium.

Lithographed and Engraved

1970, Sept. 1   Perf. 13½   Wmk. 329

553	A127	50s yel, red & pur	15	7
554	A127	1.50b ultra, grn & dk red	30	15
555	A127	3b gold, blk & dk red	75	35
556	A127	5b brt grn, ultra & dk red	1.50	85

6th Asian Games, Bangkok.

Children Writing Letters—A128
Designs: 1b, Woman writing letter. 2b, Two women reading letters. 3b, Man reading letter.

1970, Oct. 4   Photo.   Perf. 13½

557	A128	50s blk & multi	15	10
558	A128	1b blk & multi	30	20
559	A128	2b blk & multi	50	30
560	A128	3b blk & multi	75	40

Issued for International Letter Writing Week, Oct. 6–12.

Royal Palace, Bangkok, and U.N. Emblem
A129

Photogravure

1970, Oct. 24   Perf. 13½   Wmk. 329

| 561 | A129 | 50s multi | 25 | 10 |

25th anniversary of the United Nations.

Heroes of Bangrachan—A130
Designs: 1b, Monument to Thao Thepkrasatri and Thao Srisunthorn. 2b, Queen Suriyothai riding elephant. 3b, Phraya Phichaidaphak and battle scene.

1970, Oct. 25   Engraved   Perf. 13½

562	A130	50s pink & vio	15	9
563	A130	1b vio & mar	25	18
564	A130	2b rose & brn	40	30
565	A130	3b bl & grn	75	45

Heroes from Thai history.

Teakwood Type of 1968
Design: 2b, Rubber plantation.

1970, Nov. 1   Engraved

| 566 | A102 | 2b car, brn & grn | 45 | 25 |

Issued to publicize rubber export.

King Bhumibol Lighting Flame
A131

1970, Dec. 9   Photo.   Wmk. 329

| 567 | A131 | 1b multi | 25 | 10 |

Opening of 6th Asian Games, Bangkok.

Woman Playing So Sam Sai—A132
Women Playing Classical Thai Musical Instruments: 2b, Khlui Phiang-O. 3b, Krachappi. 5b, Thon Rammana.

1970, Dec. 20

568	A132	50s multi	6	5
569	A132	2b multi	40	20
570	A132	3b multi	60	30
571	A132	5b multi	90	45

Chocolate Point Siamese Cats—A133
Siamese Cats: 1b, Blue point. 2b, Seal point. 3b, Pure white cat and kittens.

Perf. 13½x14

1971, March 15   Litho.   Wmk. 356

572	A133	50s multi	15	6
573	A133	1b multi	25	12
574	A133	2b multi	50	30
575	A133	3b multi	80	45

Muang Nakhon Temple
A134

Temples: 1b, Phanom. 3b, Pathom Chedi. 4b, Doi Suthep.

THAILAND

Lithographed and Engraved
1971, Mar. 30 Perf. 13½ Wmk. 329
576	A134	50s rose, blk & brn	15	5
577	A134	1b emer, bis & pur	25	15
578	A134	3b org, brn & dk brn	60	30
579	A134	4b ultra, ocher & brn	80	50

Corn and Tractor in Field—A135
1971, Apr. 20 Engraved Wmk. 329
| 580 | A135 | 2b multi | 85 | 25 |

Export promotion.

Buddha's Birthplace, Lumbini, Nepal
A136

Designs (Buddha's): 1b, Place of Enlightenment, Bihar. 2b, Place of first sermon, Benares. 3b, Place of death, Kusinara.

1971, May 9 Engr. Perf. 13½
581	A136	50s vio bl & blk	15	6
582	A136	1b grn & blk	20	12
583	A136	2b dl yel & blk	40	30
584	A136	3b red & blk	75	50

20th anniversary of World Fellowship of Buddhists.

King Bhumibol and Subjects A137   Floating Market A138

Lithographed
1971, June 9 Perf. 13½ Unwmkd.
| 585 | A137 | 50s sil & multi | 35 | 10 |

King Bhumibol's Silver Jubilee.

1971, June 20 Photo. Wmk. 329
| 586 | A138 | 4b gold & multi | 75 | 40 |

Visit Asia Year.

Boy Scouts Saluting
A139

1971, July 1 Lithographed
| 587 | A139 | 50s org & multi | 25 | 12 |

60th anniversary of Thai Boy Scouts.

Blocks of four of Nos. 354 and 403
Overprinted in Dark Blue

a

b

Engraved
1971, Aug. Perf. 13½x13 Wmk. 334
| 588 | A57 (a) | Block of four | 1.40 | 75 |
| a. | | 80s org, single stamp | 25 | 12 |

Photo. Perf. 13x13½ Wmk. 329
| 589 | A71 (b) | Block of four | 1.40 | 75 |
| a. | | 80s dl org, single stamp | 25 | 12 |

THAILANDPEX '71, Philatelic Exhibition, Aug. 4–8.

Woman Writing Letter—A140

Designs: 1b, Women reading mail. 2b, Woman sitting on porch. 3b, Man handing letter to woman.

Lithographed
1971, Oct. 3 Perf. 13½ Wmk. 334
590	A140	50s gray & multi	15	6
591	A140	1b red brn & multi	20	12
592	A140	2b ultra & multi	40	30
593	A140	3b lt gray & multi	60	40

International Letter Writing Week, Oct. 6–12.

Wat Benchamabopit (Marble Temple), Bangkok—A141
Perf. 13½x14
1971, Oct. 24 Litho. Unwmkd.
| 594 | A141 | 50s multi | 25 | 12 |

United Nations Day, Oct. 24.

Duck Raising—A142

Designs: 1b, Raising tobacco. 2b, Fishermen. 3b, Rice winnowing.

Photogravure
1971, Nov. 15 Perf. 12½ Wmk. 329
595	A142	50s lt bl & multi	15	6
596	A142	1b multi	20	12
597	A142	2b bl & multi	40	30
598	A142	3b buff & multi	60	40

Rural occupations.

UNICEF Emblem, Mother and Child—A143
1971, Dec. 11 Perf. 13½ Wmk. 334
| 599 | A143 | 50s bl & multi | 20 | 10 |

25th anniversary of the United Nations International Children's Fund (UNICEF).

Thai Costumes, 17th Century
A144

Thai Costumes: 1b, 13th to 14th centuries. 1.50b, 14th to 17th centuries. 2b, 18th to 19th centuries.

Unwmkd.
1972, Jan. 12 Litho. Perf. 13½x14
600	A144	50s multi	9	6
601	A144	1b multi	20	12
602	A144	1.50b multi	40	25
603	A144	2b bl & multi	60	30

Globe—A145
Perf. 13x13½
1972, Apr. 1 Photo. Wmk. 334
| 604 | A145 | 75s vio bl | 20 | 10 |

Asian-Oceanic Postal Union, 10th anniversary.

King Bhumibol Adulyadej
A146
Perf. 13½x13
1972–77 Litho. Wmk. 329

Size: 21x26mm.
605	A146	10s yel grn	5	5
606	A146	20s blue	5	5
607	A146	25s rose red	5	5
608	A146	75s lilac	8	6

Engraved
609	A146	1.25b yel grn & pink	15	8
610	A146	2.75b red brn & bl grn	30	20
611	A146	3b brn & dk bl ('74)	35	25
612	A146	4b bl & org red ('73)	50	20
613	A146	5b dk vio & red brn	60	30
614	A146	6b grn & vio	75	40
615	A146	10b ver & blk	1.25	60
616	A146	20b org & yel grn	2.50	1.25
617	A146	40b dp bis & lil ('74)	5.00	2.00
618	A146	50b pur & brt grn ('77)	5.00	2.50
619	A146	100b dp org & dk bl ('77)	10.00	5.00
		Nos. 605-619 (15)	26.63	12.99

No. 608 was also issued in booklet pane of 10. See Nos. 835-838, 907-908.

Iko Women—A147

Hill Tribes: 2b, Musoe musician. 4b, Yao weaver. 5b, Maeo farm woman.

Wmk. 334
1972, May 11 Photo. Perf. 13½
620	A147	50s multi	10	6
621	A147	2b dk gray & multi	40	15
622	A147	4b multi	70	40
623	A147	5b multi	80	50

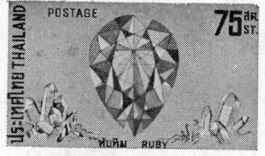

Ruby—A148

Precious Stones: 2b, Yellow sapphire. 4b, Zircon. 6b, Star sapphire.

1972, June 7 Lithographed
624	A148	75s gray & multi	15	6
625	A148	2b multi	35	15
626	A148	4b multi	70	40
627	A148	6b crim & multi	1.10	65

Prince Vajiralongkorn A149   Thai Costume A150

Perf. 13½x13
1972, July 28 Photo. Wmk. 329
| 628 | A149 | 75s tan & multi | 30 | 20 |

20th birthday of Prince Vajiralongkorn, heir apparent.

Perf. 14x13½
1972, Aug. 12 Litho. Wmk. 356

Designs: Costumes of Thai women.
| 629 | A150 | 75s tan & multi | 15 | 6 |
| 630 | A150 | 2b multi | 50 | 25 |

THAILAND

631	A150	4b yel & multi	85	40
632	A150	5b gray & multi	1.50	60
a.		Souv. sheet of 4	3.25	3.25

No. 632a contains one each of Nos. 629–632. Bright ultramarine inscription, gold ornaments and black control number in margin. Size: 120x159mm.

Rambutan—A151

Fruits: 1b, Mangosteen. 3b, Durian. 5b, Mango.

1972, Sept. 7   Perf. 13½   Wmk. 334

633	A151	75s multi	15	10
634	A151	1b multi	25	13
635	A151	3b pink & multi	60	40
636	A151	5b lt ultra & multi	1.00	45

Lod Cave, Phangnga—A152

Designs: 1.25b, Kang Krachara Reservoir. 2.75b, Erawan Waterfalls, Kanchanaburi. 3b, Nok-Kaw Cliff, Loei.

1972, Nov. 15   Litho.   Wmk. 334

637	A152	75s multi	12	10
638	A152	1.25b multi	20	15
639	A152	2.75b multi	55	35
640	A152	3b multi	60	45

International Letter Writing Week, Oct. 9–15.

Princess Mother Visiting Old People—A153

1972, Oct. 21   Photo.   Wmk. 329

641	A153	75s dk grn & ocher	35	10

72nd birthday of Princess Mother Sisangwan.

U.N. Emblem and Globe A154

Lithographed

1972, Nov. 15   Perf. 14   Wmk. 334

642	A154	75s bl & multi	25	10

25th anniversary of the Economic Commission for Asia and the Far East (ECAFE).

Educational Center and Book Year Emblem—A155

1972, Dec. 8   Perf. 13½

643	A155	75s multi	25	10

International Book Year 1972.

Crown Prince Vajiralongkorn A156

1972, Dec. 28   Photo.   Wmk. 329

644	A156	2b brt bl & multi	50	20

Investiture of Prince Vajiralongkorn Salayacheevin as Crown Prince.

Flag, Soldiers and Civilians—A157

1973, Feb. 3   Perf. 13½   Wmk. 334

645	A157	75s multi	35	10

25th anniversary of Veterans Day.

Savings Bank, Emblem and Coin A158

1973, Apr. 1   Wmk. 329

646	A158	75s emer & multi	25	10

60th anniversary of Government Savings Bank.

WHO Emblem and Deity—A159

1973, Apr. 1   Wmk. 329

647	A159	75s brt grn & multi	25	10

25th World Health Organization Day.

Water Lily—A160

Designs: Various water lilies (Thai lotus).

Perf. 11x13

1973, May 15   Litho.   Wmk. 356

648	A160	75s vio & multi	15	9
649	A160	1.50b brn & multi	25	15
650	A160	2b dl grn & multi	35	25
651	A160	4b blk & multi	60	50

King Bhumibol Adulyadej A161

Perf. 14x13½

1973–1975   Photo.   Wmk. 334

652	A161	5s purple	5	5
653	A161	20s blue	5	5
a.		Perf. 14		
654	A161	25s rose car	5	5
654A	A161	25s brn red, perf. 14 ('81)	5	5
655	A161	75s violet	10	8
a.		Perf. 14	8	8

Engraved   Perf. 13

656	A161	5b vio & brn	75	45
657	A161	6b grn & vio	90	45
658	A161	10b red & blk	1.50	75
660	A161	20b org & yel grn ('75)	3.00	1.50
		Nos. 652-660 (9)	6.45	3.43

Silversmiths—A162

1973, June 15   Litho.   Perf. 13½

Multicolored

662	A162	75s shown	15	10
663	A162	2.75b Lacquerware	45	40
664	A162	4b Pottery	70	40
665	A162	5b Paper umbrellas	85	50

Thai handicrafts.

Fresco from Temple of the Emerald Buddha—A163

Designs: Frescoes illustrating Ramayana in Temple of the Emerald Buddha.

1973, July 17   Photo.   Wmk. 329

666	A163	25s multi	5	5
667	A163	75s multi	12	10
668	A163	1.50b multi	30	20
669	A163	2b multi	40	20
670	A163	2.75b multi	55	25
671	A163	3b multi	60	25
672	A163	5b multi	90	55
673	A163	6b multi	1.10	65
		Nos. 666-673 (8)	4.02	2.25

Development of Postal Service A164

Design: 2b, Development of telecommunications.

1973, Aug. 4   Perf. 13½

674	A164	75s multi	25	10
675	A164	2b multi	50	15

90th anniversary of Post and Telegraph Department.

No. 1 and Other Stamps—A165

Designs (Various Stamps and): 1.25b, No. 147. 1.50b, No. 209. 2b, No. 244.

1973, Aug. 4   Photo. & Engr.

676	A165	75s dp rose & dk bl	20	10
677	A165	1.25b bl & dp rose	30	13
678	A165	1.50b ol & vio blk	35	30
679	A165	2b org & sl grn	50	30
a.		Souvenir sheet of 4	2.25	2.25

2nd National Philatelic Exhibition, THAIPEX '73, Aug. 4–8. No. 679a contains 4 stamps with simulated perforations similar to Nos. 676–679. Multicolored margin with commemorative inscription and black control number. Size: 190x95mm.

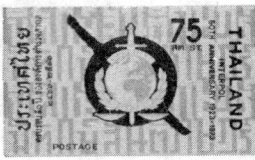

INTERPOL Emblem—A166

1973, Sept. 3   Photogravure

680	A166	75s gray & multi	35	10

50th anniversary of International Criminal Police Organization.

"Lilid Pralaw"—A167

Wmk. 368

Designs: Scenes from Thai literature.

Wmkd. JEZ Multiple (368)

1973, Oct. 7   Litho.   Perf. 11x13

681	A167	75s grn & multi	15	10
682	A167	1.50b bl & multi	30	20
683	A167	2b multi	40	20
684	A167	5b bl & multi	1.00	50
a.		Souvenir sheet of 4	2.75	2.75

International Letter Writing Week, Oct. 7–13. No. 684a contains one each of Nos. 681–684, perf. 13x14. Black marginal inscription and lilac stripes; black control number. Size: 165x104mm.

Scott's International Album provides spaces for an extensive representative collection of the world's postage stamps.

THAILAND

Wat Suan Dok, Chiangmai; UN Emblem
A168

1973, Oct. 24   Perf. 13x11
685 A168 75s bl & multi   25   10
United Nations Day.

Schomburgk's Deer—A169
Photogravure
1973, Nov. 14 Perf. 13½ Wmk. 329
Multicolored
686 A169 20s shown   5   5
687 A169 25s Kouprey   5   5
688 A169 75s Gorals   10   8
689 A169 1.25b Water buffalos 18   10
690 A169 1.50b Javan rhinoceros 30 15
691 A169 2b Eld's deer   40   18
692 A169 2.75b Asiatic two-horned rhinoceros 60 30
693 A169 4b Serows   85   40
     Nos. 686-693 (8)   2.53 1.31
Protected animals.

Human Rights Flame—A170

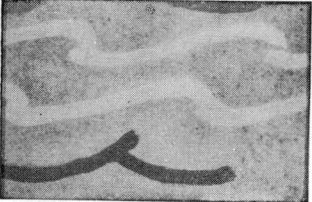

Wmk. 371
Watermarked Wavy Lines (371)
1973, Dec. 10 Litho. Perf. 12½
694 A170 75s multi   25   10
25th anniversary of the Universal Declaration of Human Rights.

Children and Flowers
A171
Perf. 13
1974, Jan. 12 Litho. Wmk. 371
695 A171 75s multi   25   10
Children's Day.

Siriraj Hospital and Statue of Prince Nakarin—A172
Perf. 13x13½
1974, Mar. 17 Photo. Wmk. 368
696 A172 75s multi   25   10
84th anniversary of Siriraj Hospital, oldest medical school in Thailand.

Phala Piang Lai
A173
Designs (Classical Thai Dances): 2.75b, Phra Lux Phlaeng Rit. 4b, Chin Sao Sai. 5b, Charot Phra Sumen.
Perf. 14
1974, June 25 Litho. Wmk. 334
697 A173 75s pink & multi   15   6
698 A173 2.75b gray bl & multi 50   20
699 A173 4b gray & multi   75   30
700 A173 5b yel & multi   90   45

Large Teak Tree in Uttaradit Province—A174
1974, July 5 Perf. 12½ Wmk. 329
701 A174 75s multi   25   10
15th Arbor Day.

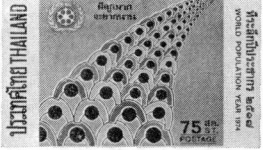

People and WPY Emblem—A175
Perf. 10½x13
1974, Aug. 19 Litho. Wmk. 368
702 A175 75s multi   25   10
World Population Year, 1974.

Ban Chiang Painted Vase—A176
Designs: 75s, Royal chariot. 2.75b, Avalokitesavara Bodhisattva. 3b, King Mongkut, Rama IV.

1974, Sept. 19 Perf. 12½ Wmk. 262
703 A176 75s bl & multi   15   6
704 A176 2b blk, brn & bis   35   25
705 A176 2.75b blk, brn & tan 40   30
706 A176 3b blk & multi   60   40
Centenary of National Museum. Inscribed "BATH" in error.

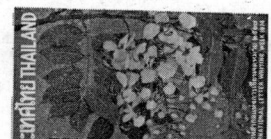

Purging Cassia—A177
1974, Oct. 6 Perf. 11x13 Wmk. 368
Multicolored
707 A177 75s shown   10   6
708 A177 2.75b Butea   40   25
709 A177 3b Jasmine   45   30
710 A177 4b Lagerstroemia   60   40
  a. Souvenir sheet of 4   2.75 2.75
International Letter Writing Week, Oct. 6-12. No. 710a contains one each of Nos. 707-710, marginal inscription, globe and control number. Size: 167x100mm.

"UPU" and UPU Emblem—A178
1974, Oct. 9 Perf. 12½ Wmk. 371
711 A178 75s dk grn & multi   25   10
Centenary of Universal Postal Union.

Wat Suthat Thepvararam—A179
Perf. 13
1974, Oct. 24 Photo. Wmk. 329
712 A179 75s multi   25   10
United Nations Day.

Elephant Roundup—A180
Perf. 12½
1974, Nov. 16 Engr. Wmk. 371
713 A180 4b multi   75   40
Tourist publicity.

Vanda Coerulea—A181
Orchids: 2.75b, Dendrobium aggregatum. 3b, Dendrobium scabrilingue. 4b, Aerides falcata.

Perf. 11x13
1974, Dec. 5 Photo. Wmk. 368
714 A181 75s red & multi   15   10
715 A181 2.75b multi   35   25
716 A181 3b ol & multi   50   35
717 A181 4b grn & multi   65   45
  a. Souvenir sheet of 4   3.00 3.00
No. 717a contains one each of Nos. 714-717, black marginal inscription. Perf. 13½x14. Size: 136x105mm.
See Nos. 745-748.

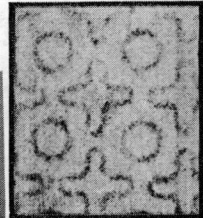

Boy
A182
Wmk. 374
Wmkd. Circles and Crosses (374)
1975, Jan. 11 Litho. Perf. 14x13½
718 A182 75s ver & multi   15   10
Children's Day.

Democracy Monument—A183
Designs: 2b, Mother with children and animals, bas-relief from Democracy Monument. 2.75b, Workers, bas-relief from Democracy Monument. 5b, Top of Democracy Monument and quotation from speech of King Rama VII.

Wmkd. "Harrison & Sons, London." in Script (233)
1975, Jan. 26   Perf. 14x14½
719 A183 75s dl grn & multi   10   6
720 A183 2b multi   30   20
721 A183 2.75b bl & multi   40   25
722 A183 5b multi   75   45
Movement of Oct. 14, 1973, to re-establish democratic institutions.

Marbled Tiger Cat
A184
1975, Mar. 5 Perf. 13½ Wmk. 334
Multicolored
723 A184 20s shown   5   5
724 A184 75s Gaurs   15   6
725 A184 2.75b Asiatic elephant 40 25
726 A184 3b Clouded tiger   50   30
Protected animals.

White-eyed River Martin
A185

THAILAND

Birds: 2b, Paradise flycatchers. 2.75b, Long-tailed broadbills. 5b, Sultan tit.

Perf. 12½
1975, Apr. 2 Litho. Wmk. 371
727	A185	75s ocher & multi	10	6
728	A185	2b lt bl & multi	25	18
729	A185	2.75b lt vio & multi	45	30
730	A185	5b rose & multi	75	50

King Bhumibol Adulyadej and Queen Sirikit—A186

Design: 3b, King and Queen, different background design.

Perf. 10½x13
1975, Apr. 28 Photo. Wmk. 368
| 731 | A186 | 75s vio bl & multi | 12 | 8 |
| 732 | A186 | 3b multi | 45 | 30 |

25th wedding anniversary of King Bhumibol Adulyadej and Queen Sirikit.

Round-house Kick—A187

Thai Boxing: 2.75b, Reverse elbow. 3b, Flying knee. 5b, Ritual homage.

Perf. 12½
1975, May 20 Litho. Wmk. 371
733	A187	75s grn & multi	10	6
734	A187	2.75b bl & multi	35	25
735	A187	3b org & multi	50	30
736	A187	5b org & multi	75	45

Tosakanth Mask A188

Masks: 2b, Kumbhakarn. 3b, Rama. 4b, Hanuman.

1975, June 10 Litho. Wmk. 371
737	A188	75s dk gray & multi	10	6
738	A188	2b dl vio & multi	25	18
739	A188	3b pur & multi	50	30
740	A188	4b multi	60	40

Thai art and literature.

THAIPEX 75 Emblem A189

Designs (THAIPEX 75 Emblem and): 2.75b, Stamp designer. 4b, Stamp printing plant. 5b, Stamp collector.

1975, Aug. 4 Perf. 12½ Wmk. 371
741	A189	75s yel & multi	10	6
742	A189	2.75b org & multi	40	25
743	A189	4b lt bl & multi	60	35
744	A189	5b car & multi	75	45

THAIPEX 75, Third National Philatelic Exhibition, Aug. 4–10.

Orchid Type of 1974
Orchids: 75s, Dendrobium cruentum. 2b, Dendrobium parishii. 2.75b, Vanda teres. 5b, Vanda denisoniana.

Perf. 11x13
1975, Aug. 12 Photo. Wmk. 368
745	A181	75s ol & multi	10	6
746	A181	2b multi	25	15
747	A181	2.75b scar & multi	40	20
748	A181	5b ultra & multi	70	35
a.		Souvenir sheet of 4	2.25	2.25

No. 748a contains one each of Nos. 745–748, perf. 13½. Black marginal inscription and control number. Size: 136x105 mm.

Mytilus Smaragdinus—A190

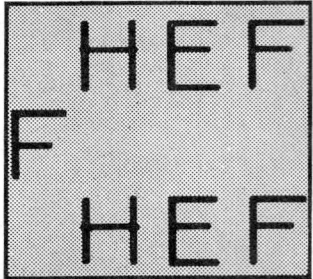

Wmk. 375
Wmkd. Letters (375)

Sea Shells: 1b, Turbo marmoratus. 2.75b, Oliva mustelina. 5b, Cypraea moneta.

1975, Sept. 5 Litho. Perf. 14x14½
749	A190	75s yel & multi	10	6
750	A190	1b ver & multi	15	8
751	A190	2.75b bl & multi	35	15
752	A190	5b grn & multi	85	40

Yachting and Games Emblem A191

Designs: 1.25b, Badminton. 1.50b, Volleyball. 2b, Target shooting.

Perf. 11x13
1975, Sept. 20 Litho. Wmk. 368
753	A191	75s ultra & blk	10	8
754	A191	1.25b brt rose & blk	25	10
755	A191	1.50b red & blk	40	15
756	A191	2b ap grn & blk	60	20
a.		Souvenir sheet of 4	2.00	2.00

8th SEAP Games, Bangkok, Sept. 1975. No. 756a contains one each of Nos. 753–756, perf. 13½. Multicolored margin with black control number. Size: 118x133 mm.

Pataya Beach—A192

Views: 2b, Samila Beach. 3b, Prachuap Bay. 5b, Laem Singha Bay.

1975, Oct. 5 Perf. 12½ Wmk. 371
757	A192	75s org & multi	15	6
758	A192	2b org & multi	25	15
759	A192	3b org & multi	30	25
760	A192	5b org & multi	75	40

International Letter Writing Week, Oct. 6–12.

"U N" U.N. Emblem, Food and Education for Children—A193

1975, Oct. 24 Litho. Wmk. 371
| 761 | A193 | 75s ultra & multi | 25 | 10 |

United Nations Day.

Morse Telegraph—A194

Design: 2.75b, Teleprinter and radar.

Perf. 14x14½
1975, Nov. 4 Litho. Wmk. 334
| 762 | A194 | 75s multi | 15 | 8 |
| 763 | A194 | 2.75b bl & multi | 50 | 25 |

Centenary of telegraph system.

Sukhrip Khrong Mueang Barge A195

Designs: 1b, Royal escort barge Anekchat Phuchong. 2b, Royal barge Anantanakarat. 2.75b, Krabi Ran Ron Rap barge. 3b, Asura Wayuphak barge. 4b, Asura paksi barge. 5b, Royal barge Sri Suphanahong. 6b, Phali Rang Thawip barge.

Perf. 12½
1975, Nov. 18 Litho. Wmk. 371
764	A195	75s multi	15	6
765	A195	1b multi	20	8
766	A195	2b lil & multi	30	15
767	A195	2.75b multi	40	20
768	A195	3b yel & multi	45	20
769	A195	4b multi	55	50
770	A195	5b gray & multi	70	60
771	A195	6b bl & multi	85	50
		Nos. 764-771 (8)	3.60	2.29

Thai ceremonial barges.

Thai Flag, Arms of Chakri Royal Family A196 — King Bhumibol Adulyadej A197

Perf. 15x14
1975, Dec. 5 Litho. Wmk. 375
| 772 | A196 | 75s multi | 15 | 6 |
| 773 | A197 | 5b multi | 60 | 45 |

King Bhumibol's 48th birthday.

Shot Put and SEAP Emblem—A198

Designs: 2b, Table tennis. 3b, Bicycling. 4b, Relay race.

1975, Dec. 9 Perf. 11x13 Wmk. 368
774	A198	1b org & blk	15	10
775	A198	2b brt grn & blk	30	20
776	A198	3b ocher & blk	45	30
777	A198	4b vio & blk	60	40
a.		Souvenir sheet of 4	2.25	2.25

8th SEAP Games, Bangkok, Dec. 9–20. No. 777a contains one each of Nos. 774–777, perf. 13½. Multicolored margin with black inscription and control number. Size: 118x130mm.

IWY Emblem and Globe—A199

Perf. 14x14½
1975, Dec. 20 Wmk. 375
| 778 | A199 | 75s blk, org & vio bl | 25 | 10 |

International Women's Year 1975.

Children Writing on Slate A200

Perf. 13x14
1976, Jan. 10 Litho. Wmk. 368
| 779 | A200 | 75s lt grn & multi | 25 | 10 |

Children's Day.

Macrobrachium Rosenbergii—A201

THAILAND

731

Designs: 2b, Penaeus merguiensis. 2.75b, Panulirus ornatus. 5b, Penaeus monodon.

Perf. 11x13
1976, Feb. 18   Litho.   Wmk. 368
780	A201	75s multi	15	8
781	A201	2b multi	30	15
782	A201	2.75b multi	45	30
783	A201	5b multi	75	50

Shrimp and lobster exports.

Golden-backed Three-toed Woodpecker — A202

Ban Chiang Vase — A203

Birds: 1.50b, Greater green-billed malcoha. 3b, Pomatorhinus hypoleucos. 4b, Green magpie.

Perf. 12½
1976, Apr. 2   Litho.   Wmk. 371
784	A202	1b multi	15	10
785	A202	1.50b multi	25	15
786	A202	3b yel & multi	50	35
787	A202	4b rose & multi	60	55

Perf. 14½x14
1976, May 5   Litho.   Wmk. 375

Designs: Ban Chiang painted pottery, various vessels, Bronze Age.
788	A203	1b ol & multi	15	10
789	A203	2b dp bl & multi	25	15
790	A203	3b grn & multi	50	35
791	A203	4b org red & multi	60	35

Mailman, 1883 — A204

Designs: 3b, Mailman, 1935. 4b, Mailman, 1950. 5b, Mailman, 1974.

Wmkd. Interlocking Circles (377)
1976, Aug. 4   Litho.   Perf. 12½
792	A204	1b multi	15	8
793	A204	3b multi	45	25
794	A204	4b multi	75	40
795	A204	5b multi	90	50

Development of mailmen's uniforms.

Kinnari — A205

Thai Mythology: 2b, Suphan-mat-cha. 4b, Garuda. 5b, Naga.

Lithographed
1976, Oct. 3   Perf. 11x13 Wmk. 368
796	A205	1b grn & multi	15	12
797	A205	2b ultra & multi	25	18
798	A205	4b gray & multi	60	40
799	A205	5b sl & multi	75	50

International Letter Writing Week.

U.N. Emblem, Drug Addicts, Alcohol, Cigarettes, Drugs — A206

Wmk. 329
1976, Oct. 24   Photo.   Perf. 13½
| 800 | A206 | 1b ultra & multi | 25 | 12 |

United Nations Day.

Old and New Telephones — A207

Wmk. 375
1976, Nov. 10   Litho.   Perf. 14x14½
| 801 | A207 | 1b multi | 25 | 15 |

Centenary of first telephone call by Alexander Graham Bell, Mar. 10, 1876.

Sivalaya-Mahaprasad Hall — A208

Royal Houses: 2b, Cakri-Mahaprasad. 4b, Mahisra-Prasad. 5b, Dusit-Mahaprasad.

Lithographed
1976, Dec. 5   Perf. 14x15   Wmk. 375
802	A208	1b multi	15	12
803	A208	2b multi	25	18
804	A208	4b multi	60	35
805	A208	5b multi	75	50

Banteng — A209

Designs: 2b, Tapir and young. 4b, Sambar deer and fawn. 5b, Hog deer family.

Perf. 11
1976, Dec. 26   Litho.   Wmk. 334
| 806 | A209 | 1b multi | 15 | 12 |
| 807 | A209 | 2b multi | 25 | 18 |

Wmk. 368
| 808 | A209 | 4b multi | 60 | 35 |
| 809 | A209 | 5b multi | 75 | 55 |

Protected animals.

Child Casting Shadow of Man — A210

Wmk. 329
1977, Jan. 8   Photo.   Perf. 13½
| 810 | A210 | 1b multi | 25 | 10 |

National Children's Day 1977.

Alsthom's Electric Engine — A211

Locomotives: 2b, Davenport's electric engine. 4b, Pacific's steam engine. 5b, George Egestoff's steam engine.

Perf. 11x13
1977, Mar. 26   Litho.   Wmk. 368
811	A211	1b multi	15	12
812	A211	2b multi	25	18
813	A211	4b multi	60	40
814	A211	5b multi	75	50

80th anniversary of State Railroad of Thailand.

Chulalongkorn University Auditorium — A212

1977, Mar. 26   Photogravure
| 815 | A212 | 1b multi | 15 | 10 |

Chulalongkorn University, 60th anniversary.

Flags of AOPU Members — A213

Lithographed
1977, Apr. 1   Perf. 12½   Wmk. 371
| 816 | A213 | 1b multi | 15 | 10 |

Asian-Oceanic Postal Union (AOPU), 15th anniversary.

Invalid in Wheelchair and Soldiers — A214

Photogravure
1977, Apr. 2   Perf. 13½   Wmk. 329
| 817 | A214 | 5b multi | 90 | 50 |

Sai-Jai-Thai Day, to publicize Sai-Jai-Thai Foundation which helps wounded soldiers.

Phra Aphai Mani and Phisua Samut — A215

Puppets: 3b, Rusi and Sutsakhon. 4b, Nang Vali and Usren. 5b, Phra Aphai Mani and Nang Laweng's portrait.

Wmk. 368
1977, June 16   Photo.   Perf. 11x13
818	A215	2b multi	30	15
819	A215	3b multi	35	25
820	A215	4b multi	60	40
821	A215	5b multi	75	50

Thai plays and literature.

Drum Dance — A216

Designs: 3b, Dance of dip nets. 4b, Harvest dance. 5b, Kan dance.

1977, July 14   Photo.   Perf. 13x11
822	A216	2b rose & multi	30	15
823	A216	3b lt grn & multi	35	25
824	A216	4b yel & multi	60	40
825	A216	5b lt vio & multi	75	50

Thailand No. 609, Various Stamps and Thaipex Emblem — A217

Wmk. 377
1977, Aug. 4   Litho.   Perf. 12½
| 826 | A217 | 75s multi | 20 | 10 |

THAIPEX 77, 4th National Philatelic Exhibition, Aug. 4–12.

A218

Designs: Scenes from Thai literature.

Perf. 11x13
1977, Oct. 5   Photo.   Wmk. 368
827	A218	75s multi	15	12
828	A218	2b multi	25	18
829	A218	5b multi	60	40
830	A218	6b multi	75	55

International Letter Writing Week, Oct. 6–12.

Old and New Buildings, UN Emblem — A219

1977, Oct. 5   Litho.   Perf. 11x13
| 831 | A219 | 75s multi | 15 | 10 |

United Nations Day.

THAILAND

King Bhumibol as Scout Leader, Camp and Emblem—A220

1977, Nov. 21   Photo.   Wmk. 368
| 832 | A220 | 75s multi | 25 | 10 |

9th National Jamboree, Nov. 21–27.

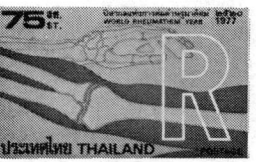

Diseased Hand and Elbow—A221

1977, Dec. 20 Perf. 11x13 Wmk. 368
| 833 | A221 | 75s multi | 15 | 10 |

World Rheumatism Year.

Map of South East Asia and ASEAN Emblem—A222   Wmk. 377

1977, Dec. 1   Litho.   Perf. 12½
| 834 | A222 | 5b multi | 70 | 40 |

Association of South East Asian Nations (ASEAN), 10th anniversary.

King Type of 1972–74 Redrawn
Lithographed
1976   Perf. 12½x13   Wmk. 377
Size: 21x27mm.
| 835 | A146 | 20s blue | 3.25 | 15 |
| 836 | A146 | 75s lilac | 3.25 | 15 |

Engraved
| 837 | A146 | 10b ver & blk | 1.25 | 1.00 |
| 838 | A146 | 40b bis & lil | 4.00 | 2.00 |

Numerals are taller and thinner and leaves in background have been redrawn.

Children Carrying Flag of Thailand—A223   Wmk. 329

1978, Jan. 9   Photo.   Perf. 13½
| 839 | A223 | 75s multi | 20 | 10 |

Children's Day.

Dendrobium Heterocarpum A224

Orchids: 1b, Dendrobium pulchellum. 1.50b, Doritis pulcherrima. 2b, Dendrobium heroglossum. 2.75b, Aerides odorata. 3b, Trichoglottis fasciata. 5b, Dendrobium wardianum. 6b, Dendrobium senile.

1978, Feb.   Perf. 11x14   Wmk. 368
840	A224	75s multi	8	5
841	A224	1b multi	10	8
842	A224	1.50b multi	15	12
843	A224	2b multi	20	15
844	A224	2.75b multi	28	24
845	A224	3b multi	35	30
846	A224	5b multi	55	50
847	A224	6b multi	80	60
Nos. 840-847 (8)			2.51	2.04

9th World Orchid Conference.

Census Chart, Symbols of Agriculture A225   Wmk. 377

1978   Lithographed   Perf. 12½
| 848 | A225 | 75s multi | 15 | 10 |

Agricultural census, April 1978.

Anabas Testudineus—A226

Fish: 2b, Datnioides microlepis. 3b, Kryptopterus apogon. 4b, Probarbus Jullieni.

Perf. 11x13
1978, Apr. 13   Photo.   Wmk. 368
849	A226	1b multi	10	8
850	A226	2b multi	25	15
851	A226	3b multi	45	25
852	A226	4b multi	60	40

Birth of Prince Siddhartha—A227

Murals: 3b, Prince Siddhartha cuts his hair. 5b, Buddha descending from Tavatimsa Heaven. 6b; Buddha entering Nirvana.

Wmk. 329
1978, June 15   Photo.   Perf. 13½
853	A227	2b multi	25	15
854	A227	3b multi	35	25
855	A227	5b multi	60	40
856	A227	6b multi	80	50

Story of Gautama Buddha, murals in Puthi Savan Hall, National Museum, Bangkok.

Bhumibol Dam—A228

Dams and Reservoirs: 2b, Sirikit dam. 2.75b, Vajiralongkorn dam. 6b, Ubol Ratana dam.

Perf. 14x14½
1978, July 28   Litho.   Wmk. 233
857	A228	75s multi	15	6
858	A228	2b multi	30	15
859	A228	2.75b multi	40	20
860	A228	6b multi	70	45

Idea Lynceus—A229

Butterflies: 3b, Sephisa chandra. 5b, Charaxes durnfordi. 6b, Cethosia penthesilea methypsia.

Wmk. 368
1978, Aug. 25   Litho.   Perf. 11x13
861	A229	2b lil, blk & red	25	15
862	A229	3b multi	35	25
863	A229	5b multi	60	40
864	A229	6b multi	80	50

Chedi Chai Mongkhon Temple A230

Mother and Children, UN Emblem A231

Temples: 2b, That Hariphunchai. 2.75b, Borom That Chaiya. 5b, That Choeng Chum.

Perf. 13x11
1978, Oct. 8   Litho.   Wmk. 368
865	A230	75s multi	15	6
866	A230	2b multi	25	15
867	A230	2.75b multi	35	20
868	A230	5b multi	60	40

International Letter Writing Week, Oct. 6–12.

Wmk. 375
1978, Oct. 24   Litho.   Perf. 14½x14
| 869 | A231 | 75s multi | 15 | 10 |

United Nations Day.

Boxing, Soccer, Pole Vault—A232

Designs: 2b, Javelin, weight lifting, running. 3b, Ball games and sailing. 5b, Basketball, hockey stick and boxing gloves.

Lithographed
1978, Oct. 24   Perf. 14x14½   Wmk. 233
870	A232	75s multi	10	6
871	A232	2b multi	25	20
872	A232	3b multi	30	30
873	A232	5b multi	60	40

8th Asian Games, Bangkok.

Five Races and World Map—A233
1978, Nov.
| 874 | A233 | 75s multi | 15 | 10 |

Anti-Apartheid Year.

Children Painting Thai Flag—A234

Children and Children's SOS Village, Tambol Bangpu A235

1979, Jan. 17   Perf. 14x14½
| 875 | A234 | 75s multi | 15 | 8 |
| 876 | A235 | 75s multi | 15 | 8 |

International Year of the Child.

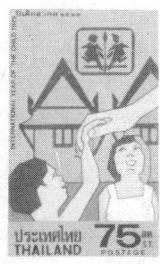

Matuta Lunaris A236

Crabs: 2.75b, Matuta planipes fabricius. 3b, Portunus pelagicus. 5b, Scylla serrata.

Lithographed
1979, Mar. 22 Perf. 12½ Wmk. 377
877	A236	2b multi	25	15
878	A236	2.75b multi	35	20
879	A236	3b multi	40	25
880	A236	5b multi	60	40

Sweetsop A237

Fruit: 2b, Pineapple. 5b, Bananas. 6b, Longans (litchi).

Perf. 12½
1979, June 25   Litho.   Wmk. 377
881	A237	1b multi	15	8
882	A237	2b multi	25	10
883	A237	5b multi	60	25
884	A237	6b multi	75	30

THAILAND

Young Man and Woman Planting Tree A238

Perf. 13x11

1979, July 10 Litho. Wmk. 368

| 885 | A238 | 75s multi | 15 | 10 |

20th Arbor Day.

Pencil, Pen, Thaipex '79 Emblem A239

Designs (Thaipex '79 Emblem and): 2b, Envelopes. 2.75b, Stamp album. 5b, Magnifying glass and tongs.

Perf. 11x13

1979, Aug. 4 Litho. Wmk. 368

886	A239	75s multi	10	6
887	A239	2b multi	25	15
888	A239	2.75b multi	35	20
889	A239	5b multi	60	38

Thaipex '79, 5th National Philatelic Exhibition, Bangkok, Aug. 4–12.

Floral Arrangement A240   United Nations Day A241

Designs: Decorative arrangements.

Wmk. 233

1979, Oct. 7 Litho. Perf. 14½×14

890	A240	75s multi	10	6
891	A240	2b multi	25	15
892	A240	2.75b multi	35	20
893	A240	5b multi	60	38

International Letter Writing Week, Oct. 8–14.

1979, Oct. 24 Litho. Perf. 14½×14

| 894 | A241 | 50s multi | 15 | 10 |

For well over a century collectors have been identifying and evaluating their stamps with the Scott Catalogue and housing their collections in Scott albums.

Frigate Makut Rajakumarn—A242

Thai Naval Ships: 3b, Frigate Tapi. 5b, Fast strike craft, Prabparapak. 6b, Patrol boat T-91.

1979, Nov. 20 Photo. Perf. 13½

895	A242	2b multi	20	16
896	A242	3b multi	30	24
897	A242	5b multi	50	40
898	A242	6b multi	60	48

 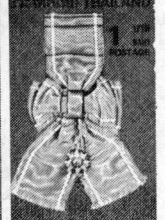

Rajamitrabhorn Order
A243   A244

Thai Royal Orders (Medallions and Ribbons): Nos. 901-902, House of Chakri. Nos. 903-904, The nine gems. Nos. 905-906, Chula Chom Klao. Stamps of same denomination printed se-tenant.

Wmk. 368

1979, Dec. 5 Litho. Perf. 13×11

899	A243	1b multi	10	8
900	A244	1b multi	10	8
901	A243	2b multi	20	15
902	A244	2b multi	20	15
903	A243	5b multi	50	38
904	A244	5b multi	50	38
905	A243	6b multi	60	45
906	A244	6b multi	60	45
	Nos. 899-906 (8)	2.80	2.12

King Type of 1972-77

Wmk. 329

1979, Dec. 23 Litho. Perf. 13½×13

Size: 21×26mm.

Engraved

| 907 | A146 | 50s ol grn | 15 | 10 |
| 908 | A146 | 2b org red & lil | 25 | 16 |

Rice Planting—A245

Children's Day: No. 910, Family in rice field.

Wmk. 368

1980, Jan. 12 Litho. Perf. 13×11

| 909 | A245 | 75s multi | 15 | 10 |
| 910 | A245 | 75s multi | 15 | 10 |

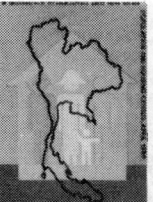 

Family, House,   Gold-fronted
Map of Thailand   Leafbird
A246   A247

1980, Feb. 1 Litho. Perf. 15×14

| 911 | A246 | 75s multi | 20 | 10 |

National Population and Housing Census, Apr.

1980, Feb. 26 Multicolored Perf. 13x11

912	A247	75s shown	10	6
913	A247	2b Yellow-cheeked tit	25	15
914	A247	3b Chestnut-tailed siva	35	22
915	A247	5b Scarlet minivet	60	38

International Commission for Bird Preservation, 9th Conference of Asian Section, Chieng-mai, Feb. 26-29.

Smokers and Lungs, WHO Emblem—A248

1980, Apr. 7 Wmk. 329 Perf. 13½

| 916 | A248 | 75s multi | 15 | 10 |

World Health Day; fight against cigarette smoking.

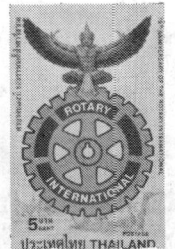

Garuda and Rotary Emblem—A249

1980, May 6 Wmk. 368 Perf. 13x11

| 917 | A249 | 5b multi | 50 | 40 |

Rotary International, 75th anniversary.

Sai Yok Falls, Kanchanaburi—A250

1980, July 1 Litho. Perf. 14x15

918	A250	1b shown	15	8
919	A250	2b Punyaban Falls, Ranong	25	15
920	A250	5b Heo Suwat Falls, Nakhon Ratchasima	60	38
921	A250	6b Siriphum Falls, Chiang Mai	75	45

Queen Sirikit—A251

Family with Cattle, Ceres Medal (Reverse)—A252

Design: No. 924, Ceres medal (obverse), weavers.

Wmk. 329, 368 (5b)

1980, Aug. 12 Litho. Perf. 13½, 11x13 (5b)

922	A251	75s multi	8	6
923	A252	5b multi	50	38
924	A252	5b multi	50	38

Queen Sirikit's 48th birthday.

Khao Phanomrung Temple, Buri Ram—A253

International Letter Writing Week, Oct. 6-12 (Temples): 2b, Prang Ku, Chailyaphum. 2.75b, Phimai, Nakhon Ratchasima. 5b, Sikhoraphum, Surin.

Wmk. 368

1980, Oct. 5 Litho. Perf. 11x13

925	A253	75s multi	8	6
926	A253	2b multi	20	15
927	A253	2.75b multi	28	20
928	A253	5b multi	50	38

Princess Mother   Golden Mount, Bangkok
A254   A255

Wmk.

1980, Oct. 21 Litho. Perf. 15x14

| 929 | A254 | 75s multi | 15 | 10 |

Princess Mother, 80th birthday.

1980, Oct. 24

| 930 | A255 | 75s multi | 15 | 10 |

United Nations Day.

733

THAILAND

King Bhumibol Adulyadej—A256

1980, Dec. 5		Wmk. 368 Litho.		Perf. 11x13	
933	A256	25s salmon		15	5
933A	A256	50s ol grn ('81)		5	5
934	A256	75s lilac		15	6
936	A256	1.25b yel grn ('81)		18	12

1983, Dec. 5		Wmk. 329 Engr.		Perf. 13	
939	A256	3b brn & dk bl ('83)		24	20
941	A256	5b pur & brn ('83)		40	32
942	A256	6b dk grn & pur ('83)		50	40
944	A256	8.50b grn & brn org ('83)		70	55
945	A256	9.50b ol & dk grn ('83)		80	65

King Rama VII Monument
Inauguration—A257

1980, Dec. 10			Perf. 15x14	
946	A257	75s multi	15	10

Bencharongware Bowl—A258

1980, Dec. 15		Wmk. 368		Perf. 11x13	
947	A258	2b shown		20	15
948	A258	2.75b Covered bowls		28	20
949	A258	3b Covered jar		30	24
950	A258	5b Stem plates		50	38

King Vajiravudh
Birth Centenary
A259

Children's Day
A260

1981, Jan. 1			Perf. 15x14	
951	A259	75s multi	8	6

1981, Jan. 16		Wmk. 368	Perf. 13x11	
952	A260	75s multi	8	6

Hegira, 1500th Anniv.—A261

1981, Jan. 18		Litho.	Perf. 12½	
953	A261	5b multi	50	38

Dolls in Native Costumes—A262

1981, Feb. 6		Wmk. 368 Litho.	Perf. 13½	
954	A262	75s Palm-leaf fish mobile	8	6
955	A262	75s Teak elephants	8	6
956	A262	2.75b shown	28	20
957	A262	2.75b Baskets	28	20

CONEX '81 International Crafts Exhibition.

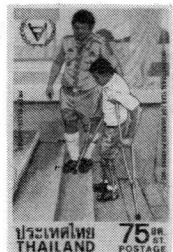

Scout Leader and Boy on
Crutches—A263

1981, Feb. 28			Perf. 13x11	
958	A263	75s shown	15	10
959	A263	5b Diamond cutter in wheelchair	50	38

International Year of the Disabled.

Dindaeng-Tarua Expressway
Opening—A264

1981, Oct. 29			Perf. 13½	
960	A264	1b Klongtoey	10	8
961	A264	5b Vipavadee Rangsit Highway	50	40

Ongkhot, Khon Mask—A265

Designs: Various Khon masks.

1981, July 1		Litho.	Perf. 13x11	
962	A265	75s shown	8	6
963	A265	2b Maiyarab	20	15
964	A265	3b Sukrip	30	24
965	A265	5b Indrajit	50	38

Exhibition Emblem, No. 83—A266

1981, Aug. 4		Litho.	Perf. 12	
966	A266	75s shown	8	6
967	A266	75s No. 144	8	6
968	A266	2.75b No. 198	28	20
969	A266	2.75b No. 226	28	20

Luang Praditphairo,
Court Musician,
Birth Centenary
A267

THAIPEX '81 Intl. Stamp Exhibition.

1981, Aug. 26			Perf. 15x14	
970	A267	1.25b multi	12	10

25th Intl. Letter
Writing Week, Oct.
6-12—A268

Designs: Dwarfed trees.

1981, Oct. 4		Wmk. 329		
971	A268	75s Mai hok-hian	8	6
972	A268	2b Mai kam-ma-lo	20	15
973	A268	2.75b Mai khen	28	20
974	A268	5b Mai khabuan	50	40

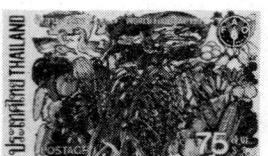

World Food Day—A269

1981, Oct. 16		Litho.	Perf. 12	
975	A269	75s multi	8	6

United Nations Day—A270

1981, Oct. 24		Wmk. 368	Perf. 13½	
976	A270	1.25b Samran Mukhamat Pavilion	18	12

King Cobra—A271

1981, Dec. 1		Wmk. 329	Perf. 13½	
977	A271	75s shown	8	6
978	A271	2b Banded krait	20	15
979	A271	2.75b Thai cobra	28	20
980	A271	5b Malayan pit viper	50	40

Children's Day
A272

Scouting Year
A273

1982, Jan. 9			Perf. 12	
981	A272	1.25b multi	12	10

1982, Feb. 22				
982	A273	1.25b multi	12	10

Bicentenary of Bangkok (Thai
Capital)—A274

Chakri Dynasty kings. (Rama I-Rama IX).

1982, Apr. 4		Wmk. Litho.	Perf. 12	
983	A274	1b Buddha Yod-Fa (1736-1809)	10	8
984	A274	1.25b shown	12	10
985	A274	2b Buddha Lert La Naphalai (1767-1824)	20	16
986	A274	3b Nang Klao (1787-1851)	30	24
987	A274	4b Mongkut (1804-1868)	40	32
988	A274	5b Chulalongkorn (1853-1910)	50	40
989	A274	6b Vajiravudh (1880-1925)	60	48
990	A274	7b Prachathipok (1893-1941)	70	55
991	A274	8b Ananda Mahidol (1925-1946)	80	65
992	A274	9b Bhumibol Aduldej (b. 1927)	90	72
a.		Souv. sheet of 9		
b.		Souv. sheet of 9		
		Nos. 983-992 (10)	4.62	3.70

Nos. 992a-992b each contain Nos. 983, 985-992; black control number. Size of No. 992a: 205x142mm; No. 992b, 195x180mm.

THAILAND

TB Bacillus Centenary—A275

1982, Apr. 7   Wmk. 368   Litho.   Perf. 13½
993 A275 1.25b multi   12   10

Local Flowers—A276

1982, June 30   Wmk. 233   Perf. 14x14½
994 A276 1.25b Quisqualis indica   12   10
995 A276 1.50b Murraya aniculata   15   12
996 A276 6.50b Mesua ferrea   65   52
997 A276 7b Desmos chinensis   70   55

Buddhist Temples in Bangkok—A277

1982, Aug. 4   Wmk. 368   Perf. 13½
998   A277 1.25b shown   12   10
999   A277 4.25b Wat Pho   42   34
1000 A277 6.50b Mahathat Yuwarat
             Rangsarit   65   52
1001 A277 7b Phra Sri Rattana
             Satsadaram   70   55
 a.   Souvenir sheet of 4   2.00 1.75

BANGKOK '83 Intl. Stamp Exhibition, Aug. 4-13, 1983. No. 1001a contains Nos. 998-1001 (perf. 12½); blue and silver margin, black control number. Size: 160x140mm.

See Nos. 1025-1026.

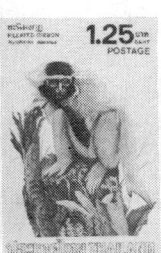   

LANDSAT Satellite A278 / Prince Purachatra of Kambaengbejra (1882-1936) A279

1982, Aug. 9   Wmk. 329   Perf. 12
1002 A278 1.25b multi   12   10

2nd UN Conference on Peaceful Uses of Outer Space, Vienna, Aug. 9-21.

1982, Sept. 14   Wmk. 233   Perf. 14
1003 A279 1.25b multi   12   10

26th Intl. Letter Writing Week, Oct. 6-12—A280

Sangalok Pottery.

1982, Oct. 3   Wmk. 329   Perf. 13½
1004 A280 1.25b Covered glazed jar   12   10
1005 A280 3b Painted jar   30   24
1006 A280 4.25b Glazed plate   42   34
1007 A280 7b Painted plate   70   55

UN Day—A281

1982, Oct. 24
1008 A281 1.25b Loha Prasat Tower   12   10

Musical Instruments—A282

1982, Nov. 30   Wmk. 329   Perf. 12
1009 A282 50s Chap, ching   5   5
1010 A282 1b Pi nai, pi nok   10   8
1011 A282 1.25b Klong that, taphon   12   10
1012 A282 1.50b Khong mong, krap   15   12
1013 A282 6b Khong wong yai   60   48
1014 A282 7b Khong wong lek   70   55
1015 A282 8b Ranat ek   80   65
1016 A282 9b Ranat thum   90   72
      Nos. 1009-1016 (8)   3.42 2.75

Pileated Gibbon A283 / ASEAN Members' Flags A284

1982, Dec. 26
1017 A283 1.25b shown   12   10
1018 A283 3b Pig-tailed macaque   30   24
1019 A283 5b Slow loris   50   40
1020 A283 7b Silvered leaf monkey   70   55

1982, Dec. 26
1021 A284 6.50b multi   65   50

15th Anniv. of Assoc. of Southeast Asian Nations.

Children's Day—A285

Wmk. 233
1983, Jan. 8   Litho.   Perf. 14½x14
1022 A285 1.25b multi   12   10

First Anniv. of Postal Code—A286

Wmk. 329 (#1024)
1983, Feb. 25   Litho.   Perf. 13½
1023 A286 1.25b Codes   12   10
1024 A286 1.25b Code on envelope   12   10

BANGKOK '83 Type of 1982

Design: Old General Post Office.

1983, Feb. 25   Wmk. 368   Photo.
1025 A277 7b multi   70   55
1026 A277 10b multi   1.00   80
 a.   Souvenir sheet of 2   1.75

No. 1026a contains Nos. 1025-1026 (perf. 12½); black control number. Size: 142x100mm.

25th Anniv. of Intl. Maritime Org.—A287

Wmk. 233
1983, Mar. 17   Litho.   Perf. 14x14½
1029 A287 1.25b Chinese junks   12   10

Civil Servants' Day A288 / Prince Sithiporn Kridakara (1883-1971) A289

1983, Apr. 1   Wmk. 329   Perf. 12
1030 A288 1.25b multi   12   10

1983, Apr. 11   Wmk. 233   Perf. 14½x14
1031 A289 1.25b multi   12   10

Domestic Satellite Communications System Inauguration—A290

Wmk. 368
1983, Aug. 4   Litho.   Perf. 13½
1032 A290 2b Map, dish antenna,
             satellite   20   15

BANGKOK '83 Intl. Stamp Show, Aug. 4-13—A291

1983, Aug. 4   Wmk. 329   Perf. 12
1033 A291 1.25b Mail collection   12   10
1034 A291 7.50b Posting letters   75   55
1035 A291 8.50b Mail transport   85   65
1036 A291 9.50b Mail delivery   95   75
 a.   Souvenir sheet of 4   2.75 2.25

No. 1036a contains Nos. 1033-1036; black control number. Size: 162x141mm.

THAILAND

Prince Bhanurangsi Memorial Statue—A292

Wmk. 233
1983, Aug. 4   Litho.   Perf. 15x14
1037 A292 1.25b multi   12   10

Malaysia/Thailand/Singapore Submarine Cable Inauguration—A293

Wmk. 368
1983, Sept. 27   Litho.   Perf. 12
1038 A293 1.25b multi   12   10
1039 A293 7b multi   70   50

Intl. Letter Writing Week—A294

Wmk. 329
1983, Oct. 6   Perf. 13½
1040 A294 2b Acropora asper   20   15
1041 A294 3b Platygyra lamellina 30   20
1042 A294 4b Fungia   40   30
1043 A294 7b Pectinia lactuca   70   50

Prince Mahidol of Songkhla—A295

Unwmkd.
1983, Oct. 10   Litho.   Perf. 12
1044 A295 9.50b multi   95   70

Siriraj Hospital Faculty of Medicine and Rockefeller Foundation, 60th Anniv. of cooperation.

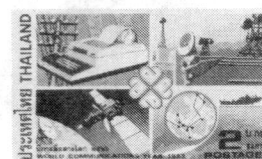

World Communications Year—A296

Design: 3b, Telecommunications equipment, diff.

1983, Oct. 24   Litho.   Perf. 14x14½
1045 A296 2b multi   20   15
1046 A296 3b multi   30   20

United Nations Day—A297

1983, Oct. 24   Litho.   Perf. 14x14½
1047 A297 1.25b multi   12   10

Thai Alphabet, 700th Anniv.—A298

Designs: 3b, Painted pottery, Sukothai period. 7b, Thai characters, reign of King Ramkamhaeng. 8b, Buddha, Sukothai period. 9b, Mahathat Temple, Sukothai province.

Wmk.
1983, Nov. 17   Litho.   Perf. 12
1048 A298 3b multi   30   20
1049 A298 7b multi   70   50
1050 A298 8b multi, vert.   80   60
1051 A298 9b multi, vert.   90   65

National Development Program—A299

Designs: No. 1052, King and Queen initiating Royal Projects. No. 1053, Technical aid. No. 1054, Terrace farming, Irrigation dam. No. 1055, Gathering grain. No. 1056, Receiving the peoples' gratitude.

Wmk.
1983, Dec. 5   Litho.
1052 A299 1.25b multi   12   10
1053 A299 1.25b multi   12   10
1054 A299 1.25b multi   12   10
1055 A299 1.25b multi   12   10
1056 A299 1.25b multi   12   10
      Nos. 1052-1056 (5)   60   50

Children's Day—A300

Wmk. 329
1984, Jan. 14   Litho.   Perf. 13½
1057 A300 1.25b multi   10   8

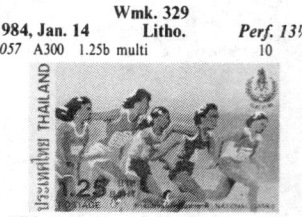

17th Natl. Games, Jan. 22-28—A301

1984, Jan. 22
1058 A301 1.25b Running   10   8
1059 A301 3b Soccer   24   18

5th Rheumatology Congress, Jan. 22-27—A302

1984, Jan. 22   Wmk. 233   Perf. 14x15
1060 A302 1.25b Rheumatic joints 10   8

Armed Forces Day—A303

1984, Jan. 25   Perf. 15x14
1061 A303 1.25b King Naresuan, tanks, jet, ship   10   8

50th Anniv. of Royal Institute—A304

1984, Mar. 31   Wmk. 233   Perf. 15x14
1062 A304 1.25b multi   10   8

Thammasat University, 50th Anniv.—A305

Wmk. 233
1984, June 27   Litho.   Perf. 14x15
1063 A305 1.25b Dome Building   10   8

THAILAND

For the advanced collector. We buy and sell specialized material.

George Alevizos
2716 Ocean Park Blvd. Ste. 1020
Santa Monica, CA 90405
Telephone: 213/450-2543

THAILAND

SEMI-POSTAL STAMPS.

Nos. 164–175 Overprinted in Red

		1918	Perf. 14	Unwmkd.	
B1	A21	2s org brn		65	50
B2	A21	3s emerald		65	50
B3	A21	5s rose red		90	65
B4	A21	10s blk & ol		1.00	1.00
B5	A21	15s blue		1.25	1.25
B6	A21	1b bl & gray blk		7.00	7.00
B7	A22	2b car rose & brn		9.00	9.00
B8	A22	3b yel grn & blk		14.00	14.00
B9	A22	5b dp vio & blk		27.50	27.50
a.		Double ovpt.		500.00	500.00
B10	A22	10b ol grn & vio brn		135.00	135.00
B11	A22	20b sea grn & brn		400.00	400.00
		Nos. B1-B11 (11)		596.95	596.40

Excellent counterfeit overprints are known.
These stamps were sold at an advance over face value, the excess being given to the Siamese Red Cross Society.

Stamps of 1906-1919 Overprinted

1920
On Stamps of 1912-17.

B12	A21	2s (+3s) org brn	22.50	22.50
B13	A21	3s (+2s) grn	22.50	22.50
B14	A21	15s (+5s) bl	30.00	30.00

On Stamp of 1905.

B15	A15	1t (+25s) dp bl & org	110.00	110.00

On Provisional Stamps of 1919.

B16	A21	5s on 6s (+20s) car rose	22.50	22.50
a.		Ovpt. inverted		
B17	A21	10s on 12s (+5s) gray blk & brn	22.50	22.50
		Nos. B12-B17 (6)	230.00	230.00

Stamps of 1906-20 Overprinted

On Stamps of 1912-17.

B18	A21	2s (+3s) org brn	22.50	22.50
B19	A21	3s (+2s) grn	22.50	22.50
a.		Pair, one without ovpt.		
B20	A21	15s (+5s) bl	55.00	55.00

On Stamp of 1905.

B21	A15	1t (+25s) dp bl & org	140.00	140.00

On Provisional Stamp of 1919.

B22	A21	10s on 12s (+5s) gray blk & brn	22.50	22.50

On Stamp of 1920.

B23	A23	5s (+20s) rose, pale rose	22.50	22.50
		Nos. B18-B23 (6)	285.00	285.00

Stamps of 1920 Overprinted in Blue or Red

B24	A23	2s brn, yel	22.50	22.50
B25	A23	3s grn, grn (R)	22.50	22.50
B26	A23	5s rose, pale rose	22.50	22.50
B27	A23	10s blk & org (R)	22.50	22.50
B28	A23	15s bl, bluish (R)	22.50	22.50
B29	A23	25s chocolate	55.00	55.00

B30	A23	50s ocher & blk (R)	110.00	110.00
		Nos. B24-B30 (7)	277.50	277.50

Nos. B12 to B30 were sold at an advance over face value, the excess being for the benefit of the Wild Tiger Corps. Counterfeits exist.

Nos. 170 to 172 Surcharged in Red

		1939	Perf. 14.	Unwmkd.	
B31	A22	5s +5s on 1b bl & gray blk		12.50	12.50
B32	A22	10s +5s on 2b car rose & brn		17.50	17.50
B33	A22	15s +5s on 3b yel grn & blk		17.50	17.50

Issued in honor of the 75th anniversary of the founding of the International Red Cross Society.

No. 214 Surcharged in Carmine

		1952	Perf. 12½	Unwmkd.	
B34	A25	80s +20s bl & blk		5.00	4.00
		New constitution.			

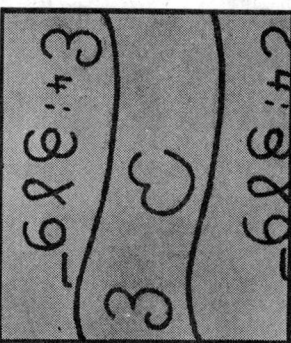

Red Cross and Dancer
SP1

Wmk. Thai Characters and Wavy Lines. (299)
Lithographed, Cross Typographed.
1953, Apr. 6   Perf. 11
Cross in Red, Dancer Dark Blue.

B35	SP1	25s +25s yel grn	1.50	1.50
B36	SP1	50s +50s brt rose	3.00	3.00
B37	SP1	1b +1b lt bl	4.00	4.00

Issued to commemorate the 60th anniversary of the founding of the Siamese Red Cross Society.

Nos. B35-B37 Overprinted with Year Date "24 98," in Black
1955, Apr. 3
Cross in Red, Dancer Dark Blue

B38	SP1	25s +25s yel grn	6.00	6.00
B39	SP1	50s +50s brt rose	8.00	8.00
B40	SP1	1b +1b lt bl	11.00	11.00

Counterfeits exist.

Red Cross Centenary Emblem
SP2   SP3

Lithographed

		1963	Perf. 13½	Wmk. 334	
B41	SP2	50s +10s gray & red		30	20
B42	SP3	50s +10s gray & red		30	20

Issued to commemorate the centenary of the International Red Cross. Nos. B41-B42 printed in alternating vertical rows.

Nos. B41-B42 Surcharged
1973, Feb. 15

B43	SP2	75s +25s on 50s +10s	45	40
B44	SP3	75s +25s on 50s +10s	45	40

Red Cross Fair, Feb. 15-19. See note after No. B42.

Nos. B41-B42 Surcharged   1973

1974, Feb. 2

B45	SP2	75s +25s on 50s +10s	40	35
B46	SP3	75s +25s on 50s +10s	40	35

Red Cross Fair, Feb. 1974. See note after No. B42. Position of surcharge reversed on No. B46.

Nos. B41-B42 Surcharged   1974

1975, Feb 11

B47	SP2	75s +25s on 50s +10s	40	35
B48	SP3	75s +25s on 50s +10s	40	35

Red Cross Fair, Feb. 1975. See note after No. B42. Position of surcharge reversed on No. B48.

Nos. B41-B42 Surcharged   1975

1976, Feb. 26

B49	SP2	75s +25s on 50s +10s	40	35
B50	SP3	75s +25s on 50s +10s	40	35

Red Cross Fair, Feb. 16-Mar. 1. Position of surcharge reversed on No. B50. See note after No. B42.

Nos. B41-B42 Surcharged   2520-1977

1977, Apr. 6 Perf. 13½ Wmk. 334

B51	SP2	75s +25s on 50s +10s	40	35
B52	SP3	75s +25s on 50s +10s	40	35

Red Cross Fair 1977. See note after No. B42.

  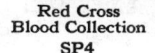 

Red Cross Blood Collection
SP4

Eye and Blind People
SP5

Wmk. 329
1978, Apr. 6   Photo.   Perf. 13

B53	SP4	2.75b +25s multi	50	35

"Give blood, save life."

Perf. 14x13½
1979, Apr. 6   Litho.   Wmk. 368

B54	SP5	75s +25s multi	40	25

"Give an eye, save new life." Red Cross Fair. Surtax was for Thai Red Cross.

Extracting Snake Venom, Red Cross—SP6

Wmk. 368
1980, Apr.   Litho.   Perf. 11x13

B55	SP6	75s +25s multi	35	25

Red Cross Fair. Surtax was for Thai Red Cross.

Nurse Helping Victim—SP7

1981, Apr. 6   Litho.   Perf. 12½

B56	SP7	75 +25s red & gray grn	10	8

Red Cross Fair (canceled). Surtax was for Thai Red Cross.

Red Cross Fair—SP8

Wmk. 329
1983, Apr. 6   Litho.   Perf. 13x13½

B57	SP8	1.25b +25s multi	15	10

Surtax was for Thai Red Cross.

No. B53 Overprinted and Surcharged.

Wmk. 329
1984, Apr.   Photo.   Perf. 13

B58	SP4	3.25b +25s on 2.75b +25s	28	25

Red Cross Fair. Surtax was for Thai Red Cross. Overprint translates: Red Cross Donation.

738 THAILAND—THRACE

AIR POST STAMPS.

Garuda—AP1

Engraved

		1925	Perf. 14, 14½		Unwmkd.
C1	AP1	2s brn, yel		1.25	10
C2	AP1	3s dk brn		1.25	12
C3	AP1	5s green		2.50	12
C4	AP1	10s blk & org		15.00	20
C5	AP1	15s carmine		4.00	30
C6	AP1	25s dk bl		1.75	25
C7	AP1	50s brn org & blk		12.50	1.50
C8	AP1	1b bl & brn		10.00	2.00
	Nos. C1-C8 (8)			48.25	4.59

Nos. C1-C8 received this overprint ("Government Museum 2468") in 1925, but were never issued. The death of King Vajiravudh caused cancellation of the fair at which this set was to have been released. They were used during 1928 only in the interdepartmental service for accounting purposes of the money-order sections of various Bangkok post offices, and were never sold to the public. Price for canceled set, $15.

1929-37			Perf. 12½	
C9	AP1	2s brn, yel	50	15
C10	AP1	5s green	50	12
C11	AP1	10s blk & org	2.00	12
C12	AP1	15s carmine	3.50	8
C13	AP1	25s dk bl	1.00	20
a.	Vert. pair, imperf. between		350.00	
C14	AP1	50s brn org & blk	2.25	50
	Nos. C9-C14 (6)		9.75	1.34

Monument of Democracy, Bangkok—AP2

Engraved

1942-43			Perf 11	
C15	AP2	2s dk org brn ('43)	60	40
C16	AP2	3s dk grn ('43)	6.00	3.50
C17	AP2	5s dp cl	75	30
a.	Horiz. pair, imperf. between		50.00	
b.	Vert. pair, imperf. between		70.00	
C18	AP2	10s car ('43)	75	45
a.	Vert. pair, imperf. between		60.00	60.00
C19	AP2	15s dk bl	1.00	50
	Nos. C15-C19 (5)		9.10	5.15

Garuda and Bangkok Skyline AP3

1952-53			Perf. 13x12½	
C20	AP3	1.50b red vio ('53)	60	15
C21	AP3	2b dk bl	90	20
C22	AP3	3b gray ('53)	1.25	25

OFFICIAL STAMPS

O1

		Perf. 10½ Rough		
1963, Oct. 1		Typo.	Unwmkd.	
O1	O1	10s pink & dp car	15	10
O2	O1	20s brt grn & car rose	20	15
O3	O1	25s bl & dp car	30	35
O4	O1	50s dp car	85	1.00
O5	O1	1b sil & car rose	1.00	1.30
O6	O1	2b brnz & car rose	1.75	1.60
	Nos. O1-O6 (6)		4.25	4.50

Issued as an official test from Oct. 1, 1963, to Jan. 31, 1964, to determine the amount of mail sent out by various government departments.

1963		Without Gum		
O7	O1	20s green	50	40
O8	O1	25s blue	50	60
O9	O1	1b silver	1.00	1.00
O10	O1	2b bister	2.75	3.50

THRACE
(thrās)

LOCATION—In southeastern Europe between the Black and Aegean Seas.
GOVT.—Former Turkish Province.
AREA—89,361 sq. mi. (approx.).

Thrace underwent many political changes during the Balkan Wars and World War I. It was finally divided among Turkey, Greece and Bulgaria.

100 Lepta = 1 Drachma
40 Paras = 1 Piastre
100 Stotinki = 1 Leva (1919)

Giumulzina District Issue.

ΕΛ. ΔΙΟΙΚ.

Turkish Stamps of 1909 Surcharged in Blue or Red

ΓΚΙΟΥΜΟΥ ΛΤΖΙΝΑΣ ΛΕΠΤΑ 25

1913		Perf. 12, 13½	Unwmkd.	
1	A21	10 l on 20pa rose (Bl)	11.50	9.50
2	A21	25 l on 10pa bl grn (R)	17.50	15.00
3	A21	25 l on 20pa rose (Bl)	13.00	13.00
4	A21	25 l on 1pi ultra (R)	20.00	17.50

Counterfeits exist of Nos. 1-4.

Turkish Inscriptions
A1   A2

1913		Lithographed.	Imperf.	
		Laid Paper.		
		Control Mark in Rose.		
5	A1	1pi blue	4.00	4.00
6	A1	2pi violet	6.00	6.00
		Wove Paper.		
7	A2	10pa vermilion	4.00	4.00
8	A2	20pa blue	4.00	4.00
9	A2	1pi violet	4.00	4.00
	Nos. 5-9 (5)		22.00	22.00

Turkish Stamps of 1908-13 Surcharged in Red or Black

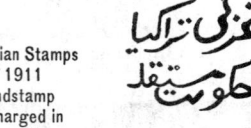

1913			Perf. 12	
10	A22	1pi on 2pa ol grn (R)	9.00	9.00
10A	A22	1pi on 2pa ol grn (Bk)	8.00	8.00
11	A22	1pi on 5pa ocher (Bk)	12.00	11.00
11A	A22	1pi on 5pa ocher (R)	13.00	12.00
12	A22	1pi on 20pa rose (R)	20.00	20.00
13	A21	1pi on 5pi dk vio (R)	85.00	70.00
13A	A21	1pi on 5pi dk vio (Bk)	85.00	70.00
14	A21	1pi on 10pi dl red (Bk)	165.00	150.00
15	A19	1pi on 25pi dk grn (Bk)	250.00	225.00
	Nos. 10-15 (9)		647.00	575.00

On Nos. 13-15 the surcharge is vertical, reading up. No. 15 exists with double surcharge, one black, one red.
Nos. 10-15 exist with forged surcharges.

Bulgarian Stamps of 1911 Handstamp Surcharged in Red or Blue

1913				
16	A20	10pa on 1s myr grn (R)	3.00	1.50
17	A21	20pa on 2s car & blk (Bl)	6.00	3.00
18	A23	1pi on 5s grn & blk (Bl)	10.00	5.00
19	A22	2pi on 3s lake & blk (Bl)	13.50	7.50
20	A24	2½pi 10s dp red & blk (Bl)	20.00	10.00
21	A25	5pi on 15s brn bis (Bl)	25.00	20.00
	Nos. 16-21 (6)		77.50	47.00

Same Surcharges on Greek Stamps.
On Issue of 1911.

1913		Serrate Roulette 13½		
22	A24	10pa on 1 l grn (R)	20.00	20.00
23	A24	10pa on 1 l grn (Bl)	20.00	20.00
25	A25	10pa on 25 l ultra (R)	25.00	25.00
26	A25	20pa on 2 l car rose (Bl)	15.00	15.00
27	A21	1pi on 3 l ver (R)	15.00	15.00
28	A26	2pi on 5 l grn (R)	30.00	30.00
29	A24	2½pi on 10 l car rose (Bl)	35.00	35.00
30	A25	5pi on 40 l dp bl (R)	50.00	40.00
	Nos. 22-30(8)		210.00	200.00

On Occupation Stamps of 1912.

31	O1	10pa on 1 l brn (Bl)	6.00	6.00
32	O1	20pa on 1 l brn (Bl)	6.00	6.00
33	O1	1pi on 1 l brn (Bl)	6.00	6.00

These surcharges were made with handstamps, two of which were required for each surcharge. One or both parts may be found inverted, double or omitted.
Nos. 16-33 exist with forged surcharges.

OCCUPATION STAMPS.
Issued under Allied Occupation.

Bulgarian Stamps of 1915-19 Handstamped in Violet Blue

THRACE INTERALLIÉE

	Perf. 11½, 11½x12, 14.		
1919		Unwmkd.	
N1	A43	1s black	55	55
N2	A43	2s ol grn	55	55
N3	A44	5s green	30	30
N4	A44	10s rose	30	30
N5	A44	15s violet	42	42
N6	A26	25s ind & blk	42	42
	Nos. N1-N6 (6)	2.54	2.54

The overprint on Nos. N1-N6 is frequently inverted and known in other positions.

Bulgarian Stamps of 1911-19 Handstamp Overprinted in Red or Black

THRACE INTERALLIÉE

1919				
N7	A43	1s blk (R)	5	5
N8	A43	2s ol grn	5	5
N9	A44	5s green	5	5
N10	A44	10s rose	5	5
N11	A44	15s violet	12	7
N12	A26	25s ind & blk	5	5
N13	A29	1 l chocolate	2.25	1.50
N14	A37a	2 l brn org	4.00	2.50
N15	A38	3 l claret	6.00	5.00
	Nos. N7-N15 (9)		12.62	8.75

Overprint is vertical, reading up, on Nos. N9-N13.
The following varieties are found in the setting of "INTERALLIEE": Inverted "V" for "A," second "L" inverted, "F" instead of final "E."

Bulgarian Stamps of 1919 Overprinted

Thrace Interalliée

1920				
N16	A44	5s green	5	5
N17	A44	10s rose	5	5
N18	A44	15s violet	5	5
N19	A44	50s yel brn	35	40

The varieties: "Interaliiee" and final "e" inverted are found on all values.

THRACE

Bulgarian Stamps of 1919 Overprinted

OCCIDENTALE

1920			Perf. 12x11½.	
N20	A44	5s green	5	5
a.	Inverted overprint		1.00	
N21	A44	10s rose	5	5
a.	Inverted overprint		1.00	
N22	A44	15s violet	5	5
N23	A44	25s dp bl	5	5
N24	A44	50s ocher	6	6
		Imperf.		
N25	A44	30s chocolate	25	30
	Nos. N20-N25 (6)		51	56

No. N25 is not known without overprint.

Issued under Greek Occupation.

For Use in Western Thrace.

Greek Stamps of 1911-19 Overprinted

Διοίκησις
Δυτικῆς
Θράκης

Serrate Roulette 13½.

1920 Lithographed. Unwmkd.

N26	A24	1 l green	15	15
a.		Inverted overprint	1.00	
N27	A25	2 l rose	10	10
N28	A24	3 l vermilion	10	10
N29	A26	5 l green	20	20
N30	A24	10 l rose	20	20
N31	A25	15 l dl bl	20	20
a.		Inverted overprint	4.00	4.00
b.		Double overprint, one inverted	4.50	4.50
N32	A25	25 l blue	1.50	1.00
N33	A26	30 l rose	15.00	15.00
N34	A25	40 l indigo	3.00	2.00
N35	A26	50 l vio brn	3.00	2.00
N36	A27	1d ultra	5.00	4.00
N37	A27	2d vermilion	7.00	7.00

Engraved.

N38	A25	2 l car rose	1.00	1.00
N39	A24	3 l vermilion	1.00	1.00
N40	A27	1d ultra	22.50	22.50
N41	A27	2d vermilion	9.00	9.00
N42	A27	3d car rose	8.00	8.00
N43	A27	5d ultra	12.50	12.50
N44	A27	10d dp bl	15.00	14.00
		Nos. N26-N44 (19)	104.45	99.95

Nos. N42–N44 are overprinted on the reissues of Greece Nos. 210–212. See footnote below Greece No. 213. Counterfeits exist of Nos. N26–N84.

Overprinted

ΔΙΟΙΚΗΣΙΣ
ΔΥΤΙΚΗΣ
ΘΡΑΚΗΣ

N45	A28	25d dp bl	25.00	25.00

This overprint reads: "Administration Western Thrace."

With Additional Overprint

Lithographed.

N46	A24	1 l green	25	25
N47	A25	2 l rose	25	25
a.		Inverted overprint	1.00	
N48	A24	10 l rose	25	25
N49	A25	20 l slate	1.50	1.50
N50	A26	30 l rose	1.50	1.50

Engraved.

N51	A27	2d vermilion	7.00	7.00
N52	A27	3d car rose	7.00	7.00
N53	A27	5d ultra	12.50	12.50
N54	A27	10d dp bl	13.00	13.00
a.		Double overprint	22.50	22.50
		Nos. N46-N54 (9)	43.25	43.25

For Use in Eastern and Western Thrace.

Greek Stamps of 1911-19 Overprinted

Διοίκησις
Θρακης

1920 Lithographed

N55	A24	1 l green	10	10
a.		Pair, one without overprint	3.00	
N56	A25	2 l rose	10	10
N57	A24	3 l vermilion	10	10
a.		Double overprint	3.00	
N58	A26	5 l green	20	20
a.		Pair, one without overprint	3.00	
N59	A24	10 l rose	20	20
a.		Double overprint	4.00	
N60	A25	20 l slate	20	20
a.		Inverted overprint	3.00	
N61	A25	25 l blue	2.00	1.10
N62	A25	40 l indigo	3.00	2.00
N63	A26	50 l vio brn	3.00	1.50
N64	A27	1d ultra	11.50	11.50
N65	A27	2d vermilion	8.00	7.00

Engraved.

N66	A24	3 l vermilion	1.00	1.00
N67	A25	20 l gray lil	4.00	4.00
N68	A28	25d dp bl	45.00	45.00
		Nos. N55-N68 (14)	78.40	74.00

This overprint reads "Administration Thrace".

With Additional Overprint

Lithographed.

N69	A25	2 l car rose	10	10
N70	A26	5 l green	1.50	1.50
N71	A25	20 l slate	2.00	2.00
N72	A26	30 l rose	2.00	2.00

Engraved.

N73	A27	3d car rose	8.00	8.00
N74	A27	5d ultra	13.00	13.00
N75	A27	10d dp bl	12.00	12.00
		Nos. N69-N75 (7)	38.60	38.60

Turkish Stamps of 1916-20 Surcharged in Blue, Black or Red

Υπάτη Αρμοστεία
Θρακης
5 Λεπτὰ 5

1920 ***Perf. 11½, 12½.***

N76	A43	1 l on 5pa org (Bl)	80	80
N77	A32	5 l on 3pi bl (Bk)	80	80
N78	A30	20 l on 1pi bl grn (Bk)	1.60	1.60
N79	A53	25 l on 5pi on 2pa Prus bl (R)	1.60	1.60
N80	A49	50 l on 5pi bl & blk (R)	1.60	1.60
N81	A45	1d on 20pa dp rose (Bl)	2.50	2.50
N82	A22	2d on 10pa on 2pa ol grn (R)	2.50	2.50
N83	A57	3d on 1pi dp bl (R)	5.00	5.00
N84	A23	5d on 20pa rose (Bk)	7.00	7.00
		Nos. N76-N84 (9)	23.40	23.40

Nos. N77, N78 and N84 are on the 1920 issue with designs modified. Nos. N81, N82 and N83 are on stamps with the 1919 overprints.

Varieties found on some values of this issue include: inverted surcharge, double surcharge with one inverted, and surcharge on both face and back.

POSTAGE DUE STAMPS.

Issued under Allied Occupation.

Bulgarian Postage Due Stamps of 1919 Handstamp Overprinted

THRACE INTERALLIÉE

1919 ***Perf. 12x11½*** **Unwmkd.**

NJ1	D6	5s emerald	30	30
NJ2	D6	10s purple	30	30
NJ3	D6	50s blue	60	60

Type of Bulgarian Postage Due Stamps of 1919–22 Overprinted

THRACE
OCCIDENTALE

1920 ***Imperf.***

NJ4	D6	5s emerald	12	12
NJ5	D6	10s dp vio	60	60
NJ6	D6	20s salmon	18	18
NJ7	D6	50s blue	38	38

Perf. 12x11½

NJ8	D6	10s dp vio	38	38
		Nos. NJ4-NJ8 (5)	1.66	1.66

TIBET

(tĭ·bĕt′; tĭb′ĕt)

LOCATION—A high tableland in Central Asia.

GOVT. — A semi-independent state, nominally under control of China (under Communist China since 1950–51).

AREA—463,200 sq. mi.

POP.—1,500,000 (approx.).

CAPITAL—Lhasa.

Tibet's postage stamps were valid only within its borders.

In 1965 Tibet became an autonomous region of the People's Republic of China.

6⅔ Trangka = 1 Sang

All stamps issued without gum.

A1

Lion

A2

Typographed.

1912 ***Imperf.*** **Unwmkd.**

Native Paper.

1	A1	⅙t green	17.00	17.00
2	A1	⅓t ultra	22.50	22.50
3	A1	½t purple	22.50	22.50
4	A1	⅔t carmine	37.50	37.50
a.		"POTSAGE"	110.00	110.00
5	A1	1t vermilion	45.00	45.00
6	A1	1s sage grn	100.00	100.00
		Nos. 1-6 (6)	244.50	244.50

1914

7	A2	4t dp bl	275.00	250.00
8	A2	8t carmine	175.00	150.00

In some 1920–30 printings of Nos. 1–8, European enamel paint was used instead of ink. It has a glossy surface.

A3

Thin White Native Paper

1932 ***Imperf., Pin-perf.***

9	A3	½t orange	27.50	27.50
10	A3	⅔t dk bl	27.50	27.50
11	A3	1t rose car	35.00	35.00
12	A3	2t vermilion	40.00	40.00
13	A3	4t emerald	30.00	30.00
		Nos. 9-13 (5)	160.00	160.00

Heavy Toned Native Paper

1934 ***Imperf.***

14	A3	½t yellow	5.00	5.00
a.		½t org	12.50	12.50
15	A3	⅔t dk bl	5.00	5.00
16	A3	1t org ver	5.00	5.00
a.		1t car	10.00	10.00
17	A3	2t red	6.50	6.50
a.		2t org ver	5.00	5.00
18	A3	4t ol grn	5.00	5.00
a.		25x25mm instead of 24x24mm	22.50	22.50
		Nos. 14-18 (5)	26.50	26.50

Excellent counterfeits of Nos. 1–18 exist. Numerous shades of all values.

Nos. 14–18 are also known pin-perf., but not believed to have been regularly issued in this form.

The ½t and 1t exist printed on both sides.

OFFICIAL STAMPS.

O1

O2

Various Designs and Sizes Inscribed "STAMP"

Sizes: No. O1, 32½x32½mm.
No. O2, 38x28½mm.
No. O3, 34x33mm.
No. O4, 44x44mm.
No. O5, 66x66mm.

Typographed.

1945 ***Imperf.*** **Unwmkd.**

Native Paper

O1	O1	½t brnz grn	*800.00*	*800.00*
O2	O2	⅓t sl blk	13.00	13.00
O3	O1	⅔t redsh brn	13.00	13.00
O4	O1	1⅓t ol grn	35.00	35.00
O5	O1	1s dk gray bl	85.00	85.00
		Nos. O1-O5 (5)	*946.00*	*946.00*

After 1952, Nos. O1–O5 became available for use as regular postage stamps.

TIMOR

(tē·mōr′)

LOCATION—The eastern part of Timor island, Malay archipelago.

GOVT.—Portuguese Overseas Territory.

AREA—7,330 sq. mi.

POP.—660,000 (est. 1974).

CAPITAL—Dili.

The Portuguese territory of Timor was annexed by Indonesia May 3, 1976.

1000 Reis = 1 Milreis
78 Avos = 1 Rupee (1895)
100 Avos = 1 Pataca
100 Centavos = 1 Escudo (1960)

Stamps of Macao Overprinted in Black or Carmine

TIMOR

1885 ***Perf. 12½, 13½*** **Unwmkd.**

1	A1	5r blk (C)	1.75	1.25
a.		Double overprint	8.50	8.50
b.		Triple overprint		
2	A1	10r green	3.00	2.50
a.		Overprint on Mozambique stamp	*20.00*	*20.00*
b.		Overprinted on Portuguese India stamp	*125.00*	*125.00*
3	A1	20r rose	5.00	4.00
a.		Double overprint		
b.		Perf. 13½	6.00	4.00
4	A1	25r violet	1.00	75
a.		Perf. 13½	20.00	12.50
5	A1	40r yellow	3.00	2.75
a.		Double overprint		
b.		Inverted ovpt.		
c.		Perf. 13½	15.00	12.50
6	A1	50r blue	2.00	1.00
a.		Perf. 13½	15.00	12.50
7	A1	80r slate	4.50	2.50
8	A1	100r lilac	2.00	1.00
a.		Double overprint		
b.		Perf. 13½	8.00	3.50
9	A1	200r orange	3.00	2.50
a.		Perf. 12½	12.50	3.00

TIMOR

10	A1	300r brown	3.00	2.50
		Nos. 1-10 (10)	28.25	20.75

The 20r brown, 25r rose and 50r green were prepared for use but not issued.

The reprints are printed on a smooth white chalky paper, ungummed, with rough perforation 13½, and on thin white paper with shiny white gum and clean-cut perforation 13½. Price of lowest-cost reprints, $1 each.

King Luiz — A2   King Carlos — A3

1887   Embossed.   Perf. 12½.

11	A2	5r black	1.75	1.50
12	A2	10r green	2.00	2.00
13	A2	20r brt rose	2.50	2.00
14	A2	25r violet	6.00	2.25
15	A2	40r chocolate	8.50	3.00
16	A2	50r blue	8.50	3.00
17	A2	80r gray	10.00	4.00
18	A2	100r yel brn	10.00	4.50
19	A2	200r gray lil	15.00	10.00
20	A2	300r orange	17.50	10.00
		Nos. 11-20 (10)	81.75	42.25

Reprints of Nos. 11, 16, 18 and 19 have clean-cut perforation 13½. Price $1.50 each.

TIMOR
Macao No. 44 Surcharged in Black
30
Without Gum

1892   Perf. 12½, 13

21	A7	30r on 300r org	4.00	5.00

1894   Typographed.   Perf. 11½

22	A3	5r yellow	1.00	75
23	A3	10r red vio	1.10	90
24	A3	15r chocolate	1.50	1.00
25	A3	20r lavender	1.50	1.00
26	A3	25r green	1.50	1.00
27	A3	50r lt bl	2.75	2.50
a.		Perf. 13½	110.00	100.00
28	A3	75r rose	3.50	3.00
29	A3	80r lt grn	3.50	3.00
30	A3	100r brn, *buff*	3.50	3.00
31	A3	150r car, *rose*	11.00	5.00
32	A3	200r dk bl, *lt bl*	11.00	6.25
33	A3	300r dk bl, *sal*	12.50	7.50
		Nos. 22-33 (12)	54.35	34.90

1 avo
Stamps of 1887 Surcharged in Red, Green or Black
PROVISORIO 仙壹

1895   Without Gum.   Perf. 12½

34	A2	1a on 5r blk (R)	1.00	75
35	A2	2a on 10r grn (Bk)	1.25	75
a.		Double surcharge		
36	A2	3a on 20r brt rose (G)	1.75	1.25
37	A2	4a on 25r vio (Bk)	1.75	1.00
38	A2	6a on 40r choc (Bk)	2.50	1.75
39	A2	8a on 50r bl (R)	2.75	1.75
40	A2	13a on 80r gray (Bk)	6.25	5.00
41	A2	16a on 100r yel brn (Bk)	6.25	5.00
42	A2	31a on 200r gray lil (Bk)	17.50	10.00
43	A2	47a on 300r org (G)	20.00	15.00
		Nos. 34-43 (10)	61.00	42.25

5 avos
No. 21 Surcharged
PROVISORIO 仙伍
Without Gum.

1895   Perf. 12½, 13.

44	A7	5a on 30r on 300r org	4.50	4.50

Vasco da Gama Issue.
Common Design Types

1898   Engraved.   Perf. 14 to 15.

45	CD20	½a bl grn	1.25	1.25
46	CD21	1a red	1.25	1.25
47	CD22	2a red vio	1.50	1.50
48	CD23	4a yel grn	1.25	1.25
49	CD24	8a dk bl	2.00	1.75
50	CD25	12a vio brn	2.75	2.00
51	CD26	16a bis brn	3.25	3.25
52	CD27	24a bister	4.00	3.25
		Nos. 45-52 (8)	17.25	15.50

400th anniversary of Vasco da Gama's discovery of the route to India.

King Carlos — A5   A6

1898-1903   Typo.   Perf. 11½
Name and Value in Black Except No. 79.

53	A5	½a gray	35	30
a.		Perf. 12½	2.50	1.75
54	A5	1a orange	35	30
a.		Perf. 12½	2.50	1.75
55	A5	2a lt grn	35	30
56	A5	2½a brown	1.50	1.25
57	A5	3a gray vio	1.50	1.25
58	A5	3a gray grn ('03)	1.50	1.00
59	A5	4a sea grn	1.50	1.25
60	A5	5a rose ('03)	1.50	1.00
61	A5	6a pale yel brn ('03)	1.50	1.00
62	A5	8a blue	1.75	1.25
63	A5	9a red brn ('03)	1.50	1.00
64	A5	10a sl bl ('00)	1.75	1.25
65	A5	10a gray brn ('03)	1.50	1.00
66	A5	12a rose	3.25	2.75
67	A5	12a dl bl ('03)	8.00	7.00
68	A5	13a violet	3.00	2.50
69	A5	13a red lil ('03)	2.50	2.00
70	A5	15a gray lil ('03)	3.50	2.50
71	A5	16a dk bl, *bl*	3.00	2.50
72	A5	20a brn, *yelsh* ('00)	3.50	3.00
73	A5	22a brn org, *pink* ('03)	4.00	4.00
74	A5	24a brn, *buff*	3.50	2.75
75	A5	31a red lil, *pnksh*	3.75	3.00
76	A5	31a brn, *straw* ('03)	3.50	3.00
77	A5	47a dk bl, *rose*	5.50	4.00
78	A5	47a red vio, *pink* ('03)	4.00	3.25
79	A5	78a blk & red, *bl* ('00)	7.50	4.50
80	A5	78a dl bl, *straw* ('03)	10.00	8.00
		Nos. 53-80 (28)	85.05	66.90

Most of Nos. 53-80 were issued without gum.

Common Design Types
pictured in section at front of book.

1899   Black Surcharge.

81	A6	10a on 16a dk bl, *bl*	2.50	2.50
82	A6	20a on 31a red lil, *pnksh*	2.50	2.50

5 avos
Surcharged in Black
5 AVOS

1902   On Issue of 1887.

83	A2	5a on 25r vio	2.00	1.75
84	A2	5a on 200r gray lil	3.00	2.50
85	A2	6a on 10r bl grn	100.00	85.00
86	A2	6a on 300r org	2.75	2.50
87	A2	9a on 40r choc	3.25	2.75
88	A2	9a on 100r yel brn	3.25	2.50
89	A2	15a on 20r rose	4.00	3.25
90	A2	15a on 50r bl	100.00	85.00
91	A2	22a on 80r gray	8.50	6.50

Reprints of Nos. 83-88, 90-91, 104A have clean-cut perf. 13½. Price $1 each.

On Issue of 1894.

92	A3	5a on 5r yel	1.25	1.00
a.		Inverted surcharge	17.50	17.50
93	A3	5a on 25r grn	1.10	75
94	A3	5a on 50r lt bl	1.50	1.25
95	A3	6a on 20r lav	1.50	1.25
96	A3	9a on 15r choc	1.50	1.25
97	A3	9a on 75r rose	1.50	1.25
98	A3	15a on 10r red vio	2.00	1.75
99	A3	15a on 100r brn, *buff*	2.00	1.75
100	A3	15a on 300r bl, *salmon*	2.00	1.75
101	A3	22a on 80r lt grn	4.75	3.25
102	A3	22a on 200r bl, *blue*	4.75	3.25

On Newspaper Stamp of 1893.

103	N2	6a on 2½r brn	75	75
a.		Inverted surcharge	17.50	17.50
		Nos. 92-103 (12)	24.60	19.25

Nos. 93-97, 99-102 were issued without gum.

Stamps of 1898 Overprinted in Black   PROVISORIO

104	A5	3a gray vio	1.25	1.00
104A	A5	12a rose	3.75	3.00

Reprint noted after No. 91.

No. 67 Surcharged in Black
10 AVOS

1905

105	A5	10a on 12a dl bl	2.50	2.00

Stamps of 1898-1903 Overprinted in Carmine or Green

1911

106	A5	½a gray	30	30
a.		Inverted ovpt.	3.50	3.50
107	A5	1a orange	30	30
a.		Perf. 12½	1.50	1.50
108	A5	2a lt grn	35	30
109	A5	3a gray grn	35	30
110	A5	5a rose (G)	35	30
111	A5	6a yel brn	35	30
112	A5	9a red brn	60	60
113	A5	10a gray brn	60	60
114	A5	13a red lil	50	50
115	A5	15a gray lil	1.25	1.25
116	A5	22a brn org, *pink*	1.25	1.25
117	A5	31a brn, *straw*	1.50	1.25
118	A5	47a red vio, *pink*	3.00	2.50
119	A5	78a dl bl, *straw*	3.75	3.75
		Nos. 106-119 (14)	14.45	13.50

Preceding Issues Overprinted in Red    Republica

1913   Without Gum
On Provisional Issue of 1902.

120	A3	5a on 5r yel	1.00	1.00
121	A3	5a on 25r grn	1.00	1.00
122	A3	5a on 50r lt bl	4.00	4.00
123	N2	6a on 2½r brn	4.00	4.00
124	A3	6a on 20r lav	1.50	1.50
125	A3	9a on 15r choc	1.50	1.50
126	A3	15a on 100r brn, *buff*	2.50	2.50
127	A3	22a on 80r lt grn	4.00	4.00
128	A3	22a on 200r bl, *bl*	4.00	4.00

On Issue of 1903.

129	A5	3a gray grn	4.00	4.00

On Issue of 1905.

130	A5	10a on 12a dl bl	1.50	1.50
		Nos. 120-130 (11)	29.00	29.00

Overprinted in Green or Red   REPUBLICA

1913
On Provisional Issue of 1902.

131	A3	9a on 75r rose (G)	2.50	2.50
132	A3	15a on 10r red vio (G)	2.50	2.50
		Inverted ovpt.		
133	A3	15a on 300r bl, *sal* (R)	3.75	3.75
a.		"REUBPLICA"	12.50	12.50
b.		"REPBLICAU"	12.50	12.50

On Issue of 1903.

134	A5	5a rose (G)	2.50	2.50

Stamps of 1898-1903 Overprinted in Red   REPUBLICA

1913

135	A5	6a yel brn	1.25	1.25
136	A5	9a red brn	1.25	1.25
137	A5	10a gray brn	1.25	1.25
138	A5	13a violet	1.50	1.50
a.		Inverted ovpt.	7.50	7.50
139	A5	13a red lil	1.50	1.50
140	A5	15a gray lil	2.25	2.25
141	A5	22a brn org, *pnksh*	3.00	3.00
142	A5	31a red lil, *pnksh*	3.00	3.00
143	A5	31a brn, *straw*	4.50	4.50
144	A5	47a bl, *pink*	3.50	3.50
145	A5	47a red vio, *pink*	3.50	3.50
146	A5	78a dl bl, *straw*	4.50	4.50

No. 79 Overprinted in Red   REPUBLICA

147	A5	78a blk & red, *bl*	6.00	6.00
		Nos. 135-147 (13)	37.00	37.00

Vasco da Gama Issue of 1898 Overprinted or Surcharged in Black:
REPUBLICA
REPUBLICA   10 A.
     a   *b*

1913

148	CD20	½a bl grn	75	75
149	CD21	1a red	75	75

TIMOR

150	CD22	2a red vio	75	75
151	CD23	4a yel grn	75	75
152	CD24	8a dk bl	1.50	1.50
153	CD25	10a on 12a vio brn	2.50	2.50
154	CD26	16a bis brn	2.00	2.00
155	CD27	24a bister	2.00	2.00
	Nos. 148-155 (8)		11.00	11.00

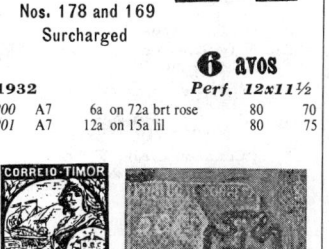

Ceres
A7

Typographed.
1914-23 *Perf. 15x14, 12x11½.*
Name and Value in Black.

156	A7	½a ol brn	15	10
157	A7	1a black	15	10
158	A7	1½a lt yel grn ('23)	60	50
159	A7	2a bl grn	20	10
160	A7	3a lil brn	1.00	75
161	A7	4a carmine	1.00	75
162	A7	6a lt vio	1.00	75
163	A7	7a lt grn ('23)	1.25	1.00
164	A7	7½a ultra ('23)	2.00	1.25
165	A7	9a bl ('23)	2.00	1.50
166	A7	10a dp bl	1.00	1.00
167	A7	11a gray ('23)	2.00	1.50
168	A7	12a yel brn	1.50	1.50
169	A7	15a lil ('23)	4.00	3.00
170	A7	16a slate	1.50	1.25
171	A7	18a dp bl ('23)	5.50	3.00
172	A7	19a gray grn ('23)	5.50	3.00
173	A7	20a org brn	13.50	6.00
174	A7	36a turq bl ('23)	5.50	3.50
175	A7	40a plum	6.00	3.50
176	A7	54a choc ('23)	5.50	3.50
177	A7	58a brn, *grn*	7.50	6.00
178	A7	72a brt rose ('23)	12.00	8.50
179	A7	76a brn, *rose*	7.50	6.00
180	A7	1p org, *sal*	11.00	7.50
181	A7	3p grn, *bl*	25.00	16.50
182	A7	5p car rose ('23)	45.00	25.00
	Nos. 156-182 (27)		168.85	107.05

Preceding Issues
Overprinted in
Carmine

1915 *Perf. 11½*
On Provisional Issue of 1902.

183	A3	5a on 5r yel	45	35
184	A3	5a on 25r grn	45	35
185	A3	5a on 50r lt bl	45	35
186	A3	6a on 20r lav	45	35
187	A3	9a on 15r lav	45	35
188	A3	9a on 75r rose	50	35
189	A3	15a on 10r red vio	50	35
190	A3	15a on 100r brn, *buff*	60	45
191	A3	15a on 300r bl, *sal*	60	45
192	A3	22a on 80r lt grn	2.00	1.50
193	A3	22a on 200r bl, *bl*	3.00	1.75

On No. 103.

194	N2	6a on 2½r brn, perf. 13½	35	30
a.		Perf. 12½	1.25	90
b.		Perf. 11½	2.50	1.75

On No. 104.

195	A5	3a gray vio	35	30

On No. 105.

196	A5	10a on 12a dl bl	60	50
	Nos. 183-196 (14)		10.75	7.70

Type of 1915 with
Additional Surcharge
in Black

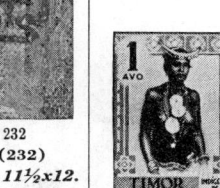

199	A3	½a on 5a on 50r lt bl	5.00	4.50
a.		Perf. 11½	9.00	6.00

Nos. 178 and 169
Surcharged

1932 *Perf. 12x11½*

200	A7	6a on 72a brt rose	80	70
201	A7	12a on 15a lil	80	75

"Portugal"
and Vasco
da Gama's
Flagship
"San Gabriel"
A8 Wmk. 232

1935 Typographed. *Perf. 11½x12.*

202	A8	½a bister	15	10
203	A8	1a ol brn	15	10
204	A8	2a bl grn	15	10
205	A8	3a red vio	40	20
206	A8	4a black	40	40
207	A8	5a gray	40	40
208	A8	6a brown	50	40
209	A8	7a brt rose	50	40
210	A8	8a brt bl	80	60
211	A8	10a red org	80	60
212	A8	12a dk bl	80	60
213	A8	14a ol grn	80	60
214	A8	15a maroon	80	60
215	A8	20a orange	80	60
216	A8	30a ap grn	80	60
217	A8	40a violet	3.75	1.75
218	A8	50a ol bis	3.75	1.75
219	A8	1p lt bl	7.50	6.00
220	A8	2p brn org	17.50	8.00
221	A8	3p emerald	25.00	10.00
222	A8	5p dk vio	40.00	17.50
	Nos. 202-222 (21)		105.75	51.30

Common Design Types
Engraved.

1938 *Perf. 13½x13.* Unwmkd.
Name and Value in Black.

223	CD34	1a gray grn	20	15
224	CD34	2a org brn	20	15
225	CD34	3a dk vio brn	20	15
226	CD34	4a brt grn	20	15
227	CD35	5a dk car	20	15
228	CD35	6a slate	30	20
229	CD35	8a rose vio	30	20
230	CD37	10a brt red vio	30	20
231	CD37	12a red	45	35
232	CD37	15a orange	60	35
233	CD36	20a blue	65	45
234	CD36	40a gray blk	1.75	1.25
235	CD36	50a brown	2.50	1.25
236	CD38	1p brn car	7.50	5.00
237	CD38	2p ol grn	12.50	5.00
238	CD38	3p bl vio	15.00	9.00
239	CD38	5p red brn	40.00	16.00
	Nos. 223-239 (17)		82.85	40.00

Mozambique
Nos. 273, 276, 278,
280, 282 and 283
Surcharged in Black

1946 *Perf. 13½x13*

240	CD34	1a on 15c dk vio brn	5.00	5.00
241	CD34	4a on 35c brt grn	5.00	5.00
242	CD35	8a on 50c brt red vio	5.00	5.00
243	CD36	10a on 70c brn vio	5.00	5.00
244	CD36	12a on 1e red	5.00	5.00
245	CD37	20a on 1.75e bl	5.00	5.00
	Nos. 240-245 (6)		30.00	30.00

Nos. 223–227 and 229–234
Overprinted "Libertacao."

1947

245A	CD34	1a gray grn	14.00	7.00
245B	CD34	2a org brn	25.00	14.00
245C	CD34	3a dk vio brn	10.00	6.00
245D	CD34	4a brt grn	10.00	6.00
245E	CD35	5a dk car	5.00	2.50
245F	CD35	8a rose vio	2.50	1.25
245G	CD37	10a brt red vio	5.00	2.50
245H	CD37	12a red	5.00	2.50
245I	CD37	15a orange	5.00	2.50
245J	CD36	20a blue	60.00	35.00
m.		Invtd. ovpt.		
245K		40a gray blk	13.00	8.00
	Nos. 245A-245K (11)		154.50	87.25

Timor Woman   U.P.U. Symbols
A9   A10

Designs: 3a, Gong ringer. 4a, Girl with basket. 8a, Aleixo de Ainaro. 10a, 1p, 3p, Heads of various chieftains. 20a, Warrior and horse.

1948 Lithographed *Perf. 14*

246	A9	1a aqua & dk brn	70	40
247	A9	3a gray & dk brn	1.25	80
248	A9	4a pink & dk grn	1.50	1.00
249	A9	8a red & bl blk	60	50
250	A9	10a bl grn & org	1.00	60
251	A9	20a ultra, aqua & bl	70	50
252	A9	1p org, bl & ultra	20.00	14.00
253	A9	3p vio & dk brn	25.00	14.00
a.		Sheet of eight	50.00	50.00
	Nos. 246-253 (8)		50.75	31.80

No. 253a contains one each of Nos. 246–253; black marginal inscription. Size: 129x99mm. Sold for 5p.

Lady of Fatima Issue.
Common Design Type

1948, Oct.

254	CD40	8a sl gray	6.00	5.00

U. P. U. Issue.

1949 *Perf. 14.* Unwmkd.

255	A10	16a brn & buff	7.00	6.00

Issued to commemorate the 75th anniversary of the formation of the Universal Postal Union.

Blackberry Lily
A13

Designs: Various flowers.
Lithographed.

1950 *Perf. 14½* Unwmkd.
Various Flowers.

260	A13	1a gray, red, pink, yel & grn	30	30
261	A13	3a ol brn, yel & dk grn	1.75	1.50
262	A13	10a dk bl, rose, yel & grn	1.75	1.50
263	A13	16a choc, red, yel & grn	5.00	2.50
264	A13	20a dk grnsh bl, gray, yel & grn	3.75	2.50
265	A13	30a ind, red, grn & yel	2.00	1.50
266	A13	70a dp cl, red, yel & grn	2.50	2.00
267	A13	1p dk grn, red, pink, yel & grn	5.50	4.50
268	A13	2p dk car rose, gray, yel, grn & brn	8.00	6.50
269	A13	5p blk, grn, red, pink & yel	14.00	10.00
	Nos. 260-269 (10)		44.55	32.80

Holy Year Extension Issue
Common Design Type

1951 *Perf. 14.*

270	CD43	86a bl & pale bl	1.75	1.50

Medical Congress Issue.
Common Design Type
Design: Weighing baby.

1952 Lithographed. *Perf. 13½.*

271	CD44	10a ol blk & brn	80	70

St. Francis Xavier Issue.

Statue of
St. Francis Xavier
A14

1952, Oct. 25 *Perf. 14*
Dated "1552-1952."

272	A14	1a black	15	15
273	A14	16a blk brn & brn	1.10	70
274	A14	1p dk car & gray	3.75	2.00

Issued to commemorate the 400th anniversary of the death of St. Francis Xavier.

Madonna   Stamp of Portugal
and Child   and Arms of
                 Colonies
A15   A16

Holy Year Issue.
Common Design Types

1950, May *Perf. 13x13½*

258	CD41	40a green	1.75	1.50
259	CD42	70a blk brn	2.50	2.25

Craftsman   Timor Woman
A11   A12

1950 *Perf. 14½.*

256	A11	20a dl vio bl	1.25	80
257	A12	50a dl red	2.50	1.25

741

TIMOR

1953 Perf. 13x13½
275	A15	3a dk brn & dl gray	12	8
276	A15	16a dk brn & cr	80	60
277	A15	50a dk bl & dl gray	1.75	1.35

Issued to commemorate the Exhibition of Sacred Missionary Art held at Lisbon in 1951.

Stamp Centenary Issue.
1953 Photogravure. Perf. 13.
Stamp and Arms Multicolored.
278	A16	10a gray & lil	1.25	1.25

Sao Paulo Issue
Common Design Type
1954 Lithographed Perf. 13½
279	CD46	16a dk brn red, bl & blk	70	60

See note after Macao No. 382.

Map of Timor
A17

1956 Perf. 14x12½ Unwmkd.
Inscription and design in brown, red, green, ultramarine & yellow.
280	A17	1a pale sal	10	5
281	A17	3a pale gray bl	15	5
282	A17	8a buff	30	15
283	A17	24a pale grn	30	15
284	A17	32a lemon	50	15
285	A17	40a pale gray	80	40
286	A17	1p yellow	2.50	1.50
287	A17	3p pale bl	5.50	2.00
		Nos. 280-187 (8)	10.15	4.45

Brussels Fair Issue.

Exhibition Emblems and View—A18

1958 Perf. 14½
288	A18	40a multi	60	50

Tropical Medicine Congress Issue
Common Design Type
Design: Calophyllum inophyllum.
1958 Perf. 13½
289	CD47	32a multi	3.00	2.50

Symbolical Globe A19 — Carved Elephant Jar A20
Lithographed
1960 Perf. 13½ Unwmkd.
290	A19	4.50e multi	50	35

Issued to commemorate the 500th anniversary of the death of Prince Henry the Navigator.

Nos. 280-287 Surcharged with New Value and Bars
1960 Perf. 14x12½ Unwmkd.
Inscription and design in brown, red, green, ultramarine & yellow.
291	A17	5c on 1a pale sal	10	7
292	A17	10c on 3a pale gray bl	10	7
293	A17	20c on 8a buff	10	9
294	A17	30c on 24a pale grn	15	7
295	A17	50c on 32a lem	15	7
296	A17	1e on 40a pale gray	40	18
297	A17	2e on 40a pale gray	50	20
298	A17	5e on 1p yel	80	50
299	A17	10e on 3p pale bl	2.00	1.50
300	A17	15e on 3p pale bl	2.50	1.75
		Nos. 291-300 (10)	6.80	4.50

1961 Lithographed Perf. 11½x12
Native Art: 10c, House on stilts. 20c, Madonna and Child. 30c, Silver rosary. 50c, Two men in boat (horiz.). 1e, Silver box in shape of temple. 2.50e, Archer. 4.50e, Elephant. 5e, Man climbing tree. 10e, Woman carrying pot on head. 20e, Cockfight. 50e, House on stilts and animals.

Multicolored Designs
301	A20	5c pale vio	10	10
302	A20	10c pale grn	10	10
a.		Value & legend inverted		
303	A20	20c pale bl	20	15
304	A20	30c rose	40	18
305	A20	50c pale grnsh bl	20	15
306	A20	1e bister	80	20
307	A20	2.50e pale ol bis	50	20
308	A20	4.50e lt sal	50	20
309	A20	5e lt gray	90	25
310	A20	10e gray	1.75	50
311	A20	20e yellow	4.00	1.25
312	A20	50e lt bluish gray	11.00	3.00
		Nos. 301-312 (12)	20.45	6.28

Sports Issue
Common Design Type
Sports: 50c, Duck hunting. 1e, Horseback riding. 1.50e, Swimming. 2e, Gymnastics. 2.50e, Soccer. 15e, Big game hunting.
1962, Mar. 22 Perf. 13½ Unwmkd.
Multicolored Designs
313	CD48	50c gray & bis	10	10
314	CD48	1e ol bis	60	20
315	CD48	1.50e gray & bl grn	45	30
316	CD48	2e buff	45	30
317	CD48	2.50e gray	60	45
318	CD48	15e salmon	2.00	1.25
		Nos. 313-318 (6)	4.20	2.60

Anti-Malaria Issue
Common Design Type
Design: Anopheles sundaicus.
1962 Lithographed Perf. 13½
319	CD49	2.50e multi	75	60

Issued for the World Health Organization drive to eradicate malaria.

National Overseas Bank Issue
Common Design Type
Design: 2.50e, Manuel Pinheiro Chagas.
1964, May 16 Perf. 13½ Unwmkd.
320	CD51	2.50e grn, gray, yel, lt bl & blk	75	60

Issued to commemorate the centenary of the National Overseas Bank of Portugal.

ITU Issue
Common Design Type
1965, May 17 Litho. Perf. 14½
321	CD52	1.50e multi	1.50	90

Issued to commemorate the centenary of the International Telecommunication Union.

National Revolution Issue
Common Design Type
Design: 4.50e, Dr. Vieira Machado Academy and Dili Health Center.
1966, May 28 Litho. Perf. 11½
322	CD53	4.50e multi	1.25	75

40th anniversary of National Revolution.

Navy Club Issue
Common Design Type
Designs: 10c, Capt. Gago Coutinho and gunboat Patria. 4.50e, Capt. Sacadura Cabral and seaplane Lusitania.
1967, Jan. 31 Litho. Perf. 13
323	CD54	10c multi	20	20
324	CD54	4.50e multi	1.75	75

Centenary of Portugal's Navy Club.

Sepoy Officer, 1792 A21 — Our Lady of Fatima A22

Designs: 1e, Officer, 1815. 1.50e, Infantry soldier, 1879. 2e, Infantry soldier, 1890. 2.50e, Infantry officer, 1903. 3e, Sapper, 1918. 4.50e, Special forces soldier, 1964. 10e, Paratrooper, 1964.
1967, Feb. 12 Photo. Perf. 13½
325	A21	35c multi	30	20
326	A21	1e multi	1.75	50
327	A21	1.50e multi	40	20
328	A21	2e multi	40	20
329	A21	2.50e multi	40	25
330	A21	3e multi	60	25
331	A21	4.50e multi	80	40
332	A21	10e multi	1.50	60
		Nos. 325-332 (8)	6.15	2.60

1967, May 13 Litho. Perf. 12½x13
333	A22	3e multi	60	30

50th anniversary of the apparition of the Virgin Mary to three shepherd children at Fatima, Portugal.

Cabral Issue

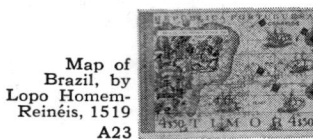

Map of Brazil, by Lopo Homem-Reinéis, 1519
A23

1968, Apr. 22 Litho. Perf. 14
334	A23	4.50e multi	80	50

See note after Macao No. 416.

Admiral Coutinho Issue
Common Design Type
Design: 4.50e, Adm. Coutinho and frigate Adm. Gago Coutinho.
1969, Feb. 17 Litho. Perf. 14
335	CD55	4.50e multi	1.00	75

View of Dili, 1834
A24

1969, July 25 Litho. Perf. 14
336	A24	1e multi	30	20

Bicentenary of Dili as capital of Timor.

da Gama Medal in St. Jerome's Convent A25 — Emblem of King Manuel, St. Jerome's Convent A26

Vasco da Gama Issue
1969, Aug. 29 Litho. Perf. 14
337	A25	5e multi	40	30

Issued to commemorate the 500th anniversary of the birth of Vasco da Gama (1469–1524), navigator.

Administration Reform Issue
Common Design Type
1969, Sept. 25 Litho. Perf. 14
338	CD56	5e multi	40	25

King Manuel I Issue
1969, Dec. 1 Litho. Perf. 14
339	A26	4e multi	40	25

Issued to commemorate the 500th anniversary of the birth of King Manuel I.

Capt. Ross Smith, Arms of Great Britain, Portugal and Australia, and Map of Timor
A27

1969, Dec. 9
340	A27	2e multi	50	40

Issued to commemorate the 50th anniversary of the first England to Australia flight of Capt. Ross Smith and Lt. Keith Smith.

Marshal Carmona Issue
Common Design Type
Design: 1.50e, Antonio Oscar Carmona in civilian clothes.
1970, Nov. 15 Litho. Perf. 14
341	CD57	1.50e multi	20	15

See note after Macao No. 422.

Lusiads Issue

Sailing Ship and Monks Preaching to Islanders—A28

1972, May 25 Litho. Perf. 13
342	A28	1e brn & multi	20	20

4th centenary of publication of The Lusiads by Luiz Camoëns.

TIMOR

Olympic Games Issue
Common Design Type
Design: 4.50e, Soccer, Olympic emblem.
1972, June 20   Perf. 14x13½
| 343 | CD59 | 4.50e multi | 50 | 30 |

20th Olympic Games, Munich, Aug. 26–Sept. 11.

Lisbon-Rio de Janeiro Flight Issue
Common Design Type
Design: 1e, Sacadura Cabral and Gago Coutinho in cockpit of "Lusitania."
1972, Sept. 20   Litho.   Perf. 13½
| 344 | CD60 | 1e multi | 25 | 25 |

WMO Centenary Issue
Common Design Type
1973, Dec. 15   Litho.   Perf. 13
| 345 | CD61 | 20e multi | 1.75 | 1.35 |

Centenary of international meteorological cooperation.

AIR POST STAMPS.
Common Design Type
1938   Perf. 13½x13.   Unwmkd.
Engraved.
Name and Value in Black.
C1	CD39	1a scarlet	60	60
C2	CD39	2a purple	60	60
C3	CD39	3a orange	60	60
C4	CD39	5a ultra	60	60
C5	CD39	10a lil brn	1.25	80
C6	CD39	20a dk grn	2.50	1.50
C7	CD39	50a red brn	5.00	3.75
C8	CD39	70a rose car	5.25	5.25
C9	CD39	1p magenta	10.00	5.00
		Nos. C1-C9 (9)	26.40	18.70

No. C7 exists with overprint "Exposicao Internacional de Nova York, 1939–1940" and Trylon and Perisphere.

Mozambique Nos. C3, C4, C6, C7 and C9 Surcharged in Black

1946   Perf. 13½x13.   Unwmkd.
C10	CD39	8a on 50c org	4.00	2.50
C11	CD39	12a on 1e ultra	4.00	2.50
C12	CD39	40a on 3e dk grn	4.00	2.50
C13	CD39	50a on 5e red brn	4.00	2.50
C14	CD39	1p on 10e mag	4.00	2.50
		Nos. C10-C14 (5)	20.00	12.50

Nos. C1–C9 Overprinted "Libertacao."
1947
C15	CD39	1a scarlet	17.50	9.00
C16	CD39	2a purple	17.50	9.00
C17	CD39	3a orange	17.50	9.00
C18	CD39	5a ultra	17.50	9.00
C19	CD39	~10a lil brn	5.00	3.25
C20	CD39	20a dk grn	5.00	3.25
C21	CD39	50a red brn	5.00	3.25
C22	CD39	70a rose car	17.50	6.50
C23	CD39	1p magenta	7.00	3.25
		Nos. C15-C23 (9)	109.50	55.50

POSTAGE DUE STAMPS.

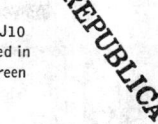

D1

1904   Perf. 12   Unwmkd.
Without Gum
Name and Value in Black.
J1	D1	1a yel grn	50	50
J2	D1	2a slate	50	50
J3	D1	5a yel brn	1.50	1.50
J4	D1	6a red org	1.50	1.50
J5	D1	10a gray brn	2.00	2.00
J6	D1	15a red brn	2.75	2.75
J7	D1	24a dl bl	5.50	5.50
J8	D1	40a carmine	5.50	5.50
J9	D1	50a orange	7.50	7.50
J10	D1	1p dl vio	13.00	13.00
		Nos. J1-J10 (10)	40.25	40.25

Overprinted in Carmine or Green
REPUBLICA

1911
Without Gum
J11	D1	1a yel grn	25	25
J12	D1	2a slate	25	25
a.		Inverted overprint		
J13	D1	5a yel brn	25	25
J14	D1	6a dp org	35	35
J15	D1	10a gray brn	60	60
J16	D1	15a brown	1.50	1.50
J17	D1	24a dl bl	2.00	2.00
J18	D1	40a car (G)	2.50	2.50
J19	D1	50a orange	2.50	2.50
J20	D1	1p dl vio	7.50	7.50
		Nos. J11-J20 (10)	17.70	17.70

Nos. J1–J10 Overprinted in Red or Green
REPUBLICA

1913
Without Gum
J21	D1	1a yel grn	5.50	5.50
J22	D1	2a slate	5.50	5.50
J23	D1	5a yel brn	2.75	2.75
J24	D1	6a dp org	2.75	2.75
a.		Inverted surch.		
J25	D1	10a red brn	3.75	3.75
J26	D1	15a red brn	3.75	3.75
J27	D1	24a dl bl	3.75	3.75
J28	D1	40a car (G)	3.75	3.75
J29	D1	50a orange	7.00	7.00
J30	D1	1p gray vio	7.00	7.00
		Nos. J21-J30 (10)	45.50	45.50

Common Design Type
Photogravure and Typographed.
1952   Perf. 14.   Unwmkd.
Numeral in Red, Frame Multicolored.
J31	CD45	1a chocolate	15	15
J32	CD45	3a brown	15	15
J33	CD45	5a dk grn	15	15
J34	CD45	10a green	15	15
J35	CD45	30a purple	40	35
J36	CD45	1p brn car	1.00	1.00
		Nos. J31-J36 (6)	2.00	1.95

WAR TAX STAMP.
2 AVOS
TAXA DE GUERRA

Regular Issue of 1914 Surcharged in Red
1919   Perf. 15 x14.   Unwmkd.
Without Gum
| MR1 | A7 | 2a on ½a ol brn | 8.00 | 4.00 |

See note after Macao No. MR2.

NEWSPAPER STAMPS.

King Luiz
N1

Stamps of Macao Surcharged in Black
Without Gum
1892   Perf. 12½   Unwmkd.
P1	N1	2½r on 20r brt rose	1.50	75
a.		"TIMOR" inverted		
P2	N1	2½r on 40r choc	1.50	75
a.		"TIMOR" inverted		
b.		Perf. 13½	4.50	3.00
c.		As "a," perf. 13½		
P3	N1	2½r on 80r gray	1.50	75
a.		"TIMOR" inverted		
b.		Perf. 13½	10.00	6.00

N2

N3

Perf. 11½, 13½
1893–95 Typographed.
P4	N2	2½r brown	50	40
a.		Perf. 12½	2.00	1.50
P5	N3	½a on 2½r brn ('95)	45	30

POSTAL TAX STAMPS.
Pombal Issue.
Common Design Types
1925   Perf. 12½.   Unwmkd.
RA1	CD28	2a lake & blk	45	45
RA2	CD29	2a lake & blk	45	45
RA3	CD30	2a lake & blk	45	45

Type of War Tax Stamp of Portuguese India Overprinted in Red
Instrução
D. L. n.º 7 de 3 2-1934
1934-35   Perf. 12.
| RA4 | WT1 | 2a grn & blk | 3.00 | 2.50 |
| RA5 | WT1 | 5a grn & blk | 5.00 | 2.50 |

Surcharged in Black.
| RA6 | WT1 | 7a on ½a rose & blk ('35) | 5.00 | 3.00 |

The tax was for local education.

Type of War Tax Stamp of Portuguese India Overprinted in Black
Assistência
D. L. n.º 72
1936   Perf. 12 x11½.
| RA7 | WT1 | 10a rose & blk | | 2.50 |

1937   Perf. 11½
| RA8 | WT1 | 10a grn & blk | 2.50 | 2.50 |

PT1   PT2

Typographed.
Without Gum
1948   Perf. 11½   Unwmkd.
| RA9 | PT1 | 10a dk bl | 2.50 | 1.75 |
| RA10 | PT1 | 20a green | 3.00 | 2.00 |

The 20a bears a different emblem.

Without Gum
1960   Perf. 11½
| RA11 | PT2 | 70c dk bl | 80 | 80 |
| RA12 | PT2 | 1.30e green | 1.50 | 1.50 |

Type of 1960 Redrawn
Without Gum
1967   Typographed   Perf. 10½
| RA13 | PT2 | 70c dp bl | 1.00 | 75 |
| RA14 | PT2 | 1.30e emerald | 1.75 | 1.35 |

The denominations of Nos. RA13–RA14 are 2mm. high. They are 2½mm. high on Nos. RA11–RA12. Other differences exist. The printed area of No. RA13 measures 18x31mm.; "Republica" 16mm.

Type of 1960 Serif Type Face
1967
| RA14A | PT2 | 70c dp bl | 1.75 | 1.50 |

Type of 1960, 2nd Redrawing
Without Gum
1967-68   Typographed   Perf. 10½
| RA15 | PT2 | 70c vio bl | 80 | 80 |
| RA16 | PT2 | 1.30e bluish grn ('68) | 1.50 | 1.50 |

The printed area measures 13x30mm. on Nos. RA15–RA16; "Republica" measures 10½mm.

743

TIMOR—TOGO

Woman and Star
PT3

1969-70		Lithographed	Perf. 13½	
RA17	PT3	30c vio bl & lt bl ('70)	10	10
RA18	PT3	50c dl org & mar	10	10
RA19	PT3	1e yel & brn	20	15

The 2.50e and 10e in design PT3 were revenue stamps.

Nos. RA15–RA16 Surcharged in Red or Carmine

.$30

1970		Typographed	Perf. 10½	
		Without Gum		
RA20	PT2	30c on 70c vio bl	7.00	5.00
RA21	PT2	30c on 1.30e bluish grn	7.00	5.00
RA22	PT2	50c on 70c vio bl	10.00	6.00
RA23	PT2	50c on 1.30e bluish grn	7.00	5.00
RA24	PT2	1e on 70c vio bl (C)	25.00	25.00
RA25	PT2	1e on 1.30e bluish grn	8.50	6.00

POSTAL TAX DUE STAMPS.
Pombal Issue.
Common Design Types

1925		Perf. 12½	Unwmkd.	
RAJ1	CD31	4a lake & blk	50	50
RAJ2	CD32	4a lake & blk	50	50
RAJ3	CD33	4a lake & blk	50	50

TOGO
(tō′gō)

LOCATION—In Western Africa, bordering on the Gulf of Guinea.
GOVT.—Republic.
AREA—20,400 sq. mi.
POP.—2,350,000 (est. 1977).
CAPITAL—Lomé.

The German Protectorate of Togo was occupied by Great Britain and France in World War I, and later mandated to them. The British area became part of Ghana. The French area was granted internal autonomy in 1956 and achieved independence in 1958. See "Togo" in Vol. I for British issues.

100 Pfennig = 1 Mark
12 Pence = 1 Shilling
100 Centimes = 1 Franc

German Protectorate.
AREA—34,934 sq. mi.
POP.—1,000,368 (1913).

A1   A2

Stamps of Germany Overprinted in Black.

1897		Perf. 13½x14½	Unwmkd.	
1	A1	3pf dk brn	5.75	9.00
a.		3pf yel brn	5.75	7.50
b.		3pf redsh brn	20.00	22.50
2	A1	5pf green	5.50	2.75
3	A2	10pf carmine	5.50	3.00
4	A2	20pf ultra	6.75	17.50
5	A2	25pf orange	45.00	67.50
6	A2	50pf red brn	45.00	67.50

Kaiser's Yacht, the "Hohenzollern"
A3   A4

1900		Typographed.	Perf. 14	
7	A3	3pf brown	1.10	1.10
8	A3	5pf green	17.50	90
9	A3	10pf carmine	45.00	90
10	A3	20pf ultra	1.40	1.75
11	A3	25pf org & blk, yel	1.40	11.50
12	A3	30pf org & blk, sal	1.75	11.50
13	A3	40pf lake & blk	1.40	11.50
14	A3	50pf pur & blk, sal	1.75	11.50
15	A3	80pf lake & blk, rose	3.00	17.50

Engraved.
Perf. 14½x14

16	A4	1m carmine	3.50	57.50
17	A4	2m blue	5.75	90.00
18	A4	3m blk vio	8.00	150.00
19	A4	5m sl & car	135.00	600.00
	Nos. 7-19 (13)		226.55	965.65

Counterfeit cancellations are found on Nos. 10–19 and 22.

Typographed.
Perf. 14
Wmkd. Lozenges (125)

20	A3	3pf brn ('19)	1.10	
21	A3	5pf green	1.50	2.25
22	A3	10pf car ('14)	1.75	115.00

Engraved.
Perf. 14½x14

| 23 | A4 | 5m sl & car ('15) | 22.50 | |

Nos. 20 and 23 were never placed in use.

Stamp issued under British Occupation, Nos. 33–91, are listed in Volume I.

Issued under French Occupation.
Stamps of German Togo Surcharged:

TOGO
Occupation
franco-anglaise
c

05   **05**   **05**
d   e   f

10   **10**   **10**
g   h   i

Wmkd. Lozenges (5pf and 10pf). (125)
Unwmkd. (other values).

1914		Perf. 14, 14½		
151	A3(c+d)	5c on 3pf brn	30.00	30.00
152	A3(c+e)	5c on 3pf brn	30.00	30.00
153	A3(c+f)	5c on 3pf brn	30.00	30.00
154	A3(c+g)	10c on 5pf grn	12.00	12.00
a.		Double surch.	750.00	750.00
155	A3(c+h)	10c on 5pf grn	13.00	13.00
156	A3(c+i)	10c on 5pf grn	17.00	17.00
158	A3(c)	20pf ultra	37.50	37.50
a.		3½mm between "TOGO" and "Occupation"	300.00	300.00
159	A3(c)	25pf org & blk, yel	40.00	40.00
160	A3(c)	30pf org & blk, sal	60.00	55.00
161	A3(c)	40pf lake & blk	450.00	325.00
162	A3(c)	80pf lake & blk, rose	450.00	325.00
	Nos. 151-162 (11)		1,169.50	914.50

Surcharged or Overprinted in Sans-Serif Type:

TOGO   **TOGO**
Occupation   **Occupation**
franco anglaise **franco anglaise**
05   k   l

1915				
164	A3	5c on 3pf brn	850.00	3,500.
165	A3	5pf green	300.00	300.00
166	A3	10pf carmine	900.00	300.00
a.		Inverted overprint		13,500.
167	A3	20pf ultra	1,100.	650.00
168	A3	25pf org & blk, yel	6,000.	4,750.
169	A3	30pf org & blk, sal	6,000.	4,750.
170	A3	40pf lake & blk	5,500.	4,750.
171	A3	50pf pur & blk, sal	8,500.	6,750.
172	A4	1m carmine		
173	A4	2m blue		15,000.
174	A4	3m blk vio		15,000.
175	A4	5m sl & car		

TOGO

Stamps of Dahomey,
1913-17,
Overprinted

Occupation
franco-
anglaise

1916-17		Perf. 13½x14.	Unwmkd.	
176	A5	1c vio & blk	12	12
a.		Double overprint	15.00	
177	A5	2c choc & rose	12	12
178	A5	4c blk & brn	12	12
a.		Double Ovpt.	110.00	110.00
179	A5	5c yel grn & bl grn	30	30
180	A5	10c org red & rose	22	22
181	A5	15c brn org & dk vio	50	50
a.		"Ooccupation"		
182	A5	20c gray & choc	32	32
183	A5	25c ultra & dp bl	32	32
184	A5	30c choc & vio	32	32
185	A5	35c brn & blk	50	50
186	A5	40c blk & red org	50	50
187	A5	45c gray & ultra	32	32
188	A5	50c choc & brn	32	32
189	A5	75c bl & vio	3.00	3.00
190	A5	1fr bl grn & blk	4.50	4.50
191	A5	2fr buff & choc	5.25	5.25
192	A5	5fr vio & dp bl	7.00	7.00
	Nos. 176-192 (17)		23.73	23.73

All values of the 1916–17 issue exist on chalky paper and all but the 15c, 25c and 35c on ordinary paper.

French Mandate
AREA—21,893 sq. mi.
POP.—780,497 (1938).

Type of Dahomey,
1913-39,
Overprinted   **TOGO**

1921				
193	A5	1c gray & yel grn	6	6
a.		Overprint omitted	90.00	
194	A5	2c bl & org	8	8
195	A5	4c ol grn & org	12	12
196	A5	5c dl red & blk	12	12
a.		Ovpt. omitted	225.00	
197	A5	10c bl grn & yel grn	30	30
198	A5	15c brn & car	30	30
199	A5	20c brn & org	45	45
200	A5	25c sl & org	28	28
201	A5	30c dp rose & ver	30	30
202	A5	35c red brn & yel grn	45	45
203	A5	40c bl grn & ol	75	75
204	A5	45c red brn & ol	75	75
205	A5	50c dp bl	38	38
206	A5	75c dl red & ultra	75	75
207	A5	1fr gray & ultra	90	90
208	A5	2fr ol grn & rose	2.75	2.75
209	A5	5fr org & grn	3.00	3.00
	Nos. 193-209 (17)		11.56	11.56

Stamps and Type of 1921 Surcharged:

60   **60**
═   ═

1922-25				
210	A5	25c on 15c ol brn & rose red ('25)	12	12
211	A5	25c on 2fr ol grn & rose ('24)	22	22
212	A5	25c on 5fr org & blk ('24)	22	22
213	A5	60c on 75c vio, pnksh ('22)	45	45
a.		"60" omitted	80.00	80.00
214	A5	65c on 45c red brn & ol ('25)	75	75
a.		"TOGO" omitted	80.00	
215	A5	85c on 75c dl red & ultra ('25)	80	80
	Nos. 210-215 (6)		2.56	2.56

Coconut Grove
A6

Cacao Trees
A7

Oil Palms
A8

1924-38			Typographed	
216	A6	1c yel & blk	6	6
217	A6	2c dp rose & blk	5	5
218	A6	4c dk bl & blk	8	8
219	A6	5c dp org & blk	8	8
220	A6	10c red vio & blk	8	8
221	A6	15c grn & blk	10	10
222	A7	20c gray & blk	10	10
223	A7	25c grn & blk, yel	30	30
224	A7	30c gray grn & blk	10	10
225	A7	30c brn & lt grn ('27)	12	12
226	A7	35c lt brn & blk	40	40
227	A7	35c dp bl grn & grn ('38)	12	12
228	A7	40c red org & blk	8	8
229	A7	45c car & blk	15	15
230	A7	50c ocher & blk, bluish	8	8
231	A7	55c vio bl & car rose ('38)	32	32

TOGO

232	A7	60c vio brn & blk, *pnksh*	8	8
233	A7	60c dp red ('26)	15	15
234	A7	65c gray lil & brn	15	15
235	A7	75c bl & blk	30	30
236	A7	80c ind & dl vio ('38)	50	38
237	A7	85c brn org & brn	40	40
238	A7	90c brn red & cer ('27)	50	50
239	A8	1fr red brn & blk, *bluish*	38	38
240	A8	1fr bl ('26)	15	15
241	A8	1fr gray lil & grn ('28)	1.50	1.25
242	A8	1fr dk red & red org ('38)	18	15
243	A8	1.10fr vio & dk brn ('28)	3.00	2.50
244	A8	1.25fr mag & rose ('33)	50	40
245	A8	1.50fr bl & lt bl ('27)	15	15
246	A8	1.75fr bis & pink ('33)	5.25	1.40
247	A8	1.75fr vio bl & ultra ('38)	50	50
248	A8	2fr bl blk & blk, *bluish*	50	50
249	A8	3fr bl grn & red org ('27)	65	65
250	A8	5fr red org & blk, *bluish*	1.00	1.00
251	A8	10fr ol brn & rose ('26)	90	90
252	A8	20fr brn red & blk, *yel* ('26)	1.10	1.10
		Nos. 216-252 (37)	20.06	15.09

No. 240 Surcharged with New Value and Bars in Red.

1926

| 253 | A8 | 1.25fr on 1fr lt bl | 22 | 22 |

Colonial Exposition Issue.
Common Design Types
1931, Apr. 13   Engr.   Perf. 12½
"TOGO" Typo. in Black

254	CD70	40c dp grn	2.75	2.75
255	CD71	50c violet	2.75	2.75
256	CD72	90c red org	2.75	2.75
257	CD73	1.50fr dl bl	2.75	2.75

Paris International Exposition Issue.
Common Design Types
1937   Perf. 13

258	CD74	20c dp vio	1.10	1.10
259	CD75	30c dk grn	1.10	1.10
260	CD76	40c car rose	1.10	1.10
261	CD77	50c dk brn	1.10	1.10
262	CD78	90c red	1.10	1.10
263	CD79	1.50fr ultra	1.10	1.10
		Nos. 258-263 (6)	6.60	6.60

Colonial Arts Exhibition Issue.
Souvenir Sheet.
Common Design Type
1937   Imperf.

| 264 | CD77 | 3fr Prus bl & blk | 3.00 | 3.00 |

Issued in sheets measuring 118x99mm. containing one stamp.

Caillié Issue
Common Design Type
1939, Apr. 5   Perf. 12½x12

265	CD81	90c org brn & org	45	45
266	CD81	2fr brt vio	45	45
267	CD81	2.25fr ultra & dk bl	45	45

Issued to commemorate the centenary of the death of René Caillié, French explorer.

Common Design Types
pictured in section at front of book.

New York World's Fair Issue.
Common Design Type
1939, May 10

| 268 | CD82 | 1.25fr car lake | 45 | 45 |
| 269 | CD82 | 2.25fr ultra | 45 | 45 |

Togolese Women
A9   A12

Mono River Bank—A10

Hunters—A11

1941   Engraved   Perf. 12½

270	A9	2c brn vio	5	5
271	A9	3c yel grn	5	5
272	A9	4c brn blk	6	6
273	A9	5c lil rose	5	5
274	A9	10c lt bl	6	6
275	A9	15c chestnut	6	6
276	A10	20c plum	5	5
277	A10	25c vio bl	5	5
278	A10	30c brn blk	10	10
279	A10	40c dk car	5	5
280	A10	45c dk grn	10	10
281	A10	50c chestnut	15	15
282	A10	60c red vio	15	15
283	A11	70c black	38	38
284	A11	90c lt vio	50	50
285	A11	1fr yel grn	28	28
286	A11	1.25fr cerise	50	50
287	A11	1.40fr org brn	30	30
288	A11	1.60fr orange	38	38
289	A11	2fr lt ultra	38	38
290	A12	2.25fr ultra	65	65
291	A12	2.50fr lil rose	50	50
292	A12	3fr brn vio	45	45
293	A12	5fr vermilion	50	50
294	A12	10fr rose vio	70	70
295	A12	20fr brn blk	1.50	1.50
		Nos. 270-295 (26)	8.00	8.00

Mono River Bank and Marshal Pétain
A12a

1941   Engraved   Perf. 12½x12

| 296 | A12a | 1fr green | 32 | |
| 297 | A12a | 2.50fr blue | 32 | |

Nos. 296-297 were issued by the Vichy government, and were not placed on sale in Togo. This is also true of nine stamps of types A9-A12 without "RF," issued in 1942-44.

Nos. 231, 238, 284 Surcharged with New Values in Various Colors

1 fr. 50
a

4 fr.
b
Perf. 14x13½, 12½.

1943-44   Unwmkd.

301	A7 (a)	1.50fr on 55c vio bl & car rose (Bk)	38	38
302	A7 (a)	1.50fr on 90c brn red & cer (Bk)	38	38
303	A11 (b)	3.50fr on 90c lt vio (Bk)	30	30
304	A11 (b)	4fr on 90c lt vio (R)	30	30
305	A11 (b)	5fr on 90c lt vio (Bl)	60	60
306	A11 (b)	5.50fr on 90c lt vio (Br)	75	75
307	A11 (b)	10fr on 90c lt vio (G) ('44)	75	75
308	A11 (b)	20fr on 90c lt vio (R)	1.00	1.00
		Nos. 301-308 (8)	4.46	4.46

Extracting Palm Oil
A13

Hunter   Cotton Spinners
A14   A15

Village of Atakpamé
A16

Red-fronted Gazelles
A17

Houses of the Cabrais
A18
Perf. 12½

1947, Oct. 6   Engr.   Unwmkd.

309	A13	10c dk red	5	5
310	A13	30c brt ultra	5	5
311	A13	50c bluish grn	6	6
312	A14	60c lil rose	12	6
313	A14	1fr chocolate	12	12
314	A14	1.20fr yel grn	15	15
315	A15	1.50fr brn org	32	32
316	A15	2fr olive	32	22
317	A15	2.50fr gray blk	65	65
318	A16	3fr slate	32	22
319	A16	3.60fr rose car	45	40
320	A16	4fr Prus grn	32	22
321	A17	5fr blk brn	80	20
322	A17	6fr ultra	80	70
323	A17	10fr org red	1.00	20
324	A18	15fr dp yel grn	1.10	32
325	A18	20fr grnsh blk	1.10	45
326	A18	25fr lil rose	1.10	50
		Nos. 309-326 (18)	8.83	4.89

Military Medal Issue.
Common Design Type
Engraved and Typographed.
1952, Dec. 1   Perf. 13

| 327 | CD101 | 15fr multi | 3.00 | 3.00 |

Gathering Palm Nuts
A19

1954, Nov. 29   Engraved

| 328 | A19 | 8fr vio & brn | 60 | 55 |
| 329 | A19 | 15fr ind & dk brn | 75 | 38 |

Goliath Beetle—A20

1955, May 2

| 330 | A20 | 8fr blk & grn | 1.40 | 90 |

Issued in connection with the International Exhibition for Wildlife Protection, Paris, May 1955.

FIDES Issue.
Common Design Type
Design: 15fr, Teacher and children planting tree.

1956   Perf. 13x12½   Unwmkd.

| 331 | CD103 | 15fr dk vio brn & org brn | 3.00 | 1.50 |

Republic

Woman Holding Flag
A21

TOGO

1957, June 8   Engr.   **Perf. 13**
| 332 | A21 | 15fr dk bl grn, sep & red | 65 | 18 |

Konkomba Helmet—A22

Teak Forest—A23

Design: 4fr, 5fr, 6fr, 8fr, 10fr, Buffon's kob.

1957, Oct.   Unwmkd.
333	A22	30c vio & cl	6	5
334	A22	50c ind & bl	6	5
335	A22	1fr pur & lil rose	6	5
336	A22	2fr dk brn & ol	5	5
337	A22	3fr blk & grn	6	6
338	A22	4fr bl & gray	55	22
339	A22	5fr bluish gray & mag	55	22
340	A22	6fr crim rose & bl gray	55	22
341	A22	8fr bluish gray & vio	55	22
342	A22	10fr grn & red brn	55	22
343	A23	15fr multi	28	18
344	A23	20fr vio, mar & org	35	18
345	A23	25fr ind & bis brn	40	28
346	A23	40fr dk brn, ol & dk grn	65	35
	Nos. 333-346 (14)		4.72	2.35

See Nos. 350–363.

Flags, Dove and U.N. Emblem
A24

1958, Dec. 10   Engr.   **Perf. 13**
| 347 | A24 | 20fr dk grn & rose red | 45 | 40 |

Universal Declaration of Human Rights, 10th anniversary.

Flower Issue.
Common Design Type

Designs: 5fr, Flower of Bombax tree (kapok). 20fr, Tectona grandis (teakwood) flower (horiz.).

1959, Jan. 15   Photo.   Unwmkd.
Perf. 12 x 12½, 12½ x 12
| 348 | CD104 | 5fr dp bl, rose & grn | 15 | 10 |
| 349 | CD104 | 20fr blk, yel & grn | 20 | 10 |

Types of 1957 Inscribed: "Republique du Togo."
Designs as Before.

1959, Jan. 15   Engr.   **Perf. 13**
350	A22	30c ultra & gray	5	5
351	A22	50c org & brt grn	6	5
352	A22	1fr red lil & lt ol grn	5	5
353	A22	2fr ol & bl grn	7	5
354	A22	3fr vio & rose car	10	8
355	A22	4fr lil rose & pale pur	35	15
356	A22	5fr grn & brn	35	22
357	A22	6fr ultra & gray bl	35	22
358	A22	8fr sl grn & bis	35	18
359	A22	10fr vio & lt brn	35	18
360	A23	15fr dk brn, bis & cl	22	18
361	A23	20fr blk, bl grn & brn	35	15
362	A23	25fr sep, red brn, ol & vio	60	35
363	A23	40fr dk grn, org brn & bl	60	38
	Nos. 350-363 (14)		3.85	2.29

"Five Continents," Ceiling Painting, Palais des Nations, Geneva
A25

1959, Oct. 24   Engr.   **Perf. 12½**
Centers in Dark Ultramarine.
364	A25	15fr brown	25	20
365	A25	20fr purple	30	25
366	A25	25fr dk org	40	35
367	A25	40fr dk grn	55	50
368	A25	60fr car rose	70	65
	Nos. 364-368 (5)		2.20	1.95

Issued for United Nations Day, Oct. 24.

Skier—A26

Bicyclist—A27

Sports: 50c, Ice Hockey. 1fr, Tobogganing. 15fr, Discus thrower (vert.). 20fr, Boxing (vert.). 25fr, Runner.

1960   **Perf. 13**   Unwmkd.
369	A26	30c sl grn, car & bl grn	12	10
370	A26	50c red & blk	12	10
371	A26	1fr red, blk & emer	25	20
372	A27	10fr brn, ultra & sl	35	15
373	A27	15fr dk red brn & grn	35	15
374	A27	20fr dk grn, gldn brn & brn	55	25
375	A27	25fr org, mag & brn	75	30
	Nos. 369-375 (7)		2.49	1.25

Nos. 369–371 commemorate the 8th Winter Olympic Games, Squaw Valley, Calif.; Nos. 372–375 commemorate the 17th Olympic Games, Rome.

Prime Minister Sylvanus Olympio and Togo Flag
A28

1960, Apr. 27   Lithographed
Center in Green, Red, Yellow & Brown.
376	A28	30c blk & buff	5	5
377	A28	50c brn & buff	5	5
378	A28	1fr lil & buff	5	5
379	A28	10fr bl & buff	12	6
380	A28	20fr red & buff	20	12
381	A28	25fr grn & buff	30	20
	Nos. 376-381 (6)		77	53

Issued to commemorate the proclamation of Togo's full independence, Apr. 27, 1960. See also C31–C33.

Flags of "Big Four," and British Flag
A29

Flags, "Big Four" and: 1fr, U.S.S.R. 20fr, France. 25fr, U.S.A.

1960, May 21   **Perf. 14x14½**
382	A29	50c beige, bl & red	6	5
383	A29	1fr bl grn, bl & red	12	6
384	A29	20fr gray, bl & red	32	25
385	A29	25fr lt bl, bl & red	40	30

Issued to commemorate the Summit Conference of France, Great Britain, United States and Russia in Paris, May 16.

Flag of Togo and U.N. Emblem
A30

1961, Jan. 6   **Perf. 14½x15**
Flag in red, olive green and yellow.
386	A30	30c red	5	5
387	A30	50c brown	6	5
388	A30	1fr ultra	5	5
389	A30	10fr maroon	10	6
390	A30	25fr black	30	15
391	A30	30fr violet	40	25
	Nos. 386-391 (6)		96	61

Togo's admission to United Nations.

Crowned Cranes over Map
A31

Augustino de Souza
A32

1961, Apr. 1   **Perf. 14½x15**
392	A31	1fr multi	10	5
393	A31	10fr multi	20	10
394	A31	25fr multi	50	25
395	A31	30fr multi	65	40

Lithographed
1961, Apr. 27   **Perf. 15**   Unwmkd.
396	A32	50c yel, red & blk	5	5
397	A32	1fr emer, brn & blk	5	5
398	A32	10fr grnsh bl, vio & blk	20	6
399	A32	25fr sal, org & blk	40	15
400	A32	30fr rose lil, bl & blk	60	30
	Nos. 396-400 (5)		1.30	61

Issued to commemorate the first anniversary of independence and to honor "Papa" Augustino de Souza, leader of the independence movement.

Daniel C. Beard—A33

Designs: 1fr, Lord Baden-Powell. 10fr, Togolese Scout and emblems. 25fr, Togolese Scout and flag (vert.). 30fr, Symbolic tents and fire (vert.). 100fr, Three hands of different races giving Scout sign.

Photogravure
1961, Oct. 7   **Perf. 13**   Unwmkd.
401	A33	50c brt rose & grn	5	5
402	A33	1fr dp vio & car	5	5
403	A33	10fr dk gray & brn	15	6
404	A33	25fr multi	40	8
405	A33	30fr grn, red & org brn	60	20
406	A33	100fr rose car & bl	1.50	60
	Nos. 401-406 (6)		2.70	99

Issued in honor of the Togolese Boy Scouts and to commemorate the 20th anniversary of the deaths of Daniel C. Beard and Lord Baden-Powell.
Four imperf. souvenir sheets each contain the six stamps, Nos. 401–406. Two sheets have a solid background of bright yellow, two a background of pale grayish brown. One yellow and one brown sheet have simulated perforations around the stamps. Size: 120x145mm. "REPUBLIQUE DU TOGO" is inscribed in white on bottom sheet margin. Price, each $3.

Plane, Ship and Part of Map of Africa—A34

Designs (Part of Map of Africa and): 25fr, Electric train and power mast. 30fr, Tractor and oil derricks. 85fr, Microscope and atomic symbol.

1961, Oct. 24   Lithographed
Black Inscriptions; Map in Ochre
407	A34	20fr vio bl, org & yel	25	10
408	A34	25fr gray, org & yel	35	10
409	A34	30fr dk red, yel & org	50	12
410	A34	85fr bl, yel & org	1.00	35
a.	Souv. sheet of 4		3.25	2.75

Issued to honor the United Nations' Economic Commission for Africa. No. 410a contains one each of Nos. 407–410, imperf., printed without separating margin between the individual stamps to show a complete map of Africa. Black marginal inscription. Size: 90x85mm.

TOGO

Children Dancing around Globe
A35

Cmdr. Alan B. Shepard
A36

Design: UNICEF Emblem, children and globe.

1961, Dec. 9 Perf. 13½ Unwmkd.
Black Inscription;
Multicolored Design.

411	A35	1fr ultra	5	5
412	A35	10fr red brn	10	5
413	A35	20fr lilac	20	10
414	A35	25fr gray	35	18
415	A35	30fr brt bl	60	20
416	A35	85fr dp lil	1.20	60
	Nos. 411-416 (6)	2.50	1.18

Issued to commemorate the 15th anniversary of the United Nations International Children's Emergency Fund.
Nos. 411-416 assembled in two rows show the globe and children of various races dancing around it.

1962, Feb. 24 Perf. 15x14

Design: 1fr, 30fr, Yuri A. Gagarin.

417	A36	50c green	8	5
418	A36	1fr car rose	14	5
419	A36	25fr blue	30	20
420	A36	30fr purple	40	25

Issued to honor the astronauts of 1961.
Issued in sheets of 50 and in miniature sheets of 12 stamps plus four central labels showing photographs of Alan B. Shepard (USA), Virgil I. Grissom (USA), Yuri A. Gagarin (USSR), Gherman S. Titov (USSR).

No. 417 Surcharged: "100F COL. JOHN H. GLENN USA VOL ORBITAL 20 FEVRIER 1962" and Bars in Black.

1962, March

421	A36	100fr on 50c grn	1.50	1.00
a.	Carmine surch.	1.50	1.00

Issued to commemorate the orbital flight of Lt. Col. John H. Glenn, Jr., USA, Feb. 20, 1962.

Independence Monument, Lomé
A37

Woman Carrying Fruit Basket
A38

Lithographed

1962, Apr. 27 Perf. 13½x14

422	A37	50c multi	5	5
423	A38	1fr grn & pink	5	5
424	A37	5fr multi	10	5
425	A38	20fr pur & yel	25	12
426	A37	25fr multi	40	15
427	A38	30fr red & yel	45	25
a.	Souv. sheet of 3	90	90
	Nos. 422-427 (6)	1.30	67

2nd anniversary of Togo's independence. No. 427a contains one each of Nos. 424, 425 and 427, imperf. Gray background, inscriptions white. Size: 127x140mm.

Malaria Eradication Emblem
A39

1962, June 2 Perf. 13½x13
Multicolored Design

428	A39	10fr yel grn	20	8
429	A39	25fr pale lil	40	12
430	A39	30fr ocher	50	20
431	A39	85fr lt bl	1.10	45

Issued for the World Health Organization drive to eradicate malaria.

Capitol, Pres. John F. Kennedy and Pres. Sylvanus Olympio
A40

1962, July 4 Perf. 13 Unwmkd.
Inscription and Portraits in Slate Green

432	A40	50c yellow	6	5
433	A40	1fr blue	6	5
434	A40	2fr vermilion	8	5
435	A40	5fr lilac	15	6
436	A40	25fr pale vio	45	15
437	A40	100fr brt grn	1.75	80
a.	Souv. sheet	7.50	7.50
	Nos. 432-437 (6)	2.55	1.16

Issued to commemorate the visit of President Sylvanus Olympio of Togo to the United States, March, 1962.
No. 437a contains one imperf. No. 437. Marginal design shows White House, Washington, and President's Residence, Lomé, in slate green, American and Togolese flags in original colors. Size: 104x75mm.

Mail Coach and Stamps of 1897
A41

Designs: 50c, Mail ship and stamps of 1900. 1fr, Mail train and stamps of 1915. 10fr, Motorcycle truck and stamp of 1924. 25fr, Mail truck and stamp of 1941. 30fr, DC-3 and stamp of 1947.

1963, Jan. 12 Photo. Perf. 13

438	A41	30c multi	5	5
439	A41	50c multi	6	5
440	A41	1fr multi	8	7
441	A41	10fr vio, dp org & blk	15	8
442	A41	25fr dk red brn, blk & yel grn	30	20
443	A41	30fr ol brn & lil rose	45	30
	Nos. 438-443, C34 (7)	2.34	1.35

Issued to commemorate the 65th anniversary of Togolese mail service.
For souvenir sheet see No. C34a.

Hands Reaching for FAO Emblem
A42

1963, Mar. 21 Perf. 14

444	A42	50c bl, org & dk brn	5	5
445	A42	1fr ol grn, org & dk brn	5	5
446	A42	25fr brn, dk brn & org	45	20
447	A42	30fr vio, dk brn & org	60	25

Issued for the "Freedom from Hunger" campaign of the U.N. Food and Agriculture Organization.

Togolese Flag and Lomé Harbor
A43

1963, Apr. 27 Litho. Perf. 13x12½
Flag in Red, Green and Yellow

448	A43	50c red brn & blk	5	5
449	A43	1fr dk car rose & blk	5	5
450	A43	25fr dl bl & blk	40	20
451	A43	50fr bis & blk	70	40

3rd anniversary of independence.

Centenary Emblem
A44

1963, June 1 Photo. Perf. 14
Flag in Red, Olive Green, Yellow.

452	A44	25fr br, blk & red	30	20
453	A44	30fr dl grn, blk & red	45	28

International Red Cross centenary.

Abraham Lincoln, Broken Fetters, Maps of Africa and United States
A45

1963, Oct. Perf. 13x14 Unwmkd.

454	A45	50c multi	5	5
455	A45	1fr multi	6	5
456	A45	25fr multi	40	18

Issued to commemorate the centenary of the emancipation of the American slaves. See No. C35 and souvenir sheet No. C35a.

U.N. Emblem and "15"
A46

Hibiscus
A47

1963, Dec. 10 Photo. Perf. 14x13

457	A46	50c ultra, dk bl & rose red	5	5
458	A46	1fr yel grn, dk bl & rose red	5	5
459	A46	25fr lil, dk bl & rose red	35	18
460	A46	85fr gold, dk bl & rose red	1.25	50

Issued to commemorate the 15th anniversary of the Universal Declaration of Human Rights.

1964 Perf. 14 Unwmkd.

Designs: 50c, Orchid. 2fr, Butterfly. 5fr, Hinged tortoise. 8fr, Ball python. 10fr, Bunea alcinoe (moth). 20fr, Octopus. 25fr, John Dory (fish). 30fr, French angelfish. 40fr, Hippopotamus. 60fr, Bohor reedbuck. 85fr, Anubius baboon.

Size: 22½x31mm.

461	A47	50c multi	5	5
462	A47	1fr yel, car & grn	5	5
463	A47	1fr lil, yel & blk	5	5
464	A47	5fr gray & multi	6	5
465	A47	8fr cit, red brn & blk	12	5
466	A47	10fr multi	15	5
467	A47	20fr dl bl, yel & brn	30	10
468	A47	25fr dl bl, grn & yel	35	12
469	A47	30fr multi	45	15
470	A47	40fr grn, red brn & blk	60	20
471	A47	60fr grnsh bl & red brn	90	30
472	A47	85fr lt grn, brn & org	1.25	50
	Nos. 461-472 (12)	4.33	1.67

See also Nos. 511-515, C36-C40, J56-J63.

Nos. 454-456 Overprinted Diagonally: "En Mémoire de / JOHN F. KENNEDY / 1917-1963"

1964, Feb. Perf. 13x14

473	A45	50c multi	5	5
474	A45	1fr multi	6	5
475	A45	25fr multi	35	10

Issued in memory of John F. Kennedy. See No. C41 and note on souvenir sheets following it.

Isis of Kalabsha
A48

Designs: 25fr, Head of Ramses II. 30fr, Colonnade of Birth House at Philae.

1964, Mar. 8 Litho. Perf. 14

476	A48	20fr blk, pale grn & red	25	10
477	A48	25fr blk & lil rose	35	15
478	A48	30fr blk & cit	45	20
a.	Souv. sheet of 3	1.50	1.50

Issued to publicize the UNESCO world campaign to save historic monuments in Nubia. No. 478a contains three imperf. stamps similar to Nos. 476-478 with simulated perforations. Gray margin with black inscription. Size: 112x78mm.

Phosphate Mine, Kpeme
A49

Designs: 25fr, Phosphate plant, Kpeme. 60fr, Phosphate train. 85fr, Loading ship with phosphate.

1964, Apr. 27 Perf. 14 Unwmkd.

479	A49	5fr brn & bis brn	7	5
480	A49	25fr dk pur & brn car	35	20

TOGO

481	A49	60fr dk grn & ol	90	35
482	A49	85fr vio blk & Prus bl	1.25	45

Fourth anniversary of independence.

African Breaking Slavery Chain, and Map
A50

1964, May 25 Photo. Perf. 14x13

483	A50	5fr dp org & brn	7	5
484	A50	25fr ol grn & brn	35	12
485	A50	85fr rose car & brn	1.25	30

Issued to commemorate the first anniversary of the meeting of African heads of state at Addis Ababa. See No. C42.

Pres. Nicolas Grunitzky and Butterfly—A51

Designs (President and): 5fr, Dove. 25fr, 85fr, Flower.

1964, Aug. 18 Litho. Perf. 14

486	A51	1fr pink, cl & dl vio	5	5
487	A51	5fr bis brn & dk brn	7	5
488	A51	15fr grnsh bl, dk bl & vio	40	18
489	A51	45fr mar, org, vio & mag	70	25
490	A51	85fr yel grn & sl grn	1.25	50
		Nos. 486-490 (5)	2.47	1.03

National Union and Reconciliation.

Soccer—A52

Designs: 5fr, Runner. 25fr, Discus.

1964, Oct. Photo. Perf. 14

491	A52	1fr gray grn	5	5
492	A52	5fr dk bl	7	5
493	A52	25fr rose lake	40	20
494	A52	45fr bl grn	65	35
		Nos. 491-494, C43 (5)	2.67	1.25

Issued to commemorate the 18th Olympic Games, Tokyo, Oct. 10–25. For souvenir sheet see No. C43a.

Cooperation Issue
Common Design Type

1964, Nov. 7 Engraved Perf. 13

495	CD119	25fr mag, dk brn & ol bis	40	20

Dirigible and Balloons—A53

Designs: 25fr, 45fr, Otto Lilienthal's glider, 1894; Wright Brothers' plane, 1903; Boeing 707.

1964, Dec. 5 Photo. Perf. 14x13

496	A53	5fr org lil & grn	8	5
497	A53	10fr brt grn, dl bl & dk red	15	6
498	A53	25fr bl, vio bl & org	35	15
499	A53	45fr brt pink, vio bl & grn	65	25
a.		Souv. sheet of 4	2.50	2.50
		Nos. 496-499, C44 (5)	2.73	1.11

Issued to commemorate the inauguration of the national airline "Air Togo." No. 499a contains four imperf. stamps similar to Nos. 497–499 and No. C44 with simulated perforations and gray margin with white inscription. Size: 136x120mm.

Orbiting Geophysical Observatory and Mariner—A54

Space Satellites: 15fr, 25fr, Tiros, Telstar and Orbiting Solar Observatory. 20fr, 50fr, Nimbus, Syncom and Relay.

1964, Dec. 12 Litho. Perf. 14

500	A54	10fr dp rose, bl & yel	15	6
501	A54	15fr multi	20	6
502	A54	20fr yel, grn & vio	30	8
503	A54	25fr multi	35	10
504	A54	45fr brt grn, dk bl & yel	65	15
505	A54	50fr yel, grn & org	75	20
a.		Souvenir sheet of 4	2.50	2.50
		Nos. 500-505 (6)	2.40	65

Issued to publicize the International Quiet Sun Year. No. 505a contains 4 imperf. stamps similar to Nos. 502–505. Orange and green margin. Size: 202x122 mm.

Togo Olympic Stamps Printed in Israel
A55

Arms of Israel and Togo—A56

Designs (Pres. Nicolas Grunitzky of Togo and): 20fr, Church of the Mount of Beatitudes. 45fr, Ruins of Synagogue at Capernaum.

Perf. 13½x14½, 14x13½

1964, Dec. 26 Photogravure

506	A55	5fr rose vio	6	5
507	A56	20fr grnsh bl, grn & dl pur	22	12
508	A56	25fr red & bluish grn	35	18
509	A56	45fr dl yel, ol & dl pur	90	50
510	A56	85fr mag & bluish grn	75	25
a.		Souvenir sheet of 4	5.25	5.25
		Nos. 506-510 (5)	2.28	1.10

Issued to honor Israel-Togo friendship. No. 510a contains 4 imperf. stamps similar to No. 510. Gray margin with white inscription. Size: 138x102½mm.

Type of Regular Issue, 1964

1965, June Perf. 14 Unwmkd.

Designs: 3fr, Morpho aega butterfly. 4fr, Scorpion. 6fr, Bird-of-paradise flower. 15fr, Flap-necked chameleon. 45fr, Ring-tailed palm civet.

Size: 23x31mm.

511	A47	3fr bis & multi	5	5
512	A47	4fr org & bluish blk	7	5
513	A47	6fr multi	8	5
514	A47	15fr brt pink, yel & brn	20	5
515	A47	45fr dl grn, org & brn	65	20
		Nos. 511-515 (5)	1.05	40

Syncom Satellite, Radar Station and ITU Emblem—A57

1965, June Perf. 13x14

516	A57	10fr Prus bl	15	10
517	A57	20fr ol bis	30	12
518	A57	25fr brt bl	40	18
519	A57	45fr crimson	65	32
520	A57	50fr green	75	35
		Nos. 516-520 (5)	2.25	1.07

Issued to commemorate the centenary of the International Telecommunication Union.

Abraham Lincoln Discus Thrower, Flags of Togo and Congo
A58 A59

1965, June 26 Photo. Perf. 13x14

521	A58	1fr magenta	5	5
522	A58	5fr dl grn	6	5
523	A58	20fr brown	30	12
524	A58	25fr slate	40	18
		Nos. 521-524, C45 (5)	2.56	1.00

Issued to commemorate the centenary of the death of Abraham Lincoln. For souvenir sheet see No. C45a.

1965, July Perf. 14x13 Unwmkd.

Designs (flags and): 10fr, Javelin thrower. 15fr, Handball player. 25fr, Runner.

Flags in Red, Yellow and Green

525	A59	5fr dp mag	8	5
526	A59	10fr dk bl	15	6
527	A59	15fr brown	25	9
528	A59	25fr dk pur	40	18
		Nos. 525-528, C46 (5)	2.38	98

Issued to commemorate the First African Games, Brazzaville, July 18–25.

Winston Churchill and "V"
A60

Stalin, Roosevelt and Churchill at Yalta—A61

Perf. 13½x14, 14x13½

1965, Aug. 7 Photogravure

529	A60	5fr dl grn	5	5
530	A61	10fr brt vio & gray	15	6
531	A60	20fr brown	30	17
532	A61	45fr Prus bl & gray	75	35
		Nos. 529-532, C47 (5)	2.65	1.23

Issued in memory of Sir Winston Spencer Churchill (1874–1965), British statesman and World War II leader. For souvenir sheet see No. C47a.

Unisphere and New York Skyline
A62

Designs: 10fr, Togolese dancers and drummer, Unisphere. 50fr, Michelangelo's Pieta and Unisphere.

1965, Aug. 28 Photo. Perf. 14

533	A62	5fr grnsh bl & vio blk	6	5
534	A62	10fr yel grn & dk brn	15	7
535	A62	25fr brn org & dk grn	35	15
536	A62	50fr vio & sl grn	65	35
537	A62	85fr rose red & brn	1.25	60
a.		Souv. sheet of 2	2.00	2.00
		Nos. 533-537 (5)	2.46	1.22

Issued to commemorate the New York World's Fair, 1964–65. No. 537a contains two imperf. stamps similar to Nos. 536–537 with simulated perforations. Light brown margin with brown inscription. Size: 140x96mm.

TOGO

749

"Constructive Cooperation" and Olive Branch—A63

Designs: 25fr, 40fr, Hands of various races holding globe and olive branch. 85fr, Handclasp, olive branch and globe.

1965, Sept. 25 Perf. 14 Unwmkd.
538	A63	5fr vio, lt bl & org	7	5
539	A63	15fr brn, org & gray	18	10
540	A63	25fr bl & org	35	15
541	A63	40fr dp car, gray & org	55	25
542	A63	85fr grn & org	1.20	60
		Nos. 538-542 (5)	2.35	1.15

International Cooperation Year, 1965.

Major White and Gemini 4—A64

Design: 25fr, Lt. Col. Alexei Leonov and Voskhod 2.

1965, Nov. 25 Photo. Perf. 13½x14
543	A64	25fr dp bl & brt car rose	35	15
544	A64	50fr grn & brn	75	30

Issued to commemorate the "Walks in Space" of Lt. Col. Alexei Leonov (USSR), and Major Edward H. White (USA). Printed in sheets of 12 with ornamental borders.

Adlai E. Stevenson and U.N. Headquarters—A65

Designs: 5fr, "ONU" and doves. 10fr, U.N. emblem and headquarters. 20fr, "ONU" and orchids.

1965, Dec. 15 Perf. 14x13½
545	A65	5fr dk brn, yel & lt bl	7	5
546	A65	10fr org, dk bl & grn	15	6
547	A65	20fr dk grn, yel grn & org brn	30	12
548	A65	25fr brt yel, dk bl & bluish grn	40	18
		Nos. 545-548, C48 (5)	2.42	1.01

Issued to commemorate the 20th anniversary of the United Nations and in memory of Adlai E. Stevenson (1900-1965), U.S. ambassador to the U.N. For souvenir sheet see No. C48a.

A particular stamp may be scarce, but if few want it, its market potential may remain relatively low.

Pope Paul VI, Plane and U.N. Emblem—A66

Designs: 15fr, 30fr, Pope addressing U.N. General Assembly and U.N. emblem (vert.). 20fr, Pope and New York skyline with U.N. Headquarters.

1966, March 5 Litho. Perf. 12
549	A66	5fr bl & multi	7	5
550	A66	15fr lt vio & multi	20	7
551	A66	20fr bis & multi	30	15
552	A66	30fr lt ultra & multi	45	20
		Nos. 549-552, C49-C50 (6)	3.02	1.02

Issued to commemorate the visit of Pope Paul VI to the United Nations, New York City, Oct. 4, 1965.

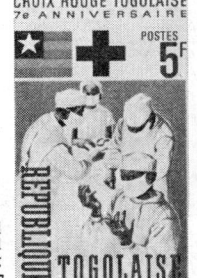

Surgical Operation and Togolese Flag A67

Designs (Togolese Flag and): 10fr, 30fr, Blood transfusion. 45fr, Profiles of African man and woman.

1966, May 7 Litho. Perf. 12
553	A67	5fr multi	6	5
554	A67	15fr multi	15	5
555	A67	15fr multi	20	10
556	A67	30fr multi	45	20
557	A67	45fr multi	75	30
		Nos. 553-557, C51 (6)	3.26	1.20

Togolese Red Cross, 7th anniversary.

Talisman Roses and WHO Headquarters, Geneva A68

Designs: Various flowers and WHO Headquarters.

1966, May Litho. Perf. 12
558	A68	5fr lt yel grn & multi	6	5
559	A68	10fr pale pink & multi	15	5
560	A68	20fr dl yel & multi	20	7
561	A68	20fr pale gray & multi	30	15
562	A68	30fr tan & multi	45	25
		Nos. 558-562, C52-C53 (7)	3.26	.92

Issued to commemorate the inauguration of World Health Organization Headquarters, Geneva.

Nos. 543-544 Overprinted or Surcharged in Red

1966, July 11 Photo. Perf. 13½x14
563	A64	50fr grn & brn, (Envolée Surveyor 1)	75	15
564	A64	50fr grn & brn, (Envolée Gemini 9)	75	15
565	A64	100fr on 25fr dp bl & brt car rose, (Envolée Luna 9)	1.65	30
566	A64	100fr on 25fr dp bl & brt car rose, (Envolée Venus 3)	1.65	30

Issued to publicize United States and Russian achievements in Space. Sheets of 12 of Nos. 543-544 received two different overprints each, creating 6 se-tenant pairs of Nos. 563-564 and of Nos. 565-566 each. The sheet margins were overprinted with additional commemorative inscriptions.

Wood Carver A69   Togolese Dancer A70

Arts and Crafts: 10fr, Basket maker. 15fr, Woman weaver. 30fr, Woman potter.

1966, Sept. Photo. Perf. 13x14
567	A69	5fr bl, yel & dk brn	6	5
568	A69	10fr emer, org & dk brn	15	6
569	A69	15fr ver, yel & dk brn	20	10
570	A69	30fr lil, dk brn & yel	45	20
		Nos. 567-570, C55-C56 (6)	3.11	.96

1966, Nov. Photogravure Perf. 13x14

Designs: 5fr, Togolese man. 20fr, Woman dancer from North Togo holding branches. 25fr, Male dancer. 30fr, Male dancer from North Togo with horned helmet. 45fr, Drummer.

571	A70	5fr emer & multi	8	5
572	A70	10fr dl yel & multi	15	6
573	A70	20fr lt ultra & multi	30	10
574	A70	25fr dp org & multi	35	14
575	A70	30fr red vio & multi	45	18
576	A70	45fr bl & multi	65	30
		Nos. 571-576, C57-C58 (8)	3.63	1.48

Soccer Players and Jules Rimet Cup A71

Various Soccer Scenes.

1966, Dec. 14 Photo. Perf. 14x13
577	A71	5fr bl, brn & red	6	5
578	A71	10fr brick red & multi	15	6
579	A71	20fr ol, brn & dk grn	30	8
580	A71	25fr vio, brn & org	35	10
581	A71	30fr ocher & multi	45	17

582	A71	45fr emer, brn & mag	65	30
		Nos. 577-582, C59-C60 (8)	3.61	1.31

Issued to commemorate England's victory in the World Soccer Cup Championship, Wembley, July 30. For souvenir sheet see No. C60a.

African Mouthbreeder and Sailboat—A72

Designs: 10fr, Yellow jack and trawler. 15fr, Banded distichodus and seiner. 25fr, Jewelfish and galley. 45fr, like 5fr.

**1967, Jan. 14 Photo. Perf. 14
Fish in Natural Colors**
583	A72	5fr lt ultra & blk	6	5
584	A72	10fr brn org & brn	15	5
585	A72	15fr brt rose & dk bl	20	10
586	A72	25fr ol & blk	35	18
587	A72	30fr grnsh bl & blk	45	25
		Nos. 583-587, C61-C62 (7)	3.21	1.33

African Boy and Greyhound A73

(UNICEF Emblem and): 10fr, Boy and Irish setter. 20fr, Girl and doberman.

1967, Feb. 11 Photo. Perf. 14x13½
588	A73	5fr org, plum & blk	8	5
589	A73	10fr yel grn, red brn & dk grn	15	5
590	A73	15fr brt rose, brn & blk	20	8
591	A73	20fr bl, vio bl & blk	30	12
592	A73	30fr ol, sl grn & blk	45	15
		Nos. 588-592, C63-C64 (7)	3.18	1.15

Issued to commemorate the 20th anniversary (in 1966) of UNICEF (United Nations Children's Fund).

French A-1 Satellite A74

Designs: 5fr, Diamant rocket (vert.). 15fr, Fr-1 satellite (vert.). 20fr, 40fr, D-1 satellite. 25fr, A-1 satellite.

Perf. 14x13½, 13½x14

1967, March 18 Photogravure
593	A74	5fr multi	6	3
594	A74	10fr multi	15	5
595	A74	15fr multi	20	5
596	A74	20fr multi	30	7

TOGO

597	A74	25fr multi	40	10
598	A74	40fr multi	65	20
		Nos. 593-598, C65-C66 (8)	4.11	1.23

French achievements in space.

Duke Ellington, Saxophone, Trumpet, Drums—A75

Designs: (UNESCO Emblem and): 5fr, Johann Sebastian Bach and organ. 10fr, Ludwig van Beethoven, violin and clarinet. 20fr, Claude A. Debussy, piano and harp. 30fr, like 15fr.

1967, Apr. 15 Photo. Perf. 14x13½

599	A75	5fr org & multi	6	5
600	A75	10fr multi	15	6
601	A75	15fr multi	20	10
602	A75	20fr lt bl & multi	30	12
603	A75	30fr lil & multi	45	18
		Nos. 599-603, C67-C68 (7)	3.16	1.11

Issued to commemorate the 20th anniversary (in 1966) of UNESCO (United Nations Educational, Scientific and Cultural Organization).

EXPO Emblem, British Pavilion and Day Lilies—A76

Designs: 10fr, French pavilion and roses. 30fr, African village and bird-of-paradise flower.

1967, May 30 Photo. Perf. 14

604	A76	5fr brt pink & multi	6	5
605	A76	10fr dl org & multi	15	6
606	A76	30fr bl & multi	45	15
		Nos. 604-606, C69-C72 (7)	4.96	1.86

Issued to commemorate EXPO '67 International Exhibition, Montreal, Apr. 28–Oct. 27.

Lions Emblem—A77

Designs: 20fr, 45fr, Lions emblem and flowers.

1967, July 29 Photo. Perf. 13x14

607	A77	10fr yel & multi	15	5
608	A77	20fr multi	30	10
609	A77	30fr grn & multi	45	15
610	A77	45fr bl & multi	75	30

50th anniversary of Lions International.

Montagu's Harriers—A78

Designs: 5fr, Bohor reedbucks. 15fr, Zebras. 20fr, 30fr, Marsh harriers. 25fr, Leopard.

1967, Aug. 19 Photo. Perf. 14x13½

611	A78	5fr lil & org brn	6	5
612	A78	10fr dk red, yel & dl bl	15	5
613	A78	15fr grn, blk & lil	20	6
614	A78	20fr dk brn, yel & dl bl	30	8
615	A78	25fr brn, ol & yel	35	12
616	A78	30fr vio, yel & dl bl	45	18
		Nos. 611-616, C79-C80 (8)	3.06	1.09

Stamp Auction and Togo Nos. 16 and C42 A79

Designs: 10fr, 45fr, Exhibition and Nos. 67 (British) and 520. 15fr, 30fr, Stamp store and No. 230. 20fr, Stamp packet vending machine and No. 545.

1967, Oct. 14 Photo. Perf. 14x13

Stamps on Stamps in Original Colors

617	A79	5fr purple	6	5
618	A79	10fr dk brn	15	5
619	A79	15fr dp bl	30	8
620	A79	20fr sl grn	40	10
621	A79	30fr red brn	55	17
622	A79	45fr Prus bl	75	25
		Nos. 617-622, C82-C83 (8)	5.61	1.65

Issued to commemorate the 70th anniversary of the first Togolese stamps. For souvenir sheet see No. C82a.
See Nos. 853-855, C205.

Monetary Union Issue
Common Design Type

1967, Nov. 4 Engraved Perf. 13

623	CD125	30fr dk bl, vio bl & brt grn	45	15

Issued to commemorate the 5th anniversary of the West African Monetary Union.

Broad Jump, Summer Olympics Emblem and View of Mexico City A80

Designs: 15fr, Ski jump, Winter Olympics emblem and ski lift. 30fr, Runners, Summer Olympics emblem and view of Mexico City. 45fr, Bobsledding, Winter Olympics emblem and ski lift.

1967, Dec. 2 Photo. Perf. 13x14

624	A80	5fr org & multi	6	5
625	A80	15fr multi	13	8
626	A80	30fr multi	45	18
627	A80	45fr multi	65	30
		Nos. 624-627, C84-C85 (6)	3.54	1.41

Issued to publicize the 1968 Olympic Games. For souvenir sheet see No. C85a.

Nos. 604-606 Overprinted:
"JOURNÉE NATIONALE / DU TOGO / 29 SEPTEMBRE 1967"

1967, Dec. Perf. 14

628	A76	5fr multi	6	5
629	A76	10fr multi	15	5
630	A76	30fr bl & multi	50	15
		Nos. 628-630, C86-C89 (7)	5.11	1.57

National Day, Sept. 29, 1967.

The Gleaners, by François Millet and Phosphate Works, Benin A81

Design: 20fr, 45fr, 90fr, The Weaver at the Loom, by Vincent van Gogh, and textile plant, Dadia.

1968, Jan. Photo. Perf. 14

631	A81	10fr ol & multi	10	5
632	A81	20fr multi	30	8
633	A81	30fr brn & multi	45	15
634	A81	45fr multi	65	25
635	A81	60fr dk bl & multi	90	25
636	A81	90fr multi	1.35	50
		Nos. 631-636 (6)	3.75	1.28

Industrialization of Togo.

Togolese Women Brewing Beer A82

The Beer Drinkers, by Edouard Manet A83

Design: 45fr, Modern beer bottling plant.

1968, Mar. 26 Litho. Perf. 14

637	A82	20fr emer & multi	30	10
638	A83	30fr dk car & multi	45	15
639	A82	45fr org & multi	65	20

Publicity for local beer industry.

Symbolic Water Cycle, Flower and Cogwheels A84

1968, Apr. 6

640	A84	30fr multi	45	20

Issued to publicize the Hydrological Decade (UNESCO), 1965-74. See No. C90.

Viking Ship and Portuguese Brigantine—A85

Designs: 10fr, Fulton's steamship and modern steamship. 20fr, Harbor activities and map of Africa.

1968, Apr. 26 Photo. Perf. 14x13½

641	A85	5fr brt grn & multi	6	5
642	A85	10fr dp org & multi	15	5
643	A85	20fr grn & multi	30	8
644	A85	30fr yel & multi	45	17
		Nos. 641-644, C91-C92 (6)	2.96	95

Inauguration of Lomé Harbor.

Adenauer and 1968 Europa Emblem A86

1968, May 25 Photo. Perf. 14

645	A86	90fr ol grn & brn org	1.20	35

Issued in memory of Konrad Adenauer (1876-1967), chancellor of West Germany (1949-63).

Adam and Eve Expelled from Paradise, by Michelangelo A87

Paintings: 20fr, The Anatomy Lesson of Dr. Tulp, by Rembrandt. 30fr, The Anatomy Lesson, by Rembrandt (detail). 45fr, Jesus Healing the Sick, by Raphael.

1968, June 22 Photo. Perf. 14

646	A87	15fr crim & multi	20	6
647	A87	20fr multi	30	10
648	A87	30fr grn & multi	45	15
649	A87	45fr multi	65	25
		Nos. 646-649, C93-C94 (6)	3.85	1.21

Issued to commemorate the 20th anniversary of the World Health Organization.

Olympic Monument, San Salvador Island, and Wrestling—A88

Olympic Monument, San Salvador Island, Bahamas and: 20fr, Boxing. 30fr, Japanese wrestling. 45fr, Running.

1968, July 27 Perf. 14x13½

650	A88	15fr org, red org & brn	20	8

TOGO

651	A88	20fr ver & multi		30	10
652	A88	30fr emer & multi		45	15
653	A88	45fr multi		65	25
		Nos. 650-653, C95-C96 (6)		3.85	1.23

Issued to commemorate the 19th Olympic Games, Mexico City, Oct. 12–27.

Chick Holding Lottery Ticket A89 **Scout Before Tent** A90

Design: 45fr, Lottery ticket, horseshoe and four-leaf clover.

1968, Oct. 5   Litho.   Perf. 14

654	A89	30fr dk grn & multi	45	15
655	A89	45fr multi	65	25

2nd anniversary of National Lottery.

1968, Nov. 23

Designs: 10fr, 45fr, Scout leader training cub scouts (horiz.). 20fr, First aid practice (horiz.). 30fr, Scout game.

656	A90	5fr dp org & multi	6	5
657	A90	10fr emer & multi	13	5
658	A90	20fr multi	30	10
659	A90	30fr multi	45	20
660	A90	45fr bl & multi	65	30
		Nos. 656-660, C97-C98 (7)	3.84	1.55

Issued to honor the Togolese Boy Scouts.

Adoration of the Shepherds, by Giorgione—A91

Paintings: 20f, Adoration of the Magi, by Pieter Brueghel. 30fr, Adoration of the Magi, by Botticelli. 45fr, Adoration of the Magi, by Durer.

1968, Dec. 28   Litho.   Perf. 14

661	A91	15fr grn & multi	20	8
662	A91	20fr multi	30	10
663	A91	30fr multi	45	15
664	A91	45fr multi	65	25
		Nos. 661-664, C100-C101 (6)	3.85	1.33

Christmas 1968.

Martin Luther King, Jr. A92

Portraits and Human Rights Flame: 20fr, Professor René Cassin (author of Declaration of Human Rights). 45fr, Pope John XXIII.

1969, Feb. 1   Photo.   Perf. 13½x14

665	A92	15fr brn org & sl grn	20	12
666	A92	20fr grnsh bl & vio	30	18
667	A92	30fr ver & sl bl	35	25
668	A92	45fr ol & car rose	60	30
		Nos. 665-668, C102-C103 (6)	3.30	1.70

International Human Rights Year 1968.

Omnisport Stadium and Soccer A93

Designs (Stadium and): 15fr, Handball. 20fr, Volleyball. 30fr, Basketball. 45fr, Tennis.

1969, Apr. 26   Photo.   Perf. 14x13½

669	A93	10fr emer, dp car & dk brn	8	5
670	A93	15fr org, ultra & dk brn	18	10
671	A93	20fr yel, ol & dk brn	28	15
672	A93	30fr dl grn, bl & dk brn	35	20
673	A93	45fr org, lil & dk brn	65	30
		Nos. 669-673, C105-C106 (7)	4.09	1.60

Opening of Omnisport Stadium, Lomé.

Lunar Module Eagle Landing on Moon A94

Designs: 20fr, 45fr, Astronaut and Eagle on moon, earth and stars in sky.

1969, July 21   Litho.   Perf. 14

674	A94	1fr grn & multi	5	5
675	A94	20fr brn & multi	30	8
676	A94	30fr scar & multi	40	15
677	A94	45fr ultra & multi	70	25
		Nos. 674-677, C107-C108 (6)	3.05	1.43

Issued to commemorate man's first landing on the moon, July 20, 1969. U.S. astronauts Neil A. Armstrong and Col. Edwin E. Aldrin, Jr., with Lieut. Col. Michael Collins piloting Apollo 11.

1969, Aug. 16   Litho.   Perf. 14

678	A95	5fr red, gold & multi	5	5
679	A95	10fr multi	10	6
680	A95	20fr grn, gold & multi	20	10
681	A95	30fr multi	40	18
682	A95	45fr pur, gold & multi	60	30
		Nos. 678-682, C109 (6)	2.85	1.29

Nos. 665–668 Overprinted

EN MEMOIRE
DWIGHT D. EISENHOWER
1890-1969

1969, Sept. 1   Photo.   Perf. 13½x14

683	A92	15fr brn org & sl grn	15	7
684	A92	20fr grnsh bl & vio	20	10
685	A92	30fr ver & sl bl	35	15
686	A92	45fr ol & car rose	50	20
		Nos. 683-686, C110-C111 (6)	2.70	1.20

Issued in memory of Gen. Dwight D. Eisenhower (1890–1969), 34th President of the U.S.

African Development Bank and Emblem A96

Designs: 45fr, Bank emblem and hand holding railroad bridge and engine.

1969, Sept. 10   Photo.   Perf. 13x14

687	A96	30fr ultra, blk gold & grn	40	15
688	A96	45fr grn, dk bl, gold & dk red	65	20

Issued to commemorate the 5th anniversary of the African Development Bank. See No. C112.

Louis Pasteur and Help for 1968 Flood Victims—A97

Designs: 15fr, Henri Dunant and Red Cross workers meeting Biafra refugees at airport. 30fr, Alexander Fleming and help for flood victims. 45fr, Wilhelm C. Roentgen and Red Cross workers with children in front of Headquarters.

1969, Sept. 27   Litho.   Perf. 14

689	A97	15fr red & multi	15	10
690	A97	20fr emer & multi	20	15
691	A97	30fr pur & multi	35	20
692	A97	45fr brt bl & multi	65	25
		Nos. 689-692, C113-C114 (6)	3.05	1.55

Issued to commemorate the 50th anniversary of the League of Red Cross Societies.

Glidji Agricultural Center A98

Designs (Emblem of Young Pioneer and Agricultural Organization and): 1fr, Corn harvest. 3fr, Founding meeting of Agricultural Pioneer Youths, Mar. 7, 1967. 4fr, Class at Glidji Agricultural School. 5fr, Boys forming human pyramid. 7fr, Farm students threshing. 8fr, Instruction in gardening. 10fr, 50fr, Cooperative village. 15fr, Gardening School. 20fr, Cattle breeding. 25fr, Chicken farm. 30fr, Independence parade. 40fr, Boys riding high wire. 45fr, Tractor and trailer. 60fr, Instruction in tractor driving.

1969–70   Litho.   Perf. 14

693	A98	1fr multi ('70)	5	5
694	A98	2fr multi	5	5
695	A98	3fr multi ('70)	5	5
696	A98	4fr multi ('70)	5	5
697	A98	5fr ultra & multi	8	5
698	A98	7fr multi ('70)	8	5
699	A98	8fr red & multi	10	5
700	A98	10fr bl & multi ('70)	12	5
701	A98	15fr red & multi ('70)	18	7
702	A98	20fr lil & multi	25	9
703	A98	25fr multi ('70)	30	12
704	A98	30fr brt bl & multi	35	13
705	A98	40fr brt yel & multi	50	18
706	A98	45fr rose lil & multi	55	18
707	A98	50fr bl & multi	60	20
708	A98	60fr org & multi	65	25
		Nos. 693-708, C115-C119 (21)	18.31	5.97

Books and Map of Africa A99

1969, Nov. 27   Litho.   Perf. 14

| 709 | A99 | 30fr lt bl & multi | 33 | 12 |

Issued to commemorate the 12th anniversary of the International Association for the Development of Libraries in Africa.

Christmas Issue

Nos. 674–675, 677 Overprinted "JOYEUX NOEL"

1969, Dec.   Lithographed   Perf. 14

710	A94	1fr grn & multi	30	20
711	A94	20fr brn & multi	1.10	50
712	A94	45fr ultra & multi	1.85	1.00
		Nos. 710-712, C120-C121 (5)	8.00	3.20

George Washington A100

Portraits: 20fr, Albert Luthuli. 30fr, Mahatma Gandhi. 45fr, Simon Bolivar.

Perf. 14x13½

1969, Dec. 27   Photogravure

713	A100	15fr dk brn, emer & buff	20	6
714	A100	20fr dk brn, org & buff	30	15
715	A100	30fr dk brn, grnsh bl & ocher	40	20
716	A100	45fr dk brn, sl grn & dl yel	50	30
		Nos. 713-716, C122-C123 (6)	3.45	1.71

Issued to honor leaders for world peace.

751

TOGO

Plower, by M. K. Klodt and
ILO Emblem—A101

Paintings and ILO Emblem: 10fr, Gardening, by Camille Pissarro. 20fr, Fruit Harvest, by Diego Rivera. 30fr, Spring Sowing, by Vincent van Gogh. 45fr, Workers, by Rivera.

1970, Jan. 24 Litho. Perf. 12½x13

717	A101	5fr gold & multi	8	5
718	A101	10fr gold & multi	12	5
719	A101	20fr gold & multi	20	12
720	A101	30fr gold & multi	40	18
721	A101	45fr gold & multi	60	25
		Nos. 717-721, C124-C125 (7) 2.95		1.50

Issued to commemorate the 50th anniversary of the International Labor Organization.

Togolese Hair Styles—A102

Designs: Various hair styles (20fr, 30fr, vertical).

Perf. 13x12½, 12½x13

1970, Feb. 21

722	A102	5fr multi	5	5
723	A102	10fr ver & multi	12	8
724	A102	20fr pur & multi	25	12
725	A102	30fr yel grn & multi	35	25
		Nos. 722-725, C126-C127 (6) 2.27		1.40

Togo No. C127 and Independence
Monument, Lomé—A103

Designs: 30fr, Pres. Etienne G. Eyadéma, Presidential Palace and Independence Monument. 50fr, Map of Togo, dove and Independence Monument (vert.).

Perf. 13x12½, 12½x13

1970, Apr. 27   Lithographed

726	A103	20fr multi	20	9
727	A103	30fr multi	30	13
728	A103	50fr multi	55	20

Issued to commemorate the 10th anniversary of independence. See No. C128.

U.P.U. Headquarters, Bern—A104

1970, May 30 Photo. Perf. 14x13½

| 729 | A104 | 30fr org & pur | 35 | 13 |

Issued to commemorate the inauguration of the new Universal Postal Union Headquarters in Bern. See No. C129.

Soccer, Jules Rimet Cup and Flags
of Italy and Uruguay—A105

Designs (Various Scenes from Soccer, Rimet Cup and Flags of): 10fr, Great Britain and Brazil. 15fr, U.S.S.R. and Mexico. 20fr, Germany and Morocco. 30fr, Romania and Czechoslovakia.

1970, June 27 Litho. Perf. 13x14

730	A105	5fr ol & multi	8	5
731	A105	10fr pink & multi	12	5
732	A105	15fr yel & multi	25	8
733	A105	20fr multi	30	12
734	A105	30fr emerald	45	20
		Nos. 730-734, C130-C132 (8) 3.90		1.90

Issued to commemorate the 9th World Soccer Championships for the Jules Rimet Cup, Mexico City, May 30–June 21, 1970.

Lenin
and
UNESCO
Emblem
A106

1970, July 25 Litho. Perf. 12½

| 735 | A106 | 30fr fawn & multi | 35 | 18 |

Issued to commemorate the centenary of the birth of Lenin (1870–1924), Russian communist leader. See No. C133.

EXPO '70 Emblem and View of
U.S. Pavilion—A107

Designs: 2fr, Paper carp flying over Sanyo pavilion. 30fr, Russian pavilion 50fr, Tower of the Sun pavilion. 60fr, French and Japanese pavilions.

1970, Aug. 8 Litho. Perf. 13

Size: 56½x35mm.

736	A107	2fr gray & multi	5	5

Size: 50x33mm.

737	A107	20fr bl & multi	25	10
738	A107	30fr lil & multi	35	15
739	A107	50fr bl & multi	65	25
740	A107	60fr bl & multi	75	30
		Nos. 736-740 (5) 2.05		85

Issued to commemorate EXPO '70 International Exhibition, Osaka, Japan, Mar. 15–Sept. 13. Nos. 737-740 printed se-tenant in sheet with continuous view of EXPO. See No. C134.

Neil A.
Armstrong,
Michael
Collins
and Edwin E.
Aldrin, Jr.
A108

Designs: 2fr, U.S. flag, moon rocks and Apollo 11 emblem. 20fr, Astronaut checking Surveyor 3 on moon, and Apollo 12 emblem. 30fr, Charles Conrad, Jr., Richard F. Gordon, Jr., Alan L. Bean and Apollo 12 emblem. 50fr, U.S. flag, moon rocks and Apollo 12 emblem.

1970, Sept. 26

741	A108	1fr multi	5	5
742	A108	2fr multi	5	5
743	A108	20fr multi	25	10
744	A108	30fr multi	35	15
745	A108	50fr multi	70	25
		Nos. 741-745, C135 (6) 3.65		1.85

Moon landings of Apollo 11 and 12.

Nos. 741–745 Inscribed:
"FELICITATIONS / BON RETOUR
APOLLO XIII"

1970, Sept. 26

746	A108	1fr multi	5	5
747	A108	2fr multi	5	5
748	A108	20fr multi	25	10
749	A108	30fr multi	35	15
750	A108	50fr multi	70	25
		Nos. 746-750, C136 (6) 3.65		1.85

Safe return of the crew of Apollo 13.

Forge of Vulcan, by Velazquez, and
ILO Emblem—A109

Paintings and Emblems of U.N. Agencies: 15fr, Still Life, by Delacroix, and FAO emblem. 20fr, Portrait of Nicholas Kratzer, by Holbein, and UNESCO emblem. 30fr, U.N. Headquarters, New York, and U.N. emblem. 50fr, Portrait of a Little Girl, by Renoir, and UNICEF emblem.

1970, Oct. 24 Litho. Perf. 12½x13

751	A109	1fr car, gold & dk brn	5	5
752	A109	15fr ultra, gold & blk	15	8
753	A109	30fr grnsh bl, gold & dk grn	20	10
754	A109	30fr lil & multi	35	15
755	A109	50fr org brn, gold & sep	65	30
		Nos. 751-755, C137-C138 (7) 3.25		1.68

United Nations, 25th anniversary.

Euchloron Megaera—A110

Butterflies and Moths: 2fr, Cymothoe chrysippus. 30fr, Danaus chrysippus. 50fr, Morpho.

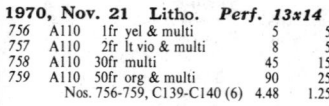

1970, Nov. 21 Litho. Perf. 13x14

756	A110	1fr yel & multi	5	5
757	A110	1t vio & multi	8	5
758	A110	30fr multi	45	15
759	A110	50fr org & multi	90	25
		Nos. 756-759, C139-C140 (6) 4.48		1.25

Nativity, by Botticelli—A111

Paintings: 20fr, Adoration of the Shepherds, by Veronese. 30fr, Adoration of the Shepherds, by El Greco. 50fr, Adoration of the Kings, by Fra Angelico.

1970, Dec. 26 Litho. Perf. 12½x13

760	A111	15fr gold & multi	12	8
761	A111	20fr gold & multi	15	10
762	A111	30fr gold & multi	30	15
763	A111	50fr gold & multi	55	25
		Nos. 760-763, C141-C142 (6) 2.92		1.33

Christmas 1970.

Nos. 715, C123, 714 Surcharged
and Overprinted:
"EN MEMOIRE / Charles De Gaulle /
1890–1970"

1971, Jan. 9 Photo. Perf. 14x13½

764	A100	30fr multi	45	15
765	A100	30fr on 90fr multi	45	15
766	A100	150fr on 20fr multi	2.10	70

"Aerienne" obliterated with heavy bar on No. 765. See No. C143.

De Gaulle
and
Churchill
A112

Designs (De Gaulle and): 30fr, Dwight D. Eisenhower. 40fr, John F. Kennedy. 50fr, Konrad Adenauer.

1971, Feb. 20 Photo. Perf. 13x14

767	A112	20fr blk & brt bl	25	10
768	A112	30fr blk & crim	32	15
769	A112	40fr blk & dp grn	60	20
770	A112	50fr blk & multi	65	25
		Nos. 767-770, C144-C145 (6) 4.07		1.45

Nos. 764-770 issued in memory of Charles de Gaulle (1890–1970), President of France.

Resurrection,
by
Raphael
A113

Designs: 30fr, Resurrection, by Master of Trebon. 40fr, like fr.

TOGO

Lithographed
1971, Apr. 10   Perf. 10½x11½
771	A113	1fr gold & multi	5	5
772	A113	30fr gold & multi	30	15
773	A113	40fr gold & multi	40	20
	Nos. 771-773, C146-C148 (6)		3.50	1.60

Easter, 1971.

Cmdr. Alan B. Shepard, Jr.—A114

Designs: 10fr, Edgar D. Mitchell and astronaut on moon. 30fr, Stuart A. Roosa, module on moon. 40fr, Take-off from moon, and spaceship.

1971, May   Lithographed   Perf. 12½
774	A114	1fr bl & multi	5	5
775	A114	10fr grn & multi	10	5
776	A114	30fr dl red & multi	30	15
777	A114	40fr dk grn & multi	40	20
	Nos. 774-777, C149-C151 (7)		4.35	2.17

Apollo 14 U.S. moon landing, Jan. 31–Feb. 9.

Cacao Tree and Pods—A115

Designs: 40fr, Sorting and separating beans and pods. 50fr, Drying cacao beans.

1971, June 6   Litho.   Perf. 14
778	A115	30fr multi	45	15
779	A115	40fr ultra & multi	50	20
780	A115	50fr multi	50	25
	Nos. 778-780, C152-C154 (6)		4.05	1.85

International Cacao Day, June 6.

Control Tower and Plane—A116

1971, June 26
781	A116	30fr multi	35	15

10th anniversary of the Agency for the Security of Aerial Navigation in Africa and Madagascar (ASECNA). See No. C155.

Great Market, Lomé—A117

Designs: 30fr, Bird-of-paradise flower and sculpture of a man. 40fr, Aledjo Gorge and anubius baboon.

1971, July 17
782	A117	20fr multi	20	10
783	A117	30fr multi	30	15
784	A117	40fr multi	40	20
	Nos. 782-784, C156-C158 (6)		3.00	1.47

Tourist publicity.

Great Fetish of Gbatchoume—A118

Designs: 30fr, Chief Priest in front of Atta Sakuma Temple. 40fr, Annual ceremony of the sacred stone.

1971, July 31   Litho.   Perf. 14½
785	A118	20fr multi	20	9
786	A118	30fr multi	30	13
787	A118	40fr multi	40	18
	Nos. 785-787, C159-C161 (6)		2.75	1.35

Religions of Togo.

No. 777 Overprinted in Silver:
"EN MEMOIRE / DOBROVOLSKY - VOLKOV - PATSAYEV / SOYUZ 11"

1971, Aug.   Perf. 12½
788	A114	40fr multi	40	18

In memory of the Russian astronauts Lt. Col. Georgi T. Dobrovolsky, Vladislav N. Volkov and Victor I. Patsayev, who died during the Soyuz 11 space mission, June 6–30, 1971. See Nos. C162-C164.

Sapporo '72 Emblem and Speed Skating—A119

Sapporo '72 Emblem and: 10fr, Slalom skiing. 20fr, Figure skating, pairs. 30fr, Bobsledding. 50fr, Ice hockey.

1971, Oct. 30   Perf. 14
789	A119	1fr multi	5	5
790	A119	10fr multi	10	5
791	A119	20fr multi	22	10
792	A119	30fr multi	30	15
793	A119	50fr multi	50	25
	Nos. 789-793, C165 (6)		3.17	1.35

11th Winter Olympic Games, Sapporo, Japan, Feb. 3–13, 1972.

Toy Crocodile and UNICEF Emblem—A120

Toys and UNICEF Emblem: 30fr, Fawn and butterfly. 40fr, Monkey. 50fr, Elephants.

1971, Nov. 27
794	A120	20fr multi	20	10
795	A120	30fr vio & multi	30	15
796	A120	40fr grn & multi	40	20
797	A120	50fr bis & multi	50	25
	Nos. 794-797, C167-C168 (6)		2.90	1.33

25th anniversary of the United Nations International Children's Fund (UNICEF).

Virgin and Child, by Botticelli—A121

Virgin and Child by: 30fr, Master of the Life of Mary. 40fr, Dürer. 50fr, Veronese.

1971, Dec. 24   Perf. 14x13
798	A121	10fr pur & multi	15	5
799	A121	30fr grn & multi	30	15
800	A121	40fr brn & multi	45	20
801	A121	50fr dk bl & multi	60	25
	Nos. 798-801, C169-C170 (6)		3.20	1.58

Christmas 1971.

St. Mark's Basilica—A122

Design: 40fr, Rialto Bridge.

1972, Feb. 26   Litho.   Perf. 14
802	A122	30fr multi	30	15
803	A122	40fr multi	40	20

UNESCO campaign to save Venice. See No. C171.

No. 784 Surcharged with New Value, Two Bars and "VISITE DU PRESIDENT / NIXON EN CHINE / FEVRIER 1972"

1972, Mar.   Lithographed   Perf. 14
804	A117	300fr on 40fr multi	3.00	1.75

Visit of Pres. Richard M. Nixon to the People's Republic of China, Feb. 20–27. See No. C172.

Crucifixion, by Master MS—A123

Paintings: 30fr, Pietà, by Botticelli. 40fr, like 25fr.

1972, Mar. 31
805	A123	25fr gold & multi	25	12
806	A123	30fr gold & multi	30	15
807	A123	40fr gold & multi	40	20
	Nos. 805-807, C173-C174 (5)		2.65	1.07

Easter 1972.

Heart, Smith, WHO Emblem—A124

Designs (Heart, WHO Emblem and): 40fr, Typist. 60fr, Athlete with javelin.

1972, Apr. 4
808	A124	30fr multi	30	15
809	A124	40fr multi	35	20
810	A124	60fr multi	60	30

"Your heart is your health," World Health Day. See No. C175.

Video Telephone — A125   Grating Cassava — A126

1972, June 24   Perf. 14
811	A125	40fr vio & multi	40	20

4th World Telecommunications Day. See No. C176.

1972, June 30
Designs: 25fr, Cassava collection by truck (horiz.).
812	A126	25fr yel & multi	25	12
813	A126	40fr multi	40	20

Cassava production. See Nos. C177-C178.

Basketball — A127   Pin-tailed Whydah — A128

1972, Aug. 26   Litho.   Perf. 14
Multicolored
814	A127	30fr shown	30	15
815	A127	40fr Running	40	20
816	A127	50fr Discus	50	25
	Nos. 814-816, C180-C181 (5)		4.45	2.10

20th Olympic Games, Munich, Aug. 26–Sept. 11.

1972, Sept. 9
Birds: 30fr, Broad-tailed widowbird. 40fr, Yellow-shouldered widowbird. 60fr, Yellow-tailed widowbird.
817	A128	25fr cit & multi	25	12
818	A128	30fr lt bl & multi	35	20
819	A128	40fr multi	40	20
820	A128	60fr lt grn & multi	60	30
	Nos. 817-820, C182 (5)		2.60	1.27

TOGO

Paul P. Harris,
Rotary Emblem
A129

Design: 50fr, Flags of Togo and Rotary Club.

1972, Oct. 7   Litho.   *Perf. 14*

821	A129	40fr grn & multi	35	20
822	A129	50fr multi	50	25
a.		Souv. sheet of 2	1.00	1.00
		Nos. 821-822, C183-C185 (5)	3.00	1.75

Rotary International, Lomé. No. 822a contains 2 stamps with simulated perforations similar to Nos. 821-822. Gray margin with portrait of Paul P. Harris, black inscription and Rotary emblem. Size: 122x105mm.

Mona Lisa,
by Leonardo da Vinci
A130

Design: 40fr, Virgin and Child, by Giovanni Bellini.

1972, Oct. 21

823	A130	25fr gold & multi	30	12
824	A130	40fr gold & multi	40	20
		Nos. 823-824, C186-C188 (5)	3.20	1.62

West African Monetary Union Issue
Common Design Type

Design: 40fr, African couple, city, village and commemorative coin.

1972, Nov. 2   Engraved   *Perf. 13*

825	CD136	40fr red brn, rose red & gray	35	20

10th anniversary of West African Monetary Union.

Presidents Pompidou and Eyadema,
Party Headquarters—A131

1972, Nov. 23   Litho.   *Perf. 14*

826	A131	40fr pur & multi	45	20

Visit of Pres. Georges Pompidou of France to Togo, Nov. 1972. See No. C189.

Anunciation,
Painter Unknown
A132

Paintings: 30fr, Nativity, Master of Vyshchibrod. 4fr, Like 25fr.

1972, Dec. 23

827	A132	25fr gold & multi	25	12
828	A132	30fr gold & multi	30	15
829	A132	40fr gold & multi	40	20
		Nos. 827-829, C191-C193 (6)	3.75	1.82

Christmas 1972.

Raoul Follereau and Lepers—A133

1973, Jan. 23   Photo.   *Perf. 14x13½*

830	A133	40fr vio & grn	40	20

World Leprosy Day and 20th anniversary of the Raoul Follereau Foundation. See No. C194.

WHO Emblem   Christ on
A134   the Cross
                    A135

1973, Apr. 7   Photo.   *Perf. 14x13*

831	A134	30fr bl & multi	30	15
832	A134	40fr dp yel & multi	40	20

25th anniversary of World Health Organization.

1973, Apr. 21   Lithographed   *Perf. 14*
Multicolored

833	A135	25fr *shown*	25	12
834	A135	30fr *Pietà*	30	15
835	A135	40fr *Ascension*	40	20

Easter 1973. See No. C195.

Eugene Cernan, Ronald Evans,
Harrison Schmitt, Apollo 17
Badge—A136

Design: 40fr, Lunar rover on moon.

1973, June 2   Litho.   *Perf. 14*

836	A136	30fr multi	30	15
837	A136	40fr multi	40	20

Apollo 17 U.S. moon mission, Dec. 7-19, 1972. See Nos. C196-C197.

Scouts Pitching   Nicolaus
Tent   Copernicus
A137   A138

Designs: 20fr, Campfire (horiz.). 30fr, Rope climbing. 40fr, Like 10fr.

1973, June 30

838	A137	10fr multi	10	5
839	A137	20fr multi	20	10
840	A137	30fr vio & multi	30	15
841	A137	40fr ocher & multi	40	20
		Nos. 838-841, C198-C199 (6)	4.35	2.10

24th Boy Scout World Conference (1st in Africa), Nairobi, Kenya, July 16-21.

1973, July 18

Designs: 10fr, Heliocentric system. 30fr, Seated figure of Astronomy and spacecrafts around earth and moon. 40fr, Astrolabe.

842	A138	10fr multi	10	5
843	A138	20fr multi	20	10
844	A138	30fr multi	30	15
845	A138	40fr lil & multi	40	20
		Nos. 842-845, C200-C201 (6)	3.00	1.55

500th anniversary of the birth of Nicolaus Copernicus (1473-1543), Polish astronomer.

Red Cross Ambulance Crew
A139

1973, Aug. 4

846	A139	40fr multi	40	20

Togolese Red Cross. See No. C202.

Teacher and Students—A140

Designs: 40fr, Hut and man reading under tree (vert.).

1973, Aug. 18   Litho.   *Perf. 14*

847	A140	30fr multi	30	15
848	A140	40fr multi	40	20

Literacy campaign. See No. C203.

African Postal Union Issue
Common Design Type

1973, Sept. 12   Engraved   *Perf. 13*

849	CD137	100fr yel, red & cl	1.10	50

INTERPOL   Weather Vane and
Emblem and   WMO Emblem
Headquarters   A142
A141

1973, Sept. 29   Photo.   *Perf. 13½x14*

850	A141	30fr yel, brn & gray grn	30	15
851	A141	40fr yel grn, bl & mag	40	20

50th anniversary of International Criminal Police Organization.

1973, Oct. 4   *Perf. 14x13*

852	A142	40fr yel, dp brn & grn	40	20

Centenary of international meteorological cooperation. See No. C204.

Type of 1967

Designs: 25fr, Old and new locomotives, No. 795. 30fr, Mail coach and bus, No. 613. 90fr, Mail boat and ship, Nos. C61 and 469.

1973, Oct. 20   Photo.   *Perf. 14x13*

853	A79	25fr multi	30	12
854	A79	30fr pur & grn	40	15
855	A79	90fr dk bl & multi	1.00	45

75th anniversary of Togolese postal service. See No. C205.

John F. Kennedy   Virgin and Child,
and Adolf   Italy, 15th
Schaerf   Century
A143   A144

Designs: 30fr, Kennedy and Harold MacMillan. 40fr, Kennedy and Konrad Adenauer.

1973, Nov. 22   Litho.   *Perf. 14*

856	A143	20fr blk, gray & vio	20	17
857	A143	30fr blk, rose & brn	30	20
858	A143	40fr blk, lt grn & brn	40	28
		Nos. 856-858, C206-C208 (6)	4.90	2.60

10th anniversary of the death of Pres. John F. Kennedy (1917-1963).

No. 758 Surcharged with New Value, 2 Bars and Overprinted in Ultramarine:
"SECHERESSE
SOLIDARITE AFRICAINE"

1973, Dec.   Photo.   *Perf. 13x14*

859	A110	100fr on 30fr multi	1.10	75

African solidarity in drought emergency.

1973, Dec. 22   Litho.   *Perf. 14*

Design: 30fr, Adoration of the Kings, Italy, 15th century.

860	A144	25fr gold & multi	25	17
861	A144	30fr gold & multi	35	20

Christmas 1973. See Nos. C210-C211.

TOGO

No. 821 Overprinted:
"PREMIERE CONVENTION / 210eme DISTRICT / FEVRIER 1974 / LOME"

1974, Feb. 21 Lithographed Perf. 14

| 862 | A129 | 40fr grn & multi | 40 | 28 |

First convention of Rotary International, District 210, Lomé, Feb. 22–24. See Nos. C212–C213.

Soccer and Games' Cup
A145

Designs: Various soccer scenes and games' cup.

1974, Mar. 2 Lithographed Perf. 14

863	A145	20fr lt bl & multi	20	10
864	A145	30fr yel & multi	35	17
865	A145	40fr lil & multi	40	20
		Nos. 863-865, C214-C216 (6)	4.95	2.27

World Soccer Championships, Munich, Germany, June 13–July 7.

Nos. 812-813 Overprinted and Surcharged: "10e ANNIVERSAIRE DU P.A.M."

1974, Mar. 25 Litho. Perf. 14

| 866 | A126 | 40fr multi | 45 | 25 |
| 867 | A126 | 100fr on 25fr multi | 1.10 | 65 |

10th anniversary of World Food Program. Overprint on No. 866 is in one line; 2 lines on No. 867 and 2 bars through old denomination.

Girl Before Mirror, by Picasso
A146

Paintings by Picasso: 30fr, The Turkish Shawl. 40fr, Mandolin and Guitar.

1974, Apr. 6

868	A146	20fr vio bl & multi	20	10
869	A146	30fr mar & multi	30	15
870	A146	40fr multi	40	20
		Nos. 868-870, C217-C219 (6)	4.90	2.40

Pablo Picasso (1881–1973), Spanish painter.

Kpeme Village and Wharf
A147

Design: 40fr, Tropicana tourist village.

1974, Apr. 20

| 871 | A147 | 30fr multi | 30 | 15 |
| 872 | A147 | 40fr multi | 35 | 20 |

See Nos. C220-C221.

Mailman, UPU Emblem
A148

Design: 40fr, Mailman, different uniform.

1974, May 10 Litho. Perf. 14

| 873 | A148 | 30fr sal & multi | 30 | 15 |
| 874 | A148 | 40fr multi | 40 | 20 |

Centenary of Universal Postal Union. See Nos. C222-C223.

Map and Flags of Members
A148a

1974, May 29 Litho. Perf. 13x12½

| 875 | A148a | 40fr bl & multi | 40 | 28 |

15th anniversary of the Council of Accord.

Fisherman with Net
A149

Design: 40fr, Fisherman casting net from canoe.

1974, June 22 Litho. Perf. 14

876	A149	30fr multi	35	15
877	A149	40fr multi	40	20
		Nos. 876-877, C224-C226 (5)	4.00	2.15

Lagoon fishing.

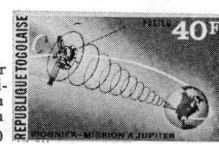

Pioneer Communicating with Earth
A150

Design: 30fr, Radar station and satellite (vert.).

1974, July 6 Rouletted, Imperf.

| 878 | A150 | 30fr multi | 30 | 17 |
| 879 | A150 | 40fr multi | 40 | 20 |

U.S. Jupiter space probe. See Nos. C227-C228.

No. 811 Overprinted with INTERNABA Emblem in Silver Similar to No: C229

1974, July

| 880 | A125 | 20fr multi | 1.50 | 75 |

INTERNABA 1974 International Philatelic Exhibition, Basel, June 7–16. See No. C229.

Tympanotomus Radula
A151

Designs: Seashells.

1974, July 13 Litho. Perf. 14
Multicolored

881	A151	10fr shown	20	5
882	A151	20fr Tonna galea	25	12
883	A151	30fr Conus mercator	35	15
884	A151	40fr Cardium costatum	50	20
		Nos. 881-884, C230-C231 (6)	2.85	1.42

Groom with Horses
A152

Design: 40fr, Trotting horses.

1974, Aug. 3 Litho. Perf. 14

| 885 | A152 | 30fr multi | 30 | 14 |
| 886 | A152 | 40fr multi | 40 | 20 |

Horse racing. See Nos. C232-C233.

Leopard
A153

1974, Sept. 7 Litho. Perf. 14
Multicolored

887	A153	20fr shown	20	10
888	A153	30fr Giraffes	25	17
889	A153	40fr Elephants	35	20
		Nos. 887-889, C236-C237 (5)	2.50	1.42

Wild animals of West Africa.

1974, Oct. 14

| 890 | A153 | 30fr Herding cattle | 25 | 12 |
| 891 | A153 | 40fr Milking cow | 35 | 20 |

Domestic animals. See Nos. C238-C239.

Churchill and Frigate
F390 A154

Design: 40fr, Churchill and fighter planes.

1974, Nov. 1 Photo. Perf. 13x13½

| 892 | A154 | 30fr multi | 30 | 12 |
| 893 | A154 | 40fr multi | 40 | 20 |

Centenary of the birth of Winston Churchill (1874–1965). See Nos. C240-C241.

Chlamydocarya Macrocarpa
A155

Flowers of Togo: 25fr, Strelitzia reginae (vert.). 30fr, Storphanthus sarmentosus (vert.). 60fr, Clerodendrum scandens.

1975, Feb. 15 Litho. Perf. 14

894	A155	25fr multi	20	10
895	A155	30fr multi	25	13
896	A155	40fr multi	35	22
897	A155	60fr multi	50	25
		Nos. 894-897, C242-C243 (6)	3.70	1.85

No. 821 Overprinted:
"70e ANNIVERSAIRE / 23 FEVRIER 1975"

1975, Feb. 23 Litho. Perf. 14

| 898 | A129 | 40fr grn & multi | 45 | 20 |

Rotary International, 70th anniversary. See Nos. C244-C245.

Radio Station, Kamina
A156

Designs: 30fr, Benedictine Monastery, Zogbegan. 40fr, Causeway, Atchinedji. 60fr, Ayome Waterfalls.

1975, Mar. 1 Photo. Perf. 13x14

899	A156	25fr multi	20	12
900	A156	30fr multi	25	15
901	A156	40fr multi	35	22
902	A156	60fr multi	50	30

Jesus Mocked, by El Greco
A157

Paintings: 30fr, Crucifixion, by Master Janoslet. 40fr, Descent from the Cross, by Bellini. 90fr, Pietà, painter unknown.

1975, Apr. 19 Litho. Perf. 14

903	A157	25fr blk & multi	25	10
904	A157	30fr blk & multi	30	15
905	A157	40fr blk & multi	40	20
906	A157	90fr blk & multi	75	45
		Nos. 903-906, C246-C247 (6)	4.10	2.15

Easter 1975.

Stilt Walking, Togolese Flag
A158

Design: 30fr, Flag and dancers.

1975, Apr. 26 Litho. Perf. 14

| 907 | A158 | 25fr multi | 25 | 12 |
| 908 | A158 | 30fr multi | 30 | 18 |

15th anniversary of independence. See Nos. C248-C249.

Rabbit Hunter with Club
A159

Design: 40fr, Beaver hunter with bow and arrow.

1975, May 24 Photo. Perf. 13x13½

| 909 | A159 | 30fr multi | 25 | 13 |
| 910 | A159 | 40fr multi | 35 | 22 |

See Nos. C250-C251.

Pounding Palm Nuts
A160

Design: 40fr, Man extracting palm oil (vert.).

1975, June 28 Litho. Perf. 14

| 911 | A160 | 30fr multi | 30 | 20 |
| 912 | A160 | 40fr multi | 35 | 20 |

Palm oil production. See Nos. C252-C253.

Apollo-Soyuz Link-up—A161

1975, July 15

| 913 | A161 | 30fr multi | 25 | 15 |
| | | Nos. 913, C254-C258 (6) | 4.25 | 2.10 |

Apollo Soyuz space test project (Russo-American cooperation), launching July 15; link-up July 17.

TOGO

Women's Heads, IWY Emblem
A162

1975, July 26 Litho. *Perf. 12½*
914 A162 30fr bl & multi 25 13
915 A162 40fr multi 35 22

International Women's Year 1975.

Dr. Schweitzer and Children—A163

1975, Aug. 23 Litho. *Perf. 14x13½*
916 A163 40fr multi 35 25

Dr. Albert Schweitzer (1875–1965), medical missionary and musician. See Nos. C259–C261.

Merchant Writing Letter, by Vittore Carpaccio
A164

Virgin and Child, by Mantegna
A165

1975, Oct. 9 Litho. *Perf. 14*
917 A164 40fr multi 35 25

International Letter Writing Week. See No. C262.

No. 797 Overprinted:
"30ème Anniversaire / des Nations-Unies"

1975, Oct. 24 Litho. *Perf. 14*
918 A120 50fr multi 45 30

United Nations, 30th anniversary. See Nos. C263–C264.

1975, Dec. 20 Litho. *Perf. 14*
Paintings of the Virgin and Child: 30fr, El Greco. 40fr, Barend van Orley.
919 A165 20fr red & multi 20 10
920 A165 30fr bl & multi 30 15
921 A165 40fr red & multi 40 20
Nos. 919–921, C267–C269 (6) 4.05 1.95

Christmas 1975.

Crashed Plane and Pres. Eyadema
A166

1976, Jan. 24 Photo. *Perf. 14*
922 A166 50fr multi 75 50
923 A166 60fr multi 40 60

Airplane crash at Sara-kawa, Jan. 24, 1974, in which Pres. Eyadema escaped injury.

Frigates on the Hudson—A167

Design: 50fr, George Washington, by Gilbert Stuart, and Bicentennial emblem (vert.).

1976, Mar. 3 Litho. *Perf. 14*
924 A167 35fr multi 30 20
925 A167 50fr multi 40 30
Nos. 924–925, C270–C273 (6) 4.15 2.27

American Bicentennial.

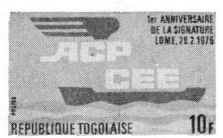

ACP and CEE Emblems
A168

Design: 50fr, Map of Africa, Europe and Asia.

1976, Apr. 24 Photo. *Perf. 13x14*
926 A168 10fr org & multi 10 6
927 A168 50fr pink & multi 40 40

First anniversary of signing of treaty between Togo and European Common Market, Lomé, Feb. 28, 1975. See Nos. C274–C275.

Cable-laying Ship
A169

Design: 30fr, Telephone, tape recorder, speaker.

1976, Mar. 10 Photo. *Perf. 13x14*
928 A169 25fr ultra & multi 20 16
929 A169 30fr pink & multi 25 18

Centenary of first telephone call by Alexander Graham Bell, Mar. 10, 1876. See Nos. C276–C277.

Blind Man and Insect
A170

Marine Exhibition Hall
A171

1976, Apr. 8 Perf. 14x13
930 A170 50fr brt grn & multi 40 25

World Health Day: "Foresight prevents blindness." See No. C278.

Air Post Type, 1976, and Type A171

1976 Lithographed *Perf. 14*
Design: 1cfr, Pylon, flags of Ghana, Togo and Dahomey.
931 A171 5fr multi 5 5
932 AP19 10fr multi 10 5
933 A171 50fr multi 40 30

Marine Exhibition, 10th anniversary (5fr, 50fr); Ghana-Togo-Dahomey electric power grid, 1st anniversary (10fr). See No. C279.

Issue dates: 50fr, May 8; 5fr, 10fr, August.

Running—A172

Designs (Montreal Olympic Emblem and): 30fr, Kayak. 50fr, High jump.

1976, June 15 Photo. *Perf. 14x13*
934 A172 25fr multi 20 12
935 A172 30fr multi 25 15
936 A172 50fr multi 40 25
Nos. 934–936, C284–C286 (6) 3.85 2.19

21st Olympic Games, Montreal, Canada, July 17–Aug. 1.

Titan 3 and Viking Emblem—A173

Design: 50fr, Viking trajectory, Earth to Mars.

1976, July 15 Litho. *Perf. 14*
937 A173 30fr bl & multi 25 15
938 A173 50fr rose & multi 40 25
Nos. 937–938, C287–C290 (6) 4.15 2.35

U.S. Viking Mars missions.

Young Routy at Celeyran, by Toulouse-Lautrec
A174

Paintings by Toulouse-Lautrec: 20fr, Model in Studio. 35fr, Louis Pascal, portrait.

1976, Aug. 7 Litho. *Perf. 14*
939 A174 10fr blk & multi 10 5
940 A174 20fr blk & multi 15 10
941 A174 35fr blk & multi 30 18
Nos. 939–941, C291–C293 (6) 3.20 1.81

Henri Toulouse-Lautrec (1864–1901), French painter, 75th death anniversary.

No. 846 Overprinted:
"Journée / Internationale / de l'Enfance"

1976, Nov. 27 Litho. *Perf. 14*
942 A139 40fr multi 30 20

International Children's Day. See No. C294.

Adoration of the Shepherds, by Pontormo—A175

Paintings: 30fr, Nativity, by Carlo Crivelli. 50fr, Virgin and Child, by Jacopo da Pontormo.

1976, Dec. 18
943 A175 25fr multi 20 12
944 A175 30fr multi 25 15
945 A175 50fr multi 40 25
Nos. 943–945, C295–C297 (6) 3.85 2.19

Christmas 1976.

Mohammed Ali Jinnah, Flags of Togo and Pakistan
A176

1976, Dec. 24 Litho. *Perf. 13*
946 A176 50fr multi 40 25

Mohammed Ali Jinnah (1876–1948), first Governor General of Pakistan, birth centenary.

No. 936 Overprinted:
"CHAMPIONS OLYMPIQUES / SAUT EN HAUTEUR / POLOGNE"

1976, Dec. Photo. *Perf. 14x13*
947 A172 50fr multi 40 25

Olympic winners. See Nos. C298–C299.

Kpeme Phosphate Mine, Sarakawa Crash
A177

1977, Jan. 13 Photo. *Perf. 13x14*
948 A177 50fr multi 40 25

10th anniversary of presidency of Etienne Eyadema. See Nos. C300–C301.

Gongophone
A178

Musical Instruments: 10fr, Tamtam (vert.). 25fr, Dondon.

1977, Feb. 7 Litho. *Perf. 14*
949 A178 5fr multi 5 5
950 A178 10fr multi 10 5
951 A178 25fr multi 20 12
Nos. 949–951, C302–C304 (6) 2.35 1.10

Victor Hugo and his Home
A179

1977, Feb. 26 Perf. 13x14
952 A179 50fr multi 40 25

Victor Hugo (1802–1885), French writer, 175th birth anniversary. See No. C305.

Beethoven and Birthplace, Bonn
A180

Design: 50fr, Bronze bust, 1812, and Heiligenstadt home.

TOGO

1977, Mar. 7   *Perf. 14*

| 953 | A180 | 30fr multi | 25 | 15 |
| 954 | A180 | 50fr multi | 40 | 25 |

Ludwig van Beethoven (1770–1827), composer, 150th death anniversary. See Nos. C306–C307.

Benz, 1894, Germany—A181

Early Automobiles: 50fr, De Dion Bouton, 1903, France.

1977, Apr. 11   *Litho.*   *Perf. 14*

955	A181	35fr multi	30	18
956	A181	50fr multi	40	25
		Nos. 955-956, C308-C311 (6)	4.15	2.48

Lindbergh, Ground Crew and Spirit of St. Louis—A182

Design: 50fr, Lindbergh and Spirit of St. Louis.

1977, May 9

957	A182	25fr multi	25	12
958	A182	50fr multi	50	25
		Nos. 957-958, C312-C315 (6)	4.10	1.57

Charles A. Lindbergh's solo transatlantic flight from New York to Paris, 50th anniversary.

No. 952 Overprinted:
"10ème ANNIVERSAIRE DU / CONSEIL INTERNATIONAL / DE LA LANGUE FRANCAISE"

1977, May 17   *Litho.*   *Perf. 14*

| 959 | A179 | 50fr multi | 50 | 35 |

10th anniversary of the International French Language Council. See No. C316.

African Slender-snouted Crocodile—A183

Design: 15fr, Nile crocodile.

1977, June 13

960	A183	5fr multi	5	5
961	A183	15fr multi	15	10
		Nos. 960-961, C317-C320 (6)	4.70	1.36

Endangered wildlife.

Agriculture School, Tove A184

1977, July 11   *Litho.*   *Perf. 14*

| 962 | A184 | 50fr multi | 50 | 35 |

Agricultural development. See Nos. C321–C323.

Landscape with Cart, by Rubens—A185

Rubens Painting: 35fr, Exchange of the Princesses at Hendaye, 1623.

1977, Aug. 8

| 963 | A185 | 15fr multi | 15 | 8 |
| 964 | A185 | 35fr multi | 35 | 18 |

Peter Paul Rubens (1577–1640), Flemish painter, 400th birth anniversary. See Nos. C324–C325.

Orbiter 101 on Ground—A186

Designs: 30fr, Launching of Orbiter (vert.). 50fr, Ejection of propellant tanks at take-off.

1977, Oct. 4   *Litho.*   *Perf. 14*

965	A186	20fr multi	20	10
966	A186	30fr multi	30	15
967	A186	50fr multi	50	25
		Nos. 965-967, C326-C328 (6)	4.90	1.53

Space shuttle trials in the U.S.

Lafayette Arriving in Montpelier, Vt. A187

Design: 25fr, Lafayette, age 19 (vert.).

1977, Nov. 7   *Perf. 14x13, 13x14*

| 968 | A187 | 25fr multi | 25 | 12 |
| 969 | A187 | 50fr multi | 50 | 25 |

200th anniversary of the arrival of the Marquis de Lafayette in North America. See Nos. C329–C330.

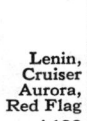 

Lenin, Cruiser Aurora, Red Flag A188

1977, Nov. 7   *Litho.*   *Perf. 12*

| 970 | A188 | 50fr multi | 50 | 25 |

60th anniversary of Russian October Revolution.

Virgin and Child, by Lorenzo Lotto A189

Virgin and Child by: 30fr, Carlo Bellini. 50fr, Cosimo Tura.

1977, Dec. 19   *Perf. 14*

971	A189	20fr multi	20	10
972	A189	30fr multi	30	15
973	A189	50fr multi	50	25
		Nos. 971-973, C331-C333 (6)	4.90	1.53

Christmas 1977.

Edward Jenner A190

Design: 20fr, Vaccination clinic (horiz.).

Perf. 14x13, 13x14

1978, Jan. 9   *Lithographed*

| 974 | A190 | 5fr multi | 5 | 5 |
| 975 | A190 | 20fr multi | 20 | 10 |

Worldwide eradication of smallpox. See Nos. C334–C335.

Orville and Wilbur Wright—A191

Design: 50fr, Wilbur Wright flying at Kill Devil Hill, 1902.

1978, Feb. 6   *Litho.*   *Perf. 14*

976	A191	35fr multi	35	18
977	A191	50fr multi	50	25
		Nos. 976-977, C336-C339 (6)	7.15	2.26

75th anniversary of first motorized flight.

John, the Evangelist and Eagle A197

Evangelists: 10fr, Luke and ox. 25fr, Mark and lion. 30fr, Matthew and angel.

1978, Mar. 20   *Litho.*   *Perf. 13½x14*

988	A197	5fr multi	5	5
989	A197	10fr multi	10	5
990	A197	25fr multi	25	12
991	A197	30fr multi	30	15
a.		Souvenir sheet of 4	80	80

No. 991a contains one each of Nos. 988–991 with simulated perforations; multicolored margin shows signs of Evangelists. Size: 114x106mm.

Anchor, Fishing Harbor, Lomé A199

1978, Apr. 26   *Photo.*   *Perf. 13*

| 997 | A199 | 25fr multi | 25 | 12 |

See Nos. C340–C342.

Venera I, USSR   Soccer
    A200   A201

Designs: 30fr, Pioneer, USA (horiz.). 50fr, Venera, fuel base and antenna.

1978, May 8   *Litho.*   *Perf. 14*

998	A200	20fr multi	20	10
999	A200	30fr multi	30	15
1000	A200	50fr multi	50	25
		Nos. 998-1000, C343-C345 (6)	4.90	1.58

U.S. and U.S.S.R. Pioneer and Venera space missions.

1978, June 5   *Perf. 14*

Design: 50fr, Soccer players and Argentina '78 emblem.

1001	A201	30fr multi	30	15
1002	A201	50fr multi	50	25
		Nos. 1001-1002, C346-C349 (6)	7.20	2.13

11th World Cup Soccer Championship, Argentina, June 1–25.

Celerifère, 1818 A202

Design: 50fr, First bicycle sidecar, c. 1870 (vert.).

Perf. 13x14, 14x13

1978, July 10   *Photogravure*

1003	A202	25fr multi	25	12
1004	A202	50fr multi	50	25
		Nos. 1003-1004, C350-C353 (6)	4.10	1.64

History of bicycle.

Thomas A. Edison,   Dunant's Birth
Sound Waves   Place, Geneva
    A203   A204

Design: 50fr, Victor's His Master's Voice phonograph, 1905, and dancing couple.

1978, July 8   *Photo.*   *Perf. 14x13*

1005	A203	30fr multi	30	15
1006	A203	50fr multi	50	25
		Nos. 1005-1006, C354-C357 (6)	7.20	2.15

Centenary of the phonograph, invented by Thomas Alva Edison.

1978, Sept. 4   *Photo.*   *Perf. 14x13*

Designs: 10fr, Henri Dunant and red cross. 25fr, Help on battlefield, 1864, and red cross.

1007	A204	5fr Prus bl & red	5	5
1008	A204	10fr red brn & red	10	5
1009	A204	25fr grn & red	25	12

Henri Dunant (1828–1910), founder of Red Cross, birth sesquicentennial. See No. C358.

TOGO

Threshing, by Raoul Dufy—A205

Painting: 50fr, Horsemen on Seashore, by Paul Gauguin.

1978, Nov. 6   Litho.   Perf. 14

1010	A205	25fr multi	25	12
1011	A205	50fr multi	50	25
		Nos. 1010-1011, C359-C362 (6)	4.95	2.47

Eiffel Tower, Paris — A206

Virgin and Child, by Antonello da Messina — A207

1978, Nov. 27   Photo.   Perf. 14x13

| 1012 | A206 | 50fr multi | 30 | 15 |

Centenary of the Congress of Paris. See Nos. C365-C367.

1978, Dec. 18   Litho.   Perf. 14

Paintings (Virgin and Child): 30fr, by Carlo Crivelli. 50fr, by Cosimo Tura.

1013	A207	20fr multi	20	10
1014	A207	30fr multi	30	15
1015	A207	50fr multi	50	25
		Nos. 1013-1015, C368-C370 (6)	4.90	2.45

Christmas 1978.

Capt. Cook's Ship off New Zealand — A208

Entry into Jerusalem — A209

Design: 50fr, Endeavour in drydock, N.E. Coast of Australia (horiz.).

1979, Feb. 12   Litho.   Perf. 14

1016	A208	25fr multi	25	12
1017	A208	50fr multi	50	25
		Nos. 1016-1017, C371-C374 (6)	4.95	2.47

200th death anniversary of Capt. James Cook.

1979, Apr. 9

Designs: 40fr, The Last Supper (horiz.). 50fr, Descent from the Cross (horiz.).

1018	A209	30fr multi	30	15
1019	A209	40fr multi	40	20
1020	A209	50fr multi	50	25
		Nos. 1018-1020, C375-C377 (6)	4.80	2.40

Easter 1979.

Einstein Observatory, Potsdam
A210

Design: 50fr, Einstein and James Ramsay MacDonald, Berlin, 1931.

1979, July 2   Photo.   Perf. 14x13

| 1021 | A210 | 35fr multi | 35 | 18 |
| 1022 | A210 | 50fr multi | 50 | 25 |

Albert Einstein (1879-1955), theoretical physicist.

Children and Children's Village Emblem — A211

Man Planting Tree — A212

Designs: 10fr, Mother and children. 15fr, Map of Africa, Children's Village emblem (horiz.). 20fr, Woman and children walking to Children's Village (horiz.). 25fr, Children sitting under African fan palm. 30fr, Map of Togo with location of Children's Villages.

1979, July 30   Photo.   Perf. 14x13

1023	A211	5fr multi	5	5
1024	A211	10fr multi	10	5
1025	A211	15fr multi	15	8
1026	A211	20fr multi	20	10
1027	A211	25fr multi	25	12
1028	A211	30fr multi	30	15
a.		Souvenir sheet of 2		60
		Nos. 1023-1028 (6)	1.05	55

International Year of the Child. No. 1028a contains Nos. 1027-1028; multicolored margin shows children. Size: 110x90mm.

1979, Aug. 13   Perf. 14x13

| 1029 | A212 | 50fr lil & grn | 50 | 25 |

Second Arbor Day. See No. C384.

Rowland Hill
A213

Designs: 30fr, French mail-sorting office, 18th century (horiz.). 50fr, Mailbox, Paris, 1850.

1979, Aug. 27

1030	A213	20fr multi	20	10
1031	A213	30fr multi	30	15
1032	A213	50fr multi	50	25
		Nos. 1030-1032, C385-C387 (6)	4.90	2.45

Sir Rowland Hill (1795-1879), originator of penny postage.

Norris Locomotive, 1843 — A214

Design: 35fr, Stephenson's "Rocket," 1829 (vert.).

1979, Oct. 1   Litho.   Perf. 14

1033	A214	35fr multi	35	18
1034	A214	50fr multi	50	25
		Nos. 1033-1034, C388-C391 (6)	5.30	2.65

Olympic Flame, Moscow 80 Emblem, Slalom — A215

1980 Olympic Emblems, Olympic Flame and: 30fr, Yachting 50fr, Discus.

1979, Oct. 18   Litho.   Perf. 13½

1035	A215	20fr multi	20	10
1036	A215	30fr multi	30	15
1037	A215	50fr multi	50	25
		Nos. 1035-1037, C392-C394 (6)	4.90	2.45

13th Winter Olympic Games, Lake Placid, N.Y., Feb. 12-24, 1980. (90fr); 22nd Summer Olympic Games, Moscow, July 19-Aug. 3, 1980.

Moslems Praying
A216

Design: 50fr, Catholic priests.

1979, Oct. 29   Perf. 13x14

| 1038 | A216 | 30fr multi | 30 | 15 |
| 1039 | A216 | 50fr multi | 50 | 25 |

Religions in Togo. See Nos. C396-C397.

Astronaut Walking on Moon — A217

Design: 50fr, Space capsule orbiting moon.

1979, Nov. 5

1040	A217	35fr multi	35	18
1041	A217	50fr multi	50	25
		Nos. 1040-1041, C397-C400 (6)	7.15	3.58

Apollo 11 moon landing, 10th anniversary.

Telecom 79 — A218

1979, Nov. 26   Photo.   Perf. 13x14

| 1042 | A218 | 50fr multi | 50 | 25 |

3rd World Telecommunications Exhibition, Geneva, Sept. 20-26. See No. C402.

Holy Family
A219

Rotary Emblem
A220

Designs: 30fr, Virgin and Child. 50fr, Adoration of the Kings.

1979, Dec. 17   Litho.   Perf. 14

1043	A219	20fr multi	20	10
1044	A219	30fr multi	30	15
1045	A219	50fr multi	50	25
		Nos. 1043-1045, C402-C404 (6)	4.90	2.45

Christmas 1979.

1980, Jan. 14

Rotary Emblem and: 30fr, Anniversary emblem. 40fr, Paul P. Harris, Rotary founder.

1046	A220	25fr multi	25	12
1047	A220	30fr multi	30	15
1048	A220	40fr multi	40	20
		Nos. 1046-1048, C405-C407 (6)	4.85	2.42

Rotary International, 75th anniversary.

Biathlon, Lake Placid '80 Emblem — A221

1980, Jan. 31   Litho.   Perf. 13½

| 1049 | A221 | 50fr multi | 50 | 25 |

13th Winter Olympic Games, Lake Placid, N.Y. Feb. 12-24. See Nos. C409-C412.

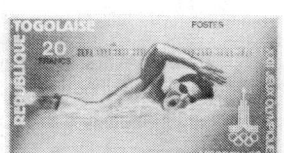

Swimming, Moscow '80 Emblem — A222

TOGO

1980, Feb. 29	Litho.	Perf. 13½
1050 A222 20fr shown		20 10
1051 A222 30fr Gymnastics		30 15
1052 A222 50fr Running		50 25
Nos. 1050-1052, C413-C415 (6)		7.00 3.50

22nd Summer Olympic Games, Moscow, July 19-Aug. 3.

Christ and the Angels, by Andrea Mantegna—A223

Easter 1980 (Paintings by): 40fr, Carlo Crivelli. 50fr, Jacopo Pontormo.

1980, Mar. 31		Perf. 14
1053 A223 30fr multi		30 15
1054 A223 40fr multi		40 20
1055 A223 50fr multi		50 25
Nos. 1053-1055, C416-C418 (6)		4.80 2.40

Jet over Map of Africa—A224

1980, Mar. 24	Litho.	Perf. 12½
1056 A224 50fr multi		50 35

ASECNA (Air Safety Board), 20th anniversary. See No. C419.

12th World Telecommunications Day—A225

1980, May 17	Photo.	Perf. 14x13½
1057 A225 50fr multi		50 35

See No. C420.

Red Cross over Globe Showing Lomé, Togo—A226

1980, June 16	Photo.	Perf. 14x13
1058 A226 50fr multi		50 35

Togolese Red Cross. See No. C421.

Slip cases are available for most Scott albums.

Jules Verne—A227

1980, July 14	Litho.	Perf. 14
1059 A227 30fr shown		30 15
1060 A227 50fr Shark (20,000 Leagues Under the Sea)		50 25
Nos. 1059-1060, C422-C425 (6)		5.20 2.60

Jules Verne (1828-1905), French science fiction writer.

Baroness James de Rothschild, by Ingres—A228

Paintings by Jean Auguste Dominique Ingres (1780-1867): 30fr, Napoleon I on Imperial Throne. 40fr, Don Pedro of Toledo and Henri IV.

1980, Aug. 29	Litho.	Perf. 14
1061 A228 25fr multi		25 12
1062 A228 30fr multi		30 15
1063 A228 40fr multi		40 20
Nos. 1061-1063, C426-C428 (6)		4.85 2.42

Minnie Holding Mirror for Leopard—A229

Disney Characters and Animals from Fazao Reserve: 2fr, Goofy (Dingo) cleaning teeth of hippopotamus. 3fr, Donald holding snout of crocodile. 4fr, Donald dangling over cliff from horn of rhinoceros. 5fr, Goofy riding water buffalo. 10fr, Monkey taking picture of Mickey. 100fr, Mickey as doctor examining giraffe with sore throat. No. 1071, Elephant giving shower to Goofy. No. 1072, Lion carrying Goofy by seat of his pants. 200fr, Pluto in party hat. No. 1072A, Pluto.

1980, Sept. 15		Perf. 11
1064 A229 1fr multi		5 5
1065 A229 2fr multi		5 5
1066 A229 3fr multi		5 5
1067 A229 4fr multi		5 5
1068 A229 5fr multi		5 5
1069 A229 10fr multi		10 5
1070 A229 100fr multi		1.00 50
1070A A229 200fr multi		2.00 1.00
1071 A229 300fr multi		3.00 1.50
Nos. 1064-1071 (9)		6.35 3.30

Souvenir Sheets

1072 A229 300fr multi	3.00 1.50
1072A A229 300fr multi	3.00 1.50

No. 1072 has multicolored margin showing glen. Size: 126x101mm.

50th anniversary of the Disney character Pluto. No. 1072A has multicolored margin showing scene from "Lend a Paw." Size: 126½x102mm.

Market Activities, Women Preparing Meat—A230

1980, Mar. 17		Perf. 14
1073 A230 1fr Grinding savo		5 5
1074 A230 2fr shown		5 5
1075 A230 3fr Truck going to market		5 5
1076 A230 4fr Unloading produce		5 5
1077 A230 5fr Sugar cane vendor		5 5
1078 A230 6fr Barber curling child's hair, vert.		5 5
1079 A230 7fr Vegetable vendor		8 5
1080 A230 8fr Sampling mangos, vert.		8 5
1081 A230 9fr Grain vendor		10 5
1082 A230 10fr Spiced fish vendor		10 5
1083 A230 15fr Clay pot vendor		15 8
1084 A230 20fr Straw baskets		20 10
1085 A230 25fr Selling lemons and onions, vert.		25 12
1086 A230 30fr Straw baskets, diff.		30 15
1087 A230 40fr Shore market		40 20
1088 A230 50fr Women carrying produce, vert.		50 25
Nos. 1073-1088 (16)		2.47 1.40

See Nos. 1105-1106, C440-C445, J68-J71.

Commemorative Wreath—A231

Famous Men of the Decade: 40fr, Mao Tse-tung (vert.).

1980, Feb. 11		Perf. 14x13
1089 A231 25fr multi		25 12
1090 A231 40fr emer grn & dk grn		40 20
Nos. 1089-1090, C429-C431 (5)		4.55 2.27

World Tourism Conference, Manila, Sept. 27—A232

1980, Sept. 15	Litho.	Perf. 14
1091 A232 50fr Hotel tourism emblem, vert.		50 25
1092 A232 150fr shown		1.50 75

Map of Australia and Human Rights Flame—A233

1980, Oct. 13	Photo.	Perf. 13x14
1093 A233 30fr shown		30 15
1094 A233 50fr Europe and Asia map		50 25

Declaration of Human Rights, 30th anniversary. See Nos. C432-C433.

Melk Monastery, Austria, 18th Century—A234

1980, Dec. 22	Litho.	Perf. 14½x13½
1095 A234 20fr shown		20 10
1096 A234 30fr Tarragon Cathedral, Spain, 12th cent.		30 15
1097 A234 50fr St. John the Baptist, Florence, 1964		50 25
Nos. 1095-1097, C435-C437 (6)		5.50 2.75

Christmas 1980.

African Postal Union, 5th Anniversary—A235

1980, Dec. 24	Photo.	Perf. 13½
1098 A235 100fr multi		1.00 50

February 2nd Hotel Opening—A236

1981, Feb. 2	Litho.	Perf. 12½x13
1099 A236 50fr multi		50 25

See No. C437B.

TOGO

Rembrandt's Father—A237

Easter 1981 (Rembrandt Paintings): 40fr, Self-portrait. 50fr, Artist's father as an old man. 60fr, Rider on Horseback.

1981, Apr. 13   **Litho.**   **Perf. 14½x13½**
1101	A237	30fr multi	30	15
1102	A237	40fr multi	40	20
1103	A237	50fr multi	50	25
1104	A237	60fr multi	60	30

Nos. 1101-1104, C438-C439 (6)   4.80   2.40

Market Type of 1980
Designs: Various market scenes.

1981, Mar. 8   **Litho.**   **Perf. 14**
1105	A230	45fr multi	45	22
1106	A230	60fr multi	60	30

Nos. 1105-1106, C440-C445, J68-J71 (12)   23.35   11.67

Inscribed 1980.

Red-headed Rock Fowl—A238

1981, Aug. 10   **Litho.**   **Perf. 13½x14½**
1107	A238	30fr shown	30	15
1108	A238	40fr Splendid sunbird	40	20
1109	A238	60fr Violet-backed starling	60	30
1110	A238	90fr Red-collared widowbird	90	45

Nos. 1107-1110, C446-C447 (6)   3.70   1.85

African Postal Union Ministers, 6th Council Meeting, July 28-20—A239

1981, Aug. 31   **Litho.**   **Perf. 12½**
1111	A239	70fr Dish antenna	70	35
1112	A239	90fr Computer operator, vert.	90	45
1113	A239	105fr Map	1.05	55

Intl. Year of the Disabled—A240

1981, Aug. 31   **Perf. 14**
1114	A240	70fr Blind man	70	35

See Nos. C448-C449A.

Woman with Hat, by Picasso, 1961—A241

Picasso Birth Centenary: Sculptures.

1981, Sept. 14   **Perf. 14½x13½**
1116	A241	25fr shown	25	12
1117	A241	50fr She-goat	50	25
1118	A241	60fr Violin, 1915	60	30

Nos. 1116-1118, C450-C452 (6)   5.25   2.62

Aix-la-Chapelle Cathedral, Germany—A242

World Heritage Year: 40fr, Geyser, Yellowstone Natl. Park. 50fr, Nahanni Natl. Park, Canada. 60fr, Stone crosses, Ethiopia.

1981, Sept. 28   **Perf. 13½x14½**
1119	A242	30fr multi	30	15
1120	A242	40fr multi	40	20
1121	A242	50fr multi	50	25
1122	A242	60fr multi	60	30

Nos. 1119-1122, C453-C454 (6)   4.80   2.40

20th Anniv. of Alan Shepard's Flight—A243

Space Anniversaries: 25fr, Yuri Gagarin's Vostok I, 20th. 60fr, Lunar Orbiter I, 15th.

1981, Nov.   **Perf. 14**
1123	A243	25fr multi	25	12
1124	A243	50fr multi	50	25
1125	A243	60fr multi	60	30

Nos. 1123-1125, C455-C456 (5)   3.25   1.62

Christmas 1981—A244

Rubens Paintings: 20fr, Adoration of the Kings. 30fr, Adoration of the Shepherds. 50fr, St. Catherine.

1981, Dec. 10   **Litho.**   **Perf. 14½x13½**
1126	A244	20fr multi	20	10
1127	A244	30fr multi	30	15
1128	A244	50fr multi	50	25

Nos. 1126-1128, C457-C459 (6)   7.00   3.50

15th Anniv. of Natl. Liberation—A245

1982, Jan. 13   **Litho.**   **Perf. 12½**
1129	A245	70fr Dove, flag	70	35
1130	A245	90fr Citizens, Pres. Eyadema, vert.	90	45

See Nos. C462-C463.

Scouting Year—A246

1982, Feb. 25   **Litho.**   **Perf. 14**
1131	A246	70fr Pitching tent	70	35

Nos. 1131, C464-C467 (5)   5.45   2.73

Easter 1982—A247

Designs: The Ten Commandments.

1982, Mar. 15   **Perf. 14x14½**
1132	A247	10fr multi	10	5
1133	A247	25fr multi	25	12
1134	A247	30fr multi	30	15
1135	A247	45fr multi	45	22
1136	A247	50fr multi	50	25
1137	A247	70fr multi	70	35
1138	A247	90fr multi	90	45

Nos. 1132-1138, C469-C470 (9)   5.45   2.74

Papilio Dardanus—A248

1982, July 15   **Litho.**   **Perf. 14½x14**
1139	A248	15fr shown	15	8
1140	A248	20fr Belenois calypso	20	10
1141	A248	25fr Palla decius	25	12

Nos. 1139-1141, C474-C475 (5)   2.55   1.27

1982 World Cup—A249

Designs: Various soccer players.

1982, July 26   **Perf. 14x14½**
1142	A249	25fr multi	25	12
1143	A249	45fr multi	45	22

Nos. 1142-1143, C477-C479 (5)   6.75   3.36

Christmas 1982—A250

Design: Madonna of Baldacchino, by Raphael. Nos. 1144-1148 show details; No. 1149 entire painting. (Size: 120x159mm.).

1982, Dec. 24   **Litho.**   **Perf. 14½x14**
1144	A250	45fr multi	45	22
1145	A250	70fr multi	70	35
1146	A250	105fr multi	1.05	52
1147	A250	130fr multi	1.30	65
1148	A250	150fr multi	1.50	75

Nos. 1144-1148 (5)   5.00   2.49

Souvenir Sheet
Perf. 14x14½
1149	A250	500fr multi, vert.	5.00	2.50

Nos. 1142-1143, C477-C480
Overprinted:
VAINQUER / COUPE DU MONDE / FOOTBALL 82 / "ITALIE"

1983, Jan. 31   **Litho.**   **Perf. 14x14½**
1150	A249	25fr multi	25	12
1151	A249	45fr multi	45	22
1152	A249	105fr multi	1.05	52
1153	A249	200fr multi	2.00	1.00
1154	A249	300fr multi	3.00	1.50

Nos. 1150-1154 (5)   6.75   3.36

Souvenir Sheet
1155	A249	500fr multi	5.00	2.50

Italy's victory in 1982 World Cup. Nos. 1152-1155 airmail.

TOGO

20th Anniv. of West African Monetary Union (1982)—A251

1983, May		Litho.		Perf. 12½x12	
1156	A251	70fr Map		70	35
1157	A251	90fr Emblem		90	45

Visit of Pres. Mitterand of France, Jan. 13-15—A252

1983, Jan. 13		Litho.		Perf. 13	
1158	A252	35fr Sokode Regional Hospital		35	18
a.		Souvenir sheet		35	18
1159	A252	45fr Citizens joining hands		45	22
a.		Souvenir sheet		50	25
1160	A252	70fr Soldiers, vert.		70	35
a.		Souvenir sheet		75	35
1161	A252	90fr Pres. Mitterand, vert.		90	45
a.		Souvenir sheet		1.00	50
1162	A252	105fr Pres. Eyadema, Mitterand, vert.		1.05	52
a.		Souvenir sheet		1.05	52
1163	A252	130fr Greeting crowd		1.30	65
a.		Souvenir sheet		1.30	65
		Nos. 1158-1163 (6)		4.75	2.37

Nos. 1161-1163 airmail. Souvenir sheets imperf. Size: 104x80mm.

Easter 1983—A253

Paintings: Mourners at the Death of Christ, by Bellini. 70fr, Crucifixion, by Raphael (vert.). 90fr, Descent from the Cross, by Carracci. 500fr Christ, by Reni.

1983		Litho.		Perf. 13½x14½	
1164	A253	35fr multi		18	10
1165	A253	70fr multi		35	18
1166	A253	90fr multi		45	22

Souvenir Sheet
Perf. 14½x13½

| 1167 | A253 | 500fr multi | | 2.50 | 1.25 |

90fr, 500fr airmail. Size of No. 1167: 101x77mm.

Folkdances—A254

1983			Perf. 14½x14	
1168	A254	70fr Kondona	35	18
1169	A254	90fr Kondona, diff.	45	22
1170	A254	105fr Toubole	52	26
1171	A254	130fr Adjogbo	65	32

90fr, 105fr, 130fr airmail.

World Communications Year—A255

1983, June 20		Litho.	Perf. 14x14½	
1172	A255	70fr Drummer	35	18
1173	A255	90fr Modern communication	45	22

90fr airmail.

Christmas 1983—A256

1983, Dec.			Perf. 13½x14½	
1174	A256	70fr Catholic Church, Kante	35	18
1175	A256	90fr Altar, Dapaong Cathedral	45	22
1176	A256	105fr Protestant Church, Dapaong	52	26

Souvenir Sheet

| 1177 | A256 | 500fr Ecumenical Church, Pya | 2.50 | 1.25 |

No. 1177 has multicolored margin showing nativity. Size: 110x85mm. 90fr, 105fr, 500fr airmail.

Sarakawa Presidential Assassination Attempt, 10th Anniv.—A257

1984, Jan. 24		Litho.	Perf. 13	
1178	A257	70fr Wrecked plane	35	18
1179	A257	90fr Plane, diff.	45	22
1180	A257	120fr Memorial Hall	60	30
1181	A257	270fr Pres. Eyadema statue, vert.	1.35	65

120fr, 270fr airmail.

20th Anniv. of World Food Program (1983)—A258

1984, May 2		Litho.		Perf. 13	
1182	A258	35fr Orchard		18	10
1183	A258	70fr Fruit tree		35	18
1184	A258	90fr Rice paddy		45	22

Souvenir Sheet

| 1185 | A258 | 300fr Village, horiz. | | 1.50 | 75 |

No. 1185 has multicolored margin continuing design. Size: 105x81mm.

25th Anniv. of Council of Unity—A259

1984, May 29			Perf. 12	
1186	A259	70fr multi	35	18
1187	A259	90fr multi	45	22

TOGO

SEMI-POSTAL STAMPS.
Curie Issue
Common Design Type
Engraved.

		1938		Perf. 13.	Unwmkd.
B1	CD80	1.75fr + 50c brt ultra		11.00	11.00

French Revolution Issue.
Common Design Type

1939   Photogravure.
Name and Value Typo. in Black.

B2	CD83	45(c) + 25(c) grn	3.75	3.75
B3	CD83	70(c) + 30(c) brn	3.75	3.75
B4	CD83	90(c) + 35(c) red org	3.75	3.75
B5	CD83	1.25fr + 1fr rose pink	3.75	3.75
B6	CD83	2.25fr + 2fr bl	3.75	3.75
	Nos. B2-B6 (5)		18.75	18.75

French Revolution, 150th anniversary. Surtax for defense of the colonies.

Stamps of 1927-41   **SECOURS**
Surcharged   **+ 1 fr.**
in Red or Black   **NATIONAL**

1941   Perf. 14 x 13½, 12½.

B7	A10	50c + 1fr chnt (Bk)	75	75
B8	A7	80c + 2fr ind & dl vio (Bk)	3.00	3.00
B9	A8	1.50fr + 2fr bl & lt bl (Bk)	3.00	3.00
B10	A11	2fr + 3fr lt ultra (R)	3.00	3.00

Common Design Type and

Togolese Militiaman SP1

Military Infirmary SP2

1941   Photogravure   Perf. 13½

B10A	SP1	1fr + 1fr red	45
B10B	CD86	1.50fr + 3fr mar	45
B10C	SP2	2.50fr + 1fr bl	45

Nos. B10A-B10C were issued by the Vichy government, and were not placed on sale in Togo.

Nos. 296-297 were surcharged "OEUVRES COLONIALES" and surtax (including change of denomination of the 2.50fr to 50c). These were issued in 1944 by the Vichy government and were not placed on sale in Togo.

Tropical Medicine Issue
Common Design Type

1950   Engraved.   Perf. 13.

B11	CD100	10fr + 2fr ind & dk bl	2.25	2.25

The surtax was for charitable work.

Republic

Patient on Stretcher SP3   Uprooted Oak Emblem SP4

Designs: 30fr+5fr, Feeding infant. 50fr+10fr, Blood transfusion.

1959   Engraved.   Perf. 13

B12	SP3	20fr + 5fr multi	60	50
a.		Souvenir sheet of 4	2.50	2.50
B13	SP3	30fr + 5fr bl, car & brn	60	50
a.		Souvenir sheet of 4	2.50	2.50
B14	SP3	50fr + 10fr emer, brn & car	60	60
a.		Souvenir sheet of 4	2.50	2.50

Issued for the Red Cross.
Nos. B12a, B13a, B14a have carmine marginal inscriptions. Size: 77x106mm.
Exist imperf.; same prices.

1960   Perf. 13   Unwmkd.

Design: No. B16 similar to No. B15, with emblem on top.

B15	SP4	25fr + 5fr dk bl, brn & yel grn	40	40
B16	SP4	45fr + 5fr dk bl, brn & ol grn	65	65

Issued to publicize World Refugee Year, July 1, 1959–June 30, 1960. The surtax was for aid to refugees.

AIR POST STAMPS.
Common Design Type
Engraved

1940   Perf. 12½x12   Unwmkd.

C1	CD85	1.90fr ultra	12	12
C2	CD85	2.90fr dk red	12	12
C3	CD85	4.50fr dk gray grn	22	12
C4	CD85	4.90fr yel bis	38	22
C5	CD85	6.90fr dp org	50	40
	Nos. C1-C5 (5)		1.34	98

Common Design Type
Inscribed "Togo" across top

1942

C6	CD88	50c car & bl	5
C7	CD88	1fr brn & blk	15
C8	CD88	2fr grn & red brn	8
C9	CD88	3fr dk bl & scar	18
C10	CD88	5fr vio & brn red	18

Frame Engraved,
Center Typographed.

C11	CD89	10fr ultra, ind & org	18
C12	CD89	20fr rose car, mag & gray blk	18
C13	CD89	50fr yel grn, dl grn & lt vio	60	75
	Nos. C6-C13 (8)		1.60

There is doubt whether Nos. C6 to C12 were officially placed in use.

Elephants—AP1

Plane—AP2

Plane—AP3

Post Runner and Plane—AP4

1947, Oct. 6   Engraved.   Perf. 12½

C14	AP1	40fr blue	2.50	1.65
C15	AP2	50fr lt ultra, & red vio	1.10	65
C16	AP3	100fr emer & dk brn	2.25	1.20
C17	AP4	200fr lil rose	4.00	2.00

UPU Issue
Common Design Type

1949, July 4   Perf. 13

C18	CD99	25fr multi	3.75	3.75

Issued to commemorate the 75th anniversary of the formation of the Universal Postal Union.

Liberation Issue
Common Design Type

1954, June 6

C19	CD102	15fr ind & pur	2.25	2.75

Liberation of France, 10th anniversary.

Freight Highway AP5

1954, Nov. 29

C20	AP5	500fr ind & dk grn	17.50	15.00

Republic

Independence Allegory—AP6
Engraved.

1957, Oct. 29   Perf. 13   Unwmkd.

C21	AP6	25fr bl, ol bis & ver	50	50

Issued to commemorate the first anniversary of Togo's autonomy.

Flag and Torch—AP7

Great White Egret—AP8

1957, Oct. 29

C22	AP7	50fr multi	75	40
C23	AP7	100fr multi	1.50	60
C24	AP7	200fr multi	3.00	1.00
C25	AP8	500fr ind, lt bl & grn	9.00	4.00

Types of 1957 inscribed:
"Republique du Togo" and

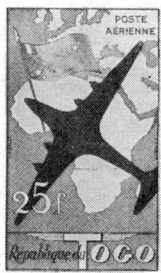

Flag, Plane and Map AP9

1959, Jan. 15   Engraved   Perf. 13

C26	AP9	25fr ultra, emer & vio brn	25	10
C27	AP7	50fr dk bl, dl grn & red	50	25
C28	AP7	100fr multi	1.25	40
C29	AP7	200fr dk grn, red & ultra	2.50	90
C30	AP8	500fr blk brn, rose lil & grn	7.00	1.35
	Nos. C26-C30 (5)		11.50	3.00

Hotel Le Benin—AP10

Eagle and Map of Togo AP11

Perf. 14½x15, 15x14½

1960, Apr. 27   Litho.   Unwmkd.

C31	AP10	100fr crim, emer & yel	1.10	25
C32	AP10	200fr multi	2.50	40
C33	AP11	500fr grn & gldn brn	6.00	35

Issued to commemorate the proclamation of Togo's full independence, Apr. 27, 1960.

Type of Mail Service Issue, 1963.
Design: 100fr, Boeing 707 and stamps of 1960.

1963, Jan. 12   Photo.   Perf. 13

C34	A41	100fr multi	1.25	60
a.		Souv. sheet of 4	2.50	2.50

Issued to commemorate the 65th anniversary of Togolese mail service.
No. C34a contains 4 stamps similar to Nos. 441-443 and C34, with simulated perforations. Gray sheet margin; colorless inscriptions. Size: 140x95mm.

Type of Emancipation Issue, 1963.

1963, Oct. *Perf. 13x14* Unwmkd.

C35	A45	100fr multi	1.25	60
a.		Souv. sheet of 4	1.80	1.50

Issued to commemorate the centenary of the emancipation of the American slaves. No. C35a contains 4 imperf. stamps similar to Nos. 454–456 and C35. Black marginal inscription. Size: 131x102½ mm.

Type of 1964 Regular Issue

Designs: 50fr, Black-bellied seed-cracker. 100fr, Blue-billed mannikin. 200fr, Red-headed lovebird. 250fr, African gray parrot. 500fr, Yellow-breasted barbet.

1964–65 Photogravure *Perf. 14*

Size: 22½x31mm.

Birds in Natural Colors

C36	A47	50fr yel grn	60	35
C37	A47	100fr ocher	1.25	45
C38	A47	200fr dl bl grn	2.25	1.25
C39	A47	250fr dl rose ('65)	3.00	1.50
C40	A47	500fr violet	6.00	2.25
		Nos. C36-C40 (5)	13.10	5.80

No. C35 Overprinted Diagonally: "En Mémoire de / JOHN F. KENNEDY / 1917–1963"

1964, Feb. *Perf. 13x14*

C41	A45	100fr multi	1.25	65

Issued in memory of John F. Kennedy.

Same overprint was applied to stamps of No. C35a, with black border and commemorative inscription added. Two sheets exist: with and without gray silhouetted head of Kennedy covering all four stamps.

Liberation Type of 1964

1964, May 25 *Perf. 14x13*

C42	A50	100fr dl bl grn & dk brn	1.25	60

Issued to commemorate the first anniversary of the meeting of African chiefs of state at Addis Ababa.

Olympic Games Type of Regular Issue, 1964.

Design: 100fr, Tennis.

1964, Oct. Photo. *Perf. 14*

C43	A52	100fr pale brn	1.50	60
a.		Souv. sheet of 3	2.00	2.00

Issued to commemorate the 18th Olympic Games, Tokyo, Oct. 10–25. No. C43a contains 3 imperf. stamps similar to Nos. 493–494 and C43. Gray margin with black inscription. Size: 105x113mm.

Flag of Togo and Jet—AP12

1964, Dec. 5 *Perf. 14x13* Unwmkd.

C44	AP12	100fr multi	1.50	60

Issued to commemorate the inauguration of the national airline "Air Togo." For souvenir sheet see No. 499a.

Lincoln Type of Regular Issue, 1965

1965, June Photo. *Perf. 13½x14*

C45	A58	100fr ol gray	1.75	60
a.		Souv. sheet of 2	1.85	1.85

Issued to commemorate the centenary of the death of Abraham Lincoln. No. C45a contains two imperf. stamps similar to Nos. 524 and C45. Tan margin with olive gray inscription. Size: 120x88mm.

Sports Type of Regular Issue, 1965

Design: 100fr, Soccer player, flags of Togo and Congo.

1965, July *Perf. 14x13* Unwmkd.

C46	A59	100fr multi	1.50	60

Issued to commemorate the First African Games, Brazzaville, July 18–25.

Churchill Type of Regular Issue

1965, Aug. 7 Photo. *Perf. 13½x14*

C47	A60	85fr car rose	1.40	60
a.		Souv. sheet of 2	2.00	2.00

Issued in memory of Sir Winston Spencer Churchill (1874–1965), British statesman and World War II leader. No. C47a contains two imperf. stamps similar to Nos. 532 and C47. Gray margin with carmine rose inscription. Size: 135x88mm.

U.N. Type of Regular Issue, 1965

Design: 100fr, Apple, grapes, wheat and "ONU."

1965, Dec. 15 *Perf. 14x13½*

C48	A65	100fr dk bl & bis	1.50	60
a.		Souv. sheet of 2	2.00	2.00

Issued to commemorate the 20th anniversary of the United Nations and in memory of Adlai E. Stevenson (1900–1965), U.S. ambassador to the U.N. No. C48a contains two imperf. stamps similar to Nos. 548 and C48 with simulated perforations. Yellow margin with dark blue quotation by President Lyndon B. Johnson. Size: 90x129mm.

Pope Type of Regular Issue

Designs: 45fr, Pope speaking at U.N. rostrum, world map and U.N. emblem. 90fr, Pope, plane and U.N. emblem.

1966, March 5 Litho. *Perf. 12*

C49	A66	45fr emer & multi	65	20
C50	A66	90fr gray & multi	1.35	35
a.		Souv. sheet of 2	2.25	1.75

Issued to commemorate the visit of Pope Paul VI to the United Nations, New York City, Oct. 4, 1966. No. C50a contains one each of Nos. C49–C50. Gray margin with red inscription. Size: 100x117mm.

Red Cross Type of Regular Issue

Design: 100fr, Jean Henri Dunant and Togolese Flag.

1966, May 7 Litho. *Perf. 12*

C51	A67	100fr multi	1.65	50

Togolese Red Cross, 7th anniversary.

WHO Type of Regular Issue

Flowers: 50fr, Daisies and WHO Headquarters. 90fr, Talisman roses and WHO Headquarters.

1966, May Litho. *Perf. 12*

C52	A68	50fr lt bl & multi	75	15
C53	A68	90fr gray & multi	1.35	20
a.		Souv. sheet of 2	2.10	1.75

Issued to commemorate the inauguration of World Health Organization Headquarters, Geneva.

No. C53a contains one each of Nos. C52–C53. Green marginal inscription. Size: 149x100mm.

Air Afrique Issue

Common Design Type

1966, Aug. 31 Photo. *Perf. 13*

C54	CD123	30fr brt grn, blk & lem	45	15

Issued to commemorate the introduction of DC-8F planes by Air Afrique.

Arts and Crafts Type of Regular Issue

Designs: 60fr, Basket maker. 90fr, Wood carver.

1966, Sept. *Perf. 13x14*

C55	A69	60fr ultra, org & blk	90	25
C56	A69	90fr brt rose, yel & blk	1.35	30

Dancer Type of Regular Issue

Designs: 50fr, Woman from North Togo holding branches. 60fr, Man from North Togo with horned helmet.

1966, Nov. Photo. *Perf. 13x14*

C57	A70	50fr multi	75	30
C58	A70	60fr ol & multi	90	35

Soccer Type of Regular Issue

Designs: Different Soccer Scenes.

1966, Dec. 14 Photo. *Perf. 14x13*

C59	A71	50fr org, brn & pur	75	25
C60	A71	60fr ultra, brn & org	90	30
a.		Souv. sheet of 3	2.25	2.00

Issued to commemorate England's victory in the World Soccer Cup Championship, Wembley, July 30. No. C60a contains 3 imperf. stamps similar to Nos. 582, C59–C60. Yellow margin and dark blue inscription. Size: 156x110mm.

Fish Type of Regular Issue

Designs: 45fr, Yellow jack and trawler. 90fr, Banded distichodus and seiner.

1967, Jan. 14 Photo. *Perf. 14*

Fish in Natural Colors

C61	A72	45fr org & brn	65	25
C62	A72	90fr emer & dk bl	1.35	45

UNICEF Type of Regular Issue

Designs (UNICEF Emblem and): 45fr, Girl and miniature poodle. 90fr, African boy and greyhound.

1967, Feb. 11 Photo. *Perf. 14x13½*

C63	A73	45fr yel, red brn & blk	65	25
C64	A73	90fr ultra, dk grn & blk	1.35	45
a.		Souv. sheet of 2	2.10	1.75

Issued to commemorate the 20th anniversary (in 1966) of UNICEF (United Nations Children's Emergency Fund). No. C64a contains 2 imperf., lithographed stamps with simulated perforations similar to Nos. C63–C64. Pink margin with brown inscription. Size: 85x125mm.

Satellite Type of Regular Issue

Designs: 50fr, Diamant rocket (vert.). 90fr, Fr-1 satellite (vert.).

1967, Mar. 18 Photo. *Perf. 13½x14*

C65	A74	50fr multi	85	25
C66	A74	90fr multi	1.50	45
a.		Souv. sheet of 2	2.25	1.75

Issued to honor French achievements in space. No. C66a contains 2 imperf. stamps similar to Nos. C65–C66 with simulated perforations. Light gray margin with dark gray inscription. Size: 90x120mm.

Musician Type of Regular Issue

Designs (UNESCO Emblem and): 45fr, Johann Sebastian Bach and organ. 90fr, Ludwig van Beethoven, violin and clarinet.

1967, Apr. 15 Photo. *Perf. 14x13½*

C67	A75	45fr multi	65	20
C68	A75	90fr pink & multi	1.35	40
a.		Souv. sheet of 2	2.00	1.65

Issued to commemorate the 20th anniversary (in 1966) of UNESCO. No. C68a contains 2 imperf. stamps similar to Nos. C67–C68 with simulated perforations and black marginal inscription. Size: 90x120 mm.

EXPO '67 Type of Regular Issue

Designs (EXPO '67 Emblem and): 45fr, French pavilion and roses. 60fr, British pavilion and day lilies. 90fr, African village and bird-of-paradise flower. 105fr, United States pavilion and daisies.

1967, May 30 Photo. *Perf. 14*

C69	A76	45fr multi	65	20
C70	A76	60fr multi	90	30
C71	A76	90fr yel & multi	1.25	50
a.		Souv. sheet of 3	3.00	2.25
C72	A76	105fr multi	1.50	60

Issued to commemorate EXPO '67 International Exhibition, Montreal, Apr. 28–Oct. 27. No. C71a contains 3 imperf. stamps similar to Nos. C69–C71. Buff margin with dark brown inscription. Size: 159x109mm.

Mural by José Vela Zanetti

AP13

The designs are from a mural in the lobby of the United Nations Conference Building, New York. The mural depicting mankind's struggle for a lasting peace is shown across 3 stamps twice in the set: on the 5fr, 15fr, 30fr and 45fr, 60fr, 90fr.

1967, July 15 Litho. *Perf. 14*

C73	AP13	5fr multi	6	5
C74	AP13	15fr org & multi	20	6
C75	AP13	30fr multi	40	10
C76	AP13	45fr multi	60	20
C77	AP13	60fr car & multi	90	25
C78	AP13	90fr ind & multi	1.35	35
a.		Souv. sheet of 3	2.75	2.25
		Nos. C73-C78 (6)	3.51	1.01

Issued to publicize general disarmament. No. C78a contains one each of Nos. C76–C78 with blue marginal inscription. Size: 160x110mm.

Animal Type of Regular Issue, 1967

Designs: 45fr, Lion. 60fr, Elephants.

1967, Aug. 19 Photo. *Perf. 14x13½*

C79	A78	45fr bl & bis brn	65	25
C80	A78	60fr bis brn, blk & pale grn	90	30

African Postal Union Issue, 1967

Common Design Type

1967, Sept. 9 Engraved *Perf. 13*

C81	CD124	100fr bl, brt grn & ol brn	1.50	60

Stamp Anniversary Type of Regular Issue

Designs: 90fr, Stamp auction and Togo Nos. 16 and C42. 105fr, Father and son with stamp album and No. 474.

1967, Oct. 14 Photo. *Perf. 14x13*

Stamps on Stamps in Original Colors

C82	A79	90fr olive	1.40	40
a.		Souv. sheet of 3	3.00	2.25
C83	A79	105fr dk car rose	2.00	55

Issued to commemorate the 70th anniversary of the first Togolese stamps. No. C82a contains 3 imperf. stamps similar to Nos. 621–622 and C82 with simulated perforations. Yellow margin with brown olive inscription. Size: 120x89mm.

Pre-Olympics Type of Regular Issue

Designs: 60fr, Runners, Summer Olympics emblem and view of Mexico City. 90fr, Broad jump, Summer Olympics emblem and view of Mexico City.

1967, Dec. 2 *Perf. 13x14*

C84	A80	60fr pink & multi	90	30
C85	A80	90fr multi	1.35	50
a.		Souv. sheet of 3	3.00	2.50

1968 Olympic Games.

No. C85a contains 3 imperf. stamps similar to Nos. 627 and C84–C85. Pale yellow margin with red inscription. Size: 89x120mm.

Nos. C69–C72 Overprinted: "JOURNÉE NATIONALE / DU TOGO / 29 SEPTEMBRE 1967"

1967, Dec. Photo. *Perf. 14*

C86	A76	45fr multi	65	20
C87	A76	60fr multi	90	22
C88	A76	90fr yel & multi	1.35	40
C89	A76	105fr multi	1.50	50

Issued for National Day, Sept. 29, 1967.

Hydrological Decade Type of Regular Issue

1968, Apr. 6 Litho. *Perf. 14*

C90	A84	60fr multi	90	25

Hydrological Decade (UNESCO), 1965–74.

Ship Type of Regular Issue

Designs: 45fr, Fulton's and modern steamships. 90fr, U.S. atomic ship Savannah and atom symbol.

1968, Apr. 26 Photo. *Perf. 14x14½*

C91	A85	45fr yel & multi	65	20
C92	A85	90fr bl & multi	1.35	40
a.		Souv. sheet of 2	2.50	2.00

Issued to commemorate the inauguration of Lomé Harbor. No. C92a contains 2 imperf. stamps similar to Nos. C91–C92 with simulated perforations. Bright green margin with commemorative inscription. Size: 75x100mm.

WHO Type of Regular Issue

Paintings: 60fr, The Anatomy Lesson, by Rembrandt (detail). 90fr, Jesus Healing the Sick, by Raphael.

1968, June 22 Photo. *Perf. 14*

C93	A87	60fr multi	90	25
C94	A87	90fr pur & multi	1.35	40
a.		Souv. sheet of 2	2.25	1.75

Issued to commemorate the 20th anniversary of the World Health Organization. No. C94a contains 2 imperf. stamps similar to Nos. C93–C94 with simulated perforations. Pink margin with purple and white inscription. Size: 75x100mm.

Olympic Games Type of Regular Issue

Olympic Monument, San Salvador Island, Bahamas and: 60fr, Wrestling. 90fr, Running.

1968, July 27 *Perf. 14x13½*

C95	A88	60fr multi	90	25
C96	A88	90fr multi	1.35	40
a.		Souv. sheet of 2	2.25	1.75

Issued to commemorate the 19th Olympic Games, Mexico City, Oct. 12–27. No. C96a contains 2 imperf. stamps similar to Nos. C95–C96 with simulated perforations. Buff margin with light brown inscription. Size: 75x100mm.

Boy Scout Type of Regular Issue

Designs: 60fr, First aid practice (horiz.). 90fr, Scout game.

1968, Nov. 23 Litho. *Perf. 14*

C97	A90	60fr ol & multi	90	35
C98	A90	90fr org & multi	1.35	50
a.		Souv. sheet of 2	2.25	1.75

Issued to honor the Togolese Boy Scouts. No. C98a contains 2 imperf. stamps with simulated perforations similar to Nos. C97–C98. Olive margin with green inscription. Size: 75x100mm.

PHILEXAFRIQUE Issue

The Letter, by Jean Auguste Franquelin
AP14

1968, Nov. 9 Photo. *Perf. 12½x12*

C99	AP14	100fr multi	1.50	1.25

Issued to publicize PHILEXAFRIQUE Philatelic Exhibition in Abidjan, Feb. 14–23. Printed with alternating light ultramarine label.

Christmas Type of Regular Issue

Paintings: 60fr, Adoration of the Magi, by Pieter Brueghel. 90fr, Adoration of the Magi, by Dürer.

1968, Dec. 28 Litho. *Perf. 14*

C100	A91	60fr red & multi	90	30
C101	A91	90fr multi	1.35	45
a.		Souv. sheet	2.25	1.75

No. C101a contains 2 imperf. stamps similar to Nos. C100–C101 with simulated perforations. Light violet margin with gold inscription. Size: 75x100mm.

Human Rights Type of Regular Issue

Portraits and Human Rights Flame: 60fr, Robert F. Kennedy. 90fr, Martin Luther King, Jr.

1969, Feb. 1 Photo. *Perf. 13½x14*

C102	A92	60fr brt rose lil & vio bl	75	35
C103	A92	90fr emer & brn	1.10	50
a.		Souv. sheet	2.50	1.50

Issued for International Human Rights Year 1968. No. C103a contains 2 imperf. stamps similar to Nos. C102–C103 with simulated perforations. Buff margin with white inscription. Size: 100x75mm.

2nd PHILEXAFRIQUE Issue

Common Design Type

Design: 50fr, Togo No. 16 and Aledjo Fault.

1969, Feb. 14 Engraved *Perf. 13*

C104	CD128	50fr red brn, grn & car rose	65	65

Issued to commemorate the opening of PHILEXAFRIQUE, Abidjan, Feb. 14.

Sports Type of Regular Issue

Designs (Stadium and): 60fr, Boxing. 90fr, Bicycling.

1969, Apr. 26 Photo. *Perf. 14x13½*

C105	A93	60fr bl, red & dk brn	90	30
C106	A93	90fr ultra, brt pink & dk brn	1.65	50
a.		Souv. Sheet	1.85	1.50

Opening of Omnisport Stadium, Lomé.
No. C106a contains 2 imperf. stamps similar to Nos. C105–C106 with simulated perforations. Dull orange margin with white inscription. Size: 75x99½mm.

Lunar Type of Regular Issue

Designs: 60fr, Astronaut exploring moon surface. 100fr, Astronaut gathering rocks.

1969, July 21 Litho. *Perf. 14*

C107	A94	60fr dk bl & multi	60	30
C108	A94	100fr multi	1.00	60
a.		Souv. sheet	8.50	7.50

See note after No. 677. No. C108a contains 4 imperf. stamps with simulated perforations similar to Nos. 676–677 and C107–C108. Magenta margin with commemorative inscription. Size: 98½x138 mm. No. C108a also exists with colors of 30fr and 100fr stamps changed, and margin in orange. Price $6.

Painting Type of Regular Issue

Painting: 90fr, Pentecost, by El Greco.

1969, Aug. 16 Litho. *Perf. 14*

C109	A95	90fr multi	1.50	60
a.		Souv. sheet	1.75	1.25

No. C109a contains two imperf. stamps with simulated perforations similar to Nos. 682 and C109. Light blue and gold margin with commemorative inscription in black and carmine. Size: 95x92mm.

Nos. C102–C103 Overprinted Like Nos. 683–686

1969, Sept. 1 Photo. *Perf. 13½x14*

C110	A92	60fr brt rose lil & vio bl	60	28
C111	A92	90fr emer & brn	90	40
a.		Souv. sheet of 2	4.25	3.50

Issued in memory of Gen. Dwight D. Eisenhower (1890–1969), 34th President of the U.S.
No. C111a is No. C103a with Eisenhower overprint.

Bank Type of Regular Issue

Design: 100fr, Bank emblem and hand holding cattle and farmer.

1969, Sept. 10 Photo. *Perf. 13x14*

C112	A96	100fr multi	1.20	60

Issued to commemorate the 5th anniversary of the African Development Bank.

Red Cross Type of Regular Issue

Designs: 60fr, Wilhelm C. Roentgen and Red Cross workers with children in front of Togo Headquarters. 90fr, Henri Dunant and Red Cross workers meeting Biafra refugees at airport.

1969, Sept. 27 Litho. *Perf. 14*

C113	A97	60fr brn & multi	70	35
C114	A97	90fr ol & multi	1.00	50
a.		Souv. sheet of 2	2.00	1.50

Issued to commemorate the 50th anniversary of the League of Red Cross Societies. No. C114a contains 2 imperf. stamps with simulated perforations similar to Nos. C113–C114. Dark red margin with black ornament and gold and white inscriptions. Size: 75x97mm.

Type of Regular Issue, 1969

Designs (Emblem of Young Pioneer and Agricultural Organization and): 90fr, Manioc harvest. 100fr, Instruction in gardening. 200fr, Corn harvest. 250fr, Marching drum corps. 500fr, Parade of Young Pioneers.

1969–70 Litho. *Perf. 14*

C115	A98	90fr multi	1.10	40
C116	A98	100fr org & multi	1.25	45
C117	A98	200fr multi ('70)	2.50	75
C118	A98	250fr ol & multi	3.25	1.25
C119	A98	500fr multi ('70)	6.25	1.50
		Nos. C115-C119 (5)	14.35	4.35

Christmas Issue

Nos. C107–C108, C108a Overprinted: "JOYEUX NOEL"

1969, Dec. Lithographed *Perf. 14*

C120	A94	60fr multi	2.00	60
C121	A94	100fr multi	2.75	90
a.		Souvenir sheet of 4	12.50	12.50

Peace Leaders Type of Regular Issue

Portraits: 60fr, Friedrich Ebert. 90fr, Mahatma Gandhi.

1969, Dec. 27 Litho. *Perf. 14x13½*

C122	A100	60fr dk brn, dk red & yel	85	40
C123	A100	90fr dk brn, vio bl & ocher	1.20	60

Issued to honor leaders for world peace.

ILO Type of Regular Issue

Paintings and ILO Emblem: 60fr, Spring Sowing, by Vincent van Gogh. 90fr, Workers, by Diego de Rivera.

1970, Jan. 24 Litho. *Perf. 12½x13*

C124	A101	60fr gold & multi	90	35
C125	A101	90fr gold & multi	1.65	50
a.		Souvenir sheet of 2	1.75	1.35

Issued to commemorate the 50th anniversary of the International Labor Organization.
No. C125a contains two stamps similar to Nos. C124–C125, with simulated perforations. Black commemorative inscription and gold marginal ornament. Size: 137x 100mm.

Hair Styles Type of Regular Issue

Designs: Various hair styles (45fr, vertical. 90fr, horizontal).

Perf. 12½x13, 13x12½

1970, Feb. 21

C126	A102	45fr car & multi	50	30
C127	A102	90fr multi	1.00	60

Independence Type of Regular Issue

Design: 60fr, Togo No. C33 and Independence Monument, Lomé.

1970, Apr. 27 Litho. *Perf. 13x12½*

C128	A103	60fr yel & multi	70	30

10th anniversary of Independence.

U.P.U. Type of Regular Issue

1970, May 30 Photo. *Perf. 14x13½*

C129	A104	50fr grnsh bl & dk car	60	25

Issued to commemorate the inauguration of the new Universal Postal Union Headquarters, Bern.

Soccer Type of Regular Issue

Designs (Various Scenes from Soccer, Rimet Cup and Flags of): 50fr, Sweden and Israel. 60fr, Bulgaria and Peru. 90fr, Belgium and Salvador.

1970, June 27 Litho. *Perf. 13x14*

C130	A105	50fr multi	65	35
C131	A105	60fr lil & multi	80	45
C132	A105	90fr multi	1.25	60
a.		Souvenir sheet of 4	3.00	3.00

Issued to commemorate the 9th World Soccer Championships for the Jules Rimet Cup, Mexico City, May 30–June 21 1970. No. C132a contains 4 stamps similar to Nos. 734, C130–C132, but imperf. with simulated perforations. Prussian blue margin with commemorative inscription. Size: 139x108mm.

Lenin Type of Regular Issue

Design: 50fr, Lenin Meeting Peasant Delegation, by V. A. Serov, and UNESCO emblem.

1970, July 25 Litho. *Perf. 12½*

C133	A106	50fr multi	75	30

Issued to commemorate the centenary of the birth of Lenin (1870–1924), Russian communist leader.

EXPO '70 Type of Regular Issue

Souvenir Sheet

Design: 150fr, Mitsubishi pavilion and EXPO '70 emblem.

1970, Aug. 8 Litho. *Perf. 13*

C134	A107	150fr yel & multi	1.75	70
a.		Inscribed "AERINNE"		

Issued to commemorate EXPO '70 International Exhibition, Osaka, Japan, Mar. 15–Sept. 13. No. C134 contains one stamp (size: 86x33mm.); view of Osaka and EXPO in margin. Size: 145x100mm.

Astronaut Type of Regular Issue

Design: 200fr, James A. Lovell, Fred W. Haise, Jr. and Tom Mattingly (replaced by John L. Swigert, Jr.) and Apollo 13 emblem.

1970, Sept. 26

C135	A108	200fr multi	2.25	1.25
a.		Souv. sheet of 3	2.75	2.25

Space flight of Apollo 13.
No. C135a contains 3 stamps similar to Nos. 741, 744 and C135, with simulated perforations. Gold margin with blue emblems of Apollo 11, 12 and 13. Size: 126x99mm.

Nos. C135, C135a Inscribed: "FELICITATIONS / BON RETOUR APOLLO XIII"

1970, Sept. 26

C136	A108	200fr multi	2.25	1.25
a.		Souvenir sheet of 3	2.75	2.25

Safe return of the crew of Apollo 13.

U.N. Type of Regular Issue

Paintings and Emblems of U.N. Agencies: 60fr, The Mailman Roulin, by van Gogh, and U.P.U. emblem. 90fr, The Birth of the Virgin, by Vittore Carpaccio, and WHO emblem.

1970, Oct. 24 Litho. *Perf. 13x12½*

C137	A109	60fr grn, gold & blk	75	40
C138	A109	90fr red org, gold & brn	1.10	60
a.		Souvenir sheet of 4	2.75	2.25

United Nations, 25th anniversary. No. C138a contains one each of Nos. 754–755 and C137–C138 with simulated perforations. Blue margin with black inscription. Size: 138x100mm.

Moth Type of Regular Issue

Moths: 60fr, Euchloron megaera. 90fr, Pseudacraea boisduvali.

1970, Nov. 21 Photo. *Perf. 13x14*

C139	A110	60fr multi	1.25	30
C140	A110	90fr multi	1.25	40

Christmas Type of Regular Issue

Paintings: 60fr, Adoration of the Shepherds, by Botticelli. 90fr, Adoration of the Kings, by Tiepolo.

1970, Dec. 26 Litho. *Perf. 12½x13*

C141	A111	60fr gold & multi	70	30
C142	A111	90fr gold & multi	1.10	45
a.		Souvenir sheet of 2	2.00	1.50

Christmas 1970. No. C142a contains one each of Nos. C141–C142 with marginal inscription and design showing Three Kings. Size: 183x114mm.

No. C122 Surcharged and Overprinted: "EN MEMOIRE / Charles De Gaulle / 1890–1970"

1971, Jan. 9 Photo. *Perf. 14x13½*

C143	A100	200fr on 60fr	3.00	1.25

De Gaulle Type of Regular Issue

Designs: 60fr, De Gaulle and Pope Paul VI. 90fr, De Gaulle and satellite.

1971, Feb. 20 Photo. *Perf. 13x14*

C144	A112	60fr blk & dp vio	90	30

C145 A112 90fr blk & bl grn 1.35 45
a. Souvenir sheet of 4 3.50 2.25

Nos. C143–C145 issued in memory of Charles De Gaulle (1890–1970), President of France. No. C145a contains 4 imperf. stamps similar to Nos. 769–770, C144–C145. Gray margin with black inscription. Size: 103x144mm.

Easter Type of Regular Issue

Paintings: 50fr, Resurrection, by Matthias Grunewald. 60fr, Resurrection, by Master of Trebon. 90fr, Resurrection, by El Greco.

Lithographed

1971, Apr. 10 ***Perf. 10½x11½***

C146 A113 50fr gold & multi 65 25
C147 A113 60fr gold & multi 90 35
C148 A113 90fr gold & multi 1.20 60
a. Souvenir sheet of 4 3.25 2.25

Easter, 1971. No. C148a contains one each of Nos. 773, C146–C148. Yellow ornamental margin with black inscription. Size: 151x196mm.

Apollo 14 Type of Regular Issue

Designs: 50fr, 200f, Apollo 14 badge. 100fr, Take-off from moon, and spaceship.

1971, May Lithographed ***Perf. 12½***

C149 A114 50fr grn & multi 50 22
C150 A114 100fr multi 1.00 50
C151 A114 200fr org & multi 2.00 1.00
a. Souv. sheet of 4 4.50 3.50

Apollo 14 U.S. moon landing, Jan. 31–Feb. 9. No. C151a contains 4 stamps similar to Nos. 777 and C149–C151 with simulated perforations. Green margin with inscription. Size: 145x100mm.

Cacao Type of Regular Issue

Designs: 60fr, Ministry of Agriculture. 90fr, Cacao tree and pods. 100fr, Sorting and separating beans from pods.

1971, June 6 **Litho.** ***Perf. 14***

C152 A115 60fr multi 60 30
C153 A115 90fr multi 90 45
C154 A115 100fr multi 1.10 50

International Cacao Day, June 6.

ASECNA Type of Regular Issue

1971, June 26

C155 A116 100fr multi 1.10 50

See note after No. 781.

Tourist Type of Regular Issue

Designs: 50fr, Château Viale and antelope. 60fr, Lake Togo and crocodile. 100fr, Old lime furnace, Tokpli, and hippopotamus.

1971, July 17

C156 A117 50fr multi 50 22
C157 A117 60fr multi 60 30
C158 A117 100fr multi 1.00 50

Tourist publicity.

Religions Type of Regular Issue

Designs: 50fr, Mohammedans praying in front of Lomé Mosque. 60fr, Protestant service. 90fr, Catholic bishop and priests.

1971, July 31 **Litho.** ***Perf. 14½***

C159 A118 50fr multi 45 25
C160 A118 60fr multi 50 30
C161 A118 90fr multi 90 40
a. Souvenir sheet of 4 2.50 2.00

Religions of Togo.
No. C161a contains one each of Nos. 787, C159–C161. Yellow margin, black inscription. Size: 125x100mm.

Nos. C149–C151 Overprinted and Surcharged in Black or Silver: "EN MEMOIRE / DOBROVOLSKY - VOLKOV - PATSAYEV / SOYUZ 11"

C162 A114 90fr on 50fr multi 90 40
C163 A114 100fr multi (S) 1.00 45
C164 A114 200fr multi 2.00 75
a. Souvenir sheet of 4 4.00 3.50

See note after No. 788.
No. C164a contains one each of Nos. 788, C162–C164. Green margin. Size: 145x100mm.

Olympic Type of Regular Issue

Design: 200fr, Sapporo '72 emblem and Ski jump.

1971, Oct. 30 **Litho.** ***Perf. 14***

C165 A119 200fr multi 2.00 75
a. Souvenir sheet of 4 3.00 2.75

11th Winter Olympic Games, Sapporo, Japan, Feb. 3–13, 1972. No. C165a contains 4 stamps with simulated perforations similar to Nos. 791–793 and C165 printed on glazed paper. Lilac margin with snowflake design and black inscription. Size: 126x98mm.

African Postal Union Issue, 1971

Common Design Type

Design: 100fr, Adjogbo dancers and UAMPT Building, Brazzaville, Congo.

1971, Nov. 13 Photo. ***Perf. 13x13½***

C166 CD135 100fr bl & multi 1.10 60

UNICEF Type of Regular Issue

Toys and UNICEF Emblem: 60fr, Turtle. 90fr, Parrot.

1971, Nov. 27 **Litho.** ***Perf. 14***

C167 A120 60fr lt bl & multi 60 28
C168 A120 90fr multi 90 35
a. Souvenir sheet of 4 2.75 2.75

25th anniversary of the United Nations International Children's Fund (UNICEF). No. C168a contains 4 stamps with simulated perforations similar to Nos. 796–797 and C167–C168. Violet margin with black inscription and UNICEF emblem. Size: 114x96mm.

Christmas Type of Regular Issue

Virgin and Child by: 60fr, Giorgione. 100fr, Raphael.

1971, Dec. 24 ***Perf. 14x13***

C169 A121 60fr ol & multi 60 40
C170 A121 100fr multi 1.10 65
a. Souvenir sheet of 4 3.00 2.50

Christmas 1971. No. C170a contains 4 stamps with simulated perforations similar to Nos. 800–801, C169–C170. Dark blue and white margin with commemorative inscription. Size: 129x172mm.

Venice Type of Regular Issue

Design: 100fr, Ca' d'Oro, Venice.

1972, Feb. 26 Lithographed ***Perf. 14***

C171 A122 100fr multi 1.10 65
a. Souvenir sheet of 3 2.10 2.10

UNESCO campaign to save Venice. No. C171a contains 3 stamps similar to Nos. 802–803, C171 with simulated perforations. Greenish blue decorative margin with UNESCO emblem and black inscription. Size: 98x130mm.

No. C156 Overprinted "VISITE DU PRESIDENT / NIXON EN CHINE / FEVRIER 1972"

1972, Mar. **Lithographed** ***Perf. 14***

C172 A117 50fr multi 50 30

Visit of Pres. Richard M. Nixon to the People's Republic of China, Feb. 20–27.

Easter Type of Regular Issue

Paintings: 50fr, Resurrection, by Thomas de Coloswa. 100fr, Ascension by Andrea Mantegna.

1972, Mar. 31

C173 A123 50fr gold & multi 70 20
C174 A123 100fr gold & multi 1.00 40
a. Souvenir sheet of 4 3.00 2.75

Easter 1972. No. C174a contains 4 stamps similar to Nos. 806–807, C173–C174 with simulated perforations. Olive gray and black decorative margin. Size: 119x147mm.

Heart Type of Regular Issue

Design: 100fr, Heart, WHO emblem and smith.

1972, Apr. 4

C175 A124 100fr multi 1.00 60
a. Souvenir sheet of 2 1.85 1.75

"Your heart is your health," World Health Day. No. C175a contains 2 stamps similar to Nos. 810 and C175 with simulated perforations. Blue gray margin with WHO emblem and black and white inscription. Size: 76x90mm.

Telecommunications Type of Regular Issue

Design: 100fr, Intelsat 4 over Africa.

1972, June 24 ***Perf. 14***

C176 A125 100fr multi 1.10 45

4th World Telecommunications Day.

Cassava Type of Regular Issue

Designs: 60fr, Truck and cassava processing factory (horiz.). 80fr, Children, mother holding tapioca cake.

1972, June 30

C177 A126 60fr multi 70 35
C178 A126 80fr multi 80 40

Cassava production.

No. C133 Surcharged in Deep Carmine: "VISITE DU PRESIDENT / NIXON EN RUSSIE / MAI 1972"

1972, July 15 **Litho.** ***Perf. 12½***

C179 A106 300fr on 50fr multi 4.00 2.00

President Nixon's visit to the U.S.S.R., May 1972. Old denomination obliterated with 6x5mm rectangle.

Olympic Type of Regular Issue

1972, Aug. 26 **Litho.** ***Perf. 14***

Multicolored

C180 A127 90fr *Gymnastics* 1.00 50
a. Souv. sheet of 2 1.85 1.60
C181 A127 200fr *Basketball* 2.25 1.00

20th Olympic Games, Munich, Aug. 26–Sept. 11. No. C180a contains 2 stamps with simulated perforations similar to Nos. 816 and C180. Light green margin with black inscription. Size: 135x97½mm.

Bird Type of Regular Issue

Bird: 90fr, Rose-ringed parakeet.

1972, Sept. 9

C182 A128 90fr multi 1.00 50
a. Souvenir sheet of 4 2.75 2.25

No. C182a contains 4 stamps similar to Nos. 818–820, C182 with simulated perforations. Lilac and black margin. Size: 108x133mm.

Rotary Type of Regular Issue

Designs (Rotary Emblem and): 60fr, Map of Togo, olive branch. 90fr, Flags of Togo and Rotary Club. 100fr, Paul P. Harris.

1972, Oct. 7 **Litho.** ***Perf. 14***

C183 A129 60fr brn & multi 50 25
C184 A129 90fr multi 75 50
C185 A129 100fr multi 90 55

Rotary International, Lomé.

Painting Type of Regular Issue, 1972

Designs: 60fr, Mystical Marriage of St. Catherine, by Assistant to the P. M. Master. 80fr, Self-portrait, by Leonardo da Vinci. 100fr, Sts. Mary and Agnes by Botticelli.

1972, Oct. 21

C186 A130 60fr gold & multi 60 30
C187 A130 80fr gold & multi 70 40
C188 A130 100fr gold & multi 1.20 60
a. Souvenir sheet of 4 3.50 2.25

No. C188a contains 4 stamps with simulated perforations similar to Nos. 824, C186–188. Green margin. Size: 111x139 mm.

Presidential Visit Type of Regular Issue

Design: 100fr, Pres. Pompidou and Col. Etienne Eyadema, front view of party headquarters.

1972, Nov. 23 **Litho.** ***Perf. 14***

C189 A131 100fr multi 1.20 60

Visit of Pres. Pompidou to Togo.

Goethe
AP15

1972, Dec. 2 **Photo.** ***Perf. 13x14***

C190 AP15 100fr grn & multi 1.20 65

140th anniversary of the death of Johann Wolfgang von Goethe (1749–1832), German poet and dramatist.

Christmas Type of Regular Issue

Paintings: 60fr, Nativity, by Master Vyshchibrod. 80fr, Adoration of the Kings, anonymous. 100fr, Flight into Egypt, by Giotto.

1972, Dec. 23 **Litho.** ***Perf. 14***

C191 A132 60fr gold & multi 70 30
C192 A132 80fr gold & multi 90 45
C193 A132 100fr gold & multi 1.20 60
a. Souvenir sheet of 4 3.00 3.00

Christmas 1972. No. C193a contains 4 stamps with simulated perforations similar to Nos. 829, C191–C193. Multicolored margin. Size: 123x140mm.

Leprosy Day Type of Regular Issue

Design: 100fr, Dr. Armauer G. Hansen, apparatus, microscope and Petri dish.

1973, Jan. 23 Photo. ***Perf. 14x13½***

C194 A133 100fr rose car & bl 1.10 60

World Leprosy Day and centenary of the discovery of the Hansen bacillus, the cause of leprosy.

Easter Type of Regular Issue

1973, Apr. 21 Lithographed ***Perf. 14***

Multicolored

C195 A135 90fr *Christ in Glory* 90 50
a. Souvenir sheet of 2 1.50 1.50

Easter 1973. No. C195a contains one each of Nos. 835 and C195 with simulated perforations. Yellow margin with gold and black inscription. Size: 90x99mm.

Apollo 17 Type of Regular Issue

Designs: 100fr, Astronauts on moon and orange rock. 200fr, Rocket lift-off at Cape Kennedy and John F. Kennedy.

1973, June 2 **Litho.** ***Perf. 14***

C196 A136 100fr multi 1.10 55
C197 A136 200fr multi 2.25 90
a. Souvenir sheet of 2 3.50 3.00

Apollo 17 U.S. moon mission, Dec. 7–19, 1972. No. C197a contains 2 stamps similar to Nos. C196–C197 with simulated perforations. Light blue decorative margin with inscription. Size: 107x100mm.

Boy Scout Type of Regular Issue

Designs: 100fr, Canoeing (horiz.). 200fr, Campfire (horiz.).

1973, June 30 **Litho.** ***Perf. 14***

C198 A137 100fr bl & multi 1.10 60
C199 A137 200fr bl & multi 2.25 1.00
a. Souvenir sheet of 2 3.50 3.00

24th Boy Scout World Conference, Nairobi, Kenya, July 16–21. No. C199a contains 2 stamps similar to Nos. C198–C199 with simulated perforations. Yellow, olive and black margin with commemorative inscription. Size: 107x98mm.

Copernicus Type of Regular Issue

Designs: 90fr, Heliocentric system. 100fr, Nicolaus Copernicus.

1973, July 18

C200 A138 90fr multi 90 45
C201 A138 100fr bis & multi 1.10 60
a. Souvenir sheet of 2 2.25 2.00

500th anniversary of the birth of Nicolaus Copernicus (1473–1543), Polish astronomer. No. C201a contains one each of Nos. C200–C201. Yellow, bister and black margin. Size: 121½x107½mm.

Red Cross Type of Regular Issue

Design: 100fr, Dove carrying Red Cross letter, sun, map of Togo.

1973, Aug. 4

C202 A139 100fr multi 1.00 50

Togolese Red Cross.

Literacy Type of Regular Issue

Design: 90fr, Woman teacher in classroom.

1973, Aug. 18 **Litho.** ***Perf. 14***

C203 A140 90fr multi 90 50

Literacy campaign.

WMO Type of Regular Issue

1973, Oct. 4 Photo. *Perf. 14x13*

C204	A142	200fr dl bl, pur & brn	2.25	90

Centenary of international meteorological cooperation.

Type of Regular Issue 1967

Design: 100fr, Early and contemporary planes, Nos. 758 and C36.

1973, Oct. 20 Photo. *Perf. 14x13*

C205	A79	100fr multi	1.20	50
a.		Souvenir sheet of 2	2.40	2.10

75th anniversary of Togolese postal service. No. C205a contains 2 stamps similar to Nos. 855 and C205 with simulated perforations. Light gray margin with black inscription and multicolored design. Size: 125x90mm.

Kennedy Type of Regular Issue

Designs: 90fr, Kennedy and Charles De Gaulle. 100fr, Kennedy and Nikita Krushchev. 200fr, Kennedy and model of Apollo spacecraft.

1973, Nov. 22 Litho. *Perf. 14*

C206	A143	90fr blk & pink	90	50
C207	A143	100fr blk, lt bl & bl	1.10	55
C208	A143	200fr blk, buff & brn	2.00	90
a.		Souvenir sheet of 2	3.25	3.00

10th anniversary of the death of John F. Kennedy (1917–1963). No. C208a contains 2 stamps similar to Nos. C207–208 with simulated perforations. Black margin with head of JFK and candles. Size: 114x72mm.

Human Rights Flame and People
AP16

1973, Dec. 8 Photo. *Perf. 13x14*

C209	AP16	250fr lt bl & multi	2.75	1.25

25th anniversary of the Universal Declaration of Human Rights.

Christmas Type of Regular Issue

Paintings: 90fr, Virgin and Child. 100fr, Adoration of the Kings. Both after 15th century Italian paintings.

1973, Dec. 22 Litho. *Perf. 14*

C210	A144	90fr gold & multi	90	40
C211	A144	100fr gold & multi	1.10	50
a.		Souvenir sheet of 2	2.40	2.25

Christmas 1973. No. C211a contains 2 stamps with simulated perforations similar to Nos. C210–C211. Yellow and brown margin with black inscription. Size: 121x 86mm.

Nos. C183 and C185 Overprinted:
"PREMIERE CONVENTION / 210eme DISTRICT / FEVRIER 1974 / LOME"

1974, Feb. 21 Lithographed *Perf. 14*

C212	A129	60fr brn & multi	60	30
C213	A129	100fr multi	90	50

First convention of Rotary International, District 210, Lomé, Feb. 22–24.

Soccer Type of Regular Issue

Designs: Various soccer scenes and games' cup.

1974, Mar. 2 Lithographed *Perf. 14*

C214	A145	90fr multi	90	45
C215	A145	100fr multi	1.10	50
C216	A145	200fr multi	2.00	85
a.		Souvenir sheet of 2	3.25	3.00

World Soccer Championships, Munich, Germany. No. C216a contains 2 stamps with simulated perforations similar to Nos. C215–C216. Green margin with black inscription. Size: 68x111mm.

Picasso Type of 1974

Paintings: 90fr, The Muse. 100fr, Les Demoiselles d'Avignon. 200fr, Sitting Nude.

1974, Apr. 6 Litho. *Perf. 14*

C217	A146	90fr brn & multi	90	45
C218	A146	100fr pur & multi	1.10	50
C219	A146	200fr multi	2.00	1.00
a.		Souvenir sheet of 3	5.25	4.25

Pablo Picasso (1881–1973), Spanish painter. No. C219a contains 3 stamps similar to Nos. C217–C219 with simulated perforations. Yellow brown margin with signature and portrait of Picasso. Size: 153x103mm.

Coastal Views Type of 1974

Designs: 90fr, Fishermen on Lake Togo. 100fr, Mouth of Anecho River.

1974, Apr. 20

C220	A147	90fr multi	90	35
C221	A147	100fr multi	1.00	45
a.		Souvenir sheet of 2	2.00	1.75

No. C221a contains 2 stamps similar to Nos. C220–C221 with simulated perforations; pale green margin with black inscription. Size: 73x76½mm.

UPU Type of 1974

Designs: Old mailmen's uniforms.

1974, May 10 Litho. *Perf. 14*

C222	A148	50fr multi	60	25
C223	A148	100fr multi	1.10	50
a.		Souvenir sheet of 2	15.00	12.50

Centenary of Universal Postal Union.
No. C223a contains 2 stamps similar to Nos. C222–C223, rouletted. Yellow margin with brown and black inscription. Size: 111x78mm.

Fishing Type of 1974

Designs: 90fr, Fishermen bringing in net with catch. 100fr, Fishing with rod and line. 200fr, Fishing with basket (vert.).

1974, June 22 Litho. *Perf. 14*

C224	A149	90fr multi	75	40
C225	A149	100fr multi	85	40
C226	A149	200fr multi	1.65	1.00
a.		Souvenir sheet of 3	3.50	3.25

Lagoon fishing. No.C226a contains 3 stamps with simulated perforations similar to Nos. C224–C226. Gray green margin with lilac fish design. Size: 192x116mm.

Jupiter Probe Type of 1974

Designs: 100fr, Rocket take-off (vert.). 200fr, Satellite in space.

1974, July 6 *Perf. 14*

C227	A150	100fr multi	1.00	50
C228	A150	200fr multi	2.00	1.00
a.		Souvenir sheet of 2	7.50	5.50

U.S. Jupiter space probe. No. C228a contains 2 stamps similar to Nos. C227–C228 with simulated perforations; imperf. or rouletted. Multicolored margin. Size: 83x94mm.

No. C176 Overprinted

1974, July *Perf. 14*

C229	A125	100fr multi	2.50	1.00

INTERNABA 1974 International Philatelic Exhibition, Basel, June 7–16.

Seashell Type of 1974

1974, July 13 Litho. *Perf. 14*

C230	A151	90fr *Alcithoe ponsonbyi*	75	40
C231	A151	100fr *Casmaria iredalei*	80	50
a.		Souvenir sheet of 2	1.85	1.60

No. C231a contains 2 stamps similar to Nos. C230–C231 with simulated perforations. Green decorative margin with black inscription. Size: 115x75mm.

Horse Racing Type of 1974

Designs: 90fr, Steeplechase. 100fr, Galloping horses.

1974, Aug. 3 Litho. *Perf. 14*

C232	A152	90fr multi	90	40
C233	A152	100fr multi	1.10	50
a.		Souvenir sheet of 2	2.25	1.75

Horse racing. No. C233a contains one each of Nos. C232–C233 with simulated perforations. Brown decorative margin with brown inscription. Size: 99x78mm.

Nos. C180, C180a and C181 Overprinted:
"COUPE DU MONDE / DE FOOTBALL / VAINQUEURS / REPUBLIQUE FEDERALE / d'ALLEMAGNE"

1974, Aug. 19

C234	A127	90fr multi	90	40
a.		Souvenir sheet of 2	1.75	1.75
C235	A127	200fr multi	1.75	1.00

World Cup Soccer Championship, Munich, 1974, victory of German Federal Republic. For description of No. C234a see note after No. C181.

Animal Type of 1974

1974, Sept. 7 Litho. *Perf. 14*

C236	A153	90fr *Lions*	80	45
C237	A153	100fr *Rhinoceroses*	90	50
a.		Souvenir sheet of 3	2.40	2.00

Wild animals of West Africa. No. C237a contains 3 stamps similar to Nos. 889, C236–C237 with simulated perforations, yellow and purple decorative margin. Size: 107x86mm.

1974, Oct. 14

C238	A153	90fr *Herd at waterhole*	75	40
C239	A153	100fr *Village and cows*	80	50
a.		Souvenir sheet of 2	2.25	1.75

Domestic animals. No. C239a contains 2 stamps with simulated perforations similar to Nos. C238–C239. Violet decorative margin. Size: 84x77mm.

Churchill Type of 1974

Designs: 100fr, Churchill and frigate. 200fr, Churchill and fighter planes.

1974, Nov. 1 Photo. *Perf. 13x13½*

C240	A154	100fr multi	90	45
C241	A154	200fr org & multi	1.75	90
a.		Souvenir sheet of 2	3.25	2.75

Centenary of the birth of Winston Churchill (1874–1965).
No. C241a contains 2 stamps similar to Nos. C240–C241; perf. or imperf. Pale olive green margin showing Churchill tank. Size: 111x88mm.

Flower Type of 1975

Flowers of Togo: 100fr, Clerodendrum thosonae. 200fr, Gloriosa superba.

1975, Feb. 15 Litho. *Perf. 14*

C242	A155	100fr multi	80	40
C243	A155	200fr multi	1.60	75
a.		Souvenir sheet of 2	4.75	3.75

No. C243a contains one each of Nos. C242–C243, perf. 13x14, green and multicolored margin. Size: 97x78mm. Exists imperf.; same price.

Nos. C184–C185 Overprinted:
"70e ANNIVERSAIRE / 23 FEVRIER 1975"

1975, Feb. 23 Litho. *Perf. 14*

C244	A129	90fr multi	75	40
C245	A129	100fr multi	85	50

Rotary International, 70th anniversary.

Easter Type of 1975

Paintings: 100fr, Christ Rising from the Tomb, by Master MS. 200fr, Holy Trinity (detail), by Dürer.

1975, Apr. 19 Litho. *Perf. 14*

C246	A157	100fr multi	80	40
C247	A157	200fr multi	1.60	85
a.		Souvenir sheet of 2	2.50	2.00

Easter 1975. No. C247a contains 2 stamps similar to Nos. C246–C247 with simulated perforations. Multicolored margin showing Christ in Glory and inscription. Size: 106x88mm.

Independence Type of 1975

Designs: 50fr, National Day parade, flag and map of Togo (vert.). 60fr, Warriors' dance and flag of Togo.

1975, Apr. 26 Litho. *Perf. 14*

C248	A158	50fr multi	40	15
C249	A158	60fr multi	50	20
a.		Souvenir sheet of 2	1.35	75

15th anniversary of independence. No. C249a contains 2 stamps similar to Nos. C248–C249 with simulated perforations; multicolored margin with black inscription. Size: 114x108mm.

Hunt Type of 1975

Designs: 90fr, Running deer. 100fr, Wild boar hunter with shotgun.

1975, May 24 Photo. *Perf. 13x13½*

C250	A159	90fr multi	75	35
C251	A159	100fr multi	80	40

Palm Oil Type of 1975

Designs: 85fr, Selling palm oil in market (vert.). 100fr, Oil processing plant, Alokoegbe.

1975, June 28 Litho. *Perf. 14*

C252	A160	85fr multi	70	35
C253	A160	100fr multi	80	40

Palm oil production.

Apollo-Soyuz Type of 1975 and

Soyuz Spacecraft
AP17

Designs: 60fr, Donald K. Slayton, Vance D. Brand and Thomas P. Stafford. 90fr, Aleksei A. Leonov and Valery N. Kubasov. 100fr, Apollo-Soyuz link-up, American and Russian flags. 200fr, Apollo-Soyuz emblem and globe.

1975, July 15

C254	AP17	50fr yel & multi	40	15
C255	A161	60fr lil & multi	50	20
C256	A161	90fr bl & multi	70	35
C257	A161	100fr grn & multi	80	55
C258	A161	200fr yel & multi	1.60	70
a.		Souvenir sheet of 4	4.25	3.00
		Nos. C254-C258 (5)	4.00	1.95

See note after No. 913. No. C258a contains one each of Nos. C255–C258; green and bister margin with black inscription. Size: 150x105mm.

Schweitzer Type of 1975

Designs (Dr. Schweitzer): 80fr, playing organ (vert.). 90fr, with pelican (vert.). 100fr, and Lambarene Hospital.

1975, Aug. 23 Litho. *Perf. 14x13½*

C259	A163	80fr multi	65	40
C260	A163	90fr multi	75	45
C261	A163	100fr multi	80	50

Dr. Albert Schweitzer (1875–1965), medical missionary and musician.

Letter Writing Type of 1975

Design: 80fr, Erasmus Writing Letter, by Hans Holbein.

1975, Oct. 9 Liitho. *Perf. 14*

C262	A164	80fr multi	65	40

International Letter Writing Week.

Nos. C167–C168a Overprinted:
"30ème Anniversaire / des Nations-Unies"

1975, Oct. 24 Litho. *Perf. 14*

C263	A120	60fr multi	50	20
C264	A120	90fr multi	70	40
a.		Souvenir sheet of 4	2.10	1.65

United Nations, 30th anniversary. No. C264a contains one each of No. 796 (with overprint), and Nos. 918, C263–C264. Size: 114x196mm.

Nos. C198-C199 Overprinted:
"14ème JAMBOREE / MONDIAL / DES ECLAIREURS"

1975, Nov. 7

C265 A137 100fr multi 80 40
C266 A137 200fr multi 1.60 75
a. Souvenir sheet of 2 2.50 2.25

14th World Boy Scout Jamboree, Lillehammer, Norway, July 29–Aug. 7. No. C266a contains one each of Nos. C265–C266 with simulated perforations. Size: 107x98mm.

Christmas Type of 1975

Paintings of the Virgin and Child: 90fr, Nativity, by Federico Barocci. 100fr, Bellini. 200fr, Correggio.

1975, Dec. 20 Litho. *Perf. 14*

C267 A165 90fr bl & multi 75 35
C268 A165 100fr red & multi 80 40
C269 A165 200fr bl & multi 1.60 75
a. Souvenir sheet of 2 2.75 2.25

Christmas 1975. No. C269a contains one each of Nos. C268–269; multicolored margin showing Virgin and Child. Size: 127x95mm.

Bicentennial Type of 1976

Paintings (and Bicentennial Emblem): 60fr, Surrender of Gen. Burgoyne, by John Trumbull. 70fr, Surrender at Trenton, by Trumbull (vert.). 100fr, Signing of Declaration of Independence, by Trumbull. 200fr, Washington Crossing the Delaware, by Emil Leutze.

1976, Mar. 3 Litho. *Perf. 14*

C270 A167 60fr multi 50 25
C271 A167 70fr multi 55 32
C272 A167 100fr multi 80 40
C273 A167 200fr multi 1.60 80
a. Souvenir sheet of 2 2.50 2.50

American Bicentennial. No. C273a contains one each of Nos. C272–C273; yellow margin with black inscription, blue border and red and blue Bicentennial emblem. Size: 138x95mm. No. C273a also exists imperf.; same price.

Common Market Type of 1976

Designs: 60fr, ACP and CEE emblems. 70fr, Map of Africa, Europe and Asia.

1976, Apr. 24 Photo. *Perf. 13x14*

C274 A168 60fr lt bl & multi 50 25
C275 A168 70fr yel & multi 55 32

First anniversary of signing of treaty between Togo and European Common Market, Lomé, Feb. 28, 1975.

Telephone Type of 1976

Designs: 70fr, Thomas A. Edison, old and new communications equipment. 105fr, Alexander Graham Bell, old and new telephones.

1976, Mar. 10 Photo. *Perf. 13x14*

C276 A169 70fr multi 55 32
C277 A169 105fr multi 85 50
a. Souvenir sheet of 2 1.50 1.35

Centenary of first telephone call by Alexander Graham Bell, Mar. 10, 1876.
No. C277a contains one each of Nos. C276–C277; green and multicolored margin. Size: 130x100mm.
Exists imperf.; same price.

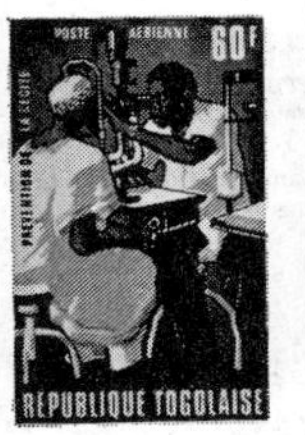

Eye Examination
AP18

Pylon, Flags of Ghana, Togo, Dahomey
AP19

1976, Apr. 8 *Perf. 14x13*

C278 AP18 60fr dk red & multi 50 28

World Health Day: "Foresight prevents blindness."

1976, May 8 Litho. *Perf. 14*

C279 AP19 60fr multi 50 28

Ghana-Togo-Dahomey electric power grid, 1st anniversary. See No. 932.

Nos. C270–C273, C273a, Overprinted:
"INTERPHIL / MAI 29–JUIN 6, 1976"

1976, May 29

C280 A167 60fr multi 50 25
C281 A167 70fr multi 55 32
C282 A167 100fr multi 80 40
C283 A167 200fr multi 1.60 85
a. Souvenir sheet of 2 2.50 2.25

Interphil 76 International Philatelic Exhibition, Philadelphia, Pa., May 29–June 6. Overprint on No. C281 in 3 lines; overprint on No. C283a applied to each stamp.

Olympic Games Type of 1976

Designs (Montreal Olympic Emblem and): 70fr, Yachting. 105fr, Motorcycling. 200fr, Fencing.

1976, June 15 Photo. *Perf. 14x13*

C284 A172 70fr multi 55 32
C285 A172 105fr multi 85 50
C286 A172 200fr multi 1.60 85
a. Souvenir sheet of 2 2.75 2.50

21st Olympic Games, Montreal, Canada, July 17–Aug. 1. No. C286a contains one each of Nos. C285–C286, perf. 14; light green, brown and black margin showing athlete. Size: 133x116mm.

Viking Type of 1976

Designs: 60fr, Viking landing on Mars. 70fr, Nodus Gordii (view on Mars). 105fr, Lander over Mare Tyrrhenum. 200fr, Landing on Mars.

1976, July 15 Litho. *Perf. 14*

C287 A173 60fr bis & multi 50 28
C288 A173 70fr multi 55 32
C289 A173 105fr bl & multi 85 50
C290 A173 200fr multi 1.60 85
a. Souvenir sheet of 2 2.75 2.50

U.S. Viking Mars missions.
No. C290a contains one each of Nos. C289–C290, perf. 14x13½; multicolored margin showing descent of capsule on Mars. Size: 120x107mm.

Toulouse-Lautrec Type, 1976

Paintings: 60fr, Carmen, portrait. 70fr, Maurice at the Somme. 200fr, "Messalina."

1976, Aug. 7 Litho. *Perf. 14*

C291 A174 60fr blk & multi 50 28
C292 A174 70fr blk & multi 55 35
C293 A174 200fr blk & multi 1.60 85
a. Souvenir sheet of 2 2.50 2.25

Henri Toulouse-Lautrec (1864–1901), French painter, 75th death anniversary. No. C293a contains one each of Nos. C292–C293, perf. 13½x14; olive green margin with black inscription and artist's portrait. Size: 122x82mm.

No. C202 Overprinted:
"Journeé / Internationale / de l'Enfance"

1976, Nov. 27 Litho. *Perf. 14*

C294 A139 100fr multi 80 50

International Children's Day.

Christmas Type of 1976

Paintings: 70fr, Holy Family, by Lorenzo Lotto. 105fr, Virgin and Child with Saints, by Jacopo da Pontormo. 200fr, Virgin and Child with Saints, by Lotto.

1976, Dec. 18

C295 A175 70fr multi 55 32
C296 A175 105fr multi 85 50
C297 A175 200fr multi 1.60 85
a. Souvenir sheet of 2 2.75 2.50

Christmas 1976. No. C297a contains one each of Nos. C296–C297; olive margin showing Virgin and Child, and gold and black inscription. Size: 150x107mm.

No. C284 Overprinted:
"CHAMPIONS OLYMPIQUES / YACHTING-FLYING DUTCHMAN / REPUBLIQUE FEDERALE ALLEMAGNE"

No. C286 Overprinted:
"CHAMPIONS OLYMPIQUES / ESCRIME-FLEURET PAR EQUIPES / REPUBLIQUE FEDERALE ALLEMAGNE"

1976, Dec. Photo. *Perf. 14x13*

C298 A172 70fr multi 55 30
C299 A172 200fr multi 1.60 90
a. Souvenir sheet of 2 2.75 2.50

Olympic winners. No. C299a (on No. C286a) contains Nos. C285 and C299.

Eyadema Anniversary Type of 1977

Designs: 60fr, National Assembly Building. 100fr, Pres. Eyadema greeting people at Aug. 30th meeting.

1977, Jan. 13 Photo. *Perf. 13x14*

C300 A177 60fr multi 50 20
C301 A177 100fr multi 80 45
a. Souvenir sheet of 2 1.40 1.25

10th anniversary of regime of Pres. Eyadema. No. C301a contains one each of Nos. C300–C301; light blue and black decorative margin. Size: 129x100mm.

Musical Instrument Type of 1977

Musical Instruments: 60fr, Atopani. 80fr, African violin (vert.). 105fr, African flutes (vert.).

1977, Feb. 7 Litho. *Perf. 14*

C302 A178 60fr multi 50 20
C303 A178 80fr multi 65 28
C304 A178 105fr multi 85 40
a. Souvenir sheet of 2 1.75 1.50

No. C304a contains one each of Nos. C303–C304; brown margin with black inscription shows drummer. Size: 120x85 mm.

Victor Hugo Type of 1977

Design: 60fr, Victor Hugo in exile on Guernsey Island.

1977, Feb. 26 *Perf. 13x14*

C305 A179 60fr multi 50 28
a. Souvenir sheet of 2 1.00 90

Victor Hugo (1802–1885), French writer, 175th birth anniversary. No. C305a contains one each of Nos. 952 and C305; tan, brown and black margin. Size: 130x100 mm.

Beethoven Type of 1977

Designs: 100fr, Beethoven's piano and 1818 portrait. 200fr, Beethoven on his deathbed and Holy Trinity Church, Vienna.

1977, Mar. 7 *Perf. 14*

C306 A180 100fr multi 80 50
C307 A180 200fr multi 1.65 1.00
a. Souvenir sheet of 2 2.50 2.50

Ludwig van Beethoven (1770–1827), composer, 150th death anniversary. No. C307a contains one each of Nos. C306–C307; multicolored margin showing musical instruments. Size: 130x99mm.

Automobile Type of 1977

Early Automobiles: 60fr, Cannstatt-Daimler, 1899, Germany. 70fr, Sunbeam, 1904, England. 100fr, Renault, 1908, France. 200fr, Rolls Royce, 1909, England.

1977, Apr. 11 Litho. *Perf. 14*

C308 A181 60fr multi 50 28
C309 A181 70fr multi 55 32
C310 A181 100fr multi 80 45
C311 A181 200fr multi 1.60 1.00
a. Souvenir sheet of 2 2.50 2.50

No. C311a contains one each of Nos. C310–C311; light green, brown and black margin showing Thomas Rickett's steam car, 1858. Size: 144x96mm.

Lindbergh Type of 1977

Designs: 60fr, Lindbergh and son Jon, birds in flight. 85fr, Lindbergh home in Kent, England. 90fr, Spirit of St. Louis over Atlantic Ocean. 100fr, Concorde over New York City.

1977, May 9

C312 A182 60fr multi 60 25
C313 A182 85fr multi 85 30
C314 A182 90fr multi 90 30
C315 A182 100fr multi 1.00 35
a. Souvenir sheet of 2 2.00 1.20

Lindbergh's solo transatlantic flight, 50th anniversary. No. C315a contains one each of Nos. C314–C315; brown and black margin. Size: 120x95mm.

No. C305 Overprinted:
"10ème ANNIVERSAIRE DU / CONSEIL INTERNATIONAL / DE LA LANGUE FRANCAISE"

1977, May 17 Litho. *Perf. 14*

C316 A179 60fr multi 60 30

10th anniversary of the French Language Council.

Wildlife Type of 1977

Designs: 60fr, Colobus monkeys. 90fr, Chimpanzee (vert.). 100fr, Leopard. 200fr, West African manatee.

1977, June 13

C317 A183 60fr multi 60 20
C318 A183 90fr multi 90 25
C319 A183 100fr multi 1.00 28
C320 A183 200fr multi 2.00 50
a. Souvenir sheet of 2 3.25 1.85

Endangered wildlife. No. C320a contains one each of Nos. C319–C320; multicolored margin shows chimpanzee's head. Size: 153x120mm.

Agriculture Type of 1977

Designs: 60fr, Corn silo. 100fr, Hoeing and planting by hand. 200fr, Tractor on field.

1977, July 11 Litho. *Perf. 14*

C321 A184 60fr multi 60 20
C322 A184 100fr multi 1.00 28
C323 A184 200fr multi 2.00 50
a. Souvenir sheet of 2 3.25 1.85

Agricultural development. No. C323a contains one each of Nos. C322–C323, perf. 13x14; light green and multicolored margin. Size: 116x95mm.

Rubens Type of 1977

Paintings: 60fr, Heads of Black Men, 1620. 100fr, Anne of Austria, 1624.

1977, Aug. 8

C324 A185 60fr multi 60 20
C325 A185 100fr multi 1.00 28
a. Souvenir sheet of 2 1.80 1.00

Peter Paul Rubens (1577–1640), Flemish painter, 400th birth anniversary. No. C325a contains one each of Nos. C324–C325, perf. 14x13; dull lilac and black margin shows Rubens' self-portrait. Size: 150x96mm.

Orbiter Type of 1977

Designs: 90fr, Retrieval of unmanned satellite in space (vert.). 100fr, Satellite's return to space after repairs. 200fr, Manned landing of Orbiter.

1977, Oct. 4 Litho. *Perf. 14*

C326 A186 90fr multi 90 25
C327 A186 100fr multi 1.00 28
C328 A186 200fr multi 2.00 50
a. Souvenir sheet of 2 3.25 1.85

Space shuttle trials in the US. No. C328a contains one each of Nos. C327–C328; multicolored margin shows space shuttle. Size: 111½x139mm.

Lafayette Type of 1977

Designs: 60fr, Lafayette landing in New York, 1824. 105fr, Lafayette and Washington at Valley Forge.

1977, Nov. 7 *Perf. 13x14*

C329 A187 60fr multi 60 20
C330 A187 105fr multi 1.05 28
a. Souvenir sheet of 2 1.80 1.00

200th anniversary of the arrival of the Marquis de Lafayette in North America. No. C330a contains one each of Nos. C329–C330; bister and olive margin. Size: 130x 100mm.

Christmas Type of 1977

Virgin and Child by: 90fr, 200fr, Carlo Crivelli (different). 100fr, Bellini.

1977, Dec. 19 *Perf. 14*

C331 A189 90fr multi 90 25
C332 A189 100fr multi 1.00 28
C333 A189 200fr multi 2.00 50
a. Souvenir sheet of 2 3.25 1.85

Christmas 1977. No. C333a contains one each of Nos. C332–C333; multicolored margin shows angel holding olive branch. Size: 132x102mm.

Jenner Type of 1978

Designs: 50fr, Edward Jenner. 60fr, Smallpox vaccination clinic (horiz.).

1978, Jan. 9 *Perf. 14x13, 13x14*

C334 A190 50fr multi 50 18
C335 A190 60fr multi 60 20
a. Souvenir sheet of 2 1.20 75

Worldwide eradication of smallpox. No. C335a contains 2 stamps with simulated perforations similar to Nos. C334–C335; multicolored margin shows smallpox hospital near Pancras. Size: 130x100mm.

Wright Brothers' Type of 1978

Designs: 60fr, Orville Wright's 7½-minute flight. 70fr, Orville Wright injured in first aircraft accident, 1908. 200fr, Wrights' bicycle shop, Dearborn, Mich. 300fr, First flight, 1903.

1978, Feb. 6 Litho. *Perf. 14*

C336	A191	60fr multi	60	20
C337	A191	70fr multi	70	28
C338	A191	200fr multi	2.00	50
C339	A191	300fr multi	3.00	85
a.		Souvenir sheet of 2	5.25	3.00

75th anniversary of first motorized flight. No. C339a contains one each of Nos. C338-C339 with simulated perforations; pale lilac and brown margin shows Wright brothers and inscriptions. Size: 137x118mm.

Port of Lomé Type, 1978

Designs (Anchor and): 60fr, Industrial harbor. 100fr, Merchant marine harbor. 200fr, Bird's-eye view of entire harbor.

1978, Apr. 26 Photo. *Perf. 13*

C340	A199	60fr multi	60	20
C341	A199	100fr multi	1.00	32
C342	A199	200fr multi	2.00	50
a.		Souvenir sheet of 2	3.25	1.85

No. C342a contains one each of Nos. C341-C342; multicolored margin shows lighthouse and ship. Size: 130x101mm.

Space Type of 1978

Designs: 90fr, Module camera (horiz.). 100fr, Module antenna. 200fr, Pioneer, USA, in orbit.

1978, May 8 Litho. *Perf. 14*

C343	A200	90fr multi	90	30
C344	A200	100fr multi	1.00	28
C345	A200	200fr multi	2.00	50
a.		Souvenir sheet of 2	3.25	1.85

U.S. and U.S.S.R. Pioneer and Venera space missions. No. C345a contains Nos. C344-C345, perf. 13½x14; multicolored margin shows Mariner 2. Size: 140x114½ mm.

Soccer Type of 1978

Designs: Various soccer scenes and Argentina '78 emblem.

1978, June 5 *Perf. 14*

C346	A201	60fr multi	60	20
C347	A201	80fr multi	80	28
C348	A201	200fr multi	2.00	50
C349	A201	300fr multi	3.00	75
a.		Souvenir sheet of 2	5.50	3.25

11th World Cup Soccer Championship, Argentina, June 1-25. No. C349a contains Nos. C348-C349, perf. 13½x14. Multicolored margin shows soccer player and flags. Size: 133x96mm.

Bicycle Type of 1978

History of Bicycle: 60fr, Bantam, 1896 (vert.). 85fr, Fold-up bicycle for military use, 1897. 90fr, Draisienne, 1816 (vert.). 100fr, Penny-farthing, 1884 (vert.).

Perf. 14x13, 13x14

1978, July 10 Photogravure

C350	A202	60fr multi	60	20
C351	A202	85fr multi	85	32
C352	A202	90fr multi	90	35
C353	A202	100fr multi	1.00	40
a.		Souvenir sheet of 2	2.00	1.25

No. C353a contains Nos. C352-C353, violet and black margin shows Opel tandem bicycle. Size: 125x115mm.

Phonograph Type of 1978

Designs: 60fr, Edison's original phonograph (horiz.). 80fr, Emile Berliner's phonograph, 1888. 200fr, Berliner's improved phonograph, 1894 (horiz.). 300fr, His Master's Voice phonograph, 1900 (horiz.).

Photogravure

1978, July 8 *Perf. 13x14, 14x13*

C354	A203	60fr multi	60	20
C355	A203	80fr multi	80	30
C356	A203	200fr multi	2.00	50
C357	A203	300fr multi	3.00	75
a.		Souvenir sheet of 2	5.25	3.00

Centenary of the phonograph, invented by Thomas A. Edison. No. C357a contains Nos. C356-C357; salmon and brown margin shows Edison with his phonograph. Size: 116x90mm.

Red Cross Type of 1978

Design: 60fr, Red Cross and other pavilions at Paris Exhibition, 1867.

1978, Sept. 4 Photo. *Perf. 14x13*

C358	A204	60fr pur & red	60	30
a.		Souvenir sheet of 2	1.00	60

Henri Dunant (1828-1910), founder of Red Cross. No. C358a contains Nos. 1009 and C358; multicolored margin shows Red Cross and Nobel Peace Prize medal awarded 1901. Size: 146x99mm.

Paintings Type of 1978

Paintings: 60fr, Langlois Bridge, by Vincent van Gogh. 70fr, Witches' Sabbath, by Francisco Goya. 90fr, Jesus among the Doctors, by Albrecht Dürer. 200fr, View of Arco, by Dürer.

1978, Nov. 6 Litho. *Perf. 14*

C359	A205	60fr multi	60	30
C360	A205	70fr multi	70	35
C361	A205	90fr multi	90	45
C362	A205	200fr multi	2.00	1.00
a.		Souvenir sheet of 2	3.00	1.75

Birth and death anniversaries of famous painters.

No. C362a contains Nos. C361-C362. Multicolored margin shows picture frame around stamps. Size: 102x132mm.

Philexafrique II—Essen Issue

Common Design Types

Designs: No. C363, Warthog and Togo No. C36. No. C364, Firecrest and Thurn and Taxis No. 1.

1978, Nov. 1 Litho. *Perf. 13x12½*

C363	CD138	100fr multi	1.00	50
C364	CD139	100fr multi	1.00	50

Nos. C363-C364 printed se-tenant.

UPU Type of 1978

Designs: 60fr, Mail ship "Slieve Roe" 1877, and post horn. 105fr, Congress of Paris medal. 200fr, Locomotive, 1870. All horizontal.

1978, Nov. 27 Photo. *Perf. 14x13*

C365	A206	60fr multi	60	30
C366	A206	105fr multi	1.05	52
C367	A206	200fr multi	2.00	1.00
a.		Souvenir sheet of 2	3.25	1.85

Centenary of Congress of Paris. No. C367a contains Nos. C366-C367. Multicolored margin shows UPU emblem. Size: 116x88mm.

Christmas Type of 1978

Paintings (Virgin and Child): 90fr, 200fr, by Carlo Crivelli (diff.). 100fr, by Cosimo Tura.

1978, Dec. 18

C368	A207	90fr multi	90	45
C369	A207	100fr multi	1.00	50
C370	A207	200fr multi	2.00	1.00
a.		Souvenir sheet of 2	3.25	1.85

Christmas 1978. No. C370a contains Nos. C369-C370; multicolored margin. Size: 123x90mm.

Capt. Cook Type of 1979

Designs: 60fr, "Freelove," Whitby Harbor (horiz.). 70fr, Trip to Antarctica, 1773 (horiz.). 90fr, Capt. Cook. 200fr, Sails of Endeavour.

1979, Feb. 12 Litho. *Perf. 14*

C371	A208	60fr multi	60	30
C372	A208	70fr multi	70	35
C373	A208	90fr multi	90	45
C374	A208	200fr multi	2.00	1.75
a.		Souvenir sheet of 2	3.00	1.75

200th death anniversary of Capt. James Cook. No. C374a contains Nos. C373-C374; green and black margin shows Capt. Cook with map. Size: 141x98mm.

Easter Type of 1979

Designs: 60fr, Resurrection. 100fr, Ascension. 200fr, Jesus appearing to Mary Magdalene.

1979, Apr. 9

C375	A209	60fr multi	60	30
C376	A209	100fr multi	1.00	50
C377	A209	200fr multi	2.00	1.00
a.		Souvenir sheet of 2	3.25	1.85

Easter 1979. No. C377a contains Nos. C376-C377; multicolored margin.

UPU Emblem, Drummer—AP20

Design: 100fr, UPU emblem, hands passing letter, satellites.

1979, June 8 Engr. *Perf. 13*

C378	AP20	60fr multi	60	30
C379	AP20	100fr multi	1.00	50

Philexafrique II, Libreville, Gabon, June 8-17.

Einstein Type of 1979

Designs: 60fr, Sights and actuality diagram. 85fr, Einstein playing violin (vert.). 100fr, Atom symbol and formula of relativity (vert.). 200fr, Einstein portrait (vert.).

Perf. 14x13, 13x14

1979, July 2 Photogravure

C380	A210	60fr multi	60	30
C381	A210	85fr multi	85	42
C382	A210	100fr multi	1.00	50
C383	A210	200fr multi	2.00	1.00
a.		Souvenir sheet of 2	3.25	

Albert Einstein (1879-1955), theoretical physicist. No. C383a contains Nos. C382-C383; violet and black margin with Einstein portrait. Size: 127x91mm.

Tree Type of 1979

Design: 60fr, Man watering tree.

1979, Aug. 13 *Perf. 14x13*

C384	A212	60fr blk & brn	60	30

Second Arbor Day.

Rowland Hill Type of 1979

Designs: 90fr, Bellman, England, 1820. 100fr, "Centercycles" used for parcel delivery, 1883 (horiz.). 200fr, French P.O. railroad car, 1848 (horiz.).

1979, Aug. 27 Photogravure

C385	A213	90fr multi	90	45
C386	A213	100fr multi	1.00	50
C387	A213	200fr multi	2.00	1.00
a.		Souvenir sheet of 2	3.25	3.25

Sir Rowland Hill (1795-1879), originator of penny postage. No. C387a contains Nos. C386-C387; multicolored margin shows inscription and coach. Size: 139x116mm.

Train Type of 1979

Historic Locomotives: 60fr, "Le General," 1862. 85fr, Stephenson's, 1843. 100fr, "De Witt Clinton," 1831. 200fr, Joy's "Jenny Lind," 1847.

1979, Oct. 1 Litho. *Perf. 14*

C388	A214	60fr multi	60	30
C389	A214	85fr multi	85	42
C390	A214	100fr multi	1.00	50
C391	A214	200fr multi	2.00	1.00
a.		Souvenir sheet of 2	3.25	3.25

No. C391a contains Nos. C390-C391. Violet and black margin shows "Le General."

Size: 118½× 95mm.

Olympic Type of 1979

1980 Olympic Emblems and: 90fr, Ski jump. No. C393, Doubles canoeing, Olympic flame. No. C394, Rings. No. C395a, Bobsledding (horiz.). No. C395b, Gymnast (horiz.).

1979, Oct. 18 Litho. *Perf. 13½*

C392	A215	90fr multi	90	45
C393	A215	100fr multi	1.00	50
C394	A215	200fr multi	2.00	1.00
a.		Souvenir sheet of 2	3.25	3.25

Souvenir Sheet

C395		Sheet of 2	3.25	3.25
a.		A215 100fr multi	1.00	50
b.		A215 200fr multi	2.00	1.00

13th Winter Olympic Games, Lake Placid, N.Y., Feb. 12-24, 1980; 22nd Summer Olympic Games, Moscow, July 19-Aug. 3, 1980. No. C395 has multicolored margin, yellow inscription. Size. 96×91mm.

Religion Type of 1979

1979, Oct. 29 *Perf. 13x14*

Designs: 60fr, Native praying (vert.). 70fr, Protestant ministers.

C396	A216	60fr multi	60	30
C397	A216	70fr multi	70	35
a.		Souvenir sheet of 2	1.50	

Religions in Togo. No. 397a contains Nos. 396-C397; multicolored margin, black inscription. Size: 116½x89mm.

Apollo 11 Type of 1979

Designs: 60fr, Astronaut leaving Apollo 11. 70fr, U.S. flag. 200fr, Sun shield. 300fr, Lunar take-off.

1979, Nov. 5

C398	A217	60fr multi	60	30
C399	A217	70fr multi	70	35
C400	A217	200fr multi	2.00	1.00
C401	A217	300fr multi	3.00	1.50
a.		Souvenir sheet of 2	5.50	5.50

Apollo 11 moon landing, 10th anniversary. No. C401a contains Nos. C400-C401; multicolored margin shows Apollo 11 emblem. Size 142×105mm.

Telecom Type of 1979

Design: 60fr, Telecom 79, dish antenna.

1979, Nov. 26 Photo. *Perf. 14×13*

C402	A218	60fr multi	60	30

3rd World Telecomunications Exhibition, Geneva, Sept. 20-26.

Christmas Type, 1979

Designs: 90fr, Adoration of the Kings. 100fr, Presentation of Infant Jesus. 200fr, Flight into Egypt.

1979, Dec. 17 Litho. *Perf. 14*

C403	A219	90fr multi	90	45
C404	A219	100fr multi	1.00	50
C405	A219	200fr multi	2.00	1.00
a.		Souvenir sheet of 2	3.25	1.75

Christmas 1979. No. C405a contains Nos. C404 and C405. Multicolored margin shows Mother and Child, gold inscription. Size: 133½×104½mm.

Rotary Type, 1980

3-H Emblem and: 90fr, Man reaching for sun. 100fr, Fish, grain. 200fr, Family, globe.

1980, Jan. 14

C406	A220	90fr multi	90	45
C407	A220	100fr multi	1.00	50
C408	A220	200fr multi	2.00	1.00
a.		Souvenir sheet of 2	3.25	1.75

Rotary International, 75th anniversary; 3-H program (health, hunger, humanity). No. C408a contains Nos. C407 and C408. Violet and black margin shows Rotary emblem. Size: 132½×132mm.

Winter Olympic Type, 1980

1980, Jan. 31 Litho. *Perf. 13½*

C409	A221	60fr *Downhill skiing*	60	30
C410	A221	100fr *Speed skating*	1.00	50
C411	A221	200fr *Cross-country skiing*	2.00	1.00

Souvenir Sheet

C412		Sheet of 2	3.00	1.50
a.		A221 100fr *Ski jump*, horiz.	1.00	50
b.		A221 200fr *Hockey*, horiz.	2.00	1.00

13th Winter Olympic Games, Lake Placid, N.Y., Feb. 12-24. No. C412 has multicolored margin showing Lake Placid '80 Emblem. Size: 104x83½mm.

Olympic Type of 1980

1980, Feb. 29 Litho. *Perf. 13½*

C413	A222	100fr *Fencing*	1.00	50
C414	A222	200fr *Pole vault*	2.00	1.00
C415	A222	300fr *Hurdles*	3.00	1.50
a.		Souvenir sheet of 2	5.00	2.50

22nd Summer Olympics, Moscow, July 19—Aug. 3. No. C415a contains Nos. C414—C415; multicolored margin shows Moscow '80 emblem. Size 110½×82m

TOGO

Easter Type of 1980

Easter 1980 (Paintings by): 60fr, Lorenzo Lotto. 100fr, El Greco. 200fr, Carlo Crivelli.

1980, Mar. 31			Perf. 14	
C416	A223	60fr multi	60	30
C417	A223	100fr multi	1.00	50
C418	A223	200fr multi	2.00	1.00
a.		Souvenir sheet of 2	3.00	1.50

No. C418a contains Nos. C417-C418; multicolored margin shows Crucifixion. Size: 127x109½mm.

ASECNA Type of 1980

1980, Mar. 24		Litho.	Perf. 12½	
C419	A224	60fr multi	60	30

ASECNA (Air Safety Board), 20th anniversary.

Telecommunications Type of 1980

1980, May 17		Photo.	Perf. 13½x14	
C420	A225	60fr "17 MAI", vert.	60	30

12th World Telecommunications Day.

Red Cross Type of 1980

1980, June 16		Photo.	Perf. 14x13	
C421	A226	60fr Nurses, patient	60	30

Togolese Red Cross.

Jules Verne Type of 1980

1980, July 14		Litho.		Perf. 14	
C422	A227	60fr	Rocket (From Earth to Moon)	60	30
C423	A227	80fr	Around the World in 80 Days	80	40
C424	A227	100fr	Rocket and moon (From Earth to Moon)	1.00	50
C425	A227	200fr	Octopus (20,000 Leagues Under the Sea)	2.00	1.00
a.			Souvenir sheet of 2	3.00	1.50

Jules Verne (1828-1905), French science fiction writer. No. C425a contains Nos. C424-C425 perf. 13½x14; multicolored margin shows Verne portrait. Size: 121x99mm.

Ingres Type of 1980

Ingres Paintings: 90fr, Jupiter and Thetis. 100fr, Countess d'Hassonville. 200fr, "Tu Marcellus Eris."

1980, Aug. 29		Litho.	Perf. 14	
C426	A228	90fr multi	90	45
C427	A228	100fr multi	1.00	50
C428	A228	200fr multi	2.00	1.00
a.		Souvenir sheet of 2	3.00	1.50

No. C428a contains Nos. C427-C428; multicolored margin shows portrait of Ingres. Size: 127x95mm.

Famous Men Type of 1980

Designs: 90fr, Salvador Allende (vert.). 100fr, Pope Paul VI (vert.). 200fr, Jomo Kenyatta (vert.).

1980, Feb. 11		Litho.	Perf. 14x13	
C429	A231	90fr ultra & lt bl grn	90	45
C430	A231	100fr pur & pink	1.00	50
C431	A231	200fr brn & yel bis	2.00	1.00
a.		Souvenir sheet of 2	3.00	1.50

No. C431a contains Nos. C430-C431; light blue green and dark blue margin shows world map. Size: 115x118mm.

Human Rights Type of 1980

1980, Oct. 13		Photo.	Perf. 13x14	
C432	A233	60fr Map of Americas	60	30
C433	A233	150fr Map of Africa	1.50	75
a.		Souvenir sheet of 2	2.25	1.00

Declaration of Human Rights, 30th anniversary. No. C433a contains Nos. C432-C433 multicolored margin with black inscription. Size: 100½x113½mm.

American Order of Rosicrucians Emblem—AP21

1980, Nov. 17		Litho.	Perf. 13	
C434	AP21	60fr multi	60	30

General Conclave of the American Order of Rosicrucians, meeting of French-speaking countries, Lome, Aug.

Christmas Type of 1980

1980, Dec. 22			Perf. 14½x13½	
C435	A234	100fr Cologne Cathedral, Germany, 13th cent.	1.00	50
C436	A234	150fr Notre Dame, Paris, 12th cent.	1.50	75
C437	A234	200fr Canterbury Cathedral, England, 11th cent.	2.00	1.00
a.		Souvenir sheet of 2	3.50	1.75

Christmas 1980. No. C437a contains Nos. C436-C437; multicolored decorative margin. Size: 136x102½mm.

Hotel Type of 1981

1981, Feb. 2		Litho.	Perf. 12½x13	
C437B	A236	60fr multi	60	30

Easter Type of 1981

Rembrandt Paintings: 100fr, Artist's Mother. 200fr, Man in a Ruff.

1981, Apr. 13		Litho.	Perf. 14½x13½	
C438	A237	100fr multi	1.00	50
C439	A237	200fr multi	2.00	1.00
a.		Souvenir sheet of 2	3.00	1.50

No. C439a contains Nos. C438-C439; light brown and light blue margin. Size: 141x102mm.

Market Type of 1980

1981, Mar. 8		Litho.	Perf. 14	
C440	A230	90fr multi	90	45
C441	A230	100fr multi	1.00	50
C442	A230	200fr multi	2.00	1.00
C443	A230	250fr multi	2.50	1.25
C444	A230	500fr multi	5.00	2.50
C445	A230	1000fr multi	10.00	5.00

Bird Type of 1981

1981, Aug. 10		Litho.	Perf. 13½x14½	
C446	A238	50fr Violet-backed sunbird	50	25
C447	A238	100fr Red bishop	1.00	50
a.		Souvenir sheet of 2	1.50	75

No. C447a contains Nos. C446-C447; multicolored margin shows tree. Size: 140x102mm.

IYD Type of 1981

1981, Aug. 31			Perf. 14	
C448	A240	90fr Carpenter	90	45
C449	A240	200fr Basketball players	2.00	1.00

Souvenir Sheet

C449A	A240	300fr Weaver	3.00	1.50

No. C449A has multicolored margin showing painter. Size: 125x90mm.

Picasso Type of 1981

1981, Sept. 14			Perf. 14½x13½	
C450	A241	90fr Violin and Bottle on Table, 1916	90	45
C451	A241	100fr Baboon and Young	1.00	50
C452	A241	200fr Mandolin and Clarinet, 1914	2.00	1.00
a.		Souvenir sheet of 2	3.00	1.50

No. C452a contains Nos. C451-C452; multicolored margin. Size: 140x101mm.

World Heritage Year Type of 1981

1981, Sept. 28			Perf. 13½x14½	
C453	A242	100fr Cracow Museum, Poland	1.00	50
C454	A242	200fr Goree Isld., Senegal	2.00	1.00
a.		Souvenir sheet of 2	3.00	1.50

No. C454a contains Nos. C453-C454; olive green margin shows Heritage Year emblem. Size: 140x102mm.

Space Type of 1981

1981, Nov.			Perf. 14	
C455	A243	90fr multi	90	45
C456	A243	100fr multi	1.00	50

Souvenir Sheet
Perf. 13x14

C456A	A243	300fr multi, vert.	3.00	3.00

10th anniv. of Soyuz 10 (90fr) and Apollo 14 (100fr). No. C456A has multicolored margin showing astronaut on space walk. Size: 110x86mm.

Christmas Type of 1981

Rubens Paintings: 100fr, Adoration of the Kings. 200fr, Virgin and Child. 300fr, Virgin giving Chasuble to St. Idefonse.

1981, Dec. 10		Litho.	Perf. 14½x13½	
C457	A244	100fr multi	1.00	50
C458	A244	200fr multi	2.00	1.00
C459	A244	300fr multi	3.00	1.50
a.		Souvenir sheet of 2	5.00	2.50

No. C459a contains C458-C459; multicolored margin shows Landscape with Steen Castle, by Rubens. Size: 121x93mm.

West African Rice Development Assoc.—AP22

1981, Dec. 21		Litho.	Perf. 12½	
C460	AP22	70fr lt grn & multi	70	35
C461	AP22	105fr yel & multi	1.05	52

Liberation Type of 1982

1982, Jan. 13		Litho.	Perf. 12½	
C462	A245	105fr Citizens holding hands, Pres. Eyadema, vert.	1.05	52
C463	A245	130fr Hotel	1.30	65

Scouting Year Type of 1982

1982, Feb. 25		Litho.	Perf. 14	
C464	A246	90fr Semaphore	90	45
C465	A246	120fr Tower	1.20	60
C466	A246	130fr Scouts, canoe	1.30	65
C467	A246	135fr Scouts, tent	1.35	68

Souvenir Sheet
Perf. 13x14

C468	A246	500fr Baden-Powell	5.00	2.50

No. C468 has multicolored margin showing emblem, sign. Size: 108x84mm.

Easter Type of 1982

1982, Apr.			Perf. 14x14½	
C469	A247	105fr multi	1.05	55
C470	A247	120fr multi	1.20	60

Souvenir Sheet

C471	A247	500fr multi	5.00	2.50

No. C471 has violet and light blue margin. Size: 114x89mm.

PHILEXFRANCE '82 Intl. Stamp Exhibition, Paris, June 11-21—AP23

1982		Litho.	Perf. 13	
C472	AP23	90fr shown	90	45
C473	AP23	105fr ROMOLYMPHIL '82, vert.	1.05	52

Issue dates: 90fr, June 11; 105fr, May 19.

Butterfly Type of 1982

1982, July 15			Perf. 14½x14	
C474	A248	90fr Euxanthe eurionome	90	45
C475	A248	105fr Mylothris rhodope	1.05	52

Souvenir Sheet

C476	A248	500fr Papilio zalmoxis	5.00	2.50

No. C476 has multicolored margin showing butterfly on flower. Size: 134x102mm.

World Cup Type of 1982

1982, July 26			Perf. 14x14½	
C477	A249	105fr multi	1.05	52
C478	A249	200fr multi	2.00	1.00
C479	A249	300fr multi	3.00	1.50

Souvenir Sheet

C480	A249	500fr multi	5.00	2.50

No. C480 has multicolored margin continuing design. Size: 121x88mm.

Pre-Olympics, 1984 Los Angeles—AP24

1983, Oct. 3		Photo.	Perf. 12½	
C481	AP24	70fr Boxing	35	18
C482	AP24	90fr Hurdles	45	22
C483	AP24	105fr Pole vault	52	26
C484	AP24	130fr Runner	65	32

Souvenir Sheet

C485	AP24	500fr Runner, diff.	2.50	1.25

Green and multicolored margin shows various players and events. Size: 112x80mm.

TOGO—TRANSCAUCASIAN FEDERATED REPUBLICS—TRIESTE

AIR POST SEMI-POSTAL STAMPS.

V4

Stamps of the design shown above and type of Cameroun V10 inscribed "Togo" were issued in 1942 by the Vichy Government, but were not placed on sale in the colony.

POSTAGE DUE STAMPS.

Postage Due Stamps of Dahomey, 1914
Overprinted **TOGO**

		1921 Perf. 14x13½	Unwmkd.	
J1	D2	5c green	38	38
J2	D2	10c rose	38	38
J3	D2	15c gray	75	75
J4	D2	20c brown	1.50	1.40
J5	D2	30c blue	1.50	1.40
J6	D2	50c black	95	75
J7	D2	60c orange	1.10	90
J8	D2	1fr violet	2.75	2.25
		Nos. J1-J8 (8)	9.31	8.21

Cotton Field
D3

		1925 Typographed	Unwmkd.	
J9	D3	2c bl & blk	6	6
J10	D3	4c dl red & blk	6	6
J11	D3	5c ol grn & blk	8	8
J12	D3	10c cer & blk	18	18
J13	D3	15c org & blk	18	18
J14	D3	20c red vio & blk	28	28
J15	D3	25c gray & blk	38	38
J16	D3	30c ocher & blk	18	18
J17	D3	50c brn & blk	30	30
J18	D3	60c grn & blk	38	38
J19	D3	1fr dk vio & blk	50	50
		Nos. J9-J19 (11)	2.58	2.58

Type of 1925 Issue Surcharged **2f**

1927				
J20	D3	2fr on 1fr rose red & vio	2.25	2.25
J21	D3	3fr on 1fr org brn, blk & ultra	2.25	2.25

Mask | Carved Figures
D4 | D5

1941		Engraved	Perf. 13	
J22	D4	5c brn blk	5	5
J23	D4	10c yel grn	6	6
J24	D4	15c carmine	6	6
J25	D4	20c ultra	22	22
J26	D4	30c chestnut	22	22
J27	D4	50c ol grn	70	70
J28	D4	60c violet	22	22
J29	D4	1fr bl brn	50	50
J30	D4	2fr org ver	32	32
J31	D4	3fr rose vio	50	50
		Nos. J22-J31 (10)	2.85	2.37

Stamps of type D4 without "R F" monogram were issued in 1942 to 1944 by the Vichy Government, but were not placed on sale in the colony.

1947				
J32	D5	10c brt ultra	5	5
J33	D5	30c red	5	5
J34	D5	50c dp yel grn	6	6
J35	D5	1fr chocolate	12	12
J36	D5	2fr carmine	18	18
J37	D5	3fr gray blk	18	18
J38	D5	4fr ultra	38	38
J39	D5	5fr sepia	50	50
J40	D5	10fr dp org	45	45
J41	D5	20fr dk bl vio	65	65
		Nos. J32-J41 (10)	2.62	2.62

Republic

Konkomba Helmet
D6 | D7

1957		Engraved	Perf. 14x13	
J42	D6	1fr brt ultra	5	5
J43	D6	2fr brt org	10	10
J44	D6	3fr dk gray	12	12
J45	D6	4fr brt red	14	14
J46	D6	5fr ultra	15	15
J47	D6	10fr dp grn	38	38
J48	D6	20fr dp cl	55	55
		Nos. J42-J48 (7)	1.49	1.49

1959			Perf. 14x13	
J49	D7	1fr org brn	5	5
J50	D7	2fr lt bl grn	5	5
J51	D7	3fr orange	10	10
J52	D7	4fr blue	12	12
J53	D7	5fr lil rose	12	12
J54	D7	10fr vio bl	35	35
J55	D7	20fr black	50	50
		Nos. J49-J55 (7)	1.29	1.29

Type of Regular Issue, 1964.
Shells: 1fr, Conus papilionaceus. 2fr, Marginella faba. 3fr, Cypraea stercoraria. 4fr, Strombus latus. 5fr, Costate cockle (sea shell). 10fr, Cancellaria cancellata. 15fr, Cymbium pepo. 20fr, Tympanotomus radula.

Photogravure

1964-65		Perf. 14	Unwmkd.	
		Size: 20x25½mm.		
J56	A47	1fr gray grn & red brn ('65)	8	8
J57	A47	2fr tan & ol grn ('65)	8	8
J58	A47	3fr gray, brn & yel ('65)	8	8
J59	A47	4fr tan & multi ('65)	15	15
J60	A47	5fr sep, org & grn	22	22
J61	A47	10fr sl bl, brn & bis	32	32
J62	A47	15fr grn & brn	90	90
J63	A47	20fr sl, dk brn & yel	95	95
		Nos. J56-J63 (8)	2.78	2.78

Tomatoes
D8

1969-70		Litho.	Perf. 14	
J64	D8	5fr yel & multi	8	8
J65	D8	10fr bl & multi	18	18
J66	D8	15fr multi ('70)	28	22
J67	D8	20fr multi ('70)	30	28

Market Type of 1980

1981, Mar. 8		Litho.	Perf. 14	
Size: 23x32mm.		32x23mm.		
J68	A230	5fr Millet (vert.)	5	5
J69	A230	10fr Packaged goods	8	8
J70	A230	25fr Chickens	15	15
J71	A230	50fr Ivory vendor	30	15

TRANSCAUCASIAN FEDERATED REPUBLICS

(Armenia, Georgia, Azerbaijan)

LOCATION—In southeastern Europe, south of the Caucasus Mountains between the Black and Caspian Seas.
GOVT.—Former republic.
AREA—71,255 sq. mi.
POP.—5,851,000 (approx.).
CAPITAL—Tiflis.

The Transcaucasian Federation was made up of the former autonomies of Armenia, Georgia and Azerbaijan. Its stamps were replaced by those of Russia.

100 Kopecks = 1 Ruble

Russian Stamps of 1909-17 Overprinted in Black or Red

1923		Perf. 14½x15.	Unwmkd.	
1	A15	10k dk bl	4.00	6.00
2	A14	10k on 7k lt bl	4.00	6.00
3	A11	25k grn & gray vio	5.00	7.00
4	A11	35k red brn & grn (R)	5.00	7.00
a.		Dbl. ovpt.	60.00	60.00
5	A8	50k brn red & grn	5.00	7.00
6	A9	1r pale brn, brn & org	8.00	15.00
7	A12	3½r mar & lt grn	20.00	

No. 7 was prepared but not issued.

Imperf.

| 8 | A9 | 1r pale brn, brn & red org | 4.00 | 8.00 |

Overprinted on Stamps of Armenia Previously Handstamped:

a   c

Perf. 14½x15.

| 9 | A11 (c) | 25k grn & gray vio | 225.00 | 375.00 |
| 10 | A8 (c) | 50k vio & grn | 110.00 | 275.00 |

Perf. 13½.

| 11 | A9 (a) | 1r pale brn, brn & org | 60.00 | 60.00 |
| 12 | A9 (c) | 1r pale brn, brn & org | 85.00 | 65.00 |

Imperf.

| 13 | A9 (c) | 1r pale brn, brn & red org | 60.00 | 60.00 |

Counterfeit overprints exist.

Oil Fields—A1

Soviet Symbols—A2

1923			Perf. 11½	
14	A1	40,000r red vio	1.00	1.50
15	A1	75,000r dk grn	1.00	1.50
16	A1	100,000r blk vio	1.00	1.50
17	A1	150,000r red	1.00	1.50
18	A2	200,000r dl grn	1.00	1.50
19	A2	300,000r blue	1.00	2.00
20	A2	350,000r dk brn	1.00	2.00
21	A2	500,000r rose	1.00	2.00
		Nos. 14-21 (8)	8.00	13.50

Nos. 14-15 Surcharged in Brown

700 000 РУБ.

1923				
22	A1	700,000r on 40,000r red vio	4.00	6.00
a.		Imperf., pair	20.00	
23	A1	700,000r on 75,000r dk grn	4.00	6.00
a.		Imperf., pair	20.00	

Types of Preceding Issue with Values in Gold Kopecks

1923, Oct. 24				
25	A2	1k orange	1.00	2.50
26	A2	2k bl grn	1.00	2.50
27	A2	3k rose	1.00	2.50
28	A2	4k gray brn	1.00	2.50
29	A2	5k dk vio	1.00	2.50
30	A1	9k dp bl	1.00	2.50
31	A1	18k slate	1.00	2.50
		Nos. 25-31 (7)	7.00	17.50

Nos. 14-21, 25-31 exist imperf. but are not known to have been issued in that condition. Price $12.50 each.

TRIESTE

(trĕ-ĕst')

A free territory (1947-1954) on the Adriatic Sea between Italy and Jugoslavia. In 1954 the territory was divided, Italy acquiring the northern section and seaport, Jugoslavia the southern section (Zone B).

ZONE A.

Issued jointly by the Allied Military Government of the United States and Great Britain.

Stamps of Italy 1945-47 Overprinted in Black:

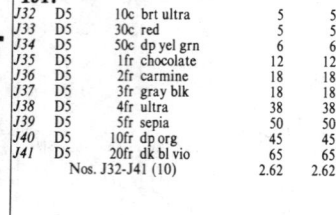

A.M.G.   **A.M.G.**
F.T.T.   **F.T.T.**
a   b

A.M.G.
F.T.T.
c

1947		Perf. 14	Wmk. 277	
1	A259 (a)	25c brt bl grn	5	5
2	A255 (a)	50c dp vio	5	5
3	A257 (a)	1 l dk grn	5	5
4	A258 (a)	2 l dk cl brn	5	5
5	A259 (a)	3 l red	5	5
6	A259 (a)	4 l red org	5	5
7	A256 (a)	5 l dp bl	6	5
8	A257 (a)	6 l dp vio	9	5
9	A255 (a)	10 l slate	15	5
10	A257 (a)	15 l dp bl	20	7
11	A259 (a)	20 l dk red vio	15	5
12	A260 (b)	25 l dk grn	70	1.25
13	A260 (b)	50 l dk vio brn	1.10	75

Perf. 14x13½

| 14 | A261 (a) | 100l car lake | 2.00 | 1.75 |
| | | Nos. 1-14 (14) | 4.75 | 4.32 |

The letters "F. T. T." are the initials of "Free Territory of Trieste."

TRIESTE

Italy Nos. 486-488
Overprinted Type "a" in Black.

			Perf. 14	
1948				
15	A255	8 l dk grn	75	1.50
16	A256	10 l red org	2.25	5
17	A259	30 l dk bl	17.50	90

Italy Nos. 495 to 506
Overprinted in Black

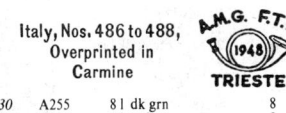

1948, July 1				
18	A272	3 l dk brn	7	18
19	A272	4 l red vio	5	18
20	A272	5 l dp bl	18	18
21	A272	6 l dp yel grn	25	38
22	A272	8 l brown	7	30
23	A272	10 l org red	38	18
24	A272	12 l dk gray grn	30	1.00
25	A272	15 l gray blk	5.50	6.00
26	A272	20 l car rose	11.00	6.00
27	A272	30 l brt ultra	18	1.00
28	A272	50 l violet	4.75	10.00
29	A272	100 l bl blk	22.50	40.00
	Nos. 18-29 (12)		45.23	65.40

Italy, Nos. 486 to 488,
Overprinted in Carmine

30	A255	8 l dk grn	8	18
31	A256	10 l red org	8	18
32	A259	30 l dk bl	1.25	1.40
	Nos. 30-32, C17-C19 (6)		2.13	3.21

The overprint is embossed.

Italy, No. 507,
Overprinted Type "d" in Carmine.

| 33 | A273 | 15 l dk grn | 50 | 65 |

Italy, No. 508,
Overprinted in Green

| 34 | A274 | 15 l dk brn | 45 | 60 |

Italy, No. 509, Overprinted Type "d" in Red.

1949		Perf. 14.	Wmk. 277	
35	A275	20 l dk brn	2.50	85

27th Milan Trade Fair, April 1949.

Italy, Nos. 510 to 513,
Overprinted in Black

Buff Background.

36	A276	5 l red brn	25	50
37	A276	15 l dk grn	6.00	10.00
38	A276	20 l dp red brn	2.25	1.00
39	A276	50 l dk bl	10.00	8.50

Issued to commemorate the 50th anniversary of the Biennial Art Exhibition of Venice.

Italy, No. 514, Overprinted Type "d" in Red.

| 40 | A277 | 50 l brt ultra | 1.50 | 3.00 |

Issued to commemorate the 75th anniversary of the formation of the Universal Postal Union.

Italy, No. 518, Overprinted Type "d" in Red.

| 41 | A279 | 100 l brown | 50.00 | 85.00 |

Centenary of the Roman Republic.

Italy, Nos. 515-517, Overprinted Type "f" in Black.

42	A278	5 l dk grn	6.00	10.00
43	A278	15 l violet	9.00	20.00
44	A278	20 l brown	15.00	20.00

European Recovery Program.

Italy, Nos. 519 and 520, Overprinted Type "e" in Carmine.

45	A280	20 l gray	3.00	2.50
46	A281	20 l brown	2.25	2.50

No. 45, erection of monument to Giuseppe Mazzini, Italian patriot and revolutionary.
No. 46, bicentenary of birth of Vittorio Alfieri, dramatist.

Italy, No. 521 AMG-FTT
Overprinted in Green g

| 47 | A282 | 20 l brn red | 1.75 | 1.25 |

Issued to publicize the Trieste election, June 12, 1949.

Italy, No. 522, Overprinted Type "f" in Carmine.

| 49 | A283 | 20 l violet | 12.00 | 3.00 |

Issued to commemorate the second World Health Congress, Rome, 1949.

Italy, No. 523 Overprinted Type "e", without Periods, in Black.

| 50 | A284 | 20 l vio bl | 2.25 | 2.00 |

Issued to commemorate the 500th anniversary of the birth of Lorenzo de Medici.

Italy, No. 524 Overprinted Type "f" in Black.

| 51 | A285 | 20 l violet | 12.00 | 10.00 |

Issued to commemorate the 400th anniversary of the death of Andrea Palladio.

Italy, No. 525, Overprinted Type "d" in Green.

| 52 | A286 | 20 l red | 2.25 | 2.50 |

Issued to publicize the 13th Levant Fair, Bari, September, 1949.

Italy Nos. 526 and 527 Overprinted AMG-FTT h

Photogravure.

1949		Perf. 14.	Wmk. 277	
53	A287	20 l rose car	1.00	2.00
54	A288	50 l dp bl	4.75	10.00

Issued to commemorate the 150th anniversary of the invention of the Voltaic Pile.

Same Overprint on No. 528.

| 55 | A289 | 20 l dp grn | 2.75 | 6.00 |

Issued to publicize plans to reconstruct Holy Trinity Bridge, Florence.

Same Overprint on No. 529.

| 56 | A290 | 20 l brt bl | 1.50 | 1.75 |

Issued to commemorate the 2,000th anniversary of the death of C. Valerius Catullus, lyric poet.

Same Overprint in Red on No. 530.

| 57 | A291 | 20 l vio blk | 1.50 | 1.50 |

Issued to commemorate the bicentenary of the birth of Domenico Cimarosa, Italian composer.

Same Overprint in Black on Italian Stamps of 1945-48.

1949-50		Photogravure.		
58	A257	1 l dk brn	5	5
59	A258	1 l dk cl brn	5	5
60	A259	3 l red	5	5
61	A256	5 l dp bl	6	5
62	A257	6 l dp vio	5	5
63	A255	8 l dk grn	2.50	6.00
64	A256	10 l red org	7	5
65	A257	15 l dp bl	42	25
66	A259	20 l dk red vio	15	8
67	A260	25 l dk grn ('50)	5.00	1.00
68	A260	50 l dk vio brn ('50)	10.00	50

Engraved.

| 69 | A261 | 100 l car lake | 20.00 | 1.75 |
| | Nos. 58-69 (12) | | 38.40 | 9.88 |

Italy, No. 531, Overprinted Type "g" in Carmine

1950				
70	A292	20 l brown	1.00	80

Issued to publicize the 28th Milan Fair, 1950.

Same Overprint in Carmine on Italy, No. 532.

| 71 | A293 | 20 l vio gray | 90 | 90 |

Issued to publicize the 32nd International Automobile Show, Turin, May 4-14, 1950.

Same Overprint in Carmine on Italy, Nos. 533 and 534.

72	A294	20 l ol grn	1.00	1.50
73	A295	55 l blue	3.50	11.50

Issued to commemorate the 5th General Conference of the United Nations Educational, Scientific and Cultural Organization.

Italy, Nos. 535 and 536, Overprinted Type "h" in Black.

74	A296	20 l violet	1.00	1.50
75	A296	55 l blue	3.50	11.00

Holy Year, 1950.

Italy, No. 537, Overprinted Type "g" in Carmine.

| 76 | A297 | 20 l gray grn | 1.50 | 1.50 |

Issued to honor Gaudenzio Ferrari, painter.

Same Overprint in Carmine on Italy, Nos. 538-539.

77	A298	20 l purple	2.50	4.00
78	A298	55 l blue	7.50	20.00

Issued to commemorate the International Shortwave Radio Conference, Florence, 1950.

Italy, No. 540, Overprinted Type "h" in Black.

| 79 | A299 | 20 l brown | 1.50 | 1.50 |

Issued to commemorate the 200th anniversary of the death of Ludovico A. Muratoriano, writer.

Italy, No. 541 AMG FTT Overprinted in Carmine i

| 80 | A300 | 20 l dk grn | 1.50 | 1.50 |

Issued to commemorate the 900th anniversary of the death of Guido d'Arezzo, music teacher and composer.

Italy, No. 542, Overprinted Type "g" in Black.

| 81 | A301 | 20 l chnt brn | 1.25 | 1.50 |

Levant Fair, Bari, Sept., 1950.

Italy, Nos. 473A and 474, Overprinted in Black

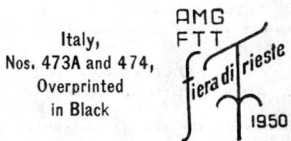

82	A257	15 l dp bl	25	60
83	A259	20 l dk red vio	25	60

Issued to publicize the Trieste Fair.

Italy, No. 543, Overprinted Type "i" in Carmine.

| 84 | A302 | 20 l indigo | 50 | 50 |

Issued to honor the pioneers of the Italian wool industry.

Italy, Nos. 544-546, Overprinted Type "h" in Black.

1950		Perf. 14.	Wmk. 277	
85	A303	5 l dp cl & grn	80	1.00
86	A303	20 l brn & grn	3.25	2.00
87	A303	55 l dp ultra & brn	22.50	32.50

Issued to publicize the European Tobacco Conference, Rome, 1950.

Same, in Black, on Italy No. 547.

| 88 | A304 | 20 l ol brn & red brn | 1.00 | 1.00 |

Issued to commemorate the 200th anniversary of the founding of the Academy of Fine Arts, Venice.

Same, in Black, on Italy No. 548.

| 89 | A305 | 20 l cr & gray blk | 1.10 | 1.00 |

Issued to commemorate the centenary of the birth of Augusto Righi, physicist.

Italy, Nos. 549 to 565, Overprinted Type "g" in Black.

90	A306	50c vio bl	5	5
91	A306	1 l dk bl vio	5	5
92	A306	2 l sepia	5	5
93	A306	5 l dk gray	5	5
94	A306	6 l chocolate	15	5
95	A306	10 l dk grn	15	5
96	A306	12 l dp bl grn	22	40
97	A306	15 l dk gray bl	22	6
98	A306	20 l bl vio	38	5
99	A306	25 l brn org	60	5
100	A306	30 l magenta	22	22
101	A306	35 l crimson	1.20	1.00
102	A306	40 l brown	30	30
103	A306	50 l violet	30	22
104	A306	55 l dp bl	30	30
105	A306	60 l red	2.50	2.00
106	A306	65 l dk grn	20	30

Italy Nos. 566 and 567 AMG-FTT Overprinted in Black k
Engraved.
Perf. 14, 14x13½.

107	A306	100 l brn org	1.50	10
108	A306	200 l ol brn	1.50	3.25
	Nos. 90-108 (19)		9.94	8.55

Italy Nos. 568 and 569 Overprinted Type "k" in Black.

1951		Photo.	Perf. 14	
109	A307	20 l red vio & red	1.00	2.00
110	A307	55 l ultra & bl	1.00	4.50

Issued to commemorate the centenary of Tuscany's first postage stamp.

Italy No. 570 Overprinted Type "g" in Black.

| 111 | A308 | 20 l dk grn | 1.10 | 1.50 |

Issued to publicize the 33rd International Automobile Exhibition, Turin, April 4-15, 1951.

Same, on Italy No. 571.

| 112 | A309 | 20 l bl vio | 85 | 1.75 |

Issued to publicize the consecration of the Altar of Peace at Redipuglia Cemetery, Medea.

Italy Nos. 572 and 573 Overprinted

113	A310 (h)	20 l brown	1.00	2.50
114	A311 (g)	55 l dp bl	1.75	4.50

International Sample Fair, Milan.

Italy Nos. 574 to 576 Overprinted Type "h" in Black.
Fleur-de-Lis in Red.

115	A312	5 l dk grn	5.00	11.00
116	A312	10 l Prus grn	5.00	11.00
117	A312	15 l vio bl	5.00	11.00

Issued to publicize the International Gymnastic Festival and Meet, Florence, 1951.

Italy No. 577 AMG-FTT Overprinted in Black m

| 118 | A313 | 20 l purple | 85 | 1.50 |

Issued to publicize the 10th International Exhibition of Textile Art and Fashion, Turin, May 2-16, 1951.

Italy No. 578 Overprinted Type "h" in Black.

| 119 | A314 | 20 l Prus grn | 1.50 | 3.00 |

Issued to commemorate the 500th anniversary of the birth of Columbus.

Italy Nos. 579-580 Overprinted Type "g" in Black.

120	A315	20 l violet	35	75
121	A315	55 l brt bl	1.10	2.50

Issued to commemorate the reconstruction of the Abbey of Montecassino.

TRIESTE

Nos. 94, 98 and 104 Overprinted in Black

FIERA di TRIESTE 1951

1951
122	A306	6 l chocolate	18	50
123	A306	20 l bl vio	22	50
124	A306	55 l dp bl	25	60

Issued to publicize the Trieste Fair, 1951.

Italy No. 581 Overprinted in Black

AMG FTT
n

125	A316	20 l brn & red brn	55	75

Issued to commemorate the 500th anniversary of (in 1950) of the birth of Pietro Vanucci, painter.

Italy Nos. 582 and 583 Overprinted Types "n" and "h" in Red.

126	A317 (n)	20 l grnsh gray & blk	65	75
127	A318 (h)	55 l vio bl & pale sal	1.40	3.00

Issued to publicize the Triennial Art Exhibition, Milan, 1951.

Italy No. 584 Overprinted Type "g" in Carmine.

128	A319	25 l gray blk	45	60

Issued to publicize the World Bicycle Championship Races, Milan, Aug.-Sept., 1951.

Overprint "g" in Black on Italy No. 585.

129	A320	25 l dp bl	45	60

Issued to publicize the 15th Levant Fair, Bari, September, 1951.

Italy No. 586 Overprinted Type "h" in Red.

130	A321	25 l dk brn	45	60

Issued to commemorate the centenary of the birth of Francesco Paolo Michetti, painter.

Italy Nos. 587-589 Overprinted in Blue

AMG o FTT

131	A322	10 l dk brn & gray	25	75
132	A322	25 l rose red & bl grn	38	75
133	A322	60 l vio bl & red org	65	1.50

Sardinia stamp centenary.

Italy Nos. 590-591 Overprinted in Black

AMG p FTT

Photogravure.
Overprint Spaced to Fit Design.

134	A323	10 l green	38	75
135	A324	25 l vio gray	38	75

Issued to publicize the 3rd Industrial and the 9th General Italian Census.

Italy Nos. 592-593 Overprinted Type "k" in Black.

136	A325	10 l ol & dl grn	40	1.00
137	A326	25 l dl grn	40	60

Issued to publicize the Italian Festival of Trees.

Italy Nos. 594-596 Overprinted Types "k" or "p" in Black.
Overprint "p" Spaced to Fit Design.

138	A327 (p)	10 l vio brn & dk grn	25	75
139	A327 (k)	25 l red brn & dk brn	38	75
140	A327 (p)	60 l dp grn & ind	65	1.50

Issued to commemorate the 50th anniversary of the death of Giuseppe Verdi, composer.

Italy No. 597 Overprinted Type "p" in Black.

1952 Perf. 14. Wmk. 277
Overprint Spaced to Fit Design.

141	A328	25 l gray & gray blk	38	42

Issued to commemorate the 150th anniversary of the birth of Vincenzo Bellini, composer.

Italy No. 598 Overprinted Type "k" in Black.

142	A329	25 l dl grn & ol bis	38	42

Issued to honor Luigi Vanvitelli, architect.

Same on Italy No. 599.

143	A330	25 l brn & sl blu	38	30

Issued to publicize Italy's first International Exhibition of Sports stamps.

Same on Italy No. 600.

144	A331	60 l ultra	1.25	2.75

Issued to publicize the 30th International Sample Fair, Milan.

Same on Italy No. 601.

145	A332	25 l dp org	8	12

Issued to commemorate the 500th anniversary of the birth of Leonardo da Vinci.

Stamps of Italy Overprinted "AMG FTT" in Various Sizes and Arrangements.

On Nos. 602-603.
1952 Perf. 14. Wmk. 277

146	A333	25 l blk & red brn	38	50
147	A333	60 l blk & ultra	65	1.50

Issued to commemorate the centenary of the first postage stamps of Modena and Parma.

On No. 604.

148	A334	25 l brt bl	22	45

Issued to honor the Overseas Fair at Naples and Italian Labor throughout the world.

On No. 605.

149	A335	25 l blk & yel	45	45

Issued to publicize the 26th Biennial Art Exhibition, Venice.

On No. 606.

150	A336	25 l bl gray, red & dk bl (R)	30	45

Issued to publicize the 30th International Sample Fair of Padua.

On No. 607.

151	A337	25 l dp grn, dk brn & red	45	50

Issued to publicize the 4th International Sample Fair of Trieste.

On No. 608.

152	A338	25 l dk grn	45	38

16th Levant Fair, Bari Sept. 1952.

On No. 609 in Bronze.

153	A339	25 l purple	45	38

Issued to commemorate the 500th anniversary of the birth of Girolamo Savonarola.

On No. 610.

154	A340	25 l gray	45	38

Issued to publicize the National Exhibition of the Alpine Troop, Oct. 4, 1952.

On No. 611.

155	A341	60 l vio bl & dk bl	1.25	3.00

Issued to publicize the first International Civil Aviation Conference, Rome, Sept. 1952.

On No. 612.
Perf. 13.

156	A342	25 l brn & dk brn	45	38

Issued to commemorate the centenary of the establishment of the first Catholic mission in Ethiopia.

On Nos. 613-615.
Perf. 14.

157	A343	10 l dk grn	10	25
158	A344	25 l blk & dk brn	15	18
159	A344	60 l blk & bl	25	55

Issued to publicize Armed Forces Day, Nov. 4, 1952.

On No. 616.

160	A345	25 l dk grn	30	38

Issued to commemorate the centenary of the birth of Antonio Mancini, painter.

On No. 617.

161	A346	25 l brown	30	38

Issued to commemorate the centenary of the birth of Vincenzo Gemito, sculptor.

On No. 618.

162	A347	25 l gray blk & dk bl (Bl)	45	38

Issued to commemorate the deaths of the five Martyrs of Belfiore.

On Nos. 601A-601B.

163	A332a	60 l ultra (G)	1.00	2.50
164	A332	80 l brn car	75	65

Issued to commemorate the 500th anniversary of the birth of Leonardo da Vinci.

1953

On No. 621.

165	A349	25 l car lake	45	38

Issued to commemorate the Messina Exhibition of the paintings of Antonello and his 15th century contemporaries.

On No. 622.

166	A350	25 l violet	45	42

20th 1,000-mile automobile race.

On No. 623.

167	A351	25 l violet	30	38

On No. 624.

168	A352	25 l dk brn	30	38

Issued to commemorate the 300th anniversary of the birth of Arcangelo Corelli, composer.

On No. 625.

169	A353	25 l brn & dl red	30	38

Issued to commemorate the 700th anniversary of the death of St. Clare of Assisi.

1953-54 **On Nos. 626-633.**

170	A354	5 l gray	5	5
171	A354	10 l org ver	7	5
172	A354	12 l dl grn	10	18
172A	A354	13 l brt lil rose ('54)	8	18
173	A354	20 l brown	12	8
174	A354	25 l purple	15	5
175	A354	35 l rose car	30	60
176	A354	60 l blue	35	70
177	A354	80 l org brn	40	80
	Nos. 170-177 (9)		1.62	2.69

Italy, Nos. 554, 558 and 564 Overprinted in Red or Green

V FIERA DI TRIESTE
AMG † FTT
1953

1953

178	A306	10 l dp grn (R)	20	42
179	A306	25 l brn org	22	35
180	A306	60 l red	28	65

Issued to publicize the 5th International Sample Fair of Trieste.

Stamps of Italy Overprinted "AMG-FTT" in Various Sizes and Arrangements.

On No. 634.

181	A355	25 l bl grn	45	38

Issued to publicize the Festival of the Mountain.

On Nos. 635-636.

182	A356	25 l dk brn	20	35
183	A356	60 l dp bl	30	65

Issued to publicize the International Exposition of Agriculture, Rome, 1953.

On Nos. 637-638.

184	A357	25 l org & Prus bl	2.00	2.00
185	A357	60 l lil rose & dk vio bl	6.75	11.00

Issued to commemorate the 4th anniversary of the signing of the North Atlantic Treaty.

On No. 639.

186	A358	25 l dk brn & dl grn	30	38

Issued to publicize the opening of an exhibition of the works of Luca Signorelli, painter.

On No. 640.

187	A359	25 l dk gray & brn	45	38

Issued to publicize the 6th International Microbiology Congress, Rome, Sept. 6-12, 1953.

1954 **On Nos. 641-646.**

188	A360	10 l dk brn & red brn	15	30
189	A361	12 l lt bl & gray	18	45
190	A361	20 l brn org & dk brn	20	35
191	A360	25 l dk grn & pale bl	22	25
192	A361	35 l cr & brn	25	60
193	A361	60 l bl grn & ind	35	75
	Nos. 188-193 (6)		1.35	2.70

On Nos. 647-648.

194	A362	25 l dk brn & choc	20	30
195	A362	60 l bl & ultra	30	65

Issued to commemorate the 25th anniversary of the signing of the Lateran Pacts.

On Nos. 649-650.

196	A363	25 l purple	25	35
197	A363	60 l dp bl grn	50	1.25

On No. 651.

198	A364	25 l purple	45	25

Issued as propaganda for the payment of taxes.

On No. 652.

199	A365	25 l gray blk	45	42

Issued to publicize the experimental transportation of mail by helicopter, April, 1954.

On No. 653.

200	A366	25 l gray, org brn & blk	30	35

Issued to commemorate the 10th anniversary of Italy's resistance movement.

On No. 654.

201	A367	25 l dk grnsh gray	30	30

Issued to commemorate the centenary of the birth of Alfredo Catalani, composer.

On Nos. 655-656.

202	A368	25 l red brn	22	35
203	A368	60 l gray grn	50	1.10

Issued to commemorate the 700th anniversary of the birth of Marco Polo.

With Additional Overprint in Black

FIERA DI TRIESTE 1954

On Nos. 644, 646.

204	A360	25 l dk grn & pale bl	15	25
205	A361	60 l bl grn & ind	20	45

Issued to publicize the International Sample Fair of Trieste.

Stamps of Italy Overprinted "AMG-FTT" in Black.

On No. 657.

206	A369	25 l dp grn & red	30	35

Issued to commemorate the 60th anniversary of the foundation of the Italian Touring Club.

TRIESTE

207	A370	25 l rose red	18	35
208	A370	60 l blue	22	45

Issued to publicize the 23rd general assembly of the International Criminal Police, Rome, 1954.

OCCUPATION AIR POST STAMPS.

Air Post Stamps of Italy, 1945-47, Overprinted Type "c" in Black.

1947, Oct. 1   Perf. 14   Wmk. 277

C1	AP59	2 l sl bl	5	5
C2	AP60	2 l dk bl	6	6
C3	AP60	5 l dk grn	40	90
C4	AP59	10 l car rose	40	90
C5	AP60	25 l brown	40	90
C6	AP59	50 l violet	2.50	1.10
		Nos. C1-C6 (6)	3.81	3.91

Italy, Nos. C116 to C121, Overprinted Type "b" in Black.

1947, Nov. 19

C7	AP61	6 l dp vio	25	50
C8	AP61	10 l dk car rose	25	45
C9	AP61	20 l dp org	1.75	1.50
C10	AP61	25 l aqua	25	60
C11	AP61	35 l brt bl	25	60
C12	AP61	50 l lil rose	1.75	45
		Nos. C7-C12 (6)	4.50	4.10

Italy, Nos. C123 to C126, Overprinted Type "f" in Black.

1948

C13	AP65	100 l green	11.50	2.00
C14	AP65	300 l lil rose	11.50	11.00
C15	AP65	500 l ultra	11.50	12.00
C16	AP65	1000 l dk brn	100.00	165.00

Italy, No. C110, C113 and C114, Overprinted in Black

(Reduced Illustration)

1948, Sept. 8

C17	AP59	10 l car rose	12	25
C18	AP60	25 l brown	30	60
C19	AP59	50 l violet	30	60

The overprint is embossed.

Italy Air Post Stamps of 1945-48 Overprinted Type "h" in Black.

1949-52

C20	AP59	10 l car rose	6	6
C21	AP60	25 l brn ('50)	12	25
C22	AP59	50 l violet	18	25
C23	AP65	100 l green	22	25
C24	AP65	300 l lil rose ('50)	4.00	6.50
C25	AP65	500 l ultra ('50)	4.00	7.00
C26	AP65	1000 l dk brn ('52)	9.50	17.50
		Nos. C20-C26 (7)	18.08	31.81

No. C26 is found in two perforations: 14 and 14x13.

OCCUPATION SPECIAL DELIVERY STAMPS.

Special Delivery Stamps of Italy 1946-48 Overprinted Type "c" in Black.

1947-48   Perf. 14   Wmk. 277

E1	SD9	15 l dk car rose	15	15
E2	SD8	25 l brt red org ('48)	5.00	4.00
E3	SD8	30 l dp vio	40	90
E4	SD9	60 l car rose ('48)	4.00	10.00

Italy No. E26, Overprinted Type "d."

1948

E5	A272	35 l violet	2.00	3.00

Italy No. E25, Overprinted Type "h."

1950

E6	SD9	60 l car rose	1.00	75

Italy No. E32 Overprinted Type "k."

1952

E7	SD8	50 l lil rose	1.00	75

OCCUPATION AUTHORIZED DELIVERY STAMPS.

Authorized Delivery Stamp of Italy, 1946 Overprinted Type "a" in Black.

1947   Perf. 14   Wmk. 277

EY1	AD3	11 dk brn	6	6

Italy, No. EY7 Overprinted in Black

EY2	AD4	8 l brt red	1.50	45

Italy, No. EY8, Overprinted Type "a" in Black.

1949

EY3	AD4	15 l violet	3.00	50

Same, Overprinted Type "h" in Black.

EY4	AD4	15 l violet	50	5

Italy No. EY9 Overprinted Type "h" in Black.

1952

EY5	AD4	20 l rose vio	65	6

OCCUPATION POSTAGE DUE STAMPS.

Postage Due Stamps of Italy, 1945-47, Overprinted Type "a" in Black.

1947   Perf. 14   Wmk. 277

J1	D9	1 l red org	12	18
J2	D10	2 l dk grn	6	6
J3	D9	5 l violet	60	18
J4	D9	10 l dk bl	80	25
J5	D10	20 l car	4.00	30
J6	D10	50 l aqua	60	5
		Nos. J1-J6 (6)	6.18	1.02

Same Overprint on Postage Due Stamps of Italy, 1947.

1949

J7	D10	1 l red org	15	25
J8	D10	3 l carmine	45	85
J9	D10	4 l brown	2.50	5.00
J10	D10	5 l violet	15.00	5.00
J11	D10	6 l vio bl	4.75	10.00
J12	D10	8 l rose vio	4.75	10.00
J13	D10	10 l dp bl	18.00	75
J14	D10	15 l gldn brn	4.75	10.00
J15	D10	20 l lil rose	4.25	25
		Nos. J7-J15 (9)	54.60	42.10

Postage Due Stamps of Italy, 1947-54, Overprinted Type "h" in Black.

1949-54

J16	D10	1 l red org	5	5
J17	D10	2 l dk grn	5	5
J18	D10	3 l car ('54)	8	20
J19	D10	5 l violet	10	10
J20	D10	5 l violet	10	10
J21	D10	6 l vio bl ('50)	8	8
J22	D10	8 l rose vio ('50)	8	7
J23	D10	10 l dp bl	5	5
J24	D10	12 l gldn brn ('50)	50	25
J25	D10	20 l lil rose	75	18
J26	D10	25 l dk red ('54)	3.00	2.00
J27	D10	50 l aqua ('52)	1.10	5
J28	D10	100 l org yel ('52)	1.75	18
J29	D10	500 l dp bl & dk car ('52)	10.00	6.50
		Nos. J16-J29 (13)	17.64	9.76

OCCUPATION PARCEL POST STAMPS.

These stamps were used by affixing them to the waybill so that one half remained on it following the parcel, the other half staying on the receipt given the sender. Almost all obtainable used copies are right halves. Complete stamps were obtainable canceled, probably to order.

Both unused and used prices are for complete stamps.

Parcel Post Stamps of Italy, 1946-48, Overprinted in Black:

A.M.G.   A.M.G.
F.T.T.   F.T.T.

1947-48   Perf. 13½   Wmk. 277

Q1	PP4	1 l gldn brn	25	40
Q2	PP4	2 l lt bl grn	35	50
Q3	PP4	3 l red org	40	60
Q4	PP4	4 l gray blk	50	75
Q5	PP4	5 l lil rose ('48)	1.40	2.00
Q6	PP4	10 l violet	2.75	4.00
Q7	PP4	20 l lil brn	4.00	6.00
Q8	PP4	50 l rose red	6.50	9.00
Q9	PP4	100 l sapphire	8.00	11.50
Q10	PP4	200 l grn ('48)	325.00	450.00
Q11	PP4	300 l brn car ('48)	160.00	225.00
Q12	PP4	500 l brn ('48)	95.00	140.00
		Nos. Q1-Q12 (12)	604.15	849.75

Halves Used

Q1-Q4		5
Q5		20
Q6-Q7		10
Q8		15
Q9		30
Q10		7.50
Q11		6.00
Q12		2.50

Parcel Post Stamps of Italy, 1946-54, Overprinted in Black:

AMG-FTT   AMG-FTT

1949-54

Q13	PP4	1 l gldn brn ('51)	80	1.00
Q14	PP4	2 l lt bl grn ('51)	15	25
Q15	PP4	3 l red org ('51)	15	25
Q16	PP4	4 l gray blk ('51)	20	30
Q17	PP4	5 l lil rose	28	35
Q18	PP4	10 l violet	35	25
Q19	PP4	20 l lil brn	40	25
Q20	PP4	30 l plum ('52)	50	60
Q21	PP4	50 l rose red ('50)	60	25
Q22	PP4	100 l saph ('52)	1.50	2.00
Q23	PP4	200 l green	16.00	22.50
Q24	PP4	300 l brn car ('50)	47.50	65.00
Q25	PP4	500 l brn ('51)	20.00	27.50

Perf. 13x13½

Q26	PP5	1000 l ultra ('54)	95.00	135.00
		Nos. Q13-Q26 (14)	183.43	255.50

Halves Used

Q13-Q16, Q18, Q20		5
Q17		5
Q19, Q22		8
Q21		6
Q23		10
Q24		70
Q25		80
Q26		1.50

Pairs of Q18 exist with 5mm between overprints instead of 11mm. Price $90.

PARCEL POST AUTHORIZED DELIVERY STAMPS.

For the payment of a special tax for the authorized delivery of parcels privately instead of through the post office.

Both unused and used prices are for complete stamps.

Parcel Post Authorized Delivery Stamps of Italy 1953 Overprinted in Black:

AMG-FTT   AMG-FTT

1953   Wmk. 277

QY1	PAD1	40 l org red	5.00	10.00
QY2	PAD1	50 l ultra	5.00	10.00
QY3	PAD1	75 l brown	5.00	10.00
QY4	PAD1	110 l lil rose	5.00	10.00

Halves Used

QY1		15
QY2		20
QY3-QY4		35

ZONE B.
Issued by the Jugoslav Military Government.

100 Centesimi = 1 Lira
100 Paras = 1 Dinar (1949)

Issues for Istria and the Slovene Coast (Zone B) of 1945-47 are listed following Jugoslavia.

Stylized Gymnast and Arms of Trieste
A1

Lithographed.

1948   Perf. 10½x11   Unwmkd.

1	A1	100 l dp car, yel (Italian inscriptions)	2.75	3.25
2	A1	100 l dp car, yel (Croatian inscriptions)	3.00	3.25
3	A1	100 l dp car, yel (Slovene inscriptions)	3.00	3.25
a.		Strip of 3 (#1-3)	15.00	16.00

May Day. Nos. 1-3 printed se-tenant.

Clasped Hands, Hammer and Sickle
A2

1949   Photogravure   Perf. 11½x12½

4	A2	10 l grnsh blk & ol grn	60	45

Issued to publicize Labor Day, May 1, 1949.

"V.U.J.A. S.T.T." are the initials of "Vojna Uprava Jugoslovenske Armije, Slobodna Teritorija Trsta" (Military Administration Jugoslav Army, Free Territory of Trieste).

Stamps of Jugoslavia, 1945-47 Overprinted in Carmine or Ultramarine

STT VUJA

1949, Aug. 15   Perf. 12½

5	A22	50p ol gray	18	18
6	A22	1d bl grn	18	18
7	A24	2d scar (U)	18	18
8	A25	3d dl red (U)	35	45
9	A24	4d dk bl	22	28
10	A25	5d dk bl	22	28
11	A26	9d rose vio (U)	35	45
12	A23	12d ultra	1.75	1.40
13	A22	16d blue	1.50	65
14	A23	20d org ver (U)	2.75	90
		Nos. 5-14 (10)	7.68	4.95

The letters of the overprint are set closer and in one line on Nos. 7 and 9.

Jugoslavia Nos. 266 and 267 Overprinted in VUJA - STT
Carmine
Burelage in Color of Stamp.

1949

15	A58	5d blue	9.00	11.00
16	A58	12d brown	9.00	11.00

Issued to commemorate the 75th anniversary of the formation of the Universal Postal Union.

Jugoslavia, Nos. 269 to 272, Overprinted in Carmine VUJA - STT

1950

17	A60	2d bl grn	45	65
18	A60	3d car rose	75	1.10
19	A60	5d blue	2.50	2.75
20	A60	10d dp org	8.00	4.50

TRIESTE

Workers Carrying Tools and Flag
A3

Peasant on Ass
A4

1950, May 1			Photogravure		
21	A3	3d violet		45	65
22	A3	10d carmine		75	1.10

Issued to publicize Labor Day, May 1, 1950.

1950 Perf. 12½. Unwmkd.
Designs: 1d, Cockerel. 2d, Goose. 3d, Bees and honeycomb. 5d, Oxen. 10d, Turkey. 15d, Goats. 20d, Silkworms.

23	A4	50p dk gray	6	20
24	A4	1d brn car	10	28
25	A4	2d dp bl	15	32
26	A4	3d org brn	35	55
27	A4	5d aqua	30	60
28	A4	10d brown	90	80
29	A4	15d violet	6.00	10.00
30	A4	20d dk grn	1.50	2.50
		Nos. 23-30 (8)	9.36	15.25

1951 Designs as before
31	A4	1d org brn	15	10
32	A4	3d rose brn	15	10

Worker
A5

1951, May 1				
33	A5	3d dk red	90	90
34	A5	10d brn ol	1.25	1.35

Labor Day.

Pietro Paolo Vergerio
A7

Bicycle Race
A8

1951, Oct. 21			Lithographed	
37	A7	5d blue	1.25	65
38	A7	10d claret	1.25	65
39	A7	20d sepia	1.25	65

Types of Jugoslavia, 1951, Overprinted "STT VUJA."
1951, Nov.
40	A81	10d brn org (V)	1.50	1.35
41	A81	12d grnsh blk (C)	1.50	1.35

1952 Photogravure.
Designs: 10d, Soccer. 15d, Rowing. 28d, Sailing. 50d, Volleyball. 100d, Diving.

42	A8	5d brown	30	22
43	A8	10d bl grn	38	45
44	A8	15d car rose	45	55
45	A8	28d vio bl	1.25	70
46	A8	50d claret	1.50	75
47	A8	100d dk bl gray	3.00	3.00
		Nos. 42-47 (6)	6.88	5.67

Marshal Tito
A9   A10

1952, May 25			Perf. 11½	
48	A9	15d dk brn	1.25	90
49	A10	28d red brn	1.50	1.35
50	A9	50d dk gray grn	1.75	1.75

60th birthday of Marshal Tito.

Types of Jugoslavia 1952 Overprinted in Carmine "STT VUJNA."
1952, July 26 Perf. 12½
51	A90	5d dk brn & sal, cr	90	1.40
52	A90	10d dk grn & grn	90	1.40
53	A90	15d dk brn & bl, lil	90	1.75
54	A90	28d dk brn & buff, cr	2.00	3.00
55	A90	50d dk brn & buff, yel	8.00	7.50
56	A90	100d ind & lil, pink	15.00	22.50
		Nos. 51-56 (6)	27.70	37.55

Issued to publicize the 15th Olympic Games, Helsinki, 1952. Nos. 52, 54 and 56 are inscribed in Cyrillic characters. The added "N" in "VUJNA" stands for "Narodna" (Peoples'). See note after No. 4.
Nos. 51-56 exist imperf. Price of set, $375.

Jugoslavia Nos. 365 to 367 Overprinted in Carmine "STT VUJNA."
1952, Sept. 13
57	A91	15d dp cl	90	1.25
58	A91	28d dk brn	1.40	1.50
59	A91	50d gray	5.50	3.75

Issued to commemorate the 10th anniversary of the formation of the Jugoslav navy.

Jugoslavia No. 358 Overprinted "STT VUJA" in Blue.
1952, June 22
| 60 | A89 | 15d brt rose | 1.25 | 65 |

Children's Week.

Jugoslavia Nos. 369-372 Overprinted "VUJNA STT" in Blue or Carmine
1952, Nov. 4
61	A93	15d red brn (Bl)	90	1.00
62	A93	15d dk vio bl	90	1.00
63	A93	15d dk brn	90	1.00
64	A93	15d bl grn	90	1.00

Issued to publicize the 6th Jugoslavia Communist Party Congress, Zagreb, 1952.

Anchovies and Starfish
A11
Photogravure.

1952 Perf. 11x11½ Unwmkd.
65	A11	15d red brn	1.50	2.25
a.	Souvenir sheet, imperf.		11.50	16.50

Capodistria Philatelic Exhibition, Nov. 29-Dec. 7, 1952.
No. 65a contains a 50d dark blue green stamp, type A11, imperf. Ornaments and inscriptions in lower margin. Size: 48½x 69½mm. Sold for 85d.

Stamps or Types of Jugoslavia Overprinted "STT VUJA" in Various Colors.
1953, Feb. 3 Perf. 12½
66	A94	15d brn car (Bl)	45	22
67	A94	30d chlksy bl (R)	1.10	45

Issued to commemorate the 10th anniversary of the death of Nikola Tesla.

1953
68	A68	1d gray	3.00	2.25
69	A68	2d car (V)	60	65
70	A68	3d rose red (R)	60	45
71	A68	5d orange	60	65
72	A68	10d emer (G)	60	65
73	A68	15d rose red	1.25	1.10
74	A68	30d bl (Bl)	2.50	2.25
75	A68	50d grnsh bl (Bl)	4.75	3.00
		Nos. 68-75 (8)	13.90	11.00

Nos. 69, 71 and 73 are lithographed.

1953, Apr. 21 Perf. 11½
76	A95	15d dk ol grn (O)	45	65
77	A95	30d dk chlky bl (O)	45	65
78	A95	50d hn brn	1.40	1.35

Issued in honor of the United Nations.

Automobile Climbing Mt. Lovcen—A12

1953, June 2 Perf. 12½
79	A12	15d ocher & choc	45	22
80	A12	30d lt bl grn & ol grn	45	45
81	A12	50d sal & dp plum	75	90
82	A12	70d bl & dk bl	1.50	1.50

Issued to publicize the International Automobile and Motorcycle Races, 1953.

Stamps or Types of Jugoslavia Overprinted "STT VUJNA" in Various Colors.
1953, July 8 Engraved
| 83 | A97 | 50d grnsh gray (C) | 2.50 | 1.80 |

Issued to commemorate Marshal Tito's election to the presidency, January 14, 1953.

1953, July 31
| 84 | A98 | 15d gray & grn (C) | 2.50 | 3.25 |

Issued to publicize the 38th Esperanto Congress, Zagreb, July 25–Aug. 1, 1953. See No. C21.

1953, Sept. 5
| 85 | A101 | 15d bl (C) | 7.50 | 8.00 |

Issued to commemorate the 10th anniversary of the liberation of Istria and the Slovene coast.

1953, Oct. 3
| 86 | A102 | 15d gray | 1.50 | 2.25 |

Issued to commemorate the centenary of the death of Branko Radicevic, poet.

1953, Nov. 29 Perf. 12½x12
87	A103	15d gray vio (V)	60	55
88	A103	30d cl (Br)	1.00	90
89	A103	50d dl bl grn (Dk Bl)	1.75	2.00

Issued to commemorate the 10th anniversary of the first republican legislative assembly of Jugoslavia.

1954, Mar. 5 Perf. 12½
90	A68	5d org (V)	75	45
91	A68	10d yel grn (C)	45	35
92	A68	15d rose red (G)	75	45

Types of Jugoslavia, 1954, Overprinted in Carmine "STT VUJNA."
1954 Photogravure. Perf. 11½
93	A104	2d red brn, sl & cr	25	22
94	A104	5d gray & dk yel brn	25	20
95	A104	10d ol grn & dk org brn	25	28
96	A104	15d dp bl grn & dk org brn	28	25
97	A104	17d gray brn, dk brn & cr	25	30
98	A104	25d bis, gray bl & org yel	50	55
99	A105	30d lil & dk brn	50	75
100	A105	35d rose vio & bl blk	50	75
101	A105	50d yel grn & vio brn	1.10	90
102	A105	65d org brn & gray blk	2.75	2.00
103	A105	70d bl & org brn	5.50	5.50
104	A105	100d brt bl & blk brn	16.00	15.00
		Nos. 93-104 (12)	28.13	26.72

Types of Jugoslavia 1954 Overprinted "STT VUJNA" in Various Colors.
1954, Oct. 8 Perf. 12½
105	A107	15d mar, red, ocher & dk bl (Bk)	30	30
106	A107	30d dk bl, grn, sal buff & choc (G)	60	60
107	A107	50d brn, bis & red (G)	1.50	1.40
108	A107	70d dk grn, gray grn & choc (R)	2.00	2.25

Issued to commemorate the 150th anniversary of the first Serbian insurrection.

AIR POST STAMPS.

AP1

Perf. 12½x11½
1948, Oct. 17 Photo. Unwmkd.
C1	AP1	25l gray	1.00	1.00
C2	AP1	50l orange	1.00	1.00

Issued to publicize an Economic Exhibition at Capodistria, October 17–24.

Fishermen
AP2

Farmer and Pack Mule
AP3

Mew over Chimneys
AP4

1949, June 1 Perf. 11½
C3	AP2	1l grnsh bl	30	45
C4	AP3	2l red brn	21	65
C5	AP2	5l blue	45	65
C6	AP2	10l purple	2.00	1.75
C7	AP2	25l brown	2.50	2.00
C8	AP3	50l ol grn	1.50	1.40

TRIESTE—TRIPOLITANIA

C9	AP4	100 l dk vio brn	2.50	3.25
		Nos. C3-C9 (7)	9.70	10.90

Italian inscriptions on Nos. C5 and C6, Croatian on C7, Slavonic on No. C8.
Nos. C3–C4 exist imperf. Price, each $135.

Nos. C3 to C9 Surcharged "DIN", or New Value and "DIN" in Various Colors

1949, Nov. 5

C10	AP2	1d on 1 l grnsh bl (Bk)	15	22
C11	AP3	2d on 2 l red brn (Br)	15	22
C12	AP2	5d on 5 l bl (Bl)	30	22
C13	AP3	10d on 10 l pur (V)	45	45
C14	AP2	15d on 25 l brn (Br)	6.00	7.50
C15	AP3	20d on 50 l ol grn (Gr)	1.50	1.40
C16	AP4	30d on 100 l dk vio brn (Bk)	2.25	1.50
		Nos. C10-C16 (7)	10.80	11.51

On Nos. C14 and C15 the original value is obliterated by a framed block, on No. C16 by four parallel lines.

Souvenir Sheet.
Jugoslavia No. C33 Overprinted "VUJA - STT" in Carmine and Lilac Rose Network.

1950 Perf. 11½x12½

C17	AP15	10d lil rose, sheet	55.00	65.00
a.		Imperf.	55.00	65.00

Main Square, Capodistria
AP5

Lighthouse, Pirano
AP6

Design: 25d, Hotel, Portorose.

Photogravure.

1952 Perf. 12½. Unmkd.

C18	AP5	5d brown	17.50	17.50
C19	AP6	15d brt bl	12.00	13.50
C20	AP7	25d green	9.00	13.50

Issued to commemorate the 75th anniversary (in 1949) of the formation of the Universal Postal Union.

Type of Jugoslavia, 1953
Overprinted "STT VUJNA" in Carmine.

1953, July 31

C21	AP21	300d vio & grn	200.00	150.00

38th Esperanto Congress, Zagreb, July 25–Aug. 1, 1953.
Sheets of 12 (12,000 stamps) and sheets of 8 (3,000 stamps in light violet and green).
A private red overprint was applied marginally to 250 sheets of 8: "Esperantski Kongres—38—a Universala Kongreso de Esperanto—Congresso del Esperanto."

Air Post Stamps of Jugoslavia in New Colors Overprinted "STT VUJNA" in Various Colors.

1954 Engraved.

C22	AP16	1d dp pur gray	5	7
C23	AP16	2d brt grn (G)	7	8
C24	AP16	3d red brn (Br)	10	8
C25	AP16	5d chocolate	12	10
C26	AP16	10d bl grn	12	18
C27	AP16	20d brn (Br)	45	32
C28	AP16	30d blue	60	55
C29	AP16	50d ol blk	90	80
C30	AP16	100d scar (R)	2.25	1.40
C31	AP16	200d dk bl vio (Bl)	4.50	3.50

Perf. 11x11½

C32	AP17	500d org (Br)	12.00	16.00
		Nos. C22-C32 (11)	21.16	23.08

POSTAGE DUE STAMPS.
Jugoslavia Nos. J51 to J55 Overprinted "S T T VUJA" in Two Lines in Ultramarine or Carmine.

1949 Perf. 12½ Unwmkd.

J1	D7	50p dp org	30	45
J2	D7	1d orange	30	45
J3	D7	2d dk bl (C)	60	45
J4	D7	3d yel grn (C)	90	45
J5	D7	5d brt pur (C)	1.50	90
		Nos. J1-J5 (5)	3.60	2.70

Croakers
D1

Anchovies
D2

1950 Photogravure

J6	D1	50p brn org	30	45
J7	D1	1d dp ol grn	1.25	1.80
J8	D2	2d dk grnsh bl	1.75	2.75
J9	D1	3d dk vio bl	1.25	1.80
J10	D2	5d plum	6.00	9.00
		Nos. J6-J10 (5)	10.55	15.80

Jugoslavia Nos. J67-J74 Overprinted "STT VUJNA" in Blue or Carmine.

1952

J11	D7	1d brn (Bl)	12	18
J12	D7	2d emerald	12	18
J13	D7	5d blue	60	45
J14	D7	10d scar (Bl)	25	28
J15	D7	20d purple	30	28
J16	D7	30d org yel (Bl)	42	45
J17	D7	50d ultra	90	90
J18	D7	100d dp plum (Bl)	2.10	1.75
		Nos. J11-J18 (8)	4.81	4.47

POSTAL TAX STAMPS.
Jugoslavia No. RA5 Surcharged in Blue "VUJA S.T.T. 2 L"

1948 Perf. 12½ Unwmkd.

RA1	PT4	2 l on 50p brn & scar	7.50	8.00

Obligatory on all mail from May 22 to 30, 1948.

Jugoslavia No. RA7 Overprinted "VUJA STT" in Black

1950, July 3

RA2	PT6	50p red & brn	90	90

Jugoslavia No. RA9 Overprinted in Black "STT VUJA."

1951

RA3	PT8	50p vio bl & red	7.50	10.00

Jugoslavia No. RA10 Overprinted "STT VUJNA" in Carmine.

1952

RA4	PT9	50p gray & car	45	45

Type of Jugoslavia, 1953, Overprinted "STT VUJNA" in Blue.

1953

RA5	PT10	2d org brn & red	60	90

The tax of Nos. RA1-RA5 was for the Red Cross.

POSTAL TAX DUE STAMPS.
Jugoslavia No. RAJ2 Surcharged Like No. RA1 in Scarlet.

1948 Perf. 12½ Unwmkd.

RAJ1	PT4	2 l on 50p bl grn & scar	125.00	180.00

Jugoslavia No. RAJ4 Overprinted "VUJA STT" in Black.

1950, July 3

RAJ2	PT6	50p red & vio	1.25	1.75

Jugoslavia No. RAJ6 Overprinted in Black "STT VUJA."

1951

RAJ3	PT8	50p emer & red	125.00	180.00

Jugoslavia No. RAJ7 Overprinted "STT VUJNA" in Carmine.

1952

RAJ4	PTD3	50p gray & car	90	90

Type of Jugoslavia, 1953, Overprinted "STT VUJNA" in Blue.

1953

RAJ5	PT10	2d lil rose & red	90	1.35

TRIPOLITANIA
(trē'pō-lê-tä'nyä)

LOCATION — In northern Africa, bordering on Mediterranean Sea.
GOVT. — A former Italian Colony.
AREA — 350,000 sq. mi. (approx.).
POP. — 570,716 (1921)
CAPITAL — Tripoli.

Formerly a Turkish province, Tripolitania became part of Italian Libya. See Libya.

100 Centesimi = 1 Lira

Propaganda of the Faith Issue.
Italian Stamps of 1923 Overprinted **TRIPOLITANIA**

1923, Oct. 24 Perf. 14 Wmk. 140

1	A68	20c ol grn & brn org	1.75	6.50
2	A68	30c cl & brn org	1.75	6.50
3	A68	50c vio & brn org	1.25	5.00
4	A68	1 l bl & brn org	1.25	5.00

Fascisti Issue.
Italian Stamps of 1923 Overprinted in Red or Black **TRIPOLITANIA**

1923, Oct. 29 Unwmkd.

5	A69	10c dk grn (R)	1.10	4.50
6	A69	30c dk vio (R)	1.10	4.50
7	A69	1 l brn car	1.10	4.50

Wmkd. Crown. (140)

8	A70	1 l blue	1.10	4.50
9	A70	2 l brown	1.10	4.50
10	A71	5 l blk & bl (R)	2.00	13.00
		Nos. 5-10 (6)	7.50	35.50

Manzoni Issue.
Stamps of Italy, 1923, Overprinted in Red **TRIPOLITANIA**

1924, Apr. 1 Perf. 14 Wmk. 140

11	A72	10c brn red & blk	50	2.25
12	A72	15c bl grn & blk	50	2.25
13	A72	30c blk & sl	50	2.25
14	A72	50c dp grn & blk	50	2.25
15	A72	1 l bl & blk	10.00	35.00
16	A72	5 l vio & blk	250.00	500.00
		Nos. 11-16 (6)	262.00	544.00

On Nos. 15 and 16 the overprint is placed vertically at the left side.

Victor Emmanuel Issue.
Italy Nos. 175-177 Overprinted **TRIPOLITANIA**

1925-26 Perf. 11, 13½. Unwmkd.

17	A78	60c brn car, perf. 11	30	1.75
18	A78	1 l dk bl, perf. 13½	1.25	9.00
a.		Perf. 11	35	1.75
19	A78	1.25 l dk bl, perf. 13½ ('26)	60	5.50
a.		Perf. 11	250.00	350.00

Saint Francis of Assisi Issue.
Italy Nos. 178-180 Overprinted **TRIPOLITANIA**

1926, Apr. 12 Perf. 14 Wmk. 140

20	A79	20c gray grn	75	2.25
21	A80	40c dk vio	75	2.25
22	A81	60c red brn	75	2.25

Italy No. 182 and Type of A83 **Tripolitania**
Overprinted in Red Unwmkd.

23	A82	1.25 l dk bl	75	2.25
24	A83	5 l +2.50 l ol grn	3.00	9.00
		Nos. 20-24 (5)	6.00	18.00

Volta Issue.
Type of Italy, 1927, **Tripolitania** Overprinted

1927, Oct. 10 Perf. 14 Wmk. 140

25	A84	20c purple	2.00	5.50
26	A84	50c dp org	2.00	3.50
a.		Dbl. ovpt.	12.00	
27	A84	1.25 l brt bl	3.50	9.00

Monte Cassino Issue.
Types of Italy, 1929, Overprinted in Red or Blue **TRIPOLITANIA**

1929, Oct. 14

28	A96	20c dk grn (R)	1.25	4.50
29	A96	25c red org (Bl)	1.25	4.50
30	A98	50c +10c crim (Bl)	1.25	4.50
31	A98	75c +15c ol brn (R)	1.25	4.50
32	A96	1.25 l +25c dk vio (R)	3.50	9.00
33	A98	5 l +1 l saph (R)	3.50	9.00

Overprinted in Red **Tripolitania**
Unwmkd.

34	A100	10 l +2 l gray brn	3.50	9.00

Royal Wedding Issue.
Type of Italy, 1930, **TRIPOLITANIA** Overprinted

1930, Mar. 17 Wmk. 140

35	A101	20c yel grn	50	1.75
36	A101	50c +10c dp org	60	3.25
37	A101	1.25 l +25c rose red	65	4.00

Ferrucci Issue.
Types of Italy, 1930, Overprinted in Red or Blue **TRIPOLITANIA**

1930, July 26

38	A102	20c vio (R)	60	1.50
39	A103	25c dk grn (R)	60	1.50
40	A103	50c blk (R)	60	1.50
41	A103	1.25 l dp bl (R)	60	1.50
42	A104	5 l +2 l dp car (Bl)	1.50	2.75
		Nos. 38-42 (5)	3.90	8.75

Virgil Issue.
Types of Italy, 1930, Overprinted in Red or Blue **TRIPOLITANIA**

1930, Dec. 4 Photogravure

43	A106	15c vio blk	30	1.75
44	A106	20c org brn	30	1.75
45	A106	25c dk grn	30	1.40
46	A106	30c lt brn	30	1.75
47	A106	50c dl vio	30	1.40
48	A106	75c rose red	30	1.75
49	A106	1.25 l gray bl	30	1.75

TRIPOLITANIA

50	A106	51 +1.50 l dk vio	2.00	5.50
51	A106	10 l +2.50 l ol brn	2.00	5.50
		Nos. 43-51 (9)	6.10	22.55

Engraved.
Unwmkd.

Saint Anthony of Padua Issue.
Types of Italy, 1931,
Overprinted in Blue or Red
TRIPOLITANIA

1931, May 7   Photo.   Wmk. 140

52	A116	20c brn (Bl)	50	2.25
53	A116	25c grn (R)	50	2.25
54	A118	30c gray brn (R)	50	2.25
55	A118	50c dl vio (Bl)	50	1.40
56	A120	1.25 l sl bl (R)	50	2.25

Overprinted **Tripolitania**
in Red or Black
Engraved.
Unwmkd.

57	A121	75c blk (R)	50	2.25
58	A122	51 +2.50 l dk brn (Bk)	3.00	10.00
		Nos. 52-58 (7)	6.00	22.65

Native Village Scene — A14

Wmk. 140

1934, Oct. 16 Wmkd. Crowns. (140)

73	A14	5c ol grn & brn	1.50	4.25
74	A14	10c brn & blk	1.50	4.25
75	A14	20c scar & ind	1.50	4.25
76	A14	50c pur & brn	1.50	4.25
77	A14	60c org brn & ind	1.50	4.25
78	A14	1.25 l dk bl & grn	1.50	4.25
		Nos. 73-78 (6)	9.00	25.50

Issued to commemorate the 2nd Colonial Arts Exhibition, Naples. See Nos. C43-C48.

SEMI-POSTAL STAMPS.

Many issues of Italy and Italian Colonies include one or more semipostal denominations. To avoid splitting sets, these issues are generally listed as regular postage, airmail, etc., unless all values carry a surtax.

Holy Year Issue.
Italian Stamps of 1924
Overprinted in Black or Red
TRIPOLITANIA

1925   Wmkd. Crowns. (140)   Perf. 12

B1	SP4	20c +10c dk grn & brn	1.00	3.50
B2	SP4	30c +15c dk brn & vio	1.00	3.50
B3	SP4	50c +25c vio & brn	1.00	3.50
B4	SP4	60c +30c dp rose & brn	1.00	3.50
B5	SP8	1 l +50c dp bl & vio (R)	1.00	3.50
B6	SP8	5 l +2.50 l org brn & vio (R)	1.00	3.50
		Nos. B1-B6 (6)	6.00	21.00

Colonial Institute Issue.

Peace Substituting Spade for Sword—SP1

1926, June 1   Typo.   Perf. 14

B7	SP1	5c +5c brn	20	1.75
B8	SP1	10c +5c ol brn	20	1.75
B9	SP1	20c +5c bl grn	20	1.75
B10	SP1	40c +5c brn red	20	1.75
B11	SP1	60c +5c org	20	1.75
B12	SP1	1 l +5c bl	20	1.75
		Nos. B7-B12 (6)	1.20	10.50

The surtax was for the Italian Colonial Institute.

Fiera Campionaria Tripoli
See Libya for stamps with this inscription.

Types of Italian Semi-Postal Stamps of 1926
Overprinted **TRIPOLITANIA**

1927, Apr. 21 Perf. 11 Unwmkd.

B19	SP10	40c +20c dk brn & blk	1.00	3.50
B20	SP10	60c +30c brn red & ol brn	1.00	3.50
B21	SP10	1.25 l +60c dp bl & blk	1.00	3.50
B22	SP10	5 l +2.50 l dk grn & blk	1.50	7.25

The surtax was for the charitable work of the Voluntary Militia for Italian National Defense.

Allegory of Fascism and Victory — SP2

1928, Oct. 15   Wmk. 140

B29	SP2	20c +5c bl grn	60	2.25
B30	SP2	30c +5c red	60	2.25
B31	SP2	50c +10c pur	60	2.25
B32	SP2	1.25 l +20c dk bl	60	2.25

Issued to commemorate the 46th anniversary of the Societa Africana d'Italia. The surtax aided that society.

Types of Italian Semi-Postal Stamps of 1928
Overprinted **TRIPOLITANIA**

1929, Mar. 4   Perf. 11   Unwmkd.

B33	SP10	30c +10c red & blk	1.00	3.50
B34	SP10	50c +20c vio & blk	1.00	3.50
B35	SP10	1.25 l +50c brn & bl	1.50	5.50
B36	SP10	5 l +2 l ol grn & blk	1.50	5.50

The surtax on these stamps was for the charitable work of the Voluntary Militia for Italian National Defense.

Types of Italian Semi-Postal Stamps of 1926, Overprinted in Black or Red
TRIPOLITANIA

1930, Oct. 20

B50	SP10	30c +10c dp grn & bl grn (Bk)	2.25	9.00
B51	SP10	50c +10c dk grn & vio (R)	2.25	9.00
B52	SP10	1.25 l +30c blk brn & red brn (R)	2.75	13.00
B53	SP10	5 l +1.50 l ind & grn (R)	9.00	35.00

Ancient Arch — SP3

1930, Nov. 27 Photo. Wmk. 140

B54	SP3	50c +20c ol brn	90	3.50
B55	SP3	1.25 l +20c dp bl	90	3.50
B56	SP3	1.75 l +20c grn	90	3.50
B57	SP3	2.55 l +50c pur	1.40	5.75
B58	SP3	5 l +1 l dp car	1.40	5.75
		Nos. B54-B58 (5)	5.50	22.00

Issued in commemoration of the 25th anniversary of the Italian Colonial Agricultural Institute. The surtax was for the benefit of that institution.

AIR POST STAMPS.
Ferrucci Issue.
Type of Italian Air Post Stamps of 1930
Overprinted in Blue or Red
TRIPOLITANIA

1930, July 26 Perf. 14 Wmk. 140

C1	AP7	50c brn vio (Bl)	1.40	3.50
C2	AP7	1 l dk bl (R)	1.40	3.50
C3	AP7	5 l +2 l dp car (Bl)	4.50	10.00

Virgil Issue.
Types of Italian Air Post Stamps, 1930
Overprinted in Red or Blue
TRIPOLITANIA

1930, Dec. 4   Photogravure

C4	AP8	50c dp grn	90	2.25
C5	AP8	1 l rose red	90	2.25

Engraved. Unwmkd.

C6	AP8	7.70 l +1.30 l dk brn	1.75	9.00
C7	AP8	9 l +2 l gray	1.75	9.00

Airplane over Columns of the Basilica, Leptis — AP1

Arab Horseman Pointing at Airplane — AP2

1931-32   Photogravure.   Wmk. 140

C8	AP1	50c rose car	28	12
C9	AP1	60c red org	45	2.25
C10	AP1	75c dp bl ('32)	65	2.25
C11	AP1	80c dl vio	1.40	3.25
C12	AP2	1 l dp bl	40	18
C13	AP2	1.20 l dk brn	1.40	3.25
C14	AP2	1.50 l org red	1.40	2.25
C15	AP2	5 l green	1.40	2.75
		Nos. C8-C15 (8)	7.38	16.30

Airplane over Ruins — AP3

1931, Dec. 7

C16	AP3	50c dp bl	1.40	4.50
C17	AP3	80c violet	1.40	4.50
C18	AP3	1 l gray blk	1.40	4.50
C19	AP3	2 l dp grn	1.75	9.00
C20	AP3	5 l +2 l rose red	4.50	22.50
		Nos. C16-C20 (5)	10.45	45.00

Graf Zeppelin Issue

Mercury, by Giovanni da Bologna, and Zeppelin—AP4

Designs: 31, 121, Mercury. 101, 201, Guido Reni's "Aurora." 51, 151, Arch of Marcus Aurelius.

1933, May 5

C21	AP4	3 l dk brn	7.50	20.00
C22	AP4	5 l purple	7.50	20.00
C23	AP4	10 l dp grn	7.50	20.00
C24	AP4	12 l dp bl	7.50	20.00
C25	AP4	15 l carmine	7.50	20.00
C26	AP4	20 l gray blk	7.50	20.00
		Nos. C21-C26 (6)	45.00	120.00

North Atlantic Flight Issue

Airplane, Lion of St. Mark — AP7

1933, June 1

C27	AP7	19.75 l blk & ol brn	18.00	60.00
C28	AP7	44.75 l dk bl & lt grn	18.00	60.00

Type of 1931 Overprinted

and Surcharged with New Values (except C31).

1934, Jan. 20

C29	AP2	2 l on 5 l org brn	2.25	6.50
C30	AP2	3 l on 5 l grn	2.25	6.50
C31	AP2	5 l ocher	2.25	6.50
C32	AP2	10 l on 5 l rose	2.25	6.50

For use on mail to be carried on a special flight from Rome to Buenos Aires.

Types of Libya 1934 Airmail Issue
Overprinted in Black or Red   CIRCUITO DELLE OASI TRIPOLI MAGGIO 1934-XII

1934, May 1   Wmk. 140

C38	AP4	50c rose red	3.50	7.25
C39	AP4	75c lemon	3.50	7.25
C40	AP4	5 l +1 l brn	3.50	7.25
C41	AP4	10 l +2 l dk bl	150.00	325.00
C42	AP5	25 l +3 l pur	165.00	325.00
		Nos. C38-C42 (5)	325.50	671.75

"Circuit of the Oases".

TRIPOLITANIA—TUNISIA

Plane Shadow on Desert
AP11

Designs: 25c, 50c, 75c, Plane shadow on desert.
80c, 1 l, 2 l, Camel corps.

1934, Oct. 16   Photogravure

C43	AP11	25c sl bl & org red	1.50	4.25
C44	AP11	50c dk grn & ind	1.50	4.25
C45	AP11	75c dk brn & org red	1.50	4.25
C46	AP11	80c org brn & ol grn	1.50	4.25
C47	AP11	1 l scar & org	1.50	4.25
C48	AP11	2 l dk bl & brn	1.50	4.25
	Nos. C43-C48 (6)		9.00	25.50

Second Colonial Arts Exhibition, Naples.

AIR POST SEMI-POSTAL STAMPS.

King Victor Emmanuel III
SPAP1

1934, Nov. 5   Perf. 14   Wmk. 140

CB1	SPAP1	25c +10c gray grn	1.25	3.50
CB2	SPAP1	50c +10c brn	1.25	3.50
CB3	SPAP1	75c +15c rose red	1.25	3.50
CB4	SPAP1	80c +15c blk brn	1.25	3.50
CB5	SPAP1	1 l +20c red brn	1.25	3.50
CB6	SPAP1	2 l +20c brt bl	1.25	3.50
CB7	SPAP1	3 l +25c pur	13.00	35.00
CB8	SPAP1	5 l +25c org	13.00	35.00
CB9	SPAP1	10 l +30c rose vio	13.00	35.00
CB10	SPAP1	25 l +2 l dp grn	13.00	35.00
	Nos. CB1-CB10 (10)		59.50	161.00

Issued in commemoration of the 65th birthday of King Victor Emmanuel III, and for the non-stop flight from Rome to Mogadiscio.

AIR POST SEMI-POSTAL OFFICIAL STAMP.

Type of Air Post Semi-Postal Stamps, 1934
Overprinted Crown and
"SERVIZIO DI STATO" in Black.

1934   Perf. 14.   Wmk. 140

CBO1	SPAP1	25 l +2 l cop red		1,500.

AIR POST SPECIAL DELIVERY STAMPS.

Type of Libya 1934   CIRCUITO DELLE OASI
Overprinted in Black   TRIPOLI
                                 MAGGIO 1934-XII

1934, May 1   Perf. 14   Wmk. 140

CE1	APSD1	2.25 l red org	3.50	7.25
CE2	APSD1	4.50 l +1 l dp rose	3.50	7.25

"Circuit of the Oases."

AUTHORIZED DELIVERY STAMP.

Authorized Delivery Stamp of Italy 1930,
Overprinted   **TRIPOLITANIA**

1931, Mar.   Perf. 14   Wmk. 140

EY1	AD2	10c dk brn	2.75	3.00

TUNISIA

(tů-nĭsh′ĭ-à ; —nĭsh′à)

LOCATION — In northern Africa bordering the Mediterranean Sea.
AREA — 63,362 sq. mi.
GOVT. — Republic.
POP. — 6,070,000 (est. 1977).
CAPITAL — Tunis.

This former French Protectorate became a sovereign state in 1956 and a republic in 1957.

100 Centimes = 1 Franc
1000 Millimes = 1 Dinar (1959)

Coat of Arms
A1

Perf. 14x13½

1888, July 1   Typo.   Unwmkd.

1	A1	1c blue	1.75	1.25
2	A1	2c pur brn, buff	1.75	1.25
3	A1	5c grn, grnsh	10.00	5.25
4	A1	15c bl, grysh	27.50	10.00
5	A1	25c rose	52.50	32.50
6	A1	40c red, straw	47.50	30.00
7	A1	75c car, rose	52.50	35.00
8	A1	5fr gray vio, grysh	275.00	185.00

All values exist imperforate.

Reprints were made in 1893 and some values have been reprinted twice since then. The shades usually differ from those of the originals and some reprints have white gum instead of grayish. All values except the 15c and 40c have been reprinted from retouched designs, having a background of horizontal ruled lines.

      A2   A3

1888-1902

9	A2	1c lil bl	75	30
10	A2	2c pur brn, buff	75	30
11	A2	5c grn, grnsh	3.75	45
12	A2	5c yel grn ('99)	3.50	45
13	A2	10c lav ('93)	3.75	30
14	A2	10c red ('01)	2.75	38
15	A2	15c bl, grysh	27.50	45
16	A2	15c gray ('01)	5.00	55
17	A2	20c red, grn ('99)	8.50	60
18	A2	25c rose	11.50	80
19	A2	25c bl ('01)	6.75	75
20	A2	35c brn ('02)	22.50	75
21	A2	40c red, straw	6.00	75
22	A2	75c car, rose	55.00	55.00
23	A2	75c dp vio, org ('93)	11.00	3.75
24	A3	1fr ol, ol	15.00	3.75
25	A3	2fr dl vio ('02)	85.00	67.50
26	A3	5fr red lil, lav	100.00	45.00
	Bar cancellation			30

Quadrille Paper.

27	A2	15c bl, grysh ('93)	25.00	30
	Nos. 9-27 (19)		424.00	182.13

No. 27 Surcharged **25** in Red

1902

28	A2	25c on 15c bl	1.75	1.40

Mosque at Kairouan   Plowing
A4   A5

Ruins of Hadrian's Aqueduct
A6

Carthaginian Galley
A7

1906-26   Typographed

29	A4	1c blk, yel	5	5
30	A4	2c red brn, straw	5	5
31	A4	3c lt red ('19)	6	5
32	A4	5c grn, grnsh	8	5
33	A4	5c org ('21)	8	5
a.	Booklet pane of 10		5.00	
34	A5	10c red	8	5
35	A5	10c grn ('21)	6	5
36	A5	15c vio, pnksh	45	5
a.	Imperf. (pair)			
37	A5	15c brn, org ('23)	8	5
38	A5	20c brn, pnksh	8	5
	Booklet pane of 10		7.50	
39	A5	25c dp bl	70	12
a.	Imperf. (pair)			
40	A5	25c vio ('21)	22	6
	Booklet pane of 10			
41	A6	30c red brn & vio ('19)	38	35
42	A5	30c pale red ('21)	45	30
43	A6	35c ol grn & brn	5.25	55
44	A6	40c blk brn & red brn	3.00	22
45	A5	40c blk, pnksh ('23)	55	30
46	A5	40c gray grn ('26)	6	5
47	A5	50c bl ('21)	38	28
48	A6	60c ol grn & vio ('21)	30	18
49	A6	60c ver & rose ('25)	20	12
50	A6	75c red brn & red	38	22
51	A6	75c ver & dl red ('26)	10	12
52	A7	1fr red & dk brn	45	15
53	A7	1fr ind & ultra ('25)	12	6
54	A7	2fr brn & ol grn	2.00	75
55	A7	2fr red & red, pink ('25)	28	18
56	A7	5fr vio & bl	5.00	2.75
57	A7	5fr gray vio & grn ('25)	42	7.50
	Nos. 29-57 (29)		21.31	7.66

Stamps and Type of 1888-1902 Surcharged **10**

1908, Sept.

58	A2	10c on 15c gray, lt gray (R)	80	80
59	A3	35c on 1fr ol, ol (R)	90	90
60	A3	40c on 2fr dl vio (Bl)	3.50	3.50
61	A3	75c on 5fr red lil, lav (Bl)	2.50	2.50

No. 36 Surcharged

1911

62	A5	10c on 15c vio, pnksh	75	22

15c.

No. 34 Surcharged

1917, Mar. 16

63	A5	15c on 10c red	45	7
a.	"15c" omitted		10.00	
b.	Double surcharge		25.00	

20c.

No. 36 Surcharged

1921

64	A5	20c on 15c vio, pnksh	45	6

Arab and Ruins of Dougga
A9

1922-26   Typo.   Perf. 13½x14

65	A9	10c green	7	5
a.	Booklet pane of 10		7.50	
66	A9	10c rose ('26)	6	5
67	A9	30c rose	45	45
68	A9	30c lil ('26)	10	5
69	A9	50c blue	30	30
	Nos. 65-69 (5)		98	91

Stamps and Type of 1906 Surcharged in Red or Black:

50
10
   a   b

1923-25

70	A4 (a)	10c on 5c grn, grnsh (R)	12	12
a.	Double surch.		22.50	
71	A5 (b)	20c on 15c vio (Bk)	55	5
72	A5 (b)	30c on 20c yel brn (Bk) ('25)	6	6
73	A5 (b)	50c on 25c bl (R)	60	5

Arab Woman Carrying Water   Grand Mosque at Tunis
A10   A11

Mosque, Tunis   Roman Amphitheater, El Djem (Thysdrus)
A12   A13

TUNISIA

Typographed.
1926-46   Perf. 14x13½

74	A10	1c lt red	5	5
75	A10	2c ol grn	5	5
76	A10	3c sl bl	5	5
77	A10	5c yel grn	5	5
78	A10	10c rose	5	5
78A	A12	10c brn ('46)	5	5
79	A11	15c gray lil	8	5
80	A11	20c dp red	6	5
81	A11	25c gray grn	12	10
82	A11	25c lt vio ('28)	42	5
83	A11	30c lt vio	10	10
84	A11	30c bl grn ('28)	8	6
84A	A12	30c dk ol grn ('46)	6	5
85	A11	40c dp brn	6	5
85A	A12	40c lil rose ('46)	6	5
86	A11	45c emer ('40)	45	45
87	A11	50c black	8	5
88	A12	50c ultra ('34)	22	5
a.		Bklt. pane of 10		
88B	A12	50c emer ('40)	6	5
88C	A12	50c lt bl ('46)	5	5
89	A12	60c red org ('40)	6	6
89A	A12	60c ultra ('45)	5	5
90	A12	65c ultra ('38)	30	12
91	A12	70c dk red ('40)	12	12
92	A12	75c vermilion	20	15
93	A12	75c lil rose ('28)	45	5
94	A12	80c bl grn	45	28
94A	A12	80c blk brn ('40)	12	12
94B	A12	80c emer ('45)	15	15
95	A12	90c org red ('28)	12	5
96	A12	90c ultra ('39)	4.50	4.50
97	A12	1fr brn vio	42	5
97A	A12	1fr rose ('40)	6	5
98	A13	1.05fr dl bl & mag	22	22
98A	A13	1.20fr blk brn ('45)	6	5
99	A13	1.25fr gray bl & dk bl	30	22
100	A13	1.25fr car rose ('40)	65	65
100A	A13	1.30fr bl & vio bl ('42)	12	12
101	A13	1.40fr brt red vio ('40)	42	42
102	A13	1.50fr bl & dp bl ('28)	60	15
102A	A13	1.50fr rose red & red org ('42)	12	12
102B	A12	1.50fr rose lil ('46)	6	5
103	A13	2fr rose & ol brn	75	12
104	A13	2fr red org ('39)	8	5
104A	A12	2fr Prus grn ('45)	8	5
105	A13	2.25fr ultra ('39)	45	45
105A	A13	2.40fr red ('46)	12	12
106	A13	2.50fr grn ('40)	45	45
107	A13	3fr dl bl & org	90	18
108	A13	3fr vio ('39)	7	7
108A	A13	3fr blk brn ('46)	6	5
108B	A13	4fr ultra ('45)	30	30
109	A13	5fr red & grn, *grnsh*	1.20	18
110	A13	5fr dp red brn ('40)	50	50
110A	A13	5fr dk grn ('46)	10	6
110B	A13	6fr dp ultra ('45)	22	12
111	A13	10fr brn red & blk, *bluish*	4.00	90
112	A13	10fr rose pink ('40)	45	45
112A	A13	10fr ver ('46)	12	12
112B	A13	10fr ultra ('46)	22	12
112C	A13	15fr rose lil ('45)	30	30
113	A13	20fr lil & red, *pnksh* ('28)	1.10	50
113A	A13	20fr dk grn ('45)	28	22
113B	A13	25fr ultra ('46)	42	30
113C	A13	50fr car ('45)	75	28
113D	A13	100fr car rose ('45)	90	30
		Nos. 74-113D (66)	25.59	15.46

See also Nos. 152A-162, 185-189, 199-206.

No. 99 Surcharged
with New Value and Bars in Red.

1927, Mar. 24

| 114 | A13 | 1.50fr on 1.25fr gray bl & dk bl | 30 | 18 |

Stamps of 1921-26 Surcharged

≡ 3c

1928, May 1

115	A4	3c on 5c org	6	5
116	A5	10c on 15c brn, *org*	12	12
117	A9	25c on 30c lil	22	12
118	A12	40c on 80c bl grn	28	22
119	A12	50c on 75c ver	30	20
		Nos. 115-119 (5)	98	71

No. 83 Surcharged
≡ 10

1929

| 120 | A11 | 10c on 30c lt vio | 90 | 60 |

No. 120 exists precanceled only. The price in first column is for a stamp which has not been through the post and has original gum. The price in the second column is for a postally used, gumless stamp. See also No. 199a.

No. 85 Surcharged
with New Value and Bars.

1930

| 121 | A11 | 50c on 40c dp brn | 2.50 | 22 |

A14    *A15*

A16    *A17*

Perf. 11, 12½, 12½x13.

1931-34   Engraved.

122	A14	1c dp bl	5	5
123	A14	2c yel brn	5	5
124	A14	3c black	6	5
125	A14	5c yel grn	6	5
126	A14	10c red	6	5
127	A15	15c dl vio	28	12
128	A15	20c dl brn	5	5
129	A15	25c rose red	5	5
130	A15	30c dp grn	6	5
131	A15	40c red org	6	5
132	A16	50c ultra	6	5
133	A16	75c yellow	90	90
134	A16	90c red	30	30
135	A16	1fr ol blk	5	5
136	A16	1fr dk brn ('34)	8	8
137	A17	1.50fr brt ultra	28	28
138	A17	2fr dp brn	22	15
139	A17	3fr bl grn	5.50	5.50
140	A17	5fr car rose	11.00	10.00
a.		Perf. 12½	15.00	7.50
141	A17	10fr black	22.50	20.00
142	A17	20fr dk brn	30.00	27.50
		Nos. 122-142 (21)	71.67	65.38

Stamps of 1928-34 Surcharged in Red or Black:

1f75

■ 0,65

c   *d*

1937   Perf. 14x13½

143	A12	65c on 50c ultra (R)	30	12
a.		Bklt. pane of 10		
b.		Dbl. surch.	37.50	35.00
144	A13	1.75fr on 1.50fr bl & dp bl (R)	2.75	75
a.		Double surch.	35.00	35.00

≡ 3c

≡ 65

e   *f*

1938

| 145 | A12 | 65c on 50c ultra (Bk) | 45 | 12 |
| 146 | A13 | 1.75fr on 1.50fr bl & dp bl (R) | 4.00 | 3.00 |

Stamps of 1938-39 Surcharged in Red or Carmine:

25c   **1 FR.**

≡   **≡**

g   *h*

1940

| 147 | A12 | 25c on 65c ultra (C) | 8 | 5 |
| 148 | A12 | 1fr on 90c ultra (R) | 22 | 12 |

Stamps of 1938-40 Surcharged in Red or Black:

25c   **1F.**

≡   **≡**

i   *k*

1941

149	A12	25c on 65c ultra (R)	12	10
150	A13	1fr on 1.25fr car rose (Bk)	8	8
151	A13	1fr on 1.40fr brt red vio (Bk)	8	7
152	A13	1fr on 2.25fr ultra (R)	8	6

Types of 1926 Without RF.

1941-45   Typo.   Perf. 14x13½

152A	A11	30c car ('45)	10	10
152B	A11	1.20fr int bl ('45)	6	6
153	A12	1.50fr brn red ('42)	28	28
154	A12	2.40fr car & brt pink ('42)	12	12
155	A13	2.50fr dk bl & lt bl	12	12
156	A13	3fr lt vio ('42)	5	5
157	A13	4fr blk & bl vio ('42)	10	10
158	A13	4.50fr ol grn & brn ('42)	10	10
159	A13	5fr brn blk ('42)	10	10
160	A13	10fr lil & dl vio	28	10
161	A13	15fr hn brn ('42)	2.00	2.00
162	A13	20fr lt vio & car	1.10	55
		Nos. 152A-162 (12)	4.41	3.68

One Aim Alone—Victory
A18

Mosque and Olive Tree
A19

1943   Lithographed   Perf. 12

| 163 | A18 | 1.50fr rose | 8 | 8 |

1944-45   Perf. 11½   Unwmkd.

Size: 15½x19 mm.

165	A19	30c yel ('45)	5	5
166	A19	40c org brn ('45)	5	5
168	A19	60c red org ('45)	5	5
169	A19	70c rose pink ('45)	5	5
170	A19	80c Prus grn ('45)	5	5
171	A19	90c vio ('45)	8	8
172	A19	1fr red ('45)	5	5
173	A19	1.50fr dp bl ('45)	5	5

Size: 21¼x26½ mm.

175	A19	2.40fr red	10	10
176	A19	2.50fr red brn	10	10
177	A19	3fr lt vio	10	10
178	A19	4fr brt bl vio	10	10
179	A19	4.50fr ap grn	10	10
180	A19	5fr gray	10	10
181	A19	6fr choc ('45)	25	25
182	A19	10fr brn lake ('45)	28	28
183	A19	15fr cop brn	28	28
184	A19	20fr lilac	38	38
		Nos. 165-184 (18)	2.22	2.22

Types of 1926
1946-47   Typo.   Perf. 14x13½

185	A12	2fr emer ('47)	5	5
186	A12	3fr rose pink	5	5
187	A12	4fr vio ('47)	5	5
188	A13	4fr vio ('47)	5	5
189	A12	6fr car ('47)	5	5
		Nos. 185-189 (5)	25	25

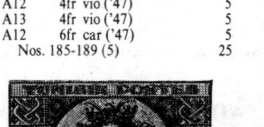

Neptune, Bardo Museum
A20

1947-49   Engraved.   Perf. 13.

190	A20	5fr dk grn & bluish blk	38	38
191	A20	10fr blk brn & bluish blk	22	6
192	A20	18fr dk bl gray & Prus bl ('48)	55	30
193	A20	25fr dk bl & bl grn ('49)	70	22

Detail from Great Mosque at Kairouan—A21

1948-49

194	A21	3fr dk bl grn & bl grn	38	30
195	A21	4fr dk red vio & red vio	30	22
196	A21	6fr red brn & red	8	8
197	A21	10fr pur ('49)	22	5
198	A21	12fr hn brn	38	22
198A	A21	12fr dk brn & org brn ('49)	30	18
198B	A21	15fr dk red ('49)	30	18
		Nos. 194-198B (7)	1.96	1.20

See also No. 225.

Types of 1926.
1947-49   Typo.   Perf. 14x13½

199	A12	2.50fr brn org	7	5
a.		2.50fr brn	60	20
200	A12	4fr brn org ('49)	30	18
201	A12	4.50fr lt ultra	12	5
202	A12	5fr bl ('48)	30	28
203	A12	5fr lt bl grn ('49)	30	12
204	A13	6fr rose red	8	5
205	A12	15fr rose red	30	30
206	A13	25fr red org	50	42
		Nos. 199-206 (8)	1.97	1.55

No. 199a is known only precanceled. See note after No. 120.

TUNISIA

Dam on the Oued Mellegue
A22

Perf. 13

1949, Sept. 1   Engr.   Unwmkd.
207   A22   15fr grnsh blk   1.10   22

U. P. U. Symbols and Tunisian Post Rider
A23

Berber Hermes at Carthage
A24

1949, Oct. 28   Bluish Paper
208   A23   5fr dk grn   75   75
209   A23   15fr red brn   75   75

Universal Post Union, 75th anniversary.
Nos. 208–209 exist imperf. See No. C13.

1950-51
210   A24   15fr red brn   50   35
211   A24   25fr ind ('51)   50   35
212   A24   50fr dk grn ('51)   1.00   35

Horse, Carthage Museum
A25

1950, Dec. 26   Typo.   *Perf. 13½x14*
Size: 21½x17½mm.
213   A25   10c aqua   5   5
214   A25   50c brown   5   5
215   A25   1fr rose lil   5   5
216   A25   2fr gray   12   5
217   A25   4fr vermilion   12   10
218   A25   5fr bl grn   18   10
219   A25   8fr dp bl   28   18
220   A25   12fr red   50   22
221   A25   15fr car rose ('50)   28   10
Nos. 213-221 (9)   1.63   97

See also Nos. 222–224, 226–228.

1951-53   Engraved.   *Perf. 13x14.*
Size: 22x18mm.
222   A25   15fr car rose   42   22
223   A25   15fr ultra ('53)   42   22
224   A25   30fr dp ultra   70   22

Type of 1948–49
1951, Aug. 1   *Perf. 13.*
225   A21   30fr dk bl   60   30

Horse Type of 1950.
1952   Typographed.   *Perf. 13½x14.*
226   A25   3fr brn org   12   10
227   A25   12fr car rose   50   22
228   A25   15fr ultra   28   12

Charles Nicolle
A26

Flags, Pennants and Minaret
A27

1952, Aug. 4   Engr.   *Perf. 13.*
229   A26   15fr blk brn   60   42
230   A26   30fr dp bl   60   42

Issued to commemorate the 50th anniversary of the founding of the Society of Medical Sciences of Tunisia.

1953, Oct. 18
231   A27   8fr blk brn & choc   60   60
232   A27   12fr dk grn & emer   60   60
233   A27   15fr ind & ultra   60   60
234   A27   18fr dk pur & pur   60   60
235   A27   30fr dk car & car   60   60
Nos. 231-235 (5)   3.00   3.00

First International Fair of Tunis.

Courtyard at Sousse
A28

Sidi Bou Maklouf Mosque
A29

Designs: 1fr, Courtyard at Sousse. 2fr, 4fr, Citadel, Takrouna. 5fr, 8fr, View of Tatahouine. 10fr, 12fr, Ruins at Matmata. 15fr, Street Corner, Sidi Bou Said. 20fr, 25fr, Genoese fort, Tabarka. 30fr, 40fr, Bab-El-Khadra gate. 50fr, 75fr, Four-story building, Medenine.

Perf. 13½x13 (A28), 13
1954, May 29
236   A28   50c emerald   5   5
237   A28   1fr car rose   5   5
238   A28   2fr vio brn   8   8
239   A28   4fr turq bl   8   8
240   A28   5fr violet   7   5
241   A28   8fr blk brn   12   12
242   A28   10fr dk bl grn   18   8
243   A28   12fr rose brn   28   8
244   A28   15fr dp ultra   80   8
245   A29   18fr chocolate   60   50
246   A29   20fr dp ultra   55   12
247   A29   25fr indigo   60   12
248   A29   30fr dp cl   55   22
249   A29   40fr dk Prus grn   65   30
250   A29   50fr dk vio   90   12
251   A29   75fr car rose   2.00   1.40

Perf. 14x13½.
Typographed
252   A28   15fr ultra   30   12
Nos. 236-252 (17)   7.80   3.57

Imperforates exist.
See also Nos. 271–287.

Mohammed al-Amin, Bey of Tunis
A30

1954, Oct.   *Perf. 13*
253   A30   8fr bl & dk bl   40   40
254   A30   12fr lil gray & ind   40   40
255   A30   15fr dp car & brn lake   40   40
256   A30   18fr red brn & blk brn   40   40
257   A30   30fr bl grn & dk bl grn   80   80
Nos. 253-257 (5)   2.40   2.40

Theater Drapes, Dove and Sun
A31

1955
258   A31   15fr dk red brn, bl & org   45   45

Essor, Tunisian amateur theatrical society.

Rotary Emblem, Map and Symbols of Punic, Roman, Arab and French Civilizations
A32

1955, May 14   Unwmkd.
259   A32   12fr vio brn & blk brn   45   45
260   A32   15fr vio gray & dk brn   45   45
261   A32   18fr rose vio & dk pur   45   45
262   A32   25fr bl & dp ultra   45   45
263   A32   30fr dk Prus grn & ind   70   70
Nos. 259-263 (5)   2.50   2.50

Issued to commemorate the 50th anniversary of the founding of Rotary International.

Bey of Tunis
A33

Embroiderers
A34

1955   Engraved   *Perf. 13½x13*
264   A33   15fr dk bl   35   8

1955, July 25   *Perf. 13*
Designs: 15fr, 18fr, Potters. 20fr, 30fr, Florists.
265   A34   5fr rose brn   45   45
266   A34   12fr ultra   45   45
267   A34   15fr Prus grn   55   55
268   A34   18fr red   55   55
269   A34   20fr dk vio   55   55
270   A34   30fr vio brn   55   55
Nos. 265-270 (6)   3.10   3.10

Independent Kingdom

Types of 1954 Redrawn with "RF" Omitted.

Perf. 13½x13, 13 (A29)
1956, Mar. 1
271   A28   50c emerald   5   5
272   A28   1fr car rose   5   5
273   A28   2fr vio brn   5   5
274   A28   4fr turq bl   15   5
275   A28   5fr violet   6   5
276   A28   8fr blk brn   10   8
277   A28   10fr dk bl grn   10   5
278   A28   12fr rose brn   10   5
279   A28   15fr dp ultra   65   8
   a. Bklt. pane of 10
280   A29   18fr chocolate   20   15
281   A29   20fr dp ultra   25   6
282   A29   25fr indigo   25   6
283   A29   30fr dp cl   1.10   15
284   A29   40fr dk Prus grn   95   15
285   A29   50fr dk vio   70   6
286   A29   75fr car rose   1.00   75

Typographed.
Perf. 14x13
287   A28   15fr ultra   10   6
Nos. 271-287 (17)   5.86   1.95

Mohammed al-Amin Bey of Tunis
A35

Farhat Hached
A36

Designs: 12fr, 18fr, 30fr, Woman and Dove. 5fr, 20fr, Bey of Tunis.

1956   Engraved.   Unwmkd.
Perf. 13.
288   A35   5fr dp bl   35   25
289   A35   12fr brn vio   40   25
290   A35   15fr red   45   35
291   A35   18fr dk bl gray   55   35
292   A35   20fr dk grn   65   25
293   A35   30fr cop brn   1.10   35
Nos. 288-293 (6)   3.50   1.80

Issued to commemorate Tunisian autonomy.

1956, May 1
294   A36   15fr rose brn   35   35
295   A36   30fr indigo   45   45

Issued in honor of the memory of Farhat Hached, nationalist leader.

Grapes
A37

Fruit Market—A38

Designs: 15fr, Hand holding olive branch. 18fr, Wheat harvest. 20fr, Man carrying food basket ("Gifts for the wedding").

1956-57   Engraved.   Unwmkd.
Perf. 13
296   A37   12fr lil, vio & vio brn   55   30
297   A37   15fr ind, dk ol grn & red brn   55   30
298   A37   18fr brt vio bl   65   35
299   A37   20fr brn org   65   35
300   A38   25fr chocolate   75   50
301   A38   30fr dp ultra   85   50
Nos. 296-301 (6)   4.00   2.30

Habib Bourguiba
A39

Farmers and Workers
A40

TUNISIA

		Perf. 14 (A39), 11½x11 (A40)		
		1957, Mar. 20		
302	A39	5fr dk bl	20	20
303	A39	12fr magenta	25	20
304	A39	20fr ultra	45	25
305	A40	25fr green	50	20
306	A39	30fr chocolate	60	45
307	A40	50fr crim rose	1.00	70
		Nos. 302-307 (6)	3.00	2.00

First anniversary of independence.

Dove and Handclasp
A41

Labor Bourse, Tunis
A42

		1957, July 5	Engraved	Perf. 13	
308	A41	18fr dk red vio		45	45
309	A41	20fr crimson		50	50
310	A41	25fr green		55	55
311	A42	30fr dk bl		60	60

Issued to commemorate the fifth World Congress of the International Federation of Trade Unions, Tunis, July 5-13.

Republic

Officer and Soldier
A43

		1957, Aug. 8 Typographed Perf. 11		
312	A43	20fr rose pink	12.00	12.00
313	A43	25fr lt vio	12.00	12.00
314	A43	30fr brn org	12.00	12.00

Proclamation of the Republic.

Bourguiba in Exile, Ile de la Galité
A44

		1958, Jan. 18 Engraved Perf. 13		
315	A44	20fr bl & dk brn	45	35
316	A44	25fr lt bl & vio	50	35

Issued to commemorate the 6th anniversary of Bourguiba's deportation.

Map of Tunisia
A45

Designs: 25fr, Woman and child. 30fr, Hand holding flag.

		1958, Mar. 20	Perf. 13	
317	A45	20fr dk brn & emer	40	20
318	A45	25fr bl & sep	40	25
319	A45	30fr red brn & red	50	30

Issued to commemorate the second anniversary of independence, March 20, 1958. See also No. 321.

Andreas Vesalius and Abderrahman ibn Khaldoun
A46

		1958, Apr. 17	Unwmkd.	
320	A46	30fr bis & sl grn	50	30

World's Fair, Brussels, Apr. 17-Oct. 19.

Redrawn Type of 1958.

		1958, June 1 Engraved Perf. 13		
321	A45	20fr brt bl & ocher	40	35

Date has been changed to "1 Juin 1955-1958." Issued to commemorate the third anniversary of the return of Pres. Habib Bourguiba.

Gardener
A47

A48

		1958, May 1		
322	A47	20fr multi	45	40

Issued for Labor Day, May 1, 1958.

		1958, July 25 Perf. 13 Unwmkd.		
		Blue Paper		
323	A48	5fr dk vio brn & ol	50	25
324	A48	10fr dk grn & yel grn	50	25
325	A48	15fr org red & fan lake	50	25
326	A48	20fr vio, ol grn & yel	50	25
327	A48	25fr red lil	50	25
		Nos. 323-327 (5)	2.50	1.25

First anniversary of the Republic.

Pres. Habib Bourguiba
A49

Fishermen Casting Net
A50

		1958, Aug. 3 Perf. 13 Unwmkd.		
328	A49	20fr vio & brn lake	35	18

Issued in honor of Pres. Bourguiba's 55th birthday.

		1958, Oct. 18 Engraved Perf. 13		
329	A50	25fr dk brn, grn & red	50	40

6th International Fair, Tunis.

UNESCO Building, Paris
A51

		1958, Nov. 3		
330	A51	25fr grnsh blk	50	35

Issued to commemorate the opening of UNESCO (U. N. Educational, Scientific and Cultural Organization) Headquarters in Paris, Nov. 3.

Woman Opening Veil
A52

Hand Planting Symbolic Tree
A53

Habib Bourguiba at Borj le Boeuf
A54

		1959, Jan. 1 Engraved Perf. 13		
331	A52	20m grnsh bl	40	25

Emancipation of Tunisian women.

		1959, Mar. 2 Perf. 13 Unwmkd.		

Designs: 10m, Shield with flag and people holding torch. 20m, Habib Bourguiba at Borj le Boeuf, Sahara.

332	A53	5m vio brn, car & sal	25	20
333	A53	10m multi	35	30
334	A53	20m blue	40	35
335	A54	30m grnsh bl, ind & org brn	75	65

Issued to commemorate the 25th anniversary of the founding of the Neo-Destour Party at Kasr Helal, March 2, 1934.

"Independence"—A55

		1959, Mar. 20		
336	A55	50m ol, blk & red	75	50

3rd anniversary of independence.

Map of Africa and Drawings
A56

		1959, Apr. 15 Litho. Perf. 13		
337	A56	40m lt bl & red brn	80	60

Africa Freedom Day, Apr. 15.

Camel Camp and Mosque, Kairouan
A57

Horseback Rider
A58

Olive Picker
A59

Open Window
A58a

Designs: ½m, Woodcock in Ain-Draham forest. 2m, Camel rider. 3m, Saddler's shop. 4m, Old houses of Medenine, gazelle and youth. 6m, Weavers. 8m, Woman of Gafsa. 10m, Unveiled woman holding fruit. 12m, Ivory craftsman. 15m, Skanes Beach, Monastir, and mermaid. 16m, Minaret of Ez-Zitouna University, Tunis. 20m, Oasis of Gabès. 25m, Oil, flowers and fish of Sfax. 30m, Modern and Roman aqueducts. 40m, Festival at Kairouan (drummer and camel). 45m, Octagonal minaret, Bizerte (boatman). 50m, Three women of Djerba island. 60m, Date palms, Djerid. 70m, Tapestry weaver. 75m, Pottery of Nabeul. 90m, Le Kef (man on horse). 100m, Road to Sidi-bou-Said. 200m, Old port of Sfax. ½d, Roman temple, Sbeitla. 1d, Farmer plowing with oxen, Beja.

Engraved.

		1959-61 Perf. 13 Unwmkd.		
338	A58	½m emer, brn & bl grn ('60)	15	12
339	A58	1m lt bl & ocher	12	8
340	A58	2m multi	12	8
341	A58	3m sl grn	12	8
342	A57	4m red brn ('60)	15	8
343	A58	5m gray grn	15	6
344	A58	6m rose vio	25	15
345	A58	8m vio brn ('60)	50	20
346	A58	10m ol, dk grn & car	20	8
347	A58	12m vio bl & ol bis ('61)	40	20
348	A57	15m brt bl ('60)	35	8
349	A57	16m grnsh blk ('60)	35	20
350	A58a	20m grnsh bl ('60)	90	35
351	A58	20m grnsh blk, ol & mar ('60)	2.00	50
352	A57	25m multi ('60)	35	25
353	A58a	30m brn, grnsh bl & ol	50	10
354	A59	40m grp grn ('60)	85	35
355	A58a	45m brt grn ('60)	60	40
356	A58a	50m Prus grn, dk bl & rose ('60)	75	25
357	A58a	60m grn & red brn ('60)	80	45
358	A59	70m multi ('60)	90	70
359	A59	75m ol gray ('60)	1.00	75
360	A58a	90m brt grn, ultra & choc ('60)	1.00	75
361	A59	95m multi	1.40	1.20
362	A58a	100m dk bl, ol & brn	1.50	1.20
363	A58a	200m brt bl, bis & car	3.00	2.75
363A	A59	½d lt brn ('60)	10.00	6.50
363B	A58a	1d sl grn & bis ('60)	18.00	13.00
		Nos. 338-363B (28)	46.91	30.91

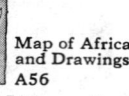

TUNISIA

U.N. Emblem and Clasped Hands A60
Dancer and Coin A61

1959, Oct. 24
364 A60 80m org brn, brn & ultra 1.00 85

Issued for United Nations Day, Oct. 24.

1959, Nov. 4
365 A61 50m grnsh bl & blk 90 90

Central Bank of Tunisia, first anniversary.

Uprooted Oak Emblem A62
Doves and WRY Emblem A63

1960, Apr. 7 Engraved Perf. 13
366 A62 20m bl blk 60 40
367 A63 40m red lil & dk grn 80 60

Issued to publicize World Refugee Year, July 1, 1959–June 30, 1960.

Girl, Boy and Scout Badge A64
Cyclist A65

Designs: 25m, Hand giving Scout sign. 30m, Bugler and tent. 40m, Peacock and Scout emblem. 60m, Scout and campfire.

1960, Aug. 9
368 A64 10m lt bl grn 30 25
369 A64 25m grn, red & brn 35 30
370 A64 30m vio bl, grn & mar 45 45
371 A64 40m blk, car & bl 60 50
372 A64 60m dk brn, vio blk & lake 1.00 80
 Nos. 368-372 (5) 2.70 2.30

Issued for the 4th Arab Boy Scout Jamboree, Tunis, August, 1960.

1960, Aug. 25
Designs: 10m, Olympic rings forming flower. 15m, Girl tennis player and minaret. 25m, Runner and minaret. 50m, Handball player and minaret.
373 A65 5m dk brn & ol 30 30
374 A65 10m sl, red vio & emer 45 45
375 A65 15m rose red & rose car 45 45
376 A65 25m grnsh bl & gray bl 50 50
377 A65 50m brt grn & ultra 1.00 1.00
 Nos. 373-377 (5) 2.70 2.70

Issued to commemorate the 17th Olympic Games, Rome, Aug. 25–Sept. 11.

Symbolic Forest Design A66
National Fair Emblems A67

Designs: 15m, Man working in forest. 25m, Tree superimposed on leaf. 50m, Symbolic tree and bird.

1960, Aug. 29
378 A66 8m multi 25 18
379 A66 15m dk grn 30 22
380 A66 25m dk pur, crim & brt grn 50 40
381 A66 50m Prus grn, yel grn & rose lake 85 70

Issued to commemorate the Fifth World Forestry Congress, Seattle, Washington, Aug. 29–Sept. 10.

1960, June 1
382 A67 100m blk & grn 1.00 70

Issued to publicize the Fifth National Fair, Sousse, May 27–June 12, 1960.

Pres. Bourguiba Signing Constitution A68

1960, June 1
383 A68 20m choc, red & emer 40 25

Promulgation of the Constitution.

Pres. Habib Bourguiba A69

1960, June 1
384 A69 20m grysh blk 25 5
385 A69 30m bl, dl red & blk 35 12
386 A69 40m grn, dl red & blk 40 20

U.N. Emblem and Arms A70
Dove and "Liberated Tunisia" A71

1960, Oct. 24 Engraved Perf. 13
387 A70 40m mag, ultra & gray grn 90 70

15th anniversary of the United Nations.

1961, March 20 Perf. 13
Design: 75m, Globe and arms.
388 A71 20m mar, bis & bl 35 30
389 A71 30m bl, vio & brn 40 35
390 A71 40m yel grn & ultra 80 65
391 A71 75m bis, red lil & Prus bl 1.00 85

5th anniversary of independence.

Map of Africa, Woman and Animals A72
Mother and Child with Flags A73

Map of Africa: 60m, Negro woman and Arab. 100m, Arabic inscription and Guinea masque. 200m, Hands of Negro and Arab.

1961, Apr. 15 Engr. Unwmkd.
392 A72 40m bis brn, red brn & dk grn 50 40
393 A72 60m sl grn, blk & org brn 55 45
394 A72 100m sl grn, emer & vio 1.00 75
395 A72 200m dk brn & org brn 2.00 1.75

Africa Freedom Day, Apr. 15.

1961, June 1 Perf. 13 Unwmkd.
Designs: 50m, Tunisians. 95m, Girl with wings and half-moon.
396 A73 25m pale vio, red & brn 40 25
397 A73 50m bl grn, sep & brn 60 35
398 A73 95m org vio, rose lil & ocher 80 60

Issued for National Feast Day, June 1.

Dag Hammarskjold A74
Arms of Tunisia A75

1961, Oct. 24 Photo. Perf. 14
399 A74 40m ultra 50 35

Issued on United Nations Day in memory of Dag Hammarskjold, Secretary General of the United Nations, 1953–61.

1962, Jan. 18 Perf. 11½
Arms in Original Colors
400 A75 1m blk & yel 5 5
401 A75 2m blk & pink 5 5
402 A75 3m blk & lt bl 10 8
403 A75 6m blk & gray 20 15

Issued to commemorate the 10th anniversary of Tunisia's campaign for independence.

Mosquito in Spider Web and WHO Emblem A76

Designs: 30m, Symbolic horseback rider spearing mosquito. 40m, Hands crushing mosquito (horiz.).

1962, Apr. 7 Engraved Perf. 13
404 A76 20m chocolate 60 40
405 A76 30m red brn & sl grn 50 40
406 A76 40m dk brn, mar & grn 60 55

Issued for the World Health Organization drive to eradicate malaria.

Boy and Map of Africa A77
African Holding "Africa" A78

1962, Apr. 15 Photo. Perf. 14
407 A77 50m brn & org 60 45
408 A78 100m blk, blk & org 90 55

Issued for Africa Freedom Day, Apr. 15.

Farm Worker A79
Industrial Worker A80

1962, May 1 Unwmkd.
409 A79 40m multi 45 35
410 A80 60m dk red brn 55 45

Issued for Labor Day, 1962.

TUNISIA

"Liberated Tunisia" A81 — Woman of Gabès A82

1962, June 1 Typo. Perf. 13½x14
411 A81 20m sal & blk   40   30

Issued for National Feast Day, June 1.

1962-63   Photo.   Perf. 11½
Designs (Women in costume of various localities): 10m, Mahdia. 15m, Kairouan. 20m, 40m, Hammamet. 25m, Djerba. 55m, Ksar Hellal. 60m, Tunis.

412	A82	5m multi	50	35
413	A82	10m multi	70	50
414	A82	15m multi ('63)	80	65
415	A82	20m multi	90	70
416	A82	25m multi ('63)	90	70
417	A82	30m multi	1.00	90
418	A82	40m multi	1.25	90
419	A82	50m multi	1.30	1.10
420	A82	55m multi ('63)	1.50	1.30
421	A82	60m multi ('63)	2.25	1.90
		Nos. 412-421 (10)	11.10	9.00

The six stamps issued in 1962 (July 25) commemorate the 6th anniversary of Tunisia's independence. The four issued in 1963 (June 1) commemorate National Feast Day. See also Nos. 470-471.

U.N. Emblem, Flag and Dove A83 — Aboul-Qasim Chabbi A84

Designs: 30m, Leaves and globe (horiz.). 40m, Dove and globe.

1962, Oct. 24   Unwmkd.
422	A83	20m gray, blk & scar	40	30
423	A83	30m multi	50	40
424	A83	40m cl brn, blk & bl	80	60

Issued for United Nations Day, Oct. 24.

1962, Nov. 20   Engr.   Perf. 13
425 A84 15m purple   30   20

Issued to honor Aboul-Qasim Chabbi (1904-34), Arab poet.

Pres. Habib Bourguiba A85 — Hached Telephone Exchange A86

1962, Dec. 7 Photo. Perf. 12½x13½
426	A85	20m brt bl	20	10
427	A85	30m rose cl	25	15
428	A85	40m green	35	20

1962, Dec. 7   Lithographed
Designs: 10m, Carthage Exchange. 15m, Sfax telecommunications center. 50m, Telephone operators. 100m, Symbol of automatization. 200m, Belvedere Central Exchange.

429	A86	5m multi	40	25
430	A86	10m multi	40	30
431	A86	15m multi	60	35
432	A86	50m blk, red brn & buff	1.00	70
433	A86	100m blk, brt bl & mag	2.50	1.50
434	A86	200m multi	3.25	2.50
		Nos. 429-434 (6)	8.15	5.60

Issued in connection with the first Afro-Asian Philatelic Exhibition and to commemorate the automation of the telephone system.

Dove over Globe A87 — "Hunger" A88

1963, Mar. 21   Engr.   Perf. 13
| 435 | A87 | 20m brt bl & brn | 30 | 25 |
| 436 | A88 | 40m bis brn & dk brn | 50 | 35 |

Issued for the "Freedom from Hunger" campaign of the U.N. Food and Agriculture Organization.

Runner and Walker A89 — Centenary Emblem A90

1963, Feb. 17 Lithographed Perf. 13
437 A89 30m brn, blk & grn   35   25

Issued for Army Sports Day, and to commemorate the 13th C.I.S.M. cross country championships.

1963, May 8   Engraved   Perf. 13
438 A90 20m brn, gray & red   30   20

Centenary of International Red Cross.

"Human Rights" A91 — Hand Raising Gateway of Great Temple of Philae A92

1963, Dec. 10 Perf. 13 Unwmkd.
439 A91 30m grn & dk brn   35   25

Issued to commemorate the 15th anniversary of the Universal Declaration of Human Rights.

1964, March 8   Engraved
440 A92 50m red brn, bis & bluish blk   55   45

Issued to publicize the UNESCO world campaign to save historic monuments in Nubia.

Sunshine, Rain and Barometer A93 — Mohammed Ali A94

1964, March 8 Perf. 13 Unwmkd.
441 A93 40m brn, red lil & sl   50   35

4th World Meteorological Day, Mar. 23.

1964, May 15   Engraved
442 A94 50m sepia   40   25

Issued to commemorate the 70th anniversary of the birth of Mohammed Ali (1894-1928), labor leader.

Map of Africa and Symbolic Flower A95 — Pres. Habib Bourguiba A96

1964, May 25   Photo.   Perf. 13x14
443 A95 60m multi   55   45

Issued to commemorate the first anniversary of the Addis Ababa charter on African Unity.

Engraved
1964, June 1   Perf. 12½x13½
| 444 | A96 | 20m vio bl | 15 | 5 |
| 445 | A96 | 30m black | 20 | 10 |

"Ship and Torch" A97

1964, Oct. 19 Photo. Perf. 11½x11
446 A97 50m blk & grn   40   30

Issued to publicize the Neo-Destour Congress, Bizerte. "Bizerte" in Arabic forms the ship and "Neo-Destour Congress 1964" the torch of the design.

Communication Equipment and ITU Emblem—A98

1965, May 17   Engraved   Perf. 13
447 A98 55m gray & bl   50   30

Issued to commemorate the centenary of the International Telecommunication Union.

Carthaginian Coin A99

Perf. 12½x14
1965, July 9   Photo.   Unwmkd.
448	A99	5m grn & blk brn	6	5
449	A99	10m bis & blk brn	30	20
450	A99	75m bl & blk brn	80	35

Festival of Popular Arts, Carthage.

Girl with Book A100

1965, Oct. 1   Engraved   Perf. 13
451	A100	25m brt bl, blk & red	40	25
452	A100	40m blk, bl & red	45	30
453	A100	50m red, bl & blk	55	35
a.		Souv. sheet of 3	4.00	4.00

Issued to publicize the Girl Students' Center and education for women. No. 453a contains one each of Nos. 451-453. Blister outline of schoolhouse in margin. Size: 129x130mm. Sold for 200m. Issued perf. and imperf.; same price.

Links and ICY Emblem A101 — Man Pouring Water A102

1965, Oct. 24
454 A101 40m blk, brt bl & rose lil   45   30

International Cooperation Year, 1965.

1966, Jan. 18 Photo. Perf. 13x14
Symbolic Designs: 10m, Woman and pool. 30m, Woman pouring water. 100m, Mountain and branches.

Inscribed "Eaux Minerales"
455	A102	10m gray, ocher & dk red	20	20
456	A102	20m multi	25	20
457	A102	30m yel, bl & red	35	25
458	A102	100m ol, bl & yel	1.00	55

Issued to publicize the mineral waters of Tunisia.

President Bourguiba and Hands A103

TUNISIA

"Promotion of Culture"
A104

Designs: 5m, like 10m. 25m, "Independence" (arms raised), flag and doves. 40m, "Development" (horiz.).

1966, June 1   Engraved   Perf. 13

| 459 | A103 | 5m dl pur & vio | 20 | 15 |
| 460 | A103 | 10m gray grn & sl grn | 30 | 20 |

Photogravure   Perf. 11½

461	A104	25m multi	30	20
462	A104	40m multi	60	30
463	A104	60m multi	80	30
		Nos. 459-463 (5)	2.20	1.15

10th anniversary of independence.

Map of Africa through View Finder, Plane and U.N. Emblem
A105

1966, Sept. 12   Engraved   Perf. 13

464	A105	15m lil & multi	25	20
465	A105	35m bl & multi	35	25
466	A105	40m multi	50	30
a.		Souv. sheet of 3	10.00	10.00

Issued to publicize the 2nd United Nations Regional Cartographic Conference for Africa, held in Tunisia, Sept. 12–24.
No. 466a contains one each of Nos. 464–466. Sold for 150m. Size: 129x 100mm. Issued perf. and imperf.; same price.

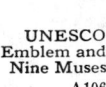 

UNESCO Emblem and Nine Muses
A106

1966, Oct. 24   Perf. 13

| 467 | A106 | 100m blk & brn | 1.00 | 45 |

Issued to commemorate the 20th anniversary of UNESCO (United Nations Educational, Scientific and Cultural Organization).

Runners and Mediterranean Map
A107

1967, March 20   Engraved   Perf. 13

| 468 | A107 | 20m dk red, brn ol & bl | 30 | 20 |
| 469 | A107 | 30m brt bl & blk | 35 | 25 |

Mediterranean Games, Sept. 8–17.

Types of 1962–63 and 1965–66 with EXPO '67 Emblem and Inscription and

Symbols of Various Activities
A108

Designs: 50m, Woman of Djerba. 75m, Woman of Gabes. 155m, Pink flamingoes.

Photogravure; Engraved (A108)
1967, Apr. 28   Perf. 11½, 13 (A108)

470	A82	50m multi	40	20
471	A82	75m multi	60	30
472	A108	100m dk grn, sl bl & blk	80	40
473	A108	110m dk brn, ultra & red	1.00	50
474	AP6	155m multi	1.25	60
		Nos. 470-474 (5)	4.05	2.00

Issued to commemorate EXPO '67, International Exhibition, Montreal, Apr. 28–Oct. 27.

Tunisian Pavilion, Pres. Bourguiba and Map of Tunisia—A109

Designs: 105m, 200m, Tunisian Pavilion and bust of Pres. Bourguiba.

1967, June 13   Engr.   Perf. 13

475	A109	65m red lil & dp org	60	30
476	A109	105m multi	80	45
477	A109	120m brt bl	1.00	65
478	A109	200m red, lil & blk	1.60	90

Tunisia Day at EXPO '67.

"Tunisia" Holding 4-leaf Clovers
A110

Woman Freeing Doves
A111

1967, July 25   Litho.   Perf. 13½

| 479 | A110 | 25m multi | 25 | 15 |
| 480 | A111 | 40m multi | 35 | 20 |

10th anniversary of the Republic.

Tennis Courts, Players and Games' Emblem—A112

Designs: 10m, Games' emblem and sports emblems (vert.). 15m, Swimming pool and swimmers. 35m, Sports Palace and athletes. 75m, Stadium and athletes.

1967, Sept. 8   Engraved   Perf. 13

481	A112	5m sl grn & hn brn	20	7
482	A112	10m brn red & multi	20	10
483	A112	15m black	30	20
484	A112	35m dk brn & Prus bl	50	30
485	A112	75m dk car rose, vio & bl grn	80	50
		Nos. 481-485 (5)	2.00	1.17

Mediterranean Games, Tunis, Sept. 8–17.

Bird, Punic Period
A113

"Mankind" and Human Rights Flame
A114

History of Tunisia: 20m, Sea horse, medallion from Kerkouane. 25m, Hannibal, bronze bust, Volubilis. 30m, Stele, Carthage. 40m, Hamilcar, coin. 60m, Mask, funeral pendant.

1967, Dec. 1   Litho.   Perf. 13½

486	A113	15m gray grn, pink & blk	30	20
487	A113	20m dp bl, red & blk	30	20
488	A113	25m dk grn & org brn	35	20
489	A113	30m grnsh gray, pink & blk	35	20
490	A113	40m red brn, yel & blk	40	25
491	A113	60m multi	50	35
		Nos. 486-491 (6)	2.20	1.40

1968, Jan. 18   Engr.   Perf. 13

| 492 | A114 | 25m brick red | 40 | 25 |
| 493 | A114 | 60m dp bl | 50 | 30 |

International Human Rights Year 1968.

Computer Fantasy
A115

1968, Mar. 20   Engraved   Perf. 13

494	A115	25m mag, bl vio & ol	40	20
495	A115	40m ol grn, red brn & brn	40	20
496	A115	60m ultra, sl & brn	50	30

Issued to publicize the introduction of electronic equipment for postal service.

Physician and Patient
A116

Arabian Jasmine
A117

1968, Apr. 7   Engraved   Perf. 13

| 497 | A116 | 25m dp grn & brt grn | 40 | 20 |
| 498 | A116 | 60m mag & car | 50 | 30 |

Issued for the 20th anniversary of the World Health Organization.

1968-69   Photogravure   Perf. 11½

Flowers: 5m, Flax. 6m, Canna indica. 10m, Pomegranate. 15m, Rhaponticum acaule. 20m, Geranium. 25m, Madonna lily. 40m, Peach blossoms. 50m, Caper. 60m, Ariana rose. 100fr, Jasmine.

Granite Paper

499	A117	5m multi ('69)	25	20
500	A117	6m multi ('69)	25	20
501	A117	10m multi ('69)	30	20
502	A117	12m multi	35	20
503	A117	15m multi ('69)	35	25
504	A117	20m multi ('69)	40	25
505	A117	25m multi ('69)	45	35
506	A117	40m multi ('69)	65	35
507	A117	50m multi	75	40
508	A117	60m multi	1.10	60
509	A117	100m multi	1.75	90
		Nos. 499-509 (11)	6.60	3.90

Issue dates: 12m, 50m, 60m, 100m, Apr. 9, 1968. Others, Mar. 20, 1969.

Flower with Red Crescent and Globe
A118

Flutist
A119

Design: 25m, Dove with Red Crescent and globe.

1968, May 8   Engraved   Perf. 13

| 510 | A118 | 15m Prus bl, grn & red | 25 | 20 |
| 511 | A118 | 25m brt rose lil & red | 30 | 25 |

Issued to honor the Red Crescent Society.

1968, June 1   Litho.   Perf. 13

| 512 | A119 | 20m vio & multi | 35 | 25 |
| 513 | A119 | 50m multi | 45 | 30 |

Issued for Stamp Day 1968.

Jackal
A120

Animals: 8m, Porcupine. 10m, Dromedary. 15m, Dorcas gazelle. 20m, Desert fox (fennec). 25m, Desert hedgehog. 40m, Arabian horse. 60m, Boar.

1968-69   Photogravure   Perf. 11½

514	A120	5m dk brn, lt bl & bis	20	15
515	A120	8m dk vio brn & yel grn	30	20
516	A120	10m dk brn, lt bl & ocher ('69)	45	25
517	A120	15m dk brn, ocher & yel grn ('69)	50	30
518	A120	20m dl yel & dk brn ('69)	60	45
519	A120	25m blk, tan & brt grn ('69)	85	45
520	A120	40m blk, lil & pale grn ('69)	1.10	70
521	A120	60m dk brn, buff & yel grn	1.50	1.10
		Nos. 514-521 (8)	5.50	3.60

Issue dates: 5m, 8m, 20m, 60m, Sept. 15, 1968. Others, Jan. 18, 1969.

TUNISIA

Worker and
ILO Emblem
A121

Design: 60m, Young man and woman holding banner.

1969, May 1   Engraved   Perf. 13

| 522 | A121 | 25m Prus bl, blk & bis | 30 | 20 |
| 523 | A121 | 60m rose car, bl & yel | 50 | 30 |

Issued to commemorate the 50th anniversary of the International Labor Organization.

Veiled Women and Musicians
with Flute and Drum
A122

1969, June 20   Litho.   Perf. 14x13½

| 524 | A122 | 100m dp yel grn & multi | 75 | 45 |

Issued for Stamp Day 1969.

Tunisian	Symbols of
Coat of Arms	Industry
A123	A124

1969, July 25   Photo.   Perf. 11½

525	A123	15m yel & multi	25	20
526	A123	25m pink & multi	30	25
527	A123	40m gray & multi	35	25
528	A123	60m lt bl & multi	35	25

1969, Sept. 10   Perf. 13x12

| 529 | A124 | 60m blk, red & yel | 45 | 30 |

Issued to commemorate the 5th anniversary of the African Development Bank.

Lute	Nurse and
A125	Maghrib Flags
	A126

Musical Instruments: 25m, Zither (horiz.). 70m, Rebab (2-strings). 90m, Drums and flute (horiz.).

1970, Mar. 20   Photo.   Perf. 11½
Granite Paper

530	A125	25m multi	35	20
531	A125	50m multi	45	25
532	A125	70m multi	60	35
533	A125	90m multi	70	40

1970, May 4   Photo.   Perf. 11½

| 534 | A126 | 25m lil & multi | 30 | 20 |

Issued to publicize the 6th Medical Seminar of Maghrib Countries (Morocco, Algeria, Tunisia and Libya), Tunis, May 4–10.

U.P.U. Headquarters Issue
Common Design Type

1970, May 20   Engraved   Perf. 13

| 535 | CD133 | 25m dl red & dk ol bis | 40 | 30 |

Inauguration of new Universal Postal Union headquarters, Bern, Switzerland.

Mail
Service
Symbol
A127

Design: 35m, Mailmen of yesterday and today (vert.).

1970, Oct. 15   Litho.   Perf. 12½x13
Size: 37x31½mm.

| 536 | A127 | 25m pink & multi | 25 | 20 |

Size: 22x37½mm.   Perf. 13x12½

| 537 | A127 | 35m blk & multi | 35 | 25 |

United Nations, 25th anniversary.

Dove,
Laurel
and
U.N.
Emblem
A128

1970, Oct. 24   Photo.   Perf. 13x12½

| 538 | A128 | 40m multi | 45 | 30 |

United Nations, 25th anniversary.

Jasmine Vendor	Lenin, after
and Veiled	N. N. Joukov
Woman—A129	A130

Scenes from Tunisian Life: 25m, "The 3rd Day of the Wedding." 35m, Perfume vendor. 40m, Fish vendor. 85m, Waiter in coffeehouse.

1970, Nov. 9   Photo.   Perf. 14

539	A129	20m dk grn & multi	15	15
540	A129	25m multi	25	20
541	A129	35m multi	35	20
542	A129	40m dp car & multi	40	25
543	A129	85m brt bl & multi	65	40
a.	Souvenir sheet of 5		5.00	5.00
	Nos. 539-543 (5)		1.80	1.20

No. 543a contains one each of Nos. 539–543 with deep claret and gold margin with commemorative inscription. Size: 138x125mm. Sold for 500m. Issued perf. and imperf.; same price.

Common Design Types
pictured in section at front of book.

1970, Dec. 28   Engraved   Perf. 13

| 544 | A130 | 60m dk car rose | 45 | 25 |

Centenary of the birth of Lenin (1870–1924), Russian communist leader.

Radar, Flags and	U.N.
Carrier Pigeon	Headquarters,
A131	Symbolic
	Flower—A132

1971, May 17   Litho.   Perf. 13x12½

| 545 | A131 | 25m lt bl & multi | 40 | 30 |

Coordinating Committee for Post and Telecommunications Administrations of Maghrib Countries.

1971, May 10   Photo.   Perf. 12½x13

| 546 | A132 | 80m brt rose lil, blk & yel | 50 | 40 |

International year against racial discrimination.

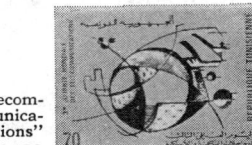

"Telecommunications"
A133

1971, May 17   Perf. 13x12½

| 547 | A133 | 70m sil, blk & lt grn | 55 | 40 |

3rd World Telecommunications Day.

Earth,
Moon,
Satellites
A134

Design: 90m, Abstract composition.

1971, June 21   Photo.   Perf. 13x12½

| 548 | A134 | 15m brt bl & blk | 40 | 25 |
| 549 | A134 | 90m scar & blk | 60 | 35 |

Conquest of space.

"Pottery
Merchant"
A135

Life in Tunisia (stylized drawings): 30m, Esparto weaver selling hats and mats. 40m, Poultry man. 50m, Dyer.

1971, July 24   Photo.   Perf. 14x13½

550	A135	25m gold & multi	25	20
551	A135	30m gold & multi	30	20
552	A135	40m gold & multi	35	25
553	A135	50m gold & multi	40	25
a.	Sheet of 4		4.25	4.25

No 553a contains one each of Nos. 550–553, Perf. 13½, gold and blue green margin. Size: 99x128mm. Sold for 500m. Issued perf. and imperf.; same price.

Pres. Bourguiba sick in 1938
A136

Designs: 25m, Bourguiba and "8" (vert.). 50m, Bourguiba carried in triumph (vert.). 80m, Bourguiba and irrigation dam.

Perf. 13½x13, 13x13½

1971, Oct. 11

554	A136	25m multi	20	12
555	A136	30m multi	20	15
556	A136	50m multi	25	20
557	A136	80m blk, ultra & grn	55	20

8th Congress of the Neo-Destour Party.

Shah Mohammed
Riza Pahlavi and
Stone Head 6th
Century B.C.
A137

Designs: 50m, King Bahram-Gur hunting, 4th century. 100m, Coronation, from Persian miniature, 1614.

Granite Paper

1971, Oct. 17   Perf. 11½

558	A137	25m multi	25	20
559	A137	50m multi	35	25
560	A137	100m multi	70	40
a.	Souvenir sheet of 3		3.50	3.50

2500th anniversary of the founding of the Persian empire by Cyrus the Great. No. 560a contains one each of Nos. 558–560. Gold marginal inscription. Size: 102x82 mm. Sold for 500m. Issued perf. and imperf.; same price.

Pimento
and
Warrior
A138

Designs: 2m, Mint and farmer. 5m, Pear and 2 men under pear tree. 25m Oleander and girl. 60m, Pear and sheep 100m, Grapefruit and fruit vendor.

1971, Nov. 15   Litho.   Perf. 13

561	A138	1m lt bl & multi	5	5
562	A138	2m gray & multi	5	5
563	A138	5m cit & multi	8	5
564	A138	25m lil & multi	25	20
565	A138	60m multi	50	30
566	A138	100m buff & multi	90	50
a.	Souvenir sheet of 6		4.00	4.00
	Nos. 561-566 (6)		1.83	1.15

Fruit, flowers and folklore. No. 566a contains one each of Nos. 561–566. Gold margin with black inscription. Size: 131x 165mm. Sold for 500m. Issued perf. and imperf.; same price.

Dancer and
Musician
A139

TUNISIA

1971, Nov. 22   Photo.   *Perf. 11½*
567   A139   50m bl & multi   40   30
Stamp Day.

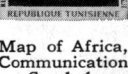

Map of Africa, Communication Symbols   **UNICEF Emblem, Mother and Child**
A139a   A140

Lithographed
1971, Nov. 30   *Perf. 13½ x 12½*
568   A139a   95m multi   60   40
Pan-African telecommunications system.

1971, Dec. 6   Photo.   *Perf. 11½*
569   A140   110m multi   60   35
25th anniversary of the United Nations International Children's Fund (UNICEF).

Symbolic Olive Tree and Oil Vat   **Gondolier in Flood Waters**
A141   A142

1972, Jan. 9   Litho.   *Perf. 13½*
570   A141   60m multi   35   25
International Olive Year.

1972, Feb. 7   Photo.   *Perf. 11½*
Designs: 30m, Young man and Doge's Palace. 50m, Gondola's prow and flood. 80m, Rialto Bridge and hand holding gondolier's hat (horiz.).
571   A142   25m lt bl & multi   20   20
572   A142   30m blk & multi   40   20
573   A142   50m yel grn, gray & blk   35   25
574   A142   80m bl & multi   55   35
UNESCO campaign to save Venice.

Man Reading and Book Year Emblem   **"Your Heart is Your Health"**
A143   A144

1972, Mar. 27   Photo.   *Perf. 11½*
Granite Paper
575   A143   90m brn & multi   60   40
International Book Year 1972.

1972, Apr. 7   *Perf. 13 x 13½*
Design: 60m, Smiling man pointing to heart.
576   A144   25m grn & multi   35   25
577   A144   60m red & multi   45   30
World Health Day.

"Only one Earth" Environment Emblem
A145

1972, June 5   Engr.   *Perf. 13*
578   A145   60m lem & sl grn   45   35
U.N. Conference on Human Environment, Stockholm, June 5–16.

Hurdler, Olympic Emblems
A146

1972, Aug. 26   Photo.   *Perf. 11½*
Multicolored
579   A146   5m *Volleyball*   20   15
580   A146   15m *shown*   25   20
581   A146   20m *Athletes*   25   20
582   A146   25m *Soccer*   30   20
583   A146   60m *Swimming, women's*   40   30
584   A146   80m *Running*   60   40
   a.   Souv. sheet of 6   4.00   4.00
       Nos. 579-584 (6)   2.00   1.45
20th Olympic Games, Munich, Aug. 26–Sept. 11. No. 584a contains 6 imperf. stamps similar to Nos. 579-584. Gold marginal inscription. Size: 129x95mm. Sold for 500m.

Chessboard and Pieces   **Fisherman**
A147   A148

1972, Sept. 25   Photo.   *Perf. 11½*
585   A147   60m grn & multi   50   35
20th Men's Chess Olympiad, Skoplje, Jugoslavia, Sept.–Oct.

1972, Oct. 23   Litho.   *Perf. 13½*
Multicolored
586   A148   5m *shown*   20   15
587   A148   10m *Basket maker*   30   20
588   A148   25m *Musician*   30   20
589   A148   30m *Married Berber woman*   40   30
590   A148   60m *Flower merchant*   40   30
591   A148   80m *Festival*   60   35
   a.   Souvenir sheet of 6   3.00   3.00
       Nos. 586-591 (6)   2.20   1.50
Life in Tunisia. No. 591a contains one each of Nos. 586-591, exists perf. & imperf. Brown marginal inscription. Size: 133x135mm. Sold for 500m.

Post Office, Tunis
A149

Lithographed and Engraved
1972, Dec. 8   *Perf. 13*
592   A149   25m ver, org & blk   30   20
Stamp Day.

Dome of the Rock, Jerusalem
A150

1973, Jan. 22   Photo.   *Perf. 13½*
593   A150   25m multi   40   30

Globe, Pen and Quill   **Family**
A151   A152

1973, Mar. 19   Photo.   *Perf. 14x13½*
594   A151   25m gold, brt mag & brn   30   20
595   A151   60m bl & multi   40   30
9th Congress of Arab Writers.

1973, Apr. 2   *Perf. 11½*
Design: 25m, profiles and dove.
596   A152   20m grn & multi   25   20
597   A152   25m lil & multi   30   20
Family planning.

"10" and Bird Feeding Young
A153

Design: 60m, "10" made of grain and bread, and hand holding spoon.
1973, Apr. 26   Photo.   *Perf. 11½*
598   A153   25m multi   30   20
599   A153   60m multi   40   30
World Food Program, 10th anniversary.

Roman Head and Ship
A154

Designs (Drawings of Tools and): 25m, Mosaic with ostriches and camel. 30m, Mosaic with 4 heads and 4 emblems. 40m, Punic stele to the sun (vert.). 60m, Outstretched hand and arm of Christian preacher; symbols of 4 Evangelists. 75m, 17th century potsherd with Arabic inscription (vert.).

1973, May 6
600   A154   5m multi   20   10
601   A154   25m multi   30   20
602   A154   30m multi   40   30
603   A154   40m multi   40   30
604   A154   60m multi   40   25
605   A154   75m multi   50   25
   a.   Souvenir sheet of 6   5.00   5.00
       Nos. 600-605 (6)   2.20   1.50
UNESCO campaign to save Carthage. No. 605a contains 6 imperf. stamps similar to Nos. 600-605. Dark gray marginal inscription. Size: 143x100mm. Sold for 500m.

Overlapping Circles   **Map of Africa as Festival Emblem**
A155   A156

Design: 75m, Printed circuit board.
1973, May 17   Photo.   *Perf. 14x13½*
606   A155   60m yel & multi   35   20
607   A155   75m vio & multi   45   25
5th International Telecommunications Day.

1973, July 15   Photo.   *Perf. 13½x13*
Design: 40m, African heads, festival emblem in eye.
608   A156   25m multi   25   20
609   A156   40m multi   30   20
Pan-African Youth Festival, Tunis.

Scout Emblem and Pennants
A157

1973, July 23   Litho.   *Perf. 13½x13*
610   A157   25m multi   40   30
International Boy Scout Organization.

Crescent-shaped Racing Cars—A158
1973, July 30   *Perf. 13x13½*
611   A158   60m multi   50   30
2nd Pan-Arab auto race.

Highway Cloverleaf
A159

Traffic Lights and Signs   **Stylized Camel**
A160   A161
Perf. 12½x13, 13x12½
1973, Sept. 28   *Lithographed*
612   A159   25m lt bl & multi   30   20
613   A160   30m multi   40   30
Highway safety campaign.

TUNISIA

1973, Oct. 8 Photo. *Perf. 13½*
Design: 10m, Stylized bird and philatelic symbols (horiz.).
614	A161	10m multi	20	15
615	A161	65m multi	45	35

Stamp Day 1973.

Copernicus
A162

African Unity
A163

Lithographed and Engraved
1973, Oct. 16 *Perf. 13x12½*
616	A162	60m blk & multi	40	30

500th anniversary of the birth of Nicolaus Copernicus (1473–1543), Polish astronomer.

1973, Nov. 4 Photo. *Perf. 14x13½*
617	A163	25m blk & multi	40	35

10th anniversary of the Organization for African Unity.

Handshake and Emblems
A164

1973, Nov. 15 Litho. *Perf. 14½x14*
618	A164	65m yel & multi	45	30

25th anniversary of International Criminal Police Organization.

Globe, Hand Holding Carnation
A165

1973, Dec. 10 *Perf. 11½*
619	A165	60m blk & multi	50	40

25th anniversary of Universal Declaration of Human Rights.

WMO Headquarters and Emblem—A166

Design: 60m, Globe and emblem.
1973, Dec. 24 Litho. *Perf. 14x14½*
620	A166	25m multi	30	20
621	A166	60m multi	40	35

Centenary of international meteorological cooperation.

Bourguiba in the Desert, 1945
A167

Scientist with Microscope
A168

Portraits of Pres. Habib Bourguiba: 25m, In exile aboard the "Galite," 1954. 60m, Addressing crowd, 1974. 75m, In Victory Parade, 1955. 100m, In 1934.

1974, Mar. 2 Photo. *Perf. 11½*
622	A167	15m plum & multi	20	15
623	A167	25m multi	30	20
624	A167	60m multi	40	25
625	A167	75m multi	50	30
626	A167	100m multi	60	40
a.	Souvenir sheet of 5		3.00	3.00
	Nos. 622-626 (5)		2.00	1.30

40th anniversary of the Neo-Destour Party. No. 626a contains one each of Nos. 622–626 with slate green marginal inscription. Size: 154x63mm. Sold for 500m. Issued perf. and imperf.; same price.

1974, Mar. 21 *Perf. 14*
627	A168	60m multi	45	30

6th African Congress of Micropaleontology, Mar. 21–Apr. 3.

Woman with Telephones and Globe
A169

Design: 60m, Telephone dial, telephones, wires.
1974, July 1 Photo. *Perf. 11½*
628	A169	15m multi	25	20
629	A169	60m multi	45	30

Introduction of international automatic telephone dialing system.

WPY Emblem and Symbolic Design
A170

1974, Aug. 19 Photo. *Perf. 11½*
630	A170	110m multi	70	40

World Population Year, 1974.

Pres. Bourguiba and Sun Flower Emblem
A171

Designs: 60m, Bourguiba and cactus flower (horiz.). 200m, Bourguiba and verbena (horiz.).
1974, Sept. 12 Photo. *Perf. 11½*
631	A171	25m blk, ultra & grnsh bl	30	20

632	A171	60m red, car & yel	40	25
633	A171	200m blk, brt lil & grn	1.00	70
a.	Souvenir sheet of 3		2.50	2.50

Congress of the Socialist Destour Party. No. 633a contains 3 imperf. stamps similar to Nos. 631–633, black marginal inscription. Size: 134x66mm.

Jets Flying over Old World Map
A172

1974, Sept. 23 Litho. *Perf. 12½*
634	A172	60m brn & multi	40	25

25th anniversary of Tunisian aviation.

Symbolic Carrier Pigeons
A173

Handshake, Letter, UPU Emblem
A174

1974, Oct. 9 Photo. *Perf. 13*
635	A173	25m multi	30	25
636	A174	60m multi	40	25

Centenary of Universal Postal Union.

Le Bardo, National Assembly
A175

Pres. Bourguiba Ballot
A176

1974, Nov. 3 Photo. *Perf. 11½*
637	A175	25m grn, bl & blk	40	40
638	A176	100m org & blk	70	40

Legislative (25m) and presidential elections (100m), Nov. 1974.

Mailman with Letters and Bird
A177

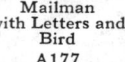
Water Carrier
A178

1974, Dec. 5 Litho. *Perf. 14½x14*
639	A177	75m lt vio & multi	50	35

Stamp Day.

1975, Feb. 17 Photo. *Perf. 13½*
Multicolored
640	A178	5m *shown*	10	10
641	A178	15m *Perfume vendor*	12	12
642	A178	25m *Laundresses*	20	20
643	A178	60m *Potter*	35	35
644	A178	110m *Fruit vendor*	60	35
a.	Souvenir sheet of 5		2.50	2.50
	Nos. 640-644 (5)		1.37	97

Life in Tunisia. No. 644a contains one each of Nos. 640–644; red orange margin with black inscription. Size: 125x118mm. Sold for 500m. Issued perf. and imperf.; same price.

Steel Tower, Skyscraper
A179

Geometric Designs and Arrow
A180

Perf. 14x13½, 13½x14
1975, Mar. 17 Photogravure
645	A179	25m yel, org & blk	25	20
646	A180	65m ultra & multi	40	25

Union of Arab Engineers, 13th Conference, Tunis, Mar. 17–21.

Brass Coffeepot and Plate
A181

Designs: 15m, Horse and rider. 25m, Still life. 30m, Bird cage (vert.). 40m, Woman with earrings (vert.). 60m, Design patterns.
1975, Apr. 14 *Perf. 13x14, 14x13*
647	A181	10m blk & multi	10	10
648	A181	15m blk & multi	15	15
649	A181	25m blk & multi	20	15
650	A181	30m blk & multi	25	15
651	A181	40m blk & multi	30	20
652	A181	60m blk & multi	35	25
	Nos. 647-652 (6)		1.35	1.00

Artisans and their works.

Communications and Weather Symbols
A182

1975, May 17 Photo. *Perf. 11½*
653	A182	50m lt bl & multi	30	20

World Telecommunications Day (communications serving meteorology).

Youth and Hope
A183

TUNISIA

Design: 65m, Bourguiba arriving at La Goulette, Tunis (horiz.).
1975, June 1   Photo.   Perf. 11½
| 654 | A183 | 25m multi | 20 | 20 |
| 655 | A183 | 65m multi | 35 | 25 |

Victory (independence), 20th anniversary.

Tunisian Woman, IWY Emblem
A184
1975, June 19 Litho.   Perf. 14x13½
| 656 | A184 | 110m multi | 60 | 40 |

International Women's Year 1975.

Children Crossing Street
A185
1975, July 5   Photo.   Perf. 13½x14
| 657 | A185 | 25m multi | 25 | 20 |

Highway safety campaign, July 1–Sept. 30.

Djerbian Minaret, Hotel and Marina, Jerba
A186

Old and new Tunisia: 15m, 17th century minaret and modern hotel, Tunis. 20m, Fortress, earring and hotel, Monastir. 65m, View of Sousse, hotel and pendant. 500m, Town wall, mosque and palms, Tozeur. 1d, Mosques and Arab ornaments, Kairouan.

1975, July 12 Litho.   Perf. 14x14½
658	A186	10m multi	20	20
659	A186	15m multi	20	20
660	A186	20m multi	20	20
661	A186	65m multi	40	30
662	A186	500m multi	3.00	1.50
663	A186	1d multi	5.50	2.75
		Nos. 658-663 (6)	9.50	5.15

Victors
A187

Symbolic Ship
A188
1975, Aug. 23   Photo.   Perf. 13½
| 664 | A187 | 25m ol & multi | 25 | 20 |
| 665 | A188 | 50m bl & multi | 35 | 30 |

7th Mediterranean Games, Algiers, Aug. 23–Sept. 6.

Flowers in Vase, Birds Holding Letters
A189
1975, Sept. 29 Litho.   Perf. 13½x13
| 666 | A189 | 100m bl & multi | 50 | 30 |

Stamp Day.

Sadiki College, Young Bourguiba
A190
Engraved and Lithographed
1975, Nov. 17   Perf. 13
| 667 | A190 | 25m sep, org & ol | 25 | 20 |

Sadiki College, centenary.

Duck
A191

Vergil
A192

Designs (Mosaics): 10m, Fish. 25m, Lioness (horiz.). 60m, Head of Medusa (horiz.). 75m, Circus spectators.

1976, Feb. 16   Photo.   Perf. 13
668	A191	5m multi	10	5
669	A191	10m multi	15	5
670	A192	25m multi	30	20
671	A192	60m multi	35	20
672	A192	75m multi	40	30
673	A192	100m multi	50	40
a.		Souvenir sheet of 6	3.00	3.00
		Nos. 668-673 (6)	1.80	1.20

Tunisian mosaics, 2nd–5th centuries. No. 673a contains one each of Nos. 668–673, olive green margin with white inscription. Size: 100x127½mm. Sold for 500m. Issued perf. and imperf.; same price.

Telephone
A193
1976, Mar. 10 Litho. Perf. 14x13½
| 674 | A193 | 150m bl & multi | 70 | 40 |

Centenary of first telephone call by Alexander Graham Bell, Mar. 10, 1876.

Pres. Bourguiba and "20"
A194

Designs (Pres. Bourguiba and): 100m, "20" and symbolic Tunisian flag. 150m, "Tunisia" rising from darkness, and 20 flowers.

1976, Mar. 20   Photo.   Perf. 11½
675	A194	40m multi	25	20
676	A194	100m multi	45	30
677	A194	150m multi	70	35

Souvenir Sheets
Perf. 11½, Imperf.
678	A194	Sheet of 3, multi	2.40	2.40
a.		50m like 40m	18	10
b.		200m like 100m	80	40
c.		250m like 150m	1.00	50

20th anniversary of independence. No. 678 has gray margin with white inscription. Size: 130x95mm.

Blind Man with Cane
A195

Procession and Buildings
A196
1976, Apr. 7   Engr.   Perf. 13
| 679 | A195 | 100m blk & red | 50 | 25 |

World Health Day: "Foresight prevents blindness."

1976, May 31 Photo. Perf. 12x11½
| 680 | A196 | 40m multi | 30 | 10 |

Habitat, U.N. Conference on Human Settlements, Vancouver, Canada, May 31–June 11.

Face and Hands Decorated with Henna
A197

Designs: 50m, Sponge fishing at Jerba. 65m, Textile industry. 110m, Pottery of Guellala.

1976, June 15 Photo. Perf. 13x13½
681	A197	40m multi	18	18
682	A197	50m multi	22	20
683	A197	65m multi	30	20
684	A197	110m multi	50	25

Old and new Tunisia.

The Spirit of 76, by Archibald M. Willard—A198
1976, July 4   Perf. 13x14
| 685 | A198 | 200m multi | 1.00 | 65 |

Souvenir Sheet
Perf. 13x14, Imperf.
| 686 | A198 | 500m multi | 3.00 | 3.00 |

American Bicentennial. No. 686 contains one stamp; light brown margin with black inscription showing stylized Paul Revere and flag. Size: 135x105mm.

Running
A199

Designs (Montreal Olympic Games Emblem and): 75m, Bicycling. 120m, Peace dove.

1976, July 17   Photo.   Perf. 11½
687	A199	50m gray, red & blk	30	20
688	A199	75m red, yel & blk	40	25
689	A199	120m org & multi	60	35

21st Olympic Games, Montreal, Canada, July 17–Aug. 1.

Child Reading
A200

Heads and Bird
A201

1976, Aug. 23   Litho.   Perf. 13
| 690 | A200 | 100m brn & multi | 50 | 25 |

Books for children.

1976, Sept. 30   Litho.   Perf. 13
| 691 | A201 | 150m org & multi | 70 | 35 |

Non-aligned Countries, 15th anniversary of 1st Conference.

Mouradite Mausoleum, 17th Century
A202

Designs: 100m, Minaret, Kairawan Great Mosque and psalmodist. 150m, Monastir Ribat monastery and Alboracq (sphinx). 200m, Barber's Mosque, Kairawan and man's bust.

1976, Oct. 25   Photo.   Perf. 14
| 692 | A202 | 85m multi | 40 | 20 |
| 693 | A202 | 100m multi | 50 | 25 |

TUNISIA

694	A202	150m multi		70	40
695	A202	200m multi		1.00	60

Cultural heritage.

Globe and Emblem
A203

1976, Dec. 24 Photo. *Perf. 13x14*
696	A203	150m multi		70	40

25th anniversary of United Nations Postal Administration.

Electronic Tree and ITU Emblem
A204

1977, May 17 Photo. *Perf. 14x13½*
697	A204	150m multi		80	60

9th World Telecommunications Day.

"Communication," Sassenage Castle, Grenoble
A205

1977, May 19 Litho. *Perf. 13½x13*
698	A205	100m multi		60	35

10th anniversary of International French Language Council.

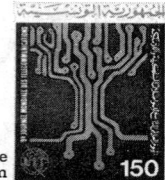

Soccer
A206

1977, June 27 Photo. *Perf. 13½*
699	A206	150m multi		80	50

Junior World Soccer Tournament, Tunisia, June 27–July 10.

Gold Coin, 10th Century
A207

Cultural Heritage: 15m, Stele, Gorjani Cemetery, Tunis, 13th century. 20m, Floral design, 17th century illumination. 30m, Bird and flowers, glass painting, 1922. 40m, Antelope, from 11th century clay pot. 50m, Gate, Sidi Bou Said, 20th century.

1977, July 9 Photo. *Perf. 13*
700	A207	10m multi		5	5
701	A207	15m multi		7	5
702	A207	20m multi		10	5
703	A207	30m multi		20	10
704	A207	40m multi		25	10
705	A207	50m multi		30	20
a.	Miniature sheet of 6			1.50	1.50
	Nos. 700-705 (6)			97	55

No. 705a contains one each of Nos. 700–705. Size: 136x37mm.

"The Young Republic" and Bourguiba
A208

Designs (Habib Bourguiba and): 100m, "The Confident Republic" and 20 doves. 150m, "The Determined Republic" and 20 roses.

1977, July 25 Photo. *Perf. 13x13½*
706	A208	40m multi		30	20
707	A208	100m multi		50	30
708	A208	150m multi		75	40
a.	Souvenir sheet of 3			2.75	2.75

20th anniversary of the Republic. No. 708a contains one each of Nos. 706–708; lilac margin with white inscription and coat of arms. Sold for 500m. Exists imperf.

Symbolic Cancellation, APU Emblem
A209

1977, Aug. 16 Litho. *Perf. 13x12½*
709	A209	40m multi		30	20

Arab Postal Union, 25th anniversary.

Diseased Knee, Gears and Globe
A210

1977, Sept. 26 Photo. *Perf. 14x13½*
710	A210	120m multi		70	40

World Rheumatism Year.

Farmer, Road, Water and Electricity—A211

1977, Dec. 15 Photo. *Perf. 13½*
711	A211	40m multi		30	20

Rural development.

Factory Workers
A212

Pres. Bourguiba, Torch and "9"
A213

Designs: 20m, Bus driver and trains (horiz.). 40m, Farmer driving tractor (horiz.).

1978, Mar. 6 *Perf. 13x14, 14x13*
712	A212	20m rose red & multi		20	20
713	A212	40m blk & grn		25	20
714	A212	100m multi		55	30

5th development plan, creation of new jobs.

1978, Apr. 9 Engr. *Perf. 13*
		Design: 60m, Pres. Bourguiba and "9."			
715	A213	40m multi		25	20
716	A213	60m multi		30	20

40th anniversary of first fight for independence, Apr. 9, 1938.

Policeman
A214

Tunisian Goalkeeper
A215

1978, May 2 Photo. *Perf. 13x13½*
717	A214	150m multi		80	50

6th Regional African Interpol Conference, Tunis, May 2–5.

1978, June 1 Photo. *Perf. 13x14*

Designs: 150m., Soccer player, maps of South America and Africa, flags.
718	A215	40m multi		25	20
719	A215	150m multi		80	50

11th World Cup Soccer Championship, Argentina, June 1–25.

Destruction of Apartheid, Map of South Africa—A216

Design: 100m, White and black doves flying in unison.

1978, Aug. 30 Litho. *Perf. 13½x14*
720	A216	50m multi		25	15
721	A216	100m multi		50	30

Fight against Apartheid.

"Pollution is a Plague"
A217

"Eradication of Smallpox"
A218

Designs: 50m, "The Sea, mankind's patrimony." 120m, "Greening of the desert."

1978, Sept. 11 Photo. *Perf. 14x13*
722	A217	10m multi		5	5
723	A217	50m multi		25	20
724	A217	120m multi		60	40

Protection of the environment.

1978, Oct. 16 Litho. *Perf. 12½*
725	A218	150m multi		75	50

Global eradication of smallpox.

Jerba Wedding
A219

Designs: 5m, Horseman from Zlass (vert.). 75m, Women potters from the Mogods. 100m, Dove over Marabout Sidi Mahrez cupolas, Tunis. 500m, Plowing in Jenduba. 1d, Spring Festival in Tozeur (man on swing).

1978, Nov. 1 Photo. *Perf. 13*
726	A219	5m multi		5	5
727	A219	60m multi		30	20
728	A219	75m multi		40	25
729	A219	100m multi		50	35
730	A219	500m multi		2.75	1.25
731	A219	1d multi		5.00	2.25
	Nos. 726-731 (6)			9.00	4.35

Traditional Arab calligraphy.

Lenin and Red Banner over Kremlin
A220

Farhat Hached, Union Emblem
A221

1978, Nov. 7 *Perf. 13½*
732	A220	150m multi		75	50

60th anniversary of Russian October Revolution.

1978, Dec. 5 Photo. *Perf. 14*
733	A221	50m multi		25	20

Farhat Hached (1914–1952), founder of General Union of Tunisian Workers.

Family
A222

Sun with Man's Face
A223

1978, Dec. 15 Photo. *Perf. 13½*
734	A222	50m multi		30	20

Tunisian Family Planning Association, 10th anniversary.

1978, Dec. 25 *Perf. 14*
735	A223	100m multi		60	40

Sun as a source of light and energy.

The only foreign revenue stamps listed in this Catalogue are those authorized for prepayment of postage.

TUNISIA

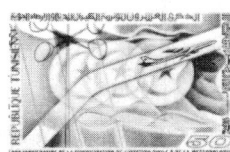

Plane, Weather Map and Instruments
A224

1978, Dec. 29
736 A224 50m multi   25   20

Tunisian civil aviation and meteorology, 20th anniversary.

Habib Bourguiba and Constitution
A225

1979, May 31   Photo.   Perf. 14x13½
737 A225 50m multi   25   12

20th anniversary of Constitution.

El Kantaoui Port
A226

1979, June 3   Perf. 13½x14
738 A226 150m multi   75   35

Development of El Kantaoui as a resort area.

View of Korbous—A227

Landscapes: 100m, Mides.

1979, July 14   Photo.   Perf. 12½x13½
739 A227 50m multi   25   12
740 A227 100m multi   50   25

Bow Net Weaving— A228

Design: 50m, Beekeeping.

1979, Aug. 15   Photo.   Perf. 11½
741 A228 10m multi   5   5
742 A228 50m multi   25   12

For all your Philatelic needs, see the yellow pages.

Pres. Bourguiba, "10" and Hands— A229

1979, Sept. 5
743 A229 50m multi   25   12

Socialist Destour Party, 10th Congress.

Modes of Communication, ITU Emblem
A230

1979, Sept. 20   Litho.   Perf. 11½
744 A230 150m multi   75   40

3rd World Telecommunications Exhibition, Geneva, Sept. 20-26.

Arab Achievements—A231

1979, Oct. 1   Perf. 14½
745 A231 50m multi   25   15

Children Crossing Street, IYC Emblem
A232

IYC Emblem and: 100m, Child and birds.

1979, Oct. 16   Perf. 14x13½
746 A232 50m multi   25   12
747 A232 100m multi   50   25

International Year of the Child.

See "Special Notices" at the front of this volume for data on the listing methods of this Catalogue, abbreviations, condition, prices and examination.

Dove, Olive Tree, Map of Tunisia   Woman Wearing Crown
A233   A234

1979, Nov. 1   Litho.   Perf. 12
748 A233 150m multi   75   40

2nd International Olive Oil Year.

1979, Nov. 3   Perf. 14½
749 A234 50m multi   25   20

Central Bank of Tunisia, 20th anniversary.

Children and Jujube Tree—A235

1979, Dec. 25   Litho.   Perf. 15x14½
750 A235 20m shown   10   5
751 A235 30m Peacocks   15   8
752 A235 70m Goats   35   18
753 A235 85m Girl, date palm   42   22

Postal Code Introduction—A236

1980, Mar. 20   Photo.   Perf. 14
754 A236 50m multi   25   12

Fight Against Cigarette Smoking—A237

1980, Apr. 7
755 A237 150m multi   75   38

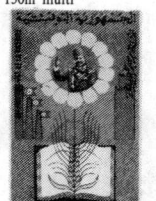

Pres. Bourguiba in Flower, Open Book—A238

1980, June 1   Photo.   Perf. 11½
756 A238 50m shown   25   12
757 A238 100m Dove, Bourguiba, mosque   50   25

Victory (independence), 25th anniversary.

Butterfly and Gymnast—A239

1980, June 3   Photo.   Perf. 12x11½
Granite Paper
758 A239 100m multi   50   25

Turin Gymnastic Games, June 1-7.

Artisans
A240   A241

1980, July 21   Photo.   Perf. 13½
759 A240 30m multi   15   8
760 A241 75m multi   38   20

ibn-Khaldun (1332-1406), Historian— A242

1980, July 28   Perf. 14
761 A242 50m multi   25   12

Avicenna (Arab Physician), Birth Millenium— A243

1980, Aug. 18   Engraved   Perf. 12½x13
762 A243 100m redsh brn & sep   50   25

Arab Achievements— A244

1980, Aug. 25   Photo.   Perf. 13½x14
763 A244 50m multi   25   12

Port Sidi bou Said— A245

TUNISIA

1980, Sept. 4			Perf. 14
764	A245	100m multi	50 25

World Tourism Conference, Manila, Sept. 27—A246

1980, Sept. 27		Photo.	Perf. 14
765	A246	150m multi	75 38

Wedding in Jerba, by Yahia (1903-1969)—A247

1980, Oct. 1			Perf. 12
766	A247	50m multi	25 12

Tozeur-Nefta International Airport Opening—A248

1980, Oct. 13		Photo.	Perf. 13x13½
767	A248	85m multi	42 20

Eye and Text—A249

1980, Oct. 26		Litho.	Perf. 13½x14
768	A249	100m multi	50 25

7th Afro-Asian Ophthalmologic Congress,

Hegira, 1500th Anniv.—A250

1980, Nov. 9

769	A250	50m Spiderweb	25 12
770	A250	80m City skyline	40 20

Film Strip and Woman's Head—A251

1980, Nov. 15		Photo.	Perf. 14x13½
771	A251	100m multi	50 25

Carthage Film Festival,

Orchid—A252

1980, Nov. 17   Perf. 13½x14

772	A252	20m shown	10 5
773	A252	25m Wild cyclamen	12 6

Size: 39x27mm.   Perf. 14

774	A252	50m Mouflon	25 12
775	A252	100m Golden eagle	50 25

Campaign to Save Kairouan Mosque—A253

1980, Dec. 29		Photo.	Perf. 12
		Granite Paper	
776	A253	85m multi	42 20

Heinrich von Stephan—A254

1981, Jan. 7

| 777 | A254 | 150m multi | 75 38 |

Heinrich von Stephan (1831-1897), founder of UPU.

Blood Donors' Association, 20th Anniversary—A255

1981, Mar. 5		Litho.	Perf. 14x13½
778	A255	75m multi	38 20

Pres. Bourguiba and Flag—A256

1981, Mar. 20		Photo.	Perf. 12x11½
		Granite Paper	
779	A256	50m shown	25 12
780	A256	60m Dove, "25"	30 15
781	A256	85m Doves	42 20
782	A256	120m Victory on winged horse	60 30
a.		Souvenir sheet of 4	2.50 1.25

25th anniversary of independence. No. 782 contains Nos. 779-782; blue margin. Size: 96x131mm. Sold for 500m. Exists imperf.

Pres. Bourguiba and Flower A257

1981, Apr. 10		Photo.	Perf. 12x11½
783	A257	50m shown	25 12
784	A257	75m Bourguiba, flower, diff.	38 20

Destourien Socialist Party Congress.

Mosque Entrance, Mahdia A258

1981, Apr. 20			Perf. 13½
785	A258	50m shown	25 12
786	A258	85m Tozeur Great Mosque, vert.	42 20
787	A258	100m Needle Rocks, Tabarka	50 25

13th World Telecommunications Day A259

Youth Festival A260

1981, May 17		Litho.	Perf. 14x15
788	A259	150m multi	75 38
1981, June 2		Photo.	Perf. 11½
		Granite Paper	
789	A260	100m multi	50 25

Kemal Ataturk (1881-1938) First President of Turkey A261

1981, June 15		Photo.	Perf. 14
790	A261	150m multi	75 38

Skifa, Mahdia—A262

1981, July 15		Photo.	Perf. 11½x12
791	A262	150m multi	75 38

Mohammed Tahar Ben Achour (1879-1973), Scholar—A263

1981, Aug. 6			Perf. 13
792	A263	200m multi	1.00 50

25th Anniv. of Personal Status Code (Women's Liberation)—A264

1981, Aug. 13

793	A264	50m Woman	25 12
794	A264	100m shown	50 25

Intl. Year of the Disabled—A265

1981, Sept. 21		Photo.	Perf. 13½
795	A265	250m multi	1.25 60

TUNISIA 791

Pilgrimage to Mecca
A266

World Food Day
A267

1981, Oct. 7		Photo.		Perf. 13½
796	A266	50m multi	25	12
1981, Oct. 16		Litho.		Perf. 12
		Granite Paper		
797	A267	200m multi	1.00	50

Traditional Jewelry—A268

Designs: 150m, Mneguech silver earrings (vert.). 180m Mahfdha (silver medallion worn by married women). 200m, Essalta gold headdress (vert.).

1981, Dec. 7		Photo.		Perf. 14
798	A268	150m multi	75	38
799	A268	180m multi	90	45
800	A268	200m multi	1.00	50

Bizerta Bridge—A269

1981, Dec. 14	**Granite Paper**		Perf. 12x11½
801	A269	230m multi	1.15	60

Chemist Compounding Honey Mixture, Manuscript Miniature, 1224—A270

1982, Apr. 3		Photo.		Perf. 13
802	A270	80m multi	40	20

Arab Chemists' Union, 16th anniv.

Oceanic Enterprise Symposium, Tunis, May 12-14
A271

The Productive Family Employment Campaign
A272

1982, May 12		Photo.		Perf. 13½
803	A271	150m multi	75	38
1982, June 26	**Granite Paper**		Perf. 12½
804	A272	80m multi	40	20

25th Anniv. of Republic
A273

Scouting Year
A274

Pres. Bourguiba and Various Women.

1982, July 25		Litho.		Perf. 14x13½
805	A273	80m multi	40	20
806	A273	100m multi	50	25
807	A273	200m multi	1.00	50
1982, Aug. 23			Perf. 14½x14, 14x14½
808	A274	80m multi	40	20
809	A274	200m multi	1.00	50

75th anniv. of scouting and 50th anniv. of scouting in Tunisia (80m).

30th Anniv. of Arab Postal Union
A275

ITU Plenipotentiaries Conference, Nairobi
A276

1982, Sept. 29			Perf. 14x13½
810	A275	80m Woman, envelopes	40	20
		Size: 23x40mm.	
811	A275	200m Woman, buildings	1.00	50
1982, Oct. 1		Photo.		Perf. 12
		Granite Paper		
812	A276	200m multi	1.00	50

World Food Day
A277

Tahar Haddad (1899-1935), Social Reformer
A278

1982, Oct. 16		Litho.		Perf. 13
813	A277	200m multi	1.00	50
1982, Oct. 25		Engr.		
814	A278	200m dk brn	1.00	50

TB Bacillus Centenary
A279

Folk Songs and Stories
A280

1982, Nov. 16		Litho.		Perf. 13½
815	A279	100m multi	50	25
1982, Nov. 22		Photo.		Perf. 14
816	A280	20m Dancing in the Rain	10	5
817	A280	30m Woman Sweeping	15	8
818	A280	70m Fisherman and the Child	35	18
819	A280	80m Rooster and the Oranges	40	20
820	A280	100m Woman and the Mirror, horiz.	50	25
821	A280	120m The Two Girls, horiz.	60	30
	Nos. 816-821 (6)		2.10	1.06

Intl. Palestinian Solidarity Day—A281

1982, Nov. 30		Litho.		Perf. 13x12
822	A281	80m multi	40	20

Farhat Hached (1914-1952)
A282

Bourguiba Dam Opening
A283

1982, Dec. 6		Engr.		Perf. 13
823	A282	80m brn red	40	20
1982, Dec. 20		Litho.		Perf. 13½
824	A283	80m multi	40	20

Environmental Training College Opening—A284

1982, Dec. 29		Photo.		Perf. 11½
		Granite Paper		
825	A284	80m multi	40	20

World Communications Year—A285

1983, May 17		Litho.		Perf. 13½x14
826	A285	200m multi	1.00	50

20th Anniv. of Org. of African Unity—A286

1983, May 25		Photo.		Perf. 12
827	A286	230m ultra & grnsh bl	1.15	58

30th Anniv. of Customs Cooperation Council—A287

1983, May 30		Litho.		Perf. 13½
828	A287	100m multi	50	25

Aly Ben Ayed (1930-1972), Actor—A288

1983, Aug. 15		Engr.		Perf. 13
829	A288	80m dk car, dl red & gray	40	20

TUNISIA

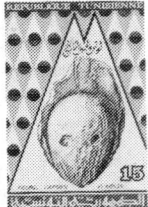

Stone – carved Face, El-Mekta—A289

Pre-historic artifacts: 20m, Neolithic necklace, Kel el-Agab. 30m, Mill and grindstone, Redeyef. 40m, Orynx head rock carving, Gafsa. 80m, Dolmen Mactar. 100m, Acheulian Bi-face flint, El-Mekta.

1983, Aug. 20	Photo.	Perf. 11½x12
830	A289 15m multi	5 5
831	A289 20m multi	10 5
832	A289 30m multi	15 8
833	A289 40m multi	20 10
834	A289 80m multi	40 20
835	A289 100m multi	50 25
	Nos. 830-835 (6)	1.40 73

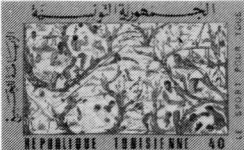

Sports for All—A290

1983, Sept. 27	Litho.	Perf. 12½
836	A290 40m multi	20 10

World Fishing Day—A293

1983, Oct. 17		Perf. 14½
837	A291 200m multi	1.00 50

Evacuation of French Troops, 20th Anniv.—A292

1983, Oct. 17	Litho.	Perf. 14x13½
838	A292 80m multi	40 20

Tapestry Weaver, by Hedi Khayachi (1882-1948)—A293

1983, Nov. 22	Photo.	Perf. 11½
	Granite Paper	
839	A293 80m multi	40 20

Natl. Allegiance
A294

Jet, Woman's Head, Emblem
A295

1983, Nov. 30	Litho.	Perf. 14½
840	A294 100m Children, flag	50 25

1983, Dec. 21		Perf. 13½
841	A295 150m multi	75 38

Pres. Bourguiba
A296

4th Molecular Biology Symposium
A297

Destourien Socialist Party, 50th Anniv.: Portraits of Bourguiba. 200m, 230m horiz.

1984, Mar. 2 Photo.	Perf. 12½x12, 12x12½
	Granite Paper
842	A296 40m multi	20 10
843	A296 70m multi	35 18
844	A296 80m multi	40 20
845	A296 150m multi	75 38
846	A296 200m multi	1.00 50
847	A296 230m multi	1.15 60
	Nos. 842-847 (6)	3.85 1.96

1984, Apr. 3		Perf. 13½x13
848	A297 100m Map, diagram	50 25

TUNISIA

SEMI-POSTAL STAMPS.

No. 36
Overprinted in Red ✚
Perf. 14x13½.

			1915, Feb.		Unwmkd.
B1	A5	15c vio, *pnksh*		45	38

No. 32
Overprinted in Red ✚

			1916, Feb. 15		
B2	A4	5c grn, *grnsh*		60	60

Types of Regular Issue of 1906,
Printed in New Colors and Surcharged
✚ 10 c.

1916, Aug.
B3	A5	10c on 15c brn vio, *bl*	45	45
B4	A5	10c on 20c brn, *org*	45	45
B5	A5	10c on 25c bl, *grn*	1.75	1.75
B6	A6	10c on 35c ol grn & vio	3.25	3.25
B7	A6	10c on 40c bis & blk	1.50	1.50
B8	A6	10c on 75c vio brn & grn	3.75	3.75
B9	A7	10c on 1fr red & grn	1.50	1.50
B10	A7	10c on 2fr bis & bl	42.50	42.50
B11	A7	10c on 5fr vio & red	65.00	65.00
	Nos. B3-B11 (9)		120.15	120.15

Nos. B3 to B11 were sold at their face value but had a postal value of 10c only. The excess was applied to the relief of prisoners of war in Germany.

Types of Regular Issue of 1906 15c
Printed in New Colors and Surcharged in Carmine ✚ ═

1918
B12	A5	15c on 20c grn	60	60
B13	A5	15c on 25c dk bl *buff*	60	60
B14	A6	15c on 35c gray grn & red	80	80
B15	A6	15c on 40c brn & lt bl	1.50	1.50
B16	A6	15c on 75c red brn & blk	2.75	2.75
B17	A7	15c on 1fr red & vio	9.00	9.00
B18	A7	15c on 2fr bis brn & red	37.50	37.50
B19	A7	15c on 5fr vio & blk	75.00	75.00
	Nos. B12-B19 (8)		127.75	127.75

The different parts of the surcharge are more widely spaced on the stamps of types A6 and A7. These stamps were sold at their face value but had a postal value of 15c only. The excess was intended for the relief of prisoners of war in Germany.

Types of
1906-22
Surcharged
AFF^t 0^c

1923
B20	A4	0c on 1c bl	28	28
B21	A4	0c on 2c ol brn	28	28
B22	A4	1c on 3c grn	28	28
B23	A4	2c on 5c red vio	28	28
B24	A9	3c on 10c vio, *bluish*	28	28
B25	A5	5c on 15c ol grn	28	28
B26	A5	5c on 20c bl, *pink*	60	60
B27	A5	5c on 25c vio, *bluish*	60	60
B28	A9	5c on 30c org	60	60
B29	A6	5c on 35c bl & vio	80	80
B30	A6	5c on 40c bl & brn	80	80
B31	A9	10c on 50c blk, *bluish*	80	80
B32	A6	10c on 60c ol brn & bl	80	80
B33	A6	10c on 75c vio & lt grn	2.00	2.00
B34	A7	25c on 1fr mar & vio	2.00	2.00
B35	A7	25c on 2fr bl & rose	8.50	8.50
B36	A7	25c on 5fr grn & ol brn	37.50	37.50
	Nos. B20-B36 (17)		56.68	56.68

These stamps were sold at their original values but had postal franking values only to the amounts surcharged on them. The difference was intended to be used for the benefit of wounded soldiers.

This issue was entirely speculative. Before the announced date of sale most of the stamps were taken by postal employees and practically none of them were offered to the public.

Mail Delivery
SP1

Type of Parcel Post Stamps, 1906, with Surcharge in Black

1925, June 7   Perf. 13½x14.
B37	SP1	1c on 5c brn & red, *pink*	22	22
a.	Surch. omitted		45.00	
B38	SP1	2c on 10c brn & bl, *yel*	22	22
B39	SP1	3c on 20c red vio & rose, *lav*	45	45
B40	SP1	5c on 25c sl grn & rose, *bluish*	45	45
a.	Surcharge omitted			
B41	SP1	5c on 40c rose & grn, *yel*	45	45
B42	SP1	10c on 50c vio & bl, *lav*	85	85
B43	SP1	10c on 75c grn & ol, *grnsh*	60	60
B44	SP1	25c on 1fr bl & grn, *bluish*	60	60
B45	SP1	25c on 2fr rose & vio, *pnksh*	3.75	3.75
B46	SP1	25c on 5fr red & brn, *lem*	22.50	22.50
	Nos. B37-B46 (10)		30.09	30.09

These stamps were sold at their original values but paid postage only to the amount of the surcharged values. The difference was given to Child Welfare societies.

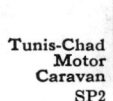

Tunis-Chad Motor Caravan
SP2

1928, Feb.   Engr.   Perf. 13½
B47	SP2	40c + 40c org brn	50	50
B48	SP2	50c + 50c dp vio	50	50
B49	SP2	75c + 75c dk bl	60	60
B50	SP2	1fr + 1fr car	60	60
B51	SP2	1.50fr + 1.50fr brt bl	60	60
B52	SP2	2fr + 2fr vio	70	70
B53	SP2	5fr + 5fr red brn	70	70
	Nos. B47-B53 (7)		4.20	4.20

The surtax on these stamps was for the benefit of Child Welfare societies.

Regular Issue of 1931 Surcharged in Black:

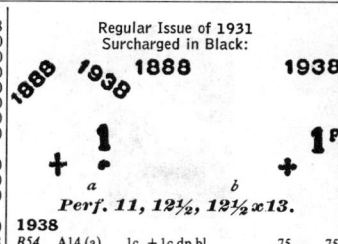

1938
B54	A14 (a)	1c + 1c dp bl	75	75
B55	A14 (a)	2c + 2c yel brn	75	75
B56	A14 (a)	3c + 3c blk	75	75
B57	A14 (a)	5c + 5c yel grn	75	75
B58	A14 (a)	10c + 10c red	75	75
B59	A15 (a)	15c + 15c dl vio	75	75
B60	A15 (a)	20c + 20c dl brn	75	75
B61	A15 (a)	25c + 25c org red	75	75
B62	A15 (a)	30c + 30c dp grn	75	75
B63	A15 (a)	40c + 40c org	75	75
B64	A16 (a)	50c + 50c ultra	75	75
B65	A16 (a)	75c + 75c yel	75	75
B66	A16 (a)	90c + 90c red	75	75
B67	A16 (a)	1fr + 1fr ol blk	75	75
B68	A17 (b)	1.50fr + 1fr brt ultra	75	75
B69	A17 (b)	2fr + 1.50fr dp brn	1.50	1.50
B70	A17 (b)	2fr + 2fr dk grn	1.50	1.50
B71	A17 (b)	5fr + 3fr car rose	9.00	9.00
a.	Perf. 12½		50.00	
B72	A17 (b)	10fr + 5fr blk	22.50	22.50
B73	A17 (b)	20fr + 10fr dk brn	35.00	35.00
	Nos. B54-B73 (20)		80.75	80.75

50th anniversary of the post office.

Stamps of 1939-40 Surcharged in Black, Blue or Red

SECOURS NATIONAL

1941

Perf. 14x13½.

1941
B74	A11	1fr on 45c emer (Bk)	30	30
B75	A13	1.30fr on 1.25fr car rose (Bl)	30	30
B76	A13	1.50fr on 1.40fr brt red vio (Bk)	30	30
B77	A13	2fr on 2.25fr ultra (R)	30	30

The surcharge measures 11x14 mm. on No. B74.

British, French and American Soldiers
SP3

1943   Lithographed   Perf. 12
B78	SP3	1.50fr + 8.50fr crim	12	12
	Liberation of Tunisia.			

V1

Stamps of the design shown above were issued in 1944 by the Vichy Government, but were not placed on sale in the colony.

Native Scene
SP4

Surcharge in Black: " + 48frcs / pour nos / Combattants"

			1944		Perf. 11½
B79	SP4	2fr + 48fr red		45	45

The surtax was for soldiers.

Sidi Mahrez Mosque
SP5

Ramparts of Sfax—SP6

Fort Saint—SP7

Sidi-bou-Said—SP8
Lithographed.

		1945	Perf. 11½	Unwmkd.
B80	SP5	1.50fr + 8.50fr choc & red	30	30
B81	SP6	3fr + 12fr dk bl grn & red	30	30
B82	SP7	4fr + 21fr brn org & red	30	30
B83	SP8	10fr + 40fr red & blk	30	30

The surtax was for soldiers.

France No. B193 Overprinted in Black **TUNISIE**
a

1945   Perf. 14x13½
B84	SP147	2fr + 1fr red org	22	22

The surtax was for the aid of tuberculosis victims.

Same Overprint on Type of France, 1945
1945   Engraved   Perf. 13
B85	SP150	2fr + 3fr dk grn	30	30

Issued to commemorate Stamp Day.

TUNISIA

Same Overprint on France No. B192.
1945
B86 SP146 4fr + 6fr dk vio brn 22 22
The surtax was for war victims of the P.T.T.

Types of 1926 Surcharged in Carmine

1945 Typographed. *Perf. 14x13½.*
B87 A10 4fr + 6fr on 10c ultra 30 30
B88 A12 10fr + 30fr on 80c dk grn 30 30

The design of type A12 is redrawn, omitting "RF." The surtax was for war veterans.

Tunisian Soldier
SP9
Engraved

1946 *Perf. 13.* *Unwmkd.*
B89 SP9 20fr + 30fr grn, red & blk 75 75

The surtax aided Tunisian soldiers in Indo-China.

Type of France, 1946, Overprinted Type "a" in Carmine.
1946
B90 SP160 3fr + 2fr dk bl 45 45
Issued to commemorate Stamp Day.

Stamps and Types of 1926-46 Surcharged in Carmine and Black

1946 *Perf. 14x13½*
B91 A12 80c + 50c emer 30 30
B92 A12 1.50fr + 1.50fr rose lil 30 30
B93 A12 2fr + 2fr Prus grn 30 30
B94 A13 2.40fr + 2fr sal pink 30 30
B95 A13 4fr + 4fr ultra 30 30
     Nos. B91-B95 (5) 1.50 1.50

The two parts of the surcharge are more widely spaced on stamps of type A13.

Type of France, 1947, Overprinted Type "a" in Carmine.
1947 *Perf. 13*
B96 SP172 4.50fr + 5.50fr sep 45 45

On Type of France, 1946, Surcharged in Carmine with New Value and Bars.
B97 SP158 10fr + 15fr on 2fr + 3fr brt ultra 45 45

Type of 1926 Surcharged in Carmine
SOLIDARITE 1947

1947 Typographed *Perf. 14x13½*
B98 A13 10fr + 40fr blk 60 60

Feeding Young Bird
SP10

1947 Engraved. *Perf. 13.*
B99 SP10 4.50fr + 5.50fr dk bl grn 60 60
B100 SP10 6fr + 9fr brt ultra 60 60
B101 SP10 8fr + 17fr dp car 60 60
B102 SP10 10fr + 40fr dk pur 60 60

The surtax was for child welfare.

Type of Regular Issue of 1948 Surcharged in Blue

1948
B103 A21 4fr + 10fr ol grn & org 50 50

The surtax was for anti-tuberculosis work.

Arch of Triumph, Sbeitla
SP11

1948
B104 SP11 10fr + 40fr ol grn & ol 60 60
B105 SP11 18fr + 42fr dk bl & ind 60 60

The surtax was for charitable works of the army.

Arago Type of France, 1948, Overprinted in Carmine

1948
B106 SP176 6fr + 4fr brt car 60 60
Stamp Day, Mar. 6-7.

Sleeping Child—SP12
1949, June 1
B107 SP12 25fr + 50fr dk grn 1.30 1.30
The surtax was for child welfare.

Neptune Type of 1947 Surcharged in Black with Lorraine Cross and "F F L + 15F".
1949, Dec. 8
B108 A20 10fr + 15fr dp ultra & car 60 60

The surtax was for the Tunisian section of the Association of Free French.

Type of France, 1949, Overprinted in Carmine
1949, Mar. 26
B109 SP180 15fr + 5fr ind 85 85
Stamp Day, Mar. 26-27.

Type of France, 1950, Overprinted Type "b" in Ultramarine.
1950, Mar. 11 *Perf. 13* *Unwmkd.*
B110 SP183 12fr + 3fr dk grn 80 80
Stamp Day, Mar. 11-12.

Tunisian and French Woman Shaking Hands
SP13

1950, June 5
B111 SP13 15fr + 35fr red 80 80
B112 SP13 25fr + 45fr dp ultra 70 70

The surtax was for Franco-Tunisian Mutual Assistance.

Arab Soldier
SP14

1950, Aug. 21 Engraved
B113 SP14 25fr + 25fr dp bl 1.00 1.00
The surtax was for old soldiers.

Type of France, 1951, Overprinted Type "a" in Black.
1951, Mar. 10
B114 SP186 12fr + 3fr brnsh gray 55 55
Stamp Day, Mar. 10-11.

Mother Carrying Child
SP15
1951, June 19 Engr. *Perf. 13*
B115 SP15 30fr + 15fr dp ultra 1.30 1.30
The surtax was for child welfare.

National Cemetery of Gammarth
SP16
1952, June 15
B116 SP16 30fr + 10fr bl 1.30 1.30
The surtax aided orphans of the military services.

Type of France 1952 Overprinted Type "c" in Lilac.
1952, Mar. 8 *Unwmkd.*
B117 SP190 12fr + 3fr pur 60 60
Stamp Day, Mar. 8.

Stucco Work, Bardo   Boy Campers
SP17   SP18
1952, May 5 Engraved *Perf. 13*
B118 SP17 15fr + 1fr ultra & ind 65 65
The surtax was for charitable works of the army.

1952, June 15
B119 SP18 30fr + 10fr dk grn 1.00 1.00
The surtax was for the Educational League vacation camps.

Type of France, 1952, Surcharged Type "a" and Surtax.
1952, Oct. 15
B120 A226 15fr + 5fr bl grn 70 70

Issued to commemorate the centenary of the creation of the French Military Medal.

Type of France, 1953, Overprinted Type "a".
1953, Mar. 14
B121 SP193 12fr + 3fr ver 60 60
Issued to commemorate the "Day of the Stamp."

Type of France, 1954, Overprinted Type "a".
1954, Mar. 20
B122 SP196 12fr + 3fr ind 60 60
Stamp Day.

Balloon Post, 1870
SP19
1955, Mar. 19
B123 SP19 12fr + 3fr red brn 60 60
Stamp Days, Mar. 19-20.

Independent Kingdom

Francois de Taxis
SP20
1956, Mar. 17
B124 SP20 12fr + 3fr dk grn 60 60
Stamp Days, Mar. 17-18.

Republic

No. 246 Surcharged in Red
1957, Aug. 8 Engraved
B125 A29 20fr + 10fr dp ultra 60 60

15th anniversary of the army.

Florist Type of 1955 with Added Inscriptions, Surcharged in Red.
1957, Oct. 19 *Perf. 13*
B126 A34 20fr + 10fr dk vio 50 50

No. B126 is inscribed "5e. Foire Internationale" at bottom and lines of Arabic at either side.

TUNISIA

 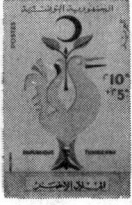

| Mailman Delivering Mail SP21 | Ornamental Cock SP22 |

Engraved.

1959, May 1 Perf. 13 Unwmkd.
B127 SP21 20fr +5fr dk brn & org brn 60 60

Issued for the Day of the Stamp. The surtax was for the Post Office Mutual Fund.

1959, Oct. 24 Lithographed Perf. 13
B128 SP22 10m +5m yel, lt bl & red 40 40

The surtax was for the Red Crescent Society.

| Mailman on Camel Phoning SP23 | Dancer of Kerkennah Holding Stamp SP24 |

1960, Apr. 16 Engraved. Perf. 13
B129 SP23 60m +5m ol, org & ultra 90 90

Issued for the Day of the Stamp, 1960.

1961, May 6 Perf. 13 Unwmkd.
Designs: 15+5m, Mail truck (horiz.). 20+6m, Hand holding magnifying glass and stamps. 50+5m, Running boy, symbols of mail.
B130 SP24 12m +4m cl, vio & ol 50 50
B131 SP24 15m +5m ol, cl & vio bl 55 55
B132 SP24 20m +6m multi 60 60
B133 SP24 50m +5m multi 75 75

Issued for Stamp Day.

Nos. B130-B133 Overprinted 1963 O.N.U

1963, Oct. 24
B134 SP24 12m +4m cl, vio & ol 35 35
B135 SP24 15m +5m cl & vio bl 45 45
B136 SP24 20m +6m multi 50 50
B137 SP24 50m +5m multi 80 80

Issued for United Nations Day.

| Old Man, Red Crescent SP25 | Nurse Holding Bottle of Blood SP26 |

Design: 75m+10m, Mother, child and Red Crescent.

1972, May 8 Engraved Perf. 13
B138 SP25 10m +10m pur & dk red 40 40
B139 SP25 75m +10m bis brn & dk red 50 50

Tunisian Red Crescent.

1973, May 10 Engr. Perf. 13
Design: 60m+10m, Red Crescent and blood donors' arms (horiz.).
B140 SP26 25m +10m multi 30 20
B141 SP26 60m +10m gray & car 50 45

Red Crescent appeal for blood donors.

| Blood Donors SP27 | Man Holding Scales with Balanced Diet SP28 |

Design: 75m+10m, Blood transfusion, symbolic design.

1974, May 8 Photo. Perf. 14x13
B142 SP27 25m +10m multi 30 30
B143 SP27 75m +10m multi 50 50

Red Crescent Society.

1975, May 8 Photo. Perf. 11½
B144 SP28 50m +10m multi 35 35

Tunisian Red Crescent fighting malnutrition.

Blood Donation, Woman and Man SP29

1976, May 8 Photo. Perf. 11½
B145 SP29 40m +10m multi 40 30

Tunisian Red Crescent Society.

Litter Bearers and Red Crescent SP30

1977, May 8 Photo. Perf. 13½x14
B146 SP30 50m +10m multi 35 35

Tunisian Red Crescent Society.

Blood Donors SP31

1978, May 8 Photo. Perf. 13x14
B147 SP31 50m +10m multi 30 30

Blood drive of Tunisian Red Crescent Society.

Hand and Red Crescent SP32

1979, May 8 Photo. Perf. 13½
B148 SP32 50m +10m multi 35 30

Tunisian Red Crescent Society.

Tunisian Red Crescent Society—SP33

1980, May 8 Photo. Perf. 13½
B149 SP33 50m +10m multi 30 25

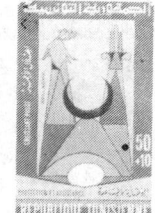

Red Crescent Society—SP34

1981, May 8 Photo. Perf. 14½x13½
B150 SP34 50m +10m multi 30 15

Dome of the Rock, Jerusalem—SP35

1981, Nov. 29 Photo. Perf. 13½
B151 SP35 50 +5m multi 28 14
B152 SP35 150 +5m multi 80 40
B153 SP35 200 +5m multi 1.05 55

Intl. Palestinian Solidarity Day.

Red Crescent Society—SP36

1982, May 8 Photo. Perf. 13½
B154 SP36 80m +10m multi 45 22

Red Crescent Society—SP37

1983, May 8 Litho. Perf. 14x13½
B155 SP37 80m +10m multi 45 22

Sabra and Chatilla Massacre—SP38

1983, Sept. 20 Photo. Perf. 13
B156 SP38 80 +5m multi 45 22

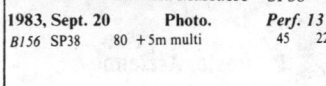

TUNISIA

AIR POST STAMPS.
No. 43 Surcharged in Red

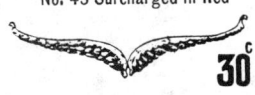

1919, Apr. Perf. 14x13½ Unwmkd.

C1	A6	30c on 35c ol grn & brn	60	60
a.		Inverted surcharge	65.00	65.00
b.		Double surcharge	65.00	65.00
c.		Double inverted surcharge	70.00	70.00
d.		Double surcharge, one inverted	65.00	65.00

Type A6, Overprinted in Rose

b

1920, Apr.

| C2 | A6 | 30c ol grn, bl & rose | 30 | 30 |

Nos. 53 and 55 Overprinted in Red

c

1927, Mar. 24

| C3 | A7 | 1fr ind & ultra | 38 | 38 |
| C4 | A7 | 2fr grn & red, *pink* | 1.50 | 1.25 |

Nos. 51 and 57 Surcharged in Black or Red

d

| C5 | A6 | 1.75fr on 75c ver & dl red (Bk) | 45 | 30 |
| C6 | A7 | 1.75fr on 5fr gray vio & grn (R) | 1.75 | 1.50 |

1928, Feb.
Overprinted on Type A13 in Blue.

C7	A13 (c)	1.30fr org & lt vio	2.25	1.10
C8	A13 (c)	1.80fr gray grn & red	2.75	60
C9	A13 (c)	2.55fr lil & ol brn	1.25	60

1930, Aug.
Surcharged on Type A13 in Blue.

C10	A13 (d)	1.50fr on 1.30fr org & lt vio	1.60	60
C11	A13 (d)	1.50fr on 1.80fr gray grn & red	2.50	45
C12	A13 (d)	1.50fr on 2.55fr lil & ol brn	5.00	1.25

UPU Type of Regular Issue
1949, Oct. 28 Engr. Perf. 13 Bluish Paper.

| C13 | A23 | 25fr dk bl | 1.10 | 1.10 |

Universal Postal Union, 75th anniversary. Exists imperf.; price $35.

Bird from Antique Mosaic, Museum of Sousse
AP2

1949 Unwmkd.

| C14 | AP2 | 200fr dk bl & ind | 3.50 | 90 |

(Arabic on one line)
AP3

1950-51

| C15 | AP3 | 100fr bl grn & brn | 1.60 | 45 |
| C16 | AP3 | 200fr dk bl & ind ('51) | 3.50 | 1.75 |

Monastir
AP4

Coast at Korbous
AP5

Design: 1000fr, Air view of Tozeur mosque.

1953-54

C17	AP4	100fr dk bl, ind & dk grn ('54)	1.50	45
C18	AP4	200fr cl, blk brn & red brn ('54)	3.00	90
C19	AP5	500fr dk brn & ultra	16.00	9.00
C20	AP5	1000fr dk grn	26.50	17.50

Imperforates exist.

Independent Kingdom
Types of 1953-54 Redrawn with "RF" Omitted.

1956, March 1

C21	AP4	100fr sl bl, ind & dk grn	1.20	55
C22	AP4	200fr multi	2.00	1.00
C23	AP5	500fr dk brn & ultra	5.25	4.00
C24	AP5	1000fr dk grn	10.00	7.50

Republic

Desert Swallows
AP6

Birds: No. C26, Butcherbird. No. C27, Cream-colored courser. 100m, European chaffinch. 150m, Pink flamingoes. 200m, Barbary partridges. 300m, European roller. 500m, Bustard.

1965-66 Photo. Perf. 12½ Size: 23x31mm.

C25	AP6	25m multi	75	35
C26	AP6	55m blk & lt bl	90	60
C27	AP6	55m multi ('66)	1.10	75

Perf. 11½ Size: 22½x33mm.

C28	AP6	100m multi	1.40	85
C29	AP6	150m multi ('66)	3.00	1.75
C30	AP6	200m multi ('66)	4.25	2.00
C31	AP6	300m multi ('66)	6.75	3.75
C32	AP6	500m multi ('66)	8.50	6.00
		Nos. C25-C32 (8)	26.65	15.05

See No. 474.

AIR POST SEMI-POSTAL STAMP.

Window, Great Mosque of Kairouan
SPAP1
Engraved.

1952, May 5 Perf. 13. Unwmkd.

| CB1 | SPAP1 | 50fr + 10fr blk & gray grn | 1.25 | 1.25 |

The surtax was for charitable works of the army.

POSTAGE DUE STAMPS.

Regular postage stamps perforated with holes in the form of a "T", the holes varying in size and number, were used as postage due stamps from 1888 to 1901.

D1 D2
Typographed.

1901-03 Perf. 14x13½. Unwmkd.

J1	D1	1c black	5	5
J2	D1	2c orange	6	6
J3	D1	5c blue	15	15
J4	D1	10c brown	22	15
J5	D1	20c bl grn	1.50	35
J6	D1	30c carmine	85	38
J7	D1	50c brn vio	70	38
J8	D1	1fr ol grn	55	38
J9	D1	2fr car, *grn*	1.75	75
J10	D1	5fr *yellow*	27.50	12.00
		Nos. J1-J10 (10)	33.33	25.12

No. J10 Surcharged in Blue

1914, Nov.

| J11 | D1 | 2fr on 5fr yel | 60 | 55 |

In January, 1917 regular 5c postage stamps were overprinted "T" in an inverted triangle and used as postage due stamps.

1922-49

J12	D2	1c black	12	8
J13	D2	2c *yellow*	12	8
J14	D2	5c vio brn	12	8
J15	D2	10c blue	12	8
J16	D2	10c yel grn ('45)	5	5
J17	D2	20c org, *red*	12	8
J18	D2	30c brn ('23)	5	5
J19	D2	50c rose red	35	22
J20	D2	50c bl vio ('45)	5	5
J21	D2	60c vio ('28)	35	22
J22	D2	80c bis ('28)	12	12
J23	D2	90c org red ('28)	55	40
J24	D2	1fr green	6	6
J25	D2	2fr ol grn, *straw*	42	15
J26	D2	2fr car rose ('45)	5	5
J27	D2	3fr vio, *pink* ('29)	15	15
J28	D2	4fr grnsh bl ('45)	15	15
J29	D2	5fr violet	42	28
J30	D2	10fr cer ('49)	15	15
J31	D2	20fr ol gray ('49)	45	15
		Nos. J12-J31 (20)	3.97	2.65

Inscribed: "Timbre Taxe."

1950 Perf. 14x13½ Unwmkd.

| J32 | D2 | 30fr blue | 70 | 45 |

Independent Kingdom

Grain and Fruit
D3

1957, Apr. 1 Engr. Perf. 14x13

J33	D3	1fr brt grn	15	15
J34	D3	2fr org brn	18	18
J35	D3	3fr bluish grn	30	30
J36	D3	4fr indigo	35	35
J37	D3	5fr lilac	30	30
J38	D3	10fr carmine	30	30
J39	D3	20fr chocolate	1.00	1.00
J40	D3	30fr blue	1.25	1.25
		Nos. J33-J40 (8)	3.83	3.83

Republic
Inscribed "Republique Tunisienne"

1960-77

J41	D3	1m emerald	5	5
J42	D3	2m red brn	5	5
J43	D3	3m bluish grn	8	8
J44	D3	4m indigo	8	8
J45	D3	5m lilac	22	22
J46	D3	10m car rose	30	30
J47	D3	20m vio brn	55	55
J48	D3	30m blue	70	70
J49	D3	40m lake ('77)	18	18
J50	D3	100m bl grn ('77)	42	42
		Nos. J41-J50 (10)	2.63	2.51

PARCEL POST STAMPS.

Mail Delivery Gathering Dates
PP1 PP2
Typographed.

1906 Perf. 13½x14 Unwmkd.

Q1	PP1	5c grn & vio brn	15	10
Q2	PP1	10c grn & red	60	15
Q3	PP1	20c dk brn & org	75	18
Q4	PP1	25c bl & brn	1.00	18
Q5	PP1	40c gray & rose	1.40	15
Q6	PP1	50c vio brn & bl	1.00	15
Q7	PP1	75c bis brn & bl	1.75	15
Q8	PP1	1fr red brn & red	1.40	15
Q9	PP1	2fr car & bl	3.75	18
Q10	PP1	5fr vio & vio brn	10.00	45
		Nos. Q1-Q10 (10)	21.80	1.87

1926

Q11	PP2	5c pale brn & dk bl	15	12
Q12	PP2	10c rose & vio	15	12
Q13	PP2	20c yel brn & blk	20	15
Q14	PP2	25c org brn & blk	35	20
Q15	PP2	40c dp rose & dp grn	90	35

TUNISIA—TURKEY

Q16	PP2	50c lt vio & blk	90	35
Q17	PP2	60c ol & brn red	1.00	50
Q18	PP2	75c gray vio & bl grn	1.00	15
Q19	PP2	80c ver & ol brn	90	15
Q20	PP2	1fr Prus bl & dp rose	90	15
Q21	PP2	2fr vio & mag	1.75	15
Q22	PP2	4fr red & blk	2.25	15
Q23	PP2	5fr red brn & dp vio	3.00	28
Q24	PP2	10fr dl red & grn, *grnsh*	6.00	40
Q25	PP2	20fr yel grn & dp vio, *lav*	10.00	65
		Nos. Q11-Q25 (15)	29.45	3.87

Parcel post stamps were discontinued July 1, 1940.

TURKEY
(tŭr'kĭ)

LOCATION — In southeastern Europe and Asia Minor, between the Mediterranean and Black Seas.
GOVT.—Republic.
AREA—296,500 sq. mi.
POP.—42,130,000 (est. 1977).
CAPITAL—Ankara.

The Ottoman Empire ceased to exist in 1922, and the Republic of Turkey was inaugurated in 1923.

- 40 Paras = 1 Piastre
- 40 Paras = 1 Ghurush (1926)
- 40 Paras = 1 Kurush (1929)
- 100 Kurush = 1 Lira

Turkish Numerals

"Tughra," Monogram of Sultan Abdul-Aziz
A1   A2

A3   A4

Lithographed.
1863   Imperf.   Unwmkd.
Red Band: 20pa, 1pi, 2pi.
Blue Band: 5pi.
Thin Paper.

1	A1	20pa *yellow*	70.00	30.00
a.		Tête bêche pair	250.00	250.00
b.		Without band	90.00	
c.		Green band		

2	A2	1pi *dl vio*	80.00	40.00
a.		1pi gray	80.00	
b.		Tête bêche pair	300.00	300.00
c.		Without band	85.00	
d.		Design reversed		350.00
e.		1pi yel (error)	300.00	250.00
4	A3	2pi *grnsh bl*	90.00	45.00
a.		2pi ind	90.00	
b.		Tête bêche pair	300.00	300.00
c.		Without band	100.00	
5	A4	5pi *rose*	140.00	65.00
a.		Tête bêche pair	550.00	550.00
b.		Without band	150.00	
c.		Green band	190.00	
d.		Red band	190.00	

Thick, Surface Colored Paper.

6	A1	20pa *yellow*	110.00	60.00
a.		Tête bêche pair	700.00	700.00
b.		Design reversed	550.00	550.00
c.		Without band	70.00	70.00
d.		Paper colored through	150.00	150.00
7	A2	1pi *gray*	130.00	85.00
a.		Tête bêche pair	700.00	700.00
b.		Design reversed		
c.		Without band		
d.		Paper colored through	250.00	250.00

The 2pi and 5pi had two printings. In the common printing, the stamps are more widely spaced and alternate horizontal rows of 12 are inverted. In the first and rare printing, the stamps are more closely spaced and no rows are tête bêche.

Crescent and Star, Symbols of Turkish Caliphate
A5

Surcharged

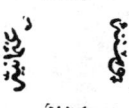

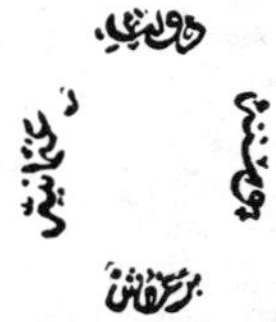

The bottom characters of this and the following surcharges denote the denomination. The characters at top and sides translate, "Ottoman Empire Posts."

1865   Typographed.   Perf. 12½

8	A5	10pa dp grn	4.00	5.00
b.		Imperf., pair	90.00	90.00
c.		"1" instead of "10" in each corner	225.00	225.00
9	A5	20pa yellow	1.00	1.25
a.		Star without rays	1.50	1.50
b.		Imperf., pair	90.00	90.00
10	A5	1pi lilac	3.00	3.00
a.		Star without rays	2.50	2.50
b.		Imperf., pair	70.00	70.00
c.		Half used as 20pa on cover		
11	A5	2pi blue	1.00	1.75
a.		Imperf., pair	70.00	70.00
b.		Half used as 1pi on cover		
12	A5	5pi carmine	1.00	1.75
b.		Imperf., pair	85.00	85.00
c.		Half used as 2½pi on cover		200.00
d.		Inverted surcharge		275.00
13	A5	25pi red org	140.00	130.00
a.		Imperf., pair	500.00	500.00

Surcharged

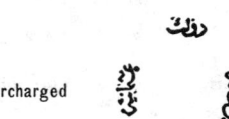

1867

14	A5	10pa gray grn		1.25
a.		Imperf., pair		50.00
15	A5	20pa yellow		2.75
a.		Imperf., pair		70.00
16	A5	1pi lilac		4.50
a.		Imperf., pair		85.00
b.		Imperf., with surcharge of 5pi		12.50

17	A5	2pi blue	1.25	1.75
a.		Imperf.		
b.		Half used as 1pi on cover		
18	A5	5pi rose		65	3.00
a.		Imperf.		
b.		Half used as 2½pi on cover		
19	A5	25pi orange	800.00	

Nos. 14, 15, 16 and 19 were never placed in use.

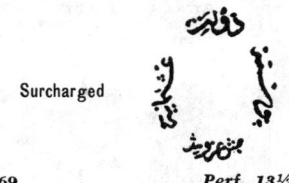

Surcharged

1869   Perf. 13½

20	A5	10pa dl vio	12.50	1.00
a.		Printed on both sides		
b.		Imperf., pair	60.00	60.00
c.		Inverted surcharge		70.00
d.		Double surcharge		
e.		10pa yel (error)		175.00
21	A5	20pa pale grn	37.50	65
a.		Printed on both sides	70.00	70.00
22	A5	1pi yellow	30	30
b.		Half used as 20pa on cover		
c.		Inverted surch.	60.00	60.00
d.		Double surcharge		
e.		Surcharged on both sides		
f.		Printed on both sides		110.00
23	A5	2pi org red	8.00	1.25
a.		Half used as 1pi on cover		
b.		Imperf., pair	100.00	100.00
c.		Printed on both sides	100.00	
d.		Inverted surcharge	50.00	50.00
e.		Surcharged on both sides		110.00
24	A5	5pi blue		20	30
25	A5	5pi gray	7.50	5.50
26	A5	25pi dl rose	20.00	17.50

Pin-perf., Perf. 5 to 11 and Compound.

1870-71

27	A5	10pa lilac	130.00	25.00
28	A5	10pa brown	45.00	2.50
29	A5	20pa gray grn	11.00	75
a.		Printed on both sides		
30	A5	1pi yellow	27.50	75
a.		Invtd. surch.	75.00	60.00
b.		Without surcharge		
31	A5	2pi red	60	60
a.		Imperf.	15.00	15.00
b.		Printed on both sides		25.00
c.		Surcharged on both sides		
32	A5	5pi blue	40	90
a.		5pi grnsh bl	2.00	2.00
33	A5	5pi slate	6.00	6.00
b.		Printed on both sides		
c.		Surcharged on both sides		25.00
34	A5	25pi dl rose	15.00	13.00

1873   Perf. 12, 12½

35	A5	10pa dk lil	35.00	2.25
a.		Inverted surcharge		70.00
36	A5	10pa ol brn	42.50	2.50
		10pa bis	32.50	3.00
37	A5	2pi vermilion	60	60
a.		Surcharged on both sides	16.50	16.50

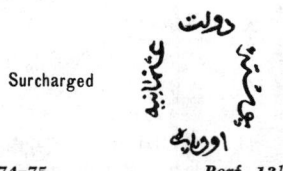

Surcharged

1874-75   Perf. 13½

38	A5	10pa red vio	10.00	1.00
a.		Imperf., pair	50.00	37.50

39	A5	20pa yel grn	12.50	1.00
a.		Half used as 10pa on cover		
b.		Inverted surch.	22.50	10.00
c.		Double surcharge		
40	A5	1pi yellow	15.00	2.00
a.		Imperf., pair	75.00	60.00
b.		Half used as 20pa on cover		

Perf. 12, 12½

41	A5	10pa red vio	22.50	7.50
a.		Inverted surch.	35.00	45.00

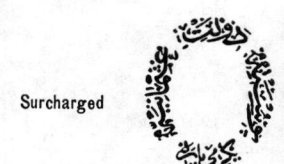

Surcharged

1876, April   Perf. 13½

42	A5	10pa red lil	25	20
a.		Imperf., pair	70.00	
b.		Imperf., pair	15.00	15.00
43	A5	20pa pale grn	25	20
a.		Half used as 10pa on cover		
b.		Inverted surcharge	70.00	
c.		Imperf., pair	15.00	15.00
44	A5	1pi yellow	25	20
a.		Imperf., pair	27.50	27.50
46	A5	5pi gray bl	225.00	
47	A5	25pi dl rose	225.00	

Nos. 46 and 47 were never placed in use.

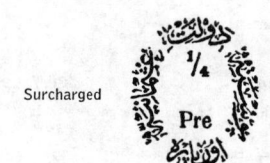

Surcharged

1876, Jan.

48	A5	¼pi on 10pa vio	70	1.00
49	A5	½pi on 20pa yel grn	1.35	1.50
50	A5	1¼pi on 50pa rose	40	55
a.		Imperf., pair	60.00	
51	A5	2pi on 2pi redsh brn	10.50	4.00
52	A5	5pi on 5pi gray bl	1.75	4.00

The surcharge on Nos. 48-52 restates in French the value originally expressed in Turkish characters.

A7

1876, Sept.   Typo.   Perf. 13½

53	A7	10pa blk & rose lil	20	30
54	A7	20pa red vio & grn	22.50	2.50
55	A7	50pa bl & yel	35	50
56	A7	2pi blk & redsh brn	20	50
a.		Half used as 1pi on cover		
57	A7	5pi red & bl	1.25	1.75
b.		Half used as 2½pi on cover		
c.		Cliché of 25pi in plate of 5pi	325.00	300.00
58	A7	25pi cl & rose	13.00	13.00
a.		Imperf.	125.00	

Nos. 56-58 exist perf. 11½, but were not regularly issued.

1880-84   Perf. 13½

59	A7	5pa blk & ol ('81)	20	15
a.		Imperf.	45.00	
60	A7	10pa blk & grn ('84)	20	15
61	A7	20pa blk & rose	30	15
62	A7	1pi blk & bl (*piastres*)	20	20
		1pi blk & gray bl	25	
b.		Imperf.	60.00	

63	A7	1pi blk & bl (piastre) ('81)	10.00	2.75

A cliché of No. 63 was inserted in a plate of the Eastern Rumelia 1pi (No. 13), but this "error" is found only in the remainders.
Nos. 60–61 and 63 exist perf. 11½, but were not regularly issued.

1881-82

Surcharged like April, 1876, Issue.

64	A5	20pa gray	25	20
a.		Inverted surch.	20.00	
b.		Imperf., pair	40.00	
65	A5	2pi pale sal	25	20
a.		Inverted surcharge	35.00	

1884-86 *Perf. 11½, 13½*

66	A7	5pa lil & pale lil ('86)	55.00	45.00
a.		Imperf.	115.00	
67	A7	10pa grn & pale grn	20	15
a.		Imperf.	20.00	
68	A7	20pa rose & pale rose	20	15
a.		Half used as 10pa on cover		
b.		Imperf.	20.00	
69	A7	1pi bl & lt bl	20	15
a.		Half used as 20pa on cover		
b.		Imperf.	20.00	
70	A7	2pi ocher & pale ocher, perf. 11½	20	15
71	A7	5pi red brn & pale brn, perf. 11½	40	75
a.		Half used as 2½pi on cover		
c.		5pi ocher & pale ocher (error)	8.00	8.00
73	A7	25pi blk & pale gray ('86)	150.00	150.00
a.		Imperf.	300.00	

1886 *Perf. 13½*

74	A7	5pa blk & pale gray	20	15
a.		Imperf.	20.00	
75	A7	2pi org & lt bl	15	15
a.		Half used as 1pi on cover		
b.		Imperf.	20.00	
76	A7	5pi grn & pale grn	35	80
a.		Half used as 2½pi on cover		
b.		Imperf.	20.00	
77	A7	25pi bis & pale bis	14.00	14.00
a.		Imperf.	40.00	

Stamps of 1884–86, bisected and surcharged as above, 10pa, 20pa, 1pi and 2pi or surcharged "2" in red are stated to have been made privately and without authority. With the aid of employees of the post office, copies were passed through the mails.

1888 *Perf. 13½*

83	A7	5pa grn & yel	10	10
a.		Imperf.	20.00	
84	A7	2pi red lil & bl	20	10
a.		Imperf.	20.00	
85	A7	5pi dk brn & gray	20	20
a.		Imperf.	20.00	
86	A7	25pi red & yel	14.00	13.00
a.		Imperf.	45.00	

Nos. 74–86 exist perf. 11½, but were not regularly issued.

1890 *Perf. 11½, 13½.*

87	A7	10pa grn & gray	10	10
a.		Imperf.	20.00	
88	A7	20pa rose & gray	10	10
a.		Imperf.	20.00	
89	A7	1pi bl & gray	10	10
a.		Imperf.	25.00	
90	A7	2pi yel & gray	35	25
a.		Half used as 1pi on cover		
b.		Imperf.	30.00	
91	A7	5pi buff & gray	90	1.00
a.		Imperf.	40.00	

Arms and Tughra of "El Gazi" (The Conqueror) Sultan Abdul Hamid
A10 A11

A12 A13

A14 A15

1892–98 **Typo.** *Perf. 13½*

95	A10	10pa gray grn	20	5
96	A11	20pa vio brn ('98)	15	5
a.		20pa dk pink	25	5
b.		20pa pink	5.00	50
97	A12	1pi pale bl	4.00	6
98	A13	2pi brn org	12	5
a.		Tête bêche pair	3.00	3.00
99	A14	5pi dl vio	3.00	1.50
a.		Turkish numeral in upper right corner reads "50" instead of "5"	25.00	25.00

1897 **Red Surcharge.**

100	A15	5pa on 10pa gray grn	25	20
a.		"Cniq" instead of "Cinq"	15.00	15.00

A16 A17

1901 **Typographed** *Perf. 13½*

For Foreign Postage

102	A16	5pa bister	40	8
103	A16	10pa yel grn	15	8
104	A16	20pa magenta	15	6
a.		Perf. 12	1.00	20
105	A16	1pi vio bl	20	6
106	A16	2pi gray bl	40	18
107	A16	5pi ocher	1.75	80
108	A16	25pi dk grn	20.00	14.00
109	A16	50pi yellow	55.00	35.00
		Nos. 102-109 (8)	78.05	50.26

For Domestic Postage

Perf. 12, 13½.

110	A17	5pa purple	5	5
111	A17	10pa green	5	5
112	A17	20pa carmine	5	5
113	A17	1pi blue	15	5
a.		Imperf.	11.00	
114	A17	2pi orange	25	5
115	A17	5pi lil rose	55	5
116	A17	25pi brn, perf. 13½	3.50	1.25
a.		Perf. 12	10.00	2.50
117	A17	50pi yel brn, perf. 13½	10.00	3.00
a.		Perf. 12	12.50	6.00
		Nos. 110-117 (8)	14.60	4.55

Nos. 110–113 exist perf. 12x13½.

A18 A19

1905

Perf. 12, 13½ and Compound.

118	A18	5pa ocher	6	6
119	A18	10pa dl grn	6	6
a.		Imperf.	6.00	5.00
120	A18	20pa carmine	6	6
a.		Imperf.	6.00	5.00
121	A18	1pi blue	8	8
122	A18	2pi slate	10	6
123	A18	2½pi red vio	25	6
a.		Imperf.	16.00	14.00
124	A18	5pi brown	30	6
125	A18	10pi org brn	70	25
126	A18	25pi ol grn	2.00	80
127	A18	50pi dp vio	10.00	4.50
		Nos. 118-127 (10)	13.61	5.99

Overprinted in Carmine or Blue ب

1906

128	A18	10pa dl grn (C)	25	8
129	A18	20pa car (Bl)	25	8
130	A18	1pi bl (C)	25	8
131	A18	2pi sl (C)	3.50	1.50

Stamps bearing this overprint were sold to merchants at a discount from face value to encourage the use of Turkish stamps on foreign correspondence, instead of those of the various European powers which maintained post offices in Turkey. The overprint is the Arab "B," for "Béhié," meaning "discount."

1908

132	A19	5pa ocher	8	5
133	A19	10pa bl grn	8	5
134	A19	20pa carmine	5.00	5
135	A19	1pi brt bl	1.50	5
a.		1pi ultra	22.50	3.25
136	A19	2pi bl blk	1.25	6
137	A19	2½pi vio brn	30	6
138	A19	5pi dk vio	4.50	12
139	A19	10pi red	9.00	60
140	A19	25pi dk grn	4.50	2.00
141	A19	50pi red brn	11.00	6.50

Overprinted in Carmine or Blue ب

142	A19	10pa bl grn (C)	1.25	40
143	A19	20pa car (Bl)	1.60	60
144	A19	1pi brt bl (C)	2.50	1.25
145	A19	2pi bl blk (C)	6.00	1.75
		Nos. 132-145 (14)	48.56	13.54

A20

1908, Dec. 17

Perf. 12, 13½ & Compound

146	A20	5pa ocher	25	10
a.		Imperf.	3.50	3.50
147	A20	10pa bl grn	25	10
a.		Imperf.	4.00	4.00
148	A20	20pa carmine	60	25
a.		Imperf.	5.50	5.50
149	A20	1pi ultra	80	30
a.		Imperf.	3.50	3.50
150	A20	2pi gray blk	7.50	3.00
		Nos. 146-150 (5)	9.40	3.75

To commemorate the granting of a Constitution, the date of which is inscribed on the banderol: "324 Temuz 10" (July 24, 1908).

Tughra and "Reshad" of Sultan Mohammed V
A21

1909, Dec.

151	A21	5pa ocher	5	5
152	A21	10pa bl grn	5	5
a.		Imperf.	3.50	3.50
153	A21	20pa car rose	5	5
154	A21	1pi ultra	10	5
a.		1pi brt bl	50	5
155	A21	2pi bl blk	20	5
156	A21	2½pi dk brn	11.00	9.50
157	A21	5pi dk vio	2.25	35
158	A21	10pi dl red	4.00	65
159	A21	25pi dk grn	80.00	40.00
160	A21	50pi red brn	42.50	35.00
		Nos. 151-160 (10)	140.20	85.75

The 2pa olive green, type A21, is a newspaper stamp, No. P68.
Two types exist for the 10pa, 20pa and 1pi. In the second type, the damaged crescent is restored.

Overprinted in Carmine or Blue ب

161	A21	10pa bl grn (C)	30	10
a.		Imperf.		
162	A21	20pa car rose (Bl)	30	10
a.		Imperf.		
163	A21	1pi ultra (C)	35	15
a.		Imperf.	8.00	
b.		1pi brt bl	45	
164	A21	2pi bl blk (C)	10.00	5.00
a.		Imperf.		

Stamps of 1901-05 Overprinted in Carmine or Blue

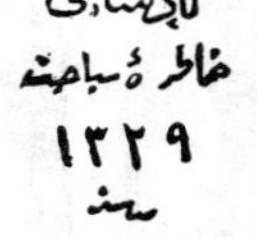

MONASTIR

The overprint was applied to 18 denominations in four settings with change of city name, producing individual sets for each city: "MONASTIR," "PRISTINA," "SALONIKA" and "USKUB."

1911, June 26 *Perf. 12, 13½.*

165	A16	5pa bister	60	
166	A16	10pa yel grn	60	
167	A16	20pa magenta	3.50	
168	A16	1pi vio bl	3.50	
169	A16	2pi gray bl	3.50	
170	A16	5pi ocher	25.00	
171	A16	25pi dk grn	35.00	
172	A16	50pi yellow	45.00	
173	A17	5pa purple	60	
174	A17	10pa green	60	
175	A17	20pa carmine	3.50	
176	A17	1pi blue	3.50	
177	A17	2pi orange	3.50	
178	A17	5pi lil rose	25.00	
179	A17	25pi chocolate	35.00	
180	A17	50pi yel brn	45.00	
181	A18	2½pi red vio	27.50	
182	A18	10pi org brn	32.50	
		Nos. 165-182 (18)	293.40	

Nos. 165–182 were intended to commemorate the Sultan's visit to Macedonia. The Arabic overprint reads: "Souvenir of the Sultan's Journey, 1329".

Price for Salonika and Uskub sets, each $325.
See also Nos. P69–P81.

General Post Office, Constantinople
A22

1913, Mar. 14 *Perf. 12*

237	A22	2pa ol grn	5	5
238	A22	5pa ocher	6	5
239	A22	10pa bl grn	5	5
a.		Booklet pane of 6	30.00	

TURKEY

240	A22	20pa car rose	5	5
a.		Booklet pane of 6	20.00	
241	A22	1pi ultra	5	5
a.		Booklet pane of 6	50.00	
242	A22	2pi indigo	10	5
243	A22	5pi dl vio	30	20
244	A22	10pi dl red	1.75	80
245	A22	25pi gray grn	5.00	2.25
246	A22	50pi org brn	17.50	16.00
	Nos. 237-246 (10)		24.91	19.55

Overprinted in Carmine or Blue ب

247	A22	10pa bl grn (C)	10	8
248	A22	20pa car rose (Bl)	12	8
249	A22	1pi ultra (C)	40	15
250	A22	2pi ind (C)	2.25	1.50

Nos. 237-240 and 249 exist imperf.

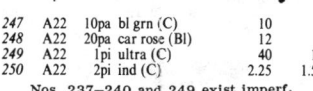

Mosque of Selim, Adrianople
A23

1913, Oct. 23 — Engraved

251	A23	10pa green	50	30
252	A23	20pa red	85	50
253	A23	40pa blue	1.50	1.00

This issue was to commemorate the recapture of Adrianople (Edirne) by the Turks. See also Nos. 592, J59-J62.

Obelisk of Theodosius in the Hippodrome A24 — **Column of Constantine** A25

Leander's Tower
A26

One of the Seven Towers
A27

Fener Bahçe (Garden Lighthouse)
A28

The Castle of Europe on the Bosporus
A29

Mosque of Sultan Ahmed
A30

Monument to the Martyrs of Liberty
A31

Fountains of Suleiman
A32

Cruiser "Hamidie"
A33

View of Kandili on the Bosporus
A34

War Ministry (Later Istanbul University)
A35

Sweet Waters of Europe Park
A36

Mosque of Suleiman
A37

The Bosporus
A38

Sultan Ahmed's Fountain
A39

Sultan Mohammed V
A40

Designs A24-A39: Views of Constantinople.

1914, Jan. 14 — Lithographed.

254	A24	2pa red lil	5	5
255	A25	4pa dk brn	5	5
256	A26	5pa vio brn	5	5
257	A27	6pa dk bl	15	5

Engraved.

258	A28	10pa green	8	5
a.		Bklt. pane of 4		
259	A29	20pa red	30	5
a.		Booklet pane of 6		
b.		Bklt. pane of 4		
260	A30	1pi blue	35	10
a.		Booklet pane of 4	1.00	
b.		Bklt. pane of 2 + 2 labels		
261	A31	1½pi car & blk	60	20
262	A32	1¾pi sl & red brn	20	10
263	A33	2pi grn & blk	1.25	10
264	A34	2½pi org & ol grn	80	10
265	A35	5pi dl vio	2.50	50
266	A36	10pi red brn	6.50	80
267	A37	25pi ol grn	30.00	4.00
268	A38	50pi carmine	6.00	3.50
269	A39	100pi dp bl	50.00	20.00
		Cut cancellation		1.00
270	A40	200pi grn & blk	450.00	225.00
		Cut cancellation		17.50
	Nos. 254-270 (17)		548.88	254.70

See Nos. 590-591, 593-598.

Stamps of Preceding Issue Overprinted ★ in Red or Blue.

271	A28	10pa grn (R)	20	6
272	A29	20pa red (Bl)	1.75	65
273	A30	1pi bl (R)	40	5
275	A32	1¾pi sl & red brn (Bl)	60	50
276	A33	2pi grn & blk (R)	12.00	1.50
	Nos. 271-276 (5)		14.95	2.76

No. 261 Surcharged

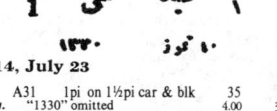

1914, July 23

277	A31	1pi on 1½pi car & blk	35	35
a.		"1330" omitted	4.00	3.00
b.		Double surcharge		
c.		Triple surch.	7.50	7.50

This stamp was issued to commemorate the seventh anniversary of the Constitution. The surcharge reads "10 July, 1330, National fête" and has also the numeral "1" at each side, over the original value of the stamp.

Stamps of 1913 Overprinted in Black or Red

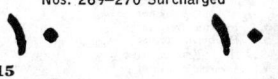

278	A26	5pa vio brn (Bk)	60	30
279	A28	10pa grn (R)	80	40
280	A29	20pa red (Bk)	1.60	70
281	A30	1pi bl (R)	4.00	1.00
282	A33	2pi grn & blk ('R)	3.00	60
283	A35	5pi dl vio (R)	20.00	4.00
284	A36	10pi red brn (R)	40.00	22.50
	Nos. 278-284 (7)		70.00	29.50

This overprint reads "Abolition of the Capitulations, 1330", which the stamps were intended to commemorate.

Nos. 269-270 Surcharged

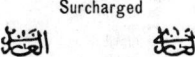

1915

286	A39	10pi on 100pi dp bl	19.00	6.50
a.		Inverted surcharge	150.00	150.00

Surcharged

287	A40	25pi on 200pi grn & blk	11.00	4.50

Preceding Issues Overprinted in Carmine or Black

1915

On Stamps of 1892.

288	A10	10pa gray grn	6	5
a.		Inverted ovpt.	7.50	7.50
289	A13	2pi brn org	8	5
a.		Inverted overprint	7.50	7.50
290	A14	5pi dl vio	1.50	20
a.		On No. 99a	15.00	15.00

On Stamp of 1897.

291	A15	5pa on 10pa gray grn	5	5
a.		Inverted ovpt.	7.50	7.50
b.		On No. 100a	4.00	1.75

On Stamps of 1901.

292	A16	5pa bister	10	7
293	A16	1pi vio bl	40	25
294	A16	2pi gray bl	25	12
295	A16	5pi ocher	3.00	50
296	A16	25pi dk grn	20.00	10.00
297	A17	5pa purple	6	6
298	A17	10pa green	10	8
299	A17	20pa carmine	10	5
a.		Inverted ovpt.	7.50	7.50
300	A17	1pi blue	25	6
a.		Inverted overprint	7.50	7.50
301	A17	2pi orange	50	10
a.		Inverted overprint	7.50	7.50
b.		Double overprint (R and Bk)	7.50	7.50
302	A17	5pi lil rose	25	8
303	A17	25pi brown	3.00	2.00

On Stamps of 1905.

304	A18	5pa ocher	12	12
305	A18	10pa dl grn	10	6
a.		Inverted overprint	7.50	7.50
306	A18	20pa carmine	10	6
a.		Inverted overprint	7.50	7.50
307	A18	1pi brt bl	40	10
a.		Inverted overprint	7.50	7.50
308	A18	2pi slate	45	15
a.		Inverted overprint	7.50	7.50
309	A18	2½pi red vio	25	10
a.		Inverted overprint	7.50	7.50
310	A18	5pi brown	15	6
a.		Inverted overprint	7.50	7.50

799

TURKEY

311	A18	10pi org brn	2.50	25
312	A18	25pi ol grn	13.00	3.00

On Stamps of 1906.

313	A18	10pa dl grn	18	6
314	A18	2pi slate	60	15
a.		Inverted overprint	7.50	7.50

On Stamps of 1908.

314B	A19	2pi bl blk	40.00	22.50
315	A19	2½pi vio brn	50	10
315A	A19	5pi dk vio	20.00	15.00
315B	A19	10pi red	4.00	1.50
316	A19	25pi dk grn	4.50	1.10
a.		Inverted overprint	25.00	25.00

With Additional Overprint ۖ

316B	A19	2pi bl blk	3.50	1.10

On Stamps of 1909.

317	A21	5pa ocher	5	5
a.		Inverted overprint	7.50	7.50
b.		Double overprint	7.50	7.50
318	A21	20pa car rose	5	5
a.		Inverted overprint	7.50	7.50
319	A21	1pi ultra	20	5
a.		Inverted overprint	7.50	7.50
320	A21	2pi bl blk	30	6
a.		Inverted overprint	7.50	7.50
321	A21	2½pi dk brn	32.50	12.00
322	A21	5pi dk vio	25	10
a.		Inverted overprint	10.00	10.00
323	A21	10pi dl red	4.00	25
324	A21	25pi dk grn	275.00	250.00

With Additional Overprint ۖ

325	A21	20pa car rose	25	10
a.		Inverted ovpt.	7.50	7.50
326	A21	1pi ultra	25	10
327	A21	2pi bl blk	35	12

On Stamps of 1913.

328	A22	5pa ocher	5	5
a.		Inverted overprint	7.50	7.50
329	A22	10pa bl grn	10	5
a.		Inverted overprint	7.50	7.50
330	A22	20pa car rose	5	5
a.		Inverted overprint	7.50	7.50
331	A22	1pi ultra	10	5
a.		Inverted overprint	7.50	7.50
332	A22	2pi indigo	60	10
a.		Inverted overprint	7.50	7.50
333	A22	5pi dl vio	50	30
334	A22	10pi dl red	2.75	35
a.		Invtd. ovpt.	15.00	15.00
335	A22	25pi gray grn	13.00	4.25

With Additional Overprint ۖ

336	A22	10pa bl grn	12	10
337	A22	20pa car rose	18	12
338	A22	1pi ultra	30	12
339	A22	2pi indigo	1.00	60
a.		Inverted ovpt.	10.00	10.00

See also Nos. P121–P133.

Stamps of 1901-13 Overprinted طرابلس

1916

340	A17	5pa purple	15	10
a.		5pa pur, No. P43	70.00	70.00
341	A17	10pa green	20	10
a.		Double overprint	10.00	10.00
b.		10pa yel grn, No. 103	70.00	70.00
342	A21	20pa car rose, No. 153	25	10
a.		20pa car rose, No. 162	70.00	70.00
343	A21	1pi ultra	45	15
344	A22	5pi dl vio	7.00	1.50

Occupation of the Sinai Peninsula.

Old General Post Office of Constantinople
A41

1916, May 29 Litho. Perf. 12½, 13½

345	A41	5pa green	40	8
346	A41	10pa carmine	20	10
347	A41	20pa ultra	35	8
348	A41	1pi vio & blk	55	8
349	A41	5pi yel brn & blk	11.50	85
		Nos. 345-349 (5)	13.00	1.19

Issued to commemorate the 50th anniversary of the introduction of postage in Turkey.

Stamps of 1892-1905 Overprinted ١٠ تموز

1916 ١٣٣٢

350	A10	10pa gray grn (R)	1.50	80
351	A18	20pa car (Bl)	1.50	80
352	A18	1pi bl (R)	2.00	80
353	A18	2pi sl (Bk)	4.50	80
354	A18	2½pi red vio (Bk)	4.50	80
		Nos. 350-354 (5)	14.00	4.00

National Fête Day. Overprint reads "10 Temuz 1332" (July 23, 1916).

Preceding Issues Overprinted or Surcharged in Red or Black:

a   *b*

1916

On Stamps of 1892-98

355	A10 (a)	10pa gray grn	15	10
355A	A11 (a)	20pa vio brn	15	8
b.		Inverted overprint	7.50	7.50
356	A12 (a)	1pi gray bl	15.00	15.00
357	A13 (a)	2pi brn org	1.50	1.00
358	A14 (a)	5pi dl vio	11.00	11.00

On Stamp of 1897.

359	A15 (a)	5pa on 10pa gray grn	8	8

On Stamps of 1901.

361	A16 (a)	5pa bister	12	8
a.		Double overprint	7.50	7.50
362	A16 (a)	10pa yel grn	25	25
363	A16 (a)	20pa magenta	10	10
364	A16 (a)	1pi vio bl	25	10
a.		Inverted overprint	10.00	10.00
365	A16 (a)	2pi gray bl	80	70
366	A16 (b)	5pi on 25pi dk grn	15.00	15.00
367	A16 (b)	10pi on 25pi dk grn	15.00	15.00
368	A16 (a)	25pi dk grn	15.00	15.00
369	A17 (a)	5pa purple	11.00	11.00
370	A17 (a)	10pa green	40	10
371	A17 (a)	20pa carmine	20	6
a.		Inverted overprint	7.50	7.50
372	A17 (a)	1pi blue	20	8
a.		Inverted overprint	7.50	7.50
373	A17 (a)	2pi orange	40	10
374	A17 (b)	10pi on 25pi brn	1.75	1.00
375	A17 (b)	10pi on 50pi yel brn	2.25	1.50
376	A17 (a)	25pi brown	2.25	50
377	A17 (a)	50pi yel brn	3.25	1.10

On Stamps of 1905.

378	A18 (a)	5pa ocher	8	8
379	A18 (a)	20pa carmine	12	7
a.		Inverted overprint	7.50	7.50
380	A18 (a)	1pi brt bl	18	6
a.		Inverted overprint	7.50	7.50
381	A18 (a)	2pi slate	60	30
382	A18 (a)	2½pi red vio	80	30
383	A18 (b)	10pi on 25pi ol grn	3.50	1.00
384	A18 (b)	10pi on 50pi dp vio	3.50	1.00
385	A18 (a)	25pi ol grn	75	
386	A18 (a)	50pi dp vio	3.00	1.00

On Stamps of 1906.

387	A18 (a)	10pa dl grn	35	15
388	A18 (a)	20pa carmine	25	15
389	A18 (a)	1pi brt bl	40	10

On Stamps of 1908.

390	A19 (a)	2½pi vio brn	11.00	11.00
391	A19 (b)	10pi on 25pi dk grn	3.00	3.00
392	A19 (b)	10pi on 50pi red brn	15.00	15.00
393	A19 (b)	25pi on 50pi red brn	15.00	15.00
394	A19 (a)	25pi dk grn	2.50	2.00
395	A19 (a)	50pi red brn	11.00	11.00

With Additional Overprint ۖ

396	A19 (a)	2pi bl blk	11.00	11.00

On Stamps of 1908-09

397	A20 (a)	5pa ocher	11.00	11.00
398	A21 (a)	5pa ocher	10	8
399	A21 (a)	10pa bl grn	11.00	11.00
400	A21 (a)	20pa car rose	11.00	11.00
401	A21 (a)	1pi ultra	60	15
402	A21 (a)	2pi bl blk	55	15
403	A21 (a)	2½pi dk brn	12.50	12.50
404	A21 (a)	5pi dk vio	12.50	12.50

With Additional Overprint ۖ

405	A21 (a)	1pi ultra	10.00	10.00
406	A21 (a)	2pi bl blk	10.00	10.00

On Stamps of 1913.

407	A22 (a)	5pa ocher	10	10
408	A22 (a)	20pa car rose	40	30
409	A22 (a)	1pi ultra	50	15
410	A22 (a)	2pi indigo	60	85
411	A22 (b)	10pi on 50pi org brn	2.50	80
412	A22 (a)	25pi gray grn	3.00	50
413	A22 (a)	50pi org brn	3.50	1.00

With Additional Overprint ۖ

414	A22 (a)	1pi ultra	40	10

On Commemorative Stamps of 1913.

415	A23 (a)	10pa green	25	15
416	A23 (a)	20pa red	40	15
417	A23 (a)	40pa blue	80	30

On Commemorative Stamp of 1916.

418	A41 (a)	5pi yel brn & blk	60	20

No. 277 Surcharged in Blue

419	A31	60pa on 1pi on 1½pi car & blk	60	40
a.		"1330" omitted	7.50	7.50

See also Nos. P134–P152, J67–J70.

Turkish Artillery—A42

Mosque at Orta Köy, Constantinople
A43

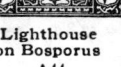

Lighthouse on Bosporus A44   **Monument to Martyrs of Liberty** A45

Map of the Dardanelles; Sultan Mohammed V A46

Map of the Dardanelles A47

Istanbul Across the Golden Horn A48

Pyramids of Egypt A49

Dolma Bahçe Palace and Mohammed V—A50

Sentry and Shell A51   **Sultan Mohammed V** A52

Perf. 11½, 12½.

1916-18   Typographed.

420	A42	2pa violet	10	5
421	A43	5pa orange	10	5
424	A44	10pa green	10	5

800

TURKEY

		Engraved.			
425	A45	20pa dp rose		30	5
426	A46	1pi dl vio		20	5
		Typographed.			
428	A47	50pa ultra		25	10
429	A48	2pi org brn & ind		30	8
430	A49	5pi pale bl & blk		6.00	1.60
		Engraved.			
431	A50	10pi dk grn		1.10	60
432	A50	10pi dk vio		3.00	60
433	A50	10pi dk brn		1.75	40
434	A51	25pi car, straw		70	50
437	A52	50pi carmine		3.00	1.25
438	A52	50pi indigo		60	60
439	A52	50pi grn, straw		6.00	5.00
		Nos. 420-439 (15)		23.50	10.98

Preceding Issues Overprinted or Surcharged in Red, Black or Blue:

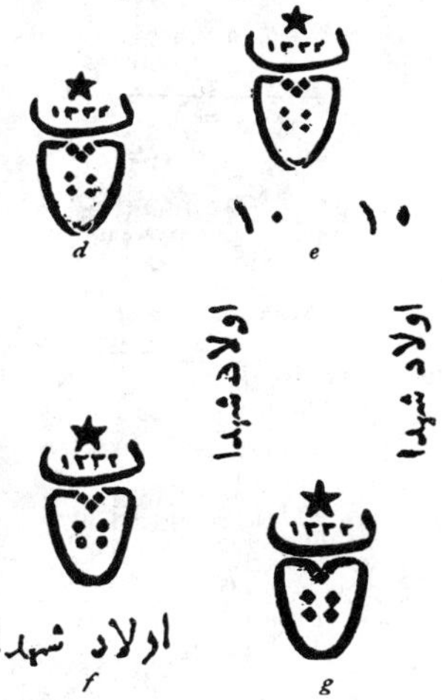

1917

On Stamps of 1865.
446	A5 (d)	20pa yel (R)	20.00	20.00
a.		Star without rays (R)	20.00	20.00
447	A5 (d)	1pi pearl gray (R)	20.00	20.00
a.		Star without rays (R)	20.00	20.00
448	A5 (d)	2pi bl (R)	20.00	20.00
449	A5 (d)	5pi car (Bk)	20.00	20.00

On Stamp of 1867.
450	A5 (d)	5pi rose (Bk)	20.00	20.00

On Stamps of 1870-71
451	A5 (d)	2pi red (Bl)	40.00	40.00
452	A5 (d)	5pi bl (Bk)	20.00	20.00
453	A5 (d)	25pi dl rose (Bl)	20.00	20.00

On Stamp of 1874-75.
454	A5 (d)	10pa red vio (Bl)	20.00	20.00

On Stamps of April, 1876.
455	A5 (d)	10pa red lil (Bl)	20.00	20.00
a.		10pa red vio (Bl)	20.00	20.00
457	A5 (d)	20pa pale grn (R)	20.00	20.00
458	A5 (d)	1pi yel (Bl)	20.00	20.00

On Stamps of January, 1876.
459	A5 (d)	¼ on 10pa rose lil (Bl)	20.00	20.00
460	A5 (d)	½ on 20pa yel grn (Bl)	20.00	20.00
461	A5 (d)	1¼ on 50pa rose (Bl)	20.00	20.00

On Stamps of September, 1876.
462	A7 (d)	50pa bl & yel (R)	20.00	20.00
464	A7 (d)	25pi cl & rose (Bk)	20.00	20.00

On Stamps of 1880-84.
465	A7 (d)	5pa blk & ol (R)	20.00	20.00
466	A7 (d)	10pa blk & grn (R)	20.00	20.00

On Stamps of 1881-82.
467	A5 (d)	20pa gray (Bl)	20.00	20.00
468	A5 (d)	2pi pale sal (Bl)	20.00	20.00

On Stamps of 1884-86.
469	A7 (d)	10pa grn & pale grn (Bk)	20.00	20.00
470	A7 (d)	2pi ocher & pale ocher (Bk)	20.00	20.00
471	A7 (d)	5pi red brn & pale brn (Bk)	20.00	20.00

On Stamps of 1886.
472	A7 (d)	5pi blk & pale gray (R)	10	10
a.		Inverted overprint	15.00	15.00
473	A7 (d)	2pi org & bl (Bk)	60	60
a.		Inverted overprint	15.00	15.00
474	A7 (d)	5pi grn & pale grn (R)	20.00	20.00
475	A7 (d)	25pi bis & pale bis (Bk)	20.00	20.00

On Stamp of 1888.
476	A7 (d)	5pi dk brn & gray (Bk)	20.00	20.00

On Stamps of 1892-98.
477	A11 (d)	20pa vio brn (R)	75	75
478	A13 (d)	2pi brn org (R)	1.10	1.10
a.		Tête bêche pair	20.00	20.00

On Stamps of 1901.
479	A16 (d)	5pa bis (R)	90	90
a.		Inverted overprint	15.00	15.00
480	A16 (d)	20pa mag (Bk)	25	25
a.		Inverted overprint	15.00	15.00
481	A16 (d)	1pi vio bl (R)	75	75
a.		Inverted overprint	15.00	15.00
482	A16 (d)	2pi gray bl (R)	1.25	1.25
483	A16 (d)	5pi ocher (R)	20.00	20.00
484	A16 (e)	10pi on 50pi yel (R)	25.00	25.00
485	A16 (d)	25pi dk grn (R)	20.00	20.00
486	A17 (d)	5pa pur (Bk)	20.00	20.00
487	A17 (d)	10pa grn (R)	1.00	1.00
488	A17 (d)	20pa car (Bk)	35	35
a.		Inverted overprint	15.00	15.00
489	A17 (d)	1pi bl (R)	25	20
490	A17 (d)	2pi org (Bk)	75	75
a.		Inverted overprint	15.00	15.00
491	A17 (d)	5pi lil rose (R)	20.00	20.00
492	A17 (e)	10pi on 50pi yel brn (R)	20.00	20.00
493	A17 (d)	25pi brn (R)	1.25	1.25

On Stamps of 1905.
494	A18 (d)	5pa ocher (R)	10	8
a.		Inverted overprint	15.00	15.00
495	A18 (d)	10pa dl grn (R)	20.00	20.00
496	A18 (d)	20pa car (Bk)	5	5
a.		Double overprint, one inverted	15.00	15.00
b.		Inverted overprint	15.00	15.00
497	A18 (d)	1pi bl (R)	6	5
a.		Inverted overprint	15.00	15.00
498	A18 (d)	2pi sl (R)	75	75
499	A18 (d)	2½pi red vio (R)	1.00	75
a.		Inverted overprint	15.00	15.00
500	A18 (d)	5pi brn (R)	20.00	20.00
501	A18 (d)	10pi org brn (R)	20.00	20.00
502	A18 (e)	10pi on 50pi dp vio (R)	20.00	20.00
503	A18 (d)	25pi ol grn (R)	20.00	20.00

On Nos. 128-131
504	A18 (d)	10pa dl grn (R)	12	12
a.		Inverted overprint	15.00	15.00
505	A18 (d)	20pa car (Bk)	20	20
a.		Double overprint, one inverted	15.00	15.00
b.		Inverted overprint	15.00	15.00
506	A18 (d)	1pi brt bl (Bk)	35	18
a.		Inverted overprint	15.00	15.00
507	A18 (d)	1pi brt bl (Bk)	65	65
a.		Inverted overprint	15.00	15.00
508	A18 (d)	2pi sl (Bk)	20.00	20.00

On Stamps of 1908.
509	A19 (d)	5pa ocher (R)	90	90
510	A19 (d)	10pa bl grn (R)	20	15
510A	A19 (d)	1pi brt bl (R)	110.00	110.00
511	A19 (d)	2pi bl blk (R)	20.00	20.00
512	A19 (d)	2½pi vio brn (R)	90	90
512A	A19 (d)	10pi red (R)	110.00	110.00
513	A19 (e)	10pi on 50pi red brn (R)	20.00	20.00
514	A19 (d)	25pi dk grn (R)	20.00	20.00

With Additional Overprint
514A	A19 (d)	10pa bl grn (Bk)	30.00	30.00
515	A19 (d)	1pi brt bl (Bk)	20.00	20.00
516	A19 (d)	2pi bl blk (Bk)	1.25	1.25
516A	A19 (d)	2pi bl blk (Bk)	20.00	20.00

On Stamps of 1908-09
517	A20 (d)	5pa ocher (R)	40	40
518	A21 (d)	5pa ocher (R)	20	20
a.		Double overprint	15.00	15.00
b.		Double overprint, one inverted	15.00	15.00
519	A21 (d)	10pa grn (R)	20	20
520	A21 (d)	20pa car rose (Bk)	20	20
a.		Double overprint	15.00	15.00
521	A21 (d)	1pi ultra (R)	20	20
a.		1pi brt bl (R)	30.00	30.00
522	A21 (d)	2pi bl blk (Bk)	85	85
523	A21 (d)	2½pi dk brn (R)	20.00	20.00
524	A21 (d)	5pi dk vio (R)	20.00	20.00
525	A21 (d)	10pi dl red (R)	20.00	20.00

With Additional Overprint
525A	A21 (d)	10pa bl grn (R)	110.00	110.00
526	A21 (d)	1pi brt bl (R)	3.50	3.50
527	A21 (d)	1pi ultra (R)	20	20
a.		1pi brt bl (R)	30.00	30.00
528	A21 (d)	2pi bl blk (Bk)	14.00	14.00

On Stamps of 1913.
529	A22 (d)	5pa ocher (R)	35	35
530	A22 (d)	10pa bl grn (R)	20.00	20.00
531	A22 (d)	20pa car rose (Bk)	35	35
532	A22 (d)	1pi ultra (R)	35	35
533	A22 (d)	2pi ind (R)	1.25	1.25
534	A22 (d)	5pi dl vio (R)	20.00	20.00
535	A22 (d)	10pi dl red (R)	20.00	20.00

With Additional Overprint
536	A22 (d)	10pa bl grn (Bk)	35	35
a.		Inverted overprint	15.00	15.00
537	A22 (d)	1pi ultra (Bk)	1.25	1.25
a.		Inverted overprint	15.00	15.00
538	A22 (d)	2pi ind (Bk)	20.00	20.00

On Commemorative Stamps of 1913.
539	A23 (d)	10pa grn (R)	85	85
a.		Inverted overprint	15.00	15.00
540	A23 (d)	40pa bl (R)	85	85
a.		Inverted overprint	15.00	15.00

On Stamp of 1914, with Addition of New Value.
541	A31	60pa on 1 pi on 1½pi car & blk (Bk)	1.50	1.50
a.		"1330" omitted	25.00	25.00

On Stamps of 1916-18.
541B	A51 (f)	25pi car, straw	1.10	1.10
541C	A52 (g)	50pi carmine	8.00	7.00
541D	A52 (g)	50pi indigo	12.50	7.50
541E	A52 (g)	50pi grn, straw	8.00	7.00

Overprinted on Eastern Rumelia No. 12.
542	A4 (d)	20pa blk & rose (Bl)	20.00	20.00

Overprinted on Eastern Rumelia Nos. 15-17.
543	A4 (d)	5pa lil & pale lil (Bk)	20.00	20.00
544	A4 (d)	10pa grn & pale grn (Bk)	20.00	20.00
545	A4 (d)	20pa car & pale rose (Bk)	20.00	20.00

Some experts question the status of Nos. 510A, 512A and 525A. See also Nos. J71-J86, P153-P172.

Soldiers in Trench A52a

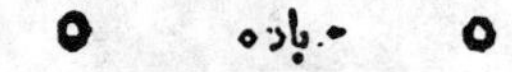

1917
545A	A52a	5pa on 1pi red	10	8

It is stated that No. 545A was never issued without surcharge. See No. 548f.

Turkish Artillery A53

1917   Typo.   Perf. 11½, 12½
546	A53	2pa Prus bl	27.50	

In type A42 the Turkish inscription at the top is in one group, in type A53 it is in two groups. It is stated that No. 546 was never placed in use. Copies were distributed through the Universal Postal Union at Bern.

Surcharged

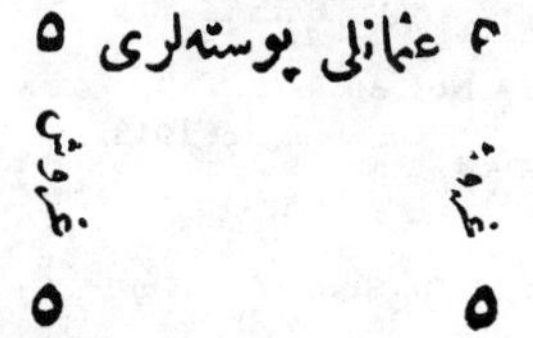

547	A53	5pi on 2pa Prus bl	45	10
a.		Inverted surcharge	15.00	15.00
b.		Turkish "5" omitted at lower left		

Surcharged

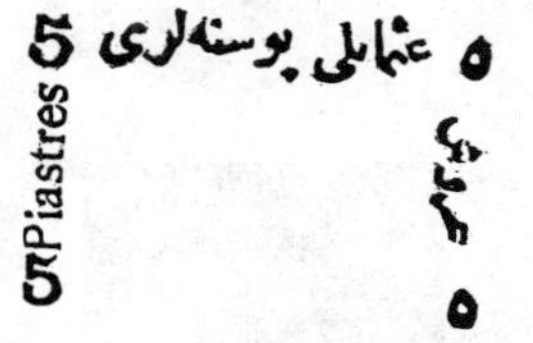

1918
548	A53	5pi on 2pa Prus bl	60	20
g.		Inverted surcharge	15.00	15.00

Top line of surcharge on Nos. 547-548 reads "Ottoman Posts."

No. 545A Surcharged

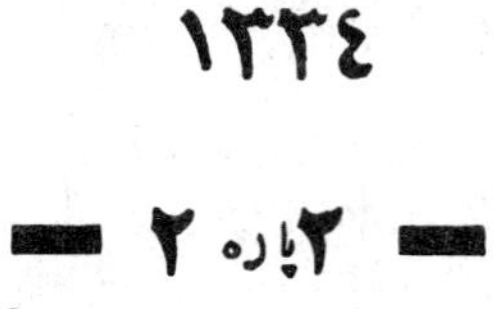

1918

548A	A52a	2pa on 1pi red	10	8
b.		Double surcharge	5.00	5.00
c.		Inverted surcharge	5.00	5.00
d.		Double surcharge inverted	5.00	5.00
e.		Double surcharge, one inverted	5.00	5.00
f.		In pair with No. 545A	10.00	10.00

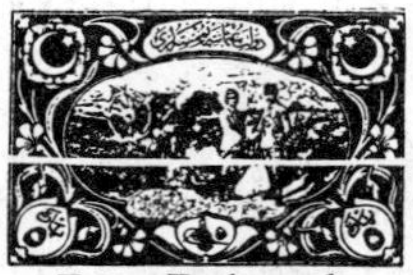

Enver Pasha and Kaiser Wilhelm II on Battlefield
A54

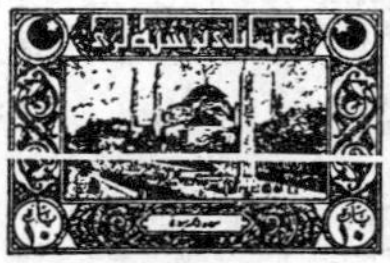

Sancta Sophia and Obelisk of the Hippodrome
A55

1918 Typographed. *Perf. 12, 12½.*

549	A54	5pa brn red	15.00
550	A55	10pa gray grn	15.00

The stamps, of which very few saw postal use, were converted into paper money by pasting on thick yellow paper and reperforating.

Armistice Issue.

Overprinted in Black or Red

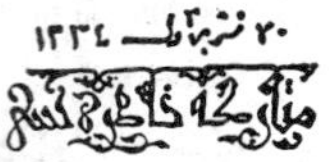

1919, Nov. 30

On Stamps of 1913.

552	A34	2½pi org & ol grn	50.00	45.00
553	A38	50pi carmine	50.00	45.00

On Stamps of 1916-18.

554	A46	1pi dl vio (R)	1.00	1.00
555	A47	50pa ultra (R)	65	65
556	A48	2pi org brn & ind	25	25
557	A49	5pi pale bl & blk (R)	25	25
558	A50	10pi dk grn (R)	1.00	1.00
559	A51	25pi car, *straw*	1.00	1.00
560	A52	50pi grn, *straw* (R)	1.00	1.00

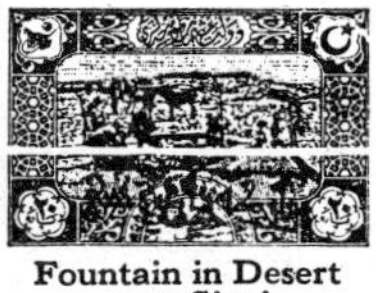

Fountain in Desert near Sinai
A56

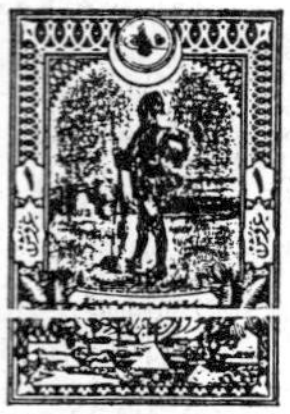

Sentry at Beersheba
A57

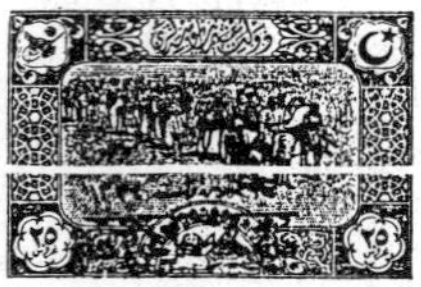

Turkish Troops at Sinai
A58

Typographed.

562	A56	20pa claret	25	25
563	A57	1pi bl (R)	50.00	45.00
564	A58	25pi sl bl (R)	50.00	45.00
		Nos. 552-564 (12)	205.40	185.40

The overprint reads: "Souvenir of the Armistice, 30th October 1334." Nos. 562 to 564 are not known to have been regularly issued without overprint.
See also No. J87.

Stamps of 1911-19 Overprinted in Turkish "Accession to the Throne of His Majesty, 3rd July 1334-1918", the Tughra of Sultan Mohammed VI and sometimes Ornaments and New Values.

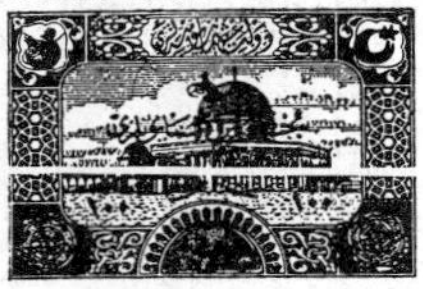

Dome of the Rock, Jerusalem
A59

1919

565	A42	2pa violet	15	15
566	A43	5pa orange	10	10
567	A21	5pa on 2pa ol grn	10	10
a.		Inverted surcharge	5.00	5.00
568	A22	10pa on 2pa ol grn	8	8
569	A44	10pa green	20	20
a.		Inverted overprint	5.00	5.00
570	A45	20pa dp rose	20	8
a.		Inverted overprint	10.00	10.00
571	A46	1pi dl vio	20	20
572	A47	60pa on 50pa ultra	30	30
573	A48	60pa on 2pi org brn & ind	25	25
574	A48	2pi org brn & ind	25	25
574A	A34	2½pi org & ol grn	10.00	10.00
575	A49	5pi pale bl & blk	25	25
576	A56	10pi on 20pa cl	30	30
577	A50	10pi dk brn	1.00	1.00
578	A51	25pi car, *straw*	1.25	1.25
579	A57	35pi on 1pi bl	1.00	1.00
579A	A52	50pi carmine	10.00	10.00
580	A52	50pi grn, *straw*	5.00	5.00
581	A59	100pi on 10pa grn	4.00	4.00
582	A58	250pi on 25pi sl bl	5.50	5.50
		Nos. 565-582 (20)	40.13	40.01

See also Nos. J88–J91.

Surcharged ١٩١٩-١٣٣٥
Ornaments and New Values.
Perf. 11½, 12½.

583	A56	20pa claret	25	25
584	A57	1pi dp bl	25	25
585	A59	60pa on 10pa grn	25	20
586	A58	25pi sl bl	1.90	1.90
a.		Inverted overprint		150.00

Nos. 576, 579, 581, 582 and 583 to 586 inclusive were prepared in anticipation of the invasion and conquest of Egypt by the Turks. They were not issued at that time but subsequently received various overprints in commemoration of Sultan Mehmet Sadi's accession to the throne (Nos. 565 to 582) and of the first anniversary of this event (Nos. 583 to 586).

Designs of 1913 Modified.

1920 Lithographed. *Perf. 11, 12.*

590	A26	5pa brn org	5	5

Engraved.

591	A28	10pa green	5	5
592	A23	20pa rose	7	6
593	A30	1pi bl grn	60	5
594	A32	3pi blue	10	10
595	A34	5pi gray	5.50	50
596	A36	10pi gray vio	65	30
597	A37	25pi dl vio	1.25	65
598	A38	50pi brown	2.25	1.25
		Nos. 590-598 (9)	10.52	3.01

On most stamps of this issue the designs have been modified by removing the small Turkish word at right of the tughra of the Sultan. In the 3pi and 5pi the values have been altered, while for the 25pi the color has been changed.

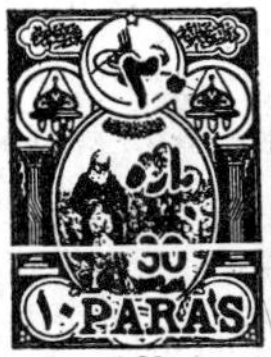

A60

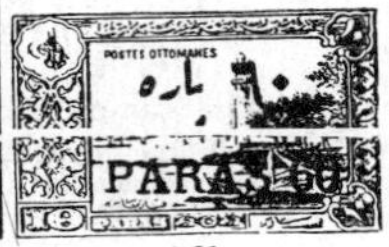

A61

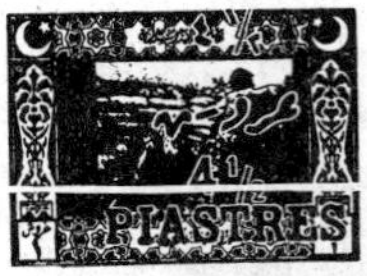

A62

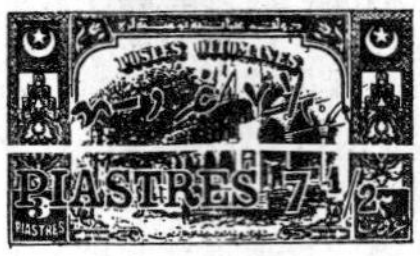

A63

Black Surcharge

1921-22

600	A60	30pa on 10pa red vio	20	10
a.		Double surcharge	5.00	5.00
b.		Imperf.		
601	A61	60pa on 10pa grn	20	10
a.		Double surcharge	5.00	5.00
602	A62	4½pi on 1pi red	80	50
a.		Inverted surcharge	10.00	10.00
603	A63	7½pi on 3pi bl	1.75	80
604	A63	7½pi on 3pi bl (R) ('22)	5.00	1.00
a.		Double surcharge	20.00	20.00
		Nos. 600-604 (5)	7.95	2.50

Issues of the Republic.

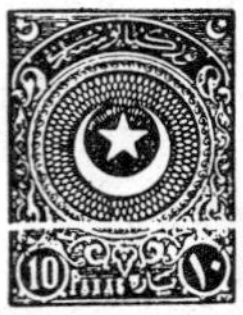

Crescent and Star
A64

TWO PIASTRES.
Type I. "2" measures 3½x1⅗mm.
Type II. "2" measures 2⅘x1½mm.
FIVE PIASTRES.
Type I. "5" measures 3½x2¼ mm.
Type II. "5" measures 3x1¾ mm.

Perf. 11, 12, 13½, 13½x12.

1923-25 Lithographed.

605	A64	10pa gray blk	30	5
606	A64	20pa citron	40	5
607	A64	1pi dp vio	45	5
a.		Slanting numeral in lower left corner	1.00	30
608	A64	1½pi emerald	30	10
609	A64	2pi bluish grn (I)	1.40	5
a.		2pi dp grn (II)	2.25	10
610	A64	3pi yel brn	70	6
611	A64	3¾pi lil brn	70	10
612	A64	4½pi carmine	1.25	6
613	A64	5pi pur (I)	2.75	10
a.		5pi vio (II)	5.00	10
614	A64	7½pi blue	1.50	5
615	A64	10pi slate	2.75	6
a.		10pi bl	7.00	50
616	A64	11¼pi dl rose	1.25	45
617	A64	15pi brown	5.00	30
618	A64	18¾pi myr grn	2.50	55
619	A64	22½pi orange	3.50	55
620	A64	25pi blk brn	10.00	15
621	A64	50pi gray	27.50	60
622	A64	100pi dk vio	50.00	60
624	A64	500pi dp grn	350.00	80.00
		Cut cancellation		2.00
		Nos. 605-624 (19)	464.50	84.03

Nos. 605–610, 612–617 exist imperf. and part perf.

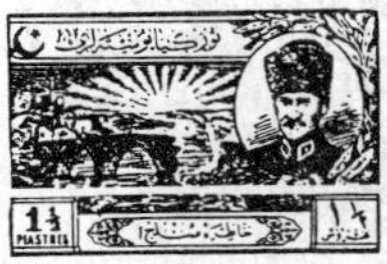

Bridge of Sakarya and Mustafa Kemal
A65

1924, Jan. 1 ***Perf. 12***

625	A65	1½pi emerald	70	30
626	A65	3pi purple	70	30
627	A65	4½pi pale rose	1.50	1.25
628	A65	5pi yel brn	90	30
629	A65	7½pi dp bl	90	40
630	A65	50pi orange	18.00	10.00
631	A65	100pi brn vio	30.00	25.00
632	A65	200pi ol brn	60.00	45.00
		Nos. 625-632 (8)	112.70	82.55

Signing of Treaty of Peace at Lausanne.

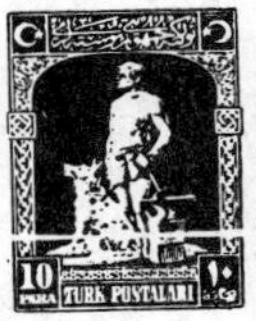

The Legendary Blacksmith and his Gray Wolf
A66

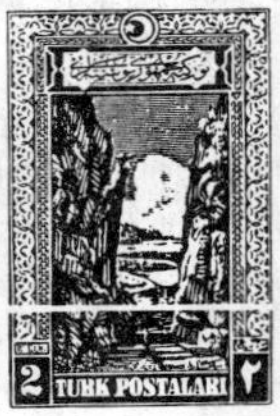

Sakarya Gorge
A67

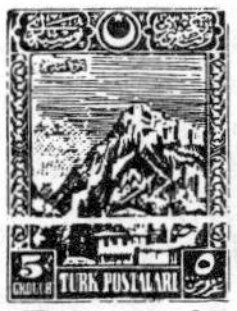

Fortress of Ankara
A68

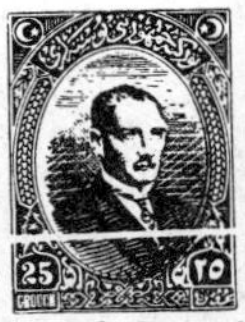

Mustafa Kemal Pasha
A69

1926 Engraved

634	A66	10pa slate	10	5
635	A66	20pa orange	15	5
636	A66	1g brt rose	18	6
637	A67	2g green	30	6
638	A67	2½g gray blk	30	6
639	A67	3g cop red	40	6
640	A68	5g lil gray	70	6
641	A68	6g red	1.00	6
642	A68	10g dp bl	90	7
643	A68	15g dp org	3.50	7
644	A69	25g dk grn & blk	7.00	8
645	A69	50g car & blk	10.50	20
646	A69	100g ol grn & blk	18.00	1.00
647	A69	200g brn & blk	45.00	2.00
		Nos. 634-647 (14)	88.03	3.88

TURKEY

Stamps of 1926 Overprinted in Black, Silver or Gold

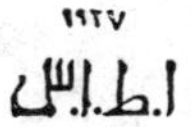

1927, Sept. 9

648	A66	1g brt rose	15	8
649	A67	2g green	15	10
650	A67	2½g gray blk	30	20
651	A67	3g cop red	45	25
652	A68	5g lil gray	75	35
653	A68	6g red	30	15
654	A68	10g dp bl	2.75	1.00
655	A68	15g dp org	2.75	1.00
656	A69	25g dk grn & blk (S)	7.50	4.50
657	A69	50g car & blk (S)	15.00	7.50
658	A69	100g ol grn & blk (G)	42.50	35.00
	Nos. 648-658 (11)		72.60	50.13

Issued in connection with an agricultural and Industrial exhibition at Izmir, September 9-20, 1927. The overprint reads: "1927" and the initials of "Izmir Dokuz Eylul Sergisi" (Izmir Exhibition, September 9).

Second Izmir Exhibition Issue.

Stamps of 1926 Overprinted in Red or Black

1928, Sept. 9

659	A66	10pa sl (R)	15	8
660	A66	20pa org (Bk)	15	10
661	A66	1g brt rose (Bk)	25	10
662	A67	2g grn (R)	25	10
663	A67	2½g gray blk (R)	70	15
664	A67	3g cop red (Bk)	45	30
665	A68	5g lil gray (R)	1.10	75
666	A68	6g red (Bk)	75	15
667	A68	10g dp bl (Bk)	1.40	60
668	A68	15g dp org (Bk)	2.50	60

Overprinted

928

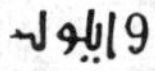

669	A69	25g dk grn & blk (R)	7.50	2.75
670	A69	50g car & blk (Bk)	20.00	6.00
671	A69	100g ol grn & blk (R)	40.00	16.00
672	A69	200g brn & blk (R)	60.00	25.00
	Nos. 659-672 (14)		135.20	52.53

The overprint reads "Izmir, September 9, 1928".

Stamps of 1926 Surcharged in Black or Red

2 ½ kuruşlur

1929

673	A66	20pa on 1g brt rose (Bk)	45	10
a.	Inverted surcharge		7.00	7.00
674	A68	2½k on 5g lil gray (R)	75	20
a.	Inverted surcharge		15.00	15.00
675	A68	6k on 10g dp bl	10.00	50

Railroad Bridge over Kizil Irmak
A70

A71

A72

A73

Latin Inscriptions. Without umlaut over first "U" of "CUMHURIYETI."

1929   Engraved.

676	A70	2k gray blk	75	10
677	A70	2½k green	75	10
678	A70	3k vio brn	75	10
679	A71	6k dk vio	10.00	10
680	A72	12½k dp bl	16.00	1.10
681	A73	50k car & blk	27.50	80
	Nos. 676-681 (6)		55.75	2.30

Sakarya Gorge
A74

Mustafa Kemal Pasha
A75

With umlaut over first "U" of "CUMHURIYETI."

1930

682	A71	10pa green	5	5
683	A70	20pa gray vio	8	5
684	A70	1k ol grn	25	6
685	A71	1½k ol blk	12	6
686	A70	2k dl vio	1.75	5
687	A70	2½k dp grn	30	5
688	A70	3k brn org	3.00	6
689	A71	4k dp rose	4.50	6
690	A72	5k rose lake	3.00	6
691	A71	6k indigo	3.50	5
692	A74	7½k red brn	25	5
694	A72	12½k dp ultra	70	5
695	A72	15k dp org	75	5
696	A74	17½k dk gray	85	30
697	A72	20k blk brn	15	60
698	A74	25k ol brn	1.50	10
699	A72	30k yel brn	2.50	10
700	A74	40k red vio	1.50	20
701	A75	50k red & blk	2.10	25
702	A75	100k ol grn & blk	4.50	30
703	A75	200k dk grn & blk	5.50	90
704	A75	500k choc & blk	22.50	4.50
	Nos. 682-704 (22)		59.35	7.90

Issue of 1930 Surcharged in Red or Black:

Sivas
D. Y.
30 ag. 930
1 K.
a

D. Y. Sivas
30 ag. 930
10 P.
b

Sivas
D. Y.
30 ag. 930
40 K.
c

1930, Aug. 30

705	A71 (a)	10pa on 10pa grn (R)	10	10
706	A70 (b)	10pa on 20pa gray vio	10	10
707	A70 (b)	20pa on 1ku ol grn	12	10
708	A71 (b)	1k on 1½k ol blk (R)	20	10
709	A70 (b)	1½k on 2k dl vio	30	10
710	A70 (b)	2k on 2½k dp grn (R)	55	15
711	A70 (b)	2½k on 3k brn org	55	15
712	A71 (b)	3k on 4k dp rose	75	15
713	A72 (a)	4k on 5k rose lake	1.50	30
714	A71 (a)	5k on 6k ind (R)	45	30
715	A74 (a)	6k on 7½k red brn	75	20
716	A72 (a)	7½k on 12½k ultra (R)	90	15
717	A72 (a)	12½k on 15k dp org	2.25	30
718	A74 (b)	15k on 17½k dk gray (R)	2.25	75
719	A72 (b)	17½k on 20k blk brn (R)	2.75	75
720	A72 (b)	20k on 25k ol brn (R)	2.75	75
721	A72 (b)	25k on 30k yel brn	2.75	75
722	A74 (b)	30k on 40k red vio	3.75	90
723	A75 (c)	40k on 50k red & blk	3.75	75
724	A75 (c)	50k on 100k ol grn & blk (R)	32.50	4.50
725	A75 (c)	100k on 200k dk grn & blk (R)	37.50	7.00
726	A75 (c)	250k on 500k choc & blk (R)	40.00	4.50
	Nos. 705-726 (22)		136.52	22.85

Issued in commemoration of the inauguration of the railroad between Ankara and Sivas.
There are numerous varieties in these settings as: "309", "390", "930" inverted, no period after "D", no period after "Y", and raised period before "Y".

No. 685 Surcharged in Red

1 Kuruş

1931, Apr. 1

| 727 | A71 | 1k on 1½k ol blk | 1.50 | 20 |

Olive Tree with Roots Extending to All Balkan Capitals—A76

1931, Oct. 20   Engr.   Perf. 12

728	A76	2½k dk grn	20	10
729	A76	4k carmine	20	12
730	A76	6k stl bl	25	5
731	A76	7½k dl red	25	12
732	A76	12k dp org	30	10
733	A76	12½k dk bl	45	10
734	A76	30k dk vio	1.25	15
735	A76	50k dk brn	2.25	45
736	A76	100k brn vio	5.25	2.00
	Nos. 728-736 (9)		10.40	3.19

Second Balkan Conference.

A77

A78

Mustafa Kemal Pasha (Kemal Atatürk)
A79

1931-42   Typo.   Perf. 11½, 12

737	A77	10pa bl grn	5	5
738	A77	20pa dp org	10	5
739	A77	30pa brt vio ('38)	10	5
740	A78	1k dk sl grn	10	5
740A	A77	1½k mag ('42)	1.00	15
741	A78	2k dk vio	10	5
741A	A77	2k yel grn ('40)	25	5
742	A77	2½k green	10	5
743	A78	3k brn org ('38)	15	5
744	A78	4k slate	10	5
745	A78	5k rose red	15	5
745A	A78	5k brn blk ('40)	70	5
746	A78	6k dp bl	45	5
746A	A78	6k rose ('40)	40	5
747	A77	7½k dp rose ('32)	30	5
747A	A78	8k brt bl ('38)	40	5
b.		8k dk bl ('36)	40	8
748	A77	10k blk brn ('32)	6.00	5
748A	A77	10k dp bl ('40)	3.75	15
749	A77	12k bis ('32)	75	5
750	A79	12½k ind ('32)	45	5
751	A77	15k org yel ('32)	55	6
752	A77	20k ol grn ('32)	55	6
753	A77	25k Prus bl ('32)	75	10
754	A77	30k mag ('32)	1.00	5
755	A79	100k mar ('32)	2.00	25
756	A79	200k pur ('32)	3.50	30
757	A79	250k choc ('32)	14.00	75
	Nos. 737-757 (27)		37.75	2.77

See also Nos. 1015-1033, 1117B-1126.

The lack of a price for a listed item does not necessarily indicate rarity.

TURKEY

Symbolizing 10th Anniversary of Republic—A80

President Atatürk—A81

1933, Oct. 29   *Perf. 10*

758	A80	1½k bl grn	75	25
759	A80	2k ol brn	75	30
760	A81	3k red brn	75	25
761	A81	6k dp bl	75	40
762	A80	12½k dk bl	2.75	2.00
763	A80	25k dk brn	5.00	3.75
764	A81	50k org brn	11.00	10.00
		Nos. 758-764 (7)	21.75	16.95

Issued in commemoration of the tenth year of the Turkish Republic. The stamps were in use for three days only.

Stamps of 1930
Overprinted or Surcharged in Red:

İzmir 9 Eylûl 934 Sergisi
a

İzmir 9 Eylûl 934 Sergisi 2 Kurus
b

1934, Aug. 26   *Perf. 12*

765	A71	10pa green	30	15
766	A71	1k on 1½k ol blk	45	15
767	A74	2k on 25k ol brn	75	15
768	A74	5k on 7½k red brn	2.00	55
769	A74	6k on 17½k dk gray	4.00	55
770	A72	12½k dp ultra	6.00	1.50
771	A72	15k on 20k blk brn	55.00	27.50
772	A74	20k on 25k ol brn	50.00	22.50
773	A75	50k on 100k ol grn & blk	50.00	22.50
		Nos. 765-773 (9)	166.50	75.75

Izmir Fair, 1934.

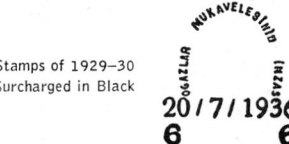

Stamps of 1929-30
Surcharged in Black

1936, Oct. 26

775	A74	4k on 17½k dk gray	1.50	55
a.		"1926" in ovpt.	5.50	5.50
776	A74	5k on 25k ol brn	1.50	55
a.		"1926" in ovpt.	5.50	5.50
777	A73	6k on 50k car & blk	1.50	55
a.		"1926" in ovpt.	5.50	5.50
778	A75	10k on 100k ol grn & blk	2.25	75
a.		"1926" in ovpt.	7.00	7.00
779	A75	20k on 200k dk grn & blk	8.50	2.00
a.		"1926" in ovpt.	15.00	15.00
780	A75	50k on 500k choc & blk	15.00	3.50
a.		"1926" in overprint	40.00	40.00
		Nos. 775-780 (6)	30.25	7.90

Re-militarization of the Dardanelles.

Hittite Bronze Stag
A82

Thorak's Bust of Kemal Atatürk
A83

1937, Sept. 20   *Litho.*   *Perf. 12*

781	A82	3k lt vio	1.10	60
782	A83	6k blue	1.50	90
783	A82	7½k brt pink	3.00	2.00
784	A83	12½k indigo	5.25	3.00

Issued in commemoration of the Second Turkish Historical Congress held at Istanbul, September 20th to 30th, 1937.

Arms of Turkey, Greece, Romania and Jugoslavia
A84

1937, Oct. 29   *Perf. 11½*

785	A84	8k carmine	12.50	4.00
786	A84	12½k dk bl	27.50	7.50

Issued in commemoration of the Balkan Entente.

Street in Izmir—A85

Fig Tree
A87

Designs: 30pa, View of Fair Buildings. 3k, Tower, Government Square. 5k, Olive branch. 6k, Woman with grapes. 7½k, Woman picking grapes. 8k, Izmir Harbor through arch. 12k, Statue of President Atatürk. 12½k, President Atatürk.

1938, Aug. 20   *Photo.*   *Perf. 11½*

Inscribed: "Izmir Enternasyonal Fuari 1938."

789	A85	10pa dk brn	25	10
790	A85	30pa purple	25	10
791	A87	2½k brt grn	85	10
792	A87	3k brn org	40	15
793	A87	5k ol grn	75	30
794	A85	6k brown	2.50	50
795	A87	7½k scarlet	2.50	90
796	A87	8k brn lake	1.25	60
797	A87	12k rose vio	2.00	1.25
798	A87	12½k dp bl	4.25	2.75
		Nos. 789-798 (10)	15.00	6.75

Izmir International Fair.

President Atatürk Teaching Reformed Turkish Alphabet
A95

1938, Nov. 2

799	A95	2½k brt grn	40	20
800	A95	3k orange	40	20
801	A95	6k rose vio	60	20
802	A95	7½k dp rose	60	60
803	A95	8k red brn	1.00	60
804	A95	12½k brt ultra	2.25	1.25
		Nos. 799-804 (6)	5.25	3.05

Issued in commemoration of the 10th anniversary of the reform of the Turkish alphabet.

Army and Air Force
A96

Atatürk Driving Tractor
A98

Designs: 3k, View of Kayseri. 7½k, Railway bridge. 8k, Scout buglers. 12½k, President Atatürk.

Inscribed: "Cumhuriyetin 15 inc yil donumu hatirasi."

1938, Oct. 29

805	A96	2½k dk grn	25	15
806	A96	3k red brn	30	15
807	A98	6k bister	35	25
808	A96	7½k red	80	40
809	A96	8k rose vio	3.00	2.00
810	A98	12½k dp bl	2.00	1.25
		Nos. 805-810 (6)	6.70	4.20

15th anniversary of the Republic.

Stamps of 1931-38
Overprinted in Black   21-11-1938

1938, Nov. 21   *Perf. 11½x12*

811	A78	3k brn org	40	25
812	A78	5k rose red	40	25
813	A78	6k dp bl	40	30
814	A77	7½k dp rose	75	40
815	A78	8k dk bl	90	65
a.		8k brt bl	18.50	15.00
816	A79	12½k indigo	1.50	1.25
		Nos. 811-816 (6)	4.35	3.10

Issued in honor of President Kemal Atatürk (1881-1938). The date is that of his funeral.

Turkish and American Flags
A102

Presidents Inönü and F. D. Roosevelt and Map of North America
A103

Designs: 3k, 8k, Inonu and Roosevelt. 7½k, 12½k, Kemal Ataturk and Washington.

1939, July 15   *Photo.*   *Perf. 14*

817	A102	2½k ol grn, red & bl	40	25
818	A103	3k dk brn & Bl grn	40	25
819	A103	6k pur, red & bl	40	25
820	A103	7½k org ver & bl grn	75	30
821	A103	8k dp cl & bl grn	1.10	55
822	A103	12½k brt bl & bl grn	2.00	1.75
		Nos. 817-822 (6)	5.05	3.35

U.S. constitution, 150th anniversary.

Anavatana Hatayın Kavuşması 23/7/1939 3 3

Stamps of 1930
Surcharged in Black

1939, July 23   *Perf. 13*   *Unwmkd.*

823	A74	3k on 25k ol brn	20	20
824	A75	6k on 200k dk grn & blk	30	30
825	A74	7½k on 25k ol brn	40	30
826	A75	12k on 100k ol grn & blk	55	30
827	A75	12½k on 200k dk grn & blk	75	45
828	A75	17½k on 500k choc & blk	1.40	1.00
		Nos. 823-828 (6)	3.60	2.50

Annexation of Hatay.

Railroad Bridge
A105

Locomotive
A106

Track Through Mountain Pass
A107

Design: 12½k, Railroad tunnel, Atma Pass.

Perf. 11½

1939, Oct. 20   *Typo.*   *Unwmkd.*

829	A105	3k lt org red	1.50	1.00
830	A106	6k chestnut	2.50	2.00
831	A107	7½k rose pink	3.00	2.25
832	A107	12½k dk bl	4.50	3.75

Issued in commemoration of the completion of the Sivas to Erzerum link of the Ankara-Erzerum Railroad.

TURKEY

Atatürk Residence in Ankara
A109

Kemal Atatürk
A110

A111

Designs: 5k, 6k, 7½k, 8k, 12½k, 17½k, Various portraits of Ataturk, "1880-1938."

1939-40   Photogravure
833	A109	2½k brt grn	15	10
834	A110	3k dk bl gray	20	15
835	A110	5k chocolate	25	20
836	A110	6k chestnut	25	20
837	A110	7½k rose red	40	40
838	A110	8k gray grn	30	40
839	A110	12½k brt bl	60	25
840	A110	17½k brt rose	1.75	1.25
	Nos. 833-840 (8)		3.90	2.95

Souvenir Sheet.
841   A111   100k bl blk   45.00   35.00

Death of Kemal Ataturk, first anniversary. Size of No. 841: 90x120mm. Issue dates: 2½, 6 and 12½ku, Nov. 11, 1939. Others, Jan. 3, 1940.

Namik Kemal
A118

Arms of Turkey, Greece, Romania and Jugoslavia
A119

1940, Jan. 3
842	A118	6k chestnut	40	30
843	A118	8k dk ol grn	60	35
844	A118	12k brt rose red	1.75	60
845	A118	12½k brt bl	2.00	1.50

Issued in commemoration of the centenary of the birth of Namik Kemal, poet and patriot.

     Perf. 11½
1940, Jan. 1   Typo.   Unwmkd.
846	A119	8k lt bl	2.50	75
847	A119	10k dp bl	2.50	75

Issued in commemoration of the Balkan Entente.

Nos. 703-704 Surcharged in Red or Black

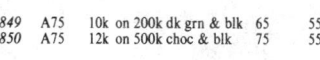

1940, Aug. 20   Perf. 12
848   A75   6k on 200k dk grn & blk   45   30
     (R)

849	A75	10k on 200k dk grn & blk	65	55
850	A75	12k on 500k choc & blk	75	55

13th International Izmir Fair.

Map of Turkey and Census Figures
A120

1940, Oct. 1   Typo.   Perf. 11½
851	A120	10pa dk bl grn	15	10
852	A120	3k orange	25	20
853	A120	6k car rose	45	40
854	A120	10k dk bl	1.25	75

Census of Oct. 20, 1940.

Runner
A121

Pole Vaulter
A122

Hurdler—A123

Discus Thrower
A124

1940, Oct. 5
855	A121	3k ol grn	1.10	75
856	A122	6k rose	4.00	2.50
857	A123	8k chnt brn	2.75	1.10
858	A124	10k dk bl	4.50	3.00

11th Balkan Olympics.

Mail Carriers on Horseback
A125

Postman of 1840 and 1940
A126

Old Sailing Vessel and Modern Mailboat
A127

Design: 12k, Post Office, Istanbul.

1940, Dec. 31   Typo.   Perf. 10
859	A125	3k gray grn	25	15
860	A126	6k rose	45	40
861	A127	10k dk bl	1.50	1.00
862	A127	12k ol brn	1.50	75

Centenary of the Turkish post.

Harbor Scene
A129

Statue of Atatürk
A132

Designs: 3k, 6k, 17½k, Various Izmir Fair buildings. 12k, Girl picking grapes.

1941, Aug. 20   Litho.   Perf. 11½
Inscribed: "Izmir Enternasyonal Fuari 1941."

863	A129	30pa dl grn	5	5
864	A129	3k ol gray	10	8
865	A129	6k sal rose	15	9
866	A132	10k blue	25	15
867	A129	12k dl brn vio	30	20
868	A129	17½k dl brn	75	55
	Nos. 863-868 (6)		1.60	1.12

Izmir International Fair, 1941.

 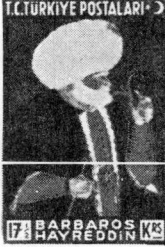

Tomb of Barbarossa II
A135

Barbarossa II (Khair ed-Din)
A137

Barbarossa's Fleet in Battle
A136

1941
869	A135	20pa dk vio	10	10
870	A136	3k lt bl	15	12
871	A136	6k rose red	30	22
872	A136	10k dp ultra	50	15
873	A136	12k dl brn & bis	1.25	45
874	A137	17½k multi	2.75	2.00
	Nos. 869-874 (6)		5.05	3.04

400th anniversary of death of Barbarossa II (Khair ed-Din).

President Inönü
A138   A138a

1942-45   Perf. 11½x11, 11
875	A138	0.25k yel bis	5	5
876	A138	0.50k lt yel grn	6	5
877	A138	1k gray grn	8	5
877A	A138	1k brt vio ('45)	60	5
878	A138	2k bluish grn	8	5
879	A138	4k fawn	10	5
880	A138	4½k slate	10	5
881	A138	5k lt bl	12	6
882	A138	6k sal rose	15	5
883	A138	6¾k ultra	18	5
884	A138	9k bl vio	1.10	5
885	A138	10k dk bl	15	5
886	A138	13½k brt pink	15	8
887	A138	16k Prus blu	30	10
888	A138	17½k rose lake	30	5
889	A138	20k brn vio	75	10
890	A138	27½k orange	40	5
891	A138	37k buff	45	12
892	A138	50k purple	1.25	20
893	A138	100k ol bis	3.25	90
894	A138a	200k brown	11.00	1.25
	Nos. 875-894 (21)		20.62	3.58

Ankara
A139

Antioch
A141

Designs: 0.50k, Mohair goats. 1½k, Ankara Dam. 2k, Oranges. 4k, Merino sheep. 4½k, Train. 5k, Tile decorating. 6k, Atatürk statue, Ankara. 6¾k, 10k, President Ismet Inonu. 13½k, Grand National Assembly. 16k, Arnavutkoy, Istanbul. 17½k, Republic monument, Instanbul. 20k, Safety monument, Ankara. 27½k, Post Office, Istanbul. 37k, Monument at Afyon. 50k, "People's House," Ankara. 100k, Atatürk and Inonu. 200k, President Inonu.

1943, Apr. 1   Perf. 11
896	A139	0.25k citron	5	5
897	A139	0.50k brt grn	45	5
898	A141	1k dp vio	6	5
899	A141	1½k dp vio	8	5
900	A139	2k brt bl grn	55	5
901	A141	4k cop red	1.00	10
902	A139	4½k black	80	5
903	A141	5k sapphire	60	15
904	A139	6k car rose	20	5
905	A139	6¾k brt ultra	15	5
906	A139	10k dk bl	25	5
907	A141	13½k brt red vio	30	10
908	A141	16k myr grn	1.50	20
909	A139	17½k brn org	60	15
910	A139	20k sepia	75	15
911	A139	27½k dk org	1.50	45
912	A139	37k lt yel brn	75	15
913	A141	50k purple	3.75	15
914	A139	100k dk ol grn	6.00	40
915	A139	200k dk brn	9.00	60
a.	Souvenir sheet		30.00	22.50
	Nos. 896-915 (20)		28.34	3.05

No. 915a contains one stamp similar to No. 915, perf. 13½ and printed in sepia. Size: 89x119mm. Issued Apr. 20.

TURKEY

Girl with Grapes—A158

Entrance to Izmir Fair—A159

Fair Building—A160

1943, Aug. 20   Litho.   **Perf. 11½**

916	A158	4½k dl ol	20	12
917	A159	6k car rose	18	12
918	A160	6¾k blue	20	15
919	A159	10k dk bl	25	15
920	A158	13½k sepia	75	30
921	A160	27½k dl gray	75	45
		Nos. 916-921 (6)	2.33	1.29

Izmir International Fair.

Soccer Team on Parade
A161

Turkish Flag and Soldier
A162

Designs: 6¾k, Bridge. 10k, Hospital. 13½k, View of Ankara. 27½k, President Inonu.

Perf. 11x11½, 11½x11

1943, Oct. 29
Inscribed: "Cumhuriyetin 20 nci Yildonomu Hatirasi."

922	A161	4½k lt ol grn	90	45
923	A162	6k rose red	25	10
924	A161	6¾k ultra	20	10
925	A161	10k vio bl	25	20
926	A161	13½k olive	40	25
927	A162	27½k lt brn	85	75
		Nos. 922-927 (6)	2.85	1.85

20th anniversary of Republic.
Nos. 922-927 exist imperf.

No. 905 Surcharged with New Value in Red.
1945   **Perf. 11**

| 928 | A139 | 4½k on 6¾k brt ultra | 20 | 10 |

Recording Census Data
A167

President Ismet Inönü
A169

1945, Oct. 21   Litho.   **Perf. 11½**

929	A167	4½k ol blk	60	45
930	A167	9k violet	60	45
931	A167	10k vio bl	60	45
932	A167	18k dk red	1.25	1.00

Souvenir Sheet.
Imperf.

| 933 | A167 | 11 chocolate | 20.00 | 11.00 |

Census of 1945.
No. 933 measures 89x122mm. and contains marginal inscriptions and double-line frame around stamp.

Perf. 11½ to 12½

1946, Apr. 1   **Unwmkd.**

934	A169	0.25k brn red	7	5
935	A169	1k dk sl grn	12	5
936	A169	1½k plum	12	5
937	A169	9k purple	33	5
938	A169	10k dp bl	90	8
939	A169	50k chocolate	2.75	20
		Nos. 934-939 (6)	4.29	48

U.S.S. Missouri—A170

1946, Apr. 5

940	A170	9k dk pur	25	10
941	A170	10k dk chlky bl	25	15
942	A170	27½k ol grn	90	45
a.		Imperf., pair	20.00	

Issued to commemorate the visit of the U.S.S. Missouri to Istanbul, April 5, 1946.

Sower
A171

Dove and Flag-Decorated Banderol
A172

1946, June 16

943	A171	9k violet	10	10
944	A171	10k dk bl	10	10
945	A171	18k ol grn	25	20
946	A171	27½k red org	70	45

Issued to commemorate the passing of legislation to distribute state lands to poor farmers.

1947, Aug. 20   Photo.   **Perf. 12**

947	A172	15k vio & dk bl	12	10
948	A172	20k bl & dk bl	20	12
949	A172	30k brn & gray blk	25	12
950	A172	11 ol grn & dk grn	1.10	90

Izmir International Fair.

Victory Monument, Afyon Karahisar
A173

Ismet Inönü as General
A174

Kemal Atatürk as General
A175

1947, Aug. 30

951	A173	10k dk brn & pale brn	12	8
952	A174	15k brt vio & gray	12	8
953	A175	20k dp bl & gray	12	10
954	A173	30k grnsh blk & gray	25	15
955	A174	60k ol gray & pale brn	45	25
956	A175	11 dk grn & gray	1.25	60
		Nos. 951-956 (6)	2.31	1.26

Issued to commemorate the 25th anniversary of the Battle of Dumlupinar, August 30, 1922.

Grapes and Istanbul Skyline
A176

1947, Sept. 22

957	A176	15k rose vio	20	12
958	A176	20k dp bl	30	25
959	A176	60k dk brn	90	60

International Vintners' Congress, Istanbul.

Approaching Train, Istanbul Skyline and Sirkeci Terminus
A177

1947, Oct. 9

960	A177	15k rose vio	55	15
961	A177	20k brt bl	85	30
962	A177	60k ol grn	1.50	1.25

International Railroad Congress, Istanbul.

President Ismet Inönü
A178   A179

Engraved.
1948   **Perf. 12, 14.**   **Unwmkd.**

963	A178	0.25k dk red	5	5
964	A178	1k ol blk	5	5
965	A178	2k brt rose lil	5	5
966	A178	3k red org	6	5
967	A178	4k dk grn	8	5
968	A178	5k blue	12	5
969	A178	10k chocolate	20	5
970	A178	12k dp red	20	6
971	A178	15k violet	25	6
972	A178	20k dp bl	40	6
973	A178	30k brown	1.00	20
974	A178	60k black	1.75	25
975	A179	11 ol grn	4.00	70
976	A179	21 dk brn	30.00	2.25
977	A179	51 dp plum	20.00	4.50
		Nos. 963-977 (15)	58.21	8.43

President Ismet Inönü and Lausanne Conference
A180

Conference Building
A180a

1948, July 23   Photo.   **Perf. 11½**

978	A180	15k rose lil	20	10
979	A180a	20k blue	25	10
980	A180a	40k gray grn	40	30
981	A180	11 brown	1.40	75

25th anniversary of Lausanne Treaty.

Statue of Kemal Atatürk, Ankara
A181

1948, Oct. 29

982	A181	15k violet	20	10
983	A181	20k blue	25	10
984	A181	40k gray grn	40	35
985	A181	11 brown	1.75	1.25

Issued to commemorate the 25th anniversary of the proclamation of the republic.

A182   A183

Wrestlers—A184

TURKEY

Wrestlers—A185

1949, June 3
986	A182	15k rose lil	2.00	1.50
987	A183	20k blue	4.00	2.00
988	A184	30k brown	4.00	2.50
989	A185	60k green	6.00	4.00

Issued to commemorate the fifth European Wrestling Championships, Istanbul, June 3–5, 1949.

Ancient Galley—A186

Galleon Mahmudiye A187

Monument to Khizr Barbarossa A188

Designs: 15k, Cruiser Hamidiye. 20k, Submarine Sakarya. 30k, Cruiser Yavuz.

1949, July 1
990	A186	5k violet	30	10
991	A187	10k brown	35	10
992	A186	15k lil rose	40	20
993	A186	20k gray bl	50	30
994	A186	30k gray	90	55
995	A188	40k ol gray	1.25	1.10
		Nos. 990-995 (6)	3.70	2.35

Fleet Day, July 1, 1949.

A189

U. P. U. Monument, Bern A190

Photogravure.
1949, Oct. 9 Perf. 11½ Unwmkd.
996	A189	15k violet	30	15
997	A189	20k blue	40	30
998	A190	30k dl rose	60	40
999	A190	40k green	1.25	75

Issued to commemorate the 75th anniversary of the formation of the Universal Postal Union.

Istanbul Fair Building A191

1949, Oct. 1 Litho. Perf. 10
1000	A191	15k brown	15	10
1001	A191	20k blue	25	15
1002	A191	30k olive	75	40

Istanbul Fair, Oct. 1–31.

Boy and Girl and Globe A192

Aged Woman Casting Ballot A193

Kemal Atatürk and Map—A194

1950, Aug. 13 Perf. 11½
1003	A192	15k purple	25	15
1004	A192	20k dp bl	40	30

2nd World Youth Council Meeting, 1950.
No. 1004 exists imperf. Price $3.

1950, Aug. 30
1005	A193	15k dk brn	15	15
1006	A193	20k dk bl	25	15
1007	A194	30k dk bl & gray	40	25

Election of May 14, 1950.

Hazel Nuts A195

Symbolical of 1950 Census A196

Designs: 12ku, Acorns. 15ku, Cotton. 20ku, Symbolical of the fair. 30ku, Tobacco.

1950, Sept. 9
1008	A195	8k gray grn & buff	30	12
1009	A195	12k magenta	45	15
1010	A195	15k brn blk & lt brn	75	35
1011	A195	20k dk bl & aqua	1.25	60
1012	A195	30k brn blk & dl org	2.00	1.00
		Nos. 1008-1012 (5)	4.75	2.22

Izmir International Fair, Aug. 20–Sept. 20.

1950, Oct. 9 Litho. Perf. 11½
1013	A196	15k dk brn	20	12
1014	A196	20k vio bl	40	25

Issued to publicize the general census of 1950.

Atatürk Types of 1931–42.
Perf. 10 x 11½, 11½ x 12.

1950–51 Typographed
1015	A77	10p dl red brn	5	5
1016	A77	10p ver ('51)	5	5
1017	A77	20p bl grn	8	5
1018	A78	1k ol grn	20	5
1019	A78	2k plum	35	5
1020	A78	2k dp yel ('51)	60	5
1021	A78	3k yel org	60	5
1022	A78	3k gray ('51)	45	5
1023	A78	4k grn ('51)	45	5
1024	A78	5k blue	40	5
1025	A78	5k plum ('51)	3.00	5
1026	A77	10k brn org	1.50	5
1027	A77	15k purple	1.75	5
1028	A77	15k brn car	13.50	5
1029	A77	20k dk bl	10.00	12
1030	A77	30k pink ('51)	12.00	15
1031	A79	100k red brn ('51)	1.50	55
1032	A79	200k dk brn	6.00	55
1033	A79	200k rose vio ('51)	3.50	75
		Nos. 1015-1033 (19)	55.98	2.52

16th Century Flight of Hezarfen Ahmet Celebi A197

Plane over Istanbul A198

Design: 40k, Biplane over Taurus Mountains.

1950, Oct. 17 Litho. Perf. 11
1034	A197	20k dk grn & bl	60	25
1035	A197	40k dk brn & bl	90	45
1036	A198	60k pur & bl	1.50	75

Issued to publicize the regional meeting of the International Civil Aviation Organization, Istanbul, Oct. 17, 1950.

Farabi—A199

1950, Dec. 1 Perf. 11½ Unwmkd.
Multicolored Center.
1037	A199	15k blue	75	45
1038	A199	20k bl vio	1.50	60
1039	A199	60k red brn	3.75	2.00
1040	A199	1l gold & bl vio	5.25	4.25

Issued to commemorate the millenary of the death of Farabi, Arab philosopher.

Mithat Pasha and Security Bank Building A200

Design: 20k, Agricultural Bank.

1950, Dec. 21 Photogravure
1041	A200	15k rose vio	50	30
1042	A200	20k blue	70	40

Issued to publicize the 3rd Congress of Turkish Cooperatives, Istanbul, December 25, 1950.

Floating a Ship—A201

Lighthouse—A202

Designs: 20ku, Steamship. 30ku, Diver Rising.

1951, July 1
1043	A201	15k blue	45	25
1044	A201	20k dp ultra	45	25
1045	A201	30k ol gray	90	60
1046	A202	1l gray grn	1.25	1.25

Issued to commemorate the 25th anniversary of the recognition of coastal rights in Turkish waters to ships under the Turkish flag.

Mosque of Sultan Ahmed A203

Henry Carton de Wiart A204

Designs: 20ku, Dolma Bahce Palace. 60ku, Rumeli Hisari Fortress.

1951, Aug. 31 Photo. Perf. 13½
1047	A203	15k dk grn	40	25
1048	A203	20k dp ultra	40	25
1049	A204	30k brown	60	40
1050	A203	60k pur brn	1.50	1.10

Issued to publicize the 40th Interparliamentary Conference, Istanbul, 1951.

TURKEY

Allegory of Food and Agriculture
A205

Designs: 20k, Dam. 30k, United Nations Building. 60k, University, Ankara.
Inscribed:
"Akdeniz Yetistirme Merkezi. Ankara 1951."

1952, Jan. 3		Perf. 14	Unwmkd.	
1051	A205	15k green	75	20
1052	A205	20k bl vio	90	25
1053	A205	30k blue	1.40	70
1054	A205	60k red	3.50	2.75
a.		Souv. sheet of 4	60.00	50.00

U.N. Mediterranean Economic Instruction Center.
No. 1054a contains one each of Nos. 1051-1054, imperf., with inscriptions in dark blue gray. Size: 132x102mm.

Abdulhak Hamid Tarhan
A206

1952, Feb. 5		Photo.	Perf. 13½	
1055	A206	15k dk pur	12	10
1056	A206	20k dk bl	20	10
1057	A206	30k brown	40	20
1058	A206	60k dk ol grn	1.00	60

Issued to commemorate the centenary of the birth of Abdulhak Hamid Tarhan, poet.

Ruins, Bergama   **Tarsus Cataract**
A207   A208

Designs: 2k, Ruins, Milas. 3k, Karatay Gate, Konya. 4k, Kozak plateau. 5k, Urgup. 10k, 12k, 15k, 20k, Kemal Ataturk. 30k, Mosque, Bursa. 40k, Mosque, Istanbul. 75k, Rocks, Urgup. 1 l, Palace, Istanbul. 2 l, Pavilion, Istanbul. 5 l, Museum interior, Istanbul.

1952, Mar. 15			Perf. 13½	
1059	A207	1k brn org	5	5
1060	A207	2k ol grn	5	5
1061	A207	3k rose brn	5	5
1062	A207	4k bl grn	5	5
1063	A207	5k brown	6	5
1064	A207	10k dk brn	20	7
1065	A207	12k brt rose car	25	10
1066	A207	15k purple	25	7
1067	A207	20k chlky bl	90	7
1068	A207	30k grnsh gray	45	7
1069	A207	40k sl bl	90	10
1070	A208	50k olive	1.00	10
1071	A208	75k slate	1.10	45
1072	A208	1 l dp pur	1.25	40
1073	A208	2 l brt ultra	2.50	60
1074	A208	5 l sepia	20.00	6.00
		Nos. 1059-1074 (16)	29.06	8.28

Imperfs, price, set $60.

No. 1059 Surcharged with New Value in Black.

1952, June 1				
1075	A207	0.50k on 1k brn org	15	7

Technical Faculty Building
A209

1952, Aug. 20			Perf. 12x12½	
1076	A209	15k violet	40	20
1077	A209	20k blue	55	25
1078	A209	60k brown	1.50	1.20

Issued to publicize the 8th International Congress of Theoretic and Applied Mechanics.

Turkish Soldier   **Pigeons Bandaging Wounded Hand**
A210   A212

Designs: 20k, Soldier with Turkish flag. 30k, Soldier and child with comic book. 60k, Raising Turkish flag.

1952, Sept. 25			Perf. 14	
1079	A210	15k Prus bl	40	20
1080	A210	20k dp bl	40	25
1081	A210	30k brown	75	40
1082	A210	60k ol blk & car	1.50	90

Issued to publicize Turkey's participation in the Korean war.

1952, Oct. 29			Perf. 12½x12	

Design: 20k, Flag, rainbow and ruined homes.

Dated "1877-1952."

| 1085 | A212 | 15k dk grn & red | 75 | 45 |
| 1086 | A212 | 20k bl & red | 1.50 | 75 |

Issued to commemorate the 75th anniversary of the foundation of the Turkish Red Crescent Society.

Relief From Panel of Aziziye Monument
A213

Aziziye Monument
A214
Design: 40k, View of Erzerum.

1952, Nov. 9			Perf. 11	
1087	A213	15k purple	40	20
1088	A214	20k blue	50	30
1089	A214	40k ol gray	90	75

Issued to commemorate the 75th anniversary of the Battle of Aziziye at Erzerum.

Rumeli Hisari Fortress
A215

Troops Entering Constantinople   **Sultan Mohammed II**
A216   A217

Designs: 8k, Soldiers moving cannon. 10k, Mohammed II riding into sea, and Turkish armada. 12k, Landing of Turkish army. 15k, Ancient wall, Constantinople. 30k, Mosque of Faith. 40k, Presenting mace to Patriarch Yenadios. 60k, Map of Constantinople, c. 1574. 1 l, Tomb of Mohammed II. 2.50 l, Portrait of Mohammed II.

1953, May 29		Photo.	Perf. 11½	

Inscribed:
"Istanbulun Fethi 1453-1953."

1090	A215	5k brt bl	8	5
1091	A215	8k gray	10	6
1092	A215	10k blue	12	7
1093	A215	12k rose lil	15	10
1094	A215	15k brown	25	15
1095	A216	20k vermilion	30	10
1096	A216	30k dl grn	90	15
1097	A215	40k vio bl	90	30
1098	A215	60k chocolate	90	45
1099	A215	1 l bl grn	2.25	75

Perf. 12.

1100	A217	2 l multi	5.25	3.00
1101	A217	2.50 l multi	6.75	4.00
a.		Souvenir sheet	65.00	40.00
		Nos. 1090-1101 (12)	17.95	9.18

Issued to commemorate the 500th anniversary of the conquest of Constantinople by Sultan Mohammed II.
No. 1101a measures 100x125mm. and contains a single copy of No. 1101, imperf. with ornamental border and inscription in gold.

Ruins of the Odeon, Ephesus
A218

Designs: 15k, Church of St. John the Apostle. 20k, Shrine of Virgin Mary, Panaya Kapulu. 40k, Ruins of the Double Church. 60k, Shrine of the Seven Sleepers. 1 l, Restored house of the Virgin Mary.

1953, Aug. 16		Litho.	Perf. 13½	

Multicolored Centers.

1102	A218	12k sage grn	25	10
1103	A218	15k lilac	25	10
1104	A218	20k dk sl bl	30	15
1105	A218	40k lt grn	75	30
1106	A218	60k vio bl	1.00	55
1107	A218	1 l brn red	3.00	2.00
		Nos. 1102-1107 (6)	5.55	3.20

Pres. Celal Bayar, Mithat Pasha. Herman Schulze-Delitzsch and People's Bank
A219

Design: 20k, Pres. Bayar, Mithat Pasha and University of Ankara.

1953, Sept. 2		Photo.	Perf. 10½	
1108	A219	15k org brn	50	30
1109	A219	20k Prus grn	1.00	60

Issued to publicize the 5th International People's Circuit Congress, Istanbul, September 1953.

Combined Harvester
A220

Kemal Atatürk
A221

Designs: 15k, Berdan dam. 20k, Military parade. 30k, Diesel train. 35k, Yesilkoy airport.

1953, Oct. 29			Perf. 14	
1110	A220	10k ol bis	10	10
1111	A220	15k dk gray	15	10
1112	A220	20k rose red	25	10
1113	A220	30k ol grn	50	25
1114	A220	35k dl bl	35	25
1115	A221	55k dl pur	1.10	75
		Nos. 1110-1115 (6)	2.45	1.55

Issued to commemorate the 30th anniversary of the formation of the Turkish Republic.

Kemal Atatürk and Mausoleum at Ankara
A222

1953, Nov. 10				
1116	A222	15k gray blk	40	30
1117	A222	20k vio brn	1.00	50

Issued to commemorate the 15th anniversary of the death of Kemal Ataturk.

Type of 1931-42.
Without umlaut over first "U" of "CUMHURIYETI."
Perf. 11½x12, 10x11½

1953-56		Typographed	Unwmkd.	
1117B	A77	20p yellow	15	5
1118	A78	1k brn org	10	5
1119	A78	2k rose pink ('53)	10	5
1120	A78	3k yel brn ('53)	10	5
1120A	A78	4k sl ('56)	35	5
1121	A78	5k blue	50	5
1121A	A78	8k vio ('56)	15	6
1122	A77	10k dk ol ('53)	15	6
1123	A77	12k brt car rose ('53)	20	8
1124	A77	15k fawn	30	6
1125	A77	20k rose lil	4.00	6
1126	A77	30k lt bl grn ('54)	1.50	20
		Nos. 1117B-1126 (12)	7.65	81

Compass and Map
A223

TURKEY

Designs: 20k, Globe, crescent and stars. 40k, Tree symbolical of 14 NATO members.

1954, Apr. 4   Photo.   **Perf. 14**

1127	A223	15k brown	2.25	2.00
1128	A223	20k vio bl	3.00	2.00
1129	A223	40k dk grn	25.00	20.00

Issued to commemorate the 5th anniversary of the formation of the North Atlantic Treaty Organization.

Industry, Engineering and Agriculture
A224

Justice and Council of Europe Flag
A225

1954, Aug. 8   Litho.   **Perf. 10½**

1130	A224	10k brown	6.00	5.00
1131	A225	15k dk grn	5.50	4.00
1132	A225	20k blue	6.00	4.00
1133	A224	30k brt vio	30.00	25.00

Issued to commemorate the fifth anniversary of the formation of the Council of Europe.

Flag Signals to Plane
A226

Amaury de La Grange and Plane
A227

Design: 45k, Kemal Ataturk and air fleet.

1954, Sept. 20   **Perf. 12½**

1134	A226	20k blk brn	25	10
1135	A227	35k dl vio	45	30
1136	A227	45k dp bl	90	45

Issued to publicize the 47th congress of the International Aeronautical Federation, Istanbul 1954.

Souvenir Sheet

A228

1954, Oct. 18   **Imperf.**

1137	A228	Sheet of three	10.00	8.00
a.		20k aqua	1.00	1.00
b.		30k vio bl	1.00	1.00
c.		1 l red vio	2.00	2.00

First anniversary of Law of Oct. 17, 1953, reorganizing the Department of Post, Telephone and Telegraph. Size: 105x132 mm.

Ziya Gokalp
A229

Kemal Atatürk
A230

1954, Oct. 25   **Perf. 11**

1138	A229	15k rose lil	15	10
1139	A229	20k dk grn	25	20
1140	A229	30k crimson	60	35

Issued to commemorate the 30th anniversary of the death of Ziya Gokalp, author and historian.

1955, Mar. 1   **Perf. 12½**

1141	A230	15k car rose	15	5
1142	A230	20k blue	20	5
1143	A230	40k dk gray	35	6
1144	A230	50k bl grn	55	8
1145	A230	75k org brn	70	15
		Nos. 1141-1145 (5)	1.95	39

Relief Map of Dardanelles
A231

Artillery Loaders
A232

Designs: 30k, Minelayer Nusrat. 60k, Colonel Kemal Atatürk.

1955, Mar. 18   **Perf. 10½**

1146	A231	15k green	10	10
1147	A231	20k org brn	15	10
1148	A231	30k ultra	30	25
1149	A232	60k ol gray	90	70

Battle of Gallipoli, 40th anniversary.

Aerial Map
A233

1955, Apr. 14   **Perf. 11**

1150	A233	15k gray	15	10
1151	A233	20k aqua	20	10
1152	A233	50k brown	40	25
1153	A233	1 l purple	1.10	45

City Planning Congress, Ankara, 1955.

Carnation
A234

Flowers: 15k, Tulip. 20k, Rose. 50k, Lily.

1955, May 19   Litho.   **Perf. 10**

1154	A234	10k rose red & dk grn	45	20
1155	A234	15k yel & grn	30	15
1156	A234	20k rose & dk grn	40	20
1157	A234	50k grn & yel	3.00	2.00

National Flower Show, Istanbul, May 20–Aug. 20.

Battle First Aid Station—A235

Design: 30k, Gulhane Military Hospital, Ankara.

1955, Aug. 28   **Perf. 12**   **Unwmkd.**

1158	A235	20k red, lake & gray	30	15
1159	A235	30k dp grn & yel grn	60	30

Issued to commemorate the XVIII International Congress of Military Medicine, Aug. 8–Sept. 1, 1955, Istanbul.

Soccer Game—A236

Emblem and Soccer Ball
A237

Design: 1 l, Emblem with oak and olive branches.

1955, Aug. 30   **Perf. 10**

1160	A236	15k lt ultra	75	20
1161	A237	20k crim rose	60	20
1162	A236	1 l lt grn	2.00	1.50

Issued to commemorate the International Military Soccer Championship games, Istanbul, Aug. 30, 1955.

Sureté Monument, Ankara
A238

Designs: 20k, Dolma Bahce Palace. 30k, Police College, Ankara. 45k, Police Martyrs' Monument, Istanbul.

1955, Sept. 5   **Perf. 10**

Inscribed: "Enterpol Istanbul 1955"

1163	A238	15k bl grn	15	8
1164	A238	20k brt vio	25	12
1165	A238	30k gray blk	45	30
1166	A238	45k lt brn	1.10	70

Issued to commemorate the 24th general assembly of the International Criminal Police, Istanbul, Sept. 5–9, 1955.

Early Telegraph Transmitter
A239

Modern Transmitter
A240

Perf. 13½x14, 14x13½

1955, Sept. 10   **Photogravure**

1167	A239	15k olive	20	10
1168	A240	20k crim rose	25	10
1169	A239	45k fawn	75	25
1170	A240	60k ultra	80	55

Centenary of telecommunication.

Academy of Science, Istanbul
A241

Designs: 20k, University. 60k, Hilton Hotel. 1 l, Kiz Kulesi (Leander's Tower).

1955, Sept. 12   **Perf. 13½x14**

1171	A241	15k yel org	35	10
1172	A241	20k crim rose	40	20
1173	A241	60k purple	60	30
1174	A241	1 l dp bl	1.10	75

Issued to commemorate the tenth meeting of the governors of the International Bank of Reconstruction and Development and the International Monetary Fund, Istanbul, Sept. 12–16, 1955.

Surlari, Istanbul
A242

Mosque of Sultan Ahmed
A243

Congress Emblem
A244

TURKEY

Designs: 30k, Hagia Sophia. 75k, Map of Constantinople, by Christoforo Buondelmonti, 1422.

1955, Sept. 15   Litho.   Perf. 11½

1175	A242	15k grnsh blk & Prus grn	50	30
1176	A243	20k ver & org	40	25
1177	A242	30k sep & vio brn	40	25
1178	A243	75k ultra	1.10	75

Issued to publicize the 10th International Congress of Byzantine Research, Istanbul, Sept. 15-21, 1955.

1955, Sept. 26   Perf. 10½x11

Inscribed: "Beynelmiel X. Vol Kongresi Istanbul 1955"

Designs: 30k, Chalet in Istanbul. 55k, Bridges.

1179	A244	20k red vio	20	10
1180	A244	30k dk grn & yel grn	25	20
1181	A244	55k dp bl & brt bl	90	60

10th International Transportation Congress.

Map of Turkey, Showing Population Increase
A245

1955, Oct. 22   Perf. 10   Unwmkd.

Map in Rose.

1182	A245	15k lt & dk gray & red	40	10
1183	A245	20k lt & dk vio & red	25	10
1184	A245	30k lt & dk ultra & red	30	20
1185	A245	60k lt & dk bl grn & red	75	35

Census of 1955.

Waterfall, Antalya
A246

Alanya and Seljukide Dockyards—A247

Designs: 30k, Theater at Aspendos. 45k, Ruins at Side. 50k, View of Antalya. 65k, St. Nicholas Church at Myra (Demre) and St. Nicholas.

Perf. 14x13½, 13½x14

1955, Dec. 10   Photo.   Unwmkd.

1186	A246	18k bl, ol grn & ultra	25	10
1187	A247	20k bl, ultra & brn	20	10
1188	A247	30k dl grn, ol bis & grn	35	10
1189	A246	45k yel grn & brn	1.50	55
1190	A246	50k Prus grn & ol bis	40	25
1191	A247	65k org ver & blk	60	45
		Nos. 1186-1191 (6)	3.30	1.55

Kemal Atatürk
A248

1955-56   Litho.   Perf. 12½

1192	A248	0.50k carmine	5	5
1193	A248	1k yel org	5	5
1194	A248	2k brt bl	5	5
1195	A248	3k scarlet	5	5
1196	A248	5k lt brn	6	5
1197	A248	6k lt bl grn	8	5
1198	A248	10k bl grn	12	5
1199	A248	18k rose vio	15	5
1200	A248	20k lt vio bl	20	5
1201	A248	25k ol grn	25	5
1202	A248	30k violet	30	5
1203	A248	40k fawn	40	5
1204	A248	75k sl bl	1.00	10
		Nos. 1192-1204 (13)	2.76	70

Issue dates: 3k, 1955. Others, 1956.

Tomb at Nigde
A249

Zubeyde Hanum
A250

1956, Apr. 12   Perf. 10½

1205	A249	40k vio bl & bl	25	10

Issued to commemorate the 25th anniversary of the Turkish History Society. The tomb of Hüdavent Hatun, a sultan's daughter, exemplifies Seljukian architecture of the 14th century.

1956, May 13   Perf. 11

1206	A250	20k pale brn & dk brn	20	10

Imperf.

1207	A250	20k lt grn & dk grn	70	40

Issued to commemorate Mother's Day 1956, and to honor Zubeyde Hanum, mother of Kemal Ataturk.

Shah and Queen of Iran
A251

1956, May 15   Perf. 11   Unwmkd.

1208	A251	100k grn & pale grn	1.75	1.50

Imperf.

1209	A251	100k red & pale grn	11.00	9.00

Issued to commemorate the visit of the Shah and Queen of Iran to Turkey, May 15, 1956.

Erenkoy Sanitarium
A252

1956, July 31   Perf. 11

1210	A252	50k dk bl grn & pink	70	30

Issued to publicize the Anti-Tuberculosis work among PTT employees.

Symbol of Izmir Fair
A253

A254

1956, Aug. 20   Perf. 11

1211	A253	45k brt grn	25	10

Souvenir Sheet
Imperf.

1212	A254	Sheet of two	1.60	1.25
a.		50k rose red	35	35
b.		50k brt ultra	35	35

Issued to commemorate the 25th International Fair at Izmir, Aug. 20-Sept. 20. No. 1212 measures 103x52mm. See No. C28.

Hands Holding Bottled Serpent
A255

1956, Sept. 10   Litho.   Perf. 10½

1213	A255	25k multi	20	10

Issued to publicize the 25th International Anti-Alcoholism congress, Istanbul Sept. 10-15.

Printed both in regular sheets (300,000) and in sheets with alternate vertical rows inverted (200,000), providing 100,000 tête bêche pairs.

Medical Center at Kayseri
A256

1956, Nov. 1   Perf. 12½x12

1214	A256	60k vio & yel	30	10

Issued to commemorate the 750th anniversary of the first medical school and clinic in Anatolia.

Sariyar Dam
A257

1956, Dec. 2   Litho.   Perf. 10½

1215	A257	20k vermilion	20	10
1216	A257	20k brt bl	20	10

Inauguration of Sariyar Dam.

Freestyle Wrestling
A258

Mehmet Akif Ersoy
A259

Design: 65k, Greco-Roman wrestling.

1956, Dec. 8   Perf. 10½   Unwmkd.

1217	A258	40k brt yel grn & brn	45	35
1218	A258	65k lt bluish gray & dp car	60	40

Issued to commemorate the 16th Olympic Games in Melbourne, Nov. 22–Dec. 8, 1956.

1956, Dec. 26

1219	A259	20k brn & brt yel grn	15	10
1220	A259	20k rose car & lt gray	15	10
1221	A259	20k vio bl & brt pink	15	10

Issued to commemorate the 20th anniversary of the death of Mehmet Akif Ersoy, author of the Turkish National Anthem.

Each value bears a different verse of the anthem.

Theater in Troy
A260

Trojan Vase
A261

Design: 30k, Trojan Horse.

Perf. 13½x14, 14x13½

1956, Dec. 31   Photo.   Unwmkd.

1222	A260	15k green	1.40	75
1223	A261	20k red vio	1.40	75
1224	A260	30k chestnut	1.40	75

Excavations at Troy.

Mobile Chest X-Ray Unit
A262

Kemal Atatürk
A263

1957, Jan. 1   Litho.   Perf. 12

1225	A262	25k ol brn & red	25	15

Issued to publicize the fight against tuberculosis.

TURKEY

1956-57			Perf. 12½	
1226	A263	½k bl grn	5	5
1227	A263	1k yel org	5	5
1228	A263	3k gray ol	5	5
1229	A263	5k violet	6	5
1230	A263	6k rose car	6	5
1231	A263	10k rose vio	8	5
1232	A263	12k fawn	8	5
1233	A263	15k lt vio bl	8	5
1234	A263	18k carmine	10	5
1235	A263	20k lt brn	10	5
1236	A263	25k lt bl grn	12	5
1237	A263	30k sl bl	12	5
1238	A263	40k olive	20	7
1239	A263	50k orange	30	8
1240	A263	60k brt bl	30	8
1241	A263	70k Prus grn	90	10
1242	A263	75k brown	50	10
	Nos.1226-1242 (17)		3.15	1.03

Pres. Heuss of Germany
A264

1957, May 5 Perf. 10½ Unwmkd.
1243 A264 40k yel & brn 25 15

Issued to commemorate the visit of Pres. Theodor Heuss of Germany to Turkey May 5. See No. C29.

View of Bergama and Ruin
A265

Design: 40k, Dancers in kermis at Bergama.

1957, May 24
1244 A265 30k brown 15 10
1245 A265 40k green 20 10

Issued to publicize the 20th anniversary of the kermis at Bergama (Pergamus).

Symbols of Industry and Flags
A266

1957, July 1 Photo. Perf. 13½x14
1246 A266 25k violet 30 10
1247 A266 40k gray bl 35 15

Issued to commemorate the tenth anniversary of Turkish-American collaboration.

Osman Hamdi Bey
A267

Hittite Sun Course from
Alaca Höyük—A268

1957, July 6 Perf. 10½
1248 A267 20k beige, pale brn & blk 25 12
1249 A268 30k Prus grn 30 15

Issued to commemorate the 75th anniversary of the Academy of Art. The 20k exists with "cancellation" omitted.

King of Afghanistan
A269

1957, Sept. 1 Litho. Perf. 10½
1250 A269 45k car lake & pink 25 15

Issued to commemorate the visit of Mohammed Zahir Shah, King of Afghanistan, to Turkey. See No. C30.

Medical Center, Amasya
A270

Design: 65k, Suleiman Medical Center.

1957, Sept. 29 Perf. 10½ Unwmkd.
1251 A270 25k ver & yel 10 10
1252 A270 65k brt grnsh bl & cit 35 20

Issued to commemorate the 11th general meeting of the World Medical Association.

Mosque of Suleiman
A271

Architect Mimar
Koca Sinan
(1489-1587)
A272

1957, Oct. 18 Perf. 11
1253 A271 20k gray grn 15 10
1254 A272 100k brown 45 30

Issued to commemorate the 400th anniversary of the opening of the Mosque of Suleiman, Istanbul.

No. 1073 Surcharged with New Value and
"ISTANBUL Filatelik n. Sergisi 1957"

1957, Nov. 11 Photo. Perf. 13½
1255 A208 50k on 2J brt ultra 30 15

1957 Istanbul Philatelic Exhibition.

Forestation Map of Turkey
A273

Design: 25k, Forest and hand planting tree (vertical).

1957, Nov. 18 Litho. Perf. 10½
1256 A273 20k grn & brn 20 12
1257 A273 25k emer & bl grn 20 12

Centenary of forestry in Turkey.
Nos. 1256-57 each come with two different tabs attached (four tabs in all) bearing various quotations.

Fuzuli—A274

1957, Nov. 23
1258 A274 50k pink, vio, red & yel 50 30

Issued to commemorate the 400th anniversary of the death of Fuzuli (Mehmet Suleiman Ogiou), poet.

Benjamin
Franklin
A275

1957, Nov. 28 Photo. Perf. 14x13½
1259 A275 65k dk Prus bl 40 25
1260 A275 65k rose vio 40 25

Issued to commemorate the 250th anniversary of the birth of Benjamin Franklin.

Green Dome,
Tomb of Mevlana,
at Konya
A276

Konya Museum—A277

Mevlana—A278

Perf. 11x10½, 10½x11
1957, Dec. 17 Litho. Unwmkd.
1261 A276 50k grn, bl & vio 25 20
1262 A277 100k dk bl 50 35

Miniature Sheet
Imperf.

1263 A278 100k multi 1.50 1.50

The 750th anniversary of the birth of Jalal-udin Mevlana (1207-1273), Persian poet and founder of the Mevlevie dervish order.
No. 1263 measures 54x103mm. (stamp measures 32x42mm.) with marginal border in citron.

Kemal Atatürk
(Double Frame; Serifs)
A279

1957 Perf. 11½ Unwmkd.
Size: 18x22mm.

1264	A279	½k lt brn	5	5
1265	A279	1k lt vio bl	5	5
1266	A279	2k blk vio	5	5
1267	A279	3k orange	5	5
1268	A279	5k bl grn	5	5
1269	A279	6k dk sl grn	5	5
1270	A279	10k violet	6	5
1271	A279	12k brt grn	8	5
1272	A279	15k dk bl grn	8	5
1273	A279	18k rose car	10	5
1274	A279	20k brown	10	5
1275	A279	25k brn red	10	5
1276	A279	30k brt bl	10	5
1277	A279	40k sl bl	10	5
1278	A279	50k yel org	15	6
1279	A279	60k black	20	6
1280	A279	70k rose vio	20	20
1281	A279	75k gray ol	30	20

Size: 21x29mm

1282	A279	100k carmine	60	15
1283	A279	250k olive	1.75	45
	Nos. 1264-1283 (20)		4.22	1.82

College Emblem   View of Adana
A280   A281

1958, Jan. 16 Litho. Perf. 10½x11

1288 A280 20k bis, ind & org 10 8
1289 A280 25k dk bl, bis & org 15 10

"Turkiye" on top of 25k.
Issued to commemorate the 75th anniversary of the College of Economics and Commerce, Istanbul.

TURKEY

1958-60 Photogravure.   Perf. 11½
Size: 26x20½mm.

1290	A281	5k org brn (Adana)	5	5
1291	A281	5k lil rose (Adapazari)	5	5
1292	A281	5k ver (Adiyaman)	5	5
1293	A281	5k choc (Afyon)	5	5
1294	A281	5k emer (Amasya)	5	5
1295	A281	5k brt bl (Ankara)	5	5
1296	A281	5k bl grn (Antakya)	5	5
1297	A281	5k ol grn (Antalya)	5	5
1298	A281	5k vio (Artvin)	5	5
1299	A281	5k org (Aydin)	5	5
1300	A281	5k lil (Balikesir)	5	5
1301	A281	5k ol (Bilecik)	5	5
1302	A281	5k brn blk (Bingol)	5	5
1303	A281	5k brt vio bl (Bitlis)	5	5
1304	A281	5k rose vio (Bolu)	5	5
1305	A281	5k brn ol (Burdur)	5	5
1306	A281	5k ol grn (Bursa)	5	5
1307	A281	5k brt ultra (Canakkale)	5	5
1308	A281	5k lil (Cankiri)	5	5
1309	A281	5k dk bl (Corum)	5	5
1310	A281	5k bl (Denizli)	5	5
1311	A281	5k org (Diyarbakir)	5	5

Size: 32½x22mm.

1312	A281	20k dp brn (Adana)	20	15
1313	A281	20k rose pink (Adapazari)	20	15
1314	A281	20k crim (Adiyaman)	20	15
1315	A281	20k brn (Afyon)	20	15
1316	A281	20k brt grn (Amasya)	20	15
1317	A281	20k dk bl (Ankara)	20	15
1318	A281	20k brt grnsh bl (Antakya)	20	15
1319	A281	20k grn (Antalya)	20	15
1320	A281	20k bl vio (Artvin)	20	15
1321	A281	20k dp org (Aydin)	20	15
1322	A281	20k lil (Balikesir)	20	15
1323	A281	20k ol grn (Bilecik)	20	15
1324	A281	20k bluish blk (Bingol)	20	15
1325	A281	20k brt vio (Bitlis)	20	15
1326	A281	20k choc (Bolu)	20	15
1327	A281	20k ol gray (Burdur)	20	15
1328	A281	20k grn (Bursa)	20	15
1329	A281	20k brt ultra Canakkale)	20	15
1330	A281	20k lil (Cankiri)	20	15
1331	A281	20k dk gray bl (Corum)	20	15
1332	A281	20k bl (Denizli)	20	15
1333	A281	20k red org (Diyarbakir)	20	15
		Nos. 1290-1333 (44)	5.50	4.40

(1959)
Size: 26 x 20½ mm.

1334	A281	5k vio blk (Edirne)	5	5
1335	A281	5k gray ol (Elazig)	5	5
1336	A281	5k brt grnsh bl (Erzincan)	5	5
1337	A281	5k red org (Erzurum)	5	5
1338	A281	5k yel grn (Eskisehir)	5	5
1339	A281	5k ol grn (Gaziantep)	5	5
1340	A281	5k ultra (Giresun)	5	5
1341	A281	5k bl (Gumusane)	5	5
1342	A281	5k rose lil (Hakkari)	5	5
1343	A281	5k lil rose (Isparta)	5	5
1344	A281	5k ultra (Istanbul)	5	5
1345	A281	5k brt ultra (Izmir)	5	5
1346	A281	5k Prus bl (Izmit)	5	5
1347	A281	5k lil (Karakose)	5	5
1348	A281	5k emer (Kars)	5	5
1349	A281	5k car rose (Kastamonu)	5	5
1350	A281	5k dl grn (Kayseri)	5	5
1351	A281	5k chnt (Kirklareli)	5	5
1352	A281	5k dp org (Kirsehir)	5	5
1353	A281	5k vio bl (Konya)	5	5
1354	A281	5k vio (Kutahya)	5	5
1355	A281	5k org brn (Malatya)	5	5

Size: 32½ x 22mm.

1356	A281	20k sl blk (Edirne)	20	15
1357	A281	20k gray ol (Elazig)	20	15
1358	A281	20k brt bl (Erzincan)	20	15
1359	A281	20k red org (Erzurum)	20	15
1360	A281	20k dp yel grn (Eskisehir)	20	15
1361	A281	20k dp yel grn (Gaziantep)	20	15
1362	A281	20k brt bl (Giresun)	20	15
1363	A281	20k dl bl (Gumusane)	20	15
1364	A281	20k lil (Hakkari)	20	15
1365	A281	20k red lil (Isparta)	20	15
1366	A281	20k brt vio bl (Istanbul)	20	15
1367	A281	20k brt ultra (Izmir)	20	15
1368	A281	20k bl grn (Izmit)	20	15
1369	A281	20k brt vio (Karakose)	20	15
1370	A281	20k emer (Kars)	20	15
1371	A281	20k car rose (Kastamonu)	20	15
1372	A281	20k grn (Kayseri)	20	15
1373	A281	20k chnt brn (Kirklareli)	20	15
1374	A281	20k brn org (Kirsehir)	20	15
1375	A281	20k dp ultra (Konya)	20	15
1376	A281	20k bl vio (Kutahya)	20	15
1377	A281	20k org brn (Malatya)	20	15
		Nos. 1334-1377 (44)	5.50	4.40

(1960)
Size: 26 x 20½ mm.

1378	A281	5k dk sl grn (Manisa)	5	5
1379	A281	5k red lil (Maras)	5	5
1380	A281	5k brn car (Mardin)	5	5
1381	A281	5k brt bl grn (Mersin)	5	5
1382	A281	5k yel grn (Mugla)	5	5
1383	A281	5k gray ol (Mus)	5	5
1384	A281	5k brt yel grn (Nevsehir)	5	5
1385	A281	5k rose brn (Nigde)	5	5
1386	A281	5k dk bl (Ordu)	5	5
1387	A281	5k dp vio (Rize)	5	5
1388	A281	5k rose cl (Samsun)	5	5
1389	A281	5k brn (Siirt)	5	5
1390	A281	5k dk bl (Sinop)	5	5
1391	A281	5k grn (Sivas)	5	5
1392	A281	5k brt grnsh bl (Tekirdag)	5	5
1393	A281	5k crim (Tokat)	5	5
1394	A281	5k bl vio (Trabzon)	5	5
1395	A281	5k org (Tunceli)	5	5
1396	A281	5k choc (Urfa)	5	5
1397	A281	5k dk sl grn (Usak)	5	5
1398	A281	5k dk car rose (Van)	5	5
1399	A281	5k brt rose (Yozgat)	5	5
1400	A281	5k brt bl (Zonguldak)	5	5

Size: 32½ x 22 mm.

1401	A281	20k sl blk (Manisa)	20	15
1402	A281	20k red lil (Maras)	20	15
1403	A281	20k rose brn (Mardin)	20	15
1404	A281	20k dp bl grn (Mersin)	20	15
1405	A281	20k emer (Mugla)	20	15
1406	A281	20k gray grn (Mus)	20	15
1407	A281	20k yel grn (Nevsehir)	20	15
1408	A281	20k brt rose brn (Nigde)	20	15
1409	A281	20k dk bl (Ordu)	20	15
1410	A281	20k bl vio (Rize)	20	15
1411	A281	20k cl (Samsun)	20	15
1412	A281	20k sep (Siirt)	20	15
1413	A281	20k dk bl (Sinop)	20	15
1414	A281	20k ol grn (Sivas)	20	15
1415	A281	20k grnsh bl (Tekirdag)	20	15
1416	A281	20k brt red (Tokat)	20	15
1417	A281	20k bl vio (Trabzon)	20	15
1418	A281	20k red org (Tunceli)	20	15
1419	A281	20k dk red brn (Urfa)	20	15
1420	A281	20k sl (Usak)	20	15
1421	A281	20k dk car rose (Van)	20	15
1422	A281	20k rose red (Yozgat)	20	15
1423	A281	20k brt bl (Zonguldak)	20	15
		Nos. 1378-1423 (46)	5.75	4.60

Ruins at Pamukkale
A282

Designs: 25k, Travertines at Pamukkale.

1958, May 18   Litho.   Perf. 12

1424	A282	20k brown	10	8
1425	A282	25k blue	20	12

"Industry"
A283

Symbolizing New Europe
A284

1958, Oct. 10   Perf. 10½   Unwmkd.

1426	A283	40k sl bl	20	10

National Industry Exhibition.

Europa Issue
1958, Oct. 10

1427	A284	25k vio & dl pink	20	15
1428	A284	40k brt ultra	40	20

Letters—A285

1958, Oct. 5

1429	A285	20k org & blk	12	7

Issued for International Letter Writing Week, Oct. 5–11.

Flame and Mausoleum
A286

Kemal Atatürk
A287

1958, Nov. 10   Perf. 12

1430	A286	25k red	10	7
1431	A287	75k bl grn	25	15

Issued to commemorate the 20th anniversary of the death of Kemal Ataturk. Nos. 1430–1431 printed in alternate rows in sheet.

Emblem—A288

1959, Jan. 10   Litho.   Perf. 10

1432	A288	25k dk vio & yel	15	10

Issued to commemorate the 25th anniversary of the Agricultural Faculty of Ankara University.

Blackboard and School Emblem
A289

1959, Jan. 15   Perf. 10½

1433	A289	75k blk & yel	30	15

Issued to commemorate the 75th anniversary of the establishment of a secondary boys' school in Istanbul.

State Theater, Ankara
A290

Design: 25k, Portrait of Sinasi.

TURKEY

1959, Mar. 30 Perf. 10½ Unwmkd.

| 1434 | A290 | 20k red brn & emer | 10 | 8 |
| 1435 | A290 | 25k Prus grn & org | 15 | 10 |

Issued to commemorate the centenary of the Turkish theater, and to honor Sinasi, writer of the first Turkish play in 1859.

Globe and Stars—A291

1959, Apr. 4 Perf. 10

| 1436 | A291 | 105k red | 40 | 30 |
| 1437 | A291 | 195k green | 75 | 60 |

Issued to commemorate the 10th anniversary of the North Atlantic Treaty Organization.

Aspendos Theater—A292

1959, May 1 Litho. Perf. 10½

| 1438 | A292 | 20k bis brn & vio | 10 | 8 |
| 1439 | A292 | 20k grn & ol bis | 15 | 8 |

Issued to publicize the Aspendos (Belkins) Festival.

No. B70 Surcharged in Ultramarine

AVRUPA KONSEYİ

1959, May 5

| 1440 | SP25 | 105k on 15k+5k org | 55 | 45 |

Council of Europe, 10th anniversary.

Basketball
A293

1959, May 21 Perf. 10

| 1441 | A293 | 25k red org & dk bl | 25 | 15 |

Issued to commemorate the 11th European and Mediterranean Basketball Championship.

"Karadeniz"
A294

Telegraph Mast   Kemal Atatürk
A295   A296

Designs: 1k, Turkish Airlines' SES plane. 10k, Grain elevator, Ankara. 15k, Iron and Steel Works, Karabück. 20k, Euphrates Bridge, Birecik. 25k, Zonguldak Harbor. 30k, Gasoline refinery, Batman. 40k, Rumeli Hisari Fortress. 45k, Sugar factory, Konya. 55k, Coal mine, Zonguldak. 75k, Railway. 90k, Crane loading ships. 100k, Cement factory, Ankara. 120k, Highway. 150k, Harvester. 200k, Electric transformer.

Perf. 10½, 11, 11½, 12½, 13½
1959–60 Lithographed Unwmkd.

1442	A294	1k indigo	5	5
1443	A294	5k brt bl ('59)	15	5
1444	A294	10k blue	8	5
1445	A294	15k brown	25	5
1446	A294	20k sl grn	10	5
1447	A294	25k violet	15	5
1448	A294	30k lilac	30	5
1449	A294	40k blue	25	5
1450	A294	45k dl vio	25	5
1451	A294	55k ol brn	35	5
1452	A295	60k green	85	6
1453	A295	75k gray ol	2.75	8
1454	A295	90k dk bl	3.75	10
1455	A295	100k gray	3.00	10
1456	A295	120k magenta	2.25	10
1457	A294	150k orange	3.75	20
1458	A295	200k yel grn	3.75	25
1459	A295	250k blk brn	3.75	50
1460	A296	500k dk bl	8.25	70
		Nos. 1442-1460 (19)	34.03	2.59

All denominations were issued in 1960 except the 5k.

Postage Due Stamps of 1936 Surcharged **20=20**

1959, June 1 Perf. 11½

1461	D6	20k on 20pa brn	14	10
1462	D6	20k on 2k lt bl	14	10
1463	D6	20k on 3k brt vio	14	10
1464	D6	20k on 5k Prus bl	14	10
1465	D6	20k on 12k brt rose	14	10
		Nos. 1461-1465 (5)	70	50

Anchor Emblem
A297

Design: 40k, Sea Horse emblem.

1959, July 4 Perf. 11

| 1466 | A297 | 30k multi | 12 | 10 |
| 1467 | A297 | 40k multi | 18 | 15 |

Issued to commemorate the 50th anniversary of the Merchant Marine College.

11th Century Warrior
A298

1959, Aug. 26 Litho. Perf. 11

| 1468 | A298 | 2½l rose lil & lt bl | 1.10 | 1.00 |

Battle of Malazkirt, 888th anniversary.

Ornament—A299

Ornament   Kemal Atatürk
A300   A301

Design: 40k, Mosque.

1959, Oct. 19 Perf. 12½ Unwmkd.

1469	A299	30k blk & red	15	10
1470	A299	40k lt bl, blk & ocher	20	15
1471	A300	75k dp bl, yel & red	40	30

Turkish Artists Congress, Ankara.

Lithographed; Center Embossed
1959, Nov. 10 Perf. 14

| 1472 | A301 | 500k dk bl | 2.25 | 1.25 |
| a. | | Miniature sheet of 1, red, imperf. | 2.50 | 1.50 |

No. 1472a measures 53x74 mm.

School of Political Science,
Ankara—A302

Emblem   Crossed Swords
A303   Emblem
                 A304

1959, Dec. 4 Photo. Perf. 13½

1473	A302	40k grn & brn	20	10
1474	A302	40k red brn & bl	15	10
1475	A303	1 l lt & dk vio & buff	55	25

Issued to commemorate the centenary of the Political Science School, Ankara.

Inscribed:
"Kara Harbokulunum 125 Yili"
Design: 40k, Bayonet and flame.

1960, Feb. 28 Litho. Perf. 10½

| 1476 | A304 | 30k ver & org | 15 | 10 |
| 1477 | A304 | 40k brn, car & yel | 25 | 10 |

Issued to commemorate the 125th anniversary of the Territorial War College.

Window on World   Carnations
and WRY Emblem   A306
A305

Design: 150k, Symbolic shanties and uprooted oak emblem.

1960, Apr. 7

| 1478 | A305 | 90k brt grnsh bl & blk | 40 | 25 |
| 1479 | A305 | 105k yel & blk | 55 | 40 |

Issued to publicize World Refugee Year, July 1, 1959—June 30, 1960.

1960, June 4 Photo. Perf. 11½

Flowers: 40k, Jasmine. 75k, Rose. 105k, Tulip.

Granite Paper

1480	A306	30k multi	20	15
1481	A306	40k gray, grn & yel	35	15
1482	A306	75k bl, red & grn	60	40
1483	A306	105k pink, grn & dk vio	90	55

Spring flower festival.

Atatürk Square, Nicosia
A307

Design: 105k, Map of Cyprus.

1960, Aug. 16 Litho. Perf. 10½

| 1484 | A307 | 40k bl & pink | 20 | 12 |
| 1485 | A307 | 105k bl & yel | 50 | 25 |

Independence of the Republic of Cyprus.

Women and Nest—A308

Design: 30k, Globe and emblem.

1960, Aug. 22 Photo. Perf. 11½

| 1486 | A308 | 30k lt vio & yel | 15 | 10 |
| 1487 | A308 | 75k grnsh bl & gray | 45 | 25 |

Issued to commemorate the 16th meeting of the Women's International Council.

Soccer
A309

Sports: No. 1489, Basketball. No. 1490, Wrestling. No. 1491, Hurdling. No. 1492, Steeplechase.

1960, Aug. 25

1488	A309	30k yel grn	25	20
1489	A309	30k black	25	20
1490	A309	30k sl bl	25	20
1491	A309	30k purple	25	20
1492	A309	30k brown	25	20
a.		Sheet of 25, #1488-1492	8.00	8.00
		Nos. 1488-1492 (5)	1.25	1.00

Issued to commemorate the 17th Olympic Games, Rome, Aug. 25–Sept. 11. Printed in sheets of 25 (5x5) with every horizontal and every vertical row containing one of each design. Also printed in normal sheets of 100.

Europa Issue, 1960.
Common Design Type

1960, Sept. 19
Size: 33x22mm.

| 1493 | CD3 | 75k grn & bl grn | 75 | 60 |
| 1494 | CD3 | 105k dp bl & lt bl | 1.40 | 90 |

Common Design Types
pictured in section at front of book.

TURKEY

| Agah Efendi and Front Page of Turcamani Ahval A310 | U.N. Emblem and Torch A311 |

1960, Oct. 21   Photo.   Perf. 11½
| 1495 | A310 | 40k brn blk & sl | 15 | 10 |
| 1496 | A310 | 60k brn blk & bis brn | 25 | 20 |

Centenary of Turkish journalism.

1960, Oct. 24   Unwmkd.
Design: 105k, U.N. headquarters building and U.N. emblem forming "15" (horiz.).
| 1497 | A311 | 90k brt bl & dk bl | 35 | 25 |
| 1498 | A311 | 105k lt bl grn & brn | 40 | 35 |

15th anniversary of the United Nations.

Army Emblem A312

Tribunal A313

Design: 195k, "Justice" (vert.).

1960, Oct. 14   Litho.   Perf. 13
1499	A312	40k vio & bis	15	10
1500	A313	105k red, gray & brn	45	25
1501	A313	195k grn, rose red & brn	80	40

Issued to commemorate the trial of ex-President Celal Bayar and ex-Premier Adnan Menderes.

| Revolutionaries and Statue A314 | Prancing Horse, Broken Chain A315 |

Designs: 30k, Atatürk and hand holding torch. 105k, Youth, soldier and broken chain.

1960, Dec. 1   Photo.   Perf. 14½
1502	A314	10k gray & blk	5	5
1503	A314	30k purple	15	10
1504	A315	40k brt red & blk	15	10
1505	A314	105k bl blk & red	40	30

Revolution of May 27, 1960.

Faculty Building A316

Sculptured Head of Atatürk A317

Designs: 40k, Map of Turkey and sun disk.

1961, Jan. 9   Litho.   Perf. 13
1506	A316	30k sl grn & gray	12	10
1507	A316	40k brn blk & bis brn	15	10
1508	A317	60k dk grn & buff	25	20

Issued to commemorate the 25th anniversary of the Faculty of Languages, History and Geography, University of Ankara.

Communication and Transportation A318

Designs: 40k, Highway construction, telephone and telegraph. 75k, New parliament building, Ankara.

1961, Apr. 27   Perf. 13   Unwmkd.
1509	A318	30k dl vio & blk	15	10
1510	A318	40k grn & blk	30	15
1511	A318	75k dl bl & blk	55	30

Issued to commemorate the 9th conference of ministers of the Central Treaty Organization (CENTO), Ankara.

| Flag and People A319 | Legendary Wolf and Osman Warriors A320 |

Design: 60k, "Progress" (Atatürk showing youth the way).

1961, May 27   Lithographed
1512	A319	30k multi	12	10
1513	A320	40k sl grn & yel	25	15
1514	A319	60k grn, pink & dk red	40	25

First anniversary of May 27 revolution.

Rockets—A321

Designs: 40k, Crescent and star emblem, "50" and Jet. 75k, Atatürk, eagle and jets (vert.).

1961, June 1
1515	A321	30k brn, org yel & blk	25	15
1516	A321	40k vio & red	30	25
1517	A321	75k sl blk & bis	75	55

50th anniversary of Turkey's air force.

Europa Issue, 1961
Common Design Type

1961, Sept. 18   Perf. 13
Size: 32x22mm.
1518	CD4	30k dk vio bl	1.40	1.40
1519	CD4	40k gray	1.40	1.40
1520	CD4	75k vermilion	1.50	1.50

| Tulip and Cogwheel A322 | Open Book and Olive Branch A324 |

Torch, Hand and Cogwheel A323

Lithographed

1961, Oct. 21   Perf. 13   Unwmkd.
| 1521 | A322 | 30k sl, pink & sil | 12 | 10 |
| 1522 | A323 | 75k ultra, org & blk | 35 | 25 |

Issued to commemorate the centenary of technical and professional schools.

1961, Oct. 29
| 1523 | A324 | 30k red, blk & ol | 12 | 10 |
| 1524 | A324 | 75k brt bl, blk & grn | 35 | 25 |

Inauguration of the new Parliament.

| Kemal Atatürk |
| A325   A326 |

1961-62 Lithographed Perf. 10x10½
Size: 20x25mm.
1525	A325	1k brn org ('62)	10	5
1526	A325	5k blue	15	5
1527	A325	10k sepia	30	5
1528	A326	10k car rose	20	5
1529	A325	30k dl grn ('62)	1.75	25

Size: 21½x31mm.
| 1530 | A325 | 10l vio ('62) | 6.00 | 1.50 |
| | | Nos. 1525-1530 (6) | 8.50 | 1.95 |

| NATO Emblem and Dove A327 | Scouts at Campfire A328 |

Design: 105k, NATO emblem (horiz.).

1962, Feb. 18   Perf. 13   Unwmkd.
| 1545 | A327 | 75k dl bl, blk & sil | 40 | 25 |
| 1546 | A327 | 105k crim, blk & sil | 55 | 40 |

Issued to commemorate the 10th anniversary of Turkey's admission to NATO (North Atlantic Treaty Organization).

1962, July 22   Lithographed
Designs: 60k, Scouts with flag. 105k, Scouts saluting.
1547	A328	30k lt grn, blk & red	15	10
1548	A328	60k gray, blk & red	35	25
1549	A328	75k tan, blk & red	55	45

Turkish Boy Scouts, 50th anniversary.

| Soldier Statue A329 | Oxcart from Victory Monument, Ankara A330 |

Design: 75k, Atatürk.

1962, Aug. 30   Perf. 13   Unwmkd.
1550	A329	30k sl grn	15	10
1551	A330	40k gray & sep	25	10
1552	A329	75k gray blk & lt gray	45	35

40th anniversary of Battle of Dumlupinar.

Europa Issue, 1962
Common Design Type

1962, Sept. 17
Size: 37x23mm.
1553	CD5	75k emer & blk	40	30
1554	CD5	105k red & blk	55	45
1555	CD5	195k bl & blk	1.40	1.10
Brown imprint.

| Virgin Mary's House, Ephesus A331 | 20pa Stamp of 1863 A332 |

Designs: 40k, Inside view after restoration (horiz.). 75k, Outside view (horiz.). 105k, Statue of Virgin Mary.

1962, Dec. 8   Photo.   Perf. 13½
1556	A331	30k multi	25	10
1557	A331	40k multi	30	15
1558	A331	75k multi	40	25
1559	A331	105k multi	60	35

1963, Jan. 13   Perf. 13x13½
Designs (issue of 1863): 30k, 1pi. 40k, 2pi. 75k, 5pi.
1560	A332	10k yel, brn & blk	10	5
1561	A332	30k rose, lil & blk	20	10
1562	A332	40k lt bl, bluish grn & blk	30	20
1563	A332	75k red brn, rose & blk	55	40

Centenary of Turkish postage stamps. See No. 1601, souvenir sheet.

TURKEY

Starving People—A333
Designs: 40k, Sowers. 75k, Hands protecting Wheat Emblem, and globe.

1963, Mar. 21   Perf. 13   Unwmkd.
1564	A333	30k dp bl & dk bl	20	10
1565	A333	40k brn org & brn	25	20
1566	A333	75k grn & dk grn	45	30

Issued for the "Freedom from Hunger" campaign of the U.N. Food and Agriculture Organization.

Julian's Column, Ankara — A334
Ethnographic Museum — A335

Designs: 10k, Ankara Citadel. 30k, Gazi Institute of Education. 50k, Atatürk's mausoleum. 60k, President's residence. 100k, Ataturk's home, Cankaya. 150k, Parliament building.

1963   Lithographed   Perf. 13
1568	A334	1k sl grn & yel grn	5	5
1569	A334	1k purple	5	5
1570	A335	5k sep & buff	8	5
1571	A335	10k lil rose & pale bl	25	5
1573	A335	30k blk & vio	60	5
1574	A335	50k bl & yel	1.25	10
1575	A335	60k dk bl gray	40	10
1576	A335	100k ol brn	90	12
1577	A335	150k dl grn	4.00	25
	Nos. 1568-1577 (9)		7.58	82

Map of Turkey and Atom Symbol A336
Designs: 60k, Symbols of medicine, agriculture, industry and atom. 100k, Emblem of Turkish Atomic Energy Commission.

1963, May 27   Perf. 13   Unwmkd.
1584	A336	50k red brn & blk	30	20
1585	A336	60k grn, dk grn, yel & red	40	25
1586	A336	100k vio bl & bl	85	60

Issued to commemorate the first anniversary of the Turkish nuclear research center.

Meric Bridge A337
Sultan Murad I A338

Designs: 10k, Üçserefeli Mosque. 60k, Summerhouse, Edirne Palace.

1963, June 17
1587	A338	10k dp bl & yel grn	10	5
1588	A337	30k red org & ultra	10	8
1589	A337	60k dk bl, red & brn	25	15
1590	A338	100k multi	95	40

Issued to commemorate the 600th anniversary of the conquest of Edirne (Adrianople).

Soldier and Rising Sun A339

1963, June 28
| 1591 | A339 | 50k red, blk & gray | 20 | 10 |
| 1592 | A339 | 100k red, blk & ol | 45 | 25 |

600th anniversary of the Turkish army.

Plowing A340

Mithat Pasha A341
Design: 50k, Agriculture Bank, Ankara.

Perf. 13x13½, 13½x13
1963, Aug. 27   Photo.   Unwmkd.
1593	A340	30k brt yel grn, red brn & grn	15	8
1594	A340	50k pale vio & Prus bl	25	10
1595	A341	60k gray & grn	40	30

Centenary of Agriculture Bank, Ankara.

Sports and Exhibition Palace, Istanbul and No. 5 A342

Designs: 50k, Sultan Ahmed Mosque and Turkey in Asia No. 22. 60k, View of Istanbul and Turkey in Asia No. 87. 100k, Rumeli Hisari Fortress and No. 679. 130k, Ankara Fortress and No. C2.

1963, Sept. 7   Lithographed   Perf. 13
1596	A342	10k blk, yel & rose	10	5
	a.	Rose omitted		
1597	A342	50k grn, blk & rose lil	25	10
1598	A342	60k dk brn, dk bl & blk	40	15
1599	A342	100k dk vio & lil rose	55	35
1600	A342	130k brn, tan & dp org	75	55
	Nos. 1596-1600 (5)		2.05	1.20

Issued to commemorate the "Istanbul 63" International Stamp Exhibition.

Souvenir Sheet
Type of 1963 Inscribed: "F.I.P. GÜNÜ"

Designs (issues of 1963): 10k, 20pa. 50k, 1pi. 60k, 2pi. 130k, 5pi.

Lithographed
1963, Sept. 13   Imperf.   Unwmkd.
1601		Souvenir sheet of 4	1.75	1.75
	a.	A332 10k yel, brn & blk	15	10
	b.	A332 50k lil, pink & blk	25	20
	c.	A332 60k bluish grn, lt bl & blk	35	30
	d.	A332 130k red brn, pink & blk	45	35

Issued to honor the International Philatelic Federation. No. 1601 has bluish green and red brown marginal inscription and black and red emblem. Size: 88x116 mm.

Europa Issue, 1963
Common Design Type
1963, Sept. 16
Size: 32x24mm.
| 1602 | CD6 | 50k red & blk | 50 | 35 |
| 1603 | CD6 | 100k bl grn, blk & bl | 85 | 65 |

Atatürk and First Parliament Building—A343

Designs (Atatürk and): 50k, Turkish flag. 60k, New Parliament building.

1963, Oct. 29   Photo.   Perf. 13½
1604	A343	30k blk, gold, yel & mar	25	15
1605	A343	50k dk grn, gold, yel & red	35	25
1606	A343	60k dk brn, gold & yel	40	30

40th anniversary of Turkish Republic.

Atatürk A344

1963, Nov. 10
| 1607 | A344 | 50k gold, grn & brn | 25 | 15 |
| 1608 | A344 | 60k red, gold, bl & brn | 35 | 25 |

25th anniversary of the death of Atatürk.

NATO Emblem—A346
Designs: 130k, NATO emblem and olive branch.

1964, Apr. 4   Litho.   Perf. 13
| 1610 | A346 | 50k grnsh bl, vio bl & red | 40 | 25 |
| 1611 | A346 | 130k red & blk | 75 | 55 |

Issued to commemorate the 15th anniversary of NATO (North Atlantic Treaty Organization).

12 Stars and Europa with Torch A347
Design: 130k, Torch and stars.

1964, May 5   Litho.   Perf. 12
| 1612 | A347 | 50k red brn, yel & vio bl | 45 | 25 |
| 1613 | A347 | 130k vio bl, lt bl & org | 85 | 55 |

15th anniversary of Council of Europe.

Recaizade Mahmut Ekrem, Writer A348

Portraits: 1k, Hüseyin Rahmi Gürpinar, novelist. 5k, Ismail Hakki Izmirli, scientist. 10k, Sevket Dag, painter. 60k, Gazi Ahmet Muhtar Pasha, commander. 100k, Ahmet Rasim, writer. 130k, Salih Zeki, mathematician.

1964   Litho.   Perf. 13½x13
1614	A348	1k red & blk	7	5
1615	A348	5k dl grn & blk	7	5
1616	A348	10k tan & blk	15	5
1617	A348	50k ultra & dk bl	70	10
1618	A348	60k gray & blk	75	10
1619	A348	100k grnsh bl & dk bl	80	15
1620	A348	130k brt grn & dk grn	3.25	25
	Nos. 1614-1620 (7)		5.79	75

Haghia Sophia A349
Kiz Kulesi, Mersin A350

Designs: No. 1622, Zeus Temple, Silifke. No. 1623, View of Amasra. No. 1625, Augustus' Gate and minaret, Ankara.

1964, June 11   Perf. 13   Unwmkd.
1621	A349	50k gray ol & yel grn	30	10
1622	A349	50k cl & car	35	15
1623	A349	50k dk bl & vio bl	35	15
1624	A350	60k sl grn & dk gray	45	25
1625	A350	60k dk brn & org brn	45	25
	Nos. 1621-1625 (5)		1.90	90

Kars Castle A351
Alp Arslan, Conqueror of Kars, 1064 A352

1964, Aug. 16   Perf. 13   Unwmkd.
| 1626 | A351 | 50k blk & pale vio | 20 | 15 |
| 1627 | A352 | 130k blk, gold, sal & pale vio | 55 | 40 |

900th anniversary of conquest of Kars.

TURKEY

Europa Issue, 1964
Common Design Type
1964, Sept. 14   Litho.   Perf. 13
Size: 22x33mm.
| 1628 | CD7 | 50k org, ind & sil | 50 | 50 |
| 1629 | CD7 | 130k lt bl, mag & cit | 1.00 | 1.00 |

Fuat, Resit and Ali Pashas
A353
Design: 60k, Mustafa Resit Pasha (vert.).

1964, Nov. 3   Perf. 13
Sizes: 48x33mm. (50k, 100k); 22x33mm. (60k).
1630	A353	50k multi	30	30
1631	A353	60k multi	45	40
1632	A353	100k multi	75	60

125th anniversary of reform decrees.

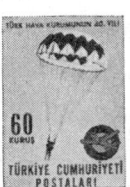

Parachutist
A354
Designs: 90k, Glider (horiz.). 130k, Ataturk watching squadron in flight.

1965, Feb. 16   Litho.   Perf. 13
1633	A354	60k lt bl, blk, red & yel	25	15
1634	A354	90k bis & multi	50	25
1635	A354	130k lt bl & multi	75	45

Issued to commemorate the 40th anniversary of the Turkish Aviation League.

Emblem
A355
Designs: 50k, Radio mast and waves (vert.). 75k, Hand pressing button.

1965, Feb. 24   Perf. 13   Unwmkd.
1636	A355	30k multi	15	10
1637	A355	50k multi	25	15
1638	A355	75k multi	40	30

Issued to commemorate the telecommunications meeting of the Central Treaty Organization, CENTO.

Coast of Ordu
A356
Designs: 50k, Manavgat Waterfall, Antalya. 60k, Sultan Ahmed Mosque, Istanbul. 100k, Hali Rahman Mosque, Urfa. 130k, Red Tower, Alanya.

1965, Apr. 5   Lithographed
1639	A356	30k multi	25	10
1640	A356	50k multi	40	15
1641	A356	60k multi	40	25
1642	A356	100k multi	70	40
1643	A356	130k multi	1.00	50
	Nos. 1639-1643 (5)		2.75	1.40

ITU Emblem, Old and New Communication Equipment
A357

1965, May 17   Perf. 13
| 1644 | A357 | 50k multi | 25 | 15 |
| 1645 | A357 | 130k multi | 75 | 40 |

Issued to commemorate the centenary of the International Telecommunication Union.

ICY Emblem
A358

1965, June 26   Litho.   Unwmkd.
| 1646 | A358 | 100k red org, red brn & brt grn | 45 | 30 |
| 1647 | A358 | 130k gray, lil & ol grn | 65 | 45 |

International Cooperation Year.

Hands Holding Book
A358a

Map and Flags of Turkey, Iran and Pakistan—A358b

1965, July 21   Perf. 13   Unwmkd.
| 1648 | A358a | 50k org brn, yel & dk brn | 40 | 20 |
| 1649 | A358b | 75k dl bl, red, grn blk & org | 55 | 25 |

Issued to commemorate the first anniversary of the signing of the Regional Cooperation Development Pact by Turkey, Iran and Pakistan.

Kemal Ataturk
A359

1965   Lithographed   Perf. 12½
1650	A359	1k brt grn	10	5
1651	A359	5k vio bl	15	5
1652	A359	10k blue	40	5
1653	A359	25k gray	90	6
1654	A359	30k magenta	70	8
1655	A359	50k brown	90	15
1656	A359	150k orange	2.00	20
	Nos. 1650-1656 (7)		5.15	64

Europa Issue, 1965
Common Design Type
1965, Sept. 27   Perf. 13
Size: 32x23mm.
| 1665 | CD8 | 50k gray, ultra & grn | 75 | 75 |
| 1666 | CD8 | 130k tan, blk & grn | 1.10 | 1.10 |

Map of Turkey and People
A360
Designs: 50k, "1965." 100k, "1965," symbolic eye and man (vert.).
Lithographed

1965, Oct. 24   Perf. 13   Unwmkd.
1667	A360	50k multi	10	5
1668	A360	50k grn, blk & lt yel grn	20	15
1669	A360	100k org, sl & blk	50	30

Issued to publicize the 1965 census.

Plane over Ankara Castle
A361
Designs: 30k, Archer and Ankara castle. 50k, Horsemen with spears (ancient game). 100k, Three stamps and medal. 150k, Hands holding book (vert.).

1965, Oct. 25
1670	A361	10k brt vio, yel & red	10	5
1671	A361	30k multi	20	10
1672	A361	50k lt gray ol, ind & red	25	20
1673	A361	100k gray & multi	55	40

Souvenir Sheet
Imperf.
| 1674 | A361 | 150k multi | 1.75 | 1.50 |

Issued to publicize the First National Postage Stamp Exhibition "Ankara 65." No. 1674 contains one stamp; gray margin shows various Turkish stamps. Size: 50x 95mm.

Resat Nuri Guntekin, Novelist
A362
Portraits: 5k, Besim Omer Akalin, M.D. 10k, Tevfik Fikret, poet. 25k, Tanburi Cemil, composer. 30k, Ahmet Vifik Pasha, playwright. 50k, Omer Seyfettin, novelist. 60k, Kemalettin Mimaroglu, architect. 150k, Halit Ziya Usakligil, novelist. 220k, Yahya Kemal Beyatli, poet.

1965   Lithographed   Perf. 13½x13
Black Portrait and Inscriptions
1675	A362	1k rose	7	5
1676	A362	5k blue	7	5
1677	A362	10k buff	15	5
1678	A362	25k dl red brn	40	5
1679	A362	30k gray	40	5
1680	A362	50k orange	1.00	5
1681	A362	60k red lil	1.00	10
1682	A362	150k lt grn	1.10	15
1683	A362	220k tan	1.50	15
	Nos. 1675-1683 (9)		5.69	70

Training Ship Savarona
A363
Designs: 60k, Submarine "Piri Reis." 100k, Cruiser "Alpaslan." 130k, Destroyer "Gelibolu." 220k, Destroyer "Gemlik."

1965, Dec. 6   Photo.   Perf. 11½
1684	A363	50k bl & brn	40	25
1685	A363	60k bl & blk	55	30
1686	A363	100k bl & blk	85	45
1687	A363	130k bl & vio blk	1.25	80
1688	A363	220k bl & ind	2.00	1.25
	Nos. 1684-1688 (5)		5.05	3.05

First Congress of Turkish Naval Society.

Kemal Ataturk   Halide Edip Adivar, Writer
A364   A365
Imprint: "Apa Ofset Basimevi"

1965   Lithographed   Perf. 13½
Black Portrait and Inscriptions
1689	A364	1k rose lil	8	5
1690	A364	5k lt grn	10	5
1691	A364	10k bl gray	15	5
1692	A364	50k ol bis	40	6
1693	A364	150k silver	1.10	15
	Nos. 1689-1693 (5)		1.83	36

See also Nos. 1724-1728.

1966   Lithographed   Perf. 13½
Portraits: 25k, Huseyin Sadettin Arel, writer and composer. 30k, Kamil Akdik, graphic artist. 60k, Abdurrahman Seref, historian. 130k, Naima, historian.
1694	A365	25k gray & brn blk	50	5
1695	A365	30k rose vio & blk brn	40	5
1696	A365	50k bl & blk	60	10
1697	A365	60k lt grn & blk brn	60	10
1698	A365	130k lt vio bl & blk	1.20	15
	Nos. 1694-1698 (5)		3.30	45

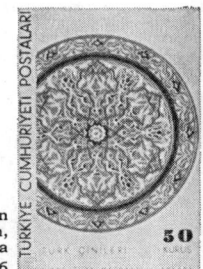

Tiles, Green Mausoleum, Bursa
A366
Tiles: 60k, Spring flowers, Hurrem Sultan Mausoleum, Istanbul. 130k, Stylized flowers, 16th century.

1966, May 15   Litho.   Perf. 13½x13
1699	A366	50k multi	45	25
1700	A366	60k multi	80	60
1701	A366	130k multi	1.00	75

On No. 1700 the black ink was applied by a thermographic process and varnished, producing a shiny, raised effect to imitate the embossed tiles of the design source.

Volleyball   View of Bodrum
A367   A368
1966, May 20   Perf. 13x13½
| 1702 | A367 | 50k tan & multi | 45 | 25 |

Issued to commemorate the 4th International Military Volleyball Championship.

Perf. 13x13½, 13½x13
1966, May 25
Views: 30k, Kusadasi. 50k, Anadolu Hisari, Istanbul (horiz.). 90k, Marmaris. 100k, Izmir (horiz.).
| 1703 | A368 | 10k multi | 10 | 5 |
| 1704 | A368 | 30k multi | 70 | 40 |

TURKEY 817

1705	A368	50k multi	20	12
1706	A368	90k multi	40	25
1707	A368	100k multi	45	30
		Nos. 1703-1707 (5)	1.85	1.12

Keban Dam
A369

Design: 60k, View of Keban Dam area.

1966, June 10   Perf. 13½

1708	A369	50k multi	20	10
1709	A369	60k multi	70	25

Inauguration of Keban Dam.

King Faisal of Saudi Arabia
A370

1966, Aug. 29 Litho. Perf. 13½x13

1710	A370	100k car rose & dk car	75	35

Visit of King Faisal.

Symbolic Postmark and Stamp
A371

Designs: 60k, Flower made of stamps. 75k, Stamps forming display frames. 100k, Map of Balkan states, magnifying glass and stamp.

1966, Sept. 3   Perf. 13½x13

1711	A371	50k multi	20	10
1712	A371	60k multi	25	20
1713	A371	75k multi	55	30

Souvenir Sheet
Imperf.

1714	A371	100k multi	1.50	1.10

Issued to commemorate the 2nd "Balkanfila" stamp exhibition, Istanbul. No. 1714 contains one stamp and has gold ornamental border. Size: 75x50mm.

Sultan Suleiman on Horseback
A372

Designs: 90k, Mausoleum, Istanbul. 130k, Sultan Suleiman.

1966, Sept. 6   Perf. 13½x13

1715	A372	60k multi	30	25
1716	A372	90k multi	75	55
1717	A372	130k multi	1.25	75

Issued to commemorate the 400th anniversary of the death of Sultan Suleiman the Magnificent (1496?-1566). On No. 1717 a gold frame was applied by raised thermographic process.

Europa Issue, 1966
Common Design Type

1966, Sept. 26 Litho. Perf. 13x13½
Size: 22x33mm.

1718	CD9	50k lt bl, vio bl & blk	1.25	80
a.		Blk. (inscriptions & imprint) omitted	125.00	
1719	CD9	130k lil, dk red lil & blk	1.50	1.00

Symbols of Education, Science and Culture
A373

1966, Nov. 4 Litho. Perf. 13

1720	A373	130k brn, bis brn & yel	60	35

Issued to commemorate the 20th anniversary of UNESCO (United Nations Educational, Scientific and Cultural Organization).

University of Technology
A374

Designs: 100k, Atom symbol. 130k, design symbolizing sciences.

1966, Nov. 15

1721	A374	50k multi	25	15
1722	A374	100k multi	45	30
1723	A374	130k multi	75	45

Issued to commemorate the 10th anniversary of the Middle East University of Technology.

Ataturk Type of 1965
Imprint: "Kiral Matbaasi—Ist"

1966 Lithographed Perf. 12½
Black Portrait and Inscriptions

1724	A364	25k yellow	12	5
1725	A364	30k pink	20	5
1726	A364	50k rose lil	1.00	7
1727	A364	90k pale brn	45	8
1728	A364	100k gray	65	10
		Nos. 1724-1728 (5)	2.42	35

Statue of Ataturk, Ankara
A375

Equestrian Statues of Ataturk: No. 1729A, Statue in Izmir. No. 1729B, Statue in Samsun.

Without Imprint

1967 Lithographed Perf. 13x12½
Size: 23x16mm.

1729	A375	10k blk & yel	20	7

Inscribed "1967"
Imprint: Kiral Matbaasi
Size: 22x15mm.

1729A	A375	10k blk & sal	15	7
1729B	A375	10k blk & lt grn	15	7

Issued for use on greeting cards. See Nos. 1790-1791A, 1911.

Perf. 13x13½, 13½x13

1967, March 30 Lithographed

1730	A376	50k multi	40	20
1731	A376	60k multi	60	40
1732	A376	90k multi	80	45
1733	A376	100k multi	1.00	60

Issued to publicize the International Tourist Year, 1967. On No. 1733 the black ink was applied by a thermographic process and varnished, producing a shiny, raised effect.

Woman Vaccinating Child, Knife and Lancet
A377

Fallow Deer
A378

1967, Apr. 1   Perf. 13x13½

1734	A377	100k multi	60	35

Issued to commemorate the 250th anniversary of smallpox vaccination in Turkey. The gold was applied by a thermographic process and varnished, producing a shiny, raised effect.

1967, Apr. 23 Litho. Perf. 13x13½

Designs: 60k, Wild goat. 100k, Brown bear. 130k, Wild boar.

1735	A378	50k multi	25	15
1736	A378	60k multi	35	20
1737	A378	100k multi	60	35
1738	A378	130k multi	90	50

Soccer Players and Emblem with Map of Europe—A379

Design: 130k, Players at left, smaller emblem.

1967, May 1   Perf. 13

1739	A379	50k multi	40	25
1740	A379	130k yel & multi	90	65

20th International Youth Soccer Championships.

Sivas Hospital
A380

1967, July 1 Litho. Perf. 13

1741	A380	50k multi	40	20

750th anniversary of Sivas Hospital.

Selim Sirri Tarcan
A381

Design: 60k, Olympic Rings and Baron Pierre de Coubertin.

1967, July 20

1742	A381	50k lt bl & multi	50	35
1743	A381	60k lil & multi	50	35

Issued to commemorate the first Turkish Olympic competitions. Nos. 1742-1743 are printed in vertical rows in sheets of 100, forming 50 horizontal se-tenant pairs.

Ahmed Mithat, Writer
A382

Portraits: 5k, Admiral Turgut Reis. 50k, Sikullu Mehmet, statesman. 100k, Nedim, poet. 150k, Osman Hamdi, painter.

1967 Lithographed Perf. 12½

1744	A382	1k grn & blk	5	5
1745	A382	5k dp bis & blk	8	5
1746	A382	50k brt vio & blk	60	5
1747	A382	100k cit & blk	1.00	15
1748	A382	150k yel & blk	1.50	30
		Nos. 1744-1748 (5)	3.23	60

Ruins of St. John's Church, Ephesus
A383

Design: 130k, Inside view of Virgin Mary's House, Ephesus.

1967, July 26   Perf. 13

1749	A383	130k multi	50	40
1750	A383	220k multi	1.00	60

Issued to commemorate the visit of Pope Paul VI to the House of the Virgin Mary in Ephesus, July 26, 1967.

Plate on Firing Grid and Ornaments
A384

1967, Sept. 1

1751	A384	50k pale lil, blk, ind & bl	40	20

5th International Ceramics Exhibition.

View of Istanbul and Emblem
A385

1967, Sept. 4 Litho. Perf. 13

1752	A385	130k dk bl & gray	50	40

Issued to commemorate the 9th Congress of the International Commission of Large Dams.

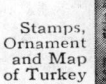 

Stamps, Ornament and Map of Turkey
A386

Design: 60k, Grapes and stamps.

1967

1753	A386	50k multi	25	15
1754	A386	60k multi	35	20
a.		Souvenir sheet of 2	1.25	1.25

Issued to commemorate the International Trade Fair, Izmir. No. 1754a contains one each of Nos. 1753-1754. Gray patterned margin with gold inscription. Size: 100x52mm.

818 TURKEY

Kemal
Ataturk
A387

Symbolic Water
Cycle
A388

1967		Litho.		Perf. 11½x12	
1755	A387	10k blk & lt ol grn		20	5
a.		Bklt. pane of 10		2.50	
b.		Bklt. pane of 25		6.00	
1756	A387	50k blk & pale rose		65	10
a.		Bklt. pane of 2		1.40	
b.		Bklt. pane of 9 + label (5 Nos. 1755, 4 Nos. 1756)		4.50	

Nos. 1755–1756 were issued in booklets only.

1967, Dec. 1 Lithographed Perf. 13
1757	A388	90k lt grn, blk & org	45	35
1758	A388	130k lil, blk & org	60	45

Hydrological Decade (UNESCO), 1965–74.

Child and Angora Cat,
Man with Microscope
A389

Design: 60k, Horse and man with microscope.

1967, Dec. 23 Perf. 13
1759	A389	50k multi	30	25
1760	A389	60k multi	40	30

Issued to commemorate the 125th anniversary of Turkish veterinary medicine.

Human
Rights
Flame
A390

1968, Jan. 1 Perf. 13x13½
1761	A390	50k rose lil, dk bl & org	25	15
1762	A390	130k lt bl, dk bl & red org	55	30

International Human Rights Year 1968.

Archer on Horseback—A391

Miniatures, 16th Century: 50k, Investiture. 60k, Sultan Suleiman the Magnificent receiving an ambassador (vert.). 100k, Musicians.

Perf. 13x13½, 13½x13
1968, Mar. 1 Lithographed
1763	A391	50k multi	30	20
1764	A391	60k multi	35	25
1765	A391	90k multi	70	40
1766	A391	100k multi	90	60

Kemal
Ataturk
A392

1968 Lithographed Perf. 12½
1767	A392	1k dk & lt bl	12	5
1768	A392	5k dk & lt grn	25	5
1769	A392	50k org brn & yel	1.25	10
1770	A392	200k dk brn & pink	3.25	40

Law Book
and Oak
Branch
A393

Mithat
Pasha and
Scroll
A394

1968, Apr. 1 Perf. 13
1771	A393	50k multi	25	20
1772	A394	60k multi	35	25

Centenary of the Court of Appeal.

1968, Apr. 1
Designs: 50k, Scales of Justice. 60k, Ahmet Cevdet Pasha and scroll.
1773	A393	50k multi	25	20
1774	A394	60k multi	35	25

Centenary of the Supreme Court.

Europa Issue, 1968
Common Design Type
1968, May 6 Litho. Perf. 13
Size: 31½x23mm.
1775	CD11	100k pck bl, yel & red	1.00	1.00
1776	CD11	130k grn, yel & red	1.75	1.75

Yacht Kismet   "Fight Usury"
     A395   A396

1968, June 15 Litho. Perf. 13
1777	A395	50k lt ultra & multi	35	25

Issued to commemorate the round-the-world trip of the yacht Kismet, Aug. 22, 1965–June 14, 1968.

1968, June 19
1778	A396	50k multi	40	10

Centenary of the Pawn Office, Istanbul.

Sakarya Battle and Independence
Medal—A397

Design: 130k, National anthem and reverse of medal.

1968, Aug. 30 Perf. 13x13½
1779	A397	50k gold & multi	25	15
1780	A397	130k gold & multi	55	40

Issued to honor the Turkish Independence medal. The gold on Nos. 1779–1780 was applied by a thermographic process and varnished, producing a shiny, raised effect.

Ataturk and Galatasaray
High School—A398

Designs: 50k, "100" and old and new school emblems. 60k, Portraits of Beyazit II and Gulbaba.

1968, Sept. 1 Lithographed
1781	A398	50k gray & multi	30	20
1782	A398	60k tan & multi	45	30
1783	A398	100k lt bl & multi	85	50

Centenary of Galatasaray High School.

Charles de Gaulle
A399

1968, Oct. 25 Litho. Perf. 13
1784	A399	130k multi	1.25	75

Issued to commemorate the visit of President Charles de Gaulle of France to Turkey.

Kemal   Ataturk and
Ataturk   his Speech to
A400   Youth
             A401

Designs: 50k, Ataturk's tomb and Citadel of Ankara. 60k, Ataturk looking out a train window. 250k, Framed portrait of Ataturk in military uniform.

1968, Nov. 10
1785	A400	30k org & blk	35	10
1786	A400	50k brt grn & sl grn	35	10
1787	A400	60k bl grn & blk	42	10
1788	A401	100k blk, gray & brt grn	85	25
1789	A401	250k multi	1.60	60
		Nos. 1785–1789 (5)	3.57	1.15

Issued to commemorate the 30th anniversary of the death of Kemal Ataturk.

Ataturk Statue Type of 1967
Equestrian Statues of Ataturk: No. 1790, Statue in Zonguldak. No. 1791, Statue in Antakya. No. 1791A, Statue in Bursa.

Imprint: Kiral Matbaasi 1968
Size: 22x15mm.

1968–69 Litho. Perf. 13x12½
1790	A375	10k blk & lt bl	12	5
1791	A375	10k blk & brt rose lil	12	5

Perf. 13½
Imprint: Tifdruk Matbaacilik Sanayii
A. S. 1969
Size: 21x16½mm.
1791A	A375	10k dk grn & tan ('69)	10	5

Ince Minare   ILO Emblem
Mosque, Konya   A403
    A402

Historic Buildings: 10k, Doner Kumbet (tomb), Kayseri. 50k, Karatay Medresse (University Gate), Konya. 100k, Ortakoy Mosque, Istanbul. 200k, Ulu Mosque, Divriki.

1968–69 Photo. Perf. 13x13½
1792	A402	1k dk brn & buff ('69)	5	5
1793	A402	10k plum & dl rose ('69)	25	5
1794	A402	50k dk ol grn & gray	50	5
1795	A402	100k dk & lt grn ('69)	1.00	10
1796	A402	200k dp bl & lt bl ('69)	1.75	35
		Nos. 1792-1796 (5)	3.55	60

1969, Apr. 15 Litho. Perf. 13
1797	A403	130k red & blk	45	30

Issued to commemorate the 150th anniversary of the International Labor Organization.

Sultana
Hafsa
A404

1969, Apr. 26 Litho. Perf. 13½x13
1798	A404	60k multi	45	25

Issued in memory of Sultana Hafsa, medical pioneer.

TURKEY

Europa Issue, 1969
Common Design Type
1969, Apr. 28   Perf. 13
Size: 32x23mm.
1799	CD12	100k dl vio & multi	85	85
1800	CD12	130k gray grn & multi	1.10	1.10

Kemal Ataturk A405   Map of Istanbul A407

Ataturk and S.S. Bandirma A406

1969, May 19   Litho.   Perf. 13
1801	A405	50k multi	25	15
1802	A406	60k multi	30	20

Issued to commemorate the 50th anniversary of the landing of Kemal Ataturk at Samsun.

1969, May 31
1803	A407	130k vio bl, lt bl, gold & red	55	40

Issued to publicize the 22nd Congress of the International Chamber of Commerce, Istanbul.

Educational Progress A408

Agricultural Progress A409

Designs: 90k, Pouring ladle and industrial symbols. 100k, Road sign (highway construction). 180k, Oil industry chart and symbols.

1969   Lithographed   Perf. 13½x13
1804	A408	1k blk & gray	5	5
1805	A408	1k blk & bis brn	5	5
1806	A408	1k blk & lt grn	5	5
1807	A408	1k blk & lt vio	5	5
1808	A408	1k blk & org red	5	5
1809	A409	50k brn & ocher	35	5
1810	A409	80k blk & grnsh gray	55	10
1811	A409	100k blk & org red	80	15
1812	A408	180k vio & org	1.50	25
		Nos. 1804-1812 (9)	3.45	80

Issue dates: 1k, 100k, Apr. 8; 50k, June 11; 90k, 180k, Aug. 15.

Sultan Suleiman Receiving Sheik Abdul Latif A410   Kemal Ataturk A411

Designs: 80k, Lady Serving Wine, Safavi miniature, Iran. 130k, Lady on Balcony, Mogul miniature, Pakistan.

1969, July 21   Litho.   Perf. 13
1813	A410	50k yel & multi	35	20
1814	A410	80k yel & multi	60	35
1815	A410	130k yel & multi	1.10	70

Issued to commemorate the 5th anniversary of the signing of the Regional Cooperation for Development Pact by Turkey, Iran and Pakistan.

1969, July 23
Design: 60k, Ataturk monument and bas-relief showing congress.
1816	A411	50k blk & gray	25	20
1817	A411	60k blk & grnsh gray	30	20

50th anniversary, Congress of Erzerum.

Sivas Congress Delegates A412

Design: 50k, Congress Hall.

1969, Sept. 4   Litho.   Perf. 13
1818	A412	50k dk brn & dp rose	30	20
1819	A412	60k ol blk & yel	35	25

Issued to commemorate the 50th anniversary of the Congress of Sivas (preparation for the Turkish war of independence).

Bar Dance—A413

Folk Dances: 50k, Candle dance (çaydaçira). 60k, Scarf dance (halay). 100k, Sword dance (kiliç-kalkan). 130k, Two male dancers (zeybek) (vert.).

1969, Sept. 9
1820	A413	30k brn & multi	25	20
1821	A413	50k multi	35	25
1822	A413	60k multi	50	40
1823	A413	100k yel & multi	70	40
1824	A413	130k multi	1.25	80
		Nos. 1820-1824 (5)	3.05	2.05

1914 Airplane "Prince Celaleddin" A414

Design: 75k, First Turkish letter carried by air.

1969, Oct. 18   Litho.   Perf. 13
1825	A414	60k dk bl & bl	35	20
1826	A414	75k lil & bis	50	35

Issued to commemorate the 55th anniversary of the first Turkish mail transported by air.

"Kutadgu Bilig" A415

1969, Nov. 20   Litho.   Perf. 13
1827	A415	130k ol bis, brn & gold	45	30

Issued to commemorate the 900th anniversary of "Kutadgu Bilig," a book about the function of the state, compiled by Jusuf of Balasagun in Tashkent, 1069.

Ataturk's Arrival in Ankara, after a Painting—A416

Design: 60k, Ataturk and his coworkers in automobiles arriving in Ankara, after a photograph.

1969, Dec. 27   Litho.   Perf. 13
1828	A416	50k multi	35	20
1829	A416	60k multi	50	35

Issued to commemorate the 50th anniversary of Kemal Ataturk's arrival in Ankara, Dec. 27, 1919.

Bosporus Bridge, Map of Europe and Asia—A417

Design: 60k, View of proposed Bosporus Bridge and shore lines.

1970, Feb. 20   Litho.   Perf. 13
1830	A417	60k gold & multi	80	60
1831	A417	130k gold & multi	1.60	1.25

Issued to commemorate the foundation ceremonies for the bridge across the Bosporus linking Europe and Asia.

Kemal Ataturk and Signature A418   Kemal Ataturk A419

1970   Litho.   Perf. 13
1832	A418	1k dp org & brn	5	5
1833	A418	5k sil & blk	5	5
1834	A419	30k cit & blk	15	5
1835	A419	50k lt ol & blk	40	8
1836	A419	50k pink & blk	30	8
1837	A419	75k lil & blk	60	10
1838	A419	100k bl & blk	80	15
		Nos. 1832-1838 (7)	2.35	56

Education Year Emblem A420   Turkish EXPO '70 Emblem A421

1970, Mar. 16
1839	A420	130k ultra, pink & rose lil	50	35

International Education Year 1970.

1970, Mar. 27
Design: 100k, EXPO '70 emblem and Turkish pavilion.
1840	A421	50k gold & multi	25	15
1841	A421	100k gold & multi	40	30

Issued to publicize EXPO '70 International Exhibition, Osaka, Japan, Mar. 15–Sept. 13.

Opening of Grand National Assembly A422

Design: 60k, Session of First Grand National Assembly, 1920.

1970, Apr. 23
1842	A422	50k multi	25	15
1843	A422	60k multi	40	20

Turkish Grand National Assembly, 50th anniversary.

Emblem of Cartographic Service A423

Map of Turkey and Gen. Mehmet Sevki Pasha—A424

Designs: 60k, Plane and aerial mapping survey diagram. 100k, Triangulation point in mountainous landscape.

Perf. 13½x13 (A423), 13x13½ (A424).

1970, May 2   Lithographed
1844	A423	50k bl & multi	20	10
1845	A424	60k blk, gray grn & brick red	30	15
1846	A423	100k multi	50	30
1847	A424	130k multi	80	60

Issued to commemorate the 75th anniversary of the Turkish Cartographic Service.

Europa Issue, 1970
Common Design Type
1970, May 4   Perf. 13
Size: 37x23mm.
1848	CD13	100k ver, blk & org	60	60
1849	CD13	130k dk bl grn, blk & org	1.00	1.00

TURKEY

U.P.U. Headquarters, Bern
A425

1970, May 20

| 1850 | A425 | 60k blk & dl bl | 30 | 20 |
| 1851 | A425 | 130k blk & dl ol grn | 50 | 35 |

Issued to commemorate the inauguration of the new Universal Postal Union Headquarters in Bern.

Lady with Mimosa, by Osman Hamdi (1842–1910)
A426

Paintings: No. 1853, Deer, by Seker Ahmet (1841–1907). No. 1854, Portrait of Fevzi Cakmak, by Avni Lifij (–1927). No. 1855, Sailboats, by Nazmi Ziya (1881–1937); horiz.

1970   Lithographed   Perf. 13

Size: 29x49mm.

| 1852 | A426 | 250k multi | 1.00 | 70 |
| 1853 | A426 | 250k multi | 1.00 | 70 |

Size: 32x49mm.

| 1854 | A426 | 250k multi | 1.00 | 70 |

Size: 73½x33mm.

| 1855 | A426 | 250k multi | 1.00 | 70 |

Issue dates: Nos. 1852–1853, June 15. Nos. 1854–1855, Dec. 15.

Turkish Folk Art
A427

1970, June 15

| 1856 | A427 | 50k multi | 20 | 10 |

Issued to publicize the 3rd National Stamp Exhibition, ANKARA 70, Oct. 28–Nov. 4. Pane of 50, each stamp se-tenant with label. This 50k, in pane of 50 without labels, was re-issued Oct. 28 with Nos. 1867–1869.

View of Fethiye
A428

Designs: 80k, Seeyo-Se-Pol Bridge, Esfahan, Iran. 130k, Saiful Malook Lake, Pakistan.

1970, July 21   Litho.   Perf. 13

1857	A428	60k multi	20	15
1858	A428	80k multi	25	20
1859	A428	130k multi	40	30

Issued to commemorate the 6th anniversary of the signing of the Regional Cooperation for Development Pact by Turkey, Iran and Pakistan.

Sultan Balim's Tomb
A429

Haci Bektas Veli
A430

Designs: 30k, Tomb of Haci Bektas Veli (horiz.).

1970, Aug. 16   Litho.   Perf. 13

1860	A429	30k multi	15	10
1861	A429	100k multi	35	20
1862	A430	180k multi	65	40

Issued to commemorate the 700th anniversity of the death of Haci Bektas Veli, mystic.

Hittite Sun Disk and "ISO"
A431

1970, Sept. 15

| 1863 | A431 | 110k car rose, gold & blk | 30 | 15 |
| 1864 | A431 | 150k ultra, gold & blk | 45 | 30 |

Issued to commemorate the 8th General Council Meeting of the International Standardization Organization, Ankara.

U.N. Emblem, People and Globe
A432

Stamp 'Flower' and Book
A433

Design: 100k, U.N. emblem and propeller (horiz.).

1970, Oct. 24   Litho.   Perf. 13

| 1865 | A432 | 100k gray & multi | 40 | 20 |
| 1866 | A432 | 220k multi | 80 | 50 |

25th anniversary of the United Nations.

1970, Oct. 28

Designs: 60k, Ataturk monument and stamps (horiz.). 1.30k, Abstract flower.

| 1867 | A433 | 10k multi | 10 | 10 |
| 1868 | A433 | 60k bl & multi | 30 | 15 |

Souvenir Sheet

| 1869 | A433 | 130k dk grn & org | 1.25 | 1.25 |

Issued for the 3rd National Stamp Exhibition, ANKARA 70, Oct. 28–Nov. 4. No. 1869, contains one stamp; gray and gold margin. Size: 78x108mm. See note below No. 1856.

Inönü Battle Scene—A434

Design: No. 1871, Second Battle of Inönü.

1971   Lithographed   Perf. 13

| 1870 | A434 | 100k multi | 45 | 20 |
| 1871 | A434 | 100k multi | 45 | 20 |

First and Second Battles of Inönü, 50th anniversary.
Issue dates: No. 1870, Jan. 10. No. 1871, Apr. 1.

Village on River Bank, by Ahmet Sekür—A435

Painting: No. 1872, Landscape, Yildiz Palace Garden, by Ahmet Ragip Bicakcilar.

1971, Mar. 15   Litho.   Perf. 13

| 1872 | A435 | 250k multi | 90 | 70 |
| 1873 | A435 | 250k multi | 90 | 70 |

See Nos. 1901–1902, 1909–1910, 1937–1938.

Campaign Against Discrimination
A436

1971, Mar. 21   Litho.   Perf. 13

| 1874 | A436 | 100k multi | 25 | 15 |
| 1875 | A436 | 250k gray & multi | 70 | 40 |

International Year against Racial Discrimination.

Europa Issue, 1971
Common Design Type

1971, May 3 Lithographed   Perf. 13
Size: 31½x22½mm.

| 1876 | CD14 | 100k lt bl, cl & mag | 90 | 90 |
| 1877 | CD14 | 150k dp org, grn & red | 1.10 | 1.10 |

Kemal Ataturk
A437   A438

1971

1878	A437	5k gray & ultra	8	5
1879	A437	25k gray & dk red	8	5
1880	A438	25k brn & pink	8	5
1881	A437	100k gray & vio	35	8
1882	A438	100k grn & sal	35	8
1883	A438	250k bl & gray	1.00	15
1884	A437	400k tan & ol grn	1.00	20
		Nos. 1878-1884 (7)	2.94	66

Pres. Kemal Gürsel
A439

Mosque of Selim, Edirne
A440

1971, May 27   Litho.   Perf. 13

| 1885 | A439 | 100k multi | 45 | 20 |

Revolution of May 27, 1960, and to honor Kemal Gürsel (1895–1966), president.

1971, July 21   Litho.   Perf. 13

Designs: 150k, Religious School, Chaharbagh, Iran. 200k, Badshahi Mosque, Pakistan (horiz.).

1886	A440	100k multi	35	20
1887	A440	150k multi	50	25
1888	A440	200k multi	70	35

Regional Cooperation by Turkey, Iran and Pakistan, 7th anniversary.

Alp Arslan and Battle of Malazkirt—A441

Design: 250k, Archers on horseback.

1971, Aug. 26 Litho.   Perf. 13x13½

| 1889 | A441 | 100k multi | 50 | 25 |
| 1890 | A441 | 250k red, org & blk | 85 | 55 |

900th anniversary of the Battle of Malazkirt, which established the Seljuk Dynasty in Asia Minor.

Battle of Sakarya—A442

1971, Sept. 13

| 1891 | A442 | 100k vio & multi | 45 | 20 |

50th anniversary of the victory of Sakarya.

Turkey-Bulgaria Railroad
A443

Designs: 110k, Ferry and map of Lake Van. 250k, Turkey-Iran railroad.

1971

1892	A443	100k multi	75	25
1893	A443	110k multi	75	25
1894	A443	250k yel & multi	1.50	75

Turkish railroad connections with Bulgaria and Iran. Issue dates: 110k, 250k, Sept. 27; 100k, Sept. 30.

Netball and Map of Mediterranean
A444

Designs: 200k, Runner and stadium (vert.). 250k, Shot put and map of Mediterranean. (vert.)

1971, Oct. 6

| 1895 | A444 | 100k dl vio & blk | 40 | 20 |
| 1896 | A444 | 200k brn, blk & emer | 60 | 40 |

Souvenir Sheet
Imperf.

| 1897 | A444 | 250k ol bis & sl grn | 1.25 | 1.25 |

Mediterranean Games, Izmir. No. 1897 contains one stamp. Pale green margin with sport scenes. Size: 49x94mm.

TURKEY

Tomb of Cyrus the Great—A445

Designs: 100k, Harpist, Persian mosaic (vert.). 150k, Ataturk and Riza Shah Pahlavi.

1971, Oct. 13
1898	A445	25k lt bl & multi	12	10
1899	A445	100k multi	35	20
1900	A445	150k dk brn & buff	55	35

2500th anniversary of the founding of the Persian empire by Cyrus the Great.

Painting Type of 1971

Paintings: No. 1901, Sultan Mohammed I and his Staff. No. 1902, Palace with tiled walls.

1971, Nov. 15   Litho.   Perf. 13
| 1901 | A435 | 250k multi | 90 | 60 |
| 1902 | A435 | 250k multi | 90 | 60 |

Yunus Emre A446

1971, Dec. 27   Litho.   Perf. 13
| 1903 | A446 | 100k brn & multi | 45 | 25 |

650th anniversary of the death of Yunus Emre, Turkish folk poet.

First Turkish World Map and Book Year Emblem—A447

1972, Jan. 3   Perf. 13
| 1904 | A447 | 100k buff & multi | 45 | 25 |

International Book Year, 1972.

Doves and NATO Emblem A448

Fisherman, by Cevat Dereli A449

1972, Feb. 18   Litho.   Perf. 13
| 1905 | A448 | 100k dl grn, blk & gray | 1.00 | 35 |
| 1906 | A448 | 250k dl bl, blk & gray | 1.25 | 90 |

Turkey's membership in NATO, 20th anniversary.

Europa Issue 1972
Common Design Type

1972, May 2   Litho.   Perf. 13
Size: 22x33mm.
| 1907 | CD15 | 110k bl & multi | 90 | 90 |
| 1908 | CD15 | 250k brn & multi | 1.25 | 1.25 |

Painting Type of 1971

Paintings: No. 1909, Forest, Seker Ahmet. No. 1910, View of Gebze, Anatolia, by Osman Hamdi.

1972, May 15   Lithographed
| 1909 | A435 | 100k multi | 90 | 50 |
| 1910 | A435 | 250k multi | 90 | 50 |

Ataturk Statue Type of 1967

Design: 25k, Ataturk Statue in front of Ethnographic Museum, Ankara.
Imprint: Ajans—Turk/Ankara 1972
Perf. 12½x11½

1972, June 12   Lithographed
Size: 22x15½mm.
| 1911 | A375 | 25k blk & buff | 5 | 5 |

1972, July 21   Litho.   Perf. 13
Paintings: 125k, Young Man, by Abdur Rehman Chughtai (Pakistan). 150k, Persian Woman, by Behzad.
1912	A449	100k gold & multi	40	30
1913	A449	125k gold & multi	60	40
1914	A449	150k gold & multi	70	50

Regional Cooperation for Development Pact among Turkey, Iran and Pakistan, 8th anniversary.

Ataturk and Commanders at Mt. Koca—A450

Designs: No. 1916, Battle of the Commander-in-chief. No. 1917, Turkish army entering Izmir. 110k, Artillery and cavalry.

1972   Litho.   Perf. 13x13½
1915	A450	100k lt ultra & blk	35	20
1916	A450	100k pink & multi	40	20
1917	A450	100k yel & multi	40	20
1918	A450	110k org & multi	45	25

50th anniversary of fight for establishment of independent Turkish republic. Issue dates: Nos. 1915, 1918, Aug. 26; No. 1916, Aug. 30; No. 1917, Sept. 9.

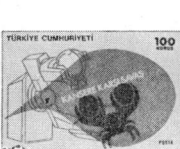

"Cancer is Curable" A451

International Railroad Union Emblem A452

1972, Oct. 10   Litho.   Perf. 12½x13
| 1919 | A451 | 100k blk, brt bl & red | 40 | 20 |

Fight against cancer.

1972, Dec. 31   Litho.   Perf. 13
| 1920 | A452 | 100k sl grn, ocher & red | 35 | 20 |

International Railroad Union, 50th anniversary.

Kemal Ataturk A453

1972-76   Litho.   Perf. 13½x13
Size: 21x26mm.
1921	A453	5k gray & bl	5	5
1922	A453	25k org ('75)	5	5
1923	A453	100k buff & red brn ('73)	40	5
1924	A453	100k lt gray & gray ('75)	20	5
1925	A453	110k lt bl & vio bl	15	5
1926	A453	125k dl grn ('73)	55	10
1927	A453	150k tan & brn	60	10
1928	A453	150k lt grn & grn ('75)	25	10
1929	A453	175k yel & lil ('73)	60	15
1930	A453	200k buff & red	65	15
1931	A453	250k pink & pur ('75)	45	15
1931A	A453	400k gray & Prus bl ('76)	70	20
1932	A453	500k pink & vio	1.40	30
1933	A453	500k gray & ultra ('75)	85	30

Perf. 13
Size: 22x33mm.
| 1934 | A453 | 101 pink & car rose ('75) | 1.75 | 50 |
| | | Nos. 1921-1934 (15) | 9.00 | 2.30 |

See Nos. 2060-2061.

Europa Issue 1973
Common Design Type

1973, Apr. 4   Lithographed   Perf. 13
Size: 32x23mm.
| 1935 | CD16 | 110k gray & multi | 55 | 55 |
| 1936 | CD16 | 250k multi | 1.10 | 1.10 |

Painting Type of 1971

Paintings: No. 1937, Beyazit Almshouse, Istanbul, by Ahmet Ziya Akbulut. No. 1938, Flowers, by Suleyman Seyyit (vert.).

1973, June 15   Litho.   Perf. 13
| 1937 | A435 | 250k multi | 90 | 50 |
| 1938 | A435 | 250k multi | 90 | 50 |

Helmet, Sword and Oak Leaves A454

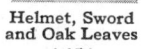

Mausoleum of Antiochus I A455

Design: 100k, Helmet, sword and laurel.

1973, June 28   Perf. 13x12½
| 1939 | A454 | 90k brn, gray & grn | 35 | 20 |
| 1940 | A454 | 100k brn, lem & grn | 35 | 20 |

Army Day.

Foreign postal stationery (stamped envelopes, postal cards and air letter sheets) lies beyond the scope of this Catalogue which is limited to adhesive postage stamps.

1973, July 21   Litho.   Perf. 13
Designs: 100k, Colossal heads, mausoleum of Antiochus I (69-34 B.C.), Commagene, Turkey. 150k, Statue, Shahdad Kerman, Persia, 3000 B.C. 200k, Street, Mohenjo-daro, Pakistan.
1941	A455	100k lt bl & multi	30	20
1942	A455	150k ol & multi	40	25
1943	A455	200k brn & multi	50	35

Regional Cooperation for Development Pact among Turkey, Iran and Pakistan, 9th anniversary.

Minelayer Nusret A456

Designs: 25k, Destroyer Istanbul. 100k, Speedboat Simsek and Naval College. 250k, Two-masted training ship Nuvid-i Futuh.

1973, Aug. 1
Size: 31½x22mm.
1944	A456	5k Prus bl & multi	5	5
1945	A456	25k Prus bl & multi	10	5
1946	A456	100k Prus bl & multi	40	20

Size: 48x32mm.
| 1947 | A456 | 250k bl & multi | 1.00 | 50 |

abu-al-Rayhan al-Biruni A457

Emblem of Darussafaka Foundation A458

1973, Sept. 4   Litho.   Perf. 13½x12½
| 1948 | A457 | 250k multi | 75 | 40 |

Millennium of the birth of abu-al-Rayhan al-Biruni (973-1048), philosopher and mathematician.

1973, Sept. 15   Perf. 13
| 1949 | A458 | 100k sil & multi | 40 | 20 |

Centenary of the educational and philanthropic Darussafaka Foundation.

BALKANFILA IV Emblem A459

Designs: 110k, Symbolic view and stamps. 250k, "Balkanfila 4."

1973   Lithographed   Perf. 13
1950	A459	100k gray & multi	40	20
1951	A459	110k multi	25	20
1952	A459	250k multi	55	35

BALKANFILA IV, Philatelic Exhibition of Balkan Countries, Izmir, Oct. 26-Nov. 5.
Issue dates: 100k, Sept. 26; 110k, 250k, Oct. 26.

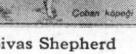

Sivas Shepherd A460

Kemal Ataturk A461

TURKEY

Design: 100k, Angora cat.
1973, Oct. 4			
1953 A460	25k blk, bl & buff	15	5
1954 A460	100k brn, yel & bl	45	15

1973, Oct. 10 Litho. *Perf. 13*
| 1955 A461 | 100k gold & blk brn | 35 | 15 |

35th anniversary of the death of Kemal Ataturk.

Flower and "50" A462   Ataturk A463

Designs: 250k, Torch and "50". 475k, Grain and cogwheel.

1973, Oct. 29
1956 A462	100k pur, red & bl	25	15
1957 A462	250k multi	75	40
1958 A462	475k brt bl & org	1.10	70

Souvenir Sheet *Imperf.*
| 1959 A463 | 500k multi | 1.75 | 1.75 |

50th anniversary of the Turkish Republic. No. 1959 contains one stamp with simulated perforations; multiple flower and inscription design in margin. Size: 78x108 mm.

Bosporus Bridge A464

Design: 150k, Istanbul and Bosporus Bridge.

1973, Oct. 30 *Perf. 13*
| 1960 A464 | 100k multi | 40 | 20 |
| 1961 A464 | 150k multi | 60 | 40 |

Inauguration of the Bosporus Bridge from Istanbul to Üsküdar, Oct. 30, 1973.

1973, Oct. 30

Design: 200k, Bosporus Bridge, children and UNICEF emblem (vert.).
| 1962 A464 | 200k multi | 70 | 40 |

United Nations International Children's Fund (UNICEF). Children from East and West brought closer through Bosporus Bridge.

Mevlana's Tomb and Dancers A465   Jalal-udin Mevlana A466

1973, Dec. 1 *Perf. 13x12½*
| 1963 A465 | 100k blk, lt ultra & grn | 30 | 20 |
| 1964 A466 | 250k bl & multi | 60 | 40 |

700th anniversary of the death of Jalal-udin Mevlana (1207–1273), poet and founder of the Mevlevie dervish order.

Cotton and Ship A467

Export Products: 90k, Grapes. 100k, Figs. 250k, Citrus fruits. 325k, Tobacco. 475k, Hazelnuts.

1973, Dec. 10 Litho. *Perf. 13*
1965 A467	75k blk, gray & bl	18	10
1966 A467	90k blk, ol & bl	25	15
1967 A467	100k blk, emer & bl	35	15
1968 A467	250k blk, brt yel & bl	1.00	35
1969 A467	325k blk, yel & bl	1.00	40
1970 A467	475k blk, org brn & bl	1.40	55
Nos. 1965-1970 (6)		4.18	1.70

Pres. Inönü A468   Hittite King, 8th Century B.C. A469

1973, Dec. 25 Litho. *Perf. 13*
| 1971 A468 | 100k sep & buff | 35 | 20 |

Ismet Inönü, (1884–1973), first Prime Minister and second President of Turkey.

Europa Issue 1974

Design: 250k, Statuette of a Boy, (2nd millennium B.C.).

1974, Apr. 29 Litho. *Perf. 13*
| 1972 A469 | 110k multi | 1.00 | 1.00 |
| 1973 A469 | 250k lt bl & multi | 1.75 | 1.75 |

Silver and Gold Figure, 3000 B.C. A470   Child Care A471

Archaeological Finds: 175k, Painted jar, 5000 B.C. (horiz.). 200k, Vessels in bull form, 1700–1600 B.C. (horiz.). 250k, Pitcher, 700 B.C.

1974, May 24 Litho. *Perf. 13*
1974 A470	125k multi	30	18
1975 A470	175k multi	40	20
1976 A470	200k multi	50	30
1977 A470	250k multi	70	50

1974, May 24
| 1978 A471 | 110k gray bl & blk | 35 | 20 |

75th anniversary of the Sisli Children's Hospital, Istanbul.

Anatolian Rug, 15th Century A472

Designs: 150k, Persian rug, late 16th century. 200k, Kashan rug, Lahore.

1974, July 21 Litho. *Perf. 12½x13*
1979 A472	100k bl & multi	30	20
1980 A472	150k brn & multi	50	30
1981 A472	200k red & multi	90	40

10th anniversary of the Regional Cooperation for Development Pact among Turkey, Iran and Pakistan.

Dove with Turkish Flag over Cyprus A473

1974, Aug. 26 Litho. *Perf. 13*
| 1982 A473 | 250k multi | 1.00 | 50 |

Cyprus Peace Operation.

Wrestling A474

Designs: 90k, 250k, various wrestling holds (horiz.).

1974, Aug. 29
1983 A474	90k multi	20	15
1984 A474	100k multi	30	15
1985 A474	250k multi	55	35

World Freestyle Wrestling Championships.

Arrows Circling Globe A475

Designs (UPU Emblem and): 110k, "UPU" in form of dove. 200k, Dove.

1974, Oct. 9 Litho. *Perf. 13*
1986 A475	110k bl, gold & dk bl	30	15
1987 A475	200k grn & brn	45	25
1988 A475	250k multi	75	45

Centenary of Universal Postal Union.

"Law Reforms" A476

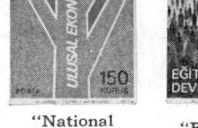

"National Economy" A477   "Education" A478

1974, Oct. 29
1989 A476	50k bl & blk	15	8
1990 A477	150k red & multi	30	20
1991 A478	400k multi	80	60

Works and reforms of Kemal Ataturk.

Arrows Pointing Up A479   Cogwheel and Map of Turkey A480

1974, Nov. 29 Lithographed *Perf. 13*
| 1992 A479 | 25k brn & blk | 10 | 5 |
| 1993 A480 | 100k brn & gray | 25 | 15 |

Third Five-year Development Program (No. 1992), and industrialization progress (No. 1993).

Volleyball A481

Designs: 175k, Basketball. 250k, Soccer.

1974, Dec. 30
1994 A481	125k bl & blk	30	20
1995 A481	175k org & blk	40	20
1996 A481	250k emer & blk	60	30

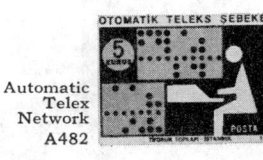

Automatic Telex Network A482

Postal Check A483

Radio Transmitter and Waves A484

1975, Feb. 5 Litho. *Perf. 13*
1997 A482	5k blk & yel	5	5
1998 A483	50k ol grn & org	15	5
1999 A484	100k bl & blk	30	15

Post and telecommunications.

Child Entering Classroom A485

Designs: 50k, View of village. 100k, Dancing children.

1975, Apr. 23 Litho. *Perf. 13*
2000 A485	25k multi	5	5
2001 A485	50k multi	12	5
2002 A485	100k multi	25	12

Children's paintings.

TURKEY

Karacaoglan Monument in Mut, by Huseyin Gezer A486

1975, Apr. 25
2003 A486 110k dk grn, bis & red   30   20

Karacaoglan (1606–1697), musician.

Europa Issue 1975

Orange Harvest in Hatay, by Cemal Tollu—A487

Design: 250k, Yoruk Family on Plateau, by Turgut Zaim.

1975, Apr. 28
2004 A487 110k bis & multi   35   35
2005 A487 250k bis & multi   55   55

Porcelain Vase, Turkey A488

Designs: 200k, Ceramic plate, Iran (horiz.). 250k, Camel leather vase, Pakistan.

Perf. 13½x13, 13x13½
1975, July 21   Lithographed
2006 A488 110k multi   40   30
2007 A488 200k multi   60   40
2008 A488 250k ultra & multi   90   60

Regional Cooperation for Development Pact among Turkey, Iran and Pakistan.

Horon Folk Dance—A489

Regional Folk Dances: 125k, Kasik. 175k, Bengi. 250k, Kasap. 325k, Kafkas (vert.).

1975, Aug. 30   Litho.   Perf. 13
2009 A489 100k bl & multi   20   10
2010 A489 125k grn & multi   35   15
2011 A489 175k rose & multi   45   25
2012 A489 250k multi   70   40
2013 A489 325k org & multi   90   50
Nos. 2009-2013 (5)   2.60   1.40

Knight Slaying Dragon A490   **The Plunder of Salur Kazan's House A491**

Design: 175k, Two Wanderers (horiz.).

1975, Oct. 15   Litho.   Perf. 13
2014 A490 90k multi   20   8
2015 A490 175k multi   40   30
2016 A491 200k multi   50   35

Illustrations for tales by Dede Korkut.

Common Carp A492

1975, Nov. 27 Litho. Perf. 12½x13
Multicolored
2017 A492 75k Turbot   20   8
2018 A492 90k shown   25   10
2019 A492 175k Trout   50   20
2020 A492 250k Red mullet   60   35
2021 A492 475k Red bream   1.25   55
Nos. 2017-2021 (5)   2.80   1.28

Women's Participation A493   **Insurance Nationalization A494**

Fine Arts A495

1975, Dec. 5 Perf. 12½x13, 13x12½
2022 A493 100k bis, blk & red   20   10
2023 A494 110k vio & multi   30   15
2024 A495 250k multi   45   35

Works and reforms of Ataturk.

Europa Issue 1976

Ceramic Plate A496

Design: 400k, Decorated pitcher.

1976, May 3   Litho.   Perf. 13
2025 A496 200k pur & multi   75   75
2026 A496 400k multi   1.25   1.25

Sultan Ahmed Mosque A497

1976, May 10
2027 A497 500k gray & multi   1.00   60

7th Islamic Conference, Istanbul.

Lunch in the Field A498

Children's Drawings: 200k, Boats on the Bosporus (vert.). 400k, Winter landscape.

1976, May 19   Litho.   Perf. 13
2028 A498 50k multi   8   5
2029 A498 200k multi   32   16
2030 A498 400k multi   64   32

Samsun 76, First National Junior Philatelic Exhibition, Samsun.

Storks, Sultan Marsh A499

Designs (Conservation Emblem and): 200k, Horses, Manyas Lake. 250k, Borabay Lake. 400k, Manavgat Waterfall.

1976, June 5
2031 A499 150k multi   1.50   75
2032 A499 200k multi   40   16
2033 A499 250k multi   60   25
2034 A499 400k multi   90   35

European Wetland Conservation Year.

Nasreddin Hodja Carrying Liver A500   **Montreal Olympic Emblem and Flame A501**

Designs: 250k, Friend giving recipe for cooking liver. 600k, Hawk carrying off liver and Hodja telling hawk he cannot enjoy liver without recipe.

1976, July 5   Litho.   Perf. 13
2035 A500 150k multi   30   12
2036 A500 250k multi   45   25
2037 A500 600k multi   1.25   50

Turkish folklore.

1976, July 17

Designs: 400k, "76", Montreal Olympic emblem (horiz.). 600k, Montreal Olympic emblem and ribbons.

2038 A501 100k red & multi   20   8
2039 A501 400k red & multi   70   40
2040 A501 600k red & multi   1.25   60

21st Olympic Games, Montreal, Canada, July 17–Aug. 1.

Kemal Ataturk A502

Designs: 200k, Riza Shah Pahlavi. 250k, Mohammed Ali Jinnah.

1976, July 21   Litho.   Perf. 13½
2041 A502 100k multi   16   8
2042 A502 200k multi   35   16
2043 A502 250k multi   45   20

Regional Cooperation for Development Pact among Turkey, Pakistan and Iran, 12th anniversary.

"Ataturk's Army" A503

Ataturk's Speeches A504

"Peace at Home and in the World" A505

1976, Oct. 29   Litho.   Perf. 13
2044 A503 100k blk & red   25   8
2045 A504 200k gray grn & multi   32   16
2046 A505 400k bl & multi   65   40

Works and reforms of Ataturk.

Hora A506

1977, Jan. 19   Litho.   Perf. 13
2047 A506 400k multi   75   40

MTA Sismik 1 "Hora" geophysical exploration ship.

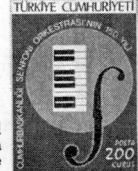

Keyboard and Violin Sound Hole A507

1977, Feb. 24   Litho.   Perf. 13x13½
2048 A507 200k multi   40   25

Turkish State Symphony Orchestra, sesquicentennial.

Ataturk and "100" A508

Design: 400k, Hand holding ballot.

TURKEY

1977, Mar. 21   Litho.   Perf. 13

2049	A508	200k blk & red	32	16
2050	A508	400k blk & brn	75	40

Centenary of Turkish Parliament.

Europa Issue 1977

Hierapolis (Pamukkale) A509

Design: 400k, Zelve (mountains and poppies).

1977, May 2   Litho.   Perf. 13½x13

2051	A509	200k multi	55	55
2052	A509	400k multi	1.00	1.00

Terra Cotta Pot, Turkey A510

Designs: 225k, Terra cotta jug, Iran. 675k, Terra cotta bullock cart, Pakistan.

1977, July 21   Litho.   Perf. 13

2053	A510	100k multi	16	8
2054	A510	225k multi	45	20
2055	A510	675k multi	1.10	50
a.		Souvenir sheet of 3	1.75	1.75

Regional Cooperation for Development Pact among Turkey, Iran and Pakistan, 13th anniversary. No. 2055a contains one each of Nos. 2053–2055 and blue label showing RCD emblem.; gold border. Size: 108x78 mm.

Finn-class Yacht A511

Designs: 200k, Three yachts. 250k, Symbolic yacht.

1977, July 28

2056	A511	150k lt bl, bl & blk	25	15
2057	A511	200k ultra & bl	40	20
2058	A511	250k ultra & blk	50	30

European Finn Class Sailing Championships, Istanbul, July 28.

Ataturk Type of 1972

1977, June 13   Litho.   Perf. 13½x13

2060	A453	100k olive	16	8
2061	A453	200k brown	30	8

Kemal Ataturk A512

Imprint: "GUZEL SANATLAR MATBAASI A.S. 1977"

1977, Sept. 23   Litho.   Perf. 13
Size: 20½x22mm.

2062	A512	200k blue	25	8
2063	A512	250k Prus bl	30	8

Imprint: "TIFDRUK-ISTANBUL 1978"

1978, June 28   Photo.   Perf. 13
Size: 20x25mm.

2065	A512	10k brown	5	5
2066	A512	50k grnsh gray	5	5
2067	A512	1 l fawn	10	5
2068	A512	2½ l purple	25	5
2069	A512	5 l blue	50	10
2072	A512	25 l dl grn & lt bl	2.00	40
2073	A512	50 l dp org & tan	3.50	1.50
		Nos. 2065-2073 (7)	6.45	2.20

No. 1832 Surcharged with New Value and Wavy Lines

1977, Aug. 17

| 2078 | A418 | 10k on 1k dp org & brn | 5 | 5 |

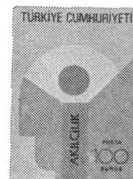
"Rationalism" A513

"National Sovereignty" A514

"Liberation of Nations" A515

1977, Oct. 29   Litho.   Perf. 13

2079	A513	100k multi	16	8
2080	A514	200k multi	32	16
2081	A515	400k multi	60	30

Works and reforms of Ataturk.

Mohammad Allama Iqbal A516

Trees and Burning Match A517

1977, Nov. 9   Perf. 13x12½

| 2082 | A516 | 400k multi | 65 | 20 |

Mohammad Allama Iqbal (1877–1938), Pakistani poet and philosopher, birth centenary.

1977, Dec. 15   Litho.   Perf. 13
Design: 250k, Sign showing growing tree.

2083	A517	50k grn, blk & red	5	5
2084	A517	250k gray, grn & blk	20	10

Forest conservation.

Wrecked Car A518

Passing on Wrong Side A519

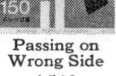
Traffic Sign, "Slow!" A520

Two types of 50k:
I. Number on license plate.
II. No number on plate.

Designs: 250k, Tractor drawing overloaded farm cart. 800k, Accident caused by incorrect passing. 10 l, "Use striped crossings."

1977–78   Perf. 13½x13, 13x13½

2085	A518	50k ultra, blk & red, II	30	5
a.		Type I	30	5
2086	A519	150k red, gray & blk ('78)	15	6
2087	A518	250k ocher, blk & red ('78)	35	12
2088	A520	500k gray, red & blk	30	25
2089	A520	800k multi ('78)	1.00	40
2090	A520	10 l dl grn, blk & brn ('78)	1.40	50
		Nos. 2085-2090 (6)	3.50	1.38

Traffic safety.

Europa Issue

Ishak Palace, Dogubeyazit—A521

Design: 5 l, Anamur Castle.

1978, May 2   Litho.   Perf. 13

2091	A521	2½ l multi	40	40
2092	A521	5 l multi	80	80

Riza Shah Pahlavi A522

1978, June 16   Litho.   Perf. 13x13½

| 2093 | A522 | 5 l multi | 80 | 30 |

Riza Shah Pahlavi (1877–1944) of Iran, birth centenary.

Yellow Rose, Turkey A523

Designs: 3½ l, Pink roses, Iran. 8 l, Red roses, Pakistan.

1978, July 21   Litho.   Perf. 13

2094	A523	2½ l multi	20	8
2095	A523	3½ l multi	35	12
2096	A523	8 l multi	80	40

Regional Cooperation for Development Pact among Turkey, Iran and Pakistan.

Apartheid Emblem A524

1978, Aug. 14   Litho.   Perf. 13½x13

| 2097 | A524 | 10 l multi | 1.00 | 40 |

Anti-Apartheid Year.

View of Ankara A525

Design: 5 l, View of Tripoli (horiz.).

Perf. 13x12½, 12½x13

1978, Aug. 17

2098	A525	2½ l multi	20	10
2099	A525	5 l multi	50	20

Turkish–Libyan friendship.

Souvenir Sheet

Bridge and Mosque—A526

1978, Oct. 25   Imperf.

| 2100 | A526 | 15 l multi | 1.25 | 1.25 |

Edirne '78, 2nd National Philatelic Youth Exhibition, No. 2100 has light blue margin showing stamps. Size: 71½x52 mm.

Independence Medal A527

Latin Alphabet A529

Speech Reform A528

Perf. 13x13½, 13½x13

1978, Oct. 29

2101	A527	2½ l multi	20	8
2102	A528	3½ l multi	25	12
2103	A529	5 l multi	40	20

Ataturk's works and reforms.
See Nos. 2120-2122.

TURKEY

House on Bosporus, 1699—A530

Turkish Houses: 2½ l, Izmit, 1774 (vert.). 3½ l, Kula, 17th century. (vert.). 5 l, Milas, 18th–19th centuries (vert.). 8 l, Safranbolu, 18th–19th centuries.

    Perf. 13x12½, 12½x13
1978, Nov. 22
2104	A530	1 l multi	10	5
2105	A530	2½ l multi	20	8
2106	A530	3½ l multi	35	12
2107	A530	5 l multi	50	20
2108	A530	8 l multi	1.00	40
	Nos. 2104-2108 (5)		2.15	85

Europa Issue 1979

Carrier Pigeon, Plane, Horseback Rider, Train—A531

Designs: 5 l, Morse key, telegraph and Telex machine. 7½ l, Telephone dial and satellite.

1979, Apr. 30   *Litho.*   *Perf. 13*
2109	A531	2½ l multi	25	25
2110	A531	5 l org brn & blk	45	45
2111	A531	7½ l brt bl & blk	65	65

Plowing, by Namik Ismail—A532

Paintings: 7½ l, Potters, by Kamalel Molk, Iran. 10 l, At the Well, by Allah Baksh, Pakistan.

1979, Sept. 5   *Litho.*   *Perf. 13½×13*
2112	A532	5 l multi	30	12
2113	A532	7½ l multi	50	20
2114	A532	10 l multi	80	35

Regional Cooperation for Development Pact among Turkey, Pakistan and Iran, 15th anniversary.

Colemanite—A533

1979, Sept. 17   *Perf. 13*
Multicolored
2115	A533	5 l shown	30	16
2116	A533	7½ l Chromite	50	25
2117	A533	10 l Antimonite	80	32
2118	A533	15 l Sulphur	1.00	48

10th World Mining Congress.

8-Shaped Road, Train Tunnel, Plane and Emblem—A534

1979, Sept. 24
2119	A534	5 l multi	30	16

European Ministers of Communications, 8th Symposium.

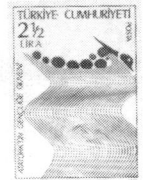

Youth—A535

Secularization—A536

Design: 5 l, National oath.

1979, Oct. 29   *Perf. 13×12½, 12½×13*
2120	A535	2½ l multi	15	6
2121	A536	3½ l multi	25	10
2122	A535	5 l blk & org	40	24

Ataturk's works and reforms.

Poppies   **Kemal Ataturk**
A537   A538a

1979, Nov. 26   *Litho.*   *Perf. 13×13½*
2123	A537	5 l shown	20	8
2124	A537	7½ l Oleander	30	12
2125	A537	10 l Late spider orchid	40	15
2126	A537	15 l Mandrake	80	35

See Nos. 2154-2157.

1979-81   *Litho.*   *Perf. 12½x11½*
2127	A538	50k ol ('80)	5	5
2128	A538	1 l grn, grnsh	5	5
2129	A538	2½ l purple	10	5
2130	A538	2½ l bl grn ('80)	8	5
2131	A538	2½ l org ('81)	8	5
2132	A538	5 l ultra, gray	20	8
a.	Sheet of 8		1.75	1.75
2133	A538	7½ l brown	30	8
2134	A538	7½ l red ('80)	20	8
2135	A538	10 l rose car	40	20
2136	A538	20 l gray ('80)	55	30
	Nos. 2127-2136 (10)		2.01	99

5 l sheet of 8 for Ankara '79 Philatelic Exhibition, Oct. 14-20, ultramarine marginal inscription. Size: 123x57mm.

1980, Dec. 10   *Photo.*   *Perf. 13½*
2137	A538a	7½ l red brn	8	5
c.	Sheet of 4 ('82)		50	25
2137A	A538a	10 l brown	14	5
2138	A538a	20 l lilac	25	5
2138A	A538a	30 l gray	30	12
2139	A538a	50 l org red	65	10
2140	A538a	75 l brt grn	1.00	20
2141	A538a	100 l blue	1.40	50

7½ l sheet of 4 for ANTALYA '82 4th Natl. Junior Stamp Show. Issue dates: 7½ l, July 15, 1981; 7½ l sheet, Oct. 3, 1982; 30 l, Sept. 23, 1981.

Turkish Printing, 250th Anniversary
A539

1979, Nov. 30   *Litho.*   *Perf. 13*
2142	A539	10 l multi	50	10

2nd International Olive Oil Year—A540

1979, Dec. 20   *Litho.*   *Perf. 12½x13, 13x12½*
2143	A540	5 l shown	16	5
2144	A540	10 l Globe, oil drop (vert.)	45	15

Uskudarli Hoca Ali Riza Bey (1857-1930), Painter—A541

Designs: 15 l, Ali Sami Boyar (1880-1967), painter. 20 l, Dr. Hulusi Behcet (1889-1948), physician, discovered Behcet skin disease.

1980, Apr. 28   *Perf. 13*
2145	A541	7½ l multi	15	5
2146	A541	15 l multi	30	30
2147	A541	20 l multi	40	40

Forest   **Earthquake**
Conservation   **Destruction**
A542   A543

1980, July 3   *Perf. 13½x13*
2148	A542	50k ol grn & red org	5	5

1980, Sept. 8   *Perf. 13*
2149	A543	7½ l shown	15	5
2150	A543	20 l Seismograph	40	20

7th World Conference on Earthquake Engineering, Istanbul.

Games' Emblem,   **Hegira**
Sports
A544   A545

1980, Sept. 26   *Perf. 13x13½*
2151	A544	7½ l shown	20	5
2152	A544	20 l Emblem, sports, diff.	50	15

First Islamic Games, Izmir.

1980, Nov. 9
2153	A545	20 l multi	35	15

Plant Type of 1979

1980, Nov. 26   *Perf. 13*
2154	A537	2½ l Manisa tulip	5	5
2155	A537	7½ l Ephesian bellflower	10	5
2156	A537	15 l Angora crocus	25	10
2157	A537	20 l Anatolian orchid	35	15

Avicenna Treating Patient—A546

Avicenna (Arab Physician), Birth Millenium: 20 l, Portrait (vert.).

1980, Dec. 15
2158	A546	7½ l multi	10	5
2159	A546	20 l multi	25	15

Balkanfila VIII Stamp Exhibition, Ankara—A547

1981, Jan. 1   *Litho.*   *Perf. 13*
2160	A547	10 l red & blk	20	8

Kemal Ataturk—A548

1981, Feb. 4
2163	A548	10 l lil rose	20	8

Ataturk Type of 1980

1983, Nov. 30
2164	A538a	15 l grnsh bl ('83)	10	5
2167	A538a	65 l bluish grn ('83)	40	10
2169	A538a	90 l lil rose ('83)	55	15

825

TURKEY

Sultan Mehmet the Conqueror
(1432-1481)—A549

1981, May 3   Litho.   Perf. 13x12½

| 2173 | A549 | 10 l | | 14 | 9 |
| 2174 | A549 | 20 l | | 25 | 15 |

Gaziantep (Folk Dance)—A550

Antalya—A551

1981, May 4   Litho.   Perf. 13

2175	A550	7½ l shown	10	5
2176	A550	10 l Balikesir	14	8
2177	A550	15 l Kahramanmaras	20	15
2178	A551	35 l shown	45	45
2179	A551	70 l Burdur	90	90
		Nos. 2175-2179 (5)	1.79	1.63

Nos. 2178-2179 show CEPT (Europa) emblem.

Nos. C40, 1925, 1931A, 2089 Surcharged
in Black
with New Value and Wavy Lines

1981, June 3   Perf. 13½x13

2179A	AP7	10 l on 60k multi		15	8
2180	A453	10 l on 110k lt bl & vio bl		15	8
2181	A453	10 l on 400k gray & Prus bl		15	8
2182	A520	10 l on 800k multi		15	8

22nd Intl. Turkish
Folklore Congress
A552

1981, June 22   Perf. 13x12½

2183	A552	7½ l Rug, Bilecik	10	5
2184	A552	10 l Embroidery	14	5
2185	A552	15 l Drum, zurna players	20	10
2186	A552	20 l Embroidered napkin	25	15
2187	A552	30 l Rug, diff.	40	20
		Nos. 2183-2187 (5)	1.09	55

Kemal Ataturk—A553

1982, May 19   Litho.   Perf. 14x15

2188	A553	2½ l No. 1801	5	5
2189	A553	7½ l No. 1816	5	5
2190	A553	10 l No. 1604	14	8
2191	A553	20 l No. 804	25	12
2192	A553	25 l No. 777	32	16
2193	A553	35 l No. 1959	40	20
		Nos. 2188-2193 (6)	1.21	66

Souvenir Sheet

2194		Sheet of 6	6.50	3.00
a.	A553	12½ l like 2½ l	15	8
b.	A553	37½ l like 7½ l	45	22
c.	A553	50 l like 10 l	62	30
d.	A553	100 l like 20 l	1.25	60
e.	A553	125 l like 25 l	1.60	75
f.	A553	175 l like 35 l	2.25	1.00

Souvenir Sheet

Balkanfila VIII Stamp Exhibition,
Ankara—A554

1981, Aug. 8   Litho.   Perf. 13

2195		Sheet of 2	1.25	75
a.	A554	50 l No. B68	62	30
b.	A554	50 l No. 733	62	30

Size: 105x82mm.

5th General Congress of European
Physics Society—A555

1982, Sept. 7   Perf. 12½x13

| 2196 | A555 | 10 l red & multi | 14 | 8 |
| 2197 | A555 | 30 l bl & multi | 40 | 20 |

World Food Day—A556

1981, Oct. 16

| 2198 | A556 | 10 l multi | 14 | 8 |
| 2199 | A556 | 30 l multi | 40 | 20 |

Constituent Assembly
Inauguration—A557

1981, Oct. 23   Perf. 13

| 2200 | A557 | 10 l multi | 14 | 8 |
| 2201 | A557 | 30 l multi | 40 | 20 |

Ataturk—A558

Portraits of Ataturk.

1981-82   Perf. 11½x12½

2202	A558	1 l green	5	5
2203	A558	2½ l purple	5	5
2204	A558	2½ l gray & org	5	5
2205	A558	5 l blue	5	5
2206	A558	10 l orange	14	6
2207	A558	35 l brown	40	10
		Nos. 2202-2216 (15)	74	36

Issue dates: No. 2204, Dec. 10, 1981; others, Jan. 27, 1982.

Literacy Campaign
A559

Energy Conservation
A560

1982, Dec. 24   Perf. 13½

| 2217 | A559 | 2½ l Procession | 5 | 5 |

1982, Jan. 11   Perf. 13

| 2218 | A560 | 10 l multi | 10 | 5 |

Magnolias, by
Ibrahim Calli
(b. 1882)
A561

Europa 1982
A562

1982, Mar. 17   Perf. 13x13½, 13½x13

2219	A561	10 l shown	10	5
2220	A561	20 l Fishermen, horiz.	20	6
2221	A561	30 l Sewing Woman	30	8

1982, Apr. 26   Perf. 13x12½

2222	A562	30 l Sultanhan Caravanserai	30	8
2223	A562	70 l Silk Route	70	20
a.	Miniature sheet of 4 (2 each #2222-2223)	2.00	75

Nos. 2222-2223 se-tenant. Size of No. 2223a: 78x80mm.

1250th Anniv. of Kul-Tigin Monument,
Kosu Saydam, Mongolia—A563

1982, June 9   Perf. 13

| 2224 | A563 | 10 l Monument | 10 | 5 |
| 2225 | A563 | 30 l Kul-Tigin (685-732), Gok-Turkish commander | 30 | 8 |

Pendik Shipyard Opening—A564

1982, July 1   Perf. 12½x13

| 2226 | A564 | 30 l Ship, emblem | 30 | 8 |

Mountains of Anatolia—A565

1982, July 17   Perf. 13

2227	A565	7½ l Agri Dagi, vert.	8	5
2228	A565	10 l Buzul Dagi	10	5
2229	A565	15 l Demirkazik, vert.	15	5
2230	A565	20 l Erciyes	20	6
2231	A565	30 l Kackar Dagi, vert.	30	8
2232	A565	35 l Uludag	35	10
		Nos. 2227-2232 (6)	1.18	39

Beyazit State Library Centenary—A566

1982, Sept. 27

| 2233 | A566 | 30 l multi | 30 | 8 |

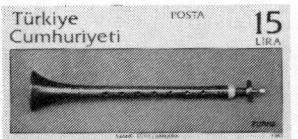

Musical Instruments of Anatolia—A567

1982, Oct. 13

2234	A567	7½ l Davul	8	5
2235	A567	10 l Baglama	10	5
2236	A567	15 l shown	15	5
2237	A567	20 l Kemence	20	6
2238	A567	30 l Mey	30	8
		Nos. 2234-2238 (5)	83	29

Roman Temple Columns, Start—A568

1982, Nov. 3

| 2239 | A568 | 30 l multi | 30 | 8 |

Family Planning and Mother-Child
Health—A569

1983, Jan. 12   Litho.   Perf. 13

| 2240 | A569 | 10 l Family on map | 10 | 5 |
| 2241 | A569 | 35 l Mother and child | 35 | 10 |

TURKEY

30th Anniv. of Customs Cooperation Council—A570

1983, Jan. 26
| 2242 | A570 | 45 l multi | 45 | 14 |

1982 Constitution—A571

1983, Jan. 27
| 2243 | A571 | 10 l Ballot box | 10 | 5 |
| 2244 | A571 | 30 l Open book, scale | 30 | 8 |

Manastirli Bey A572

1983, Mar. 16 Litho.
| 2245 | A572 | 35 l multi | 35 | 10 |

Manastirli Hamdi Bey (1890-1945), telegrapher of news of Istanbul's occupation to Ataturk. 1920.

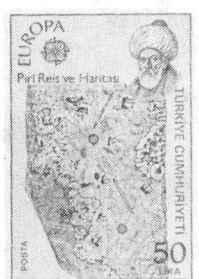

Europa 1983—A573

1983, May 5 Litho. Perf. 12½x13
| 2246 | A573 | 50 l Piri Reis, geographer | 50 | 14 |
| 2247 | A573 | 100 l Ulug Bey (1394-1449), astronomer | 1.00 | 30 |

Youth Week—A574

1983, May 16
| 2248 | A574 | 15 l multi | 15 | 5 |

World Communications Year—A575

1983, May 16 Perf. 13
2249	A575	15 l Carrier pigeon, vert.	15	5
2250	A575	50 l Phone lines	50	14
2251	A575	70 l Emblem, vert.	70	20

50th Anniv. of State Civil Aviation—A576

1983, May 20 Litho. Perf. 13
| 2252 | A576 | 50 l Plane, jet | 50 | 14 |
| 2253 | A576 | 70 l Airport | 70 | 20 |

18th Council of Europe Art Exhibition—A577

Designs: 15 l, Eros, 2nd cent. BC (vert.). 35 l, Two-headed duck, Hittite, 14th cent BC. 50 l, Zinc jugs, plate, 16th cent. (vert.) 70 l, Marcus Aurelius and his wife Faustina the Young, 2nd cent.

1983, May 22 Perf. 13
2254	A577	15 l multi	15	5
2255	A577	35 l multi	35	8
2256	A577	50 l multi	50	14
2257	A577	70 l multi	70	20

Council of Europe's "The Water's Edge" Campaign—A578

Coastal Views.

1983, Jun 1 Litho. Perf. 13x12½
2258	A578	10 l Olodeniz	10	5
2259	A578	25 l Olympus	25	8
2260	A578	35 l Kekova	35	8

Nos. 2127, 2148 Overprinted.

1983, June 8 Perf. 12½x11½, 13½x13
| 2261 | A538 | 5 l on 50k ol | 5 | 5 |
| 2262 | A542 | 5 l on 50k ol grn & red org | 5 | 5 |

Kemal Ataturk—A579

1983, June 22 Perf. 13
2263	A579	15 l bl grn & bl	15	5
		Sheet of 5 plus label	75	20
2264	A579	50 l grn & bl	50	14
2265	A579	100 l org & bl	1.00	30

Aga Khan Architecture Award—A580

1983, Sept. 4 Photo. Perf. 11½
| 2266 | A580 | 50 l View of Istanbul | 50 | 14 |

60th Anniv. of the Republic—A582

1983, Oct. 29 Perf. 13½x13
| 2268 | A582 | 15 l multi | 15 | 5 |
| 2269 | A582 | 50 l multi | 50 | 14 |

Columns, Aphrodisias—A583

1983, Nov. 2 Perf. 13
| 2270 | A583 | 50 l multi | 50 | 14 |

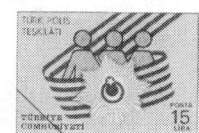

UNESCO Campaign for Istanbul and Goreme—A584

1984, Feb. 15 Litho. Perf. 13
2271	A584	25 l St. Sophia Basilica	15	5
2272	A584	35 l Goreme	22	6
2273	A584	50 l Istanbul	30	8

Natl. Police Org. Emblem—A585

1984, Apr. 10 Litho. Perf. 13
| 2274 | A585 | 15 l multi | 8 | 5 |

Europa (1959-84)—A586

1984, Apr. 30 Perf. 13½x13
| 2275 | A586 | 50 l bl & multi | 30 | 8 |
| 2276 | A586 | 100 l gray & multi | 60 | 16 |

TURKEY

For the advanced collector.
We buy and sell specialized material.

George Alevizos
2716 Ocean Park Blvd. Ste. 1020
Santa Monica, CA 90405
Telephone: 213/450-2543

TURKEY

SEMI-POSTAL STAMPS.

Regular Issues Overprinted in Carmine or Black

Overprint reads: "For War Orphans".

1915   Unwmkd.
Perf. 12, 13½ and Compound

On Stamps of 1905.
B1	A18	10pa dl grn (#119)	5	5
B2	A18	10pi org brn	3.00	15

On Stamp of 1906.
B3	A18	10pa dl grn (#128)	7.50	3.00

On Stamps of 1908.
B4	A19	10pa bl grn	25	10
B5	A19	5pi dk vio	17.50	5.00

With Additional Overprint
B6	A19	10pa bl grn	37.50	17.50

On Stamps of 1909.
B7	A21	10pa bl grn	5	5
a.		Inverted overprint	7.50	7.50
b.		Double overprint, one inverted	7.50	7.50
B8	A21	20pa car rose	10	5
a.		Inverted overprint	7.50	7.50
B9	A21	1pi ultra	20	5
B10	A21	5pi dk vio	1.50	5

With Additional Overprint
B11	A21	10pa bl grn	10	5
b.		Double overprint, one inverted	7.50	7.50
B12	A21	20pa car rose	12	5
B13	A21	1pi ultra	1.25	5

On Stamps of 1913.
B14	A22	10pa bl grn	12	10
a.		Inverted overprint	7.50	7.50
B15	A22	1pi ultra	20	5
a.		Double overprint	7.50	7.50

With Additional Overprint
B16	A22	10pa bl grn	15	10
a.		Inverted overprint	7.50	7.50

On Newspaper Stamp of 1908.
B17	A19	10pa bl grn	60.00	35.00

On Newspaper Stamp of 1909
B18	A21	10pa bl grn	25	10

1916

Regular Issues Overprinted in Carmine or Black

On Stamps of 1901.
B19	A17	1pi blue	15	7
B20	A17	5pi lil rose	3.00	20

On Stamps of 1905.
B21	A18	1pi brt bl	12	7
B22	A18	5pi brown	3.50	80

On Stamp of 1906.
B23	A18	1pi brt bl	40	8

On Stamps of 1908.
B24	A19	20pa carmine (Bk)		80.00
B25	A19	10pi red	90.00	60.00

With Additional Overprint
B26	A19	20pa carmine	20	20
B27	A19	1pi brt bl (C)	40.00	10.00

On Stamps of 1909.
B28	A21	20pa car rose	8	5
B29	A21	1pi ultra	15	5
B30	A21	10pi dl red	35.00	30.00

With Additional Overprint
B31	A21	20pa car rose	30	20
B32	A21	1pi ultra	15	10

On Stamps of 1913.
B33	A22	20pa car rose	5	5
B34	A22	1pi ultra	20	5
a.		Inverted overprint	7.50	7.50
B35	A22	10pi dl red	15.00	6.00

With Additional Overprint
B36	A22	20pa car rose	15	6

On Newspaper Stamps of 1901
B37	A16	5pi ocher	2.00	1.00
a.		5pa bis, No. P37	200.00	150.00

Regular Issues Surcharged in Black

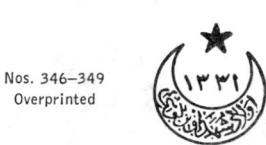

On Stamp of 1899.
B38	A11	10pa on 20pa vio brn	10	8

On Stamp of 1905.
B39	A18	10pa on 20pa car	6	6

On Stamp of 1906.
B40	A18	10pa on 20pa car	15	12

On Newspaper Stamp of 1893-99.
B41	A11	10pa on 20pa vio brn	10	10

Nos. 346–349 Overprinted

B42	A41	10pa carmine	8	6
a.		Inverted overprint	7.50	7.50
B43	A41	20pa ultra	8	6
a.		Inverted overprint	7.50	7.50
B44	A41	1pi vio & blk	8	8
a.		Inverted overprint	7.50	7.50
B45	A41	5pi yel brn & blk	60	15
a.		Inverted overprint	12.50	12.50

Nos. B42 to B45 formed part of the Postage Commemoration issue of 1916.

A Soldier's Farewell
SP1

1917, Feb. 20   Engr.   Perf. 12½
B46	SP1	10pa red vio	10	8

Stamp of Same Design Surcharged

B47	SP1	10pa on 20pa car rose	12	10

Badge of the Society
SP9

School Teacher
SP10

Carrie Chapman Catt
SP16

Kemal Atatürk
SP23

Designs: 2k+2k, Woman farmer. 2½k+2½k, Typist. 4k+4k, Aviatrix and policewoman. 5k+5k, Women voters. 7½k+7½k, Yildiz Palace, Istanbul. 12½k+12½k, Jane Addams. 15k+15k, Grazia Deledda. 20k+20k, Selma Lagerlof. 25k+25k, Bertha von Suttner. 30k+30k, Sigrid Undset. 50k+50k, Marie Sklodowska Curie.

1935, Apr. 17   Photo.   Perf. 11½

Inscribed: "XII Congres Suffragiste International."

B54	SP9	20pa + 20pa brn	50	30
B55	SP10	1k + 1k rose car	60	30
B56	SP10	2k + 2k sl bl	60	30
B57	SP10	2½k + 2½k yel grn	60	40
B58	SP10	4k + 4k bl	80	70
B59	SP10	5k + 5k dl vio	1.25	80
B60	SP10	7½k + 7½k org red	2.00	1.75
B61	SP16	10k + 10k org	3.50	2.75
B62	SP16	12½k + 12½k dk bl	10.00	8.00
B63	SP16	15k + 15k vio	10.00	8.00
B64	SP16	20k + 20k red org	17.50	12.50
B65	SP16	25k + 25k grn	30.00	25.00
B66	SP16	30k + 30k ultra	65.00	65.00
B67	SP16	50k + 50k dk sl grn	125.00	120.00
B68	SP23	100k + 100k brn car	115.00	110.00
	Nos. B54-B68 (15)		382.35	355.80

Issued in commemoration of the 12th Congress of the Women's International Alliance.

Katip Chelebi
SP24

Perf. 10½

1958, Sept. 24   Litho.   Unwmkd.
B69	SP24	50k + 10k gray	25	20

Issued to honor Mustafa ibn 'Abdallah Katip Chelebi Hajji Khalifa (1608–1657), Turkish author.

Road Building Machine
SP25

Kemal Atatürk
SP26

Ruins, Göreme
SP27

Design: 25k+5k, Tanks and planes.

1958, Oct. 29
B70	SP25	15k + 5k org	10	5
B71	SP26	20k + 5k lt red brn	12	8
B72	SP25	25k + 5k brt grn	15	15

The surtax went to the Red Crescent Society and to the Society for the Protection of Children.

1959, July 8   Litho.   Perf. 10
B73	SP27	105k + 10k pur & buff	50	40

Issued for tourist publicity.

Istanbul
SP28

1959, Sept. 11
B74	SP28	105k + 10k lt bl & red	40	30

15th International Tuberculosis Congress.

Manisa Asylum—SP29

Merkez Muslihiddin
SP30

Design: 90k+5k, Sultan Camii Mosque, Manisa. (vert.).

1960, Apr. 17   Perf. 13   Unwmkd.
B75	SP29	40k + 5k brn & lt bl	20	10
B76	SP29	40k + 5k vio & rose lil	20	10
B77	SP29	90k + 5k dp cl & car rose	40	25
B78	SP30	105k + 10k multi	60	50

Issued to publicize the kermis at Manisa.

Census Chart
SP31

Census Symbol
SP32

TURKEY

1960, Sept. 23   Photo.   Perf. 11½
Granite Paper
| B79 | SP31 | 30k +5k bl & rose pink | 15 | 10 |
| B80 | SP32 | 50k +5k grn, dk bl & ultra | 25 | 15 |

Issued for the 1960 Census.

Old Observatory   Fatin Gökmen
SP33   SP34

Designs: 30k+5k, Observatory emblem. 75k+5k, Building housing telescope.

1961, July 1   Perf. 13   Unwmkd.
B81	SP33	10k +5k grnsh bl & grn	10	5
B82	SP33	30k +5k vio & blk	15	10
B83	SP34	40k +5k brn	25	15
B84	SP33	75k +5k ol grn	50	40

Kandilli Observatory, 50th anniversary.

Anti-Malaria Work
SP35

Designs: 30k+5k, Mother and infant (horiz.). 75k+5k, Woman distributing pasteurized milk.

1961, Dec. 11   Perf. 13   Unwmkd.
B85	SP35	10k +5k Prus grn	10	10
B86	SP35	30k +5k dl vio	20	10
B87	SP35	75k +5k dk ol bis	40	30

Issued to commemorate the tenth anniversary of UNICEF (U.N. International Children's Emergency Fund).

Malaria Eradication Emblem, Map and Mosquito
SP36

1962, Apr. 7   Lithographed
| B88 | SP36 | 30k +5k dk & lt brn | 15 | 10 |
| B89 | SP36 | 75k +5k blk & lil | 30 | 25 |

Issued for the World Health Organization drive to eradicate malaria.

Poinsettia   Wheat and Census Chart
SP37   SP38

Flowers: 40k+10k, Bird of paradise flower. 75k+10k, Water lily.

1962, May 19   Perf. 12½x13½
Flowers in Natural Colors
B90	SP37	30k +10k lt bl & blk	20	15
B91	SP37	40k +10k lt bl & blk	30	25
B92	SP37	75k +10k lt bl & blk	70	60

Inscribed: "Umumi Ziraat Sayimi"
1963, Apr. 14   Photo.   Perf. 11½
Design: 60b+5k, Wheat and chart (horiz.).
| B93 | SP38 | 40k +5k gray grn & yel | 20 | 15 |
| B94 | SP38 | 60k +5k org yel & blk | 25 | 20 |

Issued to publicize the 1961 agricultural census. Two black bars obliterate "Kasim 1960" inscription.

Red Lion and Sun, Red Crescent, Red Cross and Globe—SP39

Designs: 60k+10k, Emblems in flowers (vert.). 100k+10k, Emblems on flags.

1963, Aug. 1   Perf. 13
B95	SP39	50k +10k bl, lt brn, gray & red	30	25
B96	SP39	60k +10k multi	40	35
B97	SP39	100k +10k grn, gray & red	60	50

Centenary of International Red Cross.

Angora Goat   Olympic Torch Bearer
SP40   SP41

Animals: 10k+5k, Steppe cattle (horiz.). 50k+5k, Arabian horses (horiz.). 60k+5k, Three Angora goats. 100k+5k, Montofon cattle (horiz.).

1964, Oct. 4   Litho.   Perf. 13
B98	SP40	10k +5k multi	15	10
B99	SP40	30k +5k multi	20	15
B100	SP40	50k +5k multi	30	20
B101	SP40	60k +5k multi	40	25
B102	SP40	100k +5k multi	50	40
		Nos. B98-B102 (5)	1.55	1.10

Issued for Animal Protection Day.

1964, Oct. 10   Unwmkd.
Designs: 10k+5k, Running (horiz.). 60k +5k, Wrestling. 100k+5k, Discus.
B103	SP41	10k +5k org brn, blk & red	15	15
B104	SP41	50k +5k ol, blk & red	30	25
B105	SP41	60k +5k bl, blk & red	50	35
B106	SP41	100k +5k vio, blk, red & sil	70	60

18th Olympic Games, Tokyo, Oct. 10–25.

Map of Dardanelles and Laurel
SP42

Designs: 90k+10k, Soldiers and war memorial, Canakkale. 130k+10k, Turkish flag and arch (vert.).

1965, Mar. 18   Litho.   Perf. 13
B107	SP42	50k +10k vio, yel & gold	25	20
B108	SP42	90k +10k vio bl, yel & grn	40	35
B109	SP42	130k +10k dk brn, red & yel	75	75

50th anniversary of Battle of Gallipoli.

Tobacco Plant   Goddess, Basalt Carving
SP43   SP44

Designs: 50k+5k, Tobacco leaves and Leander's tower (horiz.). 100k+5k, Tobacco leaf.

1965, Sept. 16   Perf. 13   Unwmkd.
B110	SP43	30k +5k brn, lt blk & grn	30	20
B111	SP43	50k +5k vio bl, ocher & pur	40	30
B112	SP43	100k +5k blk, ol grn & ocher	75	60

Second International Tobacco Congress.

Perf. 13½x13, 13x13½
1966, June 6   Lithographed
Designs (from Archaeological Museum, Ankara): 30k+5k, Eagle and rabbit, ivory carving (horiz.). 60k+5k, Bronze bull. 90k+5k, Gold pitcher.
B113	SP44	30k +5k multi	25	20
B114	SP44	50k +5k multi	40	30
B115	SP44	60k +5k multi	55	40
B116	SP44	90k +5k multi	75	60

Grand Hotel, Ephesus
SP45

Designs: 60k+5k, Konak Square, Izmir (vert.). 130k+5k, Izmir Fair Grounds.

1966, Oct. 18   Litho.   Perf. 12
B117	SP45	50k +5k multi	20	20
B118	SP45	60k +5k multi	35	30
B119	SP45	130k +5k multi	70	50

Issued to publicize the 33rd Congress of the International Fair Association.

Europa Issue, 1967
Common Design Type
1967, May 2   Litho.   Perf. 13x13½
Size: 22x33mm.
B120	CD10	100k +10k multi	60	60
a.		Dark bl ("Europa") omitted		
B121	CD10	130k +10k multi	80	80

Cloverleaf Crossing, Map of Turkey
SP46

Design: 130k+5k, Highway E5 and map of Turkey (vert.).

1967, June 30   Litho.   Perf. 13
| B122 | SP46 | 60k +5k multi | 50 | 40 |
| B123 | SP46 | 130k +5k multi | 95 | 60 |

Inter-European Express Highway, E5.

WHO Emblem
SP47

1968, Apr. 7   Litho.   Perf. 13
| B124 | SP47 | 130k +10k lt ultra, blk & yel | 55 | 40 |

Issued to commemorate the 20th anniversary of the World Health Organization.

Efem Pasha, Dr. Marko Pasha and View of Istanbul
SP48

Designs: 60k+10k, Omer Pasha, Dr. Abdullah Bey and wounded soldiers. 100k+10k, Ataturk and Dr. Refik Say in front of Red Crescent headquarters (vert.).

1968, June 11   Litho.   Perf. 13
B125	SP48	50k +10k multi	40	30
B126	SP48	60k +10k multi	50	40
B127	SP48	100k +10k multi	90	65

Centenary of Turkish Red Crescent Society.

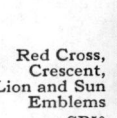

NATO Emblem and Dove
SP49

Design: 130k+10k, NATO emblem and globe surrounded by 15 stars, symbols of the 15 NATO members.

1969, Apr. 4   Litho.   Perf. 13
| B128 | SP49 | 60k +10k brt grn, blk & lt bl | 35 | 30 |
| B129 | SP49 | 130k +10k bluish blk, bl & gold | 75 | 60 |

Issued to commemorate the 20th anniversary of NATO (North Atlantic Treaty Organization).

Red Cross, Crescent, Lion and Sun Emblems
SP50

Design: 130k+10k, Conference emblem and Istanbul skyline.

1969, Aug. 29   Litho.   Perf. 13
| B130 | SP50 | 100k +10k dk & lt bl & red | 50 | 30 |
| B131 | SP50 | 130k +10k red, lt bl & blk | 70 | 50 |

Issued to publicize the 21st International Red Cross Conference in Istanbul.

Erosion Control
SP51

Designs: 60k+10k, Protection of flora (dead tree). 130k+10k, Protection of wildlife (bird of prey).

1970, Feb. 9   Litho.   Perf. 13
B132	SP51	50k +10k multi	40	40
B133	SP51	60k +10k multi	75	75
B134	SP51	130k +10k multi	1.50	1.25

1970 European Nature Conservation Year.

TURKEY

Globe and Fencer
SP52

Design: 130k+10k, Globe, fencer and folk dancer with sword and shield.

1970, Sept. 13   Litho.   Perf. 13
B135 SP52 90k +10k bl & blk   40   30
B136 SP52 130k +10k ultra, lt bl,
           blk & org   60   40

International Fencing Championships.

"Children's Protection"
SP53

Designs: 100k+15k, Hand supporting child (vert.). 110k+15k, Mother and child.

1971, June 30   Litho.   Perf. 13
Star and Crescent Emblem in Red
B137 SP53 50k +10k lil rose & blk   25   20
B138 SP53 100k +15k brn, rose & blk 40   30
B139 SP53 110k +15k org brn, bis
           & blk   50   40

50th anniversary of the Child Protection Association.

UNICEF Emblem   **"Your Heart is your Health"**
SP54   SP55

1971, Dec. 11
B140 SP54 100k +10k multi   40   25
B141 SP54 250k +15k multi   80   60

25th anniversary of UNICEF.

1972, Apr. 7   Litho.   Perf. 13
B142 SP55 250k +25k gray, blk & red 85   60

World Health Day, 1972.

Olympic Emblems, Runners
SP56

Designs: 100k+15k, Olympic rings and motion emblem. 250k+25k, Olympic rings and symbolic track ('72).

1972, Aug. 26
B143 SP56 100k +15k multi   40   25
B144 SP56 110k +15k multi   55   35
B145 SP56 250k +25k multi   80   60

20th Olympic Games, Munich, Aug. 26–Sept. 11.

Emblem of Istanbul Technical University
SP57

1973, Apr. 21   Lithographed   Perf. 13
B146 SP57 100k +25k multi   35   25

Bicentenary of the Istanbul Technical University.

Dove and "50"
SP58

1973, July 24   Litho.   Perf. 12½x13
B147 SP58 100k +25k multi   35   25

Peace Treaty of Lausanne, 50th anniversary.

Population Year Emblem
SP59

1974, June 15   Litho.   Perf. 13
B148 SP59 250k +25k multi   70   50

World Population Year.

Guglielmo Marconi
SP60

1974, Nov. 15   Litho.   Perf. 13½
B149 SP60 250k +25k multi   70   50

Birth centenary of Guglielmo Marconi (1874–1937), Italian electrical engineer and inventor.

Dr. Albert Schweitzer   **Africa with South-West Africa**
SP61   SP62

1975, Jan. 14   Lithographed   Perf. 13
B150 SP61 250k +50k multi   1.00   70

Dr. Albert Schweitzer (1875–1965), medical missionary and music scholar, birth centenary.

1975, Aug. 26   Litho.   Perf. 13x12½
B151 SP62 250k +50k multi   70   50

Namibia Day (independence for South-West Africa).

Ziya Gökalp   **Spoonbill**
SP63   SP64

1976, Mar. 23   Litho.   Perf. 13
B152 SP63 200k +25k multi   40   20

Ziya Gökalp (1876–1924), philosopher, birth centenary.

1976, Nov. 19   Litho.   Perf. 13
Birds: 150k+25k, European roller. 200k+25k, Flamingo. 400k+25k, Hermit ibis (horiz.).
B153 SP64 100k +25k multi   25   20
B154 SP64 150k +25k multi   35   25
B155 SP64 200k +25k multi   60   40
B156 SP64 400k +25k multi   1.00   60

Decree by Mehmet Bey, and Ongun Holy Bird
SP65

1977, May 13   Litho.   Perf. 13
B157 SP65 200k +25k grn & blk   40   30

700th anniversary of Turkish as official language.

Energy Conference Emblem
SP66

Design: 600k+50k, Conference emblem and globe with circles.

1977, Sept. 19   Litho.   Perf. 12½
B158 SP66 100k +25k multi   30   25
B159 SP66 600k +50k multi   1.00   75

10th World Energy Conference.

Running
SP67

Designs: 2½ l+50k, Gymnastics. 5 l+50k, Table tennis. 8 l+50k, Swimming.

1978, July 18   Litho.   Perf. 13
B160 SP67 1 l +50k multi   15   10
B161 SP67 2½ l +50k multi   20   10
B162 SP67 5 l +50k multi   50   20
B163 SP67 8 l +50k multi   75   30

GYMNASIADE '78, World School Games, Izmir.

Ribbon and Chain
SP68

Design: 5 l+50k, Ribbon and flower (vert.).

Perf. 12½x13, 13x12½
1978, Sept. 3   Lithographed
B164 SP68 2½ l +50k multi   40   20
B165 SP68 5 l +50k multi   60   30

European Declaration of Human Rights, 25th anniversary.

Children, Head of Ataturk
SP69

Designs (IYC Emblem and): 5 l+50k, Children with globe as balloon. 8 l+50k, Kneeling person and child, globe.

1979, Apr. 23   Litho.   Perf. 13x13½
B166 SP69 2½ l +50k multi   30   12
B167 SP69 5 l +50k multi   50   20
B168 SP69 8 l +50k multi   80   40

International Year of the Child.

Black Francolin—SP70

Designs: No. B170, Great bustard. No. B171, Crane. No. B172, Gazelle. No. B173, Mouflon muffelwild.

1979, Dec. 3   Litho.   Perf. 13x13½
B169 SP70 5 l +1 l multi   40   20
B170 SP70 5 l +1 l multi   40   20
B171 SP70 5 l +1 l multi   40   20
B172 SP70 5 l +1 l multi   40   20
B173 SP70 5 l +1 l multi   40   20
     Nos. B169-B173 (5)   2.00 1.00

European Wildlife Conservation Year. Nos. B169-B173 se-tenant in continuous design.

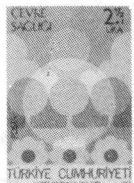

Flowers, Trees and Sun—SP71

Environment Protection: 7½ l+1 l, Sun, water. 15 l+1 l, Industrial pollution, globe. 20 l+1 l, Flower in oil puddle.

1980, June 4   Litho.   Perf. 13
B174 SP71 2½ l +1 l multi   10   8
B175 SP71 7½ l +1 l multi   25   15
B176 SP71 15 l +1 l multi   45   30
B177 SP71 20 l +1 l multi   55   35

Rodolia Cardinalis—SP72

Useful Insects: 7½ l + 1 l, Bracon hebetor; 15 l + 1 l, Calosoma sycophanta; 20 l + 1 l, Deraeocoris rutilus.

1980, Dec. 3   Litho.   Perf. 13
B178 SP72 2½ l +1 l multi   6   5
B179 SP72 7½ l +1 l multi   12   6
B180 SP72 15 l +1 l multi   22   10
B181 SP72 20 l +1 l multi   28   15

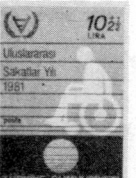

Intl. Year of the Disabled—SP73

1981, Mar. 25   Litho.   Perf. 13
B182 SP73 10 l + 2½ l multi   18   10
B183 SP73 20 l + 2½ l multi   30   15

Insect Type of 1980

Useful Insects: 10 1 + 2½ 1, Cicindela campestris. 20 1 + 2½ 1, Syrphus vitripennis. 30 1 + 2½ 1, Ascalaphus macaronius. 40 1 + 2½ 1, Empusa fasciata. Nos. B184-B187 horiz.

1981, Dec. 16 Litho. Perf. 13

B184	SP72	10 + 2½ l multi	15	8
B185	SP72	20 + 2½ l multi	25	14
B186	SP72	30 + 2½ l multi	35	20
B187	SP72	40 + 2½ l multi	45	30

TB Bacillus Centenary—SP74

Portraits of Robert Koch.

1982, Mar. 24 Perf. 13x12½

B188	SP74	10 + 2½ l multi	15	8
B189	SP74	30 + 2½ l multi	35	20

Insect Type of 1980

Useful Insects: 10 + 2½ 1, Eurydema spectabile. 15 + 2½ 1, Dacus oleae. 20 + 2½ 1, Klapperichicen viridissima. 30 + 2½ 1, Leptinotarsa decemlineata. 35 + 2½ 1, Rhynchites auratus. Horiz.

1982, Aug. 18 Litho. Perf. 13

B190	SP72	10 + 2½ l multi	15	8
B191	SP72	15 + 2½ l multi	20	10
B192	SP72	20 + 2½ l multi	25	14
B193	SP72	30 + 2½ l multi	35	20
B194	SP72	35 + 2½ l multi	40	25
	Nos. B190-B194 (5)		1.35	77

Richard Wagner (1813-1883), Composer—SP75

1983, Feb. 13

B195	SP75	30 l + 5 l multi	35	22

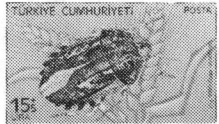

Eurygaster Intergriceps Put—SP76

Harmful Insects 25+5l, Phyllobius nigrofasciatus Pes. 35+5l, Cercopis intermedia Kbm. 50+10l, Graphosoma lineatum (L). 75+10l, Capnodis miliaris (King).

1983, Sept. 14 Litho. Perf. 13

B196	SP76	15 + 5l multi	20	10
B197	SP76	25 + 5l multi	30	15
B198	SP76	35 + 5l multi	40	20
B199	SP76	50 + 10l multi	60	30
B200	SP76	75 + 10l multi	85	45
	Nos. B196-B200 (5)		2.35	1.20

TURKEY

AIR POST STAMPS.
Regular Issue of 1930 Overprinted or Surcharged in Brown or Blue:

		1934, July 15	Perf. 12	Unwmkd.	
C1	A74	7½k red brn (Br)		25	15
C2	A72	12½k on 15k dp org (Br)		35	20
C3	A74	20k on 25k ol brn (Br)		40	30
C4	A74	25k ol brn (Bl)		60	40
C5	A74	40k red vio (Br)		1.25	1.00
		Nos. C1-C5 (5)		2.85	2.05

Regular Stamps of 1930 Surcharged in Brown

		1937			
C6	A74	4½k on 7½k red brn		1.50	1.00
C7	A72	9k on 15k dp org		40.00	35.00
C8	A74	35k on 40k red vio		7.50	7.00

Regular Stamps of 1930 Surcharged in Black

		1941, Dec. 18			
C9	A74	4½k on 25k ol brn		1.50	1.00
C10	A75	9k on 200k dk grn & blk	8.00	6.50
C11	A75	35k on 500k choc & blk	6.00	5.00

Plane over Izmir—AP1

Designs: 5k, 40k, Plane over Izmir. 20k, 50k, Plane over Ankara. 30k, 1 l, Plane over Istanbul.

		1949, Jan. 1	Photo.	Perf. 11½	
C12	AP1	5k gray & vio		10	10
C13	AP1	20k bl gray & brn		45	10

C14	AP1	30k bl gray & ol brn	60	20
C15	AP1	40k bl & dp ultra	80	20
C16	AP1	50k gray vio & red brn	90	40
C17	AP1	1 l gray bl & dk grn	1.50	1.00
		Nos. C12-C17 (6)	4.35	2.00

Plane Over Rumeli Hisari Fortress
AP2

		1950, May 19		Unwmkd.	
C18	AP2	2½ l gray bl & dk grn		20.00	16.50

Nos. C12, C14 and C16 Overprinted in Red
SANAYI KONGRESI
9-NISAN-1951

		1951, Apr. 9		Perf. 11½	
C19	AP1	5k gray & vio		1.00	80
C20	AP1	30k bl gray & ol brn		1.25	1.00
C21	AP1	50k gray vio & red brn		1.50	1.25

Issued to publicize the Industrial Congress at Ankara, April 9, 1951.

Yesilkoy Airport and Plane
AP3

Designs: 20k, 45k, Yesilkoy Airport and plane in flight. 35k, 55k, Ankara Airport and plane. 40k, as No. C22.

		1954, Nov. 1	Perf. 14	
		Designs in Blue		
C22	AP3	5k red brn	40	15
C23	AP3	20k brn org	15	8
C24	AP3	35k dk grn	20	10
C25	AP3	40k dp car	20	10
C26	AP3	45k violet	40	30
C27	AP3	55k black	75	40
		Nos. C22-C27 (6)	2.10	1.13

Symbol of Izmir Fair
AP4
Lithographed.

		1956, Aug. 20	Perf. 10½	Unwmkd.	
C28	AP4	25k redsh brn		20	15

Issued to commemorate the 25th International Fair at Izmir, Aug. 20–Sept. 20.

Type of Regular Issue, 1957.
1957, May 5
C29	A264	40k sal pink & mag	20	15

Visit of Pres. Heuss of Germany.

Type of Regular Issue, 1957
1957, Sept. 1
C30	A269	25k grn & lt grn	15	10

Visit of Mohammed Zahir Shah, King of Afghanistan, to Turkey.

Hawk Crane
AP5 AP6

Birds: 40k, 125k, Swallows. 65k, Cranes. 85k, 195k, Gulls. 245k, Hawk.
Lithographed.

		1959, Aug. 13	Perf. 10½	Unwmkd.	
C31	AP5	40k brt lil		20	10
C32	AP5	65k bl grn		30	20
C33	AP5	85k brt bl		40	20
C34	AP5	105k yel & sep		40	20
C35	AP6	125k brt vio		60	25
C36	AP6	155k yel grn		80	20
C37	AP6	195k vio bl		80	50
C38	AP6	245k brn & brn org		1.60	90
		Nos. C31-C38 (8)		5.10	2.75

De Havilland
Rapide Biplane Kestrel
AP7 AP8

Designs: 60k, Fokker Friendship transport plane. 130k, DC9-30. 220k, DC-3. 270k, Viscount 794.

		1967, July 13	Litho.	Perf. 13½x13	
C39	AP7	10k pink & blk		40	7
C40	AP7	60k lt grn, red & blk		40	10
C41	AP7	130k bl, blk & red		90	20
C42	AP7	220k lt brn, blk & red		1.25	40
C43	AP7	270k org, blk & red		1.75	55
		Nos. C39-C43 (5)		4.70	1.32

1967, Oct. 10 Litho. Perf. 13
Birds: 60k, Golden eagle. 130k, Falcon. 220k, Sparrow hawk. 270k, Buzzard.

C44	AP8	10k brn & sal	40	5
C45	AP8	60k brn & yel	50	10
C46	AP8	130k brn & lt bl	1.00	15
C47	AP8	220k brn & lt grn	1.75	40
C48	AP8	270k org brn & gray	2.25	60
		Nos. C44-C48 (5)	5.90	1.30

F-104 Jet Plane
AP9

Turkish Air Force Emblem and Jets
AP10

Designs: 200k, Victory monument, Afyon, and Jets. 325k, F-104 jets and pilot. 400k, Bleriot XI plane with Turkish flag. 475k, Flight of Hezarfen Ahmet Celebi from Galata Tower to Usküdar.

		1971, June 1 Lithographed	Perf. 13	
C49	AP9	110k multi	40	15
C50	AP9	200k multi	60	25
C51	AP10	250k gold & multi	1.00	20
C52	AP9	325k multi	1.40	45
C53	AP10	400k multi	1.75	40
C54	AP10	475k multi	2.25	70
		Nos. C49-C54 (6)	7.40	2.15

The gold ink on No. C51 is applied by a thermographic process which gives a raised and shiny effect.

F-28 Plane
AP11

Design: 250k, DC-10.

		1973, Dec. 11	Litho.	Perf. 13	
C55	AP11	110k blk, bl & red		30	20
C56	AP11	250k blk, bl & red		60	40

POSTAGE DUE STAMPS.
Same Types as Regular Issues of Corresponding Dates.

1863 Imperf. Unwmkd.
Blue Band.

J1	A1	20pa red brn	70.00	30.00
a.		Tête bêche pair	325.00	325.00
b.		Without band	40.00	
c.		Red band	95.00	45.00
J2	A2	1pi red brn	80.00	40.00
a.		Tête bêche pair	325.00	325.00
b.		Without band	40.00	
J3	A3	2pi red brn	200.00	75.00
a.		Tête bêche pair	1,000.	700.00
J4	A4	5pi red brn	140.00	70.00
a.		Tête bêche pair	650.00	650.00
b.		Without band	100.00	
c.		Red band	130.00	

1865 Perf. 12½.

J6	A5	20pa brown	20	30
J7	A5	1pi brown	20	20
b.		Half used as 20pa on cover		
c.		Printed on both sides	25.00	
J8	A5	2pi brown	80	1.00
a.		Half used as 1pi on cover		
J9	A5	5pi brown	60	60
a.		Half used as 2½pi on cover		
J10	A5	25pi brown	12.00	12.00

The 10pa brown is an essay. Exist imperf. Prices, $60 to $100.

1867

J11	A5	20pa bis brn	2.50	12.50
J12	A5	1pi bis brn	1.50	
a.		With surcharge of 5pi	20.00	
b.		Imperf., pair	100.00	
J13	A5	2pi fawn	9.00	
J14	A5	5pi fawn	7.00	
J15	A5	25pi bis brn	3,500.	

Nos. J12–J15 were not placed in use.

1869 Perf. 13½.
With Red Brown Border.

J16	A5	20pa bis brn	3.00	1.50
a.		Without surcharge		

TURKEY 833

J17	A5	1pi bis brn	125.00	6.00
a.		Without surcharge		
J18	A5	2pi bis brn	175.00	7.00
J19	A5	5pi bis brn	40	1.00
b.		Without border		
c.		Printed on both sides	20.00	
J20	A5	25pi bis brn	15.00	17.50

With Black Brown Border

J21	A5	20pa bis brn	25.00	12.50
a.		Inverted surcharge		
b.		Without surcharge		
J22	A5	1pi bis brn	175.00	17.50
a.		Without surcharge		
J23	A5	2pi bis brn	275.00	25.00
b.		Inverted surcharge		
J24	A5	5pi bis brn	20	1.25
b.		Without surcharge		
J25	A5	25pi bis brn	17.50	30.00

1871 *Pin-perf., Perf. 5 to 11 and Compound*

With Red Brown Border.

J26	A5	20pa bis brn	85.00	15.00
J27	A5	1pi bis brn		500.00
J28	A5	2pi bis brn	15.00	9.00
J29	A5	5pi bis brn	75	2.50

With Black Brown Border

J31	A5	20pa bis brn	17.50	75
a.		Half used as 10pa on cover		
b.		Imperf., pair		25.00
c.		Printed on both sides	60.00	60.00
J32	A5	1pi bis brn	20.00	50
a.		Half used as 20pa on cover		
c.		Inverted surcharge	75.00	50.00
d.		Printed on both sides		
J33	A5	2pi bis brn	40	80
a.		Half used as 1pi on cover		
c.		Imperf., pair		25.00
J34	A5	5pi bis brn	10	1.00
a.		Half used as 2½pi on cover		
c.		Printed on both sides		
J35	A5	25pi bis brn	12.50	15.00
a.		Inverted surchage		

1888 *Perf. 11½ and 13½.*

J36	A7	20pa black	15	30
a.		Imperf.	22.50	
J37	A7	1pi black	20	30
a.		Imperf.	22.50	
J38	A7	2pi black	20	30
a.		Imperf.	22.50	
b.		Diagonal half used as 1pi		

1892 *Perf. 13½.*

J39	A11	20pa black	80	40
J40	A12	1pi black	1.25	60
a.		Printed on both sides		
J41	A13	2pi black	70	60

1901

J42	A11	20pa *dp rose*	20	20

1901

J43	A17	10pa *dp rose*	80	40
J44	A17	20pa *dp rose*	60	40
J45	A17	1pi *dp rose*	30	25
J46	A17	2pi *dp rose*	30	25

1905 *Perf. 12*

J47	A18	1pi *dp rose*	70	50
J48	A18	2pi *dp rose*	80	70

The so-called overprint "T" in circle on postage stamps of 1905 is a cancellation.

1908 *Perf. 12, 13½ and Compound.*

J49	A19	1pi *dp rose*	3.50	70
J50	A19	2pi *dp rose*	50	90

1909

J51	A21	1pi *dp rose*	1.50	1.50
J52	A21	2pi *dp rose*	35.00	30.00
a.		Imperf.	100.00	

1913 *Perf. 12.*

J53	A22	2pa *dp rose*	10	8
J54	A22	5pa *dp rose*	10	8
J55	A22	10pa *dp rose*	10	8
J56	A22	20pa *dp rose*	10	8
J57	A22	1pi *dp rose*	1.00	80
J58	A22	2pi *dp rose*	2.50	1.75
		Nos. J53-J58 (6)	3.90	2.87

Adrianople Issue.

Nos. 251-253 Surcharged in Black, Blue or Red

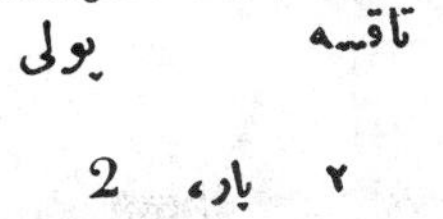

1913

J59	A23	2pa on 10pa grn (Bk)	40	20
J60	A23	5pa on 20pa red (Bl)	60	40
J61	A23	10pa on 40pa bl (R)	1.00	80
J62	A23	20pa on 40pa bl (Bk)	3.00	1.60

D1 D2

D3 D4

1914 Engraved.

J63	D1	5pa claret	40	30
J64	D2	20pa red	40	30
J65	D3	1pi dk bl	70	40
J66	D4	2pi slate	1.50	1.00

Nos. J59 to J62 Surcharged in Red or Black

1916

J67	A23	10pa on 2pa on 10pa grn (R)	15.00	15.00
J68	A23	20pa on 5pa on 20pa red (Bk)	15.00	15.00
J69	A23	40pa on 10pa on 40pa bl (Bk)	15.00	15.00
J70	A23	40pa on 20pa on 40pa bl (R)	15.00	15.00

Preceding Issues Overprinted in Red, Black or Blue

1917

On Stamps of 1865.

J71	A5	20pa red brn (Bl)	20.00	20.00
J72	A5	1pi red brn (Bl)	20.00	20.00
J73	A5	2pi bis brn (Bl)	20.00	20.00
J74	A5	5pi bis brn (Bl)	20.00	20.00
J75	A5	25pi dk brn (Bl)	20.00	20.00

On Stamp of 1869.

Red Brown Border.

J76	A5	5pi bis brn (R)	20.00	20.00

On Stamp of 1871.

Black Brown Border.

J77	A5	5pi bis brn	60.00	60.00

On Stamps of 1888.

J78	A7	1pi blk (R)	20.00	20.00
J79	A7	2pi blk (R)	20.00	20.00

On Stamps of 1892.

J80	A11	20pa blk (R)	1.00	1.00
J81	A12	1pi blk (R)	1.00	1.00
J82	A13	2pi blk (R)	1.00	75

Adrianople Issue.

On Nos. J59 to J62 with Addition of New Value.

J83	A23	10pa on 2pa on 10pa grn (R)	45	45
J84	A23	20pa on 5pa on 20pa red (Bk)	45	45
J85	A23	40pa on 10pa on 40pa bl (Bk)	75	45
a.		"40pa" double		
J86	A23	40pa on 20pa on 40pa bl (R)	1.00	75

Nos. J71–J86 were used as regular postage stamps.

Armistice Issue.

No. J65 Overprinted

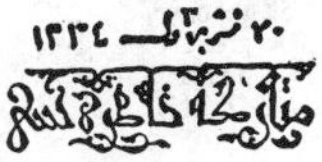

1919, Nov. 30

J87	D3	1pi dk bl	47.50	47.50

Accession to the Throne Issue

Postage Due Stamps of 1914 Overprinted in Turkish "Accession to the Throne of His Majesty, 3rd July, 1334-1918."

1919

J88	D1	10pa on 5pa cl	7.50	7.50
J89	D2	20pa red	7.50	7.50
J90	D3	1pi dk bl	7.50	7.50
J91	D4	2pi slate	7.50	7.50

Railroad Bridge over Kizil Irmak D5 — Kemal Atatürk D6

1926 Engraved.

J92	D5	20pa ocher	60	40
J93	D5	1g red	80	50
J94	D5	2g bl grn	1.00	70
J95	D5	3g lil brn	1.00	90
J96	D5	5g lilac	1.75	1.40
		Nos. J92-J96 (5)	5.15	3.90

1936 Lithographed. *Perf. 11½.*

J97	D6	20pa brown	5	5
J98	D6	2k lt bl	8	5
J99	D6	3k brt vio	10	6
J100	D6	5k Prus bl	20	10
J101	D6	12k brt rose	45	40
		Nos. J97-J101 (5)	88	66

Surcharged stamps, type D6, are listed as Nos. 1461-1465.

Local Issues.

During the years 1869-82 Turkish stamps with the above overprints were used for local postage in Constantinople and Mount Athos.

MILITARY STAMPS.

For the Army in Thessaly.

Tughra and Bridge at Larissa
M1

1898, Apr. 21 *Perf. 13* Unwmkd.

M1	M1	10pa yel grn	3.00	2.00
M2	M1	20pa rose	3.00	2.00
M3	M1	1pi dk bl	3.00	2.00
M4	M1	2pi orange	3.00	2.00
M5	M1	5pi violet	3.00	2.00
		Nos. M1-M5 (5)	15.00	10.00

Issued for Turkish occupation forces to use in Thessaly during the Greco-Turkish War of 1897–98.

Forgeries of Nos. M1–M5 are perf. 11½.

OFFICIAL STAMPS.

O1

Perf. 10 to 12 and Compound

1948 Typographed Unwmkd.

O1	O1	10pa rose brn	5	5
O2	O1	1k gray grn	5	5
O3	O1	2k rose vio	10	5
O4	O1	3k orange	20	5
O5	O1	5k blue	6.00	5
O6	O1	10k brn org	4.00	5
O7	O1	15k violet	1.25	5
O8	O1	20k dk bl	1.25	5
O9	O1	30k ol bis	1.75	10
O10	O1	50k black	1.50	6
O11	O1	1 l bluish grn	2.00	10
O12	O1	2 l lil rose	3.50	20
		Nos. O1-O12 (12)	21.65	86

Regular Issue of 1948 Overprinted

Type "a" in Black

a

1951

O13	A178	5k blue	20	18
O14	A178	10k chocolate	35	5
O15	A178	20k dp bl	70	10
O16	A178	30k brown	1.00	15

Overprint "a" is 15½mm. wide. Points of crescent do not touch star. The 0.25ku (No. 963) exists with overprint "a" but its status is questionable.

b c

Overprinted Type "b" in Dark Brown

1953

O17	A178	0.25k dk red	10	5
O18	A178	5k blue	25	5
O19	A178	10k chocolate	40	5
O20	A178	15k violet	70	5
O21	A178	20k dp bl	2.00	10
O22	A178	30k brown	1.00	12
O23	A178	60k black	1.50	20
		Nos. O17-O23 (7)	5.95	62

Overprint "b" is 14mm. wide. Lettering thin with sharp, clean corners.

834 TURKEY

Overprinted Type "c" in Black and Green Black

1953–54

O23A	A178	0.25k dk red (G Bk) ('53)	8	8
f.		Black overprint	50	50
g.		Violet overprint ('53)	30	30
O23B	A178	10k chocolate	5.00	1.00
O23C	A178	15k violet	5.00	50
O23D	A178	30k brown	3.00	1.00
O23E	A178	60k black	4.50	1.00
		Nos. O23A-O23E (5)	17.58	3.58

Lettering of type "c" heavy with rounded corners.

Small Star

d

Large Star

e

Overprinted or Surcharged Type "d" in Black

1955–56

O24	A178	0.25k dk red	5	5
O25	A178	1k ol blk	8	5
O26	A178	2k brt rose lil	5	5
O27	A178	3k red org	5	5
O28	A178	4k dk grn	6	5
O29	A178	5k on 15k vio	6	5
O31	A178	10k on 15k vio	12	5
O32	A178	15k violet	12	5
O33	A178	20k dp bl	22	8
O35	A179	40k on 1 l ol grn	38	10
O36	A179	75k on 2 l dk brn	1.00	75
O37	A179	75k on 5 l dp plum	5.00	5.00

Type "d" is 15x16mm. wide. Overprint on Nos. O35–O37 measures 19x22mm. Nos. O29, O31 and O35–O37 have two bars and new value added.

Overprinted or Surcharged Type "e" in Black

1955

O25a	A178	1k ol blk	5	5
O29a	A178	5k on 15k vio	10	5
O30	A178	5k blue	65	7
O31a	A178	10k on 15k vio	75	20
c.		"10" without serif	14	5
O33a	A178	20k dp bl	50	5
O34	A178	30k brown	90	8

Heavy crescent

f

Thin crescent

g

Overprinted or Surcharged Type "f" in Black

1957

O24b	A178	0.25k dk red	25	25
O38b	A178	½k on 1k ol blk	5	5
O25b	A178	1k ol blk	8	5
O31b	A178	10k on 15k vio	50	50
O35b	A179	75k on 1 l ol grn	1.00	25

Type "f" crescent is larger and does not touch wavy line. The surcharged "10" on No. O31b exists only without serifs. The overprint on O35b measures 17x22½mm.

Overprinted or Surcharged Type "g" in Black

1957

O38	A178	½k on 1 k ol blk	5	5
O39	A178	1k ol blk	5	5
O40	A178	2k on 4k dk grn	5	5
O41	A178	3k on 4k dk grn	5	5
O42	A178	10k on 12 k dp red	5	5
		Nos. O38-O42 (5)	2.13	1.35

The shape of crescent and star on type "g" varies on each value. Overprint measures 14x18mm. The surcharged stamps have two bars and new value added.

O2

O3

O4

1957 Lithographed. *Perf. 10½*

O43	O2	5k blue	5	5
O44	O2	10k org brn	5	5
O45	O2	15k lt vio	5	5
O46	O2	20k red	8	5
O47	O2	30k gray ol	12	5
O48	O2	40k brn vio	15	5
O49	O2	50k grnsh blk	18	5
O50	O2	60k lt yel grn	25	5
O51	O2	75k yel org	45	5
O52	O2	100k green	55	12
O53	O2	200k dp rose	1.10	40
		Nos. O43-O53 (11)	3.03	97

1959 *Perf. 10* Unwmkd.

O54	O2	5k rose	5	5
O55	O2	10k ol grn	5	5
O56	O2	15k car rose	8	5
O57	O2	20k lilac	8	5
O58	O2	40k blue	15	5
O59	O2	60k orange	25	5
O60	O2	75k gray	50	15
O61	O2	100k violet	70	25
O62	O2	200k red brn	1.25	60
		Nos. O54-O62 (9)	3.11	1.30

1960 Lithographed *Perf. 10½*

O63	O3	1k orange	5	5
O64	O3	5k vermilion	5	5
O65	O3	10k gray grn	45	5
O67	O3	30k red brn	15	5
O70	O3	60k green	30	5
O71	O3	1 l rose lil	40	10
O72	O3	1½ l brt ultra	1.25	10
O74	O3	2½ l violet	1.75	50
O75	O3	5 l blue	3.00	1.25
		Nos. O63-O75 (9)	7.40	2.20

1962 Typographed *Perf. 13*

O76	O4	1k ol bis	5	5
O77	O4	5k brt grn	5	5
O78	O4	10k red brn	5	5
O79	O4	15k dk bl	5	5
O80	O4	25k carmine	14	5
O81	O4	30k ultra	20	10
		Nos. O76-O81 (6)	54	35

Nos. O81 and O70 Surcharged

1963

O82	O4	50k on 30k ultra	40	10

Lithographed
Perf. 10½

O83	O3	100k on 60k grn	50	10

O5

O6

O7

1963 Lithographed *Perf. 12½*

O84	O5	1k gray	5	5
O85	O5	5k salmon	5	5
O86	O5	10k green	5	5
O87	O5	50k car rose	20	5
O88	O5	100k ultra	55	10
		Nos. O84-O88 (5)	90	30

1964 *Perf. 12½* Unwmkd.

O89	O6	1k gray	5	5
O90	O6	5k blue	5	5
O91	O6	10k yellow	5	5
O92	O6	30k red	12	5
O93	O6	50k lt grn	20	5
O94	O6	60k brown	22	6
O95	O6	80k pale grnsh bl	36	8
O96	O6	130k indigo	80	20
O97	O6	200k lilac	1.10	10
		Nos. O89-O97 (9)	2.95	69

1965 Litho. *Perf. 13*

O98	O7	1k emerald	5	5
O99	O7	10k ultra	5	5
O100	O7	50k orange	25	10

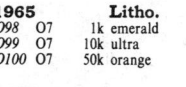

Usak Carpet Design

O8

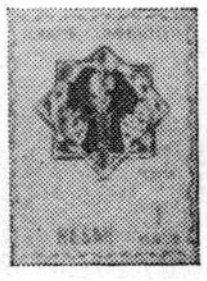

Seljuk Tile, 13th Century

O9

Leaf Design

O10

Carpet designs: 50k, Bergama. 100k, Ladik. 150k, Seljuk. 200k, Nomad. 500k, Anatolia.

1966 Lithographed *Perf. 13*

O101	O8	1k orange	5	5
O102	O8	50k green	20	5
O103	O8	100k brt pink	35	10
O104	O8	150k vio bl	55	15
O105	O8	200k ol bis	80	20
O106	O8	500k lilac	2.25	65
		Nos. O101-O106 (6)	4.20	1.20

1967 Lithographed *Perf 11½x12*

O107	O9	1k dk bl & lt bl	5	5
O108	O9	50k org & dk bl	17	5
O109	O9	100k lil & dk bl	35	10

1968 Lithographed *Perf. 13*

O110	O10	50k brn & lt grn	20	5
O111	O10	150k blk & dl yel	60	10
O112	O10	500k red brn & lt bl	2.00	30

O11

O12

O13

1969, Aug. 25 Litho. *Perf. 13*

O113	O11	1k lt grn & red	5	5
O114	O11	10k lt grn & bl	5	5
O115	O11	50k lt grn & brn	15	5
O116	O11	100k lt grn & red	35	15

1971, Mar. 1 Litho. *Perf. 11½x12*

O117	O12	5k brn & bl	5	5
O118	O12	10k vio bl & ver	5	5
O119	O12	30k org & vio bl	20	5
O120	O12	50k Prus bl & sep	30	15
O121	O12	75k yel & grn	50	20
		Nos. O117-O121 (5)	1.10	50

1971, Nov. 15 Litho. *Perf. 11½x12*

O122	O13	5k lt bl & gray	5	5
O123	O13	25k cit & lt brn	7	5
O124	O13	100k org & ol	30	5
O125	O13	200k dk brn & bis	65	5
O126	O13	250k rose lil & vio	95	15
O127	O13	500k dk bl & brt bl	1.50	70
		Nos. O122-O127 (6)	3.52	1.05

O14

O15

O16

1972, Apr. 7 Litho. *Perf. 13*

O128	O14	5k buff & bl	5	5
O129	O14	100k buff & ol	30	5
O130	O14	200k buff & car	60	20

1973, Sept 20 Litho. *Perf. 13*

O131	O15	100k vio & buff	30	10

1974, June 17 Litho. *Perf. 13½x13*

O132	O16	10k sal pink & brn	5	5
O133	O16	25k bl & dk brn	5	5
O134	O16	50k brt pink & brn	10	5
O135	O16	150k lt grn & brn	30	8
O136	O16	250k rose & brn	50	20
O137	O16	500k yel & brn	1.00	40
		Nos. O132-O137 (6)	2.00	83

O17

1975, Nov. 5 Litho. *Perf. 12½x13*

O138	O17	100k lt bl & mar	16	5

Nos. O84, O89, O98, O101, O107 Surcharged in Red or Black

Perf. 12½, 13, 11½x12

1977, Aug. 17 Lithographed

O139	O5	5k on 1k gray	5	5
O140	O6	5k on 1k gray	5	5
O141	O7	5k on 1k emer	5	5
O142	O8	5k on 1k org (B)	5	5
O143	O9	5k on 1k dk & lt bl	5	5
		Nos. O139-O143 (5)	25	25

O18

O19

1977, Dec. 29 Litho. *Perf. 13½x13*

O144	O18	250k lt bl & grn	30	30

1978 Photogravure *Perf. 13½*

O145	O19	50k pink & rose	8	5
O146	O19	2½ l buff & grnsh blk	25	15
O147	O19	4½ l lil rose & sl grn	45	15
O148	O19	5 l lt bl & pur	50	15
O149	O19	10 l lt grn & grn	1.00	20
O150	O19	25 l yel & red	2.50	40
		Nos. O145-O150 (6)	4.78	1.10

O20

1979 Litho. *Perf. 13½*

O151	O20	50k dp org & brn	8	5
O152	O20	2½ l bl & dk bl	20	5

O21

1979, Dec. 20 Litho. *Perf. 13½*

O153	O21	50k sal & dk bl	5	5
O154	O21	1 l lt grn & red	5	5
O155	O21	2½ l lil rose & red	10	5
O156	O21	5 l lt bl & mag	20	10
O157	O21	7½ l lt lil & dk bl	30	10
O158	O21	10 l yel & dk bl	40	10
O159	O21	35 l gray & rose ('81)	35	15
O160	O21	50 l pnksh & dk bl ('81)	50	20
		Nos. O153-O160 (8)	1.95	80

TURKEY

NEWSPAPER STAMPS.

N1

Black Overprint.
1879   *Perf. 11½ and 13½*   Unwmkd.
P1   N1   10pa blk & rose lil   80.00   60.00

Other stamps found with this "IMPRIMES" overprint were prepared on private order and have no official status as newspaper stamps.
Counterfeits exist of No. P1.

N2

The 10pa surcharge, type N2, on half of 20pa rose and pale rose was made privately. See note after No. 77.

Regular Issue of 1890 Handstamped in Black.

There are two types of this handstamp, varying slightly in size.

1891   *Perf. 13½, 11½*
P10	A7	10pa grn & gray	9.00	7.00
a.		Imperf.	45.00	25.00
P11	A7	20pa rose & gray	12.00	8.00
P12	A7	1pi bl & gray	45.00	27.50
P13	A7	2pi yel & gray	200.00	80.00
P14	A7	5pi buff & gray	425.00	225.00

Blue Handstamp
P10b	A7	10pa grn & gray	50.00	7.00
P11a	A7	20pa rose & gray	50.00	8.00
P12a	A7	1pi bl & gray	225.00	45.00

This overprint in red and on 2pi and 5pi in blue is considered bogus.

Same Handstamp on Regular Issue of 1892.
1892   *Perf. 13½.*
P25	A10	10pa gray grn	50.00	9.00
P26	A11	20pa rose	85.00	40.00
P27	A12	1pi pale bl	25.00	15.00
P28	A13	2pi brn org	27.50	15.00
P29	A14	5pi pale vio	300.00	200.00
a.		On #99a	1,000.	

The handstamps on Nos. P10-P29 are found double, inverted and sideways.
Counterfeit overprints are plentiful.

Regular Issues of 1892-98 Overprinted in Black
1893-98
P30	A10	10pa gray grn	20	20
P31	A11	20pa vio brn ('98)	30	30
a.		20pa dk pink	40	40
b.		20pa pale	22.50	3.00
P32	A12	1pi pale bl	20	20
P33	A13	2pi brn org	7.00	2.50
a.		Tete beche pair		35.00
P34	A14	5pi pale vio	25.00	10.00
a.		On #99a	200.00	100.00
		Nos. P30-P34 (5)	32.60	13.10

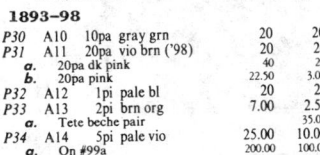

N3

1897   Black Surcharge.
P36	N3	5pa on 10pa gray grn	20	10
a.		"Cniq" instead of "Cinq"	15.00	15.00

Nos. 102-107 Overprinted in Black 
Perf. 12, 13½ and Compound.

1901
P37	A16	5pa bister	20	15
a.		Inverted overprint	80	60
P38	A16	10pa yel grn	80	60
P39	A16	20pa magenta	2.25	1.50
P40	A16	1pi vio bl	4.00	1.85
P41	A16	2pi gray bl	25.00	15.00
P42	A16	5pi ocher	40.00	20.00
		Nos. P37-P42 (6)	72.25	39.10

Same Overprint on Nos. 110-115
1901
P43	A17	5pa purple	40	15
P44	A17	10pa green	2.50	22
P45	A17	20pa carmine	25	12
a.		Overprinted on back	2.00	40
P46	A17	1pi blue	2.00	40
P47	A17	2pi orange	12.00	2.00
a.		Inverted overprint		
P48	A17	5pi lil rose	17.50	11.00
		Nos. P43-P48 (6)	34.65	13.89

Same Overprint on Regular Issue of 1905.
1905
P49	A18	5pa ocher	15	5
P50	A18	10pa dl grn	3.25	1.25
P51	A18	20pa carmine	40	8
P52	A18	1pi pale bl	25	8
P53	A18	2pi slate	12.50	3.50
P54	A18	5pi brown	12.50	6.00
		Nos. P49-P54 (6)	29.05	10.96

Regular Issue of 1908 Overprinted in Carmine or Blue 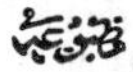
1908
P55	A19	5pa ocher (Bl)	2.25	18
P56	A19	10pa bl grn (C)	2.25	18
P57	A19	20pa car (Bl)	3.00	1.00
P58	A19	1pi brt bl (C)	5.00	1.50
P59	A19	2pi bl blk (C)	20.00	3.50
P60	A19	5pi dk vio (C)	20.00	5.50
		Nos. P55-P60 (6)	52.50	11.86

Same Overprint on Regular Issue of 1909.
1909
P61	A21	5pa ocher (Bl)	80	20
a.		Imperf.		
P62	A21	10pa bl grn (C)	1.25	25
P63	A21	20pa car rose (Bl)	9.00	1.50
a.		Imperf.		
P64	A21	1pi brt bl (C)	14.00	4.25
P65	A21	2pi bl blk (C)	35.00	17.50
P66	A21	5pi dk vio (C)	35.00	17.50
		Nos. P61-P66 (6)	95.05	41.20

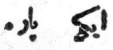

No. 151 Surcharged in Blue

Perf. 12, 13½ and Compound.
1910
| P67 | A21 | 2pa on 5pa ocher | 20 | 10 |

1911   *Perf. 12.*
| P68 | A21 | 2pa ol grn | 6 | 5 |

Newspaper Stamps of 1901-11 Overprinted in Carmine or Blue

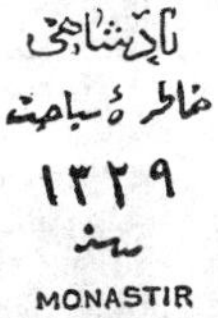

MONASTIR

The overprint was applied to 13 denominations in four settings with change of city name, producing individual sets for each city: "MONASTIR," "PRISTINA," "SALONIKA," and "USKUB."

1911   *Perf. 12, 13½*
P69	A16	5pa bister	2.50
P70	A16	10pa yel grn	2.50
P71	A16	20pa magenta	2.50
P72	A16	1pi vio bl	3.25
P73	A16	2pi gray bl	4.00
P74	A16	5pi ocher	6.50
P75	A17	5pa purple	2.50
P76	A17	10pa green	2.50
P77	A17	20pa carmine	2.50
P78	A17	1pi blue	3.25
P79	A17	2pi orange	4.00
P80	A17	5pi lil rose	6.50
P81	A21	5pa ocher	1.00
		Nos. P69-P81 (13)	43.50

Prices for each of the 4 city sets of 13 are as printed.
The note after No. 182 will also apply to Nos. P69-P81.

Preceding Newspaper Issues with additional Overprint in Carmine or Black

1915
On Stamps of 1893-98
P121	A10	10pa gray grn	30	8
a.		Inverted ovpt.	7.50	7.50
P122	A13	2pi yel brn	1.75	60
a.		Inverted ovpt.	7.50	7.50

On Stamps of 1901.
P123	A16	10pa yel grn	15	7
P124	A17	5pa purple	12	7
P125	A17	20pa carmine	45	20
P126	A17	5pi lil rose	7.50	2.00

On Stamps of 1905.
P127	A18	5pa ocher	10	10
a.		Inverted ovpt.	7.50	7.50
P128	A18	2pi slate	2.75	1.10
P129	A18	5pi brown	1.25	35

On Stamps of 1908.
P130	A19	2pi bl blk	250.00	175.00
P131	A19	5pi dk vio	6.00	60

On Stamps of 1909.
P132	A21	5pa ocher	10	10
P133	A21	5pi dk vio	35.00	10.00
		#P121-P129, P131-P133 (12)	55.47	15.27

Preceding Newspaper Issues with additional Overprint in Red or Black

1916
On Stamps of 1893-98
P134	A10	10pa gray grn	25	10
P135	A11	20pa vio brn	20	10
P136	A14	5pi dl vio	15.00	15.00

On Stamp of 1897.
| P137 | N3 | 5pa on 10pa gray grn | 15 | 10 |

On Stamps of 1901.
P138	A16	5pa bister	10	10
P139	A16	10pa yel grn	25	15
P140	A16	20pa magenta	10.00	10.00
a.		Inverted overprint	40	25
P141	A16	1pi vio bl	12.50	12.50
P142	A17	5pa purple	12.50	12.50
P143	A17	10pa green	12.50	12.50
P144	A17	20pa carmine	30	20
P145	A17	1pi blue	30	20
P146	A17	2pi orange	40	20

On Stamps of 1905.
P147	A18	5pa ocher	7	7
P148	A18	10pa dl grn	12.50	12.50
P149	A18	20pa carmine	12.50	12.50
P150	A18	1pi pale bl	50	20

On Stamps of 1908.
| P151 | A19 | 5pa ocher | 12.50 | 12.50 |

On Stamps of 1909.
P152	A21	5pa ocher	12.50	12.50
		Nos. P134-P152 (19)	93.02	91.82

Preceding Newspaper Issues with additional Overprint in Red or Black

1917
On Stamps of 1893-98
P153	A12	1pi gray (R)	40	40
P154	A11	20pa vio brn (R)	1.25	1.25

On Stamps of 1901.
P155	A16	5pa bis (Bk)	90	90
a.		Inverted ovpt.	10.00	10.00
P156	A16	10pa yel grn (R)	90	90
P157	A16	20pa mag (Bk)	90	90
P158	A16	2pi gray bl (R)	20.00	20.00
P159	A16	5pa pur (Bk)	75	60
a.		Invtd. ovpt.	7.50	7.50
b.		Double ovpt.	7.50	7.50
c.		Double ovpt., one inverted	10.00	10.00
P160	A17	10pa grn (R)	12.50	12.50
P161	A17	20pa car (Bk)	40	25
P162	A17	1pi bl (R)	90	90
P163	A17	2pi org (Bk)	90	90
P164	A17	5pi lil rose (R)	20.00	20.00

On Stamps of 1905.
P165	A18	5pa ocher (R)	10	10
a.		Inverted ovpt.	7.50	7.50
P166	A18	5pa ocher (Bk)	45	45
a.		Inverted ovpt.	7.50	7.50
P167	A18	10pa dl grn (R)	45	45
P168	A18	20pa car (Bk)	15	15
a.		Double overprint	7.50	7.50
P169	A18	1pi bl (R)	22	20
a.		Inverted ovpt.	7.50	7.50
P170	A18	2pi sl (R)	20.00	20.00
P171	A18	5pi brn (R)	20.00	20.00

On Stamp of 1908.
| P172 | A19 | 5pa ocher (R) | 20.00 | 20.00 |

Nos. P153-P172 were used as regular postage stamps.

N4   N5

1919
Blue Surcharge and Red Overprint
P173	N4	5pa on 2pa ol grn	10	10
a.		Red overprint double	7.50	7.50
b.		Blue surcharge double	7.50	7.50

1920   **Red Surcharge**
| P174 | N5 | 5pa on 4pa brn | 5 | 5 |

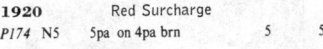

Dove and Citadel of Ankara

N6

1952-55   **Lithographed**   *Perf. 12½*
P175	N6	0.50k grnsh gray	6	5
P176	N6	0.50k vio ('53)	6	5

Perf. 10½, 10
P177	N6	0.50k red org ('54)	6	5
P178	N6	0.50k brn ('55)	6	5

POSTAL TAX STAMPS.

Map of Turkey and Red Crescent
PT1

TURKEY

1928 Typographed. Perf. 14. Unwmkd.
Crescent in Red.
RA1	PT1	½pi lt brn	15	8
RA2	PT1	1pi red vio	15	8
RA3	PT1	2½pi orange	25	15

Engraved
Various Frames
RA4	PT1	5pi dk brn	38	8
RA5	PT1	10pi yel grn	65	40
RA6	PT1	20pi slate	1.10	50
RA7	PT1	50pi dk vio	3.75	2.00
		Nos. RA1–RA7 (7)	6.43	3.29

The use of these stamps on letters, parcels, etc. in addition to the regular postage, was obligatory on certain days in each year.

Cherubs
Upholding
Star
PT2

1932
RA8	PT2	1k ol bis & red	50	10
RA9	PT2	2½k dk brn & red	35	15
RA10	PT2	5k grn & red	70	38
RA11	PT2	25k blk & red	2.50	1.75

No. RA8 Surcharged 20 para
RA12	PT2	20pa on 1k ol bis & red	20	15
RA13	PT2	3k on 1k ol bis & red	1.25	75
	a.	"3 kruus"	5.00	5.00

By a law of Parliament the use of these stamps on letters and telegraph forms, in addition to the regular fees, was obligatory from April 20th to 30th of each year. The inscription in the tablet at the bottom of the design states that the money derived from the sale of the stamps is devoted to child welfare work.

No. RA8 Surcharged 20 para
1933
RA14	PT2	20pa on 1k ol bis & red	30	15
RA15	PT2	3k on 1k ol bis & red	75	45

No. RA5 Surcharged 5 Beş Kuruş
RA16	PT1	5k on 10pi yel grn & red	90	40

PT3  PT4

1933 Perf. 11, 11½.
RA17	PT3	20pa gray vio & red	45	25
RA18	PT4	1k vio & red	30	22
RA19	PT4	5k dk brn & red	1.00	75
RA20	PT3	15k grn & red	1.25	35

Nos. RA17 and RA20 were issued in Ankara; Nos. RA18 and RA19 were issued in Izmir.

Nos. RA3, RA1 Surcharged in Black 5 Beş kuruş
1933-34
RA21	PT1	1k on 2½k org	40	20
RA22	PT1	5k on ½pi lt brn	90	40

Map of
Turkey
PT5

1934-35 Crescent in Red. Perf. 12
RA23	PT5	½k bl ('35)	20	10
RA24	PT5	1k red brn	20	10
RA25	PT5	2½k brn ('35)	30	10
RA26	PT5	5k bl grn ('35)	80	25

Frame differs on No. RA26.

Nos. RA17, RA8–RA9 Overprinted "P.Y.S." in Roman Capitals.
1936 Perf. 11, 14
RA27	PT3	20pa gray vio & red	70	40
RA28	PT2	1k ol bis & red	70	20
RA29	PT2	3k on 2½k dk brn & red	1.20	60

Type of 1934-35, Inscribed "Türkiye Kizilay Cemiyeti"
1938-46 Perf. 8½-11½
Type I. Imprint, "Devlet Basimevi". Crescent red.
Type II. Imprint, "Alaeddin Kiral Basimevi". Crescent carmine.
Type III. Imprint, "Damga Matbaasi". Crescent red.

Crescent in Red or Carmine.
RA30	PT5	½k bl (I)	20	5
a.		Type II	20	5
b.		Type III	25	10
RA31	PT5	1k red vio (I)	15	5
a.		Type II	35	10
b.		Type III	20	10
RA32	PT5	2½k org (I)	20	5
			1.25	45
RA33	PT5	5k bl grn (I)	55	12
RA33A	PT5	5k choc (III) ('42)	1.10	35
RA34	PT5	10k pale grn (I)	1.50	60
a.		Type II	1.25	60
RA35	PT5	20k blk (I)	2.25	90
RA35A	PT5	50k pur (III) ('46)	5.25	1.10
RA35B	PT5	1 l (III) ('44)	25.00	5.00
		Nos. RA30–RA35B (9)	36.20	8.22

No. RA9 Surcharged in Black 20 Para P.Y.S.
1938 Perf. 14
RA36	PT2	20pa on 2½k dk brn & red	50	30
RA37	PT2	1k on 2½k dk brn & red	75	30

No. RA9 Surcharged in Black P.Y.S. 20 Para
1938 Perf. 14. Unwmkd.
RA37A	PT2	20pa on 2½k dk brn & red	60	30
RA37B	PT2	1k on 2½k dk brn & red	75	40

No. RA9 Surcharged "1 Kurus" in Black.
1939 Perf. 14.
RA38	PT2	1k on 2½k dk brn & red	75	30

Condition is the all-important factor of price. Prices quoted are for stamps in fine condition.

Child
PT6

Nurse with Child
PT7

1940 Typographed. Perf. 12.
Star in Carmine.
RA39	PT6	20pa bluish grn	10	8
RA40	PT6	1k violet	10	8
RA41	PT7	1k lt bl	10	8
RA42	PT7	2½k pale red lil	22	15
RA43	PT6	3k black	40	15
RA44	PT7	5k pale vio	40	15
RA45	PT7	10k bl grn	1.25	30
RA46	PT6	15k dk bl	80	30
RA47	PT7	25k ol bis	3.50	1.25
RA48	PT7	50k ol gray	8.00	2.50
		Nos. RA39–RA48 (10)	14.87	5.04

Soldier and
Map of
Turkey
PT8

1941-44 Perf. 11½.
RA49	PT8	1k purple	35	10
RA50	PT8	2k lt bl	1.50	10
RA51	PT8	3k chestnut	1.75	50
RA51A	PT8	4k mag ('44)	5.00	60
RA52	PT8	5k brt rose	5.50	2.50
RA53	PT8	10k dk bl	6.50	1.75
		Nos. RA49–RA53 (6)	20.60	5.55

The tax was used for national defense.

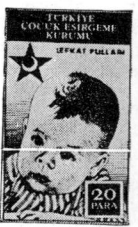

Baby Nurse and Baby
PT9 PT13

Nurse and Children
PT10

Nurse Feeding Child
PT11

Nurse and Child—PT12

Nurse and President Inönü
Child Holding Child
PT14 PT16

Children—PT15

1942 Typographed. Perf. 11½. Unwmkd.
Star in Red.
RA54	PT9	20pa brt vio	22	15
RA55	PT9	20pa chocolate	22	15
RA56	PT10	1k dk sl grn	22	15
RA57	PT11	2½k yel grn	22	15
RA58	PT12	3k dk bl	22	15
RA59	PT13	5k brt pink	30	22
RA60	PT14	10k lt bl	60	40
RA61	PT15	15k dk red brn	1.10	65
RA62	PT16	25k brown	1.75	1.00
		Nos. RA54–RA62 (9)	4.85	3.02

See also Nos. RA175, RA179–RA180.

No. RA32 Surcharged with New Value in Brown.
1942 Perf. 10.
RA63	PT5	1k on 2½k org & red (I)	20	15

Child Eating Nurse and Child
PT17 PT18

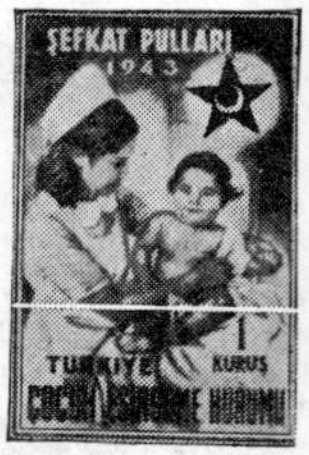

Nurse and Child
PT19

Child and President Inönü
Red Star and Child
PT20 PT21

TURKEY

Inscribed: "Sefcat Pullari 23 Nisan 1943 Cocuk Esirgeme Kurumu."

1943   Star in Red.   Perf. 11.
RA64	PT17	50pa lilac	15	8
RA65	PT17	50pa gray grn	15	8
RA66	PT18	1k lt ultra	20	8
RA67	PT19	3k dk red	22	15
RA68	PT20	15k cr & blk	90	60
RA69	PT21	100k brt vio bl	2.50	2.50
a.		Souvenir sheet	6.50	6.50
		Nos. RA64-RA69 (6)	4.12	3.49

No. RA69a contains one each of Nos. RA64–RA69, imperf. Size: 140x120mm.

Star and Crescent — PT23   Hospital — PT24

Nurse and Children — PT25   Baby — PT26

Nurse Bathing Baby — PT27   Nurse Feeding Child — PT28

Baby with Bottle — PT29   Child — PT30

Hospital — PT31

Perf. 10 to 12 and Compound.

1943-44   Star in Red
RA71	PT23	20pa dp bl	8	8
RA72	PT24	1k gray grn	8	8
RA73	PT25	3k pale gray brn	8	8
RA74	PT26	5k yel org	60	35
RA75	PT26	5k vio brn	30	15
RA76	PT27	10k red	30	20
RA77	PT28	15k red vio	50	30
RA78	PT29	25k pale vio	90	50
RA79	PT30	50k lt bl	1.50	1.00
RA80	PT31	100k lt grn	4.50	2.00
		Nos. RA71-RA80 (10)	8.84	4.74

Nurse Holding Baby — PT32   Nurse Feeding Child — PT33

Child — PT34   Star and Crescent — PT35

Lithographed.

1945-47   Perf. 11½   Unwmkd.
Star in Red.
RA81	PT32	1k lil brn	6	6
a.		1k rose vio	20	
RA82	PT33	5k yel grn	30	15
a.		5k grn	30	15
RA83	PT34	10k red brn	40	30
RA84	PT35	250k gray blk	13.00	7.00
RA84A	PT35	500k dl vio ('47)	50.00	25.00
		Nos. RA81-RA84A (5)	63.76	32.51

Imprint on No. RA82: "Kagit ve Basim Isleri A.S. Ist." On No. RA82a: "Guzel Sanatlar Matbaasi—Ankara."

Nurse and Wounded Soldier — PT36   President Inönü and Victim of Earthquake — PT37

Removing Wounded from Hospital Ship — PT38

Nurse and Soldier — PT39   Feeding the Poor — PT40

Wounded Soldiers on Landing Raft — PT41   Symbolical of Red Crescent Relief — PT42

1945   Perf. 12x10, 10x12.
Crescent in Red.
RA85	PT36	20pa dp bl & brn org	30	8
RA86	PT37	1k ol grn & ol bis	30	8
RA87	PT38	2½k dp bl & red	40	10
RA88	PT39	5k dp bl & red	1.25	22
RA89	PT40	10k dp bl & lt grn	1.25	45
RA90	PT41	50k blk & gray grn	3.50	1.10
RA91	PT42	1 l blk & yel	12.00	3.00
		Nos. RA85-RA91 (7)	19.00	5.03

See also Nos. RA181-RA182.

Ankara Sanatorium — PT43

1946   Perf. 12
RA92	PT43	20k red & lt bl	1.00	45

See also No. RA210.

Covering Sleeping Child — PT44

Designs: 1k, Mother and child. 2½k, Nurse at playground. 5k, Doctor examining infant. 15k, Feeding child. 25k, Bathing child. 50k, Weighing baby. 150k, Feeding baby.

1946   Lithographed.   Perf. 12½
Inscribed: "25ci Yil Hatirasi 1946."
Star in Carmine.
RA93	PT44	20pa brown	10	10
RA94	PT44	1k blue	10	10
RA95	PT44	2½k carmine	15	15
RA96	PT44	5k vio brn	38	30
RA97	PT44	15k violet	38	30
RA98	PT44	25k gray grn	70	40
RA99	PT44	50k bl grn	1.25	1.00
RA100	PT44	150k gray brn	4.00	3.00
		Nos. RA93-RA100 (8)	7.06	5.35

Hospital Ship — PT52

Ambulance Plane — PT53

Hospital Train — PT54

Ambulance — PT55

Boy Scout and Red Crescent Flag — PT56   Nurse and Hospital — PT58

Stretcher Bearers and Wounded Soldier — PT57

Sanatorium — PT59

1946   Perf. 11½
Crescent in Carmine.
RA101	PT52	1k bl & ind	1.40	1.00
RA102	PT53	4k sl gray & rose vio	1.40	1.00
RA103	PT54	10k Prus grn & pink	1.50	1.00
RA104	PT55	25k choc, org & bl	2.50	2.00
RA105	PT56	40k blk brn & grn	4.25	3.50
RA106	PT57	70k ol bis, blk brn & org brn	5.00	4.00
RA107	PT58	1 l vio brn, org brn & org brn	6.00	5.00
RA108	PT59	2½ l gray blk & org brn	15.00	12.50
		Nos. RA101-RA108 (8)	37.05	30.00

Souvenir Sheet

Pres. Inönü and Child — PT60

Typographed
1946   Imperf.   Unwmkd.
RA109	PT60	250k sl blk, pink & red	15.00	15.00

Turkish Society for the Prevention of Cruelty to Children, 25th anniversary. Size: 78½x105mm.

TURKEY

Nurse and
Wounded Soldier
PT61

Pres. Inönü and
Victim of
Earthquake
PT62

Nurse and
Soldier
PT64

Symbolical of
Red Crescent Relief
PT67

1946-47 Lithographed. Perf. 11½
Crescent in Red.
RA113	PT61	20pa dk bl vio & ol ('47)	10	10
RA114	PT62	1k dk brn & yel	75	45
RA115	PT64	5k dp bl & red	60	50
RA116	PT67	1 l brn blk & yel	3.00	2.50

Nurse and Wounded Soldier
PT68

PT69

Victory and Soldier
PT70

1947 Crescent in Red
RA117	PT68	250k brn blk & grn	6.00	3.50
RA118	PT69	5 l sl gray & org	10.00	6.50

Booklet Pane of One.
Perf. 11½ (top) x Imperf.
RA119	PT70	10 l dp bl	27.50	20.00

Black numerals above No. RA119 indicate position in booklet.

President Inönü
and Victim of
Earthquake
PT71

Nurse
and Child
PT72

1947 Perf. 11½
RA120	PT71	1k dk brn, pale bl & red	25	8
RA121	PT72	2½k bl vio & car	30	15

See also Nos. RA221-RA223.

Nurse Offering
Encouragement
PT73

Plant with
Broken Stem
PT74

Perf. 8½, 11½ x 10, 11 x 10½.
1948-49 Typographed. Unwmkd.
Crescent in Red.
RA122	PT73	½k ultra ('49)	65	40
RA123	PT73	1k indigo	15	8
RA124	PT73	2k lil rose	20	8
RA125	PT73	2½k org ('49)	20	8
RA126	PT73	3k bl grn	20	8
RA127	PT73	4k gray ('49)	40	30
RA128	PT73	5k blue	80	8
RA129	PT73	10k pink	1.40	25
RA130	PT73	25k chocolate	1.60	50

Perf. 10
RA130A	PT74	50k ultra & bl gray ('49)	2.25	1.50
RA130B	PT74	100k grn & pale grn ('49)	5.00	2.00
		Nos. RA122-RA130B (11)	12.85	5.35

Nurse and
Children
PT75

Various Scenes with Children,
Inscribed:
"1948 Cocuk Yili Hatirasi".
1948 Lithographed. Perf. 11
Star in Red.
RA131	PT75	20pa dp ultra	8	8
RA132	PT75	20pa rose lil	8	8
RA133	PT75	1k dp Prus bl	15	12
RA134	PT75	3k dk brn vio	45	30
RA135	PT75	15k sl blk	1.50	1.00
RA136	PT75	30k orange	3.00	2.00
RA137	PT75	150k yel grn	5.00	4.00
RA138	PT75	300k brn red	7.00	6.00
		Nos. RA131-RA138 (8)	17.26	13.58

No. RA136 is arranged horizontally.
See also Nos. RA199-206.

Nos. RA101 to RA108
Overprinted
in Carmine

Şefkat pulu

1949 Perf. 11½.
RA139	PT52	1k bl & ind	30	30
RA140	PT53	4k sl gray & rose vio	50	50
RA141	PT54	10k Prus grn & pink	1.00	80
RA142	PT55	25k choc, org & bl	2.00	1.50
RA143	PT56	40k blk brn & grn	3.00	2.00
RA144	PT57	70k ol bis, blk brn & org brn	5.00	4.00
RA145	PT58	1 l vio brn, org brn & vio	7.00	6.00
RA146	PT59	2½ l gray blk & org brn	30.00	30.00
		Nos. RA139-RA146 (8)	48.80	45.60

Ruins and Tent
PT76

"Protection"
PT77

Booklet Panes of One.
1949 Perf. 10 (top) x Imperf.
RA149	PT76	5k gray, vio gray & red	35	25
RA150	PT76	10k red vio, sal & red	50	35

Black numerals above each stamp indicate its position in the booklet.

No. RA124 Surcharged in Black.
1950 Perf. 8½ Unwmkd.
RA151	PT73	20pa on 2k lil rose & red	20	12

Postal Tax Stamps of 1944-48
Surcharged with New Value
in Black or Carmine.
Perf. 8½ to 12½ and Compound
1952
RA152	PT73	20pa on 3k bl grn	20	10
RA153	PT73	20pa on 4k gray	20	10
RA154	PT72	1k on 2½k bl vio & car (C)	25	15
RA155	PT44	1k on 2½k car	25	15
RA156	PT25	1k on 3k pale gray brn	25	15
		Nos. RA152-RA156 (5)	1.15	65

Various Symbolical Designs
Inscribed "75 iNCi" etc.
1952 Typographed. Perf. 10
Crescent in Carmine.
RA157	PT77	5k bl grn & bl	1.00	75
RA158	PT77	15k yel grn, bl & cr	1.00	75
RA159	PT77	30k bl, grn & brn	1.00	75
RA160	PT77	1 l blk, bl & cr	1.50	1.25
a.		Souvenir sheet	15.00	15.00

Printed in sheets of 20 containing one horizontal row of each value.
No. RA160a measures 96 x 117½mm., and contains one each of Nos. RA157 to RA160, imperforate, with marginal inscriptions in carmine and gray.

Nurse and Children
PT78

Design: 1ku, Nurse and baby.
1954 Lithographed. Perf. 10½
Star in Red.
RA161	PT78	20pa aqua	10	5
RA162	PT78	20pa yellow	10	5
RA163	PT78	1k dp bl	10	5

Globe and
Flag
PT79

Designs: 5k, Winged nurse in clouds.
10k, Protecting arm of Red Crescent.
1954
RA164	PT79	1k multi	5	5
RA165	PT79	5k multi	12	5
RA166	PT79	10k car, grn & gray	25	12

See also Nos. RA208, RA211-RA213.

Florence
Nightingale
PT80

Selimiye
Barracks
PT81

Portrait: 30k, Florence Nightingale, full-face.
1954, Nov. 4
Crescent in Carmine.
RA167	PT80	20k gray grn & dk brn	60	50
RA168	PT80	30k dl brn & blk	60	50
RA169	PT81	50k buff & blk	1.25	1.25

Issued to commemorate the centenary of the arrival of Florence Nightingale at Scutari.

Type of 1942 and

Children
Kissing
PT82

Nurse
Holding Baby
PT83

1955, Apr. 23 Star in Red
RA170	PT82	20pa chlky bl	6	6
RA171	PT82	20pa org brn	6	6
RA172	PT82	1k lilac	6	6
RA173	PT82	3k gray bis	12	7
RA174	PT82	5k orange	12	6
RA175	PT12	10k green	60	30
RA176	PT83	15k dk bl	30	12
RA177	PT83	25k brn car	80	40
RA178	PT83	50k dk gray grn	2.00	1.50
RA179	PT12	2½ l dl brn	50.00	35.00
RA180	PT12	10 l rose lil	120.00	100.00
		Nos. RA170-RA180 (11)	174.12	137.63

Types of 1945
Inscribed: "Turkiye Kizilay Dernegi"
Lithographed.
1955 Perf. 10½x11½, 10½
Crescent in Red
RA181	PT36	20pa vio brn & lem	10	5
RA182	PT41	1 k blk & gray grn	10	5

Nurse
PT85

Nurses on Parade
PT86

TURKEY

Design: 100k, Two nurses under Red Cross and Red Crescent flags and U. N. emblem.

Lithographed.

1955, Sept. 5   Perf. 10½   Unwmkd.
Crescent and Cross in Red.
RA183	PT85	10k blk & pale brn	1.00	70
RA184	PT86	15k dk grn & pale yel grn	1.00	70
RA185	PT85	100k lt ultra	2.25	1.25

Issued in connection with the meeting of the board of directors of the International Council of Nurses, Istanbul, Aug. 29, Sept. 5, 1955.

Nos. RA92 and RA130B Surcharged "20 Para"

1955
RA186	PT43	20p on 20k red & lt bl	20	10

Typographed
RA187	PT74	20p on 100k grn, pale grn & red (surch. 11½x2mm)	30	10
c.	Surcharge 13½x2½ mm		30	10

No. RA164 Surcharged with New Value and Two Bars

1956   Perf. 10½   Litho.
RA187A	PT79	20p on 1k multi	10	10
RA187B	PT79	2.50k on 1k multi	10	10

Woman and Children
PT87

Designs: 10k, 25k, 50k, Flag and building. 250k, 5l, 10l, Mother nursing baby.

1956   Lithographed   Perf. 10½
Star in Red.
RA188	PT87	20pa red org	6	6
RA189	PT87	20pa gray grn	6	6
RA190	PT87	1k purple	6	6
RA191	PT87	1k grnsh bl	6	6
RA192	PT87	3k lt red brn	30	12
RA193	PT87	10k rose car	60	40
RA194	PT87	25k brt grn	1.50	1.00
RA195	PT87	50k brt ultra	2.25	1.75
RA196	PT87	250k red lil	12.00	12.00
RA197	PT87	5l sepia	15.00	10.00
RA198	PT87	10l dk sl grn	20.00	15.00
	Nos. RA188-RA198 (11)		51.89	40.51

Stamps of 1948 Overprinted and Surcharged in Black or Red: "IV. DUNYA Cocuk Gunu 1 Ekim 1956"

1956, Oct. 1   Perf. 11   Unwmkd.
Star in Red.
RA199	PT75	20pa dp ultra (R)	5.00	5.00
RA200	PT75	20pa rose lil	5.00	5.00
RA201	PT75	1k dp Prus bl (R)	5.00	5.00
RA202	PT75	3k dk brn vio (R)	5.00	5.00
RA203	PT75	15k sl blk (R)	6.00	6.00
RA204	PT75	25k on 30k org	6.00	6.00
RA205	PT75	100k on 150k yel grn (R)	7.50	7.50
RA206	PT75	250k on 300k brn red	10.00	10.00
	Nos. RA199-RA206 (8)		49.50	49.50

The tax was for child welfare. No. RA204 is horizontal.

Type of 1954, Redrawn Type of 1946, and

Flower PT88   Children PT89

1957   Perf. 10½   Unwmkd.
Crescent in Red.
RA207	PT88	½k lt ol gray & brn	5	5
RA208	PT79	1k ol bis, blk & grn	8	5
RA209	PT88	2½k yel grn & bl grn	15	8
RA210	PT43	20k red & lt bl	30	22
RA211	PT79	25k lt gray, blk & grn	75	60
RA212	PT79	50k bl, dk grn & grn	90	60
RA213	PT79	100k vio, blk & grn	1.85	1.10
	Nos. RA207-RA213 (7)		4.08	2.70

No. RA210 inscribed "Turkiye Kizilay Cemiyeti." No. RA92 inscribed ".... Dernegi."

1957   Perf. 10½   Unwmkd.
RA214	PT89	20pa car & red	6	5
RA215	PT89	20pa grn & red	6	5
RA216	PT89	1k ultra & car	12	6
RA217	PT89	3k red org & car	40	25

"Blood Donor and Recipient" PT90   Child and Butterfly PT91

Designs: 75k, Figure showing blood circulation. 150k, Blood transfusion symbolism.

1957, May 22   Size: 24x40mm.
RA218	PT90	25k gray, blk & red	50	30

Size: 22½x37½mm.
RA219	PT90	75k grn, blk & red	80	60
RA220	PT90	150k yel grn & red	1.25	90

Redrawn Type of 1947
Inscribed: "V Dunya Cocuk Gunu."

1957   Star in Red   Perf 10½
RA221	PT72	100k blk & bis brn	1.25	1.00
RA222	PT72	150k blk & yel brn	1.25	1.00
RA223	PT72	250k blk & vio	1.50	1.25

The tax was for child welfare.

1958   Lithographed.   Unwmkd.
Designs: Various Butterflies. Nos. RA226-RA227 arranged horizontally.
RA224	PT91	20k gray & red	45	40
RA225	PT91	25k multi	45	40
RA226	PT91	50k multi	60	45
RA227	PT91	75k grn, yel & blk	75	60
RA228	PT91	150k multi	1.25	1.00
	Nos. RA224-RA228 (5)		3.50	2.85

Florence Nightingale
PT92

1958   Crescent in Red.
RA229	PT92	1l bluish grn	60	40
RA230	PT92	1½l gray	90	75
RA231	PT92	2½l blue	1.25	90

Turkey stopped issuing postal tax stamps in June, 1958. Similar stamps of later date are private charity stamps issued by the Red Crescent Society and the Society for the Protection of Children.

POSTAL TAX AIR POST STAMPS
Air Fund Issues

These stamps were obligatory on all airmail for 21 days a year. The tax benefitted the Turkish Aviation Society: 20 paras for a postcard, 1 kurush for a regular letter, 2½k for a registered letter, 3k for a telegram, 5k–50k for a package, higher values for air freight.

Postal tax air post stamps were withdrawn Aug. 21, 1934, and remainders destroyed later that year.

Biplane
PTAP1

Lithographed

1926   Perf. 11, Pin Perf.   Unwmkd.
Size: 35x25mm.
RAC1	PTAP1	20pa brn & pale grn	1.50	45
RAC2	PTAP1	1g bl grn & buff	1.50	45

Size: 40x29mm.
RAC3	PTAP1	5g vio & pale grn	3.50	90
RAC4	PTAP1	5g car lake & pale grn	25.00	6.00

PTAP2   PTAP3

1927–29   Perf. 11
RAC5	PTAP2	20pa dl red & pale grn	70	25
RAC6	PTAP2	1k grn & yel	55	20

Perf. 11½
RAC7	PTAP3	2k dp cl & yel grn	1.00	50
RAC8	PTAP3	2½k red & yel grn	7.50	2.50
RAC9	PTAP3	5k dk bl gray & org	75	75
RAC10	PTAP3	10k dk grn & rose	6.00	2.50
RAC11	PTAP3	15k grn & yel	6.00	4.75
RAC12	PTAP3	20k ol brn & yel	6.00	2.25
RAC13	PTAP3	50k dk bl & cob bl	10.00	4.50
RAC14	PTAP3	100k car & lt bl	90.00	50.00
	Nos. RAC5-RAC14 (10)		128.50	66.70

Nos. RAC1, RAC5, RAC7 and RAC11 Surcharged in Black or Red

1930–31
RAC15	PTAP1	1k ("Bir Kurus") on RAC1	90.00	80.00
RAC16	PTAP2	1k ("Bir Kurus") on RAC5	50	20
RAC17	PTAP3	100k ("Yuz Para") on RAC7 (R)	75	30
RAC18	PTAP2	5k ("Bes Kurus") on RAC5	75	30
RAC19	PTAP2	5k ("5 Kurus") on RAC5	75	30
RAC20	PTAP3	10k ("On kurus") on RAC7 (R)	2.25	90
RAC21	PTAP3	50k ("Elli kurus") on RAC7 (R)	12.50	4.00
RAC22	PTAP3	1l ("Bir lira") on RAC7 (R)	100.00	35.00
RAC23	PTAP3	5l ("Bes lira") on RAC11 (R)	500.00	400.00
	Nos. RAC15-RAC23 (9)		707.50	521.00

PTAP4   PTAP5

1931–32   Lithographed   Perf. 11½
RAC24	PTAP4	20pa black	25	15

Typographed
RAC25	PTAP5	1k brn car ('32)	50	15
RAC26	PTAP5	5k red ('32)	1.25	40
RAC27	PTAP5	10k grn ('32)	3.00	75

PTAP6

1933
RAC28	PTAP6	10pa ("On Para") grn	50	10
RAC29	PTAP6	1k ("Bir Kurus") red	1.25	25
RAC30	PTAP6	5k ("Bes Kurus") lil	2.25	1.75

Certain countries cancel stamps in full sheets and sell them (usually with gum) for less than face value. Dealers generally sell "CTO" (canceled to order) stamps for much less than postally used copies.

TURKEY IN ASIA

TURKEY IN ASIA
(Anatolia)

This designation, which includes all of Turkey in Asia Minor, came into existence during the uprising of 1919, led by Mustafa Kemal Pasha. Actually there was no separation of territory, the Sultan's sovereignty being almost immediately reduced to a small area surrounding Constantinople. The formation of the Turkish Republic and the expulsion of the Sultan followed in 1923. Subsequent issues of postage stamps are listed under Turkey (Republic).

40 Paras = 1 Piastre

Issues of the Nationalist Government.

Turkish Revenue Stamps Handstamped in Turkish "Osmanli Postalari, 1336" (Ottoman Post, 1920).

A1

The overprint on Nos. 1-13 comes in three types, varying in width from 20 to 24mm. All three types are found on Nos. 1, 2 and 6; two types on Nos. 1B, 5A and 10; one only on the others.

1920   Perf. 12.   Unwmkd.

1	A1	1pi green	100.00	50.00
1B	A1	5pi ultra	900.00	700.00
2	A1	50pi gray grn	2.50	2.50
		Cut cancellation		.25
3	A1	100pi buff	40.00	12.50
a.		100pi yel	30.00	25.00
		Cut cancellation		1.00
4	A1	500pi orange	50.00	35.00
		Cut cancellation		3.00
5	A1	1000pi brown	650.00	550.00
		Cut cancellation		60.00

A2

Black Overprint.

5A	A2	10pa green	60.00	50.00
5B	A2	1pi ultra	800.00	750.00
5C	A2	5pi rose	800.00	750.00
6	A2	50pi yellow	10.00	10.00
a.		50pi ocher	7.00	5.00
		Cut cancellation		.25
7	A2	100pi brown	32.50	32.50
		Cut cancellation		2.00
8	A2	500pi slate	100.00	80.00
		Cut cancellation		5.00

A3

Red and Black Overprints.

9	A3	50pi ocher	80.00	25.00
		Cut cancellation		2.00

A4   A5

Black Overprint.

10	A4	2pi emerald		1,750.
11	A5	100pi yel brn	160.00	60.00
		Cut cancellation		4.00

A5a

12	A5a	20pa black	550.00	550.00

A5b

13	A5b	2pi bl blk	700.00	650.00

Turkish Stamps of 1913-18 Handstamped in Black or Red

(The Surcharge reads "Post, Piastre 3.")

1921   Perf. 12, 12½.

On Stamps of 1913.

14	A24	3pi on 2pa red lil (Bk)	5.00	5.00
15	A24	3pi on 2pa red lil (R)		
16	A25	3pi on 4pa dk brn (Bk)	5.50	5.50
16A	A25	3pi on 4pa dk brn (R)	15.00	15.00
17	A27	3pi on 6pa dk bl (Bk)	12.50	12.50
18	A27	3pi on 6pa dk bl (R)	17.50	17.50

On Stamp of 1916-18.

19	A42	3pi on 2pa vio (R)	12.50	12.50
20	A42	3pi on 2pa vio (Bk)	6.50	6.50

Turkish Stamps of 1913-18 Surcharged in Black or Red

(The Surcharge reads "Angora 3 Piastres.")

On Stamps of 1913.

22	A24	3pi on 2pa red lil	1.00	1.00
a.		Additional surcharge as No. 14	8.00	8.00
23	A25	3pi on 4pa dk brn	4.50	4.50
a.		Additional blk surcharge as No. 16	9.50	9.50
b.		Additional red surcharge as No. 16A	8.00	8.00
24	A27	3pi on 6pa dk bl	12.50	12.50
a.		Additional blk surcharge as No. 17	27.50	27.50
b.		Additional surcharge as No. 18 (R)	12.50	12.50
25	A27	3pi on 6pa dk bl (R)	600.00	

On Stamps of 1916-18.

26	A42	3pi on 2pa vio (Bk)	2.00	2.00
a.		Additional red surcharge as No. 19	11.00	11.00
b.		Additional blk surcharge as No. 20		
27	A42	3pi on 2pa vio (R)		
28	A52a	3pi on 2pa on 5pa on 1pi red	42.50	42.50

Naval League Stamps Overprinted in Turkish "Osmanli Postalari, 1337" (Ottoman Post, 1921).

A6

1921   Perf. 12 x 11½.

29	A6	1pa orange	1.00	1.00
a.		Date "1327"	1.50	1.50
30	A6	2pa indigo	1.75	1.75
31	A6	5pa green	3.00	3.00
32	A6	10pa brown	25.00	25.00
33	A6	40pa red brn	20.00	20.00
		Nos. 29-33 (5)	50.75	50.75

The error "2337" occurs on all values of this issue.
The Naval League stamps have pictures of three Turkish warships. They were sold for the benefit of sailors of the fleet but did not pay postage until they were surcharged in 1921.

Turkish Revenue Stamps Overprinted "Osmanli Postalari 1337"

A7

TURKISH INSCRIPTIONS:

20 PARAS   1 PIASTRE

2 PIASTRES   5 PIASTRES

1921   Perf. 11½

34	A7	20pa on 1pi dk red & bl	7.50	5.00
35	A7	1pi on 1pi dk red & bl	50	
36	A7	2pi on 1pi dk red & bl	50	50
a.		Inverted surcharge		
37	A7	5pi on 1pi dk red & bl	1.50	1.50

No. 36 is also surcharged with the Turkish numeral "2."

A8   A9

38	A8	1pi on 1pi dk red & bl	15.00	15.00
39	A9	1pi grn & brn red	50	50
a.		Double overprint		
b.		Handstamped overprint		

The errors "1307", "1331" and "2337" occur once in each sheet of Nos. 34 to 39 inclusive.

A10

Perf. 12.

41	A10	10pa slate	5.00	5.00
a.		Handstamped overprint	7.00	7.00
b.		Double overprint		
42	A10	1pi green	3.00	3.00
a.		Invtd. ovpt.	15.00	12.00
b.		Handstamped overprint		
43	A10	5pi ultra	2.00	2.00
a.		"1337" invtd.	75.00	65.00
b.		Half used as 2½pi on cover		
c.		Handstamped overprint	14.00	14.00
43E	A10	50pi grn (handstamped overprint)	750.00	550.00

A11

44	A11	10pa green	2.00	2.00
a.		Handstamped overprint		
45	A11	1pi ultra	3.00	3.00
a.		Handstamped overprint	20.00	20.00
46	A11	5pi red	1.00	1.00
a.		Inverted ovpt.		
b.		"1337" inverted	7.00	5.00
c.		Half used as 2½pi on cover		
d.		Handstamped overprint		
46F	A11	50pi ocher	40.00	40.00
g.		Handstampd overprint	30.00	30.00

TURKEY IN ASIA

A12

With Additional Turkish Overprint in Red or Black.

47	A12	10pa grn (R)	25.00	25.00
	a.	Black overprint inverted	50.00	50.00
48	A12	1pi ultra (R)	20.00	20.00
49	A12	5pi rose (Bk)	25.00	25.00
	a.	"1337" invtd.	65.00	65.00

A13   A14

50	A13	10pa green	3.00	3.00
	a.	Overprint 21 mm long		
	b.	"131" for "1337"		
51	A13	1pi ultra	5.00	5.00
	a.	"13" for "1337"	20.00	20.00
	b.	"131" for "1337"	20.00	20.00
	c.	Invtd. ovpt.	30.00	30.00
	d.	Handstamped overprint		
52	A13	5pi red	17.50	17.50
	a.	Invtd. ovpt.	60.00	50.00
	b.	"131" for "1337"	50.00	50.00
	c.	Handstamped overprint		

Perf. 11½, 11½ x 11.

53	A14	10pa pink	50	50
	a.	Imperf.		
	b.	Date "1237"	1.00	1.00
	d.	Inverted overprint		
54	A14	1pi yellow	50	50
	a.	Overprint 18 mm long		
	b.	Date "1332"	5.00	
	c.	Date "1317"		
	d.	Inverted overprint	1.50	1.50
55	A14	2pi yel grn	75	75
	a.	Date "1237"	5.00	
	b.	Date "1317"		
	c.	Imperf.		
	d.	Inverted ovpt.	3.00	3.00
56	A14	5pi red	1.00	1.00
	a.	Imperf. vertically		
	b.	Inverted overprint	3.00	2.50
	c.	Double overprint	4.00	3.00
	d.	Date "1332"	5.00	
	e.	Half used as 2½pi on cover		
	f.	Overprint 18mm long	1.50	80

A15

Perf. 12, 12½.

57	A15	20pa black	1.50	1.50
	a.	Date 4½mm high	2.00	2.00
	b.	"337" for "1337"	2.00	2.00

A16

58	A16	2pi bl blk	12.50	12.50
	a.	Handstamped overprint		

A17

1921   Perf. 12.

59	A17	5pi green	25.00	25.00
	a.	Handstamped overprint		

A18

60	A18	1pi ultra	150.00	150.00
	a.	Handstamped overprint	175.00	175.00
61	A18	5pi dp grn	175.00	175.00
	a.	Handstamped overprint	350.00	275.00

Handstamped Overprint.

| 62 | A18 | 5pi dk vio | 550.00 | 550.00 |

The overprint variety "337" for "1337" exists on Nos. 60–62.

Turkish Stamps of 1915-20 Surcharged

اطنه

۱ كانون اول

۱۳۳۷

1921

On Stamp of 1913, Overprinted Crescent and Star in 1915

| 70 | A22 | 5pa ocher | 100.00 | 70.00 |

On Stamps of 1917-18.

71	A53	5pi on 2pa Prus bl (No. 547)	5.00	2.50
72	A53	5pi on 2pa Prus bl (No. 548)	5.00	2.50

On Stamp of 1919.

73	A57	35pi on 1pi bl (Bk)	15.00	10.00
	a.	Inverted surcharge		

On Newspaper Stamp of 1909, Overprinted Crescent and Star in 1915.

| 74 | A21 | 5pa ocher | 125.00 | 125.00 |

On No. 74 the overprint was printed vertically, reading upward on one half of the sheet and downward on the other half.

On Stamps of 1920.

75	A32	3pi blue	5.00	2.50
76	A36	10pi gray vio	5.00	2.50

اطنه

Overprinted

۱ كانون اول ۱۳۳۷

On Stamps of 1916-18.

77	A44	10pa green	5.00	2.50
78	A45	20pa dp rose	5.00	2.50
	a.	Inverted overprint	15.00	15.00
79	A51	25pi car, straw	15.00	9.00
	a.	Double overprint		
	b.	Invtd. ovpt.	25.00	25.00

On Newspaper Stamp of 1909, Overprinted Crescent and Star in 1915.

| 80 | A21 | 5pa ocher | 100.00 | 60.00 |

The overprints on Nos. 70 to 80 read "Adana-December 1st, 1921." This issue was to commemorate the withdrawal of the French from Cilicia and the return of the Kemalist National army.
On No. 73 the lines of the overprint are set further apart than on Nos. 70, 71, 72, 75 and 76.

Pact of Revenge, Burning Village at Top **Izmir Harbor**
A19   A20

Mosque of Selim, Adrianople   **Mosque of Selim, Konya**
A21   A22

Soldier   **Legendary Gray Wolf**
A23   A24

Snake Castle and Seyhan River, Adana—A25

Parliament Building at Sivas
A26

Mosque at Urfa
A27

Map of Anatolia
A28

Declaration of Faith from the Koran
A29

1922   Lithographed   Perf. 11½

82	A19	10pa vio brn	40	8
83	A20	20pa bl grn	50	8
	a.	Imperf.	4.00	4.00
84	A21	1pi dp bl	80	10
	a.	Imperf.	7.50	7.50
85	A22	2pi red brn	1.75	10
86	A23	5pi dk bl	1.75	6
	a.	Imperf.	7.50	7.50
87	A24	10pi dk brn	6.00	40
88	A25	25pi rose	7.50	20
	a.	Imperf.	42.50	42.50
89	A26	50pi indigo	6.00	1.25
	a.	Imperf.	12.50	12.50
90	A27	100pi violet	60.00	2.50
91	A28	200pi slate	120.00	20.00
92	A29	500pi green	110.00	12.50
		Cut cancellation		2.00
		Nos. 82-92 (11)	314.70	37.27

املنه

Stamps of Type A21 Overprinted

۵ كانون ثانى ۱۳۲۸

1922

93	A21	1pi dp bl	7.00	5.00
94	A21	5pi dp bl	7.00	5.00
95	A21	10pi brown	7.00	5.00
96	A21	25pi rose	7.00	5.00
97	A21	50pi slate	7.00	5.00
98	A21	100pi violet	7.00	5.00
99	A21	200pi blk vio	7.00	5.00
100	A21	500pi bl grn	7.00	5.00
		Nos. 93-100 (8)	56.00	40.00

To commemorate the withdrawal of the French from Cilicia and the return of the Kemalist National army. The overprint reads: "Adana, Jan. 5, 1922."

Nos. 93-100 without overprint were presented to some high government officials, not issued.

First Parliament House, Ankara
A30

1922		Lithographed.		
102	A30	5pa violet	40	20
103	A30	10pa green	40	25
104	A30	20pa pale red	70	40
105	A30	1pi brn org	3.25	1.00
106	A30	2pi red brn	12.50	2.25
107	A30	3pi rose	3.25	50
a.		Arabic "13" in right corner	10.00	5.00
b.		Thin grysh paper	20.00	2.00
		Nos. 102-107 (6)	20.50	4.60

Nos. 102–107 and 107b exist imperf.

A31

1923				
110	A31	50pi dk gray	6.50	4.00

In 1923 several stamps of Turkey and Turkey in Asia were overprinted in Turkish for advertising purposes. The overprint reads: "Izmir Economic Congress, 17 Feb., 1339."

POSTAGE DUE STAMPS.

Postage Due Stamps of Turkey, 1914, Overprinted:

1921		Perf. 12.	Unwmkd.	
J1	D1 (a)	5pa claret	75.00	70.00
J2	D2 (a)	20pa red	75.00	70.00
a.		Inverted overprint		
J3	D3 (b)	1pi dk bl	75.00	70.00
a.		Inverted overprint	100.00	100.00

Withdrawal of the French from Cilicia. Forged overprints exist.

D5

1922		Lithographed.	Perf. 11½.	
J4	D5	20pa dl grn	40	30
a.		Imperf.		
J5	D5	1pi gray grn	50	40
J6	D5	2pi red brn	1.75	1.25
J7	D5	3pi rose	3.25	2.50
J8	D5	5pi dk bl	4.50	4.00
		Nos. J4-J8 (5)	10.40	8.45

ΕΛΛΗΝΙΚΗ ΚΑΤΟΧΗ ΛΕΠΤΑ·50

Turkish Stamps of 1916-21 with Greek surcharge as above in blue or black are of private origin.

TUSCANY
TWO SICILIES

See Italian States preceding Italy in Vol. III.

UBANGI-SHARI
(oo·bäng′gê)
(UBANGI-SHARI-CHAD)

LOCATION—In Western Africa, north of the equator.
GOVT.—A former French Colony.
AREA—238,767 sq. mi.
POP.—833,916.
CAPITAL—Bangui.

In 1910 French Congo was divided into the three colonies of Gabon, Middle Congo and Ubangi-Shari and officially named "French Equatorial Africa." Under that name in 1934 the group, with the territory of Chad included, became a single administrative unit. See Gabon.

100 Centimes = 1 Franc

Stamps of Middle Congo Overprinted in Black

OUBANGUI-CHARI-TCHAD

1915-22 Perf. 14x13½. Unwmkd.
Chalky Paper.

1	A1	1c ol gray & brn	5	5
a.		Double overprint	75.00	
b.		Imperf.	21.00	
2	A1	2c vio & brn	8	8
3	A1	4c bl & brn	12	12
4	A1	5c dk grn & bl	8	8
5	A1	5c yel & bl ('22)	22	22
6	A1	10c car & bl	28	28
7	A1	10c dp grn & bl grn ('22)	18	18
8	A1	15c brn vio & rose	50	50
9	A1	20c brn & bl	95	95

No. 8 is on ordinary paper.

Overprinted
OUBANGUI-CHARI-TCHAD

10	A2	25c bl & grn	38	38
11	A2	25c bl grn & gray ('22)	22	22
12	A2	30c scar & grn	28	28
13	A2	30c dp rose & rose ('22)	22	22
14	A2	35c vio brn & bl	1.85	1.85
15	A2	40c dl grn & brn	2.50	2.50
16	A2	45c vio & red	2.50	2.50
17	A2	50c bl & red	70	70
18	A2	50c bl & grn ('22)	22	22
19	A2	75c brn & bl	5.50	5.50
20	A3	1fr dp grn & vio	5.50	5.50
21	A3	2fr vio & gray grn	5.50	5.50
22	A3	5fr bl & rose	17.50	17.50
		Nos. 1-22 (22)	45.33	45.33

Types of Middle Congo, 1907-22, Overprinted in Black or Red
OUBANGUI-CHARI

1922				
23	A1	1c vio & grn	15	15
a.		Overprint omitted	67.50	
b.		Imperf.	13.00	
24	A1	2c grn & sal	22	22
25	A1	4c ol brn & brn	28	28
a.		Ovpt. omitted	67.50	
26	A1	5c ind & rose	40	40
27	A1	10c dp grn & gray grn	50	50
28	A1	15c lt red & dl bl	65	65
29	A1	20c choc & sal	2.75	2.75

Overprinted
OUBANGUI CHARI

30	A2	25c vio & sal	2.50	2.50
31	A2	30c rose & pale rose	1.40	1.40
32	A2	35c vio & grn	2.50	2.50
33	A2	40c ind & vio (R)	2.25	2.25
34	A2	45c choc & vio	2.25	2.25
35	A2	50c dk bl & pale bl	1.50	1.50
36	A2	60c on 75c vio, *pnksh*	1.50	1.50
37	A2	75c choc & sal	2.50	2.50
38	A3	1fr grn & dl bl (R)	2.75	2.75
a.		Overprint omitted		
39	A3	2fr grn & sal	3.75	3.75
40	A3	5fr grn & ol brn	6.75	6.75
		Nos. 23-40 (18)	34.60	34.60

Stamps of 1922 Issue with Additional Overprint in Black, Blue or Red
AFRIQUE EQUATORIALE FRANÇAISE

1924-33

41	A1	1c vio & grn (Bl)	5	5
a.		"OUBANGUI CHARI" omitted	47.50	
42	A1	2c grn & sal (Bl)	5	5
a.		"OUBANGUI CHARI" omitted	47.50	
b.		Double ovpt.	52.50	
43	A1	4c ol brn & brn (Bl)	8	8
a.		Double overprint (Bl + Bk)	52.50	
b.		"OUBANGUI CHARI" omitted	80.00	
44	A1	5c ind & rose (Bk)	12	12
a.		"OUBANGUI CHARI" omitted	55.00	
45	A1	10c dp grn & gray grn (Bk)	12	12
46	A1	10c red org & bl ('25) (Bk)	18	18
47	A1	15c sal & dl bl (Bk)	28	28
48	A1	15c sal & dl bl (Bl) ('26)	28	28
49	A1	20c choc & sal (Bl)	22	22

On Nos. 41 to 49 the color in ( ) refers to the overprint "Afrique Equatoriale Francaise."

Overprinted
AFRIQUE EQUATORIALE FRANÇAISE

50	A2	25c vio & sal (Bl)	15	15
a.		Imperf.		
51	A2	30c rose & pale rose (Bl)	5	5
52	A2	30c choc & red ('25) (Bk)	18	18
a.		"OUBANGUI CHARI" omitted	65.00	
53	A2	30c dp grn & gray ('27) (Bk)	38	38
54	A2	35c vio & grn (Bl)	18	18
a.		"OUBANGUI CHARI" omitted		
55	A2	40c ind & vio (Bl)	22	22
56	A2	45c choc & vio (Bl)	28	28
57	A2	50c dk bl & pale bl (R)	15	15
58	A2	50c gray & bl vio ('25) (R)	50	50
59	A2	60c on 75c dk vio, *pnksh* (R)	15	15
60	A2	65c org brn & bl ('28) (Bk)	60	60
61	A2	75c choc & sal (Bl)	28	28
62	A2	75c dp bl & lt bl ('25) (R)	18	18
a.		"OUBANGUI CHARI" omitted	65.00	
63	A2	75c rose & dk brn ('28) (Bk)	60	60
64	A2	90c brn red & pink ('30) (Bk)	2.75	2.75
65	A3	1fr grn & ind (Bk+Bl)	18	18
66	A3	1fr grn & ind (R+R)	22	22
67	A3	1.10fr bis & bl ('28) (Bk)	90	90
68	A3	1.25fr mag & lt grn ('33) (Bk)	2.75	2.75
69	A3	1.50fr ultra & bl ('30) (Bk)	3.00	3.00
70	A3	1.75fr dk brn & dp buff ('33) (Bk)	3.75	3.75
71	A3	2fr grn & red (Bk)	30	30
a.		"OUBANGUI CHARI" omitted	475.00	300.00
72	A3	3fr red vio ('30) (Bk)	2.75	2.75
73	A3	5fr grn & ol brn (Bl)	1.50	1.50
		Nos. 41-73 (33)	23.38	23.38

On Nos. 65, 66 the first overprint color refers to OUBANGUI CHARI

Common Design Types
pictured in section at front of book.

Types of 1924 Issue Surcharged with New Values in Black or Red.

1925-26

74	A3	65c on 1fr vio & ol	60	50
a.		"65" omitted	45.00	
75	A3	85c on 1fr vio & ol	60	50
a.		"AFRIQUE EQUATORIALE FRANCAISE" omitted	47.50	
b.		Double surch.	62.50	
76	A3	1.25fr on 1fr dk bl & ultra (R) ('26)	40	30
a.		"1f25" omitted	60.00	60.00

Bars cover old denomination on No. 76.

Types of 1924 Issue Surcharged with New Values and Bars.

1927

77	A2	90c on 75c brn red & rose red	60	50
78	A3	1.50fr on 1fr ultra & bl	55	45
79	A3	3fr on 5fr org brn & dl red	1.00	75
80	A3	10fr on 5fr ver & vio	7.50	7.50
81	A3	20fr on 5fr vio & gray	11.00	10.00
		Nos. 77-81 (5)	20.65	19.20

Colonial Exposition Issue.
Common Design Types

1931 Engraved. Perf. 12½.
Name of Country Typographed in Black.

82	CD70	40c dp grn	2.25	2.25
83	CD71	50c violet	2.25	2.25
84	CD72	90c red org	2.25	2.25
a.		Imperforate	37.50	
85	CD731.50fr dl bl		2.25	2.25

SEMI-POSTAL STAMPS.

Regular Issue of 1915 Surcharged

1916 Perf. 14x13½. Unwmkd.
Chalky Paper.

B1	A1	10c +5c car & bl	90	90
a.		Inverted surch.	37.50	37.50
b.		Double surcharge	37.50	37.50
c.		Double surchrge, one inverted	52.50	52.50
d.		Vertical surcharge	37.50	37.50
e.		No period under "C"	4.75	4.75

Regular Issue of 1915 Surcharged in Carmine +5c

| B2 | A1 | 10c +5c car & bl | 28 | 28 |

POSTAGE DUE STAMPS.

Postage Due Stamps of France Overprinted
OUBANGUI-CHARI
A. E. F.

1928 Perf. 14x13½. Unwmkd.

J1	D2	5c lt bl	60	60
J2	D2	10c gray brn	60	60

UBANGI-SHARI—UKRAINE

J3	D2	20c ol grn	60	60
J4	D2	25c brt rose	60	60
J5	D2	30c lt red	60	60
J6	D2	45c bl grn	60	60
J7	D2	50c brn vio	90	90
J8	D2	60c yel brn	1.00	1.00
J9	D2	1fr red brn	1.25	1.25
J10	D2	2fr org red	1.75	1.75
J11	D2	3fr brt vio	1.75	1.75
	Nos. J1-J11 (11)		10.25	10.25

Landscape—D3

Emile Gentil
D4

1930 Typographed.

J12	D3	5c dp bl & ol	30	30
J13	D3	10c dk red & brn	45	45
J14	D3	20c grn & brn	60	60
J15	D3	25c lt bl & brn	60	60
J16	D3	30c bis brn & Prus bl	90	90
J17	D3	45c Prus bl & ol	1.40	1.40
J18	D3	50c red vio & brn	2.50	2.50
J19	D3	60c gray lil & bl blk	2.75	2.75
J20	D4	1fr bis brn & bl blk	1.10	1.10
J21	D4	2fr vio & brn	1.75	1.75
J22	D4	3fr dp red & brn	2.50	2.50
	Nos. J12-J22 (11)		14.85	14.85

Stamps of Ubangi-Shari were replaced in 1936 by those of French Equatorial Africa.

UKRAINE
(ū′krān)

LOCATION—In southwestern Russia, bordering on the Black Sea.
GOVT.—Republic.
AREA—170,998 sq. mi.
POP.—31,901,400 (1933).
CAPITAL—Kiev.

Following the collapse of the Russian Empire, a national assembly met at Kiev and formed the Ukrainian National Republic. On July 6, 1923, the Ukraine joined the Soviet Union and since that time the postage stamps of Soviet Russia have been in use.

200 Shagiv = 100 Kopecks =
1 Ruble (Karbovanetz)
100 Shagiv = 1 Grivna

Stamps of Russia Overprinted in Violet, Black, Blue, Red or Green

This trident-shaped device was taken from the arms of the Grand Duke Vladimir and adopted as the device of the Ukrainian Republic. The overprint was handstamped, typographed or lithographed. It was applied in various cities in the Ukraine and there are numerous types. Prices are for the most common types.

On Stamps of 1902-03.
Wmkd. Wavy Lines. (168)
1918 Perf. 13½.

1	A12	3½r blk & gray	25.00	30.00
2	A12	7r blk & yel	20.00	25.00

On Stamps of 1909-18.
Lozenges of Varnish on Face.
Perf. 14, 14½ x 15. Unwmkd.

3	A14	1k orange	5	5
4	A14	2k green	5	5
5	A14	3k red	5	5
6	A14	4k carmine	5	5
7	A14	5k claret	5	5
8	A14	7k lt bl	10	25
9	A15	10k dk bl	10	5
10	A11	14k bl & rose	10	25
11	A11	15k red brn & bl	5	5
12	A8	20k bl & car	5	5
13	A11	25k grn & gray vio	25	30
14	A11	35k red brn & grn	5	5
15	A8	50k vio & grn	5	5
16	A11	70k brn & org	5	5

Perf. 13½.

17	A9	1r lt brn, brn & org	5	30
18	A12	3½r mar & lt grn	50	1.25
19	A13	5r dk bl, grn & pale bl	10.00	45.00
20	A12	7r dk grn & pink	4.00	6.75
21	A13	10r scar, yel & gray	7.00	9.00
	Nos. 3-21 (19)		22.60	63.65

On Stamps of 1917.
Perf. 14, 14½ x 15.

41	A14	10k on 7k lt bl	5	5
42	A11	20k on 14k bl & rose	5	5

On Stamps of 1917-18.
Imperf.

43	A14	1k orange	5	5
44	A14	2k gray grn	5	5
45	A14	3k red	5	5
46	A15	4k carmine	10	10
47	A14	5k claret	30	55
51	A11	15k red brn & bl	5	5
52	A8	20k bl & car	30	90
54	A11	35k red brn & grn	5	5
55	A8	50k vio & grn	25	50
56	A11	70k brn & org	5	10
57	A9	1r pale brn, brn & red org	5	5
58	A12	3½r mar & lt grn	9	90
59	A13	5r dk bl, grn & pale bl	20	25
60	A12	7r dk grn & pink	45	65
61	A13	10r scar, yel & gray	27.50	27.50

The trident overprint was applied by favor to Russia Nos. 88-104, 110-111, the Romanov issue. It also exists on Russia No. 127, the 25k of 1917.

Republic's Trident Emblem A1

Ukrainian Peasant A2

Ukrainian Girl A3

Trident A4

Inscription of Value A5

Typographed.
1918 Thin Paper Imperf.

62	A1	10sh buff	15	20
63	A2	20sh brown	15	20
64	A3	30sh ultra	15	20
a.		30sh bl	1.00	2.00
65	A4	40sh green	15	20
66	A5	50sh red	15	20
	Nos. 62-66 (5)		75	1.00

The stamps of this issue exist perforated or pin-perforated unofficially.

Thin Cardboard.
Inscriptions on Back.
1918 Perf. 11½

67	A1	10sh buff		2.00
68	A2	20sh brown		2.00
69	A3	30sh ultra		3.00
70	A4	40sh green		2.00
71	A5	50sh red		2.00
a.		Imperf.		35.00

Nos. 67 to 71 were intended to be used as paper money but they were occasionally used for postage.

Nos. 62 and 66 Surcharged **35 K.**

1919 Imperf. Unwmkd.

72	A1	35k on 10sh buff	6.00	9.00
73	A5	70k on 50sh red	25.00	30.00
a.		Surch. invtd.		45.00

Some authorities state that Nos. 72-73 were issued by the South Russia government of Gen. Anton Denikin.

A6

1919 Lithographed.

74	A6	20gr red & grn	4.00	12.50

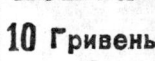

Nos. 62-66 surcharged "a" and "b" are of private origin.

Югъ Россіи.

Ukraine stamps of 1918—10, 20, 30 and 50sh—overprinted diagonally as above ("South Russia") are believed to be of private origin.

Р.О.П. и Т.

This overprint (in two sizes) was privately applied to stamps of Russian Offices in Turkey. The overprinted stamps were not issued.

A lithographed set of 14 stamps (1gr to 200gr) of these types, perf. 11½, was prepared in 1920, but never placed in use. Price, set $1.00.
All values exist imperf., some with inverted centers.

SEMI-POSTAL STAMPS.
Ukrainian Soviet Socialist Republic

"Famine"—SP1

Taras G. Shevchenko—SP2

"Death" Stalking Peasant SP3

"Ukraine" Distributing Food SP4

Perf. 14½ x 13½, 13½ x 14½.
1923, June Litho. Unwmkd.

B1	SP1	10 +10k gray bl & blk	50	3.50
a.		Imperf., pair	60.00	100.00
B2	SP2	20 +20k vio brn & org brn	50	3.50
a.		Imperf., pair	60.00	100.00
B3	SP3	90 +30k db & blk, straw	50	3.50
a.		Imperf., pair	60.00	100.00
B4	SP4	150 +50k red brn & blk	50	3.50
a.		Imperf., pair	60.00	100.00

The values of these stamps are in karbovanetz which are the rubles of the Ukraine

Wmk. 116
Wmkd. Crosses and Circles. (116)

B5	SP1	10 +10k gray bl & blk	35.00	60.00

844 UKRAINE—UPPER SENEGAL AND NIGER—UPPER SILESIA

B6	SP2	20 +20k vio brn & org brn	35.00	60.00
a.		Imperf., pair		
B7	SP3	90 +30k db & blk, straw	35.00	60.00
B8	SP4	150 +50k red brn & blk	35.00	60.00

United Arab Republic

Issues for Egypt are listed under Egypt in Vol. II.
Issues for Syria are listed at end of Syria in Vol. IV.

UPPER SENEGAL AND NIGER

(ŭp'ẽr sĕn'ė·gôl' & nĭ'jẽr)

LOCATION—In Northwest Africa, north of French Guinea and Ivory Coast.
GOVT.—A former French Colony.
AREA—617,600 sq. mi.
POP.—2,474,142.
CAPITAL—Bamako.

In 1921 the name of this colony was changed to French Sudan and postage stamps so inscribed were placed in use.

100 Centimes = 1 Franc

General Louis Faidherbe
A1

Oil Palms
A2

Dr. N. Eugène Ballay
A3

Typographed.
1906-07   Perf. 14x13½   Unwmkd.
Name of Colony in Red or Blue

1	A1	1c slate	75	75
2	A1	2c brown	75	75
3	A1	4c brn, gray bl	80	75
4	A1	5c green	2.00	1.40
5	A1	10c car (B)	2.00	1.00
6	A1	15c vio ('07)	2.25	1.75
7	A2	20c bluish gray	2.50	2.25
8	A2	25c bl, pnksh	9.00	2.00
9	A2	30c vio brn, pnksh	3.00	2.75
10	A2	35c yellow	2.00	1.50
11	A2	40c car, az (B)	3.75	2.50
12	A2	45c brn, grnsh	4.50	3.75
13	A2	50c dp vio	3.75	3.00
14	A2	75c bl, org	4.75	4.25
15	A3	1fr blk, az	12.00	8.00
16	A3	2fr bl, pink	25.00	22.50
17	A3	5fr car, straw (B)	52.50	45.00
		Nos. 1-17 (17)	131.50	104.40

Camel with Rider
A4

1914-17   Perf. 13½x14

18	A4	1c brn vio & vio	7	7
19	A4	2c gray & brn vio	8	8
20	A4	4c blk & bl	12	12
21	A4	5c yel grn & bl grn	15	15
a.		Booklet pane of 4		
22	A4	10c red org & rose	90	75
23	A4	15c choc & org ('17)	50	32
24	A4	20c brn vio & blk	50	32
25	A4	25c ultra & bl	55	50
26	A4	30c ol brn & brn	50	45
27	A4	35c car rose & vio	1.10	75
28	A4	40c gray & car rose	65	50
29	A4	45c bl & ol brn	65	60
30	A4	50c blk & grn	65	60
31	A4	75c org & ol brn	75	65
32	A4	1fr brn & brn vio	95	80
33	A4	2fr grn & bl	1.10	1.00
34	A4	5fr vio & blk	4.75	3.25
		Nos. 18-34 (17)	13.97	10.91

SEMI-POSTAL STAMP.

Regular Issue of 1914 Surcharged in Red +5c

1915   Perf. 13½x14   Unwmkd.

B1	A4	10c +5c red org & rose	45	45

POSTAGE DUE STAMPS.

Natives
D1

Numeral of Value
D2

Typographed.
1906   Perf. 14x13½   Unwmkd.

J1	D1	5c grn, grnsh	1.75	1.50
J2	D1	10c red brn	3.75	3.00
J3	D1	15c dk bl	5.25	4.50
J4	D1	20c yellow	6.00	3.00
J5	D1	50c violet	12.00	10.00
J6	D1	60c buff	8.00	7.50
J7	D1	1fr pinkish	18.00	15.00
		Nos. J1-J7 (7)	54.75	44.50

1914

J8	D2	5c green	45	45
J9	D2	10c rose	45	45
J10	D2	15c gray	60	60
J11	D2	20c brown	60	60
J12	D2	30c blue	1.00	1.00
J13	D2	50c black	60	60
J14	D2	60c orange	2.25	2.25
J15	D2	1fr violet	2.25	2.25
		Nos. J8-J15 (8)	8.20	8.20

Stamps of Upper Senegal and Niger were superseded in 1921 by those of French Sudan.

UPPER SILESIA

(ŭp'ẽr sĭ·lē'shĭ·å; -shå)

LOCATION—Formerly in eastern Germany and prior to World War I a part of Germany.

A plebiscite held under the terms of the Treaty of Versailles failed to determine the status of the country, the voting resulting about equally in favor of Germany and Poland. Accordingly, the League of Nations divided the territory between Germany and Poland.

100 Pfennig = 1 Mark
100 Fennigi = 1 Marka

Plebiscite Issues.

A1
Perf. 14x13½
1920, Feb. 20   Typo.   Unwmkd.

1	A1	2½pf slate	40	50
2	A1	3pf brown	40	50
3	A1	5pf green	20	28
4	A1	10pf dl red	45	55
5	A1	15pf violet	20	28
6	A1	20pf blue	20	28
a.		Imperf., pair	225.00	250.00
7	A1	50pf vio brn	4.50	5.75
8	A1	1m claret	4.00	5.50
9	A1	5m orange	4.00	5.50
		Nos. 1-9 (9)	14.35	19.14

Black Surcharge.

5 5 5 5
Pf. Pf. Pf. Pf.
I   II   III IV

10	A1	5pf 15pf vio (I)	11.50	22.50
a.		Type II	11.50	22.50
b.		Type III	11.50	22.50
c.		Type IV	11.50	22.50
11	A1	5pf on 20pf bl (I)	15	28
a.		Type II	20	45
b.		Type III	15	28
c.		Type IV	15	28

Red Surcharge.

10 10 10 10
Pf. Pf. Pf. Pf.
I   II   III IV

12	A1	10pf on 20pf bl (I)	18	32
a.		Type II	18	32
b.		Type III	18	32
c.		Type IV	18	32
d.		Imperf.	32.50	

Black Surcharge.

50 50 50 50 50
Pf. Pf. Pf. Pf. Pf.
I   II   III IV   V

13	A1	50pf on 5m org (I)	18.00	27.50
a.		Type II	18.00	27.50
b.		Type III	18.00	27.50
c.		Type IV	18.00	27.50
d.		Type V	25.00	30.00

Nos. 10-13 are found with many varieties including surcharges inverted, double and double inverted.

A2

Dove with Olive Branch Flying over Silesian Terrain
A3

1920, Mar. 26   Typo.   Perf. 13½x14

15	A2	2½pf gray	25	10
16	A2	3pf red brn	30	10
17	A2	5pf green	15	10
18	A2	10pf dl red	15	10
19	A2	15pf violet	15	10
20	A2	20pf blue	15	10
21	A2	25pf dk brn	25	10
22	A2	30pf orange	15	10
23	A2	40pf ol grn	15	10

Perf. 14x13½.

24	A3	50pf gray	15	10
25	A3	60pf blue	30	15
26	A3	75pf dp grn	90	55
27	A3	80pf red brn	70	40
28	A3	1m claret	42	15
29	A3	2m dk brn	42	28
30	A3	3m violet	70	28
31	A3	5m orange	1.65	1.00
		Nos. 15-31 (17)	6.94	3.81

Nos. 18-28 Overprinted in Black or Red

**Plébiscite
20 mars
1921.**

1921, Mar. 20

32	A2	10pf dl red	2.75	6.75
33	A2	15pf violet	2.75	6.75
34	A2	20pf blue	3.50	11.50
35	A2	25pf dk brn (R)	6.75	18.00
36	A2	30pf orange	6.75	18.00
37	A2	40pf ol grn (R)	6.75	18.00

Overprinted **Plébiscite
20 mars 1921.**

38	A3	50pf gray (R)	6.75	18.00
39	A3	60pf blue	9.00	18.00
40	A3	75pf dp grn	9.00	22.50
41	A3	80pf red brn	9.00	27.50
42	A3	1m claret	13.00	32.50
		Nos. 32-42 (11)	76.00	197.50

Inverted or double overprints exist on Nos. 32-33, 35-40. Counterfeit overprints exist.

Type of 1920 and Surcharged **10 M**

1922, Mar.

45	A3	4m on 60pf ol grn	80	1.40
46	A3	10m on 75pf red	1.25	2.25
47	A3	20m on 80pf org	6.00	12.50

Stamps of the above design were a private issue not recognized by the Inter-Allied Commission of Government.

OFFICIAL STAMPS.

German Stamps of 1905-20 Handstamped in Blue
Wmkd. Lozenges. (125)

1920, Feb.   Perf. 14, 14½.
On Stamps of 1906-19

O1	A22	2pf gray	1.65	2.00
O3	A22	2½pf gray	85	1.00
O4	A16	3pf brown	85	1.00

UPPER SILESIA—UPPER VOLTA

O5	A16	5pf green		85	1.00
a.		Red handstamp		15.00	20.00
O6	A22	7½pf orange		85	1.00
O7	A16	10pf car rose		85	1.00
O8	A22	15pf dk vio		85	1.00
a.		Red handstamp		10.00	13.50
O9	A16	20pf bl vio		85	1.00
a.		Red handstamp		10.00	13.50
O10	A16	25pf org & blk, yel		8.00	10.00
O11	A16	30pf org & blk, buff		85	1.00
O12	A22	35pf red brn		85	1.00
O13	A16	40pf lake & blk		85	1.00
a.		Red handstamp		30.00	40.00
O14	A16	50pf vio & blk, buff		85	1.00
O15	A16	60pf magenta		85	1.00
O16	A16	75pf grn & blk		85	1.00
a.		Red handstamp		30.00	40.00
O17	A16	80pf lake & blk, rose		10.00	12.00
O18	A17	1m car rose		1.65	2.00
O19	A21	2m gray bl		8.00	10.00

On National Assembly Stamps of 1919-20.

O25	A23	10pf car rose	1.40	1.65
O26	A24	15pf choc & bl	2.50	3.00
a.		Red handstamp	1.75	1.75
O27	A25	25pf grn & red	5.00	6.00
O28	A25	30pf red vio & red	3.75	4.50

On Semi-Postal Stamps of 1919.

O30	A16	10pf + 5pf car	10.00	12.00
O31	A22	15pf + 5pf dk vio	10.00	12.00
		Nos. O1-O31 (24)	73.00	88.15

Prices of Nos. O1-O31 are for reprints made with a second type of handstamp differing in minor details from the original (example: period after "S" is round instead of the earlier triangular form). Originals are scarce. Counterfeits exist.
Germany No. 65C with this handstamp is considered bogus by experts.

Local Official Stamps of Germany, 1920, Overprinted

C.G.H.S.

1920, Apr.   *Perf. 14.*

O32	LO2	5pf green	25	32
O33	LO3	10pf carmine	25	32
O34	LO4	15pf vio brn	25	32
O35	LO5	20pf dp ultra	25	32
O36	LO6	30pf org, buff	25	32
O37	LO7	50pf vio, buff	55	55
O38	LO8	1m red, buff	5.50	7.50
		Nos. O32-O38 (7)	7.30	9.65

Same Overprint on Official Stamps of Germany, 1920-21.

1920-21

O39	O1	5pf green	95	2.25
O40	O2	10pf carmine	5	7
O41	O3	15pf vio brn	5	7
O42	O4	20pf dp ultra	5	7
O43	O5	30pf org, buff	5	7
O44	O6	40pf car rose	5	7
O45	O7	50pf vio, buff	5	7
O46	O8	60pf red brn	5	7
O47	O9	1m red, buff	5	7
O48	O10	1.25m blk, yel	5	7
O49	O11	2m dk bl	4.50	6.75
O50	O12	5m brn, yel	12	22

1922, Feb. Wmkd. Network. (126)

O51	O11	2m dk bl	12	22
		Nos. O39-O51 (13)	6.14	10.07

This overprint is found both horizontal and vertical, reading up or down. It also exists on most values inverted, double and double, one inverted.

Methods and style of listing are detailed in "Special Notices" at the front of this volume.

A particular stamp may be scarce, but if few want it, its market potential may remain relatively low.

UPPER VOLTA
(ŭp'ẽr vŏl'tȧ)

LOCATION—In northwestern Africa, north of Ghana.
GOVT.—Republic.
AREA—105,869 sq. mi.
POP.—6,320,000 (est. 1977).
CAPITAL—Ouagadougou.

In 1919 the French territory of Upper Volta was detached from the southern section of Upper Senegal and Niger and made a separate colony. In 1933 the Colony was divided among its neighbors, French Sudan, Ivory Coast and Niger Territory. The Republic of the Upper Volta was proclaimed Dec. 11, 1958.

100 Centimes = 1 Franc

Stamps and Types of Upper Senegal and Niger, 1914-17, Overprinted in Black or Red

HAUTE-VOLTA

1920-28 *Perf. 13½x14.* Unwmkd.

1	A4	1c brn vio & vio	5	5
2	A4	2c gray & brn vio (R)	5	5
3	A4	4c blk & bl	6	6
4	A4	5c yel grn & bl grn	30	15
a.		Booklet pane of 4	7.50	
5	A4	5c ol brn & dk brn ('22)	6	6
6	A4	10c red org & rose	45	38
7	A4	10c yel org & brn ('22)	8	8
8	A4	10c cl & bl ('25)	22	22
a.		Ovpt. omitted	80.00	
9	A4	15c choc & org	45	32
10	A4	20c brn vio & blk (R)	60	50
11	A4	25c ultra & bl	60	32
12	A4	25c blk & bl grn ('22)	45	45
a.		Overprint omitted	65.00	
13	A4	30c brn & brn (R)	90	75
14	A4	30c red org & rose ('22)	30	30
15	A4	30c vio & brn red ('25)	30	30
16	A4	30c dl grn & bl grn ('27)	45	45
17	A4	35c car rose & vio	45	32
18	A4	40c gray & car rose	45	38
19	A4	45c bl & brn (R)	38	22
20	A4	50c blk & grn	1.25	1.10
21	A4	50c ultra & bl ('22)	15	15
22	A4	50c red org & bl ('25)	30	30
23	A4	60c org red ('26)	15	15
24	A4	65c bis & pale bl ('28)	45	45
25	A4	75c org & brn	32	32
26	A4	1fr brn & brn vio	55	45
27	A4	2fr grn & bl	75	65
28	A4	5fr vio & blk (R)	2.00	2.00
		Nos. 1-28 (28)	12.52	10.93

Hausa Chief A5

Hausa Woman A6

Hausa Warrior—A7

1928   Typo.   *Perf. 13½x14*

43	A5	1c ind & brn	5	5
44	A5	2c brn & lil	8	8
45	A5	4c blk & yel	15	15
46	A5	5c ind & gray bl	22	22
47	A5	10c ind & pink	50	50
48	A5	15c brn & bl	75	75
49	A5	20c brn & grn	80	80
50	A6	25c brn & yel	90	90
51	A6	30c dp grn & grn	90	90
52	A6	40c blk & pink	90	90
53	A6	45c brn & bl	1.00	1.00
54	A6	50c blk & grn	1.00	1.00
55	A6	65c ind & bl	1.40	1.40
56	A6	75c blk & bl	1.00	1.00
57	A6	90c brn red & lil	1.00	1.00

Perf. 14x13½.

58	A7	1fr brn & grn	90	90
59	A7	1.10fr ind & lil	1.10	1.10
60	A7	1.50fr ultra & grysh	1.50	1.50
61	A7	2fr grn & bl	1.75	1.75
62	A7	3fr brn & grn	2.25	2.25
63	A7	5fr brn & lil	2.25	2.25
64	A7	10fr blk & grn	8.50	8.50
65	A7	20fr blk & pink	12.00	12.00
		Nos. 43-65 (23)	40.90	40.90

Stamps and Types of 1920 Surcharged with New Value and Bars.

1924-27

33	A4	25c on 2fr grn & bl	30	30
34	A4	25c on 5fr vio & blk	30	30
35	A4	65c on 45c bl & brn ('25)	50	50
36	A4	85c on 75c org & brn ('25)	60	60
37	A4	90c on 75c brn red & sal pink ('27)	60	60
38	A4	1.25fr on 1fr dp bl & lt bl (R) ('26)	30	30
39	A4	1.50fr on 1fr dp bl & ultra ('27)	1.00	1.00
40	A4	3fr on 5fr dl red & brn org ('27)	1.25	1.25
41	A4	10fr on 5fr ol grn & lil rose ('27)	7.50	7.50
42	A4	20fr on 5fr org brn & vio ('27)	9.00	9.00
		Nos. 33-42 (10)	21.35	21.35

No. 9 Surcharged in Various Colors

$0{,}01 = 0{,}01$

1922

29	A4	0,01c on 15c choc & org (Bk)	38	38
a.		Double surch.	47.50	47.50
30	A4	0,02c on 15c choc & org (Bl)	38	38
31	A4	0,05c on 15c choc & org (R)	38	38

Type of 1920 Surcharged

$60 = 60$

1922

32	A4	60c on 75c vio, pnksh	32	32

Colonial Exposition Issue.
Common Design Types

1931   Engraved   *Perf. 12½*
Country Name Typo. in Black

66	CD70	40c dp grn	1.75	1.75
67	CD71	50c violet	1.75	1.75
68	CD72	90c red org	1.75	1.75
69	CD73	1.50fr dl bl	1.75	1.75

Common Design Types
pictured in section at front of book.

Republic

President Ouezzin Coulibaly A8

Deer Mask and Deer A9

Engraved
1959   *Perf. 13*   Unwmkd.

70	A8	25fr blk & mag	40	20

Issued to commemorate the first anniversary of the proclamation of the Republic and to honor Ouezzin Coulibaly, Council President, who died in December, 1958.

Imperforates

Most Upper Volta stamps from 1959 onward exist imperforate in issued and trial colors, and also in small presentation sheets in issued colors.

1960

Animal Masks: 1fr, 2fr, 4fr, Wart hog. 5fr, 6fr, 8fr, Monkey. 10fr, 15fr, 20fr, Buffalo. 25fr, Coba (antelope). 30fr, 40fr, 50fr, Elephant. 60fr, 85fr, Secretary bird.

71	A9	30c rose & vio	5	5
72	A9	40c buff & dp cl	5	5
73	A9	50c bl grn & gray ol	5	5
74	A9	1fr red, blk & red brn	5	5
75	A9	2fr emer, yel grn & dk grn	8	6
76	A9	4fr bl, vio & ind	8	8
77	A9	5fr ol bis, red & brn	12	10
78	A9	6fr grnsh bl & vio brn	12	10
79	A9	8fr org & red brn	15	12
80	A9	10fr lt yel grn & plum	20	15
81	A9	15fr org, ultra & brn	25	20
82	A9	20fr brn & ultra	35	20
83	A9	25fr bl, emer & dp cl	40	20
84	A9	30fr dk bl grn, blk & brn	50	20
85	A9	40fr ultra, ind & dk car	60	30
86	A9	50fr brt pink, brn & grn	70	35
87	A9	60fr org brn & bl	90	50
88	A9	85fr gray ol & dk bl	1.25	65
		Nos. 71-88 (18)	5.90	3.41

C.C.T.A. Issue
Common Design Type

1960   Engraved   *Perf. 13*

89	CD106	25fr vio bl & sl	50	50

Council of the Entente Issue

Emblem of the Entente A9a

1960   Photogravure   *Perf. 13x13½*

90	A9a	25fr multi	60	50

Council of the Entente.

UPPER VOLTA

President Maurice Yameogo
A10

1960, May 1   Engraved   Perf. 13
91   A10   25fr dk vio brn & sl   40   25

Flag, Village and Couple—A11

1960, Aug. 5   Perf. 13   Unwmkd.
92   A11   25fr red brn, blk & red   50   40

Issued to commemorate the proclamation of independence, Aug. 5, 1960.

World Meteorological Organization Emblem—A12

1961, May 4
93   A12   25fr blk, bl & red   45   40

First World Meteorological Day.

Arms of Republic
A13

1961, Dec. 8   Photo.   Perf. 12½x12½
94   A13   25fr multi   40   40

The 1961 independence celebrations.

World Meteorological Organization Emblem, Weather Station and Sorghum Grain—A14

1962, March 23   Perf. 13   Unwmkd.
95   A14   25fr dk bl, emer & brn   45   40

Issued to commemorate the United Nations Second World Meteorological Day, March 23.

Hospital and Nurse—A15

1962, June 23   Perf. 13x12
96   A15   25fr multi   50   50

Founding of Upper Volta Red Cross.

Buffalos at Water Hole
A16

Designs: 10fr, Lions (horiz.). 15fr, Defassa waterbuck. 25fr, Arly reservation (horiz.). 50fr, Diapaga reservation (horiz.). 85fr, Buffon's kob.

Perf. 12½x12, 12x12½
1962, June 30   Engraved
97   A16   5fr sep, bl & grn   15   10
98   A16   10fr red brn, grn & yel   25   15
99   A16   15fr sep, grn & yel   40   25
100   A16   25fr vio brn, bl & grn   70   30
101   A16   50fr vio brn, bl & grn   1.20   80
102   A16   85fr red brn, bl & grn   1.75 1.25
      Nos. 97-102 (6)   4.45 2.85

Abidjan Games Issue
Common Design Type

Designs: 20fr, Soccer. 25fr, Bicycling. 85fr, Boxing (all horiz.).

1962, July 21   Photo.   Perf. 12½x12
103   CD109 20fr multi   50   40
104   CD109 25fr multi   60   50
105   CD109 85fr multi   1.35   85

Abidjan Games, Dec. 24-31, 1961.

African-Malgache Union Issue
Common Design Type

1962, Sept. 8   Unwmkd.
106   CD110 30fr red, bluish grn & gold   1.10 1.00

Issued to commemorate the first anniversary of the African and Malgache Union.

Weather Map and U.N. Emblem
A17

1963, Mar. 23   Perf. 12x12½
107   A17   70fr multi   1.10   75

3rd World Meteorological Day, Mar. 23.

Basketball
A18

Amaryllis
A19

Designs: 25fr, Discus. 50fr, Judo.

1963, Apr. 11   Engraved   Perf. 13
108   A18   20fr lil, car & sep   35   20
109   A18   25fr ocher, car & sep   40   20
110   A18   50fr ultra, car & sep   80   40

Friendship Games, Dakar, Apr. 11-21.

1963   Photogravure
Flowers: 50c, Hibiscus. 1fr, Oldenlandia grandiflora. 1.50fr, Rose moss (portulaca). 2fr, Tobacco. 4fr, Morning glory. 5fr, Striga senegalensis. 6fr, Cowpea. 8fr, Lepidagathis heudelotiana. 10fr, Spurge. 25fr, Argyreia nervosa. 30fr, Rangoon creeper. 40fr, Water lily. 50fr, White plumeria. 60fr, Crotalaria retusa. 85fr, Hibiscus. Nos. 111-119 are vertical.

111   A19   50c multi   5   5
112   A19   1fr multi   5   5
113   A19   1.50fr multi   6   5
114   A19   2fr multi   8   5
115   A19   4fr multi   8   8
116   A19   5fr multi   10   8
117   A19   6fr multi   12   10
118   A19   8fr multi   18   15
119   A19   10fr multi   25   18
120   A19   15fr multi   30   22
121   A19   25fr multi   45   25
122   A19   30fr multi   50   30
123   A19   40fr multi   60   45
124   A19   50fr multi   80   55
125   A19   60fr multi   1.00   65
126   A19   85fr multi   1.40   85
      Nos. 111-126 (16)   6.02   4.06

Centenary Emblem and Globe
A20

Scroll
A21

1963, Oct. 21   Perf. 12   Unwmkd.
127   A20   25fr multi   75   30

Centenary of International Red Cross.

1963, Dec. 10   Photo.   Perf. 13x12½
128   A21   25fr dp cl, gold & bl   45   30

Issued to commemorate the 15th anniversary of the Universal Declaration of Human Rights.

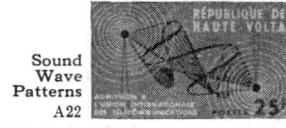

Sound Wave Patterns
A22

1964, Jan. 16   Perf. 12½x13
129   A22   25fr multi   40   30

Issued to commemorate Upper Volta's admission to the International Telecommunications Union.

Barograph and WMO Emblem
A23

1964, Mar. 23   Engraved   Perf. 13
130   A23   50fr dk car rose, grn & bl   85   60

4th World Meteorological Day, Mar. 23.

World Connected by Letters and Carrier Pigeon—A24

Design: 60fr, World connected by letters and jet plane.

1964, Mar. 29   Photo.   Perf. 13x12½
131   A24   25fr gray brn & ultra   40   30
132   A24   60fr gray brn & org   90   65

Issued to commemorate Upper Volta's admission to the Universal Postal Union.

IQSY Emblem and Seasonal Allegories
A25

1964, Aug. 17   Engraved   Perf. 13
133   A25   30fr grn, ocher & car   50   40

International Quiet Sun Year, 1964-65.

Cooperation Issue
Common Design Type

1964, Nov. 7   Perf. 13   Unwmkd.
134   CD119 70fr dl bl grn, dk brn & car   1.00   65

Hotel Independance, Ouagadougou
A26

1964, Dec. 11   Litho.   Perf. 12½x13
135   A26   25fr multi   1.50   50

Pigmy Long-tailed Sunbird
A27

Comoe Waterfall
A28

Birds: 15fr, Olive-bellied Sunbird. 20fr, Splendid Sunbird.

1965, Mar. 1   Photo.   Perf. 13x12½
       Size: 22x36mm.
136   A27   10fr multi   30   25
137   A27   15fr multi   40   30
138   A27   20fr multi   60   40
       See No. C20.

1965   Engraved   Perf. 13
Design: 25fr, Great Waterfall of Banfora (horiz.).
139   A28   5fr yel grn & bl brn   12   10
140   A28   25fr dk red, brt bl & grn 40   25

UPPER VOLTA

Soccer Abraham Lincoln
A29 A30

Designs: 25fr, Boxing gloves and ring. 70fr, Tennis rackets, ball and net.

1965, July 15   Perf. 13   Unwmkd.
141	A29	15fr brn, red & dk grn	25	20
142	A29	25fr pale org, bl & brn	45	30
143	A29	70fr dk car & brt grn	1.00	50

Issued to commemorate the First African Games, Brazzaville, July 18–25.

1965, Nov. 3   Photo.   Perf. 13x12½
144	A30	50fr grn & multi	75	55

Centenary of death of Abraham Lincoln.

Pres. Maurice Yameogo—A31

1965, Dec. 11   Photo.   Perf. 13x12½
145	A31	25fr multi	40	25

Mantis
A32

Wart Hog   Headdress
A33   A34

Designs: 1fr, Nemopistha imperatrix. 2fr, Ball python. 4fr, Grasshopper. 6fr, Scorpion. 8fr, Green monkey. 10fr, Dromedary. 15fr, Leopard. 20fr, Cape buffalo. 25fr, Hippopotamus. 30fr, Agama lizard. 45fr, Common puff adder. 50fr, Chameleon. 60fr, Ugada limbata. 85fr, Elephant.

1966   Perf. 13x12½, 12½x13
146	A33	1fr vio bl & multi	5	5
147	A33	2fr dp bl & multi	8	5
148	A32	3fr brt rose & multi	10	8
149	A32	4fr grn & multi	10	10
150	A33	5fr ocher & multi	13	10
151	A32	6fr gold, blk & brn	15	12
152	A33	8fr brt rose & multi	18	15
153	A32	10fr ultra & multi	22	10
154	A32	15fr dk bl & multi	30	15
155	A32	20fr yel grn & multi	35	25
156	A32	25fr yel & multi	45	25
157	A32	30fr gold & multi	55	30
158	A32	45fr multi	80	35
159	A33	50fr vio & multi	90	50
160	A33	60fr bl & multi	1.10	65
161	A33	85fr multi	1.35	75
	Nos. 146-161 (16)	6.81	3.95

1966, Apr. 9   Photo.   Perf. 13x12½
Designs: 25fr, Plumed headdress. 60fr, Male dancer.
162	A34	20fr yel grn, choc & red	30	20
163	A34	25fr multi	40	25
164	A34	60fr org, dk brn & red	90	50

Issued to commemorate the International Negro Arts Festival, Dakar, Senegal, Apr. 1–24.

Pô Church
A35

Design: No. 166 Bobo-Dioulasso Mosque.

1966, Apr. 15   Perf. 12½x13
165	A35	25fr multi	35	25
166	A35	25fr bl, cr & red brn	35	25

The Red Cross Helping the World
A36

1966, June   Photo.   Perf. 13x12½
167	A36	25fr lem, blk & car	35	20

Issued to honor the Red Cross.

Boy Scouts in Camp
A37

Design: 15fr, Two Scouts on a cliff exploring the country.

1966, June 15   Perf. 12½x13
168	A37	10fr multi	20	12
169	A37	15fr blk, bis brn, & dl yel	25	14

Issued to honor the Boy Scouts.

Cow Receiving Injection
A38

1966, Aug. 16   Photo.   Perf. 12½x13
170	A38	25fr yel, blk & bl	40	30

Campaign against cattle plague.

Plowing with Donkey
A39

Design: 30fr, Crop rotation, Kamboincé Experimental Station.

1966, Sept. 15   Photo.   Perf. 12½x13
171	A39	25fr multi	35	20
172	A39	30fr multi	40	25

Issued to publicize national and rural education; No. 172 also commemorates the 3rd anniversary of the Kamboincé Experimental Station.

UNESCO Emblem and Map of Africa
A40

UNICEF Emblem and Children
A41

1966, Dec. 10   Engraved   Perf. 13
173	A40	50fr brt bl, blk & red	75	40
174	A41	50fr dk vio, dp lil & dk red	75	40

Issued to commemorate the 20th anniversary of UNESCO (United Nations Educational, Scientific and Cultural Organization) and of UNICEF (United Nations Children's Emergency Fund).

 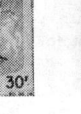

Arms of Upper Volta   Symbols of Agriculture, Industry, Men and Women
A42   A43

1967, Jan. 2   Photo.   Perf. 12½x13
175	A42	30fr multi	35	15

Europafrica Issue

1967, Feb. 4   Photo.   Perf. 12½
176	A43	60fr multi	75	45

Scout Handclasp and Jamboree Emblem
A44

Design: 5fr, Jamboree emblem and Scout holding hat.

1967, June 8   Photo.   Perf. 12½x13
177	A44	5fr multi	30	15
178	A44	20fr multi	85	60

Issued to publicize the 12th Boy Scout World Jamboree, Farragut State Park, Idaho, Aug. 1–9. See No. C41.

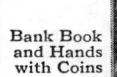 

Bank Book and Hands with Coins
A45

1967, Aug. 22   Engraved   Perf. 13
179	A45	30fr sl grn, ocher & ol	40	20

National Savings Bank.

Mailman on Bicycle
A46

1967, Oct. 15   Engraved   Perf. 13
180	A46	30fr dk bl, emer & brn	45	25

Issued for Stamp Day, 1967.

Monetary Union Issue
Common Design Type

1967, Nov. 4   Engraved   Perf. 13
181	CD125	30fr dk vio & dl bl	40	20

Issued to commemorate the 5th anniversary of the West African Monetary Union.

View of Nizier
A47

Designs (Olympic Emblem and): 50fr, Les Deux-Alps (vert.). 100fr, Ski lift and view of Villard-de-Lans.

1967, Nov. 28
182	A47	15fr brt bl, grn & brn	25	15
183	A47	50fr brt bl & sl grn	75	35
184	A47	100fr brt bl, grn & red	1.50	75

Issued to publicize the 10th Winter Olympic Games, Grenoble, France, Feb. 6–18, 1968.

White and Black Men Holding Human Rights Emblem
A48

1968, Jan. 2   Photo.   Perf. 12½x13
185	A48	20fr brt bl, gold & dp car	30	20
186	A48	30fr grn, gold & dp car	45	25

International Human Rights Year 1968.

Administration School and Student
A49

1968, Feb. 2   Engraved   Perf. 13
187	A49	30fr ol bis, Prus bl & brt grn	40	20

National School of Administration.

WHO Emblem and Sick People
A50

1968, Apr. 7   Engraved   Perf. 13
188	A50	30fr ind, brt bl & car rose	45	25
189	A50	50fr brt bl, sl grn & lt brn	70	35

Issued to commemorate the 20th anniversary of the World Health Organization.

Telephone Office, Bobo-Dioulasso
A51

UPPER VOLTA

1968, Sept. 30		Photo.	Perf. 12½x12
190	A51	30fr multi	45 25

Issued to commemorate the opening of the automatic telephone office in Bobo-Dioulasso.

Weaver
A52

1968, Oct. 30		Engraved	Perf. 13
		Size: 36x22mm.	
191	A52	30fr mag, brn & ocher	45 25

See No. C58.

Grain Pouring over World, Plower and FAO Emblem
A53

1969, Jan. 7		Engraved	Perf. 13
192	A53	30fr sl, vio bl & mar	40 20

Issued to publicize the world food program of the U.N. Food and Agriculture Organization.

Automatic Looms and ILO Emblem
A54

1969, Mar. 15		Engraved	Perf. 13
193	A54	30fr brt grn, mar & ind	40 20

Issued to commemorate the 50th anniversary of the International Labor Organization.

Smith
A55

1969, Apr. 3		Engraved	Perf. 13
		Size: 36x22mm.	
194	A55	5fr mag & blk	15 12

See No. C64.

Blood Donor
A56

1969, May 15		Engraved	Perf. 13
195	A56	30fr blk, bl & car	40 25

Issued to commemorate the 50th anniversary of the League of Red Cross Societies.

Nile Pike
A57

Fish: 20fr, Nannocharax gobioides. 25fr, Hemigrammocharax polli. 55fr, Alestes luteus. 85fr, Micralestes voltae.

1969		Engraved	Perf. 13
		Size: 36x22mm.	
196	A57	20fr brt bl, brn & yel	45 30
197	A57	25fr sl, brn & dk brn	45 30
198	A57	30fr dk ol & blk	60 40
199	A57	55fr dk grn, yel & ol	80 65
200	A57	85fr sl brn & pink	1.75 1.35
		Nos. 196-200, C66-C67 (7)	7.00 4.60

Development Bank Issue
Common Design Type

1969, Sept. 10		Engraved	Perf. 13
201	CD130	30fr sl grn, grn & ocher	35 20

Issued to commemorate the 5th anniversary of the African Development Bank.

Millet
A58

Design: 30fr, Cotton.

1969, Oct. 30		Photo.	Perf. 12½x13
202	A58	15fr dk brn, grn & yel	25 15
203	A58	30fr dp cl & brt bl	45 15

See Nos. C73–C74.

ASECNA Issue
Common Design Type

1969, Dec. 12		Engraved	Perf. 13
204	CD132	100fr brown	1.25 75

Niadale Mask
A59

Carvings from National Museum: 30fr, Niaga. 45fr, Man and woman, Iliu Bara. 80fr, Karan Weeba figurine.

1970, Mar. 5		Engraved	Perf. 13
207	A59	10fr dk car rose, org & dk brn	15 10
209	A59	30fr dk brn, brt vio & grnsh bl	40 20
211	A59	45fr yel grn, brn & bl	60 30
212	A59	80fr pur, rose lil & brn	1.10 50

African Huts and European City
A60

1970, Apr. 25		Engraved	Perf. 13
213	A60	30fr dk brn, red & bl	40 20

Issued for Linked Cities' Day.

Mask for Nebwa Gnomo Dance
A61

Designs: 8fr, Cauris dancers (vert.). 20fr, Gourmantchés dancers (vert.). 30fr, Larllé dancers.

1970, May 7		Photo.	Perf. 13
214	A61	5fr lt brn, vio bl & blk	10 8
215	A61	8fr org brn, car & blk	15 10
216	A61	20fr dk brn, sl grn & ocher	25 15
217	A61	30fr dp car, dk gray & brn	40 20

Education Year Emblem, Open Book and Pupils
A62

Design: 90fr, Education Year emblem, telecommunication and education symbols.

1970, May 14			Perf. 12½x12
218	A62	40fr blk & multi	50 30
219	A62	90fr ol & multi	1.00 50

International Education Year, 1970.

U.P.U. Headquarters Issue

Abraham Lincoln, U.P.U. Headquarters and Emblem—A63

1970, May 20		Engraved	Perf. 13
220	A63	30fr dk car rose, ind & red brn	45 25
221	A63	60fr dk bl grn, vio & red brn	75 40

See note after CD133, Common Design section.

Shipbuilding Industry
A64

Designs: 45fr, Chemical industry. 80fr, Electrical industry.

1970, June 15			
222	A64	15fr brt pink, red brn & blk	20 12
223	A64	45fr emer, dp bl & blk	50 30
224	A64	80fr red brn, cl & blk	1.00 50

1970 Hanover Fair.

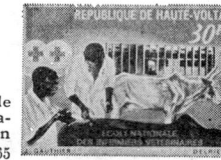

Cattle Vaccination
A65

1970, June 30		Photo.	Perf. 13
225	A65	30fr Prus bl, yel & sep	45 20

National Veterinary College.

Vaccination and Red Cross
A66

1970, Aug. 28		Engr.	Perf. 12½x13
226	A66	30fr choc & car	40 25

Issued for the Upper Volta Red Cross.

Europafrica Issue

Nurse with Child, by Frans Hals
A67

Paintings: 30fr, Courtyard of a House in Delft, by Pieter de Hooch. 150fr, Christina of Denmark, by Hans Holbein. 250fr, Courtyard of the Royal Palace at Innsbruck, Austria, by Albrecht Dürer.

1970, Sept. 25		Litho.	Perf. 13x14
227	A67	25fr multi	35 20
228	A67	30fr multi	45 25
229	A67	150fr multi	2.00 1.00
230	A67	250fr multi	3.00 1.50

Citroën
A68

Design: 40fr, Old and new Citroën cars.

1970, Oct. 16		Engraved	Perf. 13
231	A68	25fr ol brn, mar & sl grn	35 20
232	A68	40fr brt grn, plum & sl	60 30

57th Paris Automobile Salon.

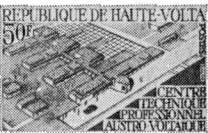

Professional Training Center
A69

1970, Dec. 10		Engraved	Perf. 13
233	A69	50fr grn, bis & brn	55 25

Opening of Professional Training Center under joint sponsorship of Austria and Upper Volta.

Upper Volta Arms and Soaring Bird
A70

1970, Dec. 10			Photogravure
234	A70	30fr lt bl & multi	35 20

Tenth anniversary of independence, Dec. 11.

UPPER VOLTA

Political Maps of Africa—A71
1970, Dec. 14   Litho.   Perf. 13½
235   A71   50fr multi   60   30

10th anniversary of the declaration granting independence to colonial territories and countries.

Beingolo Hunting Horn—A72
Musical Instruments: 15fr, Mossi guitar (vert.). 20fr, Gourounsi flutes (vert.). 25fr, Lunga drums.
1971, Mar. 1   Engraved   Perf. 13
236   A72   5fr bl, brn & car   10   6
237   A72   15fr grn, crim rose & brn   20   12
238   A72   20fr car rose, bl & gray   25   15
239   A72   25fr brt grn, red brn & ol gray   30   20

Voltaphilex I, National Philatelic Exhibition.

Four Races A73
1971, Mar. 21   Engraved   Perf. 13
240   A73   50fr rose cl, lt grn & dk brn   60   35

International year against racial discrimination.

Telephone and Globes A74
1971, May 17   Engraved   Perf. 13
241   A74   50fr brn, gray & dk pur   60   30

3rd World Telecommunications Day.

Cane Field Worker, Banfora Sugar Mill—A75   **Cotton and Voltex Mill Emblem—A76**
1971, June 24   Photo.   Perf. 13
242   A75   10fr multi   15   8
243   A76   35fr multi   40   20

Industrial development.

Gonimbrasia Hecate A77
Butterflies and Moths: 2fr, Hamanumida daedalus. 3fr, Ophideres materna. 5fr, Danaus chrysippus. 40fr, Hypolimnas misippus. 45fr, Danaus petiverana.
1971, June 30
244   A77   1fr bl & multi   5   5
245   A77   2fr lt lil & multi   5   5
246   A77   3fr multi   10   8
247   A77   5fr gray & multi   15   12
248   A77   40fr ocher & multi   70   35
249   A77   45fr multi   90   50
Nos. 244-249 (6)   1.95   1.15

Kabuki Actor A78
Design: 40fr, African mask and Kabuki actor.
1971, Aug. 12   Photo.   Perf. 13
250   A78   25fr multi   30   15
251   A78   40fr multi   45   20

Philatokyo 71, Philatelic Exposition, Tokyo, Apr. 19-29.

No. 226 Surcharged

1971   Engraved   Perf. 12½x13
252   A66   100fr on 30fr choc & car   1.00   60

10th anniversary of Upper Volta Red Cross.

Seed Preparation A79
Designs: 75fr, Old farmer with seed packet (vert.). 100fr, Farmer in rice field.
1971, Sept. 30   Photo.   Perf. 13
253   A79   35fr ocher & multi   35   20
254   A79   75fr lt bl & multi   75   32
255   A79   100fr brn & multi   1.00   50

National campaign for seed protection.

Outdoor Classroom A80
Design: 50fr, Mother learning to read.
1971, Oct. 14
256   A80   35fr multi   35   20
257   A80   50fr multi   55   25

Women's education.

Joseph Dakiri, Soldiers Driving Tractors A81
Design: 40fr, Dakiri and soldiers gathering harvest.
1971, Oct. 13   Perf. 12x12½
258   A81   15fr blk, yel & red brn   20   15
259   A81   40fr bl & multi   40   25

Joseph Dakiri (1938-1971), inaugurator of the Army-Aid-to-Agriculture Program.

Spraying Lake, Fly, Man Leading Blind Women A82
1971, Nov. 26   Photo.   Perf. 13
260   A82   40fr dk brn, yel & bl   40   25

Drive against onchocerciasis, roundworm infestation.

Children and UNICEF Emblem A84
1971, Dec. 11   Perf. 13
262   A84   45fr red, bis & blk   50   25

25th anniversary of the United Nations International Children's Fund (UNICEF).

Peulh House A85
Upper Volta Houses: 20fr, Gourounsi house. 35fr, Mossi houses. 45fr, Bobo house (vert.). 50fr, Dagari house (vert.). 90fr, Bango house, interior.
Perf. 13x13½, 13½x13
1971-72   Photogravure
263   A85   10fr ver & multi   12   8
264   A85   20fr multi   25   15
265   A85   35fr brt grn & multi   35   20
266   A85   45fr multi ('72)   50   25
267   A85   50fr multi ('72)   60   30
268   A85   90fr multi ('72)   90   50
Nos. 263-268 (6)   2.72   1.48

Town Halls of Bobo-Dioulasso and Chalons-sur-Marne—A86
1971, Dec. 23   Perf. 13x12½
269   A86   40fr yel & multi   40   22

Kinship between the cities of Bobo-Dioulasso, Upper Volta, and Chalons-sur-Marne, France.

Louis Armstrong—A87
1972, May 17   Perf. 14x13
270   A87   45fr multi   70   40

Black musician. See No. C104.

Red Crescent, Cross and Lion Emblems A88
1972, June 23   Perf. 13x14
271   A88   40fr yel & multi   50   25

World Red Cross Day. See No. C105.

Coiffure of Peulh Woman A89
Designs: Various hair styles.
1972, July 23   Litho.   Perf. 13
272   A89   25fr bl & multi   30   15
273   A89   25fr emer & multi   35   15
274   A89   75fr yel & multi   70   28

Classroom A90
Designs: 15fr, Clinic. 20fr, Factory. 35fr, Cattle. 40fr, Plowers. 85fr, Road building machinery.
1972, Oct. 30   Engraved   Perf. 13
275   A90   10fr sl grn, lt grn & choc   8   8
276   A90   15fr brt grn, brn org & brn   15   12
277   A90   20fr bl, lt brn & grn   20   15
278   A90   35fr grn, brn & brt bl   28   20
279   A90   40fr choc, pink & sl grn   32   25
Nos. 275-279, C106 (6)   1.73   1.15

2nd Five-Year Plan.

West African Monetary Union Issue
Common Design Type
1972, Nov. 2
280   CD136   40fr brn, bl & gray   40   20

10th anniversary of West African Monetary Union.

Lottery Office and Emblem A91
1972, Nov. 6   Lithographed
281   A91   35fr multi   35   18

5th anniversary of National Lottery.

UPPER VOLTA

Donkeys—A92
Domestic Animals: 10fr, Geese. 30fr, Goats. 50fr, Cow. 65fr, Dromedaries.

1972, Dec. 4 Litho. Perf. 13½x12½

282	A92	5fr multi	5	5
283	A92	10fr multi	10	5
284	A92	30fr multi	30	12
285	A92	50fr multi	50	20
286	A92	65fr multi	65	32
		Nos. 282-286 (5)	1.60	74

Mossi Woman's Hair Style, and Village—A93

1973, Jan. 24 Engraved Perf. 13

287	A93	5fr sl grn, org & choc	5	5
288	A93	40fr bl, org & choc	35	20

Eugene A. Cernan and Lunar Module A94
Designs: 65fr, Ronald E. Evans and splashdown. 100fr, Capsule, in orbit and interior (horiz.). 150fr, Harrison H. Schmitt and lift-off. 200fr, Conference and moon-buggy. 500fr, Moon-buggy and capsule (horiz.).

Perf. 12½x13½, 13½x12½

1973, Mar. 29 Litho.

289	A94	50fr multi	50	25
290	A94	65fr multi	65	32
291	A94	100fr multi	1.00	50
292	A94	150fr multi	1.50	75
293	A94	200fr multi	2.00	1.00
		Nos. 289-293 (5)	5.65	2.82

Souvenir Sheet

294	A94	500fr multi	5.00	2.50

Apollo 17 moon mission. No. 294 has multicolored margin showing moon in space. Size: 104x80mm.

No. 260 Surcharged in Red

O. M. S. 25ᵉ Anniversaire

45F

1973, Apr. 7 Photogravure Perf. 13

295	A82	45fr on 40fr multi	40	25

25th anniversary of the World Health Organization.

Scout Bugler A95

1973, July 18 Litho. Perf. 12½x13

296	A95	20fr multi	20	10
	Nos. 296, C160-C163 (5)		4.85	2.43

African Postal Union Issue
Common Design Type

1973, Sept. 12 Engr. Perf. 13

297	CD137	100fr brt red, mag & dl yel	1.00	40

Pres. Kennedy, Saturn 5 on Assembly Trailer A96

Designs (John F. Kennedy and): 10fr, Atlas rocket carrying John H. Glenn. 30fr, Titan 2 rocket and Gemini 3 capsule.

1973, Sept. 12 Litho. Perf. 12½x13

298	A96	5fr multi	5	5
299	A96	10fr multi	10	5
300	A96	30fr multi	30	15
		Nos. 298-300, C167-C168 (5)	5.45	2.75

10th anniversary of death of Pres. John F. Kennedy.

Cross-examination—A97
Designs: 65fr, "Diamond Ede." 70fr, Forensic Institute. 150fr, Robbery scene.

1973, Sept. 15 Perf. 13x12½

301	A97	50fr multi	50	25
302	A97	65fr multi	65	32
303	A97	70fr multi	70	35
304	A97	150fr multi	1.50	75

Interpol, 50th anniversary. See No. C170.

Market Place, Ouagadougou—A98

Design: 40fr, Swimming pool, Hotel Independence.

1973, Sept. 30

305	A98	35fr multi	35	18
306	A98	40fr multi	40	20

Tourism. See Nos. C171-C172.

Protestant Church—A99
Design: 40fr, Ouahigouya Mosque.

1973, Sept. 28 Perf. 13x12½

307	A99	35fr multi	35	18
308	A99	40fr multi	40	20

Houses of worship. See No. C173.

Kiembara Dancers A100
Design: 40fr, Dancers.

1973, Nov. 30 Litho. Perf. 12½x13

309	A100	35fr multi	35	18
310	A100	40fr multi	40	20

Folklore. See Nos. C174-C175.

Yuri Gagarin and Aries—A101
Famous Men and their Zodiac Signs: 10fr, Lenin and Taurus. 20fr, John F. Kennedy, rocket and Gemini. 25fr, John H. Glenn, orbiting capsule and Cancer. 30fr, Napoleon and Leo. 50fr, Goethe and Virgo. 60fr, Pelé and Libra. 75fr, Charles de Gaulle and Scorpio. 100fr, Beethoven and Sagittarius. 175fr, Conrad Adenauer and Capricorn. 200fr, Edwin E. Aldrin, Jr. (Apollo XI) and Aquarius. 250fr, Lord Baden-Powell and Pisces.

1973, Dec. 15 Litho. Perf. 13x14

311	A101	5fr multi	5	5
312	A101	10fr multi	10	5
313	A101	20fr multi	15	8
314	A101	25fr multi	20	10
315	A101	30fr multi	25	12
316	A101	50fr multi	45	22
317	A101	60fr multi	55	28
318	A101	75fr multi	65	32
319	A101	100fr multi	90	45
320	A101	175fr multi	1.60	80
321	A101	200fr multi	1.75	85
322	A101	250fr multi	2.25	1.10
		Nos. 311-322 (12)	8.90	4.42

Rivera with Italian Flag and Championship '74 Emblem—A102
Design: 40fr, World Cup, soccer ball, World Championship '74 emblem and Pelé with Brazilian flag.

1974, Jan. 15 Perf. 13x12½

323	A102	5fr multi	5	5
324	A102	40fr multi	40	20
		Nos. 323-324, C179-C181 (5)	4.70	2.38

10th World Cup Soccer Championship, Munich, June 13-July 7.

Charles de Gaulle A103
Designs: 40fr, De Gaulle memorial. 60fr, Pres. Charles de Gaulle.

1974, Feb. 4 Litho. Perf. 12½x13

325	A103	35fr multi	30	15
326	A103	40fr multi	32	18
327	A103	60fr multi	50	25

Gen. Charles de Gaulle (1890-1970), president of France. Nos. 325-327 printed se-tenant. See Nos. C183-C184.

N'Dongo and Cameroun Flag A104
Designs (World Cup, Emblems and): 20fr, Kolev and Bulgarian flag. 50fr, Keita and Mali flag.

1974, Mar. 19

328	A104	10fr multi	10	5
329	A104	20fr multi	20	10
330	A104	50fr multi	50	25
		Nos. 328-330, C185-C186 (5)	5.30	2.65

10th World Cup Soccer Championship, Munich, June 13-July 7.

Map and Flags of Members—A105

1974, May 29   Photo.   Perf. 13x12½
331 A105 40fr bl & multi   35   20
15th anniversary of the Council of Accord.

**UPU Emblem and Mail Coach
A106**
Designs (UPU emblem and): 40fr, Steamship. 85fr, Mailman.

1974, July 23   Litho.   Perf. 13½
332 A106 35fr multi   35   18
333 A106 40fr multi   40   20
334 A106 85fr multi   85   42
     Nos. 332-334, C189-C191 (6)   7.60 3.80

Universal Postal Union centenary.

**Soccer Game, Winner Italy, in
France, 1938—A107**
Designs (World Cup, Game and Flags): 25fr, Uruguay, in Brazil, 1950. 50fr, East Germany, in Switzerland, 1954.

1974, Sept. 2   Litho.   Perf. 13½
335 A107 10fr multi   10   5
336 A107 25fr multi   25   12
337 A107 50fr multi   50   25
     Nos. 335-337, C193-C195 (6)   6.85 3.42

World Cup Soccer winners.

Map and Farm Woman—A108
1974, Oct. 2   Litho.   Perf. 13x12½
338 A108 35fr yel & multi   30   20
Kou Valley Development.

Nos. 332-334 Overprinted in Red
"100ᵉ ANNIVERSAIRE DE L'UNION
POSTALE UNIVERSELLE / 9 OCTOBRE
1974"

1974, Oct. 9
339 A106 35fr multi   35   18
340 A106 40fr multi   40   20
341 A106 85fr multi   85   42
     Nos. 339-341, C197-C199 (6)   7.60 3.80

Universal Postal Union centenary.

**Flowers, by
Pierre
Bonnard
A109**
Flower Paintings by: 10fr, Jan Brueghel. 30fr, Jean van Os. 50fr, Van Brussel.

1974, Oct. 31   Litho.   Perf. 12½x13
342 A109 5fr multi   5   5
343 A109 10fr multi   10   5
344 A109 30fr multi   25   12
345 A109 50fr multi   40   20
     Nos. 342-345, C201 (5)   3.80 1.92

**Churchill as Officer of India
Hussars—A110**
Churchill: 75fr, As Secretary of State for Interior. 100fr, As pilot. 125fr, meeting with Roosevelt, 1941. 300fr, As painter. 450fr, and "HMS Resolution."

1975, Jan. 11   Perf. 13½
346 A110 50fr multi   45   22
347 A110 75fr multi   65   32
348 A110 100fr multi   85   42
349 A110 125fr multi   1.10   55
350 A110 300fr multi   2.50 1.25
     Nos. 346-350 (5)   5.55 2.76

Souvenir Sheet
351 A110 450fr multi   4.50 2.25
Sir Winston Churchill, birth centenary. No. 351 has multicolored margin showing trench warfare. Size: 115x77mm.

U.S. No. 619 and Minutemen—A111
Designs (U.S. stamps): 40fr, No. 118 and Proclamation of Independence. 75fr, No. 798 and Signing the Constitution. 100fr, No. 1003 and Surrender at Yorktown. 200fr, No. 703 and George Washington. 300fr, No. 644 and Surrender of Burgoyne at Saratoga. 500fr, Nos. 63, 68, 73, 157, 179, 228 and 1483a.

1975, Feb. 17   Litho.   Perf. 11
352 A111 35fr multi   30   15
353 A111 40fr multi   35   18
354 A111 75fr multi   65   32
355 A111 100fr multi   85   42
356 A111 200fr multi   1.75   85
357 A111 300fr multi   2.50 1.25
     Nos. 352-357 (6)   6.40 3.17

**Souvenir Sheet
Imperf.**
358 A111 500fr multi   4.50 2.25
American Bicentennial. No. 358 has multicolored margin with U.S. flags and shield. Size: 127x103mm.

**"Atlantic" No. 2670, 1904–12
A112**
Locomotives from Mulhouse, France, Railroad Museum: 25fr, No. 2029, 1882. 50fr, No. 2129, 1882.

1975, Feb. 28   Litho.   Perf. 13x12½
359 A112 15fr multi   15   8
360 A112 25fr multi   25   12
361 A112 50fr multi   50   25
     Nos. 359-361, C203-C204 (5)   3.90 1.95

**French Flag and Renault Petit
Duc, 1910—A113**
Flags and Old Cars: 30fr, U.S. and Ford Model T, 1909. 35fr, Italy and Alfa Romeo "Le Mans," 1931.

1975, Apr. 6   Perf. 14x13½
362 A113 10fr multi   10   5
363 A113 30fr multi   30   15
364 A113 35fr multi   35   18
     Nos. 362-364, C206-C207 (5)   4.25 2.13

Washington and Lafayette—A114
American Bicentennial: 40fr, Washington reviewing troops at Valley Forge. 50fr, Washington taking oath of office.

1975, May 6   Litho.   Perf. 14
365 A114 30fr multi   30   15
366 A114 40fr multi   40   20
367 A114 50fr multi   50   25
     Nos. 365-367, C209-C210 (5)   6.20 3.10

Souvenir Sheet
367A A114 500fr multi   5.00 2.50
No. 367A has multicolored margin showing White House and U.S. and Upper Volta flags. Size: 127x95mm.

Schweitzer and Pelicans—A115
Design: 15fr, Albert Schweitzer and bateleur eagle.

1975, May 25   Litho.   Perf. 13½
368 A115 5fr multi   5   5
369 A115 15fr multi   15   8
     Nos. 368-369, C212-C214 (5)   5.45 2.73

Albert Schweitzer, birth centenary.

**Apollo and Soyuz Orbiting
Earth—A116**
Design: 50fr, Apollo and Soyuz near link-up.

1975, July 18
370 A116 40fr multi   40   20
371 A116 50fr multi   50   25
     Nos. 370-371, C216-C218 (5)   6.90 3.45

Apollo-Soyuz space test project, Russo-American cooperation, launched July 15, link-up July 17.

**Maria Picasso
Lopez, Artist's
Mother
A117**
Picasso Paintings: 60fr, Self-portrait. 90fr, First Communion.

1975, Aug. 7
372 A117 50fr multi   50   25
373 A117 60fr multi   60   30
374 A117 90fr multi   90   45
     Nos. 372-374, C220-C221 (5)   7.00 3.50

Pablo Ruiz Picasso, 1881–1973.

**Expo '75 Emblem and Tanker,
Idemitsu Maru—A118**
Oceanographic Exposition, Okinawa: 25fr, Training ship, Kaio Maru. 45fr, Firefighting ship, Hiryu. 50fr, Battleship, Yamato. 60fr, Container ship, Kamakura Maru.

1975, Sept. 26   Litho.   Perf. 11
375 A118 15fr multi   15   8
376 A118 25fr multi   25   12
377 A118 45fr multi   45   22
377A A118 50fr multi   50   25
378 A118 60fr multi   60   30
     Nos. 375-378, C223 (6)   3.45 1.72

**Woman, Globe
and IWY Emblem
A119**
1975, Nov. 20   Photo.   Perf. 13
379 A119 65fr multi   55   35
International Women's Year.

UPPER VOLTA

852

Msgr. Joanny Thevenoud and
Cathedral—A120

Design: 65fr, Father Guillaume Templier and Cathedral.

1975, Nov. 20   Engr.   Perf. 13x12½
| 380 | A120 | 55fr grn, blk & dl red | 45 | 25 |
| 381 | A120 | 65fr blk, org & dl red | 55 | 30 |

75th anniversary of the Evangelization of Upper Volta.

Farmer's
Hat, Hoe
and
Emblem
A121

1975, Dec. 10   Photo.   Perf. 13x13½
| 382 | A121 | 15fr buff & multi | 12 | 8 |
| 383 | A121 | 50fr lt grn & multi | 40 | 22 |

Development of the Volta valleys.

Sledding and Olympic Emblem
A122

Designs (Innsbruck Background, Olympic Emblem and): 45fr, Figure skating. 85fr, Skiing.

1975, Dec. 16   Litho.   Perf. 13½
384	A122	35fr multi	28	15
385	A122	45fr multi	35	18
386	A122	85fr multi	70	35
	Nos. 384-386, C225-C226 (5)	4.33	2.18

12th Winter Olympic Games, Innsbruck, Austria, Feb. 4–15, 1976.

Gymnast and Olympic Emblem
A123

Designs (Olympic Emblem and): 50fr, Sailing. 100fr, Soccer.

1976, Mar. 17
387	A123	40fr multi	32	18
388	A123	50fr multi	40	20
389	A123	85fr multi	85	42
	Nos. 387-389, C228-C229 (5)	4.32	2.15

21st Olympic Games, Montreal, Canada, July 17–Aug. 1.

Olympic
Emblem and
Sprinters
A124

Designs (Olympic Emblem and): 55fr, Equestrian. 75fr, Hurdles.

1976, Mar. 25   Litho.   Perf. 11
390	A124	30fr multi	25	12
391	A124	55fr multi	45	22
392	A124	75fr multi	65	32
	Nos. 390-392, C231-C232 (5)	4.85	2.41

21st Olympic Games, Montreal.

Blind
Woman
and Man
A125

1976, Apr. 7   Engr.   Perf. 13
| 393 | A125 | 75fr dk brn, grn & org | 60 | 40 |
| 394 | A125 | 250fr dk brn, ocher & org | 2.00 | 1.20 |

Drive against onchocerciasis, roundworm infestation.

"Deutschland" over Friedrichshafen
A126

Airships: 40fr, "Victoria Louise" over sailing ships. 50fr, "Sachsen" over German countryside.

1976, May 11   Litho.   Perf. 11
395	A126	10fr multi	10	5
396	A126	40fr multi	40	20
397	A126	50fr multi	50	25
	Nos. 395-397, C234-C236 (6)	7.00	3.50

75th anniversary of the Zeppelin.

Viking Lander and Probe on
Mars—A127

Viking Mars project: 55fr, Viking orbiter in flight. 75fr, Titan rocket start for Mars (vert.).

1976, June 24   Perf. 13½
398	A127	30fr multi	25	12
399	A127	55fr multi	45	22
400	A127	75fr multi	65	32
	Nos. 398-400, C238-C239 (5)	6.35	3.16

World Map,
Arms of
Upper Volta
A128

Design: 100fr, World map, arms and dove.

1976, Aug. 19   Litho.   Perf. 12½
| 401 | A128 | 55fr brn & multi | 45 | 30 |
| 402 | A128 | 100fr bl & multi | 80 | 60 |

5th Summit Conference of Non-aligned Countries, Colombo, Sri Lanka, Aug. 9–19.

Bicentennial, Interphil 76 Emblems
and Washington at Battle of
Trenton—A129

Design: 90fr, Bicentennial, Interphil 76 emblems and Seat of Government, Pennsylvania.

1976, Sept. 30   Perf. 13½
403	A129	60fr multi	60	25
404	A129	90fr multi	80	35
	Nos. 403-404, C241-C243 (5)	7.40	3.60

American Bicentennial, Interphil 76, Philadelphia, Pa., May 29–June 6.

U.P.U. and U.N. Emblems—A130

1976, Dec. 8   Engr.   Perf. 13
| 405 | A130 | 200fr red, ol & bl | 1.60 | 1.00 |

25th anniversary of United Nations Postal Administration.

Arms of   Bronze
Tenkodogo   Statuette
A131   A132

Coats of Arms: 20fr, 100fr, Ouagadougou. 65fr, like 10fr.

1977, May 2   Litho.   Perf. 13
406	A131	10fr multi	10	7
407	A131	20fr multi	15	12
408	A131	65fr multi	50	40
409	A131	100fr multi	80	60

1977, June 13   Photo.   Perf. 13
Design: 65fr, Woman with bowl, bronze.
| 410 | A132 | 55fr multi | 45 | 30 |
| 411 | A132 | 65fr multi | 50 | 32 |

Nos. 410-411 issued in sheets and coils with black control number on every 5th stamp.

Granary, Samo   Handbag, Gouin
A133   A134

Corn Granaries: 35fr, Boromo. 45fr, Banfora. 55fr, Mossi.

1977, June 20 Photo.   Perf. 13½x13
412	A133	5fr multi	5	5
413	A133	35fr multi	30	18
414	A133	45fr multi	35	20
415	A133	55fr multi	45	28

1977, June 20
Handbags: 40fr, Bissa. 60fr, Lobi. 70fr, Mossi.
416	A134	30fr multi	25	18
417	A134	40fr multi	30	20
418	A134	60fr multi	50	32
419	A134	70fr multi	55	35

Nos. 390-392 Overprinted in Gold:
a. VAINQUEUR 1976 / LASSE VIREN / FINLANDE
b. VAINQUEUR 1976 / ALWIN SCHOCKEMÖHLE / R.F.A.
c. VAINQUEUR 1976 / JOHANNA SCHALLER / R.D.A.

1977, July 4   Litho.   Perf. 11
420	A124 (a)	30fr multi	25	12
421	A124 (b)	55fr multi	45	22
422	A124 (c)	75fr multi	60	30
	Nos. 420-422, C245-C246 (5)	4.80	2.39

Winners, 21st Olympic Games.

Crinum Ornatum   Haemanthus
A135   Multiflorus
                    A136

Hannoa
Undulata
A137

Designs: Flowers, flowering branches and wild fruits. 175fr, 300fr, horiz.

UPPER VOLTA

1977		Litho.		Perf. 12½	
		Multicolored			
423	A137	2fr	Cordia myxa	5	5
424	A137	3fr	Opilia celtidifolia	5	5
425	A135	15fr	shown	10	8
426	A136	25fr	shown	20	15
427	A135	50fr	shown	40	30
428	A135	90fr	Cochlospermum planchonii	70	50
429	A135	125fr	Clitoria ternatea	1.00	75
430	A136	150fr	Cassia alata	1.20	90
431	A136	175fr	Nauclea latifolia	1.35	1.00
432	A136	300fr	Bombax costatum	2.40	1.75
433	A135	400fr	Eulophia cucullata	3.25	2.40
		Nos. 423-433 (11)		10.70	7.93

Issue dates: 25fr, 150fr, 175fr, 300fr, Aug. 1; 2fr, 3fr, 50fr, Aug. 8; 15fr, 90fr, 125fr, 400fr, Aug. 23.

De Gaulle and Cross of Lorraine—A138

Designs: 200fr, King Baudouin of Belgium.

1977, Aug. 16		Perf. 13½x14		
434	A138	100fr multi	80	35
435	A138	200fr multi	1.60	65

Elizabeth II—A139

Designs: 300fr, Elizabeth II taking salute. 500fr, Elizabeth II after Coronation.

1977, Aug. 16				
436	A139	200fr multi	1.60	65
437	A139	300fr multi	2.40	1.00
		Souvenir Sheet		
438	A139	500fr multi	4.00	1.85

25th anniversary of reign of Queen Elizabeth II. No. 438 has multicolored margin showing Westminster Abbey and Coronation procession. Size: 104x78mm.

Lottery Tickets, Cars and Map of Upper Volta in Flag Colors—A140

1977, Sept. 16		Photo.	Perf. 13	
439	A140	55fr multi	45	35

10th anniversary of National Lottery.

Selma Lagerlöf, Literature—A141

Designs: 65fr, Guglielmo Marconi, physics. 125fr, Bertrand Russell, literature. 200fr, Linus C. Pauling, chemistry. 300fr, Robert Koch, medicine. 500fr, Albert Schweitzer, peace.

1977, Sept. 22		Litho.	Perf. 13½	
440	A141	55fr multi	45	20
441	A141	65fr multi	55	25
442	A141	125fr multi	1.00	40
443	A141	200fr multi	1.60	65
444	A141	300fr multi	2.40	1.00
		Nos. 440-444 (5)	6.00	2.50
		Souvenir Sheet		
445	A141	500fr multi	4.00	1.75

Nobel Prize winners. No. 445 has multicolored margin showing Alfred Nobel. Size: 123x85mm.

The Three Graces, by Rubens—A142

Rubens Paintings: 55fr, Heads of Black Men (horiz.). 85fr, Bathsheba at the Fountain. 150fr, The Drunken Silenus. 200fr, 300fr, Life of Maria de Medicis (different).

1977, Oct. 19		Litho.	Perf. 14	
446	A142	55fr multi	45	20
447	A142	65fr multi	55	25
448	A142	85fr multi	70	35
449	A142	150fr multi	1.20	60
450	A142	200fr multi	1.60	70
451	A142	300fr multi	2.50	90
		Nos. 446-451 (6)	7.00	3.00

Peter Paul Rubens (1577-1640), 400th birth anniversary.

Lenin in His Office—A143

Designs: 85fr, Lenin Monument, Kremlin. 200fr, Lenin with youth. 500fr, Lenin and Leonid Brezhnev.

1977, Oct. 28		Litho.	Perf. 12	
452	A143	10fr multi	10	5
453	A143	85fr multi	70	40
454	A143	200fr multi	1.60	1.00
455	A143	500fr multi	4.00	2.50

Russian October Revolution, 60th anniversary.

Stadium and Brazil No. C79—A144

Designs (Stadium and): 65fr, Brazil No. 1144. 125fr, Gt. Britain No. 458. 200fr, Chile No. 340. 300fr, Switzerland No. 350. 500fr, Germany No. 1147.

1977, Dec. 30		Litho.	Perf. 13½	
456	A144	55fr multi	45	20
457	A144	65fr multi	55	25
458	A144	125fr multi	1.00	40
459	A144	200fr multi	1.60	65
460	A144	300fr multi	2.40	1.00
		Nos. 456-460 (5)	6.00	2.50
		Souvenir Sheet		
461	A144	500fr multi	4.00	1.75

11th World Cup Soccer Championship, Argentina. No. 461 has multicolored margin showing World Cup emblem. Size: 121x82mm.

Jean Mermoz and Seaplane—A145

History of Aviation: 75fr, Anthony H. G. Fokker. 85fr, Wiley Post. 90fr, Otto Lilienthal (vert.). 100fr, Concorde. 500fr, Charles Lindbergh and "Spirit of St. Louis."

1978, Jan. 2		Litho.	Perf. 13½	
462	A145	65fr multi	55	25
463	A145	75fr multi	60	30
464	A145	85fr multi	70	30
465	A145	90fr multi	75	30
466	A145	100fr multi	80	35
		Nos. 462-466 (5)	3.40	1.50
		Souvenir Sheet		
467	A145	500fr multi	4.00	1.85

No. 467 has multicolored margin showing "Spirit of St. Louis" over Atlantic. Size: 92x118mm.

Crataeva Religiosa—A146

Designs: 75fr, Fig tree.

1978, Feb. 28		Litho.	Perf. 12½	
468	A146	55fr multi	45	35
469	A146	75fr multi	60	45

Methods and style of listing are detailed in "Special Notices" at the front of this volume.

Virgin and Child, by Rubens—A147

1978, May 24		Litho.	Perf. 13½x14	
470	A147	500fr multi	4.00	1.75

Peter Paul Rubens (1577-1640), 400th birth anniversary. No. 470 has multicolored margin with garland of flowers. Size: 88x109mm.

Antenna and ITU Emblem—A148

1978, May 30			Perf. 13	
471	A148	65fr sil & multi	55	25

10th World Telecommunications Day.

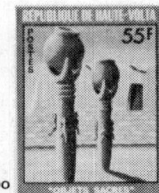

Fetish Gate of Bobo—A146

Design: 65fr, Mossi fetish.

1978, July 10		Litho.	Perf. 13½	
472	A146	55fr multi	45	20
473	A146	65fr multi	55	25

Capt. Cook and "Endeavour"—A150

Designs (Capt. Cook and): 85fr, Death on Hawaiian beach. 250fr, Navigational instruments. 350fr, "Resolution."

1978, Sept. 1		Litho.	Perf. 14½	
474	A150	65fr multi	55	25
475	A150	85fr multi	70	30
476	A150	250fr multi	2.00	1.00
477	A150	350fr multi	2.75	1.25

Capt. James Cook (1728-1779), explorer.

Nos. 436-438 Overprinted Vertically in Silver:

"ANNIVERSAIRE DU COURONNEMENT 1953-1978"

1978, Oct. 24		Litho.	Perf. 13½x14	
478	A139	200fr multi	1.60	65
479	A139	300fr multi	2.40	1.00
		Souvenir Sheet		
480	A139	500fr multi	4.00	1.75

25th anniversary of Coronation of Queen Elizabeth II. Overprint in 3 lines on 200fr, in 2 lines on 300fr and 500fr. Nos. 478-480 exist with overprint in metallic red.

UPPER VOLTA

Trent Castle, by Dürer—A151

Dürer Paintings: 150fr, Virgin and Child with St. Anne. 250fr, Sts. George and Eustachius. 350fr, Hans Holzschuher (all vertical).

Perf. 14x13½, 13½x14

1978, Nov. 20   Lithographed

481	A151	65fr multi	55	25
482	A151	150fr multi	1.25	55
483	A151	250fr multi	2.00	1.00
484	A151	350fr multi	2.75	1.00

Albrecht Dürer (1471–1528), German painter.

Human Rights Emblem A152

1978, Dec. 10   Litho.   Perf. 12½

| 485 | A152 | 55fr multi | 45 | 20 |

Universal Declaration of Human Rights, 30th anniversary.

Nos. 456–461 Overprinted in Silver

a. VAINQUEURS 1950 URUGUAY / 1978 / ARGENTINE
b. VAINQUEURS 1970 BRESIL / 1978 ARGENTINE
c. VAINQUEURS 1966 GRANDE BRETAGNE / 1978 ARGENTINE
d. VAINQUEURS / 1962 BRESIL / 1978 ARGENTINE
e. VAINQUEURS 1954 ALLEMAGNE (RFA) / 1978 ARGENTINE
f. VAINQUEURS 1974 ALLEMAGNE (RFA) / 1978 ARGENTINE

1979, Jan. 4   Litho.   Perf. 13½

486	A144(a)	55fr multi	45	20
487	A144(b)	65fr multi	55	25
488	A144(c)	125fr multi	1.00	40
489	A144(d)	200fr multi	1.60	60
490	A144(e)	300fr multi	2.40	1.00
	Nos. 486–490 (5)		6.00	2.45

Souvenir Sheet

| 491 | A144(f) | 500fr multi | 4.00 | 1.85 |

Winners, World Soccer Cup Championships 1950–1978.

Radio Station A153

Design: 65fr, Mail plane at airport.

1979, Mar. 30   Litho.   Perf. 12½

| 492 | A153 | 55fr multi | 45 | 20 |
| 493 | A153 | 65fr multi | 55 | 25 |

Post and Telecommunications Organization, 10th anniversary.

Scott's International Album provides spaces for an extensive representative collection of the world's postage stamps.

Teacher and Pupils, IYC Emblem A154

1979, Apr. 9   Perf. 13½

| 494 | A154 | 75fr multi | 62 | 30 |

International Year of the Child.

Telecommunications A155

1979, May 17   Litho.   Perf. 13

| 495 | A155 | 70fr multi | 70 | 30 |

11th Telecommunications Day.

Basketmaker and Upper Volta No. 111—A156

1979, June 8   Photogravure

| 496 | A156 | 100fr multi | 1.00 | 50 |
| 497 | A156 | 100fr multi | 1.00 | 50 |

Philexafrique II, Libreville, Gabon, June 8–17. Nos. 496, 497 each printed in sheets of 10 and 5 labels showing exhibition emblem.

Synodontis Voltae A157

Fresh-water Fish: 50fr, Micralestes comoensis. 85fr, Silurus.

1979, June 10   Litho.   Perf. 12½

498	A157	20fr multi	20	10
499	A157	50fr multi	50	25
500	A157	85fr multi	85	45

Rowland Hill, Train and Upper Volta No. 60—A158

Designs (Rowland Hill, Trains and Upper Volta Stamps): 165fr, No. 59. 200fr, No. 57. 300fr, No. 56. 500fr, No. 55.

1979, June   Litho.   Perf. 13½

501	A158	65fr multi	65	32
502	A158	165fr multi	1.65	80
503	A158	200fr multi	2.00	1.00
504	A158	300fr multi	3.00	1.50

Souvenir Sheet

| 505 | A158 | 500fr multi | 5.00 | 2.50 |

Sir Rowland Hill (1795–1879), originator of penny postage. No. 505 has multicolored margin showing Penny Black and Upper Volta stamps. Size: 120x82mm.

Wildlife Fund Emblem and Waterbuck A159

Protected Animals: 40fr, Roan antelope. 60fr, Caracal. 100fr, African bush elephant. 175fr, Hartebeest. 250fr, Leopard.

1979, Aug. 30   Litho.   Perf. 14½

506	A159	30fr multi	30	15
507	A159	40fr multi	40	20
508	A159	60fr multi	60	30
509	A159	100fr multi	1.00	50
510	A159	175fr multi	1.75	85
511	A159	250fr multi	2.50	1.25
	Nos. 506–511 (6)		6.55	3.25

Adult Students and Teacher—A160

Design: 55fr, Man reading book (vert.).

Perf. 12½x13, 13x12½

1979, Sept. 8

| 512 | A160 | 55fr multi | 55 | 28 |
| 513 | A160 | 250fr multi | 2.50 | 1.25 |

World Literacy Day.

Map of Upper Volta, Telephone Receiver and Lines, Telecom Emblem—A161

1979, Sept. 20   Perf. 13x12½

| 514 | A161 | 200fr multi | 2.00 | 1.00 |

3rd World Telecommunications Exhibition, Geneva, Sept. 20–26.

See "Special Notices" at the front of this volume for data on the listing methods of this Catalogue, abbreviations, condition, prices and examination.

King Vulture—A162

1979, Oct. 26   Litho.   Perf. 13

Multicolored

515	A162	5fr shown	5	5
516	A162	10fr Hoopoe	10	5
517	A162	15fr Bald vulture	15	8
518	A162	25fr Herons	25	12
519	A162	35fr Ostrich	35	18
520	A162	45fr Crowned crane	45	22
521	A162	125fr Eagle	1.25	62
	Nos. 515–521 (7)		2.60	1.30

Control Tower, Emblem, Jet—A163

1979, Dec. 12   Photo.   Perf. 13x12½

| 522 | A163 | 65fr multi | 65 | 32 |

ASECNA (Air Safety Board), 20th anniversary.

Central Bank of West African States A164

1979, Dec. 28   Litho.   Perf. 12½

| 523 | A164 | 55fr multi | 55 | 28 |

Eugene Jamot, Map of Upper Volta, Tsetse Fly—A165

1979, Dec. 28   Perf. 13x13½

| 524 | A165 | 55fr multi | 55 | 28 |

Eugene Jamot (1879–1937), discoverer of sleeping sickness cure.

For all your Philatelic needs, see the yellow pages.

UPPER VOLTA

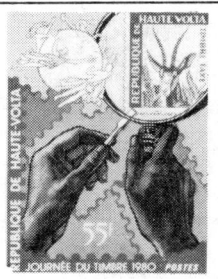

UPU Emblem, Upper Volta Type D4 under Magnifier—A166

1980, Feb. 26 Litho. Perf. 12½x13
525 A166 55fr multi 55 28

Stamp Day 1980.

World Locomotive Speed Record, 25th Anniversary—A167

1980, Mar. 30 Litho. Perf. 12½
526 A167 75fr multi 75 38
527 A167 100fr multi 1.00 50

Pres. Sangoule Lamizana, Pope John Paul II, Cardinal Pau Zoungrana, Map of Upper Volta—A168

1980, May 10 Litho. Perf. 12½
528 A168 65fr shown 65 32

Size: 21x36mm.

529 A168 100fr Pope John-Paul II 1.00 50

Visit of Pope John Paul II to Upper Volta.

12th World Telecommunications Day—A169

1980, May 17 Perf. 13x12½
530 A169 50fr multi 50 25

COLORS
Please refer to page v for a complete list of color abbreviations used in this book.

Mountains and Statue (Solar Energy)—A170

1980, June 12 Litho. Perf. 13
531 A170 65fr Sun and earth 65 32
532 A170 100fr shown 1.00 50

Downhill Skiing, Lake Placid '80 Emblem—A171

1980, June 26 Perf. 14½
533 A171 65fr shown 65 32
534 A171 100fr Women's downhill 1.00 50
535 A171 200fr Figure skating 2.00 1.00
536 A171 350fr Slalom, vert. 3.50 1.75

Souvenir Sheet
537 A171 500fr Speed skating 5.00 2.50

12th Winter Olympic Game Winners, Lake Placid, N.Y., Feb. 12-24. No. 537 has multicolored margin showing Lake Placid emblem, Olympic rings. Size: 112x87mm.

Map of Europe and Africa, Jet A172

Hand Protecting Sand Dune A173

1980, July 14 Litho. Perf. 13
538 A172 100fr multi 1.00 50

Europafrica issue.

1980, July 18

Operation Green Sahel: 55fr, Hands holding seedlings.

539 A173 50fr multi 50 25
540 A173 55fr multi 55 28

Gourmantche Chief Initiation—A174

1980, Sept. 12 Litho. Perf. 14
541 A174 30fr shown 30 15
542 A174 55fr Moro Naba, Mossi Emperor 55 28
543 A174 65fr Princess Guimbe Quattara, vert. 65 32

Gourounsi Mask, Conference Emblem—A175

1980, Oct. 6 Perf. 13½x13
544 A175 65fr multi 65 32

World Tourism Conference, Manila, Sept. 27.

Map of West Africa Showing Upper Volta, Agricultural Symbols—A176

1980, Nov. 5 Litho. Perf. 12½
545 A176 55fr shown 55 28
546 A176 65fr Transportation 65 32
547 A176 75fr Dam, highway 75 38
548 A176 100fr Industry 1.00 50

West African Economic Council, 5th anniversary.

20th Anniversary of Independence—A177

1980, Dec. 11 Perf. 13
549 A177 500fr multi 5.00 2.50

Madonna and Child, by Raphael A178

West African Postal Union, 5th Anniversary A179

Christmas 1980: Paintings of Madonna and Child, by Raphael.

1980, Dec. 22 Perf. 12½
550 A178 60fr multi 60 30
551 A178 150fr multi 1.50 75
552 A178 250fr multi 2.50 1.25

1980, Dec. 24 Photo. Perf. 13½
553 A179 55fr multi 55 28

Dung Beetle—A180

1981, Mar. 10 Litho. Perf. 13x13½, 13½x13
554 A180 5fr shown 5 5
555 A180 10fr Crickets 10 5
556 A180 15fr Termites 15 8
557 A180 20fr Praying mantis, vert. 20 10
558 A180 55fr Emperor moth 55 28
559 A180 65fr Locust, vert. 65 32
Nos. 554-559 (6) 1.70 88

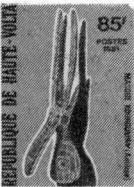

Antelope Mask, Kouroumba A181

Designs: Various ceremonial masks.

1981, Mar. 20 Litho. Perf. 13
560 A181 45fr multi 45 22
561 A181 55fr multi 55 28
562 A181 85fr multi 85 42
563 A181 105fr multi 1.05 52

Notre Dame of Kologh' Naba College, 25th Anniv. A182

1981, Mar. 30
564 A182 55fr multi 55 28

Heinrich von Stephan, UPU Founder, Birth Sesquicentennial—A183

1981, May 4 Litho. Perf. 13
565 A183 65fr multi 65 32

13th World Telecommunications Day—A184

1981, May 17 Perf. 13½x13
566 A184 90fr multi 90 45

Diesel Train, Abidjan-Niger Railroad—A185

Designs: Trains.

UPPER VOLTA

1981, July 6		Litho.	Perf. 13	
567	A185	25fr shown	25	12
568	A185	30fr Gazelle	30	15
569	A185	40fr Belier	40	20

Tree Planting Month—A186

1981, July 15				
570	A186	70fr multi	70	35

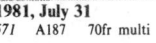

Natl. Red Cross, 20th Anniv. A187

1981, July 31			Perf. 12½x13	
571	A187	70fr multi	70	35

Intl. Year of the Disabled—A188

1981, Aug. 20		Litho.	Perf. 13x12½	
572	A188	70fr multi	70	35

View of Koudougou—A189

1981, Sept. 3		Litho.	Perf. 12½	
573	A189	35fr shown	35	18
574	A189	45fr Toma	45	22
575	A189	85fr Volta Noire	85	42

World Food Day—A190

1981, Oct. 16			Perf. 13	
576	A190	90fr multi	90	45

Elephant—A191

Desings: Various protected species.

1981, Oct. 21		Photo.	Perf. 14	
577	A191	5fr multi	5	5
578	A191	15fr multi	15	8
579	A191	40fr multi	40	20
580	A191	60fr multi	60	30
581	A191	70fr multi	70	35
		Nos. 577-581 (5)	1.90	98

Fight Against Apartheid A192

1981, Dec. 9		Litho.	Perf. 12½	
582	A192	90fr red org	90	45

1981, Dec. 15		Perf. 13x13½, 13½x13		
583	A193	20fr Papayas, horiz.	20	10
584	A193	35fr Fruits, vegtables, horiz.	35	18
585	A193	75fr shown	75	38
586	A193	90fr Melons, horiz.	90	45

Mangoes A193

Guinea Hen A194

West African Rice Development Assoc., 10th Anniv. A195

Designs: Breeding animals. 10fr, 25fr, 70fr, 250fr, 300fr horiz.

1981, Dec. 22			Perf. 13	
587	A194	10fr Donkey	10	5
588	A194	25fr Pig	25	12
589	A194	70fr Cow	70	35
590	A194	90fr shown	90	45
591	A194	250fr Rabbit	2.50	1.25
		Nos. 587-591 (5)	4.45	2.22

Souvenir Sheet

592	A194	300fr Sheep	3.00	1.50

No. 592 has blue and black margin. Size: 90x70mm.

1981, Dec. 29

593	A195	90fr multi	90	45

20th Anniv. of World Food Program—A196

1982, Jan. 18

594	A196	50fr multi	50	25

Traditional Houses—A197

1982, Apr. 23		Litho.	Perf. 12½	
595	A197	30fr Morhonaba Palace, vert.	30	15
596	A197	70fr Bobo	70	35
597	A197	100fr Gourounsi	1.00	50
598	A197	200fr Peulh	2.00	1.00
599	A197	250fr Dagari	2.50	1.25
		Nos. 595-599 (5)	6.50	3.25

14th World Telecommunications Day—A198

1982, May 17

600	A198	125fr multi	1.25	62

Water Lily—A199

1982, Sept. 22			Perf. 13x12½	
601	A199	25fr shown	25	12
602	A199	40fr Kapoks	40	20
603	A199	70fr Frangipani	70	35
604	A199	90fr Cochlospermum planchonii	90	45
605	A199	100fr Cotton	1.00	50
		Nos. 601-605 (5)	3.25	1.62

African Postal Union—A200

1982, Oct. 7

| 606 | A200 | 70fr multi | 70 | 35 |
| 607 | A200 | 90fr multi | 90 | 45 |

25th Anniv. of Cultural Aid Fund—A201

1982, Nov. 10			Perf. 12½x13	
608	A201	70fr multi	70	35

Map, Hand holding Grain, Steer Head—A202

1982			Perf. 12½	
609	A202	90fr multi	90	45

Traditional Hairstyle—A203

1983, Jan.		Litho.	Perf. 12½	
610	A203	90fr lt grn & multi	90	45
611	A203	120fr lt bl & multi	1.20	60
612	A203	170fr pink & multi	1.70	85

8th Film Festival, Ouagadougou—A204

1983, Feb. 10		Litho.	Perf. 13x12½	
613	A204	90fr Scene	90	45
614	A204	500fr Filmaker Dumarou Ganda	5.00	2.50

U.N. Intl. Drinking Water and Sanitation Decade, 1981-90—A205

1983, Apr. 21		Litho.	Perf. 13½x13	
615	A205	60fr Water drops	60	30
616	A205	70fr Carrying water	70	35

Manned Flight Bicentenary—A206

Portraits and Balloons: 15fr, J.M. Montgolfier, 1783. 25fr, Etienne Montgolfier's balloon, 1783, Pilatre de Rozier. 70fr, Charles & Roberts flight, 1783, Jacques Charles. 90fr, Flight over English Channel, John Jeffries. 100fr, Testu-Brissy's horseback flight, Wilhemine Reichardt. 250fr, Andree's Spitzbergen flight, 1897, S.A. Andree. 300fr, Piccard's stratosphere flight, 1931, August Piccard.

1983, Apr. 15		Litho.	Perf. 13½	
617	A206	15fr multi	15	8
618	A206	25fr multi	25	12
619	A206	70fr multi	70	35
620	A206	90fr multi	90	45
621	A206	100fr multi	1.00	50
622	A206	250fr multi	2.50	1.25
		Nos. 617-622 (6)	5.50	2.75

Souvenir Sheet

623	A206	300fr multi	3.00	1.50

No. 623 contains one stamp (38x47mm.). Size: 80x100mm. Nos. 621-623 airmail.

UPPER VOLTA

World Communications Year—A207

1983, May 26 **Litho.** *Perf. 12½*
624	A207	30fr	Man reading letter	30	15
625	A207	35fr	Like No. 624	35	18
626	A207	45fr	Aircraft over stream	45	22
627	A207	90fr	Girl on telephone	90	45

Fishing Resources—A208

1983, July 28 **Litho.** *Perf. 13*
628	A208	20fr	Synadontis gambiensis	10	5
629	A208	30fr	Palmotochromis	15	8
630	A208	40fr	Boy fishing, vert.	20	10
631	A208	50fr	Fishing with net	25	12
632	A208	75fr	Fishing with basket	38	18
		Nos. 628-632 (5)		1.08	53

Anti-deforestation—A209

1983, **Litho.** *Perf. 13*
633	A209	10fr	Planting saplings	5	5
634	A209	50fr	Tree nursery	25	12
635	A209	100fr	Prevent forest fires	50	25
636	A209	150fr	Woman cooking	75	38
637	A209	200fr	Prevent felling, vert.	1.00	50
		Nos. 633-637 (5)		2.55	1.30

Fresco Detail, by Raphael—A210

Paintings: 120fr, Self-portrait, by Pablo Picasso, 1901. (vert.) 185fr, Self-portrait at the palette, by Manet, 1878 (vert.). 350fr, Fresco Detail, diff., by Raphael. 500fr, Goethe, by George Oswald May, 1779 (vert.).

1983, Nov. **Litho.** *Perf. 13*
638	A210	120fr multi	60	30
639	A210	185fr multi	95	48
640	A210	300fr multi	1.50	75
641	A210	350fr multi	1.75	90
642	A210	500fr multi	2.50	1.25
		Nos. 638-642 (5)	7.30	3.68

25th Anniv. of the Republic—A211

1983, Dec. 9 **Litho.** *Perf. 14*
643	A211	90fr	Arms	45	22
644	A211	500fr	Family, flag	2.50	1.25

Council of Unity, 25th Anniv.—A212

1984, May 29 **Litho.** *Perf. 12½*
645	A212	90fr	multi	45	22
646	A212	100fr	multi	50	25

UPPER VOLTA

SEMI-POSTAL STAMPS
Anti-Malaria Issue
Common Design Type
Perf. 12½x12
1962, Apr. 7   Engr.   Unwmkd.
B1   CD108   25fr + 5fr red org   75   75
Issued for the World Health Organization drive to eradicate malaria.

Freedom from Hunger Issue
Common Design Type
1963, Mar. 21   Perf. 13
B2   CD112   25fr + 5fr dk grn, bl & brn   75   75
Freedom from Hunger campaign of U.N. Food and Agriculture Organization.

AIR POST STAMPS

Plane over Map Showing Air Routes—AP1
Designs: 200fr, Plane at airport, Ouagadougou. 500fr, Champs Elysées, Ouagadougou.

Engraved
1961, March 4   Perf. 13   Unwmkd.
C1   AP1   100fr dk bl, hn brn & lt grn   1.50   55
C2   AP1   200fr gray grn, rose brn & sep   3.00   1.10
C3   AP1   500fr multi   7.50   3.00

Air Afrique Issue
Common Design Type
1962, Feb. 17
C4   CD107   25fr brt pink, dk pur & lt grn   50   35
Issued to commemorate the founding of Air Afrique (African Airlines).

U.N. Emblem and Upper Volta Flag—AP2
Photogravure
1962, Sept. 22   Perf. 13½x12½
C5   AP2   50fr multi   75   40
C6   AP2   100fr multi   1.50   80
Admission to U.N., second anniversary.

Post Office, Ouagadougou—AP3
1962, Dec. 11   Perf. 13x12
C7   AP3   100fr multi   1.35   75

Jet Over Map AP4

1963, June 24
C8   AP4   200fr multi   3.00   1.50
First jet flight, Ouagadougou to Paris.

African Postal Union Issue
Common Design Type
1963, Sept. 8   Perf. 12½   Unwmkd.
C9   CD114   85fr dp vio, ocher & red   1.25   80

No. C8 Surcharged in Red

AIR AFRIQUE
19-11-63
50F

1963, Nov. 19   Perf. 13x12
C10   AP4   50fr on 200fr multi   90   75
See note after Mauritania No. C26.

Europafrica Issue
Common Design Type
Design: 50fr, Sunburst and Europe linked with Africa.
1964, Jan. 6   Perf. 12x13
C11   CD116   50fr multi   1.35   90

Ramses II, Abu Simbel AP5

Greek Portrait Head AP6

1964, Mar. 8   Engraved   Perf. 13
C12   AP5   25fr dp grn & choc   50   45
C13   AP5   100fr brt bl & brn   2.00   1.75
Issued to publicize the UNESCO world campaign to save historic monuments of Nubia.

1964, July 1   Perf. 13   Unwmkd.
Designs (Greek sculpture): 25fr, Seated boxer. 85fr, Victorious athlete. 100fr, Venus of Milo.
C14   AP6   15fr dk red, blk & sl grn   30   20
C15   AP6   25fr dk red, blk & sl grn   40   30
C16   AP6   85fr dk red, Prus grn & dk brn   1.25   90
C17   AP6   100fr dk red, dk brn & Prus grn   1.60   1.10
   a. Min. sheet   7.00   7.00
18th Olympic Games, Tokyo, Oct. 10–25. No. C17a contains one each of Nos. C14–C17. Size: 99½x145mm.

West African Gray Woodpecker AP7

President John F. Kennedy AP8

1964, Oct. 1   Engraved   Perf. 13
C18   AP7   250fr multi   4.00   2.75

1964, Nov. 25   Photo.   Perf. 12½
C19   AP8   100fr org, brn & lil   1.75   1.50
   a. Souv. sheet of 4   7.00   7.00
Issued in memory of Pres. John F. Kennedy (1917–1963). No. C19a contains four No. C19 with brown marginal inscription. Size: 90x128mm.

Bird Type of Regular Issue, 1965
Design: 500fr, Abyssinian roller.
Size: 27x48mm.
1965, Mar. 1   Photo.   Perf. 13
C20   A27   500fr multi   8.00   4.00

Earth and Sun—AP9
1965, Mar. 23   Engraved
C21   AP9   50fr multi   85   32
5th World Meteorological Day.

Hughes Telegraph, ITU Emblem and Dial Telephone—AP10
1965, May 17   Perf. 13   Unwmkd.
C22   AP10   100fr red, sl grn & bl grn   1.50   75
Issued to commemorate the centenary of the International Telecommunication Union.

ICY Emblem—AP10a
1965, June 21   Photo.   Perf. 13
C23   AP10a   25fr multi   50   25
C24   AP10a   100fr multi   1.35   65
   a. Miniature sheet of 4   3.75   3.75
Issued for the International Cooperation Year, 1965. No. C24a contains two each of Nos. C23–C24. Size: 135x93mm.

Early Bird Satellite over Globe AP12

Tiros Satellite and Weather Map AP13

1965, Sept. 15   Perf. 13   Unwmkd.
C27   AP12   30fr brt bl, brn & brn red   50   30
Issued to publicize space communications.

1966, March 23   Engraved   Perf. 13
C28   AP13   50fr dk car, brt bl & blk   75   50
6th World Meteorological Day.

FR-1 Satellite over Ouagadougou Space Tracking Station AP14
1966, Apr. 28   Perf. 13
C29   AP14   250fr mag, ind & org brn   4.00   2.25

WHO Headquarters, Geneva AP15
1966, May 3   Photogravure
C30   AP15   100fr yel, blk & bl   1.50   85
Issued to commemorate the inauguration of the World Health Organization Headquarters, Geneva.

Air Afrique Issue
Common Design Type
1966, Aug. 31   Photo.   Perf. 13
C31   CD123   25fr tan, blk & yel grn   45   20
Issued to commemorate the introduction of DC-8F planes by Air Afrique.

Sir Winston Churchill, British Lion and "V" Sign AP16

1965, Aug. 9   Engraved   Perf. 13
C25   AP11   60fr bl grn, sl grn & red brn   90   45
C26   AP11   85fr sl grn, red brn & brn   1.25   65

Sacred Sabou Crocodile—AP11
Design: 85fr, Lion (vert.).

UPPER VOLTA

1966, Nov. 5 Engraved *Perf. 13*

C32 AP16 100fr sl grn & car rose 1.50 80

Issued in memory of Sir Winston Spencer Churchill (1874–1965), statesman and World War II leader.

Pope Paul VI, Peace Dove, U.N. General Assembly and Emblem—AP17

1966, Nov. 5

C33 AP17 100fr dk bl & pur 1.50 80

Issued to commemorate Pope Paul's appeal for peace before the U.N. General Assembly, Oct. 4, 1965.

Blind Man and Lions Emblem AP18

1967, Feb. 28 Engraved *Perf. 13*

C34 AP18 100fr dk vio bl, brt bl & dk brn 2.00 80

50th anniversary of Lions International.

U.N. Emblem and Rain over Landscape AP19 — Diamant Rocket AP20

1967, March 23 Engraved *Perf. 13*

C35 AP19 50fr ultra, dk grn & bl grn 90 40

7th World Meteorological Day.

1967, Apr. 18 Engraved *Perf. 13*

French Spacecraft: 20fr, FR-1 satellite (horiz.). 30fr, D1-C satellite. 100fr, D1-D satellite (horiz.).

C36	AP20	5fr brt bl, sl grn & org	10	8
C37	AP20	20fr lil & sl bl	35	20
C38	AP20	30fr red brn, brt bl & emer	50	25
C39	AP20	100fr emer & dp cl	1.50	75

A little time given to study of the arrangement of the Scott Catalogue can make it easier to use effectively.

Albert Schweitzer and Organ Pipes AP21

1967, May 12 Engraved *Perf. 13*

C40 AP21 250fr cl & blk 4.00 2.25

Issued in memory of Dr. Albert Schweitzer (1875–1965), medical missionary.

World Map and 1967 Jamboree Emblem—AP22

1967, June 8 Photogravure

C41 AP22 100fr multi 1.50 85

Issued to publicize the 12th Boy Scout World Jamboree, Farragut State Park, Idaho, Aug. 1–9.

Madonna and Child, 15th Century AP23

Paintings: 20fr, Still life by Paul Gauguin. 50fr, Pietà, by Dick Bouts. 60fr, Anne of Cleves, by Hans Holbein the Younger. 90fr, The Money Lender and his Wife, by Quentin Massys (38x40mm.). 100fr, Blessing of the Risen Christ, by Giovanni Bellini. 200fr, The Handcart, by Louis Le Nain (horiz.). 250fr, The Four Evangelists, by Jacob Jordaens.

Perf. 12½x12, 12x12½, 13½ (90fr)

1967–68 Photogravure

C42	AP23	20fr multi ('68)	40	20
C43	AP23	30fr multi	45	25
C44	AP23	50fr multi	75	50
C45	AP23	60fr multi ('68)	90	50
C46	AP23	90fr multi ('68)	1.35	85
C47	AP23	100fr multi	1.50	75
C48	AP23	200fr multi ('68)	3.00	1.75
C49	AP23	250fr multi	4.00	2.00
		Nos. C42-C49 (8)	12.35	6.80

See also Nos. C70–C72.

African Postal Union Issue, 1967
Common Design Type

1967, Sept. 9 Engraved *Perf. 13*

C50 CD124 100fr brn red, dp bl & bl grn 1.25 50

Caravelle "Ouagadougou"—AP24

1968, Feb. 29 Engraved *Perf. 13*

C51 AP24 500fr bl, dp cl & blk 7.50 3.25

WMO Emblem, Sun, Rain, Wheat AP25

1968, Mar. 23 Engraved *Perf. 13*

C52 AP25 50fr dk red, ultra & gray grn 70 35

8th World Meteorological Day.

Europafrica Issue

Clove Hitch—AP25a

1968, July 20 Photo. *Perf. 13*

C53 AP25a 50fr yel bis, blk & dk red 60 30

See note after Niger No. C89.

Vessel in Form of Acrobat with Bells, Colima Culture—AP26

Mexican Sculptures: 30fr, Ballplayer, Veracruz (vert.). 60fr, Javelin thrower, Colima (vert.). 100fr, Seated athlete with cape, Jalisco.

1968, Oct. 14 Engraved *Perf. 13*

C54	AP26	10fr dk red, ocher & choc	25	15
C55	AP26	30fr bl grn, brt grn & dk grn	50	25
C56	AP26	60fr ultra, ol & mar	1.00	50
C57	AP26	100fr brt grn, bl & mar	1.50	75

Issued to commemorate the 19th Olympic Games, Mexico City, Oct. 12–27.

Artisan Type of Regular Issue
Design: 100fr, Potter.

1968, Oct. 30 Engraved *Perf. 13*
Size: 48x27mm.

C58 A52 100fr choc, cop red & ocher 1.20 55

PHILEXAFRIQUE Issue

Too Late or The Letter, by Armand Cambon AP27

C59 AP27 100fr multi 1.60 1.25

Issued to publicize PHILEXAFRIQUE, Philatelic Exhibition in Abidjan, Feb. 14–23, 1969. Printed with alternating rose claret label.

Albert John Luthuli AP28

Design: No. C61, Mahatma Gandhi.

1968, Dec. 16 Photo. *Perf. 12½*

C60	AP28	100fr dk grn, yel grn & blk	1.50	80
C61	AP28	100fr dk grn, yel & blk	1.50	80
a.		Min. sheet	6.00	6.00

Issued to honor exponents of non-violence. No. C61a contains 2 each of Nos. C60–C61 arranged checkerwise. Size: 121x160mm.

2nd PHILEXAFRIQUE Issue
Common Design Type

Design: 50fr, Upper Volta No. 59, dancers and musicians.

1969, Feb. 14 Engraved *Perf. 13*

C62 CD128 50fr pur, bl car & brn 85 85

Issued to commemorate the opening of PHILEXAFRIQUE, Abidjan, Feb. 14.

Weather Sonde, WMO Emblem, Mule and Cattle in Irrigated Field—AP29

1969, Mar. 24 Engraved *Perf. 13*

C63 AP29 100fr dk brn, brt bl & grn 1.35 75

9th World Meteorological Day.

Artisan Type of Regular Issue
Design: 150fr, Basket weaver.

1969, Apr. 3 Engraved *Perf. 13*
Size: 48x27mm.

C64 A55 150fr brn, bl & blk 1.75 90

UPPER VOLTA

Lions Emblem, Eye and Blind Man
AP30

1969, Apr. 30 Photogravure
C65 AP30 250fr red & multi 3.75 1.50

Issued to publicize the 12th Congress of District 403 of Lions International, Ouagadougou, May 2–3.

Fish Type of Regular Issue

Designs: 100fr, Phenacogrammus pabrensis. 150fr, Upside-down catfish.

1969 Engraved *Perf. 13*
Size: 48x27mm.
C66 A57 100fr sl, pur & yel 1.20 65
C67 A57 150fr org brn, gray & sl 1.75 95

Earth and Astronaut—AP31

Embossed on Gold Foil

1969 *Die-cut Perf. 10½x10*
C68 AP31 1000fr gold 12.50 12.50

Issued to commemorate the Apollo 8 mission, which put the first man into orbit around the moon, Dec. 21–27, 1968.

No. C39 Overprinted in red with Lunar Landing Module and: "L'HOMME SUR LA LUNE / JUILLET 1969 / APOLLO 11"

1969, July 25 Engraved *Perf. 13*
C69 AP20 100fr emer & dp cl 3.50 2.75

See note after Mali No. C80.

Painting Type of 1967–68

Paintings: 50fr, Napoleon Crossing Great St. Bernard Pass, by Jacques Louis David. 150fr, Napoleon Awarding the First Cross of the Legion of Honor, by Jean-Baptiste Debret. 250fr, Napoleon Before Madrid, by Carle Vernet.

1969, Aug. 18 Photo. *Perf. 12½x12*
C70 AP23 50fr car & multi 1.00 75
C71 AP23 150fr vio & multi 2.50 1.75
C72 AP23 250fr grn & multi 5.00 3.00

Issued to commemorate the 200th anniversary of the birth of Napoleon Bonaparte (1769–1821).

Agriculture Type of Regular Issue

Designs: 100fr, Peanuts. 200fr, Rice.

1969, Oct. 30 Photo. *Perf. 12½x13*
Size: 47½x27mm.
C73 A58 100fr pur & org brn 1.35 50
C74 A58 200fr dp plum & grn 2.85 1.00

Tree of Life, Symbols of Science, Agriculture and Industry
AP32

1969, Nov. 21 Photo. *Perf. 12x13*
C75 AP32 100fr multi 1.00 50

See note after Mauritania No. C28.

Lenin
AP33

Design: 100fr, Lenin Addressing Revolutionaries in Petrograd, by V. A. Serov (horiz.).

1970, Apr. 22 Photo. *Perf. 12½*
C76 AP33 20fr ocher & brn 20 12
C77 AP33 100fr blk, lt grn & red 1.00 55

Issued to commemorate the centenary of the birth of Lenin (1870–1924), Russian communist leader.

Pres. Roosevelt with Stamp Collection—AP34

Design: 10fr, Franklin Delano Roosevelt (vert.).

1970, June 4 Photo. *Perf. 12½*
C78 AP34 10fr dk brn, emer & red brn 20 6
C79 AP34 200fr vio bl, gray & dk car 2.85 90

Issued to commemorate the 25th anniversary of the death of Pres. Franklin Delano Roosevelt (1882–1945).

Soccer Game and Jules Rimet Cup
AP35

Design: 100fr, Goalkeeper catching ball and globe.

1970, June 4 Engraved *Perf. 13*
C80 AP35 40fr ol, brt grn & brn 60 30
C81 AP35 100fr blk, lil, brn & grn 1.35 60

Issued to commemorate the 9th World Soccer Championships for the Jules Rimet Cup, Mexico City, May 30–June 21, 1970.

EXPO Emblem, Monorail and "Cranes at the Seashore"
AP36

Design: 150fr, EXPO emblem, rocket, satellites and "Geisha."

1970, Aug. 7 Photo. *Perf. 12½*
C82 AP36 50fr multi 50 25
C83 AP36 150fr grn & multi 1.50 90

Issued to publicize EXPO '70 International Exhibition, Osaka, Japan, Mar. 15–Sept. 13.

U.N. Emblem, Dove and Star
AP37

Design: 250fr, U.N. emblem and doves (horiz.).

1970, Oct. 2 Engraved *Perf. 13*
C84 AP37 60fr dk bl, bl & grn 60 30
C85 AP37 250fr dk red brn, vio bl & ol 2.50 1.00

25th anniversary of the United Nations.

Holy Family—AP38

Silver Embossed

1970, Nov. 27 *Die-Cut Perf. 10*
C86 AP38 300fr silver 4.00 4.00

Gold Embossed
C87 AP38 1000fr gold 14.00 14.00

Christmas, 1970.

Family and Upper Volta Flag
AP39

Lithographed; Gold Embossed

1970, Dec. 10 *Perf. 12½*
C88 AP39 500fr gold, blk & red 5.00 3.00

Tenth anniversary of independence, Dec. 11.

U.N. "Key to a Free World"
AP40

1970, Dec. 14 Engraved *Perf. 13*
C89 AP40 40fr red, bis & bl 50 25

United Nations Declaration of Independence for Colonial Peoples, 10th anniversary.

Gamal Abdel Nasser
AP41

1971, Jan. 30 Photo. *Perf. 12½*
C90 AP41 100fr grn & multi 1.00 45

In memory of Gamal Abdel Nasser (1918–1970), president of Egypt.

Herons, Egyptian Art, 1354—AP42

Design: 250fr, Page from Koran, Egypt, 1368–1388 (vert.).

1971, May 13 Photo. *Perf. 13*
C91 AP42 100fr multi 1.00 45
C92 AP42 250fr multi 2.50 1.20

Olympic Rings and Various Sports
AP43

1971, June 10 Engraved *Perf. 13*
C93 AP43 150fr vio bl & red 1.50 90

Pre-Olympic Year, 1971.

Boy Scout and Buildings
AP44

UPPER VOLTA

1971, Aug. 12   Photo.   Perf. 12½

| C94 | AP44 | 45fr multi | 50 | 25 |

13th Boy Scout World Jamboree, Asagiri Plain, Japan, Aug. 2–10.

De Gaulle, Map of Upper Volta, Cross of Lorraine—AP45

Charles de Gaulle AP46

1971, Nov. 9   Photo.   Perf. 13x12

| C95 | AP45 | 40fr lt brn, grn & blk | 60 | 50 |

Litho.; Gold Embossed   Perf. 12½

| C96 | AP46 | 500fr gold & grn | 6.00 | 5.50 |

In memory of Gen. Charles de Gaulle (1890–1970), president of France.

African Postal Union Issue, 1971
Common Design Type

Design: 100fr, Mossi dancer and UAMPT building, Brazzaville, Congo.

1971, Nov. 13 Photo. Perf. 13x13½

| C97 | CD135 | 100fr bl & multi | 1.00 | 50 |

Gen. Sangoule Lamizana—AP47   Kabuki Actor and Ice Hockey AP48

1971, Dec. 11   Perf. 12½

| C98 | AP47 | 35fr sep, blk, gold & ultra | 35 | 17 |

Inauguration of 2nd Republic of Upper Volta.

1972, Feb. 15   Engraved   Perf. 13

| C99 | AP48 | 150fr red, bl & pur | 1.50 | 90 |

11th Winter Olympic Games, Sapporo, Japan, Feb. 3–13.

Music, by Pietro Longhi AP49

Design: 150fr, Gondolas and general view, by Ippolito Caffi (horiz.).

1972, Feb. 28   Photo.   Perf. 13

| C100 | AP49 | 100fr gold & multi | 1.00 | 50 |
| C101 | AP49 | 150fr gold & multi | 1.60 | 60 |

UNESCO campaign to save Venice.

Running and Olympic Rings AP50

1972, May 5   Engraved   Perf. 13

C102	AP50	65fr dp bl, brn & grn	90	30
C103	AP50	200fr dp bl & brn	2.85	80
a.		Miniature sheet of 2	3.25	3.25

20th Olympic Games, Munich, Aug. 26–Sept. 10. No. C103a contains one each of Nos. C102-C103. Size: 129x99mm.

Musician Type of Regular Issue

Design: 500fr, Jimmy Smith and keyboard.

1972, May 17   Photo.   Perf. 14x13

| C104 | A87 | 500fr grn & multi | 6.00 | 2.75 |

Black musician.

Red Crescent Type of Regular Issue

1972, June 23   Perf. 13x14

| C105 | A88 | 100fr yel & multi | 1.00 | 40 |

World Red Cross Day.

2nd Plan Type of Regular Issue

Design: 85fr, Road building machinery.

1972, Oct. 30   Engraved   Perf. 13

| C106 | A90 | 85fr brick red, bl & blk | 70 | 35 |

2nd Five-Year Plan.

Presidents Pompidou and Lamizana AP51

Design: 250fr, Presidents Pompidou and Lamizana, different design.

1972, Nov. 20   Photo.   Perf. 13

Size: 48x37mm.

| C107 | AP51 | 40fr gold & multi | 80 | 60 |

Photo.; Gold Embossed

Size: 56x36mm.

| C108 | AP51 | 250fr yel grn, dk grn & gold | 4.50 | 4.50 |

Visit of Pres. Georges Pompidou of France, Nov. 1972.

Skeet-shooting, Scalzone, Italy AP52

Gold-medal Winners: 40fr, Pentathlon, Peters, Great Britain. 45fr, Dressage, Meade, Great Britain. 50fr, Weight lifting, Talts, USSR. 60fr, Boxing, lightweight, Seales, U.S.A. 65fr, Fencing, Ragno-Lonzi, Italy. 75fr, Gymnastics, rings, Nakayama, Japan. 85fr, Gymnastics, Touricheva, USSR. 90fr, 110m high hurdles, Milburn, U.S.A. 150fr, Judo, Kawaguchi, Japan. 200fr, Sailing, Finn class, Maury, France. 250fr, Swimming, Spitz, U.S.A. (7 gold). 300fr, Women's high jump, Meyfarth, West Germany. 350fr, Field Hockey, West Germany. 400fr, Javelin, Wolfermann, West Germany. No. C124, Women's diving, King, U.S.A. No. C125, Cycling, Morelon, France. No. C126, Individual dressage, Linsenhoff, West Germany.

1972–73   Litho.   Perf. 12½

C109	AP52	35fr multi ('73)	28	12
C110	AP52	40fr multi	32	15
C111	AP52	45fr multi ('73)	35	18
C112	AP52	50fr multi ('73)	38	20
C113	AP52	60fr multi	45	22
C114	AP52	65fr multi	50	25
C115	AP52	75fr multi ('73)	60	30
C116	AP52	85fr multi	65	32
C117	AP52	90fr multi	70	35
C118	AP52	150fr multi ('73)	1.20	60
C119	AP52	200fr multi	1.60	75
C120	AP52	250fr multi ('73)	2.00	1.00
C121	AP52	300fr multi	2.40	1.25
C122	AP52	350fr multi ('73)	2.75	1.35
C123	AP52	400fr multi ('73)	3.25	1.60
		Nos. C109-C123 (15)	17.43	8.64

Souvenir Sheets

C124	AP52	500fr multi	3.50	2.50
C125	AP52	500fr multi ('73)	3.50	2.50
C126	AP52	500fr multi ('73)	3.50	2.50

20th Olympic Games, Munich. Nos. C124 and C125 have multicolored margins showing motion and Olympic emblem. C126 shows Olympic flame and emblem. Size: 80x104mm.

Nativity, by Della Notte—AP53

Design: 200fr, Adoration of the Kings, by Albrecht Dürer.

1972, Dec. 23   Photo.   Perf. 13

| C127 | AP53 | 100fr gold & multi | 1.00 | 45 |
| C128 | AP53 | 200fr gold & multi | 2.25 | 1.25 |

Christmas 1972.

Scott's International Album provides spaces for an extensive representative collection of the world's postage stamps.

Madonna and Child, by Albrecht Dürer AP54

Paintings: 75fr, Virgin Mary, Child and St. John, by Joseph von Führich. 100fr, The Virgin of Grand Duc, by Raphael. 125fr, Holy Family, by David. 150fr, Madonna and Child, artist unknown. 400fr, Flight into Egypt, by Gentile da Fabriano (horiz.).

1973, Mar. 22   Litho.   Perf. 12½x13

C129	AP54	50fr multi	50	25
C130	AP54	75fr multi	75	38
C131	AP54	100fr multi	1.00	50
C132	AP54	125fr multi	1.25	60
C133	AP54	150fr multi	1.50	75
		Nos. C129-C133 (5)	5.00	2.48

Souvenir Sheet

| C134 | AP54 | 400fr multi | 4.00 | 2.00 |

Christmas 1972. No. C134 has multicolored margin showing entire painting. Size: 104x80mm.

Manned Lunar Buggy on Moon AP55

Designs: 65fr, Lunakhod, Russian unmanned vehicle on moon. 100fr, Lunar module returning to orbiting Apollo capsule. 150fr, Apollo capsule in moon orbit. 200fr, Space walk. 250fr, Walk in Sea of Tranquillity.

1973, Apr. 30   Litho.   Perf. 13x12½

C135	AP55	50fr multi	50	25
C136	AP55	65fr multi	65	30
C137	AP55	100fr multi	1.00	50
C138	AP55	150fr multi	1.50	75
C139	AP55	200fr multi	2.00	1.00
		Nos. C135-C139 (5)	5.65	2.80

Souvenir Sheet

| C140 | AP55 | 250fr multi | 2.50 | 1.25 |

Moon exploration. No. C140 has multicolored margin showing astronaut making tests on moon near lunar module. Size: 104x80mm.

Giraffes AP56

African Wild Animals: 150fr, Elephants. 200fr, Leopard (horiz.). 250fr, Lion (horiz.). 300fr, Rhinoceros (horiz.). 500fr, Crocodile (horiz.).

UPPER VOLTA

	Perf. 12½x13, 13x12½		
1973, May 3		**Lithographed**	
C141	AP56 100fr multi	1.00	50
C142	AP56 150fr multi	1.50	75
C143	AP56 200fr multi	2.00	1.00
C144	AP56 250fr multi	2.50	1.25
C145	AP56 500fr multi	5.00	2.50
	Nos. C141-C145 (5)	12.00	6.00

Souvenir Sheet

C146	AP56 300fr multi	3.00	1.50

No. C146 has multicolored margins showing gazelles. Size: 104x80mm.

Europafrica Issue

Girl Reading Letter, by Jan Vermeer
AP57

Paintings: 65fr, Portrait of a Lady, by Roger van der Weyden. 100fr, Young Lady at her Toilette, by Titian. 150fr, Jane Seymour, by Hans Holbein. 200fr, Mrs. Williams, by John Hoppner. 250fr, Milkmaid, by Jean-Baptiste Greuze.

1973, June 7	**Litho.**	**Perf. 12½x13**	
C147	AP57 50fr multi	50	25
C148	AP57 65fr multi	65	30
C149	AP57 100fr multi	1.00	50
C150	AP57 150fr multi	1.50	75
C151	AP57 200fr multi	2.00	1.00
	Nos. C147-C151 (5)	5.65	2.80

Souvenir Sheet

C152	AP57 250fr multi	2.50	1.25

No. C152 has blue decorative margin. Size: 80x105mm.

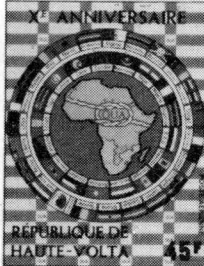

Africa Encircled by OAU Flags
AP58

1973, June 7

C153	AP58 45fr multi	45	20

10th anniversary of Organization for African Unity.

Locomotive "Pacific" 4546, 1908
AP59

Locomotives from Railroad Museum, Mulhouse, France: 40fr, No. 242, 1927. 50fr, No. 2029, 1882. 150fr, No. 701, 1885-92. 250fr, "Coupe-Vent" No. C145, 1900. 350fr, Buddicomb No. 33, Paris to Rouen, 1884.

1973, June 30	**Perf. 13x12½**		
C154	AP59 10fr multi	10	5
C155	AP59 40fr multi	40	20
C156	AP59 50fr multi	50	25
C157	AP59 150fr multi	1.50	75
C158	AP59 250fr multi	2.50	1.25
	Nos. C154-C158 (5)	5.00	2.50

Souvenir Sheet

C159	AP59 350fr multi	3.50	1.75

No. C159 has multicolored margin showing designs and emblem of museum. Size: 104x80mm.

Boy Scout Type of 1973

Boy Scouts: 40fr, Flag signaling. 75fr, Skiing. 150fr, Cooking. 200fr, Hiking. 250fr, Studying stars.

1973, July 18	**Litho.**	**Perf. 12½x13**	
C160	A95 40fr multi	40	20
C161	A95 75fr multi	75	38
C162	A95 150fr multi	1.50	75
C163	A95 200fr multi	2.00	1.00

Souvenir Sheet

C164	A95 250fr multi	2.50	1.25

No. C164 has multicolored margin showing African veldt. Size: 104x80mm.

Nos. C148 and C150 Surcharged in Silver New Value and "SECHERESSE / SOLIDARITE AFRICAINE / ET INTERNATIONALE"

1973, Aug. 16

C165	AP57 100fr on 65fr multi	1.00	50
C166	AP57 200fr on 150fr multi	2.00	1.00

Drought relief.

Kennedy Type, 1973

Designs (John F. Kennedy and): 200fr, Firing Saturn 1 rocket, Apollo program. 300fr, First NASA manned space capsule. 400fr, Saturn 5 countdown.

1973, Sept. 12	**Litho.**	**Perf. 12½x13**	
C167	A96 200fr multi	2.00	1.00
C168	A96 300fr multi	3.00	1.50

Souvenir Sheet

C169	A96 400fr multi	4.00	2.00

10th anniversary of death of Pres John F. Kennedy. No. C169 has multicolored margin showing photograph including crescent moon. Size: 80x104mm.

Interpol Type of 1973

Souvenir Sheet

Design: Victim in city street.

1973, Sept. 15	**Perf. 13x12½**		
C170	A97 300fr multi	3.00	1.50

Interpol, 50th anniversary. No. C170 has multicolored margin showing Upper Volta flag and Interpol emblem. Size: 104x80mm.

Tourism Type of 1973

Designs: 100fr, Waterfalls. 275fr, Elephant.

1973, Sept. 30

C171	A98 100fr multi	1.00	50

Souvenir Sheet

C172	A98 275fr multi	2.75	1.38

Tourism. No. C172 has multicolored margin showing road-map of Upper Volta. Size: 80x104mm.

House of Worship Type of 1973

Design: Cathedral of the Immaculate Conception.

1973, Sept. 28

C173	A99 200fr multi	2.00	1.00

Folklore Type of 1973

Designs: 100fr, 225fr, Bobo masked dancers (different).

1973, Nov. 30	**Litho.**	**Perf. 12½x13**	
C174	A100 100fr multi	1.00	50
C175	A100 225fr multi	2.25	1.10

Zodiac Type of 1973

Souvenir Sheets

Designs (Zodiacal Light and): No. C176, First four signs of Zodiac. No. C177, Second four signs. No. C178, Last four signs.

1973, Dec. 15	**Perf. 13x14**		
C176	A101 250fr multi	2.50	1.25
C177	A101 250fr multi	2.50	1.25
C178	A101 250fr multi	2.50	1.25

Nos. C176-C178 have multicolored margin showing night sky and portraits: No. C176, Louis Armstrong; No. C177, Mahatma Gandhi; No. C178, Martin Luther King. Size: 124x86mm.

Soccer Championship Type, 1974

Designs (Championship '74 emblem and): 75fr, Gento, Spanish flag. 100fr, Bereta, French flag. 250fr, Best, British flag. 400fr, Beckenbauer, West German flag.

1974, Jan. 15	**Litho.**	**Perf. 13x12½**	
C179	A102 75fr multi	75	38
C180	A102 100fr multi	1.00	50
C181	A102 250fr multi	2.50	1.25

Souvenir Sheet

C182	A102 400fr multi	4.00	2.00

10th World Cup Soccer Championship, Munich. No. C182 has multicolored margin showing Munich stadium. Size: 105x80mm.

De Gaulle Type, 1974

Designs: 300fr, De Gaulle and Concorde (horiz.). 400fr, De Gaulle and French space shot.

Perf. 13x12½, 12½x13			
1974, Feb. 4		**Lithographed**	
C183	A103 300fr multi	3.00	1.50

Souvenir Sheet

C184	A103 400fr multi	4.00	2.00

Gen. Charles de Gaulle (1890-1970), president of France. No. C184 has multicolored margin showing French satellites and rocket. Size: 80x105mm.

Soccer Cup Championship Type, 1974

Designs (World Cup, Emblems and): 150fr, Brindisi, Argentinian flag. No. C186, Kenko, Zaire flag. No. C187, Streich, East German flag. 400fr, Cruyff, Netherlands flag.

1974, Mar. 19	**Perf. 12½x13**		
C185	A104 150fr multi	1.50	75
C186	A104 300fr multi	3.00	1.50

Souvenir Sheets

C187	A104 300fr multi	3.00	1.50
C188	A104 400fr multi	4.00	2.00

10th World Cup Soccer Championship, Munich. No. C187 has multicolored margin showing soccer ball and emblem; No. C188, World Cup and emblem. Size: 80x 104mm.

UPU Type, 1974

Designs (UPU Emblem and): 100fr, Dove carrying mail. 200fr, Air Afrique 707. 300fr, Dish antenna. 500fr, Telstar satellite.

1974, July 23	**Perf. 13½**		
C189	A106 100fr multi	1.00	50
C190	A106 200fr multi	2.00	1.00
C191	A106 300fr multi	3.00	1.50

Souvenir Sheet

C192	A106 500fr multi	5.00	2.50

Universal Postal Union centenary. No. C192 has multicolored margin showing UPU emblem and Mercator map of world. Size: 104x79mm.

Soccer Cup Winners Type, 1974

Designs (World Cup, Game and Flags): 150fr, Brazil, in Sweden, 1958. 200fr, Brazil, in Chile, 1962. 250fr, Brazil, in Mexico, 1970. 450fr, England, in England, 1966.

1974, Sept. 2

C193	A107 150fr multi	1.50	75
C194	A107 200fr multi	2.00	1.00
C195	A107 250fr multi	2.50	1.25

Souvenir Sheet

C196	A107 450fr multi	4.50	2.25

World Cup Soccer Championship winners. No. C196 has multicolored margin showing Munich '74 emblem and Neuschwanstein Castle. Size: 83x107mm.

Nos. C189-C192 Overprinted in Red "100ᵉ ANNIVERSAIRE DE L'UNION POSTALE UNIVERSELLE / 9 OCTOBRE 1974"

1974, Oct. 9

C197	A106 100fr multi	1.00	50
C198	A106 200fr multi	2.00	1.00
C199	A106 300fr multi	3.00	1.50

Souvenir Sheet

C200	A106 500fr multi	5.00	2.50

Universal Postal Union, centenary.

Flower Type of 1974

Flower Paintings by: 300fr, Auguste Renoir. 400fr, Carl Brendt.

1974, Oct. 31	**Litho.**	**Perf. 12½x13**	
C201	A109 300fr multi	3.00	1.50

Souvenir Sheet

C202	A109 400fr multi	4.00	2.00

No. C202 has multicolored margin showing rays of colors. Size: 104x80mm.

Locomotive Type of 1975

Locomotives from Railroad Museum, Mulhouse, France: 100fr, Crampton No. 80, 1852. 200fr, No. 701, 1885-92. 300fr, "Forquenot," 1882.

1975, Feb. 28	**Litho.**	**Perf. 13x12½**	
C203	A112 100fr multi	1.00	50
C204	A112 200fr multi	2.00	1.00
C205	A112 300fr multi	3.00	1.50

No. C205 has multicolored margin showing Museum's emblem and galloping horse. Size: 104x80mm.

Old Cars Type, 1975

Flags and Old Cars: 150fr, Germany and Mercedes-Benz, 1929. 200fr, Germany and Maybach, 1936. 400fr, Great Britain and Rolls Royce Silver Ghost, 1910.

1975, Apr. 6	**Perf. 14x13½**		
C206	A113 150fr multi	1.50	75
C207	A113 200fr multi	2.00	1.00

Souvenir Sheet

C208	A113 400fr multi	4.00	2.00

No. C208 has multicolored margin showing five cars. Size: 115x79mm.

American Bicentennial Type of 1975

American Bicentennial: 200fr, Washington crossing Delaware. 300fr, Hessians Captured at Trenton.

1975, May 6	**Litho.**	**Perf. 14**	
C209	A114 200fr multi	2.00	1.00
C210	A114 300fr multi	3.00	1.50

Schweitzer Type of 1975

Designs (Albert Schweitzer): 150fr, Toucan. 175fr, Vulturine guinea fowl. 200fr, King vulture. 450fr, Crested corythornis.

1975, May 25	**Litho.**	**Perf. 13½**	
C212	A115 150fr multi	1.50	75
C213	A115 175fr multi	1.75	85
C214	A115 200fr multi	2.00	1.00

Souvenir Sheet

C215	A115 450fr multi	4.50	2.25

Albert Schweitzer, birth centenary. No. C215 has multicolored margin showing storks and Schweitzer's birthplace, Günsbach, Alsace. Size: 116x88mm.

Scott's editorial staff cannot undertake to identify, authenticate or appraise stamps and postal markings.

UPPER VOLTA

Apollo Soyuz Type of 1975

Designs: 100fr, Apollo and Soyuz near link-up. 200fr, Cosmonauts Alexei Leonov and Valeri Kubasov. 300fr, Astronauts Donald K. Slayton, Vance Brand and Thomas P. Stafford. 500fr, Apollo Soyuz emblem, US and USSR flags.

1975, July 18   Litho.   Perf. 13½

C216	A116	100fr multi	1.00	50
C217	A116	200fr multi	2.00	1.00
C218	A116	300fr multi	3.00	1.50

Souvenir Sheet

| C219 | A116 | 500fr multi | 5.00 | 2.50 |

Apollo Soyuz space test project, Russo-American cooperation, launched July 15, link-up, July 17. No. C219 has multicolored margin showing maps of US and USSR with linked capsules. Size: 116x 78mm.

Picasso Type of 1975

Picasso Paintings: 150fr, El Prado (horiz.). 350fr, Couple in Patio. 400fr, Science and Charity.

1975, Aug. 7

| C220 | A117 | 150fr multi | 1.50 | 75 |
| C221 | A117 | 350fr multi | 3.50 | 1.75 |

Souvenir Sheet

| C222 | A117 | 400fr multi | 4.00 | 2.00 |

Pablo Ruiz Picasso, 1881–1973. No. C222 has multicolored margin with photograph of Picasso. Size: 79x104mm.

EXPO '75 Type of 1975

Design (Expo '75 emblem and): 150fr, Passenger liner Asama Maru. 300fr, Future floating city Aquapolis.

1975, Sept. 26   Litho.   Perf. 11

| C223 | A118 | 150fr multi | 1.50 | 75 |

Souvenir Sheet
Perf. 13½

| C224 | A118 | 300fr multi | 3.00 | 1.50 |

Oceanographic Exposition, Okinawa '75. No. C224 has multicolored margin showing ancient Japanese vessels. Size: 104x77 mm.

Winter Olympic Games Type of 1975

Designs (Innsbruck Background, Olympic Emblem and): 100fr, Ice hockey. 200fr, Ski jump. 300fr, Speed skating.

1975, Dec. 15   Perf. 13½

| C225 | A122 | 100fr multi | 1.00 | 50 |
| C226 | A122 | 200fr multi | 2.00 | 1.00 |

Souvenir Sheet

| C227 | A122 | 300fr multi | 3.00 | 1.50 |

12th Winter Olympic Games, Innsbruck. No. C227 has multicolored margin showing skiers. Size: 78x103mm.

Olympic Games Type of 1976

Designs (Olympic Emblem and): 125fr, Heavyweight judo. 150fr, Weight lifting. 500fr, Sprint.

1976, Mar. 17   Litho.   Perf. 13½

| C228 | A123 | 125fr multi | 1.25 | 60 |
| C229 | A123 | 150fr multi | 1.50 | 75 |

Souvenir Sheet

| C230 | A123 | 500fr multi | 5.00 | 2.50 |

21st Olympic Games, Montreal, Canada, July 17–Aug. 1. No. C230 has multicolored margin showing Olympic flame, emblem and various games. Size: 114x 78mm.

Summer Olympic Games Type of 1976

Designs (Olympic emblem and): 150fr, Pole vault. 200fr, Gymnast on balance beam. 500fr, Two-man sculls.

1976, Mar. 25   Perf. 11

| C231 | A124 | 150fr multi | 1.50 | 75 |
| C232 | A124 | 200fr multi | 2.00 | 1.00 |

Souvenir Sheet

| C233 | A124 | 500fr multi | 5.00 | 2.50 |

21st Olympic Games, Montreal. No. C233 has multicolored margin showing Canadian flag and Olympic emblem. Size: 79x116mm.

Zeppelin Type of 1976

Airships: 100fr, Graf Zeppelin over Swiss Alps. 200fr, LZ-129 over city. 300fr, Graf Zeppelin. 500fr, Zeppelin over Bodensee.

1976, May 11

C234	A126	100fr multi	1.00	50
C235	A126	200fr multi	2.00	1.00
C236	A126	300fr multi	3.00	1.50

Souvenir Sheet

| C237 | A126 | 500fr multi | 5.00 | 2.50 |

75th anniversary of the Zeppelin. No. C237 has multicolored margin showing gasoline engine, hangar and airship pioneers: Dr. Dürr, Ferdinand von Zeppelin and Hugo Eckener. Size: 127x102mm.

Viking Mars Type of 1976

Designs: 200fr, Viking lander assembly. 450fr, Viking orbiter in descent on Mars. 450fr, Viking in Mars orbit.

1976, June 24   Litho.   Perf. 13½

| C238 | A127 | 200fr multi | 2.00 | 1.00 |
| C239 | A127 | 300fr multi | 3.00 | 1.50 |

Souvenir Sheet

| C240 | A127 | 450fr multi | 4.50 | 2.25 |

Viking Mars Project, No. C240 has multicolored margin showing Viking orbiter and lander phases. Size: 101x76mm.

American Bicentennial Type of 1976

Designs (Bicentennial and Interphil '76 Emblems): 100fr, Siege of Yorktown. 200fr, Battle of Cape St. Vincent. 300fr, Peter Francisco's bravery. 500fr, Surrender of the Hessians.

1976, Sept. 30   Litho.   Perf. 13½

C241	A129	100fr multi	1.00	50
C242	A129	200fr multi	2.00	1.00
C243	A129	300fr multi	3.00	1.50

Souvenir Sheet

| C244 | A129 | 500fr multi | 5.00 | 2.50 |

American Bicentennial and Interphil '76, Philadelphia, Pa., May 29–June 6. No. C244 has multicolored margin showing emblems and Statue of Liberty. Size: 115x 78mm.

Nos. C231–C233 Overprinted in Gold:
 a. VAINQUEUR 1976 / TADEUSZ SLU-SARSKI / POLOGNE
 b. VAINQUEUR 1976 / NADIA COMA-NECI / ROUMANIE
 c. VAINQUEUR 1976 / FRANK ET ALF HANSEN / NORVEGE

1976, July 4   Perf. 11

| C245 | A124(a) | 150fr multi | 1.50 | 75 |
| C246 | A124(b) | 200fr multi | 2.00 | 1.00 |

Souvenir Sheet

| C247 | A124(c) | 500fr multi | 5.00 | 2.50 |

Winners, 21st Olympic Games.

UPU Emblem over Globe—AP60

1978, Aug. 8   Litho.   Perf. 13

| C248 | AP60 | 350fr multi | 3.50 | 2.25 |

Congress of Paris, establishing Universal Postal Union, centenary.

The lack of a price for a listed item does not necessarily indicate rarity.

Condition is the all-important factor of price. Prices quoted are for stamps in fine condition.

Jules Verne, Apollo 11 Emblem, Footprint on Moon, Neil Armstrong
AP61

Designs: 50fr, Yuri Gagarin and moon landing. 100fr, Montgolfier hot air balloon and memorial medal, 1783; Bleriot's monoplane, 1909.

1978, Sept. 27   Litho.   Perf. 13x12½

C249	AP61	50fr multi	50	25
C250	AP61	60fr multi	60	30
C251	AP61	100fr multi	1.00	50

Space conquest.

Anti-Apartheid Emblem
AP62

1978, Oct. 12   Litho.   Perf. 13

| C252 | AP62 | 100fr bl & multi | 1.00 | 50 |

Anti-Apartheid Year.

Philexafrique II—Essen Issue
Common Design Types

Designs: No. C253, Hippopotamus and Upper Volta No. C18. No. C254, Hummingbird and Hanover No. 1.

1978, Nov. 1   Litho.   Perf. 12½

| C253 | CD138 | 100fr multi | 1.00 | 50 |
| C254 | CD139 | 100fr multi | 1.00 | 50 |

Nos. C253–C254 printed se-tenant.

Sun God Horus with Sun   Jules Verne and Balloon
AP63   AP64

Design: 300fr, Falcon with cartouches and UNESCO emblem.

1978, Dec. 4

| C255 | AP63 | 200fr multi | 2.00 | 1.00 |
| C256 | AP63 | 300fr multi | 3.00 | 1.50 |

UNESCO Campaign to safeguard monuments at Philae.

1978, Dec. 10   Engr.   Perf. 13

| C257 | AP64 | 200fr multi | 2.00 | 1.00 |

Jules Verne (1828–1905), science fiction writer.

Bicycling, Olympic Rings—AP65

1980   Perf. 14½

Designs: Bicycling scenes. 150fr, vert.

C258	AP65	65fr multi	65	32
C259	AP65	150fr multi	1.50	75
C260	AP65	250fr multi	2.50	1.25
C261	AP65	350fr multi	3.50	1.75

Souvenir Sheet

| C262 | AP65 | 500fr multi | 5.00 | 2.50 |

22nd Summer Olympic Games, Moscow, July 19–Aug. 3. No. C262 has multicolored margin showing bicycle. Size: 109x82mm.

Nos. C258–C262 Overprinted with Name of Winner and Country

1980, Nov. 22   Litho.   Perf. 14½

C263	AP65	65fr multi	65	32
C264	AP65	150fr multi	1.50	75
C265	AP65	250fr multi	2.50	1.25
C266	AP65	350fr multi	3.50	1.75

Souvenir Sheet

| C267 | AP65 | 500fr multi | 5.00 | 2.50 |

1982 World Cup—AP66

Designs: Various soccer players.

1982, June 22   Litho.   Perf. 13½

C268	AP66	70fr multi	70	35
C269	AP66	90fr multi	90	45
C270	AP66	150fr multi	1.50	75
C271	AP66	300fr multi	3.00	1.50

Souvenir Sheet

| C272 | AP66 | 500fr multi | 5.00 | 2.50 |

No. C272 has multicolored margin showing emblem, players. Size: 120x99mm.

Anniversaries and Events—AP67

1983, June   Litho.   Perf. 13½

C273	AP67	90fr Space Shuttle	45	22
C274	AP67	120fr World Soccer Cup	60	30
C275	AP67	300fr Cup, diff.	1.50	75
C276	AP67	450fr Royal Wedding	2.25	1.15

Souvenir Sheet

| C277 | AP67 | 500fr Prince Charles, Lady Diana | 2.50 | 2.50 |

UPPER VOLTA

Pre-Olympics, 1984 Los Angeles—AP68

1983, Aug. 1 Litho. Perf. 13
C278	AP68	90fr Sailing	45	22
C279	AP68	120fr Type 470	60	30
C280	AP68	300fr Wind surfing	1.50	75
C281	AP68	400fr Wind surfing, diff.	2.00	1.00

Souvenir Sheet
C282	AP68	520fr Soling Class, Wind surfing	2.50	2.50

Multicolored margin continues design. Size: 104x78mm.

Christmas 1983—AP69

Rubens Paintings.

1983 Litho. Perf. 13
C283	AP69	120fr Adoration of the Shepherds	60	30
C284	AP69	350fr Virgin of the Garland	1.75	90
C285	AP69	500fr Adoration of the Kings	2.50	1.25

1984 Summer Olympics—AP70

1984, Mar. 26 Litho. Perf. 12½
C286	AP70	90fr Handball, vert.	45	22
C287	AP70	120fr Volleyball, vert.	60	30
C288	AP70	150fr Handball, diff.	75	38
C289	AP70	250fr Basketball	1.25	65
C290	AP70	300fr Soccer	1.50	75
		Nos. C286-C290 (5)	4.55	2.30

Souvenir Sheet
C291	AP70	500fr Volleyball, diff.	2.50	1.25

Size of No. C291: 103x78mm.

Local Birds—AP71

1984, May 14 Litho. Perf. 12½
C292	AP71	90fr Phoenicopterus roseus	45	22
C293	AP71	185fr Choriotis kori, vert.	95	48
C294	AP71	200fr Buphagus erythrorhynchus, vert.	1.00	50
C295	AP71	300fr Bucorvus leadbeateri	1.50	75

POSTAGE DUE STAMPS.

Postage Due Stamps of Upper Senegal and Niger, 1914, Overprinted in Black or Red

HAUTE-VOLTA

1920 Perf. 14x13½ Unwmkd.
J1	D2	5c green	30	30
J2	D2	10c rose	30	30
J3	D2	15c gray	30	30
J4	D2	20c brn (R)	30	30
J5	D2	30c blue	38	38
J6	D2	50c blk (R)	60	60
J7	D2	60c orange	60	60
J8	D2	1fr violet	75	75
		J1-J8 (8)	3.53	3.53

Type of 1914 Issue Surcharged **2F.**

1927
J9	D2	2fr on 1fr lil rose	1.75	1.75
J10	D2	3fr on 1fr org brn	2.25	2.25

Red-fronted Gazelle
D3   D4

1928 Typographed
J11	D3	5c green	30	30
J12	D3	10c rose	30	30
J13	D3	15c dk gray	45	45
J14	D3	20c dk brn	45	45
J15	D3	30c dk bl	50	50
J16	D3	50c black	1.75	1.75
J17	D3	60c orange	2.25	2.25
J18	D3	1fr dl vio	3.25	3.25
J19	D3	2fr lil rose	5.50	5.50
J20	D3	3fr org brn	6.00	6.00
		Nos. J11-J20 (10)	20.75	20.75

Republic

1962, Jan. 31 Perf. 14x13½
Denomination in Black
J21	D4	1fr brt bl	8	8
J22	D4	2fr orange	8	8
J23	D4	5fr brt vio bl	18	18
J24	D4	10fr red lil	22	22
J25	D4	20fr emerald	50	50
J26	D4	50fr rose red	1.25	1.25
		Nos. J21-J26 (6)	2.31	2.31

OFFICIAL STAMPS

Elephant
O1

Photogravure
1963, Feb. 1 Perf. 12½ Unwmkd.
Center in Sepia
O1	O1	1fr red brn	12	12
O2	O1	5fr yel grn	12	12
O3	O1	10fr dp vio	28	28
O4	O1	15fr red org	30	30
O5	O1	25fr brt rose lil	40	40
O6	O1	50fr brt grn	65	65
O7	O1	60fr brt red	85	85
O8	O1	85fr dk sl grn	1.35	1.35
O9	O1	100fr brt bl	2.25	3.50
O10	O1	200fr brt rose	3.50	3.50
		Nos. O1-O10 (10)	9.82	11.07

URUGUAY

(ū'rōō·gwā ; ōō'rōō·gwī')

LOCATION—In South America between Brazil and Argentina and bordering on the Atlantic Ocean.
GOVT.—Republic.
AREA—72,172 sq. mi.
POP.—2,810,000 (est. 1977).
CAPITAL—Montevideo

120 Centavos = 1 Real
8 Reales = 1 Peso
100 Centesimos = 1 Peso (1859)
1000 Milésimos = 1 Peso (1898)

> Prices of early Uruguay stamps vary according to condition. Quotations for Nos. 1–17 are for fine copies. Very fine to superb specimens sell at much higher prices, and inferior or poor copies sell at reduced prices, depending on the condition of the individual specimen.

Carrier Issues.

Issued by Atanasio Lapido, Administrator-General of Posts.

"El Sol de Mayo"

A1 A1a

Lithographed.

1856, Oct. 1 ***Imperf.*** **Unwmkd.**

1	A1	60c blue	400.00	
a.		60c dp bl	500.00	
b.		60c ind	1,250.	
2	A1	80c green	400.00	
a.		80c dp grn	425.00	
3	A1	1r vermilion	400.00	
a.		1r car ver	425.00	

1857, Oct. 1

3B	A1a	60c blue	*2,500.*	
c.		60c pale bl	*2,750.*	
d.		60c dk bl	*2,750.*	

As Nos. 1-3d were spaced closely on the stone, four-margin copies are unusual. Most genuinely used specimens are pen canceled.

See Nos. 410-413, 771A.

A2

1858, Mar.

4	A2	120c blue	350.00	300.00
a.		120c dp bl	350.00	300.00
b.		120c grnsh bl	350.00	300.00
c.		Tête bêche pair	*12,000.*	
5	A2	180c green	100.00	100.00
a.		180c dp grn	200.00	250.00
b.		Thick paper	100.00	200.00
c.		Tête bêche pair	*15,000.*	
6	A2	240c dl ver	100.00	*500.00*
a.		240c dp ver	125.00	
b.		240c brn red	250.00	
c.		180c dl ver in stone of 240c		
d.		Thick paper (dl ver)	100.00	

Government Issues.

A3 A4

1859, June 26 **Thin Numerals**

7	A3	60c lilac	40.00	35.00
a.		60c gray lil	42.50	35.00
8	A3	80c yellow	350.00	65.00
a.		80c org	500.00	85.00
9	A3	100c brn lake	100.00	75.00
a.		100c brn rose	100.00	75.00
10	A3	120c blue	65.00	25.00
a.		120c sl bl	85.00	30.00
11	A3	180c green	15.00	30.00
12	A3	240c vermilion	85.00	90.00

1860 **Thick Numerals.**

13	A4	60c dl lil	25.00	10.00
a.		60c gray lil	30.00	10.00
b.		60c brn lil	30.00	15.00
c.		60c red lil	30.00	15.00
d.		As "a", fine impression (1st printing)	125.00	75.00
14	A4	80c yellow	35.00	20.00
a.		80c org	50.00	25.00
15	A4	100c rose	85.00	40.00
a.		100c car	85.00	40.00
16	A4	120c blue	40.00	20.00
17	A4	180c yel grn	175.00	150.00
a.		180c dp grn	200.00	175.00

No. 13 was first printed (1860) in sheets of 192 (16x12) containing 24 types. The impressions are very clear; paper is whitish and of better quality than that of the later printings. In the 1861–62 printings, the layout contains 12 types and the subjects are spaced farther apart.

Coat of Arms
A5

1864, Apr. 13

18	A5	6c rose	15.00	12.00
a.		6c car	25.00	20.00
b.		6c red	27.50	25.00
c.		6c brick red	35.00	30.00
20	A5	6c salmon	60.00	60.00
21	A5	8c green	25.00	20.00
a.		Tête bêche pair	600.00	
22	A5	10c yellow	35.00	30.00
a.		10c ocher	35.00	30.00
23	A5	12c blue	10.00	9.00
a.		12c dk bl	17.50	12.50
b.		12c sl bl	17.50	12.50

No. 20, which is on thicker paper, was never placed in use.

Stamps of 1864

Surcharged in Black **5** **5**

1866, Jan. 1

24	A5	5c on 12c bl	25.00	*50.00*
a.		5c on 12c sl bl	27.50	55.00
b.		Inverted surcharge	75.00	
c.		Double surcharge	40.00	
d.		Pair, one without surcharge		
e.		Triple surcharge	85.00	
25	A5	10c on 8c brt grn	25.00	*50.00*
a.		10c on 8c dl grn	25.00	50.00
b.		Tête bêche pair	300.00	
c.		Double surcharge	50.00	
26	A5	15c on 10c ocher	30.00	*90.00*
a.		15c on 10c yel	30.00	90.00
b.		Inverted surcharge	85.00	
c.		Double surcharge	45.00	
27	A5	20c on 6c rose	35.00	*75.00*
a.		20c on 6c rose red	35.00	*75.00*
b.		Inverted surcharge	75.00	
c.		Double surcharge	50.00	
d.		Pair, one withut surcharge		
28	A5	20c on 6c brick red	*200.00*	
a.		Double surcharge		

Many counterfeits exist.
No. 28 was not issued.

Coat of Arms and Numeral of Value—A7

A8 A8a

A8b A8c

ONE CENTESIMO.

Type I. The wavy lines behind "CENTESIMO" are clear and distinct. Stamps 4mm. apart.

Type II. The wavy lines are rough and blurred. Stamps 3mm. apart.

1866, Jan. 10 ***Imperf.***

29	A7	1c blk (type II)	3.00	4.00
a.		1c blk (type I)	3.00	4.00
30	A8	5c blue	5.00	2.25
a.		5c dl bl	5.00	2.00
b.		5c ultra	35.00	7.50
c.		Numeral with white flag	30.00	11.00
d.		"ENTECIMOS"	30.00	17.50
e.		"CENTECIMO"	30.00	17.50
f.		"CENTECIMOS" with small "S"	17.50	7.50
g.		Pelure paper	22.50	14.00
h.		Thick paper	35.00	14.00
31	A8a	10c yel grn	17.50	6.00
a.		10c bl grn	17.50	6.00
b.		"I" of "CENTECIMOS" omitted	45.00	17.50
c.		"CENIECIMOS"	45.00	17.50
d.		"CENTRCIMOS"	27.50	17.50
32	A8b	15c org yel	25.00	12.00
a.		15c yel	25.00	12.00
33	A8c	20c rose	30.00	12.00
a.		20c lil rose	30.00	12.50
b.		Thick paper	35.00	13.50

Engraved plates were prepared for Nos. 30 to 33 but were not put in use. The stamps were printed from lithographic transfers from the plate. In 1915 a few reprints of the 15c were made from the engraved plate by a California philatelic society, each sheet being numbered and signed by officers of the society; then the plate was defaced.

1866–67 ***Perf. 8½ to 13½***

34	A7	1c black	3.50	6.00
35	A8	5c blue	2.50	85
a.		5c dk bl	2.50	85
b.		Numeral with white flag	15.00	12.50
c.		"ENTECIMOS"	15.00	5.00
d.		"CENTECIMO"	12.50	5.00
e.		"CENTECIMOS" with small "S"	7.50	3.00
f.		Pelure paper	10.00	4.00
36	A8a	10c green	3.50	85
a.		10c yel grn	3.50	85
b.		"CENIECIMOS"	12.50	5.00
c.		"I" of "CENTECIMOS" omitted	12.50	5.00
d.		"CENTRCIMOS"	12.50	5.00
e.		Pelure paper	20.00	7.50
37	A8b	15c org yel	5.00	3.50
a.		15c yel	5.00	3.50
b.		Pelure paper	20.00	12.50
38	A8c	20c rose	7.50	3.00
a.		20c brn rose	7.50	3.00
b.		Pelure paper	27.50	15.00
c.		Thick paper	12.00	6.00
		Nos. 34-38 (5)	22.00	14.20

A9 A10

A11 A12

1877–79 **Engraved** ***Rouletted 8***

39	A9	1c red brn	85	50
40	A10	5c green	85	40
a.		Thick paper	2.75	1.75
41	A11	10c vermilion	1.00	40
42	A11	20c bister	1.50	60
43	A11	50c black	7.00	3.00
43A	A12	1p bl ('79)	40.00	17.50
		Nos. 39-43A (6)	51.20	22.40

The first printing of the 1p had the coat of arms smaller with quarterings reversed. These "error" stamps were not issued, and all were ordered burned. A copy is known to have been in a celebrated Uruguayan collection and a few others exist.

1880, Nov. 10 Litho. ***Rouletted 6***

44	A9	1c brown	20	10
a.		Imperf., pair	15.00	
b.		Rouletted 12½	3.50	

Joaquin Suárez
A13

1881, Aug. 25 ***Perf. 12½***

45	A13	7c blue	1.75	1.75
a.		Imperf., pair	13.00	13.00

Devices from Coat of Arms
A14 A14a

1882, May 15

46	A14	1c green	1.00	1.00
a.		1c yel grn	3.50	1.75
b.		Imperf. (pair)	16.50	
47	A14a	2c rose	75	75
a.		Imperf. (pair)	20.00	

These stamps bear numbers from 1 to 100 according to their position on the sheet.

Counterfeits of Nos. 46 and 47 are plentiful.

Coat of Arms
A15 A16

General Máximo Santos — A17
General José Artigas — A18

Perf. 12, 12x12½, 12x13, 13x12.

1883, Mar. 1

48	A15	1c green	1.00	75
a.		Imperf., pair	7.50	

URUGUAY

49	A16	2c red	1.25	1.00
a.		Imperf., pair	7.50	
50	A17	5c blue	1.75	1.50
a.		Imperf., pair	6.00	
51	A18	10c brown	2.50	2.00
a.		Imperf., pair	12.00	

No. 40 Overprinted in Black

1883 Provisorio

1883, Sept. 24   Rouletted 8

52	A10	5c green	90	75
a.		Double overprint	22.50	22.50
b.		Overprint reading down	8.00	8.00
c.		"Provisorio" omitted	12.00	12.00
d.		"1883" omitted	8.00	8.00

No. 52 with overprint in red is a color essay.

No. 41 Surcharged in Black

1884, Jan. 15

53	A11	1c on 10c ver	35	35
a.		Small figure "1"	3.50	3.50
b.		Inverted surcharge	3.50	3.50
c.		Double surcharge	6.00	6.00

No. 47 Overprinted in Black

PROVISORIO 1884

Perf. 12½

54	A14a	2c rose	75	75
a.		Double overprint	22.50	
b.		Imperf., pair	37.50	

A22   A23

Thick Paper.

1884, Jan. 25   Litho.   Unwmkd.

55	A22	5c ultra	1.50	1.00
a.		Imperf., pair	5.00	7.00

Thin Paper.

Perf. 12½, 13 and Compound.

56	A23	5c blue	60	60
a.		Imperf., pair	12.00	

A24   A24a

A24b

Artigas Santos
A25   A26

A27   A28

1884–88   Engraved   Rouletted 8

57	A24	1c gray	1.00	60
58	A24	1c olive	85	50
59	A24	1c green	50	25
60	A24	2c vermilion	50	25
60A	A24a	2c rose ('88)	50	25
61	A24b	5c dp bl	1.00	40
61A	A24b	5c bl, bl	1.65	75
62	A24b	5c vio ('86)	40	25
63	A24b	5c lt bl ('88)	50	25
64	A25	7c dk brn	1.75	1.10
65	A25	7c org ('88)	1.25	75
66	A26	10c ol brn	50	25
67	A27	20c red vio	1.75	60
68	A27	20c bis brn ('88)	1.25	75
69	A28	25c gray vio	2.50	1.35
70	A28	25c ver ('88)	2.50	1.00
		Nos. 57-70 (16)	18.40	9.30

Water dissolves the blue in the paper of No. 61A.

A29   A30

1887, Oct. 17   Litho.   Rouletted 9

71	A29	10c lilac	1.75	1.00
		10c gray lil	1.75	1.00

1888, Jan. 1   Engraved   Rouletted 8

| 72 | A30 | 10c violet | 60 | 35 |

No. 62 Overprinted in Black

Provisorio

1889, Oct. 14

73	A24b	5c violet	40	40
a.		Inverted overprint	6.00	6.00
b.		Inverted "A" for "V" in "Provisorio"		5.00

No. 73 with overprint in red is a color essay.

Coat of Arms   Numeral of Value
A32   A33

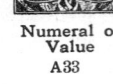

A34   A35

A36   A37

Justice   Mercury
A38   A39

A40

Perf. 12½ to 15½ and Compound.

1889–1901   Engraved

74	A32	1c green	50	25
a.		Imperf., pair	11.00	
75	A32	1c dl bl ('94)	50	25
76	A33	2c rose	50	25
77	A33	2c red brn ('94)	65	35
78	A33	2c org ('99)	50	35
79	A34	5c dp bl	50	25
80	A34	5c rose ('94)	75	25
81	A35	7c bis brn	1.00	40
82	A35	7c grn ('94)	5.00	3.00
83	A35	7c car ('00)	4.00	2.50
84	A36	10c bl grn	3.50	40
a.		Printed on both sides	25.00	
85	A36	10c org ('94)	3.50	75
86	A37	20c orange	2.50	75
87	A37	20c brn ('94)	5.00	2.00
88	A37	20c lt bl ('00)	2.50	40
a.		20c grnsh bl	3.00	40
89	A38	25c red brn	3.00	90
90	A38	25c ver ('94)	7.00	4.00
91	A38	25c bis brn ('01)	3.50	60
92	A39	50c lt bl	7.00	3.00
93	A39	50c lil ('94)	13.50	6.00
94	A39	50c car ('01)	7.00	75
95	A40	1p lilac	13.50	5.00
96	A40	1p lt bl ('94)	20.00	7.50
97	A40	1p dp grn ('01)	10.00	2.00
a.		Imperf., pair	20.00	
		Nos. 74-97 (24)	115.40	42.50

Nos. 59 and 62 Overprinted in Red:

Provisorio 1892   **Provisorio 1891**
a   b

1891-92   Rouletted 8.

98	A24 (a)	1c grn ('92)	50	50
a.		Inverted overprint	7.50	7.50
b.		Double overprint	10.00	10.00
c.		Double overprint, one inverted	5.00	5.00
d.		"PREVISORIO"	5.00	5.00
99	A24b (b)	5c violet	30	30
a.		"1391"	3.50	3.50
b.		Double overprint	3.50	3.50
c.		Inverted overprint	3.50	3.50
d.		Double overprint, one inverted	6.00	6.00

Nos. 86 and 81 Surcharged in Black or Red

UN Centésimo Provisorio 1892   **CINCO Centésimos Provisorio 1892**
c   d

Perf. 12½ to 15½ and Compound

1892

100	A37 (c)	1c on 20c org (Bk)	40	25
a.		Inverted surcharge	6.00	6.00
101	A35 (d)	5c on 7c bis brn (R)	40	25
a.		Inverted surcharge	2.00	2.00
b.		Double surcharge, one inverted	6.00	6.00
c.		Double surcharge	6.00	6.00
d.		Vertical surcharge	20.00	
e.		"PREVISORIO"	4.00	4.00
f.		"Cinco" omitted	9.00	

No. 101 with surcharge in green is a color essay.

Several surcharge errors of date and misspelling of "Centésimos" exist. Price $12.50.

A45   A46

Arms   Peace
A47   A48

1892   Engraved

102	A45	1c green	50	25
103	A46	2c rose	50	25
104	A47	5c blue	50	25
105	A48	10c orange	2.00	1.00

Issue dates: 1c, 2c, Mar. 9; 5c, Apr. 19; 10c, Dec. 15.

Liberty   Arms
A49   A50

1894, June 2

106	A49	2p carmine	30.00	15.00
107	A50	3p dl vio	30.00	15.00

Gaucho   Solis Theater
A51   A52

URUGUAY

Locomotive
A53

Bull's Head
A54

Ceres
A55

Sailing Ship
A56

Liberty
A57

Mercury
A58

Coat of Arms
A59

Montevideo Fortress
A60

Cathedral in Montevideo
A61

Perf. 12 to 15½ and Compound
1895-99

108	A51	1c bister	50	25
109	A51	1c sl bl ('97)	50	25
a.		Printed on both sides	25.00	
110	A52	2c blue	50	25
111	A52	2c cl ('97)	50	25
112	A53	5c red	50	25
113	A53	5c grn ('97)	75	20
a.		Imperf., pair	4.00	
114	A53	5c grnsh bl ('99)	60	20
115	A54	7c dp grn	7.50	2.50
116	A54	7c org ('97)	4.00	1.25
117	A55	10c brown	2.00	50
118	A56	20c grn & blk	5.00	1.10
119	A56	20c cl & blk ('97)	4.00	90
120	A57	25c red brn & blk	5.00	1.25
a.		Center inverted		2,250.
121	A57	25c pink & bl ('97)	3.00	75
122	A58	50c bl & blk	7.00	2.50
123	A58	50c grn & brn ('97)	5.00	1.25
124	A59	1p org brn & blk	10.00	5.00
125	A59	1p yel brn & bl ('97)	9.00	3.50
126	A60	2p vio & grn	27.50	15.00
127	A60	2p bis & car ('97)	9.00	2.00
128	A61	3p car & bl	27.50	15.00
129	A61	3p lil & car ('97)	10.00	2.50
		Nos. 108-129 (22)	139.35	56.65

All values of this issue exist imperforate but they were not issued in that form.

President Joaquin Suárez
A62   A63

Statue of President Suárez
A64

Perf. 12½ to 15 and Compound
1896, July 18

130	A62	1c brn vio & blk	40	25
131	A63	5c pale bl & blk	40	25
132	A64	10c lake & blk	1.00	60

Dedication of Pres. Suárez statue.

Same Overprinted in Red:

1897, Mar. 1

133	A62 (e)	1c brn vio & blk	60	40
a.		Inverted overprint	6.00	6.00
134	A63 (e)	5c pale bl & blk	60	40
a.		Inverted overprint	9.00	9.00
135	A64 (f)	10c lake & blk	1.25	90
a.		Inverted overprint	15.00	15.00
b.		Double overprint	10.00	

"Electricity"
A68

1897-99   Engraved

136	A68	10c red	1.75	60
137	A68	10c red lil ('99)	75	50

Regular Issues Overprinted in Red or Blue

1897, Sept. 26

138	A51	1c sl bl (R)	85	75
a.		Inverted overprint	5.00	5.00
139	A52	2c cl (Bl)	1.25	1.25
a.		Inverted overprint	4.00	4.00
140	A53	5c grn (Bl)	2.00	2.00
a.		Inverted overprint	7.00	7.00
141	A68	10c red (Bl)	3.00	2.50
a.		Inverted ovpt.	12.50	12.50

Commemorating the Restoration of Peace at the end of the Civil War.
Issue for use only on the days of the National Fête, September 26, 27 and 28, 1897.

Regular Issues Surcharged in Black, Blue or Red

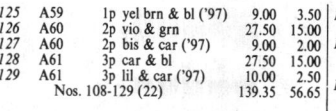

1898, July 25

142	A32	½c on 1c bl (Bk)	40	40
a.		Inverted surcharge	6.00	6.00
143	A51	½c on 1c bis (Bl)	40	40
a.		Inverted surcharge	6.00	
b.		Double surcharge	5.00	
144	A62	½c on 1c brn vio & blk (R)	40	40
145	A52	½c on 2c bl (Bk)	40	40
146	A63	½c on 5c pale bl & blk (R)	40	40
a.		Double surcharge	12.50	
147	A54	½c on 7c dp grn (R)	40	40
		Nos. 142-147 (6)	2.40	2.40

The 2c red brown of 1894 (No. 77) was also surcharged like Nos. 142 to 147 but was not issued.

Liberty
A69

Statue of Artigas
A70

1898-99   Litho.   Perf. 11, 11½

148	A69	5m rose	35	35
149	A69	5m pur ('99)	40	40

Engraved
1899-1900   Perf. 12½, 14, 15.

150	A70	5m lt bl	25	20
151	A70	5m org ('00)	25	20

No. 135 With Additional Surcharge in Black

1900, Dec. 1

152	A64(f+g)	5c on 10c lake & blk	60	40
a.		Black bar over "1897" omitted	20.00	

Cattle
A72

Girl's Head
A73

Shepherdess
A74

Perf. 13½ to 16 and Compound.
1900-10   Engraved.

153	A72	1c yel grn	50	20
154	A73	5c dl bl	50	15
155	A73	5c sl grn ('10)	50	25
156	A74	10c gray vio	60	30

Eros and Cornucopia
A75

Basket of Fruit
A76

1901, Feb. 11

157	A75	2c vermilion	40	20
158	A76	7c brn org	1.25	40

General Artigas
A78

Cattle
A79

Eros
A80

Cow
A81

Shepherdess
A82

Numeral
A83

Justice
A84

1904-05   Litho.   Perf. 11½

160	A78	5m orange	50	20
a.		5m yel	40	20
161	A79	1c green	75	20
a.		Imperf., pair	5.00	
162	A80	2c dp org	35	20
a.		2c org red	25	20
b.		Imperf., pair	5.00	
163	A81	5c blue	1.00	15
a.		Imperf., pair	5.00	
164	A82	10c dk vio ('05)	60	25
165	A83	20c gray grn ('05)	3.00	60
166	A84	25c ol bis ('05)	3.50	1.00
		Nos. 160-166 (7)	9.70	2.60

Overprinted Diagonally in Carmine or Black

Paz 1904

1904, Oct. 15

| 167 | A79 | 1c grn (C) | 60 | 40 |

URUGUAY

168	A80	2c dp org (Bk)	75	50
169	A81	5c dk bl (C)	1.25	75

Commemorating the end of the Civil War of 1904. In the first overprinting, "Paz 1904" appears at a 50-degree angle; in the second, at a 63-degree angle.

A85　　　　　A86

1906, Feb. 23　Litho.　Unwmkd.

170	A85	5c dk bl	1.25	20
a.		Imperf., pair	7.50	

1906-07

171	A86	5c dp bl	30	15
172	A86	7c org brn ('07)	60	35
173	A86	50c rose	5.00	1.00

Cruiser "Montevideo"
A87

1908, Aug. 23　Typo.　Rouletted 13

174	A87	1c car & dk grn	1.25	1.25
a.		Center inverted	450.00	450.00
b.		Imperf., pair	40.00	
175	A87	2c grn & dk grn	1.25	1.25
a.		Center inverted	450.00	450.00
b.		Imperf., pair	40.00	
176	A87	5c org & dk grn	1.25	1.25
a.		Center inverted	450.00	450.00
b.		Imperf., pair	40.00	

Issued to commemorate the independence of Uruguay, which was declared Aug. 25, 1825. Counterfeits exist.

View of the Port of Montevideo
A88

Wmk. 187
Wmkd. R O in Diamond. (187)

1909, Aug. 24　Engraved　Perf. 11½

177	A88	2c lt brn & blk	1.50	1.00
178	A88	5c rose red & blk	1.50	1.00

Issued to commemorate the opening of the Port of Montevideo, August 25, 1909.

The indexes in each volume of the Scott Catalogue contain many listings which help to identify stamps.

Centésimos
Nos. 156, 91
Surcharged

Provisorio
Perf. 14 to 16

1909, Sept. 13　Unwmkd.

179	A74	8c on 10c dl vio	60	30
a.		"Contesimos"	2.25	
180	A38	23c on 25c bis brn	1.50	75

Centaur
A89
Engraved.

1910, May 22　Perf. 11½　Wmk. 187

182	A89	2c car red	80	50
183	A89	5c dp bl	80	50

Centenary of Liberation Day, Aug. 25, 1810. The 2c in deep blue and 5c in carmine red were prepared for collectors.

Stamps of 1900-06 Surcharged:

a　　　b　　　c

Perf. 14 to 16, 11½

1910, Oct. 6　Unwmkd.

Black Surcharge.

184	A72 (a)	5m on 1c yel grn	25	15
a.		Inverted surcharge	9.00	7.50

Dark Blue Surcharge.

185	A39 (b)	5c on 50c dl red	40	30
a.		Inverted surcharge	9.00	9.00

Blue Surcharge.

186	A86 (c)	5c on 50c rose	1.00	75
a.		Double surcharge	40.00	
b.		Inverted surcharge	20.00	17.50

Artigas
A90
"Commercial Progress"
A91

1910, Nov. 21　Engr.　Perf. 14, 15

187	A90	5m dk vio	20	10
188	A90	1c dp grn	20	10
189	A90	2c org red	30	10
190	A90	5c dk bl	30	10
191	A90	8c gray blk	60	20
192	A90	20c brown	1.00	30
193	A91	23c dp ultra	1.25	60
194	A91	50c orange	3.00	1.50
195	A91	1p scarlet	7.50	1.00
		Nos. 187-195 (9)	14.35	4.00

See also Nos. 199-210.

Symbolical of the Posts
A92

1911, Jan. 6　Perf. 11½　Wmk. 187

196	A92	5c rose car & blk	90	70

Commemorating the First South American Postal Congress, at Montevideo, January, 1911.

No. 158
Surcharged in
Red or
Dark Blue

ARTIGAS 5 CENTESIMOS 1811-1911

Perf. 14 to 16

1911, May 1.　Unwmkd.

197	A76	2c on 7c brn org (R)	50	40
198	A76	2c on 7c brn org (Bl)	50	30
a.		Invtd. surch.	12.00	

Commemorating the centenary of the battle of Las Piedras, won by the forces under Gen. Jose Gervasio Artigas, May 8, 1811.

Typographed.
FOUR AND FIVE CENTESIMOS.
Type I. Large numerals about 3mm. high.
Type II. Small numerals about 2¼mm. high.

1912-15　Perf. 11½

199	A90	5m violet	20	10
a.		5m pur	20	
200	A90	5m magenta	25	10
		5m dl rose	25	10
201	A90	1c grn ('13)	20	10
202	A90	2c brn org	20	10
203	A90	2c rose red ('13)	20	10
a.		2c dp red ('14)	20	
204	A90	4c org (I) ('14)	30	10
a.		4c org (II) ('15)	30	10
b.		4c yel ('13)	25	10
205	A90	5c dl bl (I)	40	5
a.		5c bl (II)	40	
206	A90	8c ultra ('13)	60	10
207	A90	20c brn ('13)	1.50	20
		20c choc	1.50	25
208	A91	23c dk bl ('15)	3.00	75
209	A90	50c org ('14)	3.00	1.25
210	A91	1p ver ('15)	7.00	1.00
		Nos. 199-210 (12)	16.85	3.95

CENTENARIO DE LAS INSTRUCCIONES DEL AÑO XIII
Stamps of 1912-15 Overprinted

1913, Apr. 4

211	A90	2c brn org	80	60
a.		Inverted overprint	7.50	7.50
212	A90	4c yellow	80	60
213	A90	5c blue	80	60

Commemorating the centenary of the Buenos Aires Congress of 1813.

Liberty Extending Peace to the Country
A93

1918, Jan. 3　Lithographed

214	A93	2c grn & red	90	60
215	A93	5c buff & bl	90	60

Promulgation of the Constitution.

Statue of Liberty, New York Harbor
A94
Harbor of Montevideo
A95

Perf. 14, 15, 13½

1919, July 15　Engraved

217	A94	2c car & brn	50	25
218	A94	4c org & brn	60	25
219	A94	5c bl & brn	75	25
220	A94	8c org brn & ind	1.00	50
221	A94	20c ol bis & blk	2.25	1.00
222	A94	23c grn & blk	2.75	1.50
		Nos. 217-222 (6)	7.85	3.75

Peace at end of World War I.

1919-20　Lithographed　Perf. 11½

225	A95	5m vio & blk	15	8
226	A95	1c grn & blk	20	10
227	A95	2c red & blk	20	10
228	A95	4c org & blk	50	15
229	A95	5c ultra & sl	60	15
230	A95	8c gray bl & lt brn	75	25
231	A95	20c brn & blk	2.25	30
232	A95	23c grn & blk	3.50	1.00
233	A95	50c brn & bl	6.00	3.00
234	A95	1p dl red & bl	10.00	4.00
		Nos. 225-234 (10)	24.15	9.23

José Enrique Rodó
A96
Mercury
A97

1920, Feb. 28　Engr.　Perf. 14, 15

235	A96	2c car & blk	90	70
236	A96	4c org & bl	1.00	30
237	A96	5c bl & brn	1.25	90

Issued to honor José Enrique Rodó, author.

1921-22　Lithographed　Perf. 11½

238	A97	5m lilac	25	6
239	A97	5m gray blk ('22)	25	6
240	A97	1c lt grn	30	8
241	A97	1c vio ('22)	35	8
242	A97	2c fawn	40	8
243	A97	2c red ('22)	40	8
244	A97	3c bl grn ('22)	75	25
245	A97	4c orange	50	12
246	A97	5c ultra	50	6
247	A97	5c choc ('22)	75	6
248	A97	12c ultra ('22)	2.50	75
249	A97	36c ol ('22)	8.00	3.50
		Nos. 238-249 (12)	14.95	5.18

See also Nos. 254-260.

URUGUAY

Dámaso A.
Larrañaga
A98

1921, Dec. 10   **Unwmkd.**
250   A98   5c slate   1.50   1.00

Issued to commemorate the 150th anniversary of the birth of Dámaso A. Larrañaga (1771-1848), bishop, writer, scientist and physician.

Wmk. 188
Mercury Type of 1921-22.
Wmkd.
REPUBLICA O. DEL URUGUAY. (188)

1922-23
254	A97	5m gray blk	25	5
255	A97	1c vio ('23)	35	6
a.		1c red vio	35	6
256	A97	2c pale red	50	8
257	A97	2c dp rose ('23)	60	10
259	A97	5c yel brn ('23)	1.00	6
260	A97	8c sal pink ('23)	1.50	1.20
		Nos. 254-260 (6)	4.20	1.55

Equestrian Statue
of Artigas
A99
Engraved.

1923, Feb. 26   **Perf. 14**   **Unwmkd.**
264	A99	2c car & sep	40	15
265	A99	5c vio & sep	40	15
266	A99	12c bl & sep	60	30

Southern
Lapwing
A100
Size: 18x22½mm.
Wmkd. Caduceus. (189)
Perf. 12½, 11½x12½

1923, June 25   **Lithographed.**
267	A100	5m gray	10	5
268	A100	1c org yel	15	5
269	A100	2c lt vio	25	10
270	A100	3c gray grn	60	20
271	A100	5c lt bl	60	20
272	A100	8c rose red	1.00	50
273	A100	12c dp bl	1.00	50
274	A100	20c brn org	2.00	50
275	A100	36c emerald	3.50	2.00
276	A100	50c orange	7.00	3.00
277	A100	1p brt rose	35.00	20.00
278	A100	2p lt grn	35.00	20.00
		Nos. 267-278 (12)	86.20	47.10

See also Nos. 285-298, 309-314, 317-323, 334-339.

Battle of Sarandi
Monument
A101

1923, Oct. 12   **Perf. 11½**   **Wmk. 188**
279	A101	2c dp grn	90	70
280	A101	5c scarlet	90	70
281	A101	12c dk bl	90	70

Issued to commemorate the unveiling of the Sarandi Battle Monument by José Luis Zorrilla, Oct. 12, 1923.

Olympic Games Issue.

"Victory of Samothrace"
A102
Perf. 11

1924, July 29   **Typo.**   **Unwmkd.**
282	A102	2c rose	27.50	20.00
283	A102	5c mauve	27.50	20.00
284	A102	8c brt bl	27.50	20.00

Sheets of 20 (5x4).
Five hundred sets of these stamps were printed on yellow paper for presentation purposes. They were not on sale at post offices. Price per set, $225.

Lapwing Type of 1923.
Lithographed.
First Redrawing.
Size: 17¼x21½mm.
Imprint: "A. BARREIRO Y RAMOS."

1924, July 26   **Perf. 12½, 11½**
285	A100	5m gray blk	15	5
286	A100	1c fawn	20	8
287	A100	2c rose lil	60	8
288	A100	3c gray grn	40	15
289	A100	5c chlky bl	30	6
290	A100	8c pink	75	40
291	A100	10c turq bl	60	30
292	A100	12c lt bl	75	50
293	A100	15c lt vio	75	40
294	A100	20c brown	1.25	40
295	A100	36c salmon	5.00	1.50
296	A100	50c grnsh gray	7.00	2.00
297	A100	1p buff	12.00	5.00
298	A100	2p dl vio	25.00	12.50
		Nos. 285-298 (14)	54.75	23.40

Landing of the 33 "Immortals"
Led by Juan Antonio Lavalleja
A103
Perf. 11, 11½

1925, Apr. 19   **Wmk. 188**
300	A103	2c sal pink & blk	1.50	1.00
301	A103	5c lil & blk	1.50	1.00
302	A103	12c bl & blk	1.50	1.00

Issued to commemorate the centenary of the landing of the thirty-three Founders of the Uruguayan Republic.

Legis-
lative
Palace
A104

Engraved.
1925, Aug. 24   **Perf. 11½**   **Unwmkd.**
| 303 | A104 | 5c vio & blk | 1.50 | 1.00 |
| 304 | A104 | 12c bl & blk | 1.50 | 1.00 |

Dedication of the Legislative Palace.

General Fructuoso Rivera
A105
Lithographed.
1925, Sept. 24   **Perf. 11**   **Wmk. 188**
| 305 | A105 | 5c lt red | 60 | 40 |

Centenary of Battle of Rincón. See No. C9.

Battle of Sarandí—A106

1925, Oct. 12   **Perf. 11½**
306	A106	2c bl grn	1.50	1.40
307	A106	5c dl vio	1.50	1.40
308	A106	12c dp bl	2.00	1.60

Centenary of the Battle of Sarandi.

Lapwing Type of 1923.
Second Redrawing.
Size: 17½x21¾mm.
Imprint: "Imprenta Nacional."

1925-26   **Perf. 11, 11½, 10½**
309	A100	5m gray blk	40	8
310	A100	1c dl vio	40	8
311	A100	2c brt rose	50	8
312	A100	3c gray grn	50	30
313	A100	5c lt bl ('26)	75	8
314	A100	12c sl bl	2.00	90
		Nos. 309-314 (6)	4.55	1.12

The design differs in many small details from that of the 1923-24 issues. These stamps may be readily identified by the imprint and perforation.

Lapwing Type of 1923.
Third Redrawing.
Size: 17½x21¾mm.
Imprint: "Imp. Nacional" at center.

1926-27   **Perf. 11, 11½, 10½**
317	A100	5m gray	15	8
318	A100	1c lt vio ('27)	1.00	40
319	A100	2c red	75	25
320	A100	3c gray grn	1.00	50
321	A100	5c lt bl	75	10
322	A100	8c pink ('27)	1.50	75
323	A100	36c rose buff	7.00	4.00
		Nos. 317-323 (7)	12.15	6.08

These stamps may be distinguished from preceding stamps of the same design by the imprint.

Philatelic Exhibition Issue.

Post Office at
Montevideo
A107
Engraved.
1927, May 25   **Imperf.**   **Unwmkd.**
| 330 | A107 | 2c green | 6.00 | 4.50 |
| a. | | Sheet of four | 25.00 | 25.00 |

331	A107	5c dl red	6.00	4.50
a.		Sheet of four	25.00	25.00
332	A107	8c dk bl	6.00	4.50
a.		Sheet of four	25.00	25.00

Printed in sheets of 4 and sold at the Montevideo Exhibition. Lithographed counterfeits exist.

Lapwing Type of 1923.
Fourth Redrawing.
Size: 17¾x21¾mm.
Imprint: "Imp. Nacional" at right.
Perf. 11, 11½

1927, May 6   **Litho.**   **Wmk. 188**
334	A100	1c gray vio	10	5
335	A100	2c vermilion	20	10
336	A100	3c gray grn	50	35
337	A100	5c blue	30	10
338	A100	8c rose	2.00	75
339	A100	20c gray brn	4.00	1.50
		Nos. 334-339 (6)	7.10	2.85

The design has been slightly retouched in various places. The imprint is in italic capitals and is placed below the right numeral of value.

No. 292
Surcharged
in Red

Inauguración
Ferrocarril
SAN CARLOS
a ROCHA
14/1/928
5 cts. 5

1928, Jan. 13   **Perf. 11½**   **Unwmkd.**
345	A100	2c on 12c sl bl	1.25	1.00
346	A100	5c on 12c sl bl	1.25	1.00
347	A100	10c on 12c sl bl	1.25	1.00
348	A100	15c on 12c sl bl	1.25	1.00

Issued to celebrate the inauguration of the railroad between San Carlos and Rocha.

General Rivera   Artigas
(7 dots in panels below portrait.)
A108   A109

1928, Apr. 19   **Engraved**   **Perf. 12**
| 349 | A108 | 5c car rose | 40 | 20 |

Centenary of the Battle of Las Misiones.

Imprint:
"Waterlow & Sons. Ltd., Londres."
**Perf. 11, 12½, 13x13½,
12½x13, 13x12½.**

1928-43   Size: 16x19½mm.
350	A109	5m black	10	5
350A	A109	5m org ('43)	5	5
351	A109	1c dk vio	10	5
352	A109	1c brn vio ('34)	15	10
352A	A109	1c vio bl ('43)	5	5
353	A109	2c dp grn	10	5
353A	A109	2c brn red ('43)	5	5
354	A109	3c bister	25	8
355	A109	3c dp grn ('32)	15	5
355A	A109	3c brt grn ('43)	6	5
356	A109	5c red	20	5
357	A109	5c ol grn ('33)	20	10
357A	A109	5c dl pur ('43)	8	5
358	A109	7c car ('32)	20	5
359	A109	8c dk bl	30	6
360	A109	8c brn ('33)	30	8
361	A109	10c orange	45	20
362	A109	10c red org ('32)	75	50
363	A109	12c dp bl ('32)	40	8
364	A109	15c dl bl	65	15
365	A109	17c dk vio ('32)	1.00	20
366	A109	20c ol brn	85	20
367	A109	20c red brn ('33)	1.25	60
368	A109	24c car rose	1.50	60
369	A109	24c yel ('33)	1.00	50
370	A109	36c ol grn ('33)	1.50	60
371	A109	50c gray	4.00	2.25
372	A109	50c blk ('33)	5.00	2.00
373	A109	50c blk brn ('33)	4.00	1.50
374	A109	1p yel grn	9.00	4.00
		Nos. 350-374 (30)	33.69	14.35

869

URUGUAY

1929-33   *Perf. 12½.*
Size: 22 to 22½ x 28½ to 29½ mm.

375	A109	1p ol brn ('33)	6.00	3.00
376	A109	2p dk grn	12.00	7.00
377	A109	2p dl red ('32)	25.00	17.50
378	A109	3p dk bl	20.00	12.50
379	A109	3p blk ('32)	20.00	17.50
380	A109	4p violet	30.00	20.00
381	A109	4p dk ol grn ('32)	25.00	17.50
382	A109	5p car brn	40.00	30.00
383	A109	5p red org ('32)	25.00	17.50
384	A109	10p lake ('33)	90.00	60.00
385	A109	10p dp ultra ('33)	90.00	60.00
		Nos. 375-385 (11)	383.00	262.50

See also Nos. 420–423, 462. See also type A135.

Equestrian Statue of Artigas
A110

1928, May 1

386	A110	2p Prus bl & choc	15.00	7.50
387	A110	3p dp rose & blk	17.50	10.00

Symbolical of Soccer Victory
A111

General Eugenio Garzón
A112

1928, July 29

388	A111	2c brn vio	15.00	12.50
389	A111	5c dp red	15.00	12.50
390	A111	8c ultra	15.00	12.50

Issued to commemorate the Uruguayan soccer victories in the Olympic Games of 1924 and 1928. Printed in sheets of 20, divided in panes of 10 (5x2).

1928, Aug. 25   *Imperf.*

391	A112	2c red	2.00	2.00
a.		Sheet of four	12.50	12.50
392	A112	5c yel grn	2.00	2.00
a.		Sheet of four	12.50	12.50
393	A112	8c dp bl	2.00	2.00
a.		Sheet of four	12.50	12.50

Dedication of monument to Garzon. Issued in sheets of 4. Lithographed counterfeits exist.

Black River Bridge
A113

Gauchos Breaking a Horse
A114

Peace
A115

Montevideo
A116

Liberty and Flag of Uruguay
A117

Liberty with Torch and Caduceus
A118

Statue of Artigas
A124

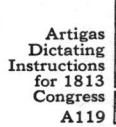

Artigas Dictating Instructions for 1813 Congress
A119

Seascape—A120

Montevideo Harbor, 1830
A121

Liberty and Coat of Arms
A122

Montevideo Harbor, 1930
A123

1930, June 16   *Perf. 12½, 12*

394	A113	5m gray blk	30	20
395	A114	1c dk brn	30	20
396	A115	2c brn rose	30	20
397	A116	3c yel grn	40	25
398	A117	5c dk bl	40	25
399	A118	8c dl red	50	30
400	A119	10c dk vio	75	50
401	A120	15c bl grn	1.00	75
402	A121	20c indigo	1.25	1.00
403	A122	24c red brn	1.75	1.00
404	A123	50c org red	5.00	3.00
405	A124	1p black	8.00	4.00
406	A124	2p bl vio	20.00	12.50
407	A124	3p dk red	30.00	20.00
408	A124	4p red org	35.00	25.00
409	A124	5p lilac	50.00	30.00
		Nos. 394-409 (16)	154.95	99.15

Issued in commemoration of the centenary of national independence and the promulgation of the constitution.

Wmk. 227
Type of 1856 Issue.
Values in Centesimos.
Wmkd. Greek Border and REPUBLICA O. DEL URUGUAY in Alternate Curved Lines. (227)

1931, Apr. 11   Litho.   *Imperf.*

410	A1	2c gray bl	4.00	4.00
a.		Sheet of 4	20.00	20.00
411	A1	8c dl red	4.00	4.00
a.		Sheet of 4	20.00	20.00
412	A1	15c bl blk	4.00	4.00
a.		Sheet of 4	20.00	20.00

Wmkd.
REPUBLICA O. DEL URUGUAY. (188)

413	A1	5c lt grn	4.00	4.00
a.		Sheet of 4	20.00	20.00

Issued in sheets containing four stamps each, in commemoration of the Philatelic Exhibition at Montevideo, April 11-15, 1931. The stamps were on sale during the five days of the exhibition only.

Juan Zorrilla de San Martín
A125

1932, June 6   *Perf. 12½ Unwmkd.*

414	A125	1½c brn vio	30	12
415	A125	3c green	40	12
416	A125	7c dk bl	50	10
417	A125	12c lt bl	1.00	50
418	A125	1p dp brn	27.50	20.00
		Nos. 414-418 (5)	29.70	20.84

Commemorating the Uruguayan poet, Juan Zorrilla de San Martin.

Semi-Postal Stamp
No. B2
Surcharged

1932, Nov. 1   *Perf. 12*

419	SP1	1½(c) on 2c+2c dp grn	40	20

Artigas Type of 1928.
Imprint: "Imprenta Nacional" at center.

1932-35   Litho.   *Perf. 11, 12½*
Size: 15¾x19¼mm.

420	A109	5m lt brn ('35)	15	8
421	A109	1c pale vio ('35)	15	8
422	A109	15m black	35	20
423	A109	5c bluish grn ('35)	60	25

Gen. J. A. Lavalleja
A126

Flag of the Race and Globe
A127

1933, July 12   Engraved *Perf. 12½*

429	A126	15m brn lake	20	8

1933, Aug. 3   *Perf. 11, 11½, 11x11½*
Lithographed

430	A127	3c bl grn	40	25
431	A127	5c rose	50	35
432	A127	7c lt bl	50	30
433	A127	8c dl red	1.00	80
434	A127	12c dp bl	60	40
435	A127	17c violet	1.50	1.00
436	A127	20c red brn	2.75	2.00
437	A127	24c yellow	3.00	2.25
438	A127	36c orange	3.50	2.75
439	A127	50c ol gray	5.00	3.00
440	A127	1p bister	12.20	8.00
		Nos. 430-440 (11)	30.95	21.10

Raising of the "Flag of the Race" and of the 441st anniv. of the sailing of Columbus from Palos, Spain, on his first voyage to America.

Sower
A128

Juan Zorrilla de San Martín
A129

1933, Aug. 28   *Perf. 11½ Unwmkd.*

441	A128	3c bl grn	30	20
442	A128	5c dl vio	50	35
443	A128	7c lt bl	40	25
444	A128	8c dp red	1.00	60
445	A128	12c ultra	1.50	1.00
		Nos. 441-445 (5)	3.70	2.40

Commemorative of the Third Constituent National Assembly.

1933, Nov. 9   Engraved *Perf. 12½*

446	A129	7c slate	20	8

Albatross Flying over Map of the Americas—A130

1933, Dec. 3   Typo.   *Perf. 11½*

447	A130	3c grn, blk & brn	3.50	2.50
a.		Sheet of six	25.00	
448	A130	7c turq bl, brn & blk	2.00	1.00
a.		Sheet of six	15.00	
449	A130	12c dk bl, gray & ver	3.00	2.00
a.		Sheet of six	20.00	

URUGUAY

450	A130	17c ver, gray & vio	6.50	3.50
a.		Sheet of six	45.00	
451	A130	20c yel, bl & grn	7.50	4.50
a.		Sheet of six	50.00	
452	A130	36c red, blk & yel	10.00	7.00
a.		Sheet of six	70.00	
		Nos. 447-452 (6)	32.50	20.50

Issued to commemorate the 7th Pan-American Conference, Montevideo. Issued in sheets of six. See also Nos. C61-C62.

General Rivera
A131

1934, Feb. Engraved *Perf. 12½*

453	A131	3c green	15	5

Stars Representing the Three Constitutions
A132

1934, Mar. 23 Typographed

454	A132	3c yel grn & grn	70	50
455	A132	7c org red & red	70	50
456	A132	12c ultra & bl	2.00	1.00

Perf. 11½.

457	A132	17c brn & rose	2.50	1.75
458	A132	20c yel & gray	3.00	2.25
459	A132	36c dk vio & bl grn	3.00	2.50
460	A132	50c blk & bl	8.00	5.00
461	A132	1p dk car & vio	20.00	11.00
		Nos. 454-461 (8)	39.90	24.50

First Year of Third Republic.

Artigas Type of 1928.
Imprint: "Barreiro & Ramos S. A."

1934, Nov. 28 Lithographed

462	A109	50c brn blk	5.00	2.00

"Uruguay" and "Brazil" Holding Scales of Justice
A133

Florencio Sánchez
A134

1935, May 30 *Perf. 11* Unwmkd.

463	A133	5m brown	75	45
464	A133	15m black	40	40
465	A133	3c green	45	35
466	A133	7c orange	50	30
467	A133	12c ultra	1.25	75
468	A133	50c yel brn	5.00	3.50
		Nos. 463-468 (6)	8.35	5.75

Visit of President Vargas of Brazil.

1935, Nov. 7

469	A134	3c green	20	10
470	A134	7c brown	30	15
471	A134	12c blue	80	50

Issued to commemorate the 25th anniversary of the death of Florencio Sanchez (1875-1910), author.

Artigas
(6 dots in panels below portrait.)
A135

Power Dam on Black River
A136

Imprint: "Imprenta Nacional" at center.

1936-44 *Perf. 11, 12½.*

474	A135	5m org brn ('37)	8	5
475	A135	5m lt brn ('39)	10	5
476	A135	1c lt vio ('37)	20	8
477	A135	2c dk brn ('37)	12	5
478	A135	2c grn ('39)	12	5
479	A135	5c brt bl ('37)	18	5
480	A135	5c bluish grn ('39)	40	8
481	A135	12c dl bl ('38)	40	8
482	A135	20c fawn	1.00	50
482A	A135	20c rose ('44)	1.00	40
483	A135	50c brn blk	2.50	75

Size: 21½x28½mm.

483A	A135	1p brown	7.00	2.50
483B	A135	2p blue	14.00	11.00
483C	A135	3p gray blk	20.00	15.00
		Nos. 474-483C (14)	47.10	30.64

See also Nos. 488, 576. See also type A109.

1937-38

484	A136	1c dl vio	25	6
485	A136	10c blue	50	15
486	A136	15c rose	1.25	75
487	A136	1p choc ('38)	7.00	2.50

Imprint: "Imprenta Nacional" at right.

1938

488	A135	1c brt vio	15	5

International Law Congress, 1889
A137

1939, July 16 Litho. *Perf. 12½*

489	A137	1c brn org	25	15
490	A137	2c dl grn	35	25
491	A137	5c rose ver	35	25
492	A137	12c dl bl	75	50
493	A137	50c lt vio	3.00	2.00
		Nos. 489-493 (5)	4.70	3.15

Issued to commemorate the 50th anniversary of the Montevideo Congress of International Law.

Artigas
A138

A138a

1939-43 Litho. Unwmkd.

Size: 15¾x19mm.

494	A138	5m dl brn org ('40)	10	5
495	A138	1c lt bl	10	5
496	A138	2c lt vio	10	5
497	A138	5c vio brn	20	5
498	A138	8c rose red	25	5
499	A138	10c green	50	8
500	A138	15c dl bl	1.00	40

Size: 24x29½mm.

501	A138	1p dl brn ('41)	3.50	1.00
502	A138	2p dl rose vio ('40)	9.00	3.50
503	A138	4p org ('43)	11.00	4.00
504	A138	5p ver ('41)	17.50	6.00
		Nos. 494-504 (11)	43.25	15.26

See also No. 578.

Redrawn: Horizontal lines in portrait background.

1940-44

Size: 17x21mm.

505	A138a	5m brn org ('41)	6	5
506	A138a	1c lt bl	6	5
507	A138a	1c lt vio ('41)	8	5
508	A138a	2c vio brn	15	5
509	A138a	8c sal pink ('44)	25	8
510	A138a	10c grn ('41)	50	12
511	A138a	50c ol bis ('42)	7.00	2.00
511A	A138a	50c yel grn ('44)	6.00	2.00
		Nos. 505-511A (8)	14.10	4.40

See also Nos. 568-575, 577, 601, 632, 660-661.

Juan Manuel Blanes
A139

Francisco Acuna de Figueroa
A140

1941, Aug. 11 Engraved *Perf. 12½*

512	A139	5m ocher	25	12
513	A139	1c hn brn	25	12
514	A139	2c green	25	15
515	A139	5c rose car	75	12
516	A139	12c dp bl	1.25	65
517	A139	50c dk vio	6.00	4.75
		Nos. 512-517 (6)	8.75	5.91

Issued in honor of Juan Manuel Blanes, artist.

1942, Mar. 18 Unwmkd.

518	A140	1c hn brn	25	20
519	A140	2c dp grn	25	20
520	A140	5c rose car	40	25
521	A140	12c dp bl	1.25	60
522	A140	50c dk vio	4.50	3.50
		Nos. 518-522 (5)	6.65	4.75

Issued in honor of Francisco Acuña de Figueroa, author of the National anthem.

No. 506 Surcharged in Red

**Valor
$ 0.005**

1943, Jan. 27

523	A138a	5m on 1c lt bl	15	12

Coat of Arms
A141

Clio
A142

1943, Mar. 12 Lithographed

524	A141	1c on 2c dl vio brn (R)	12	8
525	A141	2c on 2c dl vio brn (V)	18	12
a.		Invtd. surch.	25.00	25.00

1943, Aug. 24

526	A142	5m lt vio	30	10
527	A142	1c lt ultra	30	15
528	A142	5c brt rose	50	20
529	A142	5c buff	50	25

Issued to commemorate the 100th anniversary of the Historic and Geographic Institute of Uruguay.

Swiss Colony Monument
A143

Y. M. C. A. Seal
A144

Overprinted "1944" and Surcharged in Various Colors

1944, May 18

530	A143	1c on 3c dl grn (R)	15	8
531	A143	5c on 7c brn red (B)	30	15
532	A143	10c on 12c dk bl (Br)	60	35

Issued to commemorate the 50th anniversary of the founding of the Swiss Colony.

1944, Sept. 8

533	A144	5c blue	15	8

Issued to commemorate the 100th anniversary of the Young Men's Christian Association.

"La Educación del Pueblo"
A145

José Pedro Varela
A146

Monument
A147

Monument
A148

Perf. 11½

1945, June 13 Litho. Unwmkd.

534	A145	5m brt grn	20	10
535	A146	1c dp blk	20	10

Perf. 12½

536	A147	2c rose red	20	15
537	A148	5c blue	30	15
a.		Perf. 11½	25	10

Issued to commemorate the centenary of the birth of José Pedro Varela, author.

Santiago Vazquez
A149

Silvestre Blanco
A150

 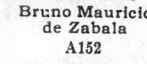

Eduardo Acevedo
A151

Bruno Mauricio de Zabala
A152

José Pedro Varela
A153

José Ellauri
A154

URUGUAY

Gen. Luis de Larrobla
A155

Engr. (5m, 5c, 10c); Litho.
1945-47   Perf. 10½, 11, 11½, 12½
538	A149	5m pur ('46)	6	5
539	A150	1c yel brn ('46)	5	5
540	A151	2c brn vio	10	8
541	A152	3c grn & dp grn ('47)	15	8
542	A153	5c brt car	17	5
543	A154	10c ultra	33	12
544	A155	20c dp grn & choc ('47)	85	40
		Nos. 538-544 (7)	1.71	83

CORREO INAUGURACIÓN DICIEMBRE, 1945
No. C86A Surcharged in Blue
20 CENTS

1946, Jan. 9   Perf. 12½
| 545 | AP7 | 20c on 68c pale vio brn | 1.25 | 90 |

Issued to commemorate the inauguration of the Black River Power Dam. See also No. C120.

Coat of Arms A156   Coat of Arms A157

Lithographed. Black Overprint.
1946-51   Perf. 12½   Unwmkd.
546	A156	5m org ('49)	8	6
a.		Inverted ovpt.		
547	A156	2c dl vio brn ('47)	12	6
548	A156	3c green	12	8
549	A156	5c ultra ('51)	12	6
550	A156	10c org brn	25	8
551	A156	20c dk grn	70	25
552	A156	50c brown	2.25	85
553	A156	3p lil rose	7.00	5.00
		Nos. 546-553 (8)	10.64	6.44

1947-48   Black Surcharge
| 554 | A157 | 2c on 5c ultra ('48) | 15 | 8 |
| 555 | A157 | 3c on 5c ultra | 15 | 8 |

Statue of Ariel A158   Bust of José Enrique Rodó A159

Bas-relief A160

Bas-relief A161

Engraved
1948, Jan. 30   Perf. 12½   Unwmkd.
Center in Orange Brown.
556	A158	1c grnsh gray	10	8
557	A159	2c purple	15	10
558	A160	3c green	20	10
559	A161	5c red vio	25	10
560	A160	10c dp org	30	15
561	A161	12c ultra	40	20
562	A158	20c rose vio	85	50
563	A159	50c dp car	3.00	1.75
		Nos. 556-563 (8)	5.25	2.98

Dedication of the Rodó monument.

View of the Port, Paysandú
A162

Arms of Paysandú
A163

1948, Oct. 9   Lithographed
| 564 | A162 | 3c bl grn | 15 | 10 |
| 565 | A163 | 7c ultra | 25 | 10 |

Issued to publicize the Exposition of Industry and Agriculture, Paysandú, October–November 1948.

Santa Lucia River Highway Bridge—A164

1948, Dec. 10
| 566 | A164 | 10c dk bl | 50 | 15 |
| 567 | A164 | 50c green | 2.25 | 1.00 |

Redrawn Artigas Types of 1940, 1936, and 1939
1948-51   Litho.   Perf. 12½
568	A138a	5m gray ('49)	10	5
569	A138a	1c rose vio ('50)	6	5
570	A138a	2c orange	12	5
571	A138a	2c choc ('50)	12	5
572	A138a	3c bl grn	12	5
572A	A138a	7c vio bl	20	5
573	A138a	8c rose car ('49)	30	8
574	A138a	10c org brn ('51)	20	5
575	A138a	12c bl ('51)	20	15
576	A135	20c violet	50	15
577	A138a	20c rose pink ('51)	60	20

Size: 18x21¾mm.
| 578 | A138 | 1p lil rose ('51) | 1.50 | 50 |
| | | Nos. 568-578 (12) | 4.02 | 1.43 |

The 2c chocolate, 3c and 7c also exist in perf. 11.

Plowing—A165

Mounted Cattle Herder A166

1949, Apr. 29   Perf. 12½   Unwmkd.
| 579 | A165 | 3c green | 20 | 10 |
| 580 | A166 | 7c blue | 30 | 10 |

Issued to commemorate the 4th Regional American Conference of Labor, 1949.

Cannon, Rural and Urban Views A167   Symbolical of Soccer Matches A168

1950, Oct. 11   Lithographed
581	A167	1c lil rose	12	6
582	A167	3c green	12	6
583	A167	7c dp bl	20	6

Issued to commemorate the 200th anniversary of the founding of Cordón, a district of Montevideo.

1951, Mar. 20
| 584 | A168 | 3c green | 75 | 25 |
| 585 | A168 | 7c vio bl | 1.50 | 50 |

Issued to publicize the 4th World Soccer Championship, Rio de Janeiro.

Gen. José Artigas A169

Flight of the People A170

Designs: 1c, 2c, 5c, Various equestrian portraits of Artigas. 7c, Dictating instructions. 8c, In congress. 10c, Artigas' flag. 14c, At the citadel. 20c, Arms of Artigas. 50c, In Paraguay. 1p, Bust.

Engraved and Photogravure.
1952, Jan. 7   Perf. 13½   Unwmkd.
586	A169	5m slate	15	6
587	A169	1c bl & blk	15	5
588	A169	2c pur & red brn	15	6
589	A170	3c aqua & dk brn	15	6
590	A169	5c red org & blk	20	10
591	A170	7c ol & blk	25	10
592	A170	8c car & blk	35	15
593	A170	10c choc, brt ultra & crim	40	15
594	A169	14c dp bl	40	15
595	A169	20c org yel, dp ultra & car	50	25
596	A169	50c org brn & blk	1.00	50
597	A169	1p bl gray & cit	3.00	1.50
		Nos. 586-597 (12)	6.70	3.13

Issued to commemorate the centenary (in 1950) of the death of Gen. José Artigas.

Plane and Stagecoach A171

1952, Oct. 9   Photo.   Perf. 13½x13
598	A171	3c bl grn	15	6
599	A171	7c blk brn	20	10
600	A171	12c ultra	25	12

Issued to commemorate the 75th anniversary (in 1949) of the formation of the Universal Postal Union.

Redrawn Artigas Type of 1940-44.
Size: 24x29½mm.
1953, Feb. 23   Litho.   Perf. 11
| 601 | A138a | 2p fawn | 6.00 | 3.50 |

Franklin D. Roosevelt A172

1953, Apr. 9   Engraved   Perf. 13½
602	A172	3c green	15	8
603	A172	7c ultra	20	10
604	A172	12c blk brn	40	20

Issued to commemorate the 5th Postal Congress of the Americas and Spain.

Ceibo, National Flower A173   Horse Breaking A174

Legislature Building A175

"Island of Seals" (Southern Sea Lions) A176   Fair Entrance A177

URUGUAY

Designs: 2c, 10c, 5p, Ombu tree. 3c, 50c, Passion Flower. 7c, 3p, Montevideo fortress. 12c, 2p, Outer gate, Montevideo.

Photo. (5m, 3c, 20c, 50c) or Engr.
Perf. 13x13½, 13½x13, 12½x13, 13x12½.

1954, Jan. 14			Unwmkd.	
605	A173	5m multi	10	5
606	A174	1c car & blk	10	5
607	A174	2c brn & grn	10	5
608	A173	3c multi	15	5
609	A175	5c pur & red brn	15	5
610	A173	7c brn & grn	10	5
611	A176	8c car & ultra	50	10
612	A174	10c org & grn	30	10
613	A175	12c dp ultra & dk brn	20	10
614	A174	14c rose lil & blk	20	10
615	A173	20c grn, brn, gray & car	75	15
616	A173	50c car & multi	1.50	30
617	A175	1p car & red brn	3.00	1.25
618	A175	2p car & blk brn	5.00	2.00
619	A173	3p lil & grn	6.00	2.50
620	A176	4p dp brn & dp ultra	15.00	7.00
621	A174	5p vio bl & grn	12.50	6.00
	Nos. 605-621 (17)		45.65	19.90

1956, Jan. 19		Litho.	Perf. 11	
622	A177	3c pale ol grn	6	5
623	A177	7c blue	8	5

Issued to publicize the First Exposition of National Products. See also Nos. C166-C168.

José Batlle y Ordonez
A178

Design: 7c, Full length portrait.
Photogravure.

1956, Dec. 15	Perf. 13½	Wmk. 90	
624	A178	3c rose red	10	5
625	A178	7c sepia	15	8

Issued to commemorate the centenary of the birth of President José Batlle y Ordonez. See also Nos. C169-C172.

Same Surcharged with New Values.
1957-58
626	A178	5c on 3c rose red ('58)	12	8
627	A178	10c on 7c sep	18	8
a.	Surcharge inverted		25.00	25.00

Diver — A179   Eduardo Acevedo — A180

Design: 10c, Swimmer at start (horiz.).
Perf. 10½, 11½

1958, Feb. 15	Litho.	Unwmkd.	
628	A179	5c brt bl grn	20	10
629	A179	10c brt bl	40	15

Issued to publicize the 14th South American swimming meet, Montevideo.

1958, Mar. 19	Perf. 11½, 10½	
630	A180	5c lt ol grn & blk	15	8
631	A180	10c ultra & blk	20	15

Issued to commemorate the centenary of the birth of Eduardo Acevedo (1856-1948), lawyer, legislator, minister of foreign affairs.

Artigas Type of 1940-44.
1958, Sept. 25	Litho.	Perf. 11	
632	A138a	5m blue	8	5

Baygorria Hydroelectric Works
A181

1958, Oct. 30	Perf. 11	Unwmkd.	
633	A181	5c yel grn & blk	8	5
634	A181	10c brn org & blk	10	8
635	A181	1p bl gray & blk	60	30
636	A181	2p rose & blk	1.25	60

Nos. 608, 610 and 605 Surcharged Similarly to

Photogravure or Engraved
1958-59   Perf. 13x13½
637	A173	5c on 3c multi ('59)	8	5
638	A173	10c on 7c brn & grn	8	6
639	A173	20c on 5m multi	20	12

Gabriela Mistral — A182   Carlos Vaz Ferreira — A183

Wmk. 327

Watermarked Coat of Arms. (327)
1959, July 6	Litho.	Perf. 11½	
640	A182	5c green	10	5
641	A182	10c dk bl	12	8
642	A182	20c red	20	10

Gabriela Mistral, Chilean poet and educator.

1959, Sept. 3		Perf. 11	
643	A183	5c blk & lt bl	5	5
644	A183	10c blk & ocher	10	5
645	A183	20c blk & ver	12	5
646	A183	50c blk & vio	35	8
647	A183	1p blk & grn	60	30
	Nos. 643-647 (5)		1.22	53

Issued to commemorate Carlos Vaz Ferreira (1872-1958), educator and author.

Dr. Martin C. Martinez — A184   Wmk. 332

Watermarked Large Sun and R O U (332)
1960, May 16	Litho.	Perf. 12	
648	A184	5c red lil & blk	5	5
649	A184	5c dp vio & blk	6	5
650	A184	10c brt bl & blk	8	5
651	A184	20c choc & blk	10	8
652	A184	1p gray & blk	40	15
653	A184	2p org & blk	85	25
654	A184	3p ol grn & blk	1.25	40
655	A184	4p yel brn & blk	2.00	1.00
656	A184	5p brt red & blk	2.25	1.25
	Nos. 648-656 (9)		7.04	3.28

Issued to commemorate the centenary of the birth of Dr. Martin C. Martinez (1859-1940), statesman.

Uprooted Oak Emblem
A185

1960, June 6	Perf. 12	Wmk. 332	
657	A185	10c dp bl & blk	20	12

Issued to publicize World Refugee Year, July 1, 1959-June 30, 1960. See No. C207.

Revolutionists and Cabildo, Buenos Aires — A186

1960, Nov. 4	Litho.	Perf. 12	
658	A186	5c bl & blk	6	5
659	A186	10c bl & ocher	8	6
	Nos. 658-659, C208-C210 (5)	94	71

Issued to commemorate the 150th anniversary of the May Revolution of 1810.

Artigas Type of 1940-44.
1960-61	Perf. 11	Wmk. 332	
660	A138a	2c gray	8	5
661	A138a	50c brn ('61)	15	10

Manuel Oribe
A187

Lithographed
1961, March 4	Perf. 12	Wmk. 332	
671	A187	10c brt bl & blk	10	8
672	A187	20c bl & blk	15	10
673	A187	40c grn & blk	20	15

Issued to honor General Manuel Oribe (1796?-1857), revolutionary leader and president of Uruguay (1835-1838).

Cavalry Charge — A188

1961, June 12	Perf. 12	Wmk. 332	
674	A188	20c bl & blk	15	8
675	A188	40c emer & blk	25	12

150th anniversary of the revolution.

Welfare, Justice and Education — A189   Gen. José Fructuoso Rivera — A190

1961, Aug. 14	Perf. 12	Wmk. 322	
676	A189	2c bis & lil	8	5
677	A189	5c bis & org	8	6
678	A189	10c bis & scar	8	5
679	A189	20c bis & yel grn	10	5
680	A189	50c bis & lt vio	15	8
681	A189	1p bis & bl	35	25
682	A189	2p bis & cit	85	50
683	A189	3p bis & gray	1.25	85
684	A189	4p bis & lt bl	1.65	1.25
685	A189	5p bis & choc	2.25	1.50
	Nos. 676-685 (10)		6.84	4.64

Issued to commemorate the Inter-American Economic and Social Conference of the Organization of American States, Punta del Este, August, 1961. See Nos. C233-C244.

Lithographed
1962, May 29	Perf. 12	Wmk. 332	
686	A190	10c brt red & blk	8	5
687	A190	20c bis & blk	12	5
688	A190	40c grn & blk	20	8

Issued to honor Gen. José Fructuoso Rivera (1790-1854), first President of Uruguay.

Scott's International Album provides spaces for an extensive representative collection of the world's postage stamps.

URUGUAY

Spade, Grain, Swiss "Scarf" and Hat	Bernardo Prudencio Berro
A191	A192

1962, Aug. 1   *Perf.* 12   Wmk. 332

| 689 | A191 | 10c bl, blk & car | 6 | 5 |
| 690 | A191 | 20c lt grn, blk & car | 10 | 6 |

Issued to commemorate the centenary of the Swiss Settlement in Uruguay. See also Nos. C245–C246.

1962, Oct. 22   Litho.   *Perf.* 12

| 691 | A192 | 10c grnsh bl & blk | 6 | 5 |
| 692 | A192 | 20c yel brn & blk | 10 | 6 |

Issued to honor Pres. Bernardo P. Berro (1803–1868).

Damaso Larrañaga
A193

1963, Jan. 24   *Perf.* 12   Wmk. 332

| 693 | A193 | 20c lt bl grn & dk brn | 6 | 5 |
| 694 | A193 | 40c tan & dk brn | 10 | 6 |

Issued to honor Damaso Antonio Larrañaga (1771–1848), teacher, writer and founder of National Library.

Rufous-bellied Thrush
A194

Birds: 50c, Rufous ovenbird. 1p, Chalk-browed mockingbird. 2p, Rufous-collared sparrow.

1963, Apr. 1   *Perf.* 12   Wmk. 332

695	A194	2c rose, brn & blk	8	5
696	A194	50c lt brn & blk	27	12
697	A194	1p tan, brn & blk	50	32
698	A194	2p lt brn, blk & gray	85	60

Thin frame on No. 696, no frame on No. 698.

UPAE Emblem—A195

1963, May 31   Lithographed

| 699 | A195 | 20c ultra & blk | 8 | 6 |

Issued to commemorate the 50th anniversary of the founding of the Postal Union of the Americas and Spain, UPAE. See also Nos. C252–C253.

Wheat Emblem	Anchors
A196	A197

1963, July 8   *Perf.* 12   Wmk. 332

| 700 | A196 | 10c grn & yel | 6 | 5 |
| 701 | A196 | 20c brn & yel | 10 | 6 |

Issued for the "Freedom from Hunger" campaign of the U.N. Food and Agriculture Organization. See also Nos. C254–C255.

1963, Aug. 16

| 702 | A197 | 10c org & vio | 6 | 5 |
| 703 | A197 | 20c dk red & gray | 10 | 6 |

Issued to commemorate the voyage around the world by the Uruguayan sailing vessel "Alferez Campora," 1960–63. See also Nos. C256–C257.

Large Intestine, Congress Emblem
A198

1963, Dec. 9   Lithographed

| 704 | A198 | 10c lt grn, blk & dk car | 5 | |
| 705 | A198 | 20c org, yel, blk & dk car | 10 | 6 |

Issued to commemorate the First Uruguayan Proctology Congress, Montevideo, Dec. 9–15.

Red Cross Centenary Emblem
A199

Imprint: "Imp. Nacional"

1964, June 5   *Perf.* 12   Wmk. 332

| 706 | A199 | 20c bl & red | 8 | 5 |
| 707 | A199 | 40c gray & red | 18 | 8 |

Centenary of International Red Cross. No. 706 exists with imprint missing.

Luis Alberto de Herrera
A200

1964, July 22   Litho.   Unwmkd.

708	A200	20c dl grn, bl & blk	6	5
709	A200	40c lt bl, bl & blk	10	6
710	A200	80c yel org, bl & blk	18	8
711	A200	1p lt vio, bl & blk	22	15
712	A200	2p gray, bl & blk	42	35
		Nos. 708–712 (5)	98	69

Issued to commemorate the 5th anniversary of the death of Luis Alberto de Herrera (1873–1959), leader of Herrerista party and member of National Government Council.

Nile Gods Uniting Upper and Lower Egypt (Abu Simbel)
A201

1964, Oct. 30   *Perf.* 12   Wmk. 332

| 713 | A201 | 20c multi | 9 | 5 |

Issued to publicize the UNESCO world campaign to save historic monuments in Nubia. See also Nos. C266–C267 and souvenir sheet No. C267a.

Pres. John F. Kennedy
A202

1965, Mar. 5   *Perf.* 11½   Wmk. 327

714	A202	20c gold, emer & blk	6	5
a.		Gold omitted		
715	A202	40c gold, redsh brn & blk	10	8
a.		Gold omitted		

Issued in memory of Pres. John F. Kennedy (1917–63). See also Nos. C269–C270.

Tete Beche Pair of 1864, No. 21a
A203

1965, Mar. 19   *Perf.* 12   Wmk. 332

| 716 | A203 | 40c blk & grn | 10 | 8 |

Issued to commemorate the First Rio de la Plata Stamp Show, sponsored jointly by the Argentine and Uruguayan philatelic associations, Montevideo, March 19–28. See also No. C271.

Benito Nardone
A204

Design: 40c, Benito Nardone before microphone (vert.).

1965, March 25   Litho.

| 717 | A204 | 20c blk & emer | 6 | 5 |
| 718 | A204 | 40c blk & emer | 8 | 6 |

Issued to commemorate the first anniversary of the death of Benito Nardone, president of the Council of Government.

Artigas Quotation
A205

Designs: 40c, Artigas bust and quotation. 80c, José Artigas.

Perf. 12x11½

1965, May 17   Litho.   Wmk. 327

719	A205	20c bl, yel & red	5	5
720	A205	40c vio bl, cit & blk	6	6
721	A205	80c brn, yel, red & bl	10	8
		Nos. 719–721, C273–C275 (6)	98	72

Issued to commemorate the bicentenary of the birth of José Artigas (1764–1850), leader of the independence revolt against Spain.

Soccer
A206

Designs: 40c, Basketball. 80c, Bicycling. 1p, Woman swimmer.

1965, Aug. 3   Litho.   Wmk. 327

722	A206	20c grn, org & blk	8	5
723	A206	40c hn brn, cit & blk	12	5
724	A206	80c gray, red & blk	15	6
725	A206	1p bl, yel grn & blk	15	8

Issued to commemorate the 18th Olympic Games, Tokyo, Oct. 10–25, 1964. See also Nos. C276–C281.

No. 572A Surcharged in Red   **10c**

1965   *Perf.* 12½   Unwmkd.

| 726 | A138a | 10c on 7c vio bl | 5 | 5 |

No. B5 Surcharged:

4c.
CINCUENTENARIO
Sociedad Arquitectos del Uruguay

1966, Jan. 25   *Perf.* 11½   Wmk. 327

| 727 | SP2 | 4c on 5c+10c grn & org | 5 | 5 |

Issued to commemorate the 50th anniversary of the Association of Uruguayan Architects.

Winston Churchill
A207

Lithographed

1966, Apr. 29   *Perf.* 12   Wmk. 332

| 728 | A207 | 40c car, dp ultra & brn | 8 | 5 |

Issued in memory of Sir Winston Spencer Churchill (1874–1965), statesman and World War II leader. See also No. C284.

Arms of Rio de Janeiro and Sugar Loaf Mountain
A208

1966, June 9   Litho.   Wmk. 332

| 729 | A208 | 40c emer & brn | 8 | 5 |

Issued to commemorate the 400th anniversary of the founding of Rio de Janeiro. See also No. C285.

URUGUAY

Army Engineer
A209

Daniel Fernandez
Crespo
A210

1966, June 17   Lithographed
730   A209   20c blk, red, vio bl & yel   8   5

Issued to commemorate the 50th anniversary of the Army Engineers Corps.

1966, Sept. 16   Perf. 12   Wmk. 332
Portraits: No. 732, Washington Beltran. No. 733, Luis Batlle Berres.
731   A210   20c lt bl & blk   5   5
732   A210   20c lt bl & dk brn   5   5
733   A210   20c brick red & blk   5   5

Issued to honor political leaders.

Old Printing Press
A211

Photogravure
1966, Oct. 14   Perf. 12   Wmk. 332
734   A211   20c tan, grnsh gray & dk brn   8   5

50th anniversary of State Printing Office.

Fireman
A212

1966   Lithographed
735   A212   20c red & blk   8   5

Issued to publicize fire prevention. Printed with alternating red and black label inscribed: "Prevengase del fuego! Del pueblo y para el pueblo."

No. 716 Overprinted in Red:
"Segunda Muestra y / Jornadas Rioplatenses de Filatelia / Abril 1966 / Centenario del Sello / Escudito Resellado"

1966, Nov. 4
736   A203   40c blk & grn   8   5

Issued to commemorate the Second Rio de la Plata Stamp Show, Buenos Aires. April, 1966, and the centenary of Uruguay's first surcharged issue. See also No. C298.

General
Leandro Gomez
A213

Designs: No. 738, Gen. Juan Antonio Lavalleja. No. 739, Aparicio Saravia, revolutionary, on horseback (horiz.).

1966, Nov. 24   Wmk. 332   Litho.   Perf. 12
737   A213   20c sl, blk & dp bl   5   5
738   A213   20c red, blk & bl   5   5
739   A213   20c bl & blk   5   5

Montevideo
Planetarium
A214

1967, Jan. 13   Perf. 12   Wmk. 332
740   A214   40c pink & blk   10   5

Issued to commemorate the 10th anniversary of the Montevideo Municipal Planetarium. See also No. C301.

Sunflower, Cow
and Emblem
A215

Church of
San Carlos
A216

1967, Jan. 13   Lithographed
741   A215   40c dk brn & yel   8   5

Issued to commemorate the 20th anniversary of the Young Farmers' Movement.

1967, Apr. 17   Perf. 12   Wmk. 332
742   A216   40c lt bl, blk & dk red   8   5

Bicentenary of San Carlos.

Eduardo
Acevedo
A217

1967, Apr. 17
743   A217   20c grn & brn   5   5
744   A217   40c org & grn   5   5

Issued to honor Eduardo Acevedo, lawyer, legislator and Minister of Foreign Affairs.

Arms of Carmelo
A218

José Enrique
Rodó
A219

1967, Aug. 11   Litho.   Perf. 12
745   A218   40c lt & dk bl & ocher   8   5

Issued to commemorate the 150th anniversary of the founding of Carmelo.

1967, Oct. 6   Perf. 12   Wmk. 332
Design: 2p, Portrait of Rodó and sculpture (horiz.).
746   A219   1p gray, brn & blk   5   5
747   A219   2p rose cl, blk & tan   12   5

Issued to commemorate the 50th anniversary of the death of José Enrique Rodó, author.

Senen M.
Rodriguez
and Locomotive
A220

1967, Oct. 26   Litho.   Perf. 12
748   A220   2p ocher & dk brn   12   6

Issued to commemorate the centenary of the founding of the first national railroad company.

Child and Map
of Americas
A221

Cocoi
Heron
A222

1967, Nov. 10   Perf. 12   Wmk. 332
749   A221   1p vio & red   5   5

Issued to commemorate the 40th anniversary of the Inter-American Children's Institute.

No. 610 Surcharged
in Red

1.00 PESO

Perf. 13x13½
1967, Nov. 10   Engr.   Unwmkd.
750   A173   1p on 7c brn & grn   5   5

Lithographed
1968–70   Perf. 12   Wmk. 332
Birds: 1p, Great horned owl. 3p, Brown-headed gull (horiz.). No. 754, White-faced tree duck (horiz.). No. 754A, Black-tailed stilts. 5p, Wattled jacanas (horiz.). 10p, Snowy egret (horiz.).
751   A222   1p dl yel & brn   10   5
752   A222   2p bl grn & blk   10   5
753   A222   3p org, gray & blk ('69)   15   5
754   A222   4p brn, tan & blk   20   6
754A   A222   4p ver & blk ('70)   20   6
755   A222   5p lt red brn, blk & yel   25   8
756   A222   10p lil & blk   50   12
Nos. 751-756 (7)   1.50   47

Concord
Bridge,
Presidents
of
Uruguay,
Brazil
A223

1968, Apr. 3
757   A223   6p brown   12   5

Issued to commemorate the opening of Concord Bridge across the Uruguay River by Presidents Jorge Pacheco Areco of Uruguay and Arthur Costa e Silva of Brazil.

Soccer
Player
and Trophy
A224

1968, May 29   Lithographed
758   A224   1p blk & yel   6   5

Issued to commemorate the victory of the Peñarol Athletic Club in the Intercontinental Soccer Championships of 1966.

St. John Bosco, Symbols of
Education and Industry
A225

1968, July 31   Perf. 12   Wmk. 332
759   A225   2p brn & blk   8   5

Issued to commemorate the 75th anniversary of the Don Bosco Workshops of the Salesian Brothers.

Sailors' Monument, Montevideo
A226

Designs: 6p, Lighthouse and buoy (vert.). 12p, Gunboat "Suarez" (1860).

1968, Nov. 12   Litho.   Perf. 12
760   A226   2p gray ol & blk   6   5
761   A226   6p grn & blk   12   8
762   A226   12p brt bl & blk   20   10
Nos. 760-762, C340-C343 (7)   1.16   63

Sesquicentennial of National Navy.

Oscar D.
Gestido
A227

1968, Dec. 6   Perf. 12   Wmk. 332
763   A227   6p brn, dp car & bl   12   5

Issued to commemorate the first anniversary of the death of President Oscar D. Gestido.

Gearwheel, Grain and Two Heads
A228

1969, Mar. 17   Litho.   Perf. 12
764   A228   2p blk & ver   8   5

25th anniversary of Labor University.

Bicyclists
A229

URUGUAY

1969, Mar. 21   **Wmk. 332**
765   A229   6p dk bl, org & emer   12   5

Issued to commemorate the 1968 World Bicycle Championships. See No. C347.

Gymnasts and Club Emblem — A230

1969, May 8   *Perf. 12*   **Wmk. 332**
766   A230   6p blk & ver   12   5

Issued to commemorate the 75th anniversary of L'Avenir Athletic Club.

Baltasar Brum — A231

Portrait: No. 768, Tomas Berreta.

1969   Lithographed   *Perf. 12*
767   A231   6p rose red & blk   12   5
768   A231   6p car rose & blk   12   6

Issued in memory of former Presidents Baltasar Brum (1883–1933) and Tomas Berreta (1875–1947).

Fair Emblem — A232

1969, Aug. 15   *Perf. 12*   **Wmk. 332**
769   A232   2p multi   8   5

Issued to publicize the 2nd Industrial World's Fair, Montevideo, 1970.

Diesel Locomotive — A233

Design: No. 770, Old steam locomotive and modern railroad cars.

1969, Sept. 19   Litho.   **Wmk. 332**
770   A233   6p car, blk & ultra   12   5
771   A233   6p car, blk & ultra   12   5

Issued to commemorate the centenary of Uruguayan railroads. Nos. 770–771 printed se-tenant with continuous design and label with commemorative inscription.

Souvenir Sheet

Diligencia Issue, 1856 — A233a

1969, Oct. 1   *Imperf.*
771A   A233a   Sheet of 3   5.00   5.00
  b.   60p bl   1.00   1.00
  c.   80p grn   1.25   1.25
  d.   100p red   1.50   1.50

Stamp Day 1969. No. 771A contains stamps similar to No. 1–3, with denominations in pesos. Buff margin with map and arms of Uruguay, and inscription. Size: 98x69½mm.

No. 771A was re-issued Apr. 15, 1972, with black overprint commemorating 15th anniversary of first Lufthansa flight from Uruguay to Germany and the Munich Olympic Games.

"Combat" and Sculptor Belloni — A234

1969, Oct. 22   *Perf. 12*   **Wmk. 332**
772   A234   6p ol, sl grn & blk   12   5

Issued to honor José L. Belloni (1882–), sculptor.

Reserve Officers' Training Center Emblem — A235

Design: 2p, Training Center emblem, and officer in uniform and as civilian.

1969, Nov. 5   Lithographed
773   A235   1p yel & dk bl   5   5
774   A235   2p dk brn & lt bl   8   5

Issued to commemorate the 25th anniversary of the Reserve Officers' Training Center.

Cobbled Street in Colonia del Sacramento — A241   Mother and Son by Edmundo Prati in Salto — A242

1970, Oct. 21   Litho.   *Perf. 12*
783   A241   5p blk & multi   10   5

Issued to commemorate the 290th anniversary of the founding of Colonia del Sacramento, the first European settlement in Uruguay.

1970, Nov. 4   Lithographed
784   A242   10p grn & blk   22   10

Issued to honor mothers.

URUEXPO Emblem — A243

1970, Dec. 9   *Perf. 12*   **Wmk. 332**
785   A243   15p bl, brn org & vio   22   12

URUEXPO '70, National Philatelic Exposition, Montevideo, Sept. 26–Oct. 4.

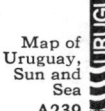

Artigas' Ancestral Home in Sauce — A238

1970, June 18   *Perf. 12*   **Wmk. 332**
777   A238   15p ver, ultra & blk   22   10

Map of Uruguay, Sun and Sea — A239

1970, July 8   Lithographed
778   A239   5p grnsh bl   8   5

Issued for tourist publicity.

EXPO '70 Emblem, Mt. Fuji and Uruguay Coat of Arms — A240

Designs (EXPO '70 Emblem, Arms and): No. 780, Geisha. No. 781, Sun Tower. No. 782, Youth pole.

1970, Aug. 5   *Perf. 12*   **Wmk. 332**
779   A240   25p grn, sl bl & yel   35   15
780   A240   25p org, sl bl & grn   35   15
781   A240   25p yel, sl bl & pur   35   15
782   A240   25p pur, sl bl & org   35   15

Issued to commemorate EXPO '70 International Exhibition, Osaka, Japan, Mar. 15–Sept. 13. Nos. 779–782 are printed se-tenant in sheets of 40.

Children Holding Hands, and UNESCO Emblem — A244

Children's Drawings: No. 786, Two girls holding hands (vert.). No. 788, Boy sitting at school desk (vert.). No. 789, Astronaut and monster.

1970, Dec. 29   Litho.   *Perf. 12½*
786   A244   10p multi   20   10
787   A244   10p multi   20   10
788   A244   10p dp car & multi   20   10
789   A244   10p bl & multi   20   10

International Education Year. Nos. 786–789 printed se-tenant in sheets of 16 in blocks of 4 with 2 labels showing Education Year and UNESCO emblems.

Alfonso Espinola — A245

1971, Jan. 13   *Perf. 12*   **Wmk. 332**
790   A245   5p dp org & blk   8   5

In memory of Alfonso Espinola (1845–1905), physician, professor and philanthropist.

Exposition Poster — A246

1971   Lithographed   *Perf. 12*
791   A246   15p multi   27   12

Uruguay Philatelic Exposition, 1971, Montevideo, March 26–Apr. 19.

5c Coin of 1840, Obverse — A247

1971, Apr. 16   *Perf. 12*   **Wmk. 332**
792   A247   25p bl, brn & blk   50   32
793   A247   25p bl, brn & blk   50   32

Design: No. 793, First coin of Uruguay, reverse.

Numismatists' Day. Printed se-tenant.

Domingo Arena — A248

1971, May 3   *Perf. 12*   **Wmk. 332**
794   A248   5p dk car   12   8

Domingo Arena, lawyer and journalist.

National Anthem — A249

1971, May 19   Lithographed
795   A249   15p bl, blk & yel   27   27

URUGUAY

José F. Arias
A250

1971, May 25 *Perf. 12* Wmk. 332
796 A250 5p sepia   12   8
José F. Arias, physician.

Eduardo Fabini, Bar from "Campo"
A251

1971, June 2   *Lithographed*
797 A251 5p dk car rose & blk   25   8
Eduardo Fabini (1882–1950), composer, and 40th anniversary of first radio concert.

José E. Rodó, UPAE Emblem
A252

1971, July 15 *Perf. 12* Wmk. 332
798 A252 15p ultra & blk   27 17
Centenary of the birth of José Enrique Rodó (1871–1917), writer, first Uruguayan delegate to Congress of the Postal Union of the Americas and Spain.

Water Cart and Faucet
A253

1971, July 17
799 A253 5p ultra & multi   12   8
Centenary of Montevideo's drinking water system.

Sheep and Cloth
A254

Design: 15p, Sheep, cloth and bale of wool.
1971, Aug. 7
800 A254 5p grn & gray   12   8
801 A254 15p dk bl, grnsh bl & gray   27 17
Wool Promotion.

José Maria Elorza and Merilin Sheep
A255

1971, Aug. 10
802 A255 5p lt bl, grn & blk   12   8
José Maria Elorza, developer of the Merilin sheep.

Criollo Horse
A256

1971, Aug. 11
803 A256 5p blk, gray bl & org   12   8

Bull and Ram
A257

1971, Aug. 13
804 A257 20p red, grn, blk & gold   35 17
Centenary of Rural Association of Uruguay; 19th International Cattle Breeding Exposition, and 66th National Cattle Championships at Prado, Aug. 1971.

Symbol of Liberty and Order
A258

Design: 20p, Policemen, flag of Uruguay and emblem.
1971
805 A258 10p gray, blk & bl   15 10
806 A258 20p dk bl, blk, lt bl & gold 35 16
To honor policemen killed on duty. Issue dates: 10p, Sept. 9; 20p, Nov. 4.

10p Banknote of 1896—A259

Design: No. 808, Reverse of 10p note.
1971, Sept. 23
807 A259 25p dl grn, gold & blk   45 27
808 A259 25p dl grn, gold & blk   45 27
75th anniversary of Bank of the Republic. Printed se-tenant in sheets of 20 stamps and 5 labels.

Farmer and Arms of Durazno
A260

1971, Oct. 11
809 A260 20p gold, bl & blk   35 16
Sesquicentennial of the founding of Durazno.

Emblem and Laurel—A261

1971, Oct. 20
810 A261 10p vio bl, gold & red   25 12
Winners of Liberator's Cup, American Soccer Champions, 1971.

Voter Casting Ballot
A262

Design: 20p, Citizens voting (horiz.).
1971, Nov. 22 *Perf. 12* Wmk. 332
811 A262 10p bl & blk   15 10
812 A262 20p bl & blk   35 16
Universal, secret and obligatory franchise.

Map of Uruguay on Globe
A263

1971, Dec. 23
813 A263 20p lt bl & vio brn   50 16
7th Littoral Exposition, Paysandu, March 26–Apr. 11.

Juan Lindolfo Cuestas
A264

1971, Dec. 27
Designs in Dull Blue and Brown
814 A264 10p shown   15 10
815 A264 10p Julio Herrera y Obes   15 10
816 A264 10p Claudio Williman   15 10
817 A264 10p José Serrato   15 10
818 A264 10p Andres Martinez Trueba   15 10
        Strip of 5, #814-818   85 85
        Nos. 814-818 (5)   75 50
Presidents of Uruguay. Nos. 814–818 printed se-tenant horizontally in sheets of 50 (10x5).

Souvenir Sheet

Uruguay No. 4, Cathedral of Montevideo and Plaza de la Constitucion—A265

1972, Jan. 17   *Imperf.*
819 A265 120p brn, bl & dp rose   85 85
Stamp Day 1971 (release date delayed). Size: 99x70mm. See Nos. 834–835, 863.

Bartolomé Hidalgo
A266

Missa Solemnis, by Beethoven
A267

1972, Feb. 28   *Perf. 12*
820 A266 5p lt brn, blk & red   6   5
Bartolomé Hidalgo (1788–1822), Uruguayan-Argentine poet.

1972, Apr. 20 *Litho.* Wmk. 332
822 A267 20p lil, emer & blk   12   8
12th Choir Festival of Eastern Uruguay.

Dove and Wounded Bird
A268

Columbus Arch, Colon
A269

1972, May 9
823 A268 10p ver & multi   15 10
To honor Dionision Diaz (age 9), who died saving his sister.

1972, June 21
824 A269 20p red, bl & blk   12   8
Centenary of Colon, now suburb of Montevideo.

No. 810 Surcharged in Silver

50

(Surcharge 69mm. wide)

1972, June 30
825 A261 50p on 10p multi   25 25
Winners of the 1971 International Soccer Cup.

Tree Planting
A270

"Collective Housing"
A271

1972, Aug. 5 *Perf. 12* Wmk. 332
826 A270 20p grn & blk   12   8
Afforestation program.

1972, Sept. 30   *Lithographed*
827 A271 10p dp bl & multi   6   5
Publicity for collective housing plan.

URUGUAY

Amethyst
A272

Uruguayan Gem Stones: 9p, Agate.
15p, Chalcedony.

1972, Oct. 7

828	A272	5p gray & multi	5	5
829	A272	9p gray bl & multi	6	5
830	A272	15p gray grn & multi	15	10

Uniform of 1830
A273

Design: 20p, Lancer.

1972, Nov. 21   Lithographed

| 831 | A273 | 10p multi | 12 | 8 |
| 832 | A273 | 20p rose red & multi | 27 | 20 |

Red Cross
and Map
of Uruguay
A274

1972, Dec. 11   Perf. 12   Wmk. 332
833   A274   30p multi   15   10

75th anniversary of the Uruguayan Red Cross.

Souvenir Sheets
Stamp Day Type of 1972.

Designs: 200p, Coat of arms type of 1864 similar to Nos. 18, 20-21, but 60p, 60p and 80p. 220p, Similar to Nos. 22-23, but 100p and 120p.

1972, Dec. 20   Imperf.

| 834 | A265 | 200p multi | 1.10 | 1.00 |
| 835 | A265 | 220p multi | 1.40 | 1.25 |

Stamp Day 1972. No. 834 commemorates the 200th anniversary of first printed cancellations; No. 835 centenary of the decree establishing regular postal service.
No. 834 has gray and green margin with view of Montevideo harbor and carmine inscription "Montevideo." No. 835 has green margin with black inscription and view of National Museum. Size of sheets: 99x70mm.

Scales of
Justice,
Olive
Branch
A275

1972, Dec. 27   Perf. 12   Wmk. 332
836   A275   10p gold, dk & lt bl   6   5

25th anniversary of the Civil Rights Law for Women.

See "Special Notices" at the front of this volume for data on the listing methods of this Catalogue, abbreviations, condition, prices and examination.

General José   Hand Holding
Artigas   Cup; Grain, Map
A276   of Americas
                 A277

       Lithographed
1972-74   Perf. 12   Wmk. 332

837	A276	5p yel ('74)	5	5
838	A276	10p dk bis ('74)	6	5
839	A276	15p emer ('74)	6	5
840	A276	20p lil ('73)	5	5
841	A276	30p lt bl ('73)	25	12
842	A276	40p dp org ('73)	25	12
843	A276	50p ver ('73)	22	13
844	A276	75p ap grn ('73)	30	22
845	A276	100p emerald	38	25
846	A276	150p choc ('73)	50	35
847	A276	200p dk bl ('73)	75	45
848	A276	250p pur ('73)	90	50
849	A276	500p gray ('73)	1.75	1.10
849A	A276	1000p bl ('73)	3.25	2.10
	Nos. 837-849A (14)	8.77	5.54

1973, Jan. 9

850   A277   30p rose red, yel & blk   12   8

30th anniversary of the International Institute for Agricultural Research.

Elbio Fernandez
and José P. Varela
A278

1973, Jan. 16

851   A278   10p dl grn, gold & blk   6   5

Centenary of the Society of Friends of Public Education.

Map of
Americas,
"1972" and
Columbus
A279

1973, Jan. 30

852   A279   50p purple   25   17

Tourist Year of the Americas 1972.

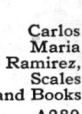 

Carlos
Maria
Ramirez,
Scales
and Books
A280

1973, Feb. 15

     Gold, Brown and Black

853	A280	10p shown	6	5
854	A280	10p Justino Jimenez de Arechaga	6	5
855	A280	10p Juan Andres Ramirez	6	5

| 856 | A280 | 10p Justino E. Jimenez de Arechaga | 6 | 5 |
| | | Strip of 4 + label | 30 | 30 |

Centenary of the Professorship of Constitutional Rights.

Nos. 853-856 were printed se-tenant in same sheet in horizontal strips of four with label centered. Label is inscribed "Jurisconsultos del Uruguay," names and dates of four honored men.

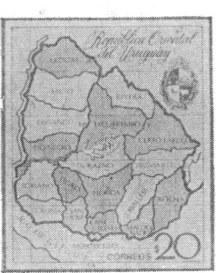

Provincial Map of Uruguay
A281

1973, Feb. 27   Litho.   Perf. 12½x12
857   A281   20p bl & multi   15   10

Francisco de los Santos
A282

1973, May 16   Perf. 12   Wmk. 332
858   A282   20p grn & blk   8   6

Soldiers' Day and Battle of Piedras. Santos was a courier who went through enemy lines.

Souvenir Sheet

No. C319 Surcharged with New Value and: "HOMENAJE AL 4 CENTENARIO DE CORDOBA . ARGENTINA . 1973"

1973, May 9   Litho.   Imperf.
859   AP57   100p on 5p multi   1.25   1.25

400th anniversary of the founding of Cordoba in Argentina. Size of No. 859: 69½x50mm.

Friar, Indians
before Church
A283

1973, July 25   Perf. 12
860   A283   20p lt ultra, pur & blk   15   10

Villa Santo Domingo Soriano, first Spanish settlement in Uruguay.

Symbolic
Fish
A284

1973, Aug. 15
861   A284   100p bl & multi   32   22

First station of Oceanographic and Fishery Service, Montevideo.

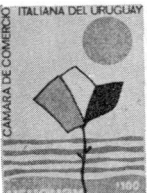

Sun over Flower
in Italian Colors
A285

1973, Sept.
862   A285   100p multi   30   22

Italian Chamber of Commerce of Uruguay.

Souvenir Sheet
Stamp Day Type of 1972

Design: 240p, Thin numeral sun type of 1859 and street scene.

     Imperf.

1973, Oct. 1   Litho.   Wmk. 332
863   A265   240p grn, org & blk   1.50   1.25

Stamp Day 1973. No. 863 contains one stamp, green margin with white inscription and black vignette. Size: 100x69mm.

Luis Alberto
de Herrera
A286

1973, Nov. 12   Perf. 12
866   A286   50p gray, brn & dk brn   25   15

Centenary of the birth of Luis Alberto de Herrera.

Emblem of
Social
Coordination
Volunteers
A287

     Perf. 12

1973, Nov. 19   Litho.   Wmk. 352
867   A287   50p bl & multi   25   15

Festival of Nations, Montevideo.

Arm with
Arteries
and Heart
A288

1973, Nov. 22
868   A288   50p blk, red & pink   25   15

3rd Congress of the Pan-American Federation of Blood Donors, Montevideo, Nov. 23-25.

Madonna, by
Rafael Perez
Barradas
A289

1973, Dec. 10   Litho.   Wmk. 332
869   A289   50p grn, gray & yel grn   25   15

Christmas 1973.

URUGUAY

Nicolaus Copernicus—A290
1973, Dec. 26 Lithographed
870   A290   50p grn & multi   25   15
500th anniversary of the birth of Nicolaus Copernicus (1473–1543), Polish astronomer.

Praying Hands and Andes
A291
Design: 75p, Statue of Christ on mountain, and flower.
1973, Dec. 26 Lithographed
871   A291   50p blk, lt grn & ultra   20   10
872   A291   75p bl, blk & org   30   20
Survival and rescue of victims of airplane crash.

OAS Emblem and Map of Americas
A292
1974, Jan. 14 Perf. 12 Wmk. 332
873   A292   250p gray & multi   1.00   70
25th anniversary of the Organization of American States (OAS).

Scout Emblems and Flame
A293
1974, Jan. 21
874   A293   250p multi   1.00   70
1st International Boy Scout Games, Montevideo, 1974.

Hector Suppici Sedes and Car
A294
1974, Jan. 28 Perf. 12
875   A294   50p sep, grn & blk   20   10
70th anniversary of the birth of Hector Suppici Sedes (1903–1948), automobile racer.

Three Gauchos
A295

1974, Mar. 20 Litho. Wmk. 332
876   A295   50p multi   20   10
Centenary of the publication of "Los Tres Gauchos Orientales" by Antonio D. Lussich.

Rifle, Target and Swiss Flag
A296
1974, Apr. 2
877   A296   100p multi   40   22
Centenary of the Swiss Rifle Association.

Map of Uruguay and Compass Rose
A297
1974, Apr. 23 Lithographed
878   A297   50p multi   20   10
Military Geographical Service.

Montevideo Stadium Tower
A298
Design: 75p, Soccer player, Games' emblem (horiz.).
1974, May 7 Perf. 12 Wmk. 332
879   A298   50p multi   20   12
880   A298   75p multi   30   20
World Cup Soccer Championship, Munich, June 13–July 7. A 1000p stamp and a 1000p souvenir card exist.

Old and New School and Founders
A299
1974, May 21
883   A299   75p blk & bis   27   20
Centenary of the Osimani-Llerena Technical School at Salto, founded by Gervasio Osimani and Miguel Llerena.

Carlos Gardel and Score
A301

Perf. 12
1974, June 24 Litho. Wmk. 332
884   A301   100p multi   45   25
Carlos Gardel (1887–1935), singer and moving picture actor.

Volleyball and Net
A302
1974, July 11 Perf. 12 Wmk. 332
885   A302   200p lil, yel & blk   60   35
First anniversary of Women's Volleyball championships, Montevideo, 1973.

"Protect your Heart"
A303
1974, July 24 Lithographed
886   A303   75p ol grn, yel & red   25   22
Heart Foundation publicity.

Eusebio Vidal, Portrait and Statue
A304

Artigas Statue, Buenos Aires, Flags of Uruguay and Argentina
A305
1974, Aug. 5
887   A304   75p dk & lt bl   20   12
Centenary (in 1973) of the founding of San José de Mayo by Eusebio Vidal.

1974, Aug. 13 Perf. 12½
888   A305   75p multi   20   12
Unveiling of Artigas monument, Buenos Aires.

Radio Tower and Waves
A306
1974, Sept. 24 Perf. 12 Wmk. 332
889   A306   100p multi   27   15
50th anniversary of Broadcasting in Uruguay.

URUEXPO 74 Emblem—A307

URUEXPO Emblem and Old Map of Montevideo Bay—A308
1974
890   A307   100p blk, dk bl & red   27   15
891   A308   300p sep, red & grn   75   27
URUEXPO 74 Philatelic Exhibition, 10th anniversary of Philatelic Circle of Uruguay (100p) and 250th anniversary of fortification of Montevideo. Issue dates: 100p, Oct. 1; 300p, Oct. 19.

Letters and UPU Emblem
A309
Design: 200p, UPU emblem, letter, and globe.
1974, Oct. 9
892   A309   100p lt bl & multi   12   8
893   A309   200p lil, blk & gold   27   15
Centenary of Universal Postal Union. See Nos. C395–C396.

Artigas Statue and Map of Lavalleja
A310
1974, Oct. 17 Perf. 12
894   A310   100p ultra & multi   12   8
Unveiling of Artigas statue in Minas, Lavalleja.

Ship in Dry Dock, Arsenal's Emblem
A312

URUGUAY

1974, Nov. 15   Litho.   Wmk. 332
896   A312   200p multi   60   40
Centenary of Naval Arsenal, Montevideo.

Globo Hydrogen Balloon—A313

1974, Nov. 20   Multicolored
897	A313	100p *shown*	25	15
898	A313	100p *Farman biplane*	25	15
899	A313	100p *Castaibert monoplane*	25	15
900	A313	100p *Bleriot monoplane*	25	15
901	A313	150p *Military and civilian pilots' emblems*	35	25
902	A313	150p *Nieuport biplane*	35	25
903	A313	150p *Breguet-Bidon fighter*	35	25
904	A313	150p *Caproni bomber*	35	25
		Nos. 897-904 (8)	2.40	1.60

Aviation pioneers. Stamps of same denomination printed se-tenant in sheets of 20 (4x5).

Sugar Loaf Mountain and Summit Cross—A314

1974, Nov. 30
905   A314   150p multi   35   25
Centenary of the founding of Sugar Loaf City.

Adoration of the Kings—A315
Designs: 150p, Three Kings.

1974   Perf. 12
906   A315   100p org & multi   12   8
907   A315   150p bl & multi   18   12
Christmas 1974. See Nos. C400–C401.
Issue dates: 100p, Dec. 17; 150p, Dec. 19.

Nike, Fireworks, Rowers and Club Emblem A316

1975, Jan. 27   Litho.   Wmk. 332
908   A316   150p gray & multi   18   12
Centenary of Montevideo Rowing Club.

Treaty Signing, by José Zorrilla de San Martin—A317

1975, Feb. 12   Perf. 12
909   A317   100p multi   12   8
Commercial Treaty between Great Britain and Uruguay, 1817.

Rose A318

1975, Mar. 18   Litho.   Wmk. 332
910   A318   150p multi   24   12
Bicentenary of city of Rosario.

"The Oath of the 33," by Juan M. Blanes—A319

1975, Apr. 16   Perf. 12
911   A319   150p gold & multi   24   12
Sesquicentennial of liberation movement.

Ship, Columbus and Ancient Map A320

1975, Oct. 9   Litho.   Wmk. 332
912   A320   1p gray & multi   1.25   75
Hispanic Stamp Day.

Leonardo Olivera and Santa Teresa Fort—A321

Artigas as Young and Old Man A322

1975   Litho.   Perf. 12   Wmk. 332
913   A321   10c org & multi   25   10
914   A322   50c vio bl & multi   1.00   50
Sesquicentennial of the capture of Fort Santa Teresa (10c) and of Uruguay's declaration of independence (50c).
Issue dates: 10c, Oct. 20; 50c, Oct. 17.

Battle of Rincon, by Diogenes Hequet—A323

Designs: No. 916, Artigas' Home, Ibiray, Paraguay. 25c, Battle of Sarandi, by J. Manuel Blanes.

1975   Lithographed
915   A323   15c ol & blk   25   15
916   A323   15c ol & multi   25   15
917   A323   25c ol & multi   50   30
Uruguayan independence. Nos. 915 and 917, 150th anniversary of Battles of Rincon and Sarandi. No. 916, 50th anniversary of school at Artigas mansion.
Issue dates: No. 915, Oct. 23; No. 916, Nov. 18; No. 917, Nov. 28.

"En Familia," by Sanchez A324

Florencio Sanchez A325

Designs (Plays by Sanchez): No. 919, Barranca Abajo. No. 920, M'Hijo el Dotor. No. 921, Canillita.

1975, Oct. 31   Perf. 12   Wmk. 332
918   A324   20c gray, red & blk   40   15
919   A324   20c bl, grn & blk   40   15
920   A324   20c red, bl & blk   40   15
921   A324   20c grn, gray & blk   40   15

922   A325   20c multi   40   15
    Block of 5 stamps + 4 labels   2.50
Florencio Sanchez (1875–1910), dramatist, birth centenary. Nos. 918–922 printed se-tenant in sheets of 30 stamps and 20 labels.

Maria Eugenia Vaz Ferreira A326

Design: No. 924, Julio Herrera y Reissig.

1975
923   A326   15c yel, blk & brn   30   15
924   A326   15c org, blk & mar   30   15
Maria Eugenia Vaz Ferreira (1875–1924), poetess, and Julio Herrera y Reissig (1875–1910), poet, birth anniversaries.
Issue dates: No. 923, Dec. 9; No. 924, Dec. 29.

Virgin and Child
A327   A328

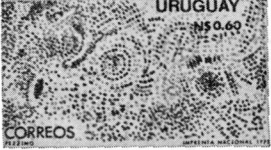

Fireworks—A329

1975
925   A327   20c bl & multi   50   20
926   A328   30c blk & multi   75   40
927   A329   60c multi   1.00   60
Christmas 1975.
Issue dates: 20c, Dec. 16; 30c, Dec. 15; 60c, Dec. 11.

Pres. Lorenzo Latorre A330

1975, Dec. 30   Perf. 12
928   A330   15c multi   18   12
Col. Lorenzo Latorre (1840–1916), president of Uruguay (1876–1880).

Nos. 840, 842–843, 849A Surcharged   **N$ 0,10**

1975
929   A276   10c on 20p lil   10   6
930   A276   15c on 40p org   15   10
931   A276   50c on 50p ver   50   30
932   A276   1p on 1000p bl   1.00   60

URUGUAY

881

Ariel, Stars, Book and Youths
A331

1976, Jan. 12   Litho.   Wmk. 332
933   A331   15c grn & multi   15   10
75th anniversary of publication of "Ariel," by Jose Enrique Rodo (1872–1917), writer.

Water Sports   Telephone
A332   A333

1976, Mar. 12   Litho.   Wmk. 332
934   A332   30c multi   30   18
23rd South American Swimming, Diving and Water Polo Championships.

1976, Apr. 9   Perf. 12
935   A333   83c multi   83   50
Centenary of first telephone call by Alexander Graham Bell, Mar. 10, 1876.

"Plus Ultra" and Columbus' Ships
A334

Wmk. 332
1976, May 10   Litho.   Perf. 12
936   A334   63c gray & multi   63   36
Flight of Dornier "Plus Ultra" from Spain to South America, 50th anniversary.

Dornier "Wal" and Boeing 727, Hourglass
A335

1976, May 24   Perf. 12
937   A335   83c gray & multi   83   50
Lufthansa German Airline, 50th anniversary.

Louis Braille
A340

1976, June 7
942   A340   60c blk & brn   60   36
Sesquicentennial of the invention of the Braille system of writing for the blind by Louis Braille (1809–1852).

Signing of U.S. Declaration of Independence
A341

1976, June 21
943   A341   1.50p multi   2.50   1.00
American Bicentennial.

Freeing of the Slaves, by P. Figari
A342

Perf. 12
1976, July 29   Litho.   Wmk. 332
944   A342   30c ultra & multi   22   12
Abolition of slavery, sesquicentennial.

Gen. Fructuoso Rivera Statue
A343

1976, Aug. 2
945   A343   5p on 10p multi   3.75   2.50
No. 945 was not issued without surcharge.

General Accounting Office
A344

Wmk. 332
1976, Aug. 24   Litho.   Perf. 12
946   A344   30c bl, blk & brn   35   20
National General Accounting Office, sesquicentennial.

Old Pump, Emblem and Flame
A345

1976, Sept. 6
947   A345   20c red & blk   15   8
First official fire fighting service, centenary.

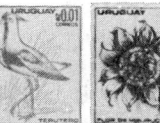  

Southern   Mburucuya   Spear-
Lapwing   Flower   head
A346   A347   A348

Figurine   The Gaucho,   Artigas
A349   by Blanes   A352
            A351

La Yerra, by J. M. Blanes
A350

Designs: 15c, Ceibo flower. 2p, 5p, 10p, Artigas, by Juan Manuel Blanes.

Wmk. 332
1976–77   Litho.   Perf. 12
948   A346   1c violet   10   5
949   A347   5c lt grn   10   5
951   A347   15c car rose   20   5
952   A348   20c gray   5   5
954   A349   30c gray bl   20   5
955   A352   45c brt bl ('79)   12   5
956   A350   50c grnsh bl ('77)   30   10
958   A351   1p dk brn ('77)   60   15
960   A352   1.75p bl grn ('79)   45   12
961   A352   1.95p gray ('79)   48   14
962   A352   2p dl grn ('77)   1.30   25
963   A352   2p lil rose ('79)   50   15
964   A352   2.65p vio ('79)   65   18
968   A352   5p dk bl   3.75   75
970   A352   10p brn ('77)   6.50   1.00
    Nos. 948-970 (15)   15.30   3.14

"Diligencia" Uruguay No. 1
A356

Lithographed
1976, Sept. 26   Perf. 12   Wmk. 332
974   A356   30c bis, red & bl   22   10
Philatelic Club of Uruguay, 50th anniversary.

Games' Emblem
A357

1976, Oct. 26   Litho.   Perf. 12
975   A357   83c gray & multi   58   25
5th World University Soccer Championships.

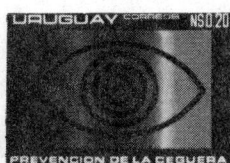

Eye and Spectrum
A358

1976, Nov. 24
976   A358   20c blk & multi   25   10
Foresight prevents blindness.

Map of Montevideo, 1748
A359

Designs: 45c, Montevideo Harbor, 1842. 70c, First settlers, 1726. 80c, Coin with Montevideo arms (vert.). 1.15p, Montevideo's first coat of arms (vert.).

Lithographed
1976, Dec. 30   Perf. 12   Wmk. 332
977   A359   30c multi   20   10
978   A359   45c multi   32   15
979   A359   70c multi   50   20
980   A359   80c multi   56   25
981   A359   1.15p multi   80   40
    Nos. 977-981 (5)   2.38   1.10
Founding of Montevideo, 250th anniversary.

Symbolic of Flight
A360

1977, May 7   Litho.   Perf. 12
982   A360   80c multi   75   20
50th anniversary of Varig airlines.

Artigas Mausoleum
A361

1977, June 17   Litho.   Perf. 12
983   A361   45c multi   45   10

Map of Uruguay   Children
and Arch   A363
A362

1977, July 5   Wmk. 332
984   A362   45c multi   45   15
Centenary of Salesian Brothers' educational system in Uruguay.

1977, Aug. 10   Litho.   Perf. 12
985   A363   45c multi   45   12
Interamerican Children's Institute, 50th anniversary.

"El Sol de Mayo"
A364

1977, Oct. 1   Litho.   Perf. 12
986   A364   45c multi   32   12
Stamp Day 1977.

URUGUAY

Windmills A365

1977, Sept. 29   **Wmk. 332**
987   A365   70c yel, car & blk   50   20
Spanish Heritage Day.

Souvenir Sheet

View of Sans (Barcelona), by Barradas—A366

1977, Oct. 7   Litho.   Perf. 12
988   A366   Sheet of 2, multi   4.50   4.00
    a.   5p, single stamp   2.00

ESPAMER '77 Philatelic Exhibition, Barcelona, Oct. 7–13. Size of No. 988: 106x87mm.

Planes, UN Emblem, Globe A367

1977, Oct. 17
989   A367   45c multi   20   8

30th anniversary of Civil Aviation Organization.

Holy Family A368

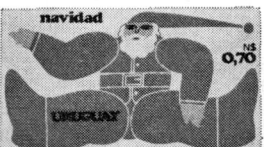

Santa Claus—A369

1977, Dec. 1   **Wmk. 332**
990   A368   45c multi   20   8
991   A369   70c blk, yel & red   30   12
Christmas 1977.

Map of Rio Negro Province A370

1977, Dec. 16
992   A370   45c multi   20   10
Rio Negro Dam; development of argiculture, livestock and beekeeping.

Mail Collection A371

1977, Dec. 21
                Multicolored
993   A371   50c shown   22   10
994   A371   50c Mail truck   22   10
995   A371   50c Post office counter   22   10
996   A371   50c Postal boxes   22   10
997   A371   50c Mail sorting   22   10
998   A371   50c Pigeonhole sorting   22   10
999   A371   50c Route sorting (seated carriers)   22   10
1000   A371   50c Home delivery   22   10
1001   A371   50c Special delivery (motorcyclists)   22   10
1002   A371   50c Airport counter   22   10
         Nos. 993-1002 (10)   2.20   1.00

150th anniversary of Uruguayan postal service. Nos. 993–1002 printed se-tenant.

Edison's Phonograph, 1877 A372

1977, Dec. 30
1003   A372   50c vio brn & yel   20   10
Centenary of invention of the phonograph.

"R", Rainbow and Emblem A373

1977, Dec. 30   **Wmk. 332**
1004   A373   50c multi   20   10
World Rheumatism Year.

Emblem and Diploma A374

1978, Mar. 27   Litho.   Perf. 12
1005   A374   50c multi   20   10
50th anniversary of Military College.

Map and Arms of Artigas Department A375

Wmk. 332
1978, June 16   Litho.   Perf. 12
1006   A375   45c multi   25   10

Souvenir Sheet

Anniversaries—A376

Designs: 2p, Papilio thoas. No. 1007b, "100." No. 1007c, Argentina '78 emblem and globes. 5p, Model T Ford.

Wmk. 332
1978, Aug. 24   Litho.   Perf. 12
1007   A376   Sheet of 4   5.00   4.00
   a.   2p multi   65   20
   b.   4p multi   1.30   40
   c.   4p multi   1.30   40
   d.   5p multi   1.60   50

Commemoration of: 75th anniversary of 1st powered flight; UREXPO '78 Philatelic Exhibition; Parva Domus social club, centenary; 11th World Cup Soccer Championship, Argentina, June 1–25; Ford motor cars, 75th anniversary. No. 1007 has multicolored marginal inscriptions. Size: 96x107mm.

Visiting Angels, by Solari—A377

Designs (Details from No. 1008b): No. 1008a, Second angel. No. 1008c, Third angel.

1978, Sept. 13   **Unwmkd.**
Sizes: Nos. 1008a, 1008c: 19x30mm.; No. 1008b, 38x30mm.
1008   Strip of 3   1.50   1.00
   a.   A377 1.50p multi   48   25
   b.   A377 1.50p multi   48   25
   c.   A377 1.50p multi   48   25
Solari, Uruguayan painter.

Bernardo O'Higgins A378

Design: No. 1010, José de San Martin and monument.

1978   **Wmk. 332**
1009   A378   1p multi   32   15
1010   A378   1p multi   32   15

Bernardo O'Higgins (1778–1842 and José de San Martin (1778–1850), South American liberators.
Issue dates: No. 1009, Sept. 13; No. 1010, Oct. 10.

Telephone Dials A379

1978, Sept. 25
1011   A379   50c multi   16   10
Automation of telephone service.

Symbolic Stamps A380

Iberian Tile Pattern A381

1978, Oct. 31
1012   A380   50c multi   16   10
1013   A381   1p multi   32   15

Stamp Day (50c) and Spanish heritage (1p).

Boeing 727 A382

1978, Nov. 27
1014   A382   50c multi   16   10

Inauguration of Boeing 727 flights by PLUNA Uruguayan airlines, Nov. 1978.

Angel Blowing Horn—A383

1978, Dec. 7
1015   A383   50c multi   16   10
1016   A383   1p multi   32   15
Christmas 1978.

URUGUAY

Horacio Quiroga
A385

Wmk. 332

1978, Dec. 27   Litho.   *Perf. 12*
1018   A385   1p blk, red & yel   32   15

Horacio Quiroga, (1868-1928), short story writer.

Sapper with Pickax, 1837
A389

Flag Flying on Plaza of the Nation
A390

Army Day: No. 1041, Artillery man with cannon, 1830.

1979, May 18   Litho.   *Perf. 12*
1040   A389   5p multi   1.60   50
1041   A389   5p multi   1.60   50

1978, Dec. 15   *Perf. 12½*
1042   A390   1p multi   32   10

Uruguay Coat of Arms
150th anniversary—A395

1979, Sept. 6
1047   A395   8p multi   2.00

Spanish Heritage Day—A401

1979, Dec. 3   *Perf. 12*
1053   A401   10p multi   2.50

Silver Coin Centenary—A402

Designs: Obverse and reverse of coins in denominations matching stamps.

Wmk. 332

1979, Dec. 26   Litho.   *Perf. 12*
1054   A402   10c multi   5
1055   A402   20c multi   6
1056   A402   50c multi   15
1057   A402   1p multi   25

Arch, Olympic Rings, Lake Placid and Moscow Emblems
A386

Design: 7p, Olympic Rings and Lake Placid '80 emblem.

Perf. 12

1979, Apr. 28   Lithographed
1019   A386   5p multi   1.60   50
1020   A386   7p multi   2.25   75

81st Session of Olympic Organizing Committee, Apr. 3-8 (5p), and 13th Winter Olympic Games, Lake Placid, N.Y., Feb. 12-24.

Salto Dam
A391

1979, June 19
1043   A391   2p multi   65

Crandon Institute Emblem, Grain
A392

1979, July 19
1044   A392   1p violet blue & blue   25

Crandon Institute (private Methodist school), centenary.

Virgin and Child
A396

Symbols, by Torres-Garcia
A397

Wmk. 332

1979, Nov. 19   Litho.   *Perf. 12*
1048   A396   10p multi   2.50

Christmas 1979; International Year of the Child.

1979, Nov. 12
1049   A397   10p yel & blk   2.50

J. Torres-Garcia (1874-1948), painter.

U.P.U. and Brazilian Postal Emblems
A398

1979, Oct. 11
1050   A398   5p multi   1.25

18th U.P.U. Congress, Rio de Janeiro, Sept.-Oct.

Souvenir Sheet

Security Agent—A403

1980, Jan. 10
1058   Sheet of 4   2.75
   a.   A403   1p *Police emblem*   25
   b.   A403   2p *shown*   50
   c.   A403   3p *Policeman, 1843*   75
   d.   A403   4p *Cadet, 1979*   1.00

Police force sesquicentennial. No. 1058 has bright blue and black margin; black control number. Size: 79½x121mm.

Map and Arms of Paysandu
A387

Map and Arms of Maldonado
A388

1979-81
1021   A387   45c shown   15
1022   A387   45c Salto   15
1023   A388   45c shown   12
1024   A387   45c Cerro Largo   12
1025   A387   50c Treinta y Tres   15
1026   A387   50c Durazno ('80)   14
1032   A388   2p Rocha ('81)   50
1033   A388   2p Flores   50
   Nos. 1021-1033 (8)   1.83

IYC Emblem, Smiling Kites—A393

Cinderella—A394

1979
1045   A393   2p multi   50
1046   A394   2p multi   50

International Year of the Child. Issue dates: No. 1045, July 23; No. 1046, Aug. 29.

Dish Antenna and Sun—A400

Wmk. 332

1979, Nov. 26   Litho.   *Perf. 12x11½*
1052   A400   10p multi   2.50

Telecom '79, 3rd World Telecommunications Exhibition, Geneva, Sept. 20-26.

Light Bulb, Thomas Edison—A404

1980, Jan. 18
1059   A404   2p multi   50

Centenary of electric light (1979).

URUGUAY

Bass and Singer
A405

1980, Jan. 30
1060		Sheet of 4	2.25
a.	A405	2p Radio waves	50
b.	A405	2p shown	50
c.	A405	2p Ballerina	50
d.	A405	2p Television waves	50

Performing Arts Society, 50th anniversary. No. 1060 has blue and black margin; black control number. Size: 80x122mm.

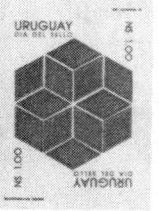 

Stamp Day — A406
La Leyenda Patria — A407

1980, Feb.
1061 A406 1p multi 25

1980, Feb. 26
1062 A407 1p multi 25

Printers' Association, 50th Anniversary — A408

1980, Feb.
1063 A408 1p multi 25

Lufthansa Cargo Container Service Inauguration — A409

1980, Apr. 12 Litho. *Perf. 12½*
1064 A409 2p multi 50

Conference Emblem, Banners — A410

1980, Apr. 28 Litho. *Perf. 12*
1065 A410 2p multi 50

8th World Hereford Conference, Punta del Este and Livestock Exhibition, Prado/Montivideo.

Man, Woman and Birds
A411

1980 Litho. *Perf. 12*
1066 A411 1p multi 25

International Year of the Child (1979).

Latin—American Lions, 9th Forum — A412

1980, May 6 Wmk. 332 *Perf. 12*
1067 A412 1p multi 30

Souvenir Sheet

Rifleman, 1814 — A413

1980, May 16
1068		Sheet of 4	2.50
a.	A413	2p shown	60
b.	A413	2p Cavalry officer, 1830	60
c.	A413	2p Private, Liberty Dragoons, 1826	60
d.	A413	2p Artigas Militia officer, 1815	60

Army Day, May 18. No. 1068 has blue and black margin with black control number. Size: 80x120mm.

Arms of Colonia — A414
Souvenir Sheet

Colonia, 1680 — A415

1980, June 17 Litho. *Perf. 12*
1069	A414	50c multi	12
1070		Sheet of 4, multi	1.00
a.	A415	1p shown	25
b.	A415	1p 1680, diff.	25
c.	A415	1p 1980	25
d.	A415	1p 1980, diff.	25

Colonia, 300th anniversary. No. 1070 has multicolored margin showing city map and gate; black control number. Size: 137x92mm.

Rotary Emblem on Globe — A416
Hand Putting Out Cigarette — A417

1980, July 8
1071 A416 5p multi 1.25

Rotary International, 75th anniversary.

1980, Sept. 8 Photo.
1072 A417 1p multi 25

World Health Day and anti-smoking campaign.

Artigas
A418

Constitution Title Page
A420

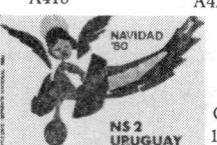

Christmas 1980 — A419

1980-82 Wmk. 332 Litho. *Perf. 12½*
1073	A418	10c bl ('81)	5
1074	A418	20c org ('80)	5
1075	A418	50c red ('80)	12
1076	A418	60c yel ('80)	15
1077	A418	1p gray ('80)	25
1078	A418	2p brn ('80)	50
1079	A418	3p grn ('80)	75
1080	A418	4p bl ('82)	1.00
1081	A418	5p grn ('82)	40
1082	A418	7p lil rose ('82)	1.75
1083	A418	10p bl ('82)	80
1084	A418	20p ('82)	1.60
1085	A418	30P lt. brn ('82)	2.40
1086	A418	50p gray bl ('82)	4.00
		Nos. 1073-1086 (14)	13.82

1980, Dec. 15 Wmk. 332 Litho. *Perf. 12*
1090 A419 2p multi 50

1980, Dec. 23 *Perf. 12½*
1091 A420 4p brt bl & gold 1.00

Sesquicentennial of Constitution.

Montevideo Stadium — A421

1980, Dec. 30 *Perf. 12*
1092	A421	5p shown	1.25
1093	A421	5p Soccer gold cup	1.25
		Size: 25x79mm.	
1094	A421	10p Flags	2.50
a.		Souvenir sheet of 3	5.50

Soccer Gold Cup Championship, Montevideo. No. 1094a contains Nos. 1092-1094. Multicolored margin shows various soccer cups; black control number. Size: 103x122mm.

Spanish Heritage Day — A422

1981, Jan. 27
1095 A422 2p multi 50

UPU Membership Centenary A423

1981, Feb. 6
1096 A423 2p multi 50

Alexander von Humboldt (1769-1859), German Explorer and Scientist
A424

1981, Feb. 19
1097 A424 2p multi 50

Intl. Education Congress and Fair, Montevideo (1980) — A425

1981, Mar. 31
1098 A425 2p multi 50

URUGUAY

Hand Holding
Gold Cup
A426

Eighth Notes
on Map of
Americas
A427

1981, Apr. 8
| 1099 | A426 | 2p multi | 50 |
| 1100 | A426 | 5p multi | 1.25 |

1980 victory in Gold Cup Soccer Championship.

1981, Apr. 28
| 1101 | A427 | 2p multi | 50 |

Inter-American Institute of Musicology, 40th anniv.

World Tourism Conference, Manila,
Sept. 27, 1980—A428

Wmk. 332
1981, June 1   Litho.   *Perf. 12*
| 1102 | A428 | 2p multi | 50 |

Inauguration of PLUNA Flights to
Madrid—A429

1981, May 12
1103	A429	2p multi	50
1104	A429	5p multi	1.25
1105	A429	10p multi	2.50

Army Day
A430

Natl. Atomic
Energy
Commission,
25th Anniv.
A431

Wmk. 332
1981, May 18   Litho.   *Perf. 12*
| 1106 | A430 | 2p Cavalry soldier, 1843 | 50 |
| 1107 | A430 | 2p Infantryman, 1843 | 50 |

1981, July 20
| 1108 | A431 | 2p multi | 50 |

Europe-South American Soccer
Cup—A432

1981, Aug. 4
| 1109 | A432 | 2p multi | 50 |

Stone Tablets, Salto Grande
Excavation—A433

1981, Sept. 10
| 1110 | A433 | 2p multi | 50 |

10th Lavalleja Week
A434

1981, Oct. 3
| 1111 | A434 | 4p multi | 1.00 |

Intl. Year of
the Disabled
A435

Wmk. 332
1981, Oct. 26   Litho. *Perf. 12*
| 1112 | A435 | 2p multi | 50 |

U.N. Environmental Law Meeting
Montevideo, Oct. 28-Nov. 6
A436

1981, Oct. 28
| 1113 | A436 | 5p multi | 1.25 |

50th Anniv. of ANCAP (Natl.
Administration of Combustible Fuels,
Alcohol and Cement)—A437

1981, Oct. 13
| 1114 | A437 | 2p multi | 50 |

Keep your collection
up to date!!
Subscribe to the
Scott Stamp Monthly
with
Chronicle of New Issues
Today!

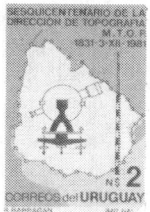
Topographical Society
Sesquicentennial—A439

1981, Dec. 5   *Perf. 12*
| 1116 | A439 | 2p multi | 50 |

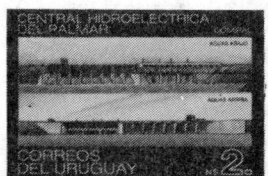
Bank of Uruguay, 85th Anniv.—A440

1981, Dec. 17   *Perf. 12½*
| 1117 | A440 | 2p multi | 50 |

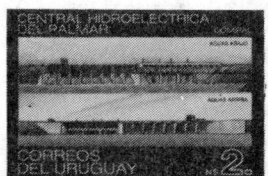
Palmar Dam—A441

1981, Dec. 22   *Perf. 12*
| 1118 | A441 | 2p multi | 50 |

Christmas 1981—A442

1981, Dec. 23
| 1119 | A442 | 2p multi | 50 |

Pres. Joaquin Suarez
Bicentenary—A443

1982, Mar. 15
| 1120 | A443 | 5p multi | 1.25 |

Artillery
Captain, 1872
Army Day
A444

Centenary
(1981) of
Pinochio, by
Carlo Collodi
A445

Wmk. 332
1982, May 18   Litho.   *Perf. 12*
| 1121 | A444 | 3p shown | 75 |
| 1122 | A444 | 3p Florida Battalion, 1865 | 75 |

1982, June 17
| 1123 | A445 | 2p multi | 50 |

2nd UN Conference on Peaceful Uses
of Outer Space, Vienna, Aug.
9-21—A446

1982, June 3
| 1124 | A446 | 3p multi | 75 |

World Food Day—A447

1982
| 1125 | A447 | 2p multi | 50 |

URUGUAY

25th Anniv. of Lufthansa's
Uruguay-Germany Flight—A448

1982, Apr. 14   **Unwmkd.**   **Perf. 12½**
1126 A448 3p Lockheed L-1049-G
              Super Constellation   75
1127 A448 7p Boeing 747   1.75

American Air Forces Cooperation
System—A449

1982, Apr. 14   **Wmk. 332**   **Perf. 12**
1128 A449 10p Emblem   2.50

Juan Zorilla de San Martin (1855-1931),
Painter—A450

1982, Aug. 18   **Perf. 12½**
1129 A450 3p Self-portrait   75

165th Anniv. of Natl. Navy—A451

1982, Nov. 15   **Perf. 12**
1130 A451 3p Navy vessel Capt.
              Miranda   25

Natl. Literacy   Stamp Day
Campaign
A452   A453

1982, Nov. 30
1131 A452 3p multi   25

1982, Dec. 23   **Perf. 12½**
1132 A453 3p like #46   25
1133 A453 3p like #47   25
    Nos. 1132-1133 se-tenant.

Christmas 1982—A454

1983, Jan. 4   **Perf. 12**
1134 A454 3p multi   25

Eduardo Fabini (1882-1950),
Composer—A455

1983, May 10
1135 A455 3p GOLD & brn   25

Army Day Type of 1982

1983, May 18
1136 A444 3p Military College
              cadet, 1885   25
1137 A444 3p 2nd Calvary Regiment
              officer, 1885   25

Visit of King Juan Carlos and Queen
Sofia of Spain, May—A456

1983, May 20
1138 A456 3p Santa Maria, globe   25
1139 A456 7p Profiles, flags   60
    Size of No. 1138: 29x39mm.

Brasiliana '83   80th Anniv. of
Emblem   First
                       Automobile in
                       Uruguay
A457   A458

Opening of   Jose Cuneo
UPAE Building,   (1887-1977),
Montevideo   Painter
A459   A460

1982 World Cup—A461

Graf Zeppelin Flight Over Montevideo,
50th Anniv. (1984)—A462

J.W. Goethe (1749-1832), 150th Death
Anniv.—A463

First Space Shuttle Flight—A464

          Wmk. 332
1983   **Litho.**   **Perf. 12**
1140 A457 3p multi   25
1141 A458 3p multi   25
1142 A459 3p multi   25
1143 A460 3p multi   25
  a. Souvenir sheet of 4   1.00
1144 A461 7p multi   60
1145 A462 7p multi   60
1146 A463 7p multi   60
1147 A464 7p multi   60
  a. Souvenir sheet of 4   2.50
    Nos. 1140-1147 (8)   3.40

No. 1143a contains stamps similar to Nos. 1140-1143. Size: 149x82mm. No. 1147a contains stamps similar to Nos. 1144-1147. Size: 82x149mm. Nos. 1143a and 1147a for URUEXPO '83 and World Communications Year. Black marginal inscriptions and control numbers.

Dates of issue: No. 1142, June 8; Nos. 1145, 1146, Sept. 29; Nos. 1143a, 1147a, June 9; No. 1140, July 22; Nos. 1144, Dec. 13; No. 1146, Sept. 20; No. 1145, Dec. 8.

Bicentenary of City of Minas—A465

              Wmk. 332
1983, Oct. 17   **Litho.**   **Perf. 12**
1148 A465 3p Founder   25

World Communications Year—A466

1983, Nov. 30
1149 A466 3p multi   25

Garibaldi Death Centenary—A467

1983, Dec. 5
1150 A467 7p multi   60

Christmas 1983—A468

Litho. & Embossed (Braille)
1983, Dec. 21   **Perf. 12½**
1151 A468 4.50p multi   36

50th Anniv. of Automatic
Telephones—A469

1983, Dec. 27   **Perf. 12**
1152 A469 4.50p multi   36

URUGUAY

SEMI-POSTAL STAMPS.

Indigent Old Man
SP1

Engraved.

		1930, Nov. 13	Perf. 12	Unwmkd.	
B1	SP1	1c + 1c dk vio		35	35
B2	SP1	2c + 2c dp grn		40	40
B3	SP1	5c + 5c red		50	50
B4	SP1	8c + 8c gray vio		50	50

The surtax on these stamps was for a fund to assist the aged. See No. 419.

Dam, Child and Rising Sun
SP2

Lithographed

		1959, Sept. 29	Perf. 11½	Wmk. 327	
B5	SP2	5c + 10c grn & org		8	8
B6	SP2	10c + 10c dk bl & org		15	15
B7	SP2	1p + 10c pur & org		50	40

Issued for national recovery. See also Nos. CB1–CB2.

AIR POST STAMPS.

No. 91
Overprinted
in Dark Blue,
Red or Green

		1921–22	Perf. 14	Unwmkd.	
C1	A38	25c bis brn (Bl)		15.00	12.00
a.		Black overprint		675.00	675.00
C2	A38	25c bis brn (R)		5.00	4.00
a.		Inverted ovpt.		90.00	90.00
C3	A38	25c bis brn (G) ('22)		5.00	4.00

This overprint also exists in light yellow green.
No. C1a was not issued. Some authorities consider it an overprint color trial.

AP2
Wmkd. REPUBLICA O. DEL URUGUAY. (188)

		1924, Jan. 2	Litho.	Perf. 11½	
C4	AP2	6c dk bl		1.50	1.25
C5	AP2	10c scarlet		2.25	1.75
C6	AP2	20c dp grn		4.00	3.50

Heron
AP3

		1925, Aug. 24		Perf. 12½	

Inscribed "MONTEVIDEO."

| C7 | AP3 | 14c bl & blk | | 30.00 | 17.50 |

Inscribed "FLORIDA."

| C8 | AP3 | 14c bl & blk | | 30.00 | 17.50 |

These stamps were used only on Aug. 25, 1925, the centenary of the Assembly of Florida, on letters intended to be carried by airplane between Montevideo and Florida, a town 60 miles north. The stamps were not delivered to the public but were affixed to the letters and canceled by post office clerks. Later uncanceled copies came on the market.

One authority believes Nos. C7–C8 served as registration stamps on these two attempted special flights.

Gaucho Cavalryman at Rincón
AP4

		1925, Sept. 24		Perf. 11	
C9	AP4	45c bl grn			9.00

Centenary of Battle of Rincon. Used only on Sept. 24. No. C9 was affixed and canceled by post office clerks.

Albatross
AP5

		1926, Mar. 3	Imperf.	Wmk. 188	
C10	AP5	6c dk bl		1.50	1.50
C11	AP5	10c vermilion		2.00	2.00
C12	AP5	20c bl grn		3.00	3.00
C13	AP5	25c violet		3.00	3.00

Excellent counterfeits of Nos. C10 to C13 exist.

		1928, June 25		Perf. 11	
C14	AP5	10c green		2.50	2.00
C15	AP5	20c orange		4.00	3.00
C16	AP5	30c indigo		4.00	3.00
C17	AP5	38c green		7.00	6.00
C18	AP5	40c yellow		8.00	6.00
C19	AP5	50c violet		9.00	7.00
C20	AP5	76c orange		17.50	15.00
C21	AP5	1p red		15.00	11.00
C22	AP5	1.14p indigo		40.00	35.00
C23	AP5	1.52p yellow		60.00	60.00
C24	AP5	1.90p violet		80.00	70.00
C25	AP5	3.80p red		200.00	150.00
		Nos. C14-C25 (12)		447.00	368.00

Counterfeits of No. C25 exist.

		1929, Aug. 23		Unwmkd.	
C26	AP5	4c ol brn		3.50	3.50

The design was redrawn for Nos. C14–C26. The numerals are narrower, "CENTS" is 1 mm. high instead of 2½ mm. and imprint letters touch the bottom frame line.

Pegasus
AP6

Size: 34x23mm.

		1929–43	Engraved.	Perf. 12½.	
C27	AP6	1c red lil ('30)		40	40
C28	AP6	1c dk bl ('32)		40	40
C29	AP6	2c yel ('30)		40	40
C30	AP6	2c ol grn ('32)		40	40
C31	AP6	4c Prus bl ('30)		70	60
C32	AP6	4c car rose ('32)		70	60
C33	AP6	6c dl vio ('30)		75	60
C34	AP6	6c red brn ('32)		75	60
C35	AP6	8c red org		3.50	3.00
C36	AP6	8c gray ('30)		4.00	3.00
C36A	AP6	8c brt grn ('43)		50	40
C37	AP6	16c indigo		2.75	2.25
C38	AP6	16c rose ('30)		3.25	3.00
C39	AP6	24c claret		3.00	2.50
C40	AP6	24c brt vio ('30)		4.00	3.25
C41	AP6	30c bister		3.25	3.00
C42	AP6	30c dk grn ('30)		2.00	1.00
C43	AP6	30c dk brn		6.00	5.00
C44	AP6	40c yel org ('30)		6.00	5.00
C45	AP6	60c bl grn		5.00	3.50
C46	AP6	60c emer ('30)		8.00	7.00
C47	AP6	60c dp org ('31)		3.00	2.00
C48	AP6	80c dk ultra		9.00	8.00
C49	AP6	80c grn ('30)		15.00	12.00
C50	AP6	90c lt bl		9.00	7.00
C51	AP6	90c dk ol grn ('30)		15.00	12.00
C52	AP6	1p car rose ('30)		7.50	5.00
C53	AP6	1.20p ol grn		22.50	20.00
C54	AP6	1.20p dk car ('30)		30.00	25.00
C55	AP6	1.50p red brn		22.50	17.50
C56	AP6	1.50p blk brn ('30)		12.00	10.00
C57	AP6	3p dp red		35.00	30.00
C58	AP6	3p ultra ('30)		25.00	20.00
C59	AP6	4.50p black		65.00	50.00
C60	AP6	4.50p vio ('30)		45.00	35.00
C60A	AP6	10p dp ultra ('43)		20.00	12.00
		Nos. C27-C60A (36)		391.25	311.40

Power Dam on Black River
AP7

Imprint: "Imp. Nacional" at center.

		1937–41		Lithographed	
C83	AP7	20c lt grn ('38)		5.00	4.00
C84	AP7	35c red brn		7.50	6.00
C85	AP7	62c bl grn ('38)		75	30
C86	AP7	68c yel org ('38)		1.85	1.35
C86A	AP7	68c pale vio brn ('41)		1.65	75
C87	AP7	75c violet		8.00	2.00
C88	AP7	1p dp pink ('38)		2.50	1.50
C89	AP7	1.38p rose ('38)		22.50	20.00
C90	AP7	3p dk bl ('40)		12.50	2.50
		Nos. C83-C90 (9)		62.25	38.40

Nos. 450, 452
Overprinted
in Red

		1934, Jan. 1		Perf. 11½	
C61	A130	17c ver, gray & vio		25.00	20.00
a.		Sheet of six		175.00	
b.		Gray omitted		200.00	
c.		Double ovpt.		200.00	
C62	A130	36c red, blk & yel		25.00	20.00
a.		Sheet of six		175.00	

Issued to commemorate the 7th Pan-American Conference, Montevideo.

Pegasus Type of 1929.

Size: 31½x21mm.

		1935	Engraved.	Perf. 12½.	
C63	AP6	15c dl yel		2.50	2.00
C64	AP6	22c brick red		1.50	1.25
C65	AP6	30c brn vio		2.50	2.00
C66	AP6	37c gray lil		1.25	1.00
C67	AP6	40c rose lake		2.00	1.25
C68	AP6	47c rose		4.00	3.50
C69	AP6	50c Prus bl		1.25	75
C70	AP6	52c dp ultra		4.00	3.50
C71	AP6	57c grnsh bl		2.00	1.75
C72	AP6	62c ol grn		1.75	75
C73	AP6	87c gray grn		5.00	4.00
C74	AP6	1p olive		3.50	2.25
C75	AP6	1.12p brn red		3.50	2.25
C76	AP6	1.20p bis brn		15.00	12.00
C77	AP6	1.27p red brn		15.00	12.50
C78	AP6	1.62p rose		10.00	9.00
C79	AP6	2p brn rose		16.00	14.00
C80	AP6	2.12p dk sl grn		16.00	14.00
C81	AP6	3p dl bl		15.00	12.50
C82	AP6	5p orange		50.00	50.00
		Nos. C63-C82 (20)		171.75	150.25

Counterfeits exist.

Plane over Sculptured Oxcart
AP8

		1939–44		Perf. 12½	
C93	AP8	20c slate		45	35
C94	AP8	20c lt vio ('43)		70	75
C95	AP8	20c bl ('44)		55	35
C96	AP8	35c red		90	70
C97	AP8	50c brn org		90	30
C98	AP8	75c dp pink		1.00	22
C99	AP8	1p dp bl ('40)		3.00	50
C100	AP8	1.38p brt vio		6.00	2.00
C101	AP8	1.38p yel org ('44)		5.50	4.00
C102	AP8	2p blue		7.50	1.25
a.		Perf. 11		7.25	
C103	AP8	5p rose lil		10.00	2.10
C104	AP8	5p bl grn ('44)		13.00	5.25
C105	AP8	10p rose ('40)		85.00	60.00
		Nos. C93-C105 (13)		134.50	77.77

Counterfeits exist.

Imprint at left.

| C91 | AP7 | 8c pale grn ('39) | | 55 | 50 |
| C92 | AP7 | 20c lt grn ('38) | | 2.10 | 1.25 |

Stamps of 1935 Surcharged in Red or Black — **$0.79**

		1944, Nov. 22			
C106	AP6	40c on 47c rose (Bk)		75	60
C107	AP6	40c on 57c grnsh bl (R)		1.00	75
C108	AP6	74c on 1.12p brn red (Bk)		1.00	75
C109	AP6	79c on 87c gray grn (Bk)		4.00	3.00
C110	AP6	79c on 1.27p red brn (Bk)		6.00	5.00
C111	AP6	1.20p on 1.62p lt rose		3.00	2.00
C112	AP6	1.43p on 2.12p dk sl grn (R)		4.00	2.75
		Nos. C106-C112 (7)		19.75	14.85

Legislature Building
AP9

Engraved.

		1945, May 11	Perf. 11	Unwmkd.	
C113	AP9	2p ultra		4.00	2.00

Type of 1929, Surcharged in Violet

		1945, Aug. 14		Perf. 12½	
C114	AP6	44c on 75c brn		1.25	75

Allied Nations' victory in Europe.

"La Eolo"
AP10

		1945, Oct. 31		Perf. 11	
C115	AP10	8c green		1.00	50

URUGUAY

Nos. C97 and C101
Surcharged in Violet, Black or Blue

1945-46			Perf. 12½.	
C116	AP8	14c on 50c brn org (V) ('46)	50	40
a.		Inverted surcharge	75.00	
C117	AP8	23c on 1.38p yel org	60	50
a.		Inverted surcharge	150.00	
C118	AP8	23c on 50c brn org	75	60
a.		Inverted surcharge	150.00	
C119	AP8	1p on 1.38p yel org (Bl)	3.00	2.50
a.		Inverted surcharge	150.00	

Issued to commemorate the victory of the Allied Nations in World War II.

No. C85 Overprinted in Black

INAUGURACION DICIEMBRE, 1945

1946, Jan. 9				
C120	AP7	62c bl grn	1.15	80

Issued to commemorate the inauguration of the Black River Power Dam.

AP11

Black Overprint.

1946-49			Lithographed	
C121	AP11	8c car rose	12	10
a.		Inverted overprint		
C122	AP11	50c brown	60	40
a.		Double ovpt.	50.00	
C123	AP11	1p lt bl	1.15	50
C124	AP11	2p ol ('49)	5.25	3.50
C125	AP11	3p lil rose	5.50	3.50
C126	AP11	5p rose car	10.00	8.00
		Nos. C121-C126 (6)	22.62	16.00

Four-Motored Plane
AP12

National Airport
AP13

1947-49			Perf. 11½, 12½	
C129	AP12	3c org brn ('49)	12	8
C130	AP12	8c car rose ('49)	18	12
C131	AP12	14c ultra	35	20
C132	AP13	23c emerald	40	25
C133	AP13	1p car & brn ('49)	2.00	30
C134	AP13	3p ultra & brn ('49)	5.00	3.00
C135	AP13	5p grn & brn ('49)	10.00	6.00
C136	AP13	10p lil rose & brn	12.00	8.00
		Nos. C129-C136 (8)	30.05	17.95

Counterfeits exist. See also Nos. C145-C164.

School of Architecture, University of Uruguay
AP14   AP15

Black Overprint

1948, June 9			Perf. 12½	
C137	AP14	12c blue	27	10
C138	AP14	24c Prus grn	50	25
C139	AP14	36c sl bl	70	40

1949, Dec. 7

Designs: 27c, Medical School. 31c, Engineering School. 36c, University.

C141	AP15	15c carmine	15	15
C142	AP15	27c chocolate	22	12
C143	AP15	31c dp ultra	40	15
C144	AP15	36c dl grn	45	15

Issued to commemorate the centenary of the founding of the University of Uruguay.

Plane Type of 1947-49

1952-59		Perf. 11, 12½.	Unwmkd.	
C145	AP12	10c blk ('54)	12	10
C146	AP12	10c lt red ('58)	12	10
a.		Imperf., pair	60.00	
C147	AP12	15c org brn	17	12
a.		Vert. pair, imperf. between	100.00	
C148	AP12	20c lil rose ('54)	20	17
C149	AP12	21c purple	27	20
C150	AP12	27c yel grn ('57)	27	6
C151	AP12	31c chocolate	40	17
C152	AP12	36c ultra	30	12
C153	AP12	36c blk ('58)	32	20
C154	AP12	50c lt bl ('57)	55	35
C155	AP12	50c bl blk ('58)	35	12
C156	AP12	62c dl sl bl ('53)	65	35
C157	AP12	65c rose ('53)	65	35
C158	AP12	84c org ('59)	80	60
C159	AP12	1.08p vio brn	1.30	65
C160	AP12	2p Prus bl	2.00	1.00
C161	AP12	3p red org	2.50	1.35
C162	AP12	5p dk gray grn	5.50	3.50
C163	AP12	5p gray ('57)	3.00	2.00
C164	AP12	10p dp grn ('55)	15.00	10.00
		Nos. C145-C164 (20)	34.47	21.51

Planes and Show Emblem
AP16

Lithographed

1956, Jan. 5		Perf. 11	Unwmkd.	
C166	AP16	20c ultra	60	30
C167	AP16	31c ol grn	70	40
C168	AP16	36c car rose	1.00	50

Issued to publicize the First Exposition of National Products.

Type of Regular Issue and

José Batlle y Ordonez
AP17

Designs: 10c, Full-face portrait without hand. 36c, Portrait facing right.

Photogravure.

1956, Dec. 15		Perf. 13½	Wmk. 90	
C169	A178	10c magenta	12	10
C170	A178	20c grnsh blk	25	12
C171	AP17	31c brown	35	25
C172	A178	36c bl grn	45	27

Issued to commemorate the centenary of the birth of President José Batlle y Ordonez.

Stamp of 1856 and Stagecoach
AP18

1956, Dec. 15			Lithographed	
C173	AP18	20c grn, bl & pale yel	65	35
C174	AP18	31c brn, bl & lt bl	75	40
C175	AP18	36c dp cl & bl	90	60

Issued to commemorate the centenary of the first postage stamps of Uruguay.

Flags of 21 American Nations Men and Torch of Freedom
AP19   AP20

Perf. 11, 11½ (No. C177)

1958, June 19			Unwmkd.	
C176	AP19	23c bl & blk	30	20
C177	AP19	34c grn & blk	40	20
C178	AP19	44c cer & blk	60	35

Issued to commemorate the 10th anniversary of the Organization of American States.

1958, Dec. 10			Perf. 11	
C179	AP20	23c blk & bl	30	12
C180	AP20	34c blk & yel grn	40	20
C181	AP20	44c blk & org red	75	40

Issued to commemorate the tenth anniversary of the signing of the Universal Declaration of Human Rights.

"Flight" from Monument to Fallen Aviators
AP21

Lithographed.

1959	Size: 22x37½mm.		Perf. 11	
C182	AP21	3c bis brn & blk	10	8
C183	AP21	8c brt lil & blk	10	8
C184	AP21	38c black	12	10
C185	AP21	50c cit & blk	17	12
C186	AP21	60c vio & blk	20	15
C187	AP21	90c ol grn & blk	32	20
C188	AP21	1p bl & blk	45	25
C189	AP21	2p ocher & blk	1.50	75
C190	AP21	3p grn & blk	1.85	1.50
C191	AP21	5p vio brn & blk	2.35	2.00
C192	AP21	10p dp rose car & blk	8.00	6.00
		Nos. C182-C192 (11)	15.16	11.23

See also Nos. C211-C222.

Alberto Santos-Dumont
AP22

1959, Feb. 13		Perf. 11½	Wmk. 327	
C193	AP22	31c multi	25	17
C194	AP22	36c multi	25	17

Issued to commemorate the airplane flight of Alberto Santos-Dumont, Brazilian aeronaut, in 1906 in France.

Girl and Waves
AP23

Designs: 38c, 60c, 1.05p, Compass and map of Punta del Este.

1959, Mar. 6			Perf. 11½	
C195	AP23	10c ocher & lt bl	12	6
C196	AP23	38c grn & bis	20	12
C197	AP23	60c lil & bis	35	25
C198	AP23	90c red org & grn	45	35
C199	AP23	1.05p bl & bis	50	40
		Nos. C195-C199 (5)	1.62	1.18

Issued to commemorate the 50th anniversary of Punta del Este, seaside resort.

Torch, YMCA Emblem and Chrismon
AP24

Lithographed.

1959, Dec. 22		Perf. 11½	Wmk. 327	
C200	AP24	38c emer, blk & gray	40	35
C201	AP24	50c bl, blk & gray	45	30
C202	AP24	60c red, blk & gray	55	55

Issued to commemorate the 50th anniversary of the Y.M.C.A. in Uruguay.

José Artigas and George Washington
AP25

Refugees and WRY Emblem
AP26

1960, Mar. 2			Perf. 11½x12	
C203	AP25	38c red & blk	25	20
C204	AP25	50c brt bl & blk	30	20
C205	AP25	60c dp grn & blk	35	25

Issued to commemorate Pres. Dwight D. Eisenhower's visit to Uruguay, Feb. 1960. No. C204 exists imperforate, but was not regularly issued in this form.

URUGUAY

No. C150 Surcharged

20 c

1960, Apr. 8   Perf. 11   Unwmkd.

C206 AP12	20c on 27c yel grn	12	10
a.	Perf. 12½	25	15

1960, June 6   Wmk. 332
Size: 24x35mm.

C207 AP26	60c brt lil rose & blk	35	30

Issued to publicize World Refugee Year, July 1, 1959–June 30, 1960.

Type of Regular Issue, 1960
Lithographed

1960, Nov. 4   Perf. 12   Wmk. 332

C208 A186	38c bl & ol grn	20	15
C209 A186	50c bl & ver	25	20
C210 A186	60c bl & pur	35	25

150th anniversary of May Revolution.

Type of 1959 Redrawn with Silhouette of Airplane Added.

1960–61   Lithographed   Perf. 12

C211 AP21	3c blk & pale vio	6	6
C212 AP21	20c blk & crim	6	6
C213 AP21	38c blk & pale bl	12	10
C214 AP21	50c blk & buff	17	12
C215 AP21	60c blk & dp grn	20	12
C216 AP21	90c blk & rose	35	20
C217 AP21	1p blk & gray	40	20
C218 AP21	2p blk & yel grn	70	40
C219 AP21	3p blk & red lil	1.15	65
C220 AP21	5p blk & org ver	1.85	1.35
C221 AP21	10p blk & yel	3.25	2.50
C222 AP21	20p blk & dk bl ('61)	6.75	4.00
	Nos. C211-C222 (12)	15.06	9.76

Pres. Gronchi and Flag Colors
AP27

1961, Apr. 17   Perf. 12   Wmk. 332

C223 AP27	90c multi	40	35
C224 AP27	1.20p multi	45	40
C225 AP27	1.40p multi	55	45

Issued to commemorate the visit of President Giovanni Gronchi of Italy to Uruguay, April, 1961.

Carrasco National Airport
AP28

1961, May 16   Perf. 12   Wmk. 332
Building in Gray

C226 AP28	1p lt vio	32	27
C227 AP28	2p ol gray	65	10
C228 AP28	3p orange	1.15	65
C229 AP28	4p purple	1.35	85
C230 AP28	5p aqua	1.65	1.00
C231 AP28	10p lt ultra	3.25	2.00
C232 AP28	20p maroon	5.50	4.25
	Nos. C226-C232 (7)	13.87	9.12

Type of Regular "CIES" Issue, 1961.

1961, Aug. 3   Litho.   Wmk. 332

C233 A189	20c blk & org	6	6
C234 A189	45c blk & grn	17	12
C235 A189	50c blk & gray	17	12
C236 A189	90c blk & plum	30	20
C237 A189	1p blk & dp rose	35	25
C238 A189	1.40p blk & lt vio	55	35
C239 A189	2p blk & bis	65	40
C240 A189	3p blk & lt bl	1.00	60
C241 A189	4p blk & yel	1.10	90
C242 A189	5p blk & lil	1.35	1.15
C243 A189	10p blk & yel grn	3.35	3.25
C244 A189	20p blk & dp pink	6.50	5.25
	Nos. C233-C244 (12)	15.55	12.70

See note after No. 685.

Swiss Flag, Plow, Wheat Sheaf
AP29

1962, Aug. 1   Perf. 12   Wmk. 332

C245 AP29	90c car, org & blk	40	30
C246 AP29	1.40p car, bl & blk	50	50

Issued to commemorate the centenary of the Swiss Settlement in Uruguay.

Red-crested Cardinal AP30

Birds: 45c, White-capped tanager (horiz.). 90c, Vermilion flycatcher. 1.20p, Great kiskadee (horiz.). 1.40p, Fork-tailed flycatcher.

1962, Dec. 5   Litho.   Perf. 12

C247 AP30	20c gray, blk & red	10	6
C248 AP30	45c multi	25	10
C249 AP30	90c crim rose, blk & lt brn	50	12
C250 AP30	1.20p lt bl, blk & yel	75	25
C251 AP30	1.40p bl & sep	1.00	30
	Nos. C247-C251 (5)	2.60	83

No frame on No. C248, thin frame on No. C251. See also Nos. C258–C263.

Type of Regular UPAE Issue, 1963.

1963, May 31   Perf. 12   Wmk. 332

C252 A195	45c bluish grn & blk	12	10
C253 A195	90c mag & blk	30	20

Issued to commemorate the 50th anniversary of the founding of the Postal Union of the Americas and Spain, UPAE.

Freedom from Hunger Issue
Type of Regular Issue, 1963

1963, July 9   Perf. 12   Wmk. 332

C254 A196	90c red & yel	30	20
C255 A196	1.40p vio & yel	35	25

Issued for the "Freedom from Hunger" campaign of the U.N. Food and Agriculture Organization.

"Alferez Campora" AP31

1963, Aug. 16   Lithographed

C256 AP31	90c dk grn & org	25	13
C257 AP31	1.40p ultra & yel	45	35

Issued to commemorate the voyage around the world by the Uruguayan sailing vessel "Alferez Campora," 1960–63.

Bird Type of 1962

Birds: 1p, Glossy cowbird (tordo). 2p, Yellow cardinal. 3p, Hooded siskin. 5p, Sayaca tanager. 10p, Blue and yellow tanager. 20p, Scarlet-headed marsh-bird. (All horizontal.)

1963, Nov. 15   Perf. 12   Wmk. 332

C258 AP30	1p vio bl, blk & brn org	27	20
C259 AP30	2p lt brn, blk & yel	65	35
C260 AP30	3p yel, brn & blk	1.00	45
C261 AP30	5p emer, bl grn & blk	1.50	95
C262 AP30	10p multi	2.50	1.25
C263 AP30	20p gray, org & blk	7.50	5.00
	Nos. C258-C263 (6)	13.42	8.00

Frame on Nos. C260-C263.

Pres. Charles de Gaulle AP32

Design: 2.40p, Flags of France and Uruguay.

1964, Oct. 9   Litho.   Perf. 12

C264 AP32	1.50p multi	60	30
C265 AP32	2.40p multi	1.25	75

Issued to commemorate the visit of Charles de Gaulle, President of France, Oct. 1964.

Submerged Statue of Ramses II AP33

Design: 2p, Head of Ramses II.

1964, Oct. 30   Litho.   Wmk. 332

C266 AP33	1.30p multi	50	20
C267 AP33	2p bis, red brn & brt bl	1.00	45
a.	Souv. sheet of 3	2.00	2.00

Issued to publicize the UNESCO world campaign to save historic monuments in Nubia. No. C267a contains three imperf. stamps similar to Nos. 713 and C266–C267. Bister marginal inscription. Size: 109x131mm.

National Flag AP34

1965, Feb. 18   Perf. 12   Wmk. 332

C268 AP34	50p gray, dk bl & yel	8.00	6.00

Kennedy Type of Regular Issue, 1965

1965, Mar. 5   Perf. 11½   Wmk. 327

C269 A202	1.50p gold, lil & blk	27	20
C270 A202	2.40p gold, brt bl & blk	50	30

Issued in memory of Pres. John F. Kennedy (1917–63).

Issue of 1864, No. 23
AP35

Designs: 6c, 8c and 10c denominations of 1864 issue.

Lithographed

1965, Mar. 19   Perf. 12   Wmk. 332

C271 AP35	Sheet of 10	1.60	1.60

"URUGUAY" at bottom

a.	1p bl & blk	15	15
b.	1p brick red & blk	15	15
c.	1p grn & blk	15	15
d.	1p ocher & blk	15	15
e.	1p car & blk	15	15

"URUGUAY" at top

f.	1p bl & blk	15	15
g.	1p brick red & blk	15	15
h.	1p grn & blk	15	15
i.	1p ocher & blk	15	15
j.	1p car & blk	15	15

Issued to commemorate the First Rio de la Plata Stamp Show, sponsored jointly by the Argentine and Uruguayan philatelic associations, Montevideo, March 19–28. No. C271 contains two horizontal rows of stamps and two rows of labels; Nos. C271a–C271e are in first row, Nos. C271f–C271j in second row. Adjacent labels in top and bottom rows. Size of sheet: 228x150mm.

National Arms AP36   **Artigas Monument** AP37

1965, Apr. 30   Perf. 12   Wmk. 332

C272 AP36	20p multi	2.25	1.50

Type of Regular Issue and AP37.
Designs: 1.50p, Artigas and wagon-train. 2.40p, Artigas quotation.

Perf. 11½x12, 12x11½

1965, May 17   Litho.   Wmk. 327

C273 AP37	1p multi	12	10
C274 A205	1.50p multi	25	17
C275 A205	2.40p multi	40	27

Issued to commemorate the bicentenary of the birth of José Artigas (1764–1850), leader of the independence revolt against Spain.

Olympic Games Type of Regular Issue

Designs: 1p, Boxing. 1.50p, Running. 2p, Fencing. 2.40p, Sculling. 3p, Pistol shooting. 20p, Olympic rings.

1965, Aug. 3   Litho.   Perf. 12x11½

C276 A206	1p red, gray & blk	12	12
C277 A206	1.50p emer, bl & blk	20	17

URUGUAY

C278	A206	2p dk car, bl & blk		27	25
C279	A206	2.40p lt ultra, org & blk		35	30
C280	A206	3p lil, yel & blk		40	35
C281	A206	20p dk vio bl, pink & lt bl		1.25	90
		Nos. C276-C281 (6)		2.59	2.09

Souvenir Sheet
Olympic Types of 1924, 1928

Designs: 5p, Stamp of 1924, No. 284. 10p, Stamp of 1928, No. 389.

C282	Sheet of 2	2.25	2.25
a.	5p buff, bl & blk	70	70
b.	10p bl, blk & rose red	1.10	1.10

Nos. C276–C282 commemorate the 18th Olympic Games, Tokyo, Oct. 10–25, 1964. No. C282 contains two stamps; blue Olympic rings in margin, black inscriptions: "HOMENAJE A LOS CAMPIONES OLYMPICOS DE FUTBOL" and "CORREOS DEL URUGUAY 1924-1928." Black control number. Size: 69x125mm.

ITU Emblem and Satellite
AP38

1966, Jan. 25 Perf. 12 Wmk. 332

| C283 | AP38 | 1p bl, bluish blk & ver | 10 | 5 |

Issued to commemorate the centenary of the International Telecommunication Union (in 1965).

Winston Churchill
AP39

1966, Apr. 29 Perf. 12 Wmk. 332

| C284 | AP39 | 2p car, brn & gold | 22 | 10 |

Issued in memory of Sir Winston Spencer Churchill (1874–1965), statesman and World War II leader.

Rio de Janeiro Type of Regular Issue
1966, June 9 Perf. 12 Wmk. 332

| C285 | A208 | 80c dp org & brn | 8 | 6 |

Issued to commemorate the 400th anniversary of the founding of Rio de Janeiro.

International Cooperation Year Emblem
AP40

1966, June 9 Lithographed

| C286 | AP40 | 1p bluish grn & blk | 8 | 5 |

U.N. International Cooperation Year.

President Zalman Shazar of Israel
AP41

1966, June 21 Wmk. 327

| C287 | AP41 | 7p multi | 50 | 40 |

Visit of Pres. Zalman Shazar of Israel.

Crested Screamer
AP42

1966, July 7 Perf. 12 Wmk. 327

| C288 | AP42 | 100p bl, blk, red & gray | 5.50 | 3.25 |

Jules Rimet Cup, Soccer Ball and Globe
AP43

1966, July 11 Lithographed

| C289 | AP43 | 10p dk pur, org & lil | 75 | 45 |

Issued to commemorate the World Cup Soccer Championship, Wembley, England, July 11–30.

Hereford Bull
AP44

Bulls: 6p, Holstein. 10p, Shorthorn. 15p, Aberdeen Angus. 20p, Norman. 30p, Jersey. 50p, Charolais.

1966 Perf. 12 Wmk. 327

C290	AP44	4p sep, dk brn & lt brn	22	12
C291	AP44	6p grn, bluish grn & blk	35	15
C292	AP44	10p grn, bluish grn & vio brn (wmk.332)	50	30
C293	AP44	15p brt red, org & blk	80	40
C294	AP44	20p yel, gray & sep	1.25	60
C295	AP44	30p sep, brn & yel	1.85	80
C296	AP44	50p bluish gray, sep & grn	3.00	1.25
		Nos. C290-C296 (7)	7.97	3.62

Issued to publicize Uruguayan cattle. Dates of Issue: 4p, 50p, Aug. 13; 6p, 30p, Aug. 29; 10p, 15p, 20p, Sept. 26.

Boiso Lanza, Early Plane and Space Capsule
AP45

1966, Oct. 14 Litho. Perf. 12

| C297 | AP45 | 25p ultra, blk & lt bl | 1.25 | 1.00 |

Issued to honor Capt. Juan Manuel Boiso Lanza, pioneer of military aviation.

No. C271 Overprinted:
"CENTENARIO DEL SELLO / ESCUDITO RESELLADO"

1966, Nov. 4 Wmk. 332

| C298 | AP35 | Sheet of 10 | 1.60 | 1.60 |

"URUGUAY" at bottom

a.	1p bl & blk	15	15
b.	1p brick red & blk	15	15
c.	1p grn & blk	15	15
d.	1p ocher & blk	15	15
e.	1p car & blk	15	15

"URUGUAY" at top

f.	1p bl & blk	15	15
g.	1p brick red & blk	15	15
h.	1p grn & blk	15	15
i.	1p ocher & blk	15	15
j.	1p car & blk	15	15

Issued to publicize the second Rio de la Plata Stamp Show, Buenos Aires, April, 1966, sponsored by the Argentine and Uruguayan philatelic associations, and commemorating the centenary of Uruguay's first surcharged issue. The addition of black numerals makes the designs resemble the surcharged issue of 1866, Nos. 24–28.
Labels in top row are overprinted "SEGUNDA MUESTRA 1966," in bottom row "SEGUNDAS JORNADAS 1966" and "CENTENARIO DEL SELLO / ESCUDITO RESELLADO" in both rows. One label each in top and bottom rows is overprinted "BUENOS AIRES / ABRIL 1966." Size of sheet: 228x150mm.

No. 613 Surcharged in Dark Blue

40 ANIVERSARIO
Club Filatélico del Uruguay

$ 1.00 aéreo

Perf. 12½x13

1966, Dec. 17 Engr. Unwmkd.

| C299 | A175 | 1p on 12c dp ultra & dk brn | 12 | 8 |

Issued to commemorate the 40th anniversary of the Philatelic Club of Uruguay.

Dante Alighieri Planetarium Projector
AP46 AP47

Lithographed

1966, Dec. 27 Perf. 12 Wmk. 332

| C300 | AP46 | 50c sep & bis | 10 | 6 |

Issued to honor Dante Alighieri (1265–1321), Italian poet.

1967, Jan. 13 Perf. 12 Wmk. 332

| C301 | AP47 | 5p dl bl & blk | 35 | 22 |

Issued to commemorate the 10th anniversary of the Montevideo Municipal Planetarium.

Archbishop Makarios and Map of Cyprus
AP48

1967, Feb. 14 Perf. 12 Wmk. 332

| C302 | AP48 | 6.60p rose lil & blk | 32 | 25 |

Issued to commemorate the visit of Archbishop Makarios, president of Cyprus, Oct. 21, 1966.

Albert Schweitzer Holding Fawn
AP49

1967, Mar. 31 Litho. Wmk. 332

| C303 | AP49 | 6p grn, blk, brn & sal | 30 | 25 |

Issued to honor Dr. Albert Schweitzer (1875–1965), medical missionary.

Corriedale Ram
AP50

Various Rams: 4p, Ideal. 5p, Romney Marsh. 10p, Australian Merino.

1967, Apr. 5

C304	AP50	3p red org, blk & gray	15	8
C305	AP50	4p emer, blk & gray	22	12
C306	AP50	5p ultra, blk & gray	27	15
C307	AP50	10p yel, blk & gray	55	40

Uruguayan sheep raising.

Flag of Uruguay and Map of the Americas
AP51

1967, Apr. 8

| C308 | AP51 | 10p dk gray, bl & gold | 45 | 32 |

Issued to commemorate the meeting of American Presidents, Punta del Este, Apr. 10–12.

Numeral Stamps of 1866, Nos. 30–31
AP52

Design: 6p, Nos. 32–33; diff. frame.

Lithographed

1967, May 10 Perf. 12 Wmk. 332

C309	AP52	3p bl, yel grn & blk	25	12
a.	Souv. sheet of 4	1.00	1.00
C310	AP52	6p bis, dp rose & blk	50	17
a.	Souv. sheet of 4	2.00	2.00

Issued to commemorate the centenary of the 1866 numeral issue. Nos. C309a–C310a each contain four stamps similar to Nos. C309 and C310 respectively (the arrangement of colors differs in the souvenir sheets). Black marginal inscriptions. Size: 93x67½mm.

Ansina, Portrait by Medardo Latorre
AP53

1967, May 17

| C311 | AP53 | 2p gray, dk bl & red | 10 | 6 |

Issued to honor Ansina, servant of Gen. José Artigas.

URUGUAY

1967, May 30
C312 AP54 10p red, bl, blk & yel 50 35

Plane Landing AP54

Issued to commemorate the 30th anniversary (in 1966) of PLUNA Airline.

Shooting for Basket AP55

Basketball Game—AP56

Basketball Players in Action: No. C314, Driving (ball shoulder high). No. C315, About to pass (ball head high). No. C316, Ready to pass (ball held straight in front). No. C317, Dribbling with right hand.

1967, June 9
C313	AP55	5p multi	25	15
C314	AP55	5p multi	25	15
C315	AP55	5p multi	25	15
C316	AP55	5p multi	25	15
C317	AP55	5p multi	25	15
		Strip of 5, #C313-C317	1.25	75

Souvenir Sheet
C318 AP56 10p org, brt grn & blk 85 85

5th World Basketball Championships, Montevideo, May 1967. No. C318 has black marginal inscription. Size: 44x62mm. Nos. C313–C317 printed se-tenant.

Souvenir Sheet

José Artigas, Manuel Belgrano, Flags of Uruguay and Argentina AP57

Lithographed
1967, June 19 *Imperf.* Wmk. 332
C319 AP57 5p bl, grn & yel 75 50

Issued to commemorate the Third Rio de la Plata Stamp Show, Montevideo, Uruguay, June 18–25. Size: 69½x50mm.

Nos. C248 and C252 Surcharged in Gold

1967, June 22 *Perf. 12*
C320	AP30	5.90p on 45c multi	32	20
C321	A195	5.90p on 45c multi	32	20

Don Quixote and Sancho Panza, Painted by Denry Torres AP58

1967, July 10
C322 AP58 8p bis brn & brn 32 17

Issued in honor of Miguel de Cervantes Saavedra (1547–1616), Spanish novelist.

Stone Axe AP59

Designs: 15p, Headbreaker stones. 20p, Spearhead. 50p, Birdstone. 75p, Clay pot. 100p, Ornitholite (ritual sculpture). Balizas (horiz.). 150p, Lasso weights (boleadores). 200p, Two spearheads.

1967-68 *Perf. 12* Wmk. 332
C323	AP59	15p gray & blk	15	8
C324	AP59	20p gray & blk	27	12
C325	AP59	30p gray & lt gray	65	22
C326	AP59	50p gray & blk	90	35
C327	AP59	75p brn & blk	1.35	55
C328	AP59	100p gray & blk	2.00	90
C329	AP59	150p gray & blk ('68)	2.65	1.10
C330	AP59	200p gray & blk ('68)	3.50	2.35
		Nos. C323-C330 (8)	11.47	5.67

Railroad Crossing AP60

1967, Dec. 4
C331 AP60 4p blk, yel & red 10 6

Issued to publicize the 10th Pan-American Highway Congress, Montevideo.

Lions Emblem and Map of South America AP61

1967, Dec. 29
C332 AP61 5p pur, yel & emer 12 8

50th anniversary of Lions International.

Boy Scout AP62

1968, Jan. 24 Lithographed
C333 AP62 9p sep & brick red 22 12

Issued in memory of Robert Baden-Powell, founder of the Boy Scout organization.

Sun, U.N. Emblem and Transportation Means AP63

1968, Feb. 29 *Perf. 12* Wmk. 332
C334 AP63 10p gray, yel, lt & dk bl 22 12

Issued for International Tourist Year.

Octopus AP64

Marine Fauna: 20p, Silversides. 25p, Characin. 30p, Catfish (vert.). 50p, Squid (vert.).

1968 *Perf. 12* Wmk. 332
C335	AP64	15p lt grn, bl & blk	27	17
C336	AP64	20p brn, grn & bl	32	22
C337	AP64	25p multi	40	27
C338	AP64	30p bl, grn & blk	50	32
C339	AP64	50p dp org, grn & dk bl	75	50
		Nos. C335-C339 (5)	2.24	1.48

Issue dates, 30p, 50p, Oct. 10; 15p, 20p, 25p, Nov. 5.

Navy Type of Regular Issue
Designs: 4p, Naval Air Force. 6p, Naval arms. 10p, Signal flags (vert.). 20p, Corsair (chartered by General Artigas).

1968, Nov. 12 Lithographed
C340	A226	4p bl, blk & red	8	5
C341	A226	6p multi	10	5
C342	A226	10p lt ultra, red & yel	22	12
C343	A226	20p ultra & blk	38	18

Sesquicentennial of the National Navy.

Rowing AP65

Designs: 50p, Running. 100p, Soccer.

1969, Feb. 11 *Perf. 12* Wmk. 332
C344	AP65	30p blk, tan & bl	50	32
C345	AP65	50p blk, tan & bl	85	55
C346	AP65	100p blk, tan & brt yel grn	1.40	90

Issued to commemorate the 19th Olympic Games, Mexico City, Oct. 12-27, 1968.

Bicycling Type of Regular Issue.
Design: 20p, Bicyclist and globe (vert.).

1969, Mar. 21 *Perf. 12* Wmk. 332
C347 A229 20p bl, pur & yel 40 22

1968 World Bicycle Championships.

"EFIMEX 68" and Globe AP66

1969, Apr. 10 *Perf. 12* Wmk. 332
C348 AP66 20p dk grn, red & bl 40 22

Issued to commemorate EFIMEX '68, International Philatelic Exhibition, Mexico City, Nov. 1-9, 1968.

Souvenir Sheet.
No. C318 Overprinted with Names of Participating Countries, Emblem, Bars, etc. and "CAMPEONATO MUNDIAL DE VOLEIBOL".

C349 AP56 10p org, brt grn & blk 27 27

Issued to commemorate the World Volleyball Championships, Montevideo, Apr. 1969.

Book, Quill and Emblem AP67   Automobile Club Emblem AP68

1969, Sept. 16 Litho. *Perf 12*
C350 AP67 30p grn, org & blk 60 35

10th Congress of Latin American Notaries.

1969, Oct. 7 *Perf. 12* Wmk. 332
C351 AP68 10p ultra & red 22 10

Issued to commemorate the 50th anniversary (in 1968) of the Uruguayan Automobile Club.

ILO Emblem AP69

1969, Oct. 29 Litho. *Perf. 12*
C352 AP69 30p dk bl & grn blk 50 30

Issued to commemorate the 50th anniversary of the International Labor Organization.

Exhibition Emblem AP70

1969, Nov. 15 *Perf. 12* Wmk. 332
C353 AP70 20p ultra, yel & grn 35 15

Issued to publicize the ABUEXPO 69 Philatelic Exhibition, San Pablo, Brazil, Nov. 15-23.

The only foreign revenue stamps listed in this Catalogue are those authorized for prepayment of postage.

URUGUAY

Rotary Emblem and Hemispheres
AP71

1969, Dec. 6   Perf. 12
C354 AP71 20p ultra, bl & bis   45   15

Issued to commemorate the South American Regional Rotary Conference and the 50th anniversary of the Montevideo Rotary Club.

Dr. Luis Morquio
AP72

1969, Dec. 22   Litho.   Wmk. 332
C355 AP72 20p org red & brn   32   15

Issued to commemorate the centenary of the birth of Dr. Luis Morquio, pediatrician.

No. C322 Surcharged
"FELIZ AÑO 1970 / 6.00 / PESOS"

1969, Dec. 24
C356 AP58 6p on 8p bis brn & brn   12   6

Issued for New Year 1970.

Mahatma Gandhi and UNESCO Emblem
AP73

1970, Jan. 26   Perf. 12   Wmk. 332
C357 AP73 100p lt bl & brn   1.40   80

Issued to commemorate the centenary of the birth of Mohandas K. Gandhi (1869–1948), leader in India's fight for independence.

Evaristo C. Ciganda—AP74   Giuseppe Garibaldi—AP75

1970, Mar. 10   Lithographed
C358 AP74 6p brt grn & brn   12   6

Issued to commemorate the centenary of the birth of Evaristo C. Ciganda, author of the first law for teachers' pensions.

1970, Apr. 7   Perf. 12   Unwmk.
C359 AP75 20p rose car & pink   17   10

Issued to commemorate the centenary of Garibaldi's command of foreign legionnaires in the Uruguayan Civil War.

Fur Seal
AP76

Designs: 20p, Rhea (vert.). 30p, Common tegu (lizard). 50p, Capybara. 100p, Mulita armadillo. 150p, Puma. 200p, Nutria.

1970–71   Perf. 12   Wmk. 332
C361	AP76	20p pur, emer & blk	45	22
C362	AP76	30p emer, yel & blk	55	32
C363	AP76	50p dl yel & brn	90	50
C365	AP76	100p org, sep & blk	1.40	80
C366	AP76	150p emer & brn	2.25	1.20
C367	AP76	200p brt rose, brn & blk ('71)	2.65	1.75
C368	AP76	250p gray, bl & blk	3.50	2.25
		Nos. C361-C368 (7)	11.70	7.04

Soccer and Mexican Flag
AP77

1970, June 2   Litho.   Perf. 12
C369 AP77 50p multi   80   45

Issued to commemorate the 9th World Soccer Championships for the Jules Rimet Cup, Mexico City, May 30–June 21.

"U.N." and Laurel
AP78

1970, June 26   Perf. 12   Wmk. 332
C370 AP78 32p dk bl & gold   45   22

25th anniversary of the United Nations.

Eisenhower and U.S. Flag—AP79

1970, July 14   Lithographed
C371 AP79 30p gray, vio bl & red   40   18

Issued in memory of Gen. Dwight David Eisenhower, 34th President of U.S. (1890–1969).

Neil A. Armstrong Stepping onto Moon—AP80

1970, July 21
C372 AP80 200p multi   2.65   1.35

Issued to commemorate the first anniversary of man's first landing on the moon.

Flag of the "Immortals"
AP81

1970, Aug. 24   Perf. 12   Wmk. 332
C373 AP81 500p bl, blk & red   6.25   6.25

The 145th anniversary of the arrival of the 33 "Immortals," the patriots, who started the revolution for independence.

Congress Emblem with Map of South America—AP82

1970, Sept. 16   Perf. 12   Unwmkd.
C374 AP82 30p bl, dk bl & yel   40   18

Issued to publicize the 5th Pan-American Congress of Rheumatology, Punta del Este.

Souvenir Sheet

Types of First Air Post Issue—AP83

1970, Oct. 1   Perf. 12½   Wmk. 332
C375 AP83 Sheet of 3   2.25   2.25
   a. 25p brn (Bl)   70   70
   b. 25p brn (R)   70   70
   c. 25p brn (G)   70   70

Issued for Stamp Day. No. C375 contains 3 stamps similar to Nos. C1–C3, but with denominations in pesos. Dark and light blue margin with map and coat of arms of Uruguay and early plane. Size: 101x70½mm.

Flags of ALALC Countries
AP84

1970, Nov. 23   Litho.   Perf. 12
C376 AP84 22p multi   40   18

For the Latin-American Association for Free Trade (Asociación Latinoamericana de Libre Comercio).

Yellow Fever, by J. M. Blanes
AP85

1971, June 8   Perf. 12   Wmk. 332
C377 AP85 50p blk, dk red brn & yel   80   45

70th anniversary of the death of Juan Manuel Blanes (1830–1901), painter.

Racial Equality, U.N. Emblem
AP86

1971, June 28   Lithographed
C378 AP86 27p blk, pink & bis   50   25

International Year Against Racial Discrimination.

Congress Emblem with Maps of Americas
AP87

1971, July 6   Perf. 12   Wmk. 332
C379 AP87 58p dl grn, blk & org   85   55

12th Pan-American Congress of Gastroenterology, Punta del Este, Dec. 5–10, 1971.

Committee Emblem
AP88

1971, Nov. 29
C380 AP88 30p bl, blk & yel   50   35

Inter-governmental Committee for European Migration.

Llama and Mountains   Munich Olympic Games Emblem
AP89   AP90

1971, Dec. 30
C381 AP89 37p multi   90   40

EXFILIMA '71, Third Inter-American Philatelic Exposition, Lima, Peru, Nov. 6–14.

1972, Feb. 1   Perf. 11½x12

Designs (Munich '72 Emblem and): 100p, Torchbearer. 500p, Discobolus.

C382	AP90	50p blk, red & org	27	15
C383	AP90	100p multi	60	45
C384	AP90	500p multi	3.00	2.00

20th Olympic Games, Munich, Aug. 26–Sept. 11.

Retort and WHO Emblem   Ship with Flags Forming Sails
AP91   AP92

URUGUAY

1972, Feb. 22   *Perf. 12*
C385 AP91   27p multi   18   12
50th anniversary of the discovery of insulin by Frederick G. Banting and Charles H. Best.

1972, Mar. 6   *Wmk. 332*
C386 AP92   37p multi   30   20
Stamp Day of the Americas.

1924 and 1928 Gold Medals, Soccer
AP93

Design: 300p, Olympic flag, Motion and Munich emblems (vert.).

1972, June 12   *Litho.*   *Perf. 12*
C387 AP93   100p bl & multi   60   45
C388 AP93   300p multi   1.75   1.10
20th Olympic Games, Munich, Aug. 26–Sept. 11.

Cross
AP94

1972, Aug. 10
C389 AP94   37p vio & gold   20   12
In memory of Dan A. Mitrione (1920–70), slain U.S. official.

Interlocking Squares and U.N. Emblem
AP95

1972, Aug. 16
C390 AP95   30p gray & multi   18   12
3rd United Nations Conference on Trade and Development (UNCTAD III), Santiago, Chile, Apr.–May 1972.

Brazil's "Bull's-eye," 1843
AP96

Perf. 12
1972, Aug. 26   *Litho.*   *Wmk. 332*
C391 AP96   50p grn, yel & bl   30   15
4th Inter-American Philatelic Exhibition, EXFILBRA, Rio de Janeiro, Aug. 26–Sept. 2.

Map of South America, Compass Rose
AP97

1972, Sept. 28
C392 AP97   37p multi   20   12
Uruguay's support for extending territorial sovereignty 200 miles into the sea.

Adoration of the Kings and Shepherds, by Rafael Perez Barradas—**AP98**

1972, Oct. 12
C393 AP98   20p lem & multi   27   20
Christmas 1972 and first biennial exhibition of Uruguayan painting, 1970. Setenant with label inscribed with name of painter and painting.

WPY Emblem
AP99

Perf. 12
1974, Aug. 20   *Litho.*   *Wmk. 332*
C394 AP90   500p gray & red   1.40   1.00
World Population Year 1974.

Soccer, Olympics and UPU Emblems
AP100

1974, Aug. 30
C395 AP100   200p grn & multi   60   35
C396 AP100   300p org & multi   80   60
Centenary of Universal Postal Union.

Mexico No. O1 and Mexican Coat of Arms
AP101

Perf. 12
1974, Oct. 15   *Litho.*   *Wmk. 332*
C399 AP101   200p multi   27   15
EXFILMEX '74 5th Inter-American Philatelic Exhibition, Mexico City, Oct. 26–Nov. 3.

Christmas Type of 1974
Design: 240p, Kings following star. 2500p, Virgin and Child.

1974
C400 A315   240p multi   27   20

Miniature Sheet
C401 A315   2500p multi   4.50   4.50
Christmas 1974. No. C401 contains one stamp; dark green margin with blue stars. Size: 100x79mm.
Issue dates: 240p. Dec. 27; 2500p, Dec. 31.

Spain No. 1, Colors of Spain and Uruguay—**AP102**

1975, Mar. 4
C402 AP102   400p multi   50   30
España 75, International Philatelic Exhibition, Madrid, Apr. 4–13.

Souvenir Sheet

Nos. C253, 893 and C402—**AP103**

Perf. 12
1975, Apr. 4   *Litho.*   *Wmk. 332*
C403 AP103   Sheet of 3, multi   6.00   6.00
  a. 1000p No. C253   1.75   1.75
  b. 1000p No. 893   1.75   1.75
  c. 1000p No. C402   1.75   1.75
España 75 International Philatelic Exhibition, Madrid, Apr. 4–13. No. C403 has gray margin with black inscription and control number. Size: 103x88½mm.

Floor Design for Capitol, Rome
AP104

1975, Aug. 15
C404 AP104   1p multi   1.25   75
500th birth anniversary of Michelangelo Buonarroti (1475–1564), Italian sculptor, painter and architect.

Sun, Uruguay No. C59 and other Stamps—**AP108**

Perf. 12
1975, Oct. 13   *Litho.*   *Wmk. 332*
C411 AP108   1p blk, gray & yel   1.75   1.00
Uruguayan Stamp Day.

Montreal Olympic Emblem and Argentina '78
AP109

Flags of U.S. and Uruguay
AP110

UPU and UPAE Emblems
AP111

Perf. 11½
1975, Oct. 14   *Litho.*   *Wmk. 332*
C412 AP109   1p multi   1.25   75
C413 AP110   1p multi   1.25   75
C414 AP111   1p multi   1.25   75
  a. Souvenir sheet of 3   17.50
EXPILMO '75 and ESPAMER '75 Stamp Exhibitions, Montevideo, Oct. 10–19. No. C414a contains 3 stamps similar to Nos. C412–C414, 2p each. Blue margin with multicolored emblems and flags, black control number. Size: 102x76mm.

Ocelot
AP112

Design: No. C416, Orchid (oncidium bifolium).

Perf. 12
1976, Jan.   *Litho.*   *Wmk. 332*
C415 AP112   50c vio bl & multi   50   30
C416 AP112   50c emer & multi   50   30

URUGUAY

AIR POST SEMI-POSTAL STAMPS
Type of Semi-Postal Stamps, 1959
Lithographed.
1959, Dec. 29   Perf. 11½   Wmk. 327
CB1	SP2	38c + 10c brn & org	30	30
CB2	SP2	60c + 10c gray grn & org	40	40

Issued for national recovery.

SPECIAL DELIVERY STAMPS.
No. 242
Overprinted **MENSAJERIAS**
1921, Aug.   Perf. 11½   Unwmkd.
E1	A97	2c fawn	75	20
a.		Double ovpt.	4.00	

Caduceus
SD1
Imprint: "IMP. NACIONAL."
Lithographed.
Wmkd.
REPUBLICA O. DEL URUGUAY.
(188)

1922, Dec. 2   Size: 21x27mm
E2	SD1	2c lt red	50	10

1924. Oct. 1
E3	SD1	2c pale ultra	50	10

1928   Perf. 11.   Unwmkd.
E4	SD1	2c lt bl	60	10

Imprint: "IMPRA. NACIONAL."
Size: 16½x19½mm.
1928-36   Wmk. 188
E5	SD1	2c blk, grn	30	10

Unwmkd.
E6	SD1	2c bl grn ('29)	30	10

Perf. 11½, 12½.
E7	SD1	2c bl ('36)	25	10

1944, Oct. 23   Perf. 12½
E8	SD1	2c sal pink	25	10

1947, Nov. 19
E9	SD1	2c red brn	20	10

No. E9 Surcharged with New Value.
1957, Oct. 30
E10	SD1	5c on 2c red brn	20	10

LATE FEE STAMPS.

Galleon and Modern Steamship
LF1
Wmkd. Crossed Keys in Sheet.
1936, May 18   Litho.   Perf. 11
I1	LF1	3c green	15	10
I2	LF1	5c violet	20	15
I3	LF1	6c bl grn	20	15
I4	LF1	7c brown	30	15
I5	LF1	8c carmine	60	40
I6	LF1	12c dp grn	90	75
		Nos. I1-I6 (6)	2.35	1.70

POSTAGE DUE STAMPS.

D1
Engraved.
Size: 21¼x18½mm.
1902   Perf. 14 to 15.   Unwmkd.
J1	D1	1c bl grn	50	25
J2	D1	2c carmine	60	25
J3	D1	4c gray vio	75	25
J4	D1	10c dk bl	1.25	50
J5	D1	20c ocher	2.00	1.00
		Nos. J1-J5 (5)	5.10	2.25

Surcharged **PROVISORIO**
in Red **UN cent'mo.**

1904
J6	D1	1c on 10c dk bl	1.00	1.00
a.		Inverted surcharge	8.00	8.00

1913-15   Lithographed.   Perf. 11½.
Size: 22½x20mm.
J7	D1	1c lt grn	35	20
J8	D1	2c rose red	35	25
J9	D1	4c dl vio	50	25
J10	D1	6c dp brn	60	40

Size: 21¼x19mm
J11	D1	10c dp bl	60	40
		Nos. J7-J11 (5)	2.40	1.50

Imprint: "Imprenta Nacional."
1922   Size: 20x17mm.
J12	D1	1c bl grn	35	20
J13	D1	2c red	35	20
J14	D1	3c red brn	50	50
J15	D1	4c brn vio	35	30
J16	D1	5c blue	60	40
J17	D1	10c gray grn	60	40
		Nos. J12-J17 (6)	2.75	2.00

Wmkd.
REPUBLICA O. DEL URUGUAY.
(188)
1926-27   Size: 20x17mm.   Perf. 11.
J18	D1	1c bl grn ('27)	25	25
J19	D1	3c red brn ('27)	50	35
J20	D1	5c sl bl	50	35
J21	D1	6c lt brn	60	50

1929   Perf. 10½, 11.   Unwmkd.
J22	D1	1c bl grn	25	15
J23	D1	10c gray grn	40	20

Figure of Value Redrawn
(Flat on sides).
1932   Wmk. 188
J24	D1	6c yel brn	60	40

Imprint:
"Casa A. Barreiro Ramos S. A."
Lithographed.
1935   Perf. 12½   Unwmkd.
Size: 20x17mm.
J25	D1	4c violet	50	30
J26	D1	5c rose	50	30

Type of 1935.
Imprint: "Imprenta Nacional"
at right.
1938
J27	D1	1c bl grn	10	5
J28	D1	2c red brn	10	5
J29	D1	3c dp pink	15	10
J30	D1	4c lt vio	15	10
J31	D1	5c blue	15	10
J32	D1	8c rose	25	10
		Nos. J27-J32 (6)	90	50

OFFICIAL STAMPS.
Regular Issues
Handstamped
in Black,
Red or Blue

OFICIAL *a*

Many double and inverted impressions exist of the handstamped overprints on Nos. O1–O83. Prices are the same as for normal stamps or slightly more.

On Stamps of 1877-79.
1880-82   Rouletted 8.   Unwmkd.
O1	A9	1c red brn	2.50	2.25
O2	A10	5c green	75	60
O3	A11	20c bister	2.00	1.75
O4	A11	50c black	14.00	12.00
O5	A12	1p blue	14.00	12.00
		Nos. O1-O5 (5)	33.25	28.60

On No. 44.
Rouletted 6
O6	A9	1c brn ('81)	1.75	1.50

On Nos. 43-43A.
Rouletted 8.
O7	A11	50c blk (R)	14.00	12.00
O8	A12	1p bl (R)	15.00	14.00

On No. 45.
Perf. 12½.
O9	A13	7c bl (R) ('81)	1.75	1.50

On No. 41.
Rouletted 8.
O10	A11	10c ver (Bl)	1.75	1.50

On No. 37a.
Perf. 13½.
O11	A8b	15c yel (Bl)	3.50	3.00

On Nos. 46-47.
1883   Perf. 12½.
O12	A14	1c green	1.75	1.50
O13	A14a	2c rose	2.25	2.00

On Nos. 50-51.
Perf. 12½, 12 x 12½, 13.
O14	A17	5c bl (R)	2.25	2.00
a.		Imperf., pair	6.00	
O15	A18	10c brn (Bl)	4.00	3.50
a.		Imperf., pair	9.00	

No. 48
Handstamped

1884   Perf. 12½.
O16	A15	1c green	30.00	20.00

Overprinted Type "a" in Black.
On Nos. 48-49.
1884   Perf. 12, 12 x 12½, 13.
O17	A15	1c green	20.00	17.50
O18	A16	2c red	10.00	9.00

On Nos. 53-56.
Rouletted 8.
O19	A11	1c on 10c ver	1.50	1.50
a.		Small "1" (#53a)	10.00	

Perf. 12½
O20	A14a	2c rose	4.00	4.00
O21	A22	5c ultra	4.00	4.00
O22	A23	5c blue	2.50	1.75

On Stamps of 1884-88.
1884-89   Rouletted 8.
O23	A24	1c gray	5.00	4.00
O24	A24	1c gray ('88)	1.25	1.00
O25	A24	1c ol grn	1.50	1.25
O26	A24a	2c vermilion	60	60
O27	A24a	2c rose ('88)	1.00	80
O28	A24b	5c sl bl	1.25	1.00
O29	A24b	5c sl bl, bl	2.75	2.25
O30	A24b	5c vio ('88)	3.50	3.00
O31	A24b	5c lt bl ('89)	2.50	2.00
O32	A25	7c dk brn	2.00	1.50
O33	A25	7c org ('89)	2.00	1.50
O34	A26	10c ol brn	1.00	85
O35	A30	10c vio ('89)	6.00	5.00
O36	A27	20c red vio	2.00	1.50
O37	A27	20c bis brn ('89)	5.00	4.00
O38	A28	25c gray vio	2.00	1.50
O39	A28	25c ver ('89)	5.00	4.00
		Nos. O23-O39 (17)	44.35	35.75

The OFICIAL handstamp, type "a," was also applied to No. 73, the 5c violet with "Provisorio" overprint, but it was not regularly issued.

On No. 71.
1887   Rouletted 9.
O40	A29	10c lilac		5.00

No. O40 was not regularly issued.

On Stamps of 1889–1899.
Perf. 12½ to 15 and Compound
1890-1900
O41	A32	1c green	35	30
O43	A32	1c bl ('95)	1.50	1.25
O44	A33	2c rose	35	30
O45	A33	2c red brn ('95)	1.75	1.50
O46	A33	2c org ('00)	90	60
O47	A34	5c dp bl	1.50	2.00
O48	A34	5c rose ('95)	2.50	1.75
O49	A35	7c bis brn	1.25	1.00
O50	A35	7c grn ('95)	35.00	
O51	A36	10c bl grn	1.25	1.00
O52	A36	10c org ('95)	35.00	
O53	A37	20c orange	1.25	1.00
O54	A37	20c brn ('95)	35.00	
O55	A38	25c red brn	1.25	1.00
O56	A38	25c ver ('95)	70.00	
O57	A39	50c lt bl	4.00	3.00
O58	A39	50c lil ('95)	4.00	3.00
O59	A40	1p lilac	6.00	4.00
O60	A40	1p lt bl ('95)	50.00	

Nos. O50, O52, O54, O56 and O60 were not regularly issued.

On No. 99.
1891   Rouletted 8
O61	A24b	5c violet	2.00	1.50
a.		"1391"	12.00	

On Stamps of 1895-99.
Perf. 12½ to 15 and Compound
1895-1900
O62	A51	1c bister	30	25
O63	A51	1c sl bl ('97)	60	50
O64	A52	2c blue	30	25
O65	A52	2c cl ('97)	90	75
O66	A53	5c red	40	30
O67	A53	5c grn ('97)	90	80
O68	A53	5c grnsh bl ('00)	1.25	1.00
a.		5c bl	1.25	90
O69	A54	7c dp grn	60	40
O70	A55	10c brown	60	40
O71	A56	20c grn & blk	85	60
O72	A56	20c cl & blk ('97)	2.50	2.00
O73	A57	25c red brn & blk	85	60
O74	A57	25c pink & bl ('97)	2.50	2.00
O75	A58	50c bl & blk	1.25	1.00
O76	A58	50c grn & brn ('97)	3.00	2.25
O77	A59	1p org brn & blk	5.00	3.00
O78	A59	1p yel brn & bl ('97)	7.00	5.00
a.		Inverted overprint		
		Nos. O62-O78 (17)	28.80	21.10

On Nos. 130-132.
1897, Sept.
O79	A62	1c brn vio & blk	1.25	1.00
O80	A63	5c pale bl & blk	1.50	1.25
O81	A64	10c lake & blk	1.75	1.50

On Nos. 136-137.
Perf. 12½ to 15 and Compound
1897-1900
O82	A68	10c red	3.00	2.50
O83	A68	10c red lil ('00)	2.00	1.75

URUGUAY

Regular Issue of 1900-01 Overprinted

OFICIAL

1901 — Perf. 14 to 16.

O84	A72	1c yel grn	35	15
O85	A75	2c vermilion	35	15
O86	A73	5c dl bl	35	20
O87	A76	7c brn org	50	40
O88	A74	10c gray vio	60	50
O89	A37	20c lt bl	5.00	4.50
O90	A38	25c bis brn	1.00	1.00
O91	A40	1p dp grn	7.00	7.00
a.		Inverted ovpt.	12.00	12.00
		Nos. O84-O91 (8)	15.15	13.90

Most of the used official stamps of 1901–1928 have been punched with holes of various shapes, in addition to the postal cancellations.

Regular Issue of 1904-05 Overprinted

OFICIAL

1905 — Perf. 11½

O92	A79	1c green	35	30
O93	A80	2c org red	35	30
O94	A81	5c dp bl	35	30
O95	A82	10c dk vio	75	60
O96	A83	20c gray grn	2.00	1.50
a.		Inverted ovpt.		
O97	A84	25c ol bis	1.50	1.00
		Nos. O92-O97 (6)	5.30	4.00

Regular Issues of 1904-07 Overprinted

OFICIAL

1907, Mar.

O98	A79	1c green	30	25
O99	A86	5c dp bl	30	25
O100	A86	7c org brn	30	25
O101	A82	10c dk vio	30	25
O102	A83	20c gray grn	50	40
a.		Inverted ovpt.	5.00	
O103	A86	25c ol bis	60	50
O104	A86	50c rose	1.00	90
		Nos. O98-O104 (7)	3.30	2.80

Regular Issues of 1900-10 Overprinted

OFICIAL 1910

1910, July 15 — Perf. 14½ to 16

O105	A75	2c vermilion	7.50	5.00
O106	A73	5c sl grn	5.00	3.00
O107	A74	10c gray vio	2.50	1.50
O108	A37	20c grnsh bl	2.50	1.50
O109	A38	25c bis brn	3.00	3.00

Perf. 11½

O110	A86	50c rose	6.00	3.00
a.		Inverted ovpt.	20.00	17.50
		Nos. O105-O110 (6)	28.50	17.00

Peace
O1

1911, Feb. 18 — Lithographed

O111	O1	2c red brn	35	35
O112	O1	5c dk bl	35	30
O113	O1	8c slate	35	30
O114	O1	20c gray brn	50	40
O115	O1	23c claret	75	60
O116	O1	50c orange	1.25	1.00
O117	O1	1p red	3.00	1.50
		Nos. O111-O117 (7)	6.55	4.45

Regular Issue of 1912-15 Overprinted

Oficial

1915, Sept. 16

O118	A90	2c carmine	50	35
O119	A90	5c dk bl	50	35
O120	A90	8c ultra	50	35
O121	A90	20c dk brn	1.50	60
O122	A91	23c dk bl	1.50	60
O123	A91	50c orange	2.50	1.50
O124	A91	1p vermilion	5.00	2.00
		Nos. O118-O124 (7)	12.00	5.75

Regular Issue of 1919 Overprinted

Oficial

1919, Dec. 25

O125	A95	2c red & blk	50	20
a.		Inverted ovpt.	3.00	
O126	A95	5c ultra & blk	60	35
O127	A95	8c gray bl & lt brn	60	35
a.		Inverted ovpt.	2.50	
O128	A95	20c brn & blk	1.25	60
O129	A95	23c grn & brn	1.25	60
O130	A95	50c brn & bl	2.00	1.50
O131	A95	1p dl red & bl	5.00	2.00
a.		Double ovpt.	10.00	
		Nos. O125-O131 (7)	11.20	5.60

Regular Issue of 1923 Overprinted

OFICIAL

1924 — Perf. 12½ — Wmk. 189

O132	A100	2c violet	30	15
O133	A100	5c lt bl	30	15
O134	A100	12c dp bl	50	15
O135	A100	20c buff	60	30
O136	A100	36c bl grn	2.00	1.50
O137	A100	50c orange	4.00	3.00
O138	A100	1p pink	7.50	6.00
O139	A100	2p lt grn	12.50	10.00
		Nos. O132-O139 (8)	27.70	21.25

Same Overprint on Regular Issue of 1924.

1926-27 — Imperf. — Unwmkd.

O140	A100	2c rose lil	15	10
O141	A100	5c pale bl	20	20
O142	A100	8c pink ('27)	35	25
O143	A100	12c sl bl	40	30
O144	A100	20c brown	1.00	60
O145	A100	36c dl rose	1.75	1.25
		Nos. O140-O145 (6)	3.85	2.70

Regular Issue of 1924 Overprinted

OFICIAL

1928 — Perf. 12½

O146	A100	2c rose lil	2.25	1.25
O147	A100	8c pink	2.25	60
O148	A100	10c turq bl	3.00	60

Since 1928, instead of official stamps, Uruguay has used envelopes with "S. O." printed on them, and stamps of many issues which are punched with various designs such as star or crescent.

NEWSPAPER STAMPS.

No. 245 Surcharged

PRENSA 3 CENTESIMOS

1922, June 1 — Perf. 11½ — Unwmkd.

P1	A97	3c on 4c org	50	35
a.		Inverted surcharge	12.00	12.00
b.		Double surcharge	5.00	5.00

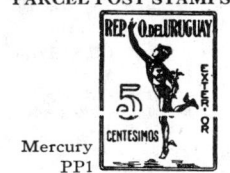

Nos. 235-237 Surcharged

1924, June 1 — Perf. 14½

P2	A96	3c on 2c car & blk	60	50
P3	A96	6c on 4c red org & bl	60	50
P4	A96	9c on 5c bl & brn	60	50

Nos. 288, 291, 293 Overprinted or Surcharged in Red:

PRENSA · **PRENSA 9 CENTESIMOS**
a · *b*

1926 — Imperf.

P5	A100	3c gray grn	40	35
a.		Double ovpt.	2.00	2.00
P6	A100	9c on 10c turq bl	60	50
a.		Double surch.	2.00	2.00
P7	A100	15c lt vio	75	60

PARCEL POST STAMPS.

Mercury
PP1

Perf. 11½

1922, Jan. 15 — Litho. — Unwmkd.

Size: 20x29½mm.
Imprint: "IMPRENTA NACIONAL."
Inscribed "Exterior."

Q1	PP1	5c grn, straw	25	15
Q2	PP1	10c grn, bl gray	50	15
Q3	PP1	20c grn, rose	2.50	75
Q4	PP1	30c grn, grn	2.25	25
Q5	PP1	50c grn, bl	4.00	40
Q6	PP1	1p grn, org	6.00	1.50
		Nos. Q1-Q6 (6)	15.50	3.20

Inscribed "Interior."

Q7	PP1	5c grn, straw	35	15
Q8	PP1	10c grn, bl gray	35	15
Q9	PP1	20c grn, rose	1.25	15
Q10	PP1	30c grn, grn	1.75	35
Q11	PP1	50c grn, bl	2.50	40
Q12	PP1	1p grn, org	7.00	1.25
		Nos. Q7-Q12 (6)	13.20	2.65

Imprint: " IMP. NACIONAL."
Inscribed " Exterior."

1926, Jan. 20 — Perf. 11½

Q13	PP1	20c grn, rose	3.00	90

Inscribed "Interior."

Perf. 11.

Q14	PP1	5c grn, yel	50	15
Q15	PP1	10c grn, bl gray	60	15
Q16	PP1	20c grn, rose	1.50	35
Q17	PP1	30c grn, bl grn	2.00	40
		Nos. Q13-Q17 (5)	7.60	1.95

Inscribed "Exterior."

1926

Q18	PP1	5c blk, straw	40	15
Q19	PP1	10c blk, bl gray	60	15
Q20	PP1	20c blk, rose	1.75	20

Inscribed "Interior."

Q21	PP1	5c blk, straw	40	15
Q22	PP1	10c blk, bl gray	50	15
Q23	PP1	20c blk, rose	1.00	20
Q24	PP1	30c blk, bl grn	1.75	35
		Nos. Q18-Q24 (7)	6.40	1.35

PP2 — Wmkd. REPUBLICA O. DEL URUGUAY. (188) — PP3

1927, Feb. 22 — Perf. 11, 11½

Q25	PP2	1c dp bl	10	5
Q26	PP2	2c lt grn	10	5
Q27	PP2	4c violet	20	5
Q28	PP2	5c red	25	5
Q29	PP2	10c dk brn	40	10
Q30	PP2	20c orange	60	30
		Nos. Q25-Q30 (6)	1.65	60

See also Nos. Q35-Q38, Q51-Q54.

1928, Nov. 20 — Perf. 11

Size: 15x20mm.

Q31	PP3	5c blk, straw	15	5
Q32	PP3	10c blk, gray bl	20	5
Q33	PP3	20c blk, rose	50	10
Q34	PP3	30c blk, grn	85	15

Type of 1927 Issue.

1929-30 — Perf. 11, 12½ — Unwmkd.

Q35	PP2	1c violet	10	5
Q36	PP2	1c ultra ('30)	10	5
Q37	PP2	2c bl grn ('30)	10	6
Q38	PP2	5c red ('30)	10	6

Nos. Q35-Q38, and possibly later issues, occasionally show parts of a papermaker's watermark.

PP4

1929, July 27 — Perf. 11 — Wmk. 188

Q39	PP4	10c orange	40	25
Q40	PP4	15c sl bl.	40	25
Q41	PP4	20c ol brn	65	40
Q42	PP4	25c rose red	75	50
Q43	PP4	50c dk gray	2.25	1.00
Q44	PP4	75c violet	10.00	8.00
Q45	PP4	1p gray grn	5.00	3.00
		Nos. Q39-Q45 (7)	19.45	13.40

Ship and Train — Numeral of Value
PP5 — PP6

1938-39 — Perf. 12½ — Unwmkd.

Q46	PP5	10c scarlet	30	10
Q47	PP5	20c dk bl	40	10
Q48	PP5	30c lt vio ('39)	75	10
Q49	PP5	50c green	1.00	15
Q50	PP5	1p brn org	1.50	20
		Nos. Q46-Q50 (5)	3.95	65

See also Nos. Q70-Q73, Q80, Q88-Q90, Q92-Q93, Q95.

Type of 1927 Redrawn.

1942-55 — Lithographed — Perf. 12½

Q51	PP2	1c vio ('55?)		
Q52	PP2	2c bl grn	15	6
Q54	PP2	5c lt red ('44)	20	6

The vertical and horizontal lines of the design have been strengthened, the "2" redrawn, etc. No. Q51 has oval "O" in CENTESIMO, 2¼mm. from frame line at right; No. Q35 has round "O" 1¾mm. from frame line.

1943, Apr. 28 — Engraved

Q55	PP6	1c dk car rose	8	5
Q56	PP6	2c grnsh blk	12	5

Parcel Post Stamps of 1929 Overprinted in Black

AÑO 1943

1943, Dec. 15 — Perf. 11 — Wmk. 188

Q57	PP4	10c orange	32	12
Q58	PP4	15c sl bl	32	27
Q59	PP4	20c ol brn	50	32
Q60	PP4	25c rose red	75	45
Q61	PP4	50c dk gray	1.50	75
Q62	PP4	75c violet	3.00	2.25
Q63	PP4	1p gray grn	4.00	3.00
		Nos. Q57-Q63 (7)	10.39	7.16

URUGUAY

Bank of the Republic PP7 — University PP8

Perf. 12½

1945, Sept. 5   Litho.   Unwmkd.
Q64 PP7   1c green   10   5
Q65 PP8   2c brt vio   10   5
See also Nos. Q77–Q79, Q84.

Custom House PP9 — Coat of Arms PP10

1946, Dec. 11   Perf. 11½
Q66 PP9   5c yel brn & bl   20   6

Red Overprint.
1946, Dec. 27   Perf. 12½
Q67 PP10 1p lt bl   1.10 27

Mail Coach PP11 — PP12

1946, Dec. 23
Q68 PP11 5p red & ol brn 11.00 4.00

Black Overprint.
1947
Q69 PP12 2c dl vio brn   6   5

Type of 1938.
1947-52   Perf. 12½   Unwmkd.
Q70 PP5   5c brn org ('52)   8   5
Q71 PP5   10c violet   15   5
Q72 PP5   20c vermilion   22   8
Q73 PP5   30c blue   32 10

1948-49   Types of 1946-47.
Black Overprint.
Q74 PP12 1c rose lil ('49) 5   5
Q75 PP12 5c ultra   6   5
Q76 PP10 5p rose car   5.00 2.00

1950   Types of 1945.
Q77 PP8   1c vermilion   5   5
Q78 PP7   2c chlky bl   6   5

1952   Perf. 11
Q79 PP7   10c bl grn   15   8

Type of 1938-39.
1954   Perf. 12½.
Q80 PP5   20c carmine   22 10

Custom House PP13

Design: 1p, State Railroad Administration Building.

Lithographed
1955   Perf. 12½   Unwmkd.
Q81 PP13 5c brown   8   5
Q82 PP13 1p lt ultra   70 45

Types of 1945 and 1955.
Design: 20c, Solis Theater.
1956-57   Perf. 11
Q83 PP13 5c gray ('57)   50 10
Q84 PP7   10c lt ol grn   10   8
Q85 PP13 20c yellow   15 10
Q86 PP13 20c lt red brn ('57) 22 10

No. Q83 Surcharged with New Value in Red.
1957
Q87 PP13 30c on 5c gray   25   8

Type of 1938-39
1957-60   Perf. 11   Wmk. 327
Q88 PP5   20c lt bl ('59)   12   6
Unwmkd.
Q89 PP5   30c red lil   12 10
Perf. 12½
Q90 PP5   1p dk bl ('60)   27 17

Nos. Q88 and Q93 are in slightly larger format—17¼x21mm. instead of 16x19½ mm.

National Printing Works PP14

1960, Mar. 23 Perf. 11 Wmk. 327
Q91 PP14 30c yel grn   15   6

Type of 1938-39
1962-63   Perf. 11   Wmk. 332
Q92 PP5   50c sl grn   15 10
Perf. 10½
Q93 PP5   1p bl grn ('63)   25 15

No. C158 Surcharged

 **$ 5.00**

ENCOMIENDAS
1965   Perf. 11   Unwmkd.
Q94 AP12 5p on 84c org   40 25
For use on regular and air post parcels.

Types of 1938-55
Design: 1p, State Railroad Administration Building.
1966   Lithographed   Perf. 10½
Q95 PP5   10c bl grn   5   5
Wmk. 327
Q96 PP13 1p brown   10   6

No. C184 Surcharged in Red

ENCOMIENDAS 1.00 PESO

1966   Perf. 11   Unwmkd.
Q97 AP21 1p on 38c blk   10   6

Plane and Bus PP15

Design: 20p, Plane facing left and bus; "Encomiendas" on top.
Lithographed
1969, July 8   Perf. 12   Wmk. 332
Q98 PP15 10p blk, crim & bl grn 18 12
Q99 PP15 20p bl, blk & yel   38 27

No. B7 Surcharged

Encomiendas $0.60

1971, Feb. 3   Perf. 11½   Wmk. 327
Q100 SP2   60c on 1p+10c pur & org 1.20 35

No. 761 Surcharged in Red

IMPUESTOS A ENCOMIENDAS $0.60

1971, Nov. 12   Perf. 12   Wmk. 332
Q101 A226 60c on 6p lt grn & blk   5   5

Nos. 770–771 Surcharged

$1 IMPUESTO A ENCOMIENDAS

1972, Nov. 6   Litho.   Perf. 12
Q102 A233 1p on 6p multi (#770) 10 5
Q103 A233 1p on 6p multi (#771) 10 5

Nos. Q102–Q103 printed se-tenant with label between each pair of stamps.

Parcels and Arrows PP16

Old Mail Truck PP17

Designs: Early means of mail transport.
Lithographed
1974   Perf. 12   Wmk. 332
Multicolored
Q104 PP16 75p shown   20   12
Q105 PP17 100p shown   35   25
Q106 PP17 150p Steam engine 45   45
Q107 PP17 300p Side-wheeler 85   70
Q108 PP17 500p Plane   1.50 1.00
Nos. Q104-Q108 (5)   3.35 2.52

Issue dates: 75p, Feb. 13. Others, Mar. 6.

VATICAN CITY
(văt′ĭ-kăn sĭt′ĭ)

LOCATION—In western Italy, directly outside the western boundary of Rome.
GOVT.— An independent state subject to certain political restrictions under a treaty with Italy.
AREA — 108.7 acres or about one-sixth square mile.
POP.—1,000 (est. 1976).

100 Centesimi = 1 Lira

Unused prices are for stamps that have been hinged.

Papal Arms Pope Pius XI
A1 A2

Engraved.
1929, Aug. 1   Perf. 14   Unwmkd.
Surface-Colored Paper.

1	A1	5c dk brn & pink	30	32
2	A1	10c dk grn & lt grn	45	40
3	A1	20c vio & lil	1.10	65
4	A1	25c dk bl & lt bl	1.50	75
5	A1	30c ind & yel	1.50	1.00
6	A1	50c ind & sal buff	1.50	1.00
7	A1	75c brn car & gray	2.25	1.50

Photogravure.
White Paper.

8	A2	80c car rose	1.00	65
9	A2	1.25 l dk bl	3.50	1.50
10	A2	2 l ol brn	8.00	3.50
11	A2	2.50 l red org	10.00	5.00
12	A2	5 l dk grn	14.00	17.50
13	A2	10 l ol blk	18.00	22.50
	Nos. 1-13, E1-E2 (15)		88.60	76.27

The stamps of Type A1 have, in this and subsequent issues, the words "POSTE VATICANE" in rows of colorless letters in the background.

No. 5
Surcharged in Red
1931, Oct. 1
| 14 | A1 | 25c on 30c ind & yel | 3.50 | 1.40 |

Arms of Pope Pius XI Vatican Palace and Obelisk
A5 A6

Vatican Gardens Wmk. 235
A7

Pope Pius XI—A8

St. Peter's Basilica—A9
Wmkd. Crossed Keys. (235)

1933, May 31   Engraved
19	A5	5c cop red	9	9
a.	Imperf., pair		225.00	325.00
20	A6	10c dk brn & blk	10	10
21	A6	12½c dp grn & blk	9	9
22	A6	20c org & blk		
a.	Vertical pair imperf. between and at bottom		175.00	175.00
23	A6	25c dk ol & blk	9	9
a.	Imperf. (pair)		125.00	185.00
24	A7	30c blk & dk brn	9	9
25	A7	50c vio & dk brn	9	9
26	A7	75c brn red & dk brn	10	10
27	A7	80c rose & dk brn	10	10
28	A8	1 l vio & blk	4.50	90
29	A8	1.25 l dk bl & blk	20.00	2.25
30	A8	2 l dk brn & blk	37.50	18.00
31	A8	2.75 l dk vio & blk	45.00	50.00
32	A9	5 l blk brn & dk grn	12	32
33	A9	10 l dk bl & dk grn	15	45
34	A9	20 l blk & dp grn	25	80
	Nos. 19-34, E3-E4 (18)		108.76	73.87

Stamps of 1929
Surcharged in Black   = 40 =
1934, June 16   Unwmkd.

35	A2	40c on 80c car rose	1.75	3.50
36	A2	1.30 l on 1.25 l dk bl	175.00	55.00
a.	Small figures "30" in "1.30"		2,000.	1,750.
37	A2	2.05 l on 2 l ol brn	225.00	12.00
a.	No comma btwn. 2 & 0		325.00	50.00
38	A2	2.55 l on 2.50 l red org	175.00	165.00
a.	No comma btwn. 2 & 5		200.00	225.00
39	A2	3.05 l on 5 l dk grn	525.00	400.00
40	A2	3.70 l on 10 l ol blk	500.00	575.00
a.	No comma btwn. 3 & 7		800.00	625.00
	Nos. 35-40 (6)		1,601.75	1,210.50

A second printing of Nos. 36–40 was made in 1937. The 2.55 l and 3.05 l of the first printing and 1.30 l of the second printing sell for more.
Forged surcharges of Nos. 35–40 are plentiful.

Tribonian Presenting Pandects to Justinian I Pope Gregory IX Promulgating Decretals
A10 A11

1935, Feb. 1   Photogravure
41	A10	5c red org	1.00	90
42	A10	10c purple	1.00	90
43	A10	25c green	8.00	5.50
44	A11	75c rose red	60.00	20.00
45	A11	80c dk brn	37.50	13.00
46	A11	1.25 l dk bl	85.00	13.00
	Nos. 41-46 (6)		192.50	53.30

Issued in commemoration of the International Juridical Congress, Rome, 1934.

Doves and Bell Allegory of Church and Bible
A12 A13

St. John Bosco St. Francis de Sales
A14 A15

1936, June 22
47	A12	5c bl grn	40	1.10
48	A13	10c black	40	45
49	A14	25c yel grn	38.50	6.75
50	A12	50c rose vio	40	90
51	A13	75c rose red	50.00	30.00
52	A14	80c org brn	70	1.75
53	A15	1.25 l dk bl	1.25	2.75
54	A15	5 l dk brn	80	2.75
	Nos. 47-54 (8)		92.45	46.45

Catholic Press Conference, 1936.

Crypt of St. Cecilia in Catacombs of St. Calixtus
A16

Basilica of Sts. Nereus and Achilleus in Catacombs of St. Domitilla—A17

1938, Oct. 12   Perf. 14
55	A16	5c bis brn	40	28
56	A16	10c dp org	60	50
57	A16	25c dp grn	60	50
58	A17	75c dp rose	7.00	10.00
59	A17	80c violet	35.00	22.50
60	A17	1.25 l blue	28.00	22.50
	Nos. 55-60 (6)		71.60	56.28

Issued in commemoration of the International Christian Archaeological Congress, at Rome, 1938.

Interregnum Issue.

Stamps of 1929
Overprinted in Black   SEDE VACANTE MCMXXXIX
1939, Feb. 20   Perf. 14
61	A1	5c dk brn & pink	55.00	6.75
62	A1	10c dk grn & lt grn	1.00	35
63	A1	20c vio & lil	1.00	35
64	A1	25c dk bl & lt bl	3.00	6.75
65	A1	30c ind & yel	1.10	70
a.	Pair, one without ovpt.		750.00	
66	A1	50c ind & sal buff	1.10	50
67	A1	75c brn car & gray	1.10	50
	Nos. 61-67 (7)		63.30	15.90

Coronation of Pope Pius XII
A18

1939, June 2   Photogravure
68	A18	25c green	2.25	75
69	A18	75c rose red	20	25
70	A18	80c violet	3.25	4.25
71	A18	1.25 l dp bl	20	25

Issued in commemoration of the coronation of Pope Pius XII, March 12, 1939.

Arms of Pope Pius XII
A19

Pope Pius XII
A20   A21

Wmkd. Crossed Keys. (235)
1940, Mar. 12   Engr.   Perf. 14
72	A19	5c dk car	8	8
73	A20	1 l pur & blk	38	35
74	A21	1.25 l sl bl & blk	22	20
a.	Imperf., pair		300.00	450.00
75	A20	2 l dk brn & blk	1.50	1.75
76	A21	2.75 l dk rose vio & blk	1.50	2.25
	Nos. 72-76 (5)		3.68	4.63

See also Nos. 91–98.

Picture of Jesus Inscribed "I have Compassion on the Multitude"
A22

VATICAN CITY

1942, Sept. 1   Photo.   Unwmkd.
77	A22	25c dk bl grn	8	5
78	A22	80c chnt brn	8	8
79	A22	1.25 l dp bl	15	30

See also Nos. 84–86, 99–101.

Consecration of
Archbishop
Pacelli by
Pope Benedict XV
A23

1942, Jan. 16
80	A23	25c myr grn & gray grn	8	8
81	A23	80c dk brn & yel brn	8	8
82	A23	1.25 l saph & vio bl	8	8
a.		Name and value panel omitted		
83	A23	5 l vio blk & gray blk	50	65

Issued to commemorate the 25th anniversary of the consecration of Msgr. Eugenio Pacelli (later Pope Pius XII) as Archbishop of Sardes.

Type of 1942
Inscribed MCMXLIII.
1944, Jan. 31
84	A22	25c dk bl grn	6	12
85	A22	80c chnt brn	6	8
86	A22	1.25 l dp bl	28	25

Raphael
Sanzio
A24

Designs: 80c, Antonio da Sangallo. 1.25 l, Carlo Maratti. 10 l, Antonio Canova.

Photogravure.
1944, Nov. 21   Perf. 14   Wmk. 235
87	A24	25c ol & grn	8	8
88	A24	80c cl & rose vio	15	18
a.		Dbl. impression of center	450.00	
89	A24	1.25 l bl vio & dp bl	15	20
a.		Imperf. (pair)	600.00	800.00
90	A24	10 l bis & ol brn	1.10	1.65

Issued to commemorate the 400th anniversary of the Pontifical Academy of the Virtuosi of the Pantheon.

Types of 1940.
1945, Mar. 5   Engraved   Unwmkd.
91	A19	5c gray	7	7
a.		Imperf., pair	160.00	
92	A19	30c brown	8	18
a.		Imperf. (pair)	120.00	
93	A19	50c dk grn	8	18
94	A21	1 l brn & blk	8	18
95	A21	1.50 l rose car & blk	8	18
a.		Imperf. (pair)	250.00	
96	A21	2.50 l dp ultra & blk	8	18
97	A20	5 l rose vio & blk	20	18
98	A20	20 l gray grn & blk	28	30
		Nos. 91-98, E5-E6 (10)	2.17	2.87

Nos. 91–96 exist in pairs imperf. between, some vertical, some horizontal. Price, each $125.

Pair imperf. vertically exist of 30c and 50c (price $60), and of 5 lire (price $90).

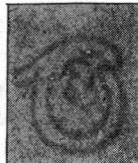

Wmk. 277

Type of 1942.
Inscribed MCMXLIV.
Wmkd. Winged Wheel. (277)
1945, Sept. 12   Photo.   Perf. 14
99	A22	1 l dk bl grn	8	8
100	A22	3 l dk car	8	8
a.		Jesus image omitted	80.00	80.00
101	A22	5 l dp ultra	20	35

Nos. 99–101 exist in pairs imperf. between, both horizontal and vertical. Price, each $100.

Pairs imperf. horizontally exist of 3 lire (price $30) and 5 lire (price $125).

Nos. 91 to 98
Surcharged with New Values and Bars
in Black or Blue.

Two types of 25c on 30c:
 I. Surcharge 16mm. wide.
 II. Surcharge 19mm. wide.

Two types of 1 l on 50c:
 I. Surcharge bars 5mm. wide.
 II. Bars 4mm. wide.

1946, Jan. 9   Perf. 14   Unwmkd.
102	A19	20c on 5c gray	10	18
103	A19	25c on 30c brn (I)	12	25
a.		Type II	25	25
b.		Inverted surch. (II)	300.00	300.00
104	A19	1 l on 50c dk grn (I)	12	25
a.		Type II	8.00	6.50
105	A21	1.50 l on 1 l brn & blk (Bl)	12	25
a.		Double surch.	150.00	
106	A21	3 l on 1.50 l rose car & blk	15	25
107	A21	5 l on 2.50 l dp ultra & blk	25	38
108	A20	10 l on 5 l rose vio & blk	35	65
109	A20	30 l on 20 l gray grn & blk	2.00	2.25
		Nos. 102-109, E7-E8 (10)	6.86	10.01

Nos. 102, 105–109 exist in horizontal pairs, imperf. between. Price, each $110.

Vertical pairs imperf. between exist of Nos. 102, 106–107 (price, each $150) and of No. 104a (price $225).

Nos. 102, 104–108 exist in pairs imperf. vertically or horizontally, or both. Price $40 to $60.

Nos. 102–108 exist in pairs, one without surcharge. Price, Nos. 102–105, each $150; Nos. 106–108, each $200.

St. Vigilio   St. Angela
Cathedral, Trent   Merici
A28   A29

Designs: 50c, St. Anthony Zaccaria. 75c, St. Ignatius of Loyola. 1 l, St. Cajetan Thiene. 1.50 l, St. John Fisher. 2 l, Christoforo Cardinal Madruzzi. 2.50 l, Reginald Cardinal Pole. 3 l, Marcello Cardinal Cervini. 4 l, Giovanni Cardinal del Monte. 5 l, Emperor Charles V. 10 l, Pope Paul III.

Perf. 14, 14x13½
1946, Feb. 21   Photo.   Unwmkd.
Centers in Dark Brown.
110	A28	5c ol bis	8	8
111	A29	25c purple	8	8
112	A29	50c brn org	8	8
113	A29	75c black	8	8
114	A29	1 l dk vio	8	8
115	A29	1.50 l red org	8	8
116	A29	2 l yel grn	8	8
117	A29	2.50 l dp bl	8	8
118	A29	3 l brt car	8	8
119	A29	4 l ocher	8	8
120	A29	5 l brt ultra	25	35
121	A29	10 l dp rose car	25	35
		Nos. 110-121, E9-E10 (14)	1.70	1.93

Issued to commemorate the 400th anniversary of the Council of Trent (1545–63).

Vertical pairs imperf. between exist of Nos. 110–111, 114, 116–117 (price, each $150); Nos. 113, 119 (price, each $100); Nos. 115, 118 (price, each $75).

Horizontal pairs imperf. between exist of No. 121 (price $150); Nos. 113, 117 (price $100).

Basilica of
St. Agnes
A40

Basilica of the
Holy Cross in Jerusalem
A41

Pope Pius XII—A42

Designs (Basilicas): 3 l, St. Clement. 5 l, St. Prassede. 8 l, St. Mary in Cosmedin. 6 l, St. Sebastian. 25 l, St. Lawrence. 35 l, St. Paul. 40 l, St. Mary Major.

Perf. 14, 14x13½, 13½x14
1949, Mar. 7   Photo.   Wmk. 235
122	A40	1 l dk brn	15	15
123	A40	3 l violet	15	15

124	A40	5 l dp org	22	15
a.		Perf. 14x13½	22.50	7.50
125	A40	8 l dp bl grn	15	15
126	A41	13 l dl grn	3.50	6.50
127	A41	16 l dk ol brn	35	30
a.		Perf. 14	50	45
128	A41	25 l car rose	6.00	1.00
129	A41	35 l red vio	21.00	16.00
a.		Perf. 13½x14	45.00	22.50
130	A41	40 l blue	30	22
a.		Perf. 14x13½	1.00	90

Engraved.
Perf. 14
131	A42	100 l sepia	3.25	5.25
		Nos. 122-131, E11-E12 (12)	65.32	50.62

Jesus   Cathedrals of
Giving St. Peter   St. Peter, St. Paul,
the Keys   St. John Lateran
to Heaven   and St. Mary Major
A43   A44

Pope Boniface VIII   Pope Pius XII
Proclaiming   in Ceremony
Holy Year   of Opening the
in 1300   Holy Door
A45   A46

Photogravure.
1949, Dec 21   Perf. 14   Wmk. 277
132	A43	5 l red brn & brn	6	6
133	A44	6 l ind & yel brn	6	6
134	A45	8 l ultra & dk grn	55	1.10
135	A46	10 l grn & sl	8	10
136	A43	20 l dk grn & red brn	1.40	60
137	A44	25 l sep & dp bl	80	80
138	A45	30 l grnsh blk & rose lil	2.50	1.50
139	A46	60 l blk brn & brn rose	1.80	3.50
		Nos. 132-139 (8)	7.25	7.72

Issued to commemorate the Holy Year, 1950.

Palatine Guard
and Statue of St. Peter
A47

1950, Sept. 12
140	A47	25 l sepia	10.00	13.00
141	A47	35 l dk grn	5.00	8.00
142	A47	55 l red brn	2.50	3.50

Centenary of the Palatine Guard.

VATICAN CITY

Pope Pius XII Making Proclamation
A48

Crowd at the Basilica of St. Peter
A49

1951, May 8   Unwmkd.
| 143 | A48 | 25 l chocolate | 3.75 | 2.00 |
| 144 | A49 | 55 l brt bl | 13.00 | 17.50 |

Issued to commemorate the proclamation of the Roman Catholic dogma of the Assumption of the Virgin Mary, November 1, 1950.

Pope Pius X
A50   A51

Perf. 14x13½

1951, June 3   Photo.   Wmk. 235

Background of Medallion in Gold.
145	A50	6 l purple	25	30
146	A50	10 l Prus grn	35	38
147	A51	60 l blue	11.00	11.00
148	A51	115 l brown	13.00	13.00

Council of Chalcedon
A52

Pope Leo I Remonstrating with Attila the Hun
A53

1951, Oct. 31   Engr.   Perf. 14x13½
149	A52	5 l dk gray grn	20	25
a.		Pair, imperf. horiz.	300.00	
150	A53	25 l red brn	1.80	2.50
a.		Horiz. pair, imperf. between	500.00	500.00
151	A52	35 l car rose	5.50	5.25
152	A53	60 l dp bl	20.00	17.50
153	A52	100 l dk brn	32.50	32.50
		Nos. 149-153 (5)	60.00	58.00

Issued to commemorate the 1500th anniversary of the Council of Chalcedon.

No. 126 Surcharged with New Value and Bars in Carmine.

1952, Mar. 15   Perf. 14
154	A41	12 l on 13 l dl grn	3.00	3.50
a.		Perf. 13½x14	3.00	3.50
b.		Pair, one without surch.	300.00	300.00

Roman States Stamp and Stagecoach
A54

1952, June 9   Engraved   Perf. 13
| 155 | A54 | 50 l sep & dp bl, cr | 8.00 | 8.50 |
| a. | | Souvenir sheet | 125.00 | 135.00 |

Issued to commemorate the centenary of the first stamp of the Papal States.

No. 155a measures 116x125mm. and contains four stamps similar to No. 155, with papal insignia and inscription in purple. Singles from the souvenir sheet differ slightly from No. 155. The colors are closer to black and blue, and the cream tone of the paper is visible on the back.

St. Maria Goretti   St. Peter
A55   A56

Perf. 13½x14

1953, Feb. 12   Photo.   Wmk. 235
| 156 | A55 | 15 l dp brn & vio | 6.00 | 4.75 |
| 157 | A55 | 35 l dp rose & brn | 4.00 | 4.75 |

Issued to commemorate the 50th anniversary of the martyrdom of St. Maria Goretti.

Perf. 13½x13, 14

1953, Apr. 23   Engraved

Designs: 5 l, Pius XII and Roman sepulcher. 10 l, St. Peter and Tomb of the Apostle. 12 l, Sylvester I and Constantine Basilica. 20 l, Julius II and Bramante's plans. 25 l, Paul III and the Apse. 35 l, Sixtus V and dome. 45 l, Paul V and facade. 60 l, Urban VIII and the canopy. 65 l, Alexander VII and colonnade. 100 l, Pius VI and the sacristy.
158	A56	3 l dk red brn & blk	5	5
159	A56	5 l sl & blk	5	5
160	A56	10 l dk grn & blk	5	5
161	A56	12 l chnt & blk	10	8
162	A56	20 l vio & blk	50	30
163	A56	25 l dk brn & blk	10	8
164	A56	35 l dk car & blk	10	8
165	A56	45 l ol brn & blk	60	70
166	A56	60 l dk bl & blk	15	18
167	A56	65 l car rose & blk	60	70
168	A56	100 l rose vio & blk	18	18
		Nos. 158-168, E13-E14 (13)	3.48	3.60

St. Clare of Assisi
A57

Photogravure

1953, Aug. 12   Perf. 13   Unwmkd.
| 169 | A57 | 25 l aqua, yel brn & vio brn | 4.00 | 1.65 |
| 170 | A57 | 35 l brn red, yel brn & vio brn | 17.50 | 18.50 |

Issued to commemorate the 700th anniversary of the death of St. Clare of Assisi.

Virgin Mary and St. Bernard
A58

1953, Nov. 10
| 171 | A58 | 20 l ol grn & dk vio brn | 1.10 | 2.25 |
| 172 | A58 | 60 l brt bl & ol grn | 12.00 | 11.00 |

Issued to commemorate the 800th anniversary of the death of St. Bernard of Clairvaux.

Peter Lombard Medal
A59

1953, Dec. 29
| 173 | A59 | 100 l lil rose, bl, dk grn & yel | 45.00 | 47.50 |

Issued to honor Peter Lombard, Bishop of Paris 1159.

Pope Pius XI and Vatican City
A60

1954, Feb. 12   Wmk. 235
| 174 | A60 | 25 l bl, red brn & cr | 3.00 | 3.00 |
| 175 | A60 | 60 l yel brn & dp bl | 4.50 | 5.00 |

Issued to commemorate the 25th anniversary of the signing of the Lateran Pacts.

Pope Pius IX—A61

Portraits: (At left)—6 l, 20 l, Pope Pius IX. (At right)—4 l, 12 l, 35 l, Pope Pius XII.

1954, May 26   Engraved   Perf. 13
176	A61	3 l violet	8	8
177	A61	4 l carmine	8	8
178	A61	6 l plum	8	8
179	A61	12 l bl grn	2.25	50
180	A61	20 l red brn	2.00	2.00
181	A61	35 l ultra	3.00	5.50
		Nos. 176-181 (6)	7.49	8.24

Issued to publicize the Marian Year, and to commemorate the centenary of the dogma of the Immaculate Conception.

St. Pius X
A62

1954, May 29   Photogravure

Colors (except background): Yellow and Plum
182	A62	10 l dk brn	25	35
183	A62	25 l violet	4.00	2.00
184	A62	35 l dk sl gray	4.75	8.00

Canonization of Pope Pius X, May 20, 1954.

Nos. 182-184 exist imperf. Price, each pair $800.

Basilica of St. Francis of Assisi
A63

1954, Oct. 1   Photo.   Perf. 14
| 185 | A63 | 20 l dk vio gray & cr | 4.00 | 2.75 |
| 186 | A63 | 35 l dk brn & cr | 2.40 | 3.75 |

Issued to commemorate the 200th anniversary of the consecration of the Basilica of St. Francis of Assisi.

St. Augustine—A64

1954, Nov. 13
| 187 | A64 | 35 l bl grn | 2.50 | 3.50 |
| 188 | A64 | 50 l redsh brn | 4.00 | 3.50 |

Issued to commemorate the 1600th anniversary of the birth of St. Augustine.

Madonna of the Gate of Dawn, Vilnius—A65

1954, Dec. 7
189	A65	20 l pink & multi	1.20	2.25
190	A65	35 l bl & multi	11.00	12.00
191	A65	60 l multi	15.00	13.00

Issued to mark the end of the Marian Year.

St. Boniface and Fulda Abbey
A66

1955, Apr. 28   Engraved   Perf. 13
192	A66	10 l grnsh gray	15	15
193	A66	35 l violet	1.25	90
a.		Imperf., pair	250.00	
194	A66	60 l brt bl grn	1.25	90

Issued to commemorate the 1200th anniversary of the death of St. Boniface.

VATICAN CITY

Pope Sixtus II and St. Lawrence
A67

Pope Nicholas V
A68

Photogravure
1955, June 27 Perf. 14 Wmk. 235
| 195 | A67 | 50 l carmine | 6.50 | 5.50 |
| 196 | A67 | 100 l dp bl | 3.25 | 5.50 |

Issued to commemorate the 5th centenary of the death of Fra Angelico (1387–1455), the painter. Design is from a Fra Angelico fresco.

1955, Nov. 28
197	A68	20 l grnsh bl & ol brn	50	55
198	A68	35 l rose car & ol brn	1.00	80
199	A68	60 l yel grn & ol brn	1.75	2.25

Issued to commemorate the 500th anniversary of the death of Pope Nicholas V.

St. Bartholomew and Church of Grottaferrata
A69

Capt. Gaspar Roust
A70

1955, Dec. 29
200	A69	10 l brn & gray	13	13
201	A69	25 l car rose & gray	1.00	1.00
202	A69	100 l dk grn & gray	3.25	3.75

900th anniversary of the death of St. Bartholomew, abbot of Grottaferrata.

1956, Apr. 27 Engraved Perf. 13
Designs: 6 l, 50 l, Guardsman. 10 l, 60 l, Two drummers.
203	A70	4 l dk car rose	8	6
204	A70	6 l dp org	8	6
205	A70	10 l dp ultra	8	6
206	A70	35 l brown	1.10	1.00
207	A70	50 l violet	1.75	1.60
208	A70	60 l bl grn	2.25	2.00
		Nos. 203-208 (6)	5.34	4.78

Issued to commemorate the 450th anniversary of the Swiss Papal Guard.

St. Rita of Cascia
A71

Pope Paul III Confirming Society of Jesus
A72

1956, May 19 Photogravure Perf. 14
209	A71	10 l gray grn	8	5
210	A71	25 l ol brn	1.00	1.25
211	A71	35 l ultra	70	80

Issued to commemorate the 500th anniversary of the death of St. Rita of Cascia.

1956, July 31 Engraved Perf. 13
| 212 | A72 | 35 l dk red brn | 65 | 90 |
| 213 | A72 | 60 l bl gray | 1.20 | 1.40 |

Issued to commemorate the 400th anniversary of the death of St. Ignatius of Loyola, founder of the Society of Jesus.

St. John of Capistrano
A73

1956, Oct. 30 Perf. 14
| 214 | A73 | 25 l sl blk & grn | 4.25 | 4.00 |
| 215 | A73 | 35 l dk brn car & brn | 1.00 | 2.00 |

Issued to commemorate the 5th centenary of the death of St. John of Capistrano, leader in the war against the Turks.

Black Madonna of Czestochowa
A74

St. Domenico Savio
A75

1956, Dec. 20
216	A74	35 l dk bl & blk	50	50
217	A74	60 l grn & ultra	1.00	1.25
218	A74	100 l brn & dk car rose	1.25	1.75

Issued to commemorate the 300th anniversary of the proclamation of the Madonna of Czestochowa as "Queen of Poland."

1957, Mar. 21 Perf. 13½ Wmk. 235
Design: 5 l, 60 l, Sts. Domenico Savio and John Bosco.
219	A75	4 l red brn	8	8
220	A75	6 l brt car	8	8
221	A75	25 l green	17	22
222	A75	60 l ultra	2.25	2.50

Issued to commemorate the centenary of the death of St. Domenico Savio.

Cardinal Capranica and College
A76

Design: 10 l, 100 l, Pope Pius XII.

1957, June 27 Engraved Perf. 13
223	A76	5 l dk car rose	8	8
224	A76	10 l pale brn	8	8
225	A76	35 l grnsh blk	45	40
226	A76	100 l ultra	1.50	1.50

Issued to commemorate the 500th anniversary of Capranica College, oldest seminary in the world.

Pontifical Academy of Science
A77

1957, Oct. 9 Photo. Perf. 14
| 227 | A77 | 35 l dk bl & grn | 90 | 90 |
| 228 | A77 | 60 l brn & ultra | 90 | 1.00 |

Issued to commemorate the 20th anniversary of the Pontifical Academy of Science.

Mariazell—A78

High Altar—A79

1957, Nov. 14 Engraved Perf. 13½
229	A78	5 l green	7	7
230	A79	15 l slate	7	7
231	A78	60 l ultra	50	50
232	A79	100 l violet	1.35	1.25

Issued to commemorate the 800th anniversary of the Mariazell shrine, Austria.

Apparition of the Virgin Mary
A80

Designs: 10 l, 35 l, Sick man and basilica. 15 l, 100 l, St. Bernadette.

1958, Feb. 21 Perf. 13x14 Wmk. 235
233	A80	5 l dk bl	10	10
234	A80	10 l bl grn	10	10
235	A80	15 l redsh brn	10	10
236	A80	25 l rose car	10	10
237	A80	35 l gray brn	10	15
238	A80	100 l violet	15	15
		Nos. 233-238 (6)	65	70

Issued to commemorate the centenary of the apparition of the Virgin Mary at Lourdes and the establishment of the shrine.

Pope Pius XII

Statue of Pope Clemens XIII by Canova
A81

Design: 60 l, 100 l, Vatican pavilion at Brussels fair.

1958, June 19 Engr. Perf. 13
| 239 | A81 | 35 l claret | 40 | 70 |

240	A81	60 l fawn	70	1.10
241	A81	100 l violet	3.25	3.25
242	A81	300 l ultra	2.25	2.50
a.		Souv. sheet of 4	21.00	25.00

Issued for the Universal and International Exposition at Brussels.
No. 242a measures 93x148mm. and contains one each of Nos. 239-242. Papal insignia and marginal inscription in violet.

1958, July 2 Perf. 14
Statues: 10 l, Clemens XIV. 35 l, Pius VI. 100 l, Pius VII.
243	A82	5 l brown	5	5
244	A82	10 l car rose	5	5
245	A82	35 l bl gray	60	50
246	A82	100 l dk bl	1.75	2.00

Issued to commemorate the bicentenary of the birth of Antonio Canova (1757-1822), sculptor.

Interregnum Issue.

St. Peter's Keys and Papal Chamberlain's Insignia
A83

Photogravure.
1958, Oct. 21 Perf. 14 Wmk. 235
247	A83	15 l brn blk, yel	4.50	4.25
248	A83	25 l brn blk	25	35
249	A83	60 l brn blk, pale vio	25	35

Pope John XXIII
A84

Pope Pius XI
A85

Design: 35 l, 100 l, Coat of Arms.
1959, Apr. 2 Photo. Perf. 14
250	A84	25 l car rose, bl & buff	10	10
251	A84	35 l multi	10	10
252	A84	60 l rose car, bl & ocher	10	10
253	A84	100 l multi	10	10

Issued to commemorate the coronation of Pope John XXIII, Nov. 4, 1958.

1959, May 25 Perf. 14 Wmk. 235
| 254 | A85 | 30 l brown | 10 | 10 |
| 255 | A85 | 100 l vio bl | 35 | 42 |

Lateran Pacts, 30th anniversary.

St. Lawrence
A86

Radio Tower and Archangel Gabriel
A87

Portraits of Saints: 25 l, Pope Sixtus II. 50 l, Agapitus. 60 l, Filicissimus. 100 l, Cyprianus. 300 l, Fructuosus.

VATICAN CITY

1959, May 25

256	A86	15 l red, brn & yel	10	8
257	A86	25 l lil, brn & yel	30	32
258	A86	50 l Prus bl, blk & yel	1.25	1.40
259	A86	60 l ol grn, brn & bis	80	75
260	A86	100 l mar, brn & yel	1.50	75
261	A86	300 l bis brn & dk brn	1.40	1.25
		Nos. 256-261 (6)	5.35	4.55

Issued to honor the martyrs of Emperor Valerian's persecutions.

1959, Oct. 27   Photo.   Perf. 14

| 262 | A87 | 25 l rose, org yel & dk brn | 15 | 22 |
| 263 | A87 | 60 l multi | 40 | 35 |

Issued to commemorate the 2nd anniversary of the papal radio station, St. Maria di Galeria.

St. Casimir, Palace and Cathedral, Vilnius—A88

1959, Dec. 14   Engraved   Wmk. 235

| 264 | A88 | 50 l brown | 25 | 25 |
| 265 | A88 | 100 l dl grn | 35 | 35 |

Issued to commemorate the 500th anniversary (in 1958) of the birth of St. Casimir, patron saint of Lithuania.

Nativity by Raphael
A89

1959, Dec. 14   Engraved   Perf. 13½

266	A89	15 l dk gray	8	8
267	A89	25 l magenta	15	22
268	A89	60 l brt ultra	50	60

| St. Antoninus | Transept of Lateran Basilica |
| A90 | A91 |

Designs: 25 l, 110 l, St. Antoninus preaching.

1960, Feb. 29   Perf. 13x14   Wmk. 235

269	A90	15 l ultra	8	6
270	A90	25 l turquoise	20	20
271	A90	60 l brown	50	40
272	A90	110 l rose cl	1.40	1.20

Issued to commemorate the 5th centenary of the death of St. Antoninus, bishop of Florence.

1960, Feb. 29   Photo.   Perf. 14

| 273 | A91 | 15 l brown | 12 | 12 |
| 274 | A91 | 60 l black | 85 | 70 |

Roman Diocesan Synod, February, 1960.

| Flight into Egypt by Fra Angelico | Cardinal Sarto's Departure from Venice |
| A92 | A93 |

Designs: 10 l, 100 l, St. Peter Giving Alms to the Poor, by Masaccio. 25 l, 300 l, Madonna of Mercy, by Piero della Francesca.

1960, Apr. 7   Perf. 14   Wmk. 235

275	A92	5 l green	8	8
276	A92	10 l gray brn	8	8
277	A92	25 l dp car	15	15
278	A92	60 l lilac	25	25
279	A92	100 l ultra	4.25	4.00
280	A92	300 l Prus grn	2.25	2.00
		Nos. 275-280 (6)	7.06	6.56

Issued to publicize World Refugee Year. July 1, 1959–June 30, 1960.

1960, Apr. 11   Engraved   Perf. 13½

Designs: 35 l, Pope John XXIII praying at coffin of Pope Pius X. 60 l, Body of Pope Pius X returning to Venice.

281	A93	15 l brown	10	10
282	A93	25 l rose car	35	30
283	A93	60 l Prus grn	60	42

Issued to commemorate the return of the body of Pope Pius X to Venice.

Feeding the Hungry
A94

"Acts of Mercy," by Della Robbia: 10 l, Giving drink to the thirsty. 15 l, Clothing the naked. 20 l, Sheltering the homeless. 30 l, Visiting the sick. 35 l, Visiting prisoners. 40 l, Burying the dead. 70 l, Pope John XXIII.

1960, Nov. 8   Photo.   Perf. 14
Centers in Brown.

284	A94	5 l red brn	5	5
285	A94	10 l green	5	5
286	A94	15 l slate	5	5
287	A94	20 l rose car	5	5
288	A94	30 l vio bl	8	8
289	A94	35 l vio brn	8	8
290	A94	40 l red org	8	8
291	A94	70 l ocher	12	10
		Nos. 284-291, E15-E16 (10)	98	96

Holy Family by Gerard van Honthorst
A95

1960, Dec. 6   Perf. 14   Wmk. 235

292	A95	10 l grn & sl blk	10	10
293	A95	15 l sep & ol blk	12	8
294	A95	70 l grnsh bl & dp bl	35	30

| St. Vincent de Paul | St. Meinrad |
| A96 | A97 |

Designs: 70 l, St. Louisa de Marillac. 100 l, St. Louisa and St. Vincent.

1960, Dec. 6

295	A96	40 l dl vio	25	25
296	A96	70 l dk gray	80	50
297	A96	100 l dk red brn	1.10	80

Issued to commemorate the 300th anniversary of the death of St. Vincent de Paul.

1961, Feb. 28   Perf. 14

Designs: 40 l, Statue of Our Lady of Einsiedeln. 100 l, Einsiedeln monastery (horiz.).

298	A97	30 l dk brn	38	20
299	A97	40 l lt vio	1.10	70
300	A97	100 l brown	1.25	1.50

Issued to commemorate the 1,100th anniversary of the death of St. Meinrad and to honor Einsiedeln Abbey, Switzerland.

Pope Leo the Great Defying Attila
A98

Photogravure

1961, Apr. 6   Perf. 14   Wmk. 235

301	A98	15 l rose brn	8	6
302	A98	70 l Prus grn	1.65	85
303	A98	300 l brn blk	5.75	3.25

Issued to commemorate the 1,500th anniversary of the death of Pope Leo the Great (St. Leo Magnus). The design is from a marble bas-relief in St. Peter's Basilica.

St. Paul Arriving in Rome, 61 A.D.—A99

Designs: 10 l, 30 l, Map showing St. Paul's journey to Rome. 20 l, 200 l, First Basilica of St. Paul, Rome.

1961, June 13   Perf. 14   Wmk. 235

304	A99	10 l Prus grn	8	6
305	A99	15 l dl red brn & gray	15	12
306	A99	20 l red org & gray	22	18
307	A99	30 l blue	75	45
308	A99	75 l org brn & gray	2.35	1.75
309	A99	200 l bl & gray	3.75	3.50
		Nos. 304-309 (6)	7.30	6.06

Issued to commemorate the 1,900th anniversary of the arrival of St. Paul in Rome.

1861 and 1961 Mastheads
A100

Designs: 70 l, Editorial offices. 250 l, Rotary press.

1961, July 4

310	A100	40 l red brn & blk	60	40
311	A100	70 l bl & blk	1.85	1.50
312	A100	250 l yel & blk	5.00	4.00

Issued to commemorate the centenary of L'Osservatore Romano, Vatican's newspaper.

| St. Patrick's Purgatory, Lough Derg | Arms of Roncalli Family |
| A101 | A102 |

Design: 10 l, 40 l, St. Patrick, marble sculpture.

Photogravure

1961, Oct. 6   Perf. 14   Wmk. 235

313	A101	10 l buff & sl grn	8	8
314	A101	15 l bl & sep	15	15
315	A101	40 l yel & bl grn	45	45
316	A101	150 l Prus bl & red brn	1.90	1.50

Issued to commemorate the 1,500th anniversary of the death of St. Patrick.

1961, Nov. 25

Designs: 25 l, Church at Sotto il Monte. 30 l, Santa Maria in Monte Santo, Rome. 40 l, Church of San Carlo al Corso, Rome (erroneously inscribed with name of Basilica of Sts. Ambrosius and Charles, Milan). 70 l, Altar, St. Peter's, Rome. 115 l, Pope John XXIII.

317	A102	10 l gray & red brn	6	6
318	A102	25 l ol bis & sl grn	13	12
319	A102	30 l vio bl & pale pur	25	22
320	A102	40 l lil & dk bl	30	22
321	A102	70 l gray grn & org brn	90	50
322	A102	115 l choc & sl	2.00	1.50
		Nos. 317-322 (6)	3.64	2.62

80th birthday of Pope John XXIII.

| "The Adoration" by Lucas Chen | Draining of Pontine Marshes Medal by Pope Sixtus V, 1588 |
| A103 | A104 |

VATICAN CITY

1961, Nov. 25
Center Multicolored

323	A103	15 l bluish grn	7	7
324	A103	40 l gray	15	18
325	A103	70 l pale lil	40	32

Issued for Christmas 1961.

1962, Apr. 7 Perf. 14 Wmk. 235
Design: 40 l, 300 l, Map of Pontine Marshes showing 18th century drainage under Pope Pius VI.

326	A104	15 l dk vio	8	8
327	A104	40 l rose car	30	20
328	A104	70 l brown	75	50
329	A104	300 l dl grn	1.75	1.40

Issued for the World Health Organization drive to eradicate malaria.

"The Good Shepherd" Wheatfield (Luke 10:2)
A105 A106

1962, June 2 Photogravure

330	A105	10 l lil & blk	20	28
331	A106	15 l bl & ocher	55	28
332	A105	70 l lt grn & blk	1.15	1.50
333	A106	115 l fawn & ocher	6.75	5.00
334	A105	200 l brn & blk	8.50	5.75
	Nos. 330-334 (5)		17.15	12.81

Issued to honor the priesthood and to stress its importance as a vocation. "The Good Shepherd" is a fourth-century statue in the Lateran Museum, Rome.

St. Catherine of Siena Paulina M. Jaricot
A107 A108

1962, June 12

335	A107	15 l brown	8	5
336	A107	60 l brt vio	1.20	1.00
337	A107	100 l blue	1.65	1.25

Issued to commemorate the 500th anniversary of the canonization of St. Catherine of Siena. The portrait is from a fresco by Il Sodoma, Church of St. Dominic, Siena.

1962, July 5
Portrait Multicolored

338	A108	10 l pale vio	6	6
339	A108	50 l dl grn	45	42
340	A108	150 l gray	2.25	1.40

Issued to commemorate the centenary of the death of Paulina M. Jaricot (1799-1862), founder of the Society for the Propagation of the Faith.

Sts. Peter and Paul
A109

Design: 40 l, 100 l, "The Invincible Cross," relief from sarcophagus.

1962, Sept. 25 Perf. 14 Wmk. 235
Photogravure

341	A109	20 l lil & brn	8	8
342	A109	40 l lt brn & blk	15	12
343	A109	70 l bluish grn & brn	15	12
344	A109	100 l sal pink & blk	30	22

Issued to commemorate the Sixth Congress of Christian Archeology, Ravenna, Sept. 23-28.

"Faith" by Raphael
A110

Designs: 10 l, "Hope." 15 l, "Charity." 25 l, Arms of Pope John XXIII and emblems of the Four Evangelists. 30 l, Ecumenical Congress meeting in St. Peter's. 40 l, Pope John XXIII on throne. 60 l, Statue of St. Peter. 115 l, The Holy Ghost as a dove (symbolic design).

Photo.; Center Engr. on 30 l
1962, Oct. 30

345	A110	5 l brt bl & blk	7	7
346	A110	10 l grn & blk	7	7
347	A110	15 l ver & sep	7	7
348	A110	25 l ver & sl	7	7
349	A110	30 l lil & blk	7	7
350	A110	40 l dk car & blk	10	8
351	A110	60 l dk grn & dp org	12	8
352	A110	115 l crimson	18	10
	Nos. 345-352 (8)		75	61

Issued to commemorate Vatican II, the 21st Ecumenical Council of the Roman Catholic Church, which opened Oct. 11, 1962. Nos. 345-347 show "the Three Theological Virtues" by Raphael.

Ethiopian Nativity Scene
A111

1962, Dec. 4
Center Multicolored

353	A111	10 l gray	5	5
354	A111	15 l brown	10	10
355	A111	90 l dl grn	50	22

Miracle of the Loaves and Fishes by Murillo Pope John XXIII
A112 A113

Design: 40 l, 200 l, "The Miraculous Catch of Fishes" by Raphael.

Photogravure
1963, Mar. 21 Perf. 14 Wmk. 235

356	A112	15 l brn & dk brn	8	6
357	A112	40 l rose red & blk	12	10
358	A112	100 l bl & dk brn	15	12
359	A112	200 l bl grn & blk	30	25

Issued for the "Freedom from Hunger" campaign of the U.N. Food and Agriculture Organization.

1963, May 8

360	A113	15 l red brn	10	10
361	A113	160 l black	80	65

Issued to commemorate the awarding of the Balzan Peace Prize to Pope John XXIII.

Interregnum Issue

Keys of St. Peter and Papal Chamberlain's Insignia
A114

1963, June 15 Perf. 14 Wmk. 235

362	A114	10 l dk brn	8	8
363	A114	40 l dk brn, yel	10	10
364	A114	100 l dk brn, vio	18	15

Pope Paul VI
A115

Design: 40 l, 200 l, Arms of Pope Paul VI.

Engraved
1963, Oct. 16 Perf. 13x14

365	A115	15 l black	6	6
366	A115	40 l carmine	15	15
367	A115	115 l redsh brn	50	40
368	A115	200 l sl bl	90	75

Issued to commemorate the coronation of Pope Paul VI, June 30, 1963.

St. Cyril African Nativity Scene
A116 A117

Designs: 70 l, Map of Hungary, Moravia and Poland, 16th century. 150 l, St. Methodius.

Photogravure
1963, Nov. 22 Perf. 14 Wmk. 235

369	A116	30 l vio blk	12	12
370	A116	70 l brown	50	50
371	A116	150 l rose cl	70	60

Issued to commemorate the 1100th anniversary of the beginning of missionary work among the Slavs by Sts. Cyril and Methodius. The pictures of the saints are from 16th century frescoes in St. Clement's Basilica, Rome.

1963, Nov. 22

372	A117	10 l brn & pale brn	5	5
373	A117	40 l ultra & brn	12	12
374	A117	100 l gray ol & brn	32	28

The design is after a sculpture by the Burundi artist Andreas Bukuru.

Church of the Holy Sepulcher, Jerusalem St. Peter from Coptic Church at Wadi-es-Sebua, Sudan
A118 A119

Designs: 15 l, Pope Paul VI. 25 l, Nativity Church, Bethlehem. 160 l, Well of the Virgin Mary, Nazareth.

1964, Jan. 4 Perf. 14 Wmk. 235

375	A118	15 l black	5	5
376	A118	25 l rose brn	8	8
377	A118	70 l brown	15	15
378	A118	160 l ultra	18	15

Issued to commemorate the visit of Pope Paul VI to the Holy Land, Jan. 4-6.

1964, March 10 Photogravure
Design: 20 l, 200 l, Trajan's Kiosk, Philae.

379	A119	10 l ultra & red brn	5	5
380	A119	20 l multi	5	5
381	A119	70 l gray & red brn	15	15
382	A119	200 l gray & multi	20	15

Issued to publicize the UNESCO world campaign to save historic monuments in Nubia.

Pietà by Michelangelo Isaiah by Michelangelo
A120 A121

Designs: 15 l, 100 l, Pope Paul VI. 250 l, Head of Mary from Pietà.

1964, Apr. 22 Perf. 14 Wmk. 235

383	A120	15 l vio bl	5	5
384	A120	50 l dk brn	10	10
385	A120	100 l sl bl	15	15
386	A120	250 l chestnut	22	15

New York World's Fair, 1964-65.

Engraved
1964, June 16 Perf. 13½x14

387	A121	10 l Michelangelo, after Jacopino del Conte	5	5
388	A121	25 l Isaiah	5	5
389	A121	30 l Delphic Sibyl	5	5
390	A121	40 l Jeremiah	10	8
391	A121	150 l Joel	15	12
	Nos. 387-391 (5)		40	35

Issued to commemorate the 400th anniversary of the death of Michelangelo Buonarroti (1475-1564). Designs of Nos. 387-391 are from Sistine Chapel.

The Good Samaritan
A122

Perf. 14x13½
1964, Sept. 22 Engraved Wmk. 235

392	A122	10 l red brn & red	5	5

VATICAN CITY

| 393 | A122 | 30 l dk bl & red | 10 | 10 |
| 394 | A122 | 300 l gray & red | 22 | 15 |

Issued to commemorate the centenary (in 1963) of the founding of the International Red Cross.

Birthplace of Cardinal
Nicolaus Cusanus
A123

Design: 200 l, Cardinal's sepulcher, Church of San Pietro in Vincoli, Rome.

1964, Nov. 16   Wmk. 235

| 395 | A123 | 40 l dl bl grn | 10 | 10 |
| 396 | A123 | 200 l rose red | 35 | 30 |

Issued to commemorate the fifth centenary of the death of the German cardinal, Nicolaus Cusanus (Nicolaus Krebs of Kues) (1401–64).

Japanese Nativity Scene by
Kimiko Koseki
A124

1964, Nov. 16   Photo.   Perf. 14

397	A124	10 l multi	5	5
a.		Yellow omitted		
398	A124	15 l blk & multi	5	5
399	A124	135 l bis & multi	25	25

Pope Paul VI and Map of India
and Southeast Asia
A125

Designs: 15 l, Pope Paul VI at prayer. 25 l, Eucharistic Congress altar, Bombay (horiz.). 60 l, Gateway of India, Bombay (horiz.).

1964, Dec. 2

400	A125	15 l dl vio	5	5
401	A125	25 l green	10	5
402	A125	60 l brown	12	10
403	A125	200 l dl vio	15	12

Issued to commemorate the trip of Pope Paul VI to India, Dec. 2–5, 1964.

Uganda Martyrs   Dante by Raphael
A126   A127

Designs: Various groups of Martyrs of Uganda.

Perf. 13½x14

1965, Mar. 16   Engraved   Wmk. 235

404	A126	15 l	Prus grn	5	5
405	A126	20 l	brown	5	5
406	A126	30 l	ultra	5	5
407	A126	75 l	black	12	10
408	A126	100 l	rose red	12	10
409	A126	160 l	violet	12	10
		Nos. 404-409 (6)		51	45

Issued to commemorate the canonization of 22 African martyrs, Oct. 18, 1964.

Photogravure and Engraved
1965, May 18   *Perf. 13½x14*

Designs: 40 l, Dante and the 3 beasts at entrance to the Inferno. 70 l, Dante and Virgil at entrance to Purgatory. 200 l, Dante and Beatrice in Paradise. (40 l, 70 l, 200 l, by Botticelli).

410	A127	10 l	bis brn & dk brn	5	5
411	A127	40 l	rose & dk brn	5	5
412	A127	70 l	lt grn & dk brn	10	10
413	A127	200 l	pale bl & dk brn	25	18

Issued to commemorate the 700th anniversary of the birth of Dante Alighieri.

St. Benedict
by Perugino
A128

Design: 300 l, View of Monte Cassino.

1965, July 2   Photo.   *Perf. 14*

| 414 | A128 | 40 l | brown | 8 | 6 |
| 415 | A128 | 300 l | dk grn | 30 | 25 |

Issued to commemorate the conferring of the title Patron Saint of Europe upon St. Benedict by Pope Paul VI, and to commemorate the restoring of the Abbey of Monte Cassino.

Pope Paul VI
Addressing
U.N. Assembly
A129

Designs: 30 l, 150 l, United Nations Headquarters and olive branch.

1965, Oct. 4   *Perf. 14*   Wmk. 235

416	A129	20 l	brown	5	5
417	A129	30 l	sapphire	5	5
418	A129	150 l	ol grn	10	10
419	A129	300 l	rose vio	15	12

Issued to commemorate the visit of Pope Paul VI to the United Nations, New York City, Oct. 4.

Peruvian Nativity   Cartographer
Scene   A131
A130

1965, Nov. 25   Engr.   *Perf. 13½x14*

420	A130	20 l	rose cl	5	5
421	A130	40 l	red brn	10	10
422	A130	200 l	gray grn	25	18

1966, Mar. 8   Photo.   *Perf. 14*

Designs: 5 l, Pope Paul VI. 10 l, Organist. 20 l, Painter. 30 l, Sculptor. 40 l, Bricklayer. 55 l, Printer. 75 l, Plowing farmer. 90 l, Blacksmith. 130 l, Scholar.

423	A131	5 l	sepia	5	5
424	A131	10 l	violet	5	5
425	A131	15 l	brown	5	5
426	A131	20 l	gray grn	6	5
427	A131	30 l	brn red	8	8
428	A131	40 l	Prus grn	10	10
429	A131	55 l	dk bl	12	12
430	A131	75 l	dk rose brn	12	12
431	A131	90 l	car rose	15	12
432	A131	130 l	black	18	18
		Nos. 423-432, E17-E18 (12)		1.53	1.47

The Pope's portrait is from a bas-relief by Enrico Manfrini; the arts and crafts designs are bas-reliefs by Mario Rudelli from the chair in the Pope's private chapel.

King
Mieszko I
and Queen
Dabrowka
A132

Designs: 25 l, St. Adalbert (Wojciech) and Cathedrals of Wroclaw and Gniezno. 40 l, St. Stanislas, Skalka Church, Wawel Cathedral and Castle, Cracow. 50 l, Queen Jadwiga (Hedwig), Holy Gate with Our Lady of Mercy, Vilnius, and Jagellon University Library, Cracow. 150 l, Black Madonna of Czestochowa, cloister and church of Bright Mountain, Czestochowa, and St. John's Cathedral, Warsaw. 220 l, Pope Paul VI blessing students and farmers.

Perf. 14x13½

1966, May 3   Engr.   Wmk. 235

433	A132	15 l	black	5	5
434	A132	25 l	violet	5	5
435	A132	40 l	brick red	8	6
436	A132	50 l	claret	8	7
437	A132	150 l	sl bl	10	9
438	A132	220 l	brown	12	10
		Nos. 433-438 (6)		48	41

Millenium of Christianization of Poland.

Pope John XXIII   Nativity,
Opening Vatican   Sculpture by
II Council   Scorzelli
A133   A134

Designs: 15 l, Ancient Bible on ornate display stand. 55 l, Bishops celebrating Mass. 90 l, Pope Paul VI greeting Patriarch Athenagoras I. 100 l, Gold ring given to participating bishops. 130 l, Pope Paul VI carried in front of St. Peter's.

1966, Oct. 11   Photo.   *Perf. 14*

439	A133	10 l	red & blk	5	5
440	A133	15 l	brn & grn	5	5
441	A133	55 l	blk & brt rose	8	8
442	A133	90 l	sl grn & blk	8	8
443	A133	100 l	grn & ocher	12	10
444	A133	130 l	org brn & brn	12	10
		Nos. 439-444 (6)		50	46

Issued to commemorate the conclusion of Vatican II, the 21st Ecumenical Council of the Roman Catholic Church, Dec. 8, 1965.

1966, Nov. 24   *Perf. 14*   Wmk. 235

445	A134	20 l	plum	5	5
446	A134	55 l	sl grn	15	15
447	A134	225 l	yel brn	15	15

St. Peter,   Cross, People
Fresco,   and Globe
Catacombs,   A136
Rome
A135

Designs: 20 l, St. Paul, fresco from Catacombs, Rome. 55 l, Sts. Peter and Paul, glass painting, Vatican Library. 90 l, Baldachin by Bernini, St. Peter's, Rome. 220 l, Interior of St. Paul's, Rome.

Perf. 13½x14

1967, June 15   Photo.   Unwmkd.

448	A135	15 l multi	6	6
449	A135	20 l multi	6	6
450	A135	55 l multi	8	8
451	A135	90 l multi	10	10
452	A135	220 l multi	15	12
	Nos. 448-452 (5)		45	40

Issued to commemorate the 1900th anniversary of the martyrdom of the Apostles Peter and Paul.

1967, Oct. 13   *Perf. 14*   Wmk. 235

| 453 | A136 | 40 l car rose | 10 | 10 |
| 454 | A136 | 130 l brt bl | 20 | 15 |

Issued to commemorate the 3rd Congress of Catholic Laymen, Rome, Oct. 11–18.

Sculpture of   Nativity, 9th
Shepherd Children   Century Painting
of Fatima   on Wood
A137   A138

1967, Oct. 13   *Perf. 13½x14*

Designs: 50 l, Basilica at Fatima. 200 l, Pope Paul VI praying before statue of Virgin of Fatima.

455	A137	30 l multi	8	8
456	A137	50 l multi	15	12
457	A137	200 l multi	15	12

Issued to commemorate the 50th anniversary of the apparition of the Virgin Mary to 3 shepherd children at Fatima.

Christmas Issue
1967, Nov. 28   Photo.   Unwmkd.

458	A138	25 l pur & multi	8	8
459	A138	55 l gray & multi	15	12
460	A138	180 l grn & multi	15	12

Pope Paul VI   Holy Infant
A139   of Prague
                     A140

VATICAN CITY

Designs: 55 l, Monstrance from fresco by Raphael. 220 l, Map of South America.

1968, Aug. 22   Perf. 14   Wmk. 235

461	A139	25 l blk & dk red brn	8	8
462	A139	55 l blk, gray & ocher	12	12
463	A139	220 l blk, lt bl & sep	18	15

Issued to commemorate the visit of Pope Paul VI to the 39th Eucharistic Congress in Bogotá, Colombia, Aug. 22–25.

Engraved and Photogravure

1968, Nov. 28   Perf. 13½x14

464	A140	20 l plum & pink	6	6
465	A140	50 l vio & pale vio	15	15
466	A140	250 l dk bl & lt bluish gray	20	20

The Resurrection, by Fra Angelico de Fiesole
A141

Pope Paul VI with African Children
A142

Easter Issue
Perf. 13½x14

1969, Mar. 6   Engraved   Wmk. 235

467	A141	20 l dk car & buff	6	5
468	A141	90 l grn & buff	15	15
469	A141	180 l ultra & buff	20	20

Europa Issue
Common Design Type
Perf. 13½x14

1969, Apr. 28   Wmk. 235
Size: 36½x27mm.

470	CD12	50 l gray & lt brn	12	10
471	CD12	90 l ver & lt brn	22	18
472	CD12	130 l ol & lt brn	22	18

Perf. 13½x14

1969, July 31   Photo.   Wmk. 235

Designs: 55 l, Pope Paul VI and African bishops. 250 l, Map of Africa with Kampala, olive branch and compass rose.

473	A142	25 l bis & brn	8	6
474	A142	55 l dk red & brn	15	12
475	A142	250 l multi	30	25

Issued to commemorate the visit of Pope Paul VI to Uganda, July 31–Aug. 2.

Pope Pius IX
A143

Mt. Fuji and EXPO '70 Emblem
A144

Designs: 50 l, Chrismon, emblem of St. Peter's Circle. 220 l, Pope Paul VI.

Perf. 13½x14

1969, Nov. 18   Engr.   Wmk. 235

476	A143	30 l red brn	8	8
477	A143	50 l dk gray	12	12
478	A143	220 l dp plum	32	25

Issued to commemorate the centenary of St. Peter's Circle, a lay society dedicated to prayer, action and sacrifice.

1970, Mar. 16   Photo.   Unwmkd.

Designs (EXPO '70 Emblem and): 25 l, EXPO '70 emblem. 40 l, Osaka Castle. 55 l, Japanese Virgin and Child, by Domoto in Osaka Cathedral. 90 l, Christian Pavilion.

479	A144	25 l gold, red & blk	8	8
480	A144	40 l red & multi	10	12
481	A144	55 l brn & multi	12	22
482	A144	90 l gold & multi	18	18
483	A144	110 l bl & multi	32	20
		Nos. 479-483 (5)	80	80

Issued to publicize EXPO '70 International Exhibition, Osaka, Japan, Mar. 15–Sept. 13.

Centenary Medal, Jesus Giving St. Peter the Keys
A145

Designs: 50 l, Coat of arms of Pope Pius IX. 180 l, Vatican I Council meeting in St. Peter's, obverse of centenary medal.

Engr. & Photo.; Photo. (50 l)

1970, Apr. 29   Perf. 13x14

484	A145	20 l org & brn	6	5
485	A145	50 l multi	15	12
486	A145	180 l ver & brn	40	30

Centenary of the Vatican I Council.

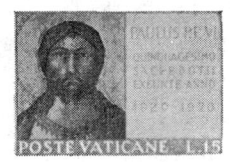

Christ, by Simone Martini
A146

Designs: 25 l, Christ with Crown of Thorns, by Rogier van der Weyden. 50 l, Christ, by Albrecht Dürer. 90 l, Christ, by El Greco. 180 l, Pope Paul VI.

Photogravure

1970, May 29   Perf. 14x13   Unwmkd.

487	A146	15 l gold & multi	5	5
488	A146	25 l gold & multi	8	8
489	A146	50 l gold & multi	12	12
490	A146	90 l gold & multi	20	20
491	A146	180 l gold & multi	40	28
		Nos. 487-491 (5)	85	73

Issued to commemorate the 50th anniversary of the ordination of Pope Paul VI.

Adam, by Michelangelo; U.N. Emblem
A147

Pope Paul VI
A148

Designs (U.N. Emblem and): 90 l, Eve, by Michelangelo. 220 l, Olive branch.

1970, Oct. 8   Photo.   Perf. 13x14

492	A147	20 l multi	5	5
493	A147	90 l multi	30	22
494	A147	220 l multi	50	50

25th anniversary of the United Nations.

Common Design Types
pictured in section at front of book.

1970, Nov. 26   Photo.   Unwmkd.

Designs: 55 l, Holy Child of Cebu, Philippines. 100 l, Madonna and Child, by Georg Hamori, Darwin Cathedral, Australia. 130 l, Cathedral of Manila. 220 l, Cathedral of Sydney.

495	A148	25 l multi	8	8
496	A148	55 l multi	15	12
497	A148	100 l multi	25	18
498	A148	130 l multi	32	25
499	A148	220 l multi	50	35
		Nos. 495-499 (5)	1.30	98

Issued to commemorate the visit of Pope Paul VI to the Far East, Oceania and Australia, Nov. 26–Dec. 5.

Angel Holding Lectern
A149

Madonna and Child by Francesco Ghissi
A150

Designs (Sculptures by Corrado Ruffini): 40 l, 130 l, Crucified Christ surrounded by doves. 50 l, like 20 l.

1971, Feb. 2   Perf. 13x14

500	A149	20 l multi	7	7
501	A149	40 l dp org & multi	10	8
502	A149	50 l pur & multi	15	12
503	A149	130 l multi	40	25

International year against racial discrimination.

1971, Mar. 26   Photo.   Perf. 14

Paintings: Madonna and Child, 40 l, by Sassetta (Stefano di Giovanni); 55 l, Carlo Crivelli; 90 l, by Carlo Maratta. 180 l, Holy Family, by Ghisberto Ceracchini.

504	A150	25 l gray & multi	8	8
505	A150	40 l gray & multi	12	12
506	A150	55 l gray & multi	15	12
507	A150	90 l gray & multi	22	15
508	A150	180 l gray & multi	32	25
		Nos. 504-508 (5)	89	72

St. Dominic Sienese School
A151

St. Stephen, from Chasuble, 1031
A152

Portraits of St. Dominic: 55 l, by Fra Angelico. 90 l, by Titian. 180 l, by El Greco.

Perf. 13x14

1971, May 25   Photo.   Unwmkd.

509	A151	25 l multi	8	8
510	A151	55 l multi	22	12
511	A151	90 l multi	22	18
512	A151	180 l multi	40	32

800th anniversary of the birth of St. Dominic de Guzman (1170–1221), founder of the Dominican Order.

1971, Nov. 25

Design: 180 l, Madonna as Patroness of Hungary, 1511.

| 513 | A152 | 50 l multi | 15 | 15 |
| 514 | A152 | 180 l blk & yel | 40 | 35 |

Millenium of the birth of St. Stephen (975?–1038), king of Hungary.

Bramante
A153

Designs: 25 l, Bramante's design for dome of St. Peter's. 130 l, Design for spiral staircase.

1972, Feb. 22   Engr.   Perf. 13½x14

515	A153	25 l dl yel & blk	7	7
516	A153	90 l dl yel & blk	25	18
517	A153	130 l dl yel & blk	32	25

Honoring Bramante (real name Donato d'Agnolo; 1444–1514), architect.

St. Mark in Storm, 12th Century Mosaic—A154

Map of Venice, 1581—A155

Design: 180 l, St. Mark's Basilica, Painting by Emilio Vangelli.

Perf. 14

1972, June 6   Photo.   Unwmkd.

518	A154	25 l lt brn & multi	45	45
519	A155	Block of 4, multi	4.00	4.00
a-d.		50 l, UL, UR, LL, LR, each	85	85
520	A154	180 l lt bl & multi	8.50	8.50
a.		Souvenir sheet	12.50	12.50

UNESCO campaign to save Venice. No. 520a contains one each of Nos. 518–520. Light blue Papal arms, inscription and border in margin. Size: 112x150mm.

Gospel of St. Matthew, 13th Century, French
A156

Designs (Illuminated Initials from): 50 l, St. Luke's Gospel, Biblia dell'Aracoeli 13th century, French. 90 l, Second Epistle of St. John, 14th century, Bologna. 100 l, Apocalypse of St. John, 14th century, Bologna. 130 l, Book of Romans, 14th century, Central Italy.

1972, Oct. 11   Perf. 14x13½

521	A156	30 l multi	8	8
522	A156	50 l multi	15	15
523	A156	90 l multi	25	25
524	A156	100 l multi	25	25
525	A156	130 l multi	75	75
		Nos. 521-525 (5)	1.48	1.48

International Book Year 1972. Illustrations are from illuminated medieval manuscripts.

VATICAN CITY

Luigi
Orione
A157

Design: 180 l, Lorenzo Perosi and music from "Hallelujah."

1972, Nov. 28 Photo. Perf. 14x13½
| 526 | A157 | 50 l rose, lil & blk | 25 | 25 |
| 527 | A157 | 180 l org, grn & blk | 50 | 42 |

Centenary of the births of the secular priests Luigi Orione (1872–1940), founder of CARITAS, Catholic welfare organization; and Lorenzo Perosi (1872–1956), composer.

Cardinal   Eucharistic
Bessarion   Congress
A158   Emblem
                 A159

Designs: 40 l, Reading Bull of Union between the Greek and Latin Churches, 1439, from bronze door of St. Peter's. 130 l, Coat of arms from tomb, Basilica of Holy Apostles, Rome.

Engraved
1972, Nov. 28 Perf. 13x14 Wmk. 235
528	A158	40 l dl grn	12	15
529	A158	90 l carmine	18	20
530	A158	130 l black	25	35

500th anniversary of the death of Johannes Cardinal Bessarion (1403(?)–1472), Latin Patriarch of Constantinople, who worked for union of the Greek and Latin Churches. Portrait by Cosimo Rosselli in Sistine Chapel.

1973, Feb. 27 Photo. Unwmkd.
Designs: 75 l, Head of Mary (Pietá), by Michelangelo. 300 l, Melbourne Cathedral.
531	A159	25 l vio & multi	8	8
532	A159	75 l ol & multi	13	13
533	A159	300 l multi	85	85

40th International Eucharistic Congress, Melbourne, Australia, Feb. 18–25.

St. Teresa   Copernicus
A160   A161

Designs: 25 l, St. Teresa's birthplace, Alençon. 220 l, Lisieux Basilica.

Engraved and Photogravure
1973, May 23 Perf. 13x14
534	A160	25 l blk & pink	8	8
535	A160	55 l blk & yel	18	18
536	A160	220 l blk & lt bl	55	50

Centenary of the birth of St. Teresa of Lisieux and of the Infant Jesus (1873–97), Carmelite nun.

1973, June 19 Engraved Perf. 14
Designs: 20 l, 100 l, View of Torun.
537	A161	20 l dl grn	8	8
538	A161	50 l brown	12	12
539	A161	100 l lilac	25	22
540	A161	130 l dk bl	50	38

500th anniversary of the birth of Nicolaus Copernicus (1473–1543), Polish astronomer.

St. Wenceslas
A162

1973, Sept. 25 Photo. Perf. 14
Multicolored
541	A162	20 l shown	8	5
542	A162	90 l Arms of Prague Diocese	30	25
543	A162	150 l Spire of Prague Cathedral	40	35
544	A162	220 l St. Adalbert	75	65

Millenium of Prague Latin Episcopal See.

St. Nerses
Shnorali
A163

Designs: 25 l, Church of St. Hripsime. 90 l, Armenian khatchkar, a stele with cross and inscription.

Engraved and Lithographed
1973, Nov. 27 Perf. 13x14
545	A163	25 l tan & dk brn	8	8
546	A163	90 l lt vio & blk	30	25
547	A163	180 l lt grn & sep	50	45

800th anniversary of the death of the Armenian Patriarch St. Nerses Shnorali (1102–1173).

Noah's Ark, Rainbow and Dove
(Mosaic)—A164

Design: 90 l, Lamb drinking from stream, and Tablets of the Law (mosaic).

1974, Apr. 23 Litho. Perf. 13x14
| 548 | A164 | 25 l gold & multi | 20 | 18 |
| 549 | A164 | 90 l gold & multi | 30 | 25 |

Centenary of the Universal Postal Union.

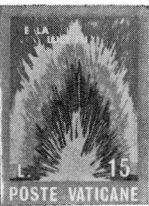 

"And There was   St. Thomas
Light"   Aquinas Teaching
A165   A166

Designs: 25 l, Noah's Ark (horiz.). 50 l, The Annunciation. 90 l, Nativity (African). 180 l, Hands holding grain (Spanish inscription: The Lord feeds his people) (horiz.). Designs chosen through worldwide youth competition in connection with 1972 International Book Year.

Photogravure
1974, Apr. 23 Perf. 13x14, 14x13
550	A165	15 l brn & multi	6	6
551	A165	25 l yel & multi	10	10
552	A165	50 l bl & multi	15	15
553	A165	90 l grn & multi	25	22
554	A165	180 l rose & multi	40	40
		Nos. 550-554 (5)	96	93

"The Bible: the Book of Books."

Engraved and Lithographed
Perf. 13x14
1974, June 18 Unwmkd.
Designs: 50 l, Students (left panel). 220 l, Students (right panel). Designs from a painting in the Convent of St. Mark in Florence, by an artist from the School of Fra Angelico.

Sizes: 50 l, 220 l, 20x36mm.. 90 l, 26x36mm.
555	A166	50 l dk brn & gold	18	18
556	A166	90 l dk brn & gold	20	20
557	A166	220 l dk brn & gold	65	65
		Strip of 3, #555-557	1.40	1.40

700th anniversary of the death of St. Thomas Aquinas (1225–1274), scholastic philosopher. Nos. 555–557 printed se-tenant in sheets of 45.

St. Bonaventure
A167

Designs (Woodcuts): 40 l, Civita Bagnoregio. 90 l, Tree of Life (13th century).

1974, Sept. 26 Photo. Perf. 13x14
558	A167	40 l gold & multi	18	12
559	A167	90 l gold & multi	28	22
560	A167	220 l gold & multi	60	45

700th death anniversary of St. Bonaventure (Giovanni di Fidanza; 1221–1274), scholastic philosopher.

Christ,   Pope Paul VI
St. Peter's   Giving his
Basilica   Blessing
A168   A169

Designs: 10 l, Christus Victor, Sts. Peter and Paul. 30 l, Christ. 40 l, Cross surmounted by dove. 50 l, Christ enthroned. 55 l, St. Peter. 90 l, St. Paul. 100 l, St. Peter. 130 l, St. Paul. 220 l, Arms of Pope Paul VI. Designs of 10 l, 25 l, are from St. Peter's; 30 l, 40 l, from St. John Lateran; 50 l, 55 l, 90 l, from St. Mary Major; 100 l, 130 l, from St. Paul outside the Walls.

1974, Dec. 19 Photo. Perf. 13x14
561	A168	10 l multi	5	5
562	A168	25 l multi	8	5
563	A168	30 l multi	10	6
564	A168	40 l multi	15	12
565	A168	50 l multi	16	12
566	A168	55 l multi	18	12
567	A168	90 l multi	28	20
568	A168	100 l multi	30	20
569	A168	130 l multi	40	28
570	A168	220 l multi	60	40
571	A169	250 l multi	70	55
		Nos. 561-571 (11)	3.00	2.15

Holy Year 1975.

Pentecost, by
El Greco
A170

1975, May 22 Engr. Perf. 13x14
| 572 | A170 | 300 l car rose & org | 70 | 55 |

Pentecost 1975.

Fountain, St. Peter's
Square—A171

Fountains of Rome: 40 l, Piazza St. Martha, Apse of St. Peter's. 50 l, Borgia Tower and St. Peter's. 90 l, Belvedere Courtyard. 100 l, Academy of Sciences. 200 l, Galleon.

Lithographed and Engraved
1975, May 22 Perf. 14
573	A171	20 l buff & blk	6	6
574	A171	40 l pale vio & blk	15	12
575	A171	50 l sal & blk	18	15
576	A171	90 l pale cit & blk	25	20
577	A171	100 l pale grn & blk	25	20
578	A171	200 l pale bl & blk	50	45
		Nos. 573-578 (6)	1.39	1.18

European Architectural Heritage Year.

Miracle
of Loaves
and Fishes,
Gilt Glass
A172

Designs: 150 l, Painting of Christ, from Comodilla Catacomb. 200 l, Raising of Lazarus. All works from 4th century.

Perf. 14x13½
1975, Sept. 25 Photo. Unwmkd.
579	A172	30 l multi	10	10
580	A172	150 l brn & multi	38	38
581	A172	200 l grn & multi	60	55

9th International Congress of Christian Archaeology.

Investiture of First Librarian Bartolomeo Sacchi by Pope
Sixtus IV—A173

Designs: 100 l, Pope Sixtus IV and books in old wooden press, from Latin Vatican Codex 2044 (vert.). 250 l, Pope Sixtus IV visiting Library, fresco in Hospital of the Holy Spirit. Design of 70 l is from fresco by Melozzo da Forlì in Vatican Gallery.

VATICAN CITY

Perf. 14x13½, 13½x14

1975, Sept. 25   Litho. & Engr.
582	A173	70 l gray & lil	15	12
583	A173	100 l lt yel & grn	28	22
584	A173	250 l gray & red	65	45

500th anniversary of the founding of the Vatican Apostolic Library.

Mt. Argentario Monastery
A174

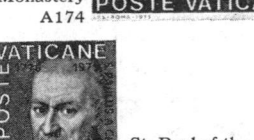

St. Paul of the Cross, by Giovanni Della Porta
A175

Design: 300 l, Basilica of Sts. John and Paul and burial chapel of Saint.

1975, Nov. 27 Photo. **Perf. 14x13½**
585	A174	50 l multi	15	15
586	A175	150 l multi	45	40
587	A174	300 l multi	90	55

Bicentenary of death of St. Paul of the Cross, founder of the Passionist religious order in 1737.

Praying Women, by Fra Angelico
A176

Design: 200 l, Seated women, by Fra Angelico.

1975, Nov. 27   **Perf. 13½x14**
| 588 | A176 | 100 l multi | 30 | 38 |
| 589 | A176 | 200 l multi | 55 | 45 |

International Women's Year 1975.

Virgin and Child in Glory, by Titian—A177

Design: 300 l, The Six Saints, by Titian.
Designs from "The Madonna in Glory with the Child Jesus and Six Saints."

1976, May 13 Engr. **Perf. 14x13½**
| 590 | A177 | 100 l rose mag | 25 | 22 |
| 591 | A177 | 300 l rose mag | 70 | 60 |

Titian (1477–1576), painter, 400th death anniversary. Nos. 590–591 printed se-tenant in sheets of 20.

Hands Holding Eucharist
A178

Designs: 150 l, Eucharist, wheat and globe. 400 l, Hungry mankind reaching for the Eucharist.

1976, July 2 Photo. **Perf. 13½x14**
592	A178	150 l gold, red & bl	35	35
593	A178	200 l gold & bl	45	45
594	A178	400 l gold, grn & brn	80	80

41st International Eucharistic Congress, Philadelphia, Pa., Aug. 1–8.

Moses Holding Tablets
A179

Details from Transfiguration by Raphael: 40 l, Transfigured Christ. 50 l, Prophet Elijah with book. 100 l, Apostles John and Peter. 150 l, Group of women. 200 l, Landscape.

1976, Sept. 30 Photo. **Perf. 13½x14**
595	A179	30 l ocher & multi	8	8
596	A179	40 l red & multi	10	10
597	A179	50 l vio & multi	12	14
598	A179	100 l multi	25	22
599	A179	150 l grn & multi	40	40
600	A179	200 l ocher & multi	50	45
		Nos. 595-600 (6)	1.45	1.39

St. John's Tower—A180

Roman Views: 100 l, Fountain of the Sacrament. 120 l, Fountain at entrance to the gardens. 180 l, Basilica, Cupola of St. Peter's and Sacristy. 250 l, Borgia Tower and Sistine Chapel. 300 l, Apostolic Palace and Courtyard of St. Damasius.

Lithographed and Engraved

1976, Nov. 23   **Perf. 14**
601	A180	50 l gray & blk	14	18
602	A180	100 l sal & dk brn	28	25
603	A180	120 l cit & dk grn	32	25
604	A180	180 l pale gray & blk	28	32
605	A180	250 l yel & brn	65	45
606	A180	300 l pale lil & mag	75	60
		Nos. 601-606 (6)	2.42	2.05

The Lord's Creatures
A181

Designs: 70 l, Brother Sun. 100 l, Sister Moon and Stars. 130 l, Sister Water. 170 l, Praise in infirmities and tribulations. 200 l, Praise for bodily death. Designs are illustrations by Duilio Cambellotti for "The Canticle of Brother Sun," by St. Francis.

1977, Mar. 10 Photo. **Perf. 14x13½**
607	A181	50 l multi	10	12
608	A181	70 l multi	22	15
609	A181	100 l multi	28	25
610	A181	130 l multi	32	30
611	A181	170 l multi	38	32
612	A181	200 l multi	45	40
		Nos. 607-612 (6)	1.75	1.54

St. Francis of Assisi, 750th death anniversary.

Sts. Peter and Paul
A182

Dormition of the Virgin
A183

Design: 350 l, Pope Gregory XI and St. Catherine of Siena. Designs are after fresco by Giorgio Vasari.

1977, May 20 Engr. **Perf. 14**
| 613 | A182 | 170 l black | 60 | 55 |
| 614 | A182 | 350 l black | 95 | 85 |

600th anniversary of the return of Pope Gregory XI from Avignon. Nos. 613–614 printed se-tenant in sheets of 50.

1977, July 5 Photo. **Perf. 13½x14**

Design: 400 l, Virgin Mary in Heaven. Both designs after miniatures in Latin manuscripts, Vatican Library.
| 615 | A183 | 200 l multi | 60 | 60 |
| 616 | A183 | 400 l multi | 95 | 95 |

Feast of the Assumption.

The Nile Deity, Roman Sculpture
A184

Sculptures: 120 l, Head of Pericles. 130 l, Roman Couple Joining Hands. 150 l, Apollo Belvedere, head. 170 l, Laocoon, head. 350 l, Apollo Belvedere, torso.

1977, Sept. 29   **Perf. 14x13½**
617	A184	50 l multi	20	20
618	A184	120 l multi	32	32
619	A184	130 l multi	32	32
620	A184	150 l multi	32	32
621	A184	170 l multi	38	38
622	A184	350 l multi	70	70
		Nos. 617-622 (6)	2.24	2.24

Classical sculptures in Vatican Museums.

Creation of Man and Woman—A185

Designs: 70 l, Three youths in the furnace. 100 l, Adoration of the Kings. 130 l, Raising of Lazarus. 200 l, The Good Shepherd. 400 l, Chrismon, Cross, sleeping soldiers (Resurrection). Designs are bas-reliefs from Christian sarcophagi, 250–350 A.D., found in Roman excavations.

1977, Dec. 9 Photo. **Perf. 14x13½**
623	A185	50 l multi	10	10
624	A185	70 l multi	18	18
625	A185	100 l multi	25	25
626	A185	130 l multi	32	32
627	A185	200 l multi	45	45
628	A185	400 l multi	85	70
		Nos. 623-628 (6)	2.15	2.00

Madonna with the Parrot and Rubens Self-portrait
A186

1977, Dec. 9   **Perf. 13½x14**
| 629 | A186 | 350 l multi | 1.00 | 1.00 |

Peter Paul Rubens (1577–1640), 400th birth anniversary.

Pope Paul VI, by Lino Bianchi Barriviera
A187

Design: 350 l, Christ's Face, by Pericle Fazzini and arms of Pope Paul VI.

1978, Mar. 9 Photo. **Perf. 14**
| 630 | A187 | 350 l multi | 80 | 65 |
| 631 | A187 | 400 l multi | 80 | 75 |

80th birthday of Pope Paul VI.

Pope Pius IX
A188

Designs: 130 l, Arms of Pope Pius IX. 170 l, Seal of Pius IX, used to sign definition of Dogma of Immaculate Conception.

Lithographed and Engraved

1978, May 9   **Perf. 13x14**
632	A188	130 l multi	38	35
633	A188	170 l multi	60	45
634	A188	200 l multi	75	60

Pope Pius IX (1792–1878), death centenary.

Interregnum Issues

Keys of St. Peter and Papal Chamberlain's Insignia
A189   A190

1978, Aug. 23 Photo. **Perf. 14**
635	A189	120 l pur & lt grn	1.00	75
636	A189	150 l pur & sal	1.00	75
637	A189	250 l pur & yel	1.00	75

1978, Oct. 12 Photo. **Perf. 14**
638	A190	120 l blk & multi	75	60
639	A190	200 l blk & multi	75	60
640	A190	250 l blk & multi	75	60

VATICAN CITY

Pope John Paul I
A191

Designs (Pope John Paul I): 70 l, Sitting on his throne. 250 l, Walking in Vatican garden. 350 l, Giving blessing (horiz.).

Perf. 13x14, 14x13

1978, Dec. 11			Photogravure	
641	A191	70 l multi	18	18
642	A191	120 l multi	50	40
643	A191	250 l multi	50	40
644	A191	350 l multi	70	65

John Paul I, Pope from Aug. 26 to Sept. 28, 1978.

Arms of Pope John Paul II
A192

Designs: 250 l, Pope John Paul II raising hand in blessing. 400 l, Jesus giving keys to St. Peter.

Lithographed and Engraved

1979, Mar. 22			Perf. 14x13	
645	A192	170 l blk & multi	45	40
646	A192	250 l blk & multi	65	60
647	A192	400 l blk & multi	1.00	90

Inauguration of pontificate of Pope John Paul II.

Martyrdom of St. Stanislas
A193

St. Basil the Great Instructing Monk
A194

Designs: 150 l, St. Stanislas appearing to the people. 250 l, Gold reliquary, 1504, containing saint's head. 500 l, View of Cracow Cathedral.

1979, May 18		Photo.	Perf. 14	
648	A193	120 l multi	25	25
649	A193	150 l multi	28	22
650	A193	250 l multi	50	45
651	A193	350 l multi	1.00	90

900th anniversary of martyrdom of St. Stanislas (1030-1079), patron saint of Poland.

Engraved and Photogravure

Design: 520 l, St. Basil the Great visiting the sick.

1979, June 25			Perf. 13½x14	
652	A194	150 l multi	32	25
653	A194	520 l multi	1.40	1.10

16th centenary of the death of St. Basil the Great.

Father Secchi, Solar Protuberance, Spectrum and Meteorograph—A195

Designs (Father Secchi, solar protuberance, spectrum and): 220 l, Spectroscope. 300 l, Telescope.

Lithographed and Engraved

1979, June 25			Perf. 14x13½	
654	A195	180 l multi	60	55
655	A195	220 l multi	75	65
656	A195	300 l multi	85	75

Father Angelo Secchi (1818–1878), astronomer.

Vatican City—A196

Papal Arms and Portraits: 70 l, Pius XI. 120 l, Pius XII. 150 l, John XXIII. 170 l, Paul VI. 250 l, John Paul I. 450 l, John Paul II.

1979, Oct. 11		Photo.	Perf. 14x13½	
657	A196	50 l multi	12	10
658	A196	70 l multi	18	12
659	A196	120 l multi	30	30
660	A196	150 l multi	38	30
661	A196	170 l multi	42	38
662	A196	250 l multi	60	50
663	A196	350 l multi	1.10	90
	Nos. 657-663 (7)		2.53	1.93

Vatican City State, 50th anniversary.

Infant, by Andrea Della Robbia, IYC Emblem—A197

IYC Emblem and Della Robbia Bas Reliefs, Hospital of the Innocents, Florence.

Engraved and Photogravure

1979, Nov. 27			Perf. 13½x14	
664	A197	50 l multi	12	10
665	A197	120 l multi	25	25
666	A197	200 l multi	40	35
667	A197	350 l multi	70	70

International Year of the Child.

Abbot Desiderius Giving Codex to St. Benedict—A198

Illuminated Letters and Illustrations, Codices, Vatican Apostolic Library: 100 l, St. Benedict writing the Rule. 150 l, Page from the Rule. 220 l, Death of St. Benedict. 450 l, Montecassino (after painting by Paul Bril).

1980, Mar. 21		Photo.	Perf. 14x13½	
668	A198	80 l multi	18	15
669	A198	100 l multi	20	18
670	A198	150 l multi	32	30
671	A198	220 l multi	45	40
672	A198	450 l multi	90	80
	Nos. 668-672 (5)		2.05	1.83

St. Benedict of Nursia (patron saint of Europe), 1500th birth anniversary.

Bernini, Medallion Showing Baldacchino in St. Peter's—A199

Gian Lorenzo Bernini (1598-1680), Architect (Self-portrait and Medallion): 170 l, St. Peter's Square with third wing (never built). 250 l, Bronze chair, Doctors of the Church. 350 l, Apostolic Palace stairway.

1980, Oct. 16		Litho.	Perf. 14x13½	
673	A199	80 l multi	20	15
674	A199	170 l multi	42	35
675	A199	250 l multi	60	50
676	A199	350 l multi	85	60

St. Albertus Magnus on Mission of Peace—A200

1980, Nov. 18		Litho.	Perf. 13½x14	
677	A200	300 l shown	75	65
678	A200	400 l As bishop	1.00	85

St. Albertus Magnus, 700th anniversary of death.

Communion of the Saints—A201

1980, Nov. 18			Perf. 14x13½	
679	A201	250 l shown	60	40
680	A201	500 l Christ and saints	1.20	95

Feast of All Saints.

Guglielmo Marconi and Pope Pius XI, Vatican Radio Emblem, Vatican Arms—A202

1981, Feb. 12		Photo.	Perf. 14x13½	
681	A202	100 l shown	20	12
682	A202	150 l Microphone, Bible text	30	22
683	A202	200 l St. Maria di Galeria Radio Center antenna, Archangel Gabriel statue	40	30
684	A202	500 l Pope John Paul II	1.00	75

Vatican Radio, 50th anniversary.

Virgil Seated at Podium, Vergilius Romanus—A203

1981, Apr. 23		Litho.	Perf. 14	
685	A203	350 l multi	70	55
686	A203	600 l multi	1.20	95

2000th birth anniversary of Virgil.

Congress Emblem—A204

Congress Emblem and: 150 l, Virgin appearing to St. Bernadette. 200 l, Pilgrims going to Lourdes. 500 l, Bishop and pilgrims.

1981, June 22			Photo.	
687	A204	80 l multi	20	20
688	A204	150 l multi	35	35
689	A204	200 l multi	50	50
690	A204	500 l multi	1.00	1.00

42nd Intl. Eucharistic Congress, Lourdes, France, July 16-23.

Intl. Year of the Disabled
A205

1981, Sept. 29		Photo.	Perf. 14x13½	
691	A205	600 l multi	1.25	1.25

Jan van Ruusbroec, Flemish Mystic, 500th Birth Anniv.
A206

1981, Sept. 29		Litho. & Engr.	Perf. 13½x14	
692	A206	200 l shown	45	45
693	A206	300 l Portrait	65	65

VATICAN CITY

1980 Journeys of
Pope John Paul II
A207

1981, Dec. 3   Photo.   Perf. 13½x14

694	A207	50 l	Papal arms	10	8
695	A207	100 l	Map of Africa	20	20
696	A207	120 l	Crucifix	25	25
697	A207	150 l	Communion	28	28
698	A207	200 l	African bishop	35	35
699	A207	250 l	Visiting sick	45	45
700	A207	300 l	Notre Dame, France	52	52
701	A207	400 l	UNESCO speech	70	70
702	A207	600 l	Christ of the Andes, Brazil	1.00	1.00
703	A207	700 l	Cologne Cathedral, Germany	1.25	1.25
704	A207	900 l	Pope John Paul II	1.65	1.65
	Nos. 694-704 (11)			6.75	6.73

700th Death Anniv. of St. Agnes of
Prague—A208

Designs: 700 l, Handing order to Grand Master of the Crosiers of the Red Star. 900 l, Receiving letter from St. Clare.

1982, Feb. 16   Photo.   Perf. 13½x14

705	A208	700 l	multi	1.25	1.25
706	A208	900 l	multi	1.50	1.50

Pueri Cantores   St. Theresa of
                        Avila
                        (1515-1582)
A209   A210

Luca Della Robbia (1400-1482), Sculptor: No. 708, Pueri Cantores (diff.) No. 709, Virgin in Prayer (44x36mm.).

1982, May 21   Photo. & Engr.   Perf. 14

707	A209	1000 l	multi	1.50	1.40
708	A209	1000 l	multi	1.50	1.40
709	A209	1000 l	multi	1.50	1.40

1982, Sept. 23   Photo.

Sketches of St. Teresa by Riccardo Tommasi-Ferroni.

710	A210	200 l	multi	30	30
711	A210	600 l	multi	90	90
712	A210	1000 l	multi	1.50	1.25

Keep your collection
up to date!!
Subscribe to the
Scott Stamp Monthly
with
Chronicle of New Issues
Today!

Christmas 1982—A211

Nativity Bas-Reliefs: 300 l, Wit, Stwosz, Church of the Virgin Mary, Cracow. 450 l, Enrico Manfrini.

1982, Nov. 23   Photo. & Engr.   Perf. 14

713	A211	300 l	multi	45	40
714	A211	450 l	multi	70	60

400th Anniv. of Gregorian
Calendar—A212

Sculpture Details, Tomb of Pope Gregory XIII, Vatican Basilica.

1982, Nov. 23   Engr.   Perf. 13½x14

715	A212	200 l	Surveying the globe	30	30
716	A212	300 l	Receiving Edict of Reform	45	45
717	A212	700 l	Presenting edict	1.10	95
a.		Souvenir sheet of 3		2.25	1.75

No. 717a contains Nos. 715-717; margin shows text from Lunar Almanac, 1582. Size: 159x109mm.

Souvenir Sheet

Greek Vase—A213

1983, Mar. 10   Litho.   Perf. 13½x14

718		Sheet of 6		3.00	1.75
a.	A213	100 l	shown	16	10
b.	A213	200 l	Italian vase	34	20
c.	A213	250 l	Female terra-cotta bust	45	28
d.	A213	300 l	Marcus Aurelius bust	50	30
e.	A213	350 l	Bird fresco	62	38
f.	A213	400 l	Pope Clement VIII vestment	70	40

Vatican Collection: The Papacy and Art-USA 1983 exhibition, New York, Chicago, San Francisco. Size: 125x170mm.

1983, June 14   Litho.   Perf. 13½x14

719		Sheet of 6		4.00	2.50
a.	A213	100 l	Horse's head, Etruscan terra cotta	16	10
b.	A213	200 l	Horseman, Greek fragment	32	20
c.	A213	300 l	Male head, Etruscan	48	30
d.	A213	400 l	Apollo Belvedere head	65	40
e.	A213	500 l	Moses, Roman fresco	80	50
f.	A213	1000 l	Madonna and Child, by Bernardo Daddi	1.60	1.00

Size: 125x171mm.

Designs: 150 l, Greek cup, Oedipus and the Sphinx. 200 l, Bronze statue of a Child, Etruscan. 350 l, Emperor Augustus, marble statue. 400 l, Good Shepherd, marble statue. 500 l, St. Nicholas Saving a Ship by Gentile da Fabriano. 1200 l, The Holy Face by Georges Rouault.

1983, Nov. 10   Litho.   Perf. 13½x14

720		Sheet of 6		4.60	2.80
a.	A213	150 l	multi	24	15
b.	A213	200 l	multi	32	20
c.	A213	350 l	multi	56	35
d.	A213	400 l	multi	65	40
e.	A213	500 l	multi	80	50
f.	A213	1200 l	multi	2.00	1.20

Extraordinary Holy Year, 1983-84
(1950th Anniv. of Redemption)—A214

Sketches by Giovanni Hajnal.

1983, Mar. 10   Photo. & Engr.

721	A214	300 l	Crucifixion	50	30
722	A214	350 l	Christ the Redeemer	62	38
723	A214	400 l	Pope	70	40
724	A214	2000 l	Holy Spirit	3.50	2.00

Theology, by Raphael
(1483-1517)—A215

Allegories, Room of the Segnatura.

1983, June 14

725	A215	50 l	shown	8	5
726	A215	400 l	Poetry	65	40
727	A215	500 l	Justice	80	50
728	A215	1200 l	Philosphy	2.00	1.25

Gregor Johann Mendel (1822-1884),
Biologist—A216

Phases of pea plant hybridization.

Photo. & Engr.

1984, Feb. 28   Perf. 14x13½

729	A216	450 l	multi	72	45
730	A216	1500 l	multi	2.40	1.50

VATICAN

Complete your collection,
we have in stock
all VATICAN stamps
mint, hinged, never hinged,
used, covers and FDC.

Good quality and fast service.
FREE PRICELIST

We also buy everything
from VATICAN

MARKOV STAMPS
5 Richmond Street East
Toronto, Ontario
M5C 1N2, Canada
tel./416/364 5931

ASDA-APS - CSDA-APHV

VATICAN CITY

SEMI-POSTAL STAMPS.
Holy Year Issue.

Cross and Orb
SP1   SP2

1933   Engraved.   *Perf. 13x13½*   Unwmkd.
B1	SP1	25c +10c grn	11.00	6.50
B2	SP1	75c +15c scar	17.50	17.50
B3	SP2	80c +20c red brn	35.00	27.50
B4	SP2	1.25 l +25c ultra	16.00	20.00

AIR POST STAMPS.

Statue of St. Peter AP1   Dove of Peace over Vatican AP2

Elijah's Ascent into Heaven AP3   Our Lady of Loreto and Angels Moving the Holy House AP4

Wmkd. Crossed Keys. (235)
1938, June 22   Engraved.   *Perf. 14.*
C1	AP1	25c brown	22	25
C2	AP2	50c green	22	25
C3	AP3	75c lake	32	35
C4	AP4	80c dk bl	45	50
C5	AP1	1 l violet	60	65
C6	AP2	2 l ultra	90	1.00
C7	AP3	5 l sl blk	3.00	3.25
C8	AP4	10 l dk brn vio	3.00	3.25
		Nos. C1-C8 (8)	8.71	9.50

Dove of Peace Above St. Peter's Basilica AP5   House of Our Lady of Loreto AP6

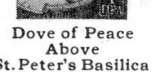

Birds Circling Cross AP7

1947, Nov. 10   Photogravure
C9	AP5	1 l rose red	6	10
C10	AP6	4 l dk brn	8	18
C11	AP5	5 l brt ultra	8	18
C12	AP7	15 l brt pur	75	1.50
C13	AP6	25 l dk bl grn	2.10	1.50
C14	AP7	50 l dk gray	4.25	3.75
C15	AP7	100 l red org	11.00	4.25
		Nos. C9-C15 (7)	18.32	11.46

Nos. C13-C15 exist imperf. Price, each pair $1,000.

Archangel Raphael and Young Tobias AP8

1948, Dec. 28   Engraved   *Perf. 14*
C16	AP8	250 l sepia	16.50	7.50
C17	AP8	500 l ultra	525.00	525.00

Angels and Globe AP9

1949, Dec. 3
C18	AP9	300 l ultra	40.00	15.00
C19	AP9	1000 l green	90.00	85.00

Issued to commemorate the 75th anniversary of the formation of the Universal Postal Union.

Franciscus Gratianus AP10   Dome of St. Peter's Cathedral AP11

1951, Dec. 20   *Perf. 14x13*
C20	AP10	300 l dp plum	250.00	275.00
C21	AP10	500 l dp bl	60.00	20.00

Issued to commemorate the 800th anniversary of the publication of unified canon laws.

1953, Aug. 10   *Perf. 13*
C22	AP11	500 l chocolate	25.00	8.00
C23	AP11	1000 l dp ultra	40.00	20.00

See also Nos. C33-C34.

Archangel Gabriel by Melozzo da Forli AP12   Obelisk of St. John Lateran AP13

Archangel Gabriel: 10 l, 35 l, 100 l, Annunciation by Pietro Cavallini: 15 l, 50 l, 300 l, Annunciation by Leonardo da Vinci.

1956, Feb. 12   Wmk. 235
C24	AP12	5 l gray blk	7	7
C25	AP12	10 l bl grn	7	7
C26	AP12	15 l dp org	8	8
C27	AP12	25 l dk car rose	33	25
C28	AP12	35 l carmine	70	80
C29	AP12	50 l ol brn	17	25
C30	AP12	60 l ultra	5.00	4.75
C31	AP12	100 l org brn	25	20
C32	AP12	300 l dp vio	65	75
		Nos. C24-C32 (9)	7.32	7.22

Type of 1953.

1958   *Perf. 13½*
C33	AP11	500 l grn & bl grn	13.00	11.00
	a.	Perf. 14	525.00	400.00
C34	AP11	1000 l dp mag	2.00	3.75
	a.	Perf. 14	2.00	3.75

1959, Oct. 27   Engr.   *Perf. 13½x14*

Obelisks, Rome: 10 l, 60 l, St. Mary Major. 15 l, 100 l, St. Peter. 25 l, 200 l, Piazza del Popolo. 35 l, 500 l, Trinità dei Monti.

C35	AP13	5 l dl vio	5	5
C36	AP13	10 l bl grn	10	10
C37	AP13	15 l dk brn	5	5
C38	AP13	25 l sl grn	10	10
C39	AP13	35 l ultra	10	10
C40	AP13	50 l yel grn	12	12
C41	AP13	60 l rose car	15	12
C42	AP13	100 l bluish blk	20	12
C43	AP13	200 l brown	35	30
C44	AP13	500 l org brn	75	65
		Nos. C35-C44 (10)	1.97	1.71

Archangel Gabriel by Filippo Valle AP14   Jet over St. Peter's Cathedral AP15

1962, March 13   Wmk. 235
C45	AP14	1000 l brown	1.75	1.50
C46	AP14	1500 l dk bl	5.25	4.50

Photogravure

1967, Mar. 7   *Perf. 14*   Wmk. 235

Designs: 40 l, 200 l, Radio tower and statue of Archangel Gabriel (like A87). 90 l, 500 l, Aerial view of St. Peter's Square and Vatican City.

C47	AP15	20 l brt vio	6	5
C48	AP15	40 l blk & pink	10	10
C49	AP15	90 l sl bl & dk gray	18	18
C50	AP15	100 l blk & sal	18	18
C51	AP15	200 l vio blk & gray	35	35
C52	AP15	500 l dk brn & lt brn	80	80
		Nos. C47-C52 (6)	1.67	1.66

Archangel Gabriel by Fra Angelico AP16

Perf. 13½x14

1968, Mar. 12   Engraved   Wmk. 235
C53	AP16	1000 l dk car rose, cr	1.75	1.50
C54	AP16	1500 l blk, cr	2.75	2.75

St. Matthew, by Fra Angelico AP17

The Evangelists, by Fra Angelico from Niccolina Chapel: 300 l, St. Mark. 500 l, St. Luke. 1000 l, St. John.

Engraved and Photogravure   *Perf. 14x13½*

1971, Sept. 30   Unwmkd.
C55	AP17	200 l blk & pale grn	75	75
C56	AP17	300 l blk & bis	1.10	1.10
C57	AP17	500 l blk & sal	3.50	3.50
C58	AP17	1000 l blk & pale lil	1.75	1.75

Seraph, Mosaic from St. Mark's Basilica, Venice AP18

Lithographed and Engraved

1974, Feb. 21   *Perf. 13x14*
C59	AP18	2500 l multi	3.75	2.75

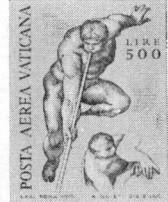

Angel with Trumpet AP19

Designs: 1000 l, Ascending figures. 2500 l, Angels with trumpets. All designs from Last Judgment, by Michelangelo.

Lithographed and Engraved

1976, Feb. 19   *Perf. 13x14*
C60	AP19	500 l sal, bl & brn	4.00	4.00
C61	AP19	1000 l sal, bl & brn	2.50	2.50
C62	AP19	2500 l sal, bl & brn	6.50	6.50

Radio Waves, Antenna, Papal Arms AP20

1978, July 11   Engr.   *Perf. 14x13*
C63	AP20	1000 l multi	1.50	1.50
C64	AP20	2000 l multi	4.50	4.50
C65	AP20	3000 l multi	5.00	5.00

10th World Telecommunications Day.

Pope John Paul II Shaking Hands, Arms of Dominican Republic—AP21

1980   Litho. & Engr.   *Perf. 14x13½*
C66	AP21	200 l *shown*	50	50
C67	AP21	300 l *Mexico*	75	75
C68	AP21	500 l *Poland*	1.25	1.25
C69	AP21	1000 l *Ireland*	2.25	2.25
C70	AP21	1500 l *United States*	3.25	3.25
C71	AP21	2000 l *United Nations*	4.50	4.50
C72	AP21	3000 l *with Dimitrios I, Turkey*	6.50	6.50
		Nos. C66-C72 (7)	19.00	19.00

Issue dates: 3000 l, Sept. 18; others June 24.

World Communications Year—AP22

Designs: 200 l, Moses Explaining The Law to the People by Luca Signarelli. 500 l, Paul Preaching in Athens, Tapestry of Raphael design.

1983, Nov. 10   *Perf. 14*

C73	AP22	200 l multi	3.50	2.00
C74	AP22	500 l multi	8.75	5.00

SPECIAL DELIVERY STAMPS.

Pius XI SD1

Photogravure.

1929, Aug. 1   *Perf. 14*   Unwmkd.

E1	SD1	2 l car rose	14.00	11.00
E2	SD1	2.50 l dk bl	11.50	9.00

Aerial View of Vatican City SD2

Engraved.

1933   Wmkd. Crossed Keys. (235)

E3	SD2	2 l rose red & brn	15	15
E4	SD2	2.50 l dp bl & brn	25	25

1945   Unwmkd.

E5	SD2	3.50 l dk car & ultra	30	40
E6	SD2	5 l ultra & grn	40	50

Nos. E5 and E6 Surcharged with New Values and Bars in Black.

1946, Jan. 9

E7	SD2	6 l on 3.50 l dk car & ultra	1.25	1.75
E8	SD2	12 l on 5 l ultra & grn	1.25	1.75

Vertical pairs imperf. between exist of No. E7 (price $150) and No. E8 (price $200).

Bishop Matteo Giberti SD3

Design: 12 l, Gaspar Cardinal Contarini.

1946, Feb. 21   Photogravure

Centers in Dark Brown.

E9	SD3	6 l dk grn	15	18
E10	SD3	12 l cop brn	25	25

See note after No. 121.
Nos. E9–E10 exist imperf. and part perforate.

Basilica of St. Peter SD5

Design: 80 l, Basilica of St. John.

1949   *Perf. 14*   Wmk. 235

E11	SD5	40 l sl gray	7.50	7.00
a.		Perf. 13½x14	11.50	9.00
E12	SD5	80 l chnt brn	9.50	16.00
a.		Perf. 13½x14	16.00	16.00

St. Peter and His Tomb SD6

Design: 85 l, Pius XII and Roman sepulcher.

Engraved.

1953, Apr. 23   *Perf. 13½x13, 14*

E13	SD6	50 l bl grn & dk brn	25	30
E14	SD6	85 l dp org & dk brn	75	80

Arms of Pope John XXIII SD7

1960   Photogravure   *Perf. 14*

E15	SD7	75 l red & brn	12	12
E16	SD7	100 l dk bl & brn	18	18

Pope Paul VI by Enrico Manfrini SD8

Design: 150 l, Papal arms.

1966, March 8   *Perf. 14*   Wmk. 235

E17	SD8	150 l blk brn	25	25
E18	SD8	180 l brown	32	32

POSTAGE DUE STAMPS.

Regular Issue of 1929 Overprinted in Black and Brown

1931   *Perf. 14*   Unwmkd.

J1	A1	5c dk brn & pink	15	30
a.		Double frame		
J2	A1	10c dk grn & lt grn	15	30
a.		Frame omitted	550.00	
J3	A1	20c vio & lil	3.00	5.50

Surcharged

J4	A1	40c on 30c ind & yel	2.75	6.25

Surcharged

J5	A2	60c on 2 l ol brn	72.50	
J6	A2	1.10 l on 2.50 l red org	10.00	27.50
		Nos. J1-J6 (6)	88.55	

In addition to the surcharges, Nos. J4 to J6 are overprinted with ornamental frame as on J1 to J3.

Papal Arms
D1   D2

Typographed.

1945   *Perf. 14.*   Unwmkd.

J7	D1	5c blk & yel	10	8
J8	D1	20c blk & lil	10	8
J9	D1	80c blk & sal	10	8
J10	D1	1 l blk & grn	10	8
J11	D1	2 l blk & bl	15	25
J12	D1	5 l blk & gray	15	25
a.		Imperf. (pair)	120.00	120.00
		Nos. J7-J12 (6)	70	82

A second type of Nos. J7-J12 exists, in which the colored lines of the background are thicker.
The 20c and 5 lire exist in horizontal pairs imperf. vertically. Price, each $30.
The 20c exists in horizontal pairs imperf. between. Price $80.

Engraved.

1954   *Perf. 13½x13*   Wmk. 235

J13	D2	4 l blk & rose	60	38
J14	D2	6 l blk & grn	1.00	1.00
J15	D2	10 l blk & yel	50	15
J16	D2	20 l blk & bl	1.25	1.75
J17	D2	50 l blk & ol brn	42	42
J18	D2	70 l blk & red brn	50	50
		Nos. J13-J18 (6)	4.27	4.20

Papal Arms D3

Photogravure and Engraved

1968, May 28   *Perf. 14*   Wmk. 235

J19	D3	10 l grysh bl	5	5
J20	D3	20 l pale bl	6	6
J21	D3	50 l pale lil rose	10	10
J22	D3	60 l gray	10	10
J23	D3	100 l dl yel	15	15
J24	D3	180 l bluish lil	28	28
		Nos. J19-J24 (6)	74	74

PARCEL POST STAMPS.

Regular Issue of 1929 Overprinted **PER PACCHI**

1931   *Perf. 14.*   Unwmkd

Q1	A1	5c dk brn & pink	20	38
Q2	A1	10c dk grn & lt grn	20	38
Q3	A1	20c vio & lil	2.50	5.00
Q4	A1	25c dk bl & lt bl	11.00	8.00
Q5	A1	30c ind & yel	12.50	8.00
Q6	A1	50c ind & sal buff	15.00	8.00
Q7	A1	75c brn car & gray	3.25	6.75

Overprinted **PER PACCHI**

Q8	A2	80c car rose	1.65	4.00
Q9	A2	1.25 l dk bl	2.50	5.50
Q10	A2	2 l ol brn	90	2.25
a.		Inverted ovpt.	325.00	450.00
Q11	A2	2.50 l red org	90	2.25
a.		Double ovpt.	225.00	
b.		Invtd. ovpt.	550.00	
Q12	A2	5 l dk grn	90	2.25
Q13	A2	10 l ol blk	90	2.25
a.		Double ovpt.	325.00	

Special Delivery Stamps of 1929 Overprinted Vertically **PERPACCHI**

Q14	SD1	2 l car rose	90	2.25
Q15	SD1	2.50 l dk bl	90	2.25
		Nos. Q1-Q15 (15)	54.20	59.51

VENEZUELA

(vĕn'ê·zwē'lȧ)

LOCATION—On the northern coast of South America, bordering on the Caribbean Sea.

GOVT.—Republic.

AREA—352,143 sq. mi.

POP.—12,740,000 (est. 1977).

CAPITAL—Caracas.

100 Centavos = 8 Reales = 1 Peso
100 Centesimos = 1 Venezolano (1879)
100 Centimos = 1 Bolivar (1880)

> Prices of early Venezuela stamps vary according to condition. Quotations for Nos. 1–21 are for fine copies. Very fine to superb specimens sell at much higher prices, and inferior or poor copies sell at reduced prices, depending on the condition of the individual specimen.

Coat of Arms
A1

Lithographed.

Fine Impression. No Dividing Line Between Stamps.

1859, Jan. 1 ***Imperf.*** **Unwmkd.**

1	A1	½r yellow	30.00	16.00
a.		½r org	35.00	18.00
b.		Greenish paper	300.00	
2	A1	1r blue	200.00	35.00
3	A1	2r red	50.00	25.00
a.		2r dl rose red	60.00	30.00
b.		Half used as 1r on cover		250.00
c.		Greenish paper	250.00	175.00

1859–60 Coarse Impression.

Thick Paper

4	A1	½r orange	12.00	6.00
a.		½r yel	600.00	40.00
b.		½r ol yel	600.00	40.00
c.		Bluish paper	750.00	
d.		½r dl rose (error)		
5	A1	1r blue	30.00	17.50
a.		1r pale bl	40.00	18.50
b.		1r dk bl	40.00	18.50
c.		Half used as ½r on cover		300.00
d.		Bluish paper	250.00	
6	A1	2r red	35.00	25.00
a.		2r dl rose	45.00	27.50
b.		Tête bêche pair	4,000.	3,000.
c.		Half used as 1r on cover		200.00
d.		Bluish paper	300.00	

In the fine impression, the background lines of the shield are more sharply drawn. In the coarse impression, the shading lines at each end of the scroll inscribed "LIBERTAD" are usually very heavy. Stamps of the coarse impression are closer together, and there is usually a dividing line between them.

Nos. 1–3 exist on thick paper and on bluish paper. Nos. 1–6 exist on pelure paper.

The greenish paper varieties (Nos. 1b and 3c) and the bluish paper varities were not regularly issued.

Arms
A2

Eagle
A3

1862 **Lithographed**

7	A2	¼c green	32.50	80.00
8	A2	½c dl lil	40.00	150.00
a.		½c vio	50.00	160.00
9	A2	1c gray brn	60.00	170.00

Counterfeits are plentiful. Forged cancellations abound on Nos. 7–17.

1863-64

10	A3	½c pale red ('64)	75.00	125.00
a.		½c red	85.00	200.00
11	A3	1c sl ('64)	85.00	150.00
12	A3	½r orange	10.00	5.00
13	A3	1r blue	30.00	15.00
a.		1r pale bl	40.00	20.00
b.		Half used as ½r on cover		150.00
14	A3	2r green	42.50	40.00
a.		2r dp yel grn	50.00	42.50
b.		Quarter used as ½r on cover		300.00
c.		Half used as 1r on cover		225.00

1865 **Redrawn.**

15	A3	½r orange	5.00	3.50
a.		½r yel	5.00	3.50

The redrawn stamp has a broad "N" in "FEDERACION". "MEDIO REAL" and "FEDERACION" are in thin letters. There are 52 instead of 49 pearls in the circle.

A4

Simón Bolívar
A5

1865–70

16	A4	½c yel grn ('67)	300.00	500.00
17	A4	1c bl grn ('67)	300.00	400.00
18	A4	½r brn vio (thin paper)	12.00	3.00
19	A4	½r lil rose ('70)	15.00	5.00
a.		½r brnsh rose	15.00	6.00
b.		Tête bêche pair	125.00	200.00
20	A4	1r vermilion	60.00	15.00
a.		Half used as ½r on cover		150.00
21	A4	2r yellow	200.00	120.00
a.		Half used as 1r on cover		425.00
b.		Quarter used as ½r on cover		500.00

This issue is known unofficially rouletted.

Overprinted in Very Small Upright Letters "Bolivar Sucre Miranda—Decreto de 27 de Abril de 1870", or "Decreto de 27 de Junio 1870" in Slanting Letters.

(The "Junio" overprint is continuously repeated, in four lines arranged in two pairs, with the second line of each pair inverted.)

1871-76 **Lithographed.**

22	A5	1c yellow	1.00	50
a.		1c org	2.00	85
b.		1c brn org ('76)	2.00	50
c.		1c pale buff ('76)	2.00	75
d.		Laid paper	3.50	1.00
23	A5	2c yellow	2.00	75
a.		2c org	5.00	75
b.		2c brn org	4.00	1.25
c.		2c pale buff ('76)	4.00	75
d.		Laid paper	4.00	1.00
e.		Frame inverted	3,750.	2,750.
24	A5	3c yellow	3.00	1.00
a.		3c org	4.00	2.50
b.		3c pale buff ('76)	7.50	3.00
25	A5	4c yellow	4.00	1.00
a.		4c org	6.00	2.25
b.		4c brn org ('76)	6.00	2.25
c.		4c buff ('76)	6.00	2.25
26	A5	5c yellow	4.00	1.00
a.		5c org	4.00	1.50
b.		5c pale buff ('76)	4.00	1.50
c.		Laid paper	9.00	1.50
27	A5	1r rose	3.50	75
a.		1r pale red	3.50	75
b.		Laid paper	7.50	1.50
28	A5	2r rose	6.00	1.25
a.		2r pale red	6.00	1.25
29	A5	3r rose	7.50	1.25
a.		3r pale red	7.50	1.25
30	A5	5r rose	7.50	1.75
a.		5r pale red	7.50	1.75
31	A5	7r rose	9.00	4.00
a.		7r pale red	9.00	4.00
32	A5	9r green	22.50	7.50
a.		9r ol grn	25.00	10.00
33	A5	15r green	45.00	15.00
a.		15r gray grn ('76)	45.00	15.00
b.		Frame inverted	7,500.	6,000.
34	A5	20r green	100.00	25.00
a.		Laid paper	125.00	50.00
35	A5	30r green	500.00	200.00
a.		30r gray grn ('76)	500.00	240.00
b.		Double overprint		
36	A5	50r green	1,000.	400.00

These stamps were made available for postage and revenue by official decree, and were the only stamps available for postage in Venezuela from March, 1871 to August, 1873.

Due to lack of cancelling stamps, the majority of specimens were cancelled with pen marks. Fiscal cancellations were also made with the pen. The prices quoted are for pen-cancelled copies.

Different settings were used for the different overprints. Stamps with the upright letters were issued in 1871. Those with the slanting letters in one double line were issued in 1872-1874. Specimens with the slanting overprint in two double lines were issued later from several different settings, those of 1876 showing much coarser impressions of the design than the earlier issues. The 7r and 9r are not known with this overprint. Stamps on laid paper are from a separate setting.

Stamps and Types of 1866–67 Overprinted in Two Lines of Very small Letters Repeated Continuously.

Overprinted

"Estampillas de Correo—Contrasena".

1873

37	A4	½r pale rose	100.00	25.00
a.		½r rose	100.00	25.00
b.		Inverted overprint	160.00	80.00
c.		Tête bêche pair	2,250.	1,750.
38	A4	1r vermilion	125.00	35.00
a.		Inverted overprint	500.00	300.00
39	A4	2r yellow	225.00	125.00
a.		Inverted overprint	500.00	300.00

Overprinted

"Contrasena—Estampillas de Correo".

1874

40	A4	1c gray lil	40.00	50.00
a.		Inverted overprint	12.50	30.00
41	A4	2c green	160.00	175.00
a.		Inverted overprint	60.00	85.00
42	A4	½r rose	100.00	20.00
a.		Inverted overprint	40.00	6.00
b.		½r pink	90.00	18.50
43	A4	1r vermilion	120.00	35.00
a.		Inverted overprint	50.00	15.00
44	A4	2r yellow	400.00	200.00
a.		Inverted overprint	175.00	100.00

Overprinted

"Contrasena—Estampilla de Correos."

1875

45	A4	½r rose	120.00	15.00
a.		Inverted overprint	150.00	30.00
b.		Double overprint	200.00	120.00
46	A4	1r vermilion	175.00	30.00
a.		Inverted overprint	250.00	110.00
b.		Tête bêche pair	3,000.	2,500.

Overprinted

"Estampillas de correo—Contrasena."

1876

47	A4	½r rose	120.00	15.00
a.		½r pink	120.00	15.00
b.		Inverted overprint	120.00	15.00
c.		Both lines of overprint read "Contrasena"	140.00	35.00
d.		Both lines of overprint read "Estampillas de correo"	140.00	35.00
e.		Double ovpt.	240.00	70.00
48	A4	1r vermilion	140.00	50.00
a.		Inverted overprint	160.00	60.00
b.		Tête bêche pair	2,150.	2,500.

On Nos. 47 and 48 "correo" has a small "c" instead of a capital. Nos. 45 and 46 have the overprint in slightly larger letters than the other stamps of the 1873–76 issues.

Simón Bolívar
A6 A7

Overprinted

"Decreto de 27 Junio 1870" Twice. One Line Inverted.

1879

49	A6	1c yellow	4.00	40
a.		1c org	5.00	1.50
b.		1c ol yel	6.00	2.00
50	A6	5c yellow	5.00	1.00
a.		5c org	4.00	1.50
b.		Double overprint	35.00	20.00
51	A6	10c blue	8.00	1.00
52	A6	30c blue	10.00	2.00
53	A6	50c blue	12.50	2.00
54	A6	90c blue	50.00	12.50
55	A7	1v rose red	100.00	17.50
56	A7	3v rose red	180.00	70.00
57	A7	5v rose red	300.00	125.00

In 1879 and the early part of 1880 there were no regular postage stamps in Venezuela and the stamps inscribed "Escuelas" were permitted to serve for postal as well as revenue purposes. Postally cancelled copies are extremely scarce. Prices quoted are for stamps with cancellations of banks or business houses or with pen cancellations. Copies with pen marks removed are sometimes offered as unused stamps, or may have fraudulent postal cancellations added.

Nos. 49–57 exist without overprint. These probably are revenue stamps.

A8

A9

1880 ***Perf. 11***

58	A8	5c yellow	2.00	20
a.		5c org	2.00	40
b.		Printed on both sides	200.00	125.00
59	A8	10c yellow	3.00	40
a.		10c org	3.00	40
60	A8	25c yellow	2.50	50
a.		25c org	3.00	65
b.		Printed on both sides	150.00	75.00
c.		Impression of 5c on back	250.00	125.00
61	A8	50c yellow	5.00	60
a.		50c org	6.00	65
b.		Half used as 25c on cover		25.00
c.		Printed on both sides	225.00	125.00
d.		Impression of 25c on back	225.00	125.00
62	A9	1b pale bl	15.00	1.50
63	A9	2b pale bl	22.50	1.75
64	A9	5b pale bl	50.00	3.00
a.		Half used as 2½b on cover		275.00
65	A9	10b rose red	275.00	100.00
66	A9	20b rose red	900.00	325.00
67	A9	25b rose red	3,750.	800.00

See note on used prices below No. 57.

Bolívar
A10

1880 **Lithographed** ***Perf. 11***

Thick or Thin Paper.

68	A10	5c blue	15.00	8.00
a.		Printed on both sides	300.00	200.00
69	A10	10c rose	25.00	15.00
a.		10c car	25.00	15.00
b.		Double impression	125.00	100.00
c.		Horizontal pair, imperf. btwn.	100.00	100.00
70	A10	10c scarlet	30.00	20.00
a.		Horiz. pair, imperf. between	100.00	100.00
71	A10	25c yellow	15.00	8.00
b.		Thick paper	30.00	15.00

72	A10	50c brown	80.00	40.00
a.		50c dp brn	80.00	40.00
b.		Printed on both sides	300.00	200.00
73	A10	1b green	120.00	60.00
a.		Horizontal pair, imperf. between	400.00	400.00
		Nos. 68-73 (6)	285.00	151.00

Nos. 68 to 73 were used for the payment of postage on letters to be sent abroad and the Escuelas stamps were then restricted to internal use.

Reprints of this issue exist in a great variety of shades as well as in wrong colors. They are on thick and thin paper, white or toned, and perforated 11, 12 and compound. They are also found tête bêche. Reprints of Nos. 68 to 72 inclusive often have a diagonal line across the "S" of "CENTS" and a short line from the bottom of that letter to the frame below it. Originals of No. 73 show parts of a frame around "BOLIVAR". This frame does not appear on the reprints.

Simón Bolívar

A11 A12

A13 A14

A15

1882 Engraved *Perf. 12*

74	A11	5c blue	1.00	40
75	A12	10c red brn	1.00	40
76	A13	25c yel brn	1.25	50
a.		Printed on both sides	75.00	40.00
77	A14	50c green	3.00	80
78	A15	1b violet	5.00	2.00
		Nos. 74-78 (5)	11.25	4.10

Nos. 75–78 exist imperf. Price, set $32.50.

A16 A17

A18 A19

A20 A21

A22 A23

1882-88

79	A16	5c bl grn	15	10
80	A17	10c brown	15	10
81	A18	25c orange	15	10
82	A19	50c blue	20	10
83	A20	1b vermilion	30	20
84	A21	3b dl vio ('88)	30	20
85	A22	10b dk brn ('88)	1.00	1.00
86	A23	20b plum ('88)	1.25	1.25
		Nos. 79-86 (8)	3.50	3.05

By official decree, dated April 14, 1882, stamps of types A11 to A15 were to be used for foreign postage and those of types A16 to A23 for inland correspondence and fiscal use.

1887-88 Lithographed. *Perf. 11.*

87	A16	5c gray grn	50	35
88	A13	25c yel brn	80.00	30.00
89	A18	25c orange	75	65
90	A20	1b org red ('88)	7.00	1.50

Perf. 14.

91	A16	5c gray grn	125.00	45.00

Stamps of type A16, perf. 11 and 14, are from a new die with "ESCUELAS" in smaller letters. Stamps of the 1887-88 issue, perf. 12, and a 50c dark blue, perf. 11 or 12, are believed by experts to be from printer's waste.

Rouletted 8.

92	A11	5c blue	50.00	30.00
93	A13	25c yel brn	25.00	15.00
94	A14	50c green	25.00	15.00
95	A15	1b purple	50.00	30.00

1887-88

96	A16	5c green	12	12
97	A18	25c orange	12	12
98	A19	50c dk bl	75	75
99	A21	3b pur ('88)	3.75	3.75

The so-called imperforate varieties of Nos. 92 to 99, and the pin perforated 50c dark blue, type A19, are believed to be from printer's waste.

Stamps of 1882–88 Handstamp Surcharged in Violet

1892 *Perf. 12.*

100	A11	25c on 5c bl	30.00	30.00
101	A12	25c on 10c red brn	12.00	12.00
102	A13	1b on 25c yel brn	12.00	12.00
103	A14	1b on 50c grn	13.50	13.50

1892

104	A16	25c on 5c bl grn	10.00	6.00
105	A17	25c on 10c brn	10.00	6.00
106	A18	1b on 25c org	12.50	7.00
107	A19	1b on 50c bl	17.50	7.00

Counterfeits of this surcharge exist.

Stamps of 1882-88 Overprinted in Red or Black:

1893

108	A11	5c bl (R)	1.00	40
a.		Inverted overprint	5.00	5.00
b.		Double overprint	25.00	25.00
109	A12	10c red brn (Bk)	1.25	1.25
a.		Inverted overprint	6.00	6.00
b.		Double overprint	25.00	25.00
110	A13	25c yel brn (R)	1.00	50
a.		Inverted overprint	8.00	8.00
b.		Double overprint	25.00	25.00
c.		25c yel brn (Bk)	185.00	185.00
111	A14	50c grn (R)	1.25	80
a.		Inverted overprint	8.00	8.00
b.		Double overprint	40.00	40.00
112	A15	1b pur (R)	3.00	1.20
a.		Inverted ovpt.	15.00	15.00
		Nos. 108-112 (5)	7.50	4.15

1893

114	A16	5c bl grn (R)	15	7
a.		Inverted overprint	5.00	5.00
b.		Double overprint	8.00	8.00
115	A17	10c brn (R)	15	15
a.		Inverted overprint	5.00	5.00
116	A18	25c org (R)	15	15
a.		Inverted overprint	5.00	5.00
117	A18	25c org (Bk)	4.50	4.00
a.		Inverted overprint	12.50	7.50
118	A19	50c bl (R)	15	15
a.		Inverted overprint	5.00	5.00
119	A20	1b ver (Bk)	90	45
a.		Inverted overprint	6.50	6.50
120	A21	3b dl vio (R)	1.20	60
a.		Double overprint	12.50	12.50
121	A22	10b dk brn (R)	3.50	3.00
a.		Double overprint	15.00	15.00
b.		Inverted ovpt.	30.00	30.00
122	A23	20b plum (Bk)	3.00	3.00
a.		Double overprint	30.00	30.00
		Nos. 114-122 (9)	13.70	11.57

Simón Bolívar

A24 A25

1893 Engraved

123	A24	5c red brn	1.40	30
124	A24	10c blue	6.00	1.50
125	A24	25c magenta	30.00	80
126	A24	50c brn vio	6.00	1.00
127	A24	1b green	8.00	1.50
		Nos. 123-127 (5)	51.40	5.10

Many shades exist in this issue, but their prices do not vary.

1893

128	A25	5c gray	12	5
129	A25	10c green	12	5
130	A25	25c blue	12	5
131	A25	50c orange	12	5
132	A25	1b red vio	40	10
133	A25	3b red	70	25
134	A25	10b dl vio	1.35	1.00
135	A25	20b red brn	4.25	3.50
		Nos. 128-135 (8)	7.18	5.05

By decree of November 28th, 1892, the stamps inscribed "Correos" were to be used for external postage and those inscribed "Instruccion" were for internal postage and revenue purposes.

After July 1, 1895, stamps inscribed "Escuelas" or "Instruccion" were no longer available for postage.

Landing of Columbus
A26

1893 *Perf. 12*

136	A26	25c magenta	20.00	1.00

Issued to commemorate the fourth centenary of the discovery of the mainland of South America, also to commemorate the participation of Venezuela in the International Exhibition at Chicago in 1893.

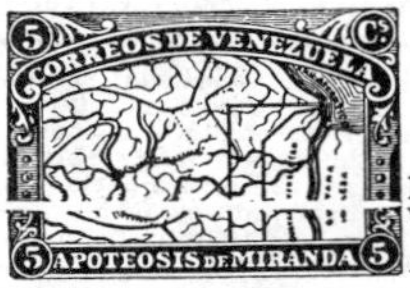

Map of Venezuela
A27

1896 Lithographed.

137	A27	5c yel grn	5.00	4.00
a.		5c ap grn	5.00	4.00
138	A27	10c blue	5.00	4.00
139	A27	25c yellow	6.00	8.00
a.		25c org	6.00	8.00
b.		Tête bêche pair	80.00	80.00
140	A27	50c rose red	80.00	40.00
a.		50c red	80.00	80.00
b.		Tête bêche pair	160.00	160.00
141	A27	1b violet	70.00	40.00
		Nos. 137-141 (5)	166.00	96.00

Issued to commemorate the 80th anniversary of the death of Gen. Francisco Antonio Gabriel de Miranda (1752-1816).

These stamps were in use from July 4 to November 4, 1896.

There are many reprints and forgeries of this issue. Some are made from new stones by transfers from the originals. They include faked errors, imperforate stamps and many tête bêche. The paper of the originals is thin, white and semi-transparent. The gum is shiny and crackled. The paper of the reprints is often thick and opaque. The gum is usually dull, smooth, thin and only slightly adhesive. Price 5 cents each.

Bolívar
A28

1899–1901 Engraved

142	A28	5c dk grn	1.50	40
143	A28	10c red	2.00	50
144	A28	25c blue	2.40	80
145	A28	50c gray blk	3.00	1.50
146	A28	50c org ('01)	2.40	75
147	A28	1b yel grn	40.00	25.00
149	A28	2b orange	500.00	375.00
		Nos. 142-147, 149 (7)	551.30	403.95

Stamps of 1899 Overprinted in Black

1900

150	A28	5c dk grn	1.50	40
a.		Inverted ovpt.	6.00	6.00
151	A28	10c red	1.50	50
a.		Inverted ovpt.	8.00	8.00
b.		Double ovpt.	16.00	16.00
152	A28	25c blue	10.00	1.50
a.		Inverted ovpt.	16.00	16.00
153	A28	50c gray blk	5.00	75
a.		Inverted ovpt.	14.00	14.00
154	A28	1b yel grn	2.00	1.00
a.		Double overprint	20.00	20.00
b.		Inverted ovpt.	14.00	14.00

VENEZUELA

155	A28	2b orange	3.50	2.50
a.		Inverted ovpt	40.00	40.00
b.		Double ovpt.	50.00	50.00
		Nos. 150-155 (6)	23.50	6.65

Initials are those of R. T. Mendoza.

Bolivar Type of 1899–1903 Issue.
Overprinted 1900

1900

156	A28	5c dk grn	250.00	250.00
157	A28	10c red	250.00	250.00
158	A28	25c blue	500.00	250.00
159	A28	50c orange	30.00	2.00
160	A28	1b slate	2.00	1.40
a.		Without overprint		4,250.

It has not been established that No. 160a was regularly issued.

Overprinted

1900

161	A28	5c green	10.00	75
a.		Inverted overprint	12.00	10.00
162	A28	10c red	8.00	1.25
a.		Inverted overprint	12.00	10.00
163	A28	25c blue	15.00	1.20
a.		Inverted ovpt.	15.00	10.00

Overprint exists on each value without "Castro" or without "1900."

A34

1904 Black Surcharge. *Perf. 12.*

230	A34	5c on 50c grn	1.00	80
a.		"Vele"	30.00	30.00
b.		Surch. reading up	1.50	75
c.		Double surcharge	30.00	30.00

General José de Sucre
A35

1904–09 Engraved

231	A35	5c bl grn	60	20
232	A35	10c carmine	80	20
233	A35	15c vio ('09)	1.25	40
234	A35	25c dp ultra	8.00	40
235	A35	50c plum	1.25	60
236	A35	1b plum	1.40	60
		Nos. 231-236 (6)	13.30	2.40

President Cipriano Castro
A37

1905 Lithographed *Perf. 11½*

245	A37	5c vermilion	6.00	6.00
a.		5c car	9.00	9.00
246	A37	10c dk red	10.00	8.00
247	A37	25c yellow	3.00	2.50

National Congress. Issued for interior postage only.
Various part-perforate varieties of Nos. 245–247 exist. Price, $15–$30.

Liberty
A38

1910, Apr. 19 Engr. *Perf. 12*

249	A38	25c dk bl	20.00	1.25

Centenary of national independence.

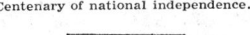

Francisco de Miranda
A39

Rafael Urdaneta   Bolívar
A40   A41

1911 Litho. *Perf. 11½x12*

250	A39	5c dp grn	60	20
251	A39	10c carmine	60	25
252	A40	15c gray	8.00	50
253	A40	25c dp bl	4.00	75
a.		Imperf., pair	60.00	75.00
254	A41	50c purple	5.00	60
255	A41	1b yellow	5.00	2.40
		Nos. 250-255 (6)	23.20	4.70

The 50c with center in blue was never issued although copies were postmarked by favor.
The centers of Nos. 250-255 were separately printed and often vary in shade from the rest of the design. In a second printing of the 5c and 10c, the entire design was printed at one time.

1913 Redrawn.

255A	A40	15c gray	6.00	4.00
255B	A40	25c dp bl	3.00	1.00
255C	A41	50c purple	3.00	1.00

The redrawn stamps have two berries instead of one at top of the left spray; a berry has been added over the "C" and "S" of "Centimos"; and the lowest leaf at the right is cut by the corner square.

Simón Bolívar
A42   A43

1914 Engr. *Perf. 13, 13½*

256	A42	5c yel grn	50.00	75
257	A42	10c scarlet	45.00	60
258	A42	25c dk bl	8.50	25

Printed by the American Bank Note Co.
Different Frames

1915–23 *Perf. 12.*

259	A43	5c green	5.00	40
260	A43	10c vermilion	16.00	75
261	A43	10c cl ('22)	16.00	1.40
262	A43	15c dl ol grn	12.00	85
263	A43	25c ultra	10.00	40
a.		25c bl	20.00	1.00
264	A43	40c ultra	30.00	15.00
265	A43	50c dp vio	8.00	1.00
266	A43	50c ultra ('23)	20.00	6.00
267	A43	75c lt bl	30.00	30.00
a.		75c grnsh bl	80.00	30.00
268	A43	1b dk gray	40.00	10.00
		Nos. 259-268 (10)	237.00	65.80

Type of 1915-23 Issue.
Printed by Waterlow & Sons, Ltd.

1924–39 Re-engraved *Perf. 12½*

269	A43	5c org brn	80	20
a.		5c yel brn	80	20
b.		Horiz. pair, imperf. between	40.00	60.00
c.		Perf. 14		2.50
270	A43	5c grn ('39)	15.00	1.60
271	A43	7½c yel grn ('39)	1.50	50
272	A43	10c dk grn	30	15
a.		Perf. 14	8.00	2.50
273	A43	10c dk car ('39)	5.00	40
274	A43	15c ol grn	3.00	75
a.		Perf. 14	10.00	4.00
275	A43	15c brn ('27)	50	15
276	A43	25c ultra	3.00	15
a.		Perf. 14	15.00	6.00
277	A43	25c red ('28)	30	15
a.		Horizontal pair, imperf. between	75.00	125.00
278	A43	40c dp bl ('25)	80	25
279	A43	40c sl bl ('39)	10.00	1.50
280	A43	50c dk bl	80	25
a.		Perf. 14	40.00	16.00
281	A43	50c dk pur ('39)	12.00	1.40
282	A43	1b black	80	40
a.		Perf. 14	50.00	30.00
283	A43	3b yel org ('25)	2.50	1.40
284	A43	3b red org ('39)	25.00	8.00
285	A43	5b dl vio ('25)	30.00	16.00
		Nos. 269-285 (17)	111.30	33.25

The re-engraved stamps may readily be distinguished from the 1915 issue by the perforation and sometimes by the colors. The designs differ in many minor details which are too minute for illustration or description.

Bolívar and Sucre
A44

1924, Dec. 1 Litho. *Perf. 12*

286	A44	25c grysh bl	5.00	1.00

Redrawn. *Perf. 11½, 12.*

286A	A44	25c ultra	6.25	1.50

Issued to commemorate the centenary of the Battle of Ayacucho.
The redrawn stamp has a whiter effect with less shading in the faces. Bolívar's ear is clearly visible and the outline of his aquiline nose is broken.

A45   A46

Revenue Stamps Surcharged in Black or Red

1926 *Perf. 12, 12½*

287	A45	5c on 1b ol grn	1.00	50
a.		Double surcharge	12.00	12.00
b.		Pair, one without surcharge	18.50	18.50
c.		Inverted surcharge	12.00	12.00
288	A46	25c on 5c dk brn (R)	1.00	60
a.		Inverted surcharge	12.00	12.00
b.		Double surcharge	12.00	12.00

View of Ciudad Bolívar and General J. V. Gómez
A47

1928, July 21 Litho. *Perf. 12*

289	A47	10c dp grn	1.25	80
a.		Imperf., pair	60.00	

Commemorative of the twenty-fifth anniversary of the Battle of Ciudad Bolívar and the foundation of peace in Venezuela.

Simón Bolívar
A48   A49

1930, Dec. 9

290	A48	5c yellow	1.50	60
a.		Imperf., pair	8.00	8.00
291	A48	10c dk bl	1.50	40
a.		Imperf., pair	10.00	10.00
292	A48	25c rose red	1.50	40
a.		Imperf., pair	16.00	16.00

Death centenary of Simón Bolívar (1783–1830), South American liberator.
Nos. 290–292 exist part-perforate, including pairs imperf. between, imperf. horiz., imperf. vert. Price range, $6–12.

Various Frames.
Bluish Winchester Security Paper.

1932-38 Engraved *Perf. 12½*

293	A49	5c violet	60	15
294	A49	7½c dk grn ('37)	1.40	60
295	A49	10c green	80	15
296	A49	15c yellow	2.00	40
297	A49	22½c dp car ('38)	5.00	1.00
298	A49	25c red	1.50	15
299	A49	37½c ultra ('36)	6.00	3.00
300	A49	40c indigo	6.25	40
301	A49	50c ol grn	6.25	60
302	A49	1b lt bl	8.00	1.25
303	A49	3b brown	50.00	25.00
304	A49	5b yel brn	70.00	32.50
		Nos. 293-304 (12)	157.80	65.20

Arms of Bolívar
A50

1933, July 24 Litho. *Perf. 11*

306	A50	25c brn red	4.00	3.00
a.		Imperf., pair	50.00	50.00

150th anniversary of the birth of Simón Bolívar.

Stamps of 1924-32 Surcharged in Black: (Blocks of Surcharge in Color of stamps)

1933

307	A43	7½c on 10c grn	80	40
a.		Double surch.	4.00	4.00
b.		Inverted surch.	5.00	5.00
308	A49	22½c on 25c red (298)	2.75	1.40
309	A43	22½c on 25c red (277)	2.50	2.50
a.		Double surcharge	15.00	15.00
310	A43	37½c on 40c dp bl	3.00	1.50
a.		Double surcharge	17.50	17.50
b.		Inverted surcharge	12.50	12.50

913

VENEZUELA

Nurse and Child
A51

River Scene
A52

Gathering Cacao Pods
A53

Cattle Raising
A54

Plowing
A55

1937, June 25   Litho.   Perf. 11½

311	A51	5c dp vio	1.00	75
312	A52	10c dk sl grn	1.00	35
313	A53	15c yel brn	2.00	1.00
314	A51	25c cerise	2.00	60
315	A54	50c yel grn	12.00	8.00
316	A55	3b red org	20.00	15.00
317	A51	5b lt brn	40.00	30.00
		Nos. 311-317 (7)	78.00	55.70

Nos. 311–317 exist imperforate. Price for set $75. Nos. 311–315 exist in pairs, imperf. between; price range, $20–$30.

No. 300 Surcharged in Black

1937   Perf. 12½

318	A49	25c on 40c ind	10.00	1.25
a.		Double surch.	25.00	25.00
b.		Inverted surch.	20.00	20.00
c.		Triple surch.	50.00	50.00

1937 Surcharged

319	A49	25c on 40c ind	325.00	275.00

A56

1937, Oct. 28   Litho.   Perf. 10½

320	A56	25c blue	2.00	80

Acquisition of the Port of La Guaira by the Government from the British Corporation, June 3, 1937. Exists imperf. See Nos. C64–C65.

A redrawn printing of No. 320, with top inscription beginning "Nacionalización..." was prepared but not issued. Price, $85.

Stamps of 1937 Overprinted in Black

RESELLADO 1937-1938

1937-38   Perf. 11½

321	A51	5c dp vio	7.50	4.00
322	A52	10c dk sl grn	2.00	1.00
a.		Inverted ovpt.	20.00	20.00
323	A51	25c cerise	1.50	85
a.		Inverted ovpt.	25.00	25.00
324	A55	3b red org	275.00	140.00

Part-perforate pairs exist of Nos. 321–322 and 324. Price range, $12.50 to $125.
See Nos. C66–C78.

Gathering Coffee Beans
A57

Simón Bolívar
A58

Post Office, Caracas
A59

1938   Engraved   Perf. 12

325	A57	5c green	60	20
326	A57	5c dp grn	60	20
327	A58	10c car rose	1.00	20
328	A58	10c dp rose	1.00	20
329	A59	15c dk vio	2.00	40
330	A59	15c ol grn	1.25	40
331	A58	15c lt bl	60	20
332	A58	25c dk bl	60	30
333	A58	37½c dk bl	12.00	5.00
334	A58	37½c lt bl	4.00	1.25
335	A59	40c sepia	30.00	10.00
336	A59	40c black	25.00	10.00
337	A57	50c ol grn	40.00	10.00
338	A57	50c dl vio	14.00	1.25
339	A58	1b dp rose	16.50	8.00
340	A58	1b blk brn	25.00	2.00
341	A57	3b orange	125.00	65.00
342	A59	5b black	22.50	10.00
		Nos. 325-342 (18)	321.65	124.60

See Nos. 400 and 412.

Teresa Carreño
A60

Bolívar Statue
A61

1938, June 12   Perf. 11½x12

343	A60	25c blue	7.00	80

Issued in honor of Teresa Carreño, Venezuelan pianist, whose remains were repatriated February 14, 1938.

1938, July 24   Perf. 12

344	A61	25c dk bl	8.00	85

Issued in honor of "The Day of the Worker".

Type of 1937 Surcharged in Black

VALE Bs. 0,40

1938   Lithographed.   Perf. 11½

345	A51	40c on 5b lt brn	16.50	6.00
a.		Inverted surch.	32.50	32.50

Gen. José I. Paz Castillo, Postmaster of Venezuela, 1859
A62

1939, Apr. 19   Engraved   Perf. 12½

348	A62	10c carmine	3.25	80

Issued to commemorate the 80th anniversary of the first Venezuelan stamp.

View of Ojeda
A63

1939, June 24   Photogravure

349	A63	25c dl bl	12.00	1.00

Founding of city of Ojeda.

Cristóbal Mendoza
A64

Diego Urbaneja
A65

1939, Oct. 14   Engraved   Perf. 13

350	A64	5c green	80	40
351	A64	10c dk car rose	80	40
352	A64	15c dl lil	2.00	60
353	A64	25c brt ultra	1.60	40
354	A64	37½c dk bl	25.00	15.00
355	A64	50c lt ol grn	25.00	10.00
356	A64	1b dk brn	12.00	8.00
		Nos. 350-356 (7)	67.20	34.80

Issued to commemorate the centenary of the death of Cristóbal Mendoza (1772–1839), postmaster general.

1940-43   Perf. 12

357	A65	5c Prus grn	75	25
357A	A65	7½c dk bl grn ('43)	1.00	35
358	A65	15c olive	1.25	40
359	A65	37½c dp bl	2.00	1.00
360	A65	40c vio bl	1.50	40
361	A65	50c violet	8.00	2.00
362	A65	1b dk vio brn	4.00	1.25
363	A65	3b scarlet	12.00	5.00
		Nos. 357-363 (8)	30.50	10.65

See Nos. 399, 408, 410 and 411.

Battle of Carabobo, 1821
A67

1940, June 13

365	A67	25c blue	8.00	80

Issued in commemoration of the 150th anniversary of the birth of General José Antonio Páez.

"Crossing the Andes" by Tito Salas
A68

1940, June 13

366	A68	25c dk bl	8.00	80

Issued in commemoration of the centenary of the death of General Francisco Santander.

Monument and Urn containing Ashes of Simón Bolívar
A69

Bed where Simón Bolívar was Born
A70

Designs: 15c, "Christening of Bolivar" by Tito Salas. 20c, Bolivar's birthplace, Caracas. 25c, "Bolivar on Horseback" by Salas. 30c, Patio of Bolivar House, Caracas. 37½c, Patio of Bolivar's Birthplace. 50c, "Rebellion of 1812" by Salas.

1940-41

367	A69	5c turq grn	45	12
368	A70	10c rose pink	45	12
369	A69	15c olive	1.00	25
370	A70	20c bl ('41)	1.75	12
371	A69	25c lt bl	1.00	18
372	A70	30c plum ('41)	2.50	38
373	A69	37½c dk bl	5.00	1.75
374	A70	50c purple	3.00	75
		Nos. 367-374 (8)	15.15	3.67

Issued in commemoration of the 110th anniversary of the death of Simón Bolívar. See Nos. 397, 398, 403, 405–407 and 409.

No. 371 Surcharged In Black

HABILITADO 1941 VALE Bs. 0,20

1941

375	A69	20c on 25c lt bl	1.00	25
a.		Inverted surch.	15.00	15.00

VENEZUELA

Nos. 311-312
Overprinted
in Black

HABILITADO
1940

1941			Perf. 11½	
376	A51	5c dp vio	3.00	75
a.		Double ovpt.	15.00	12.50
b.		Vertical pair, imperf. between	22.50	22.50
c.		Invtd. ovpt.	30.00	25.00
377	A52	10c dk sl grn	1.75	50
a.		Double ovpt.	20.00	20.00

Symbols of Industry
A77

Caracas Cathedral
A78

1942, Dec. 17		Litho.	Perf. 12	
378	A77	10c scarlet	1.50	35
a.		Imperf., pair	35.00	35.00

Grand Industrial Exposition, Caracas.

1943			Engraved	
379	A78	10c rose car	1.00	25

See No. 404.

Stamps of 1937
Overprinted in Black

Resellado
1943

1943			Perf. 11½	
380	A51	5c dp vio	18.50	12.50
a.		Invtd. ovpt.	50.00	45.00
381	A52	10c dk sl grn	7.50	5.00
a.		Invtd. ovpt.	60.00	50.00
382	A54	50c yel grn	10.00	6.00
383	A55	3b red org	55.00	27.50

Nos. 380 to 383 were issued for sale to philatelists and sold only in sets.

Stamps of 1937-38
Surcharged in Black

Habilitado
Vale
Bs. 0.20

1943			Perf. 11½, 10½, 12	
384	A51	20c on 25c cer	37.50	37.50
385	A56	20c on 25c bl	85.00	85.00
386	A60	20c on 25c dk bl	20.00	20.00
387	A61	20c on 25c dk bl	20.00	20.00
a.		Inverted surcharge		50.00

Nos. 384-387 were issued for sale to philatelists and sold only in sets.

Souvenir Sheet.

A79

1944, Aug. 22		Litho.	Perf. 12	
Flags in Red, Yellow, Blue & Black.				
388	A79	Sheet of four	40.00	40.00
a.		5c Prus grn	7.00	2.00
b.		10c rose	8.00	3.00
c.		20c ultra	8.00	4.00
d.		1b rose lake	10.00	6.00

80th anniversary of International Red Cross and 37th anniversary of Venezuela's joining. Size: 104x115mm.
No. 388 is known imperf. Price $50.

Antonio José de Sucre
A80

1945, Mar. 3		Engraved	Unwmkd.	
389	A80	5c org yel	1.50	50
390	A80	10c dk bl	2.00	1.00
391	A80	20c rose pink	2.50	1.00
Nos. 389-391, C206-C215 (13)			28.80	18.75

Issued to commemorate the 150th anniversary of the birth of Antonio de Sucre.

Andrés Bello
A81

Gen. Rafael Urdaneta
A82

1946, Aug. 24				
392	A81	20c dp bl	1.25	50
393	A82	20c dp bl	1.25	50

Issued to commemorate the 80th anniversary of the death of Andrés Bello (1780?-1865), educator and writer, and the centenary of the death of Gen. Rafael Urdaneta. See also Nos. C216-C217.

Allegory of the Republic
A83

1946, Oct. 18		Litho.	Perf. 11½	
394	A83	20c grnsh bl	1.25	50
Nos. 394, C218-C221 (5)			9.90	7.15

Anniversary of Revolution of October, 1945. Exists imperf.
See Nos. C218-C221.

Anti-tuberculosis Institute, Maracaibo
A84

1947, Jan. 12			Perf. 12	
395	A84	20c ultra & yel		
Nos. 395, C228-C231 (5)			12.75	10.10

12th Pan-American Health Conference, Caracas, January, 1947. Exists imperf. and part perf.

No. 362
Surcharged in Green

J. R. G.
CORREOS
Vale Bs. 0.15
1946

1947				
396	A65	15c on 1b dk vio brn	1.25	50
a.		Inverted surch.	9.00	7.50

See also Nos. C223-C227.

Types of 1938-40.

1947			Engraved	
397	A69	5c green	12	6
398	A70	30c black	1.50	1.00
399	A65	40c red vio	1.00	35
400	A59	5b dp org	80.00	40.00

R1

In 1947 a decree authorized the use of 5c and 10c revenue stamps of the above type for franking correspondence. Other denominations were also used unofficially.

Nos. 398 and 373
Surcharged in Red

CORREOS
Vale Bs. 0.05
1947

1947		Perf. 12	Unwmkd.	
401	A70	5c on 30c blk	60	12
a.		Inverted surcharge	7.50	7.50
402	A70	5c on 37½c dk bl	75	12
a.		Inverted surcharge	7.50	7.50

Types of 1938-43.

1947-49				
403	A69	5c brt ultra	25	10
404	A78	10c red	12	6
405	A69	15c rose car	75	12
406	A69	25c violet	60	15
407	A70	30c dk vio brn ('48)	75	25
408	A65	40c org ('48)	75	25
409	A65	50c ol grn	1.25	35
410	A65	1b dp bl	2.50	35
411	A65	3b gray	5.00	1.25
412	A59	5b chocolate	22.80	8.50
Nos. 403-412 (10)			34.77	11.38

M. S. Republica de Venezuela
A85

Imprint: "American Bank Note Company"

1948-50		Engraved	Perf. 12	
413	A85	5c blue	25	7
414	A85	7½c red org ('49)	85	45
a.		Booklet pane of 20		
415	A85	10c car rose	65	7
a.		Booklet pane of 10		
416	A85	15c gray ('50)	85	25
417	A85	20c sepia	50	12
418	A85	25c vio ('49)	85	25
419	A85	30c org ('50)	5.50	2.75
420	A85	37½c brn ('49)	2.50	2.00
421	A85	40c ol ('50)	3.75	2.50
422	A85	50c red vio ('49)	1.00	35
423	A85	1b gray grn	2.50	75
Nos. 413-423 (11)			19.20	9.56

Grand Colombian Merchant Fleet. See Nos. 632-634, C256-C271, C554-C556.

Santos Michelena
A86

Christopher Columbus
A87

1949, April 25				
424	A86	5c ultra	38	18
425	A86	10c carmine	75	25
426	A86	20c sepia	3.00	1.00
427	A86	1b green	10.00	4.50
Nos. 424-427, C272-C277 (10)			29.81	12.64

Issued to commemorate the centenary of the death of Santos Michelena, Finance Minister, and the 110th anniversary of the Postal Convention of Bogota.

1949		Engraved	Perf. 12½	
428	A87	5c dp ultra	65	18
429	A87	10c carmine	2.50	75
430	A87	20c dk brn	3.00	1.00
431	A87	1b green	7.50	3.75
Nos. 428-431, C278-C283 (10)			30.30	11.13

Issued to commemorate the 450th anniversary (in 1948) of Columbus' discovery of the American mainland.

Arms of Venezuela
A88

1948				
432	A88	5c blue	2.50	1.25
433	A88	10c red	3.00	1.50

The 20c and 1b, type A88, and six similar air post stamps were prepared but not issued. Price, set of 8, about $125.

Gen. Francisco de Miranda
A89

1950		Perf. 12	Unwmkd.	
434	A89	5c blue	38	6
435	A89	10c green	85	18
436	A89	20c sepia	1.75	75
437	A89	1b rose car	8.00	3.75

Bicentenary of birth of General Francisco de Miranda.

Map and Population Chart
A90

Alonso de Ojeda
A91

1950				
438	A90	5c blue	30	12
439	A90	10c gray	30	18
440	A90	15c sepia	45	18
441	A90	25c green	70	25
442	A90	30c red	1.00	35
443	A90	50c violet	2.00	75
444	A90	1b red brn	5.00	2.50
Nos. 438-444 (7)			9.75	4.33

Issued to publicize the 8th National Census of the Americas. See also Nos. C302-C310.

1950		Photogravure.	Perf. 11½	
445	A91	5c dp bl	35	20
446	A91	10c dp red	50	25
447	A91	15c sl gray	60	30
448	A91	20c ultra	2.50	1.00
449	A91	1b bl grn	10.00	5.00
Nos. 445-449 (5)			13.95	6.75

Issued to commemorate the 450th anniversary (in 1949) of the discovery of the Gulf of Maracaibo.
See Nos. C316-C321.

Nos. 414 and 420 Surcharged in Black

RESELLADO
"5 CENTIMOS"

1951		Perf. 12	Unwmkd.	
450	A85	5c on 7½c red org	50	25
451	A85	10c on 37½c brn	50	25
a.		Inverted surcharge	25.00	25.00

Telegraph Stamps Surcharged in Black or Red

Habilitado Correos 25 Centimos

Grayish Security Paper.

1951 Engraved.

452 5c on 5c brn 25 12
453 10c on 10c grn 50 12
454 20c on 1b blk (R) 1.00 25
455 25c on 25c car 1.25 50
456 30c on 2b ol grn (R) 1.75 1.25
Nos. 452-456 (5) 4.75 2.24

The 5c and 10c surcharges include quotation marks on each line and values are expressed "Bs. 0.05" etc.

Bolivar Statue, New York
A92

1951 *Perf. 12*

457 A92 5c green 50 10
458 A92 10c car rose 1.00 35
459 A92 20c ultra 1.00 35
460 A92 30c sl gray 1.25 60
461 A92 40c dp grn 1.75 60
462 A92 50c red brn 3.75 1.25
463 A92 1b gray blk 12.00 6.00
Nos. 457-463 (7) 21.25 9.25

Issued to commemorate the relocation of the equestrian statue of Simon Bolivar in New York City, April 19, 1951. See Nos. C322-C329.

Arms of Carabobo and "Industry"
A93

Photogravure.

1951 *Perf. 11½.* Unwmkd.

464 A93 5c green 25 10
465 A93 10c red 25 12
466 A93 15c brown 75 30
467 A93 20c ultra 1.00 50
468 A93 25c org brn 1.10 55
469 A93 30c blue 2.50 1.00
470 A93 35c purple 8.50 7.50
Nos. 464-470 (7) 14.35 10.07

Arms of Zulia and "Industry."

471 A93 5c green 35 10
472 A93 10c red 75 10
473 A93 15c brown 1.50 75
474 A93 20c ultra 2.00 1.00
475 A93 50c brn org 15.00 10.00
476 A93 1b dp gray grn 3.75 1.50
477 A93 5b rose vio 8.50 6.00
Nos. 471-477 (7) 31.85 19.45

Arms of Anzoategui and Globe.

478 A93 5c green 25 10
479 A93 10c red 30 10
480 A93 15c brown 1.50 75
481 A93 20c ultra 2.50 50
482 A93 40c red org 5.00 2.50
483 A93 45c rose vio 15.00 8.50
484 A93 3b bl gray 6.25 3.00
Nos. 478-484 (7) 30.80 15.45

Arms of Caracas and Buildings.

485 A93 5c green 85 12
486 A93 10c red 1.25 18
487 A93 15c brown 3.00 75
488 A93 20c ultra 6.25 1.50
489 A93 25c org brn 8.50 1.50
490 A93 30c blue 7.50 1.75
491 A93 35c purple 70.00 40.00
Nos. 485-491 (7) 97.35 45.80

Arms of Tachira and Agricultural Products.

492 A93 5c green 38 12
493 A93 10c red 85 38
494 A93 15c brown 1.75 65
495 A93 20c ultra 3.75 1.00
496 A93 50c brn org 225.00 35.00
497 A93 1b dp gray grn 3.75 1.50
498 A93 5b dl pur 10.00 6.25
Nos. 492-498 (7) 245.48 44.90

Arms of Venezuela and Statue of Simon Bolivar.

499 A93 5c green 75 12
500 A93 10c red 50 12
501 A93 15c brown 5.00 1.00
502 A93 20c ultra 5.00 70
503 A93 25c org brn 8.50 2.00
504 A93 30c blue 8.50 2.00
505 A93 35c purple 45.00 32.50
Nos. 499-505 (7) 73.25 38.44

1952

Arms of Miranda and Agricultural Products.

506 A93 5c green 30 12
507 A93 10c red 38 12
508 A93 15c brown 1.00 38
509 A93 20c ultra 1.25 50
510 A93 25c org brn 1.50 75
511 A93 30c blue 2.50 1.25
512 A93 35c purple 15.00 10.00
Nos. 506-512 (7) 21.93 13.12

Arms of Aragua and Stylized Farm.

513 A93 5c green 30 12
514 A93 10c red 65 12
515 A93 15c brown 1.25 25
516 A93 20c ultra 1.00 50
517 A93 25c org brn 2.25 75
518 A93 30c blue 2.50 1.25
519 A93 35c purple 13.00 10.00
Nos. 513-519 (7) 20.95 12.99

Arms of Lara, Agricultural Products and Rope.

520 A93 5c green 35 10
521 A93 10c red 35 12
522 A93 15c brown 75 50
523 A93 20c ultra 1.75 65
524 A93 25c org brn 2.00 1.50
525 A93 30c blue 3.75 1.25
526 A93 35c purple 15.00 10.00
Nos. 520-526 (7) 23.95 14.12

Arms of Bolivar and Stylized Design.

527 A93 5c green 25 6
528 A93 10c red 38 6
529 A93 15c brown 75 38
530 A93 20c ultra 1.50 50
531 A93 40c red org 6.00 2.00
532 A93 45c rose vio 15.00 10.00
533 A93 3b bl gray 7.00 5.00
Nos. 527-533 (7) 30.88 18.00

Arms of Sucre, Palms and Seascape.

534 A93 5c green 35 10
535 A93 10c red 35 10
536 A93 15c brown 1.75 38
537 A93 20c ultra 1.75 25
538 A93 40c red org 6.00 1.50
539 A93 45c rose vio 20.00 12.50
540 A93 3b bl gray 5.00 3.75
Nos. 534-540 (7) 35.20 18.58

Arms of Trujillo Surrounded by Stylized Tree.

541 A93 5c green 25 10
542 A93 10c red 35 12
543 A93 15c brown 2.50 50
544 A93 20c ultra 2.50 75
545 A93 50c brn org 14.00 8.50
546 A93 1b dp gray grn 3.75 1.50
547 A93 5b dl pur 8.50 6.25
Nos. 541-547 (7) 31.85 17.72

1953

Map of Delta Amacuro and Ship.

548 A93 5c green 25 10
549 A93 10c red 35 10
550 A93 15c brown 75 25
551 A93 20c ultra 1.25 50
552 A93 40c red org 3.75 2.50
553 A93 45c rose vio 16.00 10.00
554 A93 3b bl gray 5.00 3.75
Nos. 548-554 (7) 27.35 17.20

Arms of Falcon and Stylized Oil Refinery.

555 A93 5c green 25 10
556 A93 10c red 30 12
557 A93 15c brown 1.25 30
558 A93 20c ultra 1.25 38
559 A93 50c brn org 6.00 3.00
560 A93 1b dp gray grn 3.75 2.50
561 A93 5b dl pur 10.00 6.25
Nos. 555-561 (7) 22.80 12.65

Arms of Guarico and Factory.

562 A93 5c green 25 10
563 A93 10c red 25 10
564 A93 15c brown 1.00 50
565 A93 20c ultra 1.25 65
566 A93 40c red org 5.00 4.00
567 A93 45c rose vio 12.50 7.50
568 A93 3b bl gray 5.00 3.75
Nos. 562-568 (7) 25.25 16.60

Arms of Merida and Church.

569 A93 5c green 25 10
570 A93 10c red 25 10
571 A93 15c brown 75 50
572 A93 20c ultra 2.00 50
573 A93 50c brn org 8.00 3.75
574 A93 1b dp gray grn 2.25 1.50
575 A93 5b dl pur 8.00 5.00
Nos. 569-575 (7) 21.50 11.45

Arms of Monagas and Horses.

576 A93 5c green 25 10
577 A93 10c red 40 10
578 A93 15c brown 75 50
579 A93 20c ultra 1.00 65
580 A93 40c red org 5.00 2.00
581 A93 45c rose vio 14.00 8.50
582 A93 3b bl gray 6.25 5.00
Nos. 576-582 (7) 27.65 16.85

Arms of Portuguesa and Forest.

583 A93 5c green 18 10
584 A93 10c red 25 10
585 A93 15c brown 75 35
586 A93 20c ultra 1.50 38
587 A93 50c brn org 8.00 5.00
588 A93 1b dp gray grn 2.00 1.00
589 A93 5b dl pur 8.50 6.25
Nos. 583-589 (7) 21.18 13.18

Map of Amazonas and Orchid.

590 A93 5c green 1.25 12
591 A93 10c red 1.25 12
592 A93 15c brown 2.50 38
593 A93 20c ultra 7.50 75
594 A93 40c red org 8.00 2.50
595 A93 45c rose vio 12.50 6.25
596 A93 3b bl gray 18.50 7.50
Nos. 590-596 (7) 51.50 17.62

Arms of Apure, Horse and Bird.

597 A93 5c green 25 6
598 A93 10c red 25 12
599 A93 15c brown 75 38
600 A93 20c ultra 4.00 50
601 A93 50c brn org 5.00 3.75
602 A93 1b dp gray grn 1.75 1.50
603 A93 5b dl pur 10.00 6.25
Nos. 597-603 (7) 22.00 12.56

Arms of Barinas, Cow and Horse.

604 A93 5c green 25 10
605 A93 10c red 25 10
606 A93 15c brown 75 45
607 A93 20c ultra 5.00 75
608 A93 50c brn org 6.00 3.75
609 A93 1b dp gray grn 1.50 75
610 A93 5b dl pur 12.00 6.25
Nos. 604-610 (7) 25.75 12.15

Arms of Cojedes and Cattle.

611 A93 5c green 18 12
612 A93 10c red 38 12
613 A93 15c brown 38 18
614 A93 20c ultra 50 25
615 A93 25c org brn 2.50 75
616 A93 30c blue 3.75 1.25
617 A93 35c purple 5.00 3.00
Nos. 611-617 (7) 12.69 5.67

Arms of Nueva Esparta and Fish.

618 A93 5c green 25 10
619 A93 10c red 25 15
620 A93 15c brown 1.00 50
621 A93 20c ultra 1.25 35
622 A93 40c red org 5.00 2.00
623 A93 45c rose vio 12.50 7.50
624 A93 3b bl gray 6.25 4.00
Nos. 618-624 (7) 26.50 14.60

Arms of Yaracuy and Tropical Foliage.

625 A93 5c green 85 10
626 A93 10c red 25 10
627 A93 15c brown 75 38
628 A93 20c ultra 1.00 50
629 A93 25c org brn 1.50 75
630 A93 30c blue 1.75 65
631 A93 35c purple 3.75 2.50
Nos. 625-631 (7) 9.85 4.98
Nos. 464-631 (168) 942.46 424.15

See also Nos. C338-C553.

Ship Type of 1948-50, Redrawn.
Coil Stamps.
Imprint: "Courvoisier S.A."
Photogravure.

1952 *Perf. 11½x12.* Unwmkd.

632 A85 5c green 1.25 12
633 A85 10c car rose 2.25 12
634 A85 15c gray 7.50 12

See also Nos. C554-C556.

Juan de Villegas and Cross of Father Yepez
A94

Virgin of Coromoto and Child
A95

1952, Sept. 14 *Perf. 11½*

635 A94 5c green 50 12
636 A94 10c red 1.00 12
637 A94 20c dk gray bl 1.50 50
638 A94 40c dp org 7.00 3.75
639 A94 50c brown 3.75 2.00
640 A94 1b violet 7.50 2.50
Nos. 635-640 (6) 21.25 8.99

Issued to commemorate the 400th anniversary of the founding of the city of Barquisimeto by Juan de Villegas. See Nos. C557-C564.

1952-53 *Perf. 11½x12.*

Size: 17x26mm.

641 A95 1b rose pink 14.00 2.50

Size: 26½x41mm.

642 A95 1b rose pink ('53) 10.00 2.50

Size: 36x55mm.

643 A95 1b rose pink ('53) 5.00 2.00

Issued to commemorate the 300th anniversary of the appearance of the Virgin Mary to a chief of the Coromoto Indians.

Telegraph Stamps Surcharged in Black or Red

Correos Exposición Objetiva Nacional 1948 - 1952 5c.

1952, Nov. 24 Engr. *Perf. 12*

Grayish Security Paper.

644 5c on 25c car 50 12
645 10c on 1b blk (R) 50 12

Surcharged

CORREOS HABILITADO 1952 Bs. 0,50

1952

646 20c on 25c car 60 25
647 30c on 2b ol grn 3.75 2.50
648 40c on 1b blk (R) 1.50 75
649 50c on 3b red org 5.00 3.00

VENEZUELA

Post Office, Caracas
A96

Photogravure.

1953-54		Perf. 12½	Unwmkd.	
650	A96	5c grn ('54)	25	10
a.		Bklt. pane of 10		
651	A96	7½c brt grn	75	50
652	A96	10c rose car ('54)	50	10
a.		Bklt. pane of 10		
653	A96	15c gray ('54)	75	12
654	A96	20c ultra	50	25
655	A96	25c magenta	75	12
656	A96	30c blue	3.75	50
657	A96	35c brt red vio	1.75	50
658	A96	40c orange	2.50	75
659	A96	45c violet	3.25	1.25
660	A96	50c red org	2.50	75
		Nos. 650-660 (11)	17.75	4.94

See also Nos. C565-C575, C587-C589.

Type of 1953-54 Inscribed "Republica de Venezuela"

1955				
661	A96	5c green	18	5
662	A96	10c rose car	18	5
663	A96	15c gray	35	5
664	A96	20c ultra	50	5
665	A96	30c blue	1.25	75
666	A96	35c brt red vio	1.25	50
667	A96	40c orange	2.00	50
668	A96	45c violet	2.50	1.00
		Nos. 661-668 (8)	8.21	2.75

See also Nos. C597-C606.

Arms of Valencia and Industrial Scene
A97

Coat of Arms
A98

1955, Mar. 26		Engraved	Perf. 12	
669	A97	5c brt grn	35	12
670	A97	20c ultra	75	15
671	A97	25c redsh brn	1.25	15
672	A97	50c vermilion	2.00	50
		Nos. 669-672, C590-C596 (11)	9.48	2.92

Issued to commemorate the 400th anniversary of the founding of Valencia del Rey.

1955, Dec. 9	Perf. 11½	Unwmkd.		
673	A98	5c green	75	10
674	A98	20c ultra	1.25	10
675	A98	25c rose car	2.00	15
676	A98	50c orange	2.50	15
		Nos. 673-676, C607-C612 (10)	12.75	2.24

Issued to commemorate the First Postal Convention, Caracas, Feb. 9-15, 1954.

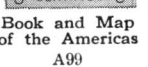

Book and Map of the Americas
A99

Simon Bolivar
A100

1957		Photogravure	Perf. 11½	
		Granite Paper		
677	A99	5c lt grn & bluish grn	15	5
678	A99	10c lil rose & rose vio	15	5
679	A99	20c ultra & dk bl	35	10
680	A99	25c gray & lil gray	50	25
681	A99	30c lt bl & bl	50	25
682	A99	40c bis brn & brn	75	35
683	A99	50c ver & red brn	1.25	50
684	A99	1b lt pur & vio	2.00	1.00
		Nos. 677-684 (8)	5.65	2.55

Issued for the Book Festival of the Americas, Nov. 15-30, 1956. See Nos. C629-C635.

Engraved, Center Embossed

1957-58		Perf. 13½	Unwmkd.	
685	A100	5c brt bl grn	15	10
686	A100	10c red ('58)	25	10
687	A100	20c lt sl bl	75	25
688	A100	25c rose lake	75	25
689	A100	30c vio bl	1.00	25
690	A100	40c red org	1.50	38
691	A100	50c org yel ('58)	2.00	1.00
		Nos. 685-691 (7)	6.40	2.33

Issued to commemorate the 150th anniversary of the Oath of Monte Sacro and the 125th anniversary of the death of Simon Bolivar (1783-1830). See Nos. C636-C642.

Hotel Tamanaco, Caracas
A101

1957-58		Engraved	Perf. 13	
692	A101	5c green	15	5
693	A101	10c carmine	15	5
694	A101	15c black	60	20
695	A101	20c dk bl	75	12
696	A101	25c dp cl	75	18
697	A101	30c dp ultra	1.25	50
698	A101	35c purple	75	25
699	A101	40c orange	1.00	38
700	A101	45c rose vio	1.25	50
701	A101	50c yellow	1.75	75
702	A101	1b dk sl grn	2.50	1.00
		Nos. 692-702 (11)	10.90	3.95

See also Nos. C643-C657.

Main Post Office, Caracas
A102

1958, May 14	Litho.	Perf. 14		
703	A102	5c emerald	10	5
704	A102	10c rose red	12	5
705	A102	15c gray	15	5
706	A102	20c lt bl	25	5
707	A102	35c red lil	35	18
708	A102	45c brt vio	2.50	1.75
709	A102	50c yellow	60	25
710	A102	1b lt ol grn	1.50	75
		Nos. 703-710 (8)	5.57	3.13

See also Nos. 748-750, C658-C670.

Main Post Office, Caracas
A103

Coil Stamps.

1958, Nov. 17	Engr.	Perf. 11½x12		
711	A103	5c green	50	5
712	A103	10c rose red	75	5
713	A103	15c black	1.00	15
		Nos. 711-713, C671-C673 (6)	4.50	57

Arms of Merida
A104

Arms of Trujillo, Bolivar Monument and Trujillo Hotel
A105

1958, Oct. 9		Photo.	Perf. 14	
714	A104	5c green	15	10
715	A104	10c brt red	15	10
716	A104	15c grnsh gray	15	10
717	A104	20c blue	30	10
718	A104	25c magenta	1.00	18
719	A104	30c violet	50	25
720	A104	35c lt pur	60	25
721	A104	40c orange	1.50	50
722	A104	45c dp rose lil	75	25
723	A104	50c brt yel	1.25	50
724	A104	1b gray grn	3.75	1.25
		Nos. 714-724 (11)	10.10	3.58

Issued to commemorate the 400th anniversary of the founding of the city of Merida. See also Nos. C674-C689.

1959		Perf. 14	Unwmkd.	
725	A105	5c emerald	10	5
726	A105	10c rose	12	5
727	A105	15c gray	15	6
728	A105	20c blue	25	6
729	A105	25c brt pink	50	16
730	A105	30c lt ultra	75	25
731	A105	35c lt pur	85	35
732	A105	45c rose lil	1.00	50
733	A105	50c yellow	1.00	38
734	A105	1b lt ol grn	2.50	1.25
		Nos. 725-734 (10)	7.22	3.13

Issued to commemorate the 400th anniversary of the founding of the city of Trujillo. See also Nos. C690-C700.

Stadium
A106

1959, Mar. 10		Litho.	Perf. 13½	
735	A106	5c brt grn	35	12
736	A106	10c rose pink	35	18
737	A106	20c blue	1.00	50
738	A106	30c dk bl	1.25	60
739	A106	50c red lil	2.00	50
		Nos. 735-739 (5)	4.95	1.90

Issued to commemorate the 8th Central American and Caribbean Games, Caracas, Nov. 29-Dec. 14, 1958. See Nos. C701-C705.

Nos. 735-739 exist imperf. Price $25 a pair.

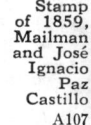 

Stamp of 1859, Mailman and José Ignacio Paz Castillo
A107

Stamp of 1859 and: 50c, Mailman on horseback and Jacinto Gutierrez. 1b, Plane, train and Miguel Herrera.

1959, Sept. 15	Engraved	Perf. 13½		
740	A107	25c org yel	75	25
741	A107	50c blue	1.25	50
742	A107	1b rose red	2.50	1.00
		Nos. 740-742, C706-C708 (6)	9.00	3.50

Centenary of Venezuelan postage stamps.

Alexander von Humboldt
A108

Newspaper, 1808, and View of Caracas, 1958
A109

1960, Feb. 9	Perf. 13½	Unwmkd.		
743	A108	5c yel grn	50	12
744	A108	30c vio bl & vio	1.25	30
745	A108	40c org & brn org	1.75	75
		Nos. 743-745, C709-C711 (6)	7.25	2.32

Issued to commemorate the centenary of the death of Alexander von Humboldt, German naturalist and geographer.

Post Office Type of 1958.

1960		Lithographed	Perf. 14	
748	A102	25c yellow	25	10
749	A102	30c blue	30	10
750	A102	40c fawn	65	25

1960, June 1		Litho.	Perf. 14	
751	A109	10c rose & blk	60	25
752	A109	20c lt bl & blk	85	30
753	A109	35c lil & blk	1.50	1.25
		Nos. 751-753, C712-C714 (6)	8.95	4.90

Issued to commemorate the 150th anniversary (in 1958) of the first Venezuelan newspaper, Gazeta de Caracas.

Agustin Codazzi
A110

National Pantheon
A111

1960, June 15	Engraved	Unwmkd.		
754	A110	5c brt grn	10	5
755	A110	15c gray	85	25
756	A110	20c blue	75	25
757	A110	45c purple	85	50
		Nos. 754-757, C715-C720 (10)	7.52	3.20

Issued to commemorate the centenary (in 1959) of the death of Agustin Codazzi, geographer.

1960, May 9		Lithographed		
		Pantheon in Bistre		
758	A111	5c emerald	15	5
759	A111	20c brt bl	75	25
760	A111	25c lt ol	1.10	30
761	A111	30c dl bl	1.25	35
762	A111	40c fawn	1.85	70
763	A111	45c lilac	1.85	70
		Nos. 758-763 (6)	6.95	2.35

See also Nos. C721-C734.

Andres Eloy Blanco
A112

1960, May 21	Perf. 14	Unwmkd.		
		Portrait in Black		
764	A112	5c emerald	30	10
765	A112	30c dl bl	50	25
766	A112	50c yellow	1.00	50
		Nos. 764-766, C735-C737 (6)	6.00	2.60

Issued to honor the poet Andres Eloy Blanco (1896-1955).

VENEZUELA

Independence Meeting of April 19, 1810, Led by Miranda
A113

1960, Aug. 19   Litho.   Perf. 13½
Center Multicolored

767	A113	5c brt grn	18
768	A113	20c blue	1.50	50
769	A113	30c vio bl	1.85	75
	Nos. 767-769, C738-C740 (6)	10.20	3.78

Issued to commemorate the 150th anniversary of Venezuela's Independence. See also Nos. 812–814, C804–C806.

Drilling for Oil
A114

1960, Aug. 26   Engraved   Perf. 14

770	A114	5c grn & sl grn	2.50	1.25
771	A114	10c dk car & brn	1.00	50
772	A114	15c gray & dl pur	1.25	60
	Nos. 770-772, C741-C743 (6)	8.30	4.05

Issued to publicize Venezuela's oil industry.

Luisa Cáceres de Arismendi
A115

Lithographed
1960, Oct. 21   Perf. 14   Unwmkd.
Center Multicolored

773	A115	20c lt bl	1.25	50
774	A115	25c citron	1.10	55
775	A115	30c dl bl	1.50	75
	Nos. 773-775, C744-C746 (6)	8.60	4.15

Issued to commemorate the 94th anniversary of the death of Luisa Cáceres de Arismendi.

José Antonio Anzoategui
A116

1960, Oct. 29   Engraved

776	A116	5c emer & gray ol	30	10
777	A116	15c ol gray & dl vio	75	10
778	A116	20c bl & gray vio	85	25
	Nos. 776-778, C747-C749 (6)	4.40	2.10

Issued to commemorate the 140th anniversary (in 1959) of the death of General José Antonio Anzoategui.

Antonio José de Sucre
A117

Lithographed
1960, Nov. 18   Perf. 14   Unwmkd.
Center Multicolored

779	A117	10c dp rose	60	25
780	A117	15c gray brn	75	35
781	A117	20c blue	1.00	50
	Nos. 779-781, C750-C752 (6)	6.80	3.41

Issued to commemorate the 130th anniversary of the death of General Antonio José de Sucre.

Bolivar Peak, Merida
A118

Designs: 15c, Caroni Falls, Bolivar. 35c, Cuacharo caves, Monagas.

1960, March 22   Perf. 14

782	A118	5c emer & grn	1.25	1.25
783	A118	15c gray & dk gray	3.75	3.75
784	A118	35c rose lil & lil	3.50	3.50
	Nos. 782-784, C753-C755 (6)	16.00	16.00

Buildings and People
A119

1961   Lithographed.   Unwmkd.
Building in Orange

785	A119	5c emerald	6	5
786	A119	10c carmine	10	5
787	A119	15c gray	15	10
788	A119	20c blue	25	10
789	A119	25c lt red brn	38	18
790	A119	30c dl bl	38	15
791	A119	35c red lil	50	18
792	A119	40c fawn	75	35
793	A119	45c brt vio	1.00	50
794	A119	50c yellow	75	30
	Nos. 785-794 (10)	4.32	1.96

Issued to commemorate the 1960 national census. See Nos. C756–C770.

Rafael Maria Baralt
A120

1961, Mar. 11   Engraved   Perf. 14

795	A120	5c grn & sl grn	15	10
796	A120	15c gray & dl red brn	50	10
797	A120	35c rose lil & lt vio	75	35
	Nos. 795-797, C771-C773 (6)	4.50	2.40

Issued to commemorate the centenary of the death of Rafael Maria Baralt, statesman.

Yellow-headed Parrot
A121

Birds: 40c, Snowy egret. 50c, Scarlet ibis.

1961, Sept. 6   Litho.   Perf. 14½

798	A121	30c multi	75	50
799	A121	40c multi	1.00	50
800	A121	50c multi	2.00	1.00
	Nos. 798-800, C776-C778 (6)	7.00	5.00

Juan J. Aguerrevere
A122

1961, Oct. 21   Perf. 14   Unwmkd.

| 801 | A122 | 25c dk bl | 25 | 12 |
| a. | Souvenir sheet | 1.75 | 1.75 |

Issued to commemorate the centenary of the founding of the Engineering Society of Venezuela, Oct. 28, 1861.
No. 801a contains one of No. 801, imperf. Size: 100x65mm. Marginal inscriptions in dark blue. Sold for 1b.
No. 801a exists with "Valor: Bs 1,00" omitted at lower left corner. Price, $3.50.

Battle of Carabobo, 1821—A123

1961, Dec. 2   Perf. 14
Center Multicolored

802	A123	5c emer & blk	15	10
803	A123	40c brn & blk	1.00	50
	Nos. 802-803, C779-C784 (8)	18.90	9.35

140th anniversary of Battle of Carabobo.

Oncidium Papilio Lindl.
A124

Orchids: 10c, Caularthron bilamellatum. 20c, Stanhopea Wardii Lodd. 25c, Catasetum pileatum. 30c, Masdevallia tovarensis. 35c, Epidendrum Stamfordianum Batem (horiz.). 50c, Epidendrum atropurpureum Willd. 3b, Oncidium falcipetalum Lindl.

Perf. 14x13½, 13½x14
1962, May 30   Litho.   Unwmkd.
Orchids in Natural Colors

804	A124	5c blk & org	12	6
805	A124	10c blk & brt grnsh bl	17	12
806	A124	20c blk & yel grn	45	18
807	A124	25c blk & lt bl	65	12
808	A124	30c blk & ol	75	25
809	A124	35c blk & yel	85	38
810	A124	50c blk & gray	1.00	50
811	A124	3b blk & vio	6.00	4.00
	Nos. 804-811 (8)	9.99	5.61

See also Nos. C794–C803.

Independence Type of 1960

Design: Signing Declaration of Independence.

1962, June   Perf. 13½
Center Multicolored

812	A113	5c emerald	35	10
813	A113	20c blue	65	25
814	A113	25c yellow	1.00	50
a.	Souv. sheet of 3	3.75	3.75
	Nos. 812-814, C804-C806 (6)	7.35	3.30

Issued to commemorate the 150th anniversary of the Venezuelan Declaration of Independence, July 5, 1811.
No. 814a contains one each of Nos. 812–814, imperf., with marginal inscriptions in brown. Size: 140x140mm. Sold for 1.50b.

Shot Put
A125

Designs: 10c, Soccer. 25c, Swimming.

1962, Nov. 30   Litho.   Perf. 13x14

815	A125	5c brt grn	12	6
816	A125	10c car rose	25	10
817	A125	25c blue	50	25
a.	Souvenir sheet of 3	3.75	3.75
	Nos. 815-817, C808-C810 (6)	5.12	3.16

Issued to commemorate the First National Games, Caracas, 1961. The stamps are arranged within the sheet so that groups of four are formed with the two pale colored edges of each stamp joining to make a border around blocks of four.
No. 817a contains one each of Nos. 815–817 imperf. with bright green marginal inscription. Size: 164x110mm. Sold for 1.40b.

Vermilion Cardinal
A126

Malaria Eradication Emblem, Mosquito and Map
A127

Birds: 10c, Great kiskadee. 20c, Glossy black thrush. 25c, Collared trogons. 30c, Swallow tanager. 40c, Long-tailed sylph. 3b, Black-necked stilt.

1962, Dec. 14   Perf. 14x13½
Birds in Natural Colors, Black Inscription

818	A126	5c brt yel grn	12	10
819	A126	10c vio bl	25	5
820	A126	20c lil rose	50	25
821	A126	25c dl brn	60	30
822	A126	30c lemon	75	35
823	A126	40c lilac	1.00	50
824	A126	3b fawn	6.25	5.00
	Nos. 818-824 (7)	9.47	6.55

See also Nos. C811–C818.

Lithographed and Embossed
Perf. 13½x14
1962, Dec. 20   Wmk. 346

| 825 | A127 | 50c brn & blk | 75 | 38 |

Issued for the World Health Organization drive to eradicate malaria. See Nos. C819–C819a.

VENEZUELA

White-tailed Deer
A128

Designs: 10c, Collared peccary. 35c, Collared titi (monkey). 50c, Giant Brazilian otter. 1b, Puma. 3b, Capybara.

Perf. 13½x14
1963, Mar. 13 Litho. Unwmkd.
Multicolored Center;
Black Inscriptions.

826	A128	5c green	10	6
827	A128	10c orange	12	8
828	A128	35c red lil	35	18
829	A128	50c blue	75	38
830	A128	1b rose brn	3.75	2.50
831	A128	3b yellow	7.50	5.00
		Nos.826-831 (6)	12.57	8.20

See also Nos. C820–C825.

Fisherman and Map of Venezuela
A129

Cathedral of Bocono
A130

1963, Mar. 21

| 832 | A129 | 25c pink & ultra | 30 | 25 |

Issued for the "Freedom from Hunger" campaign of the U.N. Food and Agriculture Organization. See Nos. C826–C827.

1963, May 30   Wmk. 346

| 833 | A130 | 50c brn, red & grn, buff | 85 | 30 |

Issued to commemorate the 400th anniversary of the founding of Bocono. See No. C828.

St. Peter's Basilica, Rome
A131

1963, June 11   Perf. 14x13½

| 834 | A131 | 35c dk bl, brn & buff | 50 | 25 |
| 835 | A131 | 45c dk grn, red brn & buff | 60 | 30 |

Issued to commemorate Vatican II, the 21st Ecumenical Council of the Roman Catholic Church. See Nos. C829–C830.

National Flag
A132

1963, July 29 Perf. 14 Unwmkd.

| 836 | A132 | 30c gray, red, yel & bl | 30 | 25 |

Issued to commemorate the centenary of Venezuela's flag and coat of arms. See also No. C831.

Lake Maracaibo Bridge
A133

Map, Soldier and Emblem
A134

Lithographed
1963   Perf. 14   Wmk. 346

837	A133	30c bl & brn	50	25
838	A133	35c bluish grn & brn	60	30
839	A133	80c bl grn & brn	1.10	60
		Nos. 837-839, C832-C834 (6)	6.80	3.50

Opening of bridge over Lake Maracaibo.

1963, Sept. 10   Unwmkd.

| 840 | A134 | 50c red, bl & grn, buff | 65 | 30 |

Issued to commemorate the 25th anniversary of the armed forces. See No. C835.

Dag Hammarskjold and World Map
A135

1963, Sept. 25   Perf. 14   Unwmkd.

| 841 | A135 | 25c dk bl, bl grn & ocher | 30 | 18 |
| 842 | A135 | 55c grn, grnsh bl & ocher | 1.25 | 60 |

Issued to commemorate the "First" anniversary of the death of Dag Hammarskjold, Secretary General of the United Nations, 1953–61. See also Nos. C836–C837a.

Dr. Luis Razetti
A136

Dr. Francisco A. Risquez
A137

1963, Oct. 20   Lithographed

| 843 | A136 | 35c bl, ocher & brn | 60 | 30 |
| 844 | A136 | 45c mag, ocher & brn | 85 | 30 |

Issued to commemorate the centenary of the birth of Dr. Luis Razetti, physician. See Nos. C838–C839.

1963, Dec. 31   Perf. 11½x12
Design: 20c, Dr. Carlos J. Bello.

| 845 | A137 | 15c multi | 25 | 12 |
| 846 | A137 | 20c multi | 30 | 15 |

Issued to commemorate the centenary of the International Red Cross. See also Nos. C840–C841.

Oil Field Workers
A138

Pedro Gual
A139

Designs: 10c, Oil refinery. 15c Crane and building construction. 30c, Cactus, train and truck. 40c, Tractor.

1964, Feb. 5 Litho. Perf. 14x13½

847	A138	5c multi	12	6
848	A138	10c multi	25	5
849	A138	15c multi	35	12
850	A138	30c multi	50	25
851	A138	40c multi	75	35
		Nos. 847-851 (5)	1.97	83

Issued to commemorate the centenary of the Department of Industrial Development. See also Nos. C842–C846.

1964, Mar. 20   Perf. 14   Unwmkd.

| 852 | A139 | 40c lt ol grn | 75 | 35 |
| 853 | A139 | 50c lt red brn | 85 | 40 |

Issued to commemorate the centenary of the death (in 1862) of Pedro Gual, statesman. See Nos. C847–C848.

Carlos Arvelo
A140

1964, Apr. 17 Engr. Perf. 13½x14

| 854 | A140 | 1b dl bl & gray | 1.50 | 75 |

Issued to commemorate the centenary of the death of Dr. Carlos Arvelo (1784–1862), chief physician of Bolivar's revolutionary army, director of Caracas Hospital, rector of Central University and professor of pathology.

Foundry Ladle and Molds
A141

1964, May 22   Perf. 14x13½

| 855 | A141 | 20c multi | 35 | 15 |
| 856 | A141 | 50c multi | 75 | 35 |

Orinoco Steel Mills. See Nos. C849–C850.

Romulo Gallegos
A142

Lithographed
1964, Aug. 3   Perf. 11½   Unwmkd.

857	A142	5c dk & lt grn	12	6
858	A142	10c bl & pale bl	18	10
859	A142	15c dk & lt red lil	35	25
		Nos. 857-859, C852-C854 (6)	2.90	1.51

Issued to commemorate the 80th birthday of novelist Romulo Gallegos.

Angel Falls, Bolivar State
A143

Designs: 10c, Tropical landscape, Sucre State. 15c, San Juan Peaks, Guarico. 30c, Net fishermen, Anzoategui. 40c, Mountaineer, Merida.

1964   **Perf. 13½x14**

860	A143	5c multi	5	5
861	A143	10c multi	18	6
862	A143	15c multi	25	12
863	A143	30c multi	50	18
864	A143	40c multi	75	25
		Nos. 860-864 (5)	1.73	66

Issued for tourist publicity.

RESELLADO

Issues of 1958–64
Surcharged in Black,
Dark Blue or Lilac

VALOR
Bs. 0,05

1965

865	A102	5c on 1b lt ol grn (#710)	75	12
866	A119	10c on 45c brt vio & org (#793)	25	15
867	A135	15c on 55c grn, grnsh bl & ocher (#842)	18	12
868	A126	20c on 3b multi (#824)	35	25
869	A110	25c on 45c pur (#757) (DB)	30	25
870	A128	25c on 1b multi (#830)	35	25
871	A128	25c on 3b multi (#831)	50	25
872	A124	25c on 3b multi (#831) (L)	30	25
873	A104	30c on 1b gray grn (#724)	35	25
874	A140	40c on 1b dl bl & gray (#854)	1.00	30
875	A133	60c on 80c bl grn & brn (#839)	1.25	50
		Nos. 865-875 (11)	4.78	2.57

Lines of surcharge arranged variously; old denomination obliterated with bars on Nos. 867, 870–72. See Nos. C856–C899.

CORREOS
Revenue Stamps of 1947 Surcharged in Red or Black
RESELLADO
VALOR
Bs. 0,05

Perf. 12, 13½ (No. 882)
1965   Engraved
Imprint: "American Bank Note Co."

876	R1	5c on 5c emer	12	6
877	R1	5c on 20c red brn	12	6
878	R1	10c on 10c brn ol	12	6
879	R1	15c on 40c grn	12	6
880	R1	20c on 3b dk bl (R)	50	25
881	R1	25c on 5b vio bl (R)	1.00	25
882	R1	25c on 5b vio bl (R)		
		(Imprint: "Bundesdruckerei Berlin")	50	25
883	R1	60c on 3b dk bl (R)	1.25	60
		Nos. 876-883 (8)	3.73	1.84

Type R1 is illustrated above No. 401.

John F. Kennedy and Alliance for Progress Emblem
A144

1965, Aug. 20 Photo. Perf. 12x11½

| 884 | A144 | 20c gray | 50 | 25 |
| 885 | A144 | 40c brt lil | 75 | 35 |

Issued in memory of President John F. Kennedy (1917–1963). See Nos. C900–C901.

VENEZUELA

Map of Venezuela and Guiana by Codazzi, 1840
A145

Protesilaus Leucones
A146

Maps of Venezuela and Guiana: 15c, by Juan M. Restrepo, 1827 (horiz.). 40c, by L. de Surville, 1778.

1965, Nov. 5 Litho. Perf. 13½
886	A145	5c multi	12	6
887	A145	15c multi	35	15
888	A145	40c multi	75	25
a.	Souv. sheet of 3		2.50	2.50
	Nos. 886-888, C905-C907 (6)		3.47	1.46

Issued to publicize Venezuela's claim to part of British Guiana.
No. 888a contains 3 imperf. stamps similar to Nos. 886–888. Black inscriptions and control number, multicolored coat of arms. Size: 158x207mm. Sold for 85c.

1966, Jan. 25 Litho. Perf. 13½x14
Various Butterflies in Natural Colors. Black Inscriptions
889	A146	20c lt ol grn	35	15
890	A146	30c lt yel grn	50	25
891	A146	50c yellow	85	35
	Nos. 889-891, C915-C917 (6)		5.95	2.85

Ship and Map of Atlantic Ocean
A147

1966, Mar. 10 Litho. Perf. 13½x14
| 892 | A147 | 60c brn, bl & blk | 1.50 | 75 |

Bicentenary of the first maritime mail.

"El Carite" Dance—A148
Various Folk Dances

Unwmkd.
1966, Apr. 5 Litho. Perf. 14
893	A148	5c gray & multi	12	5
894	A148	10c org & multi	25	10
895	A148	15c lem & multi	35	15
896	A148	10c lil & multi	50	25
897	A148	25c brt pink & multi	75	35
898	A148	35c yel grn & multi	85	50
	Nos. 893-898 (6)		2.82	1.40

See also Nos. C919–C924.

Certain countries cancel stamps in full sheets and sell them (usually with gum) for less than face value. Dealers generally sell "CTO" (canceled to order) stamps for much less than postally used copies.

Type of Air Post Stamps and

Arturo Michelena, Self-portrait
A149

Paintings: 1b, Penthesileia, battle scene. 1.05b, The Red Cloak.

Perf. 12½x12, 12x12½
1966, May 12 Litho. Unwmkd.
899	A149	95c sep & buff	1.25	1.00
900	AP74	1b multi	1.50	1.00
901	AP74	1.05b multi	1.75	1.00
	Nos. 899-901, C927-C929 (6)		9.00	6.00

Issued to commemorate the centenary of the birth of Arturo Michelena (1863–1898), painter. Miniature sheets of 12 exist.

Construction Worker and Map of Americas
A150

Designs: 20c, as 10c. 30c, 65c, Labor monument. 35c, Machinery worker and map of Venezuela. 50c, Automobile assembly line.

1966, July 6 Litho. Perf. 14x13½
902	A150	10c yel & blk	12	5
903	A150	20c lt grnsh bl & blk	38	12
904	A150	30c lt bl & vio	30	25
905	A150	35c lem & ol	45	25
906	A150	50c brt rose & cl	75	35
907	A150	65c sal pink & brn	1.00	50
	Nos. 902-907 (6)		3.00	1.52

Issued to commemorate the 2nd Conference of Ministers of Labor of the Organization of American States.

Velvet Cichlid
A151

Fish: 25c, Perch cichlid. 45c, Piranha.

1966, Aug. 31 Litho. Perf. 13½x14
908	A151	15c yel grn & multi	25	15
909	A151	25c cit & multi	35	25
910	A151	45c bl grn & multi	1.00	50
	Nos. 908-910, C933-C935 (6)		5.70	3.15

Nativity
A152

1966, Dec. 9 Litho. Perf. 14
| 911 | A152 | 65c vio & blk | 1.10 | 50 |

Christmas 1966.

Satellite, Radar, Globe, Plane and Ship
A153

1966, Dec. 28 Perf. 13½x14
| 912 | A153 | 45c multi | 75 | 35 |

Issued to commemorate the 30th anniversary of the Ministry of Communications.

Rubén Dario
A154

1967 Lithographed Perf. 14
| 913 | A154 | 70c gray bl & dk bl | 1.25 | 75 |

Issued to commemorate the centenary of the birth of Rubén Dario (pen name of Felix Rubén Garcia Sarmiento, 1867–1916), Nicaraguan poet, newspaper correspondent and diplomat.

Old Building and Arms, University of Zulia
A155

Perf. 13½x14
1967, Apr. 21 Litho. Unwmkd.
| 914 | A155 | 80c gold, blk & car | 1.25 | 75 |

Issued to commemorate the 75th anniversary of the founding of the University of Zulia.

Front Page and Printing Press
A156

1968, June 27 Photo. Perf. 14x13½
| 915 | A156 | 1.50b emer, blk & brn | 1.85 | 1.00 |

Issued to commemorate the 150th anniversary of the newspaper Correo del Orinoco.

Boll Weevil
A157

Insect Pests: 20c, Corn borer (vert.). 90c, Tobacco caterpillar.

Perf. 14x13½, 13½x14
1968, Aug. 30 Lithographed
916	A157	20c multi	50	25
917	A157	75c & multi	1.00	50
918	A157	90c multi	1.25	65
	Nos. 916-918, C989-C991 (6)		3.75	1.86

Guayana Substation
A158

Designs: 45c, Guaira River Dam (horiz.). 50c, Macagua Dam and power plant (horiz.). 80c, Guri River Dam and power plant.

1968, Nov. 8 Lithographed
919	A158	15c fawn & multi	25	12
920	A158	45c dl yel & multi	60	30
921	A158	50c bl grn & multi	85	35
922	A158	80c multi	1.25	75

Electrification program.

House and Piggy Bank
A159

1968, Dec. 6 Litho. Perf 13½x14
| 923 | A159 | 45c bl & multi | 75 | 35 |

National Savings System.

Nursery and Child Planting Tree
A160

Designs: 15c, Child planting tree (vert.; this design used as emblem on entire issue). 30c, Waterfall (vert.). 45c, Logging. 55c, Fields and village (vert.). 75c, Palambra (fish).

Perf. 14x13½, 13½x14
1968, Dec. 19 Lithographed
924	A160	15c multi	12	6
925	A160	20c multi	25	12
926	A160	30c multi	38	18
927	A160	45c multi	50	25
928	A160	55c multi	1.00	50
929	A160	75c multi	75	38
	Nos. 924-929 (6)		3.00	1.49

Issued to publicize nature conservation. See Nos. C1000-C1005.

Colorada Beach, Sucre
A161

Designs: 45c, Church of St. Francis of Yare, Miranda. 90c, Stilt houses, Zulia.

1969, Jan. 24 Perf. 13½x14
930	A161	15c multi	25	12
931	A161	45c multi	75	25
932	A161	90c multi	1.10	85
	Nos. 930-932, C1006-C1008 (6)		3.55	1.97

Tourist publicity. For souvenir sheet see No. C1007a.

Bolivar Addressing Congress of Angostura—A162

VENEZUELA

921

1969, Feb. 2   Litho.   Perf. 11
933 A162 45c multi   75   35
Issued to commemorate the sesquicentennial of the Congress of Angostura (Ciudad Bolivar).

Martin Luther King, Jr.
A163

1969, Apr. 1   Litho.   Perf. 13½
934 A163 1b bl, red & dk brn   1.00   50
Issued in memory of the Rev. Dr. Martin Luther King, Jr. (1929–1968), American civil rights leader and recipient of the Nobel Peace Prize, 1964.

Tabebuia
A164

Trees: 65c, Erythrina poeppigiana. 90c, Platymiscium.

1969, May 30   Litho.   Perf. 13½x14
935 A164 50c multi   75   35
936 A164 65c gray & multi   1.00   50
937 A164 90c pink & multi   1.50   75
     Nos. 935-937, C1009-C1011 (6)   4.22 2.06

Issued to publicize nature conservation.

Still Life with Pheasant, by Rojas
A165

Paintings by Cristobal Rojas (1858–1890): 25c, On the Balcony (vert.). 35c, The Christening. 50c, The Empty Place (family). 60c, The Tavern. 1b, Man's Arm (vert.).

Perf. 14x13½, 13½x14
1969, June 27   Litho.   Unwmkd.
Size: 32x42mm., 42x32mm.
938 A165 25c gold & multi   30   25
939 A165 35c gold & multi   55   30
940 A165 45c gold & multi   85   45
941 A165 50c gold & multi   1.00   50
942 A165 60c gold & multi   1.25   60

Perf. 11
Size: 26x53mm.
943 A165 1b gold & multi   1.75 1.00
     Nos. 938-943 (6)   5.70 3.10

ILO Emblem
A166

1969, July 28   Perf. 14x13½
944 A166 2.50b fawn & blk   3.00 2.50
Issued to commemorate the 50th anniversary of the International Labor Organization.

Charter and Coat of Arms
A167

Industrial Complex
A168

1969, Aug. 26   Litho.   Perf. 13½
945 A167 45c ultra & multi   85   35
946 A168 1b multi   1.25   60
Industrial development.

House with Arcade, Carora
A169

Designs: 25c, Ruins of Pastora Church. 55c, Chapel of the Cross. 65c, House of Culture.

1969, Sept. 8   Perf. 13x14½
947 A169 20c multi   25   12
948 A169 25c multi   38   18
949 A169 55c multi   1.00   50
950 A169 65c multi   1.25   60
400th anniversary of city of Carora.

Simon Bolivar in Madrid
A170

Designs: 10c, Bolivar's wedding, Madrid, 1802 (horiz.). 35c, Bolivar monument, Madrid.

Perf. 13½x14, 14x13½
1969, Oct. 28   Lithographed
951 A170 10c multi   15   6
952 A170 15c brn red & blk   35   15
953 A170 35c multi   60   25
  a. Souv. sheet of 2   1.75 1.75
Issued to commemorate Bolivar's sojourn in Spain. No. 953a contains 2 imperf. stamps similar to Nos. 952–953 with simulated perforation. Greenish gray background with black and white commemorative inscription; black control number. Size: 80x120mm. Sold for 75c.

"Birds in the Woods"
A171

Design: 45c, "Children in Summer Camp." Both designs are after children's paintings.

1969, Dec. 12   Litho.   Perf. 12½
954 A171 5c emer & multi   12   6
955 A171 45c red & multi   85   50
Issued for Children's Day.

Map of Great Colombia
A172

1969, Dec. 16   Litho.   Perf. 11½
956 A172 45c multi   75   35
Issued to commemorate the 150th anniversary of the founding of the State of Great Colombia.

St. Anthony's, Clarines
A173

Churches: 30c, Church of the Conception, Caroni. 40c, St. Michael's, Burbusay. 45c, St. Anthony's, Maturin. 75c, St. Nicholas, Moruy. 1b, Coro Cathedral.

1970, Jan. 15   Perf. 14
957 A173 10c pink & multi   12   6
958 A173 30c emer & multi   38   18
959 A173 40c yel & multi   75   35
960 A173 45c gray bl & multi   1.00   50
  a. Souvenir sheet   2.00 2.00
961 A173 75c yel & multi   1.25   60
962 A173 1b org & multi   1.50   75
     Nos. 957-962 (6)   5.00 2.44
Colonial architecture.
No. 960a contains one imperf. stamp with simulated perforations similar to No. 960. Black marginal inscription and control number, multicolored coat of arms and ornaments. Sold for 75c. Size: 100x60mm.

Seven Hills of Valera
A174

1970, Feb. 13   Litho.   Perf. 13x14½
963 A174 95c multi   1.25   60
Sesquicentennial of the city of Valera.

Monochaetum Humboldtianum
A175

Flowers: 25c, Symbolanthus vasculosis. 45c, Cavendishia splendens. 1b, Befaria glauca.

1970, July 29   Litho.   Perf. 14x13½
964 A175 20c multi   35   15
965 A175 25c multi   75   25
966 A175 45c multi   1.00   50
967 A175 1b multi   1.50   75
     Nos. 964-967, C1049-C1052 (8)   6.95 3.30

Battle of Boyaca, by Martin Tovar y Tovar
A176

1970, Aug. 7   Perf. 13½x14
968 A176 30c multi   50   25
150th anniversary of Battle of Boyaca.

Our Lady of Belén de San Mateo
A177

Designs: 35c, Pastoral Cross of Archbishop Silvestre Guevara y Lira, 1867. 40c, Our Lady of Valle. 90c, Virgin of Chiquinquira. 1b, Our Lady of Socorro de Valencia.

1970, Sept. 1
969 A177 35c gray & multi   60   25
970 A177 40c gray & multi   75   35
971 A177 60c gray & multi   1.10   55
  a. Souvenir sheet   1.75 1.75
972 A177 90c gray & multi   1.25   75
973 A177 1b gray & multi   1.75   85
     Nos. 969-973 (5)   5.45 2.75

The designs are from sculptures and paintings in various Venezuelan churches. No. 971a contains one imperf. stamp similar to No. 971, but with simulated perforations. Multicolored margin with inscription and control number. Size: 100x60mm. Sold for 75c.

Venezuela No. 22 and EXFILCA Emblem—A178

Designs: 20c, EXFILCA emblem and flags of participating nations (vert.). 70c, Venezuela No. C13 and EXFILCA emblem (vert.).

1970, Nov. 28   Litho.   Perf. 11
974 A178 20c yel & multi   35   12
975 A178 25c dk bl & multi   50   18
976 A178 70c brn & multi   1.00   50
  a. Souvenir sheet   2.00 2.00

Issued to publicize EXFILCA 70, 2nd Interamerican Philatelic Exhibition, Caracas, Nov. 27–Dec. 6. No. 976a contains one No. 976 with simulated perforations. The sheet is a hexagon with each side 50mm. long. Yellow green and gold margin with black inscription and control number. Sold for 85c.

Guardian Angel, by Juan Pedro Lopez
A179

1970, Dec. 1   Litho.   Perf. 14½x13½
977 A179 45c dl yel & multi   75   35
     Christmas 1970.

VENEZUELA

Jet and 1920 Plane
A180

1970, Dec. 10   Perf. 13x14
978   A180   5c bl & multi   12   6

Venezuelan Air Force, 50th anniversary.

Question Mark Full of Citizens
A181

1971, Apr. 30   Litho.   Perf. 14x13½
Lt. Green, Red & Black
979   A181   Block of 4   4.40   2.50
   a.   30c, frame L & T   1.10   45
   b.   30c, frame T & R   1.10   45
   c.   30c, frame L & B   1.10   45
   d.   30c, frame B & R   1.10   45

National Census, 1971. The frame encircles all 4 stamps of No. 979; each stamp in block has frame on 2 sides. Sheet of 20 contains 5 No. 979 and 5 blocks of 4 labels inscribed in green "Censo Nacional 1971." See No. C1054.

Battle of Carabobo
A182

1971, June 21   Perf. 13½x14
980   A182   2b bl & multi   2.50   1.50

Sesquicentennial of Battle of Carabobo.

Map of Federal District—A183

Designs: State maps. 25c, 55c, 85c, 90c, vert.

Perf. 13½x14, 14x13½
1971   Lithographed
Multicolored
981   A183   5c shown   12   6
982   A183   15c Monagas   18   6
983   A183   20c Nueva Esparta   25   12
984   A183   25c Portuguesa   30   12
985   A183   45c Sucre   45   20
986   A183   55c Tachira   65   30
987   A183   65c Trujillo   80   35
988   A183   75c Yaracuyo   1.00   50
989   A183   85c Zulia   1.25   50
990   A183   90c Amazonas   2.00   60
991   A183   1b Federal Dependencies   2.50   1.00
     Nos. 981-991 (11)   9.50   3.81

Issue dates: 5c, July 15; 15c, 20c, Aug. 16; 25c, 45c, Sept. 15; 55c, 65c, Oct. 15; 75c, 85c, Nov. 15; 90c, 1b, Dec. 15.
See also Nos. C1035-C1048.

Madonna and Child
A184

Luis Daniel Beauperthuy
A185

Design: No. 993, Madonna, and Jesus in manger.

1971, Dec. 1   Perf. 11
992   A184   25c multi   50   25
993   A184   25c multi   50   25
   Pair, #992-993   1.00   85

Christmas 1971. Nos. 992-993 printed checkerwise in same sheet.

1971, Dec. 10   Perf. 14x13½
994   A185   1b vio bl & multi   1.25   60

Dr. Luis Daniel Beauperthuy, scientist.

Globe in Heart Shape
A186

Flags of Americas and Arms of Venezuela
A187

1972, Apr. 7   Litho.   Perf. 14x13½
995   A186   1b red, ultra & blk   1.25   75

"Your heart is your health," World Health Day 1972.

1972, May 15   Litho.   Perf. 14x13½

Designs: 4b, Venezuelan flag. 5b, National anthem. 10b, Araguaney, national tree. 15b, Map, North and South America. All show flags of American nations in background.

996   A187   3b multi   3.75   2.50
997   A187   4b multi   5.00   3.75
998   A187   5b multi   6.25   5.00
999   A187   10b multi   12.50   7.50
1000   A187   15b multi   18.50   10.00
   Nos. 996-1000 (5)   46.00   28.75

"Venezuela in America."

Parque Central Complex
A188

Designs: No. 1002, Front view ("Parque Central" on top). No. 1003, Side view ("Parque Central" at right).

1972, July 25   Perf. 11½
Blue Background
1001   A188   30c yel & multi   35   25
1002   A188   30c bl & multi   35   25
1003   A188   30c red & multi   35   25
   Strip of 3, #1001-1003   1.75   1.75

Completion of "Parque Central" middle-income housing project, Caracas. Nos. 1001-1003 printed se-tenant.

Mahatma Gandhi
A189

1972, Oct. 2   Litho.   Perf. 13½x14
1004   A189   60c multi   1.00   50

103rd birthday of Mohandas K. Gandhi (1869-1948), leader in India's fight for independence, advocate of non-violence.

Children Playing Music
A190

Design: No. 1006, Children roller skating.

1972, Dec. 5   Litho.   Perf. 13½x14
1005   A190   30c multi   35   25
1006   A190   30c multi   35   25
   Pair, #1005-1006   85   85

Christmas 1972. Nos. 1005-1006 printed se-tenant.

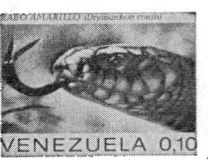

Indigo Snake
A191

Snakes: 15c, South American chicken snake. 25c, Venezuelan lance-head. 30c, Coral snake. 60c, Casabel rattlesnake. 1b, Boa constrictor.

1972, Dec. 15   Litho.   Perf. 13½x14
1007   A191   10c blk & multi   12   6
1008   A191   15c blk & multi   18   12
1009   A191   25c blk & multi   50   25
1010   A191   30c blk & multi   60   30
1011   A191   60c blk & multi   1.00   50
1012   A191   1b blk & multi   1.50   75
   a.   Nos. 1007-1012 (6)   3.90   1.98

 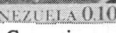

Copernicus
A192

Sun
A193

Designs: 5c, Model of solarcentric system. 15c, Copernicus' book "De Revolutionibus."

1973, Feb. 10   Litho.   Perf. 13½x14
1013   A192   5c multi   12   5
1014   A192   10c multi   25   10
1015   A192   15c multi   35   15
   Strip of 3, #1013-1015   75   75

500th anniversary of the birth of Nicolaus Copernicus (1473-1543), Polish astronomer. Nos. 1013-1015 printed se-tenant.

1973   Lithographed   Perf. 13½x14
Size: 26½x29mm.
Designs: Planetary system.
Multicolored
1016   A193   5c shown   10   5
1017   A193   5c Earth   10   5
1018   A193   20c Mars   75   15
1019   A193   20c Saturn   50   15
1020   A193   30c Planetoids   60   25
1021   A193   40c Neptune   75   30
1022   A193   50c Venus   1.00   50
1023   A193   60c Jupiter   1.25   60
1024   A193   75c Uranus   1.50   75
1025   A193   90c Pluto   1.85   85
1026   A193   90c Moon   2.00   1.00
1027   A193   1b Mercury   2.50   1.25
   Size: 27x55mm.
1028   A193   10c Orbits and Saturn   30   6
1029   A193   15c Sun, Mercury, Venus, Earth   50   10
1030   A193   15c Jupiter, Uranus, Neptune, Pluto   60   10
   Strip of 3, #1028-1030   1.50   1.50
   Nos. 1016-1030 (15)   14.30   6.16

10th anniversary of Humboldt Planetarium. Nos. 1028-1030 printed se-tenant with continuous design showing solar system.
Issue dates: Nos. 1016, 1018, 1021, 1023-1025, Mar. 15; others Mar. 30.

OAS Emblem, Map of Americas
A194

1973, Apr. 30   Litho.   Perf. 13½x14
1031   A194   60c multi   75   35

25th anniversary of the Organization of American States.

José Antonio Paez
A195

Street of the Lancers, Puerto Cabello
A196

Designs: 10c, Paez in uniform. 30c, Paez and horse, from old print. 2b, Paez at Battle of Centauro (horiz.). 10c, 2b are after contemporary paintings.

1973   Perf. 14x13½, 13½x14
1032   A195   10c gold & multi   12   6
1033   A195   30c red, blk & gold   35   18
1034   A195   50c bl, vio bl & dk brn   75   35
1035   A196   1b multi   1.50   75
1036   A195   2b gold & multi   2.50   1.50
   Nos. 1032-1036 (5)   5.22   2.84

Centenary of the death of Gen. José Antonio Paez (1790-1873), leader in War of Independence, President of Venezuela. The 1b commemorates the sesquicentenary of the fall of Puerto Cabello.
Issue dates: Nos. 1033-1034, May 6; Nos. 1032, 1036, June 13; No. 1035, Nov. 8.

VENEZUELA

José P. Padilla, Mariano Montilla, Manuel Manrique—A197

Designs: 1b, Naval battle. 2b, Line-up for naval battle.

1973, July 24		Litho.		Perf. 12½	
1037	A197	50c multi		60	30
1038	A197	1b multi		1.25	60
1039	A197	2b multi		2.50	1.25

150th anniversary of the Battle of Maracaibo.

 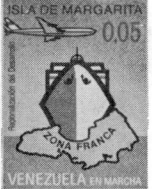

Bishop Ramos de Lora — A198

Plane, Ship, Margarita Island — A199

1973, Aug. 1	Photo.	Perf. 14x13½		
1040	A198	75c gold & dk brn	85	35

Sesquicentennial of the birth of Ramos de Lora (1722–1790), first Bishop of Merida de Maracaibo and founder of the Colegio Seminario, the forerunner of the University of the Andes.

1973, Sept. 8	Litho.	Perf. 14x13½		
1041	A199	5c multi		12	6

Establishment of Margarita Island as a free port.

Map of Golden Road and Waterfall — A200

Designs (Road Map and): 10c, Scarlet macaw. 20c, Church ruins. 50c, 60c, Indian mountain sanctuary. 90c, Colonial church. 1b, Flags of Venezuela and Brazil.

1973, Oct. 1		Litho.		Perf. 13	
1042	A200	5c blk & multi		6	6
1043	A200	10c blk & multi		12	6
1044	A200	20c blk & multi		30	12
1045	A200	50c blk & multi		75	35
1046	A200	60c blk & multi		75	35
1047	A200	90c blk & multi		1.10	50
1048	A200	1b blk & multi		1.25	60
Nos. 1042-1048 (7)				4.33	2.04

Completion of the Golden Road from Santa Elena de Uairen, Brazil, to El Dorado, Venezuela. Issue dates: 50c, 60c, Oct. 30; others Oct. 1.

Examination

The Catalogue editors cannot undertake to appraise, identify or pass upon genuineness or condition of stamps.

Gen. Paez Dam and Power Station A201

1973, Oct. 14			Perf. 14x13½	
1049	A201	30c multi	35	15

Opening of the General José Antonio Paez Dam and Power Station.

Child on Slide—A202

Designs: No. 1051, Fairytale animals. No. 1052, Children's book. No. 1053, Children disembarking from plane for vacation.

1973, Dec. 4		Litho.	Perf. 12	
1050	A202	10c multi	35	10
1051	A202	10c multi	35	10
1052	A202	10c multi	35	10
1053	A202	10c multi	35	10

Children's Foundation Festival.

King Following Star A203

Design: No. 1055, Two Kings.

1973, Dec. 5		Litho.	Perf. 14x13½	
1054	A203	30c multi	35	15
1055	A203	30c multi	35	15
		Pair, #1054-1055	85	85

Christmas 1973. Nos. 1054–1055 printed se-tenant.

Regional Map of Venezuela A204

1973, Dec. 13			Perf. 13½x14	
1056	A204	25c multi	35	12

Introduction of regionalization.

Handicraft A205

Designs: 35c, Industrial park. 45c, Cog wheels and chimney.

1973, Dec. 18			Perf. 14x13½	
1057	A205	15c bl & multi	25	10
1058	A205	35c multi	50	15
1059	A205	45c yel & multi	75	30

Progress in Venezuela and jobs for the handicapped.

Map of Carupano and Revelers—A206

1974, Feb. 22			Perf. 13½x14	
1060	A206	5c multi	12	6

10th anniversary of Carupano Carnival.

Congress Emblem A207

1974, May 20		Litho.	Perf. 13½	
1061	A207	50c multi	75	25

9th Venezuelan Engineering Congress, Maracaibo, May 19–25.

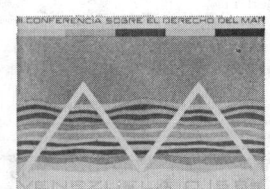

Waves and "M"—A208

Designs: Under-water photographs of deep-sea fish and marine life.

1974, June 20		Litho.	Perf. 12½	
1062	A208	15c multi	15	6
1063	A208	35c multi	30	15
1064	A208	75c multi	75	35
1065	A208	80c multi	85	50

3rd U.N. Conference on the Law of the Sea, Caracas, June 20–Aug. 29.

Pupil and New School—A209

Designs: 10c, 15c, 20c, like 5c. 25c, 30c, 35c, 40c, Suburban housing development. 45c, 50c, 55c, 60c, Highway and overpass. 65c, 70c, 75c, 80c, Playing field (sport). 85c, 90c, 95c, 1b, Operating room. All designs include Venezuelan coat of arms, coins and banknotes.

1974			Perf. 14x13½	
1066	A209	5c bl & multi	6	6
1067	A209	10c ultra & multi	12	6
1068	A209	15c vio & multi	12	6
1069	A209	20c lil & multi	15	7
1070	A209	25c multi	18	6
1071	A209	30c multi	60	30
1072	A209	35c multi	30	12
1073	A209	40c ol & multi	50	18
1074	A209	45c multi	50	25
1075	A209	50c grn & multi	50	25
1076	A209	55c multi	85	45
1077	A209	60c multi	65	30
1078	A209	65c bis & multi	1.50	75
1079	A209	70c multi	70	30
1080	A209	75c multi	75	35
1081	A209	80c brn & multi	75	35
1082	A209	85c ver & multi	75	35
1083	A209	90c multi	1.00	38
1084	A209	95c multi	2.00	1.00
1085	A209	1b multi	1.00	50
Nos. 1066-1085 (20)			12.98	6.14

"Pay your Taxes" campaign.

Bolivar at Battle of Junin—A210

1974, Aug. 6		Litho.	Perf. 13½x14	
1086	A210	2b multi	2.00	1.00

Sesquicentennial of the Battle of Junin.

Globe and UPU Emblem—AP211

Design: 50c, Postrider, sailing ship, steamer and jet.

1974, Oct. 9			Perf. 12	
1087	A211	45c dk bl & multi	50	25
1088	A211	50c blk & multi	60	30

Centenary of Universal Postal Union.

Rufino Blanco-Fombona A212

Designs: Portraits of Blanco-Fombona and his books.

1974, Oct. 16		Litho.	Perf. 12½	
1089	A212	10c gray & multi	12	6
1090	A212	30c yel & multi	30	15
1091	A212	45c multi	45	25
1092	A212	90c buff & multi	75	35

Centenary of the birth of Rufino Blanco-Fombona (1874–1944), writer.

Children A213

1974, Nov. 29		Litho.	Perf. 13½	
1093	A213	70c bl & multi	70	35

Children's Foundation Festival.

VENEZUELA

General Sucre
A214

Globe with South American Map and Flags
A215

Designs: 20c, 1b, Jesus Muñoz Tebar, first Minister of Public Works. 25c, Bridges on Caracas-La Guaira Road, 1912 and 1953. 40c, Tucacas Railroad Station, 1911, and projected terminal, 1974. 80c, Anatomical Institute, Caracas, 1911, and Social Security Hospital, 1969. 85c, Quininari River Bridge, 1804, and Orinoco River Bridge, 1967.

1974, Dec. 18   Litho.   Perf. 12½

1100	A219	5c ultra & multi	12	5
1101	A219	20c ocher & blk	35	10
1102	A219	25c bl & multi	40	10
1103	A219	40c yel & multi	35	25
1104	A219	70c grn & multi	1.25	35
1105	A219	80c multi	1.50	45
1106	A219	85c org & multi	2.00	50
1107	A219	1b red & blk	2.50	75
		Nos. 1100-1107 (8)	8.47	2.55

Centenary of the Ministry of Public Works.

Battle of Ayacucho—A216

Design: 1b, Map of South America with battles marked.

Perf. 14x13½, 13½x14

1974, Dec. 9

1094	A214	30c multi	30	15
1095	A215	50c multi	45	35
1096	A215	1b multi	1.00	50
1097	A216	2b multi	2.00	1.00

Sesquicentennial of the Battle of Ayacucho.

Adoration of the Shepherds, by J. B. Mayno
A217   A218

1974, Dec. 16   Photo.   Perf. 14x13½

1098	A217	30c gold & multi	35	25
1099	A218	30c gold & multi	35	25
		Pair, #1098-1099	1.10	1.10

Christmas 1974. Nos. 1098–1099 printed se-tenant.

Road Building, 1905 and El Ciempies Overpass, 1972
A219

Women and IWY Emblem
A220

1975, Oct. 8   Litho.   Perf. 13½x14

| 1108 | A220 | 90c multi | 75 | 50 |

International Women's Year.

Scout Emblem and Tents
A221

1975, Nov. 11   Litho.   Perf. 13½x14

| 1109 | A221 | 20c multi | 18 | 10 |
| 1110 | A221 | 80c multi | 65 | 38 |

14th World Boy Scout Jamboree, Lillehammer, Norway, July 29–Aug. 7.

Adoration of the Shepherds
A222   A223

1975, Dec. 5   Litho.   Perf. 14

1111	A222	30c multi	30	15
1112	A223	30c multi	30	15
		Pair, #1111-1112	1.00	1.00

Christmas 1975. Nos. 1111–1112 printed se-tenant.

Bolivar's Tomb
A224

Design: 1.05b, National Pantheon.

1976, Feb. 2   Engr.   Perf. 14x13½

| 1113 | A224 | 30c gray & ultra | 25 | 10 |
| 1114 | A224 | 1.05b sep & car | 75 | 35 |

Centenary of National Pantheon.

Bolivia Flag Colors
A225

1976, Mar. 22   Litho.   Perf. 13½

| 1115 | A225 | 60c multi | 50 | 25 |

Sesquicentennial of Bolivia's independence.

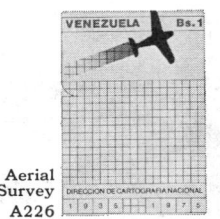

Aerial Map Survey
A226

1976, Apr. 8   Perf. 13½x12½

| 1116 | A226 | 1b blk & vio bl | 75 | 35 |

National Cartographic Institute, 40th anniversary.

Gen. Ribas' Signature
A227

José Felix Ribas
A228

1976, Apr. 26   Photo.   Perf. 12½x13

| 1117 | A227 | 40c red & grn | 35 | 15 |

Perf. 13½

| 1118 | A228 | 55c multi | 50 | 25 |

Gen. José Felix Ribas (1775–1815), independence hero, birth bicentenary.

Musicians of the Chacao School, by Armandio Barrios—A229

Lamas's Colophon
A230

1976, May 13   Litho.   Perf. 13½x14

| 1119 | A229 | 75c multi | 55 | 35 |

Photogravure
Perf. 12½x13½

| 1120 | A230 | 1.25b buff, red & gray | 90 | 55 |

José Angel Lamas (1775–1814), composer, birth bicentenary.

Bolivar, by José Maria Espinoza
A231

1976   Engr.   Perf. 12

Size: 18x22½mm.

1121	A231	5c green	5	5
1122	A231	10c lil rose	8	5
1123	A231	15c brown	10	5
1124	A231	20c black	12	5
1125	A231	25c yellow	15	6
1126	A231	30c vio bl	17	8
1127	A231	45c dk pur	25	10
1128	A231	50c orange	30	12
1129	A231	65c blue	38	15
1130	A231	1b vermilion	55	25

Size: 26x32mm.

1131	A231	2b gray	1.05	50
1132	A231	3b vio bl	1.50	75
1133	A231	4b yellow	2.10	1.00
1134	A231	5b orange	2.60	1.25
1135	A231	10b dl pur	5.25	2.50
1136	A231	15b blue	8.00	3.75
1137	A231	20b vermilion	10.50	5.00
		Nos. 1121-1137 (17)	33.15	15.71

Coil Stamps
1978, May 22   Engr.   Perf. 14 horiz.

Size: 18x22½mm.

1138	A231	5c green	5	5
1139	A231	10c lil rose	5	5
1140	A231	15c brown	8	5
1141	A231	20c black	15	5
1142	A231	25c yellow	20	6
1143	A231	30c vio bl	20	8
1144	A231	45c dk pur	30	10
1144A	A231	50c orange	35	12
1144B	A231	65c blue	40	15
1144C	A231	1b vermilion	65	25
		Nos. 1138-1144C (10)	2.43	96

Black control number on back of every fifth stamp.

Maze
A232

Central University
A233

Faculty Emblems
A234

1976, June 1   Litho.   Perf. 12½x13½

1145	A232	30c multi	25	10
1146	A233	50c yel, org & blk	35	25
1147	A234	90c blk & yel	75	50

Central University of Venezuela, 250th anniversary.

VENEZUELA

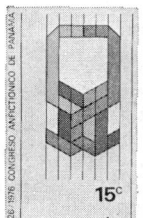

"Unity"
A235

Designs: 45c, 1.25b, similar to 15c.

1976, June 29   Litho.   Perf. 12½
1148	A235	15c multi	15	5
1149	A235	45c multi	35	10
1150	A235	1.25b multi	85	50

Amphictyonic Congress of Panama, Sesquicentennial.

George Washington, Bicentennial Emblem
A236

Designs (Bicentennial Emblem and): No. 1152, Thomas Jefferson. No. 1153, Abraham Lincoln. No. 1154, Franklin D. Roosevelt. No. 1155, John F. Kennedy.

1976, July 4   Engr.   Perf. 14
1151	A236	1b red brn & blk	80	50
1152	A236	1b grn & blk	80	50
1153	A236	1b pur & blk	80	50
1154	A236	1b bl & blk	80	50
1155	A236	1b ol & blk	80	50
	Nos. 1151-1155 (5)	4.00	2.50

American Bicentennial.

Valve
A237

Designs: Computer drawings of valves and pipelines.

1976, Nov. 8   Photo.   Perf. 13x14
1156	A237	10c multi	8	5
1157	A237	30c multi	17	12
1158	A237	35c multi	20	15
1159	A237	40c multi	22	10
1160	A237	55c multi	35	25
1161	A237	90c multi	65	35
	Nos. 1156-1161 (6)	1.67	1.02

Nationalization of the oil industry.

Nativity, by Barbaro Rivas
A238

1976, Dec. 1   Litho.   Perf. 13½x14
| 1162 | A238 | 30c multi | 50 | 10 |

Christmas 1976.

Ornament
A239

Lithographed and Embossed
1976, Dec. 15   Perf. 14x13½
| 1163 | A239 | 60c yel & blk | 50 | 25 |

Declaration of Bogota (economic agreements of Andean countries), 10th anniversary.

Coat of Arms of Barinas—A240

1977, May 25   Photo.   Perf. 12½x13
| 1164 | A240 | 50c multi | 50 | 25 |

400th anniversary of the founding of Barinas.

Crucified Christ, Patron Saint of La Grita
A241

1977, Aug. 6   Litho.   Perf. 13
| 1165 | A241 | 30c multi | 30 | 10 |

400th anniversary of the founding of La Grita (in 1976).

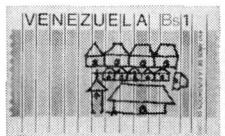

Symbolic City
A242

1977, Aug. 26   Litho.   Perf. 13½
| 1166 | A242 | 1b multi | 75 | 35 |

450th anniversary of the founding of Coro.

Communications Symbols
A243

1977, Sept. 30   Litho.   Perf. 13½x14
| 1167 | A243 | 85c multi | 75 | 25 |

9th Interamerican Postal and Telecommunications Staff Congress, Caracas, Sept. 26-30.

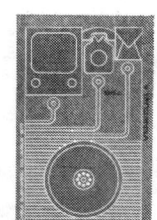

Cable Connecting with TV, Telephone and Circuit Box
A244

1977, Oct. 12   Litho.   Perf. 14x13½
| 1168 | A244 | 95c multi | 75 | 25 |

Inauguration of Columbus underwater cable linking Venezuela and the Canary Islands.

"Venezuela"
A245

Designs: "Venezuela" horizontal on 50c, 1.05b; reading up on 80c, 1.25b; reading down on 1.50b.

1977, Nov. 26   Photo.   Perf. 13½x13
1169	A245	30c brt yel & blk	20	8
1170	A245	50c dp org & blk	35	12
1171	A245	80c gray & blk	65	25
1172	A245	1.05b red & blk	75	30
1173	A245	1.25b yel & blk	85	30
1174	A245	1.50b gray & blk	1.10	38
	Nos. 1169-1174 (6)	3.90	1.43

First anniversary of nationalization of iron industry.

Juan Pablo Duarte   Nativity, Colonial Sculpture
A246   A247

1977, Dec. 8   Engr.   Perf. 11x13
| 1175 | A246 | 75c blk & lil | 60 | 25 |

Juan Pablo Duarte (1813-1876), leader in liberation struggle.

1977, Dec. 15   Litho.   Perf. 13½
| 1176 | A247 | 30c grn & multi | 20 | 8 |

Christmas 1977.

OPEC Emblem
A248

1977, Dec. 20
| 1177 | A248 | 1.05b brt & lt bl & blk | 75 | 25 |

50th Conference of Oil Producing and Exporting Countries, Caracas.

Racing Bicyclists
A249

Design: 1.25b, Bicyclist.

1978, Jan. 16   Litho.   Perf. 12½x13
| 1178 | A249 | 5c multi | 5 | 5 |
| 1179 | A249 | 1.25b multi | 85 | 30 |

World Bicycling Championships, San Cristobal, Tachira, Aug. 22–Sept. 4.

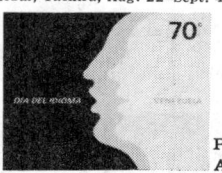

Profiles
A250

1978, Apr. 21   Litho.   Perf. 13½x14
| 1180 | A250 | 70c blk, gray & lil | 50 | 25 |

Language Day.

Magnetic Computer Tape and Satellite
A251

1978, May 17   Litho.   Perf. 14
| 1184 | A251 | 75c vio bl | 55 | 30 |

10th World Telecommunications Day.

"1777–1977"   Goya's Carlos III as Computer Print
A252   A253

1978, June 23   Litho.   Perf. 12
| 1185 | A252 | 30c multi | 15 | 8 |
| 1186 | A253 | 1b multi | 75 | 25 |

200th anniversary of Venezuelan unification.

Bolivar Bicentenary

Juan Vicente Bolivar y Ponte, Father of Simon Bolivar—A254

The Oath on Monte Sacro, Rome, by Tito Salas—A255

Designs: 30c, Bolivar as infant in nursemaid's arms (detail from design of No. 1189). No. 1189, Baptism of the Liberator, by Tito Salas, 1929.

1978, July 24   Engr.   Perf. 12½
| 1187 | A254 | 30c emer & blk | 25 | 10 |
| 1188 | A254 | 1b multi | 75 | 35 |

Souvenir Sheet
Litho.   Perf. 14
| 1189 | A255 | Sheet of 5, multi | 20.00 | 20.00 |
| a. | | 50c, single stamp | 2.00 | 2.00 |

1978, Dec. 17   Engr.   Perf. 12½
Designs: 30c, Bolivar at 25. 1b, Simon Rodriguez (Bolivar's tutor).
| 1190 | A254 | 30c multi | 15 | 8 |
| 1191 | A254 | 1b rose red & blk | 50 | 25 |

Souvenir Sheet
Litho.   Perf. 14
| 1192 | A255 | Sheet of 5, multi | 1.50 | 1.50 |
| a. | | 50c, single stamp | 25 | 25 |

Bicentenary of birth of Simon Bolivar.
Souvenir sheets have black marginal inscriptions. Size of souvenir sheet stamps: 20x24mm. Size of No 1189: 154x130mm. Size of No 1192: 130x155mm.

VENEZUELA

1979, July 24   Engr.   Perf. 12½

Designs: 30c, Alexandre Sabes Petion, president of Haiti. 1b, Bolivar's signature. No. 1195a, Partial map of Jamaica (horiz.). No. 1195b, Partial map of Jamaica (vert.). No. 1195c, Bolivar, 1816. No. 1195d, Luis Brion. No. 1195e, Petion.

| 1193 | A254 | 30c org, vio & blk | 15 | 8 |
| 1194 | A254 | 1b red org & blk | 50 | 25 |

Souvenir Sheet
Litho.   Perf. 14

| 1195 | A255 | Sheet of 5 | 1.50 | 1.50 |
| a-e. | | 50c multi, any single | 25 | 25 |

Simon Bolivar (1783-1830), revolutionary leader and statesman. No. 1195 has light blue and multicolored margin showing map of Jamaica drawn by Bolivar, 1806. Size of stamps: 26x20, 20x26mm. Size of No. 1195: 155x130mm.

Bolivar Bicentenary Type of 1978

Designs: 30c, Bolivar. 1b, Slave. No. 1198, Freeing of the Slaves, by Tito Salas. (30c, 1b, details from design of No. 1198.)

1979, Dec. 17   Engr.   Perf. 12½

| 1196 | A254 | 30c multi | 15 | 8 |
| 1197 | A254 | 1b multi | 50 | 25 |

Souvenir Sheet
Litho.   Perf. 14

| 1198 | A255 | Sheet of 5, multi | 1.50 | 1.50 |
| a. | | 50c, single stamp | 25 | 25 |

Simon Bolivar, birth centenary. Single stamps of No. 1198 show details from the Abolition of Slavery, by Tito Salas: multicolored margin shows entire painting; black marginal inscription. Size of souvenir sheet stamps: 22x28mm. Size of No. 1198: 131x 156mm.

See Nos. 1228-1230, 1264-1266, 1276-1284.

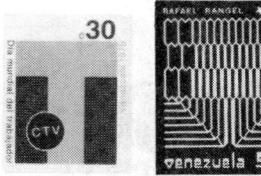

"T" and "CTV"   Symbolic Design
A256   A257

Designs: Different arrangement of letters "T" and "CTV" for "Confederacion de Trabajeros Venezolanos."

1978, Sept. 27   Photogravure   Perf. 13x13½

1199	A256	Strip of 5, multi	85	85
a.		30c, single stamp	15	8
1200	A256	Strip of 5, multi	2.50	2.50
a.		95c, single stamp	48	25

Workers' Day. Stamps of same denomination printed se-tenant.

1978, Oct. 3   Litho.   Perf. 14

| 1201 | A257 | 50c dk brn | 75 | 35 |

Rafael Rangel, physician and scientist, birth centenary.

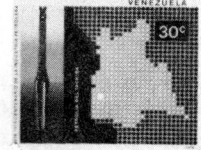

Drill Head, Tachira Oil Field Map
A258

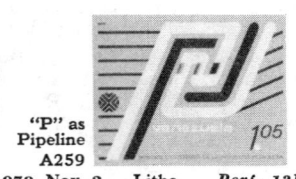

"P" as Pipeline
A259

1978, Nov. 2   Litho.   Perf. 13½

| 1202 | A258 | 30c multi | 25 | 10 |
| 1203 | A259 | 1.05b multi | 75 | 35 |

Centenary of oil industry.

Star
A260

1978, Dec. 6   Litho.   Perf. 14

| 1204 | A260 | 30c multi | 25 | 10 |

Christmas 1978.

"P T"—A261

1979, Feb. 8   Litho.   Perf. 12½

| 1205 | A261 | 75c blk & red | 38 | 20 |

Creation of Postal and Telegraph Institute.

"Dam Holding Back Water"
A262

1979, Feb. 15   Photo.   Perf. 13½

| 1206 | A262 | 2b sil, gray & blk | 1.00 | 50 |

Guri Dam, 10th anniversary.

San Martin, by E. J. Maury—A263

Designs: 60c, San Martin, by Mercedes. 70c, Monument, Guayaquil. 75c, San Martin's signature.

1979, Feb. 25   Perf. 12½x13

1207	A263	40c bl, blk & yel	25	10
1208	A263	60c bl, blk & yel	35	15
1209	A263	70c bl, blk & yel	45	25
1210	A263	75c bl, blk & yel	50	30

José de San Martin (1778-1850), South American liberator.

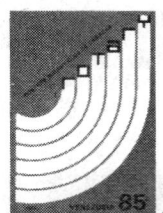

"Rotary"
A264

1979, Aug. 7   Litho.   Perf. 14x13½

| 1211 | A264 | 85c gold & blk | 42 | 22 |

Rotary Club of Caracas, 50th anniversary.

Our Lady of Coromoto Appearing to Children
A265

Engraved and Lithographed

1979, Aug. 23   Perf. 13

| 1212 | A265 | 55c blk & dp org | 28 | 15 |

25th anniversary of the canonization of Our Lady of Coromoto.

London Residence, Coat of Arms, Miranda—A266

1979, Oct. 23   Litho.
Perf. 14½x14

| 1213 | A266 | 50c multi | 25 | 12 |

Francisco de Miranda (1750-1816), Venezuelan independence fighter.

O'Leary, Maps of South America and United Kingdom—A267

1979, Nov. 6

| 1214 | A267 | 30c multi | 15 | 8 |

Daniel O'Leary (1801-1854), writer.

Boy Holding Nest, IYC Emblem—A268

IYC Emblem and: 80c, Boys in water, bridge.

1979, Nov. 20   Litho.   Perf. 14½x14

| 1215 | A268 | 70c lt bl & blk | 35 | 18 |
| 1216 | A268 | 80c mylti | 40 | 20 |

International Year of the Child.

Christmas 1979—A269

1979, Dec. 1   Litho.   Perf. 13½

| 1217 | A269 | 30c multi | 15 | 8 |

Caudron Bomber, EXFILVE Emblem
A270

EXFILVE Emblem and: No. 1219, Stearman biplane. No. 1220, UH-1H helicopter. No. 1221, CF-5 jet fighter.

1979, Dec. 15   Perf. 11x11½

1218	A270	75c multi	38	20
1219	A270	75c multi	38	20
1220	A270	75c multi	38	20
1221	A270	75c multi	38	20

Venezuelan Air Force, 59th anniversary; EXFILVE 79, 3rd National Philatelic Exhibition, Dec. 7-17. Nos. 1218-1221 printed se-tenant in sheets of 40 (blocks of 4).

IPOSTEL Emblem, World Map—A271

1979, Dec. 27   Perf. 12

| 1222 | A271 | 75c multi | 38 | 20 |

Postal and Telegraph Institute, introduction of new logo.

Queen Victoria, Hill—A272

1980, Feb. 13   Litho.   Perf. 12½

| 1223 | A272 | 55c multi | 28 | 15 |

Sir Rowland Hill (1795-1879), originator of penny postage.

Dr. Augusto Pi Suner, Physiologist, Birth Centenary—A273

1980, Mar. 14   Litho.   Perf. 12x11½

| 1224 | A273 | 80c multi | 40 | 20 |

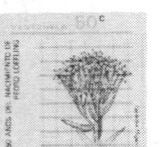

Spanish Seed Leaf—A274

1980, Mar. 27   Litho. & Engr.   Perf. 13½

| 1225 | A274 | 50c multi | 25 | 12 |

Pedro Loefling (1729-1756), Swedish botanist.

VENEZUELA

Juan Lovera (1778-1841), Artist—A275

1980, May 25		Litho.		Perf. 13½	
1226	A275	60c bl & dp org		30	15
1227	A275	75c vio & org		38	20

Bolivar Bicentenary Type of 1978

Designs: 30c, Signing of document. 1b, House of Congress. No. 1230, Angostura Congress, by Tito Salas.

1980, July 24		Engraved		Perf. 12½	
1228	A254	30c multi		15	8
1229	A254	1b multi		50	25

Souvenir Sheet

Litho.				Perf. 14	
1230	A255	Sheet of 5		1.50	1.50
a.		50c, single stamp		25	25

Simon Bolivar (1783-1830), revolutionary leader and statesman. Single stamps of No. 1230 show details of Angostura Congress, by Tito Salas; multicolored margin shows entire painting; black marginal inscription. Size of souvenir sheet stamps: 25x20mm, 20x25mm. Size of No. 1230: 156x130½mm.

Dancing Girls, by Armando Reveron A276

Bernardo O'Higgins A277

1979, Oct. 29		Litho.		Perf. 12	
1231	A276	50c shown		25	12
		Size: 25x40mm.			
1232	A276	65c Portrait		65	32

Armando Reveron (1889-1955), artist.

1980, Aug. 22	Litho. & Engr.		Perf. 13x14	
1233	A277	85c multi	85	42

Bernardo O'Higgins (1776-1842), Chilean soldier and statesman.

School Ship Simon Bolivar—A278

Frigate Mariscal Sucre—A279

		Perf. 11½ (#1234), 11x11½			
1980, Sept. 13			Lithographed		
1234	A278	1.50b shown		75	38
1235	A279	1.50b shown		75	38
1236	A279	1.50b Submarine Picua		75	38
1237	A279	1.50b Naval Academy		75	38

Workers Holding OPEC Emblem—A280

20th Anniversary of OPEC (Organization of Petroleum Exporting Countries): No. 1239, Emblem.

1980, Sept. 14		Litho.	Perf. 12	
1238	A280	1.50b multi	75	38
1239	A280	1.50b multi	75	38

Death of Simon Bolivar—A281

1980, Dec. 17		Litho.	Perf. 11x11½	
1240	A281	2b multi	1.00	50

Simon Bolivar, 150th anniversary of death.

Gen. José Antonio Sucre, 150th Anniversary of Death—A282

1980, Dec. 17 Litho. & Engr. Perf. 13x12½				
1241	A282	2b multi	1.00	50

Nativity by Rubens A283

1980, Dec. 19		Litho.	Perf. 14x13½	
1242	A283	1b multi	40	20

Christmas 1980.

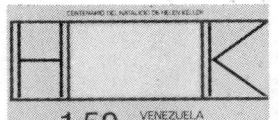

Helen Keller's Initials (Written and Braille)—A284

	Litho. & Embossed			
1981, Feb. 12			Perf. 12½	
1243	A284	1.50b multi	60	30

Helen Keller (1880-1968), blind and deaf writer and lecturer.

John Baptiste de la Salle A285

San Felipe City, 250th Anniv. A286

1981, May 15		Litho.	Perf. 11½x11	
1244	A285	1.25b multi	50	25

Christian Brothers', 300th anniv.

1981, May 1			Perf. 11½	
1245	A286	3b multi	1.00	50

Municipal Theater of Caracas Centenary—A287

1981, June 28		Litho.	Perf. 12	
1246	A287	1.25b multi	50	25

UPU Membership Centenary—A288

1981, Sept. 15		Litho.	Perf. 12	
1247	A288	2b multi	60	30

11th Natl. Population and Housing Census—A289

1981, Oct. 14		Litho.	Perf. 12	
1248	A289	1b multi	40	20

9th Bolivar Games, Barquismeto—A290

1981, Dec. 4		Litho.	Perf. 11½x12	
1249	A290	95c multi	40	20

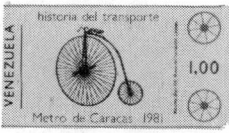

19th Cent. Bicycle—A291

1981, Dec. 5		Photo.	Perf. 13½x14½	
1250	A291	1b shown	40	20
1251	A291	1.05b Locomotive, 1926	40	20
1252	A291	1.25b Buick, 1937	50	25
1253	A291	1.50b Coach	60	30

Christmas 1981—A292

1981, Dec. 21		Litho.	Perf. 11½x12	
1254	A292	1b multi	40	20

50th Anniv. of Natural Science Society—A293

1982, Jan. 21			Perf. 12x11½	
1255	A293	1b Mt. Autana	40	20
1256	A293	1.50b Sarisarinama	60	30
1257	A293	2b Guacharo Cave	75	35

20th Anniv. of Constitution—A294

1982, Jan. 28		Photo.	Perf. 13x13½	
1258	A294	1.85b gold & blk	75	35

VENEZUELA

20th Anniv. of Agricultural Reform—A295

1982, Feb. 19   Litho.   *Perf. 13½*
1259   A295   3b multi   1.25   50

Jules Verne (1828-1905), Science Fiction Writer—A296

1982, Mar. 12   Litho.   *Perf. 13½*
1260   A296   1b bl & dk bl   20   10

Natl. Anthem Centenary (1981)—A297

1982, Mar. 26   *Perf. 12*
1261   A297   1b multi   20   10

1300th Anniv. of Bulgaria
A298

6th Natl. 5-Year Plan, 1981-85
A299

1982, June 2   Litho.   *Perf. 13½*
1262   A298   65c multi   14   8
1982, June 11
1263   A299   2b multi   40   20

Bolivar Types of 1978

1982, July 24   Engr.   *Perf. 12½*
1264   A254   30c Juan Jose Rondon   6   5
1265   A254   1b Jose Antonio Anzoategui   20   10

Souvenir Sheet
Litho.   *Perf. 14*
1266   Sheet of 5   60   60
a.-e.   A255 50c, any single   10   10

Single stamps of No. 1266 show details from Battle of Boyaca, by Martin Tovar y Tovar; multicolored margin shows entire painting, black marginal inscription. Size of souvenir sheet stamps: 19x26mm., 26x19mm. Size of No. 1266: 156x132mm.

Cecilio Acosta (1818-81), Writer—A299a

1982, Aug. 13   Litho.   *Perf. 11½*
1266F   A299a   3b multi   60   30

Aloe—A300

1982, Oct. 14   Photo.   *Perf. 13½x13*
1267   A300   1.05b shown   25   15
1268   A300   2.55b Tortoise   65   30
1269   A300   2.75b Tara armilla tree   70   32
1270   A300   3b Guacharo bird   75   35

Andres Bello (1781-1865), Statesman and Reformer—A301

1982, Nov. 20   Litho.   *Perf. 12*
1271   A301   1.05b multi   25   15
1272   A301   2.55b multi   65   30
1273   A301   2.75b multi   70   32
1274   A301   3b multi   75   35

Christmas 1982—A302

Design: Holy Family creche figures by Francisco J. Cardozo, 18th cent.

1982, Dec. 7   Photo. & Engr.   *Perf. 13½*
1275   A302   1b multi   20   10

Bolivar Types of 1978

1982-83   Engr.   *Perf. 12½*
1276   A254   30c Victory Monument, Carabobo   10   5
1277   A254   30c Monument to the Meeting plaque   10   5
1278   A254   30c Antonio de Sucre   10   5
1279   A254   1b Jose Atonio Paez   25   12
1280   A254   1b Sword hilt, 1824   25   12
1281   A254   1b Guayaquil Monument   25   12
Nos. 1276-1281 (6)   1.05   51

Souvenir Sheets
1282   Sheet of 5   1.25   1.00
a.-e.   A255 50c, any single   15   15
1283   Sheet of 5   1.25   1.00
a.-e.   A255 50c, any single   15   15
1284   Sheet of 5   1.25   1.00
a.-e.   A255 50c, any single   15   15

No. 1282: Battle of Carabobo by Martin Tovar y Tovar; No. 1283, Monument to the Meeting; No. 1284, Battle of Ayacucho, by Martin Tovar y Tovar. Size: 156x132mm.; 132x156mm. Issue dates: Nos. 1276-1277, 1279, 1282-1283, Dec. 17; others, Apr. 18, 1983.

Gen. Jose Francisco Bermudez (1782-18)—A303

Antonio Nicolas Briceno (1782-18), Liberation Hero—A304

1982, Dec. 23   Litho.   *Perf. 13x13½, 15x14*
1285   A303   3b multi   60   30
1286   A304   3b multi   60   30

25th Anniv. of 1958 Reforms—A305

1983, Jan. 23   *Perf. 10½x10*
1287   A305   3b multi   60   30

25th Anniv. of Judicial Police Technical Dept.—A306

1983, Mar. 20   Photo.   *Perf. 13½x13*
1288   A306   4b ol & red   75   40

Transportation Type of 1981

1983, March 28   Photo.   *Perf. 13½x14½*
1289   A291   75c Lincoln, 1923   10   5
1290   A291   80c Locomotive, 1889   12   6
1291   A291   85c Willys truck, 1927   15   8
1292   A291   95c Cleveland motorcycle, 1920   15   8

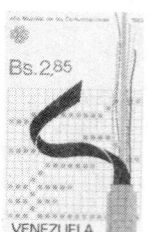

World Communications Year—A307

1983, May 17   Photo.   *Perf. 13x12½*
1293   A307   2.85b multi   50   30

Bolivar Type of 1978

Designs: 30c; Flags of Colombia, Peru, Chile, Venezuela, and Buenos Aires. 1b; Equestrian Statue of Bolivar.

Photo. & Engr. (No. 1294), Engraved (No. 1295)
1983, July 25   *Perf. 12½*
1294   A254   30c multi   6   5
1295   A254   1b multi   15   8

Souvenir Sheet
Litho.   *Perf. 14*
1296   A255 Sheet of 5   75   60
a.-e.   50c, any single   15   10

Single stamps of No. 1296 show details of "The Liberator on the Silver Mountain of Potosi" by Tito Salas; multicolored margin shows entire painting, black marginal inscription. Size of souvenir sheet stamps, 20x25mm. Size of No. 1296: 130x155mm.

9th Pan—American Games
A308   A309

Designs: No. 1303a, baseball. b, cycle wheel. c, boxing glove. d, soccer ball. e, target.

1983, Aug. 25   Litho. & Engr.   *Perf. 13*
1297   A308   2b shown   30   20
1298   A308   2b Swimming   30   20
1299   A308   2.70b Cycling   40   30
1300   A308   2.70b Fencing   40   30
1301   A308   2.85b Runners   50   32
1302   A308   2.85b Weightlifting   50   32
Nos. 1297-1302 (6)   2.40   1.64

Souvenir Sheet
1303   Sheet of 5
a.-e.   A309 1b single

No. 1303 issued for Copan '83. Size: 167x121mm.

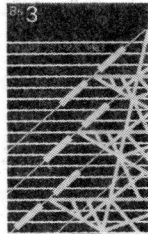

25th Anniv. of Cadafe (State Electricity Authority)—A310

1983, Oct. 27   Litho.   *Perf. 14*
1304   A310   3b multi   50   25

Bolivar Type of 1976

1983   Engr.   *Perf. 12*
Size: 26x32mm.
1305   A231   25b bl grn   4.00   2.00
1306   A231   30b brown   5.00   3.00
1307   A231   50b brt rose lil   8.00   4.00

Transportation Type of 1981

Various views of Caracas Metro.

1983, Dec.   Photo.   *Perf. 13½x14½*
1308   A291   55c multi   10   5
1309   A291   75c multi   12   6
1310   A291   95c multi   15   8
1311   A291   2b multi   30   10

VENEZUELA

Christmas 1983—A311

1983, Dec. 1		Litho.	Perf. 13x14
1312	A311	1b Nativity	16 8

Scouting Year (1982)—A312

Litho. & Eng.

1983, Dec. 14			Perf. 12½x13
1313	A312	2.25b Pitching tent	36 18
1314	A312	2.55b Planting tree	42 20
1315	A312	2.75b Mountain climbing	45 22
1316	A312	3b Camp site	50 25

Bolivar Type of 1976

Designs: No. 1317, Title page of "Opere de Raimondo Montecuccoli" (most valuable book in Caracas University Library). No. 1318, Pedro Gual, Congress of Panama delegate, 1826. No. 1319, Jose Maria Vargas (b. 1786), University of Caracas pres. No. 1320, José Faustino Sanchez Carrion, Congress of Panama delegate, 1826.

1984		Engr.	Perf. 12½
1317	A254	30c multi	5 5
1318	A254	30c multi	5 5
1319	A254	1b multi	16 8
1320	A254	1b multi	16 8

Souvenir Sheets
Litho.   Perf. 14

1321		Sheet of 5	50
a.-e.	A255	50c, any single	8
1322		Sheet of 5	50
a.-e.	A255	50c, any single	8

Single stamps of No. 1321 show details of Arts, Science and Education, fresco by Hector Poleo; 1322, Map of South America, 1829. Size of souvenir sheet stamps: 20x30mm.; 27x20mm. Sheet size: 132x156mm.

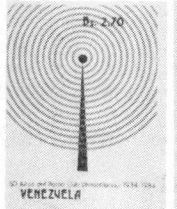 

Radio Waves   Intelligentsia for Peace
A313   A314

1983, Jan. 30		Litho.	Perf. 14x13
1323	A313	2.70b multi	45 22

Radio Club of Venezuela, 50th anniv.

1984, Jan. 31

1324	A314	1b Doves	16 8
1325	A314	2.70b Profile	45 22
1326	A314	2.85b Flower, head	50 25

SEMI-POSTAL STAMPS.

A 5c green stamp of the Cruzada Venezolana Sanitaria Social portraying Simon Bolivar was overprinted "EE. UU. DE VENEZUELA CORREOS" in 1937.
It is stated that 50,000 copies without control numbers on back were sold by post offices and 147,700 with control numbers on back were offered for sale by the Society at eight times face value.

Bolívar Funeral Carriage
SP1
Engraved.
1942, Dec. 17   Perf. 12   Unwmkd.
B1   SP1   20c +5c bl   10.00   1.25

To commemorate the centenary of the arrival of Simón Bolivar's remains in Caracas. The surtax was used to erect a monument to his memory. See Nos. CB1-CB2.

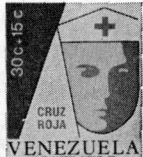
Red Cross Nurse
SP2

1975, Dec. 15		Litho.	Perf. 14
B2	SP2	30c +15c multi	50 25
B3	SP2	50c +25c multi	75 35

Surtax for Venezuelan Red Cross.

Carmen América   Children
Fernandez de   in Home
Leoni   SP4
SP3

1976, June 7   Litho.   Perf. 13½

| B4 | SP3 | 30c +15c multi | 35 25 |
| B5 | SP4 | 50c +25c multi | 65 35 |

Surtax was for the Children's Foundation, founded by Carmen América Fernandez de Leoni in 1966.

Patient
SP5

1976, Dec. 8   Litho.   Perf. 14

| B6 | SP5 | 10c +5c multi | 25 10 |
| B7 | SP5 | 30c +10c multi | 35 25 |

Surtax was for Anti-tuberculosis Society.

VENEZUELA

AIR POST STAMPS.

Air post stamps of 1930–42 perforated "GN" (Gobierno Nacional) were for official use.

Airplane and Map of Venezuela
AP1   AP2

Lithographed.

		1930	*Perf. 12.*	Unwmkd.	
C1	AP1	5c bis brn		12	5
C2	AP1	10c yellow		12	5
a.		10c sal		50.00	50.00
C3	AP1	15c gray		15	10
C4	AP1	25c lilac		15	10
C5	AP1	40c ol grn		18	10
a.		40c sl bl		60.00	
b.		40c sl grn		60.00	
C6	AP1	75c dp red		50	25
C7	AP1	1b indigo		65	25
C8	AP1	1.20b bl grn		1.00	50
C9	AP1	1.70b dk bl		1.25	60
C10	AP1	1.90b bl grn		1.50	75
C11	AP1	2.10b dk bl		2.50	1.00
C12	AP1	2.30b vermilion		2.50	75
C13	AP1	2.50b dk bl		2.50	75
C14	AP1	3.70b bl grn		2.50	1.25
C15	AP1	10b dl vio		6.25	3.75
C16	AP1	20b gray grn		12.50	7.50
		Nos. C1-C16 (16)		34.37	17.75

Nos. C1–C16 exist imperforate or partly perforated. See also Nos. C119–C126.

Bluish Winchester Security Paper

		1932	Engraved.	*Perf. 12½.*	
C17	AP2	5c brown		50	12
C18	AP2	10c org yel		50	12
C19	AP2	15c gray lil		50	12
C20	AP2	25c violet		65	12
C21	AP2	40c ol grn		1.00	12
C22	AP2	70c rose		85	12
C23	AP2	75c red org		1.65	25
C24	AP2	1b dk bl		1.85	18
C25	AP2	1.20b green		3.00	1.50
C26	AP2	1.70b red brn		6.00	1.00
C27	AP2	1.80b ultra		3.00	75
C28	AP2	1.90b green		7.50	6.25
C29	AP2	1.95b blue		8.50	5.00
C30	AP2	2b blk brn		6.25	3.75
C31	AP2	2.10b blue		12.50	10.00
C32	AP2	2.30b red		6.25	3.75
C33	AP2	2.50b dk bl		7.50	2.50
C34	AP2	3b dk vio		7.50	1.50
C35	AP2	3.70b emerald		10.00	10.00
C36	AP2	4b red org		7.50	2.50
C37	AP2	5b black		12.50	4.00
C38	AP2	8b dk car		22.50	8.00
C39	AP2	10b dk vio		42.50	14.00
C40	AP2	20b grnsh sl		95.00	42.50
		Nos. C17-C40 (24)		265.50	118.75

Pairs imperf. between exist of the 1b (price $150); the 25c and 4b (price $300 each).

Air Post Stamps of 1932 Surcharged in Black

1937 VALE POR —5— CENTIMOS

1937					
C41	AP2	5c on 1.70b red brn		25.00	17.50
C42	AP2	10c on 3.70b emer		25.00	17.50
C43	AP2	15c on 4b red org		10.00	7.50
C44	AP2	25c on 5b blk		10.00	7.50
C45	AP2	1b on 8b dk car		8.50	8.50
C46	AP2	2b on 2.10b bl		60.00	55.00
		Nos. C41-C46 (6)		138.50	113.50

Various varieties of surcharge exist, including double and triple impressions. No. C43 exists in pair imperf. between; price $30 unused, $50 used.

Allegory of Flight—AP3

Allegory of Flight AP4

National Pantheon at Caracas AP5

Airplane AP6

1937		Lithographed	*Perf. 11*	
C47	AP3	5c brn org	50	50
C48	AP4	10c org red	40	12
C49	AP5	15c gray blk	1.00	50
C50	AP6	25c dk vio	1.00	50
C51	AP4	40c yel grn	1.75	65
C52	AP3	70c red	1.75	50
C53	AP5	75c bister	4.00	1.75
C54	AP3	1b dk gray	2.50	65
C55	AP4	1.20b pck grn	10.00	5.00
C56	AP3	1.80b dk ultra	5.00	2.50
C57	AP5	1.95b lt ultra	15.00	10.00
C58	AP6	2b chocolate	6.25	3.75
C59	AP6	2.50b gray bl	20.00	15.00
C60	AP4	3b lt vio	10.00	6.25
C61	AP6	3.70b rose red	20.00	20.00
C62	AP5	10b red vio	40.00	20.00
C63	AP3	20b gray	50.00	40.00
		Nos. C47-C63 (17)	189.15	127.67

All values except 3.70b exist imperf. and part-perf.

AP7

1937, Oct. 28

C64	AP7	70c emerald	3.00	1.50
C65	AP7	1.80b ultra	5.00	2.50

Acquisition of the Port of La Guaira by the Government from the British Corporation, June 3, 1937. Exist imperf.

A redrawn printing of Nos. C64–C65, with lower inscription beginning "Nacionalización . . ." was prepared but not issued. Price, $85 each.

Air Post Stamps of 1937 Overprinted in Black

RESELLADO 1937-1938

1937–38

C66	AP4	10c org red	2.00	1.50
a.		Invtd. ovpt.	20.00	15.00
C67	AP6	25c dk vio	3.75	2.00
C68	AP4	40c yel grn	4.00	3.00
C69	AP3	70c red	3.00	2.00
a.		Invtd. ovpt.	20.00	17.50
b.		Dbl. ovpt.	30.00	25.00
C70	AP3	1b dk gray	4.00	3.00
a.		Invtd. ovt.	25.00	20.00
b.		Dbl. ovpt.	20.00	
C71	AP4	1.20b pck grn	60.00	40.00
a.		Invtd. ovpt.	100.00	
C72	AP3	1.80b dk ultra	10.00	5.00
C73	AP5	1.95b lt ultra	15.00	10.00
a.		Invtd. ovpt.	75.00	45.00
C74	AP6	2b chocolate	120.00	62.50
a.		Invtd. ovpt.	150.00	140.00
b.		Dbl. ovpt.	125.00	125.00
C75	AP6	2.50b gray bl	125.00	62.50
a.		Dbl. ovpt.	110.00	
b.		Invtd. ovpt.	160.00	125.00
C76	AP4	3b lt vio	60.00	25.00
C77	AP5	10b red vio	140.00	100.00
C78	AP3	20b gray	160.00	120.00
a.		Dbl. ovpt.	225.00	225.00
		Nos. C66-C78 (13)	706.75	436.50

Counterfeit overprints exist on Nos. C77–78.

View of La Guaira AP8

National Pantheon AP9

Oil Wells AP10

1938–39		Engraved	*Perf. 12*	
C79	AP8	5c green	1.75	1.25
C80	AP8	5c dk grn	18	12
C81	AP9	10c car rose	2.50	2.00
C82	AP9	10c scarlet	30	12
C83	AP9	12½c dl vio	1.00	1.00
C84	AP10	15c sl vio	5.00	5.00
C85	AP10	15c dk bl	1.50	18
C86	AP8	25c dk bl	5.00	2.00
C87	AP8	25c bis brn	38	12
C88	AP10	30c vio ('39)	3.00	25
C89	AP9	40c dk vio	5.00	2.00
C90	AP9	40c redsh brn	3.75	25
C91	AP8	45c Prus grn ('39)	1.75	25
C92	AP9	50c bl ('39)	1.75	15
C93	AP9	70c car rose	1.25	50
C94	AP8	75c bis brn	12.50	3.75
C95	AP10	75c ol bis	2.00	30
C96	AP10	90c red org ('39)	1.50	25
C97	AP9	1b ol & bis	10.00	3.75
C98	AP9	1b dk vio	1.75	25
C99	AP10	1.20b orange	30.00	10.00
C100	AP8	1.20b green	3.00	75
C101	AP8	1.80b ultra	3.00	1.00
C102	AP8	1.90b black	7.50	5.00
C103	AP10	1.95b lt bl	6.25	4.50
C104	AP8	2b ol gray	70.00	25.00
C105	AP8	2b car rose	2.50	1.25
C106	AP9	2.50b red brn	70.00	30.00
C107	AP9	2.50b orange	20.00	5.00
C108	AP10	3b bl grn	32.50	10.00
C109	AP10	3b ol gray	7.50	3.75
C110	AP8	3.70b gray blk	11.00	7.50
C111	AP10	5b red brn ('39)	12.50	3.75
C112	AP9	10b vio brn	40.00	5.00
C113	AP10	20b red org	140.00	62.50
		Nos. C79-C113 (35)	517.61	194.74

See Nos. C235, C236, C254 and C255.

Air Post Stamps of 1937 Surcharged in Black

1938
VALE
CINCO
CÉNTIMOS

1938, Apr. 15			*Perf. 11*	
C114	AP3	5c on 1.80b dk ultra	1.00	75
a.		Invtd. surch.	20.00	15.00
C115	AP6	10c on 2.50b gray bl	4.00	1.75
a.		Inverted surch.	17.50	15.00
C116	AP6	15c on 2b choc	1.75	1.50
C117	AP4	25c on 40c yel grn	2.00	1.75
C118	AP6	40c on 3.70b rose red	5.00	3.75
		Nos. C114-C118 (5)	13.75	9.50

Plane & Map Type of 1930. White Paper; No Imprint.

1938–39		Engraved	*Perf. 12½*	
C119	AP1	5c dk grn ('39)	38	12
C120	AP1	10c org yel ('39)	75	25
C121	AP1	12½c rose vio ('39)	1.50	1.50
C122	AP1	15c dp bl	1.25	25
C123	AP1	25c brown	1.50	25
C124	AP1	40c ol ('39)	3.75	75
a.		Imperf., pair	75.00	
C125	AP1	70c rose car ('39)	35.00	20.00
C126	AP1	1b dk bl ('39)	10.00	3.00
		Nos. C119-C126 (8)	54.13	26.12

Monument to Sucre AP11

Monuments at Carabobo
AP12   AP13

1938, Dec. 23			*Perf. 13½*	
C127	AP11	20c brn blk	80	50
C128	AP12	30c purple	1.35	50
C129	AP13	45c dk bl	1.65	38
C130	AP11	50c lt ultra	1.50	38
C131	AP13	70c dk car	32.50	22.50
C132	AP12	90c red org	2.50	1.00
C133	AP13	1.35b gray blk	3.00	1.50
C134	AP11	1.40b sl gray	12.00	5.00
C135	AP12	2.25b green	6.25	3.75
		Nos. C127-C135 (9)	61.55	35.51

Simón Bolívar and Carabobo Monument
AP14

1940, Mar. 30			*Perf. 12*	
C136	AP14	15c blue	75	25
C137	AP14	20c ol bis	65	12
C138	AP14	25c red brn	5.00	50
C139	AP14	40c blk brn	3.00	25
C140	AP14	1b red lil	8.00	75
C141	AP14	2b rose car	14.00	1.50
		Nos. C136-C141 (6)	31.40	3.37

VENEZUELA

"The Founding of Grand Colombia"
AP15

1940, June 13				
C142	AP15	15c cop brn	2.00	1.00

Issued in commemoration of the 50th anniversary of the founding of the Pan American Union.

Statue of Simón Bolívar, Caracas
AP16

1940-44				
C143	AP16	5c dk grn ('42)	40	5
C144	AP16	10c scar ('42)	40	6
C145	AP16	12½c dl pur	1.25	50
C146	AP16	15c bl ('43)	75	12
C147	AP16	20c bis brn ('44)	75	12
C148	AP16	25c bis brn ('42)	75	12
C149	AP16	30c dp vio ('43)	75	12
C150	AP16	40c blk brn ('43)	1.00	12
C151	AP16	45c turq grn ('43)	1.00	12
C152	AP16	50c bl ('44)	1.00	12
C153	AP16	70c rose pink	3.00	50
C154	AP16	75c ol bis ('43)	10.00	2.50
C155	AP16	90c red org ('43)	2.00	50
C156	AP16	1b dp red lil ('42)	1.00	12
C157	AP16	1.20b dp yel grn ('43)	3.75	1.25
C158	AP16	1.35b gray blk ('42)	15.00	7.50
C159	AP16	2b rose pink ('43)	3.00	30
C160	AP16	3b ol blk ('43)	6.00	1.25
C161	AP16	4b black	4.00	1.25
C162	AP16	5b red brn ('44)	30.00	15.00
		Nos. C143-C162 (20)	85.80	31.62

See Nos. C232 to C234 and C239 to C253.

Air Post Stamps of 1937
Overprinted in Black **Resellado 1943**

1943				
C164	AP4	10c org red	2.50	1.75
C165	AP6	25c dk vio	2.50	2.00
C166	AP4	40c yel grn	3.00	2.00
C167	AP3	70c red	2.50	2.00
C168	AP7	70c emerald	3.00	2.00
C169	AP5	75c bister	3.50	2.50
C170	AP3	1b dk gray	3.50	2.50
C171	AP4	1.20b pck grn	5.00	3.00
C172	AP5	1.80b dk ultra	4.50	2.50
C173	AP7	1.80b bl ultra	6.25	3.75
C174	AP4	1.95b lt ultra	7.50	4.50
C175	AP6	2b chocolate	7.50	6.25
C176	AP6	2.50b gray bl	8.50	6.25
C177	AP4	3b lt vio	11.00	7.50
C178	AP3	3.70b rose red	125.00	100.00
C179	AP5	10c red vio	40.00	30.00
C180	AP3	20b gray	70.00	60.00
		Nos. C164-C180 (17)	305.75	238.50

Nos. C164 to C180 were issued for sale to philatelists. Nos. C164 to C169 were sold only in sets. Nearly all are known with inverted overprint.

Flags of Venezuela and the Red Cross
AP17

Baseball Players
AP18

Lithographed.
1944, Aug. 22   Perf. 12
Flags in red, yellow, blue and black

C181	AP17	5c gray grn	18	10
C182	AP17	10c magenta	25	10
C183	AP17	20c brt bl	25	10
C184	AP17	30c vio bl	50	10
C185	AP17	40c chocolate	75	25
C186	AP17	45c ap grn	2.50	1.25
C187	AP17	90c orange	2.00	85
C188	AP17	1b gray blk	3.00	75
		Nos. C181-C188 (8)	9.43	3.50

80th anniversary of the International Red Cross and 37th anniversary of Venezuela's joining the organization. C181-C188 exist imperf. and part perf.

1944, Oct. 12
"AEREO" in dark carmine.

C189	AP18	5c dl vio brn	50	35
a.		"AEREO" double		12.50
C190	AP18	10c gray grn	60	35
C191	AP18	20c ultra	75	50
C192	AP18	30c dl rose	1.00	75
C193	AP18	45c rose vio	2.50	1.25
C194	AP18	90c red org	4.50	2.50
C195	AP18	1b dk gray	5.00	2.50
C196	AP18	1.20b yel grn	15.00	12.50
a.		"AEREO" invtd.	30.00	30.00
C197	AP18	1.80b ocher	20.00	17.50
		Nos. C189-C197 (9)	49.85	38.20

7th World Amateur Baseball Championship Games, Caracas.
Nos. C189-C197 exist imperf., and all but 1b exist part perf.

No. C134
Surcharged in Black **Habilitado 1944 VALE Bs. 0.30**

1944, Nov. 17   Perf. 13½

C198	AP11	30c on 1.40b sl gray	1.00	1.00
a.		Dbl. surch.	50.00	50.00
b.		Invtd. surch.	20.00	20.00

Charles Howarth
AP19

Antonio José de Sucre
AP20

1944, Dec. 21   Perf. 12   Unwmkd.

C199	AP19	5c black	35	25
C200	AP19	10c purple	35	25
C201	AP19	20c sepia	75	50
C202	AP19	30c dl grn	1.00	50
C203	AP19	1.20b bister	4.50	3.75
C204	AP19	1.80b dp ultra	7.50	5.00
C205	AP19	3.70b rose	10.00	8.50
		Nos. C199-C205 (7)	24.45	18.75

Centenary of founding of first cooperative shop in Rochdale, England, by Charles Howarth.
Nos. C199-C205 exist imperf. and part perf.

1945, Mar. 3   Engraved.

C206	AP20	5c orange	30	25
C207	AP20	10c violet	35	30
C208	AP20	20c grnsh blk	55	35
C209	AP20	30c brt grn	85	60
C210	AP20	40c olive	1.25	1.00
C211	AP20	45c blk brn	1.75	1.00
C212	AP20	90c redsh brn	3.00	1.25
C213	AP20	1b dp red lil	2.25	1.00
C214	AP20	1.20b black	5.00	5.00
C215	AP20	2b yellow	7.50	5.00
		Nos. C206-C215 (10)	22.80	15.75

Issued to commemorate the 150th anniversary of the birth of Antonio José de Sucre, Grand Marshal of Ayacucho.

Andrés Bello
AP21

Gen. Rafael Urdaneta
AP22

1946, Aug. 24   Perf. 12

C216	AP21	30c green	1.25	50
C217	AP22	30c green	1.25	50

See note after No. 393.

Allegory of Republic
AP23

Perf. 11½
1946, Oct. 18   Litho.   Unwmkd.

C218	AP23	15c dp vio bl	65	45
C219	AP23	20c bis brn	75	45
C220	AP23	30c dp vio	1.00	75
C221	AP23	1b brt rose	6.25	5.00

Anniversary of the Revolution of October, 1945. Exist imperf. and part perf.

Nos. 297, 371, C152 and 362
Surcharged in Black **J. R. G. AEREO Vale Bs. 0.15 1946**

1947, Jan.   Perf. 12

C223	A49	10c on 22½c dp car	30	15
a.		Inverted surcharge	6.25	6.25
C224	A69	15c on 25c lt bl	85	25
C225	AP16	20c on 50c bl	60	35
a.		Inverted surcharge	7.50	7.50
C226	A65	70c on 1b dk vio brn	1.25	1.00
a.		Inverted surch.	6.25	6.25

Type of 1938
Surcharged in Black **J. R. G. AEREO Vale Bs. 20 1946**

C227	AP10	20b on 20b org red	45.00	30.00
a.		Surcharge omitted	125.00	40.00
		Nos. C223-C227 (5)	47.80	31.75

"J. R. G." are the initials of "Junta Revolucionaria de Gobierno."

Anti-tuberculosis Institute, Maracaibo
AP24

1947, Jan. 12   Lithographed
Venezuela Shown on Map in Yellow.

C228	AP24	15c dk bl	1.00	75
C229	AP24	20c brn	1.00	60
C230	AP24	30c violet	1.00	75
C231	AP24	1b carmine	8.50	7.50

Issued to commemorate the 12th Pan-American Health Conference, held at Caracas, January, 1947.
Nos. C228-C231 exist imperf., part perf. and with yellow omitted.

Types of 1938-40.
1947, Mar. 17   Engraved

C232	AP16	75c orange	7.50	5.00
C233	AP16	1b brt ultra	1.00	35
C234	AP16	3b red brn	20.00	7.50
C235	AP16	5b scarlet	22.50	5.00
C236	AP9	10b violet	32.50	10.00
		Nos. C232-C236 (5)	83.50	27.85

On Nos. C235 and C236 the numerals of value are in color on a white tablet.

No. 370
Surcharged in Black **AEREO Vale Bs. 0.05 1947**

1947, June 20

C237	A70	5c on 20c bl	50	10
C238	A70	10c on 20c bl	50	10
a.		Inverted surcharge	7.50	7.50

Types of 1938-44.
1947-48   Engraved

C239	AP16	5c orange	12	6
C240	AP16	10c dk grn	12	6
C241	AP16	12½c bis brn	65	50
C242	AP16	15c gray	18	12
C243	AP16	20c violet	25	12
C244	AP16	25c dl grn	18	12
C245	AP16	30c brt ultra	55	18
C246	AP16	40c grn ('48)	42	18
C247	AP16	45c vermilion	85	25
C248	AP16	50c red vio	38	25
C249	AP16	70c dk car	1.85	1.00
C250	AP16	75c pur ('48)	85	38
C251	AP16	90c black	1.25	60
C252	AP16	1.20b red brn ('48)	2.00	1.25
C253	AP16	3b dp bl	3.00	1.10
C254	AP16	5b ol grn	10.00	5.00
C255	AP9	10b yellow	12.50	6.25
		Nos. C239-C255 (17)	35.15	17.42

On Nos. C254 and C255 the numerals of value are in color on a white tablet.

M. S. Republica de Venezuela
AP25

Santos Michelena
AP26

Imprint: "American Bank Note Company"

1948-50   Perf. 12   Unwmkd.

C256	AP25	5c red brn	12	6
C257	AP25	10c dp grn	12	6
C258	AP25	15c brown	18	6
C259	AP25	20c vio brn ('49)	25	6
C260	AP25	25c brn blk	30	12
C261	AP25	30c ol grn	42	18
C262	AP25	45c bl grn ('50)	75	35
C263	AP25	50c gray blk ('49)	1.00	50
C264	AP25	70c org ('49)	2.00	50
C265	AP25	75c brt ultra ('50)	3.75	65
C266	AP25	90c car lake ('49)	2.00	1.50
C267	AP25	1b purple	2.50	1.00
C268	AP25	2b gray ('49)	3.00	1.50
C269	AP25	3b emer ('49)	10.00	6.25
C270	AP25	4b dp bl ('49)	5.50	6.25
C271	AP25	5b org red ('50)	21.00	8.50
		Nos. C256-C271 (16)	52.89	27.54

Issued to honor the Grand-Colombian Merchant Fleet. See also Nos. C554-C556.

1949, Apr. 25

C272	AP26	5c org brn	30	18
C273	AP26	10c gray	38	18
C274	AP26	15c red org	1.00	60
C275	AP26	25c dl grn	2.00	1.00
C276	AP26	30c plum	2.00	1.00

C277	AP26	1b violet	10.00	3.75
		Nos. C272-C277 (6)	15.68	6.71

See note after No. 427.

Christopher Columbus
AP27

1948-49 ***Perf. 12½.*** **Unwmkd.**

C278	AP27	5c brn ('49)	50	10
C279	AP27	10c gray	65	25
C280	AP27	15c org ('49)	1.00	35
C281	AP27	25c grn ('49)	2.00	75
C282	AP27	30c red vio ('49)	2.50	1.00
C283	AP27	1b vio ('49)	10.00	3.00
		Nos. C278-C283 (6)	16.65	5.45

See note after No. 431.

Symbols of Global Air Mail
AP28

1950 ***Perf. 12***

C284	AP28	5c red brn	25	10
C285	AP28	10c dk grn	10	5
C286	AP28	15c ol brn	35	15
C287	AP28	25c ol gray	85	60
C288	AP28	30c ol grn	1.25	65
C289	AP28	50c black	75	35
C290	AP28	60c brt ultra	2.50	1.25
C291	AP28	90c carmine	3.50	1.50
C292	AP28	1b purple	3.75	1.25
		Nos. C284-C292 (9)	13.30	5.90

Issued to commemorate the 75th anniversary of the formation of the Universal Postal Union.

Araguaney, Venezuelan National Tree
AP29

1950, Aug. 25 **Photo.** ***Perf. 11½***

Foliage in Yellow.

C293	AP29	5c org brn	50	25
C294	AP29	10c bl grn	38	12
C295	AP29	15c dp plum	1.25	60
C296	AP29	25c dk gray grn	7.50	3.75
C297	AP29	30c red org	8.50	5.00
C298	AP29	50c dk gray	5.00	1.25
C299	AP29	60c dp bl	7.50	2.50
C300	AP29	90c red	15.00	5.00
C301	AP29	1b rose vio	17.50	6.25
		Nos. C293-C301 (9)	63.13	24.72

Issued to publicize Forest Week, 1950.

Census
Type of Regular Issue, 1950

1950 **Engraved** ***Perf. 12***

C302	A90	5c ol gray	25	6
C303	A90	10c green	12	6
C304	A90	15c ol grn	50	18
C305	A90	25c gray	85	75
C306	A90	30c orange	1.25	65
C307	A90	50c lt brn	75	38
C308	A90	60c ultra	75	50
C309	A90	90c rose car	3.00	1.25
C310	A90	1b violet	5.00	3.75
		Nos. C302-C310 (9)	12.47	7.58

Issued to publicize the 8th National Census of the Americas.

Signing Act of Independence—AP31

1950, Nov. 17

C311	AP31	5c vermilion	50	25
C312	AP31	10c red brn	50	25
C313	AP31	15c violet	1.00	50
C314	AP31	30c brt bl	1.50	75
C315	AP31	1b green	7.50	3.75
		Nos. C311-C315 (5)	11.00	5.50

Issued to commemorate the 200th anniversary of the birth of Gen. Francisco de Miranda.

Alonso de Ojeda
Type of Regular Issue, 1950

1950, Dec. 18 **Photo.** ***Perf. 11½***

C316	A91	5c org brn	35	10
C317	A91	10c cerise	50	25
C318	A91	15c blk brn	65	30
C319	A91	25c violet	1.25	60
C320	A91	30c orange	2.50	1.00
C321	A91	1b emerald	10.00	5.00
		Nos. C316-321 (6)	15.25	7.25

Issued to commemorate the 450th anniversary (in 1949) of the discovery of the Gulf of Maracaibo.

Bolivar Statue
Type of Regular Issue, 1951

1951, July 13 **Engraved.** ***Perf. 12***

C322	A92	5c purple	60	25
C323	A92	10c dl grn	85	25
C324	A92	20c ol gray	85	25
C325	A92	25c ol grn	1.00	30
C326	A92	30c vermilion	1.25	75
C327	A92	40c lt brn	1.25	85
C328	A92	50c gray	3.75	1.50
C329	A92	70c orange	6.25	5.00
		Nos. C322-C329 (8)	15.80	9.15

Issued to commemorate the relocation of the equestrian statue of Simon Bolivar in New York City, April 19, 1951.

Queen Isabella I
AP34

1951, Oct. 27 **Photo.** ***Perf. 11½***

C330	AP34	5c dk grn & buff	75	25
C331	AP34	10c dk red & cr	75	25
C332	AP34	20c dp bl & gray	1.25	35
C333	AP34	30c dk bl & gray	1.25	30
a.		Souvenir sheet	7.50	7.50

Issued to commemorate the 500th anniversary of the birth of Queen Isabella I of Spain.

No. C333a measures 79x100mm., and contains one each of Nos. C330–C333 with marginal inscriptions in dark blue.

Bicycle Racecourse—AP35

1951, Dec. 18 **Engraved.** ***Perf. 12***

C334	AP35	5c green	1.25	35
C335	AP35	10c rose car	1.50	40
C336	AP35	20c redsh brn	1.75	50
C337	AP35	30c blue	2.25	65
a.		Souvenir sheet	20.00	20.00

Issued to commemorate the 3rd Bolivarian Games, Caracas, December 1951.

No. C337a measures 190x150mm., and contains one each of Nos. C334–C337 together with arms and marginal inscriptions in blue. Sheets numbered in red.

Arms of Carabobo and "Industry"
AP36

1951 **Photogravure** ***Perf. 11½.***

C338	AP36	5c bl grn	50	12
C339	AP36	7½c gray grn	75	75
C340	AP36	10c car rose	25	12
C341	AP36	15c dk brn	75	35
C342	AP36	20c gray bl	1.00	50
C343	AP36	30c dp bl	4.00	60
C344	AP36	45c magenta	1.50	75
C345	AP36	60c ol brn	3.50	1.50
C346	AP36	90c rose brn	7.50	5.00
		Nos. C338-C346 (9)	19.75	9.69

Arms of Zulia and "Industry."

C347	AP36	5c bl grn	1.00	25
C348	AP36	10c car rose	25	10
C349	AP36	15c dk brn	1.25	50
C350	AP36	30c dp bl	8.50	3.75
C351	AP36	60c ol brn	5.00	1.25
C352	AP36	1.20b brn car	17.50	12.50
C353	AP36	3b bl gray	5.00	2.50
C354	AP36	5b pur brn	8.50	6.25
C355	AP36	10b violet	15.00	12.50
		Nos. C347-C355 (9)	62.00	39.60

Arms of Anzoategui

C356	AP36	5c bl grn	38	12
C357	AP36	10c car rose	30	12
C358	AP36	15c dk brn	85	38
C359	AP36	25c sepia	1.25	25
C360	AP36	30c dp bl	3.75	2.50
C361	AP36	50c hn brn	3.75	1.25
C362	AP36	60c ol brn	4.50	75
C363	AP36	1b purple	6.25	2.50
C364	AP36	2b vio gray	10.00	5.00
		Nos. C356-C364 (9)	31.03	12.87

Arms of Caracas and Buildings.

C365	AP36	5c bl grn	1.25	25
C366	AP36	7½c gray grn	3.75	1.50
C367	AP36	10c car rose	75	35
C368	AP36	15c dk brn	10.00	1.25
C369	AP36	20c gray bl	7.50	1.25
C370	AP36	30c dp bl	12.50	2.50
C371	AP36	45c magenta	7.50	1.50
C372	AP36	60c ol brn	25.00	3.75
C373	AP36	90c rose brn	15.00	12.50
		Nos. C365-C373 (9)	83.25	24.85

1952 **Arms of Tachira and Agricultural Products.**

C374	AP36	5c bl grn	60	25
C375	AP36	10c car rose	35	12
C376	AP36	15c dk brn	1.85	38
C377	AP36	30c dp bl	25.00	3.75
C378	AP36	60c ol brn	20.00	3.75
C379	AP36	1.20b brn car	18.50	12.50
C380	AP36	3b bl gray	5.00	2.50
C381	AP36	5b pur brn	11.00	6.25
C382	AP36	10b violet	16.00	12.50
		Nos. C374-C382 (9)	98.30	42.00

Arms of Venezuela and Bolivar Statue.

C383	AP36	5c bl grn	75	12
C384	AP36	7½c gray grn	1.75	1.25
C385	AP36	10c car rose	50	25
C386	AP36	15c dk brn	4.50	1.50
C387	AP36	20c gray bl	6.25	1.25
C388	AP36	30c dp bl	11.00	2.50
C389	AP36	45c magenta	5.00	1.00
C390	AP36	60c ol brn	25.00	5.00
C391	AP36	90c rose brn	17.50	12.50
		Nos. C383-C391 (9)	72.25	25.37

Arms of Miranda and Agricultural Products.

C392	AP36	5c bl grn	50	12
C393	AP36	7½c gray grn	65	65
C394	AP36	10c car rose	25	12
C395	AP36	15c dk brn	1.25	50
C396	AP36	20c gray bl	1.85	75
C397	AP36	30c dp bl	3.75	1.25
C398	AP36	45c magenta	2.50	65
C399	AP36	60c ol brn	6.25	1.75
C400	AP36	90c rose brn	30.00	20.00
		Nos. C392-C400 (9)	47.00	25.79

Arms of Aragua and Stylized Farm.

C401	AP36	5c bl grn	1.25	25
C402	AP36	7½c gray grn	65	65
C403	AP36	10c car rose	25	12
C404	AP36	15c dk brn	3.00	75
C405	AP36	20c gray bl	1.50	75
C406	AP36	30c dp bl	5.00	1.00
C407	AP36	45c magenta	3.75	75
C408	AP36	60c ol brn	7.50	1.25
C409	AP36	90c rose brn	37.50	20.00
		Nos. C401-C409 (9)	60.40	25.52

Arms of Lara, Agricultural Products and Rope.

C410	AP36	5c bl grn	1.00	25
C411	AP36	7½c gray grn	75	75
C412	AP36	10c car rose	25	12
C413	AP36	15c dk brn	1.75	38
C414	AP36	20c gray bl	2.50	65
C415	AP36	30c dp bl	6.25	1.25
C416	AP36	45c magenta	2.50	1.00
C417	AP36	60c ol brn	6.25	1.75
C418	AP36	90c rose brn	35.00	25.00
		Nos. C410-C418 (9)	56.25	31.15

Arms of Bolivar and Stylized Design.

C419	AP36	5c bl grn	7.50	75
C420	AP36	10c car rose	25	12
C421	AP36	15c dk brn	1.00	25
C422	AP36	25c sepia	75	12
C423	AP36	30c dp bl	5.00	2.50
C424	AP36	50c hn brn	3.75	1.25
C425	AP36	60c ol brn	6.25	1.50
C426	AP36	1b purple	5.00	1.25
C427	AP36	2b vio gray	10.00	5.00
		Nos. C419-C427 (9)	39.50	12.74

Arms of Sucre, Palms and Seascape.

C428	AP36	5c bl grn	75	25
C429	AP36	10c car rose	35	10
C430	AP36	15c dk brn	85	38
C431	AP36	25c sepia	18.50	50
C432	AP36	30c dp bl	6.25	2.00
C433	AP36	50c hn brn	3.00	75
C434	AP36	60c ol brn	3.75	1.50
C435	AP36	1b purple	5.00	1.25
C436	AP36	2b vio gray	10.00	5.00
		Nos. C428-C436 (9)	48.45	11.73

Arms of Trujillo Surrounded by Stylized Tree.

C437	AP36	5c bl grn	12.50	1.00
C438	AP36	10c car rose	25	12
C439	AP36	15c dk brn	3.75	25
C440	AP36	30c dp bl	15.00	3.75
C441	AP36	60c ol brn	12.50	3.00
C442	AP36	1.20b rose red	10.00	7.50
C443	AP36	3b bl gray	4.50	3.00
C444	AP36	5b pur brn	10.00	5.00
C445	AP36	10b violet	17.50	12.50
		Nos. C437-C445 (9)	86.00	36.12

1953

Map of Delta Amacuro and Ship.

C446	AP36	5c bl grn	75	10
C447	AP36	10c car rose	25	10
C448	AP36	15c dk brn	1.00	50
C449	AP36	25c sepia	1.50	75
C450	AP36	30c dp bl	5.00	2.00
C451	AP36	50c hn brn	2.50	75
C452	AP36	60c ol brn	4.00	1.25
C453	AP36	1b purple	5.00	1.85
C454	AP36	2b vio gray	10.00	8.00
		Nos. C446-C454 (9)	30.00	15.30

Arms of Falcon and Stylized Oil Refinery.

C455	AP36	5c bl grn	1.25	50
C456	AP36	10c car rose	25	10
C457	AP36	15c dk brn	1.00	35
C458	AP36	30c dp bl	10.00	2.50
C459	AP36	60c ol brn	6.25	1.50
C460	AP36	1.20b rose red	7.50	6.25
C461	AP36	3b bl gray	8.50	5.00
C462	AP36	5b pur brn	16.00	15.00
C463	AP36	10b violet	13.50	10.00
		Nos. C455-C463 (9)	64.25	41.20

Arms of Guarico and Factory.

C464	AP36	5c bl grn	75	10
C465	AP36	10c car rose	50	10
C466	AP36	15c dk brn	1.00	38
C467	AP36	25c sepia	1.50	75
C468	AP36	30c dp bl	6.25	2.50
C469	AP36	50c hn brn	3.00	1.00
C470	AP36	60c ol brn	3.75	1.75
C471	AP36	1b purple	6.25	1.75
C472	AP36	2b vio gray	10.00	6.25
		Nos. C464-C472 (9)	33.00	14.58

Arms of Merida and Church.

C473	AP36	5c bl grn	75	25
C474	AP36	10c car rose	30	12
C475	AP36	15c dk brn	1.25	25
C476	AP36	30c dp bl	10.00	2.50
C477	AP36	60c ol brn	5.00	1.25
C478	AP36	1.20b rose red	7.50	5.00
C479	AP36	3b bl gray	4.50	2.25
C480	AP36	5b pur brn	10.00	6.00
C481	AP36	10b violet	15.00	10.00
		Nos. C473-C481 (9)	54.30	27.62

Arms of Monagas and Horses.

C482	AP36	5c bl grn	75	25
C483	AP36	10c car rose	25	10
C484	AP36	15c dk brn	1.00	38
C485	AP36	25c sepia	85	25
C486	AP36	30c dp bl	8.50	2.50
C487	AP36	50c hn brn	3.75	1.25
C488	AP36	60c ol brn	4.00	1.25
C489	AP36	1b purple	6.25	1.75
C490	AP36	2b vio gray	7.50	5.00
		Nos. C482-C490 (9)	32.85	12.73

Arms of Portuguesa and Forest.

C491	AP36	5c bl grn	2.50	75
C492	AP36	10c car rose	50	10
C493	AP36	15c dk brn	1.25	50
C494	AP36	30c dp bl	8.50	3.75
C495	AP36	60c ol brn	6.25	1.25
C496	AP36	1.20b rose red	12.50	7.50
C497	AP36	3b bl gray	5.00	2.50
C498	AP36	5b pur brn	10.00	6.25
C499	AP36	10b violet	16.00	12.50
		Nos. C491-C499 (9)	62.50	35.10

Map of Amazonas and Orchid.

C500	AP36	5c bl grn	2.00	12
C501	AP36	10c car rose	50	6
C502	AP36	15c dk brn	2.00	50
C503	AP36	25c sepia	4.00	50
C504	AP36	30c dp bl	10.00	1.00
C505	AP36	50c hn brn	8.00	2.00
C506	AP36	60c ol brn	10.00	2.00
C507	AP36	1b purple	40.00	6.00
C508	AP36	2b vio gray	20.00	8.50
		Nos. C500-C508 (9)	96.50	20.68

Arms of Apure, Horse and Bird.

C509	AP36	5c bl grn	1.25	25
C510	AP36	10c car rose	25	12
C511	AP36	15c dk brn	1.25	38
C512	AP36	30c dp bl	6.25	2.50
C513	AP36	60c ol brn	5.00	1.25
C514	AP36	1.20b brn car	7.00	5.00
C515	AP36	3b bl gray	5.00	2.25
C516	AP36	5b pur brn	10.00	5.00
C517	AP36	10b violet	15.00	11.00
		Nos. C509-C517 (9)	51.00	27.75

Arms of Barinas, Cow and Horse.

C518	AP36	5c bl grn	50	25
C519	AP36	10c car rose	25	12
C520	AP36	15c dk brn	2.00	50
C521	AP36	30c dp bl	6.25	2.50
C522	AP36	60c ol brn	6.25	1.25
C523	AP36	1.20b brn car	7.00	3.75
C524	AP36	3b bl gray	5.00	2.25
C525	AP36	5b pur brn	10.00	3.75
C526	AP36	10b violet	15.00	11.00
		Nos. C518-C526 (9)	52.25	25.37

Arms of Cojedes and Cattle.

C527	AP36	5c bl grn	6.00	1.00
C528	AP36	7½c gray grn	1.25	75
C529	AP36	10c car rose	30	12
C530	AP36	15c dk brn	50	25
C531	AP36	20c gray bl	1.25	38
C532	AP36	30c dp bl	8.00	1.25
C533	AP36	45c magenta	3.00	75
C534	AP36	60c ol brn	6.00	1.00
C535	AP36	90c rose brn	7.00	3.75
		Nos. C527-C535 (9)	33.30	9.25

Arms of Nueva Esparta and Fish.

C536	AP36	5c bl grn	85	25
C537	AP36	10c car rose	30	12
C538	AP36	15c dk brn	1.50	38
C539	AP36	25c sepia	2.50	65
C540	AP36	30c dp bl	5.00	1.25
C541	AP36	50c hn brn	5.00	1.25
C542	AP36	60c ol brn	5.00	75
C543	AP36	1b purple	7.50	1.85
C544	AP36	2b vio gray	10.00	5.00
		Nos. C536-C544 (9)	37.65	11.50

Arms of Yaracuy and Tropical Foliage.

C545	AP36	5c bl grn	1.00	30
C546	AP36	7½c gray grn	15.00	15.00
C547	AP36	10c car rose	25	10
C548	AP36	15c dk brn	1.00	25
C549	AP36	20c gray bl	2.00	30
C550	AP36	30c dp bl	4.00	1.25
C551	AP36	45c magenta	3.00	75
C552	AP36	60c ol brn	3.00	1.25
C553	AP36	90c rose brn	7.00	5.00
		Nos. C545-C553 (9)	36.25	24.20
		Nos. C338-C553 (216)	1,294.03	562.71

Ship Type of 1948-50 Redrawn. Coil Stamps

Imprint: "Courvoisier S.A."

1952 ***Perf. 12x11½*** **Unwmkd.**

C554	AP25	5c rose brn	2.00	12
C555	AP25	10c org red	3.00	18
C556	AP25	15c ol brn	4.00	12

Barquisimeto Type of Regular Issue, 1952

1952, Sept. 14 Photo. ***Perf. 11½***

C557	A94	5c bl grn	50	10
C558	A94	10c car rose	25	12
C559	A94	20c dk bl	75	18
C560	A94	25c blk brn	1.00	38
C561	A94	30c ultra	1.25	30
C562	A94	40c brn org	7.50	3.75
C563	A94	50c dk ol grn	2.50	1.00
C564	A94	1b purple	10.00	5.00
		Nos. C557-C564 (8)	23.75	10.83

Issued to commemorate the 400th anniversary of the founding of the city of Barquisimeto by Juan de Villegas.

Caracas Post Office Type of Regular Issue, 1953-54

1953 ***Perf. 12½.***

C565	A96	7½c yel grn	25	25
C566	A96	15c dp plum	18	12
C567	A96	20c slate	25	10
C568	A96	25c sepia	75	12
C569	A96	40c plum	75	25
C570	A96	45c rose vio	75	25
C571	A96	50c red org	1.25	18
C572	A96	70c dk sl grn	2.50	1.25
C573	A96	75c dp ultra	3.75	1.75
C574	A96	90c brn org	2.00	1.00
C575	A96	1b vio bl	2.00	1.00
		Nos. C565-C575 (11)	14.43	6.27

See also Nos. C587-C589, C597-C606.

Simon Rodriguez

AP39

Quotation from Bolivar's Manifesto of 1824

AP40

1954, Feb. 28 ***Perf. 11½***

C576	AP39	5c bl grn	50	10
C577	AP39	10c car rose	75	12
C578	AP39	20c gray bl	1.00	15
C579	AP39	45c magenta	1.50	50
C580	AP39	65c gray grn	5.00	2.50
		Nos. C576-C580 (5)	8.75	3.37

Issued to commemorate the centenary of the death of Simon Rodriguez, scholar and tutor of Bolivar.

1954, Mar. 1 **Unwmkd.**

C581	AP40	15c blk & brn buff	25	12
C582	AP40	25c dk red brn & gray	65	25
C583	AP40	40c dk red brn & red org	1.00	25
C584	AP40	65c blk & bl	2.50	1.25
C585	AP40	80c dk red brn & rose	2.00	1.00
C586	AP40	1b pur & rose lil	3.75	85
		Nos. C581-C586 (6)	10.15	3.72

Issued to publicize the 10th Inter-American Conference, Caracas, Mar. 1954.

P.O. Type of Regular Issue, 1953

1954 **Photogravure.** ***Perf. 12½.***

C587	A96	5c orange	18	12
C588	A96	30c red brn	4.25	2.25
C589	A96	60c brt red	4.25	2.75

Valencia Arms Type of Regular Issue, 1955

1955, Mar. 26 **Engraved** ***Perf. 12***

C590	A97	5c bl grn	18	10
C591	A97	10c rose pink	25	10
C592	A97	20c ultra	35	12
C593	A97	25c gray	35	15
C594	A97	40c violet	1.00	50
C595	A97	50c vermilion	1.00	50
C596	A97	60c ol grn	2.00	50
		Nos. C590-C596 (7)	5.13	1.97

Issued to commemorate the 400th anniversary of the founding of Valencia del Rey.

P.O. Type of 1953 Inscribed: "Republica de Venezuela"

1955 **Photogravure.** ***Perf. 12½***

C597	A96	5c orange	15	10
C598	A96	10c ol brn	15	10
C599	A96	15c dp plum	25	10
C600	A96	20c slate	50	10
C601	A96	30c red brn	50	12
C602	A96	40c plum	1.50	50
C603	A96	45c rose vio	1.50	75
C604	A96	70c dk sl grn	3.75	1.75
C605	A96	75c dp ultra	2.50	1.00
C606	A96	90c brn org	1.25	50
		Nos. C597-C606 (10)	12.05	5.02

Caracas Arms Type of Regular Issue, 1955

1955, Dec. 9 ***Perf. 11½*** **Unwmkd.**

C607	A98	5c yel org	25	10
C608	A98	15c cl brn	50	12
C609	A98	25c vio blk	50	12
C610	A98	40c red	1.25	30
C611	A98	50c red org	1.25	35
C612	A98	60c car rose	2.50	75
		Nos. C607-C612 (6)	6.25	1.74

Issued to commemorate the First Postal Convention, Caracas, Feb. 9-15, 1954.

University Hospital, Caracas

AP43

Designs: 5c, 10c, 15c, 70c, O'Leary School, Barinas. 25c, 30c, 80c, University Hospital, Caracas. 40c, 45c, 50c, 1b, Caracas-La Guaira Highway. 60c, 65c, 75c, 2b, Towers of Simon Bolivar Center.

1956-57 ***Perf. 11½*** **Unwmkd.**

C613	AP43	5c orange	18	10
C614	AP43	10c sepia	18	10
C615	AP43	15c cl brn	25	12
C616	AP43	20c dk bl ('56)	25	12
C617	AP43	25c gray blk	30	18
C618	AP43	30c hn brn	75	25
C619	AP43	40c brt crim	1.00	30
C620	AP43	45c brn vio	65	25
C621	AP43	50c dp org ('56)	1.25	25
C622	AP43	60c ol grn ('56)	1.25	38
C623	AP43	65c brt bl	1.75	55
C624	AP43	70c bl grn	2.00	75
C625	AP43	75c ultra	2.25	1.00
C626	AP43	80c car rose	2.50	50
C627	AP43	1b plum	1.50	65
C628	AP43	2b dk car rose	3.00	2.00
		Nos. C613-C628 (16)	19.06	7.50

Book and Flags of American Nations

AP44

1956-57 **Granite Paper**

C629	AP44	5c org & brn ('56)	12	6
C630	AP44	10c brn & pale brn	25	10
C631	AP44	20c bl & saph	25	12
C632	AP44	25c gray vio & gray	50	18
C633	AP44	40c rose red & pale pur ('56)	75	25
C634	AP44	45c vio brn & gray brn	1.00	25
C635	AP44	60c ol & gray ol	2.00	1.00
		Nos. C629-C635 (7)	4.87	1.96

Issued for the Book Festival of the Americas, Nov. 15-30, 1956.

Type of Regular Issue, 1957-58. (Bolivar)

Engraved; Center Embossed.

1957-58 ***Perf. 13½*** **Unwmkd.**

C636	A100	5c orange	25	10
C637	A100	10c ol gray	30	10
C638	A100	20c blue	1.25	30
C639	A100	25c gray blk	1.40	38
C640	A100	40c rose red	1.25	30
C641	A100	45c rose lil ('58)	1.50	55
C642	A100	65c yel brn	2.50	1.00
		Nos. C636-C642 (7)	8.45	2.73

Issued to commemorate the 150th anniversary of the Oath of Monte Sacro and the 125th anniversary of the death of Simon Bolivar (1783-1830).

Type of Regular Issue, 1957-58 (Tamanaco Hotel)

1957-58 **Engraved.** ***Perf. 13***

C643	A101	5c dl yel	15	10
C644	A101	10c brown	15	10
C645	A101	15c chocolate	50	12
C646	A101	20c gray bl	35	12
C647	A101	25c sepia	30	18
C648	A101	30c vio bl	60	30
C649	A101	40c car rose	60	25
C650	A101	45c claret	75	25
C651	A101	50c red org	75	30
C652	A101	60c yel grn	1.50	38
C653	A101	65c org brn	3.75	2.00
C654	A101	70c slate	2.25	1.00
C655	A101	75c grnsh bl	2.50	1.25
C656	A101	1b dk cl	2.50	1.25
C657	A101	2b dk gray	3.75	1.50
		Nos. C643-C657 (15)	20.25	9.00

Type of Regular Issue, 1958. (Post Office)

1958 **Lithographed** ***Perf. 14***

C658	A102	5c dp yel	10	5
C659	A102	10c brown	10	5
C660	A102	15c red brn	12	5
C661	A102	20c lt bl	15	5
C662	A102	25c lt gray	25	10
C663	A102	30c lt ultra	25	10
C664	A102	40c brt yel grn	35	10
C665	A102	50c red org	38	12
C666	A102	60c rose pink	50	30
C667	A102	65c red	65	30
C668	A102	90c violet	1.00	50
C669	A102	1b lilac	1.25	50
C670	A102	1.20b bis brn	15.00	10.00
		Nos. C658-C670 (13)	20.10	12.22

See also Nos. C786-C792.

Coil Stamps Type of Regular Issue, 1958. (Post Office)

1958 **Engraved.** ***Perf. 11½x12***

C671	A103	5c dp yel	50	7
C672	A103	10c brown	75	7
C673	A103	15c dk brn	1.00	18

Type of Regular Issue, 1958. (Merida)

1958, Oct. 9 **Photo.** ***Perf. 13½***

C674	A104	5c org yel	15	5
C675	A104	10c gray brn	15	10
C676	A104	15c dl red brn	25	10
C677	A104	20c chlky bl	25	10
C678	A104	25c brn gray	60	25
C679	A104	30c vio bl	50	15
C680	A104	40c rose car	75	25
C681	A104	45c brt lil	75	30
C682	A104	50c red org	1.00	50

VENEZUELA

C683	A104	60c lt ol grn	75	35
C684	A104	65c hn brn	2.50	1.00
C685	A104	70c gray blk	1.50	75
C686	A104	75c brt grnsh bl	3.00	1.50
C687	A104	80c brt vio bl	1.75	75
C688	A104	90c bl grn	1.75	85
C689	A104	1b lilac	2.00	1.00
		Nos. C674-C689 (16)	17.65	8.00

Issued to commemorate the 400th anniversary of the founding of the city of Merida.

Type of Regular Issue, 1959.
(Trujillo)

1959   Photogravure.   *Perf. 14*

C690	A105	5c org yel	15	6
C691	A105	10c lt brn	15	7
C692	A105	15c redsh brn	35	15
C693	A105	20c lt bl	45	25
C694	A105	25c pale gray	60	30
C695	A105	30c lt vio bl	60	30
C696	A105	40c brt yel grn	75	35
C697	A105	50c red org	85	40
C698	A105	60c lil rose	1.25	60
C699	A105	65c vermilion	3.75	1.75
C700	A105	1b lilac	2.50	75
		Nos. C690-C700 (11)	11.40	4.98

Issued to commemorate the 400th anniversary of the founding of the city of Trujillo.

Emblem
AP45

1959, Mar. 10   Litho.   *Perf. 13½*

C701	AP45	5c yellow	25	10
C702	AP45	10c red brn	50	25
C703	AP45	15c orange	60	30
C704	AP45	30c gray	1.25	60
C705	AP45	50c green	1.50	75
		Nos. C701-C705 (5)	4.10	2.00

8th Central American and Caribbean Games, Caracas, Nov. 29-Dec. 14, 1958. Nos. C701-C705 exist imperf. Price $25 a pair.

Type of Regular Issue, 1959
(Stamp Centenary)

Stamp of 1859 and: 25c, Mailman and José Ignacio Paz Castillo. 50c, Mailman on horseback and Jacinto Gutierrez. 1b, Plane, train and Miguel Herrera.

1959, Sept. 15   Engr.   *Perf. 13½*

C706	A107	25c org yel	75	25
C707	A107	50c blue	1.25	50
C708	A107	1b rose red	2.50	1.00

Centenary of Venezuelan postage stamps.

Type of Regular Issue, 1960
(Alexander von Humboldt)

1960, Feb. 9   Unwmkd.

C709	A108	5c ocher & brn	50	10
C710	A108	20c brt bl & turq bl	1.25	30
C711	A108	40c ol & ol grn	2.00	75

Issued to commemorate the centenary of the death of Alexander von Humboldt, German naturalist and geographer.

Type of Regular Issue, 1960
(Newspaper Issue)

1960, June 11   Litho.   *Perf. 14*

C712	A109	5c yel & blk	2.50	1.50
C713	A109	15c lt red brn & blk	1.50	60
C714	A109	65c sal & blk	2.00	1.00

Issued to commemorate the 150th anniversary (in 1958) of the first Venezuelan newspaper, Gazeta de Caracas.

Type of Regular Issue, 1960
(Agustin Codazzi)

1960, June 15   Engraved

C715	A110	5c yel org & brn	12	5

C716	A110	10c brn & dk brn	25	10
C717	A110	25c gray & blk	60	15
C718	A110	30c vio bl & sl	75	25
C719	A110	50c org brn & brn	1.25	60
C720	A110	70c gray ol & ol gray	2.00	1.00
		Nos. C715-720 (6)	4.97	2.15

Issued to commemorate the centenary (in 1959) of the death of Agustin Codazzi, geographer.

Type of Regular Issue, 1960
(National Pantheon)

1960, May 9   Lithographed

Pantheon in Bistre.

C721	A111	5c dp bis	15	5
C722	A111	10c red brn	38	5
C723	A111	15c fawn	50	10
C724	A111	20c lt bl	75	25
C725	A111	25c gray	2.25	50
C726	A111	30c lt vio bl	2.50	85
C727	A111	40c brt yel grn	75	25
C728	A111	45c lt vio	1.10	30
C729	A111	60c dp pink	1.50	60
C730	A111	65c salmon	1.50	60
C731	A111	70c gray	2.25	90
C732	A111	75c chlky bl	3.75	1.50
C733	A111	80c lt ultra	3.00	1.25
C734	A111	1.20b bis brn	3.75	1.75
		Nos. C721-C734 (14)	24.13	8.95

Type of Regular Issue, 1960
(Andres Eloy Blanco)

1960, May 21   *Perf. 14*

Portrait in Black

C735	A112	20c blue	60	25
C736	A112	75c grnsh bl	1.85	75
C737	A112	90c brt vio	1.75	75

Issued to honor the poet Andres Eloy Blanco (1896-1955).

Type of Regular Issue, 1960
(Independence)

1960, Aug. 19   Litho.   *Perf. 13½*

Center Multicolored

C738	A113	50c orange	1.25	60
C739	A113	75c brt grnsh bl	1.85	1.00
C740	A113	90c purple	2.00	75

Issued to commemorate the 150th anniversary of Venezuela's Independence.

Oil Refinery
AP46

Engraved

1960, Aug. 26   *Perf. 14*   Unwmkd.

C741	AP46	30c dk bl & sl bl	75	35
C742	AP46	40c yel grn & ol	1.25	60
C743	AP46	50c org & red brn	1.50	75

Issued to publicize Venezuela's oil industry.

Type of Regular Issue, 1960
(Luisa Cáceres de Arismendi)

1960, Oct. 24   Litho.   *Perf. 14*

Center Multicolored

C744	A115	5c bister	1.00	50
C745	A115	10c redsh brn	1.25	85
C746	A115	60c rose car	1.50	75

Issued to commemorate the 94th anniversary of the death of Luisa Cáceres de Arismendi.

Type of Regular Issue, 1960
(José Antonio Anzoategui)

1960, Oct. 29   Engraved

C747	A116	25c gray & brn	75	35
C748	A116	40c yel grn & ol gray	75	75

C749	A116	45c rose cl & dl pur	1.00	55

Issued to commemorate the 140th anniversary (in 1959) of the death of General José Antonio Anzoategui.

Type of Regular Issue, 1960
(Antonio José de Sucre)

Lithographed

1960, Nov. 13   *Perf. 14*   Unwmkd.

Center Multicolored

C750	A117	25c gray	1.00	50
C751	A117	30c vio bl	1.50	75
C752	A117	50c brn org	2.00	1.00

Issued to commemorate the 130th anniversary of the death of General Antonio José de Sucre.

Type of Regular Issue, 1960

Designs: 30c, Bolivar Peak. 50c, Caroni Falls. 65c, Cuachuro caves.

1960, March 22   *Perf. 14*

C753	A118	30c vio bl & blk bl	2.50	2.50
C754	A118	50c brn org & brn	2.50	2.50
C755	A118	65c red org & red brn	2.50	2.50

Cow's Head,
Grain, Man
and Child
AP47

Arms of
San Cristobal
AP48

1961, Feb. 6   Litho.   Unwmkd.

Cow and Inscription in Black

C756	AP47	5c yellow	7	5
C757	AP47	10c brown	10	5
C758	AP47	15c redsh brn	15	7
C759	AP47	20c dl bl	25	12
C760	AP47	25c gray	30	12
C761	AP47	30c vio bl	38	18
C762	AP47	40c yel grn	50	25
C763	AP47	45c lilac	50	30
C764	AP47	50c orange	60	38
C765	AP47	60c cerise	75	38
C766	AP47	65c red org	1.00	50
C767	AP47	70c gray	1.50	75
C768	AP47	75c brt grnsh bl	1.25	60
C769	AP47	80c brt vio	1.25	50
C770	AP47	90c violet	2.00	1.00
		Nos. C756-C770 (15)	10.65	5.25

Issued to commemorate the 9th general census and the 3rd agricultural census.

Type of Regular Issue, 1961
(Rafael Maria Baralt)

Engraved

1961, March 11   *Perf. 14*

C771	A120	25c gray & sep	85	50
C772	A120	30c dk bl & vio	1.00	60
C773	A120	40c yel grn & ol grn	1.25	75

Issued to commemorate the centenary of the death of Rafael Maria Baralt, statesman.

1961, Apr. 10   Lithographed.

Arms in Original Colors

C774	AP48	50c org & blk	12	6
C775	AP48	55c red org & blk	85	42

400th anniversary of San Cristobal.

Bird Type of Regular Issue, 1961

Birds: 5c, Troupial. 10c, Golden cock of the rock. 15c, Tropical mockingbird.

1961, Sept. 6   *Perf. 14½*   Unwmkd.

C776	A121	5c multi	1.50	1.40

C777	A121	10c multi	75	75
C778	A121	15c multi	1.00	85

Charge, Battle of Carabobo
AP49

1961, Dec. 2   Litho.   *Perf. 14*

Center Multicolored

C779	AP49	50c blk & ultra	1.00	25
C780	AP49	1.05b blk & org	2.00	1.00
C781	AP49	1.50b blk & lil rose	2.50	1.00
C782	AP49	1.90b blk & lil	3.50	2.00
C783	AP49	2b blk & gray	3.75	2.00
C784	AP49	3b blk & grnsh bl	5.00	2.50
		Nos. C779-C784 (6)	17.75	8.75

140th anniversary of Battle of Carabobo.

Arms of
Cardinal Quintero
AP50

Archbishop
Rafael Arias
Blanco
AP51

1962, March 1   Unwmkd.

C785	AP50	5c lil rose	8	7
a.		Souvenir sheet	1.25	1.25

Issued to honor the first Venezuelan Cardinal, José Humberto Quintero.

No. C785a contains one of No. C785, imperf. Size: 100x75mm. Marginal inscriptions in blue. Sold for 1b.

Type of Regular Issue, 1958
(Post Office)

1962   Litho.   *Perf. 13½x14*

C786	A102	35c citron	35	18
C787	A102	55c gray ol	55	30
C788	A102	70c bluish grn	85	38
C789	A102	75c brn org	1.00	30
C790	A102	80c fawn	1.00	50
C791	A102	85c dp rose	1.50	75
C792	A102	95c lil rose	1.10	70
		Nos. C786-C792 (7)	6.35	3.11

1962, May 10   *Perf. 10½*

C793	AP51	75c red lil	1.00	50

Issued to commemorate the 4th anniversary (in 1961) of the anti-communist pastoral letter of the Archbishop of Caracas, Rafael Arias Blanco.

Type of Regular Issue, 1962
(Orchids)

Orchids: 5c, Oncidium volvox. 20c, Cycnoches chlorochilon. 25c, Cattleya Gaskelliana. 30c, Epidendrum difforme (horiz.). 40c, Catasetum callosum Lindl. 50c, Oncidium bicolor Lindl. 1b, Brassavola nodosa Lindl (horiz.). 1.05b, Epidendrum lividum Lindl. 1.50b, Schomburgkia undulata Lindl. 2b, Oncidium zebrinum.

Perf. 14x13½, 13½x14

1962, May 30   Litho.   Unwmkd.

Orchids in Natural Colors

C794	A124	5c blk & lt grn	10	10
C795	A124	20c black	25	12
C796	A124	25c blk & fawn	65	25
C797	A124	30c blk & pink	45	18
C798	A124	40c blk & vi	65	30
C799	A124	50c blk & lil	85	42
C800	A124	1b blk & pale rose	1.25	75

VENEZUELA

C801	A124	1.05b blk & dp org		3.75	2.50
C802	A124	1.50b blk & pale vio		4.25	3.00
C803	A124	2b blk & org brn		5.00	3.75
	Nos. C794-C803 (10)			17.20	11.37

Type of Regular Issue, 1960 (Independence)

Design: Signing Declaration of Independence.

1962, June 11   Perf. 13½
Center Multicolored

C804	A113	55c olive		85	35
C805	A113	1.05b brt rose		2.50	1.10
C806	A113	1.50b purple		2.00	1.00
a.	Souv. sheet of 3			6.25	6.25

Issued to commemorate the 150th anniversary of the Venezuelan Declaration of Independence, July 5, 1811.
No. C806a contains one each of Nos. C804-C806, imperf., with marginal inscriptions in brown. Size: 140x140mm. Sold for 4.10b.
A buff cardboard folder exists with impressions of Nos. 812-814, C804-C806. Perforation is simulated. Sold for 5.60b. Price $3.

No. 710 Surcharged in Rose Carmine:
"BICENTENARIO DE UPATA 1762-1962 RESELLADO AEREO VALOR Bs. 2,00"

1962, July 7   Perf. 13½x14
C807	A102	2b on 1b lt ol grn		2.50	1.30

Issued to commemorate the 200th anniversary of Upata, a village in the state of Bolivar.

Type of Regular Issue, 1962 (National Games)

Sports: 40c, Bicycling. 75c, Baseball. 85c, Woman athlete.

Lithographed
1962, Nov. 30 Perf. 13x14 Unwmkd.

C808	A125	40c gray		75	50
C809	A125	75c gldn brn		1.00	75
C810	A125	85c rose lake		2.50	1.50
a.	Souvenir sheet of 3			5.00	5.00

Issued to commemorate the First National Games, Caracas, 1961. The stamps are arranged within the sheet so that groups of four are formed with the two pale colored edges of each stamp joining to make a border around blocks of four.
No. C810a contains one each of Nos. C808-C810 imperf. with bright green marginal inscription. Size: 164x110mm. Sold for 3b.

Type of Regular Issue, 1962 (Birds)

Birds: 5c, American kestrel. 20c, Black-bellied tree duck (horiz.). 25c, Amazon kingfisher. 30c, Rufous-tailed chachalaca. 50c, Black-and-yellow troupial. 55c, White-naped nightjar. 2.30b, Red-crowned woodpecker. 2.50b, Black-moustached quail-dove.

1962, Dec. 14   Perf. 14x13½
Birds in Natural Colors;
Black Inscription

C811	A126	5c car rose		25	12
C812	A126	20c brt bl		50	25
C813	A126	25c lt gray		65	30
C814	A126	30c lt ol		75	38
C815	A126	50c violet		1.25	60
C816	A126	55c dp org		2.00	1.00
C817	A126	2.30b dl red brn		6.25	4.50
C818	A126	2.50b org yel		6.25	5.00
	Nos. C811-C818 (8)			17.90	12.15

Malaria Eradication Emblem, Mosquito and Map
AP52

Lithographed and Embossed
Perf. 13½x14
1962, Dec. 20   Wmk. 346

C819	AP52	30c grn & blk		65	38
a.	Souvenir sheet of 2			3.75	3.75

Issued for the World Health Organization drive to eradicate malaria. No. C819a contains one each of Nos. 825 and C819 imperf. on pale blue background with blue and red inscription and Venezuelan coat of arms. Size: 89x108mm. Sold for 2b.

Animal Type of Regular Issue

Designs: 5c, Spectacle bear (vert). 40c, Paca. 50c, Three-toed sloths. 55c, Great anteater. 1.50b, South American tapirs. 2b, Jaguar.

Perf. 13½x14
1963, Mar. 13 Litho. Unwmkd.
Multicolored Center;
Black Inscriptions.

C820	A128	5c yellow		25	12
C821	A128	40c brt grn		75	35
C822	A128	50c lt vio		1.00	50
C823	A128	55c brn ol		1.25	60
C824	A128	1.50b gray		3.75	2.50
C825	A128	2b ultra		6.25	3.75
	Nos. C820-C825 (6)			13.25	7.82

Type of Regular Issue, 1963 ("Freedom from Hunger")

Designs: 40c, Map and shepherd. 75c, Map and farmer.

1963, Mar. 21

C826	A129	40c lt yel grn & dl red		75	50
C827	A129	75c yel & brn		1.00	75

Issued for the "Freedom from Hunger" campaign of the U.N. Food and Agriculture Organization.

Arms of Bocono
AP53

1963, May 30 Wmk. 346
C828	AP53	1b multi		2.00	75

Issued to commemorate the 400th anniversary of the founding of Bocono.

Papal and Venezuelan Arms
AP54

1963, June 11   Perf. 14x13½
Arms Multicolored

C829	AP54	80c lt grn		1.50	65
C830	AP54	90c gray		1.50	75

Issued to commemorate Vatican II, the 21st Ecumenical Council of the Roman Catholic Church.

Arms of Venezuela
AP55

1963, July 29 Perf. 14 Unwmkd.
C831	AP55	70c gray, red, yel & bl		1.25	75

Issued to commemorate the centenary of Venezuela's flag and coat of arms.

Lake Maracaibo Bridge
AP56

Lithographed
1963, Aug. 24 Perf. 14 Wmk. 346

C832	AP56	90c grn, brn & ocher		1.60	75
C833	AP56	95c bl, brn & ocher		1.75	85
C834	AP56	1b ultra, brn & ocher		1.25	75

Opening of bridge over Lake Maracaibo

Armed Forces Type of Regular Issue
1963, Sept. 10 Unwmkd.

C835	A134	1b red & bl, buff		2.00	1.25

25th anniversary of the armed forces.

Hammarskjold Type of Regular Issue
1963, Sept. 25 Perf. 14 Unwmkd.

C836	A135	80c dk bl, lt ultra & ocher		1.25	75
C837	A135	90c dk bl, bl & ocher		1.75	1.00
a.	Souv. sheet of 4			5.00	5.00

Issued to commemorate the "First" anniversary of the death of Dag Hammarskjold, Secretary General of the United Nations, 1953-61. No. C837a contains 4 imperf. stamps similar to Nos. 841-842 and C836-C837. Multicolored marginal inscription. Size: 150x120mm. Sold for 3b.

Dr. Luis Razetti
AP57

1963, Oct. 20 Engraved
C838	AP57	95c dk bl & mag		1.60	1.00
C839	AP57	1.05b dk brn & grn		1.85	1.25

Issued to commemorate the centenary of the birth of Dr. Luis Razetti, physician.

Red Cross Type of Regular Issue

Designs: 40c, Sir Vincent K. Barrington. 75c, Red Cross nurse and child.

1963, Dec. 31 Litho. Perf. 11½x12

C840	A137	40c multi		60	50
C841	A137	75c multi		1.00	75

Centenary of the International Red Cross.

Type of Regular Issue, 1964 (Development)

Designs: 5c, Loading cargo. 10c, Tractor and corn. 15c, Oil field workers. 20c, Oil refinery. 50c, Crane and building construction.

Perf. 14x13½
1964, Feb. 5 Unwmkd.

C842	A138	5c multi		6	6
C843	A138	10c multi		12	6
C844	A138	15c multi		25	12
C845	A138	20c multi		30	12
C846	A138	50c multi		75	50
	Nos. C842-C846 (5)			1.48	86

Issued to commemorate the centenary of the Department of Industrial Development and to publicize the National Industrial Exposition.

Pedro Gual Type of Regular Issue

1964, March 20   Perf. 14x13½

C847	A139	75c dl bl grn		1.00	50
C848	A139	1b brt pink		1.25	60

Issued to commemorate the centenary of the death (in 1862) of Pedro Gual, statesman.

Blast Furnace and Map of Venezuela
AP58
Arms of Ciudad Bolivar
AP59

1964, May 22 Litho. Perf. 13½x14

C849	AP58	80c multi		1.25	60
C850	AP58	1b multi		1.60	75

Issued to publicize the Orinoco steel mills.

1964, May 22   Perf. 10½
C851	AP59	1b multi		1.75	1.25

Bicentenary of Ciudad Bolivar.

Romulo Gallegos and Book
AP60

1964, Aug. 3 Perf. 11½ Unwmkd.

C852	AP60	30c bis brn & yel		50	25
C853	AP60	40c plum & pink		75	35
C854	AP60	50c brn & tan		1.00	50

Issued to commemorate the 80th birthday of novelist Romulo Gallegos.

Eleanor Roosevelt
AP61

1964, Nov. 11 Litho. Perf. 14x13½
C855	AP61	1b org & dk vio		1.50	85

Issued to honor Eleanor Roosevelt and the 15th anniversary (in 1963) of the Universal Declaration of Human Rights.

Issues of 1947-64 Surcharged in Black, Dark Blue, Red, Carmine or Lilac with New Value and: "RESELLADO / VALOR"

1965

C856	A102	5c on 55c gray ol (C787)		12	5
C857	A102	5c on 70c bluish grn (C788)		15	10
C858	A102	5c on 80c fawn (C790)		18	12
C859	A102	5c on 85c dp rose (C791)		12	6
C860	A102	5c on 90c vio (C668)		12	6
C861	A102	5c on 95c lil rose (C792)		12	5
C862	A134	5c on 1b red & bl, buff (#C835)		75	50
C863	AP25	10c on 3b emer (#C269) (C)		25	12
C864	AP25	10c on 4b dl bl (#C270) (C)		1.00	50
C865	AP47	10c on 70c gray & blk (C) (C767)		50	25
C866	AP47	10c on 90c vio & blk (C) (C770)		35	15
C867	AP49	10c on 1.05b multi (#C780)		75	35

VENEZUELA

C868	AP49	10c on 1.90b multi (#C782)	35	25
C869	AP49	10c on 2b multi (#C783)	50	25
C870	AP49	10c on 3b multi (#C784)	50	25
C871	AP54	10c on 80c multi (#C829)	25	10
C872	AP54	10c on 90c multi (#C830)	25	10
C873	AP16	15c on 3b pb bl (#C253)	50	25
C874	A112	15c on 90c vio & blk (C737)	35	15
C875	A135	15c on 80c multi (#C836)	35	15
C876	A135	15c on 90c multi (#C837)	35	15
C877	AP59	15c on 1b multi (#C851)	50	15
C878	A101	20c on 2b dk gray (#C657) (R)	60	25
C879	AP48	20c on 55c multi (DB) (C775)	45	15
C880	A126	20c on 55c multi (#C816)	75	35
a.		25c on 55c multi (#C816)		
C881	A126	20c on 2.30b multi (#C817)	35	15
C882	A126	20c on 2.50b multi (#C818)	75	35
C883	AP55	20c on 70c multi (#C831)	75	50
C884	A110	25c on 70c gray ol & ol gray (DB) (C720)	85	40
C885	A124	25c on 1.05b multi (#C801) (L)	50	25
C886	A124	25c on 1.50b multi (#C802) (L)	50	25
C887	A124	25c on 2b multi (#C803) (L)	75	35
C888	A128	25c on 1.50b multi (#C824)	75	25
C889	A128	25c on 2b multi (#C825)	35	35
C890	AP57	25c on 95c dk bl & mag (#C838)	65	35
C891	AP57	25c on 1.05b dk brn & grn (#C839)	75	35
C892	AP53	30c on 1.05b multi (#C828)	1.00	50
C893	A113	40c on 1.05b multi (DB) (#C805)	75	35
C894	A111	50c on 65c sal & bis (#C730) (DB)	38	18
C895	A111	50c on 1.20b bis brn & bis (#C734) (DB)	1.00	50
C896	AP61	50c on 1b org & dk vio (#C855)	50	25
C897	AP56	60c on 90c multi (#C832)	1.50	75
C898	AP56	60c on 95c multi (#C833)	1.10	50
C899	A125	75c on 85c rose lake (#C810)	1.10	60
		Nos. C856-C899 (44)	24.79	12.14

Lines of surcharge arranged variously on Nos. C856-C899. Old denominations obliterated with bars on Nos. C862, C871-C873, C875-C877, C883, C885-C887, C889, C892, C896-C898. Vertical surcharge on Nos. C865-C866, C871-C873, C874, C878, C896.

Kennedy Type of Regular Issue
1965, Aug. 20 Photo. *Perf. 12x11½*

C900	A144	60c lt grnsh bl	1.00	50
C901	A144	80c red brn	1.25	60

Issued in memory of President John F. Kennedy (1917-1963).

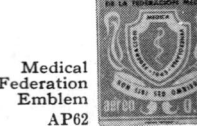
Medical Federation Emblem
AP62

1965, Aug. 24 Litho. *Perf. 13½x14*

C902	AP62	65c red org & blk	1.50	1.00

Issued to commemorate the 20th anniversary of the founding of the Medical Federation of Venezuela.

Unisphere and Venezuela Pavilion
AP63

1965, Aug. 31 *Perf. 14x13½*

C903	AP63	1b multi	1.25	60

New York World's Fair, 1964-65.

Andrés Bello
AP64

Perf. 14x13½
1965, Oct. 15 Litho. Unwmkd.

C904	AP64	80c dk brn & org	1.50	1.00

Issued to commemorate the centenary of the death of Andrés Bello (1780?-1865), educator and writer.

Map Type of Regular Issue, 1965
Maps of Venezuela and Guiana: 25c, Map of Venezuela and Guiana by J. Cruz Cano, 1775. 40c, Map stamp of 1896 (No. 140). 75c, Map by the Ministry of the Exterior, 1965 (all horiz.).

1965, Nov. 5 *Perf. 13½*

C905	A145	25c multi	50	25
C906	A145	40c multi	75	25
C907	A145	75c multi	1.00	50
a.		Souv. sheet of 3	3.75	3.75

Issued to publicize Venezuela's claim to part of British Guiana. No. C907a contains 3 imperf. stamps similar to Nos. C905-C907. Black inscriptions and control number, multicolored coat of arms. Size: 158x207mm. Sold for 1.65b.

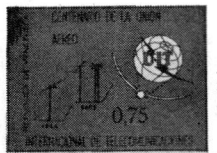
ITU Emblem and Telegraph Poles
AP65

1965, Nov. 19 Litho. *Perf. 13½x14*

C908	AP65	75c blk & ol grn	1.00	50

Issued to commemorate the centenary of the International Telecommunication Union.

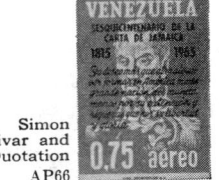
Simon Bolivar and Quotation
AP66

1965, Dec. 9 *Perf. 14x13½*

C909	AP66	75c lt bl & dk brn	1.00	50

Issued to commemorate the sesquicentennial of Bolivar's Jamaica Letter, Sept. 6, 1815.

Children riding Magic Carpet and Three Kings on Camels
AP67

Perf. 13½x14
1965, Dec. 16 Litho. Unwmkd.

C910	AP67	70c yel & vio bl	1.50	1.00

Children's Festival, 1965 (Christmas).

Fermin Toro
AP68

1965, Dec. 22 *Perf. 14x13½*

C911	AP68	1b blk & org	1.25	60

Centenary of the death of Fermin Toro (1808-1865), statesman and writer.

Winston Churchill
AP69

1965, Dec. 29 *Perf. 14½x13*

C912	AP69	1b lil & blk	1.50	75

Issued in memory of Sir Winston Spencer Churchill (1874-1965), statesman and World War II leader.

ICY Emblem, Arms of Venezuela and UN Emblem
AP70

1965, Dec. 30 *Perf. 13½x14*

C913	AP70	85c gold & vio blk	1.50	75

International Cooperation Year, 1965.

OAS Emblem and Map of America
AP71

Farms of 1936 and 1966
AP72

1965, Dec. 31 *Perf. 14x13½*

C914	AP71	70c bl, blk & gold	1.25	60

Issued to commemorate the 75th anniversary of the Organization of American States.

Butterfly Type of Regular Issue
1966, Jan. 25 Litho. *Perf. 13½x14*
Various Butterflies in Natural Colors; Black Inscriptions

C915	A146	65c lilac	1.00	50
C916	A146	85c blue	1.50	75
C917	A146	1b sal pink	1.75	85

1966, March 1 *Perf. 14x13½*

C918	AP72	55c blk, yel & emer	1.00	50

Issued to commemorate the 30th anniversary of the Ministry for Agriculture and Husbandry.

Dance Type of Regular Issue
Various Folk Dances
1966, Apr. 5 Litho. *Perf. 14*

C919	A148	40c bl & multi	1.00	50
C920	A148	50c multi	1.25	60
C921	A148	60c vio & multi	75	38
C922	A148	70c multi	1.75	85
C923	A148	80c red & multi	2.00	1.00
C924	A148	90c ocher & multi	2.25	1.25
		Nos. C919-C924 (6)	9.00	4.58

Title Page "Popule Meus"
AP73

1966, Apr. 15 *Perf. 13½x14*

C925	AP73	55c yel grn, blk & bis	75	50
C926	AP73	95c dp mag, blk & bis	1.00	75

Issued to commemorate the 150th anniversary (in 1964) of the death of José Angel Lamas, composer of national anthem.

Circus Scene, by Michelena
AP74

Paintings by Michelena: 1b, Miranda in La Carraca. 1.05b, Charlotte Corday.

Perf. 12x12½
1966, May 12 Litho. Unwmkd.

C927	AP74	95c multi	1.25	1.00
C928	AP74	1b multi	1.50	1.00
C929	AP74	1.05b multi	1.75	1.00

Issued to commemorate the centenary of the birth of Arturo Michelena (1863-1898), painter. Miniature sheets of 12 exist. See Nos. 900-901.

Abraham Lincoln
AP75

1966, May 31 *Perf. 13½x14*

C930	AP75	1b gray & blk	1.25	1.00

Issued to commemorate the centenary (in 1965) of the death of Abraham Lincoln.

Dr. José Gregorio Hernandez
AP76

1966, July 29 Litho. *Perf. 14x13½*

C931	AP76	1b brt bl & vio bl	1.75	85

Issued to commemorate the centenary (in 1964) of the birth of Dr. José Gregorio Hernandez, physician.

VENEZUELA

Dr. Manuel Dagnino and Hospital
AP77

1966, Aug. 16 Litho. Perf. 13½x14

| C932 | AP77 | 1b sl grn & yel grn | 1.50 | 75 |

Issued to commemorate the centenary of the founding of Chiquinquira Hospital.

Fish Type of Regular Issue, 1966.

Fish: 75c, Pearl hadstander (vert.). 90c, Swordtail characine. 1b, Ramirez's dwarf cichlid.

Perf. 14x13½, 13½x14

1966, Aug. 31

C933	A151	75c multi	1.50	75
C934	A151	90c grn & multi	1.50	75
C935	A151	1b multi	1.60	75

Rafael Arevalo Gonzalez AP78 — Simon Bolivar 1816 AP79

1966, Sept. 13 Litho. Perf. 13½x14

| C936 | AP78 | 75c yel bis & blk | 1.25 | 75 |

Issued to commemorate the centenary of the birth of Rafael Arevalo Gonzalez, journalist.

Imprint: "Bundesdruckerei Berlin 1966"

Bolivar Portraits: 25c, 30c, 35c, by José Gil de Castro, 1825. 40c, 50c, 60c, Anonymous painter, 1825. 80c, 1.20b, 4b, Anonymous painter, c. 1829.

1966   Multicolored Center

C937	AP79	5c lem & blk	7	5
C938	AP79	10c lt ol grn & blk	8	5
C939	AP79	20c grn & blk	15	5
C940	AP79	25c sal & blk	18	5
C941	AP79	30c pink & blk	25	12
C942	AP79	35c dl rose & blk	30	12
C943	AP79	40c bis brn & blk	25	12
C944	AP79	50c org brn & blk	50	25
C945	AP79	60c brn red & blk	50	25
C946	AP79	80c brt bl & blk	1.00	50
C947	AP79	1.20b dl bl & blk	1.50	1.00
C948	AP79	4b vio bl & blk	5.00	4.00
	Nos. C937-C948 (12)		9.78	6.56

Issued to honor Simon Bolivar. Issue dates: Nos. C937–C939, Sept. 15. Nos. C940–C942, Sept. 29. Others, Oct. 14.
See also Nos. C961–C972.

"Justice"
AP80

1966, Nov. 3 Litho. Perf. 14x13½

| C949 | AP80 | 50c pale lil & red lil | 1.00 | 50 |

Issued to commemorate the 50th anniversary of the Academy of Political and Social Sciences.

Angostura Bridge, Orinoco River
AP81

1967, Jan. 6 Litho. Perf. 13½x14

| C950 | AP81 | 40c multi | 50 | 35 |

Issued to commemorate the opening of the Angostura Bridge over the Orinoco River.

Pavilion of Venezuela
AP82

1967, Apr. 28 Litho. Perf. 11x13½

| C951 | AP82 | 1b multi | 1.25 | 60 |

Issued to commemorate EXPO '67, International Exhibition, Montreal, Apr. 28–Oct. 27, 1967.

Statue of Chief Guaicaipuro
AP83

Constellations over Caracas, 1567 and 1967
AP84

Designs: 45c, Captain Francisco Fajardo. 55c, Diego de Losada, the Founder. 65c, Arms of Caracas. 90c, Map of Caracas, 1578. 1b, Market on Plaza Mayor, 1800.

Perf. 14x13½, 13½x14

1967, July   Lithographed

C952	AP83	15c multi	12	5
C953	AP83	45c gold, car & brn	50	25
C954	AP83	55c multi	65	30
C955	AP84	60c blk, ultra & sil	75	38
C956	AP83	65c multi	85	42
C957	AP84	90c multi	1.10	55
C958	AP84	1b multi	1.25	65
	Nos. C952-C958 (7)		5.22	2.60

Issued to commemorate the 400th anniversary of the founding of Caracas (first issue). See also Nos. C977–C982 (second issue).

Two souvenir sheets each contain single stamps similar to Nos. C952-C953, but with simulated perforation. Marginal decorations and inscriptions in gray, black, gold and carmine. Sold for 1b each. Size: 80x119mm. Price $10 each.

Gen. Francisco Esteban Gomez
AP85

1967, July 31 Litho. Perf. 14x13½

| C959 | AP85 | 90c multi | 1.25 | 75 |

150th anniversary, Battle of Matasiete.

Juan Vicente González
AP86

1967, Sept. 18 Litho. Perf. 14x13½

| C960 | AP86 | 80c ocher & blk | 1.25 | 60 |

Issued to commemorate the centenary of the death (in 1866) of Juan Vicente González, journalist.

Bolivar Type of 1966
Imprint: "Druck Bruder Rosenbaum, Wien"

1967–68 Lithographed Perf. 13½x14
Multicolored Center

C961	AP79	5c lem & blk ('68)	12	6
C962	AP79	10c lem & blk	12	6
C963	AP79	20c grn & blk	12	6
C964	AP79	25c sal & blk ('68)	35	18
C965	AP79	30c pink & blk	50	18
C966	AP79	35c dl rose & blk	50	18
C967	AP79	40c bis brn & blk ('68)	75	25
C968	AP79	50c org brn & blk	1.50	75
C969	AP79	60c brn red & blk	3.00	1.75
C970	AP79	80c brt bl & blk	1.75	85
C971	AP79	1.20b dl bl & blk	2.50	1.25
C972	AP79	4b vio bl & blk	6.25	3.75
	Nos. C961-C972 (12)		17.84	9.38

Child with Pinwheel
AP87

1967, Dec. 15 Litho. Perf. 14x13½

C973	AP87	45c multi	75	35
C974	AP87	75c multi	1.00	50
C975	AP87	90c multi	1.25	65

Children's Festival.

Examination

The Catalogue editors cannot undertake to appraise, identify or pass upon genuineness or condition of stamps.

Madonna with the Rosebush, by Stephan Lochner
AP88

1967, Dec. 19

| C976 | AP88 | 1b multi | 1.75 | 1.00 |

Christmas 1967.

Palace of the Academies, Caracas
AP89

Views of Caracas: 50c, St. Theresa's Church (vert.). 70c, Federal Legislature. 75c, University City. 85c, El Pulpo highways crossing. 2b, Avenida Libertador.

Perf. 13½x14, 14x13½

1967, Dec. 28

C977	AP89	10c multi	12	6
C978	AP89	50c lil & multi	50	25
C979	AP89	70c multi	85	38
C980	AP89	75c multi	1.00	42
C981	AP89	85c multi	1.00	50
C982	AP89	2b multi	3.00	1.50
	Nos. C977-C982 (6)		6.47	3.11

Issued to commemorate the 400th anniversary of Caracas (second issue).

José Manuel Nuñez Ponte
AP90

1968, Mar. 8 Litho. Perf. 14

| C983 | AP90 | 65c multi | 75 | 50 |

Issued in memory of Dr. José Manuel Nuñez Ponte (1870–1965), educator.

De Miranda and Printing Press
AP91

Designs (Miranda Portraits and): 35c, Parliament, London. 45c, Arc de Triomphe, Paris. 70c, Portrait (vert.). 80c, Portrait bust and Venezuelan flags (vert.).

Perf. 13½x14, 14x13½

1968, June 20   Lithographed

C984	AP91	20c yel brn, grn & brn	30	15
C985	AP91	35c multi	65	25
C986	AP91	45c lt bl & multi	1.00	50
C987	AP91	70c multi	1.25	42
C988	AP91	80c multi	1.50	75
	Nos. C984-C988 (5)	4.70	2.07

Issued to commemorate the sesquicentennial of the death of General Francisco de Miranda (1750 ?–1816), revolutionist, dictator of Venezuela.

VENEZUELA

Insect Type of Regular Issue
Insect Pests: 5c, Red leaf-cutting ant (vert.). 15c, Sugar cane beetle (vert.). 20c, Leaf beetle.

Perf. 14x13½, 13½x14

1968, Aug. 30   Lithographed

C989	A157	5c multi	15	6
C990	A157	15c multi	35	15
C991	A157	20c gray & multi	50	25

Three Keys AP92

1968, Oct. 17 Litho. *Perf. 14x13½*

C992	AP92	95c yel, vio & dk grn	1.25	60

Issued to commemorate the 30th anniversary of the National Comptroller's Office.

Fencing AP93

Designs: 5c, Pistol shooting (vert.). 15c, Running. 75c, Boxing. 5b, Sailing (vert.).

Perf. 14x13½, 13½x14

1968, Nov. 6 Litho. Unwmkd.

C993	AP93	5c vio, bl & blk	8	6
C994	AP93	15c multi	50	18
C995	AP93	30c yel grn, dk grn & blk	75	35
C996	AP93	75c multi	1.50	75
C997	AP93	5b multi	7.50	3.75
		Nos. C993-C997 (5)	10.33	5.09

Issued to commemorate the 19th Olympic Games, Mexico City, Oct. 12–27.

Holy Family, by Francisco José de Lerma AP94   Dancing Children and Stars AP95

1968, Dec. 4 Litho. *Perf. 14x13½*

C998	AP94	40c multi	75	35

Christmas 1968.

1968, Dec. 13 Litho. *Perf. 14x13½*

C999	AP95	80c vio & org	1.50	70

Issued for the 5th Children's Festival.

Conservation Type of Regular Issue
Designs: 15c, Marbled wood-quail (vert.). 20c, Water birds (vert.). 30c, Woodcarvings and tools (vert.). 90c, Brown trout. 95c, Valley and road. 1b, Red-eyed vireo feeding young bronzed cowbird.

Perf. 13½x14, 14x13½

1968, Dec. 19 Lithographed

C1000	A160	15c multi	12	6
C1001	A160	20c multi	25	12
C1002	A160	30c multi	35	15
C1003	A160	90c multi	1.00	50
C1004	A160	95c multi	1.75	85
C1005	A160	1b multi	1.25	60
		Nos. C1000-C1005 (6)	4.72	2.28

Issued to publicize nature conservation.

Tourist Type of Regular Issue
Designs: 15c, Giant cactus and desert, Falcon. 30c, Hotel Humboldt, Federal District. 40c, Cable car and mountain peaks, Merida.

1969, Jan. 24   *Perf. 13½x14*

C1006	A161	15c multi	30	15
C1007	A161	30c multi	30	25
a.		Souv. sheet of 2	2.00	2.00
C1008	A161	40c multi	65	35

Issued for tourist propaganda. No. C1007a contains 2 imperf. stamps similar to Nos. 931 and C1007. Blue inscription, black control number and multicolored coat of arms in margin. Size: 119x80mm.

Tree Type of Regular Issue
Trees: 5c, Cassia grandis. 20c, Triplaris caracasana. 25c, Samanea saman.

1969, May 30 Litho. *Perf. 13½x14*

C1009	A164	5c lt grn & multi	12	6
C1010	A164	20c org & multi	35	15
C1011	A164	25c lt vio & multi	50	25

Alexander von Humboldt, by Joseph Stieler AP96   Map of Maracaibo 1562 AP97

1969, Sept. 12 Photo. *Perf. 14*

C1012	AP96	50c multi	85	35

Issued to commemorate the bicentenary of the birth of Alexander von Humboldt (1769–1859), naturalist and explorer.

Perf. 13½x13, 13x13½

1969, Sept. 30 Lithographed

Designs: 20c, Ambrosio Alfinger, Alfonso Pacheco and Pedro Maldonado (horiz.). 40c, Maracaibo coat of arms. 70c, University Hospital. 75c, Monument to the Indian Mara. 1b, Baralt Square (horiz.).

C1013	AP97	20c lil & multi	30	18
C1014	AP97	25c org & multi	38	25
C1015	AP97	40c multi	50	30
C1016	AP97	70c grn & multi	1.00	50
C1017	AP97	75c brn & multi	1.25	60
C1018	AP97	1b multi	1.50	75
		Nos. 1013-C1018 (6)	4.93	2.58

400th anniversary of Maracaibo.

Astronauts Neil A. Armstrong, Edwin E. Aldrin, Jr., Michael Collins and Moonscape AP98

1969, Nov. 18 Litho. *Perf. 12½*

C1019	AP98	90c multi	1.75	85
a.		Souv. sheet	2.50	2.50

See note after U.S. No. C76. No. C1019a contains one stamp similar to No. C1019, imperf. with simulated perforations. Multicolored margin showing Apollo 11, Venezuelan coat of arms and control number. Size: 119x80mm.

Virgin with the Rosary, 17th Century AP99

Design: 80c, Holy Family, Caracas, 18th Century.

1969, Dec. 1 Litho. *Perf. 12½*

C1020	AP99	75c gold & multi	1.00	50
C1021	AP99	80c gold & multi	1.25	60
		Pair, #C1020-C1021	3.00	2.50

Christmas 1969.
Nos. C1020–C1021 are printed se-tenant.

Simon Bolivar, 1819, by M. N. Bate AP100

Bolivar Portraits: 45c, 55c, like 15c. 65c, 70c, 75c Drawing by Francois Roulin, 1828. 85c, 90c, 95c, Charcoal drawing by José Maria Espinoza, 1828. 1b, 1.50b, 2b, Drawing by Espinoza, 183C.

1970, Mar. 16 Litho. *Perf. 14x13½*

C1022	AP100	15c multi	15	15
C1023	AP100	45c bl & multi	50	25
C1024	AP100	55c org & multi	75	35
C1025	AP100	65c multi	75	38
C1026	AP100	70c bl & multi	85	55
C1027	AP100	75c org & multi	1.10	60
C1028	AP100	85c multi	1.25	65
C1029	AP100	90c bl & multi	1.35	70
C1030	AP100	95c org & multi	1.50	75
C1031	AP100	1b multi	1.50	75
C1032	AP100	1.50b bl & multi	1.75	85
C1033	AP100	2b multi	3.75	2.50
		Nos. 1022-C1033 (12)	15.30	8.48

Issued to honor Simon Bolivar (1783–1830), liberator and father of his country.

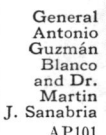 

General Antonio Guzmán Blanco and Dr. Martin J. Sanabria AP101

1970, June 26 Litho. *Perf. 13*

C1034	AP101	75c brt grn & multi	90	55

Issued to commemorate the centenary of free obligatory elementary education.

Map of Venezuela with Claim to Part of Guyana—AP102

Designs: State map and arms. 55c, 90c, vert.

Perf. 13½x14, 14x13½

1970–71 Lithographed
    Multicolored

C1035	AP102	5c shown	12	6
C1036	AP102	15c *Apure* ('71)	25	10
C1037	AP102	20c *Aragua* ('71)	30	12
C1038	AP102	20c *Anzoategui* ('71)	35	12
C1039	AP102	25c *Barinas* ('71)	35	12
C1040	AP102	25c *Bolivar* ('71)	35	12
C1041	AP102	45c *Carabobo* ('71)	65	30
C1042	AP102	55c *Cojedes* ('71)	75	35
C1043	AP102	65c *Falcon*	80	35
C1044	AP102	75c *Guárico* ('71)	1.00	40
C1045	AP102	85c *Lara* ('71)	1.25	50
C1046	AP102	90c *Merida* ('71)	1.25	60
C1047	AP102	1b *Miranda* ('71)	1.25	75
C1048	AP102	2b *Delta Amacuro* Territory ('71)	3.00	1.75
		Nos. C1035-C1048 (14)	11.67	5.64

Flower Type of Regular Issue
Flowers: 20c, Epidendrum secundum. 25c, Oyedaea verbesinoides. 45c, Heliconia villosa. 1b, Macleanita nitida.

1970, July 29 Litho. *Perf. 14x13½*

C1049	A175	20c multi	35	15
C1050	A175	25c multi	50	25
C1051	A175	45c multi	1.00	50
C1052	A175	1b multi	1.50	75

Caracciolo Parra Olmedo AP104

1970, Nov. 16 Photo. *Perf. 12½*

C1053	AP104	20c bl & multi	35	15

Sesquicentennial of birth of Caracciolo Parra Olmedo (1819–1900), professor of law, rector of University of Merida.

Census Chart—AP105

1971, Apr. 30 Litho. *Perf. 13½x14*
    Black & Multicolored

C1054	AP105	Block of 4	8.00	4.00
a.		70c, frame L & T	1.50	50
b.		70c, frame T & R	1.50	50
c.		70c, frame L & B	1.50	50
d.		70c, frame B & R	1.50	50

National Census, 1971. The frame encircles all 4 stamps in block of No. C1054; each stamp in block has frame on 2 sides. Sheet of 20 contains 5 No. C1054 and 5 blocks of 4 labels inscribed in brown "Censo Nacional 1971."

Cattleya Gaskelliana AP106

Orchids: 20c, Cattleya percivaliana (vert.). 75c, Cattleya mossiae (vert.). 90c, Cattleya violacea. 1b, Cattleya lawrenciana.

Perf. 14x13½, 13½x14

1971, Aug. 25

C1055	AP106	20c blk & multi	50	25
C1056	AP106	25c blk & multi	65	30
C1057	AP106	75c blk & multi	1.25	60

VENEZUELA

C1058	AP106	90c blk & multi	1.50	75
C1059	AP106	1b blk & multi	1.75	85
		Nos. C1055-C1059 (5)	5.65	2.75

40th anniversary of Venezuelan Society of Natural History. Issued in sheets of 5 stamps and one label with Society emblem in blue.

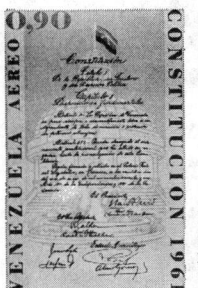

Draft of Constitution Superimposed on Capitol
AP107

1971, Dec. 29   Litho.   Perf. 13½

C1060	AP107	90c multi	1.50	75

Anniversary of 1961 Constitution.

AIR POST SEMI-POSTAL STAMPS.

King Vulture
SPAP1
Engraved.

1942, Dec. 17   Perf. 12   Unwmkd.

CB1	SPAP1	15c + 10c org brn	2.50	1.00
CB2	SPAP1	30c + 5c vio	2.50	1.25

See note after No. B1.

SPECIAL DELIVERY STAMPS.

SD1   SD2
Engraved.

1949   Perf. 12½   Unwmkd.

E1	SD1	30c red	75	35

Lithographed

1961, Apr. 5   Perf. 13½   Wmk. 116

E2	SD2	30c orange	65	38

REGISTRATION STAMPS.

Bolívar
R1
Engraved.

1899   Perf. 12   Unwmkd.

F1	R1	25c yel brn	5.00	3.75

No. F1
Overprinted in Black

1900

F2	R1	25c yel brn	3.00	3.00
a.		Inverted ovpt.	37.50	37.50
b.		Double ovpt.	50.00	50.00

OFFICIAL STAMPS.

Coat of Arms
O1

Lithographed, Center Engraved.

1898   Perf. 12   Unwmkd.

O1	O1	5c bl grn & blk	75	75
O2	O1	10c rose & blk	1.50	1.50
O3	O1	25c bl & blk	2.00	2.00
O4	O1	50c yel & blk	3.75	3.75
O5	O1	1b vio & blk	3.75	3.75
		Nos. O1-O5 (5)	11.75	11.75

1899

Nos. O4 and O5 Surcharged

5 Cms. - 5

1899   Magenta Surcharge.

O6	O1	5c on 50c yel & blk	7.00	7.00
a.		Inverted surcharge	20.00	20.00
O7	O1	5c on 1b vio & blk	27.50	27.50
a.		Inverted surcharge	55.00	55.00
O8	O1	25c on 50c yel & blk	27.50	27.50
a.		Inverted surcharge	42.50	42.50
O9	O1	25c on 1b vio & blk	16.50	16.50
a.		Inverted surcharge	70.00	70.00

Violet Surcharge.

O10	O1	5c on 50c yel & blk	8.00	8.00
a.		Inverted surcharge	27.50	27.50
O11	O1	5c on 1b vio & blk	27.50	27.50
a.		Inverted surcharge	50.00	50.00
O12	O1	25c on 50c yel & blk	27.50	27.50
a.		Inverted surcharge	55.00	50.00
O13	O1	25c on 1b vio & blk	16.50	16.50
a.		Inverted surcharge	40.00	40.00

Nos. O6-O13 exist with double surcharge. Price each $18.50-$37.50.

O3
Lithographed, Center Engraved.

1900

O14	O3	5c bl grn & blk	50	50
O15	O3	10c rose & blk	65	65
O16	O3	25c bl & blk	65	65
O17	O3	50c yel & blk	75	75
O18	O3	1b dl vio & blk	85	85
		Nos. O14-O18 (5)	3.40	3.40

O4
Imprint: "American Bank Note Co., N.Y."

1904   Engraved

O19	O4	5c emer & blk	35	35
O20	O4	10c rose & blk	75	75
O21	O4	25c bl & blk	75	75
O22	O4	50c red brn & blk	5.00	5.00
a.		50c cl & blk	5.00	5.00
O23	O4	1b red brn & blk	2.50	2.50
a.		1b cl & blk	2.50	2.50
		Nos. O19-O23 (5)	9.35	9.35

O5
Lithographed in Caracas.
Without Stars above Shield.

1912

O24	O5	5c grn & blk	38	38
O25	O5	10c car & blk	38	38
O26	O5	25c dk bl & blk	38	38
O27	O5	50c pur & blk	50	50
a.		Center double	37.50	37.50
O28	O5	1b yel & blk	1.00	1.00
		Nos. O24-O28 (5)	2.64	2.64

Perforated Initials

After 1925, Venezuela's official stamps consisted of regular postage stamps, some commemoratives and air post stamps of 1930–42 punched with "GN" (Gobierno Nacional) in large perforated initials.

A well-informed dealer has services to offer that would be helpful toward building your collection.

Use the **Yellow Pages** to fulfill your philatelic requirements.

VENEZUELA—VIET NAM

Local Stamps for the Port of Carupano.
(kä·rōō'pä·nō)

In 1902 Great Britain, Germany and Italy, seeking compensation for revolutionary damages, established a blockade of LaGuaira and seized the custom house. Carúpano, a port near Trinidad, was isolated and issued the following provisionals. A treaty effected May 7, 1903, referred the dispute to the Hague Tribunal.

A1

A2

1902		Type-set.		Imperf.
1	A1	5c pur, org	30.00	
2	A2	10c blk, org	50.00	
a.		Tête bêche pair	140.00	
3	A1	25c pur, grn	40.00	
4	A1	50c grn, yel	80.00	
5	A1	1b bl, rose	100.00	

A3

1902				
6	A3	1b blk, yel	225.00	
a.		Tête bêche pair		

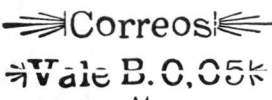

A4

1903		Handstamped		
7	A4	5c car, yel	30.00	30.00
8	A4	10c grn, yel	100.00	100.00
9	A4	25c grn, org	40.00	40.00
10	A4	50c bl, rose	40.00	40.00
11	A4	1b vio, gray	40.00	40.00
12	A4	2b car, grn	40.00	40.00
13	A4	5b vio, bl	40.00	40.00

Dangerous counterfeits exist of Nos. 1–13.

Local Stamps for the State of Guayana.
(gwī·ä'nä)

Revolutionary Steamship "Banrigh"
A1

1903		Typographed		Perf. 12
1	A1	5c gray	30.00	30.00
2	A1	10c orange	80.00	80.00
3	A1	25c pink	30.00	30.00
4	A1	50c blue	50.00	50.00
5	A1	1b straw	40.00	40.00
	Nos. 1-5 (5)		230.00	230.00

Reprints include the 10c and 50c in red.

With Control Mark in Blue Covering Four Stamps.

Coat of Arms

6	A1	5c gray	30.00	30.00
7	A1	10c red	80.00	80.00
8	A1	25c pink	30.00	30.00
9	A1	50c blue	50.00	50.00
10	A1	1b straw	40.00	40.00
	Nos. 6-10 (5)		230.00	230.00

Reprints of Nos. 1–10 printed from different settings are on papers differing in colors from the originals. All 5c on granite paper are reprints. Price 15 cents each.

Coat of Arms
A2

1903				
11	A2	5c pink	70.00	
12	A2	10c orange	80.00	
13	A2	25c gray bl	70.00	
a.		25c bl	70.00	
14	A2	50c straw	70.00	
15	A2	1b gray	50.00	
	Nos. 11-15 (5)		340.00	

Postally used examples are very scarce, and are specimens having 9 ornaments in horizontal borders. Nos. 11-20 pen canceled sell for same prices as unused.

With Control Mark in Blue, as Nos. 6 to 10.

16	A2	5c pink	70.00	
17	A2	10c orange	80.00	
18	A2	25c gray bl	70.00	
a.		25c bl	70.00	
19	A2	50c straw	70.00	
20	A2	1b gray	50.00	
	Nos. 16-20 (5)		340.00	

Nos. 1 to 20 were issued by a group of revolutionists and had a limited local use. The dates on the stamps commemorate the declaration of Venezuelan independence and a compact with Spain against Joseph Bonaparte.

Reprints exist of Nos. 11–20. Stamps with 10 ornaments in horizontal borders are reprints.

VIET NAM
(vē·ĕt·năm; vĕt'năm')

LOCATION—In eastern Indo-China.
GOVT.—Kingdom.
AREA—123,949 sq. mi.
CAPITAL—Hanoi.

Viet Nam, which included the former French territories of Tonkin, Annam and Cochin China, became an Associated State of the French Union in 1949. The Communist Viet Minh obtained control of Northern Viet Nam in 1954, and the republic of South Viet Nam was established in October, 1955.

Stamps of Indo-China overprinted "VIET NAM" and Viet Nam definitives of 1945-48 had no international validity.

100 Cents (Xu) = 1 Piaster (Dong)

Bongour Falls, Dalat
A1

Emperor Bao-Dai
A2

Designs: 20c, 2pi, 10pi, Imperial palace, Hué. 30c, 15pi, Lake, Hanoi. 50c, 1pi, Temple, Saigon.

Perf. 13x13½, 13½x13.

1951, Aug. 16		Photo.	Unwmkd.	
1	A1	10c ol grn	7	5
2	A1	20c dp plum	8	12
3	A1	30c blue	12	12
4	A1	50c red	20	15
5	A1	60c brown	12	12
6	A1	1pi chnt brn	10	6
7	A2	1.20pi yel brn	85	90
8	A1	2pi purple	30	18
9	A2	3pi dl bl	85	22
10	A1	5pi green	1.00	30
11	A1	10pi crimson	3.00	45
12	A1	15pi red brn	21.00	3.00
13	A2	30pi bl grn	12.00	3.50
	Nos. 1-13 (13)		39.69	9.17

Souvenir booklets exist comprising five gummed sheets measuring 121x97mm., containing a single copy each of Nos. 1, 2, 6, 9, and 12, together with commemorative inscriptions.

Empress Nam-Phuong
A3

Globe and Lightning Bolt
A4

1952, Aug. 15			Perf. 12½	
14	A3	30c dk pur, yel & brn	30	20
15	A3	50c bl, yel & brn	70	30
16	A3	1.50pi ol grn, yel & brn	1.25	18

1952, Aug. 24		Engr.	Perf. 13	
17	A4	1pi grnsh bl	2.00	1.35

Issued to commemorate the first anniversary of Viet Nam's admission to the International Telecommunication Union.

Coastal Scene and UPU Emblem
A5

1952, Sept. 12				
18	A5	5pi red brn	2.00	60

Issued to commemorate the first anniversary of Viet Nam's admission to the Universal Postal Union.

Bao-Dai and Pagoda of Literature, Hanoi
A6

1952, Nov. 10			Perf. 12	
19	A6	1.50pi rose vio	2.00	75

39th birthday of Emperor Bao-Dai.

Crown Prince Bao-Long in Annamite Costume
A7

Designs: 70c, 80c, 100pi, Prince in Annamite costume. 90c, 20pi, 50pi, Prince in Western uniform.

1954, June 15			Perf. 13	
20	A7	40c aqua	18	25
21	A7	70c claret	25	40
22	A7	80c blk brn	28	45
23	A7	90c dk grn	75	1.10
24	A7	20pi rose pink	4.00	4.50
25	A7	50pi violet	10.00	8.00
26	A7	100pi bl vio	18.00	18.50
	Nos. 20-26 (7)		33.46	33.20

South Viet Nam
(Viet Nam Cong Hoa)

GOVT.—Republic.
AREA—66,280 sq. mi.
POP.—19,600,000 (est. 1973).
CAPITAL—Saigon.

Mythological Turtle
A8

		Unwmkd.		
1955, July 20		Engr.	Perf. 13	
27	A8	30c claret	25	25
28	A8	50c dk grn	85	85
29	A8	1.50pi brt bl	60	35

Refugees on Raft—A9

VIET NAM

1955, Oct. 11

30	A9	70c crim rose	33	22
31	A9	80c brn vio	90	70
32	A9	10pi indigo	1.75	95
33	A9	20pi vio, red brn & org	4.75	1.50
34	A9	35pi dk bl, blk brn & yel	12.00	7.25
35	A9	100pi dk grn, brn vio & org	24.00	13.50
		Nos. 30-35 (6)	43.73	24.12

Issued to commemorate the first anniversary of the flight of the North Vietnamese.

No. 34 is inscribed "Chiên-Dich-Huynh-Dê" (Operation Brotherhood) below design. See No. 54.

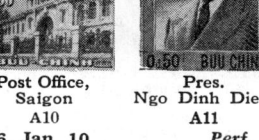

Post Office, Saigon
A10

Pres. Ngo Dinh Diem
A11

1956, Jan. 10   *Perf. 12*

36	A10	60c bluish grn	50	35
37	A10	90c violet	1.00	55
38	A10	3pi red brn	1.65	90

Fifth anniversary of independent postal service.

1956   Engraved   *Perf. 13x13½*

39	A11	20c org ver	5	5
40	A11	30c rose lil	5	5
41	A11	50c brt car	7	5
42	A11	1pi violet	13	10
43	A11	1.50pi violet	22	5
44	A11	3pi blk brn	27	6
45	A11	4pi dk bl	40	10
46	A11	5pi red brn	60	17
47	A11	10pi blue	70	25
48	A11	20pi gray blk	1.50	45
49	A11	35pi green	4.50	95
50	A11	100pi brown	7.50	3.90
		Nos. 39-50 (12)	15.99	5.78

Nos. 36-38 Công-thự Bưu-điện Overprinted

1956, Aug. 6   *Perf. 12*

51	A10	60c bluish grn	30	20
52	A10	90c violet	55	20
53	A10	3pi red brn	90	30

The overprint reads: "Government Post Office Building."

No. 34 with Black Bar over Inscription below Design.

1956, Aug. 6

| 54 | A9 | 35pi dk bl, blk brn & yel | 2.25 | 1.50 |

Bamboo
A12

Children
A13

Perf. 13x13½

1956, Oct. 26   Lithographed

55	A12	50c scarlet	12	10
56	A12	1.50pi rose vio	25	12
57	A12	2pi brt grn	30	18
58	A12	4pi dp bl	75	35

Issued to commemorate the first anniversary of the Republic, Oct. 26, 1956.

1956, Nov. 7   Engr.   *Perf. 13½x14*

59	A13	1pi lil rose	25	10
60	A13	2pi bl grn	30	17
61	A13	6pi purple	55	18
62	A13	35pi vio bl	3.00	1.75

"Operation Brotherhood."

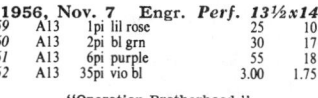

Hunters on Elephants
A14

Loading Cargo
A15

Design: 90c, 2pi, 3pi, Mountain dwelling.

1957, July 7   Photo.   *Perf. 13*

63	A14	20c yel grn & pur	13	7
64	A14	30c bis & dp mag	18	7
65	A14	90c yel grn & dk brn	22	7
66	A14	2pi grn & ultra	38	13
67	A14	3pi bl vio & brn	45	25
		Nos. 63-67 (5)	1.36	59

1957, Oct. 21   *Perf. 13½x13*

68	A15	20c rose vio	5	5
69	A15	40c lt ol grn	5	5
70	A15	50c lt car rose	8	5
71	A15	2pi ultra	20	7
72	A15	3pi brt grn	28	15
		Nos. 68-72 (5)	66	37

9th Colombo Plan Conference, Saigon.

Torch, Map and Constitution
A16

Farmers, Tractor and Village
A17

1957, Oct. 26   Litho.   *Perf. 13x13½*

73	A16	50c blk, grn & sal	8	5
74	A16	80c blk, brt bl & mag	12	5
75	A16	1pi blk, bl grn & brt car	18	6
76	A16	4pi blk, ol grn & fawn	25	12
77	A16	5pi blk, grnsh bl & cit	35	20
78	A16	10pi blk, ultra & rose	70	40
		Nos. 73-78 (6)	1.68	88

Issued to commemorate the second anniversary of the Republic of South Viet Nam.

1958, July 7   Engr.   *Perf. 13½*

79	A17	50c yel grn	10	8
80	A17	1pi dp vio	15	8
81	A17	2pi ultra	25	12
82	A17	10pi brick red	60	50

Issued to commemorate the 4th anniversary of the government of Ngo Dinh Diem.

Girl and Lantern
A18

A19

1958, Sept. 27

83	A18	30c yellow	10	10
84	A18	50c dk car rose	10	10
85	A18	2pi dp car	12	10
86	A18	3pi bl grn	30	22
87	A18	4pi lt ol grn	45	22
		Nos. 83-87 (5)	1.07	74

Issued to publicize the Children's Festival.

1958, Oct. 26   *Perf. 13½*

88	A19	1pi dl red brn	15	8
89	A19	2pi bluish grn	20	12
90	A19	4pi rose car	32	15
91	A19	5pi rose lil	65	40

Issued for United Nations Day.

Most South Viet Nam stamps from 1958 onward exist imperforate in issued and trial colors, and also in small presentation sheets in issued colors.

UNESCO Building, Paris
A20

Torch and U.N. Emblem
A21

1958, Nov. 3   *Perf. 12½x13*

92	A20	50c ultra	10	6
93	A20	1pi brt red	12	10
94	A20	3pi lil rose	25	15
95	A20	6pi violet	32	25

Issued to commemorate the opening of UNESCO (U. N. Educational, Scientific and Cultural Organization) Headquarters in Paris, Nov. 3.

1958, Dec. 10   Engr.   *Perf. 13½*

96	A21	50c dk bl	8	6
97	A21	1pi brn car	12	8
98	A21	2pi yel grn	18	10
99	A21	6pi rose vio	40	25

Issued to commemorate the tenth anniversary of the signing of the Universal Declaration of Human Rights.

Cathedral of Hué
A22

Thien Mu Pagoda, Hué
A23

National Museum
A24

Design: 50c, 2pi, Palace of Independence, Saigon.

1958-59   *Perf. 13½*

100	A22	10c dk bl gray	8	5
101	A23	30c grn ('59)	10	8
102	A24	40c dk grn ('59)	10	5
103	A24	50c grn ('59)	10	8
104	A24	2pi grnsh bl ('59)	30	15
105	A23	4pi dl pur ('59)	35	25
106	A24	5pi dk car ('59)	40	25
107	A22	6pi org brn	50	30
		Nos. 100-107 (8)	1.93	1.21

Trung Sisters on Elephants
A25

1959, Mar. 14   Photo.   *Perf. 13*

108	A25	50c multi	8	5
109	A25	2pi ocher, grn & bl	20	12
110	A25	3pi emer, vio & bis	35	15
111	A25	6pi multi	55	30

Issued to honor the sisters Trung Trac and Trung Nhi who resisted a Chinese invasion in 40-44 A. D.

Symbols of Agrarian Reforms
A26

1959, July 7   Engraved   *Perf. 13*

112	A26	70c lil rose	8	8
113	A26	2pi dk grn & Prus bl	12	12
114	A26	3pi olive	20	15
115	A26	6pi dk red & red	45	40

Issued to commemorate the fifth anniversary of Ngo Dinh Diem's presidency.

Diesel Engine and Map of North and South Viet Nam
A27

1959, Aug. 7

116	A27	1pi lt vio & grn	15	7
117	A27	2pi gray & grn	18	12
118	A27	3pi grnsh bl & grn	22	15
119	A27	4pi mar & grn	40	18

Issued to commemorate the re-opening of the Saigon-Dongha Railroad.

Volunteer Road Workers
A28

1959, Oct. 26

120	A28	1pi org brn, ultra & grn	12	5
121	A28	2pi vio, org & grn	15	12
122	A28	4pi dk bl, bl & bis	32	20
123	A28	5pi bis, brn & ocher	40	30

Issued to commemorate the 4th anniversary of the constitution, stressing communal development.

Boy Scout
A29

VIET NAM

1959, Dec.   Engraved   Perf. 13
124 A29 3pi brt yel grn   18   10
125 A29 4pi dp lil rose   30   10
126 A29 8pi dk brn & lil rose   48   27
127 A29 20pi Prus bl & bl grn 1.20   60

National Boy Scout Jamboree.

Symbols of Family and Justice
A30

1960
128 A30 20c emerald   5   5
129 A30 30c brt grnsh bl   5   5
130 A30 2pi org & mar   25   15
131 A30 6pi car & rose vio   85   50

Issued to commemorate the family code.

Refugee Family and WRY Emblem
A31

1960, Apr. 7   Engr.   Perf. 13
132 A31 50c brt lil rose   20   6
133 A31 3pi brt grn   15   15
134 A31 4pi scarlet   25   22
135 A31 5pi dp vio bl   32   25

Issued to publicize World Refugee Year,
July 1, 1959–June 30, 1960.

Henri Dunant
A32   Cross in Carmine

1960, May 8
136 A32 1pi dk bl   18   10
137 A32 3pi green   38   15
138 A32 4pi crim rose   40   25
139 A32 6pi dp lil rose   50   33

Centenary (in 1959) of the Red Cross idea.

Model Farm—A33

1960, July 7   Perf. 13
140 A33 50c ultra   10   5
141 A33 1pi dk grn   13   6
142 A33 3pi orange   28   15
143 A33 7pi brt pink   50   25

Establishment of communal rice farming.

Girl With Basket of Rice
and Rice Plant—A34

1960, Nov. 21
144 A34 2pi emer & grn   20   12
145 A34 4pi bl & ultra   42   18

Issued to commemorate the conference
of the U.N. Food and Agriculture Organization, Saigon, Nov. 1960.

Map and Flag of Viet Nam
A35

1960, Oct. 26   Engr.   Perf. 13
146 A35 50c grnsh bl, car & yel   10   5
147 A35 1pi ultra, car & yel   12   5
148 A35 3pi pur, car & yel   22   10
149 A35 7pi yel grn, car & yel   40   20

Fifth anniversary of the Republic.

Agricultural Development Center,
Tractor and Plow
A36

1961, Jan. 3   Perf. 13
150 A36 50c brt brn   8   5
151 A36 70c rose lil   10   7
152 A36 80c rose red   12   10
153 A36 10pi brt pink 50   32

Plant and   Pres. Ngo
Child   Dinh Diem
A37   A38

1961, March 23   Perf. 13
154 A37 70c lt bl   10   5
155 A37 80c ultra   12   7
156 A37 4pi ol bis   18   12
157 A37 7pi grnsh bl & yel grn   40   30

Child protection.

1961, Apr. 29   Perf. 13
158 A38 50c brt ultra 12   7
159 A38 1pi red   18   10
160 A38 2pi lil rose   25   10
161 A38 4pi brt vio   50   15

Second term of Pres. Ngo Dinh Diem.

Boy, Girl and Flaming Torch
A39

1961, July 7   Engraved   Perf. 13
162 A39 50c red   8   5
163 A39 70c brt pink 10   5
164 A39 80c ver & mar 15   6
165 A39 8pi dp cl & mag 40 30

Issued for Youth Day.

Saigon-Bienhoa Highway Bridge
A40

1961, July 28
166 A40 50c yel grn   10   5
167 A40 1pi org brn   12   5
168 A40 2pi dk bl   20   6
169 A40 5pi brt red lil 32 20

Opening of Saigon-Bien Hoa Highway.

Alexandre de Rhodes
A41

1961, Sept. 5
170 A41 50c rose car   10   7
171 A41 1pi claret   12   8
172 A41 3pi bis brn   15   10
173 A41 6pi emerald   45   25

Issued to commemorate the tercentenary of the death of Alexandre de Rhodes (1591–1660), the Jesuit missionary who introduced Roman characters to express the Viet Nam language.

Young Man   Temple Dedicated
with Torch,   to Confucius
Sage, Pagoda
A42   A43

1961, Oct. 26   Perf. 13
174 A42 50c org ver   8   7
175 A42 1pi brt grn   12   8
176 A42 3pi rose red   15   10
177 A42 4pi rose red & brn 45   22

Moral Rearmament of Youth Movement.

1961, Nov. 4   Engraved
178 A43 1pi brt grn   12   5
179 A43 2pi rose red 15   5
180 A43 5pi olive   50   20

15th anniversary of UNESCO.

Earth Scraper   Man Fighting
Preparing Ground   Mosquito and
for Model Village   Emblem
A44   A45

1961, Dec. 11   Perf. 13
181 A44 50c dk grn   8   7
182 A44 1pi Prus bl & car lake 10 8
183 A44 2pi ol grn & brn   15   15
184 A44 10pi Prus bl   50   45

Agrarian reform program.

1962, Apr. 7   Perf. 13
185 A45 50c brt lil rose   5   5
186 A45 1pi orange   10   5
187 A45 2pi emerald   12   8
188 A45 6pi ultra   35   25

Issued for the World Health Organization drive to eradicate malaria.

Postal Check   Madonna of Vang
Center, Saigon
A46   A47

1962, May 15   Engr.   Perf. 13
189 A46 70c dl grn   8   5
190 A46 80c chocolate 8   5
191 A46 4pi lil rose 20   13
192 A46 7pi rose red 45   35

Inauguration of postal checking service.

1962, July 7
193 A47 50c vio & rose red   5   5
194 A47 1pi red brn & ind   8   5
195 A47 2pi brn & rose car   12   5
196 A47 8pi grn & dk bl   55   25

Catholic shrine of the Madonna of Vang.

Armed Guards and Village
A48

1962, Oct. 26
197 A48 50c brt red   5   5
198 A48 1pi yel grn   12   5
199 A48 1.50pi lil rose 15   5
200 A48 7pi ultra   45   35

Issued to publicize the "strategic village" defense system.

Gougah Waterfall,   Trung Sisters'
Dalat   Monument and
                      Vietnamese
                      Women
A49   A50

1963, Jan. 3
201 A49 60c org red   15   7
202 A49 1pi bluish blk 22   8

Issued for the 62nd birthday of Pres. Ngo Dinh Diem and to publicize the Spring Festival.

1963, Mar. 1   Engraved
203 A50 50c green   10   7
204 A50 1pi dk car rose 17   8
205 A50 3pi lil rose   25   17
206 A50 8pi vio bl   60   38

Issued for Women's Day.

VIET NAM

Farm Woman with Grain
A51

1963, Mar. 21   *Perf. 13*
207	A51	50c red	10	5
208	A51	1pi dk car rose	12	6
209	A51	3pi lil rose	18	12
210	A51	5pi violet	30	18

Issued for the "Freedom from Hunger" campaign of the U.N. Food and Agriculture Organization.

Common Defense Emblem   Emblem
A52   A53

1963, July 7   Engraved   *Perf. 13*
211	A52	30c bister	12	6
212	A52	50c lil rose	15	8
213	A52	3pi brt grn	25	12
214	A52	8pi red	40	25

Issued to publicize the common defense effort. The inscription says: "Personalism-Common Progress."

1963, Oct. 26   *Perf. 13*
215	A53	50c rose red	10	7
216	A53	1pi emerald	15	10
217	A53	4pi purple	35	20
218	A53	5pi orange	65	50

Issued to honor the fighting soldiers of the Republic.

Centenary Emblem and Map
A54

1963, Nov. 17   Engraved
Cross in Deep Carmine
219	A54	50c Prus bl	10	8
220	A54	1pi dp car	15	12
221	A54	3pi org yel	20	18
222	A54	6pi brown	45	40

Centenary of International Red Cross.

Book and Scales
A55

1963, Dec. 10   *Perf. 13*
223	A55	70c orange	8	5
224	A55	1pi brt rose	12	5
225	A55	3pi green	15	12
226	A55	8pi ol ocher	40	25

Issued to commemorate the 15th anniversary of the Universal Declaration of Human Rights.

Danhim Hydroelectric Station
A56

1964, Jan. 15   Engraved
227	A56	40c rose red	12	5
228	A56	1pi bis brn	12	5
229	A56	3pi vio bl	18	10
230	A56	8pi ol grn	40	30

Issued to commemorate the inauguration of the Danhim Hydroelectric Station.

Atomic Reactor
A57

1964, Feb. 3   *Perf. 13*
231	A57	80c olive	10	5
232	A57	1.50pi brn org	12	6
233	A57	3pi chocolate	18	10
234	A57	7pi brt bl	35	25

Peaceful uses of atomic energy.

Compass Rose, Barograph and U.N. Emblem   South Vietnamese Gesturing to North Vietnamese; Map
A58   A59

1964, March 23   Engraved
235	A58	50c bister	8	6
236	A58	1pi vermilion	12	8
237	A58	1.50pi rose cl	15	10
238	A58	10pi emerald	45	30

4th World Meteorological Day, Mar. 23.

1964, July 20   *Perf. 13*
239	A59	30c dk grn, ultra & mar	10	5
240	A59	50c dk car rose, yel & blk	12	8
241	A59	1.50pi dk bl, dp org & blk	18	12

This "Unification" issue commemorates the 10th anniversary of the Day of National Grief, July 20, 1954, when the nation was divided into South and North Viet Nam.

Hatien Beach
A60

1964, Sept. 7   Engraved   *Perf. 13½*
| 242 | A60 | 20c brt ultra | 7 | 5 |
| 243 | A60 | 3pi emerald | 30 | 12 |

Revolutionists and "Nov. 1"
A61

Designs: 80c, Soldier breaking chain. 3pi, Broken chain and date: "1–11 1963" (vert.).

1964, Nov. 1   Engraved   *Perf. 13*
244	A61	50c red lil & ind	10	6
245	A61	80c vio & red brn	12	8
246	A61	3pi dk bl & red	22	13

Anniversary of November 1963 revolution.

Temple, Saigon
A62

Designs: 1pi, Royal tombs, Hué. 1.50pi, Fishermen and sailboats at Phan-Thiet beach. 3pi, Temple, Gia-Dhin.

1964–66   *Perf. 13*
Size: 35½x26mm.
247	A62	50c fawn, grn & dl vio	8	5
248	A62	1pi ol bis & ind	10	6
249	A62	1.50pi ol gray & dk sl grn	12	8
250	A62	3pi vio, dk sl grn & cl	28	15

Coil Stamp
Size: 23x17mm.
| 250A | A62 | 1pi ol bis & ind ('66) | 45 | 30 |

Nos. 247–250 were issued Dec. 2, 1964.

Hung Vuong and Au Co with their Children
A63

1965, Apr.   Engraved   *Perf. 13*
| 251 | A63 | 3pi car lake & org red | 35 | 30 |
| 252 | A63 | 100pi brn vio & vio | 3.50 | 2.25 |

Issued to honor the mythological founders of Viet Nam, c. 2000 B.C.

ITU Emblem, Insulator and TV Mast   Buddhist Wheel of Life and Flames
A64   A65

1965, May 17   Engraved
| 253 | A64 | 1pi ol, dp car & bis | 10 | 5 |
| 254 | A64 | 3pi hn brn, car & lil | 28 | 15 |

Issued to commemorate the centenary of the International Telecommunication Union.

1965, May 15   *Perf. 13*
Designs: 1.50pi, Wheel, lotus blossom and world map (horiz.). 3pi, Wheel and Buddhist flag.

Inscribed: "Phat-Giao" (Buddhism)
255	A65	50c dk car	7	5
256	A65	1.50pi dk bl & ocher	15	8
257	A65	3pi org brn & dk brn	18	10

Anniversary of Buddha's birth.

ICY Emblem and Women of Various Races   Ixora
A66   A67

1965, June 26
258	A66	50c bluish blk & bis	8	5
259	A66	1pi dk brn & brn	15	5
260	A66	1.50pi dk red & gray	18	10

International Cooperation Year.

1965, Sept. 10   Engraved   *Perf. 13*
Flowers: 80c, Orchid. 1pi, Chrysanthemum. 1.50pi, Lotus (horiz.). 3pi, Plum blossoms.
261	A67	70c grn, sl grn & red	5	5
262	A67	80c dk brn, lil & sl grn	5	5
263	A67	1pi dk bl & yel	10	8
264	A67	1.50pi sl grn, dl grn & gray	12	8
265	A67	3pi sl grn & org	18	15
		Nos. 261-265 (5)	53	41

Student, Dormitory and Map of Thu Duc
A68

1965, Oct. 15   *Perf. 13*
266	A68	50c dk brn	5	5
267	A68	1pi brt grn	5	5
268	A68	3pi crimson	18	10
269	A68	7pi dk bl vio	50	33

Issued to publicize higher education.

Farm Boy and Girl, Pig and 4-T Emblem
A69

Design: 4pi, Farm boy with chicken, village and 4-T flag.

1965, Nov. 25   Engraved   *Perf. 13*
| 270 | A69 | 3pi emer & dk red | 20 | 15 |
| 271 | A69 | 4pi dl vio & plum | 20 | 15 |

Issued to commemorate the tenth anniversary of the 4-T Clubs and the National Congress of Young Farmers.

Basketball
A70

Designs: 1pi, Javelin. 1.50pi, Hand holding torch, athletic couple. 10pi, Pole vault.

1965, Dec. 14   Engraved   *Perf. 13*
| 272 | A70 | 50c dk car & brn org | 8 | 5 |

944 VIET NAM

273	A70	1pi brn org & red brn	10	6
274	A70	1.50pi brt grn	15	13
275	A70	10pi red lil & brn org	45	25

Radio Tower
A71

Loading Hook and Globe
A72

Design: Radio tower, telephone dial and map of Viet Nam.

1966, Apr. 24 Engraved Perf. 13

| 276 | A71 | 3pi brt bl & brn | 12 | 10 |
| 277 | A71 | 4pi pur, red & blk | 20 | 18 |

Saigon microwave station.

1966, June 22 Engraved Perf. 13

278	A72	3pi gray & dk car rose	12	8
279	A72	4pi ol & dk pur	15	12
280	A72	6pi brt grn & dk bl	25	20

Issued in appreciation of the help given by the free world.

Hands Reaching for Persecuted Refugees
A73

1966, July 20

| 281 | A73 | 3pi brn, vio brn & ol | 12 | 10 |
| 282 | A73 | 7pi cl, vio brn & dk pur | 25 | 20 |

Issued to honor the refugees from communist oppression.

Paper Soldiers, Votive Offering
A74

Designs: 1.50pi, Man and woman making offerings. 3pi, Floating candles in paper boats. 5pi, Woman burning paper offerings.

1966, Aug. 30 Engraved Perf. 13

283	A74	50c red, blk & bis brn	6	5
284	A74	1.50pi brn, emer & grn	8	8
285	A74	3pi rose red & lake	18	12
286	A74	5pi org brn, bis & dk brn	22	15

Wandering Souls Festival.

Oriental Two-string Violin
A75

Vietnamese Instruments: 3pi, Woman playing 16-string guitar. 4pi, Musicians playing two-string guitars. 7pi, Woman and boy playing flutes.

1966 Engraved Perf. 13
Size: 35½x26mm.

287	A75	1pi brn red & brn	10	5
288	A75	3pi rose lil & pur	12	10
289	A75	4pi rose brn & brn	18	12
290	A75	7pi dp bl & vio bl	35	18

Coil Stamp
Size: 23x17mm.

| 290A | A75 | 3pi rose lil & pur | 2.00 | 65 |
| b. | Booklet pane of 5 | | 12.50 | |

Nos. 287–290 were issued Sept. 28. No. 290b contains a vertical strip of 5 with selvage at either end. These strips were also sold loose without booklet cover.

World Health Organization Building, Geneva, and Flag
A76

Designs: 50c, WHO Building and emblem (horiz.). 8pi, WHO flag and building.

1966, Oct. 12

291	A76	50c pur & car	8	5
292	A76	1.50pi red brn, vio bl & blk	12	10
293	A76	8pi grnsh bl, vio bl & brn	25	25

Opening of World Health Organization Headquarters, Geneva.

Hand Holding Spade, and Soldiers
A77

Soldier and Workers
A78

Designs: 1.50pi, Flag, workers, tractor and soldier. 4pi, Soldier and cavalryman.

1966, Nov. 1 Engraved Perf. 13

294	A77	80c dl brn & red brn	6	5
295	A77	1.50pi car rose, yel & brn	8	5
296	A78	3pi brn & sl grn	10	8
297	A78	4pi lil, blk & brn	25	15

Issued to commemorate the 3rd anniversary of the revolution against the government of Pres. Ngo Dinh Diem.

Symbolic Tree and UNESCO Emblem
A79

Designs: 3pi, Globe and olive branches. 7pi, Symbolic temple (horiz.).

1966, Dec. 15 Engr. Perf. 13
| 298 | A79 | 1pi pink, brn & dk car | 8 | 7 |

| 299 | A79 | 3pi dp bl, grn & brn org | 15 | 12 |
| 300 | A79 | 7pi grnsh bl, dk bl & red | 28 | 25 |

Issued to commemorate the 20th anniversary of UNESCO (United Nations Educational, Scientific and Cultural Organization).

Bitter Melon
A80

Designs: 50c, Cashew (vert.). 3pi, Sweetsop. 20pi, Areca nuts.

1967, Jan. 12 Engraved Perf. 13

301	A80	50c brt bl, gray grn & red	6	5
302	A80	1.50pi red brn, yel & org	8	6
303	A80	3pi dk brn, grn & brn	12	8
304	A80	20pi rose brn, sl grn & yel	45	32

Phan-Boi-Chau
A81

Designs: 20pi, Phan-Chau-Trinh portrait and addressing crowd.

1967, March 24 Engraved Perf. 13

| 305 | A81 | 1pi mar, red brn & dk brn | 10 | 5 |
| 306 | A81 | 20pi vio, sl grn & blk | 55 | 50 |

Issued to honor Vietnamese patriots.

Woman Carrying Produce
A82

Designs: 1pi, Market scene. 3pi, Two-wheeled horse cart. 8pi, Farm scene with water buffalo.

1967, May 1 Engraved Perf. 13

307	A82	50c vio bl, dk bl & ultra	5	5
308	A82	1pi sl grn & dl pur	7	5
309	A82	3pi dk car	10	8
310	A82	8pi brt car rose & pur	25	15

Issued for Labor Day.

Potter, Vases and Lamp
A83

Weavers and Potters
A84

Designs: 1.50pi, Vase and basket. 35d, Bag and lacquerware.

1967, July 22 Engraved Perf. 13

311	A83	50c red brn, grn & ultra	5	5
312	A83	1.50pi grnsh bl, car & blk	10	7
313	A84	3pi red, vio & org brn	12	10
314	A83	35pi bis brn, blk & dk red	80	60

Issued to publicize Vietnamese handicrafts.

Wedding Procession
A85

1967, Sept. 18 Engraved Perf. 13
| 315 | A85 | 3pi rose cl, dk vio & red | 22 | 15 |

Symbols of Stage, Music and Art
A86

Lithographed and Engraved
1967, Oct. 27 Perf. 13
| 316 | A86 | 10pi bl gray, blk & red | 35 | 20 |

Issued to publicize the Cultural Institute.

"Freedom and Justice"
A87

Balloting
A88

"Establishment of Democracy"
A89

1967, Nov. 1 Photogravure

317	A87	4pi mag, brn & ocher	13	6
318	A88	5pi brn, yel & blk	15	10
319	A89	30pi dl lil, ind & red	75	60

Issued for National Day and to commemorate the general elections.

Pagoda and Lions Emblem
A90

VIET NAM

1967, Dec. 5 Photo. *Perf. 13½x13*
320 A90 3pi multi   30   20

50th anniversary of Lions International.

Teacher with Pupils and Globe
A91

1967, Dec. 10 *Perf. 13x13½*
321 A91 3pi tan, blk, yel & car   30   10

International Literacy Day, Sept. 8, 1967.

Tractor and Village
A92

Designs: 9pi, Bulldozer and home building. 10pi, Wheelbarrow, tractor and new building. 20pi, Vietnamese and Americans working together.

1968, Jan. 26 Photo. *Perf. 13½*
322 A92 1pi multi   8   5
323 A92 9pi lt bl & multi   22   15
324 A92 10pi multi   35   20
325 A92 20pi yel, red lil & blk 30

Rural construction program.

WHO Emblem—A93

1968, Apr. 7 Photo. *Perf. 13½*
326 A93 10pi gray grn, blk & yel 45 20

Issued to commemorate the 20th anniversary of the World Health Organization.

Flags of Viet Nam's Allies
A94

Designs: 1.50pi, Flags surrounding SEATO emblem. 3pi, Flags, handclasp, globe and map of Viet Nam. 50pi, Flags and handclasp.

1968, June 22 Photo. *Perf. 13½*
327 A94 1pi multi   12   10
328 A94 1.50pi multi   15   12
329 A94 20pi multi   20   18
330 A94 50pi multi   90   80

Issued to honor Viet Nam's allies.

Three-wheeled Truck and Tractor
A95

Designs: 80c, Farmer, city man and symbols of property. 2pi, Three-wheeled cart, taxi and farmers. 30pi, Taxi, three-wheeled cart and tractor in field.

Inscribed: "HUU-SAN-HOA CONG-NHAN VA NONG-DAN"

1968, Nov. 1 Photo. *Perf. 13½*
331 A95 80c multi   5   5
332 A95 2pi stl bl & multi   5   5
333 A95 10pi org brn & multi 20   15
334 A95 30pi gray bl & multi 75   50

Issued to publicize private property ownership.

Human Rights Flame Men of Various Races
A96   A97

1968, Dec. 10 Photo. *Perf. 13½*
335 A96 10pi multi   35   18
336 A97 16pi pur & multi   70   25

International Human Rights Year.

UNICEF Emblem, Mother and Child—A98

Design: 6pi, Children flying kite with UNICEF emblem.

1968, Dec. 11
337 A98 6pi multi   25   18
338 A98 16pi multi 50   27

Issued to honor UNICEF (United Nations Children's Fund).

Workers and Train
A99

Design: 1.50pi, 3pi, Crane, train and map of Viet Nam.

1968, Dec. 15
339 A99 1.50pi multi   12   8
340 A99 3pi org, vio bl & grn 18   12
341 A99 9pi multi   25   15
342 A99 20pi multi   45   30

Reopening of Trans-Viet Nam Railroad.

Farm Woman
A100

Vietnamese Women: 1pi, Merchant. 3pi, Nurses (horiz.). 20pi, Three ladies.

1969, Mar. 23 Engraved *Perf. 13*
343 A100 50c vio bl, lil & ocher   7   5
344 A100 1pi grn, bis & dk brn   8   5
345 A100 3pi brn, blk & bl   10   8
346 A100 20pi lil & multi   55   40

Soldiers and Civilians
A101

Family Welcoming Soldier
A102

1969, June 1 Photo. *Perf. 13*
347 A101 2pi multi   8   5
348 A102 50pi multi   1.10 50

Pacification campaign.

Man Reading Constitution, Scales of Justice
A103

Voters, Torch and Scales
A104

1969, June 9
349 A103 1pi yel org, yel & blk   8   6
350 A104 20pi multi   55 25

Issued to publicize constitutional democracy. Phrase on both stamps: "Democratic and Governed by Law."

Mobile Post Office
A105

Designs (Mobile Post Office): 3pi, Window service. 4pi, Child with letter. 20pi, Crowd at window and postmark: "15, 12, 67."

1969, July 10
351 A105 1pi multi   8   8
352 A105 3pi multi   12   10
353 A105 4pi multi   12   10
354 A105 20pi ocher & multi 35 30

Issued to commemorate the installation of the first mobile post office in Viet Nam.

Mnong-gar Woman
A106

Designs: 1pi, Djarai woman. 50pi, Bahnar man.

1969, Aug. 29 Photo. *Perf. 13*
355 A106 1pi brt pink & multi   8   6
356 A106 6pi sky bl & multi   15   12
357 A106 50pi gray & multi   1.00 60

Issued to honor ethnic minorities in Viet Nam.

Civilians Becoming Soldiers
A107

Designs: 3pi, Bayonet training. 5pi, Guard duty. 10pi, Farewell.

1969, Sept. 20 Inscribed: "TONG BONG VIEN"
358 A107 1.50pi org & multi   8   6
359 A107 3pi pur & multi   12   8
360 A107 5pi blk, red & ocher   15   10
361 A107 10pi pink & multi   25   17

General mobilization.

ILO Emblem and Globe
A108

1969, Oct. 29 Photo. *Perf. 13*
362 A108 6pi bl grn, blk & gray 15   10
363 A108 20pi red, blk & gray   45   25

International Labor Organization, 50th anniversary.

Pegu House Sparrow—A109

Birds: 6pi, Moluccan munia. 7pi, Great hornbill. 30pi, Old world tree sparrow.

1970, Jan. 15 Photo. *Perf. 12½x14*
364 A109 2pi bl & multi   5   5
365 A109 6pi org & multi   15   10
366 A109 7pi org brn & multi   20   13
367 A109 30pi bl & multi   75   40

Burning House and Family—A110

Design: 20pi, Family fleeing burning house and physician examining child.

1970, Jan. 31 Photo. *Perf. 13*
368 A110 10pi multi   25   20
369 A110 20pi multi   50   40

Mau Than disaster, 1968.

Vietnamese Costumes—A111

Traditional Costumes: 1pi, Man, woman and priest (vert.). 2pi, Seated woman with fan. 100pi, Man and woman.

Inscribed: "Y-PHUC CO TRUYEN"

1970, Mar. 13 Photo. *Perf. 13*
370 A111 1pi lt brn & multi   5   5
371 A111 2pi pink & multi   6   5

VIET NAM

372	A111	3pi ultra & multi	8	6
373	A111	100pi multi	1.50	90

Issued for the Trung Sisters' Festival.

Building Workers, Pagodas and Bridge
A112

Design: 20pi, Concrete mixers and scaffolds.

1970, June 10   Litho. & Engr.

374	A112	6pi multi	18	9
375	A112	20pi rose lil, brn & bis	50	32

Issued to publicize the rebuilding of Hué.

Plower in Rice Field
A113

1970, Aug. 29   Perf. 13

376	A113	6pi multi	30	18

Issued to publicize the "Land to the Tiller" agricultural reform program.

New Building and Scaffold
A114

Construction Work
A115

1970, Sept. 15   Engr.   Perf. 13

377	A114	8pi pale ol & brn org	22	15
378	A115	16pi brn, ind & yel	35	18

Reconstruction after 1968 Tet Offensive.

Productivity Year Emblem
A116

1970, Oct. 3

379	A116	10pi multi	30	20

Asian Productivity Year 1970.

Nguyen-Dinh-Chieu
A117

Education Year Emblem
A118

1970, Nov. 16 Engraved   Perf. 13½

380	A117	6pi dl vio, red & brn	15	12
381	A117	10pi grn, red & dk brn	20	15

In memory of Nguyen-Dinh-Chieu (1822–1888), poet.

Lithographed and Engraved

1970, Nov. 30   Perf. 13

382	A118	10pi pale brn, yel & blk	30	15

International Education Year.

Parliament Building
A119

Dancers
A120

Design: 6pi, Senate Building.

1970, Dec.

383	A119	6pi lt bl, cit & dk brn	15	10
384	A119	10pi multi	30	15

No. 383 issued Dec. 8 for the 6th Congress and No. 384 issued Dec. 9 for the 9th General Assembly of the Asian Interparliamentary Union.

1971, Jan. 12

Designs: Various Vietnamese dancers and musicians. 6pi and 7pi horizontal.

385	A120	2pi ultra & multi	8	6
386	A120	6pi pale grn & multi	12	10
387	A120	7pi pink & multi	15	12
388	A120	10pi brn org & multi	18	15

Farmers and Law
A121

Designs: 3pi, Tractor and law, dated 26.3.1970. 16pi, Farmers, people rejoicing and law book.

1971, Mar. 26 Engraved   Perf. 13

389	A121	2pi vio bl, dk brn & dl org	8	5
390	A121	3pi pale grn, brn & dk bl	10	6
391	A121	16pi multi	45	25

Agrarian reform law.

Courier on Horseback
A122

Design: 6pi, Mounted courier with flag.

Engraved and Photogravure

1971, June 6   Perf. 13

392	A122	2pi vio & multi	8	5
393	A122	6pi tan & multi	22	10

Postal history.

Military and Naval Operations on Vietnamese Coast—A123

1971, June 19

394	A123	3pi multi	10	6
395	A123	40pi multi	90	60

Armed Forces Day. Narrow vertical yellow and red label inscribed "Mung Ngay Quan Luc / 19.6.1971" is se-tenant with each stamp.

Deer
A124

Design: 30pi, Tiger.

1971, Aug. 20   Engraved

396	A124	9pi lt grn, bl grn & dk brn	25	15
397	A124	30pi multi	75	50

Rice Harvest
A125

Designs: 30pi, Threshing and winnowing rice and rice plants. 40pi, Bundling and carrying rice.

Lithographed and Engraved

1971, Sept. 28   Perf. 13

398	A125	1pi multi	5	5
399	A125	30pi sal pink, dk pur & blk	55	30
400	A125	40pi sep, yel & grn	70	40

UPU Building, Bern
A126

1971, Nov. 9 Engraved   Perf. 13

401	A126	20pi grn & multi	38	25

Inauguration of the new Universal Postal Union Headquarters (in 1970), Bern, Switzerland.

Fish
A127

Various Fish; 2pi vertical.

1971, Nov. 16   Photo. & Engraved

402	A127	2pi multi	7	5
403	A127	10pi vio & multi	20	13
404	A127	100p lil & multi	1.90	1.35

Mailman and Woman on Water Buffalo
A128

Designs: 10pi, Bird carrying letter. 20pi, Mailman with bicycle delivering mail to villagers.

1971, Dec. 20 Engraved   Perf. 13

Inscribed: "PHAT TRIEN BUU—CHINH NONG THON"

405	A128	5pi multi	15	7
406	A128	10pi multi	25	13
407	A128	20pi multi	45	27

Rural mail.

Trawler Fishermen, and Fish
A129

Designs: 7pi, Net fishing from boat. 50d, Trawler with seine.

1972, Jan. 2   Engraved   Perf. 13

408	A129	4pi pink, blk & bl	12	7
409	A129	7pi lt bl, blk & red	18	8
410	A129	50pi multi	1.00	55

Publicity for fishing industry.

King Quang Trung (1752–1792)
A130

1972, Jan. 28   Perf. 13½

411	A130	6pi red & multi	15	6
a.		Booklet pane of 10	9.00	
412	A130	20pi blk & multi	45	25

No. 411a is imperf. horizontally.

Road Workers
A131

1972, Feb. 4

413	A131	3pi multi	10	6
414	A131	8pi multi	35	12

Community development.

Rice Farming
A132

Design: 10pi, Wheat farming.

1972, Mar. 26   Engr.   Perf. 13½

415	A132	1pi ocher, sl & red	5	5
416	A132	10pi ind & multi	35	15

Farmers' Day, March 26.

Plane over Dalat
A133

1972, Apr. 18   Engr. & Photo.

Multicolored

417	A133	10pi shown	22	12
418	A133	10pi over Ha-tien	22	12
419	A133	10pi over Hue	22	12
420	A133	10pi over Saigon	22	12
a.		Block of 4 (#417-420)	90	60
421	A133	25pi like No. 417	50	40
422	A133	25pi like No. 418	50	40
423	A133	25pi like No. 419	50	40
424	A133	25pi like No. 420	50	40
a.		Block of 4 (#421-424)	2.10	1.75

20 years Air Viet Nam. Stamps of the same denomination are printed se-tenant.

Scholar
A134

Designs: 20pi, Teacher and pupils. 50pi, Scholar and scroll.

1972, May 5   Engr. & Litho.

425	A134	5pi multi	10	5

Engraved

426	A134	20pi lt grn & multi	32	18
427	A134	50pi pink & multi	75	40

Ancient letter writing art.

VIET NAM

Armed Farmer
A135

Designs: 6pi, Civilian rifleman and Self-defense Forces emblem (horiz.). 20pi, Man and woman training with rifles.

Perf. 13

		1972, June 15	Engr. & Litho.		
428	A135	2pi brt rose & multi		5	5
429	A135	6pi multi		10	10
430	A135	20pi lt vio & multi		32	30

Civilian Self-defense Forces.

Hands Holding Safe
A136

1972, July 10

431	A136	10pi lt bl & multi	18	10
432	A136	25pi lt grn & multi	40	30

Treasury Bonds campaign.

Frontier Guard
A137

Soldier Helping Wounded Man
A138

Designs: 10pi, 3 guards and horse (horiz.). 40pi, Marching guards (horiz.).

Engraved and Lithographed

		1972, Aug. 14	Perf. 13		
433	A137	10pi ol & multi		18	12
434	A137	30pi buff & multi		42	35
435	A137	40pi lt bl & multi		60	50

Historic frontier guards.

1972, Sept. 1

Designs: 16pi, Soldier on crutches and flowers. 100pi, Veterans' memorial, map and flag.

436	A138	9pi ol & multi	15	8
437	A138	16pi yel & multi	22	15
438	A138	100pi lt bl & multi	1.25	90

Tank, Memorial, Flag and Map
A139

Soldiers and Map of Viet Nam
A140

		1972, Nov. 25	Litho.	Perf. 13	
439	A139	5pi multi		12	5
440	A140	10pi ultra & multi		30	12

Victory at Binh-Long.

Book Year Emblem and Globe
A141

Designs: 4pi, Emblem, books circling globe. 5pi, Emblem, books and globe.

1972, Nov. 30

441	A141	2pi dp car & multi	5	5
442	A141	4pi bl & multi	10	8
443	A141	5pi yel bis & multi	15	8

International Book Year 1972.

Liberated Vietnamese Family
A142

Soldiers Raising Vietnamese Flag
A143

1973, Feb. 18 Lithographed Perf. 13

444	A142	10pi yel & multi	22	15

To celebrate the 200,000th returnee.

1973, Feb. 24 Litho. Perf. 13

Design: 10pi, Victorious soldiers and map of demilitarized zone (horiz.).

445	A143	3pi lil & multi	12	8
446	A143	10pi lt grn & multi	18	15

Victory at Quang Tri.

Satellite, Storm over Viet Nam
A144

1973, Mar. 23 Litho. Perf. 12½x12

447	A144	1pi lt bl & multi	8	7

World Meteorological Day.

Farmers with Tractor, Symbol of Law
A145

Farmer Plowing with Water Buffalos
A146

Pres. Thieu Holding Agrarian Reform Law
A147

1973, Mar. 26 Litho. Perf. 12½x12

448	A145	2pi lt grn & multi	10	5
449	A146	5pi org & multi	15	10

Perf. 11

450	A147	10pi bl & multi	32.50	

3rd anniversary of the agrarian reform law and to publicize the 5-year plan for rural development. See No. 475.

INTERPOL Emblem and Headquarters
A148

Designs: 2pi, INTERPOL emblem. 25pi, INTERPOL emblem and side view of Headquarters.

1973, Apr. 8 Litho. Perf. 12½x12

451	A148	1pi ol & multi	5	5
452	A148	2pi yel & multi	5	5
453	A148	25pi ocher, lil & brn	40	25

50th anniversary of the International Criminal Police Organization (INTERPOL).

ITU Emblem and Waves
A149

Designs: 2pi, Globe and waves. 3pi, ITU emblem.

1973, May 17

454	A149	1pi dl bl & multi	7	6
455	A149	2pi brt bl & multi	7	6
456	A149	3pi org & multi	7	6

World Telecommunications Day (International Telecommunications Union).

Globe, Hand Holding House
A150

Men Building Pylon
A151

Design: 10pi, Fish in net, symbols of agriculture, industry and transportation.

1973, Nov. 6 Litho. Perf. 12x12½

457	A150	8pi gray & multi	12	5
458	A150	10pi vio bl, blk & gray	15	6
459	A151	15pi blk, org & lil rose	25	8

National development.

Water Buffalos
A152

Design: 10pi, Water buffalo.

1973, Dec. 20 Litho. Perf. 12½x12

460	A152	5pi org & multi	18	5
461	A152	10pi org & multi	28	6

Human Rights Flame, Three Races
A153

Design: 100pi, Human Rights flame, scales and people (vert.).

Perf. 12½x12, 12x12½

1973, Dec. 29

462	A153	15pi ultra & multi	25	12
463	A153	100pi grn & multi	85	42

25th anniversary of Universal Declaration of Human Rights.

"25" and WHO Emblem
A154

Design: 15pi, WHO emblem (different).

1973, Dec. 31 Perf. 12½x12

464	A154	8pi org, bl & brn	15	5
465	A154	15pi lt brn, bl & brt pink	22	13

25th anniversary of World Health Organization.

Sampan Ferry
A155

Design: 10pi, Sampan ferry (different).

1974, Jan. 13 Litho. Perf. 14x13½

466	A155	5pi lt bl & multi	12	8
467	A155	10pi yel grn & multi	18	8

Sampan ferry women.

Soldiers of 7 Nations
A156

American War Memorial
A157

Map of South Viet Nam and Allied Flags
A158

Design: No. 469, Soldiers and flags of South Viet Nam, Korea, USA, Australia, New Zealand, Thailand and Philippines. Same flags shown on 8pi and 60pi.

Perf. 12½x12, 12x12½

1974, Jan. 28

468	A156	8pi multi	8	6
469	A156	15pi lt brn & multi	15	12
470	A157	15pi multi	15	12
471	A158	60pi multi	45	30

In honor of South Viet Nam's allies.

Trung Sisters on Elephants Fighting Chinese
A159

1974, Feb. 27 Litho. Perf. 12½x12

472	A159	8pi grn, cit & blk	8	7
473	A159	15pi dp org & multi	15	12
474	A159	80pi ultra, pink & blk	60	32

Trung Trac and Trung Nhi, queens of Viet Nam, 39–43 A.D. Day of Vietnamese Women.

VIET NAM

Pres. Thieu Type of 1973 and

Farmers Going to Work
A160

Woman Farmer Holding Rice
A161

1974, Mar. 26   Litho.   Perf. 14
475 A147 10pi bl & multi   8   8

Perf. 12½x12, 12x12½
476 A160 20pi yel & multi   25   15
477 A161 70pi bl & multi   60   40

Agriculture Day. Size of No. 475 is 31x50mm, No. 450 is 34x54mm. and printed on thick paper. No. 475 has been extensively redrawn and first line of inscription in bottom panel changed to "26 THANG BA".

Hung Vuong with Bamboo Tallies
A162

Flag Inscribed: Hung Vuong, Founder of Kingdom
A163

1974, Apr. 2   Perf. 14x13½
478 A162 20pi yel & multi   25   17
479 A163 100pi ol & multi   80   60

Hung Vuong, founder of Vietnamese nation and of Hông-Bang Dynasty (2879-258 B.C.).

National Library
A164

Design: 15pi, Library, right facade and Phoenix.

1974, Apr. 14
480 A164 10pi org, brn & blk   15   8
481 A164 15pi multi   22   12

New National Library Building.

Nos. 391 and 437 Surcharged with New Value and Two Bars in Red.

1974   Perf. 13
482 A121 25pi on 16pi multi   35   20
483 A138 25pi on 16pi multi   35   20

Memorial Tower, Saigon
A165

Globe, Crane Lifting Crate
A167

Crane with Flags, Globe and Map of Viet Nam—A166

Perf. 12x12½, 12½x12
1974, June 22   Lithographed
484 A165 10pi bl & multi   8   8
485 A166 20pi multi   18   12
486 A167 60pi yel & multi   55   30

International Aid Day.

Sun and Views of Saigon, Dalat Hué
A168

Cau-Bong Bridge, Nha Trang
A169

Thien-Mu Pagoda, Hué
A170

Perf. 14x13½, 13½x14
1974, July 12
487 A168 5pi bl & multi   15   15
488 A169 10pi bl & multi   15   15
489 A170 15pi yel & multi   28   20

Tourist publicity.

Rhynchostylis Gigantea
A171

Orchids: 20pi, Cypripedium caliosum (vert.). 200pi, Dendrobium nobile.

1974, Aug. 18
490 A171 10pi bl & multi   10   6
491 A171 20pi yel & multi   13   10
492 A171 200pi bis & multi   1.65 1.35

Hands Passing Letter, UPU Emblem
A172

UPU Emblem and Woman
A173

Design: 30pi, World map, bird, UPU emblem.

Perf. 12½x12, 12x12½
1974, Oct. 9   Lithographed
493 A172 20pi ultra & multi   12   10
494 A172 30pi org & multi   18   10
495 A173 300pi gray & multi   1.75 1.20

Centenary of Universal Postal Union.

Nos. 398, 447, 451, 454, 387 Surcharged with New Value and Two Bars in Red

Litho. & Engr., Litho.
1974-75   Perf. 13, 12½x12
496 A125 25pi on 1pi multi   5.00
497 A144 25pi on 1pi multi   5.00
498 A148 25pi on 1pi multi   5.00
499 A149 25pi on 1pi multi   7.50
500 A120 25pi on 7pi multi   7.50

Issue dates: Nos. 497, 499-500, Nov. 18, 1974. Others, Jan. 1, 1975.

Hien Lam Pavilion, Hué
A174

Throne, Imperial Palace, Hué
A175

Water Pavilion, Hué
A176

1975, Jan. 5   Litho.   Perf. 14x13½
501 A174 25pi multi   15   8
502 A175 30pi multi   18   12
503 A176 60pi multi   38   25

Historic sites.

Symbol of Youth, Children Holding Flower
A177

Family and Emblem
A178

1975, Jan. 14   Perf. 11½
504 A177 20pi bl & multi   15   8

Perf. 12½x12
505 A178 70pi yel & multi   50   20

International Conference on Children and National Development.

Unicorn Dance
A179

Boy Lighting Firecracker
A180

Bringing New Year Gifts and Wishes
A181

Perf. 14x13½, 13½x14
1975, Jan. 26   Lithographed
506 A179 20pi multi   10   6
507 A180 30pi bl & multi   15   7
508 A181 100pi bis & multi   38   22

Lunar New Year, Tet.

A182

A183   A184

Designs: 25pi, Military chief from play "San Hau." 40pi, Scene from "Tam Ha Nam Duong." 100pi, Warrior Luu-Kim-Dinh.

1975, Feb. 23
509 A182 25pi rose & multi   10   8
510 A183 40pi lt grn & multi   20   10
511 A184 100pi vio & multi   75   15

National theater.

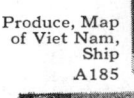 

Produce, Map of Viet Nam, Ship
A185

Irrigation Project
A186

1975, Mar. 26 Litho. Perf. 12½x12
512 A185 10pi multi   7   6
513 A186 50pi multi   50   25

Agriculture Day and 5th anniversary of Agrarian Reform Law.

Nos. 457, 464, 468 Surcharged with New Value and Two Bars in Red

1975   Perf. 12x12½, 12½x12
514 A150 10pi on 8pi multi   8.00 2.00
515 A154 10pi on 8pi multi   4.75   85
516 A156 25pi on 8pi multi   4.75 1.75

Importation Prohibited

The U.S. Treasury Department prohibited the importation of stamps of Viet Nam as of Apr. 30, 1975.

VIET NAM

SEMI-POSTAL STAMPS.

Type of 1952
Surcharged
in Carmine +50c

Perf. 12x12½
1952, Nov. 10   Unwmkd.
B1 A3 1.50pi + 50c bl, yel & brn   2.75   2.75

The surtax was for the Red Cross.

Sabers and Flag—SP1
1952, Dec. 21 Engraved *Perf. 13*
B2   SP1 3.30pi + 1.70pi dp cl   45   45

The surtax was for the Wounded Soldiers'
Aid Organization.

X-ray Camera and Patient
SP2
1960, Aug. 1   *Perf. 13*
B3   SP2 3pi + 50c bl grn & red   25   25

The surtax was for the Anti-Tuberculosis
Foundation.

AIR POST STAMPS.

AP1

AP2
Photogravure.
1952-53 *Perf. 13½x12½* Unwmkd.
C1   AP1 3.30pi dk brn red & pale yel
                grn   25   20
C2   AP1 4pi brn & yel ('53)   40   15
C3   AP1 5.10pi dk vio bl & sal pink 35   25
C4   AP2 6.30pi yel & car   35   30

Issue dates: No. C2, Nov. 24, 1953.
Others, Mar. 8, 1952.

Dragon
AP3

Fish
AP4
1952, Sept. 3   Engraved   *Perf. 13*
C5   AP3 40c red   65   40
C6   AP3 70c green   1.00   40
C7   AP3 80c ultra   1.00   45
C8   AP3 90c brown   1.00   60
C9   AP4 3.70pi dp mag   1.10   55
       Nos. C5-C9 (5)   4.75 2.40

Nos. C5–C9 exist imperforate in a souvenir booklet.

South Viet Nam

Phoenix—AP5
1955, Sept. 7
C10 AP5 4pi vio & lil rose   70   20

Crane Carrying Letter
AP6
1960, Dec. 20.   *Perf. 13*
C11 AP6 1pi olive   15   10
C12 AP6 4pi grn & dk bl 30   18
C13 AP6 5pi ocher & pur 40   28
C14 AP6 10pi dp mag   70   55

POSTAGE DUE STAMPS.

Temple Lion   Dragon
D1   D2
Perf. 13x13½
1952, June 16 Typo.   Unwmkd.
J1   D1 10c red & grn   8   8
J2   D1 20c grn & yel   8   8
J3   D1 30c pur & org   8   8
J4   D1 40c dk grn & sal rose 10   10
J5   D1 50c dp car & gray 15   15
J6   D1 1pi bl & sil   18   18
       Nos. J1-J6 (6)   67   67

South Viet Nam
1955-56
J7   D2 2pi red vio & org   18   18
J8   D2 3pi vio & grnsh bl   25   25
J9   D2 5pi vio & yel   28   25
J10 D2 10pi dk grn & car   40   30
J11 D2 20pi red & brt grn ('56) 1.10   75
J12 D2 30pi brt grn & yel ('56) 1.50 1.20
J13 D2 50pi dk red brn & yel
              ('56)   3.25 2.25
J14 D2 100pi pur & yel ('56)   6.00 5.00
       Nos. J7-J14 (8)   12.96 10.18

Nos. J11–J14 inscribed "BUU-CHINH"
instead of "TIMBRE-TAXE."

Atlas Moth
D3
Design: 3pi, 5pi, 10pi, Three butterflies.
1968, Aug. 20 Photo. *Perf. 13½x13*
J15 D3 50c multi   8   5
J16 D3 1pi multi   8   5
J17 D3 2pi multi   15   8
J18 D3 3pi multi   22   12
J19 D3 5pi multi   40   22
J20 D3 10pi multi   50   30
       Nos. J15-J20 (6) 1.43 82

Nos. J15–J18 Surcharged with New
Value and Two Bars in Red
1974, Oct. 1 Photo. *Perf. 13½x13*
J21 D3 5pi on 3pi multi   3.00
J22 D3 10pi on 50c multi   3.00
J23 D3 40pi on 1pi multi   9.00
J24 D3 60pi on 2pi multi   12.00

MILITARY STAMPS

Soldier
Guarding
Village
MF1
Lithographed
1961, June *Rouletted 7½* Unwmkd.
M1   MF1 ocher, brn, dk grn &
              blk   1.25   75

1961, Sept.   Typographed
M2   MF1 org yel, dk grn &
              brn   1.00   60

Bottom inscription on No. M1 is black,
brown on No. M2.

Battle and
Refugees
MF2
1969, Feb. 22 Litho.   *Imperf.*
M3   MF2 red & grn   3.75
  a. Booklet pane of 10

North Viet Nam

Stamps issued by the Democratic Republic of Viet Nam (Viet Nam Dan Chu Cong Hoa) are not listed. The U.S. Treasury Department (Foreign Assets Control Section) has prohibited their purchase abroad and importation.

WALLIS AND FUTUNA ISLANDS

(wŏl'ĭs & foo·too'nȧ i'lȧndz)

LOCATION—A group of islands in the South Pacific Ocean, northeast of Fiji.
GOVT.—French Overseas Territory.
AREA—106 sq. mi.
POP.—9,900 (est. 1976).
CAPITAL—Mata-Utu, Wallis Island.

100 Centimes = 1 Franc

New Caledonia Stamps of 1905-28 Overprinted in Black or Red

ILES WALLIS et FUTUNA

1920-28 *Perf. 14x13½.* Unwmkd.

1	A16	1c green	5	5
a.		Double ovpt.	32.50	
2	A16	2c red brn	8	8
3	A16	4c bl, org	8	8
4	A16	5c green	12	12
5	A16	5c dl bl ('22)	6	6
6	A16	10c rose	15	15
7	A16	10c grn ('22)	18	18
8	A16	10c red, pink ('25)	40	40
9	A16	15c violet	22	22
10	A17	20c gray brn	28	28
11	A17	25c bl, grn	30	30
12	A17	25c red, yel ('22)	30	30
13	A17	30c brn, org	45	45
14	A17	30c dp rose ('22)	30	30
15	A17	30c red org ('25)	15	15
16	A17	30c lt grn ('27)	60	60
17	A17	35c yel (R)	22	22
18	A17	40c rose, grn	30	30
19	A17	45c vio brn, pnksh	38	38
20	A17	50c red, org	30	30
21	A17	50c dk bl ('22)	30	30
22	A17	50c dk gray ('25)	15	15
23	A17	65c dp bl ('28)	1.40	1.40
24	A17	75c ol grn	60	60

ILES WALLIS et FUTUNA

Overprinted

25	A18	1fr bl, yel grn	1.40	1.40
a.		Triple ovpt.	52.50	
26	A18	1.10fr org brn ('28)	1.10	1.10
27	A18	2fr car, bl	2.10	2.10
28	A18	5fr org (R)	3.75	3.75
		Nos. 1-28 (28)	16.07	16.07

No. 9 Surcharged New Value and Bars in Various Colors

0,01

1922

29	A16	0.01c on 15c vio (Bk)	18	18
30	A16	0.02c on 15c vio (Bl)	18	18
31	A16	0.04c on 15c vio (G)	18	18
32	A16	0.05c on 15c vio (R)	18	18

Stamps and Types of 1920 Surcharged with New Values and Bars in Black or Red.

1924-27

33	A18	25c on 2fr car, bl	22	22
34	A18	25c on 5fr org	22	22
35	A17	65c on 40c red, grn ('25)	30	30
36	A17	85c on 75c ol grn ('25)	30	30
37	A17	90c on 75c dp rose ('27)	45	45
38	A18	1.25fr on 1fr dp bl (R;'26)	22	22
39	A18	1.50fr on 1fr dp bl, bl ('27)	90	90
a.		Double surcharge	70.00	
b.		Surcharge omitted	80.00	
40	A18	3fr on 5fr red vio ('27)	1.50	1.50
a.		Surcharge omitted	80.00	
b.		Double surcharge	80.00	
41	A18	10fr on 5fr ol, lav ('27)	10.00	10.00
42	A18	20fr on 5fr vio rose, yel ('27)	14.00	14.00
		Nos. 33-42 (10)	28.11	28.11

New Caledonia Stamps and Types of 1928-40 Overprinted as in 1920.
Perf. 13½, 14x13, 14x13½.

1930-40

43	A19	1c brn vio & ind	5	5
a.		Double ovpt.	45.00	
44	A19	2c dk brn & yel grn	5	5
45	A19	3c brn vio & ind ('40)	6	6
46	A19	4c org & Prus grn	6	6
47	A19	5c Prus bl & dp ol	6	6
48	A19	10c gray lil & dk brn	6	6
49	A19	15c yel brn & dp bl	6	6
50	A19	20c brn red & dk brn	6	6
51	A19	25c dk grn & dk brn	22	22
52	A20	30c gray grn & bl grn	12	12
53	A20	35c Prus grn & dk grn ('38)	22	22
		Without ovpt.	80.00	
54	A20	40c brt red & ol	12	12
55	A20	45c dp bl & red org	22	22
56	A20	45c bl grn & dl grn ('40)	15	15
57	A20	50c vio & brn	12	12
58	A20	55c bl vio & rose red ('38)	60	60
59	A20	60c vio bl & car ('40)	7	7
60	A20	65c org brn & bl	45	45
61	A20	70c dp rose & brn ('38)	22	22
62	A20	75c Prus bl & ol gray	75	22
63	A20	80c dk cl & grn ('38)	22	22
64	A20	85c grn & brn	1.25	1.25
65	A20	90c dp red & brt red	50	50
66	A20	90c ol grn & rose red ('39)	18	18
67	A21	1fr dp ol & sal red	1.25	1.25
68	A21	1fr rose red & dk car ('38)	55	55
69	A21	1fr brn red & grn ('40)	12	12
70	A21	1.10fr dp grn & brn	10.00	10.00
71	A21	1.25fr brn red & grn ('33)	75	75
72	A21	1.25fr rose red & dk car ('39)	18	18
73	A21	1.40fr dk bl & red org ('40)	18	18
74	A21	1.50fr dp bl & bl	22	22
75	A21	1.60fr dp grn & brn ('40)	32	32
76	A21	1.75fr dk bl & red org ('33)	4.00	4.00
77	A21	1.75fr vio bl ('38)	60	60
78	A21	2fr red org & brn	45	45
79	A21	2.25fr vio bl ('39)	28	28
80	A21	2.50fr brn & lt brn ('40)	40	40
81	A21	3fr mag & brn	45	45
82	A21	5fr dk bl & brn	45	45
83	A21	10fr vio & brn, pnksh	90	90
84	A21	20fr red & brn, yel	1.50	1.50
		Nos. 43-84 (42)	28.59	27.94

Common Design Types pictured in section at front of book.

Colonial Exposition Issue.
Common Design Types
1931, Apr. 13 Engr. *Perf. 12½*
Name of Country Typographed in Black.

85	CD70	40c dp grn	2.25	2.25
86	CD71	50c violet	2.25	2.25
87	CD72	90c red org	2.25	2.25
88	CD73	1.50fr dl bl	2.25	2.25

Colonial Arts Exhibition Issue.
Souvenir Sheet.
Common Design Type
1937 Imperf.

89	CD78	3fr red vio	2.50	2.50

Issued in sheets measuring 118x99 mm. containing one stamp.

New York World's Fair Issue.
Common Design Type
1939, May 10 Engr. *Perf. 12½x12*

90	CD82	1.25fr car lake	60	60
91	CD82	2.25fr ultra	60	60

Petain Issue.
New Caledonia Nos. 216A-216B Overprinted "WALLIS ET FUTUNA" in Lilac or Red.
1941 Engraved *Perf. 12½x12*

92	A21a	1fr bluish grn (L)	28	
93	A21a	2.50fr dk bl (R)	28	

Nos. 92-93 were issued by the Vichy government and were not placed on sale in the dependency.

Six stamps of New Caledonia types A19 and A21 without "RF" were overprinted "ILES WALLIS et FUTUNA" by the Vichy government and issued in 1944, but were not placed on sale in the dependency.

Stamps of 1930-40 with Additional Overprint in Black

France Libre

1941-43 *Perf. 14x13½*

94	A19	1c brn vio & ind	45	45
95	A19	2c brn & yel grn	45	45
96	A19	3c brn vio & ind	47.50	47.50
97	A19	4c org & Prus grn	45	45
98	A19	5c Prus bl & dp ol	45	45
99	A19	10c gray lil & dk brn	45	45
100	A19	15c yel brn & dp bl	45	45
101	A19	20c brn red & dk brn	90	90
102	A19	25c dk grn & dk brn	90	90
103	A20	30c gray grn & bl grn	45	45
104	A20	35c Prus grn & dk grn	45	45
105	A20	40c brt red & ol	90	90
106	A20	45c dp bl & red org	90	90
107	A20	45c bl grn & dl grn	47.50	47.50
108	A20	50c vio & brn	45	45
109	A20	55c bl vio & rose red	45	45
110	A20	60c bl vio & rose red	47.50	47.50
111	A20	65c org brn & bl	45	45
112	A20	70c dp rose & brn	45	45
113	A20	75c Prus bl & ol gray	90	90
114	A20	80c dk cl & grn	90	90
115	A20	85c grn & brn	90	90
116	A20	90c dp red & brt red	75	75
117	A21	1fr rose red & dk car	90	90
118	A21	1.25fr brn red & grn	90	90
119	A21	1.50fr dp bl & bl	60	60
120	A21	1.75fr vio bl	60	60
121	A21	2fr red org & brn	90	90
122	A21	2.50fr brn & lt brn	90.00	90.00
123	A21	3fr mag & brn	45	45
124	A21	5fr dk bl & brn	2.75	2.75
125	A21	10fr vio & brn, pnksh	27.50	27.50
126	A21	20fr red & brn, yel	40.00	40.00
		Nos. 94-126 (33)	319.70	319.70

Ivi Poo, Bone Carving in Tiki Design—A1

Photogravure.
1944 *Perf. 11½x12* Unwmkd.

127	A1	5c lt brn	5	5
128	A1	10c dp gray bl	12	12
129	A1	25c emerald	12	12
130	A1	30c dl org	12	12
131	A1	40c dk sl grn	28	28
132	A1	80c brn red	22	22
133	A1	1fr red vio	10	10
134	A1	1.50fr red	10	10
135	A1	2fr gray blk	18	18
136	A1	2.50fr brt ultra	18	18
137	A1	4fr dk pur	18	18
138	A1	5fr lem yel	22	22
139	A1	10fr chocolate	32	32
140	A1	20fr red	50	50
		Nos. 127-140 (14)	2.63	2.63

Nos. 127, 129 and 136 Surcharged with New Values and Bars in Black or Carmine.

1946

141	A1	50c on 5c lt brn	30	30
142	A1	60c on 5c lt brn	30	30
143	A1	70c on 5c lt brn	22	22
144	A1	1.20fr on 5c lt brn	22	22
145	A1	2.40fr on 25c emer	22	22
146	A1	3fr on 25c emer	22	22
147	A1	4.50fr on 25c emer	45	45
148	A1	15fr on 2.50fr brt ultra (C)	50	
		Nos. 141-148 (8)	2.43	

Military Medal Issue
Common Design Type
1952, Dec. 1 Engr. & Typo. *Perf. 13*

149	CD101	2fr multi	1.25	1.25

Wallis Islander—A2

Engraved.
1957, June 11 *Perf. 13* Unwmkd.

150	A2	3fr dk pur & lil rose	45	45
151	A2	9fr bl, dl lil & vio brn	75	75

Imperforates
Most Wallis and Futuna stamps from 1957 onward exist imperforate in issued and trial colors, and also in small presentation sheets in issued colors.

Flower Issue
Common Design Type
Design: 5fr, Montrouziera (horiz.).
1958, July 7 Photo. *Perf. 12½x12*

152	CD104	5fr multi	2.25	1.50

WALLIS AND FUTUNA ISLANDS

Human Rights Issue
Common Design Type
1958, Dec. 10   Engraved   *Perf. 13*
153   CD105   17fr brt bl & dk bl   2.75   2.75

Universal Declaration of Human Rights, 10th anniversary.

Women Making Tapa Cloth
A3

Kava Ceremony
A4

Designs: 17fr, Dancers. 19fr, Dancers with paddles.

1960, Oct. 19   Engraved   *Perf. 13*
154	A3	5fr dk brn, grn & org brn	45	45
155	A4	7fr dk brn & Prus grn	60	60
156	A4	17fr ultra, cl & grn	1.00	1.00
157	A3	19fr cl & sl	1.20	1.20

Map of South Pacific
A4a

1962, July 19   Photo.   *Perf. 13x12*
158   A4a   16fr multi   2.25   2.25

Issued to commemorate the Fifth South Pacific Conference, Pago Pago, 1962.

Triton
A5

Various Sea Shells
1962-63   Engraved   *Perf. 13*
Size: 22x36mm.
159	A5	25c dk sl grn & brn	45	45
160	A5	1fr grn & brick red	45	45
161	A5	2fr dk bl & red brn	60	60
162	A5	4fr grnsh bl & red brn	1.10	1.10
163	A5	10fr grn, org & vio ('63)	3.00	3.00
164	A5	20fr ultra & red brn ('63)	4.75	4.75
		Nos. 159-164 (6)	10.35	10.35

Red Cross Centenary Issue
Common Design Type
1963, Sept. 2   *Perf. 13*   Unwmkd.
165   CD113   12fr red lil, gray & car   1.75   1.75

Centenary of the International Red Cross.

Human Rights Issue
Common Design Type
1963, Dec. 10   Engraved
166   CD117   29fr dk red & ocher   4.50   4.50

Philatec Issue
Common Design Type
1964, Apr. 15   *Perf. 13*   Unwmkd.
167   CD118   9fr dk sl grn, grn & red   2.00   2.00

See note after Niger No. C42.

Queen Amelia and Ship "Queen Amelia"
A6

1965, Feb. 15   Photo.   *Perf. 12½x13*
168   A6   11fr multi   2.50   2.50

WHO Anniversary Issue
Common Design Type
1968, May 4   Engraved   *Perf. 13*
169   CD126   17fr bl grn, org & lil   3.00   3.00

Issued for the 20th anniversary of the World Health Organization.

Human Rights Year Issue
Common Design Type
1968, Aug. 10   Engraved   *Perf. 13*
170   CD127   19fr dk pur, org brn & brt mag   2.25   2.25

International Human Rights Year.

Outrigger Canoe
A7

1969, Apr. 30   Photo.   *Perf. 13*
171	A7	1fr multi	38	38
		Nos. 171, C31-C35 (6)	18.88	10.73

ILO Issue
Common Design Type
1969, Nov. 24   Engraved   *Perf. 13*
172   CD131   9fr org, brn & bl   2.00   2.00

U.P.U. Headquarters Issue
Common Design Type
1970, May 20   Engraved   *Perf. 13*
173   CD133   21fr lil rose, ind & ol bis   2.25   2.25

No. 157 Surcharged with New Value and Two Bars

1971   Engraved   *Perf. 13*
174   A3   12fr on 19fr cl & sl   90   90

Weight Lifting
A8

Design: 36fr, Basketball.

1971, Oct. 25
175	A8	24fr grn, ind & red brn	1.75	1.75
176	A8	36fr ol, dl red & ultra	2.75	2.75

4th South Pacific Games, Papeete, French Polynesia, Sept. 8-19. See Nos. C37-C38.

De Gaulle Issue
Common Design Type
Designs: 30fr, Gen. de Gaulle, 1940. 70fr, Pres. de Gaulle, 1970.

1971, Nov. 9   Engraved   *Perf. 13*
177	CD134	30fr bl & blk	3.75	2.75
178	CD134	70fr bl & blk	6.75	4.75

First anniversary of the death of Charles de Gaulle (1890-1970), president of France.

Child's Outrigger Canoe
A9

Designs: 16fr, Children's canoe race. 18fr, Outrigger racing canoe.

1972, Oct. 16   Photo.   *Perf. 13x12½*
Size: 35½x26½mm.
179	A9	14fr dk grn & multi	1.10	60
180	A9	16fr dk plum & multi	1.10	60
181	A9	18fr bl & multi	1.50	90

Outrigger sailing canoes. See No. C41.

Rhinoceros Beetle
A10

Insects: 25fr, Cosmopolities sordidus (beetle). 35fr, Ophideres fullonica (moth). 45fr, Dragonfly.

1974, July 29   Photogravure   *Perf. 13*
182	A10	15fr ol & multi	90	60
183	A10	25fr ol & multi	1.10	75
184	A10	35fr gray bl & multi	1.75	1.15
185	A10	45fr multi	2.75	1.75

Georges Pompidou
A11

1975, Dec. 1   Engr.   *Perf. 13*
186   A11   50fr ultra & bl   3.75   3.00

Georges Pompidou (1911-1974), president of France.

Battle of Yorktown and George Washington—A12

Design: 47fr, Virginia Cape Battle and Lafayette.

1976, June 28   Engr.   *Perf. 13*
187	A12	19fr bl, red & ol	1.10	80
188	A12	47fr bl, red & mar	2.50	2.25

American Bicentennial.

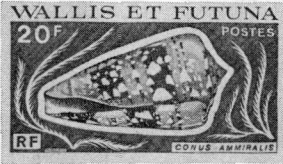

Conus Ammiralis—A13

Sea Shells: 23fr, Cypraea assellus. 43fr, Turbo petholatus. 61fr, Mitra papalis.

1976, Oct. 1   Engraved   *Perf. 13*
189	A13	20fr multi	90	75
190	A13	23fr multi	1.00	75
191	A13	43fr multi	2.25	1.10
192	A13	61fr ultra & multi	3.25	2.25

Father Chanel and Poi Church—A14

Design: 32fr, Father Chanel and map of islands.

1977, Apr. 28   Litho.   *Perf. 12*
193	A14	22fr multi	1.10	60
194	A14	32fr multi	1.40	1.00

Return of the ashes of Father Chanel, missionary.

Bowl, Mortar and Pestle
A15

Handicrafts: 25fr, Wooden bowls and leather bag. 33fr, Wooden comb, club, and boat model. 45fr, War clubs, Futuna. 69fr, Lances.

1977, Sept. 26   Litho.   *Perf. 12½*
195	A15	12fr multi	60	45
196	A15	25fr multi	1.10	75
197	A15	33fr multi	1.20	90
198	A15	45fr multi	1.75	1.30
199	A15	69fr multi	2.75	1.85
		Nos. 195-199 (5)	7.40	5.25

Post Office, Mata Utu—A16

Designs: 50fr, Sia Hospital, Mata Utu. 57fr, Administration Buildings, Mata Utu. 63fr, St. Joseph's Church, Sigave. 120fr, Royal Palace, Mata Utu.

1977, Dec. 12   Lithographed   *Perf. 13*
200	A16	27fr multi	90	80
201	A16	50fr multi	1.75	1.25
202	A16	57fr multi	2.00	1.50
203	A16	63fr multi	2.50	2.25
204	A16	120fr multi	4.75	3.25
		Nos. 200-204 (5)	11.90	9.05

Nos. 187-188 Overprinted:
"JAMES COOK / Bicentenaire de la / découverte des Iles / Hawaii 1778-1978"

1978, Jan. 22   Engr.   *Perf. 13*
205	A12	19fr multi	2.25	2.00
206	A12	47fr multi	4.50	3.00

Bicentenary of the arrival of Capt. Cook in the Hawaiian Islands.

WALLIS AND FUTUNA ISLANDS

Cruiser Triomphant—A17
Warships: 200fr, Destroyers Cap des Palmes and Chevreuil. 280fr, Cruiser Savorgnan de Brazza.

1978, June 18   Photo.   Perf. 13x12½
207	A17	150fr multi	6.75	4.50
208	A17	200fr multi	8.00	6.00
209	A17	280fr multi	11.00	8.00

Free French warships serving in the Pacific, 1940–1944.

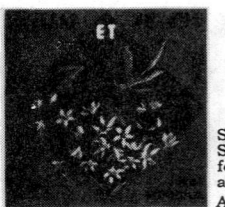
Solanum Seaforthianum A18
Flowers: 24fr, Cassia alata. 29fr, Gloriosa superba. 36fr, Hymenocallis littoralis.

1978, July 11   Photo.   Perf. 13
210	A18	16fr multi	75	60
211	A18	24fr multi	75	60
212	A18	29fr multi	90	75
213	A18	36fr multi	1.50	1.00

Gray Egret A19
Birds: 18fr, Red-footed booby. 28fr, Brown booby. 35fr, White tern.

1978, Sept. 5   Photo.   Perf. 13
214	A19	17fr multi	60	45
215	A19	18fr multi	60	45
216	A19	28fr multi	75	60
217	A19	35fr multi	1.40	1.00

Traditional Patterns—A20
Designs: 55fr, Corpus Christi procession. 59fr, Chief's honor guard.

1978, Oct. 3
218	A20	53fr multi	1.60	1.00
219	A20	55fr multi	2.00	1.25
220	A20	59fr multi	2.25	1.50

Since 1867 American stamp collectors have been using the Scott Catalogue to identify their stamps and Scott Albums to house their collections.

Human Rights Flame A21

1978, Dec. 10   Litho.   Perf. 12½
| 221 | A21 | 44fr multi | 1.50 | 90 |
| 222 | A21 | 56fr multi | 2.25 | 1.40 |

30th anniversary of Universal Declaration of Human Rights.

Fishing Boat—A22
Designs: 30fr, Weighing young tuna. 34fr, Stocking young tunas. 38fr, Measuring tuna. 40fr, Angler catching tuna. 48fr, Adult tuna.

1979, Mar. 19   Litho.   Perf. 12
223	A22	10fr multi	45	38
224	A22	30fr multi	75	60
225	A22	34fr multi	1.00	75
226	A22	38fr multi	1.25	90
227	A22	40fr multi	1.40	1.10
228	A22	48fr multi	1.75	1.25
a.		Souvenir sheet of 6	7.50	7.50
		Nos. 223-228 (6)	6.60	4.98

Tuna tagging by South Pacific Commission. No. 228a contains Nos. 223–228 and 3 labels showing fish lure, inscription and South Pacific Commission emblem. Size: 72x110mm.

Boy with Raft and IYC Emblem A23
Design: 58fr, Girl on horseback.

1979, Apr. 9   Photo.   Perf. 13
| 229 | A23 | 52fr multi | 1.40 | 1.10 |
| 230 | A23 | 58fr multi | 1.75 | 1.25 |

International Year of the Child.

Bombax Ellipticum A24
Designs: 64fr, Callophyllum. 76fr, Pandanus odoratissimus.

1979, Apr. 23   Litho.   Perf. 13
231	A24	50fr multi	1.25	90
232	A24	64fr multi	1.75	1.25
233	A24	76fr multi	2.50	1.50

Green and Withered Landscapes A25

1979, May 28   Photo.   Perf. 13
| 234 | A25 | 22fr multi | 90 | 75 |

Anti-alcoholism campaign.

Crinum A26
Flowers: 42fr, Passiflora. 62fr, Canna indica.

1979, July 16   Photo.   Perf. 12½x13
235	A26	20fr multi	60	45
236	A26	42fr multi	1.25	80
237	A26	62fr multi	1.50	1.10

Swimming—A27
Design: 39fr, High jump.

1979, Aug. 27   Engr.   Perf. 13
| 238 | A27 | 31fr multi | 1.10 | 75 |
| 239 | A27 | 39fr multi | 1.50 | 90 |

6th South Pacific Games, Suva, Fiji, Aug. 27–Sept. 8.

Flower Necklaces—A28
Design: 140fr, Coral necklaces.

1979, Aug. 27   Lithographed
| 240 | A28 | 110fr multi | 2.75 | 1.50 |
| 241 | A28 | 140fr multi | 3.75 | 2.50 |

Trees and Birds, by Sutita—A29
Paintings by Local Artists: 65fr, Birds and Mountain, by M. A. Pilioko (vert.). 78fr, Festival Procession, by Sutita.

Perf. 13x12½, 12½x13

1979, Oct. 8   Lithographed
242	A29	27fr multi	90	60
243	A29	65fr multi	1.75	1.10
244	A29	78fr multi	2.25	1.50

Marine Mantis—A30
Marine Life: 23fr, Hexabranchus sanguineus. 25fr, Spondylus barbatus. 43fr, Gorgon coral. 45fr, Linckia laevigata. 63fr, Tridacna squamosa.

1979, Nov. 5   Photo.   Perf. 13x12½
245	A30	15fr multi	45	38
246	A30	23fr multi	60	45
247	A30	25fr multi	75	45
248	A30	43fr multi	90	70
249	A30	45fr multi	1.10	85
250	A30	63fr multi	1.50	1.40
		Nos. 245-250 (6)	5.30	4.23

Transportation Type of 1979

1980, Feb. 29   Litho.   Perf. 13
251	AP32	1fr like #C87	12	5
252	AP32	3fr like #C88	12	5
253	AP32	5fr like #C89	15	8

Radio Station and Tower—A31

1980, Apr. 21   Litho.   Perf. 13
| 254 | A31 | 47fr multi | 1.25 | 75 |

Radio station FR3, 1st anniversary.

Jesus Laid in the Tomb, by Maurice Denis—A32

1980, Apr. 28   Perf. 13x12½
| 255 | A32 | 25fr multi | 90 | 60 |

Easter 1980.

Gnathodentex Mossambicus—A33

1980, Aug. 25   Litho.   Perf. 12½x13
256	A33	23fr shown	60	45
257	A33	27fr Pristipomoides filamentosus	75	60
258	A33	32fr Etelis carbunculus	75	60
259	A33	51fr Cephalopholis wallisi	1.10	90
260	A33	59fr Aphareus rutilans	1.40	1.25
		Nos. 256-260 (5)	4.60	3.80

Nos. 256-260 se-tenant.

No. 228 Surcharged:

SYDPEX 80

29 Septembre

1980		Litho.		Perf. 12	
261	A22	50fr on 48fr multi		1.25	90

Sydpex 80 Philatelic Exhibition, Sydney.

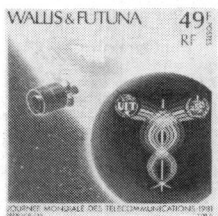

13th World Telecommunications Day—A34

1981, May 17		Litho.		Perf. 12½	
262	A34	49fr multi		90	75

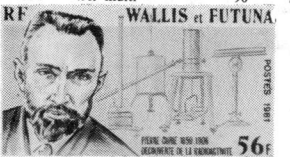

Pierre Curie and Laboratory Equipment—A35

1981, May 25		Litho.		Perf. 13	
263	A35	56fr multi		1.00	85

Pierre Curie (1859-1906), discoverer of radioactivity.

Conus Textile—A36

Designs: Marine life.

1981, June 22			Perf. 12½x13	
264	A36	28fr Favites	50	45
265	A36	30fr Cyanophycees	60	50
266	A36	31fr Ceratium vultur	60	50
267	A36	35fr Amphiprion frenatus	65	60
268	A36	40fr shown	75	65
269	A36	55fr Comatule	1.00	95
		Nos. 264-269 (6)	4.10	3.65

60th Anniv. of Anti-tuberculin Vaccine (Developed by Calmette and Guerin)—A37

1981, July 28		Litho.		Perf. 13	
270	A37	27fr multi		50	45

Intl. Year of the Disabled—A38

1981, Aug. 17					
271	A38	42fr multi		90	75

No. 245 Surcharged in Red.

1981, Sept.		Photo.		Perf. 13x12½	
272	A30	5fr on 15fr multi		15	12

Thomas Edison (1847-1931) and his Phonograph, 1878—A39

1981, Sept. 5		Engr.		Perf. 13	
273	A39	59fr multi		1.10	90

Battle of Yorktown, 1781 (American Revolution)—A40

1981, Oct. 19		Engr.		Perf. 13	
274	A40	66fr Admiral de Grasse	1.10	90
275	A40	74fr Sea battle, vert.	1.40	1.00

200-Mile Zone Surveillance—A41

1981, Dec. 4		Litho.		Perf. 13	
276	A41	60fr Patrol boat Dieppoise	1.00	90
277	A41	85fr Protet	1.75	1.40

TB Bacillus Centenary—A42

1982, Mar. 24		Litho.		Perf. 13	
278	A42	45fr multi		75	60

Flower Type of 1979 in Changed Colors

1982, May 3		Photo.		Perf. 12½x13	
279	A26	1fr like #235		5	5
280	A26	2fr like #236		6	5
281	A26	3fr like #237		8	5

PHILEXFRANCE '82 Intl. Stamp Exhibition, Paris, June 11-21—A43

1982, May 12		Engr.		Perf. 13	
282	A43	140fr #25		2.75	2.25

Acanthe Phippium—A44

Orchids and rubiaceae (83fr).

1982, May 24		Litho.		Perf. 12½x13	
283	A44	34fr shown		60	50
284	A44	68fr Acanthe phippium, diff.	1.10	1.10
285	A44	70fr Spathoglottis pacifica	1.20	1.10
286	A44	83fr Mussaenda raiateensis	1.40	1.40

Scouting Year—A45

1982, June 21			Perf. 12½	
287	A45	80fr Baden-Powell	1.35	1.10

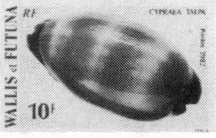

Cypraea Talpa—A46

Porcelaines shells.

1982, June 28			Perf. 12½x13	
288	A46	10fr shown	18	15
289	A46	15fr Cypraea vitellus	28	22
290	A46	25fr Cypraea argus	40	38
291	A46	27fr Cypraea carneola	45	38
292	A46	40fr Cypraea mappa	65	50
293	A46	50fr Cypraea tigris	85	60
		Nos. 288-293 (6)	2.81	2.23

Gorgones Milithea—A47

Marine Life.

1982, Oct. 1		Photo.		Perf. 13x12½	
294	A47	32fr shown		50	45
295	A47	35fr Linckia laevigata	60	50
296	A47	46fr Haxabranchus sanguineus	75	60
297	A47	63fr Spondylus barbatus	1.05	90

St. Teresa of Jesus of Avila (1515-1582)—A48

1982, Nov. 8		Engr.		Perf. 13	
298	A48	31fr multi		52	45

Traditional House—A49

1983, Jan. 20		Litho.		Perf. 13	
299	A49	19fr multi		32	20

Gustave Eiffel (1832-1923), Architect—A50

1983, Feb. 14		Engr.		Perf. 13	
300	A50	97fr multi		1.50	1.00

BANGKOK '83 Intl. Stamp Show, Aug. 4-13—A51

1983, June 28		Engr.		Perf. 13	
301	A51	92fr Thai dancer, 19th cent.	1.90	90

World Communications Year—A52

1983, Aug. 23		Litho.		Perf. 13x13½	
302	A52	20fr multi		50	30

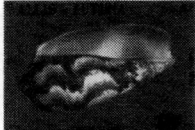

Cone Shells—A53

1983, Oct. 14 Litho. Perf. 13
303	A53	10fr Conus Tulipa	15	10
304	A53	17fr Conus Capitaneus	25	16
305	A53	21fr Conus Virgo	30	20
306	A53	39fr Conus Vitulinus	60	40
307	A53	52fr Conus Marmoreus	75	50
308	A53	65fr Conus Leopardus	1.00	65
		Nos. 303-308 (6)	3.05	2.01

Shell Type of 1983

1984 Litho. Perf. 13
309	A53	22fr Strombus lentiginosus	32	20
310	A53	25fr Lambis chiragra	38	25
311	A53	35fr Strombus dentatus	55	35
312	A53	43fr Lambis scorpius	65	45
313	A53	49fr Strombus aurisdianae	75	50
314	A53	76fr Lambis crocata	1.15	75
		Nos. 309-314 (6)	3.80	2.50

No. 298 Redrawn with Espana '84 Emblem.

1984, Apr. 27 Engr. Perf. 13
315	A48	70fr multi	1.10	70

Denis Diderot (1713-84), Philosopher—A54

1984, May 11
316	A54	100fr Portrait, encyclopedia titlepage	1.50	1.00

SEMI-POSTAL STAMPS.
French Revolution Issue
Common Design Type
Photogravure.
Name and Value Typo. in Black.

1939, July 5 Perf. 13 Unwmkd.
B1	CD83	45(c) +25(c) grn	4.50	4.50
B2	CD83	70(c) +30(c) brn	4.50	4.50
B3	CD83	90(c) +35(c) red org	4.50	4.50
B4	CD83	1.25fr +1fr rose pink	4.50	4.50
B5	CD83	2.25fr +2fr bl	4.50	4.50
		Nos. B1-B5 (5)	22.50	22.50

New Caledonia Nos. B10 and B12 Overprinted "WALLIS ET FUTUNA" in Blue or Red, and Common Design Type

1941 Photogravure Perf. 13½
B6	SP2	1fr +1fr red	60	
B7	CD86	1.50fr +3fr mar	60	
B8	SP3	2.50fr +1fr dk bl	60	

Nos. B6–B8 were issued by the Vichy government and were not placed on sale in the dependency.
In 1944 Nos. 92–93 were surcharged "OEUVRES COLONIALES" and surtax (including change of denomination of the 2.50fr to 50c). These were issued by the Vichy government and not placed on sale in Wallis and Futuna.

Red Cross Issue
Common Design Type
1944 Photo. Perf. 14½x14
B9	CD90	5fr +20fr red org	75	75

The surtax was for the French Red Cross and national relief.

AIR POST STAMPS.
Victory Issue
Common Design Type
Engraved.
1946, May 8 Perf. 12½ Unwmkd.
C1	CD92	8fr dk vio	45	45

Issued to commemorate the European victory of the Allied Nations in World War II.

Chad to Rhine Issue
Common Design Types
1946
C2	CD93	5fr dk vio	45	45
C3	CD94	10fr dk sl grn	45	45
C4	CD95	15fr vio brn	45	45
C5	CD96	20fr brt ultra	60	60
C6	CD97	25fr brn org	90	90
C7	CD98	50fr carmine	1.00	1.00
		Nos. C2-C7 (6)	3.85	3.85

Types of New Caledonia Air Post Stamps of 1948, Overprinted in Blue:

WALLIS ET FUTUNA
Perf. 13x12½, 12½x13

1949, July 4
C8	AP2	50fr yel & rose red	3.00	3.00
C9	AP3	100fr yel & red brn	4.50	4.50

The overprint on No. C9 is in three lines.

U. P. U. Issue.
Common Design Type
1949, July 4 Engraved Perf. 13
C10	CD99	10fr multi	3.75	3.75

Issued to commemorate the 75th anniversary of the formation of the Universal Postal Union.

Liberation Issue
Common Design Type
1954, June 6
C11	CD102	3fr sep & vio brn	3.25	3.25

Liberation of France, 10th anniversary.

WALLIS AND FUTUNA ISLANDS

Father Louis Marie Chanel—AP1
1955, Nov. 21   Perf. 13   Unwmkd.
C12   AP1   14fr dk grn, grnsh bl &
              ind   1.25   90

Issued in honor of Father Chanel, martyred missionary to the Islands.

View of Mata-Utu, Queen Amelia
and Msgr. Bataillon—AP2

Design: 33fr, Map of islands and sailing ship.
1960, Sept. 19   Engraved   Perf. 13
C13   AP2   21fr bl, brn & grn   2.25   2.25
C14   AP2   33fr ultra, choc & bl grn   3.75   3.75

Shell Diver—AP3
1962, Sept. 20   Perf. 13   Unwmkd.
C16   AP3   100fr bl, grn & dk red
              brn   12.50   9.50

Telstar Issue
Common Design Type
1962, Dec. 5
C17   CD111 12fr dk pur, mar & bl   2.25   2.25

Sea Shell Type of Regular Issue, 1962
Design: 50fr, Harpa ventricosa.
1963, Apr. 1   Engraved
Size: 26x47mm.
C18   A5   50fr lil rose, Prus grn &
              red brn   6.00   4.50

Javelin Thrower
AP4
1964, Oct. 10   Engraved   Perf. 13
C19   AP4   31fr emer, ver & vio brn   11.50   9.00

18th Olympic Games, Tokyo, Oct. 10–25.

ITU Issue
Common Design Type
1965, May 17   Perf. 13   Unwmkd.
C20   CD120 50fr dp lil rose, dk brn
              & brn red   12.50   11.00

Issued to commemorate the centenary of the International Telecommunication Union.

Mata-Utu Wharf—AP5
1965, Nov. 26   Engraved   Perf. 13
C21   AP5   27fr brt bl, sl grn & red
              brn   2.50   2.25

French Satellite A-1 Issue
Common Design Type
Designs: 7fr, Diamant rocket and launching installations. 10fr, A-1 satellite.
1966, Jan. 17   Engraved   Perf. 13
C22   CD121 7fr crim, red & car lake   2.50   2.50
C23   CD121 10fr car lake, red & crim 2.50   2.50
  a.   Strip of 2 + label   5.25   5.25

Issued to commemorate the launching of France's first satellite, Nov. 26, 1965. No. C23a contains one each of Nos. C22–C23 and crimson label with commemorative inscription. Each sheet contains 16 triptychs (2x8).

French Satellite D-1 Issue
Common Design Type
1966, June 2   Engraved   Perf. 13
C24   CD122 10fr lake, bl grn & red   2.25   2.25

Issued to commemorate the launching of the D-1 satellite at Hammaguir, Algeria, Feb. 17, 1966.

WHO Headquarters, Geneva, and Emblem AP6
1966, July 5   Photo.   Perf. 12½x13
C25   AP6   30fr org, mar & bl   2.75   2.75

Issued to commemorate the inauguration of World Health Organization Headquarters, Geneva.

Girl and Boy Reading; UNESCO Emblem—AP7
1966, Nov. 4   Engraved   Perf. 13
C26   AP7   50fr grn, org & choc   3.75   3.25

Issued to commemorate the 20th anniversary of UNESCO (United Nations Educational, Scientific and Cultural Organization).

Athlete and Pattern
AP8

Design: 38fr, Woman ballplayer and pattern.
1966, Dec. 8   Engr.   Perf. 13x12½
C27   AP8   32fr bl, dp car & blk   2.75   2.25
C28   AP8   38fr emer & brt pink   3.00   2.50

Issued to commemorate the Second South Pacific Games, Nouméa, Dec. 8–18.

Samuel Wallis' Ship and Coast of Wallis Island—AP9
1967, Dec. 16   Photo.   Perf. 13
C29   AP9   12fr multi   3.75   3.00

Issued to commemorate the bicentenary of the discovery of Wallis Island.

Concorde Issue
Common Design Type
1969, Apr. 17   Engraved   Perf. 13
C30   CD129 20fr blk & plum   7.50   6.00

Man Climbing Coconut Palm—AP10
Designs: 32fr, Horseback rider. 38fr, Men making wooden stools. 50fr, Spear fisherman and man holding basket with fish. 100fr, Women sorting coconuts.
1969, Apr. 30   Photo.   Perf. 13
C31   AP10 20fr multi   1.50   85
C32   AP10 32fr multi   2.50   1.25
C33   AP10 38fr multi   3.00   1.75
C34   AP10 50fr multi   4.00   2.50
C35   AP10 100fr multi   7.50   4.00
      Nos. C31-C35 (5)   18.50   10.35

No. C14 Surcharged with New Value and Three Bars
1971   Engraved   Perf. 13
C36   AP2   21fr on 33fr multi   2.50   2.50

Pole Vault—AP11
Design: 54fr, Archery.
1971, Oct. 25   Engraved   Perf. 13
C37   AP11 48fr sl grn, vio & red
              brn   3.25   2.25
C38   AP11 54fr cl, car & ultra   4.00   3.25

4th South Pacific Games, Papeete, French Polynesia, Sept. 8–19.

South Pacific Commission Headquarters, Noumea—AP12

1972, Feb. 5   Photogravure   Perf. 13
C39   AP12 44fr bl & multi   3.25   2.75

South Pacific Commission, 25th anniversary.

Round House and Festival Emblem—AP13
1972, May 15   Engraved   Perf. 13
C40   AP13 60fr dp car, grn & pur   3.75   2.75

South Pacific Festival of Arts, Fiji, May 6–20.

Canoe Type of Regular Issue
Design: 200fr, Outrigger sailing canoe race, and island woman.
1972, Oct. 16   Photo.   Perf. 13x12½
Size: 47½x28mm.
C41   A9   200fr multi   13.00   9.00

La Pérouse and "La Boussole"
AP14
Explorers and their Ships: 28fr, Samuel Wallis and "Dolphin." 40fr, Dumont D'Urville and "Astrolabe." 72fr, Bougainville and "La Boudeuse."
1973, July 20   Engraved   Perf. 13
C42   AP14 22fr brn, sl & car   1.25   90
C43   AP14 28fr sl grn, dl red & bl   1.75   1.25
C44   AP14 40fr brn, ind & ultra   2.25   1.75
C45   AP14 72fr brn, bl & pur   3.75   3.00

Charles de Gaulle—AP15
1973, Nov. 9   Engraved   Perf. 13
C46   AP15 107fr brn org & dk brn   6.25   4.75

Pres. Charles de Gaulle (1890–1970).

Red Jasmine
AP16

WALLIS AND FUTUNA ISLANDS

Designs: Flowers from Wallis.
1973, Dec. 6 Photogravure *Perf. 13*
Multicolored

C47	AP16	12fr *shown*	.90	.60
C48	AP16	17fr *Magaguabush magnifica*	.95	.60
C49	AP16	19fr *Phaeomeria magnifica*	1.20	.90
C50	AP16	21fr *Hibiscus*	1.20	.90
C51	AP16	23fr *Allamanda cathartica*	1.50	1.00
C52	AP16	27fr *Barringtonia*	1.50	1.00
C53	AP16	39fr *Flowers in vase*	3.50	2.50
		Nos. C47-C53 (7)	10.75	7.50

UPU Emblem and Symbolic Design—AP17

1974, Oct. 9 Engr. *Perf. 13*
C54 AP17 51fr multi 3.00 3.00
Centenary of Universal Postal Union.

Holy Family, Primitive Painting—AP18

1974, Dec. 9 Photogravure *Perf. 13*
C55 AP18 150fr multi 6.75 5.25
Christmas 1974.

Tapa Cloth—AP19

Designs (Tapa Cloth): 24fr, Village scene. 36fr, Fish and marine life. 80fr, Marine life, map of islands, village scene.

1975, Feb. 3 Photo. *Perf. 13*
C56	AP19	3fr multi	.45	.30
C57	AP19	24fr multi	1.40	.95
C58	AP19	36fr multi	2.00	1.40
C59	AP19	80fr multi	4.50	3.25

DC-7 in Flight—AP20

1975, Aug. 13 Engr. *Perf. 13*
C60 AP20 100fr multi 4.50 3.75
First regular air service between Nouméa, New Caledonia, and Wallis.

Volleyball—AP21

Design (Games' Emblem and): 44fr, Soccer. 56fr, Javelin. 1.05fr Spear fishing.

1975, Nov. 10 Photo. *Perf. 13*
C61	AP21	26fr dp org & multi	1.10	.75
C62	AP21	44fr lil & multi	2.00	1.10
C63	AP21	56fr lt grn & multi	2.50	1.85
C64	AP21	105fr bl & multi	6.00	4.50

5th South Pacific Games, Guam, Aug. 1–10.

Lalolalo Lake, Wallis—AP22

Landscapes: 29fr, Vasavasa, Futuna. 41fr, Sigave Bay, Futuna. 68fr, Gahi Bay, Wallis.

1975, Dec. 1 Litho. *Perf. 13*
C65	AP22	10fr grn & multi	.60	.55
C66	AP22	29fr grn & multi	1.75	.95
C67	AP22	41fr grn & multi	2.25	1.50
C68	AP22	68fr grn & multi	3.25	2.50

Concorde, Eiffel Tower and Sugar Loaf Mountain—AP23

1976, Jan. 21 Engr. *Perf. 13*
C69 AP23 250fr multi 13.00 10.00
First commercial flight of supersonic jet Concorde from Paris to Rio de Janeiro, Jan. 21.

Hammer Throw and Stadium—AP24

Design: 39fr, Diving, Stadium and maple leaf.

1976, Aug. 2 Engr. *Perf. 13*
| C70 | AP24 | 31fr multi | 1.50 | .90 |
| C71 | AP24 | 39fr multi | 2.25 | 1.40 |

21st Olympic Games, Montreal, Canada, July 17–Aug. 1.

De Gaulle Memorial—AP25

Photogravure and Embossed
1977, June 18 *Perf. 13*
C72 AP25 100fr gold & multi 4.50 3.25
5th anniversary of dedication of De Gaulle Memorial at Colombey-les-Deux-Eglises.

No. C69 Overprinted in Dark Brown:
"PARIS NEW-YORK / 22.11.77 / 1er VOL COMMERCIAL"

1977, Nov. 22 Engr. *Perf. 13*
C73 AP23 250fr multi 10.00 8.00
Concorde, first commercial flight, Paris to New York.

Balistes Niger—AP26

Fish: 35fr, Amphiprion akindynos. 49fr, Pomacanthus imperator. 51fr, Zanclus cornutus.

1978, Jan. 31 Litho. *Perf. 13*
C74	AP26	26fr multi	.75	.60
C75	AP26	35fr multi	1.10	.90
C76	AP26	49fr multi	1.75	1.50
C77	AP26	51fr multi	2.25	1.75

Map of Futuna and Alofi Islands—AP27

Design: 500fr, Map of Wallis and Uvea Islands (vert.).

1978, Mar. 7 Engraved
| C78 | AP27 | 300fr vio bl & grnsh bl | 10.00 | 9.00 |
| C79 | AP27 | 500fr multi | 16.00 | 13.00 |

Father Bataillon, Churches on Wallis and Futuna Islands—AP28

Design: 72fr, Monsignor Pompallier, map of Wallis, Futuna and Alofi Islands, outrigger canoe.

1978, Apr. 28 Litho. *Perf. 13x12½*
| C80 | AP28 | 60fr multi | 1.75 | 1.40 |
| C81 | AP28 | 72fr multi | 2.50 | 2.00 |

First French missionaries on Wallis and Futuna Islands.

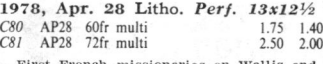

ITU Emblem—AP29

1978, May 17 Litho. *Perf. 13*
C82 AP29 66fr multi 2.25 1.50
10th World Telecommunications Day.

Nativity and Longhouse—AP30

1978, Dec. 4 Photo. *Perf. 13*
C83 AP30 160fr multi 5.25 4.00
Christmas 1978.

Popes Paul VI and John Paul I, St. Peter's, Rome—AP31

Designs: 37fr, Pope Paul VI (vert.). 41fr, Pope John Paul I (vert.).

Perf. 12½x13, 13x12½
1979, Jan. 31 Lithographed
C84	AP31	37fr multi	1.00	.75
C85	AP31	41fr multi	1.50	1.10
C86	AP31	105fr multi	3.50	2.25

In memory of Popes Paul VI and John Paul I.

Monoplane of UTA Airlines—AP32

Designs: 68fr, Freighter Muana. 80fr, Hihifo Airport.

1979, Feb. 28 *Perf. 13x12½*
C87	AP32	46fr multi	1.10	.75
C88	AP32	68fr multi	1.50	1.10
C89	AP32	80fr multi	2.25	1.50

Inter-Island transportation.

France No. 67 and Eole Weather Satellite—AP33

WALLIS AND FUTUNA ISLANDS

Designs: 70fr, Hibiscus and stamp similar to No. 25 (vert.). 90fr, Rowland Hill and Penny Black. 100fr, Birds, Kano School, Japan 17th century, and Japan No. 9.

1979, May 7	Photo.		Perf. 13
C90	AP33 5fr multi	38	22
C91	AP33 70fr multi	1.75	1.10
C92	AP33 90fr multi	2.25	1.25
C93	AP33 100fr multi	2.75	2.00

Sir Rowland Hill (1795-1879), originator of penny postage.

Cross of Lorraine and People—AP34

1979, June 18	Engr.		Perf. 13
C94	AP34 33fr multi	1.10	90

Map of Islands, Arms of France AP35

1979, July 19	Photo.		Perf. 13
C95	AP35 47fr multi	1.50	95

Visit of Pres. Valery Giscard d'Estaing of France.

Capt. Cook, Ships and Island—AP36

1979, July 28			
C96	AP36 130fr multi	3.75	3.50

Bicentenary of the death of Capt. James Cook (1728-1779).

Telecom Emblem, Satellite, Receiving Station—AP37

1979, Sept. 20	Litho.		Perf. 13
C97	AP37 120fr multi	3.25	2.50

3rd World Telecommunications Exhibition, Geneva, Sept. 20-26.

See "Special Notices" at the front of this volume for data on the listing methods of this Catalogue, abbreviations, condition, prices and examination.

Virgin and Child, by Albrecht Durer AP38

1979, Dec. 17	Engr.		Perf. 13
C98	AP38 180fr red & blk	5.25	4.00

Christmas 1979.

Rotary International, 75th Anniversary—AP39

1980, Feb. 29	Litho.		Perf. 13
C99	AP39 86fr multi	2.50	2.25

Rochambeau and Troops, U.S. Flag, 1780—AP40

1980, May 27	Engraved		Perf. 13
C100	AP40 102fr multi	2.50	2.25

Rochambeau's landing at Newport, R.I. (American Revolution), bicentenary.

National Day, 10th Anniversary—AP41

1980, July 15	Litho.		Perf. 13
C101	AP41 71fr multi	1.50	1.10

Transatlantic Airmail Flight, 50th Anniversary—AP42

1980, Sept. 22	Engraved		Perf. 13
C102	AP42 122fr multi	3.00	2.25

Fleming, Penicillin Bacilli—AP43

1980, Oct. 20			
C103	AP43 101fr multi	2.25	1.50

Alexander Fleming (1881-1955), discoverer of penicillin, 25th death anniversary.

Charles De Gaulle, 10th Anniversary of Death—AP44

1980, Nov. 9	Engraved		Perf. 13
C104	AP44 200fr sep & dk ol grn	4.50	3.00

Virgin and Child with St. Catherine, by Lorenzo Lotto—AP45

1980, Dec. 20	Litho.		Perf. 13x12½
C105	AP45 150fr multi	3.25	2.50

Christmas 1980.

Alan B. Shepard and Spacecraft—AP46

20th Anniversary of Space Flight: 44fr, Yuri Gagarin.

1981, May 11	Litho.		Perf. 13
C106	AP46 37fr multi	75	60
C107	AP46 44fr multi	90	75

Vase of Flowers, by Paul Cezanne (1839-1906)—AP47

Design: 135fr, Harlequin, by Pablo Picasso.

1981, Oct. 22	Litho.		Perf. 12½x13
C108	AP47 53fr multi	1.10	90
C109	AP47 135fr multi	2.50	2.00

Espana '82 World Cup Soccer—AP48

1981, Nov. 16	Engr.		Perf. 13
C110	AP48 120fr multi	2.25	1.75

1982	Engr.		Perf. 13
C110A	AP48 12Cfr lil, brn & ol grn	2.00	1.50

Christmas 1981—AP49

1981, Dec. 21	Litho.		Perf. 12½
C111	AP49 180fr multi	3.75	3.00

Tapestry, by Pilioho Aloi—AP50

1982, Feb. 22	Litho.		Perf. 12½x13
C112	AP50 100fr multi	1.75	1.50

Boats at Collioure, by George Braque
(1882-1963)—AP51

1982, Apr. 13	Litho.	Perf. 12½x13
C113	AP51 300fr multi	5.25 4.00

Santos-Dumont (1873-1932), Aviation Pioneer—AP52

1982, July 24
C114 AP52 95fr multi   1.75 1.40

No. C110 Overprinted with Winner's Name in Blue

1982, Aug. 26   Engr.   Perf. 13
C115 AP48 120fr multi   2.25 2.00
Italy's victory in 1982 World Cup.

French Overseas Possessions Week, Sept. 18-25—AP53

1982, Sept. 17   Litho.
C116 AP53 105fr Beach   1.75 1.50

Day of the Blind—AP54

1982, Oct. 18   Engr.
C117 AP54 130fr red & bl   2.25 1.75

Christmas 1982—AP55
Design: Adoration of the Virgin, by Correggio.

1982, Dec. 20	Litho.	Perf. 12½x13
C118	AP55 170fr multi	2.75 2.25

Wind Surfing (1984 Olympic Event)—AP56

1983, Mar. 4   Litho.   Perf. 13
C119 AP56 270fr multi   4.00 2.50

World UPU Day—AP57

1983, Mar. 30   Litho.   Perf. 13
C120 AP57 100fr multi   1.75 1.50

Manned Flight Bicentenary—AP58

1983, Apr. 25   Litho.   Perf. 13
C121 AP58 205fr Montgolfiere   3.50 3.00

Cat, 1926, by Foujita (d. 1968)—AP59

1983, May 20   Litho.   Perf. 12½x13
C122 AP59 102fr multi   2.25 1.60

Pre-Olympic Year—AP60

1983, July 5   Engr.   Perf. 13
C123 AP60 250fr Javelin   5.50 3.75

Alfred Nobel (1833-1896)—AP61

1983, Aug. 1   Engr.   Perf. 13
C124 AP61 150fr multi   3.50 2.00

Nicephore Niepce (1765-1833) Photography Pioneer—AP62

1983, Sept. 20   Engr.   Perf. 13
C125 AP62 75fr dk grn & rose vio 1.75 1.00

Raphael (1483-1520), 500th Birth Anniv.—AP63

1983, Nov. 10   Litho.   Perf. 12½x13
C126 AP63 167fr The Triumph of Galatea 2.50 1.50

Pandanus—AP64

1983, Nov. 30   Litho.   Perf. 13
C127 AP64 137fr multi   2.00 1.25

Christmas 1983—AP65

1983, Dec. 22   Litho.   Perf. 12½x13
C128 AP65 200fr Sistine Madonna, by Raphael 3.00 1.75

Steamer Commandant Bory—AP66

1984, Jan. 9   Perf. 13
C129 AP66 67fr multi   1.00 55

1984 Summer Olympics—AP67

1984, Feb. 3   Litho.   Perf. 13
C130 AP67 85fr Weight lifting 1.25 65

Frangipani Blossoms—AP68

1984, Feb. 28   Perf. 12½
C131 AP68 130fr multi   2.00 1.10

Easter 1984—AP69

1984, Apr. 17   Litho.   Perf. 12½x13
C132 AP69 190fr Descent from the Cross 3.00 1.55

WESTERN UKRAINE

AIR POST SEMI-POSTAL STAMPS.

Stamps of New Caledonia type V5 overprinted "Wallis et Futuna" and type of Cameroun V10 inscribed "Wallis et Futuna" were issued in 1942 by the Vichy Government, but were not placed on sale in the dependency.

POSTAGE DUE STAMPS.

Postage Due Stamps of New Caledonia, 1906, Overprinted in Black or Red

ILES WALLIS et FUTUNA

1920 Perf. 13½x14 Unwmkd.

J1	D2	5c ultra, *az*	38	38
J2	D2	10c brn, *buff*	38	38
J3	D2	15c grn, *grnsh*	38	38
J4	D2	20c yel (R)	38	38
a.		Double ovpt.	45.00	
J5	D2	30c car rose	45	45
J6	D2	50c ultra, *straw*	75	75
J7	D2	60c ol, *az*	1.00	1.00
a.		Double ovpt.	45.00	
J8	D2	1fr grn, *cr*	1.50	1.50
		Nos. J1-J8 (8)	5.22	5.22

Type of 1920 Issue Surcharged **2f**

1927

J9	D2	2fr on 1fr brt vio	5.25	5.25
J10	D2	3fr on 1fr org brn	5.25	5.25

Postage Due Stamps of New Caledonia, 1928, Overprinted as in 1920.

1930

J11	D3	2c sl bl & dp brn	6	6
J12	D3	4c brn red & bl grn	6	6
J13	D3	5c red org & bl blk	6	6
J14	D3	10c mag & Prus bl	6	6
J15	D3	15c dl grn & scar	8	8
J16	D3	20c mar & ol grn	22	22
J17	D3	25c bis brn & sl bl	15	15
J18	D3	30c bl grn & ol grn	32	32
J19	D3	50c lt brn & dk red	15	15
J20	D3	60c mag & brt rose	50	50
J21	D3	1fr dl bl & Prus grn	28	28
J22	D3	2fr dk red & ol grn	28	28
J23	D3	3fr vio & brn	38	38
		Nos. J11-J23 (13)	2.60	2.60

Postage Due Stamps of 1930 with Additional Overprint in Black

FRANCE LIBRE

1943

J24	D3	2c sl bl & dp brn	17.50	17.50
J25	D3	4c brn red & bl grn	17.50	17.50
J26	D3	5c red org & bl blk	17.50	17.50
J27	D3	10c mag & Prus bl	17.50	17.50
J28	D3	15c dl grn & scar	17.50	17.50
J29	D3	20c mar & ol grn	17.50	17.50
J30	D3	25c bis brn & sl bl	17.50	17.50
J31	D3	30c bl grn & ol grn	17.50	17.50
J32	D3	50c lt brn & dk red	17.50	17.50
J33	D3	60c mag & brt rose	17.50	17.50
J34	D3	1fr dl bl & Prus grn	22.50	22.50
J35	D3	2fr dk red & ol grn	22.50	22.50
J36	D3	3fr vio & brn	22.50	22.50
		Nos. J24-J36 (13)	242.50	242.50

Thalassoma Lunare
D1

Fish: 1fr, Zanclus cornutus (vert.). 5fr, Amphiprion percula.

Perf. 13x13½
1963, Apr. 1 Typo. Unwmkd.

J37	D1	1fr yel org, bl & blk	30	30
J38	D1	3fr red, grnsh bl & grn	45	45
J39	D1	5fr org, bluish grn & blk	75	75

WESTERN UKRAINE
(wĕs'tērn ū'krān)

LOCATION—In Eastern Central Europe.
GOVT.—A former short-lived independent State.

A provisional government was established in 1918 in the eastern part of Austria-Hungary but the area later came under Polish administration.

100 Shagiv (Sotykiv) = 1 Grivna
100 Heller = 1 Krone

Forgeries of almost all Western Ukraine stamps are plentiful.
Used prices are for stamps canceled to order.

Kolomyya Issue.

Укр. Н.Р.

Austrian Stamps of 1916-17 Surcharged

10

1918 Perf. 12½. Unwmkd.

1	A42	5(sh) on 15h dl red	35.00	40.00
2	A37	10(sh) on 3h vio	35.00	40.00
3	A37	10(sh) on 6h dp org	1,000.	700.00
4	A37	10(sh) on 12h lt bl	1,000.	700.00

Nos. 1-4 exist with surcharge inverted or double.

Austrian stamps of 1916-17 overprinted as illustrated were briefly used, some authorities believe. Forgeries exist.

Stanislav Issue.

Пошта Укр.Н.Реп

Austrian Stamps of 1916-18 Surcharged in Shagiv and Grivna Currency

1919

11	A37	3sh brt vio	15.00	15.00
12	A37	5sh lt grn	15.00	15.00
13	A37	6sh dp org	30.00	30.00
14	A37	10sh magenta	30.00	30.00
15	A37	12sh lt bl	30.00	30.00
16	A42	15sh dl red	30.00	30.00
17	A42	20sh dp grn	30.00	30.00
18	A42	30sh dl vio	150.00	150.00
19	A39	40sh ol grn	30.00	30.00
20	A39	50sh dk grn	30.00	30.00
21	A39	60sh dp bl	30.00	30.00
22	A39	80sh org brn	30.00	30.00
23	A39	1gr car, *yel*	42.50	42.50
24	A40	2gr lt bl	35.00	35.00
25	A40	3gr car rose	60.00	60.00
a.		3gr cl	3,750.	3,250.
26	A40	4gr yel grn	42.50	42.50
		4gr dp grn	300.00	300.00
27	A40	10gr dp vio	700.00	1,000.

The overprint exists inverted on 12sh and 80sh, double on 12sh and 10gr.
The 25sh, type A42, with this overprint is considered bogus.

Granite Paper.

28	A40	3gr car rose	42.50	42.50

Same Surcharge on Austrian Military Semipostal Stamps of 1918.
Perf. 12½x13.

31	MSP7	10sh gray grn	100.00	100.00
32	MSP8	20sh magenta	85.00	85.00
33	MSP7	45sh blue	60.00	60.00

The overprint exists inverted on Nos. 31-33, double on No. 32.

Same Surcharge on Austrian Military Stamps of 1917.
Perf. 12½.

34	M3	1sh grnsh bl	1,100.	1,100.
35	M3	2sh red org	100.00	100.00
36	M3	3sh ol gray	200.00	200.00
37	M3	5sh ol grn	350.00	350.00
38	M3	6sh violet	175.00	175.00
39	M3	10sh org brn	1,200.	1,000.
40	M3	12sh blue	700.00	700.00
41	M3	15sh brt rose	700.00	700.00
42	M3	20sh red brn	16.00	17.50
43	M3	25sh ultra	4,000.	5,000.
44	M3	30sh slate	1,150.	1,350.
45	M3	40sh ol bis	1,000.	1,000.
46	M3	50sh dp grn	10.00	10.00
47	M3	60sh car rose	900.00	900.00
48	M3	80sh dl bl	60.00	60.00
49	M3	90sh dk vio	1,200.	1,000.
50	M4	2gr rose, *straw*	20.00	27.50
51	M4	3gr bl, *grn*	30.00	35.00
52	M4	4gr rose, *grn*	30.00	35.00
53	M4	10gr dl vio, *gray*		

The overprint exists double on 2sh, 3sh and 20sh, inverted on 12sh, 50sh and 4gr.

Same Surcharge on Austrian Postage Due Stamps of 1916.

54	D5	1gr ultra	100.00	120.00
55	D5	5gr ultra	1,000.	1,100.

Surcharged on Austrian Postage Due Stamps of 1917 with two bars over "PORTO".

57	A38	15sh on 36h vio	400.00	400.00
58	A38	50sh on 42h choc	6,500.	6,500.

Same Surcharge on Postage Due Stamps of Bosnia, 1904.

61	D1	1sh blk, red & yel	30.00	30.00
62	D1	2sh blk, red & yel	10.00	16.50
63	D1	3sh blk, red & yel	10.00	16.50
64	D1	4sh blk, red & yel	100.00	100.00
65	D1	5sh blk, red & yel	2,750.	3,000.
66	D1	6sh blk, red & yel	200.00	200.00
67	D1	7sh blk, red & yel	15.00	20.00
68	D1	8sh blk, red & yel	20.00	25.00
69	D1	10sh blk, red & yel	800.00	900.00
70	D1	15sh blk, red & yel	500.00	500.00
71	D1	20sh blk, red & yel	5,000.	5,000.
72	D1	50sh blk, red & yel	200.00	200.00

Two types of surcharge on No. 61: Shagiv in singular (wara) and in plural (warib). Price the same.
The overprint exists inverted on Nos. 61, 64, 66-68.

A2

Black Surcharge on Austrian Military Stamps of 1917-18.

1919

75	A2	2gr on 2k rose, *straw*	7.00	13.00
76	A2	3gr on 2k rose, *straw*	7.00	13.00
77	A2	3gr on 3k grn, *bl*	100.00	200.00
78	A2	4gr on 2k rose, *straw*	7.00	13.00
79	A2	4gr on 4k rose, *straw*	1,100.	1,900.
80	A2	5gr on 2k rose, *straw*	7.00	13.00
a.		Inverted surch.	350.00	
81	A2	10gr on 50h dp grn (Austria type M3)	12.00	35.00

Austrian Stamps of 1916-18 Overprinted

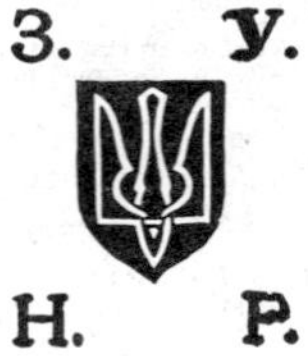

1919, May

85	A37	3h brt vio	50	1.25
86	A37	5h lt grn	50	1.25
87	A37	6h dp org	50	1.25
88	A37	10h magenta	50	1.25
89	A37	12h lt bl	50	1.25
90	A42	15h dl red	50	1.25
91	A42	20h dp grn	50	1.25
92	A42	25h blue	50	1.25
93	A42	30h dl vio	50	1.25
94	A39	40h ol grn	65	1.50
95	A39	50h dk grn	65	1.50
96	A39	60h dp bl	65	1.50
97	A39	80h org brn	75	1.75
98	A39	90h red vio	75	2.00
99	A39	1k car, *yel*	1.00	2.25
100	A40	2k lt bl	1.75	3.50
101	A40	3k car rose	2.25	5.25
102	A40	4k yel grn	5.00	6.50
103	A40	10k dp vio	7.00	8.50
		Nos. 85-103 (19)	24.95	45.50

The four letters in the overprint are the initials of Ukrainian words equivalent to "Western Ukrainian National (or Peoples) Republic." The country was formed from the eastern part of Galicia, formerly a province of the Austro-Hungarian Empire. Forged cancellations abound.

REGISTRATION STAMPS.

Kolomyya Issue

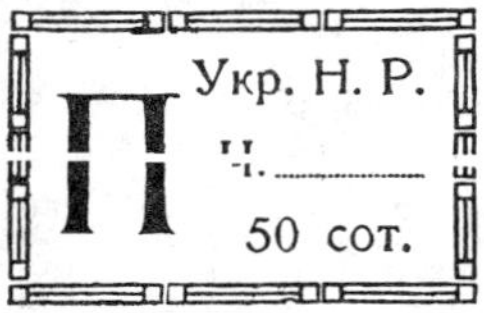

R1

Type-set.

1919 *Imperf.* **Unwmkd.**

F1	R1	30 sot *rose*	125.00	60.00
F2	R1	50 sot *dp rose*	27.50	35.00

OCCUPATION STAMPS.

Romanian Occupation of Pokutia

Austrian Stamps Surcharged in Dark Blue Black

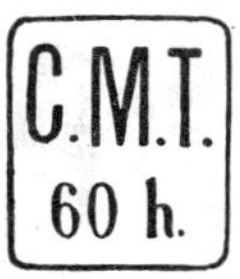

1919 *Perf. 12½* **Unwmkd.**

On Stamps of 1916-18.

N3	A37	40h on 5h lt grn
N10	A39	1k 20h on 50h dk grn
N11	A39	1k 20h on 60h dp bl
N14	A39	1k 20h on 1k car, *yel*

On Stamps of 1917–18.

N15	A42	60h on 15h dl red
N16	A42	60h on 20h dp grn
N17	A42	60h on 25h bl
N18	A42	60h on 30h dl vio

Surcharges in colors other than dark blue black are bogus or proofs.

POSTAGE DUE STAMPS.

Austrian Postage Due Stamps Surcharged like Regular Issues.

1919 *Perf. 12½.* **Unwmkd.**

On Stamps of 1916.

NJ1	D4	40h on 5h rose red
NJ5	D4	1k 20h on 25h rose red
NJ6	D4	1k 20h on 30h rose red

On Stamp of 1917.

NJ13	A38	1k 20h on 50h on 42h choc

WEST IRIAN
(Irian Barat)
(West New Guinea)

LOCATION—Western half of New Guinea, southwest Pacific Ocean.

GOVT.—Province of Indonesia.

AREA—162,927 sq. mi.

POP.—923,440 (1973).

CAPITAL—Djajapura (formerly Hollandia).

The former Netherlands New Guinea became a territory under the administration of the United Nations Temporary Executive Authority on Oct. 1, 1962.

The territory came under Indonesian administration on May 1, 1963.

100 Cents = 1 Gulden
100 Sen = 1 Rupiah

(1 rupiah = 1 former Netherlands New Guinea gulden)

Issued Under United Nations Temporary Executive Authority

Netherlands New Guinea Stamps of 1950-60 Overprinted **UNTEA**

Perf. 12½x12, 12½x13½

1962 Photogravure **Unwmkd.**

1	A4	1c ver & yel	1.00	1.00
2	A1	2c dp org	1.50	1.50
3	A4	5c choc & yel	1.15	1.15
4	A5	7c org red, bl & brn vio	1.50	1.50
5	A4	10c aqua & red brn	1.15	1.15
6	A5	12c grn, bl & brn vio	1.50	1.50
7	A4	15c dp yel & red brn	2.00	2.00
8	A5	17c brn vio & bl	2.00	2.00
9	A4	20c lt bl grn & red brn	2.00	2.00
10	A6	25c red	1.00	1.00
11	A6	30c dp bl	1.50	1.50
12	A6	40c dp org	2.50	2.50
13	A6	45c dk ol	5.00	5.00
14	A6	55c sl bl	4.00	4.00
15	A6	80c dl gray vio	25.00	25.00
16	A6	85c dk vio brn	10.00	10.00
17	A6	1g plum	8.00	8.00

Engraved

18	A3	2g redsh brn	25.00	25.00
19	A3	5g green	30.00	30.00
		Nos. 1-19 (19)	125.80	125.80

The overprint exists in four types: (1.) Size 17½mm. Applied locally and sold in West New Guinea. Top of "N" is slightly lower than the "U," and the base of the "T" is straight, or nearly so. (2.) Size 17½mm. Applied in the Netherlands and sold by the UN in New York. Top of the "N" is slightly higher than the "U," and the base of the "T" is concave. (3.) Size 14mm. Exists on eight values. (4.) Size 19mm. Exists on 1c and 10c.

Types 3 and 4 were applied in West New Guinea and it is doubtful whether they were regularly issued.

West Irian

Indonesia Nos. 454, 456, 494-501, 387, 390, 392 and 393 Surcharged and Overprinted: "IRIAN BARAT"

Perf. 12½x13½

1963, May 1 Photo. **Unwmkd.**

20	A63	1s on 70s org ver	5	5
21	A63	2s on 90s yel grn	5	5

Perf. 12x12½

22	A76	5s gray	6	6
23	A76	6s on 20s ocher	6	6
24	A76	7s on 50s dp bl	7	7
25	A76	10s red brn	10	10
26	A76	15s plum	15	15
27	A76	25s brt bl grn	25	25
28	A76	30s on 75s scar	30	30
29	A76	40s on 1.15r plum	35	35

Perf. 12½x12

30	A55	1r purple	90	90
31	A55	2r green	1.85	1.85
32	A55	3r dk bl	2.50	2.50
33	A55	5r brown	4.50	4.50
		Nos. 20-33 (14)	11.19	11.19

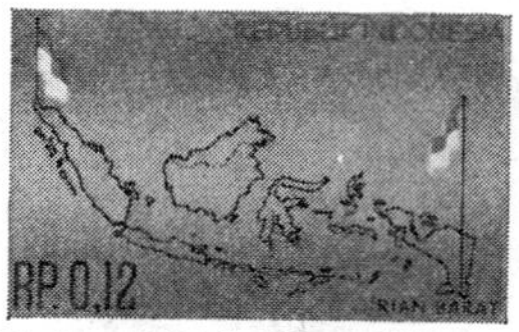

"Indonesia's Flag from Sabang to Merauke—A1

Designs: 20s, 50s, Parachutist landing in New Guinea. 60s, 75s, Bird of paradise and map of New Guinea.

1963, May 1

34	A1	12s org brn, blk & red	15	15
35	A1	17s org brn, blk & red	20	20
36	A1	20s multi	30	30
37	A1	50s multi	55	55
38	A1	60s multi	80	80
39	A1	75s multi	1.00	1.00
		Nos. 34-39 (6)	3.00	3.00

Liberation of West New Guinea.

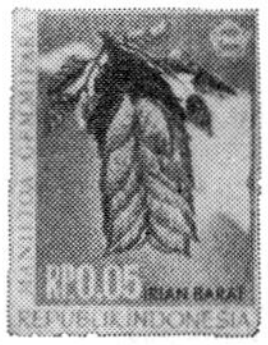

Maniltoa Gemmipara A2

Designs: 15s, Dendrobium lancifolium (orchid). 30s, Gardenia gjellerupii. 40s, Maniltoa flower. 50s, Phalanger. 75s, Cassowary. 1e, Kangaroo. 3r, Crowned pigeons.

1968, Aug. 17 Photo. *Perf. 12½x12*

40	A2	5s dl grn & vio blk	25	25
41	A2	15s emer & dk pur	25	25
42	A2	30s org & dp grn	50	50
43	A2	40s lem & brt pur	60	60
44	A2	50s rose car & blk	90	90
45	A2	75s dl bl & blk	1.25	1.25
46	A2	1r brn org & blk	2.75	2.75
47	A2	3r ap grn & blk	6.25	6.25
		Nos. 40-47 (8)	12.75	12.75

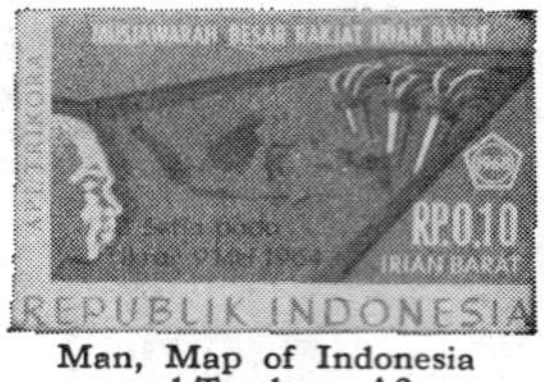

Man, Map of Indonesia and Torches—A3

1968, Aug. 17

48	A3	10s ultra & gold	10	10
49	A3	25s crim & gold	20	20

Issued to publicize the pledge of the people of West Irian to remain unified and integrated with the Republic of Indonesia.

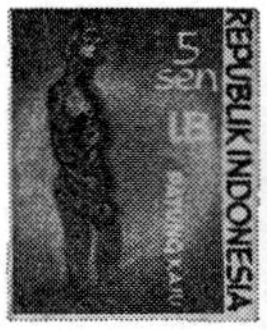

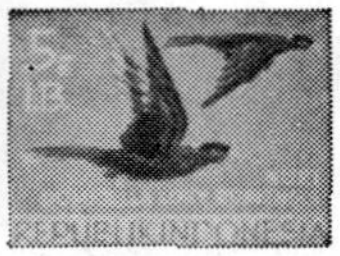

Carving, Mother and Child—A4 Black-capped Lory—A5

West Irian Wood Carvings: 6s, Shield with 3 human figures. 7s, Child atop filigree carving. 10s, Drum. 25s, Seated man. 30s, Drum (3-tiered base). 50s, Carved bamboo. 75s, Man-shaped ornament. 1r, Shield. 2r, Seated man (hands raised).

1970 Photogravure *Perf. 12½x12*

50	A4	5s multi	5	5
51	A4	6s multi	5	5
52	A4	7s multi	5	5
53	A4	10s multi	5	5
54	A4	25s multi	7	7
55	A4	30s multi	8	8
56	A4	50s multi	15	15
57	A4	75s multi	20	20
58	A4	1r multi	30	30
59	A4	2r multi	50	50
		Nos. 50-59 (10)	1.50	1.50

Issue dates: Nos. 50-54, Apr. 30; Nos. 55-59, Apr. 15.

1970, Oct. 26 Photo. *Perf. 12x12½*

Design: 10r, Bird of paradise.

60	A5	5r rose red & multi	1.00	1.00
61	A5	10r bl & multi	2.00	2.00

POSTAGE DUE STAMPS

Type of Indonesia Overprinted: "IRIAN BARAT"

Perf. 13½x12½

1963, May 1 Litho. **Unwmkd.**

J1	D8	1s lt brn	7	10
J2	D8	5s lt gray ol	10	15
J3	D8	10s lt bl	13	15
J4	D8	25s gray	30	35
J5	D8	40s salmon	50	55
J6	D8	100s bister	1.30	1.40
		Nos. J1-J6 (6)	2.40	2.70

Type of Indonesia Dated "1968" and Overprinted: "IRIAN BARAT"

1968 Photo. *Perf. 13½x12½*

J7	D9	1s bl & lt grn	5	5
J8	D9	5s grn & pink	10	10
J9	D9	10s red & gray	15	15
J10	D9	25s grn & yel	20	20
J11	D9	40s vio brn & pale grn	30	30
J12	D9	100s org & bis	50	75
		Nos. J7-J12 (6)	1.30	1.55

YEMEN

WHITE RUSSIA

Stamps of this design were not put in use and were probably propaganda labels.

WURTTEMBERG

See German States group preceding Germany in Vol. III.

YEMEN
(yĕm'ĕn)

LOCATION—Arabian Peninsula, south of Saudi Arabia and bordering on the Red Sea.
GOVT.—Kingdom.
AREA—73,300 sq. mi.
POP.—5,000,000 (est. 1958).
CAPITALS—San'a and Ta'iz.

40 Bogaches = 1 Imadi
40 Bogaches = 1 Riyal (1962)

For Domestic Postage.

Crossed Daggers and Arabic Inscriptions
A1   A2

Laid Paper.
Typographed.
Without Gum.

1926		Imperf.	Unwmkd.	
1	A1	2½b blk, *white*	20.00	20.00
2	A1	2½b blk, *org*	20.00	20.00
a.		*Wove paper*		
3	A2	5b blk, *white*	20.00	20.00

No. 2 is known rouletted 7½ or 9.
Type A1 differs from A2 primarily in the inscription in the left dagger blade.

For Foreign and Domestic Postage.

Arabic Inscriptions
A3   A4

Wmk. 127

Wmkd. Quatrefoils. (127)

1930–31		Wove paper	Perf. 14	
7	A3	½b org ('31)	20	20
8	A3	1b green	60	50
9	A3	1b yel grn ('31)	25	15
10	A3	2b ol grn	70	60
11	A3	2b ol brn ('31)	40	30
12	A3	3b dl vio ('31)	40	20
13	A3	4b red	1.20	90
14	A3	4b dp rose ('31)	80	30
15	A3	5b sl gray ('31)	1.00	70
16	A4	6b dl bl	2.00	1.50
17	A4	6b dp ultra ('31)	1.40	90
18	A4	8b lil rose ('31)	1.60	1.20
19	A4	10b lt brn	3.50	2.00
20	A4	10b brn org ('31)	2.00	1.60
21	A4	20b yel grn ('31)	7.00	4.50
22	A4	1i red brn & lt bl	15.00	12.00
23	A4	1i lil rose & yel grn ('31)	15.00	10.00
		Nos. 7-23 (17)	53.05	37.55

Some values exist imperforate.

Flags of Saudi Arabia, Yemen and Iraq
A5

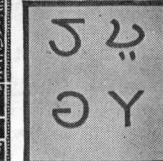

Wmk. 258

Wmkd. Arabic Characters and Y. G. Multiple. (258)

1939		Lithographed	Perf. 12½	
24	A5	4b dl rose & ultra	60	60
25	A5	6b sl bl & ultra	80	80
26	A5	10b fawn & ultra	1.10	1.10
27	A5	14b ol & ultra	2.00	2.00
28	A5	20b yel grn & ultra	3.50	3.50
29	A5	1i cl & ultra	7.00	7.00
		Nos. 24-29 (6)	15.00	15.00

Issued in commemoration of the 2nd anniversary of the Arab Alliance. Nos. 24-29 exist imperforate.

No. 7 Handstamped in Black

a

Two types of surcharge:
a. 11½x16mm.
b. 13½x15½mm.
Prices of surcharged stamps are for ordinary copies. Clear, legible surcharges command a premium.

Wmkd. Quatrefoils. (127)

1939			Perf. 14	
30	A3	4b on ½b org	4.00	2.00

A6

A7

Lithographed.

1940		Perf. 12½	Wmk. 258	
31	A6	½b ocher & ultra	15	15
32	A6	1b lt grn & rose red	25	25
33	A6	2b bis brn & vio	25	25
34	A6	3b dl vio & ultra	25	25
35	A6	4b rose & yel grn	30	30
36	A6	5b dk gray grn & bis brn	40	40
37	A7	6b ultra & yel org	40	40
38	A7	8b cl & dl bl	50	50
39	A7	10b brn org & yel grn	70	65
40	A7	14b gray grn & vio	85	65
41	A7	18b emer & blk	1.50	1.50
42	A7	20b yel ol & cer	2.25	2.00
43	A7	1i vio rose, yel grn & brn red	5.00	4.00
		Nos. 31-43 (13)	12.80	11.30

Nos. 31-34, 36 Handstamped Type "a" in Black

1945-51			Perf. 12½	
44	A6	4b on ½b	3.00	1.50
a.		Handstamp type "b" ('51)	2.50	1.50
45	A6	4b on 1b ('48)	2.25	1.25
a.		Handstamp type "b" ('49)	2.25	1.25
46	A6	4b on 2b ('48)	1.75	1.00
a.		Handstamp type "b" ('49)	1.75	1.00
47	A6	4b on 3b ('48)	2.00	1.25
a.		Handstamp type "b" ('49)	2.00	1.25
48	A6	4b on 5b ('46)	2.00	1.25
		Nos. 44-48 (5)	11.00	6.25

Forged surcharges exist.

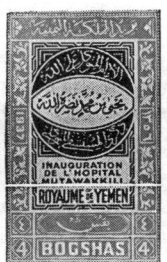

A8

1946		Frames in Emerald		
49	A8	4b black	1.40	80
50	A8	6b lil rose	1.60	1.20
51	A8	10b ultra	2.00	1.50
52	A8	4b ol grn	3.50	2.50

Opening of Mutawakkili Hospital. Exist imperforate.

Mocha Coffee Tree   Palace, San'a
A9   A10

Engraved.

1947-58		Perf. 12½	Unwmkd.	
53	A9	½b yel brn	20	8
54	A9	1b purple	60	32
55	A9	2b ultra	1.20	70
56	A10	4b red	1.10	60
57	A10	5b gray bl	60	50
58	A9	6b yel grn ('58)	1.75	1.25
		Nos. 53-58 (6)	5.45	3.45

No. 58 was printed in 1947 but not officially issued until June, 1958.
Additional values, prepared but not issued, were 10b, 20b and 1i, with views of palaces superimposed on flag, and palace square. These were looted from government storehouses during the 1948 revolution and a number of copies later reached collectors.

Nos. 9, 11, 12 and 15 Handstamped Type "a" in Black

1949		Perf. 14	Wmk. 127	
59	A3	4b on 1b yel grn	1.75	1.25
60	A3	4b on 2b ol brn	15.00	7.50
61	A3	4b on 3b dl vio	2.50	1.50
62	A3	4b on 5b sl gray	2.50	1.50

Nos. 53–55 Handstamped Type "b" and "a"

1949		Perf. 12½	Unwmkd.	
63	A9(b)	4b on ½b yel brn	2.25	2.25
64	A9(a)	4b on 1b pur	2.25	2.25
a.		Handstamp type "b"	2.25	2.25
65	A9(a)	4b on 2b ultra	4.00	3.75
a.		Handstamp type "b"	4.00	3.50

Nos. J1-J2 Handstamped Type "b" in Black

1949-53			Wmk. 258	
66	D1	4b on 1b org & yel grn	6.00	5.00
67	D1	4b on 2b org & yel grn	6.00	5.00

Three minor types of this handstamped 4b surcharge exist. Types "a" and "b" exist inverted, double or horizontal.
Forged surcharges exist.

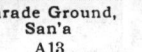

Parade Ground, San'a   Wmk. 277
A13

Mosque, San'a
A14

Designs: 5b, Flag of Yemen. 6b, Flag & eagle. 8b, Mocha coffee branch. 14b, Walled city of San'a. 20b, 1i, Ta'iz & its citadel.

YEMEN

Photogravure.
	1951-57		Perf. 14.	Wmk. 277	
68	A13	1b dk brn		15	5
69	A13	2b red brn		35	10
70	A13	3b lil rose		50	10
71	A14	5b bl & red ('56)		75	20
72	A14	6b dk pur & red		1.00	25
73	A13	8b bl bl & gray grn ('57)		1.00	30
74	A14	10b rose lil		1.25	50
75	A14	14b bl grn		2.00	75
76	A14	20b rose red		3.00	1.25
77	A14	1i violet		5.00	2.50
	Nos. 68-77 (10)			15.00	6.00

The 5b was issued and used as a 4b stamp, without surcharge. See Nos. C3-C9.

Palace of the Rock, Wadi Dhahr
A15

Design: 20b, Walls of 1bb.
Perf. 14½, Imperf.

1952		Engr. & Photo.	Unwmkd.	
78	A15	12b choc, bl & dl grn	5.00	5.00
79	A15	20b dp car, bl & brn	6.50	6.50

See Nos. C10-C11.

Flag and View of San'a (Palace in Background)—A16

1952
| 80 | A16 | 1i red brn, car & gray | 10.50 | 10.50 |

Issued to commemorate the 4th anniversary of the accession of King Ahmed, Feb. 18, 1948. See No. C12.

Palace in Foreground.
1952
| 81 | A16 | 30b red brn, car & dk grn | 9.00 | 9.00 |

Victory of Mar. 13, 1948. See No. C13.

No. 69 Handstamped Type "b" in Black.
1952		Perf. 14.	Wmk. 277	
82	A13	4b on 2b red brn	2.00	1.00

Forged surcharges exist. See also Nos. 86-87.

Leaning Minaret, Mosque of Ta'iz
A17

Yemen Gate, San'a
A18

1954 Photogravure. Unwmkd.
83	A17	4b dp org	60	25
84	A17	6b dp bl	90	50
85	A17	8b dp bl grn	1.20	60
	Nos. 83-85, C14-C16 (6)	6.85	4.75

Issued to commemorate the 5th anniversary of the accession of King Ahmed I.

Nos. 68 and 70 Handstamped Type "b" in Black
1955		Perf. 14	Wmk. 277	
86	A13	4b on 1b dk brn	1.25	1.00
87	A13	4b on 3b lil rose	1.50	1.50

1956-57		Perf. 14	Wmk. 277	
87A	A18	1b lt brn	40	10
87B	A18	5b bl grn	40	20
87C	A18	10b dk bl ('57)	75	75

Nos. 87A-87C were prepared for official use, but issued for regular postage. The 1b and 5b were used as 4b stamps. A 20b and 1-imadi of type A18 were not issued.

Arab Postal Union Issue

Globe
A19

Photogravure.
1957-58		Perf. 13½x13	Wmk. 195	
88	A19	4b yel brn	1.50	1.40
89	A19	6b grn ('58)	1.75	1.50
90	A19	16b vio ('58)	3.25	2.25

Issued to commemorate the founding of the Arab Postal Union, July 1, 1954.

Telecommunications Issue

Globe, Radio and Telegraph
A20

1959, Mar. Perf. 13x13½ Wmk. 318
| 91 | A20 | 4b vermilion | 65 | 50 |

Arab Union of Telecommunications.

United Arab States Issue

Flags of U.A.R. and Yemen
A21

1959, Mar. 13
92	A21	1b dl red brn & blk	15	15
93	A21	2b dk bl & blk	25	25
94	A21	4b sl grn, car & blk	40	40
	Nos. 92-94, C17-C19 (6)	5.75	4.35

First anniversary of United Arab States.

Arab League Center Issue

Arab League Center, Cairo
A22

Perf. 13x13½

1960, Mar. 22 Wmk. 328
| 95 | A22 | 4b dl grn & blk | 50 | 50 |

Issued to commemorate the opening of the Arab League Center and the Arab Postal Museum in Cairo.

Refugees Pointing to Map of Palestine—A23

1960, Apr. 7 Photogravure
| 96 | A23 | 4b brown | 1.10 | 1.10 |
| 97 | A23 | 6b yel grn | 1.50 | 1.50 |

Issued to publicize World Refugee Year, July 1, 1959-June 30, 1960.
In 1961 a souvenir sheet was issued containing a 4b gray and 6b sepia in type A18, imperf. Black marginal inscription, "YEMEN 1960," repeated in Arabic. Size: 103x85mm. Price $25.

Torch and Olympic Rings
A24

1960, Dec. Perf. 14x14½ Unwmkd.
98	A24	2b blk & lil rose	20	20
99	A24	4b blk & yel	40	40
100	A24	6b blk & org	70	70
101	A24	8b brn blk & bl grn	1.50	1.50
102	A24	20b dk bl, org & vio	2.75	2.75
	Nos. 98-102 (5)	5.55	5.55

Issued to commemorate the 17th Olympic Games, Rome, Aug. 25-Sept. 11.
An imperf. souvenir sheet exists, containing one copy of No. 99. Size: 100x60 mm. Price $75.

U.N. Emblem Breaking Chains
A25

1961 Perf. 14x14½ Unwmkd.
103	A25	1b violet	20	15
104	A25	2b green	25	20
105	A25	3b grnsh bl	35	25
106	A25	4b brt ultra	40	30
107	A25	6b brt lil	55	40
108	A25	14b rose brn	1.25	1.00
109	A25	20b brown	2.00	1.65
	Nos. 103-109 (7)	5.00	3.95

15th anniversary (in 1960) of U.N.
An imperf. souvenir sheet exists, containing one copy of No. 106. Blue marginal inscription. Size: 100x60mm. Price $15.

Cranes and Ship, Hodeida
A26

1961, June Litho. Perf. 13x13½
110	A26	4b multi	50	40
111	A26	6b multi	1.00	80
112	A26	16b multi	2.00	1.75

Opening of deepwater port at Hodeida.
An imperf. souvenir sheet exists, containing one each of Nos. 110-112, with marginal inscription in ultramarine. Size: 160x130mm. Price $4.

Alabaster Funerary Mask
A27

Imam's New Palace, San'a
A28

Designs (ancient sculptures from Marib, Sheba): 2b, Horned animal's head, symbolizing Moon God (limestone). 4b, Bronze head of an Emperor 1st or 2nd century. 8b, Statue of Emperor Dhamar Ali. 10b, Statue of a child, 2nd or 3rd century (alabaster). 12b, Stairs in court of Temple of the Moon God. 20b, Alabaster relief, boy riding monster. 1i, Woman with grapes, relief.

1961, Oct. 14 Photo. Perf. 11½
Granite Paper
113	A27	1b sal, blk & gray	10	10
114	A27	2b pur & gray	15	15
115	A27	4b pale brn, gray & blk	25	25
116	A27	8b brt pink & blk	60	60
117	A27	10b yel & blk	1.00	1.00
118	A27	12b lt vio bl & blk	1.50	1.50
119	A27	20b gray & blk	1.85	1.85
120	A27	1i gray ol & blk	3.50	3.50
	Nos. 113-120, C20-C21 (10)	11.05	11.05

1961, Nov. 15 Unwmkd.
Designs: 8b, Side view of Imam's palace, San'a (horiz.). 10b, Palace of the Rock (Dar al-Hajar).
121	A28	4b blk & lt bl grn	45	45
122	A28	8b blk, brt pink & grn	85	85
123	A28	10b blk, sal & blk	1.10	1.10
	Nos. 121-123, C22-C23 (5)	4.65	4.55

Exist imperf.

Hodeida-San'a Road—A29

1961, Dec. 25 Litho. Perf. 13½x13
| 124 | A29 | 4b multi | 75 | 40 |
| 125 | A29 | 6b multi | 1.10 | 60 |

YEMEN

126 A29 10b multi   1.85   1.00

Issued to commemorate the opening of the Hodeida-San'a highway. A miniature sheet exists containing one each of Nos. 124–126, imperf. with red marginal inscriptions. Size: 159x129mm. Price $3.50.

Trajan's Kiosk, Philae, Nubia — A30

1962, Mar. 1 Photo. Perf. 11x11½

127	A30	4b dk red brn	1.35	90
128	A30	6b bl grn	2.75	1.75

Issued to publicize UNESCO's help in safeguarding the monuments of Nubia.
A souvenir sheet exists, containing one each of Nos. 127–128, imperf. with black marginal inscription. Size: 100x88½mm. Price $6.

Arab League Building, Cairo, and Emblem — A31

1962, March 22   Perf. 13½x13

129	A31	4b dk grn	55	45
130	A31	6b dp ultra	70	60

Arab League Week, Mar. 22–28.
A souvenir sheet exists, containing one each of Nos. 129–130, imperf. with dark gray marginal inscription. Size: 94x80mm. Price $1.75.

Nurses, Mother and Child — A32   Malaria Eradication Emblem — A33

Designs: 4b, Nurse weighing child. 6b, Vaccination. 10b, Weighing infant.

1962, June 20 Perf. 11½ Unwmkd.

131	A32	2b multi	35	35
132	A32	4b multi	45	45
133	A32	6b multi	60	60
134	A32	10b multi	90	90

Issued for Child Welfare.

1962, July 20   Perf. 13½x13

135	A33	4b blk & dp org	40	40
136	A33	6b dk brn & grn	70	60

Issued for the World Health Organization drive to eradicate malaria. An imperf. souvenir sheet contains one each of Nos. 135–136. Black marginal inscription. Size: 95x79mm. Price $20.
No. 136 has laurel leaves added and inscription rearranged.

YEMEN

10th anniv. of Revolution—A80

1972, Nov. 25   **Photo.**   *Perf. 13*
| 301 | A80 | 7b lt bl, blk & multi | 80 | 80 |
| 302 | A80 | 10b gray, blk & multi | 1.10 | 1.10 |

See No. C40.

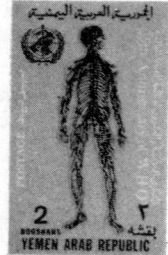
25th Anniv. of WHO—A81

1972, Dec. 1   **Litho.**
303	A81	2b lt yel grn & multi	45	45
304	A81	21b sky bl & multi	1.75	1.75
305	A81	37b red lil & multi	2.50	2.50

Burning of Al—Aqsa Mosque, 2nd Anniv.—A82

1972, Jan. 1   **Photo.**   *Perf. 13½*
| 306 | A82 | 7b lt bl, blk & multi | 45 | 45 |
| 307 | A82 | 18b lt bl, blk & multi | 1.35 | 1.35 |

See No. C41.

25th Anniv. of UNICEF—A83

1973, Jan. 15   **Photo.**   *Perf. 13*
| 308 | A83 | 7b lt bl, blk & multi | 45 | 45 |
| 309 | A83 | 10b lt bl, blk & multi | 90 | 90 |

See No. C42.

UPU Centenary—A84

1974, Nov. 20   **Photo.**   *Perf. 14*
310	A84	10b multi	45	45
311	A84	30b multi	1.35	1.35
312	A84	40b multi	1.75	1.75

10th World Hunger Program—A85

1975, Feb. 5   **Litho.**   *Perf. 13½*
313	A85	10b multi	45	45
314	A85	30b multi	1.35	1.35
315	A85	63b multi	1.75	1.75

12th Anniv. of Revolution—A86

1975, Sept. 25
| 316 | A86 | 25f Janad Mosque | 45 | 45 |
| 317 | A86 | 75f Althawra Hospital | 1.35 | 1.35 |

Nos. 301, 306 surcharged in Black with New Values and Bars.

1975, Nov. 15   **Photo.**   *Perf. 13½*
| 318 | A80 | 75f on 7b lt bl, blk & multi | 1.35 | 1.35 |
| 319 | A82 | 278f on 7b lt bl, blk & multi | 2.25 | 2.25 |

Nos. 318-319, C46-C48   6.80   6.80

Telephone Centenary—A87

1976, Mar. 10   **Litho.**   *Perf. 14½*
320	A87	25f brt pink & blk	45	45
321	A87	75f lt grn & blk	90	90
322	A87	160f lt bl & blk	1.75	1.75
a.	Souvenir sheet			

No. 322a contains No. 322; black marginal inscription. Size: 91x99mm. Exists both perf. and imperf.

Coffee bean branch—A88

1976, Apr. 25   *Perf. 14*
323	A88	1f dl lil	10	10
324	A88	3f pale gray	10	10
325	A88	5f lt bl grn	10	10
326	A88	10f bis brn	10	10
327	A88	25f gldn brn	12	12
328	A88	50f brt plum	25	25
329	A88	75f dl pink	38	38

Size: 22x30mm.   *Perf. 14½*
330	A88	1r sky bl	50	50
331	A88	1.50r red lil	75	75
332	A88	2r lt grn	1.00	1.00
333	A88	5r yel org	2.50	2.50

Nos. 323-333 (11)   5.90   5.90

2nd Anniv. of Reformation Movement—A89

1976, June 13   **Photo.**   *Perf. 12x12½*
| 334 | A89 | 75f Industrial Park | 1.35 | 1.35 |
| 335 | A89 | 135f Forestry | 1.75 | 1.75 |

Souvenir Sheet
| 336 | A89 | 135f Forestry | 2.50 | 2.50 |

No. 336 contains one stamp (32x47mm); black marginal inscription. Size: 99x105mm.

14th Anniv. of Revolution—A90

Designs: 25f, Natl. Institute of Public Administration. 75f, Housing and population census. 160f, Sanaa University emblem.

1976, Sept. 26   **Photo.**   *Perf. 12x12½*
337	A90	25f buff & multi	45	45
338	A90	75f yel bis & multi	90	90
339	A90	160f pale grn & multi	1.75	1.75

Souvenir Sheet
| 340 | A90 | 160f pale grn & multi | 3.50 | 3.50 |

No. 340 contains one stamp (33x49mm); black marginal inscription. Size: 98x105mm.

No. 306 Surcharged in Black with New Value and Bars.

1976
| 341 | A82 | 75f on 7b lt bl, blk & multi | 90 | 90 |

3rd Anniv. of Correction Movement—A91

1977   **Photo.**   *Perf. 14*
342	A91	25f Dish antenna	30	30
343	A91	75f Computer, technician	90	90
a.	Miniature sheet			

No. 343a contains No. 343; black marginal inscription. Size: 82x95mm.

15th Anniv. of September Revolution—A92

1977
344	A92	25f Sa'ada—Sa'ana Road	45	45
345	A92	75f Television, Transmitting tower	90	90
346	A92	160f like 25f	1.75	1.75
a.	Souvenir sheet		3.50	3.50

No. 346a contains No. 346; black marginal inscription. Size: 100x74mm.

25th Anniv. of Arab Postal Union—A93

1978   *Perf. 14*
347	A93	25f lt yel grn & multi	55	55
348	A93	60f bis & multi	1.25	1.25
a.	Miniature sheet		3.50	3.50

No. 348a contains No. 348; black marginal inscription. Size: 72x73mm.

President Hamdi—A94

1978   *Perf. 11½*
349	A94	25f dk grn & blk	18	18
350	A94	75f ultra & blk	55	55
351	A94	160f brn & blk	1.10	1.10
a.	Miniature sheet			

No. 351a contains No. 351; black marginal inscription. Size: 82x85mm.

YEMEN

30th Anniv. of ICAO—A95

1979, Nov. 15   **Photo.**   *Perf. 13½*
352	A95	75f multi	55	55
353	A95	135f multi	1.00	1.00
a.		Miniature sheet	1.25	1.25

No. 353a contains No. 353; black marginal inscription. Size: 80x70mm. Inscribed 1977.

Book, World Map, Arab Achievements—A96

1979, Dec. 1   *Perf. 14*
354	A96	25f multi	18	18
355	A96	75f multi	55	55
a.		Souvenir sheet	75	75

No. 355a contains No. 355; black marginal inscription. Size: 100x75mm.

12th World Telecommunications Day, May 17, 1979—A97

1980, Jan. 1
356	A97	75f multi	55	55
357	A97	135f multi, horiz.	1.00	1.00
a.		Miniature sheet	1.25	1.25

No. 357a contains No. 357; black marginal inscription. Size: 67x73mm.

Dome of the Rock—A98

1980   **Photo.**   *Perf. 14*
358	A98	5f brt bl & multi	8	8
359	A98	10f yel & multi	15	15

Palestinian fighters and their families.

Argentina World Cup—A99

Designs: World Cup emblem and various players.

1980, Mar. 30
360	A99	25f gold & multi	25	25
361	A99	30f gold & multi	30	30
362	A99	35f gold & multi	35	35
363	A99	50f gold & multi	50	50
		Nos. 360-363, C49-C52	4.55	4.55

Issued in sheets of 8.

International Year of the Child—A100

1980, Apr. 1   *Perf. 13½*
364	A100	25f Girl, bird	25	25
365	A100	50f Girl, bird, diff.	50	50
366	A100	75f Boy, butterfly, flower	75	75
		Nos. 364-366, C53-C55	4.80	4.80

Issued in sheets of 6.

World Scouting Jamboree—A101

1980, May 1   *Perf. 13½x14*
367	A101	25f Fishing	25	25
368	A101	35f Troup, aircraft	35	35
369	A101	40f Mounted bugler, flag	40	40
370	A101	50f Telescope, night sky	50	50
		Nos. 367-370, C56-C58	4.05	4.05

Issued in sheets of 6.

Argentina 1978 World Cup Winners—A102

Designs: World cup emblem and various soccer players.

1980, June 1   *Perf. 14*
371	A102	25f gold & multi	25	25
372	A102	30f gold & multi	30	30
373	A102	35f gold & multi	35	35
374	A102	50f gold & multi	50	50
		Nos. 371-374, C59-C62	4.55	4.55

Hegira, 1500th Anniv.—A102A

Designs: 160f, Outside view.

1980, July 1   *Perf. 13½*
375	A102a	25f blk & multi	25	25
376	A102a	75f car rose & multi	75	75
377	A102a	160f blk & multi	1.60	1.60
a.		Miniature sheet	2.50	2.50

No. 377a contains No. 377; black marginal inscription. Size: 89x76mm.

17th Anniv. of September Revolution
A103

A104

1980, Sept. 26   *Perf. 13½*
378	A103	25f multi	25	25
379	A104	75f multi	75	75
		Souvenir Sheet		
380		100f multi	3.00	3.00

No. 380 contains one stamp combining designs A103 and A104 (42x34mm); black marginal inscription. Size: 90x77mm.

Al Aqsa Mosque—A105

Mosques: 25f, Al-Rawda entrance. 100f, Al-Nabwi. 160f, Al-Haram.

1980, Nov. 6   **Photo.**   *Perf. 13½*
381	A105	25f dl yel, brn & multi	25	25
382	A105	75f dp ultra, emer & multi	75	75
383	A105	100f dp ultra, emer & multi	1.00	1.00
384	A105	160f dp ultra, emer & multi	1.60	1.60
		Souvenir Sheet		
385		160f dp ultra, emer & multi	3.00	3.00

Islamic Postal Systems Week and Hegira. No. 385 contains one stamp (109x47mm) combining designs of Nos. 382-384; black marginal inscription. Size 139x75mm.

Intl. Palestinian Solidarity Day—A106

1980, Nov. 29
386	A106	25f lt bl & multi	30	30
387	A106	75f ver & multi	90	90

Inscribed 1979.

9th Arab Archaeological Conference—A107

1981, Mar. 1   *Perf. 13½*
388	A107	75f Al Aamiriya Mosque	1.00	1.00
389	A107	125f Al Hadi Mosque	1.75	1.75
a.		Souvenir Sheet of 2	3.00	3.00

No. 389a contains Nos. 388-389; black marginal inscription. Size: 82x102mm.

1980 World Tourism Conference, Manila—A108

1981, Apr. 1
390	A108	25f multi	25	25
391	A108	75f multi	75	75
392	A108	100f multi, horiz.	1.00	1.00
393	A108	135f multi	1.35	1.35
394	A108	160f multi, horiz.	1.60	1.60
a.		Miniature sheet	5.00	5.00
		Nos. 390-394 (5)	4.95	4.95

No. 394a contains No. 394; black marginal inscription. Size: 89x89mm.

YEMEN

20th Anniv. of Yemen Airways—A109

1983, Apr. 1   Litho.   *Perf. 14*
395	A109	75f yel & multi	75	75
396	A109	125f red & multi	1.25	1.25
397	A109	325f bl & multi	3.25	3.25

Sept. 26th Revolution, 20th Anniv. (1982)—A111

1983, Sept. 26   Litho.   *Perf. 14*
406	A111	100f Communications	
407	A111	150f Literacy	
408	A111	325f Educational development	
a.		Souvenir sheet of 2 (#407, 408)	
409	A111	400f Independence	

Size of No. 408a: 138x77mm.

World Communications Year—A112

1983, Dec. 15
410	A112	150f lt bl & multi	
411	A112	325f lt grn & multi	
a.		Souvenir sheet	

No. 411a contains No. 411. Size: 120x81mm.

AIR POST STAMPS.

Plane over San'a—AP1
Engraved.

1947   *Perf. 12½*   Unwmkd.
C1	AP1	10b brt bl	4.50	4.50
C2	AP1	20b ol grn	6.00	6.00

View of San'a—AP2

Palace of the Rock, Wadi Dhahr—AP3

Designs: 10b, Mocha coffee branch. 16b, Palace, Ta'iz. 20b, 11, Parade Ground, San'a.

Photogravure.

1951   *Perf. 14.*   Wmk. 277
C3	AP2	6b blue	30	20
C4	AP2	8b dk brn	40	30
C5	AP2	10b dk grn	50	30
C6	AP3	12b dk bl	55	40
C7	AP2	16b lil rose	70	55
C8	AP3	20b org brn	1.10	85
C9	AP3	1i dk red	2.25	1.50
		Nos. C3-C9 (7)	5.80	4.10

Nos. C3 and C4 were used provisionally in 1957 for registry and foreign ordinary mail.

Type of Regular Issue, 1952
Designs: 12b, Palace of the Rock, Wadi Dhahr. 20b, Walls of Ibb.

Engraved and Photogravure.

1952   *Perf. 14½.*   Unwmkd.
C10	A15	12b grnsh blk, bl & brn	2.50	2.50
C11	A15	20b ind, bl & brn	3.50	3.50

Flag-and-View Type of Regular Issue, 1952
C12	A16	1i dk brn, car & brt ultra	5.00	5.00

Accession of King Ahmed, Feb. 18, 1948.

Palace in Foreground.
1952
C13	A16	30b yel grn, car & gray	4.00	4.00

Victory of Mar. 13, 1948.

Leaning Minaret, Mosque of Ta'iz — AP6

YEMEN

1954 Photogravure Perf. 14

C14	AP6	10b scarlet	75	50
C15	AP6	12b dl bl	1.00	80
C16	AP6	20b ol bis	1.75	1.25

Issued to commemorate the 5th anniversary of the accession of King Ahmed I.

Type of Regular Issue, 1959

1959 Perf. 13x13½ Wmk. 318

C17	A21	6b org & blk	1.20	80
C18	A21	10b red & blk	1.75	1.25
C19	A21	16b brt vio & red	2.00	1.50

First anniversary of United Arab States.

Type of Regular Issue, 1961 (Antiquities of Marib)

Designs: 6b, Columns, Temple of the Moon God. 16b, Control tower and spillway of 2,700-year-old dam of Marib.

Photogravure
1961, Oct. 14 Perf. 11½ Unwmkd.

C20	A27	6b lt bl grn & blk	45	45
C21	A27	16b lt bl & blk	1.65	1.65

Type of Regular Issue (Buildings)

Design: 6b, Bab al-Yemen, main gate of San'a (horiz.). 16b, Palace of the Rock (Dar al-Hajar).

1961, Nov. 15

C22	A28	6b blk, lt bl & grn	75	65
C23	A28	16b blk, rose & grn	1.50	1.50

Revolution Type of 1972

1972, Nov. 25 Photo. Perf. 13

C40	A80	21b lil, blk & multi	2.25	2.25

Al-Aqsa Mosque Type of 1973

1973, Jan. 1 Photo. Perf. 13½

C41	A82	24b lt bl, blk & multi	1.50	1.50
a.		Miniature sheet		

No. C41a contains one stamp (imperf.); black marginal inscription. Size: 84x72mm.

UNICEF Type of 1973

1973, Jan. 15 Photo. Perf. 13

C42	A83	18b lt bl, blk & multi	1.25	1.25
a.		Miniature sheet	1.25	1.25

No. C42a contains one stamp (imperf.); black marginal inscription. Size: 84x72mm.

11th Anniv. of Revolution—AP10

1973, Sept. 26 Photo. Perf. 14

C43	AP10	7b Bank	35	30
C44	AP10	10b Cement factory	55	45
C45	AP10	18b Hospital	90	75

Nos. C42, C43, C45 Surcharged in Black with New Value and Bars.

1975, Nov. 15

C46	A83	75f on 18b lt bl, blk & multi	75	75
C47	AP10	90f on 7b multi	1.10	1.10
C48	AP10	120f on 18b multi	1.35	1.35
a.		Overprinted in red		

Argentina 1978 World Cup Type of 1980

Designs: World cup emblem and various soccer players.

1980, Mar. 30 Photo. Perf. 14

C49	A99	60f gold & multi	60	60
C50	A99	75f gold & multi	75	75
C51	A99	80f gold & multi	80	80
C52	A99	100f gold & multi	1.00	1.00

Two 225f souvenir sheets exist.

IYC Type of 1980

1980, Apr. 1 Perf. 13½

C53	A100	80f Girl, bird	80	80
C54	A100	100f Boy, butterfly, flower	1.00	1.00
C55	A100	150f Boy, butterfly, flower, diff.	1.50	1.50

Two 200f souvenir sheets exist.

Scouting Type of 1980

1980, May 1 Photo. Perf. 13½x14

C56	A101	60f Bicycling	60	60
C57	A101	75f Fencing	75	75
C58	A101	120f Butterfly catching	1.20	1.20

Two 300f souvenir sheets exist.

Argentina 1978 Winners' Type of 1980

Designs: World cup emblem and various soccer players.

1980, June 1 Photo. Perf. 14

C59	A102	60f gold & multi	60	60
C60	A102	75f gold & multi	75	75
C61	A102	80f gold & multi	80	80
C62	A102	100f gold & multi	1.00	1.00

Two 225f souvenir sheets exist.

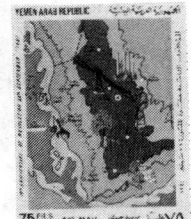

19th Anniv. of Sept. 26th Revolution (1981)—AP11

1982, Jan. 25 Litho. Perf. 14

C63	AP11	75f Map	75	75
C64	AP11	125f Map in sunset	1.25	1.25
C65	AP11	325f Dove in natl. colors	3.25	3.25
a.		Souvenir sheet (95x111mm.)	3.25	3.25
C66	AP11	400f Jets	4.00	4.00

Al-Hasan Ibn Al-Hamadani, Writer—AP12

1982, Feb. 1

C67	AP12	125f grn & multi	1.25	1.25
C68	AP12	325f bl & multi	3.25	3.25

Souvenir Sheet

C69	AP12	375f multi	3.75	3.75

No. C69 contains one stamp (36x46mm.); multicolored margin. Size: 112x90mm.

TB Bacillus Centenary—AP13

1982 Litho. Perf. 14

C70	AP13	25f multi	
C71	AP13	50f multi	
C72	AP13	60f multi	
C73	AP13	75f multi	
C74	AP13	100f multi	
C75	AP13	125f multi	
		Nos. C70-C75 (6)	

Souvenir Sheets

C76		Sheet of 4, Fruit
a.	AP13	100f, any single
C77		Sheet of 4, Flowers
a.	AP13	125f, any single

Size of Nos. C76-C77: 139x119mm.

POSTAGE DUE STAMPS.

D1

Perf. 12½

1942 Lithographed Wmk. 258

J1	D1	1b org & yel grn	20	20
J2	D1	2b org & yel grn	30	30
J3	D1	4b org & yel grn	40	40
J4	D1	6b org & brt ultra	60	60
J5	D1	8b org & brt ultra	80	80
J6	D1	10b org & brt ultra	90	90
J7	D1	12b org & brt ultra	1.20	1.20
J8	D1	20b org & brt ultra	2.00	2.00
		Nos. J1-J8 (8)	6.40	6.40

Yemen had no postage due system. Nos. J1–J8 were used for regular postage.

YEMEN (People's Republic)

YEMEN, People's Democratic Republic

LOCATION—Southern Arabia.
GOVT.—Republic
AREA—112,000 sq. mi.
POP.—1,800,000 (est. 1977).
CAPITALS—Aden and Medina as-Shaab.

The People's Republic of Southern Yemen was proclaimed Nov. 30, 1967, when the Federation of South Arabia achieved independence. It consisted of the former British colony of Aden and the Protectorates. The name was changed to People's Democratic Republic of Yemen on Nov. 30, 1970. See South Arabia, Vol. I.

1,000 Fils = 1 Dinar

People's Republic of Southern Yemen

South Arabia Nos. 3–16 Overprinted in Red or Blue

جمهورية اليمن الجنوبية الشعبية

PEOPLE'S REPUBLIC OF SOUTHERN YEMEN
a

جمهورية اليمن الجنوبية الشعبية

PEOPLE'S REPUBLIC OF SOUTHERN YEMEN
b

Perf. 14½x14

1968, Apr. 1   Photo.   Unwmkd.

Overprinted Type "a"

1	A1	5f bl (R)	8	5
2	A1	10f lt vio bl (R)	10	6
3	A1	15f bl grn (R)	15	10
4	A1	20f grn (R)	18	12
5	A1	25f org brn (B)	25	15
6	A1	30f lem (R)	30	20
7	A1	35f red brn (B)	40	30
8	A1	50f rose red (R)	45	40
9	A1	65f lt yel grn (R)	55	50
10	A1	75f rose car (B)	75	70

Overprinted Type "b"

11	A2	100f multi (B)	1.00	75
12	A2	250f multi (R)	2.25	1.65
13	A2	500f multi (R)	4.25	3.25
14	A2	1d vio & multi (R)	11.00	8.00
		Nos. 1-14 (14)	21.71	16.33

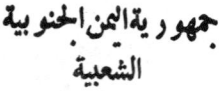

Globe and Flag — A1

Designs: 15f, Revolutionist with broken chain and flames (vert.). 50f, Aden Harbor. 100f, Cotton picking.

1968, May 25   Litho.   Perf. 13x12½

15	A1	10f multi	15	15
16	A1	15f multi	15	15
17	A1	50f multi	50	50
18	A1	100f multi	1.20	1.20

Independence Day, Nov. 30, 1967.

Girl Scouts at Campfire — A2

Designs: 25f, Three Girl Scouts (vert.). 50f, Three Girl Scout leaders.

1968, Sept. 21   Litho.   Unwmkd.   Perf. 13½

19	A2	10f ultra & sep	15	15
20	A2	25f org brn & Prus bl	25	25
21	A2	50f yel, bl & brn	60	60

Issued to publicize the Girl Scout movement in Southern Yemen, established 1966 (in Aden).

Revolutionary — A3

"Freedom-Socialism-Unity" — A4

King of Ausan, Alabaster Statue — A5

Design: 30f, Radfan Mountains where first revolutionary fell.

1968, Oct. 14   Perf. 13   Unwmkd.

22	A3	20f brn & lt bl	25	25
23	A3	30f grn & brn	35	35
24	A4	100f ver & yel	1.00	1.00

Issued for Revolution Day, commemorating the revolution of Oct. 14, 1963.

1968, Dec. 28   Litho.   Perf. 13

Antiquities of Southern Yemen: 35f, African-type sculpture of a man. 50f, Winged bull, Assyrian-type bas-relief (horiz.). 65f, Bull's head (Moon God), alabaster plaque, 230 B.C. (horiz.).

25	A5	5f ol & bis	10	10
26	A5	35f mar & lt bl	40	40
27	A5	50f bis & bl	60	60
28	A5	65f lt grnsh bl & lil	70	70

Martyr Monument, Steamer Point, Aden — A6

1969, Feb. 11   Litho.   Perf. 13

29	A6	15f yel & multi	15	15
30	A6	35f emer & multi	35	35
31	A6	100f org & multi	1.00	1.00

Issued for Martyr Day.

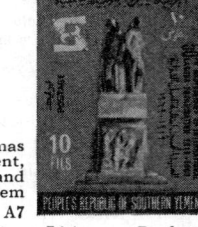

Albert Thomas Monument, Geneva, and ILO Emblem — A7

1969, June 1   Litho.   Perf. 13

32	A7	10f brt grn, blk & lt brn	10	10
33	A7	35f car rose, blk & lt brn	40	40

Issued to commemorate the 50th anniversary of the International Labor Organization, and to honor founder Albert Thomas.

Classroom — A8

1969, Sept. 8   Litho.   Perf. 13

34	A8	35f org & multi	40	40
35	A8	100f yel & multi	1.20	1.20

International Literacy Day, Sept. 8.

Mahatma Gandhi — A9

1969, Sept. 27   Litho.   Perf. 13

36	A9	35f lt ultra & vio brn	40	40

Issued to commemorate the centenary of the birth of Mohandas K. Gandhi (1869–1948), leader in India's fight for independence.

Family — A10

1969, Oct. 1

37	A10	25f lt grn & multi	30	30
38	A10	75f car rose & multi	90	90

Issued for Family Day.

U.N. Headquarters, N.Y. — A11

1969, Oct. 24   Perf. 13

39	A11	20f rose red & multi	20	20
40	A11	65f emer & multi	70	70

Issued for United Nations Day.

Map and Flag of Southern Yemen — A12

Design: 40f, 50f, Tractors and flag (agricultural progress).

1969, Nov. 30   Litho.   Unwmkd.

Size: 41x24½mm.

41	A12	15f multi	15	15
42	A12	35f multi	35	35

Size: 37x37mm.

43	A12	40f bl & multi	40	40
44	A12	50f brn & multi	60	60

Second anniversary of independence.

Map of Arab League Countries, Flag and Emblem — A13

1970, Mar. 22   Perf. 13   Unwmkd.

45	A13	35f lt bl & multi	40	40

25th anniversary of the Arab League.

Lenin — A14

Fighter — A15

1970, Apr. 22   Litho.   Perf. 13

46	A14	75f multi	90	90

Issued to commemorate the centenary of the birth of Lenin (1870–1924), Russian communist leader.

1970, May 15

Designs: 35f, Underground soldier and plane destroyed on ground. 50f, Fighting people hailing Arab liberation flag (horiz.).

47	A15	15f grn, red & blk	12	10
48	A15	35f grn, bl, red & blk	32	30
49	A15	50f grn, blk & red	60	60

Issued for Palestine Day.

U.P.U. Headquarters, Bern — A16

1970, May 22   Litho.   Perf. 13

50	A16	15f org & brt grn	20	20
51	A16	65f yel & car rose	60	60

Issued to commemorate the opening of the new Universal Postal Union Headquarters in Bern.

YEMEN (People's Republic)

Yemeni Costume — A17

Regional Costumes: 15f, 20f, Women's costumes. 50f, Three men of Aden.

1970, July 2   Litho.   Perf. 13

52	A17	10f yel & multi	10	10
53	A17	15f lil & multi	15	15
54	A17	20f lt bl & multi	20	20
55	A17	50f multi	40	40

Camel and Calf — A18

Designs: 25f, Goats. 35f, Arabian oryx. 65f, Socotra dwarf cows.

1970, Aug. 31   Litho.   Perf. 13

56	A18	15f dk brn & multi	15	15
57	A18	25f car rose & multi	25	25
58	A18	35f ultra & multi	50	50
59	A18	65f brt grn & multi	70	70

A19

Designs: 35f, National Front Organization Headquarters. 50f, Farm worker, 1970, and battle scene, 1963.

1970, Oct. 14   Litho.   Perf. 13

Size: 41½x29½mm.

| 60 | A19 | 25f multi | 30 | 30 |

Size: 56½x27mm.

| 61 | A19 | 35f multi | 50 | 50 |

Size: 41x24½mm.

| 62 | A19 | 60f multi | 60 | 60 |

7th anniversary of Oct. 14 Revolution.

U.N. Headquarters, Emblem — A20

1970, Oct. 24   Litho.   Perf. 13

| 63 | A20 | 10f org & bl | 10 | 10 |
| 64 | A20 | 65f brt pink & bl | 70 | 70 |

25th anniversary of the United Nations.

Foreign postal stationery (stamped envelopes, postal cards and air letter sheets) lies beyond the scope of this Catalogue which is limited to adhesive postage stamps.

People's Democratic Republic of Yemen

Temples at Philae — A21

1971, Feb. 1   Litho.   Perf. 13½x13

65	A21	5f vio & multi	10	10
66	A21	35f bl & multi	40	40
67	A21	65f grn & multi	80	80

UNESCO campaign to save the monuments in Nubia.

Scales, Book and Sword — A22

1971, Mar. 1   Litho.   Perf. 13x12½

68	A22	10f brt pink & multi	10	10
69	A22	15f brt grn & multi	20	20
70	A22	35f lt ultra & multi	50	50
71	A22	50f rose & multi	70	70

First Constitution, 1971.

Men of 3 Races, Human Rights Emblem — A23

1971, Mar. 21

72	A23	20f lt bl & multi	20	20
73	A23	35f grn & multi	50	50
74	A23	75f lt vio & multi	90	90

International year against racial discrimination.

Map and Flag — A24

"Brothers' Blood" Tree, Socotra Island — A25

1971–77   Litho.   Perf. 13½

75	A24	5f yel & multi	5	5
76	A24	10f grn & multi	5	5
77	A24	15f yel & multi	8	8
78	A24	20f org & multi	10	10
79	A24	25f bl & multi	15	15
80	A24	35f red org & multi	20	20
81	A24	40f vio & multi	22	22
82	A24	50f yel grn & multi	40	40
82A	A24	60f red & multi ('77)	35	35
83	A24	65f pale vio & multi	60	60
84	A24	80f org brn & multi	80	80
84A	A24	90f ol & multi ('77)	50	50

Perf. 13

84B	A25	110f brn & multi ('77)	60	60
85	A25	125f ultra & multi	1.50	1.50
86	A25	250f org & multi	2.00	2.00
87	A25	500f multi	4.00	4.00
88	A25	1d grn & multi	8.00	8.00
		Nos. 75-88 (17)	19.60	19.60

Issue dates: Nos. 82A, 84A–84B, Oct. 17, 1977. Others, Apr. 1, 1971.

Machine Gun and Map — A26

Arms with Wrench and Cogwheel — A27

Designs: 45f, Woman fighter and flame (horiz.). 50f, Fighter, factories and rainbow.

1971, June 9   Litho.   Perf. 12½x13

89	A26	15f multi	15	15
90	A26	45f grn & multi	55	55
91	A26	50f multi	70	70

Armed revolution in the Arabian Gulf.

1971, June 22

Designs: 25f, Torch, factories, symbols. 65f, Windmill.

92	A27	15f bl & multi	20	20
93	A27	25f multi	30	30
94	A27	50f multi	70	70

2nd anniversary of the revolution of June 22, 1969 (Corrective Move). A 20f picturing a fighter holding rifle and flag, with flag colors transposed, was withdrawn on day of issue.

Revolutionary Emblem — A28

Design: 40f, Map of southern Arabia and flag of republic.

1971, Sept. 26

| 95 | A28 | 10f yel & multi | 10 | 10 |
| 96 | A28 | 40f lt grn & multi | 50 | 50 |

9th anniversary of the revolution of Sept. 26.

Gamal Abdel Nasser — A29

UNICEF Emblem, Children of the World — A30

1971, Sept. 28   Litho.   Perf. 12½x13

| 97 | A29 | 65f multi | 65 | 65 |

First anniversary of the death of Gamal Abdel Nasser (1918–1970), President of Egypt.

1971, Dec. 11   Perf. 13x13½

98	A30	15f org, car & blk	15	15
99	A30	40f lt ultra, car & blk	35	35
100	A30	50f yel grn, car & blk	60	60

25th anniversary of the United Nations International Children's Fund (UNICEF).

Pigeons — A31

Birds: 40f, Partridge. 65f, Partridge and guinea fowl. 100f, European kite.

1971, Dec. 22   Perf. 13½x13

101	A31	5f bl, blk & car	10	10
102	A31	40f sal & multi	30	30
103	A31	65f brt grn, blk & car	60	60
104	A31	100f yel, blk & car	1.00	1.00

Dhow under Construction — A32

Design: 80f, Dhow under sail (vert.).

Perf. 13½x13, 13x13½

1972, Feb. 15

| 105 | A32 | 5f bl, brn & yel | 25 | 25 |
| 106 | A32 | 80f lt bl & multi | 85 | 85 |

Band — A33

Designs: 25f, 40f, 80f, Various folk dances.

1972, Apr. 8   Litho.   Perf. 13

107	A33	10f lt brn & multi	6	6
108	A33	25f org & multi	20	20
109	A33	40f red & multi	50	50
110	A33	80f bl & multi	90	90

Palestinian Fighter and Barbed Wire — A34

1972, May 15

111	A34	5f emer & multi	10	10
112	A34	20f bl & multi	20	20
113	A34	65f org ver & multi	70	70

Struggle for Palestine liberation.

Policemen on Parade — A35

Design: 80f, Militia women on parade.

1972, June 20   Litho.   Perf. 13½

114	A35	25f bl & multi	20	20
115	A35	80f bl grn & multi	80	80
		a. Souvenir sheet of 2	1.40	1.40

Police Day. No. 115a contains one each of Nos. 114 and 115. Yellow, black and red border. Size: 120x72mm. Sold for 150f.

970　　　　　　　　　　　　　　　YEMEN (People's Republic)

Designs: 15f, Parade of young women.
40f, Yemeni Guides and Scouts on parade.
80f, Acrobats (vert.).

1972, July 20　　Litho.　　Perf. 13½

116	A36	10f lt bl & multi	6	6
117	A36	15f multi	20	20
118	A36	40f buff & multi	50	50
119	A36	80f lt ultra & multi	80	80

Turtle
A37

1972, Sept. 2　　Litho.　　Perf. 13
Multicolored

120	A37	15f *Shown*	20	20
121	A37	40f *Sailfish*	50	50
122	A37	65f *Kingfish*	70	70
123	A37	125f *Spiny lobster*	1.00	1.00

Book Year Emblem
A38

1972, Sept. 9

| 124 | A38 | 40f red, ultra & yel | 50 | 50 |
| 125 | A38 | 65f org, ultra & yel | 75 | 75 |

International Book Year 1972.

Farm Couple and Fields
A39

1972, Nov. 23　　Litho.　　Perf. 13

126	A39	10f org & multi	10	10
127	A39	25f rose lil & multi	20	20
128	A39	40f red & multi	50	50

Lands Day, publicizing land reforms.

Militia—A40

Designs: 20f, Soldier guarding village.
65f, Industrial, agricultural and educational progress (vert.).

1972, Dec. 2　　Litho.　　Perf. 13

129	A40	5f multi	10	10
130	A40	20f multi	20	20
131	A40	65f multi	75	75
a.		Souvenir sheet of 3	1.20	1.20

5th anniversary of independence. No. 131a contains 3 stamps similar to Nos. 129–131 with simulated perforations. Ocher and multicolored margin. Size: 132½x140½mm.

Census Chart
A41

1973, Apr. 3　　Litho.　　Perf. 12½x13½

| 132 | A41 | 25f org, emer & ol | 25 | 25 |
| 133 | A41 | 40f rose, bl & vio | 50 | 50 |

Population census 1973.

WHO Emblem and "25"
A42

1973, Apr. 7　　Perf. 14x12½, 12½x14
Multicolored

134	A42	5f "25" and WHO emblem (vert.)	10	10
135	A42	20f *Shown*	20	20
136	A42	125f "25" and WHO emblem	1.20	1.20

25th anniversary of the World Health Organization.

Elephant Bay
A43

Views: 20f, Taweela Tanks Reservoir (vert.). 25f, Shibam Town. 100f, Al-Mohdar Mosque, Tarim.

1973, June 9　　Litho.　　Perf. 13

137	A43	20f multi	15	15
138	A43	25f multi	25	25
139	A43	40f multi	50	50
140	A43	100f multi	90	90

Tourist publicity.

Office Buildings and Slum, Aden
A44

Design: 80f, Intersection, Aden (vert.).

1973, Aug. 4　　Lithographed　　Perf. 13

| 141 | A44 | 20f multi | 20 | 20 |
| 142 | A44 | 80f multi | 80 | 80 |

Nationalization of buildings.

Army Unit
A45

Designs: 20f, Four marching soldiers. 40f, Sailors on parade. 80f, Tanks.

1973, Sept. 1

143	A45	10f multi	10	10
144	A45	20f multi	20	20
145	A45	40f multi	50	50
146	A45	80f multi	80	80

People's Army.

FAO Emblem, Loading Food—A46

Design: 80f, Workers and grain sacks.

1973, Dec. 19　　Lithographed　　Perf. 13

| 147 | A46 | 20f bl & multi | 20 | 20 |
| 148 | A46 | 80f bl & multi | 80 | 80 |

World Food Program, 10th anniversary.

Letter and UPU Emblem
A47

UPU Emblem and Yemeni Flag
A48

Map of Yemen, UPU Emblem
A49

Design: 20f, "100" formed by people, and UPU emblem.

1974, Oct. 9　　Litho.　　Perf. 12½x13½

149	A47	5f multi	10	10
150	A47	20f multi	20	20
151	A48	40f multi	50	50
152	A49	125f multi	1.00	1.00

Centenary of Universal Postal Union.

Irrigation System—A50

Designs: 20f, Bulldozer pushing soil. 100f, Tractors plowing field.

1974　　Lithographed　　Perf. 13

153	A50	10f multi	10	10
154	A50	20f multi	20	20
155	A50	100f multi	80	80

Progress in agriculture.

Lathe Operator
A51

Designs: 40f, Printers. 80f, Women textile workers (horiz.).

1975, May 1　　Litho.　　Perf. 13

156	A51	10f multi	10	10
157	A51	40f multi	50	50
158	A51	80f multi	80	80

Industrial progress.

Yemeni Woman
A52

Designs: Various women's costumes.

1975, Nov. 15　　Litho.　　Perf. 11½x12

159	A52	5f blk & ocher	8	8
160	A52	10f blk & vio	10	10
161	A52	15f blk & ol	10	10
162	A52	25f blk & rose lil	30	30
163	A52	40f blk & Prus bl	50	50
164	A52	50f blk & org brn	60	60
		Nos. 159-164 (6)	1.68	1.68

Women Factory Workers, IWY Emblem
A53

1975, Dec. 30　　Litho.　　Perf. 12x11½

| 165 | A53 | 40f blk & sal | 40 | 40 |
| 166 | A53 | 50f blk & yel grn | 60 | 60 |

International Women's Year 1975.

Soccer Player and Field
A54

Designs: Different scenes from soccer.

1976, Apr. 1　　Litho.　　Perf. 11½x12

167	A54	5f lt bl & brn	5	5
168	A54	40f yel & grn	50	50
169	A54	80f sal & vio	80	80

Rocket Take-off from Moon
A55

Designs: 15f, Alexander Satalov. 40f, Lunokhod on moon (horiz.). 65f, Valentina Tereshkova and rocket.

Perf. 11½x12, 12x11½

1976, Apr. 17　　Lithographed

170	A55	10f multi	6	6
171	A55	15f multi	9	9
172	A55	40f multi	50	50
173	A55	65f multi	70	70

Soviet cosmonauts and space program.

YEMEN (People's Republic)

Traffic Policemen
A56

1977, Apr. 16		Litho.	Perf. 14	
174	A56	25f red & blk	30	30
175	A56	60f yel & blk	70	70
176	A56	75f grn & blk	80	80
177	A56	110f dp bl & blk	1.10	1.10

Traffic change to right side of road.

APU Emblem
A57

1977, Apr. 12		Litho.	Perf. 13½	
178	A57	20f lt bl & multi	20	20
179	A57	60f gray & multi	70	70
180	A57	70f lt grn & multi	80	80
181	A57	90f bl grn & multi	90	90

Arab Postal Union, 25th anniversary.

Congress Decree and Red Star
A58

Designs: 25f, Pres. Salim Rubi'a Ali, Council members Ali Nasser Muhamed and Abdul Farta Ismail. 65f, Women's militia on parade. 95f, Aerial view of textile mill.

1977, May		Photo.	Perf. 13	
182	A58	25f grn, gold & dk brn	30	30
183	A58	35f red, gold & lt bl	50	50
184	A58	65f bl, gold & lil	70	70
185	A58	95f org, gold & grn	90	90

Unification Congress, 1st anniversary.

Afrivoluta Pringlei
A59

Shells: 60f, Festilyria duponti (vert.). 110f, Conus splendidulus. 180f, Cypraea broderipii.

1977, July 16		Litho.	Perf. 13½	
186	A59	60f multi	30	25
187	A59	90f multi	50	35
188	A59	110f multi	80	60
189	A59	180f multi	1.20	1.00

Emblem and Flag
A60

Designs: 20f, Man with broken chain. 90f, Pipeline, agriculture and industry. 110f, Flag, symbolic tree and hands holding tools.

1977, Nov. 30		Litho.	Perf. 13½	
190	A60	5f blk & multi	5	5
191	A60	20f blk & multi	10	10
192	A60	90f blk & multi	45	35
193	A60	80f blk & multi	80	50

10th anniversary of independence.

Dome of the Rock
A61

1978, May 15			Perf. 12	
194	A61	5f multi	6	6

Palestinian fighters and their families.

Congress Emblem and "CUBA"
A62

Designs: 60f, Congress emblem. 90f, Festival emblem as flower. 110f, Festival emblem, dove, young man and woman.

1978, June 22		Litho.	Perf. 14	
195	A62	5f multi	5	5
196	A62	60f multi	35	25
197	A62	90f multi	50	40
198	A62	110f multi	80	60

11th World Youth Festival, Havana.

Silver Ornaments
A63

Designs: Various silver ornaments.

1978, July 22		Litho.	Perf. 13½	
199	A63	10f blk & multi	6	6
200	A63	15f blk & multi	10	10
201	A63	20f blk & multi	12	12
202	A63	60f blk & multi	35	25
203	A63	90f blk & multi	60	45
204	A63	110f blk & multi	80	55
		Nos. 199-204 (6)	2.03	1.53

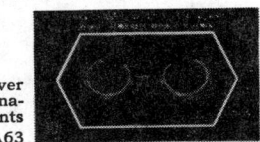

Almarfaa
A64

Yemeni Musical Instruments: 60f, Almizmar. 90f, Alqnboos. 110f, Simsimiya.

1978, Aug. 26			Perf. 14	
205	A64	35f red & multi	15	10
206	A64	60f red & multi	35	30
207	A64	90f red & multi	50	40
208	A64	110f red & multi	80	60

Attractive slip cases are available for most Scott Albums.

"V" for Vanguard
A65

Man with Palm, Factories
A66

1978, Oct. 11		Litho.	Perf. 14	
209	A65	5f multi	5	5
210	A65	20f multi	10	10
211	A65	60f multi	35	25
212	A65	180f multi	80	60

1st Conference of Vanguard Party, Oct. 11-13.

1978, Oct. 14

Designs: 10f, Palm branches, broken chains (horiz.). 60f, Candle and "15". 110f, Woman and man with rifle, "15".

213	A66	10f multi	6	6
214	A66	35f multi	15	10
215	A66	60f multi	30	20
216	A66	110f multi	50	35

15th Revolution Day.

Child, Map of Arabia and IYC Emblem
A67

1979, Mar. 20		Litho.	Perf. 13½	
217	A67	15f multi	10	10
218	A67	20f multi	10	10
219	A67	60f multi	30	20
220	A67	90f multi	45	35

International Year of the Child.

Sickle, Star, Tractor, Wheat , and Dove
A68

1979, June 22			Perf. 14	
Designs: 35f, Pylon, star, compass, wheat and hammer. 60f, Students, worker and clock. 90f, Woman with raised arms, doves and star.

221	A68	20f multi	10	10
222	A68	35f multi	15	10
223	A68	60f multi	30	20
224	A68	90f multi	45	35

Corrective Move, 10th anniversary.

Yemen No. 52, Hill—A69

Hill and: 110f, Yemen No. 56. 250f, Aden No. 12.

1979, Aug. 27		Litho.	Perf. 14	
225	A69	90f multi	45	35
226	A69	110f multi	55	45

Souvenir Sheet

| 227 | A69 | 250f multi | 1.25 | 1.25 |

Sir Rowland Hill (1795-1879), originator of penny postage. No. 227 has bright blue and black margin showing Mulready envelope. Size: 125×89mm.

Book, World Map, Arab Achievements
A70

1979, Sept. 26		Litho.	Perf. 14	
228	A70	60f multi	30	20

Party Emblem
A71

Cassia Adenesis
A72

Perf. 14½×14

| 229 | A71 | 60f multi | 30 | 20 |

Yemeni Socialist Party, 1st anniversary.

Flowers: 90f, Nerium oleander. 110f, Calligonum comosum. 180f, Adenium obesium.

1979, Nov. 30		Litho.	Perf. 13½	
230	A72	20f multi	10	10
231	A72	90f multi	45	35
232	A72	110f multi	55	40
233	A72	180f multi	90	55

First Anniv. of Iranian Revolution—A73

1980, Feb. 12		Litho.	Perf. 13½	
234	A73	60f multi	35	35

Dido—A74

1980, Mar. 5		Litho.	Perf. 13½	
235	A74	110f shown	40	40
236	A74	180f Anglia	90	55
237	A74	250f India	1.25	1.00

YEMEN (People's Republic)

Basket Maker, London 1980
Emblem—A75

1980, May 6		Litho.		Perf. 14	
238	A75	60f shown		35	35
239	A75	90f Hubble bubble pipe maker		52	52
240	A75	110f Weaver		65	65
241	A75	250f Potter		1.50	1.50

London 1980 International Stamp Exhibition, May 6-14.

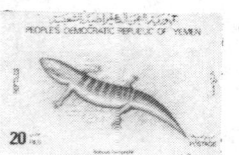
Hemprich's Skink—A76

1980, May 8		Litho.		Perf. 14	
242	A76	20f shown		12	12
243	A76	35f Mole viper		20	20
244	A76	110f Carter's day gecko		65	65
245	A76	180f Cobra		1.05	1.05

Misha and Olympic Emblem
A77

Farmers Armed
A78

1980, July 19		Litho.		Perf. 12½x12	
246	A77	110f multi		65	65

1980, Oct. 17				Perf. 13½	
247	A78	50f Armed farmers working, horiz.		30	30
248	A78	90f shown		55	55
249	A78	110f Sickle (wheat) and fist		65	65

10th anniversary of farmers' uprising.

110th Birth Anniversary of Lenin—A79

1980, Nov. 7		Litho.		Perf. 12	
250	A79	35f multi		20	20

Douglas DC-3—A80

1981, Mar. 11		Litho.		Perf. 13½	
251	A80	60f shown		35	35
252	A80	90f Boeing 707		55	55
253	A80	250f DHC Dash 7		1.50	1.50

Democratic Yemen Airlines, 10th anniversary.

Ras Boradli Earth Satellite Station—A82

1981, June 22		Litho.		Perf. 12	
257	A82	60f multi		35	35

Conocarpus Lancifolius—A83

1981, Aug. 1		Litho.		Perf. 12	
258	A83	90f shown		55	55
259	A83	180f Ficus vasta		1.10	1.10
260	A83	250f Maerua crassifolia		1.50	1.50

Supreme People's Council, 10th Anniv.—A84

1981, Aug. 18		Litho.		Perf. 15x14½	
261	A84	180f multi		1.10	1.10

Desert Fox—A85

1981, Sept. 26		Litho.		Perf. 14½	
262	A85	50f shown		30	30
263	A85	90f South Arabian leopard		55	55
264	A85	250f Ibex		1.50	1.50

No. 194 Redrawn

1981, Oct. 15		Litho.		Perf. 12	
		Size: 25x27mm.			
264A	A61	5f multi		5	5

Denomination in upper right.

Tephrosia Apollinea—A86

1981, Nov. 30		Litho.		Perf. 13½	
265	A86	50f shown		30	30
266	A86	90f Citrullus colocynthis		55	55
267	A86	110f Aloe sqarrosa		65	65
268	A86	250f Lawsonia inermis		1.50	1.50

Intl. Year of the Disabled—A87

1981, Dec. 12		Litho.		Perf. 14½	
269	A87	50f multi		30	30
270	A87	100f multi		60	60
271	A87	150f multi		90	90

TB Bacillus Centenary—A88

1982, Mar. 24		Litho.		Perf. 14½	
272	A88	50f multi		30	30

30th Anniv. of Arab Postal Union—A89

1982, Apr. 12		Litho.		Perf. 14	
273	A89	100f multi		60	60

1982 World Cup—A90

Designs: Various soccer players.

1982, June 13		Litho.		Perf. 14	
274	A90	50f multi		30	30
275	A90	100f multi		60	60
276	A90	150f multi		90	90
277	A90	200f multi		1.25	1.25
a.		Souvenir sheet of 4		3.25	3.25

No. 277a contains Nos. 274-277; gold and black margin. Size: 115x95mm.

Intl. Palestinian Solidarity Day—A92

1982, Nov. 20		Litho.		Perf. 12	
279	A92	5f multi		5	5

60th Anniv. of USSR—A93

1982, Dec. 22		Litho.		Perf. 12½x12	
280	A93	50f Flags, arms		30	30

ZAIRE

ZAIRE
(zȧ·ē′rĕ, zä′ĕr)

(formerly Congo Democratic Republic)

LOCATION—Central Africa.
GOVT.—Republic.
AREA—905,063 sq. mi.
POP.—26,380,000 (est. 1977).
CAPITAL—Kinshasa.

Congo Democratic Republic changed its name to Republic of the Zaïre in November, 1971. Issues before that date are listed in Vol. II under Congo Democratic Republic.

100 Sengi = 1 Li-Kuta
100 Ma-Kuta = 1 Zaire

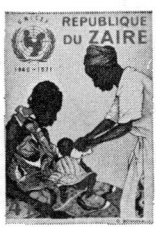

UNICEF Emblem, Child Care
A143

Designs (UNICEF Emblem and): 14k, Map of Africa showing Zaire. 17k, Boy in African village.

1971, Dec. 18   Perf. 14x13½
750	A143	4k gold & multi	20	10
751	A143	14k lt bl, gold, red & grn	60	35
752	A143	17k gold & multi	85	40

25th anniversary of the United Nations International Children's Fund (UNICEF).

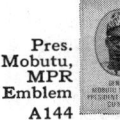

Pres. Mobutu, MPR Emblem
A144

1972   Photogravure   Perf. 11½
753	A144	4k multi	5.00	3.50
754	A144	14k multi	5.00	3.50
755	A144	22k multi	5.00	3.50

5th anniversary of the People's Revolutionary Movement (MPR).

Zaire Arms A145   Pres. Joseph D. Mobutu A146

1972   Litho.   Perf. 14
756	A145	10s red org & blk	5	5
757	A145	40s brt bl & multi	5	5
758	A145	50s cit & multi	5	5

Perf. 13
759	A146	1k sky bl & multi	5	5
760	A146	2k org & multi	10	5
761	A146	3k multi	15	6
762	A146	4k emer & multi	20	8
763	A146	5k multi	22	13
764	A146	6k multi	25	15
765	A146	8k cit & multi	42	18
766	A146	9k multi	50	20
767	A146	10k lt lil & multi	50	25
768	A146	14k multi	75	30
769	A146	17k multi	85	40
770	A146	20k yel & multi	1.00	50
771	A146	50k multi	2.50	1.20
772	A146	100k fawn & multi	5.00	2.25
Nos. 756-772 (17)			12.64	5.95

Same, Denominations in Zaires

1973, Feb. 21
773	A146	0.01z sky bl & multi	5	5
774	A146	0.02z org & multi	10	5
775	A146	0.03z multi	15	6
776	A146	0.04z multi	20	8
777	A146	0.10z multi	50	25
778	A146	0.14z multi	75	33
Nos. 773-778 (6)			1.75	82

Inga Dam
A147

1973, Jan. 25   Litho.   Perf. 13½
790	A147	0.04z multi	18	12
791	A147	0.14z pink & multi	65	40
792	A147	0.18z yel & multi	80	50

Completion of first section of Inga Dam Nov. 24, 1972.

World Map—A148

1973, June 23   Photo.   Perf. 12½x12
793	A148	0.04z lil & multi	20	8
794	A148	0.07z multi	30	12
795	A148	0.18z multi	1.00	35

3rd International Fair at Kinshasa, June 23–July 8.

The dark brown ink of the inscription was applied by a thermographic process and varnished, producing a shiny, raised effect.

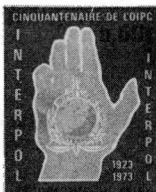

Hand and INTERPOL Emblem
A149

1973, Sept. 28   Litho.   Perf. 12½
796	A149	0.06z multi	35	10
797	A149	0.14z multi	70	30

50th anniversary of International Criminal Police Organization.

Leopard with Soccer Ball on Globe—A150

1974, July 17   Photo.   Perf. 11½x12
798	A150	1k multi	8	5
799	A150	2k multi	12	5
800	A150	3k multi	25	6
801	A150	4k multi	30	10
802	A150	5k multi	38	10
803	A150	14k multi	1.00	28
Nos. 798-803 (6)			2.13	62

World Cup Soccer Championship, Munich, June 13–July 7.

Foreman-Ali Fight
A151

1974, Nov. 9   Litho.   Perf. 12x12½
804	A151	1k multi	8	8
805	A151	4k multi	22	8
806	A151	6k multi	35	10
807	A151	14k multi	75	30
808	A151	20k multi	1.10	35
Nos. 804-808 (5)			2.50	88

World Heavyweight Boxing Championship match between George Foreman and Muhammad Ali, Kinshasa, Oct. 30 (postponed from Sept. 25).

Same, Type of 1974, Denominations in Zaires and Inscribed in Various Colors

1975, Aug.   Litho.   Perf. 12x12½
809	A151	0.01z multi (R)	5	5
810	A151	0.04z multi (Br)	15	8
811	A151	0.06z multi (Bk)	25	10
812	A151	0.14z multi (G)	65	30
813	A151	0.20z multi (Bk)	85	35
Nos. 809-813 (5)			1.95	88

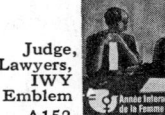

Judge, Lawyers, IWY Emblem
A152

1975, Dec.   Photo.   Perf. 11½
814	A152	1k dl blk & multi	6	5
815	A152	2k dp rose & multi	8	5
816	A152	4k dl grn & multi	25	8
817	A152	14k vio & multi	65	30

International Women's Year 1975.

Waterfall
A153

1975   Photogravure   Perf. 11½
818	A153	1k multi	5	5
819	A153	2k lt bl & multi	8	5
820	A153	3k multi	12	6
821	A153	4k sal & multi	25	8
822	A153	5k grn & multi	25	13
Nos. 818-822 (5)			75	37

12th General Assembly of the International Union for Nature Preservation (U.I.C.N.), Kinshasa, Sept. 1975.

Okapis
A154

1975
823	A154	1k bl & multi	6	5
824	A154	2k yel grn & multi	10	5
825	A154	3k brn red & multi	15	6
826	A154	4k grn & multi	20	8
827	A154	5k multi	25	13
Nos. 823-827 (5)			76	37

Virunga National Park, 50th anniversary.

Siderma Maluku Industry
A155

Designs: 1k, Sozacom apartment building (vert.). 3k, Matadi flour mill (vert.). 4k, Women parachutists. 8k, Pres. Mobutu visiting Chairman Mao (vert.). 10k, Soldiers working along the Salongo. 14k, Pres. Mobutu addressing U.N. Gen. Assembly, Oct. 1974. 15k, Celebrating crowd.

1975
828	A155	1k ocher & multi	6	5
829	A155	2k yel grn & multi	8	5
830	A155	3k multi	10	6
831	A155	4k multi	18	8
832	A155	8k dk brn & multi	38	16
833	A155	10k sep & multi	45	25
834	A155	14k bl & multi	65	32
835	A155	15k org & multi	75	40
Nos. 828-835 (8)			2.65	1.37

10th anniversary of new government.

Tshokwe Mask
A156

Designs: 2k, 4k, Seated woman, Pende. 7k, like 5k. 10k, 14k, Antelope mask, Suku. 15k, 18k, Kneeling woman, Kongo. 20k, 25k, Kuba mask.

1977, Jan. 8   Photo.   Perf. 11½
836	A156	2k multi	8	5
837	A156	4k multi	10	8
838	A156	5k gray & multi	12	10
839	A156	7k multi	18	12
840	A156	10k multi	25	15
841	A156	14k multi	35	20
842	A156	15k multi	38	22
843	A156	18k multi	45	28
844	A156	20k multi	90	30
845	A156	25k vio & multi	1.00	38
Nos. 836-845 (10)			3.81	1.88

Wood carving and masks of Zaire.

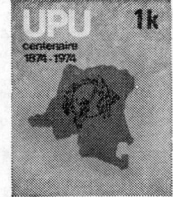

Map of Zaire, UPU Emblem
A157

1977, Apr.   Litho.   Perf. 13½
846	A157	1k org & multi	8	8
847	A157	4k dk bl & multi	20	8
848	A157	7k ol grn & multi	38	38
849	A157	50k brn & multi	4.25	4.25

Centenary of Universal Postal Union (in 1974).

Congo Stamps and Type of 1968-1971 Surcharged with New Value, Bars and "REPUBLIQUE DU ZAIRE"

Printing and Perforations as Before

1977
850	A126	1k on 10s (#642)	5	5
851	A122	2k on 9.6k (#618)	6	5
852	A140	10k on 10s (#735)	30	20
853	A134	25k on 10s (#703)	75	50
854	A127	40k on 0.6k	1.20	80
855	A135	48k on 10s (#713)	1.50	95
Nos. 850-855 (6)			3.86	2.55

No. 854 not issued without surcharge.

ZAIRE

Congo Nos. 644, 643, 635, 746 Surcharged with New Value, Bars and "REPUBLIQUE DU ZAIRE" in Black or Carmine. Zaire No. 757 Surcharged

Printing and Perforations as Before

1977
856	A126	5k on 30s	25	12
857	A126	10k on 15s (C)	25	12
858	A124	20k on 9.60k	50	25
859	A141	30k on 12k	1.00	38
860	A145	10k on 40s (C)	2.75	1.75
		Nos. 856-860 (5)	4.75	2.62

Souvenir Sheet

Adoration of the Kings, by Rubens
A158

1977, Dec. 19 Photo. Perf. 13½
861	A158	5z multi	15.00	12.50

Christmas 1977. Size: 85x100mm.

Pantodon Buchholzi
A159

Soccer Game, Argentina–France
A160

Fish: 70s, Aphyosemion striatum. 5k, Ctenopoma fasciolatum. 8k, Malapterurus electricus. 10k, Hemichromis bimaculatus. 30k, Marcusenius isidori. 40k, Synodontis nigriventris. 48k, Julidochromis ornatus. 100k, Nothobranchius brieni. 250k, Micralestes interruptus.

1978, Jan. 23 Litho. Perf. 14
862	A159	30s multi	5	5
863	A159	70s multi	5	5
864	A159	5k multi	15	8
865	A159	8k multi	25	12
866	A159	10k multi	25	15
867	A159	30k multi	75	45
868	A159	40k multi	1.00	60
869	A159	48k multi	1.25	75
870	A159	100k multi	3.25	1.50
		Nos. 862-870 (9)	7.00	3.75

Souvenir Sheet
Perf. 13½
871	A159	250k multi	6.25	6.25

No. 871 contains one stamp (46x35mm.); dark blue, light blue and red margin. Size: 80x74mm.

1978, Aug. 7 Litho. Perf. 12½

Various Soccer Games and Jules Rimet Cup: 3k, Austria–Brazil. 7k, Scotland–Iran. 9k, Netherlands–Peru. 15k, Hungary–Italy. 20k, Fed. Rep. of Germany–Mexico. 50k, Tunisia–Poland. 100k, Spain–Sweden. 500k, Rimet Cup, Games' emblem and cartoon of soccer player (horiz.).

872	A160	1k multi	5	5
873	A160	3k multi	10	6
874	A160	7k multi	18	12
875	A160	9k multi	22	15
876	A160	10k multi	25	15
877	A160	20k multi	50	30
878	A160	50k multi	1.25	75
879	A160	100k multi	2.50	1.50
		Nos. 872-879 (8)	5.05	3.08

Souvenir Sheets
880	A160	500k bl & multi	15.00	12.50
881	A160	500k red & multi	15.00	12.50

11th World Cup Soccer Championship, Argentina, June 1-25. Nos. 880-881 contain one stamp each (47x36mm.). Stamp of No. 880 has blue frameline; sheet has emerald margin with black inscription: Argentina 78 / COUPE DU MONDE. Stamp of No. 881 has red frame line and blue margin with black inscription: Finalistes Coupe du Monde 78 / ARGENTINE 3-HOLLANDE 1. Size of sheets: 104x80mm.

Mama Mobutu
A161

Pres. Joseph D. Mobutu
A162

1978, Oct. 23 Photo. Perf. 12
882	A161	8k multi	25	10

Mama Mobutu (1941–1977), wife of Pres. Mobutu.

1978 Photo. Perf. 12
883	A162	2k multi	6	5
884	A162	5k multi	8	5
885	A162	6k multi	8	5
886	A162	8k multi	12	8
887	A162	10k multi	12	8
888	A162	25k multi	25	15
889	A162	48k multi	55	40
890	A162	1z multi	1.10	85
		Nos. 883-890 (8)	2.36	1.71

Souvenir Sheet

Elizabeth II in Westminster Abbey
A163

1978, Dec. 11 Photo. Perf. 13½
891	A163	5z multi	12.50	12.50

25th anniversary of coronation of Queen Elizabeth II; multicolored margin shows interior of Westminster Abbey. Size: 72x92 mm.

Souvenir Sheet

Albrecht Dürer, Self-portrait
A164

1978, Dec. 18 Perf. 13
892	A164	5z multi	12.50	12.50

Albrecht Dürer (1471–1528), German painter and engraver; multicolored margin shows painting. Size: 72x92mm.

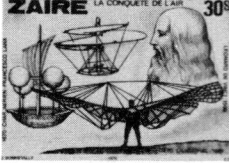

Leonardo da Vinci and his Drawings—A165

History of Aviation: 70s, Planes of Wright Brothers, 1905, and Santos Dumont, 1906. 1k, Bleriot XI, 1909, and Farman F-60, 1909. 5k, Junkers G-38, 1929, and Spirit of St. Louis, 1927. 8k, Sikorski S-42B, 1934 and Macchi-Castoldi MC-72, 1934. 10k, Boeing 707, 1960, and Fokker F-VII, 1935. 50k, Helicopter and Douglas DC-10, 1971. 75k, Apollo XI, 1969, and Concorde, 1976. 5z, Giffard's balloon, 1852, and Hindenburg LZ 129, 1936.

1978, Dec. 28 Litho. Perf. 13
893	A165	30s multi	5	5
894	A165	70s multi	5	5
895	A165	1k multi	8	5
896	A165	5k multi	12	12
897	A165	8k multi	20	20
898	A165	10k multi	25	25
899	A165	50k multi	1.25	1.25
900	A165	75k multi	1.75	1.75
		Nos. 893-900 (8)	3.75	3.72

Souvenir Sheet
Perf. 11½
901	A165	5z multi	12.50	12.50

No. 901 has multicolored margin showing U.S. Double Eagle II balloon which crossed Atlantic, Aug. 17, 1978.

Pres. Mobutu, Map of Zaire, N'tombe Dancer—A166

Designs (Pres. Mobutu and Map): 3k, Bird. 4k, Elephant. 10k, Diamond and cotton boll. 14k, Hand holding torch. 17k, Leopard's head and Victoria Regia lily. 25k, Finzia waterfall. 50k, Wagenia fisherman.

1979, Feb. Litho. Perf. 14x13½
902	A166	1k multi	5	5
903	A166	3k multi	6	6
904	A166	4k multi	8	8
905	A166	10k multi	10	8
a.		Souvenir sheet of 4	50	40
906	A166	14k multi	12	10
907	A166	17k multi	15	12
908	A166	25k multi	20	15
909	A166	50k multi	50	40
a.		Souvenir sheet of 4	3.00	2.00
		Nos. 902-909 (8)	1.26	1.04

Zaire (Congo) River expedition. No. 905a contains Nos. 902–905, No. 909a, Nos. 906–909. Multicolored margins show people and artifacts (#905a) and animals (#909a). Size: 132x101mm.

Phylloporus Ampliporus
A167

Mushrooms: 5k, Engleromyces goetzei. 8k, Scutellinia virungae. 10k, Pycnoporus sanguineus. 30k, Cantharellus miniatescens. 40k, Lactarius phlebonemus. 48k, Phallus indusiatus. 100k, Ramaria moelleriana.

1979, Mar. Photo. Perf. 13½x13
910	A167	30s multi	5	5
911	A167	5k multi	8	5
912	A167	8k multi	12	8
913	A167	10k multi	12	8
914	A167	30k multi	38	25
915	A167	40k multi	45	30
916	A167	48k multi	55	40
917	A167	100k multi	1.10	80
		Nos. 910-917 (8)	2.85	2.01

Souvenir Sheets

Pope John XXIII
A168

Popes: No. 919, Paul VI. No. 920, John Paul I.

1979, June 25 Litho. Perf. 11½
918	A168	250k multi		2.50
919	A168	250k multi		2.50
920	A168	250k multi		2.50

Pope John XXIII (1881–1963); Pope Paul VI (1897–1978); Pope John Paul I (1912–1978). Nos. 918–920 have multicolored margin showing full portraits of Popes. Size: 96x131mm.

Boy Beating Drum
A169

IYC Emblem on Map of Zaire and: 10k, 20k, Girl (diff.). 50k, Boy. 100k, Boys. 300k, Mother and child. 10z, Mother and children (horiz.).

1979, July 23 Litho. Perf. 12½
921	A169	5k multi	6	5
922	A169	10k multi	12	8
923	A169	20k multi	22	15
924	A169	50k multi	55	35
925	A169	100k multi	1.10	65
926	A169	300k multi	3.25	1.50
		Nos. 921-926 (6)	5.30	2.78

Souvenir Sheet
927	A169	10z multi		11.00

International Year of the Child. No. 927 has multicolored margin showing IYC Emblem on map of Zaire, U.N. Emblem. Size: 80x60mm.

Globe and Drummer—A170

1979, July 23
928	A170	1k multi	5	5
929	A170	9k multi	12	8
930	A170	90k multi	1.00	50
931	A170	100k multi	1.10	55

Souvenir Sheet
932	A170	500k multi	5.75	3.50

6th International Fair, Kinshasa. No. 932 contains one stamp (52x31mm.); red marginal inscription. Size: 104x62mm.

ZAIRE

Globe and School Desk—A171

1979, Dec. 24		Litho.		Perf. 13	
933	A171	10k multi		10	5

International Bureau of Education, Geneva, 50th anniversary.

Adoration of the Kings, by Memling—A172

1979, Dec. 24				Imperf.	
934	A172	5z multi		4.50	2.50

Christmas 1979.

"Puffing Billy," 1814, Gt. Britain—A173

1980, Jan. 14		Litho.		Perf. 13½x13	
935	A173	50s shown		5	5
936	A173	1.50k Buddicom No. 33, 1843, France		6	5
937	A173	5k "Elephant," 1835, Belgium		6	5
938	A173	8k No. 601, 1906, Zaire		8	5
939	A173	50k "Slieve Gullion 440," Ireland		45	25
940	A173	75k "Black Elephant," Germany		70	38
941	A173	2z Type 1-15, Zaire		1.75	1.00
942	A173	5z "Golden State," U.S.		4.50	2.50
		Nos. 935-942 (8)		7.65	4.33
		Souvenir Sheet			
943	A173	10z Type E.D.75, Zaire		9.00	6.00

No. 943 has multicolored margin showing railroad bridge and map of Zaire. Size: 79x58mm.

Hill, Belgian Congo No. 257—A174

1980, Jan. 28			Perf. 13½x14	
944	A174	2k No. 5	5	5
945	A174	4k No. 13	5	5
946	A174	10k No. 24	10	5
947	A174	20k No. 38	18	10
948	A174	40k No. 111	38	18
949	A174	150k No. B29	1.35	75
950	A174	200k No. 198	1.75	1.00
951	A174	250k shown	2.25	1.25
		Nos. 944-951 (8)	6.11	3.43
		Souvenir Sheet		
952	A174	10z No. 198	9.00	6.00

Sir Rowland Hill (1795-1879), originator of penny postage. No. 952 has black marginal inscription. Size: 84x59mm.

Albert Einstein—A175

1980, Feb. 18			Perf. 13	
953	A175	40s multi	5	5
954	A175	2k multi	5	5
955	A175	4k multi	8	5
956	A175	15k multi	12	8
957	A175	50k multi	50	30
958	A175	300k multi	2.50	1.25
		Nos. 953-958 (6)	3.30	1.78
		Souvenir Sheet		
959	A175	5z multi	4.50	2.75

Albert Einstein (1879-1955), theoretical physicist. No. 959 has different portrait; multicolored margin shows atomic symbol and Einstein's theory of relativity formula. Size: 79x68mm.

Salvation Army Brass Players—A176

Emblem and: 50s, Booth Memorial Hospital, New York. 4.50k, Commissioner George Railton sailing for U.S. mission. 10k, Mobile dispensary, Masina. 20k, Gen'l. Evangeline Booth, officer holding infant (vert.). 75k, Outdoor well-baby clinic. 1.50z, Disaster relief. 2z, Parade (vert.). 10z, Gen'l. and Mrs. Arnold Brown.

1980, Mar. 3			Perf. 11	
960	A176	50s multi	5	5
961	A176	4.50k multi	5	5
962	A176	10k multi	10	6
963	A176	20k multi	18	10
964	A176	40k multi	38	20
965	A176	75k multi	65	35
966	A176	1.50z multi	1.25	65
967	A176	2z multi	1.75	90
		Nos. 960-967 (8)	4.41	2.34
		Souvenir Sheet		
968	A176	10z multi	9.00	6.00

Salvation Army centenary in United States. No. 968 contains one stamp (53x38mm) and 2 labels. Multicolored margin shows U.S. and Salvation Army flags, emblems in French and English. Size: 152x81mm.

Souvenir Sheets

Pope John Paul II—A177

1980, May 2		Litho.	Perf. 11½	
969	A177	10z multi	6.25	3.75

Visit of Pope John Paul II to Zaire, May. Multicolored margin shows entire portrait. Size: 96x131mm.

Baia Castle, by Antonio Pitloo—A178

1980, May 5				
970	A178	10z multi	6.25	3.50

20th International Philatelic Exhibition, Europa '80, Naples, Apr. 26-May 4. Multicolored margin shows entire painting. Size: 145½x115½mm.

A179

1980, May 24		Perf. 12½x13, 13x12½ Lithographed	
971	A179	50k Woman, line-drawing	25	15
972	A179	100k Plutiarch	65	35
973	A179	500k Kneeling man, sculpture, vert.	3.25	1.75
a.		Souvenir sheet of 3	4.25	3.00

Rotary International, 75th anniversary. No. 973a contains 3 stamps similar to Nos. 971-973, size: 55x35, 35x55mm; Sepia marginal inscription. Size: 198x131. Exists imperf.

Tropical Fish—A180

1980, Oct. 20		Litho.	Perf. 14x13½	
974	A180	1k Chaetodon collaris	5	5
975	A180	5k Zebrasoma veliferum	5	5
976	A180	10k Euxiphipops xanthometapon	5	5
977	A108	20k Pomazcanthus annularis	12	8
978	A180	40k Centropyge oriculus	38	20
979	A180	150k Oxymonacanthus longirostris	90	50
980	A180	200k Balistoides niger	1.25	70
981	A180	250k Rhinecanthus aculeatus	1.50	85
		Nos. 974-981 (8)	4.30	2.48
		Souvenir Sheet		
981A	A180	5z Baliste ondule	3.25	1.50

Exhibition Emblem, Congo No. 365—A181

1980, Dec. 6		Litho.		Perf. 13	
982		Block of 4		2.75	1.75
a.		A181 1z, UR shown		65	40
b.		A181 1z, UL Belgium #511		65	40
c.		A181 1z, UR like #982b		65	40
d.		A181 1z, UR like #982a		65	40
983		Block of 4		5.25	3.00
a.		A181 2z, UR Congo #432		1.25	75
b.		A181 2z, UL Belgium #B835		1.25	75
c.		A181 2z, UR like #983b		1.25	75
d.		A181 2z, UL like #983a		1.25	70
984		Block of 4		7.75	4.25
a.		A181 3z, UR Zaire #755		1.85	1.00
b.		A181 3z, UL Belgium #B878		1.85	1.00
c.		A181 3z, UR like #984b		1.85	1.00
d.		A181 3z, UL like #984a		1.85	1.00
985		Block of 4		10.50	5.75
a.		A181 4z, UR Congo #572		2.50	1.40
b.		A181 4z, UL Belgium #B996		2.50	2.40
c.		A181 4z, UR like #985b		2.50	1.40
d.		A181 4z, UL like #985a		2.50	1.40

PHIBELZA, Belgium-Zaire Philatelic Exhibition.

Map of Africa, King Leopold I—A182

Belgian independence sesquicentennial: 75k, Stanley expedition, Leopold II. 100k, Colonial troops, Albert I. 270k, protected animals, Leopold III. Visit of King Baudouin and Queen Fabiola.

1980, Dec. 13		Photo.	Perf. 14	
986	A182	10k multi	12	8
987	A182	75k multi	50	30
988	A182	100k multi	65	40
989	A182	145k multi	90	50
990	A182	270k multi	1.65	90
		Nos. 986-990 (5)	3.82	2.18

Nos. 935, 936, 898, 939, 900, 931, 925, 951, Overprinted in Red, Silver or Black:
20e Anniversaire—Independence / 1960-1980

1980, Dec. 13			Litho.	
991	A173	50s multi	5	5
992	A173	1.50k multi	5	5
993	A165	10k multi	8	5
994	A173	50k multi	30	18
995	A165	75k multi	45	25
996	A170	100k multi (S)	65	40
997	A169	1z on 5z on 100k multi (B)	65	40
998	A174	250k multi	1.50	85
999	A169	5z on 100k multi (B)	3.25	1.75
		Nos. 991-999 (9)	6.98	3.98

20th anniversary of independence.

Nativity A183

1980, Dec. 24			Perf. 13	
1000	A183	10k Shepherds and angels	12	8
1001	A183	75k Flight into Egypt	50	30
1002	A183	80k Three kings	50	30
1003	A183	145k shown	90	50
		Souvenir Sheet		
1004	A183	10z Church, nativity	6.25	3.50

Christmas 1980. No. 1004 contains one stamp (49x33mm); gold and black decorative margin. Size: 114½x78mm. Exists imperf.

ZAIRE

Postal Clerk Sorting Mail, by Norman Rockwell—A184

Designs: Saturday Evening Post covers by Norman Rockwell.

1981, Apr. 27		Litho.		Perf. 14	
1005	A184	10k multi		8	5
1006	A184	20k multi		12	8
1007	A184	50k multi		30	18
1008	A184	80k multi		50	30
1009	A184	100k multi		65	40
1010	A184	125k multi		75	45
1011	A184	175k multi		1.10	60
1012	A184	200k multi		1.25	70
		Nos. 1005-1012 (8)		4.75	2.76

First Anniv. of Visit of Pope John Paul II—A185

Designs: Scenes of Pope's visit. 50k, 500k, vert.

1981, May 2			Perf. 13	
1013	A185	5k multi	5	5
1014	A185	10k multi	8	5
1015	A185	50k multi	38	22
1016	A185	100k multi	65	40
1017	A185	500k multi	3.25	1.75
1018	A185	800k multi	5.00	2.75
		Nos. 1013-1018 (6)	9.41	5.22

Soccer Players—A186

Designs: Soccer scenes.

1981, July 6		Litho.	Perf. 12½	
1019	A186	2k multi	5	5
1020	A186	10k multi	8	5
1021	A186	25k multi	15	6
1022	A186	90k multi	65	40
1023	A186	2z multi	1.25	70
1024	A186	3z multi	1.85	1.00
1025	A186	6z multi	3.75	2.00
1026	A186	8z multi	5.50	3.00
		Nos. 1019-1026 (8)	13≈28	7.26

		Souvenir Sheet		
1027		Sheet of 2	6.25	3.50
a.		A186 5z like #1019	3.00	1.50
b.		A186 5z like #1025	3.00	1.50

ESPAÑA '82 World Cup Soccer Championship. No. 1027 has multicolored margin showing emblem. Size: 115x80mm.

Intl. Year of the Disabled—A187

1981, Nov. 2		Litho.	Perf 14x14½	
1028	A187	2k Archer	5	5
1029	A187	5k Ear, sound waves	5	5
1030	A187	10k Amputee	5	5
1031	A187	18k Cane braille, sunglasses	8	5
1032	A187	50k Boy with leg braces	22	12
1033	A187	150k Sign language	65	38
1034	A187	500k Hands	2.25	1.25
1035	A187	800k Dove	3.50	2.00
		Nos. 1028-1035 (8)	6.85	3.95

Birth Sesquicentennial of Heinrich von Stephan, UPU Founder A188

Christmas 1981 A189

1981, Dec. 21	Photo. & Engr.	Perf. 11½x12	
1036	A188	15z purple	6.50 3.75

No. 1036 has green marginal inscription. Size: 65x85mm.

1981, Dec. 21		Litho.	Perf. 14	

Designs: 25k, 1z, 1.50z, 3z, 5z, Various children. 10z, Holy Family, horiz.

1037	A189	25k multi	12	6
1038	A189	1z multi	50	25
1039	A189	1.50z multi	65	38
1040	A189	3z multi	1.40	75
1041	A189	5z multi	2.25	1.25
		Nos. 1037-1041 (5)	4.92	2.69

		Souvenir Sheet		
1042	A189	10z multi	4.50	2.50

No. 1042 has multicolored margin continuing design. Size: 93x64mm.

13th World Telecommunications Day (1981)—A190

Designs: Symbols of communications and health care delivery.

1982, Feb. 8		Litho.	Perf. 13	
1043	A190	1k multi	5	5
1044	A190	25k multi	12	6
1045	A190	90k multi	45	22
1046	A190	1z multi	50	25
1047	A190	1.70z multi	85	42
1048	A190	3z multi	1.50	75
1049	A190	4.50z multi	2.25	1.15
1050	A190	2.50z multi	2.50	1.25
		Nos. 1043-1050 (8)	8.22	4.15

Pres. Mobutu Type of 1978

1982		Photo.	Perf. 12	
		Granite Paper		
1051	A162	10k multi	5	5
1052	A162	25k multi	12	6
1053	A162	50k multi	25	12
1054	A162	1z multi	50	25
1055	A162	2z multi	1.00	50
1056	A162	5z multi	2.50	1.25
		Nos. 1051-1056 (6)	4.42	2.23

20th Anniv. of African Postal Union (1981)—A191

1982, Mar. 8		Litho.	Perf. 13	
1057	A191	1z yel grn & gold	50	25

1982 World Cup—A192

Designs: Flags and players of finalists.

1982				
1058	A192	2k multi	5	5
1059	A192	8k multi	5	5
1060	A192	25k multi	12	6
1061	A192	50k multi	25	12
1062	A192	90k multi	45	22
1063	A192	1z multi	50	25
1064	A192	1.45z multi	70	35
1065	A192	1.70z multi	85	42
1066	A192	3z multi	1.50	75
1067	A192	3.50z multi	1.75	88
1068	A192	5z multi	2.50	1.25
1069	A192	6z multi	3.00	1.50
		Nos. 1058-1069 (12)	11.72	5.90

		Souvenir Sheet		
1070	A192	10z multi	5.00	2.50

Size of No. 1070: 111x86mm. Issue dates: Nos. 1058-1069, July 6; No. 1070, Sept. 21.

9th Conference of Heads of State of Africa and France, Kinshasa, Oct.—A193

1982, Oct. 8		Litho.	Perf. 13	
1071	A193	75k multi	36	18
1072	A193	90k multi	45	22
1073	A193	1z multi	50	25
1074	A193	1.50z multi	75	38
1075	A193	3z multi	1.50	75
1076	A193	5z multi	2.50	1.25
1077	A193	8z multi	4.00	2.00
		Nos. 1071-1077 (7)	10.06	5.03

Animals from Virunga Natl. Park—A194

1982, Nov. 5				
1078	A194	1z Lions	50	25
1079	A194	1.70z Buffalo	85	42
1080	A194	3.50z Elephants	1.75	88
1081	A194	6.50z Antelope	3.25	1.65
1082	A194	8z Hippopotamus	4.00	2.00
1083	A194	10z Monkeys	5.00	2.50
1084	A194	10z Leopard	5.00	2.50
		Nos. 1078-1084 (7)	20.35	10.20

Nos. 1083-1084 se-tenant with label showing map.

Scouting Year A195

Local Birds A196

1982, Nov. 29		Photo.	Perf. 11½	
		Granite Paper		
1085	A195	90k Camp	45	22
1086	A195	1.70z Campfire	85	42
1087	A195	3z Scout	1.50	75
1088	A195	5z First aid	2.50	1.25
1089	A195	8z Flag signals	4.00	2.00
		Nos. 1085-1089 (5)	9.30	4.64

		Souvenir Sheet		
1090	A195	10z Baden-Powell	5.00	2.50

No. 1090 has multicolored margin showing emblem. Size: 87x63mm.

1982, Dec. 6		Litho.	Perf. 13	
1091	A196	25k Quelea quelea	12	6
1092	A196	50k Ceyx picta	25	12
1093	A196	90k Tauraco persa	45	22
1094	A196	1.50z Charadrius tricollaris	75	38
1095	A196	1.70z Cursorius temminckii	85	42
1096	A196	2z Campethera bennettii	1.00	50
1097	A196	3z Podiceps ruficollis	1.50	75
1098	A196	3.50z Kaupifalco monogrammicus	1.75	88
1099	A196	5z Limnocorax flavirostris	2.50	1.25
1100	A196	8z White-headed vulture	4.00	2.00
		Nos. 1091-1100 (10)	13.17	6.58

All except 3.50z, 8z horiz.

Christmas 1982—A197

1982, Dec. 20		Photo.	Perf. 13½	
1101	A197	15z Adoration of the Magi, by van der Goes	7.50	3.75

Size: 103x66mm.

ZAIRE

Quartz—A198

**1983, Feb. 13   Photo.   *Perf. 11½*
Granite Paper**

1102	A198	2k Malachite, vert.	5	5
1103	A198	45k shown	32	16
1104	A198	75k Gold	36	18
1105	A198	1z Uraninite	50	25
1106	A198	1.50z Bournonite, vert.	75	38
1107	A198	3z Cassiterite	1.50	75
1108	A198	6z Dioptase, vert.	3.00	1.50
1109	A198	8z Cuprite, vert.	4.00	2.00
	Nos. 1102-1109 (8)		10.48	5.27

Souvenir Sheet

| 1110 | A198 | 10z Diamonds | 5.00 | 5.00 |

TB Bacillus Centenary—A199

1983, Feb. 21   Litho.   *Perf. 13*

1111	A199	80k multi	40	20
1112	A199	1.20z multi	60	30
1113	A199	3.60z multi	1.80	90
1114	A199	9.60z multi	4.80	2.40

Kinshasa Monuments—A200

1983, Apr. 25

1115	A200	50k Zaire Diplomat, vert.	25	12
1116	A200	1z Echo of Zaire	50	25
1117	A200	1.50z Messengers, vert.	75	38
1118	A200	3z Shield of Revolution, vert.	1.50	75
1119	A200	5z Weeping Woman	2.50	1.25
1120	A200	10z Militant, vert.	5.00	2.50
	Nos. 1115-1120 (6)		10.50	5.25

ITU Plenipotentiaries Conference,
Nairobi, Sept. 1982—A201

Various satellites, dish antennae and maps.

1983, June 13   Litho.   *Perf. 13*

1121	A201	2k multi	5	5
1122	A201	4k multi	5	5
1123	A201	25k multi	12	6
1124	A201	1.20z multi	60	30
1125	A201	2.05z multi	1.00	50
1126	A201	3.60z multi	1.80	90
1127	A201	6z multi	3.00	1.50
1128	A201	8z multi	4.00	2.00

Christmas 1983—A202

Raphael Paintings; No. 1129: a. Virgin and Child. b. Holy Family. c. Esterhazy Madonna. d. Sistine Madonna. No. 1130: a. La Belle Jardiniere. b. Virgin of Alba. c. Holy Family (diff.). d. Virgin and Child (diff.).

1983, Dec. 26   Photo.   *Perf. 13½x13*

1129		Sheet of 4	3.00	3.00
a.-d.		A202 10z, any single	75	75
1130		Sheet of 4	4.50	4.50
a.-d.		A202 15z, any single	1.10	1.10

Size: 89x112mm.

OFFICIAL STAMPS

Nos. 756–772
Overprinted

1975		Litho.	*Perf. 14*	
O1	A145	10s red org & blk	5	5
O2	A145	40s multi	5	5
O3	A145	50s cit & multi	5	5
		Perf. 13		
O4	A146	1k multi	5	5
O5	A146	2k org & multi	8	5
O6	A146	3k multi	12	6
O7	A146	4k multi	18	8
O8	A146	5k multi	25	12
O9	A146	6k multi	30	15
O10	A146	8k multi	38	18
O11	A146	9k multi	38	20
O12	A146	10k multi	50	25
O13	A146	14k multi	75	38
O14	A146	17k multi	90	40
O15	A146	20k yel & multi	1.00	50
O16	A146	50k multi	2.50	1.20
O17	A146	100k multi	6.50	2.25
		Nos. O1-O17 (17)	14.04	6.02

"SP" are the initials of "Service Public."

See "Special Notices" at the front of this volume for data on the listing methods of this Catalogue, abbreviations, condition, prices and examination.

ZAMBEZIA
(zăm·bē′zǐ·à ; -zhà)

LOCATION — A former district of the Mozambique Province in Portuguese East Africa.

GOVT. — Part of the Portuguese East Africa Colony.

The districts of Quelimane and Tete were created from Zambezia. Eventually stamps of Mozambique came into use. See Quelimane and Tete.

1000 Reis = 1 Milreis

King Carlos
A1   A2

Perf. 11½, 12½, 13½.

1894		Typographed.	Unwmkd.	
1	A1	5r yellow	35	30
2	A1	10r red vio	50	30
3	A1	15r chocolate	1.25	1.00
a.		Perf. 12½	22.50	15.00
4	A1	20r lavender	1.25	1.00
5	A1	25r bl grn	1.50	1.40
		Perf. 11½		
6	A1	50r lt bl	2.00	1.75
7	A1	75r carmine	4.50	4.00
a.		Perf. 11½	45.00	30.00
8	A1	80r yel grn	3.50	2.75
9	A1	100r brn, *buff*	3.50	2.50
10	A1	150r car, *rose*	4.00	3.00
11	A1	200r dk bl, *bl*	4.00	3.25
a.		Perf. 11½	200.00	150.00
b.		Perf. 13½	35.00	25.00
12	A1	300r dk bl, *sal*	9.50	7.50
a.		Perf. 11½	22.50	19.50

1898–1903			*Perf. 11½*	
		Name and Value in Black or Red (500r)		
13	A2	2½r gray	30	20
14	A2	5r orange	30	20
15	A2	10r lt grn	30	20
16	A2	15r brown	1.50	1.25
17	A2	15r gray grn ('03)	1.25	1.00
18	A2	20r gray vio	1.00	60
19	A2	25r sea grn	1.00	60
20	A2	25r car ('03)	1.50	70
21	A2	50r blue	1.75	80
22	A2	50r brn ('03)	2.75	2.25
23	A2	65r dl bl ('03)	7.50	6.00
24	A2	75r rose	8.00	4.50
25	A2	75r lil ('03)	3.50	2.50
26	A2	80r violet	5.00	3.00
27	A2	100r dk bl, *bl*	2.50	1.50
28	A2	115r org brn, *pink* ('03)	7.50	7.50
29	A2	130r brn, *straw* ('03)	7.50	6.50
30	A2	150r brn, *buff*	5.50	3.00
31	A2	200r red vio, *pnksh*	5.50	3.00
32	A2	300r dk bl, *rose*	6.50	3.00
33	A2	400r dl bl, *straw* ('03)	9.00	7.00
34	A2	500r blk, *bl* ('01)	9.00	6.00
35	A2	700r vio, *yelsh* ('01)	11.00	8.50
		Nos. 13-35 (23)	99.65	69.80

Stamps of 1894
Surcharged

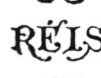

1902			*Perf. 11½, 12½*	
36	A1	65r on 10r red vio	6.00	4.50
37	A1	65r on 15r choc	6.00	4.50
38	A1	65r on 20r lav	6.00	4.50
39	A1	65r on 300r bl, *sal*	6.00	4.50
40	A1	115r on 5r yel	5.50	4.50
41	A1	115r on 25r bl grn	5.00	4.00
42	A1	115r on 80r yel grn	5.00	4.00
43	A1	130r on 75r car	6.50	3.75
44	A1	130r on 150r car, *rose*	5.50	4.00
45	A1	400r on 50r lt bl	2.00	1.75
46	A1	400r on 100r brn, *buff*	2.25	2.00
47	A1	400r on 200r bl, *bl*	2.00	1.75

Same Surcharge on No. P1.

48	N1	130r on 2½r brn	5.00	4.00
		Nos. 36-48 (13)	62.75	47.75

Stamps of 1898 Overprinted

PROVISORIO

1902			*Perf. 11½*	
49	A2	15r brown	1.60	1.25
50	A2	25r sea grn	1.60	1.25
51	A2	50r blue	1.60	1.25
52	A2	75r rose	4.50	3.00

No. 23 Surcharged in Black

50 RÉIS

1905				
53	A2	50r on 65r dl bl	5.00	3.75

Stamps of 1898-1903 Overprinted in Carmine or Green

1911				
54	A2	2½r gray	20	20
55	A2	5r orange	20	20
56	A2	10r lt grn	20	20
a.		Inverted overprint	3.00	3.00
57	A2	15r gray grn	30	30
58	A2	20r gray vio	40	30
59	A2	25r car (G)	1.00	50
60	A2	50r brown	40	40
61	A2	75r lilac	1.00	60
62	A2	100r dk bl, *bl*	1.00	60
63	A2	115r org brn, *pink*	1.00	60
64	A2	130r brn, *straw*	1.00	60
65	A2	200r red vio, *pnksh*	1.00	60
66	A2	400r dl bl, *straw*	1.50	1.10
67	A2	500r blk & red, *bl*	1.50	1.10
68	A2	700r vio, *yelsh*	1.75	1.10
		Nos. 54-68 (15)	12.45	8.40

Stamps of 1902–05 Overprinted in Carmine or Green

1914			Without Gum	
72	A2	50r on 65r dl bl	90.00	90.00
73	A1	115r on 5r yel	1.00	1.00
74	A1	115r on 25r bl grn	1.00	1.00
75	A1	115r on 80r yel grn	1.00	1.00
76	N1	130r on 2½r brn (G)	1.00	1.00
a.		Carmine overprint	10.00	10.00
77	A1	130r on 75r car	5.00	5.50
a.		Perf. 12½	6.00	5.50
78	A1	130r on 150r car, *rose*	1.00	1.00
79	A1	400r on 50r lt bl	1.75	1.75
a.		Perf. 12½	11.00	7.25
80	A1	400r on 100r brn, *buff*	1.75	1.50
81	A1	400r on 200r bl, *bl*	1.75	1.50

On Nos. 51-52.

82	A2	50r blue	1.25	1.00
83	A2	75r rose	1.25	1.00
		Nos. 73-83 (11)	13.75	12.75

Preceding Issues Overprinted in Carmine

REPUBLICA

1915				
		On Provisional Issue of 1902.		
84	A1	115r on 5r yel	50	50
85	A1	115r on 25r bl grn	50	50
86	A1	115r on 80r lt grn	50	50
87	A1	130r on 75r car	50	50
a.		Perf. 12½	4.50	2.25
88	A1	130r on 150r car, *rose*	50	50
92	N1	130r on 2½r (down)	50	50
		On No. 51.		
93	A2	50r blue	50	50
a.		"Republica" inverted		
		On No. 53.		
94	A2	50r on 65r dl bl	2.25	2.00
		Nos. 84-94 (8)	5.75	5.50

Stamps of 1898-1903 Overprinted Locally in Carmine

REPUBLICA

1917			Without Gum	
95	A2	2½r gray	1.00	1.00
96	A2	5r orange	4.50	3.25
97	A2	10r lt grn	4.50	3.25
98	A2	15r gray grn	4.50	3.25
99	A2	20r gray vio	4.50	3.25
100	A2	25r sea grn	8.50	7.50
101	A2	100r bl, *bl*	2.25	2.00
102	A2	115r org brn, *pink*	2.25	2.00
103	A2	130r brn, *straw*	2.25	2.00
104	A2	200r red vio, *pnksh*	2.25	2.00
105	A2	400r dl bl, *straw*	3.25	3.00
106	A2	500r blk & red, *bl*	3.25	3.00
107	A2	700r vio, *yelsh*	6.00	3.50
		Nos. 95-107 (13)	49.00	39.00

NEWSPAPER STAMP.

N1

Typographed

1894			*Perf. 12½*	Unwmkd.
P1	N1	2½r brown	30	25

NUMBER CHANGES
in Scott's 1985 Standard Catalogue, Vol. IV

No. in 1984 Cat.	No. in 1985 Cat.	No. in 1984 Cat.	No. in 1985 Cat.
PERU		**SWEDEN**	
790	799	43a, 44a	deleted
791-792	801-802	**THAILAND**	
793	791	1032	1031
794	790	**TUNISIA**	
795-801	792-798	769	770
802	800	770	769
ROMANIA		**TURKEY**	
J140, J142, J144, J146, J148, J150	deleted	2130A-2134	2131-2135
J141	J140	2136A-2136B	2137-2137A
J143	J141	2137-2137A	2138-2138A
J145	J142	2138-2140	2139-2141
J147	J143	**URUGUAY**	
J149	J144	1074-1075	1073-1074
RUSSIA		1076-1077	deleted
5113	deleted	1078-1079	1075-1076
5112A	5113	1082	1077
SURINAM		1084	1078
3a, 4a, 5a, 6a, 11a, 14a	deleted	1086-1089	1079-1082
		1089A-1089D	1083-1086

ADDENDA

These stamps were received too late for inclusion in their proper places in the Catalogue. Later issues will be found listed in Scott's Chronicle of New Issues.

PANAMA

Double Cup, Indian Period—A212

Pottery: 40c, Raised dish, Tonosi period. 50c, Jug with face, Canazas period (vert.). 60c, Bowl, Conte (vert.).

1984, Jan. 16		Litho.		Perf. 12	
651	A212	30c multi		60	32
552	A212	40c multi		80	45
653	A212	50c multi		1.00	60
654	A212	60c multi		1.20	80

Souvenir Sheet
Imperf.
655 A212 1b like 30c   2.00 1.25

No. 655 has black control number, marginal inscription. Size: 85x75mm.

Pre-Olympics—A213

1984, June		Litho.		Perf. 14	
656	A213	19c Baseball		38	20
657	A213	19c Basketball, vert.		38	20
658	A213	19c Boxing		38	20
659	A213	19c Swimming, vert.		38	20

PERU

25th Anniv. of FERIA Intl. of the Pacific—A304

1983
805 A304 350s multi   85 55

World Communications Year (1983)—A305

1984, Jan. 27		Litho.		Perf. 14	
806	A305	700s multi		1.75	1.15

Col. Leoncio Prado (1853-83)—A306

1984, Feb. 3		Litho.		Perf. 14	
807	A306	150s ol & ol brn		14	8

Shipbuilding and Repair—A307

1984, Feb. 22
808 A307 250s shown   22 15
809 A307 300s Mixed cargo ship 28 16

Ricardo Palma (1833-1919), Writer A308

1984 Summer Olympics A309

1984, Mar. 20
810 A308 200s purple   18 10

1984, Mar. 30
811 A309 500s Shooting 45 30
812 A309 750s Hurdles   65 45

Arms of City of Callao—A310

1984, Apr. 23
813 A310 350s dp grn   30 20

Wari Culture Pottery—A311

1984, May 9					
814	A311	100s Water jar		8	6
815	A311	150s Llama		14	8
816	A311	200s Painted vase		18	10

POLAND

POSTAGE DUE STAMPS
Type of 1950

1980, Sept. 2		Litho.		Perf. 12½	
J146	D13	1z lt red brn		10	5
J147	D13	2z gray ol		20	10
J148	D13	3z dl vio		30	15
J149	D13	5z brown		50	25

RWANDA

Souvenir Sheet

The Granduca Madonna, by Raphael—A164

1983, Dec. 19 Typo. & Engr. Perf. 11½
1166 A164 200fr multi   4.00 2.00

Christmas 1983. Size: 72x86mm.

Local Trees—A165

1984, Jan. 15		Litho.		Perf. 13½x13	
1167	A165	20c Hagenia abyssinica		5	5
1168	A165	30c Dracaena steudneri		5	5
1169	A165	50c Phoenix reclinata		5	5
1170	A165	10fr Podocarpus milanjianus		20	10
1171	A165	19fr Entada abyssinica		38	20
1172	A165	70fr Parinari excelsa		1.40	70
1173	A165	100fr Newtonia buchananii		2.00	1.00
1174	A165	200fr Acacia gerrardi, vert.		4.00	2.00

Nos. 1167-1174 (8)   8.13 4.15

SAN MARINO

Motorcross Grand Prix, Baldasserona—A259

1984, June 14 Photo. Perf. 13½x14
1067 A259 450 l multi   78 78

Souvenir Sheet

1984 Summer Olympics—A260

1984, June 14 Litho. Perf. 13x14
1068   Sheet of 2   2.75 2.75
 a. A260 550 l Man   1.00
 b. A260 1000 l Woman   1.75

Size: 150x110mm.

SEMI-POSTAL STAMP

Refugee Boy—SP6

1982, Dec. 15 Photo. Perf. 11½
B39 SP6 300 + 100 l multi   60 60

Surcharge was for refugee support.

SENEGAL

Namibia Day—A195

1983, Nov. 14   Litho.   *Perf. 13½x13*
598	A195	90fr Torch	45	22
599	A195	95fr Chain, fist	48	24
600	A195	260fr Woman bearing torch	1.30	65

West African Monetary Union, 20th Anniv. A196   Dakar Alizes Rotary Club, First Anniv. A197

Designs: 60fr, Mask emblem, Ziguinchor Agency building, Dakar (horiz.). 65fr, Monetary Union headquarters, emblem.

1983, Nov. 28   *Perf. 13½x13, 13x13½*
| 501 | A196 | 60fr multi | 30 | 15 |
| 502 | A196 | 65fr multi | 32 | 16 |

1983, Dec. 5   *Perf. 13½x13*
| 503 | A197 | 70fr grn & multi | 35 | 18 |
| 504 | A197 | 500fr bl & multi | 2.50 | 1.25 |

Customs Cooperation Council, 30th Anniv. A198   Economic Comm. for Africa, 25th Anniv. A199

1983, Dec. 23   *Perf. 12½x13*
| 605 | A198 | 90fr multi | 45 | 22 |
| 606 | A198 | 300fr multi | 1.50 | 75 |

1984, Jan. 10   *Perf. 12½*
| 607 | A199 | 90fr multi | 45 | 22 |
| 608 | A199 | 95fr multi | 48 | 24 |

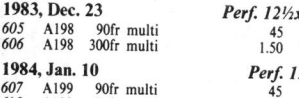
SOS Children's Village—A200

1984, Mar. 29   *Perf. 13½x13, 13x13½*
609	A200	90fr Village	45	22
610	A200	95fr Mother & child, vert.	48	24
611	A200	115fr Brothers & sisters	58	30
612	A200	260fr House	1.30	65

POSTAGE DUE STAMPS
Type of 1966

1983, Oct.   Typo.   *Perf. 14x13*
| J43 | D6 | 60fr bl & blk | 30 | 15 |
| J44 | D6 | 90fr rose & blk | 45 | 22 |

OFFICIAL STAMP
Type of 1966

1983, Oct.   Typo.   *Perf. 14x13*
| O22 | O2 | 90fr dk grn & blk ('83) | 45 | 22 |

SOMALIA

Military Uniforms—A128

Designs: a. Air Force. b. Women's Auxiliary Corps. c. Border Police. d. People's Militia. e. Army Infantry. f. Custodial Corps. g. Police. h. Navy.

1983   Litho.   *Perf. 13½x14*
| 526 | | Strip of 8, multi | 3.25 | |
| a.-h. | A128 | 3.20sh, any single | 40 | 30 |

View Type of 1980

1983
527	A117	2.80sh Barawe	35	25
528	A117	3.20sh Bur Hakaba	40	30
529	A117	5.50sh Baydhabo	68	52
530	A117	8.60sh Dooy Nuunaay	1.10	78

SPAIN
King Juan Carlos Type of 1976

1982   Photo.   *Perf. 13x13½*
| 2258 | A497 | 14p red org ('82) | 45 | 14 |

Man and the Biosphere—A651

1984, Apr. 11
| 2365 | A651 | 38p da Vinci's Study of Man | 40 | 10 |

Aragon Statute of Autonomy, 2nd Anniv.—A652

1984, Apr. 23   Litho. & Engr.   *Perf. 13x13½*
| 2366 | A652 | 16p Map | 22 | 6 |

Souvenir Sheet

King Juan Carlos—A653

Espana '84 (Spanish Royal Family): b. Sofia of Greece. c. Cristina de Borbon. d. Prince of Asturias Felipe de Borbon. e. Elene de Borbon.

1984, Apr. 27   *Perf. 12½x13*
| 2367 | | Sheet of 5 | 2.50 | 1.25 |
| a.-e. | A653 | 38p, any single | 50 | 12 |

Multicolored margin shows emblem, palace; brown control number. Size: 148x103mm.

Congress Emblem—A654

1984, May 3   Engr.   *Perf. 13x13½*
| 2368 | A654 | 38p pur & red | 50 | 12 |

World Philatelic Federation, 53rd Congress, Madrid, May 7-9.

Europa (1959-84)—A655

1984, May 5
| 2369 | A655 | 16p orange | 22 | 6 |
| 2370 | A655 | 38p dk bl | 50 | 12 |

Armed Forces Day—A656

1984, May 19   Photo.   *Perf. 13½x13*
| 2371 | A656 | 17p multi | 24 | 6 |

Design: 17p, Monument to Hunters Regiment of Caceres, by Mariano Benlliure.

Canary Islds. Statute of Autonomy—A657

1984, May 29   Litho. & Engr.   *Perf. 13*
| 2372 | A657 | 16p Arms, map | 22 | 6 |

Castilla-La Mancha Statute of Autonomy—A658

1984, May 31   *Perf. 13*
| 2373 | A658 | 17p Arms | 24 | 6 |

TURKEY
OFFICIAL STAMPS

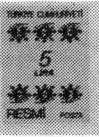
O22

1981, Oct. 23   Litho.   *Perf. 13½*
O161	O22	5l yel & red	5	5
O162	O22	10l sal & red	10	5
O163	O22	35l gray & rose	35	10
O164	O22	50l pink & dk bl	50	15
O165	O22	75l pale grn & grn	75	20
O166	O22	100l lt bl & dk bl	1.00	25
		Nos. O161-O166 (6)	2.75	80

O23

1983, Nov. 23   Litho.   *Perf.*
O167	O23	5l multi	5	5
O168	O23	15l multi	15	5
O169	O23	50l multi	50	10
O170	O23	65l multi	65	10
O171	O23	90l multi	90	15
O172	O23	125l multi	1.25	25
		Nos. O167-O172 (6)	3.50	70

URUGUAY

Simon Bolivar, Battle Scene—A470

Wmk. 332

1983, Dec.   Litho.   *Perf. 12*
| 1153 | A470 | 4.50p brn & gldn brn | | 36 |

Gen. Leandro Gomez—A471

1984, Jan. 2
1154   4.50p multi   36

American Women's Day A472

Reunion Emblem A473

1984, Feb. 18
1155 A472 4.50p Flags, emblem 36

1984, Mar.
1156 A473 10p multi 85

Intl. Development Bank Governors, 25th annual reunion, Punta del Este.

50th Anniv. of Radio Club of Uruguay (1983)—A474

1984, Apr. 16
1157 A474 7p multi 60

VATICAN CITY

St. Casimir of Lithuania (1458-1484)—A217

1984, Feb. 28   *Perf. 14*
731 A217 550 l multi   88   55
732 A217 1200 l multi   2.00 1.20

Pontifical Academy of Sciences—A218

1984, June 18   Litho. & Engr.
733 A218   150 l shown   24   15
734 A218   450 l Secret Archives   72   45
735 A218   550 l Apostolic Library 88   55
736 A218 1500 l Observatory   2.40 1.50

FOR THE RECORD

The items recorded here appeared on the stamp market in the 1960's and '70s, and have not been listed in the Scott Standard Catalogue. They are arranged chronologically and briefly described. Completeness is not claimed.

CONTENTS

Panama
Paraguay
St. Thomas and Prince Islands
Senegal
Somalia
Togo
Uruguay
Yemen, Mutawakelite Kingdom
Yemen Arab Republic

PANAMA

1963

International Red Cross centenary. *Mar. 4.* Airmail semipostal 5c+5c, 10c+10c, 31c+15c surcharged in red on Nos. C274–C276. 10c, black overprint and surcharge on 5c+5c semipostal.

Astronauts' Visit. *Aug. 21.* No. C274 overprinted **a.** "Visita / Astronautas / Glenn-Shirra / Sheppard / Cooper / a Panama" or **b.** "Habilitado". Both values surcharged 10c, No. C277a overprinted "a."

9th Winter Olympics, Innsbruck. *Dec.* ½, 1, 3, 4c; airmail, 5, 15, 21, 31c (8v). Souvenir Sheet of 2 (21, 31c) perf., imperf. 2 miniature sheets, 21, 31c (in different colors).

1964

18th Summer Olympics, Tokyo. *Apr. 1.* ½, 1c; airmail, 5, 10, 21, 50c (6v). Souvenir sheet, 50c, perf., imperf.

Space Conquest. *Apr. 21.* ½, 1c; airmail, 5, 10, 21, 50c (6v). Souvenir sheet, 50c, perf., imperf.

Aquatic Sports, Tokyo '64 Olympics. *Sept. 2.* Perf., imperf. (in different colors). ½, 1c; airmail, 5, 10, 21, 31c (6v). 6 miniature sheets, perf., imperf. Souvenir sheet, 31c, perf., imperf.

New York World's Fair. *Sept. 14.* Airmail, 5, 10, 15, 21c (4v). Souvenir sheet, 21c, perf., imperf.

Hammarskjold Memorial (United Nations Day). *Sept. 24.* Perf., imperf. (in different colors). Airmail, 21c x 2. Souvenir sheet of 2 (21c x 2).

Pope John XXIII Memorial. *Oct. 24.* Perf., imperf. (in different colors). Airmail, 21c x 2. Souvenir sheet of 2 (21c x 2) perf., imperf.

Olympic Medals and Winners, Innsbruck. *Oct. 14.* ½, 1, 2, 3, 4c; airmail, 5, 6, 7, 10, 21, 31c (11v). Souvenir sheet of 3 (10, 21, 31c) perf., imperf.

Weather Satellites. *Dec. 21.* ½, 1c; airmail, 5, 10, 21, 50c (6v). Souvenir sheet, 50c, perf., imperf.

Olympic Medals and Winners, Tokyo. *Dec. 28.* ½, 1, 2, 3, 4c; airmail, 5, 6, 7, 10, 21, 31c (11v). Souvenir sheet of 3 (10, 21, 31c) perf., imperf.

1965

Space Conquests and J. F. Kennedy. *Feb. 25.* Perf., imperf. (in different colors). ½, 1, 2, 3c; airmail, 5, 10, 11, 31c (8v). Souvenir sheet, 31c, perf., imperf.

Atomic Power for Peace. *May 12.* Perf., imperf (in different colors). ½, 1, 4c; airmail, 6, 10, 21c (6v). Souvenir sheet of 2 (10, 21c).

Galileo, 400th birth anniversary. *May 12.* Perf., imperf. (in different colors). Airmail, 10, 21c (2v). Souvenir sheet of 2 (10, 21c) perf., imperf.

J. F. Kennedy Memorial. *Aug. 23.* Perf., imperf. (in different colors). ½, 1c; airmail semipostal 10c+5c, 21c+10c, 31c+28c (5v). Souvenir sheet of 2 (1c, 31c+28c) perf., imperf.

Nobel Peace Prize. Perf., imperf. (in different colors). Airmail, 10, 21c. Souvenir sheet of 2 (10, 21c) imperf.

1966

Pope Paul VI, Visit to U.N. *Apr. 4.* ½, 1c; airmail, 5, 10, 21, 31c (6v). Souvenir sheet of 2 (5, 31c) perf., imperf.

Shakespeare, Dante and Wagner. *May 26.* ½c; airmail, 10, 31c (3v). Souvenir sheet of 2 (10, 31c) perf., imperf. (in different colors).

Master Artists. *May 26.* ½c; airmail, 10, 31c (3v). (Dürer, Raphael, da Vinci). Souvenir sheet of 2 (10, 31c) perf., imperf. (in different colors).

World Cup Soccer Championship, London. *July 11.* Perf., imperf. (in different colors). ½c x 2; airmail, 10c x 2, 21c x 2 (6v). 2 souvenir sheets of 2 (10, 21c perf.; 5, 21c imperf.).

Same, overprinted "Inglaterra vs Alemania". *Sept. 28.*

Italian Contributors to Space Research. *Aug. 12.* Perf., imperf. (in different colors). ½, 1c; airmail, 5, 10, 21c (5v). Souvenir sheet of 2 (10, 21c) imperf.

International Telecommunication Union centenary. *Aug. 12.* Perf., imperf. (in different colors). Airmail, 31c and souvenir sheet.

Religious paintings. *Oct. 24.* Perf., imperf. (in different colors). ½, 1, 2, 3c; airmail, 21c x 2 (6v) (Velazquez, Saraceni, Dürer, Orazio, Botticelli, Rubens). Souvenir sheet of 2 (21, 31c) perf., imperf.

Churchill and British Space Research. *Nov. 25.* ½c; airmail, 10, 31c (3v). Souvenir sheet of 2 (10, 31c) perf., imperf. (in different colors).

John F. Kennedy, 3rd death anniversary. *Nov. 25.* Perf., imperf. ½c; airmail, 10, 31c (3v). Souvenir sheet of 2 (10, 31c) perf., imperf. (in different colors).

Jules Verne and French Space Explorations. *Dec. 28.* Perf., imperf. (in different colors). ½, 1c; airmail, 5, 10, 21, 31c (6v). 2 souvenir sheets: 1 of 1, 31c, perf.; 1 of 2 (10, 21c) imperf.

1967

Easter paintings. *Mar. 13.* ½, 1c; airmail, 5, 10, 21, 31c (6v). (Tiepolo, Rubens, Sarto, Santi, Multscher, Grünewald). Souvenir sheet, 31c, perf., imperf.

Pre-Olympics, Mexico (Archaeological ruins). *Apr.* Perf., imperf. (in different colors). ½, 1c; airmail, 5, 10, 21, 31c (6v). 2 souvenir sheets: 1 of 1, 31c, perf.; 1 of 2 (10, 21c) imperf.

Paintings. *Aug. 23.* 5c x 3; airmail 21c x 3 (6v). (Ingres, Gainsborough, Rembrandt, Raphael, Velazquez, Dürer). 6 souvenir sheets, each 21c.

Goya paintings. *Oct. 17.* 2, 3, 4c; airmail, 5, 8, 10, 13, 21c (8v). Souvenir sheet, 50c.

1968

Life of Christ paintings. *Jan. 10.* 1c x 2, 3c; airmail, 4, 21c x 2 (6v). (Ford Madox Brown, Michelangelo, Rubens, El Greco, Van Dyck, Juan de Juanes). 6 souvenir sheets: 2 of 1, 22, 24c; 4 of 2 (1, 21c; 3, 21c; 21, 31c; 21, 31c).

Panama-Mexico Friendship. *Jan. 20.* Airmail, 50c, 1b (2v). Souvenir sheet of 2 (50c, 1b) imperf.

10th Winter Olympics, Grenoble. *Feb. 2.* ½, 1c; airmail, 5, 10, 21, 31c (6v). 2 souvenir sheets of 2 (each 10, 31c).

Sailing Ships, paintings. *May 7.* ½, 1, 3, 4c; airmail, 5, 13c (6v). Souvenir sheet, 50c, perf., imperf.

Tropical fish. *June 26.* ½, 1, 3, 4c; airmail, 5, 13c (6v). Souvenir sheet, 50c, perf., imperf.

Olympic Medals and Winners, Grenoble. *July 30.* 1, 2, 3, 4, 5, 6, 8c; airmail, 13, 30c (9v). Souvenir sheet, 70c.

Music, paintings. *Sept. 11.* 5, 10, 15, 20, 25, 30c (6v, se-tenant). (de la Hyre, ter Brugghen, Caravaggio, Tourmer, Vermeer, Memling). Souvenir sheet, 40c.

Communications by Satellite for 1968 Mexico Olympics. *Oct. 17.* Weather Satellite issue of 1964 overprinted in black or gold "Olimpiadas Mexico / Transmitidas / Via Satelite / Television Panamena." ½c; airmail, 50c (2v). 2 souvenir sheets, 50c, (in different colors).

Visit of Pope Paul VI, Latin American Eucharistic Congress. *Oct. 18.* Pope's Visit to U. N. issue of 1966 overprinted "Visita S. S. Paulo VI / Congreso Eucharistico / Latinoamerico / Transmitida ATS-3." ½c; airmail, 21c (2v). Souvenir sheet of 2 (½, 31c) perf., imperf.

Communications by Satellite. *Oct. 21.* Space Conquests and J. F. Kennedy issue of 1966 overprinted "Panama Inaugura / Communicaciones / Via Satellite / 5-Oct. 1968." ½c; airmail, 31c (2v). Souvenir sheet, 31c, perf., imperf.

Oct. 22. Churchill issue of 1966 overprinted in black or gold "Inauguracion / Communicaciones / por Satelite / Panama 5. Oct 1968." ½c; airmail, 10c (2v). Souvenir sheet of 2 (10, 31c) perf., imperf.

Hunting on horseback (paintings and tapestries). *Oct. 29.* 1, 3, 5, 10c; airmail, 13, 30c (6v).

Equestrian events, 1968 Mexico Olympics. *Oct. 29.* Airmail souvenir sheet of 2 (8, 30c) perf., imperf.

Famous race horses, paintings. *Dec. 18.* 5, 10, 15, 20, 25, 30c (6v se-tenant in miniature sheet).

International Human Rights Year (Martin Luther King, John F. and Robert F. Kennedy). *Dec. 18.* Airmail miniature sheet, 40c.

19th Summer Olympic Games, Mexico (Mexican art). 1, 2, 3, 4, 5, 6, 8c; airmail, 13, 30c, (9v). Souvenir sheet, 70c.

1969

National Philatelic and Numismatic Exposition, 1st. *Jan. 31.* Panama-Mexico Friendship issue of 1968 overprinted in black or red "la Exposicion / Filatelica y Numisma-/tica Nal. 29-8-68." Airmail, 50c, 1b (2v). Souvenir sheet of 2 (50c, 1b).

Butterflies. *Feb. 23.* Printed se-tenant in sheets checkerwise. ½, 1, 3, 4c; airmail, 5, 13c (6v). Souvenir sheet, 50c perf., imperf.

Space Exploration (international spacecraft). *Mar. 14.* Airmail, 5, 10, 15, 20, 25, 30c, 1b (7v. se-tenant). Souvenir sheet, 1b.

Red Cross, Children's Aid. *Mar. 26.* Kennedy Memorial issue of 1966 overprinted "Decreto No 112/(de 6 de marzo/de 1969)" and surcharged. Airmail, 5, 10c, 5c+5c, Red Cross issue of 1963 (3v).

Pope Paul VI's Latin American visit. *Aug. 5.* Se-tenant in sheets checkerwise. 1, 2, 3, 4, 5c; airmail, 6, 7, 8, 10c (9v). Souvenir sheet, 50c.

PARAGUAY

Sets of 1961-67 exist perf., and imperf. in different colors.

1961

Alan B. Shepard, first U. S. astronaut. *Dec. 22.* 10, 25, 50, 75c; airmail, 18.15, 36, 50g (7v). Souvenir sheet, 50c.

Europa 1961. *Dec. 31.* 50, 75c, 1, 1.50, 4.50g; airmail, 20, 50g (7v). Souvenir sheet of 5 (50, 75c, 1, 1.50, 4.50g) and souvenir sheet of 1, 4.50g.

1962

Europa 1962. *Dec. 17.* 4g; airmail, 36g (2v). Souvenir sheet of 2 (4, 36g).

Solar System. *Dec. 17.* 10, 20, 25, 30, 50c; airmail, 12.45, 36, 50g (8v). Souvenir sheet, 50g.

1963

International Sports Cooperation (Pierre de Coubertin and Olympic rings). *Feb. 16.* 15, 25, 30, 40, 50c; airmail, 12.45, 18.15, 36g (8v). Souvenir sheet, 36g.

Same, skier and Olympic rings. *May 16.* 10, 20, 25, 30, 50c; airmail, 12.45, 36, 50g (8v). Souvenir sheet, 50g.

Space Capsule and Walter M. Schirra. *Mar. 16.* 10, 20, 25, 30, 50c; airmail, 12.45, 36, 50g (8v). Souvenir sheet, 50g.

Freedom from Hunger. *May 31.* 10, 25, 50, 75c; airmail, 18.15, 36, 50g (7v). Souvenir sheet, 50g.

Space Capsule and Gordon Cooper. *Aug. 22.* 15, 25, 30, 40, 50c; airmail, 12.45, 18.15, 50g (8v). Souvenir sheet, 50g.

9th Winter Olympics, Innsbruck. *Oct. 28.* 15, 25, 30, 40, 50c; airmail, 12.45, 18.15, 50g (8v). Souvenir sheet, 50g.

1964

18th Summer Olympics, Tokyo. *Jan. 8.* 15, 25, 30, 40, 50c; airmail, 12.45, 18.15, 50g (8v). Souvenir sheet, 50g.

Red Cross centenary. *Feb. 4.* 10, 25, 30, 50c; airmail, 18.15, 36, 50g (7v). Souvenir sheet, 50g.

Space Research and 18th Summer Olympics. *Mar. 11.* 15, 25, 30, 40, 50c; airmail, 12.45, 18.15, 50g (8v). Souvenir sheet, 50g.

Rockets and satellites. *Apr. 25.* 15, 25, 30, 40, 50c; airmail, 12.45, 18.15, 50g (8v). Souvenir sheet, 50g.

United Nations. *July 30.* 15, 25, 30, 40, 50c; airmail, 12.45, 18.15, 50g (8v). Souvenir sheet, 50g.

Wernher von Braun and Rockets. *Sept. 12.* 10, 15, 20, 30, 40c; airmail semipostal, 12.45g+6g, 18.15g+9g, 20g+10g (8v). Souvenir sheet of 2 (40c, 12.45g+6g).

38th International Eucharistic Congress, Bombay. *Dec. 11.* Semipostal, 20g+10g, 30g+15g, 50g+25g, 100g+50g (4v). Souvenir sheet of 4 (20g+10g, 30g+15g, 50g+25g, 100g+50g), with and without presentation folder.

Churches and Medals. *Dec. 12.* Semipostal, 20g+10g, 30g+15g, 50g+25g, 100g+50g (4v). Souvenir sheet of 4 (20g+10g, 30g+15g, 50g+25g, 100g+50g), with and without presentation folder.

1965

Boy Scouts. *Jan. 15.* 10, 15, 20, 30, 50c; airmail, 12.45, 18.15, 36g (8v). Souvenir sheet, 36g.

Olympic and Paraguayan Medals. *Mar. 30.* 15, 25, 30, 40, 50c; airmail, 12.45, 18.15, 50g (8v). Souvenir sheet, 50g.

Scientists. *June 5.* 10, 15, 20, 30, 40c; airmail semipostal, 12.45g+6g, 18.15g+9g, 20g+10g (8v se-tenant triangles). (Newton, Copernicus, Galileo, Einstein). Souvenir sheet of 2 (40c, 12.45g+6g).

Kennedy and Churchill Memorials. *Sept. 4.* 15, 25, 30, 40, 50c; airmail, 12.45, 18.15, 50g (8v). Souvenir sheet, 50g.

International Telecommunication Union centenary. *Sept. 30.* 10, 15, 20, 30, 40c; airmail semipostal, 12.45g+6g, 18.15g+9g, 20g+10g (8v). Souvenir sheet of 2 (40c, 12.45g+6g).

Pope Paul VI, Visit to U.N. *Nov. 19.* 10, 15, 20, 30, 50c; airmail, 12.45, 18.15, 36g (8v). Souvenir sheet, 36g.

1966

Space Exploration. *Feb. 19.* (Grissom, White, McDivitt, Young) 15, 25, 30, 40, 50c; airmail, 12.45, 18.15, 50g (8v). Souvenir sheet, 50g.

Events of 1965. *Mar. 9.* 10, 15, 20, 30, 50c; airmail, 12.45, 18.15, 36g (8v). Souvenir sheet, 36g.

Pre-Olympic Games, Mexico 1968. *Apr. 1.* 10, 15, 20, 30, 50c; airmail, 12.45, 18.15, 36g (8v). Souvenir sheet, 36g.

Space Research, German Contributors. *May 16.* 10, 15, 20, 30, 50c; airmail, 12.45, 18.15, 36g (8v). Souvenir sheet, 36g.

Writers. *June 11.* 10, 15, 20, 30, 50c; airmail, 12.45, 18.15, 36g (8v) (Dante, Moliere, Goethe, Shakespeare). Souvenir sheet, 36g.

Space Research, Italian Contributors. *July 11.* 10, 15, 20, 30, 50c; airmail, 12.45, 18.15, 36g (8v). Souvenir sheet, 36g.

Moon Exploration. *Aug. 25.* 10, 15, 20, 30, 50c; airmail, 12.45, 18.15, 36g (8v). Souvenir sheet, 36g.

World Skiing Championships, Portillo, Chile, and **10th Winter Olympics,** Grenoble 1968. *Sept. 30.* 10, 15, 20, 30, 50c; airmail, 12.45, 18.15, 36g (8v). Souvenir sheet, 36g.

John F. Kennedy, 3rd death anniversary and communications satellites. *Nov. 7.* 10, 15, 20, 30, 50c; airmail, 12.45, 18.15, 36g (8v). Souvenir sheet, 36g.

Paintings. *Dec. 10.* 10, 15, 20, 30, 50c; airmail, 12.45, 18.15, 36g (8v se-tenant). (Largilliere, Rubens, Titian, Holbein, Sanchez Coello, Veronese, Mantegna, Vouet). Souvenir sheet, 36g.

1967

Holy Week, paintings. *Feb. 28.* 10, 15, 20, 30, 50c; airmail, 12.45, 18.15, 36g (8v se-tenant) (Raphael, Rubens, Bassano, El Greco, Murillo, Reni, Tintoretto, da Vinci). Souvenir sheet, 36g.

Religious paintings, 16th century. *Mar. 10.* 10, 15, 20, 30, 50c; airmail, 12.45, 18.15, 36g (8v) (Fiori, Tibaldi, El Greco, Caravaggio, Vasco, Fernandez). Souvenir sheet, 36g.

Paintings, *May 16.* 10, 15, 20, 30, 50c; airmail, 12.45, 18.15, 36g (8v se-tenant) (Chardin, Fontanesi, Cezanne, van Gogh, Renoir, Toulouse-Lautrec). Souvenir sheet, 36g.

Paintings. *July 16.* 10, 15, 20, 25, 30, 50c; airmail, 12.45, 18.15, 36g (9v) (Steen, Hals, Jordaens, Rembrandt, Desmarées, Quentin de la Tour, Nicolaes Maes, Vigée-Lebrun, Rubens, Tiepolo). 2 souvenir sheets; 1 of 1, 50g, perf.; 1 of 3 (12.45, 18.15, 36g), imperf.

John F. Kennedy, 50th birthday. *Aug. 19.* 10, 15, 20, 25, 30, 50c; airmail, 12.45, 18.15, 36g. (9v). 2 souvenir sheets: 1 of 1, 50g, perf.; 1 of 3 (12.45, 18.15, 36g) imperf.

Sculptures. *Oct. 16.* 10, 15, 20, 25, 30, 50c; airmail, 12.45, 18.15, 50g (9v).

19th Summer Olympics, Mexico (Mexican art). *Nov. 29.* 10, 15, 20, 25, 30, 50c; airmail, 12.45, 18.15, 36g (9v). 2 souvenir sheets: 1 of 1, 50g, perf.; 1 of 3 (12.45, 18.15, 36g) imperf.

1968

Madonna and Child, paintings. *Jan. 27.* 10, 15, 20, 25, 30, 50c; airmail, 12.45, 18.15, 36g (9v). Souvenir sheet of 3 (12.45, 18.15, 36g) imperf. (Bellini, Raphael, Correggio, Luini, Bronzino, Van Dyck, Vignon, de Ribera, Botticelli)

10th Winter Olympics, Grenoble. *Apr. 23.* 10, 15, 20, 25, 30, 50c; airmail, 12.45, 18.15, 36g (9v) (paintings by Pisarro, Utrillo, Monet, Breitner, Sisley, Brueghel, Anverkamp, Limbourg brothers). Souvenir sheet of 2 (36, 50g).

History of Paraguayan stamps (stamps on stamps). *June 3.* 10, 15, 20, 25, 30, 50c; airmail, 12.45, 18.15, 36g (9v). Souvenir sheet of 2 (36, 50g).

Children, paintings. *July 9.* 10, 15, 20, 25, 30, 50c; airmail, 12.45, 18.15, 36g (9v) (Russell, Velazquez, Romney, Caravaggio, Lawrence, Gentileschi, Renoir, Copley, Sessions). Souvenir sheet of 2 (36, 50g).

39th International Eucharistic Congress and Pope Paul's Visit. *Sept. 25.* 10, 15, 20, 25, 30, 50c; airmail, 12.45, 18.15, 36g (9v). Souvenir sheet of 2 (36, 50g).

Events of 1968. *Dec. 21.* 10, 15, 20, 25, 30, 50c; airmail, 12.45, 18.15, 50g (9v). 3 imperf. souvenir sheets of 3 (10, 15c, 50g; 20, 25c, 12.45c; 30, 50c, 18.15g).

1969

Gold Medal Winners, Mexico Olympics. *Feb. 13.* 10, 15, 20, 25, 30, 50c; airmail, 12.45, 18.15, 50g (9v). 3 imperf. souvenir sheets of 3 (10, 15c, 12.45g; 20, 50c, 50g; 25, 30c, 18.15g).

International Space Developments. *Mar. 10.* 10, 15, 20, 25, 30, 50c; airmail, 12.45, 18.15, 50g (9v). 3 imperf. souvenir sheets of 3 (10, 15, 20c; 25, 30c, 18.15g; 50c, 12.45, 50g).

Regional Fauna. *July 9.* Birds: 10, 15, 20, 25, 30, 50, 75c; airmail, 12.45, 18.15g (9v). Animals: 10, 15, 20, 25, 30, 50, 75c; airmail, 12.45, 18.15g (9v).

Apollo 11. *July 9.* 4 airmail souvenir sheets: 2 perf., 2 imperf., each 23.40g.

Winners of Jules Rimet Cup Soccer Championships, 1930-1966. *Nov. 26.* 10, 15, 20, 25, 30, 50, 75c; airmail, 12.45, 18.15g (9v). Souvenir sheet, 23.40g perf., imperf.

Olympic Soccer Gold Medal Winners, 1900-1968. *Nov. 26.* 10, 15, 20, 25, 30, 50, 75c; airmail, 12.45, 18.15g (9v). Souvenir sheet, 23.40g perf., imperf.

Christmas, paintings. *Nov. 29.* 10, 15, 20, 25, 30, 50, 75c; airmail, 12.45, 18.15g (9v). (Master Bertram, Procaccini, di Credi, Maitre de Flémalle, Correggio, Borgianni, Botticelli, El Greco, de Morales). Souvenir sheet, 23.40g imperf.

Goya paintings. *Nov. 29.* 10, 15, 20, 25, 30, 50, 75c; airmail, 12.45, 18.15g (9v). Souvenir sheet, 23.40g.

Space Exploration, European contributors. *Nov. 29.* Airmail souvenir sheet, 23.40g, perf., imperf.

1970

Apollo 11. *Mar. 11.* 10, 15, 20, 25, 30, 50, 75c; airmail, 12.45, 18.15g (9v). 3 souvenir sheets, each 23.40g. 1 perf., 2 imperf.

Easter. *Mar. 11.* Se-tenant checkerwise. 10, 15, 20, 25, 30, 50, 75c; airmail, 12.45, 18.15g (9v). Souvenir sheet, 23.40g.

Apollo 12. *Mar. 16.* Perf., imperf. 50c x 2; airmail, 50c x 2 (4v). 2 souvenir sheets of 2 (each 50c x 2) 1 with simulated perf., 1 imperf.

20th Summer Olympics, Munich, 1972. *Sept. 28.* 10, 15, 20, 25, 30, 50, 75c; airmail, 12.45, 18.15g (9v se-tenant) souvenir sheet, 23.40g perf., imperf.

Paintings, Pinakothek, Munich, 1972. *Sept. 28.* 10, 15, 20, 25, 30, 50, 75c; airmail, 12.45, 18.15g (9v se-tenant) (Nudes by Cranach, Baldung, Tintoretto, Rubens, Boucher, Dürer self-portrait; altar by Altdorfer). Souvenir sheet, 23.40g.

Apollo space program. *Oct. 19.* 10, 15, 20, 25, 30, 50, 75c; airmail, 12.45, 18.15g (9v se-tenant). 3 souvenir sheets, each 23.40g, 1 perf., 2 imperf.

Moon and Space Conquests, future projects. *Oct. 19.* 10, 15, 20, 25, 30 (se-tenant); 50, 75c; airmail, 12.45, 18.15g (9v). Souvenir sheet, 23.40g.

EXPO '70, Osaka, Japan, (paintings from National Museum, Tokyo). *Nov. 26.* 10, 15, 20, 25, 30, (se-tenant); 50, 75c; airmail, 12.45, 18.15, 50g (10v). 3 souvenir sheets, each 20g.

Flowers, paintings. *Nov. 26.* 10, 15, 20, 25, 30, (se-tenant) 50, 75c; airmail, 12.45, 18.15, 50g (10v) (Jawlensky, Purrmann, Vlaminck, Monet, Renoir, van Gogh, Cézanne, van Huysum, Ruysch, Walscappelle). Souvenir sheet, 20g.

Paintings, Prado, Madrid. *Dec. 16.* 10, 15, 20, 25, 30 (se-tenant), 50, 75c; airmail, 12.45, 18.15, 50g (10v). (Nudes by Titian, Velazquez, Van Dyck, Tintoretto, Rubens, Veronese; religious paintings by Goya, Murillo, El Greco). Souvenir sheet, 20g.

Dürer paintings. *Dec. 16.* 10, 15, 20, 25, 30 (se-tenant) 50, 75c; airmail, 12.45, 18.15, 50g (10v). Souvenir sheet, 20g.

Eisenhower Memorial. *Dec. 16.* Airmail souvenir sheet, 20g.

Napoleon. *Dec. 16.* Airmail souvenir sheet, 20g.

1971

20th Summer Olympics, Munich, 1972 *Mar. 23.* 10, 15, 20, 25, 30 (se-tenant) 50, 75c; airmail, 12.45, 18.15, 50g (10v). 2 souvenir sheets, each 23.40g.

Knights, paintings. *Mar. 26.* 10, 15, 20, 25, 30c (se-tenant), 50, 75c; airmail, 12.45, 18.15, 50g (10v). (Van Dyck, Titian, Walter, Orsi, David, Huguet, Perugino, Witz, Van Eyck) Souvenir sheet, 20g.

Apollo Missions. *Mar. 26.* 2 airmail souvenir sheets, each 20g.

Women, paintings, from Louvre. *Mar. 26.* 10, 15, 20, 25, 30c (se-tenant), 50, 75c; airmail, 12.45, 18.15, 50g (10v). (Boucher, de la Tour, Delacroix, Ingres, Watteau, Renoir, da Vinci). Souvenir sheet, 20g.

Paraguayan stamp centenary. *Mar. 23.* Airmail souvenir sheet, 20g.

Christmas, paintings. *Mar. 23.* 10, 15, 20, 25, 30c (se-tenant) 50, 75c; airmail, 12.45, 18.15, 50g (10v) (van der Weyden, Zeitblom, von Soest, Mayno, da Fabriano, Matirios, Memling, Poussin, Rubens, Giorgione, Batoni). Souvenir sheet, 20g.

Paintings. *Mar. 29.* 10, 15, 20, 25, 30c (se-tenant), 50, 75c; airmail, 12.45, 18.15, 50g (10v) (Botticelli, Tibaldi, Titian, Caracci, Raphael, Ricci, Delgado Rodas, Courtines, Murillo).

Paraguayan stamp centenary and Lufthansa Asuncion—Frankfurt flight. *Mar. 29.* 2 airmail souvenir sheets, each 20g.

Hunting scenes, paintings. *Mar. 29.* 10, 15, 20, 25, 30c (se-tenant), 50, 75c; airmail, 12.45, 18.15, 50g (10v) (Gozzoli, Velazquez, Uccello, Sutherland, Brun, de Vos, Vernet). 2 souvenir sheets, each 20g.

Philatokyo '71 (Japanese prints). *Apr. 7.* 10, 15, 20, 25, 30c (se-tenant), 50, 75c; airmail, 12.45, 18.15, 50g (10v). 2 souvenir sheets, each 20g.

11th Winter Olympics, Sapporo, 1972 (Japanese art). *Apr. 7.* 10, 15, 20, 25, 30c (se-tenant), 50, 75c; airmail, 12.45, 18.15, 50g (10v). 2 souvenir sheets, each 20g.

Charles de Gaulle, 1st death anniversary. *Nov. 9.* Airmail souvenir sheet, 20g.

Johannes Kepler, 400th death anniversary. *Nov. 9.* 2 airmail souvenir sheets, each 20g.

Paintings, Berlin-Dahlem Museum. *Dec. 23.* 15c and 20c (se-tenant), 10, 25, 30, 50, 75c; airmail, 12.45, 18.15, 50g (10v) (Caravaggio, De Cosimo, Cranach, Veneziano, Holbein, Grien, Dürer, Schongauer).

Napoleon I, sesquicentennial of death. *Dec. 24.* 10, 15, 20, 25, 30c (se-tenant) 50, 75c; airmail, 12.45, 18.15, 50g (10v).

Taras Shevchenko, 110th birth anniversary. *Dec. 24.* Airmail souvenir sheet, 20g.

1972

Locomotives. *Jan. 6.* 10, 15, 20, 25, 30c (se-tenant), 50, 75c; airmail, 12.45, 18.15, 50g (10v). Souvenir sheet, 20g.

11th Winter Olympics, Sapporo. *Jan. 6.* 10, 15, 20, 25, 30c (se-tenant), 50, 75c; airmail, 12.45, 18.15, 50g (10v). 2 souvenir sheets, each 20g.

American space explorations, decade. *Jan. 6.* Airmail souvenir sheet, 20g.

Racing cars. *Mar. 20.* 10, 15, 20, 25, 30c (se-tenant), 50, 75c; airmail, 12.45, 18.15, 50g (10v). Souvenir sheet, 20g.

Apollo 16. *Mar. 29.* Airmail souvenir sheet, 20g.

Olympic Games, 1896–1972. *Mar. 29.* 6 airmail souvenir sheets, each 20g.

Ancient war vessels. *Mar. 29.* 10, 15, 20, 25, 30c (se-tenant), 50, 75c; airmail, 12.45, 18.15, 50g. (10v).

Paintings, Asuncion Museum. *May 22.* 10, 15, 20, 25, 30c (se-tenant), 50, 75c; airmail, 12.45, 18.15, 50g (10v) (Holden Jara, Tintoretto, Bouchard, Italian School, Berisso, Carracci, Schiaffino, Lostow).

Paintings, Vienna Museum. *May 22.* 10, 15, 20, 25, 30c (se-tenant), 50, 75c; airmail, 12.45, 18.15, 50g (10v) (Rubens, Bellini, Carracci, Cagnacci, Spranger, Strozzi, Cranach, Coxcie, Poussin, Bronzino).

Meetings of Presidents, (Argentina, Bolivia, Brazil, Paraguay). *Nov. 18.* 10, 15, 20, 25, 30c (se-tenant), 50, 75c; airmail, 12.45, 18.15g (9v), Souvenir sheet, 23.40g.

President Stroessner, visit to Emperor of Japan. *Nov. 18.* 10, 15, 20, 25, 30c (se-tenant), 50, 75c; airmail, 12.45, 18.15g (9v), 3 souvenir sheets, each 23.40g, 2 perf., 1 imperf.

Animals, paintings. *Nov. 18.* 10, 15, 20, 25, 30c (se-tenant), 50, 75c; airmail, 12.45, 18.15g (9v) (Botke, Utamaro, Arents, Dietzsch, Brueghel, Marc, Dürer, Jakuchu, Asselyn).

Medal Winners, Sapporo Olympics, *Nov. 18.* Airmail souvenir sheet, 23.40g.

Locomotives. *Nov. 25.* 10, 15, 20, 25, 30c (se-tenant), 50, 75c; airmail, 12.45, 18.15g (9v).

South American animals. *Nov. 25.* 10, 15, 20, 25, 30c (se-tenant), 50, 75c; airmail, 12.45, 18.15g (9v).

Olympic Medals History. *Nov. 25.* 2 airmail souvenir sheets, each 23.40g.

Christmas, painting (Murillo). *Nov. 25.* Airmail souvenir sheet, 23.40g.

Civil aviation and space exploration, French contributions. *Nov. 25.* 2 airmail souvenir sheets, each 23.40g.

1973

Paintings, Florence Museum. *Mar. 13.* 10, 15, 20, 25, 30, 50, 75c; airmail, 5, 10, 20g (10v se-tenant) (Cranach, Caravaggio, Fiorentino, di Credi, Liss, da Vinci, Botticelli, Titian, del Piombo, di Michelino). 2 souvenir sheets, each 25g.

South American butterflies. *Mar. 13.* 10, 15, 20, 25, 30, 50, 75c; airmail, 5, 10, 20g (10v, se-tenant).

Apollo 17. *Mar. 13.* Airmail souvenir sheet, 25g.

IBRA 73, Munich. *Mar. 21.* Airmail souvenir sheet, 25g, imperf.

Medal Winners, Munich Olympics, *Mar. 15.* Airmail souvenir sheet, 25g.

Cats. *June 29.* 10, 15, 20, 25, 30, 50, 75c; airmail, 5, 10, 20g (10v, se-tenant).

Paintings, Flemish. *June 29.* 10, 15, 20, 25, 30, 50, 75c; airmail, 5, 10, 20g (10v, se-tenant) (Spranger, Jordaens, de Clerck, Goltzius, Rubens, Brueghel, Martin de Vos).

Copernicus, 500th birth anniversary. *June 29.* 2 airmail souvenir sheets, each 25g.

Skylab. *June 29.* Airmail souvenir sheet, 25g.

World Cup Soccer Championship, Munich, 1974. *June 29.* Airmail souvenir sheet, 25g. *Oct. 8.* 10, 15, 20, 25, 30, 50, 75c; airmail, 5, 10, 20g (10v, se-tenant). Souvenir sheet, 25g.

Venetian Women, paintings. *Oct. 8.* 10, 15, 20, 25, 30, 50, 75c; airmail, 5, 10, 20g (10v, se-tenant) (Carapaccio, Pitoni, Veronese, Tintoretto, Amigoni, Tiepolo).

Planetary exploration (Mars). *Oct 8.* 2 airmail souvenir sheets, each 25g.

Birds. *Nov. 14.* 10, 15, 20, 25, 30, 50, 75c; airmail, 5, 10, 20g (10v, se-tenant). Souvenir sheet, 25g.

Moon explorations (Apollo 11-17). *Nov. 14.* 10, 15, 20, 25, 30, 50, 75c; airmail, 5, 10, 20g (10v, se-tenant). 2 souvenir sheets, each 25g.

Picasso memorial. *Nov. 14.* Airmail souvenir sheet, 25g.

Folklore (national costumes). *Dec. 30.* 25, 50, 75c, 1, 1.50, 1.75, 2.25g (7v se-tenant).

President Stroessner, visit to Europe and Morocco. *Dec. 30.* Airmail, 5, 10, 25, 50g (se-tenant), 150g (5v). Souvenir sheet, 100g, imperf.

Flowers. *Dec. 31.* 10, 20, 25, 30, 40, 50, 75c (7v se-tenant).

1974

World Cup Soccer Championship, Munich. *Jan. 31.* Airmail, 5, 10, 20g (3v se-tenant). 2 souvenir sheets, each 25g.

Roses, paintings. *Feb. 2.* 10, 15, 20, 25, 30, 50, 75c (7v se-tenant) (Curtis, Chazal, Buchoz, Ehret, van Spaendonick).

Paintings, Gulbenkian Museum. *Feb. 4.* 10, 15, 20, 25, 30, 50, 75c; airmail, 5, 10, 20g (10v se-tenant) (Boucher, Burne-Jones, Natoire, de Vos, Bugiardini, Mabuse, Utamaro, Lawrence, Rubens).

Christmas 1973, painting (Le Nain). *Feb. 4.* Airmail souvenir sheet, 25g.

Tourism Year 1973 (emblems of 10 airlines operating in Paraguay). *Feb. 4.* Airmail souvenir sheet, 25g.

Paintings. *Mar. 20.* 10, 15, 20, 25, 30, 50, 75c; airmail, 5, 10, 20g (10v, se-tenant) (Mabuse, di Cosimo, van Haarlem, Boucher, Renoir, Dix, van Kessel, Seele, Batoni, Flamenca).

UPU centenary. *Mar. 20.* 10, 15, 20, 25, 30, 50, 75c; airmail, 5, 10, 20g (10v se-tenant). 2 souvenir sheets, each 25g.

Skylab 2. *Mar. 20.* Airmail souvenir sheet, 25g.

President Stroessner. *May 10.* Visit to France and President Pompidou: Airmail, 100g. Visit to Pope Paul VI: Airmail souvenir sheet, 200g.

World Cup Soccer Championship. *July 13.* Airmail, 4, 5, 10g (3v). Souvenir sheet, 15g.

Lufthansa-Lineas Aereas Paraguayas airlines. *July 13.* Airmail souvenir sheet, 15g.

Ships, paintings. *Sept. 13.* 5, 10, 15, 20, 25, 35, 40, 50c (8v se-tenant). Airmail souvenir sheet, 15g, imperf.

President Stroessner, visit to South Africa. *Dec. 2.* Airmail, 10g.

President Pinochet of Chile, visit to Paraguay. *Dec. 2.* Airmail, 5g.

Covers (canceled on moon). *Dec. 2.* Airmail, 4g.

UPU centenary. *Dec. 2.* 2 airmail souvenir sheets, each 15g. *Dec. 7:* Airmail 4, 5, 10g (3v).

Mariner 10. *Dec. 2 and 7.* 2 airmail souvenir sheets, each 15g.

Winter Olympics, Committee sessions. *Dec. 7.* 2 airmail souvenir sheets, each 15g.

World Cup Soccer Championship (FIFA cup; German winning team; 1973 games, Argentina). *Dec. 20.* Airmail, 4, 5, 10g (3v). 2 airmail souvenir sheets, each 15g.

1975

Paintings, Borghese Gallery, Rome. *Jan. 15.* 5, 10, 15, 20, 25, 35, 40, 50c (8v se-tenant) (Romano, Caravaggio, Domenichino, Titian, Correggio, Savoldo, da Vinci, Rubens, Piero di Cosimo). Airmail souvenir sheet, 15g.

Christmas, paintings. *Jan. 17.* 5, 10, 15, 20, 25, 35, 40, 50c (8v se-tenant) (della Robbia, David, Memling, Giorgione, French 14th century, Pulzone, van Orley, Pacher, Raphael). Airmail souvenir sheet, 15g.

OCEAN EXPO '75 International Oceanographic Exhibition, Okinawa. *Feb. 24.* Airmail, 4, 5, 10g (3v). Airmail souvenir sheet, 15g.

Summer Olympics, Montreal 1976. *Feb. 24.* Airmail souvenir sheet, 15g.

Kurt, Debus (scientist), 65th birth anniversary. *Feb. 24.* Airmail souvenir sheet, 15g.

Paintings, London National Gallery. *Apr. 25.* 5, 10, 15, 20, 25, 35, 40, 50c (8v). (Velazquez, Watteau, Correggio, Gainsborough, Cranach, Lotto, Rembrandt, Tintoretto, Pisanello) Airmail souvenir sheet, 15g.

Dogs. *June 7.* 5, 10, 15, 20, 25, 35, 40, 50c (8v). Airmail souvenir sheet, 15g.

Fauna of South America. *Aug. 20.* 5, 10, 15, 20, 25, 35, 40, 50c (8v). Airmail souvenir sheet, 15g.

Spanish Stamps, 125th anniversary, Espana '75. *Aug. 21.* Airmail, 4, 5, 10g se-tenant (3v). Airmail souvenir sheet, 15g.

Zeppelin America Flight (ZR3). *Aug. 21.* Airmail souvenir sheet, 15g.

Pioneer 11, Jupiter Flight *Aug. 21.* Airmail souvenir sheet, 15g.

Michelangelo, 500th birth anniversary. *Aug. 23.* Se-tenant in strip of 8. 5, 10, 15, 20, 25, 35, 40, 50c (8v). Airmail souvenir sheet, 15g.

Same. *Aug. 26.* Airmail, 4, 5, 10g se-tenant (3v). Airmail souvenir sheet, 15g, simulated perforation.

International Women's Year, U.N. 30th anniversary. *Aug. 26.* Airmail souvenir sheet, 15g.

Space Exploration, German contributions. *Aug. 26.* Airmail souvenir sheet, 15g.

Winter Olympics, Innsbruck. *Aug. 27.* 1, 2, 3, 4, 5g; airmail, 10, 15, 20g (8v). 2 airmail souvenir sheets, each 25g.

Summer Olympics, Montreal. *Aug. 28.* 1, 2, 3, 4, 5g; airmail, 10, 15, 20g (8v). 2 airmail souvenir sheets, each 25g.

Various Flights. *Oct. 13.* Airmail, 4, 5, 10g (3v). 3 airmail souvenir sheets; Zeppelin, World Soccer Championship, Viking, each 15g.

U.S. Bicentennial, paintings of victorious ships. *Oct. 20.* 5, 10, 20, 25, 35, 40, 50c (7v). Airmail souvenir sheet, 15g.

U.S. Bicentennial, paintings. *Nov. 20.* Se-tenant in strips of 8. 5, 10, 15, 20, 25, 35, 40, 50c (8v). (Kahill, Brackman, Catlin, Benton, Remington, Willard, Trumbull, Stuart) Airmail souvenir sheet, 15g.

U.S. Bicentennial, auto industry. *Nov. 28.* Airmail, 4, 5 and 10g se-tenant (3v).

U.S. Bicentennial, air and space technology. *Nov. 28.* Airmail souvenir sheet, 15g.

U.S. Bicentennial, flags and seals of Paraguay and U.S. *Nov. 28.* Airmail souvenir sheet, 15g.

Concorde, Lufthansa, Exfilmo '75. *Dec. 20.* Airmail, 4, 5, 10g (3v). Airmail souvenir sheet, 15g.

Schweitzer – Adenauer. *Dec. 20.* Airmail souvenir sheet, 15g.

Ferdinand Porsche, birth centenary, Vienna '75 Philatelic Exposition. *Dec. 20.* Airmail souvenir sheet, 15g.

1976

Holy Year, Christmas paintings. *Feb. 2.* Airmail, 4, 5, 10g (3v). (Raphael, del Mayno, Vignon, Ghirlandaio). Airmail souvenir sheet, 15g.

Austria, 1000th anniversary. *Feb. 2.* Airmail souvenir sheet, 15g.

World Soccer Championships, Germany 1954, 1974. *Feb. 2.* Airmail souvenir sheet, 15g.

Cats. *Apr. 2.* Se-tenant strip of 8. 5, 10, 15, 20, 25, 35, 40, 50c (8v). Airmail souvenir sheet, 15g.

Apollo-Soyuz. *Apr. 2.* Airmail souvenir sheet, 25g.

Railroads, 150th anniversary. *Apr. 2.* 1, 2, 3, 4, 5g; airmail, 10, 15, 20g (8v). Airmail souvenir sheet, 25g.

Lufthansa, 50th anniversary. *Apr. 2.* Airmail souvenir sheet, 25g.

Spanish Paintings. *Apr. 2.* 1, 2, 3, 4, 5g; airmail 10, 15, 20g (8v). (Goya, de Torres, Esquival, Murillo, Antolinez, Zuloaga, Velazquez). Airmail souvenir sheet, 25g.

Butterflies. *May 12.* Se-tenant strip of 8. 5, 10, 15, 20, 25, 35, 40, 50c (8v).

Winter Olympics, Innsbruck '76. Olympic medals and Innsbruck aerial scene. *June 15.* Airmail souvenir sheet, 25g.

July 18. Airmail souvenir sheet, 25g (Rosi Mittermaier; medals and medal-winning countries in margin.)

Domestic Animals. *June 15.* 1, 2, 3, 4, 5, 10, 15, 20g (8v).

Telephone, Bell, centenary. *June 15.* Airmail souvenir sheet, 25g.

U.S. Bicentennial & U.S. Post Office Dept. bicentenary. *June 18.* 1, 2, 3, 4, 5g; airmail, 10, 15, 20g (8v). 2 airmail souvenir sheets (Man on Moon and 1st Official Missile Mail), each 25g.

Interphil 76, seven other philatelic exhibition emblems. *May 29.* Airmail souvenir sheet, 15g.

Painting, Planets (mythology) with satellites. *July 12.* 1, 2, 3, 4, 5g; airmail 10, 15, 20g (8v, first 7 values se-tenant) (Ingres, Rubens, Tiepolo, Medina, Giordano, de la Hyre, Veronese). Airmail souvenir sheet, 25g (Satellites over Mars, Mars and Venus by Houbraken in margin).

United Nations Postal Administration, 25th anniversary, U.P.U. centenary. *July 15.* Airmail souvenir sheet, 25g. (U.N. No. 38).

Dec. 18. 25th U.P.U. anniversary, telephone centenary, 110th I.T.U. anniversary. Airmail souvenir sheet, 25g (U.N. No. 42, Geneva No. 22).

Paintings, Sailing Ships. *July 15.* 1, 2, 3, 4, 5g; airmail, 10, 15, 20g (8v, first 7 se-tenant).

Paintings, German Warships. *Aug. 20.* 1, 2, 3, 4, 5g; airmail, 10, 15, 20g (8v) (Zeeden, Wichman, Pollack, Fedeler, Seiz, Stroh, Bohrdt). Airmail souvenir sheet, Hamburg Nautical Exposition, 25g (Zeytline).

21st Summer Olympics, Montreal. Women medal winners. *Dec. 18.* 1, 2, 3, 4, 5g; airmail, 10, 15, 20g (8v, first 7 se-tenant). 3 airmail souvenir sheets, 25g (German Dressage Team; U.S. Bicentennial, Bruce Jenner, decathlon winner; list of medal-winning countries, Olympic torch.

1977

Titian, 500th birth anniversary, paintings. *Feb. 18.* 1, 2, 3, 4, 5g; airmail, 10, 15, 20g (8v, first 7 values se-tenant).

Rubens, 400th birth anniversary, paintings. *Feb. 18.* 1, 2, 3, 4, 5g; airmail, 10, 15, 20g (8v, first 7 values se-tenant). Airmail souvenir sheet (Milky Way).

U.S. Bicentennial, Space scenes. *March 3.* 1, 2, 3, 4, 5g; airmail, 10, 15, 20g (8v, first 7 values se-tenant). 2 airmail souvenir sheets, 25g. (Future space-craft on Mars).

Nobel Prize, 75th Anniversary. *June 7.* Airmail souvenir sheet, 25g (Alfred Nobel medal).

Story of Olympic Games, Athens to Montreal. *June 10.* 1, 2, 3, 4, 5g; airmail, 10, 15, 20g (8v). Airmail souvenir sheet, 25g.

LUPOSTA '77, Graf Zeppelin, trip to South America. *June 13.* 1, 2, 3, 4, 5g; airmail, 10, 15, 20g (8v). 2 airmail souvenir sheets, 25g (LUPOSTA '77), 25g (Zeppelin).

History of Aviation. *July 18.* 1, 2, 3, 4, 5g; airmail, 10, 15, 20g (8v). 2 airmail souvenir sheets, 25g (Lindbergh), 25g (Helix).

World Soccer, Argentina '78. *Oct. 28.* (First issue). 1, 2, 3, 4, 5g; airmail, 10, 15, 20g (8v, first 7 values in se-tenant strip). Airmail souvenir sheet, 25g. (Second issue) 1, 2, 3, 4, 5g; airmail, 10, 15, 20g (8v, first 7 values in se-tenant strip). Airmail souvenir sheet, 25g.

1978

Rubens, 400th birth anniversary, paintings. *Jan. 19.* 1, 2, 3, 4, 5g; airmail 10, 15, 20g (8v, first 7 values in se-tenant strip). 2 airmail souvenir sheets, 25g (gold or silver inscriptions).

World Chess Championships, Argentina 1978, Paintings. *Jan. 23.* 1, 2, 3, 4, 5g; airmail, 10, 15, 20g (8v, first 7 values in se-tenant strip) (de Cremone, L. van Leyden, H. Muelich, E. H. May, George Cruikshank, unknown). Airmail souvenir sheet, 25g.

Francisco de Goya, 150th death anniversary. *May 11.* 3, 4, 5, 6, 7, 8, 20g (se-tenant strip of 7); airmail, 10, 25g (9v).

Future Aerospace Projects. *May 16.* 3, 4, 5, 6, 7, 8, 20g (se-tenant strip of 7); airmail, 10, 25g (9v).

Racing Cars. *June 28.* 3, 4, 5, 6, 7, 8, 20g (se-tenant strip of 7); airmail, 10, 25g (9v). Airmail souvenir sheet, 25g (Ferrari).

Peter Paul Rubens, paintings. *June 30.* 3, 4, 5, 6, 7, 8, 20g; airmail, 10, 25g (9v).

Pres. Stroessner Reelection. *Aug. 15.* Airmail, 75, 500, 1000g (3v).

QEII Coronation, 25th anniversary. 2 airmail souvenir sheets, 25g (Queen with orb and scepter), 25g (Queen presenting World Soccer Cup to 1966 England team).

World Cup Soccer, Argentina 78. 3 airmail souvenir sheets. 25g (Soccer emblem and flags of 16 finalists); 25g (Stadium with flags and insignia of finalists); 25g (World Cup, Argentina champions, finals).

Christmas and New Year 1978-79, painting by Albrecht Dürer. Airmail souvenir sheet, 25g.

International Year of the Child, Grimm's "Snow White and the Seven Dwarfs." *Oct. 26.* 3, 4, 5, 6, 7, 8, 20g (se-tenant strip of 7); airmail, 10, 25g (9v).

Christmas 1978, paintings. 3, 4, 5, 6, 7, 8, 20g (se-tenant strip of 7); airmail, 10, 25g (9v). Airmail souvenir sheet, 25g (Rubens).

1979

World Cup Soccer, Argentina. 3, 4, 5, 6, 7, 8, 20g (se-tenant strip of 7); airmail, 10, 25g (9v).

Military Units. 3, 4, 5, 6, 7, 8, 20g (se-tenant strip of 7); airmail, 10, 25g (9v).

75th Anniversary, First Powered Flight. 3, 4, 5, 6, 7, 8, 20g (se-tenant strip of 7); airmail, 10, 25g (9v). Airmail souvenir sheet, 25g (Graf Zeppelin).

ST. THOMAS AND PRINCE ISLANDS

1977

Rubens, 400th birth anniversary, paintings. *June 28.* 1, 5, 10, 15, 20, 50e (6v in se-tenant strips of 3). Souvenir sheet (20, 75g).

Beethoven, 150th death anniversary, paintings. *June 28.* 20, 30, 50e (se-tenant strip of 3). (Chr. Hornemann, miniature; F. Klein, mask; F. Schimon, painting).

1978

International Organizations. *May 25.* 3, 3 (Nobel, UNACR), 5, 5 (Nobel, UNICEF), 10, 10 (Nobel, OIT), 15, 15 (Nobel, Int'l. Amnesty), 20, 20 (Nobel, Int'l. Red Cross), 35, 35d (Nobel, Int'l. Red Cross) (12v). Same denominations are se-tenant.

World Cup Soccer, Argentina 78, various teams. 3d x 4 (in se-tenant block), 25d x 3 (in se-tenant strip) (7v).

International Philatelic Exhibition, Essen 1978. *Nov. 1.* 10d x 4 (2 of each) and 10d in sheet of 9 (5v) (Paul Gauguin, Vincent Van Gogh, Henri Matisse, Georges Braque). 2 souvenir sheets, 20, 30d (Gauguin), imperf.

U.P.U. centenary. *Nov. 1.* 5, 5, 5, 5d and 15d x 4 (2 of each) in sheet of 12 (8v).

Peter Paul Rubens, Holy Family paintings. 5, 10, 25, 50, 70d (5v). Sheet of 4 containing 5, 10, 25, 70d.

Introduction of New Currency, 1st anniversary. *Dec. 15.* 5d x 4 (2 of each) and 5d in sheet of 9. 8d x 4 (2 of each) and 8d in sheet of 9 (10v).

SENEGAL

1974

International Fair, Dakar. *Nov. 28.* Airmail, 350fr (silver foil), 1500fr (gold foil) (2v).

1976

21st Summer Olympics, Montreal. *Sept. 11.* First Issue: 15, 20, 25, 50, 100fr; airmail, 400fr (6v). 6 miniature sheets of one. Airmail souvenir sheet, 400fr. Airmail embossed gold foil, 1500fr. Same, souvenir sheet, 1500fr. Second Issue: 5, 10, 60, 65, 70fr; airmail, 500fr (6v). 6 miniature sheets of same. Airmail souvenir sheet, 500fr. Airmail embossed gold foil, 1000fr. Same, souvenir sheet, 1000fr.

2nd International Fair, Dakar, Concorde. *Dec. 3.* Airmail, embossed silver foil, 500fr, embossed gold foil, 1500fr (2v).

SOMALIA

1970

U.S. Space Explorations. *Feb. 14.* 60, 80c, 1, 1.50, 1.80, 2, 2.80sh (7v). Souvenir sheet, 14sh.

TOGO

1971

Napoleon I, death sesquicentennial. *June.* Imperf., Airmail, gold foil, 1000fr and souvenir sheet.

UIPE (International Organization for the Protection of Children). *Nov. 13.* Airmail, gold foil, 1500fr.

1972

OCAM Conference (Organization of African and Malagasy Union). *Apr. 24.* Gold embossed, 1000fr.

1973

Olympic winners, 1972 Munich Games. *Jan.* Perf., imperf. Airmail, gold foil, 1500fr x 3 (3v) 3 airmail souvenir sheets, each 1500fr.

Apollo 17. *Jan.* Perf., imperf. Airmail, gold foil, 1500fr and souvenir sheet.

1974

World Cup Soccer Championship, victory of German team. Perf., imperf. Nos. C180-C181, C181a overprinted "Coupe du Monde / de Football / Munich 1974 / Vainqueur / Republique Federale / d'Allemagne".

1976

21st Summer Olympics, Montreal. *Feb. 24.* Gold foil embossed, 1000fr x 5 (5v).

1977

Elizabeth II, Silver Jubilee. *Jan. 10.* (Queen's portraits) 1000fr. Souvenir sheet, 1000fr.

1978

March. Moscow Olympic Games, 1980; World Cup Soccer, Argentina; Elizabeth II Coronation anniversary; Goya, 150th death anniversary (paintings); lunar orbit of Apollo VIII, 10th anniversary: 1000fr x 5. 5 Souvenir sheets, each 1000fr, gold foil embossed.

URUGUAY

1974

Tourism. *June 6.* Souvenir sheet, 1000p.

World Cup Soccer Championship, Munich. *June 6.* 1000p and imperf. souvenir sheet.

UPU, World Cup Soccer, Olympics. *Aug. 30.* Airmail, 500p. Airmail souvenir sheet of 3 (500p x 3).

UPU, Expo '74, Montevideo. Airmail souvenir sheet, 1000p, imperf.

1975

Pre-Olympics, Innsbruck, Montreal. *May 16.* Airmail, 400, 600p (2v). 2 airmail souvenir sheets of 2 (500, 1000p).

Apollo-Soyuz; U.S. & Uruguay Independence; UN 30th anniversary. 50th anniversary Airlines, International Women's Year. *Sept 29.* Airmail, 10, 15, 25, 50c (4v). 2 souvenir sheets of 4 (40c x 4), (20, 30, 50, 100c).

1976

Olympics, Telecommunications, UPU, UN, Soccer '78 Argentina. *June 3.* 10, 15, 25, 50c (4v). 2 airmail souvenir sheets (30, 70c, 1p) (40, 60c, 2p).

Soccer '78 Argentina, Summer Olympics, U.S. Bicentennial-Project Viking, Nobel Prize Winners. *Nov. 12.* 10, 30, 50, 80c (4v). 2 airmail souvenir sheets (20, 40, 60c, 1.50p) (35, 75, 90, 1p).

1977

Nobel Prize, 75th anniversary, World Cup Soccer, Lindbergh Transatlantic Flight, Rubens 400th birth anniversary. *July 21.* 20, 30, 50c, 1p (4v x 2 with 2 labels in se-tenant strip). 2 souvenir sheets (10, 60, 80c, 2p), (40, 90c, 1.20, 1.50p).

UREXPO '77, 150th Anniversary Uruguay Posts, 50th Anniversary Uruguay Philatelic Clubs, various emblems. *July 27.* Airmail, 8p perf., imperf. Airmail souvenir sheet, 10p.

1978

Various Events. 1979-1980 Philatelic Exhibitions and 1980 Olympic Games. Souvenir sheet of 4 (3, 4, 5, 7, 10p) perf., imperf.

Various Events. Lake Placid, 1980; Uruguay Philatelic Exhibition, 1980; World Chess Games, Buenos Aires, 1978; Sir Rowland Hill, QEII Coronation. Souvenir sheet of 4 (3, 5, 7, 10p) perf., imperf.

YEMEN, MUTAWAKELITE KINGDOM

Most sets exist perf., imperf.

1962

Nos. 98-102, 103-109, 124-126, 127-128, 129-130, 135-136 and various other issues of 1954-65 overprinted in red or black "Free Yemen Fights For God, Imam and Country" (82v).

1963

Kingdom and Flag overprinted on Republic issue of 1963. 4b, 6b x 2 (3v).

International Red Cross centenary. *Dec. 31.* $1/8$, $1/4$, $1/2$, 4b; airmail, 6b (5v).

1964

Fight Against the Republic, 1st anniversary. *Jan. 15.* Perf., imperf. Airmail, $1/2$, 1, 2, 4, 6b (5v). Souvenir sheet, 24b imperf.

British Red Cross Surgical Team. *Mar. 20.* Airmail. $1/2$ and 4b of Fight Against Republic issue overprinted "Honouring British Red Cross Surgical Team" and surcharged 10, 18b (2v).

Surcharges on Fight Against Republic issue. *Apr.* Airmail, 10, 18, 28b. *Aug.* 4b x 3 (6v).

18th Summer Olympics, Tokyo. *Sept. 1.* Perf., imperf. 2, 4b; airmail, 6b (3v). Souvenir sheet, 4b imperf.

Astronauts. *Sept. 7.* Perf., imperf. 2, 4b; airmail, 6b (3v). Souvenir sheet, 6b imperf.

1965

British Yemen Relief Committee. *Feb. 15.* Fight Against Republic surcharges of 1964 overprinted in green "Honouring British Yemen / Relief Comittee / 1963 1965" in English and Arabic (3v).

Imam's Son Memorial. *Mar. 1.* 4b.

John F. Kennedy Memorial. *Apr. 5.* Perf., imperf. $1/8$, $1/4$, $1/2$, 4b; airmail, 6b (5v). Souvenir sheet, 4b imperf.

Churchill Memorial. *Apr. 10:* Imam's Son issue overprinted in red "In Memory of Sir Winston Churchill / 1874-1965" in English and Arabic. *June 6.* (diamonds): $1/8$, $1/4$, $1/2$, 1, 2, 4b (6v). Souvenir sheet, 4b imperf.

International Telecommunication Union centenary. *May 20.* Perf., imperf. 2, 4b; airmail, 6b (3v). Imperf. souvenir sheet.

Birds. *May 30.* $1/8$, $1/4$, $1/2$, 4b; airmail, 6b (5v). Souvenir sheet, 4b imperf.

Imam, Flag and Arms. *June 28.* 1, 2, 4b; airmail, 6, 18, 24b (6v).

Mariner 4. *July 14.* Astronaut issue of 1964 overprinted "Mariner 4" in English and Arabic. (3v).

International Cooperation Year. *Sept. 15.* 2, 4b; airmail, 6b (3v). Souvenir sheet, 4b imperf.

Cats. *Oct. 1.* $1/8$, $1/4$, $1/2$, 1, 2, 4b (6v). Souvenir sheet, 4b imperf.

Gemini V. *Oct. 15.* ITU issue of 1965 overprinted "Gemini V/Gordon Cooper & Charles Conrad" in black, red or blue (3v and sheet).

Flowers. *Oct. 15.* $1/8$, $1/4$, $1/2$, 1, 2, 4b (6v). Souvenir sheet, 4b imperf.

New York World's Fair. *Oct. 4.* 2, 4, 6b (3v). Imperf. souvenir sheet.

Space Explorations. *Nov. 10.* $1/8$, $1/4$, $1/2$, 4b; airmail, 6b (5v). Souvenir sheet, 4b imperf.

Olympic Winners, 1964 Tokyo Games. *Nov. 20.* $1/8$, $1/4$, $1/2$, 2, 4b; airmail, 6b (6v). Souvenir sheet, 4b imperf.

1966

Builders of World Peace. *Feb. 1:* $1/8$, $1/4$, $1/2$, 1, 4b

(5v, se-tenant) (Nehru, Hammarskjold, Pope John 23, Churchill, J. F. Kennedy). Souvenir sheet, 4b imperf. *Apr. 16:* 1/8, 1/4, 1/2, 1, 4b (5v, se-tenant). (Lübke, de Gaulle, Pope Paul VI, L. B. Johnson, U Thant). Souvenir sheet, 4b imperf.

Surcharges on Kennedy issue of 1965. 4, 8, 10b; airmail lr (4v).

King Faisal. 1b.

19th Summer Olympics, Mexico. *May 14.* Airmail. Olympic issue of 1965 overprinted "Olympic Games Preparation / Mexico 1968" and surcharged 12, 28, 34b (3v). Souvenir sheet, 4b imperf.

Shaharah Fortress of Liberty. *May 26.* 1/2, 1, 1 1/2, 2, 4b; airmail, 6, 10b (7v). Souvenir sheet, 10b imperf.

1967

Pres. Kennedy, 3rd anniversary of death. *Jan. 1.* 12, 28, 34b (3v). Souvenir sheet, 24b imperf.

World Cup Soccer Championship Winner. *Jan 5.* Olympic Winners issue of 1965 overprinted "World Championship Cup England 1966 / England Winner" in English and Arabic. 1/8, 1/4, 1/2, 2, 4b; airmail, 6b (6v). Olympic issue of 1965 surcharged 4b x 6 (6v).

Civil War, 3rd anniversary. *Jan. 25.* 4b x 8 (8v). Souvenir sheet, 4b imperf.

Pres. Kennedy, 50th birthday. *May.* Kennedy death anniversary issue overprinted "50th Ann. / 29 / May" in English and Arabic (3v and sheet).

Rembrandt paintings. *May 15.* 2, 4, 6, 10, 12, 20b (6v). 8 souvenir sheets: 2 with gold frame; 6 with silver frame.

Paintings. *June 15.* Airmail 8, 10, 12, 14, 16, 20b (6v) (Hals, van Gogh, Rubens, Murillo, Raphael, Ucello).

Jordan Relief Fund. *Aug. 10.* Preceding issues (Flowers, cats, birds, ICY, Kennedy, Builders of World Peace) surcharged 50%.

Fish. *July:* 1/8, 1/4, 1/2, 1, 4, 6, 10b. *Oct:* Airmail, 12, 14, 16, 18, 24, 34b (13v). Souvenir sheet, 10b.

Asian paintings. *Aug. 25.* Airmail, 1/8, 1/4, 1/2, 3/4, 1, 1 1/2, 2, 3, 4, 6b (10v). Souvenir sheet, 6b imperf.

12th World Boy Scout Jamboree, Idaho. *Sept. 10.* 1/4, 1/2, 4, 6b; airmail, 1/8, 10, 20b (7v). Souvenir sheet, 20b imperf.

19th Summer Olympics, Mexico, 1968. *Oct. 8.* 1/8, 1/4, 1/2, 4, 8b; airmail, 12, 16, 20b (8v). Souvenir sheet, 16b imperf.

Moorish Art in Spain, *Dec.* 2, 4, 6, 10, 12b; airmail, 20, 22, 24b (8v). Souvenir sheet, 28b.

Queen of Sheba, Visit to King Solomon. *Dec.* 1/8, 1/4, 1/2, 4, 6, 10, 20, 24b (8v). Souvenir sheets, 28, 34b imperf.

Horses. *Dec.* 1/8, 1/4, 1/2, 4, 10b; postage due, 16b (6v).

1968

10th Winter Olympics, Grenoble. *Jan.* Fish issue of 1967 overprinted "Grenoble 1968" (13v and sheet).

Butterflies. *Feb.* Airmail, 16, 20, 40b; postage due, 4, 20b (5v).

10th Winter Olympics, Grenoble. *Feb.* 1, 2, 3, 4, 6, 10b; airmail, 12, 18, 24, 28b (10v). 2 souvenir sheets, 4, 24b imperf. Same, overprinted "Gold Medal Winner" and names of various winners (10v). 2 souvenir sheets, 4, 24b imperf.

UNESCO, 20th anniversary. *Mar.* 1/2, 1, 1 1/2, 2, 3, 4, 6, 10b (8v). Souvenir sheet, 12b imperf.

Mother's Day, paintings. *Mar. 21.* 2, 4, 6b; airmail, 24, 28, 34b (6v) (Gainsborough, Corot, Fragonard, Raphael, Titian, Bronzino). 7 souvenir sheets; 6 sheets of 1, 2, 4, 6, 24, 28, 34b; 1 sheet of 2 (24, 34b) imperf.

UNESCO Campaign to Save Venice. *Apr. 18.* 1/2, 1, 1 1/2, 24b; airmail, 28, 34b (6v) (paintings by de Pavia, Piazetta, Favretto, Tiepolo, Canaletto). Souvenir sheet, 34b imperf.

UNESCO Campaign to Save Florence. *May 3.* 2, 4, 6b; airmail, 10, 12, 18b (6v) (paintings by Raphael, Chardin, Rubens, Allori, Reni). 4 souvenir sheets, 4, 6, 19, 34b imperf.

19th Summer Olympics, Mexico. *May 15.* 1, 2, 3, 4, 6b; airmail, 10, 12, 18, 24, 28b (10v). 2 souvenir sheets, 4, 24b imperf.

Olympics, 1924–1968. *May 31.* Summer Games: 4b x 11, 12 souvenir sheets, each 4b imperf. Winter Games: 1, 2, 3, 4, 6b; airmail, 10, 12, 18, 24, 28b (21v). 12 souvenir sheets: 1, 2, 3, 4, 6, 10, 12, 18, 24b x 3, 28b imperf.

Paintings. *June 30.* 1, 2, 3, 4, 6, 10b; airmail, 12, 18, 24, 28b (10v) (Perry, Copley, Murillo, van Leyden, Chardin, Vermeer, Aylward, Sessions, Goya). 3 souvenir sheets: 2 sheets of 1, 4, 24b; 1 sheet of 2 (4, 24b) imperf.

Shah of Iran, Coronation. *July 15.* 1, 2, 3, 4b; airmail, 24, 28b (6v). 2 souvenir sheets, 24, 28b.

World Philately (Roosevelt, Ferrary, Prince Ismail, albums and catalogues). *Aug. 15.* 1, 2, 3, 4, 6b; airmail, 10, 12, 18, 24, 28b (10v). 4 souvenir sheets, each 4b imperf.

International Human Rights Year (Popes John XXIII and Paul VI, John F. Kennedy, Churchill, Martin Luther King). *Sept. 30.* 2b x 4, 4b x 4, 6b x 4 (12v). 2 souvenir sheets: 1 of 2 (4, 6b), 1 of 3 (6b x 3) imperf.

World Racial Peace (American Flag, Lincoln, Kennedy, King). *Sept. 30.* 4, 6, 18b; airmail, 10, 24b (5v). 3 souvenir sheets; 1 of 2 (10, 20b), 2 of 1, 10, 20b imperf.

Children's Day, paintings. *Oct. 1.* 1, 2, 3, 4b; airmail, 6, 10, 12, 18, 24, 28b (10v) (Renoir, Van Dyck, Velazquez, Perugino, Murillo, Lawrence). 2 souvenir sheets, 10, 18b imperf.

Gold Medal Winners, 1968 Mexico Olympics. *Oct.* Mexico Olympic issue of 1968 overprinted "Gold Medal Winner Mexico 1968" and names of winners (10v). 6 souvenir sheets, 4b x 3, 24b x 3 imperf. *Dec. 25.* 12, 18, 24, 28, 34b (5v). 2 souvenir sheets, 4, 24b imperf.

EFIMEX. *Dec. 25.* 12, 18, 24, 28, 34b (5v). 2 souvenir sheets, 4, 24b imperf.

1969

Racing Champions. *Jan. 15.* 1, 2, 3, 4, 6b; airmail, 10, 12, 18, 24, 28b (10v). 2 souvenir sheets, 4, 24b imperf.

Apollo 7 and 8. *Feb. 15.* 4b x 2, 6, 8, 10, 12, 18, 24, 28, 34b (10v). 4 souvenir sheets, 2b x 2, 28b x 2. Gold foil, 28b.

19th Summer Olympics, Mexico. Gold foil, 28b.

Imam's Mission to Pope Paul VI in Jerusalem, 5th anniversary. *May 25.* **a.** 1/8, 1/4 x 2, 1, 1 1/2, 2, 3, 4, 5, 6b (10v, se-tenant in sheets of 10). **b.** 1, 2, 3, 4, 5, 6, 7, 8, 9, 10b; airmail, 11, 12, 13, 14, 15b (15v, se-tenant in sheets of 15). **c.** 16, 17, 18, 19, 20, 21, 22, 23, 24, 25, 26, 27, 28, 29, 30b (15v, se-tenant in sheets of 15) (40v). Airmail, Gold foil, 24, 28b.

Rembrandt paintings. *June 15.* 1, 2, 4b; airmail, 6, 12b, lr (6v). Souvenir sheet, 24b imperf. Gold foil, 20b.

Paintings, *June.* 1/2, 1 1/2, 3, 5b; airmail, 10, 18, 28, 34b (9v) (Raphael, Greuze, Henner, Le Nain, Rubens, Rotari, Watteau, Murillo). Souvenir sheet, 4b imperf.

Mission to the Moon. *June 17.* 1, 2, 3, 4, 5b; airmail, 6, 7, 8, 9, 10, 11, 12, 13, 14, 15b (15v, in sheets of 15).

Apollo 10. *June 17.* 2, 4, 6, 8, 10b (5v). Souvenir sheet, 24b, perf., imperf.

Pre-Olympics, 1972, Munich. *July 28.* 1, 2, 4, 5, 6b; airmail, 10, 12, 18, 24, 34b (10v). Souvenir sheet, 4b perf., imperf.

International Animal Protection Year. *Sept. 25.* **Animals:** 1/2, 1, 2, 4b; airmail, 8, 10, 18b (8v). Souvenir sheet, 24b. **Birds:** 1/2, 1, 2, 4, 6b; airmail, 8, 10, 18b (8v). Souvenir sheet, 24b.

Apollo 11. *Oct. 1.* Airmail, 24b. Gold foil, circular embossed, 24b. Gold and silver foil (1 each) 28b. 6 souvenir sheets, 24b, 34b x 2, perf., imperf; 24b with gold foil circular embossed center, 28b x 2, 1 gold, 1 silver foil.

Save the Holy Places (Palestine). *Oct. 28.* 4b x 6, 6b x 10; airmail, 12b x 8 (24v).

Famous Men. *Nov. 10.* 4b x 4, 6b x 10; airmail, 12b x 2 (16v).

History of Outer Space Exploration. *Nov. 25.* Airmail, 6b x 32 (32v). 3 souvenir sheets, 24, 28, 34b imperf. Gold foil airmail, 24, 34b.

Olympic Sports. *Dec. 1.* 1, 2, 4, 5, 6b; airmail, 10, 12, 18, 24, 34b (10v se-tenant in sheets of 10).

World Cup Soccer Championship. *Dec. 1.* Airmail, 12b x 8 (8v).

Restoration of Al Aqsa Mosque, Jerusalem. *Dec. 21.* Semipostal, 4b+2b, 6b+3b; airmail semipostal, 10b+5b (3v).

Christmas. Gold foil airmail, 34b and imperf. souvenir sheet.

In April, 1970, an agreement between the Yemen Arab Republic and Saudi Arabia introduced Royalists into the Y. A. R. government, ending the existence of the kingdom.

YEMEN ARAB REPUBLIC

Most sets exist perf., imperf.

1962

United Nations Day. Nos. 103–109 overprinted "1945–1962" in English and Arabic (7v).

1962–63

"Y.A.R. 27.9.1962" overprinted in red or green in English and Arabic on Nos. 47–49, 111–120, 125–136, C20–C21.

1963

Yemen Arab Republic, founding. 1, 2b, 4b x 2, 6b x 2, 8, 10, 16b, 1 li (10v). 4 postage 2b to 10b (4v). 4, 6b; airmail, 8, 16b (4v). Nos. 25–29 overprinted "Airmail/Y.A.R."

Freedom From Hunger. *Mar. 21.* 4, 6b (2v). Souvenir sheet of 2 (4, 6b) imperf.

Revolution, 1st anniversary. *Sept. 26.* 2, 4, 6b (3v). Souvenir sheet of 3 (2, 4, 6b) imperf.

Red Cross centenary. *Oct.* $^1/_4$, $^1/_3$, $^1/_2$, 4, 8, 20b (6v). Souvenir sheet of 2 (4, 8b) imperf.

Astronauts, *Dec. 5.* Airmail, $^1/_4$, $^1/_3$, $^1/_2$, 4, 20b (5v). Souvenir sheet, 20b imperf.

Declaration of Human Rights, 15th anniversary. *Dec. 20.* 4, 6b (2v). Souvenir sheet of 2 (4, 6b) imperf.

1964

Olympic Sports. *Mar. 30.* $^1/_4$, $^1/_3$, $^1/_2$, 1, 1$^1/_2$b; airmail, 4, 20b, 1r (8v). Souvenir sheet, 4b imperf.

Bagel Textile Factory inauguration. *Apr. 10.* 2, 4, 6b; airmail, 16b (4v). Souvenir sheet, 16b imperf.

Hodeida Airport inauguration. *Apr. 30.* 4, 6, 10b (3v). Souvenir sheet 10b imperf.

John F. Kennedy Memorial. *May 5.* Astronaut issue of 1963 overprinted in black or red brown "John F. Kennedy / 1917 / 1963" in English and Arabic. (5v).

New York World's Fair. *May 10.* $^1/_4$, $^1/_3$, $^1/_2$, 1, 4b; airmail, 16, 20b (7v). Souvenir sheet, 20b imperf.

18th Summer Olympics, Tokyo. *June 1.* $^1/_4$, $^1/_3$, $^1/_2$, 1, 1$^1/_2$b; airmail, 4, 6, 12, 20b (9v). Souvenir sheet, 20b imperf.

Boy Scouts. *June 20.* $^1/_4$, $^1/_3$, $^1/_2$, 1, 1$^1/_2$b; airmail, 4, 6, 16, 20b (9v). 2 souvenir sheets: 16b, perf., 20b, imperf.

San'a International Airport inauguration. *June 20.* 1, 2, 4, 8b; airmail, 6b (5v). Souvenir sheet of 2 (4, 6b) imperf.

Animals. *Aug. 15.* $^1/_4$, $^1/_3$, $^1/_2$, 1, 1$^1/_2$b; airmail, 4, 12, 20b; postage due, 4, 12, 20b (11v).

Flowers. *Sept. 1.* $^1/_4$, $^1/_3$, $^1/_2$, 1, 1$^1/_2$b; airmail, 4, 12, 20b (8v).

Arab Postal Union, 10th anniversary. *Oct. 15.* 4b; airmail, 6b (2v). Souvenir sheet, 6b imperf.

Second Arab Summit Meeting. *Nov. 30.* 4, 6b (2v). Souvenir sheet of 2 (4, 6b) imperf.

Revolution, 2nd anniversary. *Dec. 30.* 2, 4, 6b (3v). Souvenir sheet, 6b, imperf.

1965

Birds. *Jan. 30.* $^1/_4$, $^1/_2$, $^3/_4$, 1, 1$^1/_2$, 4b; airmail, 6, 8, 12, 20b, 1r (11v). Souvenir sheet, 20b imperf.

Deir Yassin Massacre. *Apr. 30.* 4b; airmail, 6b (2v).

International Telecommunication Union centenary. *May 17.* 4, 6b (2v). Souvenir sheet, 6b.

Algiers Library burning. *Sept. 26.* 4b; airmail, 6b (2v). Souvenir sheet, 6b imperf.

Revolution, 3rd anniversary. *Sept. 26.* 4, 6b (2v). Souvenir sheet, 6b imperf.

International Cooperation Year. *Oct. 15.* 4, 6b (2v). Souvenir sheet, 6b, imperf.

John F. Kennedy Memorial. *Nov. 29.* $^1/_4$b x 3, $^1/_3$, $^1/_2$, 4b; airmail, 8, 12b (8v). 2 souvenir sheets, 4, 8b imperf.

Space Exploration. *Dec. 29.* $^1/_4$b x 3, $^1/_3$, $^1/_2$b; airmail, 4, 8, 16b (8v). Souvenir sheet, 16b imperf.

1966

Anti-Tuberculosis campaign. *Jan. 15.* Freedom from Hunger issue of 1963 overprinted "Tuberculous Campaign/1965" in English and Arabic (2v and sheet).

Communications. *Jan. 29.* $^1/_4$b x 3, $^1/_3$, $^1/_2$b; airmail, 4, 6, 20b (8v). Airmail souvenir sheet, 20b imperf.

Prevention of Cruelty to Animals. *Mar. 5.* Animals issue of 1965 overprinted in black or red "Prevention of Cruelty to Animals" in English and Arabic (11v). Souvenir sheet, 20b.

Third Arab Summit Meeting. *Mar. 20.* Second Meeting issue of 1965 overprinted in black or red "3rd Arab/Summit Conference/1965" in English and Arabic (2v). 2 souvenir sheets, 4, 6b imperf.

Builders of World Peace. *Mar. 25.* 1$^1/_4$b x 3, $^1/_2$, 4b; airmail, 6, 10, 12b (9v). 2 souvenir sheets, 4, 8b, imperf.

Domestic Animals. *May 5.* $^1/_4$b x 3, $^1/_3$, $^1/_2$, 4b (6v). Souvenir sheet, 22b imperf.

Butterflies. *May 5.* Airmail, 6, 8, 10, 16b (4v).

Luna 9 Moon Landing. *May 20.* Space Exploration issue of 1965 overprinted "Luna IX/3 February 1966" in English and Arabic (8v and sheet).

World Cup Soccer Championship, London. *May 29.* $^1/_4$b x 3, $^1/_3$, $^1/_2$b; airmail, 4, 5, 20b (8v). Souvenir sheet, 20b imperf.

Traffic Day. *June 30.* 4, 6b (2v). Souvenir sheet, 6b imperf.

Surveyor 1 Moon Landing. *Aug. 15.* Space Exploration issue of 1965 overprinted "Surveyor I/2 June 1966" in English and Arabic (8v and sheet).

Revolution, 4th anniversary. *Sept. 2,* 4, 6b (3v). Souvenir sheet of 2 (4, 6b) imperf.

"1965 Sana'a" overprinted in English and Arabic on World's Fair issue of 1964 (7v and sheet).

WHO Headquarters inauguration, Geneva. *Nov. 1.* $^1/_4$b x 3; airmail, 4, 8, 16b (6v). Souvenir sheet, 16b imperf.

Gemini 6–7. *Dec. 1.* $^1/_4$b x 3, $^1/_3$, $^1/_2$, 2b; airmail, 8, 12b (8v). Souvenir sheet, 12b imperf.

Gemini 9. *Dec. 25.* Gemini 6-7 issue overprinted in red "Gemini IX / Cernan-Stafford / June 1966" in English and Arabic (8v and sheet).

1967

Fruit. *Feb. 10.* $^1/_4$b x 3, $^1/_3$, $^1/_2$, 2, 4b; airmail, 6, 8, 10b; postage due, 6, 8, 10b (13v).

Further issues exist for 1967–1978

PARAGUAY

1979

International Year of the Child, Dürer's paintings. *Apr. 28.* 3, 4, 5, 6, 7, 8, 20g (se-tenant strip of 7), airmail, 10, 25g (9v). 2 airmail souvenir sheets, 25g (Christ's burial, space stations).

Winter Olympic Games, Lake Placid. *June 11.* Airmail souvenir sheet, 25g (Dorothy Hamill). *Aug. 22.* 3, 4, 5, 6, 7, 8, 20g (se-tenant strip of 7), airmail, 10, 25g (9v). Airmail souvenir sheet, 25g (Kulakova, cross-country skiing). Second issue: 3, 4, 5, 6, 7, 8, 20g (se-tenant strip of 7).

Summer Olympic Games, Moscow 1980. *Dec. 20.* Airmail souvenir sheet, 25g (Canoe race).

Electric trains. *Dec. 24.* 3, 4, 7, 8, 20g (se-tenant strip), airmail 10, 25g (9v).

Argentina '78. *Dec. 24.* Airmail souvenir sheet, 25g plus label.

1980

Composers and Paintings of young ballet dancers. 3, 4, 5, 6, 7, 8, 20g (7v). Paintings by Cydney and Degas. Composers: Rossini, Johann Strauss, Debussy, Beethoven, Chopin, Wagner, Bach.

Christmas, International Year of the Child, 3, 4, 5, 6, 7, 8, 20g (7v).

Rowland Hill, aircraft. *Apr. 8.* 3, 4, 5, 6, 7, 8, 20g (se-tenant strip), airmail 10, 25g (9v). Airmail souvenir sheet, 25g.

Maybach Automobile, DS-8 Zeppelin. *Apr. 8.* Airmail souvenir sheet 25g.

Rowland Hill. *Apr. 14.* 3, 4, 5, 6, 7, 8, 20g; airmail, 10, 25g (9v). Airmail souvenir sheets (2) 25g.

Olympic winners, Lake Placid. *June 4.* 3, 4, 5, 6, 7, 8, 20g (se-tenant strip), airmail 10, 25g (9v). Airmail souvenir sheet 25g.

Rotary Club. *July 1.* Airmail souvenir sheet, 25g.

Apollo 11, 10th anniv. *July 30.* Airmail souvenir sheet, 25g.

Christmas, Intl. Year of the Child. *Aug. 4.* 3, 4, 5, 6, 7, 8, 20g; airmail, 10, 25g (9v). Airmail souvenir sheet, 25g.

Ships, Philatelic Exhibitions '80. *Sept. 15.* 3, 4, 5, 6, 7, 8, 20g (se-tenant strip), airmail 10, 25g (9v).

Boeing 707. *Sept. 17.* 20g; airmail 100g.

Juan Carlos, ESPAMER '80. *Sept. 19.* Souvenir sheet, 25g.

Albrecht Durer. *Sept. 24.* Airmail souvenir sheet, 25g.

Espana '82 World cup soccer. *Dec. 10.* 3, 4, 5, 6, 7, 8, 20g (se-tenant), airmail 10, 25g (9v). Airmail souvenir sheet, 25g.

Chess Tournament, Mexico. *Dec. 15.* 3, 4, 5, 6, 7, 8, 20g (se-tenant), airmail souvenir sheet, 25g.

Olympics 1980. *Dec. 15.* Airmail souvenir sheet, 25g.

1981

Olympic winners. *Feb. 4.* 25, 50c, 1, 2, 3, 4, 5g (se-tenant strip), airmail 5, 10, 30g (10v). Airmail souvenir sheet, 25g.

Electric trains. *Feb. 9.* 25c, 50c, 1, 2, 3, 4, 5g (se-tenant strip), airmail 1, 5, 10, 30g (10v). Airmail souvenir sheet, 25g.

Archbishops seminar. *Mar. 26.* Airmail, 5, 10, 25, 50g (4v).

Intl. Year of the Child. *Apr. 13.* 10, 25, 50, 100, 200, 300, 400g (se-tenant strip), airmail, 75, 500, 1000g (10v). Sheet of 10, 10g, plus 2 labels.

WIPA '81. *May 22.* 4g; airmail 10g 2v).

Royal Wedding, Prince Charles and Lady Diana. *June 27.* 25, 50c, 1, 2, 3, 4, 5g (se-tenant strip of 7). Souvenir Sheet of 8, 5g, plus label.

Royal Wedding. *June 29.* Airmail, 5, 10, 30g (3v). Airmail souvenir sheet, 25g.

Traditional women's costumes, Itaipu Dam. *June 30.* 10, 25, 50, 100, 200, 300, 400g, se-tenant strip of 7.

Space travel. *Oct. 9.* Airmail, 5, 10, 30g (3v). Airmail souvenir sheets (2), 25g.

Paintings, Dominique Ingres. *Oct. 13.* 25, 50c, 1, 2, 3 (se-tenant strip), 4, 5g (7v). Souvenir sheet of 8 (4, 5g), plus label.

Espana '82, World Cup Soccer. *Oct. 15.* Airmail, 5, 10, 30g (3v). Airmail sheet of 5, 10g, plus four labels; souvenir sheet; 25g.

Paintings, Peter Paul Rubens. *July 9.* 25, 50c, 1, 2, 3, 4g (se-tenant strip), 5g (7v). Souvenir sheet of 8, 5g, plus label.

George Washington. *July 10.* Airmail, 5g. Airmail souvenir sheet, 25g.

Queen Elizabeth, 80th birthday. *July 10.* Airmail souvenir sheet of 8, 10g, plus label.

Philatokyo. *July 10.* 25g (1v). Airmail souvenir sheet, 30g.

Paintings, Pablo Picasso. *Oct. 19.* 25, 50c, 1, 2, 3, 4g (se-tenant strip), 5g (7v). Souvenir sheet of 6, 5g, plus 3 labels.

PHILATELIA '81. *Oct. 22.* 25, 50c, 1, 2, 3, 4g (se-tenant strip of 6).

ESPAMER '81, Philatelic Exhibition. *Oct. 25.* 25, 50c, 1, 2, 3, 4g (se-tenant strip of 6).

Royal Wedding. *Dec. 4.* 25, 50c, 1, 2, 3, 4g (se-tenant strip), 4g; airmail 5, 10, 30g (10v). Souvenir sheet of 8, 5g, plus label. Airmail souvenir sheets (2), 25g.

Intl. Yr of the Child. *Dec. 17.* 25, 50c, 1, 2, 3, 4g (se-tenant strip), 5g (7v). Souvenir sheet of 6, 5g, plus 3 labels.

Madonna with Child paintings. *Dec. 21.* Airmail 5, 10, 30g (3v). Airmail souvenir sheet, 25g.

Graf Zeppelin. *Dec. 21.* Airmail souvenir sheet, 25g.

1982

Intl. Yr. of the Child. *Apr. 16.* 25, 50c, 1, 2, 3, 4, 5g (se-tenant strip of 2 and 5 plus label). Souvenir sheet of 6, 5g, plus 3 labels.

Espana '82, soccer. *Apr. 19.* Airmail 5, 10, 30g (3v). Airmail sheet of 7, 10g, plus 2 labels; souvenir sheet 25g.

Scouting. *Apr. 21.* 25, 50c, 1, 2, 3, 4, 5g; Airmail 5, 10, 30g (10v). Souvenir sheet of 8, 5g, plus label. Airmail souvenir sheet, 25g.

Johann Wolfgang Van Goethe, Rembrandt painting. *Apr. 23.* Airmail souvenir sheet, 25g.

King Alfonso X, chess. *Apr. 23.* Airmail souvenir sheets (2), 25g.

PHILEXFRANCE '82. *June 11.* 25, 50c, 1, 2, 3g (5v).

Espana '82, soccer. *June 13.* 25, 50c, 1, 2, 3, 4g (se-tenant strip), 5g; airmail 5, 10, 30g (10v). Souvenir sheet of 8, 5g, plus label; sheet of 5, 10g, plus 4 labels. Airmail souvenir sheet, 25g.

PHILATELIA '82, Intl Yr. of the Child. *Sept. 12.* 25, 50c, 1, 2, 3, 4, 5g (se-tenant strips of 6 and 8, 5g, plus label).

Paintings, Raphael. *Sept. 27.* 25, 50c, 1, 2, 3, 4g (se-tenant strip), 5g (7v). Souvenir sheet of 5 plus 4 labels.

Paintings, Raphael. *Sept. 30.* 25, 50c, 1, 2, 3, 4g (se-tenant strip), 5g (7v). Souvenir sheet of 5 plus 4 labels.

Espana '82, winners world cup soccer. *Oct. 20.* Airmail, 5, 10, 30g (3v). Airmail sheet of 5, 10g, plus 4 labels; Souvenir sheet, 25g.

Paintings, Peter Paul Reubens. *Oct. 23.* Airmail, 5, 10, 30g (3v). Airmail sheet of 5, 10g, plus 4 labels; souvenir sheet, 25g.

Paintings, Albrecht Durer. *Dec. 14.* 25, 50c, 1, 2, 3, 4g (se-tenant strip), 5g (7v). Souvenir sheet of 7, 5g, plus 2 labels.

Paintings, Raphael. *Dec. 17.* Airmail, 5, 10, 30g (3v). Airmail sheet of 5, 10g, plus 4 labels; souvenir sheet, 25g.

1983

South American Trains. *Jan. 20.* 25c, 50c, 1, 2, 3, 4g (se-tenant strip), 5g (7v). Souvenir sheet of 5, 5g, plus 4 labels.

Paintings, Rembrandt. *Jan. 21.* Airmail, 5, 10, 30g (3v). Airmail sheet of 5, 10g, plus 4 labels; souvenir sheet, 25g.

Espana '82, Zeppelin. *Jan. 21.* Airmail souvenir sheet, 25g.

Racing Cars. *Jan. 23.* 25, 50c, 1, 2, 3, 4g (se-tenant strip), 5g (7v). Souvenir sheet of 5, 5g plus 4 labels.

ESPANA '82 *Zeppelin. Jan. 24.* Airmail souvenir sheet of 5, 5g plus 4 labels.

German Space Technology. *Jan. 24.* Airmail, 5, 10, 30g (3v). Airmail sheet of 5, 10g, plus 4 labels; souvenir sheets (2), 25g.

Winter Olympics. *Feb. 23.* 25, 50c, 1, 2, 3, 4g (se-tenant strip), 5g (7v). Souvenir sheet of 5, 5g, plus 4 labels.

Classic Automobiles. *July 18* 25, 50c, 1, 2, 3, 4g (se-tenant strip), airmails: 5, 10, 30g (9v). Souvenir sheet of 5, 5g, plus 4 labels. Airmail souvenir sheet, 25g, plus label.

BRASILIANA '83, FIP Congress. *July 28.* World Cup Soccer overprinted. 25, 50c, 1, 2, 3, 4g se-tenant strip of 6.

BRASILIANA '83, FIP Congress. *July 28.* Ruebens Madonnas overprinted. 25, 50c, 1, 2, 3, 4g se-tenant strip of 6.

Aircraft Carriers. 25, 50c, 1, 2, 3, 4g (se-tenant strip), 5g (7v). Souvenir sheet of 5, 5g plus 4 labels.

Flowers. Airmail. Airmail: 5, 10, 30g (3v). Souvenir sheet of 5, 10g, plus 4 labels.

Birds. *Oct. 22.* 25, 50c, 1, 2, 3, 4g (se-tenant strip), 5g (7v). Souvenir sheet of 5, 5g plus 4 labels.

PHILATELIA '83, Dusseldorf. *Oct. 28.* Trains overprinted. 25, 50c, 1, 2, 3, 4g se-tenant strip of 6.

EXFIVIA '83, Bolivia. *Nov. 5.* Durer paintings overprinted. 25, 50c, 1, 2, 3, 4g se-tenant strip of 6.

ADDENDA

ST. THOMAS and PRINCE ISLANDS

1979

World Cup Soccer Winners. *June 1.* Soccer set of 1978 overprinted with name of winning country. 7v perf. and imperf.

Flowers. *June 8.* 8d×4 (se-tenant block of 4), 1 and 25d (6v). Imperf. souvenir sheet, 50d.

Butterflies. *June 8.* 11d×4 (se-tenant block of 4), 50c and 10d (6v). Souvenir sheet, 50d.

Sir Rowland Hill, centenary of death, UPU Congress, etc. *Sept. 15.* Two souvenir sheets, 25d (Graf Zeppelin, DC3), perf., imperf.

International Year of the Child. *Oct. 4.* 1, 7, 14, 17d (4v). Souvenir sheet, 50d (One world symbol).

International Communications Day. *Oct. 4.* 1 and 11d, 14 and 17d, in strips of 2 plus label (4v).

Albrecht Dürer, 450th death anniversary. *Nov. 29.* 50c×2, 1, 7, 8, 25d (6v). Souvenir sheet, 25d (Self-portrait, father, mother).

History of Aviation, powered flight, ICAO 35th anniversary. *Dec. 21.* 50c, 1, 5, 7, 8, 17d (6v).

Nature Preservation, local birds. *Dec. 21.* 50c×2, 1, 7, 8d, airmail, 100d (6v). Souvenir sheet, 25d.

Albrecht Dürer, 450th death anniversary, International Year of the Child, Feast of the Family, Christmas 1979. *Dec. 25.* Souvenir sheet, 25d.

History of Navigation, early sailing ships. *Dec. 21.* 50c, 1, 3, 7, 8, 17d (6v). Souvenir sheet, 25d (Map).

History of Aviation, dirigibles, 1872-1910. *Dec. 28.* 50c, 1, 3, 7, 8, 17d (6v).

Nature Preservation, local fish. *Dec. 28.* 50c, 1, 3, 5, 8d, airmail, 50d (6v). Souvenir sheet, 25d.

History of Aviation, hot-air balloons, 1784-1931. *Dec. 28.* 50c, 1, 3, 7, 8, 25d (6v). Souvenir sheet, 25d.

1980

Pre-Olympic Games, 1980, Olympic stadiums. *June 13.* 50c, 11d×4 (5v), perf. and imperf. Souvenir sheet, 7d×4, perf. and imperf.

Sir Rowland Hill, death centenary. *June 13.* 50c, 1, 8, 20d (4v). Souvenir sheet, 20d.

Moon landing, 10th anniversary. *June 13.* 50c, 1, 14, 17d (4v). Souvenir sheet, 25d (three astronauts).

Independence anniversaries. *July 5.* 5d, Venezuela, Russia, India, Ghana, Russia, Algeria, Cuba, Cape Verde, Mozambique, Angola (se-tenant strip of 12 plus label). Souvenir sheet, 25d.

Intl. Yr. of the Child. *Dec. 25.* Souvenir sheet, 25d.

1981

Summer Olympics, Moscow '80. *Feb. 2.* 15, 30, 40, 50d. Souvenir sheets, 15, 40d.

United Nations, 35th Anniv. *Feb. 2.* Souvenir sheet, 25d.

Summer Olympic winners. *May 15.* 50d (1v).

Flowers. *May 22.* 50c (2), 1, 7, 8, 14d (6v). Souvenir sheet, 25d.

Shells. *May 22.* 50c (2), 1, 1.50, 11, 17d (6v). Souvenir sheet, 25d.

1981

Espana '82, World Cup Soccer. *Sept. 3.* 3d x 4, 25d x 3, Uruguay, Italy, Brazil, Germany, England, Argentina, Argentina (7v).

PHILATELIA '81. *Nov. 14.* 25d (1v). Souvenir sheet, 75d.

Tito. *Nov. 1.* 17d x 2. Souvenir sheet, 75d.

Royal Wedding, Prince Charles and Lady Diana. *Nov. 28.* 20, 30, 50d (se-tenant strip of 3).

World Chess Champion. *Dec. 10.* 30d x 2 (se-tenant). Souvenir sheet, 75d.

Pablo Picasso, I.Y.C. *Dec. 10.* 14d, 17d x 4, 20d x 2 (7v). Souvenir sheet, 75d.

TOGO

1979

People's Republic, 10th anniversary. *Dec.* Gold-foil embossed portrait of President, 1000fr. perf. (in uniform), imperf. (in civilian clothes) (2v).

1980

London, 1980, International Stamp Exhibition. *May 6.* Gold-foil embossed 1000fr single stamp and souvenir sheet of 1978 Queen Elizabeth II Coronation ovptd., "Londres, 1980," etc.

URUGUAY

1979

Various Events: International Year of the Child and Albrecht Dürer, 450th death anniversary, 70c. Powered Flight, 75th anniversary and ICAO, 1.80p. World Cup Soccer and AUF emblems ovptd. "Monumento Mondial de Futbol, Montevideo," 80c. Rowland Hill, 1980 Olympics, Lake Placid and Moscow, 1896 Greek Olympic issue, 11 stamp, 1.30p.

Albrecht Dürer, 450th death anniversary. 25c (self-portrait), airmail, 1p (horseman) (2v).

1981

Espana '82, pre-soccer championship. *Aug. 17.* Gold-foil embossed, 100fr (5), Germany, Great Britain, Brazil, Argentina, Spain. Souvenir sheets, 100fr (5), stadiums.

World Cup Soccer '78 overprinted in gold for Espana '82. 100fr single stamp and souvenir sheet.

INDEX and IDENTIFIER

See also Addenda

Entry	Page
A Certo optd. on stamps of Peru	67
Africa Occidental Espanola	611
Africa, Portuguese	181
Afrique Equatoriale Francaise	842
"Alerta" ovptd. on stamps of Peru	67
Allied Military Government, Trieste	770
Allied Occupation of Thrace	744
A.M.G./F.T.T.	770
Anatolia	840
Ancachs	66
Andalusia	550
Apurimac	67
Arabie Saoudite	496
A receber (See Portugal or Portuguese Colonies)	
Arequipa	67
Arica	44, 65
Armenia	770
Armenian stamps ovptd.	770
Army of the North	397
Army of the Northwest	397
A.R. optd. on stamps of Colombia	20
Arwad	271
Assistencia Nacionalaos Tuberculosos	181
Asturias	550
Aunus, ovptd. on Finland	397
Austrian Occupation of Romania	269
Austrian Occupation of Serbia	526
Austrian stamps surcharged (See Western Ukraine)	959
Ayacucho	67
Azerbaijan	770
Azores	175
Barcelona	552, 554
Basel	652
Béhié	798
Belgian East Africa	271
Benadir	530
Beyrouth, Russian Offices	399
Bocas del Toro	2
Bollo Postale	472
Bulgarian Occupation of Romania	270
Bureau International	682-683
Burgos	592
Buu-Chinh	940
Cadiz	593
Callao	41, 67
Canary Islands	593
Carlist	592
Carupano	940
Cataluna	592
CCCP	277
Centimos (no country name)	551
Cervantes	591
CFA ovptd. On France	196
C.G.H.S.	845
Chachapoyas	67
Chala	67
Chiclayo	67
Chilean Occupation of Peru	67
China, Russian Offices	397
C.I.H.S.	844
C.M.T.	966
Coamo	193
Colombian Dominion of Panama	1
Colon	2
Communicaciones	551
Congo, Portuguese	181
Constantinople, Romanian Offices	265
Constantinople, Russian Offices	399
Constantinople, Turkey	843
Correio	155
Correos (no country name)	69, 549, 911
Correo Submarino	556
Cote des Somalis	543
Cracow	102
Crimea	549
Cuzco	68
Danzig, Polish Offices	153
Dardanelles	399
Deficit	64
Denikin	401, 549
Diligencia	865
Distrito ovptd. on stamps of Arequipa	68
DJ optd. on Obock	543
Djibouti (Somali Coast)	543
Don Government	548
Dutch Guiana (Surinam)	611
Ekaterinodar	549
El Salvador	444
Escuelas	911
Espana, Espanola	549
Estado da India	190
Far Eastern Republic surcharged or ovptd.	530
FCFA ovptd. on France	198
Filipinas	69
Finnish Occupation of Russia	397
Franca ovptd. on stamps of Peru	67
French Colonies surcharged	508, 717
French Levant	712
French Occupation of Syria	686
French Occupation of Togo	744
French Saar	424
Frimarke (no country name)	Vol. III, 652
General Gouvernement (Poland)	152
Geneva	652
Georgia	770
German Administration of Saar	426
German Dominion of Samoa	471
German Dominion of Togo	744
German Occupation of Poland	151
German Occupation of Romania	270
German Occupation of Russia	397
German Occupation of Serbia	526
German Occupation of Ukraine	397
German Stamps Surcharged	102
Giumulzina District	738
Golfo del Guinea	595
Gorny Slask	844
Greek Occupation of Thrace	739
Greek Occ. of Turkey in Asia	842
Greek stamps overprinted	739
Groszy	108
Guayana	940
Guiana, Dutch	611
Guinea, Spanish	595
Guinea or Guiné	182, 595
Guipuzcoa	594
Gultig 9, Armee	270
Habilitado on Telegrafos	69
Hang-Khong	949
Haut Sénégal-Niger	844
Haute Silesie	844
Haute Volta	835
H B A ovptd. on Russia	530
Hejaz	492
Hejaz and Nejd	495
Helvetia (Switzerland)	648
Huacho	68
I.B. (West Irian)	960
Ierusalem	370
Ile Rouad	271
Imperio Colonial Portugues	181
Impuesto de Guerra	590
India, Portuguese	186
Industrielle Kriegswirtschaft	681
Instruccion	862
International Bureau of Education	682
International Labor Bureau	681
International Refugee Organization	683
International Telecommunication Union	684
I.O.V.R.	269
Irian Barat	960
Italian Somaliland	530
J. optd. on stamps of Peru	69
Jaffa	399
Japan (Occupation of Philippines)	100
Jedda	493
Jerusalem, Russian Offices	399
Jugoslavia (Trieste)	773
Kerassunde	399
Kilis	686
Kolomyya	957
K.S.A.	501
Kuban Government	549
K.U.K.	270
League of Nations	681
Levant, French	711
Levant, Polish	154
Levant, Romanian	270
Levant, Russian	398
Levant, Syrian (on Stamps of Lebanon)	711
Lima	41, 67
Lisboa	181
Livonia	397
Losen	652
Lublin	102
Madeira	175
Madrid	554
Malaga	594
Maluka Selatan (So. Moluccas)	548
Marruecos	Vol. III, 599
Medina	495
Metelin	400
Miller, Gen.	397
Moldavia	202
Monastir	798
Mont Athos	399, 833
Montevideo	865
Moquea, Moquegua	68
Morocco, Spanish	599
Mount Athos, Russian Offices	399
Mount Athos (Turkey)	833
M.V.iR	270
Nations Unies	683
Nejd	494
Njikolaevsk	530
Northern Poland	102
North Viet Nam	949
Novocherkasssk	548
Nowa Bb ovptd. on Bulgaria	270
O K C A (Russia)	397
Orense	594
Organisation Mondiale	683
Oriental	865
Orts-Post	652
Ostland	397
Osten	152
Ottoman	797
Oubangi Chari	842
Pacchi Postali	492, 543
Pacific Steam Navigation Co.	41
Paita	62
Panama	1
Panama (Colombian Dominion)	1
Paraguay	23
Parma	Vol. III
Pasco	68
Patzcuaro	Vol. III
PD	450
Persia	Vol. III
Peru	41
Philippines	69
Japanese Occupation	100
Philipinas	78
Pisco	68
Piura	68
Poczta Polska	101
Pohjois Inkeri	Vol. III
Pokutia	960
Poland	101
Poland, exile government in Great Britain	154
Polish Offices in Danzig	153
Polish Offices in Turkish Empire	154
Polska	101
Ponce	193
Ponta Delgada	155
Porte de Conduccion	65
Porte de Mar	Vol. III
Porte Franco	41, 180
Port Gdansk	153
Porto Rico	192
Portugal	155
Portuguese Africa	181
Portuguese Congo	181
Portuguese East Africa	Vol. III
Portuguese Guinea	182
Portuguese India	186
Posen	102
Posta	718
Poste Locale	652
Postes Serbes ovptd. on France	525
P.P.C. ovptd. on Poland	154
Priamur	530
Pristina	798
Prussia	Vol. III
P.S.N.C. (Peru)	41
Puerto Rico	192
Puno	68
Quan-Buu	949
Quelimane	194
R ovptd. on French Colonies	194
Rappan	653
Rayon	653
Reis (Portugal)	155
Réunion	194
Rio de Oro	200
Rio Muni	201
Rizeh	400
Romagna	Vol. III
Romana	203
Romania	202
Romania, Occupation, Offices	270
Romanian Occupation of Western Ukraine	960
Roman States	Vol. III
Romina	217
Rostov	548
Rouad	271
R S M (San Marino)	
Ruanda-Urundi	271
Rumania	202
Rumanien on Germany	270
Russia	273
Russia (Finnish Occupation)	397
Russia (German Occupation)	386
Russian Dominion of Poland	101
Russian Occupation of Latvia	Vol. III
Russian Occupation of Lithuania	Vol. III
Russian Offices	397
Russian stamps surcharged or ovptd.	530, 548, 770, 843
Russian Turkestan	401
Russisch-Polen ovptd. on Germany	152
Rwanda, Rwandaise	401
Ryukyu Islands	416
S A, S.A.K. (Saudi Arabia)	496
Saar, Saargebiet	422
Sahara Occidental (Espanol)	606
Ste-Marie de Madagascar	430
St. Pierre and Miquelon	430
St. Thomas and Prince Islands	438
Salamanca	551
Salonika (Turkish)	798
Salonique	399
Salvador, El	444
Samoa	471, Vol. I
San Marino	472
San Sebastian	596
Santa Cruz de Tenerife	596
Sao Tome and Principe	438
SAR	680
Sardinia	Vol. III
Sarre ovptd. on Germany and Bavaria	422
Saseno	492
Saudi Arabia	492
Saxony	Vol. III
Schleswig	508
Schleswig-Holstein	Vol. III
Senegal	502, 844
Senegambia and Niger	524
Serbia, Serbien	524, Vol. III
Seville	594
Shanghai	528

Index 4–2

S.H.S. on Bosnia and Herzegovina	Vol. III
S.H.S. on Hungary	Vol. III
Siam (Thailand)	718
Siberia	530
Silesia, Upper	844
Sinai	800
Slesvig	508
Slovenia	Vol. III
Smyrne	399
Société des Nations	681
Sociedade de Geographia de Lisboa	181
Somali, Somalia	530
Somali Coast (Djibouti)	543
Sonora	Vol. III
Soomaaliya	536
South Kasai	548
South Korea	Vol. III
South Lithuania	Vol. III
South Moluccas	548
South Russia	548
Southern Cameroons	Vol. I
Southern Poland	103
Southern Yemen	964
South Viet Nam	940
Soviet Union (Russia)	273
Spain	549
Spanish Dominion of Philippines	69
Spanish Dominion of Puerto Rico	192
Spanish Guinea	595
Spanish Morocco	599
Spanish Sahara	606
Spanish West Africa	611
Spanish Western Sahara	606
SPM ovptd. on French Cols	430
Sri Lanka	Vol. I
Stanislav	957
STT Vuja	773
Submarine mail (Correo Submarino)	556
Sumatra	Vol. III
Surinam, Suriname	611
Suvalki	Vol. III
Sverige	627
Sweden	627
Switzerland	652
Switzerland, Administration of Liechtenstein	Vol. III
Syria, Syrienne	686
Syria (Arabian Government)	713
Syrie-Grand Liban	686
T ovptd. on stamps of Peru	68
Tacna	44, 65
Tahiti	717
Tai Han (Korea)	Vol. III
Tangier, Spanish Offices	605
Tannu Tuva	717
Taxa de Guerra	181, 185, 192, Vol. III
T.C., Postalari	803
Te Betalen	617, Vol. III
Teheran	Vol. III
T.E.O. ovptd. on Turkey or France	686
Teruel	593
Tete	718
Tetuan	605
Thailand, Thai	718
Thessaly	833
Thrace	738
Thurn and Taxis	Vol. III
Tibet	739
Tical	719
Timor	739
Tjenestefrimerke	Vol. III
Tlacotalpan	Vol. III
Togo	744
Tou	Vol. III
Touva	718
Transcaucasian Federated Republics	770
Trebizonde	399
Trieste	770
Tripoli di Barberia	Vol. III
Tripoli, Fiera Campionaria	Vol. III
Tripolitania	774, Vol. III
Tsingtau	Vol. III
T. Ta. C	839
Tunisia, Tunisie, Tunis	777
Turkestan, Russian	401
Turkey, Türkiye	797
Turkey in Asia	840
Turkish Empire, Polish Offices	154
Turkish Empire, Romanian Offices	270
Turkish Empire, Russian Offices	398
Turkish stamps surcharged or ovptd.	713, 738, 840
Tuscany	Vol. III
Tuva Autonomous Region	717
Two Sicilies	Vol. III
Tyosen (Korea)	Vol. III
Ubangi, Ubangi-Shari	842
Ukraine (Ukrainia)	843
Ukraine (German Occupation)	397
Union of Soviet Socialist Republics	273, 277
United Arab Republic (UAR) Issues for Egypt	Vol. II
Issues for Palestine	Vol. II
Issues for Syria	714
United Nations European Office	714
United States, Administration of Philippines	71
Administration of Puerto Rico	193
Universal Postal Union, International Bureau	684
UNTEA ovptd. on Netherlands New Guinea	744
Upha Topa	Vol. III
Upper Senegal and Niger	844
Upper Silesia	844
Upper Volta	845
U.R.I. ovptd. on Jugoslavia	Vol. III
Uruguay	865
Uskub	798
Valladolid	551
Vatican City	897
Venezuela	911
Viet Nam	940
Viet Nam, North	949
Vilnius	Vol. III
Vojna Uprava	Vol. III
Vuja-STT	773
Walachia	202
Wallis and Futuna Islands	950
War Board of Trade	681
Warsaw	101
Wenden	397
Western Thrace (Greek Occupation)	739
Western Ukraine	959
West Irian	960
West New Guinea	960
White Russia	961
World Health Organization	683
World Meteoerological Organization	684
Wrangel Issues	400
Wurttemberg	Vol. III
Yca	68
Yemen	961
Yemen People's Republic	968
Ykp. H.P.	957
Yucatan	Vol. III
Yudenich, Gen.	397
Yugoslavia	Vol. III
Zaire	973
Zambezia	974
Zelaya	Vol. III
Zinska Pomoc ovptd. on Italy	Vol. III
Zone A (Trieste)	770
Zone B (Istria)	Vol. III
Zone B (Trieste)	773
Zurich	652

NUMERICAL INDEX OF WATERMARKS
(VOL. IV)

Wmk.	Country	Page*	Wmk.	Country	Page*	Wmk.	Country	Page*	Wmk.	Country	Page*
62	Samoa	471	172-173	Salvador	447-448	234	Poland	104	326	Poland	115
95	Romania	205	174	San Marino	472	235	Vatican City	897	327	Uruguay	873
104	Philippines	69	175	Shanghai	329	240	Salvador	450	329	Thailand	722
104-105	Spain	550	176	Thailand	719	257	Philippines	100	332	Uruguay	873
114	Schleswig	508	178	Spain	551		Ryukyu Islands	416	334	Panama	21
116	Spain	594	180-181	Sweden	627-628	258	Yemen	961		Thailand	722
	Ukraine	843	182-183	Switzerland	653-655	269	Salvador	450	337	Saudi Arabia	497
117	Salvador	445	187-189	Uruguay	868-869	276	Romania	210	339	San Marino	478
127	Yemen	961	190-191	Philippines	71	277	San Marino	474	343	Panama	7
140	San Marino	473	200	Romania	204		Vatican City	898	347	Paraguay	30
	Somalia	530	202	Surinam	613		Yemen	961	356	Thailand	724
	Tripolitania	776	204	Tannu Tuva	717	285	Saar	424	358	Romania	214
145	Poland	102	217	San Marino	473	289	Romania	212	361	Saudi Arabia	499
163-164	Romania	203	225	Romania	206	291	Syria	690	365	Panama	9
165	Romania	268	226	Russia	414	293	Russia	299	368	Thailand	728
166	Russia	273	227	Uruguay	870	299	Thailand	737	371	Thailand	729
167	Romania	204	229	Panama	16	303	San Marino	476	372	Philippines	85
168	Russia	273	230	Romania	207	307	Sweden	632	374	Thailand	728
169-171	Russia	276-277	232	Timor	741	311	Panama	7	375	Thailand	730
171	South Russia	549	233	Panama	5	319-320	Paraguay	29	377	Panama	10
				Philippines	79					Thailand	10

*Page indicates where illustration may be found.

Scott Catalogue Philatelic Marketplace

This "Yellow Pages" section of your Scott Catalogue contains advertisements to help you find what you need, when you need it...conveniently.

All Over the World...

There are reliable ASDA dealers waiting to serve you!

Dealers who care! They are constantly striving to serve you better. It makes sense to choose an ASDA dealer.

Whether you shop by mail or in person, now you can shop with confidence. Satisfaction guaranteed.

The ASDA code of ethics assures you reliable, personal service every time. So look for the ASDA symbol before you buy or sell.

American Stamp Dealer's Assoc., Inc.
5 Dakota Dr., Suite 102, Lake Success N.Y. 11042 (516) 775-3600

ACCESSORIES

WASHINGTON PRESS
See Our Display Ad Inside Front Cover
The Washington Press, Florham Park, N.J. 07932

APPROVALS

ABSP, INC. — PERSONALIZED APPROVALS
(Please Specify Interests) U.S. British and Worldwide
Box 155, Warminster, PA 18974

AUCTIONS

JACQUES C. SCHIFF, JR., INC
195 Main Street, Ridgefield Park, NJ 07660
U.S., Worldwide Stamps & Postal History

Send For Your Free Catalog

Quality Auctions, Ltd.
Box 3116, Middletown, N.Y. 10940
Telephone: (914) 343-2174

Consign all or part of your collection to a Quality auction and you'll receive professional service and.....
$ *the Highest Realization*

BUYING & SELLING

BARTLETT & FELDER
See Inside Back Cover
49 Geary, Suite 250, San Francisco, CA 94102

EDWARD D. YOUNGER CO.
See Our Display Ad in Color Section
222 Mamaroneck Ave., White Plains, NY 10605

WE WISH TO PURCHASE

Since 1923 we have been the purchaser of large holdings of U.S. & Foreign stamps, covers, coins, autographs and historic documents.

When you sell, you want top dollar. We are willing to make offers and will pay cash in currency or transfer of bank funds prior to the removal of any material purchased. We will fly anywhere immediately to view a substantial collection, dealers stock or accumulation. There is no fee involved.

WRITE - WIRE or CALL
1-800-645-3840
NYS Residents 516-354-1001
Our 400th Auction Sale
Now in Preparation.
Catalog Free on Request.

JOHN A. FOX
141 Tulip Avenue, Floral Park, N.Y. 11001

MICHAEL ROGERS

- MEMBER: ASDA, APS, GPS, BIA, AAMS
- U.S. & Foreign stamps and covers
- Our Specialties; U.S., European, British, Asia, Zeppelin Flights and Air Posts Flights
- Each price list sent for 60¢ postage.

ALWAYS BUYING

Winter Park Stamp Shop	Hours Mon-Sat 10-6 for Both Stores	Florida Stamp & Coin Co. Inc.
340 Park Avenue, North Winter Park, Florida 32789 (305) 628-1120		2507-A E. Colonial Dr. Orlando, Florida 32803 (305) 894-3021

WE BUY & SELL
AFGHANISTAN TO ZAMBEZIA
UNITED STATES   BRITISH COMMONWEALTH
We Need Specialized Collections, but We'll Look at Anything You Have to Sell.

BUY
- Collections
- Accumulations
- Covers
- Picture Postcards

Write, ship or *call collect*. All lots held intact pending acceptance of our offer.

SELL
We have an extensive stock and you can often find those elusive stamps you've been looking for. Mint, Used-Worldwide.

Bill and Celina Baehr
B. AND C. STAMP CO.
NEASDA-CASDA-FSDA—

7 West Main Street
Somerville, NJ 08876
(201) 526-8012

Sunset Galleries Inc.
72-27 S.W. 57th Court   So. Miami, FL 33143
305-666-4606

Buying and Selling
U.S., British & General Worldwide

- Auctions and Mail Sales.
- Topical & General Want Lists Filled. • Covers-U.S. & Worldwide.

—*Serious Bidders*—
Send for free Auction Catalogue

★ **Consignments Wanted** ★
Big and Small Collections or Better Single Items.
Will travel to inspect larger holdings.
FSDA   APS   ATA

GOVERNMENTS

PHILATELIC SALES BRANCH
See Our Display Ad in Color Section
Dept. B, U.S. Postal Service, Washington, DC 20265

NEW ISSUES

SPECTACULAR NEW ISSUE SERVICE
Complete Coverage of New Issues
From the Entire World
Remember our Specialty:
ALL TOPICALS AND NEW ISSUES
WANT LISTS SERVICED
Exceptionally extensive stock of worldwide 20th Century mint sets and U.S. stamps.
Top prices paid for collections.
Ask for our FREE Illustrated Topical Monthly New Issue List.

COUNTY STAMP CENTER
P.O. Box 3373
Annapolis, Maryland 21403

PHILATELIC SERVICES

JAMES H. CRUM (APS, ASDA, ANS) (Est. 1929)
Thousands of Stamps plus Personal Helpful Advice
2720 E. Gage Ave., Huntington Park, CA 90255 213-588-4467

PHILATELIC SOCIETIES

AMERICAN PHILATELIC SOCIETY
America's foremost stamp collector's society
P.O. Box 8000, State College, PA 16801

PRINTING

COSMOS PRESS
"Typesetting, Printing, Binding, Mailing"
141 East 25th Street, N.Y.C., NY 10010

SPECIAL OFFERS

WHOLESALE WHOLESALE WHOLESALE WHOLESALE
YOUR OWN SUCCESSFUL STAMP BUSINESS
Start Part-Time From Your Own Home!

America's Largest Job Lot Stamp Wholesaler Offers You The Opportunity To Start Your Own Stamp Business— Immediately and At Minimum Cost!

Take Advantage Of This Introductory Offer:
1) The Guide for Stamp Dealers - *"Secrets Of Successful Stamp Dealing"*.
2) *Our Complete Wholesale Lists* - Enormous Savings on Worldwide Sets, Singles & Packets. Great profit potential for you! **BOTH FOR $2.00**
(Refundable On Your First Order Of $10.00 Or More.)

CAMPBELL HALL CO.
America's Largest Job Lot Stamp Wholesaler
P.O. Box 295 - DEPT. SC4   EAST NORTHPORT, N.Y. 11731
Telephone 516-261-5049

Please see our 1/2 Page Ad in the Yellow Pages of Volume I.

STAMP STORES

OMEGA STAMP & COIN CO.
Brooklyn's Largest Buys & Sells U.S. & Foreign Coll.
1586 Flatbush Ave., Brooklyn, NY 11210 212-859-5086

When on the West Coast for all your Philatelic Needs.

Brewart Stamps
One of the Largest Stocks
of U.S. and Worldwide in Southern California

Brewart Stamps (store)
BOUGHT & SOLD
*Wantlists Filled Upon Request

403 W. Katella, 2 blocks from Disneyland
Anaheim, Ca. 92802
Mailing Address: P.O. Box 8580   Phone: 714-533-0400

SCOTT UNLISTED

City Hall Stamp Co. has one of the world's largest varieties of issues found in Scott's "For The Record." This includes a big selection of animals, flowers and most recent topicals such as UPU 1974, Football 1982 and many, many more. If you are an advanced collector in any topic, you will find our approval service helpful.

Do you have collections or accumulations for sale? Contact us for the best deal.

CITY HALL STAMP CO.
HIGHLY SPECIALIZED IN GOLD AND SILVER ISSUES
P.O. Box 52, East Station
Yonkers, N.Y. 10704
Tel.: 914-969-3554

TOPICALS

WESTMINSTER STAMP GALLERY, LTD
P.O. Box 456, Foxboro, MA 02035
See our full page ad in Volume 1.

Do You Collect Any Of These?

Aircraft	Churchill	Minerals	*Ships
Animals	Dogs & Cats	Military	Soccer
Antarctic	Energy	*Music	Space
Archeology	Europa	Mushrooms	Sports
Art Works	Fairy Tales	Nuclear	Sports, Winter
Astronomy	Fire & Police	*Olympics	Stained Glass
Bells	Fish	Paintings	Stamp on Stamp
Bicentennial	Flags	QE Jubilee &	& Shows
Bicycles &	*Flowers	Coronation	*Trains
Motorcycles	Food	*Red Cross	Transportation
*Birds	Horses	Religion	U.N. Related
Bridges	Insects	Reptiles	UPU 75th &
Butterflies	ITU	*Rotary	100th
Chess	Kennedy	Roosevelt	Waterfalls
Children & IYC	Lighthouses	Royal Weddings	Worldwide
*Christmas	Malaria	Scientists	Souvenir Sheets
Coins	Maps	*Scouts	Zeppelins
Costumes	Medical	Sea Shells	

If you do, try Aksarben for any of your needs. We have a strong stock of all items with * beside them. We will work want lists or send on approval with proper references. We also have a new issue service for any of the above topics and any other you may need. We also need to buy Topical and Worldwide collections for our retail sales. ATA Life Member #1578, ASDA, APS.

11035X Prairie Brook Road   **AKSARBEN**   Omaha, NE 68144

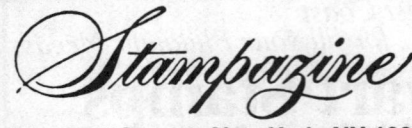

3 East 57th Street • New York, NY 10022
"The Store on the Fifth Floor"
(212) 752-5905

WE WANT YOUR WANT LIST!

There are over **400 stamp-issuing entities** listed below. Do you collect any of them? **GOOD!!! WE STOCK THEM ALL!** If you need stamps, especially those "hard-to-find" ones, send Stampazine your want-list today (by Scott numbers please). Suitable philatelic references or a deposit (checks gladly accepted) may bring you a pleasant surprise in the mail! —OR—visit Stampazine at 3 East 57th Street in the heart of New York City—across the street from Tiffany's. Stampazine stocks both unused (basically hinged) and used stamps. And our bi-monthly auctions offer many never-hinged items, sets, varieties and non-Scott listed material.

Try Stampazine—you'll love us!!
WE CAN SUPPLY STAMPS UP TO THE YEAR INDICATED–NOT LATER!

UNITED STATES (1980)
CONFEDERATE STATES
U.S. POSSESSIONS (1970)
  CANAL ZONE
  CUBA
  DANISH WEST INDIES
  GUAM
  HAWAII
  PHILIPPINES
UNITED NATIONS (1980)
GREAT BRITAIN & COLONIES (1970)
  REGIONALS
  ADEN
  KATHIRI
  QUAITI
  AITUTAKI
  ANGUILLA
  ANTIGUA
  ASCENSION
  AUSTRALIA
  A.A.T.
  BAHAMAS
  BAHRAIN
  BARBADOS
  BARBUDA
  BASUTOLAND
  BECHUANALAND
  BERMUDA
  BOTSWANA
  BR. ANTARCTIC
  BR. CENTRAL AFRICA
  BR. COLUMBIA
  BR. EAST AFRICA
  BR. GUIANA
  BR. HONDURAS
  BRUNEI
  BURMA
  CANADA
  CAPE OF GOOD HOPE
  CAYMAN ISL.
  CEYLON
  CHRISTMAS ISL.
  COCOS ISL.
  COOK ISL.
  CYPRUS
  DOMINICA
  EAST AFRICA & UGANDA
  FALKLAND ISL.
  FIJI
  GAMBIA
  GERMAN EAST AFRICA
  GHANA
  GIBRALTAR
  GILBERT & ELLICE
  GOLD COAST
  GRENADA
  GUYANA
  HONG KONG
  INDIA
    CHAMBA
    FARIDKOT
    GWALIOR
    JHIND
    NABHA
    PATIALA
    ALWAR
    BARWANI
    BHOPAL
    BUNDI
    CHARKHARI
    COCHIN
    DHAR
    DUTTIA
    HYDERABAD
    IDAR
    INDORE
    JAIPUR
    JASDAN
    JHALAWAR
    KISHANGARH
    LAS BELA
    MORVI
    NANDGAON
    NOWANUGGUR
    ORCHHA
    POONCH
    RAJASTHAN
    RAJPEEPLA
    SIRMOOR
    SORUTH
    TRAVANCORE
    TRAVENCORE COCHIN
  IONIAN ISLANDS
  IRAQ
  IRELAND
  JAMAICA
  JORDAN
  KENYA
  K.U.T.
  KUWAIT
  LABUAN
  LAGOS
  LEEWARD ISL.
  LESOTHO
  MALAWI
  MALAYA-F.M.S.
    JAHORE
    KEDAH
    KELANTAN
    MALACCA
    NEGRI SEMBILAN
    PAHANG
    PERAK
    PERLIS
    SELANGOR
    SUNGEI UJONG
    TRENGGANU
  MALAYSIA
  MALDIVE ISL.
  MALTA
  MAURITIUS
  MESOPOTAMIA
  MONTSERRAT
  NATAL
  NAURU
  NEPAL
  NEVIS
  NEW BRITAIN
  NEW BRUNSWICK
  NEWFOUNDLAND
  NEW GUINEA
  NEW HEBRIDES
  NEW REPUBLIC
  NEW SOUTH WALES
  NEW ZEALAND
  NIGER COAST PROT.
  NIGERIA
  NIUE
  NORFOLK ISL.
  NORTH BORNEO
  NORTHERN NIGERIA
  NORTHERN RHODESIA
  NORTH WEST PACIFIC ISL.
  NOVA SCOTIA
  NYASALAND
  OMAN
  ORANGE RIVER COLONY
  PAKISTAN
    BAHAWALPUR
  PALESTINE
  PAPUA NEW GUINEA
  PENRHYN ISL.
  PITCAIRN ISL.
  PRINCE EDWARD ISL.
  QATAR
  QUEENSLAND
  RHODESIA
  RHODESIA & NYASALAND
  SABAH
  ST. CHRISTOPHER
  ST. HELENA
  ST. KITTS-NEVIS
  ST. LUCIA
  ST. VINCENT
  SAMOA
  SARAWAK
  SEYCHELLES
  SIERRA LEONE
  SINGAPORE
  SOLOMON ISL.
  SOMALILAND PROT.
  SOUTH AFRICA
  SOUTH ARABIA
  SOUTH AUSTRALIA
  SOUTHERN NIGERIA
  SOUTHERN RHODESIA
  SOUTH-WEST AFRICA
  STRAITS SETTLEMENTS
  SUDAN
  SWAZILAND
  TANGANYIKA
  TANZANIA
  TASMANIA
  TOBAGO
  TOGO
  TOKELAU
  TONGA
  TRANSVAAL
  TRINIDAD
  TRINIDAD & TOBAGO
  TRISTAN DA CUNHA
  TRUCIAL STATES
  TURKS ISL.
  TURKS & CAICOS ISL.
  UGANDA
  VICTORIA
  VIRGIN ISL.
  WESTERN AUSTRALIA
  ZAMBIA
  ZANZIBAR
  ZUZULAND

AFGHANISTAN (1960)
ALAOUITES
ALBANIA (1940)
ALEXANDRETTA
ALGERIA (1960)
ALLENSTEIN
ANGOLA (1960)
ANGRA
ANNAM & TONKIN
ARGENTINA-(AIRMAILS ONLY - 1960)
AUSTRIA (1965)
  LOMBARDY-VENETIA
AZORES
BELGIAN CONGO
BELGIUM (1965)
BENIN (19th CENTURY)
BOLIVIA (1960)
BOSNIA & MERZEGOVINA
BRAZIL (19th CENTURY, & AIRMAILS - 1960)
BULGARIA (1940)
CAMBODIA (1960)
CAMEROUN (1940)
CAPE VERDE (1960)
CAROLINE ISL.
CASTELLORIZO
CENTRAL LITHUANIA
CHAD (1940)
CHILE (1960)
CHINA (19th CENTURY, & AIRMAILS - 1960)
CILICIA
COCHIN CHINA
COLUMBIA (19th CENTURY & AIRMAILS - 1960)
  ANTIOQUA
  BOLIVAR
  BOYACA
  CAUCA
  CUNDINMARCA
  SANTENDER
  TOLIMA
CORFU
COSTA RICA (1960)
CRETE
CROATIA
CUBA (1960)
CYRENAICA
CZECHOSLOVAKIA (1940)
  BOHEMIA & MORAVIA
  CARPATHO-UKRAINE
  SLOVAKIA
DAHOMEY (1940)
DALMATIA
DANZIG
DENMARK (1960)
DIEGO SUAREZ
DOMINICAN REPUBLIC (1960)
EASTERN RUMELIA
EASTERN SILESIA
ECUADOR (1960)
EGYPT (1960)
EPIRUS
ERITREA
ESTONIA
ETHIOPIA (1960)
FAR EASTERN REPUBLIC
FINLAND (1960)
FIUME
FRANCE (1970)
FRENCH COLONIES
FRENCH CONGO
FRENCH EQUATORIA AFRICA (1940)
FRENCH GUIANA (1940)
FRENCH GUINEA
FRENCH INDIA (1940)
FRENCH MOROCCO (1940)
FRENCH POLYNESIA (1940)
FRENCH SUDAN
GABON (1940)
GEORGIA
GERMAN EAST AFRICA
GERMAN NEW GUINEA
GERMAN SOUTH-WEST AFRICA
GERMAN STATES:
  BADEN
  BAVARIA
  BERGDORF
  BREMEN
  BRUNSWICK
  HAMBURG
  HANOVER
  LUBECK
  MECKLENBURG-SCHWERIN
  MECKLENBURG-STRELITZ
  OLDENBURG
  PRUSSIA
  SAXONY
  SCHLESWIG-HOLSTEIN
  THURN & TAXIS
  WURTTEMBERG
  NORTH GERMAN CONFEDERATION
GERMANY (1960)
GRAND COMORO
GREECE (1965)
GREENLAND (1960)
GUADELOUPE (1940)
GUATEMALA (1960)
HAITI (1960)
HATAY
HONDURAS (1960)
HORTA
HUNGARY (1940)
ICELAND (1960)
INDO-CHINA (1940)
INHAMBANE
ININI
ITALIAN COLONIES
ITALIAN EAST AFRICA
ITALY (1960)
IVORY COAST (1940)
JAPAN (1970)
JUGOSLAVIA (1960)
KARELIA
KIAUCHAN
KIONGA
KOREA (1955)
LAOS (1960)
LATAKIA
LATVIA
LEBANON (1960)
LIBERIA (1960)
LIBYA (1940)
LIECHTENSTEIN (1970)
LITHUANIA
LOURENCO MARQUES
LUXEMBOURG (1970)
MACAO (1960)
MADAGASCAR (1940)
MADEIRA
MARCHUKUO
MARIANA ISL.
MARIENWERDER
MARSHALL ISL.
MARTINIQUE (1940)
MAURITANIA (1940)
MAYOTTE
MEMEL
MEXICO (1960)
MIDDLE CONGO
MOHELI
MONACO (1960)
MONTENEGRO
MOZAMBIQUE (1950)
MOZAMBIQUE COMPANY
NETHERLANDS (1970)
NETHERLANDS ANTILLES (1960)
NETHERLANDS INDIES
NEW CALEDONIA (1940)
NEW HEBRIDES (1940)
NICARAGUA - AIRMAILS ONLY (1960)
NIGER (1940)
NORTH INGERMANLAND
NORWAY (1960)
NOSSI-BE
NYASSA
OBOCK
OLTRE GIUBA
PANAMA (AIRMAILS ONLY - 1960)
PARAGUAY (AIRMAILS ONLY - 1960)
PERU (AIRMAILS ONLY - 1960)
POLAND (1960)
PORTUGAL (1960)
PORTUGUESE AFRICA
PORTUGUESE CONGO
PORTUGUESE GUINEA (1960)
PORTUGUESE INDIA (1960)
QUELIMANE
REUNION (1940)
ROMANIA (1940)
RUANDA-URUNDI
RUSSIA (1940)
RYUKYU ISL.
SAAR
STE.-MARIE DE MADAGASCAR
ST. PIERRE & MIQUELON (1950)
ST. THOMAS & PRINCE ISL. (1960)
SALVADOR (AIRMAILS ONLY - 1960)
SAMOA
SAN MARINO (1960)
SCHLESWIG
SENEGAL (1940)
SENEGAMBIA & NIGER
SERBIA
SOMALIA (1940)
SOMALI COAST (1940)
SOUTH RUSSIA
SPAIN (1960)
SURINAM (1960)
SWEDEN (1960)
SWITZERLAND (1970)
SYRIA (1960)
TAHITI
TETE
THAILAND (1940)
THRACE
TIMOR (1960)
TOGO (1940)
TRANSCAUCASIAN FED. REP.
TRIESTE
TRIPOLITANIA
TUNISIA (1940)
TURKEY (1960)
UBANGI-SHARI
UKRAINE
UPPER SENEGAL & NIGER
UPPER SILESIA
UPPER VOLTA
URUGUAY (AIRMAILS ONLY - 1960)
VATICAN CITY (1975)
VENEZUELA (1960)
VIET NAM (1960)
WALLIS & FUTUNA ISL. (1940)
ZAMBESIA
WORLD-WIDE SOUV. SHEETS (1970)